THE CONCISE
OXFORD DICTIONARY
OF CURRENT ENGLISH

Edited by
H. W. FOWLER AND F. G. FOWLER

based on
The Oxford Dictionary

FOURTH EDITION
Revised by
E. McINTOSH

OXFORD
AT THE CLARENDON PRESS

Oxford University Press, Amen House, London E.C.4

GLASGOW NEW YORK TORONTO MELBOURNE WELLINGTON
BOMBAY CALCUTTA MADRAS KARACHI KUALA LUMPUR
CAPE TOWN IBADAN NAIROBI ACCRA

FIRST EDITION 1911
NEW EDITION (revised) 1929
THIRD EDITION 1934
REPRINTED 1938, 1940, 1942
1944 (with revised Addenda, etc.)
1946, 1949 (with revised Addenda, etc.)
FOURTH EDITION 1951
REPRINTED (with revised Addenda), 1952, 1954,
1955, 1956, 1958, 1959, 1960, 1961

PRINTED IN GREAT BRITAIN
AT THE UNIVERSITY PRESS, OXFORD
BY VIVIAN RIDLER
PRINTER TO THE UNIVERSITY

PREFACE TO THE FOURTH EDITION

IN this completely revised and reset edition numerous corrections and additions have been made to bring the book up to date. Thanks are due to the many correspondents who have pointed out errors or suggested improvements. Especially must I express my gratitude to Dr. Scholes, Dr. Honeyman, and Mr J. M. Wyllie for the valuable assistance given for musical terms, chemical terms, and many technical terms. The officials of the Clarendon Press too, past and present, have throughout been most helpful.

In this edition the system of pronunciation devised for the *Pocket Oxford Dictionary* has been adopted, the senses have been usually numbered, the general abbreviations have been collected into an appendix, and the swung dash has been freely employed.

Swung dash (~).

To save space the 'swung dash' or 'tilde' is very frequently used in the body of the article or the list of derivatives. It represents either the complete word at the beginning of the article or the un-infected part of that word often marked by a vertical line. As, for example, in the article **repeat**, ~ stands for *repeat* (or repeat), ~ed for *repeated*, ~edLY² for *repeatedLY*,² ~ing for *repeating*, ~ER¹ for *repeater*¹: and in the article **reverber|ate** we have ~ating, ~ate, ~atory, ~ation, ~ative, ~ant representing *reverberating*, rever-berate, reverberatory, reverberation, reverberative, rever-berant.

E. McI., 1950

From the
PREFACE TO THE THIRD EDITION

THE publication of the Supplement to the *Oxford English Diction-ary* in November 1933 makes important additions to the material which it is the aim of this book, as a dictionary of the living language, to present. Mr H. W. Fowler entrusted me with the preparation of this edition in February 1933, and until his death on the 26th December of that year I had the privilege of his guidance.

H. G. LE MESURIER, 1934

PREFACE TO THE SECOND EDITION

WHEN we began, more than twenty years ago, the work that took shape as *The Concise Oxford Dictionary*, we were plunging into the sea of lexicography without having been first taught to swim. But lexicography for us was fortunately of the minor or dependent kind; and, fortunately also, the time was one at which the major or firsthand kind was reaching greater excellence than ever before, and the *Oxford English Dictionary*, four-fifths completed, already provided popularizers with unlimited material.

The object we set before us, hinted at by the word *current* on our title-page, was to present as vivid a picture as the small dictionary could be made to give of the English that was being spoken and written at the time. The vividness was to be secured by allotting space to words more nearly in proportion to the frequency and variety of their use, and consequently to their practical value, than had been the custom; and further by an unprecedented abundance of illustrative quotation; define, and your reader gets a silhouette; illustrate, and he has it 'in the round'. That at least was our belief; and we hailed as confirmation of it one or two letters from persons unknown congratulating us on having 'produced a live dictionary', or 'treating English at last as a living language'.

A living language, however, does not remain unchanged through twenty years and a great war; our picture has needed, and received, a good deal of retouching before being again exhibited in public.

H. W. F., 1929

ACKNOWLEDGEMENTS

A DICTIONARY-MAKER, unless he is a monster of omniscience, must deal with a great many matters of which he has no firsthand knowledge. That he has been guilty of errors and omissions in some of these he will learn soon after publication, sometimes with gratitude to his enlightener, sometimes otherwise. The first letter we received after C.O.D. appeared was a demand for repayment of the book's cost, on the ground that it failed to give *gal(l)yot*, to settle the spelling of which it had been bought. Even for that announcement of an omission I am now grateful, as affording a good illustration of the less friendly form of correction, and reminding me to assure the public that to one revising for a new edition no correction is (ultimately) unwelcome; all is grist that comes to his mill. At the other end of the scale is the friend, known to me only by correspondence, who for years sent me fortnightly packets of foolscap devoted to perfecting a still contingent second edition—all this for love of the language not as a philological playground, but as the medium of exchange and bond of union among the English-speakers of the world. *Castigavit et emendavit Byron F. Caws* might have stood with justice at the foot of our title-page.

Other helpers have been many, some with systematic lists, others with a few isolated but valuable points; to all those in the list below I would fain offer—what some of them are no longer living to receive —my heartiest thanks:

Leslie J. Berlin Esq.; Major B. F. Caws; Dr R. W. Chapman; Mr S. K. N. Chaudhuri; *Sir Arthur Church K.C.V.O.; Rev. G. P. Ford; H. Gilbert-Carter Esq.; *Prof. Marcus Hartog; the Very Reverend Dr J. H. Hertz; Rev. J. Clare Hudson; Rev. F. E. Hutchinson; Lindsay Johnson M.D., F.R.S.; Rev. D. Evans Jones; Major C. V. N. Lyne; D. C. Macgregor Esq.; F. Morland Esq.; C. O. Ovington Esq.; George Pernet M.D.; Prof. Sir Flinders Petrie F.R.S.; Rev. S. de Saram; Kenneth Sisam Esq.; W. H. Thompson Esq.; B. H. Tower Esq.; F. F. Urquhart Esq.; *Rev. M. N. Walde; E. B. F. Wareing Esq.; *Dr F. H. P. van Wely; J. Beach Whitmore Esq.; Ernest W. Wignall Esq.; C. F. Williams F.G.S.; *Sir Dawson Williams C.B.E.

H. W. F.

* Those whose names are thus marked are known to me to be no longer living; and I fear the same may be true of some others, whom I have failed to reach by postal inquiries.

PREFACE TO THE FIRST EDITION

THE steady advance towards completion of the great *Oxford English Dictionary* has made it possible for the Delegates of the Clarendon Press to authorize the preparation and issue of this book, which in its own province and on its own scale uses the materials and follows the methods by which the Oxford editors have revolutionized lexicography. The book is designed as a dictionary, and not as an encyclopaedia; that is, the uses of words and phrases as such are its subject matter, and it is concerned with giving information about the things for which those words and phrases stand only so far as correct use of the words depends upon knowledge of the things. The degree of this dependence varies greatly with the kind of word treated, the difference between cyclopaedic and dictionary treatment varies with it, and the line of distinction is accordingly a fluctuating and dubious one. It is to the endeavour to discern and keep to this line that we attribute whatever peculiarities we are conscious of in this dictionary as compared with others of the same size. One of these peculiarities is the large amount of space given to the common words that no one goes through the day without using scores or hundreds of times, often disposed of in a line or two on the ground that they are plain and simple and that every one knows all about them by the light of nature, but in fact entangled with other words in so many alliances and antipathies during their perpetual knocking about the world that the idiomatic use of them is far from easy; chief among such words are the prepositions, the conjunctions, the pronouns, and such 'simple' nouns and verbs as *hand* and *way*, *go* and *put*. Another peculiarity is the use, copious for so small a dictionary, of illustrative sentences as a necessary supplement to definition when a word has different senses between which the distinction is fine, or when a definition is obscure and unconvincing until exemplified; these sentences often are, but still more often are not, quotations from standard authors; they are meant to establish the sense of the definition by appeal not to external authority, but to the reader's own consciousness, and therefore their source, even when authoritative, is not named. A third and a fourth peculiarity are the direct results of the preceding ones; if common words are to be treated at length, and their uses to be copiously illustrated, space must be saved both by the curtest possible treatment of all that are either uncommon or fitter for the encyclopaedia than the dictionary, and by the severest economy of expression—amounting to the adoption of telegraphese—that readers can be expected to put up with.

In attaching this great importance to illustration, by the need of which the relative length of articles, and our manner of expressing ourselves on every page, are governed, we are merely acting, with the exaggeration imposed on us by our limited space, upon the principles of the O.E.D. That may be said to be the first dictionary for which the ideal procedure has been possible, that is, the approaching of each article with an open mind and a collection of examples large enough to be exhaustive, and the extraction from these of classified senses—the first dictionary, to put it another way, in which quotations have served not merely to adorn or convince, but as the indispensable raw material. This procedure—first the collection of sentences from all possible sources as raw material, and then the independent classification—we have often followed even in that part of our book (A–R) in which the O.E.D., with senses already classified and definitions provided, was before us, treating its articles rather as quarries to be drawn upon than as structures to be reproduced in little; and in the later part (S–Z), where we had no longer the O.E.D. to depend upon, it has been our practice still more often; for many of the more difficult (i.e. especially the common and 'simple') words, we have collected the quotations given in the best modern dictionaries (the *Imperial*, the *Century*, the *Standard*, Cassell's *Encyclopaedic*, Webster, etc.), added to these what we could get either from other external sources or from our own heads, and then framed our articles, often without reference to the arrangement that we found in any of our authorities. Proceeding in this manner, it was almost inevitable that we should be very much alive to the inadequacy of mere definition and the need of constant illustration. That our examples have some general tendency to the colloquial, and include many usages for which room has not been found in dictionaries many times as large as this, is in harmony with our design of on the one hand restricting ourselves for the most part to current English, and on the other hand omitting nothing to which that description may fairly be applied.

VOCABULARY

The words, or senses of words, given are meant to be such only as are current; 'current', however, is an elastic term; we might, but we do not, stretch it to include all words and senses used by Shakspere or in the Bible, on the ground that the whole of Shakspere and the whole of the Bible are still commonly read; thus the archaic senses of *addition* (title), *buxom* (pliant), *owe* (own), *sad* (serious), *sort* (suit), and the archaic words *shend* (scold), *wood* (mad), familiar as they are to readers of Elizabethan literature, are not given. We do stretch it to include many words and senses that are fossilized, having in themselves no life or capacity for further

development, but kept extant by being enshrined in perhaps a single proverb or phrase that is still in use; of this sort are *coil* (confusion), preserved by 'shuffled off this mortal coil', and *scotch* (wound), preserved by 'we have scotched the snake, not killed it'.

Again, of the many thousands of old or new scientific and technical terms that have a limited currency some are carried by accident into the main stream of the language and become known temporarily or permanently, vaguely or precisely, to all ordinarily well-informed members of the modern newspaper-reading public. For the purposes of a dictionary that is not to be bulky and yet is to give a fuller treatment than is usual in dictionaries of its size to the undoubtedly current words forming the staple of the language, selection among these intruders is a difficult but very necessary task. The most that can be hoped for is that every one conversant with any special vocabulary may consider us, though sadly deficient on his subject, fairly copious on others; the meaning of many learned words that have been omitted as having no pretence to general currency may easily be gathered by reference first to the stem, which is often the subject of an article, or to another word of which the stem is clearly the same, and secondly to the suffix.

In another class of words and senses the test of currency has led us to diverge in the opposite direction from the practice usual in dictionaries of this size; if we give fewer scientific and technical terms, we admit colloquial, facetious, slang, and vulgar expressions with freedom, merely attaching a cautionary label; when a well-established usage of this kind is omitted, it is not because we consider it beneath the dignity of lexicography to record it, but because, not being recorded in the dictionaries from which our word-list is necessarily compiled, it has escaped our notice; we have not, however, consulted slang dictionaries nor made any attempt at completeness in this respect.

SPELLING

The spelling adopted is for the most part, but not invariably, that of the O.E.D. For instance, the verbs that contain the suffix *-ize* (which see), and their derivatives in *-ization* etc., are all given without the alternative forms in *-ise* etc., although these are still the commoner in British (as opposed to American) printing; but such generally established spellings as *judgment*, *rhyme*, *axe*, have not been excluded in favour of the *judgement*, *rime*, *ax*, preferred by the O.E.D., but are retained at least as alternatives having the right to exist. In dealing with verbs such as *level*, *rivet*, *bias*, whose parts and derivatives are variously spelt, the final consonant being often doubled with no phonetic or other significance, we have as far as possible fallen in with the present tendency, which is to drop the

useless letter, but stopped short of recognizing forms that at present strike every reader as Americanisms; thus we write *riveted*, *riveter*, but not *traveling*, *traveler*. On another point of varying usage—the insertion of a mute e in derivatives in *-able*, *-age*, *-ish*, etc., to indicate the 'long' sound of the stem vowel (*likable* or *likeable*, *milage* or *mileage*, *latish* or *lateish*)—we have thought ourselves justified in taking a bolder line, and have consistently omitted the -e-; it is against all analogy (or why not *smileing*, *Romeish*, *doteage*, *tideal*, *indescribeable*, *desireable*, *exciteable*?), it is used chiefly in words not familiar or important enough to have their form respected as established, it obscures the different and more valuable use by which a soft g or c is indicated as in *manageable* and *serviceable*, and it tempts bad spellers to such monstrosities as *unpalateable*, *loveable*, and *moveable*. In words of the type *ardour*, *colour*, *favour*, where the O.E.D. recognizes both *-our* and *-or*, we have excluded the latter as being (except in particular words like *horror* and *torpor*, in which it is usually the only form) entirely non-British. Words in which -y- has intruded itself without completely dispossessing a more correct -i-, as *sylvan*, *tyro*, *tyre*, we have given with the -i- form either alone or placed first.

ORDER OF SENSES

From the order in which the senses of a word are here given **no** inference must be drawn as to their historical or other relations, the arrangement being freely varied according to the requirements or possibilities of the particular word. Sense-development cannot always be convincingly presented without abundant quotation from authorities, and the historical order is further precluded by the uniform omission of obsolete senses. Occasionally, when a rare but still current sense throws light on the commoner senses that follow or forms the connecting link with the etymology, it has been placed at the beginning; but more commonly the order adopted has been that of logical connexion or of comparative familiarity or importance.

DERIVATIVES

Hence introduces one or more of the direct derivatives of the word treated; *whence* introduces such derivatives under a particular sense to which they are restricted; *so* introduces words derived from another language; *hence or cogn.*, *whence or cogn.*, introduce groups of partly English and partly foreign derivation. The suffixes of such derivatives are commonly printed in small capitals, and are thus referred to the suffix article in its alphabetical place. The numbers enclosed in brackets indicate subdivisions of the suffix article, and are often used to distinguish among the possible senses of the derivative word those in which it is chiefly current.

ETYMOLOGY.

Etymology is given in square brackets at the end of each article. Words of Teutonic origin are illustrated by all or some of the forms found in cognate languages. With words that have passed through several languages on their way to English, the forms taken in successive languages are recorded in full, with the following exceptions. (1) When OF or the like at the beginning of the etymology is not followed by the old French form written in full, it is because the latter is identical in spelling with the English or differs from it only in some unimportant detail specified in brackets. (2) The Latin form of a Greek word is usually omitted, and is to be inferred according to the rules of transliteration given below. Thus (under *pleonasm*) 'f. L f. Gk *pleonasmos*' is to be read 'f. L *pleonasmus* f. Gk *pleonasmos*'. A similar omission of a word in any other language implies absolute identity of form.

Greek words are written with the corresponding English letters (φ, χ, ψ, ῥ, ῥρ, = ph, kh, ps, rh, rrh, and ą, ῃ, ῳ, = āi, ēi, ōi), and not according to the Latin transliteration, the rules for which are as follows; Greek k = Latin c; ai = ae; ou = u; u (exc. in diphthongs) = y; ei = i or e; oi = oe (but in nom. pl. -i = i); g (before g or k) = n; also, -ŏs (nom. masc.), -ŏn, = -us, -um; -ēs, -ē, (1st decl. nom.) = -a; -ōn (nom.) = -o; -ŏs (genit.) = -is; -a (accus. sing. masc. or fem.) = -em.

French nouns of Latin origin are with few exceptions derived from the Latin accusative; but the Latin nominative is here given except when (e.g. in words in *-atio*) a change ɘf stress is involved.

Greek η (ē) and ω (ō) are regularly marked long. The accented letters (á, ǽ, etc.), in forms quoted from Old English or other Teutonic languages are long.

Greek η (ē) and ω (ō), and the e of Latin infinitives of 2nd conj. (-ēre, -ērī), are regularly marked long. The accented letters (á, ǽ, etc.) in forms quoted from Old English or other Teutonic languages are long.

F, G, etc., must not be taken to imply that the word to which they are prefixed is current, or is so spelt, in the modern language; nor does it follow from a word's being given as OF that it is obsolete.

The etymology often contains references in small capitals to words and suffixes.

The first element of a Latin or other compound word is often referred to a prefix article, and the remainder treated separately within brackets; meanings given within the bracket belong to the simple word, those of the compound being added if necessary outside it. Thus *convene* is [f. F *convenir* f. L CON(*venire vent-* come) assemble, agree, fit]. The stem *vent-* and the senses *agree*, *fit*, are here added for the purposes of *convention* and *convenience*, which are referred to *convene*. The first element of a Greek compound similarly treated is sometimes written according to the current (Latin) transliteration, to facilitate reference to the prefix article;

Greek *kakoepeia*, under *cacoepy*, accordingly appears as CACOL(*epeia*). Certain similar devices for saving needless repetition will, it is believed, explain themselves.

The etymology of all words from A to R was drawn in the first instance from the O.E.D.; but was occasionally modified after reference to Prof. Skeat's *Etymological Dictionary* (Clarendon Press, 4th edition, 1910). From S to Z Prof. Skeat's work has been our main authority, the *Century* and other dictionaries being consulted for the words that he omits.

REFERENCE BY SMALL CAPITALS

The use of small capitals for etymological purposes is explained above.

In the same way reference is made:

(1) from the word treated to another word for the purpose of contrast, distinction, correlation, or the like. Of this kind are the references from *slander* to *libel* and *scandal*, from *creationism* to *evolution* and vice versa, and from *tenon* to *mortise* and vice versa ;

(2) from any member of a group to the word under which the group is collected or further explained. *Ruby* (print.) is in this way referred to *type* ; *order* (nat. hist.) to *class*[1] ; and the *iron*[1], *golden*, and *silver ages* to *brazen*[1] ;

(3) from one or more words of a proverb or the like to that under which alone the proverb is explained. *Play*[1] and *drake*[2] contain such references to *duck*[1], *flesh* to *fish*[1] ;

(4) from a compound of the word treated to its other component for explanation. The sign (=) prefixed to such a reference indicates that the simple word treated is itself used in the sense of the compound. Thus, under *pie*[1], *sea-pie* is merely referred to *sea*; but *magpie*, besides being referred to the article *magpie*, is recorded (=MAGPIE) as one of the senses of *pie*.

June, 1911

PRONUNCIATION

Phonetic respelling is placed in round brackets immediately after such words as require it, and the symbols in the PHONETIC SCHEME are primarily intended for this purpose. But respelling is often saved by employing the same symbols in the black type of the actual word; **bănish**, for instance, has no respelling, and **dispōse** has only (-z).

Vowel symbols given in the Scheme with ¯, ˘, or ˆ, are also used without these marks to denoted a vague indeterminate sound, which is almost identical for all vowels and (except in studied elocution) has no clear relation to the corresponding vowel marked ¯ etc. (e.g, the a in *about* is like the o in *reason*, *proceed*, and is not like ă or ā.) When so used in brackets, the indeterminates are printed in italics, thus: **ago** (agō), **proceed** (prosēd), **particular** (partĭ-kūlar). Used in the actual word, they are recognized by the absence of the marks ¯, ˘, etc.; thus in **săcrament**, **cŏmmon**, **bĕggarly**, all the unmarked vowels (a, e; o; ar) are indeterminate. This does not apply to the last six vowels in the Scheme, which never have marks over them and are always distinct.

Indeterminate endings in -n, -rn, -l or -le, when they require respelling, are also represented thus: **poison** (-zn), **fusion** (-zhn), **tension** (-shn), **ŏcean** (-shn), **lĭsten** (-sn), **bosom** (bŏŏzm), **hŭstle** (-sl), **official** (-shl), **weasel** (-zl), the vowel sound being that similarly indicated by the actual spelling of *spasm*, *prism*, etc.

PHONETIC SCHEME

Consonants: b; ch (*chin*); d; dh (dhe = the); g (*go*); h; j; k; l; m; n; ng (*sing*); ngg (*finger*); p; r; s (*sip*); sh (*ship*); t; th (*thin*); v; w; y; z; zh (*vizhn* = vision).

Vowels: ā ē ī ō ū ōō (mate mete mite mote mute moot)
ă ĕ ĭ ŏ ŭ ŏŏ (rack reck rick rock ruck rook)
ār ēr ēr ōr ūr (mare mere more mure)
ăr ĕr ŏr (part pert port)
ah aw oi oor ow owr (bah bawl boil boor brow bower)

Vowels marked ◡ may be pronounced either way, e.g. pătriot (pă- or pă-). In all vowel symbols with r (ār, ār, etc., the r, besides influencing the vowel sound, has its consonantal value when followed by a vowel in the next syllable of the word or in the following word (in *fearing* but not in *fearful*, in *far away* but not in *far gone*.

ACCENT

The main accent is shown by the mark ′, usually placed at the end of the stressed syllable; but, division into syllables being arbitrary in English, positions for the accent that would disguise the pronunciation are avoided; thus **stăr′rў** but **că′rrу, wŏŏll′en** but **cōōl′lў, lŏc′al** but **vēlō′cĭtу, ŏv′er** but **cō′ver** (kŭ-). Respelling is used but **mŭd′dlе**. The placing of two accents on a word means either (*a*) that the two marked syllables are equally stressed, as in *tit′bit′*, or (*b*) that among good speakers the one accentuation has as many adherents as the other, or (*c*) that the stress varies according to position in the sentence as explained in the dictionary article-ED². In the thousands of compounds given under their first elements among the alphabetically arranged combinations, accent is thus shown: if there is no hyphen separating the parts, the accent is always given (back′bone, backslide′); if there is a hyphen, the regular usage is for the first of the compounded words to be stressed, and the accent is then

usually omitted (so **oak-apple**'); if the stress falls, contrary to this rule, on the second component, it is marked (**head-on**' adv.); if the stress is variable, each part has an accent (**high-strung**').

PRONUNCIATION WITHOUT RESPELLING

All the further information necessary for the pronunciation of any word or part of a word that is not respelt is contained in the following six paragraphs; the assumptions made in these hold unless the contrary is shown in brackets.

1. Any letter or combination in the Phonetic Scheme has the value there shown; e.g., **aw** as in *awl*, not as in **awake** (awāk') ; and **ginger**, **linger**, would be required to rhyme with *singer* unless **ginger** were followed by (-j-), and **linger** by (-ngg-).

2. The following additional symbols are used in the black type:

ê = ĭ (māk'ĕd, rély', cŏll'ĕge, prĭv'ĕt)

n̄, ūr, = ēr (bīrth, būrn)

ȳ, y̆, = ī, ĭ (ĭmplȳ', sŭnn'y̆).

3. Final e unmarked is not indeterminate, but mute (sāne, indūc'tive; cf. rê'cipê, dilĕttan'tê).

4. A doubled consonant is pronounced as single (sill'ȳ, mànn'ĭsh, bŭtt'er),
not as in crōōl'ly (-l-li) or plain'ness (-n-n-).

5. The following combinations and letters have the values shown:

Vowels.

ae = ē (aegis)

ai = ā (pain)

air = ār (fair)

au = aw (maul)

ay = ā (say)

ea, ee, = ē (mean, meet)

ear, eer, = ē (fear, beer)

eu, ew, = ū (feud, few)

ie = ē (thief)

ier = ēr (pier)

oa = ō (boat)

ou = ow (bound)

oy = oi (coy)

Consonants.

c is 'hard' and = k (cob, cry, tale), but c before **e**, **i**, **y**, is 'soft' and = s (ice, icy, city)

dg = j (judgement)

g before **e**, **i**, **y**, is 'soft' and = j (age, gin, orgy)

n before **k**, 'hard' **c**, **q**, **x**, = ng (zinc, uncle, tank, banquet, minx)

ph = f (photo)

qu = kw (quit)

tch = ch (batch)

x = ks (fox)

6. The following terminations have the values shown:

-age = -ij (garbage)

-ate = -it or -at (mandate)

-ey = -i (donkey)

-ous = -us (furious)

-sm = -zm (atheism, spasm)

-tion = -shon (salvation)

-ture = -cher as well as -tūr, esp. in common words.

INFLEXION

The rules assumed, exceptions to which are noted in a bracket placed after a word's grammatical description, are given below. The term 'sibilants' stands for words ending in -s, -x, -z, -sh or soft -ch, '-o wds' for all that end in -o, '-e wds' for all that end in mute -e, and '-y wds' for all that end in -y not preceded by a vowel (e.g. *deny, puppy*, but not *bray, donkey*).

1. Plural of nouns. Sibilants add -es (*boxes, porches*); -y wds change -y into -ies (*puppies*); the plural of -o wds is usually stated thus, **photo** n. (pl. ~s); other nouns add -s (*books*).

2. Possessive of nouns. Singular nouns take apostrophe, s (*man's, James's*); plurals, if they do not end in s, form the possessive by the same rule (*men's, geese's*), but, if they end in s, take an apostrophe only (*boys'*).

potato n. (pl. ~es); other nouns add -s (*books*).

PRONUNCIATION

3. **Comparative and superlative of adjectives and adverbs. In monosyllables and some disyllables** (e.g. those in -y add -er and -est (*bolder*), -e wds dropping the -e (*braver*), and disyllables in -y having -ier and -iest (*happier, luckiest*); in other cases prefix *more* and *most* (*more beautiful, most splendid*). Monosyllables double a final single consonant (except x) if preceded by a single vowel (*grimmer*). This may be stated in the dictionary.

4. **Third person singular present of verbs.** Sibilants and -o wds add -es (*pushes, goes*); -y wds change -y into -ies (*cries*); other verbs add -s (*sings*).

5. **Past and p.p. of verbs.** -e wds add -d (*moved*); -y wds change -y into -ied (*relied*); other verbs add -ed (*trusted, vetoed*); if the final consonant is doubled, it is stated in the dictionary, thus: **glut** v.t. (-tt-), **revel** v.i. & t. (-ll-.).

6. **Participle of verbs.** All verbs add -ing (*fishing*), -e wds dropping the -e (*dancing*); monosyllables double a final single consonant (except x) if preceded by a single vowel (*grabbing*).

7. **Archaic 2nd and 3rd singular of verbs.** The forms in -(e)st and -(e)th, being archaic, need only be mentioned, without rules; -(e)st is 2nd sing. present and past, -(e)th is 3rd sing. present; examples are *playest, dost, hear'st, madest, wouldst, saith, goeth.*

ABBREVIATIONS USED IN THE DICTIONARY

(For list of general abbreviations see Appendix I)

a., aa., adjective(s)
abbr./eviation etc.
abl./ative
abs./olute
acc., according, accusative
act./ive
adj./ective etc.
adjj., adjectives
adv./erb etc.
advv., adverbs
aeron./autics etc.
aesthet./ics etc.
AF, Anglo-French
Afr./ica(n)
alch./emy etc.
alg./ebra etc.
allus./ive etc.
alw./ays
Amer./ica(n)
anal./ogy etc.
anat./omy etc.
Anglo-Ind./ian
anion./ymous etc.
ant./iquities
anthrop./ology etc.
ap./pendix
app./arently
Arab./ic
Aram./aic
arbitr./ary
arch./aic
archaeol./ogy etc.
archit./ecture etc.
arith./metic etc.
Ass./yrian
assim./ilated etc.
assoc./iated etc.
astrol./ogy etc.
astron./omy etc.

attrib./utive etc.
augment./ative etc.
Austral./ia(n)

b./orn
back form./ation
Bibl./ical etc.
bibliog./raphy etc.
bill./iards
biog./raphy etc.
biol./ogy etc.
Boh./emian
bot./any etc.
Braz./il(ian)
Bret./on
Brit./ish
Bulg./aria(n)
Burm./ese
Byz./antine

c./entury
c./*irca*
cc., centuries
Celt./ic
cf., compare
chem./istry etc.
Chin./ese
chronol./ogy etc.
cinemat./ography etc.
cl./assical
cogn./ate
collect./ive(ly)
colloq./uial etc.
com./mon
comb./ination etc.
commerc./ial etc.
comp., compar./ative
compd., compound
compl./ement
compp., compounds

com./mon -Teut./onto
con./ics
conch./ology etc.
confus./ion
conj... conjunction, con-
    jugation
conn./ect. etc.
constr./uction etc.
contempt./uous etc.
contr./action etc.
cop./ulative
Copt./ic
Corn./ish
correl./ative etc.
corresp./onding etc.
corrupt./ion
cp., compare
crick./et
cryst./allography
cu., cub./ic, cubic
Cym./ric

d./ied
Da./nish
dat./ive
demonstr./ative
dent./istry
deriv./ative etc.
derog./atory etc.
dial./ect etc.
dict./ionary
diff./erent
different./iate etc.
dim./inutive etc.
dimm., diminutives
diplom./acy
dissim./ilate etc.
dist./inct etc.
distrib./utive etc.

dsyl./lable etc.
Dor./ic
Du./tch
dub./ious
dynam./ics etc.

E, English
eccl./esiastical etc.
EFris., East Frisian
Egyptol./ogy
E. Ind., East Indian
electr./icity etc.
ellipt./ical etc.
embryol./ogy
engin./eering etc.
Engl., England, English
entom./ology etc.
erron./eous(ly)
eschat./ology etc.
esp./ecial(ly)
eth./ics etc.
ethnol./ogy etc.
etym./ology etc.
euphem./ism etc.
Eur./ope(an)
ex./ample
exagg./eration etc.
exc./ept
exch./ange
excl., exclamation etc., ex-
    clusive etc.
excl., exclamations
expl./ain etc.
expr./essing etc.
exx., examples

F, French
f./rom
facet./ious etc.
fam./iliar etc.
fem./inine etc.
fenc./ing
fig./urative etc.
Fl./emish
foll./owing (word)
footb./all
fortif./ication
Fr./ench
Frank./ish
freq./uent(ly)
frequent./ative(ly)
Fris./ian
ft, foot, feet
fut./ure

G, German
Gael./ic
gal./lon(s)
gen., general etc., genitive
geog./raphy etc.
geol./ogy etc.
geom./etry etc.
Gk, Greek
Goth./ic
gr., gram./mar etc.
gym./nastics etc.

Heb./rew
her./aldry etc.
Hind., Hindi, Hindustani
hist./orical etc., history
hort./iculture etc.
Hung./arian, -ary
hydrost./atics etc.

i, intransitive
Icel./andic
illit./erate etc.
imit./ative etc.

imper., imperat./ive
imperf./ect
impers./onal
improp./er(ly)
impv./ive
incl./uding, -usive
Ind./ia(n)
Ind., indicative, indirect
indecl./inable
inf./initive
infl./uence etc.
instr./umental (case)
int./erjection
interrog./ative(ly)
intr./ansitive
Ir./ish
iron./ical(ly)
irreg./ular(ly)
It., Ital./ian
ital./ics

Jam./aica(n)
Jap./an(ese)
Jav./anese
Jew./ish
joc./ose, -ular(ly)

L, Latin
lang./uage
Lat., in
lexicog./raphy etc.
LG, Low German
lit./eral(ly)
Lith./uania(n)
LL, late Latin
log./ic etc.

M, middle (with languages)
magn./etism etc.
manuf./acture etc.
masc./uline
math./ematics etc.
MDu., middle Dutch
ME, middle English (1200-
    1500)
mech./anics etc.
med./icine etc.
med.L, medieval Latin
metaph./or etc.
metaphys./ics etc.
metath./esis etc.
meteor./ology etc.
Mex./ican
MHG, middle high German
mil./itary etc.
min./eralogy etc.
MIt., middle Italian
MLG, middle low German
mod./ern
monosyl./labic etc.
morphol./ogy etc.
MSw., middle Swedish
myth./ology etc.

N., noun
N. Amer., North American
nat. hist., natural history
nat. phil., natural philo-
    sophy
naut./ical etc.
nav./al etc.
neg./ative(ly)
neut./er
NF, North Frisian

nn., nouns
nom., -inative
Norm./an
north./ern
Norw./egian, -ay
N.T., New Testament
num./eral

O, old (with languages)
obj./ect etc.
obl./ique
obs./olete
obsolesc./ent
obstet./rics etc.
occas./ional(ly)
ODa., old Danish
OE, old English
OF, old French
OFris., old Frisian
OHG, old high German
OIr., old Irish
OLG, old low German
ON, old Norse
ONF, old northern French
onomat./opoeic etc.
opp., (as) opposed (to)
OPr., old Provençal
opt., optative, optics etc.
ord./inary
ornith./ology etc.
OS, old Saxon
OSl(av)., old Slavonic
OSp., old Spanish
O.T., Old Testament
OTeut., old Teutonic

p./age
paint./ing
Pal./estine
palaeog./raphy etc.
palaeont./ology etc.
parenth./etic etc.
Parl./iament(ary)
part., (present) participle
partic./iple
pass./ive(ly)
path./ology etc.
pedant./ic(ally)
perf./ect (tense)
perh./aps
Pers./ia(n)
pers./on(al)
pert./aining
Peruv./ian
Pg., Portuguese
pharm./acy etc.
philol./ogy etc.
philos./ophy etc.
Phoen./icia(n)
phon., phonet./ics etc.
phonol./ogy etc.
photog./raphy etc.
phr./ase
phren./ology etc.
phrs., phrases
phys./ics etc.
physiol./ogy etc.
pl./ural
plup./erfect
poet./ical etc.
Pol./ish, -and
pol./itics etc.
pol. econ., political eco-
    nomy
polit./ics etc.
pop./ular etc.

Port./uguese
poss./essive
P.p., past or passive participle
pp., pages
Pr./ovençal
pr./onounced etc.
prec., (the) preceding (word)
pred./icate etc.
pref./ix
prep./osition
pres./ent (tense)
pret./erite
print./ing
priv./ative
prob./able etc.
Pron., pronoun etc., pronounced etc.
pronunc./iation
prop./er(ly)
pros./ody etc.
Prov./ençal
prov., proverb etc., provincial etc.
psych./ology etc.
psycho-an./alysis
R.-C., Roman Catholic
redupl./icated etc.
ref./erence
refash./ioned etc.
refl./exive(ly)
rel./ative
repr./esent etc.
rhet./oric etc.
Rom., Roman, Romance
Rom./an Ant./iquities
Rom./an Cath./olic
Rom./an Hist./ory
Russ./ia(n)

s./ingular
S. Afr., South Africa(n)
Sax./on
sb., substantive
Sc., Scotch, Scots, Scottish
Scand./inavia(n)
schol./astic
sci./ence etc.
Scot., Scotland, Scottish
sculp./ture
Sem./itic
Serb./ian
Serv./ian
sing./ular
Skr., Sanskrit
sl./ang
Slav./onic
sociol./ogy etc.
Sp./anish
spec./ial(ly)
spirit./ualism etc.
sport./ing etc.
st./em
stat./ics etc.
subj., subject etc., subjunctive
subst./antive
suf./fix
sup., superl./ative
surg./ery etc.
surv./eying etc.
Sw./edish
syn./onym

t., transitive
tech./nical(ly)
teleg./raphy etc.
term./ination
Teut./on(ic)
theat./rical etc.

theol./ogy etc.
theos./ophy etc.
therm./ometry etc.
thr./ough
trans./itive etc.
transf., in transferred sense
transl./ation etc.
translit./eration etc.
trig./onometry etc.
Turk./ish, -ey
typ./ography etc.
ult./imate(ly)
unexpl./ained
U.S., United States
usu./al(ly)
v./erb
var., variant, various
v. aux., verb auxiliary
vb., verb
vbl., verbal
v.i., verb intransitive
voc./ative
v.refl., verb reflexive
v.t., verb transitive
vulg./ar(ly)
vv., verbs
W., Welsh
w./ith
W. Afr., West Africa(n)
wd., word
wds., words
W.Flem., West Flemish
W.Fris., West Frisian
WG, West German
W.Ind., West Indian, -ies
yd., yard
yr(s), year(s)
zoogeog./raphy etc.
zool./ogy etc.

P = proprietary term.
+, sign affixed to all forms not recorded but merely inferred, with the exception of those called Aryan or OTeut. (all of which are inferential).
* = (orig. or chiefly) U.S.
|| = not U.S.

NOTE. The addition of etc. to the completion of an abbreviation means that it may be used not only for the exact form given, but for connected words or phrases; e.g. bot./any etc. means botany, botanical, botanically, in botany; adv./erb etc. means adverb, adverbial, adverbially; transl./ation etc. means translated as well as translation. Abbreviations given in the list with initial capital have always the capital in use; but those given with initial small letter have either form according to circumstances.

ENGLISH DICTIONARY

A, letter (pl. **Æs**, **A's**, **Aes**). (Mus.) note, & the corresponding scale. (In argument) first Imaginary person or case. (Alg.) first known quantity. (Naut.) **A1** (**a'wŭn**), first-class ship in Lloyd's register; excellent, best. (colloq.) **A1** POPULATION). (Naut.) **Æ**, third-class ship at Lloyd's.

a¹, an, (a, an; emphatic, ā, an) adj. (sometimes called indefinite article. Before all consonants called silent *h*, use of a history, a historian, though some still write *an hour*; before all vowels except *eu*, *ü*, use *an*; *an ulcer*, but *a unit*, *a eulogy*; also *a one*. Placed after *many*, *such*, *what*, or any adj. preceded by *how*, *so*, *too*. Used with apparent plurals of number, a *dozen men* = a dozen of men; also with pl. adj. *few*, *good many*, *great many*). (Unemphatic substitute for) one, some, any; one like (*a Daniel*); (after all of *many of*, etc.) the same (all of a size); (distrib.) each (*£40 a year*, where a is orig. = foll.). [weakening of OE *ān* ONE]

a², prep. On to, towards, into, in. Mostly now written as pref., or oftener omitted than expressed, or confused w. **a¹**. On: *abed, afoot*. To: *ashore*. Towards: *aback, after, aside*. Into: *apart, asunder*. In: *now-a-days, twice a day*; w. vbl nouns passively, *a-building*, actively *was (a-) fighting*, and esp. w. *go*, *set*, as *he went a begging*, *they set the bells a ringing*. [weakening of OE prep. *an*, *on*]

a-, pref. f. various sources. **1.** OE *ar-* or *a-*, away, on, up, out, and so to express intensity, as *arise*; cf. **2.** OE *an*, on prep.; see prec. **3.** OE of prep., as *akin*. **4.** L *ad-* to, either directly, as *aspect*, or through F *a-* as *achieve*; many words derived in the latter way have been later assimilated to L spelling, as *ad(d)ress, at(t)grieve*. **5.** L *a, ab,* from; directly, as *avert*, or through F *a-*, as *abridge*; again occas. assimilated to L spelling, as *a(b)stain*. **6.** L *ex-* out, utterly, through AF *a-*. F. OF *e-, es-*, as *amend*. **7.** Gk *a-, an-*, not, without; directly as amorphous through L, as *acatalectic*, or through L & F, as *adamant*; compounded chiefly w. Gk words, but also w. others, as *a-moral*. [In *a*, suf. **1.** Nn. f. Gk, L & Rom. fem. sing. as *idea* (Gk), *arena* (L), *piazza* (It.), *duenna* (Sp.), esp. Nat. Hist. terms, ancient or latinized mod. (*hyena, dahlia*) Geogr. names (*Africa*), & names of women, ancient or latinized mod. (*Lydia, Hilda*) **2.** Gk & L neut. pl. nouns (*genera, pheno-mena*), esp. names, often f. mod.L, of classes of animals (*mammalia*).

aard-vark (**ärd' värk**), n. S.-African quad- ruped between armadillos & ant-eaters, f. Du. *aarde* earth + *vark* pig; cf. OE *fearh* & L *porcus* pig]

aard-wolf (**ärd' wŏŏlf**), n. S.-African carnivore between hyenas & civets, [see prec.]

Aar'on, (âr-), n. Kinds of plant, esp. **Great St John's wort.** [ref. to Ps. cxxxiii. 2]

Aar'on's rŏd (âr-), n. Kinds of plant, esp. **Great Mullein & Golden Rod.** [ref. to Num. xvii. 8]

aasvogel (**äh'sfōgl**), n. S.-Afr. vulture. [S.-A. Du. (*aas* carrion + *vogel* bird)]

ab-, pref. Away, from, off, apart. [f. L *ab*, cf. Gk *apo*, E *of, off*, G *ab-*. In L reduced to *a-* before *p, m, v*; changed to *au-* before *f*, & to *abs-* before *c, t*; in F often reduced to *a-*]

ā'ba, abaya (abä'ya), nn. Sack-like outer garment worn by Arabs. [Arab.]

abāck', adv. Backwards; (Naut.) of square sails pressed against mast by head wind; *taken ~*, of ship w. sails in that state, (fig.) surprised. [A² + BACK¹]

ăb'acus, n. (pl. -*ci*, pr. -sī). **1.** Calculating frame w. balls sliding on wires, used before adoption of the nine figures & zero, & still in China etc., & in elementary teaching. **2.** (Archit.) upper member, often square flat slab, of capital, supporting architrave. [L *abacus* f. Gk *abax -akos*]

Abad'don, n. Hell; the devil (*Rev.* ix. 11). [Heb. word, destruction (*abad* he perished)]

abaft' (-ah-), adv. & prep. (naut.) In stern half of ship; nearer the stern than aft of. [A² + *baft* = OE *be* by + OE *æftan* adv. behind]

*abalō'ne, n. Californian edible mollusc with ear-shaped shell lined with mother-of-pearl, sea-ear. [Sp., etym. dub.]

abăn'don¹, v.t. Give up to another's control or mercy; yield oneself completely to a passion or impulse; give up (a possession or habit); forsake (a person, post). [f. OF *abandoner* (à to + *bandon* jurisdiction, *mettre à bandon* meaning to put a person under any one's, including his own, control)]

abăn'don² (or as F, see Ap.), n. Careless freedom, letting oneself go. [F; see prec.]

abăn'doned (-ond), a. Profligate. [p.p. of ABANDON¹]

abăn'doned, n. Giving up or for-saking; being forsaken; self-surrender; carelessfreedom of manner, impulsiveness. [f. F *abandonnement* (ABANDON¹, -MENT)]

abáse, v.t. Lower, humiliate, make base. Hence ~MENT (-sən) n. [f. OF *abaisser* (now *abaisser*) (à to + *baisser* to lower f. LL *bassare* f. *bassus* short)]

abásh', v.t. Put out of countenance; (chiefly in pass.) be confounded. Hence ~MENT n. [f. OF *esbaïr* astound f. es- = ᴀ- (6) + *baïr* cry bah!; see -ISH² & cf. *punch* = punish]

abásk', adv. In warm light. [A² + BASK]

abáte', v.t. & i. 1. Diminish (t. & i.). 2. Do away with (nuisance); blunt (edge); lower (price); deduct (specified or unspecified part of price); mitigate (violence); weaken (energy). 3. (In law) quash (writ or action). 4. (Of flood or epidemic) grow less. So ~MENT (-tm-) n. [f. OF *abatre* (à to + *batre* f. LL *batere* f. L *batuere* beat)]

áb'atis, abátt'is, n. Defence made of felled trees w. boughs pointing outwards. Hence ab'atisᴅ² (-st) a. [F *abatis*, OF *abateïs* f. LL †*abateïcius* of throwing down; cf. OF *abatre*, see ABATE]

abattoir (see Ap.), n. Public slaughter-house. [F]

ább', n. Woof. [A-(1) + WEB]

Abb'a (ǎ-), n. Father. Used w. *Father* in invoking God (*Mark* xiv. 36). [Aram.]

ább'acy, n. Office, jurisdiction, or tenure, of an abbot. [earlier *abbatie* (see -CY) f. LL *abbatia* (abbat- nom. -as ABBOT)]

abb'átial (-shəl), a. Of an abbey, abbot, or abbess. [F, f. L *abbatialis* (*abbatia* ABBACY, -AL)]

abbé (ǎb'ā), n. Frenchman (orig. abbot) entitled to wear ecclesiastical dress, esp. without official duties. [F, f. L *abbatem* nom. -as ABBOT]

ább'ess, n. Lady superior of a nunnery. [OF *abaesse* (Pr. *abadessa*) f. LL *abbatissa* (abbat- ABBOT)]

ább'ey, n. (pl. ~s). Building(s) occupied by the monks or nuns under an abbot or abbess; the monks or nuns as a body; a church or house that was once an ~ or part of it (the A~, Westminster A~). [f. OF *abaïe*, Pr. *abadia*, f. LL *abbatia* ABBACY]

ább'ot, n. Head of abbey of monks; A~ of Misrule or of Unreason, leader in medieval burlesque festivities. Hence ~CY, ~SHIP, nn. [OE *abbod*, f. L f. Gk *abbas* -at- (ABBA)]

abbréviate¹, a. Relatively short (esp. in nat. hist.). [f. L *abbreviatus* p.p. of *abbreviare* shorten (ab off or ad to + *brevis* short)]

abbrévi'āte², v.t. Make short (chiefly now of writing part of word for whole, but also of visit, story, etc.). Hence ~ᴧᵀᴵᴼᴺ n. [f. prec.; see -ᴀᵀᴇ³]

A B C, n. The alphabet; rudiments of any subject; || alphabetical railway guide.

Ab'derite (ā-), n. The ~, Democritus (see DEMOCRITEAN). [Gk *Abdērités* (*Abdēra*, a town, -ITE¹)]

àb'dicāte, v.t. Renounce formally or by default (a power, office, right; also abs, esp. of the crown). Hence ~ᵀᴵᴼᴺ (n. also abs, ~ᴀᵀᴇᴅ) (2) a. [f. L ABdicare declare), -ᴀᵀᴇ³]

àbdóm'ēn (or ǎb'dó-), n. 1. (Anat.) belly, including stomach, bowels, & other nutritive organs. 2. (Zool.) hinder part of insects, spiders, etc. [L, etym. dub.]

abdóm'inal, a. Of the abdomen in either sense; (of fish) having the ventral fins under the belly. [f. abdomin- stem of prec. + -ᴀʟ]

àbdóm'inous, a. Corpulent. [as prec. + -ous]

àbdū'cent, a. (anat.). Drawing away (of muscles that open or pull back the part they are fixed to). [f. L *abducent-* part. st. of ABducere duct- draw)]

abdūct', v.t. Kidnap; take away (esp. a woman) by force or fraud; draw (limb etc.) from its natural position. [f. L abduct- see prec.]

abdūc'tion, n. Illegal carrying off, esp. of a child, ward; forcible carrying off of any one, as of a voter; withdrawal of limb from natural position; shrinking of sides of a wound, causing it to gape; syllogism of which the minor premiss, and therefore the conclusion, is only probable. [f. L *abductio* (prec., -ION)]

abdūc'tor, n. Person who abducts another; (also ~muscle) muscle that abducts a limb. [as ABDUCT + -OR²]

abeam', adv. (naut.). On a line at right angles to the ship's length; ~ of us, opposite our centre, abreast. [A² + BEAM¹]

abecedār'ian (ābisē'-), a. & n. 1. Arranged alphabetically, as the 119th Psalm; elementary, ignorant. 2. n. Pupil learning the alphabet (common in U.S.). [f. med. L *abecedarium* alphabet (ABCD + -ARIUM) + -AN]

abēd', adv. In bed. [A² + BED¹]

abele (ābēl', ā'bl), n. The white poplar. [f. Du. *abeel* f. OF *abel* earlier *aubel* f. LL *albellus* dim. of *albus* white]

â'belmŏsk, n. Malvaceous N.-Afr. evergreen shrub yielding musk-seeds. [ult. f. Arab. *habbu-'l-misk* grain of musk]

Aberdeen' (ǎ-), n. ~ (terrier), rough-haired Scotch terrier. [Aberdeen in Scotland]

äberdēvine', n. Birdfancier's name for the siskin. [?]

Aberdón'ian (ǎ-), a. & n. (Inhabitant, native) of Aberdeen. [-IAN]

àbergglaube (ah'berglaube), n. Excessive belief, superstition. [G]

Ab'ernĕthy (á-), n. Hard biscuit flavoured with caraway seeds. [person]

abē'rrjant (ǎ-), n. ~ (terrier). Straying from moral standard; (in nat. hist.) diverging from normal type. Hence ~ANCE, ~ANCY, nn. [f. L *aberrant-* part. st. of AB(errare stray)]

àberrā'tion, n. 1. A straying from the path, lit. & fig.; breaking of rules; moral slip; intellectual deficiency; deviation from type. 2. (Optics) non-convergence

of rays to one focus. **3.** (Aston.) displacement of heavenly body's true position to observer. [f. L *observātio*; see prec., -ATION]

abét', v.t. (-tt-). Countenance or assist (offence or offender; esp. *aid & ~*). Hence ~MENT, ~TER¹, ~T'OR¹ nn. *~ter* is the legal & the commoner general form. [f. OF *abeter* (à to + *beter* BAIT¹)]

do ĕa'trĕ, adv. From outside. [LL]

abey'ance (-bā-), n. State of suspension, dormant condition liable to revival, (of rights etc.; mostly in phr. *be in* or *fall into ~*). [f. OF *abeance* (à to + *beer* = L. *hiāre* gape)]

abhŏr', v.t. (-rr-). Regard with disgust & hatred. [f. L ABhorrēre shudder)]

abhŏ'rrence, n. Detestation; detested thing (*flattery is my ~*). [foll. -ENCE]

abhŏ'rrent, a. Inspiring disgust, hateful, inconsistent (*from*); (arch.) feeling disgust (*of*), as *the Greeks were ~ of excess*. [f. L *abhorrent*-part. st. see ABHOR]

abhŏ'rrer, n. (hist.). Nickname of those who signed addresses to Charles II in 1680. [ABHOR + -ER¹]

abī'dance, n. Continuance, dwelling (*in*), abiding (*by* rules, etc.). [ABIDE + -ANCE]

abīde', 1. Remain over; continue; dwell (~*d*). **1.** Remain over; continue; dwell (arch.); stand firm; (with *by*) remain faithful to, act upon (terms). **2.** Watt for; encounter, sustain; submit to, suffer; (negatively as *I cannot, who can, ~*) put up with (noun or infinitive). [OE *ābīdan* f. A-(1) + *bīdan* BIDE]

abī'ding, a. Permanent. Hence ~LY² adv. [part. of ABIDE]

ăbiĕt-, stem of several chemical terms. Of resin, or fir. [L *abiĕt*- noun. *abies* fir-tree]

ăb'igail, n. Lady's-maid. [character in Beaumont & Fletcher's *Scornful Lady*, perh. w. ref. to 1 Sam. XXV. 24-31]

abi'lity, n. Sufficient power, capacity (to do something); legal competency (to act); financial competency to meet a demand; cleverness, mental faculty, (general in sing., special in pl.). [f. OF *ablete* f. L *habilitas* f. *habilis* deft; in F & E it was later corrected into *habilité, hability*, whence the mod. form]

db imĭ'tio, adv. From the beginning. [L]

ăb iogĕn'esis, n. Spontaneous generation. [Allied words] **ăb'iogĕnĕt'ic** a. connected w. the doctrine; **ăb'iogĕnĕt-**ICALLY adv., by spont. gen. or according to the doctrine; **ăbiō'gĕnist** (2) n., one who believes in it; **ăbiō'gĕnous** a., so produced; **ăbiō'gĕny¹** n., = abiogenesis. [f. Gk *abios* f. A-(7) + *bios* life + GENESIS]

ăb'jĕct, a. & n. **1.** Brought low, miserable, craven, degraded, despicable. **2.** n. (Bibl. & arch.) a person of the meanest condition. Hence ~LY² adv., ~NESS n. [f. L *abiectus* p.p. of ABJicere = *jacĕre* throw)]

abjĕc'tion, n. Abasement, low estate. [F, f. L *abjectionem* (ABJECT, -ION)]

ăbjurā'tion (-joor-), n. Action or form of renunciation on oath, in all senses of ABJURE (in hist. esp. of the Stuart claim). [f. L *abjuratio* (ABJURE, -ATION)]

abjure' (-joor), v.t. Renounce on oath (an opinion, heresy, cause, claim, or claimant); swear perpetual absence from (one's country etc.). [f. F *abjurer* f. L ABjurare swear]

ăblactā'tion, n. Weaning from the mother. [f. L ABlactatio f. *lactare* suckle f. *lact*- noun. *lac* milk]

ablā'tion, n. Removal (esp. in surgery, of any part of body); (Geol.) waste of a glacier or rock by melting or water action. [f. L *ablatio* f. ABlat- p.p. st. of *ferre* carry]

āb'lative, a. & n. The case in Latin nouns that expresses source, agent, cause, instrument, of action = *from* or *by* with the noun (usu. noun); adj. with *case, sense*, etc., ~ ABSOLUTE, a construction of noun & participle in L Gram. giving time or circumstances. [F *ablatif* f. L *ablativus* brought from (ablat- see prec.]

āb'laut (-ow-), n. Vowel changes in the parent Indo-European language, arising out of differences of accent & stress, & surviving e.g. in *drive, drove, driven*. [G]

ăblāze', adv. & pred. a. On fire; glittering; excited. [A² + BLAZE]

ā'ble, a. Talented, clever; competent, having the means or power (*to*), esp. w. parts of *be* to supply the deficiencies of *can*; legally qualified; ~*-bodied seaman* (abbr. A.B.), of special class. Hence **āb'ly¹** adv. [f. OF *hable, able*, (now *habile*) f. L *habilis* handy (*habere* to hold)]

-able, suf. f. F -able f. L -a- of first conjug. +-bilis- see -BLE. In F extended to vbs of all conjug. In E now appended even to native vbs as *bearable*, nouns as *clubbable*, & phrase vbs as *get-at-able*; prob. f. confusion w. the unrelated adj. *able*. (Meaning) able to (*comfortable*), able to be (*eatable*), fit for (*salable*).

‖ āb'lĕt, āb'len, n. Name for the freshwater fish bleak. [F *ablette* f. L.L *abula*]

ăb'lings, āb'lins (-z), adv. (Sc. & north.) Possibly, perhaps. [ABLE + -LINGS]

ăblush', adv. & pred. a. Blushing. [A² + BLUSH]

ablū'tion (-loo-), n. (usu. pl.). Ceremonial washing of person, hands, or sacred vessels; ordinary personal washing; (sing.) water in which things have been washed, esp. in Catholic Ritual. Hence ~ARY¹ a. [f. L ABlutio f. *luere lut*- wash, -ION]

ăb'negāte, v.t. Deny oneself (something), renounce (a right or belief). [f. L ABnegare deny) -ATE³]

ăbnegā'tion, n. Denial; rejection (of doctrine); self-sacrifice (now oftener self-~). [f. L *abnegatio* (prec., -ATION)]

abnorm'al, a. Exceptional, irregular, deviating from type. Hence **abnorm'ITY** n., the quality or an instance of it, **~LY²** adv. [earlier & F *anormal* f. med. L *anomalus* corrupted f. Gk *anómalos* ANOMALOUS; but now regarded as f. L *abnormis*, see foll.]

abnorm'ITY. [f. L *abnormitas* f. AB(*normis* f. *norma* rule) see -TY]

aboard' (-ôrd), adv. & prep. On or into a ship (*ship* either expressed or omitted); alongside, near, esp. *close* or *hard~*. *Lay* (another ship) *~*, place one's own alongside of her to fight; *fall ~*, fall foul of (another ship). [A² +BOARD]

abode', n. Dwelling-place, house; stay, habit of dwelling, as in *make one's ~*. [vbl n. of ABIDE; cf. *ride, rode, road*]

aboil', adv. & pred. a. A-boiling, boiling. [A² +BOIL²]

abol'ish, v.t. Do away with (customs, institutions). Hence **~ABLE** a., **~ER¹**, **~MENT**, nn. [f. F *abolir* (-ISH²) f. L *abolescere* inceptive of *abolēre* become effete, destroy, AB-+*olēre* grow]

aboli'tion, n. Doing, being done, away with. In the 18th & 19th cc. w. ref. to negro slavery & the movement against it, whence also **~ISM**(3), **~IST**(2), (-shon-), nn. [f. L *abolitio* (prec., -ION)]

abom'inable, a. Detestable, odious, morally or physically loathsome; (by conscious exaggeration) unpleasant. Hence **~leNESS**, **~LY²** adv., [F (ab-, abh.), f. L *abominabilis* f. AB(*ominari* f. *omen*) deprecate; the older spelling was regularly *abh-*, due to confusion w. *homo*, & the violence of the meaning (*inhuman* instead of *ill-omened*) results from the mistake]

abom'inate, v.t. Loathe; (by exaggeration) dislike. [f. L *abominat-*; see prec.] **abom'inate²**, a. (poet.). Abominated. [f. L *abominatus* p.p., see ABOMINABLE]

abomina'tion, n. Loathing; odious or degrading habit or act; an object of disgust (*to*). [F (ABOMINATE¹, -ATION)]

aborig'inal, a. & n. 1. Indigenous, existing in a land at the dawn of history, or before arrival of colonists (of races & natural objects). 2. n. (pl. *~s*, but *aborigines* commoner) inhabitant of (rarely) native. Hence **aborig'inalLY²** adv., **~LY²** adv. [f. L *ab+origin-* nom. *origo* origin + -AL]

aborig'ines (-z), n. pl. (*aboriginal* usual for sing.; also the indefensible form *aborigine*, & rarely *aboriginia* or *-en*). First inhabitants, or those found in possession by colonists (also of native plants & animals). [L, f. phr. *ab origine* from the beginning]

abort', v.i. Miscarry, have premature delivery of a child; (Biol.) become sterile, remain undeveloped, shrink away, (of plants & animals—the race, the individual, or part of the body). Hence **~IFA'CIENT** (-àshent) a. & n., (drug or other agent) causing abortion. [f. L *abort-*, p.p. st. of AB(*orīrī* be born)]

abort'ed, a. Untimely born, undeveloped, rudimentary (*thorns are ~ branches*). [ABORT+-ED¹(2)]

abort'ion, n. Miscarriage of birth; the procuring of this, whence **~IST** (1) (-shon-) n.; arrested development of any organ; a dwarfed or mis-shapen creature; failure of a project or action. [f. L *abortio* (ABORT, -ION)]

abort'ive, a. Premature (birth etc.); fruitless, unsuccessful; rudimentary (organ etc.), arrested in development. Hence **~LY²** (-vi-) adv., **~NESS** (-vri-) n. [f. L *abortivus* (ABORT, -IVE)]

abou'lia (-ow-), **abū'lia**, n. Loss of will-power (as mental disorder). [f. Gk *a-* not +*boulomai* I will]

abound', v.i. 1. (Orig.) overflow, either of vessel or of liquid. 2. Be plentiful; be rich (*in*); teem or be infested (*with*). [f. OF *abunder, abonder, habonder*, f. L AB(*undare*, f. *unda* wave); the *h-* common in older F & E is due to confusion w. L *habēre* have]

about', adv. & prep. All round from outside, as *compass is ~*. *He is ~ my path, beat ~ the bush*; all round from a centre, *~ look* or *lay ~ you*; somewhere round, as *look ~, hang ~* (the door), *the fields ~ Oxford, people* or *objects ~ us, have not a penny ~ me*; here and there (in, or abs.), as *smallpox is ~, move* or *order ~, he put the tale ~*; *I was much put ~* (distracted), *out & ~*, restored to normal activity (after convalescence), *dotted ~ the fields, man ~ town*; near in number, scale, degree, etc., as *~ half, fifty, right, tired, midnight, my size* (occas. *much ~*); facing round, as *right~ turn* (now *~ turn!* as mil. word of command), *the wrong way ~, put* (the ship) or *go ~*; round a party, as *take turns ~, read verse ~*; occupied with, as *~ my father's business, send ~ his business, what are you ~?, go ~ to do, am ~ to do* (so all fut. participles); in connexion with, as *quarrels ~ trade, something wrong ~ it*; circuitously, as *he went a long way ~, I brought it ~, it came ~*. [OE *on-būtan* f. *on*+*būtan* without (*be* by+locative of *ūtan* out): orig. meaning is therefore *on the outside (of)*]

about'², v.t. Change the course of (ship) to the other tack. [f. ABOUT adv.]

about'-sledge, n. Largest hammer used by smiths.

above' (-ŭv), adv. & prep. 1. adv. At a higher point (w. spec. meaning acc. to context); overhead, on high; up stream, upstairs; in heaven; on the upper side; earlier in a book or article (as *was remarked ~*; *the ~-cited passages*; *the ~*); in addition (*over & ~*). 2. prep. Over, on the top of, higher than (*~ par*; *oneself* (sl.), in unusual spirits etc.; *can't get ~ C*—in music), more than (*~*

a hundred), up stream from, projecting from (head ~ water; heard ~ the tumult); earlier in hist. than (not traced ~ third century), out of reach of (~ criticism, measure, my understanding), too great or good for (~ meanness, one's station), more important than (~ all), of higher rank than. Above is also treated as a noun in from above. [f. A² + OE bufan (be by + ufan locative of uf; cf. G auf up)]

above´-board, adv. & pred. a. Undisguisedly; fair, open. [metaph. f. cards]

āb ŏv´ō, adv. (Relating tediously) from the very beginning. [L; Hor. A.P. 147]

ăbracadăb´ra, n. Spell, magic formula; gibberish. Cabbalistic word supposed when written triangularly, & worn, to cure agues, etc. [L, etym. dub.]

ăbrāde´, v.t. Scrape off, injure, (skin etc.) by violent rubbing. [f. L ABradere rās- scrape)]

Ābrahám-mǎn(ā-), n. (hist.). Wandering beggar of the 16th C.; either a lunatic or feigning lunacy; hence to sham Abram, to feign illness or madness. [Luke xvi]

ăbrănc´hial(-ngk-), **ăbrănc´hiate**(-ngk-), aa. Without gills. [A-(7) + Gk braghhia gills + -AL & -ATE²]

ăbrā´sion (-zhn), n. Scraping off (of skin etc.); the wounded place that results. So **ăbrā´sive** a. & n. (substance) capable of rubbing or grinding down, tending to graze the skin. [f. L abrasio ABRADE, -ION]

ăbreast´(-rĕst), adv. On a level & facing the same way; keeping up, not behind, (of or with progress, thought, etc., or as prep., ~ the times). [A² + BREAST¹]

ăbridge´, v.t. Shorten (interview etc.); condense or epitomize (book etc.); curtail (liberty; of limbs etc., only now w. playful archaism); deprive (person of). [f. OF abreger, abreger, f. L abbreviare ABBRE-VIATE]

ăbridge´ment, -gment, (-jm-), n. Short-ening (of time or labour), curtailment (of rights); epitome, abstract. [f. OF abrege-ment f. abreger (prec.,-MENT)]

ăbroach´, adv. & pred. a. Pierced, so as to let the liquor run (of casks). [A² + BROACH²]

ăbroad´(-rawd), adv. Broadly, widely, in different directions; in motion (there is a rumour ~; the schoolmaster is ~, educa-tion is now becoming generally acces-sible); out of doors, in or to foreign lands; in error (all ~). Also treated as a noun in from ~. [A² + BROAD a.; cf. along, at large]

ăb´rogāte, v.t. Repeal, cancel, (law or custom). So **ăbrogā´tion** n. [f. L abs. adj. abrogate f. L abrogatus p.p. of ABrogare propose law]

ăbrŭpt´, a. Sudden, hasty, disconnected; steep, precipitous; (Bot.) truncated; sud-denly cropping out (of geol. strata),

Hence ~LY² adv., ~NESS n. [f. L abruptus p.p. of ABrumpere break)]

ăbrŭp´tion, n. Breaking away of part from a mass. [f. L abruptio (ABRUPT,-ION)]

abs-, pref. From, away, off. See AB-.

ăb´scĕss (-sĕs), n. Collection of pus formed in a cavity of the body. [f. L abscessus a going away f. ABScedere cess-go)]

ăb´sciss(e) (-sĭs; pl. -es), **ăbscĭ´ssa** (-sĭ-; pl. -œ), n. Portion of given line inter-cepted between fixed point within it & ordinate drawn to it from given point without it. [L abscissa (linea) p.p. of ABscindere sciss- cut)]

ăbscĭ´ssion (-sĭshn), n. (surg.). Cutting off, violent separation. [f. L abscissio (see prec., -ION)]

ăbscŏnd´, v.i. Go away secretly, fly from the law. Hence ~ENCE, ~ER¹, nn. [f. L ABSCONdere stow, f. dare put); orig. transi-tive in E also, then refl., then intr.]

ăb´sence, n. Being away from a place; non-existence or want of; abstraction of thought (esp. ~min´ded). [f. L absentia (absent-ABSENT¹)]

ăb´sent¹, a. 1. Not present; not existing. 2. Abstracted in mind, whence ~LY² adv., ~min´dedNESS, ~NESS, nn. [F, f. L absentem nom. -ens part. of ABesse be)]

ăbsĕnt´², v.refl. Keep oneself away. [f. F absenter f. L absentare f. absent- ABSENT¹]

ăbsĕntee´, n. A person not present; a person, esp. a landlord, habitually living away from home. Hence ~ISM(2) n., practice of being an ~, practice of workers of absenting themselves from work, esp. frequently or without good reason. [ABSENT² +-EE]

ăb´sinth, n. Wormwood, the plant or its essence; a liqueur made (orig. at least) from wine & wormwood. [f. L f. Gk apsinthion]

ăb´sit ō´men, sent. May no ominous signi-ficance attach to the words, may my fears not be verified. [L]

ăb´sŏlūte (-ōōt), a. Complete, perfect, pure (as ~ alcohol), mere; unrestricted, independent; ruling arbitrarily; out of grammatical relation (ablative ~ in L, genitive ~ in Gk; ~ construction in E, noun & participle used as adverbial clause, as dinner being over we left the table; real, not merely relative or comparative; un-qualified, unconditional; self-existent & conceivable without relation to other things (the ~, as noun; ~ music, self-dependent instrumental music devoid of literary suggestions. Hence ~NESS(-tn-) n. [f. mid. F absolut (now absolu) f. L absolutus p.p. see ABSOLVE]

ăb´solutely(-ōōtlǐ), adv. Independently, in & by itself; arbitrarily, without external control; without qualification (as a without the usual accompaniments (as a

transitive vb used ~, i.e. without its obj.); unconditionally; positively; though you would not believe it; conclusively, completely; quite; at all (w. negatives); || (colloq.) quite so, yes. [f. prec.+-LY²]

absolu'tion (-ōō-), n. Formal setting free from guilt, sentence, or obligation; ecclesiastical declaration of forgiveness of sins; remission of penance; forgiveness. [F, f. L *absolutionem* (ABSOLVE, -ION)]

ăb'solutism (-ōōt-), n. (Theol.) doctrine that God acts absolutely in the affair of salvation; (Pol.) principle of absolute government. [ABSOLUTE+-ISM (3)]

ăb'solutist (also adj., as ~ *principles*); a metaphysician who identifies subject & object. [ABSOLUTE+-IST (2)]

absolve' (-s-, -z-), v.t. Set, pronounce, free (*from* blame etc., *of* sin, *from* obligation etc., or abs.); acquit, pronounce not guilty. [f. L *ab*(*solvere, solut-* loosen)]

ăb'sonant, a. Discordant, alien (*from*), unreasonable. [f. AB-+*sonant-* part. st. of L *sonare* sound on anal. of *dissonant, consonant,* & L *absonus*]

absorb' (-s-), v.t. Swallow up, incorporate (*be ~ed by,* lose one's identity in); engross the attention of; suck in (liquids); take in (heat, light, etc.) by chemical or molecular action. [f. F *absorber* f. L AB(*sorbēre sorpt-* suck in)]

absŏrb'able, a. Easily sucked in. Hence ~ABI'LITY n. [prec.+-ABLE]

absŏrbed' (-bd), a. Intensely engaged or interested. Hence ~LY² (-b'ĕdli) adv. [p.p. of ABSORB]

absŏrbĕfa'cient (-shĕnt), a. & n. Causing the absorption or drying up (e.g. of a tumour); agent that does this. [f. L *absorbĕ-*+-FACIENT]

absŏrb'ent, a. & n. 1. Having tendency to suck in (abs., or *of*). 2. n. Substance of this kind; one of the vessels in plants & animals (e.g. root tips) that absorb nutriment. [f. L *absorbent-* part. st. of *absorbēre* ABSORB]

absŏrb'ing, a. Engrossing, intensely interesting. Hence ~LY² adv. [part. of ABSORB]

absŏrp'tion, n. Disappearance through incorporation in something else; natural or medical removal of tissues; mental engrossment; sucking in of fluid, light, etc., or nutriment. [f. L *absorptio* (ABSORB, -ION)]

absquat'ulate (-ŏt-), v.i. Make off, decamp. [American-made jocular vb w. L pref. & suf.]

abstain', v.i. Keep oneself away, refrain (*from*); refrain from alcohol, whence ~ER¹ n., ~ING² (3) n. [f. F *abstenir* f. L ABS(*tinēre tent-*=*tenēre* hold)]

abstē'mious, a. Sparing, not self-indulgent, esp. in food and drink. Used of persons, habits, meals. Hence ~LY² adv., ~NESS n. [f. L ABS(*temius* f. *temum* strong drink inferred f. *temulentus, tenetum*)+-OUS]

abstĕn'tion, n. Keeping off (abs., or *from* any pleasure); esp., not using one's vote. [F (ABSTAIN, -ION)]

abstĕr'gent, a. & n. Cleansing; a cleansing substance. [f. L *abstergent-* part. st. of ABS(*tergēre ters-* wipe)]

abstĕr'sion (-shn), n. Cleansing, purgation. [F, see prec., -ION]

abstĕr'sive, a. Cleansing. [f. F (-*if, -ive*), as prec., -IVE]

ăb'stinence, n. Refraining (*from any* pleasure, or abs. in sense of continence, fasting, or, usu. *total* ~, going without alcohol); occas.=foll. [F, f. L *abstinentia* (ABSTINENT, -ENCE)]

ăb'stinency, n. Habit of refraining from pleasures, esp. food. [f. L *abstinentia* see prec. & -ENCY]

ăb'stinent, a. Practising abstinence. Hence ~LY² adv. [F, f. L *abstinent-* (ABSTAIN, -ENT)]

ăb'stract¹, a. Separated from matter, practice, or particular examples, not concrete; ideal, not practical; abstruse (with *the,* as noun) the ideal or theoretical way of regarding things (*in the* ~). Hence ~LY² adv., ~NESS n. [f. L *abstractus* p.p. of ABS(*trahere* draw)]

ăb'stract², n. Essence, summary; abstraction or abstract term. [see prec.]

abstract'³, v.t. Deduct, remove, (an obj. *much* etc. is occas. omitted); (euphemism) steal; disengage (obj. *attention* etc. occas. omitted) *from*; consider apart from the concrete; summarize. [f. ABSTRACT¹]

abstract'ed, a. Withdrawn in thought, not attending. Hence ~NESS n. [-ED¹]

abstract'edly, adv. In the abstract, ideally; separately (*from*—esp. after *consider*); in an absent-minded way. [-LY²]

abstrac'tion, n. Taking away, withdrawal; (euphemism) stealing; process of stripping an idea of its concrete accompaniments; the idea so stripped, something visionary; absence of mind. [f. f. L *abstrachionem* (ABSTRACT¹, -ION)]

abstruse' (-ōōs), a. Hard to understand, profound. Hence ~LY² (-sl) adv., ~NESS (-sn-) n. [f. L ABS(*trusus* p.p. of *trudere* push)]

absŭrd', a. Incongruous, unreasonable, ridiculous, silly. Hence ~LY² adv. [f. F *absurde* f. L *absurdus* (*ab-* utterly+*surdus* deaf, dull)]

absŭrd'ity, n. Folly, unreasonableness; an absurd statement or act. [f. F *absurdité* f. L *absurditatem* (ABSURD, -TY)]

abŭn'dance, n. Quantity more than sufficient, plenty; overflowing emotion (~ *of the heart*); many people (*there are* ~ *who*); affluence, wealth. [OF (*ab-, habr,* see ABOUND), f. L *abundantia* (as foll., -ANCE)]

abŭn'dant, a. More than sufficient, plentiful; rich (in). Hence **~ly** adv. [OF (ad-), f. L abundant- part. st. (AB(OUND), -ANT)]

ăb ŭrb'e cŏn'dĭtā, adv. (abbr. A.U.C.), Counting from the foundation of Rome (753 B.C.). [L]

abūse¹ (-z), v.t. Misuse, make bad use of; deceive (arch., but still used esp. in pass.); maltreat (arch.); revile. [f. F abuser f. L +abusare f. AB(us- p.p. st. of uti use)]

abūse² (-s), n. Misuse, perversion (of); an established unjust or corrupt practice; revilling, whence ~'ive a., ~'ively² f. L abusus n. f. abus- see prec.]

abŭt', v.i.(-tt-). Have a common boundary with, border, (upon; or occas. without prep. as trans. vb; of estates or countries); end on or against, lean on, (of parts of a building). [mixed meanings f. OF abouter place end to end (à to + bout end), & OF abuter touch with one end (à to + but end)]

abŭt'ment, n. A lateral support; (esp. in architecture) that on which an arch or bridge rests; point of junction between such support & thing supported. [ABUT + -MENT]

abŭt'ter, n. (In law) owner of the adjoining property. [ABUT + -ER¹]

abȳe'¹, v.t. (arch.: past & p.p. abought). Redeem, pay the penalty of, (an offence); usu. w. dearly, sore). [earlier abeggen, f. A-(1) away + BUY]

abȳs'm¹, n. Earlier form, still used in poetical style, of ABYSS. [OF abisme f. LL +abyssimus superl. of abyssus ABYSS]

abȳs'mal (-z-), a. Bottomless, esp. fig. as ~ ignorance. Hence **~ly²** (-z-) adv. [ABYSM¹ + -AL]

abyss', n. The primal chaos, bowels of the earth, lower world; a bottomless chasm, deep gorge; depth (~ of light). [earlier abime, abysme, f. See ABYSM, later corrected after L abyssus f. Gk abussos bottomless]

abyss'al, a. More than 300 fathoms below sea surface (water, zone, mud). [f. LL abyssalis f. abyssus: see ABYSS & -AL]

ac-, pref. to words in c-, k-, qu-. Properly the L assimilated form of AD- to, in addition. In passing through OF it became a-: this being rectified later, ac- was mistakenly written also for a- representing other pref. (see A-), e.g. OE a- (on) in acknowledge.

-ăc, suf. forming adj., which are often also (if not only) used as nouns. From Gk -akos, the modification of adj. suf. -kos appended to nouns in -ia, -ios, -ion, & imitated in L. E wds in -ac may be f. Gk (-akos), L(-acus), or F(-aque).

acā'cia (-shŏ), n. Gens of trees, of Mimosa tribe, yielding gum arabic; the Locust-tree or False A~, grown in England for ornament; gum arabic. [L, f. Gk akakia; perh. f. akē point (in ref. to its thorns)]

ăc'adēme, n. (Prop.) = Academus (see ACADEMY); (used by mistake in poetic style for) the Gk Academy, a college, university. [Gk Akadēmos see ACADEMY; mistake perh. caused by Milton's grove of Academe', P. R. iv. 244]

ăcadēm'ic, a. & n. 1. Belonging to or agreeing with the philosophic school of Plato (ACADEMY), (w. ref. to some of his successors' views) sceptical; an ancient Platonist. 2. Scholarly, (& by implication) abstract, unpractical, cold, merely logical; (as sing. noun) member of a university, one too much enslaved to the principles (in painting etc.) of an academy; (as pl. noun) merely theoretical arguments, university robes. 3. Of the two prec. [see +IX²]

ăcadēm'ical, a. Belonging to a college or university; (as pl. noun) college costume (commoner than academic). [prec. + -AL]

ăcadēm'ically, adv. Theoretically, unpractically; rarely also in any of the senses of the two prec.

ăcadēmi'cian (-shn), n. Member of an Academy or art society, esp. of the Royal Academy of Arts. [f. F académicien f. med. L academicus (foll.); see -IAN]

Acad'emy, n. 1. The garden near Athens in which Plato taught; Plato's followers or philosophical system. 2. (a~), A place of study, including universities, || but gen. used pretentiously or deprecatingly of something between a school & a university. 3. A place of training in a special art (Royal Military ~), 4. A society for cultivating literature, art, etc., of which membership is an honour, || esp. the Royal ~ of Arts; || the R.A.'s annual exhibition. [f. F académie f. L academia f. Gk akadēmeia (Akadēmos the man or demigod f. whom Plato's garden was named)]

Acā'dian, a. & n. Nova-Scotian. [f. F Acadie Nova Scotia + -AN]

ăc'ajou (-zhŏo), n. CASHEW. [F, see CASHEW]

-acăl, compd suf. = -AC + -AL. Adji. In -ac being often used as nouns also, -al was appended to distinguish the adj. (demoniac, -acal), & even when there was no noun (heliacal). In adji. -acal often differs f. -ac in suggesting looser connexion w. the orig. noun; e.g., cardiac arteries (of the heart), cardiacal herbs (having influence on the heart).

ăc'aleph (-ĕf), n. Jellyfish, medusa, sea-nettle. [Gk akalēphē nettle]

acalyc-, -ephie (-ĕf), a. Without calyx. [A-(7) + Gk kalux -ukos flower-cup]

acăn'thus, n. A genus of plants, esp. Bear's Breech or Brank-Ursine; a conventional representation of its leaf used in Gk architecture. Hence **acantho'-** comb. form. [L, f. Gk akanthos (akantha thorn f. akē point)]

acăp'sular, a. Not having capsule. [A-(7) +L capsula CAPSULE + -AR¹]

acardiac, a. (physiol.). Without a heart. [f. Gk *akardios* f. *a-* (7)+*kardia* heart+-AO]

acarpellous, a. Without carpels. [A- (7), CARPEL, -OUS]

acarpous, a. (bot.). Not producing fruit. [A- (7)+Gk *karpos* fruit+-OUS]

acatalec'tic, a. & n. (A verse) not docked of a syllable, complete. [f. LL *acatalecticus* f. Gk *akatalēktos* (see A- (7), CATA-, LECTIC)]

acat'alepsy̆, n. Incomprehensibility (philos. term), the quality in the object answering to agnosticism in the subject. So **acātalĕp'tic** a. [f. med. L f. Gk *akatalēpsia* f. *a-* (7)+*kata* thoroughly+*lēpsis* grasping (*lab-* st. of *lambanō* take)]

acaul'ous, a. (also -es'cent, -īne, -ōse), (bot.). Apparently stemless, having very short stem. [A- (7)+L *caulis* stem +-OUS]

Accād'ian, a. & n. 1. Of Accad in Shinar (*Gen.* x, 10). 2. n. A language preserved in cuneiform inscriptions. [-IAN]

accēde' (aks-), v.i. Enter upon an office; join a party; assent to an opinion, or policy. Abs, or w. *to* if the office etc. is stated, in all senses. [f. L AC(*cedere cess-* come)]

accelerran'dō (aks-), musical direction. Gradually increase speed. [It.]

accĕl'erāte (aks-), v.t. & i. Make quicker; cause to happen earlier; become swifter (of a motion or process); put on pace. [f. obs. adj. *accelerate* f. L AC(*celerare* f. *celer* swift); see -ATE²,³]

accĕl'erāted (aks-), a. (physics). Pro-gressively quicker (~ *motion*). Hence ~LY² adv. [p.p. of prec.]

accĕl'erāting (aks-), a. Causing progres-sively quicker motion (~ *force*). [-ING⁴]

accĕlerā'tion (aks-), n. 1. Making quicker; being made quicker. 2. (Phys.) rate of in-crease of velocity per time unit, as with falling bodies. 3. (Astron.) ~ *of stars*, time gained daily by them over sun; ~ *of planets*, increased velocity from aphelion to perihelion; ~ *of moon*, increase in speed of mean motion; ~ *of tides*, amount of local advance on calculated time. [f. L *acceleratio* (ACCELERATE, -ION)]

accĕl'erative (aks-), a. Tending to increase speed, quickening. [f. ACCELERATE+-IVE]

accĕl'erātor (aks-), n. Person or thing that increases anything's speed, esp. an attach-ment in motor-cars for this purpose; one of a class of nerves & muscles. [ACCELE-RATE+-OR²]

ăc'cent¹ (aks-), n. 1. Prominence given to a syllable, whether by higher musical pitch (ancient Gk & L, Swedish & Norw.), or by stress (most mod. languages, but perh. not F). Three marks called *acute* ('), *grave* ('), & *circumflex* (' or ') *accents* (systema-tically employed only in Gk, & to a less degree in F) used for various purposes, e.g. to indicate syllabic pitch (Gk), quality of vowel sound (F), etymological hist. (F, E), metrical stress, syllabic stress (dictionaries etc.), the fact of a letter's not being silent, or conventional distinc-tion between homonyms (F). 2. Indi-vidual, local, or national mode of pronun-ciation; modulation to express feeling; in pl., speech (poet.). 3. (In prosody) rhythmical stress. 4. (Mus.) stress recur-ring at intervals, regular or otherwise. 5. (Fig.) intensity, sharp distinction. [F, f. L AC(*centus -ūs = cantus* singing) lit. transl. of Gk *prosōdia* (*pros* to+*ōdē* song)]

accent²(aks-), v.t. Pronounce with accent, emphasize (word or syllable); put the written accents on; heighten, make con-spicuous. [f. obs. F *accenter* see prec.]

accen'tor (aks-), n. Kinds of bird (= WARBLER), esp. the hedge-sparrow, which name is now occas. avoided as misleading. [mod. L f. *ad* to+*cantor*, see CANTORIS]

accen'tŭal (aks-), a. Of accent; ~ *prosody* or *verse*, of which the principle is accent or stress, not quantity. Hence ~LY² adv. [f. L *accentus* ACCENT¹+-AL]

accen'tŭāte (aks-), v.t. = ACCENT², but more used than it in the fig. sense. [f. med. L *accentuare* (*accentus* ACCENT¹), -ATE³]

accentŭā'tion (aks-), n. Accenting (all senses from ACCENT. [f. med. L *accentuatio* see ACCENTUATE, -ION]

accept' (aks-), v.t. Consent to receive (gift), answer affirmatively (offer, invitation, suitor); regard with favour (esp. unfair favour, as ~ *the person of*, ~ *persons*); receive as adequate (~ *service or writ*), allow the truth of, believe; undertake (office); take responsibility for, agree to meet, (bill of exchange). Of may be added (exc. w. *service or writ*, *bill*) with a slight suggestion of formality or con-descension. Hence ~ER¹ n. [f. F *accepter* f. L *acceptare* frequent. of AC(*cipere = capere* take)]

accept'able (aks-), a. Worth accepting, pleasing, welcome. Hence or cogn.~abLY adv. ~abil'ITY, ~ableness, nn. [F, f. L *acceptabilis* (ACCEPT, -ABLE)]

accept'ance (aks-), n. Consent to receive (gift, payment, pleasure, duty); favourable reception (act. & pass.), approval, belief; ~ *of persons*, partiality; engagement to meet a bill; a bill so accepted. [OF; see ACCEPT & -ANCE]

acceptā'tion (aks-), n. A particular sense given to a word or phrase; its generally recognized meaning. [F, f. LL *accepta-tionem* (ACCEPT, -ATION)]

accept'ĕd (aks-), a. Generally recognized or believed in (*Free & A~ Masons*, see FREE¹-*mason*). Hence ~LY² adv. [-ED¹]

accept'or (aks-), n. One who accepts a bill (preferred to *accepter* in this sense). [AF *acceptour* f. L *acceptorem* (ACCEPT, -OR²)]

ăc'cĕss (-ks-; also ăksĕss', see etym.), n. Approach; addition; right or means of approaching (*to*); being approached (*easy*

of ~); advance (~ & recess); passage, channel, doorway; adhesion, growth, (usu. now *accession*); attack or outburst (of illness, anger, emotion). [The doubtful accent is due to double derivation. 1. (sense *attack*, pron. akse's) f. F *acces* f. L *accessus* n. f. Accedere *cess*- come); 2. (other senses, pron. a'kse's) direct f. L *accessus*. The two pronunciations, however, have now ceased to be significant]

accessary (akse's'-, ak'sis-), n. & pred. a. (See also ACCESSORY). Helper in any act, one privy to it (as pred. a. *be* ~, *were made* ~); accompaniment, adjunct. [f. ACCESS+ -ARY¹ formed as f. L *access*- like *accessary, adversary*; the adj. (first spelt -*ary*) being corrected later to -*ory* on L *accessorius* drew the noun after it, & the two spellings are often confused]

access'ible (-ks-), a. Able to be reached or entered (abs. or *to*); open to influence, to the influence of, (*to*). Hence ~BIL'ITY n., ~bly³ adv. [f. f. L *accessibilis* (ACCEDE, -BLE)]

accession (akse'shn), n. Coming into presence or contact; coming into an office (esp. the throne) or condition (as manhood); being added; assent; thing added, addition; (in law) improvement or natural growth of property. [F, f. L *accessionem* (ACCEDE, -ION)]

accessory (akse's'-, ak'sis-), a. & n. (see also ACCESSARY). 1. Additional, subordinately contributive (of things), adventitious. 2. n. Thing of that character, esp. in pl. the ~ies. [f. LL *accessorius* adj. (ACCEDE, -ORY)]

acciaccatura (achahkatoor'a), n. (mus.). Grace-note performed quickly before an essential note of a melody. [It.]

ac'cidence (aks-), n. The part of grammar, or a book, dealing with inflexions (i.e. the accidents or non-essentials of words); the elements of any subject. [corruption of *accidents* = F pl. n. *accidens* that befall (a word), see ACCIDENT; or perh. direct f. *accidentia* treated as fem. sing. noun]

ac'cident (aks-), n. Event without apparent cause, unexpected (so *chapter of* ~s, unforeseen course of events); unintentional act, chance, fortune, (*by* ~); mishap; irregularity in structure; a property not essential to our conception of a substance (so of material qualities of bread & wine after transubstantiation); a mere accessory. [F, f. L *accidens -entis* part. & n. f. Accidere =*cadere* fall]

acciden'tal (aks-), a. & n. 1. Happening by chance, undesignedly, or unexpectedly; occasional; not essential to a conception (so also *an* ~ as n.); subsidiary. 2. (Mus.) ~ *sharps, flats, naturals*, &c, as noun, signs attached to single notes, not in signature. 3. (Optics) ~ *colours*, those presented by subjective sensation,

not external. 4. (In painting) ~ *lights*, &c, effects of other than ordinary daylight. [F (now -*ch*), prob. f. LL *accidentalis* f. *accidens* see prec.]

acci'dentally (aks-), adv. By chance, unintentionally. [-LY²]

accip'itral (aks-), a. Hawklike; rapacious; keensighted. [f. L *accipiter*- nom. -*ter* hawk +-AL]

acclaim', v.t. Applaud loudly or enthusiastically; (w. obj. & compl.) hail as (king, winner, saviour; ~*ed him king*). [f. L Ac(clamare shout), spelling assimilated to CLAIM]

acclama'tion, n. Shout of applause. [f. prec.]

acclama'tion, n. Loud & eager assent to a proposal (*voted, carried, by* ~); shouting in a person's honour (usu. pl.). [f. L *acclamatio* (prec., -ATION)]

acclima'tion, n. = acclimatization (see foll.), or distinguished from it as a natural process, not imposed on animals by man. [f. F *acclimater* ACCLIMATIZE]

|| **accli'matize** (also, esp. U.S., ăc'li-măte), v.t. & i. Habituate (animals, plants, oneself) to new climate; (rarely) become so habituated. Hence || acclima-tiza'tion (also, esp. U.S., acclimăti-zā'tion) n. [f. F *acclimater* (à to+*climat* CLIMATE) +-IZE]

acclivity, n. Upward slope of a hill (cf. DECLIVITY). [f. L *acclivitas* f. *acclivis* (-*clivus* slope)]

accolade' (or -ahd), n. 1. Sign at bestowal of knighthood, whether embrace, kiss, or stroke on shoulder with flat of sword. 2. (Mus.) Vertical line or brace coupling staves. [F, f. It. *accollata* n. from p.p. st. of *accollare* (ac-+L *collum* neck)]

accom'modate, v.t. Adapt (thing or person to another); prove such adaptation, harmonize, (occas. w. implication of sophistry); reconcile, settle differences between; compose (quarrel); equip, supply, (person *with*); oblige, confer favour on; find lodging for. [f. obs. adj. *accommodate* f. p.p. of L Ac(commodare -dt- f. *commodus* fitting = com-+*modus* measure)]

accom'modating, a. Obliging, easy to deal with, pliable, lax. Hence ~LY² adv. [-ING²]

accommoda'tion, n. Adjustment (e.g. of eyes for various distances); adaptation of anything to a purpose or meaning different from the original; self-adaptation; settlement, compromise; serviceable thing, convenience (so in comp. as ~-*road*; ~-*ladder*, up ship's side); lodgings, entertainment; money loan (so in ~-BILL²). [F, f. L L *accommodationem* (ac-COMMODATE, -ION)]

accom'paniment (-im-), n. 1. Appendage, thing that attends another. 2. (Mus.) subsidiary part, usu. instrumental, supporting solo instrument or voice,

choir, etc. [f. F *accompagnement* (foll., -MENT)]

accom'pan|y (-ni-), v.t. **1.** Supplement (a thing *with*, as word w. blow); go with, escort, attend; coexist with (of things), characterize. **2.** (Mus.) support (singer, player, chorus) by performing subsidiary part, whence ~(y)IST (-ÿıst -ŭm-) n. After pass., *by* has almost ousted *with*. [f. OF *accompagner* (à to + *compagne* COMPANION)]

accom'plice, n. Partner, usu. subordinate, in crime. [f. earlier & F *complice* (whether by mistake from *a complice*, cf. NEWT, or by assim. to foll.) f. L *complicem* nom. *-plex* closely connected (COM- + *plic-* fold)]

accom'plish (or -ŭm-), v.t. **1.** Fulfil, perform, complete, finish. **2.** Perfect (a person) in graceful acquirements, whence ~ED¹ (-sht) a. [f. OF *acomplir* f. LL AC(*complēre* COMPLETE); see -ISH²]

accom'plishment (or -ŭm-), n. Fulfilment, completion; thing done or attained, achievement; faculty that perfects a person for society, (disparagingly) merely superficial acquirement. [f. F *accomplissement*; see prec., -MENT]

accompt, -ant, &c. arch. for ACCOUNT, -ANT. See ACCOUNT.

accôrd'¹, v.t. & i. Be in harmony or consistent (abs., or *with*; chiefly of things); grant (indulgence, request, welcome, etc.). [f. OF *acorder* f. LL AC(*cordare* f. *cor cordis* heart)]

accôrd'², n. Consent (*with one* ~), mutual agreement; treaty of peace; harmonious correspondence in colour, pitch, tone; assent (*of one's own* ~). [f. OF *acord* agreement (*acorder* ACCORD¹)]

accôrd'ance, n. Conformity, agreement, esp. in phr. *in* ~ *with*. [OF *acordance* (as prec., -ANCE)]

accôrd'ant, a. In tune, agreeing, (abs., or *with*). Hence ~LY² adv. [OF *acordant* as prec., -ANT]

accôrd'ing, adv. (only now in the compd conj. ~ *as*, & the compd prep. ~ *to*). ~ *as*: in proportion as (of a process varying w. another); in a manner depending on which of certain alternatives is true. ~ *to*: in a manner consistent with or degree proportioned to; on the authority of. [-ING²]

accôrd'ingly, adv. As the (stated) circumstances suggest; therefore: ~ *as* = *according as*. [-LY²]

accôrd'ion, n. Portable musical instrument having bellows, metal reeds, & keyboard &/or buttons. Hence ~IST (3) n. [f. It. & LL *accordare* attune see ACCORD¹; termination imitated f. CLARION]

accôst'¹, v.t. Make up to & address, open conversation with; (of prostitute) solicit. [f. F *accoster* f. LL AC(*costare* f. *costa* rib)]

accôst'², n. Greeting, opening remark. [f. prec.]

accouchement (see Ap.), n. Lying-in, delivery in child-bed. [F]

accoucheur (see Ap.), n. (fem. -*euse*). Man-midwife, midwife. [F]

account'¹, v.t. & i. Consider, regard as, (followed by obj. & compl., or inf.; ~ *him a hero, wise, to be guilty*). Be ~ed *of*, *for*, give reckoning of (money held in trust); answer for (conduct, performance of duty); explain the cause of; serve as explanation of (*that* ~s *for it*); (sport) be responsible for the death of, kill. [f. OF *aconter* f. LL *accomptare* for +AC(*computare* L = COMPUTE); the form *accompt* is due to 14th-c. correction in F passing into E, the oldest E being *acute* (see AC-²)]

account'², n. **1.** Counting, calculation, in phrr. *cast* ~s (reckon up), *money of* ~ (names not of coins, but of sums, as guinea). **2.** Reckoning of debit & credit, in money or service; statement of money received & expended, with balance; so *open* or *close an* ~ *with*, *render* or *send in*, *pay* or *settle*, *an* ~; ~ *current* (whence a/c = account), one kept going w. occasional entries; ~ *rendered*, used when a bill previously sent in, but left unpaid, is sent again; *joint* ~s, in which two persons not otherwise partners count as one; *keep* ~s, enter all expenditure for comparison w. income; *balance* or *square* ~s *with some one*, receive or pay the balance due; *cast, profit-&-loss*, etc., ~, headings of subdivision in ledger; || *sale for the* ~, on the StockExch., not for cash, but payable at next periodic settlement; *A in* ~ *with B*, having credit relations with; *for* ~ *of*, to be sold for (person); *on* ~, as interim payment; *on one's* ~, for his service; *on one's own* ~, for & at one's own purposes & risk, whence generally *on* ~ *of*, because of, & *on no* ~, by no means, certainly not. A favourable result of the reckoning, profit; *find one's* ~ *in*, profit by, *turn to* ~, make useful. Statement of administration as required by creditor; *ask, demand, yield, render, an* ~, *call* or *bring to* ~, extended from money to conduct generally, so the *great* ~, Day of Judgement, *gone to his* ~, dead; *give* ~ *of*, find cause of, explain, (in sport) *give a good* ~ *of*, dispose of (opponents, game) successfully. **3.** Estimation; person or thing *of* ~, or *held in, some* or *no* ~; *make little* ~ *of*; *take into, leave out of*, ~; *take* ~ *of*; *lay one's* ~ *with*, include in one's calculations, expect. **4.** Narration, report, description, of event, person, etc. [f. OF *acont* (à to + *cont* f. LL *computum* for *computum* f. L *computare* COMPUTE)]

account'|able, a. Bound to give account, responsible, (*for* things, *to* persons, or abs.); explicable (occas. followed by *for*). Hence ~ABI'LITY, ~ableness, nn. [f. ACCOUNT¹ +-ABLE]

account'ant, n. 1. (Law) one liable to render account; defendant in an action of account. 2. Professional keeper & inspector of accounts; ~*-general*, chief ~ in public offices. Hence **account'ancy** n., profession of an ~, **~SHIP** n., office of an ~. [F. (15th c.) *accomptant* part. of *accompter* OF *aconter* ACCOUNT¹]

accou're (-ōōter), **v.t.** (-tring, -tred). Attire, equip, esp. w. special costume (chiefly used in p.p.). [f. med. F *ac-coustrer*(now *accoutrer*) etym. dub., perh. AC-+*coustre* vestry-keeper & so rober which is perh. f. L L *custor* f. *custos* guardian]

accou'trement (-ōōter-), **n.** (usu. in pl.). Equipment, trappings; (Mil.) soldier's outfit other than arms & garments. [MF *accoustrement* (prec. ~MENT)]

accre'dit, v.t. Gain belief or influence for (adviser, advice); send out (ambassador etc.) with credentials *to* person, *to* or *at* a court; ~ thing (saying, policy) *to* person, or ~ *him with* it, put it down to him. [f. F Ac*créditer* f. *crédit* CREDIT¹]

accre'dited, a. Officially recognized (persons); generally accepted, orthodox, (beliefs). [p.p. of prec.]

accrēte', v.t. & i. Grow together or into one; form round or on *to*, as round a nucleus; attract (such additions). [f. L *accret-* p.p. st. of AC*crescere* grow)]

accrēte², a. (bot.). Grown into one with something else. [f. L *accretus* p.p. see prec.]

accre'tion, n. Growth by organic enlarge-ment; the growing of separate things (as particles) into one; the whole resulting from this; adhesion of extraneous matter to anything; the matter so added; (Law) = ACCRESSION, also increase of legacy etc. by share of failing co-legatee. [f. L *ac-cretio* (ACCRETE¹, -ION)]

accrue' (-ōō), **v.i.** Fall (*to* one, *from* a thing) as a natural growth, advantage, result; esp. of interest on invested money. Hence **~ED¹** (-ōōd) a. [f. obs. *accrue* OF *acreistre* a. f. OF *acreistre n.* f. L *accrescere* ACCRETE¹]

accū'mulate, v.t. & i. Heap up, gain by degrees, (usu. fig., a fortune, ill will, etc., or *abs.*), amass, make money; ||take (University degrees) by accumulation (obj. expressed, or *abs.*), i.e. more than one step at a time; grow numerous, form an increasing mass or heap (lit. & fig., as *dirt, disasters, had* ~*d*). [f. obs. *accumu-late* a. f. L A*ccumulare* (*cumulus* heap), -ATE²,³]

accumulā'tion, n. Collection (act, or pass.), amassing; money-making; growth of capital by continued interest; com-bination of distinct acts into one (degrees, see prec., or church services etc.); a mass (as snow, papers, property). [f. L *accu-mulatio* (prec., -ION)]

accū'mulative, a. Arising from accumu-lation (~ *proof, evidence,* now being ousted by *cumulative*); so arranged as to accumulate (sinking fund); acquisitive, given to hoarding. Hence **~IY¹**(-vli) adv. [as prec. +-IVE]

accū'mulator, n. One who collects; money-maker; ||taker of degrees by ac-cumulation; || apparatus for storing elec-tricity. [L(as prec., -OR²]

ác̄c̄ū'rate, a. Careful, precise, in exact conformity with a standard or with truth. Hence **~LY¹** adv., **~NESS** n. [f. L Ac*curare* (*cura* care), -ATE²]

accū'rse, accū'rst, v.t. Lying under a curse, ill-fated; involving misery, exe-crable, detestable. [p.p. f. obs. *accurse* earlier *acurse* (*a-* imitated as intensive f. OE *ā-* see A-¹(1))+OE *cursian* CURSE v.)]

accū'sal (-z-), **n.** Sometimes used for foll. [f. ACCUSE+-AL (2)]

ác̄c̄ūsā'tion (-z-), **n.** Accusing; being accused; a charge of offence or crime; indictment. [F, f. L *accusationem* (ACCUSE, -ION)]

accū'sative (-z-), **a. & n.** ~ *case* (or~ as n.), the grammatical case used in Gk & L for the goal of motion or obj. of action; in uninflected languages, applied to the wd that stands as obj., though with no mark of case. Hence **accusatī'vAL¹**(-z-) adj., **~IY²** (-z-; -vi) adv. [F (-*if*, -*ive*), f. L *accusativus* lit. transl. of Gk *aitiatikē* casual (also accusing), the goal or obj. being the final cause of motion or action]

accūsatō'rial (-z-), **a.** ~ *procedure* etc., in which prosecutor & judge are not the same, opposed to *inquisitorial*. [as foll. +-AL]

accūsatorȳ (-z-), **a.** ~ *language, manner,* etc., conveying or implying accusation. [f. L *accusatorius* (foll., -ORY¹)]

accūse' (-z), **v.t.** 1. Charge with a fault, indict, (person), whence p.p. as noun, *the* ~*ed*; blame, lay the fault on, (person or thing, as *the times*); ~ *as* offender, *of* of-fence. 2. Point to (subj) *evidence* etc., obj. *a person*). Hence **~ER¹**(-z-) n., **~'inglY²** (-z-) adv. [earlier *acuse* f. OF *acuser* f. L Ac(*cusare* =*causare* f. *causa* cause]

accū'stom, v.t. Habituate (oneself, per-son, or thing, *to do* or *to*; commoner in pass.). [earlier *acustom* (see AC-) f. OF *acostumer* (now *accoutumer*) (à to, CUSTOM)]

accū'stomed (-md), **a.** In vbl senses; also, usual. [p.p. of prec. in obs. sense *make usual*]

āce, n. 1. The one on dice (*ambs-*~, throw of two ones; *deuce* ~, throw of two & one, formerly two ones); throw of one or dominoes; card etc, so marked. 2. One point at rackets, lawn tennis, etc.; (Tennis) service that beats opponent. 3. The smallest possible amount, hair's-breadth, as *within an* ~ *of*. 4. (Orig. French) airman who has brought down 10 or more hostile aircraft; one who excels at something, champion; also attrib. [f. L *as* unity]

-acea (-ā'sha), L suf. freely used to form names (neut. pl. agreeing w. *animalia*) for families of animals; the names are L & pl., the sing. being supplied by E adj. in -ACEAN used as noun; so *the crustacea, a crustacean*. [f. L -*aceus* (-*ac*- + *e*-*us*) compd adj. formative]

-aceae (-ā'siē), L suf. freely used to form names (fem. pl. agreeing w. *plantae*) for families of plants. [f. -*aceus* see prec.]

-acean (-ā'shan), a. & n. suf. As adj. = -ACEOUS; as n., see -ACEA. [f. L -*aceus* see -ACEA + -AN]

Acel'dama (ak-), n. Field of bloodshed, scene of slaughter. [*Acts* i. 19]

-aceous (-ā'shus), suf. freely used to form adji. to the Nat.-Hist. nouns in -ACEA, -ACEAE, as *crustaceous, rosaceous*: [f. L -*aceus* see -ACEA + -OUS]

acephal-, stem of several bot., zool., & ecol. terms. Headless. [f. LL f. Gk *akephalos* f. A- (7) + *kephalē* head]

aceph'alous (aset'č), a. Headless; recognizing no chief; (Zool.) having no part of body specially organized as head; (Bot.) with head aborted or cut off; (in prosody), (verse) wanting the regular first syllable. [as prec. + -OUS]

ā'cerbāte, v.t. Sometimes used for EM-ACERBATE.

acerb'ity, n. Astringent sourness, harsh taste; bitterness of speech, manner, or temper. [f. F. *acerbité* f. L *acerbitatem* (*acerbus* sour-tasting, TY]

acer'vate, a. Growing in compact clusters (of spines etc.). [f. L *acervare* (*acervus* a heap), -ATE²]

aces'cent, a. Turning sour, rather sour, lit. & fig. [f. L *acescere* inceptive of *acēre* be sour (*ac*- sharp), -ENT]

acetab'ulum, n. (pl. -*la*). 1. (Rom. Ant.) cup to hold vinegar. 2. (Zool.) cup-shaped sucker of cuttle-fish etc.; socket of thigh-bone, or of joints in insects. Vinegar. [L *acetabulum* (*acetum* vinegar + -*abulum* dim. of -ceptacle]

acet'ate, n. (Of plants) used in salads. [f. L *acetaria* salad plants, neut. pl. of *acetaris* (as ACETIC, see -AR¹) + -OUS]

acet'ated, a. Treated with acetic acid. [p.p. of acetate v. (ACETIC + -ATE³) not otherwise used]

acet'ic, a. Pertaining to vinegar. [f. L *acetum* vinegar + -IC]

acet'ify, v.t. & i. Convert into vinegar; become sour. Hence ~FICA'TION, ~FIER¹ (2), nn. [as prec. + -FY]

à'cétōne, n. Colourless limpid liquid valuable as a solvent of organic compounds. [as prec. + -ONE]

à'cétous, a. Having the qualities of vinegar; sour. [as prec. + -OUS]

acet'ylēne, n. A colourless gas, burning with a bright flame. [as prec., see -YL & -ENE]

Achaean (ake'an), a. & n. (Inhabitant) of Achaea (district of the Northern Peloponnesus; also, in Homeric use, Greece generally). [f. L f. Gk *Akhaios*]

acharnement (see Ap-), n. Ferocity; gusto. [F]

Achates (akăt'ēz), n. Faithful friend of Aeneas (Virg. *Aen.*); any faithful friend.

ache¹ (āk), v.i. Suffer continuous or prolonged pain. [OE *acan*; earlier & correct spelling of the verb was *ake*]

ache² (āk), n. Continuous pain. [OE *æce* f. *acan* v.: earlier pronunciation of the noun was *ātch* (cp. *bake batch, wake watch*)]

ache³ (āch), n. Name of letter H.

Acheulian (ashūl'ian), a. Of the palaeolithic epoch represented by remains found at St Acheul in France. [-AN]

achieve', v.t. Accomplish, carry out; achieve; reach (an end). Hence ~'ABLE a. [f. F *achever* (*à chef venir* f. LL *ad caput venire* come to a head with)]

achieve'ment (-vm-), n. Completion, accomplishment; thing accomplished; escutcheon or ensign armorial in memory of a distinguished feat; = BATCHMENT. [f. F *achèvement* (*achever* ACHIEVE)]

Achilles (akĭl'ēz) **tĕn'don**. See TENDON.

achil'ous (ak-), a. (bot.). Without lips. [f. Gk *a*- not + *kheilos* lip + OUS]

achlamyd'eous (äklăm-), a. (bot.). Without calyx or corolla. [f. Gk *a*- not + *khlamus -udos* cloak + -EOUS]

āchromat'ic (-ik-), a. (opt.). Free from colour; transmitting light without decomposing it. Hence ~ICALLY adv., ~I'CITY (ak-), ~ISM (2) (akrōm²), nn., ~NE (3) (akrōm⁴) v.t. [f. Gk *akhrōmatos* (*a*- not + *khrōma -matos* colour) + -IC]

à'cid¹, a. Sour (~*drops*, kind of sweeties); (Chem.) with the essential properties of an ACID². So **acid'ITY** n. [f. L *acidus* (*acēre* be sour)]

à'cid², n. A sour substance; (Chem.) one of a class of substances that neutralize & are neutralized by alkalis, & are compounded of hydrogen & another element or elements, & turn vegetable blues to reds; ~ *test* (in which ~ is applied to test composition etc.; often fig. in morals etc.). [f. prec.]

acid'ify, v.t. & i. Make, become, sour; (Chem.) convert into an acid. Hence ~FIABLE a., ~FICA'TION, ~FIER¹ (2), nn. [as ACID, see -FY]

àcidim'ēter, n. Instrument for measuring strength of acids. [as prec., see -METER]

àcidōs'is, n. (path.). Acid condition of blood (esp. in diabetes). [hybrid formation f. ACID + -OSIS]

acid'ulāted, a. Made somewhat acid. [p.p. of acidulate v. (foll. + -ATE³), not otherwise used]

acid'ulous, a. Somewhat acid. [f. *acidulus* (dim. of *acidus* sour) + -OUS]

a'cinus, n. (pl. *acinī*). One of the small berries that make up a compound fruit such as the blackberry; the compound fruit itself; seed of a grape or berry; (Anat.) racemose gland. Hence **aci'ni-FORM** a. [L., = berry, seed]

-acious a., suf. forming adji. mean- ing 'inclined to', 'abounding in'. [f. L. *-āx -ācis*, added to vb stems to form adji. + -ous]

-acity, suf. forming nouns of quality corresponding to adji. in *-acious* directly f. L. *-acitās* or thr. F. *-acité*.

ack'-ack, a. (sl.). Anti-aircraft (gun etc.). [signallers' name for letters A-A]

ăck ěmm'a, adv. & n. (sl.). *Ante meridiem*; air-mechanic. [signallers' name for letters A.M.]

acin'ic, a. ~ *line*, magnetic equator, on which magnetic needle has no dip. [f. Gk *aktīnes* (a- not + *ktīnō* bend) + -ic]

ăc'mé, n. Highest point, point of per- fection. [Gk, = point]

ăc'ně, n. Pimple; disease marked by pimples. [perh. corrupt. of ACME]

acock', adv. (Of the hat) in cocked fashion. [A prep. + COCK² v.]

ăc'olyte, n. Inferior officer in the church; attendant; novice. [f. Gk *akolouthos* follower]

ăc'onite, n. Monk's-hood or wolf's-bane, a poisonous plant; extract from this. Hence **ăconit'ic** a., **aconiti'ne⁵** n. [f. F *aconit* f. Gk *akoniton* (etym. dub.)]

ăc'orn, n. Fruit of the oak; ~*-shell*, multi-valve cirriped, allied to barnacles. [OE *æcern*, perh. W. orig. meaning 'fruit of the open country' (OE *æcer*; confus. w. *corn*)]

acŏtyled'on, n. Plant with no distinct seed-lobes. Hence ~OUS a. [f. mod. L *acotyledonēs* f. Gk *a-* not + *kotulēdōn* cup- shaped hollow (*kotulē* cup)]

acou'chy (-ōōshi), n. Small rodent allied to guinea-pig. [f. F *acouchi*, perh. f. na- tive name in Guiana]

acous'tic (-ōō-, -ow-), a. Relating to the sense of hearing; (of a mine) that can be exploded by sound waves transmitted under water. Hence ~ICAL a., ~ICALLY² adv., ~ICIAN (-shn), ~ICS, nn. [f. F *acoustique* f. Gk *akoustikos* (*akouō* hear)]

acquaint', v.t. Make (person, oneself) aware (*of* or *with* facts, *that, how,* etc.); make oneself familiar (*with* circumstances etc.); (pass.) have personal knowledge (*with* person or thing). [f. OF *acointer* f. LL *Accointāre* f. *cognitō* p.p. st. of *cognōscere* come to know]

acquain'tance, n. Knowledge of (*with*) person etc. more than mere recognition & less than intimacy; person(s) with whom one is acquainted (pl. now usu. ~s in this sense). Hence ~SHIP (-s-sh-) n. [f. OF *acointance* (*acointer* ACQUAINT)]

acquěst', n. Thing acquired; (Law) pro- perty gained otherwise than by inheri- tance. [f. OF *acquest* f. LL *acquīstum* f. acquiescent (see ACQUIRE)]

acquiěsce', v.i. Agree tacitly; ~e *in*, accept (arrangements, conclusions). So ~ENCE n., ~ENT a. [f. MF *acquiescer* f. L Ac(quiēscere rest)]

acquīre', v.t. Gain by oneself & for oneself; (of qualities etc.) win (person a. good name etc.); come into possession of; *an ~d taste* (not natural). Hence ~MENT (-īrm-) n., ~d mental faculty. [f. OF *acquerre* f. L Ac(*quīrere quīsīt-* = *quaerere* seek)]

ăcquisi'tion (-zi-), n. Act of acquiring; thing acquired. So **acquis'ITIVE** (-zi-) a., **acquis'itiveness** (-zi- : -vn-) n. [f. L *acquīsītiō* (as prec., see -ION)]

acquit', v.t. (-tt-). Pay (a debt); declare (person) not guilty (*of* offence); discharge oneself *of* (duty, responsibility); ~ one- self (perform one's part) *well, ill,* etc. [f. OF *aquiter* f. LL Ac(*quītāre* = L *quiētāre* settle f. *quiēs -ētis* rest)]

acquit'tal, n. Discharge from debt; de- liverance from a charge by verdict etc.; performance (of duty). [prec. + -AL (2)]

acquit'tance, n. Payment of debt; re- lease from debt; receipt in full. [f. OF *acquitance* (*aquiter* ACQUIT, see -ANCE)]

ā'cre (-ker), n. Measure of land, 4,840 sq. yds; piece of tilled or enclosed land, field (only in special uses, as *broad ~s, God's ~, Long ~*). Hence (-ā'CRED² -erd) a. [f. OE *æcer, acer* (cf. OHG *achar* L *ager* acres collectively or in the abstract.

ā'creage (-ker-), n. Amount of acres; acres collectively or in the abstract. [ACRE + -AGE]

ăc'rid, a. Bitterly pungent, irritating, corrosive; of bitter temper or manner. Hence **acrid'ITY** n. [irreg. f. L *acer -cris* pungent + -ID, perh. assimilated to *acid*]

ăc'rimonȳ, n. Bitterness of temper or manner. So **ăcrimo'nious** a., **ăcrimon'- iously³** adv. [f. L *acrimōnia* pungency *acer -cris* sharp; see -MONY perh. thr. F *acrimonie*]

Ac'rita (ăk-), n. pl. (zool.). Animals with no distinct nervous system. [mod. L f. Gk *ákritos* undistinguishable (a- not + *kritos* distinguished)]

acro- in comb. Highest, topmost, ter- minal; tipped with; at the point or

extremity of. [f. Gk *akros* topmost, outermost]

ăc′robăt, n. Rope-dancer, tumbler; politician, reasoner, etc., who changes position nimbly. Hence **ăcrobăt′IC** a., **ăcrobăt′ICALLY** adv., **~ISM** n. [f. F *acrobate* f. Gk *akrobatos* walking on tiptoe, climbing aloft (ACRO- + *batos* vbl. adj. f. *bainō* go)]

ăc′rogĕn, n. (bot.). Cryptogamous plant having perennial stem with growing point at extremity, as ferns & mosses. Hence **acrō′gĕNOUS** a. [ACRO- + Gk -*genēs* born]

ăc′rolith, n. Statue with head & extremities of stone. [ACRO- + Gk *lithos* stone]

ăcrŏn′ychal (-ĭk-), a. Happening at nightfall (esp. of rising or setting of stars). Hence **~LY²** adv. [f. Gk *akronukhos* (ACRO- + *nux nuktos* night) + -AL]

acrŏp′ĕtal, a. Developing from below upwards. Hence **~LY²** adv. [ACRO- + L *petere* seek + -AL]

acrŏp′olis, n. Citadel or elevated part of a Greek city, esp. of Athens. [Gk *akropolis* (ACRO- + *polis* city)]

across′ ¹ (-aws), adv. & prep. In the form of a cross, as *with arms* ~; forming a cross with, making angles with, (object expressed or understood), as *a line drawn* ~ (*the road*); into contact with, as *came* ~ *a tiger, an instance*; from side to side (of), as *run* ~ (*the road*); on the other side (of), as *by this time he is* ~ (*the Channel*). *Put it.* ~ *a person* (sl.), get even with, impose on, deceive. [A prep. + CROSS ¹; Caxton has *in cross* f. F *encroiz*]

across′tic, n. Poem or other composition in which the initial (*single* ~), the initial & final (*double* ~), or the initial, middle, & final (*triple* ~) letters of the lines make words; word-puzzle so made; Hebrew poem of which the lines begin with the successive letters of the alphabet. Hence **across′tic** a., **across′tICALLY** adv. [ACRO- + Gk *stikhos* row, line of verse]

ăct ¹, n. Thing done, deed, this as outward sign of a condition etc. (~ *of faith, contrition*); process of doing, operation, as *in the very* ~ *of, Act of God* (operation of uncontrollable natural forces); *Acts (of the Apostles)*, N.T. book; decree passed by a legislative body etc.: ~ *& deed*, binding legal instrument (esp. *I deliver this as my* ~ *& deed* said at time of signing); main division of a play: ‖ (in Universities) thesis maintained by a candidate for a degree etc. [f. F *acte* f. L *actus* -ūs doing and f. L *actum* thing done: see foll.]

ăct ², v.t. & i. Carry out (an incident or story) in mimicry, represent, perform a play or part; personate (character in a play or in life), as ~ *Othello*, ~ *the fool*; perform actions, behave, as ~ (*behave*) *generously*, ~ (*serve*) *as interpreter*, ~ *upon* (*execute*) *a suggestion*, ~ *up to* (put into practice) *a principle*; perform special functions, as *the policeman declined to* ~

the brake refused to ~, *alcohol* ~*s on the brain*. [f. L *agere act*- do]

ăc′ting, a. & n. In vbl senses, esp.: doing duty temporarily, as *A*~ *Captain*; doing alone duties nominally shared with others, as *A*~ *Manager, Trustee*; ~ *copy* (for players' use, with stage-directions & cuts). [ACT² + -ING²·¹]

Actĭn′ia (ăk-), n. (pl. -*ae*, -*as*). Genus of Zoophytes belonging to the family Actiniadae; (pop.) sea-anemone. [mod. L f. Gk *aktis* -*inos* ray]

ăc′tinism, n. That property of the sun's rays by which chemical changes are produced, as in photography. So **actĭn′IC** to a. [as prec. + -ISM]

actĭn′ium, n. Radio-active substance found in pitchblende; an element that turns dark in sunlight. [as prec. + -IUM]

actino- in comb. = Gk *aktis* -*inos* ray, as **ăctĭnŎm′ETER** n., instrument for measuring intensity of sun's heating rays; **ăctĭnŎTHE′RAPY** n., treatment of disease by light rays.

ăc′tion, n., & v.t. 1. Process of acting, exertion of energy or influence, as *men of* ~, *put in* ~, ~ *of an acid*; thing done, act; (in drama) series of events represented; mode of acting, management of body, etc., as ~ *of a player, horse*; mechanism of piano or other instrument; legal process; engagement between troops (*A*~ *Front*), Artillery word of command. **2.** v.t. Bring a legal ~ against. [F, f. L *actionem* (as ACT² see -ION)]

ăc′tionable (-shon-), a. Affording ground for an action at law. Hence **~LY²** adv. [ACTION + -ABLE]

ăc′tĭvate, v.t. Make active (~*d sludge*, aerated sewage containing aerobic bacteria); (Phys.) make radio-active. [-ATE³]

ăc′tĭve, a. 1. Given to outward action; working, effective; energetic, diligent; acting of one's own accord, acting upon others. **2.** (Gram.) the ~ *voice* comprises all forms of intransitive verbs, & those forms of transitive verbs that attribute the verbal action to the person or thing whence it proceeds (the logical subject), as *We punished him*; not, like the forms of the passive voice, to the person or thing to whom it is directed (the logical object), as *He was punished by us*. Less correctly, verbs are themselves called ~. Hence **~LY²** (-vl-) adv. [F (-*if*, -*ive*), f. L *actīvus* (as ACT,² see -IVE); or direct f. L in theol. phr. *vita actīva*]

ăc′tĭvĭty, n. Exertion of energy; quality of being active, dilligence, nimbleness; (pl.) active forces, spheres of action. [f. F *activité* f. med. L *activitātem* (as prec., see -TY)]

ăc′ton, n. Jacket of quilted cotton worn under mail; mail-plated jacket of leather etc. [f. OF *auqueton* (mod. *hoqueton*) padding, padded jacket, f. Sp. *alcoton* (mod. *algodon*) cotton f. Arab. *al-qutun* the cotton]

ăc′tor, n. Dramatic performer, whence **ăc′tress¹** n.; (rarely) doer. [L., = doer, actor (as ACT²; see -OR¹)]

ăc′tual, a. Existing in fact, real; present, current. [f. F *actuel* f. LL *actualis* (*actus* ACT²; see -AL)]

ăctual′ity, n. Reality; (pl.) existing conditions. [f. med. L *actere* ACT²; see -ALI)]

ăc′tualize, v.t. Realize (as prec., see -IZE)

ăc′tually, adv. In actual fact, really; for the time being; even (strange as it may seem). [-LY²]

ăc′tuary, n. Expert in theory & practice of statistics, esp. of mortality, sickness, retirement, & unemployment; (formerly) registrar, notary. Hence **ăctuār′ial** a. [f. L *actuarius* amanuensis, book-keeper (*actus*; see ACTUAL & -ARY²)]

ăc′tuāte, v.t. Communicate notion to (a machine etc.); serve as motive to (person). Hence **ăctuā′TION** n. [f. med. L *actuare* (*actus* as prec., see -ATE³)]

acu′leate, a. (Zool.) having a sting; (Bot.) prickly; pointed, incisive. [f. L *aculeatus* (ACULEUS, see -ATE²)]

acu′leus, n. (pl. -i). (Zool.) sting; (Bot.) prickle. [L *aculeus* sting, dim. of *acus* needle]

acū′men, n. Keen discernment, penetration. [L *acumen –minis* anything sharp (*acuere* sharpen)]

acū′minate¹, a. (nat. hist.). Tapering to a point. [f. L *acuminare* (prec.), see -ATE²]

acū′minate², v.t. Sharpen, point; give poignancy to. Hence **acūminā′TION** n. [as prec., see -ATE³]

|| acū′shla (-ŏŏ-), n. Darling. [f. Ir. *á cuisle* O pulse (of my heart)]

acūte′, a. Sharp, pointed; (of angles) less than a right angle; (of diseases) coming sharply to a crisis, opp. to *chronic*; (of sounds) high, shrill; (of letters) bearing the ~ ACCENT. Hence ~**LY²** (-tĭ-) adv., ~**NESS** (-tn-) n. [f. L *acutus* sharpened (*acuere* acute-sharpen)]

acū′ti- in comb. Sharp, as ~*foliate* sharp-leaved, ~*lobate* sharp-lobed. [L comb. form of *acutus* ACUTE]

-acy, suf. forming nouns of state or quality from or modelled on L *-acia* or Gk *-ateia*. 1. N. of quality f. L *-aci-* f. adji. in *-aci-*: f. *fall-* deceive *fall-aci-a* f. adji. in *-aci-*: *fall-* deceive *fall-acia* f. adji. in *-aci-*: f. *fall-aci-a* deceitful *fall-aci-a* f. nouns in *-ac-* (nom. *-as, -i-* being part of stem or connecting link): med. L *primati-* primacy; & by analogy *supremacy*. 3. N. of state f. med. L *-at-i-a* f. nouns in *-atus*: *advocat-us advocat-ia* advocacy;

& by analogy *curacy*. **This formation** was extended to adji. f. L *-atus* to form nouns of state or quality. 4. N. of state, through L, f. Gk *-ateia* f. n. in *-ates* or vb in *-ateuein*.

ad-, pref. 1. f. L *ad* to, with sense of motion or direction to, change into, addition, adherence, increase, or mere intensification. Before c f g l n p q r s t, & prob. before b, *ad* was in later L assimilated; before vowels & d h j m v, it was unchanged. In OF, L *ad*, wherever recognized as such, became *a-*, even before vowels, as *adrnev* f. L *adornare*; but later the spelling was Latinized, sometimes with changed pronunciation, both in F & E, where the OF forms had still more in E. (The use of *ad-, ab-*, in pairs like *adoral, aboral, situated ad & away from mouth*, is unknown to L.) 2. The pedantic spelling *ad-* for *a-* was sometimes extended to *a-* coming not from L *ad-* but f. L *ab* (*advance* f. *avancer* f. L *abanteare*), f. OF *en-* (*adieu* OF *endette*), f. OF *es-* f. L *ex-* (*affray* OF *esfrayer*) f. OE *a-* (*accurse* ME *a-curse*, etc.; so *admiral* f. Arab. *amiral*. New native compounds with E *a-* were falsely spelt in the same way.

-ad, suf. of nouns. 1. f. Gk *-ad-* (nom. *-as*), in collective numerals (*monad, dyad, triad, chiliad, myriad*); in fem. patronymics (*Dryad, Naiad*); in names of poems (*Iliad*, & by anal. *Dunciad, Rosciad*); in family names of plants (*liliad, asclepiad*). 2. f. F *-ade*; see the more usual *-ade* ¹. 3. suf. invented to form adji. & adv. in the sense of 'towards' (the part indicated by main element of word), as *caudad* towards the tail [L *cauda* tail]

ăd′age, n. Traditional maxim, proverb. [F, f. L *adagium* (*ad* to + *agi-* root of *aio* I say)]

adā′gio (adáhl′yŏ), adv., a., n. (mus.). Slow(ly); (n.) ~ movement. [It.]

Ăd′am¹ (ă-), n. The first man (*not know one from ~*, have no knowledge of his looks); *old* ~ (unregenerate condition), ~*'s ale* or *wine* (water), ~*'s apple* (projection of the thyroid cartilage of the larynx). [Heb. *a-dām* man]

Ad′am² (ă-), a. (At first in pl.) of the decorative style created by the brothers Robert & James *Adam* in the 18th c.

ăd′amant, n. A thing impenetrably hard (*be* ~, stubbornly refuse compliance with requests); (formerly) loadstone; diamond.

Hence **adamān'tine**[2] a. [f. OF *adamaunt* f. L *adamantem* (nom. -mas) f. Gk *adamas -mantos* untamable (a- not +damaō I tame); used in Gk of the hardest metal, prob. steel; in med. L of the loadstone, from confusion with *ad-amantem* having an attraction for; from 17th cent., often a synonym for DIAMOND]

Ad'amite (ă-), n. Child of Adam, human being; unclothed man; (Eccl.) name of sects who imitated Adam in this respect; (pl.) a section of humanity supposed by some to be alone derived from Adam. [ADAM[1]+-ITE]

adapt', v.t. Fit (a thing *to* another); make suitable (*to* or *for* a purpose); modify, alter; (*plays ~ed from the French*). Hence or cogn. ~ABIL'ITY, **adapta'tion**, nn., ~ABLE, ~IVE, aa. [f. F *adapter* f. L AD(*aptare* f. *aptus* fit)]

ăd căptǎn'dum (vŭl'gus), adv. & a. (Calculated) to take the fancy (of the rabble). [L]

add, v.t. & i. Join (one thing *to* another); say *as your entreaties to mine, ~ insult to injury, this ~s to* (increases) *our difficulties, he ~ed* (stated further) *that—, ~ up* or *together* (find the sum of), *~* (perform the process of summation) *correctly, ~in* (include). [f. L AD(*dere dit*=*dare* put)]

ădd'ax, n. Large N.-African & Arabian antelope with twisted horns. [L, f. African wd]

addén'dum, n. (pl. -da). Thing to be added; appendix, addition. [L gerundive of *addere* ADD]

ădd'er, n. Small venomous snake, esp. Common Viper: *Puff, Death, Horned, A~*, species of Viperidae; *Flying A~*, dragonfly; *A~'s tongue*, kind of fern. [f. OE *nædre* (cf. OLG *nadra*, OHG *natra*) serpent: n- lost in ME by wrong division of *a naddre* into *an addre*; *nedder* survives in dial.]

addict', v.t. Devote, apply habitually, (*to* a practice), *as his tastes ~ him, he ~s himself* or *his mind, he is ~ed, to*; (Rom. Law) deliver over by sentence of a judge. So **ădd'ict** n. person ~ed to specified drug etc. (*opium ~*), **addic'tion** n. [f. L AD(*dicere dict-* say) assign]

Add'ison's disease (ă-: zěză), n. Disease characterized by progressive anaemia & debility & brown discoloration of skin. [T. Addison discoverer, 1855]

addi'tion, n. Process of adding (*in- to*, as well as); thing added (*a useful ~*). [F, f. L *additionem* (as ADD, see -ION)]

addi'tional (-shon-), a. Added, supplementary. Hence ~IY[2] adv. [prec.+-AL]

ăd'dle[1], a. *~ egg*, rotten one, one that produces no chicken; empty, vain; muddled, unsound, as *~-brained, -head, -pated*. [f. OE *adela* mud (cf. MLG *adele* G *adel*); now used only as adj.]

ăd'dle[2], v.t. & i. Muddle, confuse; (of eggs) grow addle. [f. prec.]

ăd'dled (-ld), a. Made addle. [ADDLE a. assim. to p.p. form, apparently before ADDLE v. existed]

address'[1], v.t. Direct in speech or writing (~ *remarks, a protest, petition, etc. to* person; ~ *oneself to*, speak or write to); write directions for delivery on cover of (letter, parcel, etc.); speak or write to, esp. deliver a speech to, (person, audience); apply (*oneself to* a task); (Golf) adjust club head behind (ball) before playing stroke. [f. F *adresser*=LL +AD(*drictāre* f. *drictum* for *directum* DIRECT)]

address'[2] n. Readiness, skill, dexterity, adroitness; superscription of letter, name of place to which person's letters are directed, whence ~OGRAPH (2) n. P., machine for printing ~es; act of dispatching a ship; manner, bearing, in conversation; discourse delivered to audience; (pl.) courteous approach, courtship (*pay one's ~es to*). [f. prec. & f. F *adresse* n. f. *adresser*]

addressee', n. Person to whom a letter is addressed. [ADDRESS[1]+-EE]

addu'cle', v.t. Cite as proof or instance. Hence ~e ABLE, ~'IBLE, aa. [f. L AD-(*ducere duct-* lead)]

addū'cent, a. (physiol.) (Of muscles) drawing to a common centre. [as prec. see -ENT]

ădduct', v.t. (physiol.). Draw to a common centre. [as ADDUCE]

adduc'tion, n. Act of adducing; act of adducting. [F, f. L *adductionem* (as prec, see -ION)]

-ade, suf. of nouns. **1** f. F -*ade*, the form in which Pr., Sp., or Port. wds in -*ata* f. L -*ata* (fem. sing. p.p. of verbs in -*are*) were adopted in F, often supplanting native F -*ée* direct f. L, as in *accolade* OF *acolée*. Now a living suf. both in F wds, many of which are borrowed by E (*tirade, gasconnade*), & in E (*blockade, orangeade*). E drops F *e* in *ballad, salad*. Meanings: action done (*tirade, fusillade*); body concerned in action or process (*ambuscade, cavalcade*), thing produced by action or from material (*masquerade, lemonade*). **2** f. F -*ade* f. Gk -*ada* (nom. -*as*), as *decade*; but in E usu. -AD. **3**. f. Sp. or Port. -*ado*, masc. form corresp. to 1 above, with similar meaning (*brocade*), or that of the person concerned (*renegade*).

ăd'enoids (-z), n. pl. Mass of spongy tissue between back of nose & throat, often hindering inflation of lungs. [f. Gk *adēn -enos* acorn, gland]

adept', n. & a. (One who is) thoroughly proficient (*in* anything); skilled alchemist. [f. L *adeptus* p.p. of AD(*ipisci* = *apisci* f. root *ap-*) attain, used in med. L as title by alchemists who 'had attained' the great secret]

ăd'equate, a. Proportionate (*to* the requirements); sufficient. Hence ~ACY n., ~ately[2] (-tli) adv. [f. L AD(*aequare* make equal (*aequus*), see -ATE[3])]

adēs'pota, n. pl. Literary works not attributed to (or claimed by) an author. [neut. pl. of Gk *adespotos* without owner (*a-* not + *despotēs* master)]

à deux (see Ap.), adv. & a. For two; between two. [F]

ăd ĕun'dem, adv. Admitted ~ (*gradum*), to the same (degree at another univ.). [L]

adhēre' (-h-), v.i. Stick fast, cleave, *to* (a substance, person, party, opinion). So ~ENCE (-h-) n. [f. L AD(*haerēre haes-* stick)]

adhēr'ent (-h-), a. & n. Sticking (as substance); due *to*; connected with (*to*); (n.) supporter (of party etc.). So ~ENCE (-h-) n. [f. F *adhérent* (as prec., see -ENT)]

adhē'sion (-hēzhn), n. Adhering (lit. & fig.); (Path.) unnatural union of surfaces due to inflammation. [f. F *adhésion* f, L *adhaesionem* (as ADHERE, see -ION)]

adhē'sive (-h-), a. Having the property of adhering; sticky. Hence ~LY² (-h-: -v-) adv. [f. F *adhésif, -ive* (as ADHERE, see -IVE)]

ad hŏc, a. Arranged for this purpose, special. [L]

ădiabăt'ic, a. (phys.). Impassable to heat; occurring without heat entering or leaving system. [f. Gk *adiabatos* impassable (*a-* not + *diabatos* pass)]

ădian'tum, n. Genus of ferns including the True Maidenhair; (pop.) Black Maidenhair. [L, f. Gk *adianton* maiden-hair, lit. unwetted (*a-* not + *diainō* wet)]

ădiăph'or|ism, n. Latitudinarianism. So ~IST n. [f. Gk *adiaphoros* (*a-* not + *diaphoros* different f. *dia* apart + *pherō* bear)]

adieu (adü'), int. & n. Good-bye; (pl.) take, one's ~, say good-bye. [F (*à* to + *Dieu* God)]

ăd infīnī'tum, adv. Without limit, for ever. [L]

ăd in'terim, adv. & a. For the meantime. [L]

ăd'ipocēre, n. Greyish fatty substance generated in dead bodies subjected to moisture. [f. F *adipocère* (L *adeps -ipis* fat + -o- + *cire* wax f. L *cera*)]

ăd'ipose, a. & n. Pertaining to fat, fatty; (n.) animal fat. Hence ădipŏs'ĭty n. [f. L *adeps -ipis* fat + -OSE]

ăd'it, n. Approach; (of mines) horizontal entrance; act of approaching. [f. L *aditus -ūs* (*ire it-* go)]

ăd'jacent, a. Lying near, contiguous. So ~ENCY n. [f. L AD(*jacēre* lie), see -ENT]

ăd'jective, a. & n. Additional, not standing by itself, dependent; ~ colours (not permanent without a basis); Law A~ (subsidiary part of law, procedure); (Gram.) ~, *noun* ~, the name of an attribute, added to the name of a thing to describe the thing more fully. Hence ~LY².

ădjĕctīv'al¹, a., adjectīv'alix². ~LY² (-v), adv. [f (-)j, -ive), f. L *adjectives* f. AD(*jicĕre ject-=jacĕre* throw), see -IVE]

adjoin', v.t. Join, unite, (one thing to another); be contiguous with. [f. OF *ajoindre* f. L AD(*jungere junct-* join)]

adjourn' (ajörn'), v.t. & i. Put off, postpone; break off for later resumption; (intr. of persons met together) suspend joint proceedings & separate; change the place of meeting. Hence ~MENT (ajö-) n. [f. OF *ajorner* f. LL AD(*jurnare* appoint a day (*jurnus* day, cf. It. *giorno*, F *jour*, f. L *diurnus* daily f. *dies* day)]

adjudge', v.t. Adjudicate upon (a matter); pronounce judicially (*that a thing is* or *a thing to be*); condemn (*person to* penalty or *to do*); award judicially (*thing to person*). Hence ~MENT(-jm-) n. [f. OF *ajuger* (as foll.)]

adjudicate (ajōō-), v.t. & i. (Of a judge or court) decide upon (claim etc.); pronounce (*person to be* something); (intr.) sit in judgement & pronounce sentence. Hence ~A'TION, ~ator² nn., ~A'TIVE a., (ajōō-)-. [f. L AD(*judicare* f. *judex -icis* judge), see -ATE³]

ădjŭnct, n. Subordinate or incidental thing, accompaniment (*to, of*); (Gram.) amplification of the predicate, subject, etc.; (Logic) non-essential attribute. Hence adjunc'tĬVE a., adjunc'tĬVELY² (-vi-) adv. [f. L as ADJOIN]

adjure' (ajoor'), v.t. Charge (a person) under oath or penalty of curse (*to do*); request earnestly. Hence adjura'TION (ăjoor-) n. [f. L AD(*jurare* swear) in LL sense 'put person to an oath']

adjust', v.t. Arrange, put in order; harmonize (discrepancies); adapt (*to* standard or purpose). Hence ~ABLE a., ~MENT n. [f. obs. F *adjuster* (mod. F *ajuster*) f. med. L *adjuxtare* (not, as was thought, *ad + justus* just, but) f. OF *ajuster, ad + juxta* (mod. F *ajouter*) f. LL AD(*juxtare* bring together f. *juxta* near); those meanings of OF *ajuster* that seemed connected with L *justus* being given to the new *adjuster*, formed when the conn. of OF *ajuster* with *adjuxtare* came to be concealed by the new spelling *ajouder*]

adjutage, aj- (ăjōō-), n. Mouthpiece of an artificial fountain. [f. F *ajoutage* (*ajouter* add, join; see prec. f. -AGE]

adjutant (ăjōō-), a. & n. 1. Assistant; (Mil.) army etc. officer who superior officers by communicating orders, conducting correspondence, etc., whence ~ancy n. 2. Gigantic Indian stork. [f. L *adjutare* frequent. as foll., see -ANT]

adjuvant (ăjōō-), a. & n. Helpful, auxiliary; person, thing, that helps. [f, f. L AD(*juvare juv-* help), see -ANT]

ad lib'itum, adv. (abbr. *ad lib.*). At pleasure, to any extent. [L]

admeasure (-mĕzh'er), v.t. Apportion, assign in due shares. [f. OF *amesurer* f. LL AD(*mensurare* MEASURE)]

admeasurement (-mĕzh'erm-), n. Process of admeasuring; comparison; dimensions. [f. OF *amesurement* (as prec., see -MENT)]

admin'icle, n. A help; (Law) corroboratory evidence. Hence **ădmĭnic'ŭlar**[1] a. [f. L AD(*miniculum* prop (*manus* hand)]

admin'ister, v.t. & i. Manage (affairs); dispense (justice, sacraments, *to*); tender (oath *to*); furnish, give, (thing *to*); apply (remedies *to*); (intr.) act as administrator; contribute *to* (one's comfort etc.). Hence **admin'istrable** a. [f. OF *aministrer* f. L AD(*ministrare* MINISTER)]

administra'tion, n. Management (*of business*); management of public affairs, government, the ministry, the Government; (Law) management of deceased person's estate; *Letters of A~*, authority to administer estate of an intestate, opp. *to probate; dispensation (of justice etc.); tendering (of oath); application (of remedies).* [(perh. thr. F) f. L *administratio* (as prec., see -ATION)]

admin'istrative, a. Pertaining to management of affairs; executive. Hence *~lY*[2](-vĭ) adv. [f. L *administrativus* (as prec., see -IVE)]

admin'istra͞itor, n. Manager; one capable of organizing; one who performs official duties (of religion, justice, etc.); applier or giver (*of*); one authorized to manage estates for legal owner during minority etc., or estates of one who dies without appointing competent executors. Hence *~torship* n., *~TRIX* n. (pl. *~trices*, pron. -ĭsĭz *or* -ĭs'ēz). [L, as ADMINISTER, see -OR[2]]

ăd'mirable, a. Surprisingly good, excellent. Hence *~lY*[2] adv. [F, f. L *admirabilis* (as ADMIRE, see -ABLE]

ăd'miral, n. Commander-in-chief of a country's navy (in England, formerly *Lord High A~*); naval officer of highest rank, commander of fleet or squadron; *A~ of the Fleet, A~, Vice-A~, Rear-A~*, the four grades of A~ in British Navy; privileged commander of fishing or merchant fleet; ship that carries the *~*, Flagship; *Red A~, White A~*, two European species of butterfly. Hence *~SHIP* n. [f. OF *amiral* f. Arab. *amir* Commander ad of the (*Faithful, Sea*, etc.), Latinized as *admiralis*, but refashioned (see AD-) as *admiralis*, & confused with L *admirari* wonder at, whence med. L *admirabilis mundi* ruler of the world]

ăd'miraltý, n. Office of admiral; branch of the executive that superintends the navy (in England, *Lords Commissioners of A~*); (Rhet.) command of the seas (esp. *the price of ~*); *Court of A~*, tribunal for trial & decision of maritime questions & offences. [f. OF *admiralté*; see ADMIRAL & -TY]

admira'tion, n. Pleased contemplation; (formerly) wonder; *the ~ of*, admired by; *note of ~* (!). [F, f. L *admirationem* (as foll., see -ATION)]

admire', v.t. Regard with pleased surprise or approval; (also, colloq.) express admiration of (*forgot to ~ her cat*); (formerly) wonder at, wonder. [f. F *admirer* f. L AD(*mirari* wonder at)]

admir'er, n. One that admires; lover. [ADMIRE +-ER[1]]

admiss'ible, a. (Of idea or plan) worthy to be entertained; (Law) allowable as judicial proof; capable of being admitted (*to office or position*). Hence *~BIL'TY* n. [F, f, LL *admissibilis* (as ADMIT, see -BLE]

admis'sion (-shn), n. Admitting, being admitted, (*to society of persons or class of things*); acknowledgement (of thing as true, *that* it is true). [f. L *admissio* (as foll., see -ION)]

admiss'ive, a. Tending to admit. [f. L *admissivus* (as foll., see -IVE)]

admit', v.t. & i. (-tt-). Allow (person etc.) entrance or access (*to* place, class, privileges, etc.); accept as valid or true, whence *~'t'edlY*[2] adv.; acknowledge (thing *to be, that* it is); (abs.) *this, I ~, was wrong*; (of enclosed spaces) have room for; *~ of*, leave room for (doubt, improvement). [f. F *admettre* f. L AD(*mittere miss-* let go)]

admitt'able, a. Capable of being admitted, (usu. *to* a place). [prec. +-ABLE]

admitt'ance, n. Admitting, being admitted, (usu. *to* a place). [ADMIT +-ANCE]

admix', v.t. & i. Add as an ingredient; mingle (*with* something). So *~TURE* n. [AD-+MIX; perth. due to *admixt*, really f. L *admixt-* p.p. of AD(*miscēre mixt-* MIX), but taken for a L pp.]

admon'ish, v.t. Exhort (person *to* do, *that* he should do); give advice; warn (*of* a thing); inform, remind, (*of* a thing, *that*). Hence *~MENT* n. [OE *amonest* f. OF *amonester* f. LL *admonestare* irreg. f. AD(*monēre monit-* warn); *amonest* having dropped final *-t* (supposed to be p.p. ending) became *admonish* on anal. of *abolish* abolish etc.]

admoni'tion, n. Admonishing; warning; reproof. So **admon'itory** a. [f. OF *amonition* f. L *admonitionem* (as prec., see -ION)]

ăd̄ naus'ĕăm, adv. To a disgusting extent. [L]

ădnŏm'inal, a. Belonging to an adnoun; attached to a noun. [f. L *adnomen* variant of *agnomen* in the sense (not L) 'attached to a noun' (*ad to+nomen* noun)]

ăd'noun, n. Adjective, word added to a noun substantive; adjective used substantively. [f. L *ad* to+NOUN on anal. of *adverb*]

ado (ado͞o'), n. Action, business, fuss; difficulty. [f. Norse *at* (=*to* with in-

finitive)+**do**; *much ado* prop.=*much to do*; but *much* being taken as adj., *ado* is treated as n.]

-ado, suf. of nouns, 1. f. Sp. or Port. -*ado* f. L -*ātus* p.p. of vbs in -*āre*, as *desperado* L *desperātus* (*desperāre*); sometimes changed in E to -*ade*, as *renegado*, now *renegade*. 2. Ignorant refashioning of nouns in -*ade* f. F -*ade* =Sp. -*ada*, as *crusado* Sp. *cruzado*, *scolado* Sp. *escolada*.

adŏb'e (*or* -ŏb'), n. Unburnt sun-dried brick. [Sp.]

ădōles'c̦ent, n. & a. (Person) growing up, between childhood & manhood (14 to 25) or womanhood (12 to 21). So ~ENC̦E, ~ENCY, nn. [F, f. L AD(*olescere* ult- incept. of *olere* grow), see -ENT]

Adōn'is, n. Beautiful youth loved by Venus; beau, dandy; (Bot.) genus including Pheasant's Eye; ‖ (Entom.) the butterfly Clifton Blue. [Gk, f. Phoen.]

ăd'onize, v. refl. & t. Adorn, dandify; (oneself): play the Adonis. [ADONIS +-IZE]

adŏpt', v.t. Take (person) into a relation-ship he did not previously occupy; take (idea etc.) from some one else; choose, (one of courses etc.) adopt. Hence ~ABILİTY, adŏp'TION, nn., ~ABLE a. [f. F *adopter* f. L AD(*optare* choose, frequent. of obs. *opere* opt- wish) adopt esp. child]

adŏp'tive, a. Due to adoption, as ~ *son, father*; apt to adopt. Hence ~LY² (-vl-) adv. [F (-*if*, -*ive*), f. L *adoptivus*; see prec. and -IVE]

ador'e, v.t. Regard with the utmost respect & affection; (poet.) worship as a deity; (in R. C. Church) reverence with representative honours (the Host etc.). So ~ABLE a., ~ABLY² adv., ădŏra'TION n. [f. F *adorer* f. L AD(*orare* speak f. os oris mouth) salute, worship]

ador'er, n. Worshipper; ardent admirer, lover. [prec. +-ER¹]

adŏrn', v.t. Add beauty or lustre to; fur-nish with ornaments. So ~MENT n. [f. F *adorner* a. & prep. (arch., poet.) adown =DOWN³. [f. OE of dūne off the mount (see DOWN¹ n.)]

ăd'rem, adv. & pred. a. To the point; to the purpose. [L]

ădren'alin, n. A hormone secreted by the adrenal ductless glands & affecting circula-tion & muscular action; this extracted from animals formedicinal use. [*adrenal* at the kidney (f. L *ad* at +*ren* kidney) +-IN]

adrift', adv. In a drifting condition, at the mercy of wind & tide or of circumstances; (Naut.) unfastened. [A prep. +DRIFT¹]

adroit', a. Having address, dexterous. Hence ~LY² adv., ~NESS n. [F, orig.=rightly (*à to* +*droit* right f. OF *dreit* f. LL *drictum* right; see DIRECT²)]

ădry', adv. & pred.a. Dry; thirsty. [*a-* +DRY¹ on anal. of *acold, athirst*, the prep. a² in these being misunderstood]

ăd'scr̄ipt, a. (Of serf) attached to the soil. [L]

ădscr̄ip'tious (-shi̇shus), a. Adopted from without; supplemental. [f. L AD(*scisc̆ere scit-* inceptive of *scire* know) +-ITIOUS]

ăd'ūl̆āte, v.t. Flatter basely. So ~A'TION, ~ĀTOR², nn., ~ĀTORY a. [f. L *adūlāri* fawn on, see -ATE¹]

Adŭll'amite, n. M.P. seceding from Liberal Party in 1866. [f. cave of *Adullam* (1 *Sam.* xxii. 1, 2) +-ITE¹]

adŭlt' (*or* ăd', *esp. as n*.), a. & n. (One who is) grown up; mature. [as ADOLESCENT]

adŭl'terant, a. & n. (Thing) employed in adulterating. [as foll., see -ANT]

adŭl'terate¹, a. Stained (in conception or in birth) by adultery; (of things) spurious, counterfeit. [as foll., see -ATE²]

adŭl'terāte², v.t. Falsify by admixture of baser ingredients. So ~A'TION, ~ĀTOR² nn. [f. L *adulterare* corrupt(*adulter* adul-terer, f. *ad* to +med. L *alterare* change); replaces obs. vb *adulter* f. OF]

adŭl'ter|er, n. One guilty of adultery. So ~ESS¹ n. [f. *adulter* v. (see prec. & -ER¹); obs., *adulter, avonter*, are f. OF *avoutre*]

adŭl'terine, a. Of, born of, adultery; adulterated, counterfeit; illegal, un-licensed. [f. L *adulterinus* born of adul-tery, spurious (*adulter* adulterer), see -INE²]

adŭl'ter|y, n. Voluntary sexual inter-course of married person with one of the opposite sex other than his or her spouse. So ~OUS a., ~OUSLY² adv. [f. OF *avouterie, aulterie* (L *adulter* adul-terer, see -Y¹), re-formed on F *adultère* f. L *adulterium*]

adŭm'bral, a. Overshadowing, shady. [f. AD-+L *umbra* shade +-AL]

ăd'umbrāte (*or* ădŭm'-), v.t. Represent in outline; faintly indicate; typify, fore-shadow; overshadow. Hence or cogn. ădŭmbra'TION n., adŭm'brātive a. [f. L AD(*umbrare* f. *umbra* shade), see -ATE³]

ăd'ūna'ti̇on (-nsʒw-)(fŭc'tus), a. Highly finished. [L]

ăd'ūrŏl, n. A photographic developer.

adŭst', a. Scorched, dried up, perched; sunburnt; atrabilious, gloomy. [f. L AD(*urere ust-* burn)]

ădvan̄ce' (-vah-), v.t. & i. Move or put forward; promote (plans, persons); bring forward (claims, suggestions); accelerate (events); pay (money) before it is due; lend; raise (price). 2, v.i. Move forward; make progress, as ~*d studies, ideas*. So ~MENT (-ahnsm-) n. (esp. of promotion of plan or person). [f. OF *avancer* f. LL *abantiare* (*abante* =*ab* away +*ante* before, whence F *avant*; see AD-)]

advance² (-vah-), n. Going forward; progress; personal approach, overture; rise in price; payment beforehand, loan; ~ *copy* of book etc., supplied before publication; *in* ~, before (of place or time). [f. prec. & f. F *avance* n. (as prec.)]

advan'tage¹ (-vah-), n. Better position, precedence, superiority; favourable circumstance, whence **advantá'geous** (-jus) a., **advantá'geously** (-jus) adv.; (in Tennis) next point or game won after deuce points or games; *have the* ~ *of, gain an* ~ *over*, have, acquire, a better position than (*you have the* ~ *of me*, esp. you know me & I do not know you); *take* ~ (avail oneself) *of a circumstance*; *take* ~ *of* (over-reach) *a person*; *take a person at* ~ (by surprise); *to* ~, in a way to exhibit the merits (*was seen, heard*, &c ~): ~-*ground* (usu. *vantage-*), position that gives superiority. [f. F *avantage* (*avant*; see ADVANCE v. & -AGE)]

advan'tage² (-vah-), v.t. Be beneficial to; be an advantage to; further, promote. [f. F *avantager* (*avantage*; see prec.)]

Ad'vent (ād-), n. Season before the Nativity; coming of Christ, Incarnation; second coming of Christ; (*a*~) any (important) arrival. Hence ~ISM (2) n., ~IST (2) n., (tenets of) member of a sect holding millenarian views. [f. OF *advent, avent* f.L *advent- come*]

adventi'tious (-shus), a. Coming from without; accidental, casual; || (Law, of property) coming from a stranger or by collateral, not direct, succession. Hence ~LY² adv. [f. L *adventicius* (med.L *-titius*, see -TIOUS)]

adven'ture¹, n. Risk, danger; daring enterprise; unexpected incident; commercial speculation; hazardous activity. [f. OF *aventure* f.L *adventura* (*res* thing) about to happen (as ADVENT)]

adven'ture², v.t. & i. Hazard, imperil, (oneself, thing); incur risk; dare to go or come (*into, in, upon*, a place); dare to enter on, upon, (undertaking). [f. OF *aventurer* (as prec.)]

adven'turer (-cher-), n. One who seeks adventures; soldier of fortune; speculator; one who lives by his wits. [f. F *aventurier* (as ADVENTURE¹, see -ER¹)]

adven'turesome (-cher-), a. Given to adventures. [ADVENTURE¹ +-SOME]

adven'turéss (-cher-), n. Female adventurer; woman on the look-out for a position. [f. ADVENTURER, see -ESS]

adven'turous (-cher-), a. Rash, venturesome; enterprising. Hence ~LY² adv. [f. OF *aventuros* (as ADVENTURE¹, see -OUS)]

ad'verb, n. Word that modifies or qualifies an adjective, verb, or other adverb, expressing a relation of place, time, circumstance, manner, etc. (e.g. *gently, so, now, where, why*). [f. F *adverbe* f. L AD-*verbium* (*verbum* word, verb) transl. of Gk *epirrhéma* addition to a predication]

adverb'ial, a. Pertaining to an adverb; of the nature of an adverb. Hence ~LY² adv. [f. L *adverbialis* (*adverbium*; see prec. & -AL)]

ăd vĕrb'um, adv. & a. Word for word. [L]

ăd'versary, n. Opponent, antagonist, enemy; *the A*~, the Devil. [f. OF *aversier* f. L *adversarius* opposed (as ADVERSE, see -ARY¹)]

advĕrs'ative, a. (Of words etc.) expressing opposition or antithesis. Hence ~LY² (-vi) adv. [f. L *adversativus* (*adversari* oppose, see foll. & -IVE)]

ăd'vĕrse, a. Contrary, hostile, (*to*); hurtful, injurious, (*to*); placed opposite. Hence ~LY² (-sl-) adv. [f. OF *avers* f. L AD(*vertere vers-* turn)]

advĕrs'ity, n. Condition of adverse fortune; misfortune. [f. OF *aversité* f. L *adversitatem* (as prec., see -TY)]

advĕrt', v.i. Refer *to* (in speaking or writing). [f. 14th-c. E *averte* f. F *avertir* f. LL AD(*vertĕre*=L *vertĕre* turn) draw attention to: F *avertir* (see AD-) was written *adv-* to dist. it from obs. *avertir* f.LL *avertĕre* turn away (*ab*), & E adopted this in *advert & advertise*]

ăd'vertise (-z), v.t. & i. Notify, warn, inform, (person of thing, *that*); make generally known (thing *by* circular, *in* journal, also abs.); ~ *for*, ask for by public notice. [f. F *avertir* (st. *-iss-*); see ADVERT]

advĕr'tisement (-zm-), n. Public announcement (usu. by placards or in journals). [f. F *avertissement* (as prec., see -MENT)]

advice', n. Opinion given or offered as to action, counsel; information given, news; (pl.) communications from a distance; (Commerc.) formal notice of transactions. [f. OF *avis* f. LL +*advisum* (*ad* +*visum* p.p. of *vidēre* see)]

advis'able (-z-), a. To be recommended; expedient. Hence ~LY²TY, ~ableness, nn., ~abix² adv. [f. foll. +-ABLE]

advise' (-z), v.t. & i. Offer counsel to; recommend (*the doctor* ~*s a change of air*); (Commerc.) announce; take counsel *with*. Hence **advis'ER¹** (-z-) n., esp. person habitually consulted. [f. F *aviser* f. LL *advisare* (*advisum*, see ADVICE)]

advised' (-zd), a. Deliberate, considered, whence ~LY² (-iz'édli) adv.; judicious. [p.p. of prec.]

advis'ory (-z-), a. Giving advice; consisting in giving advice. [ADVISE +-ORY]

ăd vit'am aut culpam, adv. During good behaviour. [L]

ad'vocacy, n. Function of an advocate; pleading in support of. [f. F *advocatie, -tie*, f. med. L *advocatia* (as foll., see -ACY)]

ăd'vocate¹ (-at), n. One who pleads for another; one who speaks in behalf of (proposal

etc.); professional pleader in courts of justice; *Faculty of A~s*, Scots bar; *Lord A~*, principal law-officer of crown in Scotland; *Devil's ~* (also, L., *advocatus diaboli*), one who pleads against a candidate for canonization. Hence **~SHIP** (-ts-) n. [f. F *avocat* f. L *advocatus* p.p. (as n.) of *advocare* call)]

ad'vocate², v.t. Plead for, defend, recommend publicly. [f. prec.]

|| **ad'vowson** (-z-), n. Right of presentation to a benefice. [f. OF *avoëson* f. med. L *advocationem* function of patron (as prec., see -ION)]

ād·ynăm'ia, n. Want of vital force; physical prostration. Hence **ădynăm'ic** a. [Gk *adunamia* (a- not + *dunamis* power)]

ăd'ytum, n. (pl. -ta). Innermost part of a temple; private chamber, sanctum. [L f. Gk *aduton* not to be entered (a- not + *duton* vb) adj. of *duō* enter)]

ădze, n. & v.t. Tool for cutting away surface of wood, like axe with arched blade at right angles to handle; (vb) cut with ~. [OE *adesa*, etym. dub.]

æ, ae, symbol repr. a vowel sound betw. *a* & *e*. **1**. In OE short *æ* repr. orig. Teut. short *a*, the sound of *a* in *man*; replaced after 1100 usu. by *a* sometimes by *e*. Long *æ* repr. same sound prolonged, & was replaced in 13th c. by *e* or *ee*. **2**. In 16th c. *æ* was reintroduced to repr. L *æ* & Gk *ai*; as, *ædify* (L *aedificare*), *æther* (Gk *aither*). In familiar wds *æ* gave place to *e*, (*edify*, *ether*), being kept (pron. *ē*) in some (*ædify*, *ether*); familiar wds take *æ* in Gk & L proper names *Æneas*, *Cæsar*, but *Judæa*, *Etna*), in names of Gk & Roman antiquities (*ædile*, *ægis*), & in some scientific terms [*aetiology*, *phænogamous*, but *phenomenon*, *museum*].

-æ, -ae, pl. suf. of L nouns of 1st decl. in -a.

-a, & L form of Gk -ai pl. of nouns of 1st decl. in -ē, -ē, -ēs, -as; kept in non-naturalized words (*lamina*, *larvae*), esp. in proper names (*Heraclidae*) & names of animal & plant orders (*Felidae*, *Rosidae*); varying with -as in some wds acc. to degree of familiarity (*actinias*, -ae) or of technicality (mathematical *formulae*, theological *formulas*); familiar wds take -as (*areas*, *hyenas*, *Julias*).

aed'ile, n. Roman magistrate who superintended public buildings, shows, police, etc. Hence **~SHIP** (-ish-) n. [f. L *aeditis* (*aedes* house, see -ILE)]

|| **ae'ger**, n. (In Eng. univ.) note certifying that student is ill. [L. = sick]

ae'gis, n. Protection, impregnable defence; (Myth.) shield of Zeus or Athene. [L, f. Gk *aegis*, etym. dub.]

|| **aegrō'tăt**, n. (In Eng. univ.) certificate that student is too ill to attend examination etc. [L. = he is sick (*aeger*)]

Aeō'lian, a. **1**. Of Aeolis, district of Asia Minor colonized by ancient Greeks; (Mus.) ~ *mode*, ancient Greek MODE, ninth of the church modes (with A as final & E as dominant). **2**. Of Aeolus, god of winds; ~ *harp*, stringed instrument producing musical sounds on exposure to wind. [f. L *Aeolus* (1. *Aeolis* Gk *Aiolis*; 2. *Aeolus* Gk *Aiolos*) + -AN]

Aeŏl'ic, a. & n. Aeolian (dialect). [f. L f. Gk *aiolikos* (as prec., see -IC)]

ae'olipȳle, -pile, (or ēŏl-), n. Instrument for showing force of steam escaping through narrow aperture. [f. F *æolipyle* f. L *Aeoli pylae* f. Gk *Aiolou pulai* gates of Aeolus, god of winds]

aeŏl'tropy, n. Change of physical qualities consequent on change of position. [f. Gk *aiolos* changeful + -*tropia* turning]

ae'on, ē'on, n. An age of the universe, immeasurably long period; eternity. [L *aeon* f. Gk *aiōn* age]

ā'erāte, v.t. Expose to mechanical or chemical action of air; charge with carbonic acid gas (formerly called *fixed air*). Hence **āerā'TION** n. [f. L *aer* air + -ATE³]

āēr'ial (or āēr-), a. & n. **1**. Of air, gaseous; thin as air, ethereal; immaterial, imaginary; of or in the atmosphere, atmospheric; existing, moving, in the air; ~ *railway*, *ropeway*, system of overhead cables from which cars or containers are suspended, usu. driven electrically; ~ *wire* or *antenna* as used in wireless. **2**. n. (pron. āir-). [f. L *aer*, *aereus*, f. f. *aire*, perh. f. f. *area* level ground or L *atrium* hall]

aē'riform (or āēr-), a. Of the form of air, gaseous; unsubstantial, unreal. [f. L *aer* air + -FORM]

aero- (āir'o, āēro) in comb. Air, of aircraft, as; ~*bat'ics*, feats of expert aviation; ~*dynam'ics*, the physics of gases in motion & their mechanical effects; ~*dyne*, heavier-than-air aircraft; ~*foil*, aeroplane wing, tailplane, or fin; ||~*gram*, wireless message; ~*lite*, ~*lith*, meteorite; ~*naut*, one who navigates a (lighter-than-air) flying machine; ~*naut'ic(al)* aa.; ~*naut'ics*, science, art, or practice of aerial navigation; ~*stat*, lighter-than-air aircraft; ~*statics*, physics of gases in equilibrium, science of air-navigation. [Gk comb.-form of *aēr* air]

ā'erobe, n. Any microbe that lives on free oxygen from the air. Hence **āerōb'IAN**, **āerōb'ic**, aa. [AERO-, Gk *bios* life]

|| **aerodrōme** (āir'ō), n. Large tract of open level ground, including all buildings & fixtures, for the operation of aircraft. [AERO-, -DROME]

‖ **aeroplāne** (ā°), n. Mechanically driven heavier-than-air flying machine. [AERO-, Gk *planos* wandering]

aeru'ginous (ēro͞o-), a. Of the nature or colour of verdigris, or copper-rust. [f. F *érugineux* f. L *aeruginosus* (*aerugo -inis* verdigris f. *aes aeris* brass, see -OUS]

Aescŭlāp'ius, n. God of medicine; physician. Hence ~IAN a. [L]

aes'thēte, n. Professed appreciator of the beautiful. [f. Gk *aisthētēs* one who perceives (as foll.)]

aesthět'ic, a. Belonging to the appreciation of the beautiful; having such appreciation; in accordance with principles of good taste. Hence ~ICAL a., ~ically[2] adv., ~ICISM, ~ICS, nn. [f. Gk *aisthētikos* (*aisthanomai* perceive, see -IC)]

aestho-physiŏl'ogy (z-), n. Scientific study of the organs of sensation. [irreg. f. Gk *aisth-* perceive + PHYSIOLOGY]

aes'tival, (esp. U.S.) **estival**, (ēs'tival, ēstīv'al), a. Belonging to, appearing in, summer. [F (*es-*), f. L *aestivalis* f. *aestivus* (*aestus* heat), see -IVE, -AL]

aes'tivāte (ēst°, ĕst°), v.i. Spend the summer, esp. (Zool.) in state of torpor. [f. L *aestivare*, see -ATE[3]]

aestivā'tion (ēst°, ĕst°), n. (Zool.) aestivating; (Bot.) arrangement of petals in flower-bud before expansion. [f. prec., see -ATION]

aetāt'is, **aet'āt.**, **aet.** Of or at the age of (*aet.* 17); *anno* ~ *suae* —, in the —th year of his age. [L]

aetiŏl'ogy, n. Assignment of a cause; philosophy of causation; (Med.) science of the causes of disease. So **aetiolŏ'gical** a., **aetiolŏ'gically[2]** adv. [f. L f. Gk *aitiologia* (*aitia* cause), see -LOGY]

af-, pref. = AD- before f.

afar', adv. At, to, a distance (usu. ~ *off*; *from* ~, from a distance). [f. OE *feor* FAR adv., with prepp. OF, ON]

aff'able, a. Easy of address, courteous, complaisant. Hence or cogn. **affabıl'ıty** n., **aff'ablry[2]** adv. [F, f. L L *affabilis* f. AF(*fari* speak), see -BLE]

affair', n. Thing to be done; concern; business, matter, as *that is my* ~; (pl.) ordinary pursuits of life; ~ *of honour*, duel; (colloq.) *of material things*) a *gorgeous* etc. ~. [f. OF *afaire* (*à faire* to do), cf. ADO]

affaire (*de cœur*) (see Ap.), n. Love affair. [F]

affect'[1], v.t. Practise, use, as ~ *a costume*; (of things) tend to assume (form, shape, etc.); assume (character), as ~ *the free-thinker*; pretend to have or feel (indifference etc.); pretend (*to* do). [f. F *affecter* f. L *affectare* aim at, pretend to have, frequent. of AF(*ficere fect-*=*facere* do)]

affect'[2], v.t. Attack (as disease); move, touch, (in mind), whence ~ing[LY[2]] adv.; produce (material) effect on; (pass.,

arch.) be assigned, allotted, (*to particular* service etc.). [(perh. thr. F) f. L *afficere* attach to (see prec.)]

affect'[3], n. (psych.). Feeling, emotion, desire. [f. L *affectus* disposition f. *afficere* (prec.)]

affectā'tion, n. Studied display of; artificiality of manner; pretence; (rare) declared occupation or employment (*all ships, whatever their* ~). [f. L *affectatio* pursuit after (as AFFECT[1], see -ATION)]

affec'ted, a. Artificially assumed or displayed; pretended; (of persons) full of affectation, artificial, whence ~LY[2] adv., ~NESS n.; (with adv.) disposed, inclined, (*towards* or abs.); attacked(as by disease); moved in the feelings; acted upon physically. [AFFECT[1, 2]+-ED[1]]

affec'tion, n. Affecting; mental state, emotion, whence ~AL a.; disposition (*towards*); goodwill, love, (*towards*); bodily state due to any influence; malady, disease; mode of being; property, quality, attribute. [F, f. L *affectionem* (as AFFECT[2], see -ION)]

affec'tionate (-shon-), a. Loving; fond; (of things) showing love or tenderness. Hence ~LY[2] (-tl-) adv., ~NESS (-tn-) n. [Latinized f. F *affectionné*]

affec'tive, a. Pertaining to the affections, emotional. [F (-*if*, -*ive*), f. med. L *affectivus* (as AFFECT[2] see -IVE)]

affer'ent, a. Conducting inwards or towards, as ~ *nerves*, ~ *vessels*. [f. L AF(*ferre* bring), see -ENT]

affettuo'sō (-to͞o-), adv. (mus.). Feelingly. [It.]

affi'ance[1], n. Faith, trust (*in*); pledging of faith, esp. plighting of troth in marriage. [f. OF *afiance* f. *after* trust f. LL AF(*fidare* (*fides* faith), see -ANCE]

affi'ance[2], v.t. Promise solemnly in marriage (usu. pass.). [f. OF *afiancer* f. *afiance*, see prec.]

affiche (afēsh°), n. Notice-paper affixed to wall, poster. [F, f. *afficher* post up]

affidāv'it, n. Written statement, confirmed by oath, to be used as judicial proof. (Strictly, deponent *swears* an ~, judge *takes* it; but in pop. use deponent *makes* or *takes* it) [L, = has stated on faith or oath, f. AF(*fidare*, see AFFIANCE[1]]

affil'iāte, v.t. (Of an institution) adopt (persons as members, societies as branches); attach (persons, societies) *to*, connect (them) *with*, (a society); (Law) fix paternity of (illegitimate child *on* putative father) for purpose of maintenance; ascribe (child) *to* its parent; father (a thing) *upon*, trace (it) *to*. So **affiliā'tion** n. [f. L AF(*filiare* adopt (*filius* son), see -ATE[3]]

affined' (-nd), a. Related, connected. [f. F *affind* (*affin* f. L *affinis*, see foll.) +-ED[1]; no vb in F]

affin'ity, n. Relationship, relations, by marriage; relations; kindred, in general;

structural resemblance (between animals, plants, languages); (fig.) similarity of character suggesting relationship, family likeness; liking; attraction; (Chem.) tendency of certain elements to unite with others. [f. F affinité f. L L affinitatem (AFFINIS related, lit. bordering on, f. finis end, see -TY]

affirm', v.t. & i. Assert strongly, aver; make formal declaration, (Law) make AFFIRMATION; (Logic, Gram.) state in the affirmative; confirm, ratify, (judgement). Hence ~ABLE, ~ATORY, aa. [f. OF afermer f. L L affirmare (firmus strong)]

affirma'tion, n. Affirming, esp. (Law) solemn declaration by person who conscientiously declines taking an oath. [F, f. L affirmationem (as prec., see -ATION)]

affirm'ative, a. & n. Affirming, answering yes; (Logic) expressing agreement of the two terms of a proposition; answer in the ~, answer yes, say that a thing is so. Hence ~LY² (vt) adv. [F (-f, -ive), f. L L affirmativus (as prec., see -IVE)]

affix'¹, v.t. Fix, fasten, (thing to, on); impress (seal, stamp); add in writing (signature, postscript); attach (censure, salary, etc.) [perh. thr. MF affixer, occas. refash. of OF aficher F aficher) f. med. L affixare frequent. of L L af(figere fix- fix]

affix'², n. Appendage, addition; (Gram.) addition placed at the beginning or end of root, stem, or word, to modify its meaning. [f. F affixe f. L L affigere (see prec.]

affix'ture, n. Affixing. [f. AFFIX¹ after FIXTURE; correct form (on F) would be affixure]

affla'tus, n. Communication of supernatural knowledge; divine impulse, poetic or other; inspiration. [L vbl n. f. Afflare blow)]

afflict', v.t. Distress with bodily or mental suffering. [f. 14th-c. afflict adj., f. OF aflit f. L L af(fligere fict- strike down]

afflic'tion, n. Misery, distress; pain, calamity. So ~IVE a. [F, f. L L afflictionem (as prec., see -ION]

afflu'ent¹ (-lŏŏ-), n. Tributary stream. [f. prec., prob. after F]

afflu'ent² (-lŏŏ-), a. Flowing freely, copious; abounding (esp. in riches), wealthy. Hence or cogn. ~ENCE n, ~ENTY² adv. [F, f. L L af(fluere fluc- flow), see -ENT]

af'flux (-lŏŏ-), n. Flow towards a point, esp. of humours; accession. [f. med. L affluxus -ŭs, vbl n. as AFFLUENT]

afford', v.t. (With can) have the means, be rich enough, (to do), manage to spare; furnish, bestow; (of things) yield supply of. [OE geforthian (ge- pref. implying completeness + forthian advance f. forth forward); ge- was reduced to a-, which was corrupted to af- after L (see AD-]

affo'rest, v.t. Convert into forest or hunting-ground. So ~A'TION n. [f. med. L Afforestare (foresta FOREST)]

affran'chise (-z), v.t. Free from servitude or obligation. [f. F affranchiss- lengthened st. of affranchir (à to + franchir free f. franc, see FRANK²)]

affray', n. Breach of the peace, caused by fighting or riot in a public place. [f. OF effrei f. esfreer, vb f. L L Exfridare (LL fridus f. Teut. fridu, OE frith, peace)]

affreight'ment (-rāt-), n. The chartering of a ship to carry cargo (usu. contract of ~). [f. F affréter to charter]

affright'¹ (-rīt), v.t. (arch.). Frighten. [late formation on FRIGHT v., partly due to obs.

affright'² (-rīt), n. (arch.). Alarm, terror. cf. AFRAID]

affront'¹ (-ŭnt), v.t. Insult openly; put to the blush, offend the modesty or self-respect of; face, confront. [f. OF afronter slap in the face, insult, f. L L Affrontare (frons -tis face)]

affront'² (-ŭnt), n. Open insult, as put ~ upon, offer an ~ to, feel it on ~. [f. prec.]

affu'sion (-zhn), n. Pouring on, esp. of water on the body in one kind of baptism; (Med.) pouring of water, usually 50° to 70° Fahr. upon fever patients. [f. L Af(fundere fus- pour), see -ION]

Afghan (ăf'găn), n. Native, language, of ~istan; (a~) knitted woollen coverlet. [f. prec.]

afield', adv. On or in the field (esp. of labour or battle); to the field; away from home, at a distance, as far ~. [a prep.]

afire', adv. & pred. a. On fire (lit. & fig.). [A prep.]

aflame', adv. & pred. a. In flame, in a glow of light. (lit. & fig.). [A prep.]

afloat', adv. & pred. a. In a floating condition; at sea, on board ship, in naval service; full of water; floating in the air; out of debt, paying one's way; in full swing; in general circulation, current; (Commerc.) in currency as negotiable document; unsettled, adrift. [OE on flote (ON prep.), adv. Thoroughly, fully. [F]

afoot', adv. & pred. a. On one's own feet; astir, on the move; in operation or employment. [a prep.]

afore', adv. & prep. (Naut.), in front, in front of, as ~ the mast; (arch.) previously. [f. OE on foran (on prep.+foran, adv., in front, dat. of for, which was used as noun or adj.)]

afore'-... in comb. Before, previously, as ~cited, ~going, ~named, ~said, ~thought, premeditated, as malice ~thought; ~time, previously. [prec.]

à fortiori, adv. With stronger reason, more conclusively. [L]

afraid', pred. a. Alarmed, frightened, (abs. or of); (of the consequences, & therefore unwilling to do a thing, ~ of a thing's happening, ~ lest it should happen, ~ (that) it will happen; I'm ~ (colloq.), I have to admit with regret

(I'm ~ I'm late; I'm ~ there's none left. [p.p. of obs. vb afray f. OF esfreer, see AFFRAY]

af'reet, -rit, -rite, (-rēt), n. Evil demon in Mohammedan mythology. [Arab. 'ifrīt]

afresh', adv. Anew, with fresh beginning. [A- (3) + FRESH]

Af'rican (ăf-), a. & n. (Native) of Africa. Hence ~ISM (4) n., ~IZE (3) v.t.

Afrikaans' (ăf-; -ahns), n. S.-African or Cape Dutch. [= Du. Afrikaansch]

Afrikān'(d)er (ăf-), n. & a. Native of S. Africa born of European (esp. Dutch) settlers; ~ Bond, organization for furtherance of ~ interests & ultimate formation of United States of S. Africa. [(perh. f. S.-African Du. Afrikaander) f. Du. Afrikaner n. African, altered on Englander &c.]

aft (ahft), adv. (naut.). In or near stern of ship; towards the stern; fore & ~, from stem to stern, lengthwise (also as adj. f, -&-~). [OE æftan cogn. w. Goth. aftana from behind, f. afta behind (af off + -ta superl. suf.); after, aft, are orig. compar. & superl.]

af'ter¹ (ah-), adv., prep., & conj. **1.** adv. Behind in place, later in time, (Jill came tumbling ~; look before & ~; soon, a week, ~). **2.** prep. In pursuit or quest of, as run, inquire, ~ him; about, concerning, as look ~, take care of, keep an eye on, him; for, as hanker ~; following in point of time, later than, (~ you, formula in yielding precedence; ~ you with, colloq. request for next turn at; ~ six months, when six months have or had elapsed); in view of, as ~ such behaviour; next in importance to; according to (~ a FASHION; ~ one's own heart, such as one loves); in imitation of (person), as a picture ~ Rubens; in allusion to, as named ~; ~ all, in spite of all that has happened or been said etc. (~ all, what does it matter?) or of one's exertions, expectations, etc. (he tried for an hour & failed ~ all; so you have come ~ all!). **3.** conj. In, at, the time subsequent to that at which (he ~ he went, goes, has gone, had gone. [OE æfter (af off + compar. suf. -ter) cogn. w. OHG aftar, Gk ἀπωτέρω; cf. prec.]

af'ter² (ah-), a. Later, following, as ~ years; (Naut.) hinder, posterior, as ~ cabin, masts. [f. prec.]

af'terbirth, n. Membrane enveloping the foetus in the womb, so called because its extrusion follows that of the infant. [AFTER a.]

af'ter-care, n. Attention bestowed on an individual or class after a certain period of treatment etc.; freq. attrib., as ~ association. [AFTER a.]

af'terdamp, n. Choke-damp, gas left in mine after explosion of fire-damp. [AFTER a.]

af'terglow, n. Glow in the West after sunset. [AFTER a.]

af'ter-grass, n. Grass that grows after first crop has been mown for hay, or among stubble after harvest. [AFTER a.]

af'termath, n. After-grass; (fig.) consequences, fruits, results, as the ~ of war. [AFTER a. + math mowing, OE mæth f. OTeut. root mæ MOW]

af'termost (ah-), a. (naut.). Nearest the stern, most aft. [OE æftemest, a treble superl. of af of with compar. suf. inserted, af + te (r) + me + st]

afternoon', n. The time from noon to evening, as in, during, the ~, on Wednesday ~, (fig.) the ~ of life. [AFTER prep.]

af'terpiece, n. Farce or smaller entertainment after a play. [AFTER a.]

af'terthought, n. Reflection after the act; later expedient or explanation. [AFTER a. or adv.]

af'terwards (ah-; -z), adv. Later, subsequently. [OE æftanweard, a. (æftan AFT + WARD, corrupted in OE to æfterweard, + adv. genit. suf. -ES)]

ăg-, pref. = AD- before g.

aga (ăg'a, ägah?), n. Commander, chief officer in Mohammedan countries. [Turk. agha master]

again' (or agĕn'), adv. Another time, once more; ~ & ~, time & ~, repeatedly; ever & ~, now & ~, occasionally; as much ~, twice as much; half as much ~, one-&-a-half times as much; further, besides; on the other hand, as these ~ are more expensive; back ~ (to the original position or condition); in return, as answer ~, in response, as rocks echoed ~, glasses rang ~; proportionately to specified act or condition, as the loaded table groaned ~. [OE ongēan, ongægn (on in + gagn opposite, cf. G entgegen; 12th-c. againes (see -ES) became against by confus. w. superlatives]

against' (or agĕnst'), prep. & conj. **1.** In opposition to, as fight ~, I am ~ reform; in contrast to, as ~ a dark background; in anticipation of, as ~ his coming, a rainy day; in preparation for, as warned ~ pickpockets; into collision with, as ran ~ a rock, (colloq.) ran ~ (chanced to meet) a friend; opposite to, as ~ the horsepond (usu. over ~). **2.** conj. (arch.). By the time that (be ready ~ he comes). [see prec.]

ăg'ama, n. African & Indian lizard of the iguana type. [Carib]

ăg'ami, n. Tropical American bird, the Trumpeter. [native name in Guiana]

agām'ic, a. (zool.). Characterized by absence of sexual action. [as foll. +-IC]

agămo|gĕn'esis, n. Asexual reproduction. So ~gĕnĕt'ic a., ~gĕnĕt'ICALLY adv. [as foll. + genesis birth]

agăp'ous, a. (biol.). Without (distinguishable) sexual organs. [f. L f. Gk agamos (a- not + gamos marriage) + -OUS]

agăpē¹, adv. & pred. a. On the gape; open-mouthed with wonder or expectation. [A prep.]

ăg'ăpē[2], n. Love-feast held by early Christians in connection with Lord's Supper. [Gk. = brotherly love]

Agapemon|e (ăgăpēm'onĭ), n. Love-abode (usu. with sinister implication). Hence ~ISE[1] n. & a., (member) of a sect or association founded in Somerset c. 1850, pop. believed to practise free love. [irreg. f. Gk *agapē* love + *monē* abode]

ăg'ăr-(ăg'ăr), n. Solidifying agent in culture-media for bacteria prepared from certain seaweeds. [Malay]

ăg'arĭc (or *agā*-), n. Mushroom; name of various fungi. [f. L f. Gk *agarikon*

agăs'trĭc, a. (zool.). Without distinct alimentary canal. [f. Gk a- not + *gaster*

ăg'āte, n. Name of several varieties of precious stone (semiprecious variegated chalcedonies); burnishing instrument of gold-wiredrawers'; *the printing-type called in England ruby. [f. F *agathe*(16th-c.) f. It. *agata* f. L f. Gk *akhatēs* agate]

Agā'vē, n. (bot.). Genus of plants including American Aloe. [f. L f. Gk *Agauē*, prop. name in myth.]

agāze', adv. On the gaze. [A prep.]

age[1], n. Length of life or of existence; duration of ~; time elapsed since new moon; *Moon's* ~, time required for a purpose, as *come of* ~, *full* ~ (in Eng. Law, 21 years), *of discretion* (14), *over* ~; latter part of life, as *peevishness of* ~, *before homely*, children must give precedence to their elders; a generation; BRAZEN[1] etc. ~; (Hist., Geol.) great period, as *Patriarchal* ~, *Ice* ~; (colloq.) long time, as *waiting for* ~. [f. OF *aage, edage,* f. LL *aetāticum* f. *aetās -ātis* contraction of *aevitās (aevum* an age); see -AGE]

age[2], v.t. & i. (part. *aging*). (Cause to) grow old. [f. prec.]

-age, suf. OF f. LL *-aticum* -ATIC (med. L *-agium* & adj. suf. *-āticus* -ATIC (med. L *-agium* f. F, e.g. *homagium* f. *-arium* is readopted f. F, e.g. *homagium* f. *hommage* instead of *hominaticum*); afterwards added as living suf. in F & in E. Meaning: (1) collective belongings or aggregate (of *cellarage*); (2) function, condition, (*bondage, bondage*); (3) action (*breakage*); (4) fees payable for, cost of using, (*cartage, demurrage*).

aged, a. 1. (āj'ĭd). Having lived long, old. ~NESS n. 2. (ājd). Of the age of, as *~ten* (of horses) over six years old. Hence ā'gĕd-NESS n. [f. AGE v. +-ED[1]]

āge'less (-jl-), a. Never growing old. [AGE n. +-LESS]

ā'gency, n. Active operation, action, as *moral, free,* ~; instrumentality, as *by the* ~ *of*; action personified, as *an invisible* ~; (Commerc.) office of agent; establishment for business purposes, as *Reuter's* ~. [f. med. L *agentia* (L *agere* do, see -ENCE)]

agĕn'da, n. Things to be done, items of business to be considered at a meeting; memorandum book. [L, neut. pl. of *agendum* f. *agere* do]

ā'gent, n. One who exerts power or produces an effect; (of things) efficient cause; a natural force acting on matter, as *chemical* ~; one who does the actual work, esp. one who represents a person or firm in business (*who is your* ~ *in Paris?*). So agĕn't[1UL (-shǐ) a. [as ACT[2], -ENT]

agent provocateur (see AP.), n. Person employed to detect suspected offender by tempting them to overt action. [F]

agglŏm'er|āte[2], v.t. & i. Collect into a mass; (Geol.) mass of volcanic fragments united under heat, opp. to *conglomerate*. [as prec., see -ATE[2]]

agglŏm'er|ate[2], a. & n. (Collected into a mass; (Geol.) mass of volcanic fragments united under heat, opp. to *conglomerate*. [as prec., see -ATE[2]]

Agglomeration (glomus -meris ball), see -ATE[3],

agglūt'ināte[1], v.t. Glued together; consisting of simple words combined into compounds without change of form or loss of meaning. [f. L *agglutinare* (*gluten -tinis* glue) see -ATE[2]]

agglūt'in|āte[2] (-āt-), v.t. & i. Unite as with glue; combine simple words to express compound ideas; (t. & i.) turn into glue. Hence ~A'TION n., ~ATIVE a.

ăg'grandīze, v.t. Increase the power, rank, wealth, of (person, State); exaggerate, embellish. Hence aggran'dize-MENT (-zm-) n. [f. F *agrandir* (st. *-diss*- f. *agrandire* f. L *grandis* large)]

ăg'gravāte, v.t. Increase the gravity or prob. f. It. *Aggrandire* f. L *grandis* large) asperate (person). So ~A'TION n. [f. L *aggravare* make heavy (*gravis*), see -ATE[2]]

ăg'gregāte[1], v.t. & i. Collect together (replacing obs. *aggregate* f. L *grex gregis*) (trans.) unite (individual to company). LL +*aggreviare)*

ăg'gre|gate[2], a. & n. 1. Collected into one body; collective, total; (Law) composed of associated individuals, as *corporation* ~. 2. n. Sum total; assemblage, broken stone etc. used in making concrete; (Phys.) mass of homogeneous particles; *in the* ~, as a whole. [f. L *aggregare* unite in a flock (*grex gregis*) (trans.) unite (specified total); unite amount to (specified total). Hence ~A'TION n., ~ATIVE a.

ăg'gregāte[2] (-āt-), v.t. & i. Collect together (replacing obs. *aggregate* f. L *grex gregis*) (trans.) unite (individual to company). [f. prec.]

aggress', v.i. (rare). Begin a (or the) quarrel. So ~ION (-shn),~OR[2], nn. [f. F *aggresser* f. LL *aggressus* frequent. of *aggredī gress- = gradī* step)]

aggress'ive, a. & n. Of attack; offensive; disposed to attack; *assume the* ~, begin the quarrel. Hence ~LY[2] (-vl-) adv., ~NESS (-yn-) n. [as prec., see -IVE]

aghast' (-gahst, -gȧst), a. Terrified; struck with amazement. [p.p. of obs. vb *agast* (a- (1) + *gasten*, OE *gǣstan*, alarm)]

ă'gile, a. Quick-moving, nimble, active. Hence or cogn. agil'ity n., ~LY² (-l-li) adv. [F, f. L agilis (agere do)]

ă'giŏ, n. Percentage charged on exchange of paper-money into cash, or of one currency into another more valuable; excess value of one currency over another; exchange business. [It., = ease]

ă'giotage, n. Exchange business; speculation in stocks; stock-jobbing. [F, f. agioter (prec.+connecting -t-); see -AGE]

ăgist, v.t. Take in live stock to feed; charge (land or its owner) with a public burden. Hence ~MENT n. [f. OF agister (à to +gister f. L jacitare frequent. of jacēre lie)]

ă'gitāte, v.t. Move, shake; disturb, excite, (feelings, persons); revolve mentally, discuss, debate, (plans etc.); (abs.) keep up an agitation (for). [f. L agitare move to & fro, frequent. of agere drive, see -ATE³]

ăgitā'tion, n. Moving, shaking; commotion, disturbance, (mental or physical); debate, discussion; keeping of a matter constantly before the public; public excitement. [F, f. L agitationem (as prec., see -ATION)]

ă'gitātor, n. One who agitates, esp. politically; apparatus for shaking or mixing. [L (see AGITATE & -OR²)]

dgĭta'tō (-tah-), adv. (mus.). In an agitated manner. [It.]

agley' (-ē), adv. (Sc.), Askew, awry. [A prep.+Sc. gley squint]

aglow' (-ō), adv. & pred. a. In a glow. [A prep.]

ăg'nail, n. Torn skin at root of finger-nail; (formerly) corn on toe or foot. [OE angnægl f. ang- (Goth. agguus) tight, painful, +nægl (Goth. nagls) nail (of iron etc.), hard excrescence fixed in the flesh; mod. sense, & forms hang-nail, (Sc.) anger-nail, result from false etym., nail being taken as finger-nail]

ăg'nāte, n. & a. (One who is) descended by male links (also, by male or female links) from same male ancestor; sprung from same forefather, of same clan or nation; (fig.) akin, of same nature. So ăgnat'IC² a., ăgnā'TION n. [f. L agnatus related by father's side (ad to +gnatus born p.p. of (g)nasci f. stem gen-beget)]

ăgnŏm'ĕn, n. A fourth name occasionally assumed by Romans; (loosely) nickname. [L (ad to +(g)nomen name)]

ăgnŏs'tic, n. & a. 1. One who holds that nothing is known, or likely to be known, of the existence of a God or of anything beyond material phenomena. 2. adj. Pertaining to this theory. Hence ~ISM n. [f. Gk agnōstos unknown (a- not +gnŏ- know); see -IC]

Ag'nus Căs'tus (ă-), n. Tree once held a preservative of chastity. [L, f. Gk agnos (name of tree), confused w. hagnos chaste, whence L castus is added]

Ag'nus Dē'ī (ă-), n. Part of Mass beginning Agnus Dei; figure of lamb bearing cross or flag; cake of wax stamped with such figure & blessed by Pope. [L, = lamb of God]

agō', a. & adv. (Adj., always following noun) past, gone by, as ten years ~; (adv.) long ~, long since. [orig. agone p.p. of obs. vb ago (a- forth +GO)]

agŏg', adv. & pred. a. On the move, eager, expectant. [perh. f. OF en gogues (gogue fun, etym. dub.)]

agŏn'ic, a. Making no angle; ~ line, line of no magnetic variation. [f. Gk agōnios without angle (a- not +gōnia angle) +-IC]

ăgŏnis'tic, a. Pertaining to athletic contests (esp. of Ancient Greece); (Rhet.) polemic, combative; strained, aiming at effect. Hence ~AL a., ~ally² adv. [f. Gk agōnistikos pertaining to a combatant, agōnistēs f. agō]

ăg'ŏnīze, v.t. & i. Torture; suffer agony, writhe in anguish; contend in arena, wrestle (lit. & fig.); make desperate efforts for effect. Hence ~ingLY² adv. [f. med. L agonizare f. Gk agōnizomai contend (agōn, see prec.)]

ăg'ŏny, n. Mental anguish; ~ column (in newspaper), column of advertisements for missing friends etc.; paroxysm of pleasure; pangs of death; extreme bodily suffering; struggle. [prob. formed by Wyclif on Vulgate L agonia f. Gk agōnia contest, anguish; see AGONIST(O]

ăgŏraphŏb'ia, n. Morbid dread of public places. [Gk agora assembly, -PHOBIA]

agou'ti, -ty, (-goō-), n. Genus of rodents of Cavy or Guinea-pig family, esp. a hare-like animal of W. Indies. [(thr. F) f. native Ind. aguti]

agrā'rĭan, a. & n. 1. Relating to landed property; ~ outrage (arising from discord between landlords & tenants); relating to cultivated land. 2. n. Advocate of re-distribution of landed property, whence ~ISM n., ~IZE v.t. & i. [f. L agrarius (ager agri land, see -ARY¹) +-AN]

agree', v.i. & t. Consent (to proposal, statement, to do); concur (with person that); become, be, in harmony (with person); (pl.) ~ together, cannot ~, get on with one another; suit the constitution of, as work, lobster, does not ~ with him; (Gram.) take some number, gender, case, person; (trans.) bring (balance, items of accounts) into harmony. [f. OF agréer f. LL¹ *agradare make agreeable (gradus)]

agree'able (-riabl), a. Pleasing (to or abs.); (colloq., of persons) well-disposed (to a thing, to, or to all experience, to, as ~le to all experience. Hence ~leNESS n., ~LY² adv. [f. F agréable

agree'ment, n. Mutual understanding, covenant, treaty; (Law) contract legally binding on parties; accordance in opinion; (Gram.) concord in gender, number, case, person. [OF (agreer AGREE, see -MENT)]

agréments (agré'mahn), n. pl. Agreeable qualities or surroundings; (Mus.) ornamental notes embellishing a melody. [F]

agrès'tic, a. Rural, rustic; uncouth. [f. L agrestis (ager field) +-IC]

ag'riculture, n. Cultivation of the soil. Hence agricul'tural (-cher) a., agri-cul'turalist (-cher-) nn. [(prob. thr. 17th-c. F) f. L agricultura (ager agri field +cultura CULTURE)]

ag'rimony¹, n. Kinds of plants, esp. Agrimonia Eupatoria, with small yellow flowers. [f. L agrimonia perh. f. Gk argemōnē, etym. dub.]

ag'rimotor, n. Agricultural motor tractor. [f. L ager agri field + MOTOR]

agron'omy, n. Rural economy, husbandry. So agronom'ic(AL) aa., agro-nōm'ics, ~IST, nn. [f. Gk agronomos overseer of land (agros land +nomos f. nemō dispense), see -Y¹]

aground', adv. & pred. a. Upon the bottom of shallow water, as be, run, ~ (of ships). [A prep.]

āg'ue, n. Malarial fever, with cold, hot, & sweating stages; shivering fit; quaking (lit. & fig.); ~-cake, enlargement of spleen or liver caused by ~. [(-id) a. [OF, f. L acuta sharp]

ah, int. expr. sorrow, regret, surprise, admiration, entreaty, remonstrance, dislike, contempt, mockery. [not in OE; ME has a, perh. f. OF a, ah]

aha' (ahhah'), int. expr. surprise, triumph, mockery, irony. [f. AH+HA¹; formerly written a ha]

ahead' (ahëd'), adv. & pred. a. In advance; in the direct line of one's forward motion, as breakers ~; straight forwards; forward at a rapid pace, as go ~; in advance of (lit. & fig.). [A prep.]

aheap (a-hëp'), adv. In a heap, all of a heap. [A prep.]

ahem' (a-h-), int. used to attract attention or gain time. [lengthened form of hem]

ahoy' (a-h-), int. Nautical call used in hailing. [obs. a int.+HOY²]

Ah'riman. See ZOROASTRIAN.

à huis clos (ah wē klō), adv. With closed doors, in private. [F]

ahull' (a-h-), adv. (naut.). With sails taken in & helm lashed on lee side. [A prep.+HULL²]

ai (ä'ï), n. Three-toed Sloth of S. America. [f. Braz. aí, repr. its cry]

aiblins. See ABLINS.

aid¹, v.t. Help (person to do, or abs.); promote (recovery etc.). [f. OF aider f. L adjuvare frequent. of AD(juvare jut-)]

aid², n. Help; (Law) help claimed by defendant from one who has joint-interest; (Hist.) grant of subsidy or tax to king, (later) exchequer loan; helper; material source of help (usu. pl.), as ~s & ap-pliances. [f. OF aide, aïde (Prov. ajuda) f. LL adjuta, fem. p.p. of adjuvare AID¹ used as n.]

aide (äd), n.=foll. [abbr.]

aide-de-camp (äd'ekong, & see Ap.), n. (pl. aides-de-camp pr. äd'ekongz). Officer assisting general by carrying orders etc. [F]

aide-mémoire (äd'mämwahr), n. (Book, document, serving as) an aid to the memory (esp. in diplomatic use). [F, f. aider to help+mémoire memory]

aig'rette, n. Lesser White Heron (usu. EGRET); tuft of feathers or hair; spray of gems etc. [F, dim. f. OHG heigir heron]

aig'uille (-gwë-), n. Sharp peak of rock, esp. in Alps. Hence ~ESQUE¹ a. [F, see AGLET]

aiguillette (āgwïlĕt'), n. See AGLET.

ail, v.t. & i. Trouble, afflict, as what ~s him?; be ill. Hence ail'MENT n. [f. OE eglan (cogn. w. Goth. agljan) f. egle troublesome (Goth. aglus)]

ail'eron, n. (usu. pl.). Lateral-control flap(s) at rear of aeroplane's wingtip(s). [F]

aim¹, v.t. & i. Direct (blow, missile, ad; point (gun etc.) towards (at); direct an act or proceeding against (at); (intr.) deliver blow, discharge missile, (at); take aim (abs.); form designs (abs.). [prob. f. two vbs (1) Picard. amer, OF & Prov. esmer, f. L aestimare reckon. (2) OF aesmer f. LL adaestimare; ME sense may be estimate]

aim², n. Direction of a missile at an object, as take ~; design, purpose, object, whence aim'LESS a., aim'lessLY¹ adv. [f. prec.]

aïné (ān'ā), n. Elder son (cf. CADET²). [F]

air¹, n. 1. Gaseous substance enveloping earth, mixture of oxygen & nitrogen, breathed by all land animals; atmosphere; free space overhead, as birds of the ~; unconfined space, as open ~; fresh ~, also simply ~, ~ not exhausted of its oxygen; breeze, light wind; take ~, become known; (of projects etc.) quite in the ~ (uncertain); (of opinions, feelings) in the ~, spreading about; castles in the ~ (sl.), visionary projects; give person the ~ (sl.), dismiss him; on the ~, broadcast(ing) by wireless. 2. Appear-ance, as an ~ of absurdity; mien, gesture,

as *with a triumphant* ~; affected manner (esp. in pl.), as *gave himself* ~s, ~s & *graces*, (Mus.) melody, tune, esp., in harmonized composition, predominant (usu. soprano) part. **3.** Combb.: ~*balloon*, inflated toy; ~*bed*, inflated mattress; ~*bladder*, one filled with ~, in animals or plants; ~*borne*: transported by ~; specially picked & trained for ~ operations, as *an* ~*borne division*; (of ~craft) in the ~, having taken off, as *the squadron was soon* ~*borne*; ~*brake* (worked by ~ pressure); ~*brick* (perforated for ventilation); ~*chamber* (in hydraulic machines, for equalizing pressure); *Air Force*; ~*conditioned*, (of a room, building, etc.) having the ~ in it washed & brought to standard humidity (& temperature); ~*cooled* (by a current of cool ~); ~*craft*, aeroplane(s), ~ship(s), & balloon(s); ~*craft carrier*, ship that carries & serves as a base for aeroplanes; ~*craftsman*, see *Air Force*; ~*craftswoman*, ~*cushion*; ~ *crew* (of an ~craft); *~drome*, aerodrome; ~*engine* (actuated by heated ~); ~*field*, aerodrome; *Air Force* (*the Royal Air Force*, abbr. *R.A.F.*), the ~craft service co-ordinate with Navy & Army, with officers as follows: *Marshal of the R.A.F.*, *Air Chief Marshal*, *Air Marshal*, *Air Vice-Marshal*, *Air Commodore*, *Group-Captain*, *Wing-Commander*, *Squadron-Leader*, *Flight-Lieutenant*, *Flying-Officer*, *Pilot-Officer*; the non-commissioned ranks are *warrant officer*, *flight-sergeant*, *sergeant*, *corporal*, (*leading*) ~*craftman*, ~*craftman*, ~*mechanic*; ~*frame*, body of ~craft as dist. from engine(s); ~*graph*, system of transmitting letters etc. by ~ mail in the form of microfilms to save space, letter etc. so transmitted; ~*gun* (using compressed ~ as propelling force); ~*jacket* (inflated, to support wearer in water); ~*line*, line of ~craft for public service; ~ *liner*, large passenger ~craft; ~*lock*, stoppage of flow in pump etc., caused by ~ mail (carried by ~); ~*man*, one who flies in an ~craft, esp. as pilot or member of crew; *Air Marshal*, ~*mechanic*, see *Air Force*; ~*minded*, interested in aviation; *~plane*, aeroplane; ~*pocket*, apparent vacuum in ~ causing ~craft to drop some distance; ~*port*, aerodrome, esp. one fully equipped, usu. with customs-house, at which passengers by ~ liners embark or disembark; ~*pump* (for exhausting ~ vessel of its ~); ~ *raid*, attack by ~craft (freq. attrib., as ~*raid precautions*, *warden*, *warning*); ~*screw*, propeller of ~craft; ~*ship*, flying machine lighter than ~; ~ *speed*, speed of ~craft relative to the ~ through which it is moving; ~ *strip*, strip of ground used or usable for an ~field; ~ *thermometer* (with ~ instead of mercury); ~*threads*, gossamer; ~*tight* impermeable to ~; *Air Training Corps* (formed in 1941 for youths aged 15–18; abbr. *A.T.C.*); ~ *umbrella*, a force of ~craft used to give ~ protection to a military operation; ~*way*; ventilating passage in mine; route regularly followed by ~craft; ~*worthy*, (of ~craft) fit to fly; ~*worthiness* n. [1. OF f. L *aerem*, nom. *aer* f. Gk *aēr* (*ao* breathe). **2.** perh. developed f. 1 in F; taken by E f. F about 1600]

air[2], v.t. Expose to open air, ventilate; dry at fire; (refl.) go out into fresh air; parade (qualities, grievances, theories, fine clothes). [f. prec.]

Aire'dale (ārd-), n. Large rough-coated terrier. [place in Yorks.]

air'less, a. Stuffy; breezeless, still. [AM[1] +-LESS]

air'y, a. Aerial, lofty; breezy; immaterial; of thin texture; light in movement; sprightly; graceful, delicate; unsubstantial; superficial, flippant. Hence **air'ILY**[2] adv., **air'INESS** n. [AM[1]+-Y[2]]

aisle (īl), n. Division of church, esp. one parallel to & divided by pillars from the nave, choir, or transept; passage between rows of pews. Hence **aisleD**[2] (īld) a. [f. OF *ele* f. L *ala*, contr. of *axilla* wing; confused in E with *ile* island, refash. with this as *isle*, & again modified to *aisle* after F refash. *aile* (on L *axilla*); the F spelling *aisle* (after med. L *ascella* = L *axilla*) is mere coincidence; sense *passage* from confus. of F *ala* w. OF *alée* ALLEY]

‖ **ait** (āt), n. Small isle, esp. in a river. [perh. f. OE *iggath*, *iggeoth*: *eyet*, *eyot*, are artificial spellings on *islet* & F *îlot*]

aitch, n. =ACHE[3].

‖ **aitch'bone**, n. (Cut of beef lying over) buttock or rump bone. [ME *nage* f. OF *nache*, *nage*, f. LL *natica*, adj. (L *natis* buttock) +BONE[1]; for loss of *n* (*a nage-* becoming *an age-*), cf. ADDER; pop. etym. gives H-, *ice-*, *edge-*, bone]

aja[1], adv. (Of doors) slightly open. [A prep., +*char* (OE *cyrr* a turn)]

ajar[2], adv. In a jarring state. [A prep. + JAR[4] n.]

ajutage. See ADJUTAGE.

akim'bō, adv. (Of the arms) with hands on hips & elbows turned outwards. [etym. dub.]

akin', pred. a. Related by blood; (fig.) of similar or kindred character. [A prep.]

-al, suf. **1.** Adj. f. L *-ālis* (adj. suf. varying w. *-aris* -AR[1] by dissim. f. prec. syllable, as *regularis* but *generalis*; direct or through F *-el* (since corrected to *-al* in E); now appended freely to L nouns (*cordial*), Gk nouns (*colossal*), L adjj. (*individual*), & Gk adjj. in *-kos*, *-oides*, (*comical*, *rhomboidal*); *-ical* indicates vaguer connexion w. the orig. n. than *-ic* (*comic paper*, *comical story*), cf. -ACAL; other suff. are sometimes appended, as

generality, centralize. 2. Nouns f. L -ālis, -ăl, -ăles, -ălia, parts of above used as nouns (vĭrăl, annăls, annĕals, Sătŭrnălia), with new imitations (cardĭnal, regĭmentăl); -ălia became in F -ăille, in E -ail (cŏ̄răille now espoúsăille, OF espous-aille, E sponsaille now espousal), the last now freely imitated to form vbl nn. (reprĭsal, rĕcĭtal, bestowal), partly on false anal. of BRIDAL, BURIAL.

à la (ah lah), prep. After the manner of, as à la Russe, à la Réform. [F, for à la mode]

ăl'abaster (-bah-), n. & a. 1. Name of several varieties of carbonate or sulphate of lime; (Min.) massive fine-grained sulphate of lime (Modern, Gypseous, A~), as distinct from the carbonates used by the ancients for holding unguents (Oriental, Calcareous, A~); box made of ~. 2. adj. Of ~-like ~ in whiteness or smoothness. So ălabas'trīne[1] a. [f. OF alabaustre f. L alabaster f. Gk alabast(r)os, etym. dub.]

à la carte (ah lah kart), adv. By the bill of fare. [F]

ălăck', int. (arch.) expressing regret or surprise, esp. in phr. ~-a-day. [perh. f. a int.+lăk LACK]

ălăc'rity, n. Briskness, cheerful readiness. [f. L alacritas (alacer brisk, see -TY)]

Aladd'in's lămp, n. Talisman enabling holder to gratify any wish. [Arabian Nights]

à la mŏde, à la mŏde (ah lah mōd), adv. & a. In the fashion, fashionable; ~ beef, piece of beef larded & stewed; ~ silk (also as n., alamode), a thin glossy black silk. [F (à la mode), = in the fashion]

ăl'ar[2], a. Pertaining to wings; winglike, wing-shaped; (Bot. & Physiol.) axillary. [f. L alaris (ala wing, see -AR[1])]

ălãrm'[1], n. Call to arms; warning sound giving notice of danger; warning, as give, take, the ~; excited anticipation of danger; (Fencing) stamp on ground made with advancing foot; ~-post, place for troops to assemble at in case of ~; alarum-clock, one with appara-tus that rings at appointed hour; alar(um)s & excursions (joc.), noise & bustle. [f. OF alarme f. It. alarme (all' arme!) to arms!]

ălãrm'[2], v.t. Arouse to sense of danger; disturb; agitate, excite with fear. Hence ălãrm'ĭng[1]ly[2] adv. [f. prec.]

ălãrm'ĭst, n. One who raises alarms on slight grounds (often attrib., as these ~ist reports); panic-monger. So ~ĭsm n. [ALARM +-IST]

ălã'rum, n. See ALARM n.

ăl'ary, a. Pertaining to wings or wing-like parts. [f. L alarius (ala wing, see -ARY[1])]

ălăs' (-ahs), int. expressing grief, pity, concern. [f. OF ha las (mod. F hélas) f. ha ah+las lasse wretched f. L lassus weary]

Alăs'tor (-ahs-), n. Avenging deity, nemesis. [Gk (a- not+last- f. lath- forget)]

ăl'āte, ăl'āted, a. Having wings or wing-like appendages. [f. L ālatus (ala wing, see -ATE[2])]

ălb, n. White vestment reaching to feet, worn by priests, & by some consecrated kings. [f. LL alba (tunica) white (tunic)]

ăl'bacore, n. Large species of Tunny; other fish of same genus. [f. Port. albacor (f. Arab. al the+bukr young camel, heifer)]

Albān'ian (ăl-), a. & n. (hist.). (Native) of Scotland. [f. med. L Albania Scotland (L Alban gen of Albai)]

ălbāt'a, n. White metal, German silver. [f. L alba(ta) whitened (albus white)]

ăl'batross, n. Family of birds allied to Petrels, inhabiting Pacific & Southern Oceans; esp. great A~, largest of sea-fowls, (17th-c. algatross, perh. f. obs. alcatras f. Arab. alqadus the bucket, Arab. name of Pelican, from its supposed water-carrying habit); -b- under influence of l. albus white)]

ălbē'it (awl-), conj. Though, as ~ that he failed, ~ he failed, he tried ~ without success. [=all though it be that]

ăl'bert, n. (Also A~ chain) kind of watch-chain. [f. Prince Albert consort of Queen Victoria]

Albert Hall, in Kensington, used for con-certs, demonstrations, etc. [as prec.]

ălbēs'cent, a. Growing white, shading into white. [f. L albescere (albus white), see-ENT]

Albĭgĕn'sēs (ăl-, -z), n.pl. Heretics of 12th-14th cc. in S. France. [L Albĭga in S. France, -ENE]

ălbī'nō (-bē-), n. (pl. -ōs). Human being marked by congenital absence of colour-ing pigment in skin & hair, which are white, & eyes, which are pink & unable to bear ordinary light; any animal so distin-guished; plant lacking the normal colour-ing. Hence ălbī'ness[1] (-bē-), ăl'bĭnĭsm, nn. [Port., orig. of white negroes, f. L albus white]

Al'bĭon (ăl-), n. (poet.). (Greek & Roman name for) Britain. [etym. dub., cf. L albus white]

ăl'bĭte, n. White or soda feldspar. [f. L albus white+-ITE[1]]

ăl'bum, n. Book for insertion of auto-graphs, photographs, etc. [L, neut. sing. of albus white]

ălbū'men, n. White of egg; a constituent of animal solids & fluids, of seeds, & of tuberous or fleshy roots, found nearly pure between skin & embryo of many seeds, usu. the eatable part. Hence ~ĭnŏsE, ~ĭnoŭs, aa. [L albumen -minis white of egg (albus white) see -MEN]

ǎlbūm'enīze, v.t. (photog.). Coat (paper) with an albuminous solution. [prec. +-IZE]

ǎlbūm'inoid, a. & n. Like albumen; (n. pl.) proteins, class of organic compounds forming chief part of organs & tissues of animals & plants. Hence **ǎlbūminoid'AL** a. [f. ALBUMEN +-OID]

ǎlbūminū'ria, n. Presence of albumen in the urine, usu. as symptom of kidney disease. [ALBUMEN, URINE]

ǎlbūr'num, n. Recently formed wood in exogenous trees, sap-wood. Hence ∼OUS a. [L alburnum (albus white)]

‖ **alcahest**. See ALKAHEST.

Alcā'ic (ǎ-), a. & n. Pertaining to Alcaeus (Gk lyric poet, 600 B.C.), or to the metre he invented; (n. pl.) ∼ strophes. [f. L f. Gk Alkaïkos (Alkaios)]

alcalde (ǎhlkǎh'ldǎ), n. Magistrate in Spanish, Portuguese, or Spanish-American town. [Sp., ult. f. Arab. qādi judge]

ǎlchĕm'ic (-k), a. Pertaining to alchemy. Hence ∼AL (-k) a., ∼ALrY² (-k) adv. [f. med. L. alchimicus or F alchimique: see ALCHEMY and -IC]

ǎl'chĕmist (-k-), n. One who studies or practises alchemy. Hence **ǎlchemis'tɪc** (-AL) (-k-) aa. [f. OF alquemiste; see ALCHEMY and -IST]

ǎl'chemīze (-k-), v.t. Change as by alchemy; transmute. [back-formation on prec.]

ǎl'chemy (-k-), n. Chemistry of the middle ages; esp., pursuit of the transmutation of baser metals into gold (also fig.). [f. OF alquimie f. med. L alchimia f. Arab. al-kīmīa, al the +kīmīa, apparently =khēmīa (Gk form of native name of Egypt, but confused with Gk khumeia pouring f. khu- perf. st. of kheō pour, whence the spelling alchymy)]

ǎl'cohŏl, n. Pure spirit of wine; any liquor containing this; (Chem.) large class of compounds of same type as spirits of wine. Hence ∼ATE²(3) n., **ǎl-cohŏl'ɪc** a. [med. L, f. Arab. al the +koh'l powder for staining eyelids (kaḥala v. stain)]

ǎl'cohŏlism, n. Action of alcohol on human system. [prec. +-ISM]

ǎl'cohŏl|īze, v.t. Saturate with alcohol; subject to alcoholic influence. Hence ∼īzā'TION n. [ALCOHOL +-IZE]

ǎlcohŏlŏm'ēter, n. Instrument for measuring alcoholic strength of spirits. Hence ∼M'ETRY n. [f. ALCOHOL +-O-+METER]

Alcoran (ǎlkorahn', ǎl'¢), n. Koran, sacred Mohammedan book. Hence ∼IC (-ǎn'¢) a. [(thr. F) f. Arab. al-qorān the reading (qara'a v. read)]

ǎl'cōve, n. Vaulted recess in room-wall, esp. (in Spain) recess for bed; recess in garden wall or hedge; summer-house. [F, f. Sp, alcova, -ba, f. Arab. al-qobbah the vault (qubba v. vault)]

al'dehȳde, n. Colourless volatile fluid of suffocating smell, obtained by oxidation of alcohol; class of compounds of this type. Hence **ǎldehȳd'ɪc** a. [abbr. of L alcohol dehydrogenatum (deprived of hydrogen)]

al'der (awl-), n. Tree related to Birch; other trees not related, as Black, White, Red, ∼. [OE alor, aler (cf. ON ölr, elrir, OHG elira, mod. G erle, eller w. phonetied)]

al'derman (awl-), n. Councillor in English & Irish cities & boroughs, next in dignity to Mayor. Hence ∼IC (-mǎn'¢) n. [f. OE aldor patriarch (add old +-orn noun suf.)+-MAN]

al'dermanrȳ (awl-), n. Ward, district of a borough having its own alderman; rank of alderman. [prec.+-RY]

Al'derney (awl-), a. & n. **1.** Of cattle bred in ∼ (one of the Channel Islands); (pop.) of cattle bred in the Channel Islands. **2.** n. Individual of either kind.

Al'dershot (awl-), n. (Used for) the permanent military camp at ∼ in Hampshire.

Al'dine (awl-), a. Printed by Aldus Manutius, Venetian printer of 16th cent., who introduced italic type; name of certain style of type. [f. Aldus +-INE¹]

Al'dis (awl-), a. ∼ lamp (for signalling); ∼ lens (for hand cameras); ∼ unit sight (for aircraft). [A. C. W. Aldis, inventor]

ale (awl-), n. Liquor made from an infusion of malt by fermentation, flavoured with hops etc.; ‖ merry-making at which ∼ was drunk; alecost, costmary; ∼-house, one at which ∼ is retailed; ∼-wife: woman who keeps an ∼-house; American fish allied to herring. [OE alu]

ale'atory, a. Depending on the throw of a die or on chance. [f. L aleatorius (aleator dice-player f. alea die)]

āle-cŏnner (ālk-), n. (hist.) Inspector of ale & ale-measures (now a titular office only). [ALE+CON¹+-ER¹]

alee', adv. & pred. a. On the lee or sheltered side of ship; to leeward. [f. ON á on +lē shelter; see LEE]

āl'egar, n. Sour ale; malt vinegar. [f. ALE+egre=F aigre sour, on anal. of vinegar]

alĕm'bɪc, n. Apparatus formerly used in distilling; also fig., as ∼ of fancy. [f. F alambic f. Arab. al the +ambiq still f. Gk ambix -ikos cup; lembick, limbeck, were usu. in 15th-17th cc.]

alĕrt', a. & n. **1.** Watchful, vigilant; lively, nimble. **2.** n. Warning call, alarm; (period of) air-raid warning; on the ∼, on the look-out. [f. F alerte, earlier allerte, à l'airte, t. It. all' erta (alla to the +erta look-out, watch-tower, fem. p.p. of ergere f. L erigere ERECT)]

aleur'on, aleur'ōne, (-lūr-), n. Albuminoid substance found in seeds of plants etc. [Gk aleuron flour]

Alexan'drine (ăl-), a. & n. ~ (verse), iambic line of six feet or twelve syllables. [F, f. *Alexandrin*, of doubtful orig.]

alex'in, n. One of a class of substances found in blood serum capable of destroying bacteria. [G, f. Gk *alexō* ward off, -IN].

alexiphar'mic, a. & n. (Having the quality of) an antidote. [earlier -ac f. F *alexipharmaque* f. Gk *alexipharmakon* remedy for poison (*alexō* keep off + *pharmakon* poison)]

alfal'fa, n. Lucerne. [Sp. f. Arab.]

alfres'co, adv. & a. In the open air; open-air, as ~ *lunch*. [f. It. *al fresco* in the fresh (air)]

al'ga, n. (pl. ~ae, pr. -jē). Sea-weed. Hence ~AL, ~OID, ~olō'gical, aa., ~IST nn.

al'gebra, n. Investigation of the properties of numbers by means of general symbols; quadruple aa., ~a'ically² adv. ~(ĭst un. [Lt., f. Arab, *aljebr* reunion of broken parts (*jabara* reunite)]

al'gid, a. Cold, esp. of cold stage of ague. Hence **algid'ity** n. [f. F *algide* f. L *algidus* (*algere* be cold, see -ID)]

al'gorism, n. Arabic (decimal) notation; cipher in ~, 0, mere dummy. [f. OF *augorisme* f. med. L *algorismus* f. Arab. *al-Khowarazmi* the man of Khiva, surname of a mathematician; mod. misspelling ~*ithm* by confusion w. Gk *arithmos* number]

aiguazil' (-gw-), n. Spanish warrant-officer or sergeant. [Sp. (now -*cil*) f. Arab. *al-wazir* the vizier, minister]

al'ias, adv. & n. (pl. ~es). (Name by which one is called) on other occasions. [L, adv.]

al'ibi, adv. & n. (The plea that when an alleged act took place one was) elsewhere; *excuse (colloq.). [L, adv.; old locative of *alius* another]

alicy'clic, a. (chem.). Combining the properties of aliphatic & cyclic compounds. [f. *aliphatic* + *cyclic*]

al'idade, -ād, n. Index of astrolabe, quadrant, etc., showing the degrees cut off on the arc. [F (-*ide*), f. med. L *alhidada* f. Arab. *al-'idada* the revolving radius ('*add* upper arm)]

a'lien, a. & n. 1. Not one's own; foreign, under foreign allegiance; differing in nature (*from*); repugnant (*to*). 2. n. Stranger; non-naturalized foreigner; one excluded *from*; (Law) ~*friend*, ~*enemy*, alien owing allegiance to friendly, hostile, country. Hence ~ISM (2) n., study & treatment of mental diseases, ~ISM² n., specialist in such diseases. [OF, f. L *alienus* belonging to another (*alius*)]

a'lien², v.t. (Poet.) estrange; (Law) transfer ownership of. Hence ~ABLE a., ~ABIL'ITY n. [f. OF *aliéner* f. L *alienare* (as prec.)]

a'lienate, v.t. Estrange; transfer owner-ship of; turn away, divert (*from*). Hence ~OR² n. [f. L as prec., see -ATE²]

aliena'tion, n. Estrangement; trans-ference of ownership; diversion to different purpose; (*mental*) ~, insanity. [f. MF *aliénacion* f. L *alienationem* (as prec., see -ATION)]

a'lienee', n. One to whom transfer of property is made. [ALIEN²+-EE]

a'liform, a. Wing-shaped. [f. L *ala* wing+-FORM]

alight¹ (-ït), v.i. Dismount (*from horse*), descend (*from carriage*); settle, come to earth, from the air. [OE *alihtan* (A- (1) + *lihtan* light)]

alight² (-ït), a. Kindled; on fire; lighted up. [p.p. of obs. *alight* kindle; now only used predicatively, on anal. of *a-blaze* & other adv. compds]

align' (-în), **aline'**, v.t. & i. Place, lay, in a line; bring into line; esp. bring three or more points into a straight line, as ~ *the sights* (of rifle) & *bull's-eye*; (intr.) form in line (as troops). Hence ~MENT (-ïn'm-) n. [f. F *aligner* (à to + *ligner* f. L *lineare* (*linea* line)]

alike', pred. a. & adv. Similar, like; (adv.) in like manner. [OE *gelic* a., *gelīce* adv.]

al'iment, n. Food; (fig.) support, mental sustenance. Hence ~al² (-TAL) a., ali-men'tarly² adv. [f. L *alimentum* (*alere* nourish, see -MENT)]

alimen'tary, a. Nourishing; performing functions of nutrition, as ~ *canal*; providing maintenance. [f. L *alimen-tarius* (as prec., see -ARY²)]

alimenta'tion, n. Nourishment; main-tenance. [f. med. L *alimentatio* (*alimen-tare*, as ALIMENT, see -ATION)]

al'imony, n. Nourishment; maintenance; allowance due to wife from husband's estate, on separation from certain causes. [f. L *alimonia* nutriment (*alere* nourish, see -MONY)]

aliphat'ic, a. (chem.). Of fat (as epithet of certain organic compounds). [f. Gk *aleiphar -atos* unguent, -IC]

al'iquot, a. & n. ~ (*part*), part contained by the whole an integral number of times, integral factor. [f. F *aliquote* f. L *aliquot* some, so many]

-ality, compd noun-suf. = -AL+-TY. Qual-ity, or instance of it, as (a) *generality*,

alive', adv., & pred. a. In life, living; fully susceptible to (an idea etc.); active, brisk, as (colloq.) *look ~*, be brisk; swarming *with*, as *river ~ with boats*; *any man ~* (whatever); *man ~!* (colloq. expletive). [f. A prep. + ME *live*, OE *līf* dat. of *līf* LIFE; = on life]

aliz'arin, n. Red colouring matter of madder. [f. F *alizari* madder prob. f. Arab. *al* the + *açarah* extract ('*açara* v. press); see -IN]

al'kahĕst, n. Alchemist's supposed universal solvent (also fig.). [sham Arab., prob. invented by Paracelsus]

alkalĕs'c|ent, a. & n. Incipiently or slightly alkaline (substance). Hence ~ENCE, ~ENCY, nn. [f. foll., see -ESCENT]

al'kali, n. (pl. ~s, ~es). (Chem.) series of compounds called bases, including soda, potash, & ammonia, highly soluble in water, producing caustic or corrosive solutions that neutralize strong acids, & turn vegetable yellows to brown, reds to blue, purples to green; (Commerce). caustic soda, caustic potash, other alkaline products. Hence ~fi'ABLE a., ~FY v.t. [f. F *alcali* f. Arab. *al-qaliy* calcined ashes (*qalay* fry)]

alkalim'etry, n. Measurement of strength of alkalis. [ALKALI + -METRY]

al'kaline, a. Of alkalis; of the nature of an alkali; those whose hydroxides are alkalis. [f. ALKALI + -INE[1]]

al'kaloid, n. Nitrogenous basic substance; esp. *vegeto-*~s, vegetable alkalis. Hence **alkaloid'AL a.** [f. ALKALI + -OID]

al'kanĕt, n. (Plant whose root yields) a red dye. [f. Sp. *alcana* (f. Arab. *al-henna* the henna shrub) + dim. suf. to dist. this shrub from henna]

all (awl), a., n., & adv. **1. adj.** (w. noun etc. expressed or understood). The whole amount, quantity, or extent of, as ~ *day*, ~ *England*, ~ *his life*, & ~ *that, take it* ~, ~ *whom I saw*; the greatest possible, as ~ *speed*; (w. pl.) the entire number of, as ~ *men*, *the others*; ~ *kind(s) of*, every kind of; any whatever, as *renounce* ~ *connexion*; ~ *the* TIME[1]. **2. n.** ~ *men*, as ~ *were agreed*; (in scoring at games) for both sides (*the score was two to two*; *love* ~, no score to either side); (w. of) the whole, every one, as ~ *of it*, ~ *of us*; everything (*that is* ~; ~ *is lost*); one's whole property, as *he lost his* ~; ~ *along of* (vulg.), owing to; ~ *but*, everything short of (used adv.), as ~ *but impossible*, *he was* ~ *but drowned*; ~*in*, inclusive of ~, as ~*in wrestling*, ~ *in*, ~, of all; everything unrestricted style; *in* ~, of paramount or exclusive importance; ~ *one*, just the same, as *it is* ~ *one to me*; *very fine or well*, colloq. formula of dissatisfaction, as ~ *very fine, but I shall stand it no longer*; *at* ~, in any way, as *not at* ~, *did you speak at* ~? (not in affirmative sent.); ~ *in* ~, in total number; *one & ~, & some* (arch.), ~ *& sundry*, individually

& collectively. **3. adv.** Wholly, quite, as *dressed* ~ (orig. an adj.) *in white*, ~ *covered with mud*, ~ *the better*, ~ *at once*, ~ *too soon*; ~*clear*, signal that danger is over, esp. from enemy aircraft; *~-fired* (sl.), extreme(ly), excessively; ~ *in*, exhausted; ~*out*, involving ~ one's strength or resources, as *he was going* ~ *out*, at full speed; ~ OVER; ~*overish* (colloq.), indisposed ~ over the body; ||~*red*, (of cable, line, etc.) British throughout; ~ *right*, (adv.) as desired, satisfactorily, (pred. a.) safe & sound, in good state, satisfactory, (sent.) I consent, ~ is well, (also iron. in threats, as ~ *right! you shall repent this*); ~*round* adj., having ability in many departments, as *an ~round sportsman*, so ~*rounder*, n.; ~ *there* (colloq.), sane, in one's senses, as *he's not quite ~ there*; ~ *the same*; just the same, making no difference, (*it's* ~ *the same to me whether he comes or not*; *if it's* ~ *the same to you*, if you don't mind); ~ *the same though*, notwithstanding, however, (*he was punished* ~ *the same*, in spite of extenuating circumstances etc.; ~ *the same I wish you hadn't done it*). **4.** Combb.: *All-father*, Odin, God; *All Fool's Day*, first of April; *All Hallows* (arch.), *All Saints' Day*, general celebration of saints, November 1st; *All Souls' Day*, day of supplication for souls of faithful deceased, Nov. 2nd. *All* is prefixed to many adjj., as ~*bountiful*, ~*righteous*, ~*sufficient*, & esp. to partt., as ~*suffering*, ~*seeing*, ~*knowing*. [com.-Teut.: OHG *al*, ON *allr*]

Allah (ăl'a) n. Name of God among Mohammedans. [Arab. *allah* contr. of *al-ilah* (*al* the + *ilah* god = Heb. *eloah*)]

allay', v.t. Put down, repress (pain etc.); diminish (pleasure etc.). [f. A- (1) + LAY v.; confused with obs. *allege* alleviate & obs. *allay* alloy]

ăllēgā'tion, n. Alleging; assertion (esp. one not proved). [f. F *allégation* f. L *allegationem* (*allegare* allege, see -ATION)]

allēge', v.t. Affirm; advance as argument or excuse. [f. *adlegiare* E Latiniz. of OF *esligier*, Norm. *alegier*, f. LL *exlitigare* clear at law; but treated as repr. L *allegare* cite, adduce, which would give *alleaque* (cf. F *alléguer*)]

allē'giance (-jans), n. Duty of subject to sovereign or government; loyalty (lit. & fig.). [ME *ligeaunce* f. OF *ligeance* (LIEGE); *a-* added in E perh. thr. confusion with obs. *allegeance*, n. f. prec.]

ăllēgŏ'ric, a. Pertaining to, of the nature of, allegory. Hence ~AL a., ~ALLY[2] adv. [f. F f. L f. Gk *allēgorikos* (as foll., see -IC)]

ăl'légŏrīze, v.t. & i. Treat as an allegory, make allegories. Hence ~IST n. [f. F *allégoriser* f. L *allegorizare* (as foll., see -IZE)]

ăll'égŏry, n. Narrative description of a subject under guise of another sugges-

tively similar; emblem. [f. L f. Gk *allegoria* (*allos* other + *-agoria* assembly)]

allegrétt'ō, adv. (mus.). Somewhat brisk-ly. [It.]

allégr'ō, (-lā-), a., adv., n. (mus.). Lively, gay; (movement) in brisk time. [It.]

allelú'ia (-lōōyà), n. Song of praise to God. [f. L f. (Septuagint) Gk *allēloúia* f. Heb. *halleluyah* praise ye Jehovah]

all'ergy, n. (med.). Changed reactivity produced by a subsequent inoculation or treatment with the same thing, (more widely) sensitiveness to the action of particular foods, pollens, insect-bites, etc. Hence **allér'gic** a., relating to or charac-terized by ~, (colloq.) sensitive (esp. antipathetic) to, ~. [f. Gk *allos* other, after ENERGY]

allév'iāte, v.t. Relieve, mitigate. Hence ~ĀTION, ~ātor, nn., ~ātive, ~ātory, aa. [f. LL *alleviare* lighten (*levis* light), see -ATE³]

all'ey, n. (pl. ~s). Walk, passage, esp. in park or garden; narrow street; blind ~, one closed at end; enclosure for skittles etc. [f. OF *alee*, F *allée*, walking, passage, f. *aler* go, etym. dub.]

alli'ance, n. Union by marriage; relation-ship; confederation (esp. between States); community in nature or qualities; (Bot.) group of allied families. [f. OF *aliance* (as ALLY, see -ANCE)]

Allèyn'ian (alēn-), n. Member of Dulwich College. [E. *Alleyn*, founder]

All-hall'ow(s) (-ō, -ōz), n. All saints (in heaven), as *All hallows' day, Allhallow-mass.* [ALL+*hallow* f. OE *hálga* saint]

ā'lia ceous (-shus), a. Of the genus *Allium*, including garlic, onions, & leeks; smelling, tasting, of garlic etc. [f. L *Allium* garlic + -ACEOUS]

all'igātor, n. Genus of saurian reptiles of crocodile family, found in America; other large American saurians; ~ *apple, pear,* fruit of W. Indian trees; ~ *tortoise,* snapping turtle, [corrupt. of Sp. *el lagarto* the lizard f. L *lacerta*]

allit'erate, v.i. (Use words that) begin with the same letter. Hence ~IVE a., ~iver'y² (-vĭ) adv. [f. L *ad* to+*litera* letter : -ATE³, on anal. of *obliterate*.]

allitera'tion, n. Commencement of words in close connexion (esp. in early Teut. poetry, of accented syllables) with the same letter. [f. prec.+-ATION]

all'ocāte, v.t. Assign, devote, (to person or object); locate. Hence ~ABLE a., ~A'TION n. [f. med. L *Allocare* (*locus* place), see -ATE³]

allocü'tion, n. Formal hortatory address esp. one delivered by the Pope. [f. L *allocutio -onis* f. *alloqui* exhort]

al(l)ōd'ium, n. Estate held in absolute ownership, without acknowledgement to a superior (opp. to *feudum*). Hence ~AL a., ~ally² adv., ~alism, ~alist, nn. [f. med. L f. OLG f. G +*aláod* entire property (ALL + *allod*) ; sometimes written *allod, allody*]

allōg'amy, n. (bot.). Cross-fertilization. [f. Gk *allos* other + -GAMY]

allōp'athǐ̄y, n. Curing of a diseased action by inducing another action of a different kind (opp. to *homoeopathy*). Hence ~IST n. [f. Gk *allos* other + -PATHY]

allōphyl'ian, a. & n. (One whose native tongue is) neither Aryan nor Semitic. [f. L f. Gk *allophulos* (*allos* other + *phulē* tribe) + -IAN]

allōt', v.t. (-tt-). Distribute by lot or with authority; assign (to). [f. OF *aloter* (*à* to + *loter* divide by lot f. *lot*, Teut. wd, OE *hlot*)]

allōthe'ism, n. Worship of strange gods. [f. Gk *allos* other + *theos* god + -ISM]

allōt'ment, n. Apportioning; lot in life; share allotted to one; || small portion of land let out for cultivation. [f. *allot-ment* (*aloter*, see ALLOT & -MENT)]

allōt'ropǐ̄y, n. Variation of physical pro-perties without change of substance. Hence **allōtrop'ǐc**ally² adv., ~ISM n. [f. Gk *allotropia* f. *allotropos* (*allos* other + *tropos* manner f. *trepō* turn)]

allōttee', n. One to whom allotment is made. [f. ALLOT + -EE]

allōw', v.t. & i. Admit (thing to be, that); 'form the opinion (that) ; permit (practice, person *to* do); (refl.) indulge oneself in (conduct); (intr.) admit *of*; give (limited periodical sum), as ~ *him £200 a year*; add, deduct, in consideration of some-thing; ~ *for*, take into consideration, make addition or deduction correspond-ing to; ~ *me* (formula in offering ser-vices). Hence ~ABLE a., ~ABLY² adv.; ~EDLY² adv., admittedly. [f. OF *alouer* (1) L *Allaudare* praise, (2) L *Allocare* place]

allōw'ance¹, n. Permission; tolerance (*of*) ; limited portion, esp. yearly income; deduction, discount; make ~ *for*, allow for. [f. OF *alouance* (as prec., see -ANCE)]

allōw'ance², v.t. Make allowance to (per-son) ; supply (thing) in limited quantities. [f. prec.]

allōy'¹ (or ǎl'oi), n. Standard, quality, (of gold or silver) ; inferior metal mixed esp. with gold or silver (also fig.) ; mixture of metals. [orig. *allay* f. OF *aley* (F *aloi*) f. *aleier* combine f. L *Alligare* bind; meaning influenced by confusion with F *à loi* to law]

allōy'², v.t. Mix with baser metal; mix (metals) ; debase; moderate. [f. F *aloyer* f. OF *aleier*, see prec.]

all'seed (awl-), n. Name of various plants producing much seed.

all'spice (awl-), n. Jamaica pepper, *Pimenta*, supposed to combine flavour of cinnamon, nutmeg, and cloves; other

aromatic shrubs, as *Carolina A~*, *Japan A~*, *Wild A~*.

al'lude' (-ōō-, -ŭ-), v.i. Refer covertly, indirectly, *to*; (improp.) ~ *to*, mean. [f. L Al(*ludere lus-* play)]

al'lure', v.t., & n. Tempt, entice, win over, (*to, from*, person, place, conduct); fascinate, charm; (n.) charm, attractiveness. Hence ~MENT (-ūr'm-) n. [f. OF *aleurrer* attract (*à* to + *leurre* LURE)]

al'lu'sion (-lōōzhn, -ŭt-), n. Covert, implied, indirect, reference (*to*). [f. L *allusio* (-lōōs-, -lūs-), a. Containing an allusion (*to*); abounding in allusions (Her.); (canting) *arms*. Hence ~LY² (-vl-) adv., ~NESS (-vn-) n. [as prec, see -IVE]

alluv'ion (-ōō-, -ū-), n. Wash of sea, river, against shore, banks; flood; matter deposited by flood; (Law) formation of new land by water's action. [F, f. L *alluvionem* (nom. -*vio*) f. *luere* wash]

alluv'ium (-ōō-, -ū-), n. (pl. ~*a*, ~*ums*). Deposit of earth, sand, etc., left by flood. Hence ~AL a. [L, neut. of adj. *Alluvius* (*luĕre* wash)]

ally¹, v.t. Combine, unite, for special object *to, with*, (esp. of marriage & alliance with foreign states); (of things) *allied to*, connected with. [f. OF *alier* f. L *alligare* bind]

ally'² (or āl'ī), n. Person, state, etc., allied with another. [f. prec.]

āl'ly³, *āll'ey, n. Choice playing-marble of marble or alabaster. [perh. dim. of *alabaster*]

āl'ma(h), n. Egyptian dancing-girl. [Arab. '*almah* knowing ('*alama* know)]

āl'magēst, n. Great astronomical treatise of Ptolemy; other books on astrology & alchemy. [f. F f. Arab. *al* the +*majistī* =Gk *megistē* greatest]

āl'ma Māt'er (ā-), n. Name used of Universities & schools. [L, = bounteous mother]

al'manāc (awl-), n. Annual calendar of months & days, with astronomical & other data. [med. L, etym. dub.]

al'mandine, āl'mandine, n. A garnet of violet tint. [corrupt. of obs. *alabandine* f. L *alabandina* (*Alabanda*, city in Caria)]

almī'ghty (awlmit'ī), a. & adv. All-powerful, esp. *A~ God, the A~*; (sl.) great, (adv.) exceedingly. Hence almī'ghti-NESS n. [OE *ælmeahtig* (ALL adv.+ MIGHTY)]

almīr'ah (-ȧ), n. (Anglo-Ind.). Wardrobe, movable cupboard. [Hind., ult. thr. Port., f. L *armarium* (see AMBRY)]

alm'ond (ahm-), n. Kernel of a stone-fruit borne by two trees (*sweet, bitter*, ~) allied to plum & peach; anything ~ shaped; *A~* (*Trumbler*), kind of pigeon. [f. OF *almande* f. L f. Gk *amugdalē; al-* perh. by confus. w. Arab. *al* the]

al'moner (or ahm'ner), n. Official distri-

butor of alms; *Hereditary Grand A~, Lord High A~*, (officers in royal household of Great Britain); medico-social worker attached to a hospital. [f. OF *aumoner* f. LL *almosinarius =eleemosynarius* (as ALMS, see -ARY¹)]

al'most (awl-), adv. Very nearly (qualifying v., adv., adj.; also noun, as *his ~ impudence*). [f. ALL +MOST adv.]

alms (ahmz), n. (usu. as sing.). Charitable relief of the poor; donation; ~*folk, almsman*, (supported by charity); ~*giving*; ~*house*, || one founded by charity for reception of poor. [OE *ælmysse* f. L f. Gk *eleēmosunē* compassionateness (*eleēmōn* adj. f. *eleos* compassion)]

āl'mŭg. See ALGUM.

āl'ōe, n. Genus of plants with erect spikes of flowers & bitter juice; (pl.) purgative drug procured from juice of ~s; other plants, as *American A~*, Agave. [OE *aluue* f. L f. Gk *aloē*]

ālōĕt'ic, a. & n. (Medicine) containing aloes. [f. Gk *aloē* aloe on false anal. of *diuretic* etc.]

alŏft' (or -aw-), adv. & pred. a. High up (lit. & fig.); upward. [f. ON *á* on, to, +*lopt* sky, loft]

alōne', pred. a. & adv. Solitary; standing by oneself (*in opinion* etc.); LET, *leave*, ~ abstain from interfering with; (adv.) only, exclusively. [f. ALL adv. +ONE]

alŏng', adv. & prep. From end to end of; through any part of the length of; onward, as *get ~; ~ with*, in company with, in conjunction with; *all ~*, all the time; (*all*) ~ *of* (vulg.), owing to; || ~*ships*, directed fore & aft; ~*shore*, ~ by the shore, & on the shore; ~*side*, close to side of ship; ~*side of*, side by side with (lit. & fig.). [OE *and-long* (*and-* against, facing, +*lang* long), orig. adj.]

alŏof', adv. & pred. a. Away, apart, (lit. & fig.), as *stand, keep, hold ~; (Naut.) away to windward, as *spring ~* (cf. LUFF). Hence ~NESS n. [f. A prep.+LUFF]

ălōpē'cia, n. (med.). Baldness. [L, f. Gk *alōpekia* fox-mange f. *alōpēx* fox]

aloud', adv. Loudly; not in a whisper; (colloq.) palpably, as *reeks ~*. [f. A prep. +LOUD; cf. foll.]

alow' (-ō), adv. (naut.). In, into, lower part of vessel. [f. A prep.+LOW a.]

ălp, n. Mountain-peak; (in Switzerland) green pasture-land on mountain-side; *Alps*, mountain range separating France & Italy. [(pl) f. L *Alpes* prop. n., etym. dub.]

ălpăc'a, n. Kind of llama with long woolly hair; its wool; fabric thence made. [f. Sp. (Arab. *al* the +*paco*, native Peruv. name)]

ăl'penstŏck, n. Long iron-shod staff used in climbing Alps etc. [G, =stick of the Alps]

ăl'pha, n. Greek letter A (A, α); *A~ and Omega*, beginning & end.; (Astron.) chief

star of constellation; ~ rays, helium nuclei emitted by radio-active substances (orig. regarded as rays). [Gk, f. Heb. aleph ox, leader]

al'phabet, n. Set of letters used in a language; first rudiments. Hence **älpha-bět'ic** a. [f. L alphabetum (Gk alpha, bēta, first two letters of alphabet)]

alphabět'ical, a. Of the alphabet, as ~ order. Hence ~LY² adv. [as prec. +-ICAL]

Al'pine (ǎ-), a. Of the Alps or any lofty mountains. [f. L Alpinus (Alpes, see ALP & -INE²)]

Al'pinist (ǎ-), n. Alpine climber. [f. F alpiniste (as prec., see -IST)]

already (awlrěd'i), adv. Beforehand; by this time, thus early. [f. ALL adv. +READY]

Alsatia (ălsǎsh'ǔ), n. Province west of Rhine, receded by Germany to France 1919; White Friars in London, once sanctuary for lawbreakers. Hence ~AN (-shǎn) a.; ~an (wolf-hound), a breed of dog. [Alsike in Sweden]

al'sō (awl-), adv. In addition, besides; ~ run (sl.), person(s) etc. that failed to win distinction. [f. ALL+SO: orig. in antecedent & relat. as well as demonstr. functions, now superseded in relat. by its shortened form AS, & in antec. by AS & SO]

ält, n. (Mus.) high note, esp. in ~, in octave above treble stave beginning with G; (fig.) in ~, in an exalted frame of mind; ~-horn, brass wind-instrument of saxhorn type. [Pr., f. L altum high]

al'tar (awl-), n. Flat-topped block for offerings to deity; Communion Table; lead to the ~, marry; ~-cloth, (prop.) linen cloth used at Communion or Mass, (loosely) silk frontal & super-frontal; ~-piece, reredos, esp. a painting. [f. L altare (altus high)]

al'tarwise (awl-), adv. In the manner of an altar.

ältäz'imuth, n. Instrument for determining altitude & azimuth of heavenly bodies. [alt- for altitude+AZIMUTH]

al'ter (awl-), v.t. & i. Change in character, position, etc. Hence or cogn. ~ABIL'ITY, ~A'TION, nn. ~ABLE a. [f. 14th-c. F altérer f. med. L alterare (L alter other)]

al'terative (awl-), a. & n. Tending to alter; (n.) medicine, treatment, that alters processes of nutrition. [prec. +-ATIVE]

al'tercāte (ălt-, awlt-), v.i. Dispute hotly, wrangle, (with). So ~A'TION n. [f. L altercari, see -ATE³]

ǎl'ter ĕg'ō, n. One's other self, intimate friend. [L, =second I]

ältĕrn'ant, n. (Biol.) of alternating layers; (n.) quantity. [F, part. of alterner f. L alternare ALTERNATE]

ältĕrn'āte¹ (awl-), a. (Of things of two kinds) coming each after one of the other kind; (Biol.) ~ generation (by ~ processes, as first by budding, next by sexual

reproduction); ~ leaves, angles (placed alternately on the two sides of stem, line). Hence ~LY² adv. [f. L alternare (alternus, see ~ATE²]

al'ternāte² (awl-), v.t. & i. Arrange, perform, (two sets of things) alternately; interchange (one thing) alternately with, by, another; (of two things) succeed each other by turns; (of a whole) consist of alternate things; (of one class of things) appear alternately with another. So ~A'TION n.; ~ātor² (2) n., dynamo giving an ~ating current (reversing its direction at regular intervals). [f. prec.]

ältĕrn'ative (awl-), a. & n. 1. (Of two things) mutually exclusive. 2. n. (Strictly) permission to choose between two things; (loosely) either of two possible courses, as I had no (other) ~; one of more than two possibilities. Hence ~LY² (-vī-) adv. [f. med. L alternativus (as prec., see -ATIVE) f. ALTERNATE]

although (awldhō'), conj. Though. [f. ALL adv. +THOUGH]

ältĭm'ĕter, n. Aeronautical aneroid for showing height above sea level. [L altus high, -METER]

al'titude, n. Height; depth; (Geom.) length of perpendicular from vertex to base; height above sea level; (usu. in pl.) high place; (fig.) eminence. [f. L altitudo (altus high), see -TUDE]

ält'ō, n. (mus.). Highest male voice, counter-tenor; its musical part; female voice of similar range, contralto; its part; singer with ~ voice; tenor violin; ~ clarinet, -trombone, instruments similar to the clarinet, trombone. [It. alto (canto) high (singing)]

altogether (awltogědh'er), adv. & n. Totally; on the whole; (n.) an ~, a whole; the ~ (collog.), the nude. [ALL adv.]

ǎl'tō-rēliev'ō (-lē-), n. (sculp.). High relief. [It. alto-rilievo]

ǎl'truĭsm (-rŏŏ-), n. Regard for others as a principle of action. Hence ~IST n., ~is'tIc a., ~is'tICALLY adv. [f. F al-truisme (It. altrui others', f. L alteri huic to this other, see -ISM)]

ăl'um, n. A double sulphate of alumi-nium & potassium; series of salts including this; family of compounds including these; (Min.) various native minerals, alums proper & pseudo-alums. [OF, f. L alumen]

alum'ina (-lōō-), n. One of the earths, the only oxide of aluminium. [L alumen alum, on type of soda etc.]

ălūmĭn'ium, *alūm'ĭnum, n. White light sonorous ductile malleable metal, not tarnished by air, used for instruments & as an alloy; ~ bronze, alloy of ~ & copper. [f. ALUMINA; formerly aluminum, aluminium]

alum'inous (-lōō-), a. Of the nature of alum or alumina. [f. F alumineux f. L aluminosus (alumen ALUM, see -OUS)]

alūm'n|us, n. (pl. ~ī; fem. ~a, pl. ~ae). (Former) pupil or student. [L, = foster-child]

ālvě'olate, a. Honeycombed, pitted with small cavities. [f. L *alveolatus* f. foll., see -ATE²]

ālvě'ol|us, n. Small cavity; socket of tooth, whence ~AR¹ a.; cell of honeycomb; conical chamber of a belemnite. [L, dim. of *alveus* cavity]

always (awl'wiz), adv. At all times; on all occasions (~ *exceeding, provided*, etc., legal formulae). [f. ALL a. + WAY : *away* (now arch. or poet. for ~) orig. meant 'all the way, continually'; ~ (gen. case) having prob. the sense 'on every occasion']

am. See BE.

āmadavat', āv-, n. Small Indian songbird. [native name]

ăm'adou (-ōō), n. German tinder, prepared from fungi, used as a match & styptic. [F f. Pr. (OPr. *amador*), f. L *amatorem* lover (*amare*, see -OR²)]

ămain', adv. (arch., poet.). Vehemently; in all haste. [A prep. + *main*, OE *mægn*, force]

amāl'gam, n. Mixture of a metal with mercury, as *gold* ~; plastic mixture of any substances (also fig.). [f. F *amalgame*, med. L *amalgama*, perh. f. L f. Gk *malagma* an emollient (*malassō*, st. *malak-*, soften)]

amāl'gamate¹, a. Combined, esp. of languages. [f. med. L *amalgamare* (as prec., see -ATE⁵]

amāl'gamāte², v.t. & i. Mix; unite (classes, societies, companies, ideas, etc.); (of metals) combine with mercury. Hence ~ATION n., ~ating or being ~ated, merging of two or more business concerns into one; ~ātor² n., ~ātive a. [f. prec., see -ATE³]

amănū̆en'sis, n. (pl. -nsēs). One who writes from dictation. [L, adj. used as n., f. (*servus*) *a manu* secretary + -ensis belonging to]

ăm'arant(h), n. Imaginary unfading flower; genus, including Prince's Feather & Love-lies-bleeding; purple colour. Hence ămarăn'th(ine)¹ a. [f. F *amarante* f. L f. Gk *amarantos* everlasting, name of a flower (*a-* not + *maran-* st. of *marainō* fade); *h* by confusion with Gk *anthos* flower]

ămarýl'lis, n. Kinds of bulbous plant. [L, f. Gk *Amaryllis*, name of a country girl]

amăss', v.t. Heap together; accumulate (esp. riches). [f. 12th-c. F *amasser* (*à* to + *masser* f. *masse* MASS²)]

ăm'ateur (-tŭr, -těr), n. One who is fond of; one who cultivates a thing as a pastime. Hence ămateur'ISH a., ămateur'ISHly² adv., ămateur'ishNESS,

ămateur'ISM n. [F, f. L *amatorem* (*amare* love, see -OR²)]

Amati (ahmah'tē), n. Violin or violoncello made by a member of the *Amati* family of Cremona (fl. c. 1570 onwards)

ăm'ative, a. Disposed to loving. Hence ~NESS (-vn-) n. [f. L *amare* love, see -ATIVE]

ăm'atŏl, n. High explosive made from TNT & ammonium nitrate. [irreg. f. AM(MONIUM) + (TRINITRO)TOL(UENE)]

ăm'atory, a. Pertaining to a lover or to sexual love. Hence ămatōr'IAL a. [f. L *amatorius* (*amare* love, see -ORY)]

ămaurō'sis (-or-), n. Partial or total loss of sight from disease of optic nerve. Hence ~ŏr'IC a. [Gk, f. *amauroō* darken (*amauros* dark), see -OSIS]

amāze', v.t. Overwhelm with wonder. Hence ~'edly², ~'ingly², adv., ~e'MENT (-zm-) n. [A- (1) + *maze* v., etym. dub.]

amāze'², n. (poet.). = AMAZEMENT. [f. prec.]

Am'azon (ă-), n. Fabulous race of female warriors in Scythia; female warrior (lit. & fig.); masculine woman. Hence Amazōn'IAN (ă-) a. [f. L f. Gk (prob. foreign word, but explained by Greeks as *a-* not + *mazos* breast, from destruction of right breast to facilitate use of bow)]

ămbā'ges (-jēz), n.pl. Roundabout ways. [L *amb-* about + *ag-* f. *agere* drive); 16th-c. E had *am'bage*, pl. *am'bages*]

ăm'bān, n. Chinese resident official in Tibet. [Manchu, = minister]

ămbăss'ador, n. Minister sent by one sovereign or State on mission to another (usu. *A~ extraordinary*); minister permanently representing sovereign or State at foreign court (*Ordinary, Resident, A~*; formerly *A~ Leger*); *A~ Plenipotentiary* (with full power to sign treaties etc.); official messenger. Hence ămbăssa-dōr'ial a. [f. F *ambassadeur* f. OSp. *ambaxador* f. med. L + *ambactiador* agent-noun of *ambactiare* f. *ambactia* office f. Celt. *ambactus* servant (*ambi* about + *ag-* drive, cogn. w. L *agere*)]

ămbăss'adress, n. Female ambassador; ambassador's wife. [f. prec. + -ESS¹]

ăm'ber, n. Yellow translucent fossil resin, found chiefly on S. shore of Baltic; ~ *Fauna, Flora*, animals, plants, of which remains are found in ~. [f. F *ambre* f. Arab. *'anbar* ambergris, to which the name orig. belonged]

ăm'bergris (-ēs), n. Wax-like substance found floating in tropical seas, & in intestines of sperm-whale, odoriferous & used in perfumery, formerly in cookery. [f. F *ambre gris* grey amber]

ămbidĕx'ter, a. & n. (Person) able to use left hand as well as right; double-dealing. Hence ămbidĕxtĕr'rITY n. [med. L (*ambi-* on both sides + *dexter* right-handed)]

ămbidĕx't(e)rous, a. = prec. Hence ~LY² adv., ~NESS n. [as prec. + -OUS]

am'bient, a. Surrounding, circumfused. [f. L *ambiens -entis* part. of *ambire* go about (*amb-* on both sides + *ire* go)]

ambigu'ity, n. Double meaning; expression capable of more than one meaning. [f. med. L *ambiguitas* (as foll., see -TY)]

ambig'uous, a. Obscure; of double meaning; of doubtful classification; of uncertain issue. Hence ~LY² adv., ~NESS n. [f. L *ambiguus* doubtful f. *ambigere* (*amb-* both ways + *agere* drive) + -OUS]

am'bit, n. Precincts; bounds; compass, extent. [f. L *ambitus* a going round (*ambire*, see AMBIENT)]

ambi'tion, n. Ardent desire for distinction; aspiration (*to be, to do*); object of such desire. [F, f. L *ambitionem* (*ambire* -ib-, canvass for votes, see AMBIENT & -TON)]

ambi'tious (-shus), a. Full of ambition; strongly desirous (*of* a thing, *to do*; showing ambition, as *an ~ attempt*. Hence ~LY² adv., ~NESS n. [f. L *ambitiosus* (as prec., see -OUS)]

ambiv'alent, a. Having either or both of two contrary values or qualities. [f. L *ambo* both, after *equivalent*]

am'ble, v.i. (Of horses etc.) move by lifting two feet on one side together; ride an ambling horse, ride at an easy pace; move in a way suggesting an ambling horse. [f. F *ambler* f. L *ambulare* walk]

am'ble², n. Pace of an ambling horse; easy pace. [f. F *amble* f. *ambler*, see prec.]

amblyo'pia, n. Impaired vision. Hence ~ōp'ıc a. [Gk. f. *amblyōpos* a. (*amblus* dull + *ōps ōpos* eye)]

am'bo, n. (pl. ~s, ~nes pr. -ōn'ēs), Pulpit in early Christian churches. [Ll, f. Gk *ambōn*]

amboy'na (wood), n. Finely marked wood of an Asiatic tree. [*Amboyna* Island]

ambro'sia (-zıă, -zhyă), n. (Myth.) food of the gods; anything delightful to taste or smell; bee-bread. [f. L f. Gk, fem. of *ambrosios* of the immortals f. *ambrotos* (*a-* not + (m)*brotos* mortal)]

ambro'sial (-zıăl, -zhyăl), a. Divinely fragrant; divine. Hence ~LY² adv. [f. L f. Gk *ambrosios*, see prec. & -AL]

ambs-ace (āmz ās'), n. Both aces, lowest throw at dice; bad luck; worthlessness. [f. OF *ambes as* f. L *ambas as*, see ACE; also written *ames-*]

am'bulance, n. Moving hospital following army; conveyance for sick or wounded persons. [F (L *ambulare* walk, see -ANCE)]

am'bulant, a. (path.). (Of a disease) shifting from one part of the body to another, not confining patients to bed; (of treatment) involving exercise on part of patient. [f. part. of L *ambulare* walk, see -ANT]

am'bulatory, a. & n. **1.** Pertaining to walking; adapted for walking; movable; arcade, cloister. **2.** n. Place for walking. [f. L *ambulatorius* (as prec., see -ORY)]

ambuscade'¹, n. Ambush. [f. F *embuscade* f. It. *imboscata* or Sp. *emboscada* (*imboscare*, see AMBUSH v. and -ADE)]

ambuscade'², v.t. & i. Life, conceal, in ambush. [f. prec.]

am'bush¹ (-ŏosh), n. Concealment of troops, troops concealed, in a wood etc.; (generally) lying in wait; *make lay, an ~, lie in ~*. [f. OF *embusche* (as foll.); *am-*, perh. due to AMBAGES]

am'bush² (-ŏosh), v.t. & i. Conceal (troops, only in p.p.); lie in wait for; (intr.) lie in wait. [f. OF *embuscher* (Sp. *emboscar*, It. *imboscare*) f. Ll *imboscare* (*boscus* BUSH); see prec.]

âme damnée (see AD.), n. Tool, devoted adherent. [F]

ameer', amir' (-ēr), n. Title of various Mohammedan rulers in Scinde & Afghanistan. [Arab. *amir* commander (*amara* command)]

ame'lior|āte, v.t. & i. (Cause to) become better. Hence ~A'TION, ~ātor², nn., ~ātıve a. [f. F *améliorer* f. OF *ameillorer* (à to + *meillorer* f. Ll *meliorare* f. *melior* better)]

âmen' (ā-, ah-), int. So be it. [f. L f. Gk f. Heb. *amen* certainly, certainly (*aman* strength)]

ame'n|able, a. (Of persons) responsible (to law etc. or abs.); (of things) liable *to*; capable of being tested by (*to*); responsive, tractable. Hence ~aux'ıty, ~able-NESS, nn., ~abLY² adv. [AF, f. *amener* bring to (à to + *mener* bring f. L f. L *minare* threaten), see -ABLE]

amend', v.t. & i. Abandon evil ways; (arch.) improve in health; correct an error in (legal document), make professed improvements in (measure before Parliament); make better. Hence ~ABLE a., ~MENT n. [f. OF *amender* f. L *Emendare* free from faults (*menda* fault)]

amende honorable (see AP.), n. Public apology & reparation. [F]

amends' (-z), n. Reparation, restitution, compensation, as *make ~*. [f. OF *amendes* f. *amender* AMEND; pl. now treated in E as sing.]

ameni'ty, n. Pleasantness (of places, persons, etc.); (pl.) pleasant ways. [f. L *amoenitas* (*amoenus* conn. w. *amare* love, see -TY)]

â mer'să et tö'rö, adv. From board & bed. [L]

amen'tia (-she), n. Imbecility. [L, f. *amens* (*a*= *ab* + *mens mentis* mind)]

amen'tum, amen't, n. Catkin. Hence ~ACEOUS, ~IFEROUS, ~IFORM, aa. [L, = thong]

amerce', v.t. Fine; (loosely) punish. Hence **amer'ciable** a., **~ment** (-sm-), **amer'ciament**, nn. [orig. *amercy* f. AF *amercier* (à at +*merci* MERCY)]

Ame'rican, a. & n. **1.** Belonging to continent of America or to United States; || *~ cloth, leather*, glazed cloth used for covering tables etc.; *~ organ*, small organ with suction-operated reeds instead of blown pipes. **2.** n. Native of America of European descent; citizen of United States. [-AN]

Ame'ricanism, n. Word or sense or phrase peculiar to, or extending from United States; attachment to, sympathy with, United States. [prec. +-ISM]

Ame'ricanize, v.t. & i. Naturalize as an American; make American in character; become American in character; use Americanisms. [as prec. +-IZE]

ames-ace. See AMBS-ACE.

am'ethyst, n. Precious stone, kind of quartz, purple or violet; *Oriental A~*, rare violet variety of sapphire. Hence **amethys'tine¹** a. [f. OF *ametiste* f. L f. Gk *amethustos* not drunken (*a-* not +vbl adj. f. *methuskō* intoxicate f. *methu* wine), the stone being supposed to prevent intoxication]

Amha'ric (ä-), n. Official & court language of Abyssinia. [f. *Amhara*, Abyssinian province]

am'iable, a. Feeling & inspiring friend-liness; lovable. Hence **amiabi'lity**, **~ness**, nn., **am'iably²** adv. [OF, f. L *amicabilis* AMICABLE; confused with OF *amable* (mod. F *aimable*) f. L *amabilis* lovable (*amare* love, see -BLE)]

am'ianth(us), n. Mineral variety of asbestos, splitting into flexible fibres; green fibrous chrysolite. [L, f. Gk *amiantos* undefiled (*a-* not +vbl adj. f. *miainō*), i.e. purified by fire, being in-combustible; for -*h*- cf. AMARANTH]

am'ic, a. (chem.). Pertaining to ammonia. [f. AM(MONIA) +-IC]

am'icable, a. Friendly; done in a friendly spirit. Hence **~abi'lity**, **~able-ness**, nn., **~ably²** adv. [f. L *amicabilis* (*amicare* make friendly f. *amicus*, see -BLE)]

am'ice¹, n. Square of white linen worn by celebrant priests, formerly on head, now on shoulders. [earlier *amyt* f. OF *amit* f. L *amictus* garment; -*ce*, or -*s*, perh. due to confus. w. foll.]

am'ice², n. Cap, hood, cape, of religious orders; badge worn by French canons on left arm. [f. OF *aumusse*, perh. f. Arab. *al* the +G *mütze* cap; early confused w. prec.]

amic'us cur'iae, n. Friend of the court, disinterested adviser. [L]

amid', **amidst'**, prep. In the middle of. [OE *on midden* (dat. of *mid*) in the middle, followed by genitive; see also -ES]

am'ide, n. (chem.). Compound formed from ammonia by replacing one or more hydrogen atoms by an acid radical. [f. AM(MONIA) +-IDE]

am'idin, n. Soluble matter of starch; starch in state of solution. [f. *amid-*com-Rom. form of L *amylum* starch +-IN]

am'idol, n. A photographic developer. [P; perh. f. *di(amid(ophenol*, of which it is a salt]

amid'ships, adv. In middle of ship. [AMID+SHIP+-ES]

am'idar, n. Native revenue-collector in India. [f. Pers.]

am'ine, n. (chem.). Compound formed from ammonia by replacing one or more hydrogen atoms by alcohol or other base-radicals. [f. AM(MONIA) +-INE⁵]

amir. See AMEER.

amiss', adv. & pred. a. Not up to the mark; out of order; wrongly; untowardly, as *come ~*; *take ~*, take offence at; *not ~*, appropriate. [A prep.+MISS n.]

am'ity, n. Friendship; friendly relations. [f. F *amitié*, earlier *amisté*, f. pop. L *amicitadem* (*amicus* friend, see -TY)]

am'meter, n. Instrument for measuring electric current in amperes. [f. AM(PERE) +-METER]

am'mo, n. (sl.). Ammunition. [abbr.]

am'monal, n. High explosive made from ammonium nitrate & aluminium. [f. AMMON(IUM) +AL(UMINIUM)]

ammon'ia, n. A colourless gas with pungent smell & strong alkaline reaction, spirit of hartshorn; *liquid ~*, (Chem.) *liquefied ~*; *~ liquor*, solution of *~* in water. [f. foll.]

ammon'iac, a. & n. Of the nature of ammonia; *Sal A~*, hard white crystalline salt, said to have been prepared from camels' dung near temple of Jupiter Ammon; *Gum A~* (also *A~*), a gum resin used in medicine & as cement. Hence **ammoni'acal** a. [F, f. L f. Gk *ammōnia-kon* belonging to Ammon]

ammon'iated a. Combined with ammonia. [f. prec.+-ATE¹ (3) +-ED¹]

am'monite, n. Fossil genus of Cephalo-pods. [after med. L *cornu Ammonis* horn of (Jupiter) Ammon, see -ITE (2)]

ammon'ium, n. Hypothetical radical of ammonia salts; *~ chloride*, *Sal* AMMONIAC; *~ carbonate*, rock ammonia (see SAL VOLATILE)

ammuni'tion, n. Military stores (for-merly of all kinds, now of powder, shot, shell, etc.); || *~ books, bread, hat* (supplied to soldiers). [f. F *ammunition*, vulg. *amonition*, by confus. of *la munition* (see MUNITION) with *l'amonition*]

am'nesia, n. Loss of memory. [Gk, = forgetfulness]

am'nesty, n. & v.t. Intentional overlook-ing; act of oblivion, general pardon; (v.t.) give *~* to. [f. L f. Gk *amnéstia* oblivion f. *amnéstos* a. (*a-* not +*mnē-* remember)]

ăm'nĭŏn, n. (pl. -ĭă). Innermost membrane enclosing foetus before birth. [Gk.]

amoeb'a (-mē-), n. Microscopic animalcule perpetually changing shape. Hence ~ĬFORM, ~OID, aa. [f. Gk amoibē change]

amoebaean (ămēbē'an), a. Alternately answering. [f. L f. Gk amoibaios inter-changing (amoibē change), see -AN]

amŏk. See AMUCK.

among(st)' (-mŭ-), prep. In the assemblage of, surrounded by; in the number of; within the limits of (collectively or distributively), as five shillings ~ us, divided ~ us; in comparison with, as one ~ many; by joint action of, as kill him ~ you; reciprocally, as quarrelled ~ themselves. [OE on gemang (on in.+gemang assemblage f. gemengan mingle) foll. by gen. case; see -ES]

Amontillado (ăhmŏntĭlyah'dō), n. (For-merly) a specially dry sherry; (now) sherry of a matured type; (fig. attrib.) of dry speech or manner. [Sp., f. Montilla (in Spain)+ado (= -ATE²)]

ăm'ŏral, a. Unconcerned with, out of the sphere of, morals, non-moral. [A-(7)]

ăm'orous, a. Inclined to love; in love; of, pertaining to, love. Hence ~LY² adv., ~NESS n. [OF, f. L amorosus (amor love, see -OUS)]

amorph'ous, a. Shapeless; anomalous; (Min., Chem.) uncrystallized; unorgan-ized. Hence ~ISM, ~OUSNESS, nn. [f. Gk amorphos shapeless (a- not+morphē form)]

amŏrt'īze, v.t. Alienate in mortmain; extinguish (debt, usu. by means of sink-ing fund), whence ~īZA'TION n. [f. F *amortir (st.- iss) bring to death f. LL +admortīre (ad mortem to death)]

amount', v.i. Come to (so much); be equivalent in significance) to. [f. OF amonter f. amont upward (à mont hillward f. L ad montem]

amount², n. Total to which a thing amounts; full value, significance, etc.; quantity, as a considerable ~ (of). [f. prec.]

amour' (-oor), n. Love-affair; intrigue, [F.=love f. L amorem, nom. -or, f. amare]

amourette' (-oor-), n. Petty love-affair. [F., dim. of amour]

amour-propre (ăm'oor-prŏp'r), n. Self-esteem. [F]

ampelŏp'sis, n. Kinds of vine-creeper. [Gk ampelos vine, opsis appearance]

ăm'pere (-ĕr, -âr), n. (electr.). Current that one volt can send through one ohm, unit of current. [name (Ampère) of physicist]

ămpersănd', n. The sign & (and, L et). [also ampus-, ampussy-, ampussy-, cor-rupt. of 'and per se & (= by itself and')

amphi- in comb. Both, of both kinds, on both sides, around. [Gk, prep.]

Amphĭb'ĭa (ă-), n. pl. Division of Verte-brata, intermediate between reptiles & fishes, as frogs, newts, etc. [f. L f. Gk amphibia (zōa) (animals) living in both elements (AMPHI-+bios life)]

amphĭb'ĭan a. & n. (Animal) living both on land & in water; an aircraft designed to rise from & alight on either land or water. [as prec.+-AN]

amphĭbĭol'ogȳ, n. Branch of zoology treating of Amphibia. [prec.+-LOGY]

amphĭb'ĭous, a. Living both on land & in water; connected with both land & water; having two lives, connected with two classes, etc. Hence ~LY² adv. [f. AMPHIBIA+-OUS]

ăm'phĭgăm, n. (bot.). Plant with no dis-tinct sexual organs. Hence ămphĭg'-amous a. [f. F amphigame (AMPHI-+Gk gamos marriage)]

ăm'phĭgourȳ'ī (-oorĭ), ăm'phĭgorȳ, n. Nonsensical composition. [?]

ămphĭmix'ĭs, n. (biol.). Mingling of two individuals, or of their germs, as in sexual reproduction. [AMPHI-+Gk mixis mingling]

amphĭox'us, n. The fish Lancelet. [f. AMPHI-+Gk oxus sharp]

amphĭp'oda, n. pl. Order of Crustacea, with feet of two kinds. Hence ăm'-phĭpod n. [AMPHI-+Gk pous podos foot]

amphĭp'rostȳle, a. With portico at both ends. [F, f. L f. Gk amphiprostulos (AMPHI-+prostulos PROSTYLE)]

ămphĭsbaen'a, n. Fabulous serpent with head at each end; (Zool.) genus of worm-like lizards. [L, f. Gk amphisbaina (amphis both ways+bainō go)]

ăm'phĭtheatre (-ter), n. Oval or circular building, with seats rising behind & above each other round a central open space; part of a theatre; (fig.) scene of a contest. Hence amphithea'trical a. [f. L f. Gk amphitheatron (see AMPHI- & THEATRE)]

Amphĭt'rȳon (ă-), n. Host, entertainer. [Molière, Amphitryon, iii. 5]

ăm'phora, n. (pl. -ae, -as). Greek or Roman two-handled vessel. [L, f. Gk amphoreus for AMPHI(phoreus f. pherō bear]

amphŏr'ĭc, a. (med.). Like the sound produced by blowing into large vessel with small mouth. [f. prec.+-IC]

ăm'ple, a. (-er, -est). Spacious; extensive; abundant; copious; quite enough. Hence ăm'plȳ² adv., ~NESS (-ln-) n. [F, f. L amplus]

ăm'pliative, a. (logic). Extending a simple conception. [f. L *ampliare* widen (*amplus*), see -ATIVE]

ămplĭfĭcā'tion, n. Extension, enlargement; making the most of a thing. [f. L *amplificatio* (as foll., see -ATION)]

ăm'plĭfÿ, v.t. & i. Enlarge; enhance; expatiate. Hence ~**IER**[1] **n.,** (esp.) appliance increasing loudness of sounds, strength of wireless signals, etc. [f. F *amplifier* f. L *amplificare* (as AMPLE, see -FY)]

ăm'plĭtūde, n. Breadth; abundance; wide range; dignity; (Astron.) space by which celestial body rises, sets, wide of due east, west. [F, f. L *amplitudo* (as AMPLE, see -TUDE)]

ăm'poule (-ꝏl), **n.** Small glass vessel for containing esp. hypodermic injection. [F, cf. foll.]

ămpŭll'a, n., (pl. *-ae*). Roman two-handled flask; vessel for sacred uses; (Biol.) dilated end of vessel, canal, duct, in an animal. Hence **ămpŭll'aceous** (-āshŭs) **a.** [L, etym. dub.]

ăm'pŭtāte, v.t. Cut off (part of animal body etc. or abs.). Hence ~**A'TION,** ~**ātor,** ămŏk, ămŏk, adv. *Run ~*, run about in frenzied thirst for blood (also fig.). [f. Malay *amoq* rushing in frenzy]

ăm'ūlĕt, n. Thing worn as charm against evil (lit. & fig.). [f. L *amuletum*, etym. dub.]

amūse' (-z), v.t. Divert from serious business (*with* trifles, *by* trifling); tickle the fancy of; *be ~ed with, by, at.* So ~**ABLE,** ~**IVE, aa.** [f. OF *amuser* cause to MUSE[2] (causal *à* to +*muser* stare)]

amūse'ment (-zm-), **n.** Pleasant diversion; excitement of risible faculty; pastime. [f. F *amusement* (*amuser*, see prec. and -MENT)]

ămÿgdăl'ic, a. Of almonds, as ~ *acid.* [f. L *amygdala* ALMOND +-IC]

amÿg'daloid, a. & n. (Igneous rock containing mineral nodules) of almond shape. [f. Gk *amugdalē* ALMOND +-OID]

ămÿ'l, n. (chem.). The radical of various alcohols some of which are constituents of fusel oil. Hence **amÿl'o a.** [f. L *am(ylum)* starch +-YL; named as discovered in distilling fusel oil from starch]

ămÿlā'ceous (-shŭs), **a.** Of starch, starchy. [f. L *amylum* starch +-ACEOUS]

ăm'ÿloid, a. & n. Starchy (food). [as prec.+-OID]

ămÿlŏp'sĭn, n. Ferment of the pancreatic juice that converts starch into sugar. [f. Gk *amulon* starch, after pepsin]

an[1], **a.** See A, adj.

an[2], conj. (arch.). If, [weakening of *&* an[1]; cf. AND]

an[3] = *an* before *n*, see AD-. **3.** f, L *an*- = *ambi-*, as in *anfractuosity.* **4.** f. Gk ANA-. **5.** f. Gk *an-* = *a-* not (before vowel), as in *anarchy.*

-an, suf. of adj. (often used as nn.), f. L *-anus* direct or through F *-ain* (the early E form, retained in *certain, captain, chaplain*) or *-en,* or It., Sp., Port., *-ano,* & freely used in new words; added esp. to names of place, system, zool. order, or founder (*Chilian, Anglican, reptilian, Lutheran*); often as E termination in L adj. in *-tus,* giving -IAN as a mere phonetic variant (cf. *Christ-ian, Moham-med-an*). See also -ANE.

ăn'a, n. (With pl. ~*s*) collection of person's memorable sayings: (collect. pl.) anecdotes, lit. gossip, about a person. [=-ANA]

ăna-, pref. = Gk *ana* up, back, again, anew; before a vowel *an-.*

-ana, suf. Neut. pl. of L adjj. in *-anus* (see -AN) appended in 16th-c. F to names = the sayings of; in E from 18th c., now including anecdotes about, publications bearing on, places or persons, as *Tun-brigiana, Shakespeariana.*

ănabăp'tism, n. Re-baptism; doctrine of anabaptists. [f. L f. Gk *anabaptismos* (ANA-+*baptismos* BAPTISM)]

ănabăp'tist, n. One who baptizes over again; (opprobriously) =BAPTIST. Hence ~**is'TICAL a.** [as prec., see -IST]

ăn'abăs, n. Genus of fishes that leave water & ascend trees, [Gk part. of *anabainō* walk up]

anăb'asĭs, n. Up-country march, esp. that of Cyrus the younger into Asia, narrated by Xenophon. [Gk, = ascent f. ANA(*bainō* go)]

ănăb'ŏlism, n. (biol.). Constructive metabolism (opp. KATABOLISM). So **ănăbŏl'ĭc a.,** [f. Gk *anabolē* ascent+-ISM]

** an'abranch** (-ahn-), **n.** A stream that turns out of, &, lower down, re-enters, a river, [ANA-+BRANCH]

anăchrŏn'ic (-k-), **a.** Involving anachronism; out of date. [f. ANA-+Gk *khronos* time+-IC]

anăch'ronĭsm (-k-), **n.** Error in computing time: thing out of harmony with the present. So ~**is'tic a.** [f. F *anachronisme* f. L f. Gk *anakhronismos* t. *anakhronizō* (as prec.)]

ănaclăs'tĭc, a. Pertaining to refraction; springing back with crackling sound, as ~ *glasses.* [f. Gk *anaklastos* refracted f. ANA-(*klaō* bend)]

ănacolū'thon, n. (pl. *-tha*). Sentence, words, lacking grammatical sequence. [f. Gk *anakolouthon.* (AN- (5) +*akolouthos* following f. *a-* copul.+*keleuthos* road)]

ănacŏn'da, n. Large snake of Ceylon; large S.-American Boa; any large snake that crushes its prey. [?]

anăcrĕŏn'tĭc, a. & n. (Poem) in the manner or metre of Anacreon's lyrics; convivial & amatory. [f. L *Anacreon-ticus* (Gk *Anakreōn*, name of poet)]

ānacrus'is (-ōō), n. (pros.). Unstressed syllable at beginning of verse. [f. Gk *anakrousis* (ANA(*krousis* strike up)]

anād'romous, a. (Of fishes) ascending rivers to spawn. [f. Gk ANA(*dromos* running)+-OUS]

anaem'|ia, n. (med.). Lack of blood, un-healthy paleness. Hence ~**ic** a. [f. Gk *anaimia* (AN-(6)+*haima* blood)]

anaerobe (anǎ'erōb), n. Minute organism that can live without free oxygen. Hence **anāerōb'IAN, anāerōb'ic,** aa. [f. AN-(6)+Gk *aēr* air+*bios* life]

anaesthe'sia, n. Insensibility (lit.). [f. Gk *anaisthēsia* (AN-(6)+*aisthē-* perceive)]

anaesthet'ic, a. & n. (Agent) that produces insensibility. Hence ~**ICALLY** adv. [f. as prec.+-IC]

anaes'thetize, v.t. Render insensible (lit. & fig.). Hence ~**IST** (1), ~**IZA'TION**, nn. [as prec.+-IZE]

an'aglyph, n. Embossed ornament in low relief; (Photog.) composite stereoscopic picture printed in superimposed com-plementary colours. Hence **anaglyph'ic** a. [f. Gk ANA(*gluphē* (*gluphō* carve)]

ǎnagnō'risis, n. Dénouement in a drama. [L f. Gk, f. *anagnōrizō* recognize]

ǎnagō'gē, n. Spiritual or allegorical interpretation. So **ǎnagō'gic(AL)** aa. **ǎnagō'gically** adv. [L f. Gk *anagōgē* f. *anagō* lead up (AN-4)]

an'agram, n. Transposition of letters of word or phrase, to form new word or phrase. Hence **ǎnagrammat'ic(AL)** aa., **ǎnagrammat'ically** adv. [f.F *ana-gramme* f. Gk ANA(*grapphō* write), see -M] **anagrammatize**, v.t. Form into an anagram. Hence ~**ISM**, ~**IST**, nn. [f. Gk *anagrammatizō* (as prec., see -IZE)]

an'al, a. Pertaining to, situated near, the anus. [f. ANUS+-AL]

ǎn'alects, ǎnalĕc'ta, n. pl. Literary gleanings. [L f. L f. Gk *analekta* things gathered (ANALegō pick up)]

ǎnalĕp'tic, a. & n. Restorative (medi-cine). [f. Gk *analēptikos* f. ANA(*lambanō* take) restore, see -IC]

ǎnalgē'si|a, n. Absence of pain. So **ǎnal-gĕt'ic**, (irreg.) **ǎnalgĕs'ic**, aa., giving ~, & nn., such drug. [Gk (-*gēs-*), f. *an-*(5), *algēs* feel pain]

anal'ogic, a. Of analogy. [f. L f. Gk *analogikos* (as ANALOGY, see -IC)]

anal'ogist, n. One occupied with ana-logies; philosopher who saw in words images of the things they expressed. [as foll.; see -IST]

anal'ogize, v.t. & i. Represent by ana-logy; show to be analogous; employ analogy; be in harmony (*with*). [f. ANALOGY+-IZE]

anal'ogous, a. Similar, parallel, (*to*). Hence ~**LY2** adv., ~**NESS** n. [f. L f. Gk *analogos* (*ana* up to+*logos* proportion)+-OUS]

an'alogue (-ǒg), n. Analogous, parallel, word or thing. [F f. Gk *analogon* neut. adj., see prec.]

anal'ogy, n. (Math.) proportion; agree-ment, similarity, (*to, with, between*); analogue; (Logic) process of reasoning from parallel cases; (Lang.) imitation of inflexion or construction of existing words in forming inflexions or construc-tions of others, without intervention of the formative steps through which these at first arose: (Nat. Hist.) resemblance of form or function between organs essen-tially different. [f. L f. Gk *analogia* proportion (as ANALOGOUS)]

an'alyse (-z), v.t. Examine minutely the constitution of; (Chem., Phys.) ascer-tain the elements of (a compound); find, show, the essence of (treatise etc.); (Gram.) resolve (sentence) into its gram-matical elements. Hence ~**ABLE** a. [f. F *analyser* (*enalyse*, as foll.); also -*yze* in E by assim. to vbs in -IZE]

anal'ysis, n. (pl. -*yses*). Resolution into simple elements (in all senses of prec.); *bouting* ~, register of the result of each ball. [f. L f. Gk *analusis* f. ANA(*luō* loose)]

an'alyst, n. One skilled in (usu. chemical) analysis. [f. F *analyste* f. *analyser* ANALYSE, on anal. of nouns in -*iste* -IST f. vbs in -*iser* -IZE]

ǎnalÿt'ic, a. Pertaining to analysis. Hence **ǎnalÿt'ics** n. [f. med. L f. Gk *analutikos* (as ANALYSIS, see -IC)]

ǎnalÿt'ical, a. Employing the analytic method; (Lang.) using separate words instead of inflexions. Hence ~**LY2** adv. [prec.+-AL]

ǎnamnēs'is, n. Recollection (esp. of a previous existence). [Gk (ANAmimnēskō remind)]

ǎnamŏrph'osis, n. Distorted drawing appearing regular from one point; (Bot.) abnormal transformation. [Gk *anamor-phōsis* (ANAmorphoō transform f. *morphē* form, see -OSIS)]

anān'as (or -ahn-), n. Pineapple. [prob. f. Peruv. *Nanas*; also *anana*, -s being taken for plural]

anān'drous, a. (bot.). Without stamens. [f. Gk *anandros* husbandless (AN-(5)+*anēr andros* male)+-OUS]

ǎn'apaest, n. (Prosody) foot consisting of two short syllables followed by one long. Hence **ǎnapaes'tic** a. [f. L f. Gk *anapaistos* reversed (ANA-+*paiō* strike) bear?]

anaph'ora, n. Repetition of word or phrase in successive clauses. [L f. Gk *anaphora*=carrying back f. ANA(*pherō* bear)]

an'arch (-k), n. (poet.). Leader of revolt, or... [f. Gk ANA(*pherō*? anarchos*)]

anarc'hic(al) (-k-), aa. Lawless. Hence anarc'hically² adv. [as prec. +-IC, -ICAL]

an'archist (-k-), n. Advocate of anarchy. So ~ISM (-k-) n. [as prec. +-IST]

an'archy (-k-), n. Absence of government; disorder; confusion. [f. Gk *anarkhia* (as prec.)]

anar'throus, a. (Gk Gram.) used without the article; (Physiol.) jointless. [f. AN- (5) + Gk *arthron* joint, article, +-OUS]

ănăsâr'c|a, n. A dropsical affection. Hence ~OUS a. [f. Gk *ana* up + *sarka* (nom. *sarx*) flesh]

ănăstăt'ic, a. In relief; ~ *printing* (from reliefs on zinc plates). [f. Gk *anastatos* set up (ANASta- stand up) +-IC]

ănăstigmăt'ic, a. Free from astigmatism (used esp. of photographic lenses in which this error is corrected). So (by backformation thr. G) anastig'măt n., lens, or lens-system, so corrected. [AN- (5) + ASTIGMATIC]

anăs'tomōse (-z), v.i. Communicate by anastomosis. [f. F *anastomoser* (*anastomose* = foll.)]

anăstomōs'is, n. (pl. -osēs). Cross connexion of arteries, branches, rivers, etc. [Gk, f. *anastomoō* furnish with mouth (*stoma*), see -OSIS]

anăth'ema, n. Accursed thing; curse of God; curse of the church, excommunicating a person or denouncing a doctrine; Imprecation. [L, = excommunicated person, excommunication, f. Gk *anathema* thing devoted, (later) accursed thing (ANATItHēmi set up)]

anăth'ematize, v.t. & i. Curse. [f. F *anathématiser* f. L f. Gk *anathematizō* (as prec., see -IZE)]

anatŏm'ical, a. Belonging to anatomy; structural. Hence ~LY³ adv. [f. L f. Gk *anatomikos* (as ANATOMY, see -IC)]

anăt'omist, n. Dissecter of bodies; (fig.) analyser. [f. F *anatomiste*, see foll. & -IST]

anăt'omize, v.t. & i. Dissect; (fig.) analyse. [f. med. L *anatomizare* f. *anatomia* ANATOMY, as if f. a Gk *anatomizō*]

anăt'omy, n. Dissection; science of bodily structure; anatomical structure; analysis; (pop.) skeleton, mummy, emaciated creature. [f. F *anatomie* f. L f. Gk *anatomia* abstr. n. = ANA(*tomē* f. *temnō* cut)]

anăt'ta, -tō, n. Orange-red dye, used for colouring cheese. [?]

ăn'bury, ămb-, n. Soft tumour on horses & oxen; disease of turnips & allied plants. [perh. = *ang-berry* (OE *ang-* painful, cf. AGNAIL)]

-ance, suf. forming nn. of quality or action, chiefly thr. F -ance f. L -antia & -entia f. L pres. part. in -ant-, -ent- (nom. -ans, -ens). OF gave -ance both for existing L-antia, -entia, & for wds formed in F on same model; thus, *assistance, nuisance*, where L would have -entia. Later

F followed L vowel; *élegance, tempérance* (L -antia), but *diligence, prudence* (L -entia). E adopted F forms of both kinds, & usu. retains F form; but after 1500 -ence was in some wds restored where L would have -entia, & mod. formations follow L vowel. F -ance also became living suf. in E on native vbs as *furtherance, forbearance, riddance*.

ăn'cestor, n. Any of those from whom one's father or mother is descended, forefather. Hence ~RESS¹ n. [f. OF *ancestre, ancessor,* f. L *antecessor, -oren,* f. ANTE-(*cedere cess-* go), see -OR²]

ănces'tral, a. Belonging to, inherited from, ancestors. [f. OF *ancestrel* (*ancestre,* see prec. & -AL)]

ăn'cestry, n. Ancestral lineage; ancient descent; ancestors. [f. OF *ancesserie* (as ANCESTOR, see -Y³)]

anchithere (ăng'kithē?), n. Fossil animal, size of small pony, regarded as ancestor of the horse. [f. Gk *agkhi* near + *thērion* wild beast]

ănc'hor¹ (-k-), n. Heavy iron, composed of long shank, with ring at one end to which cable is fastened, & at other end two barbed arms, used for mooring ship to bottom of sea etc.; *sheed, bower, kedge,* ~, (largest, middle, smallest size); (fig.) source of confidence; *cast, weigh,* ~, *let down, take up,* ~; *at* ~, anchored; *come to (an)* ~, anchor; ~-*plate,* heavy piece of timber or metal serving as point of support for cables of suspension-bridge etc.; ~-*stroke* (Bill.), a kind of cannon; ~-*watch,* watch set while ship lies at ~. [OE *ancor* f. L *ancora* (not *anch-*) perh. cogn. w. or adoption of Gk *agkura* (St. *agk-* hook)]

ănc'hor² (-k-), v.t. & i. Secure (ship) with anchor; (fig.) fix firmly; (intr.) cast anchor, come to anchor. [perh. f. F *ancror* f. *ancre* anchor]

ănc'horage (-k-), n. Anchoring; lying at anchor; ~-*ground;* (fig.) thing to depend upon; ~-*dues.* [prec. +-AGE]

ănc'horess, ănc'ress, (-k-), n. Female anchoret. [f. obs. *anchor* (OE *ancra,* short form of L *anachoreta,* see foll.) +-ESS¹]

ănc'horet, -rite, (-k-), n. Hermit; person of secluded habits. Hence ănchorĕt'ic (-k-) a. [f. F *anachorète* f. L *anachoreta* (med. L -*īta*) f. Gk *anakhōrētēs* (ANAkhōreō retire, see -ETE), influenced by OE *ancra,* see prec.]

ănchŏv'y (or ăn'cho-), n. Small fish of herring family; ~-*paste* & ~-*sauce,* ~-*toast,* (made, spread, with anchovies); ~-*pear,* W.-Indian fruit eaten like mango. [f. Sp. *anchova* perh. f. Basque *anchua* (perh. = *antzua* dry)]

anchusa (ăngkūs'a), n. Kinds of hairystemmed plant, such as alkanet & bugloss. [L]

ănc'hylose (-klōz), v.t. & i. (Of joints, bones) stiffen, unite. [f. foll.]

anchylós'is (ăngkĭ-), n. Formation of stiff joint by consolidation of articulating surfaces. [f. Gk * agkulōsis* (*agkuloō* crook +-OSIS); *-ch-* for *-c-* to preserve hard sound]

ancien régime (see Ap.), n. Time before French Revolution. [F]

ân'cient[1] (-shĕnt), a. & n. Belonging to times long past (esp. before fall of Western Roman Empire); having existed, lived, long (*~ lights*, window that neighbour may not deprive of light by building; *the ~ of Days*, God; *the ~s*, civilized peoples of antiquity). Hence ~LY[2] adv., ~NESS n. [f. F *ancien* f. LL *antianus* (*ante* before, see -AN); *-t* by confus. w. -ENT]

ân'cient[2] (-shĕnt), n. (arch.). = ENSIGN. [corrupt.]

ân'cientry (-shĕn-), n. Ancientness; old-fashioned style. [ANCIENT[1] +-RY]

ancill'ary (*or* ăn̄'-), a. Subservient, sub-ordinate, (*to*). [f. L *ancillarius* (*ancilla* handmaid, see -ARY[1])]

ancle. See ANKLE.

ancon (ăng'kŏn), n. (Physiol.) elbow; (Archit.) quoin of wall or rafter, console, pretended support to cornice; *A~ sheep*, race with long bodies & short legs, the fore-legs crooked. [L, f. Gk *agkōn* bend, elbow]

-ancy, suf. Mod. E different, f. -ANCE (see -Y[3]), usu. denoting only quality or state, as opposed to *-ance*, which has besides this meaning that of action or process.

and (and, *emphat.* ănd), conj. connecting words, clauses, and sentences, as *cakes ~ buns, black ~ brown bread, buy ~ sell.* Special uses: *four ~ twenty* (but *twenty four*); *two hundred ~ forty*, *two thousand ~ forty* (but *two thousand four hundred*); *two ~ ten pence, two pounds ~ ten pence* (but *two pound ten*); *miles ~* (= innumer-able) *miles; nice ~* (= nicely) *thin; try ~* (to) *come, mind ~* (= bring) *there are books ~* (different kinds of, good & bad) *books; two ~ two, by twos; stir, ~* (= if *you stir*) *you are a dead man; and/or*, formula allowing reader to take either or both of two expressions (*contributions in money and/or garments*). [OE & prep. =against, end conj. f. OTeut. +*anda*, +*andi*]

Andalu'sian (ăndalōō'shn), n. & a. (Native) of Andalusia, a province of Spain; (*~ wool*, fine soft kind; *~ (fowl)*, bluish-black domestic fowl. [-AN]

andan'te, adv. & n. (mus.). [Movement] In moderately slow time. [It.]

dndanti'nō (-tē-), adv. & n. (Movement) rather quicker than *andante*. [It., dim. of prec.]

An'derson shel'ter (ăn-), n. Portable arched corrugated-steel air-raid shelter. [Sir J. *Anderson*, Home Secretary (1939-40)]

ân'diron (-īrn), n. Firedog for supporting burning wood on hearth. [f. OF *andier* (mod. F *landier*, etym. dub.]

ăndroe'cium (-rē-), n. (bot.). The stamens taken collectively. [f. Gk *andro-* male + *oikion* house]

ăndrŏg'ynous, a. Hermaphrodite, (Bot.) with stamens & pistils in same flower or on same plant. [f. L f. Gk *androgunos* (*anēr andros* male +*gunē* woman) +-OUS]

-āne, suf. 1. Variant of -AN, usu. w. differentiation (*germane, urbane, humane*), but sometimes alone (*mundane*). 2. (Chem.) formed to give a series with Gk -ENE, -INE, -ONE, for naming hydrocarbon types.

ăn'ecdŏtage, n. Anecdotes; (joc.) garru-lous old age. [-AGE]

ăn'ecdŏte, n. Narrative of detached in-cident; (pl. *~a*) unpublished details of history. Hence ~IST n., ~AL, ănecdŏt'ICAL) aa. [f. med. L f. Gk *anekdota* things unpublished (AN- (5) + *ekdotos* f. *ekdidōmi* give out)]

ăneļe', v.t. (arch.). Anoint; give extreme unction to. [orig. *anelien* (AN- (1) + *eten* oil f. OE *ele*, n. f. L *oleum*)]

ăněm'oĭgraph (-ah̄f), n. Instrument for recording on paper the direction & force of wind. Hence ~graph'ĭc a. [f. Gk *anemos* wind +-GRAPH]

ănĕmŏm'ĕter, n. Instrument for measur-ing force of wind, whence ănĕmŏmĕt'ric a., ănĕmŏm'ĕtry n.; apparatus for showing wind-pressure in organ. [as prec. +-METER]

ănĕm'oně, n. Genus of plants, esp. *A~ nemorosa* (also called *Wind-flower*); *Sea A~*, popular name of various actinoid zoophytes. [f. L f. Gk *anemōnē* daughter of the wind (as prec. +-*ōnē* patronymic suf.)]

ănĕmŏph'ilous, a. Wind-fertilized. [f. Gk *anemos* wind, see -PHIL]

anĕnt', prep. (arch., Sc.). Concerning. [OE has *on efen* on a level with]

-ânĕous (-nē-), suf. f. L adjj. in *-aneus* (*-an- +-eo-*) +-OUS.

ăn'eroid, a. & n. *~ (barometer)*, one that measures air-pressure by its action on elastic lid of box exhausted of air, not by height of fluid column. [f. F *anéroïde* (Gk *a-* not + *nēros* wet, see -OID)]

ăn'eurysm, -ĭsm (-nūr-), n. Morbid dilatation of an artery; abnormal enlarge-ment. Hence ăneurys'mAL, -is'mAL (-nūrĭz-), a. [f. Gk *aneurusma* (*aneurunō* widen out f. *eurus* wide)]

anew', adv. Again; in a different way. [A- (3) +NEW]

ănfrăctūŏs'ĭty, n. Circuitousness, in-tricacy, (lit. & fig.); (usu. pl.) winding passage. [f. F *anfractuosité* f. L *anfrac-tuosus* f. *anfractus* f. *an*- about +*frangere fract-* break), see -OSE & -TY]

ăng'ary (-ngɛr-), n. (law). Belligerent's right (subject to compensation) of seizing or destroying neutral property under stress of military necessity. [f. med. L

angaria f. Gk *aggareia* (*aggaros* Persian courier)]

ān'gel (-j-), n. Divine messenger; *visits, like those of ~s, short & far between*; *entertain an ~ unawares*, do service to one who proves to be an important person etc. (*Heb.* xiii. 2); lovely or innocent being; minister of loving offices; old English gold coin (in full *~noble*), from 6s. 8d. to 10s., showing Michael piercing dragon; *good, evil, ~, attendant spirits*; *~ (messenger) of death*; *~fish*, kind of shark; *~s, devils, -on-horseback*, savoury of oysters wrapped in slices of bacon. [f. L *angelus* f. Gk *aggelos* messenger, used to transl. Heb, *mal'āk* messenger (of Jehovah)]

angēl'ic (-j-), a. Pertaining to angels; like an angel, of superhuman qualities; *A~ Doctor*, Thomas Aquinas. Hence ~AL a., ~ALl Y adv. [f. F *angélique* f. L f. Gk *aggelikos* (as prec., see -IC)]

angēl'ica (-j-), n. Aromatic plant, used in cooking & medicine; candied ~ root. [f. med. L (*herba*) *angelica* angelic herb]

angēlol'atrÿ (-j-), n. Angel-worship. [f. Gk *aggelos*, see ANGEL & -LATRY]

angēlol'ogy (-j-), n. Doctrine as to angels. [as prec. +-LOGY]

ān'gĕlus (-j-), n. Devotional exercise commemorating Incarnation, said by Roman Catholics at morning, noon, & sunset, at sound of bell (*~-bell* or ~). [f. opening words *Angelus domini*]

ăng'er (-ngg-), n. Rage, hot displeasure. [f. ON *angr* trouble (root *ang* strait)]

ăng'er² (-ngg-), v.t. Make angry, enrage. [f. ON *angra* vex (as prec.)]

An'gévin (-jĕvĭ-), a. & n. Of Anjou, of the Plantagenets, including English kings from Henry II to Richard II; (n.) a Plantagenet. [F]

ăngīn'a (-j-), n. Quinsy; *~ pěc'toris*, spasm of chest resulting from over-exertion when heart is diseased. [L *angina* quinsy (formerly thought to be *angēna*, whence usu. E pronunc.), cf. *angēre* choke &[Gk *agchonē* strangling]

ăn'giō- (-j-) in comb. = Gk *aggeion* vessel dim. of *aggos* chest, chiefly in terms relating to seed- or blood-vessels.

ăngle¹ (ăng'gl), n. Space between two meeting lines or planes; inclination of two lines to each other; ACUTE, OBTUSE, RIGHT, ~; corner; sharp projection; (fig.) point of view; *~iron*, L-shaped piece of iron to strengthen framework; *~-wise*, angularly. Hence (-)ăngLED² (ăng'gld) a. [F, f. L *angulus* dim. of +*angus*, cf. Gk *agkos* bend]

ăngle² (ăng'gl), n., & v.i. Fish-hook (obs. exc. in *brother of the ~*, angler); (vb) fish with hook & bait (*for* or abs.), lit. & fig. [OE *angul* cogn.w. OHG *angul* mod. G *angel*, cf. L *uncus* & *angulus*, see prec.]

Angle³ (ăng'gl), n. (Pl.) Low-German tribe settled in Northumbria, Mercia, & E. Anglia. [f. L *Anglus* f. OTeut. *angli-* (OE *engel*) f. *Angul* a district of Schleswig-Holstein (as prec.)]

Ăng'lican (ăngg-), a. & n. (Adherent) of the reformed church of England, esp. of High Church principles; *~ chant*, short harmonized melody in two or more phrases each beginning with a reciting note, for singing to unmetrical words (psalms, canticles). Hence ~ISM n. [f. med. L *Anglicanus* (*Anglicus* f. *Angli* English)]

Anglicē (ăng'glisē), adv. In English. [L]

Ăng'licism (ăngg-), n. English idiom; English political principles. [f. foll, see -ISM]

Ăng'licize (ăngg-), v.t. Make English in form or character. [f. L *Anglicus* English + -IZE]

Ăng'lo- (ăngg-) in comb. English, as *~Catholic*; of English origin, as *~American*; half English & half ~, as *~French* (entente etc.); *~Indian* a. & n., of British birth but living or having lived long in India, (in Eurasian use) Eurasian. [comb. form of L *Anglus* Eng. or Eurasian.]

Ănglo-Căth'olic, a. & n. (Member) of the party that insists on the catholicity of the Church of England & repudiates the epithet *protestant*. [prec.]

Ănglomān'ia (ăngg-), n. Excessive admiration of English customs. So **Ăng'lo-PHIL, Ăng'loPHOBE, ĂngloPHOB'IA**, (ăngg-), nn. [prec. + -MANIA]

Ănglo-Săx'on, n. & a. English Saxon (as distinct from Old Saxons of the continent); Old English (people, language) before Norman Conquest (in this dictionary called OE); of English descent (wherever found), whence ~DOM n. [f. L *Anglo-Saxones* (pl.)]

Ănglo-Săx'onism (ăngg-), n. Belief in claims of the Anglo-Saxon race. [prec. + -ISM]

ăngōr'a, ăngōr'a, (-ngg-), n. Fabric made from wool of angora goat; *~ cat* (long-haired variety). [f. *Angora* (L *Ancyra*, Gk *Agkura*), town in Asia Minor, corrupted to *angola*]

ăngostūr'a, ăngŭs-, (-ngg-), a. & n. Bark used as febrifuge & tonic, as *~ bitters*. [f. *Angustura*, town on the Orinoco, now Ciudad Bolivar]

ăng'rÿ (-ngg-), a. Enraged, wrathful, resentful, (*at, about, thing, at, with, person*); irritable, passionate; (of wound, sore, etc.) inflamed, painful. Hence ~ILŸ² adv. [f. ANGER n. +-Y²]

Ăng'ström (ăng'strŏm) **ŭn'ĭt**, n. A hundred-millionth of a centimetre, used in expressing short wave-lengths (abbr. A.U.). [A. J. Ångström, Swedish physicist]

ăng'uine (-ngw-), a. Snake-like. [f. L *anguis* snake, see -INE[1]]

ăng'uish (-ngwsh), n. Severe bodily or mental pain. [f. OF *anguisse*, *angoisse* choking (It. *angoscia*) f. L *angustia* tightness (*angustus*, cf. ANGINA)]

ăng'ular (-ngg-), a. Having angles; sharp-cornered ; placed in, at, an angle; measured by angle, as ~ *divergence*; wanting plumpness; wanting suavity. Hence ăngulă'rĭtў (-ngg-) n., ~lў[2] adv. [f. L *angularis* (*angulus* ANGLE, see -AR[1])]

ăng'ulate (-ngg-), a. Formed with corners. Hence ~ATE[2](-ngg-) v.t., ~A'TION (-ngg-) n. [f. L *angulatus*, see -ATE[2]]

ăngŭs'tī- (-ngg-) in comb. With narrow ~, as *-foliate*, *-rostrate*, (leaves, beak). [L *angustus* narrow]

ănhȳd'rous, a. (chem.). Without water +*hudōr* water)+-OUS] of crystallization. [f. Gk *anudros* (AN- (5)

ăn'icŭt, ann-, n. (Anglo-Ind.). River-dam in S. India, built for irrigation purposes. [f. Tamil *anai-kaṭṭu* dam-building]

ănīgh (anī'), adv. & prep. Near. [mod. Sham archaism, after *afar*]

ăn'il, n. Indigo (shrub & dye). [F, = Sp. *&c.* f. Arab. *an-nīl* (*al* the +*nīl* f. Skr. *nīla* indigo)]

ăn'īle, a. Old-womanish; imbecile. [f. L *anīlis* (*anus* old woman, see -ILE)]

ăn'ilīne, n. A chemical base, the source of many dyes, obtained originally from indigo, now chiefly from coal-tar. [ANIL +-INE[5]]

ănī'lĭtў, n. Dotage. [f. L *anīlitas* (ANILE, see -TY)]

ănimadvĕr'sion (-shn), n. Criticism; censure. [f. L *animadversio* (*animadver-tere* -vers-, see foll. and -ION)]

ănimadvĕr't, v.i. Pass criticism or censure on (conduct, fault, etc.). [f. L *animadvertere* f. *animus* mind +ADVERTERE]

ăn'imal, n. & a. 1. Organized being endowed (more or less perceptibly) with life, sensation, & voluntary motion; other ~ than man; quadruped; a brutish man. 2. adj. Pertaining to the functions of ~s, as ~ *spirits* (natural buoyancy), ~ *magnetism* (mesmerism); pertaining to ~s as opp. to vegetables; carnal. Hence ~IX[2] adv. [L, f. *animale* neut. of *animalis* having breath (*anima* breath, see -AL); the adj. orig. f. L adj.]

ăn'imal'cūle, n. Microscopic animal. [f. L *animalculum* (*animal*, see prec. & -CULE)]

ăn'imal'cūlĭsm, n. Reference of physiological phenomena to agency of animalcules. So ~ISM n. [f. prec. +-ISM]

ăn'imalism, n. Animal activity; sensuality; doctrine that men are mere animals. [ANIMAL +-ISM]

ăn'imăl'ĭtў, n. Animal nature or system; merely animal nature; the animal world. [f. F *animalité* (*animal* a., see -ITY)]

ăn'imalĭz|e, v.t. Convert into animal substance, sensualize. Hence ~A'TION n. [ANIMAL+-IZE]

ăn'imate[1], a. Living; lively. [f. L *animare* quicken, see -ATE[2]]

ăn'imate[1], v.t. Breathe life into; enliven, make lively, as in ~*ed discussion*; inspirit (esp. in p.p.); inspire, actuate; give life to. Hence ~**ēdlў**[2] adv., ~ā'tion n. [f. prec., see -ATE[2]]

ăn'imē (-mā), n. A W. Indian resin used in making varnish; other resins. [F, = animated (by the many insects contained)]

ăn'imĭsm, n. Doctrine of the *anima mundi* (that phenomena of animal life are produced by an immaterial soul); attribution of living soul to inanimate objects & natural phenomena; spiritualism (as opposed to materialism). Hence ~IST n., ~ĭs'tĭc a. [f. L *anima* life, soul +-ISM]

ăn'imos'ĭtў, n. Active enmity (*against*, *between*). [f. F *animosité* f. L *animositatem* (*animosus* spirited f. foll., see -OSE & -TY)]

ăn'imus, n. (no pl.). Animating spirit; animosity. [L, = soul, mind, mental impulse]

ăn'ĭon, n. Electro-negative element evolved at anode during electrolysis (opp. CATION). [Gk, = going up (ANA-, *eimi* go)]

ăn'īse, n. Umbelliferous plant with aromatic seeds. [f. F *anis* f. L f. Gk *anīson*, *anēthon*, anise, dill]

ăn'īseed, n. Seed of anise, used as a carminative.

ăn'isĕtte' (-z-), n. Liqueur flavoured with aniseed. [F, dim. of *anis* anise]

ănĭs|o- in comb. Unequal, as ~*ōm'erous*, unsymmetrical, ~*osthĕn'ic*, of unequal strength. [f. Gk *anīsos* (AN- (5)+*īsos* equal)]

ănk'er, n. Measure of wine & spirits in Holland, N. Germany, Denmark, Sweden, Russia, & formerly in England (8½ imp. gals) ; cask holding the quantity. [Du., etym. dub.]

ănkh (ăngk), n. (Egypt. ant.). Key-like cross as symbol of enduring life & generative energy. [Egyptian, = life]

ănk'le, ănc'le, (ăng'kl), n. Joint connecting foot with leg; slender part between this & calf. [earlier *ankel* (Du. *enkel*, G *enkel*) f. root *ank-* bend (cf. L *angulus*); OE has *anclēow* perh. f. Du. *anklaauw* (ending assim. to *klaauw* claw)]

ănk'lĕt, n. Ornament or support for ankle. [prec. +-LET]

ănn'a, n. Indian scallop-edged nickel coin, the sixteenth part of a rupee (see PIE[4] & PICE). [Hind. *ana*]

ǎnn'alist, n. Writer of annals. Hence **annalis'tɪc** a. [f. foll. +-IST]

ǎnn'als (-z), n. pl. Narrative of events year by year; historical records. [f. L *annales* (*libri*) yearly (books) f. *annus* year, -AL]

ǎnn'ātes (-ts), n. pl. (Rom. Cath.) first year's revenue of see or benefice, paid to Pope. [f. F *annate* f. med. L *annata* year's proceeds (*annus*, see -ADE)]

anneal' (-ēl), v.t. Toughen by gradually diminishing heat, temper (lit. & fig.). [f. AN- (1) + OE *ǣlan* burn, bake; partly also f. OF *neeler* enamel f. LL *nigellare* blacken (*nigellus*, dim. of *niger*)]

annĕc'tent, a. Connecting, as ~ link. [f. L as ANNEX, see -ENT]

Annĕl'ida, n. pl. (zool.). The class of segmented worms. Hence **ǎnn'elɪd**[3] n., **annĕl'idan** a. [mod. L, f. L F *annelés* ringed (OF *annel* ring f. L *a(n)nellus* dim. of *anulus* ring) +*ida*, cf. -ID[3]]

annĕx', v.t. Add as subordinate part; append (to book etc.); take possession of (territory etc.); attach as an attribute, addition, or consequence. Hence or cogn. ~ABLE a., **annĕxA'TION** n. [f. F *annexer* f. *annexe* thing joined f. L AN-(*nectere nex-* bind)]

annĕx(e)', n. Addition to a document; supplementary building. [F (-*xe*), see prec.]

anni'hɪlate (-nīl-), v.t. Blot out of existence. Hence ~or[2] n. [f. L ANnihilare (*nihil* nothing), see -ATE[2]]

annihilā'tion (-nīl-), n. Utter destruction; (Theol.) destruction of soul as well as body, whence ~ISM, ~IST, nn. [F (*annihiler* f. L as prec, see -ATION)]

ǎnnivĕrs'arỹ, n. Yearly return of a date; celebration of this. [f. L *anniversarius* (*annus* year + *versus* turned, see -ARY[1])]

dǎnn'ō aetāt'is suǎ'ae, phr. In the — year of his or her age. [L]

Ann'ō Dŏm'ini (ǎ-), phr. In the year of our Lord, of the Christian era, (usu. *A.D.*); || (colloq., as n.) advancing age (~ *is the trouble*). [L]

ǎnn'otāte, v.t. & i. Furnish with notes (book, author); (v.i.) make notes (*on*). So ~A'TION, ~ātor[3] nn. [f. L ANnotare (*nota* mark), see -ATE[3]]

announce', v.t. Proclaim; intimate the approach of; make known (without words) to senses or mind. Hence ~MENT (-sm-), **announ'cer**[1] (esp, of items to be broadcast), nn. [f. OF *anoncer* f. L ADnuntiare (*nuntius* messenger)]

annoy'[1], n. (arch., poet.). Annoyance. [f. OF *anoi, enoi* (OSp. *enoyo*, OVenet. *inodio*) f. L phr. *in odio* in hatred, hateful, -n- doubled by assim. to *ennoble* etc.]

annoy'[2], v.t. Irritate; molest, harass. [f. OF *anoier, enoier*, f. com.-Rom. *inodiare* (as prec.)]

annoy'ance, n. Molestation; vexation; disgust. [f. OF *anoiance, enoiance* (*anoier*, see prec. & -ANCE)]

ǎnn'ūal, a. & n. Reckoned by the year; recurring yearly; lasting for a year; (book etc.) published in yearly numbers. Hence ~LY[2] adv. [f. OF *annuel* f. L *annualis* = class. L *annalis* (*annus* year, see -AL)]

ǎnn'ūitant, n. One who holds an annuity. [f. foll. +-ANT, by assim. to *accountant* etc.]

annū'ity, n. Sum payable in respect of a particular year; yearly grant; investment of money entitling investor to series of equal annual sums; *life, terminable, perpetual,* ~ (ceasing at death of investor, after specified term, on repayment of principal); *immediate, deferred or reversionary,* ~ (commencing at end of first interval of payment after investment, after specified interval or event). [f. F *annuité* f. med. L *annuitatem* (*annuus* yearly, see -TY)]

annul', v.t. (-ll-). Annihilate; abolish; cancel; declare invalid. Hence ~MENT n. [f. OF *annuler* (mod. F *annuler*) f. LL ANnullare (*nullus* none)]

ǎnn'ūlar, a. Ring-like; ~ *space* (between inner & outer surface of cylinder); ~ *ligament* (girding wrist & ankle); ~ *eclipse* (of sun (when moon, projected on sun's disk, leaves ring of light visible). Hence ~LY[2] adv. [f. L *an(n)ularis* (*an(n)ulus* ring, see -AR[1])]

ǎnn'ūlate, -āted, aa. Furnished, marked, with rings; formed of rings. Hence **ǎnnūlā'TION** n. [f. L *annulatus* (as foll., see -ATE[2])]

ǎnn'ūlet, n. Small ring; (Archit.) small fillet encircling column. [f. L *annulus* ring +-ET[1]]

ǎnn'ūloid, a. Ring-like. So **ǎnnūlōse**[1] a. [as prec. +-OID]

annūn'ciāte (-shɪ-), v.t. Proclaim; intimate as coming or ready. [f. L *annuntiare* ANNOUNCE, see -ATE[3]]

annŭncia'tion (-sɪ-), n. Announcement; (A~) that of the incarnation, made by the angel Gabriel to the Virgin Mary, festival commemorating this, Lady-day, March 25th. [f. F *annonciation* f. L *annuntiationem* (as prec., see -ATION)]

annūn'ciātor (-shɪ-), n. Announcer; indicator showing in which direction attendance summoned by bell or telephone is needed. [f. L *annuntiator* (as prec., see -OR[2])]

ǎn'o-, pref. = Gk *anō* adv., upward; in scientific terms, as ~*car'pous*, (of ferns) having fructification on upper part of frond; ~*gén'ic*, developed upwardly or inwardly.

ǎn'ōde, n. (Electr.) positive pole (cf. CATHODE). [f. Gk *anodos* way up (*ana* up +*hodos* way)]

ǎn'odyne, a. & n. (Medicine, drug) able to assuage pain; (anything) mentally soothing. [f. L f. Gk *anōdunos* painless (AN- (5) + *odunē* pain)]

ănoĕt'ic, a. (psych.). Characterized by but without thought. [f. AN- (5) + Gk *noētos* perceptible + -IC]

anoint', v.t. Apply ointment, oil, to (esp. as religious ceremony at baptism or on consecration as priest or king); moisten, rub; *the Lord's Anointed*, Christ, (also) king by divine right. [f. obs. adj. *anoint*, f. OF *enoint* p.p. of *enoindre* f. L *inungere* *unct*-)]

anomalis'tic, a. (astron.). ~ *year*, time earth takes to pass from perihelion to perihelion; ~ *month*, time moon takes to pass from perigee to perigee. [f. Gk *anomalos* ANOMALOUS + -IST + -IC]

anŏm'alous, a. Irregular; abnormal. Hence ~LY² adv., ~NESS n. [f. L f. Gk *anōmalos* (AN- (5) + *homalos* even)]

anŏm'aly, n. Unevenness of motion etc.; irregularity. (Astron.) angular distance of planet or satellite from its last perihelion or perigee. [f. L f. Gk *anōmalia* (*anōmalos* see prec.)]

an'omon- in comb. Irregular, as ~*carp'ous*, bearing unusual fruit, ~*phyll'ous*, with leaves irregularly placed. [f. Gk *anomos* without law (a- not + *nomos*)]

anŏn', adv. Soon, presently; (of contrast) now again; *ever &* ~, every now & then. [OE *on an* into one, *on one* in one (body, mind, state, way), movement, moment)]

ănŏn'a. see ANNONA.

ănona'ceous (-â'shus), a. Pertaining to the custard-apple family *Annonaceae* (formerly *Anonaceae*). [-ACEOUS]

ăn'onym, n. Person who remains nameless; pseudonym. [f. F *anonyme* (as foll.)]

ănonym'ity, n. State of being anonymous. [as foll., see -TY]

anŏn'ymous, a. (abbr. *anon*.). Of unknown name; of unknown authorship. Hence ~LY² adv., ~NESS n. [f. Gk *anōnumos* nameless (AN- (5) + *onoma* name)]

anŏph'eles (-z), n. Kinds of (esp. malarial) mosquito. [Gk; = hurtful (a- not, *ophelos* benefit)]

anŏs'mia, n. Loss of sense of smell. [mod. L f. AN- (5) + Gk *osmē* smell]

anoth'er (-ŭdh-), pron. & a. (pl. *other* a., *others* pron.). An additional (one), as *try* ~, *pear, try* ~ ; || unnamed additional party to legal action (X *versus* Y & ~); || (in list of cricket eleven etc., written *A. N. Other*) anonymous player or one still to be selected; a counterpart to, as ~ *Solomon*; *such* ~, of the same sort; a different (one), as *take this towel away & bring me* ~ ; (contrasted or coupled with *one*) *one man's meat is* ~ *man's poison, taken one with* ~ ; ONE ~. [AN + OTHER; in OE *other* was used by itself,

an not yet being weakened to indef. article]

anour'ous (-oor-), a. Tailless. [f. AN- (5) + Gk *oura* tail + -OUS]

anscluess (än'shlöös), n. Union. [G]

answer (ähn'ser), n. Reply; defence; solution; thing done in return. [orig. = solemn affirmation to rebut a charge; OE *andswaru* f. OTeut. *andsward-* (*and-* against + *-swaru* affirmation f. *swarian*, OE *swerian* swear)]

answer² (ähn'ser), v.t. & i. Reply to or to, *as* ~ *me, my question, to me, to my question; ~ to* (acknowledge, have) the name of X; ~ (summons to) *the door*; reply to (charge); ~ *for* (be responsible *for* person or thing); ~ (correspond to, also ~ *to*) *my hopes, your description*; ~ (fulfil) *my purpose; will not* ~ (do, succeed); ~ *back* (vulg.), ~ rebuke sanctily. [OE *and-swarian* (as prec.)]

answerable (ähn'ser-), a. Responsible (*to* person, *for* act); (arch.) corresponding (*to*). [prec. + -ABLE]

ănt, n. A small social hymenopterous insect celebrated for industry, emmet, pismire; ~*bear*, the great ~-*eater*; ~*eggs*, larvae of ~s; ~-*catcher*, ~-*thrush*, bird of thrush family living on ~s; ~-*eater*, name of various animals that live on ~s; ~-*fly*, winged ~, used as bait in angling; ~-*hill*, mound over ~s'*nest*, conical nest of termites; *White Ant*, termite, destructive social insect of neuropterous order. [OE *ǣmete, ēmete,* cogn. w. WG *āmaitjō* (ā off + *maitan* cut); *ǣmete* became *ant, ēmete* EMMET]

-ant, suf. forming adj. (& nn.) f. F *-ant* (or direct) f. L *-antem, -entem, -ěntem,* accus. of pres. part. (nom. *-ans, -ens*). OF levelled all L partt. under ending *-ant,* though later F preserved L *-ent-*. E adopted F *-ant* as *-aunt,* which on loss of accent reappeared as *-ant* (*defiant* L *diffidentem, pliant* L *plicentem, serjeant* L *servientem, tenant* L *tenentem, serjeant* L *servientem, pliant* L *plicentem,* Most old wds retain *-ant,* but since 1500 some have been refash., universally (*apparant* or partly (*dependent, -ant*); *belligerant* (L *belligerans*) is wrongly changed to *-ent* on L *gerěre.* Mod. wds in *-ant* are f. L *-ant-,* direct or thr. F, or on L anal. (rarely where no vb exists, as *benignant* on anal. of *malignant*). Noun meanings: (1) personal agent, (2) thing, esp. producing effect.

antă'cid, a. & n. Preventive of acidity (esp. in stomach). [ANT- + ACID]

ăntăg'onism, n. Active opposition (*to, against, with*); opposing principle; *come into* ~ *with*; *between two*; *come into* ~. [f. Gk *antagōn-isma* (as foll., see -ISM)]

antag'on|ist, n. Opponent, adversary; (Phys.) counteracting muscle. Hence ~is'tic a., ~is'tically adv. [f. Gk *antagōnistēs* (as foll., see -IST)]

antag'onize, v.t. (Of a force etc.) counteract, tend to neutralize, (another); evoke hostility in, provoke to opposition, make into an enemy; 'oppose', resist. [f. Gk ANTagōnizomai (*agōn* contest, see -IZE)]

antal'kali, n. Substance that counteracts analkali. Hence ~NE[1] a. [ANT-+ALKALI]

antaphrodis'iac (-z-), a. & n. Preventive of venereal desire. [f. ANT-+APHRO-DISIAC]

antarc'tic, a. Southern, of south polar regions; A~ *Pole*, S. pole of earth or heavens; A~ *Circle*, parallel of 66° 32' S. [refash. f. OF *antartique* f. L f. Gk ANT(*arktikos* ARCTIC)]

an'te, n., & v.t. Stake put up by poker-player before drawing new cards; (v.t.) put up (an ~) ; ~ *up*, (transf.) to bet, stake, pay up. [L, = before]

an'te-, pref. = L *ante* before, prep. & adv., used esp. in E to form adj. with or without adj. ending, as ~*reformation(al)*; ~*bellum*, (L phr. =) before the war (used attrib. or as adj.); ~*Communion Service* to end of prayer for the 'Church militant'; ~*post*, (of racing bets) made before the runners' numbers are hoisted on the board.

anteced'ence, n. Precedence, priority, (in time or causal relation); (Astron.) retrograde motion. [f. L *antecedentia* (as foll., see -ENCE)]

anteced'ent, a. & n. 1. Previous (*to*); presumptive, a priori. 2. n. Preceding thing or circumstance; (Logic) the part of a conditional proposition on which the other depends; (Gram.) noun, clause, sentence, to which a following (esp. relative) pronoun or adverb refers; (Math.) first term of a ratio; (pl.) past history (esp. of persons). Hence ~LY[2] adv. [f. F *antécédent* f. L ANTE(*cedere* go), see -ENT]

an'techamber, n. Room leading to chief apartment. [f. F *antichambre* (*anti-* for ANTE-+*chambre* CHAMBER)]

an'techapel, n. Outer part at west end of chapel. [ANTE-+CHAPEL]

an'tedate, n. Date before the true time (esp. of writing). [ANTE-+DATE[2] n.]

antedate[2], v.t. Affix, assign, an earlier than the true date to (document, event); precede; antedate. [f. prec.]

antediluv'ian (-lōō-), a. & n. Belonging, referring, appropriate, to the time before the flood; (n.) old-fashioned person, (also) very old person. [f. ANTE-+L *diluvium* DELUGE+-AN]

an'telope, n. Deer-like ruminant genus of animals. [f. OF *antelop* f. L *anthalopus* f. Gk *antholops*, etym. dub.]

an'te merid'iem, phr. (abbr. *a.m.*). Between midnight & noon, as 7.30 *a.m.* [L]

antemun'dane, a. Existing, occurring, before creation of world. [f. ANTE-+L *mundus* world+-ANE]

antenat'al, a. Previous to birth. [ANTE-+NATAL]

antenn|a, n. (pl. ~ae). Sensory organ found in pairs on heads of insects & crustacea, feeler; (Bot.) irritable processes in male flower of some orchids; (Wireless) = AERIAL n. Hence ~AL, ~ARY[1], ~IF'EROUS, ~IFORM, aa. [L, = sail-yard, perh. f. Gk *anateinō* stretch out]

antenup'tial (-shl), a. Born, occurring, etc., before marriage. [ANTE-+L *nuptiae* nuptials+-AL]

antepen'dium, n. Veil for front of altar. [f. L ANTEpendium (*pendēre* hang]

antepenult', a. & n. Last but two (orig. & usu. of syllables. [abbr. of L (*syllaba*) antepaenultima, see foll.]

antepenul'timate, a. & n. = prec. [f. L ANTEpaenultimus (*paene* almost+*ultimus* last)+-ATE[2]]

antepran'dial, a. Before-dinner. [f. ANTE-+L *prandium*+-AL]

ante'rior, a. More to the front; prior (*to*). Hence **anteriō'rity** n., ~LY[2] adv. [L, = fore, former, f. *ante* before]

an'te-room, n. Room leading to another; (Mil.) sitting-room in officers' mess. [ANTE-+ROOM]

anth- pref. = ANTE- before aspirate.

anthel'ion, n. (pl. -*ia*). Luminous ring projected on cloud or fog bank opposite to sun. [late Gk, neut. of *anthēlios* opposite to sun (ANTH-+*hēlios* sun)]

anthelmin'tic, a. & n. (Medicine) of use against intestinal worms. [f. ANTH-+Gk *helmins -minthos* worm+-IC]

an'them, n. Composition for church use sung antiphonally; non-metrical composition (usu. from Scriptures or Liturgy) set to sacred music; song of praise or gladness. [OE *antefne* f. Rom. *antefana* f. LL *antiphona*, see ANTI-PHON, E development being *antef'ne*, *antem'ne*, *an'tem*, *an'them*]

an'ther, n. (bot.). Part of stamen containing pollen; ~-*valve*, opening by which pollen is shed. Hence ~AL, ~IF'EROUS, ~OID, aa. [f. F *anthère* f. L *anthera* medicine extracted from flowers f. Gk *anthēra* flowery, fem. adj. f. *anthos*]

anthol'og|y, n. Collection of small choice poems, esp. epigrams, (orig. Greek); literary collection. Hence ~IST n. [f. L f. Gk *anthologia* (*anthos* flower+-*logia* collection f. *legō* gather]

An'thony (ǎn'to-), n. St ~, patron of swineherds; ~, smallest pig of litter; (*St*) ~'s fire, erysipelas.

For other compounds of *ante-* see ANTE-.

ǎn'thracēne, n. Complex hydrocarbon obtained in the distillation of coal-tar, the ultimate source of synthetic alizarin. [f. Gk *anthrax -akos* coal +-ENE]

ǎn'thracīte, n. Non-bituminous variety of coal. Hence ~ĬT'IC, ~ĬTOUS, aa. [f. f. Gk *anthrakitēs* coal-like (*anthrax -akos* coal)]

ǎn'thrǎx, n. Malignant boil; splenic fever of sheep & cattle; malignant pustule caused in man by infection from animals so affected. [f.f. Gk *anthrax -akos* coal]

ǎn'thrōpo- in comb. =Gk *anthrōpos* man, as: ~ocen'tric, centring in man; ~og'eny, study of origin of man; ~ŏg'raphy, science of geographical distribution of mankind; ~ŏlite, ~ŏlith, (-ōp-), fossil man; ~ŏm'etry, measurement of human body; ~ŏph'a-gous, ~ŏph'agy, man-eating.

ǎn'thropoid, a. & n. Man-like; (n.) being that is human in form only, esp. ~ ape. [f. Gk *anthropoeidēs* (ANTHROPO-, see -OID)]

ǎnthrōpŏl'ogy, n. Whole science of man; physiological & psychological science of man; study of man as an animal. Hence **ǎnthrōpōlǒ'gǐcal** a., **ǎnthrōpŏl'ogist** n. [+-LOGY]

ǎnthrōpomŏrph'ic, a. Of the nature of anthropomorphism. [as foll.+-IC]

ǎnthrōpomŏrph'ize, v.t. Attribute human form or personality to (God etc. or abs.). Hence ~ISM, ~IST, nn. [as foll. +-IZE]

ǎnthrōpomŏrph'ous, a. Of human form. [f. Gk ANTHROPOMORPHos (*morphē* form) +-OUS]

anti-, pref. =Gk *anti* (before unaspir. vowel *ant-*, before aspirate *anth-*) oppo-site, against, in exchange; instead, rival-ling; in words f. Gk, & as living pref. in E (1) combining with nouns to form nouns, *anti-* having adj. force = rival (*-pope*, *-king*), opposing, counter (*-chorus*, *-league*), reverse of (*-climax*); (2) forming adj. on nouns governed by *anti-* (*-slavery society*, *-vaccination league*) or on adj. implying a noun so governed (*-national*, *-ritualistic*), with sense 'opposed to'; many of these are also nouns, esp. names of medicines (*-dysenteric*); (3) forming derivative nouns & adj. by addition of a suf., esp. *-ist*, (*-alcoholist*, *-tobacconist*, *-sabbatarian*) with sense 'one opposed to', also corresponding abstract nn. in *-ism* (*-Darwinism*).

ǎnti-air'craft (-ah-), a. ~ gun etc. (for shooting down hostile aircraft). [prec.]

ǎn'tiar, n. Upas tree of Java; poison thence obtained. [Jav. *anṭjar*]

ǎntibǐl'ious, a. Of use against biliousness. [ANTI- (2)]

ǎn'tibŏdy, n. (physiol.). Kinds of substance in the blood tending to neutralize others that are harmful. [ANTI- (1)]

For other compounds of *anti-* see ANTI-.

ǎn'tic, a. & n. 1. (arch.) Grotesque, bizarre. 2. n. Grotesque posture (usu. pl.); (arch.) mountebank, clown. [f. It. *antico* f. L *antiquus* ancient, apparently from ascription of GROTESQUE work to the ancients]

ǎn'tichrist (-k-), n. Enemy of Christ; (A~, the A~) great personal opponent of Christ expected by early church to appear before end of world. [f. OF *antecrist* f. L *antechristus* f. Gk *antichristos* (ANTI- (1) + *khristos* CHRIST)]

ǎntichris'tian (-k-), a. Pertaining to Anti-christ; opposed to Christianity. Hence ~ISM (-k-) n. [f. prec., with extended meaning]

ǎntic'ipāte, v.t. Use in advance; fore-stall (person or thing); accelerate, as ~*date* one's *ruin*; discuss, consider, realize, beforehand; look forward to, expect, before (event, *that* it will happen,... [f. L *anticipare* (*anti-* for ANTE-+*capere* take; see -ATE²]

ǎnticipā'tion, n. Action of anticipating (in senses of the vb); *thanking you in* ~, closing formula in letter of inquiry or request; (Med.) occurrence of phenomena before usual time; (Mus.) introduction beforehand of part of chord about to follow. [f. L *anticipatio* (as prec., see -ATION]

ǎntic'ipātor, n. One who anticipates. Hence ~ORY a. [L (as prec., see -OR²)]

ǎnticli'max, n. Opposite of climax, addition of a particular that weakens the effect; descent contrasting with previous rise. [ANTI- (1)]

ǎnticli'nal, a. (Geol.) forming ridge on which strata lean against each other, & from which they slope down in opposite directions; (Anat.) with upright spine towards which spines on both sides incline. [f. ANTI-+Gk *klinō* lean+-AL]

ǎnticy'clone, n. Rotary outward flow of air from atmospheric area of high pressure; whole system of pressure & outward flow. [ANTI- (1)]

ǎn'tidote, n. Medicine given to counter-act poison or disease (*against*, *for*, *to*). Hence ~AL a. [f. L f. Gk *antidoton* neut. of ANTIDOTOS given against]

ǎn'tigēn, n. Substance introduced into the blood to stimulate production of antibodies. [ANTI(BODY)+-GEN (1)]

ǎntigrŏp'ĕlŏs (-z), n., pl. Waterproof leggings. [perh. for *antihygropēlos* (ANTI- (2)+Gk *hugros* wet+*pēlos* mud]

ǎnti-Jac'obin, a. & n. (One) opposed to the Jacobins (revolutionary party in France, 1789) or the French revolution. [ANTI- (2)]

ǎntilog'arithm, n. Number to which a logarithm belongs, as *100 is the* ~ *of 2*. [ANTI- (1)]

ǎntil'ogy, n. Contradiction in terms. [f. Gk *antilogia* (ANTI-+*-logia* speaking)]

ănti·macăss'ar, n. Covering thrown over chairs etc., as protection from grease or as an ornament. [ANTI- (2)]

ăn'ti·masque, -mask, (-mȧsk), n. Grotesque interlude between acts of masque. [ANTI- (1)]

ănti·monȧrc'hical (-k-), a. Opposed to monarchy. [ANTI- (2)]

ăn'ti·monỹ, n. Brittle metallic substance, bluish-white, of flaky crystalline texture. [f. med. L antimonium, prob. of Arab. orig.]

ănti·nŏm'ian, a. & n. 1. Opposed to the obligatoriness of moral law; pertaining to ∧~s. 2. n. (∧~) one who maintains that the moral law is not binding on Christians. [f. L Antinomi, name of sect in Germany (1535) alleged to hold above opinion (ANTI- +Gk nomos law) +-AN]

ănti·n'omỹ, n. Contradiction in a law, or between two laws; conflict of authority; paradox. [f. L f. Gk ANTInomia (nomos law)]

ănti·pathĕt'ic, a. Opposed in nature or disposition (to). Hence ∧AL a., ∧ALlУ adv. [f. Gk ANTIpatheō (as ANTIPATHY), see -ETIC]

ănti·păth'ic, a. Of contrary character (to); (Med.) having, producing, contrary symptoms. [f. F antipathique f. anti-pathie (as foll.)]

ănti·păth'ỹ, n. Constitutional or settled aversion (against, to, between persons). [f. L f. Gk antipatheia f. ANTIpathēs opposed in feeling (pathos -eos)]

ănti·pėrsonnėl', a. (Of bombs etc.) designed to kill or injure human beings. [ANTI- (2)]

ănti·phlogīs'tic, a. & n. (Medicine, paste, etc.) reducing inflammation. So ∧INE[1] n. P. [ANTI- (2)]

ăn'ti·phon, n. Verse of psalm etc. intoned or sung responsively by alternating choirs during Divine Office before or after psalm; similar passage sung independently. [f. F antiphone f. med. L antiphona, fem. sing. f. Gk ANTIphōna (neut. pl. of antiphōnos) things sounding in response (phōnē vocal sound)]

ănti·ph'onal, a. & n. Sung alternately; responsive; (n.) collection of antiphons. Hence ∧LY[2] adv. [OF (antiphone, see prec. & -AL)]

ănti·ph'onary, n. Book of antiphons. [f. med. L antiphonarium (as ANTIPHON, see -ARY[1])]

ănti·ph'onỹ, n. Antiphon; antiphonal singing; response, echo. [f. Gk anti-phōnos, see ANTIPHON & -Y[1]]

ănti·p'odēs (-z), n. pl. Place(s) diametrically opposite (to each other), esp. region opposite to our own; (sing. ăn'ti·pŏde) exact opposite (of, to). Hence ∧AL, ∧ᴇ'AN, aa. [f. L f. Gk antipodes having the feet opposite, pl. of ANTIpous adj. (pous podos foot)]

ăn'ti·pōle, n. Opposite pole; direct opposite. [ANTI- (1)]

ăn'ti·pōpe, n. Pope elected in opposition to one (held to be) canonically chosen. [f. F antipape f. med. L antipapa; assim. to pope]

ănti·pyrĕt'ic, a. & n. (Drug) allaying or preventing fever. So **ănti·pỹr'in** n. P, a particular ∧~. [ANTI- (2); see PYRETIC]

ănti·quār'ian, a. & n. Connected with study of antiquities; large size of drawing paper; antiquary, whence ∧ISM n., ∧IZE v.i. [as foll.+-AN]

ăn'ti·quary, n. Student, collector, of antiquities. [f. L antiquarius (antiquus ancient, see -ARY[1])]

ăn'ti·quāte, v.t. Make obsolete (esp. in p.p.), abolish as out of date; make antique. [f. obs. adj. antiquate (L anti-quare f. antiquus ancient, see -ATE[2])]

ăn'ti·que (-ēk), a. & n. 1. Of old times; existing since old times; old-fashioned; after the manner of the ancients; archaic. 2. n. Relic of ancient art or of old times; the ∧~, ∧~ style. Hence ∧NESS (-kn-) n. [f. L antiquus, anticus, former, ancient (ante before; cf. posticus), whence also ANTIC]

ănti·q'uitỹ, n. Ancientness; old times, esp. time before middle ages; the ancients; (pl.) customs, events, precedents, of ancient times; (usu. pl.) ancient relics. [f. F antiquité f. L antiquitatem (antiquus, see prec. & -TY)]

ănti·ráb'ic, a. Counteracting the rabies virus. [irreg. f. ANTI- (1)+RABIES +-IC]

ănti·rrhīn'um (-rī-), n. Genus of plants, Snap-dragon. [L f. Gk antirrhinon (anti counterfeiting+rhis rhinos nose)]

ănti·sâbbatār'ian, a. & n. (Person) opposed to observance of Sabbath. [ANTI- (3)]

*ănti·salōōn', a. Opposed to the existence of drinking-saloons; A~ League (founded in 1893 to suppress these saloons). [ANTI- (2)]

ănti·scôrbūt'ic, a. & n. (Medicine) against scurvy. [ANTI- (2)]

ănti·scrip'tural (-chŏŏ-), a. Opposed to Scripture. [ANTI- (2)]

ănti·Sĕm'ı̄te, a. & n. (Person) hostile to Jews. So **ănti·Sĕmit'ic** a., ∧ITISM n. [ANTI-]

ănti·sĕp'tic, a. & n. (Agent) counteracting putrefaction (lit. & fig.). Hence ∧ICALLY adv. [f. ANTI- (3)+Gk sēptikos putrefying (sēpnos adj. f. sēpō rot, see -IC)]

ănti·sō'cial (-shl), a. Opposed to principles on which society is based. [ANTI- (2)]

ănti·stroph'e, n. (Lines recited during) returning movement from left to right in Greek choruses; inverse relation. [L f. Gk, = turning about (ANTIstrephō turn against)]

ănti·stroph'ic, a. Pertaining to antistrophes. [f. Gk antistrophikos (as prec., see -IC)]

ăn′ti-tănk, a. (Of gun etc.) for use against tanks. [ANTI- (2)]

ăntĭthē′sĭst, n. One opposed to or in existence of a God. Hence ~ISM n. [ANTI- (3)]

antĭth′ĕsĭs, n. (pl. -*theses*). Contrast of ideas expressed by parallelism of strongly contrasted words; opposition, contrast, (*of, between,* two things); direct opposite (*of, to*). [LL f. Gk (vbl n. f. ANTITHĒMĪ set against)]

ăntĭthĕt′ĭc, a. Of the nature of antithesis; contrasted; consisting of two opposites. Hence ~AL a., ~ALLY² adv. [f. Gk *antithetikos* (as prec., see -IC)]

ăntĭtŏx′ĭn, n. A serum serving to neutralize a toxin. So ~IC a. [ANTI-]

ăn′ti-trāde, a. & n. ~ (*wind*), one that blows in opposite direction to trade wind. [ANTI- (2)]

ăntĭtrĭnĭtā′rĭan, a. & n. (One) opposed to doctrine of the Trinity. Hence ~ISM n. [ANTI- (3)]

ăn′tĭtype, n. That which a type or symbol represents. Hence **ăntĭtŷp′ĭcAL** a. [f. Gk ANTI*tupos* responding as an instrument to the die (*tupos* stamp f. st. *tup-* strike)]

ăntĭvĕnēne′, n. Antitoxin, esp. a snake-poison antidote. [f. ANTI- + L *venenum* poison]

ănt′ler, n. Branched horn, branch of a horn, of stag or other deer. Hence ~ED² (-*lerd*) a. [f. OF *antoillier* f. LL *antocularem* (*ramum*) (branch) in front of the eyes (ANTE- + *oculus* eye); orig. = lowest branch]

ăntonomā′sĭa (-z-), n. Substitution of epithet etc. for proper name (e.g. *the Iron Duke*); use of proper name to express general idea (e.g. *a Solomon*). [L f. Gk, f. ANTONOMAZŌ name instead (*onoma* name)]

ăn′tonym, n. A word of contrary meaning to another, as *bad* to *good* (opp. *synonym*). [ANTI- + (SYN)ONYM]

ăn′trum, n. (pl. -*tra*). Cavity in the body (esp. one in the upper jaw-bone). [L, f. Gk *antron* cave]

Ant′wĕrp (ä-), n. ~ (*pigeon*), kind of homing or carrier pigeon. [*Antwerp* in Belgium]

ā′nus, n. Posterior opening of alimentary canal in animals. [L]

ăn′vĭl, n. Block (usu. iron) on which smith works metal; (Physiol.) a bone of the ear. [OE *onfilti*, etym. dub.]

anxĭ′etў (ăngz-), n. Uneasiness, concern; solicitous desire (*for* a thing, *to* do). [f. L *anxietas* -*ātis* (as foll., see -TY)]

anx′ĭous (ăngk′shŭs), a. Troubled, uneasy (*about*); earnestly desirous (*for* a thing, *to* do); causing anxiety, as *an* ~ *business*. Hence ~LY² adv. [f. L *anxius* (*angere* choke) +-OUS]

any(ĕn′ĭ), a., pron. & adv. (With interrog.) one, some, (no matter which), as *have*

you ~ *wool? have you* ~ *of them? were* ~ *Frenchmen there?*; (after negative expr. or implied) *cannot see* ~ *difference, to prevent* ~ *loss, cannot find* ~ *of them*; (in affirmative sent.) whichever (of all) is chosen, every, as ~ *chemist will tell you, at* ~ *rate; anyone* (pron.), whatever individual is chosen; ~ *one or anyone* (adj.), ~ person, anybody; (adv., w. compar. in neg. or interrog. context) at all, in ~ degree, (*is that* ~ *better?; without being* ~ *the wiser*). [OE *ǣnig* (oogn. w. OHG *einic*, mod. G *einig*, Du. *eenig*) f. AN ONE + -*ig* adj. ending (see -Y²), here perh. dim.]

an′ybody (ĕn-), n. or pron. Any person; *if you wish to be* ~ (of any importance); *two or three anybodies* (ordinary people). Hence ~ n.

an′yhow (ĕn-), adv. & conj. In any way whatever; in any case, at any rate; at haphazard, as *does his work* ~, *things are all.*~

an′ything (ĕn-), pron. & n. Whatever thing; a thing, no matter which; a thing of any kind.

an′yway (ĕn-), adv. & conj. =ANYHOW.

an′ywhere (ĕn′hwār), adv. In any place. In no limitation. [Gk Gram.] ~ (*tense*), one denoting simply occurrence (in indicative, with AUGMENT), past), without limitations as to continuance etc. So **āor′ist′ĭc** a. [f. Gk *aoristos*]

an′ywise (ĕn-; -z), adv. In any wise.

Ăn′zăc (ā-), n. & a. (Pl.) The Australian & New Zealand Army Corps in the war of 1914–18; (sing.) member of the ~s; (adj.) of the ~s. [=A. & N.-Z. A. C.]

ā′orist, a. & n. (Gram.) Indefinite, implying

aor′ta, n. Great artery or trunk of the arterial system, issuing from left ventricle of heart. Hence ~IC a. [f. med. L f. Gk *aortē* that which is hung (*aeirō* lift)]

à outrance (see Ap.), phr. To the death. [F]

ap- =AD- before *p*.

apăce′, adv. Swiftly, quickly. [A prep. + PACE¹]

apache′ (-ahsh), n. Violent street ruffian in Paris; (*A*~, pr. *apăch′i*) member of N.-Amer. tribe. [native, lit. = enemy]

ăp′anage, ăpp-, n. Provision for maintenance of younger children of kings etc. (orig. province or lucrative office); perquisite; (of territory) dependency; natural accompaniment or attribute. [F, f. *apaner* endow with means of subsistence f. med. L *appanare* (*panis* bread), see -AGE]

apărt′, adv. Aside, separately, independently, (*from*); set ~, devote, reserve (*for*); *jesting* ~ (laid aside). [f. F *à part* (*à* to, *part* side)]

apărt′ment, n. Single room of a house; (pl., & arch. sing.) set of rooms. [f. F

For other compounds of *anti-* see ANTI-.

appartement f. med. L *appartimentum* (Appartire apportion, see -MENT]

apathet'ic, a. Insensible to emotion; indifferent. Hence ~ICALLY adv. [f. foll. after PATHETIC]

ap'athy, n. Insensibility to suffering; passionless existence; indolence of mind. [f. F *apathie* f. L f. Gk *apatheia* f. *apathēs* without feeling (a- not + *pathos* -eos suffering]

ape, n. Tailless monkey (gorilla, chimpanzee, orang-outan, gibbons); imitator, mimic; *play the* ~, mimic; *Sea Ape,* fish (Sea Fox). [OE *apa* masc. *ape* fem. (Du. *aap,* OHG *affo,* MHG *affe*)

ape', v.t. Imitate, mimic. [f. prec.]

apeak' (-ēk), adv. & pred. a. (naut.). Vertical, as *oars* ~. [f. F *à pic* (à to, at, *pic,* summit, see PEAK)]

apep'sy, n. Lack of digestive power. [f. Gk *apepsia* (a- not + *peptō* digest)]

aperçu (see Ap.), n. Summary exposition, conspectus. [F, p.p. of *apercevoir* perceive]

ape'rient (or -ēr-), a. & n. Laxative (medicine). [f. L *aperire* open, see -ENT]

ape'ritif (or ahpārētēf'), n. Alcoholic appetizer. [F (-ēr-), f. med. L *aperitivus* variant of *apertivus* (L *aperire* open, see -IVE)]

ape'ritive, a. & n. = APERIENT. [f. F *apéritif* (prec.)]

ap'erture, n. Opening, gap; space through which light passes in optical instruments. [f. L *apertura* (as prec., see -URE)]

ap'ery, n. Mimicry; apish performance; ape-house. [APE n. + -RY]

apet'alous, a. Without petals. [f. Gk *apetalos* leafless (a- not + *petalon* leaf) + -OUS]

ap'ex, n. (pl. -ices, -exes). Tip, top, peak; vertex (of triangle, cone). [L, = small rod at top of flamen's cap, peak, tip, perh. as APT; cf. *vertex* f. *vertere*]

aphas'ia (-zya), n. Loss of speech, as result of cerebral affection. Hence **aphas'ic** (-z-) a. & n. [Gk, f. *aphatos* speechless (a- not + *pha-* speak)]

aphe'lion, n. (pl. -ia). Point farthest from sun (of planet's or comet's orbit). [Graecized f. mod. L *aphelium* f. Gk *aph' hēliou* from the sun]

aphe'liotrop'ic, a. (bot.). Turning from the sun. Hence ~ICALLY adv.; **apheliot'ropism** n. [f. Gk as prec. + *tropikos* turning (*tropē*)]

aph'esis, n. Gradual loss of unaccented vowel at beginning of word, as in *esquire.* [Gk, = letting go, f. *aphiēmi* (*apo* away + *hiēmi* send)]

aphet'ic, a. Pertaining to aphesis. Hence **aph'etīze** v.t. [f. Gk *aphetos* vbl adj. (as prec.) + -IC]

aph'is, n. (pl. *aph'idēs*). Plant-louse, minute insect, the food of ladybirds, & tended by ants for the honey-dew it yields. Hence **aphid'IAN** a. [?]

aphon'ia, n. Total loss of voice. [Gk, f. *aphōnos* voiceless (a- not + *phōnē* voice)]

aph'orism, n. Short pithy maxim; definition. Hence or cogn. **aphoris'mic,** **aphoris'tic** [-IST], aa., **aphoris'tically** adv. [f. Gk *aphorizō* (APO-+*horizō* f. *horos* boundary), see -ISM]

aphrodis'iac (-z-), a. & n. Venereal; (drug) producing venereal desire. [f. Gk *aphrodisiakos* f. *aphrodisios* (*Aphroditē* Venus), see -AC]

aphyll'ous, a. (bot.). Naturally leafless. [f. Gk *aphullos* (a- not + *phullon* leaf) + -OUS]

apiār'ian, a. Pertaining to bee-keeping. [as foll. + -AN]

ap'iarÿ, n. Place where bees are kept. Hence ~IST n. [f. L *apiarium* (*apis* bee, see -ARY[1])]

ap'ical, a. Belonging to an apex; placed at the tip. Hence ~LY[2] adv. [f. L *apex -icis* + -AL]

ap'iculture, n. Bee-keeping. [f. L *apis* bee + CULTURE]

apiece', adv. Severally, each, as *five pounds* ~. [orig. *a piece*]

ap'ish, a. Of the nature, appearance, of an ape; ape-like in manner, silly. Hence ~LY[2] adv., ~NESS n. [f. APE n. + -ISH]

aplanat'ic, a. (photog.). Symmetrical achromatic doublet lens comparatively free from spherical aberration. So **āplanā'tIo** (-ā-, (of lens) free from certain aberrations. [G, f. Gk a- not + *planaō* wander ; adj. f. Gk *aplanētos* free from error + -IC]

aplomb' (see Ap.), n. Perpendicularity; self-possession. [F, = *à plomb* according to plummet]

ăpnoe'a (-nēa), n. Suspension of breathing. [mod. L, f. Gk *apnoia* f. *azpnoos* breathless (a- not + *pnoē* breath)]

ăpo-, pref. (before unaspirated vowel *ap-*, before aspirate *aph-*), = Gk *apo* prep. off, from, away, un-, quite; in compds f. Gk, & in mod. scientific wds (not on Gk anal.) with sense 'detached, separate'.

apoc'alypse, n. Revelation, esp. that made to St John in island of Patmos; book recording this. So **apocalyp'tIc(AL),** aa., **apocalyp'tically** adv. [f. L f. Gk *apokalupsis* (Apokaluptō uncover)]

apoc'ope, n. Cutting off of last letter or syllable of word. [Gk (Apokoptō cut off)]

apoc'rypha, n. Books of Old Testament included in Septuagint & Vulgate, but not originally genuine in Hebrew, nor counted genuine by Jews, & excluded from Canon at Reformation. [LL *apocrypha (scripta)* hidden writings f. Gk *apokruphos* (Apokruphō hide away); treated in E as sing, with pl. *-as*]

apoc'ryphal, a. Of the apocrypha; of doubtful authenticity; sham, false. [as prec. + -AL]

ăp'ŏd, n. Bird, reptile, fish, without (or with undeveloped) feet or ventral fins.

Hence **ăp'odal** a. [f. Gk *apous* footless (*a-* not + *pous podos* foot)]

ăpodic'tic, ăpodeic'tic (-dī-), a. Of clear demonstration; clearly established. Hence **ăpodic'tically** adv. [f. L f. Gk *apodeiktikos* (*apodeiknumi* show, see -IC)]

ăpod'osis, n. (pl. *-dosēs*). Concluding clause of sentence (cf. PROTASIS); consequent clause of conditional sentence, wherever placed. [L, f. Gk (*apodidōmi* give back)]

ăp'ogee, n. Point (in orbit of moon or any planet) farthest from earth; greatest distance of sun from earth when latter is in aphelion; (fig.) most distant spot, highest point. Hence **ăpogē'an** a. [f. F *apogée* f. L f. Gk *apogaion* (neut. adj.) away from earth (*gaia, gē,* earth)]

ăpolaus'tic, a. Self-indulgent. [f. Gk *apolaustikos* (*apolauō* enjoy, see -IC)]

Apŏllinā'ris, n. Mineral water exported from the ~ spring in Rhenish Prussia.

Apŏll'ō, n. (pl. *-os*), Greek sun-god; (poet.) the sun; man of great beauty. [L, f. Gk *Apollōn*.]

Apŏll'yon, n. The Devil. [f. Gk *apollūōn* part. of *apolluō* (*apo-* + *olluō* destroy)]

ăpologĕt'ic, a. & n. Regretfully acknowledging, excusing, fault or failure; (n., usu. pl.) argumentative defence, esp. of Christianity. Hence ~AL a., ~**ally²** adv. [f. F *apologétique* f. L f. Gk *apologētikos* (*apologeomai* speak in defence, see APOLOGY & -IC)]

ăpologī'a, n. Written defence of the conduct or opinions of the writer. [Gk; see APOLOGY]

ăpol'ogist, n. One who defends (esp. Christianity) by argument. [f. F *apologiste* f. Gk *apologia*, see APOLOGY & -IST]

ăpol'ogīze, v.i. Make an apology (*for*). [f. APOLOGY + -IZE]

ăp'ologue (-ŏg), n. Moral fable. [F, f. L f. Gk *apologos* (*apo* off + *logos* speech)]

ăpol'ogy, n. Regretful acknowledgement of offence; assurance that no offence was intended; explanation, vindication; ~ *for*, poor or scanty specimen of (*this ~ for a letter*). [f. L f. Gk *apologia* (*apo* away + *-logia* speaking)]

ăp'ophthegm (-othĕm, -ŏthĕm), n. Terse saying; pithy maxim. Hence ~**ăt'ic** (-othĕg-, -ŏthĕg-) a., ~**ăt'ically** adv. [f. Gk *apophthegma -matos* (*apophtheggomai* speak out)]

ăp'oplĕc'tic, a. Pertaining to, causing, apoplexy; suffering from, tending to, apoplexy. Hence ~**ically** adv. [f. L f. Gk *apoplēktikos* (*apoplēssō* strike completely, see -IC)]

ăp'oplĕxy, n. Malady arresting powers of sense & motion, usu. caused by effusion of blood or serum in brain. [f. F *apoplexie* f. L f. Gk *apoplēxia* (as prec.)]

ăposiopē'sis, n. (rhet.; pl. *pēsēs*). Sudden breaking-off in speech. [L, f. Gk f. *Apo*(*siōpaō* keep silent)]

ăpŏs'tasy, n. Abandonment of religious faith, vows, principles, or party. [f. L f. Gk *apostasia* (*aposta-* withdraw)]

ăpŏs'tate, n.&a. (One) guilty of apostasy. So **ăpostăt'ical** a. [f, f. L f. Gk *apostatēs* (*aposta-* withdraw)]

ăpŏs'tatīze, v.i. Become an apostate (*from one to another*). [f. LL *apostatizare* (as APOSTATE, see -IZE)]

ā pŏsteriō'rī, adv. & adj. phr. (Reasoning) from effects to causes; inductive. [L, = from what comes after]

ăpŏs'til, n. Marginal note. [f. F *apostille*, etym. dub.]

ăpŏs'tle (-sl), n. Messenger, esp. of the twelve whom Christ sent forth to preach Gospel; first successful Christian missionary in a country, as ~ *of Germany*; leader of reform, as ~ *of temperance*; ~ *spoons* (with figures of ~s on handles). Hence ~SHIP n. [f. OF *apostle, apostre* (mod. *apôtre*) f. L f. Gk *apostolos* (*apostellō* send away); OE had *apostol*]

ăpŏs'tolate, n. Apostleship; leadership in a propaganda. [f. L *apostolatus* (as prec., see -ATE¹)]

ăpostŏl'ic, a. Pertaining to the Apostles; of the character of an apostle; of the Pope, papal, as *A~ See, succession*. Hence ~AL a., ~**ally²** adv. [f. F *apostolique* f. L f. Gk *apostolicus* (as APOSTLE, see -IC)]

ăpŏs'trophe¹, n. Sign of omission of letter, or of possessive case, (e.g. *can't, boy's*). Hence **ăpostrŏph'ic** a. [contused w. prec., but prop. three syllables (-strŏfē), f. F f. L f. Gk (*hē*) *apostrophos* (*prosōidiā*) (the accent) of elision (*apostrephō* turn away)]

ăpŏs'trophe², n. (rhet.), Exclamatory address, in course of public speech or in poem, to particular person (often dead or absent). Hence **ăpostrŏph'ic** a., -IZE v.t. & i. [L f. Gk, lit. turning away (as foll.)]

ăpŏth'ecāry, n. (arch.), Druggist, pharmaceutical chemist, as *Apothecaries' Company*. [f. OF *apotecaire* f. LL *apothecarius* f. L *apotheca* f. Gk *apothēkē* store-house (*apotithēmi* lay away), see -ARY¹]

ăpothēō'sis, n. (pl. *-osēs*). Deification (lit. & fig.); canonization; deified ideal; (loosely) release from earthly life. Hence **ăpŏth'eosīze** v.t. [L, f. Gk (*apotheoō* make a god of, f. *theos* god, see -OSIS]

ăppal' (-awl), v.t. (-ll-). Dismay, terrify, make pale; but cf. PALL v.]

Hence ~**l'ingly²** adv. [perh. f. OF *apalir*]

ăp'panage. See APANAGE.

ăpparā'tus, n. (pl. *-uses*). Mechanical requisites, an appliance, for doing something; organs by which natural processes are carried on; ~ *criticus*, materials for textual study of document. [L (*apparare* make ready for, see -ATE¹)]

ăppā'rel, v.t. (-ll-). Attire, dress. [f. OF *apareiller* f. Rom.+*apparticulare* make fit (*particulus* dim. of *par* equal)]

appa'rel², n. Ornamental embroidery on ecclesiastical vestments; (arch.) clothing, dress. [f. OF *aparail* f. *apareiller*, see prec.]

appa'rent (or -âr-), a. Manifest, palpable; seeming; *heir* ~ (whose right cannot be superseded by birth of nearer heir, cf. PRESUMPTIVE). Hence ~LY² adv. [f. OF *aparant* f. L as APPEAR, see -ENT]

ǎpparǐ'tion, n. Appearance, esp. of a supernatural being; ghost. [F, f. L *apparitionem* (as APPEAR, see -ION)]

appa'ritor, n. Public servant of Roman magistrate; officer of civil or ecclesiastical court; herald, usher. [L (as prec., see -OR²)]

appeal'¹ (-ēl), v.i. & t. Call to (higher tribunal for deliverance from decision of lower (also abs.); || ~ *to the country* (i.e. from parliament), dissolve parliament; remove (case) to higher court; call attention (*to evidence*); make earnest request (*to person, for thing or to do*); *pictures* ~ (address themselves) *to the eye, do not* ~ (prove attractive) *to me*. [f. OF *apeler* f. L Appellare address]

appeal'² (-ēl), n. Act of appealing; right of appealing; *Court of A*~ (hearing cases previously tried in inferior courts). [f. OF *apel* (as prec.)]

appeal'able (-ēl-), a. That can be appealed against; that can be appealed *to*. [APPEAL v.+-ABLE]

appear', v.i. Become, be, visible; present oneself formally, publicly; be published; be manifest; seem. [f. *aper*- st. of OF *apareir* f. L Apparēre -vit- come in sight]

appear'ance, n. Act of appearing in vbl senses; *put in an* ~, show oneself; look, aspect; semblance; *to all* ~ (so far as can be seen); *save, keep up,* ~s (out-ward show etc.); apparition, phantom. [f. OF *aparance* f. L apparentia (as prec., see -ENCE)]

appease' (-z), v.t. Pacify, quiet, (strife, anger, person); soothe; satisfy (appetite, prejudice). So ~'ABLE (-z-) a., ~e'MENT (-zm-) n. [f. OF *apeser, apaiser* (à to + *pais* peace f. L pacem, nom. pax)]

appell'ant, a. & n. **1.** Appealing; (Law) concerned with appeals. **2.** One who appeals to higher court. [F as APPEAL¹, see -ANT]

appell'ate, a. Taking cognizance of appeals, as ~ *jurisdiction*. [f. L as foll., see -ATE²]

ǎppellā'tion, n. Name, title; nomenclature. [F, f. L as APPEAL¹, see -ATION]

appell'ative, a. & n. (Of words) designating a class, common (as opp. to *proper*); common noun, applicable to any member of a class; appellation. Hence ~LY² (-vl-) adv. [f. L as APPEAL¹, see -ATIVE]

appe'nd', v.t. Hang on, annex; add in writing. [f. L Appendere]

appe'ndage, n. Thing attached; addition; accompaniment. [prec. +-AGE]

appe'ndant, a. & n. (Possession, thing, person) attached in subordinate capacity (to another). [F, part. of appendre f. L appendēre (for -êre) hang to (intr.)]

appe'ndix, n. (pl. ~ices, ~ixes). Subsidiary addition (to book or document); small process developed from surface of any organ, esp. *vermiform* ~*ix* (of the intestine), whence ~ICIT'IS n. [Lappendix -icis (Appendēre hang to, trans.)]

ǎpperceive' (-sēv), v.t. (psych.). Unite and assimilate (a perception) to a mass of ideas already possessed, & so comprehend & interpret it. [f. OF *aperceveir* (LL apercipere f. AP-+L percipere perceive)]

ǎppercep'tion, n. Mind's perception of itself; mental perception; (Psych.) action or fact of becoming conscious by subsequent reflection of a perception already experienced; process by which the mind apperceives. [f. F aperception (LL apper-cipere -cept-, as prec., see -ION)]

ǎppertain', v.i. Belong as possession or right to; be appropriate to; relate to. [f. OF apartenir f. LL Ap(pertinēre PERTAIN]

ǎpp'etence, -cy, n. Longing after, desire, (of, for, after); affinity (for). [f. F appé-tence f. L appetentia (Appetere seek after) see -ENCE, -ENCY]

ǎpp'etent, a. Eagerly desirous (after, of). [f. L appetere, see prec. & -ENT]

ǎpp'etite, n. Desire, inclination, (for); desire to satisfy natural necessities, esp. hunger; relish. So ǎppē'titUS a. [f. OF apetit f. L appetitus (as prec., see -TE²)]

ǎpp'etīze, v.t. (Of things) give appetite (only in part. ~ing). Hence~ER² (2) n. [f. F Appétissant part. as if f. L appetitare (as prec.), assim. to vbs in -IZE]

applaud', v.i. & t. Express approval loudly, as by clapping hands; (v.t.) express approval of, praise. [f. L AP-plaudere plaus- clap hands]

applause (-z), n. Approbation loudly expressed; marked approval. Hence ~'IVE (-s-), a., ~'ively² (-sivli) adv. [f. L applausus, -ûs (as prec.)]

ǎp'ple, n. Round firm fleshy fruit of a rosaceous tree; (Bot.) any inferior fleshy many-celled fruit; ~ *of discord*, golden ~ contended for by Juno, Minerva, & Venus; ~ *of Sodom, Dead Sea* ~, fruit dissolving into ashes; ~ *of the eye*, the pupil, any cherished object; ~ *brandy*, spirit distilled from cider; ~ *butter*, sauce of ~s stewed in cider; ~-*cart* (upset person's ~-cart, spoil his plans); ~ *cheese*, compressed ~ *pomace*; ~ *dumpling*, ~ cooked in paste; ~ *green*, a colour; ~ *pomace*, pulp remaining after juice is expressed; ~-*jack*, Amer. name for ~ brandy; ~-*john*, kind of ~ said to keep two years & to be best when withered; ~-*pie bed*, one with sheets so folded that one's legs cannot get down; ~-*pie order*, perfect order; *~ *sauce* (sl), insincere

flattery (also as int.=nonsense!). [comp.-Teut.; OE *æppel*, OHG *aphul*, mod. G *apfel*.]

appli´ance, n. Applying; thing applied as means to an end. [f. APPLY + -ANCE]

app´licable, a. Capable of being applied; having reference, appropriate, (*to*). Hence ~BIL´ITY n. [f. L as APPLY, see -ABLE]

app´licant, n. One who applies (*for*). [as prec., see -ANT]

applica´tion, n. Putting of one thing to another; employment of means; (application of) plaster, liniment, etc.; applying (of a general rule etc.) to bear upon particular case; relevancy; diligence; making of a request; request made, (*for*). [f. L *applicationem* (as APPLY, see -ATION)]

appliqué (àplē´kā), n. & v.t. Ornamental work cut out from one material & applied to the surface of another (esp. in dressmaking); (vb) ornament thus. [F, p.p. of *appliquer* apply (L *applicare*)]

apply´, v.t. & i. Put close (*to*); administer (remedy etc. *to*); devote (*to*); make use of; use as relative or suitable (*to*), set oneself closely (*to* task, *to do*); have reference (*to*); attend closely (*to*); address oneself (*for* help etc. *to*); make application (*for* situation). [f. OF *aplier* f. L *applicare* fold, fasten to]

appoggiatura´a (-ŏjätoorá), n. (mus.). A grace consisting of the note above the principal note, interpolated before it & momentarily taking its place in the rhythm of the passage. [It.]

appoint´, v.t. Fix (time, place, *for* purpose); prescribe (thing, *that*); (Law) declare the destination of (property, also abs.); nominate, as ~ *him governor*, *to govern*, *to be governor*, ~ *him*; (p.p.) *well*, *badly*, ~*ed*, so equipped. Hence ~EE´ n. [f. OF *apointer* (à *point* to the point)]

appoint´ment, n. Appointing; engagement, assignation; decree, ordinance; office assigned; (usu. pl.) outfit; *keep*, *break*, *an* ~, appear, fail to appear, at fixed place & time. [f. OF *apointement* (as prec., see -MENT)]

apport´, n. Material thing produced by occult means at spiritualist seance. [AP-+(ex)port, (im)port]

appor´tion, v.t. Assign as due share (*to*); portion out. Hence ~MENT (-shon-) n. [f. OF *apportionner* (à to + *portionner* f. *portion*)]

app´osite (-z), a. Well put; appropriate (*to*). Hence ~LY² (-tli) adv., ~NESS(-tn-) n. [f. L AP(*ponere* posit- *pon*)]

apposi´tion (-z-), n. Application (of seal); placing side by side; (Gram.) placing of word in syntactic parallelism with another, esp. addition of one noun to another. Hence ~AL (-zĭsho-) a. [f. L *appositio* (as prec., see -ION)]

apprais´e´ (-z), v.t. (esp. of official valuer) fix price for; estimate. Hence ~AL (-z-), ~eMENT (-zm-), nn., ~ABLE (-z-) a. [f.

PRAISE v. (formerly used in the same sense), perh. on anal. of APPRIZE.]

appré´ciable(-sha-), a. Capable of being estimated; perceptible, sensible. Hence ~LY² adv. [as foll., see -BLE]

appré´ciate (-shi-), v.t. & i. Estimate worth, quality, amount, of; estimate aright; be sensitive to; esteem highly; raise in value; rise in value. Hence ~ATIVE, ~ATORY, (-shǒ-), aa., ~ativeLY² appraise [as prec. see -ATE³]

apprécia´tion (or -shĭ-), n. Estimation, judgement; perception; adequate recognition; rise in value; critique. [f. F *appréciation* f. *apprécier* (as prec., see -ATION)]

apprehend´, v.t. Seize, arrest; perceive (by senses or intellect); understand; fear (thing, *that*). [f. F *appréhender* f. L AP-(*prehendere* -hens- lay hold of), whence also F *apprehender* learn]

apprehen´sible, a. Capable of being grasped (by senses or intellect). Hence ~BIL´ITY n. [f. L *apprehensibilis* (as prec.,

see -BLE)]

apprehen´sion (-shn), n. Seizure, arrest; grasping (of ideas), conception; understanding; dread. [f. L *apprehensio* (as prec., see -ION)]

apprehen´sive, a. Pertaining to sensuous or mental perception; perceptive (*of*); intelligent; uneasy, fearful, (*of* thing, *that* it may happen, *for* person, *for* his safety). Hence ~LY² (-vi-) adv., ~NESS (-vn-) n. [f. med. L *apprehensivus* (as prec., see -IVE)]

appren´tice, n. Learner of a craft, bound to serve, & entitled to instruction from, his employer for specified term; tiro. Hence ~SHIP (-sSH-) n. [f. OF *apprentis* f. *apprendre* (see APPREHEND), suggested by words in -*tis*, -*tif*, f. L -*tivus*]

appren´tice², v.t. Bind as apprentice. [f. prec.]

apprise´ (-z), v.t. Inform; (pass.) be aware of. [f. F *appris* -*ise* p.p. of *apprendre* learn, teach, (see APPREHEND)]

apprize´, v.t. (arch.). Appraise; appreciate. [f. OF *apriser* (à to + *prisier* PRAISE)]

|| **ap´pro**, n. *On* ~, (of goods supplied) to be returned if not satisfactory. [=approval or approbation.]

approach´¹, v.t. & i. Come nearer(, (*to*)); (Golf) play the approach shot; approximate in character etc. *to*; come near *to*; approximate *to*; (Commerce,) make overtures or proposals *to*; (Mil.) make approaches to. Hence ~ABLE a. [f. OF *approcher* f. LL AD(*propriare* draw near (*propius* compar. of *prope* near)]

approach´², n. Act of approaching; approximation; access, passage, (lit. & fig.); (Golf) stroke, not from a tee, played for the green; (Mil.) entrenchments enabling besiegers to approach. [f. prec.]

*ăpp'rŏbāte, v.t. Approve formally; sanction. [f. L L AP(probare test f. probus good) see -ATE³]

ăpprŏbā'tion, n. Sanction; approval. So ăpprŏbā'tory a. [F, f. L L approbationem (as prec., see -ATION)]

apprŏp'riate¹ a. Belonging, peculiar, (to); suitable, proper, (to, for). Hence ~LY² (-ĭ-) adv., ~NESS (-tn-) n. [f. L L Appropriare (proprius own), see -ATE²]

apprŏp'riate² v.t. Take possession of; take to oneself; devote to special purposes. Hence or cogn. ~A'TION, ~ātor², nn., ~ative a. [f. prec., see -ATE³]

approv'al (-ōō-), n. Approbation; sanction. [f. foll.+-AL (2); rare before 1800, -ance being used instead]

approve' (-ōōv), v.t. & i. Give evidence of (quality); (refl.) show oneself to be; pronounce, sanction; commend; (p.n.~) of, pronounce, consider, good; (p.p.) pronounced satisfactory, accepted, (of persons, reasons, etc.; ~d society, under Nat. Insurance Act). [f. OF aprover f. L as APPROBATE]

approv'er (-ōō-), n. One who approves; one who turns King's evidence. [f. prec. +-ER¹]

approx'imate¹, a. Very near; closely resembling; fairly correct. Hence ~LY² (-tl-) adv. [f. L L arproximare (proximus very near), see -ATE¹]

approx'imāte² v.t. & i. Bring, come, near (to thing), esp. in quality, number, etc.). Hence ~A'TION n., ~ative a., ~ativery² adv. [f. prec., see -ATE³]

appui' (-wē), n (Mil.) defensive support; point of ~ (F point d'~), fixed object on which troops commence formation into line. [F, f. appuyer f. LL Appodiare (podium support f. Gk podion base f. pous podos foot)]

appŭr'tenance, n. Belonging; appendage: accessory. [f. AF apurtenance (OF aper-, apar-) f. LL appertinentia (as APPERTAIN, see -ANCE)]

appŭr'tenant, a. & n. (Thing) belonging, appertaining, pertinent, (to). [f. OF apartenant part. as APPERTAIN]

āp'ricŏt, n. Orange-coloured stone-fruit allied to plum. [(also earlier apricock) f. Sp. abar(b)coque f. Arab. al the+burqua f. Gk praikokion prob. f. L praecoquum variant of praecox early-ripe; -cot by assim. to F abricot]

Ap'ril (ā-), n. Fourth month of year; ~fool, one sportively imposed upon on ~-fool-day (April 1). [f. OF avril f. L aprilis]

ā prior'i, adv. & a. (Reasoning) from cause to effect; deductively; (loosely) presumptively, as far as one knows. Hence ā- prio'rity n. [L, =from what is before]

āp'ron, n. Garment worn in front of body to protect clothes; official dress, as bishop's, dean's, freemason's, ~; leather covering for legs in open carriage; skin covering stuffing of roast goose or duck; tied to ~-strings of (wife, mother, etc.), unduly controlled by; (Theatr.) advanced strip of stage for playing scenes before curtain. Hence ~ED²(-nd) a., ~FUL(-ŏŏl) n. [f. OF naperon dim. of nape table-cloth f. L mappa napkin; for loss of n-(an apron=a napron) cf. adder]

ăprŏpos' (-pō), adv., a., n. To the purpose; in respect of; appropriate(ness). [F, à to+propos PURPOSE]

āpse, n. Semi-circular or polygonal recess, arched or dome-roofed, esp. in church. [f. APSIS]

ăp'sidal, a. Of the form of an apse; of the apsides. [f. foll.+-AL]

ăp'sis, n. (pl. āp'sidēs, ăpsī'dēs). Aphelion, perihelion, of planet; apogee, perigee, of moon; line of apsides, straight line joining these. [L, f. Gk (h)apsis -idos fastening, felloe of wheel, vault, (hapto join)]

ăpt, a. Suitable, appropriate; having a tendency (to do or be); quick-witted (at). Hence ~'LY² adv., ~'NESS n. [f. L aptus fitted p.p. of +apere fasten]

ăp'terous, a. Wingless; (Bot.) having no membranous expansions. [f. Gk apteros (a- not+pteron wing)+-OUS]

ăp'teryx, n. New-Zealand bird with rudimentary wings & no tail. [f. Gk a- not +pteryx wing]

ăp'titūde, n. Fitness; natural propensity (for); ability. [F, f. f. L aptitudinem (as APT, see -TUDE)]

ā'qua, n. (chem.). Liquid, solution, as ~ fort'is, nitric acid, ~ re'gia, mixture of nitric & hydrochloric acids, able to dissolve gold & platinum. [L, =water]

ăquamarine' (-ēn), n. Bluish-green beryl; bluish green (also as adj.). [f. L aqua marina sea-water]

ā'quaplāne, n., & v.i. (Ride on) plank towed behind speedboat. [f. L aqua water+PLANE³]

ăquarelle', n. Kind of painting with Chinese ink & thin water-colours. [F, f. It. acquarella water-colour dim. of acqua f. L aqua water]

aquā'rium, n. (pl. -iums, -ia). Artificial pond or tank for the keeping of live aquatic plants & animals; place of public entertainment containing such tanks. [L (aqua water, see -ARIUM]

Aquā'rius, n. Zodiacal constellation; eleventh sign of Zodiac, which sun enters on Jan. 21. [L, =water-carrier (as prec., see -ARY¹)]

aquăt'ic, a. & n. (Plant, animal) growing, living, in or near water; (of sports) conducted in or upon water. [f. F aquatique f. L aquaticus (aqua water, see -ATIC)]

ăʼquatint, n. Method of engraving on copper by use of a resinous solution & nitric acid. [f. F aqua-tinte, It. aqua tinta, f. L aqua tincta dyed water (tingere dye)]

aqua-vit'ae, n. Ardent spirits, esp. of the first distillation. [L, = water of life]

ā'quéduct, n. Artificial channel, esp. elevated structure of masonry, for conveyance of water; conduit; (Physiol.) small canal, esp. in head of mammals. [f. L *aquæ ductus* conveyance of water (*ducere* duct- lead)]

ā'queous, a. Of water, watery; (Geol.) produced by water, as ~ *rocks*. [as f. a L *aquæus* (*aqua* water) +-OUS]

āquilē'gia, n. (Kinds of) plant of buttercup type; columbine. [etym. dub.]

ā'quiline, a. Of an eagle; eagle-like, as ~ *nose* (hooked). [f. L *aquilinus* (*aquila* eagle, see -INE)]

aquos'ity, n. Wateriness. [f. med. L *aquositas* (*aquosus* (*aqua* water), see -OSE & -TY]

ar-, pref. = AD- before *r*.

-ar¹, suf. (1) f. L *-aris* (varying with *-alis* -AL), adj. suf. taken direct or thr. F, or imitated with L nouns. (2) noun suf. f. F wds have *-aire*; E corrects *-er* (*scholar*) but sometimes uses -ARY² instead of *-ar* for *-tire* (*military*). (2) noun suf, f. L *-are, -ar*, neut. of above (*altar, exemplar*)

-ar², suf. Occas. (for regular -ER², -ARY³) (*bursar*) or F *-tire* (*vicar*).

-ar³, suf. Variant for regular -ER¹, -OR², in nouns (*beggar, liar*), perh. on anal. of *scholar* (-AR³).

A'rab (ă-), n. & a. Native of Arabia; ~ *horse; street arab,* homeless child; (adj.) Arabian. [f. F *Arabe* f. L *Arabem* (nom. *-bs*) f. Gk *Araps -abos*]

ārabesque' (-k), n. & a. Arabian; fantastic. 2. n. Decoration in colour or low relief, with fanciful intertwining of leaves, scroll-work, etc.; (Mus.) florid melodic figure, composition based on such figures. [F, = Arabian, see -ESQUE]

Arāb'ian, a. & n. 1. Of Arabia; ~ *nights,* collection of fabulous stories; ~ *bird,* phoenix. 2. n. = Arab. [f. Arabia +-AN]

A'rabic, a. & n. 1. Arabian; *gum* ~ (exuded by some kinds of acacia); ~ *numerals,* 1, 2, 3, etc. 2. n. Language of the Arabs. [f. OF *Arabic* f. L *Arabicus* (*Arabs* ARAB, see -IC)]

A'rabist (ă-), n. Student of Arabic. [ARAB +-IST]

ā'rable, a. & n. (Land) fit for tillage. [f. L *arabilis* (*arare* plough, see -BLE)]

arāc'hnid (-k-), n. (zool.). Member of the *Arachnida,* class comprising spiders, scorpions, & mites. [f. Gk *arakhnē* spider +-ID³]

arāc'hnoid (-k-), a. & n. 1. (Bot.) covered with long cobweb-like hairs. 2. n. Serous membrane lining the dura mater, & enveloping brain & spinal cord. [f. Gk *arakhnoeidēs* (*arakhnē* cobweb, see -OID)]

Aramā'ic (ă-), a. & n. (Language) of Aram or Syria; northern branch of Semitic family of languages, including Syriac & Chaldee. [f. L f. Gk *Aramaios* of Aram +-IC]

Aranē'idan (ă-), a. & n. (Member of the *Aranëida* or spiders. [f. L *aranea* spider, see -ID³]

ārapai'ma (-pī-), n. S.-American food-fish (largest freshwater fish). [Brazilian]

Araucā'ria (ă-), n. Genus of trees including monkey-puzzle. [*Arauco,* name of province]

arb'alèst, ārb'last (-ah-), n. Crossbow. [f. OF *arbaleste* f. L *arcubalista* (*arcus* bow +*ballista* military engine)]

arb'iter, n. Judge; one appointed by two parties to settle dispute, umpire; one who has entire control (*of*). [L, perh. f. *ar-* = *ad* to +*bitere* go, one who goes to see)]

arb'itrage, n. Traffic in bills of exchange or stocks to take advantage of different prices in other markets. [F, f. *arbitrer* as ARBITRATE, see -AGE]

arb'itral, a. Pertaining to arbitration. [f. f. L *arbitrālis,* see ARBITER & -AL]

arb'itrament, -ement, n. Deciding of dispute by arbiter; authoritative decision. [f. OF *arbitrement* (*arbitrer,* see ARBITRAGE & -MENT)]

arb'itrar'y, a. Derived from mere opinion; capricious; unrestrained; despotic; (Law) discretionary. Hence ~ily² adv., ~iNESS n. [f. L *arbitrarius,* see ARBITER & -ARY¹]

arb'itrāte, v.t. & i. Decide by arbitration. [f. L *arbitrari* judge, see ARBITER & -ATE³]

arbitrā'tion, n. Settlement of a dispute by an arbiter; ~ *of exchange,* determination of rate of indirect exchange between two currencies. [OF, f. L *arbitrationem* (as ARBITRATE, see -ION)]

arb'itrātor, n. (Now the legal term for) arbiter. Hence ~sHiP n. [f. OF *arbitratour* by-form of *arbitreur* f. L *arbitrātorem* (as prec., see -OR³)]

arb'itress, n. Female arbiter, mediatress; absolute mistress. [f. OF *arbitresse* fem. of *arbitre* f. L ARBITER, see -ESS¹]

arb'or, n. Main support of machine; axle or spindle on which wheel revolves. [f. F *arbre* tree, axis, f. L *arbor;* refissh. on L]

arb'orā'ceous (-shus), a. Tree-like; wooded. [f. L *arbor* tree, see -ACEOUS]

Arb'or Day (ă-), n. Day set apart annually in U.S., S. Australia, & elsewhere for public tree-planting. [L *arbor* tree]

arbor'eal, a. Of, living in, connected with, trees. [f. L *arboreus* (*arbor* tree, see -AL]

arbor'eous, a. Wooded; arboreal; arborescent. [as prec., see -OUS]

arbores'cent, a. Tree-like in growth or general appearance; (Archit.) branching out. Hence ~ENCE n., ~ENTly² adv. [f. L *arborescens* grow into a tree (*arbor*), see -ENT]

arbor'eum, n. (pl. -ta). A botanical tree-garden. [L, f. *arbor* tree]

ar'bori|culture, n. Cultivation of trees & shrubs. Hence ~**cul'tural** a., ~**cul'turist** n. [f. L *arbor -oris* tree + CULTURE]

arboriza'tion, n. Tree-like appearance (Min., Chem.) in aggregation of crystals, (Anat.) from distension or injection of capillary vessels. [as prec. +-IZE +-ATION]

ar'bor vi'tae, n. Popular name of several evergreens. [L.=tree of life]

ar'bour (-er), n. Bower, shady retreat with sides & roof formed by trees or lattice-work covered with climbing plants. Hence ~ED² (-erd) a. [orig. *(h)erber* f. OF *(h)erbier* grass lawn f. L *herbarium* (*herba* grass, herb, see -ARIUM), phonetic change to *ar-* being assisted by assoc. with L *arbor* tree]

ar'bu'tus, n. Genus of evergreens including strawberry-tree. [L]

arc, n. Part of circumference of circle or other curve; *diurnal, nocturnal,* ~, part of circle that a heavenly body appears to pass through above, below, horizon; belt contained between parallel curves; (Electr.) luminous bridge formed between two separate carbon poles; ~*lamp, -light,* using this. [OF, f. L *arcus* bow, curve]

arcade', n. Passage arched over; any covered walk, esp. with shops along one or both sides; (Archit.) series of arches on same plane. Hence **arcad'ED²** a. [F. f. It. *arcata* arch f. med. L *arcata* (L *arcus* bow), see -ADE]

Arcades am'bo (ài'kādēz), sent. Blackguards both (cf. Byron *D. Juan.* iv. 93). [facet. application of Virg. *Ecl.* vii. 4]

Arcad'ian (ài'-), a. & n. Ideal(ly) rustic. [f. L *Arcadius* (Gk *Arkadia* mountain district in Peloponnese) +-AN]

Arc'ady, Arcad'ia, (ài'-), n.(poet.). Ideal rustic paradise. [f. Gk *Arkadia,* see prec.]

arcan'um, n. (Usu. in pl. *-na*) mystery, secret. [L, neut. of *arcanus* arcane chest, see -AN]

arch¹, n. Curved structure supporting bridge, floor, etc., or merely ornamental; curve; curvature in shape of ~, as *fallen* ~ (of foot); vault; *Court of Arches,* ecclesiastical court, of appeal for the province of Canterbury, orig. held in the church of St. Mary-le-Bow (or 'of the Arches'); ~*way,* vaulted passage, arched entrance. Hence ~WISE adv. [f. OF *arche* (L L *arca* chest, but confused with *arc* f. L *arcus* bow]

arch², v.t. & i. Furnish with an arch; form into an arch; overarch, span; (intr.) form an arch. [f. OF *archer* (as prec.)]

arch³, a. (sup. *-est*). Chief, pre-eminent, as ~ *rogue, knave, impostor,* (but now usu. ~-); cunning, clever, innocently roguish, whence ~LY² adv., ~NESS n. [= foll.]

arch-, pref. = Gk *arkhi-, arkh-, arkhe-,* comb. form of *arkhos* chief cogn. w. *arkhō* begin (OE *erce-, arce-,* OF *arce,* later *arche;* whence Gk *erce-,* Du. *aarts*); in mod. literary wds f. Gk *archi-* is used, as *arch-deacon* but *archidiaconal.* Meaning: (1) in titles of office etc. 'chief, superior', as *archbishop, -duke,* esp. in titles of Holy Roman or German empire, as *-butler, -chamberlain;* (2) 'pre-eminent, leading', as *-antiquary, -builder, -prophet, -wag;* esp. 'extreme, worst', as *-buffoon, -knave, -liar;* (3) rarely= 'first, original', as *-founder, -messenger;* (4) of things, 'chief', as *-diocese.*

archae'an (-kē-), a. Of the earliest geological period. [f. Gk *arkhaios* ancient (*arkhē* beginning) +-AN]

archae'ol'ogy (-ki-), n. Study of antiquities, esp. of the prehistoric period. So ~**ol'ogic** (-k-) (-kio-) aa., ~**ol'ogically²** adv., ~**ol'ogist** (-ki-) n. [f. Gk *arkhaiologia* (as prec., see -LOGY)]

archaeop'teryx (-ki-), n. Oldest known (fossil) bird, a link between birds & reptiles. [f. Gk *arkhaios* ancient+ *pteruæ* wing]

archa'ic (-k-), a. Primitive, antiquated; (of language) no longer in common use, though retained for special purposes. Hence ~ICALLY adv. [f. Gk *arkhaikos* (as prec., see -IC)]

arc'ha|ism (-k-), n. Retention, imitation, of what is old or obsolete (esp. in language & art); archaic word or expression. Hence ~IST n., ~IS'TIC a., (-k-). [f. Gk *arkhaismos* (*arkhaizō,* see foll. & -ISM)]

arc'haïze (-k-), v.t. & i. Imitate, affect, the archaic; (trans.) render archaistic. [f. Gk *arkhaizō* copy the ancients (*arkhaios* ancient, see -IZE]

arc'hángel (-k-), n. Angel of highest rank; kind of dead-nettle; kind of pigeon. Hence **arc'hángel'ic** (-k-) a. [OF, f. L L *arkhaggelos* (see ARCH- & ANGEL)

arch'bish'op, n. Chief bishop; metropolitan. Hence **arch'bish'opric** n. [f. L L *archiepiscopus* (see ARCH- & BISHOP)]

arch'deac'on, n. Ecclesiastical dignitary next below bishop, superintending rural deans & holding lowest ecclesiastical court, with power of spiritual censure. Hence **arch'deac'onship** n. [OE *arce-diacon* f. L f. Gk *arkhidiakonos* (see ARCH- & DEACON)]

arch'deac'onry, n. Jurisdiction, rank, residence, of archdeacon. [prec. + -RY]

arch'di'ocèse, n. See of an archbishop. [ARCH- (4)]

arch'dúch'ess, n. Wife of an archduke; daughter of Emperor of Austria. [f. F *archiduchesse* (see ARCH- & DUCHESS)]

arch'dúke, n. Son of Emperor of Austria. So **archdú'càl** a., **arch'DUCHY** n. [f. OF *archeduc* (see ARCH- & DUKE)]

arch'-én'émy, n. Chief enemy; Satan. [ARCH- (2)]

arch'|er, n. One that shoots with bow & arrows; Sagittarius, ninth zodiacal constellation. So ~ERY (2) n. [AF, f. OF *archier* f. L *arcuarius* (*arcus* bow, see -ARY¹)]

ar'chetȳp|e (-ki-), n. Original model, prototype. Hence ~**ally²** adv. [f. L f. Gk *arkhetupon* (*arkhe-* ARCH-(2) + *tupos* stamp)]

arch'-fiend', n. Satan. [ARCH-(2)]

‖ **arch'ibald** (-awld). See ARCHIE.

archideac'onal (-ki-), a. Pertaining to an archdeacon. [f. L as ARCHDEACON + -AL]

arch'ie, -ibald, nn. (sl.). Anti-aircraft gun. [f. name in pop. song]

archiepis'copal (-ki-), a. Pertaining to an archbishop. [f. L as ARCHBISHOP + -AL]

arch'il (or -ki-), n. (Violet dye from) various kinds of lichen. [corrupt. of *orchil* f. OF *orcell* f. It. *orcella*, etym. dub.]

archima̍n'drite (-ki-), n. Superior of monastery or convent in Greek church. [f. med. L *archimandrita* f. late Gk *arkhimandrites* (*arkhi-* ARCH- + *mandra* monastery)]

Archimēd'ean (ăr-), a. Of Archimedes (Greek mathematician); ~ *screw*, instrument raising water by tube in form of screw wound round cylinder. [f. L *Archimedeus* + -AN]

archipel'agō (-ki-), n. (pl. ~**s**), Aegean sea; sea with many islands; group of islands. [f. It. *arcipelago* (*arci-* ARCH-(4) + *pelago* gulf, pool, f. L f. Gk *pelagos* sea)]

ar'chitect (-ki-), n. Professor of building, who prepares plans & superintends work; designer of complex structure, esp. the Creator; (fig.) achiever, as ~ *of his own fortunes.* [f. F f. L *architectus* f. Gk *arkhitektōn* (*arkhi-* ARCH- + *tectōn* builder); some derivatives formed as if L *-tectus* were p.p. of *tegere* cover]

architecton'ic (-ki-), a. Of architecture or architects; constructive; controlling; pertaining to systematization of knowledge, whence ~**ICS** n., ~**ICAL** a. [f. L f. Gk *arkhitektonikos* (as prec., see -IC)]

ar'chitecture (-ki-), n. Science of building; thing built, structure; style of building; construction. Hence **architec'tural²**, **architec'turally²** adv. [F, f. L *architectura* (*architectus* ARCHITECT, see -URE)]

ar'chitrave (-ki-), n. Epistyle, main beam resting immediately on the abacus on capital of column; the various parts surrounding doorway or window; moulding round exterior of arch. [f. *archi-* ARCH- + L *trabs -bis* beam]

ar'chive (-ki-), n. (usu. pl. ~**s**, pr. -kivz). Place in which public records are kept; records so kept. [F (-*if*, -*ive*), f. L L *archī(v)um* f. Gk *arkheion* public office (*arkhē* government)]

ar'chivist (-ki-), n. Member of archives. [f. prec. + -IST]

ar'chivolt (-ki-), n. Under curve of arch from impost to impost; mouldings decorating this. [f. It. *archivolto*, *arcovolta* (*arco* f. L *arcus* arch + *volta* VAULT, *volto* arched)]

ar'chon (-k-), n. One of nine chief magistrates in ancient Athens; ruler, president. Hence ~**SHIP** n. [Gk, = ruler (part. of *arkhō*)]

arc'tic, a. Of the north pole, northern; *A~ Circle* (of earth), parallel of 66° 32' N. [f. OF *artique* f. L f. Gk *arktikos* (*arktos* bear, Ursa Major, see -IC)]

Arctū'rus (ār-), n. Brightest star in constellation Boötes. [L, f. Gk *arktouros* (*arktos* bear + *ouros* guardian)]

arc'uate, -ated, aa. Bent like a bow; arched. [f. L *arcuatus* (*arcuare* f. *arcus* bow): see -ATE²]

ar'cus senil'is, n. Narrow yellowish-white band gradually encircling the cornea with advancing age. [L, = bow of old age]

-ard, suf. forming nouns, usu. of censure (*sluggard*, *drunkard*), but cf. *standard* (orig. *stander*), *placard*; also spelt *-art* (*braggart*). [ME & OF, f. G *-hart*, *-hard*, hardy, in proper names]

ar'dent, a. Burning, red-hot; parching; ~ *spirits* (prop. = inflammable, now understood of their taste), alcoholic spirits; eager, zealous; fervent (of persons & feelings). Hence **ar'dency** n., ~**LY²** adv. [ME & OF, f. L *ardentem* (*ardēre* burn), see -ANT]

ar'dour (-der), n. Fierce heat; warm emotion; fervour, zeal, (*for*). [OF, f. L *ardorem* (*ardēre* burn, see -OR²)]

ar'duous, a. Steep, hard to climb; hard to achieve, laborious; strenuous, energetic. Hence ~**LY²** adv., ~**NESS** n. [f. L *arduus* steep, difficult + -OUS]

are¹ (ār), n. French metric unit of square measure, square whose side is 10 metres (119¼ sq. yds). [F, f. L *area*]

are². See BE.

ār'ĕa, n. Vacant ground; level space; sunk court railed off from pavement & giving access to basement of house, as (fig.) scene of conflict; region, tract; scope, range. [L, = vacant piece of ground in town]

ar'eca, n. Genus of palms; ~*nut*, astringent seed of a species of ~. [Port., f. Tamil *adaikay* (*adai* close-clustering + *kay* nut)]

arēn'a, n. (pl. ~**s**). Central part of amphitheatre, in which combats take place; (fig.) scene of conflict, sphere of action. [L (h)*arena* sand, sand-strewn place of combat]

ār̆ēna'ceous (-shus), a. Sand-like; sandy. So **ār̆ēnōse¹** a. [f. L *arenaceus* (as prec., see -ACEOUS)]

ar̆e'ola, n. (pl. ~**ae**). Very small area, as that between veins of a leaf; interstice in tissue; circular spot, as that surrounding the human nipple; (Biol.) cell-nucleus of plant. Hence ~**AR¹**, ~**ATE²**, aa., ~**A'TION** n. [L, dim. of AREA]

Arēŏp'agīte (ǎ-, -g-), n. Member of the court of Areopagus. [f. L f. Gk *areiopagītēs* (see foll. & -ITE)]

Areop'agus (ă.), n. Hill at Athens where highest judicial court sat. [L, f. Gk *Areios pagos* Mars' hill]

arête (ărāt'), n. Sharp ascending ridge of mountain. [F, f. L *arista* ear of corn]

ar'gala, n. Adjutant-bird, gigantic Indian stork. [Hind. *hargila*]

ar'gali, n. Asiatic wild sheep. [Mongol]

ar'gand, n. Lamp with tubular wick; gas-burner on same principle. [inventor]

ar'gent, n. & a. Silver (colour), esp. in armorial bearings. [F, f. L *argentum*]

argentif'erous, a. Yielding silver. [f. L *argentum* + -FEROUS;

ar'gentine, a. & n. Of silver; silvery; imitation silver; silvery lamellae on scales of fish; (Zool.) genus of small fishes; (Min.) slate-spar. [f. F *argentin* f. L *argentinus* of silver(*argentum*, see -INE[1])]

ar'gil, n. Clay (esp. potter's). So ~lA'CEOUS a. [f. F *argille* f. L *argilla* f. Gk *argillos* (*argēs* white)]

ar'gle-bar'gle, v.i., & n. (joc.). Debate. [corrupt. & redupl. of *argue*]

ar'gol, n. Tartar deposited from fermented wines, which when purified becomes cream of tartar. [?]

ar'gon, n. (chem.). A gas, an inert constituent of the atmosphere. [neut. of Gk *argos* idle (A- (7), *ergon* work)]

Ar'gonaut, n. 1. (Pl.) legendary heroes who sailed with Jason in the Argo for the golden fleece. 2. Genus of cephalopod molluscs including paper nautilus. [f. L (-*ta*) f. Gk *Argonautēs* sailor in the *Argo*]

ar'gosy, n. (hist., poet.). Large merchant-vessel, esp. of Ragusa & Venice; (poet.) ship, venture. [earlier *ragusye* (*nave*) Ragusan (vessel)]

ar'got (-gō), n. Jargon, slang; of a class, esp. of thieves. [F, etym. dub.]

ar'gue, v.t., v.t. & i. Prove, indicate, as *it ~s him (to be) a rogue, that he is a rogue, roguery in him*; maintain by reasons (*that*), reasoning, ~ *it away*, get rid of it by argument; ~ (persuade) *a person into, out of*; reason (*with, against*, person, *for, against, about,* thing). [f. OF *arguer* f. L *argutare* frequent. of *arguere* make clear, prove, accuse]

ar'gument, n. Reason advanced (*for, against*, proposition or course); (Logic) middle term in syllogism; reasoning process; debate; summary of subject-matter of book; ~ (usu. *argumen'tum) adhominem*, one that takes advantage of character or situation of particular opponent, *ad crumenam*, of his avarice, *ad ignorantiam*, of his ignorance of the facts. [F, f. L *argumentum*]

argumenta'tion, n. Methodical reasoning; debate. [F, f. L *argumentationem* f. *argumentari* (as prec.), see -ATION]

argumen'tative, a. Logical; fond of arguing. Hence ~LY[2] (-vi-) adv., ~NESS (-vn-) n. [F (-f, -ive), as prec, see -ATIVE]

Ar'gus (ăr'-), n. Fabulous person with a hundred eyes; watchful guardian; ~ eyed, vigilant; ~ -shell, oculated porcelain-shell. [L, f. Gk *Argos*]

ar'gute', a. Sharp, shrewd; (of sounds) shrill. [f. L *argutus* p.p. of *arguere*, see ARGUE]

argy-, argyro-, in comb. = Gk *arguros* silver, as *argy'ria* silver-poisoning, *argyran'thous*, with silvery flowers, *argyrophyll'ous*, silvery-leaved.

ar'ia, n. (mus.). Extended song in three sections common in 18th-c. opera & oratorio. [It.]

Ar'ian (ăr'-), a. & n. (Holder) of the doctrine of Arius of Alexandria (4th c.), who denied consubstantiality of Christ. Hence ~ISM (ăr'-) n., ~IZE (ăr'-), v.t. & i. [f. L *Arianus* (*Arius* f. Gk *Areios, Areios*, see -AN]

-ăr'ian, suf. forming adj. & nn. chiefly denoting (member) of a sect etc. (*veget-, trinit-, human-*), or (person) of an age given by L numerals (*octogen-*). [L -*arius* + -AN; first sense perh. w. ref. to ARIAN]

ăr'id, a. Dry, parched, (lit. & fig.); (of ground) barren, bare. Hence **arid'iTY**, ~NESS, nn. [f. L *aridus* (*arēre* be dry)]

ar'iel, n. Species of gazelle in Western Asia & Africa. [f. Arab. *aryil* var. of *aiyil* stag]

Aries (ăr'iēz), n. The Ram, first zodiacal constellation. [L, =ram]

aright' (-ĭt), adv. Rightly. [A prep. + RIGHT n.]

ă'ril, n. Accessory seed-covering in certain plants. [f. mod. L *arillus* f. med. L *arilli* dried grapes]

-ar'ious, compd adj. suf. = L -*arius* (-ARY[1]) + -OUS.

arise' (-z), v.i. (arōse, arĭsen, pr. -z, -z-). (Arch.) rise, get up; (poet.) rise from the dead; (arch.) be heard (of sounds); originate; be born; come into notice; result (*from*); present itself. [A- (1) + RISE v.]

aris'ta, n. (pl. -*ae*). Awn, beard, of grain & grasses. [L]

aris'tate, a. Awned, bearded. [f. L *aristatus* (ARISTA, see -ATE[2])]

aristoc'racy, n. Government by the best citizens; supremacy of privileged order, oligarchy; state so governed; ruling body of nobles; class from which ruling body is drawn, nobles; the best representatives of (intellect etc.). [f. L, f. Gk *aristokratia* (*aristos* best + -*kratia* rule)]

ă'ristocrăt, n. One of a ruling oligarchy; one of the class of nobles. Hence **ăristōc'ratism** n. [f. F *aristocrate* (as foll.)]

ăristocrăt'ic, a. Pertaining to, attached to, aristocracy; grand, stylish. Hence ~AL a., ~ALLY[2] adv. [f. F *aristocratique* f. Gk *aristokratikos* (as ARISTOCRACY, see -IC)]

Aristotēlĭan, -ŏtelĕ'an, (ă-), aa. & nn. (Disciple or student) of the Greek philosopher Aristotle. [f. LL *Aristotelēs*, -*lēos* Aristotle + -IAN; -*lean* f. Gk -*leios* aa. + -AN]

arĭth'mĕtic, n. Science of numbers; arithmetical knowledge, computation; treatise on computation. Hence **arĭthmĕ'tĭcĬAN** (-ĭshn) n. [f. OF *arismetique* f. LL *arismetica* for L *arithmetica* f. Gk *arithmētikē* (*tekhnē*) (art) of counting f. *arithmos* number, see -IC; corrupted in ME to *arsmetrike*, as if f. L *ars metrica* art (of measure)]

arĭthmĕ'tĭcal, a. Of arithmetic; ~ *progression*, (series of numbers showing increase, decrease, by a constant quantity (e.g. 1, 2, 3, 4, etc., 9, 7, 5, 3, etc.). Hence ~ly adv. [prec.+-AL]

arĭthmŏm'ĕter, n. Calculating-machine. [f. F *arithmomètre* (Gk *arithmos* number + -METER)]

-ār'ium, noun suf. f. L neut. of adjj. in *-ārius* (-ARY), chiefly in antiquarian words as *sacrārium*, *oecas*, popularized, as *aquarium*.

ärk, n. Chest, box; *Ark of the Covenant*, *Ark of Testimony*, wooden coffer containing tables of Jewish law; covered floating vessel in which Noah was saved at the Deluge; *Noah's* ~, toy ~ with animals. [com.-Teut.; OE *arc*, f. L *arca* chest]

arles (ärlz), n. pl. (dial.). Earnest-money. [see EARNEST[2]]

ärm[1], n. Upper limb of human body from shoulder to hand; *fore*~ (from elbow to hand); fore limb of an animal; large branch of tree; sleeve; thing resembling branch of tree; sleeve; thing resembling ~, as ~ *of the sea*, ~*-chair* (with side supports), ~ *of lever, balance* (part from fulcrum to point of application of power or weight); ~*hole* in garment, hole through which ~ is put; ~*-pit*, hollow under ~ at shoulder; ~*in-*~ (of two persons with ~s interlinked); *infant in* ~s (too young to walk); *with open* ~s, cordially; *keep at* ~'s *length*, avoid familiarity with; *secular* ~, authority of secular tribunal. Hence **ärm'fUL** (-ŏŏl) n. [com.-Teut.

ärm'lĕss[1], a. [com.-Teut. cf. Gk *harmos* joint f. Aryan root *ar-* join]

ärm[2], n. (usu. pl.). Weapon(s); *fire*~s (requiring explosive); *small* ~s, portable fire-arms, rifles, pistols, light machine guns, sub-machine guns, etc.; *stand of* ~s, set for one soldier; (sing.) particular kind of weapon; *take up* ~s, arm oneself (often fig.); *bear* ~s, serve as soldier; *lay down* ~s, cease hostilities; *in* ~s, armed; *up in* ~s, actively engaged in rebellion etc. (also fig.); *under* ~s, in battle array; military profession; (sing, & pl.) each kind of troops, infantry, cavalry, etc.; heraldic devices, as *coat of* ~s; *King-of-Arms*, Chief Herald.

Hence **ärm'lĕss[2]** [-LESS] a. [f. F *armes* f. L *arma* arms, fittings, f. root *ar-* join]

ärm[3], v.t. & i. Furnish with arms; ~*ed neutrality* (of nations prepared for war); furnish with tools or other requisites; plate (*with anything*); furnish (magnet) with an armature; (intr.) ~ oneself, take up arms. [f. F *armer* f. L *armāre* (arma)]

ärmā'da, n. Fleet of ships of war, esp. *the* (*Invincible*) *A*~ sent by Philip II of Spain against England in 1588. [Sp., f. L *armāta* fem. p.p. of *armāre* ARM[3], see -ADE]

ärmādĭl'lō, n. (pl. -os). Burrowing animal of S. America, with body encased in bony armour, & habit of rolling itself into ball when captured; genus of small terrestrial Crustacea with same habit, allied to wood-louse. [Sp., dim. of *armado* one armed f. L as ARM[3], see -ADO]

Ärmagĕdd'on, n. (Scene of) supreme conflict between the nations. [*Rev.* xvi. 16]

ärm'ament, n. Force (usu. naval), equipped for war; military equipments, esp. great guns on man-of-war; process of equipping for war. [f. L *armamentum* (as ARM[3], see -MENT)]

ärm'ature, n. Arms, armour; defensive covering of animals or plants; piece of soft iron placed in contact with poles of magnet, increasing its power; essential part of a dynamo. [f. L *armatura* (as prec., see -URE)]

arme blanche (see AD.), n. Cavalry sword or lance; cavalry. [F. = white arm] (*armé bl.*), a. & n. 1. Of Armenia; bole, red = earth, used medicinally; ~ *stone*, blue carbonate of copper. 2. n. Native of Armenia; adherent of ~ church. [-AN]

ärmĭg'er, n. Esquire, one entitled to bear heraldic arms. [L, = bearing arms (*arma* arms + *gerere* bear)]

ärmĭl'lary, a. Pertaining to bracelets; ~ *sphere*, skeleton celestial globe of metal rings representing equator, tropics, etc. [f. L *armilla* bracelet, see -ARY[1]]

Ärmĭn'ĭan (ă-), a. & n. (Adherent) of the doctrine of Arminius, Dutch protestant theologian, who opposed the views of Calvin, esp. on predestination. Hence ~ISM (-ĭzm) n. [f. *Arminius*, Latiniz, of *Harmensen* +-AN]

ärm'istice, n. Cessation from hostilities (lit. & fig.); short truce; *A*~ *Day*, 11th Nov., kept as anniversary of the ~ (1918) that ended hostilities in the war of 1914–18. [f. L *arma* arms + *-stitium* (*sistere* -*stit*- stop)]

ärm'lĕt, n. Band worn round arm; small inlet of sea or branch of river. [ARM[1] + -LET]

ärmō'rĭal, a. & n. (Book) pertaining to heraldic arms. [ARMORY+-AL(1)]

ärm'or(ỹ, n. Heraldry. Hence ~IST n. [f. OF *armoirie* f. *armoier* blazoner f. L *arma* arms]

ȧrm'our¹ (-mer), n. **1.** Defensive covering for the body worn in fighting (~-*bearer*, one who carries another's ~). **2.** Metal sheathing of ship of war, composed of ~-*plates* (~-*clad*, furnished with this); steel plates etc. protecting cars, tanks, etc. from projectiles; armoured vehicles collectively, e.g. tanks, armoured cars, etc. **3.** Diver's suit. **4.** Protective covering of animals or plants. **5.** Heraldic insignia. [f. OF *armeüre* f. L *armatūra* ARMATURE]

ȧrm'our² (-mer), v.t. Furnish with protective covering; ~*ed* CRUISER; ~*ed car*, *train*, etc., one supplied with armoured plates of steel etc. & (usu.) guns; ~*ed column*, *corps*, *division*, *force*, etc., one equipped with ~*ed* cars, tanks, etc. [f. prec.]

ȧrm'ourer (-mer-), n. Manufacturer of arms; official in charge of ship's, regiment's, arms. [f. AF *armurer*, OF -*urier*, f. *armeüre*, see prec. & -ER²]

ȧrm'oury (-mer-), n. Place where arms are kept, arsenal; *armourer's workshop. [perh. as ARMORY, but treated as f. ARMOUR + -Y¹]

ȧrm'y, n. Organized body of men armed for war; *standing ~*, one of professional soldiers permanently in existence; *the ~*, the military service; vast host; organized body of men, as *Salvation A~*, *Church A~*, *Blue Ribbon A~*; ~ *broker*, *contractor* (carrying on business in connexion with the ~); ~ *corps*, main subdivision of in the field consisting usu. of two or three divisions with technical, administrative, supply, etc. formations; ~-*list*, official list of officers. [f. -ADE] f. L *armāta* fem. p.p. of *armāre* arm]

ȧrn'ica, n. Genus of plants including mountain tobacco; medicine, esp. tincture, prepared from this. [?]

aroint', -**oy**, v. or int. (arch.), ~ *thee*, begone. [?]

arom'a, n. (pl. -*as*). Fragrance, sweet smell; subtle pervasive quality. [earlier (& OF) *aromat* f. L *arōmata* (pl.) f. Gk *arōma -matos*]

ȧromăt'ic, a. Fragrant; spicy. [f. F *aromatique* f. L f. Gk *arōmatikos* (AROMA, see -IC)]

arose. See ARISE.

around', adv. & prep. **1.** On every side, in every direction; *about, here & there, at random, as *fool ~*. **2.** prep. On, along, the circuit of; about, enveloping. [f. A-(2) + ROUND]

arouse' (-z), v.t. Awaken; stir up into activity. [A- + ROUSE², on anal. of *rise*, *arise*]

ȧrpe'ggio (-ějō), n. (pl. -*os*), (mus.). Striking of notes of chord in (usu. upward) succession; chord so struck. [It.]

arquebus. See HARQUEBUS.

ȧ'rrack (or arăk'), n. Eastern name for any native spirituous liquor, esp. that

distilled from the coco-palm, or from rice & sugar. [f. Arab. *'araq* juice]

ȧ'rrah (-ra), int. An Anglo-Irish expletive.

arraign' (-ăn), v.t. Indict before a tribunal; accuse; find fault with, call in question, (action, statement). So ~MENT (-ăn-). [f. AF *arrainer* f. OF *araisnier* f. L *Ad*rationare reason, talk reasonably (*ratio -ōnis* reason, discourse)]

arrange', v.t. & i. Put into order, adjust; draw up (army); (Mus.) adapt (composition) for new medium, instrumental or vocal; settle (dispute etc.); settle beforehand the order, manner, of; (intr.) take steps, form plans, give instructions, (~ *to be there*, *for the cab to be there*; ~ *about, about thing, to do, that,* or abs.). [f. OF *arangier* (à to + *rangier* f. *rang* RANK)]

arrange'ment (-jm-), n. Arranging; thing arranged; settlement of dispute etc.; (pl.) plans, measures, as *make your own* ~s. [-MENT]

ȧ'rrant, a. Notorious, downright, thorough-paced, as ~ *knave, dunce, hypocrite, nonsense.* Hence ~LY² adv. [variant of ERRANT, orig. in phr. like ~ (= out-lawed, roving) *thief*]

ȧ'rras, n. Rich tapestry; hanging screen of this formerly hung round walls of rooms (often not too closely to admit person). Hence ~ED² (-st) a. [*Arras*, town in Artois famous for the fabric]

array', v.t. Marshal, dispose, (forces); (Law) impanel (a jury); dress, esp. with display; (refl.) dress *oneself* up; adorn; (fig.) clothe (in qualities etc.). [f. AF *arayer* = OF *areyer*, *aredar*, early Rom. *arredare* f. *ad* to + *redo* (OF *rei, rai*) order, preparation, f. LG *rēde*, Goth. *garaids* ready]

array'², n. Order, as *battle* ~; (Hist.) arming of militia, as *Commission of A~*; military force; imposing series of persons or things; order of impanelling jury; (poet.) outfit, dress. [f. AF *araī*=OF *arei* f. *areyer*, see prec.]

arrear', n. (arch.). Rear part, esp. of procession; (pl.) outstanding debts; *in* ~*s* or ~ *of*, behind. [orig. adv. f. OF *arere* (mod. F *arrière*) f. LL *ad retro* (*ad* to + *retro* backwards): first used in phr. *in* ~]

arrear'age, n. Backwardness; unpaid balance; thing in reserve; (pl.) debts. [f. OF *arerage* f. *arere*, see prec. & -AGE]

arrĕct', a. (Of the ears) pricked up; (fig.) on the alert. [f. L *arrectus* p.p. of ARRigere raise up (*regere* straighten)]

arrěst'¹, v.t. Stop (person, cannon-ball, decay); (Law) ~ *judgement*, stay proceedings after verdict, on ground of error; seize (person), esp. by legal authority; catch (attention); ~ *attention*; catch attention. Hence ~IVE a., ~MENT n. [f. OF *arester* (Prov. *arestar*) f. LL *Ad*restare remain, stop (intr.)]

arrest², n. Stoppage, check; ~ *of judge-ment* (see prec.); seizure; legal appre-hension; imprisonment; *under* ~ (legal restraint). [f. OF *arest* f. *arester*, see prec.]

arrêt (arã'), n. (hist.). Authoritative sentence or decree of the King or Parlia-ment of France; (loosely) judgement, order. [F., f. OF *arest*]

arride, v.t. (arch.). Please, gratify. [f. L *arridēre* smile upon, be pleasing to]

arrière-ban (ă'rĭer-), n. Summoning of vassals to military service by Frankish king; body thus summoned or liable to be summoned; noblesse; (improp.) sum-moning of inferior (*arrière-*) vassals. [F. f. OF *arière-ban* for (*h*)*ari-ban* f. OHG *hari* army +*ban* edict, altered in form & sense by pop. etym. whence *ban et arrière-ban* summoning of superior & inferior vassals]

arrière-pensée (see Ap.), n. Ulterior motive; mental reservation. [F]

arris, n. Sharp edge formed by angular contact of two plane or curved surfaces, as ~*-gutter* (V-shaped), ~*-wise*, ridge-wise. [f. F *areste* (mod. *arête*) f. L *arista* ear of corn]

arrival, n. Act of coming to end of journey or destination (lit. & fig.); ap-pearance upon scene; person, thing, that has arrived; (colloq.) new-born child; cargo to be delivered when ship arrives. [f. OF *arriver* f. LL (2)]

arrive, v.i. Come to destination (lit. & fig.); or end of journey (*at* Bath, *in* Paris, *upon* scene, *at* conclusion); (as Gallicism) establish one's repute or position; (of things) be brought; (of time) come; (of events) come about. [f. OF *ariver* f. LL *arribare* f. L *Advigare* come to shore(*ripa*)]

arrogant, a. Overbearing; presump-tuous; haughty. Hence or cogn. ~ANCE, ~ANCY, nn., ~antry² adv. [F (as foll., see -ANT)]

arrogate, v.t. Claim unduly (thing, *to* oneself a thing); claim unduly that one possesses (a quality); claim unduly for (*to*) some one else. [f. L AR(*rogare* ask), see -ATE¹]

arrogation, n. Unjust claim (*of* or abs.); unwarrantable assumption. [f. L *arro-gatio* (as prec., see -ATION)]

arrondissement, n. Administra-tive subdivision of French department. [F]

arrow (-ō), n. Pointed missile shot from bow; index, pin, ornament, of similar shape; || ~ or *broad* ~*-head*, mark distin-guishing British Government stores; ~*stitch*, triangular set of stitches securing whale-bone in stays; ~*-headed characters*, cuneiform; ~*root*, plant from which a nu-tritious starch is prepared. Hence ~y² (-ōi) a. [OE *earh, arwe*, f. OTeut. Goth. *arhuzana* thing belonging to the bow (*arhuz* cogn. w. L *arcus* bow)]

arse, n. (not now in polite use). But-tocks, rump. [com.-Teut. cogn. w. Gk *orrhos*]

arsenal, n. Public establishment for storage or manufacture of weapons & ammunition (also fig.). [f. It. *arsenale* earlier *arzenà* f. Arab. *dar accinā'ah* (*dar* house +*al* the+*çinā'ah* art f. *çana'a* fabricate); *d-* dropped perh. by confus. w. *de* prep.; -*de* added in It.]

arsenic¹, n. (Chem.) brittle steel-grey semi-metallic substance, crystallising in rhombohedrons, & volatilising without fusion with odour of garlic; (pop.) tri-oxide of ~, white mineral substance, a violent poison; *flowers of* ~, same sublimed. Hence **arsenic¹al** a. [OF, f. L f. Gk *arsenikon* yellow orpiment (identi-fied with *arsenikos* male, from belief that metals were of different sexes, but in fact f. Arab. *az-zernikh* the orpiment f. Pers. *zerni* (*zar* gold)]

arsenic², a. Of, belonging to, arsenic; esp. (Chem.) applied to compounds in which arsenic combines as a pentad. [f. prec., -*ic* being identified with -IC (1)]

arsenious, a. Containing arsenic; esp. applied to compounds in which arsenic combines as a triad. [f. ARSENIC n. + -IOUS; see also -OUS]

arsis, n. (pl. *arsés*). Accented syllable in English scansion (cf. *thesis*). [L f. Gk, =lifting f. *airō* lift; in what sense, & whether orig. of voice or foot (in beating time), is disputed]

arson, n. Wilful setting on fire of another's house or similar property or one's own when insured. [OF, f. LL *arsionem* (*arsus ars-* burn, intr., see -ION)]

art¹, v. See BE.

art², n. Skill, esp. human skill as opposed to nature; skilful execution as an object in itself; skill applied to imitation & design, as in painting etc.; (attrib.) of artistic design etc. (chiefly shop use ~ *needlework, carpet, curtain*); thing in which skill may be exercised; esp. (pl.) certain branches of learning serving as intellectual instruments for more ad-vanced studies, as *Bachelor, Master, of Arts*, one who has obtained standard of proficiency in these; *black* ~, magic; practical application of any science; in-dustrial pursuit, craft; guild, company of craftsmen; *fine* ~*s*, those in which mind & imagination are chiefly concerned; knack; cunning; stratagem; ~ *& (or) part*, design & (or) execution, as *be* ~ *& part in* (accessary in both respects). [OF, f. L *artem*, nom. *ars*, prob. f. *ar-* fit]

artefact, arti-, n. A product of human art & workmanship; (Archaeol.) a product of prehistoric art as dist. from a similar object naturally produced. [f. L

arte (abl. of *ars* art) +*factum* (neut. p.p. of *facere* make)]

artel', n. Association or guild of workers in Russia. [Russ.]

arter'ial, a. Belonging to, of the nature of, resembling, an artery (now freq. of important main roads, & lines of transport or communication, as ~ *railway, road, traffic*). [F (*artère* ARTERY, see -AL)]

arter'ialize, v.t. Convert venous into arterial (blood) by exposure to oxygen in lungs; furnish with arterial system. Hence ~A'TION n.

arteriosclero'sis, n. Hardening of the arteries, esp. as concomitant of old age. [see ARTERY, SCLER(O)-, -OSIS]

arter'iotomy, n. Opening of artery for blood-letting; dissection of arteries. [f. Gk *artēriotomia* (as foll., see -TOMY)]

art'ery, n. Tube forming part of system by which blood is conveyed from heart (cf. VEIN) to all parts of body (also fig.). Hence ~TRIS n. [f. L f. Gk *artēria* prob. f. *airō* raise]

arte'sian (~zhn), a. ~ *well*, perpendicular boring into strata, producing constant supply of water rising spontaneously to surface. [f. F *artésien* (*Artois*, old French province)]

art'ful, a. Cunning, crafty, deceitful, (of persons & actions). Hence ~LY² adv., ~NESS n. [ART +-FUL]

arthri'tis, n. Inflammation of joint; gout. So ~it'ic a. [L f. Gk (*arthron* joint, see -ITIS)]

arthro-, comb. form of Gk *arthron* joint, as in *arthropathy*, painful affection of joints, *arthrō'sis*, articulation.

art'ichoke, n. Plant (of which bottom of flower & bases of its scales are edible) allied to thistles, native of Barbary; *Jerusalem* (corrupt. of *girasole*, sunflower) ~, species of sunflower with edible tuberous roots. [f. It. *articiocco* corrupt. of +*alcarcioffo* (mod. It. *carciofo*, OSp. *alcarchofa*) f Arab. *alkharshuf*]

art'icle¹, n. Separate portion of anything written; separate clause (of agreement etc.) as *Thirty-nine A~s, A~s of war, Apprenticeship, Association*; literary composition forming part of magazine etc. but independent; *leading* ~ in newspaper, ~ expressing editorial opinion; particular; particular thing, as *the next* ~; (Gram.) *definite* ~, 'the', *indefinite* ~, 'a, an'; *in the* ~ (*moment*) *of death*, (usu. *in artic'ulo mortis*). [F, f. L *articulus*, dim. of *artus* limb]

art'icle², v.t. Set forth in articles; indict; bind by articles of apprenticeship. [f. prec.]

artic'ular, a. Pertaining to the joints. [f. L *articularis* (as ARTICLE¹, see -AR¹)]

artic'ulate¹, a. & n. Jointed; distinctly jointed, distinguishable, as ~ *speech*; (n.) animal. Hence ~LY²(-tli-) adv., ~NESS (-tn-) n. [f. L *articulatus* (as prec., see -ATE²)]

artic'ulate², v.t. & i. Connect by joints, mark with apparent joints (usu. base); divide into words, pronounce distinctly; (intr.) speak distinctly. Hence ~ORY a. [f. prec., see -ATE³]

articula'tion, n. Act, mode, of jointing: joint; articulate utterance, speech; consonant. [F, f. L *articulationem* (*articulare* joint as ARTICLE¹, see -ATION)]

art'ifice, n. Device, contrivance; address, skill. [F, f. L *artificium* (*ars artis* art +-*ficium* making f. *facere* make)]

art'ificer, n. Craftsman; inventor (of). [f. prec.+-ER¹]

artific'ial (-shl), a. Made by art; not natural; not real, as ~ *flowers*; real, but produced by art, as ~ *ice*. Hence **artific'ial'ITY** (-shi-), ~NESS, nn., ~IZE v.t., ~LY² adv. [F, f. L *artificialis* (as ARTIFICE, see -AL)]

artill'ery, n. Anti-aircraft, anti-tank, field, medium, heavy, & mountain guns used by an army; branch or arm of the service that uses these; ~*train*, ordnance mounted on carriages & ready for marching. Hence **artill'erist**, ~**man**, nn. [f. F *artillerie* f. *artiller* maker of ~ f. LL +*articularius* (*articula* dim. of *ars* art, see -ARY²)]

artisan' (-z-), n. Mechanic, handicraftsman. [F, perh. f. It. *artigiano* f. LL +*artitianus* (*artitus* p.p. of *artire* instruct in arts, see -AN)]

art'ist, n. One who practises one of the fine arts, esp. painting; ~'s *proof*, copy of engraving taken for ~'s approval or correction & valued as fresher than ordinary copies; one who makes his craft a fine art (~ *in words* etc.). Hence **artis'tic(AL)** aa., **artis'tically²** adv., ~RY n. [f. F *artiste* f. It. f. LL *artista* (*ars artis* art, see -IST)]

artiste' (-tē-), n. Professional singer, dancer, etc. [F, see prec.]

art'less, a. Unskilful, uncultured; clumsy; natural; guileless, ingenuous. Hence ~LY² adv., ~NESS n. [ART +-LESS]

art'y, a. (colloq.). Pretentiously artistic; ~-&-*crafty*, (joc., usu. of furniture) remarkable rather for specially artistic style than for usefulness or comfort (after the *Arts & Crafts Exhibition Society*). [-Y²]

ar'um, n. Genus of monocotyledonous plants including Wake-Robin; ~ *lily* (tall & white-spached). [L, f. Gk *aron*]

-ary¹, suf. forming adjj. & nn. f. L -*arius* taken directly or thr. mod. F -*aire*, or imitated w. L nn. (rarely in E words as *bloomary*); as *arbitrary*; nouns = -*arius*, as *actuary*, = -*arium*, as *dictionary*, =-*aria*, as *fritillary*; words taken thr. OF have sometimes -ER² instead, as *primer*.

-ary², suf. Sometimes in adjj. suf. L -*aris*

instead of regular -AR¹, owing to passage
thr. F -aïve, as exemplary.

Ar'yan (ār-), a. & n. **1.** Applied by some to
family of languages (also called Indo-
European, Indo-Germanic) that includes
Sanskrit, Iranian, Greek, Latin, Celtic,
Teutonic, Slavonic, with their modern
representatives, by others only to the
Indo-Iranian portion of these. **2.** n.
Member of ~ family; in Nazi Germany
esp. contrasted with SEMITE. [f. Sk. ārya
noble (in earlier use a national name comprising worshippers of the gods of the
Brahmans); earlier Arian is f. L Ariānus
of Aria (f. Gk Areia eastern Persia)]

as¹ (āz, az) adv. conj. rel. pron. **1.** adv.
(in main sentence, foll. by as in subord.
clause expressed or understood) in the
same degree, as I come as soon as I could,
I know that as well as you, you might as
well help me, as FAR¹ as. **2.** rel. adv. or
conj. in subord. clause, with or without
antecedent as, so, expressing manner,
degree, etc., of the principal sentence;
(degree) you are as good as he, it is not so
(or as) easy as you think, quick as thought
he jumped out, fair as (=though) she is;
(manner) do as you like, according as we
decide, he looks as if he had seen a ghost,
treat him as a stranger, you are, as it were
(=as if it were actually so), compromised,
they rose as one man, late as usual, he
smiled, as who should say (=as a man
would smile who); (time) it struck me as
I was speaking; (reason) as you are not
ready, we must go on; (result) he so arranged matters as to suit everyone, be so
good as to come; (illustration) cathedral
cities, as Norwich. **3.** rel. pron. That, who,
which, as I had the same trouble as you,
such countries as Spain; (with antecedent inferred from main sentence) he
was a foreigner, as (which fact) they perceived from his accent. **4.** Special phrases:
as from (in formal dating, as cod. will be
decontrolled as from 31st March); as
regards, so far as it concerns; as to, with
respect to (said nothing as to hours, as to
when he would come; as to you, I despise
you); as yet, up to this time; I thought as
much, I thought so; as well (as), in addition (to); as good as dead, practically
dead. **5.** Phrases in (as) . . . as expressing
by reference to a proverbial type the
highest or a high degree of some quality,
& in alliterative or punning phr.
modelled on these: bald as a coot, black as
pitch, blind as a bat, bold as brass, brave as
a lion, bright as a button, bright as a new
pin, brown as a berry, busy as a bee, cold
as charity, common as dirt, cool as a
cucumber, cross as two sticks, dead as a
doornail, dead as mutton, deaf as a post,
drunk as a fiddler, drunk as a lord, dry as
a bone, dull as ditch-water, easy as ABC,
easy as lying, fit as a fiddle, flat as a pancake, good as gold (of children's conduct),
good as a play (amusing), hard as nails,
heavy as lead, hungry as a hunter, jolly as
a sandboy, keen as mustard, large as life,
light as air, mad as a hatter, mad as a
March hare, meek as Moses, merry as a
grig, old as the hills, pale as a ghost, plain
as a pikestaff, pleased as Punch, plentiful
as blackberries, plump as a partridge,
proud as a peacock, proud as Lucifer,
quick as thought, quiet as a mouse, rich as
a Jew, right as a trivet, right as rain,
safe as a house, sharp as a needle, silent as
the grave, snug as a bug in a rug, soft as
butter, soft as velvet, sound as a bell, stiff
as a poker, straight as a die, strong as a
horse, stubborn as a mule, sure as fate,
thick as thieves, thin as a lath, tight as a
drum, true as steel, ugly as sin, warm as (a)
toast, weak as a rat, weak as water, white
as a sheet. [OE alswā (later also, als)

as², n. Roman copper coin, orig. weighing
12 oz., but finally reduced to ⅓ oz. [L']

as-, pref. = AD- before s.

ăsaïoet'ida (-fēt-) n. Concreted resinous
gum with strong smell of garlic used in
medicine and cookery. [med. L (asa f.
Pers. aza mastic + foetida stinking)]

asbēs'tine (āz-), a. Of, like, asbestos,
incombustible (lit. & fig.). [f. L f. Gk
asbestinos f. foll., see -INE²]

asbēs'tŏs (āz-), n. Fibrous mineral that
can be woven into an incombustible
fabric (also fig.). Hence ~IC, ~OID, aa.
[L f. Gk, = unquenchable (a- not + sbestos
f. sbennumi quench)]

ascĕnd', v.t. & i. Go, come, up; (of
things) rise, be raised; slope upwards,
lie along ~ing slope; rise in thought,
rank, degree of quality; (of sounds) rise
in pitch; go back in point of time; (trans.)
go up, climb; ~ a river, go along it towards its source; mount upon, as ~ the
throne. [f. L ascendere, AD(scendere scans-
= scandere climb)]

ascĕn'dancy, -ency, n. Dominant control, sway, (over). [f. foll., see -ANCY]

ascĕn'dant, -ent, a. & n. **1.** Rising;
(Astron.) rising towards zenith; (Astrol.)
just above eastern horizon; predominant.
2. n. Horoscope; point of ecliptic or degree
of zodiac that (esp. at birth of child) is just
rising above eastern horizon; house of the
~ (from 5 degrees below it); lord of the ~, any
planet within this; in the ~, supreme,
dominating; (improp.) rising; supremacy;
ancestor. [f. OF (-ant) f. L as prec., see
-ENT]

ascĕn'sion (-shon), n. Act of ascending;
ascent of Christ on fortieth day after
resurrection; A~-day, Holy Thursday,
on which this is commemorated; A~-tide,
period of ten days from A~-day to
Whitsun Eve; rising of a celestial body,
as right ~ (celestial longitude). Hence
~AL a. [f. L ascensio (as ASCEND, see -ION)]

ascen'sive, a. Rising, progressive; (Gram.) intensive. [as prec., see -IVE]

ascent', n. Act of ascending; upward movement, rise, (lit. & fig.); way by which one may ascend, slope, flight of steps. [f. ASCEND on anal. of descent]

ascertain', v.t. Find out (for certain), get to know. Hence ~ABLE a., ~MENT n. [f. OF acertener, st. acertaine- (à to +CERTAIN)]

ascet'ic, a. & n. Severely abstinent, austere; (n.) one who practises severe self-discipline, esp. (Eccl. Hist.) one who retired into solitude for this purpose. Hence ~AL a., ~ALLY² adv., ~ISM (-sizm) n. [f. Gk askētikos f. askeēs monk (askeō exercise), see -ETIC and -IC]

ascid'ium (asid-), n. Genus of molluscs with leathery enveloping tunic, regarded as link in development of Vertebrata. [f. Gk askidion dim. of askos wine-skin]

Asclep'iad, n. (Gk and Lat. Prosody) verse consisting of a spondee, two or three choriambi, & an iambus. Hence ~ē'AN a. [f. L f. Gk Asklēpiadeios (Asklēpiades, Greek poet, the inventor)]

As'cot (ǎ-), n. Race-course on ~ Heath, Berks.; race-meeting at ~.

ascribe', v.t. Attribute, impute, (to) consider as belonging (to person or thing). Hence or cogn. ascrib'ABLE a., ascrip'-TION n., (esp.) preacher's words ascribing praise to God at end of sermon. [earlier ascrive f. OF ascrit- st. of ascrive f. L AD(scribere script- write)]

As'dic (ǎz-), n. Device for detecting submarine, [f. initials of Allied Submarine Detection Investigation Committee]

asē'ity, n. (metaphys.). Underived existence, the being uncreate. [f. L a se from oneself +-ITY]

asep'sis, n. Absence of putrefactive matter or harmful bacteria; the aseptic method in surgery. [A- (7) + Gk sēpsis decay (sēpō, see foll.)]

asep'tic, a. & n. Free from putrefaction or blood-poisoning; surgically sterile, sterilized, (of wounds, instruments, dressings); (of method etc.) seeking the absence (rather than counteraction, cf. antiseptic) of septic matter; (n.) non-putrescent substance, [f. Gk a- not + sēptikos putrefying (sēpō rot, see -IC)]

asex'üal¹, a. (Biol.) without sex. Hence asexüal'ITY n. [A- (7) + SEXUAL]

ash¹, n. Forest-tree with silver-grey bark, pinnate foliage, & close-grained wood; wood of this; ~-flu, ~-grub, (found on ~ & used by anglers); ~-key, winged seed of the ~; ~-leaf, an early potato; moun-tain ~, rowan-tree. [com.-Teut.; OE æsc, G esche]

ash², n. (usu. pl.). Powdery residue left after combustion of any substance; (pl.) remains of human body after cremation (lit. & fig.); lay in ~es, burn to the ground; sackcloth & ~es (symbol of repentance); ∥ bring back the ~es (Crick.), wipe out defeat; ~-fire, low fire used in chemical operations; ~-furnace (used in glassmaking); Ash Wednesday, first day of Lent (from Rom. Cath. custom of sprinkling ~es on penitents' heads). [com.-Teut.; OE asce, axe, Da. aske]

ashāmed' (-md), pred. a. Abashed, disconcerted, by consciousness of guilt; ~ of (conduct); ~ for (on account of) you; ~ to do (implying reluctance, but not always abstention). [p.p. of obs. vb ashame (a- (1) +OE scamian SHAME]

ǎsh'en¹, a. Pertaining to an ash-tree; made of ash. [ASH¹+-EN⁵]

ǎsh'en², a. Of ashes; ash-coloured, pale. [ASH²+-EN⁵]

ǎsh'ět, n. (Sc.). Big (usu. oval) plate. [f. F assiette]

Ashkenazim (ǎshkinahz'im), n. pl. Polish-German Jews (as dist. from SEPHARDIM). [mod. Heb., f. Askenaz (Gen. x. 3)]

ǎsh'lar, n. Square hewn stone(s); similar masonry as facing to rubble or brick wall. [f. OF aiseler f. L axillaris (axilla dim. of axis, assis, axle, board, see -AR¹)]

ǎsh'laring, n. Short upright boarding in garrets, cutting off acute angle formed by rafters with floor; ashlar masonry. [prec. +-ING¹]

ashōre', adv. To, on to, on, shore. [A prep.]

ǎsh'y, a. Of ashes; covered with ashes; ash-coloured, pale. [ASH²+-Y²]

Asiāt'ic (ǎshǐ-), a. & n. (Native) of Asia. [f. L f. Gk Asiātikos (Asiātēs f. Asia, see -IC]

aside', adv. & n. 1. To, on, one side, away; set ~, quash (verdict); speak ~ (apart, in privacy). 2. n. Words spoken ~, esp. spoken by an actor & supposed not to be heard by other performers; indirect effort. [orig. on side, see A prep.]

ǎs'inine, a. Pertaining to asses; stupid. Hence ǎsinin'ITY n. [f. L asininus (asinus ass, -INE¹)]

-asis, suf. forming names of diseases, [L -asis f. Gk -āsis in nouns of state f. vbs in -aō]

ask (ah-), v.t. & i. Call for an answer to, ~ (him) a question, ~ (him) this, ~ (him) who it is, ~ him the time, ~ a question of a person, ~ him about a thing; make a request (for), ~ a favour of him, ~ (him) a favour, ~ (him) for it, ask (abs.), ~ him to do it, ~ that it may be done, ~ to dinner etc., ~ to dinner one; invite (person to dinner etc., or out); (of things) demand, require, as it ~s (for) attention; ~ (publish) the banns; (top,) be ~ed in church, have one's banns called; ~ for trouble, ~ for it (sl.), court trouble. [com.-Teut.; OE āscian, ME ax ax ax ask esk ask ass, etc.; ax was usu. literary form to 1600]

askance', -ânt', adv. Sideways, asquint; with indirect meaning; look ~ at, view suspiciously. [?]

aŝkar'i (-ahr-), n. European-trained African native soldier. [Arab. *'askarî* soldier; pl. occas. as sing.]

askew', adv. & pred. a. Obliquely; *look ~* (not straight in the face); (adj.) oblique. [etym. dub., cf. SKEW]

aslant' (-ahnt), adv. & prep. Obliquely; (prep.) slantingly across, athwart. [A prep.+SLANT]

asleep', adv. & pred. a. In, into, a state of sleep (lit. & fig.); (of limbs) benumbed; (of top) spinning without apparent motion. [A prep.+SLEEP]

aslope', adv. & pred. a. Sloping, cross-wise. [prob. f. OE *aslopen* p.p. of *aslopan* slip away]

asp[1], n. (also **aspen**). Kind of poplar with specially tremulous leaves. [com.-Teut.; OE *æspe, æps*, G *espe*]

asp[2], n. Small venomous hooded serpent of Egypt and Libya; (poet.) any venomous serpent. [f. L.f. Gk *aspis*]

aspa'ragus, n. Plant, whose vernal shoots are a table delicacy. [L, f. Gk *asparagos*, etym. dub.; earlier *sperage, sparagus, sparrow-grass*]

as'pĕct, n. Way of looking; a looking, fronting, in a given direction; side so fronting; phase; look, expression; appearance (esp. to the mind). [f. L *aspectus -ûs* (*aspicere -spect-* look at)]

as'pĕn, a. & n. Of, like, the asp (tree); quivering; (n.) = ASP[1]. [ASP[1]+-EN[?]; wrongly taken as noun used attrib. in *aspen leaf* etc.]

aspergill'um, n. Brush for sprinkling holy water. [L, f. *aspergere* (*ad* to+*spargere* sprinkle)+*-illum* dim. suf.]

aspĕr'itý, n. Roughness; rough excrescence; severity (of weather); harshness, sharpness, (of temper). [f. OF *asperité* f. L *asperitatem* (*asper* rough, see -TY)]

aspĕrse', v.t. Besprinkle (*with*); bespatter (person, character, *with* damaging reports); calumniate. So **aspĕr'sion** (-shn) n. [f. L *aspergere -ers-*, see ASPER-GILLUM]

aspĕrsoir'ium, n. Vessel for holy water. [med. L (as prec., see -ORY)]

as'phält[1], n. A smooth hard bituminous substance; mixture of bitumen, pitch, & sand, for pavements etc.; similar mixture of coal-tar with sand etc. Hence **asphält'ic** a. [f. Gk *asphaltos*, of foreign orig.]

as'phält[2], v.t. Lay (road) with asphalt. [f. prec.]

as'phod'el, n. Genus of liliaceous plants; (poet.) immortal flower in Elysium. [f. L f. Gk *asphodelos*, etym. dub.; earlier *affodil*, whence DAFFODIL]

asphyx'ia, -x'ÿ, n. Suspended animation due to lack of oxygen in blood, suffocation. Hence **~AL** a., **~ATE**[2] v.t. [f. Gk *asphuxia* (*a-* not+*sphuxis* pulse)]

asp'ic[1], n. (poet.). = ASP[2]. [F, f. L *aspi-dem*, nom. *-îs*, w. unexpl. *-îc*]

asp'ic[2], n. Savoury meat jelly with cold game, eggs, etc., in it. [F, etym. dub.]

aspidis'tra, n. Foliage plant with broad taper leaves. [mod. L f. Gk *aspis* shield]

as'pirant (or aspîr-), a. & n. (One) who aspires (*to, after, for*). [F, as foll., see -ANT]

asp'irate[1], a. & n. (Consonant) pronounced with a breathing, blended with sound of *h*; the sound of *h*. [f. L *aspirare*, see ASPIRE and -ATE[2]]

asp'irate[2], v.t. Pronounce with a breathing; draw out (gas) from vessel. [as prec., see -ATE[3]]

aspira'tion, n. Drawing of breath; desire (*for, after*); action of aspirating. [f. L *aspiratio* (as prec., see -ATION)]

asp'irator, n. Apparatus for drawing air, gas, through tube; instrument for drawing pus from abscesses; winnowing machine. [f. L *aspirare*, see foll. and -OR[2]]

aspire', v.i. Desire earnestly (*to, after, at, to* do, or abs.); mount up (usu. fig.). [f. L *aspirare* breathe)]

asp'irin, n. An analgetic & febrifuge. [P]

asquint', adv. & pred. a. (With *look* or similar vb) obliquely, out at the corner of the eyes (esp. through defect in the eyes), *astinus*]

ass[1] (or ahs), n. Quadruped of horse family with long ears & tuft at end of tail (used esp. as type of ignorance, stupidity, etc.); *make an ~ of*, stultify (oneself, or another); *Asses' bridge* (Pons Asinorum, Euclid I. 5. [OE has isolated form *assa*, as well as *esol* for com.-Teut. *esil* f. L *asinus*]

ass[2] **agai, -segai**, (-gi), n. Slender spear of hard wood, esp. a missile of S. African tribes. [f. F *azagaie* f. Arab. *azzaghayah* (*al* the+Berber word *zaghayah*)]

assai', (-sah-ê), adv. (mus.). Very. [It.]

assail', v.t. Make hostile attack upon (lit. & fig.); approach resolutely (task); overwhelm (*with* questions etc.). Hence **~ABLE** a., **~ANT** n. [f. OF *asalir, assaillir*, f. med.L *assalire* (L *assilire -sult-* leap at)]

assas'sin, n. One who undertakes to kill treacherously; (Hist.) Moslem fanatic in time of Crusades, sent by the Old Man of the Mountains to murder Christians. [F, f. med. L *assassinus* f. Arab. *hashshash, hashishiyy* hashish-eater]

assas'sinate, v.t. Kill by treacherous violence. Hence **~ATION, ~ATOR**[2], nn. [f. med. L *assassinare* (*assassinus*), see prec. and -ATE[3]]

assault', n. Hostile attack (lit. & fig.); *~ of, at, arms*, attack in fencing, display of military exercises; rush against walls of fortress etc., as *carry by ~*; (Law) unlawful personal attack (including menacing words), as *~ & battery*. [f. OF *assaut* f. LL *adsaltus* (as ASSAIL)]

assault'², v.t. Make violent attack upon (lit. & fig.); assail; attack (fortress) by sudden rush. Hence ~ABLE a. [f. OF *asauter* f. Rom. *assaltare* spring at, for L AD*sultare* frequent. of *salire salt-* leap)]

assay'¹, n. Trial of metals, esp. of fineness of coin or bullion; metal to be so tried; (arch.) attempt. [OF, f. L *exagium* weighing (*exigere*, *-agere*, weigh, try)]

assay'², v.t. & i. Try the purity of (precious metals, also fig.); attempt (anything difficult, *to do*). Hence ~ABLE a. [f. OF *asayer*, *essayer*, f. LL *exagiare* (*exagium*, see prec.)]

assem'blage, n. Bringing, coming, together; concourse of persons; collection. [F (*assembler*, see foll. and -AGE]

assem'ble, v.t. & i. Gather together, collect; (Mech.) fit together the parts of (machine, structure). [f. OF *asembler* f. L *assimulare* in the (late) sense of bring together (*simul*)]

assem'bly, n. Gathering together, concourse, esp. deliberative body, legislative council, (*Indian Legislative A~*, lower chamber of Indian legislature); military call by drum or bugle; assembling a machine or its parts; ~ *room*: room in which balls etc. are given; (also ~ *shop*) place where a machine or its parts are assembled. [f. OF *asemblée* fem. p.p. of *asembler*, see prec.]

assent'¹, v.i. Agree (*to* proposal), sanction, (*to* a desire); express agreement (*to* statement or opinion, or abs.). Hence ~OR² n. [f. OF *asenter* f. L *assentari*, irreg. frequent. of *assentiri* agree to (*sentire* think)]

assent'², n. (Official) concurrence, sanction, as *royal ~* (of sovereign to bill passed by Parliament); mental acceptance. [F, OF *asente* (*asenter*, see prec.)]

assenta'tion, n. Obsequious concurrence. [F, f. L *assentationem* (as ASSENT, see -ATION)]

assen'tient (-shi-), a. & n. (Person) that assents. [f. L as ASSENT, see -ENT]

assert', v.t. Vindicate a claim to (rights); ~ *oneself*, insist upon one's rights; declare. Hence ~ABLE, ~IVE, aa., ~IVELY² (-vl-) adv., ~IVENESS (-vn-) n. [f. L AS(*serere sert-* join) put one's hand on slave's head to free him (whence obs. sense 'free' in E) or claim him, claim, affirm]

asser'tion, n. Insistence upon a right; *self-~*, insistence on recognition of one's claims; affirmation, positive statement. [f. L *assertio* (as prec., see -ION)]

assert'or, n. One who asserts; champion, advocate, (*of*). [L (as prec., see -OR²]

assess', v.t. Fix amount of (taxes, fine); fix amount of & impose (*upon* person or community); fine, tax, (person, community, property, *in*, *at*, so much); estimate value of (property) for taxation. Hence ~ABLE a., ~ABLY² adv., ~MENT n.

[f. OF *assesser* f. LL *assessare* frequent. of AS(*sidēre sess-* = *sedēre* sit)]

assess'or, n. One who sits as assistant, adviser, to judge or magistrate; one who assesses taxes or estimates value of property for taxation. [f. OF *assessour* f. L *assessorem* assistant-judge (as prec., see -OR²]

ass'ets, n. pl. (sing. *-et*). (Law) enough goods to enable heir to discharge debts & legacies of testator; property liable to be so applied; effects of insolvent debtor; property of person or company that may be made liable for debts; (sing.) item of this in balance-sheet, (loosely) any possession, (improp.) any useful quality. [f. AF *asetz* f. OF *asez* enough f. LL *ad satis* to sufficiency]

assěv'erⁱāte, v.t. Solemnly declare. So ~A'TION n. [f. L *asseverare* (*severus* serious), see -ATE³]

assib'ilāte, v.t. Give a hissing sound to. Hence ~A'TION n. [f. L *assibilare* hiss, see -ATE³]

assidu'ity, n. Close attention; (pl.) constant attentions. [f. L *assiduitas* (*assiduus*, see foll. and -TY]

assid'uous, a. Persevering, diligent. Hence ~LY² adv., ~NESS n. [f. L *assiduus* (as ASSESS) +-OUS]

assign'¹ (-īn), v.t. Allot as a share (*to*); make over (esp. personal property, *to*); appoint (place etc. *to*); fix, specify; ascribe, refer, (event *to* date); ascribe (reason *to*, *for*, thing). Hence ~ABLE (-īn-) a., ~MENT (-īn-) n. [f. OF *assigner* f. L *assignare* mark out to (*signum* sign)]

assign'² (-īn), n. One to whom property, right, is legally transferred. [ME *assigne* (three syllables) f. F *assigné* p.p. of *assigner* (see prec.) gives both *assim* & *assignee*]

ass'ignāt, n. Paper money issued by revolutionary government of France. [F, f. L *assignatum*, neut. p.p. of *assignare* assign]

assignā'tion, n. Apportionment; formal transference; appointment (of time & place); attribution of origin. [f. OF *assignacion* f. L *assignationem* (as ASSIGN¹, see -ATION)]

assignee' (-īn-), n. One appointed to act for another; assign; ~ *in bankruptcy*, persons charged with management of bankrupt's estate. [f. OF *a(s)signé*, see ASSIGN n.]

assign'ment (-īn-), n. Allotment; legal transference; document effecting this; attribution; statement (of reasons); *task* allotted to person. [f. OF *assignement* f. med. L *assignamentum* (as ASSIGN¹, see -MENT)]

assim'ilⁱāte, v.t. & i. Make like (*to*, *with*); compare (*to*, *with*); absorb into the system (lit. & fig.); (intr.) be so absorbed. Hence or cogn. ~ABIL'TY², ~A'TION, ~ātOR², nn., ~ABLE, ~āTIVE, ~ātORY, aa. [f. L AS*simulare* (*similis* like), see -ATE³]

assist', v.t. & i., & n. 1. Help (person, process, person in doing), whence ~ANT a. & n., ~ANCE n. 2. v.i. Take part (in); be present (at). 3. n. *(Baseball) score credited to fielder who stops & throws in the ball to player nearest the base to which an opponent is running, so helping to put him out. [f. F assister f. L assistere take one's stand by]

assize', n. Statutory price (of bread and ale); trial in which sworn assessors decide questions of fact; ||esp. periodical sessions in each county of England for administration of civil & criminal justice; great ~, last judgement. [f. OF assise, fem. sing. p.p. (as n.) of asseoir sit at f. L assidēre, cf. ASSESS]

assō'ciable (-sha-), a. That can be connected in thought (with). Hence ~ABILITY n. [f. f. associer (as foll., see -ABLE)]

assō'ciate[1] (-shi-), a. & n. 1. Joined in companionship, function, or dignity; allied. 2. n. Partner; companion; colleague; subordinate member of an association; thing connected with another. Hence ~SHIP n. [f. L. Associare (socius sharing, allied), see -ATE[2]]

assō'ciate[2] (-shi-), v.t. & i. Join (persons, things, or one with another); connect in idea; make oneself a partner in (a matter); (intr.) combine for common purpose; have intercourse (with). Hence ~IVE, ~ONY, &a., ~OR[2] n. [as prec., see -ATE[3]]

associā'tion, n. Act of associating (in all senses); organized body of persons; || deed of ~, document giving particulars of limited liability company; fellowship, intimacy; ~ of ideas, mental connexion between an object & ideas related to it; || ~ football (abbr. soccer), kind played with round ball, which must not be handled (cf. RUGBY). Hence ~ associātio (as prec., see -ATION)]

assoil', v.t. (arch.). Absolve from sin, pardon; acquit; release; atone for. [f. OF assoil, assoille, pres. ind. & subj. of assoudre f. L AB(solvere loose); Sc. has assoilzie (pron. -yī) still used in sense 'acquit')]

ass'onance, n. Resemblance of sound between two syllables; rhyming of one word with another in the accented vowel & those that follow, but not in the consonants (e.g. sonnet, porridge); partial correspondence. So ~ANT a. [f., f. L Assonare respond to (sonus sound), see -ANCE]

assort', v.t.&i. Classify, arrange in sorts; group with others; furnish (store, shop) with an assortment; (intr.) associate with; fall into a class; suit well or ill with. [f. OF assortir (à to +sorte SORT)]

assort'ment, n. Assorting; assorted set of goods of one or several classes. [-MENT]

assuage' (-sw-), v.t. Calm, soothe, (person, feelings, pain); appease (appetite, desire). Hence ~MENT (aswāj'm-) n. [f. OF assouager f. L +Assuaviare (suavis sweet)]

assume', v.t. Take upon oneself (aspect, air); ~ing, taking much upon oneself, arrogant; undertake (office, duty); usurp; simulate; take for granted, suppose; thing to be, that). Hence ~MME a., ~ABLY adv. [f. L AS(sumere sumpt- take)]

assump'tion, n. Act of assuming (in all senses); (A~) reception of Virgin Mary into heaven, feast in honour of this; thing assumed; arrogance. [f. L assumptio (as ASSUME, see -ION)]

assump'tive a. Taken for granted; arrogant. [f. L assumptivus (as prec., see -IVE)]

assur'ance (ashoor-), n. Formal guarantee; positive declaration; (Law) securing of a title; compact securing value of property in the event of its being lost, or payment of specified sum on person's death (usu. life~, fire~, marine~, insurance); certainty (make ~ double sure, remove all possible doubt, Shaksp., Macb. IV. i. 83); self-confidence; impudence. [f. OF aseürer f. LL ADsecurare, see foll. & -ANCE]

assure' (ashoor-), v.t. Make safe; ~ life (see prec.); make certain, ensure the happening etc. of; make (person) sure (of fact); tell (person) confidently (of a thing, of its being so, that it is so). Hence assur'ēDLY[2] adv., assur'EDNESS n. (securus safe)]

assur'gent, a. Rising; (Bot.) rising obliquely; aggressive. [f. L Assurgere rise, see -ENT]

Assyriŏl'ogy, n. Study of language, history, antiquities, of Assyria. Hence ~L'OGIST n. [f. L f. Gk Assuriā +-LOGY]

astat'ic, a. Not tending to keep one position; ~ galvanometer, one in which the effect on the needle of the earth's magnetic field is greatly reduced; ~ needle (unaffected by earth's magnetism). [f. Gk astatos unstable (a- not +sta- stand) +-IC]

ås'ter, n. Genus of plants with showy radiated flowers; China ~, flower allied to this. [f. L, f. Gk astēr star]

ås'terisk, n. Mark (*) used to mark words for reference or distinction; v.t. mark with ~. [f. L f. Gk asteriskos dim of astēr]

ås'terism, n. Cluster of stars; three asterisks (***), calling attention. [f. Gk asterismos (ASTER, see -ISM)]

astern', adv. (naut.). In, at, the stern; away behind; ~ of, behind (a ship, boat); backwards. [A prep. +STERN[2]]

ås'teroid, n. & a. 1. Star-shaped. 2. n. Name of small planets revolving round

sun between orbits of Mars and Jupiter; kind of firework. Hence ~AL (-oid²) a. [f. Gk *asteroeidēs* (ASTER, see -OID)]

ăsth'ma (-sm-), n. A disease of respiration, characterized by difficult breathing, cough, etc. [Gk *asthma -matos* (*azō* breathe hard, see -M)]

ăsthmăt'ic (-sm-), a. & n. Pertaining to, suffering from, good against, asthma; (n.) person suffering from asthma. Hence ~AL a., ~ALlY² adv. [f. Gk *asthmatikos* (as prec., see -IC-)]

‖**ăsthŏre'**, n. (voc.). Darling. [Ir., voc. of *stór* treasure]

astig'matism, n. Structural defect in the eye or a lens, preventing rays of light from being brought to common focus. So **ăstigmăt'ic** a. [f. Gk *a-* not + *stigma -matos* point + -IC]

astir', adv. & pred. a. In motion; out of bed; in excitement. [A prep. + STIR n.]

astŏn'ish, v.t. Amaze, surprise; *astonished* (arch. p.p. of *astony*, see etym.), dazed, dismayed. Hence ~MENT n. [altered f. obs. *astony* unexpl. form of obs. *astone* apparently f. OF *estoner, estuner* (mod. *étonner*), stupefy, shock, f. L *EXtonare (cf. L *ăttonare* strike with thunderbolt, stun); relation to STUN and G *staunen* is uncertain]

astound', v.t. Shock with alarm or surprise; amaze. [f. obs. *astound* a. = *astoned* p.p. of obs. *astone*, see prec.]

astrăd'dle, adv. & pred. a. In a straddling position. [A prep. + STRADDLE v.]

ăs'tragal, n. (Archit.) small moulding round top or bottom of columns; (Gunnery) ring round cannon near mouth. [f. foll.]

astrăg'alus, n. Ball of ankle-joint; genus of leguminous plants including milk-vetch. [L, f. Gk *astragalos* huckle-bone, moulding, plant]

ăstrakhăn' (-kăn), n. Skin of young lambs from Astrakhan in Russia, with wool like fur.

ăs'tral, a. Connected with, consisting of, stars; ~ *spirits* (supposed to live in stars); ~ *body*, spiritual appearance of the human form; ~ *hatch*, dome-shaped window in aircraft through which the navigator takes astronomical observations; ~ *lamp* (throwing no shadow on table below). [f. L *astralis* (*astrum* star, see -AL)]

astray', adv. or pred. a. Out of the right way (lit. & fig.). Out of *estraié* p.p. of *estraier* f. L *extravagare wander out of bounds; but confused w. forms like *a-float, a-sleep*; no early noun *stray*]

astrict', v.t. (rare). Bind tightly; make costive; bind morally, legally; restrict (*to*). So **astric'tion** n. [f. L *astringere -ict-* (*ad* to + *stringere* bind)]

astric'tive, a. Tending to contract organic tissue; astringent, styptic. [as prec., see -IVE]

astride', adv., pred. a., & prep. In striding position; with legs on each side (*of*); ~ *of the road* etc., (Mil.) posted across it; (prep.) ~ *of*. [A prep. + STRIDE n.]

astringe' (-nj), v.t. Bind together; compress; constipate. [as ASTRICT]

astrin'gent (-nj-), a. & n. Binding, styptic; severe; austere; (n.) ~ medicine. Hence ~LY² adv., **astrin'gENCY** n. [as prec., see -ENT]

astro-, in comb. = Gk *astron* star; in wds f. Gk, as ASTRONOMY, & mod. formations as **astróg'onÿ**, stellar cosmogony, **ăstro-lĭthŏl'ogÿ**, study of meteoric stones; **ăs'trodōme**, **ăs'trohătch**, = ASTRAL *hatch*; **ăstrophўs'ics**, branch of astronomy dealing with the physical properties & chemical composition of the heavenly bodies.

ăs'troïte, n. Gem known to the ancients; kind of madrepore. [f. L *astroïtes* (see prec. and -ITE)]

ăs'trolābe, n. Instrument formerly used for taking altitudes etc. [f. OF *astrelabe* f. med. L *astrolabium* f. Gk ASTRO- (*lab-* take)]

astrŏl'ogÿ, n. (Formerly) practical astronomy (also called *natural* ~); art of judging of reputed occult influence of stars upon human affairs (*judicial* ~). So **astrŏl'ogER** n., **astrŏlŏ'gic(AL)** aa., **astrŏlŏ'gicallÿ²** adv. [f. F *astrologie* f. L f. Gk ASTRO(*logia* -LOGY)]

astrŏn'omÿ, n. Science of the heavenly bodies. So ~ER¹ (3) n., student of ~y, **astronŏm'IC(AL)** aa. (~*ical figures, distances*, as enormous as those familiar to ~ers), **astronŏm'icallÿ²** adv. [f. OF *astronomie* f. L f. Gk *astronomia* f. ASTRO-*nomos* a. star-arranging (*nemō* arrange)]

astūte', a. Shrewd, sagacious; crafty. Hence ~LY² (-tl-) adv., ~NESS (-tn-) n. [f. L *astutus* length. form of *astus* crafty]

asŭn'der, adv. (Of two or more things) apart in motion or position); *tear* ~, tear to pieces. [OE *on sundram*, see A prep. & SUNDER]

asȳl'um, n. Sanctuary, place of refuge, esp. for criminals or debtors; shelter, refuge; institution for shelter & support of afflicted or destitute persons, esp. lunatics (now *mental home*). [L, f. Gk *asulon* neut. of adj. *asulos* inviolable (*a-* not + *sulē* right of seizure)]

asȳm'metrȳ, n. Want of symmetry. [A- (7) + SYMMETRY]

ăsȳmptōte, n. Line that approaches nearer & nearer to given curve but does not meet it within a finite distance. [f. Gk *asumptōtos* not falling together (*a-* not + *sum-* together + *ptōtos* falling f. *piptō*)]

asȳn'dĕton, n. (pl. *-ta*). A rhetorical figure that omits the conjunction. [f. Gk *asundeton* unconnected (*a-* not + *sundetos* f. *sundeō* bind together)]

ăt¹ (or ăt), prep. **1.** Expressing exact, approximate, or vague position, lit. &

fig., as *meet at a point, wait at the corner*; *at the top, at Bath* (or any town except London and that in which the speaker is), *at school, at sea, at a distance, at arm's length, out at elbows, at work, at dinner, play at fighting, good at repartee, at daggers drawn, at a disadvantage, at his mercy, at all events, annoyed at finding, impatient at delay*; *at 10 High Street*, = c/o Mr. A., 10 High Street. 2. Expr. motion towards, lit. & fig., as *arrive at a place, get, rush, shoot, laugh, grumble, hint, snatch, aim, at*. 3. *At all*, in any degree (in neg. contexts); *at best, worst*, assuming best, worst, result etc.; *at one*, in harmony or agreement (*with*); *at that*, at that estimate (*will take it at that*, accept that account of the matter); moreover, into the bargain (*lost it, & at that*). [com.-Teut., but lost in G & Du.; OE *æt*, cogn. w. L *ad*]

||**At²** (ät), n. (colloq.). Member of the (Women's) Auxiliary Territorial Service. [f. initials A.T.S. (äts) treated as pl.]

at-, pref. = AD- before t.

ă'taraxy, -ăx'ia, n. Stoical indifference. [Gk *ataraxia* (*a-* not + *tarassō* disturb)]

ătaun'tō, adv. (naut.). With all sails set; *all* ~, shipshape & Bristol fashion. [f. F *autant à*?]

ă'tavism, n. Resemblance to remote ancestors, reversion to earlier type; recurrence of disease after intermission of generations. Hence **ătavis'tic** [-IST, -IC] a. [f. F *atavisme* f. L *atavus* great-grandfather; see -ISM]

ătăx'ic, a. Characterized by ataxy.

ătăx'y, n. Irregularity of animal functions; *locomotor* ~, constitutional unsteadiness in use of legs, arms, etc. [f. Gk *ataxia* (*a-* not + *taxis* order f. *tassō* arrange)]

ate. See EAT.

-ate¹, suf. forming nn. orig. f. L *-ātus* (gen. *-ūs*) in nouns of state from p.p. stems of vbs, in OF became *-é* (*-ée*), but in learned words, & later in many reformed words, *-at*, as *prelāt, primāt, magistrāt*. E having adopted *-at* afterwards added *-e* to mark quantity of α, & later words took *-āte* at once. E also formed wds either directly on L as *curvāte* or by anal. as *aldermanāte*. Most nn. in *-āte* are (1) nn. of office, as *marquisāte, syndicāte*, (2) participial nn. as *legāte* one formed; (3) chem. terms denoting salts formed by action of an acid on a base, as *nitrāte, sulphāte*.

-ate², suf. forming adji. (1) chiefly (thr. F) f. L L p.p. in *-ātus* (1st conjug.), which (cf. prec.) became successively *-at, -āte*, as *desolāte*. Many such adji. formed

causative vbs (see foll.) & served as p.p. to them, till later the native *-ed* was added; *-ated* also appears without intervention of vb, as *annulated*, and as alternative form to *-ate*; (2) L participial adji. were also formed on nn. as *caudatus* tailed, & on adji. as *candidatus* white-robed; these were largely adopted in E, & others formed on anal. Many nouns in -ATE¹ were orig. adji. In *corslate, ornate*, etc., the sense is 'shaped like'.

-ate³, suf. forming vbs to correspond to adji. in -ATE² and subsequently to repr. the corresp. L vb in *-are* (p.p. *-ātus*), as *separāte, aggravāte*. As these vbs usu. have F equivalents in *-er, -āte* was further used to form vbs on model of F vbs in *-er* as *isolate* (F *isoler*). *-āte* was also used to form vbs that L might have formed, but did not, on nouns, as *felicitate* (L *felicitas -ātis*), & even vbs on nouns not of L orig., as *camphorate*.

atelier (see AP.) n. Workshop, studio. [F]

ăt'elo- in comb. = Gk *atelēs* imperfect (*a-* not + *telos* end). as *-glossia, -gnathia, -stomia*, imperfect development of tongue, jaws, mouth.

Athana'sian (ă-, -shn), a. Of Athanasius (archbishop of Alexandria in reign of Constantine), as ~ *creed* (that beginning *Whosoever will*). [f. *Athanasius* + -AN]

ăth'eism, n. Disbelief in the existence of a God; godlessness. So ~IST n., ~IS'TIC a., ~IS'TICALLY adv. [f. F *athéisme* f. Gk *atheos* without God (*a-* not + *theos* God), see -ISM]

athirst', pred. a. Thirsty; eager (*for, after*). [OE *ofthyrst* for *ofthyrsted* p.p. of *ofthyrstan* be thirsty]

ăth'lēte, n. Competitor in physical exercises; robust, vigorous, man. [f. L *athlēta* f. Gk *athlētēs* f. *athleō* contend for prize (*athlon*, see -ETE]

ăthlēt'ic, a. & n. Pertaining to athletes; physically powerful; (n. pl.) practice of physical exercises. Hence ~ICALLY adv., ~ICISM n. [f. L f. Gk *athlētikos* (as prec.)]

at-hōme', n. Reception of visitors within certain hours during which host or hostess or both have announced that they will be at home.

athwart' (-ôrt), adv. & prep. Across from side to side (usu. oblique); crosswise, perversely; in opposition to; (of ship) ~ *hawse*, across stem of another ship at anchor. [A prep. + THWART]

-atic, adj. suf. (=F *-atique*) f. L *-āticus* (orig. *-at-* of p.p. stems + -IC, but extended to nouns as *fanaticus* f. *fanum*, which gives also -AGE; in many nouns formations, as *lunatic, lymphatic*; but in many apparent exx. (*dramatic, piratic*) the suf. is -ic, & *-at-* part of the stem.

-atile, adj. suf. like -ATIO in orig., & use =-*at*-+-ILE, as *volatile, fluviatile.*

a-tilt', adv. Tilted; *run, ride,* ~ (in encounter on horseback with thrust of lance, usu. fig.). [A prep.+TILT]

-a'tion, suf. (=-*at*- of L 1st conj. p.p. stems +-ION) forming abstract nouns on L 1st conj. vbs as *agitation*, Gk vbs in -*izō* (L -*izare* -IZE) as *organization*, F vbs in -*er* as *filtration*, & rarely E vbs as *starvation*, the last on false anal. f. *vexation* etc., formed on L *vexare*, not on E *vex*. The great preponderance of -*ation* over -*ition* etc. is due to F adoption of the -*er* vb (=L 1st conj.) as the type for all new vbs. Wds taken f. OF have often -*ison*, -*son*, (*orison, reason*) instead of -*ation*. Most wds have vb in -*ate* corresp. (*creation*), many a shortened vb f. L 1st conj. (*plantation, plant*, not *plantate*; *modify*, not *modificate*), a few no vb (*duration*). Meanings: (1) vbl action; (2) instance of this; (3) resulting state; (4) concrete result (*plantation*).

-ative, adj. suf. =-*at*-+-IVE (cf. -ATIO): most exx. are f. vbs in -*ate* as *demonstrative*, or L 1st conj. as *affirmative*, some f. nouns in -TY (L st. -*tat*-) as *authoritative*, & some on E vbs as *talkative*.

atlan'tes (-ēz) n. pl. (archit.). Sculptured male figures serving as pillars. [Gk, pl. of ATLAS]

Atlan'tic, a. & n. 1. Pertaining to mount Atlas in Libya; hence applied to sea near western shore of Africa, & later to whole ocean between Europe & Africa on east & America on west. 2. n. ~ ocean. [f. L f. Gk *Atlantikos* f. ATLAS]

atlan'tosaur'us, n. (palaeont.). (Kinds of) gigantic fossil reptile. [f. ATLAS+Gk *sauros* lizard]

at'las, n. Volume of maps; large size of drawing paper; (Physiol.) uppermost cervical vertebra, supporting skull. [*Atlas -antos* (1) Greek god of the older family, who held up pillars of universe; (2) the mountain in Libya, regarded as supporting the heavens]

atmo- in comp.=Gk *atmos* vapour, as *atmŏl'ogў*, science of aqueous vapour, *atmŏl'ysis*, separation of vapours, *atmŏm'ēter* (for measuring evaporation).

at'mosphere, n. Spheroidal gaseous envelope surrounding heavenly body; that surrounding earth; one surrounding any substance; mental or moral environment; air (in any place); (w. pl.) pressure of 15 lb. on square inch (that exerted by ~ on earth's surface). Hence **ătmosphē'rĭc(al)** aa., **ătmosphē'rĭcalLY²** adv.; **ătmosphē'rĭcs** n. pl., interference with wireless reception due to electric disturbance in ~. [f. ATMO-+Gk *sphaira* ball]

atŏll' (or ăt'ŏl), n. Ring-shaped coral reef enclosing lagoon. [Maldive *atollon, atoll*, Drob.=Malayalam *adal* closing]

at'om, n. 1. Body too small to be divided; *physical* ~, supposed ultimate particle of matter (now held to consist of a positively charged nucleus, in which is concentrated most of the mass of the ~, round which revolve negatively charged electrons); *chemical* ~s, smallest particles in which elements combine with themselves or with each other; ~ *bomb*, ATOMIC *bomb*. 2. Minute portion; small thing. [f. F *atome* f. L f. Gk *atomos* indivisible (*a*- not+-*tomos* cut f. *temnō*]

atŏm'ĭc, a. Of, relating to, an atom or atoms; ~ *bomb* (deriving its destructiveness from the disintegration and partial conversion into energy of uranium *atoms*); ~ *number*, (of a chemical element) number of unit positive charges carried by the nucleus of its atom; ~ *philosophy*, doctrine of formation of all things from indivisible particles endued with gravity & motion; (Chem.) ~ *theory* (that elemental bodies consist of indivisible atoms of different elements unite with each other in fixed proportions, which determine the proportions in which elements & compounds enter into chemical combination); ~ *weight*, (now usu.) ratio between the weight of one atom of the element & $\frac{1}{16}$ of the weight of an atom of oxygen, (formerly) weight of an atom of the element as compared with that of an atom of hydrogen. Hence ~**AL** a., ~**alLY²** adv. [prec.+-IC]

ătŏmĭc'ĭtY, n. The number of atoms in the molecule of an element; (formerly) =VALENCY. [f. prec., see -TY]

ăt'omĭsm, n. Atomic philosophy; doctrine of action of individual atoms. [ATOM+-ISM]

ăt'omĭst, n. Holder of atomic theory or philosophy. Hence ~**ĭs'tĭc** a. [ATOM+-IST]

ăt'omĭze, v.t. Reduce to atoms. Hence ~**A'TION** n. (med.). [ATOM+-IZE]

ăt'omĭzer, n. Instrument for reducing liquids to fine spray. [prec.+-ER¹]

ăt'omў¹, n. Skeleton; emaciated body. [f. ANATOMY, *an-* being taken as article]

ăt'omў², n. Atom, tiny being. [f. *atomi* pl. of L *atomus* ATOM]

atŏn'al, a. (mus.). Not conforming to any system of key or mode. [A- (7)+TONAL]

atŏne', v.i. & t. 1. Make amends (esp. ~ *for*, explate). 2. v.t. (arch.). Reconcile (enemies), compose (quarrel). Hence ~**MENT** (-nm-) n. (*Day of Atonement*, most solemn religious fast of Jewish year.) [AT+ONE, =set at one, unite]

atŏn'ĭc, a. & n. Unaccented, unstressed word (esp. in Gk Gram.). [f. med. L *atonicus* f. Gk *atonos* toneless (*a*- not+*tomos* TONE, see -IC]

atŏp', adv. On the top (of). [A prep.]

ătrăbĭlˈious (-lyus), a. Affected by black bile; melancholy; acrimonious. Hence ~NESS n. [f. L atra bilis black bile +-OUS; after L biliosus bilious]

ātˈrip, adv. (Of anchor) just lifted from ground in weighing. [A prep.+TRIP]

āˈtrium, n. (pl. -a, -ums). Central court of Roman house; covered portico, esp. before church door. [L]

atrōˈcious (-shus), a. Heinously wicked; very bad, as ~ pun. Hence ~LY² adv., ~NESS n. [f. L atrox -ocis (ater black)+-OUS]

atrōˈcity, n. Heinous wickedness; atrocious deed; bad blunder. [f. L atrocitas (as prec., see -TY)]

ātˈrophy, n. Wasting away through imperfect nourishment; emaciation (lit. & fig.). Hence ātˈrophy v.t. & i. [f. F atrophie f. L f. Gk atrophiā f. atrophos ill-fed (a- not+trophē food)]

ătˈropine, n. Poisonous alkaloid found in deadly nightshade. [f. atropa deadly nightshade f. Gk Atropos inflexible, name of one of the Fates, see -INE⁵]

ătˈta, n. The common wheaten flour or meal of India. [Punjabi]

*ătˈtaboy, int. Exclamation expressive of encouragement or admiration. [corrupt, of that's the boy!]

attăch', v.t.& i. Fasten (thing to another); join oneself (to person, company, expedition); bind in friendship, make devoted, (has the gift of ~ing people to him; is deeply ~ed to her); affix (immaterial things, name, liability, etc., to); attribute (importance etc. to); (Law) seize (person, property) by legal authority; adhere, be incident, as no blame ~es to. Hence ~ABLE a. [f. OF atachier (mod. attacher, Genevese tache, Sp. and Port. tacha, nail, TACK]

attachē' (otǎsh'ā), n. One attached to ambassador's suite; ~ case, small rectangular valise ostensibly for carrying documents. [F, p.p. of attacher (as prec.)]

attăch'ment, n. Act of attaching; thing attached; means of attaching; affection; legal seizure, esp. foreign ~ (of foreigner's goods, to satisfy his creditors). [f. F attachement (attacher ATTACH, see -MENT)]

attăck'¹, v.t. Fall upon, assault, (lit. & fig.); (of physical agents or diseases) act destructively upon. Hence ~ABLE a. [f. F attaquer f. It. attaccare, see ATTACH]

attăck'², n. Act of attacking (lit. & fig.); offensive operation. [f. prec.]

attāin', v.t. & i. Arrive at, reach; gain, accomplish; (intr.)~ to, arrive at. Hence ~ABILˈITY n., ~ABLE a., ~ableness n. [f. OF ataign- st. of ataindre f. L attingere (tangere touch)]

attāin'der, n. Consequences of sentence of death or outlawry (forfeiture of estate, corruption of blood, extinction of civil rights). [OF ataindre ATTAIN used as n.:

meaning influenced by confus. w. OF taindre TAINT]

attāin'ment, n. Act of attaining; thing attained, esp. personal accomplishment. [ATTAIN+-MENT]

attāint', v.t. Subject to attainder; (of diseases etc.) strike, affect; infect; sully. [f. obs. attaint a. f. OF atteint p.p. as ATTAINT; confused in meaning with TAINT]

ăt'tar, n. Fragrant essential oil from rose-petals. [f. Pers. 'aṭar(-gul) essence (of roses) f. Arab. 'uṭur aroma f. 'aṭara breathe perfume]

attĕm'per, v.t. Quality by admixture; modify temperature of; soothe, mollify; accommodate to; attune to; temper (metal). Hence ~MENT n. [f. OF atemprer f. L attemperare]

attĕmpt'¹, v.t. Try (thing, action, to do); try to master (enemy, fortress); ~ the life of, try to kill. Hence ~ABLE a. [f. OF attempter, f. L attemptare strive after]

attĕmpt'², n. Attempting; endeavour. [f. prec.]

attĕnd', v.t. & i. Turn the mind to; apply oneself (to or abs.); be present (at); wait upon; (trans.) wait upon; escort, accompany; be present at (lecture etc.), [f. OF atendre f. L attendere -tent- stretch]

attĕn'dance, n. Act of attending (upon person, at lecture); dance ~ on, attend the convenience of; body of persons present. [f. OF atendance (as prec., see -ANCE)]

attĕn'dant, a. & n. 1. Waiting (upon) accompanying, as ~ circumstances; present, as ~ crowd. 2. n. Servant, satellite. [OF, part. as ATTEND]

attĕn'tion, n. & int. Act of attending, as pay, give, ~; faculty of attending, as attract, call, ~; consideration, care; (pl.) ceremonious politeness (pay one's ~s to, court); come to, stand at, ~ (military attitude; A~!, order to assume it). [f. L attentio (as ATTEND, see -ION)]

attĕn'tive, a. Heedful, observant; polite, assiduous. Hence ~LY² (-vl-) adv., ~NESS (-vn-) n. [F (-if, -ive), f. L as ATTEND]

attĕn'uāte¹, v.t. Make slender; make thin in consistence; reduce in force or value. So ~A'TION n. [f. L attenuare (tenuis thin), see -ATE³]

attĕn'uate², a. Slender; rarefied. [as prec., see -ATE²]

attĕst', v.t. & i. Testify, certify; put (person) on oath or solemn declaration; administer oath of allegiance to (recruit); (intr.) bear witness to. Hence ~OR² n. [f. F attester f. L attestari (testis witness)]

ăttestā'tion, n. Act of testifying; testimony; evidence; formal confirmation by signature, oath, etc.; administration of an oath. [F, f. L attestatio (as prec., see -ATION)]

Att'ic¹ (ăt-), a. & n. Of Athens or Attica;~ (dialect), Greek spoken by the Athenians

~ *salt*, *wit*, refined wit; ~ *order*, square column of any of the five ORDERS. [f. L f. Gk *Attikos*]

attĭc², n. Structure consisting of small order placed above another of greater height (usu. *Attic*); highest storey of house; room in this. [f. F *attique*, as prec.]

ăt'ticism, n. Style, idiom, of Athens; refined amenity of speech; attachment to Athens. So ~IZE (2) v.i. [f. Gk *attikismos*]

attire', v.t., & n. Dress, array. [(n. f. vb) f. OF *atirer* (*à* to +*tire*, see TIER)]

ăt'titude, n. Disposition of figure (in painting etc.); posture of body, as *strike an* ~ (assume it theatrically); settled behaviour, as indicating opinion; ~ *of mind*, settled mode of thinking. [F, f. It. *attitudine* fitness, posture, f. med. L *aptitudinem* (*aptus* fit, see -TUDE)]

ăttitūd'inize, v.i. Practise attitudes; speak, write, behave, affectedly. [f. prec. + -IZE]

attorn' (-ẽrn), v.t. & i. (law). Transfer; make legal acknowledgement of new landlord. Hence ~MENT n. [f. OF *atorner* (*à* to +*tourner* TURN)]

attorn'ey' (-tẽr-), n. One appointed to act for another in business or legal matters; *A~ General*, legal officer empowered to act in all cases in which the State is a party; *abuse plaintiff's* ~ (iron. advice to lawyer with a weak case). Hence ~SHIP n. [f. OF *atorné* p.p. as ATTORN]

attorn'ey² (-tẽr-), n. *Letter, warrant, of* ~ (by which person appoints another to act for him); *power of* ~, authority thus conferred. [f. OF *atorné* fem. p.p., see prec.]

attract', v.t. Draw to oneself (esp. of physical forces); excite the pleasurable emotions of (person); draw forth & fix upon oneself (attention etc.). Hence ~ABIL'ITY n., ~ABLE a. [f. L *attrahere tract-* draw)]

attrac'tion, n. Act, faculty, of drawing to oneself (lit. & fig.); drawing force; thing that attracts (fig.); ~ *of gravity* (existing between all bodies, & varying directly as their masses, inversely as the square of their distance apart); *magnetic, molecular* ~ (between molecules of bodies, acting only at infinitesimal distances); *capillary* ~ (by which liquid is drawn up through hairlike tube). [f. L *attractionem* (as prec., see -ION)]

attrac'tive, a. Attracting, capable of attracting (esp. fig.). Hence ~LY² (-vl-) adv., ~NESS (-vn-) n. [F (-*if*, -*ive*), as prec., see -IVE]

ăt'tribute¹, n. Quality ascribed to anything; material object recognized as appropriate to person or office; characteristic quality; (Gram.) attributive word. [f. L *attribuere -ut-* assign)]

attrĭb'ute², v.t. Ascribe as belonging or appropriate *to*; refer (effect *to* its cause); assign (*to* time or place). Hence ~ABLE a. [as prec.]

attrĭbū'tion, n. Act of attributing; authority granted (*to* a ruler etc.). [F, f. L *attributionem* (as prec., see -ION)]

attrĭb'ūtive, a. & n. **1.** (Logic) assigning an attribute to a subject; (Gram.) expressing an attribute (e.g. *old in the old dog but not in the dog is old*). **2.** n. Word denoting an attribute (usu. an adjective or its equivalent). Hence ~LY² (-vl-) adv. [F (-*if*, -*ive*), as ATTRIBUTE¹, see -IVE]

attrĭt'ed, a. Worn by friction. [f. L AT- (*terere trit-* rub)]

attrĭt'ion, n. Friction; wearing out (*war of* ~, turning on which side can last longest); abrasion; (Theol.) sorrow for sin (short of *contrition*). [f. L *attritio* (as prec., see -ION)]

attūne', v.t. Bring into musical accord (*to*, lit. & fig.); tune (instrument). [AT- + TUNE v.]

atyp'ical, a. Not conforming to type. [A- (7) +TYPICAL]

aubade (ōbahd'), n. Musical announcement of dawn. [F]

auberge (ōbãrzh'), n. Inn. [F]

aubriet'(i)a (ōbrēsh'a, ōbrēsh'a), (erron.) **-retia**, n. (Kinds of) spring-flowering dwarf perennial plant. [f. Claude Aubriet (French artist), see -IA¹]

aub'urn (-ẽrn), a. Golden-brown (usu. of hair). [f. OF *auborne* f. L *alburnus* whitish]

au courant (ō kŏŏ'rahn), pred. a, Acquainted *with* what is going on; well-informed. [F]

auc'tion, n. Public sale in which articles are sold to the highest of successive bidders; *Dutch* ~, sale in which price is reduced by auctioneer till a purchaser is found; ~ *bridge*, form of bridge in which players bid for right to play the hand. [f. L *auctio* increase, auction (*augēre auct-*, see -ION)]

auc'tioneer' (-shon-), n., &v.i. (One whose business is to) conduct auctions. [-EER]

audā'cious (-shus), a. Daring; bold; impudent. Hence ~LY² adv., ~NESS n., **audā'city** (-ăs-) n. [f. L *audax* (*audēre* dare, see -ACIOUS)]

aud'ible, a. Perceptible to the ear. Hence ~LY² adv., **audĭbil'ity**, ~leNESS (-ln-), nn. [f. med. L *audibilis* (*audīre* hear, see -BLE)]

aud'ience, n. Hearing; *give* ~, listen; formal interview; persons within hearing; assembly of listeners; (of a book) readers. [F (refash. on L), f. OF *oïance* f. L *audientia* (*audīre* hear, see -ENCE)]

aud'ile, a. & n. (Usu. of supernormal phenomena) received through the auditory nerves; (person) specially sensitive to auditory impressions. [irreg. f. L *audīre* hear + -ILE]

audióme'eter, n. Instrument for testing hearing-power. [f. L *audire* hear+-o-+-METER]

audi'phone, n. Instrument that, pressed against upper teeth, assists hearing. [improp. f. L *audire* hear+Gk *phōnē* sound, on *telephone*]

audi't, n. Official examination of accounts; searching examination, esp. Day of Judgement; periodical settlement of accounts between landlord & tenants; ~ *ale* (of special quality, brewed in English universities, orig. for use on day of ~); ~*house*, *-room* (attached to Cathedral for transaction of business). [f. L *auditus -ūs* hearing (*audire -it-*)]

audi't, v.t. Examine (accounts) officially. [f. prec.]

audi'tion, n. Power of hearing; listening; trial hearing of applicant for employment as singer etc. [f. L *auditio* (*audire -it-*, see -ION)]

audi'tive, a. Concerned with hearing. [f. (*-if, -ive*), as prec., see -IVE]

audi'tor, n. Listener; one who audits accounts. Hence ~ORSHIP, ~RESS¹, nn. [f. AF *auditour* f. L *auditor* (as prec., see -OR²)]

audito'rial, a. Connected with an audit. [f. L *auditorius* (as prec., see -ORY)+-AL]

audi'tory, a. & n. 1. Connected with hearing; received by the ear. 2. n. Assembly of hearers, audience; (now usu. **audito'rium**) part of building occupied by audience. [f. L *auditorius, -um* (as prec., see -ORY)]

au fait (ō fã'), pred. a. Conversant, instructed; *put a person* ~ *of*, instruct him in. [F]

au fond (ō fawn), adv. At bottom (cf. *à fond*). [F]

Auge'an, a. Filthy, like the stables of Augeas, which Hercules cleansed by turning river Alpheus through them. [f. L *Augeas* f. Gk *Augeias*+-AN]

auge'r (-g-), n. Tool for boring holes in wood, having long shank with cutting edge & screw point, & handle at right angles; instrument for boring in soil or strata, with stem that can be lengthened. [OE *nafugār* (*nafu* NAVE+*gār* piercer), cf. G *nāber*, Du. *avegaar*; for loss of *n*- cf. ADDER]

aught (awt), n. & adv. Anything; (adv., arch.) in any degree or respect. [OE *āwiht* (*ā* ever+*wiht* wight, whit); later OE *āht*, gives mod. *ought*, now less usu. form]

aug'ment, n. Vowel (in Sanskrit *a*, in Greek *ē*) prefixed to past tenses in the older Aryan languages. [F, f. L *augmentum* increase (*augēre*, see -MENT]

augme'nt¹, v.t. & i. Make greater, increase; prefix the augment to; (intr.) increase. [f. F *augmenter* f. L *augmentare* increase (*augmentum*, see prec.)]

augmenta'tion, n. Enlargement; growth, increase; addition; (Mus.) repetition of a passage in notes longer than those of the original. [OF, f. L *augmentationem* (*augmentare*, see prec. and -ATION]

augme'ntative, a. & n. Having the property of increasing; (Gram., of affixes or derived words) increasing in force the idea of the original word; (n.) ~ word. [F (*-if, -ive*), f. L as AUGMENT², see -ATIVE]

au grand sérieux (see Ap.), adv. Quite seriously (*take it, him*, etc., ~). [F]

aug'ur¹ (-er), n. Roman religious official who foretold future events by omens derived from the actions of birds, appearance of victims' entrails, celestial phenomena, etc.; soothsayer. Hence ~SHIP n. [L, perh. f. *avis* bird+*gar*, conn. w. *garrire* talk, Skr. *gar* shout, make known]

aug'ur², v.t. & i. Forebode, anticipate; ~ *well, ill*, have good or bad expectations of, for; *it* ~s (promises) *ill*. [f. prec.]

aug'ural, a. Pertaining to augurs; significant of the future. [f. L *auguralis* (AUGUR¹, see -AL)]

aug'ury, n. Divination by flight of birds etc.; augural ceremony; omen; presentiment; promise. [f. OF *augurie* f. L *augurium* (AUGUR¹)]

augu'st¹, a. Majestic, venerable. Hence **augu'st**LY² adv., ~NESS n. [f. L *augustus* consecrated; august, venerable, prob. f. AUGUR]

Aug'ust², n. Eighth month of year, named after Augustus Caesar. [earlier *Aust* f. OF *aoust* f. L *augustus* (see prec.), refash. on L]

Augu's'tan, a. & n. Connected with reign of Augustus Caesar, best period of Latin literature; (of any national literature) classical; ~ *confession* (drawn up by Luther & Melanchthon at Augusta Vindelicorum or Augsburg); (n.) writer of the ~ age of any literature. [f. L *Augustanus*, see -AN]

auk, n. Northern sea-bird, with short wings used only as paddles. [cogn. with Swed. *alka*, Da. *alke*, f. ON *álka*]

aul'ic, a. Pertaining to a court; *A~ Council*, (in old German empire) personal council of emperor, (later) council managing Austrian war-department. [f. F *aulique* f. L f. Gk *aulikos* (*aulē* court, see -IC)]

aum'bry, var. of AMBRY.

au naturel (see Ap.), adv. or pred. a. (Cooked) in the simplest way. [F]

aunt (ahnt), n. Father's, mother's, sister; uncle's wife; *A~ Sally*, game at fairs, in which players throw sticks at pipe in mouth of wooden woman's head. [f. OF *aunte* (Prov. *amda*) f. L *amita*; E up to 17th c. had also *naunt* (*my naunt* = *mine aunt*), still used in dial.; F *tante* perh. = *ta ante*]

au pair (ō pãr'), a. (Of arrangements between two parties) paid for by mutual services (no money passing). [F]

au pied de la lettre (ō pyã de lah lĕtr'), adv. Literally. [F]

aur'a, n. Subtle emanation (from flowers etc.); atmosphere diffused by or attending a person etc. (esp. in mystical use as a definite envelope of body or spirit); (Electr.) current of air caused by discharge of electricity from a sharp point; (Path.) sensation as of current of cold air rising from some part of body to head, premonitory symptom in epilepsy & hysterics. Hence aur'al¹ [-ᴀʟ] a. [L f. Gk, = breeze, breath]

aur'al², a. Pertaining to organ of hearing; received by the ear. Hence ~ʟʏ² adv. [f. L auris ear +-ᴀʟ]

aure'lia, n. (Formerly) chrysalis, esp. of butterfly; (Zool.) genus of phosphorescent marine animals. [It., = silkworm, fem. of aurelio golden f. L aurum gold]

aurel'ian, a. & n. Of an aurelia; golden; (n.) collector, breeder, of insects. [prec. +-ᴀɴ¹]

aure'ola, n. Aureola. (prop.) gold disk surrounding head in early pictures; circle of light depicted round head; oblong glory surrounding divine figures; actual halo, esp. that seen in eclipses. [f. prec.]

au revoir (ō revwahr'), adv. (Good-bye) till we meet again. [F]

auric'le, n. External ear of animals; process shaped like lower lobe of ear; either of the two upper cavities of the heart. Hence ~ᴇᴅ² (-ld) a. [f. foll.]

auric'ula, n. Species of primula, bear's-ear; genus of molluscs. [L, = external ear, dim. of auris ear]

auric'ular, a. Pertaining to the ear; told privately in the ear, as ~ confession; ~ witness, one who tells what he has heard; pertaining to auricle of heart; shaped like an auricle. Hence ~ʟʏ² adv. [f. L auricularis (AURICULA, see -ᴀʀ¹)]

auric'ulate, a. With ear-shaped projections. [as prec., see -ᴀᴛᴇ²]

aurif'erous, a. Yielding gold. [f. L aurifer (aurum gold +-fer producing) +-ᴏᴜs]

Auri'ga, n. Northern constellation, the Waggoner. [L, =charioteer]

Aurigná'cian (-shn), a. Of the palaeolithic epoch represented by remains found in the Aurignac cave of the Pyrenees. [-ᴀɴ]

auri'lave, n. Instrument for cleaning ears. [f. L auris ear + lavare wash]

aur'ist, n. Ear specialist. [as prec. +-ɪsᴛ]

aurochs (owr'öks, aw-), n. Extinct wild ox; (improp.) European bison. [G; OTeut. +urus, etym. dub., +ochs ox]

auror'a, n. Luminous atmospheric (prob. electrical) phenomenon radiating from earth's northern (~ boreāl'is) or southern (austrāl'is) magnetic pole; dawn; colour of sky at sunrise; A~, Roman goddess of dawn. Hence auror'ᴀʟ a. [L, = dawn, goddess of dawn]

aur'ous, a. (chem.). In which gold is monovalent. [f. L aurum +-ᴏᴜs]

aur'um, n. Gold; ~ fŭl'minǎns, fulminate of gold; ~ mosā'icum, bisulphide of tin, bronze-powder; ~ potāb'ǐlè, drinkable gold (once in repute as a cordial). [L]

auscultā'tion, n. Act of listening, esp. (Med.) to movement of heart, lungs, etc. So aus'cultator² n., auscul'tatory a. [f. L auscultare listen to (etym. dub.), see -ᴀᴛɪᴏɴ]

Ausgleich (see Ap.), n. (hist.), Political agreement between Austria & Hungary, renewable every tenth year. [G]

aus'picate, v.t. & i. Inaugurate, initiate; (intr.) augur. [f. L auspicari (auspex -ǐcis observe) see -ᴀᴛᴇ³]

aus'pice, n. Observation of birds for purposes of taking omens; prognostic; prosperous lead, patronage, as under the ~s of, [f. L auspicium (auspex, see prec.)]

auspi'cious (-shus), a. Of good omen, favourable; prosperous. Hence ~ʟʏ² adv.,~ɴᴇss n. [as prec.+-ᴏᴜs]

Auss'ie, n. (sl.), Australia(n). [abbr.]

austere', a. Harsh, stern; stringently moral, strict, severely simple; harsh in flavour. Hence ~ʟʏ² (-rl) adv., ~ɴᴇss (-rn-) n., auste'rity n. (also attrib., severely simple). [f. L f. Gk austēros drying, harsh (auō v. dry)]

aus'tral, a. Southern. [f. L australis (Auster south wind, see -ᴀʟ)]

Australā'sian (-shn), a. & n. (Native) of Australasia (Australia & adjoining islands). [f. Australasia f. F Australasiae (L australis, see prec. +Asia)+-ᴀɴ]

Austrā'lian, n. & a. Native of, colonist or resident in, Australia; (adj.) of Australian. [f. F Australian f. L as AUSTRAL]

aut'archy¹ (-ki), n. Absolute sovereignty. [f. Gk autarkhia (AUTO-, arkhō rule)]

aut'arky, aut'archy² (-ki), n. Self-sufficiency. [f. Gk autarkeia (AUTO-, arkeō suffice)]

authen'tic, a. Reliable, trustworthy; of undisputed origin, genuine; (Mus., of ecclesiastical modes) having their sounds comprised within an octave from the final. Hence ~ɪᴄᴀʟʟʏ adv., ~ɪ'cɪᴛʏ n. [f. OF autentique f. L f. Gk authentikos f. authentēs one who does a thing himself (AUTO-+hentēs, cf. sunentēs fellow-worker), see -ɪᴄ]

authen'ticāte, v.t. Establish the truth of; establish the authorship of; make valid. Hence ~ᴀᴛɪᴏɴ, ~ᴀᴛᴏʀ², nn. [f.

med. L *authenticare* (*authenticus*), see prec. and -ATE[3]]

auth'or, n. Originator (*of a condition of things, event, etc.*); writer of book, treatise, etc.; (*loosely*) ~'s writings. Hence ~'ESS[1] n., auth'orIAL a. [f. AF *autour* f. OF *autor* f. L *auctor* (*augère* *auct-*) increase, originate, promote, see AUCT-; *auth-* at first a scribal var. of *aut-*]

-OR[3]); *auth-* at first a scribal var. of *aut-*]

authori'tarian, a. & n. (Esp. Pol.) favouring obedience to authority as opp. to individual liberty; (n.) supporter of this principle. [-ARIAN]

autho'ritative, a. Commanding, imperative; possessing authority; proceeding from competent authority. Hence ~LY[2] (-vi-) adv., ~NESS (-vn-) n. [f. foll. + -ATIVE]

autho'rity, n. Power, right, to enforce obedience; delegated power (*to do, for an act, or abs.*); person having authority; personal influence, esp. over opinion; weight of testimony; book, quotation, considered to settle a question; evidence, declaration, that may be cited in support of a statement (*on the ~ of Plato*); person whose opinion is accepted, esp. expert in (*on*) a subject. [f. F *autorité* f. L *auctoritatem*, see AUTHOR and -TY]

auth'orize, v.t. Sanction; give ground for, justify, (*thing*); give authority to, commission, (*person to do*). *Authorized Version* (abbr. A.V.), the Bible of 1611. Hence ~ABLE a., ~A'TION n. [f. F *autoriser* f. med. L *auctorizare* (*auctor*, see AUTHOR and -IZE)]

auth'orship, n. Occupation, career, as a writer; origin (*of book*). [-SHIP]

auto- in comp.=Gk *auto-* (*autos* self), in sense 'self, one's own, by oneself, independently', in wds f. Gk & new formations, as *-car³pous*, consisting of pericarp alone, *-gamy*, self-fertilization. *-genous*, self-producing, *-geny*, *-gony*, spontaneous generation, *-plagious*, *-phagy*, feeding on oneself (by absorption of tissues, during starvation), *-plasty*, repair of wounds with tissue from same body; *-suggestion*, hypnotic suggestion proceeding from the subject himself.

aut'obahn, n. (pl.~*en*). German arterial road. [G (*auto* motor-car, *bahn* road)]

autobiog'rapher, n. One who writes his own history. [AUTO-]

autobiograph'ic, a. Pertaining to, engaged in, autobiography. Hence ~AL a., ~ally[2] adv. [AUTO-]

autobiog'raphy, n. Writing the story of one's own life; story so written. [AUTO-]

aut'ocar, n. Road vehicle driven by mechanical power. [AUTO-]

autoceph'alous, a. Having its own head; (of bishop, church) independent. [f. Gk *autokephalos*(AUTO-+*kephalē* head)+-OUS]

autoch'thon (-k-), n. (usu. pl.; *-ōnĕs*, *-ons*). Original, earliest known, inhabitants; aborigines. Hence ~AL, autochthón'ic, ~ous, aa., ~ISM, ~Y[1], nn. [Gk, = sprung from that land itself (AUTO-+ *khthōn onos* land)]

autoc'racy, n. Absolute government; controlling influence. [f. AUTOCRAT]

aut'ocrat, n. Absolute ruler; ~ *of all the Russias* (title of the Czar). So autocrat'ic(AL) aa., autocrat'ically[2] adv. [f. F *autocrate* f. Gk *autokratēs* (AUTO-+ *kratos* might)]

auto'cratrix, n. Female autocrat, title of empresses of Russia ruling in their own right. [Latinized fem. of Gk *autokratōr*, =AUTOCRAT]

aut'o-da-fé' (-dahfā), n. (pl. *autos-da-fé*). Sentence of the Inquisition; execution of this, esp. burning of heretic. [Port., =act of the faith; also Sp. *-de-fé*]

aut'o-e'rotism, n. Spontaneous sexual emotion generated without external stimulus. [AUTO-+*erotism* (=sexual excitement), see EROTIC]

aut'ogir'ō, n. Kind of GYROPLANE. [patented name; AUTO-, GYRO-]

aut'ograph[1] (-ahf), n. Author's own manuscript; person's own handwriting, esp. signature; copy produced by autography. Hence autograph'ic(AL) aa., autograph'ically[2] adv. [f. L f. Gk *auto-graphos* neut. of *autographos* (AUTO-+ *-graphos* written)]

aut'ograph[2] (-ahf), v.t. Write with one's own hand; copy by autography; sign. [f. prec.]

autog'raphy, n. Writing with one's own hand; author's own handwriting; lithographic reproduction of writing or drawing. [as prec., see -Y[1]]

aut'oharp, n. Kind of zither with mechanical contrivance making playing of chords possible. [AUTO-]

autol'ysis, n. Destruction of cells of the body by the action of its own serum. [f. AUTO-+Gk *lusis* dissolution]

automat'ic, a. & n. 1. Self-acting; working of itself, (of a firearm) having mechanism for loading, firing, & ejecting until the ammunition is exhausted, or until the pressure on the trigger etc. is released; (n.) ~ firearm. **2.** Mechanical, unconscious; unintelligent, merely mechanical. **3.** (Psych.) performed unconsciously or subconsciously. Hence ~AL a., ~ally[2] adv., automat'icIty n. [f. ATOMATON+-IC]

autom'atism, n. Involuntary action; doctrine attributing this to animals; unthinking routine; (Psych.) action performed unconsciously or subconsciously. action or motion; (Psych.) faculty of originating action or motion; [f. foll. +-ISM]

For other words in *auto-* see AUTO-.

autŏm'at|on, n. (pl. ~a, ~ons). Thing endued with spontaneous motion; living being viewed materially; piece of mechanism with concealed motive power; living being whose actions are involuntary or without active intelligence. Hence ~OUS a. [f. Gk AUTOmaton, neut. adj., acting of itself]

*automobile' (-ēl), n. Motor-car. [F]

autŏn'omous, a. Of, possessed of, autonomy. [f. Gk AUTO(nomos law)+-OUS]

autŏn'omy̆, n. Right of self-government; personal freedom; freedom of the will (in Kantian doctrine); a self-governing community. So **autonŏm'ĭc** a., ~IST n. [f. Gk autonomia, as prec.]

autŏp'sy̆ (or awt'-), n. Personal inspection; post-mortem examination; (fig.) critical dissection. So **autŏp'tĭc**(AL) aa. [f. Gk autopsia f. autoptos (AUTO-)+op-see]

autotŏx'|in. Poisonous substance produced by changes within the organism. So ~IO a., ~ICA'TION n., poisoning by a virus generated within the body. [AUTO-, TOXIN, TOXIC]

aut'otype, n. Facsimile; photographic printing process for reproducing in monochrome. Hence **aut'otype** v.t. [AUTO-]

aut'umn (-m), n. Third season of the year, August, September, October (Astron., Sept. 21 to Dec. 21; (pop., esp. U.S.) September, October, November; (fig.) season of incipient decay. [f. OF automne f. L autumnus, etym. dub.]

autŭm'nal, a. Of autumn; ~ equinox, time when sun crosses equator as it proceeds southward (Sept. 23); maturing, blooming, in autumn; past prime of life. [f. L autumnalis (as prec., see -AL)]

auxănŏm'ēter, n. Instrument for measuring growth in plants. [f. Gk auxanō increase +-o- +-METER]

auxil'iar|y̆ (-lya-), a. & n. (One who is) helpful to; (Mil.) ~y troops, ~ies, foreign or allied troops in a nation's service; (Gram.) ~y (verb), one used to form tenses, moods, voices, of other verbs. [f. L auxiliarius (auxilium help, see -ARY¹)]

avadavat. See AMADAVAT.

avail'able, a. Capable of being used, at one's disposal, within one's reach. Hence ~BIL'ITY, ~BLE·NESS (-ln-), nn., ~BLY² adv. [AVAIL v. +-ABLE]

ăv'alanche (-ahnsh), n. Mass of snow, earth, & ice, descending swiftly from mountain (also fig.), [F, dialect. form of avalance f. avaler descend (à val to the valley), see -ANCE]

ăvani'a (-nēa), n. (Extortionate) tax levied by Turks. [etym. dub.; common in Levant]

avant-courier (avŏng'-kŏŏr'ĭer), n. One who runs, rides, before; esp. (pl.) scouts, advance-guard. [f. F avant-courier (avant before +coureur runner f. courir)]

ăv'arice, n. Greed of gain, cupidity; (fig.) eager desire to get or keep. Hence **ăvarī'cious** (-shus) a., **ăvarī'ciously²** adv. [OF, f. L avaritia (avarus greedy, see -ICE)]

avast' (-ahst), int. (naut.). Stop; cease. [prob., f. Du. houd vast hold fast]

ăv'atăr, n. (Hind. Myth.) descent of deity to earth in incarnate form; incarnation; manifestation; display; phase. [f. Skr. avatara descent (ava down+tar- pass over)]

avaunt', int. (arch., joc.). Begone. [f. F avant forward f. LL ab-ante before (L ab from+ante before)]

ăv'ē, int. & n. Welcome; farewell; shout of welcome or farewell; Ave Maria (Hail, Mary), devotional recitation (Luke i. 28, 42) & prayer to the Virgin; ~bell, rung when this is to be said. [L, 2nd sing. imper. of avēre fare well]

avĕnge' (-j), v.t. Inflict retribution, exact satisfaction, on behalf of (person, violated right, etc.); be ~d, oneself; take vengeance for (injury). [f. OF avengier (à to+vengier f, L vindicare)]

ăv'ens (-nz), n, Wood ~, herb bennet; water ~, plant of same genus, [f. OF avence etym. dub.]

avĕn'turīne, -in, n. Brownish glass with copper crystals, manufactured first at Murano near Venice; variety of quartz resembling this. [F, f. It. avventurino (avventura chance, from its accidental discovery)]

ăv'ēnŭe, n. Way of approach (usu. fig.); approach to country house bordered by trees; roadway marked by trees or other objects at regular intervals; (esp. in U.S.) wide street. [F, fem. p.p. (used as n.) of avenir f. L avenire come to]

aver', v.t. (-rr-). Assert, affirm; (Law) prove (a plea). Hence ~RABLE a. [f. F avérer f. LL* adverare verify (verus true)]

ăv'erage¹, n. Generally prevailing rate, degree, or amount; ordinary standard; medial estimate, as on the or an ~; apportionment of loss of ship, cargo, or freight, through unavoidable accident (particular ~) or through intentional damage to ship or sacrifice of cargo (general ~), among the owners or insurers. [etym. dub.; f Avarie, Sp. averia, Du. avarij, haverij, G havarie; perh. conn. w. OF aveir goods, see AVOIRDUPOIS]

ăv'erage², a. Estimated by average; of the usual standard. Hence ~LY² (-jl-), adv. [f. prec.]

ăv'erage³, v.t. Estimate the average of (by dividing the aggregate of several quantities by the number of quantities);

estimate the general standard of; amount on an average to; ~ (work, on an average) six hours a day. [as prec.]

aver'ment, n. Positive statement, affirmation; (Law) offer to prove, proof of, a plea. [f. F *averement* (as AVER)]

averrunc'ator (-tingk-), n. Instrument for cutting off branches of trees high above head. [f. obs. vb *averruncate*, f. L *averruncare* (ā off + *verruncare* turn), but wrongly explained as f. *eruncare* weed out]

averse', a. Opposed, disinclined, (to, from;) unwilling (to do). Hence ~NESS (-sn-) n. [f. L as AVERT]

aver'sion (-shn), n. Dislike, antipathy, (to, from, for;) unwillingness (to do); object of dislike, as pet ~. [f. L *aversio* (as AVERT, see -ION)]

avert', v.t. Turn away (eyes, thoughts, from;) ward off. Hence ~IBLE, ~ABLE, aa. [f. F *avertir* f. LL *avertere*, L -*tĕre* (ā away + *vertere* vers- turn); cf. ADVERT]

A'vian, a. Pertaining to birds. [f. L *avis* bird + -AN]

a'viary, n. Place for keeping birds. [f. L *aviarium* (as prec., see -ARIUM)]

a'viate, v.i. Manage or travel in aircraft. So ~A'TION, ~ATOR², nn. [f. L *avis* bird, -ATE³]

avifau'na, n. Birds (of district, country) collectively. [f. L *avis* bird + FAUNA]

avi'so (-zō), n. Advice-boat. [Sp., f. L *advisum*, see ADVICE]

av'id, a. Eager, greedy (of, for). Hence ~ITY² adv. [f. L *avidus* (*avēre* crave)]

avid'ity, n. Ardent desire, greed. [f. F *avidité*, L *aviditātem* (as prec., see -TY)]

avizan'dum, n. (Sc. Law.) Private consideration. [med. L, gerund of *avizare* consider.]

avoca'do (-ah-), n. (Also ~ pear) pear-shaped tropical fruit, the ALLIGATOR pear. [Sp., = advocate (pop. rendering of Mex. *ahuacatl*)]

avoca'tion, n. Distraction; minor occupation; vocation, calling. [f. L *avocatio* (*avocare* call away, see -ATION]

av'ocet, -set, n. Wading bird allied to snipe. [f. F *avocette* f. It. *avocetta*]

avoid', v.t. Shun, refrain from (thing, doing;) escape, evade; (Law) defeat (pleading), quash (sentence). Hence ~ABLE a. [f. AF *avoider* f. OF *evuider* clear out, get quit of (*es* out + *vuider* f. *vuit, vuide*, VOID)]

avoid'ance, n. Act of avoiding; vacancy (of office, benefice). [prec. + -ANCE]

avoirdupois (ăvérdūpoiz'), a. & n. ~ (weight), system of weights used in Great Britain for all goods except precious metals & stones, & medicines; ~ pound contains 7,000 grains; *weight, heaviness. [recent corrupt. of *avoir-de-pois* f. AF, OF, *aveir de peis* (*aveir, avoir*, goods, property, f. L *habēre* have + *de* of + *pois, peis*, weight, f. L *pensum*)]

avouch', v.t. & i. Guarantee; affirm; confess. Hence ~MENT n. [f. OF *avochier* f. L Advocare (in legal use) call upon as defender]

avow', v.t. Admit, confess; (refl. & pass.) admit oneself to be, as ~*ed himself the author, the* ~*ed author*. Hence avow'al n., avow'edly² adv. [f. F *avouer* (ā to + *vouer* f. LL *votāre* frequent. of *votēre* vow)]

avul'sion (-shn), n. Tearing away; (Law) sudden removal of land by flood etc. to another person's estate. [f. L *avulsio* (*vellere* -vuls- pluck away)]

avinc'ular, a. Of, resembling, an uncle. [f. L *avunculus* maternal uncle (dim. of *avus* grandfather) + -AR¹]

await' (a-), v.t. Wait for; (of things) be in store for. [f. ONF *awaitier* (ā to + *waitier*)]

awake¹ (a-), v.t. & i. (past *awoke*, p.p. *awoke*, rarely ~d). ~ *to*, become conscious of; rouse from sleep (lit. & fig.). [(1) OE *awæcnan, awóc, awæcen*, (a- prob. = on) of which present tense was early treated as weak vb, with past *awæcnede*, whence AWAKEN, *awakened*; (2) OE *awæcian, awócode*, in sense = *awæcnan*; (3) in OE these were intr., the trans. sense being given by *awæc(e)an*, ME *aweche*, G *erwecken*, ousted by *awake*, trans. before 1300]

awake² (a-), pred. a. Roused from sleep; not asleep; vigilant; ~ *to*, aware of. [short for *awaken*, orig. p.p. of prec.]

awāk'en (a-), v.t. & i. = AWAKE¹ (lit. & fig.) esp. (fig.) arouse (to a sense of). [see AWAKE¹]

award¹ (awórd'), v.t. Adjudge; grant, assign. Hence awar'der f. OF *esguarder* f. Rom. *Exguardare, -guardare*, f. OLG *warden*, OHG *warten*, watch; cf. WARD] n.,

award² (awórd'), n. Judicial decision; payment, penalty, assigned by this. [AF, f. OF *esguart, esguart*, f. *esguarder*, see prec.]

aware' (a-), pred. a. Conscious, knowing (of, that). Hence ~NESS (awăr'ĭ-) n. [OE *gewær* (G *gewahr*) f. ge- quite + *wær* wary]

awash' (-wŏ-), pred. a. Flush with or washed by the waves. [a- (2)]

away' (a-), adv. To, at, a distance from the place, person, thing, in question (lit. & fig.), as *go* ~, *throw* ~, *give* ~, *he is* ~, *waste* ~, *fool* ~, *explain* ~; *out of* ~ *as fire* ~; ~ = go away (imper.); ~ *with* (imper.); *go* ~ *with*, *take* ~; (cannot) ~ *with*, get on with, tolerate; *make* ~ *with*, destroy; quasi-adj. in ~ *game, match, win*. [OE *onweg* (phr. *on weg* on one's way, onward, along), in early E used as separable vbl prefix]

awe¹, n. Reverential fear or wonder, as *stand in ~ of, hold, keep, in ~*; *~'struck*, struck with ~. Hence ~'LESS (awl-), ~'SOME (aws-), aa. [f. ON *agi*; OE has *ege*; both f. *agan* v. fear]

awe², v.t. Inspire with awe. [f. prec.]

awe³, n. One of the float-boards of an undershot water-wheel. [?]

awful, a. Inspiring awe; worthy of profound respect; solemnly impressive; (arch.) reverential; (sl.) notable in its kind, as ~ *scrawl, bore, relief, something* ~. Hence ~LY² adv., (also, sl.) extremely, ~NESS n. [AWE¹ + -FUL]

awhile (awīl'), adv. For a short time. [OE *āne hwīle* a while]

awk'ward, a. Ill-adapted for use; clumsy (person, thing); bungling; embarrassing; difficult, dangerous, to deal with. Hence ~ISH¹(2) a., ~LY² adv., ~NESS n. [f. obs. adj. *awk* backhanded, untoward (prob. f. ON *afug* turned the wrong way) + -WARD]

awl, n. Small tool for pricking, pricker, esp. that used by shoemakers. [OE *æl*, cf. OHG *āla*, G *āhle*]

awn, n. Spinous process, beard, terminating grain-sheath of barley, oats, etc. Hence ~ed¹ (-nd) [-ED²], ~'LESS. aa. [prob. f. ON *ögn* pl. *agnar*; cf. OHG *agana*, G *ahne*]

awn'ing, n. Canvas roof, esp. above deck of vessel; (Naut.) poop-deck beyond bulkhead of cabin; shelter. Hence **awned²**(-nd) [-ED²] a. [perh. f. F *auvent*, etym. dub.]

awry (arī'), adv. & a. Crookedly, askew; *look ~*, look askance (lit. & fig.); amiss, improperly; *go, run, tread, ~*, do wrong; (adj., usu. pred.) crooked (lit. & fig.). [A prep. + WRY]

axe, ăx, n., & v.t. Chopping-tool, usually iron with steel edge & wooden handle; *put the ~ in the helve*, solve a puzzle; (orig., U.S. pol.) *an ~ to grind*, private ends to serve; *the Geddes ~*, (vast reductions of public expenditure advised by) the Geddes Committee appointed 1921; (v.b) cut down (costs, services). [com.-Teut.; OE *æx*, OHG *acchus*, G *ax, axt*; akin to Gk *axīnē* & perh. L *ascia*]

ax'ial, a. Forming, belonging to, an axis; round an axis. Hence **ăxiäl'ITY** n., ~LY² adv. [f. AXIS + -AL]

ax'il, n. Upper angle between leaf & stem it springs from, or between branch & trunk. [f. L *axilla* armpit]

ax'ile, a. (bot., physiol.) Belonging to the axis. [f. AXIS, see -IL]

ax'illary¹, a. Pertaining to the armpit; (Bot.) in, growing from, the axil. [f. F *axillaire* f. L *axillaris* (as AXIL)]

ax'iom, n. Established principle; maxim; self-evident truth. [f. F *axiome* f. L *axioma*. Gk *axiōma* (*axioō* hold worthy f. *axios*, see -M)]

ăxiomăt'ic(al), aa. Self-evident; characterized by axioms; full of maxims, aphoristic. Hence **ăxiomăt'icalLY²** adv. [f. Gk *axiomatikos* (*axiōma -matos*), see prec. & -IC, -AL]

ăx'is, n. (pl. *axēs*). **1.** Imaginary line about which a body rotates, or by revolution about which a plane is conceived as generating a solid (sphere, cone, cylinder); line dividing regular figure symmetrically. **2.** Straight line from end to end of a body, as ~ *of equator* (polar diameter of earth). **3.** (Bot.) central column of inflorescence or other whorl of growth. **4.** (Opt.) ray passing through centre of eye or lens, or falling perpendicularly on it. **5.** (Physiol.) central core of organ or organism. **6.** (Pol.) agreement between two or more countries intended to form a centre round which like-minded nations may rally; *the Axis* (hist., orig. *the Rome–Berlin Axis*), (pact between) Germany & Italy, later extended to include Japan (*Rome–Berlin–Tokyo Axis*); attrib., as *Axis intrigues, powers, propaganda*, [L, = axle, pivot]

ăx'le, n. Spindle upon or with which wheel revolves; (in carriages, prop.) slender end of ~-*tree* (whole bar connecting wheels), (loosely) ~-*tree*; *wheel & ~*, a MECHANICAL power; ~-*journal*, polished end of ~ revolving under bearing in ~-*box*. Hence **ă'xlED²** (-ld) a. [first found in *axle-tree*, ON *öxul-tre* (ON *öxull* = Goth. *ahsuls* f. OTeut. *ahsō*, cogn. w. Skr. *akshas*, Gk *axōn*, L *axis*]

Ax'minster (-i-), a. ~ *carpet*, kind formerly hand-woven at ~, now made at Wilton.

ăx'olotl, n. Newt-like amphibian found in Mexican lakes. [Aztec, = servant (*axolotl*) of water (*atl*)]

ay(e), int. & n. (pl. *ayes*). Yes; (n.) affirmative answer; *the ayes have it*, affirmative voters are in majority. [?]

ayah (ī'a), n. Native Indian nurse or lady's maid. [Ind. vernacular *āya* f. Port. *aia* nurse, fem. of *aio* tutor]

aye (ā), adv. Ever, always; on all occasions; *for ~*, for ever. [ME *āy, ai, ei*, f. ON *ei, ey*, cogn. w. Goth. *aiw* f. OTeut. *aiwoz*, cogn. w. L *aevum* age; cf. Gk *aei* always]

aye-aye (ī'ī), n. Squirrel-like animal of the size of a cat, found only in Madagascar. [F., f. Malagasy *aiay*]

Azal'ea, n. Genus of flowering shrubby plants, natives of northern hemisphere, [f. Gk *azaleos* fem. of *azaleos* dry (from its dry wood or the dry soil in which it flourishes)]

ăz'arole, n. Fruit of the Neapolitan medlar. [f. F *azerole* (Sp. *azarolla*) f. Arab. *az-zu'rūr* (*al* the + name of the fruit)]

Azil'ian, a. Of the transitional period between the palaeolithic & neolithic

ages. [f. Mas d'Azil in French Pyrenees, where remains were found]

ăz′ĭmŭth, n. Arc of the heavens extending from the zenith to the horizon, which it cuts at right angles; ~-circle, one of which this is a quadrant, passing through zenith & nadir; true ~ of a heavenly body, arc of horizon intercepted between north & point of horizon intercepted between north & the point where its great circle passing through the body cuts the horizon: magnetic ~, arc intercepted between this circle & magnetic meridian. Hence **ăzĭmŭth′ăl** a., **ăzĭmŭth′ăl⋅ly²** adv. [f. F azimut f. Arab. assumut (al the+sumut pl. of samt way, direction)

azö′ic, a. Having no trace of life; (Geol.) containing no organic remains. [f. Gk azōos (a- not+zöē life)+-IC]

ăzō′te, n. Former name of nitrogen. Hence **azō′tĬc** a., **ăz′ōtīze**(3) v.t. [F, f. Gk a- not+zōē (for zoē) live, from its inability to support life]

Az′tĕc (ă-), a. & n. (One) of the Mexican tribe dominant till the conquest of Cortes (1519).

ā′zure (-zher, -zhyer), n. & a., & v.t. **1.** Sky blue; (Her.) blue; unclouded vault of heaven; bright blue pigment; lapis lazuli. **2.** adj. Sky-blue, (fig.) cloudless, serene. **3.** v.t. Make ~. [f. OF azur f. med. L azura f. Arab. al the+lazward f. Pers. lazhward lapis lazuli]

ăz′ygŏus, a. & n. (physiol.). (An organic part) not existing in pairs. [f. Gk azugos unyoked (a- not+zugon yoke)+-OUS]

B

B (bē), letter (pl. Bs, B's, Bees), (Mus.) seventh note in scale of C major (B flat, B flat); jocular euphem. for bug. (In argument) second hypothetical person or thing. (Alg.) second known quantity.

baa (bah), n., & v.i. (baaing, baaed or baa'd). = BLEAT. ~-lamb, nursery name for lamb. [imit.]

Bā′al, n. (pl. ~im). Phoenician god; (transf.) a false god. Hence ~ISM (3).

baas (bahs), n. (S. Africa). Master (freq. as form of address). [Du., see BOSS¹]

ba′bacŏŏte (bah-), n. Species of lemur (Madagascar). [Malagasy babakóto]

Băb′ĭtt-mēt′al, n. Soft alloy of tin, antimony, & copper. [inventor's name]

băb′ble¹, v.i. & t. Talk half articulately, incoherently, or excessively; murmur (of streams etc.); repeat foolishly; let out (secrets). Hence ~MENT (-lm-) n. [imit. of infant's ba, ba, +-LE (3); cf. F babiller, LG babbelen, G pappeln]

băb′ble², n. Imperfect speech; idle talk; murmur of water etc. [prec.]

băb′bler, n. Chatterer; teller of secrets; Long-legged Thrush. [-ER¹]

bābe, n. (poet.). Young child, baby; inexperienced or guileless person (in pl. often ~s & sucklings). [imit. of BABE]

bāb′el, n. (B~) the tower in Shinar (Gen. xi); a high structure; visionary plan; scene of confusion, noisy assembly; meaningless noise. [perh. f. Ass. bab-ilu gate of God]

băbīrous′sa, -rus′sa, (-rōō-), n. E.-Asiatic wild hog with upturned horn-like tusks. [Malay bābi hog+rusa deer]

Bāb′ism (bah-), n. Doctrine of a Persian mystical & pantheistic sect (Bābi) founded in 1844. [f. Pers. Bāb-ed-Din, gate (=intermediary) of the Faith, whence the founder's usual title of (the) Bāb]

bă′bōo (bah-), n. (As Hindoo title) Mr; Hindoo gentleman; Indian English clerk; (contemptuous) half anglicized Hindoo. [Hind. bābū]

băb′oon, n. Large African & S.-Asiatic monkey. [f. 13th-c. F babuin etym. dub.]

băbŏuche′ (-ōosh), n. Oriental slipper. [f. F Arab. babush f. Pers. paposh (pa foot+posh covering; for p=b cf. posha & bashaw]

Băb′ylon, n. Capital of Chaldean empire; any great empire or luxurious city; Rome, the papacy (ref. to Rev. xvii etc.), London, etc. Hence **Băbylōn′IAN** a. & n. [L, f. Gk Babulōn f. Heb. Bābel BABEL]

băb′ul (-ool), n. Gum-arabic tree of India and Arabia. [Hind. & Pers.]

bāb′y, n. Very young child; childish person, whence ~ISH¹ a., ~ISHNESS, ~ISM (2), nn.; thing small of its kind; *girl, sweetheart, (sl.); ~ car, motor-car of small size and power; ~-farmer, one who contracts to keep babies; ~ grand, small grand piano; ~-jumper, hanging frame in which child is fastened to exercise limbs; hold the ~, carry the ~, (be left to) assume an undesired responsibility. Hence ~HOOD n. [BABE, -Y³]

băccalaur′eate, n. University degree of bachelor. [f. med. L baccalaureatus (baccalaureus corrupted after bacca lauri laurelberry) f. baccalarius BACHELOR; see -ATE¹]

băc′cara(t) (-rah), n. Gambling card game. [F]

băc′cate, a. (bot.). Bearing berries, berry-shaped. [f. L baccatus berried (bacca berry, -ATE²)]

Băc′chanal (-ka-), a. & n. **1.** Of, like, Bacchus or his rites; riotous, roystering. **2.** n. Priest, priestess, votary, of Bacchus; drunken reveller; dance or song in honour of Bacchus. [f. L bacchanalis (L f. Gk Bakkhos god of wine, -AL)]

Bacchanā′lia (-ka-), n. pl. Festival of Bacchus; drunken revelry. [L neut. pl. of bacchanalis =prec.]

Bacchanā′lian (-ka-), a. & n. **1.** Of Baccha-nals; riotous, drunken; (n.) a Bacchanal,

tippler. [f. L *bacchanalis* BACCHANAL + -AN]

Băc'chant (-kə-), n. masc. or fem., & a.; **Bacchante** (băk'ant, bəkănt', băkăn'ti), n. fem. Priest, priestess, votary of Bacchus; Bacchus-worshipping, wine-loving. Hence **Bacchān'tic** (-kə-) a. [(*vide* F) f. L *bacchari* (-ANT) f. Gk *bakkheuō* celebrate Bacchic rites]

Băc'chic (-kĭk), a. =BACCHANAL (adj. meanings). [f. L f. Gk *bakkhikos* of Bacchus]

Băc'chus (-kəs), n. Greek god of wine. [L, f. Gk *Bakkhos*]

băcci'ferous, băcc'iform, băcci'v'orous (băks-), aa. Berry-bearing, -shaped, -eating. [L *baccifer* (-FEROUS); L *bacca* berry + -FORM, -VOROUS]

||**băc'cy** (-k-), n. (colloq.) Tobacco. [abbr.]

băch'elor, n. Young knight serving under another's banner (hist.); hence now, *knight*, simple knight not belonging to a special order; man or woman who has taken the university degree below Master; unmarried man. ~'s *buttons*, various button-shaped flowers esp. double buttercup, also small ratafia biscuits, also buttons attacheable without sewing; ~ *girl* (unmarried and living independently); ~ (*seal*), young male fur-seal with no mate. Hence ~HOOD, ~SHIP, ~ISM(4), nn. [f. OF *bacheler* f. L *+baccalaris*; cf. *baccalaria* piece of land, *baccalarius* farm-labourer, perh. f. *bacca* LL for L *vacca* cow]

bacill'ary, a. Of little rods (tissue, membrane; connected with bacilli (disease, research). [BACILLUS + -ARY]

bacill'iform, a. Rod-shaped. [foll. + -FORM]

bacill'us, n. (pl. -*lī*). A rodlike bacterium, esp. one of the various types that cause disease by entering and multiplying in animal and other tissues. [LL dim. of L *baculus* stick]

băck, n. & a. 1. Hinder surface of human body (*at the ~ of,* behind in support, pursuit, or concealment; BEHIND one's~; *give, make, a ~,* bend down at leapfrog; *turn* one's ~ *upon,* run away from, abandon; *on* one's~, laid up; *with* one's ~ *to wall,* hard pressed); body as needing clothes (~ *& belly,* clothing & food) or as weight-carrier (~ *equal to burden,* have *on* one's~, be burdened with; *put, get, set,* person's ~ *up,* make him angry; *break* one's~, overburden him, & see BREAK[1]); surface of things corresponding to human ~ (less visible, active, or important; ~ *of hand, leg, door, book, knife*); upper surface of animal's body, surface corresponding to this (ridge-shaped, etc.; ~ *of hill, skip* esp. in *broke her ~*; *on the ~ of,* in addition to); football player stationed behind (*full, three-quarter, half, ~*); *the ~ Backs,* grounds on the Cam at the ~ of

certain Colleges at Cambridge, of noted beauty; ~*band,* over cart-saddle to keep shafts up; ~*board,* at ~ of cart, also strapped across child's ~ to straighten it; ~*bone,* spine (whence ~BONED[2] (-nd) a.; *to the ~bone,* thoroughly), main support, axis, watershed, chief strength, firmness of character; ~*fall,* throw on ~ in wrestling; ~*sword,* with only one edge, also singlestick. 2. adj. (no comp., superl.~*most*). Situated behind, remote, inferior, (*take* ~ *seat,* humble oneself); overdue (~ *rent*); reversed, counter, (~ *current*); ||~*bench(er),* (occupant of) a seat in the House of Commons or similar assembly used by a member not entitled to a front-bench seat (~*bench* freq. used attrib.); ||~*blocks,* (Austral.) land in the remote & sparsely-inhabited interior; ~*chat* (sl.) retort(s), recrimination; ~*cloth* (Theatr.) painted cloth at ~ of stage as main part of scenery; ~*door,* lit., & fig. secret means or approach, (adj.) clandestine, underhand; ||~*end,* late autumn; ~*fire,* premature explosion in the cylinder of an internal-combustion engine (also as vb); ~ *formation,* making from a supposed derivative (as *lazy, banting*) of the non-existent word (*laze, bant*) from which it might have come); ~*ground,* part of scene, picture, or description, that serves as setting to chief figures or objects & foreground, (adj.) obscurity, retirement; ~*hand(ed),* delivered with ~ of hand or in direction counter to the usual, indirect, unexpected, (~*hander,* such blow, indirect attack, extra glass got by bottle's travelling wrong way); ~*marker,* scratch man in race etc.; ~ *number* (of magazine etc.), (sl.) out-of-date method or person; ~*set,* counter-current, check, reverse; ~*side, posterior, rump; ~*sight,* that nearer stock of rifle etc., (Surv.) sight taken backwards; ~ *slang,* form of low slang in which words are spelt & pronounced backwards (e.g. *yannep* for *penny*); ~ *stairs* n. & a., ~*stair* a., as ~*door* above; ~*stays,* ropes slanting abaft from mast-head to a lower point; ~*stroke,* motion of backhand stroke; ~*wash,* motion of receding wave (lit. & fig.); ~*water,* water dammed back, currentless water beside stream & fed by its backflow, stagnant condition of things, creek communicating with sea by barred outlets, water cast from ship's paddles, loss of power caused by this; ~*way,* bypath (lit. & fig.); ~*woods* n. & a., (connected with) remote uncleared forest land (so ~*woodsman*). [a. f. n., OE *bæc*; Teut. cf. comm. Scand. *bak*]

băck, v.t. & i. Put, or be, a back, lining, support, or background, to; assist with countenance, money, or argument, bet upon, whence ~ER[1] n.; (of sporting dogs) follow suit to one that points; ~ *up,*

help by subordinate action, esp. in cricket; ride upon, break in to the saddle; countersign, endorse; cause to move back (horse, boat, engine, etc.; ~ *a sail*, *yard*, lay it aback, i.e. to face wind; ~ *water*, reverse boat's forward motion with oars); go backwards; (of wind) change counter-sunwise (cf. VEER); ~ *out* (*of*), withdraw (from undertaking etc.); ~ *down*, abandon claim. [f. prec.]

bāck³, adv. To the rear (often with omission of vb, esp. in imperative; away from what is considered the front (*push the bolt* ~); away from a promise (*go from* or *upon one's word*); into the past, into or in an earlier position or condition; home; in return (*answer* = retort; *pay* ~); at a distance (~ *from the road*); in a checked condition (*keep* ~); = ago; reckoning backwards (*for years* ~); behind-hand; ~ *& forth* = to & fro; ~ *of*, = behind; ~*bite*, slander, speak ill of, whence ~*biter*¹ n.; ~*lash*(*ing*), irregular recoil of wheels in machinery due to defects or sudden pressure; ~*pedal*, work pedal backwards; ~*slide*¹ v.i., relapse into sin, whence ~*slider*¹, n.; ~*slid*ing¹, nn.; ~*stitch* n. & v.t. & i., sewing(ing) with overlapping stitches. [for ABACK]

bāck⁴, n. Shallow vat used in brewing, dyeing, etc. [f. Du. *bak* tub f. F *bac* punt cf. med. L *baccus* ferryboat]

bāckgămm'on, n. Game played on special double board with draughts & dice; most complete form of win in this, [BACK³ (because pieces go back or re-enter); GAME¹]

bāck'ing, n. In vbl senses; esp.: body of supporters; material used to form thing's back or support. [BACK², -ING¹]

backsheesh. See BAKSHEESH.

bāck'ward(s), adv. , **bāck'ward**, a. 1. Away from one's front (*look, lean*, etc.); back foremost (*walk* etc.); back to start-ing-point (*flow, roll*, etc.; not of living things exc. in ~ *& forwards*); into the reverse way (*spell* etc.; *ring the bells* ~, from bass upwards). 2. adj. Directed to rear or starting-point; reversed; re-luctant, shy, behindhand, dull, whence **bāck'wardness** n. [orig. for *abackward*, later referred to BACK³; see -WARDS]

bāckwardā'tion, n. (St. Exch.). Per-centage paid by seller of stock for right of delaying delivery (cf. CONTANGO). [f. prec. used as vb +-ATION on anal. of *retardation*]

bāc'on, n. Cured back & sides of pig (*save one's* ~, escape death or injury; *bring home the* ~ (sl.), succeed in one's undertaking. [OF, f. OHG *bacho* MHG *bache* buttock cf. BACK¹]

Bācon'ian, a. & n. Of Francis Bacon or his philosophy, experimental, inductive; (n.) follower of Bacon; believer in ~ authorship of Shakspere's plays. [Bacon + -IAN]

bāc'ony, a. Like bacon (esp. ~ *liver*, a disease, fatty degeneration). [BACON + -Y¹]

bāctēri|ol'ysis, n. Artificial liquefaction of solid sewage by bacterial agency; destruction of bacteria by a serum. So ~olyt'ic a., capable of destroying bac-teria. [f. foll. + Gk *lusis* dissolution (adj.)]

bāctēr'ium |lum, n. (pl. -ria). Kinds of micro-scopic unicellular organism found almost everywhere, some of which cause disease. Hence ~IAL a., ~IOl'OGY, ~IOl'OGIST, nn. [mod. L, f. Gk *baktērion* dim. of *baktēron* stick]

bāc'üline, a. Of the stick or flogging (esp. ~ *argument*). [f. L *baculum* stick + -INE²]

bād, a. (worse, worst) & n. 1. (Negatively) worthless, inferior, deficient, of poor quality, incorrect, not valid, (~ *air*, corrupt; ~ *coin*, debased; ~ *debt*, not recoverable; ~ *food*, not nourishing; *~ *lands*, extensive barren uncultivable tracts; *go* ~, decay; *with* ~ *grace*, reluctantly; ~ *shot*, wrong guess; ~ *law*, not sustainable; ~ *form*, want of breeding; ~ *pre-eminence*, disrepute; *in a* ~ *sense*, unfavourable; ~ *success*). 2. (Positively) noxious, depraved, vicious, offensive, painful, (~ *blood*, ill feeling; ~ *for*, injurious to; in ill health, injured, in pain, (*she is* ~, *worse, to-day; a* ~ *leg*); (colloq. of things in no case good) notable, decided, pronounced, (~ *blunder, head-ache, falling-off*). 3. n. Ill fortune (*take the* ~, take the good, wrong side of account (£500 *to the* ~); ruin (*go to the* ~). Hence **bād'ISH**¹ (2) a. [ME *badde*, perh. f. OE *bǣddel* hermaphrodite, womanish man; -INF]

bāde. See BID¹.

bādge, n. Distinctive mark, formerly of knight, now worn as sign of office or licensed employment or membership of a society; symbol, something that betrays a quality or condition. [ME etym. dub.]

bādge², v.t (dial.). Hawker, esp. of pro-visions. [?]

bādg'er¹, n. Grey-coated strong-jawed nocturnal hibernating plantigrade quad-ruped between weasels & bears; fishing-fly, & painting-brush, made of its hair; ~*-baiting,-drawing*, setting dogs to draw it from its burrow or a cask; ~*-legged*, with legs of unequal length (popular error). [mod. E (older *brock* or *bauson*) perh. f. BADGE +-ARD (earlier *bageard, badgerd*) with ref. to its white forehead mark]

bādg'er², v.t. Bait like a badger, worry, tease. [f. prec.]

bŏd'inage (-ahzh), n. Light raillery. [F (badiner banter f. badin silly f. LL badare gape)]

bad'ly, adv. (worse, worst). Defectively, unsuccessfully, faultily, wickedly, cruelly, dangerously, by much (beaten), very much (want a thing ~). [-LY²]

badmash (bŭd'mahsh), bŭd', n. (Anglo-Ind.). Rascal, bad character. [Pers. & Urdu]

băd'minton, n. A summer drink (claret, soda, sugar); game with net, rackets, & shuttlecocks. [Duke of Beaufort's seat]

băd'ness, n. Poor quality or condition; faultiness, invalidity; wickedness, noxiousness, adverseness. [-NESS]

Baed'eker (bād.), n. Guide-book published by firm founded by Karl Baedeker; ~ raids, German reprisal air-raids in 1942 on (cathedral) cities in England starred in...

ba'el, n. Indian tree, the orange-like fruit of which is a specific for diarrhoea etc. [f. Hind. bel]

baf'fle, v.t., & n. Foil, reduce to perplexity, bar progress of, (person, curiosity, faculties, efforts, ship); baffling winds, variable, preventing a straight course; (n.) ~ or ~plate, plate hindering or regulating passage of fluid through outlet or inlet (e.g. a damper). Hence ~r n., = ~plate. [perh. f. F beffler mock f. bafouer hoodwink, both perh. f. Pr. bafar mock perh. f. baf interj. of contempt]

bāff'y, n. Wooden golf club for lofting. [cf. Sc. baff a blow]

bag¹, n. Receptacle of flexible material with opening at top (green or blue ~, barrister's for briefs; hyphened with nouns showing contents or purpose, as mail-~, travelling-~; also alone for such compp., e.g. for money-~, so ~s = wealth, or for game-~, also for g.~'s contents or all a sportsman has shot or caught; ~ of bones, lean creature; whole ~ of tricks, every device, everything, all the lot; in bottom of ~, as last resource; in the ~ (colloq.), in one's possession or power, (as good as) secured; let cat out of ~, reveal secret, esp. involuntarily; ~ & baggage, with all belongings, esp. of utter expulsion), whence ~g'ING¹ (3) n.; cow's udder; sac in body containing honey, poison, etc.; baggy place under eyes etc.; (sl.)~s, trousers; ~ fox, one brought, not found; ~man, commercial traveller, also = fox; ~pipe(s), reed-pipe wind instrument with bag as receptacle for air, melody pipe (chanter), & fixed-note pipes (drones), used in Scotland &, with variations, in Ireland & N. England; ~sleeve, loose sleeve at wrist; ~wig, 18th-c. wig with back hair enclosed in ~. Hence ~'FUL (2), ~'pipe(s) etc. [ON baggi etym. dub.; no evidence for connexion with BELLY, BELLOWS (OHG balg)]

bag², v.i. & t.(-gg-). Swell, bulge;(Naut.) drop away from course; hang loosely, put in a bag, secure (game, whether lit. bagged or not), take possession of (euphem.) steal; (school sl.) claim on the ground of being first to claim (I ~, but usu.~s I or ~s, first innings!). [prec.]

băg³, v.t. (-gg-.). Cut (wheat etc.) with a hook. [also badge; etym. dub.]

bagasse', n. Refuse products in sugar-making, [F; perh. = bagage lumber]

băgatelle', n. Trifle, negligible amount; short unpretentious piece of music; minor game of billiard kind. [F. f. It. bagatella dim. perh. f. baga BAGGAGE]

băgg'age, n. Belongings with which one travels (now ousted exc. in U.S. by luggage); portable equipment of army; good-for-nothing woman (now only used playfully, saucy girl. [f. OF bagage f. baguer tie up or bagues bundles pl. of bague=It. & LL baga chest]

băgg'ly (-g-), a. Puffed out, hanging in loose folds. Hence ~INESS n. [BAG¹+-Y¹]

bagnio (băn'yō), n. Bathing-house (now only in Italy & Turkey); oriental prison; brothel. [f. It. bagno f. L balneum bath]

bah, int. of contempt. [F]

Bahadur (bohahd'er), n. Title of respect appended in India to a person's name (& other titles); (Anglo-Ind. sl.) consequential official. [Hind.,=gallant]

baignoire (bĕnwahr'), n. Box at theatre on level of stalls. [F]

bail¹, n. Security for prisoner's appearance, on giving which he is released pending trial (forfeit one's ~, fail to appear; save one's ~, appear); (joc.) give leg~, run away; person(s) who become(s) surety for prisoner's appearance (be, become, go, ~ for, guarantee truth of anything; magistrate accepts, admits to, allows, holds to, takes, ~; prisoner gives, offers, surrenders to his, ~; his ~ surrender, render, bring in, produce, him). [OF bail custody f. baillier take charge of f. L bajulare bear a burden (bajulus porter)]

bail², v.t. 1. Deliver (goods) in trust. 2. Admit to bail, release on security given for appearance, (of magistrate; arch.); secure liberation of, by becoming bail or security for (~ out if already in prison). [sense 1 f. F bailler deliver; sense 2 f. BAIL¹]

bail³, n. 1. (Hist.) outer line of fortification, formed of stakes; wall of castle court, or court itself. 2. (Mod.) bar separating horses in open stable; swinging ~, slung from manger to ceiling; (cricket) one of the cross pieces (orig. one, not two) over stumps. [OF bail perh. f. baillier enclose, or f. L bacalum stick]

bail⁴, n. Half-hoop for supporting wagon-tilt etc.; hoop-handle of kettle etc.; (Australia) frame holding cow's head at milking. [ME beyl f. ON beygla sword-guard etc.=(beygva=OE bēgan to bend)]

bail[5], v.t. Confine (arch.); ‖ (Australia)
~ up, secure (cow; see prec.; (of bush-
rangers) make hold up the arms to rob,
(intr. of victim) throw up the arms. [f.
OF *baillier* enclose perh. same as in prec.
& BAIL[2]]

bail[6], **bale**, v.t. & i. Throw water out of
boat with pails etc. (~ *under out*, ~ *out*
parachute descent esp. from damaged
aircraft. Hence **bail'er**[1] [-ER[1] (2)] n. [f.
obs. n. *bail* bucket f. F *baille*, f. LL *bacula*
dim. of *baca*, *bacca*, water-vessel]

bail'able, a. Admitting of bail (offence).
[BAIL[1,2]+-ABLE]

bailee', n. One to whom goods are entrusted for a purpose. [BAIL[2]+-EE]

bail'er[2], n. Ball that hits bails at cricket.
[BAIL[3]+-ER[1]]

bai'ley, n. Outer wall of castle; also any
of its inner defensive circuits, or any of
the courts enclosed between these; *Old
B~*, London Central Criminal Court,
standing in ancient ~ of city wall. [ME
variant of BAIL[3] perh. f. med. L form
ballium]

‖bail'ie(-li), n. Scottish municipal magi-
strate=Eng. alderman. [ME *baili* f. OF
baillis BAILIFF]

bail'iff, n. (Orig.) King's representative
in a district (including mayor, sheriff,
etc.), esp. chief officer of a hundred (still
in *High-B~ of Westminster, B~ of Dover
Castle*, etc.); used as Eng. equivalent of
F *bailli*, G *landvogt*, Channel-I. *bailly* or
first civil officer); officer under sheriff for
writs, processes, arrests; agent of lord
of manor; landholder's steward. [ME
& OF *baillif* obj. case of *baillis* f. LL
bajulivus (L *bajulus* porter)]

bail'iwick, n. District, jurisdiction, of
bailie or bailiff. [BAILIE+-WICK[1]]

bail'ment, n. Delivery of goods in trust;
bailing of prisoner.   [OF *baillement* see
BAIL[2] &-MENT]

bail'or, n. One who delivers goods to another for a stated purpose. [BAIL[2]+-OR[2]]

bails'man (-z-), n. One who gives bail for
another. [f. *bail's* (BAIL[1])+MAN]

bain'-marie (bān'marē'), n. Vessel of hot
water in which stewpans are stood to
warm. [F, f. L *balneum Mariae* bath of
the Virgin perh. from gentleness of
process]

Bairam (bīraͪm'), n.   Mohammedan
festival (twice a year, Lesser & Greater).
[Turk. & Pers.]

bairn, n. Child (Sc. form now borrowed in
literary Eng., the E *berne* having perished,
& *bearne* become dialectal). [OE *bearn*,
com.-Teut. f. *bera* BEAR[3]]

bait[1], v.t. & i. (Orig.) cause to bite. 1.
Worry (chained animal) by setting dogs
at it (*with dogs, or abs.*; also of the dogs),
whence (*bears, bull*, etc.). -**baiting**[1] n.;
torment (helpless person) with jeers etc.
2. Give food to, take food, (of horses on

journey); stop at inn (orig. to feed
horses, then also for rest or refreshment).
3. Put food (real or sham) on or in (hook,
trap, fishing-place). [sense 3 prob. f.
foll.; ME *beyten* & ON *beita* cause to bite
(*bíta* BITE v.); cf. OF *beter*]

bait[2], n. Food to entice prey (*live ~*,
small fish so used; (fig.) an allurement,
temptation; halt in journey for refreshment or rest. [partly f. prec.; partly f.
ON *beit* food, & *beita* BAIT[1]]

baize, n. Coarse woollen stuff with long
nap used for coverings. [f. F *baies* pl.
fem. of *bai* f. L *badius* chestnut-coloured,
BAY[1]; treated by mistake as sing. cf.
BODICE]

bake, v.t. & i. Cook by dry heat in closed
place or on hot surface (not by direct exposure to fire), whence **bak'ing**[1] (5) n.;
harden by heat; *half~d*, immature,
half-witted; (of sun) ripen (fruit), tan
(skin); (intr.) undergo the process, be
cooked, hardened, tanned, by heat; ‖~
house, house or room for baking bread,
or for making loaf-sugar; ~*stone*, flat
stone, slate, or iron plate, on which cakes
are baked in oven; *baking-powder*, substitute for yeast. [OE *bacan*; com.-Teut.
& cf. Gk *phōgō* roast]

bak'elite, n. Widely-used synthetic resin
or plastic made from formaldehyde &
phenol. [G *bakelit*; f. L. H. *Baekeland*
inventor; P]

bak'er, n. Professional breadmaker (*pull
devil, pull ~*, encouragement to both
sides; ~*'s dozen*, thirteen, 13th loaf being
huckster's profit; ~*-legged*, knock-kneed);
(Fishing) kind of artificial fly. Hence
~*ess*[1], **bak'ery** (3), nn. [OE *bæcere* (*bacan*
BAKE+-ER[1])]

baksheesh, **bakshish** (-ē-), n. Gratuity, tip, (article not used). [Pers., f. *bakh-
shīdan* give]

Balaam (-lām), n. Disappointing prophet
or ally; ‖ (journalism) matter kept in
stock to fill up gaps in newspaper (*Numb.*
xxii. 28 or 38; ~*-box*, receptacle for this).
[name corresponding seventh sign of zodiac. 2. The weighing of actions or
opinions, the wavering of fortune or
chance, power to decide (*hold the ~*);
counterpoise, set-off; equilibrium (~ *of
power*, no State greatly preponderant);
(Art) harmony of design & proportion;
(Art) harmony of design & proportion;
steady position (*lose one's ~*, fall physi-

bala'nce, n. 1. Weighing-apparatus with
central pivot, beam, & two scales; spring
or lever substitute for this; regulating
gear of clock or watch; zodiac constellation (usu. *Libra* or *The Scales*), & (not
now corresponding seventh sign of zodiac.

balalai'ka (-līka), n. Triangular guitar-
like musical instrument, popular in Slav
countries.   [Russ.]

Balacla'va (-ahva), n. Site of Crimean
battle; ‖ ~ *helmet*, woollen covering for
head & shoulders worn esp. by soldiers
etc. on active service.

bäk'sheesh, **bäk'shish** (-ē-), n. Gratuity, tip, (article not used). [Pers., f. *bakh-
shīdan* give]

cally or be upset mentally; ~-wheel, in watch, regulating the beat); preponderat-ing weight or amount (the ~ of advantage lies with him). **3.** (Accounts) difference between Cr & Dr, statement of this (strike a ~, determine it; ~-sheet, written state-ment of it with details); ~ of trade, difference between exports & imports; ~ in hand, amount over after realizing assets & meeting liabilities; ~ due, deficiency; on ~, taking everything into consideration; (sl.) the remainder of anything, [F, =It. bilancia f. L (libra) BI(lanc-lancis plate) two-scaled (balance)]

bal'ance², v.t. & i. **1.** Weigh (a question, two arguments etc. against each other; match (thing) with, by, against, another; bring (thing, oneself) into, or keep in, equilibrium; equal or neutralize weight of, make up for; oscillate, waver; (Danc-ing) move conversely with one's partner. **2.** (Accounts) compare Dr & Cr, make the entry necessary to equalize them; account ~s, two sides are equal; settle (account) by paying deficit. [f. F balancer (balance = prec.)]

bal'as, n. Red spinel resembling ruby. [f. OF balais ult. f. Pers. Badakhshan district of origin]

Bālbrig'gan, n. Knitted cotton fabric used in hose, underwear, etc. [~ in Ireland]

bal'con|y, n. Outside balustraded plat-form with access from upper-floor win-dow; (Theatre) tier of seats generally between dress-circle & gallery. Hence ~ied² (-nid) a. [f. It. balcone (balco f. OHG balcho=BALK¹+-one -OON]

bald (bawld), a. With scalp wholly or partly hairless (go ~-headed (sl.), stake everything, disregard consequences); (of animals etc.) hairless, featherless, tree-less, leafless, napless; (of horses) marked with white, esp. on face; (of style) meagre, dull, jejune, monotonous, (of bad qualities) undisguised, whence ~'LY² adv.; ~'head, ~'pate, (person) with ~ head, kinds of duck (pate only) & pigeon. Hence ~'NESS n. [earlier balled perh. f. obs. ball white spot (cf. W (ceffyl) bal (horse) with white forehead, Ir. & Gael. bal spot, +-ED²)]

bal'dachin (-k-), -quin, n. (Orig.) rich brocade; (now) canopy projecting, sus-pended, or on pillars, over altar, throne, etc. [F & Sp. baldaquin f. It. baldacchino (Baldacco It. form of Bagdad, place of origin]

bald-coot, bald'icoot, (bawl-), n. The coot, from its bare white forehead; bald person.

bal'derdash (bawl-), n. (Formerly) frothy liquid, mixture of liquors; (now) jumble of words, nonsense; foul language. [?]

baldmoney (bawld'mǐnǐ), n. Yellow-flowered umbelliferous plant. [?]

bal'dric (bawl-), n. Belt for sword, bugle,

etc., hung from shoulder to opposite hip. Hence ~-WISE adv. [earlier baudry f. OF baudrei cf. MHG balderich perh. f. L balteus BELT]

bâle¹, n. Evil, destruction, woe, pain, misery, (poet. & arch.). Hence ~FUL (-lf-) a., ~'fully² adv. [OE, OSax., & OFris. balu f. OTeut. †balwom neut. adj. evil]

bâle², n., & v.t. (Make up into) package of merchandise usu. done up in canvas & corded or metal-hooped. [ME (perh. through Flem.) f. OF bale, balle, f. It. balla, palla, either from OHG balla, palla, BALL², or f. Gk palla ball]

bâle³. See BAIL⁶.

baleen¹, n. & a. Whalebone. [ME baleyne f. OF baleine f. L balaena whale]

bâle'fire (-lf-), n. Great fire in the open; funeral pyre; beaconfire (fire added only in 19th c.); bonfire. [f. OE bæl & ON bál great fire f. OTeut. bælom (cf. Skr. bhadas lustre, Gk phalos shining) +FIRE]

balk¹, baulk, (bawk), n. Ridge left un-ploughed; stumbling-block, hindrance; sanctuary area on billiard table (make a ~, utilize this); roughly squared timber beam; tie-beam of a house; headline of fishing-net. [OE balca ridge & perh. ON bálkr beam]

balk², baulk, (bawk), v.t. & i. Shirk, miss, (topic, turn, duty, chance); jib, shy, pull up; hinder, thwart, disappoint, discourage, startle. [f. prec.]

Bal'kan (bawl-), a. Of the peninsula bounded by the Adriatic, Aegean, and Black Seas, or of its peoples and countries. So ~IZE (3) v.t., divide (an area) into small antagonistic states.

ball¹ (bawl), n. Solid or hollow sphere; (with distinctive adj.) any of the heavenly bodies; hard or soft, inflated or solid, large or small, sphere used in games; (Cricket) single delivery of it by bowler (no ~, delivery breaking rules); solid missile (not always spherical) for cannon, rifle, pistol, etc. (load with ~, opposed to blank cartridge); =BALLOT n., & see BLACK¹; ~ of eye, eye within lids; ma-terial gathered or wound in round mass, as snow, medicine (veterinary), wool, or string; ~ of foot, rounded part at base of great toe, so ~ of thumb. (Phr.) keep the ~ at one's feet, see one's way to suc-cess; keep up the ~, keep the ~ rolling, do one's part in talk etc.; the ~ is with you, it is your turn; ~ & socket, joint with greatest possible freedom; ||three ~s, pawnbroker's sign; ~-firing, with ~ car-tridge; ~-PROOF; ~-bearings, axle fittings avoiding friction by use of small ~s; ~-cock, -tap, automatic cistern-tap with floating ~; ~-flower, archit. ornament. [ME ball f. ON bǫllr f. OTeut. balluz]

ball² (bawl), n. Social assembly for danc-ing (so ~-room; give a ~, of the enter-tainer; open the ~, lead first dance, fig.

commence operations). [f. F *bal* f. *baler, baller*, = Pr. *balar*, It. & LL *ballāre* to dance perh. f. Gk *balliző* dance]

ball³ (bawl), v.t. & i. Squeeze or wind into a ball; ~ *up* (sl.), muddle; grow into a lump or lumps. [BALL¹]

ball'ad, n. Simple song, esp. sentimental composition of several verses, each sung to same melody, with accompaniment; merely subordinate; poem in short stanzas narrating popular story. Hence ~RY (6), n. [ME & OF *balade* (F *ball-*) f. Pr. *balada* dancing-song f. *balar* (BALL²)-ADE (1)]

ballade´ (bǎlahd´), n. Poem of one or more triplets of seven-lined or eight-lined stanzas, each ending with same refrain line, & envoy; poem of equal (usu. seven or eight line) stanzas; ~ *royal*, stanzas of seven (or of line) stanzas (also *rhyme royal*). [earlier spelling & pron. prec., now used technically]

ballast¹, n. Heavy material placed in ship's hold to secure stability; *in* ~, in the hold, (of ship) laden with ~ only or unladen, (of material) as ~; experience, principles, etc., that give stability to character; slag etc. used to form bed of railroad or substratum of road. [so in most Eur. langg.; perh. OSw. & ODa. *barlast* (now *bal-*) show origin, *bar* bare, mere, +*last* load]

ballast², v.t. Furnish with, render steady by means of, ballast (lit. & fig.); fill in (railroad bed) with ballast. Hence ~ING¹(3) n. [f. prec.]

ballerī´na (-ēnah), n. Dancing-woman, ballet-girl. [It.]

ball'et (-lā), n. Combined performance of professional dancers on the stage. [F, dim. of *bal* BALL²]

ballis´ta, n. (pl. *-ae*). Ancient military engine for hurling great stones etc. [L, f. Gk *balliō* throw]

ballis´tic, a. Of projectiles, of hurling-power. Hence ~ICS n. [prec. +IC]

ballon d'essai (see Ap.), n. Experiment to see whether the public, or foreign States, will tolerate a new departure in policy etc. [F]

ball'onét, n. Air-compartment in envelope of balloon or airship. [F (-*nnet*) as foll.]

balloon´¹, n. (Archit.) large ball crowning pillar, spire, etc.; (Chem.) large hollow glass globe used in distillations; round or pear-shaped airtight envelope inflated with gas lighter than air & rising sky-wards, whence ~IST (3) n.; anything hollow & inflated; shape into which, or frame on which, trees & plants are trained; ~ *barrage*, anti-aircraft barrier of steel cables supported in an almost vertical position each by a captive ~ (*barrage* ~); ~ *tire*, low-pressure motor tire of large section. [f. It. *ballone* large ball (*balla* see BALE²+-*one* see -OON)]

balloon´², v.i. Ascend in balloon, whence ~ER¹ n.; swell out like balloon (gowns etc.). [f. prec.]

ball'ot¹, n. (Small ball, ticket, or paper—also ~*paper*—used in) secret voting; votes so recorded; lot-drawing (whether by balls or not); ~*box*, used in voting or lot-drawing. [f. It. *ballotta* dim. of *balla* ball see BALE²]

ball'ot², v.i. Give secret vote; draw lots (officials etc.) by secret vote; draw lots (*for* precedence, esp. in H. of Commons for right of moving resolutions etc.). [f. It. *ballottare* (*ballotta* BALLOT¹)]

ball'ot³, n. Small bale of 70 to 120 lb. [f. dim. of *balle* BALE¹]

ball'otage, n. French second ballot, between two highest candidates with less than legal majority. [F, f. *ballotter* = BALLOT²; see -AGE]

Ball(haus)platz (bahl'howsplahts), n. Foreign Office of late Austro-Hungarian Empire. [~ in Vienna]

∥**ball'y**, a. & adv. (sl.) expr. speaker's disgust or satisfaction (*stung by a* ~ *wasp*; *too* ~ *tired*; *whose* ~ *fault is that?*; *won the* ~ *lot*). [pronunciation of *bl—y* = *bloody*]

bally'hōō´, n. (orig. U.S.). Trumped-up publicity of a vulgar or misleading kind. [?]

ball'yrag, v.t. & i. (sl.; -*gg*-). Maltreat by hustling, jeering, or playing practical jokes on; indulge in horseplay. Hence ~RING¹(-*g*-)n. [etym. dub.; also *bullyrag*, prob. by pop. etym.]

balm (bahm), n. Fragrant & medicinal exudation from certain trees; ointment for anointing, soothing pain, or healing; perfume, fragrance; healing or soothing influence, consolation; tree yielding ~ (Asia & N. Africa); *B~ Gentle* or *B~-mint, Bastard B~, Field B~*, fragrant herbs; *B~ of Gilead* or *of Mecca*, golden oleo-resin once much used as antiseptic, artificial imitation of this. [ME & OF *basme* f. L *balsamum* BALSAM; the ME has been variously corrected on the L (e.g. *balsme, balm-*) whence the mod. *l-*]

balm-cricket (bahm-), n. Cicada. [earlier *baum-*; mistransl. of G *baumgrille* tree-cricket]

balmō´ral, n. Kinds of laced boot, petti-coat, Scotch cap. [*B~ Castle*, royal residence in Scotland]

balm'y (bahm'i), a. Yielding balm; fragrant, soft, mild, soothing, healing; (sl.) = BARMY. Hence ~ily² adv., ~INESS n. [BALM+-Y¹]

balneol'ogy, n. Scientific study of bath-ing and medicinal springs. [f. L *balneum* bath+-o-+-LOGY]

bal'sam (bawl-), n. Resinous product = BALM; *True B~* or *B~ of Mecca* = BALM *of Gilead*; other medicinal oleo-resins (*Canada B~*, used in mounting for micro-scope; artificial oily or resinous ointment, esp. various substances dissolved in oil or turpentine, e.g. *B~ of Aniseed*; (fig.)

healing or soothing agency; (Chem.) compounds of resins & volatile oils, insoluble in water; tree yielding ~ ; flowering plant of genus *Impatiens*; *B~ Apple*, gourdlike plant with highly coloured fruit. Hence **balsăm′ic** (bawl- or bal-) a., **balsăm′ICALLY** adv., **balsămIF′EROUS** a., ~Y² (bawl-) a. [f. L *balsamum*; from c. 1000 to 1600 either variants of *basme* were used, or the full L; *balsam* before & after those dates]

băl′timŏre (bawl-), n. N.-Amer. orange & black starling. [colours of Lord Baltimore's (proprietor of Maryland) coat of arms]

băl′uster, n. Short pillar, slender above, pear-shaped below; post helping to support rail; (pl.) set of these supporting handrail of staircase (now usu. *banisters*). [f. F *balustre* f. It. *balaustra* f. L f. Gk *balaustion* wild-pomegranate flower (from shape of its calyx-tube)]

băl′ustrĭade (-ā-), n. Row of balusters with rail or coping as ornamental parapet to terrace, balcony, etc. Hence ~ād′ED² a. [PREC., -ADE]

băm, v.t. & n. (sl., arch.). Hoax. [from 18th c.; etym. dub.]

bămbī′nō (-ō-), n. (pl. *-ni*). Image of infant Jesus in swaddling-clothes shown in Italian churches at Christmas. [It., = baby]

bămbōō′, n. (pl. *-oos*). Genus of tropical giant grasses; the stem, used as stick or material. [*bamba* now in Java & Sumatra, but perh. not native]

bămbōō′zle, v.t. (sl.). Hoax, mystify, cheat *into* doing something or *out of* property etc. Hence ~MENT (-zelm-) n. [from c. 1700; etym. dub.; cf. BAM, also F *bambocher* play the fool, *bamboche* puppet f. It. *bamboccio* simpleton (*bambo* fool + *-occio*)]

băn¹, v.t. & i. (-nn-). Curse (t. & i., arch.); prohibit, interdict. [OE *bannan* summon & ON *banna* curse f. OTeut. *bannan* proclaim f. root *ba-* (cf. L *fa-*, Gk *pha-*) speak] **băn²**, n. Ecclesiastical anathema, interdict; curse supposed to have supernatural power; angry execration (arch.); formal prohibition; sentence of outlawry, esp. *Ban of the (Holy Roman) Empire* (*under a~*). [OF, f. LL *bannum* f. Teut. banning proclamation with penalties (*bannan* BAN¹)]

băn³, n. Viceroy of districts in Hungary, Croatia, etc., commanding in war. [Pers., = lord]

băn′al, a. Commonplace, trite. [F (BAN², -AL); orig. a feudal word; the use of the lord's mill was compulsory for all tenants (*bannal mill*), whence the sense *common to all*]

banăl′ĭty, n. Triteness; a commonplace. [f. F *banalité* f. prec., see -ALITY]

bana′na (-nah-), n. Tropical & subtropical fruit-tree; its fruit, finger-shaped with yellow rind, in clusters (*hand of* ~s, bunch). [Port. or Sp. f. the native name in Guinea]

‖ **Băn′bury̆ cake**, n. Spiced cake made at Banbury, Oxfordshire.

banc (băngk), **banco** (băngk′ō), n. Used in phrases *in banc, in banco, = on the bench, applied to sittings of a Superior Court of Common Law as a full court (not *Nisi Prius* or circuit). [*banco* L abl. of *bancus* bench; see BANK⁵]

bănd¹, n. 1. Thing that restrains, binds together; connects or unites (chiefly arch., now ousted by the orig. identical BOND); (Bookbinding) straps at back holding sheets together; ~*stone*, one passing through dry-stone wall & binding it. 2. Flat strip of thin material; hoop round anything (of iron, elastic, etc.); strap forming part of a garment (shirt, dress, hat, etc.), (pl.) development of neckband or collar into two pendent strips (clerical, legal); *reef-* ~, strip sewn on sail at eyelet holes for strength; (Mech.) belt connecting wheels; stripe of colour or distinguishable material on object; ~*box*, of paper-covered chip or cardboard for millinery (orig. for clerical ~s; *look as if one came out of* ~*box*, of extreme neatness); ~*saw*, endless saw running over wheels; ~*wheel*, worked by strap from another. 3. Organized company of armed men, robbers, persons with common object (*B~ of Hope*, total-abstinence association), body of musicians, esp. wind-instrument performers (*brass* ~; *military* ~; *dance* ~; ~*master*, conductor; ~*stand*, platform; ~*s′man*, member of ~). [all meanings ult. f. OTeut. *bindan* BIND¹, but 1, 2, 3, with different hist. (1) (tie), ME *band* f. ON *band* f. OTeut. (hence also BOND); (2) (strip), late ME *bande* f. F *bande, bende*, = Pr. & It. *banda* f. OHG *binda* f. OTeut.; (3) (company), 15th-c. *bande* f. F *bande* = Pr., Sp., It., *banda* ribbon or LL *bandum* banner both f. Teut.]

bănd², v.t. Put a band on; mark with stripes; form into a league (usu. refl. or pass.). [f. F *bander* f. *bande*, see prec.]

băn′dagle, n., & v.t. Strip of material for binding up limb, wound, etc., or anything used for blindfolding; (vb) tie up with ~e, whence ~ING³ (3) n. [F, f. *bande* BAND¹, see -AGE]

băndănn′a, -ăn′a, n. Richly coloured yellow or white spotted (orig. always silk) handkerchief. [Hind. *bāndhnu* method of spot-dyeing]

băn′dar (bŭn-), n. (Anglo-Ind.). The rhesus monkey; ~*log*: the whole race of monkeys; (fig.) irresponsible chatterers. [Hind.; *log* = people]

băndeau′ (-dō), n. (pl. -x, pr. -z). Fillet for binding woman's hair; fitting-band inside woman's hat. [F]

bän'der̃öl(e), n. Long narrow flag with cleft end flown at masthead; ornamental streamer on knight's lance; ribbon-like scroll (Archit. stone band) with inscription; sometimes = BANNEROL. [F *bande-role* dim. of *bandière* BANNER]

bän'dicoot, n. (India), rat as large as cat; (Australia) insectivorous marsupial. [f. Telugu *pandi-kokku* pig rat]

bän'dit, n. (pl. -ts, -tti'), Outlaw; law-less robber, brigand, (usu. in organized gangs); *a banditto*, pl. -tti p.p. of *bandire* = med. L *banire* proclaim see BAN[1]]

‖ **bän'dög**, n. Chained dog; mastiff, bloodhound. [earlier *band-dog* f. BAND[1]]

bändoleer', -ier' (-ër̃), n. Shoulder-belt with cartridge-loops. [f. 17th-c., F *bandoulière* f. It. *bandoliera* (*bandola* dim. of *banda* BAND)]

ban'dy[1], v.t. Throw, strike, pass, to & fro (ball, or fig. stories, epithets, etc.); often ~ *about*; discuss (names etc.); give & take (blows etc.), exchange (something with some one). [cf. F *bander* (something with some one). Tennis' perh. f. *bande* side] v unex-plained.]

ban'dy[2], n. (Orig.) special form of tennis; (now also ~*ball*) hockey; the stick, curved at end, used in the game. [perh. f. prec.]

bän'dy[3], n. Indian cart or buggy. [f. Telugu *bandi*]

bän'dy[4], a. Wide apart at the knees (of legs); ~*-legged*, (of persons or animals) having ~ legs. [perh. f. BANDY[2] curved stick]

bane, n. Poison (lit. now only in comb., as *rat's*~); cause of ruin, esp. *the* ~ *of*; ruin, woe, (poet.). Hence ~'FUL (-nf-) a., ~'fully[2] adv., ~'fulNESS n. [OE *bana* death, murder, cf. OHG *bano*; also Gk *phonos* slaughter]

bäng[1], v.t. & i. Strike (t. & i.) noisily; shut (t. & i. of door) with noise; make sound of blow or explosion; thrash; (sl.) surpass. [from 16th c.; cf. ON *banga* to hammer, LG *bangen* strike]

bäng[2], n. Sounding blow, sound of a blow, report of gun. [f. prec.]

bäng[3], adv. & int. With sudden impact, abruptly, completely, explosively; *go* ~, explode; conventional imitation of gun-fire. [f. BANG[1]]

bäng[4], v.t.& n. Cut (front hair) straight across forehead; (n.) fringe resulting; ~*-tail*, horse with tail cut straight across. [f. prec.]

bangle (bäng'gl), n. Ring bracelet or anklet. Hence ~ED (-ld) a. [f. Hind. *bangrī*, glass wrist-ring]

bän'ian, bän'yan, n. Hindoo trader; (Bengal) native broker to European house; Indian flannel jacket; (Naut.) ~*day*, on which no meat is served out; ~*-hospital*, for animals; ~*-tree* (or ~), Indian Fig, branches of which root them-selves over great extent. [Port. *banian* f. Arab. *banyan* f. Gujarati *vaniyo* man of trading caste, = ? *day*, *hospital*, from caste reverence for animal life; ~*-tree*, E name used first of a specimen under which Banians had built pagoda]

ban'ish, v.t. Condemn to exile (person from place, or double obj. as ~*ed him the court*, or obj. of person only); dismiss from one's presence or mind. Hence ~MENT n. [f. OF *banir* (-ISH[2]) f. LL]

ban'ister = BALUSTER.

bän'jö, n. (pl. -os, -oes) Stringed musical instrument with guitar neck & head, tambourine body, played with fingers. Hence ~IST (3) n. [negro corruption of BANDORE ult. f. Gk *pandoura*]

bänk[1], n. 1. Raised shelf of ground, slope, elevation in sea or river bed; artificial slope enabling car etc. to maintain speed round a curve; flat-topped mass of cloud, snow, etc. 2. Sloping margin of river, ground near river (*right*, *left*, ~ *to one looking down stream*); edge of hollow place (e.g. top of shaft in mining). [ME *banke* cf. OIcel. *bakki* in same senses f. OTeut. *bankon* cf. BANK[2]]

bänk[2], v.t. & i. Contain as a bank, confine with bank(s); (of car or aeroplane or its occupant) travel with one side higher; confine watch-escapement (of ~*ing-pins*), strike against the ~*ing-pins* (or a.ös.; of escapement); ~ *up*, heap or rise into banks (of snow, clouds), pack tightly (fire, for slow burning). [f. prec.]

bänk[3], n. Establishment for custody of money, which it pays out on customer's order; ‖ *the B~, B~ of England*, managing the public debt, receiving the revenue, issuing legal-tender notes, & having the Government for chief customer; (Gam-ing) amount of money before Keeper of table; ~*-book*, containing customer's private copy of his account with ~; ~*-credit*, arrangement by which customer may overdraw on security given; ‖ ~*-holiday*, day on which ~s are legally closed, usu. kept as general holiday also; ‖ ~*-note*, banker's promissory note payable to bearer on demand & serving as money; *B~ of England* is prepared to discount bills. [f. F *banque* f. It. *banca* f. Teut.

bänk[4], v.t. & i. Keep bank, trade in money (~*ing-house*, commercial firm that does some ~*ing*); keep money at bank; convert into

money; (Gaming) hold table fund; ~ (*upon*, base one's hopes on, count upon, reckon reliable. [f. prec.]

bănk⁵, n. Galley-rower's bench; tier of *oars* in galley; row of organ keys; working-table in some trades. [ME *bannck* f. OF *banc* f. Teut. *bank* f. OTeut. *bankis* BENCH f. *bankon*]

bănk'able, a. That will be received at a bank (securities etc.). [BANK³+-ABLE]

bănk'er¹, n. Proprietor or partner of private bank, governor, director, etc., of joint-stock bank, (*let me be your* ~, lend or give the money you need); (Gaming) keeper of the bank; dealer in some games of chance; a gambling game of cards. [BANK³+-ER¹]

bănk'er², n. Labourer (Eastern counties); (Hunting) horse that jumps on & off banks too large to clear. [BANK¹+-ER¹]

bănk'er³, n. Wooden or stone bench for trimming bricks or stone on; mason's sign manual (formerly engraved on a dressed stone before it left the ~). [perh.=It. *banco* statuary's bench]

bănk'ĕt, n. Auriferous conglomerate like pudding-stone found in S. Africa, [Du., =kind of hardbake (BANQUET)]

bănk'ing, n. In vbl senses of BANK ²,⁴; also, fishing on a sea bank (esp. Newfoundland). [BANK¹]

bănk'rŭpt¹, n. (Law) insolvent person whose effects, on creditors' or his own petition to Bankruptcy Court, are administered & distributed for benefit of all creditors; (pop.) insolvent debtor. [earlier *bankroud* etc. f. It. *banca rotta* broken bank (BANK³, L *rupt-* p.p. of *rumpere* break) corrected to *-rupt* on L]

bănk'rŭpt², v.t. Reduce to bankruptcy. [f. prec.]

bănk'rŭpt³, a. Under legal process because of insolvency; insolvent; bereft (*of* some quality etc.). [perh. the short p.p. of prec.]

bănk'ruptcy̆, n. Being declared bankrupt, being insolvent; utter loss (of something, e.g. reputation). [prec.+-CY, irreg. for *-ruptcy*]

bănk'sia (-sha), n. Australian flowering shrub now grown in Europe. [Sir J. *Banks*, -IA¹]

bănks'man, n. Coal-mine overlooker above ground. [BANK¹]

bănn'er, n. Cloth flag on pole used as standard of emperor, king, lord, knight, for war; flag of a country etc. (*join, follow, the ~ of*; now chiefly fig.); ensign (esp. in frame, or with two poles) borne in religious or political demonstrations; anything used as symbol of principles; *~-screen*, fire screen hung from standing pole or mantelpiece; (attrib.) prominent, conspicuous, as ~ *headline* (in newspaper). Hence ~ED² (-erd) a. [f. OF *baniere* f. LL +*bandaria* f. LL *bandum* f. Goth. *bandwa* perh. f. root of *band, bind*]

bănn'erĕt, n. Knight having vassals under his banner; one knighted on the field for valour. [ME & OF *banered* (*baniere* see prec. +-*ed* =-ATE²) lit. bannered]

bănn'erŏl, n. Banner borne at great men's funerals & placed over tomb;= BANDEROLE [var. of BANDEROLE]

bănn'ock, n. Scotch & N.-Eng. home-made loaf, usu. unleavened, flat, & round or oval. [f. Gael. *bannach* perh. f. L *panicium* (*panis* bread)]

bănns (-z), n. pl. Notice in church of intended marriage, thrice read to give opportunity of objection (*ask, publish, put up, forbid, the* ~). [var. of BAN²]

bănq'uĕt¹, n. Sumptuous feast; dinner with speeches in celebration of something or to further a cause. [F, dim. of *banc* bench BANK⁵]

bănq'uĕt², v.t. & i. Regale (person); feast, carouse, whence ~ER¹ n. [f. F *banqueter* (*banquet*=prec.)]

banquette' (-kēt), n. Raised way behind rampart etc. for firing from; bench behind driver in French diligence. [F, f. It. *banchetta* dim. of *banca* bench see BANK³]

băn'shee, n. Spirit whose wail portends death in a house (Irish & Scotch). [Ir. *bean sidhe* f. OIr. *ben side* woman of the fairies]

bănt, v.i. See BANTING.

băn'tam, n. Small kind of domestic fowl, of which the cock is very pugnacious; small but spirited person (~ *battalion*, of men below normal standard enrolled for the war of 1914-18); ~-*weight* (Boxing) see BOX'*ing weights*. [f. *Bantam* in Java whence they were perh. brought, though perh. orig. Japanese]

băn'ter, n. & v.t. & i. Humorous ridicule, good-humoured personalities; (vb) make fun of, rally; talk jestingly. [f. 17th c.; etym. dub.]

băn'ting, n. Treatment of obesity by abstinence from sugar, starch, & fat; also **bănt** v.i., adopt this. [for *Banting's method*]

băn'tling, n. Young child, brat. [perh. corrupted f. G *bänkling* bastard f. *bank* (bench-begotten, cf. BASTARD); or f. BAND² swathe f.+-LING³(2)]

Bantu (băhntoō'), n. & a. Used to include many related African languages & races. [native, = people]

bănk'ring, n. Javanese squirrel-like insectivorous animal. [Javanese *bangsring*]

băn'yan. See BANIAN (used esp. for the tree).

bănzai' (-zī), int. Form of greeting by Japanese to their Emperor, cheer used in battle, etc. [Jap. = ten thousand years (of life to you)]

bă'obăb, n. African tree called also Monkey-Bread with enormously thick stem. [mentioned 1592]

băp, n. (Sc.), Small loaf or roll of bread. [?]

báp'tism, n. Religious rite of immersing (person) in, or sprinkling with, water in sign of purification & (with Christians) of admission to the Church, generally accompanied by name-giving; (fig.) ~ of blood, martyrdom, ~ of fire, soldier's first battle; naming of church bells & ships. Hence **baptis'mal** (-z-) a., **baptis'mally** adv. [ME baptesme f. OF baptesme f. L f. Gk baptismos (baptizō BAPTIZE)]

báp'tist, n. One who baptizes, esp. John the B~; one of a sect (formerly called ANABAPTISTS by opponents) objecting to infant baptism, & practising immersion. [f. OF baptiste, f. L baptista f. Gk baptistēs (baptizō BAPTIZE)]

báptis'tery, n. Part of church (or formerly separate building) used for baptism; (in Baptist chapel) immersion receptacle. [f. OF baptisterie f. L f. Gk baptistērion]

báptize', v.t. Immerse in or sprinkle with water, as sign of purification or initiation, esp. into the Christian Church; christen; (abs.) administer baptism; (fig.) purify; elevate; name or nickname. [f. F baptiser f. L baptizare f. Gk baptizō bathe (baptō dip)]

bar¹, n. 1. Long-shaped piece of rigid material (metal, wood, soap, etc.; ~-bell, iron ~ with ball at each end used in gymnastics, cf. dumb-bell; ~wood, red wood from Gaboon imported in ~s for dyeing etc.). 2. Slip of silver below clasp of medal as additional distinction; band of colour etc. on surface, (Her.) two horizontal parallel lines across shield (~ sinister, by mistake for BEND or BARON supposed sign of illegitimacy). 3. Rod or pole used to confine or obstruct (window, door, grate, gate, ~); barrier of any shape (Temple Bar, toll~); harbour~, of sand across mouth). 4. (Mus.) vertical line across stave dividing piece into sections of equal time-value, such sections; immaterial barrier; (Law) plea arresting action or claim; moral obstacle. 5. Barrier with some technical significance, as, in lawcourt, place at which prisoner stands; hence ~ of conscience, opinion, etc.; || trial at ~, in King's-Bench division; a particular court (practise at parliamentary, Chancery, etc., ~); || be called to the ~ (i.e. that in Inns of Court separating benchers), be admitted a barrister; || be called within the ~ (i.e. that in courts within which K.C.s plead), be appointed King's Counsel; the ~, barristers, profession of barrister. 6. || (Parl.) rail dividing off space to which non-members may be admitted on business. 7. (In an inn etc.) counter across which refreshments are handed, space behind or room containing it; ||~man, ~maid, attendants at such counter. [ME & OF barre f. LL barra etym. dub.]

bar², v.t. (-rr-). Fasten (door etc.) with

bar(s); keep (person) in or out (~ring-out, schoolboy rebellion); obstruct (path etc.; exclude from consideration, e.g. ~ one in imperative used as prep., e.g. ~ one in betting); (sl.) object to, dislike, (person, habit, etc.); mark with stripe(s). [ME barren f. OF barrer (barre BAR¹)]

bar³, n. Large European sea-fish. [F]

bar'alip'ton, n. See BARBARA.

bárathe'a, n. Fine cloth made from wool (with or without silk or cotton). [?]

bárath'rum, n. Pit at Athens into which criminals were thrown; abyss. [L, f. Gk barathron]

barb¹, n., & v.t. 1. Beardlike feelers of barbel etc.; chin-piece of nun's head-dress; lateral filament branching from shaft of feather; subordinate recurved point of arrow, fish-hook, etc.; (fig.) sting. 2. v.t. Furnish (arrow etc.) with ~; ~ed wire, for fences & esp. as obstruction in war, with wire prickles at intervals. [f. F barbe f. L barba beard]

barb², n. Breeds of horse & pigeon imported from Barbary. [f. F barbe (Barbarie)]

barb'ara, first word of the scholastic mnemonic lines for figures & moods of the syllogism (some of these, esp. barbara, barbara celarent, baralipton, are used allusively for logic or logical training). [f. L]

bárbár'ian, n. & a. (Foreigner) differing from speaker in language & customs, esp. in hist., (a) non-Greek, (one) outside the Roman Empire, (a) non-Christian; rude, wild, or uncultured (person). [f. F barbarien (BARBAROUS, -IAN)]

barbár'ic, a. Rude, rough, like or of barbarians & their art or taste. Hence ~ICALLY adv. [f. OF barbarique f. L f. Gk barbarikos (barbaros BARBAROUS, & see -IC)]

bárb'arism, n. Mixing of foreign or vulgar expressions in talk or writing; such an expression; absence of culture, ignorance & rudeness; instance of this. [f. F barbarisme f. L f. Gk barbarismos (barbarizō speak like a foreigner f. barbaros BARBAROUS, -IZE)]

barbár'ity, n. Savage cruelty; instance of it; barbaric style or taste, instance of it. [usu. barbarism)]

bárb'arize, v.t. & i. Make or become barbarous; corrupt (language). Hence ~A'TION n. [f. L barbarus BARBAROUS + -IZE]

bárb'arous, a. (Lang.) not Greek, not Greek or Latin, not pure, illiterate; (people) non-Greek, beyond Roman Empire, non-Christian, outlandish; uncivilized; cruel; coarse. Hence ~ly adv., ~NESS n. [f. L f. Gk barbaros foreign (perh. imit. of gibberish) +-OUS]

Bárb'ary ape, n. Large tailless monkey of N. Africa and Gibraltar. [Barbary,

barb'ate, a. (bot., zool.). Having hairy tufts. [f. L *barbatus* bearded (*barba* beard, -ATE²)]

barb'ecue, n. Large wooden or iron framework for smoking or broiling; hog, ox, etc., roasted whole, whence **barb'e-cue** v.t.; *large entertainment with whole-roasting; floor for drying coffee-beans. [f. Sp. *barbacoa* f. Haitian *barba-cóa* crate on posts]

barb'el, n. Large European fresh-water fish with fleshy filaments hanging from mouth; such filament in any fish, whence ~(l)ED² a. [f. OF *barbel* f. LL *barbellus* dim. of *barbus* barbel (*barba* beard)]

barb'er, n. One who shaves & trims customers' beards & hair (now usu. *hair-dresser*); ~'s *block*, for making & dis-playing wigs; ~'s *itch*, skin disease said to be communicated in shaving; ~'s *pole*, spirally painted & used as sign. [ME & AF *barbour* f. OF *barbeor* f. L +*barbatorem* (*barbæ* beard), see -OR³]

barb'er(r)y, ber-, n. Shrub with spiny shoots, yellow flowers, & oblong red berries; its berry. [f. med. L *barbaris*, *berberis*, etym. dub.]

barb'ét, n. Bird with bristle-tufts at base of bill. [perh. OF *barbet* adj. = *barbu* bearded]

barbette', n. Platform within fort or in ship from which guns fire over parapet etc. without embrasure. [F dim. of *barbe* beard (F *barbette* = also linen up to throat showing above dress)]

barb'ican, n. Outer defence to city or castle, esp. double tower over gate or bridge. [f. F *barbacane* etym. dub.; Arab.-Pers. *bab-khanah* gate-house is suggested]

Barb'izon, n. Village near Fontaine-bleau; ~ *School*, coterie of French natura-listic painters (19th c.).

Barcelon'a, n. Spanish city; ~ (*nut*), hazel-nut imported from Spain.

barb'ol'a, n. (Also ~ *work*) the embellish-ment of small articles by attachment of coloured models of flowers, fruit, etc. made from a plastic paste. [?]

barb'ule, n. Filament branching from barb (of feather) as barb from shaft. [f. L *barbula* dim. of *barba* beard]

barb'car'ole, -ôlle, n. Song of gondolier; imitation of it. [f. F *barcarolle* f. It. *bar-caruola* boat-song (*barca* boat)]

bard¹, n. Celtic minstrel; (Wales) poet recognized at Eisteddfod, whence ~'ro a.; early poet; lyric poet; poet, whence ~'LING² n. [f. Gael. & Ir. *bard*]

bard², n. Armour for breast & flanks of warhorse. Hence ~ED² a. [f. F *barde* horse-armour perh. = Sp. & Port. *albarda* (f. Arab.?) packsaddle]

bare¹, a. Unclothed, undisguised, un-covered, bald, unfurnished, unprotected, threadbare, unsheathed, ill-provided, empty, unadorned, scanty, mere; ~ *back* a. & adv., ~ed a., with ~ back, on unsaddled horse; ~faced, without beard etc., without mask, also undisguised, shameless, or impudent, whence **bare-fa'cedly²** adv., **barefa'cedness** n.; ~foot a. & adv., ~footed a., without shoes or stockings; ~headed a., without hat or cap. Hence **bar-'ish²(2)** a. [OE *bær*; com-Teut., cf. G & Du. *baar*]

bare², v.t. Uncover, unsheathe, reveal, strip. [f. prec.]

barège' (-äzh), n. & a. (Of) silky gauze. [orig. made at Barèges]

barely (bā-'lī), adv. Openly, explicitly; merely; only just; scarcely. [BARE¹ + -LY²]

bare'ness (-rn-), n. Lack of covering, un-adorned state. [BARE¹ + -NESS]

bare'sark (-rs-), n. & adv. Wild Norse warrior; (adv.) without armour. [lit. bare shirt (SARK); mod. form embodying sup-posed etym. of BERSERKER]

barg'ain¹ (-gin), n. Agreement on terms of give and take, compact, thing acquired by bargaining (*good, bad,* ~, result cheaply or dearly bought; *a* ~, thing ac-quired or offered cheap; *into the* ~, beyond the strict terms, moreover; *strike a* ~, come to terms; *make best of bad* ~, take mis-fortune etc. cheerfully). [f. OF *bargaine, -caigne*, f. LL +*barcaneum* (*barca* see foll.)]

barg'ain² (-gin), v.i. & t. Haggle (*with* someone, or abs.) over terms of give & take; stipulate *with* person *for* thing or *to* receive, give, etc.; ~ *for*, be prepared for, expect, (usu. with neg. or *more than*); ~ (trans.) ~ *away*, part with for a con-sideration. Hence ~ER¹ n. [f. OF *bar-gaigner* f. LL *barcaniare* perh. f. *barca* 'barge which carries goods to & fro', giving sense either of 'off & on' or of trading]

barge, n. & v.i. 1. Flat-bottomed freight-boat for canals & rivers, with or without sails; second boat of man-of-war, for use of chief officers; large ornamental oared vessel for state occasions, house-boat (e.g. *College* ~); ~*pole* (for fending; *would not touch with a* ~*pole*, regard with loathing). 2. v.i. (sl.). Lurch or rush heavily *into, against, about*; ~ *in*, intrude. [OF, prob.=BARK³]

barge'-, comb. form in architecture = gable. ~*couple*, two gable beams; ~*course*, roof projecting beyond them; ~*board*, ornamental screen to them; ~*stones*, forming sloping or stepped line of gable. [f. med. L *barpus* gallows]

|| **barg'ee**, n. Man in charge of barge; *swear like a* ~, fluently, forcibly; *lucky* ~ (colloq.) lucky fellow. [-EE]

bar'ic, a. Of or containing barium. [BARIUM + -IC]

barill'a, n. Plant (*Salsola Soda*) in Spain, Sicily, Canaries; impure alkali made by burning either this or kelp. [Sp.]

baritone, var. of BARYTONE in mus. sense.

bar'ium, n. (chem.). White metallic element, basis of alkaline earth baryta. [BARYTA +-IUM]

bark[1], n. Outer sheath of tree trunks & branches; tan; quinine (also *Peruvian* or *Jesuits'* ~); (sl.) skin; ~*bed*, hot-bed of tan; ~*bound*, hindered in growth by tight ~; ~*pit*, of ~ & water for tanning; ~*tree*, E name of cinchona. [f. Scand.]

bark[2], v.t. Strip bark from (tree), kill (tree) by ring-cutting bark (also *ring-*~); abrade (one's knuckles etc.); encrust. [f. prec.]

bark[3], barque (-ärk), n. Three-masted vessel with fore & main masts square-rigged, mizen fore-&-aft rigged (usu. *barque*); any ship or boat (poet., usu. *bark*). [f. F 15th-c. *barque* f. Pr., Sp., or It., *barca* f. L *barca* ship's boat prec. f. Celt.]

bark[4], n. Usual cry of dogs, foxes, squirrels; (fig.) sound of gunfire, or of cough; ~ *worse than bite*, of testy harmless person. [f. foll.]

bark[5], v.i. & t. Utter sharp explosive cry (of dogs & some other animals); speak (& ~ *out*, say) petulantly, imperiously; ~ *at*, abuse; ~ *up the wrong tree*, denounce wrong person etc. (sl.) cough. [OE *beorcan* cf. ON *berkja*; perh. variant of BREAK]

bark'er, n. Noisy assailant; shop or auction or travelling-show tout; (sl.) pistol, cannon. [f. prec.]

bar'ley, n. (pl.~s). Hardy awned cereal used as food & in making malt liquors & spirits; its grain; *pearl* ~, the grain ground small; ~*broth*, strong ale; ~*corn*, grain of ~ (*John Barleycorn*, malt liquor personified), its length as measure, ⅓ inch, top of fore-sight on rifle; ~*mow*, stack; ~ *sugar*, twisted sweetmeat; ~*water*, soothing decoction of pearl~ for invalids. [OE *bærlic*; for *bær-* cf. obs. *bear* barley f. OTeut. *bariz*; *-lic* = -LY[1] (as if cog. an adj.)]

***bar'low** (-ō), n. (Also ~ *knife*) large single-bladed pocket-knife. [B~, orig. maker]

barm, n. Froth on fermenting malt liquor, yeast, leaven. [OE *beorma*; prob. com.-Teut., cf. G *bärme*]

Barm'ecide, n. & a. (Giver of benefits that are) illusory, imaginary, disappointing. [name of Arabian-Nights prince whose feast to beggar was rich dish-covers with nothing below]

barm'y, a. Full of barm; frothy; (sl. also ~ *on the crumpet*) wrong in the head, cracked. [-Y[2]]

barn, n. Covered building for storing grain etc.; (contempt.) unadorned building; ~*dance*, (orig. U.S.) dance in which partners advance side by side & then dance a schottische step; ~*door*, lit., & fig. target too large to be missed, also adj. of fowls =reared at the ~-door; ~-*owl*, = White, Church, Screech, Owl; ~-*stormer*, strolling player; ~-*yard*, farm-yard. [OE *bere-ern* (*bere* barley +-*ern* place)]

Barn'aby, n. (Saint) Barnabas; ~ *bright*, St. Barnabas' day, 11th June (longest day in Old Style reckoning). [f. F *Barnabé*]

barn'acle[1], n. (usu. pl.) pincers placed on horse's nose to coerce him into quiet for shoeing etc.; (sl.) pl.) spectacles. [ME *bernak* f. OF *bernac* muzzle, w. dim. ending see -LE]

barn'acle[2], n. 1. Arctic goose visiting Britain in winter (also *bernacle* for distinction from 2). 2. Stalked cirriped clinging by fleshy foot-stalk to ship's bottom; follower who cannot be shaken off. [ME *bernekke*, *bernake*, = OF *bernaque* etym. dub.: (*Hibernicula* (Irish goose), *perna* (a shellfish), *bare* +*neck*, are suggested; pop. mythol. represented the goose as developed out of the shellfish]

bar'ograph (-ahf), n. Self-recording aneroid. [f. Gk *baros* weight +-GRAPH(2)]

barol'ogy, n. Science of weight. [as prec. +-LOGY]

barom'eter, n. Instrument measuring atmospheric pressure used for forecasting weather & ascertaining height above sea-level; *common*, *siphon*, *wheel*, *aneroid*, etc., various systems; (fig.) ~ *of opinion*, etc. Hence **barometric(al)** a., **baro-met'rically[2]** adv., **barom'etry** n. [as prec. +-METER]

bā'ron, n. 1. (hist.). One who held by military or other honourable service from the king or other superior (restricted later to *king's~s*, & again to those, *Great Barons*, attending Great Council or summoned to Parliament; hence, peer). 2. (mod.) One of the lowest order of nobility; holder of foreign title (called *Baron ——*); holder like English ~, *Lord ——*); (orig. U.S.) a great merchant in a (designated) commodity (*beef~*; *beer~*); ~ *of beef*, double sirloin undivided. [ME & OF *barun* f. LL *baronem* nom. *baro* man (as in *king's ~ man*), freeman, husband, male, perh. f. L *baro -onis* dunce]

bā'ronage, n. Barons or great vassals of Crown collectively; the nobility; book with list of peers & comments. [ME & OF *baronage* f. LL +*baronaticum* f. *baro*]

bā'roness, n. Baron's wife; lady holding baronial title in her own right. [f. OF *baronesse* see BARON, -ESS[1]]

bā'ronet[1], n. Member of lowest hereditary titled order, commoner with precedence of all knights exc. K.G.s; abbr. *Bart*. [dim. of BARON; see -ET]

bā'ronet[2], v.t. Raise to rank of baronet.

bă'ronĕtage, n. Baronets collectively; book with list of them & comments. [-AGE; cf. BARONAGE].

bă'ronĕtcy, n. Baronet's patent or rank. [-CY]

barōn'ial, a. Of, belonging to, befitting, baron(s). [foll.+-AL]

bă'rony, n. Baron's domain, rank, tenure; (Ireland) division of county; (Scotland) large manor. [f. OF *baronie* f. LL *baronia*; see BARON & -Y¹]

baroque' (-ŏk), a. & n. 1. (Of) certain stylistic tendencies in 17th–18th c. arts. 2. Grotesque, whimsical. [F, f. Port. *barroco*, Sp. *barrueco* rough pearl, etym. dub.]

barouche' (-ōōsh), n. Four-wheeled carriage with collapsible half-head, for four occupants & driver. [f. G (dial.) *barutsche* f. It. *baroccio* f. L *birotus* (BI- 1 a +*rota* wheel) perh. after *carroccio* chariot]

barque, n. See BARK³.

barquentine, bark-, (bärk'entēn), n. Vessel with foremast square-rigged, main & mizen fore-&-aft rigged. [f. BARK³ after BRIGANTINE]

bă'rrack, n., & v.t. 1. Permanent building(s) in which soldiers are lodged (usu. pl.); (transf.) building in which others (e.g. children) are similarly herded together; building of severely dull or plain appearance. 2. v.t. Place in ~s; hoot, jeer at, (players in cricket-match etc.). [f. F *baraque* f. It. *baracca* or Sp. *barraca* 'souldier's tent' (1617) etym. dub.]

barracōōn', n. Set of sheds or enclosure for slaves, convicts, etc. [f. Sp. *barracon* (as prec.; see -OON)]

bă'rracŭd'a (-ōōd-), -cōōt'a, -cout'a (-ōōt-), n. Large W.-Ind. sea-fish. [f. Sp.]

bă'rr'age, n. 1. Damming; dam (esp. of those in Nile). 2. (Mil., freq. bă'räzh) barrier to offensive or defensive action on the part of an enemy usu. in the form of a line, area, or volume into which a large number of guns fire shells either continuously or for pre-arranged periods (*anti-aircraft*~, barrier of shellfire against hostile aircraft; BALLOON ~; *box* ~, one laid down usu. on three sides in order to isolate a particular area; *creeping* ~, one laid down in front of & moving with one's own advancing troops); attrib., as ~ BALLOON. [F, f. *barre* BAR¹; see -AGE]

bă'rrator, -er, n. (legal). Vexatious litigant; malicious raiser of discord. [f. OF *barateor* trickster (*barat* fraud) perh. f. Celtic, cf. OIr. *mrath*, W *brad*; meaning influenced by ON *barátta*, strife]

bă'rratrў, n. (Marine law) fraud or gross negligence of master or crew to prejudice of ship's owners; (Law) vexatious litigation or incitement to it. Hence ~OUS a. [f. OF *baraterie* (*barat* see prec., -ERY)]

bă'rrel, n. Flat-ended cylindrical wooden vessel of hooped staves, cask; varying measure of capacity (~*bulk*, 5 cub. ft); revolving cylinder in capstan, watch, & other machines; cylindrical body or trunk of an object, belly & loins of horse, etc.; metal tube of gun; *barrel-*, cylindrical or semi-cylindrical, as ~*drain*, *-vault*; ~*organ*, with pin-studded cylinder turned by handle & mechanism opening the pipes as required. [f. F *baril* perh. f. LL *barra* BAR¹]

bă'rrel', v.t. (-ll-). Put in barrel(s); ~*led*, (also) =*barrel-shaped*. [f. prec.]

bă'rren, a. (-est), & n. Not bearing, or incapable of bearing, children, young, fruit, vegetation, or produce; meagre, unprofitable, dull; (n.) ~ tract of land; *~wort*, purple-&-yellow-flowered wood plant. Hence ~LY² adv., ~NESS n. [f. OF *baraine* (fem.), *brahain*, *brehaina*, etc., etym. dub.]

bă'rrĕt, n. Flat cap, esp. the biretta. [f *barrette* BIRETTA]

bărricāde'¹, (now rarely) -ā'dō, n. Hastily erected rampart across street etc. of barrels, carts, stones, furniture; any barrier, litt. or fig. [f. F *barricade* or Sp. *barricada* (-ADO) f. F *barrique* or Sp. *barrica* cask]

bărricāde'², (now rarely) -ā'dō, v.t. Block (street etc.) with barricade; defend (place or person) with barricade. [f. prec.]

bă'rrier¹, n. Fence barring advance or preventing access; (ancient chariot-races) barred starting-cells; (foreign towns) gate at which customs are collected; (tilting) the lists or enclosing palisade, also railing parallel to which, but on opposite sides, tilters charged reaching their lances across; any obstacle, boundary, or agency that keeps apart. [ME & AF *barrere* f. OF *barrière* f. LL *barraria* (*barra* BAR¹) later assim. to F spelling]

bă'rrier², v.t. Close or shut in with barrier (usu. with *off*, *in*). [f. prec.]

bă'rring, prep. Except, not including. [part. of BAR²]

‖ bă'rrister, n. Law student called to bar & having right of practising as advocate in superior courts (in full, ~-*at-law*); *revising* ~, one appointed to revise lists of voters at parliamentary elections, [f. BAR¹ (orig. the bar in Inn of Court, later connected with that in lawcourts); *-ister* (formerly *-ester*, *-aster*) unexplained; perh. f. form *barre* +-STER]

bă'rrow¹ (-ō), n. (In local names) hill; (Archaeol.) grave-mound, tumulus. [OE *beorg*; com.-Teut., cf. G *berg* mountain f. OTeut. *bergoz* f. Aryan *bhergh* height]

bă'rrow² (-ō), n. (Also *hand-*~) rectangular frame with short shafts used by two or more men for carrying loads on, stretcher, bier; (also *wheel-*~) shallow box with shafts & one wheel for similar use by one

man : ‖(also *coster's* ~) two-wheeled handcart ; a ~ful. [ME *barewe* f. OTeut. *berwā* f. *beran* BEAR[3]]

bâ′rrow[3] (-ō), n. (dial.). Castrated boar. [OE *bearg*; com.-Teut., cf. G *barch*]

bâtt′er[1], v.t. & i. Exchange (goods or immaterial things) *for* other goods (occas. *away*) ; part with for a (usu. unworthy) consideration (usu. *away*), whence ~ER[1] n. : trade by exchange. [prob. f. obs. *barat* defraud see BARRATOR +-ER[5]]

bâtt′er[2], n. Traffic by exchange, truck, (also fig., e.g. *of* talk) : (Arith.) reckoning of quantity of one commodity to be given for another, values being known. [f. prec.]

bâr′tizan′, n. Battlemented parapet, or overhanging battlemented corner turret, at top of church tower or castle. [mod. form (Scott) prob. f. *bertisene* illit. spelling of *bratticing* see BRATTICE]

bâr′ton, n. Farmyard ; farm not let with rest of manor, but retained by owner. [OE *bere-tūn* (*bere* barley +*tūn* enclosure see TOWN)]

Bâr′ts, n. St. Bartholomew's Hospital in London. [abbr.]

bary′t[a, n. Protoxide of barium, alkaline earth of great weight. Hence ~O a, ~O- comb. form. [f. foll.]

bary′tes (-z), n. Native sulphate of barium, called also *heavy spar*, used as white paint. [f. Gk *barus* heavy, or perh. more translit. of *barutēs* weight, with pronunc. assim. to mineral names in -ITES]

bâ′rytone, n. & a. (Voice, singer with voice, music suited to voice) between tenor & bass ; euphonium or saxhorn in B flat or C ; (Gk gr.) (word) with grave or no accent on last syllable. [f. F *baryton* or It. *baritono* f. (gram. meaning direct f.) Gk *barutonos* (*barus* heavy +*tonos* TONE]

bâs′al, a. Of, at, or forming, the base ; fundamental. [f. BASE[1] +-AL]

basalt′ (*bās′awlt, bəsawlt*′), n. Dark green or brown igneous rock often in columnar strata, whence basal′tic, basal′tiform, (-sawl-), aa. : black porcelain invented by Wedgwood. [f. L *basaltes* f. an African word]

bâs′an (-z-), bâz′an, n. Sheepskin tanned in oak or larch bark (also *basil*). [f. F *bazane* f. Pr. *bazana* f. Sp. *badana* f. Arab. *bitanah* lining]

bas bleu (see Ap.), n. Bluestocking. [F]

bâs′cule, n. Lever apparatus used in ~-*bridge*, kind of drawbridge raised & lowered with counterpoise. [F, formerly *bacule* see-saw (*battre* bump or *bas* down +*cul* buttocks)]

base[1], n. 1. That on which anything stands or depends, support, bottom, foundation, principle, groundwork, starting-point (~*ball*, U.S. national game, more elaborate rounders, also ball used in it). 2. (Archit.) part of column between

shaft & pedestal or pavement. 3. (Bot. & Zool.) end at which an organ is attached to trunk. 4. (Geom.) line or surface on which plane or solid figure is held to stand. 5. (Chem.) correlative of ACID, substance capable of combining with an acid to form a salt (including, but wider than, ALKALI). 6. (Mil.) town or other area in rear of an army where drafts, stores, hospitals, etc., are concentrated (also ~ *of operations*). 7. (Surv.) known line used as geometrical ~ for trigonometry. 8. (Math.) starting-number for system of numeration or logarithms (as 10 in decimal counting). [F, f. L f. Gk *basis* (*bainō* step, stand)]

base[2], v.t. Found (something) *on* ; establish (with adv., as *firmly*) ; ~ oneself *on*, rely upon (in argument etc.). [f. prec.]

base[3], a. (Orig.) of small height (now only in plant names as ~*rocket*) ; morally low, cowardly, selfish, mean, despicable, whence ~′LY[2(-sl-)] adv. ; menial ; ‖(Law) ~ *tenure*, *estate*, *fee*, not absolute, but determinable on fulfilment of contingent qualification ; (Lang.) not classical (~ *Latinity*) ; ~-*born*, of low birth, illegitimate ; ~-*court*, outer court of castle or court behind farmhouse ; ~ *metals*, opposed to precious ; ~ *coin*, spurious, alloyed. Hence ~′NESS (-sn-) n. [f. F *bas* etym. dub.]

base′less (-sl-), a. Groundless, unfounded. Hence ~NESS n. [BASE[1] -LESS]

base′ment (-sm-), n. Lowest or fundamental part of structure ; inhabited storey sunk below ground level. [BASE n. or v. +-MENT]

bâsh, v.t. Strike heavily so as to smash in (often *in*). [perh. imit. cf. *bang*, *smash*; or = Sw. *basa* flog; Da. *baske* cudgel]

bâsh′aw, n. Earlier form of PASHA.

bâsh′ful, a. Shy ; shamefaced, sheepish. Hence ~LY[2] adv., ~NESS n. [f. obs. *bash* vb for ABASH +-FUL]

bâshi-bazouk′ (-ō̄ōk), n. Mercenary of Turkish irregulars, notorious for pillage & brutality. Hence ~ERY (4, 5) n. [mod. Turk., lit. brain-turned]

bâs′ic, a. Of, at, forming, base ; fundamental ; (Chem.) having the properties of or containing a base ; (Min.) slightly silicated (igneous rock) ; prepared by non-siliceous process (steel) ; B~ *English*, select vocabulary of 850 words ; ~ *slag*, fertilizer containing phosphates produced as by-products in the ~ process of steel manufacture. [BASE[1] +-IC]

bas′il[1] (-z-), n. An acid's relative power of combining with bases. [prec. +-IL]

bâs′il[2], n. Kinds of aromatic herb, esp. *Common* or *Sweet B~* & *Lesser B~*, both culinary. [f. OF *basile* f. L *basilisca* (*basiliscus* BASILISK), the Gk

name *basilicon* (=royal) being misinterpreted as antidote for basilisk's venom]

bas·il² (-z-), n. Corruption of BASAN.

bas·il·ic, a. (Of vein) starting from elbow & discharging into axillary vein. [f. F *basilique* f. L f. Gk *basilikos* royal (as formerly thought of special importance)]

bas·il·i·ca, n. (Orig.) royal palace; hence, oblong hall with double colonnade & apse used for lawcourt & assemblies; such a building used as Christian church; (in Rome) one of the seven churches founded by Constantine. [L, f. Gk *basilikē* (*oikia, stoa*) royal (house, portico) f. *basileus* king, -IC]

bas·il·i·con, -um, n. Kinds of ointment. [-on Gk, -um L, f. Gk *basilikos* as in prec.; so called as a 'sovereign' remedy]

bas·i·lisk (-z-), n. Fabulous reptile (also *cockatrice*) hatched by serpent from cock's egg, blasting by its breath or look; (fig.) ~*glance* etc., evil eye, person or thing that blasts (reputation etc.); (Zool.) small American lizard with hollow crest inflated at will. [f. L f. Gk *basiliskos* kinglet, serpent, golden-crested wren]

bas·in, n. Hollow round metal or pottery vessel, less deep than wide, & contracting downwards, for holding water etc., bowl; hollow depression; dock with flood-gates; land-locked harbour; tract of country drained by river & tributaries; circular or oval valley; (Geol.) formation with strata dipping towards centre, the deposit (e.g. coal) contained in this. Hence ~FUL (2) n. [ME & OF *bacin* (F *bassin*) f. LL *bacchinus* perh. for *baccinus* (*bacca* water-vessel]

bas·inet, bas·net, n. Light steel head-piece. [f. OF *bacinet* dim. of *bacin* BASIN]

bas·is, n. (pl. *bases*). = BASE¹ (chiefly in fig. senses); main ingredient, foundation, beginning, determining principle; common ground for negotiation etc.; military base. [L = BASE¹]

bask (bah-), v.i. Revel in warmth & light (usu. *in the sun*, firelight, etc.); ~*ing-shark*, largest species of shark (also *Sun-fish & Sailfish*). [prob. f. ON *bathask* (cf. *or* = other) refl. of *batha* BATHE¹]

bas·ket¹ (bah-), n. Wicker vessel of osiers, cane, rushes, etc.; the quantity contained in it (also ~*ful*); wicker singlestick hand-guard; *pick of the* ~, best of the lot; ~*ball*, game played with large inflated ball, a goal being scored when it is thrown into a ~ fixed 10 ft above ground at opponents' end; *basket-*, of ~ shape as ~*-hilt*, of ~ material or fashion as ~*-carriage, -work*. Hence ~RY(5) n. [etym. dub.; *bascauda* is mentioned by Martial as a British utensil]

bas·ket² (bah-), v.t. Put in a basket, waste-paper or other. [f. prec.]

bas·on¹, n. = BASIN.

bas·on², n., & v.t. Bench for felting hat material.; (vb) felt. [perb. =BASIN]

basque (bahsk), n. & a. **1.** Biscayan, (native or language) of Western Pyrenees (*B~*). **2.** Short continuation of bodice below waist; bodice having this. [f. f. LL *Vasco -onis*; whether 2 is from 1 is not known]

bas-relief', bâss-, n. (Piece of) shallow carving or sculpture on background (less than half the true depth). [f. F *bas-relief* f. It. *basso-rilievo* low RELIEF²; see BASE³]

bass¹, n. Common Perch; *Black B~*, Perch of Lake Huron; European sea-fish (also *Sea-wolf* and *Sea-dace*). [earlier *barse* f. OE *bærs*; com.-Teut. f. root *bars-* bristle]

bass², n. Inner bark of lime, used for mats, hassocks, & baskets, & for tying plants, flowers, etc.; ~*-broom*, coarse fibre broom for rough work; ~*-wood*, Amer. lime, its wood. [corruption of BAST]

bass³, a. & n. Deep-sounding; (of, suited to) lowest part in harmonized music (man with) ~ *voice*; *thorough-~, figured* ~, part with shorthand indications below of the proper harmony, hence theory of harmony; ~*-viol, viola da gamba* or violoncello. [ME *bas* base see BASE³; now *bass* after It. *basso*]

Bāss⁴, n. ~*'s beer*, bottle of this (*a small* ~). [*Bass*, brewer; P]

bass·et', n. Short-legged badger-dog. [F, dim. of *bas basse* low; see BASE³]

bass·et², n. Obsolete card-game. [f. It. *bassetta* f. *bassetto* dim. of *basso* BASE³]

bass·et³, n., & v.i. (vb). Edge of stratum cropping out; (vb) crop out. [?]

bass·et-horn, n. Tenor clarinet. [transl. of F *cor de bassette* f. It. *bassetto* see BASSET²]

bassinet', n. Hooded wicker cradle or perambulator. [F, dim. of *bassin* BASIN]

bass·o, n. = BASS³ (second and third senses); ~ *profundo* (or -*on*-), (singer with) specially deep bass voice. [It., =(deep) bass]

bassoon', n. Wooden double-reed instrument used as bass to oboe; organ & harmonium stop of similar quality. Hence ~IST(3) n. [f. F *basson* (*bas* BASE³ +-*on* -OON, or *bas son* deep sound]

basso-relievo (-lyā-), n. (pl. -*os*). = BAS-RELIEF. [It.]

bast, n. Inner bark of lime (see BASS²); other flexible fibrous barks. [OE *bæst*; com.-Teut., etym. dub.]

bas·tard, n. & a. (Child) born out of wedlock or of adultery, illegitimate; (of things) unauthorized, hybrid, counterfeit; ~ *file* (with serrations of medium coarseness); ~ *slip*, sucker of tree (also fig., = *bastard* n.); (Bot.) nearly resembling another species (~ BALM); (Zool.) ~-*wing*, rudimentary extra digit with quill-feathers. [OF, f. *bast* (BÂT-) packsaddle (used as bed by muleteer) +-ARD; cf. BANTLING]

bās'tardĭz|e, v.t. Declare illegitimate.
Hence ~ĀTION n. [prec. +-IZE]
bäs'tardȳ, n. Illegitimacy; ~ order, for
support of illegitimate child by putative
father. [f. AF & OF *bastardie*; see
BASTARD, -Y¹]

bāste¹, v.t. Stitch together, tack, (as
prelim. to regular sewing). [f. OF *bastir*
(now *bâtir*) perh. f. LL *bastire* construct,
build; but cf. also BAST]

bāste², v.t. Moisten (roasting meat) with
fat to prevent burning; pour melted wax
etc. on (wicks in candlemaking). [?]

bāste³, v.t. Thrash, cudgel. [perh. =Sw.
basa flog (*basti, bust, buist*, as past or p.p.
in early exx.; cf. HOIST¹, ²); or fig. use of
prec. (cf. 'dry basting' Shaksp.)]

bastille' (-ēl), n. Fortress; Paris prison-
fortress destroyed 1789; prison. [F. f. LL
bastilla pl. of *bastile* f. *bastire* build]

bastinād'ō, n. (pl. ~es), & v.t. (Punish
with) caning on soles of feet. [f. Sp.
bastonada (*baston* stick) see -ADO(2)]

bās'tion, n. Projecting part of fortification, irregular pentagon with its base in
the line (or at an angle) of the main
works. Hence ~ED¹ (-nd) a. [F, f. It.
bastione f. LL *bastire* build perh. f. same
root as *baston* BATON]

bât¹, n. Nocturnal mouse-like quadruped
with fingers extended as frame of membranous wings; *have* ~*s in the belfry*, be
crazy or eccentric; *blind* ~, often = purblind.
[f. 1575, displacing ME *bakke* f. Scand.]

bât², n., & v.i. & t. 1. Implement for
striking ball in cricket, baseball, etc.
(*off one's own* ~, in cricket, also fig.
unaided; *carry one's* ~, be not out at
end of innings); ~*sman* (*a good etc.* ~);
~*s'man* (-an), performer with cricket etc.
~, also one who signals with ~*s* in his
hands to guide aircraft landing on ship's
deck. 2. vb. (-tt-). Use ~, have innings;
strike (as) with ~. [f. OF *batte* club
(*battre* strike, see ABATE)]

bât³, n. (sl.). Pace of stroke or step (*went
off at a rare* ~). [?]

bât⁴ (baht), n. (Anglo-Ind., colloq.). *The*
~, spoken language (orig. of India, now
extended); *sling the* ~ (Army sl.), speak
the lingo (in this use freq. pron. bāt).
[Hind., = speech, word]

bât⁵, v.t. (U.S. & dial.). To wink (*never
~ted an eyelid*, did not sleep a wink).
[var. of obs. *bate* to flutter]

bât-, bât- (bah, baht), comb. form. For
officers' baggage on campaign; ~-*horse*
(for carrying baggage); ~ *man* (orig.
one who looked after a baggage animal,
∥(now esp.) an officer's servant generally;
∥~*-pay*, baggage allowance. [f. F *bât*
packsaddle f. OF *bast* = LL *bastum* perh.
f. Gk *bastazō* lift]

bâtat'a (-ahtə), n. W.-Indian plant,
Sweet or Spanish potato. [Sp. & Port. f.
native American]

Batā'vian, a. & n. (Inhabitant) of ancient

Batavia (between Rhine & Waal) or of
modern Holland, Dutch(man); of, in
habitant of, Batavia in Java. [f. L *Batavia* (*Batavi* pl.)]

bätch, n. Loaves produced at one baking;
quantity or number of anything coming
at once or treated as a set. [ME *bache*
(*bacan* BAKE) cf. *wake watch*]

bāte¹, v.t. & i. Let down (~ *hope* etc.), restrain (~*d breath*); deduct (part of; usn.
with neg., *not* ~ *a jot of*); fall off
in force. [for ABATE]

bāte², n. & v.t. Alkaline lye for suppling
hides; (vb) steep in this. [= Sw. *beta* to
tan, G *beize* maceration f. *beizen* cause
to bite BAIT¹]

∥ bāte³, bait³, n. (sl.). Rage (*was in an
awful* ~). [perh. = obs. *bate* var. of *debate*;
or f. BAIT¹ = state of baited person]

bâth¹ (bahth), n. (pl. *pr. ~s* -dhz), Bath. n. 1.
Washing; immersion in liquid, air, etc.; (*air-
~, sun~*, exposure of naked body to air,
sun; *mud~*, of mud for rheumatism; ~
of blood, carnage); water etc. for bathing,
wash, lotion, surrounding medium; vessel
(*etc.~*), like HIP-~ but with broad flat
bottom [G *stichad* sitting bath]; *sponge
~*, esp. of broad flat saucer shape to facilitate sponging), room (also *~-room*, or
building, for bathing in (see TURKISH);
~, ~*s*, town resorted to for medical bathing.
2. Order of knighthood (*B~*; for C.B.,
K.C.B., G.C.B., see abbreviations) named
from the ~ preceding installation. 3.
Town in Somerset named from hot
springs (*B~ brun*; *B~ Oliver*, biscuit
invented by Dr. W. Oliver of B~, d.
1764.; *B~ brick*, preparation for cleaning
metal; ∥*B~ chair*, wheeled for invalid;
∥*B~ chap*²; *B~ stone*, oolite building-
stone). [OE *bæth*; com. Teut., cf. G *bad*
f. OTeut. *bathom* perh. f. *bajo-* foment cf.
L *fovēre* keep warm]

bâth² (-ah- or -ā- *in all parts*), v.t. Subject to washing in bath (child or invalid,
of nurse etc.). [f. prec.]

bäthe¹ (-dh), v.t. & i. Immerse (in
liquid, air, light, etc.); (of person or river,
liquid, etc.) moisten all over; (of sunlight
etc.) envelop; take a bath or bathe, so
~*ing-costume*, ∥*-drawers*; ~*ing-machine*,
wheeled dressing-box drawn into sea for
~*ing* from. [OE *bathian* (-dh-); com.
Teut., cf. G *baden*; for *bathe* (-dh), *bath*,
cf. *graze, grass*]

bäthe² (-dh), bäthï'er (-dh-), nn. Taking
taker, of a bath, esp. in sea, river, swimming-bath. [f. prec. in infr. sense]

bathet'ic, a. Marked by bathos. [irreg. f.
Gk BATHOS on false anal. of *pathetic* (f.
pathētos, not pathos)]

bathom'eter, n. Spring balance used in
ascertaining depth of water. [f. Gk *bathos*
depth +-METER.]

Bathō'nian, a. & n. (Inhabitant) of Bath.
[mod. L *Bathonia* Bath, -AN]

bâth'ŏs, n. Fall from sublime to ridiculous;

anticlimax; performance absurdly below occasion. [Gk. = depth]

bathyb′ius, n. Slimy gelatinous substance dredged from great ocean depths (once believed to be protoplasmic, now known to be inorganic). [f. Gk *bathus* deep+*bios* life]

bathymētr-, stem of scientific words. Of depth-measurement. [f. Gk *bathus* (translit. *-us*) deep+-METER]

bath′ysphere, n. Large strong submersible sphere for deep-sea observation. [f. Gk *bathus* deep+SPHERE]

băt′ik, n. Method (orig. Javan) of printing coloured designs on textiles by waxing parts not to be dyed. [Javanese ′*mbatik* drawing]

băt′ing, prep. Except. [partic. of BATE[1]]

batiste′ (-ēst), n. & a. (Of) fine light fabric like cambric in texture. [F, f. *Baptiste* of Cambrai, first maker]

băt′on, n., & v.t. Staff of office, esp. *Marshal's* ~; constable's truncheon (vb, strike with this); (Her.) truncheon in shield (= *sinister*, badge of bastardy); (Mus.) conductor's wand for beating time. [f. F *bâton* f. OF *baston* etym. dub.]

batrā′chian (-k-), a. & n. Of frogs; (one) of the *Batrachia*, or animals that discard gills & tail. [f. Gk *batrakheios* (*batrakhos* frog)+-AN]

băt′ta, n. (Anglo-Ind.). (Orig.) subsistence allowance; (now) any extra allowance to officers or soldiers, esp. in the field. [etym. dub.; perh. f. Hind. *bhatt* advance without interest]

battal′ion (-yon), n. Large body of men in battle array (*God is for the big* ~s, force prevails); unit of infantry composed of several companies & forming part of regiment or brigade. [f. F *battaillon* (now *bata-*) f. It. *battaglione* f. *battaglia* BATTLE[1]]

‖ **băt′els**, n. pl. College account at Oxford for board & provisions supplied, or for all college expenses. [perh. f. obs. vb *battle* fatten f. obs. adj. *battle* nutritious cf. BATTEN[4]]

băt′en[1], n. Board (6 ft or more long, 7 in. × 2½ or less broad & thick) used for flooring; bar of wood used for clamping boards of door etc.; strip of wood carrying electric lamps; (Naut.) strip of wood nailed on spar to save rubbing, or securing hatchway tarpaulin. Hence ~ING[4](6) n. [var. of BATON[1]]

băt′en[2], v.t. Strengthen with battens; (Naut.) ~ *down*, close the hatches (see BATTEN[4]). [f. prec.]

băt′en[3], n. Bar in silk-loom striking in the weft. [f. F *battant* (*battre* strike, -ANT)]

băt′en[4], v.i. Feed gluttonously *on*, revel *in*, (often implying morbid taste); grow fat. [perh. f. ON *batna* get better (*bati* advantage cf. BOOT[2])]

băt′er, v.t. & i. Strike repeatedly so as to bruise or break (person, thing, or abs.; also with adv. *about*, *down*, *in*; & intr.

~ *at the door*); operate against (walls etc.) with artillery; (fig.) handle severely (theories, persons); beat out of shape, indent; (Printing) deface (type) by use; ~*ing-charge*, full charge of powder for cannon; ~*ing-ram*, swinging beam anciently used for breaching walls, sometimes with ram's-head end; ~*ing-train*, set of siege guns. [f. obs. vb *batt*, cf. OF *batre*, f.+-ER[5]]

băt′er[2], n. Mixture of ingredients beaten up with liquid for cooking; defect in printing-type or stereotype plate. [f. prec.]

băt′er[3], v.i., & n. (Have) receding slope from ground upwards (of walls narrower at top). [perh. f *abattre* depress]

băt′ery, n. (Law) infliction of blows, or of the least menacing touch to clothes or person (esp. in phr. *assault &* ~); (Mil.) emplacement for one or more guns, artillery unit of guns & men & vehicles or horses consisting usu. of two sections & forming subdivision of regiment, (fig.) *turn a man's* ~ *against himself* (in argument); (in various sciences & arts) set of similar or connected cells, instruments, or utensils (electric, galvanic, optical, cooking); hammered brass or copper vessels. [f. F *batterie* (*battre* strike, & see -ERY)]

băt′ing, n. In vbl senses; also, cotton fibre prepared in sheets for quilts etc. [BAT[2]+-ING[1]]

băt′tle[1], n. Combat, esp. between large organized forces (*general's* ~, decided by strategy or tactics, *soldier's* ~, by courage; *pitched* ~, one fought by common consent; ~ *royal*, in which several combatants or all available forces engage, free fight); victory (*the* ~ *is to the strong*, *youth is half the* ~); ~ *join*, *give*, *refuse*, *accept*, *offer*, *do*, &c.; ~*-axe*, medieval weapon; ~*-cruiser*, heavy-gunned ship of higher speed & lighter armour than ~ *ship*; ~ *dress*, soldier's etc. uniform of belted blouse & trousers; ~*-piece*, picture or literary description of a scene; *line of* ~, troops or ships drawn up to fight; *line-of-* ~ *ship*, (obs.) of 74 or more guns; ~*-ship* (mod.), most heavily armed and armoured warship, designed to meet the most powerful ships in ~. [ME *bataile* f. OF *bataille* f. LL *battualia* neut. pl. of adj. *battualis* f. *battuere* beat]

băt′tle[2], v.i. Struggle *with* or *against* (difficulties, the waves, etc.). [f. F *batailler* (*bataille* = prec.)]

băt′tledore (-teld-), n. Wooden instrument like canoe paddle used in washing, baking, etc.; wooden, stringed, or parchmented bat used with shuttlecock in the game ~ & *shuttle-cock*. [from 1440; perh. f. Pr. *batedor* beater (*batre* beat+*-dor* =-TOR)]

băt′tlement (-tel-), n. (usu. in pl.), Indented parapet (raised parts, *cops* or

merlons; gaps, embrasures or crenelles); parapet & enclosed roof. Hence **~ED²** a. [f. OF *batailles* temporary wooden turrets; *batailler* provide with these; etym. dub.; the F v b was later identified with *bastiller* cf. BASTILLE]

battue (see AP.), n. Driving of game by beaters to the sportsmen's station; shooting party on this plan; wholesale slaughter. [F]

bâti'y, a. (sl.) Crazy. [f. BAT¹+-Y²]

bau'ble, n. Showy trinket; court fool's emblem, a stick with ass-eared head carved on it; trifle, toy, thing of no worth. [f. OF *babel* child's toy, & perh. also partly f. ME *babyll* & v b *bablyn* flicker perh. f. BOB³]

bauk. See BALK.

bauxite, n. (min.). Earthy compound containing varying proportions of alumina, the chief commercial source of aluminium. [f. *Baux* in France+-ITE²(2)]

baw'bee, n. (Sc.). Halfpenny. [?]

bawd, n. Procuress; obscene talk. [?]

bawd'ly, a. & n. Obscene (talk); **~y-house**, brothel. Hence **~INESS** n. [f. prec.]

bawl, v.t. & i. Say, speak, in a noisy way (often with *out*, also with *at*, *against*, etc.). [imit., L *baulare* bark]

∥ **bawley**, n. (dial.). Fishing smack peculiar to Essex and Kentish coasts. [?]

bawn, n. Court of a castle; cattlefold. [f. Ir. *bábhun* etym. dub.]

bay¹, n. Kind of tree or shrub; (pl.) wreath of its leaves worn by conquerors or poets, heroic or poetic fame; **~berry**, a West Indian tree (*Pimenta acris*); **~rum**, a perfume distilled from bayberry leaves. [f. OF *baie* f. L *baca* berry]

bay², n. Part of sea filling wide-mouthed opening of land; recess in mountain range; *Bay State*, Massachusetts. [f. F *baie* f. LL *baia* perh. associated with, but not from, *badaia* in foll.]

bay³, n. Division of wall between columns or buttresses; recess (*horse-~*, stall; *sick-~*, part of main deck used as hospital); space added to room by advancing window from wall line (*~window*, filling such space). (Mil.) passing-place in a trench; ∥ railway platform having a cul-de-sac & acting as starting-point or terminus for a side-line, the cul-de-sac of such a platform. (*~tine*, side-line starting from this). [f. F *baie* OF *baer*, *béer* (= L *ba-dáta*) f. *boyer* OF *baer*, *béer*, gape]

bay⁴, n. Bark of large dog, of hounds in pursuit, esp. the chorus raised as they draw close; (in phr. lit. of hounds & quarry, fig. of persecutors & victim, applied to the hunted animal) *stand or be at, turn to, hold hounds etc. at, ~*, show fight; (applied to hounds) *hold at bay, bring or drive to, ~*, come to close quarters with (quarry). [mixture of (1) OF *tenir a bay* = It. *tenere a bada* hold agape or in suspense (see *badaia* in prec.) & (2) F *être*

aux abois be at (close quarters with) the barking (OF *abai*)]

bay⁵, v.i. & t. (Of large dogs) bark; bark at, esp. *~ the moon*. [mod. *aboyer*) bark perh. f. LL *badare* gape]

bay⁶, a. & n. Reddish-brown (horse). [f. F *bai* f. L *badius*]

bayadère' (-dâr'), n. Hindu dancing-girl (esp. one attached to a S.-Indian temple); striped textile fabric. [F, f. Port. *bailadeira* ballet-dancer]

Bay'ard, n. Chivalrous person. [French hero, 'chevalier sans peur et sans reproche', 1475-1524]

bay'onet, n. Stabbing blade attachable to rifle-muzzle; *the ~*, or *~s*, military force; (with prefixed number) so many infantry (cf. SABRE); *~catch*, securing of cylindrical part in place by a turn as with the triangular *~*; *Spanish ~*, a plant, species of Yucca. [perh. f. *Bayonne* as made or first used there]

bay'onet, v.t. Stab with bayonet; *~into*, coerce by military force (or fig. by pressure) into. [f. prec.]

bayou (bī'ū), n. Marshy offshoot of river in southern N. America. [f. F *boyau* gut, f. L *botulus* sausage]

bay-salt (sawlt), n. Salt in large crystals obtained by evaporation. [perh. = sea salt f. BAY²]

bazaar' (-zâr), n. Oriental market; fancy fair in imitation of this, esp. sale of goods for charities. [f. Pers. *bazar* prob. through Turk. & It.]

bdellium (d-), n. Balsam-bearing tree; its resin. [L, f. Gk *bdellion* transl. of Heb. *b'dolakh* of uncertain meaning (carbuncle or crystal or pearl)]

be (bē, bǐ), v. substantive, copulative, & auxiliary (pres. ind.: *am*, pr. ǎm, am; *art* arch., pr. ârt, art; *is*, pr. ǐz; pl. *are*, pr. ár, ar; *was*, pr. wǒz, woz; *wast* arch., pr. wǒst, wost; pl. *were*, pr. wâr, wer; pres. subj. *be*; past subj. *were*, exc. 2 sing. *wert* arch., pr. wârt, wert; imperat. *be*; past, *being*, pr. bē'ing; p.p. *been*, pr. bēn, bin; colloq. clipped forms *'m* = am, *'s* = is, *'re* = are, *'m*, *wasn't*, *aren't* pl., *weren't*, *are* legitimate in actual or printed talk; vulgar: *ain't* for *is not, are not*, is wrong). **1.** vb subst. Exist, occur, live, (often with *there*; *God is, there is a God*; *for the time being*, temporarily; *to be or not to be*, see Haml. III. i. 56—often joc. in trivial applications); remain, continue, (*let it be, do not be long*) (with adv. or adv. phr.) occupy such a position, experience such a condition, have gone to such a place, busy oneself so, hold such a view, be bound for such a place, (*where have you been, have been to Rome, be off, how is he?, what are you at?, I am for tariff reform, for London*); *been* colloq. called here, paid a visit, (*has anyone been?, has not been for*

orders); *been and*, colloq. expletive of protest or surprise (*you have been & moved my papers!*); (with dat.) befall (*woe is me*). 2. vb cop. (With nouns, adj., or adj. phr.) belong under such a description (*I am a man, sick, of good courage*); coincide in identity with, amount to, cost, signify, (*thou art the man, twice two is four, it is nothing to me, what are these pears?*). 3. vb aux. With p.p. of trans. vbs forming passives (*this was done*); with p.p. of some intr. vbs, as *fall, come, grow*, forming perfects (*the sun is set, Babylon is fallen*); with pres. part. act. forming continuous tenses act. & pass. (*he is building a house, the house was building*); with pres. part. pass. forming continuous tenses pass. (*the house was being built*); with infin. expressing duty, intention, possibility, (*I am to inform you, he is to be there, the house is to let, he is to be hanged, it was not to be found*); *were* with infin. in hypotheses (*if I were, or were I, to tell you*). 4. Parts used as adji., advv., nouns: *may-be*, perhaps, a possibility; *the to-be*, the future; *might-have-beens*, past possibilities; *would-be*, that yearns, or fancies himself, to be; *be-all*, whole being, essence. [f. three vbs (1) Aryan *es-*, OE, L, & OTeut. *es-*, Skr. *as-*, to be; (2) OTeut. *wes-*, Skr. *vas-*, remain; (3) Skr. *bhu-*, Gk *phu-*, L *fu-*, OTeut. *beo-*. From (1) come *am* (cf. Gk *esmi*), *art* (cf. ON *est*, later *ert*), *is*, *are* (cf. ON *erum*, L *sumus*, Gk *esmes*) from (2) come *was, vast, vert, were*; from (3) come *be, being, been*]

be-, pref. f. OE *be-*, weak form of prep. & adv. *bi* BY, accented form of which appears in *by-law, by-word, bygone*, etc. The orig. meaning is *about*, which is variously developed as in *before* (about the front), *bespatter* (spatter all about), *bespeak* (speak about, making vbs trans.), *bedevil* (say devil about), *benight* (bring night about), *behead* (take the head from about), *bejewel* (put jewels about). As new vbs are constantly formed, & only the well-established or peculiar ones can be given, the chief varieties are here numbered for reference. 1. Adding notion of all over, all round, to trans. vb, as *beset, besmear*. 2. Adding notion of thoroughness, excess, to trans. vb, as *bedrug, bescorch*. 3. Making intr. vbs trans., as *bemoan, bestraddle*. 4. Forming trans. vbs = to make from adji. & nouns, as *befoul, bedim, bedizen, bedishop*. 5. Making trans. vbs = to call so & so from nouns, as *bedevil, bemadam*. 6. Making trans. vbs = to surround with, to affect with, to treat in the manner of, from nouns, as *becloud, beguile, befriend*. 7. Making adji. in -ED² from nouns, as *bevinged, behumped*, (usu. with some contempt).

beach¹, n. Water-worn pebbles or sand; sea-shore covered with these; shore between high & low water mark; ~*-comber*, white man in Pacific Islands, etc. who lives by collecting jetsam, longshore vagrant; ~*-head*, fortified position established on ~ by landing forces [after *bridge-head*]; ~*-master*, officer superintending disembarkation of troops; ~*-rest*, chairback for sitting against on ~. [?]

beach², v.t. Run (ship, boat) ashore, haul up. [f. prec.]

|| **beach-la-mar** (-lah-), n. Jargon English used in Western Pacific. [corrupt. f. Port. *bicho do mar* BÊCHE-DE-MER]

beac'on¹, n. Signal, signal-fire on pole or hill; signal station; conspicuous hill (in names); lighthouse; guide or warning; ~*age*. [OE *bēacn*. f. OTeut. *baukmom* cf. BECKON]

beac'on², v.t. Give light to, guide; supply (district) with beacons. [f. prec.]

bead¹, n. 1. (Orig.) prayer. 2. Small perforated ball for threading with others on string, used in counting one's prayers (*tell one's ~s*); the same used for ornament; drop of liquid, bubble; small knob in foresight of gun (*draw a ~ on*, take aim at); (Archit.) moulding like a bead series, or small one of semicircular section; ~*-roll*, list of names, long series, (orig. of persons bound to be prayed for); ~*s'man*, pensioner bound to pray for benefactor, almsman. [ME *bede* f. OE *gebed* (or +*bedu*) prayer, see BID¹]

bead², v.t. & i. Furnish with beads; string together; form or grow into beads. [f. prec.]

bead'ing, n. In vbl senses; also, a bead moulding. [BEAD¹; see -ING¹]

|| **bea'dle**, n. Apparitor of trades guild or company; parish officer appointed by vestry. Hence ~SHIP (-dels-). [OE *bydel* f. OTeut. *budiloz* f. *biudan* announce]

bea'dledom (-deld-), n. Stupid officiousness. [-DOM]

bead'y, a. (Of eyes) small & bright; covered with beads or drops. [BEAD¹]

bea'gle, n. The smallest English hound, used for hare hunting when field follows on foot; spy etc.; *beagling*, hunting with ~s. [perh. f. F. *bé-gueule* open throat (*béer* gape)]

beak¹, n. Bird's bill (esp. in birds of prey, & when strong & hooked); similar mandible-end of other animals, as turtle; hooked nose; projection at prow of ancient warship; spout. Hence ~ED² (-kt) a. [f. F *bec* f. LL *beccus* of Gaulish origin]

|| **beak²**, n. (sl.). Magistrate; schoolmaster. [?]

beak'er, n. Large drinking-cup; lipped glass vessel for scientific experiments. [ME *biker* cf. G *becher* perh. f. med. L *bicarium* perh. f. Gk *bikos*]

For compounds of *be-* not given consult BE-.

beam[1], n. Long piece of squared timber supported at both ends; cylinder in loom on which warp, cloth, is wound; chief timber of plough; bar of balance (*kick the ~*), prove the lighter, be defeated); shank of anchor; lever in engine connecting piston-rod & crank; (pl.) horizontal cross-timbers of ship supporting deck & joining sides (*starboard, port,* ~, right & left sides, as *land on port ~* etc.; =ship's breadth (*on her ~-ends, on her side, almost capsizing, in danger, at a loss*); ray or pencil of light, or of electric radiation (~ *system,* wireless telegraphy in which transmission in a particular direction is achieved by reflecting a short ~ from a parabolic arrangement of wires charged with static electricity); radiance, bright look, smile. [OE *béam* tree; com.-Teut., cf. G *baum*]

beam[2], v.t. & i. Emit (light, affection, etc.); shine; smile radiantly. Hence ~ING[2] a. [f. prec.]

beam'y, a. Radiant (poet., of spears etc.); huge; broad (of ships). [BEAM[1], -Y[2]]

bean, n. (Kinds of leguminous plants bearing) smooth kidney-shaped seed in long pods; similar seed of other plants, as coffee; coin (sl.; *I haven't a ~*, I'm stony-broke); *full of ~s, ~fed,* in high spirits; || OLD ~, *give one ~s* (sl.), punish or scold him. [OE *béan*; com.-Teut., cf. G *bohne,* & perh. L *faba*]

bean'feast, bean'ō (sl., pl. ~os), n. Employer's annual dinner to workpeople, fête, merry time. [?]

bear[1] (bâr), n. Heavy partly carnivorous thick-furred plantigrade quadruped; rough unmannerly person, whence ~'ISH[1] a., ~'ISHNESS n.; *Great, Little, B~,* northern constellations (St. Exch.), speculator for a fall, one who sells stock for future delivery hoping to buy it cheap meanwhile, & therefore tries to bring prices down (cf. BULL, & see foll.); heavy punching-machine; ~'s-*breech, acanthus*; scene of tumult; ~'s-*grease, pomade*; ~'-*skin,* (wrap etc.) of ~'s skin, Guards' tall furry cap; ~'-*leader,* travelling tutor. [OE *bera*; com.-Teut., cf. G *bär,* & perh. L *ferus* wild]

bear[2] (bâr), v.t. & n. (St. Exch.), Speculate for a fall; produce fall in price of (stocks etc.); (n.) this operation. [f. prec., perh. w. ref. to selling the bear's skin before killing the bear]

bear[3] (bâr), v.t. & i. (*bore, borne* or *born,* see below[4]). 1. Carry (poet. or formal, or ~ *away,* win (the palm, bell, prize); exc. in the senses or contexts following: ~ *or ~ away,* win (the palm, bell, prize); carry visibly, show, be known by, (*banner, device, arms, the marks of, name, relation or ratio to,* ~ *oneself well* etc., behave); bring at need (~ *witness, com-*

pany; ~ *a hand, help*); wield (office, rule); carry internally (~ *a grudge,* ~ *in mind,* remember); wear (~ *arms, the sword*); ~ *out, confirm; be borne away (by impulse); is borne in upon one, becomes one's conviction. 2. Sustain (weight, responsibility, cost; ~ *a part in, share*); stand (test etc.), endure (*grin & ~ it*), tolerate, put up with (*cannot ~ him*); whence ~'ABLE a.; be capable of upholding weight (*ice ~s*); be fit for (*this language won't ~ repeating*); ~ *with,* treat forbearingly (~ *up* (trans.), uphold, (intr.) be borne on the books of, paid by. 3. Thrust, strive, apply weight, tend, (~ *down,* overthrow; ~ *hard on,* oppress; ~ *upon,* be relevant to; *bring to ~, apply*; ~ *to the right, away, off,* incline; ~ *down, swoop*; ~ *up,* keep ship further away from wind; ~ *up,* change ship's course so as to sail towards). 4. Produce, yield, give birth to. ¶The P.p. is *borne,* exc. that *born* is used in pass. parts referring to human & other mammal birth, even then *borne* is used before *by* with the mother (*has borne a child*; *born 1901*; *born of, borne by, Eve*). [Aryan: OE, OHG. *beran,* cf. Gk *pherō,* L *fer-*]

beard[1], n. Hair of lower face (excluding usu. the moustache; & occas. the whiskers); chin tuft of animals; gills of oyster; attachment threads of some shellfish; beak-bristles of birds; awn of grasses (*Old-Man's-B~,* = Traveller's Joy. Hence ~'ED[2], ~'LESS, aa., ~'LESSNESS n. [com.-Teut., cf. G *bart*]

beard[2], v.t. Oppose openly, defy, (~ *the lion in his den*). [f. prec.]

bear'er (bâr'-), n. Person or thing that carries; part-carrier of coffin; (India) palanquin-carrier, body servant; bringer of letters or message, presenter of cheque; (with adj. *good* etc.) plant etc. that produces well etc.; ~ *company* (MIL.), medical unit organized to tend & bring in wounded on field service. [BEAR[3] + -ER[1]]

bear'ing (bâr'-), n. In vbl senses; also or esp.: behaviour; heraldic charge or device; relation, aspect, (*consider it in all its ~s; what is the ~ of this on the argument?*); (pl.) parts of machine that bear the friction; direction in which a place lies. (pl.) relative position (*have lost my ~s,* do not know where I am); ~*-rein,* fixed rein from bit to saddle, forcing horse to arch its neck. [BEAR[3], -ING[1]]

beast, n. Animal; quadruped; (Farming) bovine animal, esp. fatting-cattle (collect. pl. *beast*); animal for riding or driving; brutal man; person that one dislikes; *The B~,* Antichrist; *the ~,* the animal nature in man. [F. OF *beste* f. L *bestia*]

beast'liness, n. Gluttony, drunkenness, obscenity; disgusting food or drink. [f. foll.]

beast'ly, a. Like a beast or its ways;

unfit for human use, dirty; (colloq.) undesirable. [-LY¹]

beast'ly², adv. (sl.). (Intensifying adj.)
& advv. used in bad sense; cf. JOLLY) very, ~
regrettably. (~ drunk, wet; raining ~
hard). [-LY²]

beat¹, v.t. & i. (past beat; p.p. beaten, but
beat in dead-beat, often in sense surpassed,
& occas. in other senses). Strike repeatedly (t. & i.; ~ the breast, in mourning; ~ black & blue, bruise; ~ the air,
strive in vain; ~ at door, knock loudly;
~ path, make it by trampling), (inflict
blows on, (of sun, rain, wind) strike (upon
something, or abs.); *~ up (sl.), ~ (person)
severely; overcome, surpass (~ hollow,
easily; ~ cockfighting, is extremely
exhilarating), be too hard for, perplex;
move up & down (t. & i. of wings); move
rhythmically (heart etc. ~s, ~ time,
seconds, etc.); shift, drive, alter, deform,
by blows (~ down, back, away, off; ~ in,
crush; ~ down price or seller, cheapen or
bargain with; ~ up eggs etc., reduce to
froth, powder, paste; ~ or ~ out metal,
forge); (Naut.) ~ up, about, strive, tack,
against wind; strike (bushes, water) to
rouse game (~ about the bush, approach
subject slowly, shilly-shally; ~ up
recruits etc., collect; ~ up the quarters of,
visit; ~ one's brains, search for ideas;
|| ~ the bounds, mark parish boundaries
by striking certain points with rods);
play on drum (~ a parley, a retreat,
propose terms, retire); *~ it (sl.), go
away. [OE béatan; com.-Teut., cf. ON
bauta f. OTeut bautan]

beat², n. Stroke on drum, signal so
given; movement of conductor's baton;
measured sequence of strokes or sounds;
throbbing; sentinel's or constable's appointed course; one's habitual round;
sportsman's range. [f. prec.]

beat'en, a. In vbl senses; also or esp.:
worn hard, trite; shaped by the hammer;
exhausted, dejected. [p.p. of BEAT¹]

beat'er, n. In vbl senses; esp.: man employed to rouse game; implement for
beating flat. [BEAT¹+-ER¹]

beātifĭca'tion, n. Making or being
blessed; (R.-C. Ch.) first step to canonization, announcement that dead person is
in bliss. [F, f. L beātificare (prec.), -ATION]

beāt'ĭfy, v.t. Make happy; (R.-C. Ch.)
announce as in prec. [f. L (prec., -FY]

beat'ing, n. In vbl senses; esp.: a chastisement; a defeat. [f. BEAT¹]

beāt'ĭtūde, n. Blessedness; (pl.) the
blessings in Matt. v. 3-11. [F, f. L beāti-
tudo (beatus see BEATIFIC, -TUDE]

beau (bō), n. (pl. ~x, pr. bōz). Fop;
lady's-man, lover. [OF, f. L bellus

pretty perh. = ⁺benlus dim. cf. bene, bonus
good]

beau geste (bōzhèst'), n. A display of
magnanimity. [F]

beau idé'al (bō), n. One's highest type of
excellence or beauty. [F (-éal), = the
ideal Beautiful (often misconceived in E
as a beautiful ideal); see BEAU & IDEAL a.]

beau monde (see Ap.), n. Fashionable
society. [F]

Beaune (bōn) n. A red Burgundy. [place]

beaut'éous (bū-), a. Beautiful (poet.).
[ME beute BEAUTY +-OUS]

beaut'iful (bū-), a. Delighting the eye or
ear, gratifying any taste, (~ face, voice,
soup, batting); morally or intellectually
impressive, charming, or satisfactory (~
patience, organization, specimen). Hence
~LY² adv. [BEAUTY +-FUL]

beaut'ĭfy̌ (bū-), v.t. Make beautiful;
adorn. Hence ~IER¹ (1, 2) n. [BEAUTY +
-FY]

beaut'y̌ (bū-), n. Combination of qualities,
as shape, proportion, colour, in human
face or form, or in other objects, that delights the sight (~ is but skin deep, one
cannot judge by appearances; combined
qualities delighting the other senses, the
moral sense, or the intellect; a ~, beautiful person or thing (often ironical), exceptionally good specimen (here is a ~);
beautiful woman; a beautiful trait or
feature, ornament, (that's the ~ of it, the
particular point that gives satisfaction);
~ parlour (orig. U.S.), establishment in
which the art or trade of face-massage,
face-lifting, applying cosmetics, etc. is
carried on, whence *beauti'cian (bĭ-) n.,
one who runs a ~ parlour; ~-sleep, before
midnight; ~-spot, small patch placed on
lady's face as foil to complexion, beautiful
scene. [ME beatte, beute, f. OF beatte,
beaute, f. L bellus pretty; see BEAU, -TY]

beaux yeux (bōzyẽr'), n. For the ~ of,
just to gratify (person). [F, = fine eyes]

beav'er¹, n. Amphibious broad-tailed
soft-furred rodent, building huts &
dams; its fur; hat of this. [OE beofor =
LG bever, G biber, L fiber]

beav'er², n. Lower face-guard of helmet.
[ME & OF bavière bib (bave saliva)]

beav'erteen, n. Cotton twilled cloth with
pile of loops. [f. BEAVER¹ after velveteen]

bĕcalm' (-kawl), v.t. (arch. or vulg.). Call
(person) names. [BE-(2)]

bēcălm' (-ahm), v.t. 1. Make calm (sea
etc.). 2. Deprive (ship) of wind. [(1) BE-
(2)+CALM v., (2) BE-(6)+CALM n.]

became. See BECOME.

because' (-ŏz, -awz), adv. & conj. For
the reason (that & clause, arch.); by
reason, on account, (of & noun); for the
reason that, inasmuch as, since. [BY
prep.+cause n.; the conj. use arises by
omission of that]

For compounds of be- not given consult BE-.

beccafi'co (-fē-), n. (pl. -os). Small migrant bird eaten in Italy. [It. (*beccare* peck.+*fico* fig)]

bêche-de-mer, n. Sea-slug, a Chinese dainty. [F]

||**bêck¹**, n. Brook, mountain stream. [f. ON *bekkr* cf. G *bach*]

bêck², n. Significant gesture, nod, etc.; the order implied (*have at one's ~, be at person's ~ & call*, of entire dominion & obedience). [f. foll.]

bêck³, v.t. & i. Make mute signal, signal mutely to, (poet.). [shortened f. BECKON]

bêck'er, n. (naut.). Contrivance for securing loose ropes, tackle, or spars, (rope-loop, hook, bracket, etc.). [?]

bêck'on, v.t. & i. Summon, call attention of, by gesture; make mute signal (to person). [OE *bīecnan* f. OTeut. *baukmo-* BEACON]

becloud', v.t. Cover with clouds; obscure. [BE-(6)+CLOUD n.]

bécome', (-ŭm), v.i. & t. (-came, -come). Come into being; *what has ~e of* (happened to) *him?* (copulative) begin to be (followed by n. adj. or adj. phr.); suit, befit, adorn, look well on, whence ~'ING² a., ~'ingly² adv.; ~'INGNESS n. (-kti-). [OE *becuman* (BE-+*cuman* COME) arrive, attain; com.-Teut., cf. G *bekommen*]

Becquerel rays (bĕk'rel rāz), n. pl. Rays emitted by radio-active substances (now usu. called *alpha, beta, gamma, rays*). [A. H. *Becquerel*, French physicist]

bêd¹, n. 1. Thing to sleep on, mattress (*feather ~* etc.), frame-work with mattress & coverings; animal's resting place, litter; (elliptical) use of ~, being in ~; *~ & board*, entertainment, connubial relations; *narrow ~*, the grave; *~ of down, flowers, roses*, easy position; *~ of sickness*, invalid state; *brought to ~*, in child-birth, of child or abs.; *die in one's ~*, being in ~; causes; *go to ~*, retire for the night (imperat., sl., cease talking etc.); *take to, keep, one's ~*, become, be, ill; *make the ~*, arrange the coverings; *lie in the ~ one has made*, take consequences of one's acts; *got out of ~ on wrong side*, is bad-tempered for the day; ~'chamber (arch., exc. of royal, as Groom, Lady, etc., of the ~chamber), ~room, sheets, pillows, etc., of ~; ~'fellow, sharer of ~, associate; ~'gown, woman's night-dress, ||northern woman's short jacket; ~'key, wrench for (un)fastening ~stead; ~'lift, appliance for raising invalid to sitting position; ||~'maker, (wo)man tending college rooms at Oxf. & Camb.; ~'pan, invalid's chamber utensil for use in bed; ~'post, upright support of ~ (in twinkling of ~post, prob. transf. f. ~staff, loose cross-piece of old ~steads often used as handy weapon; *between you & me & the ~post*, in confidence); ~'ridden, confined to ~ by infirmity, decrepit, [OE *bedreda* (*rida* rider), -en by confusion w. P.P.]; ~'room, for sleeping in; ~'side, side of esp. invalid's (good bedside manner, of tactful doctors); ~'sore, developed in invalid by lying in ~; ~'spread, coverlet; ~'stead, framework of ~; ~'straw, kinds of plant, esp. (Our Lady's ~straw) ~tick, quadrangular bag for going to ~. 2. Flat base on which anything rests; ~'plate, metal plate forming base of machine; garden plot filled with plants, swamp with osiers; bottom of sea, river, etc. (~rock, solid rock underlying alluvial deposits etc., fig. ultimate facts or principles of a theory, character, etc.); foundation of road or railway; slates etc. of billiard table; central part of gun-carriage; stratum; layer of oysters etc. [com.-Teut. cf. G *bett* perh. f. Aryan *bhodh-* whence L *fodere* dig]

bêd², v.t. & i. (-dd-). Put or go to bed (poet. or arch. exc. of horses etc.); plant (esp. ~ *out*); cover up or fix firmly in something; arrange as, be or form, a layer. [f. prec.]

bêdăb'ble, v.t. Stain, splash, with dirty liquid, blood, etc. [BE-(1)+DABBLE]

bêdăd', int. (Irish etc. for) by gad. [BE-(1)+DAUB v.]

bêdaub', v.t. Smear with paint etc.; bedizen. [BE-(1)+DAUB v.]

bêdd'er¹, n. In vbl senses; also, plant suited for flower-bed. [-ER¹]

||**bêdd'er²**, n. (Univ. sl.). Bedroom. [BED¹+-ER-(6)]

bêdd'ing, n. In vbl senses; also: mattress, bedclothes, etc.; litter for cattle; bottom layer; (Geol.) stratification. [-ING¹]

bêdéck', v.t. Adorn. [BE-(1)+DECK v.]

bêd'éguar (-gär), n. Mosslike excrescence on rose-bush produced by insect's puncture. [f. F *bédeguar* f. Pers. *badawar* wind-brought]

||**bêd'el(l)**, n. Official at Oxf. & Camb. with duties chiefly processional. [= BEADLE]

bêdev'il, v.t. (-ll-, -l-). Treat with diabolical violence or abuse; possess, bewitch; spoil, confound; call devil. [BE-(5, 6)+DEVIL n.]

bêdev'ilment, n. Possession by devil; maddening trouble, confusion. [prec.+-MENT]

bêdew', v.t. Cover with drops, sprinkle. [BE-(6)+DEW]

||**Bêd'fordshire** (-er), n. (nursery). Bed (*go to ~*).

bêdight', (-īt), v.t. (past & p.p. bedight). Array, adorn, (arch.; usu. in p.p.). [BE-(1)+DIGHT]

bêdim', v.t. (-mm-). Make (eyes, mind) dim, [BE-(4)+DIM a.]

bêdiz'en, v.t. Dress out gaudily. [BE-(2)+DIZEN]

bĕd'lam, n. (B~) hospital of St. Mary of Bethlehem used as lunatic asylum; any madhouse; scene of uproar. [f. *Bethlehem*; hospital founded as priory 1247, converted to asylum 1547]

bĕd'lamite, n. & a. Lunatic. [-ITE¹ (1)]

Bĕd'lington, n. (Also ~ *terrier*) short-haired, narrow-headed sporting terrier. [~ in Northumberland]

bĕd'ouin (-dŏo-; or -ēn), n. (pl. same) & a. (Arab) of the desert, wandering; gipsy. [F, f. Arab. *badawin* pl. of *badawiy* dweller in the desert (*badw* desert); *-n* is prop. the pl. sign]

bĕdrăb'bled (-ld), a. Dirty with rain & mud. [BE-(1), & see DRABBLE]

bĕdrăg'gle, v.t. Wet (dress etc.) by trailing it, or so that it trails or hangs limp. [BE-(1) + DRAGGLE]

bee, n. Four-winged stinging social insect (queen, drones, & workers) producing wax & honey, allied insects (*Humble, Mason, Carpenter*, etc., *B~*); poet; busy worker; meeting for combined work or amusement (chiefly U.S., exc. *spelling-~*); *have a ~ in one's bonnet*, be mad on some point; ~-*bread*, (honey &) pollen used as food by ~s; ~-*eater*, kinds of foreign bird; ~-HIVE; ~-*line*, straight between two places; ~-*master*, ~-*mistress*, keepers of ~s; *B~ orchis*, with ~-shaped flowers; ||~-*skep*, straw hive; ~s'*wax*, secreted by ~s as comb material, (v.t.) polish with this. [OE *bēo*; com.-Teut., cf. G *biene* perh. f. Aryan *bhi-* fear, quiver]

beech, n. Smooth-barked glossy-leaved mast-bearing forest tree; its wood; ~-*fern*, kind of polypody; ~ *marten*, (also *stone marten*) white-breasted marten found in S. Europe; ~-*mast*, fruit of ~ trees. [OE *bēce*, *bōc* f. Teut. & cf. Gk *phāgos*, L *fāgus*]

beef, n. (pl. -ves). Flesh of ox, bull, or cow; (in men) size, muscle; (usu. pl.) ox(en), esp. fattened, or their carcasses; ||~-*eater*, yeoman of guard, warder of Tower of London, (f. obs. sense dependant); ~ *tea*, stewed juice for invalids; ~STEAK, ~-*wood*, red timber of various trees. [f. OF *boef* f. L *borem* nom. *bos* ox = Gk *bous*, Skr. *go-*, & E COW]

beef'|y, a. Like beef; solid, muscular; stolid. Hence ~INESS n. [-Y²]

Bĕĕl'zĕbŭb, n. The Devil; a devil. [L, f. Gk *beelzeboub* f. Heb. *ba'alz'bŭb* fly-lord]

been. See BE.

beer¹, n. Alcoholic liquor from fermented malt etc, flavoured with hops etc., including ale (pale) & porter (dark); other fermented drinks, as *nettle-~*, GINGER-~; *small ~*, (lit.) weak ~, (fig.) trifling matters (*think no small ~ of*, have high opinion of); ~-*engine*, for drawing at a distance; ||~-*house*, licensed for ~, not spirits; ||~-*money*, servant's allowance in lieu of ~; ~-*pull*, handle of ~-engine. [OE *bēor*; com.-WG, cf. G *bier*; etym. dub.]

beer², n. One of the ends (so many threads) into which a warp is divided. [=BEER, cf. *porter* in same sense in Scotland]

beer'|y, a. Of, like, beer; esp., betraying influence of beer. [-Y²]

bees'tings (-z), n. pl. First milk after parturition. [f. obs. *beest* OE *blōst*, com.-WG, cf. G *biest*; etym. dub.]

bees'wing (-z-), n. Second crust in long-kept port; old wine. [BEE + WING, from its filmy look]

beet, n. Two plants with succulent root, *Red B~* used for salad, *White B~* for sugar-making; ||~-*root*, root of ~. [OE *bēte* f. L *bēta*]

bee'tle¹, n., & v.t. Tool with heavy head & handle for ramming, crushing, smoothing, etc. (vb, beat with this); *three-man-~*, requiring three to lift it; ~-*brain* etc., blockhead. [OE *bīetel* f. OTeut. *bautilos* f. *bautan* BEAT; see -LE(1)]

bee'tle², n. Insect having upper wings converted to hard wing-cases (pop. only of the black & large varieties, also wrongly of insects like them, as the *black-~* or cockroach); short-sighted person (cf. ~-*eyed*, *blind as a ~*); ~-*crusher*, large boot or foot. [OE *bitula* biter f. *bītan* BITE¹]

bee'tle³, a. Projecting, shaggy, scowling, (~ *brows*, ~-*browed*). [prob. f. prec. w. ref. to tufted antennae of some beetles]

bee'tle⁴, v.i. Overhang (of brows, cliffs), hang threateningly (of fate etc.). [f. prec.]

beeves. See BEEF.

beef'er, n. (sl.). Nose. [?]

befall', (-awl), v.t. & i. (-fell, -fallen). Happen; happen to (person etc.). [OE *befallan* f. BE-(2) + *fallan* FALL; cf. G *be-fallen*]

befit', v.t. (-tt-). Suit, be fitted for; be incumbent on; be right for. Hence ~t'ING² a., ~t'ingLY² adv. [BE-(2) + FIT v.]

befog', v.t. (-gg-). Envelop in fog; obscure. [BE-(6) + FOG² n.]

befool', v.t. Dupe. [BE-(5) + FOOL¹ n.]

before', adv., prep., & conj. 1. adv. Ahead (*go~*); on the front (~ *& behind*); previous to time in question, already, in the past, (*long ~*). 2. prep. In front of (~ *the mast*, of common sailors berthed forward), ahead of; under the impulse of (~ *the wind, recoil ~, carry all ~ you*); in presence of (*appear ~ judge, bow authority*; ~ *God* = as God sees me; *the question ~ us*); awaiting (*world all them*); earlier than (~ *Christ*, usu. abbr. B.C., appended to dates reckoned back-

For compounds of *be-* not given consult BE-.

wards from birth of Christ); this side the coming of (future event); farther on than; rather than; rather than the ~ lying). **3.** conj. Previous (to ~ *I lied*, rather than (*would die ~ I lied*, [OE *beforan* (BE-+*foran* adv. f. OTeut. *fora* FOR)]

before'hand (-rh-), adv. In anticipation, in readiness; *be ~ with*, anticipate, forestall; *~ with the world*, having money in hand. [orig. two wds; sense-development doubtful]

befoul', v.t. Make foul (lit. or fig.); *~ one's own* NEST¹. [BE-(4)+FOUL¹]

befriend' (-rend), v.t. Help, favour. [BE-(6)+FRIEND n.]

beg, v.t. & i. (-gg-). Ask for (food, money, etc.); (abs.) ask alms (*ask for alms* etc.); raised expectantly; (of dog) sit up with forepaws humbly (thing, *for* thing, *of* person, person *to do*, *of* person *to do*, *that* something may be done); (in formal & courteous phr.) *~ pardon, leave*; *~ off*, get (person) excused penalty etc.; *~ to do*, take leave to do, take the liberty of doing, (*I ~ to differ, enclose, announce, etc.*); *~ the question*, assume the truth of matter in dispute; *go (a-)begging* (of situations, opportunities, etc.), find no acceptor. [perh. shortened f. F *béguiner* be a *beghard* or *béguine*, lay brother of mendicant order named f. Lambert Bègue]

begad', int. =by God (in fam. speech).

began'. See BEGIN.

beget (-g-), v.t. (-tt-, -got, -gotten). Procreate (usu. of father, sometimes of father & mother, cf. BEAR³); give rise to, occasion. Hence ~('ER¹ n. [OE & Goth.]

beggar¹, n. One who begs; one who lives by begging; poor man or woman (*~s must not be choosers*, must take what is offered); (depreciatingly) fellow; (play-fully) *little ~*, youngster etc.; *a good ~* (= *begger*), good at collecting for charities etc. [perh. =*beghard* see BEG &-ARD]

beggar², v.t. Reduce to poverty; outshine, reduce to silence (*~ description*); *~ my-neighbour*, card game. [f. prec.]

beggar'ly, a. Indigent; intellectually poor; mean, sordid. Hence ~**liness** n. [BEGGAR¹+-LY¹]

beggary, n. Extreme poverty. [-Y³]

begin (-g-), v.t. & i. (-nn-, began, begun). Commence (*to do, doing, work* etc., or abs.; in pass. sense either *it has been begun to be done*, or *it has been begun*); be the first to do something; take the first step (*~ to* colloq., appear likely ever to, make any attempt to); start speaking; *~ at*, start from; *~ with*, take first; *to ~ with*, in the first place; *~ upon*, set to work at; come into being, arise; have its commencement, nearest boundary, etc. (at some point in space or time). [com-WG; OE *beginnan* cf. G & Du.

beginnen (BE-+*ginnan* perh. = OE *ginnan* gape f. Aryan *ghi-* open cf. L *hiare*]

beginn'er (-g-), n. In vbl senses; tiro.

beginn'ing (-g-), n. In vbl senses; also or esp.; time at which anything begins; source, origin; first part; *the ~ of the end*, first clear sign of final result. [-ING¹(1)]

begird' (-g-), v.t. (-t). Gird round or encircle. [BE-(1)+GIRD¹]

begone' (-awn-, -ŏn), vb imperat. = be gone (more peremptory than *go*).

begon'ia, n. Kinds of plant with coloured perianths but no petals. [Michel *Begon* o. 1680]

begor'ra, int. (Irish corruption of) God!

begot('ten). See BEGET.

begrime', v.t. Soil deeply. [BE-(6)+GRIME]

begrudge', v.t. Feel or show dissatisfaction at (thing); envy (one) the possession of. [BE-(2)+GRUDGE v.]

beguile' (-gīl), v.t. Delude; cheat (person *of*, *out of*, or *into doing*); charm, amuse; divert attention from (toil, passage of time). Hence ~'ER¹, ~e'MENT(-gīlm-), nn. [BE-(2)+obs. vb *guile*, see GUILE]

beguinage (bĕg'ĭnaĭzh), n. House of béguines. [foll. +-AGE]

béguine (-gēn), n. Member of Netherlands lay sisterhood not bound by vows. [Lambert *Bègue*, founder 1180]

begum (-gē-), n. Mohammedan queen or lady of high rank in Hindustan. [Hind. *begam* f. East Turk. *bigim* fem. of *big* prince (BEY)]

begun'. See BEGIN.

behalf' (-ahf), n. (Only in phr. 'on or in my etc. ~', 'on or in ...'s ~', 'on or in ~ of --'), on the part of, on account of, (a person); in the interest of (person or principle etc.). [mixture of earlier phr. *on his behove* & *bihalve him*, either = on his side; see HALF]

behave', v.t. & refl. (Intr., usu. with adv.) conduct oneself, act, (rarely abs., esp. to or of children) conduct oneself with propriety, *~ towards*, treat (*well* etc.); (refl., usu. of or to children, & usu. without adv.) show good manners; (of machines etc., intr. or refl.) work (*well, badly, etc.*); ~*d* p.p. (with *well-*, *ill-*,) having good, bad, manners or conduct. [BE-(2)+HAVE]

behav'iour (-yer), n. Deportment, manners; moral conduct, treatment shown to or towards others; *be on one's good ~*, do one's best under probation; way in which ship, machine, substance, etc., acts or works. [f. prec., the ending due to confusion w. obs. *aver*, *haveour*, *haveoure*, possession, = F *avoir*]

behav'iourism (-yer-), n. (psych.). Doctrine that, given adequate knowledge, all human actions admit of analysis into stimulus & response, & that ability to predict them depends on exhaustive

study of behaviour in that light. [f. prec. + -ISM]

behead' (-hĕd), v.t. Cut the head from; kill in that way. [OE *behēafdian* f. *be-* (from) about + *hēafod* HEAD n.]

beheld. See BEHOLD.

behēm'oth (or bē'i-), n. Enormous creature. [perh. Egyptian *p-ehe-mau* water-ox (hippopotamus) assimilated to Heb. pl. (of dignity) of *b'hēmah* beast, see *Job* xl. 15]

behēst', n. Command (poet.). [OE *behǣs* cf. *behātan* later *behight* to command, & G *heissen*]

behind', adv., prep., & n. In or to the rear (of), on the further side (of), hidden (by), at one's back, towards what was one's rear, further back in place or time (than), past in relation to, too late, in concealment, in reserve, in support of, in an inferior position (to), under the defence of, in the tracks of, outdone (by), in arrear (with); (n.) the posterior. Phrr.: *stay, leave, ~, after others'*; *one's own, departure or death*; *fall ~*, not keep up; *~ the scenes*, in private; *put ~ one*, refuse to consider; *go ~ one's words* etc., look for secret motives on his part; *~ time*, unpunctual; *~ the times*, antiquated. [OE *behindan* (be- + *hindan* = G *hinten* f. hind-HIND³ + -ana from)]

behind'hand, adv. & pred. a. In arrear (with payments etc.); out of date, behind time; ill-provided (with). [prec. + HAND, cf. BEFOREHAND]

behōld', v.t. (beheld). See, become aware of by sight; (abs. in imperat.) take notice, attend. Hence ~ER¹ n. [OE *bihaldan* f. BE-(2) + *haldan* HOLD v. keep (in view)]

behōld'en, pred. a. Under obligation (to). [p.p. (obs. exc. in this use) of prec. = bound]

behoof', n. (In phrr. *to, for, on ~, or the ~, of*) use, advantage. [OE *bihōf* n *bihōf-lic* useful cf. G *behuf* f. OTeut. *bihafjan* (BE- + *hafjan* HEAVE af. L *capere* take)]

behōve', *-hoove'**, v.t.impers. Be incumbent on (person) to (do something). [OE *bihōfian* f. *bihōf* see prec.]

beige (bāzh), n. Kinds of dress-material made of undyed and unbleached wool; colour of this. [F. = natural-coloured, grey or brown, cf. It. *bigio*]

be'ing, n. In vbl senses; also or esp.: existence (*in ~*, existing); constitution, nature, essence; anything that exists (*the Supreme B~*, God); a person. [BE- -ING¹·²]

belāb'our (-ber), v.t. Thrash (lit. & fig.). [BE-(3) + LABOUR v. (exert one's strength upon)]

belāt'ed, a. Overtaken by darkness; coming too late. [p.p. of obs. *belate* f. BE-(4) + LATE]

belaud', v.t. Load with praise. [BE-(2) + LAUD v.]

belay', v.t. Make fast (running rope) round cleat etc. to secure it; (sailor's sl. in imperat.) stop!, enough!; *~ing-pin*, fixed wooden or iron pin for ~ing on. [OE *belecgan* cf. G *belegen* f. BE-(1) + *lecgan* LAY³ = lay round]

běl cantō (kahn-), n. Singing characterized by full rich broad tone & accomplished technique. [It. = fine song]

bělch', v.i. & t. Emit wind noisily from throat; utter noisily or drunkenly (abusive, blasphemous, or foul talk); (of gun or volcano) send out or up. [OE *bealcian* cf. Du. *balken* bray]

bělch², n. Eructation; sound of gun, volcano; burst of flame. [f. prec.]

běl'cher, n. Parti-coloured neckerchief. [Jim B~, pugilist]

běl'dam(e), n. Old woman, hag; virago. [earlier = grandmother f. *bel-* (cf. obs. *belsire*, & see BEAU) expressing relationship + DAM mother]

beleag'uer (-ger), v.t. Besiege (lit. & fig.). [f. Du. *belegeren* camp round f. BE-(6) + *leger* a camp]

běl'emnite, n. Tapering sharp-pointed fossil bone of extinct cuttlefish. [f. Gk *belemnon* dart + -ITE¹ ²]

běl ěsprit' (-rē), n. (pl. *beaux esprits* pr. bōz ěsprē'). A wit. [F]

běl'fr'y, n. Bell tower, attached or separate; bell space in church tower. Hence ~IED² (-id) a. [by dissim. f. OF *berfrei* f. LL +*berefridus* f. Teut. (MHG *bercvrid* prob. f. *bergen* shelter & OHG *fridu* peace); orig. sense, shed or tower for cover in besieging]

Běl'ga, n. Belgian unit of exchange (= 5 francs). [L fem. of *Belgus* Belgian (sc. *pecunia*)]

Běl'gian, a. & n. (Native) of Belgium. [-AN]

Běl'gic, a. Of the Netherlands; of the ancient Belgae. [f. L *Belgicus* (Belgae, -IC)]

Běl'grāv'ia, n. Fashionable residential part of London south of Knightsbridge containing Belgrave Square.

Běl'grāv'ian, a. Of, suited to, Belgravia, fashionable London district. [f. Belgrave Square f. ground-landlord's Belgrave, Leics.]

Běl'ial, n. The devil; the spirit of evil; *man of ~*, reprobate. [f. Heb. *b'li-yaal* (b'li not + yaal use) worthlessness]

belie', v.t. (-lying). Give false notion of; fail to act up to (promise etc.); fail to justify (hope etc.). [OE *belēogan* f. BE-(3) + *lēogan* LIE²]

belief', n. Trust or confidence (*in*); acceptance of the Christian theology; acceptance as true or existing (of any fact),

For compounds of *be-* not given consult BE-

statement, etc.; *in*, or *of*, with n., *that* with clause; *to the best of my* ~, in my opinion, intuition; *thing* believed, religion, genuine opinion); *thing* believed, religion, Creed. [ME *bileve* (BE- + OE *lēafa* short-ened f. *ge-lēafa* cf. G *glaube* f. OTeut. *galaub- dear*)]

belie've', v.t. & i. Have faith *in*, trust word (of person); put trust *in* truth of a statement, efficacy of a principle, system, machine, etc., existence of any-thing; give credence to (person, state-ment, etc., or *that*-clause); be of opinion *that*; *make* ~e, pretend. Hence ~**ABLE a., ~'ER'** n., ~**'ING²** a. [ME *bileven* f. OE *gelēfan* cf. G *glauben* f. OTeut. as prec.]

belike', adv. (arch.) Probably, perhaps, (often iron.). [*be-* = BY prep. + LIKE a. (by what is likely)]

Belish'a (-ēsh) **beac'on**, n. Post with yellow globe on top marking street crossing-place for pedestrians. [L. Hore-*Belisha*, Minister of Transport 1934]

beli'ttle, v.t. Make small, dwarf; depre-ciate. [BE-(4) + LITTLE]

bell¹, n. Hollow body of cast metal in deep cup shape widening at lip made to emit musical sound when struck; (Naut.) other senses besides the acoustic; ~*-bird*, Brazilian and Austral. kinds with ~-like note; ~*-buoy*, with warning ~ rung by waves' motion; ~*-flower*, any plant of genus *Campanula*; ~*-founder*, *-founding*, -*foundry*, caster, casting, & manufactory, of ~s; ~*-glass*, ~*-shaped* as cover for plants; ~*-hanger*, artisan who puts up ~s & wires; *~-hop* (sl.), hotel page; ~-*metal*, alloy of copper & tin (more tin than in bronze) for ~s; ~*-pull*, cord or handle attached to ~-wire; ~*-ringer*, *-ringing* (of church ~s with changes etc.); ~ *on neck*, ringleader. [OE *belle*, com-LG cf. Du. *bel*]

bell², v.t. Furnish with bell(s); ~ *the cat*, take the danger of a common enterprise on oneself (fable of mice & cats). [f. prec.]

bell³, n. & v.i. (Make the) cry of stag or buck at rutting-time. [OE *bellan* cf. G *bellen* bark]

belladonn'a, n. (Bot.) Deadly Night-shade; (Med.) drug prepared from this. [mod. L f. It., = fair lady, perh. because a cosmetic is made from it]

belle, n. Handsome woman; reigning beauty (*the* ~ *of any place*). [F, f. L *bella* fem. of *bellus* pretty see BEAU]

belles-lettres (bel-lět'r'), n. Studies, writings, of the purely literary kind.

Hence **beli'ěf'rist (3)(-l-l-) n., beli'ětris't** to (-l-l-) a. [F]

beli'clōse, a. Inclined to fighting. Hence ~ōs'IT'Y n. [f. L *bellicosus* (*bellum* war, -IC, -OSE¹)]

beli'gerency, n. Status of a belligerent. [f. foll.; see -ENCY]

beli'gerent, a. & n. (Nation, party, or person) waging regular war as recog-nized by the law of nations; of such nation etc.; (loosely) any opponent en-gaged in conflict. [wrong correction of earlier *belligerant* f. F *belligérant* f. L *belligerare* wage war (*bellum* + *gerere*), -ANT]

Bellōn'a, n. War personified; woman of commanding presence. [L, = goddess of war f. *bellum* war]

bell'ow (-ō), v.i. & t., & n. **1.** Roar as a bull; shout, roar with pain; utter loudly and angrily (often *out, forth*); (of thunder, cannon, etc.) reverberate, roar. **2.** n. ~*ing sound*. [etym. dub.; cf. BELL²]

bell'ows (-ōz), n. pl. Portable or fixed contrivance for driving air into a fire or through pipes of organ, reeds of har-monium, etc.; *pair of* ~, two-handled for fire; means used to fan passion etc.; the expansible part of photographic camera, lungs(~ *to mend, of* broken-winded horse); ~ *fish*, northern form *betu, betu*) [earlier *belu bag* = BELLY; the present wd same wd as BELLOWS]

bell'y, n. Cavity of human body below diaphragm with stomach & bowels & other contents, abdomen; (externally) lower front of body; corresponding parts of animals; stomach; the body as food-consumer (cf. BACK), appetite, gluttony; the womb; cavity of anything; bulging part (concave or convex); front, inner, or lower surface; surface of violin etc. across which strings pass; ~*-band* (below horse's, ~, checking play of shafts); ~*-worship,* gluttony; ~*-ache,* colic. Hence **-bèll'ied²(-id) a.** [ME *bali, belÿ,* f. OE *bælġ* f. OTeut. *baljiz bag* f. *belgan swell*]

bell'yful (-ŏŏl), n. As much as one wants of anything, esp. of fighting. [-FUL(2)]

belŏng', v.i. Pertain, be proper, *to* (as duty, right, possession, natural or right accompaniment, example in classifica-tion, characteristic, part, member, in-habitant, appendage); be rightly a mem-ber of club, coterie, household, grade of society, etc.; *~be resident in*, connected *with*; ~ *under* or *in*, be rightly classified among; ~ *here* etc., live here, be rightly placed under this heading etc. [ME (-2) + obs. vb *long* pertain f. OE *gelang* adj. dependent on (cf. the now dialectal 'along of ') = OHG *gilang* akin (perh. f. notion corresponding *in length*)]

belŏng'ings (-z), n. pl. A person's

property, relatives, or luggage; every-thing connected with a subject. [f. prec.]

belov'ed (-d), adj. or n. usu. -liv'rid; as vb -livd', p.p., a., & n. (Forming pass. parts of vb obs. in act.) dearly loved (followed by *of* or *by*, or abs.); (n.) darling (common in voc., & with *my, his,* etc.). [BE-(2) + LOVE v.]

below' (-ō), adv. & prep. **1.** adv. At or to lower level; on earth; in hell; downstairs (esp. Naut. *go* ~, from deck); down stream; in lower rank (*the court* ~); at foot of page, or further on in book. **2.** prep. Lower than (~*stairs* now rare, downstairs); too low to be affected by (~ *flattery*); down stream from; on inferior side of dividing line (~ *par, ~ the gang-way*); at or to greater depth than; covered by; lower in amount, degree, etc., than (~ *one's breath,* less audibly than); of lower rank etc. than; unworthy of. Cf. BENEATH, UNDER. [*be-* = BY + LOW a.]

belt¹, n. Encircling strip of leather etc. worn round waist or baldric-wise to con-fine or support clothes or weapons etc. (*hit below the* ~, fight unfairly); cincture of earl or knight; strip of colour, special surface, trees, etc., round or on anything; zone or district (*cotton, wheat, fever,* ~); endless strap connecting wheels; row of armour plates under water-line; *Great & Little B~,* channels into Baltic. [com-Teut., cf. OHG *balz* perh. f. L *balteus*]

belt², v.t. Put belt round (~*ed cruiser,* with belt & metal-covered deck); fasten on with belt; mark with belt of colour etc.; thrash with belt. [f. prec.]

bel'vedere, n. Raised turret to view scenery from. [It. (*bel* beautiful, see BEAU, + *vedere* see)]

bely'ing. See BELIE.

bem'a, n. Platform in ancient Athenian public assembly. [Gk]

bemire', v.t. Cover or stain with mud; (pass.) be stuck in the mud. [BE-(6) + MIRE n.]

bemoan', v.t. Weep or express sorrow for or over. [OE *bemēnan* f. *mǣnan* MOAN]

bemuse' (-z), v.t. Stupefy. [BE-(2) + MUSE v.]

||bēn (Sc.). Inner room (usu. of two-roomed cottage); *but & ~,* the outer & inner room (i.e. the whole house). [ellipt. use of *ben* adv., within (OE *binnan*)]

bench, n., & v.t. **1.** Long seat of wood or stone; boat-thwart; judge's seat, office of judge, law-court (*King's, Queen's, B~*); (collect.) judges, magistrates; ||(Parl.) seats appropriated to certain groups etc. (*Treasury,* FRONT¹, CROSS³, bishops, ~es); *be raised to, be on, the* ~, be (made) a judge or bishop; working-table of carpenter etc.; ledge in masonry or earthwork; ~*-table,* stone seat in cloister etc.; ~*-mark,* cut by surveyors to mark point in line of levels; ~*-warrant,* one issued by a judge (opp. justice's war-rant). **2.** v.t. Exhibit (dog) at show. [com.-Teut.: OE *benc,* cf. Sw. *bänk,* G *bank,* f. OTeut. *bankiz;* same wd as BANK¹·⁵, which came through Rom.]

||bēn'cher, n. Senior member, sharing management, of Inn of Court. [-ER¹]

bend¹, n. (Naut.) knot of various kinds (*fisherman's, weaver's,* etc.); (Her.) parallel lines from dexter chief to sinister base (~ *sinister* in opposite direction, sign of bastardy); shape (half BUTT) in which hides are tanned (~*leather,* the thickest, used for soles). [earlier meaning *band, bond,* which wds have taken its place in most senses: OE *bend* f. OTeut. *band-* st. of *bindan* BIND¹; identified with OF *bende, bande,* BAND¹(2)]

bend², n. Bending, curve; bent part of anything; *the ~s* (colloq.), caisson disease. [f. foll.]

bend³, v.t. & i. (past *bent,* p.p. *bent* exc. in ~*ed knees*). Force out of straightness, impart to (rigid object) or receive a curved or angular shape; arch (brows); tighten up, bring to bear, (energies etc.); (pass.) be determined (*on* with gerund or noun); attach with knot (cable, sail); turn (t. & i.) in new direction (steps, eyes); incline (t. & i.) from the perpendi-cular (head), bow, stoop, submit, (*to* or *before*), force to submit (will etc.). Hence ~²ER¹ n., esp. (sl.) || sixpenny bit, *spree, [OE *bendan* prob. = ON *benda* join, strain, f. OTeut. *band-*(cf. BAND¹); sense is stringing the bow]

beneaped' (-pt), a. Left aground by neap-tide. [p.p. f. unused *beneap* see BE-(6) & NEAP]

beneath', adv. & prep. Below, under, underneath, (poetic, arch., & literary, but usual in) ~ *contempt* etc., not worth despising etc., = one, unworthy of him. [OE *beneothan* = BE- + *neothan* cf. G *nieden* f. OTeut. *nithar* NETHER + -*ana* from]

benedi'cite, n. Blessing invoked; grace at table; *the B~,* one of the canticles. [L, = *bless ye,* imperat. of *benedicere -dict-* = *bless* (*bene* well + *dicere* speak)]

ben'edick, n. Newly married man, esp. confirmed bachelor who marries. [Shaksp., *Much Ado*]

Bénédic'tine, a. & n. (Monk) of the order founded 529 by St Benedict, black monk; a liqueur. [f. F *bénédictin* f. L *benedictus* p.p. see BENEDICITE]

benedic'tion, n. Utterance of a blessing, generally at table, at end of church ser-vice, or as special R.-C. service; a bless-

For compounds of *be-* not given consult BE-.

ing, blessedness. [f. L benedictio (BENEDI-CTE², -ION)]

bènèdic'tory¹, a. Of, expressing, benediction. [f. med. L benedictorius see prec. and -ORY(1)]

Bènèdic'tus, n. One of the canticles. [first word in L version; see BENEDICTINE]

bènèfac'tion, n. Doing good; gift for charitable purpose. [f. L benefactio (BENE-FY¹, -TON)]

bèn'èfac'tor, n. Person who has given one friendly aid; patron of or donor to a cause or charitable institution. Hence ~ress¹ n. [f. M.L benefactor (bene well + facere a doing)]

bènèfic'ial (-shl), a. Advantageous; (Law) of, having, the usufruct of property. Hence ~ly² adv. [F bénéficial f. L beneficialis (BENEFICE, -AL)]

bèn'èfice, n. Church living. Hence ~D² (-st) a. [f. L beneficium (bene well & see -FIC, -ENCE)]

bènèf'icence, n. **benèf'icent**, a. Doing good, (showing) active kindness. Hence bènèf'icently² adv. [f. L beneficentia n. & beneficus a., comparat. beneficentior] cricketer, etc. who is taking a benefit, [F]

bènèfic'iary (-shar-), a. & n. (Law) holder, holding or held, by feudal tenure; holder of a living; receiver of benefits. [f. L beneficiarius, see BENEFICE, -ARY¹]

bèn'èfit¹, n. Advantage (for the ~ of, on behalf of; the ~ of the doubt, assuming innocence rather than guilt); allowance, pension, attendance, to which person is entitled under Nat. Insurance Act or as member of benefit society etc. (maternity, medical, ~); exemption from ordinary courts by the privilege of one's order (~ of CLERGY, peerage); performance at theatre, game, etc. of which proceeds go to particular players (~ s ~, ~-night, ~-match); ~-club, -society, for mutual insurance against illness or age; (Sl., Iron.) fine time, job, (had no end of a ~ getting things straight). [ME & AF benfet f. L benefactum neut. p.p. of benefacere do well]

bèn'èfit², v.t. & i. Do good to; receive benefit (by thing). [f. prec.]

bènèv'olence, n. Desire to do good, charitable feeling; (Eng. Hist.) forced loan. [f. OF benivolence f. L benevolentia f. benevolens -entis = foll.]

bènèv'olent, a. Desirous of doing good, charitable. Hence ~ly² adv. [f. OF benivolent f. L bene volentem nom. -ens well wishing (velle wish)]

Bèngal¹ (béngawl), a. ~ light, firework used for signals; ~ stripes, striped gingham, orig. from ~; ~ tiger, the tiger proper. [Indian province]

Bèngali¹, -lee, (béngawl'i), n. & a. (Native, language) of Bengal. [f. native Bangali]

bènigh'ted (-nit-), p.p. & a. (Forming pass, of vb obs. in act.) overtaken by night; involved in intellectual or moral darkness, ignorant. [BE-(6)+NIGHT]

bènign' (-in), a. Gracious; gentle; fortunate, salutary; (of diseases) mild, not malignant. Hence ~ly² adv. [f. OF benigne f. L benignus prob. = benigenus (bene well + -genus born)]

bènig'nant, a. Kind, kindly, to inferiors; gracious; salutary. Hence ~ANCY n., ~antly² adv. [recent formation f. prec. on anal. of MALIGNANT]

bènig'nity, n. Kindliness, kindness, (usu. in the old). [f. OF benignitè f. L benignitatem (BENIGN, -TY)]

bèn'ison (-zn), n. (arch.). A blessing. [= BENEDICTION, see -SON]

Bèn'jamin¹, n. Youngest child, darling; ~'s mess, large share. [Gen. xliii. 4]

bènt¹, n. Reedy rushlike stiff-stemmed grass of various kinds (with pl., or collect.); (also benned) stiff flower-stalk, old stalk, of grasses; couch-grass; Way B-, Stool B-, etc., kinds of plant; heath, uninclosed pasture, [OE beonet perh. = G binse rush]

bènt², n. Twist, inclination, bias, tendency; to the top of one's ~, to heart's content. [f. BEND³ on F anal. of descent, extent]

bènt³. See BEND³.

Bèn'thamism (-tə-), n. Greatest happiness of the greatest number as guiding principle of ethics. So ~ITE¹ (1) n. [Jeremy Bentham, 1748-1832; see -ISM (3)]

bèn'thos, n. (biol.). Flora & fauna of the sea.

bèn trovə'tō (-āh-), a. Well invented, characteristic if not true. [It.]

bènùmb' (-m), v.t. Make torpid, insensible, powerless, (usu. of cold); paralyse (mind, action). [earlier benumb (cf. dumb, numb) f. OE benuman p.p. of beniman deprive (BE-+niman cf. G nehmen)]

bèn'zène, n. An aromatic hydro-carbon got from coal-tar & represented by derivatives in all coal-tar products (formerly, & still in trade use, called benzol, -ole). [BENZO(1)+-ENE]

bèn'zine (-ēn), n. Mixture of liquid hydrocarbons got from mineral oils & used for removing grease-stains (in trade use often called benzoline or benzine). [foll.+-INE¹]

bèn'zoin (or -oin), n. (Also gum ~, benjamin) fragrant aromatic resin of Javanese tree. Hence bènzō'ïc² a. [earlier benjoin through F, Sp., It., f. Arab. luban jawi frankincense of Java (Jo- being dropped in Rom. as if the article)]

ben'zol, -ōl, n. =BENZENE. [BENZ(O)-+ -OL]

ben'zoline (-ēn, -ĭn), n. =BENZINE. [prec. +-INE³]

bequeath' (-dh), v.t. Leave (to person) by will (personalty; cf. DEVISE); transmit to posterity (example etc.). [OE becwethan f. BE-(3)+cwethan say, see QUOTH]

bequest', n. Bequeathing; thing bequeathed. [ME biquyste prob. for bicwis f. BE-+cwis saying of prec.; for -t cf. BE-HEST]

*berate', v.t. Scold. [BE-+RATE³]

berceuse (bĕrsȫz'), n. Cradle-song. [F]

Berb'er, n. & a. (Member) of the N.-African stock including the aboriginal races of Barbary, speaking allied languages. [f. Arab. barbar (barbara confusedly) or perh. f. Gk barbaros BARBAROUS]

berb'erry, n. See BARBERRY.

bereave', v.t. (~d or bereft). Rob, dispossess, of (usu. of immaterial things, as life, hope); leave desolate (esp. in p.p., usu. ~d in this sense); (of death etc.) deprive of a relation, wife, etc., whence ~MENT (-vm-) n. [com.-Teut.; OE beréafian cf. G berauben; see BE-(2), REAVE]

beret (bĕ'rā), n. Round flat cap worn by Basque peasants; similar cap worn by men & women with sports & holiday clothes; service military headdress. [F, f. LL birretum, see BIRRETTA]

berg¹, n. =ICEBERG.

‖ berg² (bĕrk), n. (S. Africa). Mountain or hill (esp. in comb.); ~wind, hot northerly wind blowing in Cape Colony in May & August. [Du.. = OE beorg]

berg'amot¹, n. Tree of orange & lemon kind; perfume extracted from its fruit. [f. Bergamo town in Italy]

berg'amot², n. Kind of pear. [f. F bergamotte f. It. bergamotta f. Turk. begarmudi prince's pear]

berg'mehl (-māl), n. Greyish-white flour-like geological deposit composed of infusorial shells, an abrasive & absorbent. [G = mountain-flour]

berg'schrund (bĕrk'shrŏŏnt), n. (mountaineering). Crevasse or gap at junction of steep upper slope with glacier or névé. [G]

berhyme' (-rīm), v.t. Write verses about, lampoon; put (matter) into rhymed form. [BE-(6)+RHYME n.]

beri'beri, n. Deficiency disease prevalent in India. [Cingalese, f. beri weakness]

Berkeleian (bärklē'an), n. & a. (Follower) of Berkeley or his philosophy, which denied the objective existence of the material world. [Bishop Berkeley, d.1753; see -AN]

Berlin', n. & a. Four-wheeled covered carriage with hooded seat behind (also berline); ~black, iron-varnish; ~iron, for casts; ~warehouse, shop for ~wool, fine dyed knitting wool; ~gloves, knitted. [~in Germany]

berm, n. Ledge in fortification between ditch & base of parapet. [f. F berme cf. ON barmr brim]

Bermūd'ian, a. & n. (Inhabitant) of the Bermudas; ~rigged, fitted with a high tapering sail. [-IAN]

Bernardine, a. & n. = CISTERCIAN.

ber'ry¹, n. (Pop.) any small roundish juicy fruit without stone; (Bot.) fruit with seeds enclosed in pulp; egg in fish-roe (in ~, of hen-lobster carrying eggs). Hence (-)ber'ried² (-id) a. [com.-Teut., cf. G beere, Goth. basi]

ber'ry², v.i. Come into berry, fill out; go gathering berries. [f. prec.]

bersagliere (see Ap.), n. pl. Crack Italian infantry, orig. riflemen. [It.]

bers'erk(er), n. Wild Norse warrior fighting with mad frenzy. [f. Icel. berserkr prob. = bear-sark, bear-coat]

berth¹, n. Convenient sea-room (give wide ~to, avoid); room for ship to swing at anchor; ship's place at wharf; proper place for anything; sleeping-place; situation, appointment. [prob. f. BEAR³ v. (make room by bearing off)+-TH¹; of same formation, but prob. later & independent, as BIRTH (early spellings coincide)]

berth², v.t. Moor (ship) in suitable place; provide sleeping-place for. [f. prec.]

berthe, a. bĕrthe, n. Deep falling (usu. lace) collar to low-necked dress. Big Bertha, German gun of vast range used in bombarding Paris in the war of 1914–18. [F (-e), the woman's name]

Berth'on boat, n. Collapsible boat. [E.L. Berthon inventor, d. 1899]

Bertill'on sys'tem, n. Method of identifying criminals by measurements. [French anthropologist d, 1914]

ber'yl, n. Precious stone, pale-green passing into light blue, yellow, & white; mineral species including also the emerald. [OF, f. L f. Gk bērullos]

beryll'ium, n. Hard white metallic element. [prec.+-IUM]

beseech', v.t. (-sought pr. -sawt). Ask earnestly for (esp. leave etc.); entreat (person, person that or to do or for thing). [BE-(2)+ME sechen, sechen, seken, SEEK]

beseech'ing, a. Suppliant (of look, tone, etc.). Hence ~LY² adv. [-ING²]

beseem', v.t. Suit, be fitting or creditable to, (abs., or with well, ill, etc.). Hence ~ingly² adv. [BE-(2)+SEEM]

beset', v.t. (-tting, past & p.p. -set). Hem in, set upon, (person); occupy & make impassable (road etc.); (of difficulties, temptations, etc.) assail, encompass,

For compounds of be- not given consult BE-.

(~ting sin, that most frequently tempts one), adv. [OE *besettan* (BE-(1), & see SET v.)]

besèt'ment, n. Besetting sin; being hemmed in. [prec.+-MENT]

beshrew' (-rōō), v.t. (Now only as mock-heroic imprecation) Plague take (me, person, or thing). [BE-(2)+ME *schrewen* to curse f. SHREW]

beside', prep. (formerly also adv.=foll.). Close to, by, near; on a level with, compared with; wide of (mark, question, etc.); ~ *oneself*, out of one's wits. [OE *be sidan* (BY, SIDE n.)]

besides' (-dz), adv. & prep. In addition (to), moreover; otherwise, else, (than) (neg. & interrog.) except. [prec.+-ES]

besiege', v.t. Invest, lay siege to; crowd round; assail with requests. Hence ~'ER¹ n. [ME *besegen* f. BE-(1)+*segen* f. OF *asegier* f. LL *assediare* (AD-+*sedium* f. L *sedere* SIT]

beslāv'er, v.t. Cover with slaver; flatter fulsomely. [BE-(1)+SLAVER v.]

beslŏb'ber, v.t.=prec.; also, kiss effusively. [BE-(1)+SLOBBER v.]

beslŭbb'er, v.t. Besmear. [BE-(1)+SLUBBER]

besmear', v.t. Smear with greasy or sticky stuff (also of the stuff as subj.). [OE *bismierwan* see BE-(1) & SMEAR v.]

besmirch', v.t. Soil, discolour; dim brightness of. [BE-(1)+SMIRCH v.]

bes'om (-z-), n., & v.t. (Sweep with) bundle of twigs tied round stick for sweeping, kind of broom. [OE *besema*, com.-WG cf. G *besen* Du. *bezem*]

besŏt', v.t. Stupefy mentally or morally. [BE-(4)+SOT]

besought'. See BESEECH.

bespangle (-ǎng'gl), v.t. Set about with spangles. [BE-(6)+SPANGLE]

bespatt'er, v.t. Spatter (object) all over; spatter (liquid etc.) about; cover with abuse or flattery. [BE-(1)+SPATTER]

bespeak', v.t. (past *-spoke*, p.p. *-spoke, spoken*). Engage beforehand; order (goods); stipulate for; speak to (poet.); suggest, be evidence of; (prop. *bespoke bookmaker* etc. (prop. *bespoke dealer*. [OE *besprecan*: com.-WG cf. G *besprechen*; see BE-(3) & SPEAK]

besprēnt', p.p. (poet.). Sprinkled (with); scattered about. [f. OE *besprengan* f. BE-(1)+OTeut. *sprangjan* causal of *springan* SPRING v.]

besprinkle (-ing'kl), v.t. Sprinkle or strew over (with; lit. & fig.; also with the liquid etc. as subj. or obj.). [ME *besprengil* frequent. of OE *besprengan*, see prec. &-LE]

Bĕs'sēmer, a. & n. ~ *process*, for removing carbon, silicon, etc. from pig-iron by passing currents of air through it when molten & so making ~ *iron*, ~ *steel*, or ~. [Sir H. ~, inventor 1856]

bĕst', a. & adv. (superl. of *good, well*). Of in, the most excellent kind, way (often, like *good, well*, used for specific adji.). Phr.: *the* ~ *part*, most; *had* ~, would find it wisest to; *one's* ~ *girl* (sl.), sweetheart; ~ *seller*, popular novel etc.; *put* ~ *leg* or *foot foremost*, go at full pace; *bad is the* ~, no good event possible; *with the* ~, as well as anyone; *do one's* ~, all one can; *be at one's* ~, in the ~ state; *one's* ~ or *Sunday* ~, ~ clothes; *have the* ~ *of it*, win in argument etc.; *make the* ~ *of things*, be contented; ~ *abused* (colloq.) most violently or generally abused (*the* ~ *abused book of the year*); *make the* ~ *of one's way*, go as fast as possible; *at* ~, on the most hopeful view; *did it for the* ~, with good intentions; *to the* ~ *of one's power* etc., as far as one's power etc. allows; *the* ~ *is the enemy of the good*, too high standard bars progress. [OE *betst*; com.-Teut. f. OTeut. *batist* cf. BETTER]

bestead' (-ĕd), v.t. & i. Avail, help. [BE-(2)+STEAD]

bĕsted', p.p. (With *ill, hard, sore*, etc.) situated, circumstanced, pressed. [ME *bistad* f. BE-(2)+*stad* f. ON *staddr* p.p. of *stedhja* stop]

bĕs'tial, a. Of, like, a beast or beasts esp. quadrupeds; brutish, barbarous; depraved, lustful, obscene. Hence or cogn. ~ITY (-ǎl²) n., ~IZE(3) v.t., ~LY² adv. [OF, f. L *bestialis* (*bestia* BEAST+-AL]

bĕs'tiary, n. Medieval moralizing treatise on beasts. [f. med. L *bestiarium* menagerie f. L *bestia* beast]

bestir', v.t.refl.(-rr-). Exert, rouse, (oneself). [OE *bestyrian* f. BE-(2)+*styrian* STIR v.]

bestow' (-ō), v.t. Deposit; provide with lodging; confer (thing) *upon* (person) as gift. Hence ~'AL(2) (-ōl) n. [ME *bistower*, see BE-(2), STOW]

bestrew' (-rōō), v.t. Strew (surface) *with*; scatter (things) about; lie scattered over. [OE *bestreowian* see BE-(1) & STREW]; p.p. *-ewn*, see BE-(3),

bestride', v.t. (past *-ode*; p.p. *-idden, -id, -ode*). Get or sit upon (horse, chair) with legs astride; stand astride over (place or fallen friend or enemy); also fig. (of rainbow etc.). [OE *bestrīdan*, see BE-(3), STRIDE v.]

bĕt', n., & v.i. & v.t. (bet). (Engagement to) risk one's money etc., risk (an amount etc.) against another's on the result of a doubtful event (*on* or *against* result or competition, *that* so-&-so will happen); (sl.) *you* ~, you may take it as certain; ABET v. (or obs. n.); whether vb or n. is prior is doubtful]

bĕt'a, n. Second letter (B, β) of Gk alphabet, used as name of second star in a

constellation, & in other numberings; ~ *rays*, fast-moving electrons emitted by radio-active substances, orig. regarded as rays. [Gk]

betake, v. refl. (-took, -taken). Commit oneself to (i.e. try) some course or means; convey oneself to (i.e. go to) a place or person. [ME; BE-, TAKE]

bē'tel, n. Leaf of *Piper betle*, which In-dians chew with areca-nut parings; (hence by mistake) ~*nut*, the areca nut. [Port. f. Malayalam *vettila*]

bête noire (bāt nwahr), n. (One's) abomi-nation. [F]

beth'el, n. Hallowed spot (*Gen.* xxviii. 19); ∥ nonconformist chapel; seamen's church (ashore or floating). [Heb. *beth-el* = house of God]

∥ **bēthĕs'da** (-z-), n. Nonconformist chapel. [*John* v, 2; Heb. = house of mercy]

bethink', v. refl. (-thought) (alw. with *self* or arch. refl. *me, him*, etc.). Reflect, stop to think; remind oneself of, *how*, or *that*: take into one's head to. [OE *bethencan*, com.-Teut. cf. G *bedenken*; see BE-(3), THINK]

betide', v.i. & t. (only in 3 sing. pres. subj.). Happen (*whate'er* ~); happen to (*woe* ~ *him* etc.). [ME *bitiden* see BE-(2), TIDE v.]

betimes' (-mz), adv. Early in day, year, life, etc.; in good time. [*by time* (ME +-ES]

bē'ton, n. (Orig. lime, now any kind of) concrete. [f. F *bēton* ult. f. L *bitumen* mineral pitch]

bet'ony, n. Purple-flowered plant. [f. F *bétoine* f. LL *betonica* f. L *vettonica* f. name of Gaulish tribe]

betook. See BETAKE.

betray', v.t. Give up treacherously (per-son or thing *to* enemy); be disloyal to; lead astray; reveal treacherously; reveal involuntarily; be evidence or symptom of. Hence ~AL(2), ~ER¹ nn. [ME *betraien* f. BE-(2) +obs. *tray* t. f. OF *traïr* t. L *tradere* (*trans* over +*dare* give)]

betrōth' (-ōdh), v.t. Bind with a promise to marry (usu. in p.p.). Hence ~AL(2) n., ~ED¹ a. & n. [ME *bitreuthien* f. BE-(6)+ *treuthe* TRUTH, later assimilated to TROTH]

bett'er¹ a., adv., & n. (comp. of *good, well*). Of, in, a more excellent kind, way (often, like *good, well*, for specific wd as more virtuous, more plentifully). Phrr.: *no ~ than*, practically; *no ~ than she should be*, (usu.) of easy virtue; *one's ~ feelings*, higher self; ~ *part*, most; one's ~ *half*, wife; *for ~ for worse*, on terms of accepting all results (see Prayer Book, Marriage Service); ~ *than* (with number etc.), above; *had* ~, would find it wiser to; *be, get*, ~, less unwell; ~ *than one's word*, more liberal than one promised to be; *one's* ~, more skilful person; *one's* ~*s*, people of higher rank; *get the* ~ *of*, defeat, outwit; *know* ~, refuse to accept statement, not be so foolish (as to do something); *think* ~ *of it*, change one's mind; *change for the* ~; ~ *off*, richer, more comfortable; *the* ~ *the day the* ~ *the deed* (retort to charge of Sabbath-breaking). [OE *betera*; com.-Teut. cf. G *besser* f. OTeut. *batizom-* f. *bat-* see BOOT³ +-ER³]

bett'er², v.t. & i. Amend, improve: sur-pass (a feat etc.); ~ *oneself*, get better situation, wages, etc. Hence ~MENT n., (also) enhanced value (of real property) arising from local improvements. [ME *beteren* cf. G *bessern* & see prec.]

bett'er³, **-or-**, n. One who bets. [BET +-ER³]

between', prep. & adv. (the orig. restric-tion to relations involving only *two* limits etc. still tends to be observed wherever AMONG is adequate for higher numbers). In, into, along, or across, a space, line, or route, bounded by (two or more points, lines, etc.); in, into, along, or across, an interval; separating; connecting; inter-mediately in place, time, or order (to); owing partly to, partaking of, shared by, (each); to & fro (*go*~); to & from (*plies London & Brighton*); reciprocally on the part of; confined to (~ *ourselves*, ~ *you & me*); by combination of; taking one & rejecting the other of (*choose*~). *Far* ~, at wide intervals; ~ *cup & lip*, of dashed hopes; ∥~*maid* (now usu. *tween'd*), ser-vant assisting two others, e.g. cook & housemaid; ~ *wind & water*, at a vulner-able point; ~ *devil & deep sea*, with no escape; *betwixt &* ~, half-&-half; *stand* ~, mediate, be protector; ~ *whiles*, in the intervals. [OE *betweonum, betwēonam*, = L *bini*, of distrib. num., = L *bīni*, (f. *seem* etc.) *twēonum* = by (seas etc.) twain]

betwixt', prep. & adv. [Poet., arch., or dial., for] BETWEEN. [earlier *betwixen* (BE-+OSax. *twisc* f. OTeut. *twiskjo-* twofold cf. G *zwischen* between)]

∥ **Beu'lah**, n. Nonconformist chapel. [*Is.* lxii. 4]

bev'el¹, n. Joiner's & mason's tool for setting off angles; a slope from the horizontal or vertical, surface so sloping; ~ *edge*, as in a chisel; ~*gear*, working one shaft from another at angle to it by ~*wheels*, cogged wheels with working face oblique to axis. [f. OF *bevel* (now *beveau*) etym. dub.]

bev'el², v.t. & i. (-ll-). Reduce (square edge) to, take, a slope. [f. prec.]

For compounds of *be-* not given consult BE-.

bĕv'erage, n. Drinking-liquor. [f. OF
bevrage (*beivre*, now *boire*, f. L *bibere*
drink +-AGE)]

Bĕv'in boy, n. Young conscript selected
by ballot for work in coal-mine. [E.
Bevin, Minister of Labour]

bĕv'y, n. Company (prop. of ladies, roes,
quails, larks). [etym. dub.; perh.=
drinking company (cf. BEVERAGE)]

bewail', v.t. & i. Wail (over), mourn (for).
[BE-(3) + WAIL v.]

bĕware', v.i. & t. (not inflected, & used
only where *be* is the vb] part required, as
I will —, but not *I —*). Be cautious, take
heed; take heed of, lest, how, that not. [as
now used, f. BE v. + OE *war* cautious, but
with traces of OE vbs *warian*, *bewarian*,
take care of, defend, (surviving in 'Ware
holes!')]

bĕwil'der, v.t. Lead astray, perplex, confuse. Hence ~ingĭy² adv., ~MENT n.
[BE-(6) + obs. *wilder*(n WILDERNESS]

bĕwĭtch', v.t. Affect by magic, put a spell
on; delight exceedingly, whence ~ING²
a., ~ingĭy² adv., ~MENT n. [ME
biwicchen f. BE-(2) + OE *wiccian* enchant f.
wicca WITCH n.]

bewray' (birā'), v.t. (arch.). Reveal, esp.
involuntarily. [BE-(2) + OE *wrēgan* accuse
cf. G *rügen*]

bey (bā), bey'lĭc (bā-), n. (Bey) Turkish
governor; (beylic) his district. [formerly
beg f. Osmanli *beg*]

beyond', adv., prep., & n. 1. At, to, the
farther side (of), past, outside, besides;
later than: out of reach, comprehension,
or range, of (~ *measure*, exceedingly);
surpassing; more than (with objective
case, as *you have prospered ~ me*); (neg. &
interrog.) except. 2. n. The ~, the future
life, the unknown; *the back of ~*, the re-
motest corner of the world. [OE *begeon-
dan* (BE- about + *geond* across + -*and*
from; cf. YON & G *jen*- that]

bĕz'ant (or bizănt'), n. Gold coin (10/-
to 20/-) current in Europe from 9th c.;
also silver (1/- to 2/-). [f. OF *besan* f. L
Byzantius (*nummus* coin) of Byzantium]

bĕz'el, n. Sloped edge of chisel etc.;
oblique faces of cut gem; groove holding
watch-glass or gem. [f. OF *besel* (now
biseau) etym. dub.]

bézique' (-ēk), n. Card-game for two or
four. [f. F *bésigue* etym. dub.]

bĕz'oar (-ōr), n. Concretion with hard
nucleus found in stomach or intestines
of certain animals (chiefly ruminants),
formerly believed antidotal. [corrupt. of
Pers. *pādzahr* antidote, Arab. *bāzahr*]

bezón'ian, n. (arch.). Rascal, beggarly
fellow. [earlier *besonio*, f. It. *bisogno*
need, want]

bhang, n. Indian hemp used as
narcotic & intoxicant (smoked, chewed,
eaten, & drunk). [earlier *bangue*, *bang*;
f. Hind. etc. *bhang*]

bhīs'tĭ, bhees'tў̆, (bēs-), n. (Anglo-Ind.).
Indian water-carrier. [Urdu *bhīstī* f.
Pers. *bihisht* paradise (prob. joc. origin)]

bī-, comb. form [f. L *bi-* (earlier *dui-*; cf. Gk *di-*,
Skr. *dvi*) twice, doubly] having two —,
freely used in English, esp. with wds f. L,
but also with E wds (*bi-weekly*). I. Adji.
(a) having two —, as *bicentral*, *bi-
cristate*; (b) doubly, in two ways, as *bi-
concave*; (c) in Bot. & Zool., twice over,
as *bipinnate*; (d) lasting for two —,
appearing every two —, as *biennial*;
(e) appearing twice in a —, as *biannual*;
bi-monthly; many wds are ambiguous
between this & the last, & *semi-*, *half-*,
would be better here; (f) joining two —,
as *bi-parietal*. 2. Nouns, double, as *bi-
millionaire*. 3. Chem. nouns & adji.
having twice the amount of acid, base,
etc., indicated by the simple wd, as
bicarbonate.

bī'as¹, n. (In bowls) lopsided form of a
bowl, its oblique course, the inserted plug
of metal or influence deflecting it;
(metaph. from bowls) inclination, predisposition (*towards*), prejudice, influence;
(Dressmaking etc.; as a, n., & adv.)
cut on the ~, *cut* obliquely across
the texture, *~ band* etc., band so cut. [f.
F *biais* oblique, obliquity, etym. dub.; L
bifacem nom. *-fax* two-faced is sug-
gested]

bī'as², n., & v.t. (-s- or -ss-). Give a bias to,
influence (usu. unfairly), inspire with
prejudice. [f. prec.]

biāx'ial, a. With two (optic) axes. [BI-
(1 a) + AXIAL]

bib¹, v.i. (-bb-). Drink much or often. [BI-
[perh. f. L *bibere* drink]

bib², n. Child's chin-cloth to keep dress-
front clean; adult's apron-top (*best ~ &
tucker*, best clothes). [perh. f. prec.]

bib³, n. A fish, the whiting-pout. [from
an inflatable membrane on head resembling prec.]

bibā'sic, a. Having two (chem.) bases.
[BI-(1) + BASI-² +-IC]

bib'ber, n., bibb'ing, n. & a. Tippler,
tippling, (usu. in comb, as *wine etc. ~*).
[BIB v., -ER¹, -ING¹, ²]

bib-cŏck', n. Tap or faucet with a bent
nozzle fixed at the end of a pipe (opp.
STOPCOCK). [perh. f. BIB²]

bibelot (bē'blō), n. Small curio or artistic
trinket. [F]

Bi'ble, n. The Scriptures of the Old &
New Testament, a copy of them, a particular edition of them (BREECHES, PRINTERS',
book; ~-*oath*, taken on the ~; ~-*reader*,
one employed to read the ~ from house
to house; ~-*Christian*, a member of sect
so called; ~-*clerk*, student at some Oxford

colleges who reads lessons in chapel. [F, f. L L f. Gk *biblia* books pl. of *biblion* dim. of *biblos* papyrus bark]

bib'lical, a. Of, concerning, contained in, the Bible. [f. med. L *biblicus* (see -IC, -AL)]

bib'lico-, comb. of BIBLICAL, as *biblico-poetical*. [-O-]

bib'lio-, comb. form of *biblion* see BIBLE. Of books or the Bible.

bibliograph-. Seefoll., & -GRAPH, -GRAPHER, -GRAPHIC, -GRAPHY.

bibliog'raphy, n. History of books, their authorship, editions, etc.; book containing such details; list of books of any author, printer, country, subject. [f. Gk *bibliographia*; see BIBLIO-, -GRAPHY]

bibliol'ater, n., **bibliol'atrous**, a., **bibliol'atry**, n. Worshipper of, worshipping, worship of, books, a book, or the Bible. [BIBLIO-, -LATRY]

bibliomán'ia, **bibliomán'iac**, nn. Rage for collecting, enthusiastic collector of, books. [see BIBLIO-, -MANIA]

bib'liophil(e), n. Book-fancier, -lover. Hence **bibliôph'ilism**(3), **bibliôph'ilist** (3), nn. [F *bibliophile* (BIBLIO-, -PHIL)]

bib'liopôle, **bibliôp'olý**, nn. Seller, selling, of (esp. rare) books. [f. L (-la) f. Gk *bibliopōlēs* (BIBLIO-, -pōlēs -seller)]

bibârb'onate. See BI-(3).

bice, n. ~ or *blue* ~, *green* ~, pigments made from blue, green, hydrocarbonate of copper; similar pigment made from smalt etc.; dull shades of blue & green given by these. [f. F *bis* dark-coloured f. It. *bigio* etym. dub.]

bicén'tenarý (*also* -ēntēn-?), a. & n. (Festival) of the two-hundredth anniversary. [BI-(1 a) +L *centenarius* CENTENARY; used of years by confusion with *centennial*]

bicénténn'ial, a. & n. Lasting, occurring every, two hundred years; (n.) = prec. [BI-(1 d) +CENTENNIAL]

bicéph'alous, a. Two-headed. [BI-(1 a) + -CEPHALOUS]

bicéps, n. (pl. ~es). Muscle with double head or attachment, esp. the upper-arm flexor; muscularity. [L, = two-headed f. BI-(1 a) +*caput* head]

bichlor'ide (*also* -kl-), n. Compound in which double amount of chlorine combines with metal etc. [BI-(3)]

bichrom'ate (*also* -kr-), n. Salt with double amount of chromic acid. [BI-(3)]

bick'er, v.i. Quarrel; (of stream, rain, etc.) brawl, patter; (of flame, light, etc.) flash, glitter. [ME *bikeren* perh. frequent. of obs. *bike* to thrust, pierce]

bicŭs'pid, a. & n. (Tooth) with two cusps. [BI-(1 a) +L *cuspis -idis* point]

bi'cýcle, n., & v.i. (Ride on) two-wheeled vehicle. Hence **bi'cýclĭst**(1) n. [F, f. BI-(1 a) +Gk *kuklos* wheel]

bid', v.t. & i. (past *bad, bade, bid*, p.p. *bidden, bid*). Command to (usu. without *to*; now literary, arch., or poet., for *tell* with *to*; also abs., as *do as you are* ~); invite (esp. in ~*den guest*); salute (person) with *welcome, farewell*, etc.; offer price, offer (a certain price) *for* (past & p.p. *bid*), whence ~d'ER[1] n.; (Bridge) make a BID[2] of or in, make a bid; proclaim (*defiance, the banns*); ~ *fair to do*, show promise of doing; ||~*ding-prayer*, inviting congregation to join. [mixture of (1) OE *bēodan* offer, proclaim, cf. G *bieten* f. OTeut. *beudan*, (2) OE *biddan* press, beg, cf. G *bitten* f. OTeut. *bidjan* f. Skr. *bādhate* press; the variety of forms is due to this confusion]

bid², n. Offer of price, esp. at auction; (Bridge) statement of number of tricks player proposes to win in specified suit or no-trumps; make a ~ *for*, (fig.) make an attempt to secure (favour, the prize, etc.). [f. prec.]

bidd'able, a. Obedient; (of hand or suit at cards) capable of being bid. [-ABLE]

bidd'ing, n. In vbl senses; esp., the offers at auction; a command. [-ING³ (1)]

biddý, n. (dial.). Chicken. [?]

bide, v.t. & i. (Arch. & poet. for ABIDE, but the regular wd in) ~ one's *time*, await best opportunity. [com.-Teut.: OE *bīdan* cf. OSax. *bīdan*, OHG *bītan*]

biénn'ial, a. & n. Lasting, recurring every, two years; (n., Bot.) plant that springs one year, & flowers, fructifies, & perishes, the next. Hence ~LY² adv. [f. L *biennis* f. BI-(1 d) +*annus* year' +-AL]

bier, n. Movable stand on which coffin (or corpse) is taken to grave. [com.-Teut.: OE *bær* cf. G *bahre* & see BARROW; mod. spelling affected by F *bière*]

biff, n., & v.t., (sl.). A smart blow; (vb) strike (person). [?]

|| **biff'in**, n. Deep-red cooking-apple. [= *beefing* f. BEEF+-ING(3) with ref. to the colour]

bif'id, a. Divided by a deep cleft into two parts. [f. L BI(*fidus* f. st. of *findere* cut)]

bifoc'al, a. Having two foci (esp. of combined distant & near vision spectacles). [BI-(1 a)]

bifôl'iate, a. Of two leaves. [BI-(1 a) +L *folium* leaf +-ATE² (2)]

bif'urcāte¹ (-ferk-), v.t. & i. Divide into two branches, fork. [f. foll., first in p.p. -ated]

bif'urcāte² (-fók-), a. Forked (esp. in Bot.). [f. med. L BI(*furcatus* f. *furca* fork, -ATE²)]

bifurcā'tion (-ferk-), n. Division into two

For words in *bi-, biw-*, not given consult BI-, BIW-.

branches: the point of division; the branches or one of them. [f. BIFURCATE¹]

big, a. & adv. Large; grown up; pregnant (~ *with young*, also ~-*bellied*, & esp. fig. as ~ *with fate, news*); important (*a* ~ *man*; *the Big Three, Five*, etc., the pre-dominant few in any affair; *get, grow, too* ~ *for one's boots*, sl., become conceited; *look* on *airs*); boastful(ly) (~ *words, looks, drum, too, game*; *Big Ben*, great bell in the Houses of Parliament; ~ *bug* (sl.), =~*wig*; ~ *business*, commerce on the grand scale (freq. with sinister implica-tion); ~ *end*, end of the connecting-rod that encircles the crank-pin; ~-*horn*, Rocky-Mountain sheep; *~ *noise* (sl.), ~*wig*, person of importance. [f.] ~NESS n. [?]

bigam'ist, n. Man (woman) with two wives (husbands). [see BIGAMY, -IST]

big'amous, a. Guilty of, involving, bi-gamy. [f. med. L *bigamus* see foll.+-OUS]

big'amy, n. Having two wives or hus-bands at once. [f. F *bigamie* (-Y¹) f. OF *bigame* bigamous f. med. L *bi(gamus* f. Gk *-gamos* -married)]

bigaroo', -ōon', n. Large white heart-cherry. [f. F *bigarreau* f. *bigarre* varie-gated]

bigem'inal, a. Arranged in two pairs. [BI-(L c)+L *geminus* twin+-AL]

big'gin¹, big'gin, n. Four-rowed barley. ON *bygg*=OE *béow* grain, cf. Skr. *bhav-*, grow]

big'gin² (bit), n. Loop of a rope; curve, recess, of coast, river, etc., bay. [OE *byht* cf. G *bucht* f. OTeut. *bugan* to BOW]

big'ot, n. One who holds irrespective of reason, & attaches disproportionate weight to, some creed or view. Hence ~ED² a. [F, etym. dub.; *Visigoth*, & Sp. *bigote* moustache, have been suggested]

big'otry, n. Conduct, mental state, act, of a bigot. [f. F *bigoterie*; see BIGOT, -RY]

bijou, n. (pl. -oux, pr. -ōo) & a. Jewel, trinket; small & elegant. [F. prob. f. Breton *bizou* ring with stone f. *biz* = Corn. *bis*, W *bys*, finger]

bijouterie (bēzhōōt'erē), n. Jewelry, trinkets, etc. [F, see prec. & -RY]

bike, n. & v.i. (Colloq. abbr. for) BICYCLE.

bilat'eral, a. Of, on, with, two sides; affecting, between, two parties. Hence ~LY² adv. [BI-(L a)+L *latus -eris* side +-AL]

bil'berry, n. Fruit of dwarf hardy N.-European shrub growing on heaths & in mountain woods (also *blaeberry, whortle-berry*). [cf. Da. *bölleber*]

bil'bō, n. (hist.; pl. -ōs). Sword. [f. Bilbao in Spain]

bil'boes (-ōz), n. pl. Iron bar with sliding shackles for prisoner. [?]

bile, n. Brownish-yellow bitter fluid secreted by the liver to aid digestion; de-

rangement of the ~; peevishness; ~*stone*, calculus in gall-bladder. [F, f. L *bilis*]

bilge¹, n. Nearly horizontal part of ship's bottom, inside or out; the foulness that collects inside the ~; (sl.) nonsense, rot; belly of barrel; ~-*keel*, timber fastened under ~ to prevent rolling; ~-*water*, stinking water collected in ~. [corrup-tion of BULGE f. OF *boulge* now *bouge*]

bilge², v.t. & i. Stave in the bilge of, spring a leak in the bilge; bulge, swell out. [f. prec.]

bilharz'ia, n. Flat-worm parasitic in the blood & bladder of residents in tropical countries (esp. Egypt). Hence ~AS'IS n., chronic disease produced by its presence. [T. *Bilharz*, discoverer]

bil'iary (-lya-), a. Of the bile. [f. F *biliaire*, see BILE, -ARY²]

bil'ing'ual (-inggwal), a. Having, speak-ing, spoken or written in, two languages. [f. L *bilinguis* f. BI-(L a)+*lingua* tongue +-AL]

bil'ious (-lyəs), a. Liable to, affected by, arising from, derangement of the bile; peevish. Hence ~LY² adv., ~NESS n. [f. F *bilieux* f. L *biliosus*; see BILE, -OSE¹, -OUS]

-bility, suf. See -BLE.

bilk, v.t. Evade payment of (creditor, bill); cheat, give the slip to. [etym. dub.; perh.=BALK; earliest use in cribbage, = spoil opponent's score]

bill¹, n. Obsolete weapon, halberd; (also ~'*hook*) concave-edged lopping imple-ment for pruning etc. [com-WG cf. G *bille*]

bill², n. Bird's beak (esp. when slender, flattened, or weak, & in pigeons & web-footed birds); muzzle of platypus; narrow promontory (*Portland B~* etc.); point of anchor-fluke. Hence ~ED² (-ld) a. [OE *bile* etym. dub.]

bill³, v.i. Stroke bill with bill (of doves); exchange caresses (esp. ~ *& coo*). [f. prec.]

bill⁴, n. Draft of proposed Act of Parlia-ment; (Law) written statement of (esp. plaintiff's) case (*find a true* ~, *ignore the* ~; forms by which Grand Jury sends, does not send, case for trial); note of charges for goods delivered or services rendered; poster, placard, programme of entertainment; (also ~ *of exchange*) written order by drawer to drawee to pay sum on given date to drawer or to named payee (if drawn not against value received, but to raise money on credit, the ~ is known as an *accommo-dation* ~); ~ *of fare*, list of dishes to be served, menu, (fig.) programme; ~ *of health*, certificate regarding infectious disease on ship or at time of sail-ing (*clean* ~ *of health*, no disease); ||~ *of lading*, ship-master's detailed receipt to consignor; ||~ *of quantities*, detailed statement of work, prices, dimensions,

etc., involved in the erection of a building; ~ of sale, transferring personal property; or authorizing its seizure by lender of money if payment is delayed; ~s of mortality (hist.), weekly return of deaths in London & district (within the ~s of mortality, in or near London); ~poster, ~sticker, man who pastes up placards; ~broker, -discounter, dealer in, dis-counter of, ~s of exchange. [ME bille f. L bulla amulet in medieval sense of seal, papal bull, document]

bill[5], v.t. Announce, put in the pro-gramme; ~ed to appear etc., announced as going to; plaster with placards. [f. prec.]

bill'abŏng, n. (Austral.). Branch of river that comes to a dead end. [native]

bill'et[1], n. Order requiring person to board & lodge the soldier etc. bearing it (every bullet has its ~, hits only by provi-dential order), place where troops etc. are lodged; destination; appointment; situation. [ME billette dim. of bille BILL[4]]

bill'et[2], v.t. Quarter (soldiers etc.) on (town, householder, etc.), in, at; (of house-holder) provide (soldier etc.) with board & lodging. Hence ~EE, ~OR[2] (1), nn. [f. prec.]

bill'et[3], n. Thick piece of firewood; small bar of metal; short roll inserted at intervals in Norman moulding (Norman archit.). [f. F billette & billot dim. of bille tree-trunk etym. dub.]

billet-doux (bĭlĭdoō'), n. Love-letter (jocular). [F]

bill'iards (-lyardz), n. pl. Game played with cues & ivory balls on cloth-covered table; billiard-marker, attendant keeping the score. [f. F billard cue dim. of bille see BILLET[3]]

bill'ingsgate (-z-), n. Abuse, violent invective. [from the scolding of fish-women in Billingsgate market]

bill'ion (-yon), n. A million millions; (in U.S. & France) a thousand millions. [F, coined in 16th c. out of BI- & million to denote the second power of a million; meaning afterwards changed in France (so U.S.) but not in England]

bill'ow[1] (-ō), n. Great wave; (poet.) the sea; (fig.) anything that sweeps along, as sound, troops. Hence ~Y[2] (-ōi) a. [f. ON bylgja f. com.-Teut. belgan swell]

bill'ow[2] (-ō), v.i. Rise, move, in billows. [f. prec.]

bill'y, n. (Austral.). Tin can used as kettle etc. in camping out. [prob. the male name]

‖ bill'yboy, n. River or coasting trading barge. [?]

‖ bill'ycŏck, n. Round-crowned hard felt hat, bowler. [said to have been orig. designed for William Coke 1850]

bill'y-goat, n. Male goat. [Billy male name]

bill'y-(h)o, n. (Colloq., used in the inten-sive phr.) like ~; raining like ~ (fiercely). [?]

bilŏb'ate, a. With two lobes. [BI-(1 a, & see LOBE, -ATE[2](2)]

bil'tong, n. Strips of sun-dried meat. [S.-Afr. Du. f. bil buttock (from which it is cut) + tong tongue (which it looks like)]

Bīn, n. (colloq.). Inhabitant of Barbados.

bim'anal, bim'anous, aa., bim'āne, n. (Individual) of the Bimana or two-handed order of mammalia, two-handed. [bimane F f. BI-(1 a) + L manus hand, & see -AL, -OUS]

bimbash'i (-ah-), n. Turkish military captain or commander; British officer in Egyptian service. [Turk., = head of a thousand]

bimetall'ic a., bimět'allism, n., bi-mět'allist, n. & a. Of, system of, advo-cate of, using both gold & silver for use as legal tender to any amount at fixed ratio to each other. [f. F bimétallique 1869; see BI-(1 a), METALLIC, -ISM(3), IST(2)]

bin, n. Receptacle (orig. of wicker, now usu. fixed, of wood) for corn, coal, dust, bottled wine, etc.; wine from a special ~; ‖ canvas receptacle used in hop-picking. [OE binn perh. f. LL benna hamper cf. It. benna wicker sleigh]

bin-, sometimes used for BI- before vowels, perh. on anal. of F binocle (f. L bini, not bi-, oculi) & of a an, co- con-; for mean-ings see BI-.

bin'ary (-z-), a. Dual, of or involving pairs; (Mus.) ~ measure, of two beats to bar; ~ form, of movement in two sections; (Astron.) ~ system, two stars revolving round common centre or each other; (Chem.) ~ compound, of two elements, ~ theory, making all acids compounds of hydrogen, all salts similar compounds with metal; (Math.) ~ scale, with 2 (not 10) as base of notation. [f. L binarius f. bini two together]

bin'ate, a. In pairs. [f. L bini two to-gether + -ATE[2](2)]

binaur'al, a. Of, used with, both ears, as ~ stethoscope. [BIN- + AURAL]

bind[1], v.t. & i. (bound, p.p. bow-; also arch. p.p. in bounden duty). Tie; fasten, attach, to, on; put in bonds, restrain; fasten or hold together; be obligatory, exercise authority, impose constraint or duty, upon, (pass.) be required by duty to (do something); subject to legal obliga-tion (esp. ~ over to appear, to good behaviour, to keep the peace; fig., I'll be bound, go bail for statement), indenture as apprentice; ratify (~ the bargain); make costive; bandage (usu. ~ up); wreathe (head etc.) round, (material) round, about, on; edge with braid, iron, etc.; cohere (of snow etc.); (Bookbind) fasten

For words in bi-, bīn-, not given consult BI-, BIN-.

(sheets) into stiff, esp. leather, cover (half-*bound*), with leather at back & corners only). *~ up*, together in one vol. [com. Teut.]. OE *bindan* cf. G *binden* f. Aryan *bhendh*]

bind, n. Indurated clay between coal strata; (Mus.) curved line between two notes to be held as one; = BINE. [f. prec.]

bind'er, n. In vbl senses; also or esp. book-~; obstetric apparatus; long fencing-withe; tie-beam; through-stone in wall; wisp of straw, part of reaping machine, for sheaf-binding; loose cover for unbound newspapers etc. [-ING¹]

bind'ing¹, a. Obligatory (*on*). [-ING²]

bind'ing², n. In vbl senses; also, book-cover; braid etc. for protecting raw edges. [-ING¹]

bind'weed, n. Kinds of convolvulus & other climbing plants. [BIND¹+WEED]

bine, n. Flexible shoot; stem of climbing plant, esp. the hop. [orig. dial. form of BEND², now adopted in its place]

binge (-j), n. (sl.). Drinking-bout, spree. [orig. dial. = soak]

bin'nacle, n. Box on deck holding compass. [earlier *bittacle* f. Sp. *bitácula* f. L *habitāculum* lodge (*habitāre* dwell f. *habēre* hold); confusion with BIN]

binŏc'ular, a. & n. (Field or opera glass) adapted for two eyes (n. now usu. pl.). [f. L *bini* two together+*oculus* eye+-AR¹]

binō'mial, a. & n. Consisting of two terms; ~ *theorem*, formula for finding any power of a ~ without multiplying at length; (n.) algebraic expression of two terms joined by + or −. [f. LL *binomius* (= L *binominis*) having two names, f. BI-(1 a)+*nomen* name]

binō'minal, a. Of two names (esp. *system*, of scientific nomenclature by genus & species). [f. L *binominis* see prec.+-AL¹]

bin'turong, n. S.-Asian prehensile-tailed civet. [Malay]

bī'ō-, comb. form of Gk *bios* (course of) life, which meaning it has in actual borrowings f. Gk, as *biography*; in mod. formations it is extended to include organic life (Gk *zōē*).

biochem'istry (-kĕ-), n. Study of the chemical or physico-chemical processes & products involved in the life phenomena of plants & animals. [prec.]

biogen'esis, n. Hypothesis that living matter arises always from living matter. [prec.+Gk GENESIS]

bī'ograph (-ahf), n. Early form of cinematograph. [trade name of U.S. machine exhibited in London in 1897]

biog'raphee, n. Person whose life is written. [formed as correl. to *biographer*; see foll. & -EE]

biog'raphy, n. Written life of a person; branch of literature dealing with persons' lives; life-course of a living being. So **biog'rapher** n., **biograph'ic(al)** aa., **bio-gräph'ically²** adv. [f. late Gk *biographia* see BIO-, -GRAPHY]

bīol'ogy, n. Science of physical life, dealing with the morphology, physiology, origin, & distribution, of animals & plants. So **biolŏ'gic(al)** aa., **biolŏ'gically²** adv., **bīŏl'ogist** n. [BIO-, -LOGY]

biŏm'etry, n., **biomĕt'rics**, n. pl. Science of the application of statistical methods to biological facts. So **biomĕt'ric(al)** aa., **biomĕtr'ician** n. [BIO-, -METRY]

bionom'ics, n. pl. Science of the application of the laws of biology dealing with the habits of life of organisms in their natural surroundings, relationship of forms of life to one another, etc. (cf. OECOLOGY). [f. BIO-, after ECONOMICS]

bī'oplasm (-zm), **bī'oplăst**, nn. The germinal matter, a small separate portion of it, from which all living things spring. [BIO-+Gk *plasma*, thing moulded, *plastos* moulded (*plassō* to mould)]

bī'oscope, n. = BIOGRAPH. [BIO-, -SCOPE]

bīpar'tite, a. 1. (Bot., of leaves) divided into two parts. 2. (Law, of treaties, contracts, etc.) drawn up in two corresponding parts. [BI-, PARTITE]

bip'ĕd, a. & n., **bip'ĕdal**, a. Two-footed (animal). [f. L *bipēs -edis* f. BI-(1 a)+*pes pedis* foot]

bipin'nate, a. Having lobes that themselves have lobes. [BI-(1 c)+PINNATE]

bip'lane, n. Two-planed aeroplane. [BI-]

bipō'lar, a. With two poles or extremities. [BI-(1 a)]

Bīpŏn'tine, a. Printed at Zweibrücken (editions of classics). [Bi- two +L *pons pontis* bridge (transl. of the name) +-INE¹]

biquadrăt'ic, a. & n. (Number) of the fourth power, square or a square; ~ (*equation*), in which the unknown quantity is ~. [BI-(1 b)]

birch, n. Kinds of smooth-barked slender-branched northern forest tree; (also ~-*rod*) bundle of its twigs used for flogging schoolboys etc. Hence ~EN⁵ a. [OE *berc* = ON *bjork* (whence northern *birk*), & OE *beorce* = OHG *bircha*, f. Aryan *bhergo*- cf. Skr. *bhurjá*]

birch², v.t. Flog with a birch. [f. prec.]

bird, n. Feathered vertebrate; *game* ~, esp. the partridge; (sl.) girl; *little* ~, unnamed informant, *old* ~, wary person; ~ *s of a feather*, people of like character; ~ *in hand, in bush*, certainty, contingency; ~ *is flown*, prisoner etc. escaped; *kill two* ~*s with one stone*, gain two ends at once; *give one, get, the* ~ (sl.), hiss him, be hissed; ~ *of Jove*, eagle, *of Juno*, peacock, *of paradise*, New Guinea family

with beautiful plumage, of passage, migratory (also fig. of sojourner, of prey, member of orders Raptores & Accipitres, as hawk, eagle, owl; ~-cage, for ~ or ~s; ~-fancier, one who knows about, collects, breeds, or deals in, ~s; ~-lime, sticky stuff spread on twigs to catch ~s; ~-seed, special seeds given to caged ~s; ~'s-eye, kinds of plant with small bright round flowers as Mealy Primrose or Germander Speedwell, (tobacco) in which ribs are cut as well as fibre, ~'s-eye view, conspectus of town, district, etc., as seen from above, or résumé of subject, (of pattern etc.) marked with spots; ~'s-foot, kinds of vetch, fern, trefoil, & starfish; ~'s mouth, re-entrant angle cut in wood or stone; ~'s nest, ~-nest, nest of ~, kinds of plant as Wild Carrot, ~-nest orchid, (v.i., esp. in gerund) hunt for nests, (of horse) turn head from side to side. [OE brid; excl. E, etym. dub.]

brd'ie, n. (golf). Hole done in one under par or bogey. [prec. + -y³]

bir'ême, n. Ancient galley with two banks of oars. [f. L biremis f. BI-(1 a) + remus oar]

birětt'a, n. Square cap worn by R.-C. & some Anglican clerics. [f. It. berretta f. LL birrettum (birrus silk or wool cape prob. f. Gk purrhos flame-coloured)]

Bir'rel(l)ism, n. Passing comment on life, pungent yet kindly, of a type characteristic of the writings & sayings of Augustine Birrell, English wit & essayist (d. 1933). [-ISM]

bîrth, n. Bringing forth of offspring (so many at a ~); coming into the world (give ~ to); origin, beginning; parentage, descent, inherited position; noble lineage, high-born people; new ~, regeneration; ~-control, methods of preventing undesired sexual conception, practice of these, policy of popularizing this; ~-day, (anniversary of) day of one's ~ (~day present, given on this; ~day book, for entering friends' ~days; ~day suit facet., one's skin; ~day honours, knighthoods etc. given on King's ~day); ~-mark, on one's body at or from ~ (so ~-blindness etc.); ~-place, at which one was born; ~-rate, births per mille of population; ~-right, rights belonging to one as eldest son, as born in a certain station or country, or as a human being. [ME byrthe prob. f. ON byrthr f. OTeut. *gabuirthiz f. beran BEAR³ + -TH¹]

bis¹, adv. 1. (Mus.) over again, repeat. 2. Twice (calling attention to a double occurrence in references etc.). [F & It.]

bis'cuit (-kit), n. & a. || Piece of un-leavened bread of various materials, usu. crisp, dry, hard, & in small flat thin cakes; porcelain etc. after baking but before glazing & painting; || half-piece or third of soldier's mattress; (of) light-brown colour; ~-throw (Naut.), short-distance. [earlier bisket (now assim. to mod. F.) f. OF bescoit (L bis, coctus p.p. of coquere cook)]

bis dắt quĩ citŏ dắt, sent. He gives twice who gives quickly. (formula in charity appeals.) [L]

bise (bēz), n. Keen dry N. wind in Switzerland, S. France, etc. [F]

bisèct', v.t. Cut or divide into two (usu. equal) parts. Hence bisèc'TION n. [BI-, L secāre sect- cut]

bisèc'tor, n. Bisecting line. [-OR²]

bisèx'ual, a. Of two sexes; having both sexes in one individual. [BI-(1 a) + SEXUAL]

bish'op, n. Clergyman consecrated as eccl. governor of a diocese; ~ in partibus (infidelium), having the title, & competent to confirm etc., but with no diocese (the nominal one being in heathen possession); mitre-shaped piece in chess; mulled & spiced wine; Bishops' Bible, version of 1568; ~'s-cap, -had, -leaves, -weed, various plants. [OE biscop f. L f. Gk episkopos overseer (epi on + -skopos -looking)]

bish'opric, n. Office of bishop. [OE bisceoprice (prec. + -rīce realm cf. G reich)]

bisk, n. Rich soup made by boiling down birds etc. [f. F. bisque crayfish soup]

Bis'ley (-z-), n. (Used for) the ranges or the shooting competitions of the Nat. Rifle Association at ~ in Surrey.

Bismil'lah (-ä), int. In the name of Allah! (common ejaculation of Moslems before action). [Arab. bi-'sm-illāhi]

bis'muth (-z-), n. A reddish-white metal. [G (now wismut), etym. dub.]

bis'on, n. Wild ox of two species, (also aurochs) formerly over Europe, & still in Lithuania, (also buffalo) about Rocky Mountains. [f. L bison -ontis f. OTeut. wisand cf. OE wesend, OHG wisunt]

bisque¹ (-k), n. (Tennis) right of scoring one point without winning it at any time in the set; (Croquet) right of playing extra turn; (Golf) stroke to be taken when desired. [F, etym. dub.]

bisque² (-k), n. Unglazed white porcelain used in statuettes. [f. BISCUIT]

bissex'tile, a. & n. (Year) containing the bis sextus dies or doubled 24th Feb. (vi Kal. Mart.) [f. L bis(s)extilis (annus), (year) containing the bis sextus dies or doubled 24th Feb. (vi Kal. Mart.]

bis'tort, n. Herb with cylindrical spike of flesh-coloured flowers. [f. L bistorta (bis twice + torta fem. p.p. of torquēre twist) w. ref. to twisted form of root]

bis'toury (-torĭ), n. Surgeon's scalpel. [f. F bistouri etym. dub.]

bis'tre (-ter), n. & a. Brown pigment prepared from soot; colour(ed) like this. [F, perh. f. OF behistre=besistre=BISSEXTILE, etc.]

For words in bi-, bin-, not given consult BI-, BIN-.

the meaning *gloomy* from notion of un-lucky day]

bit[1], n. Something to eat (a ~ & a *sup*); boring-piece of drill, cutting-iron of plane, nipping-part of pincers etc, part of key that grips lock-lever; mouthpiece of bridle, (fig.) control, (draw ~, slacken pace; *take* ~ *between teeth*, reject, control). [OE *bita*, com.-Teut. n.; cf. BITE]

bit[2], n. Morsel of food (*daintily*, *tit-*, ~); small piece of anything (~ *by* ~, gradually; *give a* ~ *of one's mind*, speak candidly; *do one's* ~, contribute service or money to a cause); piece of scenery etc.; ~ *s of*, poor little (*children*, *furniture*); a ~ *of a*, rather a (*coward etc.*); a ~, rather, *not a* ~, (of) not at all, *every* ~, quite as; a short time (*wait a* ~); small coin (U.S., of fractions of Spanish dollar; in Engl., *three-penny* ~ etc.). [OE *bita* com.-Teut. f. OTeut. *biton-* (cf. *G bisse*) f. *bitan* to BITE]

bit[3], v.t. (*-tt-*). Put bit into mouth of (horse); accustom to the bit; restrain. [f. BIT[1]]

bitch, n. Female of dog, fox, wolf, (*tsu.* ~ *fox*, ~ *wolf*); harlot. [OE *bicce* etym. dub.]

bite[1], v.t. & i. (past *bit*; p.p. *bitten* sometimes *bit*). Cut into or nip with the teeth; (with off etc.), detach with the teeth; snap at; (of serpents, fleas, etc.) sting, suck; accept bait (lit. & fig.); (of sword etc.) penetrate; cause glowing, smarting, etc, pain to (*frost-bitten*); corrode; (of wheels, anchor, etc) grip; (now only in pass.) take in, swindle, (*were you bitten* ?); ~ *the dust or ground*, fall & die; ~ *one's lips*, to control anger etc.; ~ *off more than one can chew*, attempt too great a task; ~ *bitten with*, infected with (a mania, enthusiasm, etc.). [OE *bitan*; com.-Teut. cf. *G beissen* f. OTeut. *bitan* cf. Skr. *bhid-*, L *fid-* (*findere* cut)]

bite[2], n. Act of, wound made by, piece detached by, biting; food to eat (~ & *sup*); taking of bait by fish; grip, hold, (lit. & fig.); herbage for cattle; (fig.) incisiveness, pungency. [f. prec.]

bit[1]er, n. In vbl senses; also, swindler (now only in *the* ~ *bit*). [-ER[1]]

bit[1]ing, a. In vbl senses; esp., pungent, stinging, sarcastic. Hence ~LY[2] adv. [part. of BITE[1]]

bit[1]ter, a., adv., & n. **1.** Tasting like worm-wood or quinine, opposite to sweet (~ *cup*, cup of quassia wood giving ~ tonic property to liquid drunk from it): unpalatable to the mind, full of affliction; virulent, relentless; biting, harsh; pierc-ingly cold (also as adv., *it was* ~ *cold*); *to the* ~ *end*, last extremity; hence ~NESS n. **2.** n. ~NESS (*the* ~ *with the sweet*, *the* ~ *s of life*); (pl.) liquors impregnated with wormwood etc.

taken as stomachics; ~ *beer*; ~ *sweet*, sweet(ness) with ~ after-taste or element (lit. & fig.), Woody Nightshade. [OE *biter*; com.-Teut. prob. f. *bitan* to BITE; the ~ *end* may be f. Naut., where the *wds* mean the last part of a cable left round the BITTS when the rest is overboard, *bitter* being the turn at any moment on the bitts]

bit[1]ering, n. Small carp-like freshwater fish of Central Europe. [G, f. *bitter* bitter +*ling* LING[1]]

bit[1]ern, n. Kinds of marsh bird allied to herons, esp. one known for its booming note. [ME *botor* f. OF *butor* ETYM. dub.]

‖ **bit[1]ock**, n. (dial.). Little bit. [IR[2]+ -OCK]

bitts, n. pl. Pair of posts on deck for fastening cables etc. [etym. dub.; f. most European langs.; perh. f. *bitan* BITE]

bitu[1]lith[1]ic (-*yoo-*), n. & a. (Pavement) composed of broken stone & bitumen or asphalt. [f. *bitu(men)* + *lith(ic)*]

bit[1]u[m]en, n. Mineral pitch, asphalt; kinds of native oxygenated hydrocarbon, as naphtha, petroleum. Hence ~INIZE, **bitu[m][i]nous**, aa. [L, genit. EROUS, **bitum[i]inors**, aa. *-minis*, cf. Skr. *gutu* gum]

bitu[m][i]nize (-*yoo-*), v.t. Convert into, impregnate or varnish with, bitumen. Hence ~ATION n. [prec. +-IZE (3, 5)]

bi[1]valent, a. = DIVALENT.

bi[1]valve, a. & n. **biv[1]alved** (-*vd*), **bival[1]vular**, aa. With two valves; (mollusc) with hinged double shell; oyster. [(1 a) + VALVE; *valved*; & see -ULE, -AR[1]]

bi[1]vouac (-*oo-*), v.i. & n. (*-acking*, *-acked*). (Remain, esp. for the night, in) temporary encampment without tents; *bivouacked*, in ~, see -ED[1] (2). [F. prob. f. G *beiwacht* (BY, WATCH) additional guard at night (in Argau & Zürich)]

biz, n. (colloq.). Business. [abbr.]

bizarre (*-rē*), a. Eccentric, fantastic, grotesque, mixed in style, half barbaric. So ~ ′erie (*-rē*) [-ERY] n. [F; cf. Sp. *bizarro* handsome, brave, It. *bizzarro* choleric perh. f. Basque *bizarra* beard]

blab, v.t. & i. (*-bb-*), & n. **1.** Talk or tell foolishly or indiscreetly, reveal, let out, (secrets etc, or abs.); hence ~b′ER[1] n. **2.** n. Person who ~*s*. [etym., & related to vb to n.& to older obs. vb *blabber*, doubtful]

black[1], a. **1.** Opposite to white, colourless from the absence or complete absorption of all light; so near this as to have no distinguishable colour; very dark-coloured (~ *in the face*, purple with strangulation or passion); dark-skinned; dark-clothed; (of sky, deep water, etc.) dusky, gloomy; (of hands, linen) dirty; (as specific epithet) *~bear*, *currant*, *snake*, *heart-cherry*; deadly, sinister, wicked, hateful, (*~-hearted*; ~ *ingratitude*; *crimes of* ~*est dye*); dismal (~ *despair*); angry,

sulky, threatening, (~-browed; ~ looks; look ~); implying disgrace or condemnation (~ mark; of discredit against one's name; ~ book, list, of persons suspect, tabooed, etc.; deep in one's ~ books, quite out of his favour). 2. = ∂ blue, discoloured with bruise; ~ & tan, (dog) so coloured; B~ & Tans, ex-service recruits of the R.I.C. against Sinn-Feiners 1921 named from mixture of military & constabulary uniforms; ~ & white, ink drawing (down in ~ & white, recorded in writing or print); ~ art, magic [~ partly in sense wicked, partly by assoc. w. med. L nigromantia corrupt. of NECROMANCY]; ~ ball, used to reject candidate in club ballot, whence ~-ball v.t.; ~ beetle, cockroach; ~ berry, bramble or its fruit (plentiful as ~ berries, as can be; ~ berrying, gathering them); ~ bird, European song-bird, kidnapped negro on slave-ship (~ birding, trade in these); ~ board, in lecture-room for demonstrations in chalk; ~ bottom, an American dance; ∥ ~ cap, put on by judge in sentencing to death; ~ cap, kinds of bird, esp. the B~ Warbler; ~ CATTLE ∥ ~-coat worker, clerk etc. (opp. industrial employee); ~-cock, male (opp. grey-hen) of B~ Grouse; ~ COFFEE (without milk, usu. strong); ∥ B~ Country, smoky district in Staffs. etc.; ~ dog, sulks; ~ draught, an aperient; ~ eye, discoloured with bruise, also with dark iris whence ~-eyed² (-id) a.; ~ face, dark-faced sheep; ~ fellow, Australian aboriginal; ~-fish, a species, also salmon just after spawning; ~ flag, used by pirates, also signal of execution completed; Black'foot (pl. -feet), member of a tribe of N.-Amer. Indians; ~ friar, Dominican; ~ frost, hard frost without snow or rime; ~ game, B~ Grouse (& see ~ cock); ~ guard¹ (blăg'ărd), n. (& a.) scoundrel(ly), foul-mouthed (person), whence ~ guardiy¹ (-ăg²)a., (v.t.) call ~ guard, abuse scurrilously [orig. collect. n., applied at various times to menials of royal household, camp-followers, body-guard, criminal class, & vagrants]; B~ Hand, secret organization of Italian ~ mailers & thugs in U.S.; ~ head, kinds of bird, esp. kind of gull, (also) kind of pimple on the skin; ~ hole, military lock-up (so B~ Hole of Calcutta); ~ jack, tarred-leather wine-bottle, also pirates' ~ flag, also flexible loaded life-preserver; ~ lead, (polish with) PLUMBAGO [named from marking like lead]; ~ leg, swindler esp. on turf, ∥ workman who works for master whose men are on strike (v.i. & t., act as ~ leg, betray or injure thus) [orig. of senses unknown]; ~ letter, old type like the German; ~ list (of persons under suspicion, liable to punishment, etc.); ~-list (v.t.), enter name of (person) on ~ list; ~ mail, (Hist.) tribute exacted by freebooters for protection & immunity, (mod. v.t. & n.) (force to make) payment

for not revealing discreditable secrets etc., whence ~ mail'ER¹ n. [obs. mail rent, OE măl f. ON măl agreement perh. = OHG mahal assembly]; ~ Maria, vehicle for taking prisoners from & to gaol, (also, army sl.) large shell exploding with much smoke; ~ marked, illegitimate traffic in officially controlled goods or currencies or in commodities in short supply (~ marketeer, one who engages in this), place where this traffic is carried on; ~ mass, travesty of the mass said to be used in the cult of Satanism (also Eccl. a Requiem Mass); ~ monk, Benedictine; ~ pudding, sausage-shaped of blood, suet, etc.; ∥ B~ Rod, gentleman usher of Lord Chamberlain's department, House of Lords, & Garter; ~ sheep, scoundrel; ~-shirts, fascists; ~ smith, smith working in Iron (cf. WHITESMITH); ~ thorn, thorny shrub bearing white flowers before leaves & small plums or sloes (~ thorn winter, time of its flowering, cold with NE winds); cudgel or walkingstick of this; ∥ B~ Watch, 42nd Highlanders [f. orig. uniform]; ~-water fever, tropical disease with bloody urine etc. Hence ~¹ISH¹ (2) a., ~¹NESS n. [OE blæc, blac, = OHG blah-a., perh. cogn. w. Gk phlegō burn]

blăck². n. Black colour; black paint, dye, varnish; black speck; fungus, smut, in wheat etc.; particle of soot; black cloth(es); negro or negrito, whence ~¹Y³ n. [f. prec.]

blăck³, v.t. Make black; polish with BLACKING; ~ out: obliterate or obscure; obscure (windows etc.) to prevent any light being seen from outside, esp. from the air, also abs.; ~ing out or ~ out being ~ ed out (also attrib., as ~-out material, offences, time); (fig.) condition of obscuration; temporary complete failure of memory; in flying, temporary blindness etc. resulting from centrifugal force when a sudden turn is made (v.i., suffer this). [f. BLACK¹]

blăck'amōōr, n. Negro; dark-skinned person. [BLACK¹ + MOOR²]

blăck'avised (-īzd) a. (arch.). Dark-complexioned. [BLACK + F vis face]

blăck'en, v.t. & i. Make, grow, black or dark; speak evil of (person's character). [ME blaknen (BLACK¹, -EN⁵)]

blăck'ing, n. In vbl senses; also, paste or liquid for blacking boots. [-ING¹]

blăd'der, n. Membranous bag in human & other animal bodies (esp. the urinary ~, also gall, air, swimming, ~); the same or part of it prepared for various uses, inflated etc.; (fig.) anything inflated & hollow, wordy man, windbag; inflated pericarp or vesicle in plants & seaweeds (~-wrack, common sea-weed with these in its fronds). Hence ~Y² a. [OE blǣdre, com.-Teut. cf. G blatter f. OTeut. blǣdrōn- f. v̄b blǣ- BLOW¹ + -drōn instr. suf. cf. Gk -tron]

blade, n. (Vague & poet.) leaf; flat lanceolate leaf esp. of grass & cereals; whole of such plants before ear comes (in the ~); (Bot.) expanded part of leaf apart from foot-stalk; flattened part of instrument, as oar, bat, spade, paddle-wheel; cutting-piece of edged tool, as sword, chisel, knife; sword; (also ~bone) flat bone, esp. shoulder~ as joint of meat or otherwise; fellow (usu. with epithet), gay, etc., fellow (usu. with epithet, jovial, etc., bold, hectoring, etc.). Hence (-)**blad'ED**[2] a. [OE blæd; com.-Teut., cf. G blatt, perh. partic. form with -do-, Aryan -to-, f. OTeut. vb st. bló-BLOW[3] cf. L flos; OE not using blæd, but blæf, in the vegetable sense, it is likely that the mod. use is a retransfer f. sword-~, helped by med. L bladum, OF bled (now blé, corn)]

¶ blae'berry (blā-), n. = BILBERRY. [blae livid, dark-blue, the direct descendant of the OTeut. blæwoz cf. G blau f. which blue comes indirectly through F bleu]

blague (-ahg), n. Humbug, claptrap. [F]

***blah**, n. (colloq.) Hyperbolic & frothy talk or writing. [?]

blain, n. Inflamed sore on skin, pustule. [OE blegen cf. Du. blein]

blame[1], v.t. Find fault with (for offence etc.); fix the responsibility on; be to ~e, deserve censure. Hence ~ABLE a., ~ably[2] adv. [f. OF blâmer, blasmer, f. L as BLASPHEME]

blame[2], n. Censure; responsibility for bad result (lay the ~ on, bear the ~). [f. OF blâme cf. prec.]

blame'ful (-mf-), a. (Rare) conveying, deserving, censure. [-FUL]

blame'less (-ml-), a. Innocent. Hence ~ly[2] adv., ~NESS n. [-LESS]

blame'worthy (-mwerth-), a. Deserving blame. Hence ~INESS n.

blanch[1], v.t. & i. Make white by withdrawing colour, peeling (almonds), or depriving of light (plants); make or grow pale with fear, cold, etc.; ~ over, palliate by misrepresentation. [f. F blanchir (blanc BLANK)]

blancmange (blamahnzh?), n. Opaque white jelly of isinglass, gelatine, or corn-flour, & milk. [f. OF blancmanger white food (blanc BLANK + manger eat f. L mandu-care MANDUCATE)]

bland, a. Gentle, polite, in manner; ironical; balmy, mild. Hence ~ly[2] adv., ~NESS n. [f. L blandus]

blan'dish, v.t. Flatter, coax. Hence ~MENT n. (usu. in pl.). [f. F blandir (-ISH[2]) f. L blandiri (blandus)]

blank[1], a. Not written or printed on (of paper); (of document) with spaces left for signature or details (in ~, drawn in blank), so prepared; ~ cheque, with amount left for payee to fill in, hence = CARTE BLANCHE); empty, not filled, (~ space etc.; ~ cartridge, without ball); void of interest, incident, result, or expression; look ~, nonplussed; unrelieved, sheer; unrhymed (~ verse, esp. the five-foot iambic). Hence ~NESS n. [f. F blanc (blanch f. OTeut. blankon shining cf. BLINK, blanco f. OHG blanch shining cf. BLINK]

blank[2], n. Lottery ticket that gains no prize; space left to be filled up in document, empty surface (one's mind, memory etc., is a ~, has no sensations etc.); words printed in italics in Parl. bills; time without incident, thing without meaning; coin-disk before stamping; = ~cartridge (20 rounds of ~); dash written instead of word or letter, whence ~ ~y, ~ed, as substitutes for abusive nouns and adji. [uses of prec.]

blank'et, n. & a. [1] Large woollen sheet used for bed covering, for horse-cloth, & by savages for clothes; wet ~, person who extinguishes conversation; born on wrong side of ~, illegitimate. *2. adj. General rather than individual, covering all cases or classes. [f. OF blanquette (blanc BLANK + -ETTE)]

blank'et[2], v.t. Cover with a blanket; stifle, keep quiet, (scandal, question, etc.); toss in a blanket as punishment; take wind from sails of (another craft) by passing to windward. [f. prec.]

blank'ly, adv. Without expression, vacantly, (look ~ etc.); flatly (deny ~ etc.). [BLANK[1] + -LY[2]]

blanquette (blahnket?), n. (cookery). White dish, such as a fricassee with white sauce. [F]

blare, v.i., t., & n. (Make) sound of trumpet; utter loudly. [perh. imit.; cf. MDu. blaren, G blärren]

blar'ney, n. & v.t. & i. (Use, assail with) cajoling talk. [Blarney, Irish castle with stone conferring a cajoling tongue on whoever kisses it]

blasé (-ahz'ā), a. Cloyed, tired of pleasure. [F]

blaspheme', v.i. & t. Talk impiously; utter profanity about, revile. So ~ER[2](4). Hence ~NESS n. [f. OF blasfemer f. L blasphemare f. Gk blasphēmeō f. blasphēmos (blas-etym. dub.; -phēmos speaking)]

blas'phemous[1], n., blas'phemous a. LME blasphemous adv. [ME blasphemous a.

blas'phemy[2] adv.

blast[1] (-ah-), n. Strong gust of wind; sound of wind-instrument; current of air in smelting etc. (in, out of, ~, of furnace working or not); quantity of explosive used in blasting operation; destructive wave of highly compressed air spreading outwards from an explosion; ~furnace, smelting furnace into which compressed hot air is driven by engine. [OE blæst com.-Teut. f. OTeut. blæstus, f. L blæsum]

blast[2] (-ah-), v.t. Blow up (rocks etc.) with explosives; wither, shrivel, blight, (plant, animal, limb, prosperity, charac-ter; esp. with subj. God understood, in curses, whence ~ed, damnable). [f. prec.]

~ blow see BLAZE[2]

blasto-, first element in many biological terms, meaning germ, bud. [f. Gk *blastos* sprout]

blas'tŏdĕrm, n. Disk of cells found in the early segmentation of a fertilized ovum (as differentiated from *blastula*, hollow ball of cells, & *morula*, solid ball). [prec.+Gk *derma* skin (*derō* flay, -M)]

blā'tant, a. Noisy, vulgarly clamorous. Hence ~LY² adv., **blā'tANCY** n. [prob. invented by Spenser, (*F.Q.*, V. xii. 37, ~ *beast*) perh. in sense *bleating*]

blather(skite). See BLETHER.

blāze¹, n. Bright flame or fire (*in a* ~, *on fire*); (sl.) ~s = hell (*go to* ~s, *what the* ~s!; *like* ~s, impetuously); violent outburst (~ *of passion* etc.); glow of colour; bright display; full light (~ *of publicity*). [OE *blæse*, *blǣse* torch, cf. G *blass* pale, & BLAZE²]

blāze², v.i. Burn with flame (~ *up*, burst into blaze); be brilliantly lighted; burn with excitement etc. (~ *up*, burst out in anger); show bright colours; emit light; ~ *away*, fire continuously with rifles etc. work enthusiastically at anything; *blazing indiscretion*, rash & conspicuous piece of candour; (Hunting) *blazing scent*, very strong (opp. to *cold scent*). [f. prec.]

blāze³, n. White mark on horse's or ox's face, or made on tree by chipping bark to mark route. [from 17th c.; = ON *blesi* star on horse's forehead, cf. G *blässe* in same sense & G *blass* pale]

blāze⁴, v.t. Mark (tree, & so path) by chipping bark. [f. prec.]

blāze⁵, v.t. Proclaim as with trumpet, esp. ~ *abroad*, spread (news) about. [prob. f. ON *blāsa* blow f. OTeut. *blæsan* f. root *blæ-* cf. L *flare* BLOW¹]

blāz'er, n. Coloured jacket for boating, golf, etc.; (sl.) outrageous lie. [BLAZE² +-ER¹]

blāz'on¹, n. Heraldic shield, coat of arms, bearings, or banner; correct description of these; record, description, esp. of virtues etc. [f. F *blason* etym. dub.; orig. meaning *shield* in lit. sense]

blāz'on², v.t. Describe or paint (arms) heraldically; inscribe (object) with arms, names, etc., in colours or ornamentally; give lustre to; set forth in fitting words; proclaim. Hence **blāz'onMENT** n. [f. prec. partly confused in sense with BLAZE⁵]

blāz'onry̆, n. (Art of describing or painting) heraldic devices, armorial bearings; brightly coloured display. [prec.+-RY]

L 3rd-conj. or p.p. stems, -*able* elsewhere; to this confusion, incurable at present, is added that between -*able* & -*eable*; each is necessary after soft -*c*, -*g*, (cf. *navigable*, *manageable*; it is also used arbitrarily in some wds to affect the vowel of the previous syllable (*tameable*, See also -ABLE, -IBLE. The E meaning in new wds is always passive, in old ones (*capable*) often active. From adj. ~s -*ble* are formed nouns in -*bility* (L -*bilitas*, see -TY) as well as in -*bleness*.

bleach, v.t. & i. Whiten by exposure to sunlight or by chemical process; ~*ing-powder*, (so-called) chloride of lime. Hence ~ER¹ n.; one who ~es (esp. textiles); vessel or chemical used in ~ing; *(usu. pl.) outdoor uncovered plank-seat for spectators at sports grounds. [OE *blǣcan*; com.-Teut. f. OTeut. *blaikjan* cf. OE *blāc* pale]

bleak¹, n. Small river fish, & allied sea-fish, of various species. [prob. f. ON *bleikja* f. OTeut. *blaikjōn* white cf. prec.]

bleak², a. Wanting colour; bare, exposed, windswept; chilly; dreary. [perh. northern form of obs. *bleach*, *bleche*, OE *blǣo* variant of *blǣc* see BLEACH]

blear, a., & v.t. (Make) dim-sighted, dull, filmy, (eyes or mind); (make) indistinct in outline; ~-*eyed*, having ~ eyes or wits. Hence ~Y² a. [ME *blere* adj., etym. dub.]

bleat, v.i. & t., & n. (Make) sheep's, goat's, or calf's, cry; speak (&~ *out*, say) feebly or foolishly. [OE *blǣtan*, com.-WG cf. Du. *blaten*, G *blöken*]

blĕb, n. Small blister or bubble on skin, in water or glass. [imit. of making bubble with lips, cf. *blab*, *blubber*]

bleed, v.i. & t. (bled). Emit blood (*heart* ~s, is in acute distress); suffer wounds or violent death (often *for* cause etc.); (of plants) emit sap; part with money, pay lavishly, suffer extortion; draw blood surgically from; extort money from; ‖(part., vulg. euphem., cf. *blinking*, *blooming*, for) *bloody*; ~*ing heart*, pop. name of various plants, as Wallflower. Hence ~ER¹ n., person inclined to ~ excessively from a slight injury. [OE *blēdan* f. OTeut. *blōdjan* (cf. G *bluten*) f. *blōdom* BLOOD]

blĕm'ish¹, v.t. Mar, spoil the beauty or perfection of, sully. [f. OF *blemir* (-ISH²) f. *blaisme*, *blesme*, *blême*, pale, etym. dub.]

blĕm'ish², n. Physical or moral defect, stain, flaw. [f. prec.]

blĕnch, v.i. & t. Start aside, flinch, quail; close the eyes to, disguise from oneself. [there is OE *blencan* cheat, & prob. connexion & confusion with BLINK]

blĕnd¹, v.t. & i. (~ed or blend). Mix (things) together (esp. sorts of tea, spirit, to get certain quality); mingle (t. & i. element) intimately *with*; mix (components) so as to be inseparable & indistinguishable; become one, form harmonious compound;

pass imperceptibly into each other (esp. of colours). [there is OE *blandan* mix; but ME *blendes* is prob. f. ON *blanda*]

blend², n. Mixture made of various sorts of tea, spirits, etc. [f. prec.]

blende, n. Native sulphide of zinc. [G, *blendende Erz* deceiving ore 'because while often resembling galena it yielded no lead']

Blen'heim (-nim), n. & a. Kind of spaniel; || ~ *Orange*, golden-coloured apple. [Duke of Marlborough's seat at Woodstock]

blenno-, **blenn-**, stem of many wds in pathology. Of mucus. [Gk *blennos* mucus]

blen'ny, n. Small spiny-finned sea-fish. [as prec. (through L *blennius*) from mucous coating of its scales]

blent. See BLEND¹.

bleph'aro-, stem of pathological words. Of the eyelids. [f. Gk *blepharon* eyelid]

bles'bok, n. Large S.-African antelope. [Du. f. *bles* BLAZE³ (from white mark on forehead) + *bok* goat]

bless, v.t. (past & p.p. ~ed, sometimes *blest*, & see under BLESSED). Consecrate (esp. food; *not a penny to ~ oneself with*, w. ref. to cross on silver penny); call holy, adore, (God); attribute good fortune to (esp. one's stars); pronounce words that bring supernatural favour upon (of father, priest, etc.); invoke God's favour on: make happy or successful (abs. or *with* something); *God ~ me, ~ me, God ~ you, ~ you, ~ the boy, ~ my soul, I'm blest*, exclamations of surprise or indignation; (euphem.) = damn, curse, etc. [OE *bledsian*, *blétsian*, *blédsian*; excl. E, but formed on O'Teut. *blōdisōjan* f. *blōdom* BLOOD (consecrate by sacrifice); meaning influenced (1) by the word's being used at the Eng. conversion to translate L *benedicere*, (2) by confusion with the independent BLISS]

bless'ed, **blest**, (for pronunc. see under etym.), a. Consecrated; revered; fortunate; ~ *with*, fortunate in the possession of (esp. iron.); in paradise (esp. as n., *the ~*); blissful, bringing happiness (~ *ignorance* etc.); (euphem.) cursed. [p.p. of prec.: as p.p. & past tense *blessed* is usu. monosyl., as adj. disyl.; of the adj. forms *blessed* is the ordinary, *blest* the poet., also used in some phr. as *Isles of the Blest*]

bless'edness, n. Happiness; enjoyment of divine favour; *single ~*, jocular phr. for being unmarried (perversion of Shakesp. *M.N.D.*, I. i. 78). [prec. + -NESS]

bless'ing, n. Declaration, invocation, or bestowal, of divine favour; grace before or after food (*ask a ~*): gift of God, thing one is glad of; ~ *in disguise*, unwelcome but salutary experience etc. [BLESS + -ING¹]

bleth'er, **blath'er**, (-dh-), v.i., & n. (Talk) loquacious nonsense. Hence **bleth'er-skite**, **blath'erskate**, nn. (dial.), ble-thering person. [ME *blather* f. ON *blathra* talk nonsense (*blathre* nonsense); *blether* is prob. the Scotch form adopted from Burns etc.]

blew¹ (-ōō-), n. A late edible mushroom with lilac stem. [prob. f. *blue*, cf. dial. name *blue-legs*]

blew² (-ōō-), past of BLOW¹,³.

blight¹ (-īt), n. Disease of unknown or atmospheric origin affecting plants; plant disease caused by fungoid parasites, mildew, rust, smut; species of aphis; hazy close state of atmosphere; any obscure malignant influence. [from 17th c., etym. dub.]

blight² (-īt), v.t. Exert baleful influence on, nip in the bud, wither, mar. Hence ~ER¹ (-īt-) n., esp. (sl.) annoying person. [f. prec.]

|| **Bligh'ty** (-ī-), n. (army sl.), England, home, after foreign service (*a ~ one*, wound that ensures return to~). [Anglo-Ind. corruption of Hind. *vilāyatī*, *bilātī*, European, English (*vilāyat* country, cf. Turk. VILAYET)]

|| **blim'ey**, int. (vulg.) of surprise etc. [= God blind me!]

blimp, n. 1. Small non-rigid airship. 2. (Col.) *Blimp*, character invented by the cartoonist David Low (b. 1891), representing a pompous, obese, elderly figure pop. interpreted as type of diehard or reactionary. Hence ~ERY (4), ~'ISHNESS, nn. [?]

blind¹, a. Without sight (~ *of an eye*, having one eye ~; *turn a* or *one's ~ eye to*, affect not to see); without foresight, discernment, or moral or intellectual light (~ *to*, incapable of appreciating; *one's ~ side*, direction in which one is unguarded); reckless; mechanical, not ruled by purpose, (~ *forces*); hard to trace (~ *track*); (Post Office) ~ *letter*, *man*, *reader*, of ill-addressed letters & the officials dealing with them; concealed (~ *ditch*; ~-*stitch*, sewing visible only on one side, also as v.t. & i. sew thus); ~ *door* etc., walled up; closed at one end (~ *alley*; ~-*alley occupations*, such as fail to fit one for anything further); (sl.) drunk (also ~ *drunk*, ~ *to the world*); ~ *flying*, flying without sight of the ground, or guidance from (directional) wireless signals; ~ *man's-buff*, game in which blindfold player tries to catch others, who push him about [f. obs. *buff* = *buffet*]; ~ *stamping*, *tooling* (in bookbinding without use of ink or goldleaf); ~-*story*, triforium below clerestory admitting no light; ~ *man's holiday*, time before candles are lighted; ~ *coat*, burning without flame, anthracite; ~-*worm*, = SLOW-*worm* (f. small size of eyes). [com-Teut.]

blind², v.t. & i. Deprive of sight permanently or temporarily; rob of judge-

ment, deceive; (v.i., sl.) go blindly or heedlessly (chiefly of reckless motorists); ~ing (vbl n.), process of covering newly made road with fine material to fill interstices, material used for this purpose. [f. prec.]

blind³, n. Obstruction to sight or light; screen for windows, esp. on roller (Venetian ~, of laths running on webbing; (Fortif.) = foll.; pretext, stalking-horse. [f. prec.]

blind'age, n. Screen for troops in fortification, sieges, etc. [-AGE]

blind'fold¹, v.t. Deprive (eyes, person) of sight with bandage (also fig.). [corruption (through notion of folding) of ME blindfellen (FELL v.) strike blind, chiefly used in p.p., whence the -d, which helped the confusion]

blind'fold², a. & adv. With eyes bandaged; without circumspection. [p.p., earlier blindfelled see prec.]

blind'ly, adv. Without seeing, gropingly; recklessly. [-LY²]

blind'ness, n. Want of sight; want of intellectual or moral sense, folly, recklessness. [-NESS]

blink¹, v.i. & t. Move the eyelids; look with eyes opening & shutting; shut the eyes for a moment; shine with unsteady light, cast momentary gleam; ignore, shirk consideration of, (esp. the fact); (part., vulg. euphem., cf. bleeding, blooming, foot) bloody. [ME blinken, more usu. blenken; cf. Du. & G blinken perh. f. stem blik- shine]

blink², n. Momentary gleam or glimpse; (also ice-~) whiteness about horizon, reflection of distant ice-fields. [f. prec.]

blink'er, n. In vbl senses; also, (usu. pl.) screen(s) preventing horse from seeing sideways. [-ER¹]

bliss, n. Gladness, enjoyment; perfect joy, blessedness; being in heaven. Hence ~'FUL a., ~'fully² adv., ~'fulNESS n. [OE bliths (blithe BLITHE + OTeut. suf. -sid-); the sense has shifted from earthly to heavenly joy by confusion with BLESS]

blis'ter, n., & v.t. & i. 1. Vesicle on skin filled with serum, caused by friction, burning, etc.; similar swelling on surface of plant, metal, painted wood; (Med.) anything applied to raise a ~; 2. vb. Raise ~ on; become covered with ~s; poison gas causing ~s on skin. 2, vb. [ME blester perh. f. OF blestre f. ON blāstr swelling (blāsa blow)]

blithe (-dh), a. Gay, joyous, (chiefly poet.). Hence ~'LY² (-dhl-) adv., ~'SOME (-dhs-) adj. [OE blithe, com.-Teut., cf. OHG blîdi perh. f. vb st. bli- shine]

blith'ering (-dh-), a. (colloq.). Senselessly talkative; consummate (~ idiot); contemptible. [part. of blither, var. of BLETHER]

blitz, n., & v.t., (colloq.). 1. Intensive (esp. air) attack. 2. v.t. Damage or destroy in ~ (esp. in pass., as ~ed areas, cities). [abbr. of foll.]

blitz'krieg (-krēg), n. A violent campaign intended to bring about speedy victory. [G. = lightning war]

blizz'ard, n. Blinding snow-storm. [first common in U.S. newspapers in severe winter 1880-1; imit., cf. blow, blast, blind, & see -ARD]

bloat¹, v.t., **bloat'er**, n. Cure (herring) by salting & smoking slightly into bloated herring or bloater. [f. obs. adj. bloat ME blote perh.=ON blautr soaked]

bloat², v.t. & i., **bloat'ed**, a. Inflate, swell (t. & i.); (chiefly in p.p. as adj.) puffed up, esp. with gluttony, overgrown, too big, pampered (esp. bloated aristocrat, armaments). [t. obs. adj. bloat ME blout, blout, perh. variant of ME blote see prec.]

blob, n. Drop of liquid; small roundish mass; spot of colour; (Cricket) = duck's egg. [imit., cf. BLEB]

blobb'er-lipped (-ipt), a. With thick protruding lips. [imit., cf. BLEB; blabber, blubber, are found in same sense]

bloc, n. Combination of parties to support a government; (transf.) combination of nations, groups, etc., to foster a particular interest, as sterling ~ (of countries with currencies tied to sterling). [F, = BLOCK¹]

block, n. 1. Log of wood, tree-stump, (chip of old ~, child like his father esp. in character; cut ~s with razor, waste ingenuity etc.); large piece of wood for chopping or hammering on (the ~, death by beheading) or mounting horse from; mould for shaping hats on, shape; barber's ~, wooden head for wigs. 2. Pulley, system of pulleys mounted in case. 3. Piece of wood engraved for printing. 4. Bulky piece of anything; unhewn lump of rock; prepared piece of building-stone. 5. Compact mass of buildings bounded by (usu. four) streets (~-buster sl., huge bomb capable of destroying this). 6. Stolid or hard-hearted person, whence ~'ISH¹ a. 7. Obstruction, (Parl.) notice that a bill will be opposed, which prevents its being taken at certain times & so often kills it; ‖(Traffic) jammed vehicles unable to proceed; ~ system on railways, by which no train may enter a section till it is clear. 8. (Cricket) spot on which batsman blocks ball & rests bat before playing. 9. Tract of land offered to individual settler by government. 10. Large quantity of shares etc. 11. (Austral.) fashionable city promenade. 12. ~-chain, kind of endless chain used in bicycle etc.; ~'head, dolt; ~'house, detached fort (orig. one blocking passage), sometimes one of connected chain of posts, also one-storeyed timber building with loopholes, also house of squared logs; ‖ letters,

writing (with each letter separate as in print, & in capitals); ~ tin, refined tin cast in ingots. [prob. f. F *bloc*, which is perh. f. OHG *bloh* (G *block*)]

block², v.t. Obstruct (passage etc.); put obstacles in way of (progress etc.); ~ *up*, confine in. (Parl.) announce opposition to (bill; see prec.); (Cricket) stop (ball with bat; shape (hats); emboss (book cover); ~ *out*, *in*, sketch roughly, plan, (work). [f. F *bloquer* f. *bloc* see prec.]

blockāde'², n. Shutting-up, total or on land or sea side, of a place by hostile forces in order to starve it into surrender or prevent egress & ingress (*paper* ~, one declared but not made effective; *raise* ~, cease blockading; compel blockaders to cease; *run* ~, evade blockading force); ~*runner*, ship, captain, etc. [f. prec. on anal. of F wds in -ADE] Hence **blockāde'²**, v.t. Subject to blockade (see prec.). ~ER¹ n. [f. prec.]

blōke, n. (colloq.) Man, fellow, chap; *the* ~ (Nav. sl.), ship's commander. [?]

blond, blonde (see etym.), a. & n. (Of hair) light-auburn-coloured; (of complexion) fair (n., person with such hair & skin). (also ~ *lace*) silk lace of two threads in hexagonal meshes (orig. of raw-silk colour, now white or black). [f. F *blond* fem. *blonde* cf. It. *biondo*; OE *blonden-feax* grizzled (*blandan* blend), & the ancient-German custom of dyeing hair yellow, suggest a deriv.; *blonde* is used of the lace, & of the adj. & n. as applied to a woman, *blond* elsewhere]

blood¹ (blŭd), n. 1. Red liquid circulating in veins of higher animals, corresponding liquid in lower animals, (*flesh & ~; the* ~, animal nature; *let* ~, surgically); (fig.) sap, grape-juice, etc. 2. Taking of life, murder, sacrifice, guilt of bloodshed. 3. Passion, temperament, mettle, (*bad* ~, ill feeling; *his* ~ *is up*, he is in fighting mood; ~ *out of a stone*, pity from the pitiless; *in cold* ~, deliberately). 4. Race (*blue* ~, high birth; *fresh* ~, new members admitted to family, society, etc.; ~ *royal*, royal blood; *Prince etc. of the* ~ *royal* or *of the* ~, of royal race; *runs in the* ~, is a family trait). 5. Relationship, relations, (*own flesh & ~; is thicker than water*, the tie of kindred is real); descent, good parentage, (of men, horses, etc.; *bit of* ~, thoroughbred). 6. Dandy, man of fashion, (*young* ~, either in this sense, or as personal form of party). 7. ~ *& iron*, relentless use of force (esp. as motto of Bismarckian policy); ~ *ally*, red-veined ALLY³; ~ *feud*, between families of which one has split the other's ~; ~*guilty*, responsible for murder or death; ~*heat*, ordinary heat

of ~ in health, 98·4° F.; ~*hound*, large keen-scented dog with which cattle, slaves, etc., used to be tracked, detective, spy; ~*letting*, surgical removal of some of patient's ~, (facet.) ~*shed*; ~*money*, reward to witness for securing capital sentence, fine paid to next of kin for slaughter of relative; ~ *orange*, with red juice; ~*poisoning*, state resulting from introduction of septic matter into ~ esp. through wound; ~*red*, red as ~; ~*relations*, one related by ~, not marriage; ~*shed*, spilling of ~, slaughter [f. phr. *to shed* ~] (see *things bloodshed*, find incitements to slaughter or traces of ~ in them); ~*stained*, stained with ~, disgraced by bloodshed; ~*stone*, kinds of precious stone spotted or streaked with red, esp. Heliotrope; ~*stock*, thoroughbred horses collectively; ~*sucker*, leech, extortioner; ~*thirsty*, eager for ~shed, whence ~THIRSTINESS n.; ~*vessel*, flexible tube (vein or artery conveying ~; ~*worm*, bright-red kind used in fishing; ~*wort*, kinds of plant with red roots or leaves, esp. Bloody Dock. [OE *blod*, com.-Teut.; cf. G *blut* f. OTeut. *blōdom*]

blood² (blŭd), v.t. (Surg.) remove a little of the blood of (usn. *bleed*); allow first taste of blood to (hound; also fig. of inciting persons). [f. prec.]

blood'less (-ŭ-), a. Without blood; unfeeling; pale; without bloodshed, whence ~LY² adv. [-LESS]

bloody¹ (blŭd'ĭ), a. & adv. Of, like, running or smeared with, blood (~ *nose*, bleeding; ~*flux*, dysentery; red (~*hand*, armorial device of baronet); involving, loving, resulting from, bloodshed; (also ~*minded*) sanguinary, cruel; || (in foul language) = damned etc., or as mere intensive (*not a* ~ *one*); || (similarly as adv.) = confoundedly, very; (in pop. plant names) B~ *Finger*, Foxglove. Hence **blood'ĭLY²** adv., **blood'ĭNESS** n. [OE *blōdig*, com.-Teut. cf. G *blutig*; see BLOOD, -Y¹]

bloody², v.t. Make bloody, stain with blood. [f. prec.]

bloom¹, n. Flower, esp. of plants grown or admired chiefly for the flower, florescence (*in* ~); prime, perfection, flush, glow; powdery deposit on grapes, plums, etc., freshness, (*take the* ~ *off*, stale); kind of raisin. [ME *blom* f. ON *blóm* cf. G *blume* f. OTeut. *blōmon-* f. vb st. *blo-* BLOW³+suf. *-mon-*]

bloom², v.i. Bear flowers, be in flower; come into, be in, full beauty; culminate, flourish. [f. prec.]

bloom³, n. Mass of puddled iron hammered or squeezed into thick bar. [OE *blóma* in same sense]

bloom⁴, v.t. Make (puddled iron) into a BLOOM³. [f. prec.]

bloōm'er[1], n. & a. (Female costume) of short skirt & trousers (as n., usu. pl.); (n. pl.) knickerbockers worn by girls & women for cycling, games, etc., with or without skirt. [Mrs B~, American inventor]

bloōm'er[2], n. (sl.). Blunder. [=*blooming* (see foll.) *error*; -ER[1]]

bloōm'ing, a. In vbl senses (BLOOM[3]); also sl., euphemistic substitute for vulgar BLOODY. [-ING[2]]

Bloōms'bury (-zberi), n. Part of London containing British Museum, formerly a fashionable residential (& now a literary) quarter.

bloss'om[1], n. Flower, esp. as promising fruit; mass of flowers on fruit-tree etc. (*in* ~); early stage of growth, promise; ~-*faced*, *-nosed*, bloated. Hence ~Y[2], ~LESS, aa. [OE *blōstm* prob. f. same root as BLOOM[1] (*blo-* extended to st. *blos-*, cf. L *flos*, or with double suf. *-st-+-m*]

bloss'om[2], v.i. Open into flower (lit., & fig., as ~ *out into a statesman*). [OE *blōstmian* cf. prec.]

blot[1], n. Spot of ink etc., dark patch; disfigurement, blemish, defect; disgraceful act or quality in good character. [f. 14th c., etym. dub.; cf. ON *blettr*, Da. *plet*; there was 16th-c. F *blotte* clod, *blotter* to stain]

blot[2], v.t. & i. (-tt-). Spot with ink; smudge; (of pen, ink) make blots; cover with worthless writing; sully, detract from, (fair fame); ~ *out*, obliterate (writing), exterminate, destroy; dry with ~*ting-paper*, absorbent paper for drying wet ink-marks (~*ting-book, -case, -pad*, arrangements of this), whence ~t'ER[1](2) n. [f. prec.]

blot[3], n. Exposed piece in backgammon; weak point in strategy etc. [etym. dub.; cf. Da, *blot* naked, G *bloss*]

blotch, n. Inflamed patch, boil, etc., on skin; dab of ink or colour. Hence ~ED[2](-cht), ~Y[2], aa. [f. 1600; excl. E, perh. compounded f. blot & botch or patch]

blottésque' (-sk), a. & n. (Piece of painting or description) done with heavy blotted touches. [-ESQUE]

blot'tō, a. (sl.). Fuddled with drink. [?]

blouse (-owz), n. Workman's loose linen or cotton upper garment usu. belted at waist (chiefly French); woman's loose light bodice visible only to waist, & there belted. [F, etym. dub.]

blow[1](-ō), v.i. & t. (blew pr. bloō; ~n, & in sense 'cursed', ~ed). (Of wind, air, 'it') move along, act as air-current, (~ *great guns*, violent gale); send strong air-current from mouth (~ *hot & cold*, vacillate), puff, pant; make or shape (bubble, glass) by ~ing; (of whales) eject air & water; (of electr. fuse) melt when overloaded; cause air-current by means of (~ *bellows*); work bellows of (organ);

exhaust of breath (esp. in pass.); send out by breathing (~ *air into*; ~ *off steam*, get rid of superfluous energy; (with advv. & prepp.) drive, be driven, by ~ing (~ *over*, pass off; ~ *in* sl., come in operadly, drop in); sound (wind instrument, note or signal *on* or *with* it, or with it as subject to *blow* t. or i.; ~ *one's own trumpet*, praise oneself); direct aircurrent at (~ *fingers, fire*; ~ *out*, extinguish); clear by air-current (nose, egg); break *in* or send flying *off* or *out* or *up* by explosion (~ *out* one's *brains*, shoot him, or usu. oneself); ~ *up*, inflate, shatter or be shattered by explosion, reprove; (sl.) betray; (of flies) deposit eggs in; (sl.) curse, confound, (I'll be ~*ed if* etc.; ~ *the expense*, spend recklessly); (sl.) squander, spend (sum) recklessly; ~*upon*, stale, discredit, tell tales of; ~'*ball*, seed-head of dandelion etc.; ~'*fly*, the Meat fly; ~'*hole*, nostril of whale etc., vent for air, smoke, etc., in tunnel etc.; ~'*lamp* (for directing condensed heat on a selected spot); ~'*pipe*, tube for heating flame by blowing air or other gas into it, tube used in glass-blowing, Amer.-Ind. dart tube. [OE *blāwan* cf. OHG *blāhan* f. OTent. *blæjan* cf. L *flare*]

blow[2](-ō), n. Blowing, taste of fresh air; blowing of flute, one's nose, etc.; =FLY[1]. *blow*; ~-*out*, burst in a pneumatic tire, (Electr.) blowing of a fuse, (sl.) abundant meal or feed. [f. prec.]

blow[3](-ō), v.i. (blew pr. blō, ~n). Burst into, be in, flower. [OE *blōwan* cf. OHG *blaojan*, G. *blühen*, f. OTeut. *blōjan* cf. L *flos*]

blow[4](-ō), n. Blossoming (in full ~ etc.). [f. prec.]

blow[5](-ō), n. Hard stroke with fist, instrument, etc.; disaster, shock; (*come to, exchange*, ~s, fight; *strike a* ~ *for, against*, help, oppose; *at one* ~, in one operation. [f. 15th c., etym. dub.]

blow'er(-ōer), n. In vbl senses of BLOW[1,3]; also: apparatus for increasing a fire's draught, esp. sheet of iron before grate-front; escape of gas, or fissure allowing it, in coal mine. [BLOW1, -ER[1]]

blow'y (-ōi), a. Windy, wind-swept. [BLOW[1], -Y[2]]

blowzed (-zd), blowz'y, aa. Red-faced, coarse-looking, dishevelled. [f. obs. n. *blowze* beggar's wench, etym. dub., but suggesting *blush* & *blow*]

blub, v.i. (-bb-; sl.). Shed tears. [short for BLUBBER[3]]

blubb'er[1], n. Whale fat; jelly-fish (sailor's name); weeping. [ME *biober*; prob. imit. (obs. meanings *foaming, bubble*); cf. BLEB, BUBBLE]

blubb'er[2], a. Swollen, protruding, (of lips). [as prec.]

blubb'er[3], v.t. & i. Utter with sobs, weep noisily; wet, disfigure, swell, (face) with weeping. [as prec.]

bluchers (bloō'kerz), n. pl. Old-fashioned low boots or high shoes. [named after the Prussian Field Marshal Blücher.]

bludg'eon (-ŭjn), n., & v.t. (Strike repeatedly with) heavy-headed stick. [etym. dub.; from 18th c. only]

blue¹ (bloō), a. Coloured like the sky or deep sea (also of things much paler, darker, etc., as smoke, distant hills, moonlight, bruise; & qualified by or qualifying other colours etc., as ~black, deep ~, NAVY ~, Prussian ~); livid, nervous, depressed (things looked ~, depressing); ~ funk, uncontrollable fear; true ~, faithful; dressed in ~ (Foot Guards B~); the B~ (Squadron), one of three divisions (Red, White, B~) of Navy; belonging to a particular political party, usu. Tory; (of women) learned (see BLUESTOCKING); (of talk etc.) Indecent; drink till all 's ~, to drunkenness. ~bell, (Scotland & N. Eng.) light-blue-flowered Campanula growing in dry places & flowering in summer & autumn, harebell, (S. Eng.) wild hyacinth with blue or white flower growing in moist places & flowering in spring; ~ blood, high birth; ~book, ||Parliamentary or Privy-Council report, ||book giving personal details of U.S. government officials; ~bottle, B~ Cornflower, Meat fly or Blowfly; ~coat boy, scholar in charity school, esp. Christ's Hospital; ~ devils, depression; ~ gum, kind of eucalyptus tree; ||~jacket, seaman in Navy; *~ laws, severe Puritanic laws alleged to have been in force among early colonists of Connecticut; ~ light, flare with bluish light used for signals; B~ Mantle, one of four pursuivants of College of Arms; once in a ~ moon, very rarely; ~ mould, in certain cheeses when mature; ~ murder (colloq. in intensive phr. as like ~ murder), at top speed; B~nose (colloq.), Nova-Scotian; ~ pencil, used in marking corrections, obliterations, etc.; ~pencil v.t., mark etc. with a ~ pencil, make cuts in, censor; B~ Peter, ~ flag with white square, hoisted before sailing; ~ pill, mercurial & antibilious; ~ print, photographic print representing final stage of engineering or other plans, (fig.) plan, scheme; ~ ribbon, ribbon of the Garter, greatest honour in any sphere, sign of teetotalism; ~ rock, kind of pigeon; ~ ruin, bad gin; ~ stocking, woman having or affecting literary tastes & learning [Blue Stocking Society (in sense 'not in full evening dress') name given to meetings about 1750 at houses of Mrs. Montague etc. to talk on literature etc. instead of playing cards; blue-worsted, i.e. ordinary, stockings were worn by some of the men attending instead of black silk]; ~stone, sulphate of copper; ~ water, open sea; ~water school, strategists regarding the fleet as sufficient defence for Gt Britain. Hence blu'ISH¹ (2) (bloō-) a., ~NESS (-oōn-) n. [ME bleu f. OF bleu f. OHG blāw f. OTeut. blēwoz, cf. L flavus]

blue² (bloō), n. B~ colour (Oxford ~ dark; Cambridge ~, light; the light, dark, ~s, representatives or supporters of Cambridge, Oxford, in sporting contests); ~ cloth etc.; the sky (bOIN from the ~); the sea; (pl.) the Royal Horseguards; the Blues trot, dance of fox-trot kind; colour, member, of a political party; || (badge given to) one who has represented his university in athletics etc.; = BLUE¹ stocking; (pl.) the dumps. [f. prec.]

blue³ (bloō), v.t. Make blue; treat with laundress's blue; (sl.) squander (money). [f. BLUE¹]

Blue'beard (bloō-), n. Husband of many wives. [hero of popular story, who hung up in locked chamber the bodies of his murdered wives]

bluff¹, a. With perpendicular broad front (of ship's bows, cliffs); (of person, manner) abrupt, blunt, frank, hearty. Hence ~(r)y² adv., ~NESS n. [haut. wd, etym. dub., but cf. MDu. blaf, flat, broad]

bluff², n. Headland with perpendicular broad face. [f. prec., & see foll.]

bluff³, v.t. & i. (Game of poker) impose upon (opponent) as to value of one's hand & induce him to throw up his cards; treat (political opponents or rival States) so; practise this policy. [earlier meaning, hoodwink (lit.); the prec. n. also meant earlier horse's blinker; etym. dub.]

bluff⁴, n. Overbearing demeanour, threats designed to operate without action. [f. prec.]

blun'der, v.i. & t. Move blindly, stumble, (often on, along); ~ upon, find by fluke; make gross mistake; mismanage (a business etc.); ~ out, utter thoughtlessly; ~ away, waste by mismanagement. Hence ~ER¹ n., ~ingly² adv. [ME blondren, perh. f. obs. blond, bland, mix, cf. BLEND.]

blun'derbuss, n. Ancient short gun with large bore firing many balls. [perverted f. Du. donderbus thunder gun (orig. box cf. G. büchse)]

blun'derhead (-hĕd), n. = DUNDERHEAD (cf. prec.)

blunge (-j), v.t. (Pottery) mix (clay, flint-powder, etc.) up with water by revolving machinery. [latter plunge, blend]

blunt¹, a. & n. 1. Dull, not sensitive; without edge or point; plain-spoken, hence ~ISH¹ (2) a. 2. n. Short thick needle; (sl.) ready money. [?]

blunt², v.t. Make less sharp or sensitive.

blunt'ly, adv. Obtusely (shaped etc.); rudely, curtly. [-LY²]

blunt'ness, n. Dullness of point or edge; outspokenness. [-NESS]

blur¹, n. Smear of ink etc.; dimness, confused effect. [etym. dub., perh. formed on *blear* & *blot*]

blur², v.t. & i. (-rr-). Smear (clear writing etc.) with ink etc.; sully, disfigure; make indistinct; efface; dim (perception etc.). [as prec.]

blurb, n. Publisher's eulogy of book printed on jacket or in advertisements elsewhere. [orig. U.S. sl.]

blurt, v.t. Burst out with, utter abruptly. [imit. after *blow*, *spurt*, etc.]

blush, v.i. Become red (in the face; also with *face* etc. as subj.) with shame or other emotion (*at* sight or word, *with* or *for* joy or shame, *for* another); be ashamed (*~ to own* etc.); be red, pink. Hence ~ingLY² adv. [ME *blusche*, *blosche*, *blysche*, OE *āblūscan*; cf. wds in ON & LG pointing to a st. *blusi-* f. vb root *blus-* glow (Du. *blozen* blush)]

blush², n. Glance, glimpse, (*at the first ~*, prima facie); reddening of face in shame etc. (*put to the ~*); rosy glow, flush of light; ~, pink, rosy, (~-rose, ~-tint, etc.). [f. prec.]

blus'ter¹, v.i. & t. Storm boisterously (of wind, waves, persons); (trans. with *out*, *forth*) utter overbearingly; (refl.) storm (*oneself*) *into* (anger etc.). Hence ~ER¹ n., ~ingLY² adv. [perh. imit. on *blow*, *blast*, etc.; ME *blostre* stray is prob. separate]

blus'ter², n. Boisterous blowing, noisy self-asserting talk, threats. Hence ~OUS, ~Y², aa. [f. prec.]

bo¹, **boh** (bō), int. used to startle (*can't say bo to a goose*, of shy or timid person).

*bō², n. (Hailing word corresponding to) mate, old chap. [?]

bō'a, n. S.-Amer. genus of large non-poisonous snakes killing by compression (pop. extended to Old-World pythons; so also ~ *constrictor*, prop. a Brazilian species of ~); lady's long fur or feather throat-wrap. [?]

Boaner'gēs (-z), n. Loud-voiced preacher or orator. [Gk. f. Heb. *b'ney regesh* sons of thunder (*Mark* iii. 17)]

boar (bōr), n. Male uncastrated pig; its flesh; ~'s head, esp. as dish at Christmas or on festive occasion. [OE *bār* cf. G *bär* etym. dub.]

board¹ (bōrd), n. **1.** Long thin usu. narrow piece of sawn timber (strictly, over 4 in. broad, under 2½ thick); wooden slab (of one or more 2½ thick); wooden slab (of one or more ~ bare or covered with leather etc.) used for various purposes, as in games, for posting notices, etc.; (pl.) the stage (*on the ~s*, employed as actor); thick stiff paper used in bookbinding (covered with paper, 'in ~s', or cloth, 'cloth ~s'), & for other purposes. **2.** Table (only in spec. senses or contexts); *above ~*, open(ly); *sweep the ~*, take all the cards or stakes; table spread for meals (*bed & ~*, conjugal relations; *groaning ~*, plentiful meal); food served, daily meals provided at contract price or in return for services (~money, ~wages, servant's pay in lieu of food; esp. ~ & *lodging*); council-table, councillors, committee; ‖B~ *of Trade*, B~ (now *Ministry*) *of Education*, *Local Government B~*, government departments; *Road B~*, for construction & improvement of roads; ~-school (before 1902), managed by ~ according to Elementary Education Act of 1870. **3.** Ship's side (only in spec. phrases, cf. *over~*), *go by the ~*, (of masts etc.) fall over~, *on ~* = ABOARD (in various senses), usu. now on or into ship (orig. meaning within the side, not on the deck), train, coach, etc. **4.** Tack (naut.). [OE *bord* mixture of two com.-Teut. words meaning (1) board (2) border, respectively f. OTeut. *bordom* & *bordoz*; the second was further adopted in F & returned with spec. developments]

board² (bōrd), v.t. & i. **1.** (f. prec.=wood) cover with boards (~ *up*, close with ~s). **2.** (f. prec. = table) provide (lodger or daily guest) with, receive, stated meals at fixed rate; examine before a medical board (~-*out* v.t., invalid out of army etc.); ~ *with*, be entertained for pay in the house of. **3.** (f. prec. = ship's side) come alongside (usu. to attack); force one's way on board (ship or abs.); embark on. **4.** (Of ship) tack. [f. prec., with influence of F *aborder*]

board'er (bōr-), n. One who boards with someone (prec. 2), esp. schoolboy at boarding-school. [prec. + -ER¹]

board'ing (bōr-), n. In vbl senses; also or esp.: erection of boards; ~-house, -school, in which persons, boys, board (BOARD, 2); ‖~-*out*, (intr.) feeding elsewhere than at home, (trans.) placing (destitute children) in families; ~-*ship* (examining neutrals for contraband). [BOARD¹,² + -ING¹]

boast¹, v.i. Vain-glorious statement; self-exaltation in words; fact one is proud of; *make ~*, announce proudly. Hence ~FUL a., ~fulLY² adv., ~fulness n. [ME *bost* etym. dub.]

boast², v.i. & t. Extol oneself (also refl.), brag *of* or *about*; vaunt, brag of, brag *that*; possess as thing to be proud of. Hence ~ER¹ n. [ME *bosten* as prec.]

boat¹, n. Small open oared or sailing vessel, fishing-vessel, mail packet, or small steamer (*take ~*, embark; *have oar in everyone's ~*, of busybodies; *in the same ~*, with like risks etc.); ~-shaped utensil for sauce etc.; ~-hook, long pole with hook & spike; ~-house, shed at water's edge for keeping ~s; *ship's ~*, carried on board ship; ~-train, timed to catch or meet steam packet; ~-fly, water-bug swimming on water on its

boat, n. (~man, hirer-out or seller of ~ for hire; ~, S.-Amer. heron; ~-race, between rowing boats; ~swain (bō'sn), ship's officer in charge of sails, rigging, etc., & summoning men, often with whistle [late OE *bátsuegen*, cf. Icel. *sveinn* & see SWAIN]. Hence ~AGE (4), ~FUL (2), nn. [OE *bát* cf. ON *beit* and (f. the OE) *bátr*; borrowed in other Teut. langs.; f. these, & possibly in Rom. also (F *bateau* etc.)]

boat, v.i. & t. Go in a boat, amuse oneself so (~ing man); place, carry, in a boat. Hence ~ER[1] n., hard straw hat (as worn in ~ing). [f. prec.]

bob[1], n., & v.t. (-bb-). Weight on pendulum, plumb-line, or kite-tail; knot of hair, tassel-shaped curl (~wig, also ~, with short curls, opp. to full-bottomed; cf. CHERRY-bob); horse's docked tail; bunch of lob-worms; (Metre) short line at end of stanza: (vb) cut (woman's hair) to hang short of shoulders (wear it ~bed). [etym. dub.]

bob[2], v.i. (-bb-). Fish (for eels) with bunch of lob-worms.

bob[3], v.i. (-bb-). Move up & down, dance, rebound (~ up like a cork, become active or conspicuous again after defeat; catch with the mouth (for cherries etc. floating or hanging); curtsy. [etym. dub.; cf. BOB[4]]

bob[4], n. Jerk, bounding movement; curtsy: (Bellringing) kinds of change in long peals (treble ~ in which treble bell has a dodging course, ~ minor on 6 bells, triple on 7, major on 8, royal on 10, maximus on 12). [f. prec.]

bob[5], n. Dry, wet-, ~, cricketing, boating, Etonian; tight-~, soldier of light infantry. [prob. =Robert]

bob[6], v.t. (-bb-; pl. same). Shilling. [etym. dub.]

bob[7], n. (sl.; pl. same). Rap, jerk. [ME boben. etym. dub.]

Bob adil, n. Braggart. [Jonson, Every Man in his Humour]

bob'b'ery, n. & a. 1. Disturbance, row, fuss. 2. adj. Noisy, troublesome, skittish, (~ pack, scratch pack of hounds & dogs of various breeds, usu. for hunting jackals). [Hind. bap re O father! int. of dismay]

bob'bin, n. Cylinder for holding thread, yarn, wire, etc., & giving it off as wanted, reel, spool; small bar & string for raising door-latch. [f. F bobine]

bob'binet, n. Machine-made cotton net imitating lace made with bobbins on pillow. [prec. net]

bob'bish, a. (sl.). Brisk, well, (esp. pretty ~). [BOB[3] +-ISH[2] irregularly appended to vb]

bob'by, n. (sl.). Policeman. [esp. pretty ~, -y[3] (Sir Robert Peel, Home Sec. 1828)]

***bob'cat**, n. American lynx. [BOB[1] (from shortness of tail)]

bob'olink, n. N.-Amer. songbird. [imit., cf. cuckoo]

bob'sled, **-sleigh** (slā), n. Two short sleighs coupled, used for drawing logs, & in tobogganing. [U.S. & Canadian wd]

bob'stay, n. Rope holding bowsprit down. [?]

bob'tail, n. & a. Docked tail; with this; horse or dog with this; tag-rag & ~, the rabble. [BOB[1]]

boca'rdo, n. Logical formula, see BAR-BARA.

Bôche (-sh), n. & a. (sl.). (Contempt. for) German. [F, perh. abbr. of *Alboche* in contempt for other endings]

bock, n. Strong dark-coloured German beer; (loosely) a glass of (any) beer. [F, f. G *bock* (in full *bockbier* f. *Einbecker bier* f. *Einbeck* in Hanover]

bode, v.t. & i. Foresee, foretell, (evil); portend, foreshow; promise well or ill. Hence **bôd'ingly**[2] adv., ~MENT(-dm-) n. [OE *bodian* f. *boda* messenger, cf. ON *botha*]

bode'ful(-df-), a. Ominous. [mod. formation f. prec. or obs. n. *bode* omen +-FUL(1)]

bod'ice, n. Close-fitting upper part of woman's dress, down to waist; also, inner vest over stays. [orig. *pair of bodices* (cf. *pair of stays*), being a whalebone corset; now spelt & understood as sing.; cf. BAIZE &c (perh). ACCIDENCE]

bod'ied (-did), a. Possessed of body or a body, embodied; esp. in comb., as *full-~*, *able-~*. [BODY[1]+-ED[2]]

bod'iless, a. Incorporeal; separated from the body. [-LESS]

bod'ily[1], a. Of, affecting, the human body or physical harm. [BODY[1]+-LY[1]]

bod'ily[2], adv. In the body; in person; with the whole bulk, as a whole. [BODY,

bod'kin, n. Pointless thick needle with large eye for drawing tape etc. through hem; long pin for fastening hair; person squeezed between two others (*ride, sit,*~). [etym. dub.; earlier *boydekin*]

Bodleian (-lē'an, a. & n. The ~ (*library*), the Oxford University Library, founded by Sir Thomas *Bodley*. [-IAN]

body, n. 1. Man or animal as material organism (*keep ~ & soul together*, remain alive); corpse (~-snatcher, exhumer of corpses for dissection); ~ of Christ, sacramental bread; ~-servant, valet; ~-guard, (rarely, member of) dignitary's retinue, escort, personal guard. 2. Trunk, main portion (stem, hull, nave, etc., acc. to context); upper garment (minus sleeves & collar, or = bodice); document minus preamble etc.; majority. 3. Human

being, person, (heir of) one's ~, good sort of ~, any, etc.); ~-line bowling (Cricket), fast bowling delivered persistently on the leg side. **4.** Aggregate of persons or things (in a ~, all together; ~ politic, State); society, league, military force; collection of precepts, information, etc. **5.** Piece of matter (heavenly ~, sun, star, etc.), quantity; comparative solidity or substantial character (~-colour, opaque; wine of good ~), thing perceptible to senses. [OE bodig; now excl. E, unless = G bottich cask, referred to med. L butica f. Gk apothēkē see APOTHECARY]

bŏd′y², v.t. **1.** Provide with body (rare). **2.** (Usu. with forth) give mental shape to; exhibit in outward shape; typify. [f. prec.]

Boeotian (bēō′shn), a. & n. Crass, dull, (person). [of Gk nation derided by Athenians]

Bō′er (or boor), n. & a. (Of) Dutch or Dutch-descended S.-African(s). [Du., = peasant, farmer, cf. G bauer & see BOOR]

Bō′fors (-orz), n. ~ (gun), light antiaircraft gun. [~ in Sweden]

bŏg¹, n. (Piece of) wet spongy ground, morass (in many plant names as ~ violet, BUTTERWORT, ~-berry, cranberry); ~ butter; ~ oak, ancient preserved in black state in peat; ~-trotter, Irishman. Hence ~g′y¹ (-g-) a., ~g′INESS (-g-) n. [f. Ir. or Gael. bogach (bog soft)]

bŏg², v.t. (-gg-). Submerge in bog (usu. in pass.).

bŏg³, n. A privy (vulgar).

bŏg′ey (-gi), **Colonel Bogey, n.** Score that good golf-player should do hole or course in. [f. BOGY as imaginary person?]

bŏg′gle, v.i. Start with fright, shy; hesitate, demur, at or about; equivocate; fumble. [var. of BOGLE used as vb]

‖**bŏg′ie** (-gi), n. Under-carriage with two or more wheel-pairs, pivoted below end of locomotive or railway-car; ~-car etc., fitted on these. [northern dial. wd, etym. dub.]

bō′gle, n. Phantom, goblin; bugbear; scarecrow. [introduced f. Scotch writers; etym. dub.; earlier bog in same sense, & bug (now only in BUGBEAR), may be f. W bwg ghost]

bō′gus, a. Sham, fictitious. [U.S. wd, etym. dub.]

bŏg′y̆, **-gey** (-gi), n. (pl. -ies, -eys). The devil; goblin (nursery, the ~ man); bugbear. [quoted f. 1840 only; etym. dub. see BOGLE]

bōhea′ (-hē), n. Black tea of lowest quality (last crop of season). [f. Chin. Wu-i name of district]

Bōhē′mian, a. & n. Socially unconventional (person); of free-&-easy habits, manners, & sometimes morals (esp. of

artists etc.). Hence **Bōhē′ianISM**(2) n., **bōhē′ianIZE**(4) v.i. [f. F bohémien gipsy]

*****bŏhŭnk′**, n. (sl.). Central European labourer of inferior class; rough. [?]

boil¹, n. Hard inflamed suppurating tumour. [OE bȳl, ME bile; com.-Teut., cf. G beule f. root bul- blow]

boil², v.t. & i. Bubble up, undulate, (of liquid at the heat that converts it to gas; also of containing vessel); ~ over (of liquid or vessel), overflow or be overflowed thus; seethe, be agitated, like boiling water or its vessel (of sea etc., feelings, feeling person); bring (liquid, vessel) to heat at which it boils; subject to heat of ~ing water, cook thus; undergo cookery by ~ing; ~ down, away, reduce, convert to vapour, by ~ing; ~ing; keep the pot ~ing, get a living; ~ing hot, ~ing, (colloq.) very hot; blood ~s, with indignation; ~ed shirt (sl.), cotton or linen shirt with starched front. [f. OF boillir (now bouillir) f. L bullīre (bulla bubble)]

boil³, n. = boiling, boiling-point, (esp. on, at, to, the ~).

boil′er, n. One who boils; vessel for boiling, esp. large vessel of riveted wrought-iron plates for making steam in engine; tank attached to kitchen range; laundry vessel; vegetable etc. suited to boiling; ~-iron, -plate, rolled iron ¼ to ½ in. thick; ~-tube, internal air-pipe carrying heat through ~. [-ER¹]

boil′ing, n. In vbl senses; esp.: the whole ~ (sl.), all the lot; ~-point, temperature at which anything boils (water at sea-level, 212° F., 100° C.), high excitement. [-ING¹]

bois de rose (bwah de rō′z), n. Shades of brown. [F, = rose-wood]

bois′terous, a. Violent, rough, (wind, sea, behaviour, speech, persons): noisily cheerful. Hence ~LY² adv. [earlier boistous (also -eous, -uous) etym. dub.; AF boistous (OF boisteus now boiteux lame) does not suit sense]

bŏl′as, n. (sing. & pl.). S.-Amer. missile consisting of balls connected by a strong cord (when thrown bringing down quarry by entangling limbs). [Sp., pl. of bola ball]

bōld, a. Courageous, enterprising, confident: make (so) ~ (as), presume, venture; forward, immodest; vigorous, free, well-marked, clear, (imagination, drawing, description, features, headland, etc.). Hence ~LY² adv., ~NESS n. [OE bald; com.-Teut. cf. G bald quickly]

bōle, n. Stem, trunk. [f. ON bolr cf. G bohle plank]

bōlec′tion, a. & n. (Moulding) raised above panel etc. [?]

boler′o (-ā′rō), n. Spanish dance: (freq. pr. bŏl′erō) woman's short jacket with or without sleeves resembling zouave jacket. [Sp.]

bolide, n. Large meteor, fire-ball. [F, f. L f. Gk *bolis -idos* (*ballō* throw)]

boll, n. Rounded seed-vessel, as in flax or cotton; ~-weevil, small destructive insect infesting cotton-plant. [=BOWL¹]

bollard, n. Post on ship or quay for securing ropes to. [perh. f. BOLE+-ARD]

bolometer, n. Radiation-measurer. [Gk *bolon ray+-o-+-METER]

*****bolōney,** n. (sl.) Humbug, nonsense, trash. [?]

Bol′shevik, n. Advocate of proletarian dictatorship in Russia by soviets, Russian communist; (pop.) any revolutionary. Hence ~ISM n., ~IST n. & a. [f. Russ. *bolsheviki* n. pl. majority party]

Bol′shy (sl.) n. & a. [f. prec.]

bol′ster¹, n. Long stuffed (esp. under-) pillow of bed or couch; pad or support in many machines & instruments. [OE]

bol′ster², v.t. & i. (Usu. with *up*) support with bolster, prop, aid & abet, countenance, preserve from (merited) destruction; pad; (with schoolboys) belabour with bolster, (intr.) have bolster-fight. [f. prec.]

bolt¹, n. Short heavy arrow of crossbow, quarrel, (*fool's ~ soon speaks* & is soon silenced); discharge of lightning (~ *from the blue*, complete surprise); door-fastening of sliding bar & staple, sliding piece or lock; headed metal pin for holding things together, usu. riveted or with nut; (as measure) roll of canvas etc.; bundle of osiers; ~-*line*, -*position*, (Mil.) defensive position at angle to main position to prevent a successful attack on some point of the main position from spreading farther; ~-*rope* (round sail-edge to prevent tearing; [cf. G *bolz*, Du. *bout*; etym. dub.]

bolt², v.i. & t. Dart of or away, (horse) break from control; gulp down un-chewed; fasten (door etc.) with bolt, ~ *in* or *out*, shut in, exclude, by ~ing door; fasten together with bolts. [f. prec.]

bolt³, n. Sudden start; running away. [f. prec.]

bolt⁴, adv. (With *upright*) = as a bolt, quite.

bolt⁵, boult (bōlt), v.t. Sift; investigate. [f. OF *buter*=It. *burattare* (*buratto* sieve; perh. f. *bura* kind of cloth see BUREAU)]

bolter, n. In vbl senses of BOLT⁵; esp.: horse given to bolting; (also *boulter*) sieve, sifting machine. [-ER¹]

bolus, n. Large pill. [mod. L, f. Gk *bōlos* clod]

bomb (-ŏm), n., & v.t. & i. 1. A high-explosive or incendiary or smoke or gas etc. projectile fired from a mortar, or thrown or deposited by hand, or dropped from an aeroplane, & exploded by percussion or by time mechanism; ATOMIC, FLYING, ~; ~-*bay*, compartment in aircraft for holding ~s; ~-*disposal*, removal & detonation of unexploded & delayed-action ~s; ~-*load*, weight of ~s carried by aircraft; ~-*proof*, (shelter) strong enough to resist ~s; ~-*shell*, artillery ~ (now usu. *shell* exc. in similes, as *fell like a ~-shell* etc.); ~-*sight*, device in aircraft for aiming ~s. 2. v.t. & i. Assail with ~s, throw ~s at, drive by ~s out of a building etc.; ~ *up*, load (aircraft) with ~s. Hence ~′ER¹ (-mer) n., soldier trained in, aircraft used for, ~ing (also *attrib.*, as *Bomber Command*). [f. F *bombe* f. Sp. *bomba* f. L f. Gk *bombos* hum]

bombard′, v.t. Batter with shot & shell (esp. of warships attacking town); (fig.) assail persistently with abuse, argument, etc. Hence ~MENT n. [f. F *bombarder* discharge *bombarde* f. med. L *bombarda* stone-throwing engine prob. f. L f. Gk *bombus* hum]

bombardier′ (or bŏm-), n. 1. ‖ Artillery non-commissioned officer below sergeant. 2. *Bomb-aimer in aircraft. [F, see prec.]

bom′bardon, n. Low-pitched brass instrument or organ stop imitating this. [It. (-*one*), f. *bombardo*+-*one*, see BOM-BARD, -ON]

bom′basine (-ŏm- or -ēm- or -ēn), n. Twilled dress-material of worsted with silk, with cotton, or alone, much used for mourning. [f. F *bombasin* f. LL *bombycinus* silken (*bombyx -ycis* silk or silk-worm f. Gk *bombux* see prec.]

bŏm′bast, n. Turgid language, tall talk. Hence bombas′tic a., bombas′tically adv. [earlier & OF *bombace* (-t phonetic, cf. *behest*) f. LL *bombacem* nom. -*ax* cotton (& so padding) corruption of *bombyx* see prec.]

Bŏm′bay dùck, n. Small fish of S. Asiatic coasts, eaten dried with curry. [corrupt. of *bombil*, native name of fish]

bombe (bawmb), n. (cookery). Any cone-shaped dish or confection, as *apricot, fish, ~*. [F]

bon, bonne, (F; see Ap.), a. French for *good*, common in some senses & phrases. [f. L *bonus*]

bon′a fïd′e, a. & adv. (Genuine(ly), sincere(ly). [L abl. s. of foll.; as adj. it may be hyphened, not as adv.]

bon′a fïd′ēs, n. (legal). Honest intention, sincerity. [L, =good faith; not hyphened]

bonanza, n. & a. (Prop.) prosperity, good luck; (pop.) greatly prospering, a large output (esp. of mines), worked with all best appliances (*a ~ farm*), a run of luck (*in ~*). [U.S. f. Sp., =fair weather f. L *bonus* good]

bon-bon (see Ap.), n. Sweetmeat. [BON]

‖**bonce,** n. Large playing-marble. [?]

bond¹, n. Thing restraining bodily freedom, imprisonment, (rare, only in pl., esp. *in ~s*); fagot-withe; restraining or uniting force; binding engagement, agree-

ment; deed by which A binds himself & his heirs etc. to pay a sum to B & his; government's or public company's documentary promise to pay borrowed money, debenture, (~holder, person holding such document); (Customs, of goods) in ~, 'bonded warehouse' till importer pays duty (take out of ~); (Bricklaying) various methods (English ~, Flemish ~, etc.) of holding wall together by making bricks overlap; ~ (paper) superior kind of writing-paper (suitable for ~s & similar documents); ~-stone, stone or brick running through wall. [ME var. of BAND¹]

bond², v.t. Bind together (bricks etc., see prec.), put customable goods into bond (see prec.), whence ~ER¹ n., person who puts goods into bond, binding stone or brick; encumber with bonded debt (see BONDED). [f. prec.]

bond³, n. League, confederation, (see AFRIKANDER). [Du., cf. G band f. binden BIND]

bond⁴, a. In slavery, not free, (arch.). Hence ~man, ~maid, ~servant, ~service, ~slave, nn. [influenced in sense by, but orig. separate f., BOND¹; f. OE n. bonda, bunda, husbandman f. ON bónda=bóande part. n. f. búa, boa, dwell; after the conquest, the bonde sank into a serf, & the wd changed in sense]

bon'dage, n. Serfdom, slavery; confinement; subjection to constraint, influence, obligation, etc. [ME f. AF; see prec. & -AGE]

bond'ed, a. (Of goods) placed in bond, (of warehouse) for such goods, (BOND³); (of debt) secured by bonds (BOND²). [BOND¹, -ED²]

bonds'man, n. Villein, serf; slave (lit. & fig.). [var. of bondman (BOND⁴) as though f. bond's genit. of BOND¹]

Bond Street, n. A London street, esp. as resort of fashionable loungers (a exquisite).

bone¹, n. One of the parts making up vertebrate animal's skeleton; (pl.) the body (my old ~s etc.), its remains (his ~s were laid); the body's hard, solid, or essential part (flesh & ~; skin & ~, thin person; horse with plenty of ~; well developed frame; bred in the ~, ineradicable; to the ~, penetrating, of cold, wound, etc.); material of which ~s consist; similar substance, as ivory, dentine, whalebone; thing made of ~, as (pl.) dice, castanets, stay-ribs; a small or nearly finished joint of meat (knuckle-~, broiled ~s); subject of dispute (~ of contention, ~ to pick with someone; make no ~s of, about, or to, not hesitate; will never make old ~s, live long; feel in one's ~s, be quite sure; ~-dry, quite dry; (of country etc.) teetotal; ~-head (sl.), blockhead; ~-setter, one who sets broken or dislocated bones, esp. without being qualified surgeon; ~-shaker, bicycle without rubber tires; ~-spavin, callous growth in horse's leg becoming as hard as ~, in most langg. the meaning is leg as well as bone]

bone², v.t. 1. Take out the bones from (meat, fish). 2. (sl.) Steal. [1 f. prec., & perh. 2 (as dog makes off with bone)]

bone³, v.t. (surveying). Take or test the level of (usu. as part.); boning rod, wooden rod used in levelling operations. [?]

bon'fire, n. Large open-air fire in celebration of some event; fire for consuming rubbish (make a ~ of, destroy). [earlier bonefire f. BONE n., bones being the chief material formerly used]

bon'go (-ngg-), n. Large striped African antelope. [native]

bonhomie (bŏn'ŏmē), n. Geniality. [F]

Bon'iface, n. Innkeeper. [Farquhar, Beaux' Stratagem]

bon'ism, n. Doctrine that the world is good, but not the best possible. So ~IST (2) n. [f. L bonus good +-ISM, after OPTIMISM of which it is the positive form]

bŏnit'ŏ (-ē-), n. (Kinds of) large mackerel-shaped fish, the striped tunny. [Sp., etym. dub.]

bon mot (bawn mō), n. (pl. bons mots). Witty saying. [F (BON +mot saying f. L multum a grunt]

bonne, n. (French) nursemaid, maid. [BON]

bonne bouche (-ōōsh), n. Tit-bit, esp. to end up with. [F (BON, bouche mouth f. L bucca cheek perh.=POUCH); phr. not used in this sense in F]

bonnes fortunes (see Ap.), n. Ladies' favours, as a thing to boast of or pride oneself on. [F]

bonn'et¹, n. (Man's) Scotch cap; woman's out-door head-dress without brim, with strings, & covering no part of forehead; ~ rouge (F, pr. bŏnā rōōzh), red cap as revolutionary symbol; (Naut.) additional canvas laced to sail-foot; cowl of chimney etc., protective cap in various machines; || hinged cover over motor of car; (Gaming, Auctions, etc.) accomplice, decoy; BEE in ~, an eccentricity; ~-laird (Sc.), petty landowner (who wore a ~, & not the hat of the gentry). Hence ~ED² a. [ME bonet f. OF bonet short for chapel de ~ cap (of med. L) bon(n)etus an unknown material]

bonn'et², v.t. Put bonnet on (person); crush down hat over the eyes of (person). [f. prec.]

bonn'y, a. (chiefly Sc.). Comely, healthy-looking; satisfactory. Hence ~ILY² adv. [etym. dub., perh. f. BON]

bon'spiel, n. (Sc.). Curling-match (usu. between clubs). [perh. f. Du. bond league, spel game]

bon ton (see Ap.), n. Good breeding; the fashionable world, (arch.). [F]

bon'us, n. Something to the good, into the bargain; extra dividend to shareholders of company, distribution of profits to insurance-policy-holders, gratuity to workmen beyond their wages. [jocular or ignorant use of L *bonus* good (masc.)]

bon vivant (see Ap.), n. Gourmand. [F]

bon'y, a. Of, like, bone(s); big-boned; with little flesh. [BONE¹+-Y¹]

bonze, n. Japanese or Chinese Buddhist priest. [F, f. Port. *bonzo* perh. f. Jap. *bonzō* f. Chin. *fan seng* religious person]

bon'zer, a. (Austral. sl.). Excellent, first-rate. [perh. f. BONANZA]

boo, int., n. & v.t. & i. (Make) sound of disapproval or contempt; hoot (speaker, announcement, etc.). [imit. of cow's lowing]

•**boob**, n. Simpleton. [contr. of foll.]

boob'y, n. Silly dull-witted fool, lout; kinds of Gannet; (~ *prize*, awarded to the last or lowest scorer in a contest of any kind; ~ *trap*, things placed on top of door ajar to fall on first opener, (Mil.) kinds of apparently harmless device concealing an explosive charge designed to go off when tampered with; ~ *hutch*). v.t. & i. Hence ~ISH¹ a. [prob. f. Sp. *bobo* (both fool & bird) perh. f. L *balbus* stammering]

boo'dle, n. Crowd, pack, lot, (the whole ~ or *caboodle*); money for political bribery etc.; a card-game. [now U.S., cf. obs. *buddle*]

boohoo', n., & v.i. (Make) sound of noisy weeping. [imit.]

book¹, n. 1. Portable written or printed treatise filling a number of sheets fastened together (forming roll, or usu. with sheets sewn or pasted lengthwise & enclosed in cover); literary composition that would fill such a set of sheets (or several) if printed; (fig.) anything from which one may learn, also imaginary record, list, etc., (~ *of fate*; ~ *of life*, list of those who shall be saved); the Bible (esp. *swear on the* ~); main division of treatise or poem (*Bk* I etc.), or of Bible (*B~ of Genesis*); = LIBRETTO; back-hinged set of blank sheets for writing accounts, notes, exercises, etc., in (pl., merchant's accounts); (Turf) one's bets on a race or at a meeting (*won't suit my* ~; transf., is inconvenient); set of tickets, stamps, cheques, tricks at whist, etc., bound up or collected. 2. ~ *of reference*, not read continuously but used intermittently for information; *speak like a* ~, in formal phrases, *by the* ~, with correct information; *take a leaf out of* ...'s ~, imitate him; *without* ~, from memory; (so *take one's name off the* ~(s), entered in list of members etc.); *in* ——'s *bad* or *black*, *good*, ~s, in disfavour or favour with him; *bring to* ~, call to account. 3. ~binder, -ding, binder, binding, ~s; ~case (-k-k-), case containing ~shelves; ~ends, pair of ornamental props used to keep a row of unshelved ~s upright; ~keeper, -ping, one who keeps, art of keeping, the accounts of a merchant, public office, etc.; ~learning, or -lore, -learnèd, mere theory, knowing ~s but not life, so ~ISH¹ a., ~ishly¹ adv., ~ishness n.; ~maker, -king, compiler, compiling, of ~s (esp. for mercenary motives), also professional betting man or ~ie [-Y¹] n., his profession; ~man, literary man; ~muslin, the kind folded in ~like way when sold; ~plate, label with owner's name, crest, etc., for pasting into ~s; ~rest, adjustable support for ~ on table; ~seller, -slide, expanding stand for a few ~s, ||~stall (of ~s exposed for sale out of doors); ~token, voucher for a sum of money to buy ~(s); ~value, value of a commodity as entered in a firm's ~s (opp. *market value*); ~work, study of rules or text~s (opp. to working sums, chemical analysis, etc.); ~worm, maggot eating its way through ~s, person devoted to reading. Hence ~LET n. [OE *bóc*; com.-Teut. cf. G *buch*; the supposed connexion with BEECH (as providing bark or tablets) is doubtful]

book², v.t. Enter in book or list; engage (seat, etc.) by previous payment, (guest, supporter, etc.) for some occasion; enter name of (person engaging seat etc.), issue railway ticket to; || take railway ticket; give, take down, address of (goods to be transmitted); etc.; *I'm* ~ed, caught, cannot escape; |~ing-clerk, -office, person, place, for buying tickets from. [f. prec.]

book'land, n. (hist.). Part of common land granted by charter (under the sovereign's orders) to a private owner. [OE *bóclánd*, f. *bóc* document]

boom¹, n. Long spar with one end attached stretching sail-foot; floating barrier of timber across river or harbour mouth. [Du. ~; cf. BEAM]

boom², v.i. & n. (Make) deep resonant sound; hum, buzz; (make) bittern's cry. [imit.]

boom³, v.t. & i. & n. (Show) sudden activity, development, (esp. of commercial ventures, prices, etc., cf. SLUMP); (win) sudden popularity for (an invention, cause, etc.) by advertising etc., launch with éclat. [U.S. wd, perh. f. prec. (cf. *make things hum*)]

boom'er, n. Large male kangaroo; (trappers' name for) N.-Amer. Mountain Beaver. [?]

boom'erang, n. Australian curved hardwood missile with convex edge returning to its thrower; (fig.) argument or proposal that recoils on its author. [native name, perh. modified]

boon[1], n. Request, thing asked for; favour, gift; blessing, advantage. [f. ON *bón*=OE *bén* prayer; the change f. prayer to gift prob. helped by confusion with foll.]

boon[2], a. Bounteous, benign, (poet.; of nature, air, life, etc.); congenial, jolly, (~ *companion*). [f. BON; from 14th c.]

boor, n. Peasant; clumsy or ill-bred fellow. Hence ~ISH[1] a., ~ISHLY[2] adv., ~ISHNESS n. [either f. OE *gebúr* dweller f. *búr* BOWER[1] & cf. NEIGHBOUR, or f. the cognate LG *búr*, Du. BOER]

boost, v.t. & n. 1. (colloq.). Shove, hoist. 2. Increase the reputation, value, etc. of (person, scheme, commodity, etc.) by advertising etc., boom. 3. (Mech.) raise the electromotive force in (electric circuit, battery, etc.), whence ~ER[1] (2) n. 4. n. Scheme of advertisement; resulting advance in value etc. [etym. dub.; orig. U.S. sl.]

boot[1], n., & v.t. 1. Outer foot-covering, usu. all or partly of leather, coming above ankle; (Hist.) instrument of torture, luggage-receptacle in coach under guard's & coachman's seat; ~ *is on the other leg*, truth or responsibility just the other way round; *like old* ~s (sl.), tremendously; *over shoes over* ~s, as well risk much as little; *heart in* one's ~s, in terror; *die in* one's ~s, not in bed; ~ *& saddle* [perversion of F *boute-selle*, place saddle], cavalry signal to mount; ~*jack*, for pulling ~s off; ||~*lace*, string or leather strip for lacing ~s; ~*legger*, liquor-smuggler in U.S.; ~*maker*; ~*trees*, moulds for keeping ~s in shape; (sl.) *get*, *give*, *the* ~, be dismissed, dismiss, from employment. 2. v.t. Kick; (sl.) kick (person) *out* (of the house, of employment, etc.). Hence ~ED[2] a. [ME *bote* f. OF *bote* (now *botte*), etym. dub.]

boot[2], n. Good, advantage, (now only in *to* ~, as well, as, *what* ~*s* (*it*) *to*, (*it*) *little* ~*s*, (*it*) ~*s* (*me*) *not*. [ME *boten* f. *bót* BOOT[2]]

boot[3], v.t. (arch.; usu. impers. & abs.). Do good (*to*), avail, as, *what* ~*s* (*it*) *to*, (*it*) *little* ~*s*, (*it*) ~*s* (*me*) *not*. [ME *boten* f. *bót* BOOT[2]]

bootee, n. Kind of lady's boot; infant's wool boot. [cf. *coatee*, see -EE]

booth (-dh), n. Temporary shelter of canvas etc.; covered stall in market, tent at fair, etc.; *polling*-~, for voting at elections. [ME *bothe* cf. Da., Sw., *bod*, f. East Norse *bóa* dwell]

boot'less, a. Unavailing. [OE *bótléas*, see BOOT[2], -LESS]

boots, n. Hotel-servant who cleans boots, conveys luggage, etc.

boo'ty, n. Plunder or profit acquired in common & to be divided; gain, a prize; *play* ~, act as decoy for confederates, practise collusion. [perh. f. F *butin* f. ON

býti barter, influenced in form by *bót* BOOT[2]]

booze, v.i., & n. Drink deeply, go on drinking; (n.) drink, a drinking-bout. [earlier *bouse*, *bowse*, ME *bousen* perh. f. MDu. *búsen* (*búse* drinking-cup)]

boo'zy, a. Addicted to drink; fuddled. [prec.+-Y[2]]

bo-peep, n. Game of hiding & suddenly appearing to child; *play* ~, of elusive politicians, arguers, etc. [BO+PEEP v.]

bōr'a[1], n. Cold dry N.-E. wind blowing seasonally in the upper Adriatic. [dial. It., f. L BOREAS]

bōr'a[2], n. Mohammedan trader or hawker. [Hind. *bohra*]

bōra'cic, a. Of borax (~ *acid*, = BORIC acid). [-IC]

bo'rage (bŭ-), n. Blue-flowered hairy-leaved plant used to flavour claret-cup etc. [f. med. L *borrago* or F *bourrache*; cf. perh. LL *burra* shaggy garment]

bōr'ax, n. A native salt, in white powder or crystal when pure. [ME & OF *boras* f. med. L *borax* f. Arab. *baurag* prob. f. Pers. *burah*]

Bōr'deaux' (-dō), n. Southern French wine, claret. [place]

bōrd'er, n. & a. Side, edge, boundary or part near it; frontier of country, (pl. after *within*, *out of*, etc.) territory; *the B*~, boundary & adjoining districts between England & Scotland, *frontier of civilization, (also *Border* adj. in these senses); continuous bed round garden or part of it, distinct edging for strength or ornament or definition round anything; ~*land*, district on either side of ~, (fig.) intermediate condition (as between sleeping & waking), debatable ground. [ME & OF *bordure* f. *bordura* f. *bordare* f. *bordus* f. Teut. *bord* BOARD[1]]

bōrd'er[2], v.t. & i. Put or be a border to, whence ~ING[4] (3) n.; adjoin (trans., or intr. with *on*, *upon*), resemble. [f. prec.]

bō'rdereau' (-rō), n. Memorandum of contents, docket. [F, = memorandum, invoice; came into English use during the Dreyfus Affair (1894–1906)]

bōrd'erer, n. Dweller on or near frontier, esp. that of England & Scotland. [BORDER n.+-ER (4)]

bōre[1], v.t. & i. 1. Make hole in usu. with revolving tool, hollow out evenly (tube etc.), whence **bōr'ING[1]** (2) n.; make (a hole, one's way) by boring, persistent pushing, or excavation. 2. (Of horse) thrust the head out; (Racing) push (another) out of the course. [OE *borian*; com.-Teut. cf. OE & ON *bor* anger, & L *forare* bore, Gk *pharos* plough]

bōre[2], n. Hollow of gun-barrel; diameter of this, calibre; small deep hole made in earth to find water etc. [f. prec.]

bōre[3], n. Nuisance (usu. as pred.), tiresome person, twaddler. [f. 1750, etym.

dub; early quotations imply F deriv.;
bourrer stuff, satiate?]

bōre⁴, v.t. Weary by tedious talk or dullness. [etym., & relation to prec. & to
BORE¹, doubtful; of same date as BORE³;
bore (BORE¹) one's *ears* = gain a hearing
by emphasis or repetition occurs over a
hundred years earlier]

bōre⁵, n. Great tide-wave with precipitous front moving up some estuaries.
[perh. f. ON *bára* wave]

bŏr´eal, a. Of the North or north wind.
[f. L *borealis* (foll. -AL)]

Bŏr´eãs, n. (God of) the north wind. [L,
f. Gk]

bōre´cŏle (-ōĺk-), n. = KALE. [f. Du
boerenkool peasant's cabbage]

bōre´dom (-ōŕd-), n. Being bored, ennui.
[BORE⁴+-DOM]

bŏr´er, n. Person, tool, or machine, that
bores holes; horse that bores; kinds of
boring insect. [BORE¹+-ER¹]

bŏr´ic, a. Of boron (~ *acid*, a preservative & mild antiseptic). [-IC]

born, p.p. & a. Be~, come into the world
by birth; ~ *of*, owing origin to; ~ *again*,
regenerate; (with compl.) destined to be
(~ *rich*, *tired*, *to be hanged*, *a poet*; cf. also
~ *orator*, *an orator* ~, etc.); ~ *with silver
spoon in mouth*, *under lucky star*, destined
to wealth, good luck; *in all my* ~ *days*,
my life; ~ *fool*, *idiot* (utter, hopeless)
often in comb. with adjj. & advv., as *base,
first*, ~. [p.p. of BEAR³]

bŏrne. See BEAR³.

bŏrné (bôrnā), a. Having limitations, of
limited ideas, narrow-minded. [F]

bŏro-, comb. form of roll.

bŏr´on, n. Non-metallic solid element (a
dark-brown powder). [f. BORAX with
ending of *carbon*, which it resembles in
some respects]

bŏr´ough (bŭr´ŏ), n. ‖(Munic.) town with
corporation & privileges conferred by
royal charter; (Parl.) town sending mem-
ber(s) to parliament; *the B~*, of Southwark; (Hist.) own, buy~, power of controlling election of member, close, pocket,
~, so controlled, *rotten* ~, no longer (before
1832) having real constituency. [OE *burg,
burh*; com.-Teut., cf. G *burg* castle, prob.
f. OTeut. *bergan* to shelter; Sc. form,
burgh]

borough-Eng´lish (bŭr´ŏ ingg-), n.
Tenure in some parts of England, by
which all lands & tenements fall to youngest son. [f. AF *tenure en Burgh Engleys*
(i.e. not French, but existing in some
English boroughs]

bŏr´row (-ō), v.t. & i. Get temporary use
of (money etc. to be returned; *of* or *from*
person); adopt, use without being the
true or original owner or inventor, derive
from another, import from an alien
source; (Golf) play ball up-hill to roll
back, (also) allow for wind or slope; ~*ed*

light, internal window; ~*ed*, PILfERS;
~*pit* (from which material has been
taken for filling or embanking). Hence
~ER¹, ~ING²(2), nn. [OE *borgian* f. *borg,
borh*, pledge, f. OTeut. *bergan* protect, cf.
G *borgen* borrow; orig. meaning, take on
pledge]

bŏr´sch (-sh), n. Highly seasoned Russian
soup of various ingredients including
beetroot. [Russ. *borshch*]

Bŏr´stal, n. ~ *system*, of imprisonment
for young criminals, based on the INDE-
TERMINATE sentence; ~ *Association*, for
help of ~ prisoners on discharge; ~ *Institution*, formerly ~ *Prison*, at ~ in Kent.
[place]

bŏrt, n. Diamond fragments made in
cutting. [perh. f. OF *bort* bastard]

bŏrzoi, n. Russian wolf-hound. [f. Russ.
borzoy a., swift, & n.]

‖bŏs, bŏss, n., & v.t. & i., (sl.), (Also
~-*shot*) bad shot or guess, miss; bungle,
mess; ‖~-*eyed* (sl.), blind in one eye,
cross-eyed, crooked, one-sided; (vb; -ss-)
miss, bungle. [?]

bŏs´cage, -kage, n. Masses of trees
or shrubs. [ME *boskage* f. OF *boscage*
(LL *boscum* wood & see -AGE)]

bŏsh¹, n. & int. (sl.). Nonsense, foolish
talk, folly. [Turk., = empty; introduced
by Morier's novel *Ayesha*]

‖bŏsh², v.t. (school sl.). Make a fool of,
tease. [f. prec.]

bŏsh³, n. Lower sloping part of blast-
furnace shaft, from belly to hearth.
[etym. dub.; cf. G *böschen* to slope]

bŏsk, bŏs´ket, -quet (-k-), nn. Thicket,
plantation. [*bosk* prob. mod. back-
formation f. BOSKY (but cf. ME *bosk* var.
of *busk* BUSH¹); *bosket* f. F *bosquet* f.
BOTQUET]

bŏs´ky, a. Wooded, bushy. [f. BOSK not
recorded betw. 14th & 19th cc.+-Y²]

bŏs´om (bŏŏ´zm), n. Person's breast; enclosure formed by breast & arms (*wife of
one's* ~; breast of dress, space between
dress & breast, old equivalent of pocket
(*put in one's* ~); ~*shirt-front*; surface of
lake, ground, etc.; the midst (~ *of one's
family*, *of the church*); the heart, thoughts,
desires, etc. (*comes home to one's* ~; ~
friend). [OE *bōsm* f. G *busen*, etym. dub.]

bŏss¹, n. Protuberance; round metal
knob or stud on centre of shield or ornamental work; (Archit.) projection at inter-
secting-point of vault-ribs; (Mech.) enlarged part of shaft. Hence ~ED² (-st),
a. [ME & OF *boce* (now *bosse*)
= It. *bozza* ulcer]

bŏss², n. (sl.). Master, person in authority;
*manager of political organization;
person or thing that is best at any thing,
champion. [U.S. wd f. Du. *baas* uncle,
master, cf. G *base* female cousin]

bŏss³, v.t. (sl.). Be master or manager
of (~ *the show*, make all arrangements).
[f. prec.]

Bŏs'ton, n. Variation of the waltz. [~ in U.S.]

Bŏs'well (-z), n. Biographer like James ~, writer of Johnson's life. Hence Boswéll'IAN a., ~ISM(3) n., ~IZE(4) v.i.

bŏt, bŏtt, n. Parasitic worm; *the botts*, horse disease caused by it. [?]

bŏt'anist, n. Student of botany. [f. F *botaniste*, see BOTANY, -IST(3)]

bŏt'anize, v.i. Study plants, esp. by seeking them as they grow. [f. Gk *botanizō* gather plants, see BOTANY, -IZE]

bŏt'any[1], n. Science of plants. Hence botán'ICAL a. (also botán'IC in names of old societies), botán'ICALLY adv. [historically *botanic* is the parent word. f. med. L f. Gk *botanikos* (*botánē* plant f. *boskō* feed); *botany* on anal. of *astronomy* -ic etc.; see -Y[1]]

Bŏt'any[2], a. & n. ~ (wool), Australian wool; ~ yarn, yarn made from this. [f. ~ Bay, early convict settlement in N.S. Wales named from the variety of its flora]

botăr'gō, n. (pl. -oes, -os). Relish of mullet or tunny roe. [It., f. Arab. *buṭarkhah* f. Copt. *outarakhon* (Copt. *ou*-indef. art. + Gk *tarikhion* pickle)]

bŏtch, n., & v.t. & i. (Make a) clumsy patch; bungle(d) work; repair badly. Hence ~ER[1] n. [etym. dub.; cf. PATCH & G *batzen*]

bŏth, a., pron., & adv. 1. adj. The two —— s & not only one, as ~ (the) *brothers are dead* (*have it* ~ *ways*, choose now one now the other of alternatives or contra-dictories to suit one's argument etc.). 2. pron. The two & not only one (a) with no n., as ~ *are dead*; (b) with *of* & n. or pron., as ~ *of them* (or *of the brothers*) *are dead*; (c) with n. or pron. as subj., & ~ in the pred. in apposition, as *they* (or *the brothers*) *are* ~ *dead, they were gentlemen* ~. 3. adv. With equal truth in two cases (a) where ~ might still be held pronominal, as ~ *brother & sister are dead*; (b) clearly adv., as *she is* ~ *dead & buried*; (c) of more than two nouns etc., as ~ *God & man & beast*. [earlier *bo*, OE *bā*; ME *bathe* f. ON *bāthar* cf. G *beide*; *bāthar* perh. resulted f. the addition of the def. art. (*both the*)]

bŏth'er[1] (-dh-), v.t. & i. Pester, worry; be troublesome; worry oneself, take trouble; (subjunct. as mild imprecation) confound. [etym. dub.; first in Irish writers, Swift, Sterne, etc.]

bŏth'er[2] (-dh-), n. Worry, fuss. [f. prec.]

bŏthĕrā'tion (-dh-), n. & int.=prec.;(int.) confound it! [BOTHER v. + -ATION]

bŏth'ersome (-dh-), a. Annoying, trou-blesome. [-SOME]

bŏth'y̆, -ie, n. (Sc.). Hut, cottage; one-roomed building in which workmen are lodged. [etym. dub.; cf. BOOTH]

bō'tree, n. Sacred pipal tree of India, beneath which Gautama, by enlighten-ment, became the Buddha. [Cingalese *bo* corrupted f. Pali & Skr. *bodhi* perfect knowledge]

bŏt'tle[1], n. Narrow-necked vessel, usu. of glass, for storing liquid; the amount of liquid in it; *the* ~, drinking, *over a* ~, while drinking; *bring up on the* ~ of child not fed from the breast; ~-brush, cylin-drical brush for cleaning ~s, kinds of plant as Horsetail; ~-glass, coarse dark-green glass; ~-green, dark green; ~-holder, pugilist's attendant at prizefight, second, supporter, understrapper; ~-khana (kahn'a), (Anglo-Ind.) pantry [f. Hind. *khana* house, place]; ~-neck, nar-row stretch or restricted outlet of road, (fig.) anything obstructing an even flow of production etc.; ~-nose, swollen nose, ~-nosed whale; ~-party, to which each guest brings a bottle of wine etc. (freq. extended to any gathering at which the licensing laws are defied); ~-washer, factotum, underling. [f. OF *bouteille* f. LL *baticula* dim. of *butis* BUTT[1]]

bŏt'tle[2], v.t. Store in bottles; (sl.) nab, catch, (offender, person for duty etc.); ~ up, conceal, restrain for a time, (resent-ment etc.). [f. prec.]

bŏt'tle[3], n. Bundle of hay or straw (*look for needle in* ~ *of hay*, of hopeless search). [f. OF *botel* dim. of *bot* (*botte* bundle)]

bŏt'tle[4], n. Blue, White, Yellow, B~, B~ of all sorts, kinds of plant. [partly corrup-tion of *buddle, bothel*, etym. dub., partly from shape of ovary or calyx]

bŏtt'om[1], n. & a. 1. Lowest part, part on which thing rests (*stand on own* ~, be independent; ~ *up*, upside-down; the posterior; seat (of chair); ground under water of lake etc. (*go, send, to the* ~, sink; *touch* ~, be at the lowest point or on firm facts; *to, from,* ~ *of heart*, genuinely, pro-foundly; river-basin etc., low-lying land; less honourable end of table, class, etc., person occupying this; farthest or inmost point (~ *of bay*); keel, horizontal part near keel, hull, ship esp. as cargo-carrier (*in British* ~s); foundation, basis, origin, (*be at the* ~ *of*, cause); essential character, reality, (*search to the* ~, *get to the* ~ *of*; *at your* ~ *dollar, stake all*); ‖ ~ GEAR; ~ stamina. 2. adj. Lowest, last (*bet your* ~ *dollar, stake all*); ‖ ~ GEAR; fundamental; hence ~MOST (-m-m-) a. [OE *botm* f. WG *bothm (G *bodem*), cf. Gk *puthmēn*, Skr. *budhnā*, L *fundus* (for *fudnus*)]

bŏtt'om[2], v.t. & i. Put bottom to (sauce-pan, chair); base (argument etc.) *upon*; touch bottom of sea etc.; touch bottom of, sound, find the extent or real nature of. [f. prec.]

bŏtt'omless, a. Without bottom (chair etc.); unfathomable. [-LESS]

bŏtt'omry[1], n. System of lending money to shipowner for purposes of voyage on security of ship, lender losing the money if ship is lost. [BOTTOM n.=ship+-RY after Du. *bodmerij*]

bŏt′omrў[2], v.t. Pledge (ship; see prec.). [f. L *botulus* sausage, -ISM]

bŏt′ulism, n. (med.). Sausage-poisoning. [f. L *botulus* sausage, -ISM]

boudoir (bōōd′wär), n. Lady's small private room. [F., = sulking-place f. *bouder* sulk, etym. dub.; termin. as in PARLOUR (F -*oir*)]

Bou′gainvillae′a, -*vil′ia*, (bōōgan-), n. Tropical plant with large bright-coloured bracts. [*Bougainville*, French navigator, c. 1750]

bough (-ow), n. Tree-branch (if on tree, one of the chief branches). [OE *bóg*, *bóh*; com.-Teut. (in etym. but not in sense) cf. G *bug*, Du. *boeg*, shoulder, bow of ship; also Skr. *bahus*, Gk *pēkhus* arm; Bow[2] of ship is same wd adopted separately. f. Scand. or LG]

bought(-ow). See BUY.

bougie (bōō′zhē), n. Wax candle; thin flexible surgical instrument for exploring, dilating, etc., the passages of the body. [F., f. Arab. *Būjiyah* Algerian town with wax trade]

bouillabaisse (bōōlyabās′), n. French (esp. Marseilles) dish, rich fish-stew. [F]

bouilli (bōōlyē′), n. Stewed or boiled meat. [F]

bouillon (see Ap.), n. Broth, soup; (Dress) puffed fold. [F, f. *bouillir* BOIL]

boul′der (bōl-), n. Water-worn rounded stone, cobble; large erratic block of weather-worn stone (in mining, of detached ore); ~*clay*, *-drift*, *-formation*, *-period*, geol. terms w. ref. to the Ice Age. [short for *boulderstone*, ME *bulderston*, cf. Sw. dial. *bullersten* large stone in stream (*buller* noise)]

Boule (bōō′lē) n. Legislative council of ancient Greece; modern Greek legislature. [Gk *boulē* senate (*bouloma*i choose)]

bou′levard (bōō′lvahr), n. Broad street with rows of trees. [F, f. G *bollwerk* BULWARK orig., promenade on demolished fortification]

boul′ter (bōl-), n. Long fishing-line with many hooks. [?]

bounce[1], v.i. & t. Rebound; throw oneself about; burst noisily, angrily, etc. *into* or *out of* (room), *in* or *out*; talk big; hustle (person) by bluff or assumptions *into* doing or *out of* (something); *bouncing girl* etc., big, hearty, bustling, noisy. [ME *bunsen* thump (a now arch. sense of *bounce*); perh. imit. of sound cf. G dial. *bums* for gunfire etc.]

bounce[2], n. Rebound; boast, exaggeration, swagger. [f. prec.]

bounce[3] adv. Suddenly, noisily, (*come ~ against* etc. cf. BANG). [as prec.]

boun′cer, n. In vbl senses; also; unblushing lie; thing big of its kind. [*chucker-out* (sl.) [-ER[1]]

bound[1], n. Limit of territory or estate; (usu. pl.) limitation, restriction, (*out of*

~*s*, beyond limits set by school rules; *go beyond the* ~*s of reason*, *put* ~*s to*). [f. OF *bodne*=med. L *bodena* earlier *butina*]

bound[2], v.t. Set bounds to, limit, (esp. in pass., with *by*); be the boundary of. [f. prec.]

bound[3], v.i. (Of ball etc.) recoil from wall or ground, bounce; (of living thing, wave, etc.) spring, leap, advance lightly. [f. F *bondir* (only of sound till 16th c.) perh. f. L *bombitāre* (*bombus* hum)]

bound[4], n. Springy movement upward or forward; (*advance by leaps &* ~*s*, with startling speed); (of ball etc.) recoil (on *the first* ~, between first two touchings of ground). [f. prec.]

bound[5], a. Ready to start, having started, ~*for* (or with preceding adv., as *homeward* ~). [ME *boun*, f. ON *búinn*, Norw. *buen*, p.p. of *búa* get ready; *-d* is due to the ME form's not looking like a p.p.]

bound[6], p.p. of BIND. In vbl senses; esp. ~ *up with*, having the same interests as, closely connected with; ~ *to win* etc., certain.

boun′dary, n. Limit-line; (Cricket) hit to limit of field scoring 4 or 6 runs. Hence ~. [BOUND[1]+-ARY[1]]

boun′den. See BIND[1].

boun′der, n. In vbl senses of BOUND[2],[3]; esp. (sl.) cheerfully or noisily ill-bred person. [-ER[1]]

bound′less, a. Unlimited. Hence ~*NESS* n. [BOUND[1]+-LESS]

boun′teous, a. Beneficent, liberal; freely bestowed. Hence ~LY[2] adv., ~NESS n. [ME *bontivous* f. OF *bontif* (*bonté* BOUNTY) +-OUS, altered later as though f. BOUNTY +-OUS]

boun′tiful, a.=prec. (*lady* ~, beneficent lady of a neighbourhood); also, ample. Hence ~LY[2] adv. [foll.+-FUL]

boun′tў, n. Munificence, liberality in giving; gift (*King's*, *Queen's*, B~), grant made to mother of triplets; *Queen Anne's B~*, fund for augmenting poor benefices; gratuity to soldiers & sailors on joining etc.; sum paid to merchants etc. to encourage trade enterprise (~*-fed products*). [f. OF *bonté* f. L *bonitātem* f. *bonus* good]

bouquet′ (bōōkā′), n. Bunch of flowers; perfume of wine. [F., = It. *boschetto* BOSKET]

bouquetin (bōōkĕ+′), n. The Alpine ibex. [F]

***bour′bon** (bĕr-, boor-),n. Kind of whisky distilled from Indian corn & rye. [f. *Bourbon County*, Ky, where first made]

bour′don (boor-), n. Low-pitched (16 ft) stop in organ; similar stop in harmonium; lowest bell in peal of bells; drone pipe of bagpipes. [F., = bagpipe-drone, perh. imit.]

bourgeois[1] (boorzh′wah), n. & a. (Member) of shop-keeping middle class, (person) of humdrum middle-class ideas. [F,

f. LL *burgensis* (*burgus* town f. WG *burg* BOROUGH]

bourgeois² (berjois'), n. & a. (Printing type) between long primer & brevier. [perh. a French printer's name]

bourgeoisie (boorzhwahzē'), n. The middle class. [F]

bourgeon. See BURGEON.

bourn¹ (boorn), n. Small stream. [southern var. of BURN¹]

bourn(e)² (boorn), n. Limit, goal. [t. F *borne* f. OF *bodne* BOUND¹]

bourse (boors), n. Foreign money-market, esp. that of Paris. [F]

boustrophe'don, a. & adv. (Written) from right to left & from left to right in alternate lines. [Gk, adv. = as ox turns in ploughing (f. *bous* ox, *-strophos* turning, *-don* adv. suf.]

bout, n. Spell of or turn at work or exercise; fit of drinking or illness; trial of strength; *this* ~, on this occasion. [perh. = obs. *bought*, which was perh. (being only from 15th c.) assim. of BIGHT to BOW³]

boutonnière (bōōtōnyaŕ), n. (Spray of flowers worn in) buttonhole. [F]

bouts rimés (bōō rēmā'), n. pl. Rhymed ends; versifying to set rhymes. [F]

bō'vine a. Of, like, an ox; inert, dull. [f. L *bovinus* (*bos bovis* ox, see COW)]

‖ **bō'vril,** n. A meat extract used like beef tea. [P]

bow¹ (bō), n. Curve; rainbow; weapon for shooting arrows (*bend, draw, the* ~; *two strings to one's* ~, more resources than one; *draw the long* ~, exaggerate); = SADDLE~; rod with stretched horse-hair for playing violin etc., single passage of this across strings; = BAIL⁴; = BOW-WINDOW; slipknot with single or double loop, ribbon etc. so tied; ~s, ~-compass(es), compass with jointed legs; ~-head, Greenland whale; ~-legged, bandy; ~-saw, narrow saw stretched like bow-string on wooden frame; ~'shot, distance to which ~ can send arrow; ~-string, (strangle with) string of (Turkish method of execution). [OE *boga*; com-Teut. cf. G *bogen* f. *bug-* st. of OTeut. *beugan* bend]

bow² (bō), v.t. Use the bow on (violin etc.; also abs.). [f. prec.]

bow³, v.i. & t. Submit (*to the inevitable* etc.), bend or kneel in sign of submission or reverence *to* or *before* (often with *down*) incline head in salutation, assent, etc.; ~*ing acquaintance*, that stops at this, slight); express (thanks etc.), usher *in* or *out*, by ~ing; cause to bend (lit. & fig., *knee, back* etc. for burden, *will*); ~ *down*, crush, make stoop, (esp. ~*ed down by care* etc.). [OE *būgan* f. OTeut. *beugan* f. st. *bug-* cf. Skr. *bhuj-* bend, L *fugere*, Gk *pheugō* flee; *bow* has also taken the senses of obs. *bey* its causal form f. OTeut. *'augjan*]

bow⁴, n. Bending of head or body in salutation, respect, consent, etc.; *make one's* ~, retire. [f. prec.]

bow⁵, n. Fore-end of boat or ship from where it begins to arch inwards (often pl.); *on the* ~, of objects within 45° of the point right ahead; rower nearest the ~ (~-*oar*, his oar or himself); ~*chaser*, see CHASE¹. [only from 1600; = LG *bug*, Du. *boeg*, Da. *boug*, shoulder, ship's bow; OE had *bóg, bóh*, shoulder, bough, but without the naut. sense; see BOUGH]

Bow bells (bō), n. *Within the sound of* ~, in City of London. [f. *St. Mary le Bow*]

bowd'ler¦ize, v.t. Expurgate (book, author). Hence ~ISM(3), ~izA'TION, nn. [T. *Bowdler* 1818, expurgator of Shakspere, +-IZE (4)]

bow'el, n. Division of alimentary canal below stomach, intestine, gut, (sing. only in med. use); (pl.) entrails, inside of body; pity, tender feelings, (~*s of mercy* etc.); interior of anything. [ME *buel* f. OF *boel* = t. LL *budello* f. LL *botellus* dim. of *botulus* sausage]

bow'er¹, n. Dwelling, abode, (poet.); inner room, boudoir, (poet.); place closed in with foliage, arbour, summerhouse, whence ~Y² a.; ~*bird*, Australian bird of the bird-of-paradise family constructing elaborate runs adorned with feathers, shells, etc. [OE *būr* dwelling (cf. G *bauer* birdcage) f. OTeut. *būrom* f. Aryan *bhurom* f. *bhu* (Teut. *bu-*) dwell]

bow'er², n. (Also ~-*anchor, -cable*) either of two anchors (*best & small*) carried at ship's bow or of their cables. [BOW⁵ +-ER¹]

bow'er³, n. One of two cards (*right* ~, knave of trumps, *left* ~, knave of same colour) at euchre. [f. G *bauer* peasant, knave at cards, see BOER]

bow'ie-knife (bō'ī-), n. Long knife with 10-15 in. blade double-edged at point used as weapon in wild parts of U.S. [Col. J. *Bowie*]

bowl¹ (bōl), n. Basin (hist., deep-shaped basin; now differing only as more dignified or poetic wd); drinking-vessel (*the* ~, convivality); contents of a ~; ~-shaped part of tobacco-pipe, spoon, balance, etc. Hence ~FUL(2) (bōl'fōōl) n. [var. of BOLL OE *bolla*; com-Teut. f. *bul-* swell]

bowl² (bōl), n. **1.** Wooden ball made slightly out of spherical shape or weighted on one side to make it run curved course (BIAS). **2.** Flattened or spherical wooden ball at skittles. **3.** pl. Game played with ~s (sense 1) on grass, or with round balls in room. **4.** pl. Skittles (dial). [ME & F *boule* f. L *bulla* bubble; *bowl²* has taken its pronunc. f. *bowl¹*, & *bowl¹* its spelling f. *bowl²*]

bowl³ (bōl), v.t. & i. Play bowls; trundle (ball, hoop, etc.) along or along ground; go along by revolving or by means of wheels, esp. ~ *along*, go fast & smoothly; (Cricket)

deliver (*ball, over,* or *abs.*), knock off (balls) or down (wicket), dismiss (bats-man; *out* or *abs.*), whence **bowl'er¹** [-ER¹] n.; ~ *over*, knock down, (fig.) dis-concert, render helpless. [f. prec.]

‖ **bowl'er²** (bō-), n. = BILLYCOCK. [f. B~, hatter, who designed it 1850]

bowl'ine (bō'lĭn), n. Rope from weather side of square sail to bow; (also ~*-knot*) a simple but very secure knot. [in all Teut. langs; connected with BOW⁵, but found in E centuries before that, & now with different pronunc.]

bowl'ing (bō-), n. In vbl senses; esp.: ~-*crease*, line from behind which bowler de-livers ball; ~-*alley*, long enclosure for playing skittles; ~-*green*, lawn for play-ing bowls. [-ING¹]

bow'man¹ (bou'-), Archer. [BOW¹]

bow'man², n. (pl. *-men*). Oarsman nearest the bow. [BOW⁵]

bow'sprit (bō-) n. Spar running out from ship's stem, to which forestays are fastened. [earlier recorded than BOW⁵, & with its first part very various (*bore, boar, bolt-, bole-, bow-*); therefore prob. not an E compd, but borrowed entire; cf. Du. *boegspriet* see BOW⁵, SPRIT]

Bow-street (bō-), n. & a. Street near Covent Garden with chief metropolitan police-court; *B~ runner, -officer,* old names for police officer.

bow win'dow (bō-, -dō), n. Curved (not angular) bay window; (sl.) large belly. Hence ~ED²(-ŏd) a. [BOW¹]

bow-wow' (-), int. & n. Dog's bark; imita-tion of it; (nursery talk etc.) dog; *the (big) ~ style,* dogmatic manner in talk or writing.

bow'yer (bō-), n. Maker, seller, of bows. [BOW¹+-YER]

bŏx¹, n. 1. Kinds of small dark evergreen shrub, esp. one with small dark leathery leaves, much used in garden borders; (also ~-*wood*) its wood, used by turners & en-gravers; (with qualification) similar plant, (*Bustard B~* etc.). [f. L *buxus,* cf. Gk *puxos*]

bŏx², n. 1. Receptacle (usu. lidded, rect-angular or cylindrical, for solids) of wood, cardboard, metal, etc. (*in the same case* in various machines; protective *~,* i.e. predicament); driver's seat (from the ~ under it); ~*jud* as quantity; *money~* (*put in the ~*); separate com-partment at theatre, in tavern, etc., in stable or railway truck for horse (*loose ~,* in which it can move about); = JURY-~; WITNESS~; hut for sentry or signalman; house for such temporary uses; protective case in various machines; *in the wrong ~,* awkward position. 2. ~BARRAGE; ~*bed,* sliding panels, also bed made to fold up & look like ~; ~*cloth,* close-woven cloth like buff; ~*coat,* heavy overcoat (for

boy, n. Male child (strictly till puberty, loosely till 19 or 20, 'the ~s' also of grown-up sons of a family); person who retains tastes or simplicity of boyhood; servant, slave, native labourer, male native, in various countries with subject races (cf. POST²~ etc.); (familiar voc.) *old, my, ~;* ~ often =male (~*friend*), young (~*husband*); ~ SCOUT¹; ‖~'*s-love,* Southern-wood. [cf. Elfris. *boi* young gentleman perh. = Du. *boef* knave f. MHG *buobe* (G *bube*)]

boy'cott, v.t., & n. 1. Punish, coerce, (person, class, nation) by systematic refusal of social or commercial relations; combine in abstaining from (goods etc.) with this aim. 2. n. Such treatment. [Capt. *B~,* Irish land-agent so treated; f. 1880]

boy'hood, n. Boyish age; boys. [-HOOD]

driving); ~-*drain,* of quadrangular sec-tion; ~-*iron,* for ironing, hollow for reception of heater; ~-*keeper,* attendant on theatre ~es; ~-*kite,* scientific kite consisting of two light rectangular boxes secured together horizontally; ~-*office,* in theatre etc. for booking seats; ~-*pleat,* double fold in cloth; ~*spanner* (with socket head); ~-*wallah* (Anglo-Ind. colloq.); pedlar, (sl.) European commer-cial man (in derogatory sense). Hence ~FUK(2) n. [either=prec., or f. L *buxum* boxwood, or f. L Gk *puxis* PYX]

bŏx³, v.t. Provide with, put into, a box; ~ *up,* confine uncomfortably, squeeze to-gether; ~ *lodge* (document) in Law Court; divide off from other compartments; (old sl.) ~*the watch,* overturn watchman in his box; ~*the compass,* (Naut.) rehearse the points in correct order, (fig.) make complete revolution & end where one be-gan (in politics, argument, etc.). [f. prec.]

bŏx⁴, v.i. Slap with hand *on the ear(s).* [?]

bŏx⁵, v.t. & i. Slap person's ears; fight (someone, or intr.) with fists (usu. in pad-ded gloves & merely for exercise); ~-*ing-gloves;* ~*ing-weights,* Heavy, Lt. Heavy (or Cruiser) Middle, Welter, Light, Feather, Bantam, Fly, ~*weight,* divisions being, over 12 st, 6, at 12 st. 6, 11 st. 6, 10 st. 7 (*145 lb. & below), 9 st. 9, 9 st., 8 st. 6, 8 st. See also addenda. [f. prec.]

bŏx'er, n. Pugilist; (*B~*) member of Chinese anti-foreign secret society. [BOX⁵, -ER¹]

bŏx'haul, v.i. Veer ship round on her keel (for want of room). [BOX³]

‖ **Bŏx'ing-day**, n. First week-day after Christmas [on which Christmas-boxes are given, f. obs. sense of BOX² f. (money-BOX²]

bŏx and Cŏx, n. Two persons who are never together, never at home at the same time. [name of play]

bŏx'calf'(-kahf), n. Chrome-tanned calf-skin with hatched grain. [after Joseph Box, London bootmaker]

boy'ish, a. Proper to boys; as of a boy, spirited, puerile. Hence ~LY² adv., ~NESS n. [-ISH¹ (1)]

brab'ble, v.t. & n., (arch.). (Engage in) paltry noisy quarrel. [etym. dub., but cf. Du. *brabbelen* jabber, stammer]

brace¹, n. Thing that clasps, tightens, unites, secures; ‖ (pl.) suspenders for trousers; thong for tuning drum; ‖ strap connecting carriage-body from springs; connecting mark in printing (}); pair, couple, (dogs, game, contempt. persons; pl. *3, 20,* etc., *brace*); strengthening piece of iron or timber in building; ~ *& bit,* revolving tool for boring, screw-driving, etc.; (Naut.) rope attached to yard for trimming sail (*splice the* MAIN³ ~). [f. OF *brace, brasse,* the two arms, f. L *brachia* (pl.) arms; the naut. meaning is perh. f. F *bras* arm]

brace², v.t. Fasten tightly, stretch, string up, give firmness to, (~ *oneself up,* ~ *one's energies,* etc.; *bracing air*); support; couple together; (Naut.) move (sail) by braces. Hence *brăc'er¹ n. (sl.), pick-me-up. [partly f. OF *bracier* embrace, partly f. prec.; the naut. perh. f. F *brasser*]

brace'let (-sl-), n. Ornamental band, chain, etc., for wrist or arm; wrist-fetter. Hence ~ED² a. [OF, dim. of *bracel* f. L *brachiale* (*brachium* arm) see -AL (2)]

brac'er², n. Wrist-guard in archery & fencing. [f. OF *brasseüre* as f. L *brachia-tura* (*brachium* arm), see -URE & cf. BORDER¹]

brach, n. (arch.). Bitch hound. [f. OF *brachet* dim. of *brac* f. OHG *braceo* hound hunting by scent]

brach'ial (-āk-), a. Of the, like an, arm. [f. L *brachialis* (*brachium* arm) see -AL]

brach'iate (-āk-), a. (bot.). With branches in pairs at right angles to stem, each pair at right angles to the last. [f. L *brachiatus* armed see prec. & -ATE² (1)]

brach'y- (-k-), comb. form of Gk *brakhus* short, in many scientific terms.

brăch'ycephăl'ic (-kīsĕ-), a. Short-headed (of skulls with breadth at least four-fifths of length; or of person or race with such skull). [prec. +СЕРНАЛС]

brach'ylogy (-ki-), n. Conciseness of speech, condensed expression, incorrect-ness of speech due to excessive condensa-tion. [f. Gk *brakhulogia*, see BRACHY-, -LOGY]

‖ **brăck'en**, n. A fern abundant on heaths etc.; any large fern; (collect.) mass of ferns. [ME (northern) *braken* cf. Sw. *bräken*]

brăck'et¹, n. Flat-topped projection from wall serving as support to statue, arch, etc.; shelf with slanting under-prop for hanging against wall; wooden or metal angular support supporting trunnion; support projecting from wall of gas or other lamp; pairs of marks, ( ), [ ], { } (cf. BRACE²)

used for enclosing words, figures, etc. [earlier *bragget* f. Sp. *bragueta* dim. of *braga* f. L *braccae* breeches, meaning affected by confusion with L *brachium* arm]

brăck'et², v.t. Enclose in brackets as parenthetic, spurious, (Math.) having spec. relations to what precedes or follows, etc.; couple (names etc.) with a brace, imply connexion or equality between (~*ed*, equal); (Mil.) drop two shots one short of & one beyond (target) in range-finding. [f. prec.]

brăck'ish, a. Between salt & fresh (of water). [f. obs. adj. *brack* f. Du. *brak*, -ISH¹]

brăct, n. Small leaf or scale below calyx. So **brăc'teal**, **brăc'teate²**(2), aa. [f. L *bractea* thin plate, gold leaf]

brad, n. Thin flat slightly-headed nail. [earlier *brod* prob. f. ON *broddr*=OE *brord* spike]

brăd'awl, n. Small non-spiral boring-tool. [perh. f. prec. +AWL]

brăd'bury, n. (obs. sl.). Currency note, esp. for £1. [f. signature of Permanent Sec. to Treasury]

‖ **Brăd'shaw**, n. (Used for) ~'s *Railway Guide*, a time-table of all passenger trains running in Great Britain. [orig. issued in 1839 by George *Bradshaw*, printer]

brăd'y-, comb. form of Gk *bradus* slow, as ~*pepsy* slow digestion.

‖ **brae** (-ā), n. Steep bank, hill-side. [Sc. wd used by E writers, f. ON *brá*=OE *brǣw* brow]

brăg, n., & v.i. & t. (-gg-). (Indulge in) boastful talk; boast of or of, boast *that*; card-game like poker. [etym. dub.; F *braguer* etc. later]

brăggădō'cio (-shiō), n. Empty vaunt-ing. [formed by Spenser(meaning *booster*) on prec. & It. augmentative -*occhio*]

brăgg'art, n. & a. (Person) given to brag-ging. [f. F *bragard* f. *braguer* BRAG+-ARD]

brahmapoōt'ra, **brah'ma**, n. Kind of domestic fowl. [river *Brahmapūtra*, whence brought]

brah'min, **-man**, n. Member of Hindu priestly caste. Hence **brahmin'ic**(-AL), **-măn'ıc**(AL), aa., **brah'mĭnısm**(3), **-manısm**(3), n. [f. Skr. *brahmaṇa* f. *brahman* worship]

brahminee'¹, n. Female brahmin. [f. Skr. *brahmaṇī* fem. see prec.]

brah'minee², a. Belonging to brahmin caste etc.; ~ *bull, ox,* sacred (humped) cattle, immune from slaughter. [f. BRAHMIN on anal. of *Bengalee* etc.]

Brah'mōism, n. Reformed theistic Hinduism. So **Brah'mō(ıst)** n., adherent of ~. [f. *Brahmo* in *Brahmo Samaj* (religious society founded in 1830). -ISM]

braid¹, n. Entwined hair, plait; band etc.

entwined with the hair; silk, thread, etc., woven into a band. Hence ~ING¹(3, 6) n. [see foll.]

braid², v.t. Platt, interweave, (hair, flowers, thread); arrange (hair) in braids; confine (hair etc.) with ribbon etc.; trim, edge, with braid. [OE *bregdan* com-Teut. move to & fro, move suddenly sideways]

Braid'ism, n. =HYPNOTISM, [first scientifically applied & explained by Dr J. *Braid*, 1842; -ISM (3)]

brail, n., & v.t. (Haul up with) small rope(s) on sail-edges for trussing sails before furling. [OF, f. L L *bracile* waist-belt (*bracae* breeches) see -AR(2)]

braille (-āl), n. System of writing & printing for the blind. [M.*Braille*, French inventor, 1834]

brain, n., & v.t. Convoluted nervous substance in skull of vertebrates (sing. of the whole as an organ, pl. of the substance; *blow out one's ~s*, shoot him in the head); centre of sensation, thought, etc. (usu. pl. sing. with dignified or exalted effect; *cudgel* etc. *one's ~s*, think hard; *have something on the ~*, be crazy about it; *turn one's ~*, make him vain & silly; intellectual power (*such, pick, one's ~*, extract & use his ideas); *~fag*, nervous exhaustion; *~fever*, inflammation of the ~; *~fever bird*, Indian cuckoo (with maddeningly persistent cry sounding like "*~-fever*"); *~-pan*, skull; *~ sauce*, intelligence; *~-sick*, mad; *~-storm*, temporary mental upset marked by uncontrolled emotion & violent action; *~wave*, (colloq.), sudden inspiration or bright idea; hence ~LESS a. (Vb) dash out ~s of. [OE *brægen*=Du. *brein*, cf. perh. Gk *brekhmos* forehead]

brain'y, a. Clever. [-Y²]

braird, n., & v.i. (Come up in) fresh shoots. [f. OE *brerd* brim cf. *brord* see BRAD]

braise (-z), v.t. Stew (prop. with fire above & below) tender with bacon, herbs, etc. [f. F *braiser* (*braise* hot charcoal)]

brake¹, n. =BRACKEN. [perh. borrowed though pl. ending]

brake², n. Thicket, brushwood. [cf. MLG *brake* tree-stumps (*breken* BREAK v.)]

brake³, n. Toothed instrument for braking flax & hemp; (also *~-harrow*) heavy harrow; instrument for peeling off willowbark. [=MLG *brake* or ODu. *braeke* flaxbrake. f. Du. *breken* BREAK¹]

brake⁴, v.t. Crush (flax, hemp) by beating. [f. prec.]

brake⁵, n. Apparatus for checking wheel's motion; (also *~-van*) railway-carriage

containing this, guard's compartment. Hence ~'LESS (-kl-) a. [etym. dub.; perh. f. obs. or techn. *brake* = lever f. OF *brac*

brake⁶, v.t. Apply brake to (wheel, car, train). [f. prec.]

brake⁷. See BREAK³.

‖**brakes'man** (-ks-), n. Man in charge of BRAKE⁵.

Brām'ah- (Look, press, pen, etc.) invented by J. *Bramah* c. 1790.

brām'ble, n. Rough prickly shrub with long trailing shoots; blackberry-bush (Sc.); blackberry. Hence **brām'bl'y²** a. [OE *brembel* earlier *bremel* (for -b- cf. *humble, number*) dim. of OTeut. wd=OF *bromm* BROOM cf. G *brom-bere* blackberry]

brām'bling, n. The Mountain Finch. [prec. +-LING¹(1)]

brān, n. Husks of grain separated from flour after grinding. *~ pie*, form of LUCKY-*bag*. [f. OF *bren* etym. dub.]

brān'card (-ngkǎ-), n. A horse-litter. [F. =litter (foll. -ARD)]

branch¹ (-ah-), n. Limb springing from tree or bough (*bough, ~, twig*, is the order; but *~* sometimes for either of the others); lateral extension or subdivision of mountain-range, river, road, family, genus, subject of knowledge, argument, legislature, bank or other business, etc.; *root & ~, root d- ~ adj., root & ~ adv.*, thorough(ly), radical(ly). Hence (-~)ED¹ (-cht), ~LESS, aa., ~Y² a. [f. F *branche* branch f. L L *branceo* paw]

branch² (-ah-), v.i. Put branches out, forth; spread forth, tend away or off, diverge into. [f. prec.]

brănc'hiae, -ia, (-ngk-), n. pl. Gills. Hence ~AL, ~ATE²(2), ~FEROUS, ~FORM aa., ~o- comb. form. [L *branchia*, pl. -ae]

brăn'chiy (-ah-), a. With many branches [-Y²]

brănd¹, n. Burning or charred log or stick (*~ from the burning*, rescued person, convert), torch (poet.); mark made by hot iron; stigma (*the ~ of Cain*, bloodguiltiness); trade-mark, particular kind of goods; iron stamp for burning a mark in; kind of blight (leaves etc. with burnt look); sword (poet.; perh. as flashing) [conn.-Teut., f. OTeut. *brandoz* (*bran*- pret. st. of *brinnan* BURN²+suf. -do as in WORD)]

brănd², v.t. Burn with hot iron (surgically, penally, or showing ownership or quality); impress on memory; stigma [f. prec.]

brăn'dish, v.t. Wave about, flourish (weapon, threat) as preliminary to action or in display. [f. F *brandir* (-ish²) f. Teut. BRAND¹ sword]

brănd'ling, n. Red worm with brighter rings used as bait. [BRAND¹+-LING¹(1)]

brand-new', **brān-**, a. Conspicuously new. [f. BRAND¹, as if freshly stamped]

brăn'dré̄th, n. Wooden stand for cask, hay-rick, etc. [f. ON *brandreidh* grate (*brandr* BRAND¹+*reith* carriage)]

brăn'dy̆, n. Strong spirit distilled from wine; ||~-*ball*, kind of sweet; ||=*pawnee* [Hind. *pani* water], ~ & *water*; ~-*snap*, gingerbread wafer. [earlier *brandewine*, *brandewine*, f. Du. *brandewijn* = burnt (distilled) wine]

brănk-ŭrs'ine (-ngk-), n. Bear's breech, acanthus. [f. med. L *branca ursina* bear's claw cf. BRANCH]

brăn-new. See BRAND-NEW.

brănt(-goose). See BRENT.

brăsh, n. Loose broken rock or ice; hedge refuse, clippings, etc. [perh. f. F *brèche* breach]

*brăsh², a. (colloq.). Rash, cheeky, saucy. [?]

brass (-ahs), n., a., & v.t. & i. **1.** (Hist.) alloy of copper with tin, zinc, or other base metal; (mod.) yellow alloy of copper with ½ zinc (cf. BRONZE); inscribed sepulchral table of ~; *the* ~, *the* ~ *instruments of a band*; (sl.) money; effrontery, shamelessness. **2.** adj. Made of ~; ~ *band*, set of musicians with ~ instruments, esp. *don't care a* ~ *farthing*, least possible amount, esp. farthing; ||~ *hat*, (army sl.) officer of high rank; ||~ *plate*, on door, gate, or window-ledge, with name, trade, etc.; ||~ *rags*, sailors' cleaning cloths, as *part* ~ *rags* (Naut. sl.), dissolve intimacy *with*; ~ *tacks*, (sl.) actual details, real business, esp. *get down to* ~ *tacks*. **3.** v.t. & i. (sl.) Pay up. [OE *bræs* etym. dub.]

brass'age, n. Mint-charge for coining money. [F, f. *brasser* stir melted metals together; see -AGE]

brassărd, n. Badge worn on arm. [F (*bras* arm & see -ARD)]

brasserie, n. Beer-saloon or beer-garden (usu. supplying eatables also). [F, =brewery (*brasser* brew)]

brassière (bras'yār), n. Woman's underbodice worn to support breasts. [F]

brass'y̆ (-ah-), a. & n. **1.** Like brass in colour, sound, taste; impudent; pretentious; hence ~lY² adv., ~INESS n. **2.** n. (Also ~ie) brass-soled golf-club. [-Y²]

brat, n. Child (usu. contempt.), etym. dub., but cf. obs. or dial. *brat* cloth, applied in OW (*brith* pl.) to swaddling-clothes]

brătt'ice, **brătt'icing**, nn. (Coal-mining) wooden partition or shaft-lining. [formerly wooden parapet on fortress; ME *brutaske* f. ONF *breteske* perh. f. G *brett* board + Rom. suf. -esca -ESQUE]

brava'dō (-vah-, -vä-), n. (pl. -oes, -os). Show of courage, bold front. [f. Sp. *bravada*, f *bravade*; see foll., ADO(2), -ADE(1)]

brăve¹, a. & n. **1.** Courageous (*the* ~, men); (archaic-literary) finely dressed, showy, worthy, honest, admirable; hence ~lY²(-v¹-) adv. **2.** n. Red-Indian warrior. [F, f. It. *bravo* etym. dub.; L *rabidus*, mad, & *barbarus*, have been suggested]

brăve², v.t. Defy, encounter with courage; ~ *it out*, carry oneself defiantly under suspicion or blame. [f. F *braver* see prec.]

brāv'ery, n. Daring; splendour, ostentation, finery. [prob. f. F *braverie* f. *braver* see prec. (orig. E sense *bravado*); -ERY]

bra'vō¹ (-ah-), n. (pl. -oes, -os). Hired assassin, desperado. [It., see BRAVE¹]

bra'vō² (-ah-), n. & int. Cry of approval, esp. to actors etc. (sometimes *brava, bravi*, to actress, company; also *bravissimo* superl). [It.=BRAVE¹]

bravu'ra (-oora), n. Brilliant or ambitious execution, forced display; style of (esp. vocal) music requiring exceptional powers. [It.]

brawl, v. i., & n. Squabble, (engage in) noisy quarrel; (of streams) murmur. Hence ~ER¹ n. [quoted from 1375, etym. dub.; cf. mod. Du. & G *brallen* brag, shout]

brawn, n. Muscle; pickled or potted boar's flesh. [f. OF *braon* flesh f. WG *brādo* (*brāddan* roast cf. OE *brēdan* burn); sense boar's flesh is excl. E]

brawn'y̆ [ỹ, a. Strong, muscular. Hence ~INESS n. [-Y²]

brăx'y̆, n. & a. (Sc.). Splenic apoplexy in sheep; (adj.) suffering from ~, (of meat) of a ~ sheep (also abs. as n., = meat). [etym. dub.; cf. OE *bræc* catarrh]

bray¹, n., & v.i. & t. (Make) the cry, or a sound like the cry, of ass or trumpet; ~ *out*, utter harshly. [f. F *braire* cf. L *fragor* crackling noise]

bray², v.t. Pound, beat small, esp. with pestle & mortar. [f. OF *breier* (now *broyer*) etym. dub.]

brāze¹, v.t. Colour like brass. [perh.= OE *brasian* (*bræs* BRASS) make of brass (not found betw. 1000 and 1550), but prob. mod. form on *glass, glaze*]

brāze², v.t. Solder with alloy of brass & zinc. [perh. f. F *braser* solder f. ON *brasa* expose to fire]

brā'zen¹, a. Made of brass; strong, yellow, or harsh-sounding, as brass; (also ~-*faced*) shameless, whence ~lY² adv.; ~ *age*, third stage in human deterioration (golden, silver, ~, iron). [OE *bræsen* (*bræs* BRASS +-EN⁵)]

brā'zen², v.t. ~ *out*, carry off impudently ('it', matter, deed); make shameless. [f. prec.]

brā'zier¹ (-zher), n. Worker in brass. Hence **brā'ziery(1)** n. [BRAZE¹+-IER, cf. GLAZIER, GRAZIER]

brā'zier² (-zher), n. Pan for holding lighted charcoal. [f. F *brasier* (*braise* hot coal)]

Brazil', n. & a. (Also ~-*wood*) kinds of hard red S.-Amer. wood yielding dyes; ~-*nut*, large three-sided nut. [etym. dub.; orig. Sp., Port., & F name of E.-Ind. wood, transferred to S.-Amer. similar species & thence to the country]

breach¹, n. (Naut.) breaking of waves (*clear* ~, rolling over without breaking; *clean* ~, carrying away of masts & everything on deck); breaking or neglect (of rule, duty, contract, someone's privileged rights, or promise, esp. to marry); ~ *of close*, trespass, *of the peace*, riot or affray; breaking of relations, separation, alienation, quarrel; broken state; gap, esp. in fortifications made by artillery (*stand in the* ~, bear brunt of attack, lit. or fig.); whale's leap clear out of water. [OE *bryce* (f. OTeut. st. *brek-* see BREAK) gave ME *bruche*; ME *breche* (f. F *brèche* f. same Teut.) combined with & has displaced *bruche*, but ~ has dissociated itself from BREAK, as *speak speech*]

breach², v.t. & i. Break through, make gap in; (of whale) leap clear out of water. [f. prec.]

bread (-ĕd), n. Flour moistened, kneaded, & baked, usu. with leaven (*white*, BROWN, *black*, ~; *standard* ~, wheaten of mixed flours; *break* ~, take food, join in Lord's supper; ~ *& butter*, necessary food, a livelihood, ~-&-*butter letter*, ROOFER; ~-&-*butter miss*, school-girl; ~ *& scrape*, stingily buttered bread; *ship's* ~ (Naut.), hard biscuit; ~ *& cheese*, simple food, a livelihood; ~ *& milk*, broken ~ in boiling milk; ~ *& wine*, Lord's supper; ~ *of life* (see *John* vi. 35); *know which side one's* ~ *is buttered*, where one's interest lies; ~ *buttered on both sides*, easy prosperity; *take the* ~ *out of one's mouth*, take away his living by competition etc.; *eat the* ~ *of idleness*, affliction, etc.; *daily* ~, livelihood; *make one's* ~, earn a living; ~-*basket*, (sl.) stomach; ~-*crumb*, inner part of loaf, ~ crumbled for use in cooking; ~-*fruit*, *-tree*, South-Sea tree with farinaceous fruit; ~-*line*, queue of poor people waiting to receive food; ~-*stuffs*, grain, flour; ~-*ticket* (entitling to ration); ~-*winner*, person (also art, trade, tool) that supports a family. Hence ~LESS a. [OE *brēad* (cf. G *brod*, *brot*) f. OTeut. *braude*; orig. sense prob. *fragment* or *piece*, loaf being the

breadth (-ĕd-), n. Broadness, measure from side to side, (*to a hair's* ~, exactly); piece (of cloth etc.) of full ~; extent, distance, room; largeness (of mind, view, etc.), liberality, catholicity, toleration; bold effect. Hence ~WAYS, -WISE, advv. [formed on obs. *brede*, OE *brǣdu*, in same sense. +-TH² on anal. of *length* etc.]

break¹ (-āk), v.t. & i. (*broke* & in Bible *broke*; *broken* sometimes *broke* see BROKE²). **1.** (Of a whole) make or become discontinuous otherwise than by cutting, divide into two or more parts, (~ BULK¹; ~ *a set*, sell parts separately; ~ *up*, dismiss, depart; ~ *small*, (of person) become feeble, show signs of decay;

gap in; (of whale) leap clear out of water. [f. prec.]

it when run up from its trussed state; ~ *a lance with*, argue against; ~ *bread with*, be entertained by; ~ *Priscian's head*, use bad grammar; ~ *person on wheel*, waste power; ~ *ground*, plough, begin siege, or fig. any, operations; ~ *the ice*, get over initial shyness or reserve; ~ *the ranks*, disorder by leaving them; *troops* ~, disperse in confusion; *clouds* ~, show gap); crack, graze, (~ *a head*); shatter; dislocate (neck; ~ *the neck or back of*, kill, dispose of); make by separating obstacles (a *way* etc.); penetrate by ~ing (~ *open*); interrupt, change, (gloom, journey, silence, one's *fast*; *voice* ~s, with emotion or at manhood; ~ *off*, bring to an end, cease); disrupt (*broken bonds* etc.); solve (a cipher); (Boxing, etc.) clinch; ~ *out*, open up (receptacle & remove contents (esp. Naut., of cargo), come out of a bough from tree, person of habit; ~ *with*, have breach or cease relations with; ~ *an officer*, dismiss; ~ *piece of* ill, bring changes from its course, *back* from off, in from leg, side). **3.** Make a way, come, produce, with effort, suddenness, violence, etc., (~ *into house*, *out of prison*, *through obstacles*; ~ *in*, intrude, interpose; ~ *news*, *disease*, *war*, ~ *out*; ~ *out*, exclaim; ~ *news*, *a jest*, reveal it; ~ WIND¹; *dog* ~s; *abscess* ~s); escape, emerge from, (prison, bounds, covert; ~ *free* or *loose*; ~ *away from*). **4.** Make or become weak, disable, discourage, ruin, destroy, cease, exhaust, (~ *the heart*, *heart* ~s; *frost*, *weather*, ~s; ~ *bank*, exhaust its resources; *merchant* ~s, is bankrupt; ~ *blow*, *fall*, weaken its effect; ~ *doom*, demolish, collapse, fall); tame, discipline, overpower, (with *in*, *to*, or abs.; ~ *a horse*, ~ *a horse to the rein*; ~ *in child*; ~ *one's will*, *spirit*; ~ *resistance*, *a rebellion*); make of no effect, transgress, violate, neglect, (law, Sabbath, contract, promise, one's *word*). Hence ~ABLE a. (also as n. pl. things easily broken), ~AGE(3) n. [OE *brecan* cf. G *brechen* t. f. OTeut. st. *brek-* = L *frag-*]

break² (-āk), n. Breaking; ~ *of day*, dawn; (Cricket) deviation of ball on pitching (~-*back*, f. off side); (Billiards) points scored continuously; gap, broken place, interruption of continuity; short spell of recreation between lessons (colloq.) a chance; (Mus.) point of separation between different registers of voice; irregularity; *a bad* ~ (colloq.), unfortunate remark or ill-judged action. [f. prec.]

break³ (-āk), n. Carriage-frame with no body for breaking in young horses; large wagonette. [f. BREAK¹ (= ~-*horse*¹), or f. obs. n. *brake*=curb, bridle, which may be special use of BRAKE²]

break-down, n. Collapse, stoppage; failure of health or power; negro dance (brǎk′down).

break′er[1] (-āk-), n. In vbl senses (esp. in comb. as horse-∼); also, heavy ocean-wave breaking on coast or over reefs. [-ER[1]]

break′er[2] (-āk-), n. (naut.). Small keg. [f. Sp. *barrica* cask]

break′fast (brěk-), n., & v.i. & t. (Take, entertain at) first meal of day. Hence ∼LESS a. [BREAK[1] interrupt +FAST n.]

break′-neck (-ākn-), a. Dangerous (∼ *pace, road, climb*).

break′-up, n. Disintegration, decay, collapse, dispersal. [f. phr. *to break up*]

break′water (-ākwaw-), n. Object breaking, mole etc. built to break, force of waves.

bream[1], n. Yellowish arch-backed fresh-water fish: (also *sea-*∼) a salt-water variety of this. [ME *breme* f. F *brême* OF *bresme* f. Teut. (WG *brahsm-, brehsm-*, perh. f. st. of *brehvan* glitter)]

bream[2], v.t. Clear (ship's bottom) by singeing with burning furze etc. [perh. f. Du. *brem* BROOM, furze]

breast[1] (-ěst), n. Either milk-secreting organ in woman, corresponding rudiment in man, (sometimes of beast's dug); (fig.) source of nourishment; upper front of human body or of coat, dress, etc.; corresponding part of animals; heart, emotions, thoughts, (*make clean ∼ of, confess*); ∼*bone*, thin flat vertical bone in chest connecting ribs; ∼*drill, -hoe, etc., pushed with* ∼; ∼*harness*, with ∼ band instead of collar; ∼*high*, high as the ∼, (of submerged) to the ∼, (of scent) so strong that hounds race with heads up; ∼*pin*, jewelled etc., worn in tie; ∼*plate*, piece of armour covering ∼, lower shell of turtle, tortoise, etc., inscription-plate on coffin; ∼*wall*, confining a bank of earth; ∼*wheel*, water-wheel with water admitted near axle; ∼*work*, temporary defence or parapet a few feet high. Hence ∼ED[2] a. [OE *brēost* f. OTeut. *breustom* cf. G *brust*; perh. related to OSax. *brustian* to bud]

breast[2] (-ěst), v.t. Oppose the breast to, face, contend with, (waves, hill). [f. prec.]

breast′summer (-ěst-), **brěss′ummer**, n. Beam across broad opening, sustaining superstructure. [BREAST[1] + *summer* beam f. F *sommier* f. L *sagmarius* (*sagma* packsaddle)]

breath (-ěth), n. Exhalation as perceptible to sight or smell; slight movement of air; whiff of perfume etc.: air taken into and expelled from lungs (*draw* ∼, breathe, live; *a* ∼ *of fresh air; spend, waste,* ∼, talk vainly; *keep* ∼ *to cool porridge,* abstain from talk; ∼ *of life, nostrils,* a necessity; *take away person's* ∼, render him breathless with astonish-

ment); respiration (*catch, hold,* one's ∼, in fear or absorbing emotion); one respiration (*say inconsistent things in one or the same* ∼); power of breathing (*out of* ∼, not able to breathe quick enough; *take* ∼, pause, rest); whisper, murmur, (*not a* ∼ *heard; also below* one's ∼, in a whisper). [OE *brǣth* smell of burning f. OTeut. *brǣthoz* f. Aryan *bhrēto-* (*bhre-*burn)]

breathe (-ēdh), v.i. & t. Use the lungs; live; seem alive; take breath, pause, (∼ *again, freely,* recover from fear etc., be at ease); sound, speak, (of wind) blow softly (∼ *upon,* tarnish, taint); send out (*new life into; fragrance; ∼* one's *last breath or last,* die); take in (∼ *foul, wholesome, air*); utter softly, also passionately (∼ *strife*), exhibit (∼ *simplicity*); allow to ∼, give rest to; force to ∼, exercise, tire. [ME *brethen* f. prec.]

breath′er (-ēdh-), n. In vbl senses; esp., short spell of exercise; brief pause for rest. [-ER[1]]

breath′ing[1] (-ēdh-), n. In vbl senses; esp.; (Gk Gram.) *rough, smooth,* ∼, signs (‘), (’), indicating that initial vowel is or is not aspirated; ∼*space,* time to breathe, pause. [-ING[1]]

breath′ing[2] (-ēdh-), a. In vbl senses; esp., lifelike (*statue* etc.). [-ING[2]]

breath′less (-ěth-), a. Lifeless; panting; holding the breath; unstirred by wind. [-LESS]

breath′lessly (-ěth-), adv. Pantingly; in suspense. [-LY[2]]

breath′ly (-ěth-), a. (Of singing-voice) not clear-cut at beginning of sound, using breath before vocal chords are tense. Hence ∼INESS n. [-Y[3]]

brěc′cia (-cha), n. Rock of angular stones etc. cemented by lime etc. [It. ∼ gravel or rubbish of broken walls cf. F *brèche* f. Teut.=BREAK]

bred. See BREED[1].

breech, n., & v.t. 1. pl. ∼*es* (-ĭch′ĭz) or *pair of* ∼*es,* short trousers fastened below knee (*Breeches Bible,* Geneva Bible of 1560 with ∼*es* for *aprons* in Gen. iii. 7) and (now) used only for riding or in court costume etc. (cf. KNICKERBOCKERS); (loosely) trousers or knickerbockers; *wear the* ∼*es,* of wife ruling her husband; (sing., arch.) posterior. 2. (Gunnery) part of cannon behind bore, back part of rifle or gun barrel; ∼*block,* closing ∼ aperture in guns; ∼*loader, -loading,* (gun) loaded at breech, not through muzzle; ∼*es-buoy,* lifebuoy with canvas ∼*es* for user's legs. 3. v.t. (arch.). Put (boy) into ∼*es* instead of petticoats. Hence ∼ED[2] a., (-ĭcht) wearing ∼*es,* (-ěcht) having a ∼. [OE *brēc* pl., f. OTeut. *brōks* loin & thigh garment; *breeches* a double pl., *breech* being a pl. like *feet*]

breech′ing (-ĭch-), n. Leather strap round shaft-horse's hind-quarters for

pushing back; (Naut.) rope securing gun to ship's side. [f. prec.+-ING¹]

breech'less (-ich-), a. Without breeches. [-LESS]

breed, v.t. & i. (bred). Bear, generate, (offspring); cherish in womb or egg; propagate; be pregnant; yield, produce, result in; make propagate, raise, (cattle); train up; fit for being, adapt to, (~ *him a lawyer, to the law*); bring up; arise, spread; ~ *in & in*, always marry near relations; *what is bred in the bone*, hereditary traits. Hence ~ER¹ n. [OE *brēdan* cf. G *brüten* see BROOD]

breed, n. Race, stock, strain; family with hereditary qualities. [f. prec.]

breed'ing, n. In vbl senses; esp. result of training, behaviour, good manners. [-ING¹]

breeze¹, n. Gad-fly. [OE *briosa*, dub.]

breeze², n. Gentle wind; wind off land, or sea, at certain hours; (sl.) quarrel, display of temper. Hence ~'LESS (-zl-) a. [earlier *brize* f. OSp. *briza* NE wind perh. = F *bise, bise,* N wind; F *brise* is later]

breeze³, n. Small cinders used with cement in making ~ *blocks* (light-weight concrete building blocks). [perh. f. F BRAISE, cf. BRAZIER²]

breez'y, a. Wind-swept; pleasantly windy; fresh, lively, jovial. Hence ~'ILY² adv., ~'INESS n. [-Y²]

Bre'hon, n. & a. Ancient Irish judge; ~ *law*, Irish code abolished under James I. [f. OIr. *brithem* judge]

brent(-goose), brant², n. Smallest species of wild goose, visiting Britain in winter. [etym. dub.; cf. G *brandgans*]

bren, n. (U.S. negro dial. contraction for) brother (esp. in beast-fable personifications, as *B~, Fox, Rabbit*).

bress'ummer. See BREASTSUMMER.

breth'ren (-edh'rin). See BROTHER.

Bret'on, a. & n. (Native of) Brittany in France. [F. = BRITON]

Brétwal'da (-ôl-), n. Lord of the Britons, title given to Egbert & Old Eng. Kings of various States who held nominal or real supremacy over the rest.

brève, n. (Hist.) authoritative letter from sovereign or pope; (Mus.) note = two semibreves now rarely used; short prosody mark (‿) in printing. [var. of BRIEF¹]

brève't, n. & v.t. Document conferring a privilege from sovereign or government, esp. rank without corresponding pay in army (~ *rank*, ~ *major*); honorary, nominal, position; (vb) confer ~ rank on. [F. = note, dim. of *bref* BRIEF¹]

brēv'i-, comb. form in scientific terms of L *brevis* short, as *brevirostrāte* short-beaked.

brēv'iary, n. (R.-C. Ch.) book containing the Divine Office for each day, to be recited by those in orders. [f. L *brevi-ārium* summary (*brevis* short, -ARY²)]

brēv'ier, n. Printing-type size between bourgeois & minion. [used in *breviaries*]

brēv'ity, n. Shortness of expression, conciseness; short span (*of life*). [f. AF *brevete* f. L *brevitātem* (*brevis* short, -TY)]

brew¹ (-ōō), v.t. & i. Make (beer etc.) by infusion, boiling, & fermentation (*drink as you have ~ed*, take consequences); make (tea, punch) by infusion or mixture; undergo these processes; concoct, bring about, set in train, grow to ripeness, fester, gather force, (usu. of evil results; *mischief is ~ing*, ~ *rebellion*); ~*house*, ~'ER¹, ~'ERY(3), (-ōō-), nn. [OE *brēowan*, com.-Teut., cf. G *brauen*; perh. also L *defrūtum* new wine boiled down]

brew² (-ōō), n. Process of brewing; amount brewed at once; quality of stuff brewed. [f. prec.]

brew'age (-ōō-), n. Concocted drink; process or result of concoction (lit. & fig.).

brew'is (-ōō-), n. Broth (arch. & dial.). [ME *brewes* f. OF *brouetz* nom. of *brouet* dim. of *bro* f. OHG *brod* BROTH]

Brew'ster Séssions (-ōō-), n. Sessions for issue of licences to trade in alcoholic liquors. [f. obs. *brewster* (orig. female) brewer, see -STER]

briar. See BRIER.

Briar'eus, n. Many-handed person. [Gk mythol.]

bribe, n. Money etc. offered to procure (often illegal or dishonest) action in favour of the giver. [perh. f. OF *bribe* piece of bread given to beggar, etym. dub.]

bribe², v.t. Pervert by gifts or other inducements the action or judgement of; (abs.) practise bribery. Hence ~'ER¹, ~'EE', ~aBIL'ITY, nn., ~'ABLE a. [f. prec.]

bric-à-brac, n. Curiosities, old furniture, china, fans, etc. [F, perh. = *de bric et de broc* by hook or by crook]

brick, n. & a. 1. Clay kneaded, moulded, & baked by fire or sun; block (usu. rectangular & about 9 in. × 4⅝ × 2⅝) of this (*like a hundred of ~s* colloq., with crushing weight or force); ~-shaped loaf, block of tea, etc.; child's wooden toy building-block; (sl.) generous or kind person; *drop a ~* (sl.), commit an indiscretion; ~-*dust*, piece of ~, esp. as missile [BAT¹]; ~-*field, -kiln*, in which ~s are made, baked; ~-*layer*, workman building in

~work, building in ~; hence (rare) ~ER³ a. 2. adj, Built of ~; (prob. f.F brique broken piece f. Teut. brek-BREAK] [f. prec.]

brick', v.t. ~ up, block (window etc.) with brickwork (& used with other adv.). [f. prec.]

brick'y, a. Littered with, coloured or looking like bricks. [-Y²]

bric'ole (-ikl), n. Stroke off wall or cushion in tennis & billiards. [F, etym. dub.]

brid'al, n. & a. **1.** Wedding-feast, wedding. **2.** adj. Of bride or wedding (~cheer, veil); hence ~LY² adv. [=bride ALE or festivity; OE brȳd-ealo; the prevailing adj. use results f. confusion with -AL]

bride², n. Delicate network connecting the patterns in lace; bonnet-string. [F, = BRIDLE¹, f. Teut.]

bride'groom (-dg-), n. Man at or soon before or after his marriage. [OE had brȳdguma (guma man cf. L homo) common. Teut.: guma becoming obs. in ME, perh. groom was substituted by mistake; but as there is more than a century's gap between instances of the old & new form, the latter may be independent=bride lad (bride in 15th & 16th cc. being of either sex)]

brides'maid (-dz-), n. Unmarried woman (usu. one of several) attending bride at wedding. [earlier bridemaid, altered when the attrib, sense of bride was missed]

brides'man (-dz-), n. Bridegroom's attendant, best man. [earlier brideman, cf. prec.]

‖ **bride'well** (-dw-), n. House of correction, gaol. [St Bride's Well, near the London ~]

bridge¹, n. (northern form, in writers for local colour, brig). Structure carrying road or path across stream, ravine, road, etc. (~ of boats, over boats moored abreast; ~ of gold, golden ~, easy retreat provided for beaten enemy); (in command; upper bony part of nose; movable piece over which strings of violin etc. are stretched; (Billiards) support for cue formed with left hand; ~head, post held on far side of frontier river giving one access to enemy's territory; ~train, Mil. Engineers with material for building floating ~s. Hence ~LESS (-jl-) a. [OE brycg; com.-Teut. cf. G brücke]

bridge², v.t. Span as, with, or as with, a bridge. [OE brycgian see prec.]

bridge³, n. Card-game of Russian origin resembling whist, in which a player looks on while his exposed hand is played by his partner; AUCTION ~; CONTRACT¹ ~. [?]

bri'dle, n. Head-gear of harness, including head-stall, bit, & rein (give horse the ~, lay ~ on his neck, abandon control; horse going well up to ~, willing goer); restraint, curb; (Naut.) mooring-cable; (Physiol.) ligament checking motion of a part; ~bridge, ~path, ~road, etc., fit for riders but not for vehicles. [OE bridel f. bregdan twitch see BRAID² + -LE (1)]

bri'dle, v.t. & i. Put bridle on (horse etc.); curb, hold in, bring under control; express offence, vanity, etc., by throwing up head & drawing in chin (often ~ up). [OE bridlian see prec.]

bridoon', n. Snaffle & rein of military bridle. [f. F bridon (BRIDE², -OON]

Brie (brē), n. A cream cheese. [~, in France]

brief¹, n. Pope's letter on matter of discipline to person or community (less formal than bull); ‖(Law) summary of facts & law-points of a case drawn up for counsel (hold ~ for, be retained as counsel for, argue in favour of); size of writing-paper, typewriter, etc.; (R.A.F.) instructions given to air crews; watching~, of barrister who watches case for client indirectly concerned; ‖ ~-bag, small leather hand-bag; ‖ a ~-piece of employment for barrister, whence ~'LESS a. [ME & OF bref f. L breve dispatch, note, neut. of brevis short]

brief², v.t. (Law) reduce (facts etc.) to a brief; instruct (barrister) by brief, employ; instruct (air crews) with regard to raid etc. (~ing-room, where such instructions are given). [f. prec.]

brief³, a. & n. Of short duration; concise; be ~, speak shortly; in ~, in short. Hence ~'LY² adv., ~'NESS n. [ME & OF bref f. L brevis short]

bri'er¹, bri'ar, n. (also brere arch.). Prickly bush, esp. of wild rose; Sweet B~, wild rose with fragrant leaves & flowers; B~-rose, Dog-rose. Hence ~Y² a. [OE brēr, brǣr, etym. dub.: cf. frere, FRIAR]

bri'er², bri'ar, n. The White Heath, of which the root is used for tobacco pipes. [at first (the material was introduced only c. 1859) bruyer f. F bruyère heath]

brig¹, n. Two-masted square-rigged vessel, but with additional lower fore-& aft sail on gaff & boom to mainmast. [abbr. of BRIGANTINE, f. which the type of ship was developed]

brig², See BRIDGE¹.

brigade¹, n. **1.** Subdivision of army, varying in different countries & times; infantry unit consisting usu. of 3 battalions (with freq. a regiment of field artillery) & forming part of a division; corresponding armoured unit; ‖ the B~ (of Guards). **2.** Organized or uniformed band of workers (Boys', Church, etc., B~, organizations on military model for disciplining & occupying boys etc.). [F,

f. It. *brigata* company (*brigare* brawl f. LL *briga* strife); see -ADE]

brigade'², n., v.t. Form into brigade or brigades; join (regiment etc.), with others into a brigade. [f. prec.]

brigadier', n. (Formerly *Brigadier-General*) officer commanding a brigade; (titular rank granted to) staff officer of similar standing. [MF.]

brig'and, n. Bandit, robber. Hence or cogn. ~AGE(3), ~ISM(2), nn., ~ISH¹ a. [ME. f. OF., prob. f. It. *brigante* (*brigare*)]

brig'antine (-ēn), n. Two-masted vessel with square-sailed fore-mast & fore-&-aft mainmast. [f. F *brigantin* (*brigant* see BRIGADE¹)]

bright'¹ (-īt), a. Emitting or reflecting much light, shining; lit up with joy, hope, etc.; vivid (~ *red* etc.); illustrious, vivacious, quick-witted, (often iron.). Hence ~'EN⁵ v.t. & i., ~'ISH¹ (2) a., ~'LY² adv. ~'NESS n., (-it-). [OE *beorht*]

bright'² (-īt), adv. = brightly (*shine* ~, ~ *beaming*, etc.). [OE *beorhte* with adv. -e now lost; see prec.]

Bright's disease (-īts: -zēz), n. Granular degeneration of the kidneys. [Dr R. Bright, 1827]

brill, n. Flat-fish resembling turbot. [?]

brill'iant¹ (-lya-), a. Bright, sparkling; illustrious, striking; talented, showy. Hence ~ANCE, ~ANCY, nn., ~antly² adv., (-lya-). [f. F *brillant* part. of *briller* shine referred to LL *berillare* (BERYL)]

brill'iant² (-lya-), n. Diamond of finest cut & brilliance (~ *shape* has two horizontal tables, joined by facets); a size of TYPE. [f. F as prec. used as n.]

brill'iantine (-lyantēn), n. Cosmetic for hair. [f. F *brillantine* see BRILLIANT¹ +-INE¹]

brim¹, n. Edge or lip of cup, bowl, or hollow; projecting edge of hat; ~-*full*, to the ~. Hence ~'LESS, ~'MED (-md), aa. [ME *brimme* etym. dub.; cf. G *brime*]

brim², v.t. & i. (-mm-). Fill, be full, to the brim (lit. & fig.; ~ *over*, overflow). [f. prec.]

brim'mer, n. Full cup. [BRIM²+-ER¹]

brim'stone, n. (|| ~& *treacle*, nursery medicine); fuel of hell-fire; ~ *butterfly, moth*, sulphur-coloured species. Hence **brim'stony²** a. [ME (*bernen, brimnen*, BURN²+STONE)]

brin'ded (-did), **brin'dle**, a. Brownish or tawny with streaks of other colour. [earlier *brinded* (perh. p.p. of a possible vb *brenden* f. BRAND¹ burning) has been ousted by *brindled* (perh. with dim. sense); f. which *brindle* is perh. a mistaken back-formation]

brine, n. Salt water; the sea; tears (poet.); ~-*pan*, iron vessel or shallow pit for getting salt by evaporation. Hence

brin'y² a. (the *briny*, sl., the sea). [OE *bryne* etym. dub.; cf. Du. *brijn*]

brine, v.t. Steep or pickle in, or wet with, brine. [f. prec.]

bring, v.t. & i. (brought, pr. -awt). 1. Cause to come, come with or conveying or attracting, (whether by carrying, leading, impelling, or sponding notions with *go* for *come*); cause, result in; prefer (charge), adduce (argument); ~ *home to*, cause to realize, convict or convince of; ~ *into play*, cause to operate; ~ *into world*, give birth to; cause to become (~ *low*); ~ *to bear*, apply (influence etc.); ~ *to mind*, recall; ~ *to pass*, cause to happen; persuade (*cannot ~ myself to believe*). 2. ~ *about*, cause to happen, reverse (ship); ~ *back*, call to mind; ~ *down*, kill or wound, cause penalty to alight on, abase, lower (price), continue (record) to a point, (Theatr.) ~ *down the house*, elicit tumultuous applause; ~ *forth*, give birth to, cause; ~ *forward*, carry sum of page's figures to next page; ~ *in*, introduce (custom), produce as profit, adduce, pronounce (*guilty, not g.*); ~ *off*, rescue from wreck etc., conduct (enterprise) to success; ~ *on*, lead to, cause discussion of; ~ *out*, express, exhibit clearly, introduce (girl) to society, publish; ~ *over*, convert; ~ *round*, restore to consciousness; ~ *through*, save (sick person); ~ *to*, check motion of, come to a stop, restore to consciousness; ~ *under*, subdue; ~ *up*, educate, rear, sue in court, anchor (ship), come to a stop, call attention again to, cause (M.P.) to rise & speak, continue (accounts etc.) to a further point; ~ *up the rear*, come last. [com.-Teut. cf. G *bringen*]

brink, n. Edge of steep place or abyss (*on ~ of grave*, soon to die); border of water, esp. when steep (*shiver on the ~*, hesitate to plunge); verge (*of discovery, ruin, eternity*, etc.). [ME. prob. f. Scand., cf. Da. *brink* precipice]

brio (-ēō), n. Vivacity. [It.]

briquette' (-kĕt), **bri'quet** (-kĕt), n. Block of compressed coal-dust. [F (-ette), dim. of *brique* BRICK]

brise-bise (brēz' bēz), n. Curtain stretched across lower part of window. [F]

brisk, a. Active, lively, (usu. of movement; ~ *pace, trade, wind*, etc.); enlivening, keen, (champagne, air, etc.). Hence ~'LY² adv., ~'NESS n. [f. 16th c., perh. f. W *brisg* quick-footed or F. perh. *brittle*, or perh. = F BRUSQUE]

brisk, v.t. & i. Make or become brisk (usu. with *up*). [f. prec.]

brisk'et, n. Breast of animals (esp. as joint of meat). [etym. dub.; there is F *brechet* in same sense]

bris'tle (-isl), n. One of stiff short hairs on hog's back & sides; short stiff hair of other

animals, man's short-cropped beard, or plants; *set up* one's, another's, ~s, show or rouse temper. Hence **bri'stly²** (-isl), a. [ME *bristel* f. OE *byrst* & see -LE(1); f. OTeut. *bors-*]

bri'stle² (-isl), v.i. & t. (Cause to) stand upright (hair etc.), raise or rise like bristles or into roughness, (often with *up*); show temper, prepare for fight; be thickly set *with* hair, difficulties, etc. [f. prec.]

bris'(t)ling, n. A small sardine-like fish. [?]

Bris'tol, n. (attrib.) ~ *board*, kind of cardboard for drawing on; (*ship*s*hape &*) ~ *fashion* (Naut., & transf.), with all in good order; ~ *milk* P, kind of sherry.

Brit'ain (-tn), n. (Also *Great~*) England, Wales, & Scotland, the British Empire; *North* ~, Scotland; *Greater* ~ (descriptive, not official), Gt ~ & the dominions & colonies. [ME *Bretayne* f. OF *Bretaigne* f. L *Brittannia* or *Brittania* (L *Britannia* would have produced F *Bri-, Breaigne*]

Britānnia (-yǎ), n. Personification of Britain; ~ *metal*, alloy of tin & regulus of antimony resembling silver. [L *Britannia*, *Brittannia*, *Brittania*, = Gk *Brettanía* f. *Brittanī* or *Brittanī*, = Gk *Brettanoí*]

Britānnic. a. Of Britain (chiefly in phr. *Her* or *His~Majesty*). [prob. f. F *britan-nique* f. L *Britannicus*]

Brit'icism, n. = BRITISHISM. [U.S. wd, non-existent *Britic*+-ISM(4)]

Brit'ish, a. Of the ancient Britons; of Great Britain or its inhabitants (esp. in political or imperial connexion, & in botany etc.); *the* ~, soldiers, people, etc.; ~ *Academy*, chartered body of 200 for promotion of moral & political sciences; ~ *Association* (for advancement of science); ~ *Expeditionary Force* (abbr. B.E.F.), army of Great Britain or the British Empire (poet., melodramatic, etc.); *North* ~, Scotsman. [ME & F *breton* f. L *Brittomern* nom. *Britto*, f. the native name, which displaced *Brittannī* after the Roman conquest]

brit'tle, a. Apt to break, fragile. Hence ~NESS (-tn-) n. [ME *britul* cf. OE *bréotan* break]

riage with calash top & space for reclining. [f. Pol. *bryczka* dim. of *bryka* wagon]

brize (-ëz). = BREEZE².

broach¹, n. Roasting-spit; church spire rising from tower without parapet. boring-bit. [ME & F *broche*=It. *brocca* cf. L *brocci dentes* projecting teeth; var. of BROOCH]

broach², v.t. Pierce (cask) to draw liquor, begin drawing (liquor); open & start using (bale, box, cargo, etc.); begin discussion of, moot, (subject). [f. prec.]

broach³, v.t. & i. (Usu. ~ *to*) veer or cause (ship) to veer & present side to wind & waves. [perh. f. obs. use of prec. = turn on the spit]

broad (-awd), a., n., & adv. **1.** Large across, wide, not narrow; = in breadth (*6 ft.*); extensive (~ *lands*); full, clear, main, explicit, (~ *daylight, facts, distinction, hint*); coarse (~ *story*); downright in sound, not mincing, (~ *Yorkshire, Scotch*); generalized (~ *rule*); tolerant (B~ *Church, churchmen* favouring comprehension & not pressing doctrines); bold in effect or style; *as* ~ *as it is long*, indifferent; || ARROW; ~ *bean*, the common flattened variety; ||~*cloth*, fine plain-wove double-width dressed black cloth [phr. in Act of Parl. 1482 kept as name for quality rather than width]; ~ GAUGE; ~-*glass*, window-glass (~*mind'ed(ness*), (the condition of) being tolerant in thought or opinion; ~*sheet*, large sheet of paper printed on one side only; ~*side*, ship's side above water between bow & quarter (~*side on, to*, with this presented), (discharge of) all guns on one side of ship, also = ~*sheet*; ~*silk*, ~*weaver*, (of) silk in piece not in ribbons; ~*sword*, ~ bladed cutting-sword. **2.** n. The ~ part (~ *of the back*); || (E. Anglia) large piece of fresh water formed by widening of river. **3.** adv. = -ly (*speak*, ~*awake*) ~*blown*, in full bloom. Hence ~EN² v.t. & i., ~*ly², *WAYS*, ~*WISE*, adv. [OE *brād*, com.-Teut. cf. G *breit*]

broad'cast (-awrdäch-), a., adv., v.t. & i. (past -*casted*, p.p. -*cast*), & n. (Of seed) scattered freely, not in drills or rows, (adv.) in this manner, (v.i. & t.) sow thus, (all also fig. of information, propaganda, etc.); (Wireless, v.t.) disseminate (news, music, any audible matter) by wireless telephony to owners of receiving-sets, (v.i.) speak, sing, play, etc., for such transmission (n., esp. attrib.) the practice etc. of ~*ing* (*to-day's* ~ *programme*). [f. prec.+*cast* p.p.]

Broad'moor (braw-), n. Asylum in Berkshire for criminal lunatics.

broad'ness (-aw-), n. (Superseded by *breadth*, exc. in sense) indelicacy (of speech). [-NESS]

Bröb'dingnag, n. Land of giants. Hence ~IAN (-äg⁴) a. [Swift, *Gulliver's Travels*]

brocāde'¹, n. Fabric woven with raised

brocade patterns; Indian cloth of gold & silver. Hence ~d(4) a. [f. Sp. & Port. *brocado* = It. *broccato* cf. BROACH[1] & see -ADE]

bróc'(c)oli, n. Cultivated cabbage with edible flower head, hardy variety of cauliflower. [It., pl. of *broccolo* cabbage-top dim. of *brocco* see BROACH[1]]

brö'ché (-shā), a. & n. (Of fabrics, esp. silk) embossed, woven with a pattern on the surface; (n.) such fabric. [F, p.p. of *brocher* stitch]

brö'chure (-shoor), n. Stitched booklet, pamphlet. [F]

brŏck, n. Badger; stinking fellow. [OE *broc* f. Celt. cf. Ir. & Gael. *broc*]

brŏck'ĕt, n. Second-year stag with straight horns. [f. F *brocart* (*broche* see BROACH[1]+-ARD]

broderie Anglaise (brōd'ri ahngglāz'), n. Open embroidery on white linen or cambric. [F, = English embroidery]

brogue[1] (-ōg), n. Rude Irish & Scotch-Highland shoe of untanned leather; *fishing-~s*, waterproof leggings with feet; nailed & goloshed shoe for golf etc. [f. Gael. & Ir. *brog* f. OIr. *broce* whence L *brucca* see BREECH]

brogue[2] (-ōg), n. Dialectal, esp. Irish, accent. [perh. f S. Gael. *barrog*, applied to cramped pronunciation.]

broid'er, v.t. **broid'ery**, n. (Poet. & arch. for) EMBROIDER(Y).

broil[1], n. Quarrel, tumult. [f. obs. vb *broil* mix, quarrel, f. F *brouiller* cf. It. *broglio* n. hurly-burly, & *brogliare* v., etym. dub.]

broil[2], v.t. & i. Cook (meat) or be cooked on fire or gridiron; make, be, very hot (of person in sun etc.). [etym. dub.; the assim. to F *brûler* burn]

broil[3], n. Broiled meat. [f. prec.]

broke[1], n. Short-stapled wool on certain parts of fleece. [OE *broc* f. *breccan* BREAK]

broke[2], p.p. of BREAK, still often used in some spec. senses, as = *ruined* (esp., sl., *stony~*), & *dismissed the service*.

brŏk'en, a. In vbl senses of BREAK[1]; also or esp. ~ *meat* etc., remains; ~ *tea*, sittings; ~ *water*, choppy; ~ *ground*, uneven; ~ *sleep*, intermittent; ~ *weather*, uncertain; ~ *English*, imperfect; ~ *numbers*, fractions; ~ *money*, small change; ~-*hearted*, crushed by grief; ~ *man*, reduced to despair; ~ REED; ~ *time*, (esp. working) time which has been reduced by interruptions; ~-*winded*, (of horse) incapacitated for hard work by ruptured air-cells. [p.p. of BREAK]

brŏk'enly, adv. Spasmodically, by jerks, with breaks. [prec.+-LY[2]]

brōk'er, n. || Dealer in second-hand furniture etc.; middleman in bargains; agent, commissioner; || person licensed to sell or appraise distrained goods. Hence ~AGE(4) n. [ME & AF *brocour* f. L +*broccatorem* nom. -*or* (see -OR[2]) broacher (BROACH) of cask, retailer of wine]

brök'ing, n. Broker's trade, acting as broker. [f. prec.]

brŏll'y, n. (sl.) Umbrella. [abbr.]

brō'mal, n. Compound produced by action of bromine on alcohol. [BROM(INE)

brŏm'ĭc, a. Containing bromine in chem. combination. Hence **brŏm'ATE(3)** n. [BROMINE, -IC]

brō'mīde, n. Compound (see -IDE) of bromine, esp. ~ *of potassium* (a common-place bore, trite remark, conventionalism. (orig. U.S., sl.); ~ *paper*, photographic printing & enlarging paper coated with silver.~ *emulsion*. [foll.+-IDE]

brō'mīne, n. Non-metallic element resembling chlorine (poisonous dark liquid with rank smell) used in various preparations as sedative. Hence **brōm'ISM(3)** n. [f. F *brome* f. Gk *brōmos* stink +-INE[5]]

brō'mo-, brŏm'-, comb. forms of bromine as in *bromobenzoic, bromacetic*, [-o-]

brŏn'chia, brŏn'chia, (-nĕk-), n. pl. ramifications of these in lungs. Hence **brŏn'chiAL** a., **bronchi...**

bronch'itis (-ngk-), n. Inflammation of bronchial mucous membrane. Hence **bronch'it'IC...**

brŏn'chocele (-ngksōsēl), n. Swelling of thyroid gland, goitre. [f. Gk *bronchokēlē*]

brŏn'cho-, brŏn'cho-, comb. forms, **bronchŏt'OMIST, -ŏt'OMY**, nn. [L, f. Gk *bronchos*]

brŏn'co (-ngk-), n. (pl. -os). Wild or half-tamed horse of California etc.; ~-*buster* (sl.), breaker in of ~s. [Sp., = rough]

Brontosaur'us, n. Genus of huge prehistoric dinosaurian reptiles of the Jurassic & Cretaceous periods. [f. Gk *brontē* thunder+*sauros* lizard]

bronze[1], n. & a. 1. Brown alloy chiefly of copper & tin (about 8:1; *the ~ age*, in which weapons and tools were made of ~); work of art made of this; colour of ~; hence **brŏnz'Y[2]** a. 2. adj. Made of, coloured like, ~. [f. F. It. *bronzo, bronzino*, f. L (*aes*) *Brundusinum* (brass) of Brundusium]

bronze[2], v.t.&i. Give bronze-like surface to; make or become brown, tan. [f. prec.]

brooch (-ō-), n. Ornamental, jewelled, etc., safety-pin for fastening some part of female dress, esp. the neck. [ME *broche* var. of BROACH[1]]

brood, n. Hatch of young birds or other eggs-produced animals; (usu. contempt.) human family, children; swarm, crew, of men, animals, or things; ~, for breeding (~-*mare, -hen*). [OE *brōd* cf. G *brut* f. Teut. vb root *bro-* warm]

brood³, v.i. Sit as hen on eggs; hang close *over* or *on* (of night etc.); meditate *on* or *over* (esp. insults, ill designs, etc.); meditate (often sullenly). [f. prec.]

brood⁴[ў, a. Wishing to sit or incubate (of hen). Hence ~INESS n. (BROOD¹+-Y²]

brook¹, n. Small stream; ~*time*, kind of Speedwell common in ditches [OE *hleomoc* name of the plant]. Hence ~LET n. [OE *broc* cf. G *bruch* moor, marsh; etym. dub.]

brook², v.t. Put up with, tolerate (in neg. context). [OE *brúcan*; com.-Teut., cf. G *brauchen* use, f. OTeut. *bruk-* use cf. L *frui fruct-*]

broom, n., & v.t. Yellow-flowered shrub growing on sandy banks etc.; genus to which it belongs; sweeping-implement usu. on long handle (vb. sweep with this); *new* ~, newly appointed official eager to sweep away abuses; ~*rape*, genus of parasitic herbs on roots of broom etc. (brown, leafless, fleshy-stemmed bracteate) [med. L *rapum* root-knob]; ~*stick*, handle of ~ (ridden on through the air by witches, & jumped over by parties to sham marriage). [OE *bróm* f. OTeut. *brēmoz* thorny shrub whence BRAMBLE]

brose (-z), n. Dish of oatmeal with boiling water or milk poured on it; *Athole* ~, mixture of whisky & honey. [=BREWIS]

broth (-ŏ-, -aw-), n. Water in which something, esp. meat, has been boiled, thin soup; (Irish) ~ *of a boy*, good fellow. [com.-Teut. f. vb root *brū-* boil, BREW, +-TH¹]

brothel, n. House of ill fame, bawdy-house. [orig.=ruined man f. OE *brothen* p.p. of *brēothan* go to ruin, foul connexion with *bordel* cabin, hut, f. OF f. It. *bordello* (med. L *borda* f. Teut. *bord* BOARD].

brother (-ŭdh-), n. (pl. ~s & in some senses *breth'ren* pr. -ĕdhrĭn, see below). Son of same parents or (strictly *half*-~) parent as another person (the latter usu. specified by *my* etc. or a possessive case; pl. abbr. *Bros*, in title of firm, as *Smith Bros & Co.*); close friend; fellow citizen, countryman, or man, equal, (*a man & a* ~, esp. of negro slaves); fellow member of religious society (pl. *brethren*); fellow member of guild, order, profession, etc. (pl. *brethren*); official of certain companies etc. (*Elder B~, Brethren*, of Trinity House); companion, associate, (pl. ~s) often with specification as *in arms, of the angle*; member of religious order (as title: either pl.); vocative of sovereigns to each other; ~ *german*, on both sides, ~ *uterine*, of same mother only; ~-*in-law*, ~ of one's husband or wife, husband of one's sister. Hence ~LESS a., ~LIKE a. & adv., ~LY¹,² a. & adv., ~INESS n. [Aryan; OE *brōthor* cf. G *bruder*, Skr. *bhrātr*, Gk *phrātēr*, L *frater*, W *brawd*]

broth'erhood (-ŭdh-), n. Fraternal tie; companionship; (members of) association for mutual help etc.; community of feeling. [OE *brotherhede* ME *brotherhede -hode*; see -HEAD]

brougham (-ōŏm, -ōŏ'am), n. One-horse (or electric) closed carriage. [Lord B~]

brought. See BRING.

brow¹, n. Arch of hair over eye (usu. in pl.; *knit, bend*, one's ~s, frown); forehead (~*ague*, megrim); edge, projection, of cliff etc., top of hill in road. Hence ~ED²(-wd) a. [OE *brū* f. OTeut. *brūs* cf. Skr. *bhrus*, Gk *ophrus*]

brow², n. (naut.). Gangway, inclined plane of planks. [perh. f. Da. *bru* bridge]

brow'beat, v.t. Bully, bear down, with looks & words. [BROW¹]

brown¹, a. Of the colour given by mixing orange, & black or by toasting bread; as distinctive epithet of species etc. (~ *bear, willow*; ~ *coal*, lignite; ~ *bread*, coarse unbolted flour; ~ *paper*, coarse unbleached kind used for parcels etc.; ~ *shirt*, a Nazi; ~ *sugar*, half refined; ~ *ware*, common sort of pottery); dark-skinned, tanned; || (sl.) *do* ~, take in, cheat; *B~ Bess*, old army flintlock musket; ~ *study*, reverie. Hence ~ISH¹ (2) a., ~NESS (-nn-) n., ~ў- comb. form. [OE *brún*; com.-Teut. cf. G *braun* f. OTeut. *brūnoz*, Aryan *bhrūnos*, root *bhru-* cf. BEAVER; Rom. wds. as F *brun*, It. *bruno*, adopted f. the Teut.]

brown², n. Brown colour; brown pigment; (ellipt. for) brown butterfly, fishing-fly; clothes; || (sl.) copper coin; || *the* ~, brown mass of flying game-birds; || *fire into the* ~, let fly into a covey without singling out a bird (also transf., fire, launch missile, indiscriminately into a mass). [f. prec.]

brown³, v.t. & i. Make or become brown by roasting, sunburn, or (gun-barrel etc.) chemical process; ||~*ed off* (sl.), bored, fed up. [BROWN¹]

brown'ie, n. Benevolent shaggy goblin haunting house & doing household work secretly; junior member (ages 8-11) of GIRL guides; (Photog.) kind of camera. [BROWN¹+-Y³]

Brown'ing, n. Kind of automatic pistol. [~ surname]

*****brown'stone**, n. Kind of reddish-brown sandstone used for building (esp. in front elevation); ~ *district*, quarter occupied by the well-to-do. [BROWN¹]

browse¹ (-z), n. Twigs, young shoots, etc., as fodder for cattle; act of browsing. [foll.]

browse² (-z), v.i. & t. Feed *on*, crop, (leaves, twigs, scanty vegetation); (abs.) feed thus, (fig.) read for enjoyment. [f. 16th c. F *brouster* vb, *broust* n. (now *broust*), f. Teut., cf. OSax. *brustian* see BREAST]

Bru'in (-ōō-), n. (Personifying name for)

bear. [MDu. = BROWN[1], name in *Reynard the Fox*]

bruise[2] (-ōoz), v.t. & i. Injure by blow that discolours skin without breaking it or any bone, contuse, (human or animal body, also fruit, plant, etc.); dint, batter, (wood, metal); (fig.) disable; pound, bray, grind small; (Hunting) ride recklessly; (with *easily* etc.), show effects of blow. [OE *brȳsan* crush combined w. AF *bruser* (now *briser*) break perh. f. Teut.]

bruis'er (-ōoz-), n. In *vbl* senses; esp., prizefighter. [-ER[1]]

bruit[1] (-ōot), n. (arch.). Report, rumour. [F, = noise (*bruire* roar perh. f. L *rugire*)]

bruit[2] (-ōot), v.t. (arch.). Spread (report) abroad, *about*, make famous, celebrate. [f. prec.]

brumby, n. (Austral. colloq.). Unbroken horse. [?]

Brümm'agem, n. & a. (Dial. & con-tempt. form of) Birmingham; (article) made at ~, counterfeit, cheap & showy. [allusion to counterfeit groats made there in 17th c., & to its plated goods]

brum'ous (-ōo-), a. Wintry, foggy. [f. L *bruma* (= *brevima* shortest day f. *brevis*) +-ous]

brunch, n. (sl.). Single meal in lieu of breakfast & lunch. [portmanteau wd]

brunette' (-ōo-), n. & a. Dark-skinned & brown-haired (woman). [F, fem. of *brunet* dim. of *brun* BROWN[1] see -ETTE]

Bruns'wick (-z-), a. From ~ in Germany; esp., ~ *line*, ~ of Eng. sovereigns from George I; ~ *black*, a varnish. [f. G *Braunschweig*]

brunt, n. Chief stress (usu. *of the attack* etc., & in phr. *bear the* ~ *of*). [etym. dub.; there is ON *bruna* to advance like fire]

brush[1], n. 1. (Arch. & U.S., Austral., etc.) brushwood or underwood, thicket, small trees & shrubs growing or (in U.S.) cut in fagots. 2. Implement of bristles, hair, wire, etc., set in wood etc. for scrubbing or sweeping; bunch of hairs etc. in straight handle, quill, etc., for painting etc.; *the* ~, art of painting; ~, painter's style, painter (*from the same* ~). 3. Tail, esp. of fox; ~-like tuft. 4. (Electr.) ~-like discharge of sparks, piece of carbon or metal ending in wires or strips securing good metallic connexion, (also) movable strip of conductible material for making & breaking connexion. 5. (Optics) bright or dark figure with vague edge. 6. Application of ~, brushing, esp. ~ *up* [f. foll.]; short smart encounter, skirmish, graze, abrasion. [f. foll.]; artist's colour~; ~-*work*, undergrowth, thicket; ~-*work*, painter's (style of) manipulation. Hence ~'Y[2] a. [(sense of ~*wood*) ME *bruschke* f. OF *brosse*, *broce*,

bubble

151

(other senses) ME *brusshe* f. OF *brosse*, *broisse*; whether *broce* & *broisse* are identical in etym. & f. Teut. (cf. G *borste* bristle, *bürste* brush), is uncertain]

brush[2], v.t. & i. Move briskly, esp. *by*, *through*, *against*; sweep or scrub clean, put in order, with brush; ~ *up*, freshen, (fig.) renew one's memory of; ~ *over*, paint lightly; graze or touch in passing; remove (*dust* etc.) with brush; ~ *aside*, *away* (fig.), ignore, pass over; injure by grazing, [partly f. prec., perh. partly f. F *brosser* dash through underwood (*brosse* brush-wood)]

brusque (-ōosk, -ūsk), a. Blunt, offhand (of or in manner, speech). Hence ~'LY[2] (-k-) adv., ~'NESS (-kn-), ~'rie (-ōoskerē) n. [F, f. It. *brusco* sour, etym. dub.]

Brüss'els (-z), a. Made or grown at, or adopted from, ~; as ~ *carpet*, *lace*, *sprouts* (edible buds of kind of cabbage).

brut'al (-ōo-), a. (Of wines) unsweetened. [F]

brut'al (-ōo-), a. Sensual, rude, coarse, savagely cruel. Hence ~ISM(-z-) n., ITY, n., ~'LY[2] adv., (-ōo-). [f. L *brutus*]

brut'alize, v.t. & i. (-ōo-). Make (*rarely* grow) brutal. Hence ~A'TION n. [prec. + -IZE(3)]

brute (-ōot), a. & n. (Beast) not gifted with reason; stupid, sensual, unspirited, beast-like, cruel, or passionate (person; & in same adj. senses of acts, motives, etc.); unconscious, merely material, (~ *force*, *matter*) lower animal; lower nature in man. Hence ~e'HOOD (-t-h-) n., ~'ISH[1](i) a., ~'ISHLY[2] adv., ~'IFY v.t., ~'IFICA'TION n., (-ōo-). [f. F *brut* f. L *brutus* dull]

brut'um ful'men (-ōo-) n. Empty threat, blank cartridge (fig.). [L]

Brut'us(-ōo-), n. Style of wig (19th cent.). [F name in honour of Roman hero]

bry'ol'ogist, -l'ogy, nn. Person learned in, the lore of, mosses. [Gk *bruon* kind of seaweed +-LOGIST, -LOGY]

bry'ony, n. Genus of climbing plants; *Red* or *White B*~, common species; *Black B*~, *Bastard B*~, plants resembling but not belonging to the genus. [f. L f. Gk *bruōnia* (*bruō* swell)]

bub'al, n. A N.-African antelope. [f. L f. Gk *boubalos* ox-like antelope]

bub'ble[1], n. Spherical or hemispherical envelope of liquid enclosing air etc.; air-filled cavity in solidified liquid, as glass, amber; unsubstantial or visionary project, enterprise, etc. (also adj.; in this sense; *prick the* ~, unmask futility, pretension, etc.); sound or appearance of boiling; ~-*&-squeak*, cold meat fried with chopped vegetables. Hence **bub'-bly**[2] a.(also ||n. sl., champagne). [f. foll.]

bub'ble[2], v.i. & t. Send up, rise in, make the sound of, bubbles (lit., & fig. as ~ *over*, ~, *with* laughter, wrath); delude

(arch.). [prob. imit. of sound of bursting bubbles, or of the action of lips in making one; cf. BLEB, BLUBBER]

‖ **bub'bly-jock**, n. Turkey-cock. [bubbly (BUBBLE¹)+jock=Jack]

bub'ō, n. (pl. -oes). Inflamed swelling in glandular part, esp. groin or armpit. Hence ~ōn'ic a. [LL, f. Gk boubōn groin]

būbón'ocele (-sēl), n. Hernia of groin. [prec., -CELE]

buccaneer', n., & v.i. (Be a) sea-rover, pirate, esp. of the Spanish-American coasts; adventurer. Hence ~ISH¹(-nēr-) a. [f. F boucanier hunter of oxen (boucan BARBECUE-frame Brazilian wd)]

buc'cinātor (būks-), n. Flat thin cheek-muscle. [L (buccinare blow the trumpet f. buccina, -TOR)]

Būcĕph'alus, n. Riding-horse (facet.). [charger of Alexander of Macedon]

Buch'manism (bŏŏk-), n. Religious system, occas. called the Oxford Group (Movement) & (in U.S.) the Moral Rearmament Movement, introduced c.1921 by F. Buchman. So ~ITE¹ ³ a. & n. [-ISM]

buck¹, n. Male of fallow-deer, reindeer, chamois, antelope, hare, rabbit; dandy (also old ~, vocative=old fellow), whence ~ISH¹ a., ~ISHLY² adv.; (attrib., sl.) male, of or for males, (~ nigger, bunch, etc.); ~-horn, as material for knife handles etc., (also ~, as ~-handled); ~hound, small variety of staghound (not now used for hunting); ~-shot, coarse shot; ~skin, (leather made of) ~'s skin, (pl.) breeches of it; ~thorn, thorny shrub with cathartic berries; ~-tooth, one that projects. [OE buc & bucca, cf. G bock he-goat; F bouc, W bwch, are f. the Teut.]

buck², v.i. & t. (Of horse) jump vertically with back arched & feet drawn together (also ~-jump, whence ~'jumper¹ n.); ~ off, throw (rider) thus. Hence ~ER¹ n. [f. prec.]

buck³, v.i. & t. (sl.). (With up) make haste, become or make vigorous or cheerful; brag (about); ~ BUCK¹ in sense dandy]

‖ *buck⁴, n. (sl.). Basket for trapping eels. [?]

‖ **buck⁵**, n. Body of cart (chiefly in comb. as ~-board, ~-cart, in various local senses). [perh. f. obs. bouk belly cf. BULK n.]

buck⁶, n., & v.i. (orig. Anglo-Ind.). Conversation, boastful talk; (v.i.) chat, swagger, brag (about); ~ stick (sl.), braggart. [f. Hind. bakná talk freely]

buck'et¹, n. Wooden or other vessel for drawing or carrying water; piston for pump; compartment of water-wheel, scoop of dredging-machine or grain-elevator; socket for whip, carbine, wooden leg, etc.; kick the ~ (sl.), die (but perh. f. obs. bucket beam, yoke); ~-shop, (orig. U.S.) office for gambling in stocks, speculating on markets, etc. [accidental; story connected with elevator of office first so called]. Hence ~FUL(2) (-ŏŏl) n. [perh. f. OE buc pitcher, or f. OF buket tub]

buck'et², v.i. & t. Ride hard (horse, or abs.); ‖ (Rowing) hurry the forward swing, row hurried stroke. [f. prec., cf. pump = exhaust]

Buck'ingham Pal'ace, n. London residence of the Sovereign. [place]

buck'le¹, n. Metal rim with hinged spiked tongue for securing strap, ribbon, etc. [f. F boucle f. L buccula cheek-strap (bucca cheek, see -ULE)]

buck'le², v.t. & i. Fasten (with to prep.) (often up, on, etc.); ~ to (with to prep.) prepare for, set about, (with to adv.) get to work, start vigorously; (cause to) give way, crumple up, under longitudinal pressure (t. & i. of wheel, saw, etc.). [f. prec.; the last sense perh. f. F boucler bulge]

buck'ler, n., & v.t. Small round shield usu. held by handle; protection, protector, (vb, protect); also technically in various naut., zool., & anat. senses. [f. OF boucler (now bouclier) f. L buccularius f. buccula BUCKLE¹, -ER²(2)]

buck'ō, a. & n. (naut. sl.). Swaggering (fellow). [f. BUCK¹]

buck'ra, a. & n. (negro dial). Characteristic of, belonging to, the white man; (n.) white man, master. [etym. dub.; perh. f. Surinam negro patois bakra master]

buck'ram, n. & a. Coarse linen or cloth stiffened with gum or paste; stiffness, stiff, (of manner); strong, strength, in appearance only; men in ~, ~ men, non-existent (1 Hen. IV, II. iv. 210-50). [f. OF boquerant or It. bucherame etym. dub.]

‖ **buck'shee**, n., a., & adv. (sl., orig. army). 1. Something in addition to the usual allowance, as extra rations. 2 adj. & adv. Gratuitous(ly), free. [corrupt. of BAKSHEESH]

buck'wheat (-wēt), n. A cereal plant with seed used for horse & poultry food, & in U.S. for breakfast cakes. [=beech wheat, from its three-cornered seeds like beech-mast; either transl. of Du. boekweit or made on obs. buckmast= beechmast]

būcŏl'ic, a. & n. Of shepherds, pastoral, rustic; (usn. pl.) pastoral poems (the B~s, those of Virgil). Hence būcŏl'ICALLY adv. [f. L f. Gk boukolikos f. boukolos herdsman (bous cow, kol- cf. L colere tend)]

bud¹, n. Rudiment of branch, leaf-cluster, or flower; flower not fully open; (Zool.) animal forming by GEMMATION, anything still undeveloped; *nip in the ~*, destroy at early stage (fig.). Hence ~'LESS a. [ME *budde*, *bodde*, etym. dub.]

bud², v.i. & t. (-dd-). Put forth buds, spring forth; begin to grow or develop (*~ding horns*, *lawyer*, *cricketer*); (Zool.) be produced by GEMMATION; (Gardening) ingraft (trans. or abs.) into alien stock. [f. prec.]

budd'ed, p.p. In vbl senses; esp. that has budded, is in bud. [f. prec.]

Buddh|a (bood'a), n. The Enlightened, title of successive teachers past & future of the Asiatic religion ~ISM(3) (bood'i-) n., but applied esp. to Sakyamuni, Gautama, or Siddartha (5th c. B.C., in N. India). Hence ~ISM(2) (bood'i-) n. & a., ~IST(ic,al) aa. [Skr., p.p. of *budh* awake]

budd'leia (-lea), n. Kinds of shrub with lilac or yellow flowers of various forms. [A. *Buddle*, botanist, -IA¹]

***budd'y**, n. (colloq.). (Usu. as familiar form of address) brother, chum, mate. [dim. of *bud*, childish pronunc. of *brother*]

budge, v.i. & t. Make the slightest movement, force to do this, (in neg. sentences). [f. F *bouger* stir perh. (cf. Pr. *bolegar*) = It. *bulicare* f. LL *bullicare* frequent. of *bullire* boil]

budg'erigar', n. The grass parakeet, or Australian love-bird. [native name]

budg'et, n. & a. Contents of a bag or bundle (mostly fig., esp. of news, & as title of newspapers); annual estimate of revenue & expenditure by Chancellor of Exchequer in House of Commons; private person's similar estimate; (v.i.) ~ *for*, allow or arrange for in ~. Hence ~ARY¹ a. [f. F *bougette* dim. of *bouge* leather bag f. L *bulga* (f. Gallic) knapsack]

buff¹, n. & a. (Of) stout velvety dull-yellow leather of buffalo or ox-hide; the human skin (*in ~*, naked); (of) dull-yellow colour (*the B~s*, East Kent Regt., from colour of the facings); (Path.) coagulated coating on blood drawn from fever patients, whence ~'y² a.; ~*coat*, -*jerkin*, formerly worn by soldiers as proof against sword-cut; ~-*stick*, -*wheel*, polishing tools covered with ~; ~-*tip*, kind of moth. [f. F *buffle* BUFFALO]

buff², v.t. Polish (metal) with buff; make (leather) velvety like buff. [f. prec.]

buff'alo, n. (pl. -oes). Kinds of ox [*Bos bubalus*, India, Asia, Europe, N. Africa; *Bos caffer*, S. Africa; incorrectly, American BISON]; amphibious tank. [prob. f. Port. *bufalo*, f. L f. Gk *boubalos* antelope]

buff'er¹, n. Apparatus for deadening the concussion, or sustaining by springs or padding, or sustaining by strength of beams etc., a concussion, esp. of railway vans; ~ *State*, small State between two large ones diminishing chance of hostilities. [f. obs. vb *buff* (prob. imit. of sound made by soft body struck, cf. PUFF & F *bouffer*)+-ER¹]

buff'er², n. (sl.). (Usu. old-)old-fashioned or incompetent fellow. [etym. dub.; Wyclif's Bible has it = stammerer,—'the tunge of bufferes swyftli shal speke']

buff'et¹, n. (Strike with) blow of the hand; (of fate etc.) knock, hurt, plague; contend with (waves); contend with. [OF. dim. of *buffe* blow (also in obs. E *buff* cf. BLIND¹-*man's-buff*)]

buff'et², n. 1. Sideboard, recessed cupboard, for china, plate, etc. 2. (pr. boof'a) refreshment bar. [F, etym. dub.; sense 2 of later introduction than 1; there is also *buffet stool*, hassock, (obs. exc. in dial. & in *Little Miss Muffet sat on a ~*)]

buffoon' (-oōn), n. & a. Burlesque, comic, mocker. Hence ~ERY(4) n. [f. F *buffon* f. It. *buffone* (*buffa* jest, *buffare* to puff), -OON]

bug, n. Flat ill-smelling blood-sucking insect infesting beds; (loosely) small insect often with defining word as *harvest*, *May*, ~; *big ~* (sl.), person of importance. Hence ~g'y² a. [?]

bug'aboo, **bug'bear** (-bar), nn. Fancied object of fear; false belief used to intimidate or dissuade. [etym. & mutual relation doubtful; cf. BOGY, BOGLE, & obs. *bug* in same sense]

bugg'er (-g-), n. & v.t. (Law) sodomite, man having unnatural intercourse with beast or man, whence **bugg'ERY(4)** n.; (in foul or low talk, abusively or humorously) fellow, beggar, chap, beast; (v.t.) ~ *about*, hound from pillar to post. [f. F *bougre* f. L *Bulgarus* 11th-c. heretic from Bulgaria, supposed capable of any crime]

bugg'y, n. Light vehicle for one or two persons (esp. now in U.S., India, colonies). [?]

bu'gle¹, n. & v.i. & t. Brass instrument like small trumpet used for military signals; (vb) sound ~, sound (call) on ~. Hence **bu'gLER¹** n. [orig. hunting-horn, short for ~-*horn* f. obs. & dial. & OF *bugle* young bull f. L *bucculus* dim. of *bos* bugle's ox see cow]

bu'gle², n. Kinds of creeping plant with blue flowers. [F, f. LL *bugula*]

bu'gle³ n. Tube-shaped glass bead sewn on dress etc. for ornament. [etym. dub.; there is Du. *beugel* ring]

bu'glet, n. Small (bicyclist's) bugle. [-ET¹]

bu'gloss, n. Kinds of plant allied with borage. [f. F *buglosse* f. L *buglossa* f. Gk *bouglossos* ox-tongued (*bous*, *glossa*), from shape & roughness of leaves]

buhl (bool), n. & a. (Inlaid with) brass, tortoise-shell, etc., cut in ornamental patterns for inlaying. [Germanized f. *Boule* name of carver (d. 1732)]

build¹ (bĭl), v.t. & i. (built). Construct by putting parts or material rightly together (house, ship, carriage, organ, engine, nest, or other structure large relatively to the builder); (abs.) be busy making one's house or nest; ~ *up, round, in,* surround (person, place, etc.) with houses etc., block up; (with material as obj.) lay *in(to* wall etc.) *in* ~ing; establish, make gradually, (often with *up*; system, empire, reputation); base (hopes etc.) *upon,* rely *upon*; *built* (with preceding adv.), of such a BUILD². [ME *bulden* f. OE *bold* dwelling f. OTeut. *buðwell,* cf. BOOTH]

build² (bĭl), n. Style of construction, make; proportions of human body (*sturdy* ~ etc.), [prec.]

buil'der (bĭl-), n. In vbl senses: esp., master-builder, contractor for building houses. [-ER¹]

buil'ding (bĭl-), n. In vbl senses: esp.: house, edifice; ~-*lease,* permitting lessee to build on the land; ǁ ~-*society,* of contributors to fund for loan to members when needing house. [-ING¹]

bŭlb¹, n. Nearly spherical underground stem of lily, onion, etc., sending roots downwards & leaves etc. upwards; leaf-bud detaching itself from stem & becoming separate plant; (Anat.) roundish swelling of any cylindrical organ, as of hair-root or spinal cord; dilated part of glass tube (~-*tube,* ending in a ~); electric-light container. Hence ~ED², (-bd),~IF EROUS, **bŭl'bi**FORM, aa., **bŭl'bo-**comb. form. [f.L *bulbus* f.Gk *bolbos* onion]

bŭlb², v.i. Swell into bulb(s). [f. prec.]

bŭl'bous, a. Of, having, like, springing from, a bulb. [BULB¹ +-OUS]

bŭlbul (bo͝ol'bo͝ol), n. Eastern song-thrush; singer, poet. [Pers. f. Arab.]

bŭlge, n. Convex part, irregular swelling, tendency to swell out, on flat or flatter surface; = BILGE; (sl.) advantage (chiefly in phr. *have,* or *get, the* ~ *on,* have, get, the advantage over). Hence **bŭl'gY²** a., **bŭl'gi**NESS n. [ME, f. OF *boulge, bouge,* (or direct) f. L *bulga* see BUDGET]

bŭlge², v.i. & t. Swell outwards irregularly & usu. faultily; extend (bag etc.) by stuffing it. [f. prec.]

bŭl'imy, bŭlĭm'ĭa, n. (Med.) morbid hunger; (fig.) voracity (for books etc.). [f. Gk *boulimia* ox- (i.e. vast) hunger (*bous* ox + *limos* hunger); latinized *buli-mia* now preferred in medical use]

bŭlk¹, n. Cargo (*break* ~, begin unloading; ~ *not equal to sample; in* ~, loose, not in package; *load in* ~, put grain etc. in loose; *sell in* ~, in large quantities, as it is in the hold); large shape, person, body; size, magnitude; great size; mass, large mass; *the* greater part or number of. [perh. f. ON *bulki* cargo, but with the meanings also of obs. *bouk* OE *buc* belly cf. G *bauch*]

bŭlk², v.i. & t. Seem in respect of size or importance (~ *large, larger*); ~ *up,* form considerable sum etc., amount *to*; pile up heaps (fish); (Customs) ascertain weight of (tea etc.) by emptying out of chest. [f. prec.]

bŭlk'head (-hĕd), n. Upright partition dividing ship's cabins or water-tight compartments; compartment, stall. [f. obs. *bulk* framework before shop, stall, perh. f. ON *balkr* BALK¹]

bŭl'kY², a. Large; too large. Hence **bŭl'ki**NESS n. [BULK¹+-Y²]

bŭll¹ (bo͝ol), n. & a. 1. Uncastrated male of ox or any bovine animal (~ *in china shop,* reckless or clumsy destroyer; *take by horns,* meet not evade difficulty); male of whale, elephant, & other large animals (usu. ~ *whale* or *whale-* etc.); constellation & sign Taurus. 2. (St. Exch.) person trying to raise prices (see BEAR¹). 3. = BULL's-eye (of target). 4. adj. Like that of a ~ (~ *head, neck, voice*: also ~ *operations* on St. Exch.). 5. ~-*calf,* male calf, simpleton; ǁ ~-*corner* (local), barred refuge, usu. at junction of fields, from ~'s attack; ~*dog,* powerful & courageous large-headed smooth-haired breed of dog, tenacious & courageous (person), ǁ University proctor's attendant, gun or pistol (esp. of a certain pattern), [f. use in ~-baiting, or f. its ~ head]; *~*doze,* v.t. (sl.), cow, coerce; *~*dozer,* powerful caterpillar tractor pushing broad steel blade in front, used for removing obstacles, levelling uneven surfaces, etc.; ~*fight,* Spanish sport of baiting ~ with horsemen etc.; ~*finch,* bird, also [perh. = *fence,* cf. *minch* dial. for *mince*] quickset hedge with ditch; ~*frog,* large Amer. species; ~*head,* small big-headed fish = Miller's thumb; ~-*headed,* obstinate, impetuous, blundering; ~-*of-the-bog,* bittern; ~-*puncher,* (Austral.) bullock-driver; ~-*pup, -bitch,* young, female, bulldog; ~-*ring,* arena for bull-fight; ~*roarer,* kind of noisy toy; ~*s-eye,* boss of glass formed at centre of blown glass sheet, hemispherical piece or thick disk of glass as light in ship's side, hemi-spherical lens, (lantern) with such lens, small circular window, centre of target, kind of sweetmeat; ~-*terrier,* cross between bulldog & terrier; ~*trout,* fish of salmon tribe. [OE *bule-,* in comb. only], cf. MLG *bulle,* prob. connected with BELLOW]

bŭll² (bo͝ol), v.i. & t. (St. Exch.) speculate for the rise; try to raise price of (stocks). [f. prec.; BULL¹,² perh. merely correl. to the more explicable BEAR¹,²]

bŭll³ (bo͝ol), n. Papal edict. [f. L *bulla* BILL⁴]

bŭll⁴ (bo͝ol), n. (Often *Irish* ~) expression containing contradiction in terms or implying ludicrous inconsistency (often

an intelligible statement made absurd by compression). [etym. dub.; f. 1630 cf. *bullfrog*, *bulltrout*, & Gk use of *bou-* (connexion with *Irish* is more recent; there is OF *boul*, *bole*, trickery)]

bull⁵ (bŏŏl), n. Drink made of water flavoured in empty spirit cask. [?]

Bull⁶ (bŏŏl), n. = JOHN *Bull*.

bull⁷ (bŏŏl), n. Deck-game in which small flat sandbags are thrown on an inclined board marked with numbered squares. [?]

bullace (bŏŏl'is), n. Wild (or semicultivated) plum tree or fruit. [f. OF *beloce* f. LL *pilota* PELLET]

bill'ate, a. (bot., physiol.). Puffy, blistered-looking. [f. L *bullatus* (*bulla* bubble, -ATE²)]

bull'et (bŏŏl-), n. Missile of lead etc., spherical or conical, used in muskets & rifles (*Dumdum*, *expanding*, *soft-nosed*, *explosive*, ~, varieties so shaped etc. as to inflict complicated wound); ~*drawer*, instrument for extracting ~ from wound; ~*head*, *-headed*, (with) round & presumably thick head; ~-PROOF. [f. F *boulette* dim. of *boule* ball f. L *bulla* knob]

bull'etin (bŏŏl-), n. Short official statement of public event or news or of invalid's condition. [F., f. It. *bulletino* dim. of *bulletta* lottery ticket dim. of *bulla* seal, BULL²]

bullion¹ (bŏŏl'yon), n. & a. Gold or silver before (or as valued apart from) coining or manufacture; (made of) solid or real gold or silver. [AF, prob. = F *bouillon* soup f. med. L *bullionem* nom. *-io* (L *bullire* BOIL+-ION); but the meanings are E only]

bullion² (bŏŏl'yon), n. Fringe of gold & silver thread twists. [f. F *bouillon*, see prec., in sense *bubble* (independent adoption)]

bull'ionist (-ŏŏlyo-), n. Advocate of metallic currency. [BULLION¹+-IST²]

bull'ock (bŏŏl-), n. Castrated bull, ox. [OE *bulluc* (-OCK)]

bull'y¹ (bŏŏl-), n. Blusterer, tyrant (esp. among boys), coward & tyrant; hired ruffian. [obs. senses *lover*, *sweetheart*, *gallant*, *fine fellow*, perh. f. Du. *boel* lover cf. G *buhle*]

bull'y² (bŏŏl-), v.t. Persecute, oppress, tease, physically or morally; frighten *into* or *out of* (*abs.*) play the bully; ~ *off*, (hockey). [f. prec.]

bull'y³ (bŏŏl-), a. & int. (esp. U.S. & colonial). Capital, first-rate; ~ *for you*, *him*, etc., = bravo. [f. BULLY¹]

‖ **bull'y⁴** (bŏŏl-), n. Scrummage in (prop. Eton) football.

bull'y⁵ (bŏŏl-), n. (Also ~ *beef*) tinned beef. [perh. = BOUILLI, or f. BULL¹]

bull'yrag (bŏŏl-), v. See BALLYRAG.

bull'rush (bŏŏl-), n. Kinds of tall rush (pop. the Cat's Tail; in Bible, papyrus).

[BOLE (strong-stemmed)?, or BULL¹ (big cf. *bullfrog*, *bulltrout*, & Gk use of *bou-*; see BULLY¹)]

bul'wark (bŏŏl-), n. Rampart, earthwork, etc.; mole, breakwater; person, principle, etc., that acts as a defence; ship's side above deck. [cf. Du. *bolwerk*, G *bolwerk*; perh. = BOLE+WORK (log-rampart)]

bum¹, n. Backside, buttocks; ‖~*bailiff* (also ~), employed for arrests (from touching debtor on the back); ~*boat*, plying with fresh provisions for ships (orig. scavenger boat). [cf. BUMP; earlier than, not contracted f., *bottom* in this sense]

*bum²**, n., a., & v.i. (sl.). 1. Habitual loafer (*go on the* ~, sponge on the community). 2. adj. Of poor quality. 3. v.i. (-mm-). Loaf, sponge, wander *around*. [perh. back-formation f. BUMMER]

‖ **büm'ble**, n. Beadle; consequential jack-in-office. Hence ~DOM (-id-) n. [name of beadle in *Oliver Twist*]

büm'ble-bee, n. Large kind of bee. [f. obs. *vb bumble* (*BOOM*+-LE)]

büm'ble-puppy, n. Whist, tennis, etc., played unscientifically; game with tennis-ball slung to post. [prop. an obs. out-of-door bagatelle; etym. dub.; there is obs. *vb bumble bungle*]

büm'bo, n. Cold rum-punch. [cf. It. *bombo* child's wd for drink]

‖ **bümf**, n. (sl.). Toilet paper; paper(s), documents. [= *bum*-*fodder*]

büm'malo, n. Small fish of S.-Asiatic coasts. [f. Mahratti *bombil*]

‖ **bümmaree'**, n. Middleman at Billingsgate fish-market. [?]

büm'mer, n. Idler, loafer. [cf. G *bummler*]

bump¹, v.t. & i., & adv. 1. Push, throw down, (box etc.) *against* or *on* (wall, person, floor, etc.); hurt (one's head etc.) by striking it (*against*, *on*, or *abs.*); seize by arms & legs & strike the posterior of (person) against floor, wall, etc.; come with a bump *against*; go along with repeated bumps; (Boat-racing, see foll.) overtake; (of cricket-ball) rise abruptly on pitching; ~ *off* (sl.), remove by violence, murder. 2. *adv.* With a bump, suddenly, violently, (*come*, *go*, etc., ~; cf. BANG, BOUNCE). [expressing the sound, or shape of swelling]

bump², n. Dull-sounding blow, knock, collision; swelling caused by it; (Phrenol.) prominence on skull, faculty indicated by it; (Boat-racing) touching of boat by next, a win for latter(~*supper*, in celebration of this); (Aviation) variation of air pressure causing irregularity in aircraft's motion, jolt experienced by aircraft in flight; ~*ball* (Cricket; pr. *büm'bawl*) ball hit hard on ground close to bat, coming with a long hop to fieldsman (so looking like a possible catch). [f. prec.]

---

bump³, n., & v.i. (Make) bittern's cry. [imit.]

bum'per, n. In vbl senses; also, brim-full glass of wine; (sl.) anything unusu. large or abundant (harvest, full theatre); (Whist) score of two games against nil; (Motoring) spring fender for mitigating collisions. [-ER¹]

bump'kin, n. Country or awkward or bashful fellow. [perh. f. Du. *boomken* little tree or MDu. *bommekijn* little barrel]

bump'tious (-shus), a. Self-assertive. Hence ~LY² adv., ~NESS n. [jocular form, on BUMP² & e.g. *fractious*]

bum'py, a. Full of bumps, causing jolts, (esp. of road or cricket pitch or air in aviation). Hence ~INESS n. [-Y¹]

bun¹, n. Small soft round sweet cake with a few currants (the usu. Eng. sense, but with local variations); *hot cross* ~, marked with cross & eaten on Good Friday; hair dressed in ~ shape. [perh. f. OF *bugne* bump, swelling, (at Lyons = fritter, whence mod. F *beignet*)]

bun², n. (Personifying name of) squirrel, rabbit. [etym. dub.; there **is** Sc. *bun*, hare's tail]

bunch¹, n. Cluster of things growing or fastened together (flowers, grapes, keys); lot (*best of the* ~); (sl.) gang, group; ~ *of fives* (sl.), fist, hand. Hence ~Y² a. [?]

bunch², v.t. & i. Make into bunch(es), gather (dress) into folds; come or cling together, (Mil., of skirmishers) fail to keep intervals. [f. prec.]

*****bunc'ō**, n., & v.t., (sl.) (To) swindle (esp. by card-sharping or the confidence trick); ~-*steerer*, swindler. [cf. Sp. *banca* a card-game]

bun'combe. See BUNKUM.

bund, n. (Anglo-Ind.). Embankment, causeway, quay. [Hind. *band*, of Persian orig.]

bun'der, n. (Anglo-Ind.). Landing-place, quay, harbour; ~-*boat* (used for coasting & harbour work). [Hind.]

bun'dle¹, n. Collection of things fastened together (esp. clothes & odds & ends in handkerchief); set of sticks, iron rods, etc., bound up; set of parallel fibres, nerves, etc.; 20 hanks of linen yarn. [perh. f. MDu. *bondel* or G *bündel* (OTent. *bindan* BIND); see -LE(1)]

bun'dle², v.t. & i. Tie in, make up into, a bundle; throw confusedly *in, to* any receptacle; go, put or send (esp. a person), in a hurry or unceremoniously *out, off, away*, etc. [f. prec.]

bun'dōōk, n. (Anglo-Ind.). Rifle, musket. [Hind. *banduq*]

bung¹, n. Stopper, esp. large cork stopping hole in cask; (sl.) He; ~-*hole*, for filling cask. [cf. MDu. *bonghe* = +*bonde* f. L *puncta* orifice (*pungere punct-* prick)]

bung², v.t. Stop (cask) with bung; *eyes* ~*ed up*, closed with swelling from blow, or sealed with rheum; (sl.) throw (stones). [f. prec.]

bung'alow (-nggalō), n. One-storeyed house, orig. lightly built or temporary. Hence ~OID a., having the style or appearance of a ~ow. [f. Hind. *bangla* belonging to Bengal]

bungle (bǔng'gl), v.i. & t., & n. (Make) clumsy work, confusion; blunder over, fail to accomplish, (task). Hence ~ER¹ n. [imit., cf. RUMBLE, BOGGLE]

bun'ion (-yon), n. Inflamed swelling on foot. [perh. f. It. *bugnone* (*bugno* boil, lump, cf. F *bugne* BUN¹,+-*one* -OON)]

bunk¹, n. Sleeping-berth. [?]

bunk², v.i., & n., (sl.). ~, *do a* ~, make off, vanish. [?]

*****bunk³**, n. (sl.). Humbug, balderdash. [contr. of BUNKUM]

bunk'er, n., & v.t. Ship's coal-bin; (Golf) sandpit or other obstruction to free dealing with balls; (Mil.) underground shelter; (v.t., usu. in p.p.) entangle in ~, (fig.) bring into difficulties. [?]

bunk'um, -combe (-km), n. Humbug, claptrap, sophistry. [anecdotic; member for Buncombe in N. Carolina speaking needlessly in Congress to impress his constituents]

bunn'ia (-ya), n. (Anglo-Ind.). Indian trader or shopkeeper. [Hind. *banya*; see BANIAN]

bunn'y, n. Pet name for rabbit; ~-*hug*, an American dance. [BUN²+-Y²]

Bun'sen('s) (bŏŏn-, bǔn-), a. Invented by Prof. *Bunsen* of Heidelberg (~ *burner, lamp*, burning air with gas for heating & blow-pipe work; ~ *battery, cell*, voltaic of spec. kind).

bunt¹, n. Cavity, baggy part, of fishing-net, sail, etc.; ~-*line* (confining ~ in furling sail). [?]

bunt², n. (Also *Smut-ball*) disease of wheat. [?]

bunt³, n., & v.t. & i. 1. (Baseball) short hit to the infield; (v.t.) stop (ball) with bat without swinging latter. 2. (Aviation) half an outside loop followed by a half roll; (v.i.) perform this. [dial.]

bunt'ing¹, n. Sub-family of birds including *Common* or *Corn B~, Yellow B~* (or *Yellow-hammer*), *Black-headed, Reed, Snow*, etc., *B~*; grey shrimp. [?]

bunt'ing², n. (Open-made worsted stuff used for) flags. [perh. = bolting-cloth (BOLT⁶) f. obs. *bunt* sift, or perh. = G *band* parti-coloured +-ING¹]

buoy¹ (boi), n. Anchored float showing navigable course or reefs etc.; (also *life-*~) something to keep person afloat; also fig. in both senses. [f. OF *boie* or MDu. *boei* f. L *boia* chain]

buoy² (boi), v.t. 1. (Usu. with *up*) keep afloat; bring to surface of water; sustain (person, courage, etc.), uplift. 2. (Without *up*, sometimes with *out*) mark with

buoy(s). [see prec., but the vb is perh. directly f. a foreign source]

buoy·age (boi-), n. Providing of buoys. [-AGE]

buoy·ancy (boi-), n. Floating power (of solid or ...); (Hydrost.) loss of weight by immersion in liquid; elasticity, recuperative power, (of spirits, also of prices, etc., afloat); [f. foll.: see -ANCY]

buoy·ant (boi-), a. Apt to float, rise, keep up, or recover, springy; able to keep things up; light-hearted. Hence ~LY² adv. [= & perh. f., Sp. *boyante*; earlier than BUOY²; see BUOY²]

bûr, n. (Any plant with) clinging seed-vessel or flower; female hop-catkin; person hard to shake off. [= Da. *borre*]

Bûrb'erry, n. A kind of waterproof cloth, coat etc. of this, made by a company of that name.

bûr'ble, v.i. Simmer (*with* rage, mirth), . . . [on *burst*, *bubble*; but cf. obs. *burble* bubble]

bûrb'ot, n. Eel-like flat-headed bearded fresh-water fish. [f. F *bourbotte* cf. *borboros* mud]

bûrd'en¹, bûrth'en (-dh-), n. (usu. -den). Load (lit., or of labour, duty, sorrow, etc.; = ~ of proof, obligation to prove falling on maker of statement); obligatory expense; ship's carrying capacity, tonnage; bearing of loads (*ship, beast, of* ~); (Bibl.) oracle, heavy fate; (= obs. senses of BOURDON) refrain, chorus of song, chief theme or gist of poem, book, speech, etc. [OE *byrthen* = OSax. *burthinnia* (st. of BEAR³+suf. -inmia): for -d- cf. *murther, murder*]

bûrd'en², bûrth'en (-dh-), v.t. Load (lit. & fig.), encumber, oppress, tax. [f. prec.]

bûrd'ensome, a. Oppressive, wearying. [-SOME]

bûrd'ock, n. Coarse plant with prickly flower-heads (BUR) & dock-like leaves. [BUR+DOCK¹]

bureau (bûrō, bū-), n. (pl. *-eaux*, pr. -ōz). Writing-desk with drawers, escritoire; office, government department. [F. = office, desk, orig. baize f. OF *bure* brown f. L *burrus* red perh. f. Gk *purrhos* red]

bureau'cracy (-rō-), n. Government by bureaux, centralization; officialism; officials. Allied wds: ~CRAT (bû'rō-), n., ~crat'ic a., ~crat'ically adv., ~'cratism(2), ~cratist(2), nn. [f. prec. +-CRACY]

burette', n. Graduated glass tube for measuring small quantities of liquid. [F, dim. of *buire* vase]

*****bûrg**, n. (colloq.). Town or city. [see BOROUGH]

‖**bûr'gage**, n. An ancient tenure (*hold in* ~). [f. med. L *burgagium* (*burgus* see BOROUGH)]

bûrg'ee', n. Swallow-tailed pennant used by yachts etc. [?]

bûr'geon, bour'geon, (ber'jn), n., & v.i. (Put forth, spring forth as) young shoot(s), bud, begin to grow, (poet. & rhet.). [ME *burion*, f. OF *burjon* etym. dub.]

bûr'gess, n. Inhabitant of borough with full municipal rights, citizen; (chiefly hist.) member of parliament for borough, corporate town, or university. [ME & OF *burgeis*=BOURGEOIS¹]

burgh (bŭr'rō), n. (Sc.). Scots chartered town (used in E in writing of Scots boroughs). [see BOROUGH]

burgher (ber'ger), n. (arch.). Citizen (chiefly of foreign towns). [f. G or Du. *burger* (*burg* fortified town), later assim. to E *burgh*]

bûrg'lar, n. One who breaks into house by night with intent to commit felony. Hence ~Y¹ n., burglār'ious a., burglar'iously adv. [f. Anglo-L *burglator*, -*atrum* f. prec., made on *burgh-breche* the native term for burglary]

bûr'gle, v.i. & t. Commit burglary; enter or rob (house) burglariously. [recent back-formation f. prec., but cf. *burgulare* 1354]

bûrg'omaster (-ah-), n. Mayor of Dutch or Flemish town. [f. Du. *burgemeester* (BOROUGH)]

bûrg'onet, n. (hist.). Visored helmet; steel cap. [f. OF *bourguignotte* f. Bourgogne Burgundy]

burgoo', n. (naut. sl.). Porridge. [?]

bûrg'undy, n. Kinds of (usu. red) wine of Burgundy in France.

bû'r(h)el, n. Himalayan wild sheep. [f. Hind. *bharal*]

bu'rial (be-), n. Depositing under earth, burying, esp. of dead body, funeral; ~-ground, cemetery; ~-service, religious form (esp. that in Ch.-of-Engl. prayer-book) at funeral. [f. ME *byriels*, OE *byrgels* (burying, cf. *bergan* cover) -s dropped as though pl., cf. PEA]

bu'rin (be-), n. Tool for engraving on copper, graver. [F, perh. f. OHG *bora* boring-tool (BORE²)]

bûr'ke, v.t. Avoid, smother, (publicity, inquiry); hush up, suppress, (rumour, book). [*Burke* executed 1829 for smothering people to sell bodies for dissection]

bûrl, n., & v.t. Knot in wool or cloth; (v.t.) clear of ~s. [F. OF *bourle*]

bûrlesque' (-k), a. & n., & v.t. Imitative, imitation, imitate, for purpose of deriding or amusing; bombast(ic), mock-serious(ness); caricature, parody, esp. (of) literary & dramatic work. [F, f. It. *burlesco* (*burla* mockery) -ESQUE]

Bûr'lington House, n. Building in London used as headquarters of the Royal Academy, British Academy, & British Association.

burl'y, a. Sturdy, corpulent. Hence ~INESS n. [ME *borlich* prob. f. an OE *borlic* handsome, fit for the BOWER¹, see -LY¹]

Burmese' (-z), a. & n. Of Burma; (n.) native (pl. same) or language. **Burm'an** a. & n. = ~. [*Burma* + -ESE, -AN]

burn¹, n. (Sc., north., poet.). Small stream. [com.-Teut., cf. Du. *born*, & S.-Engl. BOURN¹]

burn², v.t. & i. (~*ed*, occas. ~*t*). **1.** Consume, waste, by fire (t. & i., the heat, heating person, or heated thing, being subject; ~ *away*, *out*, to nothing, to extinction; ~ *up*, get rid of by fire; ~ *out*, consume contents of; ~ one's *boats*, commit oneself irrevocably to a course); blaze, glow, with fire (~ *up*, flash into blaze; ~ *down*, *low*, less vigorously as fuel fails). **2.** Give, make to give, light (lamp, candles, gas, oil, etc.; ~ *blue* etc., give blue etc. light; ~ *candle at both ends*, not husband energy; ~ *daylight*, use artificial light by day; ~ *the midnight oil*, work late). **3.** Put, be put, to death by fire. **4.** Harden, produce, (bricks, lime, charcoal) by heat. **5.** Make (hole etc.) by heat (*money* ~*s hole in pocket*, clamours to be spent). **6.** Injure, be injured, by fire or great heat (~ one's *fingers*, suffer for meddling or rashness); char, scorch, in cooking (t. & i.), adhere to saucepan etc.; cauterize, brand, (~ *in*, *into*, impress indelibly); eat, make acid etc. eat, its way (*into* material, material, or *abs.*). **7.** Parch, freckle, tan, colour, (t. & i.; *abs.* or with *brown*, *dry*, etc.). **8.** Give, feel, sensation or pain (as) of heat (~*t child dreads fire*; *ears* ~, when one is talked of; ~, get near discovery or truth, as in child's game). **9.** Make, be, hot or passionate, glow, blaze, rage, yearn; ~ *person out*, expel him by fire; ~ *the water*, spear salmon by firelight; ~*ing-glass*, convex lens or concave mirror concentrating sun's rays enough to ignite object at focus; ~*t almond* (enclosed in burnt sugar); ~*t ochre*, *sienna* (calcined); ~*t offering*, sacrifice made by ~ing. [OE *brinnan* intr., *bærnan* trans.; com.-Teut. cf. G *brennen*]

burn³ n. Sore, mark, on body made by burning. [f. prec.]

burn'er, n. In vbl senses, esp. in comb. as *brick*-~; also, part of lamp etc. that shapes the flame. [-ER¹]

burn'et, n. Kinds of brown-flowered plant. [f. obs. adj. *burnet* f. OF *burnete* see BRUNETTE]

burn'ing, a. In vbl senses; also: flagrant (~ *shame*, *disgrace*); hotly discussed, exciting, (~ *question*, *question*); ~ *scent* (in hunting) strong. [-ING²]

burn'ish, v.t. & i. Polish by friction; (with *well* etc.) take a polish. Hence ~ER¹(2) n. [f. OF *burnir* = *brunir* (brun BROWN), see -ISH²]

burnoose' (-ōos, -ōoz), n. Arab, Moorish, & lady's, hooded cloak. [F (-s), f. Arab, *barnus*]

burr¹, n. Nebulous disk round moon or star; rough ridge left on cut or punched metal or paper (~*drill*, dentist's); siliceous rock used for mill-stones; whetstone; kinds of limestone; rough sounding of letter *r* as in Northumberland; whirring sound; = BUR. [etymn. dub.; perh. four different wds; & cf. BUR]

burr², v.t. & i. Pronounce with sound of Northumbrian *r*, also of French *r*; speak without clear articulation. [cf. prec.]

*burro (boo'rō), n. (colloq.). Small donkey used as pack-animal. [Sp.]

bu'rrow (-ō), n., & v.i. & t. (Make, live in) hole excavated in earth, as of foxes, rabbits, etc.; make by excavating (hole, one's way); retire out of sight; (fig.) investigate mysteries etc. Hence ~ER¹ n. [perh. = BOROUGH]

burs'ar, n. Treasurer, esp. of a college; exhibitioner esp. in Scots University or school, whence ~Y¹ n. [f. med. L *bursarius* (*bursa* bag f. Gk = hide)]

burst¹, v.t. & i. (past & p.p. *burst*). **1.** Fly by expansion of contents, send (containing case), violently asunder, split, (powder, shell, etc.; exaggeratively, ~ *with food or emotion, heart* ~*s*). **2.** Get away from or through, make way *out* or *in*, express one's feelings, by force or suddenly (*river* ~*s banks*; ~ *in*, come into room, interrupt; ~ *out*, exclaim; ~ *into tears, out laughing*, break into tears, laughter; ~ *upon enemy's country*, overrun it). **3.** Open, come open, be opened, forcibly (*boil, bud, cloud*, ~; ~ *door, door* ~*s, in* or *open*). **4.** Fill, be full, to overflowing (*grain* ~*s granary, granary* ~*ing*; ~ *with joy, envy, pride, a secret*). **5.** Appear suddenly (~ *into flame, upon the view; sun, war, disease,* ~ *out*); suffer ~ing of (some part; ~ *a blood-vessel*, one's *heart*, *sides with laughing*, *buttons with food*; ~ *up*, explode, bring or come to utter collapse, (colloq., & often spelt *bust up*). [OE *berstan* f. OTeut. *brestan* perh. f. *brek-* BREAK; there has been double metathesis, OTeut. *brest-*, OE *berst-*, ME *brest-*, mod. *burst*]

burst², n. Bursting, split; ~*up* (often *bust-* colloq.), collapse; sudden issuing forth (~*f* of *flame*), explosion, outbreak, (lit. & fig.); spurt; continuous gallop; bout of drunkenness etc. (often vulg. *bust; on the bust*). [f. prec.]

burth'en (-dh-). See BURDEN.

burt'on (-tn), n. Light handy two-block tackle. [?]

bury (be'rĭ), v.t. Deposit in, commit to, earth, tomb, or sea (corpse); (of relatives) to have buried; ~ *d*, perform burial rites over; put under ground (~ *alive*; put ~ *the hatchet*, renounce quarrel); put

away, forget; (chiefly refl. & pass.) consign to obscurity; hide in earth (treasure etc.), cover up, submerge; with-draw from view (face in hands, hands in pockets); (p.p.) immersed (*buried in sloth*; ~*ing-ground*, -*place*, graveyard, cemetery. [OE *byrgan* cf. BURIAL]

bŭs, n. (pl. ~*es*), & v.i. 1. Omnibus; (sl.) aeroplane, motor-car, motor-cycle; (sl.) *the* ~ (sl.), lose an opportunity, fail in an undertaking; ~*man*, driver of an omnibus; (~*man's holiday*, leisure time spent in the same kind of occupation as one's regular work). 2. v.i. Go by ~. [abbr.]

‖ **bŭs'by** (-z-), n. Tall fur cap of Hussars & R.H.A. [?]

bush¹ (-ŏŏ-), n. Shrub, clump of shrubs; bunch of ivy as ancient Vintner's sign (*good wine needs no* ~); luxuriant growth of hair, whisker, etc.; woodland, untilled district, (esp. in colonies) *take to the* ~, become bush-ranger); BEAT *about the* ~; ~ in many bird, beast, & plant names; ~-*fighter*, -*ing*, (person used to) fighting in the ~, guerilla warfare; ~-*harrow*, heavy frame with bars between which branches are inserted for harrowing grass land or covering seed, (vb) harrow with this; ~*man*, aboriginal of a S.-Afr. tribe, dweller, farmer, or traveller in the Australian ~, whence **bush'manship**(3) n. [After Du. *boschjesman* (*bosch* bush)]; ~-*ranger*, Australian brigand (at first escaped convict) living in the bush; ~-*rope*, tropical wild vine netting trees together. [ME *busk* f. ON *buskr*, cf. G *busch*, Du. *bosch* (whence prob. the sense *woodland* above), f. Rom. *bosco* see BOSK]

bush² (-ŏŏ-), v.t. Set (ground) with bushes to frustrate net-poaching; bush-harrow (ground). [prec.]

bush³ (-ŏŏ-), n. & v.t. Metal lining of axle-hole or other circular orifice, perfor-ated plug; (vb) furnish with ~. [prob. f. MDu. *busse* BOX² cf. BLUNDERBUSS]

bush'el (-ŏŏ-), n. Measure of capacity (8 gal.) for corn, fruit, etc. (*not hide light or candle under* ~, set example; *measure others' corn by one's own* ~, judge others by oneself). Hence ~FUL(2) n. [ME *boschel* f. OF *boissiel* f. LL *buscellus* f. *buxis* BOX²]

Bushido (bŏŏshē'dō), n. The code of honour & morals evolved by the samurai. [Jap., = military knight way]

bush'veld (bŏŏsh'felt), n. Veld composed largely of bush; low country of Trans-vaal. [f. Du. *boschveld*, see BUSH¹ & VELD]

bush'y (-ŏŏ-), a. Abounding in bushes; growing thickly. Hence ~INESS n.

business (biz'nis), n. 1. Being busy (orig. sense, now obs. see BUSYNESS). 2. Task, duty, province, (*make it one's* ~, undertake); cause of coming (*what is your* ~?). 3. Habitual occupation, profes-sion, trade; serious work (*means* ~, is in earnest; *on* ~, with definite purpose; ~ *as usual*, things will proceed in spite of disturbing circumstances; ~ *end of* (tin-tack, point; ~ *hours*, *hours of* ~, of regular work, open shop or office, etc.). 4. Thing needing attention, agenda, (*the* ~ *of the day, meeting*, etc.); dealings with men & matters (~ *man*, one used to these, & see below; ~ *man*, agent, attorney, &c.). 5. Difficult matter (*what a* ~! *make a great* ~ *of it*). 6. Thing that concerns one, that one may meddle with, (*mind your own, go about your, send about his*, ~, no reproof or dismissal; *has no* ~ *to*, no right). 7. (Contempt.) device, machine, process, concern, course of events, (*sick of the whole* ~; *a lath-&-plaster* ~). 8. (Theatr.) action, dumb-show. 9. Buying & selling, bargaining, (*doing a great* ~; *good stroke of* ~; ~ *man*, engaged in commerce, also see below). 10. Com-mercial house, firm; *do one's* ~, kill him; *well done!* [OE *bisignis* (BUSY¹ + -NESS)]

business-like, a. Systematic, practical, prompt, well-ordered. [-LIKE]

bŭsk, n. Rigid strip stiffening corset-front. [f. F *busc* etym. dub.]

bŭs'ker, n. (sl.), Itinerant musician or actor. [f. *busk* beat about, seek (perh. f. obs. F *busquer* to prowl)]

bŭs'kin, n. Boot reaching to calf or knee; thick-soled boot lending height to Athe-nian tragic actor; the tragic vein, tragedy, (see SOCK; *put on the* ~, write or act tragedy). Hence ~ED²(-nd) a. [in many Europ. langg.; the E perh. f. OSp. *bos-zequi*, F *brosequin*, Du. *broseken*, etc., having *br-*; etym. dub.] Mlt. *borzacchino* suggests *borza* PURSE]

bŭss, n. & v.t., (arch.). Kiss. [earlier *basse* n. & v.; cf. F *baiser*, L *basiare*, *basium*]

bŭst¹, n. Sculpture of person's head, shoulders, & chest; upper front of body, bosom, esp. of woman. [f. F *buste* f. It. *busto* etym. dub.]

bŭst². See BURST¹,².

bŭst³ (-sl), n. (sl.), frog. in comb., as BLOCK¹,², BRONCO-, TANK-, ~er.

bŭst'ard, n. Genus of large swift-running birds. [perh. mixture of OF *bistarde*, *oustarde*, both f. L *avis tarda* slow bird (the inappropriate adj. unexplained)]

bŭs'tle¹ (-sl), v.i. & t. Bestir oneself; make show of activity, hurry about; make (others) hurry or work hard. [perh. f. obs. *buskle* f. obs. *busk* prepare]

bŭs'tle² (-sl), n. Excited activity. [f. prec.]

bŭs'tle³ (-sl), n. Pad or frame puffing out top of woman's skirt behind. [perh.

busy¹ (biz'i), a. & n. 1. Occupied, work-ing, engaged, with attention concen-trated, (~ *in, with, at*; also, prep. being dropped, with vb) n. now looking like

part., as *he was ~ packing*); unresting; ever employed, stirring, (*~ as a bee*); fussy, meddlesome, prying, mischievous; ~ **idle**(ness), spending energy on trifles; ~**body**, meddlesome person, mischief-maker. Hence busILY² (biz²) adv. **2.** n. (sl.). Detective. [OE *bisig*; only E & LG cf. Du. *bezig*]

busy² (biz¹), v.t. Occupy (esp. oneself, one's hands, eyes, etc.), keep busy, (*with, in, at, about*, or *with -ing*, or abs.). [OE *bisgian* see prec.]

busyness (biz²), n. State or quality of being busy. [mod. form differentiated in spelling & pronunc. f. BUSINESS]

but¹ (orig. adv. & prep. = outside, without; developed into conj., under which most mod. uses belong; but it is now adv., prep., negative rel. pron., subord. & coord. conj.; clear distinction of these is not here possible). **1.** Only (*she is ~ a child, I can ~ do it*). **2.** Except, if not, short of, except that, if it were not that, short of the condition that, (*they are all wrong ~ he, him; no one ~ me, I; never ~ once; he all ~ did it; what can he do ~ die; nothing would content him ~ I must come*). **3.** Otherwise than (*cannot choose ~, cannot ~, do it*). **4.** Who or that not (*no one ~ knows that*). **5.** Without the result etc. that (*never rains ~ it pours; justice was never done ~ someone complained*). **6.** Rather than so-&-so shall prove untrue (*it shall go hard ~ I will get there; ten to one ~ it was you*); that not (*not such a fool ~*—also *~ that, ~ what*—*he can see that; it is impossible ~ that offences will come*). **7.** To say (that) not (*not ~ that*— also *what*—*he believed it himself*); *~ for this* etc., were it not so, without this; *~ then*, ~ on the other hand (*it is hot, no doubt, ~ then the heat is dry*). **8.** (After neg.) that (*I don't deny, doubt, ~ that.* **9.** On the contrary, nevertheless, however, on the other hand, moreover, yet. [OE *be-ūtan, būtan, būta*, (BE-, OUT) outside, without]

but², n. & v.t. An objection; (vb) utter, use, (*~s; ~ me no ~s*). [uses of prec.]

butch'er¹ (boo̅-), n. Slaughterer of animals for food; dealer in meat (*the ~, the baker, the candlestick-maker*, people of all trades); judge, general, etc., who has men killed needlessly or brutally; a salmon-fry; *~'s bill*, list of killed in war; *~bird*, kind of shrike; *~'s-broom*, low spiny-leaved evergreen = *Knee Holly*; *~'s mead*, excluding poultry, game, & bacon etc. [f. OF *bochier* (*boc* BUCK¹) lit. dealer in goat's flesh]

butch'er² (boo̅-), v.t. Slaughter (people) wantonly or cruelly; ruin by bad reading or editing, damage by harsh criticism. [f. prec.]

butch'erly (boo̅-), a. Fit for, like, a butcher, coarse, brutal, bloody, [-LY¹]

butch'ery (boo̅-), n. Shambles (in bar-racks, camp, ship, etc.); (attrib.) butcher's trade (*~ trade, business*, etc.); needless or cruel slaughter of people. [f. F *boucherie* (BUTCHER¹, -Y¹)]

but'ler, n. Servant in charge of wine-cellar & plate etc., head servant. [f. AF *butuiller* t. OF *bouteillier*, see BOTTLE¹, -ER²(2)]

butt¹, n. Wine or ale cask (108-140 gals); any barrel. [f. Rom. (F & It. *botte*) f. LL *buttis*]

butt², n. Thicker end, esp. of tool or weapon (*give fish the ~, turn ~ of rod towards him for firmer hold*); trunk of tree just above ground; *~ or ~end*, remnant (*~end* also = thicker end); base of leaf-stalk; kinds of flat-fish, as sole, plaice, turbot; hide of back & flanks trimmed to rectangle, thickest leather (cf. BEND²); square end of plank meeting a similar end (also *~end*). [cf. Da. *but*, Du. *bot*, stumpy, Sw. *but* stump; whether senses belong together, & relation to other wds *bud*, doubtful]

butt³, n. Mound behind target; grouse-shooter's stand screened by low stone wall; (pl.) shooting-range; target; end, aim, object; object of (ridicule etc.); object of teasing & ridicule. [f. F *but* goal cf. foll.]

butt⁴, v.i. & t., & n. Push (v. & n.) with the head (*come ~ or full ~ against*, run *into*; *~ in*, fig., intervene, meddle); meet end to end (*~ against, upon*); come, place (timber etc.), with end flat against wall etc. [f. OF *boter, buter*, (now *bouter*) thrust, project, influenced by ABUT]

*****butte** (būt), n. Conspicuous isolated hill, esp. one with steep or cliff-like sides. [F, = knoll]

butt'er¹, n. Fatty substance made from cream by churning (*look as if ~ would not melt in mouth*, demure; *melted ~, sauce of ~*, flour, etc.); kinds of substance of similar consistence or look, as *~ of almonds*; fulsome flattery; *~ɛ-eggs*, kinds of plant with two yellows in flower, as toad-flax; *~bean*, yellow-pod kind usu. cooked in the pod unsliced, wax-pod, (also) large dried haricot bean; *~boat*, sauce-boat; *~knife*, blunt, of silver etc., for cutting ~; *~scotch*, kind of toffee; *~bur*, plant with large soft leaves; *~cup*, kinds of yellow-flowered *Ranunculus*; *~fingers, -fingered*, (person) unable to hold things, esp. a catch at cricket; *~milk*, liquid left after churning ~; *~muslin*, thin loosely-woven cloth with fine mesh, used primarily as a wrapping for ~; *~nut*, N.-Amer. oily nut (*~tree*); *~print*, wooden stamp for marking ~; *~wort*, fleshy-leaved violet-flowered bog-plant. Hence ~Y² a., ~INESS n. [OE *butere*, f. L f. Gk *bouturon* (*bous* cow, *turon* cheese, or perh. barbarian wd so accounted for)]

butt'er², v.t. Spread, cook, sauce, with butter (*fine words ~ no parsnips*, mere

professions are valueless); for other phrr. see BREAD]; (also ~ *up*) flatter. [f. prec.]

||**bütt'erbump,** n. =BITTERN. [see BUMP³]

bütt'erflÿ, n. & a. Diurnal erect-winged insect with knobbed antennae; showy or fickle (person); trifler; ~*-nut*, ~*-screw* (Mech.), with wings to be turned by thumb & finger; BREAK ~ *on wheel*. [OE *buttorfleoge* cf. Du. *botervlieg*, connexion with *butter* unexplained]

bütt'erine (-ēn), n. Imitation butter of oleo-margarine & milk. [-INE¹]

bütt'eris, n. Farrier's tool for paring hoof. [cf. F *boutoir* & obs. E *butter*]

bütt'erÿ, n. Place in colleges etc. where bread & ale, butter, etc., are kept; ~*hatch*, half-door over which provisions are issued. [f. OF *boterie*=*bouteillerie* (BOTTLE¹, -ERY)]

bütt'ock¹, n. Half of rump (usu. in pl.); manœuvre in wrestling (*buttock, cross-, running*~, etc.); ~*-steak*, = rumpsteak. [BUTT² +-OCK]

bütt'ock², v.t. Throw by using buttock. [f. prec.]

butt'on¹, n. Knob or disk sewn to garment to fasten it by passing through ~*-hole*, or for ornament (*boy in* ~s, page; *take by the* ~, detain, see ~*hole* below); bud; unopened mushroom; in plant names, as BACHELOR'S ~; knob, handle, catch, as in electric bell (*touch the* ~, produce complicated result by simple action); small bar revolving on pivot as door-fastening; small rounded body; terminal knob (on foil, making it harmless; also as ornament) *a*~*short* (colloq.), of weak intellect; ||~*-boot*, fastened with ~s; ~*hole*, slit made to receive fastening ~, (fig.) small mouth, || flower(s) worn in ~*-hole*, (vb) make ~*-holes* (in), hold by a coat or waistcoat ~, detain, (reluctant listener); [last sense by confusion with earlier ~*hold*]; ~*hook*, for pulling ~ into place; ~*-stick*, soldier's appliance for ~-polishing. Hence (~) ~ED² (nd), ~LESS, aa., ~LESSNESS n. [f. OF *boton* bud f. LL. +*bottonem* nom. -to f. *bottare* push, cf. BUTT¹]

butt'on², n. v.t.&i. Furnish with button(s); fasten (t. & i.) with buttons (often *up*); enclose within ~ed garment (person, or object carried with one; usu. *up*). [f. prec.]

butt'ons, n. Liveried page. [pl. of BUTTON¹]

bütt'onÿ, a. With many buttons. [-Y²]

butt'ress, n. & v.t. Support built against wall etc. (FLYING ~); prop (lit. & fig.); ~like projection of hill; (vb) support (lit. & fig., often with *up*) with ~, by argument, etc. [perh. f. OF *bouteret*, -*et*, flying buttress (*bouter* push cf. ABUT)]

bütt'ÿ, n. (Colloq.) mate, chum, companion; (Mining) middleman between mine-proprietor & miners; ~*-gang* (of men undertaking part of large job, sharing profits equally. [?]

bütt'yr-, bütÿro-, st. & comb. form of technical wds as *butÿra'ceous, butÿ'ric, butÿroacē'tic*; of BUTTER, esp. in its chem. aspect.

bux'om, a. Plump, comely. Hence ~NESS n. [earlier sense *pliant*; ME *buhsum* f. st. of *bēgan* BOW³ +-SOME]

buy (bī), v.t. (bought, pr. bawt), & n. 1. Obtain by paying a (usu. money) price; serve to procure (*money cannot*~); get by some sacrifice (*dearly bought*); gain over (person) by bribery etc.; *I'll* ~ *it* (sl.), I give it up, I don't know (in reply to a riddle or question); ~ *in*, ~ a stock of, withdraw at auction by naming higher price than highest offered; ~ *into*, company; ~ *off*, get rid by payment of (claim, claimant, blackmailer), get (soldier) discharged so; ~ *out*, pay person to give up post, property, etc.; ~ *over*, bribe; ~ *up*, = as much as possible of, absorb (other firm etc.) by purchase; ~ *pig in poke*, commit oneself inconsiderately. Hence ~ABLE a., ~ER¹ n., (esp.) agent who selects & purchases stock for a large shop etc. 2. n. A purchase (*a good*~, a bargain). [OE *bycgan* cf. Goth. *bugjan* etym. dub.]

büz(z)¹, int. = Stale news! [imit.]

büzz², n. Hum of bee etc.; sound of people talking, stir, general movement; *circular saw. [f. prec.]

büzz³, v.i. & t. Make humming sound; move, hover, *about* (person or abs.) annoyingly like bluebottle; (sl.) go off or *away* quickly; (of a company or place) sound confusedly; circulate (t. & i. of rumour etc.); utter by speaking together (~ *applause*); throw hard (~ *stones*).

büzz', n. Downy beetle, fishing-fly like it. [perh. as expressive, cf. FUZZY & obs. *buzz* (large bushy) *wig*]

||**büzz',** v.t. Finish (bottle of wine). [?]

büzz'ard, n. Kinds of falcon (*B*~, *Bald B*~ or osprey, *Honey B*~, *Moon B*~, etc.), [f. OF *busart* f. L *buteo* falcon +-ARD]

büzz'er, n. In vbl senses; esp. steam-whistle, (also) electric buzzing-machine for sending signals, (army sl.) signaller. [BUZZ³ -ER¹]

by, prep. & adv. 1. prep. (bī, sometimes bĭ). Near, at *or* to side of, in postal district of, about person *or* in possession of, in company of, in region of, slightly inclining to, (*Bromley-by-Bow, Coniston-by-Ambleside; come here by me; stand by*, be faithful to, help; *abide by*, accept, observe; *have not got it by me; come by*, obtain; *by oneself*, alone; *North by East*, between N & NNE; *by the head, stern*, deeper in water there; *by land & sea, adventures by flood & field*). 2. Along, in passing along, through, via, avoiding,

passing, out-stripping, (*by nearest road*; *by the way*, as one goes, parenthetically; *so by the by*, esp. as formula introducing digression; *travel by Bâle, Paris*; *pass him by*, *go by him*). **3.** During, in the circumstances of, (*by day, night, daylight*; *by the space of*, biblical for *during*). **4.** Through the agency, means, instrumentality, or causation, of, owing to, in such a manner, with, (*by oneself*, without help or prompting; *know, say, by* HEART; *multiply, divide, by*; *3 ft by 2 ft*; *lead by the hand*; *set by the ears, egg on to quarrel, go, be known, by the name of* ——; *what do you mean by that?*; *travel by rail, by all, no, means; live by bread; do it by* one's *deputy*; *have children by such a father, mother*; *authorized, hanged, made, begin, end, by* ——*ing*; *by way of a joke*; *no gas to read by*; *case goes by default*; *be by way of knowing everybody*, profess or be supposed to; *cautious by nature*; *by cheque, £6.* **5.** *4.* in Cr entries; *by chance*; *by dint of*; *by reason of*). **5.** As soon as, not later than, (*by now, next week, tomorrow*; *the time*—with or oftener without—*that*); according to, after, from, (*by time*; *by role*; *by right*; *by rights*, if right were done; *take warning, example, by*; *by your leave*; *judge by appearances*; *sell, buy, by retail, measure, the yard, packed*). **6.** With succession of, succeeding, (*by degrees, by hundreds, man by man, little by little*). **7.** To the extent of (*missed by a foot, too moral by half, better by far, much*). **8.** Concerning, in respect of, (*do one's duty by*; *French by blood, Jones by name; pull up by the rocks*). **9.** As surely as I believe in (*by God; swear by all one holds sacred; swear by vegetarianism*, declare complete belief in BY a.). **10.** Near (*stand by*, be inactive, also fig. (*bī*). Near (*stand by*, be inactive, esp. Naut.). **11.** Aside, in reserve, (*put, lay, set, by, abandon or store up*). **12.** Past (*they marched by; all that is gone by*). **13.** ~ *&* large, on the whole, everything considered, (orig. Naut., to the wind & off it). [OE *bī*, *bȳ*, *be*; cf. OHG *bī*, *bī*, (G *bei*, *be*-): in OE the prep. was sometimes *be*; in mod. E the adv. is always *bȳ*, the prep. usu. *bĭ* sometimes *bĭ*, & the pref. either *bĭ*- or BE-]

by², *bȳe*, a. Subordinate, incidental, secondary, side, out-of-the-way, secret, as *by(e) road, the by(e) effects, a by(e) consideration*; ~ ELECTION. [*by* adv. used attrib.; often hyphened with noun; usu. *by* when this is done, & *bye* as sep. wd]

by³, n. = BYE (*-e* usu. exc. in *by the by*).

by⁴, pref. **1.** Usu. with one of the meanings of BY a.; it may be written as separate wd (*by path* or *bye path*), hyphened (*by-path*), or, if the combination is often used, as one wd with the other (*bypath*). **2.** Sometimes with meanings of BY adv. as in *bystander, bygone*.

by⁵ and bȳ', adv. & n. Before long, pre-

sently; (n.) the future. [perh. f. BY prep. denoting succession (*one by one* etc.).]

bȳ'-blow (-ō), n. Side blow at someone else than the main opponent; bastard child. [BY a.]

bye, n. Something subordinate (*by the by* or *bye*, incidentally, parenthetically); (Cricket) run scored for ball that passes batsman and wicket-keeper, *leg*~; (in one that touches batsman; (Golf) hole(s) remaining after decision of match & played as a new game; (in games where competitors are paired off) odd man, being odd man. [BY¹ as n.]

bȳe'-bȳe', n. (Nursery word for) sleep, bed. [sound used in lullabies cf. *hushaby*, *lullaby*, *bye baby banking*]

bye-bȳe', int. = Good-bye. [colloq. & childish clipping of *good-bye*]

bȳ'-ênd, n. Side or secret purpose. [BY a.]

bȳ'-gone (-aw-), a. & n. Past, departed; antiquated; (pl. n.) the past, past offences (*let* ~*s be* ~*s*, forgive & forget). [BY adv.]

bȳ'-lāne, n. See BY-.

bȳ'-law, bȳe'-law (-bĭl-), n. Regulation made by local authority or corporation, as town or railway company. [prob. f. obs. *byrlaw* local custom (ON *bȳjar* genit. of *bȳr* OE *bȳ* town, cf. *Derby* etc.), but associated with BY a.]

bȳ'-nāme, n. Secondary name, sobriquet; nickname. [BY a.]

bȳ'-pass (-ah-), n., & v.t. **1.** Secondary gas-jet always alight from which main jet is lit when wanted. **2.** Road usu. passing round, or through outskirts of, town etc., & designed to relieve traffic congestion by providing an alternative route for through traffic. **3.** v.t. Furnish with a ~, make détour round (town etc.), also fig. [BY a.]

bȳ'-past (-ah-), a. Gone by, elapsed. [BY adv.]

bȳ'-path (-ah-), n. Retired path (lit. & fig.). as ~*s of history*). [BY a.]

bȳ'-play, n. Action apart from the main course of events; esp., dumb-show of minor characters on stage. [BY a.]

bȳ'-product, n. Thing produced incidentally in manufacturing something else. [BY a.]

bȳre, n. Cow-house. [OE *bȳre* perh. cogn. w. *bȳr* BOWER]

bȳ'-road, n. Little-frequented road. [BY a.]

bȳss'ŭs, n. Fine ancient textile fibre & fabric of flax; tuft of silky filaments by which some molluscs adhere to rock. Hence ~A'CEOUS, ~AL, ~IF'EROUS, ~INE², ~OID, aa. [L, f. Gk *bussos*]

bȳ'stănder, n. Spectator. [BY adv.]

bȳ'street, n. Out-of-the-way street. [BY a.]

bȳ'-way, n. Secluded road or track (often *highway &* ~; short cut; less known department of any subject. [BY a.]

bȳ'word (-wĕrd), n. Proverb; person, place, etc. taken as type of some (usu.

bad) quality (esp. *a ~ for iniquity* etc.).
[BY a.]

by'-work (-wérk), n. Work done by the way, at leisure moments. [BY a.]

Byzan'tine, a. & n. (Inhabitant) of Byzantium or Constantinople (*~ine historians*, of Eastern Empire from 6th to 15th c.); of the style in architecture etc. developed in the Eastern Empire (round arch, cross, dome, circle, mosaic). Hence ~**inesque** (-ĕsk) a., ~**inism** n., ~**inize**(4) v.t. [f. L *Byzantinus* f. L f. Gk *Buzantion*]

C

C (sē), letter (pl. *Cs, C's, Cees*). *C springs*, see CEE. *C3 population*, (Mus.) first note of natural major scale. (In argument) third hypothetical person or thing. (Alg.) third known quantity.

Caaba (kah'aboa), n. Sacred building at Mecca, Mohammedan Holy of Holies containing the black stone. [Arab. *ka'bah*]

cab¹, n., & v.i. (-bb-). (Go in a) hackney carriage esp. of brougham or hansom shape or taxi; driver's shelter on locomotive; ~'*man*, driver of ~; ||~*rank*, row of wait; ||~*runner*, -*tout*, men earning pay by fetching, or unloading luggage from, ~s. Hence ~'LESS a. [short for CABRIOLET]

‖cab², n., & v.i. (sl.; -bb-). (Use secretly in preparing lessons) a translation, crib. [short for arch. *cabbage* v. & n. pilfer(ing) perh. f. F *cabas* basket f. L *capacem* nom. ~*ax* CAPACIOUS]

cabal', n., & v.i. (-ll-). (Join in a) secret intrigue; clique, faction; (Hist.) the C~, 'Committee for Foreign Affairs' under Charles II, esp. Clifford, Arlington, Buckingham, Ashley, & Lauderdale (1672). ~'YER¹ n. [f. F *cabale(r)* f. med. L *cabala* CABBALA; not f. initials of Clifford etc., being quoted from 1646]

cabа'na (-bah-), n. Brand of cigar. [maker]

cab'aret (-ā), n. French tavern; (in England, U.S., etc.), entertainment provided in restaurant etc. while guests are at table. [F]

cabb'age, n. Kinds of cultivated vegetable with round heart or head; *Sea C~*, Small White; ~ *butterfly*, Large White or Small White; ~*net*, for boiling ~ in; ~ *rose*, double red rose with large compact round flower; ~*tree*, various trees, esp. certain palms with terminal bud eaten like ~. [earlier *cabbage-cole* head-vegetable f. ME & F *caboche* head-*regechia* f. *capo* f. L *caput*]

cabb'ala, n. Jewish oral tradition; mystic interpretation, esoteric doctrine, occult lore. Hence ~ISM(3), ~ISt(2), nn., ~is'tic a., ~is'tically adv. [med. L f. Heb. *qabbalah* tradition]

cabb'y, n. (colloq.). Cab-driver. [-Y³]

cab'er, n. Roughly trimmed pine-trunk used in Sc. Highland sport of *tossing the ~*. [f. Gael. *cabar* pole]

cab'in, n., & v.t. Small rude dwelling; room or compartment in ship for sleeping or eating in, officer's or passenger's room; ~*boy*, waiting on officers or passengers; (vb, chiefly in p.p.) confine in small space, cramp. [ME & F *cabane* f. LL *capanna*]

cab'inet, n. & a. **1.** Small private room, closet; case with drawers etc. for keeping valuables or displaying curiosities. **2.** ||(Pol.) council-room of about twelve or twenty chief ministers of state; those ministers collectively; ~ *council*, one of their meetings; ||~ *crisis*, difficulties involving change of government or resignation of some member(s) of ~; *shadow ~* (formed by Opposition leaders from prospective holders of portfolios). **3.** ||~ *edition*, between library & popular in cost etc.; ||~ *photograph*, size larger than carte-de-visite; ~ *pudding*, made of sponge-cakes, eggs, milk, etc.; ~*maker*, -*making*, skilled joiner, joinery; (also joc. of prime minister forming new government); [CABIN + -ET¹ influenced also by F *cabinet*]

ca'ble¹, n. Strong thick rope (Naut, 10 in. or more in circumf., cf. CABLET, HAWSER) of hemp or wire strands; (Naut.) rope or chain of anchor, (as measure) 100 fathoms; (Teleg.) submarine or underground line containing insulated wires, also =CABLEGRAM; (Archit. & goldsmith's work) rope-shaped ornament; ~*laid rope*, of three twisted strands. [cf. Du. *kabel* f. Rom. cf. F *câble*, It. *cappio*, f. LL *capalum* halter cf. L *capulus* hilt (*capere* take); but the F may be f. L +*catabola* kind of BALLISTA]

ca'ble², v.t. & i. Furnish, fasten, with cable; (Archit.) fill lower part of flutings of (column) with convex mouldings; transmit (message), communicate, inform (person), by cable. [f. prec.]

ca'blegram (-igr-), n. Message by submarine cable. [CABLE¹+-GRAM (hybrid on TELEGRAM)]

ca'blet, n. Cable-laid rope under 10 in. in circumference. [-ET¹]

cabochon' (-sh-), n. Gem polished but not shaped or faceted; *en ~*, (of a gem) so treated. [f. F *caboche*; see CABBAGE]

cabob's', n. pl. Meat cooked in small pieces with ginger, garlic, etc. [Arab. *kabab*]

caboo'dle, n. (sl.). *The whole ~*, all the lot (persons or things). [U.S. wd etym. dub.]

caboose', n. Cooking-room on ship's deck. [cf. Du. *kabuis* perh. =+*kaban-huys* cabin-house]

cab'otage, n. Coasting-trade; reservation to a country of traffic within its territory. [F, f. *caboter* to coast, etym. dub.]

cab'riole, n. & a. Kind of curved leg characteristic of Queen Anne & Chippendale furniture (often attrib.), [as foll., from resemblance to goat's foreleg]

cabriolet' ('-lā), n. Light two-wheeled hooded one-horse chaise; motor car with fixed sides & folding top. [F. f. *cabriole* goat's leap f. It. *capriola* (*caprio* f. L *caprum* nom.-*per* goat)]

cacā'ō, n. & a. Seed of tropical Amer. tree, giving cocoa & chocolate; the tree (also ~-*tree*). [Sp., f. Mex. *caca(uatl*-tree)]

cach'alot (-shalŏt, -shalō), n. Kinds of whale with teeth in lower jaw, esp. *Common C~*, Sperm whale. [F., = toothed (cf. Gascon *cachau* large tooth]

cache (kăsh), n. & v.t. Hiding-place for treasure, provisions, ammunition, etc., esp. as used by explorers; the hiding (*make a ~*) or stores hidden; (vb) place in ~. [F, f. *cacher* to hide f. L *co(actare* collect frequent. of *agere* bring]

cachec'tic ('-k-), a. Of, suffering from, CACHEXY. [f. Gk *kakhektikos* or CACHEXY]

cach'et ('-shā), n. Stamp (fig.), distinguishing mark, internal evidence of authenticity; (Med.) small case (made of gelatine etc.) enclosing dose of (nauseous) medicine. [obs. sense seal, cf. F *lettre de ~* letter under king's private seal (*cacher* see CACHE)]

cachex'ý ('-k-), n. Ill-conditioned state of body or mind. [f. Gk *kakhexia* (CACO-+ *hexis* habit f. *ekhō* hold, be)]

cac'hinnāte (-k-), v.i. Laugh loudly. So ~A'TION n., ~ātorý a. [f. L *cachinnare*, -ātE[3]]

cach'olong, n. Kind of opal. [f. Kalmuck *kaschilon* beautiful stone]

cach'ou (-shoō), n. = CATECHU; pill used by smokers to sweeten breath. [F, = CASHEW]

cachu'cha (-ŏō-), n. A Spanish solo dance. [Sp.]

cacique' ('-sēk'), n. W.-Indian & Amer.-Indian native chief; (Spanish pol.) political boss. Hence **caciqu'ism** (-sēk²) n., local government on Tammany lines. [Sp., f. Haytian]

caco-, pref. = Gk *kako-* (*kakos* bad; found in some wds taken direct or through L (& F) f. Gk; as prefixed in med. terms = *disease of*, as *cacophthalmia* eye-disease, or *mal-*, as *cacomorphia* malformation) usu. to Gk components, rarely to L as *cacodorous* ill-smelling.

cacodēm'on, -aem'on, n. Evil spirit; malignant person. [f. Gk *kakodaimōn* (prec.+*daimōn* spirit)]

cac'odyl, n. Stinking poisonous compound of arsenic & methyl. Hence **cáco-dȳl'ic** a. [Gk *kakōdēs* stinking (CACO-+ *od-* root of *ozō* to smell)+-YL]

caco'epy, n. Bad pronunciation (cf. ORTHO-EPY). [f. Gk CACO(*epeia* f. *epos* word, see-Y[3])]

cacŏ"ēth'es (-ēz), n. Ill habit, itch for doing something unadvisable, usu. in *scribendi ~*, scribbling-mania. [f. Gk *kakoēthes* neut. adj. (CACO-+*ēthos* disposition)]

cacog'raphy, n. Bad handwriting or spelling. Hence cacŏG'RAPHER n., cáco-GRAPHIC(AL) aa. [CACO-, -GRAPHY]

cacol'ogy, n. Bad choice of words or pronunciation. [f. Gk *kakologia* vituperation (*caco-, -logos*-speaking f. *legō* speak]

cacŏŏn', n. Large flat polished bean of tropical shrub with 6-8ft pods. [African?]

cacŏph'onous, a. Ill-sounding. [Gk CACO-(*phōnos*-sounding f. *phōnē* sound)+-OUS]

cacŏph'ony, n. Ill sound (cf. EUPHONY); discord (lit. & fig.). [f. F *cacophonie* f. Gk *kakophōnia* as prec. & see -Y[1]]

cac'tus, n. Kinds of succulent plant with thick fleshy stem, usu. no leaves, & clusters of spines. Hence ~A'CEOUS (-shus), ~AL, ~OID, aa. [L, f. Gk *kaktos* cardoon]

cad, n. Person of low manners; person guilty or capable of ungentlemanly conduct, blackguard, whence ~d'ISH[1] a.; member of lower classes; hanger-on employed about (esp. school & college) games; (obs.) omnibus conductor. [quoted f. 1831; prob. short for CADET[2] (cf. CADDIE) & started at Eton & Oxford as name for townsmen]

cadás'tral, a. Of, showing, the extent, value, & ownership, of land for taxation (esp. ~ *survey*). [F, f. *cadastre* f. L *capitastrum* register of *capita* (*caput* head) units made for Roman *capitatio terrena* land-tax]

cadāve'ric, a. (med. & physiol.). Characteristic of a corpse. [L *cadaver* corpse (perh. f. *cadere* fall)+-IC]

cadāv'erous, a. Corpse-like; deadly pale. [f. F *cadavéreux* f. L *cadaverosus* (prec., -OSE[2])]

cadd'ie, n. Golf-player's attendant for carrying clubs etc. [Sc. (also *cadie*) f. F CADET[2]]

cadd'is, -ice, n. Larva of May-fly etc., living in water & making cylindrical case of hollow stems etc., used as bait; also **cădd'ỹ-worm**. [also *cad, cod*, etym. dub.]

cadd'y, n. Small box for holding tea. [f. Malay *kati* weight=1⅓ lb.]

cad'ence, n. Rhythm; measured movement, esp. of sound; fall of voice, esp. at end of period; intonation; close of musical phrase. Hence (~)căd'encED[2] (-st) a. [F, f. It. *cadenza* (L *cadere* fall.-ENCY]

cad'ency, n. Descent of younger branch, cadetship. [as prec., -ENCY]

cadĕn'za (-tsa), n. (mus.). Flourish of voice or instrument at close of movement. [It.]

cadet¹, n. Younger son; student in naval or military or air force college, whence ~SHIP n.; member of Russian Constitutional-Democratic party; ~ corps, company of schoolboys receiving elementary military training. [f. foll. f. 15th-c. capdet f. Rom. †capitello dim. of L caput head = little chief]

cadet²' (-dā), n. (Appended to surname of distinction, cf. AÎNÉ) the younger brother (as Coquelin ~). [F]

cad'i (kah-, kā-), n. Civil judge, usu. of town etc., among Turks, Arabs, Persians. [Arab.]

Cadmē'an. See VICTORY.

cād'mium, n. Bluish-white metal resembling tin; ~-yellow, intense yellow pigment. Hence cādmĪF'EROUS, cād'mic, aa. [f. obs. cadmia CALAMINE f. L f. Gk kadmia (gē) Cadmean (earth), -IUM]

cadre (kah'dr), n. Framework, scheme; (Mil.) permanent establishment of regiment forming nucleus for expansion at need. [F f. It. quadro f. L quadrum SQUARE]

cadū'cēus, n. (pl. -ēi), Ancient herald's wand, esp. as carried by messenger-god Hermes. [L, f. Gk karukion (kērux herald)]

cadū'city, n. (pl. -ēi), a. Fleeting (nature); perishable(ness); (Zool. & Bot., of organs & parts) falling off (n. & a.) when work is done. [n. thr. F caducité (-TY), a. f. L caducus falling (cadere fall) + -OUS]

caec'um (sē-), n. (pl. -ca). The blind gut, first part of large intestine in mammals etc.; any tube with closed end. Hence ~AL, ~IFORM, aa., ~ALLY² adv., ~ITIS n. [L, for intestinum caecum f. caecus blind]

Caes'ar (sēz'ar), n. Roman Emperor from Augustus to Hadrian; heir presumptive of later Roman Emperor; (loosely) any Roman Emperor; an autocrat; the civil power (Matt. xxii. 21); ~'s wife, person required to be above suspicion. [L, family name of C. Julius]

Caesā'rean, -ian, (sēz-) a. & n. Of Caesar or the Caesars; imperial; ~ birth, operation, delivery of child by cutting walls of abdomen (as with Julius); (n.) adherent of Caesar or an autocratic system. [f. L Caesarianus see -IAN]

caes'arism, -ist, (sēz-), nn. (Believer in) autocracy. [-ISM(3), -IST(2)]

caes'ious (sēz-) a. (bot.). Bluish or greyish green. [f. L caesius +-OUS]

caes'ium (sēz-), n. (chem.). An 'alkali-metal. [as prec. f. its spectrum lines]

caesūr'|a (sēz-), n. (Cl. prosody) break between words within a metrical foot; (Eng. prosody) pause about middle of line. Hence ~AL a. [L (caedere caes- cut, -URE)]

café¹ (kǎf'ā), n. Coffee-house, restaurant (esp. foreign); ~ chantant (see Ap.), with music & entertainments, often in open air). [F. = coffee(-house)]

café² (kǎfā'), n. Coffee; ~ au lait(ō lā), with milk; ~ noir(nwar), without milk. [F]

caffé'ic, a. (chem.) Of coffee (esp. ~ acid). [f. F caféique, see prec.]

•**cafété'ria,** n. Restaurant in which customers fetch what they want from the counters. [Sp., = coffee-shop]

caffé'ine, n. Vegetable alkaloid found in coffee & tea plants. [f. F caféine (CAFÉ1,2 -INE5)]

Caffre. See KAFIR.

căf'tan (also kǎftahn'), n. Eastern long under-tunic with waist girdle. [f. Turk. qaftan]

cāge, n., & v.t. Fixed or portable prison, of wire or barred, esp. for birds or beasts; prison (lit. or fig.); (Mining) frame for hoisting & lowering cars; open framework of various kinds; (vb) place or keep in ~. [F, f. L cavea(cavus hollow) cf. cage]

caïman. See CAYMAN.

Cain, n. Fratricide, murderer; raise ~, make a disturbance. [Gen. iv]

cainozō'ic (kin-), a. (geol.). Of the third geological period (= tertiary, cf. palaeozoic, mesozoic). [f. Gk kainos new +zōōn animal + -IC]

caïque (ka-ēk'), n. Light Bosporan row-boat; Levantine sailing-ship. [F, f. Turk. kaïk]

cairn, n. Pyramid of rough stones as memorial, sepulchre, landmark, etc.; (also ~ terrier) small short-legged long-bodied shaggy-coated terrier (from its being used to hunt among ~s). [f. Gael. carn]

cairngǒrm', n. (Also ~ stone) yellow or wine-coloured precious stone. [found on C~, Scotch mountain (Gael. carn gorm blue cairn)]

caiss'on, n. Ammunition chest or wagon; large water-tight case used in laying foundations under water; boat-shaped vessel used as dock gate; ~ disease (of workers in compressed air, as in ~s etc.). [F (caisse f. L capsa CASE² -OON)]

cait'iff, n. & a. (poet. & arch.). Base, despicable, (person); coward(ly). [f. ONF caitif f. L captivus CAPTIVE]

cajole', v.t. Persuade or soothe by flattery, deceit, etc. (also ~e person into doing, out of something; or ~e something out of person). Hence ~e'MENT(-1m-), ~'ER¹, ~'ERY(4), nn., ~'ingLY² adv. [f. F cajoler etym. dub.; Cotgrave has also cageoler 'jangle like a jay', whence it has also been referred to cage]

cake, n., & v.i. & t. Small flattish loaf of bread (arch., as in king Alfred & the

~s); thin oaten bread (Sc. & north.; also *oat~*; *land of* ~s, Scotland). (usu. Eng. sense) bread with other ingredients besides flour, as currants, spice, eggs, sugar —the substance (~) or (*a* ~) a portion of it baked in a thick disk or ornamental shape—; flattish compact mass of other food (*fish-*~, PAN-~) or of any compressed substance (~ *of soap, wax, tobacco*); ~s *& ale*, merry-making; ~*-walk*, kinds of dance developed from negro contest in graceful walking with ~ for prize; *a piece of*~ (colloq.), something easy or pleasant; *take the* ~, carry off the honours; *cannot eat your* ~ *and have it*, do mutually exclusive things; hence **căk'y²** a. **2.** v.t. & i. Form into compact flattish mass. [prob. f. ON *kaka* cf. G *kuche* etym. dub. (not cogn. with L *coquere* cook)]

calabaŕ' bean, n. Poisonous seed of African climbing plant yielding an extract valuable in medicine & surgery. [*Calabar* on W. coast of Africa]

căl'abăsh, n. Kinds of gourd whose shell serves for holding liquid; fruit of American ~-tree, so used; pipe etc. made from these or of like shape. [f. F *calebasse* f. Sp. *calabaça*, Sicil. *caravuzza*, perh. f. Pers. *kharbuz* melon]

cǎl'aber, -ar, n. Fur of grey squirrel. [prob. f. F *Calabre* Calabria]

***cǎlabōose' (-z), n. Common prison, lock-up. [f. Sp. *calabozo* dungeon]

calamăn'cō, n. Glossy Flemish woollen stuff much used in 18th c. [etym. dub.; f. Du. *kalamink*, F *calmande*]

cǎlamăn'der, n. Hard cabinet wood of Ceylon & India. [etym. dub.; perh. f. *Coromandel*]

cǎl'amarý, n. Kinds of cuttlefish with pen-shaped internal shell. [f. L *calamarius* (*calamus* pen, -ARY²)]

cǎl'amine, n. A zinc ore found in England. [F, f. med. L *calamīna* (L *cadmia* (CADMIUM]

cǎl'amint, n. Kinds of aromatic herb. [ult. f. Gk *kalaminthē*]

calǎsh', n. Light low hooded carriage; carriage hood; (Canada) two-wheeled one-seated vehicle with driver's seat on splash-board; woman's hooped silk hood. [f. F *calèche* f. Slav. (Boh. *koléša* etc.]

cǎl'amitous, a. Marked by, causing, calamity. Hence ~LY² adv. [f. F *calamiteux* f. L *calamitosus* see foll., -OUS]

calǎm'itý, n. Adversity, deep distress; grievous disaster. [f. F *calamité* f. L *cala-mitatem* (-TY) cf. *incolumis* safe]

cǎlǎn'dō, mus. direction. Diminish tone & pace gradually. [It.]

cǎl'amite, n. Fossil plant allied to Mare's Tail. [f. L *calamus* reed +-ITE(2)]

---

calcĕ'ĕous, -ĭous, a. Of, containing, carbonate of lime or limestone. Hence **calcaŕ'ĕo-**, comb. form. [f. L *calcarius* (CALC-, -ARY²) +-OUS; first spelling wrong but usu.]

calcĕolāŕ'ia, n. Kinds of plant with flower shaped like slipper. [f. L *calceolus* dim. of *calceus* shoe + fem. of *-arius* -ARY¹]

cǎl'cĕolāte, a. (bot.). Slipper-shaped. [as prec., -ATE²]

cǎl'cĭc, a. Of calcium. [-IC]

calcĭf'erous, a. Yielding carbonate of lime. [CALC-, -I-, -FEROUS]

cǎl'cĭfý, v.t. & i. Convert, be converted, into lime; harden by lime; harden by deposit of salts of lime; petrify. Hence ~IF'ĬC a., ~ĬFICA'TION n. [CALC-, -I-, -FY]

cǎl'cĭmine, n., & v.t. White or tinted wash for ceilings & walls; (vb) distemper with ~. [f. L *calx-cis* lime]

cǎl'cĭne, v.t. & i. Reduce to quick-lime or friable substance by roasting or burning; desiccate; refine by consuming grosser part; burn to ashes; (intr.) suffer these processes. Hence ~A'TION, ~ER¹(2), nn. [f. med. L *calcinare* reduce to lime. [f. L *calx-cis* lime]

cǎl'cĭte, n. Native carbonate of lime. [f. L *calx-cis* lime + -ITE¹]

cǎl'cĭum, n. Chemical element, white metal, the basis of lime (in many compd terms, as ~ *chloride*). Hence **cǎl'cĭo-** comb. form. [as prec.+-IUM]

cǎl'cŭlable, a. That may be reckoned, measured, computed, or relied upon. Hence ~ABIL'ĬTY n. [f. L *calculare* (foll., -ABLE]

cǎl'cŭlāte, v.t. & i. Compute (w. noun or clause, or abs.) by figures (~*ating-machine*, that does sums automatically); ascertain beforehand (event, date, etc.) by exact reckoning; plan deliberately (t. & i., esp. in intr. sense, with *upon*); (t. & i., esp. ish); (usu. pass.) arrange, adapt, (conduct, apparatus, etc.) *for* (purpose), *to* (do); (in p.p.) fit, suitable; (in U.S.) believe, suppose, believe. Hence ~ATIVE a. [f. L *calculare* (CALCULUS), -ATE³]

cǎlcŭlā'tion, n. (Result got by) reckoning; forecast. [f. F, L *calculationem* (prec., -ATION]

cǎl'cŭlātor, n. In vbl senses; also: set of tables for use in calculation; calculating-machine. [L (CALCULATE, -OR²]

cǎl'cŭlous, a. Of, suffering from, stone or calculus. [f. L *calculosus* (foll., -OSE³]

cǎl'cŭlus, n. (pl. *-lī*, in math. sense freq. ~*es*). **1.** (Med.) Stone, concretion in some part of body (*renal* etc. ~ f. the particular part; *uric acid* etc. ~ f. its composition). **2.** (Math.) particular method of calculation, as *differential, integral*, ~. [L, = small stone (*calx -cis* stone, -ULE) used in reckoning on abacus]

căldaŕ'ĭum, n. (archaeol.). Roman hot bath room. [f. L *caldārius* hot, see -ARY¹]

caldron. See CAULDRON.

Caledōn'ian, a. & n. (Native) of ancient

Scotland (also used in mod. titles of clubs etc. & joc. =Scotch or Scot). [f. L *Caledonia* northern Britain, -AN]

calefa'cient (-shent), a. & n. (Medical agent) producing warmth. [f. L *calefacere* (*calere* be warm, *facere* make), -ENT, -ANT]

calefac'tory, a. & n. Producing warmth; (Archaeol.) warm room in monastery. [f. L *calefactorius* see prec.]

cal'endar¹, n. System by which beginning, length, & subdivision, of civil year is fixed, esp. the Gregorian ~; used in Engl. from 1752; table(s) with months, weeks, & festivals etc., of a given year, or with dates important for certain classes, as *Gardener's* ~; register, list, esp. of canonized saints, prisoners for trial, or documents chronologically arranged with summaries; ~ MONTH. [f. OF *calendier* f. L *calendarium* account-book (CALENDS, -ARY¹)]

calen'dar², v.t. Register, enter in list; arrange, analyse, & index (documents), whence ~ER¹ n. [f. prec.]

cal'ender¹, v.t. & n. Press (cloth, paper, etc.) in a ~ or roller-machine to smooth it; steam mangle; (arch.) person who ~s. Hence cal'endry n. [f. F *calandre(r)* f. med. L *calendra* f. L f. Gk *kulindros* roller]

cal'ender², -r, n. pl. First of month in Roman calendar; *on the Greek ~s*, never. [f. L *kalendae* (*cal-* cf. *calare*, Gk *kaleō*, proclaim)]

calen'ture, n. Tropical fever or delirium in which sailors etc. leap into sea. [f. Sp. *calentura* fever f. part. st. of L *calere* be hot, -URE]

calf¹ (kahf), n. (pl. -ves). Young of bovine animal, esp. domestic cow, for first year (*cow in, with,* ~; pregnant; *slip her* ~; suffer abortion); *golden* ~; wealth as object of worship (*Ex.* xxxii); stupid fellow; ~ child (so ~*love*, childish love affair); (also ~*skin*)=~*leather*, esp. in bookbinding (~*bound*) & shoemaking (*willow*~, superior brown leather used in shoemaking); young of elephant, whale, deer, etc.; *sea*~, seal; (Naut.) floating piece of ice; ~*knee*, knock-knee; ||~'*s teeth*, milk teeth; *calves-foot jelly*. Hence ~HOOD n., ~ISH¹(1) a. [com.-Teut., cf. G *kalb*]

calf² (kahf), n. (pl. -ves). Fleshy hinder part of leg-shank; ~ part of stocking. Hence ~'LESS, -CALVED² (kahvd), aa. [f. ON *kálfi* etym. dub.]

Cal'iban, n. Man of degraded bestial nature. [Shaksp., *Tempest*, & see CANNI-BAL]

cal'ibrate, v.t. Find calibre of; calculate irregularities of (tube, gauge) before graduating. Hence ~A'TION n. [foll. +-ATE³]

cali̇bre (-er), **cal'iber**, n. Internal diameter of gun or any tube; weight or character, standing, importance. Hence -cāl'ibred² (-erd) a. [F (-*bre*), f. It. *calibro* perh. f. Arab. *qāḷib* mould]

cal'icle, n. (biol.). Small cup-like body. So calic'ular a. [f. L *caliculus* dim. of *calix* cup]

cal'ico, n. & a. (pl. ~es). ||(Of) cotton cloth, esp. plain white unprinted, bleached or unbleached (~*ball*, dance at which only cotton dresses are worn); ~*printer*, -*ting*, cotton production, of coloured patterns on ~. [orig. *Calicut-cloth* f. town on Malabar coast]

cal'iology, n. Study of birds' nests. [f. Gk *kalia* hut, nest, -o-, -LOGY]

cal'ipash, **cal'ipee**, nn. Gelatinous substances in turtle regarded as dainties (~*ash*, dull green next upper shell; -*ee*, light, yellow next lower shell). [perh. W.-Ind.: perh. ~*ash* = CARAPACE, & -*ee* formed for distinction f. it]

cal'iph, -**if**, n. Successor of Mohammed, chief civil & religious ruler. Hence cāl'iphate¹ n. [f. F *calife* f. Arab. *khalīfah* successor]

calix, n. (anat.; pl. -ices). Cup-like cavity or organ. [L, = cup, often confused w. L CALYX]

calk¹ (kawk), v.t., & n. (Provide with) sharp iron to prevent horse-shoe or boot from slipping. [f. L *calx calcis* heel, cf. CALKIN]

calk² (kawk), v.t. Trace by colouring back of design & pressing along outlines. [f. F *calquer* f. It. *calcare* tread.]

cal'kin (kaw-, also kăl-), n. Turned-down heels of horse-shoe, also turned edge in front, esp. when sharpened in frost; iron guards on boots or shoes. [perh. f. OF *calcain* heel f. L *calcaneum* (*calx calcis* heel)]

call¹ (kawl), v.t. & i. 1. Cry, shout, speak loudly, (lit. & fig. etc., as): (bird, trumpet, etc.) utter characteristic note; cry out; cry to (person); signal (*for trumps*); pay brief visit (*at house, on person*); read over (names to ascertain presence); ~ *for*, order, demand, need, go & fetch; ~ *on*, invoke, appeal to; put off (engagement etc.). 2. Summon (lit. & fig. etc., as): demand presence of (cab, witness, actor after curtain); broadcast (to); (Cards) direct opponent to play (exposed or other card); ~ *into play*, give scope for; ~ *in question*, dispute; ~ *to mind* etc., also ~ *up*, recollect; ~ *away, off*, divert, distract; ~ *in* money lent, doctor etc. for advice; ~ *forth*, ~*out*, elicit, challenge to duel, summon (troops) esp. to aid the civil authorities; ~ *over the* COALS; ~ *up*, imagine, summon to talk by telephone, summon to serve in army etc.; rouse from sleep; fix the moment for (~*case in law*-

court; ~ a hall; ~ a meeting; urge, invite, nominate, (duty, pleasure, ~s; many are ~ed; || ~ to the BAR¹, ministry; ~ attention to; ~ to witness). **3.** (With n. or adj. as compl.) name, describe as, (~ a SPADE a spade; ~ him John, ~ him by the name of John; ~ person names, abuse him; ~ COUSINs with); consider, regard as, (~ that mean); ~ (thing) one's own, possess; ~ down (colloq.), reprimand, challenge. [f. ON *kalla*, conn.-Teut. cf. Du. *kallen*]

call² (kawl), n. Shout, cry; (also ~-over) =ROLL-~; special cry of bird etc., imitation of this, instrument imitating it; signal on bugle etc., signalling-whistle; looking-in on business (so house of ~); short formal visit (pay ~, make one); invitation, summons, (to actor for applause; || to the BAR¹; from God, conscience, or congregation, to be pastor); duty, need, occasion, (no ~ to blush); demand for money, esp. for unpaid capital from company shareholders. (St. Exch.) option of claiming stock at given date; (Bridge) player's right or turn to make a bid, bid thus made; ~-loan, money, lent subject to recall without notice; ~-boy, within, ~ ready for orders; prompter's attendant summoning actors; ~-day, -night, at Inns of Court, for calling students to bar; ~-over (Betting) reading aloud a list of prices (in sporting club etc.); roll-~ at schools. [f, prec.]

call'a, n. (bot.). (Also ~-lily) marsh plant of N. Europe, bog arum. [?]

call'er¹ (kaw-), n. In vbl senses: esp. person who pays call or visit. [-ER¹]

call'er², a. (Sc.). Fresh, not decaying, (of herring etc.); cool (of air). [?]

callig'raphy̆, n. Beautiful handwriting; handwriting. So callig'RAPHER, ~IST(1), nn., calliGRAPH'IC a. [ult. f. Gk *kalligraphia* (*kallos* beauty, -GRAPH)]

call'ing (kaw-), n. In vbl senses; also or esp.: divine summons to salvation or self-devotion; impulse to do something as right, occupation, profession, trade; persons following a particular business. [-ING¹]

calli'ope, n. Steam-organ. [Gk *Kalliopē* beautiful-voiced (Muse)]

call(i)'iper, n., & a., & v.t. ~ compasses or ~s, compasses with bowed legs for measuring diameter of convex bodies, or with out-turned points for measuring calibre; ~-square, rule with movable cross-heads for taking internal or external diameters; (vb) measure with ~s. [prob.=CALIBRE]

callisthen'ic, a. Suitable for producing strength with beauty (esp. of girls' gymnastics). Hence ~ICS n. [f. Gk *kallos* beauty + *sthenos* strength +-IC]

callos'ity, n. Abnormal hardness & thickness of skin; hardened insensible part, lump, (from friction, or natural as on horses' legs). [f. F *callosité* f. L *callositatem* (see foll.-TY)]

call'ous, a. (Physiol., Zool.) hardened, hard, (of parts of skin); (of person, heart, etc.) unfeeling, insensible, unmoved. ~NESS n. [f. L *callosus* (*callum* or CALLUS, -OSE¹)]

call'ow (-ō), a. Unfledged; downy like young birds; raw, inexperienced; (Irish, Sc., & n.) low-lying, often flooded, (meadow). [OE *calu* f. WG *kalwo-* (cf. G *kahl*) perh. f. L *calvus* bald]

call'us, n.(physiol.,path.,bot.). Thickened part of skin or soft tissue; bony material formed while bone-fracture heals. [L]

calm¹ (kahm), n. Stillness, serenity, (of weather, air, sea, the mind, social or political conditions); a ~, windless period. [f. F *calme* f. It., Sp., or Port., *calma* perh. (with infl. of L *calor* heat) f. Gk *kauma* heat (*kaiō* burn)]

calm² (kahm), a., & v.t. & i. **1.** Tranquil, quiet, windless, (lit. & fig.); (colloq.) impudent (*pretty ~ of him*); hence ~'LY² adv., ~'NESS n. **2.** v.t. Make ~, pacify; (v.i.; alw. w. *down*) become ~. [f. F *calme* n. & a., see prec.]

calm'ative (also kawm-), a. & n. (med.). Calming (agent), sedative. [prec. +-ATIVE]

cal'omel, n. (med.). Mercurous chloride used as purgative. [F, f. Gk *kalos* fair, *melas* black (explained anecdotically in various ways)]

calores'cence, n. (physics). Change of heat-rays to light-rays. [for *calescence* (L *calescere* grow hot) by confusion w. foll.]

calori-, comb. form of L *calor* heat in Physics & Physiol. Hence calo'ri-FACIENT, calorif'IC, calo'riFER(RIC(AL), aa., calorif'ICALLY adv., calo'rifica'TION, calorif'ETER, -METRY, nn., calo'rify v.t. calo'ric n. Heat; ~-engine, driven by hot air. [f. F *calorique* (L *calor* heat, -IC)]

cal'orie, n. (physics). Unit of quantity of heat; *large* or *great* or *food ~*, amount of heat required to raise one kilogram of water 1° C. [F, f. L *calor* heat +-ie (-y)]

calotte', n. Skull-cap of priests etc. [F, dim. of *calte* CAUL]

calp, n. Irish dark-grey limestone. [?]

cal'trop, n. Four-spiked iron ball thrown on ground to maim cavalry horses; kinds of plant, as Star-thistle. [found earliest as plant name: but prob. transf. f. the iron: f. L *cala -cis* heel + LL *trappa* f. OHG *trapo* TRAP]

cal'umet, n. Amer.-Ind. clay-bowled reed-stemmed tobacco-pipe; symbol of peace; *smoke the ~ together*, make peace. [F, esp. Fr.-Canadian form of *chalumet* tube f. L *calamellus* dim. of *calamus* reed]

calum'niate, v.t. Slander. Hence or cogn. ~ATION, ~ATOR², nn., ~ATORY a. [f. L *calumniari*, see -ATE³]

calum'nious, a. Given to, marked by, calumny. Hence ~LY² adv. [f. L *calumniosus* (see foll., -OUS)]

cal'umny̆, n. Malicious misrepresenta-

tion; false charge; slanderous report. [f. L *calumnia* (& F *calomnie*) f. *calvi* deceive]

Cal'vary, n. Place, (R.-C. Ch.) representation, of Crucifixion. [f. L *calvaria* skull, f. *calvus* bald; transl. of *Golgotha*, *Matt.* xxvii. 33]

calve (kähv), v.i. & t. Give birth to a calf; (esp. in pass. of calf) give birth to; (of iceberg etc.) throw off mass of ice. [OE *cealfian* (CALF¹)]

calved. See CALF¹.

Cal'vinism, n. Calvin's theology (esp. the doctrines of Particular election & redemption, Moral inability in a fallen state, Irresistible grace, Final perseverance); adherence to this. So ~IST(2) n. & a., ~IS'TIC(AL) aa., ~is'tically adv. [f. *John Calvin,* 1509–1564]

calx, n. (pl. *cal'cēs*). Powder or friable substance left when a metal or mineral has been burnt, residuum. [L, genit. *calcis,* lime]

calyc-, calyci-, calyci-, **calci-flor'al, -flor'ate², -flor'ous,** aa., with stamens & petals inserted in calyx; **cal'yciform** a.; **calyc'inal, cal'ycine³, cal'yciñe¹** a., on the calyx; **calyc'inal** a., = -al, also (of flower) double by increase of calyx-lobes; **cal'ycoid, caly-coid** EOUS, aa.

cal'ycle, n. (bot.). Row of bracts surrounding calyx-base; adherent crown of seed. Hence or cogn. ~ED¹(-id), **calyc'u-**LAR¹, **calyc'ulate²** aa. [f. L *calyculus* dim. of CALYX (-ULE)]

calyp'tra, n. (bot.). Row of bracts surrounding calyx-base; adherent crown of seed. Hence or cogn. ~ED¹(-id), **calyc'u-**LAR¹, **calyc'ulate²** aa. [f. L *calyculus* dim. of CALYX (-ULE)]

calyp'tra, st. of bud, forms=having, like, a hood. [f. Gk *kaluptra* veil (*kaluptō* to cover)]

ca'lyx, n. (pl. -*yces, -yxes*). (Bot.) whorl of leaves (SEPAL) forming outer case of bud (for derivatives see CALYC-); (Physiol. & Biol.) = CALIX. [L, f. Gk *kalux* (cf. *kaluptō* to cover) case of bud, husk]

cam, n. Projecting part of wheel etc. in machinery, grooved, toothed, or otherwise adapted to convert circular into reciprocal or variable motion. [var. of COMB, cf. Du, Da., Sw., *kam*, G *kamm*]

camarade'rie (-ahder'i), n. The intimacy, mutual trust, & sociability, of comrades. [F]

cam'ber (CAMERA)³ f. L *camerare* to vault. [F]

cam'ber, n. & v.i. & t. Slight convexity above, arched form, (of beam, deck, road, etc.); (also ~*beam*) slightly arched beam; small dock or tidal basin; (vb) have, impart to (beam etc.), such convexity. [f. F *cambre(r)* f. L *camera* (see CHAMBER)]

cam'bist, n. Expert in, manual of, exchanges; dealer in bills of exchange. [f. F *cambiste* f. L *cambium* exchange]

cam'brel. See CAMBER.

cam'bric, a. & n. ~ *blue,* light blue. [f. W *cambren* (*cam* crooked + *pren* wood)]

Cam'brian, a. & n. Welsh(man); (Geol.) (of) palaeozoic rocks lying above the archaean in Wales & Cumberland. [f. L *Cumbria* var. of *Cumbria* f. Celt. *Cymry* Welshman or *Cymru* Wales (OCelt. *Com-broges* compatriots)]

Cam'bridge, n. ~ *blue,* light blue. [f. place of making]

cam'bric, a. & n. Fine white linen; handkerchiefs. [*Cambray,* orig. place of making]

cam'bric, n. Grooved slip of lead used in lattice windows. [cf. Sc. *calm* casting-mould]

came¹. See COME.

cam'el, n. Large hornless ruminant long-necked cushion-footed quadruped with (Arabian) one hump or (Bactrian) two humps; thing hard to believe or put up with (*Matt.* xxiii. 24); machine for floating ship over shoals etc.; ∥ ~*brown,* fish-ing-fly; ~'*s-hair,* made of ~'s hair or (paint-brushes) of squirrel's tail hairs. [OE, f. L f. Gk *kamēlos* f. Semit. (cf. Heb. *gāmāl* camel, Arab. *jamala* carry)]

camel'ēer, n. Camel-driver. [-EER]

camel'ia, n. Flowering evergreen from China & Japan. [*Kamel,* Jesuit & botanist, -IA¹]

cam'elopard (or käm'e-), n. = the now usu. GIRAFFE. [f. L *camelopardus* f. Gk *kamēlo-pardalis* (CAMEL, PARD)]

cam'elry, n. Troops on camels. [-RY]

Cam'embert(-âr), n. Small soft rich Norman cheese. [name of village]

cam'eo, n. (pl. ~s). Piece of relief-carving in stone (sardonyx, agate, etc.) with colour-layers utilized to give background (cf. INTAGLIO). [f. It. *cameo* cf. med. L *cammaeus* etym. dub.]

cam'era, n. In *camerā* (Lat.), in the judge's private room, not in open court; (orig. ~ *obscura*) photographing-apparatus; ~ *öbscūr'a, tū'cida* (L, = dark, light, chamber), two kinds of apparatus projecting on paper, for tracing, image of distant object. [L, = vault, cf. Gk *kamara* anything with arched cover]

cam'erling'o (-nggō), -*lēn-,* n. The Pope's chamberlain & financial secretary; treasurer of the Sacred College. [It. (-*ingo*); see CHAMBERLAIN]

Cam'eron'ian, a. & n. (Follower) of Richard Cameron or his doctrines; Scottish reformed presbyterian; ∥ (pl.) both battalions of the Scottish Rifles (formed orig. of ~*s*). [-IAN]

∥ **cam'i-knick'ers,** n. pl. Woman's under-garment of camisole & knickers combined. [*camisole + knickers* (*bockers*)]

cam'ion, n. Low flat four-wheeled horse or motor truck. [F]

cam'biun, n. Cellular tissue, below bark of exogens, in which annual growth of wood & bark occurs. [L, = exchange]

cam'brel, n. Butcher's bent wood or iron for slinging carcasses by ankles. [perh. f. W *cambren* (*cam* crooked + *pren* wood)]

camisole, n. Under-bodice, usu. embroidered etc. [F, f. Sp. *camisola* (*camisa* CHEMISE)]

cam'let, n. Light cloth of various materials for cloaks etc. [orig. a costly Eastern stuff of silk & camel's hair; f. F *camelot* perh. f. CAMEL, perh. f. Arab. *khaml* nap]

camm'ock, n. Rest-harrow; kinds of yellow-flowered plant. [OE *cammoc* etym. dub.]

cam'omile, ch- (pr. k-), n. Aromatic creeping composite plant with daisy-like flowers used as tonic; allied kinds of plant, *Dog's, Stinking, Purple, C~; ~ tea,* infusion of the flowers. [f. F *camomille* f. L *chamomilla* f. Gk *khamaimēlon* earth-apple]

Camo'rra, n. Secret society in Naples etc. [It.]

cam'ouflage (-ooflahzh), n., & v.t. Disguise of guns, ships, etc., effected by obscuring outline with splashes of various colours; use of smoke-screens, boughs, etc., for same purpose; (transf.) means of throwing people off the scent; (vb) hide by ~. [F, f. *camoufler* smoke-puff] **camouflet** (kahmooflā'), n. Subterranean cavity formed by bomb exploding beneath surface of earth. [F]

camp[1], n. Place where troops are lodged in tents etc.; army on campaign; military life (*courts & ~s*); temporary quarters of nomads, gypsies, travellers; camping-out; persons camping out; adherents of a doctrine; *~-bed, -chair, -stool,* folding & portable; *~-colour,* flag used in marking out; *~-fever,* esp. typhus; *~-follower,* non-military hanger-on of camp, male or female; *~-meeting,* American religious open-air or tent meeting lasting several days. [F, f. It. or Sp. *campo* (cf. F *champ* direct) f. L *campus* level ground, esp. the Campus Martius, exercising-ground]

camp[2], v.i. & t. Encamp, lodge in camp; (also *~ out*) lodge in tent or the open, take up quarters; station (troops) in camp. [f. F *camper* (prec.)]

Campa'gna (-ahn'nya), n. *The ~,* Italian plain S.E. of Tiber. [f. L *Campania* (CAMP[1])]

campaign[2] (-ān), n., & v.i. **1.** Series of military operations in a definite theatre or with one objective or from taking the field to a temporary or final cessation of hostilities (*the Burma, Moscow, 1704, ~*); organized course of action, esp. (Pol.) attempt to rouse public opinion for or against a policy. **2.** v.i. Serve on a ~; hence ~ER[1] n. (*old ~er,* person practised in adapting himself to circumstances). [f. F *campagne* open country, campaign, f. It. CAMPAGNA (cf. F *champagne* CHAMPAIGN)]

campanil'e (-nē-), n. Bell-tower, usu. detached. [It., f. *campana* bell]

campanol'ogy, n. The subject of bells (founding, ringing, etc.). Hence ~ōl'oGER, ~ōl'oGIST, nn., ~olŏG'ICAL a. [f. LL *campana* bell +-LOGY]

campan'ula, n. Kinds of plant with bell-shaped flowers, usu. blue or white, as Canterbury Bell. Hence ~A'CEOUS a. [mod. L, dim. of *campana* bell]

campan'ulate, a. (zool. & bot.). Bell-shaped. [as prec. +-ATE[2]]

cam'phor, n. Whitish translucent crystalline volatile substance with aromatic smell & bitter taste. Hence **cam-phō'rrо** a. [f. F *camfre,* med. L *camphora,* f. Arab. *kafur* f. Malay *kapur* chalk]

cam phorāte, v.t. Impregnate or treat with camphor. [+-ATE[2]]

cam'pion, n. Kinds of flowering plant, esp. the Red & the White C~. [?]

cam'pō stsur'tō, n. Cemetery in Italy. [It., = sacred field]

‖**camp'shed, v.t.** Face with campshot. ‖**camp'shot,** ‖**camp'shedding,** ‖**camp'sheeting,** nn. Facing of piles & boarding to resist water-action on, or out-thrust of, a bank. [etym. dub.; cf. WAINSCOT]

*__cam'pus, n.__ Grounds of a school or college; the college as a teaching etc. institution. [L, = field]

cam pylo-, comb. form in bot. terms = bent-. [f. Gk *kampulos*]

cam'wood, n. Hard red W. African wood yielding dye. [native name *kambi*?]

can[1], n., & v.t. ‖Vessel for liquids, usu. of metal, esp. tin, & with handle over top, whence ~FUL(2) n.; *~-buoy,* large conical buoy over sands etc.; *~-dock,* water-lily; *(put in a) tin-plate box for hermetic sealing (meat, fish, fruit, etc.), whence (-)~ER[1] n., ~n'ERY (3) n., ~ning-factory; ~ned (sl.), drunk. [com.-Teut.: OE *canne* f. WG *kanna* cf. G *kanne*]

can[2], v.aux. (2 s., *canst;* 3 s., neg., *cannot, can't* (kahnt); past & condit., *could* (kood), *couldst* or *couldest;* infin., part., & p.p., wanting; defective parts supplied f. *be able to*). Be able to; have the right to; be permitted to (*you ~ go;* also as mild imperat.); *could,* feel inclined to (*could laugh for joy; really couldn't think of it*); *~not AWAY with;* (with ellipse) *will do what I ~.* [OE *cunnan,* com.-Teut.: cf. G *können,* OTeut. sense know, cogn. w. KEN, KNOW, & W. L (*gnosco,* Gk *gignoskō,* learn; as in DARE, MAY, MUST, the tense used as pres., is an old past, *could* being a later development; *could* (earlier *cothe, couthe, coud*) has -*l*- merely on anal. of *would, should;* infin. *can* is now obs. or a conscious archaism or jocular exc. in Sc.; part. *cunning* now only as adj., preserving orig. sense know]

Can'aan (-nyan, -nan), n. Land of promise, paradise. [O.-T. name of Palestine]

Can'ada, a. Of, from, ~ (in names of plants, animals, products, as ~ BALSAM).

Canād'ian, a. & n. (Native) of Canada. [-IAN]

canaille (kanah'ĕ, -nāl'), n. The rabble. [F]

canal', n., & v.t. (-ll-). Duct in plant or animal body for food, liquid, air, etc.; artificial watercourse for inland navigation (~s of Mars, markings of doubtful nature on planet Mars); artificial irrigation channel; (Zool.) groove in shell for protrusion of breathing-tube; (v.t.) make ~; through; provide with ~s. [F, f. L canalis]

cănălic'ŭlate, -āted, aa. (nat. hist.). With longitudinal groove(s); striated. [f. L canaliculatus dim. of CANAL]

Canarese. See KANARESE.

cănăl'īze, v.t. = CANAL vb.; convert (river) into canal by embanking, straightening course, locks, etc.; (fig.) give desired direction etc. to. Hence ~liza'TION n. [prob. f. F canaliser (CANAL+-IZE)]

căn'apé (-ă), n. Piece of fried bread with anchovies etc. [F]

cănăr'd (or kăn'ăr), n. False report, hoax. [F, = duck, false report]

cănăr'ý, a. & n. From the C~ Islands; (also ~-bird) yellow-feathered song-bird (green in wild state); (also C~-wine) a favourite wine in 16th–18th cc.; yellow fishing-fly; ~-coloured, bright yellow; C~ creeper, yellow-flowered used esp. in window-boxes; ~-seed, used as food for window-bird. [f. F Canarie f. Sp. & L Canaria (canis dog), one of the islands being noted in Roman times for large dogs]

cănăs'ter, n. Tobacco prepared by coarsely breaking the dried leaves, originally the rush basket used for packing it; f. Sp. canastro f. +L f. Gk kanastron basket see CANISTER]

cancan (see Ap.), n. High-kicking dance. [F]

căn'cel, v.t. & i. (-ll-). Obliterate, cross out, annul, make void, abolish, countermand, neutralize, balance, make up for, leaves; (v.i. ~ out or ~, of items) neutralize each other; (Math.) strike out (same factor) from numerator & denominator, from two sides of equation, etc. Hence ~LA'TION n. [f. F canceller f. L cancellare (cancelli cross-bars, lattice)]

căn'cel, n. Countermand; suppression & reprinting of leaf or leaves set up, the suppressed or the substituted leaf or leaves; (pair of) ~s, pincers for punching tickets. [f. prec.]

căn'cellate, -āted, aa. (bot. & zool.). Marked with crossing lines, reticulated; (of bone) formed of interlacing fibres & plates with cavities, porous. [f. L cancellatus (CANCEL, -ATE² -³)]

căn'cellous, a. (Of bone)=prec. [-OUS]

căn'cer, C~, n. Zodiacal constellation the Crab (C~); fourth sign of zodiac (C~); TROPIC of C~; malignant tumour eating the part it is in, spreading indefinitely, &

tending to recur when removed, (fig.) evil (sloth, bribery, etc.) acting similarly, whence ~ED² (erd), ~OUS, aa. [OE (later CANKER, corrected to -cer for disease or 1600) f. L cancer-cri crab, cancer; tumour named from swollen veins, like crab's limbs]

cănc'roid, a. & n. 1. Crab-like; like cancer. 2. n. Crustacean of crab family; disease like cancer. [as prec.+-OID]

cằndēlāb'rum, n. (pl. -bra; also sing. -bra, pl. -bras), Large, usu. branched, candlestick or lampstand. [L (-um), f. candela CANDLE]

căndes'cient, a. Glowing (as) with white heat. Hence ~ENCE n. [f. L candescere (candère be white, -ESCENT)]

căn'did, a. Unbiased; not censorious; frank; ~ friend, nominal friend glad to tell home-truths. Hence ~LY¹ adv. ~NESS n. [f. L candidus white, see prec.]

căn'didate, n. One who puts himself or is put forward for appointment to an office or honour; person thought likely to gain any position. [f. L candidatus, as prec., -ATE² (2), orig. white-robed (Roman ~s wearing white)]

căndida'ture, n. Standing for election, being candidate. [F, as prec.+-URE]

căn'died (-dĭd). See CANDY (p.p.).

căn'dle, n. Cylinder of wax, tallow, spermaceti, etc., enclosing wick, for giving light; (also ~-power) unit of light-measurement; Roman ~, firework, tube discharging coloured balls; can't, is not fit to, hold a ~ to, by auction, last bid before small ~ expires winning; BELL, book & ~; game not worth the ~, result not justifying the cost or trouble; BURN² ~ at both ends; hide ~ under BUSHEL; ~ myrtle (N.-Amer.), ~berry-tree (Moluccas), ~-tree, ~-berry &c nut-kernels used for ~s; ~-ends, remnants of ~, odds-&-ends hoarded by the stingy; ~-light, light of ~s, any artificial light, evening; ~-stick, support for (usu. single) ~; ~-tree, Amer. with ~-like fruit some feet long. [OE candel f. L candela (candère shine)]

Cằn'dlemas (-lm-), n. Feast of purification of Virgin Mary; (as date) 2nd Feb.; Sc. quarter-day. [OE Candelmæsse (CANDLE, MASS²)]

căn'dour (-der), n. Open-mindedness, impartiality; freedom from malice; frankness. [f. L candor whiteness (candère shine, -OR²)]

căn'dý, n., & v.t. & i. 1. Crystallized sugar made by repeated boiling & slow evaporation (also sugar-~); (w. pl.) sweety. 2. vb. Preserve by coating with ~; form (t. & i.) into crystals; (p.p.) glistening, (arch.) honeyed, flattering. [f. F (sucre) candi f. Arab.-Pers., candy crystallized sugarcane juice cf. Skr. khanda piece]

căn'dytuft, n. Plant with white, pink, or

purple flowers in flat tufts. [f. obs. *Candy* (*Candia* Crete)+TUFT]

cane¹, n. Hollow jointed stem of giant reeds & grasses (bamboo, sugar ~) or solid stem of slender palms (rattan, Malacca, etc.) collectively & as material (~), or with pl. (*a* ~, ~*s*) of the stem or a length of it used for walking-stick or instrument of punishment; ~-*brake*, genus of grasses, (also) tract of land overgrown with ~s; ~-*chair*, with seat of woven ~ strips; ~-*sugar* (obtained from the sugar~). Hence **cán'Y'a**, [OF (now *canne*), f. L f. Gk *kanna* reed perh. f. Semit. cf. Heb. *qaneh*]

cane², v.t. Beat with cane, whence **cān'ING¹** (1) n.; drive (lesson) *into* (person) with cane; insert cane into (chair-frame etc.). [f. prec.]

canéph'orus, n. (pl. **-rī**). Sculptured Greek youth or maid bearing basket on head at feast of Demeter. [L, f. Gk *kanēphoros* (*kaneon* basket, *pherō* carry)]

cangue (káng), **cāng**, n. Heavy wooden board worn round neck by Chinese criminals. [F (*-gue*), f. Port. *cango* cf. *canga* yoke]

cān'ine (also *kanin'*), a. & n. ~ *tooth* or *dogs* = *tooth* or ~, one of the four strong pointed teeth between incisors & molars. [f. L *caninus* (*canis* dog, -INE¹)]

cān'ister, n. Small box usu. of metal for tea, shot, etc.; (R.-C. Ch.) vessel holding wafers before consecration; ~-*shot* or ~, = CASE²-*shot*. [f. L *canistrum* f. Gk *kanastron* wicker basket (*kanna* CANE¹)]

cank'er, n., & v.t. 1. Ulcerous disease of human mouth; disease of horse's foot; disease of fruit-trees; (fig.) corrupting influence, rotten tendency; ~-*worm* or ~, caterpillar or larva destroying leaves or buds; ~-*rash*, variety of scarlet fever with ulcerated throat; hence ~OUS a. 2. v.t. Consume with canker; infect, corrupt; (p.p.) soured, malignant, crabbed. [f. ONF *cancre* f. L *cancrum* nom, CANCER]

cann'a, n. Plant with bright yellow, red, or orange flowers & ornamental leaves. [L (CANE¹)]

cann'el, n. (Also ~-*coal*) bituminous coal burning with bright flame & used in making coal oils & gas. [perh. f. CANDLE]

cann'ibal, n. & a. 1. Man who eats human flesh; animal feeding on its own species; hence ~ISM(2) n., ~**is'tīc** a. adj. Of, having, these habits. [16th-c. E & Sp. *Canibales* pl., var. of Carib name of W.-Ind. nation; *Caliban* is prob. another variant]

cann'ikin, n. Small can. [-KIN]

cann'on¹, n. 1. (Now *gun*) piece of ordnance, gun of the kind that needs mounting, (collect. sing. usu. instead of pl.); aircraft's heavy automatic gun, firing

explosive shell; ~-*ball*, projectile; ~-*bone*, tube-shaped bone between hough & fetlock; ~-*clock*, fired at noon by burning-glass; ~-*fodder*, men regarded as material to be consumed in war. 2. (Mech.) hollow cylinder moving independently on shaft; watchkey barrel. 3. (Also ~-*bit*) smooth round bit for horse. 4. || (Billiards) hitting of two balls successively by player's ball. 5. (Also ~-*curl*) sausage-shaped, prop. horizontal, ~-*curl*. [in 16th c. also *canon* f. F *canon* cf. It. *cannone* great tube (*canna* CANE¹, -OON) sense 4 is corruption of obs. *carom* short for *carambole* (F, f. Sp. *carambola* etym. dub.); sense 5 = obs. *canion* f. Sp. *cañon* ornamental roll on breeches-legs (*canna* as above)]

cann'on², v.i. || Make a cannon at billiards (of player or ball); come into collision, strike obliquely, *against, into, with*. [f. prec.]

cannonáde', n., & v.t. & i. Continuous gunfire; (vb) fire continuously; bombard, fire fast at. [CANNON¹+-ADE]

cannot. See CAN².

cann'y, a. Shrewd, worldly-wise; natural, safe to meddle with, (esp. w. neg.); thrifty; gentle, quiet, circumspect, (*ca'* ~-*y*, Sc. for *drive* or *go gently*, as name for trade-union policy of limiting output); sly, pawky. Hence ~ILY² adv., ~INESS n. [Sc. wd (w. senses differing f. above) f. CAN² know +-Y¹]

canoe' (-ōō), n., & v.i. (Go in, paddle) boat propelled with paddle(s). Hence **canoe'IST**(3) (-nōō-) n. [f. Sp. & Haytian *canoa*]

căn'on, n. Church decree; ~ *law*, eccl. law; general law governing treatment of a subject; criterion; list of Bible books accepted by Church; part of Mass containing words of consecration; (Mus.) piece with different parts taking up same subject successively in strict imitation; (Typ.) largest size of type with specific name; metal loop on bell for hanging it; member of cathedral CHAPTER, whence ~RY(2) n.; MINOR ~. [OE.f. L f. Gk *kanōn* rule (*kanna* CANE¹); in last sense short for CANONIC, meaning (person) living (with others) according to rule]

cañon. See CANYON

canŏn'ical, a. & n., **canŏn'ic**, a. (arch.). Appointed by canon law (~ *hours*, for prayer, or for celebration of marriage, 8 a.m. to 3 p.m.; ~ *dress*, of clergy, also ~s at 8 a.m. on pl.); included in canon of Scripture; C~ *Epistles*, the seven of Peter, James, John, Jude; authoritative, standard, accepted; (Mus.) in canon form; of a cathedral chapter or a member of it. Hence *canŏn'ically*² adv. [f. med. L *canonicalis* f. *canonicus* (CANON, -IC)+-AL]

canŏn'icate, n. = CANONRY². [f. med. L *canonicatus* (as prec., -ATE¹)]

cǎnoni'city, n. Status as canonical book. [f. *canonicus* CANONICAL, -TY]

căn'onist, n. Canon-lawyer. Hence ~ĭs'tĭc(AL) aa. [f. F canoniste (CANON, -IST)]

căn'onīze, v.t. Admit formally to calendar of saints; regard as a saint; recognize (book) as canonical; sanction by church authority. So ~ā'TION n. [f. med. L canonizare (CANON, -IZE)]

• canō'dle, v.i. & t. (sl.). Cuddle, fondle. [?]

Canō'pic, a. Of Canopus, town of ancient Egypt; ~ jar, vase, urn used for holding the entrails of an embalmed body in ancient Egyptian burial. [f. L Canopicus]

căn'opy, n. & v.t. Covering suspended or held over throne, bed, person, etc. (also fig., of any overhanging shelter, sky, etc.; (Archit.) roof-like projection over niche etc.; (vb) supply, be, such a covering to. [f. F canapé (now) couch f. med. L canopeum f. Gk kōnōpeion mosquito-net (kōnōps gnat)]

canō'rous, a. Melodious, resonant. [f. L canorus (canor song f. canere sing)+-OUS]

cănt, n. Bevel, oblique face, of crystal, bank, etc.; push, toss, movement, that partly or quite upsets; tilted or sideways position; ~board, sloping board. [cf. Du. kant, OF cant, It. canto, corner, edge, etc., perh. f. L f. Gk kanthos corner of eye]

cănt², v.t. & i. (Trans.) bevel off; tilt; turn over, turn upside down; push, pitch sideways.; (v.i.) take inclined position; lie aslant; (Naut.) swing round; ~hook, iron hook at end of long handle, used for rolling logs. [f. prec.]

cănt³, n. & a., & v.i. 1. Peculiar language of class, profession, sect, etc.; jargon; temporary catchwords (esp. as adj.; ~ phrase etc.); words used for fashion without being meant, unreal use of words implying piety; hypocrisy. 2. v.i. Use talk of these kinds; (Her.) ~ing arms, heraldry, coat, containing allusion to name of bearer; hence ~ER¹ n. [earlier of musical sound, of intonation, & of religious mendicants; prob. f. L cantus song, cantare frequent. of canere sing]

can't (kahnt). See CAN².

Cănt'āb, n. (Cantabrī'gian, n. & a. (Member) of Cambridge University. [f. L Cantabrigia Cambridge +-AN]

can'taloup (-oop), n. Kind of melon. [F, f. It. Cantaluppo in Italy]

căntăn'kerous, a. Cross-grained, quarrelsome. Hence ~LY² adv., ~NESS n. [perh. of ME contak contention on anal. of rancorous, f.?]

cănta'ta (-tah-), n. (mus.). Choral work, kind of short oratorio, or lyric drama set to music but not acted; (formerly) elaborate vocal solo. [It. (cantare sing, -ata -ADE)]

Cănta'te (-ahtē), n. Psalm xcviii (O sing—) as a canticle. [L, = sing ye]

cāntatri'ce (-ě'chā, -ēs'), n. Professional woman singer. [It. & F]

cănteen', n. || Provision & liquor shop in camp or barracks (drij, wet, ~), without, chiefly for, liquor); box of cooking utensils for use in camp, soldier's mess-tin; soldier's water-vessel of tin, wood, etc.; bar, lunch-counter, etc. at outdoor entertainments & in large public & private institutions; case or chest of plate & cutlery for domestic use. [f. F cantine f. It. cantina cellar etym. dub.]

cănter, n. & v.i. & t. 1. Easy gallop (win in a ~ easily). 2. Vb. Go at this pace (of horse or rider); make (horse) go thus. [short for Canterbury pace, gallop, trot, etc., f. easy pace of Canterbury pilgrims]

Căn'terbury, n. Stand with partitions for music etc. [f. bells of Canterbury Campanula. [f. bells of Canterbury pilgrims' horses]

cănthā'rĭdēs (-z), n. pl. (med.). Dried Spanish Fly. [L, pl. of L f. Gk kantharis blister-fly]

căn'tĭcle, n. Little song, hymn; one of the Prayer-Book hymns, as the Benedicite, Nunc Dimittis, Te Deum; Canticles, Song of Solomon. [f. L canticulum dim. of canticum song (cantus song f. canere sing)]

căn'tĭlĕver, n. Bracket (of length many times breadth & more than twice depth) projecting from wall to support balcony etc.; ~ bridge, with piers each of which has two ~s, with long girders connecting ~s of adjacent piers. [prob. f. CANT¹ & LEVER]

căn'tle, n. || Piece, slice, cut off; hind-bow of saddle. [f. ONF cantel dim. of CANT¹]

căn'tō, n. (pl. -os). Division of long poem. [It., = song, as CANT³]

can'ton (also kănton'), n. Subdivision of country; State of Swiss confederation; (Her.) square division less than a quarter in upper corner of shield. Hence ~AL a. [OF, = corner (CANT¹, -OON)]

canton'² (also -tōōn'), v.t. Divide into cantons (-tŏn); (-tōōn) quarter (soldiers). [f. prec.]

canton'ment (-tōōn-, -ŏn-), n. Lodging assigned to troops (in India also permanent military station). [prec. +-MENT]

cantor'ial, a. Of the precentor, of N. side of choir (cf. DECANAL). [f. L as foll. +-AL]

cân'toris, mus. direction. To be sung by cantorial side in antiphonal singing. [L, genit. of cantor precentor (canere cant-sing, -OR)]

căn'trip, n. (Sc.). Witch's trick; piece of mischief, playful act. [?]

Canuck', n. & a. (sl.). French Canadian; *Canadian. [U.S. word]

căn'vas, n. Strong unbleached cloth of hemp or flax, for sails, tents, painting on; open kind used as basis for tapestry & embroidery; under ~, in tent(s), with sails spread; racing-boat's covered end; picture; ~back, N.-Amer. duck (f. colour

of back feathers), [ME & ONF canevas f. LL †cannabaceus (Lf. Gk kannabis hemp, -ACEOUS)]

can'vass, v.t. & i., &n. Discuss thoroughly; solicit votes, solicit votes from (constituency), ascertain sentiments of, ask custom of, whence ~ER¹ n.; (n.) ~ing for votes. [f. prec., orig. sense being toss in a sheet, & so shake up, agitate, etc.]

can'yon, cañon (kăn'yon), n. Deep gorge with stream. [f. Sp. cañon tube (caña f. L canna CANE²)]

canzonet' (-et), n. Short light song; kind of madrigal. [f. It. canzonetta (canzone f. L cantionem f. canere sing)]

caoutchouc (kowch'ōōk), n. & a. (Of) unvulcanized rubber. [F, f. Carib. cahuchu]

cap¹, n. Head-dress (woman's, esp. of muslin etc. worn indoors, but also now, like man's or boy's, for out-door use, brimless & of cloth or soft material; ~ in hand, humbly; ~ fits, person feels that general remark is true of him; set one's ~ at, try to attract as suitor); special head-dress (college or square ~; steel ~; helmet; Scotch ~, part of Highland costume; football ~, of velvet etc.; ‖ sign of inclusion in team; ~ of MAINTENANCE; ~ of liberty, conical, given to Roman slave on emancipation, now Republican symbol; ~ & bells, jester's insignia; FOOL'S ~); caplike covering, natural (mushroom top, knee~, etc.), or added for various purposes (windmill top, toe~, inner watch-case; percussion ~, for igniting explosive in cartridges etc.); (Naut.) doubly pierced block for lengthening mast by extra spar; conical paper bag, cornet; (Fox-hunting etc.) recognized payment by non-subscriber for day's hunting (collected in ~), whence ~p'ER¹ n., the authorized collector; ~-paper, whity-brown for packing, also a size of writing-paper; ~-stone, top stone, coping. [OE cæppe f. LL cappa, the Rom. forms of which meant cloak, cape, cope; cape, cope, are separate E adoptions of the same wd through Rom. or in its med. L form capa]

cap², v.t. & i. (-pp-). Put cap upon; (Sc. Univv.) confer degree on; put percussion cap on nipple of (gun); protect (end of beam etc.) with metal etc., whence ~p'ING¹ (3) n.; lie on top of, crown; award (a player) his cap (for football etc.); outdo (~ anecdote, quotation, etc., produce a better or another apposite one; ~ verses, reply with one beginning with the last's last letter); touch or take off one's hat to (also intr. with to); injure at point (horse ~s its hocks). [f. prec.]

capabil'ity, n. Power of (action etc., acting etc.), for (being done something to), to (do something); undeveloped faculty (has ~ies). [foll., -BILITY]

cap'able, a. Susceptible (of, or abs.); having the power or fitness for (of); wicked enough for (of); gifted, able, Hence ~LY² adv. [F, f. LL capabilis irreg. for capibilis (L capere hold, -BLE); earlier sense having room (for)]

capā'cious (-shus), a. Roomy. Hence ~NESS n. [L capax (capere hold), -ACIOUS]

capā'citāte, v.t. Render capable (for, to do); make legally competent. [foll., -ATE³]

capā'city, n. Holding-power, receiving-power, (for happiness, heat, moisture; filled to ~, quite full; ~ house, packed theatre etc.); cubic content (measure of ~ for vessels & liquids, grain, etc.); mental power, faculty; capability, opportunity, to do, of doing, etc. (rare); position, relative character, (in a civil ~; in my ~ as critic); legal competency; (Electr.) power of an apparatus to store static electricity. [f. F capacité f. L capacitatem (CAPACIOUS, -TY)]

cāp-a-pie' (-apē), adv. From head to foot, (armed, ready, etc.). [f. OF cap a pié]

capă'rison, n. (often pl.), & v.t. Horse's trappings; equipment, outfit; (vb) put ~ upon. [f. F caparasson (now -çon) f. Sp. caparazon f. med. L caparo (capa CAPE¹)]

cape¹, n. Short sleeveless cloak, either as separate garment or as fixed or detachable part of longer cloak or coat. Hence cāPED² (-pt) a. [F, f. Sp. capa or It. cappa; see CAP¹]

cape², C, n. &a. Headland, promontory; the C~, of Good Hope, also = C~ Colony (C~ boy, S.-African of mixed black & white descent); & as adj. of its products (C~ wine etc.; C~ doctor, strong S.-E. wind peculiar to S. Africa; C~ gooseberry, kind of winter cherry; C~ smoke, S.-African brandy). [f. F cap f. Rom. capo f. L caput head]

cap'(e)lin, n. Small smelt-like fish used as cod-bait. [F capelan]

cap'er¹, n. Bramble-like S.-European shrub; (pl.) its flower-buds pickled (esp. ~ sauce); English ~s, seed vessels of Nasturtium pickled. [ME caperis, caperes, (sing.) f. L f. Gk kapparis; -s lost as though pl. sign cf. PEA, MACE]

cap'er², n., & v.i. (Give a) frisky movement, leap; fantastic proceeding; cut a ~, ~s, = vb. [short for CAPRIOLE]

cāpercaill'ie, -l'zie (-lyi, -lzi), n. Wood-grouse, largest European gallinaceous bird (Scotland etc.). [f. Gael. capull coille horse of the wood]

cap'erer, n. In vbl senses; esp., caddis-fly (from its flight). [CAPER², -ER¹]

cap'ful, (-ool), n. Enough to fill a cap; esp., ~ of wind, passing gust. [-FUL²]

cap'ids, n. Writ of arrest. [L, = take thou]

capillă'rity, n. (Power of exerting) capillary attraction or repulsion. [f. F capillarité see foll., -TY]

capill'ary (also kăp-d), a. & n. Of hair; hair-like, thin as a hair; (tube, blood-

vessel) of minute or hair-like diameter (e.g. one of ramified blood-vessels inter-vening between arteries & veins); so ~. ATTRACTION, REPULSION. [f. L *capillāris*]

cap'ital¹, n. Head or cornice of pillar or column. [= L *capitellum* (cf. F *chapiteau*) dim. of *capitulum* dim. of *caput* head]

cap'ital², a. & n. Involving loss of life, punishable by death, (~ *sentence, offence*); vitally injurious, fatal, (~ *error*); stand-ing at the head (~ *letter*, also ~ as noun); chief (~ *manor*, held in *capite* or direct from king; ~ *messuage*, occupied by owner of estate with several messuages; ~ *town* or *city*, or ~ as noun, head town of country, county, etc.); important, lead-ing, first-class,(~ *ship*, battleship or battle-cruiser); excellent, first-rate, (often as interj. of approval); original, principal, (~ *fund* or ~, stock with which company or person enters into business, accumu-lated wealth used in producing more, holders of this as a class, as *C~ & Labour*; *fixed* ~, machinery etc., *circulating* or *floating* ~, goods, money, etc.; so fig.; *make* ~ *out of*, turn to account). Hence ~LY² adv. [F, f. L *capitālis* (*caput* head, -AL)]

cap'italism, n. Possession or influence or system, possessor, of capital or fund used in pro-duction, (mod., Pol.) dominance of private capitalists (opp. *socialism*). Hence capi-talis'tic a. [prec., -ISM(3), -IST(3)]

cap'italize (*also* kapit-), v.t. Convert into, use as, capital; compute or realize present value of (income). Hence ~A'TION n. [-IZE(3)]

cap'itate, -ated, aa. (nat. hist.). Having distinct head; with clustered flowers etc. [f. L *capitātus* headed (*caput -tis*, -ATE²)]

capita'tion, n. (Levying of) tax or fee of so much a head; (~ *grant*, of so much for every person fulfilling conditions. [f. L *capitātio* poll-tax (*caput -tis* head, -ATION]

Cap'itol, n. Roman temple of Jupiter on Tarpeian hill (later *~ine hill* or *~ine*); *Congress or State legislature building. [f. L *capitōlium* (*caput* head)]

capit'ular, a. Of a cathedral chapter; (Physiol.) of a terminal protuberance of bone. [f. med. L *capitulāris* (L *capitulum* CHAPTER, -AR²)]

capit'ulary, n. Collection of ordinances, esp. of Frankish kings. [f. med. L *capitu-larius* (as prec., -ARY²)]

capit'ulate, v.i. Surrender on terms. [f. med. L *capitulāre* draw up under heads (see CHAPTER)]

capitula'tion, n. Stating heads of sub-ject; agreement, conditions, (esp. the *C~s*, by which foreign residents in Turkey had exterritoriality); surrender on terms, instrument containing these. [F, f. med. L *capitulātiōnem* (prec. -ATION)]

cap'on, n. Castrated cock. Hence ~IZE(3) v.t. [OE *capun* f. L *capōnem*, nom. *capo*]

caponier', n. Covered passage across ditch of fort. [f. F *caponnière* f. Sp. *caponera* orig. a capon-cote (see prec.)]

cap'oral (-ahl), n. A French tobacco. [F]

capôt', n. & v.t. (-tr-). (In piquet) win-ning of all tricks by one player; (vb) do this against (opponent). [F]

capōte', n. Soldier's, traveller's, etc., long cloak with hood. [F, dim. of *cape* CAPE¹]

cap'ric, a. (chem.). ~ *acid*, obtained from butter, coco-nut oil, etc. [f. L *caper* goat]

capric'cio (-ècho), n. Lively (usu. short) musical composition. [It., see foll.]

caprice' (-ès), n. Unaccountable change of mind or conduct, fancy, freak; in-clination to these; work of sportive fancy in art etc. [F f. It. *capriccio* sudden start (*capro* goat, f. L *caper -pri*)]

capri'cious (-shus), a. Guided by whim, inconstant, irregular, incalculable. Hence ~LY² adv., ~NESS n. [f. F *capricieux* f. It. *capriccioso* (prec., -OUS)]

Cap'ricorn, n. Zodiacal constellation (Goat; tenth sign of zodiac; TROPIC of ~. [f. L *capricornus* (*caper -pri* goat, *cornu* horn]

caprifica'tion, n. Hastening of ripeness in figs by subjecting them to puncture by wild-fig grall-insects. [f. L *caprificātio* f. *caprificus* wild fig (*caper -pri* goat, *ficus* fig), -ATION]

cap'rine, a. Of, like, a goat. [f. L *caprinus* (*caper -pri*, -INE¹)]

cap'riole, n. & v.i. (Give a) leap, caper, esp. (in manège) horse's high leap & kick without advancing. [F (now *cab-*), or f. It. *capriola* dim. of L *capra* she-goat]

caprō'ic a. (chem.). ~ *acid*, found with capric & butyric acids in butter etc. [var. of *capro* for differentiation]

câps, abbr. of *capitāls* (capital letters) in direction to printers etc.

cap'sicum, n. Kinds of plant with hot capsules & seeds, Guinea Pepper etc. [f. L *capsa* CASE²]

capsize', n. & v.t. & i. Upset, overturn, (of ship, boat). Hence ~A(2) n. [perh. f. Sp. *cabezar* pitch or *cabuzar* sink by the head (*cabo* f. L *caput* head)]

cap'stan, n. Revolving barrel, worked by men walking round & pushing horizontal levers, or by steam etc., for winding cable in, hoisting heavy sails, etc. [f. Prov. *cabestan* f. L *capistrāre* (*capistrum* halter f. *capere* hold), -ANT]

cap'sule, n. (Physiol.) membranous en-velope; (Bot.) dry seed-case opening when ripe by parting of valves; (Chem.) shallow saucer for evaporating etc.; (Med.) gelatine envelope enclosing dose; metallic top for bottle. Hence ~AR, ~IFORM, aa., ~i comb. form. [F, f. L *capsula* (CASE², -ULE)]

cap'tain¹ (-tin), n. Chief, leader; great soldier, strategist, experienced commander; (Army) officer of rank next below major & above lieutenant, normally commanding a company or troop; (Navy) officer commanding man-of-war (also used, by courtesy, of commander); *C~ of the Fleet*, adjutant-general of a force, with rear-admiral's uniform; chief sailor of special gang (*~ of forecastle* etc.); Master of merchant ship; foreman; ‖ head boy (or girl) at school; leader of side in games; = Grey Gurnard; *~'s biscuit*, partly fermented ship's biscuit of superior quality. Hence ~CY, ~SHIP, nn., ~LESS a., (-tin-). [ME & OF *capitaine* f. LL *capitaneus* (a. & n.) chief (L *caput* head)]

cap'tain² (-tin), v.t. Be captain of, lead. [f. prec.]

capta'tion, n. Use of *ad captandum* arguments or appeals. [f. L *captatio* (*captare* catch at, frequent. of *capere* take, -ATION]

cap'tion, n. ‖ (Legal arrest; (Law) certificate attached to or written on document; heading of chapter, article, etc. [f. L *captio* (*capere* take, -TION); last meaning f. second]

cap'tious (-shus), a. Fallacious, sophistical; fond of taking exception, trying to catch people in their words. Hence ~LY² adv., ~NESS n. [f. L *captiosus* (prec., -OSE²)]

cap'tivate, v.t. Fascinate, charm. Hence ~A^TION n. [f. L *captivare* take CAPTIVE, -ATE³]

cap'tive, a. & n. (Person, animal) taken prisoner, kept in confinement, under restraint, unable to escape; of, like, prisoner (*~ state*); *lead, take, hold, ~*; *~ balloon*, held by rope from ground. So **captiv'ITY** n. [f. F *captif* t. L *captivus* (*capere capt-* take, -IVE)]

cap'tor, n., **cap'tress**, n. fem. One who takes a captive or prize. [-or L (as prec., -OR²); & see -ESS¹]

cap'ture, n., & v.t. Seizing, taking possession of; thing or person seized; (v.t.) take prisoner, seize as prize; hence ~ER¹ n. [F, f. L *captura* as prec., -URE]

Cap'uchin, n. & a. Franciscan (friar) of new rule of 1528; woman's cloak & hood (*~ monkey, pigeon*, kinds with head hair or feathers like cowl. [F (now -*cin*),f. It. *capuccino* (*capuccio* cowl f. *cappa* CAP²)]

cap'ut mor'tuum, n. Worthless residue. [L, = dead head; alch. term for residuum of any substance after distillation or sublimation]

capyba'ra, n. Large S.-Amer. rodent allied to guinea-pig. [Brazilian]

car¹, n. Wheeled vehicle (chiefly poet. = chariot; *~ of the sun, triumphal ~*, of Juggernaut, etc.; or with specification as JAUNTing~, MOTOR-~, tramway-~, dining-~; ‖in U.S. of any railway carriage or van; in Engl. also of motor-car, of low two-wheeled truck for hogsheads etc., & of other low heavy carts); pendant of airship or balloon holding passengers; *~'man*, driver of van or jaunting-~, carter, carrier. Hence ~FUL(2) n. [ME & ONF *carre* f. LL *carra* cf. L *carrus* four-wheeled vehicle f. Bret. *karr* cf. OW *carr*]

cärabineer', **cärb-**, n. Soldier with carbine; *The C~s*, 6th Dragoon Guards. [f. F *carabinier* (CARBINE, -IER)]

cä'racäl, n. Kind of lynx. [F, f. Turk. *qarah-qulaq* black-ear]

cä'racŏle, **-ŏl**, n., & v.i. (Execute) half-turn(s) to right or left (of horse or rider). [f. F *caracole*(-) f. It. *caracollo* f. Sp. *caracol* snail, spiral shell]

cä'racul (-ŏŏl), n. Kind of astrakhan fur; cloth imitating this. [Russ.]

carafe' (-ahf), n. Glass water-bottle for table. [F, cf. It. *caraffa*, Sp. *garrafa* perh. f. Arab. *gharrafa* draw water]

cä'ramĕl, n. Burnt sugar used for colouring spirits etc.; a sweetmeat; the colour of ~, a light brown. [F. f. Sp. *caramelo*]

cä'rapāce, n. Upper shell of tortoise & crustaceans. [F, f. Sp. *carapacho* etym. dub.]

cä'rat, n. Measure of weight for precious stones, about $3\frac{1}{3}$ grains; measure of purity of gold, pure gold being 24~. [F, f. It. *carato* f. Arab. *qirat* perh. f. Gk *keration* fruit of carob tree (dim. of *keras* horn]

caravan' (or kä⁴), n. Eastern or N.-African company of merchants, pilgrims, etc., travelling together for safety, esp. through desert; covered cart or carriage, house on wheels (esp. of menagerie etc.). [16th-c. *carouan* f. Pers. *karwan*, perh. assim. to F *caravane*]

caravan'serai (-ri), **-sera**, **-sarŷ**, n. Eastern quadrangular inn with great inner court where caravans put up. [f. Pers. *karwansarai* (prec., *sara* mansion]

cä'ravel, **cärv'el**, n. (hist.). Small light fast ship, chiefly Spanish & Portuguese of 15th-17th cc. [f. F *caravelle* f. It. *caravella*; cf. LL f. Gk *karabos*]

cä'raway (a-w-), n. Umbelliferous plant with fruit (*~seeds*) used in cakes. [f. med. L *carui* ef. Arab. *al-karawiya* & Gk *karon* cummin]

cärb-, **cärbo-**, comb. forms of CARBON. Hence **cärb'IDE** n. (often for *calcium carbide* used in making acetylene gas).

cärb'ine, **cä'ra-**, n. Short fire-arm for cavalry use. [F (*carra-*) weapon of *carabin* soldier perh. f. Calabria perh. f. med. L *chadabula* kind of ballista (Gk *katabolē* overthrow]

cärbo-hyd'rate, n. (chem.). Organic compound of carbon with oxygen & hydrogen in the proportion to form water (starch, sugar, glucose).

cärbŏl'ic, a. (chem.). *~ acid*, powerful antiseptic & disinfectant. Hence **cärb'o-IZE**(5) v.t. [CARB-, -OL, -IC]

carb'on, n. (chem.). Non-metallic element occurring as diamond, graphite, &c., in carbonic acid gas, the charcoal, & all organic compounds; (Electr.) charcoal pencil used in one form of electric lighting; ~ *printing, process, producing permanent prints in various colours;* ~ *paper,* for taking copies of letters etc.; Hence ~ATE[1](3) n. [f. F *carbone* f. L *carbonem* nom. -o charcoal]

carbona'ceous (-shes), a. Of, like, coal or charcoal; consisting of or containing carbon. [as prec., -ACEOUS]

carbona'di (-dē), n. Neapolitan secret society of republican revolutionists, impregnate with carbonic acid gas, aerate. [f. *carbonate* n. see CARBON, -ATE[3]]

carb'onate, v.t. (chem.). Form into a carbonate; impregnate with carbonic acid gas, aerate. [f. *carbonate* n. see CARBON, -ATE[3]]

carbon'ic, a. (chem.). Of carbon; ~ *acid,* the gas formed in combustion of carbon, given out in breathing, & constituting choke-damp. [-IC]

carboni'ferous, a. Producing coal; (Geol.) ~ *strata, system, formation,* palaeozoic next above Old Red Sandstone; ~ *age, era, period,* in which these strata were deposited. [CARBON, -I-, -FEROUS]

carb'onize, v.t. Convert into carbon; reduce to charcoal or coke; cover (paper) with carbon for taking copies. Hence ~A'TION n. [-IZE(3), 5)]

carbor'undum, n. Compound of carbon and silicon used for polishing by abrasion. [P.; CARBON+CORUNDUM]

carb'oy, n. Large globular glass bottle usually protected with a frame. [f. Pers. *qarâbâ.*]

carb'uncle, n. Red precious stone (formerly of many kinds, e.g. ruby; now garnet cut in bun shape); malignant tumour, anthrax, pimple on nose or face, whence ~ED[2] (-ld), **carbunc'ular,** aa. [ME & OF *charbucle* f. L *carbunculus* small coal (CARBON -UNCLE)]

carb'uret, v.t. (-tt-). Combine (any element) chemically with carbon; charge with carbon. Hence ~t'OR[2](2) or ~t'ER[1](2) n., apparatus mixing air with petrol vapour for combustion in motor engines. [CARBON, -URET]

carc'ass, -ase, n. Dead body (of human body now only with contempt); (with butchers') beast's trunk without head, limbs, or offal; mere body, dead or alive (*to save* one's ~), worthless remains (of); skeleton, framework, (of house, ship, etc.); (Mil.) kind of fire-ball from gun for igniting buildings. [ME *carcois, carcas,* partly f. 16th-c. F *carcasse* f. It. *carcassa;* etym. and mutual relations of *carcosium, carcassa,* doubtful]

carci'nōm'a, n. (pl. -ata). (med.). (A form of) cancer. [L, f. Gk *karkinōma* ulcer f. *karkinos* crab]

4895

G

card[1], n. & v.t. (Cleanse, comb, get into order, also scratch or torture, with) toothed instrument, wire-brush, or wire, set, rubber or vulcanite strip, for raising nap on cloth or preparing wool, hemp, etc.; ~ *thistle,* teasel; ~*ing-machine,* with card-strips fixed on rollers. [f. F *carde* teasel-head ult. f. L *carduus* thistle]

card[2], n. (Also *playing-*~) one of pack of 52 oblong pieces of pasteboard used in games (COURT-~); ~ *make* a ~, take trick with it; *house of* ~s, insecure scheme etc.; ~*s, card-playing; sure, safe, doubtful, queer,* ~, *such a person: throw up, show, one's* ~*s,* give up, let out, one's plan; ~ *up* one's *sleeve,* plan in reserve; *on the* ~*s,* likely, possible); flat piece of thick paper or pasteboard for various purposes (*speak by the* ~, with precision, f. obs. use as ~ = mariner's compass; ~ [POST-~; *correspondence-*~, for short notes; = ticket of admission; = invitation; ~ *or visiting-*~, with name etc., sent or left in lieu of formal visit, *so leave* a ~ *on; wedding, Christmas,* etc., ~, sent in notification or compliment to friends; *collecting-*~, for entering subscribers to charities; *programme of events at race-meetings etc.,* or of cricket scores, esp. *correct* ~; *the correct thing, what is expected;* printed or written notice, rules, etc., for hanging in window or on wall); ~*-case,* for carrying visiting-~s; ~*-basket, -rack,* for keeping visitors' ~s; ~*-board, pasteboard for cutting ~s from or making boxes etc.; ~ *index* (in which each item is entered on separate ~); ~*-sharper,* swindler at ~*-games;* || ~ *vote* (of delegates each counting for the number of his constituents). [f. F *carte* f. It. *carta* (cf. *charte* direct) f. L *charta* f. Gk *khartēs* papyrus leaf; *for -te* unexplained]

card'amom, n. Spice from seed-capsules of E.-Ind. plants. [f. L f. Gk *karda-momon* (*kardamon* cress, *amōmon* a spice plant)]

card'an, a. (engineering). ~ *joint,* UNIVERSAL *joint;* ~ *shaft* (with universal joint at one or both ends). [f. G. *Cardano,* Italian mathematician (d. 1576)]

card'iac, a. & n. Of the heart (esp. path., as ~ *symptoms,* of heart-disease); of upper orifice of stomach; (n.) heart-stimulant, cordial. [f. F (*-aque*) f. L f. Gk *kardia-kos* (*kardia* heart, -Ac)]

card'igan, n. Knitted woollen over-waistcoat with or without sleeves. [named after Earl of C— c. 1855]

card'inal, C—, a., & n. On which something hinges, fundamental, important, (~ *virtues,* the four natural & three theological, see VIRTUE; ~ *numbers,* the simple ones, as one, six, cf. ORDINAL; ~ *points* (of compass), North, S., E., W.; ~ *church,* one of principal churches in Rome,

to which others were subordinate, whence ~C~, noun, orig. person in charge of one of these, now one of seventy princes of R.-C. Ch., members of Pope's council of 6 ~ bishops, 50 ~ priests, & 14 ~ deacons; & electors of new Pope, whence ~ATE¹, ~SHIP, nn.; also prefixed to other titles, as C~-Legate; whence ~LY² adv.; of deep scarlet; woman's short hooded (orig. scarlet) cloak; small scarlet bird; (Zool.) of the hinge of a bivalve; ~flower, Scarlet Lobelia. [F; f. L cardinalis (cardo -inis hinge, -AL); sense scarlet f. Cardinal's robes]

cardio-, comb. form of Gk kardia heart.

cardoon′, n. Composite kitchen-garden plant allied to artichoke. [f. F cardon f. It. cardone (cardo f. L cardus, carduus thistle, -OON)]

care¹, n. Solicitude, anxiety; occasion for these; serious attention, heed, caution, pains, (take, have a, ~, be cautious); charge, protection, (A, c/o or ~ of B, in addresses; have the, take, ~ of; in, under, one's ~); thing to be done or seen to (~s of State etc.; that shall be my ~); ~laden, -worn, with anxieties; ~taker, person hired to take charge, esp. of house in owner's absence. [OE caru, com.-Teut. f. OTeut. karô; not related to L cura]

care², v.i. Feel concern or interest for or about; provide food, attendance, etc., for (children, invalids, etc.); (w. neg. expressed or implied) feel regard, deference, affection, for, be concerned whether etc., (often with expletive a pin, a damn, a farthing; I don't ~ if I do, am willing); be willing or wishful to (should not ~ to be seen with him; do you ~ to try them?). [OE carian f. prec.]

career, v.t. & i. Turn (ship) on one side for cleaning, caulking, etc.; (cause to) heel over. [ult. f. L carina keel]

career′age, n. Careening a ship; expense of it; place for it. [-AGE]

career′, n., & v.i. 1. Swift course, impetus, (in full, mid, etc., ~); course or progress through life; development & success of party, principle, nation, etc.; way of making a livelihood; hence ~IST (3) n., one intent mainly on personal advancement & success in life. 2. v.i. Go swiftly or wildly (often about). [f. F carrière race-course f. LL carraria (via) carriage-(road) f. L carrus car¹]

care′ful (-ărf-), a. Concerned for, taking care of; painstaking, watchful, cautious, (to do, that, what, whether, etc.); done with or showing care. Hence ~LY² adv., ~NESS n. [-FUL]

care′less (-ărl-), a. Unconcerned, light-hearted; inattentive, negligent (of), thoughtless; inaccurate. Hence ~LY² adv., ~NESS n. [-LESS]

caress′, n., & v.t. 1. Fondling touch, kiss; blandishment. 2. v.t. Bestow these on; pet, make much of; hence ~ingly² adv.

[f. F caresse(r) f. It. carezza(re) f. LL +carilia (L carus dear)]

ca′ret, n. Mark (∧) placed below line to show place of omission. [L, = it needs (carēre)]

carg′o, n. (pl. ~es). Freight of ship. [Sp., = loading f. med. L carricum f. LL carricare to load (L carrus car¹)]

Ca′rib, n. & a. (One) of aboriginal inhabitants of Southern W.-Ind. islands. So~bé′an a. [f. Sp. Caribe cf. CANNIBAL]

caribou′ (-ōō), -bōō′, n. N.-Amer. reindeer. [-ou Canad. F, prob. f. native wd]

caricatūr′e, n., & v.t. Grotesque representation of person or thing by over-emphasis on characteristic traits (pictorial, literary, or mimetic); hence ~IST(1) n.; (v.t.) make, give, a ~ of; hence ~′ABLE a. [F, f. It. caricatura (caricare to load see CARGO, -URE)]

cār′ies (-z), n. Decay (of bones or teeth). [L]

ca′rillon (-lyon), n. Set of bells sounded either from keyboard or mechanically; air played on bells; instrument (or part of organ) imitating peal of bells. [F, f. med. L quadri-lionem nom. -o quaternary (formerly four bells)]

carin′a, n. (zool. & bot.). Ridge-shaped structure. Hence ~AL, cā′rinATE², aa., ~o-comb. form. [L, = keel]

cār′ious, a. Decayed (esp. of bones, teeth). [f. L cariosus (CARIES, -OSE¹)]

cărk′ing, a. Burdensome (alw. with care). [f. obs. vb cark f. ONF carkier f. LL carricare (CARGO)]

|| **cāf̄l′ine¹**, n. (Sc.). Man. fellow. [OE in comb. as hús-carl f. ON karl cogn. w. CHURL]

|| **cāf̄l′ine¹**, n. (Sc.). Old woman. [ME & ON kerling fem. of prec.]

cāf̄l′ine², n. Genus of composite plants allied to thistle. [F, f. med. L carlina for Carolina named f. Carolus Charlemagne]

Cārl′ism, **Cārl′ist**, nn. Spanish Dogmatism, legitimist, support(er) of Don Carlos second son of Charles IV. [-ISM(3), -IST(2)]

Cărlovin′gian, **Carolin′gian**, (-j-), a. & n. (One) of second French dynasty founded by Charlemagne. [F carlovingien after mérovingien MEROVINGIAN]

Cărl′ton Clŭb, n. The chief Conservative club in England.

Cārlyl′ism, n. Principles, literary manner, a mannerism, of Carlyle. So ~E′AN, ~IAN, aa., ~ESE′ a. & n. [Thomas Carlyle 1795–1881; -ISM³(3, 4]

Cărm′agnole (-ănyōl), n. Song & dance among French revolutionists of 1793. [F]

Cārm′élite, n. & a. (Member) of mendicant order of friars (also White Friars f. their white cloak; fine woollen stuff, usu. grey. [Mt. Carmel, place of foundation (12th c.), -ITE¹(2)]

cărm'inative, a. & n. (Drug) curing flatulence. [f. L *carminare* card, -IVE; gross humours being combed out like tangled wool]

cărm'ine, n. & a. (Coloured like, colour of) crimson pigment made from cochineal. [f. F or Sp. *carmin* f. med. L *carminus* for *carmesinus* CRIMSON]

cărn'age, n. Great slaughter, esp. of men. [f. F f. It. *carnaggio* f. LL *carnaticum* (L *caro carnis* flesh, -AGE)]

cărn'al, a. Sensual, fleshly; sexual; unsanctified, worldly. Hence ~ISM(2), cărnăl'ĭTY, n. ~IZE(3) v.t., ~lȳ² adv. [f. L *carnalis* (*caro* see prec., -AL)]

cărnā'tion¹, n. & a. (Of) rosy pink colour. [orig. flesh-colour f. L *carnatio* (*caro* see CARNAGE) fleshiness]

cărnā'tion², n. Cultivated kinds of Clove-pink. [formerly also *incarnacyon, coronation, cronation*; perh. orig. *coronation* as indented like coronet, later confused w. the colour; for *corn-, carn-*, cf. foll.]

cărnē'lian, n. = CORNELIAN. [*ca-* by confusion w. L(CARNATION) as flesh-coloured]

cărn'ĭfy, v.t. & i. (path.). Change (t. & i. of bone, lungs, etc.) to structure of flesh or muscle. Hence ~FICA'TION n. [L *caro carnis* flesh, -FY]

cărn'ival, n. Half-week or week before Lent; festivities usual during this in R.-C. countries; riotous revelry; reckless indulgence in something (of; ~ *of blood-shed* etc.). [f. It. *carnevale* orig. name for Shrove Tuesday only, f. L phr. *carnem levare* put away meat]

cărniv'ŏra, n. Large order of flesh-eating mammalia, including cats, dogs, bears, etc. [L neut. pl. see CARNIVOROUS]

cărn'ivore, n. Carnivorous animal or plant. [F, as foll.]

cărniv'ŏrous, a. Feeding on flesh (esp. of the CARNIVORA, & of plants digesting animal substance). [f. L *carnivorus* (*caro carnis* flesh, -VOROUS)]

‖ cărn'ȳ, -ey, v.t.(colloq.). Coax, wheedle. [?]

cărŏb, n. Horn-like pod of Mediter-ranean ~-tree. [f. F *carobe* f. Arab. *kharrūbah* bean-pod]

cărŏl, n., & v.t. & i. (-ll-). 1. Joyous song, human or of birds, esp. Christmas hymn. 2. v.i. Utter, celebrate with, these; hence ~lER¹ n. [obs. senses *dance, ring*; ~lER¹ n. OF *carole(r)* perh. f. L *choraula* f. Gk *khoraulēs* flute-player for chorus-dancing (*khoros* chorus, *aulos* flute), or f. L co-ROLLA ring]

Că'roline, a. Of Charlemagne; of the time of Charles I & II of England. [f. L *Carolus* Charles + -INE¹]

Carolingian. See CAROLOVINGIAN.

*că'rom, n. Cannon at billiards. [see CANNON²]

cărŏt'id, a. & n. Of, near, the two great arteries carrying blood to head; (n.) one of these. [f. Gk *karōtides* pl. (*karoō* stupefy, compression of these arteries being thought to do this)]

carouse' (-z), v.i. & n. (Have, engage in) a drinking-bout; drink deep. Hence ~AL(2) n. [orig. as adv. = right out, in phr. *drink* ~ f. G *gar aus trinken*]

cărp¹, n. A fresh-water fish usu. bred in ponds. [f. OF *carpe* f. LL *carpa* cf. OHG *charpho*, G *karpfen*]

cărp², v.i. Talk querulously, find fault, (usu. *at*; esp. ~*ing tongue, criticism, captious*. [obs. senses *talk, say, sing*, prob. f. ON *karpa* to brag, but mod. sense influenced by L *carpere* pluck at, slander]

cărp'enter, n., & v.i. & t. 1. Artificer in wood-work (esp. of rough solid kinds as in ship or house building, cf. JOINER, CABINET-*maker*; *the* ~'s *son*, Jesus); ~*ant*, *-bee*, kinds boring into trees; ~*scene*, *scene*) to give ~ time for preparing elaborate scene behind: so cărp'entry n. 2. vb. Do, make by, ~'s work. [f. ONF *carpentier* (now *ch-*) f. LL *carpenta-rius* (*carpentum* wagon f. Celt.)]

cărp'ĕt, n., & v.t. 1. Thick fabric, usu. woollen & patterned, for covering floor & stairs (at first of table-covering, whence *on the* ~; *under discussion*; & as floor-covering, long a boudoir luxury, whence ~*-knight*, stay-at-home soldier, ladies' man); *on the* ~ (also, colloq.) being reprimanded; ~*bag*, travelling-bag, orig. made of ~; ~*bagger*, candi-date for election or political agitator un-connected with district; hence ~LESS a. 2. v.t. Cover (as) with a carpet, whence ~ING¹(3) n.; ‖ summon (servant etc.) into the room for reprimand, reprove. [f. OF *carpite* or It. *carpita* p.p. of *carpire* f. L *carpere* pluck, the fabric being perh. a patchwork; cf. F *charpie* lint]

cărpŏl'ŏgy, n. Delirious fumbling with bed-clothes etc. [f. Gk *karphologia* (*kar-phos* twig, *legō* pick, -Y¹)]

cărpo-¹, comb. form of CARPUS.

cărpo-², comb. form of Gk *karpos* fruit.

cărp'us, n. (anat.; pl. -pī). Part of skeleton that unites hand etc. to fore-arm, eight small bones in higher vertebrates (in man, wrist; in horse, knee). [f. Gk *karpos* wrist]

carragëen (kǎ'ragēn), n. An edible sea-weed found in N. Europe, Irish moss. [f. *Carragheen* in Ireland]

cărp'al, a. Of the CARPUS. [CARPUS, -AL]

cărp'el, n. (bot.). Pistil-cell, whether pistil is one cell or several. Hence ~lARY¹ a. [mod. dim. f. Gk *karpos* fruit, see -ʊR(2)]

ca'rriage (-rĭj), n. Conveying, transport; cost of conveying (~-FREE; || ~-forward, not prepaid); management (of enterprise etc.); passing (of Parl. motion etc.). 6. Bring to (of day's journey etc.). 7. Prolong, continue, to (~ tower to 500 ft, modesty to excess). 8. Win (prize; ~ it, the day, succeed; ~ fortress etc., capture; ~ hearers with one, persuade; win victory for (candidate; ~ one's point, a motion, bill). 9. Wear, have with one, possess, involve, (arms, a watch, etc.; ~ one's BAR²; ~ weight, authority, be influential; ~ with one, remember; loans ~ interest, principles ~ consequences). 10. Hold in a certain way (~ one's head, body, etc.). 11. Endure weight of, support, (ships ~ sail, piers ~ dome). 12. ~ away, inspire, transport, deprive of self-control, (Naut.) lose (mast. etc.) by breakage; ~ off, remove from life, win, render passable, ~ it off well, make brave show; ~ on, advance (process) a stage, continue, manage (business), (v.i.) go on with what one is doing, (colloq.) behave strangely, flirt or have amorous intrigue (with); ~ out, put (principles, instructions, etc.) in practice; ~ over (St. Exch.), keep over to next settling-day; ~ through, bring safely out of difficulties, complete. [f. ONF carier f. LL carricare (L carrus CAR²]

ca'rriageable (-ĭja-), a. Available for carriages (of road). [-ABLE]

ca'rrick bend, n. (naut.). Kind of knot or splice. [BEND¹; carrick perh.f. obs. carrack armed merchant ship]

ca'rrier, n. In vbl senses; esp. : person undertaking for hire the conveyance of parcels (common ~, legal term including also railway and steamship companies etc.); part of bicycle etc. for carrying luggage; person or animal that without catching a disease conveys its germs; = Bren~, aircraft~, etc.; ~-PIGEON; ~-nation etc., conducting oversea trade for others. [CARRY + -ER¹]

ca'rriôle, n. Small open carriage for one; covered light cart; Canadian sledge. [f. F carriole, med. L carota f. Gk karòtan perh. f. kara head]

ca'rrion, n. & a. Dead putrefying flesh; anything vile, garbage, filth; ~-crow, between raven & rook, feeding on ~, small animals, etc.; (adj.) rotten, loathsome, etc. [ME & ONF caroine perh. f. Rom. *caronada f. L caro carnis flesh]

carronade', n. (hist.). Short large-calibred ship's gun. [Carron orig. place of making + -ADE]

ca'rrot, n. (Plant with) tapering orange-coloured edible root; (pl., sl.) red hair, red-haired person, whence ~y² a. [f. F carotte f. L carota f. Gk karòton perh. f. kara head]

ca'rry, v.t. & i. 1. Convey in vehicle, ship, hand, or head (as news), or on person (also of vehicle etc., or water, wind, etc., as subject; ~ corn, from field to stack; fetch & ~, be underling; ~ all before one, succeed; ~ weight, be handicapped in horse-racing or fig.). 2. Conduct (pipes ~ water, wires ~ sound; ~ into effect; ~ one back, in fancy to earlier times; ~ off to prison). 3. Transfer (figures to column of higher notation; ~ conviction, implant one's own in other minds; ~ over, forward, entries to new page or account). 4. Propel to specified distance (of gun etc.,

with obj. usu. omitted; also intr.=go or missile). 5. Cause or enable to go to (of motive, journey-money, etc.).

ca'rt, n., & v.t. & i. 1. Strong two-wheeled vehicle (cf. WAGON) used in farming & for heavy goods, (also spring, mail, dog, ~) light two-wheeled one-horse vehicle for driving in, (put ~ before horse, reverse order, take effect for cause); in the ~ (sl.), in a fix, in an awkward or losing position; ~horse, thickset & fit for heavy work; ~ladder, rack at sides or ends for increasing capacity; ~load, ~ful, also large quantity of anything; ~-road, -way, too rough for carriages; ~-wheel, wheel of ~, large coin as crown etc., lateral somersault of street urchins (turn ~a.); ~-whip, long & heavy; ~-wright, maker of ~s; hence ~AGE(4), ~ER¹, ~FUL(2) (-ôôl). nn. 2. vb. Carry in a ~; work with a ~. [prob. f. ON kartr cart cf. OE cræt of doubtful meaning]

ca'rte, quarte (kårt), n. Fencing position (~ & tierce, sword-play). [F (q²), f. It. quarta fourth]

carte-de-visite (vĭzēt'), n. Photograph 3½in.×2½. [F, = visiting card, its orig. purpose]

carte blanche (see Ap.), n. Blank paper given to person to write his own terms on; full discretionary power. [F (CARD², BLANK)]

ca'rtel, n. Written challenge to duel; (agreement for) exchange of prisoners;

(also **kartel**) manufacturers' union to control production, marketing arrangements, prices, etc. [F. f. It. *cartello* dim. of *carta* CARD².]

Carté'sian (-zhn), a. & n. (Follower) of Descartes or his philosophy or mathematical methods. Hence ~ISM (-zizm-)(3) n. [*Cartesius* mod. L name of René Descartes, 1596–1650, -AN]

car'tilage, n. (Structure, part, in vertebrates, of) firm elastic tissue, gristle, (*temporary* ~, in the young, changing later to bone). So **cartila'ginod** a. [F. f. L *cartilago -inis*]

cartila'ginous, a. Of, like, cartilage (~ *fish*, with ~ *skeleton*). [f. L *cartilago -inis*]

carto'graphy, n. Map-drawing. So **carto'GRAPHER** n., **cartograph'ic(al)** aa. [f. F *carte* chart (CARD²)+-GRAPHY; the correct form f. Gk would have *chi-*]

car'tomancy, n. Fortune-telling by playing-cards. [f. It. *carta* CARD² -MANCY]

car'ton, n. White disk within bull's-eye of target; cardboard box for holding goods or the cardboard used for these. [f. F as foll.]

cartoon', n. & v.t. & i. 1. Drawing on stout paper as design for painting, tapestry, mosaic, etc.; full-page (or large) illustration, esp. on politics in comic paper; hence ~IST(3) n.: *animated* ~, film made from a succession of drawings simulating a cinematographic film of living persons. 2. v.b. Draw ~, represent (person etc.) in a ~. [f. F *carton* or It. *cartone* (*carta* CARD², -OON)]

cartouche' (-ōōsh), n. (Archit.) scroll ornament, e.g. volute of Ionic capital; tablet imitating, or drawing of, scroll with rolled-up ends, used ornamentally or bearing inscription; (Archaeol.) oval ring containing hieroglyphic names & titles of Egyptian kings etc. [F., f. It. *cartoccio* augmentative of *carta* CARD²]

car'tridge, n. Charge of explosive for firearms or blasting made up in case of paper, flannel, metal, etc. (*small-arm ball* ~, or ~, contains bullet also, *blank* ~ the explosive only); *brass* ~-*belt*, with sockets for ~s; ~-*paper*, thick & rough, used also for drawing & for strong envelopes. [corrupt of prec.]

car'tulary, n. Collection of records; register. [f. med. L *c(h)artularium* f. L *cartula* dim. of *c(h)arta* CARD², -ARY¹]

ca'runcle (also kar̆ŭ'-), n. Fleshy excrescence, as turkeycock's wattles. [f. 16th-c. F *caruncule* f. L *caruncula* (*caro caro* flesh, -UNCLE)]

carve, v.t. & i. (p.p. -ed, arch. -en).. Cut (flesh, etc.) into pieces, cut (meat etc.) at or for table (*carving knife*, long for this purpose); subdivide (usu. *up*); ~ *out*, take from larger whole, acquire esp. by the sword (in gen. sense now only fig., as ~ *one's way*); produce by cutting (statue, portrait, representation in relief or intaglio, inscription, design, *out of*, *in*, or *on*, material), change by cutting (material *into* something), cover or adorn (material *with* figures cut in it, cut designs etc.), whence **carv'ING**(2) n. [OE *ceorfan* f. com.-Teut. cf. Du. *kerven*, prob. cogn. w. Gk *graphō* write]

carv'el, = CARAVEL; ~-*built*, with planks flush (cf. CLINKER-BUILT).

carv'er, n. In vbl senses; also, carving knife, (pl.) carving knife & fork. [-ER¹]

caryat'id, n. Female figure used as pillar. [f. L f. Gk *karuatis -idos* priestess at...

cascade', n. & v.i. (Fall like a) waterfall, wavy fall of lace etc. [F. f. It. *cascata* (*cascare* to fall for *casicare* f. L *cas-* see CASE¹)]

casca'ra sagra'da (-ahd), n. Laxative drug from the bark of a tree. [Sp. = sacred bark]

case¹, n. 1. Instance of thing's occurring; actual state of affairs (*is*, *is not*, *the* ~, is true, false); position, circumstances, in which one is; plight, (*in good, evil,* ~, well, badly, off); (Med.) person's diseased condition; instance of any disease. 2. (Law) cause, suit, for trial; statement of facts in court's consideration (*judge states a* ~); cause that has been decided & may be cited (*leading* ~, one often cited & governing subsequent decisions); sum of arguments on one side (*that is our* ~; *make out one's* ~, prove it); (fig.) ~ *of conscience*, matter in which conscience has to decide between conflicting principles. 3. (Gram.) form of noun, adj., or pronoun, in inflected languages expressing relation to some other word in sentence (in uninflected languages, this relation itself apart from form). 4. *In* ~, if, in the event that, lest; *in* ~ *of*, in the event of; *in the* ~ as regards (*in the* ~ *of Jones an exception was made*); *put (the)* ~ *that*, suppose; *in any* ~, whatever the fact is, whatever may happen; *in that* ~, if that is true, should happen; ~-*law*, law as settled by precedent. [ME & OF *cas* f. L *casus -ūs* fall (*cadere cas-* fall)]

case², n. & v.t. 1. Enclosure of something, box, bag, sheath, etc.; frame for plant-growing; glass box for showing specimens, curiosities, etc.; outer protective covering (of watch, sausage, seed-vessel, book, etc.); box with proper contents (*dressing-*~); (Print.) receptacle with compartments (*upper* ~, capitals, *lower* ~, small letters); ~-*bottle*, square for fitting

into ~ with others; **~harden** v.t., harden surface of, esp. give steel surface to (iron) by carbonizing; (fig.) render callous; **~knife**, worn in sheath; **~shot**, or ~, bullets in tin box fired from cannon without fuse, also=SHRAPNEL; **~worm**, = CADDIS. **2** v.t. Enclose in case, surround *with*, (also with *up*, *over*); hence **cās′ING**[1] (3) n. [f. ONF *casse* (now *châsse*) f. L *capsa* (*capere* hold)]

cās′ein, n. Protein of milk, the basis of cheese. [L *caseus* cheese + -IN]

cāse′māt(e (-săt-), n. Vaulted chamber in thickness of wall of fortress, with embrasures; armoured enclosure for guns in warship. Hence **~ED¹** a. [F, f. It. *casamatta* (*casa* house, perh. *matto* mad, also pseudo-)]

cāse′ment (-zmⁿ-, -sm-), n. Metal or wooden hinged frame with glass forming (part of) window (often *~-window*) (poet. etc.) window; **~ cloth**, cotton cloth used for curtains & as dress material etc. [f. med. L *casamentum*, or f. CASE²+-MENT]

cās′eous, a. Of, like, cheese. [f. L *caseus* cheese + -OUS]

casĕrn(e (-z-), n. (Usu. pl.) small building(s) for troops between ramparts & houses of fortress. [F (-*e*), f. Sp. *caserna* (*casa* house)]

cash¹, n. (no pl.), & v.t. **1.** Ready money (*in*, *out of*, ~ having, not having, money; ~ *down*, paid on the spot); || = *on delivery* (abbr. C.O.D.), forwarding of goods against ~ to be paid to postman; (Banking etc.) specie, or specie & bank-notes; (Book-keeping) *~account*, to which only ~ is carried, & from which all payments are made, *~book*, for record of ~ received & paid; *~ payment*, in ready money; *~ price*, lowest, for ready money; *~ register*, mechanical till visibly recording amount of each purchase, totalling receipts, etc.; hence **~LESS** a. **2.** v.t. Give or obtain ~ for (note, cheque, etc.); *~in* (colloq.), die, *~ in on*, realize profit on, (fig. use of poker phr.). [f. F *casse* (now *caisse*) box f. L *capsa* CASE²]

cash², n. (pl. *cash*). Kinds of E.-Ind. & Chinese small coin, esp. a former Chinese coin perforated for stringing = $\frac{1}{1000}$ of tael. [ult. f. Tamil *kasu* a small coin by confusion with CASH¹]

cash′ew (-ōō), n. W.-Ind. etc. tree with kidney-shaped nut (*~nut*). [f. F *acajou*, f. Braz. *acajoba*]

cashier¹, n. Person in charge of bank's or merchant's cash. [f. F *caissier* (CASH¹, -IER)]

cashier′², v.t. Dismiss from service, depose; discard. [f. Flem. or Du. *casseren* cf. F *casser* f. L *quassare* (*quatere quass-* shake), with senses also of L *cassare* annul (*cassus* vain)]

cash′mere, n. (Also *~ shawl*) shawl of fine soft wool of Cashmere goat; the material; imitation of it. [place]

casi′nō (-sē-), n. (pl. -os, -oŝ). Public music or dancing room; old card-game. [It., dim. of *casa* house f. L *casa* cottage]

cask (-ā-), n. Wooden vessel (=BARREL¹); this & its contents; varying measure of capacity. [perh. f. F *casque* helmet]

cas′kĕt (-ah-), n. Small box, often of precious material & workmanship, for jewels, letters, cremated ashes, etc. [perh. dim. of prec. (-ET²), but quoted from a century earlier]

Cās′lon (-z-), n. (typ.). ~ *type*, old-face type cut in the foundry established by William ~ (d. 1766), or in imitation of this.

casque (kāsk), n. (hist., poet.). Helmet. [F, f. Sp. *casco*]

Cassăn′dra, n. Prophet of ill; unregarded prophet. [Trojan prophetess fated to prophesy truly & be unbelieved]

cassā′tion, n. Annulment; *Court of C~*, court of appeal (esp. of foreign countries). [f. LL *cassatio* (L *cassare* CASHIER², -ATION)]

cassā′va (-sah-), n. W.-Ind. etc. plant with tuberous roots; its starch or flour, bread made from these. [f. Haytian *casáví* etc.]

căss′erōle, n. A heat-proof earthenware vessel in which meat etc. is cooked & served (*en ~*, so served). [F]

cā′ssia (also -sha), n. Inferior kind of cinnamon; genus of plants yielding senna-leaves. [L f. Gk *kasia* f. Heb. *q'tsi'ah* (*qatsa'* cut off bark)]

căss′ock, n. Long close tunic worn by some Anglican clergymen under gown or short surplice, or as ordinary attire. Hence **~ED²** (-kt) a. [f. F *casaque* etym. dub., perh. f. It. *casacca* habitation, also long coat, (*casa* see CASINO); cf. CHASUBLE]

cassolĕtte′, n. Vessel for burning perfumes; perfume-box with perforated top. [F, dim. of *cassole* dim. of *casse* pan]

căss′owary (-o-w-), n. Kinds of large running bird related to ostrich. [f. Malay *casuari*]

cast¹ (-ah-), v.t. & i. (*cast*). **1.** Throw (poet. or arch. exc. in spec. uses, as: ~ *dice*; *~ a vote*, give or deposit it; ~ LOTS; ~ *ashore*; ~ *net, hook, fly*; *~ing-net*, one thrown & at once drawn in; ~ *the* LEAD¹, in sounding; ~ *anchor*; *~ in one's teeth*, reproach him with, *that*; ~ *an eye, glance, look*; *~ a spell on*, bewitch; *~ light, a shadow, on*; *~ blame, one's cares, upon*; *~ into prison*). **2.** Overthrow in a lawsuit. **3.** Throw off, get rid of, lose, (*~ not a* CLOUT *till May be out*; *~ aside*, give up using, abandon; horse casts shoe, snake, deer, slough, horns; cow, tree, ~ *calf, fruit*, drop prematurely; *~ing-net, soldier, police-man, horse*, dismiss, reject; *~ loose*, detach oneself. **4.** Reckon, calculate, (*~ accounts*, do sums; *~ a column of figures* etc., add up; *~ a* HOROSCOPE or *nativity*).

5. Arrange (~ facts into such a shape; ~ actors for parts, parts to actors). 6. Form, found, (molten metal) into some shape, (devise means, etc.) (for, to do, how); ~ away, reject, (pass., of ship) be wrecked; ~ back, revert; ~ down, depress; ~ in one's lot with, share fortunes of; ~ off, abandon, (Knitting) close loops & make selvedge, (Naut.) loose & throw off (rope etc.), (Printing) estimate space taken in print by MS. copy; ~ up, calculate. [f. ON kasta perh. cogn. w. L gerere gest-; it displaced OE weorpan, & has been displaced in ordinary literal use by throw]

cast² (-ah-), n. 1. Throw of missile etc., distance so attained, (arch.); throw, number thrown, at dice, whence chance or try; throw of net, sounding-lead, or fishing-line (also in fishing the fly with hook & gut; ~ & good, bad, etc. place for casting). 2. Casual lift in cart etc. 3. Undigested food thrown up by hawk, owl, etc. 4. Calculation, adding of columns in account. 5. Set of actors taking the parts in play, or the distribution among them. 6. Form into which any work is thrown; model made by running molten metal or pressing soft material into mould (also the negative mould itself), (~ in eye, slight squint). 8. Tinge, shade, of colour. 9. Type, quality, (esp. ~ of features, ~ of mind). [f. prec.]

Cas'tal¹y, n. Fount of poesy. So Cas-ta'lian a. [f. L f. Gk Kastalía fountain of the Muses + -AN]

cas'tanet (or -ĕt'), n. (Usu. pl.) hard-wood or ivory instrument(s) used in pairs to rattle in time with dancing. [f. Sp. castañeta dim. of castaña f. L castanea chestnut]

cast'away (kahsta-), n. & a. Reprobate; shipwrecked (person). [p.p. of CAST¹, AWAY]

caste (-ah-), n. Indian hereditary class, with members socially equal, united in religion, & usu. following same trade, having no social intercourse with persons of other ~s; hereditary more or less ex-clusive class elsewhere; this system, the position it confers (lose, renounce, ~; de-scend in social scale). Hence ~'LESS (-tl-) a. [f. Sp. & Port. casta lineage perh. orig. fem. of casto CHASTE]

cas'tellan, n. Governor of castle. [ME & ONF castelain f. L castellanus]

cas'tellated, a. Castle-like; battlemented; (of district etc.) having castles. [f. med. L castellatus (CASTLE, -ATE²)]

cas'tigate, v.t. Chastise, punish with blows or words; correct & emend (book etc.). Hence ~A'TION, n., ~ātor², n., ~ātory a. [f. L castigare (see -ATE³) perh. = castum agere make CHASTE]

Cas'tile' (-ēl) soap, n. Hard soap, usu. mottled, made with olive oil & soda. [Castile, in Spain]

cast'ing-vote (-ah-), n. Vote that decides between two equal parties, [part. of CAST¹ in obs. sense, cf. CASTOR²]

cast iron, n., cast-iron, a. Iron shaped by being run into mould; (adj.) made of ~; hard, unfiring, rigid, unadaptable.

castle¹ (kah'sl, kâ'sl), n. Large fortified building or set of buildings, stronghold; mansion that was once such; (Ireland) The C~, government system (f. Dublin C~, seat of vice-regal court & govern-ment); Englishman's house his ~, none may force entrance; (Chess) piece made with battlemented top, also Rook; ~ in the air, or as Gallicism ~ in Spain, vision-ary project, day-dream, (so ~-builder). Hence ca'stlED² (-ld) a. ~WISE (-lw-) adv. [f. ONF castel f. L castellum dim. of castrum fort]

ca'stle² (kah'sl, kâ'sl), v.t. & i. (chess). Move castle next king and king round castle (~ the king, or abs.). [f. prec.]

cas'tor¹ (-ah-), n. Substance obtained from beaver used in medicine & per-fumery; (sl.) hat. [obs. wd for beaver, F, f. L f. Gk kastōr]

cas'tor², -er², (-ah-), n. 1. Condiment-bottle for table, (pl.) cruet-stand; ~ sugar, white, finely granulated. 2. Small swi-velled wheel on leg of chair, table, etc. [CAST¹ + -OR², -ER²; sense 1 orig. of per-forated-top bottle for casting pepper etc.; sense 2 f. obs. sense of CAST¹= veer, turn]

cas'tor³ (-ah-), n. Horny external knob inside horse's leg (also chestnut), [perh. = obs. castane chestnut ONF castanie f. L castanea]

cas'tor oil (-ah-), n. Nauseous vegetable oil used as purgative (cold-drawn ~, ex-pressed from seeds without heat) & lubri-cant. [etym. dub.; perh. so called as having succeeded CASTOR¹ in med. use]

castrametā'tion, n. (archaeol.). Laying out of camps. [f. F castramétation f. L castra camp, metari measure, -ATION]

ca'strāte, v.t. Remove testicles of, geld; deprive of vigour; expurgate (book). Hence ~A'TION n. [f. L castrare, -ATE³]

ca'sual (-zhoo-, -zū-), a. & n. Accidental; irregular; undesigned; unmethodical; careless; ~ labourer, who works when the chance comes; ~ ward, who sometimes need poor-relief (also ~ as noun); ~ water (i.e. not one of the recognized hazards of the course). Hence ~LY² adv., ~NESS n. [f. F casuel f. L casualis (casus CASE¹, -AL)]

ca'sualty (-zhoo-, -zū-), n. Accident, mishap, disaster, esp. (pl.) list or number of killed, wounded, & invalided, in a battle, march, war, etc. (sing.) wounded etc. person. [f. L casualitas (prec., -TY) on anal. of royalty etc.]

casuarin'a (also -ēn-ȧ), n. (Kinds of) quick-growing Australian & E.-Indian tree with jointed leafless branches resembling gigantic horse-tails. [f. mod. L *casuarius* cassowary (from resemblance between branches & feathers)]

ca'suist (-zhōō-, -zū-), n. Person, esp. theologian, who lays down application of ethical rules to special cases, weighs conflicting obligations, classifies exceptions, & draws distinctions; sophist, quibbler. Hence ~is'tic(AL) aa., ~is'tically² adv., ~istry n. [f. F *casuiste* f. L *casus* CASE, -IST(3)]

ca'sus, L n. ~ *bell'i*, act justifying war; ~ *foed'eris* (fēd-), circumstances contemplated in treaty as requiring the action of the parties when they arise.

cāt¹, n. 1. Small domesticated carnivorous quadruped (male, *Tom-~*); *Wild Cat*, larger native British kind; spiteful woman, scratching child; (Zool.) any member of genus *Felis*, as lion, tiger, panther, leopard (esp. *the Cats, the great Cats*); ~-like animal of other species (*civet, musk, -~*). 2. (Hist.) pent-house in sieges. 3. (Also ~*head*) horizontal beam from each side of ship's bow for raising & carrying anchor. 4. (Also ~*o'-nine-tails*) rope whip with nine knotted lashes formerly used for flogging sailors & soldiers, & still ordered by magistrates sentencing for certain criminal offences. 5. Six-legged tripod always standing on three of its legs. 6. Tapered short stick in game tip-~. 7. *Turn ~ in pan*, change sides, be turncoat; ~ *may look at king*, rebuke to the exclusive; *care killed the ~* (for all its nine lives; therefore be cheerful); *wait for the ~ to jump, see which way the ~ jumps, cult of the jumping ~*, etc., of politician refusing to advise until public opinion has declared itself; *fight like Kilkenny ~s*, to mutual destruction; *BELL² the ~*; *not room to swing a ~*, confined space; ~-*&-dog life* etc., full of quarrels, esp. that of husband & wife; || ~-*&-mouse Act* (sl.), that enabling hunger-strikers to be released temporarily; *rain ~s & dogs*, very hard. 8. *~bird*, Amer. thrush; || ~*burglar* (who enters by climbing); ~*call*, shrill whistle (sound or instrument) expressing disapproval at theatre etc. (also as v.i. & t., use, reprove with, this); ~*eyed*, able to see in dark; ~*fish*, of various kinds, esp. large Amer. river-fish; ~*head*, see sense 3; ~*ice*, milky-looking, bubbly, not solid, irregular; || ~*lap*, slops, tea, etc.; ~*mint*, blue-flowered aromatic plant; ~*nap*, *sleep*, brief, in chair etc.; ~*'s-cradle*, child's game with transfers of string between fingers of two players; ~*'s-eye*, precious stone of Ceylon & Malabar; ~*'s-foot*, ground-ivy; || ~*'s-meat*, horse-flesh prepared & hawked as food for ~s; ~*'s-paw*, person used as tool by another; slight

breeze rippling water in places; ~*'s-tail*, various plants, as Reed-mace; ~*walk*, narrow footway along a bridge, among large engines, etc.; || ~*whisker*, fine adjustable wire in crystal wireless receiver. Hence ~*HOOD* n., ~*LIKE* a. [com.-Europ. f. L *catta*]

cāt², v.i. & t. (-tt-), || Vomit (colloq.); (Naut.) raise (the anchor) from the surface of the water to the cathead. [f. prec.]

cata-, cat-, cath-, pref. in wds taken from Greek, & in others formed with Gk materials or on Gk analogy; meanings: down, away, wrongly, mis-, entirely, down, upon, according to, alongside of, thoroughly. [f. Gk *kata* prep.]

cătachrē'sĭs (-k-), n. Perversion, improper use, of words. So ~ĕs'tic(AL) aa., ~ĕs'tically² adv. [L, f. Gk CATA- (*khrēsis* f. *khraomai* use)]

cat'aclasm, n. Violent break, disruption. [f. Gk CATA(*klasma* f. *klaō* to break)]

cat'aclysm, n. Deluge (esp. in Geol. as required by theory of school that believed in repeated destructions of all life followed by new creations); political or social upheaval. Hence ~AL, ~IC, aa., ~ist(3) n., *(all iz-)*. [f. F *cataclysme* t. Gk CATA(*klusmos* flood f. *kluzō* wash)]

cat'acomb (-kōm), n. Subterranean cemetery (orig. that under basilica of St Sebastian near Rome, supposed burying-place of Peter & Paul); (usu. pl.) the many Roman subterranean galleries with recesses excavated in sides for tombs; similar works elsewhere (in Paris, worked-out stone-quarries with bones from emptied churchyards); wine-cellar. [etym. dub.; the ~s generally, while in use, were not so called; that of St Sebastian was, *catacumbas* (Gk CATA- *kumbas* at the boats?) being possibly name of district or an inn]

catād'romous, a. (zool.). Descending to lower river or sea to spawn. [f. Gk CATA- (*dromos* -running) +-OUS]

cat'afălque (-k), n. Decorated stage for coffin or effigy of distinguished person during funeral service; open hearse. [F, f. It. *catafalco* etym. dub.; but cf. F *chafaud* SCAFFOLD]

Cat'alan, a. & n. (Native, language) of Catalonia.

cătalĕc'tic, a. Wanting a syllable in last foot (of verse). [f. LL f. Gk CATA(*lēktikos* ceasing f. *lēgō* cease)]

cat'alĕpsy, n. Suspension of sensation & consciousness accompanied by rigidity of the body. [f. med. L *catalepsia* f. Gk CATA(*lēpsis* seizure) see foll.]

cătalĕp'tic, a. & n. Of, subject to, the disease catalepsy (n., ~ person):(Philos.) of mental apprehension. [f. LL *catalepticus* f. Gk CATA(*lēptikos* seizing f. *lambanō* seize)]

cat'alŏgue (-g), n. & v.t. (Enumerate, enter in, a) complete list, usu. alpha-

betical or under headings, & often with particulars added to items; ~e raisonné (-zonǎ'), descriptive ~e arranged according to subjects or branches of subject. Hence ~ER¹ n. [F, f. LL f. Gk *katálogos* f. CATA- (*légō* choose) enroll]

catál'pa, n. Kinds of tree with heart-shaped leaves & trumpet-shaped flowers. [W.-Ind.]

catál'ysis, n. (chem.). Effect produced by a substance that without undergoing change itself aids a chemical change in other bodies. So cat'alyt'ic a. [f. ~, catalyt'ica... f. Gk CATA(*lusis* loosing f. *luō* to loose) dissolution]

cátamarán', n. Raft or float of logs tied side by side, longest in middle, used for communication with shore or short voyage; raft of two boats fastened side by side; quarrelsome woman. [f. Tamil *kattu-maram* tied tree]

cat'amite, n. Sodomite's minion. [f. L *cadamitus* f. Gk *Ganumēdēs* cup-bearer of Zeus]

cátamoun'tain (-tin), cát-o'-m-, n. Leopard; wild quarrelsome person. ...

cat'aplasm, n. (med.). Poultice. [f. F *cataplasme* f. L f. Gk *kataplasma* (*kata-plassō* spread, smear over)]

cat'apult, n., & v.t. & i. Ancient engine worked by lever & ropes for discharging darts, stones, etc.; || boy's shooting contrivance of forked stick & elastic; mechanical contrivance usu. employing explosive charge for launching aircraft from deck of ship etc., or abs.) with ~, launch (aircraft). [f. L *catapulta* f. Gk *kata-pultē*, CATA- + *pallō* hurl]

cat'aract, n. Waterfall (prop. large & sheer, cf. CASCADE); downpour of rain, rush of water; (Path.) eye-complaint producing partial blindness; (Mech.) steam-engine governor acting by flow of water. [f. F *cataracte* & L *cataracta*, f. Gk *katarrhaktēs* f. CATA(*russō* dash) or CATA-(*rhēgnumi* break); the Path. sense prob. f. obs. sense *portcullis*]

catarrh' (-ár), n. Inflammation of mucous membrane, a cold. Hence catár'rhal (-rǎ) a. [f. F *catarrhe* f. LL *catarrhus* f. Gk CATA(*rheō* flow)]

cat'arrhine (-rīn), a. & n. (zool.). (Monkey) having nostrils close together, oblique, & directed downwards, & opposable thumbs on all limbs. [f. Gk CATA, *rhinos* nostril]

catás'trophē, n. Dénouement of drama; disastrous end, ruin; event subverting system of things, esp. in Geol. (cf. CATA-CLYSM, UNIFORMITARIAN), whence cátas-tróph'ic(-ǎl) aa., ~ISM(3), ~IST(2), nn.; sudden, widespread, or signal disaster. [f. Gk CATA(*strophē* turning f. *strephō* to turn)]

Cataw'ba, n. U.S. grape & wine. [river ~]

cat'boat, n. Sailing-boat with single mast placed well forward, carrying one sail only. [prob. f. obs. *cat(t)*, vessel formerly used on the N. E. coast]

catch¹, v.t. & i. (caught pr. kawt). 1. Capture, ensnare (~ CRAB¹), overtake (also ~ up; caught in storm), lay hold of (also ~ hold of; ~ a TARTAR; ~ up habit etc., adopt), be in time for (train etc.). 2. Surprise, detect, (at or in, or doing; ~ me!, him!, you may be sure we shall not). 3. Hit (usu. with part specified; caught him on the nose; also caught him a blow or one). 4. (Of fire or combustible) ignite, be ignited, (~ fire or ~). 5. Be entangled, take hold, (usu. ~ in a thing; bolt ~es); ~ up, become popular. 6. Snatch (esp. ~ up, away; ~ at, often fig. = be glad to get). 7. Intercept motion of (nail ~es dress; at cricket, ~ ball, prevent its touching ground off bat, also ~ or ~ out batsman, dismiss by doing this); ~ out, (fig.) ~ in a mistake etc., ~ napping. 8. Check suddenly, interrupt). 9. Receive, incur, be infected with, (cold, a cold, a fever; be scolding, thrashing, or 'it'; enthusiasm, a habit, an accent; ~ one's DEATH; pond etc. ~es, is coated with ice). 10. Grasp with senses or mind (meaning, sound, tune; ~ glimpse of, see for a moment; don't ~ on, fail to see meaning). 11. Arrest, captivate, (attention, eye, fancy; ~ Speaker's eye, succeed in being called on to speak in H. of Commons). 12. ~a-~-can, Lancashire wrestling style; ~-drain, along hillside to prevent water's running off; || ~'em-alive-o, sticky flypaper; ~-fly, a sticky-stemmed plant; ~'penny (adj.), clap-trap, intended merely to sell; ~'weed, Goosegrass; ~'word, word so placed as to draw attention, e.g. first of dictionary article, rhyming word in verse, last word (cue) of actor's speech, first word of page anticipated at foot of previous one, also influential temporary phrase in politics, religion, etc. Hence ~ABLE a., (~)~ER¹(1, 2 n. [catch & CHASE are respectively f. ONF *cachier* & OF *chacier* (now *chasser*) both f. LL *captiare* (L *captus* captive f. *capere* take); the gen. sense of catch (take, not pursue) is excl. E.

catch², n. 1. Act of catching; amount of fish caught. 2. Chance of, success in, catching at cricket (also a good, safe, ~, one skilful at it). 3. Cunning question, deception, surprise; (~out, act of catching out, circumstance that upsets calculations. 4. Contrivance for checking motion of door etc. 5. Thing or person caught, or worth catching (no ~, bad bargain, unwelcome acquisition). 6. (Mus.) composition for three or more equal voices, occas-

so devised as to produce punning or other humorous verbal combinations. [f. prec.]

catch'ing, a. In vbl senses; esp.: infectious, attractive. [-ING²]

catch'ment, n. ~*basin*, ~*area*, from which rainfall flows into river etc. [CATCH¹, -MENT]

catch'pole, -poll, n. Sheriff's officer; bum-bailiff. [f. med. L *cacepollus* cf. OF *chacepol* chase-fowl (CHASE, L *pullus* fowl)]

catch'up, mis-spelling of KETCHUP.

catch'y, a. Attractive; easily caught up (of tune etc.). [CATCH¹ + -Y²]

cate, n. (Arch.; usu. pl.) choice food. [for obs. *acate* f. OF *acat* purchase f. *acater* now *acheter* buy f. LL *ad*(*captare* frequent of L *capere* take) catch at]

catéchét'ical (-kě-), aa. Of, by, oral teaching; according to a, or the Church, catechism; consisting of, proceeding by, question & answer. Hence **catéchét'i**cally² adv. [f. L f. Gk *katěkhětikos* f. *katěkhětēs* oral teacher (*katěkheō* CATE-CHIZE), -IC]

cat'echism (-k-), n. Instruction by question & answer; published example of this, esp. on religious doctrine (*Church C*~, the Anglican; *Longer & Shorter C*~, of Presbyterians); series of questions put to anyone. Hence **catěchis'mAL** (-k-), a. [f. L *catechismus* (foll., -ISM)]

cat'echize (-k-), v.t. Instruct by question & answer, or by use of Church Catechism; put questions to, examine. Hence or cogn. ~ist(1), ~izer¹, (-k-), nn. [f. L *catechizare* f. Gk *katěkhizō* f. CAT(*ěkhěō* sound) make hear]

catégó'rical, a. (Logic: of proposition) unconditional, absolute; explicit, direct, plain-speaking; (Ethics) ~ *imperative*, bidding of conscience as ultimate moral law. Hence ~LY² adv. [f. L f. Gk *katěgorikos* f. CAT(*ěgoros* -speaking) + -AL]

cat'egorỹ, n. (Orig. Gk meaning, statement) one of a possibly exhaustive set of classes among which all things might be distributed (the ~ies of Aristotle are: substance, quantity, quality, relation, place, time, posture, possession, action, passion); one of the *a priori* conceptions applied by the mind as frames to material supplied by sense; class, division. [f. L f. Gk *katěgoria* statement as prec.]

caten'a, n. Connected series. [L, = chain] f. Gk *katěgoria* statement as prec.]

caten'ary, cátenar'ian, aa. & nn. (Like) curve formed by uniform chain hanging freely from two points not in one vertical line (~ *bridge*, suspension, hung from such chains). [f.L *catenarius*(prec.,-ARY¹,-AN)]

cat'enate, v.t. Connect like links. So ~A'TION n. [f. L *catenare* as prec. -ATE³]

cat'er¹, n. (obs.). The four of cards or dice. [f. F *quadre* f. L *quatuor* four]

cat'er², v.i. Purvey food (usu. *for*); provide amusement etc. *for*. Hence ~ER⁴ n. [f. obs. noun *cater* (now *caterer*) = obs. *acater* f. OF *acateor* buyer (CATE, -OR²)]

cat'eran, n. (Sc.). Highland fighting-man, marauder, cattle-lifter. [f. Gael. *ceath-airne* peasantry]

cat'er-cousin (kŭz-), n.(arch.). Intimate; *be* ~*s*, on good or familiar terms. [perh. f. CATER² as feeding together]

cat'erpillar, n. Larva of butterfly or moth; rapacious person; (Mech.) endless articulated steel band passing round & worked by two wheels of a tank, tractor, or vehicle required to cope with rough ground. [perh. f. OF *chatepelose* lit. hairy-cat, with **-s** dropped as pl. sign, & spelling influenced by vb *pill* rob, strip]

cat'erwaul, v.i., & n. (Make) cat's screaming; quarrel like cats. [CAT¹, WAUL]

cat'gut, n. Material used for strings of fiddle etc. made of twisted intestines of sheep, horse, or ass (not cat); stringed instruments. [expl. of *cat* doubtful]

cath-. See CATA-.

cathar'sis, n. (Med.) purgation; outlet to emotion afforded by drama (ref. to Arist., *Poet.* 6). [f. Gk *katharsis* (*kathairō* cleanse f. *katharos* clean)]

cathar'tic, a. & n. (med.). Purgative (medicine). [f. L f. Gk *kathartikos* as prec.]

Cathay', n. (Arch. & poet. for) China. [Kitah, race name]

cathěd'ral, a. & n. (Also *C*~ *church*) principal church of diocese, with bishop's throne; ~ *utterance* etc., delivered ex CATHEDRA. [f. med. L *cathedralis* f. L f. Gk CAT(*hedra* chair f. *hed*-sit), -AL]

Cáth'erine-wheel, n. Circular spoked window or window-compartment; rotating firework; lateral summersault (*turn* ~*s*). [spiked wheel in St Catherine's martyrdom]

cáth'eter, n. (med.). Tubular instrument for passing into bladder. [L, f. Gk *kathetēr* f. CAT(*hiěmi* send)]

cáth'ode, n. (electr.). Negative pole of current. [f. Gk CAT(*hodos* way) descent or use to all men; all-embracing, of wide sympathies, broad-minded, tolerant; *C*~ *Epistles*, encyclical (those of James, Peter, Jude, & John—2 & 3 *John* being irregularly included—; cf. CANONICAL). **2.** (Eccl.) *C*~ *Church*, whole body of Christians; ~, belonging (a) to this, (b) to the church before separation into Greek or Eastern & Latin or Western, (c) to the Latin church after that separation (cf. ORTHODOX), (d) to the part of the Roman obedience that remained under the Latin obedience after the reformation, (e) to any

cáth'olic, a. & n. **1.** Universal; of interest

church (as the Anglican) claiming continuity with (b); orthodox, in accord with the church in any of above senses, esp.=ROMAN CATHOLIC as (d) in contrast with Protestant, Reformed, Lutheran, etc.; C~ *King*, *his* C~ *Majesty*, of Spain; hence cathŏl′icALLY, ~LY², advv.; cathŏl′icĭsM(2, 3) n., cathŏl′icĭzM(3), v.t., cathŏli′co- comb. form. **3.** n. Member of the church in above senses; a Roman Catholic (cf. C~ *emancipation* etc., i.e. of dub.) = OMENTUM. [f. F *cale* small cap etym. warn]

cathŏli′city, n. Comprehensiveness, freedom from prejudice; wide prevalence; agreement with Catholic or R.-C. Church doctrine, catholicism. [prec., -ITY]

cathŏl′icŏn, n. Panacea. [F, f. Gk *katholikon* neut. CATHOLIC]

Căt′illine, n. Profligate conspirator. [*Catilina* Roman noble d. 63 B.C.]

căt′ion, n. Electro-positive element evolved at cathode in electrolysis (opp. ANION). [Gk.; = going down (CAT-, *eimi* go)]

căt′king, n. Downy hanging inflorescence of willow, hazel, etc. [f. Du. *katteken*]

căt′ling, n. Small cat; fine cat-gut; amputating knife. [-LING¹(2); surg. sense unexpl.]

catŏp′tric, a. Of mirror, reflector, or reflexion. Hence -ICS n. [f. Gk *katoptrikos* (*optron* f. *op-* see, -tron instr. suf.)]

căt′sup. Var. of KETCHUP.

cătt′y, aa. Catlike; (esp. fig.) sly and spiteful. [CAT¹]

căt′tle, n. Live stock; oxen (as ~ & sheep); (sl.) horses; *black* ~, oxen of Scotch & Welsh highland breeds, orig. black; contemptible persons; ~-*feeder*, machine regulating amount of food for ~; ~-*leader*, nose-ring; ~-*lifter*, ~-*stealer*; ~-PEN¹; ~-*piece*, picture with ~; ~-*plague*, contagious disease of ~, rinderpest; ~-*rustler*, ~-*thief*. [ME & ONF *catel* f. L *capitale* neut. CAPITAL in sense *chief property*; cf. CHATTEL, to which the orig. meaning of ~ now belongs]

Caucă′sian (-shn), a. & n. (Member) of the white race, Indo-European. [the *Caucasus*, supposed starting-place, + -IAN]

cauc′us, n., & v.t. & i. 1. ‖ Local political (usu. elective party committee for fighting elections, defining party policy, etc. (gen. used only of opponents' organization); *the* ~, ~ *system* as a political power; hence ~-DOM n. 2. vb. Use the ~ system; organize, dictate to, by its means; hence ~-ER¹ n. [U.S. wd (in sense *meeting*) perh. f. Algonkin = elder]

caud′al, a. Of, at, like, tail. Hence or cogn. ~LY² adv., caud′ATE² a. [f. L *cauda* tail + -AL]

caud′le, n. Warm gruel with spice, sugar, & wine, for invalids, esp. women in childbed. [f. ONF *caudel* f. med. L *caldellum* dim. f. L *cal(i)dum* hot drink (*calidus* warm)]

caught. See CATCH¹.

caul, n. Plain part at back of woman's cap; membrane enclosing foetus; portion of this occas. found on child's head (good omen, & charm against drowning); = OMENTUM. [f. F *cale* small cap etym. warn]

caul′dron, căl′, n. Large boiling-vessel (usu. of deep basin shape with hoop handle & removable lid). [f. ONF *cauderon* f. L *caldarium* hot bath (L *calidus* warm, -ARY¹), -OON]

caules′cent, a. (bot.). With visible stem. [f. L *caulis* stalk after *arborescent* etc.]

caul′iflower (kŏl-), n. Cabbage with large fleshy flower-head. [f. F *choufleri* (now -*fleur*) f. L *caulis* stem + f P p. of L *florere* to flower, w. assim. in E to L *caulis* & E *flower*]

caul′ine, a. (bot.). Of, on, stem. [f. L *caulis* stem]

caulk (kawk), v.t. Stop up seams of (ship), stop up (seams), with oakum & melted pitch (or, in iron ship, by striking plate-junctions with blunt chisel). Hence ~ER¹ n. (in vbl senses, &c, sl., = final dram). [f. OF *cauquer* squeeze f. L *calcare* tread (*calx* heel)]

caulo-, comb. form of Gk *kaulos* or L *caulis* stem. [-o-]

caus′al (-z-), a. Of, acting as, expressing, due to, a cause or causes; of the nature of cause & effect. Hence ~LY² adv. [f. L *causalis* (*causa*), -AL]

causal′ity (-z-), n. The being, having, or acting as, a cause; relation of cause & effect, doctrine that all things have causes, whence ~ISM(3), ~IST(2), nn. [f. L *causalitas*]

causā′tion (-z-), n. Causing, producing an effect; relation of cause & effect; doctrine that all things have causes, pretext, w. sense f. med. L *causare* to cause (L *causa*). [prec., -ATION]

caus′ative (-z-), a. Acting as cause, productive of; ((Gram.) expressing cause. Hence ~LY² adv. [f. F *causatif* f. L *causativus* (*causari* give as pretext, -IVE)]

cause (-z), n. 1. What produces an effect; antecedent(s) invariably & unconditionally followed by a certain phenomenon; person who, agent that, occasions something; ground, reason, motive, for action; adequate motive or justification (esp. *show* ~); *efficient* ~, producing force, *material* ~, the requisite matter, *formal* ~, the idea or definition, *final* ~, purpose; *First C*~, the Creator. 2. (Law, & from law) matter about which person goes to law; his case (*plead a* ~); law-suit; side of any dispute espoused by person or party, militant movement, propaganda

(make common ~ with); ||-list, of cases awaiting trial. [F, f. L causa]

cause² (-z), v.t. Effect, bring about, produce; induce, make, (person or thing to do, to be done something to). Hence **caus**ᴇʀ¹ n. [f. med. L causare (cf. L causari plead causes, give as pretext)]

cause célèbre (kōz sělě'br), n. (pl. **causes célèbres**, pr. as sing.). Law-suit that excites much attention. [F]

cause'less (-zl-), a. Fortuitous; without natural cause; unjustifiable, groundless, whence ~LY¹ adv. [-LESS]

causerie (kōzerē'), n. (pl. -s, pr. as sing.). Newspaper article (or spoken address) of an informal or conversational kind, esp. on literary subjects. [F]

causeuse (kōzĕz'), n. (pl. -s, pr. as sing.). Small sofa for two. [F]

cause'way (-zw-), **caus'ey** (-z-), n., & v.t. Raised road across low or wet place or piece of water; raised footway by road; (v.t.) provide with ~. [causeway=causey ONF caucie f. LL calciāta trodden f. L calcāre f. calx -cis heel]+WAY]

caus'tic, a. & n. (Substance) that burns or corrodes organic tissue (*Common* or *Lunar~ic*, nitrate of silver for surg. use); sarcastic, biting, whence ~ICALLY adv.; (Math.) (surface, curve) formed by intersection of rays reflected from or refracted from curved surface. Hence ~I'CITY n. [f. L f. Gk *kaustikos* (*kaustos* burnt f. *kaiō* burn, -IC)]

caut'erize, v.t. Sear with hot iron or caustic; (fig.) make callous. Hence ~IZA'TION n. [f. F *cautériser* f. LL *cauterizare* f. Gk *kautērion* branding-iron (*kaiō* burn)]

caut'er³, n. Metal instrument for searing tissue; cauterizing. [f. L f. Gk *kautērion* see prec.; second sense on anal. of nouns in -ERY]

cau'tion, n., & v.t. 1. Prudence, taking care, avoidance of rashness, attention to safety, (|| = money, deposited as security for good conduct, esp. at Universities & Inns of Court); whence **cau'tious** (-shus), a., **cau'tiously²** adv.; warning (in drill, preliminary word of command), fact that acts as warning, warning with reprimand (*dismissed with a ~*), whence ~ARY¹(-sho-), a.; (sl.) extraordinary thing, hideous or strange person. 2. v.t. Warn (person, often *against*, *to* or *not to* do); warn & reprove. [F, f. L *cautionem* (*cavēre* caut-take heed, -ION]

cavalcade', n. Company of riders. [F, f. Pr. *cavalcada* f. *cavalcar* ride f. LL *cavalcare* f. L *caballus* horse; see -ADE]

cavalier', n. & a. 1. Horseman; courtly gentleman, gallant, esp. as escorting a lady, whence **cavalier** v.t.: 17th-c. royalist. 2. adj. Off-hand, curt, supercilious, whence ~LY² adv. [earlier -*liero*, -*liero*, f. Sp.; present form F, f. It. *cavaliere* (*cavallo* see CAVALRY, -IER)]

cavall'y, n. Kinds of tropical fish, horse-mackerel. [f. Sp. *cavalla* mackerel]

cav'alry, n. Horse-soldiers (usu. w. pl. vb). [f. F *cavalerie* f. It. *cavalleria* (*cavallo* f. L *caballus* horse, -ERY)]

cavati'na (-tē-), n. Short simple song; similar piece of instrumental music, usu. slow & emotional. [It.]

cave¹, n. Underground hollow usu. with horizontal opening, den; IDOLS *of the* ~; || (Pol.) secession of part of party on some question (ADULLAMITE), the seceders; ~*dweller*, esp. of prehistoric men living in ~s; ~*fish*, *-man*, *-rat*, *-spider*, *-swallow*, kinds living in ~s (also ~*bear* etc. of extinct kinds whose remains are found in ~s); ~*man*, (in modern use) man of primitive passions, instincts, & behaviour. Hence ~LET (-vl-) n. [F, f. L *cava* neut. pl. of *cavus* adj. hollow]

cave², v.t. & i. Hollow out, make into a cave; || form political party; ~ *in*: subside, recede, (of earth etc. over hollow; of wall yielding inwards cf. BULGE); yield to pressure, submit, withdraw opposition; smash in (esp. person's hat or head), spoil shape of, (f. prec.; but ~ *in* may be f. obs. *calve* fall in cf. Flem. *inkalven* Du. *af-kalven*, in similar sense)]

cave³, int. (schoolboy sl.). Look out! (warning of master's approach). [L, = beware]

cav'eat, n. 1. (Law) process to suspend proceedings (*enter, put in, a* ~). 2. Warning; proviso. [L, = let him beware]

cav'eat émp'tor, (= let the buyer see to it) disclaiming responsibility for buyer's disappointment.

cav'endish, n. Tobacco softened, sweetened, & pressed into cake, negro-head. [?]

cav'ern, n. Underground hollow (rhet.). [f. F *caverne* f. L *caverna* (*cavus* hollow)]

cav'erned (-nd), a. Like, in, with, cavern(s). [-ED²]

cav'ernous, a. Full of caverns; as of, huge or deep as, a cavern (~ *darkness*, *mouth*, *eyes*); porous. [f. L *cavernosus* (CAVERN, -OSE²)]

cav'es(s)on, n. Strong nose-band used in breaking in troublesome horses. [f. F *cavesson* f. It. *cavezzone* augment. of *cavezza* halter (perh. conn. w. L *capistrum* halter)]

cavia'r(e)º (or kăv-), n. Sturgeon-roe pickled, eaten as relish; ~ *to the general*, good thing unappreciated by the ignorant. [16th-c. It., has *caviale*, etym. dub.]

cav'il, v.i. (|| -ll-), & n. (Raise) captious objection(*at*, *about*). Hence ~IER¹, n. [f. OF *caviller* f. L *cavillari* (*cavilla* mockery)]

cav'ity, n. Empty space within solid body. [f. F *cavité* (L *cavus* hollow, -TY)]

*cavo'rt, v.i. (sl.). Prance. [?]

cav'y, n. Amer. rodent. [f. *cabiai* native name in French Guiana]

caw, n. & int. Cry of rook's, crow's, raven's, cry; ~ *out*, utter in cawing tone. [imit.]

Cax'ton, n. Book printed by W. ~ (first Engl. printer, d. 1492); printing-type in imitation of ~'s.

cay, n. Insular bank or reef of coral, sand, etc., cf. KEY². [= QUAY]

cayenne (kāĕn'), n. (Also ~ **pepper**) pungent red pepper of capsicum. [f. Braz. *kyinha assīnu*, to Cayenne capital of French Guiana]

cay'man, cai'man, n. Kinds of large saurian of crocodile family (prop. an American genus with round short muzzle). [prob. f. Carib *acayoumau*]

‖**cd**, ‖ **cmd**, = COMMAND²

ce, = OE.

céanoth'us, n. A flowering shrub. [Gk]

cease¹, v.i. & t. Desist *from*; (of feelings, actions) come to an end; bring to an end (strife, endeavours, etc.); (Mil.) ~ *fire*, discontinue firing. [ME *cessen* f. F *cesser* f. L *cessare* frequent. of *cedere cess-* yield]

cease² n. Ceasing (obs. exc. in *without* ~, ~'**lessly** adv., ~'**lessness** n. [f. OF *ces* (cesser see prec.)]

cěc'ity, n. Blindness (usu. fig.). [f. L *caecitas* (*caecus* blind, -TY)]

ced'ar, n. Kinds of cone-bearing tree including C~ *of Lebanon*, *Atlas* C~, & *Deodar*; various trees resembling ~; ~-**wood**. Hence (poet.) ~**n** [-EN³] a. [ME f. OF *cedre* f. L f. Gk *kedros*]

cēde, v.t. Give up, grant, admit, surrender (territory). [f. L *cedere cess-*]

cēdil'a, n. Mark (¸) written under ç to show that it is sibilant. [Sp., f. It. *zediglia*, dim. of *zeta* Gk name of Z]

cee, n. The letter C; ~ *spring*, *C-spring*, spring so shaped supporting carriage body.

ceil (sēl), v.t. Line roof of (room). Hence **ceil'ing**¹(²) n.: such lining; (Aviation) maximum altitude a given aeroplane can attain, maximum altitude in particular weather conditions; upper limit of prices, wages, etc. [prob. f. F *ciel* heaven, ceiling, f. L *caelum* heaven, w. inf. of L *caelare* emboss]

cel'adon, n. & a. Willow green. [F, perh. f. name of character in D'Urfé's *Astrée*]

cel'andine, n. Two yellow-flowered plants, *Greater* C~, & *Lesser* C~ (Pilewort, Fig-wort). [f. OF *celidoine* f. L *chelidonia* f. Gk *khelidonion* (*khelidon* swallow): for -n- cf. *passenger*]

célanèse' (-z), n. Kind of artificial silk. [P]

-cele (sēl), in medical compound words, = tumour of the—. [f. Gk *kēlē* tumour]

cěl'ebrant, n. Officiating priest, esp. at Eucharist. [f. L *celebrare* (foll.), -ANT]

cěl'ebrāte, v.t. & i. Perform publicly & duly (religious ceremony etc.); officiate at Eucharist; observe, honour, with rites, festivities, etc. (festival, event); publish abroad, praise, extol, (p.p.) famous, célébrity. Hence ~ATION n. [f. L *celebrāre* (*celeber -bris* frequented, celebrated, famous), -ATE²·³]

célěb'rity, n. Being famous; well-known person (also attrib., as ~ *concert*). [f. L *celebritas* (*celeber* see prec., -TY)]

cěl'eriāc, n. Turnip-rooted celery. [f. CELERY, -ac unexplained]

cělér'ity, n. Swiftness, dispatch (of living movement or agency). [f. *célérité* f. L *celeritatem* (*celer* swift, -TY)]

cěl'ery, n. Plant of which blanched stem is used as salad & vegetable. [f. F *céleri* f. L *celeri*]

céleste' n. & a. Sky blue; (also *voix* ~) organ & harmonium stop; (adj.) sky-blue. [f. F *céleste* f. L *caelestis* (*caelum* heaven)]

céles'tial, a. & n. Of the sky (~ *globe*, *map*); heavenly, divine, divinely good, beautiful, etc., whence ~**ly**² adv.; C~ *Empire*, China (transl. of native title; so C~ = Chinese, a. & n.). [OF (L *caelestis* see prec., -AL)]

cěl'ibate, a. & n. (Person) not married, bound or resolved not to marry; unmarried (of life, habits). So **cěl'ibacy** n. [f. L *caelibatus* (*caelebs* unmarried +-ATE¹²)]

cell, n. 1. Dependent nunnery or monastery (hist.); anchoret's one-roomed dwelling; cottage (poet.); grave (poet.); single person's small room in monastery or prison (*condemned* ~, for one condemned to death); compartment in bees' comb; (Electr.) voltaic apparatus with only one pair of metallic elements, organism or mineral (~*s of brain*, various faculties); (Biol.) portion of protoplasm usu. enclosed in membrane, ultimate element of organic structures; (Zoophytes) cup-like cavity of individual polype in compound polypidom; (fig., of persons) centre or nucleus of (revolutionary) propaganda. Hence (-**celled**²) (-ld), ~**FORM**, aa. [f. OF *celle* f. L *cella* small room]

cěll'ar, n., & v.t. (Put, store, in an underground room; (also *wine-*~) place in which wine is kept, one's stock of wine (*keeps a good* ~); ~-*flap*, trapdoor into ~; ~-*plate*, in pavement over hole into coal-~. Hence ~AGE n. [f. OF *celier* f. L *cellarium* (prec., -AR²·-ARY¹)]

cěll'arer, n. Monastic keeper of wine & provisions. [f. OF *celerier* (*celier* see prec., -ER²)]

cěllarět', n. Case or sideboard for keeping winebottles in dining-room. [-ET¹]

cěll'ō (ch-), n. (pl. -os). (Short for) vioLONCELLO. Hence **cěll'ist** (³) n.

cěll'ophane, n. Transparent wrapping material made from viscose, used for rooms or compartments or cavities; ~

shirt etc. (of open texture); (Physiol.) consisting of cells (as ~ *tissue*); ~ *plant*, without distinct stem, leaves, etc. Hence **cĕllŭlā′rĭty** n. [as foll., -AR¹]

cĕll′ūle, n. (anat.). Cell or cavity (see CELL, 2; the derivatives are formed from *cellule*, not *cell*). Hence or cogn. ~ATE², -ātĕd, ~ĭF′EROUS, ~OUS, aa., ~A′TION n., ~o- comb. form. [f. L *cellula* (*cella* CELL, -ULE)]

cĕll′ūloïd, a. & n. Like cells; (n.) plastic made from camphor & cellulose nitrate. [irreg. f. CELLULOSE²+-OID]

cĕll′ūlōse¹, a. Consisting of cells. Hence **cĕllūlōs′ĭty** n. [CELLULE, -OSE¹]

cĕll′ūlōse², n. (chem.). Substance forming solid framework of plants; (in pop. usage for) ~ acetate or ~ nitrate, solutions of which give the ~ finish used in varnishing metal, woodwork, etc., (also v.t., treat with ~). [F, f. L *cellula* CELLULE, -OSE²]

Cĕl′sĭus. See CENTIGRADE.

Cĕlt¹, Kĕlt, n. Member of one of the peoples akin to the ancient Galli (Bretons, Cornish, Welsh, Irish, Manx, Gaels). [f. F *Celte* f. L *Celta*; cf. Gk *Keltoi, Keltai*, pl.]

cĕlt², n. (archaeol.). Bronze or stone (or iron) chisel-edged prehistoric implement. [wd founded on a perh. false reading in Vulgate of *Job* xix. 24—*stylo ferreo, et plumbi lamina, vel celte* (v.l. *certe*) *sculpantur*]

Cĕl′tic, K-, a. & n. (Language) of the Celts; *the ~ fringe,* the Scots, Irish, Welsh, & Cornish, in relation to the U.K. Hence **Cĕl′tĭcALLY** adv., **Cĕl′tĭcĬSM**(2, 4) n., **Cĕl′tĭcĬZE**(2, 3) v.i. & t. [f. L *celticus* (CELT¹, -IC)]

cĕlto-, comb. form of CELT¹. Hence **Cĕl′-tŏl′OGIST, Cĕl′tophĭl,** nn. [-o-]

cĕmĕnt′, n., & v.t. **1.** Substance applied as paste & hardening into stony consistence for binding together stones or bricks & for forming floors, walls, etc., strong mortar of calcinated lime & clay (*hydraulic ~*), hardening under water); any substance applied soft for sticking things together; (fig.) principle of union; substance for stopping teeth; bony crust of tooth-fang. **2.** v.t. Unite (as) with ~; apply ~ to, line or cover with ~. [ME *cyment* f. OF *ciment* f. L *caementum* for *caedimentum* (*caedere* cut, -MENT) chippings of stone]

cĕm′eterў, n. Place for burials, not being a churchyard. [f. L t. Gk *koimētērion* dormitory (*koimaō* put to sleep)]

cĕn′obīte. See COENOBITE.

cĕn′otaph (-ahf), n. Sepulchral monument to person whose body is elsewhere; *the C~,* that in Whitehall commemorating the dead of the 1914–18 war; tomb from which one has risen. [f. F *cénotaphe* f. L t. Gk *kenotaphion* (*kenos* empty, *taphos* tomb)]

cĕnse, v.t. Perfume, worship, with burning incense. [f. obs. *cense* noun short for INCENSE²]

cĕn′ser, n. Vessel in which incense is burnt. [f. OF (*en*)*censier* f. L *incensum* INCENSE¹, -ER²(2)]

cĕn′sor, n., & v.t. **1.** Ancient-Roman magistrate drawing up register or census of citizens & supervising public morals; person expressing opinions on others' morals & conduct. **2.** Official licensing, or suppressing as immoral, seditious, or inopportune, books, plays, news, or military intelligence (vb, exercise such control over, make excisions or changes in). **3.** Various university officials. **4.** (Psychoanal.) ~(*ship*), a power by which elements of the Unconscious are inhibited from emerging into the consciousness. Hence or cogn. **cĕnsōr′ĭAL** a., ~SHIP n. [L, f. *censēre* tax, -OR²]

cĕnsōr′ious, a. Fault-finding, over-critical. Hence ~LY² adv., ~NESS n. [f. L *censorius* (CENSOR, -ORY) +-OUS]

cĕn′sur|e (-sher), n., & v.t. **1.** Adverse judgement, expression of disapproval, reprimand. **2.** v.t. Blame, criticize unfavourably, reprove; hence ~ABLE a. [f. F *censure*(r) f. L *censura* (*censēre* tax, -URE]

cĕn′sus, n. Official numbering of population with various statistics (in Gt Britain taken every ten years); ~*paper,* form left at every house to be filled up with names, ages, etc., of inmates. [L, f. *censēre* to rate]

cĕnt, n. *Per ~,* for, to, in, every hundred (in stating proportion, esp. of interest): *three* etc. *per ~s,* public securities at 3% etc.; *per ~,* interest equal to principal; (U.S. etc.) hundredth of a dollar; typical small coin (*don't care a ~*). [f. F *cent* or L *centum* hundred]

cĕn′tal, n. Weight of 100 lb. used for corn. [f. L *centum* hundred, perh. after QUINTAL]

cĕn′taur (-tôr), n. Horse with human body, arms, & head, taking the place of its neck & head; hybrid creation, person or thing of double nature; (C~) name of a constellation; perfect horseman. Hence ~ESS¹ n. [f. L f. Gk *kentauros* etym. dub.]

cĕn′taurў, n. Name of various plants. [ult. f. Gk *kentaurion* (*kentauros* see prec.) said to have been used medicinally by centaur Chiron]

cĕntenā′r′ian, a. & n. (Person) a hundred years old. [as foll.+-AN]

cĕntēn′arў (*also* sĕn′tĕn-), a. & n. **1.** Of a hundred years. **2.** n. Space of a hundred years reckoned from any point in a century; centennial anniversary, celebration of it. [f. L *centenarius* (*centeni* a hundred each, -ARY¹]

cĕntĕnn′ial, a. & n. Of, having lived or lasted, completing, a hundred years; (of)

the hundredth anniversary. [f. L *centum* hundred, & as BIENNIAL]

centés'imal, a. Reckoning, reckoned, by hundredths. Hence ~LY² adv. [f. L *centesimus* hundredth (*centum* hundred) +-AL]

cĕn'ti-, comb. form of L *centum* hundred, = 1/100 of the denomination in the metric system. Hence ~METRE (-mēter), n.

cĕn'tigrade, a. Having a hundred degrees (of Celsius's thermometer, with freezing-point 0° & boiling-point 100°). [F., f. L *centum* a hundred + *gradus* step]

‖**centil'lion** (-yon), n. Hundredth power of a million (1 with 600 ciphers). [(prec.), BILLION]

centime (săhntēm'), n. French coin = 1/100 of a franc. [F]

cĕn'tipĕde, n. Many-footed wingless crawling animal. [f. L *centipeda* (*centum* hundred, *pes pedis* foot)]

cĕnt'ner, n. German weight, about 1 cwt. [G., f. L *centenarius* CENTENARY]

cĕn'tō, n. (pl. -os). Composition made up of scraps from other authors. [L., =patchwork garment]

cĕn'tral, a. Of, in, at, from, containing, the centre; leading, principal, dominant; C~ *Empires, Powers*, (hist.), Germany & Austria-Hungary; ~ *heating*, method of warming a building by hot water or steam conveyed by pipes from ~ source. Hence cĕntrăl'ITY n., ~LY² adv., ~NESS n. [f. L *centralis* (*centrum* CENTRE, -AL)]

cĕn'tralism, cĕn'tralist, nn. (Upholder of) a centralizing system. [prec. +-ISM(3), -IST(2)]

cĕn'tralize, v.i. & t. Come, bring, to a centre; concentrate (administration) at single centre; subject (State etc.) to this system. Hence ~A'TION n. [CENTRAL, -IZE(3)]

cĕn'tre¹ (-ter), n. & a. **1.** Middle point (strictly, equidistant from all points in periphery of irregular surface or body). **2.** Point, pivot, axis, of revolution (in lathe, conical adjustable bearing to hold revolving object). **3.** Point of concentration or dispersion, nucleus, source. **4.** (Fenians etc.) organizer, leader, (esp. *head* ~). **5.** (Hit on) part of target between bull's-eye & outer. **6.** (Archit.) wooden mould for arch or dome while building. **7.** (Mil.) main body of troops between wings. **8.** (Pol.; orig. f. French *the C~*), men of moderate opinions (*left ~, left*, radical grades; *right ~, right*, reactionary). **9.** (Assoc. footb., Hockey) middle player in forward line (also ~ *forward*), kick or hit from wing to ~. **10.** ~ *of attraction*, (Physics) to which bodies tend by gravity, (fig.) drawing general

attention; ~ *of gravity*, that point in body which being supported body remains at rest in any position; ~ *of mass*, point (in relation to body) any plane passing through which divides body into two parts of equal weight; DEAD ~; ~*piece*, ornament for middle of table; ~*rail*, third rail on mountain railways for cogged wheel etc.; ~*second*(*s*), seconds hand mounted on centre arbor of clock or watch; ~*bit*, boring-tool with ~ point & side cutters; ~*board*, (flat-bottomed boat with) board for lowering through keel to prevent lee-way; hence ~LESS, ~MOST (-ōst.) aa., cĕn'trically² adv., ~: hence [f. (-re), f. Lf. Gk *kentron* spike (*kenteō* to prick)]

cĕn'tre² (-ter), **cĕn'ter**, v.i. & t. Be concentrated in, on, at, round, about; place in centre; mark with a centre; concentrate in etc.; find centre of; (Assoc. footb., Hockey) kick or hit (ball) from wing to centre. [f. prec.]

cĕn'tre(ing (-ter-), n. Temporary framing used to support arch, dome, etc., while under construction. [CENTRE¹+-ING¹]

centrif'ugal, a. Flying, tending to fly, from centre; ~ *force*, with which body revolving round centre tends to fly off, inertia; ~ *machine* etc., in which ~ force is utilized; (Bot.) ~ *inflorescence*, in which end flower opens first & side ones in downward order. Hence ~LY² adv. [f. L *centrum* CENTRE¹+ *fugus* -flying (*fugere* flee)+-AL]

centrif'é'tal, a. Tending towards centre; ~ *force, machine* etc.; *inflorescence*, opposite of CENTRIFUGAL. Hence ~LY² adv. [f. L -*petus* -seeking (*petere* seek) & as prec.]

cĕn'tri-, comb. form of L *centrum* CENTRE¹, = centre-, central, centrally.

cĕn'tuple, a., n., & v.t. Hundredfold; (vb) multiply by a hundred. [f. Ll. *centuplus* for L *centuplex* (*centum* hundred, *plic-* fold)]

cĕn'tuplicate, a. & n. (-at), & v.t. (-āt). = prec., esp. *in* ~, of things of which a hundred copies are produced. [f. L *centuplicare* as prec., -ATE²;³]

centŭr'ion, n. Commander of century in Roman army. [f. L *centurio -onis* (foll.)]

cĕn'tury, n. **1.** (Rom. hist.) company in army, orig. of 100 men; political division for voting. **2.** A hundred of something (esp. 100 runs at cricket); one of the hundred-year periods counting from a received epoch, esp. from birth of Christ (*first* ~, 1-100, *nineteenth* ~ 1801-1900, etc.); any hundred successive years, centenary. [f. L *centuria* (*centum* hundred)]

cephal'ic, a. Of, in the head. [f. F *céphalique* f. L f. Gk *kephalikos* (*kephalē* head, -IC)]

-cephal'ic, = -CEPHALOUS.

ceph'alo-, comb. form = -CEPHALOUS, -0-] [see CEPHALIC, -0-]

cĕph'alopŏd, n. Mollusc with distinct tentacled head. [prec. + Gk *pous podos* foot]

cĕphalŏthōr'ăx, n. Coalesced head & thorax of spider, crab, etc. [CEPHALO-, THORAX]

-cĕph'alous, last element esp. of anthropological terms = -headed, as *brachy~*, with short head. [f. Gk *kephalē* head + -OUS]

cĕrām'ic, k~, a. Of the art of pottery. Hence *~ICS*, **cĕ'ramist**(2), nn. [f. Gk *keramikos* (*keramos* pottery, -IC)]

cĕrăs'tes (-ēz), n. The horned viper of N. Africa. [L.f. Gk *kerastēs* (*keras* horn)]

cĕrăs'tium, n. Kinds of herb with horn-shaped capsules. [mod. L, f. Gk *kerastēs* horned (*keras* horn)]

cĕ'rato-, comb. form of Gk *keras -atos* horn, = horn-&- —, horny-, & esp. of the cornea.

Cĕrb'erus, n. Three-headed dog guarding entrance to Hades (*sop to ~*, something to propitiate an official, guard, etc.). [L, f. Gk *Kerberos*]

cĕre, n. Naked wax-like membrane at base of some birds' beaks. [f. F *cire* f. L *cera* wax]

cĕr'ēal, a. & n. Of corn or edible grain; (n., usu. pl.) kind(s) of grain used for human food; *article of diet made from wheat, maize, or other ~ (usu. as breakfast dish). [f. L *Cerealis* (*Ceres* goddess of corn, -AL)]

cĕrĕbĕll'um, n. Little or hinder brain. [L, dim. of CEREBRUM]

cĕr'ēbral, a. Of the brain; ~ *letter*, consonant sounded by turning tongue-tip to top of palate. [f. F *cérébral* (CEREBRUM, -AL)]

cĕrēbrā'tion, n. Working of the brain, esp. *unconscious ~*, of results reached without conscious thought. [CEREBRUM + -ATION]

cĕr'ēbrum (sĕrĭ-), n. The brain proper, in front of & above the cerebellum. Hence **cĕr'ēbro-** comb. form; *cerebro-spin'al*, of brain & spine (*cerebro-spinal meningitis*, spotted fever). [L]

cĕre'cloth (sērĭklaw-), n. Cloth impregnated with wax etc., used as waterproof covering or (esp.) winding-sheet. [orig. CERED *cloth*]

cĕre'ment (sēr'm-), n. (usu. pl.) Graveclothes. [f. F *cirement* (*cirer* to wax, wrap in waxed cloth, see CERE)]

cĕrēmōn'ial, a. & n. 1. With or of ritual or ceremony, formal; hence *~ISM*(3), *~IST*(2), nn. *~LY²* adv. **2.** n. System of rites; formalities proper to any occasion; observance of conventions; (R.-C. Ch.) book of ritual. [f. L *caerimonialis* (CEREMONY, -AL)]

cĕrēmōn'ious, a. Addicted or showing addiction to ceremony, punctilious. Hence *~LY²* adv., *~NESS* n. [f. L *caerimoniosus* (foll., -OUS)]

cĕr'ēmonÿ, n. Outward religious rite or polite observance; empty form; stately usage; formalities; punctilious behaviour (*without ~y*, off-hand; *stand upon ~y*, insist on conventions, keep one's distance); *Master of the C~ies*, superintending forms observed on state or public occasions. [prob. f. OF *cerymonie* f. L *caerimonia* cf. Skr. *karman* work, rite, (*kri* do)]

cĕrise' (-ēz), a. & n. (Of) a light clear red. [F, = CHERRY]

cĕr'ium, n. A metallic element. Hence **cĕr'IC**(1), **cĕr'ous,** aa. [f. planet *Ceres*, discovered (1801) just before, + -IUM]

cēro-, comb. form of L *cera* or Gk *kēros* **wax**.

cēroplăs'tic, a. Modelled, of modelling, in wax. Hence *~ICS* n. [f. Gk *kēro-* OERO(*plastikos* adj. f. *plassō* to mould)]

cĕrt, n. (sl.) Event or result certain to happen. [abbr. *certain*]

cĕrt'ain (-tn, -tin), a. Settled, unfailing; unerring, reliable; sure to happen; indisputable; convinced (*of, that*); destined, undoubtedly going, *to* do; that might but need not or should not be specified (*a ~ person, lady of a ~ age*), some though perhaps not much (*felt a ~ reluctance*), existing but probably unknown to hearer (*~ John Smith*); *for ~, assuredly.* [OF (L *certus* orig. p.p. of *cernere* decide, -AN)]

cĕrt'ainly (-tn-), adv. Indubitably; infallibly; confidently; admittedly; (in answers) I admit it, no doubt, yes. [prec. + -LY²]

cĕrt'aintÿ (-tn-), n. Undoubted fact (*bet on a ~*, usu. dishonestly with secret knowledge of result), indubitable prospect; thing in actual possession; absolute conviction (*of, that*); *to, for, a ~*, beyond possibility of doubt. [f. OF *certaineté* (CERTAIN, -TY)]

cĕrt'ēs (-z), adv. (arch.). Assuredly, I assure you. [OF, also *a certes* perh. f. L *a certis* from sure (grounds)]

certif'icate, n. & v.t. 1. (-ĭt). Document formally attesting a fact, esp. the bearer's status, acquirements, fulfilment of conditions, right to company shares, etc.; || *bankrupt's ~*, stating that he has satisfied legal requirements & may recommence business. **2.** v.t. (-āt). Furnish with, license by, ~; hence **cĕrtIFICA'TION** n. [f. med. L *certificatum* neut. p.p. (foll.)]

cĕrt'ifÿ, v.t. Attest formally, declare by ~ || (of doctor) officially declare (person) insane, whence *~IABLE* a.; inform certainly, assure. Hence *~IER¹* n. [f. F *certifier* f. med. L *certificare* (CERTAIN, -FY)]

cĕr'tiorā'rī (-shī-), n. Writ from higher court for records of case tried in lower. [L, *wd* in writ]

cĕrt'itūde, n. Feeling certain, conviction. [F, f. LL *certitudinem* (CERTAIN, -TUDE)]

cerul'ean (-ōō-), a. Deep-blue. [f. L *caeruleus* prob. for *caeluleus* (*caelum* sky)]

cerum'en (-ōō-), n. Ear-wax. So **cerum'inous** a. [f. L *cera* wax on anal. of *albumen*]

cer'use (-ōōs), n. (Also *white lead*,) a white paint from carbonate & hydrate of lead, esp. as cosmetic. [f. L *cerussa* prob. f. a Gk *kērōussa* fem. of *kērōeis* waxy (*kēros*)]

cer'vical (or servī'k-), a. (physiol.), Of the neck. So **cer'vic'o-** comb. form. [f. L *cervix -īcis* neck+-AL]

cer'vine, a. Of, like, deer. [f. L *cervīnus* (*cervus* deer+-INE)]

Césá rèvitch, -witch, (-ž-), n. Tsar's eldest son: ||=(-wī-) horse-race run annually at Newmarket. [Russ.]

||**cèss**, n. Tax, rate, (now displaced by *rate* in Engl., but used in various senses in Ireland, Scotland, & India). [prop. *assess* for obs. *assess* n. see ASSESS]

cessá'tion, n. Ceasing; pause. [f. L *cessātiō* (*cessāre* CEASE¹, -ATION)]

cèss'er, n. (legal), Coming to an end, cessation (of term, liability, etc.). [CEASE¹, -ER²]

cèss'ion (-shn), n. Ceding, giving up, (of rights, property, or esp. of territory by State). [F, f. L *cessiōnem* (*cedere cess-* go away, -ION)]

cèss'ionary (-shon-), n. =ASSIGN². [f. med. L *cessiōnārius* as prec.+-ARY¹]

cèss'pit, n. Midden. [see foll.]

cèss'pool, n. Well sunk for soil from water-closet etc., retaining solids & letting liquid escape (also fig., as ~ *of iniquity*). [prob. f. It. *cesso* privy f. L *secessus* SECESSION]

cēs'tus, n. Loaded bull-hide hand-covering worn by Roman boxers. [L *caestus* (*caedere* strike)]

cèt-, comb. form. of spermaceti, in chem. names. [f. L *cētus -ī* f. Gk *kētos -eos* whale]

cetā'cean (-shn), n. & a. (Member) of the mammalian order containing whales. So **cetā'ceous** (-āshus) a. [as prec., -ACEAN]

cēt'eosaur (-ōr), **-saur'us**, n. Fossil saurian. [f. Gk *kētos -eos* whale & *sauros* lizard]

cèt'erich (-k), n. Kinds of fern with frond-backs covered with scales. [med. form. dub.]

cet'eris pa'ribus, adv. Other things being equal. [L]

Chablis (shåb'lē), n. A French white wine. [place name]

Chad'band, n. Unctuous hypocrite. [person in Dickens's *Bleak House*]

chafe, v.t. & i., & n. 1. Rub (skin, to restore warmth); make, become, sore by rubbing; (of beast, river) rub itself against (bars, rocks); irritate; show irritation, fume, fret. 2. n. (Sore made by) friction; state of irritation, pet, (*in a* ~). [f. OF *chaufer* f. L *calefacere* (*calēre* be hot, *facere* make)]

CHAFER. [OE *cefer* cf. G *käfer* perh. f. *kef-* gnaw cf. JOWL]

chaff (-ahf), n., & v.t. 1. Separated grain-husks; chopped hay & straw; bracts of grass-flower; spurious substitute (*caught with* ~, easily deceived or trapped); worthless stuff; ~-*cutter*, machine chopping fodder; hence ~y². [OE *ceaf*]

chaff, v.t. & n. Banter (n. & v.t.). [OE *ceaf* cf. OHG *cheva* perh. f. *kef-* gnaw cf. JOWL; sense 2 may be fig. use of 1 (starting with noun), or (starting with v) be = CHAFE (anger playfully)]

chaff'er, v.i. & t., & n. 1. Haggle, bargain (~ *away*). = BARGAIN (*away*); hence ~ER¹. 2. n. =~ing. [ME *ch(e)apfare* f. OE *cēap* see CHAPMAN+*faru* FARE]

||**chaff'inch**, n. Common British small bird. [CHAFF (f. haunting barndoor)+FINCH]

chaf'ing-dish, n. Vessel with burning charcoal etc. inside for keeping warm things placed on it. [f. obs. sense of CHAFE=warm]

chagrin (shagrēn'?), n., & v.t. (Affect with) acute disappointment or mortification. [f. F *chagrin(er)* f. Turk. *saghri* rump of horse, prepared hide, SHAGREEN; sense by metaphor f. use of shagreen for friction]

chain, n., & v.t. 1. Connected series of metal or other links (ENDLESS ~); fetters, confinement, restraining force; necklace, watchguard, etc. 2. Sequence, series, set, (of proof, events, posts, mountains; *ladies'* ~, movement in quadrille). 3. Jointed metal-rod measuring-line, its length (66 ft). 4. (Also ~-*shot*) two balls or half balls joined by ~ for cutting masts etc. 5. (Naut.) fastening for shrouds below CHANNEL² (also ~-*plate*), the ~s, ~ (of convicts ~ed together, or forced to work in ~s; ~-*letter*, a letter of which the recipient is asked to make copies to be sent to a (named) number of others (those doing the like in their turn); ~-*moulding*, archit, ornament with link carvings; ~ *reaction*, chem. reaction forming intermediate products which react with the original substance & are repeatedly renewed; ~-*smoker* (who lights another cigarette or cigar from the stump of the one last smoked); ~-*stitch*, ornamental sewing (in sewing machine) simple sewing

chair (cf. LOGE³-*stitch*); *~-store*, one of a series of shops owned by one firm & selling the same goods; *~-wale*, = CHANNEL²; *~-wheel*, transmitting power by *~* fitted to its edge; hence *~'LESS* a., *~'LET* n. 7. v.t. Secure, confine, with chain (lit. & fig.). [f. OF *chaîne* f. L *catena*]

chair, n., & v.t. 1. Separate seat for one, of various forms (ARM¹ or elbow, BATH¹, CURULE, DECK¹, EASY¹; *take a ~*, sit down). 2. Seat of authority; professorship; ‖ mayoralty (*past or above the C~*, *below the C~*, of alderman who has, has not, been mayor). 3. Seat, office, of person presiding at meeting, public dinner, etc. (*take, leave, the ~*, begin, end, the proceedings); chairman (*address, appeal to, the ~*; *chair! chair!*; protest against disorder). 4. (Railway) iron or steel socket holding rail in place. 5. (Hist.) = SEDAN. 6. *Electric ~*. 7. v.t. Install in chair of authority; ‖ place in chair & carry aloft (winner of contest, election, etc.). [f. OF *chaire* f. L f. Gk *kathedra* (CATHEDRAL)]

chair'man, n. (pl. *-men*; fem. *chair-woman*). Person chosen to preside over meeting, permanent president of committee, board, etc. (*C~ of Committees*, in Houses of Parl., presiding instead of Lord Chancellor & Speaker when House is in Committee), whence *~SHIP* n.; one who keeps or propels a Bath chair; (Hist.) one of two sedan-bearers.

chaise (shāz), n. Pleasure or travelling carriage of various shapes, usu. now low, four-wheeled, & open, with one or two ponies; POST-*~*. [F, var. of *chaire* f. OF *chaire* CHAIR]

chalcēd'ony (k-), **cal-**, n. Precious stone of quartz kind with many varieties as agate, cornelian, chrysoprase. [f. L *chalcedonius* f. Gk *khalkēdōn* etym. dub.]

chālco- (k-), comb. form esp. in mineralogical terms = copper, brass. [f. Gk *khalkos*]

chalcog'raphy (k-), n. Art of engraving on copper. [prec.,-GRAPHY]

chālcopyr'īte (k-; -īr-), n. A copper ore, yellow or copper pyrites. [CHALCO-, PYRITE]

Chaldē'an, **Chaldee'**, (kāl-), a. & n. (Native) of Chaldea or Babylon; soothsayer, astrologer. [f. L f. Gk *khaldaios* + -AN]

chald'ron (-awl-), n. Coal measure, 36 bushels. [f. OF *chauldron* as CAULDRON]

chalet (shăl'ā), n. Swiss mountain dairyhut; Swiss peasant's wooden cottage; villa in this style; street lavatory. [F. Swiss wd perh. dim. of *casella* dim. of It. *casa* house]

chăl'ice, n. Goblet; eucharistic wine-cup (*mixed ~*, with water ceremonially added); (poet.) flower-cup, whence **chăl'iced²** (-st) a. [OF (now *calice*), f. L CALIX]

chalk¹ (-awk), n. White soft earthy

limestone used for burning into lime & for writing & drawing; coloured preparation of like texture used in crayons for drawing; *as like as ~ & cheese*, unlike in essentials; *by a long ~*, *by long ~s*, by far (f. use of *~* to score points in games); *~-bed*, stratum of *~-pit*, quarry; *~-stone*, gouty concretion like *~* in tissues & joints esp. of hands & feet. [OE *cealc*, com.-WG, cf. G *kalk*, f. L *calx -cis* lime]

chalk² (-awk), v.t. Rub, mark, draw, write, write *up*, with chalk; *~ out*, sketch, plan as thing to be accomplished (often *for oneself*). [f. prec.]

chalk'ly (-awk-), a. Abounding in, white as, chalk; like or containing chalk-stones. Hence *~'NESS n. [-Y¹]

chǎll'enge¹ (-j), n. Calling to account (*sentry's ~*, 'Who goes there?'); exception taken (e.g. to juryman); summons to trial or contest, esp. to duel, defiance. [f. OF *chalenge* f. L *calumnia* CALUMNY]

chǎll'enge²(-j), v.t. Call to account (of sentry, & fig.); take exception to (evidence, juryman), dispute, deny; claim (attention, admiration, etc.); invite to contest, game, or duel, defy. Hence *~EABLE a., *~ER¹ n. [f. OF *chalenger* f. LL *calumniare* (CALUMNY)]

chǎll'is, n. Lady's-dress fabric. [?]

chalyb'ēate (ka-), a. Impregnated with iron (of mineral water or spring). [irreg. for *chalybäte* f. L f. Gk *khalups -ubos* steel + -ATE³]

cham (kăm), n. *Great ~*, autocrat (of dominant critic etc., esp. Dr Johnson). [obs. form of KHAN]

chamade (shamahd'), n. Signal for retreat on drum or trumpet. [F, f. Port. *chamada* (*chamar* f. L *clamare* call, -ADE)]

chamar', n. Member of the very low Indian caste of leather-workers; tanner, shoemaker. [Hind.]

chăm'ber, n. Room, esp. bedroom (but or arch.; but *~ music*, for small instrumental combinations; *~ concert*, of such music; *~ orchestra*, *organ*, small); (pl.) set of rooms in larger building, esp. in Inns of Court, let separately, judge's room for hearing cases not needing to be taken in court; (hall used by) deliberative or judicial body, one of the houses of a parliament; *C~ of Commerce, Agriculture*, a board organized to forward these in a district; (also *~-pot*) vessel for urine; *~ counsel*, lawyer giving opinions in private, not practising in court; *~-maid*, housemaid at inn; enclosed space in body of animal or plant, or in machinery etc. (esp. part of gun-bore, of larger diameter in some guns, separate in revolver, that contains charge). Hence (-)*~ED²* (-erd) a., *~ING¹* n. (arch.), licentiousness. [f. F *chambre* f. L *camera* f. Aryan *kam-* cover over cf. Gk *kamara* vault]

chăm'berlain (-lin), n. Officer managing household of sovereign or great, noble;

Lord Great C~ of England, hereditary holder of ceremonial office; Lord C~ of the Household, with part management of Royal Household, & licenser of plays. Hence ~SHIP n. [OF. f. Teut. + camera (OHG chamarling) f. kamara f. L camera; see prec.]

chaméľeon (kə-), n. Small prehensile-tailed long-tongued lizard with power of changing colour & of living long without food; inconstant person. Hence ~ON'IC a., ~on-like, a. & adv. [F. f. L f. Gk khamaileōn (khamai on ground, leōn lion)]

chám'fer, v.t., & n. Bevel symmetrically (right-angled edge or corner); (n.) surface so given (hollow or concave ~, one with gouge instead of chisel); channel, flute. [v.t. & n.). [f. OF chanfrein (CANT, L frangere) lit. break-corner]

chamois (shăm'wah, in sense 2 shăm'i), n. 1. Wild mountain antelope of goat size. 2. (Also ~-leather, shammy, shammy-leather) soft pliable leather from sheep, goats, deer, etc. [F. prob. f. Swiss Rom.; cf. It. camozza, also G gemse (OHG gamz]

chám'omile, = CAMOMILE.

chámp, v.t. & i., & n. Munch (fodder) noisily; work (bit) noisily in teeth; (make) chewing action or noise. [prob. imit.]

champagne (shămpān'), n. Kinds of wine from E. France (usu. white & sparkling). [name of province, = foll.]

chám'paign (-ān), [n. (law). The offence of assisting a party in a suit in which one is not naturally interested with a view to receiving a share of the disputed property. So ~ous a. [f. F champart feudal lord's part of produce, f. L campus field, pars part]

chám'pion, n. & a., & v.t. 1. Person who fights, argues, etc., for another or for a cause (King's, Queen's, C~; or C~ of England, hereditary official at corona-tions). 2. Athlete etc., animal, plant, etc., that has defeated all competitors (often as adj. ~ boxer, ~ turnip); (as adj. or adv., dial. or vulg.) first-class, prime, top-hole, splendidly. Hence ~LESS a., ~SHIP n. 3. v.t. Maintain the cause of. [OF, f. LL campionem nom. -io fighter (L campus CAMP')]

champlevé (shămp'lĕvā), a. & n. ~ enamel or ~, enamel in which the colours are filled into hollows made in the surface (cf. CLOISONNÉ) [F, = raised field]

chance¹ (-ahns), n. & a. 1. Way things fall out, fortune; undesigned occurrence; opportunity; (Cricket) opportunity of dismissing a batsman given to a fields-man (esp. in phr. give a ~); possibility, probability (esp. in pl., as the ~s are against it); absence of design or discover-able cause; course of events regarded as a power, fate; by ~, as it falls or fell out, without design; on the ~, in view of the possibility (of, that); take one's ~, let what comes; the main ~, that of getting rich; stand a (good, fair) ~, have a pros-pect; stand a ~, by ~, as~-soum tree, ing). [f. OF cheance f. LL cadentia n. (L cadere fall. -ENCE)]

chance² (-ahns), v.i. & t. Happen (arch. in abs. use, getting rare in constr. it ~d that, he ~d to do); ~ upon, happen to find, meet, or come upon; (colloq.) risk (esp. ~ it); ~ one's arm (colloq.), take one's chance of doing something success-fully (prob. orig. Army sl., from a N.C.O.'s risking the loss of his stripes). [f. prec.]

chan'cel (-ah-), n. Eastern part of church reserved for clergy, choir, etc., & usu. railed off. [OF, f. L cancelli f. L cancelli lattice-bars]

chan'cellory (-ah-), **-ory**, n. Position, staff, department, official residence, of a chancellor; office attached to embassy or consulate. [f. OF chancelerie (chanceler see foll.]

chan'cellor (-ah-), n. State or law official of various kinds; Lord C~ (also C~ of England, Lord High C~), highest judge, presiding in H. of Lords & in Chancery Div. of Supreme Court; C~ of EXCHEQUER; C~ of Duchy of Lancaster, member of government (legally representative of King as Duke of Lancaster), often Cabinet minister who does not desire departmental work; C~ of bishop or diocese, bishop's law officer; C~ of Garter or other order, who seals commissions etc.; titular head of university (Vice-C~ performing duties); (Germany, Austro-Hungary) chief minister of State. Hence ~SHIP n. [ME (h)anceler f. OF (h)anceler (-OR⁴) f. L cancellarius law-court usher

chance-méd'ley (-ah-), n. (Law) action, esp. homicide, mainly but not entirely unintentional; inadvertency. [AF chance medlé (see MEDDLE) mixed chance]

chan'cery (-ah-), n. (C~) Lord Chancel-lor's court, a division of High Court of Justice (formerly a separate court of equity for cases with no remedy in common-law Courts, whence the meaning, still in U.S. & in literature, of court of equity); office for public records; (Boxing) in ~, with head held under opponent's arm being pommelled (from difficulty of getting clear of old Court of C~). [short-ened f. CHANCELLERY]

chancre (shănk'er), n. Venereal ulcer. [F, = CANCER]

chan'cy (-ah-), a. Uncertain, risky. [CHANCE¹, -Y²]

chandelier (sh-), n. Branched hanging support for several lights. [F see foll.]

chand'ler (-ah-), n. Dealer in candles, oil, soap, paint, & groceries (corn-~, in corn; ship-~, in cordage, canvas, etc.). Hence

chand'lier(y1) (-ah-) n. [f. OF chandelier (L candela CANDLE, -ARY¹)]

change¹ (-j), n. Alteration; substitution of one for another, variety (for a ~); whence ~'FUL(I) (-jf-), ~'LESS (-jl-), aa.; Change (now usu. but wrongly 'Change) place where merchants meet (on C~, engaged there); arrival of moon at fresh phase (prop. at new moon only); ~ of clothes, second outfit in reserve; lower coins given for higher one or for foreign money; money returned as balance of that tendered for article (take one's, the, ~ out of, avenge oneself on); get no ~ out of (a person), fail to get the better of him (in business, argument, etc.); (Bell-ringing, usu. pl.) different orders in which peal can be rung (ring the ~s fig., exhaust ways of putting or doing thing); ~-over, alteration from one working system to another, reversal (of the situation in affairs, of opinions, etc.). [OF, f. LL cambium (cambire CHANGE²)]

change² (-j), v.t. & i. Take another instead of (~ one's coat); resign, get rid of, for; give or get smaller or foreign coin for (money); put on different clothes; go from one to another of (thing ~s hands, passes to different owner; also abs.=~trains, boats, etc.); give & receive, exchange, (~ places with, ~ ~d places); make or become different (often to, into, from), (moon) arrive at fresh phase, esp. become new moon; ~ colour, turn pale or blush; ~ one's feet (colloq.), put on other shoes etc.; ~ front, take new position in argument etc.; ~ one's condition, marry; ~ one's mind, adopt new plan or opinion; ~ one's note or tune, become more humble, sad, etc.; ~ step, foot, feet, time other foot to drum in marching. [f. OF changer f. LL cambiare (cambium f. L cambire barter cf. Gk kambos turn back)]

change'able (-ja-), a. Irregular, inconstant; alterable. Hence or cogn. ~BIL'ITY (-ja-), ~bleNESS (-ja-: -ln-), nn. [F, see prec., -ABLE]

change'ling (-jl-), n. Thing or child substituted for another by stealth, esp. elf-child thus left by fairies. [CHANGE² + -LING¹]

chann'el¹, n., & v.t. (-ll-). 1. Natural or artificial bed of running water; (Geog.) piece of water, wider than strait, joining two larger pieces, usu. seas (|| the C~, English C~); tubular passage for liquid; course in which anything moves, direction, line; medium, agency; groove, flute; ~ iron (or bar), rolled iron bar or beam flanged to form a ~ on one side. 2. v.t. Form ~s in, groove; cut out (way etc.). [f. OF chanel var. of CANAL]

chann'el², n. Broad thick plank projecting horizontally from ship's side abreast of mast to broaden base for shrouds; (mod. sing. or pl.) level of deck (rolling ~s under). [for chainwale, (WALE) cf. gunnel for gunwale]

chant(-ah-), n., & v.i.&t. 1. Song; (Mus.) short musical passage in two or more phrases each beginning with reciting note, for singing to psalms & canticles (single, double, quadruple, as one, two, four, verses are sung to it); measured monotonous song; sing-song intonation in talk. 2. vb. Sing; utter musically; intone, sing to a ~; ~ the praises of, constantly praise; ~ horses, sell fraudulently. [f. F chant(er) song, sing, f. L cantus -ūs, cantare, (canere cant- sing)]

chant'age (-ah-), n. Blackmailing. [F]

chanterelle (-ah-), n. Yellow edible fungus. [F, dim. f. L f. Gk kantharos drinking-cup]

chant'icleer (-ah-), n. (Personal name for) domestic cock. [f. OF chantecler (CHANT, CLEAR; name in Reynard the Fox]

chant'ress (-ah-), n. Female singer (arch. or poet.). [f. OF chanteresse, see CHANTER, -ESS¹]

chant'ry (-ah-), n. Endowment for priest(s) to sing masses for founder's soul; priests, chapel, altar, so endowed. [f. OF chanterie (chanter CHANT, -ERY]

chant'y (-ah-), **shan'ty**, n. Sailors' song (with alternating solo by ~man, & chorus) in heaving. [prob. f. F chantez, imperat. pl. of chanter see prec.]

cha'os (kā-), n. Formless void or great deep of primordial matter (C~, this personified as eldest of the gods); utter confusion. Hence (irreg.) chāŏt'ic a., chāŏt'ICALLY adv. [L, f. Gk khaos; -otic on false anal. of erotic etc.]

chap¹, v.t. & i. (-pp-), & n. 1. Crack (t. & i.) in fissures (usu. of skin, by wind etc., also of dried-up earth etc.). 2. n. (Usu. pl.) crack(s), open seam(s), esp. in skin; hence ~p'y² a. [ME chappen, cf. MDu. cappen, & CHIP, CHOP]

chap², chŏp, n. (Pl.) jaws, esp. of beasts (lick one's ~s, w. relish or anticipation), cheeks (fat-chops, fat-faced person); (sing.) lower jaw or half of cheek, esp. of pig as food (Bath chap; ~fallen, with jaw hanging down, dispirited, dejected); chops of the Channel, entrance from Atlantic to Channel. [f. prec.]

chap³, n. (colloq.). Man, boy, fellow. [short for CHAPMAN cf. customer]

chaparejos (chahporā'hŏs), n. pl. Cowboy's leather or sheepskin overalls for legs. [Mex. Sp.; often abbr. as **chaps** (ch- or sh-)]

*chaparral', n. (Thicket of) dwarf evergreen oak; ~cock, fast-running bird. [Sp., f. chaparra evergreen oak]

chap'book, n. (bibliog.). Specimen of popular literature (usu. small pamphlet of

tales, ballads, tracts) formerly hawked by chapmen. [mod. wd, see CHAPMAN]

chape, n. Metal cap of scabbard-point; back-piece of buckle attaching it to strap etc.; ∥ sliding loop on belt or strap. [F, f. LL *cappa* CAP¹]

chapeau-bras (shapō-brah´), n. (hist.), Three-cornered flat silk hat of 18th c., carried under arm. [F, = arm-hat]

chap'el, n. Place of Christian worship other than parish church or cathedral, esp. one attached to private house or institution (~ *royal*, or *royal palace*); oratory in larger building, with altar, esp. compartment of cathedral etc. separately dedicated (*Lady-*~, dedicated to Virgin; usu. E. of high altar); subordinate Anglican church, esp. ~ *of ease*, for convenience of remote parishioners; ∥ R.-C. or dissenters' place of worship in Britain; ~ *service* or attendance at ~ (*keep a* ~, be present, in colleges) ; (Print.) printing-office, journeyman printers' association or meeting. [f. OF *chapele* f. LL *cappella* dim. of *cappa* cloak (CAP²); first ~ was sanctuary in which St Martin's sacred cloak was kept by *cappellani*]

chapelle ardente (shăpĕl´ ärdahnt´), n. Chamber prepared for lying-in-state of great personage & lit up with candles, torches, etc. [F]

chap'elry, n. District served by chapel. [-RY]

chap'erŏn (sh-), n., & v.t. **1.** Married or elderly woman in charge of girl on social occasions; hence ~AGE n. **2.** v.t. Act as ~ to. [F, = hood, chaperon, dim. of *chappe* cope (CAP²]

chap'iter, n. (bibl.), Capital of column. [earlier form of CHAPTER]

chap'lain (-lĭn), n. Clergyman officiating in private chapel of great person or institution, on board ship, or for regiment etc.; nun reciting inferior services in nunnery. Hence ~CY (-lĭn-) n. [f. OF *chapelain* f. LL *cappellanus* (CHAPEL, -AN)]

chap'let, n. Wreath of flowers, leaves, gold, gems, etc., for head ; string of beads for counting prayers (one-third of rosary number), or as necklace; string of eggs in toad etc.; bead-moulding. Hence ~ED¹ a. [f. OF *chapelet* dim. of CHAPE, see -LET]

chap'man, n. (hist. ; pl. *-men*). Pedlar. cf. G *kaufmann* (*kaup* n. barter, *mann* man) & see CHEAP]

chap'pie, -y, n. (colloq.). Exquisite, man about town. [CHAP¹ + -Y³]

chap'ter, n. Main division of a book piece of narrative, esp. (fig.) limited subject, numbered as part of session's statutes for reference (5 & 6 WILL. IV. cap. 62 = Statutory Declarations Act 1835) general meeting, whole number, of canons of collegiate or cathedral church or members of monastic or knightly order (~

house, **used for such meetings**); ~ & *verse*, exact reference to passage, exact authority *for statement*; *to end of* ~, for ever; ~ *of* ACCIDENTS, [for CHAPITER f. OF *chapitre* f. L *capitulum* dim. of *caput* -*itis* head]

chăf¹, n. Hill trout of Wales etc. [?]

chăr², chär³, v.t. & i. (-rr-). Burn (t. & i.) to charcoal, scorch, blacken with fire. [prob. back-formation f. CHARCOAL]

char-à-banc(s) (shă´rǎbang, or as in Ap.), n. Long vehicle, with many seats looking forward, for holiday excursions. [F *char à bancs* = benched carriage]

chă'racter (kărĭk-), n., & v.t. **1.** Distinctive mark; (pl.) inscribed letters or figures; national writing-symbols (*in the German* ~); person's handwriting. **2.** Characteristic (esp. of species etc. in Nat. Hist.); collective peculiarities, sort, style; person's or race's idiosyncrasy, mental or moral nature. **3.** Moral strength, backbone; reputation, good reputation; description of person's qualities; testimonial; status. **4.** Known person (usu. *public* ~); imaginary person created by novelist (*in, out of,* ~, appropriate to these or not, also more widely of actions that are in accord or not with person's ~). **5.** Eccentric person (~ *actor*, who devotes himself to eccentricities). **6.** v.t. (poet. & arch.). Inscribe; describe. [f. F *caractère* f. L f. Gk *kharaktēr* stamp (*kharassō* engrave)]

charactĕris'tic (kă-), a. & n. Typical, distinctive. (trait, mark, quality), whence ~ICALLY adv.; (Math.) index of logarithm. [f. Gk *kharaktēristikos* (prec., -ISTIC)]

chă'racterize (kă-), v.t. Describe character of; describe *as*; be characteristic of, impart character to. Hence ~A´TION n. [f. med. L f. Gk *kharaktērizō* (CHARACTER, -IZE)]

chă'racterless (kă-), a. Ordinary, undistinguished; without testimonial. [-LESS]

charade (shărahd´), n. Game of guessing word from written or acted clue given for each syllable & for the whole. [F, f. Pr. *charrada* (*charrà* chatter)]

chär'coal, n. Black porous residue of partly burnt wood, bones, etc., form of carbon (occas. w. allus. to use of the fumes as method of suicide); ~*burner*, maker of this. [perh. f. CHARE + COAL in sense (*wood*) *turned coal*]

chăre, chär, n. (usu. pl.), & v.t. (-rr-). **(Do)** odd job(s); work by the day at housecleaning; ∥ *char* (colloq.), charwoman. [OE *cerr*, *cerran*, turn; U.S. *chore*]

charge¹, n. 1. Material load; **right** quantity to put into thing, esp. of explosive for gun; figurative load. **2.** (Her.) ~); price demanded for service or goods. **4.** Task, duty, commission; care, custody,

(of): nurse in ~ of child, child in ~ of nurse; CURATE in ~; ‖ give person in ~, hand over to police); take ~, (colloq., of things) get out of control (esp. with disastrous results); thing or person entrusted, minister's flock. **5.** Exhortation, directions, (parting ~, bishop's ~, judge's ~ to jury). **6.** Accusation (lay to one's ~, accuse him of; ‖ ~-sheet, record of cases at police station). **7.** Impetuous attack, rush, (return to the ~, begin again, esp. in argument); (Mil.) signal sounded for attack. [F, f. Rom. *carga* f. LL *carrica* (L *carricare* see foll.]

charge², v.t. & i. 1. Load, fill to the full or proper extent, (vessel, gun with explosive; saturate (air with vapour, water with chemicals, accumulator with electricity, memory with facts). **2.** Entrust with (~ oneself with, undertake). **3.** Command to do, exhort (esp. of bishop, judge). **4.** Accuse, impute, (person with action, fault upon person); saddle with (liability) place (liability) on. **5.** Demand (price) for (also ~ person price for). **6.** Attack (t. & i.) impetuously, esp. on horseback. **7.** Place (weapon) in position for use (~ bayonets, bring down to receive cavalry ~). [f. OF *charger*, cf. prec., f. L *carricare* (*carrus* CAR²)]

charge'able (-ja-), a. **1.** Expensive (arch.). **2.** Liable to be charged with (accused of); subject to a money demand; liable to be made an expense (~ to the parish); imputable to (on); proper to be added to an account. Hence **cha'rgeabi'lity** (-ja-) n. [f. CHARGE¹, 2 f. CHARGE², +-ABLE]

chargé (d'affaires) (shäzh'ā dafār'), n. (pl. -gés (pr. as sing.). Deputy ambassador; ambassador at minor court. [F, = one charged with affairs]

char'ger¹, n. (arch.). Large flat dish. [ME *chargeour* perh. f. CHARGE² +-OR² (loader), or f. OF +*chargeoir* (CHARGE² & as PARLOUR)]

char'ger², n. In vbl senses; esp., (Mil.) officer's horse. [-ER¹]

cha'riot, n., & v.t. Stately vehicle, triumphal car, (poet. & esp. fig. of sun's ~ etc.); 18th-c. four-wheeled carriage with back seats only; (Hist.) car used in ancient fighting & racing, whence **cha'rioteer'** n.; (vb) convey as or in ~. [OF, augment. of *char* CAR]

cha'ritable, a. Liberal in giving to the poor; connected with such giving; wont to judge favourably of persons, acts, & motives. Hence ~**leness** (-ln-), n., ~**LY²** adv. [OF (*charité* = foll, -ABLE]

cha'rity, n. Christian love of fellow men (in, out of, ~ with); kindness, natural affection, (~ begins at home), is due first to kith & kin); candour, freedom from censoriousness, imputing of good motives when possible, leniency, beneficence, liberality to the poor, alms-giving, (pl., acts of this), alms; institution for helping the helpless, help so given, (cold as ~, in allusion to mechanical administration; ‖ ~-boy, -girl, brought up in such place); Brother, Sister, of C~, member of a society devoted to relieving poor; C~ Commission(ers), board created 1853 to control charitable trusts. [f. OF *charité* f. L *caritatem* (*carus* dear, -TY)]

char'ivar'i (sh-), n. Medley of sounds, hubbub. [F, etym. dub.; prop. a serenade of pans, trays, etc., to unpopular person]

chark'a, n. Country-made Indian spinning-wheel. [Hind. *charkha*]

‖ **char'lady,** sl. var. of CHARWOMAN.

char'latan (sh-), n. & a. Impostor in medicine, quack; (of, as of) empty pretender to knowledge or skill. Hence ~**ISM¹**(1) a.. ~**ISM**(2), ~**RY**, nn. [F, f. It. *ciarladano* (*ciarlare* patter)]

Charles's Wain (-lziz), n. (Also *Plough, Great Bear*) constellation [*Ursa Major* or its seven bright stars. [OE *Carles wægn*; wain of Arcturus, neighbouring constellation, became wain of Arthur, who was confused with the other great hero Charlemagne]

Charles'ton (-lz-), n., & v.i. An American dance with side-kicks from the knee; (vb) dance this, kick thus. [f. ~ in S. Carolina]

‖ **char'ley,** n. (old colloq.). Night-watchman. [dim. of *Charles*]

char'lock, n. Field mustard. [OE *cerlic*]

char'lotte (sh-), n. Kinds of pudding made of stewed fruit with casing or layers or covering of bread, biscuits, sponge-cake, or bread-crumbs; ~ *russe*, custard enclosed in sponge cake. [F]

charm, n. Verse, sentence, word, act, or object having occult power (against), spell; thing worn to avert evil etc.; amulet; trinket on watch-chain etc.; quality, feature, exciting love or admiration (~s, beauty); attractiveness, indefinable power of delighting, (esp. as literary critics' word). [f. F *charme* f. L *carmen* song]

charm, v.t. Bewitch, influence (as) by magic, (abs. or with pred. as ~ *asleep, away*); ~ (secret, consent, etc.) out of; endow with magic power (*bear a ~ed life*); captivate, delight, (~ed with); give pleasure to (*I shall be ~ed* as polite formula); (part.) delightful, whence ~**'ingLY²** adv. [f. F *charmer* (CHARM¹)]

charm'er, n. In vbl senses; esp., beautiful woman (now joc. or arch.). [-ER¹]

charmeuse (shärmú'ĕrz), n. Soft smooth silk dress-fabric. [F]

charn'el-house, n. House or vault in which dead bodies or bones are piled. [OF *charnel* burying-place f. LL *carnale* (CARNAL)]

Char'on (k-), n. Ferryman conveying souls across Styx to Hades in Gk mythol. (~'s boat, ferry, etc., phrr. for hour of death). [f. Gk *Kharôn*]

char′poy, n. (Anglo-Ind.). Light Indian bedstead. [f. Hind. *charpāī*]

chart, n. & v.t. **1.** Navigator's sea map, with coast outlines, rocks, shoals, etc.; outline map with conspectus of special conditions, as *magnetic* ~; record by curves etc. of fluctuations in temperature, prices, etc.; sheet of tabulated information; hence ~LESS a. **2.** v.t. Make ~ of, map. [OF, f. L *carta* CARD²]

charter, n. Written grant of rights by sovereign or legislature, esp. creation of borough, company, etc. (*Great C~*, MAGNA CHARTA); deed conveying land; = CHARTER-PARTY; privilege, admitted right. [f. OF *chartre* f. L *cartula* dim. of *carta* CARD²]

char′ter, v.t. Grant charter, give privilege, to (||~*ed accountant*, member of Institute of Accountants with royal charter; ~*ed libertine*, one allowed to take liberties); hire (ship) by ~-*party*, (loosely) hire (vehicle etc.). Hence ~ER¹ n. [f. prec.]

Char′terhouse, n. Alms-house in London for aged pensioners on site of Carthusian monastery; (also ~ *School*) public school of same foundation now at Godalming. [corrupt. of CHARTREUSE]

chartog′raphy (k-), etc. See car-.

chartreuse (see Ap.), etc. Carthusian monastery; kinds (*green, yellow,* ~) of liqueur; pale apple-green colour. [made by CARTHUSIAN monks]

char′tulary (-k-). See car-.

||**char′woman** (-wŏŏ-), n. Woman hired by the day or hour for house-work. [CHARE]

char′y, a. Cautious; shy *of*, sparing *in, doing*; stingy *of* (~ *of praise*). Hence char′ily adv., char′iness n. [OE *cearig,* = OSax. *karag* f. OTeut. *karā* CARE]

chase¹, v.t. Pursue (*in* ~ *of*, pursuing; *give* ~, go in pursuit, hunting (*the* ~, hunting as sport); (also *chace*) unenclosed park-land; hunted animal or pursued ship; (Hist.) ~, ~-*port,* ~-*gun, chaser; bow-*~, *stern-*~, bow, stern, gun, port, in bow or stern for use while chasing or being chased; (Tennis) a certain stroke. [f. OF *chace* (LL *captāre* CATCH¹)]

chase², v.t. Pursue; drive *from, out of, to,* etc.; ~*r* (colloq.), tot of spirit taken after drinking neat spirits (also fig.). [see CATCH¹]

chase³, v.t. Emboss, engrave, (metal). [for poet. & arch. *enchase* = set (jewels), inlay, engrave, enshrine, f. F *enchâsser* (en in, CASE²)]

chase⁴, n. Part of gun enclosing bore; groove cut to receive pipe etc. [f. F *chas* f. LL *capsum* hollow of the chest (L *capsa* hold)]

chase⁵, n. Iron frame holding composed type for page or sheet. [f. F *châsse* CASE²]

chasm (kǎ'zm), n. Deep fissure; break of continuity, hiatus; wide difference of feeling, interests, etc., between persons or parties; void, blank. Hence (poet.) ~y² a. [f. L f. Gk *khasma* (*khaskō* . . .

chasse (shahs), n. Liqueur after coffee etc. [F]

chassé (shǎs'ā), n. & v.i. (Make) gliding step in dancing; ~ *croisé* (see Ap.; pl. -s), *double*~, (fig.) idle manoeuvring. [F]

chassepot (shǎs'pō), n. French army breech-loading rifle. [inventor's name]

chassis (shǎs'ē), n. (pl. the same). Base-frame of gun-carriage, motor-car, etc. [f. F *châssis* (LL *capsus* wagon-body f. L *capere* take)]

chaste, a. Abstaining from unlawful or immoral (also from all) sexual intercourse, pure, virgin; decent (of speech); restrained, severe, pure in taste or style, unadorned, simple. Hence ~LY² adv. [OF, f. L *castus*]

chas′ten (-sn), v.t. Discipline, correct by suffering. (usu. of God, Providence, etc., or of trouble etc.); make chaste in style etc., refine; temper, subdue, (esp. in p.p.). Hence ~ER¹ n. [prec. + -EN³]

chastise′ (-z), v.t. Punish; beat. Hence chas′tisEMENT (-zm-), ~ER¹ n. [form (later *chasty, chaste*) f. OF *chastier* . . .

chas′tity, n. Continence; virginity; celibacy; simplicity of style or taste. [f. OF *chasteté* f. L *castitātem* (*castus* CHASTE, -TY)]

chas′uble (-z-), n. Sleeveless vestment of celebrant at Mass or Eucharist with colour regulated by the feast of the day. [F, f. med. L *casubula* dim. of *casa* cottage]

chat¹, v.i. (-tt-), & n. (Indulge in) easy familiar talk. Hence ~ty² a., ~t′iness n. [short for CHATTER]

chat², n. Kinds of bird, chiefly Warblers (usu. in comb. as *Stone*~, *White*~, ~). [f. prec.]

château (shǎt'ō), n. (pl. -z, pr. -z). Foreign country house; *C*~, used attrib. in names of French wines near certain ~x. [F]

châtelaine (sh-), n. Set of short chains attached to woman's belt for carrying keys, watch, pencil, etc.; mistress of country house; (esp. in journalistic use) hostess. [F (*ché-*), . . .

chattel, n. Movable possession (usu. pl., esp. *goods &* ~*s*); *~ *mortgage*, conveyance of ~s by mortgage as security for debt. [f. OF *chatel* see CATTLE]

chatt'er, v.i., & n. **1.** (Of birds) utter quick series of short notes; (of persons) talk quickly, incessantly, foolishly, or inopportunely; (of teeth) rattle together (also of ill-adjusted parts of machine). **2.** n. Any of these sounds; ~*box*, child etc. given to ~. [imit., see -ER⁵]

chaud-froid (shō'frwal'), n. Dish of filleted poultry etc. served cold in jelly or sauce. [F, lit. hot-cold]

chauf'fer, n. Metal basket holding fire; portable furnace with air-holes. [f. F *chauffoir* f. L *calefactorius* CALEFACTORY]

chauffeur (shōf'er, shōfer'), n. Professional driver of a motor-car. Hence **chauffeuse** (shōfōz') n., female ~. [F]

chaulmoo'gra, n. East-Indian tree; ~ *oil*, vegetable fat obtained from its seeds & used in treatment of leprosy. [native name]

chaurmontel' (shō-), n. Large kind of pear. [name of French village]

chauv'inism (shōv-), n. Bellicose patriotism, foreign jingoism. So ~ist(2) n. & a., ~is'tic a. [*Chauvin*, Napoleonic veteran, person in Cogniard's *Cocarde Tricolore* 1831]

chaw, v.t., & n. (now vulg.). Chew; ~*up*, utterly defeat; ~-*bacon*, bumpkin, (n.) quid of tobacco. [var. of CHEW]

chawl, n. Large tenement house peculiar to Indian cities (esp. Bombay). [native name]

cheap, a. Inexpensive (of thing, price, shop, dealer; ~ & *nasty*, of low cost & bad quality; worth more than its cost; easily got; worthless, of little account; staled, (*hold* ~, despise); (as pred.) = cheaply (*got it* ~ etc.); *dirt* ~, very ~; *feel* ~ (sl.), be out of sorts; *on the* ~, in ~ manner; *C~ Jack*, travelling hawker; ||~ *tripper*), excursion(ist) by rail etc. at reduced fares. Hence ~LY² adv., ~'ISH¹(2) a., ~'NESS n. [f. phr. *good cheap* f. obs. *cheap* n., OE *céap* barter, price, com.-Teut. cf. G *kauf* purchase]

cheap'en, v.t. & i. Haggle for (arch.); make or become cheap, depreciate. [-EN⁶]

cheat, n., & v.t. & i. **1.** Trick, fraud; swindler, deceiver; card-game in which undetected cheating is licensed. **2.** vb. Deceive, trick (person *out of* thing); deal fraudulently; while away (time, fatigue). [ME *chete* short for ESCHEAT]

striking string twice; ~*nut*, screwed on over nut to prevent its working loose; ~*rein*, attaching one horse's rein to other's bit, also rein preventing horse from lowering head; ~*spring*, in carriage for signalling to driver to stop; ~*taker*, collector of pass tokens in theatre etc.; ~*till*, in shop, recording receipts. [f. OF *eschec* f. Arab. f. Pers. *shāh* king]

check², v.t. & i. **1.** Threaten opponent's king at chess. **2.** Suddenly arrest motion of. **3.** (Of hounds) stop on losing scent, or to make sure of it. **4.** Restrain, curb, (Mil., of superior) find fault with, rebuke. **5.** Test (statement, account, figures, employés) by comparison etc., examine accuracy of. [f. OF *eschequier* play chess, check, as prec.]

check³, n. Cross-lined pattern; fabric woven or printed with this. So ~ED² (-kt) a. [perh. short for CHEQUER]

check⁴, n. = CHEQUE.

check'er. See CHEQUER¹,².

*****check'ers**, n.pl. The game of draughts. [see CHEQUER¹]

checkmate', int. & n., & v.t. (also *mate*, now more usu. in chess but not in fig. sense). (Announcement to opponent of) inextricable check of king at chess, final defeat at chess or in any enterprise; (vb) defeat, frustrate. [f. OF *eschec mat* (see CHECK¹) f. Arab. *shāh māta* king is dead]

Chedd'ar, n. Kind of cheese. [place]

chedd'ite, n. A high explosive notable for its stability. [F f. *Chedde* (in Haute Savoie) + -ITE¹ (2)]

chee'-chee, n. (Anglo-Ind.). The minced English spoken by Eurasians (also attrib.). [Hind. *chi-chi* fie!]

cheek, n., & v.t. Side-wall of mouth, side of face below eye, (~-*tooth*, molar; ~-*bone*, that below eye; ~ *by jowl*, close together, intimate; *to one's own* ~, not shared with others); saucy speech (vb, address saucily), whence ~Y² a., ~'ILY² adv., ~'INESS n.; cool confidence, effrontery, (*have the* ~ *to*); side post of door etc.; (pl.) jaws of vice, side-pieces of various parts of machines arranged in lateral pairs. [OE *céce* cf. Du. *kaak*]

cheep, v.i., & n. (Utter) shrill feeble note as of young bird. Hence (of young partridge or grouse) ~'ER¹ n. [imit.]

cheer¹, n. Frame of mind (*what* ~?, how do you feel?; *be of good* ~, stout-hearted, hopeful); food, fare, (*make good* ~, feast; *the fewer the better* ~, more to eat); shout of encouragement or applause (*three* ~*s*, successive united hurrahs, often for person or thing honoured). [obs. sense *face*, ME & OF *chere* f. LL *cara* face perh. f. Gk *kara* head]

cheer², v.t. & i. Comfort, gladden; incite, urge on, esp. by shouts; applaud (t. & i.), shout for joy; ~ *up*, comfort, take comfort. [f. prec.]

cheer'ful, a. Contented, in good spirits, hopeful; animating, pleasant; willing, not reluctant. Hence ~LY² adv., ~NESS n. [CHEER + -FUL]

cheer'less, a. Dull, gloomy, dreary, miserable. Hence ~LY² adv., ~NESS n. at ~. [CHEER + -LESS]

cheer'ly, adv. (naut.). Heartily, with a will. [formerly adj.; CHEER¹]

cheer'y², a. Lively, in spirits, genial. Hence ~LY² adv., ~NESS n. [-Y²]

cheese¹ (-z), n. Food made of pressed curds; a ~, complete cake or ball of this within rind; green ~, immature, not yet dried; BREAD & ~; CHALK & ~; make ~s (of schoolgirls), spin round & sink suddenly, inflating petticoats; fruit of mallow; the heavy flat wooden ball used in skittles; damson, guava, ~, conserve of the fruit pressed into consistency of ~; ~-cutter, with broad curved blade; ~-cake, tartlet filled with sweet yellow compound of curds etc.; ~-hopper, maggot of ~-fly; ~-paring, stingy, stinginess, (pl.), worthless odds & ends; ~-plate, 5 or 6 in. diameter, also large coat-button; ~-rennet, name for Lady's bedstraw; ~-scoop, -taster, instrument for extracting small piece as sample; ~-straws, savoury of grated cheese etc. made up into thin strips. [OE cēse, cf. G käse f. L caseus]

cheese² (-z), n. (sl.). The ~, the correct thing. [prob. Anglo-Ind. f. Pers. & Hind. chīz thing]

cheese³ (-z), v.t. (sl.). ~ it, stop, cease, give over. (only as imper.). [?]

chees'y², (-z-), a. Like, tasting of, cheese; (sl.) stylish. Hence ~INESS n. [CHEESE¹·², -Y²]

cheet'ah, n. Kind of leopard, tamed in India & trained to hunt deer. [f. Hind. chītā f. Skr. chitraka speckled]

cheirop'teran, n., **cheirop'terous**, a. (kīr-). (Member) of mammal order with membraned hands serving as wings, the Bats. [prec. + Gk pteron wing + -AN, -OUS]

chek'a (chä-), n. (Earlier name of) OGPU. [Russ., f. initials (che, ka) of Chrezvy-chainaya Kommissiya, extraordinary commission]

chela' (chē-), n. Novice qualifying for initiation in esoteric Buddhism. [Hind. = pupil]

chel'a² (kē-), n. (pl. -lae). The prehensile claw of crabs, lobsters, scorpions, etc. Hence ~ATE², ~IFORM, aa. [f. Gk khēlē claw]

cheil(o)- (kī-). = CHIL(O)-.

cheir(o)- (kīr-). = CHIR(O)-.

chef (sh-), n. Head cook (male). [F]

chef-d'œuvre (shĕdȫ'vr), n. (pl. chefs-, same pronunc.). A, one's, master-piece. [F]

Chelt'enham College. [-AN]

chem'ical (kĕ-), a. & n. Of, made by, relating to, chemistry; ~ COMBINATION; (usu. pl.) substance obtained by or used in ~ process; heavy ~s, bulk ~s used in industry & agriculture (prop. only of manufactured ~s). Hence or cogn. ~LY² adv., chĕm'ico- comb. form. [obs. chemic or mod. L chymicus, assim. of alchimicus ALCHEMIC to supposed

chemin de fer (shemăн' de fĕr'), n. A form of baccarat. [F. lit. = road of iron, railway]

chemise (shĭmēz'), n. Woman's body under-garment. [OF, f. LL camisia shirt]

chemisette (shĕmizĕt'), n. Bodice with upper part like chemise; muslin, etc., filling up opening of dress below throat. [F, dim. of prec.]

chem'ist (kĕ-), n. Person skilled in chemistry; || dealer in medical drugs, apothecary. [f. F chimiste f. mod. L chymista see ALCHEMIST]

chem'istry (kĕ-), n. Science of the elements & compounds & their laws of combination & behaviour under various conditions: applied or practical ~, art of utilizing this knowledge; (fig.) mysterious change or process. [prec., -RY]

chem'itype (kĕ-), n. (Process for getting) relief cast of engraving. [CHEMICAL etc. +TYPE]

chenille (shĭnēl'), n. Velvety cord used in trimming dresses & furniture. [F, = caterpillar f. L canicula small dog]

cheque (-k), **check**, n. Written order to banker to pay named sum on drawer's account to bearer or named person; BLANK ~; CROSS²ed ~; ~-book, number of stamped & engraved forms for drawing ~s bound & issued to customer. [var. of CHECK¹ formerly used of counterfoils for checking forgery]

chequer (-k-), **check'er**, n. (pl.) chess-board as inn-sign; (often pl.) pattern made of squares or with alternating colours, whence chĕq'uer-WISE (-ker-), adv.; || Chequers, Prime Minister's official country house. [f. OF eschekier f. LL scaccarium chess-board, EXCHEQUER]

chĕq'uer² (-ker), **chĕck'er**, v.t. Mark with squares, esp. of alternate colours; variegate, break uniformity of, (often fig., esp. in p.p. as chequered lot, fortunes). [prob. f. prec.]

Cheil'ean (sh-), a. (archaeol.). Of the palaeolithic epoch represented by remains found at Chelles in France. [-AN]

Chĕl'sea (-sǐ), n. || ~ pensioner, inmate of the ~ Royal Hospital for old or disabled soldiers; ~ ware, kind of porcelain made at ~ in 18th c. [place]

Cheltōn'ian, a. & n. (Member) of Cheltenham College.

chĕr'ish, v.t. Foster, nurse, keep warm; value, hold in one's heart, cling to, (esp. hopes, feelings, etc.). [f. F chérir (see -ISH²) f. cher f. L carus dear]

cheroot′ (sh-), n. Cigar with both ends open. [f. Tamil *shuruṭṭu* roll]

che′rry, n. & a. Small stone-fruit; tree bearing this (also ~-*wood*, its wood (also ~-*wood*; *make two bites at a* ~, boggle, be unenterprising or formal; || ~-*bob*), two cherries with joined stems (BOB[2]); ~ *brandy*, dark-red liqueur of brandy in which cherries have been steeped; ~-*pie*, garden heliotrope; ~ *ripe*, fruit hawker's cry; (adj.) red (~*lips*, *ribbon*; || ~-*breeches*, 11th Hussars). [ME *chery* f. ONF *cherise* (*s* lost as if pl. cf. PEA) f. L f. Gk *kerasos* perh. f. town name; OE *ciris* (cf. G *kirsche*) was prob. not source of ME]

che′rsonese (k-: -ēs), n. Peninsula. [f. L f. Gk *khersonēsos* (*khersos* dry, *nēsos* island)]

chert, n. A flint-like quartz. [?]

che′rub, n. (pl. -s, -*im*). Angelic being; one of the second order of ninefold celestial hierarchy, gifted with knowledge as the first (seraphim) with love; (Art) winged (head of) child; beautiful or innocent child. Hence **cheru′bic** (-ōō-) a. [earlier *cherubin* sing., -*ins* pl., *cherubim* sing., -*ims* pl.; f. F *cherubin* through L, Gk, f. Heb. *k'rub* pl. *k'rubim*]

chervil, n. Garden herb used in soup, salad, etc. [OE *cærfille* f. L f. Gk *khaire-phullon* perh. f. *khairō* rejoice + *phullon* leaf]

Chesh′ire (-er), n. ~ *cheese*, made in ~; ~ *cat*, person with fixed grin. [place; prov. *grin like a* ~ *cat* unexpl.]

chess[1], n. Game for two players with thirty-two pieces or ~-*men* on ~-*board* chequered with sixty-four squares. [ME *ches* f. OF *esches* pl. of *eschec* CHECK[1] (lit. sense *kings*)]

chess[2], n. One of the flooring planks of a pontoon bridge. [?]

chess′el, n. Cheese-making mould. [prob. f. CHEESE[1] + WELL[1]]

chest, n. 1. Large strong box; box for sailor's belongings; *carpenter's*, *medicine*, etc., ~, holding special requisites; treasury, coffer, of institution (usu. fig. for the sums in it); *case of some commodity*, esp. tea (& so as variable measure); 2. Part of human or lower animal's body enclosed in ribs (*get thing off one's* ~ sl., say & be quit of it), whence ~-*ED[2]* a.; ~-*note*, -*voice*, of lowest speaking or singing register; ~-*protector*, flannel etc. worn on ~-*trouble*, lung disease esp. chronic. [OE *cest* f. L f. Gk *kistē*]

ches′terfield, n. Kind of overcoat, also of couch. [19th-c. Earl of C~]

chest′nut (-sn-), n. & a. Tree (also ~-*tree*, *Spanish*, ~, or *Sweet* ~) or its edible fruit; = ~-*wood*; ~ = HORSE[1]-; ~ = CASTOR[3]; stale anecdote; (of) ~-*colour*, deep reddish-brown; *horse of this colour*. [f. obs. *chesten* (f. OF *chastaigne* f. L f. Gk *kastanea* prob. f. place-name) + NUT]

cheval-glass (sh-; -ahs), n. Tall mirror swung on uprights. [f. F *cheval* horse, frame]

chevalier′ (sh-), n. Member of certain orders of knighthood, & of French Legion of Honour etc.; (Hist.) *The C~* or *C~ de St George*, Old Pretender; *The Young C~*, Young Pretender; soldier cadet of old French noblesse; ~ *of industry* (oftener in F form ~ *d'industrie*, see Ap.), adventurer, swindler. [OF (L *caballus* horse, -ARY[1] orig. sense *horseman*), cf. CAVALIER]

chevaux de frise (shevō′defrēz′), n. pl. Iron spikes set in timber etc. to repel cavalry etc. in war, or to guard palings in peace; natural protective line of hair in plants, eyelashes, etc. [F, lit. horses of Friesland, invented by 17th-c. Frisians who had no cavalry]

chevet (shevā′), n. Apse; group of apses. [F, dim. of *chef* head (L *caput*)]

che′viot, n. & a. (Wool, cloth) got, made, from sheep of C~ hills.

che′vron (sh-), n. Bent bar of inverted V shape, in escutcheons, as archit. ornament (~*moulding*, consisting of series of these), & on sleeve of Service uniform indicating *rank* (3 bars for sergeant, 2 for corporal, etc.), or || length of service. [F, = rafter, chevron, chevronné, f. L *capriōnem* nom. -*io* (L *caper* goat), as pair of rafters]

che′vrotain, **-tin**, (sh-), n. Small Musk Deer. [F, dim. of OF *chevrot* (*chèvre* goat)]

che′vy, **chiv′y**, (usu. spelt -e- & pron. -i-), n. & v.t. Chase (n. & v.), scamper (n. & v.); game of prisoners' base. [prob. f. ballad *Chevy Chase* (place-name)]

chew (-ōō), v.t. & i., & n. 1. Work about between teeth, grind to pulp or indent with repeated biting; (abs.) ~ tobacco, whence ~*ER[1]* n.; turn over in mind; meditate *upon* or *over*; ~ *the cud*, bring back half-digested food into mouth for further chewing, (fig., usu. with of reflection, fancy, etc.) meditate; ~ *the rag* (Army sl.), reiterate an old grievance, grouse; ~*ing-gum*, preparation of sweetened & flavoured gums (esp. CHICLE) used for prolonged ~*ing*. 2. n. Act of ~*ing*; quid of tobacco. [OE *cēowan* cf. G *kauen*]

Chian′ti (kiah-), n. Dry red Ital. wine. [It.]

chiaroscuro (kyároskoor′ō), n. & a. Treatment of light & shade in painting; light & shade effects in nature; variation, relief, handling of transitions, use of contrast, in literature etc.; (adj.) of ~; half-revealed. [It., = bright-dark (L *clarus*, *obscurus*)]

chias′mus (kiáz-), n. Inversion in second phrase of order followed in first (*I cannot dig, to beg I am ashamed*). Hence **chiás′tic** (ki-) a. [mod. L, f. Gk *khiasmos* cross arrangement f. *khiazō* make letter *khi* (shaped as Eng. *X*)]

chib'ol, n. (dial.). Spring onion with green stalk attached. [ult. (through F) f. L *cæpa* onion; cf. It. *cipolla*]

chibouk', -que, (-ook), n. Long Turkish tobacco pipe. [f. Turk. *chibūk* tube]

chic (sh-), n. & a. Skill, effectiveness, style, stamp of superiority; (adj.) stylish, in the fashion. [F, etym. dub. (adj. use in Engl.)]

chicane' (sh-), v.t. & i., & n. Use chicanery; cheat (person) into, out of, etc.; (n.) chicanery; (holding of) hand without any trumps in bridge. [f. F *chicaner*) perh. f. med. Gk *tzoukanizō* play polo f. Pers. *tchaugān* polo-stick]

chican'ery (sh-), n. Legal trickery, petti-fogging; sophistry. [f. F *chicanerie* (prec., -ERY)]

chick[2], chik, n. (Anglo-Ind.). Screen-blind of finely-split bamboo laced with twine. [Hind. *chīk*]

chick[1], n. Young bird before or after hatching; *the* ~s, children of a family (so ~*abīdī'ī,* term of endearment of or to child); ~ weed, small plant. [short for CHICKEN[1]]

chick'en[1], n. (pl. ~s, ~). Young bird, esp. of domestic fowl, flesh of this; youth-ful person (esp. in *no* ~); *Mother Carey's* ~, Stormy Petrel; *count one's* ~s *before they are hatched,* be over-sanguine, pre-cipitate; ~-*breast(ed)*, (having) malformed projection of breast-bone; *~-feed,* food for poultry, (fig.) poor or trifling stuff; ~-*hazard,* game at dice; ~-*heart(ed),* (with) no courage; ~-*pox,* children's mild eruptive disease. [OE *cīcen* cf. Du. *kieken* prob. cogn. w. COCK[1]]

chick'en, chik'an, n. (Anglo-Ind.). Embroidery; ~-*work,* itinerant vendor of embroidered articles. [Hind., f. Pers. *chīkīn* needlework]

chick'ling, n. Common cultivated Vetch. [earlier *chicheling* dim. of ME & OF *chiche* ult. f. L *cicer*]

chick'-pea, n. Dwarf pea. [earlier *chich-pease* as prec. +PEASE]

chic'le (-kl or -klē), n. Milky juice of the sapodilla, the basis of chewing-gum. [f. Mex. *tzictli*]

chic'ory, n. Blue-flowered plant culti-vated for its salad leaves & its root; its root ground for use with or instead of coffee. [f. F *cichorée* (now *chico-*) f. L *cichorium* f. Gk *kikhora* succory]

chide, v.t. & i. (literary; *chid, chidden* or *chid*). Make complaints, speak scoldingly, (esp. fig. of hounds, wind, etc.); scold, rebuke. [OE *cīdan*]

chief, n. & a. (Her.) upper third of shield; leader; ruler; head man of tribe, clan, etc., whence ~'ESS[1] n.; head of a depart-ment, highest official; *C~ of Staff,* senior staff officer of a commander; *C~ of the General Staff,* senior staff officer of a Commander-in-Chief (esp. in India); ‖*C~ of the Imperial General Staff,* senior

military member of the Army Council; *in* ~, most of all, especially, (*for many reasons, & this one in* ~); ~-*in-*~, supreme, as *Commander, Colonel, -in-*~, Hence ~'-DOM, ~'SHIP, nn., ~'LESS a. [f. OF *chef* f. L *caput* head]

chief', a. & adv. (-er, -est, now rare). First by title (*C~ Justice* etc.); first in importance, influence, etc.; prominent, leading; (adv.) chiefly, especially, (*but ~ or ~est of all, forget not*). [prec. used in apposition]

chief'ly[1], a. Proper for a chief. [CHIEF[1] + -LY[1]]

chief'ly[2], adv. Above all; mainly but not exclusively. [CHIEF[2] + -LY[2]]

chief'tain (-tin), n. Military leader(poet.); captain of robbers; chief of Highland clan or uncivilized tribe. Hence ~CY, ~'ESS[1], ~-RY, ~'SHIP, (-tin-), nn. [f. OF *chevetaine* CAPTAIN]

chiff-chaff, n. Bird of Warbler family. [imit.]

chiffon (see Ap.), n. (Usu. pl.) adorn-ments of female dress; (sing.) thin gauze. [F, f. *chiffe* rag]

chiffonier' (sh-), n. Movable low cup-board with sideboard top. [F (prec. -IER)]

chignon (see Ap.), n. Mass of hair on pad at back of head. [F, f. 13th-c. *chaaignon* nape of neck = *chaînon* link (*chaîne* CHAIN)]

chig'oe, n. Tropical flea, burrowing into skin. [W.-Ind.]

chil'blain, n. Itching sore on hand, foot, etc., from exposure to cold. Hence ~ED a. [CHILL+BLAIN]

child, n. (pl. chil'dren). Unborn or new-born human being (pronoun *it,* or *he, she*); boy or girl (*from a* ~, from childhood on); childish person; (sl.) *this* ~, I, me; son or daughter (at any age) of (or with any one), offspring; descendant lit. or fig. or fol-lower or adherent of (~ *of God, of the devil;* ~*ren of Izaak Walton,* anglers; *fancy's* ~; ~ *of nature*); result of; (in arch. form *childe*) youth of noble birth (*Childe Harold, Roland*); *with* ~, preg-nant; ~'s-*play,* easy task; BURNT ~ *dreads fire;* ~-*bed, -birth,* parturition; ~'*wife,* very young wife. Hence ~'LESS a. ~'less-NESS n. [OE *cild* cf. Goth. *kilthei* womb]

child'ermas, n. Festival of Holy Inno-cents, 28th Dec. [OE *cildra* (prec.) of infants+*masse* MASS[1]]

child'hood, n. Child's state; time from birth to puberty; *second* ~, dotage. [-HOOD]

child'ish, a. Of, proper to, a child; puerile, improper for a grown person. Hence ~-LY[2] adv., ~NESS n. [-ISH[1]]

child'like, a. Having good qualities of child, as innocence, frankness, etc. [-LIKE]

child'ly, a. & adv. (poet.). Like a child. [mod. revival of obs. wd; -LY[1,2]]

chile, *chil'i. Var. of CHILLI.

chil'iad (k-), n. A thousand; a thousand years. [f. L f. Gk *khilias -ados* t. *khilioi* adj. a thousand, -AD(1)]

chil'iasm, chil'iast, (k-), nn. Doctrine of or belief in, believer in, the millennium. Hence **chilias'tic** a. [f. Gk *khiliasmos, -astēs* (prec. +endings used w. vbs in -*azō* cf. -ISM, -IST)]

chill¹, n. Cold sensation, lowered temperature of body, feverish shivering, (*catch a* ~; also of special part as *liver*~); unpleasant coldness of air, water, etc. (*take* ~ *off water or claret,* warm slightly); depressing influence (*cast a* ~ *over*); coldness of manner. [OE *cele* cogn. w. COLD; but the noun, after giving CHILL²,³, was dormant 1400-1600, & revived as deriv. of CHILL³]

chill², a. Unpleasantly cold to feel; feeling cold; unfeeling, unemotional, abstract. Hence ~NESS n. [prob. f. prec.]

chill³, v.t. & i. Make, become, cold; deaden, blast, with cold; depress, dispirit; harden (molten iron) by contact of cold (iron; colloq.) take the chill off (liquid); ~*ed beef* etc., beef etc. preserved at moderately low temperature in cold storage (as distinct from frozen meat). [prob. f. CHILL¹]

chill'i, -y, n. Dried pod of Capsicum (as relish, or made into cayenne). [Mex.]

chill'y¹, a. Rather cold to feel; feeling rather cold; sensitive to cold; not genial, cold-mannered. Hence ~INESS n. [CHILL¹ +-Y¹]

chil'ly² (-I-II), adv. (rare). In cold manner (lit. & fig.). [CHILL² +-LY²]

chil(o)-, cheil(o)-, (k-), comb. form of Gk *kheilos* lip, in zool. terms as *chilopod* (having feet serving as jaws).

Chil'tern Hun'dreds (-z), n. pl. *Apply for, accept, the* ~, resign seat in House of Commons. [a Crown manor, administration of which, being titular office under Crown, requires the member to vacate his or her seat]

chime¹, n. Set of attuned bells; series of sounds given by this; harmony, melody, rhythm, sing-song; agreement, correspondence. [ME *chymbe* f. L f. Gk *kumbalon* CYMBAL]

chime², v.i. & t. Make (bell) sound; ring chimes (of person or bells); ring chimes on (bells); show (hour) by chiming (also of hour, = sound); summon by bells *to;* repeat mechanically; be in rhyme, make to rhyme; be in agreement (*together, with,* or abs.); join *in,* express eager agreement. [as prec.]

chime³, chimb, (-m), n. Projecting rim at ends of cask. [ME *chimbe* cf. Du. *kim* edge]

chimer'a, -aer'a, (kĪ-), n. 1. Monster with lion's head, goat's body, & serpent's tail. 2. Bogy; thing of hybrid character; fanciful conception; whence **chimē'r-** ICAI a., **chimē'rically¹** adv., (kī-). [f. F *chimère* f. L f. Gk *khimaira* she-goat, chimera, (*khimaros* goat)]

chimēre', n. Bishop's robe. [= OF *chamarre* etym. dub.]

chim'ney, n. Flue carrying off smoke or steam of fire, furnace, engine, etc.; (also ~*stalk, -top*) part of flue above roof; glass tube providing draught for lamp-flame; natural vent, e.g. of volcano; (Mountaineering) narrow cleft by which cliff may be climbed; ~*corner,* warm seat within old-fashioned fire-place; ~*jack,* rotating cowl; ~*piece,* = MANTEL; ~*pot,* earthenware or metal pipe added to ~*top* (||~*pot hat,* tall silk hat); ~*stack,* united group of ~*stalks;* || ~*stalk,* see above, also = tall fireplace; ||~*swallow,* common swallow; ~*sweep,* man who sweeps ~*s;* ~*sweeper,* = ~*sweep,* also=jointed ~*cleaning* brush. [f. OF *cheminée* f. LL *caminata* (perh. *camera* fireplaced (chamber) f. L *caminus* oven, -ATE²]

chimpanzee', n. African ape resembling man. [native name in Angola]

chin, n. Front of lower jaw; *up to the* ~, ~*deep,* deeply immersed. Hence ~NED² (-nd) a. [OE *cin* cf. G. *kinn,* & Gk *geneion* chin, *genus* cheek]

Chin'a (a-), **chin'a,** n. & a. 1. (C~). From China (*C~ crape, C~* ASTER, etc.; *C~ orange,* common orange, orig. from China; *Chin'aman,* (derog. for) a Chinese; *China-town,* section of a town (esp. a seaport) in which the Chinese live as a colony). 2. (c~). (Made of) a fine semi-transparent earthenware, porcelain; things made of this; whence ~MAN'IA(0) nn.; ~*closet,* for keeping or displaying one's ~; ~*clay,* KAOLIN. [not native name; found in Skr. about 1st c.]

chinchill'a, n. Small S.-Amer. rodent; its soft grey fur. [Sp., dim. of *chinche* bug f. L *cīmex -icis* (from supposed smell)]

||**Chin(o)-Chin'** int. of greeting & farewell (Anglo-Chin.); also as n. & vb). [Chin. *ts'ing ts'ing*]

chine¹, n. Backbone; animal's backbone or part of it as joint; ridge, arête. [t. OF *eschine* perh. f. OHG *scina* splinter]

chine², n. Deep narrow ravine (now only in Isle of Wight & Hampshire). [OE *cinu* cf. Du. *keen* chap in skin]

Chinese' (-z), a. & n. (pl. the same). (Native, language) of China; ~ *lantern,* collapsible of paper used esp. in Illuminating; ~ *white,* a pigment, white oxide of zinc. [China+-ESE]

chink¹, n. Crevice; long narrow opening, slit, peep-hole. [f. 16th c.; excl. E.; etym. dub., perh. f. OHNE¹, which it has re-placed]

chink², n. & v.i. & t. 1. Sound as of glasses or coins striking together; (sl.) ready money. 2. vb. Make this sound; cause (coin etc.) to make it. [imit.]

Chink³, n. (sl.) A Chinese. [abbr.]

Chino-, comb. form of *China*. [-o-]

chintz, n. & a. (Of) cotton cloth fast-printed with particoloured pattern & usu. glazed. [earlier *chints* pl. f. Hind.; for sing. use cf. BAIZE]

chip¹, n. Thin piece cut from wood or broken from stone etc.; thin slice of potato, fruit, etc.; (pl., colloq.) potato--s fried (*fish & ~s*); wood split into strips for making hats etc. (~ *bonnet, basket*); *dry as a ~*, flavourless, uninteresting; ~ (*scion*) *of*, esp. ~ *of old block*, son resembling father; place in china etc. from which a ~ has been knocked off; (sl.) counter, piece of money; ~*-shot* (Golf), short lofted approach-shot on to putting-green. [f. foll.]

chip², v.t. & i. (-pp-). Cut (wood), break (stone, crockery etc.), at surface or edge; shape thus; cut or break (piece etc.) *off, from*; be susceptible to breakage at edge; carve (inscription); crack (egg-shell; esp. of chickens); (colloq.) banter (a person); (sl.) ~ *in*, interrupt; [dim. of CHOP², cf. *drip, drop, tip top*; cf. also E.Fris. *kippen* cut]

chip³, chip⁴, n., & v.t. (-pp-). Wrestling-trick; (v.b.) trip up. [cf. Du. *kippen* ensnare]

chip'muck, chip'-- ~ink, n. North-American squirrel. [prob. Amer.-Ind.]

Chipp'endale, n. A fine and solid style of furniture. [~, 18th-century cabinet-maker]

chipp'y, a. (sl.). Dry, uninteresting; parched & queasy after drunkenness etc.; irritable. Hence ~INESS n.

Chips, n. (naut. sl.). Ship's carpenter. [pl. of CHIP¹, cf. BUTTONS]

chir(o)-, cheir(o)-, comb. form of Gk *kheir* hand, as *chirog'RAPHY* hand-writing, *chir'OMANCY* palmistry. [f. F *chirographe* f. L f. Gk *kheirographon*]

chiro'podist, chirop'ody, (kĭr-), n. Treater, treatment, of feet, toe-nails, corns, bunions, etc. [prob. f. CHIRO-, Gk *pous podos* foot, -IST(3); but there is Gk *kheiropodistēs* with chapped feet (*kheiras* chap f. *kheir* hand)]

chiroprac'tic (kīr-), n. Manipulation of spinal column as method of curing disease. Hence ~OR²n, one who prac-tises—ic. [f. CHIRO-+ Gk *praktikos* (*prassō* do, see -IC)]

chirp, v.i. & t. & n. (Make) short sharp note (as) of small bird; utter (song), express (joy etc.), thus; talk merrily; speak feebly. [imit.; from 15th c., dis-placing earlier *chirk* (OE *cearcian* creak), *cherk, chirk*]

chirp'y, a. Lively, cheerful. Hence ~INESS n. [prec., -Y¹]

chirr, v.i., & n. (Make) prolonged trilling sound (as) of grasshopper. [imit.]

chi'rrup, v.i., & n. (Make) series of chirps, twitterings; (make) imitative chirping to baby etc.; (sl.) act as paid applauder at theatre etc., whence ~ER¹ n. [form of CHIRP]

chis'el (-zl), n., & v.t. (-ll-). (Cut, shape, with) steel-edged tool with square bevelled end for shaping wood, stone, or metal (*cold ~*, all of steel or iron for trimming cold iron; ~*led features etc.* clear-cut); *the ~*, sculptor's ~, (art of) sculpture; (sl.) defraud, unfair treatment. [ONF. dim. of L -*cisum* neut. p.p. of *-cidere* (*caedere* cut)]

chit¹, n. Young child; young, small, or slender woman (depreciatingly, esp. *of a ~ girl*). [earlier = whelp; var. of *kit*, KITTEN]

chit², chit'ty, n. (orig. Anglo-Ind.). Note or written paper, esp. character given to servant; note of sum owed for drink etc.; ~*-system* (of giving vouchers in payment instead of cash down). [f. Hind. *chitthi* f. Skr. *chitra* mark]

chit'al (-ēt-), n. The Indian spotted deer. [Hind.]

chit'-chat, n. Light conversation; sub-jects of it, gossip. [redupl. of CHAT¹]

chit'in (kī-), n. Substance forming horny cover of beetles & crustaceans. Hence ~OUS a. [should be *chitine*; f. F *chitine* f. Gk *khitōn -ōnos* tunic +-IN]

chit'terling, n. (usu. pl.). Smaller in-testines of beasts, esp. as cooked for food. [etym. dub.; cf. G *kuttleln*]

chitt'y. See CHIT².

chiv'alrous, (poet. etc.) **chiv'alric** (*also* -āl-), (see foll.), a. Of, as of, the Age of Chivalry; of, as of the ideal knight, gallant, honourable, courteous, disinter-ested; quixotic. Hence chiv'alrously² adv. [f. OF *chevalerous* (CHEVALIER, -OUS)]

chiv'alry (formerly ch-; now usu. sh-, as though a recent F importation), n. Horse-men, cavalry, (arch.); gallant gentlemen; knightly skill (arch.); medieval knightly system with its religious, moral, & social code; ideal knight's characteristics; devotion to service of women; inclination to defend weaker party; *flower of ~*, pattern knight, élite of nation's soldiers. [f. OF *chevalerie* f. L *caballarius* CAVALIER, -ERY]

chive, cive (s-), n. Small herb allied to onion & leek. [F (*cive*) f. L *cepa* onion]

chiv'vy. See CHEVY.

chlor- (kl-), ~o-, [= CHLORO-¹·², used before vowel, consonant, resp.]

chlor'al (kl-), n. ~ *hydrate* or ~, a hyp-notic & anaesthetic. Hence ~IZE(6) v.t. [pop. misuse of *chloral*.

strictly a chem. substance first got by action of *chlorine* on *al(cohol)*, whence the name]

chlŏr′ide (kī-), n. (Chem.) compound of chlorine (-IDE); (pop.) kinds of bleaching agent; salt not true ~s, as ~ of *lime*, *soda*, *potash*. [CHLOR-², -IDE]

chlŏr′ināte (kī-), v.t. Impregnate with chlorine. Hence ~ATION n., treatment with chlorine (esp. in the extraction of gold from certain ores). [CHLORINE]

chlŏr′ine (kī-), n. (chem.). Non-metallic element, a yellowish-green heavy ill-smelling gas. [f. Gk *khlōros* green + -INE⁶]

chlŏro-¹, comb. form in bot. & mineral, terms of Gk *khlōros* green.

chlŏro-², comb. form in chem. terms of CHLORINE. Hence **chlŏr′ATE**²(3) n., **chlŏr′IC**(2), **chlŏr′OUS**(chem.) aa...(kī-).

chlŏr′odyne (kī-), n. Patent medicine, narcotic & anodyne. [foll. + Gk *odunē* pain]

chlŏr′ofŏrm (kī-), n., & v.t. **1.** Anaesthetic, thin colourless liquid whose inhaled vapour produces insensibility. **2.** v.t. Treat (person) with, render insensible by, ~, whence ~IST (1) n.; soak (thing) in ~. [f. F *chloroforme* f. CHLORO-² + *form(yl)* see FORMIC]

chlŏr′ophyll (kī-), n. Colouring-matter of green parts of plants. [F CHLORO-¹*phylle* f. Gk *phullon* leaf]

chlŏr′os′is (kī-), n. Green sickness, anaemic disease of young women, with greenish complexion; (Bot.) blanching of green parts, or turning green of petals etc. Hence ~OT′IC a. [CHLOR-¹, -OSIS]

chŏck¹, n. Block of wood, esp. wedge for stopping motion of cask or wheel, also in various senses on ship esp. that of wedges supporting boat on deck; (Turning; earlier form of CHUCK⁴. [perh. f. ONF *choque* log]

chŏck², v.t., & adv. Make fast with chocks; place (boat) on chocks; ~ *up*, wedge in tightly, encumber (room etc.) with furniture etc.; (adv.) closely, tightly, close up; ~*a-block*, jammed together, crammed *with*, chock-full of (orig. naut., of two blocks brought close together in a tackle); ~*full*, stuffed. [f. prec.; the var. *choke-full* for ~*full* is prob. an etym. guess & misrepresents pronunc.]

chŏc′olate, n. & a. (Cake) of cacao-seed paste; drink of this in hot milk or water; dark brown (n. & a.); ~ *cream*, sweetmeat of ~ enclosing sweet paste. [f. F *chocolat* f. Mex. *chocolatl* etym. dub. (not f. *cacao* or *cocoa*)]

chŏc′taw, n. (skating). Step from either edge to edge on other foot in opposite direction. [fancy name, cf. MOHAWK]

choice¹, n. Choosing, selection, (*make of*, select; *take* one's ~, decide between possibilities; *the girl of* one's ~; *for* ~, by preference, if one must select); power, right, faculty, of choosing (*at* ~, at

pleasure; *have* one's ~; *have no* ~, not care which; *Hobson's* ~, to take or leave the one offer); élite, flower, of.; variety to choose from; thing or person chosen; alternative (*have no* ~ *but*). [f. OF *chois* f. *choisir* choose f. Rom. *causire* f. Teut. (Goth. *kausjan* test)]

choice², a. Of picked quality, exquisite; carefully chosen, appropriate. Hence ~LY²(sī-) adv., ~NESS (-sn-) n. [perh. mixture of prec. w. obs. *chis* (OE *cīs* etym. dub.) fastidious]

choir (kwīr), n., & v.t. & i. **1.** Band of singers performing or leading in musical parts of church service; chancel of cathedral, minster, or large church; choral society, company of singers (also of birds, angels, etc.); band of dancers; ~*organ* (corruption of *chair*~), softest of three parts (*great*, *swell*, ~, *organ*) making up large compound organ, with lowest of three key-boards. **2.** v.b. Sing in chorus (intr., or with *strain*, *hymn*, etc., as obj.). [ME *quere* f. OF *cuer* f. L f. Gk *khoros* song & dance]

chōke¹, v.t. & i., & n. Stop breath of, suffocate, temporarily or finally, by squeezing throat from without, blocking it up within, or (of water, smoke, etc.) being unbreathable; (fig., of emotion) paralyse (~*pear*, fact, reproof, etc., hard to swallow); suppress (feelings); block up wholly or partly (tube by narrowing part of it; as n., the narrowed part, whence ~*bore*, of gun with bore narrowing towards muzzle; also of channel with sand, stones, etc., *stones* or ~ *up down*, swallow (food), conceal (emotion), with difficulty; ~ *off*, make (person) relinquish an attempt; ~*damp*, carbonic acid gas in mines, wells etc.; *choking coil* (Electr.), (also ~) coil of low resistance used to modify an alternating-current circuit. [OE *ācēocian* etym. dub.]

chōke², n. Centre part of artichoke. [prob. confusion of ending w. prec.]

chōk′er, n. In vbl senses: esp. clerical or stand-up collar; *white* ~, white tie (sl.). [-ER¹]

chŏk′ra, n. (Anglo-Ind.). Boy (esp. one employed as domestic servant). [Hind. *chhokra*]

‖ **chōk′y̆**, n. (orig. Anglo-Ind., sl.). Prison, lock-up. [Hind. *chaukī* shed]

chŏl′(ō)- (k-), comb. form in med. & chem. wds of Gk *kholē* gall, bile.

chŏl′er (kŏ-), n. (Hist.) one of the four HUMOURS, bile; (poet., arch.) anger, irascibility. [ME & OF *colre* f. L f. Gk *kholera* cholera perh. f. *kholē* bile]

chŏl′era (kŏ-), n. (Also *English*, *bilious*, *summer*, ~, or in L ~ *nostras* = of our

country billious summer & autumn disorder with diarrhoea & vomiting; (also *Asiatic*, *epidemic*, *malignant*, ~) non-billious often fatal disease endemic in India & epidemic in Europe; *chicken* ~, infectious disease of fowls; ~*-belt*, flannel or silk waistband worn as preventive. Hence **choleră′ic** (kŏ-) a. [L, in orig. Gk sense (prec.) of summer ~]

chol′eric (kŏ-), a. Irascible; angry. [f. F ~ *choléríque* f. L f. Gk *kholerikos* (CHOLER, -IC)]

chol′erine (kŏ-; also -ēn), n. Summer cholera; diarrhoea often prevalent at same time as Asiatic cholera. [F (-ĕ-), f cholera CHOLERA]

chol′iamb (kŏ-), n. = SCAZON. Hence ~ic (-ăm⁴) a. [f. L f. Gk *kholiambos* (*kholos* lame, *iambos* IAMBUS)]

chondri-, -o-, (kŏ-), comb. form of Gk *khondros*, in Med. & Physiol.-cartilage. -z-]

choose (-z), v.t. & i. (*chose*, *chosen*, pr. -z-). Select out of greater number; (Theol., esp. in p.p.) destine to be saved; decide (*to do* one thing rather than another); think fit, be determined, *to do*; make choice *between*; *cannot* ~ *but*, must, have to, (arch.); (with compl.) select as (*was chosen king*); (with compl.) *pick &* ~, be fastidious; *nothing to* ~ *between them*, of things nearly equal. Hence **choŏs′ER¹** (-z) n., **choŏs′(e)Y²** (-z-) a., (sl.), fastidious. [OE *cēosan* cf. G *kiesen*]

chop¹, v.t. & i. (-pp-). Cut by a blow, usu. with axe (~ *up*, ~ *into* small pieces, mince; often ~ *off*, *away*, *down*); deliver such blow *at*; make one′s way by such blows *through*; mince (esp. in p.p.); (fig.) cut (words etc.) short or into distinct parts; ~ *in*, intervene in talk; ~ *back*, reverse one′s direction suddenly, double; (of strata) ~ *up*, *out*, come to surface. [var. of CHAP¹ cf. Du & G *koppen*]

chop², n. Cutting stroke with axe etc.; thick slice of meat, esp. mutton or pork, usu. including rib (~*-house*, cheap restaurant); broken surface of water usu. due to action of wind against tide, so ~**p′y¹** [-y¹] a. [f. prec.]

chop³. See CHAP².

chop⁴, v.t. & i. (-pp-), & n. ~ *& change* (emphatic for *change*, usu. intr.), vacillate, be inconstant, (n. ~*s & changes*, variations); ~ *round*, *about*, (esp. of wind) change direction suddenly; ~ *logic*, bandy arguments. Hence ~**p′y¹** [-y¹] a. [etym. dub., but cf. CHOP¹ in some senses]

chop⁵, n. (India, China) seal, licence, passport, permit; (China) trade-mark, a brand of goods; (Anglo-Ind. & colloq.) first, second, ~, first, second, -class. [f. Hind. *chhăp* stamp]

chop-chop′, adv. & int. (Pidgin-Eng.). Quick, quickly. [f. Chin. *k′wai-k′wai*]

chopp′er, n. One who chops; large-bladed short axe; butcher′s cleaver. [CHOP¹+-ER¹]

chop′stick, n. Small slip of ivory etc. of which two held in one hand are used by Chinese as fork. [transl. of Chin. *k′wai-tsze* nimble ones f. Chin. *chop* quick +STICK]

chop-su′ey, n. Dish of fried or stewed meat or chicken flavoured with sesame oil & served with rice, onions, etc. (in Chinese restaurant). [Chin. = mixed bits]

chŏr′al¹ (k-), a. Of, sung by, choir (~ *service*, with canticles, anthems, etc., so sung; *full* ~ *service*, with versicles & responses also sung); of, with, chorus. Hence ~LY² adv. [f. med. L *choralis* (CHORUS, -AL)]

choral(e)² (korahl′), n. (Metrical hymn to) simple tune usu. sung in unison, orig. in German reformed church. [G (-), e added merely to suggest foreign accent as in *morale*, *locale*]

chord¹ (k-), n. String of harp etc. (poet.; also fig., as *touch the right* ~, appeal skilfully to emotion); (Physiol.) structure resembling string, as *vocal* ~, *spinal* ~, (also *cord*); (Math.) straight line joining ends of arc. [16th-c. correction of CORD¹ after L f. Gk *khordē*]

chŏrd² (k-), n. (Mus.) group of notes sounded together, combined according to some harmonic system (*common* ~, any note with its major or minor third, perfect fifth, & octave; *break* or *spread* ~, play its notes successively); harmonious combination of colours. [earlier *cord* for ACCORD² later confused w. prec.]

chŏr′dal (k-), a. Of, like, etc., CHORD¹·².

chore, n. & v.i. = CHARE.

chore′a (k-), n. St. Vitus′s dance. [L f. Gk *khoreia*]

choree′ (k-), n. = TROCHEE. [f. L f. Gk *khoreios* of dance]

cho′regraph etc. See CHOREOGRAPH etc.

chore′ic (k-), a. Of, having, chorea; marked by, chorees. [-IC]

cho′reograph (kŏ-; -ahf), n. Designer of ballet. So **choreŏg′RAPHER**, **choreŏg′RAPHY**, nn., **choreograph′ic** a., (kŏ-). [f. Gk *khoreia* dancing (*khoros* dancing-company)+-GRAPH]

chori(s)- (-kŏ-), pref. f. Gk *khōrĭs* apart, used in bot. terms, as *choripetalous* with separate petals.

cho′riamb′us (kŏ-; -ahmb), n. Metrical foot (-∪∪-). Hence **choriăm′bus** (kŏ-), a. [f. L f. Gk *khoriambos* (CHORUS, IAMB]

chŏr′ic (k-), a. Of, like, chorus in Greek play. [f. Gk *khorikos* (CHORUS, -IC]

chŏr′ion (k-), n. Outer membrane of foetus. [f. med. L *chorisma* (CHORUS, -IC) f. Gk *khorion*]

chŏr′ister (kŏ-), n. Member of choir, esp. choir-boy (also fig. of angels, birds). [f. L *choraista* (CHOIR, -ISTER)]

choreŏg′raphy (kŏ-), n. Describing, de-

scription, of districts (more limited than *geography*, less than *topography*). Hence or cogn. **chorŏg'rapher** n., **chorographic'al** a., (kō-). [f. F *chorographie* f. Gk *khōrographia* (*khōra* land, -GRAPHY)]

chŏr'oid (k-), a. & n. Like chorion in shape or vascularity, esp. ~ *coat* (or ~ as noun), membrane lining eye-ball. [f. Gk *khoroeidēs* wrong reading in Gk MSS. for *khorioeidēs* (CHORION, -OID)]

chorŏl'ogy (kō-), n. Local distribution of species etc. Hence **chorolŏg'ICAL** a. [f. Gk *khōra* land + -LOGY]

chŏr'tle, v.i. & n. (Utter) loud chuckle. [invented by L. Carroll; perh. f. *chuckle, snort*]

chŏr'us (k-), n., & v.t. & i. **1.** (Gk Ant.) band of dancers & singers in religious ceremonies & dramatic performances (also representing interested spectators in play; so in some Eng. plays): (one of) their utterances. **2.** Personage speaking prologue & commenting on action in Elizabethan plays. **3.** Band of singers; choir: thing sung by many at once; any simultaneous utterance of many (*in* ~, all speaking etc. together). **4.** (Mus.) composition in several (oftenest four) parts each sung by several voices; refrain of song in which audience joins. **5.** vb. Sing, speak, say, in ~. [L, f. Gk *khoros*]

chose jugée (see Ap.), n. Thing it is idle to discuss, as already settled. [F]

chose(n). See CHOOSE.

chŏt'a haz(i)ri (nahz'ri), n. (Anglo-Ind.). Light early breakfast. [Hind. (*chh-*) = little breakfast]

chou (shōō), n. Rosette or ornamental knot of ribbon, chiffon, etc., on woman's hat or dress. [F, f. L *caulis* cabbage]

chough (chŭf), n. Red-legged crow. [cf. Du. *kauw*, OF *choue*]

chow-chow, n. Chinese preserve of orange-peel, ginger, etc. [Chin.]

chow'der, n. Newfoundland & New England dish, stew of fresh fish or clams with bacon, onions, biscuit, etc. [f. F *chaudière* pot f. L *caldaria* (*calidus* hot, -ARY¹)]

Chow, a. & n. (Austral. sl.). Chinese (a. & n.); dog of a Chinese breed.

chrē'matis'tic (k-), a. Of money-making, economic. Hence ~ICS n. [f. Gk *khrēmatistikos* (*khrēmatizō* traffic f. *khrēmata* pl. money f. *khraomai* use), see -IST, -IC]

chrēstŏm'athy (k-), n. Collection of choice passages. [f. Gk *khrēstomatheia* (*khrēstos* good, *math*- st. of *manthanō* learn)]

chri'sm (k-), n. Consecrated oil, unguent, anointing, esp. in sacred rites. [OE *crisma* f. L f. Gk *khrisma* (*khriō* anoint, -M); cf. CREAM]

chris'om (k-), n. (hist.). Child's white robe at baptism, used as shroud if it died within a month; ~*child*, in its first month. [var. of prec., perh. orig. a head-cloth to keep chrism from being rubbed off]

Christ (k-), n. Messiah or Lord's anointed of Jewish prophecy; (title, now treated as name, given to) Jesus as fulfilling this; divine ruler, saviour, inspirer, (esp. *the* or *a* ~); *the* ~*child*, ~ as a child. Hence ~'HOOD n., ~'LESS, ~'LIKE, ~'LY¹, aa., ~'lessNESS, ~'likeNESS (-kn-), nn., ~'WARD(S) adv. [OE *crist* f. L f. Gk *khristos* anointed one (*khriō* anoint) transl. of Heb. see MESSIAH]

Christ-cross-row, criss-, (kris'kraws-rō), n. (arch.). The alphabet. [*Christ's cross*, a cross before alphabet in horn-books, + ROW (of letters)]

christen (kri'sn), v.t. & i. Admit as Christian by baptism; administer baptism; give name to (person at baptism, also or as nickname; ~ *him*, ~ *him John*; also ships, bells, etc., with analogous ceremony). [OE *cristnian* make Christian (*cristen* f. WG *cristān* f. L CHRISTIANUS)]

Christendom (kri'sn-), n. Christians; Christian countries. [f. *cristen* adj., see prec., -DOM]

Christian (kris'tyan), a. & n. (Person) believing in, professing, or belonging to, the religion of Christ (also as adj. of communities); of Christ or his religion; (person) showing character consistent with Christ's teaching, of genuine piety, Christ-like, (also as adj. of conduct, feelings, communities, etc.); human (person) as opposed to *brute*, *brutal*; (sl.) civilized, decent, (person); ~ *burial* (with the ceremonies of the church); ~ *name*, given at baptism; ~ *era*, reckoned from supposed birth of Christ; ~ *Science, Scientist*, (adherent of) a system of combating disease etc. without medical treatment by mental effect of patient's ~ faith. Hence or cogn. ~IZE (2, 3) v.t. & t., ~izA'TION n., ~LIKE a., ~LY¹,² a. & adv. [f. L *Christianus* (CHRIST, -T-, -AN)]

Christia'nia (k-; -ahn-), n. A swing in skiing, used to stop short (abbr. **Chris'tie**). [~ in Norway (now Oslo)]

Christian'ity (k-), n. The Christian faith, doctrines of Christ & his apostles; a Christian religious system; being a Christian, Christian quality or character. [f. L *Christianitas* (as prec., -TY)]

Chris'tie (kris'tiz), n. A sale-room in London esp. for art sales.

Christmas (kris'm-), n. (abbr. *Xmas*). (Also ~*day*) festival of Christ's birth, 25th Dec., devoted esp. to family reunion & merrymaking, & a quarter-day (*Father* ~, personification of family festivity); (also ~*tide*) week or more beginning 24th Dec. (~ *eve*); (attrib.) appropriate to ~, as ~ *book*, *card* (of greeting by post), *member* (of magazine), *present*, *pudding*;

‖ ~box (cf. BOXING-DAY), money given at ~ to postman etc. in general acknow-ledgement of indefinite or continuous services; ~tree, small tree set up in room & hung with candles, presents, etc.; ~ rose, white-flowered hellebore bloom-ing Dec.–Feb. Hence ~Y[2] a. [OE *Cristes mæsse* (MASS[1])]

Christo- (k-), comb. form of L *Christus* or Gk *Khristos* CHRIST, as ~phany (-ŏf-), manifestation of Christ. Hence Christo-L'ATRY, Christoman'IAC (-nī-), Christó-L'OGY, Christó-LOGICAL a.

Chris'ty min'strels (k-; -z), n. pl. Negro-song troupe with blacked faces. [inven-tor's name]

chromat'ic (k-), a. 1. Of, produced by, full of bright, colour (~ *printing*, from blocks inked with various colours; ~s, notes not included in diatonic scale; ~ *scale*, proceeding by semitones; ~ *sense* of colour). 2. (Mus.) of, having, notes not included in diatonic scale; ~ *scale*, proceeding by semitones; ~ *interval*, interval between note & its flat or sharp. Hence chromat'ICALLY adv. [f. Gk *khrōmatikos* (*khrōma -atos* colour, -IC)]

chrom'atin (k-), n. (biol.). Tissue that can be stained. [as CHROMO-+-IN]

chrom'ato-, chrom'o-, (k-), comb. forms of Gk *khrōma -atos* colour, as in *chroma-topsy*, abnormally coloured vision, *chromo-photograph(y)*, *photograph(y)* in the natural colours, *chromosphere*, red gaseous envelope of sun.

chrom'atrope (k-), n. Lantern slide of two circular disks, one rotating in front of other, giving kaleidoscopic movement of colours. [irreg. f. prec. + Gk -*tropos* -turning (*trepō*)]

chrōme (k-), n. (Also ~ *yellow*) yellow pigment & colour got from chromate of lead; ~ *green, orange, red*, pigments from other compounds of chromium. [F, orig. name of chromium, f. Gk *khrōma* colour]

chrŏm'ic (k-), a. Of chromium. [prec. +-IC]

chrŏm'ium (k-), n. (chem.). Metallic ele-ment. Hence chrŏm'ATE[3] n. [CHROME

chromo-[1], comb. form of prec.

chromo-[2]. See CHROMATO-.

chrŏm'ograph (k-; -ahf), n., & v.t. (Reproduce with) gelatine copying apparatus in which aniline dye is used for ink. [CHROMO-[2] -GRAPH]

chrōmolith'ograph (-ahf), **chrŏm'ō** (pl. -os), n. Picture printed in colours from stone. So chromolithŏg'RAPHER, chromolithŏG'RAPHY n., chrŏm'oli'-thograph'IC a. [CHROMO-[2]+LITHOGRAPH]

chrŏm'osome (k-), n. [CHROMO-[2] sōma body)] rods or threads into which the chromatin of the cell-nucleus is transformed before cell-division occurs. [f. G *chromosom* (CHROMO-+Gk *sōma* body)]

chrŏn'ic (k-), a. Lingering, lasting, in-veterate, (of disease, cf. ACUTE; ~ *invalid* with ~ *complaint*; also of other states as ~ *doubt, rebellion*); ‖ (vulg.) bad, intense, severe. Hence chrŏn'ICALLY adv., chronic'ITY n. [f. F *chronique* f. L f. Gk *khronikos* (*khronos* time, -IC)]

chrŏn'icle (k-), n., & v.t. (Enter, relate, in a) continuous register of events in order of time; *Chronicles*, two books of O.T.; ~ narrative, account; C~, newspaper name. Hence chrŏn'ICLER n. [f. OF *cronique* f. med. L *cronica -æ* f. L f. Gk *khronika* neut. pl., see prec.]

chroniqúe scandaleúse (see Ap.), n. Body of scandalous gossip current at any time & place. [F]

chrŏn'ogram (k-), n. Phrase etc. of which the Roman-numeral letters added give a date, as LorD haVe MerCIe Vpon Vs = 50+500+5+1000+100+1+5+5 = 1666. Hence chronogrammat'ic a. [f. Gk *khronos* time + GRAM- -*matic* after Gk *grammatikos* adj. f. *gramma*]

chrŏn'ograph (k-; -ahf), n. Instrument recording time with extreme accuracy; stop-watch. Hence chrŏnoGRAPH'IC a. [as prec. + GRAPH]

chronol'ogY(k-), n. Science of computing dates; arrangement of events with dates, table or treatise displaying this. Hence chronolŏG'ICAL a., chronolŏg'ICALLY adv., ~ÓL'OGIZE(3) v.t. [as prec. +-LOGY]

chronŏm'eter (k-), n. Time-measuring instrument, esp. one with extreme pro-vision against disturbance by tempera-ture, used for fixing longitude at sea, etc. [as prec. + -METER]

chronŏm'etry (k-), n. Scientific time-measurement. So chronomÉT'RIC(AL) aa., -MÉT'RICALLY[2] adv. [as prec. + -METRY]

chrŏn'opher (k-), n. Apparatus for dis-tributing electric time-signals. [as prec. + Gk -*phoros* -bearing (*pherō* bear)]

chrŏn'oscope (k-), n. Apparatus measur-ing velocity of projectiles. [as prec. + -SCOPE]

chrys- (k-), comb. form of Gk *khrūsos* gold, = yellow in chem. & mineral. wds, of gold, golden, yellow, etc., in general wds.

chrys'alïs, -ïd, (k-), n. (pl. -ïses, -ïds, chrysál'idës). Form taken by insect in the torpid stage of passive development between larva (caterpillar etc.) & imago (butterfly etc.); case then enclosing it; (fig.) preparatory or transition state. [f. L f. Gk *khrūsallis -idos* lit. golden thing, see prec.]

chrysán'themum (k-), n. (Bot.) genus including Corn Marigold; (Gardening) cultivated varieties of this brought from Japan & blooming in Nov. & Dec.; *land of the ~*, Japan. [f. L f. Gk *khrūsanthe-mon* (CHRYS- -*anthemon* flower)]

chrysélephan'tine (k-), a. Overlaid with gold & ivory as by ancient Greek sculp-

tors. [f. Gk khruselephantinos (CHRYS-, ELEPHANT, -INE²)]

chrýso- (k-). = CHRYS-.

chrýsobé'ryl (k-), n. Yellowish-green gem. [f. L f. Gk khrusobērullos (CHRYSO-, BERYL)]

chrýs'olite (k-), n. (Formerly) green gem of various kinds; (now) olivine. [f. OF crisolite f. L f. Gk khrusolithos (CHRYSO-, lithos stone)]

chrýs'opráse (k-; -z), n. (N.T.) prob. a golden-green variety of beryl; (now) apple-green variety of chalcedony. [f. OF crisopace f. L f. Gk khrusoprasos (CHRYSO-, prason leek)]

chub, n. Thick coarse-fleshed river fish of the carp family, dusky green above. [ME chubbe, etym. dub.]

chŭbb'ȳ, a. Round-faced, plump. Hence ~INESS n. [CHUB+-Y²]

chŭck¹, int., n., & v.i. (Make) call of fowl or person calling fowls or urging horse. [imit.]

chŭck², n. Term of endearment. Hence ~Y³ n. [prob. var. of CHICK]

chŭck³, v.t., & n. Jerk under the chin (n. & v.); fling, throw, (n. & v.) with contempt, carelessness, ease, (the ~, sl. dismissal, as give one the ~; ~ away, waste, lose (chance etc.); ~ up the sponge, give up contest or attempt; ~ out, expel (troublesome person) from meeting, music-hall, etc., whence ||~ER-out n.; (sl.) ~ it, cease; ~-farthing, kind of quoit game with coins, also pitch and toss. [in 16th c. chock, perh. f. F choc, choquer]

chŭck⁴, n. Contrivance in lathe & the like for holding work to be operated on; (vb) fix (wood etc.) to this. [var. of CHOCK¹]

chŭck⁵, n. (sl.) Food, grub; ~-wagon, provision-cart accompanying pioneers etc. [?]

chŭc'kle, v.i., & n. (Indulge in) suppressed laughter, laugh with closed mouth; (show) signs of glee; exult over; (make) hen's call. [imit. & cf. CHUCK¹, -LE³]

chŭc'kle-head (-hĕd), n. Dolt(ish); stupid (fellow). [f. obs. chuckle adj. hulking cf. CHUCK¹, CHOCK¹]

chŭdd'ar, n. (Anglo-Ind.). Large sheet, worn as shawl or head-covering by Indian women. [Hind. chadar]

chŭg, n. Characteristic sound of oil-engine or small petrol-engine when running slowly (also as v.i., esp. of exhaust gases). [imit.]

chŭkk'er, n. (polo). Each of the periods into which the game is divided. [Hind. chakar]

chŭm, v.i. (-mm-), & n. 1. Occupy rooms together, whence ~m'ERY(3) n.; be intimate; ~ up (colloq., form intimacy (with). 2. n. Familiar friend (esp. now among boys); (Australia) new ~, recent immigrant, greenhorn. [from 1684; etym. dub.]

chŭmp, n. Short thick lump of wood; || thick end, esp. of loin of mutton (so ~ chop); (colloq.) head, || esp. off one's ~, mad with excitement etc.; (sl.) fool, blockhead. [mod. wd perh. on chop & lump]

chŭnk, n. (colloq.). Thick lump cut off (wood, bread, cheese, etc.). [prob. var. of CHUCK⁴]

chupătt'ȳ, n. (Anglo-Ind.). Small flat cake of coarse unleavened bread. [Hind. chapdti]

chŭrch¹, n. Building for public Christian worship, || esp. according to established religion of country; all Christians (~ militant, Christians on earth warring against evil); an organized Christian society of any time (primitive C~), place (C~ of Scotland), or distinguishing principle (reformed C~); C~ of England, English or Anglican C~, English branch of Western or Latin Church rejecting Pope's supremacy since reformation; Established C~, recognized by State, as C~ of England, Scotland; organization, clergy & other officers, of a religious society or corporation; clerical profession (go into the C~, take holy orders); HIGH, LOW¹, BROAD, C~, parties with different views of doctrine & discipline, whence ~'man, ~'ISM(3), nn.; public worship (go to, after, ~; ~-time; ~-goer, -going); C~ Army, C.E. mission to working classes founded by Preb. Carlile in 1882; ~'man, ~'woman, ~'manship, member, membership, of ~; poor as a ~ mouse, of poor person; ||~-rate, levied by vestry for maintenance of parish ~ & its services; ~ service, public worship, || book with Common Prayer, proper lessons, etc.; ~-text, black letter in monumental inscriptions; ~-warden, elected lay representative of parish (usu. one of two, elected one by incumbent, one by parishioners); ~-yard, enclosed ground in which ~ stands, sometimes used for burial (||~-yard cough, heralding death; fat ~-yard, many deaths). Hence ~'LESS a., ~'WARD(S) adv. [OE circe f. WG kirika f. LG kuriakon (perh. dōma) Lord's (house) f. kurios lord. -AC]

chŭrch², v.t. Bring (woman) to church to have thanks offered for delivery of child. [f. prec.]

chŭrch'lȳ, a. Obtrusively or intolerantly devoted to church or opposed to dissent. Hence ~IFY v.t., ~INESS n. [-Y²]

chŭrl, n. Person of low birth (gentleman or ~); peasant, boor; ill-bred fellow; cross-grained or niggardly person, whence ~'ISH¹ a., ~'ishIY² adv., ~'ishNESS n. [OE ceorl f. WG kerl man]

chŭrn, n., v.t. (Agitate milk or cream, produce butter, in) butter-making

machine; work this machine; stir (liquid) about, make it froth; (of sea etc.) wash to and fro, foam, seethe; ~dash(er), ~staff, appliance for agitating milk in ~; a ~ing, amount of butter made at once. [OE cyrin com- Teut. cf. Du. karn]

churr, v.i., & n. (Make) deep trill as of night-jar. [imit., cf. chirr]

chut, int. of impatience. [imit.]

chute (shoot), n. Smooth rapid descent of water over slope; sloping channel, slide, with or without water, for conveying things to lower level (also shoot); slope for shooting rubbish down; toboggan-slide. [mixture of F chute=It. caduta (L cadere fall) & shoot]

chut'ney (pl. ~s), n. Hot Indian condiment of fruits, chillies, etc. [f. Hind. chatni]

chyle (kil), n. White milky fluid formed by action of pancreatic juice & bile on chyme. [F, f. L f. Gk khūlos juice (khu- pour)]

chylo- (-ki-), comb. form of Gk khūlos

chyme (kim), n. Food converted by gastric secretion into acid pulp. [f. L f. Gk khūmos juice (khu- pour); khūmos & khūlos, synonyms, were differentiated by Galen]

chym'istry). Old spelling of CHEMIST(RY).

chymo- (ki-), comb. form of Gk khūmos so shaped]

cicad'a, cica'la, ciga'la, (-ah-), n. Transparent-winged shrill-chirping insect. [(-cada It.), f. L cicada, f. F (-gale) f. L f. (-dal)]

cibor'ium, n. (Archit.) canopy, canopied shrine; receptacle for reservation of Eucharist, shaped like shrine, or cup with arched cover. [f. med. L f. Gk kibōrion seed-vessel of water-lily, cup

cica'trice, cica'trix, n. (-ix, pl. -ices, L form in scientific use). Scar of healed wound; scar on tree bark; (Bot.) mark left by fall of leaf etc., hilum of seed. Hence **cicatri'cial** (-shl), **cica'tricose,** aa. [F (-ice), f. L cicatricem nom. -ix]

cica'tricule, n. (Biol.) germ of chick, round white spot on yolk, tread; (Bot.) = prec. [f. L cicatricula (prec., -ULE)]

cic'atrize, v.t. & i. Heal, skin over, (t. & i.); mark with scars. Hence ~A'TION n. [f. F cicatriser f. L cicatricare (CICATRICE)]

cic'ely, n. Kinds of umbelliferous plant (Sweet, Wild, Rough, C~). [f. L f. Gk seselis SESELI w. assim. to the woman's name (=Cecilia)]

cicerone (chiche-), n. (pl. -oni pr. -ōnē), & v.t. (Conduct traveller etc. as) guide who understands & explains antiquities etc. [It., f. L Ciceronem (next)]

Cicero'nian, a. & n. Eloquent, classical, or rhythmical, as Cicero's style; (n.)

ci'der, n. Fermented drink from apple-juice; ~-cup, for squeezing juice from apples. [f. OF sidre f. LL f. Gk sikera f. Heb. shekar strong drink (shakar drink deeply)]

ci-devant (see Ap.), a. or adv. Former(ly, that has been (with the earlier name or state). [F]

cigala. See CICADA.

cigar', n. Roll of tobacco-leaf for smoking; ~-shaped, cylindrical with pointed end(s); ~-holder, mouthpiece holding ~. [f. Sp. cigarro perh. f. cigarra cicada (of similar shape)]

cigarette', n. Small cylinder of cut tobacco or of narcotic or medicated substance rolled in paper for smoking. [dim. of prec.]

cil'ia, n. pl. Eyelashes; similar fringe on leaf, insect's wing, etc.; (Physiol.) hair-like vibrating organs on animal & vegetable tissue, serving many lower water animals for locomotion. Hence ~ARY[1], ~ATE[2], ~ATED, aa., ~A'TION n. [pl. of L cilium eyelash]

cil'ice, n. (Garment of) hair-cloth. [F also OE cilic, f. Gk kilikion (Kilikia Cilicia]

person learned in or admiring Cicero. Hence ~ISM(3, 4) n. [f. L Ciceronianus (prec., -IAN)]

cicisbeo (chichizbā'ō), n. (pl. -bei pr. -bāē). Recognised gallant of married woman. So **cicisbe'ism**(3) n. [It.]

Cid, n. The ~, title (lord) of Ruy Diaz, 11th-c. Christian champion against Moors, & of epic relating his deeds. [Sp., f. Arab. saiyid]

-cide, suf. forming nouns meaning (1) slayer of (F, f. L -cida) or (2) slaughter of (F, f. L -cidium) both f. L caedere kill; taken f. L as parricide, or formed on L as regicide, or facetiously on E m. as birdicide.

Cimmē'rian, a. Thick, gloomy, (of darkness, night, etc.). [f. L f. Gk kimmerios (of Cimmerii, people in perpetual night) +-AN]

cinch, n. Saddle-girth used in Mexico etc.; (sl.) sure thing, a certainty. [Sp. cincha]

cincho'na (-kō-), n. Kinds of evergreen tree yielding cinchona bark or Peruvian bark & quinine; the bark, drug made from it & highly esteemed as tonic & febrifuge. Hence **cinchon'ic**(DROUS a., **cin'chonINE**[5], **cin'chonISM**(5), nn., **cin'chonIZE**(5) v.t., (-ko-). [Countess of Chinchon, introducer of drug in Spain 1640]

Cincinnat'us, n. Great man in retirement who can be called upon in a crisis. [Roman hero called from plough to dictatorship]

cinc'ture, n. & v.t. (Surround with or as with a) girdle, belt, fillet, border. [f. L cinctura (cingere cinct- gird, -URE)]

cin'der, n. Slag; residue of coal, wood, etc., that has ceased to flame (whether

cold or not) but has still combustible matter in it; (loosely in pl.) ashes; ~ *path*, running-track laid with fine ~s; ~ *sifter*, for separating ~s from ashes. Hence ~Y² a. [OE *sinder* cf. G *sinter*, Sw. *sinder*, w. assim. to the unconnected F *cendre* & L *cinis-eris*]

Cinderĕll'a, n. Person of unrecognized merit or beauty; ~ *dance* or ~, dance closing at twelve o'clock. [allusions to fairy-tale]

cin'e̅, comb. form of CINEMA; so: ~ *camera* (for taking cinematographic photographs); ~-*film*; ~-*projector*; ~-*variety*, vaudeville entertainment including a cinema show.

cin'ema, n. Cinematograph theatre; *the* ~, cinematography, moving pictures. [abbr. of foll.]

cinĕmăt'ograph (-ahf), n., & v.t. & i. 1. Apparatus producing pictures of motion by the rapid projection on a screen of a great number of photographs taken successively on a long film; = prec. 2. v.t. Make ~ film of (scene), film; (v.i.) use ~. Hence **cinĕmăt'ograph¹⁰** a., **-ĭcally²** adv., **cinĕmătŏg'raphy¹** n. [f. F *cinématographe* f. Gk *kīnēma -atos* movement (*kineō* move), see -GRAPH]

cinerā'ria, n. Bright-flowered composite plant, grown chiefly under glass. [f. L *cinerarius* of ashes f. *cinis-eris* ashes (ash-coloured down on leaves)]

cinerā'rium n. Recess in which a cinerary urn is deposited. [as prec.]

cin'erary, a. Of ashes (esp. ~ *urn*, holding ashes of dead after cremation). [as prec.]

cinĕr'eous, a. Ashen-grey (esp. of birds or plumage). [f. L *cinereus* (*cinis-eris* ashes) +-OUS]

Cingalēse' (-nggalez), **Sin(g)halēse'** (-z), a. & n. (Native, language) of Ceylon. [f. Skr. *sinhalas*]

cing'ulum (-ngg-), n. Belt (used technically in Surg., Anat., Zool., etc.). [L]

cinn'abar, (n. & a.). Red mercuric sulphide, vermilion, (n. & a.). [f. L *cinnabaris* f. Gk *kinnabari* f. Oriental source]

cinn'amon, n. & a. (E.-Ind. tree yielding) aromatic inner bark used as spice; ~-colour(ed), (of) yellowish-brown; ~ *bear*, ~-coloured variety of the common N.-American black bear; ~-*stone*, brown or yellow garnet. Hence or cogn. **cinn'a-MATE¹⁰** n., **cinnamŏm'IC**, **cinna-mŏn'IC**, aa. [f. F *cinnamome* f. L f. Gk *kinnamōmon* f. Semit. (Heb. *qinnā-mōn*)]

cinque, cinq, (sink), n. The five at dice & cards. [f. OF *cink* f. L *quinque* five]

cinquecen'tō, cinquecen'tist, (chink-wichě-), nn. Italian style of art, artist, of the 16th c. (15-) with reversion to classical forms. [It. (-*o*, -*ista*) with omission (in It.) of *mil*]

cinq(ue)'foil (sǐnkf-), n. Kinds of plant with compound leaf of five leaflets;

(Archit.) five-cusped ornament in circle or arch. [thr. OF f. L *quinquefolium* five-leaf]

Cinque Ports (sink), n. pl. Certain ports (orig. five only) on SE coast with ancient privileges. [f. OF *cink porz* five ports]

ciph'er¹, cȳ-, n. Arithmetical symbol (0) of no value in itself but multiplying number it is placed after, and dividing decimal number it is placed before, by ten; person or thing of no importance; any Arabic figure; secret writing, thing so written, key to it; interlaced initials of person, company, etc., monogram; continued sounding of organ-note owing to defective valve. [f. OF *cyfre* f. Arab. *çifr* zero (orig. adj.=empty)]

ciph'er², cȳ-, v.i. & t. Do arithmetic; work (ususout) by arithmetic, calculate; put into secret writing (cf. DECIPHER); (of organ-note) go on sounding when not pressed. [f. prec.]

cip'olin, n. Italian white-&-green marble. [f. f. It. *cipollino* (*cipolla* onion) from resemblance of structure to coats of onion]

circ'a, circ'iter, prepp. (abbr. *c.* or *circ.*). About (with dates). [L]

Circă'ssian (-shn), a. & n. (Member, language) of a group of tribes of Caucasian race living in the Kuban province of Russia. [f. *Circassia* f. Russ. *Tcherkess*]

Cir'ce (-si), n. Enchantress, temptress. Hence **Circē'AN¹** a. [proper name in Gk myth.]

cir'cinate, a. (bot.). (With leaves) rolled up from apex to base, as in most ferns. [f. L *circinare* make round (*circinus* compasses, -ATE³)]

cir'cle¹, n. 1. (Line enclosing) perfectly round plane figure (*square the* ~, find square of same area as given ~, attempt impossibilities; *great, small,* ~, ~ on surface of sphere whose plane passes, does not pass, through sphere's centre; POLAR, ARCTIC, ANTARCTIC, ~); (loosely) roundish enclosure; orbit of planet; ring; curved tier of seats at theatre etc. (*dress* ~, *upper* ~, more & less expensive); (Archaeol.) ring of stones as at Stonehenge. 2. Period, cycle, round, (*come full* ~, end at starting-point); circling-feat in gymnastics; complete series. 3. (Logic, often *vicious* ~) fallacy of proving proposition from another that rests on it for proof. 4. Action & reaction that intensify each other (often *vicious* ~). 5. Persons grouped round centre of interest; set, coterie, class, (*first, upper,* ~s; ~s *in which*, one moves). 6. Area of influence, action, etc., sphere. Hence ~WISE (-lw-) adv. [OE *circul* (ME *cercle* f. F) f. L *circulus* dim. of *circus* ring]

cir'cle², v.t. & i. Encompass (poet.); encompass round, about; move in a circle *round, about*; (Gym.) revolve round bar in various ways; be passed round (of

wine etc.); (Mil.) sweep round on moving flank (of cavalry, cf. WHEEL²); (p.p.) rounded, marked with circles. [f. prec.]

circ'let, n. Small circle; circular band, esp. of gold, jewelled, etc., worn on head or elsewhere. [f. F *cerclet* (CIRCLE, -ET)]

circs., n. pl. (colloq.). Circumstances. [abbr.]

circ'uit (-kit), n. Line enclosing an area, distance round; area enclosed; round-about journey; sequence of changes, acts, etc.; chain of theatres, cinemas, etc., under a single management; journey of judge in particular district to hold courts, this district (eight in Eng. & Wales), the barristers (*member of a* ∼) making the ∼; group of local Methodist churches form-ing a minor administrative unit (∼ *rider*, itinerant preacher serving a ∼); (Electr.) path of current (*short* ∼, faulty shortening of ∼ by defective insulation). [F, f. L *circuitus* (*circum-ire* go)]

circu'itous, a. Roundabout, indirect. Hence ∼LY² adv., ∼NESS n. [f. LL *circuitosus* (CIRCUIT, -OSE²)]

circ'ular, a. & n. Round in superficies; moving in a circle (∥∼ *tour*, ending where it began by different route, ∼ *ticket*, for this); (Logic) of, using, the *vicious* CIRCLE¹; addressed to a circle of persons, customers, etc. (∼ *note*, banker's letter of credit in traveller's favour to several foreign bankers; ∼ *letter* or ∼, notice, advertisement, etc., reproduced for dis-tribution; of, like, the geometrical circle; ∼ *saw*, toothed disk revolving by machinery for sawing. Hence **circ'ular-I·TY n., ∼LY² adv. [f. OF *circuler* f. L *circularis* (CIRCLE, -AR²)]

circ'ularize, v.t. Send circulars to. [-IZE(1)]

circ'ulate, v.i. & t. Go round (blood ∼es through veins, water in pipes, wine on table, newspaper to circle of readers); (of decimals) = RECUR; send round, give currency to, (book, report, scandal, etc.); ∼*ing library*, with books taken by sub-scribers in succession; ∼*ing medium*, notes, gold, etc., used in exchange. [f. L *circulare* (CIRCLE¹), -ATE³)]

circula'tion, n. Movement of blood from and to heart, similar movement of sap etc.; movement to and fro (∼ *of under*, *atmosphere*, etc.); transmission, distri-bution, (of news, books, etc.); number of copies sold, esp. of newspapers; currency (*in*, *out of ∼*); of coin, etc. [F, f. L *circulationem* (*circulare* see prec., -ATION)]

circ'ulative, a. Inclined to, promoting, circulation. [as prec.-IVE]

circ'ulator, n. One who circulates coin, etc. [as prec.-OR²]

circ'ulatory, a. Of circulation of blood or sap. [f. L *circulatorius* (as prec., -ORY)]

circum-, pref. = L *circum* round, about, used (1) adverbially, as *circumnavigant* wandering round or about; (2) prepositionally, as *circummacular* sur-rounding the eye. E wds are some f. L (direct, as *circumscribe* or thr. F as *circumcise*), some formed in E on L elements as *circumambient*, & some facetious hybrids as *circumbending*.

circumam'bient, a. Surrounding (esp. of air or other fluid). Hence ∼ENCY n. [CIRCUM-(1) + AMBIENT]

circumam'bulate, v.t. & i. Walk round (place etc.); walk about; beat about the bush. Hence ∼A'TION n.,∼ATORY a. [f. L CIRCUM(*ambulare* walk), -ATE³]

circumben'dibus, n. (joc.). Round-about method; circumlocution. [CIRCUM-(1), BEND, ending of L abl. pl. case]

circ'umcise (-z), v.t. Cut off foreskin of (as Jewish or Mohammedan rite, or surgically); purify (∼ *the heart, passions,* etc.). [f. OF *circonciser* f. L *circumcidere -cis-* = *caedere* cut)]

circumci'sion (-izhn), n. Act or rite of, spiritual purification by, circumcising; (Bibl.) *the* ∼, the Jews; (Eccl.) festival of C∼ of Christ, 1st Jan. [f. OF *circum-cision* f. L *circumcisionem* (as prec., -ION)]

cir'cumference, n. Encompassing boun-dary, esp. of figure enclosed by curve, as circle; distance round. So **circum-feren'tial** (-shl) a. [f. L CIRCUM(*ferentia* f. *ferent-* part. st. of *ferre* bear, & see -ENCE)]

cir'cumflex, a. & n. & v.t. ∼ (*accent*), mark (∼ or ^ in Gk, ^ elsewhere) placed over vowel to indicate contraction, length, or special quality (vb. mark thus); (Anat.) curved, bending round something else, (∼ *artery, muscle, etc.*). [f. L CIRCUM-(*flexus* -x- f. *flectere* bend) transl. of Gk *perispōmenos*]

cir'cumfluent (-lŏŏ-), a. Flowing round, surrounding. Hence ∼ENCE n. [f. L CIR-CUM(*fluens* f. *fluere* flow)]

circum'fluous (-lŏŏ-), a. = prec.; sur-rounded by water. [f. L CIRCUM(*fluus*]

cir'cumfuse (-z), v.t. Pour (fluid) *about or round* (object); surround, bathe, (object *with*, or of fluid as subj.). So **circumfu'sion** (-zhn) n. [f. L CIRCUM(*undere* e *fus-* pour]

cir'cumjacent, a. Situated around. [f. L CIRCUM(*jacent-* part. st. of *jacēre* lie)]

circumlit'toral, a. Bordering the shore. [CIRCUM-(2) + L *littus -oris* shore + -AL]

circumlocu'tion, n. Use of many words where few would do; evasive talk; a roundabout expression; C∼ *Office*, dila-tory Government expression. Hence ∼AL, ∼IST(1) (-shon-), **circumloc'utory**, aa.. [CIRCUM(*locutio LOCUTION)]

cir'cum-merid'ian, a.(astron.). Near the meridian (of observations taken of star etc. when so placed). [CIRCUM-(2)]

circumnav′igate, v.t. Sail round (esp. *the globe or world*). Hence ~**or²** n. [f. L CIRCUM (*navigare* NAVIGATE)]

circumnūt′āte, v.i. (bot.). Bend towards all points of compass successively (of growing parts of plant). Hence ~**A′TION** n. [CIRCUM-(1), NUTATE]

circumor′al, a. (physiol.). Placed round mouth. [CIRCUM-(2), L *os oris* mouth, -AL]

circumpō′lar, a. (Astron.).~ *star, motion,* etc., above horizon throughout diurnal course; (Geog.) about, near, one of the earth's poles. [CIRCUM-(2), L *polus* POLE², -AR¹]

circ′umscrībe, v.t. Draw line round; (Geom.) describe (figure) round another touching it at points, but not cutting it; lay down limits of, confine, restrict; define logically; sign (round robin); whence **circumscrib′ER¹** n. [f. L CIRCUM(*scribere script-* write)]

circumscrip′tion, n. Having, marking out, or imposing, of limits; boundary; limited district; definition; (Geom.) circumscribing (see prec.); inscription round coin etc. [f. L *circumscriptio* (prec.), -TION]

circumsōl′ar, a. Revolving round, being near, the sun. [CIRCUM-(2), SOL¹, -AR¹]

circ′umspect, a. Cautious, wary, taking everything into account. Hence or cogn. **circumspēc′tion**, ~NESS, nn., ~IVE a., ~LY² adv. [f. L CIRCUM(*spectus* p.p. of *-spicere* look at) considered, of act, & transf. of persons]

circ′umstance, n. 1. (Pl.) time, place, manner, cause, occasion, etc., surroundings, of an act; external conditions affecting or that might affect an agent (*in, under, the* ~*s,* owing to or making allowance for them; *under no* ~*s,* not whatever happens, never); material welfare (*in good, bad, easy, reduced, straitened,* ~*s*). 2. (Sing.) full detail in narrative; ceremony, fuss, (*without* ~, unceremoniously; *pomp &* ~); incident, occurrence, fact (esp. *the* ~ *that*). Hence **circ′umstanced²**(-st) a. [OFf.L CIRCUM-(*stantia* f. part. of *stare* stand) surrounding state]

circumstan′tial (-shl), a. Depending on subordinate details (~ *evidence,* establishing the doubtful main fact by inference from facts otherwise hard to explain); adventitious, incidental; with many details (~ *story*). Hence **circumstantiāl′ITY** (-shl-) n., ~**LY²** (-shal-) adv. [as prec. + -AL¹]

circumvall′āte, v.t., **circumvalla′tion,** n. (Surround with) rampart or entrenchment, process of doing this. [f. L CIRCUM(*vallare* f. *vallum* rampart), see -ATE³, -ATION]

circumvent′, v.t. Entrap; overreach; outwit. So ~**vēn′tion** n. [f. L CIRCUM-(*venire vent-* come)]

circumvolu′tion (-lōo-), n. Rolling

round; coil; period; sinuous movement. [f. L CIRCUM(*volvere volut-* roll), -TION]

circ′us, n. Rounded or oval arena lined with tiers of seats for equestrian & other exhibitions; amphitheatre of hills; || open circle with streets converging on it; travelling show of horses, riders, etc. [L, = ring]

cirque (-k), n. Arena, natural amphitheatre, (chiefly poet. & rhet.). [F, f. L as prec.]

cirrhō′sis (sirō-), n. Disease of liver, chiefly alcoholic. [Gk *kirrhos* tawny, -OSIS]

cirri-, cirro-, comb. form of CIRRUS. Hence **cirri′FEROUS, ci′rriFORM,** aa. & names of cloud-forms as *cirro-cūm′ulus.* [-I-, -O-]

ci′rripĕd, -ēde, n. Marine animal in valved shell attached to other bodies, with legs like curl of hair. [f. F CIRRI(*pĕde* f. L *pes pedis* foot)]

ci′rrus, n. (pl. -*rī*). (Bot.) tendril; (Zool.) slender appendage, as beard of fishes, feet of cirripeds; (Meteor.) form of cloud with diverging filaments like lock of hair or wool. Hence **cirrōSE¹, ci′rrOUS,** aa.

cis-, pref.= on this side of, opp. to *trans-* or *ultra-,* retaining in some orig. L wds the Roman sense (*cispādāne, cisalpine,* S. or Rome-wards of Po, Alps); but usu. w. ref. to speaker's or majority's position (*cismontāne,* N. of Alps or non-Italian; *cis-Leithan,* W. of Leitha, Austrian, non-Hungarian; *cis-pontine,* in London, on northern or better-known side of bridges or Thames); prefixed to the adj. form of the second element; often used in wds made for the nonce in opposition to wds in *trans-* or *ultra-* (*transatlantic & cisatlantic*); also of time as *cis-Eliza-bethan.* [L prep.]

ciss′y, sī-, n. (sl.). Effeminate person. [ult. f. SISTER]

cist, n. (archaeol.). Prehistoric stone or hollowed-tree coffin; round receptacle used esp. for sacred purposes. [f. Ll f. Gk *kistē* box]

Cistēr′cian (-shn), n. & a. (Monk) of order founded 1098 at Cistercium or Cîteaux, stricter offshoot of Benedictines, also called *Bernardine* as patronized by St Bernard of Clairvaux. [-AN]

cis′tern, n. Reservoir for storing water, usn. on upper storey with pipes supplying taps on lower levels (also fig., of pond). [f. OF *cisterne* f. L *cisterna* (*cista* see CIST)]

ci′stus, n. Kinds of shrub with large white or red short-lived flowers. [f. Gk *kistos*]

cit, n. (arch.). Citizen (usn. in derogatory sense). [abbr. of *citizen*]

cit′adel, n. Fortress, esp. one guarding or dominating city; last retreat of hardpressed party, belief, etc. [f. F *citadelle* f.

It., *cittadella* dim. of *cittade* f. L *civitāda* CITY]

cite, v.t. Summon to appear in law-court; quote (passage, book, author) in support of a position; mention as example. Hence or cogn. *mention in an official dispatch. [f. F *citer* f. L *citāre* frequent. of *ciēre* set moving]

cith'ern, **cit'tern**, n. (arch. or poet.), Wire-stringed lute-like instrument usu. played with plectrum. [f. L Gk *kithara* harp with seven to eleven strings]

cit'izen, n. Burgess, freeman, of city; townsman; civilian; member, native or naturalized, of a State (usu. of; ~ *of the world*, cosmopolitan); inhabitant of. Hence ~HOOD, ~SHIP, nn. [ME *citesein* (-s- perh. on anal. of DENIZEN) f. OF *citeain* (CITY, -AN¹)]

cit'rate¹, n. (hist.).= CITHERN(N).

cit-, comb. form of foll. Hence **cit'RATE¹** f. L *citrus*, -INE¹]

cit'ric, a. (chem.). Of citron (esp. ~ *acid*).
[f. L *citrus* CITRON + -IC]

cit'rine, a. Lemon-coloured. [f. F *citrin*]

citro- = CITR-.

cit'ron, n. (Tree bearing) lemon-like but larger, less acid, & thicker-skinned fruit; lemon colour. [F, f. It. *citrone* (L *citrus*, -ONE)]

cit'rus, n. The genus including the citron, lemon, lime, orange, etc. [L]

citronell'a, n. Fragrant ethereal oil obtained from a tropical grass, used for keeping insects away. [mod. L, as CITRON]

cit'y, n. (Loosely) Important town; (strictly) town created city by charter, esp. as containing cathedral (but not all cathedral towns are cities, nor vice versa);~ *of* REFUGE | *Holy* C~, Jerusalem, Heaven;~ *Eternal* C~, Rome; *Celestial* C~, *Heavenly* C~, ~ *of God*, Paradise; | the C~, part of London governed by Lord Mayor & Corporation, business part of this, commercial circles, || (C~ *man*, in commerce or finance; C~ *article*, in newspaper representing ancient trade-guild); C~ *editor*, one who deals with the financial news of a daily or weekly journal;~ *state*, a city that is also an independent sovereign state. Hence (-)CITIED² (-tid), ~LESS, aa. [f. OF *cité* f. L *civitātem* (*civis* citizen, -TY)]

civ'et, n. (Also ~-*cat*) carnivorous quadruped between fox & weasel in size & look; strong musky perfume got from anal glands of this. [f. F *civette* f. Arab. *zebad*]

civ'ic, a. Of, proper to, citizens (~ *crown*,

oak-garland, Roman honour to one who saved fellow-citizen's life in war); of city, municipal; of citizenship, civil, (~ *virtues*, *activity*), whence **CIV'ICS** n. Hence **civ'ICALLY adv.** [f. L *civicus* (*civis* citizen, -IC)]

civ'(v)ies (-viz), n. pl.(sl.), Civilian clothes. [abbr.]

civ'il, a. 1. Of gregarious men (~ *society*, *life*); of a citizen community (~ *institutions*; ~ *war*, confined to this, between fellow-citizens, *The* C~ *War*, in Engl., between Charles I & Parliament, in U.S., War of Secession);~ *disobedience* (India), refusal to pay taxes, obey laws, etc. as part of a political campaign; of, becoming, a citizen(~ *rights*, *liberty*;~ *spirit*). 2. Polite, obliging, not rude, (*make a* ~ *tongue*, with pl.= *favours*). **civ'il'ITY n. 3.** Not naval, military, etc.(~ *defence*, wartime civilian organization for dealing esp. with air raids;~ ENGINEER¹; C~ *Service*, all non-warlike branches of State administration, whence ~ *Servant*, member of one of them). 4. Not ecclesiastical (~ *magistrates*, & formerly as ~ *marriage*, solemnized as ~ contract without religious ceremony). 5. Not criminal (~ *law*, concerning questions of private rights merely). 6. Not natural or astronomical (~ *day*, *year*, as recognized for dating etc.). 7. C~ *Law*, Roman law (so D.C.L.; & see above); || ~ *list*, Parliamentary allowance for King's household & royal pensions. Hence ~IZ² adv. [F, f. L *civilis* (*civis* citizen, -IL)]

civil'ian (-yan), n. & a. (Person) not in or of navy or army or air force; (also *Indian* C~) member of Indian Civil Service.[arch. sense, one learned in Civil Law, f. OF *civilien* as prec.,-IAN]

civiliza'tion, n. Making or becoming civilized; stage, esp. advanced stage, in social development; civilized States. [f. foll.,+ -ATION]

civ'ilize, v.t. Bring out of barbarism, enlighten, refine;~ *e* a~*aa*, get rid of (barbarous habits etc.). Hence ~ABLE a., ~ER¹ n. [f. F *civiliser*, see CIVIL, -IZE(3)]

civ'ly Street, n.(sl.), Civilian life. [abbr.]

clack, n. & v.i. 1. Sharp sound as of boards struck together; flap-valve in pumps etc.; clatter of tongues. 2. v.i. Chatter loudly; make sound as of clogs on stone. [prob. imit.; cf. F *claque(r)*, Du. *klakken*]

clad. See CLOTHE.

clad'o(-), comb. form of Gk *klados* young shoot, in bot. terms as *cladocarp'ous* with fruit on lateral branchlets.

claim, v.t. Demand as one's due (recognition etc., *to be*, *that* one should be, recognized etc.); represent oneself as having (~ *the victory*, *accuracy*);(of things) (be the owner, *have* told the truth); demand recognition of the fact that; contend, assert; (of things) deserve (esp.

attention). Hence ~ABLE a., ~'ANT(1) n. [f. OF cla(i)mer f. L clamare call out]

claim(2), n. Demand for something as due (lay ~ to); right, title, to thing, right to make demand on person; (Mining etc.) piece of land allotted: *~jumper, one who appropriates a mining ~ already taken by another. [f. OF claime see prec.]

clairaud'ience, n., ~ant a. & n.=foll. with 'hearing' for 'sight' 'seeing'. [after foll. f. L audio hear]

clairvoy'ance, n. Faculty of seeing mentally what is happening or exists out of sight; exceptional insight. [F (L clarus clear, vidēre see, -ANCE); first sense given in E]

clairvoy'ant, n. (occas. fem. -te), & a. (Person) having clairvoyance. [F, as prec., -ANT]

clam(1). See CLAMP(1).

clam(2). n. Various bivalve shell-fish, esp. the N.-Amer. Hard or Round, & Soft or Long, C~, used for food. [orig. ~shell f. clam-=CLAMP(1)]

clam'ant, a. Noisy, insistent; urgent. [f. L clamare cry out, -ANT]

clam'ber, v.i. & n. Climb with hands & feet; climb with difficulty or labour. [prob. f. CLIMB+-ER(5), but cf. CLAMP(1) & G sich klammern hook oneself on]

clamm'y, a. Moist, usu. cold, & sticky or slimy (of the hand, ill-baked bread, any surface). Hence ~ILY(2) adv., ~INESS n. [perh. f. OE clām clay]

clam'our (-mer), n., & v.i. & t. Shout(ing); (make) loud appeal, complaint, or demand (abs., or for, against, to do; also as v.t., ~ down, silence, ~ out of, into, force by ~); (make) confused noise. So **clam'orous** a., **clam'orously**(2) adv. [f. OF f. L clamor (clamare call out)]

clamp(1), n., & v.t. (also clam in some technical uses of n.). 1. Brace, clasp, or band, usu. of iron, for strengthening other materials or holding things together; various appliances or tools with opposite sides connected by screw for holding or compressing. 2. v.t. Strengthen, fasten together, with ~ or ~s. [f. 15th c.; there was OE clam in same sense]

clamp(2), n., & v.t. 1. Pile (of bricks for burning, potatoes etc. under straw & earth, turf, peat, garden rubbish, etc.). 2. v.t. Pile (bricks etc.) up. [perh.=prec.; cf. Du. klamp a heap]

clan, n. Scottish Highlanders with common ancestor, esp. while under patriarchal control (~s'man, member, fellow member, of ~); tribe; family holding together, whence ~n'ISH(1) a., ~n'ishry(2) adv., ~n'ishNESS n.; party, coterie; genus, species, class. [f. Gael. clann f. L plantā]

clandes'tine, a. Surreptitious, secret. Hence ~LY(2)(-nI-) adv. [f. L clandestīnus (clam secretly, cf. intestine, matutine)]

clang, n., & v.i. & t. Loud resonant metallic sound (esp. of trumpet, arms, large bell, some bodies); (vb) make, cause (thing) to make, this. [f. L clangere cf. Gk klang-]

clang'our (-ngger), n. Succession, prevalence, of clanging noises. Hence **clang'orous** a., **clang'orously**(2) adv. (-ngg-). [f. L clangor (prec., -OR(3)]

clank, n. & v.i. & t. Sound as of heavy chain rattling; (vb) make, cause (bucket, chain, etc.) to make, this. [f. 17th c., perh. on clang, clink; but cf. Du. klank]

clan'ship, n. The clan system; division into mutually jealous parties; devotion to a leader. [-SHIP]

clap(1), n. Explosive noise (of thunder, of hand-palms struck together); slap, pat, (arch.). [perh. f. foll.]

clap(2), v.i. & t. (-pp-). ~ one's hands, ~ (t. & i.), applaud by striking palms together loudly (also, usu. w. hands, strike them for warmth, as signal etc.); ~ on the back, slap so in encouragement or congratulation; put, place, quickly or energetically (spurs to horse, person in prison, duty on goods; ~ on all sail; ~ up peace, bargain, make hastily or carelessly; ~ eyes on, catch sight of, esp. w. neg.); ~-ned, fowler's or entomologist's, shut by pulling string. [cf. G klappen, ON klappa]

clap(3), n. (not in decent use). Venereal disease, gonorrhoea. [?]

*__clap'board__ (-bord), n. = WEATHER-board. [anglicized f. LG klappholt cask-stave]

clapp'er, n. Tongue or striker of bell; hand or wind rattle for scaring birds. [CLAP(2)+-ER(1)]

clapp'erclaw, v.t. Scratch & hit; abuse, criticize spitefully. [prec., CLAW]

clap'trap, n. & a. Language, sentiment, meant to catch applause; showy. [CLAP, TRAP]

claque (-ahk), **claqueur'** (-kër'), nn. Hired body of applauders, hired applauder. [F]

clar'abella (-ahr-), n. Powerful fluty organ-stop. [f. L clarus clear, bellus pretty]

clar'ence, n. Four-wheeled close carriage with seats for four inside & two on box, four-wheeler cab. [Duke of C~ (William IV)]

clar'encieux (-sū), n. Second KING(1). [AF (-ceux), f. Clarence (Clare in Suffolk), dukedom of Lionel son of Edw. III]

clar'endon, a. & n. (typog.). Thick-faced (type), thus, of various sizes.

clar'et, n. & a. Kinds of red French wine imported from Bordeaux (usu. blends of light wine with Benicarlo); (sl.) blood (tap one's ~, make his nose bleed with blow of fist); ~-colour(ed), reddish-violet; artificial salmon-fly so coloured; ~-CUP(1). [OF (vin ~), =claret dim. of

clair f. L *clarus* clear (orig., of light red wines between white & red.]

cla'rify, v.t. & i. Make clear (observe subject, mind, sight); free from impurities, make transparent, (liquid, butter, air, etc.); become transparent (lit., & fig. of literary style etc.). [f. OF *clarifier* f. L *clarificare* (*clarus* clear, -FY)]

cla'rinet (also -ĕt'), n. Wood-wind instrument with single-reed mouthpiece, holes, & keys; organ-stop of like quality. So **cla'rinĕt'tĭst**(3) n. [f. F *clarinette* dim. of *clarine*=foll.]

clā'rion, n. & a. Shrill narrow-tubed trumpet formerly used in war; rousing sound; organ-stop of ~ quality; (adj.) clear & loud. [f. OF *claron* f. med. L *clarionem* nom. *-io* (CLEAR)]

clārionĕt', n. = CLARINET. [prec., -ET']

clā'rĭty, n. Clearness. [ME & OF *clarté* f. L *claritatem* (*clarus* clear, -TY)]

clā'rk'ia, n. Kinds of plant with showy flowers. [W. *Clarke*, U.S. explorer]

clā'ry, n. Kind of pot-herb. [OE *sclarie* f. med. L *sclarea* etym. dub.]

clăsh, v.i. & t. & n. (Make) loud broken sound as of collision, striking weapons, cymbals, bells rung together; encounter, conflict, (v.i., & n.) disagree(ment); be at variance *with*; *colours* ~, are discordant; rush or charge (vb) *into*, *against*, *upon*; ring (bells) all together. [prob. imit.]

clasp¹ (-ah-), n. Contrivance of interlocking parts for fastening, buckle, brooch; metal fastening of book-cover; embrace, reach; grasp, handshake; bar of silver on medal-ribbon with name of occasion (in campaign commemorated by medal) at which wearer was present; ~-*knife*, folding, with catch fixing blade when open. [f. 14th c.; exc. E; etym. dub.; var., *clapse*, cf. *hasp/haspe*, *ask/ax*]

clasp² (-ah-), v.t. & i. Fasten (clasp); fasten (t. & i.) with or as clasp; encircle, hold closely, embrace; grasp (another's hand; ~ *hands*, shake hands emotionally; make common cause; ~ *one's hands*, interlace fingers). [f. prec.]

clas'per (-ah-), n. In vbl senses: esp. (pl.) appendages of some male fish & insects for holding the female. [-ER¹]

class (-ah-), n. & v.t. **1.** Rank, order, of society (*higher*, *upper*, *middle*, *lower*, *working*, ~*es*; *the* ~*es*, the rich or educated, opp. *the masses*); ~-*conscious*(*ness*), esp. realizing & taking part in the conflict between the labouring & other ~es; caste system. **2.** Set of students taught together, their time of meeting, their course of instruction, *all college students of same standing, (~*fellow*, ~*mate*, present or past member of same ~ with one; ~*book*, used by ~; ~-*room*, where ~ is taught). **3.** (In foreign armies) all the recruits of a year (*the* 1946 ~). **4.** || Division of candidates after examination (*take* a ~, gain honours; so ~'*man* opp. to *pass-man*; || ~-*list*, issued by examiners. **5.** Division according to quality (so *high*, *low*, *first*, *second*, etc., ~, as adj. of praise or depreciation, & *first*, *second*, *third*, ~, of railway carriages etc.; *no* ~, quite inferior). **6.** Number of individuals having common name as like in any respect. **7.** (Nat. Hist.) highest division (~, *order*, *family*, *genus*, *species*) of animal, vegetable, or mineral kingdom. **8.** Distinction, high quality (also attrib.), **9.** v.t. Place in a ~; hence ~ABLE a. [f. F *classe* f. L *classis* assembly (*calare* convoke)]

clăs'sic, a. & n. **1.** Of the first class, of allowed excellence; of the standard ancient Latin & Greek authors, art, or culture; of Latin & Greek antiquity; in the ~ style, simple, harmonious, proportioned, & finished (cf. ROMANTIC); having literary associations (~ *ground*); *Derby, Oaks, St Leger, Two & One Thousand Guineas*, are the ~ *races*, Two & One Thousand Guineas). **2.** n. Writer or artist of admitted excellence; ancient Greek or Latin writer; Latin and Greek scholar; follower of ~ models (cf. ROMANTIC); (pl.) classical studies. [f. L *classicus* (prec. -IC) of the first class]

clăs'sical, a. Standard, first-class, esp. in literature; of ancient Greek or Latin standard authors or art; learned in these; based on these (~ *education*); in, following, the restrained style of ~ antiquity (as prec., cf. ROMANTIC). Hence ~ISM(3), ~ITY(4), n. [as prec. + -AL]

clăs'sicism, -ist, n. Following, follower of classic style; classical scholar(ship); advocacy, advocate, of classical education; (-ism) a Latin or Greek idiom. [-ISM(3, 4), -IST(2, 3)]

clăs'sicize, v.t. & i. Make classic; imitate the classical style. [-IZE(2, 3)]

clăs'sico-, comb. form of L *classicus* w. senses of CLASSIC. Hence **clăssicŏl'ATRY**

clăss'ify, v.t. Arrange in classes; assign to a class. So ~fĭABLE a., ~fĭcā'TION, ~fĭcĀTOR(1), aa., ~icĀTŎRy, ~FĬER¹ nn. [f. Gk *klastos* (*klaō* break)]

clas'sy, a. (sl.). Superior. [-Y²]

clătt'er, v.i. & t., & n. (Make) dry confused sound as of many plates struck together; (resound with) noisy talk; ~ *along*, *down*, etc., move, fall, with a ~; (v.t.) cause (plates etc.) to ~. [OE *clatrung* cf. Du. *klateren*]

clause (-z), n. Short sentence; (Gram.) subordinate words including subject & predicate but syntactically equivalent to noun, adj., or adv.; single proviso in treaty, law, or contract. [OF, f. LL *clausa* = L *clausula* conclusion (*claudere* shut, -ULE)]

claus'tral, a. Of the cloister, monastic, narrow. [f. LL *claustralis* (CLOISTER, -AL)]

claustrophōb′ia, n. Morbid dread of closed places. [f. L *claustrum* (see CLOISTER) +-PHOBIA]

clăv′āte, a. (bot.). Club-shaped. [f. L *clava* club +-ATE²]

clăv′ichŏrd (-k-), n. Predecessor of piano, first string-instrument with key-board. [f. 15th-c. L *clavichordium* (L *clavis* key, CHORD¹)]

clăv′icle, n. Collar-bone. So **clavic′ŭlar¹** a. [f. L *clavicula* dim. of *clavis* key]

clăv′iform, a. Club-shaped. [L *clava*, -FORM]

claw¹, n. Pointed horny nail of beast's or bird's foot (*pare, cut, the ~ s of*, disarm); foot so armed, pincers of shellfish; (contempt.) hand; contrivance for grappling, holding, etc. (*~hammer*, with bent split end for extracting nails; *~hammer coat*, dress coat). Hence **(-)clawED²** (-awd) a. [OE *clawu* f. obl. cases of *clēa* of *clee* still dial.; cf. Du. *klaauw*, G *klaue*]

claw², v.t. & i. Scratch, tear, seize or pull towards one, with claws or hands (*~ me & I'll ~ thee*, of mutual flattery f. obs. sense, still So., *scratch gently*); (Naut.) beat to windward, esp. *~ off*, away from shore. [f. prec.]

clay, n. Stiff tenacious earth, material of bricks, pottery, etc.; (material of) human body (*wet, moisten*, one's *~*, drink); (also *~ pipe*) tobacco-pipe made of *~* (*yard of ~*, long one); *~-cold*, cold as *~* (usu. of the dead). Hence (with -e- to separate *vy*, & comp. *more, most*) **clāy′ey²** a. [OE *clǣg*, com.-Teut. cf. Du. & G *klei*, f. Idic-to stick cf. Gk *gloios*, L *gluten*]

clay′more, n. Ancient Scottish two-edged broadsword; (incorrectly) basket-hilted often single-edged broadsword introduced in 16th c. [f. Gael. *claidheamh mòr* great sword]

clean¹, a. 1. Free from dirt, unsoiled, clear, (land of weeds, ship of barnacles, paper of writing; printing-proof of corrections; *~* BILL⁴; *~ hands*, *~-handed*, *~-handedness*, innocence, innocent; *~-fingered*, unbribed; *~ slate*, fig., freedom from all commitments; *~ tongue*, abstinence from foul talk; *~* BREAST¹; *show ~ pair of heels*, escape by speed; *~-bred*, thoroughbred); (Bibl.) free of ceremonial defilement or of disease; (of beasts etc.) fit for food (esp. *~ fish*, not at or soon after spawning). 2. Hostile to dirt (*~ servant*), cleanly. 3. Well-formed, shapely, (joints, figure, so *~-limbed*; *~ ship*, with tapering lines). 4. Smart, adroit, not bungling, (*~ fielding*). 5. Even, unobstructed, clear-cut, complete, (*~ sweep*, complete riddance; *~ timber*, without knots). 6. Free from impropriety, esp. *keep it ~* (colloq.). Hence **~′NESS n.** [OE *clǣne*; cf. G *klein* small]

clean², adv. Completely, right, outright, altogether, simply, absolutely, (*~ gone*, *~ bowled, cut~through, ~mad, ~wrong*);

~-cut, sharply outlined. [OE *clǣne* adv. f. prec.]

clean³, v.t., v.t. & n. 1. Make clean (of dirt etc.); empty (one's plate); make oneself, make oneself, become, clean (also *~ up*); *~ up*, put things tidy, put (things) tidy, clear (mess) away, (colloq.) acquire as gain or profit; *~ out*, empty, strip, (esp. sl., person of his money); *~ down*, *~* by brushing or wiping; hence *~′ABLE a.*, (-)*~′ER¹* (1, 2), n. 2. n. *~ing* (*give it a ~*). [f. CLEAN¹]

clean′ly¹, adv. In clean way. [OE CLEAN¹]

clean′li² (-ĕn-), a. Habitually clean; attentive to cleanness. Hence *~′liINESS n., (-ĕn-).* [OE *clǣnlic* (CLEAN¹ +-LY²)]

cleanse (-ĕnz), v.t. Make clean (now formal or arch., for *clean* in lit. sense) purify (of sin etc., or with *sin* etc. as obj.); (Bibl.) cure (leper etc.). [OE *clǣnsian* (*clǣne* CLEAN¹)]

clear¹, a. & adv. 1. Unclouded, transparent, not turbid, lustrous, unspotted, (so *~-starch v.t.*, = starch well; *~ conscience*, feeling that one is innocent); distinct, unambiguous, intelligible, not confused, manifest, (*in ~*, not in cipher or code); discerning, penetrating, (so *~-sighted, ~-sightedness*, usu. fig.); confident, decided, certain, (*on point, of fact, that*); easily audible; without deduction, net; rid *of*; complete (*three ~ days*); open, unobstructed, (*coast is ~*, no one about to see or interfere); unengaged, free, unencumbered by debt. 2. adv. Clearly (*speak loud & ~*; *~-cut*, well defined; *show, shine, ~*); quite (*~ away, off, out, through*; *three feet ~*); apart, without, contact, (*stand, hang, steer, get, ~*). [ME & OF *cler* (now *clair*) f. L *clarus*]

clear², v.t. & i. Make, become, clear (of; *~ the air*, lit. of sultriness, fig. of suspicion, constraint, sulks, etc.; one's *~ throat*, by slight coughing); show or declare innocent (of); free from or of obstruction (*~ the decks for action*, make ready to fight; *~ land*, cut down trees etc. before cultivating; remove (obstruction, esp. *~ out of the way*); melt away (also sl. of persons, go away); empty, become empty; pass over or by without touching (esp. in jumping, *~ 6 ft, 22 ft, a gate*); (Naut.) free (ship); defray (prospective charges) by single payment; make (sum) as net gain; *~ away*, remove, remove meal from table, (of mist etc.) disappear; *~ off, get rid of*, melt away, (of intruders) go away; *~ out*, empty, make off; *~ up*, solve (mystery), make tidy, (of weather etc.) grow clear. [f. prec.]

clear′ance, n. Making clear; removal of obstructions; passing of cheques through Clearing-House; (certificate of) clearing of ship at Custom-House; permit to leave

government employ; (Mech.) space allowed for the passing of two parts; ‖~ *sale* (held to effect ~ of superfluous stock). [prec. + -ANCE]

clear′cōle, n. (Paint with) size and whiting or white-lead as first coat in house-painting. [f. F *claire colle* clear glue]

clear′ing, n. In vbl senses; esp.: piece of land in primeval forest cleared for cultivation; C~ *Hospital*, field hospital for temporary reception and treatment of sick and wounded; C~-*House*, banker's institution in London at which cheques & bills are exchanged, the balances only being paid in cash. [CLEAR² -ING¹]

clear′ly, adv. Distinctly to, with, senses or mind; manifestly; undoubtedly, (in answers) yes, no doubt. [CLEAR¹, -LY²]

clear′ness, n. Transparence; distinctness to, of, senses or mind; freedom from obstruction. [CLEAR¹, -NESS]

cleat, n. Wedge; projecting piece bolted on spar, gangway, etc., to give footing or prevent rope from slipping; piece of wood or iron bolted on for fastening ropes to. [cf. Du. *kloot* ball; cogn. w. CLOT]

cleav′age, n. Way in which thing (mineral, party, opinion, State) tends to split (esp. *lines, planes, of* ~). [foll. + -AGE]

cleave¹, v.t. & i. (*clove* or *cleft*; *cloven* or *cleft*). Split (often *asunder, in two*); chop, break, or come, apart, esp. along the grain or line of cleavage (*cleft palate, malformation in mouth; in a cleft stick,* in tight place allowing neither retreat nor advance; *cloven hoof,* of ruminant quadrupeds, & of god Pan, & so of devil, whence *show the cloven hoof,* reveal an evil nature); make way through (water, air); hold (ground, persons) apart (of chasm lit. & fig.). Hence cleav′ABLE a. [OE *clēofan,* com.-Teut. cf. G *klieben,* also Gk *gluphō*=carve]

cleave², v.i.(~d or *clave*;~d). Stick fast, adhere, *to* (arch. exc. in fig. sense of be *faithful*). [OE *clifan* & *clifian,* com.-Teut., cf. G *kleben* f. *kli-* stick]

cleek, n. Iron-headed golf-club. [Sc., cogn. w. ME *cleche* to clutch]

clef, n. One of the three symbols (C, F, or G; or *alto; G* or *treble; F* or *bass*) indicating pitch of stave in music. [F, f. L *clavis* key]

cleft¹, n. Fissure, split. [earlier *clift, chift,* cf. Du. & G *kluft,* cogn. w. CLEAVE¹]

cleft², see CLEAVE¹.

‖ cleg, n. Large grey fly, horse-fly. [f. ON *kleggi*]

cleav′ers (z), cliv′, n. (used as sing. or pl.). Goose-grass, creeper sticking to clothes. [earlier -*er*: perh. f. CLEAVE²+ -ER¹]

cleistogam′ic (klī-), a. (bot.), Permanently closed & self-fertilizing (of certain flowers). [Gk *kleistos* closed (*kleiō*)+ -*gamos* -married]

‖ clem, v.t. & i. (northern; -mm-). [cf. Du. & G *klemmen* pinch, & CLAM¹]

clem′atis, n. Kinds of climbing shrub (British wild species, Traveller's Joy or Old Man's Beard). [L, f. Gk *klēmatis*]

clem′ency, n., clem′ent, a. Mild(ness) of temper or weather: (showing) mercy. [f. L *clementia, clemens -entis*]

clench, clinch, v.t. & i. & n. (choice between & *t* as indicated). 1. Secure (nail, rivet) by driving point sideways when through (e, l); close (f, s, *t* of teeth (of boxers) come to quarters too close for full-arm blow (l); (Naut.) fasten (rope) with special bend (e, l); confirm, settle (argument, bargain) conclusively (l, e). 2. n. Any of above actions or the resulting state. [OE *clenc(e)an,* cf. OHG *klenken,* cogn. w. CLING, W. causal sense]

Clē′o·pat′ra's nee′dle, n. Egyptian obelisk on Thames embankment.

clep′sydra, n. Ancient time-measuring device worked by flow of water. [L, f. Gk *klepsudra* (*klepsō* steal, *hudōr* water)]

clere′story (-ēr-), n. Part of wall of cathedral or large church, with series of windows, above aisle roofs. [perh. f. CLEAR¹+STOR(E)Y]

cler′gy, n. The clerical order, all persons ordained for religious service (*the* ~ usu. as pl. vb; *a* ~, i.e. the ~ of a country or church, has usu. sing. vb);~men (30 or were *present*): (Hist.) membership of, learning proper *to,* ~ (*benefit of* ~, exemption from trial by secular court, & later from sentence for first conviction, enjoyed by all who could read); ~*man,* ordained minister, esp. of Established Church; ~*man's week, fortnight,* holiday including ~*man's week,* i.e. ~*woman, wife, daughter,* etc., of ~*man,* esp. if dominating days of ~ on ~ 2, 3, Sundays; ~*woman, wife, daughter,* etc., of ~*man,* esp. if dominating church). [OF *clergie* (*clerc* f. LL *CLERICUS, -Y*)]

cler′ic, a. (arch.), & n. Clergyman; = CLERGYMAN. Hence clē′rico- comb. form. [f. LL f. Gk *klērikos* (*klēros* lot, *Acts* i. 17, *Deut.* xviii. 2)]

cler′ical, a. & n. Of clergy, clergyman, or clergymen; of, made by, clerk(s) (~ *error,* in writing out; ~ *duties, staff*); (n.) member of ~ party in a parliament etc. Hence ~ISM(3), ~IST(2), nn., ~IZE(3) v.t., ~LY² adv. [f. LL *clericalis* (prec.-AL)]

clē′rihew, n. Short witty, comic, or nonsensical verse, usu. in four lines of varying length. [E. *Clerihew* Bentley's names]

clerk (||klâk, *klēak), n. (Also ~ *in holy orders*) clergyman (arch., legal & sometimes appended to signature to show status of writer); lay officer of parish church with various duties; (no) *great* ~,

(no) scholar (arch.); officer in charge of records etc., secretary, man of business, of town (*Town C~*), corporation, etc. (usu. a lawyer); person employed in bank, office, shop, etc., to make entries, copy letters, keep accounts, etc.; *shop-assistant; *C~ of the Weather*, personifica-tion of meteorology; *~ of the works*, over-seer of materials etc. in buildings done by contract. Hence ~DOM, ~ESS¹, ~SHIP(1, 3), nn., ~LY¹ a. [OE *cleric, clerc*, as CLERIC]

clev'er, a. Adroit, dexterous, neat in movement; (*~ horse*, good fencer; skilful, talented; ingenious (of doer or thing done). Hence ~ISH¹(2) a., ~LY² adv., ~NESS n. [etym. dub.; *cliver* occurs 1220 = quick at seizing; cf. EFris. *cliifer*, & ME *clivers* claws]

clev'is, n. U-shaped iron at end of beam for attaching tackle. [perh. cogn. w. CLEAVE¹]

clew (-ōō), n., & v.t. **1.** Ball of thread or yarn; this as used in mythol. story to guide through labyrinth; = CLUE. **2.** (Naut.) small cords suspending hammock; lower or aft corner of sail by which it is extended. **3.** v.t. *~ up*, draw lower ends of (sails) to upper yard or mast ready for furling. [OE *cliwen, cliwe* n. prob. dim. of OHG *kliu*; CLUE is a var. spelling merely, but the two are now usu. differentiated]

cliché (klēsh'ā), n. Metal cast esp. stereo or electro duplicate; hackneyed literary phrase. [F]

click, n., & v.i. (Make) slight sharp sound as of cocking gun; catch in machinery acting with this sound; (of horse) touch shoes of fore & hind feet (n., this fault) (S.-Afr. langg.) (make) sharp non-vocal smacking sound as articulation. So ~ER¹ n., foreman shoemaker who cuts out the leather and gives out work, || (Printing) foreman of a companionship of com-positors who distributes the copy etc. [imit., cf. Du. *klikken*, F *cliquer*]

click², v.i. (sl.). Have luck, secure one's object; (of two persons) get along well together, fall in love with each other. [perh. f. dial. vb=snatch, as CLEEK]

cli'ent, n. (Rom. Ant.) plebeian under protection of noble; (arch.) dependant, hanger-on; employer of lawyer; employer of any professional man, customer. Hence ~AGE, ~SHIP, nn., ~LESS a. [f. L *cliens -entis* (*cluere* hear, obey), ~ENT]

cli'entèle, n. **1.** Person's dependants, following. **2.** Customers, supporters, (of physician, shop, theatre, etc.). [f. L *clientela* as prec. in sense 1, but dropped & later readopted f. F in sense 2, & often pronounced & written *-tèle*) as F]

cliff, n. Steep rock-face, usu. overhanging sea; *~s'man*, skilled climber. [OE, cf. Du.; *clif*]

climac'teric (or -ĕr'-), a. & n. **1.** Con-stituting a crisis, critical; (Physiol. & Med.) occurring at period of life (45-60) at which vital force begins to decline. **2.** n. Critical period in life (multiples of 7, odd multiples of 7, etc.; *grand ~*, 63rd year). [f. L f. Gk *klimaktērikos* f. *klimak-tēr* rung of ladder (*klimax*), -IC]

clim'ate, n. (Region with certain) condi-tions of temperature, dryness, wind, light, etc. Hence **climat'IC** a., **climati-CALLY** adv., **clim'atE/OGY** n., **clim'ato-LO'GICAL** a. [f. F *climat* f. LL f. Gk *klima -at-* (*klinō* slope, -M)]

clim'ax, n., & v.i. & t. **1.** Ascending scale; series of ideas or expressions so arranged; last term in these; culmination, apex; hence (irreg.) **climac'tIc** a. **2.** vb. Come, bring, to a *~*. [L, f. Gk *klimax -akos* ladder, climax]

climb (-īm), v.t. & i. (past *~ed* & arch. *clomb* pr. -ōm), go up, (t. & i.) esp. with help of hands; *go up*, (t. & i.) esp. with help of hands; *~ down* (t. & i.), descend (clif etc., or abs.) similarly, (intr.) retreat from position taken up, give in; (of plants) get support etc.) go slowly up; (of plants) get support by tendrils or twining from tree, trellis, etc.; slope upwards; rise by effort in social rank, intellectual or moral strength, etc.; *~ing-iron*, spikes attachable to boot for *~ing* trees or ice slopes; hence **cli'mb-ABLE** (-īma-) a. **2.** n. Piece of *~ing* (*~ down*, abandonment of declared inten-tion), place (to be) *~ed*. [cf. G *klimmen*. prob. cogn. w. CLEAVE²]

cli'mber (-īmer), n. In vbl senses; esp.: climbing plant; kinds of bird, usu. with two forward & two backward toes; person climbing socially. [-ER¹]

clime, n. (poet.). Tract, country, (with or without ref. to climate). [f. LL as CLI-MATE]

clinch. See CLENCH.

clin'cher, clen'cher, n. In vbl senses; esp., remark, argument, that triumph-antly settles a question; *clincher-built=* CLINKER-BUILT. [prec. +-ER¹]

cling, v.i. (clung). *~ together*, remain in one body or in contact, resist separation; stick, adhere *to*, (whether by stickiness, suction, grasping, or embracing; *~ing garments*, showing form of body or limbs) remain faithful *to* (friend, habit, idea) *~stone*, kind of peach or nectarine in which flesh adheres to stone. [OE *clingan* cf. EFris. *klingen* shrink, Sw. *klänge* climb, tendril]

clin'ic, n. Teaching of medicine or surgery at the hospital bed-side; class, institution, so taught, conducted. [f. F *clinique* f. Gk *klīnikē* (*tekhnē*) CLINICAL (art)]

clin'ical, a. (med.). Of, at, the sick-bed (esp. of lectures, teaching, so given; *~ thermometer*, for taking patient's tem-perature). Hence ~LY¹ adv. [f. L f. Gk *klinikos* (*klīnē* bed) +-AL]

clink¹, n., & v.i. & t. (Make, cause *glasses* etc. to make) sharp ringing sound; ||*~ing*

clink'er² (sl. as a. & adv.), exceedingly (good, fine), as *a ~ing*, or *~ing good, race*; *~ stone*, kinds of felspar (f. ringing like iron when struck). Hence **clink'er²** [~'er² [-ER¹] n. (sl.), ~ing specimen. [imit.; cf. Du. *klinken*]

clink², n. (sl.), Prison, lock-up. (esp. *in ~*). [name of a Southwark prison; prob. = CLINCH]

clink'er², n. Very hard yellow Dutch brick; brick with surface vitrified by great heat; mass of bricks fused together or of slag or lava. [f. Du. *klinckaerd* (now *klinker*) f. *klinken* CLINK¹]

clink'er-built, a. (Of boats) made with external planks overlapping downwards & fastened with clinched copper nails. [f. obs. *clink*, *clink* vb = CLINCH]

clinom'eter, n. Instrument for measuring slopes. [f. Gk *klīnō* to slope, -o-, -METER]

Cli'ō, n. (The Muse of) history. [f. Gk *Kleiō* (*kleiō* celebrate)]

clip¹, v.t. (-pp-), & n. 1. Surround closely, grip tightly. 2. n. Appliance for holding things together or for attachment to object as mark; brooch; set of attached cartridges for magazine rifle. [OE *clyppan* embrace cf. ON *klypa* pinch]

clip², v.t. (-pp-), & n. 1. Cut with shears or scissors, trim thus, take away part of (hair, wool) thus, remove hair or wool of (sheep, person) thus, (~ one's *wings*, disable him from pursuing his ambition); pare edge of (coin); omit (letter etc.) syllables of (words); omit letters or ~ *his* g's). 2. n. Operation of shearing or hair-cutting; quantity of wool clipped from sheep, flock, etc.; smart blow with the hand, cut with the whip, etc. [prob. f. ON *klippa*]

clipp'er, n. In vbl senses; also or esp.: instrument for clipping hair; swift mover (esp. of horse or ship); ship with forward-raking bows & aft-raking masts; trans-oceanic flying-boat P; (sl.) thing excellent of its kind. [CLIP²,-ER¹]

clipp'ing¹, n. In vbl senses; esp., piece clipped off. [CLIP²,-ING¹]

clipp'ing², a. In vbl senses; esp., (sl.) first-rate. [CLIP²,-ING²]

clique (-ēk), n. Small exclusive party, set, coterie. Hence **cli'quish¹** (-ēk-), aa., **cli'quishness**, **cli'quey²** (-ēk), aa., **cli'quism(2)**, (-ēk-), nn. [F, f. *cliquer* CLICK¹ cf. CLAQUE]

clit'oris, n. Rudimentary internal part of female genitals analogous to penis. [Gk *kleitoris*]

clivers. See CLEAVERS.

cloā'ca, n. (pl. -ae), Sewer; excrementory cavity in birds, reptiles, etc.; gathering-place of moral evil. Hence **cloā'cal**, a. [L]

cloak, (arch.) **clōke**, n., & v.i. & t. 1. Loose usu. sleeveless outdoor upper garment; covering (~ *of snow*); pretence, pretext, (*under the ~ of*); *~-room*, for leaving ~s, hats, etc., or any luggage.

clō'che (klōsh), n. ~ (*lid*), woman's bell-shaped hat. [F, = bell]

clock¹, n., & v.i. & t. 1. Time-measuring instrument periodically wound up, kept in motion by springs or weights acting on wheels, & recording hours, minutes, etc., by hands on a dial (*o'clock* now usu. only appended to the actual hour, as *six o'clock*, but *quarter to six, six fifteen, 7.25*; *what o'clock is it?*, what is the time?; *of the clock* still in formal or facetious use); (sl.) stop-watch; downy head of dandelion etc.; *~'wise, counter-~'wise*, moving in curve from left to right, right to left, as seen by spectator at centre; *~-work*, mechanism on ~ principle (*like ~-work*, regularly, automatically), (attrib.) regular, mechanical. 2. v.i. *~ in, on, out, off*, register one's entry or exit by means of an automatic ~; (v.t.; sl.) time (race) with stop-watch. [f. MDu. *clocke* (cf. G *glocke* bell), or ONF *cloke* f. LL *cloca* cf. CLOAK; orig. meaning *bell*, prob. in init. of the sound]

clock², n. (shop pl., formerly, *cloc*). Pattern worked in silk etc. on side of stocking. Hence (-)~ED¹ a. [?]

clock'ing, a. ~ *hen*, one sitting on eggs. [part. of dial. vb *clock*=CLUCK]

clod, n., & v.t. (-dd-). Lump of earth etc., soil, land, mere matter; (also *~'hopper, ~'pole*) bumpkin, lout, (so *~'hopping, loutish*), whence *~'dish¹* a., *~'dishness* n.; coarse part of neck of ox as meat. [var. of CLOT now differentiated]

clog¹, n. Block of wood fastened to leg to impede motion; impediment, encumbrance; woman's wooden-soled over-shoe for wet ground; wooden rim etc. with metal rim; *~-dance*, performed in ~s. [?]

clog², v.t. & i. (-gg-). Confine (animal) with clog; be an encumbrance to, burden; impede, hamper; choke up, obstruct by stickiness; fill up with choking matter; stop or act badly from being choked up. [f. prec., & cf. dial. vb *clag* stick]

clogg'y (-g-), a. Lumpy, knotty; sticky. [-Y²]

cloisonné (klwazŏnā'), a. & n. ~ *enamel* or ~, enamel in which colours of pattern are kept apart by thin outline plates. [F]

clois'ter, n., & v.t. (Enclose, shut *up, in*) convent, monastic house, (*the~*), monastic seclusion); covered walk, often round quadrangle with wall on outer & colonnade or windows on inner side, esp. of convent, college, cathedral buildings; whence *~ED¹* (-erd) a. Hence **clois'tral**, a. [ME & OF *cloistre* f. L *claustrum* (*claudere* shut, *-trum* instr. suf.)]

2. vb. Put on one's ~; put ~ on (oneself or another); conceal, disguise. [f. ONF *cloque* f. med. L *cloca* horseman's cape named from its bell shape (CLOCK¹)]

cloke. See CLOAK.

clon'us, n. (path.). Spasm with violent successive muscular contractions & relaxations. Hence **clon'ic** a. [f. Gk *klonos*]

cloop, n., & v.i. (Make) sound (as) of cork being drawn. [imit.]

close¹, a. & adv. **1.** Shut; (of vowels) pronounced with lips or mouth cavity contracted (e.g. *o* in *not* is open, in *note* ~); narrow, confined, contracted, stifling, (~ *siege, prisoner, air*); covered, concealed, secret, given to secrecy, (*keep, lie,* ~, be in hiding; ~-*stool*, chamber-pot mounted in stool with cover) niggardly (so ~-**fist¹**ED² a., ~-**fist'ed**NESS n.); restricted, limited, (~ *corporation* etc.; ‖ ~ *scholarship*, not open to all; ~ BOROUGH); under prohibition (‖ ~ *season, time,* in which something is forbidden, esp. killing of game etc.). **2.** Near; dense, compact, with no or slight intervals, (~ *texture, thicket, writing;* ~ *order, combat;* ~ *quarters,* immediate contact; ~ *reasoner, argument, analysis,* leaving no gaps or weak spots, coherent; also adv., as *shut* ~, *ranked;* ~-*grained,* without visible interstices; *stand, sit,* ~); in or nearly in contact (~ *proximity; a* ~ *shave,* near the skin, also fig., narrow missing of collision etc.; ~-*hauled,* with sail-tacks hauled ~ to side to windward; SAIL ~ *to the wind);* esp. in adv. or prep. phrr. ~ *by,* ~ *to, upon,* as *he was* ~ *by,* ~ *to the road,* ~ *upon two hundred);* fitting exactly (~ *cap,* ~ *resemblance; near & dear;* nearly equal (~ *contest);* concentrated (~ *examination, attention);* ~ *call* (colloq.), a near thing, something almost fatal; ~-*up* n., part of cinema film taken at short range and showing person(s) etc. on large scale. Hence ~'**LY²** (-sl-) adv., ~'**NESS** (-sn-) n. [f. F *clos* f. L *claudere claus-* shut]

close², n. Enclosed place (*break one's* ~, legal, trespass on his land); precinct of cathedral; school playground; (Sc.) entry from street to court at back. [f. F *clos* f. L *clausum* neut. p.p. as prec.]

close³ (-z), v.t. & i., & n. **1.** Shut (t. & i. of lid or box, door or room or house; lit, or = declare or be declared not open, at which shops etc. stop business; ~ *upon,* of place of business etc.; *closing-time,* at hand, box, etc., grasp or imprison, also of eyes, lose sight of by shutting); ~*d shop,* a trade etc. restricted to members of a (particular) trade union. **2.** Be the boundary of, conclude, bring or come to an end, complete, settle, (~ *one's days, die;* ~ *bargain;* abs. stop speaking, often *with the remark* etc.). **3.** Bring or come into contact (~ *the ranks* or, intr., ~ *up;* ~ *electric current* or *circuit,* give it continuity), come within striking distance, grapple with, (Naut., as v.t.) approach or come alongside of (other

ship etc.); (Mil., as v.i., to men in rank) *right* ~, *left* ~, move sideways to right, left. **4.** Express (often eager) agreement with (offer, terms, or person offering them). **5.** ~ *in,* enclose, come nearer, (of days) get successively shorter; ~ *up,* block, fill, coalesce. **6.** n. Conclusion, end; grappling of combatants; (Mus.) cadence. [f. OF *clos-* st. of *clore* f. L *claudere* shut]

clos'et (-z), n., & v.t. Private or small room, esp. for private interviews (so vb, *be* ~*ed with, together,* hold consultation) or for study (~ *play,* to be read not acted; ~ *strategist* etc., theoretical); cupboard, as *china-*~; = WATER-~. [OF (CLOSE³, -ET¹)]

clō'sure (-zher), n., & v.t. **1.** Closing, closed condition. **2.** (Parl.) decision by vote of House of Commons, under certain restrictions, to put the question without further debate; (v.t.) apply ~ to (motion, speakers, etc.). [OF, f. L *clausura* (*claudere claus-,* -URE¹)]

clot, n., & v.i. & t. (-tt-). **1.** Mass of material stuck together; semi-solid lump of coagulated liquid, esp. of blood (~ *of blood,* pop. name for THROMBOSIS). **2.** vb. Form (t. & i.) into ~*s* (~*ted hair,* stuck together in locks; ~*ted cream,* got by scalding milk; ~*ted nonsense,* utter absurdity). [cf. G *klotz* & CLEAT, CLOD]

cloth (-awth, *pl.* -awdhz, -ôths), n. (*pl.* ~s, & in differentiated sense CLOTHES). (Piece, used for any purpose, of) woven or felted stuff; (also *table-*~) covering for table, esp. of linen at meals (*lay the* ~, prepare table for meal); woollen woven fabric as used for clothes; each of the breadths of canvas in a sail; *duster;* ~ *of gold, silver,* tissue of gold or silver threads interwoven with silk or wool; ‖ *American* ~, enamelled ~ like leather; *cut coat according to* ~; adapt expenditure to resources; profession as shown by clothes, esp. clerical (*respect due to his* ~; also *the* ~, clergy); ~-*binding,* cover of book in linen or cotton ~ (Hist.); ~-*yard shaft,* arrow a yard long. [OE *cláth* (earliest sense a ~) cf. G *kleid,* prob. f. *clt-* stick cf. CLAY]

clothe (-dh), v.t. (~*d* or, arch. & literary, *clad*). Provide with clothes, put clothes upon; cover like or as with clothes or a cloth (*leaves* ~ *trees;* ~*d with righteousness, with plantations; body* ~*s soul;* also ~ *face in smiles, ideas in words*). Hence **clŏth¹ING¹**(4) (-dh-) n. [OE *clathian,* whence *clothe* & *clatham,* whence *clad,* f. *cláth* CLOTH; cf. G *kleiden*]

clothes (-ôz, -ôdhz), n. pl. Wearing-apparel; BED¹,~; linen etc. to be washed (~-*bag, -basket,* for conveying this; ~-*horse,* for airing it on; ~-*line,* ~*post,* ‖ -*prop,* ‖ -*peg,* rope, supports of rope, wooden clip on rope, for drying it after washing); ~-*brush;* ~-*moth,* destructive to ~; ~-*press,* cupboard with shelves for

~; (old.)~-man, dealer in usu. old ~. [the orig. pl. of CLOTH, *cloths* being modern]

clōthier (-dh-), n. (Formerly) maker of cloth; dealer in cloth or clothes. [orig. *clother*, see -ER[1]]

clou (klōō), n. Point of greatest interest, chief attraction, central idea. [F, = nail, peg]

cloud, n., & v.t. & i. 1. (Mass of) visible condensed watery vapour (see CIRRUS, CUMULUS, NIMBUS, STRATUS) floating high above general level of ground (~-*drift*, in motion; ~-*rack*, pile of broken ~s; ~-*burst*, violent rainstorm; ~-*capped*, of hill with top hidden by ~; ~-*scape*, picture, picturesque grouping, of ~s; ~-*kissing*, of high hill or building); unsubstantial or fleeting thing; mass of smoke or dust (~-*compeller*, smoker, facet. use of Greek epithet of Zeus); local dimness or vague patch of colour in or on liquid or transparent body; great number of birds, insects, horsemen, arrows, moving together; light woollen scarf; obscurity (*under a* ~ *of night*; a ~ *of words*); in the ~s, mystical, unreal, imaginary, (so ~-*castle*, daydream; ~-*land*, ~-*world*, utopia, fairyland), (of person) abstracted, inattentive; state of gloom, trouble, suspicion, louring or depressed look, (~ *on brow*; *under a* ~, out of favour, discredited); ~-*berry*, mountain shrub with white flower & orange-coloured fruit; C~-*cuckoo-town*, ideal realm [transl. of Gk *Nephelokōkkugia* (*nephelē* cloud + *kokkux* cuckoo) in Aristophanes' *Birds*]; hence ~'LESS a., ~'lessly[2] adv., ~'lessNESS, ~'WARD(s) adv. 2. v.b. Overspread, darken, with ~s, gloom, or trouble; become over-cast or gloomy (~ *up, over*). [prob. f. OE *clūd*, meaning & cogn. w. CLOT]

clough (kluf), n. Ravine, steep valley (usu. with torrent bed. [cf. Gk *klēugē*]

clout, n., & v.t. (arch. & dial.). Patch (n. & v.); a cloth (esp. *dish-~*); piece of clothing; rap, knock, (n. & v., esp. on head with knuckles); iron plate on boot etc. to save wear, (also ~-*nail*) broad-headed nail for attaching this; (Hist.) canvas on frame as target at archery (*in the* ~, *a hit*). [OE *clūt* cogn. w. CLOT]

clōve[1], **clōven**. See CLEAVE[1].

clōve[2], n. One of small bulbs making up compound bulb of garlic, shallot, etc. (usu. *of*). [OE *clufu* cogn. w. CLOT]

clōve[3], n. (Pungent aromatic dried bud of) tropical tree (*oil of* ~s, extracted from ~s & used in medicine; (also ~-*gilly-flower*) ~-scented Pink, original of carnation & other double pinks. [ME *clou(e*) f. F *clou* (*de girofle*; *girofle* (see GILLYFLOWER) f. F *clou* (*de girofle*) was orig. name of the spice; *clou* (f. L *clāvus* nail) *de girofle* was used of it w. ref. to its shape, transferred to

the similarly shaped bud of Pink, & later divided into *clove* for the spice, & *gilly-flower* for the Pink]

clōve hitch, n. Hitch by which rope is secured at any intermediate part round spar or rope that it crosses at right angles. [perh. old p.p. of CLEAVE[1], as showing parallel separate lines]

clō'ver, n. Kinds of trefoil used for fodder (*be, live, in* ~, in ease & luxury]. [OE *clāfre* cf. Du. *klaver*, G *klee*]

clown, n., & v.i. 1. Rustic; ignorant or ill-bred man, whence ~'ısh[1] a., ~'ıshly[2] adv., ~'ıshNESS n.; jester, esp. in panto-mime or circus, whence ~'ERY(4) n. 2. v.i. Play the ~. [prob. cogn. w. CLOT, &=lump; cf. Icel. *clunni*]

cloy, v.t. Satiate, weary, by richness, sweetness, sameness, excess, of food or pleasure (usu. *with*). [f. obs. *accloy* choke (put nail into) f. OF *encloyer* (AC-) f. LL *inclāvāre* f. L *clāvus* nail)]

clōxe. See CLOCK[2].

---

club[1], n. 1. Stick with one thick end as weapon (*Indian* ~s, pair swung to develop muscles; ~-*law*, rule by physical force); kinds of stick used in games, esp. golf; structure or organ in Bot. etc. with knob at end; ~-*footed*, (with) congenitally distorted foot; ~-*moss*, kind with upright spikes of spore-cases; ~-*root*, disease of turnips etc.; playing-card of suit bearing black trefoil (~s, the suit). 2. Association of persons united by some common interest, meeting periodically for co-operation (*Alpine, golf, yacht*, BENEFIT, ~) or conviviality; body of persons with purposes & having premises (~-*house*) for resort, meals, temporary residence, etc. (||~-*land*, St. James's in London, where ~s cluster), whence ~'DOM n., ~'LESS a. [ME *clubbe* perh. f. ON *clubba* by assim. f. *clumba*=CLUMP; sense 2 prob. =knot of persons]

club[2], v.t. & i. (-bb-). Beat with club; use butt of (gun) as club; bring, come, into a mass; contribute (money, ideas) to common stock; (v.i.) combine *together*, with, for joint action, making up a sum, etc.; (Mil.) get (one's men) into a confused mass. [f. prec.]

clŭbb'able, a. Fit for membership of a club. [CLUB[1],-ABLE]

club'haul, v.t. Tack (*ship*, or abs.) by anchoring & cutting cable, as device for getting off lee-shore when there is not room to wear. [?]

clŭck, n., & v.i. (Make) guttural cry of hen. Hence ~'y[2] a., = CLOCKING. [cf. obs. & dial. *clock* (OE *cloccian*); imit.]

clue (-ōō), n. Fact or principle that serves as guide, or suggests a line of inquiry, in any problem, investigation, or study; thread of story, train of thought; (also rarely in other senses of) CLEW. Hence ~'LESS (-ōō-) a. [=CLEW]

clŭm′ber, n. Kind of spaniel. [*C~* in Notts.]

clŭmp, n., & v.i. & t. **1.** Cluster of trees or shrubs (usu. *of*); (also *~-sole*) extra thickness of leather added to sole, usu. nailed on. **2.** vb. Tread heavily; heap or plant together; provide (boot) with ~. [cf. G *klumpen*, Du. *klomp*, ON *clumba* & *clubba* CLUB]

clŭm′s|y̆ (-z-), a. Awkward in movement or shape, ungainly; ill-contrived; without tact. Hence ~**ly̆²** adv., ~**ĭness** n. [f. obs. *clumse* be stiff with cold; cf. Norw. *klumsa* paralyse, & CLEM, CLAMMY]

clŭnch, n. Soft white limestone used for internal carving-work. [perh. var. of CLUMP, cf. *lump bunch*, *hump hunch*]

clŭng. See CLING.

clŭs′ter, n., & v.t. & i. **1.** Group of similar things, esp. such as grow together, bunch; swarm, group, of persons, animals, etc. **2.** vb. Bring or come into, be in, a ~ or ~s (*~ed columns*, *pillars*, *shafts*, several close together, or disposed round or half detached from pier). [OE *clyster* prob. cogn. w. CLOT]

clŭtch¹, v.t. & t. Seize eagerly, grasp tightly; snatch *at*. [OE *clyccean* f. OTeut.(foll.)]

clŭtch², n. Tight grasp; (pl.) grasping hands, cruel grasp; a grasping *at*; (Mech.) arrangement for throwing working parts into or out of action, gripping-piece of crane. [ME *cloke* claw. n. f. OTeut. *kluk-*]

clŭtch³, n. Set of eggs; brood of chickens. [earlier *cletch* f. *cleck* to hatch f. ON *klekja*]

clŭt′ter, n., & v.i. & t. (Bustle, run, with) confused noise or movement, loss of self-possession; confused mass, untidy state, litter n. & (esp. in *~ed up with*) v.t. [var. of obs. *clotter* (CLOT, *-ER⁵*]

Clȳdesdāle (klīdz′dāl), a. & n. (Of) a breed of heavy draught-horses (orig. from *Clyde* district in Scotland).

clȳp′e|ŭs, n. Shield-like part of insect's head. Hence ~**al**, ~**āte²**, ~**ĭform**, aa., **~o-** comb. form. [L, = shield]

clȳs′ter, n., & v.t., (med., now rare). = EN-EMA; (vb) treat with ~. [L, f. Gk *klustēr* syringe (*kluzō* wash)]

‖ **cmd.** =OD.

co-, pref. **I.** Short form of *com-* (*cum* prep. with), used in L only before vowels, **h**, **gn**, & (in the correct classical form) **n**, but in E as living pref. before any letter. **1.** Prefixed to vbs.= with other subjects (*cooperate*) or objects (*co-adjust*); to adji. & advv., = jointly, together, mutually, (*coeternal*, *coadjacent*); & to nouns, = joint, mutual, (*coheir*, *coequality*). **2.** In some math. words, short for *complement*, = 'of the complement'; *complement of* as *cosine*, *co-declination*. In unfamiliar words, a hyphen or diaeresis is used to indicate pronunciation, and the three

methods (cooperate, co-operate, coöperate) are employed arbitrarily.

cōăcerva′tion, n. Heaping together, pile. [f. L L co(*acervāre* f. *acervus* f. *acervus* heap, see -ATION)]

coach, n., & v.t. & t. **1.** State carriage; (also *stage-~*) large four-wheeled & usu. four-horsed close carriage with seats inside and on the roof carrying passengers at fixed rates & times with stoppages for meals & relays of horses; HACKNEY-~; MOURNING-~; SLOW-~; (official name for) railway carriage; (Naut.) room near stern of man-of-war; private tutor; trainer of athletic team etc.; *drive ~ & six through Act of Parliament*, stultify it; *~-box*, driver's seat; *~-built*, (of motorcar bodies) built of wood by craftsmen; *~-dog*, = CARRIAGE-*dog*; *~-house*, outhouse for carriages; *~′man*, driver of any carriage, whence ~′**manship(3)** n.; hence ~′**ful(2)** n. **2.** vb. Travel in, go by, stage-~ (*in the old ~ing days*); tutor, train, (pupil for examination, crew for race); give hints to, prime with facts; (intr.) read with tutor. [f. F *coche* f. Hung. *kocsi* adj. f. *Kocs* place-name]

cōăd′jŭtor (-ōō-; *also* -ăjōō̆-), n. Assistant (esp. to bishop or other ecclesiastic). [f. OF *coadjuteur -jut-* help, -OR²)]

cōăd′ūnate, a. (physiol. & bot.). Congenitally united. [f. L L co(*adunātus* p.p. of *apenāre* make one f. *unus* one)]

cōăg′ulāte, v.t. & i. Change (t. & i.) from fluid to more or less solid state, clot, curdle, set, solidify. Hence or cogn., ~**A′TION**, ~**ātor²(2)**, ~**ANT(2)**, nn. [f. obs. *coagulate* adj. f. L L *coagulāre* f. *coagulum* n. f. co(*agere* bring) usu. *cogere* collect; -ATE²,³]

coai′ta (kōi′-), n. Small S.-Amer. monkey (Red-faced Spider-monkey). [f. Braz. *coatá*]

coal, n., & v.t. & i. **1.** Hard opaque black or blackish mineral of carbonized vegetable matter found in seams or strata below earth's surface & used as fuel & in manufacture of gas, tar, etc. (~s, pieces of it ready for supplying fire; chief kinds, ANTHRACITE, BITUMINOUS, LIGNITE; *heap ~s of fire*, return good for evil, cf. *Rom.* xii. 20; *blow the ~s*, fan flame of passion etc.; *haul*, *call*, *over the ~s*, reprimand; *~s to Newcastle*, superfluous action); *~-bed*, *-seam*, stratum of ~; *~-black*, quite; *~-box*, *-scuttle*, ‖ (vulg.) *-vase*, receptacle for~ to supply room fire (*~-scuttle bonnet*, with front projection as of inverted ~ box); *~-BUNKER*; *~-dust*, small *~s*; ‖ *~-factor*, middleman between ~-owners & customers; *~-field*, district with series of ~ strata; *~-fish*, black cod; ‖ *~-flap*, *-plate*, cover of *~-cellar* opening in pavement; *~-gas*, mixed gases extracted from

For compounds of *co-* not given consult OO-.

~ & used for lighting & heating; ~ of *heaver*, man employed in moving ~; whence ~'ie [-i⁴] n.; ~hole, || small ~ cellar; ~master, owner or lessee of ~mine or ~pit=COLLIERY; ~measures (Geol.), series of rocks formed by seams of ~ & intervening strata; ~sack, black patch in Milky Way (esp. one near Southern Cross); ~screen, frame for parting large from small ~s; ~tar, TAR extracted from bituminous ~ & yielding paraffin, naphtha, benzene, creosote, & aniline dyes; ~tit, = COALMOUSE; ~ *whipper*, man, machine, raising ~ from ship's hold; hence ~'LESS (-l-), ~'Y² aa. 2. vb. Put ~ into (ship etc.); take in supply of ~. [OE *col*, cf. G *kohle*]

coalesce', v.i. Come together & form one (of material or immaterial things); combine in a coalition (of statesmen, parties). So ~'cence n., ~'cent a. [f. L *coalescere coalit-* (prec., ~ION)]

coali'tion, n. Union, fusion; ||(Pol.) temporary combination for special ends between parties that retain distinctive principles. Hence ~IST(1) (-sho-) n. [f. L *coalitio* (prec., ~ION)]

coal'mouse, cole-, n. Small dark-coloured bird (also COAL-tit). [ME *colmose* f. OE *colmāse* (*col* coal+*māse* f. WG *maisa* kinds of small bird)]

coam'ing, n. Raised border round hatches etc., of ship to keep out water. [?]

coarse, (kôrs), a. Common, inferior, (~ *fish, fare*); rough, loose, or large, in texture, grain, or features; not delicate in perception, manner, or taste, unrefined; rude, uncivil, vulgar; obscene (of language); ~*fibred*, ~*grained*, lit. of things, also fig. of persons = without grain. Hence ~'LY² (-sl-) adv., ~'NESS (2) n. [phr. *in ~ or of course*=ordinary, cf. sense of *mean* (average, low) & *plain* (ordinary, ugly)]

coast¹, n. (Also *sea~*) border of land near sea, sea-shore; CLEAR¹ ~; (U.S. & Canada) toboggan slide; (hence through coast²) downhill run on bicycle with feet up or still; ~*guard(sman)*, Admiralty ~ police(man); ~*line*, the line of the sea-shore esp. with regard to its configuration (*the rugged ~line of the island*); || ~ *waiter*, custom-house officer who deals with goods carried ~wise. Hence ~AL a., ~WARD(S) adv., ~'WISE a. & adv. [ME & OF *coste* (now *côte*) f. L *costa* rib, side]

coast², v.i. Sail along coast, trade between ports on same coast; slide down hill on toboggan, bicycle down hill without pedalling. Hence ~ER¹ n., ~*ing vessel*, silver tray for decanter, rest for the foot on front fork of bicycle. [f. OF *costier* (now *côtoyer*) f. Rom. **costicare* as prec.]

coat, n., & v.t. 1. Man's sleeved usn. cloth body garment (*dress-~*, with swallow tails for the evening; ~ of MAIL; FROCK-~; ~ *gread~*, *top~*, out-door, worn over another; *red ~*, traditional uniform of British soldier; so *red~*, soldier; ~ *of arms*, herald's tabard, gentleman's heraldic bearings or shield; ~ *armour*, blazonry, heraldic arms; ~*card*, now usn. *court*, playing-card with coated figure, king, queen, or knave; ~ *trail one's ~tails*, for someone to tread on, = seek to pick quarrel; *dust one's ~*, beat him; *turn one's ~*, change sides, desert; *wear the king's ~*, serve as soldier); woman's stout buttoned overcoat, (also, esp. in ~ & *skirt*) shorter tailor-made garment falling over skirt; petticoat (arch. & dial.; in literature esp. in KILT one's ~s). 2. Covering compared to garment; beast's hair, fur, etc. of organ; skin, rind, husk, layer of onion; hence (~)~ED², ~LESS, aa. 3. v.t. Put or (with *paint* etc., as subj.) be ~ of paint, tin, etc., *upon*, (p.p.) covered over *with* dust etc. [f. OF *cote* (now *cotte* petticoat) f. med. L *cotta* cf. OHG *chozza* (garment) of shaggy woollen stuff]

coatee', n. Short-tailed (esp. mil.) coat. [-EE]

coa'ti (-ah-), n. American carnivorous mammal like civet & racoon with long flexible snout. [Braz. (*cua* cincture, *tim* nose)]

coat'ing, n. Layer of paint etc.; material for coats. [-ING¹]

coax, v.t. & i. Persuade by blandishments (*to do, into doing or good temper* etc.; ~ *thing out of person*; ~ *fire to light, key into lock*, etc.); ~ *away, out*, etc., entice; practise wheedling. Hence ~ER¹ n. [=fool vb f obs. *cokes* fool n. perh. cogn. W. COCKNEY]

coax'al, -ial, a. (math.). Having common axis. [CO-, AXIS, -AL]

cob¹, n. Male swan; stout short-legged riding-horse, whence ~b'Y² a.; (also ~*nut*) large kind of hazel-nut; roundish lump of coal etc.; round-headed loaf; *corn~*. [?]

|| **cob²**, n. Composition of clay, gravel, & straw, used for building walls. [?]

cob'alt (-awlt-), n. Silvery-white metal similar in many respects to nickel; deep-blue pigment made from it. Hence **cobal'tic**, ~IFEROUS, **cobal'tous** (chem.), aa., **cobal'to-** comb. form. [-awl-). [G, prob. = *kobold* goblin of mines]

cob'ble¹, n., & v.t. (Also ~*-stone*) water-worn rounded stone of size used for paving (vb. pave with these); (pl.) coals of this size. [cf. COB¹]

cob'ble², v.t. Put together roughly; mend, patch *up*, (esp. shoes). [etym. dub.; foll. is quoted a century earlier]

cob'bler, n. Mender of shoes; clumsy workman; (often *sherry ~*) iced drink of wine, sugar, lemon, sucked through straw

(origin unknown; from U.S.); ~'s wax, resinous substance used for waxing thread. [?]

Cob'denism, n. Policy based on Free Trade, international cooperation, & retrenchment, peace, non-intervention, and opposition to Empire. Hence ~ITE¹(†) a. & n. [R. Cobden, d. 1865, -ISM]

co'ble, n. Kinds of fishing-boat in Scotland & N.E. England. [cf. W ceubal, Bret. caubal]

cŏb'ra (dĕ capĕll'ō), n. The venomous Hooded Snake of India, with neck dilated like hood under irritation. [Port.; cobra t. L colubra snake, capello hood, = F chapeau]

cob'wĕb, n. & a. Spider's network, material of it, thread of this; thing of flimsy texture (so adj., thin, flimsy) subtle fanciful reasoning; musty rubbish (esp. fig. as ~s of antiquity; blow away the ~s, take an airing); entanglement, mesh. Hence ~BED¹(-bd), ~BY², aa., ~BERY(5) n. [obs. cob spider is prob. f. cobweb; but cf. Flem. cobbe, coppe, spider]

cŏc'a, n. (Leaves of) Bolivian shrub (chewed as stimulant). [Sp., f. Peruv. cuca]

cocaine', n. Drug from coca producing local insensibility. Hence ~IZE(5) v.t., ~IZA'TION, ~ISM(5), nn. [-INE¹]

cŏc'cagee (-gē), n. A cider apple, cider from it. [f. Ir. cac a ghéidh goose dung (so coloured)]

cŏc'cyx (-ks-), n. Small triangular bone ending spinal column in man; analogous part in birds etc. Hence or cogn. **cŏccy'gĕal** a., **cŏccy'gĕo-**, **cŏc'cyg(o)-**, (-ks-), comb. forms. [L, f. Gk kokkux -ugos cuckoo, (like its bill)]

cŏch'in-chin'a, n. & a. (Fowl) of Cochin China breed. [place]

cŏch'ineal, n. Dried bodies of insect reared on cactus in Mexico etc., used for making scarlet dye & carmine. [f. F cochenille f. It. cocciniglia (coccino f. L coccinum scarlet robe f. coccum scarlet, orig. berry)]

cŏch'lea (-k-), n. (pl. -leae), Spiral cavity of internal ear. [L, = snail]

cŏck¹, n. 1. Male bird (alone of domestic fowl, as below, also of BLACK~; of other birds only when aided by context; in comb, in bird-names, as PEACOCK, WOOD~, & prefixed = male as ~ robin; ~ sparrow, male sparrow, small lively sparrow, pugnacious person; ~ of the wood, caperaillye; || ~ of the north, brambling; ~-nest, built by some ~s, as wren, to roost in); (short for) woodcock (w. collect. sing. for pl.); male of domestic fowl (~-a-doodle-doo, its crow, child's name for ~); GAME¹~; ~-o'-bull story, idle invention, incredible tale; ~-crow, -crowing, dawn; ~-fighting, setting ~s to fight as sport; this beats ~-fighting, is inexpressibly delightful; live like fighting ~s, on best of fare; that ~ won't fight, that plea, plan, will not do; ~ lobster, male; ~-shot, -shy, object set up to be thrown at with sticks, stones, etc., as formerly ~s at Shrovetide, a throw at this; ~s'-comb, crest of ~, Yellow Rattle & other plants, & see COXCOMB; ~s'foot, a pasture grass; ~s'head, kinds of trefoil; ~-spur, ~'s spur, gas-burner of same shape; ~ of the walk, dominant person (so ~ of the school among boys); old ~, familiar vocative. 2. Tapped spout, tap, (~-metal, two parts copper to one of lead); (not decent) penis; lever in gun raised ready to be released by trigger (at half, full, ~, of gun half-ready or ready to be let off); indicating-tongue of balance. [OE cocc, cf. F coq. LL coccus; prob. imit. from its cluck; sense 2 perh. f. resemblance of tap to ~'s head & comb]

cŏck², v.t. & i. Erect, stick or stand up, jauntily or defiantly (~ the ears, in attention; ~ one's nose, in contempt; a SNOOK; ~ one's eye, glance knowingly, wink); ~ one's hat, set it on aslant, also turn up the brim (~ed hat, formerly, with brim fixed so, now, brimless triangular hat pointed before, behind, & above, of various uniform costumes; knock into a ~ed hat, out of shape or recognition); raise cock of (gun) in readiness for firing. [f. prec. n. ref. to cock's comb, crowing-attitude, etc.]

cŏck³, n. Upward bend (of nose etc.); significant turn (of eye); way of cocking hat; cocked state of gun (see COCK²). [f. prec.]

cŏck⁴, n., & v.t. (Heap hay, rarely corn, into) small conical heap(s) in the field. [cf. Norw. kok a heap, ON kökkr lump]

cockabon'dy (-tn-), n. Kind of fishing-fly. [f. W cock a bon ddu red with black trunk]

cockā'de¹, n. Rosette etc. worn in hat as badge of office or party or part of livery, esp. black leather rosette (badge of House of Hanover) worn by servants of persons serving Crown. Hence ~ED³ a. [f. F cocarde fem. of 16th-c. coquard pert (coq COCK¹, -ARD)]

cŏck-a-hoop', a. & adv. Exultant(ly), with boastful crowing. [orig. doubtful; there were inn-signs Hart, Swan, Cock, etc., on the Hoop; early quotations do not suggest the bird; an explanation (1670) is that the spigot (cock) being taken out and laid on hoop of barrel, the running of the ale produced jollity]

Cockaigne' (-ān), **-ayne'** n. Imaginary land of idleness and luxury; (punningly) w. ref. to COCKNEY London. [f. OF

For compounds of co- not given consult co-.

coquīnus perh. = cake-land (L *coquere* cook).]

cŏck´-a-leek´ie. = COOKY-LEEKY.

cŏckalŏr´um, n. (colloq.) Self-important little man; || high ~, boy's game of leap-frog type. [arbitrary form, f. COCK¹]

cŏckatoo´, n. Kinds of parrot with mov-able crest. [f. Malay *kakatūa* w. assim. to COCK¹]

Cŏck´atrice, n. = BASILISK. [f. OF *cocatris*, f. L †*calcātricem* nom. *-tor* treader, transl. of Gk *īchneumōn* ichneumon (*ichneuō* trace)]

cŏck´boat, n. Small ship's boat. [f. obs. *cock,* cf. OF *coque,* Du. *kog,* etym. dub.]

cŏck´chafer, n. Greyish-chestnut beetle flying with loud whirring sound. [COCK¹]

cŏck´er¹, v.t. Indulge, pamper, coddle, (child, invalid, etc.; usu. *up*). [perh. f. obs. *cock* vb in same sense, & cf. etym. of COCKNEY]

Cŏck´er², n. *According to* ~, exact, correct. [E.]

cŏck´er³, n. Breed of spaniel, [COCK¹ (as starting woodcock etc.) + -ER¹]

cŏck´erel, n. Young cock; pugnacious youth. [dim. of COCK¹, cf. *pickerel, mongrel*]

cŏck´-eyed (-īd), a. (sl.). Squinting; crooked, set aslant, not level; stupid. [COCK¹?]

cŏck´-horse, adv. (Also *a-cock-horse*, see A²) astride, mounted. [in 16th c.= toy horse]

cŏck´le¹, n. (Also *Corn~*) purple-flowered plant growing among corn, esp. wheat; disease of wheat turning grains black. [OE *coccel*; exl. E.; perh. f. a L dim. of *coccum* berry]

cŏck´le², n. An edible bivalve; its shell; ~*s of the heart*, one's feelings (*delight, warm, the ~s* etc.). [f. F *coquille* shell f. L *conchȳlia* pl. of L f. Gk *kogkhulion* dim. of *koghkha* mussel]

cŏck´le³, v.i. & t., & n. (Make to) bulge, curl up, pucker; (n.) bulge or wrinkle in paper, glass, etc. [cf. F *coquiller* blister (of bread)]

cŏck´le⁴, n. Radiating-stove for heating room. [perh. f. Du. *kakel* f. G *kachel* stove-tile]

cŏck´-loft (-aw), n. Small upper loft. [?]

cŏck´ney, n. & a. (pl. ~s). (Characteristic of a) native of London (usn. contemp-tuous, ~ *accent*). Hence ~DOM (-nĭd-), ~ESE´ (-nĭēz´), nn., ~FY (-nĭ-), ~ISH² a., ~ISM(2, 4) n., (-nĭĭ-), ~IZE(3) v.t. & i. [ME *coken-ey* f. OE *æg*); orig. etym. (*coken* gen. pl., *eg* f. OE *ǣg*) orig. senses egg in dial., cf. G *hahnenei*); obs. senses prob. small or ill-shaped egg (still *cock's egg*), 'one made by other animals'; (vb) are 'child that sucketh long'; one made a wanton or nestle-cock of; townsman, the limitation to London being later]

cŏck´pit, n. Place made for cockfights; arena of any struggle (~ *of Europe,* Bel-gium); after part of man-of-war's orlop deck, quarters of junior officers, used in action as hospital; (Aeronaut.) space for pilot etc. in fuselage of aeroplane.

cŏck´roach, n. Nocturnal voracious dark-brown beetle-like insect (also *black-beetle*) infesting kitchens. [f. Sp. *cucaracha* etym. dub.]

cŏck´-sure´ (-shoor), a. Certain to happen, undoubtedly about to do; quite con-vinced *of, about*; self-confident, dogmatic, presumptuous. Hence ~NESS (-rn-) n. [COCK¹ used intensively; SURE]

cocksy, coxy, coxiness. = COOKY etc.

cŏck´y, cŏck´sy, cŏck´tailed (-ld), a. (Horse) with docked tail, of racing stamp but not thorough-bred; (person) placed above his birth or breeding; kind of beetle; drink of spirit with bitters, sugar, etc. (origin doubtful; from U.S.). [tail like that of cock, or that cocks up; sense *half-bred* f. docking of hunters & stage-coach horses]

cŏck´up, n. (typog.). Initial letter much taller than the rest. [COCK²]

cŏck´y, cŏck´sy, coxy, etc. a. Conceited, pert. Hence **cŏck´ily², cŏx´i-,** adv., **cŏck´INESS, cŏx´i-,** n. [COCK¹, -Y²]

cŏck´y-leek´y, n. Scotch soup of cock boiled with leeks.

cŏckŷōll´ŷbīrd, n. (Nursery phr. for) bird. [COCK¹]

cŏc´ō (pl. ~os), **cŏc´ōa¹** (-kō), **cŏk´er,** n. (Also ~-*nut,* ~-*tree,* ~-*nut-tree*) tropical palm-tree; *coco-nut,* its large ovate brown hard-shelled seed with edible white lining enclosing whitish liquid (~-*nut milk*), (sl.) human head; *that accounts for the milk in the* (joc.) now all is explained; ~-*nut butter,* the solid oil obtained from the lining of a ~-nut, used in soap, candles, ointment, etc.; ~-*nut matting,* made from fibre of nut's outer husk; *double* ~-*nut,* much larger two-lobed seed of Seychelles palm. [~a added f. confusion w. foll.; f. Port. & Sp. *coco* grimace; *coker* chiefly in commerce, use to avoid ambiguity]

cŏc´ōa² (-kō), n. Powder made from crushed cacao seeds often with other ingredients; drink made from this or from the seeds; ~ *bean,* cacao seed; ~ *nib,* cotyledon of this; ~ *powder,* kind of gunpowder. [corruption of CACAO]

cŏcoon´, n. & v.t. & i. Silky case spun by larva to protect it as chrysalis, esp. that of silkworm, whence ~ERY(3) n.; similar structure made by other animals; (vb) form, wrap (oneself, thing etc.) in, ~. [f. F. *cocon* dim. of *coque* shell]

cŏcŏtte´, n. Member of the Parisian demi-monde; fashionable prostitute. [F]

cŏd¹, n. Large sea fish (also ~-*fish*); ~-*bank,* submarine bank frequented by it; ~-*liver oil,* used as medicine. [exsl. E, etym. dub.]

cod², v.t. & i. (sl.; -dd-). Hoax, fool. [?]

cod'a, n. (mus.). Independent and often elaborate passage introduced after the natural conclusion of a movement (also fig.). [It., f. L *cauda* tail]

cod'dle, v.t., v.i., & n. Treat as invalid, keep from cold & exertion, feed *up*; (n.) person who coddles himself or others. [perh.=CAUDLE]

code, n., & v.t. 1. Systematic collection of statutes, body of laws so arranged as to avoid inconsistency & overlapping, whence **cod'ify** v.t., **cod'ifier**, **cod'ifica'tion**, nn.; set of rules on any subject; prevalent morality of a society or class (esp. ~ *of honour*); system of mil. etc. signals; (Telegr.) set of letter or figure or word groups with arbitrary meanings for brevity or secrecy. 2. v.t. (Also *codify*) put (message) into ~ words, whence **cod'er**¹ n. [F, f. L CODEX]

co-declina'tion, n. (astron.). Complement of the declination, North-Polar distance. [CO-(2)]

cod'eine, n. Alkaloid in opium used as hypnotic. [f. Gk *kōdeia* poppy-head + -INE³]

cod'ex, n. (pl. *-dicēs*). Manuscript volume, esp. of ancient Bible or classical texts. [L, earlier *caudex* tree-trunk, tablet, book]

codg'er, n. (colloq.). Fellow, buffer, queer old person. [perh. var. of CADGER]

cod'icil, n. Supplementary addition, esp. modifying or revoking will. So **codicill'-ary¹** a. [f. L *codicillus* (usu. pl.) dim. of CODEX]

cod'ling¹, n. Small cod-fish. [-LING¹(2)]

cod'lin(g)², n. Kinds of apple of long tapering shape; ~*s-&-cream*, willow-herb. [earlier *querdling* perh. f. Ir. *cueirt* apple + -LING¹]

*****co'-ed'**, n. (colloq.). Girl or woman student at co-educational institution. [abbr.]

co-ēdūca'tion, n. Education of boys & girls together. Hence ~AL(-sho-) a. [CO-]

coeffi'cient (-shnt), n. Joint agent or factor; (Alg.) number placed before and multiplying another quantity known or unknown; (Physics) multiplier that measures some property (~ *of friction, expansion*, etc.); *differential* ~, quantity measuring rate of change of a function of any variable with respect to that variable. [CO-]

coel'iac (sēl-), a. (physiol.). Of the belly. [f. L f. Gk *koiliakos* (*koilia* belly f. *koilos* hollow)]

coel'o(-) (sēl-), **coel'o-** (sel-), in comb. = Gk *koilos* common.

coen'obite (sēn-), **cēn'**, n. Member of monastic community. Hence **c(o)eno-**

bit'ı'c(al) aa., **c(o)en'obitısm**(3) n., (sēn-). [f. LL *coenobīta* f. LL f. Gk *koinobion* convent (COENO-, *bios* life)]

coĕq'ual, a. & n. (Arch., theolog., or emphatic, for) equal. Hence **cŏēqual'ıty** (-kwŏl-) n., ~ly² adv. [CO-]

coĕrce', v.t. & i. Forcibly constrain or impel (person) into quiet, obedience, or any course (*into*, rarely *to do*, or abs.); use force, secure by force (*a* ~*d obedience*). Hence **cŏēr'cıble** a. [f. L co(*ercēre* excit-=*arcēre* shut up)]

coĕr'cıon (-shn), n. Controlling of voluntary agent or action by force; government by force, esp. of Ireland by suspension of ordinary liberties (*C~ Act, Bill*, with such exceptional provisions). Hence ~ary¹ a., ~ıst(2) n. & a., (-sho-). [f. OF *coercion* f. L *coerc(ō)tionem* (COERCE, -ION)]

coĕr'cıve, a. Of, acting by, exercising, coercion. Hence ~ly² (-vl-) adv., ~NESS (-vn-) n. [irreg. f. COERCE +-IVE]

coĕssen'tial (-shl), a. Of the same substance or essence. [CO-]

coĕtān'eous, a. = COĒVAL a. [f. LL co(*aetaneus* f. L *aetas* age)+-OUS]

coĕtĕrn'al, a. Alike eternal. So ~ıty² n., ~ly² adv. [CO-]

coĕv'al, a. & n. (Person) of same date or origin, of same age, existing at same epoch, of same duration. Hence ~ıty n. (-āl-), ~ly² adv. [f. L co(*aevus* f. *aevum* age)]

co-exĕc'ūtor, cō-exĕc'ūtrıx, (-gz-), nn. Joint executor, executrix. [CO-]

coĕxıs|t', v.i. Exist together or *with*. So ~tent a., ~tence n. [CO-]

coĕxtĕn'sıve, a. Extending over same space or time. [CO-]

cŏff'ee (-fı), n. Drink made from seeds of a shrub roasted & ground; light meal with ~, ~ *as final course at dinner*; the shrub, its seeds raw, roasted, or ground; ~-*beam*, the seed; ~-*cup*, of special shape or size; ~-*grounds*, sediment after infusion; ~-*house, -palace*, refreshment house; ~-*mill*, for grinding seeds; ~-*pot*, for making or serving ~ in; ~-*room*, public dining-room of hotel; ~-*tavern*, temperance refreshment house. [f. Turk. f. Arab. *qahweh* the drink]

cŏff'er, n. Box, esp. for valuables; (pl.) treasury, funds; sunk panel in ceiling etc.; ~-*dam*, water-tight case in bridge-building, caisson. [f. OF *cofre* f. L f. Gk *kophinos* basket; cf. *cofre*, F. *ordre*, L *ordinem*]

cŏff'ın, n., & v.t. 1. Chest in which corpse is buried; *drive nail into* one's ~, hasten his, one's, death by annoyance, intemperance, etc.; unseaworthy ship; horse's hoof below coronet (~-*bone*, last phalangeal bone of foot; ~-*joint* at top of hoof; ~-*plate*, of metal in lid with deceased's

For compounds of *co-* not given consult *co-*.

cog¹, n. One of series of projections on edge of wheel or side of bar transferring motion by engaging with another series; ~*-wheel*. [f. ?]

coffle, n. Train of beasts, slaves, etc., fastened together. [f. Arab. *qāfilah* caravan]

cog², v.t. (-gg-). ~ *dice*, fraudulently control the way they fall (~*ged dice* for loaded dice is a mistake of modern archaists). [?]

co'gent, a. Forcible, convincing, (of argument, &, usu. now playfully as though by transf. from this, of motive, compulsion, etc.). Hence **co'GENCY** n., ~**LY²** adv. [F, f. L *cogere*=*coagere* drive), *cogent-*]

co'gitable, a. Able to be grasped by reason, conceivable. [f. L *cogitabilis* (foll., -ABLE)]

co'gitate, v.i. & t. Ponder, meditate; devise; (Philos.) form conception of. Hence or cogn. ~**ATION** n., ~**ATIVE** a., ~**ATIVENESS** n. [f. L *cogi-tare*=*co(agitare* AGITATE) think.]

cognac (kŏn'yăk), n. French brandy, prop. that distilled from ~ wine. [place-name]

co'gnate, a. & n. 1. Descended from common ancestor (cf. AGNATE), akin in origin, nature, or quality; a. relative. 2. (Philol.) of same linguistic family; representing same original word; of parallel development in different allied languages (*father* is ~ with L *pater*, *paternal* is derived from it); a. ~ *word*. 3. (Gram.) object or accusative, one of kindred meaning to vb, used adverbially, not as true object (in *die the death*, *death* is ~, in *her slew death* it is object). Hence ~**NESS** (-tn-) n. [f. L *co(gnatus* born usu. *natus*]

cognā'tion, n. Cognate relationship, now esp. in philology. [f. L *cognatio* (prec., -ION)]

cognĭ'tion, n. (philos.). Action or faculty of knowing, perceiving, conceiving, as opposed to emotion & volition; a perception, sensation, notion, or intuition. So ~**AL** (-she-), **co'gnitive**, aa. [f. L *cognitio* f. *co(gnoscere* -gnit- apprehend f. *gno*- KNOW, usu. *noscere*]

co'gnizable (also kŏn'iz-), a. 1. Being aware, notice, sphere of observation, (*have* ~ *of*); within the jurisdiction of a court etc. Hence ~**LY²** adv. [f. foll.+-ABLE]

co'gnizance (also kŏn'i-), n. 1. Knowledge; perception; notice, esp. in a legitimate or official way; *take* ~ *of*, attend to, not allow to go unobserved; *fall within*, *be beyond*, *one's* ~, of things that fairly concern, do not

concern, one). 2. (Right of) dealing with a matter legally or judicially (with phr. as above in legal sense). 3. Distinctive mark; as crest, coat of arms, badge. [f. OF *conois(sance* var. of *conoissance* f. L *co-gnoscent*- part. st. of *cognoscere* see COGNI-TION, -ANCE; -z- (cf. the later COGNIZE]

cog'nizant (also kŏn'i-), a. Having know-ledge, being aware, *of*; (Philos.) having cognition. [f. prec., see -ANT]

cognize', v.t. (philos.). Have cognition of. [on anal. of COGNIZANCE & RECOGNIZE & of vbs rightly ending in -IZE]

cognō'men, n. Nickname; surname; name; (Rom. Ant.) third or family name, as *Cicero*, *Caesar*, or fourth name or personal epithet, as *Africanus*. [L, co-(gnomen name f. st. of *(g)noscere* KNOW]

cognoscente (kŏnyŏshĕn'ti), n. (pl. -ti). Connoisseur. [It., = one who knows]

cognō'scible, a. Capable of being known (esp. Philos.). [f. L *cognoscere* see COGNI-TION + -IBLE]

cognō'vit, n. (legal). Defendant's ac-knowledgement, to save expense, that plaintiff's cause is just. [L, = he has acknowledged]

cohā'bit, v.i. Live together, esp. as husband & wife (usu. of persons not married). So ~**ATION** n. [f. L *co(habitare* dwell frequent. of *habēre* hold)]

coheir', **coheir'ess**, (kōăr'-), nn. Male, female, joint heir. [co-]

cohere', v.i. Stick together, remain united, (of parts or whole); be consistent, well knit, (of arguments, style, etc.). Hence **coher'ER** n., detector of electric waves consisting of a glass cylinder con-taining metal filings which ~ when struck by a wave. [f. L *co(haerēre* -haes- stick)]

coher'ent, a. Cohering; consistent, easily followed, not rambling or inconsequent, (of argument, narration, etc.). So ~**ENCE**, ~**ENCY**, nn., ~**ently²** adv. [f. F *cohérent* f. L (prec., -ENT)]

cohē'sion (-zhn), n. Sticking together, force with which molecules cohere; tendency to remain united. So **cohē'sive** a., **cohē'sive'ly²** (-v-) adv., **cohē'sive-NESS** (-vn-) n. [f. F *cohésion* (L *cohaes*- see COHERE, -ION)]

cohō'rt, n. Division of Roman army; band of warriors; persons banded to-gether. [f. F *cohorte* f. L *cohortem* nom. -ors (co-, *hort*- enclose, cf. L *hortus* garden, E GARTH, GARDEN)]

coif, n. (hist.). Close cap covering top, back, and sides, of head; serjeant-at-law's white cap. [f. OF *coife* f. MHG *kupfe*]

coiffeur (see Ap.), n. Hair-dresser. [F]

coiffure (see Ap.), n. Way one's hair is dressed. [F]

coign (koin), n. ~ *of vantage*, place

affording good view of something. [old form of COIN, QUOIN, preserved by *Macb.* I. vi.7]

coil², v.t. & i. Dispose (rope etc.) in concentric rings; twist (t. & i., often *up*) into circular or spiral shape; move sinuously. [perh. = F *cueillir* f. L COL-*ligere = legere* gather]

coil², n. Length of coiled rope, spring, etc.; arrangement, thing arranged, in concentric circles; single turn of coiled thing, e.g. snake; lock of hair twisted & coiled; wire, piping, etc., in circles or symmetric curves; (Electr.) spiral wire for passage of current. [f. prec.]

coil³, n. (arch. & poet.). Disturbance, much ado, noise, (*this mortal ~*, turmoil of life). [?]

coin¹, n. Piece of metal made into money by official stamp; metal money; money; *false ~*, imitation in base metal etc., (fig.) anything spurious; *pay one in his own ~*, give tit for tat. Hence ~'LESS a. [F = wedge, corner (cf. COIGN, QUOIN), stamping-die, f. L *cuneus*]

coin², v.t. Make (money) by stamping metal (~ *money*, get money fast); make (metal) into money by means of (one's *brains* etc.); invent, fabricate, (esp. new word). [f. OF *coignier* f. *coin* see prec.]

coin'age, n. Coining; coins; system of coins in use (*decimal ~*, in which each value is ten times the next below); fabrication (*the ~ of one's brain*), invention, coined word. [f. OF *coignaige* see prec., -AGE]

coincide', v.i. Occupy same portion of space; occur at and occupy same time; agree together or *with*; concur in opinion etc. [f. F *coïncider* f. med. L co-IN(*cidere* = *cadere* fall]

coin'cidence, n. (Instance of) being co-incident; notable concurrence of events or circumstances without apparent causal connexion. [F, see foll., -ENCE]

coin'cident, a. Coinciding. Hence ~LY² adv. [f. F, see COINCIDE, -ENT]

coincidén'tal, a. Of the nature of (a) coincidence. [f. prec. +-AL]

coin'er, n. In vbl senses; esp., maker of counterfeit coins. [COIN²+-ER¹]

coir (kol'er), n. Coco-nut fibre, used for ropes, matting, etc. [f. Malayalam *kayar* cord]

coi'tion, n. Sexual copulation. [f. L *coitio* f. co(*ire it- go*)]

cōke, n., & v.t. (Convert *coal* into) solid substance left when volatile parts have been distilled from coal. [prob. f. obs. *colk* core cf. OFris. & LG *kolk* hole]

coker(nut). See COCO.

cōl, n. Depression in mountain-chain. [F, = neck, col, f. L *collum* neck]

col-, form taken by COM- before *l*.

col'a, k-, n. W.-Afr. tree; (also ~*nut*, ~*seed*), its seed, used as condiment, tonic, and antidote to alcohol. [W.-Afr.]

col'ander (kŭl-), **cull'ender**, n., & v.t. (Pass through a) perforated vessel used as strainer in cookery; similar appliance for casting shot. [corruption of med. L *colatorium* (*colare* strain, -ORY)]

cō-lăt'itude, n. (astron.). Complement of latitude, difference between it & 90°. [CO-(2)]

|| **cŏlcánn'on**, n. Irish dish of cabbage and potatoes pounded and stewed. [?]

cŏl'chicum (-ki-), n. Meadow-saffron; drug extracted from it used for gout. [L, f. Gk *kolkhikon* neut. adj. (*Kolkhis* on Black Sea, -IC]

cōl'cothar, n. Red peroxide of iron used in polishing glass etc. [f. Arab. *qolqotar*]

cōld¹, a. 1. Of low temperature, esp. when compared with human body or with that usual in things like the one in question (*ice, key, stone, ~*, as these; ~*-blooded*, of fish & reptiles, also fig. of sluggish persons, & see below; ~*-livered*, un-emotional; ~ *steel*, sword, bayonet, etc., opposed to fire-arms, *inch or few* etc. *inches of ~ steel*, thrust). 2. Not heated or having cooled after heat (~ *water*: *throw ~ water on plan*, discourage it; ~ *in death*; or ~, dead; ~ *pig*, water thrown on sleeper to wake him, also ~*pig* as v.t.; ~-*hammer*, work metal in ~ state; ~-CHISEL; ~ *without*, sugarless spirit & water; ~ *meat*, that has cooled after cooking; ~ *shoulder*, ~*shoulder to*, *give the ~ shoulder to*, entertain poorly, show distaste for company of, also ~-*shoulder* as v.t.; *in ~ blood*, without the excuse of heat or excitement, of cruelty etc., whence ~'blood'ED²a., ~'blood'ed-NESS n.); feeling ~; slow to absorb heat (of clayey soil). 3. Without ardour, friendliness, or affection, undemonstra-tive, apathetic, (so ~'heart'ED² a., ~'-heart'edNESS n., ~'heart'ediY²adv.; ~ *idea leaves one* ~, unmoved, not im-pressed). 4. Chilling, depressing, un-interesting, (~ *comfort*, *counsel*, *news*). 5. Faint (of scent in hunting), ~ *colours*, blue, grey, etc., opp. red, yellow, etc.; ~-*drawn* CASTOR OIL; ~ *coil*, tube coiled round inflamed part with ~ water running in it; ~ *blast*, of ~ air forced into furnace; ~ *feet*, (orig. army sl.) funk, disinclination to fight or go to or remain at the front; ~ *snap*, sudden spell of ~ weather; *have person* ~ at one's mercy); ~. Hence ~'ISH¹(2) a., ~'LY² adv., ~'NESS n. [OE *cald*, com.-Teut. cf. G *kalt*, cogn. w. L *gel-*]

cōld², n. Prevalence in atmosphere, or rarely in any object, of low temperature (*left out in the ~*, not looked after);

For compounds of *co-* not given consult co-.

inflamed state of mucous membrane, with hoarseness, running at nose, sore throat, etc. (CATCH¹ ~; often ~ *in the head.*) Hence ~PROOF a. [OE *cald* neut. adj; see prec.]

cold'-short', a. Brittle in its cold state (of iron). [f. Scand. (Da. *kold-skjör*) *skjör* brittle w. assim. to *short* as in *shortbread*]

côle, n. (Old name, now rare exc. in comb., for) kinds of cabbage etc., as Rape, Sea-kale; ~seed, plant from which colza oil is got. [f. L *caulis* stem, cabbage]

côleóp'terous, a. Of the order of *Coleoptera* or beetles, with front wings converted into sheaths for hinder. [f. Gk *koleopteros* (*koleos* sheath, *pteron* wing) + -OUS]

•**côle-slaw** (-ls-), n. Salad of sliced cabbage. [f. Du. *koolsla* = *kool-salade* (*kool* cabbage)]

côl'ic, n. Severe griping pains in belly. Hence ~KY² a. [f. F *colique* f. L f. Gk *kolikos* (COLON¹, -IC)]

colī'tis, n. Inflammation of the lining of the colon. [COLON¹+-ITIS]

collăb'oráte, v.i. Work in combination (*with*, or abs.) esp. at literary or artistic production; co-operate treacherously with the enemy. So ~A'TION, ~ātor², nn. [f. L col(*labor are* LABOUR²), -āte²]

collăpse', n. & v.i. (Undergo, experience, a) failing in, sudden shrinking together, giving way, prostration by loss of nervous or muscular power, breakdown of mental energy, loss of courage. [(n. f. L *collapsus -ûs*) f. col(*labi laps-* slip)]

collăp'sible, -able, a. So made as to collapse when required for packing etc. [-IBLE]

collăr'¹, n. Neckband, upright or turned over, of coat, dress, shirt, etc.; band of linen, lace, etc., completing upper part of costume; || neck-chain of order of knighthood; || ~ *of SS* or *esses*, formerly badge of House of Lancaster, still in some officials' costume; leather or metal band round dog's or prisoner's neck; roll round horse's neck bearing weight of draught (~-*harness*, opp. BREAST¹-*harness*); ~-*work*, hard pulling esp. up hill, & fig. of severe effort, so also *against the* ~; restraining or connecting band, ring, pipe, in machines etc.; arrangement connecting several fishing-flies; coloured stripe round animal's neck; piece of meat, brawn, fish, tied in roll; ~*beam*, horizontal beam connecting two rafters and forming with them an A-shaped roof-truss; ~-*bone*, joining breast-bone & shoulder-blade, clavicle. Hence (-)~ED² (-rd), ~LESS, aa. [f. OF *colier* f. L *collare* (*collum* neck, -AR¹)]

collăr'², v.t. Seize (person) by the collar, capture; (Footb.) lay hold of and stop (opponent holding ball); (sl.) appropriate; press (meat etc.) into roll. [f. prec.]

collarĕtte', n. Woman's collar of lace, fur, etc. [f. F *collerette* (*collier* COLLAR¹, -ETTE)]

collāte', v.t. Compare in detail (copies of text, or document, one copy *with* another); (Bibliog.) verify order of (sheets) by signatures; appoint (clergyman) to benefice (only of the Ordinary). So ~ on² n. [f. L col(*lat-* p.p. st. of *ferre* bring)]

collăt'eral, a. & n. Side by side, parallel; subordinate but from same source, contributory, connected but aside from main subject, course, etc.; of common descent but by different line (so as noun = ~ kinsman); ~ *security* or ~; properly pledged as guarantee for repayment of money (opp. *personal* giving right of action for recovery). Hence ~LY² adv. [f. med. L col(*lateralis* L *latus -eris* side)]

collā'tion, n. In vbl senses of COLLATE; also: (R.-C. Ch.) light repast in evening of fast-day; light meal (usu. *cold* ~) often at exceptional time. [OF. f. L *collationem* (COLLATE, -ION); sense *repast* from Benedictine monastery readings of Lives of the Fathers (*collationes patrum*; *collatio* also of the reading & debate on it) followed by light repast]

côl'league (-ēg), n. One of two or more holders of joint office (usu. with *my* etc.). [f. F *collègue* f. L col(*lega* f. *legere* choose)]

côl'lect¹, n. Short prayer of Common Prayer Book, esp. one of those appropriated to days or seasons & read before Epistle & in morning & evening prayer. [f. F *collecte* f. L *collecta* fem. p.p. of *colligere* COLLECT²; orig. sense perh. summing up (of thought appropriate to occasion); for noun use of p.p. cf. e.g. *army*]

collĕct'², v.t. & i. Assemble, accumulate, bring or come together; get (taxes, contributions) from a number of people; secure (specimens, books, etc.) for addition to a set; regain control of, concentrate, recover, (*oneself, one's thoughts, energies, courage*; ~*edly adv.*, not distracted, cool, whence ~édly² adv.; ~ *a horse*, keep him in hand, not let him sprawl); infer, gather, conclude. Hence ~ABLE, -IBLE, a. [f. obs. *collect* adj. f. L *collectus* p.p. of col(*ligere* = *legere* pick)]

collĕctānē̆a, n. pl. Collected passages, miscellany. [L, neut. pl. adj.]

collĕc'tion, n. Collecting; collecting of money, money collected, at meeting or Church service for charitable or religious purpose; accumulation of water, dust, etc.; group of things collected & belonging together (literary materials, specimens, works of art, etc.); || (pl.) college terminal examination at Oxford etc. [OF. f. L *collectionem* (COLLECT², -ION)]

collĕc'tive, a. & n. Formed by, constituting a, collection, taken as a whole, aggregate, (~ *fruit*, resulting from many

flowers, **as** mulberry); **of, from,** many individuals, common, (~ *note*, signed by several States; ~ *ownership*, of land, means of production, etc., by all for benefit of all, whence **collec'tivism, collec'tivist,** nn.); (Gram. & Log.) ~ *noun*, ~ *idea*, or ~, used in sing. to express many individuals, as *cattle, troop, duck*. Hence ~LY² (-vl-) adv., **collec'tiv'ITY** n. [f. L *collectivus* (as prec., -IVE)]

collec'tor, n. One who collects (specimens, curiosities, railway tickets at station, money due, esp. taxes, rent, & subscriptions); collecting-apparatus in various machines; (I.C.S.) chief official of district collecting revenue & holding magisterial powers, whence (office & district) ~ATE¹ -OR.²]

|| **colleen',** n. (Anglo-Ir.). Girl. [Ir. *cailín*, dim. of *caile* country-woman]

coll'ege, n. Body of colleagues with common functions & privileges (*Sacred C~, ~ of cardinals*, the Pope's council of 70; *Herald's C~, or C~ of Arms; C~ of Physicians, Preceptors*, etc.); || independent corporation of scholars in university, usu. with master, fellows, scholars, & students not on foundation; || similar foundation outside university (as Eton, Dulwich); small degree-giving university; institution for higher education affiliated to university; place of professional study (army, naval, of agriculture, etc.); || large public secondary school (Marlborough); (pretentious name for) private school; buildings of any of these; || ~ *living*, benefice in gift of a ~; ~ *pudding*, small plum pudding for one person. Hence **colle'GIAL** a. [f. OF *college* f. L *collegium* (*collega* COLLEAGUE)]

|| **coll'eger,** n. One of seventy foundation scholars at Eton. [-ER¹]

colle'gian, n. Member of a college; || (old sl.) inmate of a prison. [-AN¹]

colle'giate¹ a. Constituted as, belonging to, a college or body of colleagues, corporate; ~ *church*, endowed for chapter but with no see, (Sc. & U.S.) under joint pastorate; ~ *school*, of high pretensions. Hence ~LY² (-tl-) adv. [f. L *collegiatus* (COLLEGE, -ATE²)]

colle'giate², v.t. Make collegiate. [as prec., -ATE³]

coll'et, n. Encompassing band, ferrule, socket, flange holding gem, bezel. [F, dim. of col]

collide', v.i. Come into collision; be in conflict. [f. L *collidere lis-* = *laedere* hurt]

coll'ie, -ў, n. Scotch sheep-dog. [cf. obs. adj. *colly*=*coaly*; perh. as orig. black]

coll'ier (-yer), n. Coal-miner; coal-ship; sailor on this. [COAL, -IER²]

coll'igate, v.t. Bring into connexion (esp. isolated facts by a generalization). So ~A'TION n. [f. L col(*ligare* bind), see -ATE³]

coll'imate, v.t. Adjust line of sight of (telescope etc.), make parallel (telescopes, rays). Hence ~A'TION n. [*collimare* false reading in Cicero for col(*lineare* f. *linea* line)]

coll'imator, n. Small attached telescope for collimating an instrument; tube in spectroscope throwing parallel rays on prism. [-OR³]

collin'ear, a. In same straight line. [COL-¹]

|| **coll'ins,** (-z), n. (colloq.). = ROOF-¹. [Jane Austen, *P. & P.*, ch. xxxii]

colli'sion (-zhn), n. Dashing together, violent encounter of moving body, esp. ship or railway train, with another; (fig.) clashing of opposed interests etc. (esp. *in ~, come into ~ with*); (Naut.) ~*mat*, ready for putting over hole made by ~. [f. L *collisio* (COLLIDE, -ION)]

coll'ocate, v.t. Place together; arrange; station, set in particular place. So ~A'TION n. [f. L col(*locare* f. *locus* place) station]

coll'ocutor, n. Partaker in talk, as *my ~ said*. [LL, f. col(*loqui locut-* talk), -OR²]

collo'd'ion, n. Solution of gun-cotton in ether filming when exposed, used in photography & surgery. Hence ~ED³ (-nd) a., ~IZE(5) v.t., **collo'd'io-** comb. form. [f. Gk *kollōdēs* (*kolla* glue, -ODE)]

collogue' (-g), v.i. Talk confidentially (with suggestion of plotting, an obs. sense). [cf. F *colloque* conference, & obs. *colleague* vb plot]

coll'oid, a. & n. Gluey (substance); (Path.) ~ *tissue* etc., degenerated into homogeneous gelatinous consistence (also ~, such substance); (Chem.) (substance) of non-crystalline semi-solid kind suspended or dispersed in some medium, e.g. gelatine & starch. Hence **colloid'AL** a. [Gk *kolla* glue, -OID]

coll'op, n. Slice of meat; (Bibl.) fold of skin in fat person or animal. [f. 14th c., orig. sense *fried ham and eggs*, etym. dub.]

collo'quial, a. In or of talk, oral; belonging to familiar speech, not used in formal or elevated language. Hence ~ISM(3, 4), ~IST(1), nn., ~LY² adv. [COLLOQUY, -AL]

coll'oquist, n. Interlocutor. [foll., -IST(1)]

coll'oquy, n. Converse; a conversation; judicial and legislative court in Presbyterian Church. [f. L col(*loquium* f. *loqui* speak)]

coll'otype, n. Thin plate of gelatine etched by actinic rays & then printed from (~ *plate, process*, etc.). [f. Gk *kolla* glue+TYPE]

collude' (-ōō-), v.i.(arch.). Practise collusion. [f. L col(*ludere lus-* play)]

For compounds of co- not given consult co-.

collu'sion (-ōōzhn), n. Fraudulent secret understanding, esp. between ostensible opponents as in law-suit. Hence collu'-IVE (-ōō-) a., collu'sivelY adv. [F f. L collusionem (prec., -ION)]

colly'rium, n. (pl. -ia). Eyesalve; suppository. [L f. L f. Gk kollurion poultice]

coll'ywobbles (-lz), n. pl. (colloq.). Rumbling in the intestines. [imit.]

Col'ney Hatch, n. (Used for) ~ Lunatic Asylum for County of London. [place]

coll'ocynth, n. Bitter-apple, gourd plant with bitter-pulped fruit used as purgative drug; the drug. [f. L f. Gk kolokunthis]

côlon¹, n. (anat.). Greater part of larger intestine, from caecum to rectum. Hence ~TIS n. [L, f. Gk kolon]

COLONY, -ATE†)

côlon²‚ n. Punctuation-mark (:) used between period and semicolon, & used esp. to mark antithesis, illustration, or (often with dash :—) quotation; in Greek (·), [L, f. Gk kōlon limb, clause]

colonelate, n. Serf system in later Roman Empire. [f. L L L colonatus (L colonus, see COLONY)]

colonel (kèrn'ĕl), n. Highest regimental officer; (short for) lieutenant~; C~ Commandant, honorary rank of senior officers of R.A., R.E., etc. Hence ~CY (kêrn'·) n. [corrected f. coronel f. F coronel f. It. colonnello (colonna column)]

colonelship (kêrn'-), n. Being a colonel (cf. colonelcy, ordinary word for the office).

colonial, a. & n. (Inhabitant) of a colony, esp. of a British self-governing or Crown Colony ; C~ Office, State department in charge of the Colonies. Hence ~ISM(2, 4) n. [-IAL]

colonist, n. Settler in, part-founder of a colony. [COLONIZE, -IST]

colonize, v.t. & i. Establish colony in ; establish in a colony ; plant voters in a district for party purposes. Hence ~A'TION, ~ER¹, n. [f. L colonus farmer (colere till) +-IZE]

colonnade', n. Series of columns with entablature; row of trees. Hence ~ED² a. [F (colonne COLUMN, -ADE)]

col'ony, n. (Gk hist.) Independent city founded by emigrants; (Rom. hist.) settlement usu. of veterans in conquered territory acting as garrison; settlement, settlers, in new country forming community fully or partly subject to mother State; their territory; people of one nationality or occupation in a city, esp. if living in a special quarter (so of animals, ~ of sparrows etc.); (Biol.) aggregate of animals as in coral. [f. L colonia (colonus farmer f. colere till)]

col'ophon, n. Tail-piece in old books, often ornamental, giving information now placed on title-page (from title-page to ~, from cover to cover). [L L, f. Gk kolophōn summit]

coloph'ony, n. Dark resin distilled from turpentine & water. Hence colŏph'ŏn-ATE³(3) n., colŏph-‚ colŏph'ony-‚ comb. forms. [L f. Gk kolophōnia (resina resin) of Colophon in Lydia]

col'oquin'tida, n. = COLOCYNTH.
Colora'do-bee'tle(-rab-), n. Yellow-black-striped beetle, destructive to potatoes. [Colorado in U.S.]

colora'tion (kŭ-‚ kŏ-), n. Colouring, method of putting on or arranging colour; natural, esp. variegated, colour of living; of other things. [F, f. L L COLOUR², -ATION]

coloratu'ra (-ahtoor'a), n. Florid passages in vocal music (often attrib., as ~ soprano). [It., f. L colorare to colour]

colŏrif'ic (also Kŭ-), a. Producing colour; highly coloured. [f. F colorifique(COLOUR¹, -FIC)]

colŏrim'eter (also kŭ-), n. Instrument for measuring intensity of colour. [L color, -I-‚ -METER]

coloss'al·a‚ a. Of, like, a colossus; gigantic, huge; (colloq., f. G) remarkable, splendid, delightful. Hence ~IY² adv. [foll.+-AL]

coloss'us, n. (pl. -i, -uses). Statue of person or personified empire etc., esp. much more than life size; gigantic person (esp. C~ of Rhodes) as standing astride over dominions. [L, f. Gk kolossos]

col'ŏtomy, n. (surg.). Incision in COLON¹ to provide artificial anus in stricture etc. [COLON¹, -TOMY]

colour¹ (kŭl'er), n. 1. Sensation produced on eye by rays of decomposed light (cf. black, effect produced by no light or by surface reflecting no rays, & white, effect produced by rays of undecomposed light). 2. A particular hue, one, or any mixture, of the constituents into which light decomposes as in spectrum, including loosely black, white (ACCIDENTAL ~); complementary ~, that combined with given ~ makes white: fundamental, primary, simple, ~s, red, green & violet, or with painters red, blue, & yellow, giving all others by mixture; secondary ~, mixture of two primary; ~-blind, unable to distinguish certain colours, see DALTONISM, also fig. in U.S., impartial between whites & blacks, whence ~-blindness n.; ~ scheme, ~-design on which the furnishing and decoration of a room or the planting of a flower garden is based; ~-wash, coloured distemper (also as v.t.); see the ~ of one's money, receive some payment from him; man, woman, etc., of ~, of non-white race, esp. negro (~ bar, legal or social distinction between whites & people of~). 3. Ruddiness of face (lose, gain, ~; change ~, turn pale or red). 4. Appearance, light, (paint in bright, dark, ~s; see the ~ in its true ~s; put false ~s upon). 5. (Art) colouring, ~-perception, effects as of ~ got

by light and shade in engraving, whence ~IST(3) (kŭl'er) n., ~IS'TIC a.; pigment, paint, (~-box, of assorted artists' paints; WATER-~s; ~-man, dealer in paints). **6.** (Pl.) coloured ribbon, dress, etc., worn as symbol of party, membership of club, etc. (|| *get* one's, *give* one *his*, ~s, of inclusion in athletic team; *show* one's ~s, one's party or character); flag of ship, pair of silken flags (*King's* or *Queen's* ~, *regimental* ~) carried by regiment (TROOP*ing of the* ~ or ~s; *with the* ~s, serving in army; *sail under false* ~s, fig. of hypocrite or impostor; *come off with flying* ~s, win credit; *nail* ~s *to mast*, persist, refuse to climb down; ~-*sergeant*, senior sergeant of infantry company, now *Company Sergeant-Major* or *Quartermaster Serjt.* dresses. **7.** Show of reason, pretext, false plea, (*give no* ~ *for saying*; *under* ~ *of*). **8.** (Mus.) timbre, quality, also variety of expression. **9.** (Gen.) character, tone, quality, mood, shade of meaning, (*take one's* ~ *from*). **10.** (Literature) picturesqueness, ornate style, (*local* ~, use of details giving verisimilitude, background, or atmosphere). Hence ~FUL (kŭl'er) a., full of ~, bright, gay (often fig.). [f. OF *color* f. L *colorem* nom. -*or*]

colour² (kŭl'er), v.t. & i. Give colour to; paint, stain, dye; disguise; misrepresent (*highly* ~*ed details*); imbue with its own colour (*motive* ~s *act*); take on colour; blush; ~*ed person* (not wholly of white descent). [f. OF *colorer* f. L *colorare* (color COLOUR¹)]

col'ourable (kŭler-), a. Specious, plausible; counterfeit. Hence ~LY¹ adv. [f. OF *colorable* (as prec., -ABLE)]

col'ouring (kŭler-), n. In vbl senses; esp., style in which thing is coloured, or in which artist employs colour. [-ING¹]

col'ourless (kŭler-), a. Without colour; pale; dull-hued; wanting in character or vividness; neutral, impartial, indifferent. Hence ~LY¹ adv., ~NESS n. [-LESS]

col'oury (kŭleri), a. (commerce.) Having the colour that goes with good quality (of hops, coffee, etc.). [-Y¹]

colporteur' (-tĕr; also kŏl²), n. Bookhawker, esp. one employed by society to distribute Bibles. [F (*colporter* vb f. L *collum* neck, *porter* carry, -OR²)]

colt¹, n., & v.t. Young male of horse from when it is taken from dam to age of 4 (with thoroughbreds 5); inexperienced person, (esp. cricket professional in first season; (Naut.) rope used for chastisement (vb, thrash with ~); ~s'*food*, common large-leaved yellow-flowered weed; ~'s *tail*, ragged-edged cloud. Hence ~HOOD n., ~'ISH¹ a. [?]

Colt², n. (Used for) ~ revolver, automatic gun, or pistol. [S. ~, inventor]

*col'ter. See COULTER.

col'ubrine, a. Snake-like; esp., of, like, the *coluber* (genus of harmless snakes). [f. L *colubrinus* (coluber snake)]

columbar'ium, n. (pl. -*ia*). (In mod. use) building with tiers of niches for reception of cinerary urns. [L, = pigeon-house]

col'umbine¹, n. Garden plant with flower like five clustered pigeons, kind of aquilegia. [f. F *columbine* f. med. L *columbina* f. L *columba* dove, -INE¹]

Col'umbine², n. Mistress of Harlequin in pantomime. [f. It. *Columbina* character in comedy, proper name f. L as prec.]

col'umn (-*um*) n. **1.** (Archit.) long vertical often slightly tapering cylinder usu. supporting entablature or arch, or alone as monument, (fig.) support; ~-shaped object, organ in Anat. or Bot., part of machine, etc. (~ *of water, mercury*, confined vertical cylindrical mass; ~ *of smoke*, rising straight). **2.** Vertical division of page for figures etc., or to reduce length of lines in newspapers (also part of newspaper, sometimes more or less than ~, devoted to special subject, as AGONY ~, *advertisement* ~; *our* ~s, *the* ~s *of The Times*, contents of newspaper), whence *~IST n., journalist who regularly contributes to a newspaper a~ of miscellaneous comment on people and events. **3.** Narrow-fronted deep arrangement of troops in successive lines (*in* ~ *of sections, platoons, companies*, with one section etc. forming each line & one section's etc. length between lines; *quarter* ~, with 6 paces between lines; FIFTH ~; body of ships, esp. following one another. Hence or cogn. colim'nar¹, ~ED² (-*umd*), colum'niform, aa. [f. OF *colompne* f. L *columna* (col *celsus* high)]

colure', n. One of two great circles intersecting rectangularly at poles & dividing equinoctial & ecliptic into four equal parts, one passing through equinoctial, & one through solstitial, points of ecliptic. [f. L f. Gk *kolouros* truncated]

col'za, n. = COLE-seed; ~-oil, made from it & used in lamps. [F, f. LG *kôlsât* COLE-seed]

com-, pref. = L *cum* in comb., retained as *com*- before b, p, m, & rarely before vowels, changed to *cor*- before r, *col*- before l, *co*- before vowels, h, & gn, & *con*- before other consonants; *com*- occurs in E also before f (*comfort*). Meaning, *with, together, altogether, completely.*

com'a¹, n. Unnatural heavy sleep, stupor, lethargy. Hence ~TOSE a. [f. Gk *kôma -atos* cf. *koimaô* put to sleep]

com'a², n. (pl. -*ae*). (Bot.) tuft of silky hairs at end of seed; (Astron.) nebulous envelop round nucleus of comet. [L, f. Gk *komê* hair of head]

For compounds of *co*- not given consult co-.

comb¹ (-m), n. Toothed strip of horn, metal, ivory, etc., for arranging, cleaning, or confining the hair; = CURRY²-*comb*; thing of same shape, look, or purpose, in many machines, esp. for dressing wool, or collecting electricity, or in animal structure; red fleshy crest of fowl esp. cock, analogous growth in other birds, (*cut the ~ of*, humiliate); crest of bill or wave; = HONEYCOMB¹; *~ing out*. Hence (-)cōmbED¹. [com-Teut., cf. Du. *kam*, G *kamm*; also Gk *gomphos* pin, Skr. *gambhas* tooth]

cōmb² (-m), v.t. & i. Draw comb through (hair), curry (horse), dress (wool, flax) with comb; (of wave) curl over; *~ out*, secure or get rid of (as) by *~ing* (esp. of getting recruits from among those previously exempted from service). [earlier *kemb*; present vb f. prec.]

com'bat (kŭ- or kŏ-), n. & v.t. & i. (Do) battle; *single ~*, duel; (engage in) contest, struggle; oppose, strive against. [F, f. LL *combat & combative* f. LL (*com-, battere*, fight)]

com'bative (kŭ- or kŏ-), a. Pugnacious. Hence ~LY² adv., ~NESS n. [COMBAT v. +-IVE]

combe. See COOMB.

cōmb'er (-mer), n. In vbl senses: esp.: machine for combing cotton or wool very fine; long curling wave, breaker. [-ER¹]

cōmbinā'tion, n. Combining; combined state (*in ~ with*); combined set of things or persons; (Math., pl.) different collections possible of given number of individuals in groups of given smaller number; (Chem.) union of substances in compound with properties differing from theirs; united action; || (pl.) single under-garment for body & legs; motor-cycle with side-car attached (in full *motor-cycle ~*); *~ (lock)*, complicated locking arrangement used for safes, strong rooms, etc.; *~-room*, at Cambridge = COMMON-*room*. [OF f. LL *combinationem* (COMBINE, -ATION)]

combine¹, v.t. & i. **1.** Join together (persons, or things material or other); possess (esp. qualities usu. separate) together; (cause to) coalesce in one substance, form chemical compound; co-operate; *~d operation* (in which the fighting services co-operate). **2.** n. (usu. kŏm¹-). Combination of persons, esp. to raise prices or obstruct course of trade; (pr. kŏm¹-) *~d* reaping and threshing machine. So **cŏm'binATIVE** a. [f. LL *combinare* f. *bini* two together]

cōm'bing (-mi-), n. In vbl senses; (pl.) hairs combed off. [-ING¹]

combus'tible, a. & n. **1.** (Matter, thing) capable of or used for burning; excitable. Hence ~BILITY n. [f. LL *combustibilis* f. *comburere* f. COM-+*urere* burn (-b- unexplained)]

head; the work, till luck, ~s to me). **7.** Happen (*how ~s it that—?; to ~*; pred. adj. future; *~ for a year to ~; the to-~*, the future; *~ what may*, whatever happens). **8.** Become present from future (*~ to pass; the time will ~ when*). **9.** Spring of, be the result of, (*that's what ~s of grumbling; ~ of noble parents*). **10.** Enter, be brought, *into* (collision, play, prominence; *~ to harm*, be injured). **11.** Amount *to* (*~s to 2/6; it ~ to this, that—*, is as much as to say that). **12.** Take form (*the butter will not ~*). **13.** Find oneself under compulsion or in a position *to* (*have ~ to believe, has ~ to be used*). **14.** (With cogn. obj.) traverse, accomplish, (*have ~ 3 miles, a long way*). **15.** Play a part (sl.; *~ the bully over; ~ it too strong, show vigour; ~ it too strong, over-do something, exaggerate*). **16.** Become, get to be, prove, (*string ~s untied, things ~ right, he came alive; ~s expensive, easy, true, natural*). **17.** (Imperat. as exclamation) now then (encouraging; think again, don't be hasty. **18.** *~ about*, happen; *~ across*, meet with; *~ along*, (colloq.) make haste; *~ at*, reach, discover, get access to; *~ away*, get detached; *~ back*, recur to memory, *retaliate or retort (sl.); (as n., *~-back*) a return to, reinstatement in, one's former position (*stage a ~-back*); *~ by* (prep.) obtain, (adv.) pass; *~ down*, extend downwards to, be handed down by tradition, fall, be humbled (esp. *in the world*, lose caste); *~ down upon*, rebuke, punish, exact reparation from; *~ down with*, pay (money); *~ forward*, present oneself,

combus'tion (-schn), n. **1.** Destruction by fire (SPONTANEOUS ~). **2.** (Chem. etc.) development of light & heat going with chemical combination; oxidation of organic tissue. [OF, f. LL *combustionem* (prec., -ION²)]

come¹ (kŭm), v.i. (came, come). **1.** Start, move, arrive, towards or at a point, time, or result (often not specified because obvious, while point of departure, if it matters, is always specified; cf. go; *~ into world*, be born; *~ of AGE; ~ to an end*, cease; *~ to hand*, of letter etc., be delivered; *~ SHORT; ~ to a point*, taper; *by ~ & go*, pass to & fro, pay brief visit, be transitory; *let 'em all ~!*, sl. announcement of readiness; *light ~ light go*, what is easily won is soon lost; *coming nineteen*, in nineteenth year; *two years ~ Christmas*, including time from now to Christmas). **2.** Be brought (*the dinner came; ~ under notice, before judge*). **3.** Fall, land, on (*came on my head*). **4.** Move relatively by motion of beholder etc. towards one (*~ into sight, to one's knowledge, in one's way; ~ to light*, be revealed). **5.** Reach point with hand, instrument, or missile. **6.** Occur, fall to lot of, (*~s on such a page; one ~s before, after, another; ~ into one's*

answer appeal; ~ *in*, enter house or room, begin innings, take such a place in race etc. (~ *in third*), be elected, come to power, be received as income, become seasonable or fashionable, serve a purpose (esp. ~ *in useful*), find a place (*where does the joke ~ in?; where do I ~ in?* how are my interests advanced?); ~ *in for*, get share of, get; ~ *into*, receive possession of; ~ *near doing*, narrowly escape or fail; ~ *off*, be detached, extricate oneself from contest etc. in such state (*with flying* COLOURS, *badly*), be accomplished, fulfilled; ~ *on*, (prep.) = ~ *upon*, (adv.) continue coming, advance esp. to attack, progress, thrive, supervene (of wind, storm, disease), arise to be discussed, appear on stage, begin to bowl, (imperat.) follow me, I defy you; ~ *out*, go on strike, emerge from examination etc. with such success, emerge from clouds, be found out, be solved, show itself (of photograph, smallpox, arrogance), be published (~*s out on Saturdays*), make debut on stage or in society; ~ *out of that*, sl. order to clear out or desist; ~ *out with*, utter; ~ *over*, (prep.) master as an influence; (adv.) ~ *from some distance or across obstacle* (*came over with the Conqueror, over from London to see us*), change sides or opinion; ~ *round*, look in for casual visit, recover from ill temper, swoon, etc.; ~ *to*, (prep.) inherit, return to (oneself, one's senses from fainting-fit or from folly), (adv.) cease moving, revive; ~ *under*, be classed as or among, be subjected to (influence); ~ *up*, || join university, approach person for talk, get abreast with, spring out of ground, become fashionable, be mooted, be equal to standard etc., (imperat. to horse) go faster; ~ *upon*, attack by surprise, strike or lay hold of (mind), make demand on, [OE *cuman*, com.-Teut. cf. Du. *komen*, G. *kommen*; cogn. also w. Skr. *gam*, Gk *bainō*, L *venire*]

come² (kŭm), n. ~-*t'-go*, passing to & fro; ~-*down*, downfall, degradation. [f. prec.]

come-at'-able (kŭm-), a. Accessible. [-ABLE]

comēd'ian, n. Actor, writer, of comedies. [f. F *comédie* f. L *comoedia* COMEDY +-AN]

comédienne', n. Comedy actress. [F]

comédiett'a, n. Short or slight comedy. [It., dim. of *comedia* COMEDY]

com'edist, n. Writer of comedies. [foll. -IST(3); to avoid ambiguity of COMEDIAN]

com'edy, n. Stage-play of light, amusing, & often satirical character, chiefly representing everyday life, & with happy ending (cf. TRAGEDY); branch of drama concerned with ordinary persons & employing familiar language; life, or an incident in it, regarded as a spectacle; *Old, Middle, New, C*~, classification of ancient Greek ~, the first farcical & largely political, the last corresponding to modern ~, & the second transitional. [f. F *comédie* f. L f. Gk *kōmōidia* f. *kōmō(i)dos* f. *kōmos* revel, *aoidos* singer]

come'ly (kŭm'li), a. Pleasant to look at (usu. of personal appearance, sometimes of behaviour or conduct). Hence ~i-NESS n. [OE *cȳmlic* (*cȳme* fine f. WG *kāmi-*, -LY²)]

com'er (kŭm-), n. One who comes (usu. qualified, as *first* ~); *all* ~*s*, any one who applies, takes up a challenge, etc. [-ER¹]

comes'tible, n. (usu. pl.). Thing to eat. [f., f. LL *comestibilis* (*comest*- var. of *comes*- p.p. st. of L *comedere* eat up)]

com'et, n. Body with star-like nucleus & train or tail of light moving round sun in elliptical or towards & from it in parabolic course; ~-*year*, in which conspicuous ~ comes; ~-*wine*, made in ~-*year*, supposed of superior quality. Hence ~-ARY¹, comēt'IC, aa. [f. L f. Gk *komētēs* long-haired (star) f. *komaō* wear hair long (*komē* hair)]

com'fit (kŭm-), n. Sweetmeat, sugar-plum. [f. OF *confit* f. L CON(*fectum*=*factum* neut. p.p. of *facere* make)]

com'fort (kŭm-), n., & v.t. 1. Relief in affliction, consolation, being consoled; person who consoles one or saves one trouble; cause of satisfaction; conscious well-being, being comfortable; possession of ~*s*, things that make life easy; *creature* ~*s*, good food, clothes, etc. 2. v.t. Soothe in grief, console; make comfortable; ~ *the king's enemies* (arch.), give them aid. [f. OF *confort(er)* f. L CON(*fortare* f. *fortis* strong)]

com'fortable (kŭm-), a. Such as to obviate hardship, save trouble, & promote content, ministering to comfort; at ease, free from hardship, pain, & trouble; tranquil, with easy conscience; *the C~ Words*, the four scriptural passages following the Absolution in the Communion Office. Hence **com'fortably²** (kŭm-) adv. [f. AF *confortable* (prec. -ABLE)]

com'forter (kŭm-), n. One who comforts (*the C*~, Holy Ghost; *Job's* ~, professed consoler who depresses); || baby's dummy teat; || woollen scarf. [-ER¹]

com'fortless (kŭm-), a. Dreary, without provision for comfort. [-LESS]

com'frey (kŭm-), n. (pl. ~*s*). Tall rough-leaved ditch plant with clusters of whitish or purplish bells. [f. OF *confire* etym. dub.]

com'fy (kŭm-), a. (colloq.). Comfortable. [abbr.]

com'ic (kŭm-), a. & n. 1. Of comedy (~ *opera*, with ~ treatment & much spoken dialogue, also mere burlesque set to music);

For compounds of *co-* not given consult *co-*.

mirth-provoking, laughable or meant to be so, facetious, burlesque, funny; (~ *song*, *paper*; ~ *history of Rome* etc.; ~ *strip*, set of drawings, forming part of a series, appearing regularly in a journal, usu. broadly humorous). **2.** n. (colloq.). Music-hall comedian (also, in F form, *comique*). Hence ~o- comb. form. [f. L f. Gk *kōmikos* f. *kōmos* revel]

cŏm'ical, a. Mirth-provoking, laughable; odd, queer. Hence ~ITY (-ăl'-) n., ~LY² adv. [as prec. + -AL]

Cŏm'intern, n. Third INTERNATIONAL. [f. first elements of Russ. forms of Com-(munist) International).]

cŏmităd'ji, n. Member of band of irregular soldiery in the Balkans. [Turk., ult. f. L as COUNTY]

cŏm'ity, n. Courtesy; ~ *of nations*, friendly recognition as far as practicable of each other's laws & usages. [f. L *comitas* (*comis* courteous)]

cŏmm'a, n. Punctuation-mark (,) of the least separation indicated between parts of sentence, also used to separate figures etc.; (Mus.) definite minute interval or difference of pitch; *inverted* ~s, raised or superior ~s used to begin & to end a quotation, the first (or first pair) inverted (the said 'no' or 'no'); ~ *bacillus*, ~-shaped found in cholera. [f. L f. Gk *komma* clause (*koptō* cut, -MT)]

command'¹ (-ah-), v.t. & i. Order, bid, (*what God* ~s, ~s *us*, ~s *us to do*, ~s *that we should do*, ~s *to be done*; also ellipt., *let us do as God* ~s; & abs., *God* ~s & *man obeys*); have authority over, control of; be supreme; be in command; be in command of (ship, forces, etc.); ~ *in chief*, be commander-in-chief of, or abs.; restrain, master, (passions, oneself); have at disposal or within reach (sum, skill, person; so *yours to* ~, obediently); deserve & get (sympathy etc.); dominate (strategic position) from superior height, look down over. [f. OF *comander* f. LL *com-(mendare* entrust)]

command'² (-ah-), n. Order, bidding, (*word of* ~), customary order for movement in drill; *at* or *by one's* ~, in pursuance of his bidding); ~ *paper* (usn. abbr. *Cmd.*, formerly *Cd.*, with register number, as *Cd. 5723*), paper laid by ~ of the Crown before Parliament etc.; exercise or tenure of authority, esp. naval or military (*in* ~ *of*, commanding; *under* ~ *of*, commanded by); control, mastery, possession, (*great* ~ *of language*, skill in speech; *at* ~, ready to be used *at will*; ~ *of the passes* etc.); body of troops etc., district, under command (*the Nore, Southern, Bomber, C*~); ~-*in-chief*, supreme ~; ‖ ~ *night*, with theatrical etc. performance given by royal ~; ‖ ~ *performance*, theatrical etc. performance given by royal ~; *the High(er)*~ [f. ¹ or as prec.]

cŏmmandănt', n. Commanding officer, esp. governor of fortress. Hence ~SHIP n. [F (COMMAND², -ANT)]

commandeer', v.t. Impress (men), seize (stores), for military service. [f. S. Afr. Du. *kommanderen* (-ār-) f. as prec.]

comman'der (-ah-), n. In vbl senses; also or esp.: *C~ of the Faithful*, title of Caliph; *C~, Lieut.-C~*, naval OFFICERS; *Wing-C~*, AIR¹-*force officer*; member of higher class in some Orders of Knighthood; large wooden mallet; *C~-in-Chief*, (Army) of portion of them quartered in colony, or (Navy) of all ships on a station. Hence ~SHIP(1) n. [f. OF *comandere* (COMMAND¹)]

comman'ding (-ah-), a. In vbl senses; esp.: exalted, impressive, (of persons, looks, ability, etc.); with wide view (of hill, position). [-ING²]

command'ment (-ah-), n. Divine command (*the ten* ~s, Mosaic decalogue; *eleventh* ~, any precept jestingly classed with these). [f. OF *comandement* (COMMAND¹, -MENT)]

comman'dō (-ah-), n. (pl. ~s), Party called out for military service, body of troops; (C~) British and Imperial shock-troops in the 1939-45 war. [Port., f. *commandare* COMMAND, f. familiarized in Boer war]

comme il faut (kǒm ēl fō), pred. a. Well-bred. [F]

commĕm'orāte, v.t. Celebrate in speech or writing; preserve in memory by some celebration; (of things) be a memorial of. Hence ~IVE a. [f. L *commemorare* bring to remembrance, see -ATE³]

commĕmorā'tion, n. Act of commemorating; service, part of service, in memory of saint or sacred event; ‖ (Oxford Univ.) annual celebration in memory of founders. [f. OF *commemoration* (as prec., see -ATION)]

commĕnce', v.t. & i. Begin (work, doing, to do); (arch.) start, set up, as (lawyer etc.); ‖ take the full degree of (M.A. etc.). [f. OF *comencer* f. LL +*comitiāre* (see INITIATE)]

commĕnce'ment (-sm-), n. In vbl senses; also, ceremony when degrees of Master & Doctor are conferred at Cambridge, Dublin, & U.S. Univs. [OF (*commencer*, see prec. & -MENT)]

commĕnd', v.t. Entrust for safe keeping (arch. exc. in ~ *one's soul to God*, ~ *to person's care*; praise; (arch.) ~ *me to*, remember me kindly to (person); ~ *me*, to give me by choice (often iron.). [f. L *commendare*=*mandare* entrust, see MAN-DATE]

commĕnd'able, a. Praiseworthy. Hence ~leNESS (-ln-) n., ~LY² adv. [OF, f. L *commendābilis* (prec., -BLE)]

commĕn'dam, n. Tenure of benefice in absence of regular incumbent. [med. L (*in*) *commendam* (*depositum*) given in

commendā'tion, n. Praise; act of commending person to another's favour. [OF, f. L commendationem (as COMMEND, see -ATION)]

commen'datory, a. Commending, holding, held, in commendam. [f. LL commendatorius (as prec., see -ORY)]

commen'sal, a. & n. (One) who eats at the same table; (animal, plant) living as another's tenant & sharing its food (cf. PARASITE). Hence ~ISM, **commensal'-ITY**, nn. [F, f. med. L COM(mensalis f. mensa table, see -AL)]

commen'surable (-sher-), a. Measurable by the same standard (with, to); (of numbers) divisible without remainder by the same quantity; proportionate to. Hence ~ABIL'ITY, ~ableness, nn., ~ablY² adv., ~(sher-). [f. L COM(mensurabilis, as MEASURE, see -BLE)]

commen'surate (-sher-), a. Coextensive (with); proportionate (to, with). Hence ~lY² (-tl-) adv., ~NESS (-tn-) n. [f. L COM(mensurātus, prec., -ATE²)]

comm'ent², n. Explanatory note or remark; criticism; (fig., of events etc.) Illustration. [OF, = comment, neut. p.p. of COM(miniscī f. root men- cf. mens mind)]

comm'ent², v.i. Write explanatory notes (upon a text); make (esp. unfavourable) remarks (upon). [f. prec.]

comm'entary, n. Expository treatise; set of running comments on a book or remarks on a speech or performance; comment. [f. L commentarius a. (COMMENT¹, -ARY¹)]

commentā'tion, n. Making of comments. [f. L commendatio (commentārī discuss, frequent. of comminiscī, see COMMENT & -ATION)]

comm'entātor, n. Writer of commentary; eyewitness whose description of a ceremony, sporting event, etc., is broadcast by wireless. [L (as prec., see -OR³)]

comm'erce, n. Exchange of merchandise, esp. on a large scale; CHAMBER of ~; intercourse (esp. sexual); card game; ~-destroyer, warship harrying enemy's merchant-ships. [F, f. L COM(mercium f. merx mercis merchandise)]

commer'cial (-shl), a. & n. Of, engaged in, bearing on, commerce; ~ (traveller), trader's agent, showing samples & soliciting orders; ∥ ~ room (in hotel for ~ travellers). Hence ~ISM, ~IST, (-sha-), ~ITY (-shiáli), nn., ~IZE v.t., ~lY² adv., (-sha-). [f. L commercium COMMERCE + -AL]

comminā'tion, n. Threatening; denunciation, recital of divine threats against sinners in Anglican Liturgy. [F.f. L commīnātionem f. COM(minārī threaten), see -ATION]

comm'inatory, a. Threatening, denun-

ciatory. [f. L comminatorius (as prec., see -ORY)]

commin'gle (-nggl), v.t. & i. Mingle together. [COM-]

comm'inūte, v.t. Reduce to small fragments; divide (property) into small portions. So **comminū'tion** n. [f. L COM(minuere -ūt- f. minor less)]

commis'erāte (-z-), v.t. & i. Feel, express, pity for; condole with. Hence² cogn. ~A'TION n., ~ATIVE a., ~ativelY² adv. [f. L COM(miserārī f. MISER¹), -ATE³]

commis'sar', n. (Former name of) head of a government department of the U.S.S.R. [Russ. kommissar f. F commissaire (as COMMISSARY)]

commissā'rial, a. Of a commissary. [-AL]

commissā'riat, n. Department (esp. Mil.) for supply of food etc.; a department of the Soviet Republic Civil Service. [as foll., see -ATE¹]

comm'issarY, n. Deputy, delegate; representative of a bishop in part of his diocese, or of absent bishop; officer charged with supply of food etc. for body of soldiers; C~ general, chief ~, esp. (Mil.) chief of a commissariat service. Hence ~SHIP n. [f. med. L commissārius person in charge (COMMIT, -ARY¹)]

commi'ssion¹ (-shn), n. 1. Command, instruction; authority, body of persons having authority, to act; ∥ ~ of the peace, (authority given to) Justices of the Peace; on the ~, having this. 2. Warrant conferring authority, esp. that of officers in the army, navy, and air force from lieutenant or pilot officer upwards. 3. In ~, (of persons) having delegated authority, (of an office) placed by warrant in charge of a body of persons instead of the constitutional administrator, (of ship of war) manned, armed, & ready for sea. 4. Entrusting of authority etc. to a person; charge, matter, entrusted to person to perform. 5. Authority to act as agent for another in trade, as have goods on ~; pay of a ~-agent, percentage on amount involved. 6. Committing (of crime etc.); ∥ ~-day, opening day of assizes, when judge's ~ is read. [F, f. L commissionem (as prec., -ION]

commi'ssion² (-shn), v.t. Empower by commission: give (officer) command of ship; order (ship) for active service; (of officer) assume command of (ship); give (artist etc.) a commission for piece of work. [f. prec.]

commissionaire' (-shonár), n. ∥ Member of the corps of C~s organized in London for employment as messengers etc.; uniformed door attendant at theatres, cinemas, large shops, etc. [as COMMISSIONER]

commi'ssioned (-shond), a. Authorized;

For compounds of co- not given consult co-.

(of officers) holding rank by commission; (of ships) put in commission. [-ED¹]

commi'ssioner (-sho-), n. One appointed by commission; member of a commission, esp. of government boards etc., as *Charity, Civil Service, C~*; representative of supreme authority in a district, department, etc.; *High C~*, chief representative in London of a British Dominion or of India. Hence ~SHIP n. [f. F *commissionnaire* f. med. L *commissionarius* (COMMISSION, -ARY)]

co'mmissure, n. Juncture, seam; joint between two bones; line where lips, eyelids, meet; bands of nerve substance connecting hemispheres of brain, two sides of spinal cord, etc. So co'mmissu'RAL a. [f. L *commissura* junction (as foll., see -URE)]

commi't, v.t. (-tt-). Entrust, consign, for treatment or safe keeping (*to* person, his care, his judgement, *to* writing, memory, earth, the flames); ~ (*to* prison) consign officially to custody; refer (bill) to committee; perpetrate (crime, blunder), whence ~TABLE a.; compromise, involve, (character, honour, oneself); bind oneself *to* (a course). Hence ~'t'AL n. (~ting to prison, reference to committee, ~ting of oneself), ~MENT n. (esp. engagement that restricts freedom of action). [f. L *committere* miss- send) join, entrust]

commi'ttee (-ti), n. Body of persons appointed for special function by (& usu. out of) a (usu. larger) body, as *House resolves itself into a C~, goes into C~, is in C~, C~ of the whole House; Standing C~* (permanent during existence of appointing body); *Joint C~* (of members nominated by different bodies); ~man, member of a ~; (Law, pron. komitē') person entrusted with charge, as ~s *for lunatics*. [late AF for F *commis* p.p. of *commettre*, as prec.]

commi'x, v.t. & i. (arch., poet.). Mix. So ~TURE n. [back-formation on *commixt*, see MIX]

commo'de, n. Chest of drawers; chiffonier; (esp. *night-~*) close-stool. [F, f. L *commodus* measure) convenient]

commo'dious, a. Roomy; (arch.) handy. Hence ~LY² adv., ~NESS n. [f. F *commodieux* f. med. L *commodiosus*, irreg. f. L *commodum* (neut. adj. as n.), see prec.]

commo'dity, n. Useful thing; article of trade (*staple ~*); (arch.) convenience. [f. F *commodité* f. L *commoditatem* (COMMODE, -TY)]

commo'dore, n. Naval officer above captain and below rear-admiral (in Brit. navy a temporary rank); *Air C~*, officer of AIR¹ *Force*; (courtesy title) senior captain when three or more ships cruise together, captain of pilots, president of

yacht-club; senior captain of a shipping line; ~'s ship. [17th c. (*-mand-*) f. L *commandator* COMMANDER]

commo'n, a. (-er, -est). 1. Belonging equally to, coming from, or done by, more than one, as *our ~ humanity, ~ cause, ~ consent.* 2. Belonging to, open to, affecting, the public, as ~ *crier, jail, alehouse, nuisance, scold.* 3. Of ordinary occurrence, as *a ~ experience* (~ or garden, sl.), of the familiar kind); ordinary, of ordinary qualities, as ~ *honesty, no ~ mind*; without rank or position, as ~ *soldier, the ~ people*; of the most familiar type, as *C~ Nightshade, Snake.* 4. Of inferior quality; vulgar. 5. (Math.) belonging to two or more quantities, as ~ *factor, multiple*; (Gram.) ~ *noun*, name applicable to any one of a class, ~ *gender*, masculine or feminine; (Pros.) of variable quantity; (Mus.) ~ *time, measure*, two or four beats in bar, ~ CHORD. 6. ~ *ground*, basis for argument etc., accepted by both sides; ~ *law*, unwritten law of England, administered by the King's courts, purporting to be derived from ancient usage; ~ *metre*, hymn stanza of 4 lines (with 8, 6, 8, 6 syllables); *Court of C~ Pleas* (for trial of civil causes, abolished 1875); *C~ Prayer*, liturgy set forth in Book of C. P. of Edward VI; ~ *room* (at Oxford), room to which fellows retire after dinner; ~ *sense*, normal understanding, good practical sense in everyday affairs, general feeling (of mankind or community), philosophy of ~ *sense* (accepting primary beliefs of mankind as ultimate criterion of truth); ~ *weal, weal,* arch., public welfare, (also) = COMMONWEALTH. Hence ~NESS (-n-n-) n. [f. OF *comun* f. L *communis*]

commo'n², n. +*mun's* bound, obliged, or +*unus* one)] land, condition of land, held in common; commonalty. [-AGE]

commo'nable, a. (Of animals) that may be pastured on common land; (of land) that may be held in common. [f. obs. vb *common* f. OF *comuner* (as COMMON²)

commo'nage, n. Right of common; land, condition of land, held in common; commonalty. [-AGE]

commo'nalty, n. The common people; general body (of mankind etc.); body corporate. [f. OF *comunalté* f. commun f. L *communalis* (*commune* neut. adj. as n., see COMMON¹ & -AL), see -TY]

||**commo'ner**, n. One of the common people (below rank of peer); (rarely) member of House of Commons, esp. the *great C~*, elder Wm Pitt, *First C~*, the Speaker; (at Oxford University) student

not on foundation; one who has right of common. [COMMON² & obs. vb *common* (see COMMONABLE) +-ER¹]

commoney, n. Inferior playing-marble. [COMMON¹+-Y³]

common'ly, adv. Usually; to an ordinary degree, as ~ *honest*; meanly, cheaply. [-LY²]

comm'onplace¹, n. & a. 1. Notable passage, entered for use in a ~*book*; ordinary topic; everyday saying; platitude: anything common or trite. 2. adj. Lacking originality, trite. Hence ~NESS (sn-) n. [=L *locus communis*=Gk *koinos topos* general theme.]

comm'onplace², v.t. & i. Extract commonplaces from; enter in commonplace-book; utter commonplaces. [f. prec.]

comm'ons (-z), n. pl. The common people; third estate in English or other similar constitution, represented by Lower House of Parliament (*House of C~*); provisions shared in common; common table, as DOCTORS' COMMONS; ∥ (Oxf., Camb,) definite portion of food supplied at fixed charge; daily fare, as *short* ~. [pl. of COMMON²]

comm'onwealth (-wel-), n. Body politic, independent community; republic (also fig., as ~ *of learning*); republican government in England, 1649-60; title of federated Australian States; *British C~ of Nations* (term coined by Gen. Smuts in 1919 for) British Empire; company of actors sharing receipts; (formerly) public welfare. [COMMON¹+WEALTH, cf. F *bien public*, L *res publica*]

commo'tion, n. Physical disturbance; bustle, confusion; tumult, insurrection. [f. OF *comocion* f. L *commotionem* (as foll, see -ION)]

commove' (-ōov), v.t. Move violently (lit. & fig.); excite. [f. F *commovoir* f. L COM(*movere mot-* move)]

comm'unal, a. Of a commune; of the Paris Commune; of the commonalty, of or for the community, for the common use; (India) of the antagonistic religious and racial communities in a district (~ *voting, elections, disturbances*, etc.). [F. f. med. L *communalis* (as COMMUNE, see -AL]

comm'unalism, n. Theory of government by local autonomy. So ~IST n., ~is'TIC a. [prec.+-ISM]

comm'unalize, v.t. Make (thing) the property of a local community. Hence ~A'TION n. [-IZE]

comm'une¹, n. French territorial division, smallest division for administrative purposes; similar division elsewhere; *The C~ (of Paris)*, (1) usurping body during the Reign of Terror, (2) communalistic government in 1871. [F. f. med. L *communa* f. LL *communia* (neut. pl. adj. as noun), see COMMON¹]

commune² (or kŏm'-), v.i. Hold intimate intercourse (*with* person, one's own heart, *together*; *receive Holy Communion. [f. OF *comuner* (as COMMON¹)]

commun'icable, a. That can be imparted; communicative. Hence ~ABIL'TTY, ~ABLENESS, nn., ~ABLY adv. [prob. F (as foll, see -BLE]

commun'icant, n. One who (esp. regularly) receives Holy Communion; one who imparts information. [as foll, see -ANT]

commun'icate, v.t. & i. Impart, transmit, (heat, motion, feeling, news, a discovery, *to*); share (a thing) *with*; receive, administer, Holy Communion; hold intercourse *with*; (of rooms etc.) have common door (*with*). [f. L *communicare* (as COMMON¹ +-*ic-* factitive suf.), see -ATE³]

communica'tion, n. Act of imparting (esp. news); information given; intercourse; common door or passage or road or rail or telegraph or other connexion between places, (Mil., pl.) connexion between base & front. [f. OF *comunicacion* f. L *communicationem* (prec., -ATION)]

commun'icative, a. Ready to impart; open, talkative. Hence ~LY² adv., ~NESS n. [F (-*if*, -*ive*), as COMMUNICATE, see -IVE]

commun'icator, n. Person, thing, that communicates; part of telegraph instrument used in sending message; contrivance for communicating with guard or driver of train. [L (as prec., see -OR²)]

commun'ion (-yon), n. Sharing, participation; fellowship (esp. between branches of Catholic Church); body professing one faith; intercourse; participation in Lord's Supper (also *Holy C~*); *close, open, ~*, exclusion from, admission to, ~ of persons not baptized according to Baptist principles; ~*-cloth, -cup* (used at Holy C~); ~*-rail* (in front of ~*-table* in some churches); ~*-table* (used for Holy C~). [F. f. L *communionem* (as COMMON¹, see -ION]

comm'unionist (-yon-), n. *Close, open, ~, fellow-~*, adherent of close, open, communion; *fellow-~*, member of same communion. [-IST]

communiqué (see Ap.), n. Official intimation. [F]

comm'unism, n. Vesting of property in the community, each member working according to his capacity and receiving according to his wants. Hence ~IST n., ~is'TIC a. [f. F as COMMON¹+-ISM]

communitä'rian, n. Member of community practising communism. [-ARIAN]

comm'unity, n. Joint ownership, as ~ *of goods*; identity of character; fellowship (~ *of interest* etc.; also attrib., as ~ *singing*, in which all present join);

For compounds of *co-* not given consult CO-.

organized political, municipal, or social body; body of men living in same locality; body of men having religion, profession, etc., in common, as *the* ~, *the mercantile* ~, *the Jewish* ~; *the* ~, the public; monastic, socialistic, or other body practising ~ of goods. [f. OF *com-muneté* f. L *communitatem* (as COMMON¹, see -TY)]

commū'nize, v.t. Make (land etc.) common property. Hence ~ā'TION n. [f. L as COMMON¹+-IZE]

commutā'tion, n. Commuting; money paid by way of ~; *C~ Act* (for ~ of tithes in England, 1836); *~-ticket,* season ticket. [F., f. L *commutationem* (as foll., see -ATION)]

commūt'ative (also kŏm'ūtāt-), a. Relating to or involving substitution. [f. med. L *commutativus* (as foll., see -ATIVE)]

commūt'ātor, n. Person, thing, that commutes; contrivance for altering course of electric current. [as foll., see -OR²]

commūte', v.t. & i. Interchange (two things); buy off (one obligation) for (*into*) another; change (punishment *into* another less severe); change (one kind of payment *into, for,* another); *buy and use a season (*commutation*) ticket for travelling, esp. daily to and from work in a city, whence *~ER. [f. L com-*mūtāre* exchange]

cōmōse', a. Having a COMA²; hairy, downy. [f. L *comosus* (COMA² see -OSE¹)]

com'pact¹, n. Agreement between parties; *general* ~, common consent; FAMILY, SOCIAL, ~. [f. L COM(*pacisci pact-* covenant)]

compact'², a. & n. 1. Closely or neatly packed together; (of style) condensed, terse. Hence ~LY² adv., ~NESS n. 2. n. [kŏm'pakt). Miniature flat vanity case, or refill for it. [f. L COM(*pingere pact-*=*pangere* fasten)]

compact'³, v.t. Join firmly together; condense; make up, compose, (*of*). [f. prec.]

compā'gēs, n. Framework, complex structure (lit. & fig.). [L *compăges* f. *pangere* fix]

compā'ginate, v.t. Join firmly together. So ~ā'TION n. [f. LL *compagināre* (com-*pago=-inis*=prec.), see -ATE³]

compan'ion¹ (-yon), n. & v.t. & i. One who accompanies another; associate *in,* ~ *of his retreat;* title of handbooks, as *Gardener's C~;* || member of order of C-s of *Honour;* person (usu. woman) paid to live with another; thing that matches another (also adj., as ~ *volume*); (v.t.)

accompany; (v.i.) consort *with.* Hence ~ATE² a. (~*āte marriage,* marriage with legalized birth-control & provision for divorce by mutual consent). [f. OF *compaignon* f. LL com(*panionem* f. *panis* bread)]

companion² (-yon), n. (naut.). Raised frame on quarter-deck for lighting cabins etc. below; ~*-hatch,* wooden covering over ~*-way;* ~*-hatchway,* opening in deck leading to cabin; ~*-ladder* (from deck to cabin); ~*-way,* staircase to cabin. [cf. Du. *kompanje,* It.(*camera della*) *compagna* = storeroom = LL *compagnia* (*panis* bread)]

companionable (-nyo-), a. Sociable. Hence ~LY² adv., ~bLENESS (-in-) n. [com-PANION¹+-ABLE]

companionship (-nyo-) n. State of being companion(s).

com'pany (kŭm-), n., & v.t. & i. Companionship; *in* ~, not alone; *bear, keep, a person* ~, accompany him; *part (with), part (from); weep for* ~ (because one's companion weeps); *keep* ~, associate as lovers; number of persons assembled; one's usual associates, as *addicted to low companion);* social party; guests; *I sin in good* ~, better men have done the same; *~manners,* the artificial behaviour put on before strangers; body of persons combined for common (esp. commercial) object, as JOINT² *Stock C~,* ||*Limited Liability C~* (liability of each member limited usu. to amount subscribed by him), *John C~*(*East India C~*); partner(s) not named in title of firm, as *Smith & Co.;* party of players; subdivision of infantry battalion usu. commanded by major or captain (cf. TROOP, BATTERY; ~ *officer,* captain or lower commissioned officer; ~ *sergeant-major,* senior non-com. officer of ~); unit of R.A.S.C., R.E., etc.; *ship's* ~, entire crew; (v.t., arch.) accompany; (v.i.) consort *with.* [vb f. OF com-*paignier*) f. OF *compaignie* formed on *compagnon* COMPANION¹]

com'parable, a. That can be compared (*with*); fit to be compared (*to*). [F., f. L *comparabilis* (as COMPARE¹, see -BLE¹]

compa'rative, a. & n. 1. Of or involving comparison, as *the* ~ *method,* esp. of sciences, as ~ *anatomy;* (Gram.) expressing a higher degree of the quality denoted by the simple word; estimated by comparison, as *the* ~ *merits of;* perceptible by comparison, as *in* ~ *comfort.* 2. n. ~ degree. Hence ~LY² adv. [f. L *comparativus* (foll., -ATIVE)]

compare'¹, v.t. & i. Liken, pronounce similar, (*to*), esp. with negative, as *not to be* ~*d to;* estimate the similarity of (one thing *with, to,* another); two things

together); **observe** the similarity or relation between (passages of book etc.; abbr. *cp.*); ~ *notes*, exchange views; (Gram.) form comparative & superlative degrees of (adjective, adverb); (v.i.) bear comparison, as *no lady can ~ with Sally*. [f. L *comparāre* (*par* equal)]

compa're², n. Comparison, as *beyond, without, past, ~*. [f. prec.; prob. arising f. obs. *compare*=COMPEER, misunderstood in *without ~*]

compa'rison, n. Act of comparing; simile, illustration; *in ~ with*, compared to; *degrees of ~*, positive, comparative, superlative, (of adjectives & adverbs). [f. OF *comparaison* f. L *comparationem* (as COMPARE¹, see -SON)]

compa'rt, v.t. Divide into compartments. [f. L *compartīrī* (*pars partis* part)]

compa'rtment, n. Division separated by partitions esp. of railway carriage; water-tight division of ship; ‖ (Pol.) separate portion of a bill, or business in hand, for discussion of which a limit of parliamentary time is allotted by Government. [f. F *compartiment* f. LL *compartimentum* (as prec., see -MENT)]

com'pass¹ (kŭm-), n. (*Pair of*) ~*es*, with two legs connected at one end by movable joint; *beam-~es* (with sliding sockets, for large circles); *bow-~es* (with legs jointed to bend inwards); circumference, boundary; area, extent, (also *fig.*, as *beyond my ~*); range of a voice; roundabout way, as *fetch, go, a ~*; instrument showing magnetic meridian or one's direction with respect to it (*Mariner's ~*); BOX³ *the ~*; *~-plane* (convex, for planing concave surfaces); *~-saw* (with narrow blade, for curves); *~ window*, semicircular bay window. [f. F *compas* f. med. L *compassus* pair of compasses (perh. *passus* step); sense-history of *compassus* and vb *compassare* is obscure]

com'pass² (kŭm-), v.t. Go round; hem in; grasp mentally; contrive; accomplish. Hence ~ABLE a. [f. F *compasser* measure, contrive, f. LL †*compassare*, see prec.]

compa'ssion (-shn), n. Pity inclining one to spare or help, as *have ~ on us*. [F, f. LL *compassionem* f. COM(*pati pass-* suffer), see -ION]

compa'ssionate¹ (-sho-), a. Sympathetic, pitying; ‖ *~ allowance* (granted when an ordinary pension or allowance is not admissible under official rules); ‖ *~ leave* (granted out of compassion). Hence ~LY² (-tl) adv., ~NESS (-tn-) n. [f. F *compassionné* p.p. of *compassionner* as prec.), -ATE²]

compa'ssionate² (-sho-), v.t. Regard, treat, with compassion. [f. prec.]

compa'tible, a. Consistent, able to co-exist, (*with*). Hence or cogn. ~BIL'ITY n.,

~**bly²** adv. [F, f. med. L *compatibilis* (*compati* suffer with, -BLE)]

compa'triot, n. Fellow-countryman. Hence ~ŌT'IC a. [f. F *compatriote* f. L COM(*patriota* PATRIOT)]

compeer', n. Equal, peer; comrade. [f. OF COM(*per* PEER¹)]

compel', v.t. (-ll-). Constrain, force, (*to do, to a course*); bring about (an action) by force, as *~ submission*; (poet.) drive forcibly. Hence ~l'ABLE a. [f. OF *compeller* f. L COM(*pellere puls-* drive)]

com'pend, n.=COMPENDIUM.

compe'ndious, a. Brief but comprehensive (of works & authors). Hence ~LY² adv., ~NESS n. [f. OF *compendieux* f. L *compendiosus* (foll., see -OUS)]

compe'ndium, n. (pl. *-ums, -a*). Abridgement; summary; abstract. [L, lit. what is weighed together f. *compendere* weigh]

com'pensate, v.t. & i. 1. Counterbalance; make amends (*for* thing, *to* person, *with, by*, another thing, or abs.). 2. (Mech.) recompense (person *for* thing). 2. (Mech.) provide (pendulum etc.) with mechanical compensation. Hence **com'pensa·tive** a. & n., ~OR² n., **compen'satory** a. [f. L COM(*pensare* frequent. of *pendere pens-* weigh)]

compensa'tion, n. Compensating; thing given as recompense; *~-balance, ~-pendulum*, of chronometer (neutralizing effect of temperature). Hence ~AL a. [f. L *compensatio* (as prec., see -ATION)]

com'père (-pâr), n. Organizer of cabaret or broadcast entertainment who introduces the artistes, comments on the turns, etc. [F, = gossip]

compe'te, v.i. Strive (*with* another *for* thing, *in doing*, or abs.; vie *with* another *in* a quality). [f. L COM(*petere -tit-* seek), in class. L=coincide, be fitting]

com'petence, -cy, nn. Sufficiency of means for living, easy circumstances; ability (*to do, for* a task); (of court, magistrate, etc.) legal capacity, right to take cognizance. [f. F *compétence* f. L *competentia* (as prec., see -ENCE, -ENCY)]

com'petent, a. Properly qualified (judge, court, witness); (of things) belonging, permissible, *to*, as *it was ~ to him to refuse*. Hence ~LY² adv. [f. F *compétent* (as COMPETE, see -ENT)]

competi'tion, n. Act of competing (*for*), by examination, in market, etc.; (Anglo-Ind.) *~-wallah*, member of I.C.S. chosen by ~. [f. L *competitio* (as foll., see -TION)]

compe'titive, a. Of, by, offered for, competition. Hence ~LY¹ (-vl) adv. [f. L (as COMPETE, see -IVE)]

compe'titor, n. One who competes, rival. Hence ~ORY a., ~RESS¹ n. [L (as prec., see -OR²)]

For compounds of *co-* not given consult *co-*.

compilā'tion, n. Compiling; thing compiled. [F, f. L *compilationem* (foll., -ATION)]

compile', v.t. Collect (materials) into a volume; make up (volume) of such materials; (Cricket sl.) score (so many runs). [f. F *compiler* (perh.) f. L *compilāre* plunder (*pilāre* plunder)]

complā'cence, -cy, nn. Tranquil pleasure; self-satisfaction. [f. med. L *complacentia*, whence F *complaisance*, f. L COM(*placēre* please), see -ENCE, -ENCY]

complā'cent, a. Self-satisfied. Hence ~LY² adv. [f. L as prec., see -ENT]

complain', v.i. Express dissatisfaction with (of); announce that one is suffering from (of a headache etc.); state a grievance (to an authority for offence or offence), whence ~ANT (1) n., plaintiff in certain suits; (poet.) emit mournful sound. [f. F *complaindre* (st.-*aign*-) f. LL COM(*plangere planct*- beat the breast) bewail]

complaint, n. Utterance of grievance; formal accusation; *plaintiff's case in civil action; subject, ground, of ~; bodily ailment. [f. F *complainte*, f. fem. p.p. as prec.]

complaisance (-plīz-; *or* kŏm²), n. Obligingness; politeness; deference. So **complaisant** a. [F (see COMPLACENCE)]

cóm'plement¹, n. That which completes; (Gram.) ~ *of* (words completing) *the predicate*; full number required (to man ship, fill conveyance, etc.); (Math.) ~ *of an angle*, its deficiency from 90° (cf. SUPPLEMENT). Hence **cómplemén'tal** a., **plemén'taly²** adv. [f. L *com-plementum* (COMPLETE¹, -MENT)]

cómplemén'tal², v.t. Complete, form complement to. [f. prec.]

complemén'tary, a. Serving to complete (making up 90°); ~ COLOURS. [-ARY¹]

complete¹, a. Having all its parts, entire; finished; unqualified, as ~ *surprise*; (arch. of persons) accomplished, as ~ *horseman*. Hence ~LY² (-tl-) adv., ~NESS (-tn-) n. [f. L *completus* p.p. of *complēre* fill up]

complete², v.t. Finish; make whole or perfect; make up the amount of. So **comple'tion** n., **comple'tive** a. [f. prec.]

cóm'plex¹, n. Complex whole; (Psych.) kind of mental abnormality set up by suppressed tendencies or by obsession. [f. L *complexus* -*ūs* (as foll.)]

cóm'plex², a. Consisting of parts, composite; complicated; ~ *sentence*, one containing subordinate clause(s). Hence **complex'ity** n. ~LY² adv. [f. L com-(*plectere plex*- plait) embrace]

complé'xion (-kshn), n. Natural colour, texture, & appearance, of the skin (esp. of face); (fig.) character, aspect, as *his*

complī'cate, v.t. Mix up (with other things); make intricate (esp. in p.p.). [f. L *complicāre* fold, see -ATE³]

complicā'tion, n. Involved condition; complicating circumstance, as *here is a further* ~. [f. L *complicatio* (as prec., see -ATION)]

compli'city, n. Partnership in an evil action. [f. L COM(*plex -plicis* f, *plic-* fold), see -ITY]

cóm'pliment¹, n. Polite expression of praise, as *pay, make, a* ~; *as* implying praise; (pl.) formal greetings, as *make, pay, send*, one's ~*s*, (as accompaniment to message, note, present, etc.) *with Mr—'s* ~*s*; ~*s of the season*; (arch.) gift, gratuity. Hence ~ARY¹(-ĕn-) a. [F. It. *compli-mento* f. Sp. *cumplimiento* fulfilment of the duties of courtesy f. L as COMPLEMENT; cf. COMPLY]

cóm'pliment², v.t. Pay a compliment to (person on thing); present (person with thing) as mark of courtesy. [f. F *com-plimenter* (prec.)]

cóm'pline¹, n. (Eccl.) last service of the day. [ME *cumplie* f. OF *complie* f. L *completa* (*hora*) see COMPLETE; -*in* unexplained; mod. E often uses pl., after F *complies*; -*es* is mod.]

comply', v.i. Act in accordance (with wish, command, etc., or abs.). [f. It. *complire* f. Sp. *cumplir* COMPLETE, cf. COMPLEMENT]

cóm'po, n. (pl. -os). Abbr. of COMPOSITION, esp. =stucco, plaster.

compō'nent, a. & n. 1. Contributing to the composition of a whole. 2. n. ~ part. [f. L COM(*ponere* put), -ENT]

compo'rt, v.t. & i. Conduct, behave, oneself; ~ *with*, suit, befit. [f. L COM-(*portare* carry)]

compōse' (-z), v.t. (Of elements) make up, constitute, (esp. pass., *be* ~*ed of*); construct in words, produce in literary form, (poem etc., or abs.); (Mus.) invent & put into proper form; set (words) to music; (Print.) set up (type) to form words & blocks of words, set up (article etc.) in type; put together, arrange, artistically; adjust (dispute etc.); arrange in specified or understood manner, or for specified purpose, as ~*e your countenance*, ~*e your*

conduct wears another ~. Hence -ED² (-kshond), ~LESS, aa. [f. f. L *complexio-nem* (as prec., see -ION); orig.= combination of supposed qualities determining nature of a body]

complī'ance, n. Action in accordance with request, command, etc.; *in* ~ *with*, according to (wish etc.); base submission. [COMPLY, -ANCE]

complī'ant, a. Disposed to comply, yielding. Hence ~LY² a. [-ANT]

cóm'plicacy, n. Complexity; compli-cated structure. [f. L as foll. see -ACY]

thoughts for action; tranquillize (*oneself*, passions, etc.), esp. in p.p., whence ~**ĕd.ly**² adv., ~**ĕd·ness** n., (~z-), [f. F COM(*poser* f. LL *pausāre* cease, lie or lay down, see POSE; confused with & replacing in compounds *pōndre* f. L *pōnere posit-* place]

compŏs·er (-z-), n. One who composes (usu. music). [prec. + -ER¹]

compŏs·ing (-z-), n. In vbl senses; ~**stick**, metal instrument of adjustable width in which type is set. [-ING¹]

cŏm·posite (-zĭt- *or* -zī-), a. & n. (Thing) made up of various parts; (Archit.) fifth classical ORDER, Ionic & Corinthian mixed; (plant) of the Natural Order *Compositae*, in which the so-called flower is a head of many flowers (as daisy, dandelion, etc.); (of ships) built of both wood and iron; ‖ ~ (railway) *carriage*, one with compartments of different classes; ~ *candle* (of stearic acid & stearin or coco-nut oil); ~ *photograph* (produced by accurately superimposing several portrait-heads). Hence ~**ly**² adv., ~**ness** n. [f. L COM(*pōnere posit-* put)]

composi·tion (-z-), n. 1. Act of putting together; formation, construction; formation of words into a compound word; construction of sentences, art of literary production; act, art, of composing music; setting up of type. 2. Mental constitution, as *a touch of madness in his* ~. 3. Arrangement (of the parts of a picture etc.); thing composed, mixture; piece of music or writing. 4. Agreement for cessation of hostilities; compromise. 5. Compound artificial substance, esp. one serving the purpose of a natural one (often attrib., as ~ *billiard-balls*. 6. Agreement for payment of sum in lieu of larger sum or other obligation, as *made a* ~ *with his creditors*. [F, f. L *compositiōnem* (as prec., see -ION)]

composi·tive (-z-), a. Combining. [f. L *compositīvus* (as prec., see -IVE)]

composi·tor (-z-), n. Type-setter. [f. AF *compositour* f. L *compositōrem* (as prec., see -OR²)]

cŏm·pŏs (*mĕn·tĭs*), a. In one's right mind; *non* ~, not in one's right mind. [L]

compŏs·sible, a. Able to coexist (*with*). [F, f. med. L COM(*possibilis* POSSIBLE)]

cŏm·pŏst¹, n. Compound manure; combination. [OF, f. L as COMPOSITE]

cŏm·pŏst², v.t. Treat with, make into, compost. [f. OF *composter* (prec.)]

compŏ·sure (-zher), n. Tranquil demeanour, calmness. [f. COMPOSE + -URE]

compota·tion, n. Tippling together. So **cŏm·potātor²** n. [f. L *compotātio* f. +COM(*pōtāre* drink) see -ATION]

cŏm·pote (-pŏte, -ōt), n. Fruit preserved in syrup. [F, f. OF *composte* f. L fem. p.p. as COMPOSITE]

compound¹, v.t. & i. 1. Mix (ingredients, lit. & fig.); combine (verbal elements) into a word; make up (a composite whole). 2. Settle (matter by mutual concession, debt by partial payment, subscription by lump sum, or abs.). 3. Condone (liability, offence) for money etc.; ~ *a felony*, forbear prosecution on private motive. 4. v.i. Come to terms (*with* person *for* forgoing claim etc. *for* offence). Hence ~**ABLE** a. [ME *compounen* f. OF *compoundre* f. L COM(*pōnere* put), whence obs. *compone*]

cŏm·pound², a. & n. 1. Made up of several ingredients; consisting of several parts; combined, collective; ~ *fracture* (complicated with skin wound); ~ *addition, subtraction*, etc. (dealing with various denominations); ~ INTEREST¹; (Zool., Bot.) consisting of a combination of organisms, or simple parts, as ~ *animal*, ~ *flower*; ‖ ~ *householder* (whose rates are paid *by* landlord & included in rent). 2. n. Mixture of elements, ~ thing, esp. ~ word. [orig. p.p. of *compoun*, see prec.]

cŏm·pound³, n. (In India, China, etc.) enclosure in which house or factory stands. [perh. f. Malay *kampong*]

comprādō·r, n. (In China) chief native servant in European house of business. [Port., = buyer, f. LL *comparātōrem* f. COM(*parāre* furnish), see -OR²]

comprehĕnd·, v.t. Grasp mentally, understand; (person, thing) include, take in. [f. L COM(*prehendere* -*hens-* grasp)]

comprehĕn·sible, a. That may be understood; that may be comprised. Hence ~**ibi·l·ity** n., ~**ibly**² adv. [f. L *comprehensibilis* (as prec., see -BLE)]

comprehĕn·sion (-shn), n. Act, faculty, of understanding; inclusive power, as *a term of wide* ~; toleration of divergent opinions (esp. Eccl.). [f. L *comprehensiō* (as prec., see -ION)]

comprehĕn·sive, a. Of understanding, as ~ *faculty*; including much, as ~ *term*, ~ *grasp* (fig. & lit.). Hence ~**ly**² adv., ~**ness** (-vn-) n. [f. L *comprehensīvus* (as prec., see -IVE)]

comprĕss·¹, v.t. Squeeze together; condense (air, language, thoughts). Hence ~**IVE** a. [f. OF *compresser* f. L *compressāre* f. COM(*primere press-* = *premere* press)]

cŏm·press², n. Soft pad of lint etc. for compressing artery etc.; piece of wet cloth covered with waterproof bandage, for relief of inflammation. [f. F *compresse* f. L fem. p.p. as prec.]

comprĕss·ible, a. That may be compressed. Hence ~**ibi·l·ity** n. [COMPRESS¹ + -IBLE, as if on L *comprimere*, not *compressāre*]

For compounds of *co-* not given consult co-.

compre'ssion (-shn), n. Squeezing together, condensation, (lit. & fig.). So
COMPRESS'OR² n. [F., f. L compressionem
(as COMPRESS¹, see -ION)]

compris'e' (-z), v.t. Include, comprehend; consist of, as the house ~es 9 bed-
rooms etc.; condense (within limits etc.).
Hence ~ABLE (-z-) a. [f. F compris (p.p.
compriser) f. L as COMPREHEND, prob. after
ENTERPRISE]

còm'promise¹ (-z), n. Settlement of
dispute by mutual concession; adjustment of (between) conflicting opinions,
courses, etc., by modification of each.
[f. F compromis f. L com(promittere
PROMISE)]

còm'promise² (-z), v.t. & i. Settle (dispute) by mutual concession; (v.i.) make
a compromise; bring (person, oneself)
under suspicion by indiscreet action. [f.
prec.]

comprovin'cial (-shl), a. & n. (Person,
esp. bishop) of the same (esp. archiepiscopal) province. [f. med. L com-
provincialis (COM-, PROVINCE, -AL)]

comptroll'er (kont-), n. Mis-spelling of
CONTROLLER in some titles, as C~ of
accounts.

compul'sion (-shn), n. Constraint, obligation; under, upon, ~, because one is
compelled. [F, f. L compulsionem (as
COMPEL, see -ION)]

compul'sive, a.   Tending   to compel.
Hence ~LY² adv. [f. L as COMPEL, -IVE]

compul'sor¡ly, a. (Of action, agent)
enforced; compelling (~ry legislation etc.).
opp. permissive.   Hence ~ILY² adv.
~INESS n. [as prec., -ORY]

compůnc'tion, n. Pricking of conscience;
slight regret, scruple, as without ~ion.
Hence ~IOUS (-shus) a., ~IOUSLY² (-shus-)
adv. [OF, f. L compunctionem f. COM-
(pungere punct- prick), see -ION]

compůrga'tion, n. Clearing from a
charge, vindication, esp. (Eng. Hist.)
trial & purgation by oath. So còm'-
půrgator² n., compůrga'tory a. [f. L
compurgatio f. com(purgare purify) see
-ATION]

compůte', v.t. Reckon (number or
amount often at figure, that, or abs.). So
~ABLE (or kom̆'-), ~ATIVE (or kom̆'-), aa.,
còmpůta'TION n. [f. F computer f. L
com(putare reckon)]

comrade (kŭm'rid, kŏ'-), n. Mate or fellow
in work or play or fighting, equal with
whom one is on familiar terms, (usu. of
males, cf. companion); (as prefix) fellow
member of trade union, benefit society,
etc. (C~ Smith). Hence ~SHIP (-dsh-) n.
[f. F camarade f. Sp. camarada chamber-
mate, lit. chamberful (camara room f. L
camera, see -ADE); -o- prob. to repr. sound
of Sp. a]

• Còm'stŏckerÿ n. Opposition to naked
realism in art or literature. [A. Comstock,
U.S. neo-Puritan (d. 1915)]

Còm't,ism, n. = POSITIVISM. So ~IST n.
[Auguste Comte, founder (d. 1857), + -ISM]
cŏn¹ (-ŭn-), v.t. ~ (over), study, learn by
heart, [earlier spelling and pron. cun, a
differentiation of CAN² (pres. st, cun-)]
cŏn² *cŏnn, v.t. (-nn-). Direct steering
of (ship, or abs.); conning-tower, armoured
pilot-house of warship, superstructure for
submarine from which steering, firing,
etc., are directed when it is on or near
the surface. [perh. weakened form of
cond, conduce, f. F conduire f. L conducere
CONDUCT v.]

cŏn³, prep. (It.). With (esp. Mus.), as ~
brio (spirit), espressione (expression),
fuoco (fire), moto (spirited movement).

*cŏn⁴, v. See CONTRA.

*cŏn⁵, n. & v.t. (In attrib. use) confidence
(~ game, CONFIDENCE trick); (v.t.) swindle,
dupe, [abbr.]

con-, pref. = L cum (see COM-) before c d l
g j l m n p q s t v.

con'acre (-ker) n. (In Ireland) letting by
tenant of small portions of land prepared
for crop. [CORN¹ + ACRE]

con amo're (-rĭ), adv. Zealously. [It.]

cona'tion, n. (philos.). The exertion of
willing that desire or aversion shall issue
in action. Hence cŏn'ATIVE a. [f. L
conationem (conari to try)]

concat'en|āte (-n-k-), v.t. Link together
(fig.). So ~A'TION n. [f. L CON(catenare
f. catena chain), see -ATE³]

cŏn'cāve, a. & n. With outline or surface
curved like interior of circle or sphere
(cf. CONVEX); (n.) ~ surface, esp. vault
of heaven. Hence or cogn. ~LY² (-vl-)
adv., cŏncāv'ITY n. [F, f. L CON(cavus
hollow)]

concāv'ō-, in comb. Concavely, concave
&c., as ~-concave, concave on both sides,
~-convex, concave one side, convex the
other. [-o-]

conceal', v.t. Keep secret (from); hide.
Hence ~MENT n. [f. OF conceler f. L
CON(celare)]

concēde', v.t. Admit, allow, (statement,
that); grant (right, privilege, points or
start in game etc.; to person); (Sport,
sl.) lose (game etc.). [f. F conceder f. L
CON(cedere -cess- yield)]

conceit' (-sēt), n. Personal vanity; fanciful notion, far-fetched comparison or
other euphuism: in my own ~ (judgement); out of ~, no longer pleased with.
[f. CONCEIVE on deceit]

conceit'ed (-sēt-), a. (arch.). Imagine;
persuade oneself (that). [f. prec.]

concēiv'ed (-sēt-), a. Vain (orig. self-~).
Hence ~LY² adv. [CONCEIT¹ + -ED²]

concēiv'able (-sēv-), a. That can be
(mentally) conceived.   Hence ~ABIL'ITY,
~ableNESS, nn., ~ably² adv., (-sēv-). [f.
foll. + -ABLE]

conceive' (-sēv), v.t. & i. Become pregnant with; become pregnant; form in
the mind, imagine, (also ~ of); fancy,

think, (*that*); formulate, express, (usu. pass., as ~d *in plain terms*). [f. OF *conceiver* (st. *conceiv-*) f. L CON(*cipere cept-* = *capere* take)]

concél'ebráte, v.i. (R.-C. Ch., of newly ordained priest) celebrate mass with ordaining bishop. Hence ~A'TION n. [f. L CON(*celebrate* CELEBRATE)]

cón'centráte, v.t. & i. Bring together to one point (troops, power, attention); (Chem.) increase strength of (liquid etc.) by contracting its volume, (fig. in p.p. of hate etc.) intense; (v.i.) employ all one's power or attention (*upon*). Hence **concentrA'TION** n. (~*ion camp*, for the accommodation of political prisoners, internees, etc.); ~**iveness**, ~**or**² nn. ~IVE a., [as f. a L CON(*centrare* f. *centrum* CENTRE), -ATE²]

concén'tre (-ter), v.t. & i. Bring, come, to a common centre. [f. F *concentrer* (as prec.)]

concén'tric, a. Having a common centre (*with* or abs.); (Mil.) ~ *fire*, firing concentrated on a point. Hence ~**ICALLY** adv., **concéntri'city** n. [f. med. L CON-(*centricus*, as CENTRE)]

cón'cept, n. Idea of a class of objects, general notion. [f. L as CONCEIVE]

concép'tion, n. Conceiving (in all senses); thing conceived, idea. Hence ~**AL** (-sho-) a. [f., f.L conceptionem (as prec., -ION)]

concép'tive, a. Conceiving (mentally), of conception. [f.L *conceptivus* (as prec., see -IVE)]

concép'tual, a. Of mental conceptions. [f. med. L *conceptualis* (*conceptus* -ūs as prec., -AL]

concép'tualism, n. Doctrine that universals exist as mental concepts (only); doctrine that the mind can form ideas corresponding to abstract terms. So ~**IST** n. [-ISM]

concérn'¹, v.t. Relate to; affect; interest oneself (*with, in, about, matter, to do*); be ~*ed* (take part) *in*; *I am not* ~*ed, it is not my business* (*to*); (in p.p.) troubled, as a ~*ed air, am* ~*ed to hear, as, for person, about;* ~*ing* (prep.), about. [f. F *concerner* f. L CON(*cernere* sift, regard), in med. L = have regard to]

concérn'², n. Relation, reference, (*with*); *have no* ~ (nothing to do) *with*; *have a* ~ (interest, share) *in*; anxiety, solicitous regard, as *asked with deep* ~; matter that affects one, as *no* ~ *of mine*; (pl.) affairs, as *meddling in my* ~*s*; business, firm, as *a flourishing* ~; (colloq.) thing, as *smashed the whole* ~. [f. prec.]

concérn'ment, n. Affair, business; importance, as *of vital* ~; being concerned (*with*); anxiety. [-MENT]

cón'cert¹, n. Agreement, union, as *work in* ~ (*with*); *the C~ of Europe*, chief Powers acting together occasionally from

1815; combination of voices or sounds, as *voices raised in* ~; musical entertainment; ~ *grand*, grand piano of largest size for ~s; ~ *pitch* (slightly higher than the ordinary; transf., state of unusual efficiency or readiness). [F, f. It. *concerto*, as foll.]

concért'², v.t. Arrange (by mutual agreement, also of one person). [f. F *concerter* f. It. *concertare* accord together; connexion with L *concertare* contend, doubtful]

concért'ed, a. In vbl senses; also (Mus.) arranged in parts for voices or instruments. [-ED¹]

cōncerti'na (-tē-), n. Portable musical instrument consisting of a pair of bellows with a set of studs at each end. [CONCERT¹ +-INA¹]

concert'ō (-chār-), n. (pl. -os). Composition (usu. in three movements) for solo instrument(s) accompanied by orchestra. [It., see CONCERT¹]

concé'ssion (-shn), n. Act of conceding; thing conceded, esp. (Diplom.) grant to CONCESSIONAIRE, piece of territory of which the occupation & use is granted to a State, company, or person. Hence ~**ARY**¹ (sho-) a. [F, f.L *concessionem* (as CONCEDE, see -ION)]

concéssion(n)aire' (-sho-), n. Holder of concession, grant, etc., esp. of monopoly given by government to foreigner. [F (-*nn-*), prec., -ARY¹]

concéss'ive, a. Of, tending to, concession; (Gram.) expressing concession. [f. L *concessivus* (as CONCEDE, see -IVE)]

concett'ism (-chět-), n. Use of fanciful turns (It. *concetti*) in literature. [-ISM]

cónch (-ngk), n. Shell-fish; shell of a mollusc, esp. (Rom. Myth.) as trumpet of a Triton; (Archit.) domed roof of semicircular apse; (also *concha*) external ear, its central concavity; (Naut. sl., C~) native of Bahamas. [f. L *concha* shell f. Gk *koŋkhē* mussel etc.]

cónchif'erous (-ngk-), a. (zool., geol.). Shell-bearing. [as prec., see -FEROUS]

cónchŏ'logǐ'y (-ngk-), n. Study of shells & shell-fish. So **cónchŏlō'gical** a.,~**IST** n. [as CONCH, see -LOGY]

|| **cón'chy**, n. (sl.). Conscientious objector. [abbr.]

concierge (see Ap.), n. (In France etc.) door-keeper, porter, (esp. of flats etc.). [F]

concil'iar, a. Of ecclesiastical councils. [f. L *concilium* COUNCIL+-AR¹]

concil'iāte, v.t. Gain (esteem, goodwill); pacify; win over (*to* one's side etc.); reconcile (discrepant theories). Hence or cogn. ~**ATIVE**, ~**ATORY**, (-lyǎ-), aa.,~**ātor**², ~**atoriness** (-lyǎ-), nn. [f.L *conciliare* (as prec.), see -ATE³]

conciliā'tion, n. Reconcilement; use of conciliating measures; *Court of* ~ (offer-

For compounds of co- *not given consult* co-.

ing parties a voluntary settlement). [f. L *concilidio* (as prec., see -ATION)]

concin'nity, n. Elegance, neatness, of literary style. [f. L *concinnitas* (*concinnus* well-adjusted, etym. dub., see -TY)]

concise', a. Brief in expression (of speech, style, person). Hence ~NESS (-s-) n., ~ly² (-sĭ-) adv. [f. L *concidere cis-* = *caedere* cut]

conci'sion (-zhn), n. Mutilation (in *Phil.* iii. 2. = circumcision, contemptuously); conciseness. [F, f, L *concisionem*]

côn'clave, n. Meeting-place, assembly, of cardinals for election of Pope; private assembly, as *in ~*. [F, f, L *conclave* lock-up place f. *clavis* key]

conclude' (-n-klood), v.t. & i. Bring to an end, arrange, settle, (of ~, *with* remark etc.) one's speech etc., or things) come to an end; infer (*from* premisses etc.); resolve (*to do*). [f. L *concludere* shut]

conclu'sion (-n-klōōzhn), n. Termination (*in* ~, lastly, to conclude; final result; decision; (Logic) proposition deduced from previous ones, esp. last of three forming a syllogism; *try ~s with*, engage in a trial of skill etc. with; settling, arrangement, (of peace etc.); [f. L *clusionem* (as prec., see -ION)]

conclu'sive, (-n-klŏŏ-), a., Decisive, convincing. Hence ~IY² (-vĭ-) adv., ~NESS (-vn-) n. [f. LL *conclusivus* (as prec., see -IVE)]

concoct', v.t. Make up of mixed ingredients (soup, drink, story, plot). Hence **concoc'tion, concoc'tor²,** nn., **concoc'TIVE** a. [f. L CON(*coquere coct-* cook)]

concol'orous (-kŭl-), a. (nat. hist.), Of uniform colour. [f. L CON(*color* colour) + -OUS]

concom'itance, -cy, (-n-k-), n. Coexistence, esp. (-cence) of body & blood of Christ in each of the eucharistic elements. [f. L *concomitantia* (as foll., see -ANCE, -ANCY)]

concom'itant (-n-k-), a. & n. Going together, as ~ circumstances; (n.) accompanying thing. Hence ~ly² adv. [f. L CON(*comitari* f. *comes -mitis* companion), see -ANT]

côn'cord, n. Agreement, harmony, between persons or things; treaty; (Mus.) chord satisfactory in itself without others to follow; (Gram.) agreement between words in gender, number, etc. [f. F *concorde* f. L *concordia* f. CON(*cors* f. *cordis* heart) being of one mind]

concord'ance, n. Agreement; alphabetical arrangement of chief words (*verbal ~*) or subjects (*real ~*) occurring in a book (esp. the Bible) or author, with citations of the passages concerned. [F, f. LL *concordantia* (foll., -ANCE)]

concord'ant (-n-k-), a. Agreeing, harmo-

---

nious, (*with* or abs.); in musical concord. Hence ~ly² adv. [F, f, L *concordare*]

concord'at, n. (see CONCORD and -ANT)

con'course (-ôrs), n. Crowd; confluence of *concours*... as fortuitous ~ of atoms. [f. OF *concours* f. L *concursus -ūs* (as CONCUR)]

con'crescence, n. (biol.), Coalescence, growing together. [f. L *concrescentia* (as foll., see -ENCE)]

côn'crete¹, a. & n. 1. (Gram., of noun) denoting a thing as opposed to a quality, state, or action, not ABSTRACT; existing in material form, real; *in the ~*, in sphere of reality. 2. n. ~ thing; composition of gravel, cement, etc., for building, (attrib.) made of this. Hence ~ly² (-tl-) adv. [f. L CON(*crescere cret-* grow)]

concrete², v.t. & i. (-n-krēt') form into a mass, solidify; (konk') treat with concrete. [f. prec.]

concre'tion (-n-k-), n. 1. Coalescence; concrete mass, esp. (Path.) morbid formation in the body, (Geol.) mass formed of solid particles, whence ~ARY¹ (-n-krēsho-) a.; embodiment in concrete form. [f. L *concretio* (as CONCRETE¹, see -ION)]

concu'binage (-n-k-), n. Cohabiting of man and woman not legally married; having, being, a concubine. [F, as foll.]

côn'cubine, n. Woman who cohabits with a man, not being his wife; (among polygamous peoples) secondary wife. [F, f, L CON(*cubina* f. *cubare* lie)]

concu'piscence (-n-k-), n. Sexual appetite; (N.T.) desire for worldly things. [f. L *concupiscentia* (as foll., see -ENCE)]

concu'piscent (-n-k-), a. Lustful, eagerly desirous. [f. L *concupiscere* inceptive of CON(*cupere* desire), see -ENT]

concur' (-n-k-), v.i. (-rr-), Happen together, coincide; (of circumstances etc.) co-operate (*with* or abs.); agree in opinion (*with*). So **concu'rrence** (-n-k-) n. [f. L CON(*currere curs-* run)]

concu'rrent (-n-k-), a. & n. Running together, as parallel lines; existing together; co-operating; agreeing; ~ *lease* (made before the former expires); ~ *insurance* (of which the risk is definitely proportioned among several companies); (n.) ~ circumstance. Hence ~ly² adv. [as CONCUR, see -ENT]

concuss' (-n-k-), v.t. Shake violently, agitate, (usu. fig.); intimidate. [f. L *concuss-* = *quatere* shake)]

concu'ssion (-n-kŭshn), n. Violent shaking; shock; (Surg.) injury to brain etc. caused by heavy blow etc.; ~-*bellows*, self-acting reservoir regulating wind in

organ; ~*fuse* (in shell, ignited by ~). [f. L *concussio* (as prec., see -ION)]

condemn' (-m), v.t. Censure, blame; give judgement against; bring about conviction of, as *his looks* ~ *him*; doom (*to death, to be beheaded; also fig. to toilet etc.); ~*ed cell, pew, sermon* (for ~*ed* persons); pronounce forfeited (smuggled goods etc.), unfit for use, incurable. Hence **condem'-NABLE** (-mn-) a. [f. OF *condemner* f. L CON(*damnare* = *damnare* damage, condemn)]

condemnā'tion, n. Censure; judicial conviction; ground for condemning, as *his own conduct is his* ~. [f. L *condemnatio* (as prec., see -ATION)]

condem'natory, a. Expressing condemnation. [f. L as CONDEMN, see -ORY]

condensā'tion, n. Act of condensing (t. & i.); condensed mass. [f. L *condensatio* (as foll., see -ATION)]

condense', v.t. & i. Compress; ~*ed milk* (reduced by evaporation); concentrate (rays of light); increase intensity of (electricity); reduce, be reduced, from gas or vapour to liquid; compress into few words, make concise. Hence or cogn. ~**ABIL'ITY** n., ~**ABLE** a. [prob. thr. F *condenser*) f. L CON(*densare* f. *densus* thick)]

conden'ser, n. In vbl senses; esp. chamber in steam-engine in which steam is condensed on leaving cylinder; apparatus for accumulating electricity; lens, system of lenses, concentrating light. [-ER[1]]

condescend', v.i. Deign, stoop, (*to an act, to do*); waive one's superiority (*to a person*); || (Sc.) ~ *upon*, specify (particulars). [f. F *condescendre* f. L CON(*descendere* DESCEND)]

condescend'ing, a. Showing condescension, esp. patronizing. Hence ~**LY[2]** adv. [prec. + -ING[2]]

condescen'sion (-shn), n. Affability to inferiors; patronizing manner. [f. L *condescensio* (as CONDESCEND, see -ION)]

condign' (-in), a. Adequate (~ *punishment, vengeance*). Hence ~**LY[2]** (-inl-) adv. [f. F *condigne* f. L CON(*dignus* worthy)]

con'diment, n. Thing used to give relish to food. Hence ~**AL** (-ēn[2]) a. [f. F, f. L *condimentum* (*condire* pickle, see -MENT)]

condi'tion[1], n. Stipulation, thing upon the fulfilment of which depends that of another, (~ *precedent*, that must be fulfilled before a bequest etc. becomes valid); *on* ~ *that*, if, provided that; (Gram.) clause expressing a ~; (pl.) circumstances, esp. those essential to a thing's existence, as *the* ~*s of equilibrium, favourable* ~*s, under existing* ~*s*; state of being, as *eggs arrived in good* ~, *persons of humble* ~; *in, out of,* ~, in good, bad, ~; *change* one's ~, marry. [f. OF *condicion*

f. L *condicionem* f. CON(*dicere*, weak st. *dic-*, say) agree upon, see -ION]

condi'tion,[2] v.t. Stipulate (*that*); agree by stipulation (*to do*); (of things) be essential to; (of persons) make fit (esp. dogs, horses, etc.). [f. OF *condicionner* f. med. L *condicionare* (as prec.)]

condi'tional (-sho-), a. & n. Not absolute, dependent (*on or abs.*); (Gram.) ~ *clause*, one expressing a condition, PROTASIS; ~ *mood,* in French and Italian verbs, that used in the apodosis; (n.) ~ word, conjunction, mood, clause. Hence ~**LY[2]** adv. [f. L *condicionalis* (as CONDITION[1], see -AL)]

condi'tioned (-shond), a. 1. Having a (specified) disposition, as *ill, well,* ~; in a (specified) condition, as *well-ground, cattle*; circumstanced. 2. Subject to conditions. 3. ~ *reflex*, reflex action responding, through habit or training, to a stimulus not naturally connected with it, e.g. watering of dog's mouth at sound of feeding-bell. [CONDITION[1,2] + -ED[2,1]]

condōl'atory, a. Expressing condolence. [f. foll. on anal. of *consolatory* etc.]

condōle', v.i. Express sympathy (*with or abs., upon* loss etc.). Hence **condol'ENCE** n. [f. L CON(*dolēre* suffer)]

con'dom, n. Contraceptive sheath. [inventor]

condomin'ium, n. (diplom.). Joint control of a State's affairs vested in two or more other States. [CON-, L *dominium* DOMINION]

condōne', v.t. Forgive, overlook, (offence, esp. matrimonial infidelity); (of actions) atone for (offence). So **condōna'TION** n. [f. L CON(*donare* give)]

con'dor, n. Large S.-Amer. kind of vulture. Hence ~**ive** a., **condū'civeness** (-vn-) n. [f. L CON(*ducere* lead)]

con'duct, n. Leading, guidance, (cf. SAFE-*conduct*); ~*money* (paid to a witness for travelling expenses); manner of conducting (business etc.); (Art) mode of treatment; behaviour (esp. in its moral aspect, as *good, bad*, ~); *regimental, company,* ~ *sheet,* record of a soldier's offences and punishments. [partly f. F *conduite* f. LL.[+]*conducta* (fem. p.p. as noun), partly f. F *conduit* (whence also CONDUIT) f. L *conductus* -ūs; both as foll.]

For compounds of co- not given consult CO-.

conduct'², v.t. & i. Lead, guide, *to*; (of road) lead *to*; command (army); direct, manage, (business etc.); ~ *oneself*, behave (*a* ~). [f. L CON(*ducere duct-* lead); re-fash. on L in 16th c.]

conduct'ible, a. Capable of conducting (heat etc.) or (rarely) being conducted. Hence ~BIL'ITY n. [f. prec., see -BLE]

conduc'tion, n. Transmission (of heat by contact etc.); conducting (of liquid through pipe etc.), esp. of natural processes). So ~IVE a., **conductiv'ity** n. [f. L *conductio* (as CONDUCT² see -ION)]

conduc'tor, n. Leader, guide; manager; director of orchestra, choir, etc.; official in charge of passengers on omnibus, tram, or (U.S.) train; warrant officer of a military department; thing that conducts or transmits (esp. heat etc., as *good, bad, non-,* ~); *lightning-*~, rod at top of building, conducting electricity away into earth. Hence ~SHIP, **conduc'tress¹**, nn. [f. F *conducteur* f. L *conductorem* (as CONDUCT² see -OR²)]

con'duit (kŭn'dĭt, kŏn'), n. Channel or pipe for conveying liquids (or fig.); tube or trough for protecting insulated electric wires, length of this; ~ *system*, (electr. traction) with conductor in underground in lead piping. [see CONDUCT²]

condu'plicate, a. (bot.) Folded lengthwise along middle. [f. L CON(*duplicare* DUPLICATE)]

cŏn'dyle, n. (anat.) Rounded process at end of bone, forming articulation with another bone. Hence ~oid a. [F, f. L f. Gk *kondulos* knuckle]

Con'dy's fluid, n. A solution of sodium permanganate as disinfectant. [maker]

cône, n., & v.t. & i. **1.** Solid figure with circular (or other curved) base, tapering to a point (generated by straight line that always passes through a fixed point, and describes any fixed curve); fruit of pine or fir; marine shell of genus *Conus*; ~-*shaped thing*, esp. (Meteorol.) foul-weather signal; ~s, fine flour used by bakers for dusting troughs. **2.** v.t. Shape like ~; (pass., of aircraft) be picked up or illuminated by many (hostile) search-lights simultaneously; (v.i.) bear ~s. [vb f. n.] f. L f. Gk *kōnos*]

cŏn'ey. See CONY.

confab', n. & v.i. Colloq. abbr. of CONFABULATION or foll.

confab'ulate, v.i. Converse, chat, (*with* ~, or abs.). Hence or cogn. ~A'TION n., ~atory a. [f. L CON(*fabulari* f. *fabula* tale), see -ATE³]

confec'tion, n. & v.t. Mixing, compounding; thing compounded, esp. preserve, sweetmeat, whence ~ary¹ (-sho) a.; ready-made article of (usu. female) dress, mantle, wrap, etc.; (v.t.) prepare, make, (*a* ~). [vb f. n.] F, f. L *confectionem* f.

confec'tioner (-sho-), n. Maker of sweetmeats, pastry, etc. (usu. for sale). Hence ~y² (2) n. [-ER¹]

confed'eracy n. League, alliance; conspiracy; collusion; body of confederate persons or States, as *Southern C~, Confederate States of America*. [as foll., see -ACY (3)]

confed'erate¹, a. & n. **1.** Allied (lit. & fig.); *C~ States of America* (seceding from the Union, 1860-5). **2.** n. Ally, esp. in bad sense, accomplice. [f. L ... *foedus, -eris* league), see -ATE²]

confed'erate², v.t. & i. Bring (person, State, oneself), come, into alliance (*with*). So ~A'TION n. [as prec., see -ATE³]

con'fer¹, v. (imperat.). Compare (abbr. *cf.*). [L]

confer'², v.t. & i. (-rr-). Grant, bestow, (title, degree, favour, etc., *on*); (v.i.) converse, take counsel, (*with* or abs.). Hence ~ment n. [f. L CON(*ferre* bring)]

cŏn'ference, n. Consultation; annual assembly of Methodist Church. So **conferen'tial** (-shl) a. [f. med. L *conferentia* (as prec., see -ENCE)]

confess', v.t. & i. Acknowledge, as *I ~ my fault, that I did it, to doing it, to having done it, to a dread of spiders*; formally declare one's sins, esp. to a priest, whence ~ANT n.; (of priest) hear (penitent). Hence ~edly² adv. [f. OF *confesser* f. LL *confessare* f. L CON(*fitēri fess-*)]

confe'ssion (-shn), n. Acknowledgement of offence, fact, etc.; *auricular* ~ (of sins to priest), whence ~ary¹ (-sho) a.; thing confessed; ~ *of faith*, declaration of religious doctrine, creed, statement of one's principles in any matter; (formerly) tomb of CONFESSOR. (as prec., see -ION)]

confe'ssional (-sho-), a. & n. Of confession; (n.) stall in which priest hears confession, as *secrets of the C~*. [(adj.) prec. +AL; (n.) F, f. med. L *confessionale* (neut. adj. as n.)]

confe'ssionist (-sho-), n. Adherent of a creed, esp. of the Augsburg Confession (Lutheran). [f. F *confessioniste* -IST]

confe'ssor (-sho-), n. One who confesses; one who avows his religion in face of danger, but does not suffer martyrdom; *The C~, King Edward the C~*; priest who hears confession. [L (as CONFESS, see -OR²)]

confet'ti, n. pl. Plaster bonbons, bits of coloured paper, used as missiles in the carnival, at weddings, etc. [It. =sweet-meats]

confi'dant, n. (fem. ~e, pron. -ănt, love). Person trusted with private (usu.

affairs. [18th c.; perh. meant to repr. sound of F *confident*, -*ente* (as foll., see -ANT)]

confide', v.t. & i. Repose confidence *in*, (part.) unsuspicious; impart (secret *to*); entrust (object of care, task, *to*). [f. L CON(*fidere* trust)]

con'fidence, n. Firm trust; assured expectation; boldness; impudence; imparting of private matters (*in* one's ~, allowed to know his private affairs); thing so imparted; *told in* ~ (as a secret) || ~ *trick*, persuading victim to entrust valuables to one as sign of ~. [f. L con-*fidentia* (as prec., see -ENCE)]

con'fident, a. & n. Trusting, fully assured (*that, of,* or abs.), bold; impudent; (n.) confidant, sharer of (secret). Hence ~LY² adv. [as CONFIDE, see -ENT]

confiden'tial (-shl), a. Spoken, written, in confidence; entrusted with secrets; charged with secret service. Hence ~RY (-shiǎl²), ~NESS, nn., ~LY² adv., (-sha-). [as CONFIDENCE + -AL]

configūrā'tion, n. Mode of arrangement, conformation, outline, (Astron.) relative position of planets etc. [f. L *configuratio* (foll., -ATION)]

config'ure (-ger), v.t. Give shape to (usu. fig.). [f. L CON(*figurare* FIGURE)]

con'fine¹, n. (usu. pl.). Border-land, esp. (fig.) between two classes of ideas etc. [f. F *confins* pl. f. med. L CON(*fines* pl. adj. f. *finis* end, limit)]

confine'², v.t. & i. Keep (person, thing, oneself, *within, to,* limits); imprison; (pass.) be in childbed, be brought to bed; (rarely) ~ *with*, be adjacent to. [f. F *confiner* f. It. *confinare* (*confino* f. L as prec.)]

confine'ment (-nm-), n. Imprisonment; being confined, esp. in childbed; limitation. [F (-MENT)]

confirm', v.t. Establish more firmly (power, possession, person *in* possession); ratify (treaty); possession, title, to person); corroborate (statement, evidence); whence ~ATIVE, ~ATORY, aa., ~ativeiy² adv.; establish, encourage, (person *in* habit, opinion, etc.); administer religious rite of confirmation to, whence confirm-and'[-ND⁴] (candidate for ~ation), côn-firmEE', nn.; a~ed (inveterate) drunkard, disease. [f. OF *confermer* f. L CON(*firmare* f. *firmus* firm)]

confirmā'tion, n. Act of confirming; corroboration; rite administered to baptized persons in various Christian Churches. [OF, f. L *confirmationem* (as prec., see -ATION)]

con'fiscāte, v.t. Appropriate to the public treasury (by way of penalty); seize as by authority. So **confis'cable**, aa., ~OR², L CON-(*fiscāre* f. *fiscus* treasury), see -ATE³]

confiscā'tion, n. Act of confiscating;

(colloq.) legal robbery with sanction of ruling power. [f. L *confiscatio* (prec., -ATION)]

confit'eor, n. (eccles.). Form of prayer or confession of sins. [L, = I confess (con-*fitēri*)]

conflagrā'tion, n. Great & destructive fire (lit. & fig.). [f. L *conflagratio* (CON-*flagrare* burn up, see FLAGRANT)]

confla'tion, n. Fusing together esp. fig. of two variant readings into one. [f. L con-*flatio* f. CON(*flare* blow), see -ATION)]

con'flict¹, n. Fight, struggle, (lit. & fig.); collision; clashing (*of* opposed principles etc.); *in* ~, discrepant (often *with*). [f. L *conflictus* -*ūs* (as foll.)]

conflict'², v.i. Struggle (*with* or abs., usu. fig.); clash, be incompatible, whence **conflic'tion** n. [f. L CON(*fligere flict-* strike)]

con'fluent (-ōoent), a. & n. 1. Flowing together, uniting, (of streams, roads, etc., ~ *with*); & *smallpox* (-ōens) n.; ~ *smallpox* (when vesicles run together). 2. n. Stream flowing with another (prop. of same size). [f. L CON(*fluere flux-* flow), -ENT]

con'flux (-ks), n. Confluence. [as f. a L con-*fluxus* -*ūs* (as prec.)]

conform', v.t. & i. Form according to a pattern, make similar (*to*); adapt oneself *to*; (v.i.) comply with (*to*), be conformable (*to* or abs.). Hence ~ANCE n. [f. F *con-former* f. L CON(*formare* f. *forma* shape]

conform'able, a. Similar (*to*); consistent, adapted (*to*); tractable. Hence ~ABIL'ITY n., ~ABLY² adv. [-ABLE]

conformā'tion, n. Manner in which a thing is formed, structure; adaptation (*to*). [f. L *conformatio* (as CONFORM, see -ATION)]

|| **conform'ist**, n. One who conforms to usages of Church of England. [-IST]

conform'ity, n. Likeness (*to, with*); compliance (*with, to*). [f. F *conformité* f. L CON(*formis* f. *forma* shape), see -TY]

confound', v.t. Defeat (plan, hope); (mild oath) ~ *it, you,* (= God ~), esp. in p.p. whence o~EDLY² adv.; (Bibl.) put to shame; throw into perplexity; throw (things) into disorder; mix up; confuse (in idea). [f. OF *confondre* f. L CON-(*fundere fus-* pour) mix up]

confrater'nity, n. Brotherhood (esp. religious or charitable); body, gang. [F (-*té*), f. L CON(*fraternitatem* FRATERNITY)]

con'frère (see Ap.), n. Fellow member of profession, scientific body, etc. [F]

confront' (-frŭnt), v.t. Meet face to face, stand facing; be opposite to; face in hostility or defiance; (of difficulties etc.) oppose; bring (person) face to face with (accusers etc.); compare. Hence côn-fronta'TION n. [f. F *confronter* f. med. L CON(*frontari* f. *frons -ntis* face)]

For compounds of *co-* not given consult *co-*.

Confū'cian (-shn), a. & n. (Follower) of Confucius, the Chinese Philosopher. Hence ~ISM (-sha-) n. [f. *Confucius*, latiniz. of *K'ung Fū tsze* K'ung the master; +-AN]

confū'se (-z), v.t. Throw into disorder; mix up in the mind; abash, perplex (usu. pass.). Hence ~EDLY² adv., ~EDNESS n. (-z-). [f. L as CONFOUND]

confū'sion (-zhn), n. Act of confusing; confused state; tumult; (as imprecation) ~!, *drink* ~ *to*; ~ *worse confounded*, made worse than it was. [OF, f. L *confusionem* (as prec., see -ION)]

confū'te, v.t. Convict (person) of error by proof; prove (argument) false. So **cŏn'futā'TION** n. [f. L *con(fūtāre* perh. f. same root as *fundere* pour)]

congé (see Ap.), n. Dismissal without ceremony; (arch.) bow, esp. at parting; (F) *congé d'élire* (dăler²), royal permission to elect bishop. Hence **con'gé, ~gée**, v.t. & i. [ME *conge* f. OF *congied* f. L *commeātus* -ūs leave of absence f. L *com(meāre* go) & come; now usu. treated as mod. F]

congeal (-j-), v.t. & i. Freeze, solidify by cooling; coagulate (t. & i. of blood etc. or fig.). Hence **~MENT** n. [f. OF *congeler* f. L *con(gelāre* f. *gelu* frost)]

congelā'tion (-j-), n. Congealing; congealed state; congealed substance. [f. L *congelatio* (as prec., see -ATION)]

con'gener (-j-), n. & a. One of the same kind as (*of* another; *adj.*) akin, allied, (*to*). [(n. thr. F *congénère*) f. L *con(genus -eris* kind)]

congene'ric (-j-), a. Of same genus, kind, race; allied in nature or origin. [-IC]

conge'nerous (-j-), a. Of same genus or (loosely) family; of same kind; ~ *muscles* (concurring in same action). [-OUS]

congē'nial (-j-), a. (Of persons, characters, etc.) kindred, sympathetic, (*with, to*); suited, agreeable, (*to*). Hence **~ITY²** (-ălĭ-), n., **~LY²** adv. [CON-+GENIAL]

congē'nital (-j-), a. Belonging to (*with*) one from birth (esp. of diseases, defects, etc.). Hence **~LY²** adv. [f. L con-(*genitus* p.p. of *gigno* beget)+-AL]

cŏng'er (-nggr-), n. Large sea eel (also ~ *eel*). [f. OF *congre* f. L *conger -gri* f. Gk *goggros*]

cŏng'eries (-jĕrĭéz), n. (pl. same). Collection, mass, heap. [L (as foll.)]

congĕst' (-j-), v.t. & i. (Intr.) accumulate to excess (esp. in p.p.); affect with congestion; ~*ed district*, area of land too crowded to support its population (esp. in Ireland and Scotland) (Med.). [f. L *congerere gest-* bring]

congĕs'tive a.

conge'stion (-jschon), n. Abnormal accumulation of blood in a part of the body (fig. of population, traffic, etc.). [F, f. L *congestionem* (as prec., see -ION)+-AL]

cŏn'globāte (-n-g-), v.t. & i. & n. Form into a ball; (adj.) so formed. So ~ATION n. [f. L CON(*globāre* f. *globus*), see -ATE²,³]

conglōbe' (-n-g-), v.t. & i. = prec. [as prec.]

conglŏm'erate¹ (-n-g-), a. & n. Gathered into a round mass; (Geol.) (pudding-stone, water-worn fragments of rock) cemented into a mass (cf. AGGLOMERATE). [f. L CON-(*glomerāre* f. *glomus -eris* ball), see -ATE²]

conglŏm'erāte² (-n-g-), v.t. & i. Collect into a coherent mass (lit. & fig.). So **conglŏm'erā'TION** n. [as prec., see -ATE³]

conglu'tināte (-n-glōō-), v.t. & i. Stick together (as) with glue. So ~ATION n. [f. L *con(glūtināre* (*glūten -inis* glue), see -ATE³]

cŏng'ou (-nggoō, -ō), n. Kind of black Chinese tea. [f. Chin. *kung-fu(-ch'a* labour (tea)]

congrā'tulāte (-ng-gr-), v.t. Address (person) with expressions of sympathetic joy (*on* an event); ~ *oneself*, think oneself happy (*on*). Hence ~ANT a. & n., ~ATIVE, ~ATORY, aa., ~ATOR n., (-n-g-). [f. L *con(grātulārī* f. *grātus* pleasing), see -ATE³]

congrā'tulā'tion (-n-g-), n. Congratulating; (pl.) congratulatory expressions. [f. L *con(grātulātio* (as prec., see -ATION)]

con'gregāte (-ng-gr-), v.t. & i. Collect, gather, into a crowd (of persons) or mass (of things). [f. L *con(gregāre* f. *grex gregis* flock), see -ATE³]

congregā'tion (-ng-gr-), n. Collection into a body or mass; assemblage; || general assembly of (qualified) members of university; (Bibl.) collective body of Israelites in wilderness, also, (whole body) body assembled for religious worship; permanent committee of Roman College of Cardinals, as *the C~ de propaganda fide*. [f. F *congregation* f. L *congregationem* (as prec., see -ATION)]

congregā'tional (-ng-gr-; -sho-), a. Of a congregation; (C~) of, adhering to, Congregationalism. [(C~) of Congregationalism. [-AL]

Congregā'tionalism (-ng-gr-; -sho-), n. System of ecclesiastical polity that leaves legislative, disciplinary, and judicial functions to the individual church. So ~IST n., ~IZE v.t. [prec. +-ISM]

cŏng'ress (-ngr-), n. Coming together, meeting; formal meeting of delegates for discussion, esp. of envoys or persons engaged in special studies, as *Church C~*, annual meeting of Church of England, *Social Science C~*, etc.; (C~) national legislative body of U.S. or S. & Central Amer. republics; its session; *C~-man*, member of *C~*; (C~) Indian political party, founded 1885. [f. L *congressus -ūs* f. *con(gredi gress-*=*gradi* walk)]

congrē'ssional (-ngrĕssho-), a. Of a congress. [f. L *congressio* (as prec., see -ION) +-AL]

Cŏng'rĕve (-ngg-), a., & n. ~ (match), kind of friction match; ~ (rocket), kind formerly used in war. [Sir W. ~, inventor]

cŏng'ruence (-nggrōoĕns), -cў, n. Agreement, consistency, (of one with another, between two). [f. L congruentia (as foll., see -ENCE, -ENCY)]

cŏng'ruent (-nggrōo-), a. Suitable, accordant, (with). [f. L CON(gruere not otherwise found), see -ENT]

cŏng'ruous (-nggrōo-), a. Accordant, conformable, (with); fitting. Hence or cogn. congru'ITY (-nggrōo-) n., ~LУ² adv. [f. L congruus (as prec.) +-OUS]

cŏn'ic, a. & n. Cone-shaped; of a cone, as ~ section; (n. pl.) study of plane ~ sections. Hence ~AL a., ~ALLУ² adv., ~alNESS n. [f. Gk kōnikos (CONE, -IC)]

cŏn'ico-, in comb. With a conical tendency, as ~-cylindrical. [as prec.]

cŏn'ifer, n. Cone-bearing plant. Hence conif'EROUS a. [L (as CONE, see -FEROUS)]

cŏn'ifŏrm, a. Cone-shaped. [CONE, -FORM]

cŏn'ine, cŏn'iine, n. An alkaloid, the poisonous principle of hemlock. [f. L conium f. Gk kōneion hemlock +-INE⁵]

conjec'tural (-cher-), a. Involving, given to, conjecture. Hence ~LУ² adv. [f. L conjecturalis (as foll. see -AL)]

conjec'ture¹, n. Formation of opinion without sufficient grounds, guessing, esp. in textual criticism, of a reading not in the text; a ~, a guess, proposed reading. [F, f. L conjectura f. conjicere jec- = jacĕre throw), see -URE]

conjec'ture², v.t. & i. Guess; propose (a conjectural reading); (v.i.) make a guess. Hence ~ABLE a., ~ablУ² adv., (-kcher-). [f. F conjecturer (prec.)]

conjoin', v.t. & i. Join (t. & i.); combine. [f. F conjoindre f. L CON(jungere junct-)]

conjoint', a. United; associated. Hence ~LУ² adv. [F, p.p. as prec.]

cŏn'jugal (-ōō-), a. Of marriage, as rights; of husband and/or wife, as affection. Hence ~ITY (-ăl²) n., ~LУ² adv. [f. L conjugalis f. CON(jux jugis f. root of jungere join) consort, see -AL]

cŏn'jugate¹ (-ōō-), v.t. & i. (Gram.) inflect (verb) in voice, mood, tense, number, person; (v.i.) unite sexually; (Biol.) become fused. [f. L CON(jugare f. jugum yoke) yoke together, see -ATE³]

cŏn'jugate² (-ōō-), a., & n. Joined together, esp. coupled; (Gram.) derived from same root; (Math.) joined in a reciprocal relation; (Biol.) fused; (n.) word or thing. [as prec., see -ATE²]

conjuga'tion (-ōō-), n. Joining together; (Gram.) schema of verbal inflexion; (Biol.) fusion of two (apparently) similar cells for reproduction. Hence ~AL (-ōō-sho-) a. [f. L conjugatio (as prec., see -ATION)]

conjunct', a. & n. Joined together; combined; associated, joint; (n.) ~ person or thing. Hence ~LУ² adv. [f. L as CONJOIN]

conjunc'tion, n. 1. Union, connexion; in ~, together (with). 2. (Astrol., Astron.) apparent proximity of two heavenly bodies. 3. Combination of events or circumstances; number of associated persons or things. 4. (Gram.) uninflected word used to connect clauses or sentences, or to co-ordinate words in same clause. Hence ~AL a., ~LУ² adv., (-sho-). [OF, f. L conjunctionem (as prec., see -ION)]

conjuncti'va, n. Mucous membrane connecting inner eyelid & eye-ball. Hence conjunctivi'TIS (-ītis) n. [mod. L (for membrana~) as foll.]

conjunc'tive, a. & n. 1. Serving to join, as ~ tissue. 2. (Gram.) of the nature of a conjunction; uniting sense as well as construction, cf. DISJUNCTIVE; ~ mood of another verb, cf. SUBJUNCTIVE. 3. n. ~ word or mood. Hence ~LУ² (-IVE) adv. [f. L conjunctivus (as CONJOIN, see -IVE)]

conjunc'ture, n. Combination of events, posture of affairs. [f. F conjoncture f. L as CONJOIN, see -URE]

cŏnjura'tion (-ōō-), n. Solemn appeal; incantation. [OF, f. L conjurationem (foll., -ATION)]

conjure, v.t. & i. 1. (konjoor'). Appeal solemnly to (person to do). 2. (kŭn'jer). Constrain (spirit) to appear by invocation (also ~ up, down, out of person); effect, bring out, convey away, by juggling; juggle, produce magical effects by natural means, perform marvels (a name to ~ with, of vast influence; ~ up, cause to appear to the fancy. [f. OF conjurer f. L CON(jurare swear) band together by oath]

con'jurer, -or, (kŭn'jerer), n. One who practises legerdemain, juggler; unusually clever person, as he is no ~. [(-er) f. prec. +-ER¹; (-or) f. OF conjurer f. L conjuratorem (as prec., see -OR²)]

cŏnk¹, n. (sl.). Nose. Hence ~У² a. & n, big-nosed (person). [perh. =CONCH]

cŏnk², v.i. (colloq.). Break down, give out (usu. of mechanism etc.). [?]

cŏnk'ers (-z), n. pl. Boys' game played with horse-chestnuts (orig. with small-shells) through which a string is threaded, the object being to break that held by opponent. [dial. conker snail-shell]

cŏnn'āte, a. Born with a person, innate; (of two or more qualities etc.) born together, coeval in origin; (Bot., Zool.) congenitally united (of leaves united at base etc.). [f. L CON(nascī nāt- be born)]

cŏnna'tural (-cher-), a. Innate, belonging naturally, (to); of like nature. Hence ~LУ² adv. [f. med. L CON(naturalis NATURAL)]

connect', v.t. & i. Join (two things, one with, to, another); make coherent (argu-

For compounds of co- not given consult co-.

ments etc.); (pass.) have practical rela- tions *with*; associate mentally; unite *with* others in relationship etc. (usu. pass., or refl.); (v.i.) join on (*with*). Hence ~ER²(2), -OR² n., ~IBLE a. [f. L CONnectere *nec- bind*]

connec'ted, a. In vbl senses, esp.: joined in sequence, coherent, whence ~LY² adv., ~NESS n.; related, as *well* ~ (with persons of good position). [-ED¹]

connec'tive, a. Serving, tending, to con- nect; ~ *tissue* of the body, fibrous tissue connecting & supporting the organs. [-IVE]

connec'xion (-kshon), **connec'tion**, n. Act of connecting; state of being connected (*cut the* ~ separate things, have no more to do with something); relation of thought, as *in this* ~; connecting part, as *hot water* ~s; personal intercourse; sexual relation, as *criminal* ~; (abbr. *conn.*); family relationship; relative; religious body, whence ~AL (-sho-) a.; body of customers etc., as *business with a good* ~; *in* ~ *with*, connected with, esp. of trains, boats, etc., taking on passengers from others. [f. L *connexio* (as CONNECT, see -ION)]

conning tower. See CON².

***connip'tion**, n. (sl.). (Usu. ~ *fit*) fit of rage or hysteria. [etym. dub.]

conni'vance, n. Conniving (*at, in*); tacit permission, as *done with his* ~; (earlier *-ence*, f. L *conniventia* (as foll., see -ENCE, -ANCE)]

connive', v.i. Wink *at* (what one ought to oppose), at a sign, *nudere* wink.] Hence ~ANCE, etc. [f. L CON(*nivere*, cf. *nicere* make a sign, *nudere* wink)]

connive'nt, a. (nat. hist.). Gradually con- vergent. [as CONNIVE, see -ENT]

connoisseur (kŏnosẽr'), n. Critical judge (of, in, matters of taste). Hence ~SHIP n. [F, f. L *cognoscere* f. L COGnoscere become acquainted with]

connote', v.t. (Of words) imply in ad- dition to the primary meaning; (of facts etc.) imply as a consequence or condition (Logic) imply the attributes while de- noting the subject; (loosely) mean. Hence or cogn. CONNOTA'TION n., ~ATIVE a., ~ATIVELY² adv. [f. L CON(*notare* f. *nota* mark) mark together]

connu'bial, a. Of marriage; of husband and/or wife. Hence ~ITY (-āl²) n., ~LY² adv. [f. L *connubialis* f. CON(*nubium* f. *nubere* marry) see -AL]

cō'noid, a. & n. Cone-shaped; (n.) solid generated by revolution of a conic section about its axis, also, any more or less cone- shaped body. Hence **conoi'd**AL a. [f. Gk *kōnoeidēs* (as CONE, see -OID)]

cônq'uer (-nker), v.t. & i. Overcome by force; get the better of (habit, passion, etc.); *stoop to* ~, use indirect means for gaining one's end; acquire, subjugate, (land). Hence ~ABLE a. [f. OF *conquerre* f. L CON(*quaerere* seek, get)]

cônq'ueror (-nker), n. One who con- quers; *the* C~, William I; (colloq., *play the* ~ (decisive game); ∥ horse-chestnut that has broken others in boys' game of CONKERS. [f. OF *conqueror* f. L †con- *quaerentorem* (*conquerere* for -*ĕre*, see prec.)]

cônq'uest, n. Subjugation (of country etc.); *the* (*Norman*) C~, acquisition of English crown by William of Normandy, 1066; conquered territory; person whose affections have been won; *make a* ~ (*of*), win (person's) affections. [f. OF (1) *con- quest* being acquired by ~; (2) *conquest* action of ~, f. L *conquerre*, fem. p.p. of *conquirere* (-*quaerere*) CONQUER]

consang'uine (-nggwin), a. Of the same blood, akin. [f. L CON(*sanguineus* f. *sanguis -inis* blood) +-OUS]

consanguin'eous (-nggw-), a. Of the same blood, akin. [f. L CON(*sanguineus* f. *sanguis -inis* blood) +-OUS]

consanguin'ity (-nggw-), n. Blood- relationship (also fig.). [f. F *consanguinité* f. L *consanguinitatem* (as prec., see -TY)]

con'science (-shens), n. Moral sense of right & wrong; *good* or *clear*, *bad* or *guilty*, ~, consciousness that one's actions are right, wrong; *have on one's* ~, feel guilty about; *in all* ~, *upon one's* ~, (forms of asseveration); *have the* ~ *to*, have the im- pudence to; *for* ~ (or ~) *sake*, to satisfy one's ~; ~ *clause* in act, one ensuring re- spect for the ~s of those affected; ~ *money* (sent to relieve the ~, esp. in pay- ment of evaded income-tax). Hence ~LESS a. [f. L *conscientia* f. CON(*scire* know) be privy to, see -ENCE]

consciĕn'tious (-shi-: -shĕs), a. Obedient to conscience, scrupulous, (of persons or conduct); ~ *objector*, person who avails himself of CONSCIENCE clause, man (often abbr. *c.o.*) who pleads conscience & objects to military service. Hence ~LY² adv., ~NESS n. [f. F *consciencieux* (as prec., see -OUS)]

con'scious (-shus), a. Aware, knowing, (of fact, of external circumstances, that, or abs.) with mental faculties awake; (of actions, emotions, etc.) realized by the actor etc. (*with* ~ *superiority*); *a hardly* ~ *movement*); ~ SELF-CONSCIOUS. Hence ~LY² adv. [f. L *conscius* f. CON(*scire* know)]

con'sciousness (-shus-), n. State of being conscious; totality of a person's thoughts & feelings, or of a class of these, as *moral* ~; perception (*of, that*). [-NESS]

conscribe', (now rare), **conscript¹**, v.t. Enlist by conscription. [f. L CON(*scribere script-* write) enrol]

con'script¹, a. & n. (Recruit) enrolled by conscription; ~ *fathers* (collective title of Roman senators). [as prec.]

conscrip'tion, n. Compulsory enlistment for military or naval or air force service (esp. enrolment by lot); ~ *of wealth*,

taxation or confiscation of property for war purposes to impose equality of sacrifice on non-conscripts. [f. L conscriptio (as prec., see -ION)]

con'secrate¹, a. Consecrated. [f. L CON-secrare=sacrare f. sacer -cri sacred), see -ATE¹]

con'secrate², v.t. Set apart as sacred (to); devote to (purpose); sanctify. So ~OR² n., ~ORY a. [prec., -ATE³]

consecra'tion, n. Act of consecrating, dedication, esp. of church, churchyard, etc., by bishop; ordination to sacred office, esp. of bishop; devotion to (a purpose). [f. L consecratio (as prec., see -ATION)]

consec'tary, n. Deduction, corollary. [f. L consectarium (neut. adj. as n.) f. consectari frequent. as foll.]

consecu'tion, n. Logical sequence; sequence of events; (Gram.) sequence of words, tenses, etc. [f. L consecutio f. con-(sequi secut- pursue) overtake, see -ION]

consec'utive, a. Following continuously; (Gram.) expressing consequence, as ~ clause; (Mus.) ~ intervals (of the same kind, occurring adjacently between the same two parts, esp. fifths or octaves). Hence ~LY² (-vl-) adv., ~NESS (-vn-) n. [f. F consécutif, -ive (as prec., see -IVE)]

conse'nescence, n. General decay by age. [f. L CON(senescere grow old f. senex).-ENCE]

consen'sual (-su-, -shoo-), a. (physiol.). Caused by sympathetic action. [f. foll. +-AL]

consen'sus, n. Agreement (of opinion, testimony, etc.); (Physiol.) agreement of different organs in effecting purpose. [L as foll.)]

consent'¹, v.i. Acquiesce, agree, (to a thing, to do, that, or abs.). [f. OF consentir f. L CON(sentire sens- feel) agree]

consent'², n. Voluntary agreement, compliance; permission; age of ~ (at which ~, esp. of girl to seduction, is valid in law); (prov.) silence gives ~; with one ~, unanimously. [f. OF consente (as prec.)]

consentan'eous, a. Accordant, suited, (to, with); unanimous, concurrent. Hence consentan'erry, ~NESS, nn., ~LY² adv. [f. L consentaneus (as CONSENT²) +-OUS]

consen'tient (-shnt), a. Agreeing; concurrent; consenting (to). [f. L as CON-SENT¹, see -ENT]

con'sequence, n. Result of something preceding; take the ~s, accept whatever results from one's choice or act); logical inference; in ~, as a result (of); importance; of (no), (un)important; social distinction, rank, as persons of ~. [f. F consequence f. L consequentia (as foll., -ENCE)]

con'sequent¹, n. Event that follows another; second part of conditional proposition, dependent on the antecedent; (Math.) second of two numbers in a ratio, second & fourth of four proportionals. [as foll.]

con'sequent², a. Following as a result (on); following logically; logically consistent. [f. F consequent f. L CON(sequi follow), see -ENT]

consequen'tial (-shl), a. Following as a result or inference; following or resulting indirectly, as ~ damages; self-important. Hence ~ITY (-shial-), n., ~LY²(-shial-) adv. [f. L as CONSEQUENCE +-AL]

con'sequently, adv. & conj. As a result; therefore. [-LY²]

‖ **conser'vancy**, n. Commission, court, controlling a port, river, etc., as Thames C~; official preservation (of forests etc.). [f. L as CONSERVE², see -ANCY]

conserva'tion, n. Preservation; ~ of energy, principle that total quantity of energy of any system of bodies (including the universe) is invariable. [f. L conser-vatio (as prec., -ATION)]

conser'vative (a. & n.) 1. Preservative (a. & n.); (C~ party, English political party) disposed to maintain existing institutions; (improp., of estimate) moderate, cautious, purposely low. 2. n. One so disposed, (C~) member of the C~ party. So con-ser'vatism n. [F (-if, -ive), f. med. L conservativus (as foll., see -IVE)]

conservatoire' (-twahr), n. Public school of music & declamation (on Continent). [F., f. L conservatorium (as foll., see -ORY)]

con'servator, n. Preserver; official custodian (of museum etc.); ‖~s of the peace, the King, Lord Chancellor, etc.; ~s of a river (see CONSERVANCY). [f. F conservateur f. L conservatorem (as foll., see -OR²)]

conser'vatory, n. Greenhouse for tender plants; =CONSERVATOIRE. [f. L conserva-torius a. (as foll., see -ORY)]

conser'vatory¹, n. (usu. pl.). Confection, preserve. [F., f. med. L conserva (as foll.)]

conserve², v.t. Keep from harm, decay, or loss. [f. F conserver f. L CON(servare keep)]

consid'er, v.t. & i. Contemplate mentally; weigh the merits of (course, claim, etc.); reflect (that, whether, etc., or abs.), reckon with, make allowance for; be of opinion (that); regard as, as ~ him (to be) a knave, ~ yourself under arrest; (arch.) ~ think over. [f. F considérer f. L CON(siderare perh. f. sidus -eris star) examine]

consid'erable, a. Worth considering; (of persons) notable, important; (of immaterial things) much, no small, (trouble, annoyance, pleasure), whence ~LY² adv. [f. med. L considerabilis (as prec., see -ABLE)]

consid'erate, a. Thoughtful for others; (arch.) careful. Hence ~LY² (-tl-) adv., ~NESS (-tn-) n. [as prec., -ATE²]

For compounds of co- not given consult co-.

considerā'tion, n. Act of considering; meditation; take into ~, consider; under ~, being considered; in ~ of, in return for, on account of; fact, thing, regarded as a reason, as that is a ~, on no ~; compensation, reward, as for a ~; (Law) thing given, done, as is equivalent by person to whom a promise is made; thoughtfulness for others; importance (now rare). [F, f. L consideratio f. L consideration f. (as prec., see -ATION)]

consid′ering, prep. In view of, as it is excusable ~ his age, how young he is, (that) he has no experience; (ellipt.) that is not so bad, ~ (the circumstances). [-ING²]

consign′ (-īn), v.t. Hand over, deliver, to (misery, watery grave, person, person's care); transmit, send by rail etc., to (person), whence consignēe′, consignor², (-īn-), nn.; deposit (money in bank). Hence ~ABLE (-īn-) a. [f. L consignare mark with a seal (signum)]

consignā′tion, n. Formal payment of money to person legally appointed; act of consigning goods; to the ~ of, addressed to. [f. L consignatio (as prec., see -ATION)]

consign′ment (-īn-), n. Consigning; goods consigned. [-MENT]

consis′tent, a. (Of inductions from different phenomena) accordant. Hence ~ENCE n. [f. L ⁺CONSISTire=satire jump).

consist′, v.i. Be composed of (esp. material things); be comprised in, as virtue~s in being uncomfortable; harmonize with; (Bibl., Col. i. 17) exist. [f. L CON(sistere stop) exist]

consis′tence, -CY, n. Degree of density, as of thick liquids; firmness, solidity, (lit. & fig.); (-cy) state of being consistent, esp. of persons. [as prec., see -ENCE, -ENCY]

consis′tent, a. Compatible, not contradictory, (with); (of person) constant to same principles. Hence ~LY² adv. [as prec., -ENT]

con′sistory (also konsis'-), n. Senate composed of Pope & Cardinals; (also C~ Court) bishop's court for ecclesiastical causes & offences; Lutheran clerical board; court of presbyters. So consistō′rial a. [f. F consistoire f. L consistōrium (as CONSIST, see -ORY]

consō′ciate¹ (-shi-), a. & n. Associated(d). [f. L CON(sociare f. socius fellow), see -ATE³]

consō′ciate² (-shi-), v.t. & i. Associate. So consō′ciate² (-shi-) v.t. & i. Associate. So consōciā′tion, n. [as prec., see -ATE³]

consolā′tion, n. Act of consoling; consoling circumstance; ~ race, prize, stakes (open to competitors unsuccessful in former events). [F, f. L consolationem (as foll., see -ATION)]

consōl′atory, a. Tending, meant, to console. Hence ~iy² adv. [f.L consolatorius (as foll., see -ORY)]

consōle¹, v.t. Comfort. Hence ~ABLE a. [f. F consoler f. L consolare,

consōle², n. (Archit.) kind of bracket or corbel; frame containing keyboards, stops, etc., of organ; ~table, -mirror, (supported by bracket against wall). [F, etym. dub.]

consōl′idate, v.t. & i. Solidify (t. & i.); strengthen (usu. fig., power etc.); combine (territories, estates, companies, debts) into one whole; ||~ed annuities, consols, Government securities of Great Britain, ~ed in 1751 into a single stock at 3% (now 2½), C~ed Fund, united product of various taxes etc., whence interest of national debt etc. is paid. Hence consōlidā′tion (~ON², nn., ~ORY a. [f. L CON(solidare f. solidus), see -ATE³]

||consōls′ (-z), n. pl. See prec. [abbr.]

consommé (see Ap.). n. Strong meat soup. [F]

con′sonance, n. Recurrence of same or similar sounds in words, assonance; sounding of two notes in harmony; (Mus.) consonant interval, concord; (fig.) agreement, harmony. [F, f. L consonantia (as foll., see -ANCE]

con′sonant¹, a. Agreeable to, consistent with; harmonious; agreeing in sound; (Mus.) making concord. Hence ~LY² adv. [F, f. L CON(sonare sound f. sonus), see -ANT]

con′sonant², n. Alphabetical element other than vowel; sound that in forming a syllable is combined with vowel. Hence consonan′tal a. [F, f. L consonantem (litteram letter) sounding with another (as prec.)]

con′sort¹, n. 1. Husband or wife; queen ~, king's wife; king, prince, ~, queen's husband. 2. Ship sailing with another. [F, f. L CON(sors -rtis lot) sharer, comrade]

consort², v.t. & i. Class or bring together, keep company, (with); agree, harmonize, (with). [f. prec., and f. vb sort]

consōr′tium (-shĭum), n. Temporary co-operation of several powers or large interests to effect some common purpose. [L., = partnership (consors sharing; sharer)]

conspecī′fic, a. Of the same species. [con-]

conspec′tus, n. General view of subject, scene, etc.; tabulation of details, synopsis. [L, vbl n. f. CON(spicere look at)]

conspic′uous, a. Clearly visible, striking to the eye; attracting notice, remarkable, as ~ by its absence, for his loyalty. Hence conspicū′ity, ~NESS, nn., ~LY² adv. [f. L conspicuus (as prec.) +-OUS]

conspī′racy, n. Act of conspiring (in good or bad sense); combination for unlawful purpose; plot. [f. L conspiratio (as foll., see -ATION), with -ACY(3) substituted]

conspī′rator, n. One engaged in a conspiracy. Hence ~RESS¹ n. [f. F conspirateur f. L conspiratorem (as foll., see -OR²]

conspīre′, v.i. & t. Combine privily for unlawful purpose, esp. treason, murder,

sedition; combine, concur, (*to do*); plot, devise, as ~ *his ruin*, ~ *an attack*. [f. F *conspirer* f. L CON(*spirare* breathe) agree, plot]

conspue', v.t. (rare). Express detestation, clamour for the abandonment or abolition, of (person, policy, etc.). [f. F *conspuer* f. L CON(*spuere* spit) spit upon]

co'nstable (kŭn-), n. (Also *police* ~) policeman; ‖*Chief C*~, head of police force of county etc.; *special* ~, person sworn in to act as ~ on special occasion; *outrun the* ~, run into debt; *C~ of France*, principal officer of household of early French kings, commander-in-chief in King's absence; *C~ of England, Lord High C*~, similar officer in English Royal household (now temporary officer on special occasions). [f. OF *conestable* f. LL *comes stabuli* count of the stable]

consta'bulary, a. & n. (Organized body) of constables. [f. med. L *constabularius* (n. *-aria*) f. *constabulus* CONSTABLE, see -ARY1]

co'nstancy, n. Firmness, endurance; faithfulness; unchangingness. [f. L *constantia* (as foll., see -ANCY1]

co'nstant, a. & n. **1.** Unmoved, resolute; faithful(*to*); unchanging; unremittent, as ~ *attention, chatter*. **2.** n. (Math.) quantity that does not vary; (Phys.) number expressing a relation, property, etc., that remains the same for same substance in same conditions, as ~ *of friction*. [F., f. L CON(*stare* stand), see -ANT]

Consta'ntia (-shǎ), n. Wine from the ~ farm near Cape Town.

co'nstantly, adv. Always, often. [-LY2]

co'nstellate, v.t. & i. Form into a constellation. [f. L†CON(*stellare* f. *stella* star), see -ATE3]

constella'tion, n. Number of fixed stars grouped within an imaginary outline (also fig.). [f. L *constellatio* (as prec., see -ATION]

co'nsternate, v.t. Dismay (usu. pass.). [f. L CON(*sternare, -sternere*, throw down), see -ATE3]

consterna'tion, n. Dismay. [f. L *con-sternatio* (as prec., see -ATION]

co'nstipate, v.t. Confine (bowels); render costive. [f. L CON(*stipare* press), see -ATE3]

constipa'tion, n. Costiveness. [f. L *con-stipatio* (as prec., see -ATION]

consti'tuency, n. Body of voters who elect a representative member; place, body of residents in place, so represented; body of customers, subscribers, etc. [f. foll. see -ENCY]

consti'tuent, a. & n. **1.** Composing, making up, a whole; appointing, electing; able to frame or alter a (political) constitution, as ~ *assembly, power*. **2.** n. One who appoints another his agent; component part; member of a constituency. [as foll. see -ENT]

co'nstitute, v.t. Appoint, as ~ *him president*, ~ *oneself a judge*; establish, found; give legal form to (assembly etc.); frame, form, (esp. pass. of bodily or mental constitution); make up, be the components of. [f. L CON(*statuere -ut- = statuere* set up]

constitu'tion, n. Act, mode, of constituting; character of the body as regards health, strength, etc.; mental character; mode in which State is organized; body of fundamental principles according to which a State is governed; *written* ~ document embodying these; (Hist.) decree, ordinance, as *C~s of Clarendon* (1164). [F., f. L *constitutionem* (as prec., see -ION]

constitu'tional (-sho-), a. & n. **1.** Of inherent in, affecting, the bodily or mental constitution; essential; of, in harmony with, authorized by, the political constitution, as ~ *sovereign, government* (limited by ~ *forms*), whence ~my (-shonal2) n.; adhering to the political constitution. **2.** n. ~ walk, for health's sake. Hence ~LY2 adv. [-AL]

constitu'tionalism (-sho-), n. Constitutional government; adherence to constitutional principles. [-ISM]

constitu'tionalist (-sho-), n. Writer on the political constitution; adherent of constitutional principles. [-IST]

constitu'tionalize (-sho-), v.t. & i. Make constitutional; (intr.) take a constitutional. [-IZE]

co'nstitutive, a. Constructive, formative; essential; component. Hence ~LY2(-vl-) adv. [f. CONSTITUTE †-IVE]

constrain', v.t. Compel (person to do, *to course or state*, or abs.); bring about by compulsion; confine forcibly, imprison (lit. & fig.); (p.p.) forced, embarrassed, as ~*ed voice, manner*, whence ~edLY2 adv. [f. OF *constreindre* f. L CON(*stringere strict-* tie)]

constraint', n. Compulsion (*under* ~); confinement; restraint of natural feelings, constrained manner. [f. OF *constreinde*, fem. p.p. as n., see prec.]

constrict', v.t. Contract, compress; cause (organic tissue) to contract. So **constric'tion** n., **constric'tive** a. [f. L as CONSTRAIN]

constric'tor, n. Muscle that draws together or narrows a part; compressor (surgical instrument); BOA ~. [LL(as prec., see -OR2]

constringe' (-j), v.t. Compress; cause ~ **GENCY** n., (-j-), [as prec.]

construct', v.t. Fit together, frame, build, (also fig.); (Gram.) combine (words) syntactically; draw, delineate, as *a*

For compounds of *co-* not given consult *co-*.

triangle. [f. L CONstruere struct- pile, build)]

construc'tion, n. Act, mode, of con-structing; thing constructed; syntactical connexion between words; construing, explanation, (of words); interpretation (of conduct etc.), as *put a good, bad, ~ upon his refusal*; ~ *train* (conveying materials for the ~ or upkeep of a rail-way). Hence ~ISM (-sho-) n., artistic expression by means of mechanical struc-tures (chiefly Theatr.). [f. L *constructio* (as prec., see -ION)]

construc'tional (-sho-), a. Of construc-tion ; structural, belonging to the original structure. [-AL]

construc'tive, a. Of construct-ing, tend-ing to construct, esp. opposed to *destruc-tive* as *positive* to *negative*, as ~ *criticism*; belonging to the structure of a building; inferred, not directly expressed, virtual, as a ~ *denial, permission, blasphemy, treason*. Hence ~LY² (-vl-) adv. [f. med. L *constructivus* (as CONSTRUCT, see -IVE)]

construc'tor, n. One who constructs, esp. supervisor of naval construction. Hence ~SHIP n. [-OR²]

con'strue (-ōō, *also* konstrŏō'), v.t. & i. & n. **1.** Combine (words *with* others) gram-matically, as '*rely' is ~d with 'on'*; analyse (sentence), translate word for word; ad-mit of grammatical analysis, as *this passage does not* ~; expound, interpret, (words, actions). **2.** n. (kŏn-). Passage to be translated word for word. [as CON-STRUCT]

cŏnsubstăn'tial (-shl), a. Of the same substance, esp. of the three Persons in the Godhead. Hence ~ITY (-shiăl-) n. [f. L CONsubstantialis as SUBSTANCE, see -AL)]

cŏnsubstăn'tiate (-shi-), v.t. & i. Unite in one substance. [f. med. L CONsub-stantiare as prec., -ATE³]

cŏnsubstăntiă'tion (-shi-), n. (Doctrine of) real substantial presence of body & blood of Christ together with bread & wine in Eucharist (cf. TRANSUBSTANTIA-TION). [f. 16th-c. L *consubstantiatio* (as prec., see -ATION)]

con'suetude (-sw-), n. Custom, esp. as having legal force; social intercourse. [OF., f. L *consuetudo -inis* (cf. CUSTOM) f. consuescere accustomed p.p. of *consuescere,* see -TUDE]

cŏnsuetu'dinary (-sw-), a. & n. Custo-mary, as ~ *law*; (n.) manual of customs, esp. of monastic house, cathedral, etc. [f. L *consuetudinarius* (as prec., see -ARY)]

cŏn'sul, n. Title of two annual magistrates exercising supreme authority in Roman republic; title of three chief magistrates of French Republic 1799–1804 (*First C~,* Napoleon); State agent residing in foreign town and protecting subjects there; local representative of Cyclists' Touring Club. Hence ~SHIP n. [L (CON-

cŏn'sular, a. Of a consul; (Roman) of ~ rank. [f. L *consularis* (as prec., see -AR¹)]

cŏn'sulate, n. Office, establishment, of a (modern) consul; (period of) consular government in France; office of (Roman) consul. [f. L *consulatus* (as prec., see -ATE¹)]

cŏnsult', v.t. & i. Take counsel (*with* person or about, or abs.); seek information or advice from (person, book); ~ *one's pillow,* take a night for reflection; take into consideration (feelings, interests); ~*ing physician,* (who is called in by colleagues or applied to by patients for advice in special cases). Hence con-sul'TABLE, consul'TATIVE, aa., cŏnsulter' n. [f. L *consultare* frequent. of *consulere*]

cŏnsul'tant, n. One who consults; con-sulting physician. [as prec., see -ANT]

cŏnsultă'tion, n. Act of consulting; de-liberation; conference. [f. L *consultatio* (as prec., see -ATION)]

cŏnsum'e, v.t. & i. Make away with; use up; eat, drink, up; spend, waste, (time, trouble, etc.); (p.p.) eaten up (*with envy*); (v.i.) waste away. Hence ~'ABLE a. & n. (usu. pl.), (article) intended for consump-tion (~*able ledger,* register of receipt and issue of such items). [f. L CONsumere sumpt- take up)]

cŏnsum'edly, adv. Excessively. [prec.,

cŏnsum'er, n. In vbl senses, esp. (Pol. Econ.) user of an article, opp. to *producer;* ~(*s') goods,* things which directly satisfy human wants and desires, e.g. food and clothing. [-ER¹]

cŏnsum'ate², a. Complete, perfect, as ~ *general, skill, ass.* Hence ~LY² (-ti-) adv. [f. L CONsummare complete f. summus utmost]

cŏn'summate², v.t. Accomplish, com-plete, esp. marriage (by sexual inter-course). Hence ~IVE a., ~OR² n. [as prec., see -ATE³]

cŏnsummă'tion, n. Completion (esp. of marriage, see prec.); desired end, goal; perfection; perfected thing. [f. OF con-sommation & L consummationem (as prec., see -ATION)]

cŏnsŭmp'tion, n. Using up; destruc-tion; waste; amount consumed; wasting disease, esp. *pulmonary* ~, phthisis. [f. L *consumptio* (as CONSUME, see -ION)]

cŏnsŭmp'tive, a. & n. Tending to con-sume; tending to, affected with, con-sumption, whence ~LY² (-vl-) adv., ~NESS (-vn-) n.; (n.) ~ patient. [as CONSUME, see -IVE]

cŏntăbĕs'cence, n.(bot.). Suppression of pollen formation in anthers of flowers. So ~ENT a. [f. L CON(tabescere waste away f. tabes consumption), see -ENCE]

cŏn'tact, n. & v.t. **I.** State, condition, of touching, as *be in ~ with*; (fig.) come into

contadino, n. (fem. -na; pl. -ni pr. -nē, fem. -ne pr. -nā). Italian peasant. [It.]

conta′gion (-jn), n. Communication of disease from body to body; contagious disease; moral corruption; contagious influence (fig.). [F, f. L CON(tagionem f. tangere touch, -ION)]

conta′gionist, n. One who thinks a disease (plague, cholera, etc.) contagious. [-IST]

conta′gious (-jus), a. Communicating disease by contact (lit. & fig.); (of diseases) so communicable (fig.) catching, infectious. Hence ~LY² adv., ~NESS n., (-jus~). [f. OF contagieus f. LL contagiosus (as CONTAGION, see -OUS)]

contain′, v.t. Have, hold, as contents; comprise, include; (of a measure) be equal to, as a pound ~s 16 ounces; (pass.) be included (within a space, between limits; (Geom.) enclose, form boundary of; (of numbers) be divisible by (number) without remainder; restrain, as could not ~ himself for joy, ~ your anger; (Mil.) keep (enemy force) from moving, esp. with a view to operations elsewhere. Hence ~ABLE a., ~ER¹ n., (esp.) vessel, box, etc., designed for ~ some particular article(s). [f. OF contenir f. L CON(tinēre tend-=tenēre hold)]

contam′inate, v.t. Pollute, infect. So **contāmina′TION** n. (also, in literary criticism, the blending of two plays, tales, etc., into one). [f. L contaminare f. CON(tamen f. tag- root of tangere touch), see -ATE³]

|| **contang′o** (ŏ-nggˠ), n.(pl.-os). Percentage paid by buyer of stock for postponement of transfer (cf. BACKWARDATION); ~ (also continuation)-day, second day before settling-day. [perh. = Sp. contengo I check, stop, f. contener f. L as CONTAIN]

conte (kawnt), n. Short story (as a form of literary composition). [F]

contemn′ (-m), v.t. (literary). Despise, treat with disregard. Hence~ER¹(-mn-) n. [f. OF contemner f. L CON(temnere tempt-)]

con′templāte, v.t. & i. Gaze upon; view mentally; expect; intend, purpose; (v.i.) meditate. So ~A′TION n. (in ~ation, intended), ~ātor² n. [f. L CON(templari f. templum TEMPLE, open space for observation), see -ATE³]

con′templative (also kontĕm′pla-), a. Meditative, thoughtful; (of life in middle ages) given up to religious contemplation, opp. to active. Hence ~LY² (-vĭ-) adv., ~NESS (-vn-) n. [OF (-tĭf,-ĭve), f. L contemplātivus (prec., -IVE)]

contemporān′eous, a. Existing, occurring, at the same time (with); covering the same period; of the same period. Hence **contĕmporān′ITY**, ~NESS, nn., ~LY² adv. [f. L CON(temporaneus f. tempus -oris time, see -ANEOUS)]

contem′porary, a. & n. (Person) belonging to the same time; (person) equal in age; (newspaper) published during same period. [CON-+TEMPORARY]; in 18th c. contĕmporary was preferred

contem′porize, v.t. Make contemporary, cause to agree in time. [f. st. of prec.+-IZE]

contempt′, n. Act, mental attitude, of despising; condition of being despised; have, hold, in ~, bring, fall, into ~; (Law) disobedience to sovereign's lawful commands or to authority of Houses of Parliament or other legislative body, esp. ~ of court, disobedience to, interference with administration of justice by, courts of law. [f. L condemptus -ūs (as CONTEMN)]

contempt′ible, a. Deserving contempt, despicable; Old C~s, Sir J. French's army of 1914 (w. ref. to Kaiser's alleged 'French's ~ little army'). Hence **contempt′ibly²** adv. [f. L condemptibilis (as CONTEMN, see -BLE)]

contempt′uous (of), a. Showing contempt (of); scornful; insolent. Hence~LY² adv., ~NESS n. [as CONTEMPT +-OUS]

contend′, v.i. & t. Strive, fight, (with person for thing); struggle with (feelings, natural forces); compete, be in rivalry, as ~ing passions; argue (with); (v.t.) maintain (that). [f. L CON(tendere tend-stretch, strive)]

con′tent¹ (formerly, & still occas., kon-tĕnt′), n. 1. (pl.) ~s of, what is contained in (vessel etc., book, document); (table of) ~s, summary of subject-matter of book. 2. Capacity (of vessel), volume (of solid). 3. (sing. only). Constituent elements of a conception; substance (of cognition, art, etc.), opp. form; amount (of some particular constituent) contained (the ester~ of an oil), or yielded (the sugar ~ per acre of beet). [f. L as CONTAIN]

content², n. Contented state, satisfaction, esp. to one's heart's ~. [f. CONTENT v. or a.]

content³, a. & n. Satisfied; willing (to do); well ~, well pleased; || (House of Lords) ~, not ~, (= ay, no, in House of Commons); || (n. pl.) those who vote '~'. [F (as CONTENT⁴) orig.=bounded (in desires by what one has)]

content⁴, v.t. Satisfy; ~ oneself, be satisfied (with thing, with doing). Hence

For compounds of co- not given consult co-.

~édly² adv., ~édness, ~ment, nn. [f. F *contender* (as prec.)]

contén'tion, n. Strife, dispute, contro-versy; emulation; point contended for in argument. [F., f. L *contentionem* (as CON-TEND, see -ION)]

contén'tious (-shus), a. Quarrelsome; involving contention. Hence ~ly² adv., ~ness n. (-shus-). [f. F *contentieux* (-ENT)]

contérm'inal, a. Having a common boundary. [f. med. L *conterminalis* (as prec., see -AL)]

contérm'inous, a. Having a common boundary (*with, to*); (of two things) meeting at their ends; coextensive (in space, time, meaning). Hence ~ly² adv. [f. L *conterminus* boundary + -ous]

cón'test², n. Debate, controversy; strife; (friendly) competition. [f. foll.]

contést', v.t. & i. Debate, dispute (point, statement, etc.); strive *for*; strive in argu-ment (*with, against*); strive for (seat in Parlia-ment etc.). Hence **contés'table** a. [f. F *contester* call to witness, argue, gainsay, f. L *contestari* (*litem*) bring an action (*testis* witness)]

contestā'tion, n. Disputation; assertion contended for; *in ~,* in dispute. [f. L *contestatio* (as CONTEST², see -ATION)]

cón'text, n. Parts that precede or follow a passage & fix its meaning; *in this ~* (connexion). So **contex'tual** a., **con-tex'tually²** adv. [f. L *contextus -ûs* f. CON-(*texere* weave)]

contex'ture, n. Act, mode, of weaving together; structure; fabric; mode of literary composition. [F (as prec., see -URE)]

contigü'ity, n. Contact; proximity; (Psych.) proximity of ideas or impres-sions in place or time, as principle of association. [f. L *contiguus* (as foll., see -TY)]

contig'uous, a. Touching, adjoining, (*to*); next in order (*to*); neighbouring. Hence ~ly² adv. [f. L *contiguus* f. CONtingere = tangere touch) + -ous]

cón'tinent, a. Temperate; chaste. Hence or cogn. **cón'tinence** n., ~ly² adv. [OF f. L as CONTAIN, see -ENT]

cón'tinent², n. Continuous land, main-land; || *the C~,* mainland of Europe; one of the main continuous bodies of land (Europe, Asia, Africa, N. & S. America, Australia). [as prec.]

continén'tal, a. & n. 1. Of a continent; ~ *drift,* (Geol.) supposed slow movement of the continents on a deep-seated plastic substratum; belonging to, characteristic of, the Continent, whence ~ISM, ~IST, nn., ~IZE v.t., ~ly² adv. 2. n. Inhabitant of the Continent; *(sl.) currency note

of an early issue that rapidly depreci-ated (*I don't care a ~*). [-AL]

contin'gency (-j-), n. Uncertainty of occurrence; chance occurrence; thing that may happen hereafter; thing depen-dent on an uncertain event; thing incident to another, incidental expense etc. [f. L as foll., see -ENCY]

contin'gent (-j-), a. & n. 1. Of uncertain occurrence; accidental, incidental *to;* true only under existing conditions; non-essential, conditional. 2. n. Force contri-buted to form part of army etc. (or fig.). Hence ~ly² adv. [f. F, f. L *contingentem* = *tangere* touch), see -ENT]

contin'ual, a. Always going on; very frequent. Hence ~ly² adv. [f. OF *continuel* f. L as CONTINUOUS, see -AL]

contin'uance, n. Going on, duration (*in long ~,* lasting long); remaining, stay, (*in* place, condition, etc.). [OF (CONTINUE, -ANCE)]

contin'uant, a. (Consonant) of which the sound can be prolonged (as *f e s r*), opp. of stop or check. [f. L as CONTINUE, see -ANT]

continuā'tion, n. Carrying on, resump-tion, (of an action, course, story, book, etc.); || (Stock Exch.) carrying over an ac-count to next ~ (or CONTANGO) *day;* that by which a thing is continued, additional part; gaiters continuous with knee-breeches; (sl.) trousers; ~ *school* (for additional teaching in leisure time of those who have left primary and other schools). [F, f. L *continuatio* (as prec., see -ATION)]

contin'uātive, a. Tending, serving, to continue. [f. L *continuatives* (as prec., see -IVE)]

continuā'tor, n. One who writes con-tinuation to another's work. [f. L as foll., -OR²]

contin'ue, v.t. & i. Maintain, keep up, (action etc.); retain (person *in* office etc.); take up, resume, (narrative etc. or abs.); (Law) adjourn; remain in existence; stay (*in, at,* place, *in* a state); *if you ~e* (are still) *obstinate;* not cease (*doing, to do*). [f. F *continuer* f. L *continuare*]

continü'ity, n. State of being continuous; (Cinemat.) scenario; *law of ~* (that all changes in nature are continuous, not abrupt). [f. F *continuité* f. L *continuita-tem* (as foll., see -TY)]

contin'uous, a. (Of material things) con-nected, unbroken; uninterrupted in time or sequence; ~ *brake* of train, ~ series of carriage brakes controlled from one point; (Archit.) ~ *style* (with mullions of window continued in tracery); ~ *voyage,* one single voyage in ref. to the object with which it was undertaken. Hence ~ly² adv., ~NESS n. [f. L *continuus* f. CON-

contin′uum, n. (philos.). **An unbroken mass or tissue or course of or of matter, sensation, events, etc.** (SPACE-*time* ~). [L, neut. of *continuus*, see prec.]

cŏn′-line, n. Spiral interval between strands of rope; space between casks stowed side by side. [?]

contŏrn′iate, a. & n. (Medal) with deep furrow round disk within edge. [f. It. *contorno* contour f. *contornare* compass about f. CON- + L *tornare* turn in lathe (*tornus*)]

contŏrt′, v.t. Twist, distort. [f. L CON- (*torquēre tort-*)]

contŏr′tion, n. Twisting; twisted state (esp. of face or body). [f. L *contortio* (prec. -ION)]

contŏr′tionist (-shŏ-), n. Artist whose work, gymnast whose body, exhibits contortions. [-IST]

cŏn′tour (-oŏr), n., & v.t. Outline; line separating differently coloured parts of design; artistic quality of outline; outline of coast, mountain mass, etc.; ~ *line*, one representing horizontal ~ of earth's surface at given elevation, as in a ~ *map*; (v.t.) mark with ~ lines, carry (road) round ~ of hill. [vrb f. n.) F, f. CON- (*tourner* TURN)]

cŏn′tra, prep. & n. *Pro & ~* (usu. *con*), for & against; (*pros & cons*, arguments for & against; (Bookkeeping) opposite side of account, esp. credit side. [L, as foll.]

contra-, pref. Against; in names of mus. instruments & organ-stops, denoting a pitch of an octave below. [L]

cŏn′trabănd, n. & a. **1.** Prohibited traffic, smuggling; smuggled goods; ~ *of war*, anything forbidden to be supplied by neutrals to belligerents (*absolute*, *conditional*, ~, things that may under no, some, circumstances be supplied, as, *absolute* ~, *weapons*, *conditional* ~, *cotton*). **2.** adj. Forbidden to be imported or exported, as ~ *goods*; concerned with these, as ~ *trade*(r). [f. Sp. *contrabanda* f. It. CONTRA(*bando* proclamation f. LL *bandum* BAN)]

cŏn′trabăndist, n. Smuggler. [f. Sp. *contrabandista* (as prec., see -IST)]

cŏn′trabăss, n. = DOUBLE-*bass*. [f. It. CONTRA(*basso* BASS)]

cŏntracĕp′tive, a. & n. Preventive of uterine conception. So **cŏntracĕp′tion** n., use of ~s. [CONTRA- + (CON)CEPTION]

cŏn′trăct[1], n. Agreement between parties, States, etc.; business agreement for supply of goods or performance of work at fixed price; agreement enforceable by law (NUDE ~); accepted promise to do or forbear; formal agreement for marriage; conveyance of property; (Bridge) undertaking to make so many tricks; ~ *bridge*, a form of auction bridge in which only tricks bid and won count towards game. [OF, f. L *contractus* (as foll.)]

contrăct[2], v.t. & i. **Enter into business or legal engagement** (*to do*, *for doing*, *for piece of work*, or *abs*.); ~ *oneself out of*, ~ *out of*, or *abs*. ~ *out*, ~ for exemption or exclusion from provisions of (law etc.); ~ (enter into) *marriage*; form (friendship, habit), incur (debt); draw together (muscles, brow, etc.); make smaller, whence **contractibil′ITY** n., **contrăc′t-IBLE** a.; restrict, confine, (lit. & fig.); (Gram.) shorten (word) by combination or elision; shrink, become smaller; (p.p.) narrow, mean, (of ideas etc.). [f. L CON- (*trahere tract-* draw)]

contrăc′tile (-il, -īl), a. Capable of or producing contraction, as ~ *muscles*, *metal*, *force*. So **contractil′ITY** n. [F (as prec., see -ILE)]

contrăc′tion, n. Shrinking, contracting; restriction, confinement; shortening of word by combination or elision; contracted word; contracting (*of* debt, disease, habit). [F, f. L *contractio* (as prec., see -ION)]

contrăc′tive, a. Serving to contract. [-IVE]

contrăc′tor, n. Undertaker of contract; contracting muscle. [L (as CONTRACT[2], -OR[2])]

contrăc′tual, a. Of (the nature of) a contract. [as CONTRACT[1] + -AL]

contradict′, v.t. Deny (statement); deny the words of (person); be contrary to, as *these rumours ~ each other*. Hence or cogn. **contradic′tor** TABLE a., **contradic′tor**[2] n. [f. L CONTRA(*dicere dict-* say)]

contradic′tion, n. Denial; opposition; statement contradicting another; inconsistency; ~ *in terms*, plainly self-contradictory statement or words, as '*almost quite ready*' is a ~ *in terms*. [F, f. L *contradictionem* (as prec., -ION)]

contradic′tious (-shŭs), a. Inclined to contradict; disputatious. Hence ~LY[2] adv., ~NESS n. [-IOUS]

contradic′tor[1] y, a. & n. Making denial; mutually opposed or inconsistent; contradictious; (n.) ~y assertion. Hence ~ILY[2] adv., ~INESS n. [f. L *contradictorius* (as prec., see -ORY)]

contradistinc′tion, n. Distinction by contrast. [CONTRA-]

contradisting′uish (-nggw-), v.t. Distinguish (things, one *from* another) by contrast. [CONTRA-]

contral′tō, n. & a. (pl. -os). (Part assigned to, singer with) lowest female voice. [It. (CONTRA- + ALTO)]

contraposi′tion (-z-), n. Opposition, contrast; (Logic) a mode of conversion (*if all A is B, then by ~ all not-B is not-A, or no not-B is A*). So **contrapŏs′ĭtIVE** (-z-) a. [f. L *contrapositio* (see -ION)]

cŏn′traprŏp, n. Coaxial, oppositely rotating airscrew. [CONTRA-, PROP(ELLER)]

For compounds of *co*- not given consult CO-.

contrap'tion, n. (sl.), Queer machine, makeshift contrivance. [perh. f. *contrive*, cf. *conceive*, *-ception*]

contrapun'tal, a. Of or in counterpoint. [f. It. *contra(p)punto* COUNTERPOINT+-AL]

contrapun'tist, n. One skilled in counterpoint. [f. It. *contra(p)puntista* (as prec., -IST]

contrâr'iant, a. Opposed (to). [F, f. med. L *contrariare* (as CONTRARY, see -ANT]

contrâri'ety, n. Opposition in nature, quality, or action; disagreement, inconsistency. [f. OF *contrarieté* f. LL *contrarietatem* (as contrary, see -TY]

contrâr'ious, a. (arch.). Opposed; perverse; (of things) adverse. [f. OF *contrarius* f. med. L *contrariosus* (as prec., see -OUS]

con'trariwise (-z; *also* kontrār'i-), adv. On the other hand; in the opposite way; perversely. [foll.+WISE]

con'trary (see below), a., n., adv. [-ARY²]
1. Op-posed in nature or tendency (*to*); (of wind) impeding, unfavourable; *the* opposite (of two things); (pop., pron. kontrār'i) perverse, self-willed, whence **contrâr'iness** n.; opposite in position or direction.
2. n. *The* opposite; *on the ~* (corroborating a denial expressed or understood, as *Have you nearly done?—On the ~, I have only just begun*) interpret *by contraries*, understand Yes for No etc.; *to the ~*, to the opposite effect, as *there is no evidence to the ~*. 3. adv. In opposition to, as *act CONtrary to nature*. Hence **con'trarily²** adv. [OF *contraire* f. L *contrarius* (CONTRA, see -ARY²]

contrast'¹ (-ah-), v.t. & i. Set (two things, one *with* another) in opposition, so as to show their differences (*between*; *in ~ with*); thing showing such a difference (*to*). Hence **contras'ty²** (-ah-) a., exhibiting strong ~s (esp. of photographic negatives). [f. F *contraste* f. It. *contrasto* (see prec.)]

con'trast² (-ah-), n. Juxtaposition (esp. of forms, colours, etc.) showing striking differences (*between*; *in ~ with*); thing showing striking difference on comparison (*with*). [f. OF *contraster* (= It. *contrastare*) f. L CONTRA-(*stāre* stand)]

con'trate, a. ~*wheel*, one with teeth at right angles to its plane. [CONTRA-+ -ATE²]

contravalla'tion, n. Chain of redoubts and breastworks placed by besiegers between their camp and the town. [f. F *contrevallation* (CONTRA-, see CIRCUMVALLATION]

contravene', v.t. Infringe (law); dispute (statement); (of things) conflict with. [f. F *contrevenir* f. L CONTRA(*venire* vent-come)]

contraven'tion, n. Infringement (*in ~ of*, violating). [F (as prec., see -ION]

con'tretemps (see Ap.), n. Unlucky accident; hitch. [F]

contrib'ute, v.t. & i. Pay, furnish, (to common fund etc.); (v.i.) ~ *to*, supply (literary article etc.); (v.i.) ~ *to*, help to bring about. [f. L *contribuere* -ut- bestow]

contribu'tion, n. Act of contributing; thing, help, literary article, contributed; imposition levied for support of army in the field; *lay under ~*, *exact ~s from*. [F, f. L *contributionem* (as prec., see -ION]

contrib'utor, n. One who contributes (esp. literary articles). [f. AF *contributour* (as CONTRIBUTE, see -OR²]

contrib'utory, a. & n. That contributes (~ *negligence*, of injured person who has failed to take proper precautions against accident); (n.) person liable, when a company fails, to share in paying off its debts. [CONTRIBUTE, -ORY]

con'trite, a. Broken in spirit by sense of sin, completely penitent; (of actions) showing a ~ spirit. Hence **~ly²** (-tli) adv. [f. F *contrit* f. L CON(*terere* trit- rub)]

contri'tion, n. Being contrite, penitence. [f. OF *contricium* f. L *contritionem* (prec., -ION]

contriv'ance, n. Act of contriving; deceitful practice; invention; mechanical device; inventive capacity. [-ANCE]

contrive', v.t. Invent, devise; bring to pass, manage, (thing, to do; also of undesired event, as~*e to make matters worse*); (abs.) manage household affairs (*well* etc.), whence **~ER¹** n. Hence **~ABLE** a. [f. OF *controver* find f. L *turbare* disturb, stir up]

contról'¹, n. Power of directing, command; restraint; means of restraint, check; standard of comparison for checking inferences deduced from experiment; (Spirit), personality actuating a medium; station at which aeroplanes, motors, etc., in races are allowed time to stop for overhauling etc.; section of road in which certain instructions (as to speed etc.); (pl.) various devices in aircraft used to control altitude, direction, speed, etc. [perh. f. F *controlle* for *contrerolle* copy of a roll f. med. L CONTRA(*rotulus* see ROLL];

contról'², v.t. (-ll-), Dominate, command; hold in check (oneself, one's anger); check, verify; regulate (prices etc.). Hence **~l'ABLE** a., **~MENT** n. [f. F *controler* OF *contreroller* keep copy of roll of accounts (as prec.]

contról'ler, n. In vbl senses; also one who checks expenditure, steward, (often spelt compt-), Mint, Navy, etc. [f. OF *contre-rolleur* (as prec., see -OR²; spelling compt- by confus. w. obs. *compte* count]

controv'ersial (-shl), a. Of, open to, given to, controversy. Hence **~ISM, ~IST,** nn., **~ly²** adv.; (~sha-), **~ly²** adv. [f. L *contro-*

cŏn'trovêrsy̆, n. Disputation; *without, beyond*, ~, unquestionably. [f. L *controversia* (as foll., see -Y[1])]

cŏn'trovêrt (*also* -vêrt'), v.t. Dispute about, discuss; dispute, deny. Hence ~IST n. [f. L *controversus* turned against, opposed (*contro-* against + p.p. of *vertere* turn) whence +*controvertere* was assumed]

cŏntŭmā'cious (-sh*u*s), a. Insubordinate, disobedient, esp. to order of court. Hence or cogn. ~LY[2] adv., ~NESS, **cŏn'tūm**ACY, nn. [f. L CON(*tumax -acis* perh. f. *tumēre* swell or *temnere* despise), see -ACIOUS]

cŏntūmēl'ious, a. Opprobrious; insolent. Hence ~LY[2] adv. [f. OF *contumélieus* f. L *contumeliosus* (as foll., see -OUS)]

cŏn'tūmēly̆ (*or* -mĭ-), n. Insolent, reproachful, language or treatment; disgrace. [f. OF *contumelie* f. L *contumelia* (cf. CONTUMACIOUS)]

contūse' (-z), v.t. Injure by blow without breaking skin, bruise. So **contū'**SION (-zhn) n. [f. L CON(*tundere tus-* thump)]

conŭn'drum, n. Riddle; hard question. [?]

cŏnûrbā'tion, n. Aggregation of urban districts. [CON-, L *urbs urbis* city, -ATION]

cŏnvalĕsce', v.i. Regain health. [f. L CON(*valescere* incept. of *valēre* be well)]

cŏnvalĕs'c|ent, a. & n. (Person) recovering from sickness; *~ent hospital* (for ~ents). So ~ENCE n. [as prec., see -ENT]

convĕc'tion, n. Transportation of heat or electricity, by movement of heated or electrified substance. [f. L *convectio* f. CON(*vehere vect-* carry), see -ION]

convenance (see Ap.), n. (usu. pl.). Conventional propriety. [F]

convēn|e', v.t. & i. Assemble (t. & i.); convoke (assembly); summon (person *before* tribunal). Hence ~'ABLE a. [f. F *convenir* f. L CON(*venire vent-* come) assemble, agree, fit]

convēn'ience, n. Suitableness, commodiousness; material advantage, as *marriage of* ~; personal comfort, as *at your* ~, in a way, at a time, convenient to you; advantage, as *a great* ~; *make a* ~ *of* one, utilize him unconscionably, abuse his good nature; useful appliance; ‖ water-closet; (arch.) vehicle; (pl.) material comforts. [f. L *convenientia* (as prec., see -ENCE)]

convēn'ient, a. Suitable, commodious; not troublesome, as *if it is* ~ *to you.* Hence ~LY[2] adv. [as CONVENE, see -ENT]

cŏn'vent, n. Religious community (usu. women, cf. MONASTERY) living together; building occupied by this. [f. AF *covent* (cf. *Covent Garden*) f. OF *convent* f. L *conventus -ūs* (as prec.)]

‖ **convĕn'ticle, n.** (hist.). Clandestine religious meeting, esp. of Nonconformists or Dissenters; building used for this. [f. L *conventiculum* (place of) assembly, dim. as prec.]

convĕn'tion, n. Act of convening; formal assembly, esp. (Eng. Hist.) of Parliament without summons of King, 1660 & 1688; agreement between parties; general (often tacit) consent; practice based on this; accepted method of play (in leading, bidding, etc.) in various card games. [F, f. L *conventionem* (as CONVENE, see -ION)]

convĕn'tional (-sho-), a. Depending on convention, not natural, not spontaneous; (Art) following traditions. Hence ~ISM, ~IST, ~ITY (-ăl'-), nn., ~IZE v.t., ~LY[2] adv. [f. L *conventionalis* (as prec., -AL)]

convĕn'tionary̆ (-sho-), a. & n. (Tenant, tenure) on terms orig. fixed by convention, not by custom. [f. med. L *conventionarius* (as prec., -ARY[1])]

convĕn'tūal, a. & n. (Member, inmate) of a convent; (member) of the less strict branch of Franciscans, living in large convents. [f. med. L *conventualis* (as CONVENT, see -AL)]

convêrge', v.i. & t. (Of lines) tend to meet in a point (also fig.); (Math., of series) approximate in the sum of its terms towards a definite limit; (trans.) cause to ~. So **convêr'g**ENCE, -ENCY, nn., **convêr'g**ENT a. [f. LL CON(*vergere* VERGE)]

convêrs'ab|le, a. Easy, pleasant, in conversation; fit for social intercourse. Hence ~**le**NESS n., ~LY[2] adv. [F, f. med. L *conversabilis* (as foll., see -BLE)]

cŏn'versance, -cy̆, n. Familiarity, acquaintance, (*with*). [as foll., see -ANCE]

cŏn'versant, a. Having frequent intercourse, well acquainted, (*with* person, subject, etc.); (of things) concerned (*in, about, with*). [f. L *conversari* CONVERSE[1], see -ANT]

cŏnversā'tion, n. Talk, whence ~IST (-sho-) n.; ~ (*piece*), kind of genre painting of group of figures; sexual intercourse, as *criminal* ~ (*crim. con.*, cf. CONNEXION). [OF, f. L *conversationem* (as prec., see -ATION)]

cŏnversā'tional (-sho-), a. Fond of, good at, pertaining to, conversation. Hence ~IST n., ~LY[2] adv. [-AL]

cŏnversaziōn'ė (-ăts-), n. (pl. *-nes, -ni* pr. -nē). Soirée given by learned or art society. [It., f. L as CONVERSATION]

convêrse'[1], v.i. Talk (*with* person, *on, about*, subject). [f. F *converser* f. L *conversari* keep company (with), frequent. as CONVERT[1]]

cŏn'vêrse[2], n. (arch.). Discourse; intercourse. [f. prec.]

cŏn'vêrse[3], a. & n. **1.** Opposite, contrary. **2.** n. (Logic) converted proposition; form of words produced by transposition of some terms of another (*he had learning without wealth* is the ~ of *he had wealth without learning*); (Math.) *this proposition is the* ~ *of the former* (assumes its conclu-

sion & proves its datum). Hence ~LY² (-sĭ-) adv. [as CONVERT¹]

conver'sion (-shn), n. Transposition, inversion, esp. (Logic) of subject & predicate (*if no A is B, then by ~ no B is A*); bringing over (*to* an opinion, party, faith, etc.); turning of sinners to God; changing (*to, into*); change (of debentures, stocks, etc.), into others of different character. [F, f. L *conversionem* (as foll., see -ION)]

convert'¹, v.t. Change (*into*); cause to turn (*to* opinion, faith, etc.), cf. PERVERT; turn to godliness; (Stocks etc.) see prec.; (Logic) see prec.; (Rugby football) complete (a try) by kicking goal (also abs.). Hence ~ER¹ n. (esp.) large retort used in Bessemer steel process. [f. L *convertere* (*vers-* turn) turn about]

con'vert², n. Person converted, esp. to religious faith or life. [f. prec.]

converti·ble, a. That may be converted; exchangeable for specie; (of paper-money) exchangeable for specie; *~ terms*, synonyms; (of paper-money) *~ husbandry*, rotation of crops. Hence **converti·bi·li·ty**, **converti·bly²** adv. [F, f. LL *convertibilis* (as prec., see -BLE)]

con'vex, a. Curved like the outside of circle or sphere (cf. CONCAVE). Hence or cogn. **convex·ity** n., ~LY² adv. [f. L *convexus* p.p. of CON(*vehere* bring)]

convex·o- in comb. Convex and —, as *convexo-concave*. [as prec., see -O-]

convey' (-vā), v.t. Transport, carry; transmit (sound, smell, etc.); impart, communicate, (idea, meaning); (Law) make over (property *to*, or abs.). Hence ~ABLE (-ā'a-) a., ~ER¹(-ā'er), ~OR²(-ā'or), nn., (esp.) mechanical contrivance for ~ing heavy articles or materials (*coal*-etc.). [f. OF *conveier*, mod. *convoyer* (*voie*, *voie*, f. L *via* way)]

convey'ance (-ā'a-), n. Carrying; transmission; communication (of ideas etc.); (document effecting) transference of property; carriage, vehicle. [-ANCE]

convey'ancer (-ā'a-), n. Lawyer who prepares documents for conveyance of property. [-ER¹]

convey'ancing (-ā'a-), n. Work of prec. [-ING¹]

con'vict¹, n. Condemned criminal undergoing penal servitude. Hence ~ISM(3) n. [f. obs. adj. *convict* (as foll.)]

convict'², v.t. Prove guilty (of offence); declare guilty by verdict of jury or decision of judge; impress (person) with sense of error. Hence **convic'tive** a. [f. L con(*vincere* *vict-* conquer)]

convic'tion, n. Proving or finding guilty; *summary ~* (by judge or magistrates without jury); act of convincing; settled belief; (Theol.) awakened consciousness of sin. [f. L *convictio* (as prec., see -ION)]

convince', v.t. Firmly persuade (*of, that*; esp. pass.); produce in (person) a moral

conviction (*of* sin etc.). Hence ~e·MENT (-sm-), ~'ingNESS, nn., ~'ing·LY² adv. [as CONVICT²]

convin'cible, a. Open to conviction. [as prec., see -BLE]

convi'vial, a. Of, befitting, a feast; festive, jovial. Hence ~IST, **convivia·li·ty**, nn., ~LY² adv. [f. L *convivialis* f. con(*vivium* feast f. con(*vivere* live)]

convoca'tion, n. Calling together; assembly; ||(Ch. of Eng.) synod of clergy of province of Canterbury or York; ||legislative assembly of Oxford or Durham Univ. Hence ~AL (-sho-) a. [f. L con(*vocatio* (as foll. -ATION)]

convoke', v.t. Call together, summon to assemble. [f. F *convoquer* f. L con(*vocare* call)]

con'volute, a. & n. (bot., conch.). Rolled together, coiled; (n.) coil. [as CONVOLVULUS]

con'voluted (-ŏŏt-), a. (zool.). Coiled, twisted. [f. vb convolute (as prec., otherwise rare)]

convolu'tion (-ōō-), n. Coiling, twisting; fold, twist. [as foll., see -ION]

convolve', v.t.&i. Roll together, roll up. (esp. in p.p.). [f. L con(*volvere* *volut-* roll)]

convo'lvulus, n. (pl. *-luses*). Kinds of twining plant including bindweed. [L, as prec., with dim. suf.]

con'voy¹, v.t. (Of ship of war) escort (merchant or passenger vessel); escort with armed force; (arch.) conduct (guests, lady, etc.). [f. L con(*vehere* *vect-*)]

con'voy², n. Act of convoying; protection; escort (for honour or protection); company, supply of provisions, etc., under escort; number of merchant ships under escort or able to defend themselves. [f. F *convoi* (as prec.)]

convulse', v.t. Shake violently (lit. & fig.); throw into convulsions (usu. pass.); cause to be violently seized with laughter (usu. pass.). [f. L con(*vellere* *vuls-* pull)]

convul'sion (-shn), n. Violent irregular motion of limb or body due to involuntary contraction of muscles (usu. pl., & esp. as a disorder of infants); (pl.) violent fit of laughter; violent social or political agitation; violent physical disturbance. Hence ~ARY¹(-sho-)a. [f. L *convulsio* (as prec., see -ION)]

convul'sive, a. Attended or affected with, producing, convulsions (lit. & fig.). Hence ~LY² adv. [CONVULSE, -IVE]

con'y, **~ney**, n. (pl. *-ies, -eys*). Rabbit (now used only in statutes etc. & as shop name for the fur); (Bibl.) small pachyderm of Palestine living in clefts of rocks, hyrax; (arch.) *~catcher*, sharper. [sing. f. pl. *conies* f. OF *coniz* pl. of *conil* f. L *cuniculus* rabbit, etym. dub.; formerly pron. kŭ-]

coo, v.i.&t. & n. (Make) soft murmuring sound of or as of doves & pigeons; (till &

~, converse amorously: say ~ingly. [imit.]

coo'ee, coo'ey, n., & v.i. (Make) sound adopted as signal by Australian colonists from the aborigines. [imit.]

cook¹, n. One whose business is to cook food; *too many ~s spoil the broth*, one director is enough; ~-house, camp kitchen, outdoor kitchen in warm countries, (on ship, also ~-room) galley; ~-shop, eating-house. [OE coc f. L coquus]

cook², v.t. & i. Prepare (food or abs.) by heat; (v.i.) undergo ~ing; (also ~ up) concoct (fig.); (colloq.) tamper with (accounts etc.); || (sl., of exertion etc.) exhaust (runner etc., esp. in p.p.); ~ *his goose*, do for him, settle his hash. [prec.]

cook'er, n. Cooking-apparatus, -stove; vessel food is cooked in; fruit etc. that cooks well; one who cooks (accounts etc.) or concocts. [-ER¹]

cook'ery, n. Art, practice, of cooking; ~-book (dealing with ~). [-ERY]

cook'ie, n. (Sc.) plain bun; *small flat cake, biscuit. [prob. f. Du. koekje dim. of koek cake]

cook'y, n. (colloq.). (Usu. female) cook. [-Y³]

cool¹, a. & n. Moderately cold; (Hunt.) ~ scent (faint, weak); unexcited, calm; lacking zeal, lukewarm; wanting cordiality; calmly audacious, as a ~ hand (person); (complacently or emphat. of large sums of money) *it cost me a thousand*; (n.) ~ air, ~ place, ~ness; ~-headed, not easily excited; ~ tankard, ~ing drink of wine, water, lemon-juice, etc. Hence ~ISH¹ a., ~LY² (-l-li) adv., ~'NESS n. [OE col f. OTeut. kōluz (kal-=L gel cold]

cool², v.i. & t. Become cool (lit. & fig.; also ~ down); make cool (lit. & fig.); ~ *one's coppers*; ~ *one's heels*, be kept waiting. [OE cōlian f. OTeut. kōlōjan (as prec.)]

cool'ant, n. Liquid applied to edge of cutting tool etc. to lessen friction. [cool¹, -ANT]

cool'er, n. Vessel in which a thing is cooled, as *wine, butter, ~*; *refrigerator; (sl.) prison cell. [-ER¹]

cool'ie, -ly, n. Indian or Chinese hired labourer. [f. Hind. qulī]

cool'th, n. (colloq. or joc.). Coolness. [f. cool¹, after warmth]

coomb, || combe, (koom), n. Valley on flank of hill; short valley running up from coast. [OE cumb, etym. dub.]

coon, n. =RACOON; sly fellow; *(colloq.) a negro; *gone ~*, one whose case is hopeless. [abbr.]

coon-can', n. (Also *conquian) simple two-handed card-game (orig. Mexican). [f. Sp. con quien with whom?]

coop¹, n. Basket placed over sitting or fattening fowls; fowl-run; || basket used in catching fish. [= ME cupe basket; cf. G kufe cask]

coop², v.t. Put in coop; confine (persons; also ~ up, in). [f. prec.]

coop'er¹, n., & v.t. Maker of casks for dry goods (dry~) or liquids (wet~); white~, maker of pails, tubs, etc.; (on ship) repairer of casks etc.; (also wine~) one who samples, bottles, or retails wine; repair (cask), stow in casks, furnish up. [vb f. n. f. med. L cuparius (as prec., -ARY²)]

cooper² see COPER².

coop'erage, n. Cooper's work or workshop. So COOP'ERY(3) n. [-AGE]

co-op'erate, v.i. Work together (with person in a work, to an end); (of things) concur in producing an effect. So ~ANT a. & n., ~ātor²n. [f. L co(operari f. opus operis work), see -ATE³]

co-opera'tion, n. Working together to same end; (Pol. Econ.) co-operative combination. [f. L cooperatio (as prec., see -ION)]

co-op'erative, a. Of, tending to, co-operation; (Pol. Econ.) ~ society (for production or distribution of goods, profits being shared by members), ~ store (belonging to ~ society). Hence ~LY² (-vl-) adv. [as CO-OPERATE, see -IVE]

co-opt¹, v.t. Elect into body by votes of existing members. So cō-ōptā'TION n. [f. L co(optare choose)]

cō-ōrd'inate¹, a. & n. 1. Equal in rank, esp. (Gram.) of clauses of compound sentence (cf. SUBORDINATE); consisting of ~ things. 2. n. ~ thing, esp. (Math.) each of a system of magnitudes used to fix position of point, line, or plane. Hence ~LY² (-tl-) adv. [f. CO- + L ordinare (ordo -inis order); see -ATE²]

cō-ōrd'in|āte², v.t. Make co-ordinate; bring (parts) into proper relation. Hence ~A'TION n., ~ātīve a. [prec., -ATE³]

coot, n. Name of several swimming & diving birds, esp. the Bald C~, web-footed bird with base of bill extended to form white plate on forehead, whence *bald as a ~*. [ME cote= Du. koet, etym. dub.]

coot'ie, n. (Army sl.). Body-louse. [etym. dub., perh. f. Hind. khuthi scab]

cop¹, n. (spinning). Conical ball of thread wound upon spindle. [OE cop top]

cop², n. (sl.). Policeman. [cf. foll.]

cop³, v.t. (-pp-), & n., (sl.). 1. Catch (~ *it*, catch it, be punished). 2. n. Capture (chiefly in phr. a fair ~). [?]

copai'ba, -va, (-pī-, -vā-), n. Aromatic balsam used in medicine & the arts. [(-ba) Sp., f. Braz. cupauba]

cop'al, n. Kinds of resin used for varnish. [Sp., f. Mex. copalli incense]

For compounds of co- not given consult CO-.

copar'cenary, -erÿ, copär'cener, nn. =PARCENARY, PARCENER. [00-]

copart'ner, n. Partner, sharer, associate. Hence ~SHIP n. (labour ~ship, system designed to interest workmen in their business by means of profit-sharing). [00-]

copart'nerÿ, n. Copartnership. [f. prec., see -ERY(2)]

cope¹, n. (Eccl.) long cloak worn by ecclesiastics in processions; (fig.) (cloak) of night, ~ (canopy) of heaven; eating. ~SHIP n. [Port., prob. f. Malayalam koppara coco-nut.]

~ing; ~-stone, head stone of building, finishing touch. [f. med.L capa cap]

cope², v.t. & i. Furnish with a cope; cover (wall etc.) with coping; cover as with a vault; (v.i.) ~ over, project like a coping. [f. prec.]

cope³, v.i. Contend evenly, grapple successfully, with (person, task). [f. F couper strike (COUP)]

cope'ck, n. Russian copper coin (the hundredth part of a rouble). [f. Russ. kopeeka dim. of koppé lance]

cop'er¹, n. (Also horse-~) horse-dealer. [f. obs. cope buy, barter (as foll.)]

cop'er², coop'er² (kō-), n. Floating grogshop for North Sea fishers. [f. Flem. & Du. kooper f. koopen buy (cf. CHEAP)]

Copern'ican, a. ~ system, theory, (that the planets, including earth, move round sun). [f. Copernicus latinized f. Kopper-nik, astronomer (d. 1543)+-AN]

cop'ing, n. Top (usu. sloping) course of masonry in wall; overhanging ledge protecting wall-fruit; ~-stone (used for ~). [COPE²+-ING¹]

cop'ious, a. Plentiful; abounding in information; profuse in speech; (of language) having large vocabulary. Hence ~LY² adv., ~NESS n. [f. L copiosus (copia plenty, see -OUS]

copp'er¹, n., a., & v.t. 1. Reddish malleable ductile metal; bronze (formerly ~) coin, penny, halfpenny, farthing; cooking or laundry boiler of iron or ~; hot ~s, mouth & throat parched by drinking; cool one's ~s (by drinking); ~ beech (kind with ~-coloured leaves); ~-bit, soldering tool pointed with ~; ~-bottom v.t., sheathe the bottom (of ship) with ~ (esp. in red Indian of N. America; ~-head, venomous American snake; ~-plate, polished ~ plate for engraving or etching, print from this, (adj., of writing) neat; ~-smith, one who works in ~. 2. v.t. Cover (ship's bottom etc.) with ~. Hence ~Y² a. (esp. ~-coloured). [(vb f. n.) OE coper f. pop. L cuprum, L Cyprium (aes), Cyprian metal]

copp'er², n. (sl.) Policeman. [cf. COP¹]

copp'eras, n. Sulphate of iron, green vitriol. [f. med.L cupe(ro)sa perh. = aqua cuprosa copper water]

copp'ice, n. Small wood of underwood &

small trees, grown for periodical cutting; ~-wood, underwood. [f. OF copeïz f. LL +colpaticium f. colpare cut (colpus f. L f. Gk kolaphos blow, cuff)]

cop'ra, n. Dried kernels of coco-nut. [Port., prob. f. Malayalam koppara coco-nut]

cop'ro- in comb.=Gk kopros dung, as: -lite, fossil dung, so -lit'ic a.; -logy (-ŏjĭ), treatment of filthy subjects in literature etc.; -phagous (-ŏfă), (of beetles) dung-eating.

Copt, n. Native Egyptian Christian of Jacobite sect of Monophysites. [f. Copt. gyptios, kyptanos, f. Gk Aigyptios Egyptian]

Cop'tic, a. & n. (Language) of the Copts. [-IC]

cop'ula, n. (Logic, Gram.) verb be (as mere sign of predication); (Anat.) connecting part (bone, cartilage, ligament); (Mus.) short connecting passage. Hence ~AR¹ a. [L (cō-+ap- fasten+dim. suf.)]

cop'ulate, v.i. Unite sexually. Hence ~atory a. [f. L copulare fasten together (prec.), see -ATE³]

copula'tion, n. Sexual union; grammatical or logical connexion. [f. L f. copula-tionem (as prec., see -ION)]

cop'ulative, a. & n. Serving to connect; (Gram.) connecting words or clauses that are connected in sense (cf. DISJUNCTIVE), also, connecting subject & predicate; (Zool., Anat.) relating to sexual union; (n.) ~ conjunction or particle. Hence ~LY² adv. [F (-if, -ive), f. L copula-tivus (as prec., see -IVE)]

cop'y¹, n. Reproduction (of writing, picture, etc.); imitation; page written after model (of penmanship); || (Law) transcript of manorial court-roll, containing entries of admissions of tenants to land hence called COPYHOLD; written or printed specimen (of book etc.); rough, foul, ~, original draft; fair, clean, ~ (transcribed from rough ~); ~ of verses, short set as school exercise; fair ~, model version of this; model to be copied; manuscript or matter to be printed (in-cident etc. will make good ~, lends itself to interesting narration in newspapers etc.); ~-book, one containing copies for learners to imitate; ~-book maxims, morality (commonplace). [f. F copie f. L copia abundance, in phr. dare copiam legendi give the power of reading, i.e., give a copy]

cop'y², v.t. & i. Transcribe (from original), whence ~IST n.; make copy of; imitate; crib from neighbour in examination. [f. F copier f. med.L copiare (as prec.)]

|| **cop'yhold, n. & a.** Tenure by cory¹; (land) so held. Hence ~ER¹ n.

cŏp'yright (-rīt), n. & a., & v.t. Exclusive right given by law for term of years to author, designer, etc., or his assignee to print, publish, or sell, copies of his original work; (adj.) protected by ~ (of books etc.); (v.t.) secure ~ for (book etc.).

coque (kōk), n. Small loop of ribbon; (in mod. use, pr. kŏk, attrib.) applied to feathers used in trimming, in boas, etc. [F, = a shell]

coquet'¹ (-kĕt), a. Coquettish. [F (orig. noun, dim. of coq cock]

coquet'², coquette', (-kĕt), v.i. (-tt-.) Play the coquette; flirt (with); dally, trifle, with (matter, proposal, etc.). [f. F coqueter t, prec.]

cŏq'uetry (-kit-), n. Coquettish behaviour or act; (fig.) trifling; attractive prettiness as result of art. [f. F coquetterie (coqueter, as prec., see -ERY]

coquette' (-kĕt), n. Woman who trifles with man's affections; crested humming-bird. Hence ~ISH¹ a., ~'ISHLY² adv., (-kĕt-), [F, fem. of COQUET]

coqui'to (-kē-), n. Chilian palm-tree yielding palm-honey. [Sp., dim. of coco coco-nut]

cor-, pref. = COM- before r.

‖ cŏr'acle, n. Wicker boat covered with waterright material used on Welsh & Irish lakes & rivers. [f. W curugl f. curug = Ir. curach boat]

cŏr'aco- in comb. (anat.). Of the coracoid process (beak-shaped process extending from shoulder-blade towards breast-bone). [f. Gk korax -akos crow]

cŏr'al, n. & a. Hard calcareous substance (red, pink, white, etc.) secreted by many tribes of marine polyps for support & habitation; ~-reef, accumulation of this; ~ zone of sea-depths, that in which these abound. [f. It. corallina dim. of corallo CORAL]

cŏr'alline¹, n. Genus of seaweeds with calcareous jointed stem; (pop.) name of various plant-like compound animals; ~ zone of sea-depths, that in which these abound. [f. It. corallina dim. of corallo CORAL]

cŏr'alline² (-ī-, -ĭ), a. Coral-red; ~ ware, Italian red-paste pottery (17th–18th c.); like, composed of, coral. [f. L corallinus (CORAL, -INE¹)]

cŏr'allite, n. Fossil coral; coral skeleton of polyp; coralline marble. [-ITE¹]

cŏr'alloid, a. & n. (Organism) like, akin to, coral. [-OID]

cŏr'am, prep.(w.abl. case). In the presence of (judice, (jōōd'isi), a judge; pŏp'ŭlō, the public, etc.). [L]

cor anglais (kor ahng'glā), n. The tenor oboe. [F, = English horn]

cŏrb'el, n., & v.t. & i. (-ll-.) (Archit.) projection of stone, timber, etc., jutting out from wall to support weight, whence ~-TABLE¹ (also ~-block) short timber laid on wall or pier longitudinally under beam; ~-table, projecting course resting on ~s; (v.t. & i.) ~ out, off, (cause to) project on ~s. [(vb f. n.) OF, f. LL corvellus dim. of corvus raven]

cŏrb'ie, n. (Sc.). Raven; carrion crow; ~-steps, step-like projections on sloping sides of gable. [f. OF corb CORBEL +-Y³]

cŏrd, n., & v.t. Thin rope, thick string; (Anat.) ~-like structure in animal body, as SPINAL, UMBILICAL, ~, VOCAL ~s; ~-like rib on cloth; ribbed cloth, esp. corduroy ~s, corduroy breeches or trousers; measure of cut wood (usu. 128 cub. ft); (fig.) ~s of discipline, fourfold ~ of evidence, etc.; (v.t.) bind with ~, [(vb f. n.) f. F corde f. L f. Gk khordē gut, string of musical instrument]

cŏrd'age, n. Cords, ropes, esp. in rigging of ship. [F (as prec.+-AGE]

cŏrd'ate, a. Heart-shaped. [f. L cor cordis heart, see -ATE²]

cŏrd'ed, a. Bound with cords; furnished with cords; (of cloth etc.) ribbed. [-ED². 1]

cŏrdelier', n. Franciscan friar of strict rule (wearing knotted cord round waist). [F (cordelle dim. as CORD, see -IER)]

cŏrd'ial, a. & n. (Medicine, food, drink) that stimulates the heart, esp. (Commerc.) aromatized & sweetened spirit; hearty, sincere; warm, friendly, whence ~ITY¹ (-ăl-) n., ~LY² adv. [f. med. L cordialis (cor cordis heart, -AL]

cŏrdille'ra (-lyăr'a), n. Mountain ridge (one of parallel series), esp. of the Andes & same system in Central America & Mexico. [Sp.]

cŏrd'ite, n. A smokeless explosive. [f. CORD (from its appearance) +-ITE¹(2)]

cŏrd'on, n. Projecting course of stone in wall; chain of military posts; line or circle of police etc.; (also sanitary ~) guarded line between infected & uninfected districts; ornamental cord or braid; (pron. as F) ribbon of knightly order (~ bleu, see AP. joc., first-class cook); fruit-tree pruned to grow as single stem. [F (as CORD, see -OON]

cŏrd'ovan, a. & n. (Leather) of Cordova. [f. Sp. cordovan(o)]

cŏrd'uroy, n. & a. Coarse thick ribbed cotton stuff, orig. worn chiefly by labourers; (pl.) ~ trousers; * road, of tree-trunks laid across swamp. [perh. f. F ³corde du roi king's cord]

cŏrd'wain, n. (arch.). Spanish leather formerly used for shoes. [f. OF cordoan CORDOVAN]

For compounds of co- not given consult co-.

cord'wainer, n. Shoemaker (now only as guild-name etc.). [f. OF *cordoanier*, as prec.]

core, n. & v.t. Horny capsule containing seeds of apple, pear, etc.; central part cut out (esp. of rock in boring); bar of soft iron forming centre of electro-magnet or induction coil; internal mould filling space to be left hollow in a casting; central strand of rope; innermost part, heart; (fig.) *rotten at the ~, English to the ~*; remove ~ *from*, whence COR'ER(2) n. [Hence ~LESS (-rĭ-) a. [?]

cō-rela'tion. See CORRELATION.

cō-rel'igionist (-jo-), n. Adherent of same religion. [-IST]

coréop'sis, n. Plant with rayed usu. yellow flowers. [mod. L.f. Gk *koris* bug, *opsis* appearance, w. ref. to shape of seed]

cō-respon'dent, n. Person proceeded against together with the RESPONDENT in divorce suit. [CO-]

coíf, n. Large basket formerly used in mining; basket in which fish are kept alive in water. [cf. Du. *korf*, G *korb*, perh. f. L *corbis*]

corg'i (-gē), **-gy,** n. Small Welsh dog. [W]

cōriā'ceous (-shus), a. Like leather. [f. L *coriaceus* (*corium* leather, see -ACEOUS)]

cōrian'der, n. Annual plant with aromatic fruit (pop. called ~ seed) used for flavouring. [F, f. L *coriandrum* f. Gk *koriannon*]

Corin'thian, a. & n. (Native) of Corinth; (arch.) man of fashion & pleasure; *Epistles to the ~s*, books in N.T.; (Archit.) ~ *order*, one of the three Grecian ORDERS, having bell-shaped capital with rows of acanthus leaves, whence ~ESQUE' a. [f. L Gk *Korinthios* (*Korinthos*) +-AN]

cork, n. & a., & v.t. 1. Bark of ~ (-*tree*); piece of ~ used as float for fishing line etc. (*like a ~*, buoyant, recovering quickly from depression etc.); bottle-stopper of ~; (Bot.) inner division of the bark in higher plants; (adj.) made of ~, as ~ *jacket* (for supporting person in water; ~-*screw*, steel screw for drawing ~ from bottle, ~-*screw curl* (spirally twisted), (v.t. & i.) move spirally; ~-*wood*, name of various light porous woods. 2. v.t. Stop, stop up, (as) with ~, blacken with burnt ~. [(vb f. n.) f. Sp. *corcho* f. L *cortex -icis* bark; or f. Sp. *alcorque*, etym. dub.]

cork'age, n. Corking, uncorking, of bottles; hotel-keeper's charge for serving wine etc. not supplied by himself. [-AGE]

corked (-kt), a. Stopped with, blackened with burnt, cork; (of wine) gone bad from defective corking. [-ED¹]

cork'er, n. (sl.) Circumstance that precludes further discussion, esp. notable lie. [-ER¹]

cork'y, a. Cork-like; (colloq.) frivolous, lively, skittish, restive. [-Y²]

corm, n. (bot.) Bulb-like subterraneous stem, solid bulb. [f. Gk *kormos* trunk with boughs lopped off (*keirō* cut)]

cormo- in comb. Trunk, stem, (in terms referring to evolution of races etc.) [as prec.]

cor'morant, n. A voracious sea-bird, 3 ft in length; rapacious person. [f. F *cormo-ran* f. L *corvus marinus* sea-raven]

corn¹, n. A grain, seed, esp. of cereals (also of pepper etc.); (collect. sing.) grain, also cereal plants while growing; *maize, Indian ~*; ||~-*chandler*, retail dealer in ~; ~-*cob*, part to which grains are attached in ear of maize; ~-*cob pipe* (made of this); ~-*crake*, the bird Landrail; ~-*exchange* (tortradein~); ~-*factor*, dealer in ~; ~-*flag*, plant of genus Gladiolus; ~-*flour*, fine-ground Indian~, also, flour of rice or other grain; ~-*flower*, name of various plants growing among ~; ||~-*laws* (regulating ~-trade, esp. the English laws restricting importation, and repealed in 1846); varying with price of ~; ~-*rent* (paid in ~ or varying with price of ~); ~-*stalk* (colloq., tall person (applied as nickname to persons of European descent born in Australia, esp. in N.S.W.). [com.-Teut.; f. Aryan *grnom* (*ger*- wear down), cf. L *granum* grain]

corn², v.t. Sprinkle, preserve, with salt (esp. in p.p.). [f. prec.]

corn³, n. Horny place esp. on feet; *tread on my ~s*, hurt my feelings; ~-*plaster* (for application to ~s). [OF. f. L *cornu* horn]

corn'brash, n. (geol.). Coarse calcareous sandstone. [CORN¹+*brash* rubble, etym. dub.]

corn'ea, n. Transparent horny part of anterior covering of eyeball. [L *cornea (tela)* horny (web)]

corn'el, n. Genus including Cornelian Cherry & Common C~ or Dogwood. [ult. f. L *cornus*]

cornél'ian, car-, n. Dull red or reddish-white chalcedony. [f. F *cornaline*, etym.]

corne'ous, a. Horn-like, horny. [f. L *corneus* (*cornu* horn) +-OUS]

corn'er, n. & v.t. & i. 1. Place where converging sides or edges meet; projecting angle, esp. where two streets meet; *turn the ~*, pass round it into another street, (fig.) pass critical point (in illness etc.); *cut off a ~*, avoid it by a short cut; ||(sl.) *the C~*, Tattersall's betting-rooms (orig. near Hyde Park C~); hollow angle enclosed by meeting walls etc.; *put* (child) *in the ~* (as punishment); (fig.) *drive into a ~* (difficult position from which there is no escape). 2. Secret or remote place, as *done in a ~, hole-&-~ transactions* (underhand); region, quarter, as *all the ~s of the earth*. 3. (Commerc.) buying up the whole of any stock in the market, so as to com-

pel speculative sellers to buy from one to fulfil their engagements, (loosely) any combination to raise price by securing monopoly. **4.** (Association football and Hockey) free kick, hit, from the ~-flag given when the ball has been kicked, hit, over his own goal-line by an opponent. **5.** ~-chisel, -punch, etc. (angular, for cutting, cleaning, etc., ~s); ||~-boy, -man, street rough, loafer; ||~-man² (at either end of row of nigger minstrels, playing bones or tambourine & contributing comic effects); ~-stone, one in projecting angle of wall, (fig.) indispensable part, basis. **6. v.t.** Furnish with ~s, set in ~, drive into ~ (esp. fig.), force (dealers) or control (commodity) by means of ~. **7. v.i.** Form ~ (in commodity). [(vb f. n.) f. OF cornier ult. f. L cornu horn, see -ARY¹]

córn′et¹, n. (Also cornet-à-piston(s), cornopean) brass musical instrument of trumpet class, with valves operated by pistons; ~-player, also ~IST n.; conically-rolled piece of paper for groceries etc.; conical wafer filled with ice-cream; solo ~, echo ~, organ-stops. [OF, dim. of corn, cor, f. L cornu horn]

córn′et², n. White head-dress of Sister of Charity; || (formerly) fifth commissioned officer in cavalry troop, who carried the colours (from obs. sense pennon, standard), whence ~CY n. [f. F cornette dim. of corne f. Rom. corna f. L cornua horns]

córn′icle, n. (Archit.) horizontal moulded projection crowning a building etc., esp. uppermost member of entablature of an order, surmounting frieze; ornamental moulding round wall of room just below ceiling; (Mountaineering) overhanging mass of hardened snow at edge of precipice. Hence ~ED² (-st) a. [F, f. It., etym. dub.; L has corona cornice, corniz -icis crow]

córnif′erous, a. (geol.). Producing or containing hornstone. [f. L cornifer horn-bearing (cornu horn, see -FEROUS)]

Córn′ish, a. & n. **1.** Of Cornwall; ~ boiler, cylindrical flue-boiler; ~ Riviera, extreme South-West of England. **2. n.** The ~ language (extinct since 18th c.). [-ISH¹]

córnóp′ean. See CORNET¹.

córn′stone, n. Mottled red and green limestone, subordinate bed in Old Red Sandstone formation. [CORN¹]

córnucóp′ia, n. (pl. -as). Horn of plenty; goat's horn represented in art as overflowing with flowers, fruit, and corn; ornamental vessel shaped like this; overflowing store, whence ~AN a. [LL, f. L cornu copiae horn of plenty (that of the goat Amalthea by which Zeus was suckled)]

córnut′ed, a. Having horns or horn-like

projections. [f. obs. cornute f. L cornutus (cornu horn)+-ED¹]

córn′y², a. Of, abounding in, corn. [-Y²]

córn′y², a. Of, having, corns. [CORN²+-Y²]

coróll′a, n. (bot.). Whorl of leaves (petals), separate or combined, forming inner envelope of flower. Hence COROLL′ACEOUS (-ā′shus) a. [L, dim. of corona crown]

coróll′ary, n. Proposition appended to one already demonstrated, as self-evident inference from it; immediate deduction; natural consequence, result. [f. L corollarium money paid for chaplet, gratuity, neut. adj. f. prec., -ARY¹]

corón′a¹, n. (pl. -ae). **1.** Small disk of light round sun or moon; similar disk opposite sun, ANTHELION; halo of white light seen around disk of moon in total eclipse of sun (now known to belong to sun). **2.** Circular chandelier hung from roof of a church. **3.** (Archit.) member of cornice, with broad vertical face, usu. of considerable projection. **4.** (Anat.) various crown-like parts of body. **5.** (Bot.) appendage on top of seed or inner side of corolla. **6.** Brush discharge of electricity. [L, =crown]

coróna², n. A brand of Havana cigar. [Sp.; P]

|| **córón′ach** (-k), n. Funeral-song, dirge, in Scottish Highlands and Ireland. [Ir., =Gael. corranach (comh-together+ranach outcry)]

córón′al¹, n. Circlet (esp. of gold or gems) for the head; wreath, garland. [prob. f. AF +coronal (coroune f. CORONA²)]

córón′al² (also kó5), a. (Anat.) ~ suture, transverse suture of skull separating frontal bone (~ bone) from parietal bones; ~ of the crown of the head; (Bot.) of a corona. [F.f.L coronalis (CORONA¹, see -AL)]

có′ronate, -āted, aa. (bot. & zool.). Furnished with a corona or crown-shaped part. [f. L coronare (CORONA¹, see -ATE²)]

córóna′tion, n. Ceremony of crowning sovereign or sovereign's consort; ~-oath, taken by sovereign at ~. [OF (as prec., -ATION)]

có′roner, n. Officer of county, district, or municipality, holding inquest on bodies of persons supposed to have died by violence or accident; ~'s inquest, inquiry held by ~'s court as to cause of death; (orig.) officer charged with maintaining rights of private property of crown. Hence ~SHIP n. [f. AF corouner f. coroune CROWN, see -ER²(2)]

có′ronet, n. Small crown (implying dignity inferior to that of sovereign); fillet of precious materials, esp. as decorative part of woman's head-dress; garland; (Anat.) lowest part of horse's pastern. [f. OF coronette dim. of corone CROWN]

For compounds of ~ see co-.

co- not given consult co-.

co'roneted, a. Wearing a coronet (esp. as belonging to peerage). [f. -ED²]

coro'noid, a. (anat.). Curved like crow's beak (of processes of bones). [f. Gk korōnē crow +-OID]

corozo, n. (pl. -os). S.-American tree, from which vegetable ivory is made. [native]

corp'oral¹, a. Of the human body, as ~ punishment; personal; (arch.) ~ oath, one ratified by touching a sacred object. Hence ~LY² adv. [OF., f. L corporalis (corpus -oris body, see -AL¹)]

corp'oral², -as, n. Cloth on which consecrated elements are placed during celebration of mass. [f. med. L corporalis (palla) body-cloth (as prec.); -as f. OF corporaus, -als, nom. sing.]

corp'oral³, n. Non-commissioned officer ranking below sergeant (the little C~, Napoleon I); ~ ship's ~, officer attending to police matters under master-at-arms. [F., var. of caporal f. It. caporale prob. f. L corporalis (as prec.) confused w. capo head]

corpora'lity, n. Material existence; body; (pl.) bodily matters, wants, etc. [f. LL corporalitas (as CORPORAL², see -TY)]

corp'orate, a. Forming a body politic or corporation, as ~ body, body ~; ~ town (having municipal rights); forming one body of many individuals; of, belonging to, a body politic. Hence ~LY² (-tli) adv. [f. L corporare form into a body (corpus -oris), see -ATE²]

corpora'tion, n. United body of persons, esp. one authorized to act as an individual; artificial person created by charter, prescription, or act of the legislature, comprising many persons (~ aggregate) or one (~ sole); municipal ~, civic authorities of borough, town, or city; (colloq.) abdomen, esp. when prominent. [f. L corporatio (as prec., see -ATION)]

corp'orative, a. Of a corporation. [f. L corporativus (as prec., see -ATIVE)]

corp'orator, n. Member of a corporation. [as CORPORATE, see -OR²]

corpor'eal, a. Bodily; material; (Law) tangible, as ~ hereditament (of material objects). Hence ~ITY (-ǎl·) n., ~LY² adv. [f. L corporeus (corpus -oris body)+-AL]

corpore'ity, n. Quality of being or having a material body; bodily substance. [f. med. L corporeitas (as prec., see -TY)]

corp'osant, n. Ball of light sometimes seen on ship during storm, St Elmo's fire. [Port. corpo santo, It. corpo santo=L corpus sanctum holy body]

corps (kōr), n. (pl. same, pr. kōrz). 1. =ARMY ~. 2. Body of troops for special service. 3. A students' society in a German university. 4. ~ d'armée (dahmā), the army ~; ~ de ballet (see AP.), the company of dancers in a ballet; C~ Diploma-tique (dēplōmahtēk), all the doors & attaches of foreign states at a Court or capital. [F (as foll.)]

corpse, n. Dead (usu. human) body; ~-candle, lambent flame seen in churchyard or over grave, regarded as omen of death. [f. OF cors (mod. corps) f. L corpus body]

corp'ulent, a. Bulky (of body); fat. So ~ENCE, ~ENCY, nn. [F, f. L corpulentus (corpus body, see -ULENT)]

corp'us, n. (pl. -pora). Body, collection, of writings; ~ juris (joor'is), body of law; ~ delicti (dilik'tī), all that goes to make a breach of law; (Physiol.) structure of special character in the animal body; C~ Christi (kris'tī), Feast of the Blessed Sacrament (Thursday after Trinity Sunday). [L, = body]

corp'uscle (-sl), corp'uscule (-kūl), n. Minute body forming distinct part of the organism, esp. (pl.) those constituting large part of the blood in vertebrates; atom (esp. of electricity). [f. L corpusculum (as prec., see -CULE)]

corpu'scular, a. Of corpuscles or atoms; ~AR⁷ (EMISSION) theory of light. [as prec. +-AR²]

corral', n. & v.t. (-ll-). 1. Pen for horses, cattle, etc. (in U.S. & Span. Amer.); defensive enclosure of wagons in encampment; enclosure for capturing wild animals. 2. v.t. Form (wagons) into ~, confine in ~; [(vb f. n.) Sp. (corro ring of spectators f. correr toros give bull-fight f. L currere run).]

correct'¹, v.t. Set right, amend; substitute right text for (wrong); mark errors in (proof-sheet etc.) for amendment; admonish (person); cure (person) of fault; punish (person, fault); counteract (hurtful quality); bring into accordance with standard (reading of barometer etc.). [f. L corrigere rect-=regere guide)]

correct'², a. True, accurate; right, proper, (of conduct, manners, etc.) in accordance with a good standard (of taste etc.); the ~ card (sl.), programme of events at a sports-meeting etc., etiquette or one of its requirements. Hence ~LY² adv. ~NESS n. [as prec.]

correc'tion, n. Correcting; thing substituted for what is wrong; punishment, as house of ~ (bridewell). Hence ~AL (-sho-) a. [F, f. L correctionem (as prec., see -ION)]

correc'titude, n. Correctness esp. of conduct. [mod., = correct+rectitude]

correc'tive, a. & n. (Thing) serving, tending, to correct or counteract what is harmful. Hence ~LY² (-vl-) adv. [F (-if, -ive), as CORRECT¹, see -IVE]

correc'tor, n. One who corrects; censor, critic; ~ of the press, proof-reader; one who punishes. [f. AF correctour f. L corrector-em (as CORRECT¹), the com-...

corr'elate, n. Each of two related things (esp. so related that one implies the other). [BACK-f. L relatum p.p. of referre REFER]

có'rrĕlāte², v.i. & t. Have a mutual relation (with, to); bring (thing) into such relation (with another). [as prec.]

corrĕl'ative, a. & n. Having a mutual relation (with, to); analogous; (Gram., of words) corresponding to each other & regularly used together, e.g. either & or; (n.) ~ word or thing. Hence or cogn. corrĕlā'tion n.,~LY²(-vl-) adv., corrĕla'tiv'tY n. [COR-]

corréspónd', v.i. Be in harmony (with, to); be similar, analogous, (to); agree in amount, position, etc. (to); communicate by interchange of letters (with); ~ing member (of learned society etc.), honorary non-resident member with no voice in the society's affairs. Hence ~ingLY² adv. [f. med. L COR(respondēre RESPOND)]

corréspón'dence, n. Agreement, harmony, (with, to; between two); communication by letters; letters; ~ school (instructing by ~, and conducting ~ courses). [as prec., see -ENCE]

corréspón'dent, n. & a. One who writes letters (to person or newspaper, esp. one employed for that purpose, esp. our New York ~, war-~); person, firm, having regular business relations with another esp. in another country; (adj.) corresponding (to, with, or abs.), whence ~LY² adv. [as prec., -ENT]

có'rridōr, n. Main passage in large building, on which many rooms open; outside passage connecting parts of building; (Pol.) strip of a State's territory that runs through that of another & secures access to the sea etc. (Polish ~, through Prussia to Danzig); ‖ ~ train (with narrow passage from end to end). [F, f. It. corridore corridor for corridoio (correre run +-orio -ORY) by confus. w. corridore runner]

‖ có'rrie, n. (Sc.). Circular hollow on mountain side. [f. Gael. coire cauldron]

córrigén'dum, n. (pl. -da). Thing to be corrected (esp. fault in printed book). [L (as CORRECT¹, -ND²)]

corri'gible, a. Capable of being corrected; (of persons) submissive, open, to correction. [F (as CORRECT¹, see -BLE)]

corriv'al, n. = RIVAL. [COM-]

corrŏb'orant, a. & n. Strengthening (medicine); corroborating (fact). [F (as foll., see -ANT)]

corrŏb'orāte, v.t. Confirm formally (law etc.); confirm (person, statement) by evidence etc. Hence or cogn. ~ATIVE, ~ATORY, aa., ~ātor² n. [f. L COR(roborāre f. robur -oris hard wood), -ATE³]

corrŏborā'tion, n. Confirmation by further evidence. [F (as prec., see -ATION)]

corrŏb'oree, n. Native dance of Australian aborigines; [native]

corrōde', v.t. & i. Wear away, destroy gradually (of rust, chemical agents, diseases, & fig.); (v.i.) decay. So corrō'siōn (-zhn) n. [f. L COR(rodere rosus- gnaw)]

corrōs'ive, a. & n. (Thing) tending to corrode (lit. & fig.); ~ sublimate, (Commerc.) mercuric chloride, a strong acrid poison. Hence ~LY² (-vl-) adv., ~NESS (-vn-) n. [F (-if, -ive), as CORRODE, see -IVE]

có'rrugāte (-ōō-), v.t. & i. Contract into wrinkles or folds (b. & i.); mark with, bend into, ridges, as ~d iron. Hence có'rrugā'TION (-ōō-) n. [f. L COR(rugare f. ruga wrinkle), -ATE³]

có'rrugātor (-ōō-), n. Muscle that contracts the brow in frowning. [as prec., see -OR²]

corrupt¹, a. Rotten; depraved, wicked; influenced by bribery; (of language, texts, etc.) vitiated by errors or alterations; ~ practices, forms of bribery esp. at elections. Hence ~LY² adv., ~NESS n. [f. L COR(rumpere rupt- break)]

corrupt'², v.t. & i. Infect, taint, (lit. & fig.); bribe; destroy purity of (language); become corrupt. So corrup'tive a. [f. prec., displacing earlier corrump]

corrup'tible, a. Liable to corruption, perishable; capable of moral corruption. Hence or cogn.~BILITY n.,~biY²adv. [F, f. L corruptibilis (CORRUPT¹, -BLE)]

corrup'tion, n. Decomposition; moral deterioration; use of corrupt practices (bribery etc.); perversion (of language etc.) from its original state; (Law) ~ of blood, effect of attainder upon person attainted. [F, f. L corruptionem (as prec., see -ION)]

còrs'āc, -āk, n. (zool.). Tartar fox. [Turki]

còrs'āge (-ahzh or -ij), n. Bodice of woman's dress; bouquet (to be) worn there. [OF (cors body, see CORPSE & -AGE)]

còrs'air, n. Privateer, privateering vessel, esp. of Barbary. [f. F corsaire f. med. L cursarius (cursus -ūs inroad, f. currere run, -ARY¹)]

còrse, n. (arch., poet.). = CORPSE.

còrs'ĕt, -sĕlĕt (-sl-), n. Woman's closely fitting inner bodice stiffened with whalebone & fastened by lacing, stays. Hence ~RD² a. [F, dim. of OF cors body, see CORPSE]

còrs'lĕt, -sĕlĕt (-sl-), n. Piece of armour covering body; garment (usu. tight-fitting) covering body as distinct from limbs; (Zool.) insect's thorax, part between head & abdomen. [F (corse-), double dim. as prec.]

cortège (kôr'tāzh'), n. Train of attendants; procession. [F]

Còr'tĕs, n. pl. Two chambers making legislative assembly of Spain or Portugal. [Sp., Port.]

còr'tĕx, n. (pl. -tĭcēs). Bark; outer grey matter of brain, outer part of kidney. [L, = bark]

For compounds of co- not given consult co-.

cŏr'tical, a. (Bot.) of the bark or rind; (Anat., Zool.) forming the outer part of animal body or organ. [f. prec.+-AL]

cŏr'ticate, -āted, aa. Having bark; bark-like. [f. L *corticatus* (as prec., see -ATE²)]

corun'dum, n. Crystallized mineral of same species as sapphire & ruby, blue, grey, brown, black; mineral species of crystallized alumina. [f. Tamil *kurun-dam*]

cŏ'ruscāte, v.i. Sparkle, flash, (lit. & fig. of wit etc.). So **corus'cant** a., **corusca'-TION** n. [f. L *coruscare*, see -ATE³]

corvée (-vā), n. (feudal.) Day's work of unpaid labour due by vassal; statute labour, e.g. that exacted of French peasants before 1776. [F., f. Rom. *corvada* f. L.L *cōrrogāta* (*opera*) requisitioned (work) f. *rogare* ask]

corvětte, n. (naut.). Flush-decked war-vessel with one tier of guns (hist.); (now) small fast naval escort-vessel. [F., f. Sp. *corbeta*; cf. L *corbita* (*navis*) ship of burden (*corbis* basket)]

corvine, a. Of, akin to, the raven or crow. [f. L *corvinus* (*corvus* raven, see -INE¹)]

Cŏr'ybant, n. (pl. -s, -ēs). Priest of Phry-gian worship of Cybele, performed with extravagant dances. Hence **Cŏr̆yban'-tian, Cŏr̆yban'tic, Cŏr̆yban'tine** aa. [f. F *Corybante* f. L *Corybantem* (nom. -*as*)]

Cŏr'ydon, n. Typical rustic in pastoral poetry. [L, f. Gk *Korudōn*]

cŏr'ymb, n. (bot.). Species of inflorescence; raceme in which lower flower-stalks are proportionally longer. Hence ~OSE¹ a. [f. F *corymbe* f. L f. Gk *korum-bos* cluster]

cŏr'yphée (-fā), n. A leading dancer in a ballet. [F, as prec.]

coryphae'us, n. Leader of a chorus (also fig.). [L, f. Gk *koruphaios* (*koruphē* head)]

cory'za, n. Catarrh. [L, f. Gk *koruza* running at nose]

cos¹, n. (Also *Cos lettuce*) kind of lettuce introduced from Cos (now Stanchio). [f. Gk *Kōs*]

cos², n. Abbr. of COSINE.

cosaque (-ahk), n. Cracker bon-bon. [F]

cose (-z), v.i. Make oneself cosy. [back-formation on COSY, cf. LAZE f. *lazy*, & COZE]

cosec'ant, n. (trig.). Secant of complement of given angle (abbr. *cosec*). [co-]

cōseis'mal (-sīz-), a. & n. (Line or curve connecting points) of simultaneous shock from earthquake wave. [co-]

∥**cŏsh**, n., & v.t. (sl.). Bludgeon, life-preserver; (v.t.) strike with ~. [?]

cŏsh'er, v.t. Pamper, cocker up. [?]

cō-sig'natory, a. & n. (Person) signing jointly with others. [co-]

cō'sine, n. (trig.). Sine of complement of given angle (abbr. *cos*). [co-]

cŏs'lettize (-z-), v.t. Treat (steel, esp. cycle frames) with a special rust-prevent-ing process. [Inventor's name +-IZE]

cŏsmět'ic (-z-), a. & n. (Preparation) designed to beautify hair, skin, or complexion. [f. Gk *kosmētikos* (*kosmeō* adorn f. *kosmos* order, adornment, see -IC)]

cŏs'mic (-z-), a. Of the universe or cosmos (esp. as distinguished from the earth); ~ *philosophy*, = foll.; ~ *rays*, radiations that reach the earth equally from all directions, characterized by enormous voltages and high penetrating power. Hence **cŏs'mic(AL** a., ~**ally²** adv. [f. Gk *kos-mikos* (*kosmos* world, see -IC)]

cosmo- in comb.= Gk *kosmos* universe, as -*geny*, evolution of the universe; -*logy*, -*logist*, -*logical*, -*logically*, science of, student of, concerned with, the universe, -*plastic*, moulding the universe.

cŏsmŏg'ony (-z-), n. (Theory of) the creation of the universe. So **cŏsmŏgŏn'-IC(AL** aa., ~**IST**(3) n., -y. [f. Gk *kosmogo-nia* (COSMO-+-*gonia* f. -*gonos* -begetting)]

cŏsmŏg'raphy (-z-), n. Description, mapping, of general features of universe or earth. So **cŏsmŏg'rapher** n., **cosmographic(al)** aa., (-z-). [f. Gk *kosmographia*, see COSMO- -GRAPHY]

cŏsmŏp'olis (-z-), n. A cosmopolitan city. [f. COSMO-+Gk *polis* city]

cŏsmŏp'olitan (-z-), a. & n. Belonging to all parts of the world; (person) free from national limitations. ~**IZE** v.t. & i., (-z-). [f. foll.+-AN]

cŏsmŏp'olite (-z-), n. Citizen of the world; (adj.) free from national prejudices. Hence ~**ISM** n. [f. Gk *kosmopolitēs* (COSMO-+*politēs* citizen)]

cŏs'mos¹ (-z-), n. The universe as an ordered whole; ordered system of ideas, etc., sum-total of experience. [f. Gk *kosmos*]

cŏs'mos² (-z-), n. Plant bearing single dahlia-like blossoms of various colours. [f. Gk *kosmos* ornament.]

Cŏss'ack, n. Member of a people of south-eastern Russia, esp. as light horse in Russian army; ~ *post*, military outpost of a few mounted men. [f. Turki *quzzaq* adventurer]

cŏss'ét, n., & v.t. Pet lamb; (v.t.) pet, pamper. [(vb f. n.) perh.=OE *cotsǣta* cot-sitter (i.e. animal brought up in house)]

cost (-kaw-, kŏ-), n. Price (to be) paid for thing; *prime* ~ (also ~ *price*), that at which merchant buys; (pl.) law expenses,

cost esp. those allowed in favour of winning party; expenditure of time, labour, etc.; *at* ~, at the initial ~; *at all* ~*s*, cost what it may; *at the* ~ *of*, at the expense of losing; *count the* ~, consider the risks before action; *to a person's* ~, to his loss; ~ *accountant, clerk*, one who records every item of (esp. overhead) expenses in a business concern (with a view to checking wasteful expenditure); ~-*book* (showing expenses, profit, etc., of mine). Hence ~'LESS a. [OF (as foll.)]

cost² (kaw-, kŏ-), v.i. (*cost*). Be acquirable at, involve expenditure of, as ~ *him five shillings*, ~ *the writer infinite labour*; result in the loss of, as ~ *him his crown*; (Commerce) fix prices. No price is expressed adverbially, *in* being understood. [f. OF *coster*, *couster*, f. L CON(*stare* stand) with dative of person, locative of price]

cos'tal, a. Of the ribs. [F, f. med. L *costalis* (*costa* rib, see -AL)]

cos'tard, n. ‖ Large kind of apple; (arch.) head. [perh. f. OF *coste* rib (as prec.) +-ARD]

cos'tate, a. Ribbed, having ribs. [f. L *costatus* (as COSTAL, see -ATE²)]

‖ **cóstean'**, **-een**, v.i. (mining). Sink pits down to rock to find direction of lode. [f. Corn. *cothas stean* dropped tin]

‖ **cos'ter(monger)** (-tŭngg-), n. Man who sells fruit, fish, etc., from barrow in street. [COSTARD]

cos'tive, a. With confined bowels, constipated; (fig.) niggardly. Hence ~NESS (-vn-) n. [f. OF *costivé* f. L *constipatus* CONSTIPATED]

cost'ly (kaw-, kŏ-), a. Of great value; expensive. Hence ~INESS n. [-LY¹]

cŏs'mary, n. Aromatic perennial plant, formerly used in medicine & for flavouring ale. [OE *cost* f. L f. Gk *kostos* + (St) Mary]

cŏst'ume (also -tūm'), n., & v.t. Style, fashion of dress or attire (including way of wearing hair); complete set of outer garments; ~ *piece*, play in which actors wear historical ~; (v.t.) provide with ~. [(vb f. n.) F, f. It. *costume* f. L *consuetudinem* CUSTOM]

cŏstüm'ier, **-üm'er**, n. Maker of, dealer in, costumes. [F (-*ier*), f. *costumer* (COSTUME)]

cŏs'y (-z-), **-zy**, a. & n. Comfortable, snug, (of person or place); (n.) canopied corner seat for two (cf. F *causeuse*); *tea, egg,* ~, quilted covering to retain heat in teapot, egg. Hence **cŏs'ILY²** adv., **cŏs'INESS** n., (-z-). [?]

cŏt¹, n., & v.t. (-tt-). Small erection for shelter, as *bell-, sheep-,* ~; (poet.) cottage; (v.t.) put (sheep) in ~. [vb f. n.) OE, f. OTeut. †*kutom*]

cŏt², n. (Anglo-Ind.) light bedstead; (Naut.) swinging bed for officers, sick persons, etc.; ‖ small (usu. swinging) bed for child; bed in children's hospital. [Anglo-Ind., f. Hind. *khaṭ* bedstead, bier]

cŏt³, n. Abbr. of foll.

cotán'gent (-j-), n. (trig.). Tangent of complement of given angle (abbr. *cot*). [CO-]

côte, n. Shed, stall, shelter, esp. for animals as *dove-, hen-, sheep-,* ~. [OE, parallel to cor¹]

co-temporary etc. See CONTEMPORARY etc.

cō-ten'ant, n. Joint tenant. [CO-]

cŏt'erie, n. Circle, set, of persons associated by exclusive interests; select circle in society. [F, orig.=association of country people, f. *coster* COTTAR, see -ERY]

cothûr'nus, n. (pl. -*ni*). Buskin, thick-soled boot of Athenian tragic actor (also fig., of elevated style etc.). [L, f. Gk *kothornos*]

cō-tid'al, a. ~ *line* on map (connecting places at which high water occurs at same time). [CO-]

cotill'ion, **-llon**, (-lyon), n. Name of several dances; music for these. [F (-*llon*), =petticoat]

cŏtōneás'ter, n. (Kinds of small tree or shrub of N. Europe, resembling hawthorn and bearing rose-red berries. [f. L *cotonea* quince + ASTER]

cŏtt'a, n. Short surplice. [med. L, = tunic]

cŏtt'age, n. Labourer's or villager's small dwelling; small country residence; ~ *hospital* (in-, without resident medical staff); ~ *loaf*, loaf of bread (of two round masses, smaller on top of larger); ~ *piano* (small upright). [prob. f. AF +*cotage* (COTE + -AGE)]

cŏtt'ager (-tĭj), n. Inhabitant of a cottage. [-ER¹]

cŏtt'ar, **-er¹**, n. Scots peasant occupying cottage on farm, and labouring on farm at fixed rate when required; = COTTIER. [f. med. L *cotarius* (*cota* COTE, see -ARY¹)]

cŏtt'er², n. Key, wedge, bolt, for securing parts of machinery etc.; esp., split pin that opens after passing through hole; ~*pin*, pin to keep ~ in place. [?]

‖ **cŏtt'ier**, n. Cottager: Irish peasant holding under ~ *tenure* (letting of land in small portions at rent fixed by competition). [OF (as COTTAR)]

cŏtt'on¹, n. White downy fibrous substance clothing seeds of ~*plant*, used for making cloth, thread, etc.; ~*plant*; thread spun from ~ yarn (also *sewing*-~); cloth made of ~; GUN~; ~*cake*, compressed ~ seed as food for cattle; ~*grass*, kinds of plant with white silky hairs; ‖~*lord*, magnate of ~ trade; ~ *spinner*, workman who spins ~-

For compounds of *co-* not given consult co-.

of. ~ **mill**; ~ **tail**, common American rabbit, with white fluffy tail; ~ **waste**, refuse yarn used for cleaning machinery etc.; || ~ **wool**, raw ~, esp. as prepared for wadding; ~ **yarn**, ~ prepared for weaving into fabrics. Hence ~Y² a. [f. F. OSp. *coton* f. Arab. *qutun*]

cŏtt'on², v.i. Agree, harmonize, (*together, with each other*); ~ **up**, make friendly advances (to or abs.); become attached to; ~ **on to** (person, thing), take to him, it; ~**ed (to)**, (sl.) understand. [f. prec.]

Cŏttonŏ'polis n. (joc.), Manchester. [COTTON¹+-o-+-POLIS city]

cŏttonŏ'cracy n. The magnates of the cotton trade. So **Cŏttonŏ'polis** n. (joc.), ...

cŏtt'ony, a. [-OUS]

cotylé'don (anat.). Cup-shaped. [f. Gk *kotuloeidēs* (*kotulē* cup, see -OID)]

cotyledon (-lē-), n. Primary leaf in embryo of higher plants; seed-leaf; genus of plants including navelwort or pennywort. [f. L f. Gk *kotulēdōn* cup-shaped cavity (*kotulē* cup)]

cotylé'donous, a. Having cotyledons. [-OUS]

couch¹, n. Bed; thing one sleeps on; lounge like sofa, but with half-back and head-rest only; (Malting) bed in which grain germinates after steeping. [f. F *couche* (as foll.)]

couch² v.t. & i. Lay oneself down (now only in p.p.); (Malting) lay (grain) on floor to germinate; lower (spear etc.) to position of attack; remove (cataract); also ~ *person, person's eye*, for cataract; express (thought etc. in words); veil (meaning *under* words); (of animals) lie (esp. in lair); crouch, cower; lie in ambush. [f. F *coucher* f. L *collocare* place]

couch³ (kow-, kōō-), n. (More usu. ~-**grass**) kind of grass with long creeping roots, a common weed. [var. of QUITCH]

couch'ant, a. (her.). (Of animals) lying with body resting on legs and head raised. [F part. as COUCH²]

Couéism (kōō'āizm), n. Systematic auto-suggestion of a sanguine kind. [Emile Coué, French psychologist (d. 1926), +-ISM]

cougar (kōō-), n. Large American feline quadruped, puma. [f. F *couguar* repr. Guarani *guaçu ara*]

cough (kawf, kŏf), n. Act of coughing; tendency to cough, diseased condition of respiratory organs. [f. foll.]

cough² (as prec.), v.i. & t. Expel air from lungs with violent effort and noise produced by abrupt opening of glottis; (trans.) ~ **out, up**, eject by, say with, cough; ~ **down**, silence (speaker) by reluctance, bring out, produce. [ME *coughen*; Du. *kuchen*, cough, G *keuchen*; cf. MDu. *kuchen*]

could. See CAN².

4895

coulisse (koolēs'), n. (Usu. pl.) wings in theatre; space between two of these; groove in which sluice-gate moves. [F. f. OF *couleis* f. L *colaticius* (*colare* flow)]

couloir (koolwahr'), n. Steep gully on mountain side. [F]

coulomb (koolom'), n. Quantity of electricity conveyed in one second by current of one ampere. [de C~, French physicist]

coulter (kōl-), *cŏl-, n. Iron blade fixed in front of share in plough. [OE *culter* f. L *culter* f.]

coumarin (koo-), n. Aromatic crystalline substance found in seeds of Tonka bean &c. Hence, &c. [f. F *coumarine* (*cumarú*, name in Guiana of Tonka bean), see -IN]

council, n. Ecclesiastical assembly, as *oecumenical, diocesan,* ~; (N.T.) Jewish Sanhedrin; advisory or deliberative assembly, as (Hist.) *Great C~,* ~ of tenants-in-chief & great ecclesiastics (last summoned in 1640), CABINET ~; body of councillors, || as PRIVY ~ (*the King, C~ of Crown, in C~,* Privy C~ as issuing Orders in C~ or receiving appeal petitions from colonies etc., *C~ of State* (of foreign countries); || body assisting governor of British crown colony or dependency or local administrative body of town, city, or administrative county, as *County C~; C~ of War,* assembly of officers called (in some foreign countries); permanent military board; ~-**board**, table at which ~ sits; ~-**chamber**, -**house** (in which ~ meets); (1) in eccles. sense f. OF *cuncile* f. L *concilium* assembly, meeting (*calare* call); (2) f. OF *conseil* f. L *consilium* advisory body. COUNSEL; E confused the two words; acc. to mod. different. (begun in 16th c.) *council*=any deliberative body, *counsel*=act of counselling, advice, etc.]

councillor, n. Member of a council. [COUNCIL+-OR]

counsel, n. Consultation; *take* ~, consult (*with* or abs.); advice; (Theol.) ~ *of perfection,* injunction (orig. of Christ or Apostles) not regarded as universally binding (*Matt.* xix. 21); plan; *keep one's (own)* ~ *or another's* ~ (secret); body of legal advisers in cause; barrister; *Queen's, King's, C~* (abbr. Q.C., K.C.), ~ to the crown, taking precedence of other barristers. [f. OF *conseil* f. L *consilium* f. *sal-* jump = Skr. *sar-* go) deliberative body, plan, cf. COUNCIL]

counsel², v.t. (-ll-), Advise (person to do); recommend (thing, that). [f. F *conseiller* f. LL *consiliare* (L -ari), as prec.]

counsellor, n. Adviser; (also ~-**at-law**) advising barrister (now only in Ireland). [f. OF *conseillere, -or,* f. L *consiliator(em)* as prec., -OR²]

count¹, n. Counting; one's reckoning (*keep, lose,* ~; *be aware, fail to know, how many there have been*); sum total;

K

(Law) each charge in an indictment; || (H. of Commons) ~out, ~, adjournment when fewer than 40 members are present; ~out (Boxing), counting of 10 sec. to give fallen man time to rise, failing which he loses the match. [f. OF conte f. LL computum (as foll.)]

count³, v.t. & i. Enumerate, reckon up; repeat numerals in order; ~ up, find the sum of; ~ out, ~ while taking from a stock; (of boxer) be ~ed out, fail to rise in time (see prec.); || ~ out the House, procure adjournment (as prec.); include in reckoning; consider (a thing) to be (so & so); ~ on, upon, expect confidently; be included in reckoning, as that does not ~ for, be worth (much etc.); (Sc.) ~ kin (with), be demonstrably related (to). [f. OF conter COMPUTE]

count⁴, n. Foreign noble corresp. to earl; ~ PALATINE. Hence ~SHIP n. [f. OF conte f. L comitem (nom. -mes) companion]

count'enance¹, n. Expression of face, as ~ change (one's) ~ (from emotion), keep one's ~, maintain composure, esp. refrain from laughing; face; composure, as put out of ~, disconcert, keep (person) in ~ (usu. by show of support). [f. OF contenance bearing, aspect, f. L continentia (as CONTAIN, see -ENCE)]

count'enance², v.t. Sanction (act); encourage (person, practice, person in practice). [f. OF contenancer (as prec.)]

count'er¹, n. 1. Small (usu. round) piece of metal, ivory, etc., used for keeping account in games, esp. cards; imitation coin. 2. Banker's table; table in shop on which money is counted out & across which goods are delivered; ~-jumper, (derog.) shopman. [f. OF conteor f. L computatorium (as COMPUTE, see -ORY(2)]

count'er², n. Part of horse's breast between shoulders and under neck; curved part of stern of ship. [perth. f. COUNTER⁵]

count'er³ n. (fencing). Circular parry in which hand retains same position while point describes a circle. [f. F contre COUNTER-]

count'er⁴ n. (shoemaking). Back part of shoe or boot round heel. [abbr. of COUNTERFORT]

count'er⁵ a. Opposed; opposite; duplicate; ~ (rocking turn or rocker), skating figure (see ROCK³). [arising f. comb. w. COUNTER-]

count'er⁶, v.t. & i. Oppose, contradict; (Chess) meet with counter move; (Boxing) give (opponent, or abs.) return blow while parrying. [partly f. ENCOUNTER, partly f. COUNTER-]

count'er⁷, adv. In the opposite direction, as hunt, run, go, ~ (i.e. to direction taken by game); contrary, as act, go, ~ (to instructions etc.). [f. F contre COUNTER-]

count'er⁸, n. (Abbr. for) counter rocking turn (see ROCK³).

coun'ter-, pref. f. F contre (It. contra) f. L contra against, in return, orig. in words f. OF, F, or It., but now a living prefix of vbs., nouns, adjj., and advv., with sense (1) reciprocation, opposition, frustration, rivalry, (2) opposite position or direction, (3) correspondence, match, (of things having naturally two opposite parts), (4) duplicate, substitute.

counter-a'gent, n. Counteracting agent or force. [COUNTER-(1)]

coun'ter-approach, n. (mil.). Work constructed by besieged outside permanent fortifications to check besiegers. [COUNTER-(1)]

coun'ter-atta'ck, n., & v.t. & i. Sortie, charge, etc., in reply to attack by enemy; (v.t. & i.) make ~ (upon). [COUNTER-(1)]

coun'ter-attra'c'tion, n. Attraction of contrary tendency; rival attraction. [COUNTER-(1)]

coun'terbal'ance, n., & v.t. Weight balancing another; (v.t.) act as ~ to. [COUNTER-(1)]

coun'terblast (-ah-), n. Energetic declaration against something. [COUNTER-(1)]

coun'ter-ceiling (-sēl-), n. Layer of dry material between joists of floor. [COUNTER-(4)]

counterchange' (-j-), v.t. & i. Interchange; chequer; (v.i.) change places or parts. [f. F contrechanger (see COUNTER-(1) and CHANGE v.)]

coun'tercharge, n. Charge in opposition to another, charge against accuser. [COUNTER-(1)]

coun'tercheck, n. Check that opposes a thing; check that operates against another; (arch.) retort (the ~ quarrelsome, see As You Like It, v. iv. 85). [COUNTER-(1)]

coun'ter-claim, n. Claim set up against another; claim set up by defendant in suit. [COUNTER-(1)]

coun'ter-clock'wise (-z). See CLOCK¹.

coun'ter-es'pionage (or -ahzh?), n. Spying directed against the enemy's spy system. [COUNTER-(1)]

coun'terfeit¹ (-fit, -fēt), a. & n. (Thing) made in imitation, not genuine, (of coins, writings, persons, etc.). [f. OF contrefet, -fait, p.p. of contrefaire f. med. L CONTRA- (facere make)]

coun'terfeit² (-fit, -fēt), v.t. Imitate; forge (coin, bank-notes, handwriting); simulate (feelings); (fig.) resemble closely. [f. prec.]

coun'terfoil, n. Complementary part of bank cheque, official receipt, etc., with

For compounds of co- not given consult co-.

note of particulars, retained by drawer. [COUNTER-(3)]

coun'terfoŕt, n. Buttress supporting wall or terrace. [f. F *contrefort*(COUNTER-, FORT)]

counter-ir'ritant, n. Thing used to produce surface irritation and thus counteract disease (also fig.). So counter-irritā'tion n. [COUNTER-(1)]

countermand' (-ah-), v.t., & n. (Command); recall (person, forces, etc.) by contrary order; cancel order for (goods etc.); (n.) order revoking previous one. [f. OF *contremander*(COUNTER-(1) & CONTRA(*mandare* order)]

coun'termarch, v.i. & t., & n. (Cause to) march in the contrary direction. [COUN-TER-(2)]

coun'termark, n. Additional mark, for greater security etc.; additional mark on bale of goods belonging to several merchants; hallmark added to that of the maker. [f. F *contremarque*, see COUNTER-(3) & MARK]

coun'termine, n., & v.t. & i. (Mil.) mine made to intercept that of besiegers; submarine mine sunk to explode enemy's mines by its explosion; (fig.) counterplot; (v.t.) oppose by ~; (v.i.) make a ~, behind another as reserve defence. [f. F *contremine* (COUNTER-(2), *mine* f. L *mina* wall)]

coun'terpane (-in, -ān), n. Outer covering of bed, coverlet, quilt. [f. obs. *counter-point* f. OF *contrepointe* corrupt. of *cuilte pointe* f. L *culcita puncta* stitched QUILT; assim. to PANE in obs. sense *cloth*]

coun'terpart, n. Duplicate; person, thing, forming natural complement to another; opposite part of INDENTURE. [COUNTER-(3)]

coun'terplot, n. & v.t. & i. (-tt-), n. Plot contrived to defeat another; (vb) frustrate by ~, devise ~ (against). [COUNTER-(1)]

coun'terpoint, n. (mus.). Melody added as accompaniment to given melody; art, mode, of adding melodies as accompaniment according to fixed rules; *double, triple,* etc., ~, invertible ~, in which the melodies can be changed in position above and below one another; *strict* ~ (acc. to code of rules as academic exercise, not as actual composition). [f. OF *contrepoint* f. med. L CONTRA*punctum* pricked opposite, i.e. to the original melody (*pungere punct-* prick)]

coun'terpoise¹ (-z), v.t. Counterbalance; compensate; bring into, keep in, equilibrium (lit. & fig.). [f. OF *contrepeser* f. L *pensare* weigh]

coun'terpoise¹ (-z), n. Counterbalancing weight; thing of equivalent force etc. on opposite side; equilibrium. [f. OF *contre-pois* (*contre* COUNTER-(1) + *pois* f. L *pensum* weight]

coun'tershaft (-ah-), n. Intermediate shaft driven from main shaft to transmit motion to particular parts of a system of machinery. [COUNTER-(1)]

coun'tersign¹ (-īn), n. Watchword, pass-word, given to all men on guard (cf. PAROLE); mark used for identification etc. [f. F *contresigne* (see COUNTER-(3) & SIGN)]

coun'tersign² (-īn), v.t. Add signature to (document already signed); ratify. [f. F *contresigner* (as prec.)]

countersink, v.t. Bevel off (top of hole) to receive head of screw or bolt; sink (screw-head) in such hole. [COUNTER-(3)]

counter-tĕn'or, n. (mus.). (Part for, singer with) male voice higher than tenor, alto. [f. obs. F *contre-teneur* (see CONTRA- & TENOR)]

countervail', v.t. & i. Counterbalance (esp. in ~*ing duly*, one put on imports that are bounty-fed to give home goods an equal chance); avail against. [f. OF *contravaloir* f. L CONTRA *valēre*]

coun'terweight (-wāt), n. Counterbalancing weight. [COUNTER-(1)]

coun'terwork, n. & v.t. & i. (Mil.). work raised in opposition to those of enemy; (gen.) opposing work; (v.t.) counteract, frustrate; (v.i.) work in opposition. [COUNTER-(1)]

coun'tess, n. Wife, widow, of count or earl; lady ranking with count or earl in her own right. [f. OF *contesse* f. L.L *comitissa* fem. of *comes -itis* COUNT³]

coun'tless, a. Too many to count. [-LESS]

coun'ting-house, n. Building, room, devoted to keeping accounts; office.

coun'trified, -ryfied, (kŭn-; -īd), a. Rural, rustic, in appearance, manners, etc. [p.p. of *countrify*, else little used (COUNTRY + -FY)]

coun'try (-kŭn-), n. Region; territory of a nation; land of a person's birth, citizenship, etc., fatherland; rural districts as opp. to towns, esp. the rest of a land as opp. to the capital; (Cricket sl.) *in the ~*, far from the wickets; ~ (body of electors); ~ *club* (orig. U.S.), club with its quarters in a rural district for the sake of outdoor sports; ~ *cousin*, relation of countrified manners or appearance; ~ *house*, ~ *seat*, residence of ~ *gentleman*; ‖ ~ *note*, bank-note issued by local bank; ~ *party*, political party supporting agricultural, against manufacturing interests; ~ *-side*, parti-cular rural district, its inhabitants. [f. OF *contrée* f. LL *contrata* land lying opposite (CONTRA)]

coun'ter-reformā'tion, n. Reformation running counter to another, esp. that in Church of Rome following on Protestant Reformation. [COUNTER-(1)]

coun'terscarp, n. (fortif.). Outer wall or slope of ditch, supporting covered way. [f. F *contrescarpe* f. It. CONTRA(*scarpa* SCARP)]

coun'try dance, n. Any rural or native English dance, esp. those in which couples stand face to face in two long lines. [COUNTRY + DANCE; perverted to *contre-dance* etc.]

coun'tryman, n. (fem. *coun'trywoman*). Man of one's own (or a specified) country; person living in rural parts.

coun'ty, n. Territorial division in Great Britain and Ireland, chief unit for administrative, judicial, and political purposes; administrative division in most British colonies: *political and administrative division next below State; people of a ~; ~ PALATINE; || ~ corporate, || ~ borough, one of over 50,000 inhabitants ranking (since 1888) as administrative ~; ~ council, representative governing body of administrative ~; ~ court, || local court esp. for recovery of small debts, whence ~-court (v.t. colloq.), sue in this; || ~ family (with ancestral seat in a ~); ~ town, seat of ~ administration: || the ~, familics, so ~ attrib. [f. OF *counté* f. L *comitatus* (as COUNT², see -ATE¹)]

coup (kōō), n. Notable or successful stroke or move; (Billiards) direct holing of ball; ~ *d'état* (dētah'), violent or illegal change in government; ~ *de grâce* (de grahs), finishing stroke; ~ *de main* (see Ap.), sudden vigorous attack; ~ *d'œil* (dü'ö), comprehensive glance, general view; ~ *de théâtre* (tāah'tr), dramatically sudden or sensational act. [F. f. LL *colpus* f. L f. Gk *kolaphos* blow]

coupé (kōōp'ā), n. Four-wheeled close carriage for two inside & driver; || half-compartment at end of railway carriage. [F., p.p. of *couper* cut, as noun]

cou'ple¹ (kŭ-), n. Leash for holding two hounds together, whence (fig.) *go, hunt, run, in ~s*; pair, brace, esp. of hunting dogs (collect. sing. for pl., as *15 ~*); wedded or engaged pair; pair of partners in dance; *a ~ of*, two; pair of rafters (Dynam.) pair of equal and parallel forces acting in opposite directions. [f. OF *cople* f. L COPULA]

cou'ple² (kŭ-), v.t. & i. Fasten, link, together (often dogs in pairs); connect (railway carriages) by a coupling; unite, bring together, (persons); marry (t. & i.); associate in thought or speech (two things *together, one with another*); (v.i.) unite sexually. [f. OF *copler* (as prec.)]

coup'ler (kŭ-), n. In vbl senses; esp. contrivance for connecting two manuals, or manual with pedals, or notes with their octaves above or below (*octave ~*), of organ. [prec. + -ER¹]

coup'let (kŭ-), n. Pair of successive lines of verse. [F., dim. of COUPLE]

coup'ling (kŭ-), n. In vbl senses; esp. link connecting railway carriages; contrivance for connecting parts of machinery. [-ING¹]

coup'on (kōō-), n. Detachable ticket entitling holder to periodical payments of interest, services of excursion agency, ration under food-control, etc. (*clothing, petrol, ~*, entitling holder to ration of clothing, and petrol); ||(Pol. sl.) party leader's recognition of parliamentary candidate as deserving election; voucher given with retail purchase, a certain number of which entitle holder to a 'free gift' (so ~ *system*). [F. = piece cut off (*couper*, see COUPÉ, -OON]

cour'age (kŭ-), n. Bravery, boldness, as *take, pluck up, lose, ~*; (Gallicism) *take one's ~ in both hands*, nerve oneself to a venture; *Dutch*~ (induced by drinking); ~ *of one's opinions*, ~ to act up to them. [OF (*cœur* f. L *cor* heart, see -AGE)]

courā'geous (kŭrā'jŭs), a. Brave, fearless. Hence ~LY² adv., ~NESS n. [f. OF *corageus* f. prec., see -OUS]

cou'rier (kōō-), n. Servant employed to make travelling arrangements on continent; title of newspapers, as *Liverpool C~*; running messenger. [(1) ME *corour* f. OF *coreor* f. LL *curriörem* (*currere* currere run, see -OR³); (2) 16th-c. f. It. *corriere* (*corre* run f. L *currere*)]

cour'lan (koor-), n. Long-billed rail-like wading bird of tropical America, noted for its dismal cry; Crying Bird, limpkin. [F]

course¹ (kōrs), n. 1. Onward movement; pursuit of game esp. of hares with (grey)hounds; direction taken, as *hold, take, change, one's ~, ship's ~, a dangerous ~* (line of conduct); ~ *of events*, ~ *of nature* (ordinary procedure); (pl.) *evil ~s* (behaviour). 2. Ground on which race is run (also *race~*); channel in which water flows; golf links. 3. ~ *of* EXCHANGE. 4. Career; series (of lectures etc.); rota for duty among members of cathedral body. 5. Each of successive divisions of meal (esp. soup, fish, joint, etc.). 6. Continuous layer of stone etc. in building. 7. (Naut.) *fore, main, ~, fore, main, ~sail*. 8. *In the ~ of*, during; *by ~ of*, according to ordinary procedure of (law etc.); *in due ~*, in the natural order; *of ~*, naturally; *matter of ~*, natural thing. [partly f. F *cours* f. L *cursus-ûs* (as COURIER); partly f. F *course* fem. noun f. L p.p. of *currere* run, cf. -ADE¹]

course² (kōrs), v.t. & i. Pursue (game, as prec.); run about, run, (esp. of liquids); give (horse) a run; use (hounds) in coursing. [f. prec.]

cours'er, n. (poet.). Swift horse. [f. OF *corsier* f. L +*cursarius* (*cursus* COURSE, see -ARY¹); orig. = warhorse, charger]

court¹ (kōrt), n. 1. (Also ~'yard) space enclosed by walls or buildings; ||(Camb.

For compounds of co- not given consult co-.

Univ.) college quadrangle; subdivision of an Exhibition building, museum, etc., open to the general public; ||confined yard opening off street. 2. Enclosed quad-rangular area, open or covered, for games, as *tennis*, *fives*, ~; plot of ground marked out for lawn-tennis. 3. ||Sovereign's residence; his establishment and retinue; the body of courtiers; ||sovereign and his councillors as ruling power, as *C~ of St James's* (British sovereign's ~); assembly held by sovereign, state reception; *High C~* (assembly) *of Parliament*. 4. Assembly of judges or other persons acting as tribunal, as ~ *of law*, *law~*, ~ *of justice*, ~ *of judicature*, COUNTY, criminal, POLICE, &c. *C~ of ADMIRALTY*, *COMMON pleas*, EQUITY, etc.; place, hall, in which justice is administered; *out of ~*, (of plaintiff, and of arguments) not entitled to be heard. 5.(Meeting of) qualified members of com-pany or corporation; (in some friendly societies)=LODGE[1]. 6. Attention paid to one whose favour, affection, interest, is sought, as *pay ~ to*. 7.||*~-card* (orig. *coat-card*), king, queen, knave; ||*~ circular*, daily report of ~ doings published in newspapers; ||*~ guide*, directory contain-ing (theoretically) names of those who have been presented at ~; ~ *martial*, judicial ~ of military or naval officers, (held round upturned drum in time of war); (formerly used by ladies at for ents etc. (v.t. *~plaster*, sticking-plaster ~ *martial* ||by this; *drumhead* ~ for face-patches); ~ *roll*, manorial court register of holdings (see cory[1]). [f. OF *cort* f. L *c(h)ortem* (nom. *-ors*), yard, COHORT; the senses of assembly, judicial court, by confus. in f with L *curia*]

court (kōrt), v.t. Pay court to; make love to (also abs.); entice (person, *into*, *to*, *from*, etc.); seek to win (applause etc.); invite (inquiry etc.; *you are ~ing disaster*) [prec.]

court'eous (kō-, kĕ-), a. Polite, kind, considerate, in manner or address. Hence ~LY[2] adv., ~NESS n. [f. OF *corteis*, see COURT[1]]

courtesan, -zan (kŏrtĭzăn'), n. Prosti-tute. [f. F *courtisane* f. It. *cortigiana* fem. adj. as n. (as prec. +*-ano* -AN)]

court'esy (kō-, kĕ-), n. Courteous behaviour or disposition; *by ~*, by favour, not of right; ||*~ title*, one held by ~, having no legal validity; ||(Law) ~ *of England*, *Scotland*, husband's tenure after wife's death of certain kinds of property inherited by her; =CURTSY. [f. OF *cortesie* =It. *cortesia* (*cortese* COURTEOUS)]

court'ier (kō-, kĕ-), n. Attendant at, fre-quenter of, sovereign's court. [prob. f. OF *cortoyer*, *cortoyeur* v.b (*corte* COURT[1])]

court'ly (kō-), a. Polished, refined, in manners; obsequious, flattering. Hence ~NESS n. [-LY[1]]

cous'cous(sou) (kōō'skōōsōō), n. African dish of granulated flour steamed over broth, freq. with meat added. [F, f. Arab. *kuskus* (*kaskasa* bruise)]

cous'in (kŭzn), n. (Also *first ~*, *~german*) child of one's uncle or aunt; *my second ~*, my parent's first ~'s child; *my first ~ (second etc.) ~ once (twice etc.) removed*, child (etc.), also, my parent's (grand-parent's etc.) first (second etc.) ~; *call ~s*, claim kinship (*with*); title used by sovereign in addressing another sovereign or a nobleman of same country; ||*~ Jacky*, (nickname for) Cornishman. Hence ~HOOD, ~SHIP, nn., ~LY[1] a., (kŭzn-). [F, f. L CON(*sobrinus*, *-na*, f. *soror* sister) ~ by mother's side]

cŏüte que cŏüte (kōōtkekōōt'), adv. At all costs. [F]

couvade (kōōvahd'), n. Primitive people's custom by which husband feigns illness and is put to bed when his wife lies in. [obs. F, f. *couver* hatch]

cove[1], n. Small bay or creek; sheltered recess; (Archit.) concave arch, curved junction of wall with ceiling or floor. [com.-Teut.: OE *cofa*]

cove[2], v.t. Arch (esp. ceiling at junction with wall); slope (fireplace sides) inwards. [prec.]

cove[3], n. (sl.), Fellow, chap. [thieves' cant, etym. dub.]

cŏv'en (kŭ-), n. (Sc.), Assembly of witches. [var. of AF *covent*, see CONVENT]

cŏv'enant (kŭ-), n., & v.t. & i. Compact, bargain; (Law) contract under seal, clause of this; (Bibl.) compact between God and the Israelites, as ARK *of ~*, *land of the ~* (Canaan); *Solemn League and C~* (establishing Presbyterianism in England and Scotland, 1643); *C~ of the League of Nations*, document constituting the League, incorporated in the Treaty of Versailles & other treaties concluding the first world war (1919); (v.t. & i.) agree (*with person for thing*, *to do*, *that*). [vb f. n.) OF, part. of *convenir*, see CONVENE]

cŏv'enanted (kŭ-), a. Bound by a covenant, esp. of Indian Civil servants (*the ~ service*). [-ED[1]]

cŏv'enanter (kŭ-), n. One who covenants, esp. (Sc. Hist.) adherent of the National Covenant (1638) or Solemn League & ~. [-ER[1]]

Cŏv'ent Gàrden, n. (Used for) the fruit and vegetable market in London. [*covent*, =CONVENT]

Cŏv'entry (kŭ-), n. Town in War-wickshire; *send person to ~*, refuse to associate with him.

cŏv'er[1] (kŭ-), v.t. Overspread, overlay, (with cloth, lid, etc., also fig. *with disgrace* etc.); strew thoroughly (*with*); lie over, be a covering over; extend over, occupy the surface of; protect; *~ing letter*,

explanatory one with enclosure; (of fortress, guns, etc.) command (territory); conceal (feelings etc.); ~ with gun, present gun at; (Mil., Cricket) stand behind (front-rank man, another player to stop balls he misses); ~point, fielder ~ing point, his place); include, comprise; (Journalism) report (proceedings of a meeting, public dinner, etc.); suffice to defray (expenses); protect by insurance; (of stallion) copulate with; ~ in, complete the covering of, fill in (grave etc.) with earth; ~ up, conceal, esp. by wrapping up. Hence ~ING¹ (3) n. [f. OF *cuvrir* t. L *cooperire opert-*)]

co′ver² (kŭ-), n. Thing that covers; lid; binding of book; either board of this, as *from* ~ *to* ~; wrapper, envelope, of letter, as *address* person *under* ~ *to another*; case of bicycle tire; hiding-place, shelter, (*take* ~, Mil., utilize lie of ground for protection); protection from attack (*cloud* ~); a force of aircraft for protecting a land or sea operation (*air, fighter,* ~); screen, pretence, as *under* (*the*) ~ *of humility*; woods or undergrowth sheltering game, COVERT²; (Commerce.) funds to meet liability or secure against contingent loss; plate, napkin, etc., laid for each person at table. [f. prec.]

co′verlet, -lid, (kŭ-), n. Counterpane, quilt; covering. [earlier *coverlite* perh. f. OF +*covre-lit* (as COVER¹ + *lit* bed)]

co′vert¹ (kŭ-), a. (Of threat, glance, etc.) secret, disguised. Hence ~LY² adv. [OF (as COVER¹)]

co′vert² (kŭ′vert, -er), n. Shelter, esp. thicket hiding game; ~ *coat*, short light overcoat. [f. F *couvert* p.p. as n. (COVER²)]

co′verture (kŭ-), n. Covering, cover; shelter; condition of married woman under husband's protection. [OF (as COVER¹, see -URE)]

co′vet (kŭ-), v.t. Desire eagerly (usu. what belongs to another). Hence ~ABLE a. [f. OF *cuveitier* f. L +*cupiditare* (as CUPIDITY)]

co′vetous (kŭ-), a. Eagerly desirous (of another's property etc.); grasping, avaricious. Hence ~LY² adv., ~NESS n. [f. OF *coveitus* (as prec., see -OUS)]

co′vey (kŭ-), n. (pl. ~s). Brood of partridges; family, party, set. [f. OF *covée* f. *couver* hatch f. L *cubare*, see -ADE]

co′vin (kŭ-). n. (legal, arch.) Conspiracy, collusion. [OF, f. LL *convenium* t. CONVENE]

co′ving, n. Arched piece of building; (pl.) curved sides of fire-place. [COVE² + -ING¹]

cow¹, n. (pl. ~s, arch. *kine*). Female of any bovine animal, esp. of the domestic species (*the* ~ *with the iron tail*, pump as used in adulterating milk); female of elephant, rhinoceros, whale, seal, etc.; ~*bane,* water hemlock; ~*boy,* boy in

charge of ~s, *man in charge of grazing cattle on ranch; *~-catcher,* apparatus fixed in front of locomotive engine to remove cattle & other obstructions; ~-*fish,* (1) sea-cow, (2) Indian & American fish with horn-like spines over eyes; ~*grass,* wild species of Trefoil; ~*heel,* foot of ~ or ox stewed to jelly; ~*herd,* one who tends ~s at pasture; ~*hide,* (leather, whip, made of) ~'s hide; ~*itch,* = COWAGE; *~-puncher,* = ~-*boy; *~*shod* (Cricket sl.), violent pull made in crouching position; *~-tree,* S.-American tree with milk-like juice. Hence ~ISH¹ a. [com.-Teut.; OE *cū* t. OTeut. *kouz* t. Aryan *gwous* (Skr. *gaus,* Gk *bous,* L *bos*]

cow′age, cowh-, n. Tropical plant with stinging hairs on pod. [f. Hind. *kawānch*]

cow′an, n. (Sc.). Working but unqualified mason; (hence) intruder on a freemasons' lodge. [†]

cow′ard, n. & a. Faint-hearted, pusillanimous, (person). Hence ~LINESS n., ~LY¹ a., ~LY² adv. [f. OF *coart* = It. *codardo* (coda tail f. L *cauda*, -ARD)]

cow′ardice, n. Faint-heartedness; moral ~, fear of disapprobation. [f. OF *couardise* (as prec., see -ICE)]

cow′er, v.i. Stand, squat, in bent position; crouch, esp. from fear. [etym. dub.; cf. Icel. *kūra* sleep, Da. *kure* squat; also G *kauern*]

cowl¹, n. Monk's hooded garment; hood of this; hood-shaped covering of chimney or ventilating shaft. Hence **cowlED²** (-ld) a. [(1) OE *cugele* f. LL *cuculla* f. L *cucullus* hood of cloak; (2) OE *cuffe* cogn. w. Du. *keuvel,* conn. w. Icel. *kofl* cowl]

cowl², coul (-ow-), n. Tub for water, esp. one with two ears, carried by two men on ~-*staff.* [prob. f. OF *cuvelle* f. L *cupella* dim. of *cupa*]

cow-pox, n. Disease on teats of cows, communicated to human beings by vaccination.

cowr′ie, -ȳ, n. Shell of small gastropod found in Indian Ocean, used as money in Africa & S. Asia; the animal; kinds of gastropod including *common* ~ of British coast. [f. Hind. *kaurī*]

cow′slip, n. || Wild plant growing in pastures, with fragrant yellow flowers; (OE *cū-slyppe* prob. = cow-dung (*cū*- cow- + *slyppe* slimy substance)]

cox, n., & v.t. & i., (colloq.). = COXSWAIN, esp. of racing boat; (vb) act as ~ (of).

cox′a, n. (pl. *-ae*). Hip. Hence **cŏx′AL** a. [L]

cox′comb (-ōm), n. Conceited showy person. Hence **cŏxcomb′**ICAL (-mi-) a. [= *cock's comb*; orig. (cap worn by) professional fool]

For compounds of *co-* not given consult *co-*.

côx'comb (-kōmt), n. Foppery, behaviour of a coxcomb. [-RY]

côx'swain (-kswān, -ksn), n. (abbr. cox). Helmsman of boat; person on board ship permanently in charge of a superior officer is present) commanding, boat & crew. Hence ~LESS a., ~SHIP n. [earlier *cockswain* (cook = COCKBOAT + SWAIN)] cf. BOATSWAIN]

coxy. See COCKY.

coy, a. Modest, shy, (usu. of girl); (of place) secluded; ~ *of*, backward, reserved, in (speech etc.). Hence ~LY² adv., ~NESS n. [f. F *coi* (fem. *coite*) f. L as QUIET]

coyōt'ē (ко-, *also* kī'ōt), n. N.-American prairie-wolf. [Mex. Sp., f. Mex. *coyotl*]

coypu (koi'pŏō), n. S.-American aquatic beaver-like rodent (cf. NUTRIA). [native name]

cŏz'y̆, a. See COSY.

cŏz (kŭz), n. (arch.). Abbr. of COUSIN.

cōze, v.i. *& n.* (Have a) chat. [cvb) prob. f. F *causer*; in perh. influenced by COSY]

cō'zen (kŭ-), v.t. & i. (literary). defraud, (of, *out of*); beguile (*into doing*); act deceitfully. Hence ~AGE(3) n. [?]

crăb¹, n. Kinds of ten-footed crustacean, esp. edible species found near most seacoasts; zodiacal constellation, CANCER; machine (orig. with claws) for hoisting heavy weights; (pl.) lowest throw at hazard, two aces; whence *turn out ~s*, end in failure; *catch a ~* in rowing, get oar jammed under water by faulty stroke; ~*'s eyes*, round concretion of carbonate of lime, found in stomach of crayfish; ~(-*louse*), parasitical insect infesting human body; ~-*pot*, wicker trap for ~s. Hence ~LET n., ~LIKE a. & adv. [OE *crabba* = ON *krabbi*, Du. *krabbe*, cogn. w. LG *krabben* scratch, claw]

crăb², v.t. & i. (-bb-). (Of hawks) scratch, claw, fight with, (each other or abs.); (colloq.) cry down, pull to pieces. [prob. = LG as prec.]

crăb³, n. (Also ~-*apple*) wild apple (fruit & tree); sour person. [?]

crăbb'ĕd, a. Cross-grained, perverse; churlish, irritable; (of writings or authors) ruggedly intricate, difficult to make out; (of handwriting) ill-formed & hard to decipher; sour, harsh. Hence ~LY² adv., ~NESS n. Also (in first two senses only) **crăbb'y̆** a. [CRAB¹ + -ED²]

crăck¹, v.t. & i. & a. Sudden sharp noise (of whip, rifle, thunder); ~ *of doom*, thunderpeal of Day of Judgement; sharp blow, as *a ~ on the head*; *in a ~*, in a moment; brisk talk, (pl.) news; (sl.) = WISE¹ ~; fracture (the parts still cohering); partial breaking; (adj.; colloq.) first-rate; ~-*brained*, crazy. [f. foll.; not in OE]

crăck², v.t. & i. (Cause to) make sharp noise, as ~ *a whip, whips* ~; (utter) *a joke*; chat; ~ *up*, praise; break (nut, bottle, empty, drink it; (sl.) ~ *a crib*, break into a house; break (it, & i.) with out complete separation of parts; ~ *s, is ~ed* (becomes dissonant, esp. at age of puberty); damage, ruin, (credit etc.); decompose (heavy oils) by heat and pressure to produce lighter hydrocarbons (such as petrol); (p.-p., colloq.) crazy, insane; ~-*jaw* (colloq.), (word) difficult to pronounce. Hence ~'ABLE a. [com-Teut.; OE *cracian*, G *krachen*]

crăck'er, n. In vbl senses; also or esp. firework exploding with sharp report; explosive bon-bon; instrument for cracking, as *nut*~*s*; thin hard biscuit; *biscuit*-smash, breakdown; (school sl.) lie; *~jack* (sl.), exceptionally fine or expert (thing or person); ~s, pred. a. (sl.), crazy, mad. [-ER¹]

crăc'kle, v.i. & n. Emit slight cracking sound; (n.) such sound, (also ~-*china*, -*glass*, -*ware*) china, glass, with appearance of minute cracks. [(n. f. vb) CRACK² + -LE(3)]

crăck'ling, n. In vbl senses; also, crisp skin of roast pork. [prec. + -ING¹]

crăck'nel, n. Light crisp kind of biscuit. [prob. f. F *craquelin*]

crăcks'man, n. Burglar. [CRACK¹, MAN]

crăck'y̆, a. Full of cracks; apt to crack; (colloq.) crazy. [-Y²]

-crăcy, noun suf. added to Gk stems (and as *-ocracy* to E wds), meaning ' rule of, ruling body of, class influential by '; thus *democracy* = government by the rich, *the p.* those whose wealth gives them power; so *cottonocracy* etc. [f. F *-cratie* f. Gk *-kratia* (*kratos* power)]

crā'dle, n. & v.t. **1.** Bed, cot, for infant, mounted on rockers; *from the ~*, from infancy; (fig.) place in which thing is nurtured in earliest stage, as ~ *of an art*, *of a nation*; framework resembling ~, esp. (Naut.) that on which ship rests during construction or repairs; frame attached to scythe to lay corn evenly; (Engraving) kind of serrated chisel, rocking-tool; (Mining) trough on rockers in which auriferous earth is shaken in water; CAT'S-~. **2.** v.t. Place in (child's, ship's) ~; contain or shelter as ~, mow (corn) with ~-scythe. [OE *cradol*, etym. dub.]

crā'dling, n. In vbl senses; also (Archit.) wood or iron framework. [prec. + -ING¹]

craft (-ah-), n. Skill; cunning, deceit; art, trade, (esp. in combn., as *handi*~, *priest*~, *state*~); *the gentle ~*, angling; members of a ~; *the C*~, brotherhood of Freemasons; boat, vessel,(pl.*craft*);~*brother*, ~-*guild*, workman, guild of workmen, of

same trade; ~s'man, one who practises a ~, whence ~s'manship(3) (-ah~) n. [com-Teut., OE *cræft*, G *kraft* strength]

craf'ty¹ (-ah-), a. Cunning, artful, wily. Hence ~ily² adv., ~iness n. [com-Teut., OE *cræftig* (CRAFT, see -Y²)]

crag¹, n. Steep or rugged rock; ~s'man, skilled climber of ~s. Hence ~g'ED², ~g'y², aa., ~g'EDNESS, ~g'iNESS, nn., (-g-). [prob. Celt.; cf. Ir. *creag*]

‖**crag²**, n. (geol.). Deposits of shelly sand found in Norfolk, Suffolk, Essex, [perh. = prec.]

crake, n., & v.i. Kinds of bird including CORN-~; cry of the corn-~; (v.i.) utter this. [imit., cf. CROAK]

cram, v.t.&i.(-mm-),&n. 1. Fill overfull; force (thing *into*, *down*; ~ *down* one's *throat*, tell him repeatedly); stuff (poultry etc. *with food*); eat greedily; (fig.) prepare (t. & i.) for examination; learn, get up, (subject) for special purpose; ~-*full*, as full as ~*ming* can make it. 2. n. Crowd; ~ming for examination; (sl.) lie. [(n. f. vb) OE *crammian* f. *crimman* insert, cf. OHG *krimman*, pinch]

cram'bo, n. Game in which one player gives word to which each of the others must find rhyme; *dumb*~, game in which one side must guess word, a rhyme to which is given, by representing other rhymes to it in dumb show. [prob. f. L *crambe repetita* cabbage served up again]

cram'mer, n. In vbl senses esp.: one who crams (esp. pupils); lie. [-ER²]

cram'oisy, -m'esy, (-z-), a. & n. (arch.). Crimson (cloth). [f. It. *cremesi*, *chermesi*, f. Arab. *qirmazi* of the KERMES]

cramp¹, n. Contraction of muscles from sudden chill, strain, etc.; ~-*fish*, electric ray, torpedo. [f. OF *crampe* f. same root as CRAMP²]

cramp², n. (Also ~-*iron*) metal bar with bent ends for holding masonry etc. together; portable tool for pressing two planks etc. together; restraint, [as prec., but thr. Du.]

cramp³, a. Hard to make out, as ~ *word*, *handwriting*; contracted, cramped. Hence ~'NESS n. [f. CRAMP¹ or OF *crampe* a.]

cramp⁴, v.t. Affect with CRAMP¹; confine narrowly (also ~ *up*); (fig.) restrict (energies etc.); fasten with CRAMP². Hence ~'EDNESS n.

cram'pon, n. Metal hook, grappling-iron; iron plate with spikes for walking on ice etc. [F. f. LL *cramponem*, nom. -o, f. root of CRAM¹]

‖**cran**, n. (Sc.). Measure for fresh herrings (37½ gal.). [?]

cran'age, n. Use of crane; dues paid for this. [CRANE¹+-AGE]

cran'berry, n. Small dark-red acid berry, fruit of dwarf shrub native of Britain, N. Europe, N. America, etc. [recent in E, thr. N. Amer. colonists f. LG *krönbere*]

crane¹, n. Large wading bird with long legs, neck, and bill; machine for moving heavy weights; siphon; (also *under-*~) tube for supplying water to locomotive; ~-*fly*, daddy-long-legs; ~'*s-bill*, various species of geranium. [OE *cran*, cf. Du. *kraan*, G *kranich*]

crane², v.t. & i. Move with crane; stretch (neck), stretch neck, like crane; ~ *at*, pull up at, shrink from, (hedge, difficulty). [f. prec.]

cranio- in comb. = foll., as cranio/o'GI-CAL, -LOGIST, -LOGY (-ŏlŏ), -METRY (-ŏmĕ-).

cran'ium, n. (pl.-*ia*). Bones enclosing the brain; bones of the whole head, skull. Hence crān'iAL a. [med. L, f. Gk *kranion* skull]

crank¹, n., & v.t. 1. Part of axle or shaft bent at right angles for converting reciprocal into circular motion, or vice versa; elbow-shaped connexion in bell-hanging; revolving disk turned by criminals as punishment. 2. v.t. Bend into ~ shape, furnish or fasten with ~; ~ *up*, set (engine of motor-car) going by turning ~ (also abs.). [(vb f. n.) OE *cranc* prob. f. *crincan* (past *cranc*) rare by-form of *cringan* contract, curl up]

crank², n. Fanciful turn of speech; eccentric idea or act; eccentric person. [different. f. prec.]

crank³, a. Weak, shaky, (usu. of machinery). [f. CRANK¹]

crank⁴, a. (naut.). Liable to capsize. [?]

crankle (-äng'kl), v.i., & n. Bend in and out, twist; (n.) bend, twist. [(n. f. vb) CRANK¹ vb +-LE]

crank'y¹, a. Sickly; shaky, crazy; capricious; crochety, eccentric; full of twists; (Naut.).=CRANK⁴. Hence ~ily² adv., ~iNESS n. [CRANK¹,²,³,⁴+-Y²]

crann'og, n. Ancient lake-dwelling in Scotland or Ireland. [Ir. (*crann* tree, beam)]

crann'y, n. Chink, crevice, crack. Hence crann'iED² (-id) a. [prob. f. F *cran*, etym. dub.]

crape, n., & v.t. Gauze-like fabric with wrinkled surface, usu. of black silk or imitation silk (of other colour or material now usu. CRÊPE), used for mourning dress; band of this round hat etc. as sign of mourning; ~-*cloth*, ~-like woollen material; (v.t.) cover, clothe, drape, with ~. Hence crāp'y² a. [f. CRÊPE]

crāped (-pt), a. In vbl senses; also, crisped, crimped. [CRAPE+-ED²,¹]

*****craps**, n. pl. Game of chance played with dice; *shoot*~, play this. [etym. dub., perh. orig. F]

crap'ulent, a. Given to, suffering from effects of, resulting from, intemperance. Hence or cogn.~ENCE n., ~OUS a. [f. L *crapulentus* (*crapula* debauch f. Gk *kraipalē* drunken headache, see -LENT)]

crash¹, v.i. & t. & n. 1. Make a ~ (see n.); move, go, with a ~, (of aircraft or airman) fall to earth; (v.t.) dash in pieces,

crash, n. throw, force, drive, with a ~; go, fall, ~ (with a ~). 2. n. Noise as of broken crockery, thunder, loud music, etc., violent percussion or breakage; (fig.) ruin, collapse of mercantile credit; ~-*dive*, (of submarine) dive hastily and steeply in an emergency (also as n.);—*land*, (of aircraft or airman) land hurriedly with a ~, usu. without lowering undercarriage. [imit.]

crash[2], n. Coarse linen for towels etc. [?]

cra'sis, n. (Gk gram.). Combination of the vowels of two syllables (as *kagȏ* for *kai egȏ*). [Gk, = mixture (*kerannumi* mix)]

crass, a. Thick, gross; (fig.) gross, as ~ *stupidity*; grossly stupid. Hence ~LY[2] adv., ~NESS n. [f. L *crassus* solid, thick]

crass'itude, n. Grossness; gross stupidity. [f. L *crassitudo* (as prec., see -TUDE)]

-crat, noun suf. = supporter, member, of a -CRACY, & used & appended similarly (-*crat*, -*ocrat*). Hence -**crat'ic**(al) adj. suf. [f. F -*crate* formed f. adj. in -*cratique* (on anal. of Gk *aristokratēs* or independently) f. Gk -*kratēs* -CRACY]

cratch, n. Rack for feeding beasts out of doors. [f. OF *creche*; cf. OHG *chrippa* CRIB]

crate, n. Large open-work case on basket for carrying glass, crockery, fruit, etc. Hence ~'FUL (-t-) n. [prob. f. L *cratis* hurdle]

cra'ter, n. Mouth of volcano; bowl-shaped cavity, esp. that made by explosion of shell or bomb. Hence ~'IFORM a. [L, f. Gk *kratēr* mixing-bowl for wine (*kerannumi* mix)]

cravat', n. Neckcloth, tie, (now arch. or shop). Hence ~'ED[2] a. [f. F *cravate*, f. G *Krabate* Croatian]

crave, v.t. & i. Beg for; long for; beg, long, for. [OE *crafian*]

cra'ven, a. & n. Cowardly, abject, (person); *cry* ~, surrender. Hence ~LY[2] adv. [?]

craw, n. Crop of birds or insects. [ME *crawe* cogn. w. Du. *kraag* neck]

craw'fish. See CRAYFISH.

crawl[1], v.i. Pen in shallow water for fish, turtles, etc. [f. Du. KRAAL]

crawl[2], v.i. & n. 1. Move slowly, dragging body along close to ground, or on hands & knees; walk, move, slowly; creep abjectly; (of ground etc.) be alive with crawling things; feel creepy sensation, whence ~Y[2] a. 2. n. ~*ing*; *the* ~, a modern high-speed swimming stroke. [(n. f. vb) prob. f. Norse; cf. Da. *kravle* crawl, Sw. *krafla* gropel]

craw'ler, n. In vbl senses; esp.: baby's overall; louse; cab moving slowly in search of fare. [-ER[1]]

cray'fish, craw'fish, n. Small lobster-like fresh-water crustacean; spiny lobster. [ME & OF *crevice* f. OHG *crebiz* f. same st. as CRAB[1]]

cray'on, n. & v.t. Stick, pencil, of coloured chalk or other material for drawing; carbon point in electric arc lamp; (v.t.) draw with ~s, (fig.) sketch. [(n.) F *craie* f. L *creta* chalk, see -OON); (vb) f. F *crayonner*]

craze, v.t. & i. & n. Render insane (usu. in p.p.); produce small cracks on (pottery); (v.i.) have such cracks; (n.) insane fancy, mania, crazy condition, (*be the* ~, be generally sought or affected). [(n. *the* ~) orig. = break, shatter, perh. (direct or thr. OF *acraser* = *écraser*) f. Sw. *krasa*]

cra'zing, n. In vbl senses; ~*mill* (for crushing tin ore). [-ING[1]]

cra'zy, a. (Of ship, building, etc.) unsound, shaky; sickly; insane, mad; (colloq.) extremely enthusiastic (*about*); (of paving, quilts, etc.) made of irregular pieces fitted together. Hence ~INESS n. [CRAZE + -Y[1]]

creak, n. & v.i. Harsh strident noise, as of unoiled hinge, new boots, etc.; (v.i.) make this. Hence ~Y[2] a. [prob. imit.]

cream[1], n. Oily part of milk, which gathers on the top, & by churning is made into butter; choicest (also *Devonshire* ~; fancy dish, sweet, like or made of ~; best part of anything, esp. the point of an anecdote; part of a liquid that gathers at the top; ~ *of tartar*, purified & crystallized bitartrate of potassium, used in medicine etc.; ~ *of lime* (pure slaked); ~-like preparation, as *cold* ~ (cooling unguent); ~-coloured horse; ~ *cheese*, soft rich kind made of un-skimmed milk & ~; ~-*fruit*, a ~-like fruit of Sierra Leone; ~-*laid*, -*wove*, paper of ~ *colour*; ~ *separator*, machine for separating ~ from milk. Hence ~Y[2] a., ~INESS n. [f. F *crème* f. L as CHRISM]

cream[2], v.i. & t. (Of milk & liquids) form cream or scum; cause (milk) to ~; take cream from (milk); take the best part of (anything); add cream to (tea etc.). [f. prec.]

cream'er, n. Flat dish for skimming cream off milk; machine for separating cream. [-ER[1]]

cream'ery, n. Butter-factory; shop where milk, cream, etc., are sold. [f. F *crèmerie* (as CREAM', see -ERY)]

crease, n. & v.t. & i. Line caused by folding, fold, wrinkle; (Cricket) line defining position of bowler & batsman, as *bowling* ~ (from behind which bowler delivers ball); POPPING ~; (v.t.) make ~s in (material); (v.i.) fall into ~s. Hence **creas'y**[2] a. [?]

create', v.t. Bring into existence, give rise to; originate, as (of actor) ~ *a part*; invest (person) with rank, as ~ *a man a peer*. Hence ~IVE a., ~IVENESS n. [f. L *creare*, see -ATE[3]]

cre'atine, n. An organic base found in the juice of flesh. [f. Gk *kreas -atos* meat + -INE[5]]

crea'tion, n. Act of creating (esp. the world); investing with title, rank, etc. (~ *of peers*, ultimate means of overcoming resistance of House of Lords to will of Commons); all created things; a production of the human (esp. dressmaker's, actor's) intelligence, esp. of the imagination. [f. F *création* f. L *creationem* (as CREATE, see -ATION)]

crea'tion|ism (-sho-), n. Theory that God creates a soul for every human being at birth; theory that attributes origin of matter & species to special creation (not EVOLUTION). So ~IST n. [-ISM]

crea'tor, n. *The C~*, the Supreme Being; one who creates, whence **crea'TRESS¹** n. [OF, f. L *creatorem* (as CREATE, see -OR²)]

crea'ture, n. Created thing; animate being; animal (often as distinct from man); human being, person, (often expr. admiration, contempt, patronage, etc.); one who owes his fortune to another; mere instrument; *the ~* (often spelt as Ir., *cratur* etc.) whisky or other intoxicant; ~ *comforts*. [f. F *créature* f. L *creatura* (as prec., see -URE)]

crea'turely (-rl-), a. Of creatures. [-LY¹]

crèche (krāsh), n. Public nursery for infants. [F (as CRATCH)]

crèd'it Judae'us (*Apell'a*) (jōō-), sent. expressing incredulity. [L, =let the Jew Apella believe it, see Hor. *Sat.* I. v. 100]

crèd'ence, n. Belief; *give ~ to*, believe; *letter or ~* (introduction); small side table for eucharistic elements before consecration. [f. med. L *credentia* (*credere* believe, see -ENCE)]

crèden'tial, n. (usu. pl. ; -shalz). Letter(s) of introduction (also fig.). [as CREDENCE + -AL]

crèd'ible, a. (Of persons or statements) believable, worthy of belief. Hence or cogn. ~BIL'ITY n., ~BLY² adv. [f. L *credibilis* (as CREDENCE, see -BLE)]

crèd'it¹, n. Belief, trust; *give ~ to*, believe (story); good reputation; power derived from this; acknowledgement of merit, as *have the ~ of, get ~ for*; source of honour, as *a ~ to the school, it does him ~*; trust in person's ability & intention to pay, as *give ~, deal on ~, long ~*; reputation of solvency & honesty; sum placed at person's disposal in books of a bank etc.; *letter of ~* (authorizing person to draw money from writer's correspondent in another place); (Bookkeeping) acknowledgement of payment by entry in account, sum entered on ~ side of account (cf. DEBIT), this side; *give figures ~ for*, enter (sum) to his~; (fig.) ascribe (quality) to him. [f. F *crédit* f. L *creditum* (*credere* believe, trust)]

crèd'it², v.t. Believe; carry to credit side of account (~ *amount to person, person with amount*); (fig.) ~ *person with*, person with quality). [f. prec.]

crèd'itable, a. That brings credit or honour (to). Hence ~LY² adv. [-ABLE]

crèd'itor, n. One to whom a debt is owing; (Bookkeeping) ~ (abbr. *Cr*) side of account, right-hand side. [f. OF *creditour* f. L *creditorem* (as CREDIT¹, see -OR²)]

crèd'ō, n. (pl. -os). Creed (esp. Apostles' & Nicene, beginning in Latin with ~); musical setting of Nicene Creed. [L, =I believe]

crèd'ulous, a. Too ready to believe; (of things) showing such readiness. Hence or cogn. **crèdŭl'ITY**, ~NESS, nn., ~LY² adv. [f. L *credulus* (*credere* believe)]

creed, n. Brief formal summary of Christian doctrine, esp. *Apostles'* (also *the C~*), *Nicene, Athanasian, C~*; system of religious belief; set of opinions on any subject. Hence ~LESS a. [OE *crēda*, f. L CREDO]

creek, n. ‖ Inlet on sea-coast; small harbour; short arm of river; (U.S. & Colon.) tributary river; narrow plain between mountains. [etym. dub., prob. G; ME *crike* (cf. F *crique*), later *creke* (cf. Du. *kreke*), *crick* (cf. Sw. *krik*)]

creel, n. Large wicker basket for fish; angler's fishing-basket. [orig. Sc., etym. dub.]

creep, v.i. (crěpt), & n. **1.** Move with body, prone & close to ground; move timidly, slowly, or stealthily; ~*ing* BARRAGE; insinuate oneself *into*, come *in*, *up*, unobserved; proceed, exist, abjectly; (of plants) grow along ground, wall, etc.; *flesh* ~*s*, feels as if things were ~ing over it (result of fear, repugnance, etc.); (Naut.) drag with creeper at bottom of water; ~*mouse* (adj.), timid, shy. **2.** n. ~ing; shrinking horror, as (colloq. pl.) *gave me the ~s*; low arch under railway embankment; opening in hedge etc.; (Geol.) gradual movement of disintegrated rock due to atmospheric changes etc. [(n. f. vb) com.-Teut.; OE *crēopan*, Du. *kruipen*]

creep'er, n. In vbl senses, esp.: plant that creeps along ground or up wall; (colloq.) tea-planting pupil in Ceylon; grapnel for dragging bottom of water. [-ER¹]

creep'y, a. Having a creeping (of the flesh; productive of this); given to creeping. So ~-**crawl'y** a. [-Y²]

creese, crease, kris (-ēs, -ĭs), n. Malay dagger with wavy blade. [Malay (*k(')ris, kres*)]

crè'mate, v.t. Consume (esp. corpse) by fire. So ~A'TION, ~a'tionISM(2) (-sho-), nn. [f. L *cremare*, see -ATE³]

crèmatō'ri-um (pl. -s, -a), **crèm'atory**, nn. Person, furnace, cremating corpses or rubbish. Hence **crèmatō'ri-um** (pl. -s, -a), **crèm'atory**(2), nn. [L (as prec., see -OR²)]

crème (-ām), n. ~ *de menthe* (demahnt), peppermint liqueur; ~ *de la* ~ (-dlah-), the very pick, élite. [F]

crèmo'na, n. Violin made at C~; cromorne. [place]

crên'ate, -āted, a. (bot., zool.). With notched or toothed edge. Hence crēnā'TION n. [f. It. *crena* notch, etym. dub., see -ATE²]

crên'ature, n. Rounded tooth on edge etc. [as prec. see -URE]

crên'el, crênelle, n. Open space in embattled parapet, for shooting through etc. [OF (-el), dim. of *cren* = It. *crena* (see CRENATE)]

crên'ellāte, v.t. Furnish with battlements or loopholes. Hence crênella'TION n. [on F *créneler* (as prec.), see -ATE²]

crê'ole, n. & a. (Descendant of) European (also ~ *white*) or negro (~ *negro*) settler in W. Indies, Mauritius, etc.; (of animals etc.) natural-ized in W. Indies etc. [f. F *créole* f. Sp. *criollo* perh. f. +*criadillo* dim. of *criado* bred, domestic, f. *criar* rear, f. L *creare* CREATE]

crê'osôte, n. Colourless oily fluid distilled from wood-tar, a strong antiseptic; (Commerc.) carbolic acid. Hence crês'ot-, caustic liquid obtained by distillation of coal tar. [f. Gk *kreas* meat +*sōzō* save]

crêpe (krâp), n. Crapy fabric other than black mourning crape; ~ *de Chine* (deshin), of silk kind; ~ *rubber*, very durable rubber used for boot soles etc. [F, f. L *crispa* curled, fem. adj.]

crêp'itate, v.i. Make crackling sound; (of beetles) eject pungent fluid with sharp report. Hence ~ANT a., ~A'TION n. [f. L *crepitare* frequent. of *crepare* creak, see -ATE³]

crêp'on (krêp'ón), n. Stuff like crape, but of firmer substance. [F (as crêpe, see -ON)]

crêpt. See CREEP.

crêpus'cular, a. Of twilight; (Zool.) appearing, active, in twilight; dim, not yet fully enlightened. [f. L *crepusculum* twilight+-AR¹]

crescen'do (krêsh-), adv., n., & a. (mus.). (Passage of music to be played) with gradually increasing volume (abbr. *cres.*, *cresc.*); (fig.) progress towards a climax. [It., part. of *crescere* grow (as foll.)]

crês'cent, n. & a. 1. Increasing moon; figure of moon in first or last quarter; this as badge of Turkish Sultans; the Turkish power; the Mohammedan religion; any figure of ~ shape, ‖ esp. row of houses. 2. adj. Increasing, ~-shaped. [f. L *crescere* grow, see -ENT]

crêss, n. Name of various plants usu. with pungent edible leaves, as *Garden C~*, WATER-~. [OE *cresse*, f. root of OHG *chresan* creep]

crêss'et, n. Metal vessel for holding grease or oil for light, usu. mounted on pole; (mod.) fire-basket for lighting wharf etc. [OF (also *craisseet*), f. *graisse* GREASE]

crêst, n., & v.t. & i. 1. Comb or tuft on animal's head; ~-*fallen*, dejected, abashed; ~, with drooping plume, tuft, of feathers; (apex or) helmet; head, top, esp. of mountain; surface line or neck in animals; mane. 2. (Anat.) ridge along surface of bone, as *fronted*, *occipital*, & *skull*. 3. (Her.) device above shield & helmet on coat of arms, or separately, as on seal, notepaper, etc. 4. v.t. Furnish with ~, serve as ~ to, reach ~ of (hill, wave); (v.i., of waves) form into a ~. [vrb f. n., f. OF *creste* f. L *crista* tuft]

crêta'ceous (-shus), a. Of (the nature of) chalk. [f. L *cretaceus* (*creta* chalk, see -ACEOUS)]

crêt'ic, n. Metrical foot (-~-). [f. Gk *Krētikos* (*Krētē* Crete, see -IC)]

crêt'in, n. Deformed idiot of a kind found esp. in Alpine valleys. Hence ~ISM (2) n., ~IZE v.t., ~OUS a. [f. French f. L *Chris-tianus* CHRISTIAN in mod. Rom. sense (barely) human creature]

crêt'onne (also -ětn'), n. Stout un-glazed cotton cloth with pattern printed on one or both sides. [F]

crevasse', n. Deep fissure in ice of glacier. [F, readopted as different, f. foll.]

crêv'ice, n. Chink, fissure. [ME & OF *crevace* f. Ll *crepita* (*crepare* creak, crack)]

crew¹ (-ōō), n. Whole body of men man-ning ship or boat; associated body, com-pany, (of persons; set, gang, mob. [f. OF *creue* increase fem. p.p. (as n.) of *croistre* grow f. L *crescere*]

crew². See CROW³.

crew'el (-ōō-), n. Thin worsted yarn for tapestry & embroidery; ~-*work*, design in worsted on linen or cloth ground. [?]

crib¹, n. Barred receptacle for fodder; hovel, hut; small bed for child, with barred sides; wicker salmon-trap; frame-work lining shaft of mine; (also ~*work*) heavy crossed timbers used in founda-tions in loose soil etc.; *bin for maize, salt, etc.; set of cards given to dealer at cribbage, taken from other players' hands; (colloq.) plagiarism; translation for (esp. illegitimate) use of students; CRACK a ~; ~-*biting* (of horses), habit of seizing manager in teeth & at same time noisily drawing in breath. [com.-WG; Du. *krib*]

crib², v.t. (-bb-). Confine in small space; furnish (cowshed etc.) with cribs; pilfer; copy unfairly or without acknowledge-ment. [f. prec.]

crib'bage, n. Card game for two, three, or four persons. [f. CRIB¹+-AGE]

crib'riform, a. (anat., bot.). Having small holes, like a sieve. [f. L *cribrum* sieve +-FORM]

crick, n., & v.t. Spasmodic affection of muscles of neck, back, etc., sudden stiff-ness; (v.t.) produce ~ in (neck etc.). [prob. imit.]

crick'et¹, n. (Also *house~*) a jumping chirping insect. [f. OF *criquet* conn. w. *criquer* creak; imit.]

crick'et², n., & v.i. Open-air game played with ball, bats, & wickets, between two sides of 11 players each (|| *not ~* colloq., infringing the code of fair play between honourable opponents in any sphere); (v.i.) play ~. Hence ~ER¹ n. [etym. dub.; OF has *criquet*, a game, (also) a stick to aim at]

cric'oid, a. & n. (zool.). Ring-shaped (cartilage of larynx). [f. Gk *krikoeidēs* (*krikos* ring, -OID)]

cri'er, n. One who cries; officer who makes public announcements in court of justice or (*town ~*) in a town. [ME & OF *criere*, nom. of *crieur* (*crier* CRY, see -OR²)]

crik'ey, int. (sl.), expr. astonishment. [perh. substituted for L *Chrīstē* O Christ]

crime, n., & v.t. 1. Act (usu. grave offence) punishable by law; evil act, sin; *~-shed*, record of soldier's offences against regulations. Hence ~LESS (-ml-) a. 2. v.t. (Mil.) charge with or convict of military offence. [F., f. L *crīmen minis* judgement, offence (*cernere cred-* decide)]

crim'inal, a. & n. Of (the nature of) crime; (person) guilty of crime. Hence or cogn. (person) guilty of crime. Hence or cogn. ~ CONVERSATION, CONNEXION; (person) guilty of crime. Hence or cogn. ~ CONVERSATION, CONNEXION; **criminal'ity** n., ~LY² adv. [f. F *criminel* f. L *crīminālis* (as prec, see -AL)]

crim'inate, v.t. Charge with crime; prove (oneself etc.) guilty of crime; censure. Hence or cogn. ~A'TION n., ~ATIVE, ~ATORY, aa. [f. L *crīminārī* (*crīmen CRIME* + -o- + -LOGY)]

criminol'ogy, n. Science of crime. [f. L *crīmen -minis* CRIME + -o- + -LOGY)]

crim'inous, a. Guilty of crime, only in phr. ~ *clerk* (clergyman). [f. OF *crimineux* f. L *crīminōsus* (as prec, see -OUS)]

crimp¹, n., & v.t. Agent who entraps men for seamen or soldiers (also fig.); (v.t.) entrap thus, impress, (seamen, soldiers). [?]

crimp², v.t. Compress into plaits or folds, frill; make fluttings in, corrugate; contract (flesh of freshly-caught fish) by gashing; mould, bend, into shape. [f. same root as CRAMP¹, cf. Du. *krimpen* contract (intr.)]

crim'son (-z-), a. & n., & v.t. & i. Deep-red (colour); (v.t. & i.) turn ~. [(vb f. n.) f. Sp. *cremesin, car-*, (*carmes* CRAMOISY, -INE²)]

cringe (-j), v.i., & n. Cower servilely; behave obsequiously (*to*); (n.) fawning obeisance, cringing. [(n. f. vb) earlier *crenge* f. *cringan*, see CRANK¹]

cring'le (kring'gl), n. (naut.). Eye of rope containing thimble for another rope to pass through. [cf. G *kringel* dim. of *kring* ring f. root of CRANK¹]

crin'ite, a. (bot., zool.). Hairy. [f. L *crīnītus* (*crīnis* hair, cf. -ATE²(2)]

crink'le (kring'kl), v.t. & i., & n. Twist, wrinkle. Hence ~Y² a. [n. prob. f. vb) frequent. of OE *crincan*, see CRANK¹ & -LE(3)]

crink'um-crank'um, n. & a. (Thing) full of twists & turns (lit. & fig.). [playful f. CRANK¹]

crin'oid, a. & n. (zool.). Lily-shaped (echinoderm). Hence **crinoid'AL a.** [f. Gk *krinoeidēs* (*krinon* lily, see -OID)]

crinolette', n. Contrivance for distending back of woman's skirt. [dim. f. foll.]

crin'oline (also -ēn), n. Stiff fabric of horsehair etc. formerly used for skirts; hooped petticoat; netting round warship as defence against torpedoes. [F (L *crin's* hair + *līnum* thread)]

crio- in comb. = Gk *krios* ram, as *-sphinx* (ram-headed), *-ceratitē*, ram's-horn ammonite.

crip'ple, n., & v.t. & i. Lame person; staging for cleaning windows etc.; (v.t.) disable, impair; (v.i.) hobble, walk lamely, (*along* etc.). Hence ~DOM (-ld-), ~HOOD (-lh-), nn. [(vb f. n.) OE *crypel* f. OTeut. *krupilo-* (*krūupan* creep)]

cris-. =CREESE.

cris'is, n. (*crises*, pr. -ēz). Turning-point, esp. of disease; moment of danger or suspense in politics, commerce, etc., as *cabinet, financial*, ~. [L, f. Gk *krisis* decision (*krinō* decide)]

crisp, a., n., & v.t. & i. Hard but fragile, brittle; bracing, as *~ air*; brisk, decisive, as *~ manner, style*, etc.; (of hair etc.) curly; || (in. pl.) thin fried and dried slices of potato (marketed in packets) (v.t. & i.) curl in short stiff folds, make or become ~. Hence ~LY¹ adv., ~NESS n. [(vb f. adj.) f. L *crispus* curled]

crisp'y, a. Curly; brittle; brisk. [-Y³]

criss'-cross (-aws), n., a., adv., & v.i. & t. 1. see CHRIST-CROSS-ROW. 2. adj. In crossing lines, currents, etc. (for*~ rows* see CHRIST-CROSS-ROW). 2. adj. In cross lines (*~ pattern, traffic*). (of persons or temper) peevish. 3. adv. Crosswise, at cross purposes (*everything went~*). 4. vb. Move crosswise, work with ~ pattern. [partly f. *Christ's Cross*, partly redupl. of *cross*]

cris'tate, a. (nat. hist.). Having a crest. [f. L *cristātus* (as CREST, see -ATE²)]

criter'ion, n. (pl. *-ia*). Principle, standard, a thing is judged by. [f. Gk *kritērion*, as foll.]

crit'ic, n. One who pronounces judgement; censurer; judge of literary or artistic works; one skilled in textual criticism. Hence ~ASTER n. [f. L f. Gk *kritikos* (*kritēs* judge f. *krinō*, see -IC)]

crit'ical, a. Censorious, fault-finding; skilful, engaged, in criticism; belonging to criticism, involving risk or suspense; as ~ *condition, operation;* (Math., Physics) marking transition from one state into another, as ~ *angle, temperature.* Hence **~LY² adv.** [-AL]

crit'icism, n. Work of a critic; critical essay or remark; (dealing with the higher ~) (dealing with origin, character, etc., of texts, esp. of Biblical writings). [-ISM]

crit'icize, v.t. Discuss critically (often abs.); censure. Hence **~ABLE a.** [-IZE]

crit'ico-, in comb. = critically, critical & ~, as ~ *historical.* [CRITIC-O-]

critique (-ēk), n. Critical essay or notice; art of criticism. [F (as CRITIC)]

croak, n. & v.i. & t. Deep hoarse sound of frog or raven; (v.i.) utter ~, forebode evil, (sl.) die; (v.t.) utter dismally, *(sl.)* kill. Hence **~Y² a.** [prob. imit.]

croak'er, n. In vbl senses; esp. prophet of evil. [-ER¹]

—, as ~*historical.*

Croa'tia is named. [Slav.]

cro'ceate (-ši), a. Saffron, saffron-coloured. [f. L *croceus* (CROCUS), see -ATE²]

cro'chet (-shi), n. & v.t. (-*cheted* pr. -shïd). Knitting (material or work) done with hooked needle; (v.t.) make (shawl etc. or abs.) in ~. [(vb f. n.) F, dim. of *croche*, *croc*, hook]

cro'cidolite, n. A fibrous silicate of iron & sodium, blue asbestos; yellow mineral. [f. Gk *krokis -idos* nap of cloth + -LITE]

crock¹, n. Earthen pot or jar; ||(dial.) metal pot; broken piece of earthenware used for covering hole in flowerpot. [OE *croc, crocca,* cf. Icel. *krukka*]

crock², n. & v.i. & t. (Sl.) Inefficient or broken-down or worn-out person; broken-down horse; ||(Sc.) old ewe; (v.i., sl.) ~ *up,* break down; (v.t.) disable (usu. in p.p.). [prob. cogn. W. CRACK v.; cf. Norw. *krake* sickly beast, MDu. *kraecke* broken-down horse or house]

crock'ery, n. Earthenware vessels. [f. obs. *crocker* potter (CROCK¹), see -ERY]

crock'et, n. Small ornament (usu. bud or curled leaf) on inclined sides of pinnacles etc. [f. AF *croket* = F CROCHET]

croc'odile, n. Large amphibious reptile (esp. the Nile species); ~ *tears* (hypocritical, from belief that the crocodile wept while devouring, or to allure, its victim); ||(colloq.) girl's school walking two & two. Hence **crocodil'ian** (-yan) a. [f. l, f. Gk *krokodilos*]

Croe'sus (krēs-), n. Wealthy person. [~, king of Lydia]

||**croft** (-aw-, -ŏ-), n. Enclosed piece of (usu. arable) land; small holding of CROFTER. [etym. dub., cf. Du. *kroft* high land]

||**cro'fter** (-aw-, -ŏ-), n. One who rents a small holding, esp. joint tenant of Scotch divided farm. [-ER¹]

Cro-Magnon (-man'yon), a. Of a prehistoric tall long-headed European race, remains of which were found in ~, a cave in Dordogne, France.

crōm'lech (-k-), n. (In Wales and formerly in England) megalithic tomb; (in France) circle of upright prehistoric stones. [W (*crom* bent, *llech* flat stone)]

cromorne, cremōn'a, n. An organ reedstop. [F f. G *krummhorn* crooked horn]

crōne, n. Withered old woman; old ewe. [ult. f. ONF *caroine,* see CARRION]

crōn'y, n. Intimate friend. [?]

crook, n. & a. & v.t. & i. Shepherd's, bishop's, hooked staff; anything hooked; hook; bend, curve; act of bending; (sl.) rogue, swindler; *by* HOOK *or by~;* (sl.) *on the ~,* dishonestly; *by* HOOK *or by~;* (sl.) on *the ~,* dishonestly; ~ *back(ed),* hunchback(ed); (adj.) = CROOKED; (vb f. n. & i.) bend, curve. [(vb f. n.) ME *crok,* f. ON *krókr*]

crook'ed, a. Not straight, bent, twisted; deformed; bent with age; (fig.) not straightforward, dishonest; (of stick, pr.-ŏŏkt) having a cross handle, crutched. Hence **~LY² adv., ~NESS n.** [-ED¹]

Crookes (-ks), n. Name of Sir William ~ (d. 1919), English scientist, used attrib. (or in gen.) to designate apparatus invented by him etc. So: ~ *rays,* cathode rays; ~'*s tube,* glass vacuum tube for illustrating high rarefaction phenomena; ~'*s vacuum* (extremely high one).

crōon, v.i. & t. & n. (Hum., sing, mutter, in) low undertone. Hence **~ER¹ n.,** soft singer of highly sentimental songs. [chiefly Sc. till 19th c.; cf. Du. *kreunen* groan]

crop¹, n. Pouch-like enlargement of gullet in birds, where food is prepared for digestion; stock, handle, of whip; (also *hunting-~*) short whipstock with loop instead of lash; produce of cultivated plants, esp. cereals; *in, under, out of,* ~ (cultivation); season's total yield (of cereal etc.); entire hide of animal tanned; cropping of hair; style of wearing hair cut short; piece cut off end; name of some cuts of meat; NECK *& ~; ~-eared,* with ears (also, hair) cut short; ~*over,* annual junketings at end of the W.-Indian sugar-cane harvest. [OE, = bird's crop, rounded top of plant, cf. LG & Du. *krop,* OHG *chropf,* bird's ~; other senses developed in E]

crop², v.t. & i. (-pp-). Cut off (of animals) bite off (tops of plants); gather, reap; cut short (ears, tail, hair, nap of cloth, edges of book); sow, plant, (land with barley etc.); (v.i.) bear a crop; turn *up* un-

expectedly; ~ *out, forth,* appear; (Geol.) ~ *up, out,* come to surface. [f. prec.]

cropp'er, n. Person, thing, that crops; pigeon with large crop, pouter; plant yielding good etc. crop; (sl.) heavy fall, as *came a~.* [CROP¹·² + -ER¹]

cropp'y, n. Person with short cropped hair, esp. (Hist.) Irish rebel, sympathizer with French revolution, in 1798. [CROP¹ + -Y²]

crŏqu'et¹ (-kā), n. Game, played on lawn, in which wooden balls are driven with mallets through hoops; act of croqueting a ball. [perh. North. F, dial. form of CROCHET]

crŏqu'et² (-kā), v.t. (~*ing, ~ed,* pr. -king, -kid. (In game of croquet) drive away (opponent's ball or abs.) by placing the two together & striking one's own (cf. ROQUET). [f. prec.]

croquette' (-kĕt), n. Seasoned & fried ball of rice, potato, meat, etc. [F (*croquer* crunch)]

crōre, n. (Anglo-Ind.). Ten millions, one hundred lakhs (usu. of rupees). [f. Hind. *kror*]

crō'sier, -zier, (-zhyer), n. Bishop's, abbot's, pastoral staff; (improp.) archbishop's cross. [orig.=bearer of a crook, f. OF *crocier* f. med. L *crociarius* (*crocia* crook) confused w. F *croisier* f. L †*cruciarius* cross-bearer (*crux* cross); mod. *croisier*=~'s staff (16th c.)]

cross¹ (-aw-, -ŏ-), n. **1.** Stake (usu. with transverse bar) used by the ancients for crucifixion, esp. that on which Christ was crucified; model of this as religious emblem; *sign of* ~ made with right hand as religious act; staff surmounted with ~ & borne before archbishop or in processions, ~*-bearer,* person who carries this; monument in form of ~, esp. (also *marked-*~) one in centre of town; Christian religion. **2.** Trial, affliction; annoyance. **3.** ~-shaped thing; (*Southern*) *C*~, a constellation; *Greek* ~ (+); *Latin* ~ (†); *St Andrew's* ~ (×); *Tau*~, ~ *of St Anthony,* (T); *Maltese*~ (✱); *fiery*~, Scots signal (orig. two bloody sticks) sent through district to rouse inhabitants. **4.** Decoration in orders of knighthood (*Grand C.,* highest degree of this); decoration for distinguished valour, as *Victoria, George, Distinguished Service, Military, Distinguished Flying, C*~. **5.** Intermixture of breeds; animal resulting from this; mixture, compromise, *between* two things; (sl.) fraud, swindle; *on the* ~, diagonally. Hence ~'LET n., ~'WISE adv. [ult. f. L *crux crucis*: late OE has *cruc,* ME *cruche, crouche,* & (thr. OF) *crois*]

cross² (-aw-, -ŏ-), v.t. & i. Place crosswise, as ~ *swords* (in fighting, also fig.); make sign of cross on or over (esp. oneself, as sign of awe, to invoke divine protection, etc.); ~ *fortune-teller's hand with,* give her (coin); draw line across, as ~ *out, off, cancel,* ‖~ *cheque* (with two lines usu. filled up with *& Co.* or name of bank through whom alone it may be paid); write across (what is already written, a letter); go across (road, river, sea, or abs.); bestride (saddle, horse); carry, move, across; meet and pass (*each other* or abs.); *two persons' letters* ~ (each being dispatched before receipt of the other); ~ *one's mind,* occur to one; ~ *the path of,* meet with, thwart; thwart (person, will, plans); (cause to) inter-breed; cross-fertilize (plants). [f. prec.]

cross³ (-aw-, -ŏ-), a. Passing from side to side, transverse, ‖(=~ *bench,* in the House of Lords, for independent members who do not vote with the Government or the official Opposition; so ~*-bench,* adj., impartial, as the ~*-bench mind;* ~ *voting,* when in Parliamentary divisions etc. some of either or each side vote against their own party, as *there was no* ~ *voting);* intersecting; contrary, opposed, (to a purpose etc., or abs.); (colloq.) peevish, out of humour, as *as* ~ *as two sticks,* whence ~'LY² adv., ~'NESS n.; ~*-patch,* ill-natured person; ~ *reference* (from one part of book to another for further information); (Bookkeeping) ~ *entry* (transferring amount to different account or neutralizing previous entry); ~*-bred,* hybrid; (sl.) dishonestly, dishonestly got. [CROSS¹]

cross- in comb. **1.** f. CROSS n., objectively, as ~*-bearer,* or attrib.=having a transverse part, as CROSS-BOW, marked with a ~, as ~-BUN. **2.** f. CROSS a. = crossing, transverse, as ~*-bar, -beam, -keys, -piece, -section,* CROSS-BONES. **3.** Adv., in vbs as ~*-bred, -fertilize* (animals, plants, from individuals of different species), CROSS-EXAMINE, CROSS-QUESTION; in vbl nouns as ~*-fire,* firing in two crossing directions. **4.** Prep. = across, as ~*-country,* adj., across fields, not following roads.

cross'belt, n. Belt for cartridges etc. from shoulder to opposite hip. [CROSS-(2)]

cross'bill, n. Bird the mandibles of whose bill cross when bill is closed. [CROSS-(2)]

cross'bones, n. pl. Figure of two thigh-bones laid across each other, usu. under skull as emblem of death. [CROSS-(2)]

cross'bow (-bō), n. Bow fixed across wooden stock, with groove for the missile (stone, arrow, etc.) and mechanism for holding and releasing string. [CROSS-(1)]

cross'butt'ock, n. (boxing). Throw over the hip, in wrestling. [CROSS-(4)]

cross'-coun'ter, n. (boxing). Blow at head delivered across opponent's lead-off with the other hand. [CROSS-(4)]

cross'-cut, n. & a. Diagonal cut, path, etc.; figure in skating; adj.) adapted for cutting across the grain (chiefly in ~ *saw*). [CROSS-(2)]

crosse, n. Long racquet-like implement used in LACROSSE. [F, f. OF *croce, croc,* hook]

cross-exam'ine, v.t. Examine (esp. witness in legal action) minutely, with a view to checking previous examination or eliciting suppressed facts. Hence **cross-examina^tion** n.

cross-garnet, n. T-shaped hinge, fixed to door etc. by the long shank. [cross-]

cross-grain, n. Grain running across the regular grain. [cross-(2)]

cross-grained (-nd), a. (Of wood) with grain running irregularly or in crossing directions; (fig.) perverse, intractable. [-ED²]

cross'ing, n. [cross-(2)]

cross heading, n. (In newspaper etc.) indication of the contents of the following passage inserted here & there across the column for the reader's guidance in an article or report. [cross-(2)]

cross'ing (-aw-, -ŏ-), n. In vbl senses; also or esp.: Intersection of two roads, railways, etc., as || level ~ (of road and railway, or two railways, on same level); place where street is crossed; ~-sweeper, one who sweeps this. [-ING¹]

cross'legged (-gd), a. (Of person squatting) with legs crossed; (of person sitting on chair) with one leg laid across the other. [cross-(2)]

cross'light, n. Light that crosses another; (fig.) illustration of subject from another point of view. [cross-(2)]

cross purposes, n. pl. Contrary or conflicting purposes; name of a game; *be at ~*, misunderstand one another, (also) have conflicting plans with same object. [cross-(2)]

cross question, n. Question asked in cross-questioning; *~s & crooked answers*, game in which each question gets answer written for another.

cross-ques'tion, v.t. Question in order to elicit details or test accuracy. [cross-(3)]

cross-road, n. Road that crosses another or joins two main roads; (also *cross roads*) intersection of two roads; *at the ~s* (fig.), at a critical turning-point (in person's life etc.). [cross-(2)]

cross-ruff', n. & v.i. (Whist, Bridge). Alternate trumping by partners (see ruff⁴); (vb) play a ~. [cross-(2)]

cross-stitch, n. Stitch formed of two crossing each other; kind of needlework characterized by these. [cross-(2)]

cross-trees, n. pl. Two horizontal cross-timbers bolted to head of lower mast to support mast above. [cross-(2)]

cross'word, n. Puzzle in which words crossing vertically & horizontally according to a chequered pattern have to be filled in from clues. [cross-]

crotch, n. Bifurcation, fork (esp. of the human body). [prob. var. of crutch or crook; cf. F *croche*]

crotch'et, n. || (Mus.) black-headed note

with stem, half of minim; whimsical fancy, whence ~ERY, ~INESS, nn., ~Y¹ a.; hook. [f. F *crochet* dim. of *croc* hook]

crot'on, n. Genus of plants, from one species of which ~ *oil*, a drastic purgative, is obtained. [f. Gk *krotōn* tick, croton]

crouch, v.i., & n. Stoop, bend, esp. timidly or servilely; (n.) ~ing. [?]

croup¹ (-ōō-), n. Inflammatory disease in larynx & trachea of children, marked by sharp cough. [f. obs. vb *croup* croak (imit.)]

croup² (-ōō-), n. Rump, hindquarters, (esp. of horse). [F(-pe), f. Teut. cf. crop¹]

croup'ier (-ōō-), n. Raker in of money at gaming table; assistant chairman at public dinner. [F, orig.=rider on the croup¹]

crou'ton (krōō'tawn), n. Small piece of fried bread served with soups. [F]

crow¹ (-ō), n. Genus of birds, esp. *Carrion C.~*, large black bird; *white ~*, a rarity; *have a ~ to pluck* (fault to find) *with him; as the ~ flies, in a ~ line*, straight; *eat ~*, submit to humiliation; ~ (-bar), bar of iron (usu. with beak-like end) used as lever; ~*berry*, fruit of a small heath-like shrub; ~*bill*, forceps for extracting bullets etc.; ~*foot*, name of various plants, esp. species of buttercup, (Naut.) arrangement of small ropes for suspending awning, (Mil., also ~*'s-foot*) caltrop; ~*'s-foot*, marked with ~'s-feet; ~*'s-nest*, barrel fixed at mast-head of whaler etc. as shelter for look-out man; ~*-toe*, (usu.) = *crowfoot*. [OE *crāwe* f. *crāwan* crow³]

crow² (-ō), n. Crowing of cock; joyful cry of infant. [f. foll.]

crow³ (-ō), v.i. (past *crew* pr. krōō, or ~*ed* pr. krōd, p.p. ~*ed*). Utter loud cry of cock; (of child) utter joyful cry; exult loudly; ~ *over*, triumph over. [OE *crāwan*, cf. Du. *kraaijen*, G *krähen*; imit.]

crowd¹, n. Throng, dense multitude, (*would pass in a ~*, is not conspicuously defective); *the ~*, the masses (colloq.) company, set, lot; large number (of things); (Naut.) ~ *of sail*, large number of sails hoisted. [f. foll.]

crowd², v.i. & t. Collect (t. & i.) in a crowd; fill, occupy, cram, (space etc. *with*); (place etc., as a crowd does; force one's way *into*, *through*, etc. (confined space etc. or abs.); force (thing, person) *into* etc.; ~ *out*, exclude by ~*ing*; (Naut.) ~ *of* ship or crew) hasten on; ~ *sail*, hoist unusual number of sails. [OE *crūdan* press, drive, cf. MDu. *crūden*.]

crown, n. 1. Wreath of flowers etc. worn on head, esp. as emblem of victory, (also fig. as *martyr's ~*, *no cross no ~*). 2. Monarch's head-covering of gold etc. & jewels; (fig.) king or queen, regal power,

supreme governing power in a monarchy. **3.** Any ~-shaped ornament. **4.** (British coin worth) five shillings; foreign coin, esp.=KRONE. **5.** Top part, esp. of skull; whole head; upper part of cut gem above girdle; highest or central part of arch or arched structure, as ~ of the causeway; top of hat; part of tooth projecting from gum. **6.** Size of paper, 15"×20". **7.** ~ & anchor, popular gambling game played with dice marked with ~s, anchors, etc., and a corresponding board; ~-glass, made in circular sheets without lead or iron and chiefly for windows; || ~ land (belonging to the C~); C~ Colony (controlled by the C~); ~ Derby, kind of china made at Derby & often marked with ~ surmounting D; || ~ law, criminal law; || ~ lawyer (in service of the C~); C~ office (transacting common law business of Chancery); C~ prince, heir-apparent or designate to a sovereign throne (esp. in Germany and N. Europe); C~ princess, his wife; ~-wheel, CONTRATE wheel. [f. ONF corune f. L corona wreath, crown]

crown², v.t. **1.** Place crown on (person, head); invest (person) with regal crown or dignity (~ him, ~ him king; ~ed heads, kings & queens); (fig.) reward; occupy the head of, form chief ornament to, (lit. & fig.); put finishing touch to, as to ~ all; bring (efforts) to happy issue. **2.** (Draughts) make (piece) a king. **3.** (Dent.) ~ a tooth, protect its remains with a gold etc. cap cemented on. [f. OF coroner f. L coronare (as prec.)]

crowned (-nd), a. In vbl senses; (of hat) high, low, ~, with high, low, crown. [-ED¹,²]

crown'er¹ (-ooshn), n. = CORONER.

cru'cial (-ooshl), a. Decisive, critical, (case, point, test, etc.); (Anat.) cross-shaped, as ~ incision. [F, f. L cruz crucis cross+-AL]

cru'ciate (-oosh-), a. (zool., bot.). Cross-shaped. [f. med. L cruciatus (as CRUCIAL, -ATE²)]

cru'cible (-oo-), n. Melting-pot (usu. of earthenware); (fig.) severe trial. [f. med. L crucibulum, etym. dub.]

cru'ciferous (-oo-), a. Wearing, adorned with, a cross; (Bot.) of the family Cruci-ferae, having flowers with four equal petals arranged crosswise. [f. LL crucifer (as CRUCIAL, see -FEROUS)]

cru'cifix (-oo-), n. Image of Christ on the cross; (improp.) cross. [f. OF crucefix f. L cruci fixus one fixed to the CROSS (see FIX)]

crucifi'xion (-oo--; -kshon), n. Crucifying; the C~ (of Christ); picture of this. [f. mod. L crucifixio (L cruci figere, as prec., see -ION)]

cru'ciform (-oo-), a. Cross-shaped. [f. L cruz crucis cross, see -FORM]

cru'cify (-oo-), v.t. Put to death by fastening to a cross; (fig.) mortify (passions, sins, flesh); (Mil.) tie up (soldier) with arms out in field punishment. [f. OF crucefier f. LL †crucifīcāre (see -FY)=cruci figere, see CRUCIFIX]

crude (-oo-), a. In the natural or raw state; (of food etc.) not digested; unripe; (of diseases etc.) not matured; (fig.) ill-digested, unpolished, lacking finish; rude, blunt, (action, statement, manners); (Gram., of form of word) uninflected. Hence or cogn. ~'LY² adv., ~'NESS (-dn-), crud'TRY, nn., (-oo-). [f. L crudus raw]

cru'el (-oo-), a. Indifferent to, delighting in, another's pain; (of actions) showing such indifference; painful, distressing. Hence or cogn. ~'LY² adv., ~TY n., (-oo-). [F, f. L crudelis (crudus CRUDE)]

cru'et (-oo-), n. Small glass bottle with stopper for vinegar, oil, etc., for table; small vessel for wine or water in celebration of Eucharist; ~-stand (for ~s & castors). [f. OF †cruete dim. of cruie f. OLG crūca jug]

cruise (-ooz), v.i., & n. **1.** Sail to & fro on look-out for ships, for protection of commerce in time of war, for plunder, or for pleasure, making for no particular port (also fig.); (of aircraft) fly at cruising speed (economic travelling speed, less than top speed). **2.** n. Cruising voyage. [(n. f. vb) f. Du. kruisen or Sp., Port., cruzar, F croiser, f. L crucāre cross (crux)]

cruis'er (-ooz-), n. Warship designed for speed; armoured, (un)protected, one with(out) protective deck; ~ weight (Boxing, 'light-heavy' weight, not over 12st. 6lb. [-ER¹]

cruive (-oov), n. (Sc.). Wicker salmon-trap. [?]

crumb (-m), n., & v.t. Small fragment, esp. of bread; (fig.) small particle, atom, (of comfort etc.); soft inner part of bread; ~-cloth (laid over carpet, esp. under table); (v.t.) cover, thicken, with ~s, break into ~s. Hence ~'Y² (-mi) a. [vb f. n.) OE cruma, cf. Du. kruim]

crum'ble, v.t. & i. Break, fall, into crumbs or fragments (lit. & fig.). [earlier crimble f. OE cruma CRUMB]

crum'bly, a. Apt to crumble (intr.). [CRUMB+-LY¹, now treated as f. prec.+ -Y²]

crum'py, a. (sl.). (Of women) plump, comely; rich. [CRUMB+-Y²]

crump, v.t., & n. (colloq.). Hit (esp. cricket-ball) hard; (n.) heavy hit, heavy fall, (army sl.) bursting shell; sound of bursting bomb or shell. [imit.]

crum'pet, n. Soft cake of flour, egg, milk, etc., baked on iron plate; (sl.) head (BARMY on the ~). [?]

crŭm'ple, v.t. & i. Crush together or up into creased state; ruffle, wrinkle; become creased; (fig.) collapse, give way (usu. with up). [f. obs. *crump* v. & a. (make, become) curved + -LE(3)]

crŭnch, v.t. & i., & n. 1 Crush with teeth, esp. noisily; grind under foot (gravel etc.); make one's way (up, through, etc.) thus. 2. n. ~ing (noise). [replaces *cra(u)nch*, imit.]

crŭpp'er, n. Strap buckled to back of saddle & looped under horse's tail; hind-quarters of horse. [f. OF *cropiere* (as GROUP[1])]

crŭr'al (-oor-), a. (anat.). Of the leg. [f. L *cruralis* (*crus cruris* leg, see -AL)]

crusāde' (-ōō-), n. & v.i. (Hist.) Christian expedition to recover Holy Land from Mohammedans; war instigated by Church for alleged religious ends; (fig.) aggressive movement against public evil etc., as *Temperance* ~; (v.i.) engage in ~. Hence crusād'ER[1] n. [vb f. n.; f. 16th-c. F *croisade* & Sp. *cruzada* f. med. L *cruciata* p.p. of *cruciare* mark with CROSS[1]]

crus̄ād'ō (-ōō-), n. Portuguese coin. [f. Port. *cruzado* marked with cross]

cruse (-ōōs, -ōōz), n. (arch.). Pot, jar, of earthenware (*widow's* ~, inexhaustible supply, see 1 *Kings* xvii. 12 etc.). [cf. Du. *kroes*, G *krause*, etym. dub.]

crŭsh[1], v.t. & i. Compress with violence, so as to break, bruise, etc.; crumple (dress etc.) by rough handling; (fig.) sub-due, overwhelm, as ~*ing defeat, reply*; ~ *out*, extinguish, stamp out; ~ *a cup of wine*, drink it; (v.i.) squeeze one's way (*into* etc.). [prob. f. OF *croissir* crush, prob. f. Teut. orig.]

crŭsh[2], n. Act of crushing; crowded mass (esp. of persons); (colloq) crowded social gathering; (Austral.) fenced passage with funnel-shaped end along which cattle are driven in single file for branding; similar but shorter closed passage for dealing with sick animal; ~*room* in theatre etc. (for promenade during intervals); ~ *hat*, collapsible opera hat with spring; *have a* ~ *on* (sl.), be in love with. [f. prec.]

crŭst, n., & v.t. & i. 1. Hard outer part of bread; similar casing of anything, e.g. harder layer over soft snow (~*-hunt* n. & v.t. & i., of hunting elks etc. over a ~ that supports hunters but not quarry); hard dry scrap of bread; pastry covering pie; hard dry formation, scab, on skin; (Geol.) outer portion of earth; coating, deposit, on surface of anything; ~ *of wine*, deposit on sides of bottle; hard ex-ternal covering of animal or plant; (fig.) anything superficial. 2. v.t. Cover with, form into, ~. [(vb f. n.) f. L *crusta*, partly thr. OF *crouste*]

Crŭstā'cea (-sha), n. pl. Large class of animals, mostly aquatic, with hard shell, as crabs, lobsters, shrimps. Hence Crŭstā'cean a. & n.; crŭstā-cěoŭ'ogy n. [neut. pl. of mod. L CRUST-(*aceus* -ACEOUS)]

crŭstā'ceoŭs (-shus), a. Crust-like; (of animals) having a hard covering, esp. (Zool.) belonging to the *Crustacea*. [as prec.]

crŭst'ed, a. Having a crust; (of wine) having deposited a crust; (fig.) anti-quated, venerable, as ~ *prejudice, theory*. [-ED[2]]

crŭst'ily, adv., crŭst'iness n. [-Y[2]]

crŭst'y, a. Crust-like, hard; irritable; curt. Hence ~ILY[2] adv., ~INESS n. [-Y[2]]

crŭtch, n. Staff (usu. with crosspiece at top) for lame person (usu. *pair of* ~*es*) to support, prop (lit. & fig.); forked rest for leg in a side-saddle; fork of the human body (cf. CROTCH); (Naut.) various forked contrivances; crosspiece, whence ~*-comm.-*Teut.; cf. MHG[2] (-cht) a. [comm.-Teut.; cf. MHG[2] *kruk*, G *krücke*, f. OTeut. *kruk-bend*]

Crŭtch'ed Fri'ars, n. pl. Minor order of friars wearing a cross; site of their con-vent in London. [f. ME *crouch* CROSS[1] + -ED[2]]

crŭx, n. Difficult matter, puzzle; ~ *ansād'a*, ANKH (lit. = handled cross). [L, = cross]

crȳ[1], n. Loud inarticulate utterance of grief, pain, fear, joy, etc.; loud excited utterance of words; appeal, entreaty; proclamation of wares to be sold in streets; rumour; voice of the public; watchword, as *war~*, *battle~*; fit of weeping; yelping of hounds (also fig.), as *in full* ~ (pursuit); *within* ~, within calling distance (*of*); *a far* ~, a long way; ~*-baby*, one who cries childishly; *follow in the* ~, be in the following crowd of nobodies; *much* ~ *& little wool*, fuss to no purpose, as when pigs are shorn. [f. F *cri*, as foll.]

crȳ[2], v.t. & i. (*cried*). Utter loudly, ex-claim, (with sentence as object, or *that*); make loud utterance, as ~ *out*, ~ *to* (person etc.); announce for sale, as ~ *up*, praise, extol; ~ *off*, withdraw from bargain; claim share (*in*); ~ QUARTER, QUITS; ~ *shame upon*, protest against (act, person). [f. F *crier* f. L *quiritare* cry aloud, orig. ask aid of the citizens (*Quirites*)]

crȳ'ing, a. In vbl senses; esp. (of evils) calling for notice, flagrant. [-ING[2]]

crȳ'ogen, n. (chem.). Freezing-mixture; thing mixed with ice to make this. [f. Gk *kruos* frost + -GEN(1)]

crȳ'olite, n. Lustrous mineral of con-siderable industrial value found abun-dantly in Greenland, consisting mainly of sodium-aluminium fluoride. [f. Gk *kruos* frost + -LITE]

crypt, n. Underground cell, vault, esp. one beneath church, used as burial-place. [f. L f. Gk kruptē (kruptō hide)]

cryptaesthēs'ia, n. Supernormal knowledge, whether telepathic or clairvoyant. [CRYPTO-+ Gk aisthēsis perception +-IA¹]

cryp'tic, a. Secret, mystical. [f. L f. Gk kruptikos (as CRYPT, see -IC)]

cryp't(o)- in comb. = Gk kruptos hidden, secret, as -branchiate, with concealed gills.-Communist,secret sympathizer with Communism,-logy, enigmatical language.

crȳp'togam, n. Plant having no stamens or pistils, & therefore no proper flowers. Hence cryptogam'ic, cryptog'amous, aa., cryptog'amist(3), cryptog'amy¹, nn. [f. F cryptogame (prec.+ Gk -gamos wedded), after Linnaean class-name Cryptogamia]

cryp'togram, -graph (-ahf), nn. Thing written in cipher. So cryptog'rapher, cryptog'raphy, nn., cryptograph'ic a. [CRYPTO-+-GRAM, -GRAPH]

cryptomēr'ia, n. Evergreen tree of the cypress type: Japanese Cedar. [CRYPTO-+ Gk meros part (because the seeds are enclosed by scales)]

crȳs'tal, n.&a. 1. A clear transparent ice-like mineral; rock~, a form of pure quartz; piece of this; ~ set, simple form of receiving apparatus in broadcasting using a ~ rectifier; (poet.) any clear transparent thing, esp. water; ~gazing, concentration of one's gaze on ball of rock-~, pool of ink, etc., for the purpose of inducing a hallucinatory picture of future or distant events (~, colloq., view of the future thus obtained, prophetic utterance); (also ~ glass) glass of very transparent quality; vessel etc. of this; C~Palace, building of glass & iron built in Hyde Park for the 1851 Exhibition & re-erected at Sydenham & destroyed by fire in 1936; (Chem., Min.) aggregation of molecules with definite internal structure & external form of solid enclosed by symmetrically arranged plane faces. 2. adj. Made of, like, clear as,~. [f. OF cristal f. L cristallum f. Gk krustallos ice, crystal. f. krustainō freeze (kruos frost)]

crȳs'talline a. Made of, clear as, like, crystal; ~ heaven (in Ptolemaic system, between primum mobile & firmament, assumed to explain precession of equinox etc.); ~ lens of eye, transparent body in membranous capsule behind iris. [f. L f. Gk krustallinos (as prec., see -INE²)]

crȳs'tallize, v.t. & i. Form into crystals or (fig.) definite or permanent shape; ~ed fruit (preserved by impregnation with sugar, and coated with sugar crystals). Hence ~ABLE a.,~A'TION n. [-IZE]

crystallo- in comb. = Gk krustallos CRYSTAL, as -gen'ic, -geny, forming, formation of, crystals, -grapher, -graph'ic, -graphy, student of, pertaining to, science of, crystal structure.

crȳs'talloid, a. & n. Crystal-like: (body) of crystalline structure (cf. COLLOID). [-OID]

ctēn'oid (t-), a. & n. (Fish with scales or teeth) like a comb. [f. Gk kteis ktenos comb, see -OID]

cub, n., & v.t. &i.(-bb-). 1. Young of fox, as~-hunting; young of bear or other wild beast; unpolished youth (usu. unlicked ~); = WOLF~ (junior boy scout). 2.(vb). Bring forth (~s, or abs.). Hence ~b'ISH¹ a.,~HOOD n. [?]

cub'age, n. [Finding of] cubic content. [CUBE+-AGE]

cub'ature, n. = prec. [f. mod. L cubare -at-. (LL cubus CUBE), see -URE]

cubb'ing, n. Cub-hunting. [CUB+-ING²]

cubb'y, n. Snug place (usu. ~-hole). [f. obs. or dial. cub, stall, pen: cf. LG kübje linhay]

cube, n., & v.t. 1. Solid contained by squares; block of anything so or similarly shaped; product of a number multiplied by its square (~ of 2, alg. symbol $2^3 = 8$, ~ root of 8, alg. symbol $\sqrt[3]{8}$, = 2). 2. v.t. Find ~ of (number); find cubic content of (solid); pave with ~s. [(vb f. n.) F, f. LL f. Gk kubos cube, die]

cub'eb, n. Pungent berry of a Javan shrub, used in medicine & cookery. [f. F cubèbe f. Arab. kababah]

cub'ic, a. Cube-shaped; of three dimensions; ~ foot, inch, volume of a cube whose edge is one foot, inch; ~ content of solid, its volume expressed in ~ feet etc.; involving the cubes of numbers, as ~ equation. Hence ~AL a.,~ALLY² adv. [f. F cubique f. L f. Gk kubikos (as CUBE, see -IC)]

cub'icle, n. Small separate sleeping compartment in schools etc. [f. L cubiculum (cubare lie down)]

cub'iform, a. Cube-shaped. [-I-, -FORM]

cub'ism, n. A recent style in art in which objects are so presented as to give the effect of an assemblage of geometrical figures. So cub'IST n. [CUBE, -ISM]

cub'it, n. Ancient measure of length, 18 to 22 in. [f. L cubitus elbow, length of fore-arm]

cub'ital, a. Of the forearm or corresponding part in animals. [f. L cubitalis (prec., -AL)]

cub'oid, a. & n. Cube-shaped, like a cube, as ~ bone (of the foot); (n.) rectangular parallelepiped. Hence cuboid'AL a. [f. Gk kuboeidēs (as CUBE, see -OID)]

cuck'ing-stool, n. (hist.) Chair in which disorderly women etc. were ducked as punishment. [prob. f. obs. cuck f. ON kúka void excrement, stool]

cuck'old, n., & v.t. Husband of unfaithful wife; (v.t.) make a ~ of. [(vb f. n.) ME cokewold f. OF cucuault (cucu cuckoo); mod. F coucou cuckoo, cocu cuckold]

cu'ckoo (kōō-), n. & pred. a. 1. Migratory bird reaching British Islands in April & depositing its eggs in nests of small birds;

cut bôn'er (kŭt), sentence. [f. Cufa, city S. of Bagdad, -IC]

Cuf'ic, K-, a. & n. (Of) rude form of the Arabic alphabet found chiefly in inscriptions.

cuff², v.t., & n. 1. Strike with fist or open hand. 2. n. Such blow. [etym. dub.; Sw. has kuffa thrust]

cuff¹, n. Ornamental bottom part of sleeve; separate band of linen worn round wrist. Hence (-)**cuffed²**(-t)a. [?]

cue'ist (kū'ist), n. Billiard-player. [prec. +IST(3)]

cue², n. Pigtail (also QUEUE); long straight tapering leather-tipped rod for striking ball in billiards etc. [f. F queue (OF cue) f. L cauda tail]

cue, n. Last words of a speech in a play, serving as signal to another actor to enter or speak; (Mus.) similar guide to singer or player; hint how to act; proper course to take. [?]

cud'weed, n. Composite plant with chaffy scales round flower-heads, given to cattle that had had lost their end.

cud'gel, n. & v.t. (-ll-). 1. Short thick stick used as weapon; ~-play, contest with ~s; (fig.) take up the ~s for, defend vigorously. 2. v.t. Beat with ~, esp. fig.; ~ one's brains for, try to think of. [vb f. n.) OE cycgel, etym. dub.]

‖ **cuddy²** n. (Sc.), Donkey; fool, ass; young of the coal-fish; lever on tripod for lifting stones etc. [?]

cuddÿ¹, n. saloon of large ship; closet, cup-board. [?] (Hist.) Cabin of half-decked boat,

cud'dle, v.t. & i., & n. 1. Hug, embrace, fondle; lie close & snug; nestle together; curl oneself up. 2. n. Hug, embrace, ~ing or tempting to ~e, [?] Hence ~ESOME (-ĭs-), ~ÿ², aa., given to

cud'bear (-bâr), n. Purple or violet dyeing-powder prepared from various lichens; kind of lichen. [named by Cuthbert Gordon, patentee]

cud, n. Food that ruminating animal brings back from first stomach into mouth & chews at leisure; (fig.) chew the ~, reflect, ruminate. [OE cudu, cf. OHG chuti, quiti, glue]

cucùrb'it, n. Gourd. Hence ~A'CEOUS" (-āshus) a. [f. L cucurbita]

---

cuc'ullate, -āted, a. (bot., zool.) Shaped like, covered with, a hood. [f. LL cucul-latus (cucullus hood, see -ATE²)]

cuc'umber, n. (Creeping plant with) long fleshy fruit eaten in thin slices as salad; cool as a ~, quite cool, self-possessed. [f. F, (mod. concs-) f. L cucumerem (nom. -mis)]

simpleton; ~ clock (striking with sound like ~'s note). ~-flower, meadow plant like, common meadow flower, ladysmock; ~pint, common arum, wake-robin; ~-spit, froth exuded by the larvae of certain insects as a protection. 2. adj. (sl.). Crazy, barmy. [f. F coucou, imit.]

---

cuish, **cuisse** (kwis), n. (hist.). Thigh armour (usu. pl.), (earlier cuisses, cuissess- -es, -es, (pl.) f. OF cuissel f. L coxa hip)]

cuisine (kwizēn'), n. Kitchen arrange-ments; style of cooking. [F, = kitchen f. L coquina (coquere cook)]

cuisse (kwis), **cuish** (kw-), n. (hist.). = prec., see

cuirass' (kw-), n. Body armour, breast-plate & back-plate fastened together; woman's close-fitting sleeveless bodice. [f. F cuirasse f. L coriacea (fem. adj.) leathern (corium leather, see -ACEOUS)]

cuirassier (kwirasēr', kū-), n. Horse-soldier wearing cuirass. [F (as prec., see -EER)]

it? (i.e. who is most likely to have brought it about?); (pop.) to what purpose? [LL]

cud-de-sac (see Ap.), n. Blind alley; (Anat.) tube etc. open at one end only. [F]

-cule, dim. suf. = F -cule f. L -culus, -cula, -culum; or in full -cle, as -cule, so in full: article, corpuscule, cor-puscle, fascicula, fascicula, vesiculum.

cul'inarÿ, a. Pertaining to a kitchen or cooking; fit for cooking, as ~ plants. [f. L culinarius (culina kitchen, see -ARY")]

cull, v.t., & n. Pick (flower etc.); select; (n.) animal removed from flock (& usu. fattened) as inferior or too old for breed-ing. [f. OF cuillir (mod. cueillir) f. L as COLLECT]

cullender. See COLANDER.

cull'et, n. Refuse glass with which crucibles are replenished. [later form of COLLET now disused in this sense] ‖ **cull'ÿ**, n. (sl.). Dupe, simpleton; mate, pal. [?]

culm¹, n. Coal-dust (esp. of anthracite). [?]

culm², n. (bot.). Stem of plant (esp. of grasses). So ~IF'EROUS a. [f. L culmus]

cul'minate, v.i. Reach its highest point (in; lit. & fig.); (Astron.) be on the meri-dian. Hence ~A'TION n. [f. LL culminare (culmen top) see -ATE']

cul'pable, a. Criminal, blameworthy, as ~le negligence, hold him ~le. Hence **culpaBIL'ITY**, ~leNESS (-ĭn-), nn., ~lÿ² adv. [f. OF coupable f. L culpabilis (culpa fault)]

cul'prit, n. Offender; prisoner at the bar. [17th c.; orig. in formula Culprit, how will you be tried?, said by Clerk of Crown to prisoner pleading Not Guilty; abbr. of Culpable: prest d'averrer etc. (You are) guilty: (I am) ready to prove etc.]

cult, n. System of religious worship; devotion, homage, to person or thing (the ~ of). [f. L cultus -ūs worship (colere cult- till, worship)]

cul'tivate, v.t. Till, whence **cul'tivABLE** a.; (fig.) improve, develop, (person, mind, manners; esp. in p.p.); pay attention

to, cherish, (faculty, art, person, his acquaintance); prepare (ground) with CULTIVATOR. [f. LL *cultivare* f. *cultivus* (*terra*) tilled (land), as prec., -IVE, -ATE³]

culti·va'tion, n. Cultivating, cultivated state, (lit. & fig.). [F (as CULTIVATE, see -ATION)]

cul'tivator, n. One who cultivates; implement for breaking up ground & uprooting weeds. [-OR²]

cul'trate, a. (nat. hist.). Knife-edged. So **cul'triform** a. [f. L *cultratus* (*culter* -tri knife, -ATE²)]

cul'ture, n., & v.t. Tillage; rearing, production, (of bees, oysters, fish, silk, bacteria); set of bacteria thus produced; improvement by (mental or physical) training; intellectual development; (v.t.) cultivate (lit. & fig., chiefly in p.p. ~ed pp. -cherd). Hence ~AL a., ~ISM(2) n., (-cher-). [vb f. F *culturer* F, f. L *cultura* as CULM, -URE]

|| **cul'ver**, n. (dial.). Wood-pigeon; ~*keys*, cowslip, other plants. [OE *culfre*, etym. dub.]

cul'verin, n. (hist.). Large cannon, small firearm. [f. F *couleuvrine* snake (L *colubra*, -INE¹)]

cul'vert, n. Channel, conduit, carrying water across under road, canal, etc.; channel for electric cable. [?]

cum, prep. With; ~ *grano* (*salis*) (grān'ō sāl'is), with caution or reserve (lit. with a grain of salt); ~ *dividend* (abbr. ~ *div.*), including dividend about to be paid; also in names of combined parishes, as *Stow-~-Quy*. [L]

cum'ber, v.t., & n. Hamper, hinder; burden; (n.) hindrance, obstruction. [(vb) f. OF *combrer* f. LL *cumbrus* heap, etym. dub, perh. f. L CUMULUS; (n.) f. vb or f. G *kummer* trouble]

cum'bersome, a. Unwieldy, clumsy. Hence ~LY² (-ml-) adv., ~NESS (-ran-) n. [-SOME]

Cum'brian, a. & n. (Native) of Cumberland; of the ancient British kingdom of Cumbria. [-AN]

cum'brous, a. = CUMBERSOME. Hence ~LY² adv., ~NESS n. [CUMBER+-OUS]

cum'in, -mm-, n. Umbelliferous plant like fennel, with aromatic seed. [f. L f. Gk *kuminon*]

|| **cumm'er, kimm'er**, n. (Sc.). Godmother of one's child or godchild; female companion; woman. [f. F *commère* f. LL COM(*mater* mother)]

cumm'erbund, n. (Anglo-Ind.). Waist sash. [f. Hind. & Pers. *kamar-band* loin band]

cum'quat (-ŏt), n. Plum-sized orange-like fruit with sweet rind and acid pulp, used in preserves. [dial. form of Chin. *kin kü* golden orange]

cum'shaw, n. (pidgin Engl.). Present, tip, baksheesh. [dial. form of Chin. *ken hsieh* grateful thanks]

cum'ulate¹, a. Heaped up, massed. [us foll., see -ATE²]

cum'ulate², -v.t. &i. Accumulate. Hence ~A'TION n. [f. L *cumulare* (*cumulus* heap), see -ATE³]

cum'ulative, a. Tending to accumulate; increasing in force etc. by successive additions, as ~ *evidence*; ~ *voting*, system in which each voter has as many votes as there are representatives, & may give all to one candidate; ~ *preference shares* (entitling holder to arrears of interest before other shares receive any on current year). Hence ~LY² (-vl-) adv., ~NESS (-vn-) n. [f. prec.+-IVE]

cum'ulus, n. (pl. -*li*). Heap; set of rounded masses of cloud heaped on each other & resting on horizontal base. So **cum'ulo-, comb. form, cum'ulous a.** [L] **cun'eate**, a. Wedge-shaped. [f. L *cuneatus* (*cuneus* wedge), see -ATE²]

cun'eiform (*also* kūne'i-), a. & n. 1.Wedge-shaped. 2. n. ~ writing in ancient inscriptions of Persia, Assyria, etc. [f. L *cuneus* wedge, -FORM]

cunette', n. (fortif.). Central trench sunk in fort ditch, serving as drain. [F, f. It. *cunetta* (dim. f. L *lacuna* ditch]

cunn'ing¹, n. Artfulness, craft; (arch.) ability, dexterity. [vbl n. f. CAN²]

cunn'ing², a. Artful, crafty; (arch.) skilful, ingenious; able. Hence ~LY² adv. [part. (orig. *~tunnende* of CAN²]

cup¹, n. Drinking-vessel, with or without handle & stem, as *tea, coffee,* ~; *challenge* ~ (prize for race etc., usu. of gold or silver, esp. one held by winner only until next race etc.); rounded cavity, esp. calyx of flower, socket of some bones, etc.; cupful, as ~ *of tea, half a* ~; one's ~ *of tea* (colloq.), what interests or suits one; chalice used, wine taken, at Communion; fate, portion, experience, as *a bitter~, his~was full* (happiness, misery, was complete); *the ~s that cheer but not inebriate,* tea (Cowper *Task* iv. 39); *in one's ~s,* while (getting) drunk; wine, cider, etc., with various flavourings, as *claret-~; ~ & ball,* ~ at end of stem, with attached ball to be thrown & caught in ~ or on spiked end of stem; ~-*bearer,* one who serves wine, esp. officer of royal or noble household; ~-*moss,* lichen with ~-shaped processes arising from the thallus;~-*shake,* opening between two concentric layers of timber. Hence ~FUL (-ŏŏl) n. (pl. -*ls*). [perh. f. LL *cuppa,* whence OF *cope,* It. *coppa,* etc.]

cup², v.t. (-pp-). Bleed (person) by means of a ~-*ping-glass.* [f. prec.]

cup'board (kŭb'erd), n. Shelved closet or cabinet for crockery, provisions, etc.; SKELETON *in the* ~; ~ *love* (simulated for sake of what one can get by it). [CUP¹+BOARD]

cup'el, n., & v.t. (-ll-). Small flat circular vessel used in assaying gold or silver with lead; (v.t.) assay in ~. Hence ~LA'

TION n. [vb f n.] f. F *coupelle* f. *cupa* cask]

Cupid (kū-), n. Roman god of love; beautiful boy; ~'s *bow*, (upper edge of) upper lip, which is shaped like the conventional double-curved bow carried by ~. [f. L *Cupīdo* (*cupere* desire)]

cupid'ity, n. Greed of gain. [f. F *cupidité* f. L *cupiditatem* (*cupidus* desirous, see -TY)]

cup'ola, n. Rounded dome forming roof; ceiling of dome; (also ~*-furnace*) furnace for melting metals; revolving dome protecting mounted guns on warship. [It., f. L *cupula* dim. of *cupa* cask]

cup'reous, a. Of or like copper. [f. L *cupreus* (*cuprum* COPPER) + -OUS]

cup'ric, a. Containing copper. So **cu-pri'ferous**, a., **cup'ro-** comb. form. [f. L *cuprum*, -IC(1)]

cup'ule, n. (bot., zool.). Cup-shaped organ, receptacle, etc. [f. L as CUPOLA]

cur, n. Worthless, low-bred, or snappish dog; surly, ill-bred, or cowardly fellow. [cf. MDu. *korre*, cf. ON, Sw., *kurra* grumble]

cur'açao, -çoa, (-sō), n. Liqueur of spirits flavoured with peel of bitter oranges. [Du. island in Caribbean sea; -çoa is E mis-spelling]

cur'acy, n. Curate's office; benefice or perpetual curate. [f. CURATE, see -ACY(3)]

cur'are, -i, n. Resinous bitter substance from some S. American plants, paralysing the motor nerves, used by Indians to poison arrows. Hence **cur'arine** n, **cur'arize(t)** v.t. [corrupt. of native *wurali*]

cur'assow (-ō), n. Turkey-like bird of Central & S. America. [=CURAÇAO]

cur'ate, n. Assistant to parish priest; ~*-in-charge*, clergyman appointed to take charge of parish during incapacity or suspension of incumbent; ∥(joc.) small extra poker meant for use. [f. med. L -ATE(1)]

cur'ative, a. & n. (Thing) tending to cure (esp. disease). [F (-*if*, -*ive*), f. L *curare* CURE2, see -ATIVE]

cur'ator, n. Person in charge, manager; keeper, custodian, of museum; ∥ member of board managing property or having general superintendence in University; ∥(Sc. law; kŭr'a-) guardian of minor, lunatic, etc. Hence **cur'atorIAL** a., ~SHIP n. [L (as prec., -OR2)]

curb, n., & v.t. 1. Chain, strap, passing under lower jaw of horse, used as a check; (fig.) check, restraint; hard swelling on horse's leg, whence ~'y2 a.; frame round top of well; timber or iron plate round edge of circular structure; = KERB; ~ *roof*, one of which each face has two slopes, the lower one steeper. 2. v.t. Put ~ on (horse), (fig.) restrain. [[vb f. n.] f. F *courbe* (adj.) f. L *curvus* bent]

cur'cuma, n. Turmeric, substance used in curry-powder, as test for alkalis (~ *paper*), etc.; genus of tuberous plants yielding this & other commercial substances. [mod.L f. Arab. *kurkuma* saffron, turmeric, cf. CROCUS]

curd, n. Coagulated substance formed (naturally or artificially) by action of acids on milk, and made into cheese or eaten (often pl.; ~*s & whey*, junket); fatty substance found between flakes of boiled salmon; ~ *soap* (white, of tallow & soda). Hence ~'y2 a. [perh. f. OE as CROWD2]

cur'dle, v.t. & i. Congeal, form into curd; (fig.) ~ *the blood* (with horror), [*curd* v.t. & i.(now rare) + -LE(3)]

cure1, n. Remedy; course of medical or other treatment (esp. of specified kind, as *grape, milk,* ~); success with this; spiritual charge, as ~ *of souls*; vulcaniza-tion. Hence ~'LESS a. [f. F *cure* f. L *cura* care]

cure2, v.t. & i. Restore to health (also fig.); remedy (an evil); preserve (meat, fruit, tobacco) by salting, drying, etc. (also intr.); vulcanize (rubber), (of rubber) become vulcanized. Hence **cur'able2** a. [f. F *curer* f. L *curare* CURE take care of (*cura*)]

cure3, n. (sl.). Odd or eccentric person. [?]

curé, (see Ap.), n. Parish priest in France etc. [F]

curette', n., & v.t. & i. Surgeon's small scraping-instrument; (vb) scrape with ~. [F (as CURE1, -ETTE)]

cur'few, n. Medieval regulation for extinction of fires at fixed hour in evening; hour for this; (also ~*-bell*) bell announcing it; ringing of bell at fixed evening hour, still surviving in some towns; (under martial law etc.) signal or time after which inhabitants may not be abroad. [f. AF *coeverfu* f. OF *covrefeu* (*couvrir* cover + *feu* fire)]

cur'ia, n. One of the ten divisions of any of the three ancient Roman tribes; its place of worship; Roman senate-house; senate of ancient Italian towns; court of justice (esp. under feudal organization); the Papal court. [L]

cur'ial, a. Of a curia; of the Papal court, whence ~ISM n. [F; f. L *curialis* (CURIA, see -AL)]

cur'io, n. (pl. -os). Curious object of art. [=foll.]

curios'ity, n. Desire to know; inquisi-tiveness; strangeness; *a* ~, strange or rare object. [f. OF *curiosité* f. L *curiosi-tatem* (as foll., see -TY)]

cur'ious, a. Eager to learn; inquisitive; minutely careful, as ~ *inquiry*; strange, surprising, odd; erotic, pornographic (as euphemism in booksellers' catalogues). Hence ~LY2 adv., ~NESS n. [f. OF *curios* f. L *curiosus* f. *cura* care, see -OUS(1)]

curl¹, n. Spiral lock of hair; ~paper (used for twisting hair into ~s); anything spiral or incurved; act of curling; as ~ of the lip (expressing scorn); state of being curled, as keep the hair in ~; disease of potatoes etc. in which shoots or leaves are curled up. [f. foll.]

curl², v.t. & i. Bend, coil, into spiral shape (t. & i.); ~ up, roll up into a curl, (intr., sl.) collapse; move in spiral form (of smoke etc.); play at CURLING; ~ing-irons, -tongs, instruments (heated before use) for ~ing the hair; ~ing-pins, folding clips used (cold) for similar purpose. [f. obs. adj. croll, crull, curly; cf. Du. krollen, G krollen, krollen]

curl'ew, n. Wading bird with long slender curved bill. [f. OF courlieus perh. imit. of cry, but assim. to corliu courier f. courir run]

curl'ing, n. In vbl senses; esp. Scots game played on ice with large round stones; ~irons, -tongs, -pins, see CURL². [-ING¹]

curl'y, a. Having, arranged in, curls; ~pate, ~-headed person. Hence **curl'iness** n. [-Y²]

curmudg'eon (-jn), n. Churlish or miserly fellow. Hence ~LY¹ (-jn-) a. [?]

cur'rach (-ra), n. Coracle. [f. Ir. curach, cf. CORACLE]

cur'ragh (-ra), n. Marshy waste land; the C~, military camp and race-course near Dublin. [Ir. corrach marsh, Manx curragh fen]

cur'rant, n. Dried fruit of a seedless variety of grape grown in the Levant, much used in cookery; Red, White, Black, C~, (fruit of) species of Ribes. [orig. raisins of Corauntz (Corinth)]

cur'rency, n. Time during which a thing is current; (of money) circulation; money current in actual use in a country (|| ~ note, inconvertible legal-tender note for £1 or 10s. issued by Treasury during & after the 1914–18 war, replaced in 1928 by Bank of England notes); prevalence (of words, ideas, reports). [f. L currere run, see -ENCY]

cur'rent¹, a. In general circulation or use (of money, opinions, rumours, words); pass, go, run, ~, be generally accepted as true or genuine; (of time) now passing, as ~ week, month; belonging to the ~ time, as ~ issue (of journal); ~ handwriting, cursive. Hence ~LY² adv. [f. OF corant part. of courir f. L currere run (refash. on L)]

cur'rent², n. Running stream; water, air, etc., moving in given direction; course, tendency, (of events, opinions, etc.); transmission of electric force through a body. [prec. as n.]

cur'ricle, n. Light two-wheeled carriage (usu. for two horses abreast). [f. foll.]

curric'ulum, n. Course (of study). [L, = course, race-chariot, f. currere run]

cur'rier, n. One who dresses & colours tanned leather. [f. OF corier f. L coriarius (corium hide, leather), see -ARY¹]

cur'rish, a. Like a cur; snappish; mean-spirited. Hence ~LY² adv., ~NESS n. [-ISH¹]

cur'ry¹, n., & v.t. 1. Dish of meat etc. cooked with bruised spices & turmeric (~paste, -powder, preparations of turmeric etc. for making ~. 2. v.t. Prepare, flavour, with ~-powder. [(vb f. n.) f. Tamil kari sauce]

cur'ry², v.t. Rub down or dress (horse etc.) with ~-comb; dress (tanned leather); (fig.) thrash; ~ favour (orig. favel f. OF faveau, favel, the chestnut horse), ingratiate oneself (with person) by officiousness etc. [f. OF correier, earlier CON(reder prepare see ARRAY]

curse¹, n. Utterance of deity or person invoking deity, consigning person or thing to destruction, divine vengeance, etc. (~s come home to roost, injure the curser; under a ~, feeling or liable to its effects); sentence of excommunication; profane oath, imprecation; accursed object; evil inflicted in response to ~; great evil, bane; (Cards) = ~; nine of diamonds. [?]

curse², v.t. & i. Utter curse against; excommunicate; blaspheme; afflict with (esp. in pass.); (v.i.) utter curses. [?]

curs'ed, -st, a. & adv. In vbl senses; also: damnable, abominable; (arch.; usu. curst) cantankerous; (adv.) cursedly. Hence **curs'édly²** adv., **curs'édness** n. [p.p. of prec.]

curs'ive, a. & n. Running (writing in manuscript), opp. to UNCIAL. [f. med. L cursivus (L currere curs- run, see -IVE)]

curs'or, n. Transparent slide engraved with hair-line forming part of slide-rule. [L, as CURSIVE]

curs'ory, a. Hasty, hurried, (~y inspection). Hence ~ILY² adv., ~INESS n. [f. L cursorius of a runner (as CURSIVE, see -ORY)]

curt, a. Discourteously brief; terse, concise; (literary) short. Hence ~LY² adv., ~NESS n. [f. L curtus short]

curtail', v.t. Cut short (lit. & fig.); deprive of. Hence ~MENT n. [f. obs. curtal horse with docked tail f. OF cortald (court short f. L curtus + Teut. suf. -ald; assim. to tail]

curt'ail-step, n. Lowest step of stair, with outer end carried round. [?]

curt'ain (-tn), n., & v.t. 1. Suspended cloth used as screen; draw the ~ (back or aside to reveal objects, forward to conceal them); screen separating stage of theatre from auditorium (~ falls, drops, is dropped, at end of action, rises, is raised, at beginning; also fig.; ~!, narrator's word drawing attention to dramatic situation just described, = tableau);

fire-proof ~ in theatre; plain wall of fortified place, connecting two towers etc.; piece of plain wall not supporting a roof; partition, cover, in various technical senses; ~-*fire*, = BARRAGE (Mil.); ~ *lecture*, wife's reproof to husband in bed; ~-*raiser* in theatre, short opening piece. 2. v.t. Furnish, cover, shut off, with ~s. [vb f. n.] f. OF *cortine* f. L *cortina*, etym. dub.]

curti'lage, n. (law, dial.), Area attached to dwelling-house. [f. OF *courtillage* (*courtil* small court f. COURT +-AGE)]

cŭr'tsy, -sey, n., & v.i. 1. Feminine salutation made by bending knees & lowering body; *make, drop,* a ~. 2. v.i. Make ~ (to person). [var. of COURTESY]

cŭr'ule (-ōōl), a. Pertaining to any high civic dignity; (Rom. Ant.) ~ *chair,* one like camp-stool, inlaid with ivory; ~ *magistrate,* one entitled to this. [f. L *curulis* perh. f. *currus* chariot]

cŭr'vature, n. Curving; (of curve) form; deviation (of curved line) from straight line. [f. L *curvatura* (as foll.)]

cûrve¹, v.t. & i. Bend so as to form a curve. [f. L *curvare* (as foll.)]

cûrve², n. Line of which no part is straight; curved form or thing; (Statistics etc.) line presenting diagrammatically a continuous variation of quantity, force, etc.; graph. [f. L *curvus* bent]

cûr'vet (also kŏŏrvĕt'), n. & v.i. (-tt-, -t-). Horse's leap with fore-legs raised together & hind-legs raised with spring before fore-legs reach ground; (v.i., of horse or rider) make ~. [vb f. n.] [f. It. *corvetta* dim. of *corvo* curve (as prec.)]

cûrvili'near, a. Contained by consisting of, curved line(s). Hence ~LY² adv. [+LINEAR]

cŭs'cus, n. Aromatic root of an Indian grass, used for fans etc. [f. Hind. *khas khas*]

cū'sec, n. (Flow of) one cubic foot (of water) per second (unit in irrigation engineering). [abbr. of 'cubic foot per second']

cŭsh'at, n. (Sc., dial.), Wood-pigeon, ring-dove. [?]

cushion¹ (kŏŏ'shn), n. **1.** Mass of soft material stuffed into cloth or silk covering for sitting, kneeling, reclining, on; PIN~, **2.** Pad worn by woman under hair; pad beneath skirt of woman's dress. **3.** Elastic lining of sides of billiard table; steam left in cylinders as buffer to piston; fleshy part of buttock (of pig etc.); frog of horse's hoof; sweety in ~ shape; ~ *tire* of bicycle (rubber tubing stuffed with rubber shreds). Hence ~Y² (-sho-) a. [ME, f. F *coussin*, etym. dub.; the earlier (ME) form *cuissin* is f. OF *coissin* f. L +*coxinum* (*coxa* hip, see -URE¹)]

cushion², v.t. Furnish with cushions (also fig.); suppress quietly (complaints etc.); (Billiards) place, leave, (ball) against cushion. [f. prec.]

cush'y (kŏŏ-), a. (sl.). (Of a post, task, etc.) easy, pleasant, comfortable. [Anglo-Ind., f. Hind. *khush* pleasant]

cusp, n. Apex, peak; (Geom.) point at which two branches of curve meet & stop; (Archit.) projecting point between small arcs in Gothic tracery; (Bot.) pointed end, esp. of leaf. Hence ~ED² (-pt) a. [f. L *cuspis -idis* point]

cus'pidal, a. Of (the nature of) a cusp. So ~ate, ~ated, [-ATE²(2)] aa. [as prec., -AL]

*cus'pidor, n. Spittoon. [Port., = splitter (*cuspir* f. L *conspuere*, see -OR³)]

*cuss, n. Curse; person, creature, (often disparaging). [vulg. pron. of CURSE¹]

*cuss'edness, n. Perversity, esp. pure ~. [vulg. pron. of *cursedness*]

cus'tard, n. Mixture of eggs & milk, baked or served liquid; ~-*apple,* W. Indian fruit with pulp like ~, lorig. a kind of pie; prob. f. obs. *crustade* t. F *croustade* (as CRUST,-ADE)]

custō'dial, a. Relating to custody. [-AL]

custō'dian, n. Guardian, keeper. So ~SHIP n. [as foll. +-AN]

cus'tody, n. Guardianship, care, (*parent has ~ of child, child is in the ~ of father*); imprisonment, esp. *take into ~*, arrest. [f.L *custodia*(*custos -odis*guardian,see-Y³)]

cus'tom, n. Usual practice; (Law) established usage having the force of law; (pl.) duty levied upon imports from foreign countries; ~-*house,* office (esp. in seaport) at which ~s are collected; business patronage or support; *the C~s,* department of the Civil Service that deals with the levying of ~s. [f. OF *costume* f. L *consuetudinem* f. *consuescere* sued-]

cus'tomari'ly, a. & n. Usual; (Law) subject to, held by, custom (of the manor etc.); (n., also -*tumary*) written collection of the customs of a country. Hence ~iLY² adv., ~INESS n. [f. med. L *custumarius* = L *consuetudinarius* (as prec., see -ARY¹)]

cus'tomer, n. Buyer; (colloq.) *queer, awkward,* etc., ~ (person to deal with). [prob. f. CUSTOM +-ER¹]

cŭs'tŏs, n. Guardian, keeper; ~ *rŏtŭlōr'um*, keeper of the rolls, principal justice of the peace in a county. [L]

cŭt¹, n. Act of cutting; stroke, blow, with knife, sword, whip; ~ *de thrust*, hand-to-hand struggle; excision (of part of a play etc.); act, speech, that wounds the feelings; particular stroke in cricket, lawn tennis, croquet, etc.; refusal to recognize an acquaintance (esp. *give* one *the ~ direct*); *short ~*, crossing that shortens the distance; fashion, style, (of clothes, hair, etc.; *the ~ of* one's *jib¹*); *a ~* (degree, stage) *above*; wound made by cutting; railway cutting; narrow opening in floor of stage of theatre, by which scenes are moved up & down; = woop-*cut*; piece (esp. of meat) cut off; reduction (in wages, prices, etc.); *draw ~s*, draw lots with sticks of unequal length (prob. a different word); ~-*off*, device to prevent feeding of cartridges from magazine of rifle; ~-*out*, device in motor-car for releasing gas rapidly without passage through silencer. [f. foll.]

cŭt², v.t. & i. (*cŭt*). 1. Penetrate, wound, with edged instrument, as *the knife ~ his finger*, *he ~ his finger with a knife*, (fig.) *argument ~s both ways* (tells for both sides); (fig.) *a ~ting wind*, ~*ting report*, *it ~ him to the heart*, whence ~*t'ing*ʟʏ² adv.; divide with knife etc. *in two*, *in* or *into pieces* (~ *the knot*, fig., solve problem in irregular but efficient way, cf. GORDIAN); (fig.) ~ (renounce) *a connection*; detach by ~*ting*; carve (meat); cross, intersect, as *two lines ~ each other*; (intr.) pass *through*, *across*, etc., (sl.) run (*de run*, etc.) *away*; reduce by ~*ting* (hair etc.); reduce (wages, prices, time, etc.: ~ *it fine*, allow only the minimum; ~ *a loss*, abandon losing speculation in good time; ~ *the record*, reduce the recorded shortest time for race etc., or surpass record otherwise); shape, fashion, by ~*ting* (coat, gem, etc.); perform, execute, make, as ~ *a* CAPER, DASH, FIGURE, *joke*; divide (pack of cards, or abs.) to select dealer, prevent cheating, etc.; hit (ball, or abs.) in certain way, in cricket etc.; renounce acquaintance of (person), decline to recognize him, esp. ~ *him dead*; absent oneself from, avoid, renounce, as ~ *a lecture*, *the whole concern*; ~ *a tooth*, have it appear through gum (~ one's *eye* or *wisdom teeth*, fig., develop insight or wisdom); ~ *short*, shorten by ~*ting* (lit. & fig.), also interrupt; ~ one's *stick*, go; ~ *coat according to* cloth. 2. ~ *back* (Cinemat.), repeat, for dramatic reasons, portions of scenes already shown on screen (also as n., ~*-back*); ~ *down*, bring or throw down by ~*ting*, (fig.) reduce (expenses); ~ *in* (intr.), enter abruptly; interpose (in conversation), (Cards) join in game by taking place of player who

~ *s out*, (Motoring) obstruct path of vehicle one has just overtaken by returning to one's own side of the road too soon: ~ *no ice* (sl.), effect little or nothing; ~ *off*, remove by ~*ting*, bring to an end, intercept (supplies, communications), exclude (*from access* etc.); ~ *off with a shilling*, disinherit by bequeathing a shilling; ~ *out*, remove by ~*ting*, stop doing or using (something), (fig.) out-do or supplant (rival), fashion or shape (lit. & fig.), *detach* (animal from the herd), (Cards, intr.) be excluded from game as result of ~*ting*, (Nav.) capture (enemy ship) by getting between it & shore, (Motoring) obstruct path of oncoming vehicle by moving out from one's own side of the road, esp. in order to overtake another vehicle; ~ *up*, in pieces, destroy utterly, (fig.) criticize severely, (usu. pass.) distress greatly, ~ *up* (*well*), leave (large) fortune, ~ *up rough*, show resentment; ~*-&-come-again*, abundance; ~ *& dried* or *dry* (of opinions etc.), ready-made, lacking freshness; ~ *purse*, *thief*; ~*throat*, murderer, (adj., of competition) intensive, merciless, (of bridge, euchre, etc.) three-handed. [?]

cutā̆n'ĕous, a. Of the skin. [f. mod. or med. L *cutāneus* (*cutis* skin, see -ANEOUS)]

cŭt'-away, a. & n. (Coat) with skirt cut back from the waist.

cŭtch'ā̆, a. (Anglo-Ind.). Of poor quality; makeshift (opp. PUCKA); (of bricks) sun-dried. [Hind. *kachchā raw*]

cutche'rry̆, **cŭtch'ery̆**, n. (Anglo-Ind.). Public office, court-house; office of planter etc. [f. Hind. *kachahrī*]

cūte, a. (colloq.). Clever, shrewd; ingenious; *attractive*. Hence ~ʟʏ² (-tī-) adv., ~ɴᴇss (-tn-) n. [for ACUTE]

‖ **Cŭth'bert**, n. (sl.). Evader of military service esp. on plea of indispensability in Civil Service. [the pers. name]

cŭt'icle, n. Epidermis or other superficial skin; (Bot.) superficial film of plants. Hence **cutic'ŭlaʀ¹** a. [f. L *cuticula* dim. of CUTIS]

cŭt'is, n. (anat.). True skin, underlying the epidermis. [L, = skin]

cŭt'lăss, n. Short sword with wide slightly curved blade, esp. that used by sailors. [f. F *coutelas* augment. of *couteau* (*-tel*) knife, dim. f. L as COULTER]

cŭt'ler, n. One who makes or deals in knives & similar utensils. [f. OF *coutelier* f. *coutel* dim. as prec. f. L as -ER⁽²⁾]

cŭt'lery̆, n. Trade of the cutler; things made or sold by cutlers. [f. OF *coutelerie* (as prec., see -ERY)]

cŭt'lĕt, n. Neck-chop of mutton, small piece of veal, broiled or fried in bread-crumbs; imitation of mutton-~ in minced fish etc. [f. F *côtelette* double dim. of *côte* rib f. L *costa*]

cŭt'tĕr, n. Person, thing, that cuts; superior kind of brick that can be cut;

boat belonging to ship of war, fitted for rowing & sailing; small single-masted vessel rigged like sloop, but with running bowsprit. [-ER¹]

cut'ting, n. In vbl senses; ||excavation of high ground for railway, road, etc.; ||press ~, paragraph etc. cut from newspaper. [-ING¹]

cut'tle, n. (Usu. ~-*fish*) mollusc ejecting black fluid when pursued; ~-*bone*, its internal shell, used for polishing. [OE *cudele*, etym. dub.]

cut'water (-waw-), n. Knee of head of ship, dividing water before it reaches bow; forward edge of prow.

cut'ty, a. & n. (Sc. & north.). Cut short, abnormally short; (n.) short pipe; ~ *stool*, seat in Sc. churches where unchaste women sat to receive public rebuke during service. [CUT²-Y²]

cut'worm (-wer̄m), n. Caterpillar that cuts off young plants level with the ground.

-cy, suf., special form of the abstract suf. -Y, repr. L -*cia*, -*tia*, & Gk -*kia*, -*keia*, -*tia*, -*teia* (see -ACY, -ANCY, -ENCY). On anal. of wds in -*acy*, -*ncy*, with corresp. nn. in -*ate*, -*nt*, as *advocacy*, *advocate*, *infancy*, *infant*, -*cy* was extended to wds in -*n*, as *chaplaincy*, *captaincy*, after *incumbency*, *lieutenancy*, &c., being thus regarded as independent suf.; -*ship*, to other wds as *colonelcy*; it is even added to wds ending in -*t* (where -c- should have been substituted for -*t*-), as *bankruptcy*, *idiotcy*, normal form being *idiocy* f. Gk *idiōteia*.

cyan'ic, a. Blue; (Chem.) of, containing, cyanogen. [as foll.]

cyano- in comb. 1. Dark-blue, as -*meter*, instrument for measuring blueness of sky. 2. Of, containing, cyanogen. [f. Gk *kuanos*, a dark-blue mineral]

cyan'ogen, n. (chem.). Compound radical consisting of one atom of nitrogen and one of carbon. Hence **cy'anide,** (*cyanide process*, method of extracting a precious metal from its ore by treatment with a dilute solution of cyanide). [f. F *cyanogène* (as prec. +-GEN)]

cyano'sis, n. Blue discolouration, due to circulation of imperfectly oxygenated blood. [f. Gk *kuanōsis* (as prec., see -OSIS)]

cy'cad, n. (bot.). Kinds of palm-like plant.

cyc'lamen, n. Kinds of plant cultivated for their early-blooming flowers. [med. L, f. Gk *kuklaminos*, etym. dub.]

cy'cle, n., & v.i. 1. Recurrent period (of events, phenomena, etc.); *Metonic* or *Lunar~*, one of 19 years, used for finding date of Easter; period of a thing's completion; complete set or series; series of poems or songs (*song~*) collected round a central event or idea; bicycle, tricycle, or similar machine; ~-*car*, very light motor vehicle of simplified design with 3 (rarely 4) wheels, usu. fitted with chain drive & engine of 1 or 2 cylinders. 2. v.i. Revolve in ~s; ride ~. [f. L f. Gk *kuklos* circle]

cyc'lic, -ical, aa. Recurring in cycles; belonging to a chronological cycle; (-ic) of a cycle of poems, as ~ *poet*; (Gk Ant. -ic) ~ *chorus*, dithyrambic chorus, danced in ring round altar; (Bot., of flower) with its parts arranged in whorls; (Org. Chem. -ic) with the constituent atoms in a ring formation. [f. L f. Gk *kuklikos* (as CYCLE)]

cyc'list, n. Rider of a cycle. [CYCLE +-IST]

cyclo- in comb. = Gk *kuklos* circle, as ~*graph*, instrument for tracing circular arcs, ~*meter* (-ŏm-), instrument for measuring (1) circular arcs (2) distance traversed by bicycle etc., ~*stomous* (-ŏs-), with round mouth, ~*ra'ma* (-ah-), circular panorama.

cyc'loid, n. Curve traced by a point on a radius of a circle within (*prolate ~*), on circumference, as the circle rolls along a straight line. Hence **cycloid'al** a. [f. Gk *kukloeidēs* (as CYCLE, see -OID)]

cyc'lone, n. System of winds rotating round a centre of minimum barometric pressure; violent hurricane of limited diameter. Hence **cyclon'ic** a. [irreg. f. Gk *kuklōn* circle]

cyclop(a)ed'ia (-pēd-), n. = ENCYCLOPAE-DIA. Hence **cyclop(a)ed'ic** a. [abbr. of ENCYCLO-PAEDIA]

Cyclōpē'an, -clōp'ian, a. Of, like, a Cyclops; huge; ~ *masonry*, an ancient style made with huge irregular stones. [f. L *Cyclopeus, -pius*, f. Gk *kuklōpeios, -pios*, as foll.]

Cyc'lop(s), n. (pl. -*ops*, -*opses*, -ŏp'ĕs), (Gk Myth.), one-eyed giant; one-eyed person. [L (-s), f. Gk *kuklōps* (*kuklos* circle + *ōps* eye)]

cyc'lostȳle, n., & v.t. Apparatus printing copies of writing from stencil-plate cut by pen with small toothed wheel; (v.t.) reproduce with this. [CYCLO-]

cyc'lotron, n. (phys.). Apparatus for electro-magnetic acceleration of charged atoms, atomic nuclei, etc. [CYCLO- +(ELEC)TRON]

cy'der. See CIDER.

cyg'net, n. Young swan. [f. L *cygnus* swan +-ET¹]

cyl'inder, n. (Geom.) solid generated by straight line moving parallel to itself and describing with its ends any fixed curve, esp. circle; roller-shaped body, hollow or solid; barrel-shaped object of baked clay covered with cuneiform writing and buried under Babylonian or Assyrian temple; stone of similar shape used as seal by Assyrians; cylindrical part of various machines, esp. chamber in which steam acts upon piston; metal roller used in printing. [f. L f. Gk *kulindros* (*kulindō* roll)]

cȳlin'drical, a. Cylinder-shaped. [f. Gk *kulindrikos* (as prec., see -IC) +-AL]

cȳl'indroid, a. & n. (Figure) like a cylinder. [f. Gk *kulindroeidēs* (as prec., -OID)]

cȳm'a, n. (pl. -mas). Ogee moulding of cornice (~ *recta* with concave, ~ *reversa* with convex, curve uppermost). = CYME. [mod. L, f. Gk *kuma* wave, anything swollen]

cȳmar', n. Woman's loose light garment esp. under-garment. [f. F *simarre* OF *chimarre*, cf. CHIMERE]

cym'bal, n. One of a pair of concave brass or bronze plates, struck together to make ringing sound. Hence ~IST n. [f. L f. Gk *kumbalon* (*kumbē* cup)]

cym'balo (-lō, -os), n. = DULCIMER. [f. It. *cembalo*, as prec.]

cym'biform, a. (anat., bot.). Boat-shaped. [f. L *cymba* boat +-FORM]

cymbocephal'ic, a. With boat-shaped (i.e. long and narrow) skull. [f. Gk *kumbē* boat+*kephalē* head +-IC]

cȳme, n. (bot.). Inflorescence in which primary axis bears single terminal flower that develops first, system being continued by axes of secondary and higher orders (cf. RACEME). Hence cȳmOSE[1] a., cȳmOUS a. [F, = top (as CYMA)]

cym'ric (k-), a. Welsh. [f. W *Cymru* Wales]

cyn'ic, a. & n. 1. Of, characteristic of, the Cynic philosophers; = foll. 2. n. (C~) philosopher of sect founded by Antisthenes, marked by ostentatious contempt for pleasure. 3. Sneering fault-finder. Hence ~ISM n. [f. L f. Gk *kunikos* (*kuōn kunos* dog, nickname for Cynic)]

cyn'ical, a. Churlish; captious; incredulous of human goodness; sneering. Hence ~LY[2] adv. [-AL]

cȳno- in comb. repr. Gk *kuōn kunos* dog, dread of dogs.

cynoceph'alus, n. Fabulous dog-headed man; (Zool.) dog-faced baboon. [L, f. Gk *kunokephalos* (prec. + *kephalē* head]

cȳn'osūre (or -shoor), n. (Constellation containing) Pole-star, Little Bear; guiding star; centre of attraction or admiration. [F, f. L f. Gk *kunosoura* dog's tail, Little Bear (*kuōn kunos* dog +*oura* tail)]

cypher. See CIPHER.

cy pres (sēprā'), adv., n., & a. (Law) as near as possible to (testator's intentions); (adj.) approximate; (n.) approximation. [AF, =F *si près* so near (as etc.)]

cyp'ress, n. Coniferous tree with hard wood and dark foliage; branch of this as symbol of mourning. [f. OF *ciprès* f. LL *cypressus* f. Gk *kuparissos*]

Cyp'rian, a. & n. (Inhabitant, native) of Cyprus; licentious (person). [f. L *Cyprius* (*Cyprus*) +-AN]

Cyp'riot, -ōte, a. & n. = prec. (first sense). [-OT[2]]

Cyrēnā'ic (sīr-), a. & n. (Philosopher) of the hedonistic school of Aristippus of Cyrene. [f. L f. Gk *Kurēnaikos* (*Kurēnē*)]

Cyrill'ic, a. ~ *alphabet*, that used by Slavonic peoples of the Eastern Church. [St *Cyril*, supposed inventor, +-IC]

cyrto- (sēr-) in comb. = Gk *kurtos* curved, as ~*meter* (-ōm-), instrument measuring chest.

cyst, n. (Biol.) hollow organ, bladder, etc., in animal or plant, containing liquid secretion; (Path.) sac containing morbid matter, parasitic larva, etc.; cell containing embryos etc. [f. Gk *kustis* bladder]

cyst-, cysti-, cysto-, in comb. repr. Gk *kustis, kustē*, bladder, as *cystiform*, bladder-shaped, *cysto*CELE, -SCOPE, -TOMY. cys'tic, a. Of the urinary bladder; of the gall-bladder; of the nature of a cyst. [f. F *cystique* (as CYST, see -IC)]

cystit'is, n. Inflammation of the bladder. [CYST, -ITIS]

-cȳte, suf. in biol. wds meaning *cell*, as LEUCOCYTE. [f. Gk *kutos* vessel]

cȳto- in comb. = cell, as ~*blast*, protoplasmic nucleus of a cell. [as prec.]

cȳtol'ogy, n.(biol.). Study of cells. Hence cȳtol'ogist, cȳtol'ogic [CYTO-]

czar, tsar, tzar, (z-, ts-), n. Emperor of Russia. [f. Russ. *ts(is)ari* f. L *Caesar*]

cza'revitch, -wich, tsar-, (z-, ts-), n. Son of a czar (not now an official title; cf. CESAREWITCH). [f. Russ. *tsarevitsh*]

czarev'na, tsar-, (zah-, ts-), n. Daughter of a czar. [Russ.]

czarina, tsar-, (zahrēn'a, ts-), n. Wife of a czar, Russian empress. [f. G *czarin* f. czar]

czarit'za, tsar-, n. Russian form of prec.

Czech, -kh, (chěk), n. & a. (Native or language) of Bohemia. [f. Boh. *Cech*]

Czechoslovak (chěkōslōv'ăk) a. & n. (Native) of the State called Czechoslovakia including Bohemia, Moravia, part of Silesia, Slovakia, and formerly Carpathian Ruthenia. [*Czech, Slovak*, native race-names, -o-]

D

D (dē), letter (pl. Ds, D's, Dees); D block, trap, valve, shaped like the letter; also D=DEE; (Mus.) second note of natural major scale.

'd. Colloq. clipping of had & would, chiefly after I, we, you, he, she, they.

-d, p.p. suf. (heard etc.); see -ED[1], & cf. DEAD.

da. See DAD.

dăb[1] v.t.(-bb-). Strike lightly or undecidedly, hit feebly at, tap, peck; press but not rub (surface) with sponge etc., whence ~b'ER[1](2) n.; press (brush, dabber, etc.) against surface. [f. 1300; etym. dnb.]

dăb[2], n. Slight or undecided but sudden blow, tap, peck; brief application of

sponge, handkerchief, etc., to surface
without rubbing; moisture, colour, etc.,
so applied. [f. prec.]

dāb⁴, n. Kind of flat-fish. [?]

dāb⁵, n. (colloq.). Adept (*at* games etc.,
doing). [f. 1690; etym. dub.]

dāb'ble, v.t. & i. Wet intermittently,
slightly, or partly, soil, moisten, splash;
move the feet, hands, bill, about in
water; engage *in* or *at* pursuit etc. as a
hobby, whence **dāb'bler¹** n. [cf. Du.
dabbelen & DAB¹.]

dāb'chick, n. Water-bird, the Little
Grebe. [early forms *dap-*, *dop-*; perh.
cogn. w. DIP]

dāb'ster, n. = DAB⁴; = DAUBSTER. [-STER]

da ca'pō (dahkah-), mus. direction. [It.]

dace, n. Small fresh-water fish. [ME.
darse, f. OF *dars* DART]

dachs'hund (dahks-hoont), n. Short-
legged breed of dog. [G, = badger-dog]

dacoit', n. Member of Indian or Burmese
armed robber band. [f. Hind. *ḍakait* f.
ḍāku gang-robbery]

dacoit'y, n. (Act of) gang-robbery. [f.
Hind. *ḍakaiti* as prec.]

dăc'tyl, n. Metrical foot —‿‿. [f. L f. Gk
daktulos finger]

dăctyl'ic, a. & n. Of dactyls; (noun, usu.
pl.) ~ verse(s). [f. L f. Gk *daktulikos*

dăd, dā (dah), **dăd'a**, **dăd'dy**, nn.
(colloq.). Father (esp. as voc.); *daddy-
long'legs*, crane-fly. [f. 16th c.; infantile
sound]

dăd'ō, n. (pl. -os). Cube of pedestal between base & cornice; lower few feet of
room-wall when faced with wood or
coloured differently from upper part.
[It., = DIE¹]

Daedal'ian, -ean, a. In the manner of
Daedalus the Greek artificer; intricate;
labyrinthine. [f. L *Daedaleus* of Daedalus
(cf. Gk *daidaleos* cunningly wrought) +
-AN]

daemonic. See dem-.

daff (dah-), v.t. (arch.). Put aside, waive.
[var. of DOFF, preserved by 1 *Hen. IV*,
IV. i. 96]

dăf'fodil (also **dăff'odil'ly**, **dăff'adown-
dill'y**, in poetry etc.), n. & a. Lent Lily,
pale-yellow-flowered Narcissus (alternative to leek as Welsh national emblem);
pale yellow (n. & a.). [f. earlier *affodill*
(*d-* unexplained) f. L f. Gk *asphodelos*]

daft (dah-), a. (esp. Sc.). Foolish, reckless,
wild, crazy. [OE *gedæfte* mild, meek,
whence also DEFT; orig. sense (cf. Goth.
gadaban be fit) fitting, suitable; for change
of meaning cf. *innocent*]

dăg'ger (-g-), n. Stabbing-weapon with
short pointed and edged blade (*at ~s
drawn*, on the point of fighting, in strained

relations, *with*, person, or abs.; *look,
speak, ~s*, bitterly, so as to wound);
(Print.) (double) ~ = (double) OBELISK. [cf.
F *dague*, & ME *dag* to pierce]

*dăg'ō, n. (pl. -os). (Term of contempt
for) a Spaniard, Portuguese, or Italian.
[f. Sp. *Diego* = James]

dague'rreotype (-gĕro-), n. (Portrait
taken by) early photographic process.
[*Daguerre* 1839 inventor, -o-, TYPE]

dah, n. Burmese sword-knife. [Burmese]

dahabeeyah (dah-ha-), **-bī'ah** (-bē-), n.
Nile sailing-boat. [Arab., = the golden,
orig. sense *gilded barge*]

dahl'ia (dāl-), n. Mexican composite
plant cultivated in Europe for its many-
coloured single & double flowers (*blue ~*,
impossibility); shade of red. [*Dahl* d.
1791, botanist, -IA¹]

dai (dī), n. (Anglo-Ind.). Wet-nurse.
[Hind.; cf. Pers. *dāyah*]

Dail (Éireann) (dollyé'rǎn), n. Chamber
of Deputies in the Irish Republic legislature. [Ir., = assembly (of Ireland)]

dail'y, a., adv., & n. 1. (Recurring,
appearing, done) every day or week-day,
from day to day, constant, often; ~
bread, one's necessary food or livelihood.
2. n. A ~ newspaper (pl. *dailies*); (Ireland
loq.) non-resident maid-servant. [OE
dæglic (DAY, -LY¹)]

dain'ty², n. Choice morsel, dish, etc.,
delicacy, tit-bit, (lit. & fig.). [f. OF
dainté f. L *dignitatem* (*dignus* worthy,
-TY)]

dain'ty¹, a. Delicate, choice; tasteful,
pretty, of delicate beauty, scrupulously
clean; particular, nice, of delicate tastes
& sensibility; fastidious; inclined to
luxury. Hence ~**ily²** adv., ~**iNESS** n.

dair'y², n. Room or building for keeping
milk & cream & making butter etc.
(*~maid*, in charge of this); the milk
department in farming; shop for milk
etc. (*~man*, dealer in milk etc.); cows
of a farm. Hence (f. rare vb)) ~**iNG¹** n.
[f. obs. *dey* OE *dǣge* maid-servant cogn.
w. DOH DOUGH +-ERY]

dais (dās), n. Raised platform, esp. at
end of hall for high table, throne, etc.,
or terrace. [f. OF *deis* f. L *discus* disk
in LL sense *table*]

dais'y (-z-), n. Small European wild &
garden flower; other plants resembling
it, esp. the larger Ox-eye D~; (sl.) first-
rate specimen of anything; *~-chain*,
string of daisies fastened together; *~-
cutter*, horse lifting feet very little, ball
travelling along ground at cricket. Hence
dais'iED² (-zid) a. [OE *dǣges éage* day's
eye]

dak, dāk. See DAWK.

dal (dahl). See DHAL.

dale, n. Valley (esp. in north; also in poet. use, as *hill & ~*); ~*s'man*, inhabitant of ~s in north. [OE *dæl*, com.-Teut. cf. G *t(h)al*]

dally, v.i. & t. Amuse oneself, make sport; toy amorously (*with* or abs.); coquet *with* temptation etc.; be evasive *with* person or business; idle, loiter, delay; ~ *away*, consume (time, opportunity) to no purpose. Hence **dǎll'iance** n. [f. OF *dalier* chat]

Dalmā'tian (-shn), n. (Also ~ *dog*) spotted dog kept to run with carriage. [*Dalmatia*, -AN]

dalmǎt'ic, n. Wide-sleeved loose long vestment with slit sides worn by deacons & bishops on some occasions, & by kings & emperors esp. at coronation. [f. F *dalmatique* f. L *dalmatica* (*vestis* robe) of *Dalmatia*]

dǎl segno (sān'yō), mus. direction (abbr. D.S.). Repeat from point indicated. [It.]

dǎlt'onism (dawl-), n. Colour-blindness, esp. inability to distinguish green from red. [f. F *daltonisme* f. John *Dalton*, Eng. chemist, so affected, d. 1844, -ISM(2)]

dam¹, n., & v.t. 1. Barrier constructed to hold back water & raise its level, to form a reservoir, or to prevent flooding; causeway; water confined by ~. 2. v.t. (-mm-). Furnish or confine with ~ (usu. *up*). [com.-Teut., cf. Du. *dam*, G *damm*]

dam², n. Mother (usu. of beast); *the devil & his ~*, the powers of evil. [var. DAME]

dǎm'age, n., & v.t. 1. Harm (*to one's great ~*), injury impairing value or usefulness; (Law; pl.) sum of money claimed or adjudged in compensation for loss or injury; (sl.) cost (*what's the ~*?). 2. v.t. Injure (usu. thing) so as to diminish value; detract from reputation of (person etc.; *trying to ~ the Government*; *a damaging admission*); hence ~ABLE (-ijǝ-) a. [f. OF *damage(r)* f. *dam* loss f. L *damnum* +-AGE]

dǎm'ascene', *-skeen'*, v.t. Ornament (metal) with inlaid gold or silver; ornament (steel) with watered pattern produced in welding. [f. *Damascus*, -cene thr. L f. Gk *damaskēnos*, *-keen* thr. F & It.]

dǎm'ask, n. & a., & v.t. 1. ~ *rose*, old variety brought from Damascus; its colour; figured woven material (prop. of silk); twilled table-linen with woven designs shown by reflection of light; steel of or as of Damascus, with wavy surface-pattern due to special welding of iron & steel together. 2. adj. Coloured like ~ rose, blush-red; made of or resembling the silk, linen, or steel. 3. v.t. Weave with figured designs; = DAMASCENE; ornament with pattern; make (cheek etc.) red. [f. It. *Damasco* f. L *Damascus*]

dāme, n. (Arch., poet., or joc., for) lady; ||keeper, male or female, of Eton boarding house; (Law; ||) wife of knight or baronet (*Lady* in ordinary use; cf. D~ *Fortune*, D~ *Nature*); ||lady member of Order of British Empire (also as prefix corresp. *Sir*; D~ *Commander*, D~ *Grand Cross*, (ranks in Order); ||higher female member of Primrose League; ||~-*school*, elementary kept by old lady. [OF, f. L *domina* mistress]

dǎmn'ar, n. Resin obtained from certain Indian and Australasian coniferous trees, used in varnish-making. [Malay *damar*]

dǎmn (-m), v.t. & i., & n. 1. Condemn, censure, (~ *a person's character*); (Theatr., of audience) receive coldly, secure the withdrawal of, (play); bring condemnation upon, be the ruin of; ~ *with faint praise*, commend so frigidly as to suggest disapproval; doom to hell (so in optative, often d~, = *may God* ~ person or thing, or with object omitted; ~*ed*, or *I'll be* ~*ed*, *if I know* etc., colloq. negation); cause the damnation of; curse (person or thing, or abs.; esp.~ *your eyes*, or *impudence!*). 2. n. An uttered curse; a negligible amount (*don't care, not worth, a ~*). [f. OF *damner* f. L *damnare* (*damnum* loss, harm)]

dǎm'nable, a. Subject to, deserving, damnation; hateful, confounded, annoying. Hence ~LY² adv. [F, f. L *damnabilis* as prec., -ABLE]

dǎmnā'tion, n. & int. Damning of play; (condemnation to) eternal punishment in hell; (int.) = may ~ take a person or thing. [F, f. L *damnationem* (DAMN), -ATION]

dǎm'natory, a. Conveying, causing, censure or damnation. [f. L *damnatorius* (*damnare* DAMN, -ORY)]

dǎmned (-md), a. & adv. In vbl senses; also or esp.: *the ~*, souls in hell; damnable, infernal, unwelcome; confoundedly, extremely, (~ *or* or d~ *or damn' hot, funny*, etc.). [-ED¹]

dǎm'nify, v.t. (legal). Cause injury to. Hence ~FICA'TION n. [f. OF *damnifier* f. L *damnificare* (*damnum* loss, -FY)]

dǎmn'ing¹ (-mi-), a. In vbl senses: esp., cursing. [-ING¹]

dǎmn'ing² (-mn- -mi-), a. In vbl senses; esp.~ *evidence*, that secures conviction. [-ING²]

dǎmnō'sa heredǐ'tǎs, n. Inheritance that brings more burden than profit. [L]

Dǎm'ocles (-z), n. *Sword of* ~, imminent danger in midst of prosperity. [Greek who was feasted with sword hung by a hair over him]

Dǎm'on and Pyth'ias, n. & a. (As of) devoted friends (~ *friendship*). [Gk tale]

dǎm'osel (-z-), -zěl, n. (arch.). Var. of DAMSEL.

damp, n., a., & v.t. & i. 1. = CHOKE¹-~, (also *black*-~); FIRE¹-~; moisture in air,

on surface, or diffused through solid; dejection, chill, discouragement, (cast or
strike ~ over or into); (~proof) course,
layer of slate etc. in wall to keep ~ from
rising; hence ~PROOF a. 2. adj. Slightly
wet; hence ~EN³ v.t. & i. (chiefly U.S.),
~ISH¹(2) a., ~EN³ a., ~NESS n. 3. vb.
Stifle, choke, dull, extinguish, (~ down
combustion); (Mus.) stop vibration of
(string); discourage, depress, (zeal, hopes);
moisten; (Gardening) ~ off, rot & fall of
from ~. [vb f. adj. f. noun; cf. Du. & Da.
damp, G *dampf*, vapour]

damp'er, n. (Piano) pad silencing string
except when removed by pedal, or by
note's being struck; metal plate in flue
controlling combustion; contrivance for
wetting paper, stamps, etc.; (Austral.) unleavened cake baked in wood-ashes. [-ER¹]

dam'sel (-zl), n. (arch. & literary). Young
unmarried woman. [f. OF *damesele* f.
med. L *domnicella* dim. of L *domina*
mistress]

dam'son (-z-), n. & a. Small dark-purple
plum; ~ *plum*, larger but similar; tree
bearing it; ~ *cheese*, solid conserve of ~s
& sugar; (adj.)-coloured. [ME *damascene* f. L *damascenum* (*prunum* plum) of
Damascus]

Dan'aos. See TIMEO.

dance¹ (dah-), v.i. & t. Move with rhythmical steps, glides, leaps, revolutions,
gestures, etc., usu. to music, alone or
with a partner or set (~ *to* one's *tune* or
pipe, follow his lead); jump about, skip,
move in lively way (of heart, blood, etc.;
bob up and down on water etc. (~ *upon*
nothing, be hanged); perform (minuet,
waltz, etc.); ~ *attendance* (*upon* person),
be kept waiting (by), follow about;
cause to ~ (bears etc.); toss up & down,
dandle, (baby); ~ *away*, *off*, *into*, etc.,
lose, bring, etc., by dancing (*his head
off*, *his chance away*, *herself into favour*).
[f. OF *dancer*, *-ser*, perh. f. OHG *danson*
stretch out]

dance² (dah-), n. Dancing motion (see
prec.); some special form of this; single
round or turn of one; tune for dancing
to, or in ~ rhythm; dancing-party; *lead*
(person) *a* ~, entangle him in useless
pursuit or toil; *D~ of Death of Macabre*,
medieval picture-subject of Death leading
all ranks to grave; *St. Vitus's* ~, disorder
chiefly in children with convulsive involuntary movements. [f. prec.]

dan'cer (dah-), n. In vbl senses; esp. one
who dances in public for money; ||*merry
~s*, aurora borealis. [-ER¹]

dandy, G *dampf*, vapour]

dan'die Din'mont, n. Breed of terrier.
[character in *Guy Mannering*]

dan'dle, v.t. Dance (child) on knee or in
arms; pet. [cf. It. *dandolare* (*dandola* doll)]

dan'druff, -**iff**, n. Dead skin in small
scales among the hair; scurf. [also *dan-
druf; ending perh. Norweg. *hrufa*, Icel.
hrufa scab]

dan'dy¹, n. & a. (Person) devoted to
smartness esp. of costume, neat, smart,
decorated, whence **dandi'acal** a., **dan'-
*diFY** v.t., **dandification** n., ~ISH¹ a.,
~ISM(2) n.: *(colloq.)* very good of its
kind, splendid, first-rate; sloop with
special rig; ||(also ~*cart*) spring-cart used
by milkmen; ~*-brush, -curb* (whalebone etc.
for cleaning horse. [1780 in Scotland,
where *Dandy* also stands for *Andrew*]

dan'dy², n. = DENGUE. [negro corrupt. of
dengue; perh. w. ref. to stiff attitude caused by pain]

dan'dy', n. (Anglo-Ind.). Strong cloth
hammock slung from bamboo pole, carried shoulder-high by two or more men
(a common means of transport in hilly
districts). [Hind. *dandi* (*dand* staff]

Dane, n. Native of Denmark; (Hist.)
Northman invader of England; (also
Great ~) powerful short-haired breed of
dog. [f. Da. *Daner* f. OTeut. *Danīz* pl.]

dan'ger (-j-), n. Liability or exposure to
harm, risk, peril, (*of* one's life, *of* death
etc.); position of railway signal directing stoppage or caution (*signal is at* ~);
thing that causes peril (*a* ~ *to the peace
of Europe*, *to navigation*. So ~OUS a.,
~OUSLY² adv., (-j-). [earlier sense *power*
(*within his* ~=at his mercy), f. OF *dangier*
f. LL *dominiarium* (L *dominium* f.
dominus lord, -ARY¹)]

dan'gle (dang'gl), v.i.& t. Be suspended
& sway to & fro; hold or carry (thing)
swaying loosely; hold (hopes etc.) as
temptation before person, *in* his sight,
etc.; hover *after*, *round*, *about*, person as
a follower, lover, etc., whence ~ER¹ n.
[cf. Sw. *dank* marshy spot]

Dan'iel (-yel), n. Upright judge, person of
infallible wisdom. [*Dan.* i.-vi, & *Merchant
of Venice*, IV. i. 223, 333]

Dan'ish, a. & n. (Language) of Denmark
or the Danes. [OE *Denisc* (-ISH¹)]

dank, a. Soaked, oozy; unpleasantly or
unwholesomely damp (of air, weather,
etc.). [cf. Sw. *dank* marshy spot]

Dan'te'an, a. & n. (Student) of Dante; in
Dante's style or recalling his description.
So **Dantes'que** a., **Dan'tesq**(3) n. [-AN]

dap, v.i. & t. (-pp-), & n. Fish by letting
bait bob on water; dip lightly; make (ball)

302

bounce, (of ball) bounce, on ground; (n.)
bounce of ball. [cf. DAB¹]

daph'né, n. Kinds of flowering shrub.
[Gk (-ē) = laurel]

dapp'er, a. Neat, smart, in appearance or
movement. [cf. Du. *dapper*, G *tapfer*,
valiant]

dap'ple, v.t. & i., & n. Variegate, become
variegated, with rounded spots or patches
of colour or shade; (n.) ~d effect; ~grey,
(horse) of grey with darker spots. [perh.
= Icel. *depill* spot dim. of *dapi* pool; but
G *apfelgrau*, F. *gris-pommelé*, & other
parallels, suggest some connexion with
apple]

darb'ies (-biz), n. pl. (sl.). Handcuffs. [?]

Darb'y and Joan, n. Devoted old married
couple. [perh. f. poem 1735 in *Gentleman's Mag.*]

dare, v.t. (before expressed or implied
infin. without *to*, the 3 sing. pres. is usu.
~, the past & conditional often *durst*;
otherwise ~s, ~d; infin. without *to* is
usual only after the sense *venture* in
negative or virtually negative sentence).
Venture (to), have the courage or impudence (to), (*I ~ swear*, feel sure that;
~ he do it?; *he ~s to insult me*; *I would
if I durst* or *~d*; *they ~d* or *durst not
come*, *did not ~ to come*); attempt, take
the risks of, (*~ all things, a leap, the
event*, person's *anger*); defy (person);
challenge (person) *to do, to it*, etc.; *I ~
say* (rare exc. in 1st person; 3rd sing. in
reported speech, *he ~s to say*, past *he
~d say* or *to say*), am prepared to believe,
do not deny; ~*very likely* (often iron.).
~'devil, reckless (person). [OE *durran*
f. Aryan *dhers*- cf. Gk *tharseō* be bold;
the pres. (cf. CAN) is an old past, whence
dare as 3rd sing.]

dar'i, n. = DURRA.

dar'ing¹, a. In vbl senses; esp., adventurous courage. [-ING¹]

dar'ing², a. In vbl senses; esp., adventurous, bold. Hence ~LY² adv. [-ING³]

dark¹, a. With no or relatively little light,
unilluminated (~ *lantern*, that can have
its light covered), gloomy, sombre; of
colour more or less near black (esp. as
pref. to adj. of colour as ~*brown*; as
BLUE²s); brown(-complexioned, not fair;
evil, atrocious; cheerless (~ *side of things*);
sad, sullen (*a ~ humour*), frowning;
obscure (~ *saying*, ~ *oblivion*); secret
(*keep thing ~*; *keep ~*, remain in hiding);
little known of (~ *horse*, unexpected
winner of race, & fig. of persons); unenlightened (*in the ~est ignorance*; *the
~ ages*, Middle Ages; *the D~ Continent*
(in last two senses) Africa; ~ *room*, with
actinic rays excluded for treating photographic plates. Hence ~'ISH²(2) a., ~'LY²
adv., ~'NESS n. (*Prince of ~ness*, the
Devil). [OE *deorc*; as adj. exclusively
E, but cf. OHG *tarchanjan* to hide]

dark², n. Absence of light (esp. *in the ~*);
nightfall (*at ~*); dark colour (esp. in art,
the lights and ~s of a picture); want of
knowledge (*am in the ~ about it*; *leap in
the ~*, rash step or enterprise). Hence
~'SOME a. (poet.). [f. prec.]

dark'en, v.t. & i. Make or become DARK¹;
~ *one's door*, pay him a visit (usu. neg.);
~ *counsel*, make perplexity worse. [-EN³]

dark'le, v.i. Lie concealed; grow dark.
[mod. back-formation f. foll. misunderstood as part.]

dark'ling, adv. & a. In the dark. [-LING²]

dark'y, -ey, n. (colloq.). Negro. [-Y³]

dar'ling, n. & a. Loved, best loved,
lovable, (person or animal). [OE *deorling*
(DEAR, -LING¹)]

darn¹, v.t. & n. 1. Mend (esp. knitting)
by interweaving yarn with needle across
hole, whence ~'ING⁴(5) n.; ~'ing-ball, -last,
for stretching work during operation.
2. n. Place so mended. [perh. f. obs. vb &
adj. *dern* hide, hidden, = OHG *tarnan* hide]

darn², v.t. (sl.). Damn (as imprecation).
[deformation of DAMN]

darn'el, n. Kind of grass growing as
weed among corn. [cf. Walloon *darnelle*]

dart, n., & v.t. & i. 1. Pointed missile, esp.
light javelin, ‖ (pl.) indoor game with toy
~s & target; sting of insect etc.; sudden
rapid motion; act of throwing missile.
2. vb. Throw (missile), throw missile;
emit suddenly (glance, flash, anger); start
rapidly in some direction. [OF accus. of
dars cf. DACE]

dart'er, n. In vbl senses; also: web-
footed bird of pelican tribe; (pl.) order of
birds including kingfishers & bee-eaters;
kinds of fish. [-ER¹]

dart'le, v.t. & i. Keep on darting. [-LE(3)]

Dart'moor, n. (Used for) convict prison
near Princetown, Devon.

Dart'mouth (-mu-), n. (Used for) Royal
Naval College, ~, Devon.

Dar'tre (-ter), n. Kinds of skin disease, esp.
herpes. So **dar'trous** a. [F, etym. dub.]

Darwin'ian, a. & n. Of, person believing
in, Charles Darwin or his doctrines esp.
on evolution of species. So **Dar'win-
ISM**(3) n., **Dar'winIST**(2) n. & a., **Darwin-
is'tic** a., **Dar'winTR²**(1) n. & a., **Dar'-
winIZE**(2, 4) v.t. & i.

dash¹, v.t. & i. Shatter *to pieces* (rarely
abs., as *flowers ~ed by rain*); knock,
drive, throw or thrust, *away, off, out,
down*, etc.; fling, drive, splash, (thing or
person *against, upon, into*; bespatter
with water etc. (~*board*, of wood or
leather in front of vehicle to keep out
mud, board beneath motor-car wind-
screen containing instruments; ~*ed with
colour*) dilute, qualify, (*water with spirit,
joy with pain*); frustrate (~ *one's hopes*),
daunt, discourage, confound; write down
or throw off rapidly (composition, sketch);
underline; (sl.)=*damn* as mild imprecation; fall, move, throw oneself, with
violence; come into collision *against*,

dash, upon; ride, run, or drive *up*, move about, behave, with spirit or display, whence ~**ING**² a., ~**ING**LY² adv. [cf. Sw. *daska* drub; but perh. imit., cf. *clash, crash,* etc.; imprecatory use perh. f. use of dashes in d—d—d—d, cf. BLANK²]

dash'er, n. In vbl senses; *esp.* contrivance for agitating cream in churn. [-ER¹]

das'tard, n. Coward, skulker, *esp.* one who commits brutal act without endangering himself. Hence ~RY¹ a., ~**LINESS** n. [prob. f. *dazed* p.p.+-ARD]

dā'syūre, n. (Kinds of) small ferocious arboreal cat-like carnivorous marsupial found in Australia and Tasmania. [Gk *dasus* rough+*oura* tail]

dāt'a. See DATUM.

‖ **dāt'aller, day'taler,** n. Workman engaged and paid by the day. [-ER¹]

date¹, n. W.-Asiat. & N.-Afr. tree (also seeded berry. [OF, f. L f. Gk *daktulos* finger]

date², n. Statement in document, letter, book, or inscription, of the time (& often place) of execution, writing, publication, etc.; time at which thing happens or is to happen; *(colloq.)* engagement, appointment; period to which antiquities etc. belong; period in age, duration, term of life, (arch. or poet.); (*go*) *out of* ~ (become) obsolete; *up to* ~ (f. bookkeeping phr. for accounts completed to meeting, according to, the latest requirements or knowledge; ~*line*, meridian 180° from Greenwich, east & west of which the ~ differs. [F, f. L f. L *data* fem. p.p. of *dare* = (letter) given (at such a time & place)]

date³, a., v.t. & i. Mark (letter etc.) with date (~*d from London*), whence **dāt'ER**²(2) reckon, (*dating from the Creation*); bear date, be ~*d*; have origin *from* (*church* ~*s from the 14th c.*); (of art, style, etc.) become recognizable as of a past or particular period; be or become out of date. Hence **dāt'ABLE** a. [f. prec.]

date'less (-tl-), a. Undated; endless; immemorial. [f. DATE² ,-LESS]

dā'tive, a. & n.(-*case,* the case in nouns, pronouns, & adjs. proper to the remoter object or recipient. So **dativ'AL** a., ~**LY**² (-vi-) adv. [f. L *dativus* (*dare* dat-give, -IVE)]

dā'tum, n. (pl. -ta). Thing known or granted, assumption or premiss from which inferences may be drawn; ~*line*, fixed starting-point of scale etc. (ORDNANCE ~). [L, neut. p.p. of *dare* give]

datū'ra, n. Kinds of poisonous plant, including stramonium, yielding strong narcotic. [f. Hind. *dhatura*]

daub, v.t. & i. & n. Coat (wall etc.) *with* plaster, clay, etc. (n., the material); smear (surface; n., a smear), lay on (greasy or sticky stuff); soil, stain; paint (n., a coarse painting), whence ~**ER**¹ (n., & i.), inartistically, lay (colours) on so. Hence ~**ING**, ~**Y**² a. [f. OF *dauber* f. L DE(*albare* f. *albus* white) whitewash]

daugh'ter (dawt-), n. One's female child; female descendant, female member of family, race, etc.; woman who is the spiritual or intellectual product of person or thing; product personified as female (*Carthage* ~ *of Tyre*; *Fortune and its* ~ *Confidence*; ~*-language*, as French of Latin); ~*-in-law,* son's wife, (loosely) step~. Hence ~**HOOD** n., ~**LY**² a. [OE *dohtor,* Du. *dochter,* G *tochter,* Gk *thugatēr,* cf. Skr *duh-* to milk]

daunt, v.t. Discourage, intimidate; press (now *dompter*) f. L *domitare* frequent. of *domare* tame]

daunt'less, a. Intrepid, persevering. Hence ~**LY**² adv., ~**NESS** n. [perh. f. obs. *daunt* a check f. prec.+-LESS]

dau'phin, dauph'iness, nn. (Wife of King of France's eldest son. [family name (f. L *delphinus* DOLPHIN) of lords of Dauphiné, last of whom ceded it on condition of *dauphin*'s being accepted as French heir-apparent's title]

‖ **dāv'enport,** n. Escritoire with drawers & hinged writing-slab. [prob. maker's name]

Dā'vid and Jōn'athan, n. Any pair of devoted friends. [1 *Sam.* xviii etc.]

dā'vit, n. Crane at ship's bow for hoisting anchor clear of side; one of pair of cranes for suspending or lowering ship's boat. [formerly also *david* prob. f. the male name; cf. *jenny*]

Dā'vy (dāmp), n. Miner's wire-gauze safety lamp. [Sir H. *Davy* (d. 1820), inventor]

dā'vy, n. (sl.). *Take* one's ~, swear (*that, to* fact). [short for AFFIDAVIT]

Dā'vy Jōne's's lock'er (jōnziz), n. The deep, a watery grave (in the sea). [?]

daw, n. = JACKDAW. [cf. OHG *tāha,* G *dohle*]

daw'dle, v.i. & t., & n. Idle, dally; ~ *away* (time etc.), waste; hence ~**ER**¹ n. (n.) ~*ing* person. [cf. DODDER², & dial. *daddle* totter as baby; -LE(3)]

dawk, dāk, dak (dawk), n. (Anglo-Ind.). Post or transport by relays of men or horses; relay; ~ *bungalow,* house for travellers at ~ *station.* [Hind.]

dawn, v.i. & n. 1. Begin to appear or grow light (of day, daylight, morning,

country shone upon, things becoming
evident to mind, intelligence, civilization,
etc.); first ~ings etc., beginning; ~ing,
(lasting) for whole ~; ~out, Hawk-owl
the East; ~ upon, begin to be perceptible
to. 2. n. First light, daybreak, rise or
incipient gleam of anything. [back
formation f. dawning prob. f. ON, which
displaced dawing vbl n. f. obs. daw OE
dagian become day]

day, n. 1. Time while sun is above
horizon, (loosely) including twilights (~
& night, adv., throughout these or the
both alike; all ~, all the ~, throughout it; ~ break, break of ~, dawn; ~
dream, -ing, -er, reverie or castle in air,
indulgence, indulger, in them); dawn
(before, at, ~); daylight (by ~; was broad
~; clear as ~). 2. Twenty-four hours
(solar or astronomical ~, from noon;
civil ~, from midnight; sidereal ~, between two meridional transits of first
point of Aries, about 4' shorter than
solar; natural ~, = sidereal, also in first
sense above). 3. Civil ~ as point of time,
date, etc. (one ~, adv., on an unspecified
date past or future; the other ~, on a
not long ago; one of these ~s or fine ~s,
before long, in prophecy or promise;
some ~, at some future; on one's ~s. 4.
when he is at his best; ~ of GRACE). 4.
Date of specified festival etc. (first ~,
Sunday; Christmas ~, birth~, pay~,
last Day or Day of JUDGEMENT; the Day
or der Tag, that of victory over Gt
Britain expected by Germans). 5. Date
agreed upon (keep one's ~, be punctual;
one's ~, for being at home to guests, esp.
once a week). 6. Victory (carry, win,
lose, the ~). 7. Period (often pl., in the
~s of, the ~s of old, in ~s to come, men of
other ~s; better ~s, when one was or will
be better off; fallen on evil ~s, in misfortune; sing., at, to, this ~; present~,
adj. = modern; these ~s, adv., nowadays;
the ~, the current ~; sufficient for the ~
is the evil thereof; do not anticipate
trouble; men of the ~, persons of importance at any time; creature of a ~,
short-lived). 8. One's ~, lifetime, period
of prosperity, activity, power, etc., (also
pl. end one's ~s, die; every dog has his
~, no one always unlucky). 9. This ~
week, month, year, reckoning forward or
back from to~; ~ about, on alternate
~s; by ~, ~ after ~, from ~ to ~, every
~; advv. of daily repetition or progress;
twice etc. a ~, in each ~ (see A²); call it a
~, consider that one has done a ~'s work;
know the time of ~, be wide awake, knowing; the ~ before, after, the fair, advv., too
early, late, for opportunity. 10. ||~
boarder, schoolboy feeding but not sleeping at school; ~book in book-keeping,
book in which esp. sale transactions are
entered at once for later transfer to

ledger; ||~ boy, schoolboy living at
home; ~fly, ephemerid; ~labourer, hired
by ~ at fixed wage; ~long a. & adv.,
(lasting) for whole ~; ~out, Hawk-owl
hunting by ~; ~ room, used by ~ only,
esp. common living-room at schools;
~ school, opp. Sunday, evening, or boarding school; ~ spring, dawn (poet.); ~
ticket, covering return on same ~; ~ time,
not night, esp. in the ~time. [OE dæg,
com.-Teut., cf. Du. dag, G tag; not cogn.
w. L dies]

day'light (-līt), n. Light of day (BURN²
~); openness, publicity; let ~ into (sl.),
stab or shoot; dawn (before, at, ~);
visible interval as between boats in race,
wine & glass-rim (no ~, fill up), or rider
& saddle; ~ saving, use of fictitious time
in summer making lamps etc. needless.
[f. DAY, LIGHT]

daze, v.t., & n. 1. Stupefy, bewilder;
dazzle; hence dāz′edly² adv. 2. n.
Stupefaction, bewilderment. [ME dasen
cf. Icel. dasask refl. vb become weary]

daz′zle, v.t., & n. 1. Confuse or dim
(sight, eye, person) with excess of light,
intricate motion, incalculable number,
etc.; confound or surprise (mind, person)
by brilliant display, lit. or fig.; ~ed with
or by; ~e lamps or lights (over-bright, on
motor-car); ~e paint (so patterned on
ship as to deceive enemy about her type or
course); hence ~EMENT(-lm-) n., ~ing ly²
adv. 2. n. Glitter. [f. prec. + -LE(3)]

D-Day, n. Day (6 June 1944) on which
British and American forces invaded
N. France. [D for day]

de-, pref. From L de (prep. &) pref. =
down (depend), away (defend, orig. fend
off, deduce, deprecate), completely (declare,
denude), un- (in L oftener dis-, but also
de-, which is now a living pref. in this
sense, as decentralize, denazify, derequisi-
tion, derserve; many such E wds in
de- are also f. F in de-, which represents L
dis-, OF & Rom. des-, as well as L de-),
twice over or doubly (in chem. & bot. wds
as decomposite, decompound; a LL use).

deac'on, n. (Primitive Church) appointed
minister of charity (Acts vi. 1-6); (Episcopal) member of third order of ministry
below bishop & priest; (Baptist, Congregational, Presbyterian) officer attending to congregation's secular affairs.
Hence ~SHIP n. [f. L f. Gk diakonos
servant]

deac'oness, n. Woman in primitive &
some modern Churches with functions
analogous to deacon's. [-ESS¹]

dead (děd), a., n., & adv. 1. That has
ceased to live (the ~, n., person or
persons, or all who have ever died; from
the ~, from among these; ~ men tell no
tales, argument for killing possessor of
secret; ~ house, mortuary; ~ march,
march-like funeral music; ~ office,

For compounds of de- not given consult DE-.

funeral service; ~ as a doornail, quite ~; ~ & gone; ~ wait for ~ men's SHOES; FLOG ~ horse; ~ men or marines, empty bottles; ~ man's finger, kinds of orchid; ~ man's handle, the controlling handle in electric trains which must be held and pressed down for current to pass, so that slackening by death or ill-ness cuts the current & stops the train. 2. Benumbed, insensible, (~ to, unconscious or unappreciative of; spiritual ~; ~ to, hardened against). 3. Without effective, (~ language, one no longer in ordinary use, e.g. ancient Gk; ~ letter, law no longer observed, unclaimed or undelivered letter at post office). 5. In-animate (~ fence, of timber etc., opp. quickset; ~ matter), extinct, dull, lustre-less, without force, muffled, (~ brand, coal; ~ gold, unburnished; ~ colour, first layer in picture, cold & pale; ~-nettle, non-stinging weed like nettle; ~-alive, spiritless; ~ sound, not resonant). 6. In-active, motionless, idle, (D~ Sea; ~ point or ~ centre, least & greatest exten-sion of piston or crank, where it exerts no effective power; ~ weight, inert, of lifeless matter, also fig. of debt etc.; ~ pull, lift, at thing too heavy for one to move; ~ freight, sum paid in chartering ship for part not occupied by cargo; ~ arch, window, etc., sham; ~ end, terminus of branch line of railway etc.; ~ hand, = MORTMAIN, usu. implying ~ protest; ~ hours, still in night; ~ season, goods; ~ ball, out of play; wind falls ~ as n., = time, at ~ of night, in the ~ of winter). 7. Abrupt, complete, unre-lieved, exact, (come to a ~ stop; a ~ faint; on a ~ level; ~ heat, exact equality in race.~heed v.i.&t.; ~spit (colloq.), very counterpart of; a ~ calm; ~ loss, without compensation; be in ~ earnest; a ~ certainty; ~ on the target, quite straight, so ~ shot, unerring; ~lock, utter stand-still. 8. (Golf, of ball) very close to hole, within certain holing distance. 9. ~ alive, (of place, occupation, etc.) dull, tedious, monotonous; ~-eye (Naut.), round flat three-holed block for extending shrouds; ~-fire, St Elmo's fire, as presaging death; ~ ground, water (out of reach of a fort's guns, infantry fire, etc.); ~'head, non-paying theatre-goer or pas-senger; ~'light (Naut.), shutter inside porthole to prevent light showing out; ~ line, line beyond which it is not per-mitted or possible to go, fixed limit of time. (U.S. prisons) painted line across liable to be shot; ~ man's (or men's) fin-gers, finger-like divisions of gills in lobster or crab; ~ reckoning (Naut.), of ship's position by log, compass, etc.,when obser-vations are impossible; D~Sea APPLE. [OE

hence ~NESS n. 10. adv. Profoundly, absolutely, completely, (~ asleep, level, straight, tired, drunk; ~-beat, tired out, (Mech.) without recoil, *(n., sl.) worthless sponger; CUT²; ~ against, directly opposite to). [OE déad, com.-Teut. cf. Du. dood, G tot, f. OTeut. daudoz p.p. of vb st. dau- DIE²]

dead en (déd-), v.t. & i. Deprive of or lose vitality, force, brightness, feeling, etc.; make insensible to. [-EN⁶]

dead'ly¹ (déd-), a. Causing fatal injury; entailing damnation (~ sin); implacable, internecine; deathlike (~ paleness, faint-ness, gloom); intense (in ~ haste; ~ dullness). Hence dead'liNESS n. [OE déadlic (DEAD, -LY¹)]

dead'ly² (déd-), adv. As if dead (~ white, faint); extremely (~ tired, dull). [OE déadlíce (DEAD, -LY²)]

deaf (déf), a. Wholly or partly without hearing (the ~, ~ people; ~ of an, or in one, ear; ~ as an adder or a post; none so ~ as those that won't hear); insensible to, unappreciative of (~ to; ~ ear), not giving ear to (turn a ~ ear to); ~ mute, with no kernel; ~-&-dumb alphabet, language, etc., signs for communication by the ~; ~ mute, ~ & dumb person. Hence ~ly¹ adv.,~NESS n. [OE déaf, com.-Teut. cf. Du. doof, G taub, also Gk tuphlos blind]

deaf'en (déf-), v.t. Deprive of hearing by noise; make (sound) inaudible by louder one; make (floor etc.) impervious to sound. [-EN⁶]

deal¹, n. A great, good, ~, large, con-siderable, amount; (sl.) a ~; (same phrases used adv.) to a large, considerable, extent, (esp. with com-parative or superl.) by much, consider-ably. [OE déʒl, com.-Teut. cf. G teil part; also cogn. w. DOLE]

deal², v.t. & i. (~t pr. délt) & n. 1. Dis-tribute, give out, (gifts etc.) among several; deliver as his share or deserts to person (esp. of Providence etc.; ~t him happiness, good measure; of persons, esp. ~ a blow, abs. or with at, lit. & fig.). 2. Distribute cards to players for a game or round (n., such distribution, player's turn for it, as my ~, or round played after it); give (card, hand, etc., to player. 3. Associate with (esp. neg. as refuse to ~ with); do business with person, in goods (n., colloq., a bargain or transaction; also dishonest job); *New D~, the programme of social and economic reform planned by the Roosevelt administration of 1932 and subsequent years; raw ~ (colloq.), unfair treatment; square ~ (colloq.), justice, fair treatment. 4. Occupy one-self, grapple by way of discussion or refutation, take measures, with; (with adv.) behave (~ honourably, cruelly, esp. with or by person). Hence ~ING(1) n.

deal³, n. Piece of sawn fir or pine wood between 7 & 9 in. broad & 6 ft. long, & not over 3 in. thick; a quantity of deal fir or pine wood. [cogn. w. OE *thille* THILL, but f. LG cf. Du. *deel*, G *diele*]

deal'er, n. In vbl senses; esp.: player dealing at cards; trader, usu. in comb. as *corn-~*. [-ER¹]

deämbula'tion, n. **deäm'bulatory**, a. Walking. [f. L *deambulatio, deambulatorius*, f. DE(*ambulare* walk), -ATION, -ORY]

dean¹, n. Head of cathedral or collegiate-church chapter; || (also *rural~*) clergyman invested with jurisdiction or precedence over division of archdeaconry; (colleges) resident fellow, or one of several, with disciplinary & other functions; (foreign, Scots, & modern universities) president of a faculty; = DOYEN. [earlier sense *one set over ten. monks* f. L (Vulgate etc.) *decanus* prob. f. *decem* ten]

dean², **dêne**, n. Vale (esp. in names ending in -*dean*, -*dene*, -*den*). [OE *denu*, cogn. w. DEN]

dean'ery, n. Office, house, of dean; || group of parishes presided over by rural dean. [-ERY]

dear, a., n., adv., & int. **1.** Beloved (often as merely polite or even ironical form in talk, esp. *my ~ sir, my ~ Jones*, & now used at beginning of most letters not intended to be markedly business-like; as n., ~ or ~*est*, esp.in voc.; = ~ *one*; *a* ~, esp. in coaxing formulae). **2.** Precious *to*; one's dearest (*for ~ life*, as though life were at stake). **3.** High-priced, costly, (as adv., *sell, buy, pay, cost²* one, ~; ~ *year, shop*, in which prices run high); hence ~LY² adv., ~'NESS n. **4.** int. adv., ~ *me!, oh ~!*, expressing surprise, distress, sympathy, etc. [OE *dēore*, com.-Teut., cf. Du. *dier* loved, *diuer* costly, G *teuer*]

dearth (der²), n. Scarcity & dearness of food; scanty supply of. [ME *derthe* (prec., -TH¹)]

dear'y̆, -ie, n. (usu. voc.). Dear one. [-Y³]

death (dĕth), n. **1.** Dying (DIE² the ~; ~'-bed, on which one dies, ~*bed repentance*, fig., change of policy made too late to bear fruit; ~*rattle*, sound in dying person's throat; ~*roll*, list of the killed or dead; ~*watch*, kinds of insect whose ticking portends ~). **2.** End of life (*civil* ~, ceasing to count as citizen by out-lawry, banishment, etc.; *catch* one's ~, i.e. fatal chill etc.; ~*duties*, tax levied before property passes to heir; ~*rate*, yearly number of ~s to 1,000 of popula-tion; ~*trap*, unwholesome or dangerous place). **3.** Being killed or killing (*field of* ~, battlefield etc.; *be the* ~ *of*, kill; *do, put, stone, etc., to* ~; *war to the* ~, ~*feud*, till one kills or is killed; *it is, we make it, ~ to*, ~ is the penalty; *be in at the* ~, see *~ on* (sl.), skilful at killing game etc., or fig. at doing anything; *sick unto, tired to, ~*, to utmost limit; ~*blow*, mortal, lit. & fig.; ~*warrant*, for criminal's execution, abolition of custom etc.). **4.** Ceasing to be, annihilation, personified power that annihilates, (*at ~'s door*, soon to die; ~*'s-head*, skull as emblem of mortality, also kind of moth with skull marked on back; *sure, pale, as ~; hold on like grim* ~; *on rods*, good rat-killer, of dogs; ~*;*, archaic imprecation). **5.** Being dead (~*mask*, cast taken of dead person's face; *eyes closed in* ~). **6.** Want of spiritual life (*everlasting* ~, damnation). **7.** *Black D~*, (mod. name, transl. f. G for) great pestilence of Oriental Plague in Europe in 14th c. Hence ~*LESS a., ~*lĕss'ly² adv., ~*lĕssNESS n., ~'LIKE a. & adv., ~'LY² a. & adv., ~'WARD(S) a. & adv., (dĕth-). [OE *dēath*, com.-Teut. cf. Du. *dood*, G *tod*, f. vb st. *dau-* DIE², -*th* cogn. w. L p.p. -*tus*]

*dĕb, n. (colloq.). Débutante. [abbr.]

débâcle (dĭbā'kl), n. Break-up of ice in river; (Geol.) sudden rush of water carry-ing along blocks of stone and other debris; confused rush, rout, stampede; collapse, downfall, e.g. of a government. [F]

debâr', v.t. (-rr-). Exclude *from* admission or right (also ~ *person the crown* etc.). [f. (rare) prevent, bar, (entrance etc.). [f. 1430; F *débarrer*, OF *desbarer*, LL *debarrare*, have almost contrary sense *unbar*; cf. DE- in *defend*]

debārk', v.t. & i. = DISEMBARK. Hence debārka'tion n. [f. F *débarquer* (DE-, BARK²)]

debāse', v.t. Lower in quality, value, or character; adulterate (coin). Hence ~*MENT (-sm-) n. [DE-+ obs. *base* for ABASE]

debāt'able, a. Questionable, subject to dispute, (~ *ground* lit. or fig., for which parties contend, borderland). [OF (foll. -ABLE]

debāt'e, v.t. & i., & n. **1.** Contest, fight for, (*long ~ed the victory*); dispute about, discuss, (a question); hold argument, esp. in Parliament or public meeting (~*ing-society*, for practice); consider, ponder, (~ *it, & i.*); hence ~'ER¹ n. (esp. of one skilled rather in argument than in oratory). **2.** n. Controversy, discussion, public argument. [f. OF *débatre* & 13th-c. F *debat* (DE-, Rom. *battere* fight)]

debauch', v.t., & n. **1.** Pervert from virtue or morality; make intemperate or sensual; seduce (woman); vitiate (taste, judgement); hence ~*ABLE a., 2. n. Bout or habit of sensual indulgence; hence ~*ERY(4) n. [f. F *débaucher* entice *from* a master (DE-, perh. *bauche* workshop)]

For compounds of *de-* not given consult DE-.

debauchee' (-bosh-), n. Viciously sensual person. [f. F *débauché* p.p. see prec.]

deben'ture, n. 1. ||(Arch., or techn.) voucher given to person supplying goods to Royal Household or Government Office, entitling him to payment, Custom-House certificate to exporter of amount due to him as drawback or bounty. 2. ||(Ord. sense) sealed bond of corpora-tion or company acknowledging sum on which interest is due till principal is re-paid, esp. fixed interest constituting prior charge on assets; ||~ *stock*, ~s consoli-dated or created as stock whose nominal capital represents debt of which interest only is secured as perpetual annuity. [perh. (w. assim. to -URE) = L *debentur* are due, as initial word of vouchers]

debili'tate, v.t. Enfeeble (constitution etc.). [f. L *debilitare*, see foll.; -ATE²]

debil'ity, n. Feebleness (of health, pur-pose, etc.). [f. F *débilité* f. L *debilitatem* (*debilis* weak, -TY)]

debit (de-), n. & v.t. 1. Entry in account of sum owing; side of account (left-hand) in which these entries are made (cf. CREDIT). 2. v.t. Charge (person) *with* sum; enter (sum) *against* or *to* person. [f. L *debitum* DEBT]

déblai (dāb'lā), n. (fortif.). Earth exca-vated from the ditch (to form parapet). [F, f. *déblayer* to clear]

débonair', a. (arch.). Genial, pleasant, unembarrassed. [f. OF *debonaire* = *de bonne aire* of good disposition]

débouché' (-sht), a. (Arch. for) de-bauched.

débouch' (-oosh), v.i. Issue from ravine, wood, etc. into open ground (of troops; also of stream). So ~MENT (-oosh-) n. [f. F *déboucher* (L *dis*- see DE- + F *bouche* mouth)]

Débrétt', n. (Used for) ~'s Peerage etc. [John ~, compiler]

debris, dé-, dé-, (dā'brē, dĕ'brē), n. Scattered frag-ments, wreckage, drifted accumulation. [F (*dé-*), f. obs. *débriser* break down]

debt (dĕt), n. Money, goods, or service, owing (~ *of honour*, not legally recover-able, esp. of sum lost in gambling; ||~ *collector*, one whose business it is to collect ~s for creditors; ~ *of nature*, death; *National D~*, sum owed by State to persons who have advanced money to it; *funded* ~, the part of this converted into fund of which interest only is to be paid; *floating* ~, part of it repayable on demand, or at stated time; *small* ~, of limited amount recoverable in County Court); being under obligation to pay something (*in, out of, get into,* ~ or person's ~). [ME & OF *dette* f. L *debitum* neut. p.p. of *debēre* owe]

debt'or (dĕt-), n. One who owes money or an obligation or duty. (Book-keeping) *Debtor, Dr*, heading of left-hand or debit

side of account. [ME & OF *dettour* f. L *debitōrem* (prec., -OR)]

*débunk', v.t. (collog.). Remove the false sentiment from (person, reputation, institution, cult, etc.; remove (celebrity) from his pedestal. [DE-, BUNK¹]

débris', v.t. & i. (-ss-). Unload (men, stores) or alight from motor vehicles. [DE- + BUS, after *detrain*]

début (see Ap.), n. First appearance in society, or on stage etc. as performer. [F] **débutant, débutante,** (see Ap.) nn. Male or female performer making début; (fem.) girl coming out or being presented. [F]

déca-, dec-, pref. f. Gk *deka* ten in many technical terms as *decāg'ynous* [Gk *gunē* female] with ten pistils, *decāhē'dral* [Gk *hedra* base] ten-sided (-*hedron*, such solid), *decän'drous* [Gk *andr*- male] with ten stamens, *dēc'astyle* [Gk -*stulos*] ten-columned (portico; esp. in French metric system = ten of the specified unit (cf. DECI-), whence *dec'agram(me)*, .353 oz avoird.; *déc'alitre* (-ēter), about 2⅕ gal.; *déc'amētre* (-ēter), about 32 ft 9 in.

dec'ad(e), n. Set, series, of ten; ten years; ten books (1-10, 11-20, etc.) of Livy. So **dec'adal, decād'ic,** aa. [13th-c. f. F (-e), f. L, f. Gk *dekas -ad*- f. *deka* ten. -AD, -ADE(2)]

dec'adence, n., **dec'adent,** a. & n. Falling away, declining, deteriorating, (used esp. of a period of art or literature after cul-mination; (literary sl.) decadent, (writer or artist) affecting certain vices, obscuri-ties, & turgidities of style. [f. F *décadence* f. med. L *decadentia* (DE-, Rom. *cadere* = L *cadēre* fall. -ENCE)]

dec'agon, n. Plane figure with ten sides and angles. So **decăg'onal** a. [f. med. L DECA(*gonon* f. Gk -*gōnos* -angled)]

decal'cify, v.t. Deprive (bone etc.) of its lime. [DE-]

dec'alogue (-ŏg), n. The ten command-ments. [f. F *décalogue* f. L f. Gk *dekalogos* the D~ of Boccaccio (100 tales told by a company in ten days). [f. It. *decamerone* wrong form f. Gk -*ēmeron* in *hexaēmeron* neut. adj. of six days]

décamp', v.i. Break up or leave camp; go away suddenly, take oneself off, abscond. So ~MENT n. [f. F *décamper* (DE-, CAMP¹]

dēcan'al (or dĕk'a-), a. Of dean, deanery, or south side, on which dean sits, of choir. [f. L *decanus* DEAN¹ + -AL]

décani (-ī), mus. direction. To be sung by decanal side in antiphonal singing (cf. CANTORIS). [L genit. as prec.]

decant', v.t. Pour off (liquid of solution) by gradual inclination of vessel without disturbing sediment; pour (wine) similar-ly from bottle into decanter; (fig.) move or transfer as if by pouring. [f. F *décanter* f. med. L DE(*canthare* f. L f. Gk *kanthos* cant¹ used of lip of beaker)]

decăn'ter, n. Stoppered glass bottle in which wine or spirit is brought to table. [-ER¹]

dĕcăp'itāte, v.t. Behead (esp. as legal punishment); cut the head or end from. So ~ABLE a., ~ATION n. [f. F décapiter f. LL DE(capitare f. caput -itis head)]

dĕc'apŏd, n. Ten-footed crustacean. [f. F décapode f. Gk DECA(pous -podos foot)]

dĕcărb'onīze, v.t. Deprive of its carbon or carbonic acid. [DE-]

dĕcă'sualīze (-zhŏŏ-, -zū-), v.t. Do away with the casual employment of (labour). Hence ~ATION n. [DE-, -IZE]

dĕcăsyllăb'ic, a. & n., **dĕcăsyll'able,** n. & a. (Line) of ten syllables. [DECA-]

dĕcăthŏl'icize, v.t. Divest of its catholic character. [DE-]

decay'¹, v.i.&t. Deteriorate, lose quality, decline in power, wealth, energy, beauty, etc.; rot (t. & i.); cause to deteriorate. [f. OF decair f. Rom. DE(cadĕre for L cadĕre fall)]

decay'², n. Decline, falling off; ruinous state, wasting away (phonetic ~, wearing down of word-forms); break-up of health, decomposition; rotten tissue (remove the ~). [f. prec.]

decea'se'¹, n., & v.i. (Esp. in legal and formal use for) death, die, depart(ure) from life. Hence ~ED¹(2) (-sĕd') a. and n. (with or without the). [f. F decès f. L DE(cessus n.f. cedĕre cess- go)]

deceit' (-sēt), n. Misrepresentation, deceiving; trick, stratagem; the vice of deceitfulness; misleading appearance. Hence ~FUL¹a., ~fully² adv., ~fulness n., (-sēt-). [f. OF deceite n.f. fem. p.p. of deceveir f. L DE(cipere -cept- = capere take) deceive]

deceive' (-sēv'), v.t. & i. Persuade of what is false, mislead, (~e oneself, juggle with one's own convictions, also be mistaken); use deceit; disappoint (esp. hopes). So ~'ABLE a., ~'ER¹ n., (-sēv-). [f. OF deceveir f. L as prec.]

Decĕm'ber, n. Twelfth month of year. Hence ~RIST n, member of Russian revolutionary conspiracy in ~er 1825. [f. OF décembre f. L December (decem ten) orig. tenth month of Roman year]

decĕm'vir (-er), n. (pl. ~s, ~ī). (Rom. Hist.) member of board of ten acting as council or ruling power, esp. that appointed 451 B.C. to draw up laws of Twelve Tables; member of any ruling body of ten, as at Venice. So ~AL a., ~ATE¹ n. [L, f. decem viri ten men]

de'cencў, n. Propriety of behaviour; what is required by good taste or delicacy; avoidance of obscene language & gestures & of undue exposure of person; respecta-

bility; the ~ies, decorous observances, requirements of a decent life. [f. L decentia (decere be fitting, -ENCY)]

decĕnn'ary, a. & n. (Of) period of ten years. [f. L decennis (decem, annus) ten-year + -ARY¹]

decĕnn'iad, decĕnn'ium (pl. -ĭa), n. Ten-year period. [-ad irreg. f. L (-um) f. decennis (prec.); see -AD]

decĕnn'ial, a. Of ten-year period; recurring in ten years. Hence ~LY² adv. [f. L, decennium see prec. + -AL]

dē'cent, a. Seemly, not immodest or obscene or indelicate; respectable; passable, good enough, tolerable, whence ~ISH²(2) a.; ∥(school sl.) kind, not severe or censorious. Hence ~LY² adv. [f. L F decere beseem, -ENT]

decĕn'tralize, v.t. Undo the centralization of; confer local government on. Hence ~ATION n. [DE-]

dĕcĕp'tion, n. Deceiving, being deceived; thing that deceives, trick, sham. [f. F deception f. L deceptionem (decipere see DECEIT, -ION)]

dĕcĕp'tive, a. Apt to deceive, easily mistaken. Hence ~LY² (-vl-) adv., ~NESS (-vn-) n. [f. F déceptif(prec., -IVE]

dēchris'tianize (-krĭscha-), v.t. Divest of its christianity. [DE-]

dĕci-, pref. shortened from L decimus tenth, used (as deci-) in F) esp. in French metric system in sense ŧ̄₀ of specified unit. So **dē'cibĕl** (unit for measuring relative intensities of sounds), **dē'cigrăm(m)**, **dē'cilĭtre** (-ēter), **dē'cimĕtre** (-er), nn.

decīde', v.t. & i. Settle (question, issue, dispute) by giving victory to one side; give judgement (between, for, in favour of, against, or abs.); bring, come, to a resolution (that ~s me; ~ to do, on, for, or against doing). Hence **decīd'ABLE** a. [f. F décider f. L DE(cīdere cis- = caedere cut)]

decīd'ĕd, a. In vbl senses; also: definite, unquestionable, (a ~ difference); (of persons) of clear opinions or vigorous initiative, not vacillating. Hence ~LY² adv. [-ED¹]

decīd'er, n. In vbl senses; also, (Racing) heat in which tie is run off. [-ER¹]

decīd'ŭous, a. Shed periodically or normally (of leaves, teeth, horns, etc.); shedding its leaves annually; shedding its wings after copulation (of ants etc.); fleeting, transitory. [f. L deciduus f. DE(cidere=cadere fall)+-OUS]

dĕcĭll'ion (-yon), n. ∥Tenth power of million (1 with 60 ciphers). Hence ~TH² a. & n. [f. L decem ten & million, see BILLION]

dĕc'imal, a. & n. Of tenths or ten, proceeding by tens, (~ numeration, ordinary counting-system with ten for basis, reckoned by decades; ~ system, of

For compounds of de- not given consult DE-.

weights and measures, with denominations rising by tens; ~ *notation*, counting in tens; ~ *arithmetic*, using this notation, also called ~s, treating of ~ *fractions*; ~ *fraction* or ~, one whose denominator is a power of ten, esp. when expressed by figures written to right of the ~ *point*, or dot placed after the unit figure, & denoting tenths, hundredths, etc., according to their place; RECURRING ~; ~ COINAGE); ~ *coinage*, whence ~IZE(3) v.t.; ~IZA'TION n. [f. L *decima* tenth, tithe, but treated as f. L *decima* tenth, -AL]

dē'cimate, v.t. Put to death one in ten of (mutinous or cowardly soldiers); destroy tenth or large proportion of (esp. of epidemic or other visitation. So **decimā'TION** n. [f. L *decimare* take the tenth man (*decimus*), see -ATE³]

dē'cimō-sex'tō, see SEXTODECIMO.

dē'cimus. See PRIMUS.

deciph'er, v.t., & n. Turn into ordinary writing or make out with key (thing written in cipher); make out meaning of (bad writing, hieroglyphics, anything perplexing); (n.) interpretation of cipher document. Hence ~ABLE a., ~MENT n. [DE-]

deci'sion (-izhn), n. Settlement (of question etc.), conclusion, formal judgement; making up one's mind, resolve; resoluteness, decided character. [F (*dé-*), f. L *decisionem* (DECIDE, -ION)]

dēcī'sive, a. Deciding, conclusive, (esp. ~ *battle*); = DECIDED (~ *character*, ~ *superiority*). Hence ~LY² (-vl-) adv., ~NESS n. [f. med. L *decisivus*]

dēcī'vilize, v.t. Divest of civilization. [DE-]

deck¹, n. 1. Platform of planks or wood-covered iron extending from side to side of ship or part of it (in large ships *main*, *middle*, *lower*, ~s, also *upper* or *spar* & *forecastle* ~s, short ones in stern & bow); CLEAR² *the* ~s; *on* ~, not below; ~*chair*, camp-stool, also long-armed reclining chair, used in passenger steamers; ~*hand*, man employed on ~, in cleaning and odd jobs; vessel's ~*house*, room erected on ~. 2. Pack of cards (now chiefly U.S.), [perh. as foll. f. MDu., but found in E 160 years earlier than the corresp. Du. in same sense]

deck², v.t. Array, adorn; furnish with, cover as, a deck. [prob. f. MDu. *deken* cover as, dress, ~*s*; prob. f. MDu. *deken* whence also OE *thec* THATCH]

deck'le, n. Contrivance in papermaking-machine for limiting size of sheet (~*edge*, rough uncut edge). [f. G *deckel* dim. of *decke* cover]

declaim', v.i. & t. Speak rhetorically (often *against*, = inveigh), practise speaking or recitation; deliver impassioned or rhetorical speech; utter rhetorically. So **declaim'** f. L DE(*clamare* cry out) w. assim.

declamā'tion, n. Act or art of declaiming; rhetorical exercise, set speech; impassioned speech, harangue. So **declam'atory** a. [f. L *declamatio* (prec., -ATION)]

declar'ant, n. One who makes legal declaration. [f. L *declarare* (prec., -ANT)]

declarā'tion, n. Stating, announcing; positive, emphatic, solemn, or legal assertion, announcement, or proclamation (~ *of war*, before beginning hostilities, not now usual; ~ *of the poll*, of vote-totals of election-candidates); manifesto, written announcement of intentions, terms of agreement, etc. (D~ *of* INDULGENCE; D~ *of* RIGHTS; D~ *of Independence*, of 4th July 1776 by N. Amer. British colonies; D~ *of Paris* 1856, *of London* 1909 unratified by Gt Britain, international agreements on maritime law); (Law) plaintiff's statement of claim, affirmation in lieu of oath, Custom-House Statement (see foll.); (Cards) a bid, pass, double, etc., the winning bid. [f. L *declaratio* (foll., -ATION)]

declāre', v.t. & i. 1. Make known, proclaim publicly, formally, or explicitly, (~ *war*, *a dividend*); (abs.) *Well, I* ~ (excl. of incredulity, surprise, or vexation). 2. Pronounce (person etc.) to be something, as ~ *him (to be) an enemy to humankind*; ~ *oneself*, avow intentions, reveal character; ~ *for*, *against*, side with, against; ~ *innings closed*, or ~, elect to cease batting as though all were out; ~ *off*, break off (bargain etc. or abs.). 3. (Customs) name (dutiable goods) as in one's possession. 4. (Bridge) name the trump suit, or call 'No trumps' (other card games) announce that one holds (certain combinations of cards etc). Hence or cogn. **declā'rative**, **declā'ratory**, aa., **declā'ratively²** **declā'redly²**, adv., **declā'rER¹** n. (esp. at cards). [f. F *déclarer* f. L DE(*clarare* f. *clarus* clear)]

déclassé (dākläs'ā), a. (fem.-ée), That has lost caste or sunk in social scale. [F]

déclen'sion (-shn), n. Deviation from uprightness etc.; deterioration, decay; (Gram.) case-inflexion, one of the noun-classes distinguished by their different methods of case-inflexion, declining, [irreg. f. L DE(*clinatio* f. *-clinare* cf. Gk *klīnō* bend, -ATION)]; perh. thr. F *dé-clinaison* & a form *declin'son* corresp. to *pensison*.]

declinā'tion, n. Downward bend; (Astron.) angular distance of star etc. north or south of celestial equator, celestial latitude; (Compass) angular

deviation of needle, E. or W., from true north. Hence ~AL (-sho-) a. [f. OF *déclination* f. L *declinationem* see prec.]

decline'¹ v.i. & t. Slope downwards (usu. intr.); bend, droop, (i., & also t. as *with head ~d, ~s its blossoms*); (of day, life, etc.) draw to close; sink morally (*~ on*, descend to); fall off, decay, decrease, deteriorate; turn away from, refuse, (discussion, challenge, battle; *~ to do, doing, to be treated in such a way*); say one cannot accept (invitation etc., or abs.; *~ with thanks* freq. iron.,reject,scornfully; (Gram.) inflect, recite the cases of, whence declin'ABLE a. [f. F *décliner* f. L *decline*, *de-* in the L = *away*, in the E chiefly *down*]

decline'² n. Sinking, gradual loss of vigour or excellence, decay, deterioration; phthisis, consumption; fall in price; setting, last part of course, (of sun, life, etc.). [f. F *déclin* f. *décliner* see prec.]

declinom'eter, n. Instrument for measuring magnetic declination. [irreg. f. L *declinare* see DECLENSION +-METER]

decliv'ity, n. Downward slope. [f. L *declivitas* f. *declivis* f. *clivus* slope) +-TY]

decliv'ous, a. Sloping down (esp. in Zool. of profile). [f. L *declivus, -is*, see prec. +-OUS]

declutch', v.i. Disengage clutch esp. of motor-car. [DE-]

decoc'tion, n. Boiling down so as to extract essence; liquor resulting. [OF. f. L DE(*coctionem* f. *coquere coct-* boil, -ION)]

decode', v.t. Decipher (code telegram etc.). [DE-]

décolletage (dākŏl'tahzh), n. (Exposure of neck and shoulders by) low-cut neck of bodice. [F (DE-, *collet* collar of dress)]

décolleté (dākŏl'tā), a. (fem. *-ée*). Low-necked (of dress); wearing low-necked dress. [F]

décol'o(u)rize (-kŭler-), v.t. Deprive of colour. Hence ~A'TION, ~ER-(2), nn. [DE-, COLOUR,-IZE(3)]

dec'omplex, a. Doubly complex, having complex parts. [DE-]

décompose' (-z), a. & t. Separate into its elements (substance, light, etc.); analyse (thought, motive); rot (t. & i.). Hence ~ABLE a., ~ER-(2), décomposi'TION, nn., (-z-). [f. F *décomposer* (DE-, COMPOSE)]

decom'posite (-z), a. & n. (Substance, word, etc.) made by compounding a compound with another element, further composite. [f. LL *decompositus* transl. of Gk *parasunthetos* used of words derived from compounds; see DE-]

dec'ompound, a. & n. = DECOMPOSITE (esp. in Bot.). [DE-]

décompress', v.t. Relieve pressure on (underwater or other worker) by means of an air-lock. Hence décompré'ssION (-shn) n., ~OR² n., contrivance for relieving pressure in motor engine. [DE-]

décon'sécrate, v.t. Secularize. [DE-]

décontám'inate, v.t. Remove contamination from (esp. areas, clothes, etc., affected by poison-gas). Hence ~A'TION n. [DE-]

décontról', v.t.(-ll-), & n. Release from (esp. war-time) control by Government etc. [DE-]

décor (dākŏr'), n. All that makes up the appearance of a room or the stage. [F]

déc'orate, v.t. Furnish with adornments (esp. church with flowers etc.); serve as adornment to; invest with order, medal, etc.; *~ed* as adj. or n., (of) third English STYLE of architecture. Hence ~IVE a. [f. L *decorare* (*decus -oris* beauty), -ATE³]

déc'oration, n. In vbl senses; esp.; (pl.) flags, wreaths, etc., put up on occasion of public rejoicing; medal, star, etc., worn as honour. [f. L *decoratio* (prec., -ATION)]

déc'orator, n. In vbl senses; esp., tradesman who papers, paints, etc., houses. [-OR²]

déco'rous, a. Not violating good taste or propriety, dignified and decent. Hence ~LY² adv., ~NESS n. (*decor* f. *decēre* be fit, -OR²) +-OUS]

décor'um, n. Seemliness, propriety, etiquette; particular usage required by politeness or decency. [L, neut. adj. as prec.]

décoy', n., & v.t. (Entice, esp. by help of trained bird etc., into) pond with narrow netted arms into which wild duck may be tempted and caught; allure *into, out of, away*, etc., ensnare; bird etc. trained to entice others; (also *~-duck*) swindler's confederate, tempter; bait, enticement. [earlier *coy* f. Du. *kooi* f. WG *cavia* f. L *cavea* CAGE¹; *de-* unexplained (duck-coy n. & v. is early, but not earliest, E form)]

décrease', v.i. & t., **déc'rease,** n. **1.** Lessen, diminish, (i. & t.); hence décrease'inglY² adv. **2.** n. Diminution, lessening. [vb f. OF *descreiss-* part. st., n. f. OF *descreis-* vb st., of *descreistre* f. (Rom. *dis-*) L DE(*crescere cret-* grow)]

décree', n., & v.t. **1.** Ordinance or edict set forth by authority; decision (in other courts called *judgement*) in Admiralty cases, (in Divorce cases) order declaring nullity or dissolution or giving judicial separation (|| *~ nisi'i*, order for divorce unless cause is shown within a period, orig. six months, later six weeks); will, as shown by result, of God, Providence, Nature, etc. **2.** v.t. Ordain by ~. [f. OF *decré* f. L DE(*cretum* neut. p.p. of *cernere* sift) thing decided]

For compounds of *de-* not given consult DE-.

déc'rement, n. Decrease, amount lost by diminution or waste, (esp. as scientific term opp. INCREMENT). [f. L *decrementum* (DECREASE, -MENT)]

décrép'it, a. Wasted, worn out, enfeebled with age & infirmities, (of persons or institutions). So décrép'itude n. [f. F *décrépit* f. L DEcrepitus p.p. of *crepare* creak]

décrép'itàte, v.t. & i. Calcine (mineral or salt) till it ceases to crackle in fire; crackle under heat. Hence ~A'TION n. [DE-, L *crepitare* frequent. of *crepare* creak]

decrescen'dó (dākrěsh-). = DIMINUENDO. [It.]

décrés'cent, a. Waning, decreasing, (usu. of moon). [f. L *decrescens* (DECREASE, -ENT)]

décré'tal, n. Papal decree; (pl.) collection of these, forming part of canon law. [f. décrétal f. L *decretalis* (letter) of DECREE, -AL]

décry', v.t. Disparage, cry down. [f. F *décrier* (DE-, CRY[2])]

décû'man, a. Especially large or powerful (usu. of wave lit. or fig.). [f. L *decumanus*, used of main gate of camp where tenth cohort was quartered (*decimus* tenth, -AN)]

décûm'bent, a. (bot. & zool.). Lying along ground or body (of plant, shoot, bristles). [f. L DECumbere lie), -ENT]

déc'ûple, a., n. & v.t. & i. Tenfold (amount); (vb) multiply by ten. [F (dé-), f. L *decuplus* (*decem* ten, -*plus* cf. *duplus* DOUBLE]

décüss'ate, a. (-át), & v.t. & i. (-át). 1. X-shaped, intersecting; (Bot.) with pairs of opposite shoots, each at right angles to pair below (Rhet.) marked by intersect; hence décussa'tion n. [f. L *decussis* number ten, X, *decussare* (*decussis* number ten, -ATE[2,3])

dedans (dedahn'), n. (tennis). Open gallery at end of service-side of a court; (transf., *the* ~) spectators watching a tennis match. [F, = inside]

déd'icàte, v.t. Devote with solemn rites (to God or to sacred use; of church etc. esp. without certain forms necessary for legally consecrating ground or buildings); give up (to special purpose); inscribe (book etc.) to patron or friend. So ~OR[2], ~EE[1], nn., ~IVE[2], ~ORY, aa. [f. L DEDicare declare), -ATE[3]]

dédica'tion, n. In vbl senses; also, dedicatory inscription on building etc. or in book. [f. OF *dédicacion* f. L *dedicationem*]

dédûce', v.t. Bring down (annals etc.) from or to a time; trace descent of (person etc.) from; infer, draw as conclusion, from. So ~IBLE a. [f. L DEducere duct- lead)]

dédûct', v.t. Take away, put aside, (amount, portion, etc. *subtract* being now used of numbers) from (or abs.). [f. L *deduct*- see prec.]

dédûc'tion, n. Deducting; amount deducted; deducing, inference from general to particular, *a priori* reasoning, (cf. INDUCTION); thing deduced. [f. L *deductio* (DEDUCE, -ION)]

dédûc'tive, a. Of, reasoning by, deduction, *a priori*. Hence ~LY[2] (-vĭ-) adv. [f. L *deductivus* (DEDUCE, -IVE)]

dee, n. Letter D; D-shaped harness-ring.

deed, n. Thing done intentionally; brave, skilful, or conspicuous act; actual fact, performance, (*in word & ~; in ~ & not in name*, whence *in very ~*); (Law) written or printed instrument effecting legal disposition & sealed & delivered by disposing party (in practice now always signed also but not always delivered); ~-*poll*, deed made & executed by one party only (paper polled or cut even, not indented). Hence ~LESS a. [OE *dǣd* cf. Du. *daad*, G. *tat*, cogn. w. DO[1]]

deem, v.t. Believe, consider, judge, count, (abs. in parenthesis, *as it was, I ~ed, time to go*; ~ *highly of*, have high opinion of; ~ *it one's duty*; *was ~ed sufficient, it ~ to suffice*; ~*ed that this would do*). [OE *déman* com.-Teut. f. OTeut. *dōmjan* f. *dōma* DOOM]

deem'ster, n. One of two justices of Isle of Man. [prec., -STER]

deep[1], a. 1. Going far down from top (~ *hole, water, draught, drink, drinker, gaming, gamester*; *go (in) off the ~* END[1]; far in from surface or edge (~ *wound, shelf, border*; ~ *mourning*, expressed by wide crape etc.; ~ *plunge*; ~ *reader, thinker*). 2. Hard to fathom, profound, not superficial, penetrating, (~ *dissimulation*; ~ *a one*, sl., cunning or secretive; *the ~er causes*; ~ *insight*). 3. Heartfelt, absorbing, absorbed, (~ *feelings, interest, curses*; ~ *in a pursuit*, dead to everything else). 4. Intense, vivid, extreme, heinous, (~ *disgrace, sleep, night, sin, colour*; ~ *red* etc.). 5. Going or placed (so far down back, or in (*under 6 ft*; *ankle-~ in mud*; *drawn up six ~*; *skip ~ in the water, hands ~ in pockets*; ~ *in debt*; ~ *in the human heart*, fully versed in it). 6. Brought from far down (note, bell, voice; ~*mouthed*, full-toned, (note, bell, voice; ~*mouthed*, far down (~ *sigh*); not shrill, low-pitched, of dog). Hence ~EN[6] v.t. & i., ~LY[2] adv.; ~NESS n. (rare, for *depth*). [OE *déop, déop*, com.-Teut. cf. Du. *diep*, G. *tiep*, cogn. w. DIP]

deep[2], n. *The ~* (poet.), the sea; (Cricket, *the ~*) position of fieldsmen stationed behind the bowler at or near boundary (*the ~ field*) (usu. pl.) deep part(s) of the sea; abyss, pit, cavity; mysterious region of thought or feeling. [as prec. (neut. adj.)]

deep³, adv. Deeply, far in, (read ~ into the night; still waters run ~, real feeling or knowledge (not showy); esp. in comb. as ~-drawn (of sighs), ~-laid (of scheme, secret & elaborate), ~-rooted (esp. of prejudice), ~-seated (of emotion or disease). [OE díope, déope, (DEEP¹)]

deep'ing, n. Section, one fathom deep, of fishing-net. [-ING³]

deer, n. (collect. sing. usu. for pl.). Kinds of ruminant quadruped with deciduous branching horns (small ~, insignificant animals or things collectively, cf. King Lear III iv. 144); ~-hound, large rough greyhound; ~-forest, wild land reserved for stalking ~; ~-lick, spring or damp spot impregnated with salt etc. where ~ come to lick; ~-neck, horse's thin neck; ||~'s-foot, a fine grass; ~'skin, (made of) ~'s skin; ~'stalker, sportsman stalking ~, cloth cap peaked before and behind. [OE déor, Du. dier, G tier]

deface', v.t. Mar appearance or beauty of, disfigure; discredit; make illegible. Hence ~ABLE (-sa-) a., ~MENT (-sm-) n. [f. obs. F defacer (DE-, FACE²)]

dē̆ fac'to, a. & adv. In fact, whether by right (DE JURE) or not (king ~, the ~ king). [L]

dēr'alcāte, v.i. Commit defalcations, misappropriate property in one's charge. So ~OR² n. [f. med. L DEfalcare lop f. L fala -cis scythe]. -ATE³]

dēfalcā'tion, n. Defection, shortcoming; fraudulent deficiency of money owing to breach of trust, misappropriation, amount misappropriated. [f. med. L defalcatio (prec., -ATION)]

dēfame', v.t. Attack the good fame of, speak ill of. So **dēfam'A'TION** n., **dēfam'a-TORY** a. [f. OF diffamer f. L diffamare spread abroad (DIS-, fama report), see DE-; there are also LL defamis, -atus, infamous]

default'¹, n. Want, absence, (in ~ of, if or since such a thing is wanting; failure to act or appear, neglect, (make ~, judgement by ~, given for plaintiff on defendant's failure to plead); failure to pay, default-ing. [f. OF defaute f. defaillir see foll. & cf. FAULT]

default'², v.i. & t. 1. Make, be guilty of, default; fail to appear in court; not meet money calls, break; hence ~ER¹ n., (also MIL.) soldier guilty of military offence (~er sheet, record of such offences, now conduct sheet). 2. Declare (party) in default & give judgement against him. [f. OF defaillir (3 sing. default) f. DE-, L fallere deceive]

dēfeas'ance (-fēz-), n. Rendering null & void. [f. OF desfesance f. desfaire undo (DE-, L facere do), -ANCE]]

dēfeas'i|ble (-fēz-), a. Capable of annul-ment, liable to forfeiture. Hence ~BIL'ITY n. [as prec., -BLE]

defeat', v.t., & n. Frustrate, frustration; (Law) annul(ment); (arch.) disappoint of; overthrow (v. & n.) in contest esp. in battle. [n. prob. f. vb, which is f. OF defeit p.p. of desfaire see DEFEASANCE]

defeat'|ism, n. Conduct tending to bring about acceptance of defeat, esp. by action on civilian opinion. So ~IST n. & a. [f. F défaitisme (as prec., -ISM)]

dēfea'ture, v.t. Make unrecognizable. [f. obs. noun f. OF desfaiture (prec., -URE)]

dēf'ēcāte, v.t. Clear of dregs, refine, purify, (lit. & fig.); get rid of (irregs, ex-crement, sin). Hence ~A'TION, ~ātor²(2), nn. [f. L DEfaecare f.faex -cis dregs), -ATE³]

dēfect', n. Lack of something essential to completeness; shortcoming, falling, (has the ~s of his qualities, the particular ones that often accompany his particular virtues); blemish; amount by which thing falls short. [f. L defectus n. f. DE(facere fect- = facere do) desert, fail]

dēfec'tion, n. Falling away from allegiance to leader, party, religion, or duty; desertion, apostasy. [f. L defectio (prec., -ION)]

dēfec'tive, a. Having defect(s), incom-plete, faulty, wanting or deficient (in some respect); (Gram.) not having all the usual inflexions. Hence ~LY² (-vi-) adv., ~NESS (-vn-) n. [f. F défectif f. L defectivus as prec., -IVE]

|| dēfence', *defense'*, n. Defending from, resistance against, attack (cf. OFFENCE; best ~ is offence, advantage goes with the initiative; in cricket, guarding of one's wicket, also batting as opposed to bowl-ing; science or art of ~, boxing or fenc-ing; (Mil., pl.) fortifications (also line of ~, series of fortified posts); thing that protects; justification, vindication, speech or writing used to this end; (Law) accused party's denial, pleading, & proceedings, counsel for the ~; ||D~ of the Realm Act (abbr. D.O.R.A., joc. Dor'a), Act of August, 1914, providing Government with wide powers during war. Hence ~LESS (-sl-) a., ~lēssLY² adv., ~lēssness n. [f. OF defens f. L defensum neut., thing forbidden, & OF defense f. L defensa fem. used as noun cf. -ADE(1), both p.p. see foll.]

dēfend', v.t. 1. Forbid, avert, (arch.; still in God ~!); ward of attack from; keep safe, protect (against, from); up-hold by argument, vindicate, speak or write in favour of; (Law) make defence in court (~ oneself, conduct one's own defence), (of counsel) appear for defen-dant, conduct defence of. [f. OF defendre f. L DEfendere -fens- FEND]

dēfen'dant, n. Person sued in law-suit (cf. plaintiff); (attrib.) holding this

For compounds of de- not given consult DE-.

relation (the ~ *company*). [f. F *défendant* part. (prec., -ANT)]

défen´der, n. One who defends; D~ *of the Faith,* title of Eng. Sovereigns from Henry VIII, who received it from Pope for writing against Luther; (Sport) holder of championship etc. defending the title (opp. *challenger*). [f. OF *defendeor* f. Rom. †*defenditorem* (DEFEND, -OR²)]

defense. See DEFENCE.

défen´sible, a. Easily defended (in war or argument); justifiable. Hence ~BIL´ITY n., ~bly² adv. [f. L *defensibilis* (DEFEND, -IBLE)]

defen´sive, a. & n. 1. Serving, used, done, for defence, protective, not aggressive; hence ~LY² (-vi-) adv. 2. n. State or position of defence (esp. *be, stand, act, on the* ~). [f. F *défensif* f. med. L *defensivus* (DEFEND, -IVE)]

defer´¹, v.t. (-rr-). Put off, postpone, delay; (absol.) procrastinate, be dilatory; ~*red* ANNUITY; ~*red pay,* part of soldier's pay formerly held over to be paid at discharge or death; ~*red* SHARE²s]; procrastinate, be dilatory. Hence ~MENT n. [ME *differren* f. OF *differer* f. L *differre* carry]

defer´², v.i. (-rr-). Submit or make concessions in opinion or action to (person). [f. F *déférer* f. L DE*ferre* bring]

déf´erence, n. Compliance with advice etc. of one superior in wisdom or position (*pay* etc. ~ *to*; *in, out of,* ~ *to*); respect, manifestation of desire to comply, courteous regard, (*in* ~ *to, out of respect for authority of*). So **défèren´tial¹**(-shl) a., **déféren´tial²ly²** (-shl-) adv. [f. F *déférence* (prec., -ENCE)]

def´erent, a. (Physiol.) conveying to or (of ducts etc.); (rare for) deferential. [first sense (f. F or direct) f. L *deferens* part. of DE*ferre* carry); second f. DEFER², -ENT]

defi´ance, n. Challenge to fight or maintain cause, assertion, etc.; open disobedience, setting at naught, (*bid* ~ *to, set at* ~; *in* ~ *of*). [OF (DEFY, -ANCE)]

defi´ant, a. Openly disobedient; rejecting advice, suspicious and reserved. Hence ~LY² adv. [f. F *défiant* (DEFY, -ANT)]

defi´ciency (-ishn-), n. Being deficient; want, lack; thing wanting; amount by which thing, esp. revenue, falls short; ~ *diseases* (caused by lack of some essential element in the diet). [f. LL *deficientia*]

defi´cient (-ishnt), a. Incomplete, defective, wanting in specified quality; insufficient in quantity, force, etc.; half-witted. Hence ~LY² adv. [f. L *deficiens* (DEFECT, -ENT)]

def´icit, n. Amount by which esp. sum of money is too small; excess of liabilities over assets. [f. F *déficit* f. L *deficit* 3 sing. pres. of *deficere* see DEFECT]

défi´er, n. One who defies. [DEFY, -ER¹]

défilade´, v.t. & n. Secure (fortification) against enfilading fire; (n.) this precaution or arrangement (also *defilement*). [see DEFILADE]

defile´¹, v.i., & n. March by files in file. 2. n. Narrow way through which troops can only march so, gorge. [f. F *défiler* unthread, -ADE]

defile´², v.t. Make dirty, befoul; pollute, corrupt; desecrate, profane; make ceremonially unclean. Hence ~MENT (-lm-) n. (see DEFILADE), [earlier *defoul* f. OF *defouler* trample (DE-, L *fullo* fuller, f. OF *defiler,* which would have given E *defile²*) f. L DE*finire* f. *finis* end]

defi´nite, a. With exact limits; determinate, distinct, precise, not vague; (Gram.) ~ *article, the;* ~ *past* or *preterite* ~, simple past tense in French, as *il vint* he came. Hence ~LY² (-tl-) adv. (also, in loose colloq. use, yes, certainly), ~NESS n. [f. L *definitus* p.p. see prec.]

defini´tion, n. Stating the precise nature of a thing or meaning of a word; form of words in which this is done; making distinct, degree of distinctness, in outline (esp. of image given by lens or shown in photograph). [OF (-*cion*), f. L DE*finitio* f. *finire* f. *finis* end, -ION]

defi´nitive, a. Decisive, unconditional, final, (of answer, treaty, verdict, etc.). Hence ~LY²(-vi-) adv. [f. OF *definitif* f. L *definitivus* (prec., -IVE]

de´flagrate, v.t. & i. Burn away with rapid flame. Hence ~ATION, ~ator²(2), nn. [f. L DE*flagrare* blaze]

defla´te, v.t. Let out air etc. out of (pneumatic tire etc.); (Finance) reduce the inflation of (State's currency); (abs.) adopt this policy. Hence **defla´tion** n. [f. L DE*flare* blow away (w. changed sense), -ATE³]

deflect´, v.t. & i. Bend aside or (rarely) down, (make) deviate (*from*). Hence ~or²(2) n. [f. L DE*flectere flex-* bend]

defle´xion (-kshn), -ec´tion, n. Lateral or downward bend, deviation, (lit. & fig.; in Electr. & Magn., of needle from its zero). [f. L *deflex-* (prec. -ION)]

deflora´tion, n. Deflowering. [OF (-*cion*), f. L *defloration-* (foll. -ATION)]

deflow´er, v.t. Deprive of virginity, ravish; ravage, spoil; strip of flowers. [f. OF *deflorer* f. L DE*florare* (*flos floris* flower)]

de'fluent (-lŏŏ-), a. & n. Down-flowing (part; e.g. lower end of glacier). [f. L DE(fluere flow), -ENT]

defo'rest, v.t. = DISFOREST. [f. DE-DE(forester]

deform', v.t. Make ugly, deface; put out of shape, mis-shape, (esp. in p.p. of person with mis-shapen body or limb). [f. OF deformer f. L L DE(formare f. forma shape]

deformā'tion, n. Disfigurement; change for the worse (esp. as opponent's name for Reformation); perverted form of word (dang for damn etc.); (Physics) changed shape of. [f. L L deformatio (prec., -ATION)]

deform'ity, n. Being deformed, ugliness; disfigurement, (physical or moral); a malformation esp. of body or limb. [f. OF (-té) f. L L deformitatem f. DE(formis f. forma shape), -TY]

defraud', v.t. Cheat (person, person of, or abs.). [f. OF defrauder (DE-, L fraudare f. fraus -dis FRAUD)]

defray', v.t. Settle, discharge by payment, (cost, expense). Hence ~ABLE a., ~AL(2) n. [f. F défrayer (DE-, frai sing. of frais expenses perh.=LL fredum fine f. OHG fridu, G friede, peace)]

defrock', v.t. =UNFROCK.

deft, a. Dextrous, skilful, handling things neatly. Hence ~LY² adv., ~NESS n. [var. of DAFT]

defunct', a. Dead (the ~, way of mentioning a particular dead person), no longer existing. [f. L DE(functus p.p. of fungi perform) dead]

defy', v.t. Challenge to combat or combat or competition (arch. or joc.); challenge to do or prove something; resist openly, set at naught; (of things) present insuperable obstacles to (defies definition, capture, attack, etc.). [f. OF defier f. Rom. ⁺DIS(fidare trust f. fidus faithful)]

dégagé (dāgah'zhā), a. (fem. -ée). Easy, unconstrained. [F]

dégauss' (-gows), v.t. Neutralize the magnetization of (ship etc.) with an encircling current-carrying conductor (~ing belt), esp. as precaution against magnetic mines. [DE-, GAUSS]

degen'erate, a. & n. 1. Having lost qualities proper to race, sunk from former excellence; (Biol.) having reverted to lower type; hence degén'eracy n. 2. n. ~ person or animal. [f. L L p.p. see foll. -ATE²]

degen'erate², v.i. Become degenerate (see prec.). [f. L degenerare, f. DE(gener f. genus -eris race) ignoble, -ATE³]

degenera'tion, n. Becoming degenerate; (Path.) morbid disintegration of tissue or change in its structure (esp. fatty ~ of heart). [f. F dégénération (prec., -ION)]

degluti'tion (-glōō-), n. Swallowing. [f. F déglutition f. L DE(glutire swallow), -ION]

degrade', v.t. & i. Reduce to lower rank; depose as punishment; lower in estimation, debase morally, whence dé-grad'ING² a.; reduce (Biol.) to lower organic type, (Physics) to less convertible form (energy), (Geol.) to disintegration (rocks etc.); degenerate; || (Camb. Univ.) put off entering for honours examination for a year beyond regular time. So degrada'tion n. [f. OF degrader f. LL DE(gradare f. forma shape)]

degrade' (gradus step)

degree', n. 1. Step (as) of staircase (arch.; perh. so in 2 Kings xx. 9, & in Psalm title Song of ~s); thing placed like step in series, tier, row; stage in ascending or descending scale or process (by ~s, gradually; fine by ~s & beautifully less, see Prior, Henry & Emma, 431, often misquoted small by etc.); step in direct genealogical descent (prohibited ~s, number of these too low to allow of marriage, i.e. first, second, & third, reckoning from one party to common ancestor & down to the other). 2. Social or official rank; relative condition (each good in its ~); stage in intensity or amount (to a high or the last ~, also colloq. in latter sense to a~; in law, principal in the first, second, ~). 3. Academic rank conferred as guarantee of proficiency, or (honorary ~) on distinguished person; masonic rank. 4. (Gram.) stage (POSITIVE, COMPARATIVE, SUPERLATIVE) in comparison of adj. & adv. 5. (Geom. etc.) unit of angular or circular-arc measurement, 1/90 of right angle or 1/360 of circumference (symbol °, as 45°; ~ of LATITUDE, about 69 miles); (Therm.) unit of temperature in any scale. 6. *Third~, severe and protracted examination of accused person by the police to extract information or confession (also attrib.). Hence ~LESS a. [f. OF degré, LL DE(gradusstep)]

degre'ssion (-shn), n. A going down; (esp.) decrease in the rate of taxation on sums below a certain limit. [f. L degressus p.p. of degredi descend]

de haut en bas (de hauht en bas), adv. In a condescending or superior manner. [F]

dehisce' (-is), v.i. Gape, burst open, (esp. in Bot. of seed-vessels, & in Physiol.). So ~CENCE n., ~CENT a. [f. L DE(hiscere incept. of hiare gape)]

dehort'ative, a. & n. Dissuasive: thing meant to dissuade. [f. L DE(hortativus f. hortari exhort, -IVE]

dehūm'anize, v.t. Divest of human characteristics. [DE-]

dehyd'rate, v.t. (chem.). Deprive (substance) of water or its elements. [DE-, Gk hudōr in comb. hudr- water, -ATE³]

dehyp'notize, v.t. Rouse, release, from hypnotic state. [DE-]

de-ī'cer, n. Composition applied to aircraft's wings to prevent formation of ice.

For compounds of de- not given consult DE-.

or any mechanical or electrical device for the same purpose. So **dē-ice'** v.t., free (aircraft) from ice. [DE-]

dē'icide, n. Killer, killing, of a God. [f. L *deus* god, -i-, -CIDE]

deic'tic(dīk-), a. (philol., gram.), Pointing, demonstrative. [f. Gk *deiktikos* (*deiktos* = *legere* choose)]

dē'iform, a. Godlike in form or nature. [f. med. L *deiformis* (*deus* god, -i-, -FORM)]

dē'ify, v.t. Make a god of; make godlike; regard as a god, worship. Hence **dēi-FICA'TION** n. [f. F *déifier* f. L *deificare* (*deus* god, -FY)]

deign (dān), v.t. Think fit, condescend, to do; condescend to give (answer etc.), to or to agent. [f. F *daigner* (usu. -t) deem worthy]

dē'ism, n. Belief, believer, in the existence of a god without accepting revelation; (adherent of) natural religion. Hence **dē'ist** n. [f. F *déisme*, *déiste*, f. L *deus* god +-ISM(3), -IST(2)]

dē'ity, n. Divine status, quality, or nature; a god; *the D~*, the Creator, God. [f. F *déité* f. L *deitatem* (*deus* god, -TY)]

deject', v.t. Dispirit, depress (usu. in p.p.). Hence **~ed**LY² adv. [f. L DE(*iicere* — *-ject- = jacere* throw)]

dejec'ta, n. pl. Person's or animal's excrements. [L, neut. pl. p.p. as prec.]

dejec'tion, n. Downcast state, low spirits; (Med.) evacuation of bowels, excrement. [OF, f. L *dejectionem* (prec.)]

déjeuner (dē'zhonā), n. Breakfast; lunch, esp. of ceremonial kind. [F]

de jure (joor'i), a. & adv. Rightful, by right, (being etc.; *the ~*; *the ~ king*); cf. DE FACTO]

dekk'ō, n. (sl.). A look (*let's have a ~*). [Hind. *dekho* imp. of *dekhnā* look]

delaine', n. Light dress-fabric. [f. F (*mousseline*) *de laine* woollen (muslin)]

delate', v.t. Inform against, impeach, (person); report (offence). So **dēla'tion**, **dēlā'tor²**, n. [f. L DE(*lat-* p.p. st. of *ferre* carry)]

delay', v.t. & i. & n. Postpone(ment), defer(ring), putting off; loiter(ing); being tardy, wait; hinder, hindrance. [f. F *délai*] f. OF *deleier* perh. irreg. f. L *dilatare* frequent. of DIFFere *lat-* carry) defer]

dēlė cred'erė (-ād-), a., adv., & n. (commerc.). Under, charge made for, selling agent's guarantee that buyer is solvent. [It.]

dē'lė, printing direction (abbr. đ). Delete indicated letter, word, or passage (written in margin). [L, imperat. of *delere* DELETE]

dēlec'table, a. Delightful, pleasant, (arch. exc. in irony). [OF, f. L *delectabilis* f. DE(*lectare* frequent. of *lacere* snare) delight]

delec'tā'tion, n. Enjoyment(usu.for one's ~). [OF (prec., -ATION)]

del'ectus, n. School reading-book of selected passages. [L, n. f. DE(*ligere lect-* = *legere* choose)]

del'egacy, n. System of delegating; appointment, as delegate; body of delegates. [foll. -ACY]

del'egate¹, n. Deputy, commissioner; elected representative sent to conference; representative. [f. OF *delegat* f. L *delegatus* (foll., -ATE¹)]

del'egate² v.t. Depute (person), send as representative; commit (authority etc.), to or to agent. [f. L DE(*legare* depute)]

delėga'tion, n. Entrusting of authority to deputy; body of delegates (*Congress representatives of a single State; Austro-Hungary, *the D~s* (Hist.), two bodies appointed by Austrian & Hungarian Parliaments to deal jointly with imperial questions). [f. L DE(*legatio* LEGATION)]

delēte', v.t. Strike out, obliterate, (letter, word, passage; also fig.). So **dēlē'tion** n. [f. L DE(*lēre -let-* cf. *linere* smear)]

dēlē'ter'ious, a. Noxious physically or morally, injurious. Hence **~LY²** adv. [f. Gk *dēlētērios* f. *dēletēr* destroyer (*dēleomai* injure) +-OUS]

delf(t), n. Glazed earthenware made at *Delft* (earlier *Delf*) in Holland. [place]

delib'erate¹, a. Intentional; considered, not impulsive; slow in deciding; cautious; leisurely, not hurried, (of movement etc.). Hence **~LY²** (-tli-) adv., **~NESS** (-tn-) n. [f. L *deliberatus* (foll., -ATE²)]

delib'erate², v.i. & t. Consider, think carefully, (intr., or with indirect question *how it might be done, what to do*); take counsel, consult, hold debate, [f. L DE(*liberare* = *librare* weigh f. *libra* balance), -ATE³]

dēlibera'tion, n. Weighing in mind, careful consideration; discussion of reasons for & against; debate; care, avoidance of precipitancy; slowness of movement. [f. F *délibération* f. L *deliberationem* (prec., -ATION)]

delib'erative, a. Of, appointed for purpose of, deliberation or debate (usu. *~ assembly* or *functions*). Hence **~LY²** (-vi) adv. [f. L *deliberativus* (DELIBERATE², -IVE)]

del'icacy, n. Fineness of texture, graceful slightness, tender beauty; weakliness, susceptibility to disease or injury, need of care, discretion, or skill; nicety of perception, sensitiveness, (of persons, senses, or instruments); consideration for others' feelings; shrinking from, avoidance of, the immodest or offensive; choice kind of food, dainty; a nicety. [foll. -ACY]

del'icate, a. Delightful (poet.); palatable, dainty, (of food); sheltered, luxurious,

effeminate, (~ *living, nurture, upbringing*); fine of texture, soft, slender, slight; of exquisite quality or workmanship; subdued (of colour); subtle, hard to appreciate; easily injured, liable to illness; requiring nice handling, critical, ticklish; subtly sensitive (of persons or instruments); deft (*a ~ touch*); avoiding the offensive or immodest; considerate (esp. of actions). Hence ~LY² (-tli-) adv. [f. L *delicatus* cogn. or associated w. *delicatessen* f. F *délicatesse*]

*delicatess'en, n. pl. (Shop selling) delicacies or relishes for the table. [G *delikatessen*, see DELICIOUS]

deli'cious (-shus), a. Highly delightful, esp. to taste, smell, or the sense of humour. Hence ~LY² adv., ~NESS n. [OF, f. LL *deliciosus* f. L *deliciae* delight f. DE(*licere=lacere* allure), -OSE¹]

delict', n. Violation of law, offence, (*in flagrant ~*, = IN FLAGRANTE DELICTO). [f. L *delictum* neut. p.p. of DE(*linquere* leave) come short]

delight¹ (-īt), v.t. & i. & n. 1. Please highly (*shall be ~ed to*, in accepting invitation; *was ~ed with* or *at the result*) take, find, great pleasure in (so in p.p., *the books ~ed in by the many*); be inclined and accustomed to do. 2. n. High pleasure, thing that ~ causes it; hence ~FUL a., ~fully² adv., ~SOME a. (literary). [ME *deliten* f. OF *delitier* f. L *delectare* see DELECTABLE, now mis-spelt after *light*]

Delil'ah (-lȧ), Da-, n. Temptress, false & wily woman. [*Judges* xvi]

delim'it(āte), v.t. Determine limits or territorial boundary of. So delimit-A'TION n. [-ít thr. F *délimiter*, -itate direct, f. L DE(*limitare* f. *limes -itis* boundary), -ATE³]

delin'eāte, v.t. Show by drawing or description, portray. So ~A'TION, ~ātor², nn. [f. L DE(*lineare* f. *linea* line), -ATE³]

delinq'uency, n. Neglect of duty; guilt; a sin of omission; misdeed. [f. L *delinquentia* f. *delinquens* part. (DELICT, -ENCY)]

delin'quent, a. & n. 1. Defaulting, guilty. 2. n. Offender. [f. L *delinquens* (prec. -ENT)]

deliqu'esce', v.i. Become liquid, melt, (fig.) melt away. So ~CENT a., ~'CENCE n. [f. L DE(*liquescere* incept. of *liquēre* be liquid)]

delir'ious, a. Affected with delirium, temporarily or apparently mad, raving; wildly excited, ecstatic; betraying delirium or ecstasy. Hence ~LY² adv. [as foll.+-OUS]

delir'ium, n. Disordered state of mind with incoherent speech, hallucinations, & frenzied excitement; great excitement; ecstasy; ~ *trēm'ens* (abbr. *d.t.*), special form of ~ with terrifying delusions to which heavy drinkers are liable. [L, f. DE*lirare* (*lira* furrow)]

delites'cent, a., delites'cence, n. Latent (state). [f. L DE(*litescere* incept. of *-lītēre* =*latēre* lie hid), -ENT, -ENCE]

deliv'er, v.t. Rescue, save, set free from; disburden (woman in parturition) of child (usu. pass.; also fig. *was ~ed of a long-suppressed opinion* etc.) in discourse; give up or over, abandon, resign, hand on to another; distribute (letters, parcels, ordered goods) to addressee or purchaser (~ *the goods*, fig., carry out one's part of agreement); present, render, (account); (Law) hand over formally (esp. sealed deed to grantee, so *seal & ~*); launch, aim, (blow, ball, attack); ~ *battle*, accept opportunity of engaging; recite (*well-~ed sermon*). Hence ~ABLE a. [f. F *délivrer* f. LL *deliberare* (DE-, L *liberare* f. *liber* free)]

deliv'erance, n. Rescue; emphatically or formally delivered opinion, (in jurors' oath) verdict. [f. OF *délivrance* (prec., -ANCE)]

deliv'erer, n. In vbl senses; esp., saviour, rescuer. [f. OF *délivrere* nom. of *delivreor* f. LL *deliberatorem* (DELIVER, -OR²)]

deliv'erỹ, n. Childbirth; surrender of; delivering of letters etc., a periodical performance of this (*the first, the two-o'clock, ~*); (Law) formal handing over of property, transfer of deed (formerly essential for validity) to grantee or third party; sending forth of missile, esp. of cricket-ball in bowling, action shown in doing this (*a good, high, ~*); uttering of speech etc. (*its ~took two hours*), manner of doing this (*a telling ~*). [AF *delivrée* fem. part. used as n. of F *délivrer* DELIVER, -Y¹]

dell, n. Small hollow or valley usu. with tree-clad sides. [cf. Du. *del*, G *telle*, DALE]

Dell'a Crūs'can, a. & n. (Member) of the Florentine Academy della Crusca, a society for purifying the Italian language, which issued an authoritative dictionary; following artificial literary methods; member of a late 18th-c. artificial English school of poetry. [f. It. (*Accademia*) *della Crusca* (Academy) of the bran (i.e. sifting) +-AN]

delouse', v.t. Rid of lice, & fig. of booby-traps, mines, etc. [DE-]

Del'phian, Del'phic, aa. (As) of the oracle of Delphi; obscure, ambiguous. [-ic f. L f. Gk *Delphikos*, -ian f. L f. Gk *Delphoi* +-IAN]

Del'phin, a. The ~ *classics* or *text*, in an edition prepared for the Dauphin, son of

For compounds of *de-* not given consult DE-.

Louis XIV. [f. Gk, = dolphin; see DAUPHIN]

del′phinine, n. (chem.). A poisonous alkaloid used medically. [f. bot. L f. Gk *delphinion* (dim. of *delphin* dolphin)

delphin′ium, n. (Kinds of) ranunculaceous plant, including the larkspur. [as prec.]

del′phinoid, n. & a. (Member) of the family including dolphins, porpoises, grampuses, etc. [f. Gk *delphin* dolphin, -OID]

delta, n. Letter D (Δ, δ) of Greek alphabet; triangular (capital an equilateral triangle); triangular alluvial tract at mouth of river enclosed or traversed by its diverging branches, esp. that of Nile, whence **delta′ic** a.; ~ *metal*, alloy of copper, zinc, and ferro-manganese. [Gk]

del′toid, a. & n. Triangular; ~ *muscle* or ~, muscle of shoulder lifting upper arm; like a river delta. [f. Gk *deltoeidēs* (prec., -OID)]

delude (-ōōd, -ūd), v.t. Impose upon, deceive. [f. L DE(*ludere lus-* play)]

del′uge, n. & v.t. 1. Great flood, inundation, (*the D~*), Noah's flood); heavy fall of rain; flood of words etc. 2. vb. Flood, inundate, (lit. & fig.). [F (*dé-*), f. L *diluvium* (*diluere* DILUTE)]

delu′sion (-ōōzhn, -ūž-), n. Imposing or being imposed upon; false impression or opinion, esp. as symptom or form of madness, whence ~**AL** a. [f. L *delusio* (DELUDE, -ION)]

delu′sive (-ōō-, -ū-), a. Deceptive, disappointing, unreal. Hence ~**LY**[2] adv., ~**NESS** n. [DELUDE, -IVE]

delve, v.t. & i., & n. (arch., poet., & dial.). 1. Dig; make research in documents etc.; (of road etc.) make sudden dip. 2. n. Cavity; depression of surface, wrinkle. [OE *delfan*, com.-WG cf. Du. *delven*]

demagnetize, v.t. Deprive of magnetic quality. Hence ~**A′TION** n. [DE-]

dem′agŏgue (-g), n. Popular leader; political agitator appealing to cupidity or prejudice of the masses, factions or orator. Hence or cogn. **dēmagŏg′ic** (-gĭk) a., ~**ISM**(2), ~**Y**[1] nn., (-g̃-). [f. Gk *dēmagōgos* (DEMOS, *agōgos* leading)]

demand[1] (-ah-), n. Request made as of right or peremptorily, thing so asked, (*payable on* ~, as soon as the ~ is made); call of would-be purchasers for commodity (*laws of supply and* ~ in Pol. Econ.; *in* ~, sought after); urgent claim (*many* ~*s on my time*). [f. F *demande f. demander* see foll.]

demand[2] (-ah-), v.t. Ask for (thing) as right or peremptorily or urgently (*of or from* person; obj. a noun, infin., or *that*-clause); require, need, (*piety* ~*s it*; *task* ~*s skill*); ask to be, insist on being, told (~ *one's business, what he wants*). Hence or cogn. ~**ABLE** a., ~**ANT**(1) n. [f. F

demander f. L D(ē)*mandare* order of. MANDATE]

dēmarca′tion, n. Marking of boundary, esp. *line of* ~. Hence (by back-formation) **dē′marcate v.t.** [Sp. (-*cion*), f. *demarcar*]

dēmarche (dāmǎsh′), n. (In E diplomatic journalese) political step or proceeding. [F]

dēmater′ialize, v.t. & i. Make, become, non-material, spiritual. [DE-]

dēme, n. (Gk hist.) township of ancient Attica; (Biol.) undifferentiated aggregate of cells. [f. Gk *dēmos*]

demean′, v. refl. ~ *oneself*, behave, conduct oneself, (always w. adv. or adv. phr.). [f. OF *demener* (DE-+*mener* lead f. L *minare* threaten as in LL drive cattle)]

demean′[2], v.t. (usu. refl.). Lower in dignity. [DE-, MEAN[3], but prob. generated by misunderstanding of prec.; chiefly used by the uneducated or in imitations of them]

demean′our (-ner), n. Bearing, outward behaviour. [earlier -*ure*, -*er*; see -URE, -ER.[4] DEMEAN[1]; assim. to *honour* etc.]

dēment′, v.t. Drive mad, craze, (usu. in p.p.). Hence **dēmen′tědly**[2] adv. [f. L *dementare* f. *dēmens* out of one's mind (mens mentis)]

dēmen′ti (see AP.), n. Official denial of rumour etc. [F]

dēmen′tia (or -sha), n. (med.). Species of insanity consisting in feebleness of mind. [L (*demens* see DEMENT)]

dēmerā′ra (or -ahr′ra), n. Kind of brown raw cane sugar in large crystals from Demerara. [place]

dēmer′it, n. Ill desert; fault, defect. Hence ~**OR′IOUS** [-ORY, -OUS] a. [f. L *demeritum* neut. p.p. of *demereri* deserve; orig. sense desert (good or bad, like *meritum*; the two have now been fixed to opposite senses)]

dēmesne (-ēn or -ān), n. 1. (Law) possession (of real property) as one's own (esp. *held in* ~); an estate held in ~, all of an owner's land not held of him by freehold tenants, or all that he actually occupies himself; *Royal* ~, Crown lands; *State* ~, land held by State. 2. Sovereign's or State's territory, domain; landed property, estate; region, sphere, &c. [f. OF *demeine* f. L *dominicus* (*dominus* lord, -IC)) hyphen, still used as living pref. to form temporary words, but more or less ousted by SEMI-. Half-size, half, imperfect, partial(ly), semi-; ~-*official (letter)*, (esp. in Indian Secretariats) letter written in private form on official topics; ~-*tasse* (F), small cup (of black coffee). [F, f. L *dimidium* half (DIS-, *medius* middle)]

dēm′igŏd, n. Partly divine being, son of god and mortal, or deified man. [prec.]

dēm′ijohn (-jŏn), n. Bulging narrow-necked bottle of 3-10 gal. usu. cased in

wicker & with wicker handles. [corrupt. of F *dame-jeanne* Dame Jane; found in many langg., but earliest in F, prob. as playful personification]

demi'lune (-ōōn), n. (fortif.). Outwork protecting bastion or curtain. [F, = half moon]

dēm'i-mônde, n. Class of women on outskirts of society, of doubtful reputation & standing. Hence ~*aine* n., woman of the ~*e*. [F, = half world]

dēm'i-rep, n. Woman of suspected chastity. [abbr. for *demi-reputable*]

demise (-z), v.t., & n. Convey, grant, (estate) by will or lease (n., this process); transmit (title etc.) by death or abdication (n., this event, esp. ~ *of the Crown*; transf., death). Hence **demis'able** (-z-) a. [vb f n., prob. f. p.p. of OF *desmettre* DISMISS, in refl. abdicate]

dēm'isēmiquāv'er, n. (mus.). Note, with three-hooked symbol, equal to half a semiquaver. [DEMI-]

demi'ssion (-shn), n. Resigning, abdication, of. [f. F *démission* f. LL *dis-* for L DI(*missionem* f. *mittere miss-* send, -ION]

demit', v.t. & i. (-tt-). Resign (office, or abs.). [f. F *démettre* (DIS-+*mettre* send, put, f. L *mittere* send)]

demi'ûrge, n. Creator of world (in Platonic philosophy; also of Christian God, & of supposed subordinate agents in creation). Hence **demiûr'gic** a. [f. Gk *dēmiourgos* craftsman (*dēmios* f. DEMOS, *-ergos* -working)]

demob', v.t. (-bb-). Demobilize (esp. in p.p. of individuals released by demobilization). [abbr.]

demob'iliz|e, v.t. Release from mobilized state, disband, (troops, ships). Hence ~A'TION n. [DE-]

democ'racy, n. (State practising) government by the people, direct or representative; *the politically unprivileged class*. [f. F *démocratie* f. L f. Gk *dēmokratia* (DEMOS, -CRACY)] *(D~)* member of Democratic party. Hence **democ'ratism**(3) n. [f. F *démocrate* (prec.)]

democrat'ic, a. Of, like, practising, advocating, democracy; *D~ party*, opposed to REPUBLICAN & supporting State, local, & individual liberty against federal powers. So **democrat'ically** adv., **democ'ratize**(3) v.t. & i., **democratiza'-TION** n. [f. F *démocratique* f. med. L f. Gk *dēmokratikos* (DEMOS, -CRATIC)]

Democrité'an, a. Of Democritus, his humour, or his theory of atoms. [f. L f. Gk *Dēmokriteios* of Democritus (Gk philosopher of 5th c. B.C. called the laughing philosopher, & an atomistic physicist) +-AN]

démodé (dāmōd'ā), a. Out of fashion. [F]

Dēmogōrg'on, n. A mysterious & terrible infernal deity. [LL; perh. assim. of some Oriental name to Gk DEMOS, *gorgos* grim]

dēmog'raphy, n. Statistics of births, diseases, etc., illustrating condition of communities. Hence **dēmog'rapher** n., **dēmograph'ic** a. [DEMOS, -GRAPHY]

demoiselle (dəm'wazel'), n. The Numidian crane. [F, = DAMSEL]

demol'ish, v.t. Pull or throw down (building), destroy; overthrow (institution, theory); eat up. So **démoli'TION** n. [f.F *démolir*(-ISH²) f.L DE(*molīr* construct f. *moles* mass]

dēm'on, dae-, n. (Gk myth.; often dae-) supernatural being, inferior deity, spirit, ghost, in-dwelling or attendant spirit, genius; evil spirit (as in demoniacs); heathen deity; devil; malignant supernatural being; cruel, malignant, destructive, or fierce person (~ *bowler*, very fast; *is a ~ for work*, works strenuously); personified vice or passion. Hence **demono-** comb. form, **démonŏl'ATRY**, **démonŏl'OGY**, nn. [f. L f. Gk *daimōn* deity, w. sense also of L f. Gk *daimonion* divine (power etc.) neut. adj.]

dēmō'nétize (or -mŏt-), v.t. Deprive (metal etc.) of its status as money. [f. F *démonétiser* (DE-, L *moneta* MONEY, -IZE]

démōn'iäc, a. & n. (Person) possessed by an evil spirit; of such possession. [devilish] fiercely energetic, frenzied. [f. LL *daemoniacus* (Gk *daimonion* see DEMON, -AC)]

démoni'acal, a. = prec. adj. (esp. in phr. ~ *possession*, & in sense *devilish*). [prec.+-AL]

démŏn'ic, dae-, a. = prec.; inspired, of supernatural genius or impulses. [f. L f. Gk *daimonikos* (DEMON, -IC)]

dēm'onism, n. Belief in the power of demons. [-ISM(3)]

dēm'onīze, v.t. Make into or like, represent as, a demon. [f. med. L *daemonizare* (DEMON, -IZE)]

démōn'stra|ble (or dēm'on-), a. Capable of being shown or logically proved. Hence ~BIL'ITY n., ~bly² adv. [f. L *démonstrābilis* (foll., -ABLE)]

dēm'onstrate, v.t. & i. Show (feelings etc.); describe & explain by help of specimens or experiments, teach as a demonstrator; logically prove the truth of; be a proof of the existence of; make a military demonstration; take part in a demonstration by public meeting, whence **démōn'strant**(1) n. [f. L DE-(*monstrare* show, see MONSTER). -ATE²]

dēmonstrā'tion, n. Outward exhibition of feeling, etc.; logical proving, clear proof, (*to* ~, conclusively); thing serving as proof; exhibition & explanation of specimens or experiments as way of

For compounds of *de-* not given consult DE-.

teaching; show of military force to intimidate, to mask other operations, or in peace to show readiness for war; exhibition, esp. public meeting or procession, whence ~ISM(3) (-sho-) n. [f. L *demonstro* (-strat-)] ~AL (-sho-) a. [f. L *demonstrativus* (as prec., -IVE)]

demon'strative, a. & n. Serving to point out or exhibit (esp. in Gram., ~ *pronoun* or *adjective*, or ~ as noun, this etc.); giving proof of; logically conclusive; concerned with proof; given to or marked by open expression of feelings (~ *person, behaviour, affection, etc.*). Hence ~LY2 (-vli-) adv., ~NESS (-vn-) n. [f. F *démonstratif* f. L *demonstrativus* (as prec., -IVE)]

dēmon'strātor, n. One who demon- strates; teacher by demonstration, assis- tant to professor doing practical work with students; partaker in demonstra- tion by public meeting. [L (DEMON- STRATE, -OR²)]

dēmo'ralize, v.t. Corrupt morals of, deprave; destroy the discipline, cohesion, courage, or endurance of (esp. troops; see MORALE). Hence ~A'TION n. [f. F *démoraliser* (DE-, MORAL, -IZE)]

dē mo'rt'uis nil nisi bŏn'um, sent. Nothing but good should be spoken of the dead. [L]

Dēm'ŏs, n. Personification of the popu- lace or democracy. [Gk, = people]

Dēmosthēn'ic, a. Like Demosthenes or his oratory; eloquent, patriotic, denun- ciatory, (of speech). [f. Gk *Dēmosthenios* of Demosthenes (Attic orator 4th c. B.C.)]

*dēnō'te, v.t. Reduce to lower rank or class. Hence dēnō'TION n. [f. DE- +(PRO)MOTE]

dēmō'tic, a. Popular, vulgar; (Archaeol.) in the popular form (opp. *hieratic*) of ancient Egyptian writing. [f. Gk *dēmotikos* (*dēmotēs* one of the DEMOS +-IC)]

dēmū'lcent, a. & n. Soothing (medicine). [f. L DE(*mulcēre* soothe), -ENT]

dēmū'r, v.i. (-rr-), & n. 1. Make diffi- culties, raise scruples or objections to or at; (Law) put in a demurrer, whence dēmū'rrant(1) n. 2. n. Objecting, ob- jection, (usu. *without, no, ~*), [earlier sense tarry(ing), f. F *demeurer*) f. L DE(*morare* pop. for -*i* delay)]

dēmūre', a. Sober, grave, composed; ironically reserved; affectedly coy, prudish. Hence ~LY² (-rli-) adv., ~NESS (-rn-) n. [DE-+obs. *mure* f. OF *meur* f. L *maturus* ripe]

dēmū'rrable, a. That may be demurred to, open to objection.(esp.legal). [DEMUR, -ABLE]

dēmū'rrage, n. Rate or amount payable to ship-owner by charterer for failure to load or discharge ship within time allowed, similar charge on railway trucks; detention, delay; charge (1½d. per oz) of Bank of Engl. deducted in giving notes or gold for bullion. [f. OF *demorage* (DEMUR, -AGE)]

dēmū'rrer, n. Legal objection to rele- vance of opponent's point even if granted, which stays action till relevance is settled; exception taken. [f. OF *demurrer* infin., = DEMUR; -ER⁴]

dēmy', n. (pl. *-ies*, pr. *-iz*). Size of paper (printing, 17½ × 22¾; writing, 15½ × 20); ||scholar of Magd. Coll., Oxford (orig. w. half fellow's allowance), whence ~SHIP n. [var. of DEMI-]

dēn, n. Wild beast's lair; lurking-place of thieves etc.; small room unfit to live in; room in which person secludes himself to work etc. [OE *denn* cf. G *tenne*, Du. *denne*]

dēn'ary, a. Of ten, decimal. [f. L(prec.)]
dēnāri'us, n. (pl. *-ii*). Ancient-Roman silver coin (orig. about 8d.), whence Engl. *d.* for penny. [f. L *deni* ten each, -ARY]; *denarius (nummus)* = (coin) of ten (asses)]

dēnā'tionalize (-sho-), v.t. Deprive (nation) of its status or characteristics of, State. Hence ~A'TION n. [f. F *dénationaliser* (DE-, NATIONAL, -IZE)]

dēnā'ture, v.t. Change nature or essential qualities of (esp. tea or alcohol by adulteration). So dēnā'turant (-choŏ-) n., substance used in denaturing. [f. F *dénaturer* (DIS-, NATURE)]

dēn'drite, n. (Stone or mineral with) natural tree-like or moss-like marking. Hence dēndri'tic a. [f. Gk *dendritēs* adj. (*dendron* tree)]

dendr(o)-, -i-, comb. forms, f. Gk *dendron* tree. Hence dēn'driform, dēn'driod, aa., dēndrŏl'ogy, dēndrŏl'ogist, nn.

|| **dēne¹**, n. Bare sandy tract, low sandhill, by sea. [cf. G *dūne*, Du. *duin*, F *dune*]

dēne². See DEAN².
dēnēgā'tion, n. (arch.). Denial. [F (*dēnē-*), f. L DE(*negationem* f. *negare* deny), -ATION]

dēne-hōle, dāne-, n. (archaeol.). Arti- ficial cave in chalk entered by vertical shaft often 60 ft deep. [etym. dub.; perh.

dēng'ue (-nggā), n. Infectious eruptive fever causing acute pains in joints. [prob. f. Zanzibar name, w. assim. to Sp. *dengue* prudery w. ref. to stiffness of patient's neck & shoulders]

dēni'able, a. That one can deny. [-ABLE]
dēni'al, n. Refusal of request; = SELF- ~; statement that thing is not true (*meet charge with, flat ~*) or existent, contra- diction; disavowal of person as one's leader etc. [DENY, -AL(2)]

deni′er, n. One who denies. [DENY, -ER¹]

denier′² (-nēr), n. (arch.). Very small sum or coin. [OF, f. 1/12 of sou, f. DENARIUS]

den′igrāte, v.t. Blacken; defame, whence or cogn. ~ātor², ~ā′TION, nn. [f. L DE(nigrare f. niger black)]

de′nim, n. Twilled cotton fabric used for overalls etc. [for serge de Nim (Nîmes in France)]

denit′rāte, denit′rīfy, vv.t. Free of nitric or nitrous acid or nitrates. [DE-¹]

den′izen, n., & v.t. 1. Inhabitant, occupant, (of place); foreigner admitted to residence & certain rights; naturalized foreign word, animal, or plant; hence ~SHIP n. 2. v.t. Admit as ~ (usu. pass.). [f. AF deinzein (deinz = F dans f. L DE-, intus within, -neus see -ANEOUS)]

denom′ināte, v.t. Give name to, call or describe as so-&-so (w. obj. & compl.). [f. L DE(nominare NOMINATE)]

denominā′tion, n. Name, designation, esp. characteristic or class name: class of units in numbers, weights, money, etc. (reduce to the same ~; money of small ~s); class, kind, with specific name; religious sect, whence ~AL (-sho-) a. (~al education, according to principles of a Church or sect, whence ~ALIZE(3) (-sho-) v.t.). [OF (-cion), f. L denominationem (prec., -ATION)]

denom′inātive, a. Serving as, giving, a name, [f. L denominativus (as prec., -ATIVE)]

denom′inātor, n. Number below line in vulgar fraction, divisor. [med. L (as prec., -OR²)]

denotā′tion, n. Denoting; expression by marks or symbols; sign, indication; designation; meaning of a term; (Log.) aggregate of objects that may be included under a word (cf. CONNOTATION), extension. [f. L denotatio (DENOTE, -ATION)]

denōt′ative, a. Indicative of; (Log.) merely designating, implying no attributes, (cf. CONNOTATIVE). Hence ~LY² (-vl) adv. [DENOTE, -ATIVE]

denōte′, v.t. Mark out, distinguish, be the sign of; indicate, give to understand, (esp. that-clause); stand as name for; (Log.) be a name for, be predicated of, (the word white ~s all white things, as snow, paper, foam). Hence ~MENT (-tment-) n. [f. F dénoter f. L DE(notare mark f. nota NOTE¹)]

denouement (see Ap.), n. Unravelling of plot or complications, catastrophe, final solution, in play, novel, etc. [F (dénouer unknot, f. DE-¹, L nodare f. nodus knot, -MENT]

denounce′, v.t. Prophesy (woe, vengeance); inform against; openly inveigh against; give notice of termination of (armistice, treaty). Hence ~MENT (-sm-)

n. [f. OF denoncier f. L DE(nuntiare f. nuntius messenger perh. for noventius t. novus new)]

de nouveau (de nōŏvō′), adv. Afresh, starting again. [F]

dē nōŏ′ō, adv. = prec. [L]

dense, a. Closely compacted in substance; crowded together; crass, stupid. Hence ~LY² (-sl) adv., ~NESS (-sn-) n. [f. L densus]

den′sify, n. Closeness of substance; (Physics) degree of consistence measured by ratio of mass to volume or by quantity of matter in unit of bulk; crowded state; stupidity. [f. F densité f. L densitatem (prec., -ITY)]

dent, n., & v.t. (To mark with a) surface impression (as) from the blow of a blunt-edged instrument. [var. of DINT]

den′tal, a. & n. Of tooth, teeth, or dentistry; ~ letter or ~, made with tongue-tip against upper front teeth (as th) or front of palate (as d, t), whence ~IZE(3) v.t. [f. L dens dentis tooth +-AL]

den′tāte, a. (bot. & zool.). Toothed, with tooth-like notches. So dent-a′TION n., dentāt′o- comb. form. [f. L dentatus (prec., -ATE³)]

den′ti-, comb. form of L dens dentis tooth, as ~lingual formed by teeth & tongue. Hence ~FORM, dent′igerous, aa.

den′ticle, n. Small tooth or tooth-like projection; = DENTIL. So dentic′ūlar¹, dentic′ūlāte² (-at) or -āted, aa., denticulā′TION n. [f. L denticulus (prec., -CULE)]

den′tifrice, n. Powder, paste, etc., for tooth-cleaning. [f. L DENTI(fricum f. fricare rub)]

den′til, n. One of series of small rectangular blocks under bed-moulding of cornice in classical architecture (often ~cornice, -band, -moulding). [f. obs. F dentille dim. of dent tooth f. L dens dentis]

den′tine, n. Hard dense tissue forming main part of teeth. [f. L as prec. +-INE⁴]

den′tist, n. Dental surgeon. Hence ~RY n. [f. F dentiste f. dent see DENTIL, -IST(3)]

denti′tion, n. Cutting of teeth, teething; characteristic arrangement of teeth in animal. [f. L dentitio (dentire to teethe, -ION)]

den′ture, n. Set of (usu. artificial) teeth. [F, f. dent tooth (see DENTIL) +-URE]

dēnūde′ v.t. Make naked; strip of clothing, covering, possession, attribute; (Geol.) lay (rock, formation) bare by removal of what lies above. Hence dēnudā′TION n., dēnūd′ATIVE a. [f. L DE(nudare f. nudus naked)]

dēnunciā′tion, n. Denouncing; invective. So dēnun′ciATIVE, dēnun′ciATORY, (-sha-) aa., dēnun′ciātor² (-shi-) n. [f. L denuntiatio (DENOUNCE, -ATION)]

For compounds of de- not given consult DE-.

deny', v.t. Declare untrue or non-existent (~ *the charge, the possibility, that it is so, this to be the case*; rarely with *but* after neg., *I don't ~ but he may have thought so*); disavow, repudiate, (~ *one's word, signature, faith, leader*); refuse (person, thing, person a thing, thing to person; *I was denied this, this was denied me or to me*); ~ *oneself*, be abstinent; report as not at home, refuse access to, (person visited). [f. F *dénier* f. L Denegare say no)]

déo'dár, n. Himalayan cedar. [f. Hind. *de'odar* f. Skr. *deva-dāru* divine tree]

‖ **de'odánd**, n. (hist.) Thing forfeited to Crown to be used in alms etc. as having caused a human death. [f. L *deo dandum* thing to be given to God]

déo'dorize (or -ĭz), v.t. Deprive of odour, disinfect. Hence ~A'TION, ~ER(2), nn. [DE-, L *odor* smell -IZE]

déŏntŏ'lŏgў, n. Science of duty, ethics. So **déŏntŏlŏ'gĬcal** a., **déŏntŏ'lŏgĬST** n. [f. Gk *deont-* part. st. of *dei* it is right, -o-, -LOGY]

Dé'ŏ ŏp'tĭmŏ măx'ĭmŏ, phr. To God the best & greatest (in dedications). [L]

Dé'ŏ vŏlén'tĕ, adv. (abbr. D.V.). God willing; if nothing occurs to prevent it. [L]

dépar't, v.i. & t. (Poet., arch., etc.) go away (from), take one's leave; set out, start, leave, (esp. in time-tables, as *dep. 6.30 a.m.*); die, leave by death, (~ *from life*, ~ *this life*); diverge, deviate, (~ *from received account, custom*). [f. OF DÉpartir f. L *partire* divide)]

dépar'ted, a. & n. Bygone (~ *greatness*); deceased (person; esp. *the* ~). [-ED²(2)]

dépar'tment, n. Separate part of complex whole, branch, esp. of municipal or State administration; French administrative district; *~ *store*, large shop supplying all kinds of goods. So **départ- men'tal** a., **department'ally** adv. [f. F *département* (DEPART, -MENT)]

dépar'ture, n. Going away; deviation from (truth, standard); starting, esp. of train (the ~ *platform*); setting out on course of action or thought (esp. *new* ~). (Naut.) amount of ship's change of longitude in sailing. [OF (DEPART, -URE)]

dépa'sture (-ah-), v.t. & i. (Of cattle) graze upon, graze; put (cattle) to graze; (of land) feed (cattle). Hence ~AGE n. [DE-]

dépau'perize, v.t. Impoverish; reduce in vigour, stunt, make degenerate. So ~A'TION n. [f. med. L DEpauperare f. L *pauper* poor]

dépaup'erize, v.t. Raise from, rid of, pauperism. [DE-, PAUPER, -IZE]

depend', v.i. Hang down (poet., arch., etc.); be contingent (*it* ~*s upon himself*, etc.); be upon his efforts, skill, wisdom, etc.; also abs. in *that* ~*s*, i.e. can only be answered conditionally); be grammatically dependent (upon); rest for maintenance etc., upon (*she* ~*s upon her own efforts, her pen, her mother, my help*); reckon confidently upon (esp. in imperat., ~ *upon it, you may be sure*); be waiting for settlement (of lawsuit, Bill, etc.). [f. OF DÉpendre f. L Dependere suspend but with sense of *pendēre* be suspended)]

dépén'dable, a. That may be depended on. Hence ~LENESS (-in-) n., ~LY² adv.

dépén'dant, -ent¹, n. One who depends on another for support, retainer, servant. [f. F *dépendant* part. (DEPEND, -ANT)]

dépén'dence, n. Depending (upon), being conditioned or subordinate to; reliance, confident trust; thing relied on. [f. F *dépendance* (prec., -ANCE)]

dépén'dency, n. Something subordinate or dependent, esp. country or province controlled by another. [as prec., -ANCY]

dépén'dent², a. Depending (on), contingent, subordinate; maintained at another's cost; (Gram. of clause, phrase, or word) in subordinate relation to a sentence or word. [earlier -ant = DEPENDANT]

dépho'sphŏrĭze, v.t. Rid (ore) of phosphorus. Hence ~A'TION n. [DE-]

dépict', v.t. Represent in drawing or colours; portray in words, describe. Hence or cogn. ~'ER¹, ~'TOR², ~'TION, nn. [f. L DEpingere pict- paint)]

dépic'ture, v.t. Picture, depict. [DE- +PICTURE v.]

dépi'lāte, v.t. Remove hair from. Hence ~A'TION, ~A'TOR²(2), nn., **dépil'atory** a. & n. [f. L DEpilare f. *pilus* hair)]

dépléte', v.t. Empty out, exhaust; relieve of congestion. So **déplé'TION** n., ~IVE a. & n., ~ORY a. [f. L DEplere -plet- fill]

déplôr'e, v.t. Bewail, grieve over, regret; be scandalized by. Hence ~ABLE a., ~'ABLY² adv., ~ABIL'ITY, ~'ableNESS, nn. [f. L DEplorare bewail)]

déplŏy', v.t. & i. & n. (mil.). 1. Spread out (t. & i. of troops) from column into line; so ~MENT n. 2. n. Doing this. [f. F *déployer* f. L DISplicare fold), whence also DISPLAY]

déplume', v.t. Pluck, strip of feathers. [f. F *déplumer* (DE-, L *pluma* feather)]

dépŏl'arĭz|e, v.t. (Opt.) change direction of polarization of (ray); (Electr. & Magn.) deprive of polarity; (fig.) disturb, shake loose, dissolve, (convictions, prejudices). Hence ~A'TION, ~ER(2), nn. [DE-]

dépŏn'ent, a. & n. 1. (L. & Gk gram.) (verb) passive in form but active in sense (named from notion that they had laid

aside the pass. sense). **2.** Person making deposition under oath or giving written testimony for use in court etc. [f. L DE(*ponere posit- place*), -ENT]

dēpop′ūlāte, v.t. & i. Reduce population of; decline in population. So ~ATION n. [f. L DE(*populārī* lay waste f. *populus* people), -ATE³]

dēpôrt′, v.t. **1.** Bear or conduct oneself in such a manner. **2.** Remove, esp. into exile, banish, whence **dēpôrtā′TION** n., **dēpôrtEE′** n., person who is or has been ~ed. [sense 1 f. OF *deporter* (DE-, *porter* carry f. L *portāre*); sense 2 f. F *déporter* f. L DE(*portāre* carry)]

dēpôrt′ment, n. Bearing, demeanour, manners; way a thing (e.g. metal in chem. experiment) behaves. [OF(-*emend*), as prec. l, -MENT]

dēpōse′ (-z), v.t. & i. Remove from office, esp. dethrone, whence ~ABLE (-z-) a.; bear witness *that*, testify *to*, esp. on oath in court. [f. F *déposer* (DE-+*poser* f. LL *pausāre* PAUSE, POSE²)]

dēpōs′it¹ (-z-), n. Thing stored or entrusted for safe keeping; sum placed in bank, || usu. at interest & not to be drawn on without notice (*on ~*, so disposed of; *has a current & a~ account*); sum required and paid as pledge or earnest or first instalment; layer of precipitated matter, natural accumulation. [f. L DE(*positum* neut. p.p. of *ponere* place)]

dēpōs′it² (-z-), v.t. Lay down in a (usu. specified) place; lay (eggs; usu. with adv. etc.); (of water or natural agency) leave (layer of matter) lying; store or entrust for keeping (esp. sum at interest in bank); pay as pledge for fulfilment of contract or further payment. [f. obs. F *depositer* f. med. L *depositāre* frequent. of L *deponere* see prec.]

dēpōs′itary (-z-), n. Person to whom thing is committed, trustee. [f. L *depositārius* (DEPOSIT¹, -ARY¹)]

dēpōsi′tion (-z-), n. (Picture of) taking down of Christ from the cross; deposing from office, dethronement; (giving of) sworn evidence, allegation, (usu. dē-); depositing. [OF, f. L DE(*positionem* f. *deponere* (DEPOSIT¹, -ION), but w. senses chiefly of unconnected DEPOSE]

dēpōs′itor (-z-), n. Person who deposits money, property, etc.; apparatus for depositing some substance. [L (*deponere* see prec.), -OR²]

dēpōs′itory (-z-), n. Storehouse (lit. & fig.); = DEPOSITARY. [f. med. L *depositorium* (DEPOSIT¹, -ORY)]

dēp′ot (-ō), n. **1.** (Mil.) place for stores; recruiting, &c. headquarters of regiment not on foreign service. || part of regiment not on foreign service. **2.** Storehouse, emporium; *(pr. dē′pō)* railway station. [f. F *dépôt* f. L as DEPOSIT¹]

dēprāve′, v.t. Make bad, deteriorate, pervert, corrupt, esp. in moral character or habits. So **dēprāvā′TION** n. [f. L DE(*prāvāre* f. *prāvus* crooked)]

dēprāv′ity, n. Moral perversion, viciousness; (Theol.) innate corruption of man. [DE-+obs. *pravity* f. L *prāvitās* (prec., -TY)]

dēp′rĕcāte, v.t. Plead against (~e one's anger, beseech him not to be angry); express wish against or disapproval of (~e war, hasty action, panic). Hence or cogn. ~ingLY² adv., **dēprĕcā′TION** n., ~IVE, ~ORY, aa. [f. L DE(*precārī* pray), -ATE³]

dēprē′ciāte (-shǐ-), v.t. & i. Diminish (t. & i.) in value; lower market price of; reduce purchasing power of (money); disparage, belittle. Hence ~ingLY¹ adv., ~ORY (-shǎ-) a. [f. L DE(*pretiāre* f. *pretium* price), -ATE³]

dēprēciā′tion (-ēsǐ-, -ēshǐ-), n. Depreciating or being depreciated; allowance made in valuations, estimates, and balance sheets, for wear & tear. [prec., -ATION]

dēprĕdā′tion, n. (usu. pl.). Spoliation, ravages. [F (dē-), f. L DE(*praedationem* f. *praedārī* f. *praeda* prey, -ATION]

dēp′redātor (prec., -OR³]

dēprĕss′, v.t. Push or pull down, lower; bring low, humble; reduce activity of (esp. trade); lower (voice) in pitch; dispirit, deject; ~ed classes (Indian pol.), persons of the lowest Indian castes, untouchables. So ~IBLE a. [f. OF *depresser* f. L +DE(*pressāre* frequent. of *premere* PRESS²)]

dēprĕss′ant, a. & n. (med.). Lowering, sedative, (medicine). [prec. + -ANT]

dēprĕss′ion (-shn), n. Lowering, sinking; (Astron.) angular distance of star etc. below horizon; sunk place, hollow, on surface; reduction in vigour (esp. of trade), in pitch (of voice), vitality, or spirits; (Meteorol.) lowering of barometer or atmospheric pressure, esp. centre of minimum pressure or system of winds round it. [f. L DE(*pressio* f. *premere* press-press, -ION]

dēprĕss′or, n. (anat.). ~ muscle or ~, one pulling down some organ etc. [L (prec., -OR²]

dēprivā′tion (or -ī-), n. Loss, being deprived, of; deposition from esp. ecclesiastical office; felt loss (*that is a great ~*). [f. med. L *deprivatio* (foll., -ATION)]

dēprive′, v.t. Strip, bereave, debar from enjoyment, of; depose (esp. clergyman) from office. Hence ~ABLE a., ~AL(2) n. [f. OF DE(*priver* f. L *privāre* deprive)]

dē profun′dis, n. & adv. (Cry) from the depths of sorrow etc. [initial L wds of *Ps.* cxxxi]

For compounds of *de-* not given consult DE-.

depth, n. Being DEEP; measurement from top down, from surface inwards, or from front to back; intensity of colour, darkness, etc.; (pl.) deep water, deep place, abyss, lowest or innost part; middle (*in the ~ of winter*); deep or mysterious region of thought, feeling, etc. (*cry from the ~s, ~ of in-spiration, ~s of degradation*); *out of one's ~*, in water too deep to stand in, (fig.) engaged on too hard a task or subject; *~-charge*, bomb for dropping on submerged submarine, set to explode at desired ~. [DEEP, -TH²]

dep′ur̄āte, v.t. & i. Make, become, free from impurities. So *~ā′TION*, *~ātOR*(2), nn., depūr′ative a. & n. [f. med. L DE-*(purare* f. L *purus* pure)]

depū̆tā′tion, n. Body of persons appointed to represent others. [foll., -ATION]

depūte′, v.t. Commit (task, authority) to another or others (*by ~, by proxy; ~ tenant*, abbr. D. L., ~ of Lord Lieutenant of county); member of deputation; parliamentary representative. (*Chamber of Deputies*, lower house in French & other Parliaments); || manager ~. Hence ~SHIP(1) n. [f. F *député* p.p. of *députer* DEPUTE, -Y⁴]

derā′cin̄āte, v.t. Tear up by the roots. [f. F *déraciner* (DE-, *racine* f. LL *radicina* dim. of *radix* root), -ATE³]

derail′, v.t. & i. Cause (train etc.) to leave the rails (usu. pass.); (rarely) leave the rails. So *~MENT* n. [f. F *dérailler* (DE-, *rail* rail)]

derange′ (-j), v.t. Throw into confusion or out of gear, disorganize; cause to act irregularly; make insane (esp. in p.p.); disturb, interrupt. So *~MENT* (-jm-) n. [f. F *déranger* (DE-, *rang* rank)]

Der′by (där′-), n. 1. Annual horse-race at Epsom; *~ day*, of the race; (~ *dog*, any dog straying on course, (fig.) trivial untimely interruption. *2. (d~; pron. dĕr-) bowler hat. [Earl of ~ founder 1780]

Der′byshire (där′-; -sher), a. *~ neck*, goitre, bronchocele; *~ spar*, fluor-spar, de règle (rĕ′gl), pred. a. Customary, proper. [F]

dĕr′elict, a. & n. Abandoned, ownerless, (esp. of ship at sea); abandoned property, (esp. of ship at sea). [f. L L DE-*(relict*-see RELINQUISH)]

dĕrelic′tion, n. Abandoning, being abandoned; retreat of sea exposing new land; neglect of duty; failure in duty, short-coming. [f. L *derelictio* (prec., -ION)]

dĕrīde′, v.t. Laugh to scorn. [f. L *dērīdēre* (rīs-laugh)]

de rigueur (rēgĕr′), pred. a. Required by etiquette (*evening dress is ~*). [F]

dĕrī′sion (-zhn), n. Ridicule, mockery, (*hold, have, in ~, mock at; be in ~, be mocked at; bring into ~*); laughing-stock. [f. L *dērīsiō* (DERIDE, -ION)]

dĕrī′sive, dĕrī′sory, aa. Scoffing (*~ cheers, ironical*); (*~ory* only; of offer etc.) ridiculously futile, not to be taken seriously. Hence **dĕrī′sively**²(-vl) adv., **dĕrī′sory**²(-vl) adv. [f. L *dērīsus*-see DERIDE, +-IVE, -ORY]

dĕrīvā′tion, n. Obtaining from a source; extraction, descent; formation of word from word or root, tracing or statement of this; theory of evolution, whence ~IVE a. [f. L (*dé-*), f. L *derivationem* (DERIVE, -ATION)]

dĕrī′vative, a. & n. (Thing, word, chemical substance) derived from a source, not primitive or original. Hence *~LY*²(-vl-) adv. [f. F *dérivatif* f. L *derivativus* (foll., -IVE)]

dĕrīve′, v.t. & i. Get, obtain, (*from a source, or with the source present in thought*); have one's or its origin etc. from; gather, deduce, (knowledge, truth, ideas, etc.) *from*: (pass., refl., & intr.) be descended or have one's origin *from*; (pass., of words) be formed *from*; trace (pass.), or assert, descent, origin, or formation, of (person, thing, word) *from*. Hence *~ABLE* a. [f. F *dériver* f. L *derivare* (DE-, *rivus* stream) divert, derive]

derm, n. Skin; true skin or layer of tissue below epidermis. Hence or cogn. *~AL*, *~IC*, aa., *~at*(o)-, *~o-*, comb.forms, *~atī′tIS* n., inflammation of the skin, *~ator′ogY*, *~ator′ogist*, nn. [f. Gk *derma* skin (*derō* flay, -M)]

dernier ressort (dĕrnyā′ resor̄′), n. Last resort, desperate expedient. [F]

dĕr′ogāte, v.i. Detract, take away part, *from* (a merit, right, etc.); sink in the scale, do something derogatory. [f. L DE-*(rogare* ask), -ATE³]

dĕrogā′tion, n. Lessening or impairment of law, authority, position, dignity, etc.; deterioration, debasement. [f. L *derogationem* (prec., -ATION)]

dĕrŏg′atory, a. Tending to detract *from*, involving impairment, disparagement, or discredit, *to*; lowering, unsuited to one's dignity or position; depreciatory. [f. L *derogatorius* (DEROGATE, -ORY)]

dĕr′rick, n. Contrivance for moving or hoisting heavy weights, kind of crane with adjustable arm pivoted at foot to central post, deck, or floor; framework over oil-well or similar boring. [obs. senses *hangman, gallows*, f. name of hangman c. 1600]

dĕr′ring-dō, n. (pseudo-arch.). Desperate courage. [f. Chaucer's *In dorryng don that longeth to a knight* (in daring to

do that which belongeth etc.) misinterpreted by Spenser]

der'ringer (-j-), n. Small large-bore pistol. [U.S. inventor's name]

der'vish, n. Mohammedan friar vowed to poverty & austerity (*dancing or whirling ~, howling ~*, according to the practice of his order). [f. Pers. *darvesh* poor]

des'cant¹, n. (poet.). Melody, song; (Mus.) melodic independent treble accompaniment. [f. OF *deschant* f. med. L DIS(*cantus* CHANT)]

descant'², v.i. Talk at large, dwell freely, upon (esp. in praise, *~ upon the beauties of*). [f. OF *deschanter* (prec., L *cantare*)]

descend', v.i. & t. Come or go down, sink, fall, (*~ing letter* in Typ., with tail below line); slope downwards; make sudden attack upon; proceed in narrative etc. from earlier to later time, from greater to less (so Math., *~ing series of numbers*), from general to particular; stoop *to do*; (rare) be DESCENDED *from*; (of qualities, property, privileges), pass (*to* heir, or abs.); go down (hill, stairs). [f.F *descendre* f. L DE(*scendere=scandere* climb)]

descen'dant, n. Person or thing DE-SOENDED (*of*, or with *his* etc.) [F (prec.-ANT)]

descen'ded, p.p. Sprung, having origin, *from* ancestor or stock (*is ~* etc. usual instead of the rare *descends* etc.). [-ED²]

descen'dible, -able, a. Transmissible by inheritance. [OF (-*able*); see -BLE]

descent', n. Descending, downward motion; downward slope; way down; sudden attack, esp. from sea; decline, sinking in scale, fall; being descended, lineage; single generation (*lineal succession of four ~s*); transmission of property, title, or quality, by inheritance. [f. F *descente* (*descendre* DESCEND)]

describe', v.t. Set forth in words, recite the characteristics of; quality as (*should ~e him as a scoundrel*); mark out, draw, (esp. geom. figure); move in (such a line, curve); (abs.) deal in, give a, description. Hence ~'ABLE a. [f. L DE(*scribere script-* write)]

descrip'tion, n. Describing, verbal portrait(ure), of person, object, or event (*answers to the ~*, *has the qualities specified*), more or less complete definition; sort, kind, class, (*no food of any ~, tyrant of the worst ~*). [F, f. L *descriptionem* (DESCRIBE, -ION)]

descrip'tive, a. Serving to describe (*~ touches*), fond of describing (*~ writer*). Hence ~LY² (-vl-) adv. [f. LL *descriptivus* (DESCRIBE, -IVE)]

descry', v.t. Catch sight of, succeed in discerning (lit. & fig.). [prob. var. of DESCRIBE, & often confused in early use with DECRY]

des'ecrate, v.t. Deprive of sacred character; outrage, profane, (sacred thing); dedicate (to evil). Hence ~A'TION, ~ATOR, nn. [DE-+(CON)SECRATE]

desen'sitize, v.t. Reduce or destroy the sensitiveness of (photographic plates etc.). [DE-¹]

desert'¹ (-z-), n. Deserving, worthiness of recompense good or bad; character that deserves good, virtue, whence ~LES s.; deserving people; (pl.) acts or qualities deserving good or bad recompense, such recompense, (*reward him according to, give him, he has got, his ~s*). [OF obs. p.p. of *deservir* DESERVE]

dĕs'ert'² (-z-), a. & n. 1. Uninhabited, desolate; uncultivated, barren. 2. Waterless & treeless region, (fig.) uninteresting or barren subject, period, etc.; *~ rat* (colloq.), soldier of 7th (British) armoured division, which had a jerboa's figure as divisional sign, & which fought in the *~* campaign in N. Africa (1941-2). [f. OF (a. & n.) f. L L p.p. see foll.]

desert'³ (-z-), v.t. & i. Abandon, give up, (thing); depart from (place, haunt); forsake (person or thing having claims on one, as *wife, post, the colours, ship*); fail (*his presence of mind ~ed him*); run away (esp. from service in army or navy), whence ~ER² (-z-) n. So deSER'tion (-z-) n. [f. F *déserter* f. L L *desertus* f. DE(*serere sert-* join)]

deserve' (-z-), v.t. & i. Be entitled by conduct or qualities to (good or bad), have established a claim to be *well or ill* treated at the hands of. Hence ~'edly² (-z-) adv. [f. OF *deservir* f. L DE(*servire* serve)]

deserv'ing (-z-), a. Meritorious; worthy (*of* praise, censure, etc.). [-ING²]

déshabillé (see AP.), n. = DISHABILLE. [F]

des'iccate, v.t. Dry, dry up, (esp. milk etc. for preservation). So ~A'TION, ~ator²(2), nn., ~ATIVE a. [f. L DE(*siccare* f. *siccus* dry), -ATE³]

desid'erate, v.t. (pedant.). Feel to be missing, regret absence of, wish to have. [f. L DE(*siderare* see CONSIDER), -ATE³]

desid'erative, a. & n. (gram.). (Verb, conjugation, etc.) formed on another verb etc. & expressing desire of doing the action. [f. L *desiderativus* (prec., -IVE)]

desiderat'um, n. (pl.-ta). Thing missing, felt want. [L (neut. p.p. see DESIDERATE)]

design'¹ (-zin), n. Mental plan; scheme of attack upon (*has ~s upon me*); purpose (*whether by accident or ~*; end in view, adaptation of means to ends (*the argument from ~*, maintaining existence of a God by pointing to such adaptation); preliminary sketch for picture etc.; delineation, pattern; artistic or literary groundwork, general idea, construction,

For compounds of *de-* not given consult DE-.

plot, faculty of evolving these, invention. [f. 15th c. F *desseign* f. *desseigner* see foll.]

design² (-zīn), v.t. & i. Set (thing) apart for person; destine (person, thing) for a service; contrive, plan; purpose, intend, (*~s an attack, to do, doing, or that —*, whence ~ēdly² (-zīn-) adv.; make preliminary sketch of (picture); draw plan of (building etc. to be executed by others); be a designer; conceive mental plan for, construct the groundwork or plot of, (book, work of art). [f. F *désigner* DESIGNATE¹, with senses also of obs. F *dessigner* draw & mod. F *dessiner* draw]

dēs'ignate¹ (-z-), a. (placed after its noun). Appointed to office but not yet installed (*bishop ~* etc.). [f. L p.p. (foll.; -ATE²)]

dēs'ignate² (-z-), v.t. Specify, particularize; serve as name or distinctive mark of; style, describe as; appoint to office. [f. L DESIGNARE f. *signum* mark), -ATE³]

dēsigna'tion (-z-), n. Appointing to office; name, description, title. [f. L DESIGNATIONEM]

design'er (-zīn-), n. In vbl senses; esp. draughtsman who makes plans for manufacturers. [-ER¹]

design'ing (-zīn-), a. In vbl senses; esp. crafty, artful, scheming. [-ING²]

dēsil'verize, v.t. Extract the silver from. [DE-, SILVER, -IZE]

dēsip'ience, n. Trifling, silliness. [f. L *desipientia* f. DE(*sipere* = *sapere* be wise)]

dēsir'able (-z-), a. Worth wishing for. Hence ~BIL'ITY, ~bleness, nn., ~bly² adv. [-ABLE]

dēsire¹ (-z-), n. Unsatisfied appetite, longing, wish, craving; request; thing desired. [f. OF *desir* cf. foll.]

dēsire² (-z-), v.t. Long for, crave, wish (noun, infin., noun & infin., or *that*-clause); feel desire; ask for; pray, entreat, command, (*~ one to wait; she ~d me would wait*). [f. OF *desirer* f. L *desiderare* DESIDERATE]

dēsir'ous (-z-), pred. a. Wishful to do, ambitious of (success etc.), having the desire of doing, wishful that. [f. OF *desiros* f. LL *desiderosus* (st. of *desiderare* see prec.; +-OSE²)]

dēsist' (-zī-, -sī-), v.i. Cease (*from doing, from sin*). [f. OF *desister* f. L *desistere* (*sistere* stop)]

desk, n. Fixed or movable piece of furniture or box having (often in combination with drawers, seat, etc.) a board usu. sloped serving as rest for writing or reading at; *the ~*, clerical, office, or literary work. Hence ~FUL(2) n. [f. med. L *desca* f. L *discus* disk]

dēs'man, n. Aquatic insectivorous shrew-like mammal of Russia and the Pyrenees. [f. Sw. *desman-rätta* musk-rat]

dēs'olate¹, a. Left alone, solitary; uninhabited; ruinous, neglected, barren, dreary; forlorn, disconsolate, wretched. Hence ~LY² (-tl-) adv., ~NESS (-tn-) n. [f. L DESolare f. *solus* alone), -ATE²]

dēs'olate², v.t. Depopulate; devastate; make (person) wretched. Hence ~ōs² n.

dēsola'tion, n. Desolating; neglected, ruined, solitary, or barren state; being forsaken, loneliness; dreary sorrow. [f. L *desolatio* (as prec., -ATION)]

dēspair', n. & v.i. 1. Loss, utter want, of hope; thing that causes this, whether by badness or unapproachable excellence. 2. v.i. Lose, be without, hope (*of*, or abs.; *his life is ~ed of*); hence ~ingly² adv. [f. OF *despeir-* stressed st. of *desperer* f. L DESperare hope)]

‖ **despatch.** See disp-.

dēs'perate, a. Leaving no or little room for hope, extremely dangerous or serious, utterly impracticable; reckless from despair, violent, lawless, staking all on a small chance, whence despera'TION n.; extremely bad (*a ~ night, storm, etc.*); very great (*~ fear, a ~ fool*), whence ~LY² adv., ~NESS (-tn-) n. [f. L DESperatus

dēspera'dō, n. (pl. -oes). Person ready for or given to reckless, esp. criminal, undertakings. [OSp. (adj. only), f. L *desperatus* see foll.]

dēs'patch. See disp-.

dēspīc'able, a. Vile, contemptible. Hence ~IY² adv. [f. L *despicabilis* f. DE(*spicari* = *specere* look at), -BLE]

dēspīse' (-z), v.t. Look down upon, contemn. [f. *despis-* st. of OF *despire* f. L DE(*spicere* = *specere* look at)]

dēspīte', n. & prep. Outrage, injury, contumely, (arch.); malice, spite, offended pride (*died of mere ~*); *in ~ of, ~ of*, notwithstanding the opposition of, in the teeth of, in spite of, (also *in my* etc. *~*, in spite of my etc. efforts, arch.). Hence ~FUL a., ~fully² adv., (-ti-). [f. OF *despit* f. L *despectus -ūs* f. *despicere* see prec.]

dēspoil', v.t. Plunder, spoil, rob, deprive, (person or place; often *of*). Hence or cogn. ~ER¹, ~MENT, despolia'TION, nn. [f. OF *despoillier* (now *dépouiller*) f. L DE(*spoliare* spoil)]

dēspŏnd', v.i. & n. 1. Lose heart, be dejected; so ~ENCY(1), ~ENT a., ~ently² adv². 2. n. (Arch., only in SLOUGH of D~) dejection. [f. L DE(*spondēre* give up, resign)]

dēs'pot, n. Absolute ruler, whence ~ISM(2) n.; tyrant, oppressor. So **dēspŏt'ic** a., **despŏt'ICALLY** adv. [OF f. Gk *despotēs*]

dēs'potism, n. Arbitrary rule; State under a despot. [f. F *despotisme* (prec. -ISM)]

dēsquam'āte, v.t. & i. Strip off (in p.p., come off in scales. Hence ~A'TION n., **desquam'ative**, **desquam'atory**, aa. [f. L DE(*squamare* f. *squama* scale)]

dessërt' (-z-), n. || Course of fruit, sweetmeats, etc., at end of dinner; ~-SPOON. [F.f. desservir (des- f. L dis-, servir SERVE) clear the table]

destina'tion, n. Place for which person or thing is bound. [f. L destinātiō (foll., -ATION)]

des'tine, v.t. Appoint, fore-ordain, devote, set apart, (person or thing to do, to or for a service, achievement, etc.; of God, Fate, etc., or of persons; but chiefly in pass.); was ~d to, was, as we now know to. [f. F destiner f. L destināre prob. causative of stare stand]

des'tiny, n. Predetermined events; person's, country's, etc., appointed or ultimate lot; power that fore-ordains, invincible necessity. [f. OF destinée (prec.,-Y⁴)]

des'titute, a. Without resources, in want of necessaries; devoid of. So destitu'tion n. [f. L DE(stituere -tut- = statuere place) forsake]

des'trier, n. (hist.), War-horse. [OF f. LL dextrarius hand-led (DEXTER, -ARY¹)]

destroy', v.t. Pull down, demolish, undo, make useless, kill, annihilate, nullify, neutralize effect of. Hence ~ABLE a. [f. OF destruire ult. f. L DE(struere struct- build)]

destroy'er, n. In vbl senses; esp. as abbr. for TORPEDO-boat ~. [-ER¹]

destruc'tible, a. Able to be destroyed. Hence ~BIL'ITY n. [f. L destructibilis (DESTROY, -BLE)]

destruc'tion, n. DESTROYING or being destroyed; what destroys, cause of ruin, (is our ~). [OF, f. L DE(struction-em (DESTROY, -ION)]

destruc'tive, a. & n. 1. Destroying; deadly to, causing destruction of; (of criticism or policy) merely negative, refuting etc. without amending, not constructive; hence ~LY² (-vl-) adv., ~NESS (-vn-) n. 2. n. Person, thing, that aims at or effects destruction. [OF (-if, -ive), f. L destructivus (DESTROY, -IVE)]

|| destruc'tor, n. Refuse-burning furnace. [L, = destroyer (DESTROY, -OR²)]

dès'uetude (-swI-), n. Passing into, state of, disuse. [f. F désuétude f. L DE(suetudo f. suescere suet- be wont, -TUDE)]

desul'phurize (-fer-), v.t. Free from sulphur. Hence ~A'TION n. [DE-]

des'ultorily, a. Skipping from one subject to another, disconnected, unmethodical. Hence ~iLY² adv., ~iNESS n. [f. L desultorius f. desultor circus-rider f. DE(sult- salt- p.p. st. of salire leap)]

dēsynŏn'ymize, v.t. Differentiate in sense (synonymous words). [DE-, SYNONYM, -IZE]

detach', v.t. Unfasten & remove (from, or abs.; ~ed mind, view, etc., regarding things impartially, free from prejudice; ~ed house, not joined to another on either side; (Mil. & Nav.) send (ship, regiment, etc.) on separate mission. Hence ~ABLE a., ~édLY² adv., ~édNESS n. [f. F détacher (DE-, Rom. tacca nail, tack)]

detach'ment, n. Detaching; portion of army etc., or large body, separately employed; standing aloof from or unaffected by surroundings, public opinion, etc., independence of judgement, selfish isolation. [f. F détachement (prec., -MENT)]

dē'tail¹, n. Dealing with things item by item (in ~; go into ~, give the items separately; army beaten in ~, in small sectional engagements); minute account, number of particulars; item, small or subordinate particular, (but that is a ~, often iron, to call special attention), whence ~ED² (-Id) a., with particulars; minor decoration in building, picture, etc., way of treating this; (Mil.) distribution of orders of the day, small detachment. [f. F détail f. détailler see foll.]

dētail'², v.t. Give the particulars of, relate circumstantially; (Mil.) tell off for special duty. [f. F détailler (DE-, tailler cut, see TAILOR)]

detain', v.t. Keep in confinement; withhold (money due etc.); keep waiting, hinder. [f. OF DE(tenir f. L tinēre -tent- = tenēre hold)]

detain'er, n. (legal). Detaining of goods taken from owner for distraint etc.; keeping of person in confinement; writ by which person already arrested may be detained on another suit. [f. AF detener f. OF detenir see prec., -ER¹]

detèct', v.t. Find out (guilty person, person in doing); discover existence or presence of. Hence or cogn. detec'TABLE a., détèc'TION n. [f. L DE(tegere tect- cover)]

detèc'tive, a. & n. 1. Serving to detect. 2. n. Policeman employed to investigate special cases (private ~, person undertaking special inquiries for pay; amateur ~, person who sets up theories on police cases); ~ story etc. (that tempts readers to solve ~ problems). [prec., -IVE]

detèc'tor, n. In vbl senses; also or esp.: coherer used in wireless telegraphy; valve in wireless receiving set. [-OR²]

detènt', n. Catch by removal of which machinery is set working, (in clocks etc.) catch that regulates striking. [f. F, détente f. détendre slacken (DE-, L tendere stretch)]

détente (see Ap.), n. Cessation of strained relations between States. [F, as prec.]

dētèn'tion, n. Detaining, being detained; arrest, confinement. (House of D~, lockup); compulsory delay; (at schools) keeping in as punishment; ~ barracks, military prison. [f. L detentio (DETAIN, -ION)]

For compounds of de- not given consult DE-.

détenu (dătĕnōō'), n. Person detained in custody (esp. Indian political prisoner). [F., p.p. of *détenir* detain]

déter', v.t. (-rr-). Discourage or hinder (*from*, or abs.) by or as fear, dislike of trouble, etc. Hence **détĕr'rence** n., **détĕr'rent** a. [f. L DĒ(*terrēre* frighten)]

dētĕr'gent a. & n (Substance) wiping, cleansing (agent). [f. L DĒ(*tergēre ters-* wipe), -ENT]

dētĕrior|āte, v.t. & i. Make, grow, worse. Hence or cogn. **~A'TION** n., **~ATIVE** a³. [f. L *deteriorāre*(*deterior* worse f. *de* down), -ATE³]

dētĕr'minant, a. & n. Determining, (agent). [DETERMINE, -ANT]

dētĕr'minate, a. Limited, definite, distinct, finite, definitive. Hence **~LY²** adv., **~NESS** (-tn-) n. [f. L p.p.]

dētĕrminā'tion, n. (Law) cessation of estate or interest; conclusion of debate; judicial sentence; fixing of limit etc.; delimitation, definition; exact ascertainment of amount etc.; fixed direction, decisive bias; (~ *of blood to some part*, tendency *to flow there*); settling of purpose, fixed intention; resoluteness. [f. L *determinatio* DETERMINE -ATION]

dētĕr'minative, a. & n. (Thing) that impels in a certain direction; (attribute, mark, symbol) serving to define or qualify. [f. F *déterminatif*(toll. -IVE)]

dētĕr'min|e, v.t. & i. Bring, come, to an end (esp. in law); limit in scope, define; fix beforehand (date); settle, decide; conclude, give decision; be the deciding factor in regard to (*amount ~es supply*); ascertain precisely, fix; give an aim to, direct, impel to; decide (person) *to do*; resolve (*to do, that ~, on doing*, on a course; *be ~ed*, have resolved). Hence **~ABLE** a. [f. OF *determiner* f. L DĒ(*terminare* f. *terminus* end)]

dētĕrm'ined (-nd), a. In verbal senses; also, resolute, unflinching. [-ED¹]

dētĕrm'inism, n. Theory that human action is not free but determined by motives regarded as external forces acting on the will. So **~IST**(2) n. & a., **~IS'TIC** a. [DETERMINE +-ISM]

dētĕs'ive, a. & n. Cleansing (substance). [f. F *détersif*(DETERGENT, -IVE]

dētĕst', v.t. Abhor, dislike intensely. Hence or cogn. **~ABLE** a., **~ableness** (-lb-) n., **~ABLY²** adv. [f. F *détester* f. L DĒ(*testari* call God to witness against)]

dētĕstā'tion, n. Abhorrence (*have, hold, in ~*, abhor); detested person or thing. [F (*dé-*), f. L *detestationem* (prec., -ATION]

dēthrōne', v.t. Depose (ruler, dominant influence). Hence **~MENT**(-nm-) n. [DE-¹]

dĕt'inūe, n. (legal). *Action of ~*, suit for recovery of thing wrongfully detained. [f. OF *detenue* f. p.p. of *detenir* DETAIN]

dĕt'on|āte (or dē-), v.i. & t. (Cause to) explode with loud report. Hence or cogn. **~A'TION** n., **~ATIVE** a. [f. L DĒ(*tonāre* thunder), -ATE³]

dĕt'onātor, n. Detonating contrivance, esp. as part of bomb or shell; railway fog-signal. [-OR³]

dētour (dētoor'), **détour** (F), n. Deviation (ditour'), roundabout way, digression, (esp. *make a ~*). [F (*dé-*), f. *détourner* (DE-, TURN)]

dētract', v.t. & i. Take away (*much, something*, esp. or abs.) *from* a whole (esp. in sense *reduce the credit due to, deprecate*). Hence or cogn. **détrac'tion**, **détrac'tor²**, nn., **détrac'tive** a. [f. L DĒ(*trahere tract-* draw)]

détrain', v.t. & i. Discharge, alight, from train (troops etc.; cf. ENTRAIN, [DE- + TRAIN n.]

dĕt'riment, n. Harm, damage, (esp. *without ~ to*), [F (*dé-*), f. L DĒ(*trimentum* f. *terere trit-* rub, wear, -MENT)]

detrit'|us, n. Matter produced by detrition, as gravel, sand, silt; debris. Hence **~AL** a. [wrong use of L *détritus -ūs* = wearing down for *detritium* neut. p.p. see DETRIMENT]

de trop (de trŏ'), pred. a. Not wanted, unwelcome, in the way. [F]

deuce¹, n. The two at dice or cards; (Tennis) state of score (40 all, games all) at which either party must gain two consecutive points or games to win. [f. F *deux* f. L *duos* nom. -o two]

deuce², n. Plague, mischief; the devil (*~ take it; who, where, what*, etc., *the ~?; the ~ is it if I cannot*, I certainly can; *play the ~ with*, spoil, ruin; *the ~ to pay*, trouble to be expected; *a ~ of a mess*; *~ knows; ~ a bit*, not at all; *the ~ he isn't*, it is incredible that he is not). [perh. = prec., the two at dice being the worst throw; cf. G *daus* in same sense] **deu'ced** (dū- or -st), a. & adv. Confoundedly; great (*in a ~ hurry*). Hence **~LY²** adv. [-ED²]

Dē'us misĕrēātŭr (-z-), n. The canticle *God be merciful*, Psalm 67. [L]

dē'us ex māc'hinā (-k-), n. Power, event, that comes in the nick of time to solve difficulty; providential interposition, esp. in novel or play. [L, = god from the machinery (by which in ancient theatre gods were shown in air)]

deuteragonist (also -ăg'o-), n. Person of next importance to PROTAGONIST in drama. [f. Gk *deuteragonistēs* (DEUTERO-, *agōnistēs* actor)]

deuter'ium, n. Heavy isotope of hydrogen with mass about double that of ordinary hydrogen; so **deut'eron** n., nucleus of the ~ atom. [DEUTERO- + -IUM; *deuteron* after PROTON]

deut'ero-, comb. form of Gk *deuteros* second, as ~*Isaiah*, supposed later author of *Is.* xl-lxvi, ~*canón'ical* of Bible books, admitted later to Canon, *deuteróg'amŷ*, second marriage.

Deuterón'omist, n. Author, joint-authors, or compiler, of *Deuteronomy*. [-IST]

Deuterón'omŷ (*also* dūt-), n. Fifth book of Pentateuch. Hence **Deuteronóm'-** IC(AL) aa. [f. L f. Gk DEUTERO(*nomion* f. *nomos* law) second book of law]

deut'zia (*also* doit-), n. White-flowered shrub. [J. *Deutz* d. 1781, -IA¹]

deux-temps (see Ap.), n. Kind of waltz more rapid than the trois-temps. [F, =two-time]

dēv'astāte, v.t. Lay waste, ravage. Hence or cogn. ~A'TION, ~ātor² nn. [f. L DE(*vastare* f. *vastus* waste), -ATE³]

dēvěl'op, v.t. & i. Unfold (t. & i.), reveal, bring or come from a latent to an active or visible state; (Mil.) open (an attack); make or become fuller, more elaborate or systematic, or bigger; (Photog.) treat (plate, film) so as to make picture visible; make progress; exhibit (*has* ~*ed a tendency to*), come or bring to maturity. Hence ~ABLE a., ~ER¹ (1, 2) n. [f. F *développer* etym. dub.; cf. It. *viluppo* wrapping]

dēvěl'opment, n. Gradual unfolding, fuller working out; growth; evolution (of animal & plant races); well-grown state; stage of advancement; product; more elaborate form; developing of photograph; || ~ *area*, one suffering from or liable to severe unemployment. [-MENT]

dēvělopměn'tal, a. Incidental to growth, (~ *diseases*); evolutionary. Hence ~LY² adv. [-AL]

dēv'iāte, v.i. Turn aside, diverge, (*from* course, rule, truth, etc., or abs.), digress. [f. L DE(*viare* f. *via* way), -ATE³]

dēvia'tion, n. In vbl senses; esp.; deflexion of compass-needle by iron in ship etc.; divergence of optic axis from normal position. [-ATION]

dēvice', n. Make, look, (arch.; *things of rare, strange*, ~); (pl.) fancy, will, (*left to one's own* ~); plan, scheme, trick; contrivance, invention, thing adapted for a purpose; drawing, design, figure; emblematic or heraldic design; motto. [ME & OF *devis, devise,* f. L *divisum, -a,* neut. & fem. p.p. of *dividere* DIVIDE]

dēv'il, n. **1.** *The D*~, supreme spirit of evil, tempter of mankind, enemy of God, Satan. **2.** Heathen god; evil spirit possessing demoniac; superhuman malignant being. **3.** Wicked or cruel person; mischievously energetic, clever, knavish, or self-willed person, luckless or wretched person (usu. *poor* ~); vicious animal. **4.** Junior legal counsel working for a leader (*Attorney-General's* ~, junior Counsel to Treasury). **5.** Literary hack doing what his employer takes the credit and pay for; *printer's* ~, errand-boy in printing-office. **6.** Personified evil quality (*the* ~ *of greed* etc.); fighting-spirit, energy or dash in attack. **7.** (Name of) kinds of animal, bird, firework, & implement; devilled S.-African dust-storm (also *dust* ~); highly seasoned dish, esp. devilled bones. **8.** Phrases (see also those in DEUCE, in all of which ~ may be substituted): *a* ~ *of a* ~, one of an unwelcome or remarkable or amusing kind; —*is the* ~, a great difficulty or nuisance; *like the* ~, with great energy etc.; *go to the* ~, be ruined, (imperat.) be off; *the* ~ *l*, excl. of annoyance or surprise; ~ *a one*, not one; *the* ~ *& all*, everything bad; *between the* ~ *& the deep sea*, in a dilemma; ~*s-on-horseback*, see ANGEL; *take the hindmost* (motto of selfish competition); *give the* ~ *his DUE*; *the* ~ *to pay*, trouble ahead; *talk of the* ~ (*& he will appear*), said when one comes just after being mentioned; || *the* ~ *among the tailors, row, disturbance*; ~ *on two sticks*, older name for DIABOLO; ~'*s advocate, -acy* (one who puts) the ~'s case against canonization, (transf.) depreciator, depreciation; ~'*s bones*, dice; ~'*s books*, cards; || *D*~'*s Own*, 88th Foot, Inns of Court Volunteers; ~'*s TATTOO*; ~'*s* in many plant-names, esp. ~'*s-bit*, kind of scabious; ~'*s coach-horse*, large cocktail beetle; || ~'*s dust*, shoddy. **9.** ~*dodger*, preacher; *parson*; ~*-fish*, name of many kinds; ~*-may-care*, reckless, rollicking. Hence ~DOM, ~HOOD nn., ~WARD(S) adv. [OE *deofol* (perh. f. L) f. Gk *diabolos* slanderer (*diaballō* slander f. *dia* through, *ballō* throw)]

dēv'il², v.i. & t. (-ll-). Work as lawyer's or author's devil (usu. *for* principal); grill with hot condiments. [f. prec.]

dēv'ilish, a., & adv. **1.** Like, worthy of, the devil, damnable; hence ~LY² adv., ~NESS n. **2.** adv. (colloq.) Very. [-ISH¹]

dēv'ilism, n. Devilish quality or conduct; worship of devils. [-ISM]

dēv'ilment, n. Mischief, wild spirits; devilish or strange phenomenon. [-MENT]

dēv'ilrŷ, -trŷ, n. Diabolical art, magic; the devil and his works; wickedness, cruelty; reckless mischief, daring, or hilarity; demonology; devils. [(-*try* corrupt. of) -RY]

dēv'ious, a. Remote, sequestered; winding, circuitous, erratic; erring. Hence

For compounds of *de-* not given consult DE-.

~LY² adv., ~NESS n. [f. L DĒvius f. *via* way)]

dévir·aliz|e, v.t. Make lifeless or effete. Hence ~A'TION n. [DE-]

devit·rify, v.t. Deprive of vitreous quality, make (glass or vitreous rock) opaque & crystalline. Hence ~FICA'TION n. [DE-]

dévoid', a. Destitute, empty, of. [short p.p. of obs. *devoid* f. OF DÉvoider f. *vide* VOID)]

dévoir' (-vwahr), n. Duty, one's best, (do one's ~); (pl.) courteous attentions (pay one's ~s to). [ME *deveir* f. OF *deveir* f. L *dēbēre* owe]

dévolu'tion (-loo-), n. Descent through a series of changes; descent of property by the succession; lapse of unexercised right to ultimate owner; (Biol.) degradation of species (cf. EVOLUTION); deputing, delegation, of work or power (esp. by House of Parliament to its committees etc. [f. med. L *dēvolūtio* (foll. -TION) roll)]

dévolve', v.t. & i. Throw (duty, work), (of duties) be thrown, fall, descend, *upon*, (deputy, or one who must act for want of others); descend, fall for want (*to, upon*, or abs.). [f. L DĒ(*volvere volut-*)

Devō'nian, a. & n. (Native) of Devonshire; (Geol.) (of) the formation lying above the Silurian & below the Carboniferous. [-IAN]

Dévonshire (-er), n. ~ (i.e. clotted) cream.

devōte', v.t. Consecrate, dedicate, give up exclusively, (oneself, another, thing, esp. abilities etc.), *to* (God, person, pursuit, purpose); give over to destruction etc. Hence ~MENT (-tm-) n. [f. L DĒ(*vovēre vōt-* vow)]

dévōt'ed, a. In vbl senses; esp. zealously loyal (~ *friend*), whence ~LY² adv.; doomed (esp. ~ *head*). [-ED¹]

dévotée', n. Votary *of*, one devoted *to*, zealously or fanatically pious person. [-EE]

devō'tion, n. Devoutness; devoting; divine worship, (pl.) prayers, praying; (*tacs at his ~s*), whence ~AL a., ~ally² adv., ~ALISM(3), ~ALIST(2), nn. (-sho-); enthusiastic addiction or loyalty (*to*, or abs.). [OF (-*tion*) f. L *devotionem* (DEVOTE, -ION)]

dévour' (-own), v.t. Eat (of beasts); eat like a beast or ravenously; (Bibl.) consume recklessly, waste, destroy, pillage, (substance, property, or its owners); kill decimate, (of fire, sword, plague, etc.); engulf; take in greedily with ears or eyes (book, story, beauty or beautiful person); absorb the attention of (~*ed by anxiety*); ~ the *way* etc., go fast, esp. of horses. Hence ~ingly² adv. [f. OF *devorer* f. L DĒ(*vorare* swallow)]

dévout', a. Reverential, religious, pious, (of person, act, etc.), earnest, hearty, genuine. Hence ~LY² adv., ~NESS n.; [f. OF *devot* f. L p.p. (DEVOTE)]

dew¹, n. Atmospheric vapour condensed in small drops on cool surfaces from evening to morning; freshness, refreshing or gently stealing influence, (usu. of sleep, eloquence, youth, music, etc.) any beaded or glistening moisture, esp. tears, sweat; *mountain ~*, illicitly distilled whisky; ~*berry*, kind of blackberry; ~*claw*, rudimentary inner toe of some dogs; ~*drop*; ~*fall*, time when ~ begins to form, evening; ~*point*, temperature at which it forms; ||~*pond*, shallow, usu. artificial, pond fed by atmospheric condensation, (chiefly) found or constructed on English downs; ~*rake*, for surface of grass or stubble; ~*ret* v.t., RET by exposure to ~ instead of steeping in water; ~*worm*, large garden worm. Hence ~LESS, ~Y², aa., ~ily² adv., ~INESS n. [OE *dēaw*, com.-Teut. cf. Du. *dauw*, G *tau*]

dew², v.t. & i. (Impers.) form or fall as dew (*it is beginning to ~*); (poet.) bedew, moisten. [ME *deuen* as prec.]

déwan' (-wahn), n. Head financial minister of Indian state; prime minister of a native state. [Arab. & Pers. *dīwān* (= *dēwan*, see DIVAN)]

dew'lap, n. Fold of loose skin hanging from throat of cattle (& transf. of other animals or men). Hence ~PED²(-pt) a. [*dew-* of doubtful etym. & sense, cf. Da. *doglæd*; *-lap* f. OE *læppa* skirt, lobe]

déx'ter, a. Of or on the right-hand side (in Her., to the spectator's left). [L, comparative (cf. -THER) f. *dex-* cf. Gk *dexios*, Goth. *taíhswa*, Skr. *dakshá*]

dexter'ity, n. Manual or mental adroitness, skill, neatness of handling; right-handedness, using of right hand. [f. L DEXTER(*itas* -TY)]

déx'trin, n. (chem.). Soluble gummy substance obtained from starch & used on adhesive stamps etc. [as foll. + -IN]

déx'tro-, comb. form of L DEXTER, esp. in terms concerned w. chem. property of causing plane of polarized light ray to rotate to right (opp. LAEVO-, which see for compounds).

déx'trōse, n. (chem.). Dextro-rotatory form of glucose. [prec. -OSE²]

déx'trous, -ter-, a. Neat-handed, deft; mentally adroit, clever; using right hand by preference. Hence déx'ter(e)rously² adv. [DEXTER +-OUS; -tr- correct but -ter- less common]

Dey (dā), n. (hist.). Commander of janizaries at Algiers; governor of Algiers or Tripoli. [F, f. Turk. dāī maternal uncle]

d(h)al (dahl), n. Split pulse, a common foodstuff in India. [Hind.]

dhar'ma (dǎr-, dĕr-), n. (India). Right behaviour, virtue; (in Buddhism) the law. [Skr., = a decree, custom]

dharmsala (dǎrmsah'lǎ), n. (India). Building devoted to charitable uses (esp. a travellers' rest-house). [Skr., f. dharma custom, sālā house]

dhōb'ī (dōb-), n. Indian native washerman; ~('s) itch, troublesome oriental form of eczema. [Hind., f. dhōb washing]

dhōt'ī (dōt-), n. Loin-cloth worn by male Hindus. [Hind.]

d(h)ow (dow), n. Single-masted Arabian-Sea ship of about 200 tons; any Arab ship, esp. as used in E.-Afr. slave-trading. [etym. dub.; spelling dow more correct but rare]

d(h)u'rrie (dŭr-), n. A thick coarse durable Indian cotton cloth fringed. Square used for floor-coverings etc. [f. Hind. darī]

di-¹, pref. Form of L DIS- (which see for meaning) used before b, d, l, m, n, r, s + cons., v, usu. g, & sometimes j. In LL & Rom. often replaced by dis- (so dismiss), in OF & ME often varying with de- (so deͅfer. L f. differre). Not a living pref. in Eng.

di-², pref. f. Gk di-=dis twice, two-, double-. In many E wds, & as living pref. in Chem. with various special uses.

di-³, pref.=foll. before vowel.

di(a)-, pref. f. Gk prep. or pref. dia through, thorough(ly), apart, across. In Gk words taken direct, or through L or F & L; also in many scientific words made with Gk elements or on Gk analogy.

diabēt'ēs (-z), n. Disease with excessive glucose-charged urine, thirst, & emaciation. [L f. Gk, f. DIA(bainō go)]

diabēt'ic, a., & n. Of diabetes; (person) suffering from diabetes. [f. F diabétique f. L diabeticus (prec., -IC)]

dia'blerie (-ahblerē), n. Devil's business; sorcery; wild recklessness; devil-lore. [F (diable f, L diabolus DEVIL, -RY)]

diabōl'ical, aa. Of, having to do with, proceeding from, externally like, the devil (usu. -ic); fiendish, atrociously cruel or wicked; (usu. -ical). Hence diabōl'ically² adv. [f. F diabolique f. L f. Gk diabolikos (DEVIL, -IC) +-AL]

diab'olism, n. Sorcery; devilish conduct or nature; belief in or worship of the devil. [f. Gk diabolos DEVIL, +-ISM]

diab'olize, v.t. Make into, represent as, a devil. [as prec. +-IZE]

diab'olō (or dǐ-), n. Game with two-headed top & sticks. [mod. fancy formation; older DEVIL on two sticks]

diāc'hylon, -hylum, (-k-), **-ūlum,** n. Sticking-plaster of litharge, olive oil, & water, on linen. [med. L (-ylum) f. Gk dia khulōn by juices; -culum by confus. w., -CULE]

diāc'onal, a. Of a deacon. [f. LL diaconalis (DEACON, -AL)]

diāc'onate, n. Office of, one's time as, deacon; deacons. [f. LL (-tus), as DEACON, -ATE¹]

diacrit'ical, a. Distinguishing, distinctive, esp. ~ marks used in printing to indicate different sounds of a letter, accents, diaeresis, cedilla, etc.; capable of seeing distinctions. [f. Gk DIA(kritikos see CRITIC) +-AL]

diāctin'ic, a. Transmitting, transparent to, the actinic rays. [DI-³, Gk aktis -īnos ray, -IC]

diadel'phous, a. (bot.). With stamens united in two bundles (cf. MONADELPHOUS, POLYADELPHOUS). [DI-², Gk adelphos brother]

di'adem, n. Crown, or plain or jewelled fillet, as badge of sovereignty; wreath of leaves or flowers worn round head; sovereignty; crowning distinction or glory. Hence ~ED² (-md) a. [f. 13th-c. F dyademe f. L f. Gk DIA(dēma f, deō bind, -M]

diaer'esis, n. (pl. -esēs). Mark (as in aërate) over second of two vowels indicating that they are not one sound. [L, f. Gk diairesis (DI-³, hairéō take) separation]

diagnōse' (-z), v.t. Determine from symptoms the nature of (a disease). [f. foll.]

diagnōs'is, n. (pl. -osēs). Identification of disease by means of patient's symptoms etc., formal statement of this; classification of person's character, assignment of species etc. [L f. Gk (DIA-, gignōskō recognize)]

diagnōs'tic, a., & n. Of, assisting, diagnosis; (n.) symptom. Hence ~ICS n, ~ICALLY adv., ~I'CIAN (-shn) n. [f. Gk DIA(gnōstikos f. gnōstos known, prec., -IC)]

diag'onal, a., & n. (Straight line) joining two non-adjacent angles of rectilineal figure or solid contained by planes; obliquely placed like the ~ of a parallelogram (~ row or ~, as of the squares of the same colour on chess-board); inclined at other than a right angle, having some part so inclined (~ cloth or ~, twilled with ridges oblique to the lists). Hence ~LY² adv. [f. L diagonalis f. Gk DIA(gōnios f. gōnia angle), -AL]

di'agram, n. (Geom.) figure made of lines used in proving etc.; sketch showing the features of an object needed for exposition; symbolic representation, by lines, of process, force, etc. Hence or cogn. diagrammat'ic a., diagrammat'ically adv., diagrammat'atize(1) v.t. [f. F diagramme f. L f. Gk DIA(gramma -atos f. graphō write, -M)]

di'agraph (-ahf), n. Instrument for drawing projections, enlarging maps, etc., mechanically. [f. F *diagraphe* (prec., -GRAPH)]

di'al, n. & v.t. & i. (-ll-). 1. (Usu. sun~) instrument showing hour by sun's shadow on graduated plate; (also ~-plate) face of clock or watch; plate in steam-gauge, gas-meter, etc., on which pressure, consumption, etc., are indicated by index-finger; (sl.) face. 2. v.b. Measure, indicate, (as) with ~; (automatic telephony) make a call by moving disk from successive numbers or letters to fixed point and letting it return, ring up (number etc.) thus. [prob. f. med. L (*rota*) *dialis* daily (wheel) f. L *dies* day, -AL; hardly found outside E]

di'alect, n. Form of speech peculiar to a district, class, or person, subordinate variety of a language with distinguishable vocabulary, pronunciation, or idioms. Hence dialec'tal a., dialec'tally² adv. [f. L f. Gk *dialektos* (*dialegomai* converse) f.]

dialec'tic¹, n. (often in pl.). Art of investigating the truth of opinions, testing of truth by discussion, logical disputation; (Mod. Philos.; not in pl.) criticism dealing with metaphysical contradictions & their solutions. So dialec'tian (-shn) n. [f. OF *dialectique* f. L f. Gk *dialektike* (*tekhne* art) of debate (prec., -IC)]

dialec'tic² a. & n. Logical, of disputation; (person) skilled in critical inquiry by discussion. [f. L f. Gk *dialektikos* (-IC)]

dialec'tical, a. = DIALECTIC¹ (adj.); = DIALECTIC² (adj.); belonging to DIALECTIC¹ in mod.-philos. sense. Hence ~ly² adv. [-AL]

dialó'gic, a. In, of, dialogue. [f. med. L *dialogicus* (DIALOGUE, -IC)]

dialó'gist, n. Speaker in, writer of, dialogue. [f. L f. Gk *dialogistes* (foll., -IST)]

di'alogue (-og), n. Conversation; piece of written work in conversational form, this kind of composition (written in ~); the conversational part in a novel. [f. 13th-c. F *dialogue* f. L f. Gk *dialogos* (*dialegomai* converse)]

dialy'sis, n. (pl. -yses). Parting of colloid from crystalloid parts of mixture by filtration through parchment floating in water. Hence di'alyse (-z) v.t. [f. Gk DIA(*lusis* f. *luo* loose)]

dialy'tic, a. (chem.). Of, by, dialysis. [f. Gk DIA(*lutikos* f. *luo* loosed)]

diamägnet'ic, a. & n. Tending to lie E. & W., across the magnetic axis, when suspended freely & acted on by magnetism; of ~ic bodies or diamagnetism; a ~ic body or substance. Hence ~ally adv., diamäg'netizě(3) v.t. [DIA-]

diamäg'netism, n. Diamagnetic tendency; the diamagnetic branch of magnetism. [DIA-]

diamäg'netous a. & n. (Material) scintillating with powdered crystal etc. [F; see DIAMOND]

di'amantiferous, a. Diamond-yielding. [f. F *diamant* DIAMOND, -i-, -FEROUS]

diăm'eter, n. Straight line passing from side to side of any body or geom. figure through centre (with special geom. applications for curves), transverse measurement, width, thickness; unit of linear measurement of magnifying-power (*lens magnifying* 2000 ~*ers*). So ~TAL a., ~rally² adv. [f. OF *diametre* f. L f. Gk *diametros* (*gramme* line) measuring across f. *metron* measure]

diamět'rical, a. Of, along, a diameter; diametral; (of opposition, difference, etc.) direct, complete, like that between opposite ends of diameter. Hence ~ly² adv. [f. Gk *diametrikos* (prec., -IC) +-AL]

di'amond, n., a., & v.t. 1. Colourless or tinted precious stone of pure carbon crystallized in octahedrons & allied forms, harder than any other known substance (cut into TABLE, ROSE, & BRILLIANT²; *Bristol, Cornish*, etc., ~, kinds of rock crystal; *black* ~, dark-coloured ~; coal; *rough* ~, not yet cut, person of intrinsic worth but rough manners; ~ *cut* ~, of persons well matched in wit or cunning). 2. Glittering particle or point. 3. (Usu. *glazier's* or *cutting* ~) tool with small ~ for glass-cutting. 4. Figure shaped like section of ~, rhomb (~-*panes*, small panes so shaped set in lead), playing-card bearing this (~s, the suit; *a small* ~, one of lower cards). 5. A printing TYPE. 6. ~-*back*, kinds of moth & turtle; ~ *cement*, for setting ~s; ~-*drill*, set with ~s for boring hard substance; ~-*field*, tract yielding ~s; ~-*point*, ~-tipped stylus used in engraving, (usu. pl.) place where two lines or rails intersect obliquely; ~-*snake*, Australian & Tasmanian kinds; ~ *wedding*, 60th anniversary; hence ~IFEROUS a., ~-WISE adv. 7. adj. Made of, set with, ~ or ~s, rhomb-shaped. 8. v.t. Adorn with ~s, dewdrops, etc. [ME & OF *diamant* f. LL *adamantem* nom. -*as* f. L f. Gk *adamas* ADAMANT]

Diăn'a, n. Horsewoman, lady who hunts; woman bent on remaining single. [L, goddess of hunting & chastity]

diapā'son (-zn, -s), n. Combination of notes or parts in harmonious whole; melody, strain, esp. grand swelling burst of harmony; range, scope; fixed standard of musical pitch; *open, stopped*, ~, two chief foundation-stops in organ. [L, f. Gk DIA *pasón* (*khordon*) through all (strings) f. *pas* all]

di'aper, n., & v.t. Linen fabric with small diamond pattern; baby's napkin of this; sanitary towel; ornamental design of diamond reticulation for panels, walls, etc. (vb, decorate with this). [f. OF diapre f. Byzant. Gk diaspros adj. f. DIA-, aspros white]

diaph'anous, a. Transparent. [f. med. L diaphanus f. Gk DIA(phanēs -showing f. phainō show) +-OUS]

diaphoret'ic, a. & n. (Drug, treatment) productive of perspiration. [f. L f. Gk diaphorētikos f. DIA(phoreō carry f. pherō), -ETIC]

di'aphragm (-ăm), n. Muscular & tendinous partition separating thorax from abdomen in mammals; partition in shell-fish, plant tissues, & various instruments, esp. in optics, telephony, & wireless, disk pierced with circular hole. So diaphragmat'ic a. [f. L f. Gk DIA(phragma -atos f. phrassō hedge in, -m)]

di'archy (-kĭ), dy-, n. Government by two independent authorities, esp. the reformed Indian constitution started in 1921. [DI-², DIArchö rule; dy- less correct]

di'arist, n. One who keeps a diary. Hence diaris'tic a. [DIARY +-IST]

di'arize, v.i. & t. Keep, enter in, a diary. [DIARY, -IZE]

diarrhoe'a (-rēă), n. Excessive looseness of bowels. Hence ~AL, ~IC, aa. [L, f. Gk DIA(rrhoia f. rheō flow)]

di'ary, n. Daily record of events, journal; book prepared for keeping this in; calendar with daily memoranda esp. for persons of a particular profession. Hence diar'IAL a. [f. L diarium (dies day, -ARY¹)]

di'astase, n. (chem.). A ferment converting starch to glucose, important in digestion. So diastat'ic, (irreg.) -ăs'ic, aa. [f. Gk diastasis separation (DIA-, aa, histēmi set)]

dias'tole, n. Dilatation of heart or artery alternating with systole & with it forming pulse (systole & ~ often fig. of reaction, fluctuation, etc.). [med L f. Gk, f. DIA(stellō send)]

diatess'aron, n. Harmony of the four gospels. [f. Gk dia tessarōn by four]

diatherm'ancy, n., diatherm'anous, diatherm'ic, aa. (Having the) quality of transmitting radiant heat. [f. F diathermansie, diathermane +-OUS, dia-thermique, f. Gk DIA(thermansis f. thermainō f. thermos warm)]

di'athermy, n. Application of electric currents to produce heat in the deeper tissues of the body. [DIA- +Gk thermē heat +-Y¹]

diath'esis, n. (med.; pl. -esēs). Constitutional predisposition, habit. [Gk, f. DIA(tithēmi place)]

di'atom, n. Member of genus Diatoma, microscopic unicellular Algae found esp. at bottom of sea & forming fossil deposits. So diatoma'ceous (-āshus) a. [f. Gk DIA(tomos f. temnō cut) alluding to the cells' being connected in easily separable chains]

diatom'ic, a. (chem.). Consisting of two atoms; having two replaceable atoms of hydrogen. [DI-², ATOM-, -IC]

diaton'ic, a. (mus.). (Of scale) proceeding by notes proper to key without chromatic alteration; (of melodies & harmonies) constructed from such a scale. [f. F diatonique f. L f. Gk DIA(tonikos TONIC) with intervals of a tone]

di'atribe, n. Piece of bitter criticism, invective, denunciation. [F, f. L f. Gk (-ē)=wearing away of time, discourse, f. DIA(tribō rub)]

dib, v.i. (-bb-). =DAB.¹ [var. of DAB¹, whence also dap]

dibas'ic, a. (chem.). Having two bases or two atoms of a base. [DI-², BASE¹]

dibb'er, n. Instrument for dibbling, dibble. [f. DIB, now used thus only in dibbing-stick]

dib'ble, n., & v.t. & i. 1. Instrument for making holes in ground for seeds etc. 2. vb. Prepare (soil) with this; sow or plant thus; use a ~. [perh. f. DIB +-LE(1), but found much earlier]

dibs (-z), n. pl. (Child's game with) sheep's knuckle-bones; counters at cards; (sl.) money. [prob. f. DIB; cf. earlier dib-stones]

dic'ast, dicas'tery, nn. (Gk Ant.). (Member of) Athenian jury (-ery), which gave both verdict & sentence. [f. Gk dikastēs, dikastērion, (dikazō to judge f. dikē right)]

dice¹, n. pl. See DIE¹.

dice², v.i. & t. Play DICE¹, whence di'CER¹ n.; gamble away, at dice; chequer, mark with squares; (Cookery) cut (meat) into small squares. [f. prec.]

dice-box, n. Box of hour-glass shape from which dice are thrown; ~insulator, piece of porcelain so shaped supporting telegraph wire.

dichlamyd'eous (-k-), a. (bot.). Having calyx & corolla. [DI-² +Gk khlamus-udos cloak, -EOUS]

dichog'amous (-k-), a. (bot.). Having stamens & pistils that mature at different times, so that self-fertilization is impossible. [f. Gk dikho- asunder, -gamos -married]

dichot'om"ly (-k-), n. Division into two; binary classification. [Bot. & Zool.] repeated bifurcation. So dichotom'ic, ~OUS, aa., ~IST(1)n., ~IZE(1,3)v.t.&i.,~ OUSLY² adv., -(k-). [as prec., -TOMY]

dichro'ic (-k-), a. Showing two colours (esp. of doubly refracting crystals). [f. Gk DI²(khroos f. khrōs colour) +-IC]

dichromat'ic (-k-), a. Two-coloured (esp. of animals species of which individuals show different colorations). [DI-² +Gk khrōmatikos (khrōma -atos colour, -IC)]

dichrom'ic (-k-), a. With only two colours (esp. of colour-blind vision seeing two

of three primary colours). [Gk *dikhrōmos*

dick, n. (sl.). Take one's ~ *that* or *to it*, swear, affirm. [prob. for *declaration*]

dick'ens (~z), n. (colloq.). Devil, deuce, [from 1598; prob. use of *Dickon*=Richard, or the surname *Dickens*, as alliterative substitute for *devil*]

dick'er¹, n. (commerce.). Half-score, ten, esp. of hides. [ME *dyker* cf. G *decher* f. L *decuria* set of ten (*decem*)]

***dick'er²,** v.i. Trade by barter, chaffer, haggle. [prob. f. prec. through the barter in skins with Indians]

dick'y¹, -ey, n. (colloq. & sl.). Donkey; (also ~*bird*) small bird; false shirt-front; pinafore or apron; driver's seat; || servant's seat at back of carriage. [etym. dub.; some senses f. the male name]

dick'y², a. (sl.). Unsound, shaky. [?]

dicotyle'don, n. Flowering plant with two cotyledons. Hence ~OUS a. [DI-²]

dic'taphone, n. Machine recording, for subsequent reproduction in type, what is spoken into it. [P, f. foll. + PHONE²]

dic'tate¹, v.t. & i. Say or read aloud (matter to be written down, often to writer; also abs.); prescribe, lay down authoritatively, (terms, thing to be done; of person, also of motive etc.); lay down the law, give orders, (*will not be ~d to*). So **dicta'TION** n. [f. L *dictare* frequent. of *dicere dict-* say, -ATE³]

dic'tate², n. Authoritative direction (usu. of reason, conscience, nature, etc.; often pl.). [f. L *dictatum* neut. p.p. see foll.]

dicta'tor, n. Absolute ruler, usu. temporary or irregular, in State, esp. one who suppresses or succeeds a democratic government; person with absolute authority in any sphere; one who dictates to writer. Hence ~SHIP, **dictat'RESS¹,** nn. [L (prec. -OR²)]

dictator'ial, a. Of dictator; imperious, overbearing. Hence ~ly² adv. [f. L *dictatorius* f. prec.+-AL]

dic'tion, n. Wording & phrasing, verbal style. [f. L *dictio* (*dicere dict-* say, -ION)]

dic'tionary (-sho-), n. Book dealing, usu. in alphabetical order, with the words of a language or of some special subject, author, etc., wordbook, lexicon, (*French-English* etc., ~, of French etc. words with English etc. explanation; ~ *of architecture* or *the Bible, Shakspere* ~, etc.). [f. med. L *dictionarium*

dic'tograph (-ahf), n. Apparatus reproducing in one room the sounds made in another. [P, irreg. f. foll. + -GRAPH]

dic'tum, n. (pl. -a, -ums). Formal saying, pronouncement; (Law) judge's expression of opinion not having legal validity; maxim, current saying. [L, neut. p.p. of *dicere* say]

did. See DO¹.

didac'tic (or di-), a. Meant to instruct; having the manner of a teacher. Hence ~ALLY adv., ~ICISM n. [f. Gk *didaktikos* (*didaskō* teach)]

did'apper, n. Small diving water-fowl. [for *dive-dapper* f. earlier *divedap* f. OE *dūfedoppa* (*dūfan* dive+*doppa* cf. dip)]

did'dle, v.t. (sl.). Cheat, swindle. [perh. back-formation f. *Jeremy Diddler* in Kenney's *Raising the Wind*, 1803]

***did'ō,** n. (colloq.) (pl. -oes). Antic, caper, prank (esp. in phr. *cut(up)* ~es). [?

didst. 2 sing. past of DO¹.

didym'ium, n. (chem.). A rare metal. [f. Gk *didumos* twin+-IUM (from its being always found with lanthanum)]

die¹, n. (pl. *dice,* ~s). 1. (Pl. *dice*) cube with faces bearing 1–6 spots used in games of chance; *dice,* game played with these; *the* ~ *is cast,* course irrevocably decided; *upon the* ~, at stake (Archit.), plinth, cubic part of pedestal between base & cornice; engraved stamp for coining, striking medal, embossing paper, etc.; ~*-sinker,* engraver of ~s. [ME & OF *de* f. L *datum* neut. p.p. of *dare* give, perh. in sense *what is given by fate;* for pl. *dice* (perh. felt as collective) cf. *pence,* the orig. pl. *truce,* also *mice* etc.]

die², v.i. (dying). Cease to live, expire, (of illness, hunger, etc., by violence, the sword, one's own hand, from wound etc., in battle, for friend, cause, etc., in poverty; ~ *a beggar, martyr;* ~ *a glorious, dog's, death;* ~ *the death,* be put to death, arch. or jocular; ~ *game,* fighting, not tamely; ~ *hard,* not without struggle; ~ *in one's bed,* of age or illness, *in one's boots* or *shoes,* by violence, *in harness,* while still at work, *in last ditch,* desperately defending something; *never say* ~, notgive in, keep up courage); (Bibl.) suffer as in death (*I* ~ *daily*), suffer spiritual death, ~ *unto,* escape thraldom of (sin); *be dying for,* to do, have great desire; ~ *of laughing,* laugh to exhaustion; (of plants etc.) lose vital force, decay; come to an end, cease to exist, go out, disappear, be forgotten, fade away, (of flame, fame, sound, etc.; *secret* ~*s with one;* often *away, down, off, out*); ~*-away* adj., languishing; ~*-hard,* person who dies hard or resists compulsion etc. to the last, obstinate politician etc.; ||*Die-hards,* 57th Regiment of Foot. [ME *deghen* perh. f. ON *deyja* cf. OHG *touwan* f. OTeut. *dau-j-an*]

dielec'tric, a. & n. Insulating (medium or substance), non-conductive, non-conductor, (DI-³ + ELECTRIC = through which electricity is transmitted (without conduction)]

Diesel (dēz-), n. (attrib.), ~ *engine,* type of oil-engine invented by Dr R. ~ of

Munich, in which ignition of fuel is produced by the heat of air suddenly compressed. [person]

dī′es (-z) **ī′rae**, n. Day of Judgement; Latin hymn beginning so. [L, = day of wrath]

dī′es (-z) **nōn**, n. (Law) day on which no legal business is done; (transf.) day that does not count or cannot be used. [L, short for ~ *juridicus* non-judicial day]

dī′et[1], n., & v.t. **1.** Way of feeding; prescribed course of food, regimen, one versed in or practising dietetics (prop. *-tician*, after *physician*); one's habitual food. **2.** v.t. Feed (person, *oneself*) on special food as medical regimen or punishment. Hence ~**LY**[2] (-sha-) adv. [f. OF *diete(r)* f. L f. Gk *diaita* way of life perh. f. *zaō* live]

dī′et[2], n. Conference, congress, on national or international business; meeting of the estates of the realm or confederation (esp. as Engl. name for foreign parliamentary assemblies). [f. med. L *diaeta* DIET[1] confused with *dies* day]

di′etary, n. & a. (Course) of diet; allowance or character of food in hospital, workhouse, etc. [f. L *diaetarius -um* (DIET-, -ARY[1])]

diētēt′ic, a. Of diet. Hence ~**ICS** n., ~**ICALLY** adv. [f. L f. Gk *diaitētikos*(*diaitē*)]

dif-, pref.= DIS- before f in L wds. Sometimes changed in OF to *de-* (*defy, defer*[1]).

dif′fer, v.i. Be unlike; be distinguishable *from*; be at variance, disagree, (*from, with*, or abs.; *agree to* ~, give up attempt to convince each other). [f. F *différer* (cf. DEFER[1]) f. L DIF(*ferre* bear, tend)]

dif′ference, n. & v.t. Being different, dissimilarity, non-identity (DISTINCTION *without* ~); point in which things differ, quantity by which amounts differ, remainder after subtraction, (*split the* ~, come to compromise); change in price of stocks etc. between certain dates (*pay, meet, the* ~); disagreement in opinion, dispute, quarrel; characteristic mark distinguishing individual or species, differentia (vb, serve as distinguishing mark of, differentiate; *make a* ~ *between*, treat differently; *it makes a* ~ *great* ~, is important. [f. F *différence* f. L *differentia* (foll., -ENCE)]

dif′ferent, a. Not the same, unlike, of other nature, form, or quality, (*from, to, than*, all used by good writers past and present, *than* chiefly where a prep. is inconvenient). Hence ~**LY**[2] adv. [f. F *différent* f. L *different-* part. st. (DIFFER, -ENT)]

differen′tia (-shia), n. (pl. *-ae*). Distinguishing mark, esp. of species within a genus. [L, see DIFFERENCE]

differen′tial (-shl), a. & n. **1.** Of, exhibiting, depending on, a difference (~ duties, charges, tariff, that differ according to circumstances). **2.** Constituting a specific difference, distinctive, relating to specific differences (~ *diagnosis*). **3.** (Phys., Mech.) concerning the difference of two or more motions, pressures, etc. (~ *gear*, or ~ as n., gear enabling car's hind-wheels to revolve at different speeds in rounding corners). **4.** n. (Math.) infinitesimal difference between consecutive values of continuously varying quantity (~ *calculus*, method of calculating this). Hence ~**LY**[2] (-sha-) adv. [f. med. L *differentialis* (DIFFERENCE, -AL)]

differen′tiāte (-shi-), v.t. & i. Constitute the difference between, of, or in; develop (t. & i.) into unlikeness, specialize, (species, organs, functions, synonyms); discriminate, discriminate between. Hence ~**ATION** (-si-) n. [f. med. L DIFFERENTIare, -ATE[3]]

dif′ficile (-ēl), a. Unaccommodating, exigent, hard to deal with, persuade, etc. [F]

dif′ficult, a. Hard to do or practise, troublesome, perplexing, (often ~ *of access, to answer*, etc.); = prec. [perh. back-formation f. foll.]

dif′ficulty, n. Being hard to do (*with* ~*y*, often as adv.= not easily) or obscure; something hard or obscure; hindrance; embarrassment of affairs, esp. want of money; reluctance, demur, objection, (*make* ~*ies*, be unaccommodating). [f. L DIF(*ficultas=facultas* FACULTY]

dif′fidence, n. Self-distrust, excessive modesty, shyness. [f. L *diffidentia* (foll., -ENCE)]

dif′fident, a. Wanting in self-confidence, bashful. Hence ~**LY**[2] adv. [f. L DIF(*fidere* trust), -ENT]

dif′fluence, n., **dif′fluent**, a., (-lōō-). Flowing apart, becoming fluid; deliquescence, deliquescent. [f. L DIF(*fluere* flow), -ENT, -ENCE]

diffract′, v.t.(opt.). (Of edge of opaque body) break up (beam of light) into series of dark and light bands or coloured spectra. So **diffrac′tion** n., **diffrac′tive** a., **diffrac′tively**[2] (-vl) adv. [f. L DIF(*frangere fract-* break)]

diffuse[1] (-s), a. Spread out, diffused, not concentrated, (of light, inflammation, etc.); not concise, long-winded. Hence ~**LY**[2] (-sl-) adv., ~**NESS** (-sn-) n. [f. L DIF(*fundere fus-* pour)]

diffuse[2] (-z), v.t. & i. Send forth, shed abroad, (light, particles, heat, geniality, knowledge, rumour; (Phys.) intermingle (t. & i.) of gases or fluids) by diffusion. whence ~**IBLE** (-z-) a., ~**IBIL′ITY** (z-) n. Hence or cogn. **dif′fusion**(-zhn)n.,~**′IVE** (-s-) a., ~**′IVELY**[2] (-sivl-) adv.,~**′IVENESS** (-sn-) n. [f.L *diffus-* see prec.]

dig, v.t. & i. (dug, formerly also ~*ged*, -gg-), & n. **1.** Use spade or mattock, claws, hands, or snout, in excavating or

turning over ground; make research (for information, *into* author etc.); make way by ~*ging into, through, under*; excavator (for turn up (ground) with spade etc.); make (hole etc.) by ~*ging* (~*a pit for, fig.*, try to entrap); get by ~*ging* (potatoes); thrust (spurs, one's nails, feet, point of weapon) *into* something or *in*; poke (person *in the ribs*); ~ (-*self*, -*selves, a, abs.) *in*, prepare defensive trench or pit; ~ *out*, get, find, make, by ~*ging*; ~ *up*, break up (fallow land). **2. n.** Piece of ~*ging*; thrust, poke, (esp. *in the ribs*; also *fig.* ~ *at*, remark directed against). [prob. f. F *diguer* cf. OE. *dīc* dike; from 14th c. only, not in OE. nor directly related to *ditch*]

digamma'a, n. Sixth letter (F, in sound = w) of original Gk alphabet, later disused, but important in philology. [L f. Gk (DI-², GAMMA)]

dig'amly, n. Taking, having, a second spouse. Hence or cogn. ~IST(I) n., ~OUS a. [f. L LL Gk DI²(*gamos* f. *gamos*-married)]

digas'tric, a. & n. (anat.). With two swelling ends (of muscles); muscle of lower jaw. [DI-² Gk *gastēr*-tr- belly, -IC]

di'gest¹, n. Methodical compendium or summary, esp. of a body of laws (*the D~*), that compiled by order of Justinian). [f. L *digesta* neut. pl. p.p. see foll.]

digest'², v.t. & i. Reduce into systematic form, classify; summarize; think over, arrange in the mind; prepare (food) in stomach and bowels for assimilation (intr. of food, admit of digestion; ~s well, *will not* ~); (of drugs, wine, etc.) promote digestion of; assimilate (conquered territory etc.); brook, endure, be reconciled to, (insult, opinion); get mental nourishment from. Hence ~IBLE a., ~IBLI'ITY n., ~IBLY² adv. [f. L DI¹(*gerere gest*-carry) sort]

digest'er, n. In vbl senses; esp. in cookery, stock-pot (cf. foll.). [-ER¹]

diges'tion (-schon), n. Digesting (hard, *easily*, *of* ~) of physical or mental food; power of digesting (*a good, weak*, ~); long steeping in hot fluid to extract essence, stewing. [F, f. L L *digestiōnem* (DIGEST², -ION)]

diges'tive, a. & n. Of, promoting, digestion; substance aiding digestion; ointment to promote suppuration. Hence ~LY² (-vl) adv. [F (-*f*- -*tve*), f. L *digestīvus* (DIGEST², -IVE)]

digg'er (-g-), n. In vbl senses; also or esp. (also *gold-*~-)one who digs or searches for gold in gold-fields; (sl.) Australian; *D~s*, N.-Amer. Indians living on roots; digging-part of various machines; (also ~-*wasp*) division of *Hymenoptera*. [-ER¹]

digg'ing (-g-), n. In vbl senses; also or esp. (pl.), *occas.* ~*s*) mine or goldfield; || (pl.), colloq., also abbr. *digs*) lodgings. [-ING¹]

dight (dīt), v.t. (arch., & chiefly in p.p. esp. (pl.), *occas. a* ~*s*) mine or goldfield; || (pl.), colloq., also abbr. *digs*) lodgings. Clothe, array, adorn; make ready. [repr.

[common in ME, with many meanings; obs. exc. dial, f. 1670 to 1800; revived by Scott, & now as above: OE *dihtan* f. L *dictāre* dictate, whence also G *dichten* write poetry]

dig'it, n. Finger or toe (joc., or in Zool. or Anat.); finger's breadth; any numeral from 0 to 9; (Astron) twelfth part of sun's or moon's diameter (in measuring eclipse). So ~AL a. [f. L *digitus*]

dig'ital, a. [f. L *digitus*]

dig'itate, a. (zool.). Walking on toes, not touching ground with heel, (cf. PLANTIGRADE). [F (L *digitus*, -*t*-, *-gradus*-walking)]

dig'nify¹, v.t. Make worthy; confer dignity upon, ennoble; make stately (p.p., marked by dignity, self-respecting, stately); speak of by high-flown title (*school* ~*ied with name of college*, title of manner, proper stateliness; ~ *ball*, negro public dance (from its elaborate formality). [f. OF *dignefie* f. LL *dignificāre* (*dignus* worthy, -FY)]

dig'nitary, n. Person holding high office, esp. ecclesiastical. [f. L as foll. + -ARY¹]

dig'nity, n. True worth, excellence, (*the* ~ *of labour*); high estate or estimation (*beneath one's* ~, unfit for one to do); honourable office, rank, or title; elevation of manner, proper statelliness; ~ *worthy*, -TY); cf. DAINTY]

di'graph (or dī-), n. Group of two letters expressing one sound, as *ch, ea.* [DI-² Gk *graphē* writing]

digress' (or dī-), v.i. Diverge from the track, stray; depart from or the main subject temporarily in speech or writing. Hence or cogn. **digre'sSION** n., ~IVE a. [f. L DI¹(*gradī gress*-) walk *gress*-)]

dihed'ral, a. Having or contained by two plane faces; ~ *angle*, (esp.) angle formed by wing pairs of an aeroplane. [f. DI-² + Gk *hedra* seat, base, +-AL (1)]

dike, dyke, n. & **v.t. 1.** Ditch; || natural watercourse; || low wall esp. of turf; embankment, long ridge, dam, against flooding, esp. those in Holland against sea; causeway; (fig.) barrier, obstacle, defence; (Mining & Geol.) fissure in stratum filled with deposited matter, this matter; || ~-*reeve*, officer in charge of drains, sluices, & sea-banks, of fen district. **2. v.t.** Provide, defend, with ~(s), pond]

dilap'idate, v.t. & i. Bring, come, into disrepair or decay (building, furniture, clothing, estate, fortune). [f. L DI¹(*lapi-*

dare t, *lapis* stone) understood in E as *take stone from stone*, in L perh. *throw away like stones*]

dilapida′tion, n. Squandering; bringing or coming into, being in, disrepair; || sum charged against incumbent etc. for wear & tear during his tenancy; falling away of cliffs etc., debris resulting. [f. L *dilapidatio* (prec., -ATION)]

dilate′ (dī-, dǐ-), v.t. & i. Make or become wider or larger, expand, widen, enlarge, (*with ~ed eyes*), whence ~′ABLE a., ~AHIL′- TY n., DILATA′TION (& irreg. **dila′tion**) n.; expatiate, speak or write at large (usu. *upon*). [f. F *dilater* f. L DI′(*latare* f. *latus* wide); the L p.p. st. being *dilatat-*; *dilation* is irreg.]

dilat′or, n. (anat.). (Also ~ *muscle*) muscle that dilates an organ (cf. CON- STRICTOR). [irreg. for less used *dilatator*; see prec., -OR²]

dil′atorУ, a. Tending to, designed to cause, given to, delay. Hence ~ǏLУ² adv., ~INESS n. [f. L *dilatorius* (DI′(*dat-* p.p. st. of *differre* DEFER), -ORУ]

dilemm′a (or dī-). n. Argument forcing opponent to choose one of two alterna- tives (*horns of the~*) both unfavourable to him; position that leaves only a choice between equal evils. So **dilemmā′tic** a. [L, f. Gk Dǐ²(*lemma -atos* assumption f. *lambanō* take, -M]

dilettan′te, n. (pl. -*ti*, pr. -*tē*) & a. 1. Lover of the fine arts; amateur; smatterer, one who toys with subject or concentrates on nothing; hence ~TISH¹ a., ~TISM(1) n. 2. adj. Trifling, not thorough, amateur. [It., f. *dilettare* f. L *delectare* DELIGHT, -ANT]

dil′igence¹, n. Persistent effort or work; industrious character. [F, (DILIGENT), -ENCE]]

dil′igence² (*occas.* dēlēzhahns′), n. Foreign public stage-coach. [F, as prec.]

dil′igent, a. Hard-working, steady in application, industrious, attentive to duties. Hence ~lУ² adv. [F, f. L Dǐ²(*ligere lect-* = *legere* choose) love, take delight in, -ENT]

dill, n. Umbelliferous annual yellow- flowered herb. [OE *dile* cf. G *dill* etym. dub.]

dill′y-dally, v.i. (colloq.). Vacillate; loiter. [redupl. of DALLY]

dil′uent (*or* -ōō-), a. & n. Diluting (agent) (substance) increasing proportion of water in the blood etc. [f. L *diluere* DILUTE², -ENT]

dil′ute¹, a. Weakened by addition of water, (of colour) washed-out, faded; (fig.) watery, watered down. [f. L *dilutus* p.p. see foll.]

dilute² (dǐlōōt′, dī-), v.t. Reduce strength of (fluid) by adding water; diminish brilliance of (colour); water down (doc- trine, zeal); ~ *labour*, substitute a pro- portion of women or unskilled men

(*dilutees*′) for skilled men. So **dilu′tion** (-ōō-) n. [f. L Dǐ(*luere lut-* wash)]

dilu′vial (-ōō-, -ū-), a. 1. Of a flood, esp. ~ *theory*, *changes*, etc., depending on general deluge or catastrophic water-action, whence ~IST(2) n.; of the drift formation now called Glacial Drift. [f. L *diluvialis*]

dim, a., & v.i. & t. (-mm-). 1. Faintly luminous or visible; not bright, clear, or well-defined; obscure; seeing or seen, hearing or heard, apprehending or apprehended, indistinctly; hence ~lУ² adv., ~m′ISH¹ (2) a., ~′NESS n. 2. vb. Become or make ~, becloud, outshine. [OE, cf. OHG *timbar*]

*dime, n. Silver coin, 1/10 of dollar (~ *novel*, cheap shocker), [obs. sense *tithe*, f. OF *disme* f. L *decima* fem. of *decimus* tenth]

dimen′sion (-shn), n. Measurable ex- tent of any kind, as length, breadth, thickness, area, volume, (usu. pl.; of *great* ~*s*, very large); *the three* ~*s*, length, breadth, & thickness (point has no ~*s*, line one, surface two, body three; *fourth* ~, in math. speculations, property of matter that should be to solids as solids are to planes); (Alg.) number of unknown quantities contained as factors in a product (x^3, x^2y, xyz, all of three ~*s*). Hence ~AL, ~LESS, aa., (-sho-). [F, f. L Dǐ²(*mensionem* f. *metiri mensus* measure, -TON)]

dim′erous, a. (bot., entom.). With two parts. [Dǐ-², -MEROUS]

dim′eter, n. Verse of two measures (measure in some metres has one foot, in others two). [f. L f. Gk Dǐ²(*metros* f. *metron* measure)]

dimin′ish, v.t. & i. Make or become, actually or in appearance, less (*hide one's ~ed head*, i.e. reduced power etc.; in Mus., ~*ed*, of intervals less by a chromatic semi- tone than the full, as ~*ed fifth* etc.); (Archit.) taper (t. & i.). Hence ~ABLE a., ~inglУ² adv. [mixture of MINISH with obs. *diminue* f. F *diminuer* f. L Dǐ²(*minuere -minut-* cf. *minor* less]

diminu′endō, adv. (mus. direction (abbr. *dim.*) (cf. CRESCENDO); gradual decrease, musical passage marked by it, (also fig.). [It.]

diminu′tion, n. Diminishing, amount of it; (Mus.) repetition of passage in notes shorter than those previously used. [F, f. L *diminutionem* (DIMINISH, -ION)]

dimin′utive, a. & n. (Gram.) (word) de- noting small specimen of the thing de- noted by corresponding primitive word; remarkably small, tiny. Hence **dimin′u- tiv′**AL a. (gram.), ~lУ² (-vl-) adv., ~NESS (-vn-) n. [F (-*if*, -*ive*), f. L *diminutivus* (DIMINISH, -IVB)]

dim'issory, a. Sending away; permitting to depart; *letters* ~ (Eccl.), bishop's authorization of a candidate's ordination outside his own see. [f. L *dimissorius* (*dimittere* send away)]

dim'ity, n. Stout cotton fabric woven with raised stripes or fancy figures used for bedroom hangings etc. [f. It. *dimito* (pl. *-i*) f. LL *dimitum* f. Gk Di²*dimitos* warp-thread)]

dimorph'ic, dimorph'ous, aa. (bot., zool., chem., mineral.). Exhibiting, occurring in, two distinct forms. So **di-morph'ISM(2)** n. [f. Gk Di²(*morphos morphē* form)+-IC, -OUS]

dim'ple, n., & v.t. & i. 1. Small hollow esp. in cheek or chin; ripple in water, hollow in ground; hence **dim'ply²** a. 2. vb. Produce ~s in, show ~s, (of; perh. cogn. w. G *tümpel* pool (cf. DAPPLE) f. OHG *dumphilo*]

din, n., & v.t. & i. (-nn-). 1. Continued confused stunning or distracting noise. 2. vb. Assail with ~; repeat ad nauseam *into* person or person's *ears*; make a ~. [yb.f. n., OE *dyne* cf. ON *dynr*]

dine, v.i. & t. Take dinner (~ *out, away from home*; ~ *off* or *on*, have for dinner; ~ *with Duke Humphrey*, go without dinner—perh. w. allusion to those who walked during dinner-time in Duke Humphrey's Walk in St Paul's); entertain (persons) at dinner, (of room etc.) provide dining-accommodation for (some number; *dining-room*, used for meals. [f. F *dîner* perh. f. LL *DISjÉUNARE* f. *jējunus* fasting)]

ding-dong', adv., n., & a. (With) alternating strokes as of two bells (*hammer away at it* ~; ~ *race*, in which each has the better alternately; sound of bell(s); jingle of rhyme. [imit.]

dinghy, dingey, (ding'gi), n. Small ship's boat; small inflatable rubber boat, craft's small rowing-boat on Indian rivers. [f. Hind. *dēngī*]

dingle (ding'gl), n. Deep dell, usu. shaded with trees. [etym. dub.; perh.=DIMPLE]

ding'o (-ngg-), n. (pl. ~es). Wild or half-domesticated Australian dog. [native]

din'gy² (-i-), a. Dull-coloured, grimy, dirty-looking. Hence ~IHY² adv., ~INESS n. [perh. f. DUNG2+-Y]

dink'um, n. & n. (Austral. dial. or sl.). Genuine, real (~ *oil*, the honest truth); hard work, toil. [?]

dink'y, a. (colloq.). Pretty, neat, of engaging appearance. [cf. Sc. *dink* trim, f. 1108]

dinner, n. Chief meal of day, whether at midday or evening (formal meal with distinct courses); public feast in honour

4895

of person or event; ~*-bell, -hour, -time, -party*; ~*-claret, -sherry*, etc. (inferior to ~*-set*, of plates, dishes, etc.; ~*-wagon*, movable tray on castored legs; ~ *without grace*, ante-nuptial sexual intercourse. ||~*-jacket*, tailless dress coat; Hence ~LESS a. [f. F *dîner* DINE used as n.; -ER¹]

dino'ceras, n. Extinct elephant-sized ungulate mammal with three pairs of horns. [f. Gk *deinos* terrible + *keras* horn]

dinorn'is, n. Extinct ostrich-sized New Zealand flightless bird, the moa. [f. Gk *deinos* terrible+*ornis* bird]

dino'saur (-or), n. Extinct gigantic reptile. Hence **dinosaur'IAN** (-ōr-) a. & n. [f. Gk *deinos* terrible+*sauros* lizard]

din'othere, n. Huge extinct proboscidean quadruped. [f. Gk *deinos* terrible+*thērion* wild beast]

dint, n., & v.t. 1. (Arch.) stroke, blow, (whence, mod.) *by* ~ *of*, by force or means of; mark made by blow or pressure, dent. 2. v.t. Mark with ~s, dent. [OE *dynt*]

dio'cesan (-zn), a. & n. 1. Of a diocese. 2. n. Bishop in relation to diocese or clergy; member of diocese in relation to bishop (corresp. to *parishioner*). [f. F *diocésain* f. med. L *diocesis* f. L f. Gk Di²*dioikēsis* f. *oikeō* inhabit) administration)]

di'ocese (-ĕs, -ĭs), n. Bishop's district. [f. OF *diocise* f. med. L *dioecesis* f. L f. Gk Di²*dioikēsis* f. *oikeō* inhabit) administration)]

dioe'cious (-ēshus), a. (Bot.) having the male & female flowers on separate plants; (Zool.) with the two sexes in separate individuals. [DI-², Gk -*oikos* -housed, -OUS]

Diony'sian, a. Of Dionysus, the Greek god of wine, or his worship. [-ian f. L *Dionysius*+-AN; -iac f. L L f. Gk *Dionusiacos* f. *Dionusia* the feast of Dionysus]

diop'ter, -tre (-ter), n. Refractive power of a lens having a focal length of one metre (used as unit of refractive power; thus a lens of +5 ~s is a positive lens with a focal length of 20 cm.). [f. F *dioptre* f. L f. Gk *dioptra* (see foll.)]

diop'tric, a. & n. 1. Serving as medium for sight, assisting sight by refraction, (~*ic glass, lens, system*); of refraction, refractive; of ~*ics*; hence ~ICALLY adv. 2. n. Unit of refractive power, power of lens with focal distance one metre; (pl.) part of optics dealing with refraction (cf. CATOPTRICS). [f. Gk *dioptrikos* f. DI²*optra* (see foll.)]

diora'ma (-rah-), n. Spectacular painting in which, by changes in the colour & direction of light thrown on or through it, effects of such natural processes as sunrise are produced. Hence **diorā'mIC** a. [DI-³, Gk *horama* -*dios* (*horaō* see, -M)]

M

diŏx'ide, n. (chem.). Oxide formed by combination of two atoms of oxygen with one of metal or non-metal (*carbon* etc.). [DI-²]

dip¹, v.t. & i. (-pp-). **1.** Put or let down into liquid, immerse, (~ *one's pen in gall*, write bitterly); dye thus; make (candles) by immersing wick in hot tallow; wash (sheep) in vermin-killing liquid; take up (liquid, grain, etc.) in scoop, pan, etc. **2.** Lower (flag, sail, scale of balance) for a moment. **3.** Involve in debt (colloq.). **4.** Go under water & emerge quickly; put hand, ladle, etc., *into* to take something out (~ *into one's purse* etc., spend freely); go below any surface or level (*sun ~s below horizon; bird ~s & rises in flight; scale ~s*). **5.** Extend downwards; have downward slope (esp. of magnetic needle, & of strata; ~*ping-needle*, one so mounted as to measure magnetic dip). **6.** Make investigations (~ *deep into the future*; look cursorily or skippingly into the (book). [OE *dyppan*, cogn. w. DEEP; cf. G *taufen* baptize]

dip², n. **1.** A dipping (see prec.); quantity dipped up; (colloq.) bathe in sea etc.; amount of submergence. **2.** (Astron., Surv.) apparent depression of horizon due to observer's elevation; angle made by magnetic needle with horizon. **3.** Downward slope of stratum; depression of sky-line etc. **4.** Tallow candle. **5.** ~*needle*, = dipping-needle (see prec.); ~*net*, small fishing-net with long handle; ~*pipe*, ||-*trap*, arranged to cut off communication of gas etc. by downward bend in which liquid stands. [f. prec.]

diphther'ia, diphtherit'is, (-fth-), nn. Acute infectious disease with inflammation & exudation forming a false membrane. Hence **diphther'IAL, diphthe'rIC, diphtherit'IC, diph'theron,** aa. [f. F *diphthérie, diphthérite* (earlier name), f. Gk *diphthera* hide, -rī¹, -ītīs]

diph'thong(-fth-), n. Union of two vowels pronounced in one syllable (ou, oi); two vowels representing sound of single vowel (ea in *feat*), digraph; compound vowel character, ligature, (æ). Hence **diphthong'AL** a., ~IZE (3) v.t. (-ugg-). [f. F *diphthongue* f. L f. Gk dī²(*phthoggos* sounded f. *phthoggos* voice)]

dipl(o)-, comb. form of Gk *diploos* double, in many scientific words as **diploblas'tic** with two germinal layers, **diplocard'iac** with right & left sides of heart separate. **diplŏd'ocus,** n. Gigantic extinct N.-American herbivorous dinosaur. [f. prec. + Gk *dokos* wooden beam]

diplŏm'a, n. (pl. -s, rarely -ta). State paper, official document, charter; document conferring honour or privilege, esp. University or College certificate of degree, whence ~'d, ~ED² (-mad), ~LESS, aa. [L f. Gk (-ŏ-), f. *diploō* (*diploos* double), -M; orig. folded paper]

diplom'acy, n. Management of, skill in managing, international relations; DOLLAR ~; adroitness, artful management, tact. [f. F *diplomatie* f. *diplomate* see foll., -Y¹]

dip'lomāt, n. = DIPLOMATIST. [f. F *diplomate* back-formation f. *diplomatique* see foll.]

diplomat'ic, a. & n. (Palaeographic examination) of official or original documents, charters, etc.; of diplomacy (~ *body,* ambassadors & legation-officials at a court; ~ *agent, service*); skilled in diplomacy; proceeding by negotiation; (of statements, dealings, persons) uncandid, deceiving. Hence **diplomat'ICALLY** adv. [f. F *diplomatique* f. mod. L *diplomaticus* f. Gk DIPLOMA -*atos*, -IC]

diplŏm'atist, n. One officially engaged in diplomacy; adroit negotiator. [DIPLOMAT, -IST]

diplŏm'atize, v.i. Act as diplomatist. use diplomatic arts. [DIPLOMAT, -IZE]

dip'nŏan, a. & n. (Fish) having both gills and lungs. [f. Gk *dipnoos* with two breathing-apertures (di-² + *pnoē* breath)]

dipp'er, n. In vbl senses; also or esp. : Anabaptist or Baptist; kinds of bird, esp. water ouzel; kind of ladle; (Photog.) apparatus for immersing negatives; *the D~,* the Great Bear. [DIP¹, -ER¹]

dipp'y, a. (sl.). Crazy. [?]

dipsomān'ia, n. Morbid craving for alcohol. Hence **dipsomān'IAC** n. [Gk *dipso*-(*dipsa* thirst, -o-), -MANIA]

dip'teral, a. With double peristyle. [f. L f. Gk dī²(*pteros*-winged f. *pteron* wing), -AL] **dip'terous,** a. (Entom.) two-winged, belonging to the order *Diptera* (insects with one pair of membranous wings); (Bot.) with two wing-like appendages. [as prec. +-OUS]

dip'tych (-ĭk), n. Ancient hinged two-leaved writing-tablet with inner sides waxed; painting, esp. altarpiece, of two leaves closing like book. [f. L f. Gk dī²(*ptukha* neut. pl. of -*ptukhos* -folding f. *ptukhē* fold)]

dīre, a. Dreadful, calamitous, (~ *sisters,* the Furies). Hence ~'LY² (-rlī) adv. [f. L *dīrus*]

dĭrect'¹, v.t. & i. Address (letter, parcel, etc.; order or write to or to be conveyed to (I ~ *my remarks to you*); control, govern the movements of, (*soul ~s body,* commander troops); turn (thing, person, eyes, attention) straight *to* something; tell (person) the way (*to*; ~*ing-post,* = FINGER-*post*); guide as adviser, principle (*duty ~s my actions*), etc.; order (person) *to do,* thing *to be done*; give orders (*that* or abs.). So **dĭrec'tive** a. (also n., general instruction for the carrying out of military etc. operations). [f. L L DI(*rigere rect-=regere* put straight)]

direct'[1], a. & adv. Straight, not crooked. (ly) or round about, (the ~ road; went ~ to heaven.) ~ action, exertion of pressure on the community by strikes instead of on Parliament by votes to force political measures on the Government; ~ ray, not reflected or refracted; ~ shot, hit, without ricochet; (Astron.) proceeding from W. to E., not retrograde; (of descent) lineal(ly), not collateral(ly); (of argument) following uninterrupted chain of cause & effect etc.; diametrical (~ opposite, contrary, contradiction); (Mus.) not inverted (of interval, chord), not contrary (of motion); straightforward, frank, going straight to the point, not ambiguous; immediate(ly), personal(ly), not by proxy; (Gram.) ~ speech or oration, the words as actually spoken, not modified (cf. OBLIQUE, INDIRECT) in reporting; ~ current, electric current flowing always in the same direction; ~ tax, levied originally (income tax etc.) on person who bears the burden ultimately (cf. INDIRECT). Hence ~NESS n. [(prob. F) f. L directus p.p. see prec.]

direc'tion, n. Directing, aiming, guiding, managing; = DIRECTORATE; instruction what to do, order, (usu. pl.); address on letter or parcel; course pursued by moving body, point to which one moves or looks, (in the ~ of London, Londonwards); scope, sphere, subject, (new ~s of inquiry, improvement in many ~s); ~finder, wireless receiving device for finding bearings of transmitting stations. Hence~AL(-shon-) a. (went ~ l knew). [-IY[2]]

direc'tly, adv. & conj. In a DIRECT[2] manner; at once, without delay; presently, in no long time; (colloq.) as soon as (went ~ l knew). [-IY[2]]

Direc'toire (-twär), a. (Dressmaking) in imitation of styles prevalent during the French Directory. [F; see DIRECTORY[2]]

direc'tor, n. Superintendent, manager, esp. member of managing-board of commercial company; (Cinemat.) stage-manager and producer of a film; (Fr. Hist.) member of Directory; (Eccl.) priest acting as spiritual adviser; apparatus controlling direction in instruments etc. Hence direc'toral a., ~ship, direc'-tress[1] n. [f. F directeur (DIRECT[1], -OR[2]) or f. L. directus (DIRECT[1])]

direc'torate, n. Office of director; board of directors. [-ATE[1]]

direc'tory[1], a. Directive, advisory. (esp. of part of law advising procedure omission of which does not invalidate action). [f. L directorius (DIRECT, -ORY)]

direc'tory[2], n. Book of rules, esp. for public or private worship; book with lists of inhabitants of district, members of professions, etc., with various details; (Fr. Hist.) revolutionary executive of five directors in power 1795-9 (D~). [f. med. L directorium neut. adj. see prec.]

direc'trix, n. (pl. -ices). = DIRECTRESS; (Geom.) fixed line used in describing curve or surface. [DIRECTOR, -TRIX]

dire'ful (-rf-), a. Terrible, dread. Hence ~LY[2] adv. [DIRE, -FUL(1)]

dirge, n. Song sung at burial, or in commemoration of the dead; lament. [f. wd in Latin antiphon in Matins part of Office of the Dead]

diri'gible, a. & n. Capable of being guided (esp. of balloons); (n.) ~ balloon or airship as opp. aeroplane. [as DIRECT[1], -IBLE]

diri'ment, a. Nullifying (~ impediment, making marriage null & void from the first). [f. L dirimere(DIS-,emere take), -ENT]

dirk, n. & v.t. Kind of dagger (esp. of Highlanders); (vb) stab with this. [earlier dork (1602) perh. f. Du. dolk cf. G dolch]

dirt, n. Unclean matter that soils, wet mud (~ pie, made by children in gutters etc.); anything worthless (yellow ~, gold; cheap); scornful name for land; ~cheap, very cheap; earth, soil; dirtiness; foul talk; fling ~, talk abusively or slanderously of; anything worthless (yellow ~, gold; etc.. [ME drit excrement]]

dir'ty, a., & v.t. & i. 1. Soiled, foul, mixed with or like or connected with dirt, (D~ Shirts, 101st Foot, from fighting in shirt-sleeves at Delhi); unclean, obscene, sordid, mean, despicable; do the ~; play a shabby trick; ~ work, esp. dishonourable proceedings, (also) drudgery (do person's ~ work for him); ill-gotten (of weather) rough, squally; (of colour) not pure or clear; D~ Allen, sea-bird getting food by forcing gulls etc. to disgorge; hence dir'tiLY[2] adv., dir'ti-NESS n., ~ISH[1](2) a. 2. vb. Make, become.

dis-, pref. f. L dis- (which was changed to di-[1] or di- before certain letters; see also DIE[?]) related to bis (orig. ~ dis twice) & duo two. In wds taken direct or thr. F f. L; in wds taken f. L LL in which dis- or Rom. des- had displaced de-; & used as living pref. to modify sense of E wds. Meanings: asunder, away, apart or between, one by one, utterly (in wds already negative, as disanimal), un-, not, the reverse of, deprivation of, expulsion from.

disabil'ity, n. Thing, want, that prevents one's doing something, esp. legal disqualification. [f.obs. adj. disable (=un-able), -ITY]

disa'ble, v.t. Incapacitate from doing or for work etc.; cripple, deprive of power of

acting; disqualify legally, pronounce incapable, hinder. Hence ~MENT (-blm-) n. [DIS-, ABLE]

disabúse′(-z), v.t. Undeceive, disillusion. [DIS-]

disaccórd′, n., & v.i. Disagree(ment), (be at) variance. [DIS-]

disadvan′tage (-vah-), n. Unfavourable condition (taken at a ~); loss, injury, [f. F désavantage (DIS-, ADVANTAGE)]

disǎd′vantā′geous (-jus), a. Involving disadvantage or discredit, derogatory. Hence ~LY² adv. [DIS-]

disǎffěc′ted, a. Estranged, unfriendly, disloyal, esp. to Government. [p.p. of scarcely used vb DISaffect]

disǎffěc′tion, n. Political discontent, disloyalty. [as prec. after AFFECTION]

disaffirm′, v.t. (legal). Reverse (previous decision); repudiate (settlement). Hence disaffirmATION n. [DIS-]

disaffő′rest, v.t. ‖ Reduce from legal state of forest to ordinary land. Hence ~ATION n. [f. med. L DIS(AFFORESTARE)]

disagree′, v.i. Differ, be unlike, not correspond; differ in opinion, dissent, quarrel; differ (of food, climate, etc.) prove unsuitable, have bad effects, (with person, his health, digestion, etc.). Hence ~MENT n. [DIS-]

disagree′able (-grĭa-), a. & n. 1. Not to one's taste, unpleasant; unamiable, bad-tempered; hence ~leNESS (-ln-) n., ~LY² adv. 2. n. (Usu. pl.) unpleasant experience(s), trouble(s), worries. [f. F désagréable (DIS-, AGREEABLE)]

disallow′, v.t. Refuse to sanction or accept as reasonable or admit, prohibit. [f. OF desalouer (DIS-, ALLOW)]

disannúl′, v.t.(-ll-). Cancel, annul. [DIS-]

disappear′, v.i. Cease to be visible, vanish, die away from sight or existence, be lost. Hence ~ANCE n. [DIS-]

disappoint′, v.t. Not fulfil desire or expectation of, break appointment with, (person; ~ed at, in, of, with; agreeably etc.; ~ed, glad to find one's fears groundless); belie, frustrate, (hope, purpose, etc.). Hence ~ING² a., ~ĕdLY², ~ingLY² adv., ~MENT n., event etc. that ~s, distress resulting. [f. F désappointer (DIS-, APPOINT)]

disǎpprobā′tion, n. Disapproval. So disǎpp′robātive, disǎpp′robātory, aa. [DIS-]

disǎpprov[e′ (-ŏov), v.t. & i. Have, express, unfavourable opinion of or of. Hence ~AL(2) n., ~ingLY² adv., (-ŏo-). [DIS-]

disarm′, v.t. & i. Deprive of weapons; deprive of weapons (esp. in fencing, jerk foil etc. out of hand of); dismantle (city, ship), reduce, be reduced, to peace footing (of army), abandon or cut down military establishment, whence DISARM′A-

MENT n.; deprive of power to injure; pacify hostility or suspicions of. [f. F désarmer (DIS-, ARM²)]

disarrǎnge′ (-j), v.t. Put into disorder, disorganize. Hence ~MENT (-jm-) n. [DIS-]

disarray′, n., & v.t. (Throw into) disorder (poet.) unclothe. [DIS-]

disǎrtic′ulāte, v.t. Separate, undo the articulation of, take to pieces. Hence ~ATION n. [DIS-]

disavow′, v.t. Say one does not know or approve of, repudiate. Hence ~AL(2) n. [f. F désavouer (DIS-, AVOW)]

disassimilā′tion, n. (physiol.). Conversion of assimilated into less complex or waste substances. [DIS-]

disassociā′tion, n. = DISSOCIATION (esp. in psych. senses: ~ of a personality). [DIS-]

disas′ter (-zah-), n. Sudden or great misfortune, calamity; ill luck (a record of ~er). So ~ROUS a., ~ROUSLY² adv., (-zah-). [f. F désastre (DIS-, astre t. L f. Gk astron star)]

disbelieve′, v.t. & i. Refuse credence to (person or statement etc.); be a sceptic; have no faith in. So DISBELIEF′ n. [DIS-]

‖ disběnch′, v.t. Deprive of status of bencher. [DIS-, BENCH n.]

disbranch′ (-ah-), v.t. Strip of branches. [DIS-]

disbúd′, v.t. (-dd-). Remove (esp. the superfluous) buds of. [DIS-]

disbúrd′en, v.t. Relieve of or of a burden; get rid of, discharge, (load, thoughts). [DIS-]

disbūrse′, v.t. & i. Expend, defray; pay money. Hence ~MENT (-sm-) n. [f. OF desbourser (DIS-, BOURSE)]

disc. Now usu. spelling of DISK.

discǎl′ceāte, a. & n., discǎl′cĕāted, discǎl′cĕāted (-st), aa. Barefooted or only sandalled (friar, nun). [-ed anglicized f. L DIS(calceatus p.p. of calceare f. calceus shoe)]

discǎrd′, v.t. & i., & n. 1. Throw out or reject from hand at cards (specified card, or abs. of playing non-trump that does not follow lead); cast aside, give up, (clothes, habit, belief, etc.); dismiss, cashier. 2. n. (dis′-). ~ing at cards, ~ed card. [DIS-, CARD²]

discǎr′nate, a. Parted from the flesh, disembodied. [DIS-, (IN)CARNATE]

discern′ (-s-, -z-), v.t. & i. 1. (Arch.) distinguish, see the difference between, (good & bad, good from bad, between good & bad). 2. Perceive clearly with the mind or senses, make out by thought or by gazing, listening, etc.; so ~IBLE a.,

For compounds of dis- not given consult DIS-.

~**ibary²** adv. [f. F *discerner* f. L DIS(*cernere*, *cret-* sift)]

discern'ing (-s-, -z-), a. Having quick or true insight, penetrating. [-ING²]

discern'ment (-s-, -z-), n. Discerning; keenness of perception, penetration, insight. [-MENT]

discerp'tible, a. That can be plucked apart, not indestructibly one. Hence **discerptibil'ITY** n. [f. L DIS(*cerpere -cerpt-* = *carpere* pluck) + -IBLE]

discerp'tion, n. Pulling apart, severance; severed piece. [f. L *discerptio* (prec., -ION)]

discharge¹, v.t. & i. Relieve of load (ship etc.): *~ gun*, fire it off; *~ bankrupt*, relieve him of further liability), withdraw electricity from; dismiss, cashier; (*was ~d from*, or rarely *~d, the service*); release (prisoner), let go (patient, jury); put forth, get rid of, send out, emit, unload from ship, (cargo, missile, liquid, purulent matter, *abscess, has ~d*); (of river, refl. or intr.) disembogue; (Law) cancel (order of court); acquit oneself of, pay, perform, (duty, debt, vow); (Dyeing) remove (colour), undye (fabric). [f. OF *descharger* (DIS-, CHARGE²)]

discharg'er², n. In vbl senses; esp. appliance for producing electric discharge. [-ER¹]

disci'ple, n. One of Christ's personal followers, esp. one of the Twelve; any early believer in Christ; follower; any adherent, of any leader of thought, art, etc. Hence ~SHIP (-ŝh-) n, **discip'ular** a. [OE *discipul* f. L *discipulus* (*discere* learn)]

disciplinar'ian, n. Maintainer of discipline (*strict, good, poor, no, ~*). [as foll.+ -AN]

dis'ciplinary (also -īn-), a. Of, promoting, discipline; of the nature of mental training. [f. med. L *disciplinarius* (foll., -ARY)]

dis'cipline¹, n. Branch of instruction (arch.); mental & moral training, adversity as effecting this; military training, drill, (arch.); trained condition; order maintained among schoolboys, soldiers, prisoners, etc.; system of rules for conduct; control exercised over members of church; chastisement; (Eccl.) mortification by penance. So **dis'ciplin²** (or -īn'-) a. [F, f. L *disciplina* (*discipulus* DISCIPLE, -INE²)]

dis'cipline², v.t. Bring under control, train to obedience & order, drill, whence ~ABLE a.; chastise. [f. med. L (*-nare*) as prec.]

disclaim', v.t. & i. Renounce legal claim to, renounce claim; disown, disavow, (authorship, character). [AF *desclamer* (DIS-, CLAIM¹)]

disclaim'er, n. Act of disclaiming, renunciation, disavowal. [AF (= prec. as n., -ER¹)]

disclose' (-z), v.t. Remove cover from, expose to view, make known, reveal. [f. OF *desclore* (DIS-, L *claudere claus-* shut)]

disclō'sure (-zher), n. Disclosing; thing disclosed. [-URE]

discŏb'olus, n. (pl. -ī). Ancient quoit-thrower; statue of one in act of throwing. [L, f. Gk *diskobolos* (*diskos* stone or metal quoit, *-bolos* -throwing f. *ballō* throw)]

dis'coid, a. Disk-shaped. [f. L f. Gk *diskoeidēs* (prec., -OID)]

discol'our (-kŭler), v.t. & i. Change or spoil the colour of, stain, tarnish; become stained etc. Hence or cogn. **discolo(u)ra'-TION**(-kŭlerā'-), n. [f. OF *descolorer* f. L DIS(*colorare* COLOUR²)]

discomfit (-kŭm-), v.t. Defeat in battle; thwart, disconcert. So ~URE n. [orig. p.p. = defeated f. OF *desconfit* f. L DIS(*confectus* p.p. see CONFECTION) undone]

discom'fort (-kŭm-), n. & v.t. Uneasiness of body or mind; want of comfort; (vb) make uneasy. [f. OF *desconfort(er)* (DIS-, COMFORT)]

discommode', v.t. Put to inconvenience, incommode. So ~URE n. [DIS- + obs. *commode* f. L *commodare* (*com- modus* see COMMODE]

discommon', v.t. ‖ Debar (tradesman) from serving undergraduates; enclose (common land). [DIS-, COMMON.¹,²]

‖ **discommons** (-z), v.t. Deprive (member of college) of commons; discommon (tradesman) [DIS-, COMMONS]

discompose' (-z), v.t. Disturb composure of, ruffle, agitate. Hence ~ēdix², ~'ingix² (-z-), adv., **discompō'sure** (-zher) n. [DIS-]

disconcert', v.t. Derange, spoil, upset, (plan, concerted measures); disturb self-possession of, ruffle, fluster. Hence ~MENT n. [f. obs. F DIS(*concerter* CONCERT²)]

disconnect', v.t. Sever the connexion of (thing *from, with*, another) or between. [DIS-]

disconnec'ted, a. In vbl senses; esp. (of speech or writing) incoherent, with bad connexion or transitions, whence ~IY² adv. ~NESS n. [-ED¹]

disconnexion, -ction (-kshn), n. Disconnecting; want of connexion, disconnectedness. [DIS-]

discon'solate (-lit), a. Forlorn, inconsolable, unhappy, disappointed. Hence ~IY² (-li) adv. [f. med. L DIS(*consolatus* p.p. of L *consolari* CONSOLE¹)]

discontent', n., a., & v.t. **1.** Dissatisfaction, want of contentment; grievance. **2.** adj. (rare). Not content, dissatisfied, (*with*). **3.** v.t. (Usu. in p.p.) make dissatisfied; hence ~**EDLY**[2] adv., ~**EDNESS**, ~**MENT**, nn. [DIS-, CONTENT[2,3,4]]

discontig'uous, a. (With parts) not in contact. [DIS-]

discontin'ūe, v.t. & i. (Cause to) cease; cease from, give up, (*doing*, habit etc.); cease taking, paying (newspaper, subscription). So ~**ANCE** n. [f. F *discontinuer* f. med. L DIS(*continuare* CONTINUE)]

discontin'ūous, a. Wanting continuity in space or time, having interstices, intermittent. Hence or cogn. **discontinū'ITY** n., ~**LY**[2] adv. [f. med. L DIS(*continuous* CONTINUOUS) + -OUS]

dis'cŏrd[1], n. **1.** Disagreement, variance, strife; harsh noise, clashing sounds; whence or cogn. **discŏrd'ANT**[a], **discŏrd'ANCE** n., **discŏrd'antly**[2] adv. **2.** (Mus.) want of harmony between notes sounded together; chord unpleasing or unsatisfactory in itself & requiring to be resolved by another; any interval except unison, octave, perfect fifth and fourth, major & minor third & sixth, & their octaves; single note dissonant with another. [f. OF *descord* (foll.)]

discŏrd'[2], v.i. Disagree, quarrel, be different or inconsistent, (*with*, *from*); be dissonant, jar, clash. [f. OF *descorder* f. L *discordare* f. DIS (*cors-cord-* heart)]

dis'count[1], n. Deduction from amount due or price of goods in consideration of its being paid promptly or in advance; deduction from amount of bill of exchange etc. by one who gives value for it before it is due; discounting; allowance for exaggeration in accepting story; *at a ~*, below par, depreciated, not in demand. [f. 16th-c. F *descompte* (foll.)]

discount'[2], v.t. Give or get present worth of (bill not yet due); leave out of account; lessen, detract from; part with for immediate but smaller good; allow for exaggeration in; use up effect of (news etc.) beforehand, stale by anticipation. Hence ~**ABLE** a. [f. OF *desconter*, *-compter* f. med.L DIS(*computare* f. COMPUTE)]

discount'enance, v.t. Refuse to countenance, discourage, show disapproval of. [f. obs. F *descontenancer* (DIS-, COUNTE-NANCE[2])]

discou'ragle (-kŭ-), v.t. Deprive of courage, confidence, or energy; deter *from*; dissuade *from*. Hence ~**EMENT** n., ~**ingLY**[2] adv., (-kŭrĭj-). [f. OF *descoragier* (DIS-, COURAGE)]

dis'course[1] (-ōrs), n. Talk, conversation, (arch.); dissertation, treatise, sermon. [f. F *discours* f. L DIS(*cursus* COURSE[1])]

discourse'[2] (-ōrs), v.i. & t. Talk, con-

verse; hold forth in speech or writing on a subject (*of*, *upon*, or abs.); give forth (some kind of music; ref. to *Hamlet* III. ii. 374). [f. prec.]

discourt'ēous, a., **discourt'esў**, n.,(-kēr-, -kŏr-). Rude(ness), uncivil, incivility. [DIS-]

Hence **discourt'ēously**[2] adv. [DIS-]

disco'ver (-kŭ-), v.t. Disclose, expose to view, reveal, make known, exhibit, manifest, betray; (Chess) ~ *check*, check by removing piece or pawn; find out (fact etc., *that* etc., unknown country), suddenly realize, whence or cogn. ~**ABLE** a., ~**ER**[1] n. [f. OF *descovrir* f. med. L DIS(*cooperire* COVER[1])]

disco'vert (-kŭ-), a. (legal). Unmarried or widowed (of woman). [f. OF *descovert* p.p. (prec.)]

disco'verў (-kŭ-), n. Revealing, disclosure, (in Law, compulsory disclosure by party to action of facts or documents on which he relies; in play, poem, etc., revelation unravelling plot); finding out, making known; thing found out. [f. DISCOVER on anal. of RECOVERY (OF *recovrée*, OF for *discovery* being *descoverte*)]

discrĕd'it[1], n. Loss of repute, thing involving this; doubt, lack of credibility, (*throws* ~ *upon*); loss of commercial credit. [DIS-]

discrĕd'it[2], v.t. Refuse to believe; bring disbelief or disrepute upon. [DIS-]

discrĕd'itable, a. Bringing discredit, shameful. Hence ~**LY**[2] adv. [DIS-]

discreet', a. Judicious, prudent, circumspect, not speaking out at inopportune times. Hence ~**LY**[2] adv. [f. F *discret* f. L DIS(*cretus* p.p. of *cernere* sift) separate, with LL sense f. its derivative *discretio* discernment]

dis'crĕpant (or -rĕp'-), a. Different, inconsistent, (of stories etc.). So **discrĕp'-ANCY** n. [f. L DIS(*crepare* sound), -ANT]

dis'crēte, a. Separate, individually distinct, discontinuous, (Metaphys.) abstract, not concrete. Hence ~**NESS** (-tn-) n. [f. L *discretus* see DISCREET]

discrē'tion, n. Liberty of deciding as one thinks fit, absolutely or within limits (*it is within one's ~ to*; *at the ~ of*, to be settled or disposed of by the wish of; *at ~*, unconditionally), whence ~**ARY**[1] (-sho-) a.; discernment, prudence, judgement, (*years*, *age*, *of* ~, time at which one is fit to manage oneself—in Eng. law, 14; ~ *is the better part of valour*, used as joc. excuse for cowardice). [f. OF *discrecion* f. L *discretionem* (DISCREET, -ION)]

discrim'inate, v.t. & i. Be, set up, or observe, a difference between (also intr. with *between*), distinguish *from* another; make a distinction (~*ate against*, distinguish unfavourably, of taxes etc.), observe distinctions carefully. So ~**A'TION**

For compounds of *dis-* not given consult DIS-.

n., ~ATIVE a. [f. L *discriminare* (*discrimen* distinction f. *discernere* DISCERN)-ATE³]

discrim´inating, a. In vbl senses; esp.: discerning, acute; ~ *duty, rate*, varying in amount according to country sending goods or person rated, differential. [-ING²]

discrown´, v.t. Take crown from, depose, (sovereign lit. or fig.). [DIS-]

discur´sive, a. Rambling, digressive, expatiating; proceeding by argument, not intuitive. Hence ~LY², (-vi) adv., ~NESS (-vi-) n. [f. L DIS(*currere cursu-* run), -IVE]

dis´cus, n. Heavy disk thrown in ancient Roman & Greek athletic exercises & modern Olympic Games & other sports. [L f. Gk *diskos* quoit]

discuss´, v.t. Examine by argument, debate, whence ~IBLE a.; consume with enjoyment (food, wine, meal). [f. L DIS(*cutere -cuss- = quatere* shake)]

discu´ssion (-shn), n. Examination by argument; examination; consumption with enjoyment of food. [OF f. L *discussionem* (prec., -ION)]

disdain´, n., & v.t. Scorn, (regard with) contempt; think beneath oneself (*to do, doing*, or noun) or one's notice. Hence ~FUL a., ~fully² adv. [f. OF *desdeignen* f. L DE(*dignare* f. *dignus* worthy)]

disease´ (-zez), n. Morbid condition of body, plant, or some part of them, illness, sickness; any particular kind of this with special symptoms & name; deranged or depraved state of mind or morals. [f. OF *desaise* (AISE n.)]

diseased´ (-zēzd), a. Affected with disease; morbid, depraved. [p.p. of obs. *disease* vb f. OF *desaisier* as prec.]

disembark´, v.t. & i. Put, go, ashore. Hence disembarka´tion n. [f. F *desembarquer* (DIS-, EMBARK)]

disembā´rrass, v.t. Free from embarrassment, rid or relieve (*of*); disentangle (*from*). Hence ~MENT n. [DIS-]

disembod´y, v.t. Separate, free, (soul, idea) from body or the concrete; disband (troops). Hence ~IMENT n. [DIS-]

disembogue´ (-g), v.t. & i. (Of river etc.) pour forth at mouth (intr. or *itself*, waters, etc.); (fig.) discharge, pour forth, (f. & i. of speech, crowd, etc.). [f. Sp. *desembocar* (DIS-, en in, *boca* mouth)]

disembos´om (-ŏoz-), v.t. Disclose, reveal; unburden oneself, make confidences. [DIS-]

disembow´el, v.t.(-ll-). Remove entrails of, rip up so as to cause bowels to protrude. Hence ~MENT n. [DIS-]

disembroil´, v.t. Extricate from confusion or entanglement. [DIS-]

disenchant´ (-ah-), v.t. Free from enchantment or illusion. Hence ~MENT n. [f. F *desenchanter* (DIS-, ENCHANT)]

disencum´ber, v.t. Free from encumbrance. [f. F *desencombrer* (DIS-, ENCUMBER)]

disendow´, v.t. Strip (esp. Church) of endowments. Hence ~MENT n. [DIS-]

disengage´, v.t. & i. & n. Detach, liberate, loosen, (Fencing) pass point of sword to other side of opponent's (n. this move-ment); come apart, break contact. [DIS-]

disengaged´ (-jd), a. In vbl senses; esp.: at leisure to attend to any visitor or business that comes; vacant, not be-spoken. [-ED¹]

disengage´ment (-jm-), n. Disengaging; liberation (of chem. component); freedom from ties, detachment; easy natural manner; dissolution of engagement to marry; (Fencing) = DISENGAGE n. [-MENT]

disentail´, v.t. (legal). Free from entail, break the entail of. [DIS-]

disentan´gle (-nggl), v.t. & i. Extricate, free from complications; unravel, un-twist; come clear of tangle. Hence ~MENT (-nggelm-) n. [DIS-]

disenthral(l) (-awl), v.t. (-ll-). Free from bondage. Hence disenthral´MENT (-awl-) n. [DIS-]

disentomb´ (-ōom), v.t. Take out of tomb; unearth, find by research. [DIS-]

disequilib´rium, n. Lack or loss of equilibrium, instability. [DIS-]

disestab´lish, v.t. Undo establishment of; deprive (Church) of State connexion, depose from official position. Hence ~MENT n. [DIS-]

disesteem´ (-ver), n., & v.t. Dislike, disapproval; being disliked (*fall into, be in*, ~); (vb) regard, treat, with ~. [DIS-]

disfea´ture, v.t. Mar features of, disfigure. [DIS-]

disfig´ure (-ger), v.t. Mar beauty of, deform, deface, sully. Hence disfigura´-TION, ~MENT (-germ-), nn. [f. OF *des-figurer* (DIS-, L *figurare* f. *figura* FIGURE)]

disafforest´, v.t. = DISAFFOREST; clear of forests. [f. OF *desforester* (DIS-, FOREST)]

disfran´chise (-iz), v.t. Deprive of citizen rights; deprive (place) of right of sending, (person) of right of voting for, parliamentary representative. Hence ~MENT (-izm-) n. [DIS-, obs. *franchise* vb=ENFRANCHISE]

disfrock´, v.t. Deprive of clerical (garb &) status. [DIS-]

disgrace´¹, n. Loss of favour, downfall from position of honour; ignominy, shame; thing involving dishonour, cause of reproach. Hence ~FUL a., ~fully² adv., ~fulNESS n. (-sf-). [f. F *disgrâce* f. It. *disgrazia* f. med.L DIS(*gratia* GRACE)]

disgrace'², v.t. Dismiss from favour, degrade from position; bring shame or discredit upon; be a disgrace to. [f. F *disgracier* as prec.]

disgrŭn'tled (-ld), a. Discontented, moody. [from 17th c.; DIS-, *gruntle* obs. frequent. of GRUNT]

disguise'¹ (-gīz), v.t. Conceal identity of (~ *oneself*, person or thing, *as* someone or something else, *by doing, with* false beard etc., *in* costume etc.); misrepresent, show in false colours; conceal, cloak, (~ *one's intention, opinion*); ~*d in* or *with drink* or *liquor*, drunk. Hence ~MENT (-īzm-) n. [f. OF *desguiser* (DIS-, Rom. *guisa* GUISE)]

disguise'² (-gīz), n. Use of changed dress or appearance for concealment's sake, disguised condition (*blessing in* ~, one that seems to be a misfortune); garb used to deceive; artificial manner, deception. [f. prec.]

disgust'¹, n. Loathing, nausea, repugnance, strong aversion, (*at, for, towards, against*). [f. 16th-c. F *desgoust* (DIS-, L *gustus* taste)]

disgust'², v.t. Excite loathing, aversion, or indignation, in (~*ed with, at, by*). Hence ~ēdLY², ~īngLY² adv. [f. 16th-c. F *desgouster* (DIS-, L *gustare* taste)]

disgust'ful, a. Disgusting, repulsive; (of contempt, curiosity, etc.) inspired by, full of, disgust. [-FUL]

dish¹, n. Shallow flat-bottomed usu. oval or oblong vessel of earthenware, glass, or metal, for holding food at meals; food so held, particular kind of food (SIDE~; *made* ~, of various ingredients; *standing* ~, that appears daily, also fig.); || (arch.) cup, esp. ~ *of tea*, tea-drinking; whence ~ *of gossip*, a chat; ~-*shaped* receptacle used for any purpose; ~-*cover*, of metal etc. for keeping food in ~ hot; ~-*cloth* & (arch.) -*clout*, for washing ~es & plates; ~-*wash*, ~-*water*, in which ~es have been washed; ~-*washer*, water wagtail. [OE *disc* (cf. G *tisch* table) f. L *discus* DISK]

dish², v.t. & i. Put (food) into dish ready for serving; ~ *up*, serve meal, (fig.) present (facts, argument) attractively; make concave or dish-shaped; (of horse) move fore-feet not straight but with scooping motion; circumvent, outmanoeuvre, (esp., Pol.) defeat (opponents by adopting their policy (~*ing the Whigs*, of Reform Bill 1867). [f. prec.]

dishabille' (-sŏbēl), n. Being negligently or partly dressed, undress, (usu. *in* ~; undress garment or costume. [f. F *déshabillé* p.p. of *déshabiller* (DIS-, *habiller* clothe f. *habile* ready, ABLE)]

dishabit'ūate (-s-h-), v.t. Make (person) unaccustomed (*for* etc.). [DIS-]

dishărm'onize (-s-h-), v.t. Put out of harmony, make discordant. [DIS-]

dishărm'ony (-s-h-), n. Discord, dissonance. So **dishărmon'ious** a. [DIS-]

dishear'ten (-s-h-), v.t. Make despondent, rob of courage. Hence ~MENT n. [DIS-]

dishē'rison (-s-h-), n. Disinheriting. [f. OF *disheritison* (DIS-, *hereditare* f. *heres* heir, -ATION, -SON)]

dishēv'elled (-ld), a. With disordered hair; (of hair) loose, flung about, unconfined; (of person) untidy, ruffled, unkempt. Hence **dishēv'el**MENT n. [f. OF *descheveté* (DIS-, OF *chevel* hair f. L *capillus*, p.p. suf. -é)]

dishŏn'est (-sŏ-), a. Fraudulent, knavish, insincere, (of person, act, statement). Hence ~LY² adv. [f. OF *deshoneste* f. L DE(*honestus* HONEST)]

dishŏn'esty (-sŏ-), n. Want of honesty, knavery, deceitfulness, fraud. [f. OF *desonesté* f. L DIS*honestus* after *honestadem* HONESTY]

dishŏn'our¹ (-s-ŏner), n. State of shame or disgrace, discredit; thing that involves this; refusal to honour cheque, bill of exchange, etc. [f. OF *deshonor* (DIS-, L *honorem* HONOUR¹)]

dishŏn'our² (-s-ŏner), v.t. Treat with indignity; violate chastity of; disgrace; refuse to accept or pay (cheque, bill of exchange). [f. OF *deshonnorer* f. LL DIS-(*honorare* L=HONOUR²)]

dishŏn'ourable (-s-ŏner-), a. Involving disgrace, ignominious; unprincipled, base, against dictates of honour. Hence ~leNESS n., ~LY² adv. [DIS-]

dishŏrn' (-s-h-), v.t. Cut off horns of. [DIS-]

dishouse' (-s-h-), v.t. Deprive (population etc.) of house(s). [DIS-]

disillu'sion, n., & v.t., **disillu'sionize**, v.t., (-ōōzho-). Disenchant(ment), free(dom) from illusions. Hence ~MENT n. [DIS-, -IZE]

disinclinā'tion, n. Want of liking or willingness (*for* or *to* course, *to* do). [DIS-]

disincline', v.t. Make indisposed (*to do, for* or *to* course). [DIS-]

disincŏr'pŏrāte, v.t. Dissolve (corporate body). [DIS-]

disinfĕct', v.t. Cleanse (room, clothes, etc.) of infection. Hence or cogn. **disinfĕc'tant**(2) a. & n., **disinfĕc'tion** n. [DIS-]

disingĕn'ūous (-j-), a. Insincere, having secret motives, not candid. Hence ~LY² adv., ~NESS n. [DIS-]

disinhĕr'it, v.t. Reject as heir, deprive of inheritance. Hence ~ANCE n. [DIS-, *inherit* in obs. sense *make heir*]

disin'tĕgrāte, v.t. & i. Separate into component parts, deprive of or lose cohesion. Hence ~A'TION, ~ātor²(2), nn. [DIS-]

For compounds of *dis-* not given consult DIS-.

disinter', v.t. (-rr-). Unbury, exhume; unearth. Hence ~MENT n. [f. DIS-, INTER-¹]

disin'terest, n. [DIS-]

disin'terest, v.t. & refl. To divest of interest, (refl.) cease to concern oneself (esp. in Diplom.), renounce intention or right of intervening etc.). [DIS-]

disin'terested, a. Not biased by self-seeking, impartial; ~ management (of public house by manager who does not profit by sale of liquor). Hence ~LY adv., ~NESS n. [DIS-]

disinvest'ment, n. Realization of a country's assets abroad. [DIS-]

disjecta mēm'bra, n. pl. Fragments, scattered remains. [L]

disjoin', v.t. Separate, disunite, part. [f. OF desjoindre f. L DIS(jungere junct- join)]

disjoint', v.t. Dislocate, disturb working or connexion of (p.p., esp. of talk, incoherent, desultory, whence ~edly² adv., ~edness n.); take in pieces at the joints. [f. obs. disjoint adj. f. p.p. of OF as prec.]

disjunc'tion, n. Disjoining, separation. [f. L disjunctio (DISJOIN, -TION)]

disjunc'tive, a.&n. Disjoining, separation; (Log., Gram.) alternative (adj.), involving choice between two words etc., (n., ~) proposition or conjunction). Hence ~LY² (-vi-) adv. [f. L disjunctivus (DISJOIN, -IVE)]

disk, disc, n. Thin circular plate (e.g. coin); round flat or apparently flat surface (sun's ~) or mark; round flattened part in body, plant, etc. [f. L f. Gk diskos quoit]

dislike', v.t. & n. 1. Not like, have aversion or objection to. 2. n. Aversion (to, of, for). [DIS-]

dis'locate, v.t. Put out of joint (limb, or fig. machinery, affairs); (Geol.) make (strata) discontinuous; displace. So **dislocaᵀᴵᴼN** n. [f. med.L DIS(locare L= place), -ATE³]

dislodge', v.t. Remove, turn out, (esp. fortified enemy) from position. Hence ~(e)'MENT (-jm-) n. [f. OF desloger (DIS-, LODGE v.)]

disloy'al, a. Unfaithful to or to friendship etc.; untrue to allegiance, disaffected to government, whence ~NESS(2) n. & a. Hence or cogn. ~LY² adv., ~TY n. [f. OF desloial (DIS-, LOYAL)]

dis'mal (-z-), a., **dis'mals**, n. pl. Depressing, miserable, sombre, dreary; hence ~LY² adv., ~NESS n.; the ~ science, political economy; the ~s, low spirits, dumps. [orig. noun f. L f. dies mali ill days: these were two special days in each month in medieval calendars]

disman'tle, v.t. Strip of covering, protection, etc.; deprive (fortress, ship, etc.) of defences, rigging, equipment. Hence ~MENT (-jm-) n. [f. obs. F desmanteler (DIS-, MANTLE n.)]

dismast' (-ah-), v.t. Deprive (ship) of mast(s). [DIS-]

dismay', v.t., & n. (fill with) consternation, discouragement. [prob. thr. OF f. DIS-+OHG magan be powerful (MAY v.)]

dismĕm'ber, v.t. Tear or cut limb from limb; partition (empire, country), divide up. Hence ~MENT n. [f. OF desmembrer

dismiss', v.t. & n. Send away, disperse, disband, (assembly, army); Mil., imperat., word of command closing drill, also as n., the ~, release at end of drill); allow to go; discharge, cashier, from service or office (usu. ~ed the, or from the, army); send away from one's presence; put out of one's thoughts, cease to feel; treat (subject) summarily; (Law) send out of court, refuse further hearing to, (cease); (Cricket; of batsman) send (ball), send ball of (bowler, usu. to boundary or for four etc.), (of fielding side) put (batsman, side) out (usu. for score). Hence ~AL(2), (now rare) **dismiss'ion** (-shn), nn., ~IBLE a. [prob. f. L DI(mittere miss- send) with dis- due to obs. dismit f. OF desmettre in same sense]

dismount', v.t. & n. Alight, cause to alight, from or from horseback etc. (n. alighting); (Law) unseat, unhorse, (of horse) send (ball) ... remove (thing) from its mount (esp. gun from carriage).

disobē'dience, n., **disobē'dient**, a. Disobeying (~ to orders, master, etc.), rebellious(ness), rule-breaking. Hence **disobē'diently²** adv. [f. OF (dés-), see DIS-, OBEDIENCE, OBEDIENT]

disobey' (-bā), v.i. & t. Disregard orders, break rules; not obey (person, law). [f. F désobéir (DIS-, OBEY)]

disoblige', v.t. Refuse to consult convenience or wishes of. Hence ~ING² a., ~INGNESS n. [f. OF désobliger (DIS-, OBLIGE)]

disor'der, v.t. Disarrange, throw into confusion; put out of health, upset. [assim. to ORDER v. of earlier disordain f. OF désordener (DIS-, ORDAIN)]

disor'derly, a. 1. Untidy, confused; irregular, unruly, riotous; hence ~INESS n. 2. Constituting public nuisance (~ house, bawdy, gaming, or betting, -house). [DISORDER¹, -LY²]

disor'ganize, v.t. Destroy system etc. of, throw into confusion. Hence ~Aᵀᴵᴼn n. [f. F désorganiser (DIS-, ORGANIZE)]

disō'rientate, v.t. Place (church) with chancel not directly eastwards; confuse (person) as to his bearings (lit. & fig.). Hence ~Aᵀᴵᴼn n. [DIS-]

disown' (-ōn), v.t. Refuse to recognize, repudiate, disclaim; renounce allegiance to. [DIS-]

dispa'ragle, v.t. Bring discredit on, lower; speak slightingly of, depreciate. So ~EMENT (-ijm-) n., ~ingly² (-ij-) adv. [f. OF *desparagier* marry unequally (DIS-, *parage* equality f. L *par* equal, -AGE]

dis'parate, a. & n. 1. Essentially different, diverse in kind, incommensurable, without relation; hence ~LY² (-tl-) adv., ~NESS (-tn-) n. 2. n. (usu. pl.) Thing(s) so unlike that there is no basis for comparison. [f. L DIS(*paratus* p.p. of *parare* provide separate, influenced in sense by L *dispar* unequal]

dispa'rity, n. Inequality, difference, incongruity. [f. F DIS(*parité* PARITY]

dispärk', v.t. Convert (park-land) to other uses. [DIS-]

dispärt', n. (gunnery). Difference between semidiameters of gun at base-ring and at muzzle, to be allowed for in aiming; sight making the allowance. [?]

dispart'², v.t. & i. (poet.). Separate, part asunder, (t. & i.); go in different directions; distribute. [f. L dis(*partire* t. *pars* part) distribute]

dispa'ssionate (-sho-), a. Free from emotion, calm, impartial. Hence ~LY² (-tl-) adv., ~NESS (-tn-) n. [DIS-]

dispätch'¹, dés-, v.t. & i. Send off to a destination or for a purpose; give the death-blow to, kill; get (task, business) promptly done, settle, finish off; eat (food, meal) quickly; (arch.) make haste. [f. Sp. *despachar* expedite (DIS-, L *pactus* p.p. of *pangere* fasten); not connected w. F *dépêcher*]

dispätch'², dés-, n. Sending off (of messenger, letter, etc.); putting to death (*happy ~*, suicide as practised by Japanese); prompt settlement of business, promptitude, efficiency, rapidity; written message, esp. official communication on State affairs (~*box*, for carrying these & other documents); agency for conveying goods etc.; ~*rider*, esp. motorcyclist or horseman carrying military messages. [f. prec.]

dispel', v.t. (-ll-). Dissipate, disperse, (fears, darkness). [f. L DIS(*pellere* drive)]

dispen'sable, a. That can be relaxed in special cases (canon, law, oath); not necessary, that can be done without. [f. med. L *dispensabilis* (DISPENSE, -ABLE]

dispen'sary, n. Place, esp. charitable institution, where medicines are dispensed; apothecary's shop. [DISPENSE, -ARY¹]

dispensa'tion, n. Distributing, dealing out; ordering, management, esp. of the world by Providence; arrangement made by Nature or Providence; special dealing of Providence with community or person; religious system prevalent at a period (*Mosaic, O.T., Christian, ~*); exemption from penalty or duty laid down in esp. eccl. law (*with, from*); doing without (*with*). [f. L *dispensatio* (foll., ATION]

dispénse', v.t. & i. 1. Distribute, deal out; administer (sacrament, justice); make up & give out (medicine); grant dispensations; release *from* obligation. 2. ~ *with*: relax, give exemption from, (rule); annul binding force of (oath); do without. Hence **dispén'sER¹** n.. (esp.) professional maker-up of medical prescriptions. [f. OF *dispenser* f. L *dispensare* frequent. of DIS(*pendĕre* pens- weigh]

dispeo'ple (-pēp-), v.t. Depopulate. [f. OF *despeupler* f. L DIS(*populare* f. *populus* people]

dispérsle', v.t. & i. Scatter(t. & i.), drive, go, throw or send, in different directions, rout, dispel, be dispelled; send to or station at separate points; put in circulation, disseminate; (Opt.) divide (white light) into its coloured rays. Hence ~AL(2) n., ~ĕdLY² adv., ~IVE a., ~iveLY² adv., ~iveNESS n. [f. F *disperser* f. L DI¹(*spergere* spers- *spargere* scatter)]

dispér'sion (-shn), n. Dispersing (see prec.); *the D~*, the Jews dispersed among Gentiles after Captivity. [f. L *dispersio* (prec., -ION]

dispi'rit, v.t. Make despondent, depress. Hence ~ĕdLY² adv. [DIS-]

dispi'teous, a. Pitiless. [19th-c. revival of 16th-c. *despiteous* (DESPITE]

displace', v.t. Shift from its place (~*d persons*, (esp.) forced and slave labourers of Nazis); remove from office; oust, take the place of, put something else in the place of, replace. [f. OF *desplacer* (DIS-, PLACE n.]

displace'ment (-sm-), n. Displacing, being displaced; amount by which thing is shifted from its place; ousting, replacement by something else; amount or weight of fluid displaced by solid floating or immersed in it (*a ship with a ~ of 11,000 tons*). [prec., -MENT]

display'¹, v.t. Exhibit, expose to view, show; show ostentatiously; reveal, betray, allow to appear. [f. OF *despleier* f. L DIS(*plicare* fold) cf. DEPLOY]

display'², n. Displaying; exhibition, show; ostentation; (Print.) arrangement of type with a view to calling attention. [f. prec.]

displease' (-z), v.t. Offend, annoy, make indignant or angry, be disagreeable to; be ~*ed* (*at, with*, or abs), disapprove, be indignant or dissatisfied. Hence ~ING² a., ~ingLY² adv., (-zi-). [f. OF *desplaisir* (DIS-, L *placēre* please]

displea'sure (-lĕzher), n., & v.t. Displeased feeling, dissatisfaction, disapproval, anger; (vb) cause ~ to, annoy. [f. OF as prec., assim. to PLEASURE]

For compounds of *dis-* not given consult DIS-.

displume' (-ōōm), v.t. (poet.), Strip of feathers, lit. & fig. [DIS-]

dispôrt', v.refl. &i., &n.(arch.). 1. Frolic, gambol, enjoy oneself, display oneself sportively. 2. n. Relaxation, pastime. [f. OF desporter f. DIS-, L portare carry]

dispôs'able (-zǎ-), a. That can be disposed of, got rid of, made over, or used; at disposal. Hence ~BIL'ITY n. [DISPOSE, -ABLE]

dispôse' (-z), v.t. & i. 1. Place suitably, at intervals, or in order; bring (person, mind) into certain state (esp. in p.p. well, ill, ~d); incline, make willing or desirous, to something or to do; give (thing) tendency to; determine course of events (man proposes, God ~s). 2. ~ of: do what one will with, regulate; get off one's hands, stow away, settle, finish, kill, demolish (claim, argument, opponent), dismiss (cricket XI for certain score), consume (food); sell. [f. OF DIS(poser see POSE¹) substituted for L disponere thr. such derivatives as foll.]

disposi'tion (-zĭ-), n. 1. Setting in order, arrangement, relative position of parts; (usu. pl.) plan, preparations, stationing of troops ready for attack, defence, etc.; ordinance, dispensation, (a ~ of Providence etc.); bestowal by deed or will; control, disposal, (at one's ~); bent, temperament, natural tendency; inclination to, (f. f. L DISpositionem f. ponere posit- place]

dispossess' (-zes-), v.t. Oust, dislodge, (person); deprive of; rid (person) of or of evil spirit (obs.). Hence dispossess'ion (-shn), ~OR² (-oz-), nn. [f. OF despossesser f. L DÉpréciare DEPRECIATE]

dispraise' (-z), v.t., & n. Disparage-(ment), censure. [n.f. OF des-preisier f. L DÉpretiare DEPRECIATE]

disproof', n. Refutation; thing that disproves. [DIS-]

dispropor'tion, n. Want of proportion; being out of proportion. Hence ~ED² (-shond) a. [DIS-]

dispropor'tionate (-sho-), a. Wanting proportion; relatively too large or small. Hence ~LY² (-li) adv. [DIS-]

disprove' (-ōov), v.t. (p.p. ~d, rarely ~n). Prove false, show fallacy of, refute. [f. OF desprover (DIS-, PROVE]

dis'putable, a. Open to question, uncertain. Hence ~LY² adv. [f. L disput-abilis (DISPUTE)]

disputa'tion, n. Argument, controversy. [DIS-]

disputa'tious (-shus), a. ~tious n., ~a'tious-ly² adv., ~a'tiousness n., (-shus-). [f. L disputatio (foll., -ATION)]

dispute'¹, v.i. & t. Argue, hold disputation, (with, against, person, on, about,

subject), whence dis'putant(i) n. & a.; quarrel, have altercation, discuss (whether, how, etc.; point, question); controvert, call in question (statement, fact); resist (landing, advance, etc.); contend for, strive to win, (pre-eminence, victory, every inch of ground). [f. OF desputer f. L DIS(putare reckon)]

dispute'², n. Controversy, debate, (in ~, certainly, indisputably); heated contention, quarrel, difference of opinion. [f. prec.]

disqualifica'tion (-ŏl-), n. In vbl senses; esp., thing that disqualifies. [foll., -FICATION]

disqual'ify (-ŏl-), v.t. Unfit, disable, (for some purpose or office); incapacitate legally, pronounce unqualified. [DIS-]

disqui'et, v.t., a., & n. Deprive of peace, worry; (adj.) uneasy, disturbed, whence disqui'etUDE, ~NESS, nn.; (n.) anxiety, unrest. [DIS-]

disquisi'tion (-zĭ-), n. (Arch.) Investigation, inquiry; (mod.) long or elaborate treatise or discourse on subject. Hence ~AL¹ a. [f. L DIS(quisitio f. -quirere -quisit = quaerere seek, -ION)]

disrate', v.t. (naut.). Reduce to lower rating or rank. [DIS-]

disregärd', v.t., & n. 1. Pay no attention to, ignore, treat as of no importance. 2. n. Indifference, neglect (of, for). [DIS-]

disrel'ish, n., & v.t. Dislike, (regard with) distaste, aversion. [DIS-]

disremem'ber, v.t. (dial. etc.), Fail to remember. [DIS-]

disrepair', n. Bad condition for want of repairs (usu. is etc. in ~). [DIS-]

disrep'utable, a. Discreditable; of bad repute, not respectable in character or appearance. Hence ~LENESS (-in-) n., ~LY² adv. [DIS-]

disrepute', n. Ill repute, discredit. [DIS-]

disröbe', v.t. & i. Divest of robe or garment (also fig.); undress (refl. or intr.). [DIS-]

disroot', v.t. Uproot; dislodge. [DIS-]

disrupt', v.t. Shatter, separate forcibly. [19th-c. vb f. L disruptus see foll.]

disrup'tion, n. Bursting asunder, violent dissolution, rent condition; the D~, split in Church of Scotland 1843. So disrup'tive a. [f. L DIS(ruptio f. rumpere rupt- break, -ION]

dissat'isfy, v.t. Fail to satisfy, make discontented (dissatisfied with, at). So dissatisfac'tion n. [DIS-]

dissave', v.t. Spend one's savings. [DIS-]

disseat', v.t. Unseat. [DIS-]

dissect', v.t. Cut in pieces; anatomize, cut up, (animal, plant) to show its structure etc.; examine part by part, analyse,

criticize in detail. Hence or cogn. dis-séc'tion, dissec'tor², nn. [f. L DIS(secare sect- cut)]

disseise', -ze, (-sēz), v.t. Oust, dispossess, of estates (or fig.). [f. OF dessaisir (DIS-, SEIZE]

disseis'in, -zin, (-sēz-), n. (legal). Dis-seising, wrongful dispossession of real property. [f. OF dessaisine (DIS-, SEIZIN]

dissem'ble, v.t. & i. Cloak, disguise, con-ceal, (character, feeling, intention, act); pretend not to see, ignore, (insult etc. arch.); fail to mention (fact); conceal one's motives etc., be a hypocrite, whence ~ER¹, n. [perh. assim. to resemble of obs. dissimule f. OF dissimuler f.L DIS(simulare SIMULATE)]

dissēm'ināte, v.t. Scatter abroad, sow in various places, (lit., seed; usn. fig., doctrines, sedition, etc.). So ~A'TION, ~āTOR², nn. [f. L DIS(seminare f. semen -inis seed), -ATE³]

dissēn'sion (-shn), n. Discord arising from difference in opinion. [F, f. L DIS(sensionem f. sentire sens- feel, -ION]

dissent'¹, v.i. Refuse to assent; disagree, think differently or express such differ-ence (from), ‖ esp. in religious matters from an established church (~ing minister, nonconformist clergyman). Hence ~ing-LY² adv. [f. L DIS(sentire feel]

dissent'², n. (Expression of) difference of opinion; ‖ refusal to accept doctrines of established church, nonconformity, (col-lect.) dissenters. [f. prec.]

dissent'er, n. One who dissents, esp. from a national church; ‖ member of a sect that has separated itself from the Church of England. [-ER¹]

dissen'tient (-shi-, -shnt), a., & n. (One) disagreeing with a majority or official view. [f. L DIS(sentire feel, -ENT]

dissep'iment, n.(bot. & zool.). Partition, septum. [f. L DIS(saepimentum f. saepire f. saepes hedge, -MENT]

dissert', dissert'āte, vv.i. Discourse, give an exposition, disquisition, or dis-serta'TION n. [f. p.p. stems of L DIS(severe sert- join) & its frequent. dissertare, -ATE³]

dissērve', v.t. Do an ill turn to. So dis-SERV'ICE n. [DIS-]

dissēv'er, v.t. & i. Sever, divide. [DIS-]

diss'idence, n. Disagreement, dissent. [f. L dissidentia (foll., -ENCE]

diss'ident, a. & n. Disagreeing, at variance; dissentient (a. & n.); dissenter. [f. L DIS(sidēre = sedēre sit), -ENT]

dissight' (-īt), n. (rare). Unsightly thing, eyesore. [DIS-]

dissim'ilar, a. Unlike (to, also rarely from, with). Hence dissimilā'RITY n., ~LY² adv. [DIS-]

dissim'ilāte, v.t. (philol.). Make unlike (sounds repeating each other, as in cin-namon, orig. cinnamom). Hence ~A'TION n. [f. L DIS(similis like), after ASSIMILATE]

dissimil'itūde, n. Unlikeness. [f. L dissimilitūdo (prec., -TUDE]

dissim'ūlāte, v.t. & i. Pretend not to have or feel (cf. SIMULATE); dissemble, be hypocritical. So ~A'TION, ~āTOR², nn. [f. L DIS(simulare SIMULATE), -ATE³]

diss'ipāte, v.t. & i. Disperse, dispel or disappear, (cloud, vapour, care, fear, darkness); dissolve to atoms, bring or come to nothing; squander (money); fritter away (energy, attention); engage in frivolous or dissolute pleasures (people go there to ~e). Hence ~IVE a. [f. L DIS(sipare throw), -ATE³]

diss'ipātěd, a. In vbl senses; esp., given to dissipation, dissolute. [-ED¹]

dissipā'tion, n. Scattering, dispersion, disintegration; wasteful expenditure, of distraction, want of concentration, of faculties etc.; frivolous amusement; in-temperate or vicious living. [f. L dissi-patio (DISSIPATE, -ION]

dissō'ciālize (-sha-), v.t. Make unsocial, disincline for society. [DIS-, SOCIAL, -IZE]

dissō'ciāte (-shi-), v.t. Disconnect, sepa-rate, in thought or in fact (from); (Chem.) decompose, e.g. by heat; (Psych.) cause (person's mind) to develop more than one centre of consciousness (~āted personality, co-existence of two or more distinct personalities in the same person). So ~A'TION (-si-), n., ~ABLE, ~ATIVE, (-sha-), aa. [f. L DIS(sociare f. socius comrade), -ATE³]

diss'olūble (-ōobl; or disōl'ūbl), a. That can be disintegrated, untied, or discon-nected. Hence ~BIL'ITY (-lōō-) n. [f. L DIS(solubilis SOLUBLE]

diss'olūte (-ōōt), a. Lax in morals, licen-tious. Hence ~LY² adv., ~NESS (-tn-) n. [f. L dissolūtus p.p. (DISSOLVE]

dissolū'tion (-lōō-), n. Disintegration, de-composition; liquefaction (of ice or snow); undoing of bond, partnership, marriage, or alliance; dismissal of assembly, ‖ esp. ending of a Parliament with a view to fresh election; death; coming to an end, fading away, disappearance. [f. L dis-solutio (foll., -ION]

dissolve' (-z-), v.t. & i. Decompose (t. & i.); make or become liquid esp. by im-mersion in liquid (~ed in tears, weeping copiously); relax, enervate; vanish (~ing views, of magic lantern, one fading while another replaces it); disperse (t. & i.), ‖ esp. ~e Parliament or ~e, declare dis-SOLUTION; put an end to (partnership etc.), annul. Hence ~'ABLE a. [f. L DIS(solvere solut- loosen]

diss'olvent (-z-), a. & n. (Thing) that dissolves something (usn. of). [-ENT]

diss'onant, a. Discordant, harsh-toned, incongruous. Hence or cogn. diss'o-

For compounds of dis- not given consult DIS-.

nance n., ~ry² adv. [L. DISsonare sound.]

dissuade' (-swād), v.t. Advise against, deprecate, (action); give advice to hinder, divert, (person from). So dissua'sion (-wēzhn) n., dissua'sive (-sw-) a. [f. L DISsuadere suas- persuade.]

dissyllable etc. See disy- etc.

dissymmet'rical, a., dissymm'etrȳ n. Symmetrical, symmetry, in opposite directions, as in the two corresponding forms.

dis'taff, n. Cleft stick about 3 ft long on which wool or flax was wound for spinning by hand; corresponding part of spinning-wheel; woman's work; ~ side, female branch of family (cf. spear-side for the male). [OE distæf (LG diesse bunch of flax +STAFF)]

dis'tal, a. (anat., bot.). Away from centre of body or point of attachment. [irreg. f. DISTANT. -AL]

dis'tance, n., & v.t. 1. Being far off; remoteness; extent of space between, interval, (within striking~; near enough to deliver blow); avoidance or familiarity, reserve, (esp. keep one's~); distant point (at, to, from, a~); remoter field of vision (in the~; middle~, in painted or actual landscape, between foreground & far part); space of time (at this ~ of time; in adv. phrr.) a good this. ~ off; ~post, used in (obs.) heat-racing, from the winning-post; beaten by a~(by about that~). 2. v.t. Place or make seem far off; leave far behind in race or competition. [f. OF destance f. L distantia]

dis'tant, a. Far, or a specified distance, away or from (three miles~); remote, far apart, in position, time, resemblance, etc. (a ~ likeness, connexion; ~ ages; ~ signal on railway, one in advance of home signal to give warning; not intimate, reserved, cool. Hence ~ly² adv. [f. F f. L distant- part. st. see DISTANCE]

distaste', n. Dislike, repugnance, slight aversion. (for). [DIS-]

distaste'ful (-tf-), a. Disagreeable, repellent, (to). Hence ~NESS n. [-FUL]

distem'per¹, v.t. (arch., usu. in p.p.). Upset, derange, in health or sanity (a ~ed fancy). [f. med. L DIStemperare (a ~)]

distem'per², n. Derangement, an ailment, of body or mind; dog-disease with catarrh, cough, & weakness; political disorder. [f. prec.]

distem'per³, n., & v.t. 1. Method of painting on plaster or chalk with colours mixed with yolk of eggs, size, etc., instead of oil, used for scene-painting & internal walls (paint in~). 2. v.t. Paint (wall etc. or abs.) thus. [f. L as DISTEMPER.¹]

distend', v.t. & i. Swell out by pressure from within (balloon, vein, nostrils, etc.). So disten'sible a., disten'sibil'ity n., ten'sion (-shn), nn. [f. L DIStendere tend- stretch]

dis'tich (-k), n. Pair of verse lines, couplet. [f. L f. Gk DIstichon f. stichos line) neut. adj.]

dis'tichous (-k-), a. (bot.). (Having fruit etc.) arranged in two vertical lines on opposite sides of stem. [f. L f. Gk as prec., -OUS]

distil', v.t. & i. (-ll-). Trickle down; come or give forth in drops, exude; turn to vapour by heat, condense by cold, & recollect (liquid); extract essence of (plant etc., or fig. doctrine etc.); drive (volatile constituent) off or out by heat; make (whisky, essence) by distillation; undergo distillation. So ~la'tion n., ~la'tory a. [f. L f. L DIstillare drop)]

dis'tillate, n. Product of distillation. [as prec., -ATE²]

distill'er, n. One who distils, esp. alcoholic spirit, whence ~ERY(3) n.; apparatus for distilling salt water at sea. [-ER¹]

distinct', a. Not identical, separate, individual, different in quality or kind, unlike, (from, or abs.); clearly perceptible, plain, definite; unmistakable, decided, positive. Hence ~LY² adv., ~NESS n. [f. L distinctus p.p. see DISTINGUISH]

distinc'tion, n. Making of a difference, discrimination, the difference made (~ without a difference, a merely nominal or artificial one); being different; thing that differentiates, mark, name, title; showing of special consideration, mark of honour; distinguished character, excellence, eminence; (of literary style) individuality. [f. f. L distinctionem (DISTINGUISH)]

distinc'tive, a. Distinguishing, characteristic. Hence ~LY² adv., ~NESS [DISTINGUISH, -ION]

distingué (see Ap.), a. Of distinguished air, features, manners, etc. [F]

disting'uish (-nggw-), v.t. & i. Divide into classes etc.; be, see, or point out, the difference of (thing, thing from another; also faint, with between), differentiate, draw distinctions; characterize, be a mark or property of; make out by listening, looking, etc., recognize; make oneself prominent (often by gallantry etc.). Hence ~ABLE a., ~ABLY² adv. [f. L DI'stinguere stinct- extinguish prob. cogn. w. Gk stizō prick), with irreg. use of -ISH²]

disting'uished (-nggwisht), a. In vbl senses; esp. remarkable (for a) by quality etc.), eminent, famous, of high standing; distinc'

distort', v.t. Put out of shape, make crooked or unshapely, (actually or, as by curved mirror etc., apparently); misrepresent (motives, facts, statements). Hence or cogn. ~édly² adv., distor'tion n. (also) lack of clearness and correctness in sounds transmitted by telephone or

wireless, **distor'tional** (-sho-) a. [f. L DIS(torquēre tort- twist)]

distor'tionist (-sho-), n. Caricaturist; acrobat who distorts his body. [-IST]

distract', v.t. Divert, draw away, (attention, the mind, usu. from); draw in different directions, divide or confuse the attention of, (often p.p. with between) bewilder, perplex; (chiefly p.p.) drive mad or infuriate (~ed with, by, at). Hence ~ĕdlY², ~ingly², adv. [f. L DIS(trahere tract- draw)]

distrac'tion, n. Diversion of, thing that diverts, the mind; interruption; lack of concentration; amusement, relief from over-absorption; confusion, perplexity; internal conflict, dissension; frenzy, madness, (to ~, to a mad degree). [f. L distrachio (prec., -ION)]

distrain', v.i. (legal). Levy a distress (upon person or his goods, or abs.), seize chattels to compel person to pay money due (esp. rent) or meet an obligation, or to obtain satisfaction by sale of the chattels. Hence ~ER¹, ~OR², ~EE', ~MENT & (in same sense) **distraint'**, nn. [f. OF destreindre f. L DI¹(stringere strict- squeeze)]

distrait' (-rā) a. (fem. -te, pr. -āt), Absentminded, not attending. [F]

distraught' (-awt), a. (arch.), Violently agitated; crazy. [var. of obs. distract a. f L distrachus p.p. see DISTRACT]

distress'¹, n. Severe pressure of pain, sorrow, etc., anguish; want of money or necessaries; straits, dangerous position; exhaustion, being tired out, breathlessness; (Law) =DISTRAINT; ~-gun, -rocket, -signals from ship in danger; ~-warrant, authorizing distraint. Hence ~FUL a. (the ~ful country, Ireland). [f. OF destrece f. LL district(ia (DISTRAIN, -Y¹)]

distress'², v.t. Subject to severe strain, exhaust, afflict; cause anxiety to, vex, make unhappy. Hence ~ingLY² adv. [f. F destresser f. LL districtiare as prec.]

distrib'ŭtary, n. River branch that does not return to main stream after leaving it (as in a delta). [foll. +-ARY¹]

distrib'ŭte, v.t. Deal out, give share of to each of a number; spread abroad, scatter, put at different points; divide into parts, arrange, classify; (Log.) use (term) in its full extension so that it includes every individual of the class. Hence (orig. -er) ~OR²(1, 2) n., ~ABLE a. [f. L DIS(tribuere tribut- assign)]

distribū'tion, n. Distributing; apportionment; (Pol. Econ.) dispersal among consumers effected by commerce, also extent to which individuals or classes share in aggregate products of community; spreading abroad, dispersing, scattered situation or arrangement; division into parts, arranging, classification; (Log.) application of term to all individuals of the class. Hence ~AL (-sho-) a. [F, f. L distributionem (prec., -ION)]

distrib'ŭtive, a. & n. 1. Of, concerned with, produced by, distribution; (Log., Gram.) referring to each individual of a class, not to the class collectively. 2. n. (Gram.) ~ word (as each, neither, every). Hence ~LY² (-vl-) adv. [F (-if, -ive), f L as DISTRIBUTE, -IVE]

dis'trict, n., & v.t. 1. Territory marked off for special administrative purpose; || division of parish with its own church or chapel & clergyman; || urban or rural division of county with D~ Council; assigned sphere of operations; tract of country with common characteristics, region; ||D~ Railway, serving parts of London & suburbs; || ~ visitor, person working under clergyman's direction in section of parish. 2. v.t. Divide into ~s. [F, f. med. L districtus jurisdiction f. L district- see DISTRAIN]

distrust'¹, n. Want of trust, doubt, suspicion. Hence ~FUL a. (of), ~fulLY² adv. [DIS-]

distrust'², v.t. Have no confidence in, doubt, not rely on. [DIS-]

distûrb', v.t. Agitate, trouble, disquiet, unsettle; perplex. [f. OF destorber f. L DIS(turbare f. turba crowd)]

distûrb'ance, n. Interruption of tranquillity, agitation; tumult, uproar, outbreak; (Law) molestation, interference with rights or property. [f. OF destorbance (prec., -ANCE)]

disūn'ion (-yon), n. Separation, want of union, dissension. So **disunīTE'** v.t. & i. [DIS-]

disūse'¹ (-s), n. Discontinuance, want of use or practice, desuetude. [DIS-]

disūse'² (-z), v.t. Cease to use. [DIS-]

disyll'able, diss-, n. Word, metrical foot, of two syllables. So ~ăb'ic a., ~ăb'icalLY adv. [f. F dissyllabe (DI-², SYLLABLE); -ss- in F as sign of hard sound]

ditch, n., & v.i. & t. 1. Long narrow excavation, esp. to hold or conduct water or serve as boundary; watercourse; the D~, English Channel or North Sea (R.A.F. sl.); DIE² in last ~, stagnant in ~ (esp. dull as ~water), 2. vb. Make or repair ~es (esp. hedging & ~ing), whence ~ER¹ (1, 2) n.; provide with ~es, drain; (sl.) leave in the lurch; (sl., of airman) make forced landing on sea, bring (aircraft) down thus; (pass., of vehicle) stick in a ~. [OE dīc, whence also DIKE]

dī'theism, n. Religious dualism, belief in independent principles of good & evil [DI-²]

dith'er (-dh-), v.i., & n. Tremble, quiver; vacillate. [prob. imit.]

dith'ÿramb (-ăm), n. Greek choric hymn of wild character; Bacchanalian song;

For compounds of *dis-* not given consult DIS-.

vehement or inflated poem, speech, or writing. So **dithyrăm'bic** a. & n. [f. L f. Gk *dithurambos* etym. dub.]

dítt'any, n. A herb, formerly of medicinal repute. [f. OF f. L f. *Dikté* in Crete]

ditt'ŏ, n. & n. (abbr. dᵒ, dᵒ; pl. -os). The aforesaid, the same, (in accounts, inventories, & commerce, or colloq. talk, instead of repeating word); duplicate, similar thing, (~ *suit*, *suit of* ~s, clothes all of one material); *say* ~ *to*, agree with, endorse opinion of. [It. (now *detto*), f. L *dictus* p.p. of *dicere* say]

ditt'ŏgraphy, n. Copyist's mistaken repetition of letter, word, or phrase, cf. HAPLOGRAPHY. Hence **dittográph'ĭc** a. [f. Gk *dittos* double, -GRAPHY]

ditt'y, n. Short simple song. [ME f. OF *dité* f. L f. L *dictātum* neut. p.p. of *dictāre* DICTATE²]

ditt'y-băg, -box, nn. Sailor's, fisherman's, receptacle for odds & ends. [?]

diūrēt'ic, a. & n. (Substance) exciting discharge of urine. [f. L f. Gk *diourētikos* f. *diourēō* make water, -IC]

diūrn'al, a. (Astron.) occupying one day; (arch.) daily, of each day; of the day, not nocturnal. Hence ~LY² adv. [f. L *diurnalis* (*dies* day)]

div (dēv), n. Evil spirit in Persian mythology. [Pers. = Skr. *deva* god]

dī'va (dē-), n. Great woman singer, prima donna. [It. f. L, = goddess]

dīv'agate, v.i. Stray, digress. Hence **divaga'TION** n. [f. L (f.L di¹(*vagari* wander), -ATE³]

dī'valent, a. Combining with two atoms of hydrogen etc., having two combining equivalents. [DI-², L *valēre* be worth, -ENT]

divan', n. Oriental council of State, esp. Turkish privy council; oriental council-chamber, court of justice; long seat against room-wall; smoking-room, cigar-shop. [Turk., f. Pers. *dēwan* brochure, account-book, custom-house(see DOUANE), tribunal, senate, bench]

divă'ricate (or di), v.i. Diverge, branch (of roads, branches, etc.). Hence or cogn. ~A'TION n., ~ATE²(-āt) a. (bot., zool.). [f. L di¹(*varicare* f. *varicus* straddling), -ATE³]

dive, v.i. & n. 1. Plunge, esp. head foremost, into water etc.; (of aircraft) plunge steeply downwards, (of submarine) submerge; go down or out of sight suddenly; put one's hand into water, vessel, pocket; penetrate or search mentally into; *diving-bell*, open-bottomed box or bell in which person can be let down into deep water. 2. n. Plunge, header, swim under water; submerging of submarine, aircraft's steep descent; sudden dash out of sight; *drinking-den; a basement or underground room in which some particular commodity is sold (*oyster* ~); hiding-place or sanctuary for the disreputable; ~-*bomber*, aircraft specially designed to

aim bombs at target by diving towards it and release them while diving, so ~-*bombing* v.t. & i. [mixture of sense of OE *bomb* v.t.&i. [mixture of sense of OE *dūfan* sink with form of OE *dȳfan* immerse]

dīv'er, n. In vbl senses: esp.: person who dives for pearls, to examine sunk ships, etc.; kinds of diving bird. [-ER¹]

divērge' (or di), v.i. & t. Proceed in different directions from point or each other; go aside *from* track; differ, deviate; make ~, deflect. Hence ~GENCE, ~GENCY nn., ~GENT a., ~gently² adv. [f. L f. DI-¹, *vergere* VERGE² v.]

dīv'ers (-z), a. (arch. or joc.). Sundry, several, more than one. [OF, f. L DI-¹ *divi-*]

divērse' (or di-), a. Unlike in nature or qualities; varied, changeful. Hence or cogn. ~LY² (-sl-) adv., **divērs'ĬFORM** a. [as prec.]

divērs'ify (or di-), v.t. Make diverse, vary, modify, variegate. So ~FICA'TION n. [f. OF *diversifier* f. med. L *diversi-*]

divēr'sion (or di-; -shn), n. Deflecting, deviation; diverting of attention, manœuvre to secure this, feint; recreation, distract; entertain, amuse, whence ~ING² a., ~ingly² adv. [f. OF *divertir* f. L di¹-*vertere* & -*vers-* turn in different directions, turn away]

dívertisse'ment (dēvertēs'maht), n. Short ballet etc. between the acts of a play. [F]

Dīv'es (-z), n. (Typical name for) rich man; [[Law] ~ *costs*, costs on higher scale (opp. *pauper costs*). [L, = rich, ref. to *Luke* XVI. 19, where Vulgate has ~]

divēst' (or di-), v.t. Unclothe; strip of garment etc.; deprive, rid, of (~ *oneself of*, abandon). Hence ~MENT, ~TURE, nn. [earlier *devest* f. OF *desvestir* (DIS-, L *vestire* f. *vestis* garment)]

|| **divī'de¹** (or di-), v.t. & i. Separate (t. & i.) into parts, split or break up; make way through, make (way etc.) through; mark out actually or mentally in parts, fall into parts, make classification in, distinguish kinds of; sunder, part, cut off, (things, thing *from*); cause to disagree, set at variance, distract; share *with* others; (Math.) see how often number contains another (~ *20 by 3*), do DIVISION¹, (of number) go into (number)

without remainder; part (t. & i. of House of Parliament, meeting, etc.) into two sets in voting. [f. L DĪ(viděre -vis- ct. *vidua* WIDOW)]

divide'², n. (U.S. etc.). Watershed. [f. prec.]

div'idend, n. (Math.) number to be divided by DIVISOR; sum payable as interest on loan or as profit of joint-stock company (EX ~, CUM ~) or to creditors of insolvent estate; individual's share of it (‖~warrant, order to pay this). [f. F *dividende* f. L *dividendum* (DIVIDE¹, -ND¹)]

divid'er, n. In vbl senses; esp. (pl.) measuring-compasses, esp. those provided with screw for setting to small intervals. [-ER¹]

divi-divi'¹, n. Curved pods of a small tropical-American tree, used in tanning; this tree. [Carib]

divina'tion, n. Divining, insight into or discovery of the unknown or future by supernatural means; skilful forecast, good guess. [OF, f. L *divinationem* (DIVINE², -ATION)]

divine'¹, a. (-er, -est) & n. 1. Of, from, like, God or a god (~ *right of kings*, independent of their subjects' will); devoted to God, sacred, (~ *service*, public worship); superhumanly excellent, gifted, or beautiful; hence ~LY² (-nl-) adv. 2. n. Person (usu. cleric) skilled in theology. [f. OF *devin* f. L *divinus* cf. *divus, deus*, god]

divine'², v.t. & i. Make out by inspiration, magic, intuition, or guessing, foresee, predict, conjecture; practise divination; ~*ing-rod*, see DOWSING. Hence ~ER² (4) n. [f. F *deviner* f. L *divinare* (*divinus* DIVINE¹)]

divin'ity, n. Being divine, godhood; a god, godhead; *the D~*, God; adorable person; theology; University theological faculty; (Bookbind.) ~ *calf* (dark brown with blind TOOLING). [f. OF *devinité* f. L *divinitatem* (DIVINE¹, -TY)]

divi'nize, v.t. Deify. Hence ~A'TION n. [f. F *diviniser* f. *divin*=*devin* DIVINE¹]

divi'sible (-z-), a. Capable of being divided actually or in thought; (Math.) ~ *by*, containing (a number) some number of times without remainder. Hence DIVISIBI'LITY (-z-) n. [f. L *divisi-bilis* (DIVIDE¹, -IBLE)]

divi'sion (-zhn), n. 1. Dividing or being divided, severance; distribution, sharing, (~ *of labour*, time-saving arrangement giving different parts of manufacturing process etc. to different persons). 2. Disagreement, discord. 3. (Math.) process of dividing number by another (*long, short, ~*, methods usual with divisors greater, not greater, than 12). 4. (Log.) classification, enumeration of parts, distinction of meanings. 5. (Parl.) separation of House into two sets for counting votes. 6. Dividing line, boundary; part, section. 7. Administrative etc. district, definite part, under single command, of army or fleet, esp. (Mil.) formation of an army, commanded by a Major-General, and (*infantry ~*) usu. consisting of three infantry brigades, with cavalry (now armoured car regiment), artillery, engineers, signals, R.A.S.C., R.A.M.C., and R.A.O.C.; *airborne, armoured, parachute, ~*. 8. (Nat. Hist.) section of kingdom, order, genus, etc. 9. ‖ (Civil Service) *second*, lower grade of clerks. 10. ‖ (Prison) *1st, 2nd, 3rd, ~*, lenient, medium, severe, treatment in prison prescribed by judge. Hence ~AL(-zho-) a.,~ALLY² adv. [OF, f. L *divisionem* (DIVIDE¹, -ION)]

divis'or (-z-), n. (math.). Number by which another (the DIVIDEND) is to be divided; number that divides another without remainder. [L (DIVIDE¹, -OR²)]

divorce'¹, n. Legal dissolution of marriage (~ *à vinc'ulō matrimōn'iī*, i.e. from the bonds of marriage) opp. to judicial separation of married pair (~ *à men'sā et thŏ'rō*, i.e. from board and bed); (loosely) decree of nullity of marriage; (fig.) severance, sundering. [F, f. L *divortium* f. DĪ¹(*vortere* later *vertere* turn)]

divorce'², v.t. Legally dissolve marriage between; separate (spouse) by divorce *from*; put away, repudiate, (spouse); dissolve (union); sever (things, thing *from*). Hence di- or divo'rcer (also F *divorcé* masc., *-ée* fem.), ~MENT (-sm-), nn. [f. F *divorcer* f. med. L *divortiare* (prec.)]

div'ot, n. (Sc., north.). ‖ A turf, sod; (Golf) piece of turf cut out in making a stroke. [?]

divulge'¹ (-j), v.t. Let out, reveal. Hence ~MENT (-jm-), ~'GENCE, nn. [f. L DĪ(*vulgare* publish f. *vulgus* people]

Dix'ie('s) land, n. The U.S.A. south of Mason & Dixon's line, the former slave States. [corrupt. of *Dixon*, surveyor]

dix'y, dix'ie, n. Large iron pot in which stew, tea, etc., are made or carried on campaign. [corrupted f. Hind. *degchā* f. Pers. *degcha* (dim. of *dag* iron pot)]

diz'en (or dī-), v.t. (rare). Array with finery, deck *out* or *up*, bedizen. [cf. LG *diesse* bunch of flax, & *distaff*; from 1530]

dizz'y, a., & v.t. 1. Giddy, dazed, unsteady, tottering, confused; making giddy, (of mountain, tower, etc.) very high; (of stream, wheel, etc.) whirling rapidly; hence ~ILY² adv., ~INESS n. 2. v.t. Make ~y, bewilder. [OE *dysig* n., *dysigian* v., cf. LG *dusen* v.]

do¹ (dōō). See JIBBA(H).

do¹ (dōō), v.t. & i. & aux. (sing. pres. 2, *doest* pr. dŏŏ'ĕst as t. & i., *dost* pr. dŭst as aux.; 3, *does* pr. dŭz & arch. *doth* pr. dŏth, *doeth* pr. dŏŏ'ĕth; past *did, didst*; p.p. *done* pr. dŭn; *dŏn't, didn't*, are com-

mon for **do** not, *did* not; doesn't, & vulg. don't, for *does not.* **1.** v.t. Put (arch.) now only in *do to* (death); bestow, impart, grant, render, give, (*does me good, does credit to his intelligence; does me good, harm; did a service to his country; do justice to*); perform, carry out, effect, bring to pass, (thing, work, good, right, wrong, duty, bidding, penance; *it isn't done*, is bad form), whence **do'ing** (dōō-) n. (esp., pl.) what happens on an occasion or is done by or befalls a person, (sl.) adjuncts, things needed; (p.p. & perf.) complete, bring to an end, (*it is, I have, done*); exert, use, (*do one's endeavour, one's best, &,* sl., *one's damned -est*); produce, make, (*have done six copies*); operate on, deal with, repair, set in order, (*does the French books for the Athenæum; does one's hair*); cook, roast, etc., to the right degree (*chop done to a turn; well, over, under, -done*); solve (sum, problem); translate *into* English etc.; work at (lesson); play the part of (*did Lear, the cicerone;* hence *do the polite* etc.); exhaust, tire out, (sl.) cheat (also *do in the eye*); traverse (such a distance); (colloq.) see the sights of (city, museum); (with noun of action as compd vb) *do battle* etc., fight (term of punishment); (§sl.) provide food etc. for (*they do you very well; do oneself well,* make liberal provision for one's own comfort). **2.** v.i. (With adv., or adv. phr.) act, proceed, (*do as they do at Rome; would do wisely to withdraw*); perform deeds (*do or die*); make an end (*have done!,* cease; *let us have done with it*); fare, get on, (well, badly, etc.; of person or thing; *how do you do?* or *how d'ye do?*); be suitable, answer purpose, serve, suffice. **3.** v. substitute: (a) replacing vb and taking its construction, as *I chose my wife as she did her gown;* (b) replacing vb & obj. etc., as *if you saw the truth as clearly as I do;* (c) as elliptical auxiliary, as '*did you see him?*' '*I did*'; (d) with *so, it, which,* etc., as: *I wanted to see him, & I did so; in passing through the market, which he seldom did; if you want to tell him, do it now.* **4.** v. aux. Used with infin. for simple pres. & past (a) when special emphasis is to be laid on a fact, as *I do rather;* (b) when inversion is desired, as *do rarely does it happen that;* (c) in questions except with *have, be,* & some monosyl. vbs, as *did you recognize her?, do you dare?* or *dare you?;* (d) usual in *not* statements except with *be, have, dare, need,* etc.; also in *not* commands. **5.** Phr. etc.: *a to-do,* bustle, fuss; *well-*

to-do, rich enough, thriving; *have to do with,* be concerned or connected or have dealings with; *nothing doing,* going on; *done,* used in accepting offer or bet; *do-nothing,* a. & n., idle(r). **6.** With prep.: *do by,* treat, deal with, in such a way; *do for* (colloq.), || act as housekeeper etc. for, ruin, destroy, kill; *do to, unto,* = *do by; do with,* get on with, tolerate (joc., *could do with a drink*), find sufficient; *do without,* (with), abolish; *do in* (sl.), kill; *do up* (parcel), wrap up (parcel), tire out, restore, repair, Hence **do'ABLE** (dōō-) a., **do'ER¹** (dōō-) n. [com.-WG, OE *dōn* cf. G *tun,* f. Aryan *dhe-, dhō-;* put, cf. Gk *tithēmi,* L *-dere* in *condere* etc.]

do² (dōō), n. (sl.). Swindle, imposture, hoax; || (colloq.) entertainment, jolli-fication (*there's a big do on at No. 2*), (in pl.) share (*fair do's!* share fairly). [f. prec.]

do³ [doh, (dō), (mus.). Key-note of scale (*movable do*); the note C (*fixed do*). [arbitrary]

do⁴, abbr. of DITTO.

doat. See DOTE.

dobb'in, n. Draught or farm horse, [pet-name = Robert]

Docet'ic, a., **Docet'ist, Docet'ism**, n. (Of, holder of) the heresy that Christ's body was not human but phantasmal or of celestial substance. [med. L f. Gk *dokētikē* lit. seemers (*dokeō* seem) -IC, -IST, -ISM]

doch-an-dō'ris (döχr, see AP., döχ-), n. Stirrup-cup, last drink. [f. Gael. *deoch-an-doruis* a drink at the door]

doch'mĭac (döχ-), a. & n. Composed of dochmii (dochmius, ∪-∪-); (n., usu. pl.) line(s) so composed. [f. Gk *dokhmiakos* f. *dokhmios* adj. (*dokhmē* hand-breadth f. *dekhomai* receive)]

dō'cĭle, a. Teachable; submissive; easily managed. So **docil'ĭTY** n. [F, f. L *docilis* (*docēre* teach, -IL)]

dock¹, n. Kinds of coarse weedy herb, popular antidote for nettle stings. [OE *docce,* cf. G *docken-blätter*]

dock², n. Solid fleshy part of animal's tail; crupper of saddle or harness. [= Icel. *dockr* stumpy tail, cf. G *docke* bundle, plug]

dock³, v.t. Cut short (animal in tail, person in hair; or tail etc.); lessen, deprive of, put limits on (person, sup-plies); (Law) ~ *the entail,* cut it off; ~*-tailed,* with tail ~ed. [ME, f. prec.]

dock⁴, n. & v.t. & i. **1.** Basin with flood-gates in which ships may be loaded, unloaded, or repaired (*dry* or *graving* ~, for repairing or building, water being pumped out; *wet* ~, with water kept at high-tide level; *floating* ~, floating struc-ture usable as dry ~); (usu. pl.) range of ~ basins with wharves and offices, dock-yard. [? ship's berth, wharf; (Railway)

|| platform-enclosure in which line terminates; ~-dues, charge for use of, ~, also ~'AGE(4) n.; ~-glass (large, for wine-tasting); ~-master, superintendent of ~'yard or enclosure with ~s & all ship-building & repairing appliances; ||esp. in connexion with Navy. 2. vb. Bring (ship) (of ship) come, into ~; furnish with ~s. [cf. 16th-c. Du. docke]

dock⁵, n. Enclosure in criminal court for prisoner; || ~brief (undertaken gratis by barrister in court selected by poor prisoner in ~). [= Fl. dok rabbit-hutch]

dock'er, n. Labourer in dock⁴. [-ER¹]

dock'ét, n., & v.t. ||(Law) register of legal judgements (vb, enter in this); endorsement on letter or document showing its contents or subject (vb, endorse thus); ||Custom-House warrant certifying payment of duty; ||certificate of cotton clearing-house entitling presenter to delivery; ||permit to buy controlled or scarce goods. [f. 15th c.; etym. dub.]

dock'ize, v.t. Make (river) into range of docks. Hence ~A'TION n. [-IZE]

doc'tor¹, n. (Arch.) teacher, learned man, (D~s of the Church, certain, esp. four Eastern & four Western, early fathers; who shall decide when ~s disagree?); holder of the highest university degree in any faculty (often honorary, used as prefix to surname, usu. abbr. Dr), esp. ~ of medicine (male or female (also pop. of any medical man, M.D. or not, esp. in voc.); (Naut. sl.) ship's cook; kinds of mechanical appliance for regulating etc.; artificial fly; ~'s stuff, physic. Hence or cogn. ~AL, doctor'IAL, ~LESS, aa., ~ATE¹, ~SHIP(1, 3), ~HOOD, doc'tress¹ (joc. etc. for usu. ~ fem.), nn. [OF f. L (doc-) doctor. -OR²]

doc'tor², v.t. & i. Confer degree of doctor on; treat (patient, oneself) medically; patch up (machinery etc.); adulterate, falsify; practise as physician (esp. in gerund). [f. prec.]

Doc'tors' Comm'ons, n. pl. Common table, buildings (in which certain courts were held), of former College of Doctors of Civil Law in London (frequent literary allusions to probate, marriage-licence, & divorce business once transacted there). [COMMONS]

doctrinaire', **doctrinal'ian**, nn. & aa. 1. Pedantic theorist, person who applies principle without allowance for circumstances; hence doctrinair'ism(2), doctrinair'ianism(2), nn. 2. adj. Theoretic and unpractical. [-aire F (L doctrina DOCTRINE, -ARY¹) name of French political party 1815; -ARIAN]

doc'trinal (or dōktrīn-), a. Of, inculcating, doctrine(s). Hence ~LY² adv. [f. LL doctrīnālis (foll., -AL)]

doc'trine, n. What is taught, body of instruction; religious, political, scientific, etc., belief, dogma, or tenet (Monroe ~e, U.S. policy foreshadowed by President Monroe 1823 discountenancing European State interference in America). Hence ~ISM(1), ~IST(1), nn., ~IZE(2) v.i. [F, f. L doctrīna (DOCTOR¹, -INE³)]

doc'ument, n., & v.t. 1. Thing, esp. deed, writing, or inscription, that furnishes evidence (human ~, description, incident, etc., illustrating human nature); hence docümen'tARY¹ a., (also n., film dealing with a natural history, archaeological, industrial, travel, or similar subject, usu. accompanied by an explanatory talk). 2. v.t. Prove by, provide with, ~s or evidence; so docümenta'TION n. [OF, f. L documentum (docēre teach, -MENT]

dodd'er¹, n. Kinds of slender leafless threadlike parasitic plant. [ME doder cf. G dotter]

dodd'er², v.i. Tremble, nod, with frailty, palsy, etc. (~-grass, Quaking-grass); totter, potter, be feeble. Hence ~ER¹ n., infirm, feeble, or inept person. [?]

dodd'ered (-erd), a. Having lost the top or branches (of oaks & other trees). [prob. f. frequent. of dod poll, lop]

dōde(a)-, pref. = twelve, as dōdē'cagon, plane figure of twelve sides, dōdecahē'dron, solid figure of twelve faces, dōdecasýll'able, verse of twelve syllables. [f. Gk dōdeka twelve]

dodge¹, v.i. & t. 1. v.i. Move to & fro, change position, shuffle; move quickly round, about or behind, obstacle so as to elude pursuer, blow, etc.; play fast & loose, quibble, prevaricate; (of bell in chime) sound one place out of the normal order. 2. v.t. Baffle by finesse, trifle with; elude (pursuer, opponent, blow) by sideward deviation etc.; move (thing) to & fro; ask (person) questions in unexpected order. [?]

dodge², n. Piece of dodging, quick side-movement; trick, artifice; (colloq.) clever expedient, mechanical etc. contrivance; sounding of bell out of normal place in chimes. Hence dŏdg'Y² a. [f. prec.]

dodg'er, n. In vbl senses; esp., artful or elusive person; (colloq.) screen on ship's bridge as protection from spray etc.; *small handbill; *Indian-meal cake (corn~). [-ER¹]

dōd'ō, n. (pl. -oes, -os). Large extinct bird of Mauritius. [f. Port. doudo simpleton]

doe (dō), n. Female of fallow deer (cf. BUCK¹), hare, or rabbit; ~skin (-ŏs-), skin of ~, leather of this, fine cloth resembling it. [OE dá perh. f. L dama deer]

does, doest. See DO¹.

dŏff, v.t. Take off (hat, clothing); (rarely) abandon, discard, (custom, condition). [=do off]

dŏg¹, n. 1. Quadruped of many breeds wild & domesticated; hunting-dog (fig., ~s of war, havoc, rapine; male of ~, wolf (also ~wolf), (fem. bitch), or fox (also ~fox), 2. Worthless or surly person; fellow

(sb.), *lucky, jolly, ~; SEA-~*). **3.** (Astron.) *Greater* or *Lesser Dog*, constellations, also *Sirius* or *Procyon*, chief star in either (also *~-star*, usu. Sirius *~-days*, hottest part of year in July & Aug., variously dated according to heliacal & cosmical rising of Sirius). **4.** Kinds of mechanical device for gripping etc.; short iron bar with upturned spike at each end in common use for joining heavy timbering; (pl., also *fire-~s*) pair of metal supports for burning wood, or for grate, or for fire-irons. **5.** (Also *sea-~*) light near horizon portending storm; *sun-~*, parhelion. **6.** Phr.: *go to the ~s*, be ruined; *throw ~WORD[1] to throw away*, sacrifice; *not have love me, love my ~*; accept my friends as yours; *rain CATS & ~s*; *die like a ~*, *a ~'s death*, miserably, shamefully; *not a ~'s chance*, not even the least chance; *take hair of ~ that bit you*, drink more to cure effects of drink; *help lame ~ over stile*, be friend in need; *lead, lead one, a ~'s life*, be worried, worry another; *give ~ till name & hang him*, of power of nickname or slander; *let sleeping ~s lie*, let well alone; *put on* (colloq.), assume airs of importance; || *the ~s* (colloq.), greyhound race-meeting; *~ in the manger*, one who prevents others' enjoying what is useless to him; *~ in a blanket*, rolled currant dumpling or jam pudding. **7.** *~berry*, fruit of *~wood* or wild cornel; *~-biscuit*, for feeding *~s*; *~-cart*, two-wheeled driving-cart with cross seats back to back; *~-cheap*, very; *~-collar*, lit. & fig. of person's straight high collar; *~-faced*, epithet of kind of baboon; *~-fall*, in which wrestlers touch ground together; *~-fennel*, Stinking Camomile; *~-fight*, a fight (as) between *~s*, (colloq.) a fight between aircraft; *~-fish*, kinds of small shark & other fish; *~(s)-grass*, Couch-grass; *~-hole, -hutch*, mean room; *~ latin*, incorrect, mongrel; *~-led(ged)*, staircase, going back & forward without well-hole; *~-rose*, wild hedge rose; *~(s)-ear* n. & v.t., corner of page turned down with use, fill (book) with these; *~-shore*, wooden prop supporting ship's weight during building and cut away before launching; *~-skin*, leather of or imitating *~'s* skin used for gloves; *~-sleep*, light & fitful; *~'s letter*, r (f. snarling sound); *~-s-nose*, horseflesh, offal; *~'s-nose*, mixed drink of beer & gin; *~(s)-tail*, kind of grass; *~'s-tongue*, plants of borage kind & flowers; *~-tired*, tired out; *~-tooth*, small pyramidal ornament esp. in Norman & Early English architecture; *~-violet*, scentless kind; *~-watch* (Naut.), short half watch of two hours (4–6, 6–8, p.m.); *~-whip*, for keeping *~s* in order. Hence ~g'ISH[1], ~LESS,

~LIKE, aa., ~g'ly[1] or ~g'ie (~g-) [-Y[1]], ~HOOD, nn. [OE *dogga* etym. dub.]

dog[2], v.t. (-gg-). Follow closely, pursue, track, (person, his *steps*; of person or calamity etc.); (Mech.) grip with dog. [f. prec.]

dog'āte, n. Office of doge. [f. F *dogat* f. It. *dogato* (foll. -ATE[1])]

dōge (-j), n. (hist.). Chief magistrate of Venice, Genoa. [F f. It. f. L *ducem* nom. *dux* leader]

dogg'ed (-g-), a. Obstinate, tenacious, persistent, unyielding, (*it's ~ does it*, persistency succeeds). Hence ~LY[2] adv., ~NESS n. [-ED[2]]

dogg'er (-g-), n. Two-masted bluff-bowed Dutch fishing-boat. [f. 14th c., etym. dub.]

dogg'erel (-g-), a. & n. Trivial, mean, halting or irregular, (verse). [?]

dogg'ō, adv. (sl.). *Lie ~* (motionless, making no sign). [dog[1]]

dogg'y[1] (-g-), a. (for *doggy[1]* see dog[1]). Of dogs; devoted to dogs. Hence ~INESS n. [-Y[2]]

dŏg'ma, n. (pl. ~s, rarely ~ta). Principle, tenet, doctrinal system, esp. as laid down by authority of Church; arrogant declaration of opinion. [L f. Gk (gen. -*atos*), f. *dokeō* seem. -M]

dŏgmăt'ic, a. Of dogma(s), doctrinal; based on *a priori* principles, not on induction; (of person, book, etc.) authoritative, laying down the law, arrogant. Hence ~ICS n., ~ICALLY adv. [L f. Gk *dogmatikos* (prec. -IC)]

dŏg'matize, v.i. & t. Deal in positive unsupported assertions, speak authoritatively; express (principle etc.) as a dogma. So ~ISM(1), ~IST (1), nn. [f. F *dogmatiser* f. L f. Gk *dogmatizō* (DOGMA, -IZE)]

Dŏg'ra, n. Member of a warlike Hindu race of N.-West India (many of whom enlisted in the Indian Army).

doh, See DO[3].

doi'ly, n. Small napkin placed below finger-glass etc. [fabric named from 17th-c. inventor]

dō'ing (dōō-). See DO[1].

doit, n. Very small sum or coin; merest trifle (esp. *don't care a ~*). [f. Du. *duit* etym. dub.]

|| doit'ed, a. (Sc.). Crazed, esp. with age. [?]

doï'ce fŏr nĭ̄en'tē (-chā), n. Pleasant idleness. [It. = sweet doing nothing]

dŏl'drums (-z), n. pl. Dullness, dumps, depression; (of ship, usu. *in the ~*) becalmed state; region of calms & light baffling winds near equator. [prob. formed on *dull*, cf. *tantrums*]

dōle[1], n. & v.t. **1.** (Arch.) lot, destiny, sense prob. due to mistake] **2.** Charitable distribution; charitable (esp. sparing, niggardly) gift of food,

clothes, or money; || **the ~** (colloq.), relief claimable by the unemployed. **3. v.t.** Deal *out* sparingly, esp. as alms. [OE *dāl* cogn. w. *dǣl* DEAL¹]

dōle², n. (poet.). Grief, woe; lamentation. [revived obs. wd. f. OF *doel* (now *deuil* mourning) f. LL *dolium* grief cf. L *dolor*]

dōle'ful (-lf-), a. Dreary, dismal; sad, discontented, melancholy. Hence ~LY² adv., ~NESS n. [prec., -FUL]

dōl'erite, n. Coarse basaltic rock much used as road-metal. [F (-é-), f. Gk *doleros* deceptive (because easily confused with true greenstone)]

dōl'ichocephāl'ic (-ko-), a. Long-headed (of skull with breadth less than ⅘ of length; or of person or race with such skull). [f. Gk *dolikhos* long +-CEPHALIC]

dŏll, n., & v.t. & i. **1.** Toy baby, puppet; (*~'s house*, miniature toy house for ~s, diminutive dwelling-house); pretty silly woman (so *~'s face*). Hence ~ISH¹ a., ~ISHLY² adv., & l ~ISHNESS n. **2,** v.t. & i. (colloq.). Dress *up* smartly, deck up. [short for *Dorothy*]

dŏll'ar, n. (Orig.). English name for German thaler, also for Spanish piece of eight; unit of U.S. gold & silver coinage =100 cents, about 4s. 1½d. (symbol or ~ *sign*, $; *the almighty ~*, money, mammon); corresponding coin in Canada, etc.; || (sl.) five-shilling piece, crown; *half a ~* (sl.), half a crown; *~ diplomacy* (that seeks to further the commercial and financial interests of a country abroad and to extend its influence in international relations by means of these interests). [earlier & Du. *daler*=G *taler*, f. *Joachimstaler* gulden from silver mine of the Joachims(*tal* valley)]

dŏll'op, n. (colloq.). Clumsy or shapeless lump of food etc. [?]

dŏll'y, n. (Pet-name, esp. in voc, for) doll; kinds of appliance in clothes-washing, ore-washing, pile-driving, iron-punching, polishing, etc.; *~shop*, marine store. [-Y¹]

Dŏll'y Vard'en, n. Kinds of woman's hat & dress. [character in *Barnaby Rudge*]

dŏl'man, n. Long Turkish robe open in front; hussar's jacket worn with sleeves hanging loose; woman's mantle with flaps for sleeves. [ult. f. Turk. *dolaman*]

dŏl'mĕn, n. Cromlech. [F, perh. f. Cornish (*doll* hole, *men* stone)]

dŏl'omīte, n. Kind of rock (double carbonate of lime & magnesia); (*the D~s*, mountains of this, esp. those in Tyrol. Hence **dŏlomīt'IC** a. [*Dolomieu*, French geologist 1794, -ITE¹]

dŏl'orous, a. (usu. poet. or joc.). Distressing, painful; dismal, doleful; distressed. Hence ~LY² adv., -OUS] ~NESS n. [OF, f. LL *dolorosus* (DOLOUR, -OUS]

dolōse', a. (legal). Having criminal intent; intentionally deceitful. [f. L *dolosus* (*dolus* guile, -OSE¹)]

dōl'our (-ler), n. (poet.). Sorrow, distress. [OF, f. L *dolorem* nom. -or]

dōl'phin, n. Cetaceous mammal resembling porpoise, but with beak-like snout; (pop.) the fish dorado, which changes to many colours in dying; curved fish in heraldry, sculpture, etc.; bollard or mooring-post or buoy. [earlier *delphin* f. L *delphinus* f. Gk *delphis -inos*]

dōlt, n. Dull fellow, blockhead. Hence ~'ISH¹ a., ~'ISHNESS n. [perh.=*dulled*]

Dŏm, title prefixed to names of R.C. dignitaries, and Benedictine & Carthusian monks, and in Portugal & Brazil to Christian names of persons of the royal family, cardinals, bishops, etc. [abbr. of L *dominus* lord]

-dom, suf. forming nouns expressing rank, condition, domain, f. m. or adj. (*earldom, freedom, kingdom*), & (f. nouns) used collectively for the pl. or = the ways of (*officialdom*). [OE *dóm* cf. G *-tum* (st. of DO¹, *-m* as in *seam*]

domain', n. Estate, lands, dominions; district under rule, realm, sphere of influence: scope, field, province, of thought or action; (internat. & U.S. law) *Eminent D~*, lordship of sovereign power over all property in State, with right of expropriation. So **domāin'IAL** a. [f. F *domaine* f. L *dominicum* neut. adj. (*dominus* lord, -I0]

dōme, n., & v.t. **1.** Stately building, mansion, (poet.): rounded vault as roof, with circular, elliptical, or polygonal base, cupola; natural vault, canopy, (of sky, trees, etc.); rounded summit of hill etc.; hence **dōmed²** (-md), **dōm'IC**(AL), ~LIKE (-ml), **dōm'Y²**, aa. **2.** v.t. Cover with, shape as, (& direct) f. L *domus* house]

Domes'day (Bōōk) (dōōmz-), n. Record of Will. I's Great Inquisition of lands of England made 1086. [ME, = DOOM-*sday*, pop. name given to the book as final authority]

domĕs'tic, a. & n. **1.** Of the home, household, or family affairs; of one's own country, not foreign; native, home-made; (of animals) tame, kept by or living with man; home-keeping, fond of home; hence ~ICALLY adv. **2.** n. Household servant. [f. F *domestique* f. L *domesticus* (*domus* home)]

domĕs'ticāte, v.t. Naturalize (colonists, animals); make fond of home (esp. in p.p.); bring (animals) under human control, tame; civilize (savages). So ~ABLE a., ~ATION n. [f. med. L *domestic-care* (prec., -ATE³)]

domĕsti'cit̄y (or -dŏ-), n. Domestic character; home life or privacy; homeliness; *the ~ies*, domestic affairs; domesticated state. [-ITY]

dŏm'ĕtt, n. Fabric of wool & cotton used for shrouds etc. [?]

dom'icile (or -ĭl), n., & v.t. & i. **1.** Dwelling-place, home; (Law) place of permanent residence, fact of residing; place at which bill of exchange is made payable (v.t., make payable at a place). **2.** vb. (Also **domicil'iate**) establish, settle (t. & i.), in a place; so **domicilia'tion** n. [f. L *domicilium* f. *domus* home]

domicil'iary (-lyǎ-), a. Of a dwelling-place (~ *visit*, of officials to search or inspect private house). [as prec., -ARY¹]

dom'inant, a. & n. **1.** Ruling, prevailing, most influential; (of heights) overlooking, (of scale of any key) fifth note, as ~*chord*, *seventh*, etc.); reciting note in chant. **2.** (Mus.) fifth note in scale. **3.** (Mendelism) main characteristic appearing in the first generation of hybrids inherited from one only of the parents (adj., of this). Hence **dom'inANCE** n. [f. L *dominari* see foll., -ANT]

dom'inate, v.t. & i. Have commanding influence over (also intr. with *over*); be the most influential or conspicuous (of person, power, sound, feature of scene); (of heights) overlook, hold commanding position over. [f. L *dominari* (*dominus* lord), -ATE³]

domina'tion, n. Ascendancy, sway, control; (pl.) angelic powers of fourth rank (see ORDER¹ 1). [F, f. L *dominationem* (*domina-*)]

domineer', v.i. Act imperiously, tyrannize, be overbearing. Hence ~**ingly²** adv. [f. Du. (-*neren*) f. F *dominer* DOMINATE]

Domin'ical, a. Of the Lord (Christ; ~ *year*, date A.D.); of the Lord's day, Sunday; (~ *letter*, the one of the seven A–G denoting Sundays in any year). [f. med. L *dominicalis* f. L *dominicus*]

Domin'ican, a. & n. **1.** Of St Dominic or his order of preaching friars. **2.** n. Black or ~ friar. [f. eccl. L *Dominicanus* f. *Dominicus* L name of Domingo de Guzman +-AN]

∥ **dom'inie**, n. (Sc.). Schoolmaster. [= *domine* sir voc. of L *dominus* lord]

domin'ion (-yon), n. Lordship, sovereignty, control; domains of feudal lord, territory of sovereign or government (*D~ of Canada*, name given to Canadian colonies united 1867; *D~ of New Zealand*, title given 1907); (Law) right of possession. [OF, f. LL *dominionem* nom. -*o* f. L *dominium* (*dominus* lord)]

dom'ino, n. (pl. ~*es*). **1.** Loose cloak with half-mask worn to conceal identity esp. at masquerade, whence ~. **2.** One of 28 small brick-shaped pieces marked with pips used in game of ~*es*. [f. prob. f. L *dominus* lord, but unexplained]

don¹, n. **1.** Spanish title prefixed to Christian name (*Don Juan*, rake, liber-tine; *Don* QUIXOTE) Spanish gentleman, Spaniard. **2.** Distinguished person; adept at something. **3.** Head, fellow, or tutor, of college, whence ~**n'ish¹** a., ~**n'ishness** n. [Sp. f. L *dominus* lord]

don², v.t. (-nn-). Put on (garment). [= *do on*¹]

don'ah), n. (sl.). Woman; sweetheart. [f. Sp. *doña* or Port. *dona* f. L *domina* lady]

dona'tion, n. Bestowal, presenting; thing presented, gift, (esp. of money given to institution), whence ~**n'ish¹** a., ~**n'ishness** n. [F, f. L *donationem* (*donare*)]

don'ative (or dō-), a. & n. (Benefice) given directly, not involving presentation to or investment by the Ordinary; gift, present, esp. official largess. [f. L *donativum* (*donare* give, -IVE)]

don'atory, n. Recipient of donation. [f. med. L *donatorius* (*donare* give, -ORY)]

done (dŭn), p.p. of DO¹. ~ *brown*, duped, swindled; ~ *up*, tired.

donee', n. Recipient of gift. [as DONOR, -EE]

∥ **dŏn'ga** (-nggǎ), n. Gully, ravine. [S.-Afr.]

dŏn'jon (also dŭ-), n. Great tower of castle, keep. [arch. spelling of DUNGEON]

dŏnk'ey, n. (pl. ~*s*). (Usual word for) ass; stupid person; ~-*engine*, hauling or hoisting steam-engine on ship's deck; ~*'s years* (sl.), a very long time. [perh. f. DUN¹ with double dim. ending]

dŏn'na, n. Italian or Spanish or Portuguese lady. [It., f. L *domina* mistress]

Donn'ybrook (Fair), n. Scene of uproar, free fight. [*Donnybrook* in Ireland]

don'or, n. Giver (esp. of blood for transfusion). [f. OF *doneur* f. L *donatorem* (*donare* give, -OR²)]

don't¹. See DO¹.

don't², n. (joc.). Prohibition. [use of prec.]

dŏo'dle, v.i. & n. (Make) an aimless scrawl while one's attention is engaged elsewhere; ~-*bug*, *(larva of) tiger beetle, *unscientific device for locating minerals, *flying-bomb (colloq.). [?]

doo'lie, -**y**, n. Simple form of Indian litter used as army ambulance. [f. Hind. *doli* (Skr. *dol-* to swing)]

dōōm¹, n. (Hist.) Statute, law, decree; (arch.) decision, sentence, condemnation; fate, destiny (usu. evil); ruin, death; the Last Judgement (now only in *crack, day, of ~*, & in ~*'s day*; *till ~'sday*, for ever; the DOMESDAY). [com.-Teut.; OE *dōm* f. O'Teut. (*dōm* pō'²)]

dōōm², v.t. Pronounce sentence against, condemn to some fate, to do; consign to misfortune or destruction (esp. in p.p.); (arch.) decree (~*ed his death*). [f. prec.]

door (dōr), n. **1.** Hinged or sliding barrier usu. of wood or metal for closing entrance

to building, room, safe, etc. (*front* ~, chief ~ from house to street etc.; *lives* etc. *next* ~, in next house or room; so *three* ~s *off* etc.; *next* ~ *to* fig., nearly, almost, near to; so *at death's* ~). **2.** Entrance, access, exit. (*show* one *the* ~, expel him; *open a* ~ *to*, *close the* ~ *upon*, make possible, impossible). **3.** *Out of* ~s, abroad, in the open air; *within* ~s, in the house; *lay, lie, at the* ~ *of*, impute, be imputable to; cf. DARKEN; ~ *bell*, inside bell worked by handle outside; ||~-*case, -frame*, structure in which ~ is fitted: ||~-*keeper*, porter; ~-*mat*, for rubbing off mud from boots; ~-*money*, taken at ~ of place of entertainment; ~-*nail*, with which ~s used to be studded (*dead, deaf*, etc., *as a* ~*nail*); ~-*plate*, usu. of brass bearing occupant's name; ~-*posts*, uprights of ~-*case*; ~-*step*, leading up to usu. outer ~; ~-*stone*, slab in front of ~; ~-*way*, opening filled by ~. Hence (~)ED² (-ōrd), ~·LESS (-ōr̃-), aa. [OE *duru* cf. G *tür*, also Gk *thura*, L *fores*]

dop, n. Cheap S.-Afr. brandy; a dram of liquor. [Du.~ shell, husk]

dope, n., & v.t. **1.** Thick liquid used as food or lubricant; kinds of varnish esp. in aeroplane manufacture; narcotic, stupefying drink; *(sl.)* information about a racehorse's past performances or form, information of use to journalists etc. **2.** v.t. Administer ~ to, drug. [f. Du. *doop* sauce (*doopen* to dip)]

doppel-gänger. See DOUBLE¹-*ganger*.

dopp'er, n. (Derog. for) member of the Gereformeerde Kerk of S. Afr., in communion with the Christian Reformed Church of Holland. [f. Du. *domper* extinguisher, (fig.) stupid person]

dor, n. Insect flying with loud humming noise; black dung-beetle, cockchafer, rose-beetle, etc. [OE *dora* etym. dub.]

||**Dor'a,** n. See DEFENCE.

dora'dŏ (-äh-), n. (pl. ~s). Splendidly coloured sea-fish, dolphin. [Sp., f. L DE(*auratus* gilt f. *aurum* gold, -ATE²)]

Dor'cas, n. Meeting of ladies to make clothes for the poor. [*Acts* ix. 36]

Dor'ian, a. & n. (Inhabitant) of Doris, district of ancient Greece; (member) of one of three divisions (*Aeolian, Ionian,* ~) of ancient Greeks (~ *mode*: ancient Greek MODE, reputedly simple & solemn in character; first of eccles. modes, with D as final & A as dominant). [f. L f. Gk *Dōrios* (*Dōris* as above)+-AN]

Dŏ'ric, a. & n. **1.** = prec. adj.; ~ ORDER (also ~ as n.); (of dialect) broad, rustic. **2.** n. Dialect of ancient Greece (cf. *Attic, Ionic, Aeolic*), rustic English or esp. Scots. [f. L f. Gk *Dōrikos* (prec., -IC)]

Dŏrk'ing, a. & n. (Fowl) of the ~ breed. [~ in Surrey]

dorm'ant, a. Lying inactive as in sleep (of some animals through winter, undeveloped buds, potential faculties);

(Her, of beast) with head on paws; not acting, in abeyance, (often *lie* ~, *warrant* etc., drawn in blank); ~ *partner*, sleeping). Hence **dorm'ancy** n. [OF (*dormir* f. L *dormīre* sleep, -ANT]

dorm'er, n. (Also ~-*window*) projecting upright window in sloping roof. [f. OF *dormeor* f. L *dormītorium* (prec., -ORY)]

||**dorm'euse** (-ȫz), n. Travelling-carriage for sleeping in; kind of couch. [F, fem. of *dormeur* sleeper (DORMANT, -OR²)]

dorm'itory, n. Sleeping-room with several beds & sometimes cubicles; suburban or country district of city people's residences. [f. L (DORMER)]

dorm'ouse, n. (pl. *-mice*). Small hibernating rodent between mouse and squirrel. [perh. f. st. of F *dormir* (DORMANT)+MOUSE]

dorm'y, a. (golf). (Of player or side) as many holes ahead as there are holes to play (~ *one, five*, etc.). [?]

dŏ'rothy băg, n. Lady's open-topped handbag slung by loops from wrist. [fem. name]

Dŏ'rothy Pĕrk'ins (-z), n. Climbing rose bearing clusters of double pink flowers. [personal name]

dŏrp, n. (S. Africa). Village, small township. [Du.; cf. THORP]

dors'al, a. (Anat., Zool., Bot.) of, on, near, the back; ridge-shaped. Hence ~LY² adv. [f. med. L *dorsalis* (foll., -AL)]

dors(o)-, comb. form = back-&-, as in *dorsäbdom'inal* of back & belly, *dorsilāt'eral* of back & sides. [L *dorsum* back, -o-]

dŏrt'our (-ter), **-ter,** n. (hist.) Bedroom, dormitory, esp. in monastery. [OF (-*our*), as DORMER]

dŏr'y¹, n. (Also *John D*~) sea-fish used as food. [f. F *dorée* fem. p.p. of *dorer* gild, as DORADO]

dŏr'y², n. Flat-bottomed skiff, esp. fishing-vessel's boat in U.S. [?]

dŏs'age, n. Giving of medicine in doses; size of dose. [-AGE]

dose, n., & v.t. **1.** Amount of medicine to be taken at once (also fig, of flattery, punishment, etc.). **2.** v.t. Give physic to (person), adulterate, blend, (esp. wine with spirit). [vb f. noun, F, f. med. L f. Gk *dosis* (*didōmi* give]

||**dŏss,** n., & v.i. (sl.). Bed in ~-*house* or common lodging-house; (v.i.) sleep in this; hence ~ER¹ n. [perh. f. F *dos* f. L *dorsum* back]

dŏss'al, n. Hanging behind altar or round chancel. [f. med. L *dossale* (L *dorsum* back, -AL)]

dŏss'ier (-syā, -sier), n. Set of documents, esp. record of person's antecedents. [F, = bundle of papers (as doss, from bulging shape)]

dost. See DO¹.

dŏt¹, n. Small spot, speck, roundish penmark; (Orthogr.) period, point over *i* or

j, point used as diacritical mark; (Mus. writing) point used with various meanings; small child, tiny object; **~-&-dash,** using **~s** & dashes, as in Morse code; **~-wheel,** used for making dotted line; || **off one's ~** (sl.), half-witted, (temporarily) crazy. [OE OHG *tutto* nipple]

dot² v.t. (-tt-). Mark with dots(); place dot over (letter i; **~ the is & cross the ts,** fill in details, make meaning quite clear); (Mus.) **~ted** crotchet etc., with time value increased by half; diversity as with dots (*sea ~ted with ships*); scatter (*about, all over*) like dots; || (sl.) hit (*~ted him one in the eye*); **~ & carry** (one), child's formula for remembering to carry in addition sum; **~ & go one,** n., a., & adv., limping(ly). [f. prec.]

dot³ n. Woman's marriage portion. [F]

dot'age, n. One in his dotage. [foll., -ARD]

dôte, doat, v.i. Be silly, deranged, infatuated, or feeble-minded, esp. from age, whence **dôt'AGE**(2) n.; concentrate one's affections, bestow excessive fond-ness, (*up*)*on*. Hence **dôt'ingly²** adv. [cf. M.Du. *doten*, OF *redoter*]

doth. See DO¹.

dôtt'(e)rel, n. Kind of plover. [DOTE + -REL, named from the ease with which it is caught]

dôt'le, -tel, n. Plug of tobacco left unsmoked in pipe. [DOT¹-LE]

dôtt'y, a. Dotted about, sporadic, marked with dots; (colloq.) shaky of gait (*~ on his legs*); feeble-minded, half idiotic. [DOT¹ + -Y²]

Dou'ai, -ay, (dŏŏ'ā, dow'ā), n. **~ version, Bible,** English translation of the Bible used in the R.C. Church. The Old Testament was completed at ~ in France early in the 17th c.

dou'ane (dŏŏ'ahn), n. Foreign custom-house. [F, f. Arab. *diwan* DIVAN]

dou'ble¹ (dŭ'-), a. & adv. **1.** adj. Consisting of two members, things, layers, etc., forming a pair, twofold (**~ chin,** with roll of fat below chin proper); folded, bent, stooping much; with some part ~ (**~ ace,** with two edges, **~ eagle,** with two heads); (of flowers) with petals multiplied by conversion of stamens etc.; having twofold relation, dual, ambiguous (**~ meaning** = DOUBLE ENTENDRE); twice as much as ~ of many (of, or, with prep. wd); of twofold or extra size, strength, value, etc., (**~ ale, ~ florin**); (Mus.) lower in pitch by an octave (**~ bassoon** etc.); general use, **~-quick time**), regulation running pace; deceitful, hypocritical; (~ ENTRY) || **~-first,** (person who has taken first-class University honours in two subjects; **~ stars,** two stars so close as to seem one, esp. when forming connected pair; **~ work,** esp.

n., doub'ly² adv. **2.** adv. To twice the amount etc. (**~ as bright;** see ~, two things when there is only one, esp. of drunken man); two together (*ride ~;* two on horse; *sleep ~,* two in bed).

3. ~, a. or adv., is freely used in new or obvious compounds, as well as in the following: **~-acting,** in two ways, direc-tions, etc., esp. of engine in which steam acts on both sides of piston; **~-barrel,** = **~-barrelled,** or **~-barrelled gun; ~-barrel,** with two barrels (also fig. = ambiguous, of compliment etc.; of compound surname); **~-bass,** lowest-pitched stringed instrument; **~-bedded,** with two beds or **~ bed; ~-bitt** v.t. (Naut.), pass (cable) twice round bitts or round two pairs of bitts; **~-breasted** of coat or waistcoat, made to button on either side; ***~-cross²** (sl.), (v.t.) cheat (each of two parties, usu. by pretended collusion with both), (n.) act of this nature; hence **~-cross²~-dealer, -ting** n. & a., deceiver, deceit(ful); **~-dyed** usu. fig., deeply stained with guilt (**~-dyed scoundrel**); **~-edged,** with two cutting edges, (of argu-ment, sarcasm, etc.) telling against as well as for one; **~-faced,** insincere; **~-ginger** (-nj-), wraith [f. G *doppel-gänger* double-goer]; **~ harness** (fig.), matri-mony; **~-leaded** (-lĕd-), of printed matter with wide spaces between lines to draw attention; **~-lock** v.t., turn key of (some locks) twice; **~-quick** (see **~ time** above; also) adv., very quickly; **~-reef** v.t. (Naut.), contract spread of (sail) by two reefs; **~-refine,** refine twice over. [OF, f. L *duplus* (*duo* two, *-plus* f. pie- fill]

dou'ble² (dŭ'-), n. Double quantity, twice as much or many—or quits, game, throw, toss, deciding whether person shall pay twice his loss or debt or nothing; counter-part of thing or person; wraith; (Mil.) **at the ~,** running~ score (short whist) of five, nothing, (stake being doubled); (Lawn tennis etc.) game between two pairs; Guernsey copper coin, ¼d.; sharp turn of hunted animal, or of river. [f. prec. & foll.]

dou'ble³ (dŭ'-), v.t. & i. **1.** Make double, increase twofold, multiply by two; amount to twice as much as; (Mus.) add same note in higher or lower octave to; (of actor) **~ part(s),** play two in same piece. **2.** (Mil.) move in double time, run. **3.** Put (passenger etc.) in same quarters with another (also ~ up). **4.** Bend, turn, (paper, cloth) over upon itself (often up). **5. ~ up,** bend one's body into stooping or curled-up position, cause (another) to do this by blow, (of paper, leaf, etc.) become folded. **6.** Clench (fist). **7.** (Bill-ards) rebound, make to rebound. **8.** (Naut.) get round (headland). **9.** Turn sharply in flight, pursue tortuous course. [f. OF *doubler* f. L *duplare* (*duplus* DOUBLE¹)]

double entendre (see Ap.), n. Ambiguous expression, phrase with two meanings, one usu. indecent; use of such phrases. [from 1673; obs. F (now *double entente*, which is often needlessly substituted in E for the established ~)]

doub'let (dŭ-), n. 1. (Hist.) close-fitting body-garment worn by men with or without sleeves & short skirts (~ *& hose*, masculine attire, also light attire without cloak). 2. One of a pair, esp. one of two words of same derivation but different sense (*fashion* & *faction*). 3. pl. Same number on two dice thrown at once. 4. Two birds killed with double-barrel. 5. (Microscope etc.) combination of two simple lenses. [F (DOUBLE¹, -ET)]

dou'bleton (dŭ'blton), n. Two cards only of a suit (dealt to a player). [f. DOUBLE¹, after singleton]

doubloon' (dŭ-), n. Spanish gold coin, double pistole (orig. 33-38s., later slightly over £1). [f. F *doublon* or Sp. *doblon* (DOUBLE¹, -OON)]

doublure (dōōblūr'), n. Ornamental usu. leather lining inside book-cover. [F]

doubt¹ (dowt), n. Feeling of uncertainty (*about*), undecided frame of mind, inclination to disbelieve (*of*, *about*; *have no* ~ *that* . .), hesitation; uncertain state of things, want of full proof (*give one the benefit of the* ~, assume his innocence rather than guilt) or of clear signs for the future; *make no* ~, feel sure; *no* ~, certainly, admittedly; *without* ~, certainly. [f. OF *doute* f. douter DOUBT²]

doubt² (dowt), v.i. & t. Feel uncertain (*about*), waver; be undecided about or *about*, hesitate to believe or trust, call in question, (person, fact expressed by noun or by clause with *whether*, *if*, or, in negative or interrog. sentences, *that*, *but*, *but that*; *I* ~ *whether*, *I don't* ~ *that*, *can you* ~ *that*, *he will win*); have doubts of (esp. w. neg., as *never* ~*ed of success*); ‖ (arch. & dial.) be afraid, rather think, suspect, that (*I* ~ *we are late*). [f. OF *douter* f. L *dubitare* (dubius DUBIOUS); -*b*-inserted f. the L as correction]

doubt'ful (-owt-), a. Of uncertain meaning, character, truth, or issue, undecided, ambiguous, questionable, (~ *syllable*, *letter*, that can be either long or short); unsettled in opinion, uncertain, hesitating. Hence ~LY² adv., ~NESS n. [-FUL]

doubt'less (-owt-), adv. Certainly, no doubt, I admit, (usu. concess., cf. UN-DOUBTEDLY). [-LESS]

‖ **douce** (doos), a. (Sc.). Sober, gentle, sedate. [ME, f. OF *douz* fem. *douce* f. L *dulcis* sweet]

douceur (see Ap.), n. Gratuity; bribe. [F]

douche (doosh), n., & v.t. & i. 1. Jet of water applied to body externally or internally as form of bathing or for medicinal purpose. 2. vb. Administer ~ to, take ~. [F, f. It. *doccia* pipe ult. f. L *ductus* conduit (*ducere* lead)]

dough (dō), n. Kneaded flour, bread-paste; pasty mass; (sl.) money; ~*boy*, boiled dumpling, (sl.) U.S. infantryman; ~*nut*, cake of ~ sweetened & boiled in fat. Hence ~Y² (dō'i) a., ~'INESS (dō'i-) n. [com.-Teut.: OE *dāh*, cf. G *teig*, also Skr. *dih-* besmear, L *fig-* shape, Gk *teikhos* wall]

dough'ty (dow'-), a. (arch. or joc.). Valiant, stout, formidable. Hence ~LY² adv., ~'NESS n. [OE *dohtig* var. of *dyhtig* (cf. *dugan* be strong, & G *tüchtig*)]

Dou'khobórs (dōōko-), n. pl. Religious sect, with some likeness in doctrines to Quakers, of which large numbers migrated from Russia to Canada after persecutions for refusing military service. [f. Russ. = spirit-fighters]

doum (down, dōōm), n. (Also ~*palm*.) Egyptian palm-tree. [f. Arab. *daum*, *dūm*]

‖ **dour** (-oor), a. (Sc.). Severe, stern, obstinate. Hence ~LY² adv., ~'NESS n. [prob. f. L *dūrus* hard]

douse, dowse, v.t. (Naut.) lower (sail), close (port-hole); extinguish (light); ~ *the glim*, sl., put out the light); throw water over, drench. [?]

dove (dŭv), n. Kinds of pigeon (*cushat*, *ground*, *ring*, *rock*, *stock*, *turtle*, *wood*, ~); the Holy Spirit; type of gentleness or innocence (so ~*-eyed*); messenger of good news or peace (*Gen.* viii); darling (esp. *my* ~); ~*-colour(ed)*, (of) warm grey; ~*'s-foot*, kinds of crane's bill; ~*-hawk*, hen-harrier (from its colour); ~*-cot(e)*, pigeon-house (*flutter the* ~*-cots*, alarm quiet people). Hence ~LIKE (dŭv'l-) a. [cd. OE *tawbe*; perh. cogn. w. OE *dūfan* DIVE]

Dōv'er's powd'er, n. (pharm.). Preparation of opium, ipecacuanha, and sulphate of potash or sugar of milk, an anodyne diaphoretic. [Dr. Thos. *Dover* (d. 1742)]

dove'tail (dŭvt-), n., & v.t. & i. 1. Tenon shaped like dove's spread tail or reversed wedge, fitting into corresponding mortise & forming joint; such a joint. 2. vb. Put together with ~s; (fig.) fit together (t. & i.) compactly. [from 16th c.]

dow. See D(H)OW.

dow'ager, n. ‖ Woman with title or property derived from her late husband (often in comb. as *Queen* ~, *duchess*) (colloq.) dignified elderly lady, [f. OF *douagere* f. *douage* dower, -ER²(?)]

dowd (dowd), n., & a. (Woman) shabbily, badly, or unfashionably dressed; (of dress etc.) unattractive, unfashionable. Hence ~LY² adv.,~INESS,~YISM(2), nn.,~YISH¹ a. [f. obs. *dowd* slut, etym. dub.]

dow'el, n., & v.t. Headless pin of wood, metal, etc., for keeping two pieces of wood, stone, etc., in their relative

position; (vb) fasten with ~. [cf. G *döbel* plug, OF *doelle* barrel-stave]

dow'er, n. & v.t. 1. Widow's share for life of husband's estate; property or money brought by wife to husband, dowry; endowment, gift of nature, talent, etc. Hence ~LESS a. 2. v.t. Give dowry to; endow with talent etc. [vb f. n., OF *douaire* f. LL *dotarium* (L *dos dotis*, -ARY)]

‖ **dow'las**, n. Kind of strong calico or linen. [*Doulas* in Brittany]

down¹, n. Open high land, ‖ esp. (pl.) treeless undulating chalk uplands of S. England used for pasture; = DUNE; ‖ *The D~s*, part of sea (opposite *North D~s*) within Goodwin Sands. [OE *dūn* hill cf. ODu. *dūna* whence F *dune*]

down², n. First covering of young birds; bird's under plumage, used in cushions etc.; fine short hair, esp. first hair on face, also on fruit etc.; fluffy substance. [f. ON *dūnn*, cf. G *daune*]

down³, adv. (superl. a. or adv., ~'most, & ~s). **I.** (Motion), 1. from above, to lower place, to ground, (*come ~*,) from bedroom, *knock, fall*, ~; *sun, ship, goes* ~, sets, sinks; *food goes* ~, is swallowed; *get* ~ swallow, alight; *book* etc. *goes* ~, finds acceptance; *get, set*, ~, from carriage etc.; *brought ~ by river*; *money* ~, paying at once, as though on counter; *write, set, put, take, copy*, ~, on paper; *send ~ to Commons*; *bear* ~, sail to leeward; *run, ride, hunt*, ~, bring to bay; *shout, hiss*, ~, silence; ~ *to Norfolk* from London; ‖ *go* ~, for vacation or at end of university life; ‖ *send* ~, university punishment; *up & ~*, to & fro; (ellipt. for imperat. of) *lie, get, put*, etc., ~; *Ponto!*; ~ *helm*, put the HELM ~; & with *with*, ~ *with the aristocrats!*). **2.** (Station) in lower place (*winds were* ~; *is not* ~ *yet*, i.e. out of his bedroom); ‖ not up in capital or university; in fallen posture, prostrate, at low level, in depression, humiliation, etc. (*hit man who is* ~; *many ~ with fever*; *sun, tide, are* ~; ~ *in the mouth* or ~ or *~-hearted*, dispirited; *are we ~-hearted?*, sl. assertion of confidence; *bread is* ~, cheaper). **3.** (Order, time, quality); inclusively of lower limit in series (*from King ~ to cobbler*); from earlier to later time (*custom handed* ~); to finer consistence (*boil, grind, wear, thin*, ~); into quiescence (*calm~*). **4.** (Phrases) *be ~ on*, pounce upon, treat severely; *~ to the ground*, completely; *~ at* HEEL; *on one's* LUCK; *~ & out*, unable to resume the fight in boxing, beaten in the struggle of life, done for; *~-&-out* n.; *~-easter, New-Englander, esp. inhabitant of Maine; *~ under*, at the antipodes, in Australia etc. [OE *dūne* for *adūne* ADOWN]

down⁴, prep. Downwards along, through, or into; from top to bottom of; at a lower part of (*situated ~ the Thames*; *up & ~*, to & fro along; *~ town*, into the town; from higher or outlying part; *~ the wind*, with it (*let go ~ the wind*, abandon, discard). [f. prec.]

down⁵, a. (not compared). Directed downwards (*~ train, look*; *~ grade*, descending slope in railroad, fig. deterioration); *~-draught*, downward draught, esp. one driving down chimney into room; *~ train*, going, coming, from London, *~ platform*, for such train's departure or arrival. [f. DOWN³]

down⁶, v.t. (colloq.). Put, throw, knock, (usu. person or aeroplane) down; *~ tools*, cease work for the day etc., go on strike. [f. DOWN³]

down⁷, n. Reverse of fortune (usu. *ups & ~s*); (Dominoes) = POSE¹; *have a ~ on*, dislike, tend to be down on, (colloq.). [f. DOWN³]

down'cast¹ (-ah-), n. (Also *~-shaft*) shaft for introducing fresh air into mine. [DOWN³ + CAST²]

down'cast² (-ah-), a. (Of looks) directed downwards; dejected.

down'fall (-awl), n. Great fall of rain etc.; fall from prosperity, ruin.

down'hill, n. adj. & adv. (N., down'hil') downward slope, decline, (*~ of life*, later half); (adj., down') sloping down, declining; (adv., -hil') in descending direction, etc.

down'pour (-por), n. Heavy fall of rain.

Down'ing Street, n. Street in London containing some government offices, (home of) the Government of the day (*does not find favour in ~*; *~ disapproves*).

down'right (-rīt; downrīt' if placed late), a. & adv. **I.** (Arch.) vertical; plain, straightforward, blunt, whence ~NESS (-tt-) n.; not short of, out-&-out, (*a ~ lie, atheist*; *~ nonsense*). **2.** adv. Thoroughly, positively, quite, (*~ scared, insolent*). [DOWN³ + RIGHT a. & adv.]

downstairs', adv., **down'stair(s)**, a. Down the stairs; to, on, of, a lower floor.

down'throw (-ō), n. (geol.), Depression of strata on one side of fault.

down'trodden, a. Oppressed, kept under.

down'ward, a. & adv., **down'wards** (-z), adv. (Moving, pointing, leading) towards what is lower, inferior, or later. [OE *adūneweard* (DOWN³ -WARD)]

down'y¹, a. Like, of, downs. [DOWN¹, -Y²]

down'y², a. Of, like, covered with, down; (sl.) wide awake, knowing. So ~iy³ adv., ~INESS n. [DOWN², -Y²]

dow'ry, n. Portion woman brings to her husband; talent, natural gift. [f. OF

dows'ing (-z-), n. Searching for latent water or minerals with the ~ (or *divining*) *rod*, a forked twig held by & dipping over the right spot. [?]

dows'er (-z-) n. [?]

dox·ō'logy, n. Liturgical formula of praise to God, as *Glory be to* etc. [f. med. L f. Gk *doxologia* (*doxa* glory, -LOGY)]

dox'·ȳ¹, n. Beggar's wench, paramour. [?]

dox'·ȳ², n. Opinion, esp. on theology. [joc. use of end of *orthodoxy*, *heterodoxy*]

doyen (see Ap.), n. Senior member of a body, esp. senior ambassador at a court. [F., f. L as DEAN¹]

doyley. See DOILY.

dōze, v.i., & n. 1. Sleep drowsily, be half asleep; ~ *off*, fall lightly asleep. 2. n. Short slumber. [cf. Da. *döse* make drowsy]

dō'zen (dŭ-), n. (Pl. ~, used adjectivally or as noun, when with numeral or equivalent except *some*) twelve, as *a*, *three*, *several*, *how many*, ~ *figs* or *of the best figs*, *of these*, but *some* ~s *of people*, cf. *some* (about a) ~ (*of*) *people*, ~s *of* (= many) *times*; (pl. ~s) set of twelve, as *pack them in* ~s; *baker's*, *devil's*, *long*, *printer's*, ~, *thirteen*; || *talk nineteen to the* ~, *incessantly*. [f. OF *dozeine* (L *duodecim* twelve)]

drăb¹, n., & v.i. (-bb-). Slut, slattern; prostitute; (vb) whore. [cf. Irish *drabog*, Gael, *drabag*]

drăb², a., & n. (Of) dull light brown colour; dull, monotonous; monotony. [prob. f. obs. & F *drap* cloth]

|| **drăb'ět**, n. Drab twilled linen used for smock-frocks. [prec., -ET¹]

drăb'ble, v.i. & t. Go splashing *through*, make dirty and wet with, water or mud. [= EFris. *drabbeln* paddle]

Dracaen'a (-sēn-), n. Genus of liliaceous trees, including the *Dragon-tree* (yielding DRAGON's-blood). [mod. L f. Gk *drakaina* fem. of *drakōn* dragon]

drachm (-ăm), n. Ancient Greek silver coin, drachma; (Apoth. wt) 60 grains, ⅛ oz; (Avoird.) 27⅓ grains, ¹⁄₁₆ oz; small quantity. [f. F *drachme* f. L as foll.]

drăch'ma (-k-), n. (pl. ~s, -æ). Ancient Greek coin (see prec.); modern Greek coin. [L, f. Gk *drachmē* (*drassomai* grasp)]

Dracōn'ian, Dracōn'ic, aa. (Of laws) rigorous, harsh, cruel. [*Drakōn* Athenian legislator 621 B.C.+ -IAN, -IC]

draff (-ahf), n. Dregs, lees; hog's-wash; refuse of malt after brewing. [from 1205; ME, MDu, Icel, Sw., *draf*, cf. G *träber* husks]

draft¹ (-ahf-), n. 1. (Selection of) detachment of men from larger body for special duty, contingent, reinforcement. 2. Drawing of money by written order (*make a* ~ *on* fund etc., also fig. *on* person's confidence, friendship, etc.), bill or cheque drawn, esp. by one branch of bank on another. 3. Sketch of work to be executed; rough copy of document. 4. (Masonry) chisel-dressing along margin of stone's surface. [var. of DRAUGHT¹]

draft² (-ahf-), v.t. 1. Draw off (part of larger body, esp. of troops) for special purpose. 2. Prepare, make rough copy of, (document, esp. Parliamentary Bill), whence ~'ER¹ n. 3. (Masonry) cut draft on (stone). [f. prec.]

drafts'man (-ahf-), n. One who makes drawings or designs; one who drafts documents or Parliamentary Bills. [= DRAUGHTSMAN]

drăg¹, v.t. & i. (-gg-). Pull along with force, difficulty, or friction; allow (feet, tail, etc.) to trail; *ship* ~s *her anchor*, *anchor* ~s, anchor fails to hold; ~ *in*, introduce (subject) needlessly (*why* ~ *in Velasquez?*; also ~ *in by the head & shoulders*); (Mus.) go too slowly, be wanting in life; trail, go heavily; ~ *on*, continue (t. & i.) tediously; ~ *out*, protract; use grapnel or drag (often for drowned person or lost object), dredge, search bottom of, (river etc.) with grapnels, nets, etc.; harrow (land); apply drag to (wheel, vehicle); (colloq.) ~ *up* (child), rear roughly. [perh. var. of DRAW¹]

drăg², n. Heavy harrow; rough sledge; four-horsed private vehicle like stage coach; (also ~-*net*) net drawn over bottom of river etc. or surface of field to enclose all fish or game; apparatus for dredging or recovering drowned persons etc.; muckrake; iron shoe for retarding vehicle downhill; obstruction to progress; strong-smelling lure for hounds in lieu of fox (so ~-*hounds*), club for pursuing this sport; slow motion, impeded progress; ~-*anchor*, floating frame on hawser to check lee-way of drifting ship; ~-*chain*, used to retard vehicle by fixing wheel, (fig.) impediment. [f. prec.]

dragée (drah'zha), n. Chocolate drop, sweetmeat (often one serving as vehicle for a drug). [F; said to be ult. f. Gk *tragēmata* sweetmeats]

drăg'gle, v.t. & i. Make wet, limp, & dirty, by trailing; hang trailing; lag, straggle in rear; ~-*tail(ed)*, (woman) with ~d or untidily trailing skirts. [prob. f. DRAG¹+-LE(3)]

drăg'oman, n. (pl. -*ans*, -*en*). Interpreter, esp. in Arabic, Turkish, or Persian. [F, f. OArab. *targumān*, cf. TARGUM]

drăg'on, n. Mythical monster like crocodile or snake with wings & claws & often breathing fire; (with allusion to legends) guardian of treasure etc. or of female chastity, watchful person, duenna; (Bibl.) whale or shark, serpent, crocodile, jackal; *the old D*~, Satan; kinds of lizard & pigeon; ~-*fly*, neuropterous insect with long slender body & two pairs of large wings ~'s-*blood* bright

red gum exuding from kind of palm fruit; ~'s teeth, anti-tank obstacles resembling teeth pointing upwards. [F. f. L *draco-nem* nom. -o f. Gk *drakōn* serpent perh. f. *derkomai* see, st. *drak-*]

dragonnade, n., & v.t. (Pl.) persecutions of Protestants under Louis XIV by quartering dragoons on them; persecution carried on by means of troops; (vb) persecute thus. [F (dragon DRAGON, -ADE)]

dragoon', n., & v.t. 1. Cavalryman (orig. mounted infantryman armed with carbine called ~; later of certain cavalry regiments that were formerly mounted infantry); rough fierce fellow; kind of pigeon (also *dragon*). 2. v.t. Set ~s upon, persecute (see prec.); force *into* a course by persecution. [f. F dragon carbine, so named as breathing fire (DRAGON)]

drail, n. Fish-hook & line weighted with lead for dragging at depth through water. [perh. a mixture of *drag, trail*]

drain¹, v.t. & i. 1. Draw (liquid) off or away by conduit. ~-pipes, etc. (also fig. *the wealth of England*); drink (liquid), empty (vessel), to the dregs; dry (land-); by withdrawing moisture; (of river) carry off superfluous water of (district); deprive (person, thing *of* property, strength, etc.; trickle *through*, flow off of moisture by its flowing away (*set it there to ~*). [OE *dreahnian* cogn. w. DRY]

drain², n. Channel carrying off liquid, artificial conduit for water, sewage, etc.; (surg.) tube for constant outlet, withdrawal, demand, or expenditure (*a great ~ on my resources*); (sl.) small draught, drink. [f. prec.]

drain'age, n. Draining; system of drains, artificial or natural; ~-*basin*, district drained by river; what is drained off, sewage. [-AGE]

drain'er, n. In vbl senses: esp., vessel in which things are put to drain. [-ER¹]

drake¹, n. Kinds of ephemeral fly used in fishing (*green ~*, common day-fly). [OE *draca* f. L *draco* DRAGON]

drake², n. Male duck (*play* DUCK's *& ~s*). [cf. G dial. *draak*, perh. seen in G *enderich* earlier *endrich*, of which *end-* perh. = duck]

dram, n. A weight (see DRACHM); small draught of spirit etc. (~-*drinker*, -*ing*, tippler, -*shop*, public-house). [for DRACHM]

dra'ma (-ah-), n. Stage-play; *the ~*, the dramatic art, composition & presentation of plays; set of events having the unity & progress of a play & leading to catastrophe or consummation. [LL f. Gk (gen. *-atos*, f. *draō* do, -M]

dramat'ic, a. Of drama; as of a play-actor, theatrical; fit for theatrical representation, sudden, striking, im-

pressive; (of utterances etc.) not to be taken as one's own, representing another person's thoughts. Hence ~ICALLY adv. [f. L f. L *dramatikos* (prec., -IC)]

dramatis persōnæ, n. pl. (often with sing. constr.). (List of) characters in a play. [L]

drám'atist, n. Playwright. [DRAMA, -IST]

drám'atize, v.t. & i. Convert (novel etc.) into a play, admit of such conversion; make a dramatic scene of. Hence ~A'TION n. [DRAMA, -IZE]

drape', v.t. Cover, hang, adorn, with cloth etc.; arrange (clothes, hangings) in graceful folds. [f. F *draper* (*drap* cloth)]

dráp'er, n. Dealer in cloth, linen, etc. [f. F *drapier* (prec., -IER)]

dráp'ery, n. Cloth & linen & cotton fabrics; draper's trade; arrangement of clothing in sculpture etc.; clothing or hangings disposed in folds, whence ~IED² (-id) a. [f. F *draperie* (*drap* cloth, -ERY]

drás'tic, a. Acting strongly, vigorous, violent, esp. (Med.) strongly purgative. Hence ~ALLY adv. [f. Gk *drastikos* (*drastos* vbl adj. of *draō* do, -IC]

drat, v.t. & sing. subjunct. (vulg.). Confound, curse, bother, (as woman's imprecation). Hence ~'t'ED¹ a. [for 'od (God) rot!]

draught¹ (-ahft), n. (also *draft* in some senses, as stated). 1. Drawing, traction, (*beast of ~, ~-horse*, etc., for drawing cart, plough, etc.). 2. Drawing of net for fish etc., take of fish at one drawing. 3. Single act of drinking; amount so drunk, (also fig. *of joy, love, pain*, etc.); dose of liquid medicine (*black ~*; a purgative). 4. (Naut.) depth of water ship draws or requires to float her. 5. pl. || Game with 24 similar pieces on ~ (same as chess) -*board*. 6. Current of air in room, chimney, etc. (*forced ~*, of furnace, made by rarefying air above or compressing it below; *I feel the ~*, sl., suffer from adverse conditions), whence ~Y² a., ~INESS n. 7. Outline, preliminary drawing for work of art; plan of something to be constructed (also -*ft*); rough copy, first conception, of document (usn. -*ft*). 8. (Selection of) military detachment, party, reinforcement, (usn. -*ft*). 9. (Written order for) withdrawing of money from fund in bank etc., cheque, bill of exchange, (now -*ft*). 10. Drawing of liquor from vessel (*beer on ~*, in tapped cask; so || *~ beer*, opp. *bottled*). [ME *draht* f. *dragan* DRAW]

draught² (-ahft), v.t. Draw off (party for military service etc.) from larger body (now *draft*); make plan or sketch of (also -*aft*). [f. prec.]

draughts'man (-ahft-), n. (pl. *-men*). One who makes drawings, plans, or sketches (*good, bad, no,* ~, one who draws well etc), whence ~**ahftswō̆o̅-**) n. fem.; (usu. *draftsman*) person who drafts document, esp. Parliamentary Bill; piece in game of draughts. [*draught's +man*]

Dravid'ian, a. & n. (Member, language) of one of the non-Aryan races of Southern India and Ceylon (including Tamils & Kanarese). [f. Skr. *Dravida*, a province of S. India]

draw[1], v.t. & i. (*drew, drawn*). **1.** Pull (boat up from water, hat over face, belt tighter, pen across paper, friend aside); pull after one (plough, cart, cartload, etc.); drag (criminal) on hurdle etc. to execution; contract, distort, (*with ~n face*); haul in (net); bend (bow; ~ a BEAD[1] *on*); pull at (~ *bit, bridle, rein,* check horse, & fig. oneself); pull (curtain, veil) open or shut; ~ *cloth*, clear table after meal; (Cricket) divert (ball) to on side with bat:- (Golf) drive (ball) too much to left (of right-handed player). **2.** Attract, bring to one, take in, (*drew a deep breath;* & abs. *chimney, pipe,* ~*swell,* promotes, allows, draught; *I felt ~n to him; drew my attention;* ~ *him into talk, out of temptation;* ~s *customers,* & abs. attracts attention or custom); induce to do; be attracted, assemble, *round* or *about* some centre (*drew round the table*); bring about, entail, (*drew after it great consequences;* ~ *ruin upon oneself*). **3.** Extract (cork, tooth, gun-charge, nail, cricket-stumps from ground, card from pack; pistol, sword from sheath, also abs.:- ~ *one's sword* or *pistol;* ~ *one's sword against,* attack; ~ LOTS, also abs. = ~ *lots,* & trans. = obtain by lot, as *drew the winner*); drag (badger, fox) from hole; haul up (water) from well; bring out (liquid, blood) from vessel, body (~ *it mild,* i.e. orig. beer, now = be moderate, not exaggerate); extract essence of (~ *the tea,* also intr. *the tea* ~*s*); (of poultice) drain (gathering etc.); take, get, from a source (~ *inspiration,* one's *salary; tax* ~*s well,* ~*s from the rich only*); (Cards) cause to be played (~ *all the trumps*); bring (person) out, make him reveal information, talent, irritation, etc.; deduce, infer, (conclusion); extract something from, empty, drain (*calf* ~*s cow*), disembowel (*hanged,* ~*n, & quartered,* of criminal; ~ *fowl* before cooking); (Hunt.) search (covert) for game (~ *blank,* find none). **4.** Protract, stretch, elongate, (*long*~*n agony;* ~*plate,* hard steel plate pierced with graduated apertures through which rods or wires are ~n during manufacture; ~ *wire,* make it by pulling piece of metal through successively smaller holes); (Naut., intr. of sail) swell out with wind. **5.** Trace (furrow, figure, line;

~ *the line at,* refuse to go as far as or beyond); delineate, make (picture), represent (object), by ~ing lines, (abs.) use pencil thus; describe in words; practise delineation; frame (document) in due form, compose, (often *up, out*); formulate, institute, (comparisons, distinctions); write out (bill, cheque, draft, *on* banker etc.), (abs.) make call *on* person or his family, memory, etc.. *for* money or service. **6.** Make way, move, *towards, near, off, back,* etc., (~ *to an end* or *close*); (Racing) get further *away* to the front, come *level, gain on.* **7.** (Of doubtful origin; (of ship) require (such a depth of water) to float; ~ *game* or *battle,* part without deciding it. **8.** (With adv. in special senses); ~ *back,* withdraw from undertaking; ~ *in,* entice, persuade to join, (of day) close in, (of successive days) become shorter; ~ *off,* withdraw (troops; or intr. of troops etc.); ~ *on,* lead to, bring about, allure, approach (intr.); ~ *out,* lead out, detach, or array (troops), prolong, elicit, induce to talk, write out in proper form, (of days) become longer; ~ *up,* (refl.) assume stiff attitude, (intr.) come *up with* or *to*=overtake, come to a stand, (t. & i. of troops) bring or come into regular order, (trans.) compose (document etc.). [com.-Teut., OE *dragan,* cf. G *tragen* carry]

draw[2], n. Act of DRAWING; esp.: strain, pull; attractive effect, thing that draws custom, attention, etc.; drawing of lots, raffle; drawn game; remark etc. meant to elicit information or set person off on pet subject; act of whipping out revolver in order to shoot (*quick on the* ~); *movable part of drawbridge. [f. prec.]

draw'back, n. Amount of excise or import duty paid back or remitted on goods exported; deduction *from;* thing that qualifies satisfaction, disadvantage; ~ *lock,* with spring bolt that can be drawn back by inside knob. [DRAW[1]]

draw'bridge, n. Bridge hinged at one end for drawing up to prevent passage or to open channel. [DRAW[1]]

Drawcan'sir (-*er*), n. & a. (Person) formidable both to friend and foe; fierce swashbuckler. [name of character in Villiers's *Rehearsal*]

drawee', n. Person on whom draft or bill is drawn. [-EE]

draw'er, n. In vbl senses; also or esp.: (arch.) tapster; receptacle sliding in & out of special frame (~s or *chest of* ~s) or of table etc., for holding clothes, papers, etc., whence ~FUL(2) n.; (pl.) two-legged garment suspended from waist. [-ER[1]]

draw'ing, n. In vbl senses: esp.: art of representing by line, delineation without colour or with single colour, (*out of* ~, incorrectly drawn); product of this, black-&-white or monochrome sketch;

~-block, of detachable leaves of ~-paper adhering at edges; ~-board, for stretch-ing ~-paper on; ~-compass(es), with pen or pencil substituted for one point; ~-pin, for fastening ~-paper to ~-board. [-ING¹]

draw'ing-room, n. Room for reception of company, to which ladies retire after dinner; levee, formal reception esp. at court. [for earlier withdrawing-]

draw'l, v.i. & t., & n. 1. Speak, utter(often out), with indolent or affected slowness (of words, esp. in part.) be so uttered; hence ~'ingly² adv. 2. n. Slow utter-ance. [prob. intensive f. DRAW¹; cf. Du. dralen, LFris. draulen, loiter]

drawn, p.p. of DRAW¹; ~-work, fancy work in linen etc. done by drawing out threads.

draw-well, n. Deep well with rope and bucket. [DRAW¹]

dray, n. Low esp. brewer's cart without sides for heavy loads (~-horse, large & f. OE drǽge, brewer's driver). [t. powerful; ~-man, brewer's driver). [t. OE dragan DRAW¹, cf. Sw. drög]

dread¹(-ěd), v.t., & n. 1. Be in great fear of; shrink from, look forward to with terror; fear greatly (that, to learn etc.), be afraid (to do). 2. n. Great fear, awe, apprehension; object of fear or awe. [n. f. vb. ME dreden, adreden, cf. OE andrǽden, etym. dub.]

dread²(-ěd), a. Dreaded, dreadful; awful, revered. [ME p.p. of DREAD¹]

dread'ful(-ěd-), a. Terrible, awe-inspiring (||penny ~ ellipt. story-book full of horrors); troublesome, disagreeable, bor-ing, very bad or long, horrid. Hence ~LY² adv. [-FUL]

dread'nought (-ědnawt), n. (Cloth used for) thick coat for stormy weather; (D~) type of 20th-c. battleship greatly superior in tonnage & power to all predecessors (f. name of first built in 1907).

dream¹, n. Vision, series of pictures or events, presented to sleeping person; act, time, of seeing such vision; waking ~, similar experience of one awake; con-scious indulgence of fancy, reverie, castle in the air, (also day-~); thing (ideal, person, dress, dish, etc.) of ~-like goodness, beauty, or refinement; ~reader, inter-preter of ~s; ~-world, -land, region out-side the laws of nature. Hence ~'LESS, ~-LIKE, aa. [cf. G traum, perh. cogn. w. prec.]

dream², v.i. & t. (~t pr. -ěmt, or ~ed). Have visions in sleep; see, hear, etc., in sleep (~t a dream, did you ?, it's, ~ that . . .); imagine as in a dream, think of possible (with negative etc.); think of even in a dream, so much as contemplate possibility of, have any conception of; fall into reverie; form imaginary visions of; be inactive or unpractical (~ away one's time). Hence ~'ER¹ n. [as prec.]

dream'-hōle, n. Hole left in wall of tower etc. to admit light. [perh. f. OE dréam mirth, music (the holes letting sound of bells issue)]

dream'ȳ a. Full of dreams (rare or poet.); given to reverie, fanciful, unpractical; dreamlike, vague, misty. Hence ~ILY² adv., ~INESS n. [-Y¹]

drear'(y¹, (poet.) drear, a. Dismal, gloomy², dull. Hence ~(I)LY² adv., ~(I)-NESS n. [OE dréorig (dréor gore) prob. cogn. w. dréosan to drop & G traurig sad]

drēdge¹, n., & v.t. & i. 1. Apparatus for bringing up oysters, specimens, etc., or clearing out mud etc., from river or sea bottom. 2. vb. Bring up, clear away or out, with ~; use ~; hence drēdg'er¹ [-ER¹] (1, 2)]n. [earlier dreg perh. f. DRAG¹]

drēdge², v.t. Sprinkle with flour or other powder; sprinkle (flour etc.), over ; dredg-ing-box, =foll. f. obs. dredge sweetmeat, f. OF dragee f. L f. Gk tragēma (trōgō chew)]

drēdg'er², n. (for dredger¹ see DREDGE¹), Box with perforated lid for sprinkling flour etc. [prec., -ER¹]

drēg, n. (usu. pl.). Sediment, grounds, lees, (drink², drain, to the ~s, leaving nothing; worthless part, refuse; (sing.) small remnant (esp. not a ~). Hence ~g'y¹ (-g'-) a. [cf. Icel. dreggjar, Sw.]

Dreibund (drī'bŏŏnt), n. = TRIPLE Alliance (3). [G (drei three, bund league)]

drench¹(-), v.t. (arch.), (arch.). Draught or dose administered to animal; (arch.) large, medicinal, or poisonous draught; a soaking or down-pour. [OE drenc cogn. w. DRINK]

drench², v.t. Make to drink largely; force (animal) to take draught of medi-cine; (Sheep-washing, Tanning) steep, soak; wet all over with falling liquid (or of the liquid; ~ed with, by). [OE drencan cf. G tränken, causative of DRINK]

drěn'cher, n. In vbl senses; esp.: drench-ing shower; apparatus for giving drench to beast. [-ER¹]

Drěs'den (-z-), n. ~ china, porcelain, kind produced in Saxony esp. in 18th c.

dress¹, v.t. & i. 1. (Mil.) correct the align-ment of (companies etc. in relation to each other, or men in line); (intr.) come into correct place in line etc. (up, i.e. for-ward, back, or abs.). 2. Array, clothe, (~ed in black, serge, etc.); provide oneself with clothes (~ well etc.); put on one's clothes; put on evening dress (esp. ~ for dinner); ~ up, attire oneself, attire (an-other), elaborately or in masquerade; ~ out, attire conspicuously. 3. Deck, adorn, (ship with flags, shop-window with tempting wares; shop-window with costumes. 4. Treat (wound, wounded

man) with remedies, apply dressing to. **5.** Subject to cleansing, trimming, smoothing, etc.; brush, comb, do up, (hair); curry (horse, leather; & fig., often ~ *down*, thrash, scold). **6.** Finish surface of (textile fabrics, building-stone). **7.** Prepare, cook, (food); prune (plant); manure, [f. OF *dresser* cf. It. *dirizzare* f. L *directus* DIRECT]

dress², n. **1.** Clothing, esp. the visible part of it, costume (*full* ~, that worn on great occasions; *evening* ~, or ~, that worn at dinners or evening parties; *morning* ~, ordinary; *a* ~, lady's gown, frock). **2.** External covering, outward form, (*birds in their winter* ~, *French book appearing in English* ~). **3.** || ~ *circle*, first gallery in theatres, in which evening-tailed for evening ~; ~ *coat*, swallow-was once required; ~*guard*, on bicycle etc. to protect ~; ~*improver*, = BUSTLE³; ~*maker, king, rehearsal*, final one in costume; ~s; ~*shield, ~preserver*, piece of waterproof material fastened under the arms of a bodice. [f. prec.]

dress'er¹, n. || Kitchen sideboard with shelves for dishes etc. [f. OF *dresseur* (*dresser* DRESS³) cf. med. L *directorium*]

dress'er², n. In vbl senses: esp.: surgeon's assistant in hospital operations; whence ~SHIP(1) n.; one who helps to dress actors or actresses, looks after costumes, etc. [-ER¹]

dress'ing, n. In vbl senses; esp.: scolding or thrashing (usu. with *down*); sauce, stuffing, etc.; manure; bandages, ointments, etc., for wound; stiffening used in finishing fabrics; ~*-bell* etc., signal to dress for dinner; ~*-case*, of toilet necessaries; ~*-gown*, worn while making toilet or in dishabille; ~*-room*, attached to bedroom for toilet; ~*-table*, for looking-glass etc. [-ING¹]

drew. See DRAW¹.

drib'ble, v.t., v.i., & n. **1.** Flow, let flow, in drops or trickling stream (n., such flow); (of child, idiot, etc.) run at the mouth. **2.** (Football) work (ball) forward with slight touches of alternate or different players' feet (n., piece of ~*ing*). **3.** (Billiards) make (ball) just roll (or intr. of ball) into pocket. Hence ~ER¹ n. [frequent. of obs. *drib* v. var. of DRIP]

drib(b)'let', n. Small quantity, petty sum, (esp. *by* ~s). [f. *drib* see prec.+-LET]

dried, drier. See DRY².¹

drift¹, n. **1.** Being driven by current; slow course or current; ship's deviation due to currents (~*-anchor*, = DRAG²*-anchor*). **2.** Projectile's deviation due to rotation. **3.** || (Forest Law) driving of cattle to one place on appointed day to determine ownership etc. **4.** Natural or unperceived progress, tendency. **5.** Waiting on

events, inaction, (esp., contempt, *the policy of* ~). **6.** Purpose, meaning, tenor, or scope, of person or his words. **7.** Shower, driving mass; snow, sand, etc., accumulated by wind; (also ~*-ice, -wood*, etc.) matter driven by water: (Geol.) superficial deposit made by current of water or air (*D~*, pleistocene ice detritus, boulder clay). **8.** (Also ~*-net*) large net for herrings etc. allowed to drift with tide. **9.** (Mining) horizontal passage following mineral vein. **10.** S.-Afr. ford. **11.** Tool for enlarging or shaping hole in metal **12.** The horizontal component of the aerodynamic pressure on all exposed surfaces of an aeroplane in flight (cf. LIFT). [f. OE *drīfan* DRIVE¹]

drift², v.i. & v.t. Be carried (as) by current of air or water, (of current) carry; go passively or aimlessly; pile, be piled, by wind into drifts; cover (field, road) with drifts; form or enlarge hole (see prec.). Hence ~AGE(1) n., ~ER¹ n., (esp.) boat used in drift-net fishing (much also in mine-sweeping during the 1914-18 war). [f. prec.]

drill¹, n., & v.t. & i. **1.** Pointed steel etc. tool, or machine, for boring holes (vb, tool, or person or tool, with *metal* etc., or *hole* etc., as obj.; also intr., ~ *through*, perforate); boring shell-fish. **2.** Instruction or exercise in military evolutions (~*-serpeant*, instructor in ~, also fig.), rigorous discipline, exact routine, (vb, subject to, or undergo, such discipline; *B Company will* ~ *tomorrow*; ~ *him in what he is to say*, in Latin Grammar). [n. in sense *tool* f. Du. *dril* f. *drillen* v.; vb in sense *bore* f. n.; other n. senses f. vb]

drill², n., & v.t. Small furrow for sowing seed in, ridge with such furrow on top, row of plants so sown; machine for furrowing, sowing, & covering seed; (vb) sow (seed) thus, plant (ground) in ~s. [perh. = prec.]

drill³, n. Kind of baboon. [perh. W.-Afr.]

drill⁴, n. Coarse twilled linen or cotton fabric. [earlier *drilling* f. G *drillich* f. L *trilicem* nom. -*ix* (tri- three-, *licium* thread)]

drily. See DRY¹.

drink¹, v.t. & i. (*drănk; drŭnk* & poet. *drănk'en*). Swallow (liquid); take (*the waters at a spa*) medicinally; ~ *off, up*, ~ the whole of at once; (of plants, porous things, etc.) absorb (moisture; often *up* or *in*); (fig.) ~ *in*, contemplate, listen to, with delight; empty (vessel, *the cup of pain or delight*; spend (wages etc.) on drink; swallow liquid, take draught, (often of a source; ~ *deep*, take large draught, or be sober ~*er* as in next sense); take spirituous liquor esp. to excess, tipple, be a drunkard, (~ *hard, heavily, like a fish*; ~*ing*-BOUT; ~*-ing-water* (reserved, pure enough, for ~*ing*); ~ *oneself drunk*, to

drink (cont.) death, out of a situation; ~ *down* or *under the table*, outdrink. In retaining control of oneself while ~ing; ~ *to*, pledge, toast; to collect money for a special purpose; wish good etc. to in ~ing (~ *one's health*, ~ *success or confusion to*). Hence (-)~ER[1].

drink[2], n. Liquid swallowed or absorbed; beverage; intoxicating liquor (also *strong* ~), excessive indulgence in it, intemperance (*on the* ~, giving way to this; *in* ~, drunk); glass etc. or portion of liquor; *the* ~ (R.A.F. sl.), the sea. Hence ~LESS a. [OE *drinc* & *drinca* f. *drincan*- prec.]

drink'able, a. & n. Good to drink; (n., esp. in pl.) thing(s) to drink. [-ABLE]

drip[1], v.i. & t. (-pp-). Fall, let fall, in drops; let drops fall, be so wet (*with blood* etc.) as to shed drops (~*ping wet*, very wet). [OE *dryppan* cf. G *triefen*]

drip[2], n. Act of dripping; dripping liquid; (Archit.) projection keeping rain from parts below (so ~*moulding*, ~*stone*); ~*ping*, persistent dripping. Hence ~P'Y[2] a. [f. prec.]

drip'ping, n. In vbl senses; also: fat melted from roasting meat, & used for frying or as food.

drive[1], v.t. & i. (*drōve*, *driven*). 1. Urge in some direction by blows, threats, violence, etc. (usu. with adv. or prep. as *away*, *back*, *in*, *out*, *from*, *to*, *through*; ~ *out*, oust, take place of); chase or frighten (game, wild beasts, enemy esp. in guerrilla warfare) from over large area into small in order to kill or capture. 2. Scour (district), ‖(Forest Law) hold a DRIFT. 3. (Urge &) direct course of (animal drawing vehicle or plough, vehicle etc., or locomotive); convey in vehicle; act as driver of vehicle; travel, go, in car or carriage at one's disposal (cf. *ride* in omnibus, tram, train). 4. Impel forcibly, constrain, compel (*to*, *into*, *to small-*, *out of one's senses*); overwork (*was very hard-*~*n*). 5. Impel, carry along (of wind, water), throw, propel, send in some direction, (inanimate things); (Cricket) return (ball) from freely swung bat to or past bowler; (Golf) strike (ball, or abs.) with DRIVER from tee. 6. Force (stake, nail, etc.) into ground etc. with blow(s); bore (tunnel, horizontal cavity); (also steam or other power) set or keep (machinery) going (also of person, ~ *a bargain*, *pen*, *write*). 8. Carry on, effect, conclude, (*drove a roaring trade*, *good bargain*). 9. Defer (~ *it to the last minute*). 10. Dash, rush, hasten; work hard at. 11. Float along, drift, tend, (*driving rain*; ~ *at*, seek, intend, mean; *what is he driving at?*). [com.-Teut. OE *drīfan* cf. G *treiben*]

drive[2], n. Excursion in vehicle (see prec.); driving of game or enemy (see prec.); ...

driv'el, v.i. & t., & n. 1. Run at mouth or nose like child; talk childishly or idiotically; fritter *away*; hence ~ER[1] n. 2. n. Silly nonsense. [ME *drevelen*, *dravelen*, OE *dreflian*, prob. cogn. w. DRAFF]

driv'er, n. One who drives (DRIVE[1]), coachman (also *cab-*~, *engine-*~, etc.; *slave-*~, overseer of slave gang); (Golf) straight-faced wooden club for driving long distance from tee; (Mech.) driving wheel or other part that receives power directly; (*front*, *rear*, ~, bicycle in which power is applied to front, rear, wheel; *quill-*~. Hence ~LESS a. [-ER[1]]

driving-wheel, n. Wheel communicating motion to other parts of machine; large wheel of locomotive; cycle wheel that is directly worked.

driz'zle, v.i. & n. (Fall in, be wet with) fine dense drops of rain (subj. *it*, *the day*, *rain*, *it*). Hence **driz'zlY[2]** a. [cf. OE *dréosan* fall, -LE(3)]

dro'gher (-ger), n. W.-Ind. coasting vessel; slow heavy craft. [thr. F f. 16th-c. Du. *drogher* (*droogen* to dry) named from drying herrings]

drogue (-ōg), n. Buoy at end of harpoon line; sea anchor, a bag-like contrivance used to steady and delay the movement of a boat; = WIND[1]sock. [perh. var. of DRAG[2]]

droit (or *drwah*), n. Right, due, legal perquisite, (esp. ~*s of Admiralty*, proceeds of enemy's ships, wrecks, etc.). [f. F f. LL *directum* f. L *directum* neut. adj. = f. LL legal right (DIRECT[2])]

drôll, a., n., & v.i. Facetious, amusing; queer, odd, surprising; hence **drôll'LY[2]** (-öl-li) adv., ~NESS n.; (n., now rare) jester, wag; (v.i., now rare) play the buffoon, jest *with*, *at*, *on*. [f. F *drôle*]
-ARY]

drôll'ery, n. Jesting; a facetious composition; quaint humour. [-ERY]

drôme, n. (colloq.). Aerodrome. [abbr.]

-drôme, suf. repr. Gk *dromos* course, used in Gk compounds such as *hippodrome*, in modern words such as *aerodrome*, and (loosely) in *picturedrome*.

drom'edary (also -tim-), n. Light fleet camel bred for riding. [f. OF *dromedaire* f. LL *dromedarius* f. L f. Gk *dromas* -*ados* runner.

drom'ond, n. (hist.). Large medieval ship for war or commerce. [f. OF *dromon* f. LL f. Byz. Gk *dromon* (*dromos* race)

drone, n., & v.i. & t. [OE *drān*] ... Male of honey-bee, which does not work; idler; deep humming sound; monotonous speech or speaker; bass-pipe of bagpipe; fixed ...

continuous note emitted by this. **2.** vb. Buzz like bee or bagpipe, talk or utter monotonously, whence **drōn'ingly²** adv.; idle *away* (life etc.). [OE *dran, dræn,* (sense bee); cf. G *drohne*]

drōōl, v.i. (U.S. & dial.). Drivel, slobber. [contr. f. DRIVEL]

drōōp, v.i. & t., & n. **1.** Hang down, slope, incline, as in weariness; (of eyes) look downwards; (poet., of sun etc.) sink; languish, decline, flag, lose heart; let (head, face, eyes) fall forward or down; hence **~ingly²** adv. **2.** n. ~ing attitude, loss of spirit, fall of tone. [f. ON *drūpa* vb cogn. w. foll.]

drŏp¹, n. **1.** Round, pear-shaped, or hemispherical portion of liquid such as hangs or falls separately or adheres to surface (of water, tears, sweat, dew, rain, blood, or abs. in these senses); (Med.) smallest separable quantity of a liquid (in pl., liquid medicine to be measured by ~s); minute quantity (~ *in bucket or ocean,* infinitesimal factor); glass etc. of intoxicating liquor (*take a* ~; *has taken a* ~ *too much,* is drunk; *have a* ~ *in one's eye,* show signs of having drunk); pendant, hanging ornament, (ear-~s), sugarplum (*acid, pear* etc., ~s); hence **~'LET** n. **2.** Act of dropping, fall, social comedown, descent in prices, temperature, etc.; thing that drops or is dropped, as between acts (also ~*curtain*), (in gallows) platform withdrawn from under feet of condemned (also, distance he is allowed to fall, as ~ *of 3 ft*); abrupt fall in level of surface, amount of this; (also ~*kick*) kick at football made by dropping ball and kicking it as it rises (~*off,* ~*out,* such kick to start play after goal, try, or touchdown). **3.** ~*forging* (also *die-forging*), the system of forcing a piece of white-hot metal through an open-ended die of the required shape; ~*hammer* (also ~*press*), forging-machine using the power of a dropped weight; ~*shot* (Lawn Tennis), shot dropping abruptly after clearing net; ~*shutter,* appliance for giving instantaneous exposure in photography; ~*sulphur, -tin,* granulated by being dropped molten into water; ~*wort,* kinds of plant with tuberous root fibres. [sense 1 f. OE *dropa* cf. G *tropfen,* cogn. w. *drip; droop;* sense 2 f. foll.]

drŏp², v.i. & t. (-pp-). **1.** Fall in drops; give off moisture in drops. **2.** Fall by force of gravity from not being held etc., (fig.) be uttered casually (*the remark ~ped from him*), disappear (*a letter has ~ped out*). **3.** Sink to ground exhausted, wounded, etc. (~ *on one's knee,* kneel), (of setter) crouch at sight of game. **4.** Fall naturally asleep, (*back*) into habit etc.; die; cease, lapse, (*affair was allowed to* ~; *the correspondence ~ped*). **5.** Fall in direction, condition, amount, degree, pitch, (*prices, voices,* ~); *go down* stream; fall *behind, to the rear,* etc. **6.** Come or go casually *in* as visitor, *into* place, *across* person; ~ *on* or *across,* reprimand or punish. **7.** Let fall (liquid, tears) in drops; shed; let go, relinquish, cease to hold, (~ *anchor,* anchor ship); give birth to (esp. lambs). **8.** Utter casually as if unconsciously (esp. ~ *a hint;* so ~ *a postcard, line, note*). **9.** Lose (money, esp. in gaming), **10.** Fell with axe, blow of fist, or bullet. **11.** Set down (passenger, parcel). **12.** Omit (*letter, one's hs, syllable*) in speech. **13.** Let (eyes) droop; lower (voice); ~ CURTSY. **14.** (Football) send (ball), make (goal), by drop-kick (see prec.; also intr.=take drop-kick). **15.** Cease to associate with, have done with (~ *it,* stop that). **16.** ~*away, in,* depart, enter, one by one; ~ *off,* ~ *away,* also fall asleep. [OE *dropian,* see prec.]

drŏpp'ings (-z), n. pl. What falls or has fallen in drops, e.g. wax from candles; dung of beasts or birds. [-ING¹]

drŏp-scēne, n. = drop-curtain (DROP¹). final scene, finale, of drama in real life.

drŏp'sy, n. Disease in which watery fluid collects in cavities or tissue of body, (fig.) overswollen state. Hence **~ICAL** a., **~ICALly²** adv. [f. OF *ydropisie* f. L *hydropisis* f. Gk *hudrōps -ōpos* (*hudōr, hudr-,* water)]

drŏs(h)'ky, n. Russian low four-wheeled carriage; cab in German towns. [f. Russ. *drozhki* dim. of *drogi* wagon (*droga* perch)]

drŏss, n. Scum thrown off from metals in melting; foreign matter mixed with anything, impurities; refuse, rubbish. Hence **~'Y²** a. [OE *drōs* cf. G *drusen* husks, dregs]

drought (-owt) (poet., Sc., U.S.) **drouth,** n. (Arch.) dryness, lack of moisture, also thirst; continuous dry weather, want of rain. Hence **drought'Y²**(-owt-), **drouth²** a. [OE *drūgad* (*drūge* DRY¹, -TH¹)]

drōve¹, n. **1.** Herd, flock, being driven or moving together; crowd, multitude, shoal, large number, esp. as moving together. **2.** Mason's broad chisel. [OE *drāf* (*drīfan* DRIVE¹)]

drōve². See DRIVE¹.

drō'ver, n. Driver of droves to market, cattle-dealer. Hence **drōve³** v.t., **drōv²** ING¹ n. [DROVE¹+-ER]

drown, v.i. & t. **1.** Suffer death by suffocation in liquid (now usn. *be ~ed;* but ~*ing man* etc.); suffocate (person, animal) by submersion (subj., person etc., or the liquid); submerge, flood, drench, (esp. fig. ~*ed in tears, sleep, wine; like ~ed rat,* in soaked condition; ~ *out,* drive out by flood). **2.** Deaden (grief etc.) with or in drink; overpower (esp. of louder sound making voice etc. inaudible). [perh. f. *drumlen* p.p. of *drink,* cf. MDa. *drukne* drown f. *drucken* p.p. of *drikke* drink]

drowse (-z), v.i. & t., & n. Be dull & sleepy, half asleep; be sluggish; make drowsy; pass away (time) in drowsing; (n.) half-asleep condition. [perh. = OE *drūsian* sink, become slow, cogn. w. *drēosan* fall; but not found in 11th–15th cc.; prob. back-formation from foll.]

drow'sy (-z-), a. Sleepy, half asleep; dozing; lulling, soporific; sluggish; (-gy-*head*, sleepy person. Hence ~i-LY² adv., ~i-NESS, nn., ~i-NY² adv. [perh. = OE *drūsian* see prec.; found earlier than prec.]

drudge, n., & v.i. 1. Servile worker, slave, hack; hence ~ERY²(5) n. 2. v.i. Work slavishly at distasteful work; hence ~ING-LY² adv. [perh. f. Arab. *darb* beating]

drug, n., & v.t. & i. (-gg-). 1. Original simple medicinal substance, organic or inorganic, used alone or as ingredient (*the ~ habit*, of taking opiates etc.); unsalable commodity, thing no longer in demand (usu. ~ *in the market*); hence ~g'Y²(-g-) a. 2. v.b. Adulterate with ~, esp. with narcotic or poison; administer ~s, esp. narcotics, to; indulge in narcotics etc.; nauseate, cloy. [f. F *drogue* cf. Pr. *droga*, Sp. It., *droga*, etym. dub.]

drug'get (-g-), n. (Over-carpet or floor-cloth or) coarse woollen stuff used for floor or table coverings. [f. F *droguet*, etym. dub.]

drug'gist (-g-), n. Dealer in drugs, pharmaceutical chemist. [-IST]

Dru'id (-ōō-), n. Priest, magician, soothsayer, among Celts of ancient Gaul & Britain; officer of Welsh Gorsedd or national assembly. Hence ~ESS¹, ~ISM(3), nn. **Dru'id'(IC)AI** aa. (-ōō-), *Druid'ide* f. I pl. *druidae, -des*, f. OCelt. *druid*- magician]

drum¹, n. 1. Musical instrument sounded by striking & made of hollow cylinder or hemisphere with parchment stretched over opening(s) (*bass, tenor, big*, KETTLE, etc., ~). 2. (Zool.) natural organ giving resonance, as howling monkey's hyoid bone. 3. Sound (as) of ~, esp. bittern's cry; player of ~, drummer. 4. Cylindrical structure (~ *of ear*, hollow part of middle ear) or object, cylinder or barrel in machinery on which something is wound or for other purposes; solid part of Corinthian or composite capital; stone block forming section of shaft; cylindrical receptacle for packing dried fruit, holding oil, etc. 5. Evening or afternoon-tea party (Hist.). 6. (Also ~-*fish*) kinds of American fish able to make drumming noise. 7. ~*fire*, heavy continuous rapid artillery fire usu. heralding infantry attack; ~'*head*, skin or membrane of (~*head* COURT¹ *martial*), membrane across ~ of ear, circular top of capstan; ~ *major*, N.C.O. commanding drummers of regiment; ~'*stick*, stick with knob or pad for beating ~; lower joint of cooked fowl's leg. [cf. Du. *trom*, & MHG *trumme* orig. trumpet]

drum², v.i. & t. (-mm-). Play the drum, whence ~m'ER¹ n., player of drum, *commercial traveller; beat, tap, or thump, continuously on something (on piano, *at door; feet ~ on floor; a ~ming in the ears*); (of birds, insects) make loud hollow noise with quivering wings; summon, beat *up*, as by ~ming; ~ *out*, cashier by beat of drum; drive (person) into apathy etc., (lesson) into person, by persistence; strike (hands etc.), repeatedly as on drum. [f. prec.]

drum³, **drum'lin**, nn. (geol.). Long oval mound of drift or diluvial formation. [f. Gael. & Ir. *druim* ridge; -*lin* perh. for -LING¹]

Drúmm'ond light (lit), n. Limelight or oxyhydrogen light. [Capt. T. *Drummond*, inventor c. 1825]

drunk, pred. a. & n. (also p.p. of DRINK¹). 1. Intoxicated, overcome with liquor, (*beastly, blind, dead, half*, etc., ~; ~ *as a fiddler or lord*; also fig., ~ *with joy, success, rage*); hence ~ARD n. 2. n. (sl.). Drinking-bout, drunken fit; (from police charge-sheets) case of drunkenness (hence gen.) man charged with drunkenness.

drunk'en, a. (rarely pred., cf. prec.). Intoxicated; given to drinking, often drunk; caused by or exhibiting drunkenness (~ *frolic, brawl*). Hence ~ly adv., ~NESS n. [as prec., see -EN¹]

drupe (-ōō-), n. Stone-fruit, fleshy or pulpy fruit enclosing stone or nut with kernel, as olive, plum, cherry. Hence **drupà'CEOUS** (-ōōpā'shús) a. [f. L f. Gk *drúppa* over-ripe (olive)]

drup'el (-ōō-), **drupe'let** (-ōōpl-), nn. Small drupe in compound fruit, as blackberry. [-EL, -LET¹]

druse¹ (-ōōz), n. Crust of crystals lining rock-cavity, cavity so lined. [G. f. Boh. *druza*]

Druse² (-ōōz), n. Member of political & religious sect of Mohammedan origin about Mt Lebanon. [Ismail *al-Darazī*, founder 1040]

dry¹, a. (*drier, -est*). 1. Without moisture (~ *eyes*, free from tears; ~ *shampoo*, applied as powder); not rainy, with deficient rainfall. 2. Parched, dried up (colloq.) thirsty, (of liquid) having disappeared by evaporation, draining, wiping, etc., (of country, legislation, etc.) teetotal, prohibiting sale of intoxicants (*go ~*, accept such legislation). 3. Not yielding water, milk, etc. (*cow, well, is ~*). 4.

Without butter (~ *bread, toast*). **5.** Solid, not liquid, (~ *goods*, see below; ~ *measure*, measure of capacity for these). **6.** (Of wine) free from sweetness & fruity flavour. **7.** Unconnected with liquid (*die a ~ death*, not by drowning or bloodshed; ~ *cough*, without phlegm; ||~-BOB²). **8.** Impassive, unsympathetic, stiff, hard, cold, (~ *jest, sarcasm, humour*, expressed in matter-of-fact tone with show of unconsciousness). **9.** Meagre, plain, bare, not enlarged upon, (~ *facts, thanks*). **10.** Untinged by prejudice or interest (~ *light*). **11.** ~-*bulb thermometer*, one of pair in hygrometer with wet & ~ bulbs; ~-*clean*, clean (clothes etc.) by means of spirit etc., without using water, so ~ *cleaner*, ~-*cleaning*; ~ *cooper*, maker of casks for ~ goods; ~-*cure*, cure (meat etc.) without pickling in liquid; ~-DOCK⁴; ~-*fly* a. & v.i., (fish) with fly floating lightly on water; ~ *goods*, non-liquid goods, as corn, also (esp. U.S.) drapery, mercery, haberdashery; ~ *lodging*, without board; ~ *nurse*, tending but not suckling child, (v.t.) bring up by hand; ~ *pile*, electric pile or battery in which no liquid is used; ~-*plate*, photographic plate with sensitized film hard & ~ for convenience of keeping, developing at leisure, etc.; ~-*point*, needle for engraving without acid on bare copper plate (also v.i., use this process, & n., engraving produced so); ~-*rot*, decayed state of wood not exposed to air caused by fungi, also the fungi, (fig.) unsuspected moral or social decay; ~-*salt* v.t., ~-*cure*; ~ *salter(y)*, dealer, dealing or shop that deals, in drugs, dyes, gums, oils, pickles, tinned meats, etc.; ~-*shod* a. or adv., without wetting the feet; ~-*walling* (without mortar). Hence ~ISH¹ (2) a., ~NESS n. [OE *drīge* cf. Du. *droog*.]

dry², v.t. & i. Make or become dry by wiping, evaporation, draining, etc.; ~ *up*, cause (cow) to cease giving milk; ~ *up*, make utterly dry, (of moisture) disappear utterly, (of well etc.) cease to yield water, (colloq., esp. in imperat.) cease talking or doing something. Hence DRIER¹ (1, 2) (or ~**er**) n., (also) substance mixed with oil-paints to expedite ~ing. [OE *drȳgean* (*drīge* DRY¹)]

dry'ad, n. Nymph inhabiting tree, wood-nymph. [f. L f. Gk *druas -ados* (*drus* tree)]

Dry'asdust (-az-) n., **d-**, a. Dull laborious antiquary or historian; (adj.) very dry, uninteresting. [*Dr ~*, fictitious person (*dry as dust*) to whom Scott dedicated]

'**dst**, clipping of *wouldst, hadst*.

du'ad. n. (Incorrect for) DYAD.

du'al, a. & n. **1.** Of two, twofold, divided in two, double, (~ *ownership, skirt*); the *D~ Monarchy*, former Austro-Hungarian Empire. **2.** (Gram.) ~ *number* or ~, inflected form proper to two persons or things (additional to *singular* & *plural*). So **dua'l'ITY** n., ~IZE(3) v.t., ~LY² adv. [f. L *dualis* (*duo* two, -AL)]

du'alin, n. Powerful explosive of nitre, nitroglycerin, & sawdust. [prec. (*dual nitre*) +-IN]

du'allism, n. Duality; use of dual number; theory recognizing two independent principles (mind & matter, cf. *idealism* & *materialism*; good & evil in the universe; two personalities in Christ), so ~IST (2) n., ~IS'TIC a., ~IS'TICALLY adv. [DUAL+-ISM]

dub¹, v.t. (-bb-). **1.** Make (person) into a *knight* by striking shoulders with sword; invest with (new title), name, nickname, (person or thing, with complement) (~*name me Doctor, quack, a scribbler*). **2.** Dress (artificial fishing-fly). **3.** Smear (leather) with grease. [perh. f. OF *aduber*, com.-Rom. cf. It. *addobbare*, etym. dub.]

dubb'ing, n. In vbl senses; esp., prepared grease for leather. [f. DUB¹ +-ING¹]

dubi'ety, n. Feeling of doubt; doubtful matter. [f. LL *dubietas* (*dubius* doubtful, -TY)]

dub'ious, a. Indistinct (~ *light*), vague, unreliable (~ *friend*), of questionable value or truth (*a ~ complement*); of doubtful issue (~ *undertaking, struggle*); of suspected character (~ *gains, company*); hesitating, doubting. Hence ~LY² adv., ~NESS n. [f. L *dubiosus* (*dubius* doubtful, -OSE⁴)]

dubita'tion, n. Doubt, hesitation. [F, f. L *dubitationem* (*dubitare* DOUBT², -ATION)]

dub'itative, a. Of expressing, inclined to, doubt or hesitation. Hence ~LY² (-vl-) adv. [f. L *dubitativus* as prec.+-IVE]

duc'al, a. Of, like, bearing title of, duke. [F, f. LL *ducalis* (*dux* DUKE, -AL)]

duc'at, n. Gold coin about 9s., formerly current in most European countries; coin, (pl.) money. [F, f. It. *ducato* f. LL *ducatus* DUCHY (prob. named from Duke of Apulia 1140)]

Duce (dōō'chā), n. Chief (*Il*, or *the*, ~, Mussolini as Fascist leader). [It., f. L *dux ducis*]

duch'ess, n. Duke's wife or widow; lady holding a duchy in her own right; imposing woman; ||(sl.) costermonger's wife (abbr. *dútch*). [F (-*e*), f. LL *ducissa* (DUKE, -ESS⁴)]

duchesse (dōōshěs'), n. Kind of satin; ~ *lace*, kind of Brussels pillow-lace. [F, = duchess]

duch'y, n. Territory of reigning duke or duchess; royal dukedom of Cornwall or Lancaster, each with certain courts of its own. [f. OF *duché* f. LL *ducatus* (*dux* DUKE, -ATE²)]

duck¹, n. (pl. often ~ collective; ~s). 1. Kinds of swimming-bird, esp. the domesticated form of the mallard or wild-~ (like ~ in thunderstorm, with up-turned eyes, looking flabbergasted, faint; like water off ~'s back, producing no effect; take to anything like ~ to water; fine day for young ~s, rainy weather; lame ~, disabled person, defaulter on Stock Exchange; in two shakes of ~'s tail, in an instant); its female ~ of this (cf. DRAKE²); its flesh. 2. Darling (esp. in voc.), whence ~y³, n. (also ~y diamond, voc.). 3. (Cricket; also ~'s-egg) batsman's score of 0. 4. Bombay ~, BUMMALO; ~ water (make ~s & drakes of, play ~s etc. with, squander); ~-bill, red wheat, also = ~-billed PLATYPUS or ORNITHORHYNCHUS; ~-boards, narrow path of wooden slats in trench or over mud; ~-hawk, marsh harrier; ~-shot, of size for shooting wild ~; ~-weed, plant that carpets surface of still water. Hence ~'LING¹(2) n. (UGLY ~-ling). [OE duce cogn. w. foll.]

duck², v.i. & t., & n. 1. Plunge, dive, dip head, under water & emerge; bend quickly, bob, to avoid blow etc. or by way of bow or curtsy; plunge (person etc.) momentarily in water, or abs., whence ~'ING¹(1) n. (~ing-stool, chair at end of oscillating pole, formerly used for dip below water in bathing, or lowering ~ing scolds and other objectionable persons); lower (head) suddenly. 2. n. Quick dip below water & other objectionable ... of head. [ME d(o)uke f. OE *dūcan com-WG cf. G tauchen]

duck³, n. Strong untwilled linen or cotton fabric for small sails & outer clothing esp. of sailors; (pl. ~s) trousers of this. [prob. f. Du. doeck = G tuch cloth]

duck⁴, n. (colloq.). Amphibious landing craft. [f. DUKWS, official designation.]

duck'er¹, n. Kinds of diving-bird, esp. dabchick & water ouzel. [DUCK², -ER¹]

duck'er², n. Breeder of ducks. [DUCK¹, -ER¹]

duct'ile, a. (Of metals) malleable, flexible, not brittle, (in technical use) capable of being drawn out into wire, tough; plastic (of clay etc., or of person or character); pliable, tractable, docile. Hence ductil'-ITY n. [F, f. L ductilis (ducere see prec., -IL)].

duct, n. Conduit, tube, for conveying liquid; tube or canal in body conveying chyle, lymph, or secretions (named from function, as biliary ~, or from discoverer, as Eustachian ~, ~s of Bellini); vessel of plant's vascular tissue holding air, water, etc. Hence ~'LESS a. (~less glands, of which the secretion is not carried off by a ~, but acts directly on the blood). [f. L ductus leading, aqueduct (ducere lead)]

dud¹, n. & a. (sl.). 1. (Pl.) clothes, rags; (sing.) scarecrow (also ~'man), shell etc. that fails to go off, futile plan or person. 2. adj. Counterfeit, useless, unsatis- [-ID]

*dude, n. (sl.). Fastidious aesthetic person, often imitating English speech, dress, & manners; dandy, swell. Hence dud'ISH¹ a. [?]

dudg'eon¹ (-jn), n. Resentment, feeling of offence. (usu. in ~). [etym. dub.; obs.]

dud'(h)een (doo-), n. (Ir.). Short clay pipe. [?]

due¹, a. & adv. 1. Owing, payable, as a debt or obligation (fall, become, ~, as bill reaching maturity; that ought to be given to person (first place is ~ to Milton, (has his ~ reward), rightful, proper, ade-quate (after ~ consideration, to be looked for, calculated or foreseen (in ~ time); to be ascribed to cause, agent, etc. (the discovery is ~ to Newton; the advl use for ~ owing, as I came late ~ to an accident, is incorrect); under engagement to do some-thing (is ~ to speak tonight) or to arrive at certain time (train ~ at 7.30; already ~, exactly directly. (went ~ east, a ~ N. wind). [f. OF deü (p.p. of devoir owe) f. LL debitus for L debitus (debēre owe)]

due², n. Person's right, what is owed him, (give one, esp. the devil, his ~, not be un-just to him, even though he deserves little or is no friend); what one owes (pay one's ~s); (usu. pl.) toll, fee, legally demandable (harbour, light, tonnage, uni-versity, ~s). [f. prec.]

dü'el, n., & v.i.(-ll-). 1. Fight with deadly weapons between two persons, in pre-sence of two seconds, to settle quarrel (the ~, ~ling & its code of rules) any contest between two persons, animals, parties, causes; hence ~list(1) n. 2. v.i. Fight ~(-s). [F, f. med.L sense of arch. L duellum (duo two) orig. form of bellum war: for duel-bel- cf. BIS]

düen'na, n. Elderly woman acting as governess & companion in charge of girls (orig. & esp. in Spanish family); chaperon. [f. Sp. dueña f. L domina mistress]

düet', n. Musical composition for two voices or performers; (fig.) dialogue, scolding-match; pair, couple. Hence düet'TIST(1) n. [f. It. duetto dim. of duo]

‖ **duff'¹**, n. (Dial. etc. for) DOUGH; PLUM-~. [f. L duo two]

duff'², v.t. (sl.). Fake up (goods), give look of newness etc. to, (‖~ing, counter-feit; (Austral.) steal & alter brands on (cattle); (Golf) misbit (shot, ball). [perh. back-formation f. DUFFER]

duff'el, duff'le, n. Coarse woollen cloth with thick nap; sportsman's, camper-out's, change of clothes. [Duffel in Brabant]

duff'er, n. ‖ One who sells trash as valuable, pretending it to be smuggled, stolen, etc.; ‖ pedlar, hawker; faker of sham articles; counterfeit coin, picture, etc.; unproductive mine; thing of which no use can be made; inefficient, useless, or stupid person. [etym. dub.; first sense a century older than last, & than DUFF²]

dug¹, n. Udder of female mammals, also teat, nipple, (not now used of women exc. contempt.). [cf. Sw. dægga suckle]

dug². See DIG¹.

dug'ong (dōō-), n. (pl. often ~). Large herbivorous mammal of Indian seas. [f. Malay duyong]

dug'-out, n. Canoe made by hollowing tree-trunk; underground shelter esp. for troops in trenches; ‖ (sl.) retired officer etc. recalled to service.

duik'er, duy-, (dīk-), n. Small S.-African antelope. [Du. duiker (in full duikerbok)]

duke, n. 1. (Hist.) provincial military commander under later Roman emperors; (Bibl.) chief of tribe. 2. (In some parts of Europe) sovereign prince ruling duchy or small State; (Gt Britain & some other countries) person holding highest hereditary title of nobility outside royal family (also royal ~, who is also royal prince, with precedence); DINE with D~ Humphrey. 3. Kind of cherry. 4. (sl.) Hand, fist. [f. F duc f. L dux ducis leader]

duke'dom (-kd-), n. Territory ruled by, dignity of, duke. [-DOM]

Duk'eries (-iz), n. pl. District in Notts. containing several ducal estates. [-ERY]

Dul'äg (dōō-), n. Camp for prisoners of war in transit. [G]

dul'cet, a. Sweet, soothing, (esp. of sounds). [f. F doucet dim. of doux f. L dulcis sweet]

dul'cify, v.t. Sweeten, make gentle. Hence FICA'TION n. [f. L dulcificare (dulcis sweet, -FY)]

dul'cimer, n. Musical instrument with strings of graduated length over sounding board or box struck with hammers, prototype of piano. [f. OF doulcimer perh. f. L dulce melos (not found in required sense)]

Dulcine'a (or -sin'ĭa), n. Idolized & idealized mistress. [name of Don Quixote's mistress]

dull, a., & v.t. & i. 1. Slow of understanding, obtuse, stupid, whence ~ARD n.; (of ears, eyes, etc.) without keen perception; (of inanimate things) insensible; (of pain etc.) indistinctly felt; sluggish, slow-moving, stagnant, (of person, animal, trade); (of goods, stocks) not easily salable, not in demand; listless, depressed; tedious, monotonous; blunt (esp. of edge); (of colour, light, sound, taste) not bright, vivid, or keen; (of weather) overcast, gloomy; hence ~ISH a., dull'NESS n., dull'LY² (dŭl-lĭ) adv. 2. vb. Make ~ (~ the edge of, blunt, make less sensitive, interesting, effective); lose force, intensity, clearness, or keenness. [ME, cf. OE dol, also G toll mad]

dulse, n. Edible kind of sea-weed. [f. Ir. & Gael. duileasg]

dul'Y, adv. Rightly, properly, fitly; sufficiently; punctually. [DUE¹+-LY²]

du'ma (dōō-), n. Russian parliament, 1906–17. [previously name of elective municipal councils]

dumb¹ (-m), a. (compar. & superl., pron. -mer, -mist). Unable to speak; pron. (of human beings; the ~, the deaf & ~, as nouns) or normally (~ animals, used in pity or contempt); inarticulate, having no voice in government etc., (the ~ millions); silenced by surprise, shyness, etc. (esp. strike ~; ~ in mixed company); taciturn, reticent, (Nature is ~ on the point; English a ~ people); *stupid; without speech (~ crambo; ~ show, significant gestures, part of play given in early drama without words); unheard, giving no sound; without the voice, sound, or other property, usual in things of the name (~ piano, set of keys for exercising fingers; ~waiter, ‖ an upright with revolving shelves enabling waiter to be dispensed with in dining-room, *food-lift; ‖ ~barge, craft, without sails or motive power; ~bell, short bar sunk merely to carry off surface water); ~-iron, one of the two curved forward ends of the side-members of a motor-car chassis. Hence ~'LY² (-ml-) adv., ~'NESS (-mn-) n. [com.-Teut.; OE dumb, cf. Du. dom, G dumm, stupid]

dumb², v.t. Make dumb. [prec.]

dumbfound' (-mf-), v.t. Strike dumb, confound, nonplus. [dumb, confound]

‖ **dum'bledōre** (-ld-), n. (dial.) Bumble-bee; cockchafer. [-]

dum'dum, a. & n. ~ (bullet), kind of soft-nosed bullet that expands & inflicts laceration. [D~ in India, with cantonment & arsenal]

dumm'Y, n. & a. 1. (Whist) imaginary fourth player whose hand is turned up & played by partner (~ whist or ~, game so played; double ~, game with two such hands); (Bridge) the partner of the player who makes the first call in the accepted declaration, or his (exposed) hand. 2. Person taking no real part, or pretended one only for show, figurehead, mere tool, man of straw; dolt, blockhead. 3. Counterfeit object, sham package etc., clothes-block, lay figure, man's figure as target; baby's indiarubber teat; sell the ~ (Rugby football), deceive opponent by feigning to pass ball. 4. adj. Sham. [DUMB¹+-Y³]

dump¹, n. 1. Short thick object of various kinds; ‖ leaden counter used in games;

obs., Australian coin, (sl.) small coin (*not
worth a ~*); ∥ kind of bolt in ship-building;
rope quoit for game on board ship; kind
of skittle; kind of sweetmeat; short stout
person. [prob. back-formation f. DUMPY]

dump[2], v.t. & i., & n. 1. Shoot, deposit,
tilt down, (rubbish) ; let fall with a bump;
(Commerce), send (goods unsalable at high
price in home market) to foreign market
for sale at low price, to avoid lowering
home price & capture new market; drop
down (t. & i.) with a bump; land (superfluous immigrants) in foreign country;
hence ~ER[1] n. 2. n. Dull blow, thud;
heap of refuse, place for shooting this;
(Mil.) temporary depot of munitions.
[cf. Da. *dumpe*, Norw. *dumpa*, fall plump]

dump'ing, n. Mass of dough boiled or
baked either plain or enclosing apple etc.
[cf. LG *dump* damp, heavy, & see -LING[1]]

dumps, n. pl. Depression, melancholy,
(usu. *in the ~*). [f. 1523; etym. dub.]

dump'y, a. & n. 1. Short & stout (~*y level*,
2. n. ∥ Short-legged Scotch breed of fowls.
Hence ~INESS n. [etym. dub.; earlier than DUMP[1]]

dun[1], a. & n. (Of) dull greyish-brown
colour as of ass or mouse (~*-bird*, ∥ po-
chard ; ~ *diver*, ∥ female or young male of
goosander) ; (poet.) dark, dusky ; ~ *horse*,
kinds of artificial fishing-fly. [OE, cf. Ir.
& Gael. *donn*, W *dwn*]

dun[2] n., & v.t. (-nn-). 1. Importunate
creditor; debt-collector; demand for
payment. 2. v.t. Importune for payment
of debt; pester. [perh. var. of DIN]

dunce, n. One slow at learning, dullard,
(~*'s cap*, paper cone put on head of ~ at
school). [f. John Duns Scotus, school-
man, d. 1308, whose followers were ridiculed by 16th-c. humanists and reformers
as enemies of learning]

dun'derhead (-ĕd), n. **dun'der-headed**
(-ĕd), a. Blockhead, stupid (person), [?]
[etym. dub.]

Dundrear'y, n. ~ *whiskers*, long side
whiskers worn without beard. [~,
character in T. Taylor's comedy *Our
American Cousin*]

dune, n. Mound or ridge of loose sand
on coast. [F, f. ODu. *dūna* = OE *dūn*
DOWN[1]]

dung, n., & v.t. 1. Manure; excrement of
animals (rarely of man; ~*-beetle*, whose
larvae develop in ~; ~*-fly*, feeding in it;
~*-worm*, found in cow-~ & used as bait;
~*-cart*, *-fork*, for conveying, loading, &
spreading, manure); moral filth. 2. v.t.
Manure (land; of farmer, grazing animals,
or the manure). [OE, cf. G *dung, düngen*,
manure, & Sw. *dynga* dung]

dung'aree (-ngg-), n. Coarse Indian
calico ; (pl.) overalls etc. of ~. [f. Hind.
dungrī]

dun'geon (-jn), n., & v.t. (Now usu.
donjon) great tower of castle in innermost
court or bailey; strong subterranean cell
for prisoners ; (vb) shut *up*, imprison in

~. [f. F *donjon* f. LL *domnionem* nom. ~,
f. *domina* for L *dominus* lord; doublet of
DOMINION]

dung'hill, n. Heap of dung or refuse in
farmyard, etc., household,
parish, etc., tyrant or bully; ~ *cock* etc.,
barn-door not game, whence ~ *as adj.*,
craven].

∥ **dun'iwassal** (dōō-), n. (Sc.), Highland
gentleman of secondary rank. [Gael.
duine uasal noble]

Dunkirk', n. (Scene of) evacuation of a
defeated army by sea like that of the
British from ~ in May 1940. [port in
France]

dun'lin, n. Red-backed sand-piper.
[-LING[1]]

Dun'ker, n. (In music-hall usage) pair of
artistes (*comedy ~*). [DUN, etym. dub.;
-OCK]

∥ **dunn'ock**, n. Hedge-sparrow. [DUN[1],
-OCK]

dunt, n. Blow given to aircraft by a
vertical current of air suddenly encountered. [orig. Sc., prob. var. of DINT]

dun'nage, n. Mats, brushwood, gratings,
etc., stowed under or among cargo to
prevent moisture & chafing. [earlier *din-*,
etym. dub.]

duode̅c'imo, n. (usu. 12mo). Book-size in
which each leaf is 1/12 of printing-sheet;
book of this size; diminutive thing or
person. [L (*in*) *duodecimo* abl. see prec.]

duo̅den'ary, a. Proceeding by twelves,
in sets of twelve. [f. L *duodenarius* (*duodeni* twelve at once, -ARY[1]]

duode̅c'imal, a. & n. Of twelve or
twelfths, proceeding by twelves; (n. pl.)
cross-multiplication method used for
dimensions given in feet, inches, &
twelfths of inch, used by quantity surveyors etc. [f. L *duodecimus* twelfth +
-AL]

duo̅de̅'cimo̅, n. (usu. 12mo). Book-size in
which each leaf is 1/12 of printing-sheet;
book of this size; diminutive thing or
person. [L (*in*) *duodecimo* abl. see prec.]

duo̅de̅'num, n. (anat.). First portion of
small intestine immediately below stomach. Hence ~AL a., ~IT'IS (-īt-) n.
[med. L (*duodeni* see prec., from its
length of 12 in.)]

du'ologue (-ŏg), n. Conversation between
two persons, dramatic piece with two
actors. [irreg. f. Gk *duo* two, after *mono-
logue*]

duo̅mo̅ (dw-), n. (pl. ~s), Italian cathedral. [It.]

du'ple, n. & v.t. 1. Victim of deception,
gull ; hence ~ERY(2) n. 2. v.t. Cheat,
makes a fool of; hence ~ABILE a.,~ABIL'ITY,
~ER[1], nn. [F, etym. dub.]

du'ple, a. Double (now only in : ~ *ratio*,
that of 2 to 1 ; ~ *time*, *rhythm*, of two
beats to the bar). [f. L *duplus* (duo two,
-plus f. *ple-* fill)]

du'plex, a. Of two elements, twofold, (~
gas-burner, with two jets combining into
one flame ; ~ *lamp*, with two wicks); ~
telegraphy, by which one wire transmits
messages both ways at once. [L, gen.
-*plicis* (duo two, *plic-* fold)]

dup'licate¹, a. & n. **1.** With two corresponding parts, existing in two examples; doubled, twice as large or many; ~ *proportion, ratio*, proportion of squares in relation to that of their radicals; exactly like a thing already existing (of any number of copies or specimens). **2.** n. One of two things exactly alike, esp. that made after the other; second copy, with equal legal force, of letter or document; second copy of bill drawn in two parts, second of exchange; pawnbroker's ticket; exact correspondence between two things (*made in* ~). [f. L as foll., -ATE²]

dup'licate², v.t. Double, multiply by two; make in duplicate, make exact copy of, produce copies of, whence~ātor²(2) n. Hence~A'TION n. [f. L duplicare (DUPLEX, -ATE⁵)]

dupli'city, n. Double-dealing, deceitfulness; doubleness. [f. F duplicité f. L duplicitatem (DUPLEX, -TY)]

dūr'able, a. Lasting, not transitory; resisting wear, decay, etc. Hence dūrā-BI'LITY, ~leNESS (-ln-), nn., ~LY² adv. [F, f. L durabilis (durare f. durus hard, -ABLE]

dūrā'l'ūmin, n. An aluminium alloy remarkable for its strength and hardness, used for its strength etc. [P, f. Dür(en) in Prussia + ALUMIN(IUM)]

dūr'a mā'ter, n. (anat.). Tough outer membrane enveloping brain & spinal cord. [med. L, = hard mother, transl. of Arab. phrase]

dūrā'men, n. Heart-wood of exogenous tree. [L, f. durare harden]

dūr'ance, n. Imprisonment (usu. *in* ~ *vile*). [earlier sense endurance; F (durer f. L durare sense DURABLE, -ANCE]

dūrā'tion, n. Continuance in, length of, time; time for which thing continues (*for the* ~). Phr. common in war-time contracts). [obs. F, f. LL durationem (prec., -ATION)]

dūrb'ar, n. Indian ruler's court; public levee of Indian prince or Anglo-Ind. governor or viceroy. [f. Pers. & Hind. *darbar* court]

dūr'ess(e) (or dūrēs'), n. Forcible restraint, imprisonment; compulsion, esp. imprisonment, threats, or violence, illegally used to force person to do something (*under* ~; *plea of* ~, for voiding contract so made). [obs. F (-e), f. L durītia (durus hard, -ESS²]

dūr'ian (door²-), n. E.-Indian tree bearing a large oval fruit containing pulp notable for its fetid smell and agreeable taste; its fruit. [Malay, f. dūri thorn (from prickly rind)]

dūr'ing, prep. Throughout, at some point in, the continuance of. [part. of obs. dure last, used in abs. construction after F f. L; L vita durante, OF vie durant, E life ~ or ~life]

---

dūrm'ast (-ah-), n. Kind of oak. [etym. dub.; cf. *mast* fruit of forest tree]

dūrn, v.t. = DARN²

du'rra, dh-, (dŏŏ²-), n. Indian millet. [f. Arab. durah]

dūrst. See DARE.

dusk, n., a. & v.i. & t. **1.** Shade, gloom; darker stage of twilight. **2.** adj. (poet.). Shadowy, dim, dark-coloured, whence ~'ISH¹ a., & (in ordinary use) ~'Y² a., ~'LY² adv., ~'NESS n. **3.** vb. (poet.). Become, look, make, dim or dark or shadowy. [n. f. much earlier adj. ME *dosc* f. OE *dox*, cf. Norw. *dusk* mist]

dust¹, n. **1.** Finely powdered earth or other matter lying on ground or on surfaces or carried about in clouds by wind (*shake off the* ~ *of one's feet*, depart indignantly; *throw* ~ *in one's eyes*, mislead him by misrepresentation or diverting attention from point; *bite the* ~, fall wounded or slain). **2.** || Household refuse (~'bin, ~-hole, receptacles for this; || ~'man, scavenger who empties these). **3.** Pollen. **4.** (With *a*) cloud of ~ (*what a* ~, *a great* ~, *make or raise a* ~). **5.** Dead person's remains (*honoured* ~; *also in the* ~, *dead*); the human body, man. **6.** Humiliation (*humbled 'in, to, the* ~). **7.** Confusion, turmoil, excitement, row, contest, (~ *& heat*, the burden of a struggle). **8.** (sl.). Cash. **9.** ~-brand, disease of corn, smut; ~-cloak, -coat, -gown, -wrap, -cloth, worn or put over objects to keep off ~;~-colour, dull light brown; ~-cover, -jacket, book's jacket; ~-guard, in machine, or on bicycle to protect dress ;~man, = SANDMAN;~pan, into which ~ is brushed from floor; ~-shot, smallest-sized shot. Hence~'LESS a. [OE *dúst*, cf. MDu. *donst*, & G *dunst* vapour]

dust², v.t. & i. Sprinkle with dust or powder (intr., of birds, take dust-bath); *the eyes of*, deceive, take in); make dusty; sprinkle (dust, powder); clear of dust by brushing, wiping, or beating (~ one's *jacket*, beat him); clear away (dust etc.), clear furniture of dust. [f. prec.]

dus'ter, n. Cloth for dusting furniture etc.; person who does this. [-ER¹]

dus'ting, n. In vbl senses: esp. (sl.), thrashing, tossing in storm at sea. [-ING¹]

dūs't[ÿ, a. Full of, strewn with, finely powdered like, dust; dry as dust, uninteresting; vague, indefinite, (~ *answer*); || (sl.) *not so* ~y, fairly good; ~'miller, plant auricula, artificial fishing-fly. Hence ~'ily² adv., ~'iNESS n. [-Y²]

Dūtch¹, a. & n. **1.** (hist.). Of Germany including Netherlands (*High* ~). **2.** Of the language or people of Holland & Netherlands (~ *school*, of painters distinguished by artistic treatment of everyday subjects; *the* ~, people of Holland

& Netherlands). **3.** Coming from Holland, made or invented by the ~, (~ *clock, chair, cheese,* HOE, OVEN). **4.** Characteristic of or attributed to the ~ (~ AUCTION, COURAGE; *talk to one like a ~ uncle,* lecture him paternally; ~ *wife,* frame of cane etc. for resting the limbs in bed, long bolster similarly used). **5.** n. The German language in any of its forms (*High* ~, German; *Low* ~, Low German, including languages of Holland & other northern varieties) (Hist.). **6.** Language of Holland & Netherlands (*double* ~, gibberish). [f. MDu. *dutsch* Hollandish, Netherlandish, German, = G *deutsch* German, f. OHG *diutisc* popular, vulgar, national, (*diota* people cf. OE *theod*); in E the sense has narrowed f. *Teutonic* to *Hollandish*; in G & Du. from *Teutonic* to *German*]

||**dutch²**, n. See DUCHESS.

Dutch man, n. (pl. *-men*, fem. *-woman*). Hollander or Netherlander (or *I'm a* ~, forms of positive & negative asseveration); Dutch ship (*Flying* ~, spectral ship).

dut´eous, a. Dutiful, obedient, (of person or conduct). Hence ~LY² adv., ~NESS n. [DUTY+-EOUS]

dut´iable, a. Liable to customs or other duties. [-ABLE]

dut´iful, a. Regular or willing in obedience & service. Hence ~LY² adv., ~NESS n. [-FUL]

||**dut´y**, n. **1.** Behaviour due to superior, deference, expression of respect. **2.** Payment to public revenue levied on import, export, manufacture, or sale, of goods (CUSTOMS, EXCISE, *duties*), transfer of property (DEATH, PROBATE, *succession, stamp, duties*), licences, legal recognition of documents, etc. (~ *is* levied on article or transaction, *tax* usu. on persons). **3.** Moral or legal obligation, what one is bound or ought to do (~ *call,* visit one would rather not but feels bound to pay). **4.** Binding force of what is right. **5.** Business, office, function, performance of or engagement in these (*on, off,* ~, actually so engaged or not), (Eccl.) performance of church services (*took my* ~ *for me*). **6.** (Mech.) measure of engine's effectiveness in units of work done per unit of fuel. **7.** *Do* ~ *for,* serve or pass for (something else); ~-*paid, -free,* (of goods on which customs or excise ~ has been paid or is not leviable. [AF *dueté* (no corresp. F) see DUE¹.-TY]

duum vir (-er), n. (pl. ~*s*, ~). Member of board of two equal officials. Hence ~-ATE¹ n. [L, L, lit. man of the two]

duvet n. (see Ap.). n. Eider-down quilt. [F]

||**dux**, n. (no pl.). Top pupil in class (chiefly Sc.). [L, = leader]

dwale, n. Deadly Nightshade. [prob. f. Scand. (ON *dvöl* delay, Sw. *dvala* trance)]

dwarf (-örf), n., a., & v.t. **1.** Person, animal, or plant, much below ordinary size of species, whence ~'ISH¹ a., ~'ISHLY² adv., ~'ISHNESS n. **2.** Small supernatural being in esp. Scandinavian mythology skilled in metal-working. **3.** adj. Undersized (in many plant names); puny, stunted. **4.** v.t. Stunt in growth, or in intellect etc.; make look small by contrast or distance. [com.-Teut.: OE *dweorh*, cf. Du. *dwerg*, G *zwerg*]

dwell, v.i. (*dwelt*, & n. **1.** Keep one's attention fixed, write or speak at length, (*upon* subject; ~ *upon note, syllable,* etc., prolong it). **2.** Make one's abode, spend one's time, live, *in, at, near, on,* etc. (now usu. *live* in talk). **3.** (Of horse) be slow in raising feet, pause before taking fence. **4.** n. Slight regular pause for some purpose in motion of machine. [OE *dwellan* lead astray, delay, be delayed, cf. OHG *twellan* retard, MDu. *dwellen* stun; also Skr. *dhur* mislead]

dwell´er, n. Inhabitant, resident *in, on,* etc.; horse that DWELLS at fence. [-ER¹]

dwell´ing, n. In vbl senses; place of residence, house; ~-*house,* used as residence, not as office, warehouse, etc.; ~-*place,* = ~. [-ING¹]

dwin´dle, v.i. Become smaller, shrink, waste away; lose importance, decline, degenerate. [obs. *dwine,* cf. *dwine,* cf. ON *dvina,* Du. *verdwijnen,* vanish, +-LE³]

dy´ad, n. The number two; group of two, couple; (Chem.) atom, radical, or element, with combining-power of two atoms of hydrogen. Hence dyad´ic a. [f. L f. Gk *duas -ad-* (*duo* two, -AD)]

Dy´ak, n. Aboriginal of Borneo. [Malay, = savage]

dye¹, n. Colour produced by or as by dyeing, tinge, hue, (also fig., *crime of soundrel, s~ of blackest, deepest,* ~); matter used for dyeing, colouring-matter in solution; ~-*stuff, -ware, -wood,* yielding ~; ~-*house, -works,* where dyeing is done. [OE *déag*]

dye², v.t. & i. (~*d*; part. ~*ing*). Colour, stain, tinge; impregnate (tissue) with colouring-matter (~ *in the wool, in grain,* while material is in raw state, giving more permanent result); make (thing) such a colour (~ *cloth red, a rose colour,* etc.); (of material) take colour *well, badly,* etc. [OE *déagian* (prec.)]

dy´er, n. One who dyes cloth etc. (~*'s bugloss, broom, oak*). [-ER¹]

dy´ing, n. In vbl senses of DIE²; esp. (attrib.) connected with, at time of, death (~ *bed, declaration, wish;* ~ *oath,* made at, or with solemnity proper to, death). [-ING¹]

dyke. See DIKE.

dynam´ic, a. & n. **1.** Of motive force (or *static*), of force in actual operation (cf.

potential); active, potent, energetic; of dynamics; (Med.) functional (cf. *organic*); (Philos.) accounting for matter or mind as being merely the action of forces, so **dỹn'amism**(3), nn. 2. n. Energizing or motive force. [f. F *dynamique* f. Gk *dunamikos* (*dunamis* power, -IC)]

dynam'ical, a. Of dynamics; of force or mechanical power actively operative; (Theol., of inspiration) endowing with divine power, not impelling mechanically; of dynamism (see prec.). Hence ~LY adv. [-AL]

dynam'ics, n. pl. used as sing. **1.** Branch of mechanics that treats of motion in itself, and of the motion of bodies or matter under the influence of forces (including KINEMATICS and KINETICS: opp. STATICS), whence **dỹn'amist²** -IST(3)] (& see DYNAMIO) n.; branch (of any science) in which forces are considered (now often with a specific prefix, as in AERODynamics). **2.** Moving forces, physical or moral, in any sphere. [-ICS]

dyn'amite, n., & v.t. High explosive of nitro-glycerine mixed with inert absorbent; (vb) shatter with ~. [Gk *dunamis* force, -ITE]

dyn'amiter, -ard, nn. User of explosive esp. for revolutionary purposes. So **dynamit'ro** a., ~ISM(1), ~IST(1), nn. [prec., -ER¹; -ard after F *communard* (-ARD)]

dyn'amo-, comb. form of Gk *dunamis* power, as in ~-electric = of current (formerly *dynamic*) electricity, also = converting mechanical into electric energy.

dyn'amo, n. (pl. -os). Machine converting mechanical into electric energy by rotating coils of copper wire in magnetic field. [short for ~-electric machine, see prec.]

dynamom'eter, n. Kinds of instrument measuring energy expended by animal, engine, or mechanical force; gauge for telescope's magnifying-power. [DYNAMO-, -METER]

dyn'ast, n. Ruler, member of a dynasty. [f. LL f. Gk *dunastēs* (*dunamai* be able)]

dyn'asty, n. Line of hereditary rulers. So **dỹnas'tic** a., **dỹnas'tically** adv. [f. F *dynastie* f. LL f. Gk *dunasteia* lordship (prec.)]

dyne, n. (physics). Unit of force (the amount that, acting for one second on one-gramme mass, gives it velocity of one centimetre per second). [F, f. st. of Gk *dunamis* force]

dys-, pref. = Gk *dus-* bad-, opp. *eu-* good-, chiefly in medical or other scientific words taken f. Gk or made with Gk elements.

dys'entery, n. Disease with inflamed mucous membrane & intestinal glands, bloody griping pains, & mucous & bloody evacuations. So **dysentě'ric** a. [f. OF *dissenterie* f. LL f. Gk *dusenteria* (DYS-, *entera* bowels)]

dysgĕn'ic, a. Exerting a detrimental effect on the race (opp. EUGENIC). [f. DYS-+Gk *gen-* produce+-IC]

dyslogis'tic, a. Disapproving, opprobrious, (of sense in which term is used). Hence ~ICALLY adv. [DYS-+(EU)LOG-ISTIC]

dyspep'sia, -sy, n. Indigestion. So **dyspep'tic** a. & n., (person) subject to ~ or the attendant depression. [L, f. Gk DYS(*pepsia* f. st. of *pessō* cook)]

dyspnoe'a, n. (path.). Difficult breathing. Hence ~IC a. [L, f. Gk *duspnoia* (DYS-, *pneō* breathe)]

dysū'ria, n. Painful urination. [mod. L, f. Gk *dusouria* (DYS-+*ouron* urine)]

E

E, e, (ē), letter (pl. Es, E's), (Mus.) note, & corresp. scale; second-class ship in Lloyd's register.

e-, pref. Shortened form of EX-(1).

each, a. & pron. (Of two or more) every (one) taken separately, as *~ man has two votes, ~ of us has two votes, we have two votes ~, they cost a penny ~, ~ is worse than the one before; they hate ~ other, ~ hates the other; sides of two triangles are equal ~ to ~* (a side of one to the corresponding side of the other). [OE has (1) ǣlc (cf. OHG *eogilīh*, G *jeglich*) perh. f. +*āwon galīkō* ever alike, (2) *gehwilc* (cf. OHG *gihwelih*, & see Y-, & WHICH), (3) *ǣghwilc* (cf. OHG *eogihwelih*, & see AYE)]

eag'er (-g-), a. Full of keen desire; strongly desirous (*to do, for, after, about,* etc.); (of passions etc.) keen, impatient; (arch.) ~ (*cold*) air. Hence ~LY² adv., ~NESS n. [f. OF *aigre* keen, f. L *acrem* (nom. *acer*)]

ea'gle, n. **1.** Large bird of prey, with keen vision, & powerful flight; figure of this, esp. as ensign of Roman or French army, or as lectern in church. **2.** (Golf) hole played in two strokes under par. **3.** *Double ~, coin worth twenty dollars; ~-eyed, keen-sighted; ~-owl, largest European owl. [f. OF *aigle* f. L *aquila*]

eag'let, n. Young eagle. [f. F *aiglette* (as prec., see -ET³)]

eagre (ā'ger, ē-), n. Large tidal wave, esp. in the Humber, Trent, and Severn. [?]

-ean, suf. of adjj. & nn. (also *-aean, -eian,* with sense ' of, belonging to, like ' : = -AN w. end of stem, usu. Gk *-ai(os)*, L *-ae(us)*, or Gk *-ei(os)*, L *-ei(us)*; *-aean* chiefly in unfamiliar wds as *Ascraean, Achaean,* *-eian* (apart from Gk & L as *Pompeian* etc.) is used w. E names in *-ey, -y,* as *Bodleian, Rugbeian;* -*ean* is pron. with ē (*Tacitēan, empyrēan*), exc. in familiar adjj. as *Prōt'ean, Hercūl'ean,* (*-ĭan*), but cf. *pygmēan;* some have *-ean* incorrectly for *-ian* (*antipodēan*), & some vary betw. the two (*Aristotelean, -ĭan*).

ear¹, n. Organ of hearing, esp. external part of this; faculty of discriminating sound, as *an ~ for music*; ~-shaped thing, esp. handle of pitcher; *bring* (storm, hornets' nest, etc.) *about one's ~s*; *prick up one's ~s*, assume expectant attitude; (*for a thing, to do*); *over head and ~s*, deeply immersed in (lit. & fig.); *set* (persons), *be, by the ~s* (at variance); *a word in your ~s* (in private); *it goes in at one ~ & out at the other*, it leaves no impression; *give ~*, listen *to*; *have a person's ~* (favourable attention); *were your ~s burning last night?* (we were talking about you); *sent him away with a flea in his ~*, told him some home truths etc. 2. ~-ache, pain in drum of ~; ~mark, (n.) mark on of sheep etc. as sign of ownership, (fig.) mark of ownership, (v.t.) mark (sheep etc.) with this, (fig.) assign (fund etc.) to definite purpose; ~-phone, = HEAD-phone; ~-ring (worn in lobe of ~ for ornament); ~-shot, hearing distance, as *within, out of, ~*; ~-trumpet, tube used by persons partly deaf; ~-wax, viscid secretion in ~. Hence (-)~ED² (-rd), [OE *ēare*, G *ohr*; cogn. w. L *auris*, Gk *ous*]

ear², n. Spike, head, of corn, containing its flowers or seeds. [OE *ēar* (cf. G *āhre*), Du. *aar*, cogn. w. L *acus -eris* husk]

ear'ing, n. (naut.). Small rope (one to several) fastening upper corner of sail to yard. [EAR¹ + -ING²; or = *ear-ring*]

earl (ērl), n. (fem. *countess*). Nobleman ranking between marquis & viscount (cf. COUNT²); *E~ Marshal*, officer presiding over Heralds' College etc. Hence ~DOM (ēr-) n. [OE *eorl*, cf. ON *earl, jarl*]

ear'ly (ēr-), a. & adv. Absolutely or relatively near to the beginning of a portion of time, as *an ~ visit, ~ riser, rise ~, keep ~ hours* (rise & go to bed ~), *~ peaches* (maturing ~ in the year), *E~ English STYLE*, far, *an ~ date* (not long hence); *at your earliest convenience* (as soon as you conveniently can); *the ~ part* (beginning) of the century; *the ~ spring, morning*, etc., the ~ part of spring etc.; *~ bird*, (joc.) ~ riser (w. ref. to proverb *the ~ bird gets the worm*); *~-Victorian* a. & n., (writer etc.) of Victoria's reign, antiquated; *~ door*, theatre door admitting audience before usual hour and at an enhanced price; *earlier on*, at an earlier stage, previously (after *later on*). Hence earl'INESS (ēr-) n. [adj. f. adv.). OE *ǣrlice* (or posit. degree of *ǣr* ERE, -LY²]

earn (ērn), v.t. (Of person, action, conduct, etc.), obtain as reward of labour or merit. [OE *(ge-)earnian* f. OTeut. *azniðan* (*aznd* field-labour, cf. G *ernte* harvest)]

earn'est¹ (ēr-), a. & n. Serious, zealous, not trifling; ardent (desire etc.); *in ~*, serious(ly), not jesting(ly). Hence ~LY² adv., ~NESS n. [OE *eornost(e)* a. f.

n. (cf. G *ernst*) perh. f. root *ers* seen in obs. *erre* anger]

earn'est² (ēr-), n. Money paid as instalment, esp. to confirm contract etc.; foretaste, presage, betokening, (*is an, in, ~ of what is to come*). [prob. conn. W. *erles, arles(-penny)* f. L + *arrhāta* dim. of *arrha*.]

earn'ing (ēr-), n. In vbl senses, esp. (pl.) money earned. [-ING¹]

earth¹ (ēr-), n. (pl. only as below). 1. The ground, as *it fell to ~*; (w. pl.) hole of badger, fox, etc.; the dry land; land & sea opp. the sky; this planet; this world opp. heaven or hell (*why* etc. *on ~? why EVER?*); (w. pl.) soil, mould; (Chem., w. pl.) any of certain metallic oxides, uninflammable & having little taste or smell; || (Electr., w. pl.) communication with, as completion of circuit. 2. ~born, of mortal race, (Myth.) emerging from ~ at birth; ~closet; ~light, illumination of dark part of moon by light from ~; ~nut, pig-nut & other plants; ~work, work, bank of ~ used in fortification; ~worm, worm living in ground, (fig.) grovelling person. Hence ~WARD(S) adv. [com.-Teut.: OE *eorthe*, Du. *aarde*, G *erde*]

earth² (ēr-), v.t. & i. Cover (roots of plants) with heaped-up earth; drive (fox) to earth; (intr., of fox) run to earth; (Electr.) = GROUND². [f. prec.]

earth'en (ēr-), a. Made of earth; made of baked clay. [-EN⁵]

earth'enware (ēr-), n. (often attrib.). Vessels etc. made of baked clay; baked clay. [WARE¹]

earth'ly (ēr-), a. Like, of, earth or soil; (fig.) grossly material. Hence ~INESS n. [-Y²]

earth'quake (ēr-), n. Volcanic convulsion of earth's surface; (fig.) social or other disturbance.

earth'y (ēr-), a. Of the earth, terrestrial; (colloq.) *no ~y use, reason, chance*, no use etc., at all; ||*not an ~y* (sl.), no chance whatever. Hence ~INESS n. [-Y¹]

ear'wig (ēr-), n. & v.t. (-gg-). Insect once held to get into the head through the ear; (v.t.) influence (person) by secret communications. [vrb f. n.] OE *ēarwicga* (*ēare* EAR¹ + *wicga*)

ease¹ (ēz), n. Freedom from pain or trouble; freedom from constraint, as *at one's ~*; (Mil.) *stand at ~* (in relaxed attitude, with feet apart); relief from pain; CHAPEL of ~; facility, esp. *with ~*. Hence ~'LESS (-zl-) a. [f. OF *aise* (cf. It. *agio* etym. dub.)]

ease² (ēz), v.t. & i. Relieve from pain etc.; give mental ease to (person, oneself, one's *~*); (Mil.) rob (person of his purse etc.); relax, adjust, (what is too tight); (Naut.) slacken (rope, sail, *away, down, off*), *~ her*, reduce speed of engine; (v.i.) *off*, become less burdensome. [f. prec.] F had *aiser* = It. AD(*agiare*, see prec.)]

ease'ful (ēzʹ-), a. Comfortable, soothing; at rest; slothful. Hence ~LY² adv., ~NESS n. [-FUL]

ease'l (-z-), n. Wooden frame to support picture, blackboard, etc. [f. Du. ezel = G esel ASS]

ease'ment (-zm-), n. (Law) right of way or similar right over another's ground; supplementary building, shed, etc.; (arch.) relief from pain or burden. [f. OF aisement (as EASE², -MENT]

east, adv., n., & a. (Towards, at, near) the point of the horizon where the sun rises (90° to right of North): to the ~ (of), in an eastward direction (from); ~ (wind), wind blowing from the ~; eastern part of the world, orient; altar-end of church (whether truly oriented or not); far E~, China, Japan, etc.; middle E~, (esp.) countries from Egypt to Iran (Persia) inclusive; near E~, Turkey; E~ INDIES; ∥ E~End, eastern part of London. Hence ∥ E~WARD a. & n., ~WARD(S) adv. [OE (1) ēastan (cf. Du. oost, G osten) f. OTeut. austanô from the east (aus- seen in L aurora dawn), (2) ēast perh. shortened f. †ēaster eastwards]

Eas'ter, n. Festival of Christ's resurrection, corresponding to Passover, & observed on 1st Sunday (~ day, Sunday) after the first full moon on or after March 21 (also arch. ~tide); (also ~-week) week commencing with ~ day; ~ eggs (painted & presented to friends at ~); ~ eve, day before ~ day; ~ offering(s), customary payments made to the incumbent on ~ day (now usually the collection proceeds). [OE ēastre perh. f. Ēostre dawn-goddess (aus-, see prec.)]

eas'ting, n. (naut.). Distance to the eastward; eastward direction. [-ING¹]

eas'terly, a. & adv. In an eastern position or direction; (coming) from the east, as ~ wind. [f. obs. easter (perh. compar. of EAST)¹ -LY¹]

eas'tern, a. & n. Of, dwelling in, the east part of the world; E~ Church (Greek); E~ question, political problem relating to E~ Europe, esp. Turkey; lying towards the east; (n.) inhabitant of the East, member of E~ Church. Hence ~MOST a. [OE ēasterne (see EAST & -ERN)]

eas'y̆ (-z-), a., adv., & n. 1. Free from pain, discomfort, annoyance, anxiety, etc.; ~ circumstances, affluence; free from embarrassment or stiffness, as ~ manners, free & ~ (not stiff, not strict); not difficult (to do, or abs.; ~ of access, easily got at); easily persuaded, compliant, (lady of ~ virtue, unchaste); (Commerc., of commodity) not much in demand, (of market) not showing eager demand, (cf. TIGHT). 2. adv. In manner, as take it ~, proceed comfortably; (as command) ~!, move gently, ~ all!, stop (prop. rowing); whence am ~, a short rest; ∥ stand ~, (Mil.), permission to squad standing at ease to relax attitude further. 3. ~ chair, one designed for comfort, usu. with arms; ~-going, (of horse) having an ~ gait, (of person) fond of comfort, indolent; (of) mark (colloq.), simpleton; ~ money (not hard to earn). Hence eas'ily² adv., eas'INESS n., (-z-). [f. OF aisié p.p. of aisier EASE²]

eat, v.t. & i. (past āte, eat, pron. ĕt: p.p. eaten, pron. ĕtn). Masticate & swallow (solid food); swallow (soup): ~ one's words, retract them in humiliating manner; ∥ ~ one's terms or dinners, be studying for the bar; ~ HUMBLE pie; ~ (person) out of house & home, ruin him by ~ing (lit. & fig.) all he has; horse etc. ~s its head off, costs more to feed than it is worth; well, don't ~ me!, joc. reply to vehement protest etc.; (intr. as pass.) the cakes ~ crisp; destroy, consume, as ~ one's heart out, suffer bitterly; ~ away, destroy gradually (lit. & fig.); ~ up, consume completely, waste, (lit. & fig.), absorb, as ~en up with pride. Hence eat'ABLE a. & n. (usu. pl.). [com.-Teut.: OE etan, Du. eten, G essen]

eat'ing, n. In vbl senses; ~-house, restaurant. [-ING¹]

*eats, n. pl. (sl.). Food. [pl. of obs. eat, something edible (OE æt), or fresh formation f. vb]

eau (ō), n. ~-de-Cologne (ōdʹekolōn'), perfume made at Cologne; ~-de-Nil (-denēl'), greenish colour (supposed to resemble Nile water); ~-de-vie (-devē'), brandy; ~ sucrée (see Ap.), water and sugar. [F, = water]

eaves (ēvz), n. (now pl.). Overhanging edge of roof or thatch; ~-drop, stand under this to listen to secrets; ~-dropper, one who does this (usu. fig.). [OE efes (cf. dial. G obsen), prob. f. same root as OVER; -s being now taken as pl. eave is sometimes used for sing.]

ĕbb, n., & v.i. 1. Reflux of tide, as ~ & flow, ~-tide; decline, decay, as at a low ~. 2. v.i. Flow back, recede, decline, decay. [OE (ebbian vb f.) ebba (cf. Du. eb, ebbe), etym. dub.]

E'-boat, n. Enemy high-speed motor torpedo-boat. [E abbr. of enemy]

ĕb'on, a. (poet.). Made of, black as, ebony. [f. L f. Gk ebenos, perh. of oriental orig.]

ĕb'onite, n. = VULCANITE. [f. foll. + -ITE¹]

ĕb'on|y̆, n. & a. 1. Kinds of hard black wood. 2. adj. Made of, black as, this. Hence ~IZE(3) v.t. [ME hebenyf f. L hebeninus (perh. misread -tuus) f. Gk hebeninos EBON]

ĕbri'ĕty, n. (now rare). Drunkenness. [f. F ébriété f. L ebrietatem (as foll., see -TY]

ĕb'rious, a. (now rare). Drunk; given to, of, drunkenness. [f. L ebrius + -OUS]

ĕbull'i|ent, a. Boiling; exuberant. So ~ENCE, ~ENCY, nn. [f. L ebullire -it- boil), -ENT]

ebulli′tion, n. Boiling; effervescence; (fig.) sudden outburst (*of* passion, war, etc.). [f. L *ebullitio* (as prec., see -ION)]

écarté (ākär′tā), n. Card-game for two persons. [F (*écarter* discard)]

Ec′ce Hōm′ō (ĕksĭ), n. Picture of Christ wearing crown of thorns. [L, = behold the man (*John* xix. 5)]

eccen′tric (-ks-), a. & n. **1.** Not concentric (*to* another circle); not placed, not having its axis etc. placed, centrally; (of orbit) not circular; (of heavenly body) moving in an ∼ orbit; irregular; odd, whimsical. **2.** n. (Mech.) = contrivance for changing rotatory into backward-&-forward motion, esp. for slide-valve of steam-engine; odd, whimsical, person. Hence **eccén′-trically** adv., **eccentric′ity** n. [f. LL. *kentron* CENTRE]; see -IC]

ecclē′sia (-z-), n. (Gk. Ant.) General assembly (esp. of Athenian citizens), cf. ecclē′siast (-z-), n. Member of Athenian ecclesia; 'the Preacher', Solomon (regarded as author of *Eccles.*). [f. Gk *ekklēsiastēs* (as prec.)]

Ecclēsias′tes (ĭ-, -zĭ-, -z′), n. An O.T. book. [as ECCLESIAST]

ecclēsias′tic (-zĭ-), n. & a. Clergyman; (adj., now rare) = foll. [f. Gk *ekklēsiastikos* (as prec.)]

ecclēsias′tical (-zĭ-), a. Of the church or clergy; ∥*E∼al Commission(ers*), body administering part of Church of England revenues. Hence or cogn. ∼ally² adv., ∼ISM n. [-AL]

Ecclēsias′ticus (ĭ-, -zĭ-), n. A book of the Apocrypha. [as ECCLESIAST]

ecclēsiŏl′ogy (-zĭ-), n. Science of churches, esp. of church building & decoration. Hence **ecclēsiŏlŏ′gic(AL)** aa., **∼ist** n., **-zĭ-**. [f. ECCLESIA + -o- + -LOGY]

ec′dysis, n. (pl. -sēs). Casting off (esp. of slough in serpents etc.; also fig.); slough. [f. Gk *ekdusis* (*ekduō* put off)]

e′chelon (-sh-), n., & v.t. Formation of troops in parallel divisions, each with its front clear of that in advance; *in* ∼, so drawn up; (v.t.) draw up thus. [(vb f. n.] f. F *échelon* (*échelle* ladder f. L *scala*, see -OON)]

echī′na (-k-), n. Australian toothless burrowing animal like hedgehog. [f. Gk *ekhidna* viper]

ĕ′chinīte (-k-), n. Fossil echinoderm or sea-urchin. [f. ECHINUS + -ITE¹]

echīnodĕ′rm (kĭnĭ, ĕk′ĭn-), n. Class of animals including sea-urchins. [as foll. + DERM]

echī′nus (-k-), n. Sea-urchin, animal inhabiting spheroidal prickly shell. [f. Gk *ekhinos* hedgehog, sea-urchin]

ĕc′hō¹ (-k-), n. (pl. ∼es). Repetition of sound by reflexion of sound-waves (*cheer*

person etc. *to the* ∼, loudly); *E∼*, cause of this personified; close imitation; obsequious imitator or adherent; artifice by which last syllables of one verse are taken up by next; conventional indication given to partner at bridge or whist of the number of cards held in suit led etc. Hence ∼LESS a. [f. L f. Gk *ēkhō*, conn. w. *ēkhē* sound]

ĕc′hō² (-k-), v.i. & t. (Of places) resound with an echo; (of sounds) be repeated, resound; (Bridge etc.) play the echo (see prec.); (v.t.) repeat (sound) by echo; repeat (another's words), imitate the words or opinions of (person). [f. prec.]

ĕc′hoïsm (-k-), n. = ONOMATOPOEIA. So **ĕc′hoïst** n.

éc′lair (āk′lâr), n. Small finger-shaped cake filled with cream and iced. [F]

éclaircissement (see Ap.), n. Clearing up, explanation, (of conduct etc.). [F]

ĕclamp′sia, n. Kind of epileptic convulsions caused by anatomical lesion to which pregnant women are specially liable. [irr. f. Gk *eklampō* shine forth (visual hallucination being a symptom)]

écclat (āklah′), n. Conspicuous success, general applause, as *with great* ∼; social distinction. [F]

éclec′tic, a. & n. (Ancient philosopher) selecting such doctrines as pleased him in every school; (person) borrowing freely from various sources, not exclusive in opinion, taste, etc. Hence ∼ALLY adv., ∼ICISM(3) n. [f. Gk *eklektikos* (*eklegō* pick out, see -IC)]

éclipse¹, n. Interception of the light of a luminous body (sun, moon, etc.) by intervention of another body between it & the eye or between the luminous body and what illuminates it; ANNULAR, PARTIAL, TOTAL, ∼; deprivation of light, loss of brilliance or splendour (*in* ∼, of birds, having lost the courting plumage); periodical obscuration of lighthouse light. [OF, f. L f. Gk *ekleipsis* vbl n. f. *ekleipō* fail to appear, be eclipsed (*leipō* leave)]

éclipse², v.t. (Of a heavenly body) obscure (another) by passing between it & spectator or between it and the source of its light; intercept (light, esp. of lighthouse); (fig.) deprive of lustre, outshine, surpass. [f. prec.]

éclip′tic a. & n. Of eclipse; (n.) sun's apparent orbit. [f. L f. Gk *ekleiptikos* (ECLIPSE¹, -IC)]

éc′logue (-g), n. Short poem, esp. pastoral dialogue, such as Virgil's Bucolics. [f. L f. Gk *eklogē* selection (*eklegō* pick out)]

ĕcŏl′ogy, oec- (ē-), n. Branch of biology dealing with living organisms' habits, modes of life, and relations to their surroundings. [f. Gk. *oikos* house, -LOGY]

ĕconŏ′mic, a. & n. **1.** Of ∼s; maintained for profit, on a business footing, paying

expenses, (of rent) high enough to compensate builder, owner, etc.; connected with industrial arts; ~ *botany, geography*, etc., botany etc. studied from the utilitarian standpoint. **2.** n. pl. Practical science of the production & distribution of wealth, (also) condition of a country as to material prosperity. [f. L f. Gk *oikonomikos* (see ECONOMY & -IC)]

económ'ical, a. Saving, thrifty, not wasteful (of); relating to economics or to political economy. [-AL]

económ'ically, adv. Thriftily; from an economic point of view. [-LY²]

écon'omist, n. Manager (of money etc.); thrifty person; writer on economics or political economy. [as ECONOMY + -IST]

écon'omize, v.t. & i. Use sparingly; turn to the best account; (v.i.) practise economy, cut down expenses. Hence ~ATION n. [as foll. + -IZE]

écon'omy, n. **1.** Administration of concerns & resources of a community; *Political E~*, theory of production & distribution of wealth. **2.** Frugality. (w. pl.) instance of this. **3.** (Theol.) judicious handling of doctrine, whence (with play on sense *frugality*) ~ *of truth.* **4.** Organization; organized body, society, etc. [f. L f. Gk *oikonomia* f. *oikonomos* steward (*oikos* house + *nomos* f. *nemō* manage)]

écru' (-ōō, or as F *écru*), n. Colour of unbleached linen. [F., = unbleached]

ēc'stasize, v.t. & i. Throw, go, into ecstasies. [f. foll. + -IZE]

ēc'stasy, n. Exalted state of feeling, rapture, (esp. of delight); (Med.) morbid state of nerves in which mind is occupied solely by one idea; trance; poetic frenzy. [f. OF *extasie* f. med. L f. Gk *ekstasis* f. *existēmi* put (person) out of (his senses)]

ēcstat'ic, a. Of, subject to, producing, ecstasies (esp. of joy). Hence ~ICALLY adv. [f. Gk *ekstatikos* (as prec., see -IC)]

ēc'to- in comb. = Gk *ektos* outside, as, ~*plasm,* (Biol.) outer layer of protoplasm, supposed viscous substance exuding from body of spiritualistic medium during trance; ~*zōon,* external parasite.

ēc'todērm, n.(biol.). Outer cellular membrane investing a multicellular animal. [ECTO-, DERM]

-ectomy, suf. f. Gk *ektomē* excision, in surgical terms denoting operations in which some part is removed, as *colectomy*, excision of part of the colon.

ecuménical. See OECUMENICAL.

ēc'zēma, n. Inflammation of the skin, of several kinds. [f. Gk *ekzema* (*ek* out + *zeō* boil, see -M)]

-ed¹, (1) suf. forming p.p. of weak vbs (also -*d*, -*t*, as in *sold, bought*); -*ed* (now reduced in sound to -*d* or -*t* except in -*ded*, -*ted*, in some bibl. wds, as *blessed*, & in *learned*) was in OE -*ed*, -*od*, -*ad*, acc. to vb class, -*d* alone being the participial element, f.

OTeut. -*do-* f. Aryan -*to-* (cf. L *-tos, L p.p. -tus*); -*t* is used in vbs that shorten in p.p. a long vowel of stem, as *crept, dreamt* (dreamed if pronounced with ē), and in some ending in -*d* after *l, n, r*, are used (rarely f. intr., commonly from trans. vbs) as adjj., meaning when intr. 'that has done so-&-so' (*vanished hand, fallen idol, escaped convict*); a special use, w. resultant force, is seen in *outspoken, well-read*; sometimes it is doubtful whether adjj. in -*ed* are trans. or (intr.) p.pp. or belong to foll.: *decayed* may be *that has been decayed, that has decayed,* or *that is affected with decay*; reference to -*ED*¹(2) is made only for the rare intr. p.p. adjj.

-ed² (as prec.), suf., distinct f. prec., in OE (-*ede*), though perh. a form of the p.p. suf. in OTeut. (cf. *caudatus* tailed in L), appended to nn. to form adjj. meaning possessed of, affected with, etc., as *talented, wooded, diseased*; esp. used to make adj. out of adj. & n., usu. stressed (apart from demands of context) in attrib. use on first component (*a quick-witted lad, met'al-cornered dish*), in pred. use on second (*he seems quick-witt'ed enough*) exc. where this is more or less otiose (*ru'by, coff'ee,* etc., -*coloured* attrib. & pred.); sometimes = 'having the ways of' instead of simply 'having', as *bigoted, crabbed, dogged*; sometimes indisting. f. prec. (2).

ēdā'cious (-shus), a. (pedant.). Of eating; greedy. So **ēdā'city** n. [f. L *edax -acis* (*edere* eat, see -ACIOUS)]

Ed'am (ē-), n. Spherical Dutch cheese. [~ in Holland]

Edd'a (ē-), n. (*Older, Poetic,* ~) collection of ancient Icelandic poems; (*Younger, Prose,* ~) miscellaneous handbook (c. 1230) to Icelandic poetry. [perh. f. a name in an ON poem]

edd'y, n., & v.t. & i. **1.** Small whirlpool; wind, fog, smoke, moving like this. **2.** v.t. & i. Whirl round in ~ies. [?]

edelweiss (ād'elvīs), n. Alpine plant with white flower, growing in rocky places. [f. G *edel* noble + *weiss* white]

Ed'en (ē-), n. Abode of Adam & Eve at their creation; delightful abode; state of supreme happiness. [f. Heb. '*eden* orig. = delight]

ēden'tate, a. & n. (Animal) without incisor & canine teeth; toothless (animal). [f. L *edentatus* f. *dens -ntis* tooth, see -ATE²]

ēdge¹, n. Sharpened side of blade of cutting instrument or weapon; sharpness of this, as *the knife has no* ~; *take the* ~ *off,* blunt, weaken, dull, (appetite, argument, etc.); *be on* ~, be excited or irritable; *set* (person's) *teeth on* ~, jar his nerves, affect him with repulsion; (fig.)

critical position or moment; meeting-line of two surfaces of a solid; meeting (*do the* *inside*, *outside*, ~, skate on the inner, outer, ~ of skates; boundary-line of surface; ~ *tool*, cutting-tool (in fig. sense also *edged tool*). Hence ~'LESS (-ji-)
a. [OE *ecg* (cf. Du. *egge* edge, corner) f. root *ak*- whence L *acies*, Gk *akis*, corner)]

edge, v.t. & i. Sharpen (tool etc., also fig.); ~ *on*, = EGG² *on*; furnish with border, form border to; insinuate, push, (thing, oneself) *into*, *in*, *out*, *off*, etc.; (v.i.) advance obliquely. [f. prec.]

edge'ways, -wise, (-jwäz, -jwïz), adv. With edge uppermost or foremost; (fig.) *get a word in* ~ (in talkative person's silent interval). (of two things) edge to edge. [-WAYS, -WISE]

edg'ing, n. Border, esp. narrow one of different material; (attrib.) ~*-shears* (for trimming edges of lawn). [-ING¹]

edg'y, a. Sharp-edged; (of painting) too sharp outline; having one's nerves on edge, irritable. [-Y²]

Hence **edim'/iry** n. [f. LL *edibilis* (*edere* eat, see -BLE)]

ed'ible, a. & n. (Thing) fit to be eaten. eat, see -BLE)]

ed'ict, n. Order proclaimed by authority; *E~ of Nantes*, issued by Henry IV of France to grant toleration to Protestants and revoked by Louis XIV. Hence **edic'tal** a. [f. L *edictum* f. *Edicere* dict- say) proclaim]

ed'ifice, n. Building (esp. large one; also fig.). [f. F *édifice* f. L *aedificium* (*aedis* temple+-*ficium* f. *facere* make)]

ed'ify, v.t. Benefit spiritually; improve morally (often iron.). So **Edifica'tion** n. [f. F *édifier* f. L *aedificare* (as prec., see -FY)]

ed'it, v.t. Prepare an edition of (another's work); set in order for publication (material chiefly provided by others); garble, cook, (dispatches etc. in newspaper, etc.); act as editor of (paper etc.). [(1) f. L *Edere dit-* = *dare* give) put out; (2) back-formation f. EDITOR]

edi'tion, n. Form in which a literary work is published (*library, cabinet, popular,* ~); whole number of copies of book, newspaper, etc., issued from same types & at same time (see also IMPRESSION); (fig.) production of the same type, person, etc., resembling another (*a more charming* ~ *of her sister*). [f. F *édition* f. L *editionem* (as EDIT, see -ION)]

editio'ne luxe (see Ap.), n. Handsome edition. [F]

ed'itor, n. One who conducts a newspaper or periodical, or who prepares the work of others for publication; one who conducts edition of a book. [L]

edito'rial, a. & n. Of an editor.

2. n. Newspaper article written by or under responsibility of the editor. Hence ~'iry¹ adv. [-AL]

ed'ucate, v.t. Bring up (young persons) so as to provide intellectual & moral training to; give intellectual & moral training to; provide schooling for; train (person, oneself, a faculty, to do); train (animals). Hence ~ABIL'ITY, ~ABLE, ~ATIVE, aa. [f. L *educare* conn. w. EDUCE, see -ATE³]

educa'tion, n. Bringing up (of the young); systematic instruction; course of this, as *classical, commercial, art,* ~; development of character or mental powers; training (of animals). Hence ~AL a., ~(al)IST(³) nn., ~ally² adv. (-shon-). [f. L *educatio* (as prec., see -ATION)]

educe' (-s), v.t. Bring out, develop, from latent or potential existence; (Chem.) disengage (substance) from a compound; infer (number, principle, *from* data, *lead*). Hence **edu'CIBLE** a. [f. L *Educere* duct- lead)]

educt, n. (Chem.) body disengaged from another in which it previously existed; inference. [as prec.]

educ'tion, n. Educing; (in steam-engine) ~*-pipe, -valve,* etc., ducing; (in steam-engine) ~*-pipe, -valve,* etc. [f. L *eductio* (as prec., see -ION)]

edul'corate, v.t. Free from acrid properties or from soluble particles, purify. Hence **~ATION** n. [f. L *Edulcorare* f. *dulcor* sweetness f. *dulcis*), see -ATE³]

-ee, suf. forming nn. expr. the person affected by the vbl action, corresp. to agent nn. in *-or*, prop. in legal terms (*lessee, vendee*) on anal. of AF (*capstour, appela, summoner, summoned*), but extended to the indirect obj.; now also in non-techn. wds, & without corresp. *-or*, as *employee, payee*; & without consciousness of its meaning, as *bargee, absentee*; a few wds are adoptions f. mod. F *-é*, as *debauchee, refugee*. In *committee* (orig. a person), accent has changed with meaning. *Epopee* is not an instance; in *coatee, -ee* perh. = -Y³; in *settee, goatee, -ee* is unexplained. [AF *-é* of p.p. f. L *-atus*]

eel, n. A snake-like fish; (fig.) slippery creature; (pop.) minute animal found in vinegar & in sour paste; ||~*-BUCK'*; ~*-spear* (for transfixing ~s). Hence ~'y² a. [com.-Teut.: OE *æl*, Du. & G *aal*]

e'en. See EVEN¹,².

-eer, suf. expr. person concerned with, f. L *-arius* or *-arius* -ARY¹; f *-ter* is retained in the less familiar wds (*muleteer* but *bombardier*); *-eer* is freely used for new nn., as *auctioneer, mountaineer*, often contempt., as *sonneteer*. Vbs are also formed (*electioneer*) by back-formation on *auctioneering* etc.

e'er. See EVER.

ee'rie, -y, a. Superstitiously timid; strange, weird. Hence ~'ily² adv., ~'iness n. [ME *eri*, *etym.* dub.]

ef-, pref. = EX-(1) before f.

efface', v.t. Rub out; (fig.) obliterate, wipe out; utterly surpass, eclipse; treat, regard, oneself as unimportant. Hence ~ABLE a., ~MENT (-sm-) n. [f. F effacer f. L ex out +facies face]

effect', n. Result, consequence (cause and ~, causation; efficacy, as of no ~; combination of colour or form in picture etc., as a pretty ~; (pl.) property, as personal ~s, no ~s (written by banker on dishonoured cheque); give ~ to, take ~, make, become, operative; impression produced on spectator, hearer, etc., as calculated for ~; bring to, carry into, ~, accomplish; in ~, for practical purposes. Hence ~LESS a. [OF, f. L effectus -ūs f. EF(ficere fect- = facere make)]

effect'2, v.t. Bring about, accomplish; ~ (take out) a policy (of insurance). [f. prec.]

effec'tive, a. & n. 1. Having an effect; ~ range (of weapon), range within which it is ~; powerful in effect; striking; (of soldiers or sailors) fit for service; actual, existing. 2. n. ~ soldier, ~ part of army. Hence ~LY2 (-vl-) adv., ~NESS (-vn-) n. [F (-if, -ive), f. L effectivus f. med.L see -IVE]

effec'tual, a. Answering its purpose; valid. Hence ~LY2 adv., ~NESS n. [f. OF (-el) f. LL effectualis EFFECT1, -AL]

effec'tuate, v.t. Bring to pass, accomplish. Hence ~ATION n. [f. F effectuer (as EFFECT2), on anal. of ACTUATE]

effem'inate, a. Womanish, unmanly; voluptuous. Hence ~ACY n., ~atelY2 (-tl-) adv. [f. L EF(feminare f. femina woman), see -ATE2]

effen'di, n. Turkish title of respect applied to government officials & members of learned professions. [f. Turk. efendi lord, corrupt. of Gk authentēs (see AUTHENTIC)]

effer'ent, a. (physiol.). Conveying outwards, discharging. [f. L EF(ferre carry), see -ENT]

efferves'ce, v.i. Give off bubbles of gas, bubble, (often fig. of persons); (of gas) issue in bubbles. Hence ~CENCE, ~CENCY, nn., ~CENT a. [f. L EF(fervescere incept. of fervēre be hot)]

effête', a. Exhausted, worn out; feeble, incapable. Hence ~NESS (-tn-) n. [f. L EF(fetus worn out by breeding (fetus)]

effica'cious (-shus), a. (Of thing) producing, sure to produce, desired effect. Hence or cogn. ~LY2 adv. (arch.), ~NESS, **effic'acy,** nn. [f. L efficax (as foll., -ACIOUS)]

effi'cient (-shent), a. Productive of effect; (of persons) competent, capable; ~ CAUSE1, that which makes a thing what it is. Hence or cogn. **effi'ciency** n. (also, Mech.) the ratio of useful work performed by a machine to the total energy expended, ~LY2 adv. [f. L, as EFFECT1, see -ENT]

eff'igy, n. Portrait, image; hang, burn, (person) in ~, hang, burn, his image. [f. F effigie f. L effigies EF(fingere fashion)]

effloresce', v.i. Burst out into flower (lit. & fig.); (Chem., of crystalline substance) turn to fine powder on exposure to air, (of salts) come to the surface & there crystallize, (of ground or wall) become covered with saline particles. So ~'CENCE n., ~'CENT a. [f. L EF(florescere FLOURISH]

eff'luence (-lŏŏ-), n. Flowing out (of light, electricity, etc., or fig.); what flows out. [foll., -ENCE]

eff'luent (-lŏŏ-), a. & n. 1. Flowing forth. 2. n. Stream flowing from larger stream, lake, sewage tank, etc. [f. L EF(fluere fluct- flow), see -ENT]

efflu'vium (-lŏŏ-), n. (pl. -via, -ia). Exhalation affecting lungs or sense of smell; (supposed) stream of minute particles emitted by magnet etc. [LL, as prec.]

eff'lux (-ks), n. Flowing out (of liquid, air, gas; also fig.); that which flows out. Hence **efflu'xion** (-kshon) n. [f. L effluxus -ūs (as prec.)]

eff'ort, n. Strenuous exertion; (of oratory etc.) display of power; (colloq.) something accomplished involving concentration or special activity (that's a pretty good ~). [F, f. efforcer f. med.L EX(fortiare f. fortis strong)]

eff'ortless, a. Making no effort, passive; (of skill etc.) without effort, easy. [-LESS]

effron'terý (-tunt-), n. Shameless audacity. [f. F effronterie f. effronté f. L EX(frontatus f. frons -ntis forehead) shameless]

efful'gent, a. Radiant. Hence ~ENCE n., ~entlY2 adv. [f. L EF(fulgēre shine), see -ENT]

effuse'1 (-s), a. (Bot., of inflorescence) spreading loosely; (Conch.) with lips separated by groove. [as foll.]

effuse'2 (-z), v.t. Pour forth (liquid, air, light, smell; also fig.). [f. L EF(fundere fus- pour)]

effu'sion (-zhn), n. Pouring forth (lit. & fig.); unrestrained utterance (often contempt., of literary work). [f. L effusio (as prec., see -ION]

effus'ive, a. (Of speech or emotions) exuberant, demonstrative; (Geol., of an igneous rock) poured out when molten and later solidified. Hence ~LY2 (-vl-) adv., ~NESS (-vn-) n. [as EFFUSE2 (-z)]

eft, n. Newt. [OE efeta etym. dub.]

‖ **eftsoon(s)',** adv. (arch.). Soon afterwards. [OE eftsōna (see AFT & SOON); -s = -ES]

egad', int. By God. [prob. orig. a ah + God]

Egē'ria (ij-), n. A person's tutelary divinity. [name of a prophetic nymph of Roman legend, Numa's instructress]

egg', n. Spheroidal body produced by female of birds etc. esp. of domestic fowl, containing germ of a new indi-

vidual; ADDLE, WIND[1], ~; (sl.) bomb or grenade; (fig.) *in the* ~ in an early stage; *as full as an* ~, chock-full; *bad* ~, person, scheme, that comes to no good; *good* ~ (sl.), excellent person or thing (also as commendatory exclamation); *as sure as ~s is* ~*s*, undoubtedly; *teach your grand-mother to suck* ~*s*, offer advice to persons more experienced than yourself; *have all your* ~*s in one basket*, risk all on a single venture; ~ *& anchor, dart, tongue*, (Archit.) kinds of moulding; ~*-&-spoon race* (in which runners carry ~ in spoon); ~ *cleavage* (Biol.), process of cleavage in fertilized ~; ~*-shell*; ~*-cup* (for holding boiled ~; *bolled in shell*); ~*-dance, dance blindfold among* ~*s*, (fig.) intricate task; ~*-flip, -nog*, hot beer, cider, wine, etc., with ~s stirred in; ~*-plant*, white-fruited *Solanum esculentum*; ~*-shell*, shell of ~; *fragile thing* (~*-shell china*, very thin kind); ~*-slice*, utensil for taking omelette from pan; ~*-spoon*, small spoon for eating boiled ~s; ~*-tooth*, protuberance on bill-sheath of embryo bird for cracking shell; ~*-whisk*, utensil for beating ~s. [com.-Teut.: OE *ǣg*, Du. & G *ei*]

egg[2], v.t. Urge (person) *on* (to an act, to do). [f. ON *eggja* = EDGE v.]

egg'er, n. Kind of large moth common in Great Britain (also ~*-moth, oak* ~*-moth*). [prob. f. EGG[1]+-ER (owing to egg-like appearance of cocoon)]

eg'lantine, n. Sweet-brier. [f. F *églantine* f. OF *aiglent* prob. f. L *acus* needle, see -INT]

ĕg'ō, n. (metaphys.). The thinking subject, opp. to the non-ego or object. [L. = I]

ēgocĕn'tric, a. Centred in the ego; (loosely) self-centred, egoistic. [EGO + centric (CENTRE[1]+-IC), after *geocentric* etc.]

ĕg'ōism, n. (Ethics) theory that treats self-interest as foundation of morality; systematic selfishness; self-opinionated-ness; = foll. Hence ~**ist** n., ~**is'tic(al)** adj. [f. F *égoïsme* (as EGO, see -ISM)]

ĕg'ŏtism, n. Too frequent use of 'I' & 'me'; practice of talking about oneself; self-conceit; selfishness. Hence ~**ist** n., ~**is'tic(al)** aa., ~**is'tically** adv., ~**IZE** v.i. [f. EGO + -T- perh. on F *idiotisme* etc.]

ĕgrē'gious (-jus), a. (Arch.) surpassing; (mod.) shocking, as ~ *folly, blunder, ass*. Hence ~**LY**[2] adv., ~**NESS** n. [f. L *ēgregius -ēs* f. L *egregius* = f. *grex gregis* flock) lit. towering above the flock]

ĕg'rĕss, n. (Right of) going out; (Astron.) end of eclipse or transit; way out (lit. & fig.). [f. L *ēgressus* -ūs f. L *ēgredī gress- = gradī* step)]

ēgrĕs'sion (-shn), n. Going out or forth. [f. L *ēgressiō* (as prec., see -ION)]

ĕg'ret (ēg- or ĕg-), n. Lesser White Heron;

feathery down on seeds of dandelion, thistle, etc. [var. of AIGRETTE]

Ēgyp'tian (ĭjip'shn), a. & n. (Native of) Egypt; ~ *pound* (usu. abbr. £E, as £E10), coin worth about 20/6; ∥ ~ *tug-type* (thick-stemmed) = GIPSY. [-IAN]

Ēgyptŏl'ŏgy (ē-), n. Study of Egyptian antiquities. So ~**l'OGIST** n. [o-, -LOGY]

eh (ā), int. expr. inquiry or surprise, or inviting assent. [ME *ey*]

ei'der (ī-), n. An Arctic species of duck; ~ (*-down*), small soft feathers from breast of this (~*-down*, also, quilt stuffed with ~*-down*). [ult. f. Icel. *æðr*]

eid'ograph (ī-; -ahf), n. Instrument for enlarging or reducing drawings. [f. Gk *eidos* form + *graphō* write]

eidōl'on (ī-), n. (pl. -*ons*, -*a*). Spectre, phantom. [Gk, see IDOL]

eight (āt), a. & n. One more than seven (8, viii); (Skat.) figure of two adjacent circles; crew of ~ in rowing-boat; ∥ *the* ~*s*, boatraces at Oxford & Cambridge between such crews; ∥ *have one over the* ~ (sl.), get drunk. Hence **eighr'r**[2] (ăttr) a. & n., ~**h'ly**[2] (ăttr) adv. [com.-Teut.: OE *ahta*, Du. & G *acht*) & Aryan]

eighteen' (āt-), a. & n. One more than seventeen (18, xviii); ~*mo*, = OCTODECIMO. Hence ~**TH**[2] a. & n. [OE *eahtatēne, -tēne* (as prec., see -TEEN)]

eight'some (āt-), n. & a. ~ (*reel*), lively Scottish reel for eight dancers. [-SOME]

eight'y (āt-), a. & n. Eight times ten (80, lxxx); *the* ~*-s*, Liberal club founded in 1880. Hence **eight'ĭĔTH** (āt-) a. & n. [OE *eahtatig* (as EIGHT + *-tig* decade)]

eirēn'icŏn (ī-), n. Proposal tending to make peace. [Gk, neut. adj. (*eirēnē* peace, see -IC)]

eistĕddfod (āstĕdh'vod), n. (pl. ~*au*). Congress of Welsh bards; local gathering for musical competitions etc. [-SOME] session f. *eisteddfa* fit]

eis wool (īs; -wŏŏl) very fine glossy worsted wool of two-thread thickness. [G *eis* ice]

eī'ther (īdh-, ē-), adj., pron., & adv. (conj.). 1. Each of two, as *at* ~ *end was a lamp*, ~ *view is tenable*, ~ *is tenable*; *on or other of two, as put the lamp at* ~ *end, there is no lamp at* ~ *end, on* ~ *of you can go*. 2. adv. or conj. On one or other supposi-tion, which way you will, as *he is* ~ *drunk or mad*, ~ *come* (*or go out*; (w. neg. or interrog.) any more than the other, as *if you do not go, I shall not* ~. [OE *ǣghwæðer* f. WG *+aiwon* always + *gihwatharoz* each of two (see Y- & WHETHER)]

ējăc'ūlāte, v.t. Utter suddenly (words or abbs.); eject (fluids etc.) from the body. Hence ~**A'TION** n., ~**ATORY** a. [f. L *ējaculārī* f. *jaculum* javelin) dart]

ēject'[1], v.t. Expel *from* place, office, property; dart forth, emit. Hence or

cogn. **ejĕc'tion**, ~MENT, **ejĕc'tor**[1], nn. [f. L *ejectare* frequent., of E(*jicĕre ject-*= *jacĕre* throw]

ejĕc'tor[2], n. Something inferred, not an actual nor a conceivable object of our own consciousness. [f. L *ejectum* neut. p.p. of *ejicĕre* (see prec.)]

ejĕc'tive, a. Tending to eject; pertaining to an eject. Hence ~LY[2] (-vl-) adv. [-IVE]

ēke[1], v.t. ~ *out*: supplement (defective means etc. *with*); (improp.) contrive to make (livelihood) or support (existence). [dial. form of obs. n. *eke* (OE *ēacan*) f. OTeut. *aukan* cogn. w. L *augēre* increase; partly also f. obs. n. *eke* (OE *ēaca*) f. OE *ēac*, Du. *ook*, G *auch*]

ēke[2], adv. (arch.). Also. [com.-Teut.: OE *ēac*, Du. *ook*, G *auch*]

ĕkk'a[2], n. (Anglo-Ind.). Small one-horse Indian vehicle; similar cart drawn by bullock. [Hind.]

-el. See -LE(2).

ĕlăb'orate[1], a. Carefully or minutely worked out; highly finished. Hence ~LY[2] (-tl-) adv., ~NESS (-tn-) n. [f. L E(*laborāre* f. *labor* work), see -ATE[2]]

ĕlăb'orāte[2], v.t. Produce by labour; work out (invention, theory, etc.) in detail; (of natural agencies) produce (substance etc.) from its elements or sources. Hence or cogn. ~ATION n., ~ATIVE a. [as prec., -ATE[3]]

ĕlaeo- in comb. = Gk *elaion* oil, as ~*meter*, instrument for determining purity of oils. *ĕlan* (see Ap.), n. Vivacity; impetuous rush. [F]

ĕl'and, n. S.-African antelope of heavy build. [Du. = elk]

ĕlăpse', v.i. (Of time) pass away. [f. L E(*labi laps-* glide)]

ĕlăs'tic (or -lah-), a. & n. 1. Spontaneously resuming its normal bulk or shape after contraction, dilatation, or distortion (of solids, liquids, & gases); springy; (of feelings or persons) buoyant; flexible, adaptable, as ~ *conscience*; ~*side boots* or ~*sides*, 19th-c. boots with ~ web at sides instead of buttons or laces. 2. n. ~ cord or string, usu. woven with india-rubber. Hence **ĕlăs'tically** adv., **ĕlăstī'city** n. [f. Gk *elastikos* impulsive (*elaunō* drive, st. *ela-*)]

ĕlāte', v.t., & a. 1. Inspirit, stimulate, (esp. in p.p.); make proud. 2. adj. (arch.). In high spirits, exultant, proud. So **ĕlā'tion** n. [f. L E*ferre* ēlat- bring out, raise]

ĕl'bow[1] (-ō), n. Outer part of joint between fore & upper arm; ~-shaped bend or corner; *at one's* ~, close at hand; *up to the* ~*s*, busily engaged *in*; *out at* ~*s*, (of coat) worn-out, (of person) poor; ~*-grease*, vigorous polishing, hard work; ~*-room*, plenty of room. [com.-Teut.: OE *elnboga*, Du. *elleboog*, G *ell(en)bogen*, f. OTeut. *alino-bogon* (see ELL & BOW[1])]

ĕl'bow[2] (-ō), v.t. & i. Thrust, jostle, (person, oneself, *into, in,* etc.; also intr.). [f. prec.]

ĕl'chee (-ĭ), n. Ambassador. [f. Turk. *ilchi* representative of a tribe (*il*)]

‖ **ĕld**, n. (arch., poet., dial.). Old age; the olden time. [OE *eldo* (add OLD)]

ĕl'der[1] a. & n. 1. (The) senior (of relations, or of two indicated persons), as *his* ~ *brother, which is the* ~ ?; (Cards) ~ *hand*, first player; ‖ ~ *brother of Trinity House*, each of thirteen senior members of this corporation who sit as Nautical Assessors in navigation cases (usu. pl., ~ *brethren*). 2. n. (Pl.) persons of greater age, as *respect your* ~ *s*; person advanced in life; member of a senate; official in early Christian Church (= Gk *presbuteros*), & in some Protestant (esp. Presbyterian) churches, whence ~SHIP n.; E~ STATESMAN. [OE *eldra* (add OLD)]

ĕl'der[2], n. Low white-flowered tree; ~(*-berry*) *wine* (made from fruit of this). [OE *ellaern*, cf. MLG *ellern, alhorn*]

ĕl'derly, a. Getting old. [ELDER[1]+-LY[1]]

ĕl'dĕst, a. First-born or oldest surviving (member of family, son, daughter, etc.). [OE *eldest(a)* superl. of *add* OLD]

El Dorad'o (ĕldorahd'ō), n. (pl. ~s). Fictitious country or city abounding in gold; (Sp.) = the gilded (man)

ĕl'dritch, a. (Sc.). Weird, hideous. [?]

ĕlēcămpāne', n. Plant with bitter aromatic leaves & root; sweetmeat flavoured with this. [corrupt. of med. L *enula* (L *in-*) *campana; campana* may = of Campania, or of the fields]

ĕlĕct'[1], a. Chosen; select, choice; (Theol.) chosen by God, *as the* ~; chosen to office etc., *as bride* ~. [f. L E(*ligĕre lect-* = *legere* pick]

ĕlĕct'[2] v.t. Choose (thing, *to do*); choose (person) by vote, *as* ~ *a magistrate,* ~ *him to the magistracy,* ~ *him (to be) magistrate*; (Theol., of God) choose (persons) in preference to others for salvation. [as prec.]

ĕlĕc'tion, n. Choosing, esp. by vote; *general* ~ (of representatives, esp. members of House of Commons, throughout the country), ‖ *by-* ~ (of M.P. to fill vacancy); (Theol.) see prec. [OF, f. L *electionem* (as prec., see -ION]

ĕlĕctioneer' (-shon-), v.i., & n. Busy oneself in political elections; (n.) one who ~s. [prec. +-EER]

ĕlĕc'tive, a. (Of official, office, authority) appointed by, filled up by, derived from, election; having power to elect; (Chem.) ~ *affinity*, tendency to combine with some substances rather than others. Hence ~LY[2] (-vl-) adv. [f. F *electif -ive* (as ELECT[1], -IVE)]

ĕlĕc'tor, n. One who has right of election (esp. of M.P.); (Hist.) German Prince entitled to share in election of Emperor, Hence ~AL a., ~SHIP n. [L (as ELECT[1], -OR[2])]

ĕlĕc'torate, n. Dignity, dominions, of German Elector; body of electors. [-ATE[1]]

eléc'tress, n. Female elector; wife of German Elector. [as prec. +-ESS¹]

eléc'tric, a. & n. Of, charged with, capable of developing, electricity; ~ *chair* (used in an execution); ~ *eel*, one able to give shock; ~ *light* (produced by electricity); accumulation of electricity in Leyden jar etc.; ~ *charge*, ~ *current*; ~ *torch*, portable ~ lamp operated by a dry battery in its holder; ~ *blue*, steely blue; (n.) substance in which ~ force can be excited by friction. Hence **eléc'trically** adv.

eléc'trical, a. Relating to electricity (rare in other senses of prec.). [-AL]

electrí'city, n. 1. (Properly *static* ~) abnormal condition of the atoms or molecules of a body usu. due to an excess or deficiency of electrons; various kinds were formerly distinguished by the methods of production, as *frictional* ~ (by friction), *galvanic* ~ (by chemical action), *thermal* ~ (by heat), *magnetic* ~ (by magnetism), or by the substances in which they were produced, as *vitreous* ~ (in glass), *resinous* ~ (in resin); but only two kinds are now recognized in ordinary use, *positive* ~, a deficiency of electrons, and *negative* ~, an excess of electrons. 2. Movement of electrons or electrons moving along a conductor. 3. Science of static ~ or of electric currents. [-ITY]

electrifica'tion, n. Electrifying; conversion of steam railway into electric. [as foll., see -FICATION]

eléc'trify, v.t. Charge (body) with electricity; subject (person etc.) to electric shock; convert (railways, transport, manufactures, etc.) to electric working; (fig.) startle, excite. [f. ELECTRIC +-FY]

eléc'trize, v.t. = prec. Hence ~ATION n. [as prec. +-IZE]

eléc'tro, n., & v.t. (colloq.). = ELECTRO-*plate, type*. [abbr.]

eléc'tro- in comb. Of, pertaining to, caused by, electricity, science of the electrical phenomena of living beings; ~*chem'istry*, science of the electrical phenomena as applied to chemistry; ~*dynam'ics*, dynamics of electricity; ~*kinet'ics*, science of electricity in motion; ~*lys'is* (-ŏl-), chemical decomposition by electric action, science of this; (Surg.) breaking up of tumours or calculi by electric agency; ~*lyse* (-z), decompose thus; ~*lyte*, any liquid or solution chemically changed by passage of electric current, any substance forming such a solution with water or another liquid; ~*magnet'ic*, having both electrical and magnetic character or effects (applied esp. to waves or radiations which travel with the same velocity as light); ~*mag-netism*, production of magnetism by electric current; ~*meter* (-ŏm-), instrument measuring electricity; ~*mŏt'ive*, motion of electric current, mechanical motion produced by electricity; ~*mŏt'ive*, producing, tending to produce, an electric current; ~*mŏt'or*, machine for using electricity as motive power; ~*nēg'ative*, ~*pŏs'itive*, of negative, positive, electricity; ~*path*, ~*pathy* (-ŏp-), electrical treatment of disease; ~*phŏre*, ~*phŏrus* (-ŏf-), instrument for generating statical electricity by induction; ~*plate*, (v.t.) coat with silver by ~*lysis*, (n.) ware thus produced; ~*scŏpe*, instrument indicating presence or quality of electricity; ~*stāt'ics*, science of statical electricity; ~*therap'ia*, ~*therap'y*, cure of diseases by electrical treatment (hence ~*thē'rapist*); ~*therm'al*, relating to heat electrically derived; ~*tonus* (-ōū-), condition of motor nerve under electric current; ~*type*, (n.) model, copy, formed by deposition of copper on a mould by electrolytic action, esp. for printing, (v.t.) copy thus. [f. Gk *elektron* amber]

eléc'trode, n. Either pole (ANODE, CATHODE) of electric battery. [ELECTRO- + Gk *hodos* way]

eléc'trolier, n. Cluster of electric lamps. [f. ELECTRO- on *chandelier*]

eléc'tron, n. (physics, chem.). Indivisible unit of negative electricity and one of the fundamental constituents of matter, normally rotating (in numbers constant for each element) about the positive nucleus of every atom. Hence **eléc'trŏn'ic** a., also n. pl., branch of physics dealing with ~s & the other elementary particles (protons, neutrons, etc.) that constitute matter. [f. ELECTRIC or ELECTRO-, with Gk -*on* appended]

eléc'trum, n. Alloy of silver & gold used by the ancients; (Mineral.) native argentiferous gold. [L, f. Gk *ēlektron* amber; ~]

eléc'tuary, n. Medicinal powder etc. mixed with honey or syrup. [f. Ll *electuarium* perh. corrupt. of Gk *ekleikton* (*ekleikhō* lick out)]

elēēmŏs'ynarý (or -z-), a. Of, dependent on, alms; charitable; gratuitous. [f. med. L *eleemosynarius* (as ALMS, see -ARY¹)]

él'egant, a. & n. (Of movements, style, author, manners), graceful; tasteful; refined; (of modes of life etc.) of refined luxury; (vulg.) excellent; (n.) person with pretensions to taste & fashion. Hence or cogn. **él'egance** n., ~LY² adv. [F f. L *elegans* (as ELECT¹)]

elē'giac, a. & n. 1. (Of metre) suited to elegies, esp. ~ *couplet*, (usu. Gk or Lat.) dactylic hexameter & pentameter;

mournful. **2**, n. pl. ~ verses. [f. L f. Gk *elegeiakos* (as ELEGY, see -AC)]

el′egize, v.i. & t. Write an elegy (*upon*); write in mournful strain; write an elegy upon. [-IZE]

el′egy, n. Song of lamentation, esp. for the dead (often vaguely used of other poems); poem in elegiac metre. [f. F *élégie* f. L f. Gk *elegeia* (*elegos* mournful poem)]

el′ement, n. **1**. Component part, as *reduced to its ~s, analysed, the ~s of national wealth, there was an ~ of cant, cant was a notable ~, in his style*. **2**. (Chem.) any of the many substances that defy analysis. **3**. Any of *the four ~s*, viz. earth, water, air, fire; one of these as a being's abode or sphere, as (usu. fig.) *in, out of, his ~*. **4**. Atmospheric agencies, as *war of the ~s*. **5**, pl. Rudiments of learning (i.e. the A B O or of an art or science; *Euclid's E~s* (of Geometry). [OF, f. L *elementum*, etym. dub.]

elemen′tal, a. & n. **1**. Of the four elements; of the powers of nature, as ~ *worship*; comparable to these, as ~ *grandeur, tumult*; uncompounded; essential. **2**, n. (Theosoph.) spirit of earth, air, etc. [prec. +-AL]

elemen′tar′y, a. Rudimentary, introductory, (Chem.) not decomposable. Hence ~ILY² adv., ~INESS n. [f. L *elementarius* (as ELEMENT, see -ARY¹)]

el′emi, n. A stimulant resin used in ointments, varnish, etc. [?]

elen′chus (-ngk-), n. (pl. *-chī*). Logical refutation; *Socratic ~*, mode of eliciting truth by short question & answer. [L, f. Gk *elegkhos*]

elenc′tic (-ngk-), a. Of, given to, refutation or cross-examination. [f. Gk *elegktikos* (*elegkhō* refute, as prec., see -IC)]

el′ephant, n. Huge four-footed pachyderm with proboscis & long curved ivory tusks; *white ~*, burdensome possession (from cost of maintenance). **2**. Size of paper (28×23 in.; *double ~*, $40 \times 26\frac{1}{2}$). Hence **eleph′antoID** a. [ME *olifaund* f. OF *olifant* corrupt. f. L *elephantum* (nom. *-tus*), *-ntem* (nom. *-phas*), f. Gk *elephas -antos*, etym. dub.]

elephanti′asis, n. Skin disease causing part affected to resemble elephant's hide. [L f. Gk (as prec., see -ASIS)]

eleph′antine, a. Of elephants; ~ *epoch* (when large pachydermata abounded); as ~*mān′ia*, mad zeal for freedom, humour, task. [-INE³]

Eleusin′ian (s-), a. ~ *mysteries* (of Demeter, celebrated at Eleusis in Attica). [f.L f.Gk *Eleusinios* (*Eleusis -inos*) +-AN¹]

eleuth′ero- in comb. = Gk *eleutheros* free, as ~*phill′ous*, with distinct leaves.

el′evāte, v.t. Lift up; hold up (the Host) for adoration; raise (one's eyes, voice,

hopes); raise axis of (gun); exalt in rank etc.; raise morally or intellectually (aims, style; esp. in p.p.); (p.p., colloq.) slightly drunk. Hence ~ORY a. [f. L ELEVARE (*levis* light), see -ATE³]

elevā′tion, n. Elevating, being elevated, (in all senses); angle (esp. of gun) with horizon; height above given (esp. sea) level; drawing made in projection on vertical plane, flat drawing of front, side, or back, of house etc.; grandeur, dignity. [f. L *elevatio* (as prec., see -ATION]

el′evātor, n. Person, thing, that elevates; muscle that raises limb etc.; machine for hoisting corn etc.; lift. [L (as prec, see -OR²)]

elev′en, a. & n. One more than ten (11, xi); *an ~*, ~ persons forming side at cricket etc.; *the E~* (disciples, without Judas); ||~*s(es)* n. (colloq.), light refreshment about 11 a.m. Hence **elev′enTH¹** a. & n. (*the ~th* HOUR). [com.-Teut. OE *endleofon, Du. & G elf*, f. OTeut. *ainlif-* (*ain* ONE +*-lif-* etym. dub.)]

elf, n. (pl. *elves*). (Teut. Myth.) a supernatural being; mischievous creature; dwarf; little creature; ~*bolt*, flint arrowhead; ~*lock*, tangled mass of hair; ~*struck*, bewitched. Hence **elf′ISH¹**, **elv′ISH¹**, aa. [OE *ælf*, cf. G *alp* nightmare]

elf′in, a. & n. Of elves, elfish; (n.) dwarf, child. [f. prec., *-in* unexpl.]

elf′cit, v.t. Draw forth (what is latent, usu. fig.); educe (truths *from* data), draw out, evoke, (admission, answer *from* person). [f. L ELIicere *licit*- for *lacere* entice]

elīde′, v.t. Omit (vowel, syllable) in pronunciation. [f. L ELIdere *līs-* = *laedere* dash]

el′igible, a. Fit to be chosen (*for* office etc.); desirable, suitable. Hence ~BIL′ITY n., ~BLY² adv. [f. F *éligible* (ELECT¹ -BLE)]

elim′ināte, v.t. Remove, get rid of; (Physiol., Chem.) expel (waste matter *from* tissues, substance *from* a compound); ignore (part of question etc.); (Alg.) get rid of (quantities) from equation; (improp.) extract (desired element from compound, also fig.). So ~ABLE a., ~A′TION n., ~ātor² n., (esp.) apparatus enabling a wireless set to use mains current, so ~ating any or all of its batteries. [f. L ELImināre f. *limen -minis* threshold), see -ATE³]

elī′sion (-zhn), n. Suppression of vowel or syllable in pronouncing, (rarely) of passage in book etc. [f. L *elīsio* (as ELIDE, see -ION)]

élite (ālēt′), n. *The* choice part, *the best*, (*of*). [F, = choice]

elix′ir (-er), n. Alchemist's preparation designed to change metals into gold or (*also ~ of life*) to prolong life indefinitely; sovereign remedy; PAREGORIC ~. [med. L f. Arab. *alîksîr* the elixir (*iksîr* prob. f. late Gk *xêrion* desiccative powder)]

Elizabeth'an (-t), a. & n. (Person, writer) of the time of Queen Elizabeth I. [-AN]

elk, n. Large animal of the deer kind found in N. Europe and (also moose) N. America; species of deer & antelope; ~-hound, large Scandinavian shaggy-coated hunting dog. [etym. dub.; OE eolh; also alke, influenced by L alces, Gk alkē]

ell, n. Measure of length (English ~ = 45 in.; now obs. as measure); give him an inch (a little) & he'll take an ~ (much). [com.-Teut.: cf. OE eln, Du. el, G elle, f. OTeut. alina forearm (cogn. w. Gk ōlenē, L ulna), whence med. L alena, f anne]

ellipse', n. Regular oval; figure produced when a cone is cut by a plane making smaller angle with the base than the side of the cone makes, whence ellip'tic(al') aa., -ically' adv. [f. Gk elleipsis (-eipō leave)]

ellip'sis, ellipse'², n. (pl. -psēs, -psĕz). Omission from sentence of words needed to complete construction or sense. So ellip'tical² a., -ically² adv. [prec.]

ellip'soid, n. Solid of which all plane sections through one axis are ellipses & through the other ellipses or circles. [-OID]

elm, n. Tree with rough doubly serrated leaves. Hence ~Y² a. [OE elm (cf. Swed. alm, Da. ælm), = L ulmus]

elocu'tion (ē- or ĕ-), n. Manner, style, art, of oral delivery. Hence ~ARY¹ a., ~IST(3) n., (-shon-). [f. L elocutio f. ēloqui locū- speak), see -ION]

elope, (ēlōzh'-), n. Discourse in honour of deceased person (esp. member of French Academy, pronounced by his successor). [F]

Elō'hist (-ǒ-), n. Author(s) of the elohistic parts of the Hexateuch, marked by use of Elohim for Yahveh (Jehovah). [f. Heb.]

el'ongate (-ngg-), v.t. & i. & a. 1. (-āt). Lengthen, prolong; (Bot.) be of slender or tapering form. 2. adj. (-āt; Bot., Zool.) long, slender, tapering. [f. LL ēlongare f. longus long, see -ATE³]

ēlongā'tion (-ngg-), n. Lengthening; the part (of line etc.) produced; (Astron.) angular distance of planet from sun. [f. LL elongatio (as prec., see -ATION)]

elope', v.i. (Of woman) run away from husband or home (with paramour, lover); abscond. Hence ~MENT (-pm-) n. [AF aloper perh. f. ME *lope p.p. of *loupen (a-=and- against +LEAP), cf. G entlaufen run away]

el'oquence, n. Fluent, forcible, & apt use of language; rhetoric, as Professor of E~. So el'oquent a., el'oquently² adv. [F (é-), f. L eloquentia f. ēloqui speak, see -ENCE]

else, adv. (Following indef. or interrog. pron.) besides, in addition, as any one, anybody, anything ~, who ~? who ~'s?, whose ~?; (same constr.) what ~ could I say?; otherwise, if not, as what, (or) ~ you will be late; ~where, in, to, some other place. [OE elles f. Gmc, cogn. w. L alius, Gk allos]

ēl'ū-cidāte (-ō-, -ū-), v.t. Throw light on, explain. Hence ~A'TION, ~ATOR² nn., ~ATIVE, ~ATORY aa. [f. LL ēlucidare f. lux lucis light)]

ēlūde', v.t. (-ood, -ūd), v.t. Escape adroitly from (blow, danger, difficulty, person's grasp, person, inquiry, observation); avoid compliance with (law, request) or fulfilment of (obligation); escape from, baffle, (the understanding). So ēlū'sion (-lōzhn or -lū-), ēlū'sivenESS, n., ēlū'sIVE, ēlū'sORY, aa., ēlū'siVE'ly², ēlū'sIVE'ry² adv., (-ōō- or -ū-). [f. L ēludere lus- play)]

ēl'van, n. Hard rock of igneous origin; broad vein or dyke of this. [perh. f. Corn. elven spark]

ēl'ver, n. A young eel. [var. of eel-FARE]

Elysée (ālāzā'), n. Official residence of French President. [F]

Elysē'um (-ē-) (pedīon plain)], n. (Gk Myth.) abode of the blessed after death; place, state, of ideal happiness. Hence ~AN a. [f. L f. Gk Ēlusion (ē-) (pedīon plain)]

ēl'ytron, n. (pl. -tra). Outer hard wing-case of coleopterous insect; the vagina. [f. Gk elutron sheath (eluō roll round)]

El'zevir (ĕ-; -ēr), a. & n. (Book) printed by Elzevier family at Amsterdam, The Hague, etc.

ēm, n. The letter M; (Typog.) unit for measuring amount of printed matter in line.

em-, pref.=EN- before b, p, and (often) m.

ēmā'ciāte (-shi-), v.t. Make lean, waste, (esp. in p.p.). Impoverish (soil). So ~A'TION (-si-) n. [f. L ēmaciare f. macies leanness), see -ATE³]

ēm'anāte, v.i. Issue, originate, (from source, person, etc.); (of gases, light, etc.) proceed, issue, (from). [f. L ēmanare (from), see -ATE³]

ēmanā'tion, n. Issuing (from); thing proceeding from a source (esp. fig., of virtues, qualities, moral powers); person, thing, proceeding from the Divine Essence. So ēm'anātIVE a. [f. L ēmanatio (as prec., see -ATION)]

ēman'cipāte, v.t. (Rom. Law) release (child, wife) from power of pater familias; free from legal, social, political, intellectual, or moral restraint. Hence ~on² n., ~ORY a. [f. L ēmancipare f. capere take), see -ATE³]

ēmancipā'tion, n. Setting free, esp. from slavery or from legal disabilities, whence ~IST (-shon-) n.; setting free, freedom, from intellectual or moral

fetters. [f. F *émancipation* f. L *emancipationem* (prec. -ATION)]

||émán'cipist, n. (Austral.). Ex-convict who has served his term. [f. EMANCIPATE + -IST]

émás'culate¹, a. Castrated; effeminate. [f. L E(*masculare* f. *masculus* dim. of *mas* male), see -ATE²]

émás'cūlāte², v.t. Castrate; weaken, make effeminate; impoverish (language); weaken (literary composition) by excisions. Hence ~A'TION n., ~ātīve, ~ātory, aa. [as prec., see -ATE³]

émbalm' (-ahm), v.t. Preserve (corpse) from decay orig. with spices, now by means of arterial injection; preserve from oblivion; endue with balmy fragrance. Hence ~MENT, as BALM¹]

émbánk', v.t. Shut in, confine, (river etc.) by banks, raised stone structure, etc. Hence ~MENT n. (also) structure of earth etc. to carry a railway, road, etc. [EM-]

émbár'gō, n. (pl. ~es), & v.t. 1. Order forbidding ships of a foreign power to enter, or any ships to leave, the country's ports; suspension of (a branch of) commerce, as *be under, lay on, an ~*; impediment. 2. v.t. Lay (ships, trade) under ~; seize (ship, goods) for State service. [Sp., f. *embargar* f. LL †*imbarricare* (*barra* BAR²)]

émbárk', v.t. & i. Put, go, on board ship (*for* destination), whence émbárkA'TION n.; engage (*in, upon,* undertaking, war, etc.). [f. F *embarquer* f. LL IM(*barcare* f. *barca* BAR³)]

embarras de choix, de richesse (ahnbahrah' de shwah', de reshès'), n. More alternatives, wealth, than one knows how to deal with. [F]

émbá'rrass, v.t. Encumber, impede; (p.p.) encumbered with debts; complicate (question etc.); perplex. Hence ~ingly² adv., ~MENT n. [f. F *embarrasser* f. *embarras* n, conn. w. EM(*barrer* BAR²)]

émbássy, n. Ambassador's function or office; his residence; deputation to a sovereign etc. [f. OF *ambassée* f. L †*ambactiata* (*ambacht,* see AMBASSADOR, & cf. -ADE]

émbát'tle¹, v.t. Set (army) in battle array. [f. OF EM(*bataillier* f. *bataille* BATTLE)]

émbát'tle², v.t. Furnish (building, wall) with battlements. [EM- + obs. vb *battle* f. OF *bataillier,* see BATTLEMENT]

émbay', v.t. Lay (vessel) within a bay; (of wind) force (vessel) into a bay; enclose as in a bay, shut in. Hence ~MENT n. [EM-]

émbéd', im-, v.t. (-dd-). Fix firmly in surrounding mass (esp. in p.p.); (of the mass) surround thus. [EM-]

émbéll'ish, v.t. Beautify, adorn; heighten (narrative) with fictitious additions.

Hence ~MENT n. [f. OF EM(*bellir* f. *bel* f. L *bellus* handsome), see -ISH²]

ém'ber¹, n. (usu. pl.). Small piece of live coal or wood in dying fire (& fig.). [OE *émerge,* cf. Da. *emmer,* Sw. *mörja;* -b- phonetic]

ém'ber², a. ~ *days,* days of fasting and prayer, the Wed., Fri., & Sat., after (1) 1st Sun. in Lent, (2) Whitsunday, (3) Holy Cross Day (Sep. 14), and (4) St Lucia's day (Dec. 13). [OE *ymbren* n. perh. f. *ymbryne* period (*ymb* about + *ryne* course)]

ém'ber³, n. (Usu. ~-*goose, -diver*) an Orkney sea-fowl, the Loon. [f. Norw. *emmer*]

émbéz'zle, v.t. Divert (money etc., also abs.) fraudulently to one's own use. Hence ~MENT (-zelm-) n. [f. AF EN(*besiler* = OF *besillier* maltreat, ravage, perh. f. L *bis-* used in LL as pejorative pref.)]

émbitt'er, v.t. Make bitter (fig.); aggravate (evil); exasperate (person, feeling). Hence ~MENT n. [EM-]

émblāz'on, v.t. Portray conspicuously, as on heraldic shield; adorn (shield) with heraldic devices (also fig.); celebrate, extol. Hence ~MENT n. [EM-]

émblāz'onrẏ, n. = BLAZONRY. [EM-]

ém'blém, n., & v.t. 1. Symbol, typical representation; (arch.) pictorial parable; (of person) type (of a quality); heraldic device. 2. v.t. Symbolize, show forth by ~. [(vb f. n.) f. L f. Gk *embléma -matos* insertion f. IM(*ballō* throw)]

émblémát'ic(al), aa. Serving as a type or symbol. Hence émblémát'ically² adv. [prec. -IC]

émblém'atist, n. Maker of emblems or of allegories. [as prec.+-IST]

émblém'atīze, v.t. Serve as emblem of; represent by an emblem. [as prec. +-IZE]

ém'blément, n. (legal; usu. pl.). Profits of sown land; natural products of soil. [f. OF *emblaement* f. *emblaer* f. med. L IM(*bladare* sow with wheat (*bladum*), see -MENT]

émbod'ẏ, v.t. Clothe (spirit) with body; give concrete form to (ideas etc.); express tangibly (principles *in* actions etc.); (of things) be an embodiment of (ideas etc.); form into a body; include, comprise. Hence ~iMENT n. [EM-]

émbog', v.t. (-gg-). Plunge into, hamper in, a bog (lit. & fig.). [EM-]

émbol'den, v.t. Make bold, encourage (often *to do*). [EM- + BOLD + -EN⁴]

ém'bolism, n. Obstruction of artery etc. by clot of blood etc., esp. as cause of paralysis. [f. Gk *embolos* peg, stopper (*en* in, *ballō* throw)]

embonpoint (see Ap.), n. Plumpness (chiefly of women; usu. euphem.). [F, f. phr. *en bon point* in good condition]

émbós'om (-ooz-), v.t. Embrace; (n.p.) enclosed *in,* surrounded *with,* (trees, hills, etc.). [EM-]

emboss', v.t. Carve, mould, in relief; cause figures etc. to stand out on (surface); make protuberant. Hence ~MENT n. [prob. f. OF*EMbocer (see BOSS¹)]

embouchure (see Ap.), n. Mouth of river; opening of valley; (Mus.) part of musical instrument applied to mouth, mode of applying this. [F]

embow'el, v.t. (-ll-). Remove the bowels from (body). [f. OF ENboueler for esboueler (es- = EX-+bouel BOWEL)]

embrace', v.t. & n. 1. Fold (person etc., in pl. abs. = ~ one another) in the arms, as sign of affection; clasp, enclose; accept eagerly (offer, opportunity, etc.); adopt (course of action, doctrine, party, cause); (of persons) comprise (thing in a formula, report, etc.); take in with eye or mind. 2. n. Folding in the arms, (euphem.) sexual intercourse. Hence ~ABLE a., ~MENT (-sm-) n. [a.f.v.b f. OF embracer f. L brace'chium arm]

embran'gle (-nggl), **im-,** v.t. Entangle, confuse. Hence ~MENT (-nggelm-) n. [EM-+obs. brangle perh. suggested by brawl, wrangle]

embrasure (-zher; also Embrazhoor'), n. Bevelling off of wall at sides of door or window, splaying; opening in parapet for gun, widening from within. [F (EM- + braser splay, mod. f. F ébraser; see -URE)]

em'brocate, v.t. Bathe, foment, (limb etc.) to mitigate disease. [f. med. L embrocare f. embrocha f. Gk embrokhē f. EM(brekhō wet)]

embroca'tion, n. Liquid used for rubbing affected part. [f. prec., see -ATION]

embroid'er, v.t. Ornament (cloth etc., or abs.) with needlework; embellish (narrative) with fictitious additions. [EM- + broider f. F. broder, orig. = work on the edge (bord); -er perh. f. wrong division of foll.]

embroid'ery, n. Embroidering; embroidered work; adventitious ornament. [-ERY]

embroil', v.t. Bring (affairs, narrative, etc.) into state of confusion; involve (person) in hostility (with another). Hence ~MENT n. [f. F EMbrouiller, see BROIL(1)]

embrown', v.t. Make brown. [EM-]

em'bryo, n. & a. (pl. -os). 1. Offspring of animal before birth (or emergence from egg); thing in rudimentary stage; in ~, undeveloped. 2. adj. Undeveloped. Hence émbryŏn'ic a. [med. L embryo, -onis corrupt. of Gk EMbruŏn (en in, bruō swell, grow)]

~gén'esis, destruction of foetus in womb, formation of embryo, ~logy (-ŏl), science of the embryo, ~logy (-ŏl), cutting up of foetus in womb. || **émbus',** v.t. & i. (Mil.: -ss-). Put (men, stores) or get into motor vehicles. [EM-+ BUS, after entrain]

embusqué (ahǐbōōskā'), n. One who has escaped service at the front by securing home or base employment, a CUTHBERT. [F. p.p. of embusquer ambush]

émend', v.t. (Seek to) remove errors from (text of book etc.). Hence émenda'tion, ēn'endātor², nn., ~ATORY a. [f. L E(mendare f. menda fault)]

em'erald, n. Bright-green precious stone; colour of this; size of TYPE; E~ Isle, Ireland. Hence ~INE¹ a. [f. OF esmeralde f. Rom. +smaragdus]

emerge', v.i. Come up out of a liquid; come into view (from enclosed space etc.); issue (from state of suffering etc.); (of facts etc.) come out as result of inquiry, (of question, difficulty, etc.) crop up. So ~NCE, ~NCY nn., émer'gent a. [f. L E(mergere mers- dip)]

émer'gency, n. Sudden juncture demanding immediate action; ~y door, exit, etc., for use in ~ies only, in case of fire; ~y man, (in Ireland) bailiff's officer recruited for special service, esp. in evictions (hist.). [f. LL emergentia (as prec., see -ENCY)]

émér'itus, a. Honourably discharged from service, as ~ professor (retired). [L, p.p. of E(mereri earn)]

émer'sion (-shn), n. Emerging; reappearance of sun, moon, star, after eclipse or occultation. [as EMERGE, see -ION]

em'ery, n. Coarse corundum used for polishing metal, stones, etc.; ~cloth, ~paper, ~wheel (covered with ~ powder). [f. F émeri(l) f. LL smericulum f. Gk smeris polishing powder]

emet'ic, a. & n. (Medicine) that cause vomiting (also fig.). [f. Gk emetikos (emeō vomit, see -ETIC)]

émeute (see Ap.), n. Popular rising. [F]

em'igrate, v.i. & t. Leave one country to settle in another; (colloq.) change one's place of abode; (v.t.) assist (person to emigrate. So ~ANT a. & n., ~ATION n., ~ATORY a. [f. L E(migrare MIGRATE)]

émigré (ěm'ĭgrā), n. French emigrant, esp. Royalist who fled at French Revolution. [F]

ém'inence, n. 1. Rising ground. 2. Distinguished superiority (social, intellectual, etc.); (É~) cardinal's title. [f. L eminentia (as foll., see -ENCE)]

ém'inent, a. Exalted, distinguished; ~DOMAIN; (of qualities) remarkable in degree, whence~LY² adv. [f. L E(minēre jut, cf. minae projecting points, threats), -ENT]

émir' (or ĕ'—), n. Saracen or Arab prince or governor; descendant of Mohammed [=AMEER]

em'issary, n. Person sent on (usu.) an odious or underhand mission. [f. L *emissarius* (as EMIT, see -ARY¹)]

emi'ssion (-shn), n. Giving off or out (of light, heat, smell, etc.); thing thus given out; ~ *theory* (that light is ~ or streams of imponderable particles from luminous bodies). So **emiss'ive** a. [f. L *emissio* (as foll., see -ION)]

emit', v.t. (-tt-). Give out, send forth, (stream, light, heat, sound, opinion, paper currency, etc.). [f. L e(*mittere miss-* send)]

emm'et, n. (dial.). Ant. [see ANT]

emoll'ient (-lye-), a. & n. (Application) that softens living animal textures (also fig.). [f. L e(*mollire* t. *mollis* soft), see -ENT]

emol'ument, n. Profit from office or employment, salary. [f. L *emolumentum*, *emolu-*, t. e(*molere* grind or *moliri* work out), -MENT]

emo'tion, n. Agitation of mind, feeling; excited mental state. Hence ~LESS a. [f. L *emotio* f. E(*movere emot-* move), see -ION]

emo'tional (-shon-), a. Of the emotions; liable to emotion, whence ~ISM(1), ~ISM(2), ~ITY (-shonal²), nn., ~LY² adv. [prec. +-AL]

emo'tive, a. Of, tending to excite, emotion. Hence ~LY² (-vl-) adv. [f. L *emovere*, see EMOTION & -IVE]

empan'el, em-, v.t. (-ll-). Enter on panel, enrol, (jury). [f. AF EM(*paneller* PANEL)]

em'pathy, n. (psych.). The power of projecting one's personality into (and so fully comprehending the object of contemplation. [rendering of G *einfühlung* (*ein+fühlung* feeling) after Gk *empatheia*]

em'peror, n. (fem. **em'press**). Sovereign of Roman, Western, or Eastern Empire; head of Holy Roman Empire; sovereign (title superior in dignity to king); *Purple E~*, kind of butterfly. Hence ~SHIP n. [f. OF *empereur, -peror*, f. L *imperator, -orem*, f. IM(*perare=parare* prepare, order) command, see -OR³]

em'phasis, n. Stress laid on word(s) to indicate special significance; vigour, intensity, of expression, feeling, action, etc.; importance assigned to a thing; prominence, sharpness of contour. [L f. Gk f. EM(*phainō* show)]

em'phasize, v.t. Lay stress upon (word in speaking); bring (fact etc.) into special prominence. [f. prec. +-IZE]

emphat'ic, a. (Of language, tone, gesture) forcibly expressive; (of words) bearing the stress; (of person) expressing himself with emphasis; (of actions) forcible, significant. Hence ~ICALLY adv. [f. Gk *emphatikos* (as EMPHASIS, see -IC)]

emphyse'ma, n. (path.). Enlargement of air vesicles of the lungs; swelling caused by presence of air in connective tissues of body. [f. Gk *emphusēma*(*emphusaō* puff up)]

em'pire, n. Supreme & wide (political dominion; absolute control (*over*); government in which sovereign is (called emperor; territory of an emperor; (Hist.) *the E~*, (usu.) Holy Roman E~; *E~ Day*, May 24th, birthday of Q. Victoria, largely kept as (esp. school) holiday in British E~; *E~ City, State* (of New York). [F, f. L *imperium* conn. w. *imperare*, see EMPEROR]

empi'ric, a. & n. Based, acting, on observation & experiment, not on theory, whence ~ISM(2) n.; (person) relying solely on experiment; quack. Hence ~AL a., ~ALLY adv., ~ISM n. [f. L f. Gk EM(*peirikos* f. *peira* trial, see -IC)]

emplace'ment (-sm-), n. Situation; placing; platform for guns. [F (EM-+PLACE+-MENT)]

empläne', v.i. & t. Go or put on board aeroplane. [EM-+(AERO)*plane*]

employ', v.t., & n. **1.** Use (thing, one's power, etc., *for, in, on, about*, an object); use services of (person); keep (person) in one's service; busy, keep occupied, (oneself, others, *doing, in*, etc.). **2.** n. *In the ~ of*, *~ed by*. Hence ~ABLE a., ~ER¹ n. [(n. t. F *emploi*) f. F *employer* f. L IM-(*plicare* fold), cf. IMPLY]

employé (ömploi'ā), n. (fem. -ée). Person employed for wages. [F p.p. (prec.)]

employee', n. = prec. [-EE]

employ'ment, n. In vbl senses: esp. one's regular trade or profession. [-MENT]

empois'on (-zn), v.t. Put poison into; taint; corrupt (fig.); embitter (person's mind *against*). [f. F EM(*poisonner* POISON)]

empor'ium, n. Centre of commerce, mart; (vulg.) shop. [L f. Gk *emporion*, f. EMporos merchant (*por-* journey)]

empow'er, v.t. Authorize, license, (person to do); enable. [EM-]

em'press, n. Wife of emperor; woman governing an empire or (fig.) having absolute power. [f. OF *emperesse* fem. of *emperere* EMPEROR, see -ESS¹]

empressement (see Ap.), n. Display of cordiality. [F]

|| **emprise'** (-z), n. (arch.). (Chivalrous) enterprise. [OF, fem. p.p. as n. of *emprendre* f. LL IM(*pre(he)ndre* take)]

emp'ty¹, a. & n. **1.** Containing nothing; devoid of (qualities); (colloq.) hungry; (of house) devoid of furniture or inmates; (of van, ship, etc.) without load; (of persons, plans, etc.) lacking sense; meaningless. **2.** n. ~ truck, box, etc. **3.** ~*handed*, bringing no gift, carrying nothing away; ~*headed*, ~*pated*, witless. Hence **emp'tiness** n. [OE *ǣmetig* at leisure (*ǣmetta*, see -Y²)]

emp'ty², v.t. & i. Remove contents of (vessel etc. *upon* etc.); transfer (contents of one thing *into* etc. another); (of river) discharge itself (*into*); (v.i.) become empty. [f. prec.]

empur'ple, v.t. Make purple, redden. [EM-]

empyré'an, a. & n. (Of) the highest heaven, as the sphere of fire or as the abode of God; (of) the visible heavens. So empyré'al a. [f. med. L empyreus f. Gk EN(*puros* f. *pur* fire) + -AN]

ēn¹û, ēn'eu, n. Large Australian bird allied to the Cassowary. [perh. f. Port. *ema* crane, ostrich]

ēm'ûlate, v.t. Try to equal or excel; rival; imitate zealously. So ~ATION, ~ATOR² nn., ~ātive a. [f. L *aemulari* (as foll.), see -ATE³]

ēm'ûlous, a. Zealously, jealously, imitative (of); desirous (of renown etc.); ~ly² adv. [f. L *aemulus* + -OUS]

ēmûl'sify, v.t. Convert into an emulsion. [f. L E*mulgēre mulk-* milk) + -FY]

ēmûl'sion (-shn), n. Milky liquid with oily or resinous particles suspended in it; mixture of light-sensitive silver salts suspended in gelatine or collodion for coating photographic plates and films. Hence or cogn. ~IZE(3) v.t., ēmûl'sive a. [as prec., see -ION]

ēmûnc'tory, a. & n. Of nose-blowing; (organ, duct) conveying waste matter from the body. [f. L E*mungere munct-*), see -ORY]

ēn, n. Unit of width in printing, narrower than EM. [N]

en-, pref. 1. en-, em-, f. F en-, em- f. L IN-, IM- (*enamour, embarrass, engage*); now used to form E vbs (a) on nouns, with sense 'put (the object) into or on something' (*embed, engulf, entrust*) or 'put something into or on (the object)' (*enjewel*); (b) on nn. or adjj., w. sense 'bring into such condition' (*englad, enslave*); often with suf. -EN⁶ (*embolden, enlighten*); (c) on vbs with sense 'in', 'into', 'upon', (*enfold*) or w. intensive force (*encrimhed?*). 2. en-, em- f. Gk en- (en- before *b, m, p*; el-, er-, before *l, r*), w. sense 'in' (*energy, enthusiasm, emphasis*).

-en¹, -n, suf. forming p.p. of strong vbs (*spoken, sworn*); often obs. or arch. (*gotten, graven*); in some not recorded (*flung*); also displaced by -ed (*shaped* for *shapen*), or surviving only in adj. sense (*drunken, torn*). For adj. sense see -ED(2).

-en², suf. forming dimin., as *chicken, maiden*. [f. OTeut. -*inun*-]

-en³, suf. forming fem. (now only in *vixen*), and found in some nouns, as *burden*. [f. WG -*innjō* f. OTeut. -*inō*]

-en⁴, suf. seen in *oxen*; orig. part of stem in weak-decl. nouns, but retained only in pl., & added to other old plurals, as in *brethren, children, kine*, (earlier -*ther, -der, kyl*. [OE -*an*]

-en⁵, -n, suf. forming adjj. f. nn. usu. material; mostly obs. or arch. (*silvern*) or only in metaph. senses (*golden*), the noun being used as adj.; but *wooden, woollen*, & a few others, remain. [f. OTeut. -*ino*, cf. Gk & L -*ino*-]

-en⁶, suf. forming vv.t. & i. from adjj. (*deepen, moisten*) on anal. of a few in OE (*fasten*), & f. nouns as *listen* (OE), *happen* (14th c.), f. *heighten, hearten*, etc., (mod.).

ēnâ'blē, v.t. Authorize, empower, (person to do); supply (person etc.) with means to (do); || *Enabling Act*, esp. that of 1920 conferring on the Established Church a certain measure of autonomy subject to parliamentary veto. [EN-]

ēnâc't, v.t. 1. Ordain, decree, (thing, that), whence ēnâc'tion, ~MENT, nn.; ēnâc'tive, ēnâc'tory, aa.; ~*ing clauses* (containing new provisions). 2. Play (scene, part, on stage or in life). [ACT n. & v.]

ēnâm'el¹, n. Glass-like opaque or semi-transparent coating of metallic surfaces for ornament or as preservative lining (also fig.); any smooth hard coating; kinds of complexion-veneer; coating of teeth; painting done on ~; (poet.), smooth bright surface colouring, verdure, etc. [f. foll.]

ēnâm'el², v.t. (-ll-). Inlay, encrust, (metal etc., the face or skin) with enamel; portray (figures etc.) with enamel; adorn with varied colours. [f. AF EN(*amayller* f. OE *esmail*, cf. L *smaltum* of Teut. orig., cf. Gk *smaltim* SMELT¹)]

ēnâm'our f. (-ner), v.t. Inspire with love (of, esp. in p.p.); charm, delight, [f. OF EN(*amourer* f. *amour* love f. L *amorem*, nom.-*or*)]

ēnântiōp'athy, n. = ALLOPATHY. [f. Gk *enantios* opposite f. -PATHY]

ēnârthrō'sis, n. (anat.). Ball-&-socket joint. [Gk, f. EN(*arthros* f. *arthron* joint), -OSIS]

en bloc (ahñ), adv. In a lump, wholesale. [F]

ēncaen'ia (-sēn-), n. Dedication festival; ||(Oxf.) = COMMEMORATION. [L, f. Gk *egkainia* (EN- + *kainos* new)]

ēncâg'e (-ĝ-), v.t. Confine (as) in cage. [EN-]

ēncâmp', v.t. & i. (Of troops) settle (t. & i.) in camp; lodge (t. & i.) in the open in tents. [EN-]

ēncâmp'ment, n. In vbl senses; also, place where troops are encamped. [-MENT]

ēncâse', in-, v.t. Put into a case; surround as with a case. Hence ~MENT (-sm-) n. [EN-]

ēn'cash', v.t. Convert (bills etc.) into cash; receive in form of cash, realize. Hence ~MENT n. [EN-]

ēncaus'tic, a. & n. (Painting, art of painting) by burning in; ~ *brick, tile*, (inlaid with coloured clays burnt in). [f. Gk *egkaustikos* f. *egkaiō* (EN- + *kaiō* burn)]

-ence, suf. forming nn. of quality or action f. F -ence or direct f. L -*entia* f. L pres. part. in -*enti*- (nom.-*ens*); rarely repr. L -*entia* f. adjj. in -*lentus* (*corpulence*); see -ANCE, -ENCY.

enceinte (see Ap.), a. & n. 1. (Of women) pregnant. 2. n. Enclosure (in fortification). [F]

encéphalic, a. Of the brain. So **encéphali'tis** n., inflammation of the brain (see SICKNESS). [f. Gk *egkephalon* brain (EN-+*kephalē* head)+-IC]

enchain', v.t. Chain up, fetter; hold fast (attention, emotions). Hence ~MENT n. [f. OF EN(*chainer* CHAIN)]

enchant' (-ah-), v.t. Bewitch (lit. & fig.); charm, delight. Hence or cogn. ~ER[1], ~MENT, ~RESS[1] nn., ~ingLY[2] adv., (-ah-). [f. F *enchanter* f. L IN(*cantare* sing, frequent. of *canere* cant-)]

enchiri'dion (-k-), n. Handbook. [Gk (*egkheir-*), f. *en* in, *kheir* hand]

encir'cle, v.t. Surround, encompass, (*with*); form a circle round. [EN-]

ea clair (ahn), phr. (Of telegrams, official messages, etc.) in ordinary language (not in code or cipher). [F]

enclasp' (-ah-), v.t. Hold in clasp or embrace. [EN-]

enclave', n. Territory surrounded by foreign dominion. [F, f. *enclaver* f. LL IN(*clavare* f. *clavis* key or *clavus* nail)]

enclit'ic, a. & n. (gram.). (Word) so unemphatic as to be pronounced as part of preceding word, esp. (Gk) throwing its accent back on preceding word. Hence ~ICALLY adv. [f. L f. Gk *egklitikos* (EN-+*klinō* lean), see -IC]

enclose', **in-**, (-z), v.t. Surround, fence in, (land etc. *with, in,* walls etc.); shut up in receptacle (esp. something besides letter in envelope); bound on all sides, contain, (esp. Math.); hem in on all sides. [EN-]

enclo'sure (-zher), n. Enclosing (esp. of common land, to make it private property, as *E~ Act*); enclosing fence etc.; enclosed place; paper etc. enclosed with letter in envelope. [F (OF EN(*clore* P.P. -*clos*), see CLOSE[3] and -URE]

enclothe' (-dh), v.t. Clothe. [EN-]

encloud', v.t. Envelop in cloud. [EN-]

encō'miast, n. Composer of an encomium; flatterer. Hence **encōmiās'tic** a. [f. Gk *egkōmiastēs* (*egkōmiazō*, as foll. -*ast* = -IST(1) w. vbs in -*azō*)]

encō'mium, n. Formal or high-flown praise. [L, f. Gk *egkōmion* (EN-+*kōmos* revelry)]

encom'pass (-ŭm-), v.t. Surround (esp. with friendly or hostile intention); contain. Hence ~MENT n. [EN-+COMPASS n.]

encore (ōngkōr', & see Ap.), int., n., & v.t. 1. (Spectators' or auditor's demand for song etc. to be sung etc.) again, once more; further item given in response. 2. v.t. Demand repetition of (song etc.), summon (performer) for this. [vb f. n.) F, = still, again, (cf. It. *ancora*) perh. f. L (*in*) *hanc horam* to this hour]

encoun'ter, v.t., & n. 1. Meet hostilely; fall in with. 2. n. Meeting in conflict, falling in, (*with*). [(n. f. OF *encontre* f. OF *encontrer* f. LL IN(*contrā* f. L *contra* against)]

encou'rage(-kŭ-), v.t. Embolden; incite, advise, (person *to do*); promote, assist, (commerce, opinion, etc.). Hence or cogn. ~EMENT(-kŭrijm-) n., ~ingLY[2] adv. [f. OF EN(*corager*, as COURAGE)]

En'cratite (ĕ-), n. Member of early Christian heretical sect abstaining from meat, wine, & marriage. [f. LL f. late Gk *egkratitēs* (*egkratēs* continent, -ITE[1])]

encrim'son (-z-), v.t. Make crimson. [EN-]

encroach', v.i. Intrude usurpingly (on others' territory, rights, etc., or abs.). Hence ~MENT n. [f. OF EN(*crochier* f. *croc* hook)]

encrust', **in-**, v.t. & i. Cover with a crust; overlay (surface) with ornamental crust of precious material; (v.i.) form into a crust. Hence ~MENT n. [f. F *encruster* f. L IN(*crustare*, as CRUST); also f. EN-+CRUST]

encum'ber, v.t. Hamper (person, movement, action, *with* burden, difficulty, etc.); burden (person, estate, *with* debts); fill, block, (place *with* lumber etc., lit. & fig.). Hence ~MENT n. [f. F EN(*combrer* CUMBER)]

encum'brance, n. Burden; annoyance; impediment; *without ~*, having no children; claim, mortgage, etc., on property. [f. OF *encombrance* (as prec., see -ANCE)]

encum'brancer, n. One who has an encumbrance on another's estate. [-ER[1]]

ency', suf., mod. E different. of -ENCE (-Y), usu. denoting quality or state, not action.

encyc'lic(al), aa. & nn. (Pope's letter) for extensive circulation. [f. LL *encyclicus*, for -*ius*, f. Gk *egkuklios* (EN-+*kuklos* circle)]

encyclop(a)ed'ia (-pē-), n.(pl.-as). Book giving information on all branches of knowledge or of one subject, usu. arranged alphabetically; esp. the French ~ia of Diderot, D'Alembert, and others; general course of instruction. Hence ~IC(AL) aa., ~ISM(3), ~IST(3), nn. [LL, f. false Gk *egkuklopaideia* for *egkuklios paideia* all-round education (as prec., *paideia* f. *paideuō* educate f. *pais paidos* boy)]

encyst', v.t. Enclose in a cyst. Hence ~A'TION, ~MENT, nn. [EN-]

end[1], n. 1. Limit, as *there is no ~ to it*; extremity (of line etc.); || *East, West, End* (part of London); surface bounding a thing at either extremity, head of cask etc.; remnant, as *candle ~s, odds & ~s; rope's ~*, short piece bound at ~s with thread for flogging; *shoemaker's ~*, length of thread armed with bristle. 2. Conclusion (of period, action, state, book, etc.); latter part; destruction; death. 3. Result; purpose, as *to gain his ~s, to*

what ~?; object for which a thing exists, final cause. 4. *Place on* ~ (upright); *turn* ~ *for* ~, reverse; *word without* ~, for ever; *placed* ~, (lengthwise, continuously); ~ *on*, with its ~ fronting one; *no* ~, much, many, of; *on* ~, continuously (*for three weeks or* ~); *be at, come to, an* ~, be, become, exhausted or completed; *in the* ~, finally, after all; *at one's wits* ~, quite perplexed; *put an* ~ *to*, stop, abolish; *keep one's* ~ *up*, acquit oneself well in conversation, bargain, etc.; *go (in) off the deep* ~ (sc. of swimming-bath) fig., take risks; *make an* ~ *of*, put a stop to; *at a loose* ~, unoccupied; *make both* ~*s meet*, live within one's income; *is at the* ~ *of his tether*, knows, can do, no more; ~*iron*, movable plate changing size of grate in range; ~*paper*, blank leaf at beginning and ~ of book. [com.-Teut.: OE *ende*, Du. *einde*, G *ende*]

endám'age, v.t. (as prec.). [EN-]
endán'ger (-j-), v.t. Cause danger to. [EN-]
endéar', v.t. & i. Render (person, thing, oneself) dear (to). Hence ~ing² adv., ~MENT n. [EN-]
endéav'our (-dĕvér), v.t. & i. & n. 1. Try (to do); strive after. 2. n. Attempt (to do, at doing). [f. u.f. vb.] f. EN-+DEVOIR]
endēm'ic, a. & n. 1. Regularly found among (specified) people, in (specified) country. 2. n. ~ic disease. Hence ~ICALLY adv. [f. Gk EN-+*dēmos* people+-IC]
endérm'ic, a. Acting on the skin. Hence ~ICALLY adv. [EN-+DERM+-IC]
end'ing, n. In vbl senses, esp. latter part (of word, story, etc.). [-ING¹]
end'ive, n. Species of chicory, with curled leaves, used as salad. [F. f. L intibus]
end'less, a. Infinite; eternal; incessant; (Mech.) ~ band, cable, chain (with ends joined for continuous action over wheels endless, see END¹ and -LESS]

én'dō- in comb.=Gk *endon* within, as; ~*card'ium*, lining membrane of heart; ~*card'itis*, inflammation of this; ~*carp*, inmost layer of pericarp; ~*crine*, inner surface of skull; ~*crine*, secreting internally, ductless, of the ~crine glands; [Gk *krīnō* sift]; ~*derm*, inner layer of blastoderm; ~*gen*, plant that develops wood in interior of stem; ~*genous* (-ǒj-), growing from within; ~*lymph*, fluid in membranous labyrinth of ear; ~*mētrītis*; ~*mētrium*, (inflammation of) lining membrane of womb;

endórse', in-, v.t. Write on back of (document), esp. sign one's name on back of (bill, cheque, etc.); write (explanation, comment, on back of document) ~ *over*, make over one's rights in (bill etc. to another person, also fig.); confirm (statement, opinion), (vulg. in advertisements) confirm advertiser's praise of (~'s pills etc.); || motorist's, publican's, licence is ~*d*, has record of offence written on the back. Hence ~MENT (-sm-) n. [refash. on L; ME *endosse* f. OF *endosser* f. med. L IN(*dorsum* f. *dorsum* back)]
endōw', v.t. Bequeath, give, permanent income to (person, institution); invest (person) *with* (privileges etc.); furnish (person) *with* (ability etc.; esp. in p.p.). Hence ~MENT n. (~*ment assurance*, payment of a fixed sum to an insured person on attaining an agreed age, or to his or her estate if death occurs earlier). [f. EN-+F *douer* f. L *dotare* (as DOWER)]
endūe', in-, v.t. Put on (clothes etc., also fig.); clothe (person) *with*; (usu. pass.) furnish (person *with* qualities etc.) [f. OF *enduire* f. L IN(*duere* lead, draw), associated in sense w. *induere* put on (clothes)]
endúr'ance, n. Habit, power, of enduring; enduring. [-ANCE]
endúr'e', v.t. & i. Undergo (pain etc.); submit to; bear (*to do*, esp. w. neg.); last. Hence ~ABLE a., ~ingly² adv., ~'ing-NESS n. [f. OF *endurer* f. L IN(*dūrāre* hard, make hard f. *dūrus*)]
end'ways, end'wise (-z), adv. With the end turned towards the spectator or uppermost or foremost; end to end. [-WAYS, -WISE]
én'ēma (or inē'), n. Injection of liquid or gaseous substance into the rectum; the syringe used. [Gk *enema* f. *en-*+*hiēmi* send-), see -M]
én'émy, n. & a. 1. Hostile person; opponent (*of, to*, another); *the* E~, the Devil; member of hostile army or nation; hostile force or ship; (colloq) *how goes the* ~?, what is the time? 2. adj. Of, or belonging to, the ~ (~ *ships, aircraft*, etc.). (*an ~ is destroyed by* ~ *action*). [f. OF *enemi* f. L IN(*amicus*=*amicus* friend]

~*morph*, mineral enclosed in another; ~*pa'rasite*, internal parasite; ~*plasm*, ~*sarc*, inner soft layer of protoplasm; ~*scope*, instrument for viewing internal parts of body; ~*skěl'ěton*, internal framework of vertebrates; ~*smōse* (-ǒz'm-), passage of a fluid inwards through a porous septum; ~*sperm*, albumen enclosed with embryo in seeds; ~*spore*, inner coat of spore, spore formed in a case; ~*thel'ium*, layer of cells lining blood-vessels etc.

énérgĕt'ic, a. & n. Strenuously active; forcible, vigorous; powerfully operative;

(n. pl.) science of energy. Hence ~ICALLY adv. [f. Gk energētikos t. ergon WORK], see -IC]

éněr´gic, a. (rare). = prec. [f. ENERGY + -IC]

ěn´ergize, v.t. & i. Infuse energy into (person, work); be in active operation. [-IZE]

ěněr´gūm´ěn, n. Demoniac; enthusiast, fanatic. [f. LL f. Gk energoumenos (pass. part., see ENERGETIC)]

ěn´ergy, n. 1. Force, vigour, (of speech, action, person, etc.); active operation; (pl.) individual powers in exercise, as *devote your energies to this*; (latent) ability. 2. (Physics) *actual, kinetic, motive, ~*, a body's power of doing work by virtue of its motion (half product of mass into square of velocity); *potential, static, latent, ~*, body's power of doing work by virtue of stresses resulting from its relation to other bodies; CONSERVATION OF ~; *mass ~*, ~ which all bodies possess in virtue of their mass (half product of mass into square of velocity of light), and of which a small portion is released (as radiations etc.) in radioactivity and other types of atomic disintegration. [f. LL f. Gk energeia f. energēs f. ergon work]

ěn´ervate¹, a. Wanting in (physical, moral, literary, artistic) vigour. [f. L E(nervare f. nervus sinew), see -ATE²]

ěn´ervāte², v.t. Weaken (physically etc. as prec.). So ~A´TION n. [as prec., -ATE³]

ěnface´, v.t. Write, print, stamp (form of words) on bill etc.; do this (bill etc.). Hence ~MENT(-sm-) n. [EN-]

en famille (ahñ fămē´ye), adv. At home, among one's family. [F]

enfant terrible (see Ap.), n. Child who asks awkward questions, repeats what he has heard, etc. [F]

ěnfee´ble, v.t. Make feeble. Hence ~MENT (-belm-) n. [f. OF EN(feble as FEEBLE)]

ěnfeoff´ (-fěf´), v.t. Invest (person) with fief; (fig.) hand over. [f. OF EN(feffer (FIEF)]

ěnfeoff´ment (-fěf´-), n. Enfeoffing; document effecting this; fief. [-MENT]

en fête (ahñ fāt), adv. & pred. a. Engaged in, attired etc. for, holiday-making. [F]

ěnfětt´er, v.t. Bind in fetters (lit. & fig.) enslave (person also). [EN-]

ěnfilāde´, n., & v.t. 1. Fire from guns etc. sweeping line of works or men from end to end. 2. v.t. Subject (troops, road, etc.) to ~. [(vb f. n.) F, f. EN(filer f. fil thread), see -ADE]

ěnfōld´, ~in-, v.t. Wrap up (person etc. in, with); clasp, embrace; shape into folds. [EN-]

ěnforce´, v.t. Urge, press home, (argument, demand); impose (action, conduct, upon person etc.); compel observance of (law etc.). Hence or cogn. ~ABLE a., ~dĭy² (-sěd-) adv., ~MENT (-sm-) n. [f. OF enforcer f. LL IN(fortiare t. fortis strong]

ěnfrāme´, v.t. Set (picture etc.) in frame; serve as frame to. [EN-]

ěnfran´chĭse (-z), v.t. Set free; invest (town) with municipal rights; esp. that of representation in parliament; admit (person) to electoral franchise. Hence ~isEMENT (-zm-) n. [f. OF EN(franchir f. franc FRANK a.), see -ISH²]

ěngāgle´ (-n-g-), v.t. & i. 1. Bind by contract or promise (esp. of marriage, as ~ed couple). 2. Hire (servant); bespeak (seats, cab, etc.). 3. Pledge oneself (to do, that); ~e for, guarantee, promise. 4. Induce; attract, charm, (esp. in part.), whence ~´ingLY adv. 5. (Archit.) fasten (pillar) into wall; interlock (thing with another). 6. Hold fast (attention); employ (usu. pass.). 7. Embark in (politics etc.). 8. Bring (troops) into conflict, enter into conflict with (also with.). Hence ~e´MENT (-jm-) n. [f. F EN(gager f. GAGE²)]

en garçon (see Ap.), adv. & pred. a. As a bachelor, unmarried. [F]

ěngâr´land and (-n-g-), v.t. Put a garland upon; wreathe (with flowers etc.). [EN-]

ěngěn´der (-n-g-), v.t. Beget (now only fig.); (of situation, condition, etc.) bring about. [f. F engendrer f. L IN(generare t. GENERATE]

ěn´gine¹ (-j-), n., & v.t. 1. Mechanical contrivance consisting of several parts; = STEAM-~; FIRE-~; machine, instrument, used in war; instrument, means; ||~-driver (of steam-~, esp. locomotive); ~-lathe (worked by machinery); ~-turning, engraving of symmetrical patterns on metals by machine. 2. v.t. Fit (ship etc.) with ~(s). [(vb f. n.) f. OF engin f. L ingenium (see INGENIOUS]

ěngineer´¹ (-j-), n. 1. One who designs & constructs military works; soldier of branch of army called E~s, trained to engineering. 2. (Also civil ~) one who designs works of public utility, bridges, canals, gas-works, etc.; maker of engines. 3. One who has charge of engine; *engine-driver. Hence ~SHIP n. [f. OF engineor f. LL ingeniatorem (ingeniare, as ENGINE, see -OR²]

ěngineer´² (-j-), v.i. & t. Act as engineer; construct, manage, (bridge, work, etc.) as engineer; (colloq.) arrange, contrive, bring about. [f. prec.]

ěn´ginery (-j-), n. Engines; machinery (often fig.). [-ERY]

ěngĭr´d(le) (-n-g-), v.t. Surround with or ~ with girdle. [EN-]

|| Eng´lander (ĭngg-), n. Little ~, one opposed to imperial policy. [-ER¹]

Eng´lish¹ (ĭngg-), a. & n. 1. Of England; the ~ (people, soldiers, etc.); ~man, ~woman, one who is ~ by birth, descent, or naturalization. 2. Of, written or spoken in, the ~ language. 3. The ~

language (also *the king's, queen's,* ~ as mishandle *the king's* ~); Old ~, (ending about 1150), *Middle* ~ (ending 1500); *in plain* ~, in plain words. **4.** Size of TYPE; O'Tent. *anglisko* (*angli-* ANGLE ")]

eng'lish² (ingg-), v.t. (arch., affected). Render into English. [f. prec.]

engorge', v.t. Devour greedily; (pass.) be crammed, (Path.) be congested with blood. Hence ~MENT n. [f. F EN-]

engraft', in-, (-ah-), v.t. Insert (scion of one tree into, *upon,* another); implant (principles etc. *in* the mind etc.); incorporate (thing *into* another); add (adventitious thing *upon*). [EN-]

engrail', v.t. Indent the edge of, give serrated appearance to, (esp. Her.). [f. OF *engresler* perh. f. *gresle* hail]

engrain', in-, v.t. Cause (dye etc.) to sink deeply into a thing (usu. fig.) (p.p. cf. INGRAINED) Inveterate, *as an* ~*ed rogue.*

engrave', v.t. Inscribe, ornament, (hard surface *with* incised marks); carve (figures etc. *upon* surface); (fig.) impress deeply (*upon* memory etc.); cut (figures etc.) in lines on metal plates for printing. [EN-+ GRAVE²]

engrāv'ing, n. In vbl senses, copy of picture, etc. from engraved plate. [-ING¹]

engross', v.t. Write (document) in large letters; express in legal form; (Hist.) buy whole stock of (corn etc.) so as to get monopoly; monopolize (conversation etc.); absorb (person, his attention, time, etc.; esp. in p.p. ~*ed* subject etc.). Hence ~MENT n. [(1) f. AF *engrosser* (*grosse* f. med.L *grossa* large writing; (2) f. phr. *in gross* wholesale]

engulf, in-, v.t. Plunge into, swallow up (as) in, a gulf. Hence ~MENT n. [EN-]

enhance' (-hah-, -hâ-), v.t. Heighten, intensify (qualities, powers, etc.); exaggerate; raise (price). Hence ~MENT n. [A.F *enhauncer* prob. corrupt. of OF *enhaucier* f. LL **IN(altiare alttus* high)]

enharmon'ic, a. (mus.). Of, having, intervals smaller than semitone (esp. such intervals as that between G sharp & A flat). Hence ~ICALLY adv. [f. L f. Gk ENARMONIKOS (*harmonia* HARMONY, see -IC)]

enig'ma, n. Riddle; puzzling person or thing. Hence or cogn. ~MATIC(AL) aa., ~MAT'ICALLY adv., ~TIZE(3) v.t. [f. L f. Gk *ainigma-matos* f. *ainissomai* speak allusively (*ainos* fable)]

enisle', in-, (-īl, v.t. (poet.). Make into an isle; place on an isle; isolate. Con-tinuation of sentence beyond second line f. of couplet. [f. F *enjambement* f. EN(*jambe* leg), see -MENT]

enjoin', v.t. Prescribe, impose, (action, conduct, *on* person); command (person

---

to do); issue instructions (*that*); (Legal, esp. U.S.) prohibit by judicial order. [f. F *enjoindre* (st. *-joign-*) f. L I(*jungere* join)]

enjoy', v.t. ~ *oneself,* experience pleasure; take delight in, whence ~ABLE a., ~able-NESS n., ~ABLY² adv.; have the use of (advantages etc.); experience, *as* ~ *poor health.* Hence ~MENT n. [f. OF EN(*joir* f. *joie* JOY) give joy to, (refl.) enjoy; or f. L I(*gaudēre* rejoice)]

enkin'dle, v.t. Cause (flame, passions, war, etc.) to blaze up; inflame with passion. [EN-]

enlāce', v.t. Encircle tightly; enfold; en-twine. Hence ~MENT (-sm-) n. [f. F EN-]

enlarge', v.t. & i. Increase, extend; widen, expand, (mind, heart, ideas) (arch.) release; (Photog.) reproduce, be capable of reproduction, on larger scale. Hence ~MENT (-jm-) n., (esp.) such photographic reproduction, enlār'gER¹ n., apparatus for enlarging or reducing negatives or positives. [f. OF EN(*larger* LARGE)]

enlight'en (-it-), v.t. Instruct, inform, (person *on* subject); (poet.) shed light on (object), give light to (person); free (person) from prejudice or superstition (esp. in p.p.). Hence ~MENT (-it-) n. [EN-+ LIGHT², + -EN²]

enlink', v.t. Link together, connect closely, (*with, to*; lit. & fig.). [EN-]

enlist', v.t. & i. Engage (t. & i.) for mili-tary service; secure the co-operation or support of (persons, feelings, natural forces, sciences, etc., *in* enterprise etc.). Hence ~MENT n. [EN-]

enliv'en, v.t. Animate, inspirit, (persons, feelings, trade, etc.); brighten (picture, scene). Hence ~MENT n. [EN-]

en masse (ahñ), adv. In a mass; all to-gether. [F]

en'mity, n. Hatred; state of hostility. [f. OF *enemistie* f. LL *inimicitatem*]

en'nead, n. Set of nine (discourses, books, points). [f. Gk *enneas* nine, see -AD]

enno'ble, v.t. Make (person) a noble; make noble, elevate. Hence ~MENT n. [f. F EN(*nobler* (NOBLE)]

ennui', n. Mental weari-ness from lack of occupation or interest. Hence ~ED² (önwéd), *ennuyé* (see Ap., fem.-ée, pl. -és, -ées), aa. [F; f. L *in odio*, cf. ANNOY²]

enor'mity, n. Monstrous wickedness; crime. [f. F *énormité* f. L *enormitatem* (as foll., see -TY]

enor'mous, a. Huge, very large, ~ NESS n. [f. L E(*normis* f. *norma* pattern, stand-

enough (enŭf', (poet.) **enow'**) a., n., & adv. Not less than the required number, quantity, degree, as: (adj.) *we have apples* ~, ~ *apples, beer* ~, ~ *beer*; *he made* ~ *noise* (to justify supposition etc.), ~ *noise to wake the dead, for his purpose*; (n.) *we have* ~ *of everything except beer*, ~ *of* (stop) *this folly*, ~! (say no more), ~ *is as good as a feast, cry* ~' (acknowledge defeat), *I have had* ~ (am tired) *of him, I had* ~ *to do* (my work cut out) *to catch the tram, you have done more than* ~, ~ *and to spare*; (pred.; adj. or n.) *five men are* ~, *five quarts is not* ~; (adv.) *it is boiled* (just) ~, *he does not advertise* ~ *are you warm* ~, *he does not* ~ (usu. sufficiently) *realize the difficulties, she sings well* ~ (tolerably), *you know well* ~ (quite well) *what I mean; oddly* ~ (to justify the term oddly), *he had lost his purse; sure* ~ (to satisfy rational doubt), *there it was*. [OE *genog* (Du. *genoeg*, G *genug*) f. *geneah* it suffices f. OTeut. *ga-* pref. + *nah* f. Aryan *nak* seen in L *nancisci nact-*obtain]

énounce', v.t. Enunciate; pronounce (words). Hence ~MENT (-sm-) n. [f. F *énoncer* (as ENUNCIATE]

en passant (see Ap.), adv. By the way; (Chess) *take* (pawn that advances two squares at once) ~ (with your own pawn by which it could have been taken if it had advanced only one). [F]

en prise (ahn prēz), phr. (Chess). In a position to be taken. [F]

|| **enquire, enquiry.** See INQUIRE, INQUIRY.

enrage', v.t. Make furious (~*d at, by, with*). [f. OF ENrager (RAGE)]

en rapport (ahn rapōr'), adv. In touch (*with*). [F, see RAPPORT]

enrapt'ure, v.t. Delight intensely. [EN-]

enré'giment (-jm-), v.t. Form (men) into a regiment; discipline. [f. F EN(*régimenter* f. *régiment* REGIMENT)]

en règle (ahn rāgl), adv. In due form. [F]

enrich', v.t. Make rich; add to contents of (collection, museum, book); make richer in quality, flavour, etc. Hence ~MENT n. [f. F EN(*richir* f. *riche* RICH]

enrobe', v.t. Put a robe upon. [EN-]

enrōl', -ll, v.t. (-ll-). Write name of (person) on list, esp. of army; incorporate (person) as member (*in* society etc.); enter (deed etc.) among rolls of court of justice; record, celebrate. Hence **énrōl'-MENT** n. [f. OF ENroller f. *rolle* ROLL n.]

en route (ahn rōōt), adv. On the way (*to, for*, place etc. or abs.). [F]

ens (ĕnz), n. (pl. *entia*, pr. ĕn'shia). An entity (esp. as an abstract notion). [LL, as ENTITY]

|| **En'sa** (ĕ-), n. Organization for entertaining troops etc. [initials of *Entertainments National Service Association*]

ensam'ple, n. (arch.). = EXAMPLE. [earlier *assumple* f. OF *essample* EXAMPLE]

ensang'uined (-nggwind), a. Blood-stained, bloody, (lit. & fig.) [EN-+L *sanguis -inis* blood+-ED[1]]

ensconce', v.t. Establish (oneself etc. in secret, safe, snug, etc. place). [EN-]

ensemble (see Ap.), n. (Also *tout* ~) thing viewed as a whole; general effect; (Mus.) concerted passage in which all performers unite (*good* ~, performance of such passage in which all performers are in tune & time with one another, with blend & balance of tone). [F]

enshrine', v.t. Enclose (relic etc.) in shrine; serve as shrine for (precious thing, lit. & fig.). Hence ~MENT (-nm-) n. [EN-]

enshroud', v.t. Cover completely, hide from view. [EN-]

en'sifōrm, a. Sword-shaped; ~ *cartilage* (appended to the sternum). [f. L *ensis* sword+-FORM]

en'sign (-sin), n. **1.** Badge (of office etc.); banner, flag, || esp. (Brit. naut.) white, blue, or red, flag with union in corner (*white*~, or red, flag of Royal Navy & Royal Yacht Squadron, *blue* ~, of naval reserve etc., *red* ~, of merchant service). **2.** Standard-bearer (formerly, lowest commissioned officer of foot, cf. ANCIENT[2]), whence ~CY (-fn-) n. [f. OF *enseigne* f. L *insignia* neut. pl. of *insignis* (*signum* sign) conspicuous]

en'silage, n., & v.t. Preservation of green fodder in silo or pit without drying; fodder thus preserved; (v.t.) treat (fodder) by ~. [(vb f. n.) F (as foll., see -AGE]]

ensile, v.t. Put (fodder) into a silo. [F f. *ensiler* f. Sp. ENsilar (SILO)]

enslave', v.t. Make (person etc.) a slave (lit., or fig. *to* habit, superstition, etc.). Hence ~MENT (-vm-) n. [EN-]

enslāv'er, n. In vbl senses, esp. woman by whose charms a man is enslaved. [-ER[1]]

ensnare', v.t. Entrap (lit. & fig.). [EN-]

ensoul' (-sōl), **In-**, v.t. Infuse a soul into. [EN-]

ensphēre', v.t. Encircle, enclose. [EN-]

ensūe', v.i. & t. Happen afterwards; result (*from, on*); (Bibl.) seek after. [f. OF *ensuivre* f. LL IN(*sequere*=L *sequi* follow]

ensure' (-shoor), v.t. Make (person, thing) safe (*against, from*, risks); make certain (thing, *that* it shall happen); secure (thing *to, for*, person etc.); (formerly)=INSURE. [f. AF EN(*seurer* f. OF *seur* SURE]]

enswäthe' (-dh), v.t. Bind, wrap, in bandage (lit. & fig.). Hence ~MENT (-dhm-) n. [EN-]

-ent, suf. forming adj. & nn., repr. L *-ent-* (nom. *-ens*) of pres. part. in 2nd, 3rd, & 4th conjj. See -ANT. For noun meanings (1, 2) see -ANT.

entab'lature, n. (archit.) The part of an order above the column, including architrave, frieze, & cornice. [f. It. *intavolatura* f. IN(*tavolare* f. *tavola* TABLE), see -URE]

entab'lement (-belm-), n. Horizontal platform(s) supporting statue, above

dado & base. [F, f. ENtailler (TABLE), see -MENT]

entail¹, n. Settlement of succession of landed estate so that it cannot be bequeathed or alienated; estate so secured; (fig.) inalienable inheritance (of qualities, beliefs, etc.). [f. foll.]

entail², v.t. Settle (land etc.) as in prec.; bestow (thing) as inalienable possession (on person); necessitate, impose (expense, labour, on person); involve. Hence ~MENT n. [EN-+TAIL²]

entangle (-ngg'l), v.t. Catch in snare or among obstacles; involve (person etc.) in difficulties (lit. & fig.); tangle or (-nggelmen) n. (also, Mil.) barrier erected to impede the enemy's progress (esp. one formed of stakes and interlaced barbed wire). Hence ~MENT n. [EN-]

entasis, n. (archit.). Slight convexity of a column shaft (introduced to correct the visual illusion of concavity). [Gk, f. enteinō to stretch]

entelechy (-ki), n. (philos.). Realization, the becoming or being actual of what was potential, developed perfection, (Aristotle defines the soul, the Form or E~ of an organized body); what gives perfection, informing spirit. [f. Gk entelecheia (en telei echein to be in perfection)]

entellus, n. (Also ~ monkey) the sacred Indian bearded monkey. [proper name (Virg. Aen. v. 437–72)]

entente (see AP.), n. (diplom.). Friendly understanding between States; group of States in such relation; E~ cordiale, the Gt Britain & France 1904; the (Triple) E~, of these with Russia 1908; the Little E~, of Czecho-Slovakia, Jugo-Slavia, & Roumania 1921. [F, = understanding]

enter, v.i. & t. 1. v.i. Go, come, in, (into place, room, etc. or abs.); (3rd pers. imperat. as stage direction) come upon stage, as E~ Macbeth; ~ into, engage in (conversation, relations, agreement, inquiry etc.), sympathize with (person's feelings etc.), form part of (calculations, plans, etc.), bind oneself by (recognizances, treaty, contract); ~ (up)on, assume possession of (property), begin (process etc.), begin to deal with (subject). 2. v.t. Go, come, into (place etc.); penetrate (flesh etc.); become member of (army, church, etc.); give initial training to (dog), break in (horse); write (name, details, etc., in list, book, etc.); record name of (person) as competitor for (competition); also intr., announce oneself as competitor at a meeting etc.; (of show oneself at a meeting etc.; (of minority in deliberative body, ||esp. House of Lords) ~ a protest, record it in journals or minutes, make it; admit, procure admission for, (pupil, member of a society); ~ up, complete series of entries in (account-books etc.). Hence

~ABLE a. [f. F entrer f. L intrare (intra within)]

enteric, a. & n. Of the intestines; ~ (fever), typhoid. So **enteritis** n. [f. Gk enterikos (enteron intestine, see -IC)]

entero- in comb. = Gk enteron intestine, as ~like, stony concretion of stomach etc., ~tomy (-ŏt-) cutting open intestine.

enterprise (-z), n. Undertaking, esp. bold or difficult one; courage, readiness, to engage in ~s, as he has no ~. [f. OF entreprise f. entreprendre (entre between + prendre take f. L prehendere)]

enterprising (-z-), a. Ready to undertake enterprises. Hence ~LY² adv. [part. of arch. vb enterprise (f. prec.)]

entertain, v.t. Maintain (correspondence, discourse); amuse, occupy agreeably, (person etc., often iron., whence ~ING² a., ~ingly² adv.; receive hospitably (person etc.), whence ~ER¹ n.; cherish, welcome or consider, (idea, feeling, proposal). [f. F entretenir (INTER-, tenir hold)]

entertainment, n. In vbl senses, esp.: amusement, as much to my ~; public performance or show (||~, one levied on attendance at these). [-MENT]

enthral(l)² (-awl), v.t. Enslave (usu. fig.); charm. Hence **enthral'MENT** (-awl-) n.

enthrone', v.t. Place (king, bishop, etc.) on throne, esp. as formal induction (also fig.). Hence ~MENT (-nm-) n. [EN-]

enthroniza'tion, n. Enthronement (lit. & fig.). [f. obs. vb enthronize f. OF introniser f. L L(m-), f. Gk (EN)thronizō (EN)THRONE, -IZE)]

enthuse' (-z), v.i. (colloq.). Show enthusiasm, gush. [back-formation on foll.]

enthusiasm (-zi-), n. Ardent zeal (for, about, an object, cause, etc.), [f. L L f. Gk enthousiasmos f. enthousiazō f. enthousia-]

enthusiast (-zi-), n. One who is full of enthusiasm (for cause etc.), whence ~IC enthousiastēs god) possessed by a god]

enthusiast'ic, a. [... enthousiastikos] **enthusiastically** adv.

enthymeme, n. (logic). Syllogism in which one premiss is suppressed. [f. L f. Gk enthumēma f. enthumeomai consider (thumos mind)]

entice', v.t. Allure (person etc. from place, course of conduct, etc., into another; to do). So ~MENT (-sm-) n. [f. OF ENticer prob. lit. set on fire (L titio firebrand)]

entire', a. & n. Whole, complete; not broken or decayed; not castrated; unqualified; all of one piece, continuous; pure, unmixed; (n., hist., ||& on inn signs) blend of former ale, beer, & two-penny. Hence ~NESS (-īrn-) n. [f. OF entier f. L integer, f. tag- tangere touch]

entire'ly (-īli, -līli), adv. Wholly; solely

entire'ly (-īrtī), n. Completeness, esp. *in its ~y*; sum total (*of*); (Law) possession *by ~ies* (undivided). [f. OF *entiereté* f. L *integritatem* (as ENTIRE, see -TY)]

entir'tle, v.t. Give (book etc.) the title of (*Adam Bede* etc.); give (person) the title of (sultan etc.); (of circumstances, qualities, etc.) give (person etc.) a claim (*to a thing, to do*). [f. OF *entiteler* f. LL IN*titulare*, as TITLE)]

en'tity, n. A thing's existence, as opp. to its qualities or relations; thing that has real existence. So **en'titative** a. [f. LL *entitas* (*ens* LL part. of *esse* be, suggested by *absens*; see -TY)]

en'to- in comb. = Gk *entos* within, as *-pa'rasite*, *-zo'on*, internal parasite, *-phyte*, plant growing inside a plant or animal.

entomb' (-ōom), v.t. Place in tomb (lit. & fig.); serve as tomb for. Hence ~MENT (-ōom-m-) n. [f. OF ENtoumber (as TOMB)]

entomb'ic, a. Of insects. [as foll. + -IC]

ento'mo- in comb. Insect, as:~*lite* (-ōm²), fossil insect, ~*phagous* (-ŏf²), insect-eating, ~*philous* (-ŏf²), (Bot.) fertilized by means of insects, ~*tomy* (-ŏt²), insect anatomy. [f. Gk EN(*tomos* f. *temnō* cut) cut up, in neut. pl.=insects]

entomol'ogy, n. Study of insects. Hence **entomolo'gical** a.,~IST n.,~IZE v.i. [f. F ENTOMO(*logie* -LOGY)]

entourage (see Ap.), n. Surroundings; attendant persons. [F]

en-tout-cas (ahn tōō kah), n. Umbrella-sunshade. [F, lit. in any case]

entr'acte (see Ap.), n. (Performance in) interval between acts of play.

en'trails (-z), n. pl. Bowels, intestines; (fig.) inner parts (*of the earth* etc.). [f. OF *entraille* f. LL *intralia* (neut. pl. taken in F as fem. sing.) f. *inter* among]

entrain', v.t. & i. Put (esp. troops), get, into a train. [EN-]

entramm'el, v.t. (-ll-), Entangle, hamper. [EN-]

en'trance, n. Coming or going in; coming of actor upon stage; entering *into*, *upon* (office etc.); right of admission (in *full ~ fee*) fee paid on admission to club, school, etc.; door, passage, etc., one enters by. [OF (as ENTER, -ANCE)]

entrance'² (-ah-), v.t. Throw into a trance; overwhelm (*with* joy, fear); carry away as in trance (*from*, *to*). Hence ~MENT (-ahnsm-) n. [EN-]

en'trant, n. One who enters room, profession, etc., or *for* (race etc.). [F, part. as ENTER]

entrap', v.t. (-pp-). Catch in or as in trap; beguile (person *to* destruction etc., *into* doing). [f. OF EN(*traper* TRAP¹)]

entreat', v.t. (Also *~ of*) ask (person) earnestly (*to do*, *that*), whence ~ingly¹ adv.; (Bibl.) *evil ~*, treat ill. [f. OF EN(*traiter* TREAT)]

entreat'y, n. Earnest request. [prec. + -y⁴]

entrechat (ŏ'ntreshah), n. Striking together of the heels several times during leap from ground, in dancing. [F]

entrecôte (ŏ'ntrekōt), n. (cookery). Steak cut out of the ribs. [F]

entrée (ŏ'ntrā, & see Ap.), n. Right, privilege, of admission; || made dish served between fish & joint. [F, = ENTRY]

entremets (see Ap.), n. A side dish or dainty. [F]

entrench', **in'**, v.t. & i. Surround (post, army, town) with trench (also fig., esp. oneself); (rarely) encroach, trespass, *upon*. Hence ~MENT n. [EN-]

entre nous (see Ap.), adv. Between you & me. [F]

entrepôt (see Ap.), n. Storehouse for deposit; commercial centre for import & export, collection & distribution. [F]

entrepreneur (ahntrepronĕr'), n. Person in effective control of commercial undertaking. [F]

entresol (see Ap.), n. Low storey between first & ground floor. [F]

en'tropy, n. (physics). Measure of the unavailability of a system's thermal energy for conversion into mechanical work. [f. EN- + Gk *tropē* transformation (*trepō* turn), on *energy*]

entrust', **in-**, v.t. Charge (person) *with* (duty, object of care); confide (duty, person, thing, its safety, *to* person). [EN-]

en'try, n. 1. Coming or going in; ceremonial entrance; (Law) taking possession; place of entrance, door, gate, lobby, mouth of river. 2. Registration in records, account-books, etc.; item so entered; *bookkeeping by double, single, ~* (in which each item is entered twice, once, in ledger); list of competitors for race etc. [f. F *entrée* f. LL *intrata* (as ENTER, cf. -ADE]

entwine', **in-**, v.t. Interweave (lit. & fig.); wreathe (thing *with*, *about*, *round*, another); embrace; embrace. [EN-]

entwist', **in-**, v.t. Clasp with, form into, a twist; twist (thing) *in with* (another). [EN-]

enu'cleate, v.t. Explain, clear-up; (Surg.) extract (tumour etc.) from shell etc. Hence ~A'TION n. [f. L E(*nucleare* f. NUCLEUS)]

enum'erate, v.t. Count; specify (items). Hence or cogn. ~A'TION, ~ātor² nn., ~ātive a. [f. L E(*numerare* NUMBER²)]

enun'ciate (-shi-), v.t. Express definitely (proposition, theory); proclaim; pronounce (words). So ~A'TION (-si-),~ātor² (-shi-), nn., ~ative (-sha-) a. [f. L E(*nuntiare* announce f. *nuntius* messenger', -ATE³]

enūre', v.i. (& t.). See INURE.

enūrē'sis, n. (path.). Incontinence of urine. [f. Gk *enoureō* urinate in (*en* in + *ouron* urine)]

envel'op, v.t. Wrap up (person, thing, subject, etc., *in* garment, flames, clouds,

en'velope (or ŏn-), n. Wrapper, covering, (lit. & fig.); esp. folded & gummed cover of letter. [f. F *enveloppe* (as prec.)]

en'venom, v.t. Put poison on or into (weapon, air, etc.); infuse venom into (feelings, words, actions); corrupt (mind etc.). [f. OF *envenimer* as VENOM]

en'viable, a. Calculated to excite envy (said of desirable thing or its possessor). Hence ~LY² adv. [f. ENVY v. + -ABLE]

en'vious, a. Full of envy; feeling envy of (person, thing). Hence ~LY² adv. [f. OF *envious* f. L *invidiosus* (as ENVY¹, see -OUS)]

envi'ron, v.t. (Of persons or things) form a ring, be stationed, round; surround (person, place, etc.), hostilely, protectively, as attendants, etc.; surround (person, thing, *with* others). [f. F *environ* round]

envi'ronment, n. Surrounding; surrounding objects, region, or circumstances. [-MENT]

envi'rons (-z; or en'vironz), n.pl. District surrounding town etc. [f. OF *environ* (n. t. adv.) f. *viron* circuit, cf. *virer* VEER]

en'visage (-z-), v.t. Look in the face of; face (danger, facts); contemplate, esp. under particular aspect. Hence ~MENT (-ij-) n. [f. F *envisager* (VISAGE)]

en'voy¹, n. (arch.). (Author's) parting words, esp.) short stanza concluding certain such forms of poem (also -oi). [OF, f. *envoiier* send (*en voie* on the way) f. L *via*)]

en'voy², n. Messenger, representative; esp. minister plenipotentiary, ranking below ambassador & above *chargé d'affaires*. Hence ~SHIP n. [prob. f. F *envoyé*, p.p. as prec.]

en'vy¹, n. Grudging contemplation (of more fortunate persons, *of, at,* their advantages, or abs.; often playfully); object, ground, of this, as she, *her poodle, is the ~ of Bath*. [f. F *envie* f. L *invidia* f. *invidus* f. INVIDERE see) envy]

en'vy², v.t. Feel envy of, as *I ~ him, ~ his impudence, ~ him his impudence*. [f. F *envier* f. med.L *invidiare* (*invidia* ENVY¹)]

en'wind', v.t. (Of thing) wind itself round (another). [EN-]

en'womb' (-ōōm), v.t. Enclose (as) in womb. [EN-]

en'wrap', (in-), v.t.(-pp-). Wrap, enfold, (in; lit. & fig.). [EN-]

en'wreathe'(-dh), v.t. Surround as or (as) with wreath; interwine. [EN-]

enzoö'tic, a. & n. (Disease) regularly affecting cattle etc. in a particular district or at a particular season. [f. EN-², Gk *zōion* animal, -IC]

en'zyme, n. (chem.). An organic catalyst formed by living cells but not depending

on their presence for its action. [EN-(2) + Gk *zumē*, see ZYMOSIS]

é'ocène, a. (geol.). Of the lowest division of Tertiary strata. [f. Gk *ēōs* dawn + *kainos* new]

eolith'ic, a. Of the period preceding the PALAEOLITHIC age. [Gk *ēōs* dawn + *lithos* stone]

eon. See AEON.

ê'osin, n. Red fluorescent dye-stuff used (esp.) in microscopy and colour-photography. [f. Gk *ēōs* dawn + -IN]

-cous, suf. = L -eus + -OUS, forming adj. meaning 'of the nature of', as *ligneous*, like wood; a few are f. L nn. direct (*aqueous* f. *aqua*); some add -ous to -te (*now -ty*) as *duteous*, or are changed f. *courteous*, are by false anal.

eozoö'ic, a. (geol.). (Of strata) showing the earliest indications of animal life. [Gk *ēōs* dawn, *zōion* animal]

ep- in comb. = EPI- before unaspirated vowels.

ep'act, n. Age of moon on Jan. 1; excess of solar over lunar year. [f. F *épacte* f. L f. Gk *epaktē* f. *epagō* bring) intercalate]

ep'arch, n. Governor, bishop, of an eparchy. [f. Gk EK(*arkhos* ruler)]

ep'archy (-k-), n. Subdivision of modern kingdom of Greece; diocese in Russian (Greek) Church. [f. Gk *eparkhia* (as prec., see -Y²)]

épaule'ment(-awlm-), n. (fortif.). Breastwork (esp. as flank protection. [F, f. *épauler* protect with ~, *v.t. épaule* (as foll.)]

ép'aulette (-pol-), n. Ornamental shoulder-piece of uniform; (of private soldier) *win his ~s*, earn promotion to rank of officer. [f. F *épaulette* dim. of *épaule* shoulder f. L *spatula*]

épée (ápā), n. The sharp-pointed duelling-sword, used (blunted) in fencing. [F, = sword]

epergne(épern'),n. Centre ornament (esp. in branched form) for dinner-table to hold flowers or fruit. [?]

ép'exėgē'sis, n. Additional, addition of, words to make meaning clear (e.g. '*difficult to do*'). So ~ĚT'IC(AL) aa., ~ĚT'ically² adv. [Gk EPI-before h.]

eph-, pref. = EPI- before h.

ephē'bė', n. (Gk Antt.). Citizen aged 18 to 20. [f. L f. Gk EPHĒbos (*hēbē* early manhood)]

ephĕm'era (pl. -*rœ*), -eron (pl. -*rons*, -*ra*), nn. Insect living only a day; genus of insects including May-fly; short-lived thing. [f. Gk EPHĒMEROS lasting only a day (*hēmerŏ*)]

ephĕm'eral, a. (Of diseases) lasting only a day; (of insects, flowers, etc.) lasting a day or a few days; short-lived, transitory. Hence ~RY(-ăli-) n. [f. Gk as prec. + -AL]

ephĕm'eris, n. (pl. ~ides, pr. -ĕ'ridēz, (-ĕm-), = calendar (as prec.)] Astronomical almanac or table. [Gk

eph'od, n. Jewish priestly vestment. [Heb., f. *aphad* put on]

eph'or, n. One of five Spartan magistrates controlling the kings; (in mod. Greece) overseer. [f. Gk EPHoros (*horaō* see)]

epi-, pref. = Gk *epi* upon, at, on the ground of, in addition.

ep'iblast, n. (biol.). Outermost layer of blastoderm. [f. EPI-+Gk *blastos* sprout, germ]

ep'ic, a. & n. (Poem) narrating continuously achievements of one or more heroes, as the *Iliad & Odyssey*; fit for recital in an ~, of heroic type or scale; *E~ dialect*, form of Gk in which the ~ poems were written; *national ~*, poem, of any form, embodying nation's conception of its past history. Hence ~AL a., ~ally² adv. [f. L f. Gk *epikos* (EPOS, -IC)]

epiced'ium, n. Funeral ode. [f. L f. Gk EPI(*kēdeion* f. *kēdos* care)]

ep'icēne, a. & n. (Lat. & Gk Gram.) denoting either sex without change of gender; for, used by, both sexes; (person) with characteristics of both sexes. [f. L f. Gk EPI(*koinos* common)]

epicĕn'trum, -tre (-ter), nn. Point at which earthquake breaks out. [f. Gk EPI(*kentron* f. *kentron* as CENTRE)]

ep'iclēs'is, -klēs'is, n. Invocation, esp. of the Holy Spirit to consecrate the elements in the Eucharist. [Gk (EPI-, *kaleō* call)]

ep'icūre, n. One who is choice & dainty in eating & drinking. Hence ~ISM (2) n. [f. L f. Gk *Epikouros* Epicurus, or LL *epicurius* a.]

epicūre'an, a. & n. (Follower of) Epicurus, Athenian philosopher (300 B.C.) who taught that highest good was pleasure (i.e. practice of virtue); (person) devoted to pleasure, esp. refined sensuous enjoyment. Hence ~ISM(3) n. [f. L (-eus) f. Gk *Epikoureios* (prec.)]

ep'icÿcle, n. (Geom.) small circle rolling on circumference of a greater. Hence **epicÿc'lic** a. [f. L f. Gk EPI(*kuklos* circle)]

epicÿc'loid, n. Curve traced by point in circumference of a circle rolling on exterior of another. Hence ~AL (-oid²) a. [prec.+-OID]

epideic'tic (-dīk-), a. Meant for display. [f. Gk *epideiktikos* f. EPI(*deiknumi* show), see -IC)]

epidem'ic, a. & n. (Disease, lit. & fig.) prevalent among community at special time, cf. ENDEMIC. Hence ~AL a., ~ally² adv. [f. F *épidémique* f. *épidémie* f. LL f. Gk *epidēmia* f. *epidēmios* a. (*dēmos* people)]

epidemiol'ogÿ, n. Science of epidemics. [f. Gk as prec., -LOGY]

epidĕrm'is, n. Outer layer of skin of animals, cuticle; outer animal integument of shell; true skin of plant below cuticle. Hence ~AL, ~IC, ~OID, **epidĕr'moid'AL**, aa. [Gk (EPI-, *dermis* (DERM)]

epidi'ascōpe, n. Optical lantern projecting images of both opaque & transparent objects. [EPI-+DIA-+-SCOPE]

epigas'trium, n. Part of abdomen immediately over stomach. Hence ~IC a. [f. Gk EPI(*gastrion* (*gastēr* stomach)]

ep'igēne, a., (Geol.) produced on surface of earth; (of crystal) chemically altered since its formation. [f. F *épigène* f. Gk EPI(*genēs* born)]

epigen'ēsis, n. Formation of organic germ as a new product; *theory of ~* (that the germ is brought into existence, not merely developed, in process of reproduction). [EPI-]

ep'iglŏtt'is, n. Erect cartilage at root of tongue, depressed during swallowing to cover glottis. Hence ~IC a. [Gk EPI-(*glōttis* f. *glōtta* tongue)]

ep'igram, n. Short poem ending in witty turn of thought; pointed saying or mode of expression. So **epigrammat'IC** adv., **epigramm'at**IST(3) n., **epigramm'at**IzE(1, 2) v.t. & i. [f. F *épigramme* f. L f. Gk EPI-(*gramma* -GRAM)]

ep'igraph (-ahf), n. Inscription on stone, statue, coin, etc., whence **epig'raph¹**IC a., **epig'raph**IST (2), **epig'raphy¹**, nn.; motto. [f. Gk EPI(*graphē* f. *graphō* write)]

ep'ilepsÿ, n. Nervous disease in which patient falls to ground unconscious, with or without convulsions. [f. OF *epilepsie* f. L f. Gk *epilēpsia* f. EPI(*lambanō* take)]

epilĕp'tic, a. & n. Of epilepsy; (person) subject to epilepsy. [f. F *épileptique* f. L f. Gk *epilēptikos* (as prec.)]

epil'ogist, n. Writer, speaker, of epilogue. [f. foll.+-IST]

ep'ilŏgue (-g), n. Concluding part of literary work; speech, short poem, addressed to spectators by actor at end of play. [F, f. L f. Gk EPI(*logos* speech)]

epiph'anÿ, n. Manifestation of Christ to the Magi; manifestation of a superhuman being. [f. OF *epiphanie* f. LL *epiphania* (neut. pl. adj.) f. EPI(*phainō* show); partly also f. Gk *epiphaneia* (*epiphanēs* manifest)]

epiphĕnŏm'enŏn, n. (med., philos.; pl. -ena). Secondary symptom, mere concomitant of something else not regarded as its cause or result. [EPI-, PHENOMENON]

ep'iphÿte, n. Plant growing on (usu. not fed by) another; vegetable parasite on animal body. Hence **epiphÿt'AL**, **epiphÿt'IC**, aa. [f. EPI-+Gk *phuton* plant]

Epir'ot (-i-), n. Inhabitant of Epirus. [f. Gk *Epeirōtēs* (*Epeiros*, -OT²)]

epis'copacÿ, n. Government of church by bishops; *the ~*, the bishops. [as EPISCOPATE, -ACY]

epis'copal, a. Of bishop(s); *~ church*, constituted on principle of prec. Hence

~ISM(3) n., ~LY² adv. [f. F *épiscopal* f. LL *episcopālis* (as BISHOP, see -AL)]

epĭs̄copā'lian, a. & n. (Adherent) of epis-copacy; (member) of episcopal church. Hence ~ISM(3) n. [f. L as prec. +-AN]

epĭs̄'copate, n. Office, see, tenure, of bishop; *the* ~, the bishops. [f. L *episco-pātus* (*episcopus* BISHOP, see -ATE¹)]

ep'isode, n. Part between two choric songs in Gk tragedy (orig. interpolation); incidental narrative or series of events. Hence **episŏd'ic(AL)** aa., **episŏd'ically²** adv. [f. Gk *epeisodion* f. *eisodos* entry (*eis* into + *hodos* way)]

epispăs'tic, a. & n. (med.). Blistering (plaster, substance). [f. Gk *epispastikos* f. *epispaō* draw), see -IC]

epistemŏl'ogy, n. Theory of the method or grounds of knowledge. [f. Gk *epistēmē* knowledge +-o-+-LOGY]

epĭs'tle, n. (-sl), n. Letter (now only joc. of ordinary modern letters), esp. one of those of an apostle, part of the canon of Scripture; *the E~*, extract from apostolical ~ read in Communion service; literary work, usu. in form of letter. [OF, f. L f. Gk *epistolē* f. *epistellō* send)]

epĭs'toler, n. (eccl.). Reader (cf. GOSPEL-ER) of the Epistle. [f. F *épistolier* f. L *epistola*]

epĭs'tolary, a. Of, carried on by, suited to, letters. [f. F *épistolaire* f. L *epistolaris* (as prec., see -ARY²)]

epĭs'trophe, n. (rhet.). Ending of several sentences or clauses with same word. [Gk EPI(*strophē* turning f. *strephō*)]

ep'istyle, n. (archit.). = ARCHITRAVE. [f. L f. Gk EPI(*stulion* f. *stulos* pillar)]

ep'itaph (-ahf), n. Words (supposed to be) inscribed on tomb. [f. L f. Gk EPI(*taphion* f. *taphos* tomb), neut. adj. as n.]

epithalā'mium, n. (pl. -iums, -ia). Nup-tial song or poem. Hence ~AL adj. [L f. Gk EPI(*thalamion* f. *thalamos* bride-chamber), neut. adj. as n.]

epithē'lium, n. Tissue forming outer layer of mucous membrane; (Bot.) epi-dermis formed of young cells. Hence ~IAL a., [mod.L, f. EPI-+ Gk *thēlē* teat]

ep'ithet, n. Adjective expressing quality or attribute; significant appellation. Hence ~IC(AL) aa., ~ically² adv. (-ét-). [f. L f. Gk *epitheton* f. *epitithēmi* place)]

epĭt'ome, n. Summary, abstract, of book; condensed account; (fig.) thing that represents another in miniature, as *man, the world's ~e*. Hence ~IST(1) n., ~IZE(3) v.t. [Gk *epitomē* cut, abridge)]

epizŏ'ŏn, n. (pl. -oa). External parasite or commensal. [EPI-, Gk *zō(i)on* animal]

epizŏŏt'ic, a. & n. (Disease) temporarily prevalent among animals (cf. ENZOOTIC, EPIDEMIC). [prec., -IC]

ep'och (-k), n. Beginning of era in history, science, life, etc., as *this made an* ~, making event; date; period in history or life marked by special events. Hence ~AL(8) adj. [f. LL f. Gk *epokhē* holding]

ep'ode, n. Form of lyric poem, used by Horace; third division of Greek choral ode. [OF, f. L f. Gk *epōidos* f. EPI(*ōidē* song)]

epŏn'ym, n. One who gives his name to a people, place, or institution. So **epŏn'ymous** a. [f. L f. Gk EPI(*ōnumos* f. *onoma* name)]

ep'opee, n. Epic poem or poetry. [f. F *épopée* f. Gk *epopoiïa* f. *epopoios* (foll. + *poieō* make)]

ep'os, n. Early unwritten epic poetry; epic poem. [f. Gk *epos* word, song]

epsīl'on, n. Greek letter (E, ε) (cf. ETA). [Gk (*psīlos* bare)]

Ep'som (ě-), n. Town in Surrey; ~ *salt*, magnesium sulphate; (used for) race-course at ~, principal race-meeting there held, including Derby and Oaks.

ē'qua‚ble, a. Uniform, even, not easily disturbed. Hence ~BIL'ITY n., ~BLY² adv. [f. L *aequābilis* (as EQUATE, -BLE]

ē'qual, a. & n. 1. The same in number, size, value, degree, etc. (*to, with*, or abs.), as *twice three is = to six, the two are ~ in ability*; having strength, courage, ability, etc., adequate *to* (the occasion, a cup of tea, doing, etc.); uniform in opera-tion etc., as ~ *laws*; evenly balanced (fight etc.); ~ *to* another in rank etc., as *mix with your ~s*, or in power etc., as *he has no* ~; ~ *to* things, as *if* = *s be added to* ~*s*. [f. L *aequalis* (*aequus* even, see -AL)]

equal'ity (-ŏl-), n. Condition of being equal (*between two or more*; *usu. abs.*); *is on an* ~ *with*, is on equal terms with. [f. OF or L *aequālitas* (*aequus* even + -ITY), see -TY]

ē'qualize, v.t. & i. Make (thing etc.) equal (*to, with*); (Footb. etc.) bring score to equality with opponent's. Hence ~A'TION(3) n. [-IZE]

ē'qually, adv. In an equal degree; in equal shares; uniformly. [-LY²]

equanim'ity, n. Evenness of mind or temper; composure; resignation. [f. F *équanimité* f. L *aequanimitas* f. *aequa-nimis* (*aequus* even + *animus* mind), see -ITY]

ē‚quāte', v.t. State equality of (thing *to, with*, another); treat as equivalent. [f. L *aequare* (*aequus* equal), see -ATE³]

equā'tion, n. 1. Making equal, balancing, (of demand & supply etc.). 2. (Amount or process of) compensation for inaccuracy, as (Astron.) *personal* ~, allowance for individual slowness in noting phenomena (also fig.), ~ (difference between mean & apparent places) *of the equinoxes*. 3. (Math.) formula affirming equivalence of

two expressions connected by the sign =. Hence **~AL** a., **~ALLY²** adv., (-shon-). [f. L *aequatio* (as prec., see -ATION)]

equāt'or, n. A great circle of the earth, equidistant from the poles; = EQUINOC-TIAL; *magnetic* ~, ACLINIC line. [LL (as prec.,-OR²)]

equātor'ial, a. Of, near, the equator; ~ *telescope* (attached to axle revolving in direction parallel to plane of equator). Hence **~ly²** adv. [-AL]

|| **ĕq'uerry** (or ĭkwĕ'rĭ), n. Officer of prince or noble charged with care of horses; officer of British royal household. [f. F *écurie* f. med.L *scuria* stable f. OHG *scûr* shed; confused in E with L *equus* horse]

eques'trian, a. & n. 1. Of horse-riding; ~ *statue* (of person on horse); (Rom. Ant.) 2. n. Rider, performer, on horseback. [f. L *equestris* (*eques* horseman f. *equus* horse) +-AN]

equestrienne', n. Horsewoman; (esp.) female circus-rider. [pseudo-F, f. prec. with fem. suffix]

equi- in comb. = L *aequus* equal, as **~ångular** (-ngg-), having equal angles.

equidis'tant, a. Separated by equal distance(s). [f. F *équidistant* f. LL *aequidistantem* (see EQUI- & DISTANT)]

equilat'eral, a. Having all the sides equal. [f. LL *aequilateralis* (see EQUI- & LATERAL)]

equilĭb'rĭate, v.t. & i. Cause (two things) to balance; balance (t. & i.); counterpoise. Hence **~A'TION** n. [f. EQUI-+L *libra* balance +-ATE³]

equil'ibrist, n. Rope-walker, acrobat. [f. F *équilibriste* (*équilibre* EQUILIBRIUM]

equili'brium, n. State of balance (lit. & fig.); *a body in stable* ~ (tending to recover ~ after disturbance); neutrality of judgement etc. [L (EQUI-, *libra* balance)]

equimŭl'tiple, n. (usu. pl.). Number having a common factor with another. [EQUI-]

ĕq'uine, a. Of, like, a horse. [f. L *equinus* (*equus* horse, see -INE³)]

equinŏc'tial (-shal), a. & n. 1. Of equal day & night; ~ *line*, circle of celestial sphere whose plane is perpendicular to earth's axis; happening at or near time of equinox, as ~ *gales*; at, near, the (terrestrial) equator. 2. n. ~ *line*, (pl.) ~ *gales*. [f.L *aequinoctialis* (as foll., see -AL)]

ĕq'uinŏx, n. Time at which sun crosses equator & day & night are equal (*vernal* ~, March 20; *autumnal* ~, Sep. 22 or 23) (pl.) two points at which sun crosses equator: PRECESSION of the ~es. [f. L *aequinoctium* (*nox -ctis* night, EQUI-)]

equip', v.t. (-pp-). Furnish (ship, army, person, with requisites); provide (oneself etc.) for journey etc. Hence **~MENT** n. [f. F *équiper*, esp., prob. f. ON *skipa* man (ship) f. *skip* SHIP]

ĕq'uipage, n. Requisites for an under-taking; outfit for journey etc.; carriage & horses with attendants. [f. F *équipage* (as prec., see -AGE)]

ĕq'uipoise (-z), n., & v.t. 1. Equilibrium (often fig.); counterbalancing thing. 2. v.t. Counterbalance, hold (mind) in suspense. [EQUI-]

equipŏll'ent, a. & n. Equal in power, force, etc.; practically equivalent; (n.)~ent thing. So **~ENCE**, **~ENCY**, nn. [f. OF *equipolent* f. L *aequipollentem* (EQUI-, *pollēre* be strong)]

equipon'derate, v.t. Counterbalance. So **~ANT** a. & n. [f. med.L *aequi(ponderare* weigh f. *pondus -eris* weight), see EQUI- & -ATE³]

equipon'tial (-shl), a. (physics). In which the potential of a force is the same or constant at all points. [EQUI-]

ĕq'uitable, a. Fair, just, whence **~leness** n., **~LY²** adv.; (of claims etc.) valid in equity as opposed to law. [f. F *équitable* (as EQUITY+-ABLE]

equita'tion, n. (usu. joc.). Riding on horse; horsemanship. [f. L *equitatio* f. *equitare* f. *eques -itis* horseman f. *equus* horse, see -ATION]

ĕq'uitỹ, n. 1. Fairness; recourse to principles of justice to correct or supplement law; system of law coexisting with and superseding common and statute law. 2. ||(E~) actors' trade union, 3. pl. Stocks and shares not bearing fixed interest. [f. OF *equité* f. L *aequitatem* (*aequus* fair, see -TY]

equiv'alent, a. & n. 1. Equal in value (*to*); (of words) meaning the same; (Chem.) equal in combining value (*to*); having the same result; corresponding. 2. n. ~ent thing, amount, word, etc. So **~ENCE**, **~ENCY**, nn. [f. LL *aequi(valēre* be worth), see EQUI- & ENT]

equiv'ocal, a. Of double meaning, ambiguous; of uncertain nature; ~ *generation* (spontaneous); undecided; (of persons, character, etc.) questionable, suspicious. Hence **~ITY**(-ǎl'-), **~NESS**, nn., **~LY²** adv. [f. LL *aequivocus* (EQUI-, *vocare* call), see -AL]

equiv'ocāte, v.i. Use ambiguous words to conceal the truth, prevaricate. Hence **~A'TION**, **~ATOR**, nn. [f. LL *aequivocare* (as prec., see -ATE³]

ĕq'uivöque(-k), **-ōke**, n. Pun; ambiguity. [f. LL *aequivocus* EQUIVOCAL]

-er¹, suf. forming esp. agent nn. f. nn. & vbs. Orig.=' one who has to do with', f. OTeut. *-ârjos* (cf. L *-arius* -ARY³); so E wds as *hatter* & (after -w) *bowyer*, *sawyer*, *lawyer*, & perh. on their anal. coll00 *collier*, *grazier*, etc.; also colloq. wds of action, as *header*, *out-&-outer*, and of number, as *fiver*, *tenner*; add *Londoner*, *foreigner*, etc. As many wds so formed correspond to vbs, -er took agent sense (*clothier* one connected with cloth, one who clothes), & can now be added to any vb not other-

wise provided (correspondent, translator); -or (-our, -ier) & -er may coexist, with or without differentiation (saviour, -er; assertor, -er); some wds seem to double -er (caterer, fruiterer, poulterer); -er is occas. used to anglicize L -us (astro-nomer, geographer, perh. philosopher). Meanings: (1) person, animal, that does something; (2) instrument, machine, oc-currence, etc. (3) person concerned with thing (hatter, geographer); (4) person belonging to place etc. (Londoner, British&er); (5) sl. distortion of word with other ending (Rugger, Soccer, footer, Rugby, Association, football).

-er³, suf. in nn. & adj. f. OF, of various orig., esp.: (1) OF -er f. L L -arium, as sampler. (2) AF -er f. OF -ier f. L L -arius -eure f. L L -atura, as border. (4)

-er⁴, suf. forming comparatives; now (exc. in poetry and mannered prose) only in adj., of one syllable, or of two ending in -y, -ly, -le, -er, -ow, & a few others (esp. w. accent on last syllable; see -END², & in adv., chiefly those identical with adj., as hard; the vowel change seen in German etc. now remains only in elder, BETTER, etc. [OE: (adj.) -ra f. OTeut.]

-er⁵, suf. forming frequent. vbs f. others (wander, waver, f. wend, wave) or on sound-imitations (twitter, flicker, shimmer, slumber.

ĕr'a, n. System of chronology starting from some particular point of time, as Christian -, ~s, of the HEGIRA; historical or other period; date forming commence-ment of this. [f. L L aera number ex-pressed in figures (pl. of aes aeris money, treated as fem. sing.)]

ĕrad'ĭcāte, v.t. Tear up by roots; extir-pate, get rid of. So ~ABLE a., ~A'TION n. [f. L Eradicare f. radix -icis root.]

ĕrāse', v.t. Rub out; obliterate. Hence ĕrā'SABLE a., ĕrās'ER²(-z), ĕrā's-URE (-zher) nn. [f. L Eradere ras-scrape)]

Ĕras'tian (t), a. & n. (Adherent) of the supposed doctrines of Erastus, subordin-ating ecclesiastical to secular power. Hence ~ISM(3) n., ~ISE(3) v.t. & i. [f. Erastus, Heidelberg physician of 16th c., + -IAN]

ere (âr), prep. & conj. (poet., arch.). Before (of time); ~ long, before long; ~while (arch.), formerly. [OE ǣr (Du. eer, G eher, ehe) f. OTeut. airiz compar. of air adv. early.]

Ĕr'ĕbus (ĕ-), n. (Gk Myth.). Place of

darkness between earth & Hades. [L, f. Gk Erebos]

ĕrĕct'¹, a. Upright, not stooping, (lit. & fig.); vertical; (of hair etc.), set up, brist-ling. Hence ~LY² adv., ~NESS n. [f. L L]

ĕrect'², v.t. = regere direct) set up] Ĕrĭgere rect- = Raise, set upright, (oneself, body, etc.); build (lit. & fig.); form (per-sons, principles, etc.), into (class, system, etc.), as prec.]

ĕrec'tile, a. That can be erected: ~ tissue (in animals (capable of being distended & becoming rigid under excitement). [f. F érectile (as ERECT¹, see -IL)]

ĕrec'tion, n. Erecting; building, struc-ture, (lit. & fig.). [f. L L erectio (as prec., see -ION)]

ĕrĕmīte, n. Person, thing, that erects, as ~muscle. [-OR²]

ĕ'remīte, n. Hermit, (esp. of Christian solitaries from 3rd c. onwards). Hence ĕremĭt'ic(AL) aa. [f. L L as HERMIT]

ĕrĕthism, n. (path.). Abnormal excite-ment (of organ or tissue, fig. of mind). [f. F érethisme f. Gk erethismos (erethizō irritate, see -ISM)]

ĕrg, ĕrg'ŏn, n. (physics). Unit of work or energy. (The work done by unit force, one dyne, on a body which moves 1 cm. in the direction of action of the force.) [f. Gk ergon work]

ĕr'gatocracy, n. Rule of the workers. [f. Gk ergatēs worker, -O-, -CRACY]

ĕrg'ō, adv. (usu. joc.). Therefore. [L]

ĕrg'ŏt, n. Disease of rye etc. caused by fungus; diseased rye seed as medicine. [F, f. OF argot cock's spur, f. appearance produced]

ĕrg'otism, n. = prec.; disease produced by bread made from flour affected by this. [-ISM]

E'rĭn (ē-), n. (Ancient name of) Ireland.

ĕris'tĭc, a. & n. (Art) of disputation; (of argument or arguer) aimed or aiming at victory rather than truth. [f. Gk eristikos (eris f. eris strife, see -IC)]

ĕr'lking, n. Bearded golden-crowned giant of Teutonic folk-lore who lures little children to the land of death. [f. G erl-könig alder-king; a mistransl. of Da. eller-konge king of the elves]

ĕr'mine, n. Animal of weasel tribe, whose fur is brown in summer & white (except black tail-tip) in winter; its fur, used in robes of judges & peers (often poet. as emblem of purity), whence ~ED²(-nd) a.; (Her.) white marked with black spots. [f. OF (hermine (Prov. ermini), etym. dub.]

-ern, suf. in northern etc.a. [OE (-rо- + -ðoujo- = L -ānus.]

ĕrne, n. Sea eagle or white-tailed eagle. [OE earn (Du. arend) f. OTeut. arnuz, cf. Gk ornis bird]

ĕrōde', v.t. (Of acids, currents, etc.) gnaw away; destroy gradually, wear out. So ĕrō'SION (-zhn) n., ĕrōs'IVE a. [f. F éroder f. Ĕrōdere ros-gnaw)]

ĕrŏt'ic, a. & n. Of love, amatory; (n.) ~ poem. [f. Gk erōtikos (erōs -ōtos sexual love, see -IC)]

ĕrŏt'omān'ia, n. (path.). Melancholy madness, arising from love. [f. Gk erōs (as prec.) + -MANIA]

ĕrr, v.i. Make mistakes; (of statements etc.) be incorrect; sin. [f. F errer f. L errare]

ĕ'rrand, n. Short journey on which an inferior is sent to carry message etc., as run, go, (on) ~s, ~boy; object of journey, purpose. [OE ǣrende, cf. Da. ǣrinde, etym. dub.]

ĕ'rrant, a. & n. Roaming in quest of adventure, esp. knight~; itinerant; erring, deviating from correct standard; whence ĕ'rrancy n.; (n.) knight-~. [F (1) f. OF errer, esrer, edrer, f. vulg. L iterare (iter journey), (2) as ERR; see -ANT]

ĕ'rrantry n. Condition, notions, of a knight-errant. [-RY]

ĕrrăt'ic, a. Uncertain in movement; (of diseases) moving from one part to another; irregular in conduct, habit, opinion; (Geol.) ~ic blocks, stray masses foreign to surrounding strata. Hence ~ICALLY adv. [f. L erraticus (as ERR) see -ATIC]

ĕrrā'tum n. (pl. -ta). Error in printing or writing, esp. (pl.) errors noted in list attached to book. [L, neut. p.p. as prec.]

ĕrrōn'ĕous, a. Mistaken, incorrect. Hence ~LY² adv., ~NESS n. [f. L erroneus (erro -onis vagabond, as ERR) + -OUS]

ĕ'rror, n. Mistake, as make, commit, an ~; CLERICAL ~; condition of erring in opinion; wrong opinion; in ~, mistaken(ly), by mistake; ~ of a planet, difference between its observed & calculated positions; (Law) writ of ~ (to procure reversal of judgement on ground of ~): transgression. Hence ~LESS n. [OF, f. L errorem (as ERR, -OR²)]

ĕrsǎtz' (āŕz-.) n. & a. Substitute. [G]

Erse (ĕrs), a. & n. Highland Gaelic (dialect); (unused & disliked in Ireland for) Irish. [early Sc. form of Irish]

ĕrst, adv. (arch.). (Also ~'while) formerly, of old. [OE ǣrest superl. of ǣr, see ERE]

ĕrubĕs'cent (-rōō-), a. Reddening, blushing. [f. L E(rubescere incept. of rubēre), see -ENT]

ĕructā'tion, n. Belching (lit. & fig., esp. of volcano). [f. L eructatio (ēructare, see -ATION)]

ĕ'rudite (-rōō-), a. (Of persons & writings) learned. Hence or cogn. ~LY² (-tǐ-) adv., ĕrudī'tion n. (-rōō-). [f. L ērudīre -īt- train (rudis rude)]

ĕrŭpt', v.i. (Of teeth) break through gums; (of volcano) break out. [f. L E(rumpere rupt- break)]

ĕrŭp'tion, n. Outbreak (of volcano, whence ~AL (-shon) a.; also of geyser, disease, war, passion, mirth, wit); (Path.) breaking out (of rash, pimples, etc.); (of teeth) breaking through gums, [f. L eruptio (as prec. see -ION)]

ĕrŭp'tive, a. Bursting forth; tending to burst forth; of, formed by, forced up by, volcanic eruption. Hence ~LY¹ adv., ~NESS, ĕrŭptiv'ITY, nn. [f. F éruptif, -ive (as ERUPT, see -IVE)]

-ĕrў, -rў, suf. forming nouns, orig. after F -erie: (a) f. com-Rom. -aria = L -ario- F -ier, -er) + -ia -Y¹; F wds in -ter usu. denote person having some occupation, wds in -erie the class of goods he deals in, as draperie, his employment, as archerie, his place of work, as boulangerie; -erie was also used without existing wd in -ter, as soierie (soie) silk goods, niaiserie (niais) foolishness. (b) f. OF -ere, -eor (mod. F -eur f. L -ator + -ie. On anal. of wds thus formed, -erie was added to vb stems direct, w. sense class of actions (from-perie deceit), occupation (confiserie confectioner's business), place of this (brasserie brewery). Many E wds are f, F; others are formed on nn. in -er (bakery, fishery, pottery), or on others (knavery, slavery, popery). Meanings: (1) class of goods (drapery); (2) employment or condition (archery, deapery): (3) place of work or cultivation or breeding (brewery, vinery, piggery); (4) conduct (foolery); (5) all that has to do with (popery), things of the nature of

ĕrysip'ĕlas, n. (Also St. Anthony's fire, the rose) local febrile disease producing deep red colour on skin. [Gk erusipelas, etym. dub.]

ĕrўthēm'a, n. Superficial inflammation of the skin in patches. [f. Gk eruthēma f. eruthainō be red (eruthros)]

-es, old genit. termination used to give adv. force; appearing as -s (needs), -ce (once), & (by confus. w. superl.) -st (against); also in the emphatic absolute forms ours, yours, hers, etc. Often on false anal., as betimes, besides, nowadays.

ĕscalāde', n. Scaling of walls with ladders. [F, f. Sp. escalada f. med. L scalare (scala ladder), see -ADE¹]

ĕs'calātor, n. Moving staircase for carrying passengers up or down. [as ESCALADE, -OR¹]

ĕscallōn'ia, n. S.-Amer. genus of flowering shrubs. [Escallon, discoverer, -IA¹]

ĕscăl'op. See SCALLOP.

ĕscapāde', n. Breaking loose from restraint; flighty piece of conduct. [F, f. Sp. escapada (as ESCAPE, see -ADE]

ĕscāpe'¹, n. Act of escaping; fact of having escaped (a narrow, hairbreadth, ~); (means of) mental distraction or relief from reality (also attrib., as ~ literature, reading), whence escāp'ism n., escāp'IST n. & a.; leakage (of gas etc.); garden plant growing wild; = FIRE~; ~pipe, -valve (for ~ of steam or water); ~shaft (for ~ of miners when other shaft is blocked). [f. foll.]

ĕscāpe'² v.i. & t. Get free (from prison, person, etc.); (of steam, fluids, etc.) find

a way out; get off safely, go unpunished; (v.t.) get clear away from (person, his grasp, etc.), avoid (unpleasant thing, doing); elude notice or recollection of, as *his name had ~d me*; (of words) issue unawares from (person, his lips). [f. OF *escaper*, ONF *escaper* (Sp. *escapar*), f. LL ExCAPPare f. *cappa* cloak]

escape'ment (-pm-), n. Outlet; (of watch or clock) mechanism connecting motive power & regulator. [-MENT]

escarp', n., & v.t. 1. Steep bank immediately in front of & below rampart; similar natural formation. 2. v.t. Cut into form of ~, so ~MENT n. [f. F *escarpe* f. It. *scarpa* SCARP]

eschalot (ĕsh-). See SHALLOT.

eschatŏl'ogy (ĕsk-), n. Doctrine of death, judgement, heaven, & hell. Hence ~olŏ'ḡical a. [f. Gk *eskhatos* last + -LOGY]

escheat'¹, n. Lapsing of property to crown or lord of manor on owner's dying intestate without heirs; property so lapsing. [f. OF *eschete* f. *eschoir* f. LL ExCadere fall]

escheat'², v.t. & i. Confiscate; hand over (property) as an escheat (*to* person, *into* his hands); revert by escheat (*to* or abs.). [prec.]

eschew' (-ōō), v.t. Avoid, abstain from, (action, conduct, kind of food, etc.). [f. OF *eschiver* f. com.-Rom. *skivare*, cf. G *scheuen* & SHY¹]

eschscholtz'ia (ishōl-), n. A plant with usu. yellow flowers, Noah's nightcap. [*Eschscholtz*, explorer, -IA¹]

escort'¹ (-ōr-), n. Body of armed men acting as guard to persons, baggage, etc.; person(s) accompanying another on journey for protection or guidance, or for courtesy's sake. [f. F *escorte* f. It. *scorta* f. *scorgere* conduct f. LL ExCOrrigere f. *regere* direct]

escort'², v.t. Act as escort to; ~ carrier, aircraft carrier for ~ing convoys. [f. prec.]

escribe', v.t. (math.). Describe (circle) so as to touch one side of triangle exteriorly & the other two produced. [E-+ L *scribere* write]

escritoire (-twahr), n. Writing-desk with drawers etc. for stationery. [F (now éc-), f. LL *scriptorium* (as prec., see -ORY)]

escrow' (-ō), n. Written legal engagement to do something, kept in third person's custody until some condition has been fulfilled. [AF *escrowe* f. OF *escroue*]

escud'o, n. (pl. -os). Portuguese monetary unit & silver coin worth about 4s. 5d.

at par (applied also to various Spanish-American gold & silver coins). [Sp. & Port. f. LL *scudum* shield]

es'culent, a. & n. (Thing) fit for food. [f. L *esculentus* (*esca* food, see -LENT)]

escutch'eon (-chon), n. Shield with armorial bearings; *a blot on his ~* (stain or reputation); middle of ship's stern where name is placed; pivoted keyhole-cover. [f. ONF *escuchon* f. LL ⁺*scutionem* (L *scutum* shield, see -OON)]

-ese, suf. forming adjs. (& nn.) f. OF -*eis* = It. ~*ese* f. L ~*ensis* local suf. (usu. now -*tan*, as *Atheniensis* Athenian); applied to some foreign countries & towns (*Japanese, Milanese*), either as adj. or meaning ', inhabitant ' (pl. -*ese*) or ' language '; also used spec. (adj. or n.) of diction of mannered writers (*Carlylese*), as though a non-English language.

es'ker, -ar, n. (geol.). Long ridge of post-glacial gravel in river valleys. [Ir. *eiscir*]

Eskimo, -quimau, (ĕs'kimō), n. (pl. -os, -oes, pr. -mōz). Member of a race inhabiting the arctic coasts of America. [native]

ésotéric, a. (Of philosophical doctrines etc.) meant only for the initiated; (of disciples) initiated; private, confidential. Hence ~AL a., ~ally² adv. [f. Gk *esōterikos* (*esōterō* compar. of *esō* within, see -IC)]

éspagnolette' (-ănyŏlĕt), n. Fastening of French window. [F, dim. of *espagnol* Spanish]

espàl'ier, n. Lattice-work on which trees or shrubs are trained; tree so trained. [F, f. It. *spalliera* (*spalla* shoulder)]

espâr'to, n. (Also ~ *grass*) kinds of grass imported from Spain and N. Africa for paper-making. [Sp., f. L f. Gk *sparton* rope of the plant *spartos*]

espé'cial (-shl), a. Pre-eminent, exceptional, as *my ~ friend, thing of ~ importance*; particular (opp. to *ordinary*, cf. SPECIAL); belonging chiefly to one case (*for your ~ benefit*). Hence ~ly² (-shŏ-) adv. [OF, f. L as SPECIAL]

Esperan'tō (ĕ-), n. An artificial language designed as a medium for persons of all nations. [pen-name (f. L *spero* hope) of its inventor, Dr Zamenhof, 1887]

es'pial, n. Acting as a spy; watching; espying. [f. OF *espaille*, as ESPY, see -AL(2)]

espièglerie (see Ap.), n. Roguishness. [F]

es'pionage (see Ap.), n. Practice of spying or using spies. [f. F *espionnage* f. *espion* SPY f. It. *spione* (of Teut. orig., cf. ESPY), see -AGE]

esplanáde', n. Level piece of ground, esp. one used for public promenade; level space separating citadel of fortress from town. [F, f. Sp. *esplanada* f. *esplanar* f. L *explanare* make level (*planus*), see -ADE]

espous'al (-zl), n. (arch.). (Usu. pl.) marriage or betrothal; (fig.) espousing of

(a cause etc.). [f. OF *espousailles* f. L *sponsalia* neut. pl. (*sponsus* p.p. as foll., see -AL)]

espouse' (-z), v.t. (Usu. of man) marry; give (woman) in marriage (*to*); adopt, support, (doctrine, cause, etc.). [f. OF *espouser* f. L *sponsare* (*sponsus* p.p. of *sponsāre* betroth)]

espr̄essi'o (-ĕvō), adv. (mus.). With expression. [It.]

esprit (ĕsprē'), n. Sprightliness; wit; ~ *de corps* (de kôr), regard for honour & interests of body one belongs to; ~ *fort* (fôr), strong-minded person, free-thinker. [F, f. L as SPIRIT]

espy', v.t. Catch sight of; detect (flaw etc.). [f. OF *espier* ult. f. OHG *spehōn* SPY]

-esque, suf. forming adj., = F *-esque* f. It. *-esco* f. med. L *-iscus* in Teut. adjs.; cf. OHG *-isc* (mod. *-isch*) = -ISH¹; meaning 'after the manner of', as *arabesque, Dantesque, burlesque*.

Esquimau. See ESKIMO.

esquire', n. || Title appended to name of one regarded as gentleman by birth, position, or education, esp. in address of letter (abbr. *Esq.*); (arch.) = SQUIRE. [f. OF *esquier* f. L *scutarius* shield-bearer (*scutum* shield, -ARY¹)]

ĕss¹, n. S(-shaped thing); COLLAR¹ of -es.

-ess¹, suf. forming female n., f. F (*countess, lioness*) or the OE fem. *-ster* (now only in *spinster*) came to be regarded as masculine, & could take fem. *-ess* (*seamstress*); agent nn. in *-ter, -tor*, regularly have *-tress* (*chandress*); other exx. are *authoress* etc. (*author* etc. now preferred), *giantess, quakeress*; *governess* (formed on vb) is irreg., perh. on anal. of *sorceress* (formed on old *sorcer* not on *sorcerer*, which has double agent suf.); euphony leads to same clipping in *adventuress, murderess, -trice* (L *-trix -tricis*), though of diff. orig. [f. F *-esse* f. LL f. Gk *-issa*]

-ess², suf. in abstr. nn. f. adjj., as *duress, largess; riches, laches*, are exx., mistaken for pl. [ME & OF *-esse* = It. *-ezza* f. L *-itia* -ICE]

ĕss'ay¹, n. Attempt (*at*); a literary composition (usu. prose & short) on any subject, whence ~IST(3) n. [f. OF *essai* = ASSAY¹]

ĕssay'², v.t. &1. Try, test, (person, thing); attempt (task, *to do*, or abs.). [refash. f ASSAY² on F *essayer*]

ĕss'ē, n. Essential being or nature (often contrasted with *bene esse* well-being). [L, = to be]

ĕss'enc|e, n. An existence or entity (spiritual or immaterial); absolute being, reality underlying phenomena; all that makes a thing what it is; intrinsic nature; indispensable quality or element; extract obtained by distillation etc. (lit. & fig.); perfume, scent, whence ~ED² (-st) a. [F, f. L *essentia* f. +*essentis* fictitious part. of *esse* be, repr. Gk *ousia*]

essēne'tial (-shl), a. & n. 1. Of, constituting, a thing's essence; indispensable (*to*) ~ *proposition*, one that predicates of a subject what is implied in its definition; ~ *character* (of species, genus, etc.), marks that distinguish it from others included with it in next superior division; ~ *harmony* (belonging to one particular key); ~ *oil*, volatile oil, marked by characteristic odour etc. 2. n. Indispensable element. Hence ~ITY (shăl>) n., ~LY² (-shal-) adv. [f. LL *essentialis* (as ESSENCE, -AL)]

-ēst, suf. forming superl. adjj. & advv. (& FIRST, LAST); for limits of use see -ER³ but many adjj. can bear *-est* though not *-er*, as *awkward, barren, fragile, loyal, legible*, & many in *-id*, as *limpid*; in poetry & mannered prose *-est* is used w. almost any adj., & appended to advv. in *-ly*, as *quickliest*, [OE *-ost, -ust, -ast*, t. OTeut. *-isto- -osto-*, & OE *-est, -st*, t. OTeut. *-isto-* (compar. *-ōz-, -iz-*, +Aryan *-to-*), cf. Gk *-isto-*; *-iz-* required vowel change, now only in *eldest*, BEST]

estăb'lish, v.t. Set up (government, house of business, etc.) on permanent basis; settle (person, oneself, *in* office etc.); secure permanent acceptance for (custom, precedent, belief, etc.); place beyond dispute (fact, *that*); make (church) legally national. [f. OF *establir* (st. -ISH-, see -ISH²) f. L *stabilire* (as STABLE a.)]

estăb'lishment, n. Establishing; *Church E~, the E~*, church system established by law; organized body of men maintained for a purpose, as army, navy, civil service; *peace, war*, ~s; *reduced, increased, army* etc. in time of peace, war; staff of servants etc.; public institution, house of business; household, as *separate ~* (of man maintaining paramour). [-MENT]

estăblishmentār'ian, a. & n. (Person) adhering to, advocating the principle of, an established church. [-ARIAN]

ĕstăm'inet (-nā), n. French café selling wine, beer, & coffee, or cottage with barroom, [F]

estāte', n. 1. Order, class, forming part of body politic & sharing in government; || *the Three E~s* (in England), Lords Spiritual, Lords Temporal, Commons; *third ~*, (usu.) French bourgeoisie before Revolution; ||(Doc.) *fourth ~*, the press. 2. Person's interest in landed property (*real ~* or movables (*personal ~*), whence estāt'ED² a.; a landed property (|| *agent*, steward of, a go-between in sales of houses & land). 3. One's collective

assets & liabilities. 4. (Arch.) condition, as *the holy ~ of matrimony*. [f. OF *estat*, f. L as STATE]

esteem′, v.t., & n. 1. Think highly of; consider, as *I shall ~ it (us) a favour*. 2. n. Favourable opinion, regard, respect. [n. f. vb] f. OF *estimer* f. L as ESTIMATE]

es′ter, n. (chem.). Compound formed by replacing the hydrogen of an acid by a hydrocarbon radical of the ethyl type. [coined by the German chemist L. Gmelin]

es′timable, a. Worthy of esteem. [F. f. L *aestimabilis* (as ESTEEM, see -BLE)]

es′timate¹, n. Approximate judgement (of number, amount, etc.); quantity assigned by this; || the E~s, forecasts of national expenditure, presented annually to parliament; contractor's statement of sum for which he will undertake specified work; judgement of character or qualities. [f. L *aestimatus* -*ūs* (as foll.)]

es′tim|ate², v.t. Form an estimate of (number etc.) by estimate *at* (so much): form an opinion of. So ~ATIVE a., ~ATOR² n. [f. L *aestimare*, see -ATE³]

estima′tion, n. Judgement of worth, as *in my ~*; esteem, as *hold in ~, be in ~*. [F. f. L *aestimationem* (as prec., see -ATION)]

estival, etc. See *aest-*.

estop′, v.t. (law; -pp-). Bar, preclude, (*from thing, from doing*). Hence ~p′AGE n. [f. OF *estouper* (estoup² bung]

estōv′ers (-z), n. pl. Necessaries allowed by law (as wood for repairs or fuel taken by a tenant from his holding). [f. OF *estover* to be necessary, used subst.]

estrade′ (-ahd), n. Raised platform, dais. [F. f. Sp. *estrado* f. L *stratum* neut. p.p. of *sternere* spread (with carpets)]

estrange′ (-j), v.t. Alienate (person) in feeling (*from* another). Hence ~MENT (-jm-) n. [f. OF *estranger* f. L *extranare*]

estreat′, v.t. (law). Take out record of (fine, bail, etc.) & return it to Court of Exchequer to be prosecuted. [f. *estreat* n. record f. OF *estraite* fem. p.p. of *estraire* extract f. L EX(*trahere* draw)]

ës′tuary, n. Tidal mouth of large river. Hence ~INE¹ a. [f. L *aestuarium* neut. as n. (*aestus -ūs* tide, see -ARY¹)]

ē′sur|ient, a. (joc.). Hungry; needy & greedy. So ~ENCE, ~ENCY, nn. [f. L *ēsurire* (-*t*-, suf. forming (orig.) dimin., many not now realized as such; mostly in ME adoptions f. F (*bullet, hatchet, sonnet*); double dim. -LET (*-l- + -et*) is living suf. [OF *-et* & *-ete* (dist. only in mod. ED)=It. *-etto*, *-etta*, *-etta*, etym. dub.] *-ōt*¹, *-ēte*, suf. in agent nn. f. Gk. *-ēt* in

older or familiar wds, as *poet, comet, an-chorēt, -ēte* in newer or learned ones, as *athlete, aesthete, exegete*. [f. Gk *-ētēs* (-*-ēs*, -*ad*) agent n. as appended esp. to vbs in -*eō*, -*aō*); *epithet, paraclete*, are not exx.; *diabetes* retains full form]

ēt′a, n. Greek letter (H, η) = ē (cf. EPSILON).
[Gk]

ēr′acism (ā-), n. Pronunciation of Gk ē as English ā (cf. ITACISM). [f. Gk *ēta* letter ē, -ISM]

état-major (ātah′ mahzhō′′), n. (mil.). Staff, staff-office. [F]

et cēt′era, ètcēt′era, phr. & n. (pl. *-as*). (Abbr. *etc., &c.*) & the rest, & so on, as *I remain yours etc.*; (n. pl.) extras, sun-dries. [L]

ětch, v.t. & i. Reproduce (pictures etc.), portray (subject), by engraving metal plate etc. by means of acids or corrosives, esp. for purpose of printing copies; (v.i.) practise this art. [f. Du. *etsen* f. G *ätzen* f. OTeut. *atjan* make EAT]

ětch′ing, n. In vbl senses, esp. copy from etched plate; ~-needle, used in ~. [-ING¹]

ētēr′n|al, a. That always (has existed &) will exist, as *~ life*, *punishment*; the E~, God; *~ CITY*; (colloq.) incessant, too fre-quent, as *these~ bickerings*; *the ~ triangle*, two males & a female or *vice versa*. Hence or cogn. *ĕtĕrn′*(a)LIZE(3) v(t)., ~ly² adv. [OF, f. LL *aeternalis* (*aeternus* for *aevi-ternus* f. *aevum* age, see -AL)]

ētern′ity, n. Being eternal; immortality (pl.) eternal truths; infinite time, esp. future; the future life. [f. F *éternité* f. L *aeternitatem* (*aeternus*, see prec. & -TY)]

Etē′sian (tēzh′ăn), a. *~ winds* (blowing annually in Mediterranean from N.W. for about 40 days in summer). [f. L (Gk *etēsios* (*etos* year) + -AN]

ē′ther, n. 1. Clear sky, upper regions beyond clouds. 2. (Physics) a medium as-sumed to permeate space & fill interstices between particles of air & other matter, medium in which electro-magnetic waves are transmitted, whence ~ic a. 3. (Chem.) colourless light volatile liquid produced by action of sulphuric acid & other acids on alcohol, an anaesthetic. [f. L f. Gk *aithēr* f. root of *aithō* burn, shine]

ethē′real, -ial, a. 1. Light, airy; heaven-ly; of unearthly delicacy of substance, character, or appearance, whence ~ITY (-âl-), ~IZA′TION, nn., ~ize(3) v.t., ~ly² adv. 2. (Physics, Chem.) of like, ethereal (as prec.) + -AL]

ĕth′ic, n. Science of morals, moral principles, system of morals, as *Aristotelian ethics*; the whole field of moral science, including besides ethics proper... [f. L *ethica* f. Gk *ēthikē* (as foll.)]

ĕth′ics (as prec.) + -AL]

Gk *aitherios* (as prec.) + -AL]

êth′erize, v.t. Put (patient) under in-fluence of ether. Hence ~A′TION n. [-IZE]

ĕth'ic, a. & n. 1. (Now usu. ~*al*) relating to morals, treating of moral questions; ~ *dative* (of person indirectly interested in fact stated). 2. n. pl., & rarely sing. Science of morals, treatise on this, moral principles, rules of conduct, whole field of moral science. Hence ~AL a., ~ally² adv., ~IZE(3) v.t. [f. L f. Gk *ēthikos* (ETHOS, -IC)]

Ethiōp'ian (-ō-), a. & n. (Native) of Ethiopia, esp. (Anthropol.) as epithet of one of the races into which human species is divided. [-AN]

ĕth'moid, a. Sieve-like; ~ *bone*, square-shaped bone at root of nose, through the many perforations of which the olfactory nerves pass to the nose. [f. Gk *ēthmoeidēs* (*ēthmos* sieve)]

ĕth'nic, -ic|al, aa. Pertaining to race, ethnological, whence ~ally² adv.; (~) gentile, heathen, whence ~alism(2) n. [f. Gk *ethnikos* (*ethnos* nation, see -IC]

ĕthnŏg'raphy, n. Scientific description of races of men. So **ĕthnŏg'rapher n., ĕth-nŏgrăph'ic(al) aa., ĕthnŏgrăph'ically²** adv. [f. Gk *ethnos* nation +-GRAPHY]

ĕthnŏl'ŏgy, n. Science of races & their relations to one another & characteristics. So **ĕthnŏlŏ'gic(AL) aa.** (*-ic frontier*), corresponding to a division of races), **ĕthnŏ-lŏ'gically²** adv., **ĕthnŏl'ogist n.** [as prec. +-LOGY]

ĕt hŏc gĕn'us ŏm'nĕ, phr. And all that kind of thing (often as ornamental substitute for *et cetera*). [L]

ĕthŏl'ŏgy, n. Science of character-formation. Hence **ĕthŏlŏ'gicAL a.** [f. L f. Gk *ēthologia* (ETHOS, see -LOGY]

ĕth'ŏs, n. Characteristic spirit of community, people, or system. [Gk (ē-) = character, nature, disposition]

ĕth'yl, n. (chem.). The hydrocarbon radical present in ordinary alcohol & ether. [f. ETH(ER), -YL]

-ĕt'ic, suf. of adj|. & nn. = Gk agent suf. *-ēt-* or *-ēt-* + *ic*, in wds f. Gk or on Gk models, as *emetic* (Gk *emētikos*), *ascetic* (Gk *askētikos*)

ĕt'iolāte, v.t. Make (plant) pale by excluding light; give sickly hue to (person). Hence ~A'TION n. [f. F *étioler* f. Norm. *étieuler* make into haulm (*éteule* f. L *stipula* straw)]

ĕtiŏlŏgy. See AETIOLOGY.

ĕtiquette' (-kĕt), n. Conventional rules of personal behaviour in polite society; ceremonial of court; unwritten code re-stricting professional men in what concerns interests of their brethren or dignity of their profession, esp. *medical*, *legal*, ~. [f. F *étiquette* TICKET, ~]

Ĕt'na n. Vessel for heating small quantity of liquid by burning spirit. [f. the volcano]

Ĕt'on (ō-). n. ~ *collar* (broad, stiff, worn outside coat-collar); ~ *crop*, cutting of woman's hair short like boy's; ~ *jacket*,

boy's short coat reaching only to waist. [f. ~ College]

Etrus'can (ī-) a. & n. (Native) of ancient Etruria. [f. L *Etruscus* +-AN]

ĕt sēq|., sēquĕn'tēs (z), -*tia*, (in reference to books etc.). And the words, pages, etc., that follow. [L]

-ĕtte, suf. forming dim. nn. (rarely adj|.), repr. OF -*ette*, the fem. corresp. to -ET. (1) Older adoptions f. F now have -*et*, -*ette* appearing chiefly in wds introduced since 17th c., as *cigarette*, *etiquette*. (2) A mod. commerc. use, = 'sham', is seen in *leatherette*, *Brusselette* (carpet). (3) A mod. fem. suf., as *conductorette*, *usherette*. *étude* (ātüd'), n. A short musical composition or exercise. [F]

étui' (-wē), **étwee', n.** Small case for needles, tooth-picks, etc. [f. F *étui*, etym. dub.]

ĕtymŏl'ŏgize, v.t. & i. Give, trace, the etymology of; suggest etymology for; study etymology. [f. LL *etymologizare* (as foll., -IZE)]

ĕtymŏl'ŏgy, n. Account of, facts relating to, formation & meaning of word; branch of linguistic science concerned with this; part of grammar treating of individual words & their formation & inflexions. Hence or cogn. **ĕtymŏl'ogER, ĕtymŏl'o- gIST, nn., ĕtymŏlŏ'gic(AL) aa., ĕtymo-lŏ'gically² adv.** [f. OF *éthimologie* f. L f. Gk *etumologia* (as foll., -LOGY)]

ĕt'ymon, n. Primary word that gives rise to a derivative. [L, f. Gk *etumon* (neut. of *etumos* true) literal sense, original form, of a word]

eu- in comb. = Gk *eu* well, cf. DYS-.

eucalȳp'tus, n. Genus of plants including Australian Gum tree; ~ *oil*, a disinfectant. [f. EU-+Gk *kaluptos* covered (*kaluptō*), flower being protected by cap]

eu'charis (ūk-), n. (Also ~ *lily*) S.-Amer. bulbous plant with white bell-shaped flowers. [Gk EU(*khāris* grace) pleasing]

Eu'charist (ūk-), n. Lord's Supper; consecrated elements, esp. the bread, as *rēve, receive*, the ~. Hence ~IC(AL) -*is*² aa. (~*ic Congress*, international meeting of the Roman Catholics in veneration of the Blessed Sacrament, originally held annually, later biennially). [f. OF *eucariste* f. LL f. Gk *eukharistia* f. EU(*kharistos* f. *kharizomai* offer willingly) grateful]

euchlō'rine (ūkl-), n. Bright yellow-green compound gas discovered by Davy. [EU-+Gk *khlōros* an anal. of CHLORINE]

eu'chre (-ker), n., & v.t. 1. American card game for 2, 3, or 4 persons. 2. v.t. Gain advantage over (opponent) by his failure to take three tricks at ~ (also fig.). [?]

Eu'clid, n. Alexandrian mathematician (c. 300 B.C.); his *Elements* or treatise on geometry, a copy of this; (pop.) geometry as a science or subject; (mod.) the geometry of ordinary experience, accepting ~'s axioms as indisputable (cf.

eudaemonism (-dēm-), n. System of ethics basing moral obligation on tendency of actions to produce happiness. So **Eudaemon·ism** (-dēm-), n. System of ethics basing moral obligation on tendency of actions to produce happiness. So **eudaemon′ic(2)** n. [f. Gk *eudaimonia* happy, -ISM]

eudiom′eter, n. Graduated glass tube in which gases may be chemically combined by electric spark passing between metallic terminals at its closed end, used in chemical experiments. So **eudiom′etric** (AI) aa., **eudiom′etrical′ly** adv., **eudiom′etry**, n. [f. Gk EU(*dios*, st. of *Zeus*, gen. *Dios*, god of the sky) clear + -METER]

eugē′nic, a. & n. 1. Of the production of fine (esp. human) offspring. 2. n. pl. Science of this. So **eugen′ic(2)** n. student of -s. [f. Gk EU-+ -GEN + -IO]

euhem′erism, n. Reference of mythical or historical basis. So **~ISM(2)** n. ~**IST**(4) v.t. & i. [f. *Euhemerus*, Sicilian author c. 316 B.C., + -ISM]

eulo′gize, v.t. Extol, praise, in speech or writing. So **~ISM**(1) n., **~ist**(1) a., **~ist-ICALLY** adv. [f. foll. + -IZE]

eu′logy, n. Speech, writing, in praise of a person etc.; *as pronounce his ~, pronounce a ~ on him*; praise. [prob. f. med. L (also used as E) *eulogium* irreg. f. Gk *eu-* -logy]

eun′uch (-uk), n. Castrated male person, esp. one employed in harem, or (in Oriental courts & under Roman empire) employed in state affairs. [f. L f. Gk *eunoukhos* lit. bedchamber attendant (*eunē* bed + *okh-* st. of *ekhō* hold)]

euon′ymus, n. Genus of shrubs including spindle-tree. [f. L f. Gk EU(*onuma* f. *onoma* name) of lucky name]

eupep′tic, a. Of, having, good digestion. [f. Gk EU(*peptos* f. *pessō*, *pepō*, digest) + -IO]

euph′emism, n. Substitution of mild or vague expression for harsh or blunt one; expression thus substituted, as *' queer ' is a ~ism for ' mad '*. So **~ist′ic(1)**(2) v.t. & i. [f. Gk *euphēmismos* f. EU(*phēmos* f. *phēmi* speak, fame), see -ISM]

euphō′nium, n. (mus.). Bass instrument of saxhorn family. [mod. L, f. Gk *eu-* *phōnos* see foll.]

euph′ony, n. Pleasing sound; quality of having this (usu. of words, phrases, etc.); tendency to phonetic change for ease of pronunciation. So **euphon′ic**, **euphon′ious** aa., **euphon′ically**, **euphon′iously** adv., **euph′onize**(3) v.t. [f. F *euphonie* f. L f. Gk *euphōnia* (*phōnē* sound)]

euphor′bia, n. (Kinds of) widely-distributed herb or shrub of the spurge family. [L (-*ea*), f. *Euphorbus* physician to Juba II, -IA]

euph′rasy, n. = EYEBRIGHT. [f. med. L f.
Gk *euphrasia* cheerfulness f. *euphrainō*
gladden (*phrēn* mind)]

euph′uism, n. Artificial or affected style of writing (prop., in imitation of Lyly's *Euphues*, 1580); high-flown style. So **~IST** n., **~ist′ic(a)** a., **~ist′ically** adv. [-ISM]

Eurā′sian (ŪrĀsh'an), a. & n. (Person) of mixed European & Asiatic parentage; of Eurasia. [f. *Europe* & *Asia*]

eurē′ka (ūr-), int. & n. [The exulting exclamation] 'I have (found) it.' [f. Gk *heurēka* 1st pers. perf. of *heuriskō* find]

eurhyth′mic(ūr-), a. In or of harmonious proportion (esp. in architecture). Hence **~s** n. pl., harmony of bodily movement, esp. as developed with the aid of music into a system used in education. [f. L f. Gk *euruthmia* good rhythm (see EU-, RHYTHM) + -IO]

Europē′an (ūr-), a. & n. (Native), of Europe, happening in, extending over, Europe, *as a ~ reputation*. Hence **~ISM**(2, 3, 4), **~IZE**(3) v.t., (Ūr-). [f. F *européen* f. L f. Gk *Europaios* (L f. Gk *Europē*) + -AN]

eu′sōl, n. Antiseptic and bactericide prepared from bleaching powder. [f. initial letters of *Edinburgh University solution* of lime]

Eustā′chian (-āk-), a. Of Eustachius the anatomist (d. 1574); *~ tube*, canal leading from the pharynx to the cavity of the middle ear. [-AN]

Euter′pē, n. The Muse of music, whence **~AN** a.; genus of palms. [Gk]

euthanā′sia (-z-, -s-), n. Gentle & easy death; bringing about of this, esp. in case of incurable & painful disease. [Gk EU-+ *thanatos* death]

evac′ūāte, v.t. Empty (esp. stomach or bodily organ of contents), whence **~ANT**(2) a. & n.; withdraw from (place); remove (troops); remove (person) esp. from place considered to be dangerous, whence **~EE′** n., person so removed; discharge (excrement etc.; also fig.). So **~Ā′TION** n. [f. L *evacuare* f. *vacuus* empty]

evāde′, v.t. Escape from, avoid, (attack, pursuit, designs, adversary, blow, obstacle, etc.); avoid doing (duty etc.), answering (question), yielding to (argument etc.); defeat intention of (law etc., esp. while complying with its letter); (of things) elude, baffle. Hence **evād′ABLE** a. [f. F *évader* f. L E(*vadere vas-* go)]

evā′gināte, v.t. (physiol.). Turn (tubular organ) inside out. So **~Ā′TION** n. [f. E(*vagina* f. *vagina* sheath), see -ATE[2]]

evāl′uāte, v.t. Ascertain amount of; find numerical expression for. So **~Ā′TION** n. [f. F *évaluer* (*é-* EX-, VALUE)]

evanesce′, v.i. Fade out of sight; become effaced; disappear. [f. L *evanescere*, VANISH]

ēvanes′cent, a. (Of impression, appearance, etc.) quickly fading; (Math.) infini-

tesimal. Hence ~ENCE n., ~enty² adv. [f. F *évanescé* (as prec., see -ENT]

évan'gel (-j-), n. (arch.). The Gospel; any of the Four Gospels; doctrine, principle, (of politics etc.). [f. OF *evangile* f. eccl. L f. Gk EU(*aggelion* cf. ANGEL) fee for good news]

évangěl'ic, -ical, (-j-), aa. & nn. 1. Of, according to, the teaching of the Gospel or the Christian religion; esp. of the Protestant school maintaining that the essence of the Gospel consists in doctrine of salvation by faith, good works & sacraments having no saving efficacy, whence ~alism(3) n. **2.** n. Member of this school. Hence ~al'ly² adv. [f. LL f. eccl. Gk *euaggelikos* (as prec., see -IC, -AL)]

évan'gelism (-j-), n. Preaching of the Gospel. [= EVANGELICALISM. -ISM]

évan'gelist (-j-), n. One of the writers of the Four Gospels; preacher of the Gospel; layman doing home missionary work. [f. F *évangéliste* f. L (-*ta*) f. Gk *euaggelistēs* (as EVANGELIZE, -IST)]

évangelis'tic (-j-), a. Of the Four Evangelists; of preachers of the Gospel; =EVANGELICAL. [-IC]

évan'gelīze(-j-), v.t. Preach the Gospel to (persons, also abss.); win over (person) to Christianity. Hence ~A'TION n. [f. eccl. L *evangelizare* f. Gk *euaggelizomai* (as EVANGEL)]

évan'ish, v.i. (literary). Vanish; die away. Hence ~MENT n. [f. OF *evanir* (-ISH-) f. pop. L †*exvanire* = L *evanesce* EVANESCE]

évap'oriāte, v.t. & i. Turn (t. & i.) from solid or liquid into vapour (also fig.; esp. collog. disappear, die); remove the liquid part of; (v.i.) exhale moisture. So ~ABLE, ~ATIVE, aa., ~A'TION, ~ā'TOR² nn. [f. LL *evaporare* (as VAPOUR), see -ATE³]

évā'sion (-zhn), n.** Act, means, of evading; shuffling excuse. So **évās'īve a., évas'īveness** (-vi-) adv.; ~évas'īveness (-vn-) n. [f. F *évasion* f. LL *evasionem* (as EVADE, see -ION)]

Eve¹ (ēv), n. The first woman; *daughter of* ~, woman (often w. allusion to feminine curiosity etc.). [f. Heb. *Hawah* orig. = life, living]

ēve², n. Evening or day before (*of*) a church festival or any date or event; time just before anything, as *on the* ~ *of an election*; (arch.) evening. [=EVEN¹; for loss of -n cf. *morrow*]

évec'tion, n. Inequality in moon's longitude. [f. L *evectio* f. E(*vehere vect*- carry)]

ē'ven¹, n. (poet.). Evening; ~*song, even-ing prayer in Church of England; ~tide, evening. [OE *ǣfen, efen*, Du. *avond*, G *abend*]

ē'ven², a. (-er, -est). Level; smooth; uniform in quality; in same plane or line (*with*); equally balanced, as ~*-handed justice*; equal in number or amount; (Law, Commerce.) of ~ (same)

date; (of temper etc.) equable, unruffled; ~ *money* (Betting), even odds. **adv.** interally divisible by two, (of numbers) integrally divisible by two, opp. to ODD; ODD & ~; *be* ~ *with*, have one's revenge on. Hence ~LY² adv., ~NESS n. [com.-Teut.: OE *efen*, Du. *even, effen*, G *eben*]

ē'ven³ adv. 1. Of, according to, inviting comparison of the assertion, negation, etc., made with a less strong one that might have been made, as *he disputes* ~ *the facts* (not merely the inferences from them), *I never ~ opened* (much less read) *it, does he ~ suspect* (not to say realize) *the danger ?, ~ if my watch is right we shall be late* (later if it is slow); *this applies ~ more* (not merely equally) *to French* (than to English); (arch.) neither more nor less than, just, simply, as ~ (quite) *so*, (emphasizing identity) that is, as *God, our own God.* [OE *efne*, as prec.]

ē'ven⁴, v.t. Make even; treat as equal or comparable (*to*); ~ *up*, to balance; *~ up on*, requite, make return to (a person). [OE *efnan*, as prec.]

ē'vening (-vn-), n. Close of day, esp. sunset to bedtime; this time spent in particular way, as *musical* ~*s*; (fig.) decline of life, closing period; ~ *dress*, that prescribed by fashion to be worn in the ~; ~ *star*, Jupiter, Mercury, or other planet, & in West after sunset. [OE *ǣfnung* vbl n. f. *ǣfnian* (as EVEN¹)]

ē'vent, n. Fact of a thing's happening, as *in the* ~ *of his death, his coming*, if he dies, comes; thing that happens, esp. important thing, as *quite an* ~, whence ~FUL, ~LESS, aa.; (in doctrine of chances) any of several possible but mutually exclusive occurrences; *double* ~, combined occurrence of two ~s, esp. as subject of bets; (Sport.) something on the issue of which money is staked; result, outcome; *in any* or *either* ~, *at all* ~s, in any case. [OF, f. L *eventus -ūs* f. E(*venīre come*)]

ēven'tüal, a. That will happen under certain circumstances; ultimately resulting, whence ~ITY² adv. [f. F *éventuel* (prec., -AL)]

ēventüăl'ity, n. Possible event. [-ITY]

ēven'tüāte, v.i. Turn out (*well, ill,* etc.); result (*in* or abss.); *happen, come to pass. [f. L as EVENT, -ATE³]

ěv'er, adv. Always, at all times, (arch. exc. as foll.); *for ~ (& ~, & a day)*, for all future time, incessantly; ~*more* (in always; ~ *since*); ~ *since*, *after*, (arch.), ~ *& anon*, now & then; (w. negative, question, condition, comparison) at any time, as *nothing ~ happens, did you ~ hear such stuff ?, if I ~ catch him, the best thing I ~ heard, as good as ~, better than ~*; (strengthening *as*) *be as quick as ~ you can*; (emphasizing question, collog.) *what*

~ (also whatever) does he want?, who ~ can it be?, which ~ Brown do you mean?, when ~, where, how, ~ did I do it?, why ~ didn't you say so?; ~ so (earlier never so), very, as it is ~ so much easier; (appended to superl. as sl. ellipsis for that ~ was or were: the back-benchers were the most docile ~); did you ~? (as complete sentence), did you ~ see or hear the like? [OE ǣfre, ǣfen. dub., perh. conn. w. AYE]

*ĕv'erglāde, n. Marshy tract of land, esp. (pl.) swamp in S. Florida. [prec. +GLADE]

ĕv'ergreen, a. & n. Always green or fresh (lit. & fig.); (tree, shrub) having green leaves all the year round (cf. DECIDUOUS).

ĕverlas'ting (-ah-), a. & n. 1. Lasting for ever; lasting long; lasting too long, repeated too often; (of plants) keeping shape and colour when dried. 2. n. Eternity, as from ~; ~ flower; strong twilled woollen stuff. Hence ~lỹ² adv., ~NESS n. [EVER+LASTING]

ĕvert', v.t. (Physiol.) turn (organ etc.) inside out. So ēvĕr'siŏn n. [f. L evertere vers-turn)]

ĕv'ery (-ri), a. Each, all (w. sing. vb), as ~ word of it is false, (w. possess. pron.) it engaged his ~ thought, (of succession or alternation) he comes ~ day, ~ other (i.e. second) day, ~ three days, ~ third day; ~ now & then, ~ now & again, from time to time; ~ bit (quite) as much; ~body (else), ~ (other) person; ~day (adj.), occurring daily, worn or used on ordinary days, commonplace; ~ one, each, as ~ one of them is wrong; ~one (also ~ one), ~body, as ~one likes to have his way; ~thing, all things, as ~thing depends on that, thing of first importance, as pace is ~thing; ~ time (colloq.), without exception, without any hesitation; ~ way, in ~ way, in ~ respect; ~where, in ~ place. [OE ǣfre ǣlc EVER EACH]

ĕv'erymăn (ĕvr'-), n. The ordinary or typical human being, the 'man in the street.' [character in 16th c. morality]

ēvict', v.t. Expel (person; esp. tenant from land etc.); recover (property, title to it, of, from, person) by legal process. So ēvic'tiŏn, ēvic'tŏr², nn. [f. L ēvincere evict- conquer]

ĕv'idence, n. & v.t. 1. Clearness, obviousness, esp. in ~, conspicuous. 2. Indication, sign, (of quality, treatment, etc.); testimony, facts, making for (also of) a conclusion, esp. (pl.) the E~s of Christianity; INTERNAL, EXTERNAL, ~. 3. (Law) information (given personally or drawn from documents etc.) tending to establish fact, as call (person) in ~ (as a witness), CIRCUMSTANTIAL, PRESUMPTIVE, verbal ~; || turn King's, Queen's, &c., (of accomplice in crime) give ~ against one's accomplices; statements, proofs, ad-

missible as testimony in court. 4. v.t. Serve to indicate, attest. So ĕv'idĕn'tIAL (-shl), ĕvidĕn'tIARY¹ (-sha-) aa., ĕvi- dĕn'tIARY² (-sha-) adv. [(γb L) f. F évidence f. L ēvidentia (as foll., see -ENCE)]

ĕv'idĕnt, a. Obvious (to eyes or mind). Hence ~lỹ² adv. [f. L ēvidēre see)]

ēv'il (-vl, -vil), a., n., & adv. 1. Bad, harmful; the E~ One, the Devil; of ~ (bad) repute, an ~ (slanderous) tongue; ~ eye, malicious look, pop. believed to do material harm. 2. n. ~ thing, sin, harm, (of two ~s choose the less); ~doer; Aleppo ~, a disease of boils; = KING's ~. 3. adv. In ~ manner, as speak ~ of, (Bibl.) ~ entreat, ~-disposed. Hence ~lỹ² adv., ~NESS n. [OE yfel, Du. euvel, G übel; perh.

ēvince', v.t. Show, indicate, (quality etc., that etc.); show that one has (quality). Hence ēvin'cIVE a. [as EVICT]

ēvir'āte, v.t. Castrate (male); (fig.) deprive of manly qualities. So ~A'TION n. [f. L ēvirare f. vir man), see -ATE³]

ēvis'cerāte, v.t. Disembowel; (fig.) empty (thing) of vital contents. Hence ~A'TION n. [f. L ēviscerare (VISCERA), see -ATE³]

ēvōke', v.t. Call up (spirit from the dead, feelings, memories, energies); || summon (cause) to higher court. So ēvŏc'ative, ēvŏc'atory aa. [f. F évoquer f. L E(vocare call)]

ēvŏlu'tion (-loo-), n. 1. Opening out (of roll, bud, etc.; usu. fig.); appearance (of events etc.), in due succession; evolving, giving off, (of gas, heat, etc.). 2. Unfolding of curve; (Math.) extraction of root from any given power (cf. INVOLUTION). 3. Development (of organism, design, argument, etc.); Theory of E~ (that the embryo is not created by fecundation, but developed from a pre-existing form); origination of species by development from earlier forms, not by special creation (cf. CREATIONISM), whence ~ISM, ~IST, nn. 4. Formation of heavenly bodies by concentration of cosmic matter. 5. Change in disposition of troops or ships; wheeling about, movement, in dancing etc. Hence ~AL, ~ARY¹, aa., (-lōōshon-). [f. L ēvolutio (as EVOLVE, see -ION)]

ēvō'lutive (-loō-), a. Tending to evolution. [-IVE]

ēvolve', v.t. & i. Unfold, open out, (fig.); set forth in due sequence; give off (heat etc.); develop, deduce, (theory, facts, etc.); develop (t. & i.) by natural process; ~ from one's inner consciousness, create imaginatively (often joc., of romancing etc.). Hence ~MENT (-vm-) n. [f. L E(vol- vere volut-roll)]

evŭl'sion, n. Forcible extraction. [f. L *evulsio* f. E(*vellere vuls-* pluck), see -ION]

ewe (ū), n. Female sheep; one's ~ *lamb*, one's most cherished possession (2 *Sam.* xii); ~-*necked*, (of horses) having a thin concave neck. [com.-Aryan: OE *eowu*, Du. *ooi*, L *ovis*, Gk *ois*, Skr. *avi*]

ew'er, n. Pitcher; water-jug with a wide mouth. [f. OF *aiguiere* f. L *aquaria* fem. adj. as n. (*aqua* water, see -ARY[1])]

ewigkeit (ā'vigkīt), n. (joc.). *Into, in, the* ~, into thin air, in the unknown. [G, = eternity]

ex, prep. (commerc.). (Of goods) out of, sold from, (*ship, store*, etc.); (of stocks or shares) *ex div'idend* (abbr. *ex div.* or *x.d.*), not including next dividend. [L]

ex-, pref. **1.** = L *ex* before *h, c, p, q, s* (which is often dropped), and *f*; becoming *ef-* before *f*, *e-* before other consonants, forming vbs with sense 'out', 'forth', (*exclude, exit*), 'thoroughly' (*excruciate*), 'make so-&-so' (*exasperate*), 'remove, expel, free, from' (*expatriate, -onerate, -coriate*), and adjl. w. sense 'not having', esp. in form *e-* (*ecaudate* tailless). **2.** = Gk *ex* (= *ek* before vowels) out, as *exodus*. **3.** L *ex* is prefixed to nn. and rarely adjj. (orig. to titles of office etc.) in sense 'formerly', 'quondam', as *ex-chancellor, ex-Prime-Minister*.

exăc'erbāte, v.t. Aggravate (pain, disease, anger); irritate (person etc.). So ~A'TION n. [f. L EX(*acerbare* f. *acerbus* bitter)]

exăct'[1] (-gz-), a. Precise, rigorous, (rules, order, etc.); (of person, judgement, description, report, answer, etc.) accurate, strictly correct; ~ *sciences* (admitting of absolute precision). Hence or cogn. exăc'tirude, ~NESS, nn., (-gz-). [f. L p.p. as foll.]

exăct'[2] (-gz-), v.t. Demand & enforce payment of (money, fees, etc., *from, of*, person), insist upon (act, conduct, *from, of*), (of circumstances) require urgently. Hence or cogn. exăc'tor[2] n., (-gz-). [f. L EX(*igere act- = agere* drive)]

exăc'tion (-gz-), n. Exacting (of money etc.); sum, thing, thus exacted; illegal or exorbitant demand, extortion; arbitrary & excessive impost. [F, f. L *exactionem* as prec., see -ION]

exăct'ly (-gz-), adv. In adj. senses, esp. (as answer or confirmation) quite so, just as you say. [-LY[2]]

exa'ggerāte (igzăj-), v.t. Magnify (thing described, or abs.) beyond limits of truth; intensify, aggravate; make (physical features etc.) of abnormal size. Hence or cogn. ~ātēdly[2], ~ātive[y]2 advv., ~A'TION, ~ātor[2], nn., ~ātive a., (igzăj-). [f. L EX-(*aggerare* heap up, f. *agger* heap), see -ATE[3]]

exalt' (igzawlt), v.t. Raise, place high in rank, power, etc.; praise, extol, (often ~ *to the skies*); dignify, ennoble, (esp. in p.p.); intensify (colours etc.). [f. L EX(*altare* f. *altus* high)]

exăltā'tion (-awl-), n. Raising, lifting up, (usu. fig.); elation, rapturous emotion; intensification. [F, f. L *exaltationem* (prec., -ATION]

exăm' (-gz-), n. (colloq.). See foll.

examinā'tion (-gz-), n. Minute inspection (*of, into*): POST-MORTEM ~; (colloq. abbr. *exam*) testing of knowledge or ability (of pupils, candidates) by questions oral or written; ~-*paper*, series of such questions or of examinee's answers to them. Hence ~AL (-shon-) a. [F, f. L *examinationem* (as foll., see -ATION]

exăm'ine (-gz-), v.t. & i. Investigate, scrutinize, (accounts, person *in* or *on* subject, organ, statement, one's own conscience, *whether*); (intr.) inquire *into*. Hence ~ANT, ~EE', ~ER[1], nn., ~ator[1IAL] a., (-gz-). [f. F *examiner* f. L *examinare* (*examen*, for *exagmen*, tongue of balance, examination, as EXACT[2])]

exăm'ple (igzahl-), n., & v.t. Fact, thing, illustrating general rule; problem, exercise, designed to do this; specimen of workmanship, picture, etc.; warning to others, as *make an ~ of* (punish) *him*; precedent, as *beyond, without,* ~; conduct as object of imitation, as *give, set, a good* ~; *take ~ by*, copy; (v.t., rare exc. in p.p.) exemplify. [vb f. n.) OF f. L *exemplum* (as EXEMPT[1])]

exăn'imate (-gz-), a. Dead; lacking animation, spiritless. [f. L EX(*animare* deprive of life (*anima*), see -ATE[2]]

ex än'imō, adv. & a. Heartily, sincere(ly). [L, = from the soul]

ex'arch (-k), n. (Under Byzantine emperors) governor of distant province; (in Eastern Church) patriarch, bishop, patriarch's deputy. So ~ATE[1] (-k-) n., (-gz-). [f. L. Gk *exarkhos* f. EX(*arkhō* rule)]

exăs'perāte (-gz-), v.t. Make hollow (ill feeling, disease, pain); irritate (person; ~*ated at, by*); provoke (person *to* ill, *to do*). Hence or cogn. ~āting[l] adv., ~A'TION n., (-gz-). [f. L EX(*asperare* f. *asper* rough), see -ATE[3]]

ex cathědrā'dd, adv. & a. Authoritative(ly). [L, = from the (teacher's) chair]

ex'cavāte, v.t. Make hollow (hole, channel) by digging; dig out (soil) leaving a hole; unearth, get out, by digging. Hence or cogn. ~ING[2] a. & (arch.), ~ātor[2], nn. [f. L EX(*cavare* f. *cavus* hollow), see -ATE[3]]

exceed', v.t. & i. Do more than is warranted by (one's commission, rights, etc.); be greater than (quantity, thing, *by so much*); surpass (person etc. *in*). be pre-eminent, whence ~ING[2] a. (arch.) adv., ~ingly[2] adv.; be immoderate in feeding etc.; exaggerate. [f. F *exceder* f. L EX(*cedere cess-* go)]

excĕl', v.t. & i. (-ll-). Surpass (others *in* quality, *in doing*); be pre-eminent (*in*,

at, thing, *in quality, in doing*). [f. F *ex-celler* f. L EXcellere, cf. *celsus* lofty) in which person etc. excels. [F, f. L *excellentia* (as prec., see -ENCE)]

excellency, n. Title (*Your, His, Her, E~*) of ambassadors, governors & their wives, & some other officers. [as prec., see -ENCY]

ex'cellent, a. Pre-eminent; very good. Hence ~LY² adv. [F (as prec., see -ENT)]

excel'sior, int. & n. Higher (as trade mark etc.); *soft shavings of wood for stuffing. [L, compar. of EXCELSUS lofty]

except¹, v.t. & i. Exclude (thing) from enumeration, statement, etc., as *present company ~ed*, *~ him from the general pardon*; make objection against. So **excep'tive** a. [f. F *excepter* f. L EXcipere

except², **excep'ting**, prep. & conj. (~*ing* is required only after *not*, *without*, as *we are all fallible, except the pope*, but *not excepting the pope*; ~*ing* is also usual after *always*). 1. Not including, but, as *we all failed ~ him*, *he is everywhere ~ in the right place, never to be found ~ in the wrong place*, *it is right ~ that the accents are omitted*. 2. conj. (arch.) Unless, as *~ he be born again*. [*except* orig. p.p. (f. L as prec.) abs. constr. (~ *you*=*you being excepted*); ~*ing*, abs. use of part. of prec.]

excep'tion, n. Excepting; thing excepted, thing that does not follow the rule; *the ~ proves the rule*, (prop.) the excepting of some cases shows that the rule exists, or (pop.) the weaker my case, the stronger my conviction; *with the ~ of*, except; *take ~*, object *to*; *subject, liable, to ~* (objection), whence ~ABLE (-shon-) a. [f. AF *excepcioun* f. L *exceptionem* (EXCEPT¹-TION)]

excep'tional (-shon-), a. Forming an exception; unusual, esp. (of *advantages*, Hence ~ITY (-ǎl²-ty), ~LY² adv. [-AL]

excerpt¹ (EK'sĕrpt or ĕksĕrpt'), n. Extract from book etc., article from learned society's Transactions etc. printed off separately for private circulation. [as foll.]

excerpt², v.t. Extract, quote, (passage from book etc., or abs.). Hence or cogn. ~IBLE a., **excerp'tion** n. [f. L EX(*cerpere cerpi*=*carpere* pluck)]

excess', n. (Usu. pl.) outrage; intemperance in eating or drinking; overstepping of due limits; fact of exceeding, esp. *in ~ of*, more than; amount by which one exceeds another; *~ fare* on railway, payment due for travelling farther or in higher class than ticket warrants; *~ luggage* (over the weight for free carriage), superabundance, extreme degree, (of cruelty etc.); exceeding of the proper amount or degree, esp. *in*, *to*, *~*; *~ profits*

duty, tax, tax on profits swollen by war conditions. So ~IVE a., ~IVELY² (-vl-) adv. [f. F *excès* f. L *excessus -ūs* (as EXCEED)]

exchange¹, n. 1. Act, process, of exchanging (of goods, prisoners of war, blows, words, etc.; *~ is no robbery*, joc. excuse for unfair~). 2. Exchanging of coin for its equivalent in coin of same or another country; money-changer's trade; *par of ~*, standard value of coinage of one country in terms of that of another; (*rate, course, of*) *~*, price at which bills drawn in a foreign currency may be bought, also, difference between this & par; system of settling debts between persons (esp. in different countries) without money, *by bills of ~* (*first, second, third, of~*, separate bills of even tenor & date as security against miscarriage). 3. Thing exchanged for another. 4. Building where merchants assemble to transact business, as STOCK~. 5. Central telephone office of a district where connexions are made for local or trunk calls. [f. OF *eschange* (as foll.)]

exchange², v.t. & i. Give, receive, (thing) in place of (*for*) another; interchange (blows, words, glances, etc.); (v.i., esp. of coin) be received as equivalent *for*; pass *from* one regiment or ship *into* another) by exchange with another officer. [f. OF *eschangier* f. LL EX(*cambiāre* CHANGE²)]

exchan'geable (-jab), a. That may be exchanged (*for*), ~*ble value* (estimated by that of the goods for which a thing may be exchanged). Hence ~BIL¹TY (-jab-) n. [-ABLE]

exchéq'uer (-ker), n. ‖ Department of public service charged with receipt & custody of revenue; ‖ *Chancellor of the E~*, finance minister of United Kingdom; royal or national treasury; money of private person etc.; ‖ (also *Court of E~*) court of law, now merged in King's Bench Division (orig. using table with chequered cloth for accounts); ‖~ *bill* (issued by authority of Parliament, bearing interest at current rate). [f. OF *eschequier* f. med. L *scaccarium* chessboard (*scacchi* chess, see -ARIUM)]

excise¹ (~z), n., & v.t. 1. Duty charged on home goods during manufacture or before sale to home consumers; ‖ government office collecting ~ (now *Commissioners of Customs & E~*); officer collecting ~ & preventing infringement of ~ laws. 2. v.t. Force (person) to pay ~, overcharge (also fig.). Hence **exci'sABLE** (-z-) a. [vrb f. n.); prob. f. MDu. *excijs* f. LL +*accensum* tax (L tax (CENSUS)]

excise² (~z), v.t. Cut out (passage of book, limb, organ, etc.); (Bot., Zool.) cut out, notch. So **exci'sION** (-zhon) n. [f. L EX(*cidere cīs-* = *caedere* cut)]

excite', v.t. Set in motion, rouse up, (feelings, faculties, etc.); provoke, bring about, (action, active condition); promote activity of (bodily organs etc.) by stimulus; move (person) to strong emotion; (colloq. ellipt.) *don't ~e'*, keep cool; (Electr., Magnet.) induce activity in (substance), set (current) in motion, whence **éxcitā'TION** n.; (Photog.) sensitize (plate). Hence or cogn. **~ABIL'ITY**, **~e'MENT** (-tm-), nn., **éx'citant** a. & n., **~ed**, unbalanced), **~'ēdiy²** adv. [f. F *exciter* f. L *excitare* frequent. of EX(*ciēre* set in motion)]

exclaim', v.i. & t. Cry out, esp. from pain, anger, etc.; utter (words quoted direct or with *that*) thus; *~ against*, accuse loudly. [f. F *exclamer* f. L EX(*clamare* shout)]

exclamā'tion, n. Exclaiming; words exclaimed; *note of ~* (!). So **éxclām'atory** a. [F., f. L (prec., -ATION)]

exclude' (-ōōd), v.t. Shut out (person, thing, *from* place, society, privilege, etc.); prevent the occurrence of, make impossible, (doubt etc.); expel & shut out. So **éxclū'SION** (-lōōzhn) n. [f. L EX(*cludere clus- = claudere* shut)]

exclū'sive (-ōō-), a. Shutting out; not admitting of; desirous of excluding others, (of social circles etc.) chary of admitting members, select, whence **éxclū'ivISM**(2) (-lōō-) n.; (shop, newspaper) not to be had, not published, elsewhere; (of terms etc.) excluding all but what is specified; employed, followed, to the exclusion of all else, as *his ~ occupation*; (quasi-adv.) not counting, as *20 men, ~ of our own*. Hence **~LY²** (-lōōsivv-) adv., **~NESS** (-lōōsivn-) n. [f. med. L *exclusivus* (prec., -IVE)]

excō'gitāte, v.t. Think out, contrive. So **~ā'TION** n., **~ātive** a. [f. L EX(*cogitare* COGITATE)]

excommū'nicāte, v.t. (Eccl.) cut off (person) from participation in sacraments, or from all communication with the Church. So **éxcommūnicā'TION**, **~OR²**, nn., **~IVE**, **~ORY**, aa. [f. LL EX(*communicare* f. *communis* COMMON), see -ATE³]

excō'riāte, v.t. Remove part of skin of (person etc.) by abrasion etc.; strip, peel off, (skin). So **~ā'TION** n. [f. L EX(*coriare* f. *corium* hide), see -ATE³]

ex'crément, n. Waste matter discharged from bowels, dung, (often pl.). Hence or cogn. **~AL** (-ēn²), **~'iTOUS¹** (-ishus), aa. [f. F *excrément* f. L *excrementum* (as EXCRETE, see -MENT]

excrēs'cence, n. Abnormal or morbid outgrowth on animal or vegetable body (also fig.). So **éxcrēs'ciㅠFIAL** (-shal) a. [f. L *excrescentia* (as foll., see -ENCE)]

excrēs'cent, a. Growing abnormally; redundant; (Gram., of sound in word) due merely to euphony. [f. L EX(*crescere crēt-* grow), -ENT]

excrē'ta, n.pl. Waste expelled from body, esp. faeces & urine. [L, p.p. as foll.]

excrēte', v.t. (Of animals or plants) separate & expel (waste matters, also abs.) from system. Hence or cogn. **éxcrē'TION** n., **~'IVE**, **~'ORY**, aa. [f. L EX(*cernere crēt-* sift)]

excrū'ciāte (-krōōshi-), v.t. Torment acutely (person's senses; now esp. in part. as adj.); torture mentally (now rare). Hence or cogn. **~ingLY²** (-krōōshi-) adv., **éxcruciā'TION** (-krōō-) n. [f. L EX(*cruciare* torment f. *crux crucis* cross), see -ATE³]

ex'culpāte, v.t. Free from blame; clear (person *from* charge etc.). Hence **éxculp'ā'TION** n., **éxcul'patory** a. [f. EX- + L *culpā* blame + -ATE³]

excū'rrent, a. Running out; (of blood) flowing from heart, arterial; affording an exit; (Bot.) projecting, [as foll., see -ENT]

excū'rsie', v.i. (rare). Wander, digress (usu. fig.), make an excursion. Hence **~'IVE** a., **~'ively²** (-vi-) adv., **~'iveNESS** (-vn-) n. [f. L EX(*currere curs-* run)]

excū'rsion (-shon), n. Journey, ramble, with intention of returning (also fig.); pleasure trip of number of persons, whence **~IST** (-shon-) n., **~'train** (for ~ists, usu. at reduced rates); (arch.) sortie (*alarms & ~s*); (Astron.) deviation from regular path. Hence **~AL**, **~ARY¹**, aa., (-shon-), [f. L *excursio* (as prec., see -ION)]

excū'rsus, n. (pl. ~es). Detailed discussion of special point in book, usu. in appendix at end. [L vbl n. as EXCURSE]

excū'se¹ (-z), v.t. Attempt to lessen the blame attaching to (person, act); obtain exemption for (person, oneself, *from* duty etc.); (of things) serve as exculpation for (person, act); accept the exculpation of (person from act, person for act); release (person from a duty; dispense with obl., as *we ~e him the fee*); dispense with, as *we will ~e your presence*; *~e me* (as apology for lack of ceremony, interruption, etc.; also as form of dissent). So **~'ABLE**, **~'atORY**, aa., **~'ablY²** adv., (-z-). [f. OF *excuser* f. L EX(*causare* (*causa* CAUSE²)]

excū'se² (-s), n. Apology offered, exculpation (usu. *in ~ of*); ground of this; plea for release from duty etc. [OF (as prec.)]

ǁ **ēx'ēat**, n. (In schools, colleges, etc.) permission for temporary absence. [L, 3rd sing. subj. of EX(*īre* go)]

ex'ēcrable, a. Abominable. Hence **~LY²** adv. [f. L *execrābilis* (foll., -BLE)]

ex'ēcrāte, v.t. & i. Express, feel, abhorrence for; (v.i.) utter curses. Hence or cogn. **éxēcrā'TION** n., **~IVE**, **~ORY**, aa. [f. L EX(s)*ecrārī* (*sacrare* devote f. *sacer* sacred, accursed), see -ATE³]

exēc'ūtant (-gz-), n. One who executes, performer, (of music etc.). [f. F *exécutant*, part. as foll.]

ĕx'ĕcūte, v.t. Carry (plan, command, law, judicial sentence, will) into effect; perform (action, operation, etc.); make (legal instrument) valid by signing, sealing, etc.; ǁ convey (estate) in property; discharge (office, function); perform (musical composition); inflict capital punishment on. Hence ~ABLE a. [f. F *exécuter* f. med. L *exsecūtāre* f. L EXSEQUI; *secut-* follow)]

ĕxĕcū'tion, n. Carrying out, performance; dexterity in performing music; (of weapons) destructive effect, as *do* ~ (also fig. of personal charms etc.); seizure of property or person of debtor in default of payment; infliction of capital punishment, whence ~ER¹ (-shon) n.; ǁ *Eb~ Dock* (Hist.), place on bank of Thames near Wapping where pirates were formerly hanged. [f. F *execution* f. L *exsecūtiōnem* (as prec., -ION)]

ĕxĕc'ūtĭve (-gz-), a. & n. 1. Pertaining to, having the function of, executing. 2. *literary* ~, person charged with writer's unpublished works etc. Hence ĕxĕcū'tŏr¹ᴸᴸ a. ĕxĕc'ūtŏrsm, ĕxĕc'ūtrĭx (pl. *-trīces), nn. (-gz-). [f. AF *executōrie* f. L *exsecūtōrem* (EXECUTE, -OR²)]

position in business organization etc. [-IVE]

ĕx'ĕcutŏr, n. 1. (ĕk'sĕ-). One who carries out or performs. 2. (ĭgzĕk-). Person appointed by testator to execute his will; unpublished works etc. [Gk *exēgēsis* f. EX(*hēgeomai* lead)]

ĕxĕg'ĕsĭs, n. Exposition esp. of Scripture. So ~ĕt'ĭc(ᴬᴸ) aa., ~ĕt'ĭcally² adv. [Gk *exēgēsis* f. EX(*hēgeomai* lead)]

ĕxĕm'plăr (-gz-), n. Model, pattern; type (of a class); parallel instance. [f. OF *exem-plaire* f. LL *exemplārium* (EXAMPLE, -ARY²)]

ĕxĕm'plărӯ (-gz-), a. Fit to be imitated; typical; illustrative; serving as a warning (~y *damages* in law, exceeding amount needed for compensation). Hence ~ILY² adv., ~INESS n. [f. L *exemplāris* (as EXAMPLE, see -ARY²)]

ĕxĕm'plĭfӯ (-gz-), v.t. Illustrate by example; be an example of; make attested copy of (document) under official seal. So ~FICA'TION n. [f. med. L *exemplificāre* (EXAMPLE, -FY)]

ĕxĕmpt¹ (-gz-), a. & n. 1. Free (*from* taxation, control, failings, etc.). 2. n. Person exempted, esp. from tax; ǁ one of four officers sometimes commanding Yeomen of Guard (now usu. *exon*). [F, f. L EX(*imĕre empt-* = *emĕre* take)]

ĕxĕmpt² (-gz-), v.t. Free *from* (as prec.). So ĕxĕmp'tion (-gz-) n. [f. L *exemptāre* (prec.)]

ĕxĕn'tĕrāte, v.t. Disembowel (only fig.). So ~A'TION n. [f. L EX*enterāre* (Gk *enteron* intestine), see -ATE³]

ĕxĕq'uātur (-er), n. Recognition of a country's consul by a foreign govern-

ment; temporal sovereign's authorization of bishop under Papal authority, or of publication of Papal bulls. [L, = he may perform]

ĕx'ĕquĭes (-kwĭz), n. pl. Funeral rites. [OF, f. L *exsequiae* f. EX(*sequi* follow.)]

ĕx'ercĭse (-z), n. Employment (of organ, faculty, power, right); practice (of virtues, profession, functions, religious rites); exertion of muscles, limbs, etc., esp. for health's sake; bodily, mental, or spiritual training; task set for this purpose; (pl.) military drill, athletics, etc.; academical declamation etc. required for degree; composition set to pupils; act of worship. [f. OF *exercice* f. L *exercitium* f. *exercēre* -*cit-* = *arcēre* restrain) keep at work)]

ĕx'ercĭse (-z), v.t. & i. Employ (faculty, powers of; perplex, worry; discharge (functions); take, give (horse etc.), exercise. Hence ~ABLE a. [f. prec.]

ĕxercĭtā'tion (-gz-), n. Practice, training; literary or oratorical exercise. [f. L *exercitātiō* f. *exercitāre* frequent. as EXER-CISE¹, -ATION]

ĕx'ert⁀gue (-g; *also* ĕgzĕrg'), n. Small space usu. on reverse of coin or medal, below principal device; inscription there, Hence ĕxĕrg'uᴀᴸ (-gl) a. [F, prob. f. Gk EX-*ergon* work]

ĕxĕrt' (-gz-), v.t. Exercise, bring to bear (quality, force, influence); ~ *oneself*, strive (*to do, for* object). So ĕxĕr'tion n. (-gz-). [f. L EX(*serere sert-* bind) put forth]

Ex'ĕter Hall (ĕ- hawl), n. Building in Strand formerly used for May meetings etc. (see MAY.)

ĕxhāle', v.t. & i. Give off (fumes etc., also fig.) in vapour; be thus given off, evaporate, (*from, out of*); (Path., of animal fluids) pass off in minute quantities through blood-vessel etc.; breathe out (life, soul, words, etc.); get rid of (anger etc.) as if by blowing. [f. F *exhaler* f. L EX(*halāre* breathe)]

ĕxhalā'tion (ĕksĕ-), n. Evaporation; puff of breath; short burst (*of* anger etc.); mist, vapour; effluvium. [f. L *exhalātiō*]

ĕxhaust' (ĭgzaw-), v.t. Draw off (fumes etc.); empty (vessel of contents); consume or use up; expend the whole of; treat (subject) exhaustively; (of steam, or internal-combustion engines) expulsion or exit of motive fluid, steam, or gaseous products of combustion from cylinder after completion of power stroke by piston; similar exit of spent fluid or

gases from turbine; ~-*pipe* etc. (for this); process of exhausting vessel of air; (apparatus for) production of outward current of air by creating partial vacuum. [f. foll.]

exhaust'² (igzaw-), v.t. Draw off (air, also fig.); consume entirely; use, account for, the whole of; empty (vessel) of contents; say, find out, all that is worth knowing of (subject); drain (person, kingdom, etc.) of strength, resources, etc. esp. in p.p.; tire out. Hence ~IBIL'ITY a., ~IBLE a. [f. L EX(*haurire haust-* draw)]

exhaus'tion (igzaws'chon), n. Exhausting (in all senses); total loss of strength; arrival at a conclusion by eliminating alternatives. [-ION]

exhaus'tive (igzaw-), a. Tending to exhaust esp. a subject; comprehensive. Hence ~LY² (-vl) adv., ~NESS (-vn-) n. [-IVE]

exhib'it¹ (igzi-), n. Document or thing produced in lawcourt & referred to in written evidence; thing, collection of things, sent by person, firm, etc., to an exhibition; showing, display. [f. L neut. p.p. as foll.]

exhib'it² (igzi-), v.t. Show, display; submit for consideration; manifest (quality); show publicly (for amusement, ~; competition, etc.). So ~OR² n., ~ORY a. [f. L EX(*hibēre hibit-* = *habēre* hold)]

exhibi'tion (ĕksi-), n. 1. Showing, display, (of thing); *make an ~ of* oneself, behave so as to excite contempt; public display of works of art, etc.; *the Great E~*, first on large scale, London, 1851. 2. ||Fixed sum given to student for term of years from funds of school, college, etc., whence ||~ER¹ (ĕksĭbĭsh'ŏn-) n. (f. OF *exhibicion* f. LL *exhibitionem* (as prec., see -ION)) last use f. prec. in obs. sense ' provide maintenance']

exhibi'tionism (ĕksĭbĭsh'ŏn-), n. Tendency towards display or extravagant behaviour; (Path.) perverted mental condition characterized by indecent exposure of the person. [-ISM]

exhil'ariāte (igzi-), v.t. Enliven, gladden, (person, spirits). So ~ANT²(2) a. & n., ~A'TION n., ~ātive a., (igzi-). [f. L EX(*hilarare* f. *hilaris* cheerful), see -ATE³]

exhort' (igzŏrt'), v.t. Admonish earnestly; urge (person *to* do, *to* a course); advocate (reform etc.). So ~ative, ~atory, aa., (igzŏrt'-). [f. L EX(*hortari*, see HORTATORY)]

exhorta'tion (ĕksŏr-), n. Exhorting; formal, liturgical, address. [f. L *exhortatio* (prec., see -ATION)]

exhume' (-z), v.t. Dig out, unearth, (lit. & fig.). So ~A'TION n. [f. F *exhumer* f. L EX(*humare* f. *humus* ground)]

ex'igence, -cy, (-sĭ), nn. Urgent need; emergency. [F(-*ce*), f. L *exigentia* (foll., -ENCY)]

ex'igent, a. Urgent, pressing; requiring much, exacting; ~ *of*, demanding. [f. L EX(*igere* = *agere* drive), see -ENT]

ex'igible, a. That may be demanded or exacted (*against, from*, person). [as prec. +-BLE]

exig'uous, a. Scanty, small. Hence or cogn. **exigu'ITY,** ~NESS, nn. [f. L *exiguus* f. *exigere* (as prec.)/+-OUS]

ex'ile¹, n. Penal banishment; long absence from one's country (also fig.). [f. OF *exil* f. L EX(*silium* (*salire* leap))]

ex'ile² n. Banished person (lit. & fig.). [perh. f. prec.; L has *exsul* (as prec.)]

ex'ile² v.t. Banish (person *from*; lit. & fig.). [f. OF *exilier* f. LL *exsiliare* (as EXILE¹)]

exil'ian, a. Of the Jews' exile in Babylon. So ~IC a. [f. L as EXILE¹+-IAN]

exil'ity, n. (pedant.) Thinness; subtlety. [f. L *exilitas* (*exilis* thin, etym. dub., see -TY)]

exist' (-gz-), v.i. Have being in the domain of reality; have being under specified conditions; ~ *as* (in the form of); (of circumstances etc.) occur, be found; live; continue in being. [f. F *exister* f. L EX(*sistere* redupl. f. *stare* stand)]

exis'tence (-gz-), n. Being, existing, esp. *in* ~; life, as *a wretched, precarious,* ~; mode of existing; existing thing; all that exists. So **exisentʹTIAL** (-gz-; -shl) a. [OF, f. med. L *existentia* (as prec., see -ENCE)]

exis'tent (-gz-), a. Existing, actual, current. [-ENT]

ex'it¹, n. Departure of player from stage (also fig.); death; going out or forth; liberty to do this; passage to go out by. [f. L *exitus* -*us* going out (as foll.); partly also from foll.]

ex'it², v.i. (Stage direction) — goes off stage, as *E~ Macbeth* (also fig.). [3rd sing. pres. of L EX(*ire it-* go)]

ex-lib'ris, n. Book-plate, label with arms, crest, etc., & owner's name pasted into book. [L *ex libris* from library (of So-&-so)]

ex'o- in comb. = Gk *exō* outside as:~*dĕrm*, outer layer of blastoderm; ~*gamous*, ~*gamy*, (-ŏg-²), (of, following) custom compelling man to marry outside his own tribe; ~*gen* n., ~*genous* (-ŏj²) a., = DICO-TYLEDON(ous), w. ref. to external growth of stem; ~*pāthʹic*, (of disease) originating outside the body; ~*phagous*, ~*phagy*, (-ŏf²), not eating members of one's own tribe; ~*plasm*, outermost layer of protoplasm; ~*skelʹeton*, external integument, bony or leathery; ~*smōsʹis*, passage of a fluid outwards through a porous septum.

ex'odus, n. Departure, going forth, (esp. of body of emigrants); departure of Israelites from Egypt; (*E~*) book of O.T. relating this. [L, f. Gk EX*ODOS* (*hodos* way)]

ex offi'cio (-shĭō), adv. & a. In virtue of one's office, as ~ *members of committee*. [L]

||**ex'on,** n. See EXEMPT¹. [repr. F pron.]

exŏn'er|āte (-gz-), v.t. Exculpate; free (person) *from* (blame etc.); release (person from duty etc.). Hence or cogn. ~Ā'TION n., ~ĀTIVE a., (-gz-). [f. L EX(*onerāre* f. *onus -eris* burden), see -ATE³]

exŏph'thal'm|us, -ŏs, n. Protrusion of eyeball. Hence ~IC a. [f. Gk EX(*ophthal-mos* eye) adj.]

exŏrb'itant (-gz-), a. Grossly excessive (of price, demand, ambition, person). Hence ~ANCE n., ~ANTLY² adv., (-gz-). [f. L EX(*orbitāre* go out of the wheel-track (ORBIT), -ANT]

ĕx'orcize, a. & n. Expel (evil spirit *from, out of*), person or place) by invocation or use of holy name; clear (person, place, of evil spirits). So ~ISM⁴, ~IST⁴, nn. [f. LL *exorcizāre* f. Gk EXORCIZO (*horkos* oath)]

ĕx'ord'ium, n. (pl. *-iums, -ia*). Beginning, esp. of discourse or treatise. Hence ~AL a., ~ALLY² adv. [f. LL f. Gk *exōrtikós* compar., see EXO-, -IC]

exŏt'ic (-gz-), a. & n. 1. (Of plants, words, fashions) introduced from abroad. 2. n. ~ plant (also fig.). [f. L f. Gk *exōtikos*]

ĕxŏter'ic, a. & n. Of doctrines, modes of speech, etc., intelligible to outsiders (cf. ESOTERIC); (of disciples) not admitted to esoteric teaching; commonplace, ordinary, popular; (n. pl.) ~ doctrines or treatises. Hence ~AL a., ~ALLY² adv. [f. L f. Gk *exōterikós* (*exōterō* compar., see EXO-, -IC)]

expand' (-ē-), v.t. & i. Spread out flat (t. & i.); write out, in full (what is condensed or abbreviated, algebraical expression, etc.); develop (t. & i.); swell, dilate, increase in bulk, (t. & i.); become genial, throw off reserve; ~*ed metal*, sheet metal slit and stretched into a lattice, used (esp.) to reinforce concrete. So expansibil'ity n., expan'sible a. [f. L EX(*pandĕre pans-* spread)]

expanse', n. Wide area or extent; expansion. [as prec.]

expan'sile, a. (Capable) of expansion. [-IL]

expan'sion (-shn), n. Expanding; ~ (Commerce) of the currency; ~ (increase) of transactions; ~ (increase) n.; increase in bulk of steam in cylinder or engine; *triple-~ engine* (in which steam passes through 3 cylinders). [f. LL *expansio* (prec., -ION)]

expan'sive, a. Able, tending to expand (t. & i.); extensive; comprehensive; (of persons, feelings, speech) effusive. Hence ~LY² adv., ~NESS (-vi-), ~VENESS (-vi-), nn. [as prec., -IVE]

ĕx parte', adv. & a. (Law, & transl.). On, in the interests of, one side only; (adj., *ex-parte*) made or said thus, as *an ex-parte statement.* [L]

ĕx'patriāte (-sht-), v.t. Speak, write, copiously (*on* subject); wander unrestrained (usu. fig.). [L]

---

exŏn'er|āte n.; ~atory (-sha-) a. [f. L EX(*spatiāri* from *spatium* SPACE), -ATE³]

ĕxpā'triāte, v.t. Banish (reflexc), emigrate; (Law of Nations, refl.) renounce citizenship. Hence ~A'TION n. [f. LL EX(*patriāre* f. *patria* native land), see -ATE³]

expect' (-ē-), v.t. Look forward to, regard as likely, as *I ~ a storm, ~ to see him, ~ him to come;* ~ (*that*) *he will come, ~ him next week, don't ~ me, ~ payment today, not so bad as I ~ed (it to be), just what I ~ed of him; shall not ~ you till I etc., see you, leave you to arrive when you please; look for as due, as *I ~ you to be punctual, do you ~ pay-ment for this?;* (colloq.) think, suppose, (*that*); (abs.) *she is ~ing (colloq.), she is pregnant.* [f. L EX(*spectāre* look, freq. of *specere see*)]

expec'tancy, n. State of expectation; prospect, esp. of future possession; pro-spective chance (*of*). [f. L f. *expectāntia*]

expec'tant, a. & n. 1. Expecting (*of or* abs.; ~ *mother*, pregnant woman); having the prospect, in normal course, of posses-sion, office, etc.; characterized by waiting for events, esp. (Med.) ~ *method*. [f. L *expectans*; see -ANT]

expec'tā'tion, n. Awaiting; anticipation, as *beyond, contrary to, ~;* ground for expecting (*of*); (pl.) prospects of inheri-tance; thing expected; ~ *of LIFE;* proba-bility of a thing's happening. [f. L *expectatio* (as prec., see -ATION)]

expec'tative, a. Of reversion of benefices, reversionary. [f. LL *expectatīva* (prec., -ATIVE)]

expec'torant, a. & n. (Medicine) that promotes expectoration. [as foll., see -ANT]

expec'tor|āte, v.t. Eject (phlegm etc.) from chest or lungs by coughing or spit-ting; (abs.) spit. Hence ~A'TION n. [f. L EX(*pectorāre* relieve the mind (*pectus -oris* breast))]

expē'dient, a. & n. 1. (Usu. predic.) advantageous, suitable, as *do whatever is ~; it is ~ that he should go;* politic rather than just. 2. n. Contrivance, device, Hence or cogn. expē'dience, -ENCY, nn., ~LY² adv. [f. F *ex-pédient* (as foll., see -ENT]

ĕx'pedīte, v.t. Assist the progress of (measure, process, etc.); dispatch (busi-ness). [f. L *expedīte -dīt* lit. free feet of (*pes pedis* foot)]

ĕxpedī'tion, n. Warlike enterprise; journey, voyage, for definite purpose; men, fleet, sent on this; promptness, speed. Hence ~ARY¹ a., ~IST(?) n., (-shon). [f. L *expedītio* (as prec., see -ION)]

ĕxpedī'tious (-shus), a. Doing or done speedily; suited for speedy performance.

Hence ~LY² adv., ~NESS n., (-shus-). [f. expel', v.t. (-ll-). Eject (person from place, bullet from gun, etc.) by force; turn out (person from a community, school, etc.; also w. from omitted was ~ed the school). Hence ~lENT a. [f. L EX(pellere puls- drive)]

expend', v.t. Spend (money, care, time, on object, in doing; use up; (Naut.) wind (spare rope) round spar etc. [f. L EX(pendĕre pens- weigh)]

expen'diture, n. Laying out (of money etc.); consuming; amount expended. [as prec. (irreg. p.p. penditus), see -URE]

expense', n. Expenditure; cost; (pl.) outlay in execution of commission etc., reimbursement of this, as he paid my ~s, offered me £10 @ ~s: at the ~ (cost) of, esp. (fig.) by bringing discredit etc. on, as you defend his veracity at the ~ of his understanding, if what he says is true he is a fool; a laugh at his ~ (at him). [AF, f. LL expensa orig. fem. p.p. (as EXPEND)]

expen'sive, a. Costly. Hence ~LY² (-vl-) adv., ~NESS (-vn-) n. [EXPEND, -IVE]

experience¹, n. Actual observation of facts or events; knowledge resulting from this, whence exper'ienced² (-st) a.; event that affects one, as an unpleasant ~; fact, process, of being so affected, as I learnt by ~; (usu. pl.) state, phase, of religious emotion; ~ table, table showing expectation of life at different ages etc. compiled from the ~ of life-assurance offices. [f. F expérience f. L experientia f. EX(perīrī perit- go through), see -ENCE]

experience², v.t. Meet with, feel, undergo, (pleasure, treatment, face, etc.); learn, find, (that, how, etc.). [f. prec.]

experien'tial (-shal), a. Of experience; ~ philosophy (treating all knowledge as based on experience), whence ~ISM, ~IST, ISM, ~IST, nn.; tentative; used in experiments. Hence ~ISE(2) v.i., ~LY² adv. nn., (-shal-). Hence ~LY² (-shal-) adv. [f. L as EXPERIENCE¹, see -AL]

exper'iment¹, n. Test, trial, (of); procedure adopted on chance of its succeeding or for testing hypothesis etc. [OF, f. L experimentum (as prec., see -MENT)]

exper'iment², v.i. Make experiment (on, with). Hence ~A'TION n. [prec.]

experimen'tal, a. Based on experience, not authority or conjecture; based on experiment, as ~ philosophy, whence ~ ISM, ~IST, nn.; tentative; used in experiments. Hence ~LY² adv., ~ISM, ~IST, nn. [f. L as EXPERIENCE¹]

expert'¹, a. Trained by practice, skilful, (at, in). Hence ~LY² adv., ~NESS n. [OF, f. L as EXPERIENCE¹]

ex'pert², n. Person having special skill or knowledge (at, in), as mining ~, (attrib.) ~ evidence. [F (prec. as n.)]

exper'tō crēdĕ', sent. You may take my word for it, because I have tried. [L, =believe one who has tried]

ex'piāte, v.t. Pay the penalty of, make amends for, (sin). So ~ABLE, ~ATORY, aa., ~A'TION, ~ATOR⁴, nn. [f. L EX(piāre seek to appease f. pius devout), -ATE²]

expirā'tion (-per-), n. Breathing out (of air etc.); termination (of period, truce, etc.). [f. L expiratio (as foll., see -ATION]

expīre', v.t. & i. Breathe out (air from lungs, or abs.), whence expīr'atory a.; die; (of fire etc.) die out; (of period) come to an end; (of law, patent, truce, etc.) become void, reach its term; (of title etc.) become extinct. [f. F expirer f. L EX(spīrare breathe)]

expīr'y, n. Termination (of period, truce, etc.). [f. prec. + -Y¹]

|| expis'cāte, v.t. (Sc.). Find by scrutiny (meaning, that, how, etc.). [f. L expiscari (EX-, piscari to fish)]

explain', v.t. Make known in detail (thing, that, how, etc.); make intelligible (meaning, difficulty, etc., also abs.); account for (conduct etc.); ~ away, modify, do away with, (esp. offensive language) by explanation; ~ oneself, make one's meaning clear, (also) give an account of one's motives or conduct. Hence ~ABLE a. [f. L EX(planare f. planus flat)]

explana'tion, n. Explaining, esp. with view to mutual understanding or reconciliation; statement, circumstance, that explains. [f. L explanatio (as prec., see -ATION)]

explan'atory, a. Serving, meant, to explain. Hence ~LY² adv. [as EXPLAIN, see -ORY]

explē'tive (or iksplē⁴), a. & n. 1. Serving to fill out (esp. sentence, metrical line, etc.). 2. n. ~ thing, word, etc., esp. oath or meaningless exclamation. [f. L expletivus f. EX(plēre fill), -IVE]

ex'plicāte, v.t. Develop (notion, principle, etc.), whence ~A'TION n.; (arch.) explain, whence ~ABLE, ~ĀTIVE, ~ĀTORY, aa. [f. L EX(plicare plicāt- or plicĭt- fold) unfold, see -ATE³]

ex'plicit², a. Here ends (formerly written at end of book). [med. L; prob. abbr. of p.p. as prec., but treated as 3rd sing.]

expli'cit², a. Stated in detail, leaving nothing merely implied; definite; (of persons) outspoken; ~ faith, acceptance of doctrine with clear understanding of all it involves (cf. IMPLICIT). Hence ~LY² adv., ~NESS n. [f. L explicite (as EXPLICATE)]

explōde', v.t. & i. Expose, bring into disrepute, (theory, fallacy, etc.); (of gas, gunpowder, boiler, etc.) go off with loud noise; cause (these) to do this; magneto ~r, hand-operated portable electrical apparatus for detonating high-explosive charges. [f. L EX(ploder eplos- = plaudere clap) hiss off stage]

ex'ploit¹, n. Brilliant achievement. [f. OF esploit(e) f. L neut. & fem. p.p. as EXPLICATE]

exploit'², v.t. Work, turn to account, (mine etc.); utilize (person etc.) for one's

own ends. Hence or cogn. ~AGE, éxploità'TION, nn. [f. F *exploiture frequent. as prec.

explŏŕe´, v.t. Inquire into; examine (wound) by touch; examine (country etc.) by going through it. Hence or cogn. EXPLORA'TION, ~ER¹, nn., ~ATIVE, ~a-TORY, aa. [f. F explorer f. L explorare, =make flow f. pluere flow) search out, reconnoitre.]

explō'sion (-zhn), n. Going off with loud noise; such noise; outbreak (of anger etc.). [f. L explosio (as EXPLODE, see -ION]

explō'sive, a. & n. 1. Tending to eject something with loud noise (of consonant sound) produced by explosion of breath, stopped; tending to explode or cause explosion (lit. & fig.). 2. n. ~ agent or material, ~ letter; high ~, kinds having very violent shattering effect & used not as propellents but in shells, bombs, etc. Hence ~LY² (-vi-) adv., ~NESS (-vi-) n. [as EXPLODE, see -IVE]

expō´nent, a. & n. (Person, thing) that sets forth or interprets; executant (of music etc.); type, representative; (Alg.) Index, symbol indicating what power of a factor is to be taken, whence ex-ponēn'tial (-shal) a. [f. L EX(ponere posi-, put), see -ENT]

expŏŕt¹, v.t. Send out (goods) to another country. Hence or cogn. ~ABLE a., ~ATION n. [f. L EX(portare carry)]

ex'pŏrt², n. Exported article; (usu. pl.) amount exported; exportation; ~ duty. [f. prec.]

expōse' (-z), v.t. Leave (person, thing unprotected (esp. from weather); sub-ject to (risk etc.); (Photog.) subject (film perish; (p.p.) open to (the East etc.); exhibit, display; put up for sale; disclose (secret, project, etc.); unmask (villain, villainy). [f. F EX(poser, see COMPOSE)]

exposé (ěkspōz'ā), n. Statement of facts; showing up (of discreditable thing). [F, p.p. as prec.]

exposi´tion (-z-), n. Setting forth, de-scription; explanation; commentary; = EXPOSURE; exhibition of goods etc. [F, f. L EX(positionem (as prec., see -ION]

expos'itive (-z-), a. Descriptive; ex-planatory. So ~OR² n., ~ORY a., (-z-). [f. L expositivus (as prec., see -IVE]

ex post făc'tō, a. Acting retrospectively, as ~ law. [L, = from what is made (i.e. enacted) afterwards]

expŏs'tulate, v.i. Make friendly remon-strance; remonstrate (with person about, for, on). Hence or cogn. ~ATION n., ~atory a. [f. L EX(postulare POSTULATE)]

expō'sure (-zher), n. Exposing, being exposed, (to air, cold, danger, etc.); abandoning (of child); display, esp. of goods for sale; unmasking of imposture etc.; aspect, as southern ~; (Photog.)

action of exposing plate or film to the light, duration of this action. [-URE]

expound', v.t. Set forth in detail (doc-trine etc.); explain, interpret, (esp. Scripture). [ME expounen f. OF espondre (as EXPONENT)]

expréss´³, a., adv., & n. 1. (Of likeness) exact; definitely stated, not merely implied; done, made, sent, for special purpose; ∥ ~ train (fast, stopping at few intermediate stations); ~ rifle (discharg-ing bullet with high initial velocity & low trajectory); ~ rifle). 2. adv. ~ delivery (by special postal messenger). 2. adv. With speed, by ~ messenger or train. 3. n. ~ train, messen-ger, rifle. Hence ~LY² adv. [f. F exprès, -esse (as foll.]

expréss´¹, v.t. Squeeze out (juice, air, from, out of); emit, exude; represent by symbols, as (Math.) ~ (quantity) in terms of (another); reveal, betoken, (feelings, qualities); put (thought) into words; ~ oneself, say what one means (strongly etc., on subject, well, aptly, etc.). Hence ~IBLE a. [f. OF EX(presser PRESS²]

expréssion (-shn), n. Expressing (in all senses); wording, diction, word, phrase; (Alg.) collection of symbols expressing a quantity; aspect (of face), intonation (of voice), whence ~LESS (-shn-) a.; (Art) mode of expressing character etc., whence ~IST(2) (-shon-) n.; (Mus.) execution that expresses the feeling of a passage, ~mark, sign, word, indicating~required, ~stop (in harmonium), producing~by varied air-pressure). [f. F L expressionem f. EX(primere = premere PRESS², see -ION]

expréssional (-shon-), a. Of verbal, facial, or artistic expression. [-AL]

expréssionism (-shon-), n. Modern ten-dency among painters, dramatic authors, etc., to subordinate realism to the sym-bolic or stylistic expression of the artist's or character's inner experience; (Mus.) tendency to discard rules and conventions and thus obtain complete freedom for composer's self-expression (as in Schön-berg). [-ISM]

expréss'ive, a. Serving to express (~ of motion etc.); (of word, gesture, etc.) significant. Hence ~LY² (-vi-) adv., ~NESS (-vi-) n. [F (-if, -ive), as EXPRES-SION, see -IVE]

exprobrā'tion, n. Reproachful language. [f. L exprobratio f. EX(probrare f. probrum shameful deed), see -ATION]

exprōp'riāte, v.t. Dispossess (from estate etc.); take away (property). So ~A'TION n. [f. L L EX(propriare f. pro-prium property), see PROPER &c -ATE³]

expŭl'sion (-shon), n. Expelling. So ~IVE a. & n. (med.). [f. L expulsio (as EXPEL, see -ION]

expŭnge' (-j), v.t. Erase, omit, (name from list, passage from book, etc.). So expŭnc'-tion n. [f. L EX(pungere punct- prick]

ex′purgāte (-per-), v.t. Purify (book etc.) by removing objectionable matter; clear away (such matter). Hence or cogn. ~A′TION, ~ātor² nn., expurgatōr′IAL, expūrg′atory, aa. [f. L EX(purgare cleanse). -ATE³]

ex′quisite (-z-), a. & n. 1. Of consummate excellence or beauty; acute (~ pain, pleasure); keen (~ sensibility etc.). 2. n. Coxcomb, fop. Hence ~LY² (-tl-) adv., ~NESS (-tn-) n. [f. L EX(quirere quisit- = quaerere seek)]

exsang′uinate (-nggwin-), v.t. Drain of blood. [f. L EX(sanguinare f. sanguis -inis blood), see -ATE¹]

exsang′uine (-nggwin-), a. Lacking blood. [EX-]

exscind′, v.t. Cut out, excise, (lit. & fig.). [f. L EX(scindere cut)]

exsert′, v.t. (biol.). Put forth. [= EXERT]
‖ ex-ser′vice, a. & n. That has been but is no longer in one of the fighting services. [EX-(8)]

ex′siccāte, v.t. Dry up; drain dry. [f. L EX(siccare f. siccus dry)]

ex′tant (or ikstănt′), a. Still existing (esp. of documents etc.). [f. L EX(stare stand), see -ANT]

extasy. See ECSTASY.

extĕm′por|e, adv. & a. (Spoken, done) without preparation; off-hand; speak ~e (without notes). Hence or cogn. ~AN′EOUS, ~ARY¹, aa., ~AN′EOUSLY², ~arily², advv., ~an′eousness n. [L ex tempore from the time]

extĕm′poriz|e, v.t. & i. Compose, produce, extempore; (intr.) speak extempore. Hence ~A′TION n. [f. prec. +-IZE]

extĕnd′, v.t. & i. Lay out (esp. body, limbs, etc.) at full length; write out (shorthand etc.) at full length; (intr. & refl.) reach (to point, over, across, etc., space); cause to do this; prolong (period); enlarge (scope, meaning of word, etc.); (Mil., of line etc.) spread out into open order with regular intervals between men (trans., cause to ~); (Sport. sl.) tax powers of (horse, athlete) to the utmost (usu. pass.); stretch forth (hand, arm); accord (kindness, patronage, to); (Law) value (land etc.), seize (land etc.) for debt. Hence or cogn. extĕnsibĭl′ITY n., extĕn′sible, extĕn′sible, aa. [f. L EX(tendere tens- or tent- stretch)]

extĕn′sile, a. Capable of being stretched out or protruded. [as prec, see -ILE]

extĕn′sion (-shn), n. Extending (in all senses exc. Law); extent, range; prolongation; enlargement; additional part (of railway, plan, theory, etc.); word(s) amplifying subject or predicate; University E~, admission of non-resident students to some forms of Univ. teaching & examination. [f. L extentio, -sio, (as prec, see -ION)]

extĕn′sive, a. (Of space, purchase, operation, etc.) large; far-reaching, com-

prehensive; (of agricultural production etc.) depending on extension of area (cf. INTENSIVE). Hence ~LY² (-vl-) adv., ~NESS (-vn-) n. [f. LL extensivus (as prec, see -IVE]

extĕn′sor, n. ~ (muscle), one that straightens out part of the body. [LL, as prec, -OR²]

extĕnt′, n. Space over which a thing extends; width of application; scope, as to a great ~, to the full ~ of his power; large space, as a vast ~ of marsh; (Law) valuation (of land etc.); seizure, writ for seizure, (of land etc.). [f. AF estente p.p. of estendre (as EXTEND)]

extĕn′uāte, v.t. Lessen seeming magnitude of (guilt, offence) by partial excuse, as we must not ~e, nothing can ~e, his baseness, whence ~ORY a.; (improp.) lessen seeming guilt of, as do not ~e yourself, his conduct; (arch.) make thin or weak. Hence extĕnūa′TION n. [f. L EX(tenuare f. tenuis thin). -ATE³]

extēr′ior, a. & n. 1. Outer; situated or coming from without; ~ angle, that between side of rectilineal figure & adjacent side produced. 2. n. Outward aspect or demeanour. Hence ~ITY (-ŏ′r-) n., ~LY² adv. [L, compar. of exterus outside]

extēr′ioriz|e, v.t. Realize (conception) in outward form; attribute external existence to. Hence ~A′TION n. [-IZE]

extēr′min|āte, v.t. Root out (species, race, sect, opinion). Hence or cogn. ~A′TION, ~ātor² nn., ~ātorY a. [f. L EX(terminare TERMINUS). -ATE³]

extern′al, a. & n. 1. Situated outside; (of remedies etc.) applied to the outside of the body; (Theol.) consisting in outward acts, whence ~ISM(2) n.; belonging to the world of phenomena (~ world), outside the conscious subject; ~ evidence (derived from source independent of the thing discussed). 2. n. pl. Outward features or aspect, ~ circumstances, non-essentials. Hence extĕrnăl′ITY n., ~LY² adv. [f. L externus outward +-AL]

extĕrn′aliz|e, v.t. Give, attribute, external existence to. Hence ~A′TION n. [-IZE]

extĕrritōr′ial, a. (Of ambassadors etc.) free from jurisdiction of the territory in which one resides. So ~ITY (-ăl-) n. [EX-]

extinct′, a. (Of fire etc.) no longer burning; (of volcano) that has ceased eruption; (of life, hope, etc.) quenched; (of family, class, species) that has died out; (of office etc.) obsolete; (of title of nobility) having no qualified claimant. [f. L EX(stinguere stinct- quench)]

extinc′tion, n. Extinguishing; making, being, becoming, extinct; wiping out (of debt); annihilation. So ~IVE a. [f. L extinctio (as prec, see -ION)]

exting′uish, v.t. Put out, quench, (light, hope, life, faculties);

eclipse, obscure, (person) by superior brilliancy; reduce (opponent) to silence; destroy; wipe out (debt); annihilate. Hence ~ABLE a., ~MENT n. [as EXTINCT, see -ISH²]

exting'uisher (-nggw-), n. In vbl senses; esp. hollow conical cap for putting out candle. [-ER¹]

ex'tirpate, v.t. Root out, destroy, (tree, weed, species, nation, tumour, heresy, etc.). So ~A'TION, ~ATOR², nn. [f. L EXstirpare (stirps stem), see -ATE³]

extôl', v.t. (-ll-). Praise enthusiastically (~ him to the skies). [f. L EX(tollere raise)]

extôrt', v.t. Obtain (money, promise, etc.) by violence, intimidation, importunity, inference, from words, data). [f. L extorquere tort- twist]

extôr'tion, n. Extorting, esp. of money; illegal exaction. Hence ex-/tôr'tive a. [f. L EX(torquere tort- twist)]

extôr'tionate (-shon-), a. Using (given to, extortion; (of prices etc.) exorbitant. [-ATE²]

ex'tra, a., adv., & n. 1. Additional; larger than its name indicates, as ~ foolscap, octavo; of superior quality, as ~ calf. 2. adv. More than usually, as ~ strong; additionally; || ~-special (latest) edition (of evening paper). 3. n. ~ thing, one for which ~ charge is made, as dancing is an ~; (Crick.) run not scored off bat; additional (score); thing not included in the essence of a thing; additional (score); temporarily (for a minor part or to the one of a crowd. [prob. for EXTRAORDINARY, perh. f. F]

ex'tra- in comb. = L extra in senses 'situated outside of a thing', 'not coming within its scope'; chiefly in wds f. med. L or mod. L (L has only extra-ordinarius), as: ~atmospheric, of the space beyond the atmosphere; ~cos'mical, acting outside the universe; ~crân'ial, outside the skull; ~essen'tial, not belonging to the essence of a thing; ~judi'cial, not made in court; ~mun'dane, outside of our world or of the universe; ~mur'al, outside the walls or boundaries (of town or city), (of lecturers etc.) from outside a university; ~offi'cial, not pertaining to an office; ~parôch'ial, outside the parish; ~phys'ical, not concerned with, the not subject to physical laws; ~spec'tral, lying outside the visible spectrum; ~terres'trial, outside the earth or its atmosphere; ~territôr'ial(ity), = EXTRATERRITORIAL(ITY).

extra'ct¹, n. The tough or viscid matter got by treating a substance with solvents & then evaporating them; preparation containing the active principle of a substance in concentrated form; passage from book etc. [as foll.]

extra'ct², v.t. Copy out (passage in book etc.); make extracts from (book etc.);

take out by force (teeth, anything firmly fixed); draw forth (money, admission, etc.), against person's will; obtain (juices etc.) by suction, pressure, etc.; derive (pleasure etc. from); deduce (principle etc. from); (Math.) find (root of a number). Hence extrác'table a., ex-trác'tor² n. [f. L EX(trahere tract- draw)]

extrac'tion, n. Extracting; lineage (of Indian ~); = rude, proportion of total weight of unground wheat which is converted into flour, & not into bran or sharps, expressed as a percentage of weight unground. [f. med. L extrac-tionem (prec., -ION)]

extrác'tive, a., & n. (of extract); ~ industries (concerned with obtaining natural productions).

extra'dite, v.t. Give up (fugitive foreign criminal) to the proper authorities; obtain the extradition of. [back formation f. foll.]

extradi'table, a. Liable to, (of crime) warranting, extradition. [f. foll. +-ABLE]

extradi'tion, n. Delivery of fugitive foreign to proper authorities; (Psych.) localizing of sensation at distance from the centre of sensation. [F EX-, see TRADITION]

extrad'ôs, n. Upper or outer curve of arch. [F EXTRA(dos back f. L dorsum)]

extrâ'neous, a. Of external origin; foreign to (object to which it is attached); not belonging (to matter in hand, class). Hence ~LY² adv., ~NESS n. [f. L extraneus (extra outside) +-OUS]

extraôrd'inarily (-trôr-, -traör-), a., & n. Out of the usual course; (of officials etc.) additional, specially employed; envoy ~, diplomatic minister of second class rank-ing next to ambassador; exceptional, surprising; unusually great; (n. pl.) extra allowances to troops (arch.). Hence ~liy² adv., ~iNESS n. [f. L extraordinarius (extra ordinem outside the usual order, -ARY)]

extrapola'tion, n. (math.) The calcula-tion from known terms of a series of other terms which lie outside the range of known terms (also fig.). [EXTRA-+(INTER)-POLATION]

extrav'agance, n. Being extravagant; absurd statement or action. [F (foll. -ANCE)]

extrav'agant, a. Immoderate; exceed-ing the bounds of reason; profuse; waste-ful; (of price etc.) exorbitant. Hence ~LY² adv. [f. L EXTRA(vagari wander, see -ANT)]

extrav'aganza, n. Fantastic composition (literary, musical, dramatic, language, or behaviour. [f. It. estravaganza wander, see -ANT]

extrav'agate, v.i. (rare). Wander away (from right course, into error etc.); exceed due bounds. [as EXTRAVAGANT, see -ATE³]

extráv'asăte, v.t. & i. Force out (fluid) from its proper vessel; flow out. Hence **extravasA'TION** n. [EXTRA-, L *vas* vessel, -ATE³]

extrēme', a. & n. **1.** Outermost, farthest from centre, situated at either end; *divided in*, & *meant ratio* (the whole being to one part as that part to the other); utmost; last, as (R.-C. Ch.) ~ *unction*, anointing by priest of dying person; reaching a high degree, as ~ *old age, in* ~ *danger*; *an* ~ *case* (having some characteristic in the utmost degree); (of actions, measures, etc.) going to great lengths, opp. to *moderate*; whence ~ly. **2.** n. Thing at either end of anything, esp. (pl.) things as remote or as different as possible, as ~*s meet*; (Logic) subject or predicate in proposition, major or minor term in syllogism; (Math.) first, last, term of ratio or series; *run to an* ~, *go to* ~*s*, *take an* ~ *course*. Hence ~LY³ (-ml-) adv., ~NESS (-mn-) n. [OF², f. L *extremus* superl. of *exterus* outward]

extrēm'ity, n. Extreme point, very end; *the* ~*ies*, hands & feet; extreme adversity, embarrassment, etc., as *driven to* ~*y, what can we do in this* ~*y?*; (usu. pl.) extreme measure(s). [f. F *extrémité* f. L *extremitatem* (prec., -TY)]

éx'tricăte, v.t. Disentangle, release, (person, thing, *from* confinement, difficulty); (Chem.) liberate (gas etc.) from state of combination. Hence ~ABLE a., ~A'TION n. [f. L EX(*tricare* f. *tricae* perplexities), -ATE³]

extrin'sic, a. Lying outside, not belonging, (*to*); operating from without; not inherent or essential. Hence~ICALLY adv. [f. F *extrinsèque* f. LL (adj.) f. L (adv.) *extrinsecus* (*exter* outside + -*in* local suf. + *secus* beside)]

extrōrse', a. (bot.). (Of anthers) turned outwards. [F, f. L *extrorsus* outwards (EXTRA-+ *versus* towards)]

ex'trovĕrt, n. (psych.). Person not given to introspection (chiefly in antithesis with INTROVERT n.). [f. L *extra* outside (w. assim. to INTRO-) + *vertĕre* turn, after *convert* n.]

extrude' (-ōō-), v.t. Thrust out (person, thing, *from*). Hence **extru'sion** (-ōōzhn) n., **extru'sive** (-ōō-) a. [f. L EX(*trudere trus-* thrust)]

exūb'eriant (-gz-), a. Luxuriantly prolific (lit. & fig.); growing luxuriantly; (of health, emotions, etc.) overflowing, abounding; (of persons, actions, etc.) effusive, overflowing with spirits; (of language) copious, lavish in ornament; abundant. Hence or cogn. ~ANCE n., ~antLY² adv., (-gz-). [f. L EX(*uberare* be fruitful *uber* fertile, cf. *über* udder), -ANT]

exūb'erăte (-gz-), v.i. Abound, overflow; indulge freely in. [as prec., see -ATE³]

exūde' ('gz), v.t. & i. Ooze out, give off (moisture etc.), like sweat. Hence or cogn. **exūdA'TION** n., **exūd'ative** (-gz-) a. [f. L EX(*sudare* sweat)]

exūlt' (-gz-), v.i. Rejoice exceedingly (*at, in*, thing, *to find* etc.); triumph (*over* person). Hence or cogn. **exūlt'ANT** a., (-gz-), **exūlta'TION**, nn., **exūlt'ANTLY** a., (-gz-), **exūlt'antly²** adv., (-gz-). [f. F *exulter* f. L EX(*sultare* = *saltare* frequent. of *salire* salt- leap)]

exūv'iae, n. pl. Animal's cast skin, shell, or covering, (recent or fossil, also fig.). Hence~AI a. [L, = animal's skin, spoils of enemy, f. EX(*uere* divest oneself of)]

exūv'iăte, v.t. & i. Shed (exuviae, also fig.), slough. Hence ~A'TION n. [prec., -ATE³]

éx vōt'ō, adv. & n. (Offering made) in pursuance of a vow. [L (as adv. phr.)]

eyas (ī'as), n. Young hawk taken from nest for training, or not yet completely trained. [orig. *nyas* f. F *niais* f. L +*nidiacem* (nom. -*ax*) f. *nidus* nest; for loss of *n*- cf. ADDER]

eye [ī], n. Organ of sight; iris of this, as *blue, brown,* ~*s*; region of the ~*s*, as BLACK¹ ~; ~ *of day*, sun; EVIL ~; *in the wind's* ~ (direction of the wind); (Mil.) ~*s right, left, front*, (turn them thus); *mind your* ~, take care; (contempt.) *pipe, put one's finger in, one's* ~, weep; *beam, mole, in one's* ~ (*Matt.* vii. 3); *for* ~, retaliation (*Exod.* xxi. 24); *clap, set,* ~*s on, behold; be all* ~*s*, watch intently; *up to the* ~*s*, deeply (engaged), as *up to the* ~*s in work, mortgaged up to the* ~*s; his* ~*s are bigger than his belly* (said of a person who has helped himself to more than he can eat); *made him open his* ~*s* (stare with astonishment); *open one's* ~*s to*, make him realize; *wipe the* ~ *of* (shooter), kill game he has missed; *all my* ~ (*d-? Betty Martin*), humbug, nonsense; *my* ~(*s*)!, int. expr. astonishment; *lose an* ~, (often) lose the sight of it; *if you had half an* ~ (were not wholly blind or dull); *saw with half an* ~ (at a glance); *the* NAKED ~; *have an* ~ *to*, have as one's object; *with an* ~ (*a view*) *to; keep an* ~ *on*, keep watch on (lit. & fig.); *have an* ~ *for* (a due sense of) proportion etc.; *in the* ~*s* (judgement) *of; in the* ~ (from the point of view) *of the law; in the mind's* ~, in anticipation or imagination; *see* ~ *to* ~, agree entirely (*with*); *view with a friendly, jealous,* ~, (with such feelings); *throw* DUST *in the* ~*s of; make* ~*s* (look amorously) *at; cast* SHEEP'*s* ~*s*; thing like an ~, as spot on peacock's tail, ~ *of needle* etc. (hole for thread etc.), *hook &* ~ (kind of fastening for dress), loop of cord or rope, leafbud of potato; BULL¹'s-~; *glass* ~ (artificial, of glass etc.); APPLE *of the* ~; ~'*ball*, pupil of the ~, within lids & socket; ~-*cup*, small glass for applying lotion etc. to ~-*bath*, bolt,

bar, with ~ at end for hook etc.; ~ bright (also euphrasy), plant formerly used to state fictitiously; (p.p.) celebrated in over ~; ~ weak ~s; ~ brow, fringe of hair over ~; ~ glass, lens for assisting detection by hand or by spring on nose (cf. SPECTACLE); ~ hole, hole containing ~, of hairs, on edge of ~ lid; ~ lid, upper or lower cover of ~, (fig.) hang on by the ~ lids, have only slight hold; ~ opener, enlightening or surprising circumstance; ~ piece, lens(es) at ~-end of telescope etc.; ~ servant (working properly only under employer's ~); ~ service (performed only thus); ~ shot (of); ~ sight, power, faculty, of seeing; ~ sore, ugly object, thing that offends the sight; ~ splice (made by turning up end of rope & interlacing its strands with those of upper part); ~ strings, muscles, nerves, tendons, of ~; ~ tooth (canine, just under or next to ~, in upper or lower jaw); ~ wash, lotion for ~, (sl.) bunkum, mere professions; ~ water, tears, lotion for ~; ~ witness, one who can bear witness from his own observation. Hence (-)EYED¹ (Id), ~NESS. [OE éage, Du. oog, G auge, f. OTeut. augon, etym. dub.]

eye² (i), v.t. (part. eying or ~ing). Observe, watch, (jealously, narrowly, with disgust, ASKANCE, etc.). [f. prec.]

eye'let (Il-), n. Small hole in cloth, sail, etc., for lace, ring, rope, etc.; loophole; ~ hole, small hole to look or shoot through; small eye. [ME oilet f. F œillet dim. of œil eye f. L oculus]

eyot. See AIT.

eyre (âr), n. (hist.). Circuit, circuit court, as Justices in E~. [f. OF eire f. L errer (ERRANT 1)]

eyrie. See AERIE.

F

F (ef), letter (pl. Fs, F's). (Mus.; also fa) fourth note in diatonic scale of C major (F sharp, joc. for flea).

fa (fah), n. Fourth note of octave in solmization. [first syl. of famuli, see GAMUT]

Fā'bian, a. Employing cautious & dilatory strategy to wear out an enemy (esp. ~ policy); ~ Society (of socialists following such policy). [f. L Fabianus (Q. Fabius Cunctator (= delayer), commander against Hannibal, -AN)]

fā'ble¹, n. Story, esp. of supernatural character, not founded on fact; (collect.) myths, legendary tales; idle talk (old wives' ~s); false statement, lie; thing only supposed to exist; short story, esp. with animals for characters, conveying a moral, apologue; plot of play etc. [F, f. L fabula (fari speak)]

fā'ble², v.t. & i. (arch. & poet.). Romance, tell fictitious tales, whence fāb'lING¹ n.; state fictitiously; (p.p.) celebrated in fable, legendary, fictitious. [f. OF fabler f. L fabulari; see prec.]

fabliau (-iō), n. (pl. -x, pr. -z). Metrical tale of early French poetry. [F]

fāb'rīc, n. Thing put together; edifice, building; frame, structure, (lit. & fig.); (often textile ~) woven material; construction, texture, tissue. [f. F fabrique f. L fabrica (faber artificer)]

fāb'rīcāte, v.t. Construct, manufacture, (rare); invent (facts), forge (document). So ~ATION, ~ātor², nn. [f. L fabricare as prec., -ATE³]

fāb'ūlist, n. Composer of fables or apologues; liar. [f. F fabuliste (FABLE¹, -IST)]

fāb'ūlous, a. Given to legend (~ historians); celebrated in fable; unhistorical, legendary, incredible, absurd, exaggerated. Hence or cogn. fāb'ūlousˡy, ~NESS, nn., ~ity² adv. [f. L fabulosus (FABLE¹, -OUS)]

façade (-sahd), n. Face of building towards street or open space. [F (foll., -ADE³)]

face¹, n. 1. Front of head from forehead to chin (look one in the ~, confront him steadily; show one's ~, appear; ~ to ~, confronted; ~ to ~ with, confronting; set one's ~ against, oppose; with wind, sun, the ~ of, against, straight against one; fly in the ~ of, openly disobey; in ~ of, despite; to ~ in the ~ of, or in ~ of, opposite person's ~, openly in his presence; in the ~ of day, openly; her ~ is her fortune, beauty her only dower; ~ lifting, operation of tightening the skin and smoothing out wrinkles in order to give more youthful appearance. 2. Expression of countenance (pull, wear, a long ~, look serious or dismal); grimace (make, pull, a ~ or ~s). 3. Composure, coolness, effrontery, (have the ~, be shameless enough; save one's ~, forbear from or evade shaming him or oneself openly). 4. Outward show, aspect, (on the ~ of it, to judge by appearance; put a new ~ on, alter aspect of; put a good, bold, ~ on matter, make it look well, show courage in facing it); good name [transl. of Chin. tiu bien]. 5. Surface (from the ~ of the earth); front, façade, right side, obverse, dial-plate of clock etc., working surface of implement etc. 6. ~ ache, neuralgia; ~ card, king, queen, or knave; ~ value, nominal value as stated on coin, note, etc. Hence -FACED² (-st) a. [F, f. pop. L facia = facies (facere make, or fa- shine)]

face², v.t. & i. 1. Meet confidently or defiantly (~ matter out, carry it through; ~ opponent down, browbeat him), not shrink from, stand fronting, (~ the music, not quail at moment of trial); present itself to (the problem that ~s us). 2. Turn

(card) face upwards. **3.** (Of persons etc.) look, (of things) be situated, in a certain direction (*on..to*, or *North..Eastwards*, etc.). **4.** Front towards, be opposite to, (*to ~ page 20*). **5.** (Lacrosse, Ice hockey, etc.) place (ball, puck, etc.) between crosses, sticks, etc., of two opposing players as preliminary to commencement of game (so ~ *off*). **6.** (Mil.) turn in certain direction on one's ground (*left, about, ~*; also trans., *he ~d his men about*). **7.** Supply (garment) with FACINGS; cover (surface of; coat (tea) with colouring matter. [f. prec.]

fā'cer, n. Blow in the face: great & sudden difficulty. [FACE¹+-ER¹]

fā'cet, n. One side of a many-sided body, esp. of a cut gem; one segment of a compound eye. Hence ~ED² a. [f. F *facette* (FACE¹, -ETTE)]

face'tiae (-shiē), n. pl. Pleasantries, witticisms; (book catalogues) books of humorous or erotic character. [L (*facetus* urbane)]

face'tious (-shus), a. Addicted to or marked by pleasantry, waggish. Hence ~LY² adv., ~NESS n., (-shus-). [f. F *facétieux facetia* sing. of prec.)]

fā'cia (-sha), n. Plate over shop-front with occupier's name etc. [VAR. of FASCIA]

fā'cial (-shl), a. & n. **1.** Of the face (esp. in Anat. as ~ *artery*): ~ *angle*, that formed by two lines from nostril to (1) ear & (2) forehead. **2.** n. Face massage. [F, f. med. L *facialis* (FACE¹, -AL)]

-fācient (-shnt), suf. forming adj. representing L *-facient-* (*facere* make, -ENT) added to infin. in *-e(re)*, as *calefacere, liquefacere*, w. sense *producing the action* of the vb. L forms, on strict anal. w. L, *absorbefacient* etc., &, loosely, *abortifacient, calorifacient*, etc., where L would have vbs in *-ficare*, adj. in *-ficus* -FIC.

fā'cile, a. Easily done or won; working easily, ready, fluent; of easy temper; gentle, flexible, yielding. [F, f. L *facilis* (*facere* do)]

fā'cile prin'ceps, pred. a. Easily first. [L]

facil'itāte, v.t. Make easy, promote, help forward, (action or result). Hence ~A'-TION n. [f. F *faciliter* (FACILE, -ATE³)]

facil'itỹ, n. Being easy, absence of difficulty, unimpeded opportunity (*give ~ies for, of doing*); ease or readiness of speech etc., aptitude, dexterity, fluency; pliancy. [f. F *facilité* f. L *facilitatem* (FACILE, -TY)]

fā'cing, n. In vbl senses of FACE²; esp.: (pl.) cuffs, collar, etc., of soldier's jacket, differently coloured from rest; coating of different material, esp. of stone etc. on wall; turning in some direction (*put person through his ~s*, test his qualities, proficiency, etc.; *go through one's ~s*, be thus tested). [-ING¹]

facsim'ile, n., & v.t. Exact copy, esp. of writing, printing, picture, etc. (*reproduced in ~, exactly*); (vb) make ~ of. [L *fac* imperat. of *facere* make+neut. of *similis* like]

făct, n. Perpetration of act, occurrence of event, (now only in *before, after, the ~, confess the ~*); thing certainly known to have occurred or be true, datum of experience, (often with explanatory clause or phrase, as *the ~ that fire burns, of my having seen him; the ~s of life* (colloq.), details of animal reproduction (*his ~s are disputable*); (sing. without *a*) the true or existent, reality, (so *matter of ~*, independent of inference; MATTER¹-of-~; *in ~; as a matter of ~; in point of ~; the ~ of the matter is*); ~-finding adj., engaged in finding out ~s. [f. L *factum* neut. p.p. of *facere* do]

făc'tion, n. Self-interested, turbulent, or unscrupulous party, esp. in politics; prevalence of party spirit. Hence or cogn. ~AL (-shon-), **făc'tious** (-shus), aa., **făc'tious**LY² adv., **făc'tious**NESS n., (-shus-). [F, f. L *factionem* (*facere fact-* do, -ION) way of making (FASHION), class, clique]

-faction (-shus), suf. repr. L *-factio*, forming nn. of action related to vv. in -FY, prop. only when *-fy* represents L *facere*, F *faire*, as in *satisfaction*, but also used when *-fy* represents L *-ficare*, F *-fier*, as in *petrifaction*.

factitious (-shus), a. Designedly got up, not natural, artificial. Hence ~LY² adv., ~NESS n. (-shus-). [f. L *factitius* (*facere fact-* make)+-OUS]

făc'titive, a. (gram.), ~ *verb*, one with sense *make, call*, or *think*, that takes obj. & compl. (*he thought her mad*). [irreg. f. L *facere fact-* make, -IVE]

făc'tor, n. Agent, deputy; merchant buying & selling on commission, whence ~AGE(4) n.; ||(Sc.) land agent, steward; (Math.) one of the components that make up a number or expression by multiplication; circumstance, fact, or influence, contributing to a result; ~ *cost*, cost of product to producer; ~ *of safety* (Engineering), ratio of a material's strength to the maximum load etc. it may have to sustain. [f. F *facteur* f. L *factor* (prec., -OR³)]

făctō'rial, n. & a. (math.). Product of series of factors in arithmetical progression; product of an integer & all lower integers (adj., ~ 4, symbol $\lfloor4$ or $4\rfloor$, $= 4 \times 3 \times 2 \times 1$). [-AL]

fāc'tory, n. Merchant company's foreign trading station; manufactory, workshop, (||F~ *Acts*, regulating management in interest of the hands). [ult. f. med. L *factoria* (FACTOR, -Y¹)]

făctō'tum, n. Man of all work; servant managing his master's affairs. [med. L, as FACSIMILE+neut. of L *totus* whole]

făc'tual, a. Concerned with, of the nature of, fact. Hence ~ITY² adv. [f. FACT on false anal. of ACTUAL]

făc'tum, n. Statement of facts or points in controversy, memorial. [L, see FACT]

făc'ūl|a, n. (astron.; pl. -ae), Bright spot or streak on sun. Hence ~AR¹, ~OUS, aa. [L, dim. of *fax fac-* torch]

făc'ultative, a. Permissive; optional; contingent; of a faculty. [F (-*if, -ive*); foll. -IVE]

făc'ult|ý, n. Aptitude for any special kind of action; executive ability (chiefly U.S.); power inherent in the body or an organ; a mental power, e.g. the will, reason; || branch of art or science, department of University teaching (*the four ~ies*, Theology. Law, Medicine, Arts), Masters & Doctors in any of these (|| pop., *The F~y*, members of medical profession); liberty of doing something given by law or a superior, authorization, licence, (esp. eccl.). [f. F *faculté* f. L *facultatem* (*facilis* easy)]

făd, n. Pet notion or rule of action, craze, piece of fancied enlightenment. Hence ~'DISH¹, ~'d'Y², aa., ~'d'INESS, ~'dISH-NESS, ~'d'ISM(3), ~'dISM(2), nn. [?]

fade, v.i. & t. Droop, wither, lose freshness & vigour; (of colour etc.) grow dim or pale; cause to lose colour; disappear gradually; (Cinemat.) cause (picture) to pass gradually *in* or *out* (of view on the screen), (transf. of sound-films and broadcasting) increase or reduce (sound) from or to inaudibility, whence **făd'ING¹** vbl n. Hence ~'LESS¹ a., ~'lessLY adv. [f. OF *fader* (*fade* dull, insipid, perh. f. L *vapidus*]

fae'cēs (-z), n. pl. Sediment; excrement of the bowels. Hence **faec'AL** a. [L, pl. of *faex*]

Fā'erie -rý, n. & a. Fairyland, the fairies, esp. as represented by Spenser; (attrib.) visionary, fancied. [var. of FAIRY]

făg, v.i. & t. (-gg-), & n. 1. Toil painfully; (of occupation) tire, make weary; || (at schools, of seniors) use the service of (juniors), (of juniors) do service for seniors; (Cricket) ~ *out*, field; ~*end*, inferior or useless remnant. 2. n. || Drudgery, unwelcome task (*what a ~ !*), exhaustion (*brain-~*); || (at schools) junior who has to ~; (sl.) cigarette. [perh. corrupt. of *fag²*]

făg'ot, făg'ot, n., & v.t. & i. 1. Bundle of sticks or twigs bound together as fuel; bundle of steel rods; || dish of liver chopped, seasoned, & baked; ||~*vote*, manufactured by transferring sufficient property to unqualified person, so ~*voter*. 2. vb. Bind in ~s, make ~(s). [F (*fagot*), etym. dub.]

Fahr'enheit (-hīt), a. (abbr. F.), ~ *thermometer*, with 32° & 212° for freezing & boiling points (used esp. in giving temperatures, as 50° F.). [Prussian inventor d. 1736]

faïence (see Ap.), n. Decorated earthenware & porcelain. [f. F *faïence* f. *Faenza* Italian town]

fail¹, n. *Without ~*, for certain, irrespective of hindrances, (emphasising injunction or promise). [f. OF *faile* (*faillir* FAIL²)]

fail², v.i. & t. (strictly, intr. with ind. obj.). Be missing (see FAILING²) or insufficient, not suffice for needs of (person), run short, (*time would ~ me to tell; words ~ me, I cannot adequately describe etc.; his heart ~ed him*); neglect, not remember or not choose, to (*he ~ed to appear; don't ~ to let me know*); become extinct, die away; flag, break down; prove misleading, disappoint hopes of, (*the prophecy ~ed; the wind ~ed us*); be insufficiently equipped *in*, not succeed in the attainment of; not succeed (*in doing or to do*); miscarry, come to nothing; suspend payment, go bankrupt; be rejected as candidate, &c. [f. OF *faillir* f. pop. L *fallire* f. L *fallere* deceive]

fail'ing¹, n. In vbl senses; also, foible, shortcoming, weakness. [-ING¹]

fail'ing², prep. In default of (~ *this*, if this does not happen; *whom ~ or ~ whom* in proxy appointments). [-ING²]

faille (fāl), n. A light glossless ribbed silk dress-material. [F]

fail'ure (-yer), n. Non-occurrence, non-performance; running short, breaking down; ill success; unsuccessful person, thing, or attempt; insolvency. [earlier *failer* for F *faillir* FAIL², cf. -ER¹, -URE]

fain¹, pred. a., & adv. Willing under the circumstances to; left with no alternative but to; (adv.) *would ~*, would be glad to. [OE *fœgen* cogn. w. OHG (ʒi)*fehan* rejoice]

fain² fains (-z), n. child's formula (usu. *fains I* as v.t.) stipulating for exemption from unwelcome office etc. (~ *I wicked-keeping!*). [?]

faint¹ (see Ap.), n. & a. Idle(r), inactive (official). [F, perversion on *faire* do, *néant* nothing, of OF *faignant* sluggard (*faindre* skulk)]

faint¹, a. Sluggish; timid (~-*heart*, coward; so ~-*heart'ED²* a., ~-*heart'edly²* adv., ~-*heart'EDNESS* n.); feeble (*a ~ show of resistance*); feint, indistinct, pale (~ *or feint lines ruled ~* or *a ~ idea*, inadequate); giddy or languid with fear, hunger, etc., inclined to swoon (of air, scents, etc.) sickly, oppressive. Hence ~'ISH¹(2) a., ~'LY¹ adv., ~'NESS n. [OF p.p. of *faindre* FEIGN]

faint², v.i., & n. Lose courage, give way, (arch.) swoon (v. & n.; ~*ed away; in a dead ~*), utterly insensible). [f. prec.]

faints, n. pl. Impure spirit coming over at beginning & end of distillation. [f. FAINT¹]

fair¹, n. Periodical gathering for sale of goods, often with shows & entertainments,

at place & time fixed by charter, statute, or custom (*a day after the* ~, *too late*); FANCY ~. [f. OF *feire* (now *foire*) f. L *feria* holiday]

fair², a., n., & v.i. & t. **1.** Beautiful (*the* ~ *sex, the* ~, women; also arch. as n., *a* ~ = *a heritage*); satisfactory, abundant, (*a* ~ *heritage*); specious (~ *speeches*); blond, not dark, (*a* ~ *man, complexion, hair*, whence ~**haired²** a.); clean, clear, unblemished, (~ *water*; ~ COPY¹; ~ *fame*); just, unbiased, equitable, legitimate, (~ *& square* a. & adv., without finesse, above-board; ~ *trade*, principle that reciprocity should be the condition of free trade; *a* ~ FIELD¹ *& no favour*; *all's in love & war*; ~ *play*, equal conditions for all); of moderate quality, not bad, pretty good, whence ~ISH²(2) a.; favourable, promising, gentle, unobstructed, (~ *or foul weather*; ~*weather friends*, not good *in a* ~ *way to succeed*; *by* ~ *means*, without violence or fraud; ~*way*, navigable channel, regular course or track of ship, prepared part of golf-links free from hazards between tee and green); ‖~*light*, = FUMADE; ~*maid*, snowdrops. **2.** v.i. (Of weather) become ~; (v.t.) make ~ copy of (document). [Shipbuilding etc.) make smooth and regular. Hence ~NESS n. [com.-Teut.; OE *fæger* cf. OHG *fagar*]

fair³, adv. *Speak one* ~, address him courteously; ~*spoken*, (of person) courteous, bland; *write out* ~, as FAIR² copy; *hit, fight,* ~, according to the rules; BID ~; ~ *& softly*, gently, not so fast, (esp. as protest against assumptions etc.); (with *strike, fall,* etc.) straight, plump, clean. [OE *fægre* (prec.)]

fair'ing¹, n. Present bought at a fair. [-ING¹]

fair'ing², n. The making of an aircraft's surface smooth and streamlined; any light structure added for this purpose. [f. FAIR² as v.t. + -ING¹]

Fair Isle (īl), n. One of the Shetlands; ‖~ (*sweater, pull-over*, etc.), jersey knitted in designs said to be Moorish & to be traceable to Armada wrecks.

fair'ly, adv. In adj. senses; (also) utterly, completely, (~ *beside himself*; there is sometimes doubt between this sense & that of *rather, tolerably*, as in ~ *good*). [-LY²]

fair'|y, n. & a. **1.** Small supernatural being with magical powers; ~*y lamps* (of glass, for esp. outdoor decoration); *Fairyland*, home of ~ies, enchanted region; ~*y ring*, circular & attributed to ~y dancing; ~*ytale*, about ~ies, also account of strange incident, coincidence, marvellous progress, etc.; hence ~YDOM, ~YHOOD, ~YISM, nn. **2.** adj. Of ~ies; imaginary, fictitious; ~*y-like*, beautiful & delicate or small, whence ~ILY² adv. [f. OF *faerie* (now *féerie*) f. OF *fae* FAY]

fait accompli (see Ap.), n. Thing done & no longer worth arguing against. [F]

faith, n. Reliance, trust, *in*; belief founded on authority (*pin one's* ~ *to* or *upon*, believe implicitly); (Theol.) belief in religious doctrines, esp. such as affects character & conduct, spiritual apprehension of divine truth apart from proof; system of religious belief (*the Christian, Jewish,* ~; DEFENDER *of the F*~; *the* ~, the true religion); things (to be) believed; warrant (*on the* ~ *of*); promise, engagement, (*give, pledge, plight, keep, break, violate, one's* ~); loyalty, fidelity, (*good* ~, honesty of intention; *bad* ~, intent to deceive; *Punic* ~, treachery); ~-*cure*, -*curer, -healing, -healer*, acting by prayer, not drugs etc. [f. OF *feid* f. L *fides*]

faith'ful, a. Loyal, constant, (*to person*; one's word); conscientious; trustworthy; true to fact, the original, etc., accurate; *the* ~ (pl.), true believers, esp. Mohammedans (*Father of the* ~, Caliph). Hence ~NESS n. [-FUL]

faith'fully, adv. In adj. senses: esp.: *yours* ~, formula of rather distant tone for closing letter; *deal* ~ *with*, speak home truths to or of; *promise* ~, emphatically (colloq.). [-LY²]

faith'less, a. Unbelieving; perfidious, false to promises; unreliable. Hence ~LY² adv., ~NESS n. [-LESS]

fake¹, v.t., & n. (naut.) Coil (rope); (n.) one round of a coil. [?]

fake², v.t., & n. **1.** Do *up*, make presentable or specious, contrive out of poor material. **2.** n. Piece of faking, thing ~d up, dodge, cooked report. Hence ~MENT (-km-) n., ~ER (*fegen* sweep) [perh. f. G *fegen* sweep]

fakir' (-ēr), n. Mohammedan (or Hindu) religious mendicant, devotee. [f. Arab. *faqir* poor man]

fal'bala, n. Flounce, trimming. [?]

fal'cate, a. (anat., bot., zool.). Hooked, sickle-shaped. [f. L *falcatus* f. *falx* sickle, -ATE²(2)]

fal'cated, a. (astron.). = prec. (of moon etc.). [as prec. See -ATE²]

falchion (fawl'chon), n. Broad curved convex-edged sword. [f. OF *fauchon* f. pop. L †*falcionem* nom. -*o* (L *falx* sickle)]

fal'ciform, a. (anat.). Sickle-shaped. [f. L *falx* -*cis* sickle +-FORM]

falcon (faw'kn, fawl'kn), n. Small diurnal bird of prey, esp. as trained to hawk for sport (~ry the female only, cf. TERCEL). So ~RY(2, 5) n. [f. OF *faucon* f. LL *falconem* perh. f. L *falx* sickle]

falc'oner (faw'k-), n. Keeper and trainer of hawks; one who hunts with hawks. [f. OF *fauconnier*, see prec. -ER²(2)]

falc'onet (faw'k-), n. **1.** (Hist.) light cannon. **2.** Species of shrike. [first sense f. It. *falconetto* dim. of *falcone* FALCON; last f. FALCON +-ET¹]

falderal', n. Gewgaw, trifle. [earlier as meaningless refrain in songs]

fald'stōōl (fawl-), n. Bishop's armless chair; || movable desk for kneeling at; desk for litany to be said from. [f. med. L *faldistolium* f. OHG *faldstuol* (*faldan* to fold, STOOL)]

Falēr'nĭan, n. A famous wine of ancient Campania. [f. L (*vinum*) *Falernum* Faler- nian (wine) +-AN]

fall¹ (fawl), v.i. (*fell*; en often conjugated with *be*, see -ED¹(2), & used as adj.). 1. Descend freely (~*ing star*, meteor; drop (*the remark fell from him*; *lambs* ~, are born); come down, lose high position (*statesmen* ~; ~*en angel*, one of those cast out of heaven); *fall*, see fall. 2. Become detached, hang down; sink to lower level (*barometer prices*, ~), de- cline, slope; disembogue into; subside, ebb, abate; show dismay (*faces* ~), droop (*eyes* ~). 3. Cease to stand (~*ing sickness* arch., epilepsy), become prostrate, come to ground, sin, be overthrown, perish (~ *prostrate, flat*; *plans* ~ *to the ground*, are abandoned, fall; ~ *on one's knees*, in suicide; *wicket* ~s, batsman is out; *fortress* ~s, is taken; *woman* ~s, loses chastity; *many fell*, were killed in battle; *seven lions fell to his rifle*; ~*en on evil times*, in misfortune; ~ *a prey or sacrifice to*; ~ *into error; houses* ~, tumble in frag- ments; ~ *to pieces, in two, asunder*). 4. Take such a direction (*his eye fell upon me*), have such a place (*accent* ~s *on first syllable*), alight, come by chance etc., (*the lot fell upon me; it fell to my lot to; cost* ~s *to you; it fell in my way*; ~*amongst thieves, upon a corrupt age; subject* ~s *into three divisions*). 5. Pass into such a state (*fell into a rage, in love*), become so-&-so (~ *dumb, due*); lapse, revert, (*revenues* ~ *to the Crown*), find place (*what now* ~s *to be described*). 6. Occur, have date, (*Easter* ~s *early*). 7. With prepp.: ~ *a-* —*ing, begin; ~ *behind*, be passed by; *~ *for* (sl.), be captivated by, admire, yield to take one's place in the ranks, combine with others, (*conversation with*) begin talking to, (*habit* etc.) adopt it; ~ (*upon*, assault, come across, (one's feet or legs) get well out of difficulty; ~ *to*—*ing*, take to, begin, (also ~ *to work*); ~ *under*, be classed among, be subjected to (*observa- tion* etc.); ~ *within*, be included in. 8. With adv.: ~ *astern*, (of ship) drop behind; ~ *away*, desert, apostatize, decay, vanish; ~ *back*, retreat; ~ *back upon*, have recourse to; ~ *behind*, lag; ~ *foul of*, come into collision with, quarrel with, attack; ~ *in*, (Mil.) take or cause to take places in line, (of buildings etc.) give way inwards, (of debt etc.) become due, (of land etc.) become available, (of lease) run out; ~ *in with*, happen to meet, coincide with, humour; ~ *off*, withdraw, decrease, degenerate (so ~*ing off*, n.), (of

ship) refuse to answer helm, (of subjects) revolt; ~ *on, join battle, begin feeding; ~ *out*, quarrel, come to pass, result (*well* etc., (Mil.) leave the ranks; ~ *out of, give up (habit) etc., become insuffi- cient, (of missile) not go far enough; ~ *short of*, fail to obtain; ~ *through*, mis- carry, fail; ~ *to*, begin eating or fighting. [com.-Teut. ; f. OE *feallan* cf. G *fallen*; also

fall² (fawl), n. Act of falling (see prec.); also or esp.: amount of rain etc. that falls; (now chiefly U.S.; also ~ *of the year or leaf*) autumn; number of lambs born; cataract, cascade, (often pl.); downward trend, amount of descent; wrestling bout, throw in this, (*try a* ~, lit. & fig.); rope of hoisting-tackle; amount of timber cut down; succumbing to temptation (*the F*~ *of man*, Adam's sin and its results); kind of woman's veil. [f. prec.]

fāll'āċy, n. Misleading argument, soph- ism, (Log.) flaw that vitiates syllogism, one of the types of such flaws; delusion, error, (PATHETIC ~); unsoundness, de- lusiveness, disappointing character, (of arguments or beliefs). So fāllā'cĭous (-shus) a., fāllā'ciousŭy² adv., fāllā'- ciousness n., (-shus-). [f. L L *fallacia* (*fallax* deceiving t. *fallere* deceive) see -ACY]

fāl-lāl', n. Piece of finery. Hence fāllāl'- ERY(5) n. [contemptuous reduplication, cf. *geegaw*, perh. f. FAIRAL]

fāll'ĭble, a. Liable to err or be erroneous. Hence fāllibil'ĭty n. [f. LL *fallibilis* (fallere deceive, -BLE)]

Fallōp'ĭan, a. Of Fallopius the Italian anatomist (d. 1562); ~ *tubes*, the human oviducts. [-AN]

fāll'ow¹ (-ō), n., a., & v.t. (Ground) ploughed and harrowed but left un- cropped for a year; uncultivated (land); (vb) break up (land) for sowing or to destroy weeds. [ME *falwe* ploughed land, cf. OE *fealga* harrows]

fāll'ow² (-ō), a. Of pale brownish or red- dish yellow (now only in ~*deer*, species smaller than red deer). [OE *falu* cf. G *falb*, prob. cogn. w. L *pallidus* pale & Gk *polios* grey]

false (fawls), a. & adv. 1. Erroneous, wrong, incorrect, (~ *idea, verdict*; ~ *con- cord*, breach of agreement rules in gram- mar; ~ *quantity*, incorrect length of vowel in verse or pronunciation; ~ *note* in music; ~ *drawing*; ~ *imprisonment*, illegal; ~ *weights* etc.; ~ *pride, shame*, based on wrong notions; ~ *position*, one that tempts person to act against his prin- ciples; ~ *step, stumble, transgression*; ~ *start*, wrong start (in racing) ; lying, deceit- ful, treacherous, unfaithful to; deceptive (~ *mirror, medium*); spurious, sham, arti- ficial, (~ *coin, god, prophet, hair, teeth*; ~ *colours*, flag one has no right to, lit. & fig.); improperly so called, pseudo-, (~

acacia; ~ *bottom*, horizontal partition in vessel; ~ KEEL; ~ *pretences*, misrepresentations made with intent to deceive; hence or cogn. ~LY² (-awlsl-) adv. ~NESS (-awlsn-), **fal'sITY** (fawl-), n. **2.** adv. *Play person ~*, cheat, betray. [OE *fals* f. L *falsus* p.p. of *fallere* deceive]

false'hood (fawls-h-), n. Falsity; something untrue, contrariety to fact; lying, lie(s). [-HOOD]

falsett'ō (fawl-), n. (pl. **-os**). Head voice in men, as used by male altos (*in ~*, a tone, etc., often of sham indignation). [It., dim. of *falso* FALSE]

fal'sIfy (fawl-), v.t. Fraudulently alter (document); misrepresent; make wrong, pervert; disappoint (hope, fear, etc.). So ~ICA'TION (fawl-) n. [f. F *falsifier* f. LL *falsificare* (FALSE, -FY)]

fal'ter (fawl-), v.i. & t. Stumble, stagger, go unsteadily; stammer, speak hesitatingly, (*~ out*, utter, say, thus); waver, lose courage, flinch. Hence ~ingLY² adv. [?]

fame¹, n. Public report, rumour; reputation (*house of ill ~*, bawdy-house), good reputation; renown, celebrity. [F, f. L *fama*=Gk *phēmē* (*fa-* speak)]

fame², v.t. (Pass.) be currently reported as, for, to be or do; (p.p.) famous, much spoken of, (*for valour* etc.). [f. OF *famer* (prec.)]

famil'iar (-lyar), a. & n. **1.** Of one's family (arch. for family attrib.); intimate (*with*) in close friendship (*~ spirit*, or *~* as n., demon attending & obeying witch etc.); closely acquainted *with* (some subject); well known, no longer novel, (*to*); common, current, usual; unceremonious, free, over-free; amorously or sexually intimate (*with*). **2.** n. (R.-C. Ch.) person rendering certain services in Pope's or bishop's household; intimate friend or associate; *~ spirit*. Hence ~LY² adv. [f. OF *familier* f. L *familiaris* (FAMILY, -AR¹)]

famili'arity (-lya-), n. Close intercourse, intimacy *with* person or some subject; (pl.) caresses etc.; unceremoniousness, treating of inferiors or superiors as equals, (*~ breeds contempt*). [f. F *familiarité* f. L *familiaritatem* (prec., -TY)]

famil'iariz|e (-lya-), v.t. Make (thing) well known; make (person, person's *mind* etc., *oneself*) well acquainted with or at home *with*. Hence ~A'TION n. [-IZE]

fam'ily, n. **1.** Members of a household, parents, children, servants, etc. (*happy ~*, animals of different kinds in one cage); set of parents & children, or of relations, living together or not (*Holy F~*, the Virgin, Jesus, & often St John Baptist, & St Elizabeth, as grouped in pictures); person's children. **2.** All descendants of common ancestor, house, lineage, (*of ~*, well born); race, group of peoples from common stock. **3.** Brother-

hood of persons or nations united by political or religious ties. **4.** Group of objects distinguished by common features. **5.** Group of allied genera, usu. subdivision of ORDER. **6.** *~ butcher* etc., supplying families as opp. to the army etc.; *~ hotel*, with special terms for families; *in a ~ way*, without ceremony; || *in the ~ way*, with child; *~ Bible*, large Bible with fly-leaves for registering births etc.; || *~ coach*, large closed carriage, a game of forfeits; *F~ Compact*, in 18th c. between Bourbons of France, Spain, & Two Sicilies, esp. against England & Austria; *~ likeness*, that between relations, vague resemblance; || *~ living*, benefice in gift of head of *~ man*, one with *~*, domestic person; *~ tree*, genealogical tree. [f. L *familia* household (*famulus* servant, -IA¹)]

fam'ine, n. Extreme scarcity of food in a district etc.; dearth of something specified, as *water ~* (*~ prices*, raised by scarcity); hunger, starvation, (*die of ~*). [F, f. LL *famina* f. L *fames* hunger, -INE¹]

fam'ish, v.t. & i. Reduce, be reduced, to extreme hunger; (colloq.) be *~ing*, feel hungry. [obs. *fame* v.t. f. L *fames* hunger, -ISH²]

fam'ous, a. Celebrated (*for quality* etc.), well known; (colloq.) capital, excellent, whence ~LY² adv. [f. OF *fameus* f. L *famosus* (FAME, -OSE²)]

fam'ulus, n. (pl. **-lī**). Attendant on magician. [L, = servant]

fan¹, n. Winnowing-machine; instrument, usu. folding & sector-shaped when spread out, on radiating ribs, for agitating air to cool face; anything so spread out, as bird's tail, wing, leaf, kind of ornamental vaulting (*~ tracery*); rotating apparatus giving current of air for ventilation etc.; (Naut.) (blade of) screw, propeller; (in windmill) small sail for keeping head towards wind; ||*~light*, *~-shaped window over door*; *~-tail*, *~-shaped tail or end*, kind of pigeon; ||*~* coal-heaver's hat or sou'-wester. [OE *fann* f. L *vannus* winnowing-basket]

fan², v.t. & i. (**-nn-**). Winnow (corn), whence ~n'ER¹(2) n.; winnow away (chaff), sweep *away* (as) by wind from fan; move (air) with fan; drive current of air (as) with fan upon, to cool (face etc.) or to kindle (flame; (fig.) *the flame*, increase excitement etc.); (of breeze) blow gently on, cool; spread out (t. & i.) in fan shape. [f. prec.]

fan³, n. (sl.). Devotee of a specified amusement, as *film~s*, *football~s*. [abbr. of fan¹]

fanat'ic, a. & n. (Person) filled with excessive & mistaken enthusiasm, esp. in religion. Hence ~AL a., ~alLY² adv., ~ISM n., ~IZE(2, 3) v.t. & i. [f. L *fanaticus* (*fanum* temple, -ATIC)]

fän'cier, n. Connoisseur in some article or animal (of which the name is usu. pro-fixed, as *dog, rose,* ~). [FANCY, -IER¹]

fän'ciful, a. Indulging in fancies, whim-sical, capricious; fantastically designed, ornamented, etc., odd-looking; imagi-nary, unreal. Hence ~ly² adv., ~NESS n. [-FUL]

fän'cy, n. & a. 1. Delusion, unfounded belief; faculty of calling up things not present, of inventing imagery; mental image; arbitrary supposition; caprice, a whim; individual taste, inclination (*take a* ~ *to, for; catch the* ~ *of,* please); *the* ~, those who have a certain hobby; = *-fanciers,* esp. the patrons of boxing; art of breeding animals with certain points of excellence; ~*-free,* not in love. 2. adj. (not pred.). Ornamental, not plain, (~ *bread;* ~ *dress,* masquerade costume, so ~*-dress* or ~*-ball;* ~*-work,* ornamental sewing etc.); (of ~ *goods*); (of flowers etc.) particoloured; capricious, whimsical, extravagant, (*at a* ~ *price;* ~ *franchise,* based on complicated or arbitrary quali-fications; ~ *dog, pigeon,* etc., bred for particular points of beauty etc.); based on imagination, not fact (~ *picture*); ~ *man,* sweetheart, (sl.) man living on earnings of a prostitute. [contraction of FANTASY]

fän'cy, v.t. Picture to oneself, conceive, imagine, (~ *oneself dead;* ~ *a blue dahlia;* ~ *him to be here, that he is here;* imperat. as excl. of surprise, ~!, ~ *his believing it!*); be inclined to suppose, rather think; (colloq.) have good conceit of (*oneself,* one's *game* etc.); take a fancy to, like; breed, grow, (animals, plants) with atten-tion to certain points. [f. prec.]

fandangle (-ăng'gl), n. Fantastic orna-ment, tomfoolery. [perh. f. foll.]

fandăn'gō (-ng-), n. (pl. -oes). Lively Spanish dance; tune for this. [Sp.]

fäne, n. (poet.). Temple. [f. L *fanum*]

fän'fare (& see Ap.), n. Flourish of trum-pets, bugles, etc. [F]

fänfaronāde', n. Arrogant talk, brag; = prec. [f. F *fanfaronnade* f. *fanfaron* braggart, f. prec.]

fäng¹, n. Canine tooth, esp. of dogs & wolves; serpent's venom-tooth; spike of tool held in the stock; (prong of) root of tooth. Hence (-)~ED² (-gd), ~LESS, aa. [OE, cf. G *fangen* seize]

fäng², v.t. Prime (pump) by pouring in water to start it. [f. prec.]

fän-tän', n. Chinese gambling game in which the number of coins etc. hidden under a bowl has to be guessed; gambling game played with cards. [Chin.]

fantasia (-ăzē'ă, -ā'zĭă, -ah-²), n. Musical or other composition in which form is subservient to fancy. [It. = FANTASY]

fän'tăst, n. Visionary, dreamer. [f. med. L f. Gk *phantastēs* (*phantazomai* make a show f. *phainō* show)]

fäntăs'tic, a. Fancied (rare); extrava-gantly fanciful, capricious, eccentric, grotesque or quaint in design etc. Hence (thr. obs. ~al) ~ALLY³, ~ISM, ~IST², nn., ~ALNESS n. [f. OF f. med. L f. Gk *phantastikos* (prec., -IC)]

fäntăs'y, pl., n. Image-making faculty, esp. when extravagant or visionary; mental image; fantastic design; = FAN-TASIA; whimsical speculation. [f. OF *fantasie* f. L f. Gk *phantasia* (see FANTASY)]

Fän'tee, n. Member, language, of a Negro tribe the inhabiting the Gold Coast; *go* ~ (of European) conform to native habits. [native]

fäntoccini (-ochēnē), n. pl. Mechanically worked puppets; marionette show. [It.]

faquir. See FAKIR.

fär¹, adv. (FARTHER, -thest, FURTHER, -thest), off, (often with *away, off, out;* also fig., as ~, *so* ~, *from doing,* ~ *from it;* ~ *be it from me to,* I would on no account); to a great distance or advanced point (*driven* ~ *into the ground;* ~ *gone,* advanced (see below also); *he will go* ~, do much; *go* ~ *to effect* etc., nearly do so; by a great interval, by much, (~ *different, better, the best;* also ~ *as away*); *so* ~, to such a distance, (also *as, right to, not short of,* (place); *as or so as, in so* ~ *as,* to whatever extent, (*as* ~*-away,* remote, long-past, (of look etc.) absent, dreamy; ~*-between,* infre-quent; ~*-famed,* widely known; ~*-fetched,* (of simile, illustration etc.) studiously sought out, strained; ~*-flung* (rhet.), widely extended; ~*-gone,* very ill or mad or drunk or much in debt; ~*-off, remote;* ~*-reaching,* widely applicable, carrying many consequences; ~*-seeing, -sighted,* prescient, prudent, (*sighted*) see-ing distant things more clearly than near ones. 3. n. A distance (*do you come from* ~?); large amount (*by* ~, with compar. & superl.; *prefer, surpass,* etc.). [OE *feorr*] f. OTeut. *fer-* f. Aryan *per-* cf. Gk *peran* beyond]

fär², a. (farther, -est, further, -est). Distant, remote, (*a* ~ *cry*). [OE *feor*¹ f. prec.]

fä'rad, n. (electr.). Electro-magnetic unit of capacity. [f. *Faraday,* physicist, d. 1867]

färädă'ĭc, a. (electr.). Inductive, induced, (of current). [as prec., -IC]

färce¹, n. Dramatic work merely to ex-cite laughter; this species of drama; absurdly futile proceeding, pretence, mockery. Hence fär'cical a., fär'ci-cally² adv., färcical'ĭty n. [F, orig.= stuffing, f. L *farcire* to stuff, used metaph. of interludes etc.]

färce², v.t. (arch.). Season, spice, stuff, (in cookery, & fig. of literary composi-tions). [f. OF *farsir* f. L as prec.]

färceur' (-sö), n. Person who habitually indulges in mystifications. [F]

far′cy, n. Disease, esp. of horses, allied to glanders; ~ *bud*, *button*, small tumour in this. [f. F *farcin* f. L *farciminum* (*farcire* stuff)]

‖ **färd′el**, n. (arch.). Bundle, burden. [OF, dim. of *farde* burden perh. f. Arab. *fardaǩ*]

fāre′, n. 1. Cost of passenger's conveyance, passage-money; passenger in hired vehicle. 2. Food provided (usu. *good*, *bad*, *plentiful*, etc., ~; BILL⁴ of ~). [OE *fær* (sense 1), & *faru* (sense 2), f. st. of foll.] **fāre²**, v.i. Journey, go, travel, (poet.; so ~ *forth*, *start*); happen, turn out, (*how* ~*s it?*); get on *well*, *ill*, etc., have such luck; be entertained, be fed or feed oneself, *well*, etc. [com.-Teut.; OE & OHG *faran* f. Aryan *por-* pass through cf. Gk *poros* ford, L *portare* carry]

farewell′ (-rw-), int. & n. 1. Good-bye; Adieu!, (~ *to*, no more of). 2. n. Leavetaking, parting good wishes. [imperat. of prec. + *well*]

farin′a, n. Flour or meal of corn, nuts, or starchy roots; (Chem.) starch. Hence ‖ (Bot.) pollen; (Chem.) starch. Hence **farinā′ceous** (-ǎshus) a. [L *far* corn, -INE⁴)]

fā′rinōse, a. Mealy, sprinkled with powder. [prec., -OSE¹]

färl, n. (Sc.). Thin cake, orig. quadrantshaped, of oatmeal or flour. [for obs. *fardel* quarter (FOURTH, DEAL), cf. FARTHING]

färm¹, n. Tract of land used under one management for cultivation (orig. only of leased land; *home* ~, reserved & worked by owner of estate containing other ~*s*); (also ~*house*) dwelling-place attached to ~; tract of water used as a preserve (*oyster-*~); place where children are farmed (see foll.); ~*stead*, ~ with buildings on it; ~*yard*, enclosure attached to ~-house. [f. F *ferme* f. med. L *firma* fixed payment (*firmare* fix f. FIRMUS)]

färm², v.t. & i. 1. Take proceeds of (tax, office, etc.) on payment of fixed sum; (also ~ *out*) let out proceeds of (tax etc.) to person for fixed sum. 2. Let the labour of (persons) for hire; contract to maintain and care for (persons, esp. children) for fixed sum. 3. Cultivate, till; till the soil, be a farmer. Hence ~ER¹, ~ING¹, nn. [f. prec.]

fär′ō, n. Gambling card-game. [f. *Pharaoh* (significance doubtful)]

farouche′ (-ōosh), a. Sullen, shy. [F]

farra′go (-rah-, -rā-), n. (pl. -*os*). Medley, hotch-potch. Hence **farra′ginous** a. [L (genit. *-inis*), = mixed fodder (*far* corn)]

fā′rrier, n. Shoeing-smith; ‖ horse-doctor; N.C.O. in charge of cavalry regiment's horses. Hence **fā′rriery**(2) n. [f. OF *ferrier* f. L *ferrarius* f. *ferrum* iron, -ER²(2)]

fā′rrow (-ō), n., & v.t. & i. 1. Giving birth

to, litter of, pigs (20 *at one* ~). 2. vb. Produce (pigs), produce pigs. [vb f. n., OE *fearh* f. OTeut. *farhoz* cf. L *porcus*]

färt, n., & v.i. (indecent). Emission of, emit, wind from the anus. [Aryan, cf. Gk *perdomai*]

färth′er (-dh-) adv. & a. (used as comp. of FAR¹,²; see etymn.), & v.t. 1. To or at a more advanced point or greater extent or distance (*I'll see you* ~ or FURTHER *first*); in addition, also, besides, moreover, (now usu. *further*). 2. adj. More extended, additional, more; more distant or advanced, whence~MOST a. 3. v.t. (rare). =FURTHER, [var. of FURTHER; both used as comp. of *far*, but with tendency to restrict ~ to lit. & *further* to secondary senses]

färth′est (-dh-), a. & adv. 1. Most distant (*at the*, *at*, ~), at the greatest distance, at latest, at most). 2. adv. To or at the greatest distance. [var., now more usu., of FURTHEST]

‖ **färth′ing** (-dh-), n. Quarter of a penny; least possible amount (*doesn't matter a* ~). [OE *fēorthing* (*fēortha* FOURTH, -ING³)]

färth′ingāle (-dhingg-), n. (hist.). Hooped petticoat. [f. OF *verdugale* f. Sp. *-ado* (*verdugo* rod, -ADO)]

fäs′cēs (-z̄), n. pl. (Rom. hist.). Bundle of rods with axe in the middle carried by lictor before high magistrate; ensigns of authority. [L (pl. of *fascis* bundle)]

fascia (fǎ′shiǒ), n. (Archit.) long flat surface of wood or stone under eaves or cornice; (Anat.) thin sheath of fibrous tissue; stripe, band, fillet, belt. [L]

fä′sciāted (-shǐ-), a. (Bot.; of contiguous parts) compressed, growing, into one (so **fäsciā′TION** n.), striped. [f. obs. *fasciate* f. L *fasciare* (prec.), -ATE²]

fä′scicle, -icüle, -ic′ulus, (fǎsǐ-), n. (Bot. etc.) bunch, bundle, whence **fäs′cicled²** (-ld), **fascic′ülar¹**, **fascic′ulāte²**, -**ātěd**, aa., **fasciculā′TION** n.; one part of book published by instalments. [f. L *fasciculus* (FASCES, -CULE)]

fäs′cināte, v.t. Deprive (victim) of power of escape or resistance by one's look or presence (esp. of serpents); attract irresistibly, enchant, charm, whence~**āting²** a., ~**āting**LY² adv. Hence or cogn. ~**A′TION**, ~**ātor²**(esp., = opera-hood), nn. [f. L *fascinare* (*fascinum* spell), -ATE²]

fäscine′ (-sēn), n. Long faggot used for engineering purposes & esp. in war for lining trenches, filling ditches, etc.; ~ *dwelling*, prehistoric lake dwelling supported by cross layers of sticks sunk below surface. [F, f. L *fascina* (*fascis* bundle, -INE⁴)]

Fäs′cism (fǎshǐ-, fǎsǐ-), **fascǐ′smo** (-shēz̄mō), n. Principles & organization of the patriotic & anti-communist movement in Italy started during the 1914–18 war, culminating in the dictatorship of Benito Mussolini (d. 1945), & imitated by Fascist or blackshirt associations in other coun-

tries. So **Fäs′cist** (fäshi-, făsi-, *fȧsh′i-*) (- té) pl. *-ti* pron. *-tē*), n. [It. *fascismo* (*fascio* bundle, group, f. L as FASCES, see -ISM)]

‖ **fäsh**, v.t. & n. (Sc.). Bother, trouble, inconvenience. [n.f, vb, f. OF *fascher* (now *fâcher*)]

fä′shion (-shn), n., & v.t. **1.** Make, shape, style, pattern, manner (*after the ~ of*; like; so ; 80 : ... : -WISE, not satisfactorily, but somehow or other. **2.** Prevailing custom, esp. in dress (~*-plate*, picture showing style of dress). **3.** Conventional usages of upperclass society (*the ~, whatever is in accord with these for the time being; set the ~, give the example in changing them; the ~, (also) admired & discussed person or thing; in, out of, ~ or the ~, agreeing or not with current usage; man &c. of ~, of social standing, moving in & conforming with upper-class society); hence ~ED²(-ond) a. **4.** v.t. Give shape to, form, mould, (*into, to, or abs.*). [f. OF *façon*, f. L *factionem* (*facere* fact-, make, -ION)]

fä′shionable (-shon-), a. & n. **1.** Following, suited to, the fashion; characteristic of, treating of, or patronized by, persons of fashion. Hence ~IeNESS n., ~LY² adv.
2. n. ~le person. [prec. n., -ABLE]

fast¹ (fah-), v.i. **1.** Abstain from all or some kinds of food as religious observance or in sign of mourning (*~ing-day*); ~*ing-day*. **2.** Go without food. [com.-Teut.; OE *fæstan* cf. Goth. *fastan* = orig. keep, observe, f. OTeut. as prec.]

fast² (fah-), n. Act of fasting (prec., 1); season or (also *~-day*, *fasting-day*) day appointed for fasting; going without food (*break one's ~* = BREAKFAST v.). [prob. f. ON *fasta* f. OTeut. as prec.]

fast³ (fah-), a. **1.** Firmly fixed or attached (*stake ~ in the ground*; ~ *friend or friendship*, steady, close; *ship ~ aground*; ~ *with gout*, confined). **2.** Rapid, quick-moving, producing quick motion, (~ *train*; ~ *cricket-pitch*, *racquet-court*, *putting-green*, on which ball bounds or runs smartly; *watch is ~*, shows too advanced time; ~ *person*, dissipated, see foll.). Hence ~-ISH¹(2) a. [com.-Teut.; cf. G *fest* cogn. w. Goth. *fastan* FAST¹]

fast⁴ (fah-), adv. (-er, -est). Firmly, fixedly, tightly, securely, (*stand, sit, stick, ~*; ~ *bind*, ~ *find*, lock up what you would not lose*; *eyes ~ shut*; *sleep ~*, soundly); (poet. & arch.) close beside, by, upon, etc., quickly, in quick succession; *live ~*, live in a dissipated way, expend much energy in short time. [OE *fæste* (prec.)]

fa′sten (fah′sn), v.t. & i. Make fast, attach, fix, secure by some tie or bond, (*to, upon,*

on adv, or prep.; *together, up, in* adv, or prep.; or abs.; ~ *parcel, garment, door, etc.,* or *string, bolt, etc.; ~ off thread etc.,* secure with knot or otherwise), whence ~ING¹(4) (fah′sn-) n.; direct (look, thoughts, etc.), keenly (*upon*; fix (nickname, imputation, etc.), (*upon*; ~ *quarrel upon*, pick quarrel with; become fast (*door will not ~*); ~ (*upon*, lay hold of, single out for attack, seize upon (pretext). Hence ~ER¹(2) (fah′sn-) n. [OE *fæstnian* cf. G *festnen* (FAST³, -EN⁶)]

fäs′ti, n. pl. Chronological register of events, annals. [L, = calendar]

fastid′ious, a. Easily disgusted, squeamish, hard to please. Hence ~LY² adv., ~NESS n. [f. L *fastidiosus* (*fastidium* loathing, -OSE²)]

fastig′iäte, a.(bot.). With conical or tapering outline. [f. L *fastigium* gable + -ATE²]

fast′ness (fah-), n. In adj. senses (FAST³); also, stronghold, fortress. [-NESS]

fat, a., n., & v.t. & i. (-tt-). **1.** Fed up for slaughter, fatted; well-fed, plump, (*cut up ~*, leave much money); corpulent; thick, substantial, (esp. of printing-type); greasy, oily, unctuous, (*cut it ~*, make a display); (of coal) bituminous; (of clay etc.), sticky; fertile, rich, yielding abundantly, (~ *lands, benefice, job; a ~ lot, sl.*, a great deal usu. iron. = very little); slow-witted, indolent, (~*-head*, dolt; ~*-witted*, stupid); ‖ ~*-guts*, corpulent person; ~*-hen*, kinds of goose-foot; ~ *lime*, nearly pure lime, slaking easily; hence ~f′ISH¹(2) a., ~′NESS n. **2.** n. The ~ part of anything (*live on the ~ of the land*, have the best of everything); oily substance composing ~ parts of animal bodies (*the ~ is in the fire*, there will be an explosion); (Theatr.) part of role that enables actor to show off; (Chem.) natural ester of glycerol & acid; hence ~′NESS n. **3.** vb. = FATTEN; *kill the fatted calf for*, receive (returned prodigal) with joy. [OE *fætt(an)* cf. Du. *vet* f. OTeut. *faitjan* (*faito-* adj.-fed-).]

fa′tal, a. Like fate, inevitable, necessary; of, appointed by, destiny (~ *sisters*, the Fates; ~ *thread*, allotted length of life; ~ *shears*, death); fateful, important, decisive; destructive, ruinous, ending in death, (*to*); deadly, sure to kill; by (*exagg.*) mischievous, ill-advised. Hence ~LY² adv. [f. L *fatalis* (FATE, -AL)]

fä′talism, n. Belief that all events are predetermined by arbitrary decree; submission to all that happens as inevitable. So ~IST(2) n. & a., ~IS′TIC a., ~IS′TICALLY adv. [-ISM]

fatal′ity, n. Subjection to, supremacy of, fate, predestined liability to disaster; fatal influence; misfortune, calamity, death by accident, in war, etc. [f. F *fatalité* f. LL *fatalitas*, see FATAL, -ITY]

fa′talize, v.i. & t. Incline to fatalism; subject to government by fate. [-IZE]

fe'ta mõrga'na (fah-, -gah-), n. Kind of mirage seen esp. in strait of Messina. [It. (*fata* FAY, *Morgana* female name)]

fate, n., & v.t. 1. Power predetermining events unalterably from eternity; (Myth.) goddess, one of the three Greek goddesses, of destiny; what is destined to happen; appointed lot of person etc.; person's ultimate condition (*decide, fix, seal, one's* ~); death, destruction. 2. v.t. (usu. pass.) Preordain (*he was* ~*d to do or be; it was* ~*d that*); (p.p.) doomed to destruction. [f. L *fatum* neut. p.p. of *fari* speak]

fate'ful (-tf-), a. Prophetic; fraught with destiny, important, decisive; controlled by, showing power of, fate. Hence ~LY² adv. [-FUL]

fa'ther¹ (fahdh-), n. 1. Male parent (also fig.; *the wish is* ~ *to the thought*, one believes because one wishes to; *the child is* ~ *to the man*, lays down the lines of his development); = ~-in-law; = step-~; (also *adoptive* ~), one who has adopted a child. 2. Progenitor, forefather; originator, designer, early leader, (~ *of English poetry*; F~ *of lies*, the devil; F~ *of the* FAITHFUL; F~*s of the Church* or F~*s*, Christian writers of first five centuries). 3. One who deserves filial reverence (~ *of his country*); religious teacher. 4. God; First Person of the Trinity. 5. Confessor; priest belonging to religious order, superior of monastic house; *Right, Most, Reverend* F~ *in God*, titles of bishop, archbishop; *The Holy* F~, the Pope; = priest as prefixed title; venerable person, god, (F~ *Christmas, Thames, Time*, personifications). 6. Oldest member, doyen, (F~ *of House of Commons*, member with longest continuous service); (pl.) leading men, elders, (F~*s of the City; Conscript* F~*s*, Roman senators). 7. ~-*in-law*, = of one's wife or husband; ~-*land*, native country. Hence ~HOOD, ~SHIP, nn., ~LESS a., ~LIKE, ~LY¹,² aa. & advv., ~liness n., (fahdh-). [Aryan; OE *fæder* cf. G *vater*, L *pater*, Gk *pater*]

fa'ther² (fahdh-), v.t. Beget; be the father of; originate (statement etc.); pass as, confess oneself, the father, author, of (child, book); govern paternally; fix paternity of (child, book) *upon*. [f. prec.]

fath'om¹ (-dh-), n. (pl., often fathom). Measure of six feet, chiefly used in soundings; || quantity of wood 6 ft square in section, whatever the length. [OE *fæthm* the outstretched arms, cf. G *faden* 6 ft cogn. w. Gk *petannumi* spread]

fath'om² (-dh-), v.t. Encircle with the arms (arch.); measure with fathom-line, sound, (depth of water); (fig.) get to the bottom of, comprehend, whence ~LESS a., ~lessly² adv. [OE *fæthmian* (prec.)]

fatid'ical, a. Gifted with prophetic power. [f. L *fatidicus* (FATE, *-dicus* -saying) +-AL]

fatigue' (-ēg), n., & v.t. 1. Weariness after exertion; weakness in metals after repeated blows or long strain; task etc. that wearies; soldier's non-combatant duty (~-*party* or ~, party told off for this; so ~-*dress*). 2. v.t. Tire, exhaust, whence ~LESS (-ēgl-), fati'guing² (-ēgi-), aa.: weaken (metal; see above). [f. F *fatigue(r)* f. L *fatigare* prob. cogn. w. *fatiscere* gape]

fat'ling, n. Young fatted animal. [-LING¹]

fätt'en, v.t. & i. Make fat (esp. animals for slaughter); grow fat; enrich (soil). [-EN⁶]

fätt'y¹, a. Like fat, unctuous, greasy; consisting of fat, adipose; with morbid deposition of fat (~ *degeneration of heart or kidney*). [-Y²]

fät'uous, a. Vacantly silly, purposeless, idiotic. Hence or cogn. fatu'ITY n., ~LY² adv., ~NESS n. [f. L *fatuus* +-OUS]

faubourg (fōb'oorg), n. Suburb, esp. of Paris. [F]

fauc'al, a. & n. (phonol.). Of the throat, deeply guttural (sound). [f. L *fauces* throat +-AL]

fauc'es (-ēz), n., pl. (anat.). The cavity at the back of the mouth. [L]

fauc'et, n. (esp. U.S.). Tap for barrel. [f. F *fausset* vent-peg etym. dub.]

faugh (faw), int. of disgust.

fault, n., & v. (geol.) 1. & t. 1. Defect, imperfection, blemish, of character or of structure, appearance, etc. (*generous* etc. *to a* ~, excessively, *with all* ~*s*, at buyer's risk). 2. Transgression, offence, thing wrongly done, (Racquets etc.) ball wrongly served; *find* ~ (*with*) complain (of), whence ~finder¹ n., ~finding¹,² n. & a. 3. Responsibility for something wrong (*the* ~ *was mine; it will be our own* ~); defect that causes something (*the* ~ *is in the patient*); *in* ~, guilty, to blame, (*who is in* ~). 4. (Hunt.) loss of the scent, check so caused, (*be at* ~, also fig.; = be puzzled, not know what to do). 5. (Geol.) break in continuity of strata or vein (vb., break continuity of, show such break). 6. (Telegr.) imperfect insulation, leakage. Hence ~LESS a., ~lessly² adv., ~lessNESS n., ~Y² a., ~ILY² adv., ~INESS n. [ME & OF *faute*) f. pop. L †*fallita* fem. p.p. of *fallere* FAIL²]

faun, n. One of a class of Latin rural deities with horns & tail. [f. L *Faunus* Latin god identified w. Gk Pan]

faun'a, n. (pl. ~ae, ~as). The animals of a region or epoch; treatise upon these. Hence ~AL a., ~IST(3) n., ~is'TIC(AL) aa. [mod. L, f. name of goddess sister of Faunus, see AP.]

fauteuil (fōteui'), n. Arm-chair; theatre stall. [F]

faux pas (fō pah), n. Act that compromises one's, esp. a woman's, reputation; an offence against social convention, an indiscreet speech or action. [F, = false step]

fav'our¹ (-ver), n. **1.** Friendly regard, goodwill, (*find* ~ *in the eyes of*, be liked by; CURRY² ~), approval (*be, stand high etc., in person's* ~); kindness beyond what is due (*esteem it a* ~; *by* ~ *of* —, written on letter conveyed by friend); *do me the* ~ *of* —*ing*; *woman bestows her* ~*s on lover, yields*; **2.** Leave, pardon, (arch.; *by your* ~; *under* ~, if one may venture to say so). **3.** Partiality, too lenient or generous treatment (FEAR¹ *or* ~). **4.** Aid, furtherance, (*under* ~ *of night*); *in* ~ *of*, on person's advantage or account of, (*am, in* ~ *of the treasurer*); *cheques to be drawn in woman's suffrage* ~ *of the treasurer*). **5.** Thing given or worn as mark of ~, knot of ribbons, rosette, cockade, badge. **6.** (Arch.) looks, counte-(-erd) nance, whence *well, ill, hard, etc.,* ~*ED²*(-erd) a. [OE f. L *favorem* (*favere* show kindness to, -OR¹)]

fav'our² (-ver), v.t. **1.** Look kindly upon, approve; treat kindly, countenance; oblige *with*.. **2.** Treat with partiality, be unjust on behalf of. **3.** Aid, support; serve as confirmation of (theory etc.), prove advantageous to (person), facilitate (process etc.), whence ~ING² (-ver-) a. **4.** Resemble in features (~ *one's father*). **5.** (p.t.) Having unusual advantages (*most* ~*ed nation*, to which a State accords lowest scale of import duties); ~*ed by*, (of letter) by favour of. [f. OF *favorer* f. med. L *favorare* as prec.]

fav'ourable (-ver-), a. Well disposed, propitious; commendatory, approving; giving consent (*~le answer*); promising, auspicious, (*~le aspect*); helpful, suitable, (*to*). Hence ~LENESS n., ~LY² (-verle) adv. [f. *favorabilis* (FAVOUR¹, -ABLE)]

fav'ourite (-ver-), n. & a. (Person) preferred above others (*the* ~ *of*, *a* ~ *with or of*); (Racing) *the* ~*e*, competitor generally expected to win; person chosen as intimate by king or superior & unduly favoured, whence ~ISM²(-z-) n. [f. OF *favori* fem. *favorite*]

fawn¹, n., a., & v.i. & t. **1.** Young fallow deer, buck or doe of first year (*in* ~ *preg-* nant); ~ *or* ~*-colour(ed)*, (of) light yellow-ish brown. **2.** vb. (Of deer) bring forth (young, or abs.). [f. OF *faon* f. med. L *fetonem* nom. -o (FOETUS)]

fawn², v.i. (Of animals, esp. dog) show affection by tail-wagging, grovelling, etc. (~ *on, upon*, lavish caresses on); (of persons) behave servilely, cringe (*upon* patron, or abs.), whence ~ING² a. ['inqy² adv. [OE *fahnian* cogn. w. FAIN¹]]

fay, n. (poet.). Fairy. [f. OF *fae* f. Rom. *fata* sing. f. L *fata* pl. the fates]

fe'alty, n. Feudal tenant's or vassal's (acknowledgement of obligation of) fidelity to his lord (*do, make, receive, swear*, ~).

4895

fear¹, n. [f. OF *feaute* f. L *fidelitatem* (*fides* faith, -TY)]

fear¹, n. Painful emotion caused by impending danger or evil, state of alarm (*was in* ~), dread of; dread, *or less*; *for* ~ *of* (*that*, *lest*, in order that so-&-so may not occur; *without* ~ *or favour*, impartially; *for the safety of* (*in* ~ *of his life*); *no* ~, it is not likely. Hence ~*LESS* a. (of danger etc.), ~*lessLY²* adv., ~*lessNESS* n. [OE *fær* cf. G *gefahr* danger]

fear², v.i. & t. Be afraid (also as arch. refl. in parenthesis, *I* ~ *me*; *never* ~, there is no danger of that); be afraid of; hesi-tate to do, shrink from doing; revere (God); apprehend, have uneasy anticipa-tion of; be afraid *that* (or with *that* omitted; also *need not etc.* ~ *but or but that*). [OE *fǽran* f. prec.]

fear'ful, a. Terrible, awful; (by exagg.) annoying etc. (*in a* ~ *mess*); frightened, timid; apprehensive *of*, *lest*, (*that*); want-ing resolution *to*; reverential. Hence ~*LY²* adv., ~*NESS* n. [-FUL]

fear'nought (-awt), n. Stout woollen cloth used at sea for clothing & for pro-tecting portholes etc. [FEAR² NOUGHT]

fear'some, a. Appalling, esp. in appear-ance (usu. joc.). Hence ~*LY²* adv., ~*NESS* (-mn-) n. [-SOME]

feas'ible (-z-), a. Practicable, possible; (loosely) manageable, convenient, ser-viceable, plausible. Hence ~*BILITY* n. [OF *fais* impf. st. of *faire* f. L *facere* do + -IBLE]

feast¹, n. & v.i. & t. **1.** Joyful religious anniversary (*movable, 'immovable,* ~, recurring on different, same, date); annual village festival; sumptuous meal, esp. one given to number of guests and of public nature; (fig) gratification to the senses or mind (~ *of reason*, intellectual talk). **2.** vb. Partake of ~, fare sumptu-ously, whence ~*ER¹* n.; pass (night etc.) away in ~ing; regale (guests, one's eyes on beauty etc.). [f. OF *feste*(r) f. L *festa* neut. pl. of *festus* festal]

feat¹, n. Noteworthy act, esp. deed of valour (often ~ *of arms*); action showing dexterity or strength, surprising trick. [f. OF *fait* FACT]

‖ **feat²**, a. (arch.). Adroit, smart, dextrous, neat. Hence ~*LY²* adv. [f. OF *fait* made f. L *factus* p.p. of *facere* make]

feath'er (fedh-), n. **1.** One of the appen-dages growing from bird's skin, consisting of quill, shaft, & two vanes of barbs (*show the white* ~, betray cowardice—white ~ in game-bird's tail being mark of bad breeding; *crop one's* ~*s*, humiliate him; (collect.) plumage (*in high or full* ~, in good spirits etc.; *birds of a* ~, people of one sort); feathered game (*fur &* ~, game beasts & birds). **2.** Piece(s) or (a ~ *in one's cap*, something one may be proud

of); very light object (*could have knocked me down with a ~*); ridge of upright hair; ~like flaw in gem. **3.** (Rowing) action of feathering (see foll.). **4.** ~ *bed*, mattress stuffed with ~s; ~-*edge*, (n.) fine edge of wedge-shaped board, (v.t.) bring (board) to this; ~-*headed*, -*brained*, -*pate(d)*, silly (person); ~-*stitch*, ornamental zig-zag sewing; ~-*weight*, very light thing or person, esp. jockey not over 4 st. 7 lb., boxer 9 st. Hence (-) ~ED² (-erd), ~LESS, ~Y², aa., ~INESS, ~LET, nn., (fēdh-), ~Y³. [com.-Teut., cf. G *feder*, also Gk *pteron* wing, *petomai* fly]

feath'er² (fēdh-), v.t. & i. **1.** Furnish, adorn, line, coat, with feathers (~ *an arrow*; ~ *one's nest*, enrich oneself; TAR & ~); form featherlike ornamentation for. **2.** Float, move, or wave, like feathers. **3.** Turn (oar), turn oar, so as to pass through the air edgeways. **4.** (Shoot.) knock feathers from (bird) without kill-ling. **5.** (Hunt.: of hound) make quiver-ing motion of body & tail while seeking scent. [OE *gefithrian* f. prec.]

feath'ering (fēdh-), n. In vbl senses; esp.: plumage; feathers of arrow; feathery structure in animal's coat; (Archit.) cusps in tracery; featherlike marking in flower. [-ING¹]

fea'ture, n., & v.t. **1.** (Usu. pl.) part(s) of the face, esp. with regard to shape & visible effect; distinctive or character-istic part of a thing, part that arrests attention; distinctive or prominent article etc. in newspaper etc.; ~ *film*, ~ *picture*, cinema drama of some length in several reels. **2.** v.t. Stand as distinctive mark upon; portray, sketch the promi-nent points of; *show on cinema screen, have as chief ~, give special prominence to. Hence -**fea'tur**εd² (-cherd), ~LESS (-cherl-), aa. [f. OF *faiture* f. L *factura* (*facere fact-* make, -URE)]

feb'rifuge, n. Medicine to reduce fever, cooling drink. Hence **febrif'ug**AL a. [f. F *fébrifuge* (L *febris* fever, *fugare* drive away)]

feb'rile, a. Of fever, feverish. [F, f. L *febrilis* (prec.-IL)]

Feb'ruary (-rŏŏ-), n. Second month of year (~ *fill-dike*, name referring to its rain & snow). [f. L *Februarius* (*februa* puri-fication)]

fē'cit, fēcεr'unt, (abbr. *fec.*), v. sing. & pl. 3rd pers. (So-&-so) made this picture etc. (used with artist's signature). [L, perf. of *facere* make]

fεck'less, a. Feeble, futile, inefficient. Hence ~LY² adv., ~NESS n. [Sc. *feck* perh. for EFFECT + -LESS]

fec'ulent, a. Turbid, fetid. So ~ENCE n. [F (*f(-)* f.L *faeculentus* (FAECES, -ULENT)]

fec'und, a. Prolific, fertile; fertilizing. So **fecun'd**ITY n. [f. F *fécond* f. L *fecundus*]

fec'undāte, v.t. Make fruitful; impreg-nate. Hence ~ATION n. [L FECUNDāre, -ATE³]

fed. See FEED¹.

fed'eral, a. **1.** (Theol.) based on doctrine of Covenants. **2.** (Pol.) of the polity in which several States form a unity but remain independent in internal affairs; concerning this whole & not the separate parts. **3.** Relating to, favouring, central (as distinct from State) government. Hence ~ISM(3), ~IST(2), nn., ~IZE(3) v.t., ~IZA'TION n., ~LY² adv. [f. F *fédéral* (L *foedus-eris* covenant, cogn. w. *fides* FAITH, +-AL)]

fed'erate, v.t. & i. Band together (t. & i.) in league for some common object; organ-ize (t. & i. of States) on a FEDERAL basis. So ~ATE² (-āt), ~ATIVE, aa., ~ATIVELY² adv. [L *foederare* (prec.), -ATE³]

federā'tion, n. Federating, whence ~IST(2) (-sho-) n.; federated society, esp. federal empire or group of States; IM-PERIAL ~. [f. F *fédération* f. L *foedera-tionem* (prec. -ATION)]

fee, n., & v.t. (~d, ~d). **1.** Fief, feudal benefice, (Hist.). **2.** Inherited estate (~ *simple*, without limitation to particular class of heirs; ~*tail*, with such limitation; *hold in ~ simple* or ~, have as absolute property). **3.** Sum payable to public officer for performing his function, or remuneration of lawyer, physician, or professional man (RETAINING~); entrance money for examination, society, etc.; terminal school-money; gratuity. **4.** vb. Pay ~ to, engage for a ~. [f. OF *fé, fief, fieu*, med. L *feodum, feudum*, etym. dub.]

fee'ble, a. & n. **1.** Weak, infirm: deficient in character or intelligence; wanting in energy, force, or effect; dim, indistinct; hence ~leNESS (-ln-) n., ~ISH(2) a., ~LY² adv. **2.** n. (Fenc.) = FOIBLE. [f. OF *feble, foible*, (now *faible*) f. L *flebilis* lamentable (*flēre* weep)]

feed¹, v.t. & i. (fēd). Supply with food (~ *a cold*, eat plentifully when you have a cold); put food into mouth of (*cannot ~ himself*); gratify (cattle); gratify (*vanity* etc., also *eyes* etc.), comfort (person) *with hope* etc.; take food, eat, (*at the high table*; *well, high*, etc., often ~ *on*, con-sume); serve as food for; nourish, make grow, (~ *up*, fatten, also satiate; *fed up*, sl., having had too much of something, *bored with*); keep (reservoir, fire, etc.) supplied; supply (machine) with material (~*pipe*, doing this); use (land) as pasture (often ~ *down, close*); deal out (fodder) to animals; supply(material)(*in*)to machine; (Theatr. sl.) supply (principal comedian) with cues; (Football) give a pass to (of cattle) eat, eat *down*, (pasture); ~*ing-bottle*, for hand-fed infants. [OE *fēdan* cf. FOOD]

feed², n. **1.** Act of feeding, giving of food, (*two biscuits at one ~*; *out at ~*, turned out *to graze*; *off one's ~*, with no appetite; *on the ~*, of fish, feeding or looking out for

food); pasturage, green crops; horse's allowance of oats etc.; fodder; (colloq.) meal, feast; feeding of machine, material supplied, charge of gun; ~-tank, -trough, holding water for locomotive. [f. prec.]

feed³. See FEE.

feed′er, n. In vbl senses; esp.: ~, one who eats much etc.; child's feeding-bottle; ‖ child's bib; tributary stream (also fig.); ‖ (Rounders etc.) player who tosses ball to striker; hopper or feeding apparatus in machine; ~ line, railway, branch line linking up outlying districts with main line. [-ER¹]

feed′ing, a. In vbl senses; also, ~ storm, one that constantly increases. [-ING¹]

fee-faw-fŭm′, int. In vbl senses; also, ~ storm, child. [in Jack the Giant-Killer]

feel, v.t. & i. (fĕlt), & n. 1. Explore by touch (~ the pulse of), lit., & fig. =cautious-ly ascertain sentiments of; ~ one's way, (about) with hand after, for; try to ascertain by touch whether, if, how; (Mil.) recomoitre (ground, enemy); perceive by touch (~ a hard substance, heat, pain, a blow; I felt him move, moving, that he was cold;~ one's legs or feet, find firm stand-ing, also fig., be at ease); have sensation of touch; be conscious of (sensation, emotion, conviction; I feel it want, desidera-tum); be consciously (~well, warm, angry, CHEAP; ~ quite oneself, be fit, self-pos-sessed, etc.; ~ UP to work etc.; ~ like do-ing, have inclination to do); experience (the storm severely), be affected by, behave as if conscious of, (ship ~s her helm); be emotionally affected by, have sympathy with or compassion for, (~ the censure keenly); have vague or emotional con-viction (that); esp. ~ in one's bones). 2. n. Sense of touch (firm to the ~); testing by touch; sensation (quasi-pass.) be realized as, seem, produce impression of being, (air ~s chilly; ~s like velvet). 2. n. Sense of touch (firm to the ~); testing by touch; sensation characterizing something. [com.-WG.; OE fēlan, cf. G fühlen, f. Aryan pol-whence Gk palamē, L palma, palm of hand]

feel′er, n. In vbl senses: esp.: organ in certain animals for testing things by touch or searching for food; (pl.) scout; tentative proposal or hint, feeler d'essai. [-ER¹]

feel′ing¹, n. In vbl senses: esp.: sense of touch: physical sensation; emotion (often of hope, fear, etc.); (pl.) susceptibilities, sympathies, (hurts my ~s, offends me); readiness to feel, tenderness for others' sufferings, (good ~, avoidance of unkind-ness etc.); consciousness of (had a ~ of safety); conviction not based solely on reason; sentiment (the general ~ was against it); (Psych.; differently used by various writers &c).

feel′ing², a. In vbl senses: esp.: sensitive; sympathetic; showing emotion; heart-felt (a ~ pleasure). Hence ~LY² adv. [-ING²]

feet. See FOOT.

feign (fān), v.t. & i. Invent (excuse, story, accusation, forge (document), re-present in fiction, imagine, (arch.); simulate, pretend, (~ that one is mad, oneself mad, madness); practise simula-tion. [f. OF feindre f. L fingere]

feint² (fā-), n. & v.i. 1. Sham attack (blow, cut, thrust, or military assault) to divert attention or deceive opponent; pretence (make a ~ of doing). 2. v.i. Make ~ (at, upon, against). [f. F feinte n. (feindre FEIGN]

‖ **feint²** (fā-), a. & adv. ~ lines, ruled ~, = FAINT¹. [old spelling often kept in this use]

fĕl(d)spar, n. Kinds of crystalline white or flesh-red mineral. So **fĕl(d)spă′th′ic a.** [f. G feldspath(b) t. feld field, spat(h) spar; spelling fels-, commoner but incorrect, due to false deriv. f. G fels rock]

fĕl′ibrist, n. Member of the Félibrige, a society of Provençal poets & writers (Mistral etc.). [f. F Félibrige, -IST]

fĕl′icide, n. Cat-killing. [f. L feles cat + -CIDE]

felicif′ic, a. (eth.). Tending to happiness. [f. L felicificus (felix happy, -FIC)]

felic′itate, v.t. Make happy (rare); con-gratulate (usu. on), whence (usu. pl.) ~A′TION n. [f. L felicitare (felix happy, -ATE³]

felic′itous, a. Blissful (rare); (of expres-sion, quotation, civilities, or person in these connexions) strikingly apt, plea-santly ingenious. Hence ~LY² adv. [foll. -OUS]

felic′ity, n. Being happy, intense happi-ness; a blessing; fortunate trait; happy faculty in expression, appropriateness; well chosen phrase. [f. OF felicité t. L felicitatem (felix happy, -TY)]

fel′ine, a. & n. Of cats; catlike (~ amen-ties, veiled spite, women's innocent-seeming thrusts), whence **felin′ITY** n.; (n.) =prec. [f. L felinus (prec., -INE²)]

fell¹, n. Animal's hide or skin, with the hair (also transf. of human skin); thick or matted hair or wool, fleece, (~ of hair, un-kempt hair of head); (~ of hair, un-kempt hair of head). [com.-Teut., cf. G fell, cogn. w. MONGER, [com.-pellis; also w. FILM]

‖ **fell²,** n. Hill (in names, as Sca F~); stretch of N.-English moorland. [f. ON fiall perh. cogn. w. G fels rock]

fell³, a. (poet.). Fierce, ruthless, terrible, destructive. [f. OF fel t. pop. L fello

sensation or desire or emotion (not per-ception or thought), element of pleasure or pain in any mental state, intuitive belief; (Art) general emotional effect produced. [-ING¹]

fell¹, v.t., & n. Strike (person, animal) down by blow or cut; cut down (tree; n., amount of timber cut); stitch down (projection of seam). [causative of FALL¹, cf. G *fällen*]

fell⁵. See FALL¹.

fell'ah (-a), n. (pl. ~*een*, ~*s*). Egyptian peasant. [Arab.]

fell'oe (-l, -lō), **fell'y**, n. Outer circle (or one piece of it) of wheel, attached by spokes. [OE *felg*, cf. G *felge*]

fell'ow (-ō), n. **1.** One associated with another, comrade, (usu. in pl., as *separated from his ~s; good ~, boon companion;* HAIL³~*well-met; ~-feeling,* sympathy). **2.** Counterpart, match, other of pair, equal, one of same class, contemporary, (*stone dead hath no ~, no keeper of secrets like a dead man; shall never find his ~; passed all his ~s*). **3.** ‖ Co-opted graduate incorporated member of college (~ *commoner,* undergraduate privileged to dine at ~'s table); ‖ elected graduate holding stipend for certain years on condition of research. **4.** Member of governing body in some Universities; member of various learned Societies. **5.** Man, boy, (*poor ~!, my dear or good ~; old ~; a ~,* occas. = *one, I,* as *a ~ can't work all day long; the ~,* contemptuously). **6.** (In comb. with nn.; or ~) belonging to same class (~ *creature,* person or animal also created by God), associated in joint action (~ *soldier*), in same relation to same object (~ *citizen,* whence ~**cit'izenSHIP** n.; ~*-countryman*); ~*-traveller,* (also) non-Communist who sympathizes with aims and general policy of Communist party. [OE *féolaga* (FEE, LAY) one who lays down money in partnership]

fell'owship (-lō-), n. Participation, sharing, community of interest; companionship, intercourse, friendliness, (often *good hand of ~,* sign of admission); ‖ body of associates, company, (*right hand of ~,* sign of admission); guild, corporation; brotherhood, fraternity; ‖ dignity or income of college fellow. [-SHIP]

felly. See FELLOE.

fel'ō dē sē, n. (pl. *felonēs, felos*). Self-murderer, (no. pl.) self-murder. [Anglo-L., = FELON about himself]

fel'on¹, a. (poet.), & n. **1.** Cruel, wicked, murderous. **2.** n. One who has committed felony. [OF, f. LL *fellonem* nom. -*o* perh. f. L *fel* gall]

fel'on², n. Small abscess esp. under or near nail, whitlow. [perh. as prec.]

felon'ious, a. Criminal; (Law) of, involving, felony; who has committed felony. Hence ~LY² adv. [FELONY +-OUS]

fel'onry, n. The class or body of felons. [-RY]

fel'onў, n. Crime of kind legally graver than misdemeanour. [f. F *félonie* (FELON, -Y¹)]

felspar. See FELDSPAR.

fel'stone (-ōn), n. Compact felspar occurring in amorphous rock masses. [f. G *felsstein* (*fels* rock, *stein* stone)]

felt¹, n. A horse-disease. [?]

felt², n., & v.t. & i. **1.** Kind of cloth made by rolling & pressing wool with lees or size; (attrib.) made of this (esp. ~ *hat*); hence ~Y² a. **2.** vb. Make into ~, mat together; become matted; cover with ~. [OE; cf. Du. *vilt*, G *filz*]

felt³. See FEEL.

fel'ucca, n. Small Mediterranean coasting vessel with oars or lateen sails or both. [It., perh. f. Arab.]

fem'āle (-l), a. & n. **1.** Of the offspring-bearing sex (~ *child, slave, dog*); (of plants or their parts) fruit-bearing, having pistil & no stamens, (also used of some plants by mere metaphor suggested by their colour etc., as ~ *fern, bamboo, myrtle*); of women (~ *sex, education, suffrage, weakness*). **2.** Of inferior vigour etc. (~ *sapphire,* pale variety). **3.** (In instruments etc.) fitted to receive corresponding male part (~ *screw,* as in nuts). **4.** n. ~ person (*the law is harsh to all ~s*) or animal; (vulg.) woman, girl, (*a young ~ has called*). [ME & OF *femelle* n. f. L *femella* dim. of *femina* woman, w. assim. to male]

feme co'vert (fèm krt), **feme sõle**, nn. (legal). (*Covert*) married woman; (*sole*) spinster, widow, or married woman entirely independent of her husband as regards property. [AF (*soul*)]

feminal'itÿ, n. Female nature; female peculiarity; woman's knick-knack etc. [obs. *feminal* f. OF (L *femina* woman, -AL) +-ITY]

feminē'itÿ, n. Womanliness; womanishness. [f. L *femineus* (*femina* woman) +-ITY]

fem'inine, a. Of female sex (rare); of women; womanly; (Gram.) having the gender proper to women's names; (Pros.) ~ *rhyme,* of two syllables, the second being unstressed (orig. in F verse, of words ending in mute -*e*), ~ *ending,* of line with last accent on penult; ~ *caesura,* not immediately following stress. Hence ~LY² adv., ~NESS, feminin'ITY, nn. [f. OF *feminin* f. L *femininus* (*femina* woman, -INE¹)]

fem'inism, n. Advocacy, extended recognition, of the claims of women. So ~IST n. [f. L *femina* woman +-ISM]

feminin'itÿ, n. = FEMININITY. [f. OF *féminité* (L *femina* woman, -ITY)]

fem'iniz|e, v.t. & i. Make or become feminine. Hence ~A'TION n. [f. L as prec. +-IZE]

femme de chambre (see Ap.), n. Lady's maid; chambermaid. [F]

fēm'ur (-er), n. (pl. ~*s, fĕm'orā*). Thighbone; corresponding part of insect. So **fēm'orAL.** [L]

fēn¹, n. Low marshy or flooded tract of land (‖ the ~*s,* low-lying districts in Cambs. etc.; ~-*berry,* cranberry; ~-*fire,*

will-o'-the-wisp; ~s; ||~-reeve, officer in charge of ~-lands; ~-runners, kind of skates. Hence ~n'y² a. [OE; cf. Du. ven, G fenne]

fen²·, fens. See FAIN².

fence¹, n. Art of fencing, use of the sword (master of ~); skilled swordsman, often (fig. = good debater); (arch.) bulwark; hedge, wall, railing, etc., keeping out intruders from field etc.; (sit on the ~, remain neutral in contest, not take sides; come etc. down on right side of ~, join winner; PUT horse at ~); guard, guide, gauge, in various machines; receiver, receiving-house, of stolen goods; ||~-month, -season, -time, close time for game or fish. [for DEFENCE]

fence², v.t. & i. Practise sword-play, use the sword scientifically, (~ with question or questioner), parry, evade answering; screen, shield, protect, (from, against); repel, keep off or out; surround (as) with fence, enclose, fortify, (~d cities in O.T.); (of horse) leap fences; deal in stolen goods. Hence fen'cer¹·² n. (esp. of swordsman, also of horse). [f. prec.]

fence'less (-sl-), a. Unenclosed; (poet.) unfortified, defenceless. [FENCE¹+-LESS]

fen'cible, n. (hist.). Soldier liable only for home service. [for DEFENSIBLE]

fen'cing, n. In vbl senses; also: railing; fences; material for fences; ||~-cully,-ken, storer, store, of stolen goods. [-ING¹]

fend, v.t. & i. Ward off, keep away, repel from; provide for (usu. oneself). [for DEFEND]

fen'der, n. Thing used to keep something off, prevent collision, etc.; guard, esp. metal frame for fire to keep coals from rolling into room; ||~-stool, long foot-stool before ~. Hence ~LESS a. [-ER¹]

fenestell'a, n. (archit.). Niche in wall S. of altar holding piscina & often credence. [L, dim. of fenestra window]

fenes'trate, a. (bot., zool.). With small window-like perforations. [f. L fenestrare (prec.), -ATE²]

fenestra'tion, n. (Archit.) arrangement of windows in a building. [prec., -ATION]

Fen'ian, n. & a. 1. One of a league among the Irish in U.S. for promoting revolution & overthrowing English government in Ireland; hence ~ISM(3) n. 2. adj. Of ~s or ~ism. [f. OIr. féne name of ancient Irish people confused w. fiann guard of legendary kings]

fenks, n. pl. Fibrous parts of whale's blubber, refuse of blubber when melted. [?]

fenn'ec, n. Small N.-African fox notable for its huge pointed ears. [Moorish]

fenn'el, n. Yellow-flowered fragrant umbelliferous herb used in sauces. [OE finugl, f. L faeniculum (faenum hay, -CULE)]

fēn'ugreek, n. Leguminous plant with seeds used in farriery. [f. L faenugraecum (faenum hay, Graecus Greek)]

feoff. See FIEF.

feoffee' (fĕfē'), n. Person to whom freehold estate in land is conveyed by a feoffment; ~ in or of trust, trustee invested with such estate. [f. AF feoffé p.p. f. OF fieffer (FIEF), see -EE]

feoff'ment (fĕf-), n. Particular mode of conveying freehold estate. [as prec., -MENT]

feoff'or, -er, (fĕf-), n. One who makes feoffment to another. [as FEOFFEE, -OR²]

fĕr'al¹, a. Wild, untamed, uncultivated; brutal. [f. L fera wild beast+-AL]

fē'ral², a. = of a wild nature (animals ~). [L, = of a wild nature (hares are, the hare is, ~; wild state)]

fer de lance (fār de lahns'), n. A large and peculiarly venomous snake of tropical S. America. [F, = iron head of lance]

fē'rĕtory, n. Shrine for saint's relics, tomb; ||bier; chapel in which shrines were deposited. [ME fertre f. L feretrum f. Gk pheretron (pherō bear), w. assim. to -ORY]

fēr'ial, a. (eccl.). (Of day) ordinary, not appointed for festival or fast (~ service etc., for use on ~ day). [f. F férial f. L feriālis (feria holiday+-AL)]

fērine, a. = FERAL. [f. L ferinus (fera wild beast, -INE¹)]

Fering'hee (-inggē), n. (Indian term for) European, esp. Indian-born Portuguese. [corrupt. of FRANK¹]

fer'ment¹, n. Leaven, fermenting-agent; fermenting; fermentation; agitation, excitement, tumult. [F, f. L fermentum (fervēre boil, -MENT)]

ferment²·, v.i. & t. Suffer, subject to, fermentation; (make) effervesce; excite, stir up, foment. Hence ~ABLE a. [f. F fermenter f. L fermentāre (prec.)]

fermentā'tion, n. Process like that induced by leaven in dough, with effervescence, heat, & change of properties; agitation, excitement. Hence fermênt'ATIVE a. [f. L fermentātio (prec.-ATION)]

fern, n. One of a large group of vascular cryptogams with feathery fronds (also collect., go through heath & ~); ~-owl, Nightjar. Hence ~LESS, ~Y², aa., ~ERY(3) n. [OE fearn cf. G farn cogn. w. Skr. parna wing, feather, leaf]

fero'cious (-shus), a. Fierce, savage, cruel. Hence ~LY² (-shus-) adv. [f. L feroc-ocis+-OUS]

fero'city, n. Ferocious character or act. [f. F férocité f. L ferocitātem (prec. -TY)]

-ferous, suf. (in actual use -iferous, see -i-) forming adj., = -fer -producing or act., carrying; in adj. taken direct or [f. F fer-, L fer- bear]

thr. F -fère f. L as *auriferous*, & now a living suf., esp. in Nat. Hist., = -bearing, -having.

fě'rŏx, n. Great lake trout. [L name *Salmo ferox* fierce salmon]

fě'rrāte, n. A salt of ferric acid. [f. L *ferrum* iron +-ATE[4](3)]

fě'rrēous, a. Of, containing, iron. [f. L *ferreus* (prec.) +-OUS]

fě'rrĕt[1], n. Half-tamed variety of polecat kept for driving rabbits from burrows, killing rats, etc.; searcher, detective. Hence ~Y[2] a. [f. OF *furet* dim. of *furon* f. LL *furonem* nom. -o robber (L *fur*)]

fě'rrĕt[2], v.i. & t. Hunt with ferrets (*go ~ ing*); clear out (holes, ground), take or drive away (rabbits etc.), with ferrets (*about, away, out*, etc.); rummage, search *about*, (*for*); search out (secrets, criminals, etc.), [f. prec.]

fě'rrĕt[3], n. Stout cotton or silk tape. [f. It. *fioretti* floss-silk pl. of *floretto* dim. of *fiore* f. L *flos -oris* flower]

fě'rri-, comb. form used to indicate presence of iron in the ferric state (cf. FERRO-). [as f. L *ferrum* iron]

fě'rriage, n. Conveyance by, charge for using, ferry. [-AGE]

fě'rric, a. Of (Chem.) containing iron in trivalent form (cf. FERROUS). [as FERRI-+-IC]

ě'rriferous, a. Iron-yielding, [as prec. +-FEROUS]

Fě'rris wheel, n. Giant revolving vertical wheel supporting passenger cars on its periphery, an attraction at exhibitions etc. [G. W. G. *Ferris*, U.S. engineer]

fě'rro-, comb. form of L *ferrum* iron, as ~-*calcite*; ~-*cŏncrēte*, = REINFORCED *concrete*; (Chem.) containing iron in the ferrous state (cf. FERRI-).

fě'rro-magnĕt'ic, a. Magnetic as opp. to diamagnetic. [prec.]

fě'rrotype, n. Positive photograph taken on thin iron plate; this process. [FERRO-TYPE]

fě'rrous, a. (chem.). Containing iron as a divalent (cf. FERRIC). [as FERRO-+-OUS]

ferru'ginous, a. Of, containing, iron-rust or iron as a chemical constituent; rust-coloured, reddish-brown. [f. L *ferrugo -ginis* rust (*ferrum* iron) +-OUS)]

fě'rrule, -rel, n. Metal ring or cap strengthening end of stick or tube; band strengthening or forming joint. Hence **fě'rrulĕd[2]** (-ld) a. [earlier *verrel* f. OF *virele* f. med. L *virola* f. L *viriola* dim. of *viriae* bracelets, altered as though dim. of *ferrum* iron]

fě'rry, v.t. & i., & n. 1. Convey or pass in boat, work (boat), (of boat) pass to & fro, over river, canal, or strait; fly (aircraft) from factory to operational airfield (~ *pilot*, one who makes such flights). 2. n. Place, provision, for ~*ing*; (Law) right of ~*ing* & levying toll for it; ~*boat*; ~*man*; ~-*bridge*, large ~*boat* transporting railway train entire. [n. f. vb, OE *ferian* cogn. w. FARE]

fě'rtile (-īl, -ĭl), a. Bearing abundantly, fruitful, (lit. & fig.; ~ *of, in*). So **fertǐ'lǐry** n. [f. OF *fertil* f. L *fertilis* (*ferre* bear)]

fer'tǐlīze, v.t. Make fertile or productive (esp. soil); fecundate (individual, organ). Hence ~ABLE a., ~A'TION, ~ER[1](1, 2), nn. [-IZE]

fě'rula (-ool-), n. (Bot.) giant fennel(-ula); flat ruler with widened pierced end for punishing boys, whence **fě'rule** (-ool) v.t. [L (-a)]

fěr'vent, a. Hot, glowing; ardent, intense, (~ *soul, lover, hatred*), so **fěr'vENCY** n. Hence ~LY[2] adv. [F, f. L *fervēre* boil, -ENT]

fěr'vid, a. = prec. (poet. in first sense). [f. L *fervidus* (prec.)] Hence ~LY[2] adv.

fer'vour (-er), n. Glowing condition, intense heat; vehemence, passion, zeal. [f. OF *fervor* f. L *ferrorem* nom. -or (PERVENT-, -OR[3])]

Fěscěnnine, a. ~ *verses*, scurrilous lampoons. [f. *Fescenninus* (*Fescennia* town in Etruria, -INE[1])]

fěs'cue, n. Small stick, teacher's pointer; kinds of grass. [f. OF *festu* f. L *festuca*]

fěsse, n. (her.). Two horizontal lines as bar across middle of field. [OF, f. FASCIA]

fěs'tal, a. Of a feast; keeping holiday; gay. Hence ~LY[2] adv. [OF (FEAST, -AL)]

fěs'ter, v.i. & t., & n. 1. (Of wound or sore) generate matter, ulcerate; (of poison, disease, grief) cause suppuration, rankle; putrefy, rot; cause festering in. 2. n. ~*ing* condition. [f. obs. n. *fester* f. OF *festre* f. L FISTULA]

fěs'tival, a. (not pred.), & n. Festal day, celebration, (pl.) festive proceedings, [f. OF *festival* f. L *festivālis* (foll. -AL)]

fěs'tive, a. Of a feast; joyous; fond of feasting, jovial. Hence ~LY[2] (-ĭv-) adv. [f. L *festivus* (*festum* FEAST, -IVE)]

fěstǐv'itÿ, n. Gaiety, rejoicing; festive celebration, (pl.) festive proceedings. [f. OF *festivité* f. L *festivitātem* (prec., -TY)]

fěstōōn', n. & v.t. 1. Chain of flowers or leaves, or ribbons etc., hung in curve between two points. 2. v.t. Adorn (as with, form into, ~s. Hence ~ERY(5) n. [f. F *festoon* f. It. *festone* perh. f. *festa* feast +-OON]

fĕtch[1], v.t. & i., & n. 1. (Go for &) bring back (person or thing; ~, or *go &* ~, *a doctor*; FAR[1]~*ed*; ~ *& carry*, run backwards & forwards with things, be a servant); cause to come, draw forth, (blood, tears; ~ *up*, vomit); bring in, realize, sell for, (a price); move the feelings of, delight (whence ~ING[2] a.); or irritate; heave (sigh), draw (breath); deal (blow; usu. with ind. obj., ~ *him a box on the ears*); ~ *a* COMPASS[1]; ~ *up*, come to a stand. 2. n. Far-reaching effort

(arch.); dodge, trick; (Naut.) line of continuous extent from point to point, e.g. of a bay or of open sea. [OE *feccan*]

fetch², n. Person's wraith or double. [?]

fête (fāt), n., & v.t. 1. Festival, great entertainment. (~*-day*, appointed for ~); day of saint after whom child is named, observed in R.-C. countries like birth-day. 2. v.t. Entertain, make much of, (person). [F. F *fête*) FEAST]

fête champêtre (see Ap.). [f. F *fête*) FEAST] fête. [F]

fetial (-shl) a. & n. (Rom. ant.). 1. ~ *law*, of declarations of war & treaties of peace. 2. n. One of Roman college of priests who served as heralds. [f. L *fetialis* etym. dub.]

fetid, foe- (fĕ-) a. Stinking. Hence ~LY² adv. ~NESS n. [f. L *fetidus* (*fetere* stink)]

fetish, -ch(e) (-sh), n. Inanimate object worshipped by savages for its magical powers or as being inhabited by a spirit; principle etc. irrationally reverenced. Hence or cogn. ~EER², ~ER¹, ~ISM(3), ~ist(3), nn., ~is'tic a. [f. F *fétiche* f. Port. *feitiço* charm, orig. adj. f. FACTITIOUS]

fetlock, n. Part of horse's leg where tuft of hair grows behind pastern-joint (~*deep*, so as to cover ~*s*). [ME *fytlok* cf. G *fisstoch* etym. dub.]

fetor, n. Stench. [L, see FETID, -OR¹]

fetter, n. & v.t. 1. Shackle for the feet; bond, (pl.) captivity; check, restraint; ~*lock*, (heraldic representation of) D-shaped ~ for tethering horse by leg. 2. v.t. Bind (as) with ~s, impede, re-strain. Hence ~LESS a. [OE *feter* cf. G *fesser* f. OTeut. *fet-* cogn. w. *fôt* FOOT; also w. L *pedica*, Gk *pedē*, fetter]

fettle, n. Condition, trim, (*in good* etc. ~). [f. dial. vb *fettle* put right cf. OE *fetel* bond]

fetus. See FOETUS.

fetwa, n. Decision given by Moslem judicial authority. [Arab.]

feu, n. (Sc.). Perpetual lease at fixed rent; piece of land so held. [var. of FEE]

feud¹, n. Lasting mutual hostility (*be at ~ with*), esp. (often *deadly ~*) between two tribes, families, etc., with murderous assaults in revenge for previous injury. [ME & OF *fede* f. OHG *fēhida* = OE *fǣhthu* enmity; cogn. w. FOE]

feud², n. Fief, feudal benefice; territory held in fee. [f. med. l. as FEE]

feud'al, a. Of a feud or fief; ~ *system*, medieval European polity based on relation of vassal & superior arising from holding of lands in feud; of, resembling, according to, this system. Hence ~ISM(3), ~IST(2), nn., ~is'tic a., adv. ~IZE(3) v.t., ~IZA'TION n. [f. med. L *feudalis* (prec., -ITY)]

feudal'ity, n. Feudal system or principles; feudal holding, fief. [f. F *féudalité* (prec., -TY)]

feud'atory, a. & n. Feudally subject to, under overlordship; (n.) feudal vassal. [f. med. L *feudare* enfeoff (FEUD²), -ORY]

feu de joie (ferdezhwah'), n. Salute of guns fired on ceremonial occasions. [F]

feuilleton (see Ap.), n. Ruled-off portion at foot of (esp. French) newspapers, devoted to fiction, criticism, light literature, etc. [F. = leaflet]

fēv'er, n., & v.t. 1. Morbid condition with high temperature & excessive change & destruction of tissues; any of a group of diseases so characterized, each with distinctive name, as *scarlet*, *typhoid*, &c., nervous excitement, agitation; ~ *heat*, high temperature of body in ~; ~-*trap*, place that collects ~-*germs*. 2. v.t. Throw into ~. [OE *fēfor* f. L *febris*]

fēv'erfew, n. A herb formerly used in medicine. [OE *feferfuge* f. L *febrifugia* (prec., *fugare* drive away)]

fēv'erish, a. Having symptoms of fever; excited, fitful, restless; (of places) in-fested by fever, feverous. Hence ~LY² adv. ~NESS n. [-ISH¹]

fēv'erous, a. Infested with or apt to cause fever; feverish. [-OUS]

few, a., & n. Not many (~ is opp. to *many*, words; *he spoke a ~ words*; ~ *have such a chance*; ~, *a* ~, *of his friends remained there*; *a ~ know the truth*; *a faithful ~ remained*; the minority, the elect, etc.; *not a* ~, many; (colloq.) *a good* ~, a fair number; (of); *every ~ days* etc., once in every group of a ~ days; (sl.) *a* ~, very much, beyond a doubt. Hence ~NESS n. [com. Teut.; OE *fēawe* a, OHG *fao*; cogn. w. L *paucus* & *pauillus*, Gk *pauros*. In the use with *a* (cf. *hundred* etc.) ~ forms with the n. a collective, which however is followed by pl. vb]

fey (fā), a. (Sc.). || Fated to die, at point of death; disordered in mind (often with over-confidence etc.) like person about to die. [com.-Teut.; OE *fǣge* cf. G *feige* cowardly]

fez, n. Turkish cap, a tasselled dull-red truncated cone. [f. Turk. *fes* perh. f. *Fez*, town]

fiacre (fē'ahkr), n. French four-wheeled cab. [f. the Hôtel de St F~, Paris]

fiancé, -ée, (see Ap.), n. One's betrothed. (-ē) male, (-ée) female. [F]

Fianna Fáil (fēŭna fawl), n. Irish political organization and party which was founded in 1926 and entered Dáil Eireann in 1927. [nom. pl. of Ir. *fian* + gen. of *Fál* Ireland); lit. = armed men of Ireland]

fiāş'cō, n. (pl. -os). Failure or break-down (orig. in dramatic etc. performance); ignominious result. [It. = bottle (significance doubtful)]

fiat (-ăt, -aat), n., & v.t. Authorization; decree, order, (n., & rarely vb = authorize);

* ~ money, inconvertible paper-money made legal tender by Government decree. [L, = be it done]

fib¹, n., & v.i. (-bb-). (Tell) trivial or venial lie. Hence **~b'ER¹**, **~'SHER**, nn. [perh. f. obs. *fible-fable* nonsense, redupl. of FABLE]

fib², n., & v.t. (-bb-). A blow (vb, strike, hit about) in pugilism etc. [?]

fi'bre (-ber), n. Thread-like filament forming with others animal & vegetable tissue or textile substance; substance consisting of ~s; fibrous structure; structure, grain, character, (*man of coarse ~*); substance that can be spun, woven, or felted; small root or twig. Hence (-)**fi'bred²** (-berd), **~NESS** (-er-), **fib'riFORM**, **fib'rOUS**, aa., **fib'rOUSLY** adv., **fib'rOUSNESS** n., **fibro-** comb. form. [F, f. L *fibra* etym. dub.]

fib'ril, n. Small fibre; subdivision of fibre; ultimate subdivision of root. Hence **~lAR(Y)**, **~lATE**, **~lATED**, **~l'FORM**, **~lOSE¹**, aa., **~lA'TION** n. [also *fibrilla* mod. L dim. of prec.]

fib'rin, n. Coagulable lymph found in animal & vegetable matter. Hence **~o-** comb. form, **~OUS** a. [FIBRE + -IN]

fib'roid, a. & n. Of fibrous structure or appearance; (n.) = uterine tumour. [FIBRO- + -OID]

fib'roin, n. Chemical substance of which silk & cobweb mainly consist. [FIBRO- + -IN]

fibrom'a, n. (pl. *-ta*). Fibrous tumour. [mod. L (FIBRE, & cf. SARCOMA)]

fibrosi'tis, n. (Rheumatic) inflammation of fibrous tissue. [mod. L (FIBRE, -ITIS)]

fib'ula, n. (pl. *-ae*, *-as*). Splint bone on outer side of leg. Hence **~AR¹** a. [L, = brooch (*figere* fix)]

-fica'tion, suf. (in actual use *-ification*, see -ification (nom. *-tio*), which formed nn. of action f. vv. in *-ficare* -FY. E adopted many pairs of words, n. & vb, f. L thr. F or of F formation, as *purify*, *purification*; hence *-fication* has become the recognized means of forming nn. corresp. to vv. in *-fy* exc. when these repr. L vv. in *-facere* (see -FACTION); as a rule the formation is based only on possible L types; exceptions are *beauti~*, *Frenchi~*, *transmogri~*.

ficelle', a. String-coloured. [F. = string]

fi'chu (-shoo), n. Woman's small triangular shawl of lace etc. for shoulders & neck. [F]

fic'kle, a. Inconstant, changeable. Hence **~NESS** (-lin-) n. [OE *ficol* cf. *beficien* deceive]

fic'tile, a. Made of earth or clay by potter; of pottery. [f. L *fictilis* (*fingere* fict- fashion, -IL)]

fic'tion, n. Feigning, invention; thing feigned or imagined, invented statement or narrative; literature consisting of such narrative, esp. novels, whence **~IST** (-shon-) n.; conventionally accepted falsehood (esp. *legal*, *polite*, ~). Hence **~AL** (-shon-) a. [F, f. L *fictionem* (prec., -ION)]

ficti'tious (-shus), a. Counterfeit, not genuine; (of name or character) assumed; imaginary, unreal; of, in, novels; regarded as what it is called by legal or conventional fiction. Hence **~LY²** adv., **~NESS** n., (-shus-). [f. L *ficticius* (prec.) +-OUS]

fic'tive, a. Creating, created, by imagination. [F (*-if*, *-ive*), see FICTION, -IVE]

fid, n. 1. (Naut.) conical wooden pin used in splicing; (also *~ pin*) square wooden or iron bar for supporting topmast. 2. Small thick piece or wedge of anything. [?]

fid'dle, n., int., & v.i. & t. 1. (Fam. or contempt. for) violin (*fit as a ~*, in good condition & spirits; *hang up one's ~ when one comes home*, be witty abroad & dull at home; *play first*, *second*, ~, take leading, subordinate, position; *face as long as a ~*, dismal). 2. (Naut.) contrivance for stopping things from rolling off table. 3. **~-BOW¹**; **~-case**, for holding ~; **~-de-dee'**, int. & n., nonsense; **~-faddle**, (n.) trivial matters, idler, (adj.) petty, fussy, (int.) nonsense, (v.i.) fuss, trifle; **~-head**, carving at ship's bows; *~ pattern*, of spoons & forks with ~-shaped heads; **~stick**, (n.) = ~-bow, (also, usu. pl., as int.) nonsense! 4. int. Nonsense! 5. vb. Play the ~, play (tune etc.) on ~; be idle or frivolous, make aimless movements, (*about*, *at*, *with*, etc.); fritter away. [ME *fithele*, cf. MDu. *vedel*, G *fedel*, etym. dub.; there is med. L *vitula*, whence VIOL]

fidd'ler, n. Player on fiddle, esp. for hire (*F²'s Green*, sailor's Elysium); kind of small crab. [OE *fithelere* (prec., -ER²)]

fidd'ley, n. (naut.; pl. *~s*). Iron framework round opening of stokehole. [?]

fidd'ling, a. In vbl senses; esp. petty, futile, contemptible, inconsiderable. [-ING²]

fidel'ity, n. Faithfulness, loyalty, (*to*); strict conformity to truth or fact, exact correspondence to the original. [f. F *fidélité* f. L *fidelitadem* (*fidelis* faithful f. *fides* faith, -TY]

fidg'et, n. 1. Bodily uneasiness seeking relief in spasmodic movements (often the ~s); restless mood. 2. One who fidgets or causes others to; act of bustling etc., rustle of dress etc. Hence **~Y²** a., **~IVESS** n. [sense 1 f. obs. *fidge* to twitch, cf. G *ficken*; sense 2 f. foll.]

fidg'et², v.i. & t. Move restlessly (often *about*); be uneasy, worry; make uncomfortable, worry, (person). [f. prec.]

fid'ibus, n. Paper spill for lighting candles, pipes, etc. [?]

Fid'ō, n. Device for enabling aircraft to land by dispersing fog by means of petrol-fired flame burners heating air over runway. [initials of *Fog Investigation Dispersal Operation*]

fidū'cial (-shl), a. (surv., astron., etc.), ~ *line, point,* etc., one assumed as fixed basis of comparison etc. [f. L *fiducia* trust, AL]

fidū'ciary (-sha-), a. & n. 1. Of trust or trustee(ship); held or given in trust; (of paper currency) depending for its value on public confidence or securities. 2. n. Trustee. [f. L *fiduciarius* (as prec., ARY¹)]

fī'dus Achā'tēs (akătēz), n. Devoted follower of Aeneas in *Aeneid*.

fie (fī), int. expr. sense of outraged propriety, usu. iron. or to children (often ~ *upon you!*) [f. OF, L f *fi* excl. of disgust at stencil]

Ref [fēē]

fief, feoff (fēf), n. = FEUD².

field, n., & v.i. & t. 1. (Piece of) ground, esp. one used for pasture or tillage, & usu. bounded by hedges etc.; tract abounding in some natural product (*diamond, coal,* etc., ~). 2. Ground on which battle is fought (often *battle*-~); also fig., *left his rival in possession of the* ~; *fair* ~ *& no favour,* equal conditions in contest; *hold,* not be superseded); scene of campaign (*in the* ~, campaigning); *take, keep, the* ~, begin, continue, campaign); battle (*hard-fought, stricken,* ~); ~ *of Cloth of Gold,* scene of meeting between Henry VIII & Francis I, 1520. 3. Ground for playing cricket, football, etc.; players, partakers in outdoor contest or sport; all competitors or all except the favourite (*a good* ~, many & good competitors); (Cricket) side not batting, one of this side (see also LONG¹,~). 4. Large stretch, expanse, of sea, sky, ice, snow, etc., also fig. (*the whole* ~ *of history*). 5. (Her.) surface of escutcheon or of one of its divisions; groundwork of picture, coin, flag, etc. 6. Area or sphere of operation, observation, etc. (*each supreme in his own* ~; *filled the* ~ *of the telescope; vide* ~ *of vision; outside the magnetic* ~, not near enough to be attracted). 7. attrib. (In names of animals etc.) found in the open country (~*mouse,* ~*ash*). 8.~*allowance,* to officer on campaign to meet increased expenditure; ~*artillery, -battery, -gun* or *-piece,* light & mobile for use with armies in the ~; ~*-book* (used in ~ by surveyor for technical notes); ~*cornet,* magistrate of township in Cape Colony etc.; ~*-day,* (Mil.) manœuvring-exercise or review, (fig.) great occasion, important debate; ~ *dressing,* appliances for wound in battle; ~ *events,* athletic sports such as weight-putting, jumping, discus-throwing, etc. (cf. other than *races*); ~*-glass,* binocular telescope for outdoor use, one of the lenses of astronomical telescope or compound microscope; ~ *hospital, ambulance,* temporary hospital near battle-field; F~ *Marshal,* army officer of the highest rank; F~ *weight,* = ~*-day* (fig. sense); ~*-officer,* above captain & below general); ~*-preacher, -preaching,* in open air; ~ *punishment* (Mil.), kinds of penal servitude for offences on campaign; ~*s', ~man, ~er* at cricket; ~*-sports,* outdoor *graph,* movable for use on campaign; esp. hunting, shooting, fishing; ~ *tele-*~*work,* temporary fortification; hence ~WARD(S) adv. 9. vb. Act as ~*man* in (cricket, baseball, or rounders; stop (& return) ball; put into the ~ (of football teams etc.); (Betting) back the ~ against the favourite; hence ~ER¹ n. [com-WG; OE & G *feld*]

field'fare, n. Species of thrush spending winter in Britain. [ME *feldefare* perh.

fiend, n. The devil; evil spirit, demon; person of superhuman wickedness, esp. cruelty (often jocular, as *the interviewer* ~); (with qualifying word) devotee or addict (*fresh-air* ~, *dope* ~, *morphia* ~). Hence ~ISH¹ a., ~ishly² adv., ~'ish-NESS n., ~LIKE a. [com.-Teut., f. OE *féond* cf. G *feind* enemy, f. OTeut. vb = hate, -ND²]

fierce, a. Violent in hostility, angrily combative; raging, vehement; ardent, eager. Hence ~LY² (-sl-) adv., ~NESS (-sn-) n. [f. OF *fers* nom. of *fier* (f = prond) f. L *férus* savage]

‖ **fi'eri fā'ciās** (-shi-), n. (legal; abbr. fi. fa.). Writ to sheriff for executing judgement. [L = see that (the sum) is made]

fier'y (fīr-), a. Consisting of, flaming with, fire; (of arrows etc.) fire-bearing; looking like fire, blazing-red; (of eyes) flashing, ardent; hot as fire; acting like fire, inflaming, (~*y taste* etc.); eager, pugnacious, spirited, irritable; (of horse) mettlesome; (of gas, mine, etc.) inflammable, liable to explosions; (of cricket-pitch) making ball rise dangerously; ~*y* CROSS¹. Hence ~LY² adv., ~INESS n. [FIRE¹+-Y¹]

fiesta (fē-ěstah), n. Festivity, holiday. [Sp., = feast]

fife, n., & v.i. & t. 1. Kind of small shrill flute used with drum in military music. ~. 2. vb. Play the ~; play (air etc.) on the ~; hence fif'ER¹ n. [f. G *pfeife* PIPE, or f. F *fifre* fiféér) f. OHG *pfifri* piper]

fife-rail (-fr-), n. (naut.) Rail round mainmast with belaying-pins. [perh. f. prec. because fifer sat on it while anchor was weighing]

fifteen' (also fif'-), a. & n. One more than fourteen, 15, XV; (Rugby football) side

of 15 players; the F~, Jacobite rising of 1715. Hence ~TH² a. & n. [OE *fífte, -fíne*, (FIVE, -TEEN)]

fifth, a. & n. 1. Next after fourth (*smite under the ~rib*, kill; *~ wheel of coach etc.*, something superfluous; also as name of two horizontal half-circles sliding one over the other when a carriage-front turns); ~ *part*, one of five equal parts into which thing is or might be divided. 2. n. = ~ *part*; (Mus.) interval of which the span involves five alphabetical notes, harmonic combination of the notes thus separated; (pl.) ~*rate material*. 3. ~ *column*, organized body sympathizing with and working for the enemy within a country at war etc., (loosely) traitors, spies; ~*column activities*, organized hindrance of the national effort by subversive propaganda on the part of ~*columnists*; F~ *Monarchy*, last of the five great empires (*Dan.* ii. 44; ~*monarchy-man*, 17th-c. zealot expecting immediate second coming of Christ & repudiating all other government). [OE *fífta* (still *fíft* in diall.) cogn. w. G *fünfte*, Gk *pemptos*, L *quin(c)tus*, -th on anal. of FOURTH see -TH²]

fifth'ly, adv. In the fifth place (in enumerations). [-LY²]

fif'ty, a. & n. 1. Five times ten, 50, L, (~*y-one, -seven*, etc.; ~*y-first, -third*, etc.); (~*y-y*, half & half, equal shares (*go ~y-y; on a ~y-y basis*); large indefinite number (*have ~y things to tell you*); hence ~*yfold* a. & adv., ~IETH a. & n. 2. n. Set of ~*y* persons or things (*lid them by ~ies in a cave; the ~ies*, years between 49 & 60 in life or century). [OE *fíftig* cf. G *fünfzig* (FIVE, -TY²)]

fig¹, n. (Broad-leaved tree, usu. ~*tree*, bearing) soft pear-shaped many-seeded fruit eaten fresh (*green ~s*) or dried (esp. *Turkey* or *Smyrna ~s; pulled ~s*, superior hand-picked Turkey ~s); *under one's vine & ~tree*, safe at home; anything valueless (*don't care a ~ for*; also *a ~ for—*, as excl.); ~*-leaf*, device for concealing what is indecorous (*Gen.* iii. 7); ~*wort*, brown-flowered herb. [f. F *figue* f. pop. L **fica* f. L *ficus*]

fig², n. Dress, equipment, (*in full*); condition, form, (*in good ~*). [prob. f. foll.]

fig³, v.t. (-gg-). ~ *out* or *up* (horse), make lively; ~ *out* (person), dress up, bedizen. [= obs. *feague* perh. f. G *fegen* furbish]

fight¹ (fīt), v.i. & t. (*fought*, pr. fawt), Contend in battle or single combat (*against, with; for*, on behalf of person or to secure thing); maintain (cause, suit at law, quarrel) against opponent, contend over (question), win one's *way* by ~*ing*; contend with in battle or duel, or with the fists; set on (cocks, dogs) to ~ (~*ing-*COCK¹); manœuvre (troops, ship) in battle; ~ *off*, repel with effort; ~ (dispute etc., or *th*) *out*, settle by ~*ing*; ~ *shy of*, keep aloof from (person, undertaking, etc.); ~*ing chance*, a possibility of success if strenuous effort is made; ~*ing-top*, circular gun-platform fixed high up on warship's mast. Hence ~ER¹ (fĭt-) (esp.) n. & a., (fast aircraft) designed primarily for aerial ~*ing* (~*er-bomber*, such aircraft used as a bomber). [com. WG; OE *feohtan*, cf. G *fechten*]

fight² (fĭt), n. Act of fighting (*give, make a ~; valiant in ~*); battle; combat, esp. pugilistic or unpremeditated, between two or more persons, animals, or parties (*running ~*, kept up while one party flies & one pursues; || *sham ~*, between troops for practice or display; *stand-up ~*, open & formal); (fig.) strife, conflict; appetite or ability for fighting (*has ~ in him yet; show ~*, not yield tamely). [f. prec.]

fig'ment, n. Invented statement; thing that has no existence except in imagination. [f. L *fīgmentum* (*fig-* see FIGURE, -MENT)]

fig'urant masc., **-ante** fem., **figūrán'tè** (pl. -ti, pr. -tē), nn. Ballet-dancer. [F (first two forms) & It. (third)]

figūrā'tion (also -ger-), n. Determination to a certain form; the resulting form; shape, outline; allegorical representation; ornamentation by designs; (Mus.) use of florid counterpoint. [F, f. L *figurationem* (FIGURE², -ATION)]

fig'urative (-ger-, -gūr-), a. Emblematic, typical; pictorial or plastic; metaphorical, not literal; metaphorically so called; abounding in, addicted to, figures of speech. Hence ~LY² (-vi-) adv., ~NESS n. [F (-*if*, -*ive*), f. LL *figurātīvus* (as prec., -ATIVE)]

fig'ure¹ (-ger), n. 1. External form, shape; (Geom.) superficial space enclosed by line(s), or three-dimensional space enclosed by surface(s), any of the classes of these, as triangle, sphere; bodily shape (*has a well-developed ~; keep one's ~*, not grow stout); a person as seen (*saw a ~ leaning against the door*; *of fun*, grotesque person); a person as contemplated mentally (*the most terrible ~ in our history*); conspicuous appearance (*make or cut a brilliant, poor, ~*, produce such impression; *person of ~*, distinguished). 2. Image, likeness; representation of human form, statue, person in picture; emblem, type, simile. 3. Diagram, illustrative drawing; (abbr. for ref., *fig.*); horoscope; decorative pattern; evolution in dancing, division of set dance; (Skating) movement, series of movements, beginning & ending at centre. 4. Numerical symbol, esp. one of the ten in Arabic notation (*double ~s*, number between 9 & 100; *income of five ~s*, between £10,000 & £100,000; *reach three ~s*, in cricket, get century; *got it a lou*,

figure 443 fill

high, ~, cheap, dear). **5.** (Rhet.; also ~ *of speech*) recognized form of abnormal expression giving variety, force, etc, e.g. aposiopesis, hyperbole, metaphor, (~ *of speech* only) piece of exaggeration. **6.** (Gram.) permitted deviation from rules of construction, e.g. ellipse. **7.** (Log.) particular form of syllogism according to position of middle term. **8.** (Mus.) short succession of notes producing single impression, brief melodic or rhythmic formula out of which longer passages are developed. **9.** ~*-dance*, dance or dancing exhibition with distinct divisions; ~*-dancer*, performer in this; ~*-head*, carving, usu. bust or full-length ~ over ship's cutwater, nominal leader or president without real authority, (joc.) person's face. Hence ~LESS (-ger-) a. [F, f. L *figura* (fig- st. of *fingere* fashion, -URE]

fig'ure² (-ger), v.t. & i. Represent in diagram or picture; picture mentally, imagine, (often *to oneself*); be symbol of, represent typically; embellish with pattern (~*d satin*); mark with numbers or prices, do arithmetic, cipher (~*up*, reckon amount of); ~ *out*, give result in figures (~*s out at £46*); make appearance, appear, (~ *as*, pass for, assume character of), be conspicuous. [f. prec.]

figurine' (-ēn), n. Statuette. [F, f. It. *figurina* dim. of *figura* FIGURE]

fil'ament, n. Slender thread-like body, fibre, (esp. in animal or vegetable structure); not easily fusible conductor in electric bulb or thermionic valve, heated or made incandescent by current; (of air, light, etc.) imaginary portion of stream, row of particles following each other; (Bot.) part of stamen that supports anther. Hence ~ARY¹ (-ēn-), ~OUS (-ēn-), aa. [f. LL *filare* spin f. L *filum* thread, -MENT]

fil'ature, n. (Establishment for) reeling silk from cocoons. [F, as prec., -URE]

fil'bert, n. (Nut of) cultivated hazel. [short for ~*nut* = dial. F *noix de filbert*, ripe about St Philibert's day (Aug. 22)]

filch, v.t. Steal, pilfer. [?]

file¹, n. & v.t. **1.** Instrument usn. of steel with roughened surface(s) for reducing or smoothing objects (*bite, gnaw, ~*, attempt vain task); (sl.) artful person, dodger, (usn. *old, deep*, etc., ~), person. **2.** v.t. Smooth, reduce surface of, with ~; elaborate to perfection (esp. literary work); ~ *away* (roughnesses etc.), remove with ~. [OE *fēol* cf. Du. *vijl*, G *feile*]

file², n., & v.t. **1.** Stiff pointed wire on which documents etc. are run for keeping; kinds of appliance for holding papers arranged for reference; set of papers so kept, esp. in court of law referring to a cause; series of issues of a newspaper in order. **2.** v.t. Place (papers) on ~ or among public records. [f. F *fil* f. L *filum* thread]

file³, n. & v.t. & i. **1.** (Mil.), a front-rank man & the man or men straight behind him (*in* ~, marching with the men of a double line faced towards one of its ends; *single, Indian,* ~, similar formation of single line; RANK ~; *a* ~ *of men*, two, told off for some purpose); row of persons or things one behind another; (Chess) line of squares from player to player (cf. RANK²). **2.** vb. March in (~ *off, away,* go off by ~s; (v.t.) order (soldiers) to move off by ~s. [F (L *filare* vb f. L *filum* thread]

fil'emot, a. & n. Dead-leaf coloured, brownish yellow. [f. F *feuille morte* dead leaf]

filet (fēlā), n. Kind of net with square mesh (~ *lace*, ~ *net*). [F, = thread]

fil'ial, a. Of, due from, son or daughter. Hence ~LY² adv. [f. LL *filialis* (L *filius*, -d; son, daughter, -AL)]

fil'iate, v.t. (Rare for) AFFILIATE.

filia'tion, n. Being son's child; descent (*from*); formation of offshoots, branch of a society or language; genealogical relation or arrangement. [F, f. med. L *filiationem* (*filiare* give birth to f. L *filius* son, -ATION)]

fil'ibeg, n. (Sc.). Kilt. [f. Gael. *feileadh beag* little fold]

fil'ibuster, n., & v.i. **1.** One who engages in unauthorized warfare against foreign State; *obstructionist in legislative assembly. **2.** v.i. Act as ~. [f. F *flibustier*, Sp. *filibustero*, f. same)]

fil'igree, fil'a-, n. Ornamental work of fine gold or silver or copper wire formed into delicate tracery, fine metal open-work; anything delicate, light, showy, & frail. Hence **fil'igreed²** a. [f. F *filigrane* (L *filum* thread, *granum* grain)]

fil'ing, n. In vb¹ senses of FILE¹; also, (usu. pl.) particle(s) rubbed off by file. [-ING¹]

fill, v.t. & i., & n. **1.** Make or become full (*with*; *seals* ~, are distended with wind); stock abundantly; occupy whole capacity or extent of, spread over, pervade, (~ *the bill*, be the only conspicuous item, also in U.S., do all that is required, suffice); (of dentist) block up (hollow tooth, cavity) with gold etc, whence ~ING(4) n.; satisfy, satiate, (esp. in part., of kinds of food); hold (position, order, commission, etc.); occupy (vacant time); appoint holder of (vacant post); adulterate (esp. cotton fabrics; usn. in p.p.); ~ *in*, complete (outline), add what is wanted to complete (unfinished document, blank cheque, etc.); ~ *out*, enlarge, become enlarged, to the proper limit; ~ *up*, completely, supply vacant parts or places or deficiencies in, do away with (pond etc.) by ~ing, grow full; ~ *-dike*; hence ~'ER¹(1, 2) n. **2.** n. Full

supply of drink or food (*drink, have, etc.,* one's ~; also with intr. vbs, as *fresh* er ~); enough to ~ something (a ~ *of tobacco*). [OE *fyllan* cf. G *füllen*, cogn. w. FULL¹]

fille (fē'ye), n. ~ *de chambre* (de shahñ'br), chambermaid; ~ *de joie* (de zhwah) prostitute. [F, = daughter]

fill'et, n., & v.t. 1. Head-band, ribbon, string, or narrow band, for binding the hair or worn round head; band, bandage; thin narrow strip of anything; (pl.) animal's loins; fleshy detachable piece of meat near loins or ribs, undercut of sirloin; one of the thick slices into which a fish may be divided; middle part of leg of veal boned, rolled, & tied up; piece of beef, fish, etc., similarly prepared; (Archit.) narrow flat band separating two mouldings, small band between flutes of column; (Her.) horizontal division of shield, quarter of CHIEF¹ in depth; raised rim or ridge on any surface; (Book-bind.) plain line impressed on cover. 2. v.t. Bind (hair, person as to hair) with ~; encircle with ornamental band; divide (fish) into ~s. [f. F *filet* f. L *fīlum* thread +-ET¹]

fill'ip, n., & v.t. & i. 1. Sudden release of finger or thumb when it has been bent & checked by thumb or finger; slight smart stroke thus given; stimulus, incentive; mere trifle (*not worth a* ~). 2. vb. Propel (coin, marble, etc.) with a ~; stimulate (one's *memory* or *wits*); strike slightly & smartly; make a ~. [prob. imit., cf. FLIP]

fill'ister, n. Rabbeting-plane for window-sashes etc. [?]

fill'y, n. Female foal (cf. COLT); young lively girl. [perh. f. ON *fylja* cogn. w. FOAL]

film, n., & v.t. & i. 1. Thin skin, plate, coating, or layer; (Photog.) coating of collodion, gelatin, etc., spread on photographic paper or plate, or used instead of plate, celluloid roll used in cinematography, its contents as shown (~FAN³; ~ *star*, eminent cinema actor or actress; ~ *test*, photographic test of would-be actor; *the* ~s, cinema show); dimness over eyes; slight veil of haze etc.; fine thread or filament; hence **fil'my²** a., **fil'mily²** adv., **fil'miNESS** n. 2. vb. Cover, become covered, (as) with ~; reproduce (scene etc.) for the cinema; be (well or ill) suited for reproduction on the ~s. [OE *filmen* membrane cf. OFris. *filmene* skin, & FELL¹]

fil'oselle, n. Floss silk. [F, f. It. *filosello* perh. f. pop. L †*follicellus* cocoon, dim. of L *follis* bag, influenced by It. *filo* thread]

fils (fēs), n. The son, junior, (appended to son of same names, cf. PÈRE). [F]

fil'ter, n., & v.t. & i. 1. Contrivance for freeing liquids from suspended impurities, esp. by passing them through stratum of sand, charcoal, etc.; ~-*bed*, tank or pond with false bottom covered with sand etc. for ~ing large quantities, 2. vb. Pass (liquid), flow, through ~; (of ~) purify (liquid); make way *through, into,* etc., percolate, (of news etc.) leak *out* or come *through*; obtain by ~ing. [vb f. n., f. OF *filtre* f. med. L *fīltrum* f. Teut. st. whence FELT¹ (earliest ~ being of felt)]

filth, n. Loathsome dirt; uninviting food, garbage; vileness, pollution, obscenity; foul language. Hence **fil'thy²** a. (~y *lucre*, dishonourable gain, also joc., money), **fil'thily²** adv., **fil'thiNESS** n. [OE *fylth* FOUL¹, -TH¹)]

fil'trate², v.t.&i. = FILTER v. So ~ATION n. [f. mod. L *fīltrāre* (as prec., -ATE²)]

fim'briate, -ated, aa. (bot., zool.), Fringed, bordered with hairs etc. [f. L *fimbria* fringe +-ATE²]

fin, n. Organ for propelling & steering attached to fish & cetaceans at various parts of body (*anal, caudal, dorsal, pectoral, ventral,* etc.); (sl.) hand (*tip us your* ~, shake hands). Hence (-)~nED¹ (-nd), ~LESS, aa. [OE *finn*, cf. MDu. *vinne*, & L *pinna*]

fin'al, a. & n. 1. At the end, coming last, ultimate; putting an end to doubt, conclusive, definitive, unalterable; concerned with the purpose or end aimed at (~ CAUSE¹; ~ *clause* in Gram., introduced by *in order that, lest,* etc.); hence ~LY² adv. 2. n. Last or deciding heat or game in athletics, whence ~IST n., competitor in this; (sing. or pl.) last of a series of examinations; ||(colloq.) edition of newspaper published latest in the day; (Mus.) principal note in any mode. [F, f. L *fīnālis* (*fīnis* end, -AL)]

fina'le (-nah-), n. (Mus.) last movement of instrumental composition, piece of music closing act in opera; close of drama etc.; conclusion, final catastrophe. [It., as prec.]

final'ity, n. Principle of final cause viewed as operative in the universe; being final; belief that something is final; final act, state, or utterance. [F (-té), f. LL *fīnālitātem* (FINAL, -TY)]

finance', n., & v.t. & i. 1. (pl.) pecuniary resources of sovereign, State, company, or person; management of (esp. public) money, science of revenue. 2. vb. Furnish with ~s, find capital for; engage in financial operations. [OF (*finer* settle debt f. *fin* end: -ANCE)]

finan'cial (-shl), a. Of revenue or money matters (~ *year*, annual period for which public accounts are made up). Hence ~LY² (-sha-) adv. [prec.+-IAL]

finan'cier¹ (*also* finanser²), n. One skilled in levying & managing public money; capitalist. [F (FINANCE, -IER)]

financier² (-sēr), v.i. & t. Conduct financial operations (usu. contempt.); (~ cheat, swindle, (~ money away,) one out of). [f. prec.]

finch, n. Kinds of small bird (usu. with distinctive epithet or prefix, as *~, BULL~,). [OF finc cf. G fink]

find, v.t. (found), & n. 1. Come across, fall in with, light upon, (was found dead; we found a treasure; *St John saying; administer the law as you ~ it; found a treasure); obtain, receive, (~ favour, mercy; one's ACCOUNT² in; ~ one's feet, get the use of them, develop one's powers); recognize as present, acknowledge or discover to be so-&-so, (I ~ no sense in it, ~ the terms reasonable; how do you ~ yourself?; must take us as you ~ us, put up with us as we are); discover by trial to be or do or (that) or (has been found wanting; I ~ it im-possible, or to pay, or that it pays; ~ it im-possible, necessary, to —); discover by search; discover (game), discover game, in hunting; ~ oneself, discover one's vocation, & see below; succeed in obtaining (money, bail, sureties; can't ~ time to read; found courage to —; ~ it in my heart to —, am inclined; ~ expression, place, vent); come home to, reach the conscience of; ascertain by study or calculation or inquiry (~ one's way to, contrive to reach, arrive at); (Law) determine & declare (it, i.e. the offence, murder; person guilty etc.; that ~ABLE a. 2. n. ~ing of fox; discovery of treasure, minerals, etc.; sure ~, place where something (esp. fox) is sure to be found. [com.-Teut.; OE findan cf. Du. vinden, G finden; perh. cogn. w. L petere seek]

find'er, n. In vbl senses; esp.: small telescope attached to large one to find object; contrivance for same purpose in microscope & in photographic camera. [-ER¹]

fin de siècle (see Ap.), a. Characteristic of end of nineteenth century, advanced, modern; decadent. [F. = end of century]

fine¹, n., & v.i. & t. 1. End (now only in in ~, to sum up, finally, in short); ‖ sum of money paid by in-coming tenant in consideration of small rent; sum of money fixed as penalty for offence. 2. vb. Pay consideration for privilege or appointment; punish by a ~, whence fin'ABLE a. [ME & OF fin settlement of dispute f. L fīnis end]

fine², n., adv., & v.t. & i. 1. Of high quality; clear, pure, refined, (of gold or silver) containing specified proportion of pure metal, as gold 22 carats ~, silver 11 oz ~; delicate, subtle, exquisitely fashioned, (of feelings) elevated; of slender thread, in small particles, thin (~ pencil, of hard lead for making ~ lines); sharp (~ pen, narrow-pointed); (Athlet.) reduced to perfect condition; capable of delicate perception or dis-crimination, perceptible only with diffi-culty (a ~ distinction); excellent, of striking merit, good, satisfactory, for-tunate, of good effect, (had ~ sport; has been a ~ thing for him; often iron., as a ~ friend you have been!); well conceived or expressed; of handsome appearance or size, dignified, (~ potatoes; a man of ~ presence); bright, cloudless, free from rain, (~ weather; one ~ days, once upon a time; one of these ~ days, some day, in prophecies); ornate, showy, smart, (~ feathers make ~ birds); fastidious, dainty, affecting refinement, (of speech or writing) affectedly ornate; complimen-tary, euphemistic, (say ~ things about person, call things by ~ names); ~ arts, those appealing to sense of beauty, as poetry, music, & esp. painting, sculpture, architecture; ~ chemicals, chemicals pro-duced or used in small quantities and in a state of comparative purity (i.e. other than heavy chemicals, dyestuffs, cellulose or sugar products, etc.); ~ drawn, sew together (two pieces of cloth, rent, gar-ment) so that the join is imperceptible; ~drawn, subtle, extremely thin, (Athlet.) trained down in weight; ~ gentleman, lady, person of fashion, person who thinks himself above working; ~spun, delicate, flimsy, (of theories etc.) excessively subtle, unpractical; hence fin'ISH¹(2) a., ~ly² adv. ~NESS (-n-n-) n. 2. n. ~ weather (in rain or ~). 3. adv. ~ly (tall ~). 4. vb. Make (beer) clear (often down ~); (of liquid) become clear; ~ away, down, off, make or become ~r, thinner, less coarse, (make) dwindle, taper. [f. F fin f. Rom. finus fino prob. back formation f. finīo FINISHED]

fine champagne (see Ap.), n. Liqueur brandy. [F]

fin'ery¹, n. Smartness, stylishness (rare); showy dress or decoration. [FINE² adj.; -ERY]

fin'ery², n. Hearth where cast iron is made malleable or steel made from pig-iron. [F (-ie), f. finer refine f. Rom. fīnāre (L fīnis end). -ERY]

finesse', n., & v.i. & t. 1. Delicate manipu-lation, subtle discrimination; artfulness, cunning strategy; (Cards) attempt to take trick by inferior card, with higher one in reserve. 2. vb. Use ~; wheedle into, trick away, manage by ~; (Cards) play (card) by way of ~. [F (Rom. fino FINE²,-ESS²)]

fin'ger (-ngg-), n., & v.t. **1.** One of five terminal members of hand (*thumb*, & *fore, middle, ring, & little* ~s), or four excluding thumb (usu. now numbered thus, but cf. *fourth* ~, i.e. ring ~, in marriage service); (*done by the* ~, i.e. agency, *of God*; *more wit in his little* ~ *than in your whole body*; *lay, put, a* ~ *upon*, touch however slightly; *lay, put, one's* ~ *on* ailing part or cause of evil, point with precision to; *look through one's* ~s *at*, pretend not to see; *stir a* ~, make the least effort; *turn or twist person round one's* (*little*) ~, cajole him; *my* ~s *itch*, I long, am impatient, *to do*; *his* ~s *are all thumbs*, he is clumsy; *with a wet* ~, with ease; *have one's* ~s~s, *have a* ~ *in the pie*, take part in a matter; *let skip through one's* ~s, lose hold of; *have at one's* ~-*tips* or ~-*ends*, be versed in, know familiarly; *to the* ~-*nails*, completely); part of glove that holds ~s; ~-like object, esp. such part of a fruit etc., & in various machines; ~-*alphabet, -language*, conventional signs for talking with the deaf; ~-*bowl, -glass*, for rinsing ~s after dessert; ~-*fern*, kind of spleenwort; ~-*fish*, star-fish; ~-*plate*, fastened on door to prevent ~-marks; ~-*post*, giving directions at parting of roads; ~-*print*, impressions of person's ~s, used for identifying criminals etc.; ~-*stall*, cover of leather or rubber to protect ~ in dissections etc. or when wounded; hence ~LESS, (~)~ED² (-nggerd), aa. **2.** v.t. Touch with, turn about in, the ~s; take (bribes etc.); play upon (instrument) with the ~s, play (passage) with ~s used in particular way, mark (music) with signs showing which ~s are to be used, whence ~ING¹ (-ngg-) [-ING¹] n. [com.-Teut.; OE, OFris., Sw.-Da., *finger*; perh. cogn. w. FIVE]

fing'ering² (-ngg-), n. (for *fingering*¹ see prec.). Wool for stockings; [earlier *fin-gram, -im*, etc., perh. f. F *fin grain* fine grain, cf. GROGRAM]

‖**fing'erling** (-ngg-), n. Parr. [FINGER n., -LING¹]

fin'ial, n. (archit.). Ornament finishing off apex of roof, pediment, gable, tower-corner, canopy, etc. [var. of FINAL]

fin'ical, a. Over-nice, precise, fastidious; too much finished in details. Hence ~LY² adv., ~NESS, ~ITY (-ăl-), nn. [perh. f. FINE², or var. of foll.]

fin'icking, fin'ikin, a.=prec. [etym. dub.; cf. MDu. *fijnkens* accurately, neatly]

fin'is, n. (no pl.) (At end of book) the end; end of anything, esp. of life. [L]

fin'ish, v.t. & i., & n. **1.** Bring to an end, come to the end of (often ~ *doing*; ~ *off*, provide with an ending), complete; consume, get through, the whole or remainder of (food, book); kill, dispatch, overcome completely; perfect, put final or ~ing touches to, (~ed manners,

gentleman; also with *off, up*); complete education of; (v.i.) reach the end, cease, leave off; have done *with*; end in something or *by doing*. **2.** n. Last stage, termination, esp. of a fox-hunt (*be in at the* ~, often fig.); *fight to a* ~, till one party is completely worsted; what serves to give completeness; accomplished or completed state; mode of ~ing (esp. furniture, as *mahogany*~). [f. OF *fenir* f. L *finire* (*finis* end), -ISH¹]

fin'isher, n. In vbl senses; esp.: workman or machine doing last operation in manufacture; discomfiting thing, crushing blow, etc. [-ER¹]

fin'ite, a. Bounded, limited, not infinite; (Gram.) limited by number and person, not infinitive. Hence ~NESS (-tn-) n. [f. L *finitus* p.p. of *finire* FINISH]

Fin(n), n. One of N.-Eastern European people who call their country *Suomi*. [OE, *Finnas* pl., etym. dub.]

finn'an, n. (Also ~ *haddock*) haddock cured with smoke of green wood, turf, or peat. [f. *Findhorn* or *Findon*, Scotland]

finn'er, n. Kinds of whale, esp. rorqual, having dorsal fin. [-ER¹]

Finn'ic, a. Of the group of peoples allied to the Finns; Finnish. [-IC]

Finn'ish, a. & n. (Language) of the Finns; Finnic. [-ISH¹]

finn'y, a. Having fins; like a fin; of, teeming with, fish. [FIN+-Y²]

Fin'sen light (lit), n. (Apparatus for producing) ultra-violet light for the treatment of lupus etc. [Niels *Finsen*, Danish physician (d. 1904)]

fiord, fjord, (fy-), n. Long narrow arm of sea between high cliffs as in Norway. [Norw.]

fi'orin, n. Kind of grass. [f. Ir. *fíorthán*]

fir, n. (Also ~-*tree*) kinds of coniferous tree with needles placed singly on the shoots (*Scotch, Silver, Spruce, F~*); their wood; ~-*apple, -ball, -cone*, fruit of ~; ~-*needle*, its leaf. Hence ~RY² a. [of. Da. *fyr*, G *föhre*, prob. cogn. w. L *quercus* oak]

fire¹ (-r), n. **1.** Active principle operative in combustion, flame, incandescence, (*set a* ~, kindle; *strike* ~, elicit sparks by friction or blow; *no smoke without* ~, always some ground for rumour). **2.** State of combustion (*on* ~, burning, fig. excited: *set on* ~, ignite, excite; *set Thames on* ~, do something remarkable; *catch, take,* ~, be ignited). **3.** Burning fuel in grate, furnace, etc. (*heap* COALS *of* ~; *burnt child dreads the* ~; *out of* FRYING-*pan into* ~; FAT *is in the* ~), whence **4.** Conflagration, destructive burning, (~!, call for aid at a ~; *pour oil on* ~, add to excitement while deprecating it; *go through* ~ & *water*, face all perils; ~ & *sword*, burning & slaughter); *Greek* ~, combustible composition for igniting enemy's ships etc. **5.** Lumi-

nosity, glow, (St Elmo's ~, corposant); burning heat, fever, (St Anthony's ~, erysipelas). **6.** Vehement emotion, fervour, spirit, lively imagination, vivacity, poetic inspiration. **7.** Firing of guns (open, cease, ~; running ~, successive shots from line of troops etc., esp. fig. of criticism, objections, etc.; between two ~s, shot at from two directions; line of ~, path of bullet about to be shot; under ~, being shot at; HANG, MISS¹, ~). **8.** ~alarm, automatic arrangement for giving notice of ~; ~arm (usu. pl.), rifle, gun, pistol, etc.; ~back, Sumatran pheasant; ~ball, large meteor, globular lightning, (Mil.) ball filled with combustibles; ~balloon, made buoyant by heat of combustible burning at its mouth; ~bird, kind of bee-eater; ~blast, disease of plants; ~blight, disease of hops; ~bomb, incendiary; ~boor, fuel-chamber of steam-boiler; ~brand, piece of burning wood, person or thing kindling strife; ~brick (proof against ~, used in grates etc.); ~brigade, organized body of ~men; ~clay (kind used for ~bricks); ~control, system of regulating ~ of ship's or fort's guns; ~cross, = fiery CROSS¹; ~damp, miner's name for carburetted hydrogen, explosive when mixed in certain proportion with air; ~dog, andiron; ~drake, meteor, fiery dragon (in German myth.); ~eater, juggler who eats fire, great fighter, duellist; ~engine, machine for throwing water to extinguish ~s; ~escape, apparatus for saving people in burning house; ~eyed (poet.), with glowing eyes; ~flair, a fish, the sting-ray; ~fly, winged insect emitting phosphorescent light; ~guard, protective frame or grating in front of ~ in room, (also) = ~watcher; ~hose, hose-pipe for extinguishing ~s; ~insurance, against losses by ~; ~irons, tongs, poker, & shovel; ~light, light from fuel; ~place, prepared kindling-place; ~lock, antiquated musket in which priming was ignited by sparks; ~man, tender of furnace or steam-engine ~, man employed to extinguish ~s; ~new (arch.), = brand-new; ~office, insuring against ~; ~opal, kind of opal with internal flame-coloured reflections, GIRASOLE; ~pan, brazier; ~place, grate or hearth for room-~; ~plug (abbr. F.P.), connexion in water-main for ~hose; ~policy, ~insurance office's certificate guaranteeing compensation in case of ~; ~raising, arson; ~screen, to keep off heat of ~; ~ship, freighted with combustibles and sent adrift to ignite enemy's ships etc.; ~side, space round ~place, home life; ~step, = firing-step (FIRE²); ~stone, kind that resists ~, used for furnaces etc.; ~teazer, stoker; ~trap, building without proper exits in case of ~; ~walking, (religious) ceremony of walking barefoot

over white-hot stones, wood-ashes, etc.; ~watcher, person keeping watch for ~s esp. those caused by ~bombs; ~water, ardent spirits; ~wood, wood prepared for fuel; ~work, kinds of apparatus giving spectacular effects by use of combustibles etc., squib, rocket, etc., (fig. pl.) display of wit, passion, etc.; ~worship, treatment of ~ as a deity. Hence ~~PROOF (~IF²ᵈ), ~~LESS (-Fl-), aa. [com. WG: OE *fÿr* cf. G *feuer*; also Gk *pur*]

fire², v.t. & i. Set fire to with intention of destroying; kindle (explosives); (fig.) stimulate (the imagination), fill (person) with enthusiasm; (of explosives, mines) catch fire; become heated or excited (~ *up*, show sudden anger); redden (t. & i.) bake (pottery, bricks), cure (tea, tobacco) by artificial heat; (Farriery) cauterize; supply (furnace, engine) with fuel; cause (explosive, gun) to explode (often *off*; ~ *salute*, discharge number of guns as salute; ~ *broadside*, discharge all guns on one side of ship), (abs.) shoot, discharge gun etc. (*at*, *into*, *on*, *upon*), (fig.) *~away* begin, go ahead; (of gun etc.) go off; propel (missile) from gun etc. (fig.) *~off a postcard*, *a remark*); *~ out* or *~*, expel, dismiss, reject, (person); *firing-party*, squad detailed to ~ volleys at a military funeral or carry out a military execution; *firing-step* (on which soldier in trench stands to ~). [f. prec.]

fir'er, n. In vbl senses: esp. *single* etc. ~, gun that fires once etc. without reloading. [-ER¹]

fir'kin, n. Small cask for liquids, butter, fish, etc.; (as measure) half of kilderkin. [earlier *ferdekyn* prob. f. MDu (*vierde* fourth, -KIN)]

firm¹, n. Partners carrying on business (|| *long* ~, set of swindlers who obtain goods & do not pay). [earlier senses *signature*, *style*, f. Rom. *firma* (L *firmare* confirm); doublet = FARM¹]

firm², a., adv., & v.t. & i. **1.** Of solid or compact structure; fixed, stable; steady, not shaking; established, immutable, (of offer etc.) not liable to cancellation after acceptance; steadfast, unflinching, resolute; constant to; (Commerce, of prices, goods) maintaining their level or value; hence ~'LY² adv., ~'NESS n. **2.** adv. ~ly (*stand ~, hold ~ to*). **3.** v.t. & i. Solidify (t. & i.), compact, (soil after planting, etc. cheese); fix ~ly (plants in soil). [f. OF *ferme* f. L *firmus*]

firm'ament, n. Vault of heaven with its clouds & stars. Hence ~AL (-ĕn') a. [f. L *firmamentum* (*firmare* as prec. -MENT)]

firm'an, n. Oriental sovereign's edict, grant, licence, passport. [f. Pers. * fermān*]

first, a., n., & adv. **1.** Earliest in time or order (*at ~ sight*, *view*, or *blush*, prima facie; *F~ CAUSE¹; come in ~*, win race; *shall do it ~ thing*, colloq., before anything else; *in the ~ place*, to begin with; *the ~*

two etc., lit. or = the ~ & second etc.; often further defined, as *the ~ man you meet*, *was the ~ to do it*); foremost in position, rank, or importance (*head* etc., *with the head in front*; *the ~ men in the country*; ǁ F~ *Lord of the* TREASURY; ǁ F~ *Lord of the* Admiralty, parliamentary chief of Navy; ǁF~ *Sea Lord*, professional chief of Navy); coming next after a specified or implied time (*shall take the ~ train*; *the ~ cuckoo*); (with *the*) even one (*he doesn't know the ~ thing about it*); unsupported by others, sufficient by itself, (*obeyed at her ~ word*); basic or self-evident (*~ principles*). **2.** ~ *aid*, help given to hurt person before doctor comes; ~*-born*, eldest (child); ~-CHOP`; ~ *class*, set of persons or things grouped together as better than others, ǁ best accommodation in railway train etc., ǁ highest division in examination list, place in this; ~*-class*, (adj.) belonging to the ~ class, of best quality, very good, (adv.) ǁ by the ~ class (*travels ~class*); ~ *coat*, ǁ layer of paint; ~ *cost*, cost not including profit; ~*-day*, Sunday; ~ *floor*, ǁ the one above ground-floor, *ground-floor; ǁ~-foot (Sc.), ~ person to cross threshold in the New Year (also as vb); ~ *form*, lowest class in schools; ~ *fruit* (usu. pl.), ~ products of agriculture for the season esp. as offered to God, ~ results of work etc., (Hist.) payment to some superior by new holder of office; ~ *hand*, direct, without intermediate agency (*at ~ hand*, directly); ~ *name*, Christian name; ǁ~*-night(er)*, (habitual frequenter of) ~ performance of plays; ~*-offender* (against whom no previous conviction is recorded); ~*-rate*, of the highest class (*the ~-rate Powers*, great States of ~-rate importance), excellent, very well, (*a ~-rate machine, feeling ~rate*), (as n., Naut.) line-of-battleship of the old type, three-decker; ~ *violin*, one of the players taking the uppermost string part in orchestral music, the leader of such players, the leader of a string quartet. **3. n.** *The ~*, person or thing ~ mentioned; *from the ~*, from the beginning; *from ~ to last*, throughout; *at ~*, at the beginning; = ~ day of June etc.; ǁ *the F~* (of September, when partridge-shooting begins); (Commerc.) ~ *of exchange*, ~ of set of bills of even tenor & date; place in ~ class in examination, person who takes this; ~ place in race, winner of it; (pl.) best quality of flour, butter, etc. **4. adv.** Before anyone or anything else (often ~ *of all*, ~ *& foremost*; ~ *come ~ served*; ~ *& last*, taking one thing with another, on the whole; ~ *or last*, sooner or later); before some specified or implied event, time, etc. (*must get this done ~*; in preference, rather, (*will see him damned ~*); for the ~ time (*when did you see him ~?*). [com.-Teut.; OE *fyrst* cf. G *fürst* prince, superl. 1. st. of FOR, cf. (with different superl. suf.) FORMER]

first'ling, n. (usu. pl.). First result of anything, first-fruits; first offspring, first born of season. [-LING¹]

first'ly, adv. In the first place, first, (only in enumerating topics; & many writers still prefer *first*). [-LY²]

fifth, frith, n. Arm of sea; estuary. [So. wd prob. f. ON =*fiord*]

fisc, fisk, n. Treasury of ancient Rome, Roman emperor's privy-purse; (rare) State treasury, exchequer. [f. L *fiscus*]

fis'cal, a. & n. **1.** Of public revenue. **2. n.** Legal official in some foreign countries. (Sc.) = PROCURATOR ~. Hence ~LY² adv. [f., t LL *fiscalis* (prec., -AL)]

fish¹, n. (pl. often fish). **1.** (Pop.) animal living in the water, (strictly) vertebrate cold-blooded animal having gills throughout life & limbs (if any) modified into fins, (*pretty kettle of ~*, confusion, muddle; *~ out of water*, person out of his element; *drunk, dull, mute, as a ~*; *drink like a ~*, excessively; *feed the ~es*, be drowned, be sea-sick; *all 's ~ that comes to his net*, he takes all he can get; *there 's as good ~ in the sea as ever came out of it*, no fear of scarcity; FLAT, FLYING, GOLD, JELLY, SHELL¹, SUN, SWORD, etc., ~); person who is angled for; (colloq.) person of specified kind (*cool, loose, queer*, etc., ~); the flesh of ~ (*~, flesh, & fowl*; *neither ~, flesh, nor good red herring*, thing of indefinite character; *other ~ to fry*, more important business to attend to); *the F~* or F~es, zodiac constellation. **2.** ~*-carver*, knife for serving; ~*-globe*, for keeping gold ~ etc. in; ~*-glue*, isinglass; ~*-hook*, used for catching ~, (Naut.) part of anchor-raising tackle; ~*-kettle*, oval pan for boiling ~; ~*-knife*, of silver etc. for eating ~; ~*-pond*, in which ~ are kept, (joc.) the sea; ~*-pot*, wicker trap for eels, lobsters, etc.; ~*-slice*, carving-knife for ~, cook's implement for turning or taking out ~; ~*-sound*, ~'s swimming-bladder; ~*-tail*, shaped like ~'s tail (of jet of gas, whence ~*-tail burner*); ~*-tail wind* in rifle shooting, one blowing down range & varying in direction; ~*-torpedo*, torpedo shaped like ~ & with automatic propulsion; ~*-wife*, woman selling ~. Hence ~LET, ǁ~-MONGER, nn. [com.-Teut.; w *fisc*, cogn. w. L *piscis*]

fish², v.i. & t. Try to catch fish (*~ in troubled waters*, make one's profit out of disturbances), whence ~ERY(2, 3) n.: search for something in or under water: seek by indirect means for (secrets, compliments, etc.), whence ~ING² a.; (rare) try to catch (fish) or get (coral etc.) from below water; draw out of water, pocket, etc., *draw out*; (Naut.) ~ *the anchor*, draw flukes up to gunwale; try to catch fish in (pool etc.; *~ out*, exhaust the fish in), whence ~ABLE a.; get (fact, opinion,

secret) out; ~ing-rod, long tapering usu. jointed rod to which ~ing-line is attached. [OE *fiscian* cf. G *fischen* & see prec.]

fish³, n. & v.t. 1. (Naut.) piece of wood, convex & concave, used to strengthen mast etc.; flat plate of iron, wood, etc., strengthening beam or joint (so ~*plate*, one of two holding rails together); 2. v.t. Mend or strengthen (spar etc.), join (rails) with ~. [perh. = FISH¹ or foll.]

fish⁴, n. Piece of ivory etc. used as counter for £1. [f. signature of Permanent Sec. to Treasury]

‖ fish´er, n.(obs. sl.), Currency note, esp. = peg (*fischer* fix perh. ult. f. L *figere*) in games. [f. F *fiche* in same sense, also

fish´er¹, n. Fisherman (arch.; ~ *of men*, evangelist, see *Matt.* iv. 19); fishing animal; ~*man*, man who lives by fishing (rare) angler, fishing-boat. [OE *fiscere* (FISH¹, -ER¹)]

fish´er², n. [f. prec.]

fish´y, a. Abounding in fish; like fish's (~*y eye*, dull, vacant-looking); smelling or tasting like fish; consisting of fish (*a~y repast*); (sl.) of dubious character, questionable. Hence **fish´ILY** adv., **~iNESS** n. [-y²]

fisk. See FISC.

fissi-, fisso-, comb. forms of L *fissus* see FISSURE, as *fissidac´tyl* with digits divided, *fissip´arous* reproducing by fission.

fiss´ile, a. Cleavable, tending to split, fissionable. Hence **fissil´ITY** n. [f. L *fissilis* (-IL)]

fi´ssion (-shn), n. (biol.). Division of cell etc. into new cells etc. as mode of reproduction. [f. L *fissio* (foll., -TON)]

fi´ssure (-sher), n. & v.t. & i. Cleft made by splitting or separation of parts; (Bot., Anat.) narrow opening in organ etc., esp. depression between convolutions of brain; cleavage; (vb) split (t. & i.). [F, f. L *fissura* (*findere* fiss-cleave, -URE)]

fist, n. & v.t. 1. Clenched hand, esp. as used in boxing (~ *law*, the right of the strongest); (joc.) hand (*give us your* ~, shake hands), handwriting (*writes a good* ~; *I know his* ~). 2. v.t. Strike with ~; (Naut.) handle (sail, oar, etc.). Hence ~**ED²** a. [OE *fȳst* cf. G *faust*]

fis´tic(al), aa. (joc.), Puglistic. [-ICAL]

fis´ticuffs, n. pl. Fighting with the fists. [FIST + CUFF cf. *handiwork*]

fis´tula, n. Long-pipe-like ulcer with narrow mouth; natural pipe or spout in whales, insects, etc. Hence~**AR¹,**~**OUS,** aa. [earlier *fystel, fistle, etc.,* f. L *fistula* pipe, flute]

fit¹, n. [OE *fitt* f. OHG *fizza* list of cloth] Section of a poem.

fit², n. Paroxysm of periodic ailment, sudden transitory attack of some illness; sudden seizure, with loss of consciousness or convulsions, of hysteria, apoplexy, fainting, paralysis, or epilepsy (*give one a* ~, surprise or outrage him; *beat one into,* give one one), ~**s,** defeat him easily); sudden transitory state (*a ~ of energy,*

fit³, a. (-tt-). Well adapted or suited (*for* some purpose or status *or to* do or be; SURVIVAL *of the ~test*); good enough *for* (a *dinner ~ for a king*); becoming, proper, right, (*it is ~ that; see or think ~ to,* decide to); qualified, competent, worthy, *to* do (*not ~ to hold a* CANDLE *to*); in suitable condition, ready, *to* do or *for* (also vulg. as adv., *crying ~ to burst himself*); angry, troubled, or exhausted enough *to* (do, something violent, sink to the ground, etc.); in good athletic condition or health (~ *as a* FIDDLE). Hence ~**LY²** adv. [from 1440; etym. dub.]

fit⁴, v.t. & i. (-tt-), & n. 1. Be in harmony with, become, befit; be of right measure, shape, & size *for* (esp. of dress; often abs., *as the* CAP*~s*); fill up, exactly correspond *to,* (receptacle, fellow, etc., or this; often *in, into, on with*), make *to* do this; make suitable, adapt, *for,* *to* with n. or inf.; make competent *for or to;* ~ *on,* try on (garment); supply, furnish, (ship etc., rarely person) *with;* ~ *out, up,* equip; hence ~**ER¹** n., esp.: (Tailoring and Dressmaking) one who supervises cutting, ~*ting,* altering, etc., of garments; mechanic who ~*s* (up) all kinds of metalwork. 2. n. Adaptation, adjustment, style in which garment ~*s* (*a tight, bad, excellent,* ~); ~*-out,* equipment. [from 16th c., prob. f. prec.]

fitch, n. (Brush made of) polecat's hair. [f. MDu. *fisse* polecat]

fitch´ew (-ōō), n. Foumart, polecat. [f. OF *fissel* dim. of MDu. *fisse* (prec.)]

fit´ment, n. Piece of furniture. [FIT⁴, -MENT]

fit´ness, n. Being fit; moral worthiness; propriety (*the* ~ *of things,* what is right or appropriate). [-NESS]

fit´ting, n. In vbl senses: esp. (usu. pl.) fixture(s), apparatus, furniture; (Engin.) ~*-shop,* place where parts are put together. [-ING¹]

fit´ting², a. In vbl senses: esp. becoming, proper, right, whence ~**LY²** adv. [-ING²]

fit-up, n. (Theatr. colloq.). Temporary or portable stage and stage-fittings; ~(*company*), minor travelling theatrical troupe carrying makeshift scenery. [FIT⁴]

five, a. & n. One more than four, 5, V, (*twenty-~, ~-twenty;* ~ *o'clock; How old are you?—I*(~); the number ~ (*twice* ~ *is ten*); set of ~ things; card, die, or domino with ~ pips; (also **fiv´ER¹** n.) hit at cricket for ~ runs, ‖ £5 note; *bunch of* ~*s,* hand; (pl.) gloves, shoes, etc., of fifth size; (pl.) the *~-per-cents;* ~*-day week* (having ~ working days); ~*-finger exercise,* on piano for exercising all fingers, keeping them on same ~ notes all the

tideless, devotion, indifference, etc., whence ~**FUL** a., **´FULLY²** adv., **´FULNESS** n.: ~*s* (*as starts*), spasmodically; caprice, mood, (*when the* ~ *was on him*). [OE *fitt,* perh.—prec.]

time; ~-finger, kinds of plant, also star-fish; ||~-lined) whip, urgent summons to attend in House of Parliament (now disused); ~-o'clock tea, light afternoon meal; ~'penny (also pr. fip-), costing &c at, 5d.; (Guernsey etc.) half-franc; ~-per-cents, stock or shares paying 5%; ~-year plan (for the economic development of Russia in 5 years, inaugurated in 1928). Hence ~FOLD (vt-) a. & adv. [Aryan; OE fíf cf. G fünf, Gk pente, L quinque]

fives (-vz), n. Ball-game played with hands or bat in court with two, three, or four walls. [pl. of five used as sing.; significance unknown]

fix¹, v.t. & i. Make firm or stable, fasten, secure, implant (principles, memory, etc.) (in, on, to, etc.); direct steadily, set, (eyes, gaze, affection, attention) on or upon; (of object) attract & hold (attention, eyes, etc.); make (eyes, features) become, rigid; deprive of, lose, volatility or fluidity, congeal (t. & i.); make (colour, photographic image) fast, whence ~ER²(2) n.; single out (person) with one's eyes etc.; place definitely or permanently, station, establish; take up one's position; settle one's choice, decide, (upon; assign precise position of; refer (thing, person) to definite place or time; determine incidence of (liability etc.); settle, determine, specify, (price, date, place); arrest changes or development in (language, literature); *(freq. up) arrange, organize, prepare; ~ed focus (Photog.), best position of lens for general snapshot work. [ult. f. L fixus p.p. of figere fix; perh. thr. obs. fix a., or F fixer or med. L fixare]

fix², n. Dilemma, position hard to escape from; finding position, position found, by bearings or astronomical observations (radio ~, position of aircraft, ship, etc., found by radio). [f. prec.]

fixa'tion, n. Fixing, being fixed; process of rendering solid, coagulation; (Psychoanal.) arrested mental development. [f. med. L fixatio (fixare fix)]

fix'ative, a. & n. Tending to fix; (n.) substance used to fix colours or drawings. [-ATIVE]

fix'ature, n. Gummy preparation for fixing the hair. [as prec., -URE]

fixed (-kst), a. In vbl senses; esp.: ~ idea, one tending to become a monomania; ~ acid or oil, one not evaporable without decomposition; ~ point, where polar is permanently stationed; ~ star, one seeming to keep same relative position to others (opp. planet); ~ CAPITAL²; properly, land & houses. [-ED¹]

fix'edly, adv. In fixed manner; esp. (of looking) intently. [-LY²]

fix'edness, n. Fixed state, immobility, permanence, steadfastness. [-NESS]

*fix'ings (-z), n. pl. Apparatus, equipment; trimming of dress or dish, adjuncts. [-ING¹]

fix'ify, n. Fixed state; (Physics) property of enduring heat without being volatilized or losing weight; stability, permanence. [f. L fixus see FIX¹+-ITY]

fix'ture, n. Thing fixed or fastened in position; (Law; pl.) articles of a personal nature annexed to house or land; person or thing confined to or established in one place (chiefly in pred.. as seems to be a ~); (Athlet. etc.) (date appointed for) meet, race, etc. [changed f. obs. fixure f. LL fixūra (figere fix-, -URE)]

fiz'gig (-g-), n. & a. Giddy flirtatious young woman; kind of small firework, cracker; (adj.) flighty. [prob. f. FIZZ+gig (obs. = flighty girl)]

fizz, v.i., & n. (Make) hissing or splintering sound, whence ~Y² a.; champagne. [imit.]

fiz'zle, v.i., & n. Hiss or splutter feebly (n., this sound); ~ out, come to lame conclusion; (n.) fiasco. [f. obs. fise break wind¹+-LE(3)]

flabb'ergast (-gah-), v.t. Dumbfound, so astonish as to incapacitate. [from 1722; etym. dub.]

flabb'y, a. Hanging down, flaccid, limp, (usu. of flesh); nerveless, feeble, (of language or character). Hence ~IVESS n. [earlier flappy (FLAP, -Y²)]

flabell'ate, flabell'iform, aa. (bot. & zool.). Fan-shaped. [f. L flabellum fan (flare blow)+-ATE², -FORM]

flac'cid (-ks-), a. Hanging loose or wrinkled, limp, flabby, (usu. of flesh); relaxed, drooping; wanting vigour, feeble. Hence flâccid'ITY n. f. F flaccide f. L flaccidus (flaccus flabby)]

flag¹, n. Kinds of plant with bladed leaf growing on moist ground, esp. various species of iris; ~s or ~ collect., kind of coarse grass; long slender blade of a plant. Hence ~g'Y² (-g-) a. [cf. Du. flag]

flag², n., & v.t. (-gg-). (Also ~stone) flat slab of rock for paving, (pl.) pavement made of these, also ~g'ING¹(6) (-g-) n.; (vb) pave with ~s. [earlier sense sod, cf. Icel. flag spot whence sod has been cut, & FLAKE²]

flag³, n. (Also ~-feather) quill-feather of bird's wing. [perh. f. obs. flag drooping f. OF flac f. L flaccus flabby]

flag⁴, n., & v.t. (-gg-). 1. Piece of bunting or other stuff, usu. oblong or square, attached by one edge to staff or halyard & used as standard, ensign, or signal (black ~, pirate's ensign, also ~ hoisted outside prison to announce execution of criminal; Black Flags, irregular Chinese soldiers, orig. rebels, in Tonquin; white ~, of truce, disclaiming hostile intention; yellow ~, displayed by ship with infectious disease on board, hospital ship, or ship in quarantine; ~ of truce,

flag⁵, v.i.¹ (-gg-). Hang down, flap loosely; droop, fade, become limp; lag, lose vigour, grow languid; fall off in interest. [perh. as FLAG³]

flag'ging², n. (pl. ~s). (One) who scourges himself; given to flogging. [f. L *flagellare* (FLAGELLUM), -ANT]

flā·gellate¹, v.t. Scourge. Hence or cogn. ~ATION, ~ātor¹, nn., ~ātory a. [as prec., -ATE³]

flā·gellate², ~ātor², nn., ~ātory a. [as prec.]

flagell'um, n. (pl. ~a). (Bot.) runner, creeping shoot; (Zool.) lashlike appendage. Hence flā·gellate² [-ATE³], a. [L, = whip]

flageolet¹ (-jol-; also flăj⁴), n. Small flute blown at end. [F, dim. of OF *flajol* etym. dub.]

flageolet² (-jol-; also -lă), n. Kind of kidney-bean. [F, = *fageoled* dim. of *fageol* f. L *faseolus*]

flagi'tious (-shus), a. Deeply criminal, atrocious, heinous, villainous. Hence ~LY² adv., ~NESS n. (-shus-). [f. L *flagitiosus* (*flagitium* crime, -OSE¹)]

flag'on, n. Large vessel usu. with handle, spout, & lid, to hold liquor for table; similar vessel for Eucharist (Wine-trade) flattened globular glass bottle holding nearly two bottles. [ME *fagon* f. OF *flacon* (FLASK, -OON]

flag'rant, a. Glaring, notorious, scandalous, (of offence or offender). Hence or cogn. flag'rancy n., ~LY² adv. [f. L *flagrant-* (FRAGRANT)]

flagra'nte de'licto, in the very act. [L]

flag'TANCY n., -ANT]

flail, n. Hand threshing-implement, wooden staff at end of which a short heavy stick hangs swinging. [OE *fligel* cf. Du *wlegel*, G *flegel*, prob. f. L FLAGELLUM]

flair, n. Selective instinct for what is excellent, paying, etc. [F (*flairer* see FRAGRANT)]

flāk, n. (German) anti-aircraft fire; ~ship, f. pop. L *flagrare* = *fragrare* see FRAGRANT)]

white, indicating desire to parley; DIP¹; *lower* or *strike* one's ~, take it down as salute or sign of surrender; (Naut.) ~ carried by ~ship as emblem of admiral's rank afloat (*hoist*, *strike*, one's ~, relinquish, command); tail of setter or Newfoundland dog; ~-*boat*, serving as mark in aquatic matches; ||~-*captain*, captain of ~ship; ~-*day*, day on which money is raised for a cause by sale to passers-by etc., of ~s to be worn as evidence of having given); ~-*lieutenant*, admiral's A.D.C.; ||~-*list*, roll of ~ officers, i.e. admirals, vice-admirals, or rear-admirals; ~-*man*, signaller at races etc.; ~-*rank* (of ~officers); ~-*ship*, having admiral on board; ~-*staff*, pole on which ~ is hung; ~-*station*, where trains stop only if signalled; ~-*wagging* (sl.), signalling; ~-*waver*, agitator. 2. v.t. Place ~ on or over; mark out with ~s; inform (person), communicate (information, *that*), by ~-signals. [perh. imit., of flapping sound; in all mod. Teut. langg.; earliest in E (15th c.)]

German anti-aircraft vessel. [abbr. of *Flügerabwehrkanone*]

flāke², n. & v.i. & t. 1. Light fleecy tuft, esp. of snow; portion of ignited matter thrown off; thin broad piece peeled off; natural division of fish's flesh; layer; pigment made from white-lead in ~; hence flāk'y², a. 2. vb. Fall like, sprinkle as with snow; take, come, away or off in ~s. [perh. ult. f. Aryan *plag*- cf. Gk *plēganon* beat]

flăm, n. Sham story, trick, deception. [?]

flăm'beau (-bō), n. (pl. ~s or ~, pr. -z). Torch, esp. of several thick waxed wicks. [F, f. *flambe* FLAME¹ (= med. L *flambellum*)]

flămboy'ant, a. & n. 1. Marked by wavy flamelike lines (of French 15th & 16th c. Archit.); floridly decorated; gorgeously coloured. 2. n. Kinds of flame-coloured flower. [F, part. of *flamboyer* f. *flambe* FLAME¹]

flāme¹, n. (Portion of) ignited gas (*the ~s*, fire, esp. as consuming); visible combustion (*in ~s*; *burst into ~* or *~s*); bright light, brilliant colouring; passion, esp. of love (*fan the ~*, make it more intense); (joc.) sweetheart (*an old ~ of mine*); kinds of moth; ~-*projector* or *-thrower*, = FLAM-MENWERFER. Hence ~LESS (-ml) (poet.), flām'y², aa. [f. OF *flambe* f. L *flamma*]

flāme², v.i. & t. Emit flames, blaze, (often *away*, *forth*, *out*, *up*); (of passion) burst into anger; shine, gleam, (~ *up*, blush violently); move like flame; send (signal) by fire; ~ subject to action of flame (*sterilized by flaming*). [f. OF *flamber* as prec.]

flā'men, n. (Rom. Ant.) A god's-priest. [L]

flā'ming², a. In vbl senses; very hot (*a ~ sun*); bright-coloured; exaggerated, over-laudatory, (*a ~ description*; ~ *onions*, anti-aircraft projectile resembling a chain of fire-balls. [-ING²]

flaming'o (-nggo-), n. (pl. ~es), Large long-legged long-necked heavy-billed scarlet-feathered bird. [Port. (-engo) perh. f. Rom. *flama* flame + -*enc*- =-ING³]

flăm'mable, a. (Rare, & chiefly in non-~ for) INFLAMMABLE.

flăm'menwerfer (-vāfer), n. Machine spouting liquid fire in war. [G, = flame-thrower]

flâ'nerie (flah'nē), **flâneur** (flah'ner), nn. Idling, idler. [F]

flānge (-j), n., & v.t. 1. Projecting flat rim, collar, or rib. 2. v.t. Provide with ~, [perh. f. OF *flanche* FLANK]

flănk, n., & v.t. 1. Fleshy part of side between ribs & hip; side of building.

mountain, etc.; right or left side of army or body of troops (in ~, at the side; TURN¹ ~ *of*). **2.** v.t. Guard or strengthen on the ~, menace ~ of, take in ~, enfilade, rake; be posted or situated at ~ of; march past ~ of. [f. F *flanc* etym. dub.]

flank'er, n. Fortification guarding or menacing flank; (Mil., usu. pl.) flank skirmisher(s); thing that flanks anything. [-ER¹]

flann'el, n. & a. **1.** Open woollen stuff, usu. without nap (pl., kinds of this, ~ goods); (pl.) underclothing of ~, ~ bandages, garments esp. trousers of ~ for games, whence ~LED² (-ld) a.; piece of ~ used in washing person or cleaning floor, whence **flänn'el** (-l-) v.t.; hence ~ETTE′ (2) n., ~LY² a. **2.** adj. Made of ~. [perh. f. W *gwlanen* (*gwlân* wool)]

flap, v.t. & i. (-pp-), & n. **1.** Strike with something broad, drive (flies etc.) *away* or *off*; (of birds) strike (something) with flat of wing; swing or sway about, flutter, oscillate; move (t. & i. of wings) up & down; beat the wings. **2.** n. Light blow with something broad; motion of wing etc.; broad hanging piece hinged or attached by one side only, e.g. trapdoor, pocket-cover, hat-brim, table-leaf, valve, fish's gill-cover, piece of skin left in amputations; open mushroom-top (cf. *button*). [imit.]

flapdoo'dle, n. Nonsense, bunkum. [?]

flap'jack, n. Small cake of flour fried in grease; flat vanity case for face-powder. [FLAP+JACK¹]

flapp'er¹ n. Flat fly-killing instrument; bird-scaring clapper; young wild-duck or partridge; (sl.) girl in late teens; hinged or hanging piece, flap; broad fin; crustacean's tail; (sl.) hand; (w. ref. to Lapntans) person, thing, that jogs one's memory or wits. [-ER¹]

flare, v.t. & i. & n. **1.** (Cause to) bulge gradually upwards (of ship's sides); spread outwards gradually (as the sides of a ship, a woman's skirt, etc.); blaze with bright unsteady flame, glow as with flame, (often *about, away, out*; part, *away, out, over-conspicuous*); ~ *up*, burst into sudden blaze or anger. **2.** n. Dazzling irregular light, unshaded flame in open air; sudden outburst of flame; signal light used at sea; bright light used as signal; container of combustible material, dropped from aircraft to illuminate target area etc.; ~-*path*, area illuminated to enable aircraft to land or take off; ostentation; upward bulge in ship's sides; gradual widening (esp. of a skirt); ~-*up*, sudden breaking into flame, short brilliant popularity or display, burst of anger, uproarious merrymaking. [?]

flash, v.i. & t. Break suddenly into flame, give out flame or sparks, (~ *in the pan*, fail after showy start, like priming of old guns); emit or reflect light, gleam; send, reflect, (something) like a flash or in flashes (*eyes ~ fire, ~ back defiance*); burst suddenly into view or perception (~*ed upon me that* —); move swiftly; ~ *up* or *out*, show sudden passion; cause to gleam (~*ed his sword; had a lantern ~ed in my face*); send by telegraph (*news was ~ed over England*); (Glass-making) spread out (t. & i.) into a sheet, cover (plain glass) with coloured film; (of water) rush along, rise & flow, fill or flood (stream etc.) with water; ~-*board*, for sending more water from mill-dam into mill-race; ~-*pipe*, extra pipe with line of holes for lighting high gas-lamp; ~*ing-point*, temperature at which vapour from oil etc. may be ignited. [prob. imit. in sense *flood* etc. (the earliest)]

flash², n. Sudden transitory blaze (~ *in pan*, abortive effort; see prec.), time occupied by it, instant, (*in a ~*); ostentation; sudden short access of feeling (*a ~ of hope*); (Cinemat.) exposure of a scene, recapitulation of an earlier scene (also ~*back*); preparation for colouring spirits; rush of water let down weir to take boat over shallows, contrivance for producing this; (Mil.) coloured patch of cloth as distinguishing emblem of division etc.; ~-*light*, used for signals & in lighthouses, also for photographing by night etc., (also) electric torch; ~-*point*. (now more usu. for) FLASH¹ing-point. [f. prec.]

flash³, a. Gaudy, showy, counterfeit (~ *notes, money*); cant. slang; connected with thieves, tramps, etc. [f. prec.]

flash'ing, n. Strip of metal to obviate flooding or soaking at joint of roofing etc. [?]

flash'|y, a. Brilliant but shallow or transitory, cheaply attractive; showy, gaudy; given to display. Hence ~ILY² adv., ~i-NESS n. [-Y²]

flask (-ah-), n. (Usu. *powder*-) leather or metal case for carrying sportsman's supply of gunpowder; Italian narrow-necked wickered wine or oil bottle; traveller's pocket bottle of metal or (usu. leather-covered) glass for wine, spirit, etc. [cf. It. *fiasco*, G *fläsche*; perh. ult. f. L *vasculum* dim. of *vas* vessel]

flask'et (-ah-), n. || Long shallow basket (arch.); || clothes-basket; small flask. [f. OF *flasquet* (*fasque* FLASK, -ET²)]

flat¹, n. Storey (now rare); suite of rooms on one floor as residence; *apartment. [OE *flet* floor, cogn. w. foll.]

flat², a. & adv., n. & v.t. (-tt-). **1.** Horizontal, level; spread out, lying at full length, (*fell ~; ~ against the wall; with the ~ hand*); even, smooth, unbroken, without projection, (~ *tint*, uniform); with broad level surface & little depth; unqualified, plain, downright, (~ *denial, refusal; ~ nonsense, blasphemy; that's ~*, let there be no doubt about it); dull, life-

less, monotonous, (full ~, prove a failure, not win applause; *market is, prices are,* ~, inactive, sluggish; slow-witted; dejected, without energy, (~ *beer,* that has lost its effervescence); (Mus.) below the true pitch (*B, D, etc.,* ~, a semitone lower than *B, D, etc.,* ~); ~ *aback* (emphat. for ABACK naut. & fig.); ~ *boat,* with ~ bottom for transport in shallow water; ~ *candlestick,* with broad base & short stem for carrying about; ~*-fish,* family including sole, turbot, plaice, etc.; ~ *foot(ed)* (having) foot not normally arched; ~*-iron,* for ironing linen etc.; ~ *race,* over level ground (opp. hurdle-race or steeplechase); ~ *rate* (the same in all cases, not proportional etc.); hence ~LY[2] adv., ~NESS n. [~f'en[2] v.t. & i.(~*-ten out,* bring aircraft parallel with ground), ~t'ISH[2] a., ~WAYS, ~WISE, adv. 2. n. What is ~ (on, *from, the* ~, of drawings etc. as opposed to sculpture); ~ part of anything (*the* ~ *of the hand, with the* ~ *of his sword*); level ground, plain, low land, swamp; ~*-bottomed* boat; shallow basket; (Theatr.) section of scenery mounted on frame (*join the* ~s, make a thing into a coherent whole, resume attitude); (sl.) duffer, dupe; (Mus.) note lowered a semitone below natural pitch, sign indicating this lowering, *sharps &* ~s, black notes on piano. 3. v.t. Make ~ (chiefly in manufacturing processes; elsewhere ~*ten*). [f. ON *flatr* etym. dub.]

flättĕr, v.t. Court, fawn upon; compliment unduly, overpraise; gratify vanity of, make feel honoured; inspire with (esp. unfounded) hope; please oneself with the belief (*that*); gratify (eye, ear, etc.); ~*ing unction,* salve one administers to one's own conscience or self-esteem (*Haml.* III. iv. 145); (of portrait, painter, etc.) exaggerate good looks of. Hence ~ER[1], flätt'ERY(4, 5), nn., ~ING[2] adv. [perh. irreg. f. OF *flater* (to smooth)]

flat'us, n. Wind in stomach or bowels. [L, vbl n. (*flare* blow)]

flaunt, v.i. & t., & n. **1.** Wave (t. & i.) proudly; display oneself or one's finery; show off, parade, (oneself, finery, etc.); hence ~ing[1] adv., ~Y[2] a. **2.** n. ~*ing* motion. [?]

flav'in, n. Surgical antiseptic, & yellow dye, got from dyer's oak. [L *flavus* yellow, -IN]

flaves'cent, a. Turning yellow, yellowish. [f. L *flavescere (flavus* yellow, -ESCENT)]

flav'our (-ver), n., & v.t. & i. **1.** Aroma, mingled sensation of smell & taste, distinctive taste; undefinable characteristic quality; hence **flav'orous,** ~LESS, ~SOME, (~ver-), aa. **2.** v.t. Give ~ to, season; hence ~ING[1](3) (-ver-) n. [f. OF *flaur, fraor,* smell, perh. f. L *fragrare* be FRAGRANT]

flaw[1], n., & v.t. & i. **1.** Crack, breach, rent; imperfection, blemish; (Law) invalidating defect in document, procedure, evidence, etc.; hence ~LESS a., ~'lessly[2] adv., ~'lessNESS n. 2. v.b. Crack (t. & i.), damage, mar. [perh. f. ON *flaga* slab of.]

flaw[2], n. Squall of wind; short storm. [cf. Du. *vlaag,* Sw. *flaga:* perh. cogn. w. FLAY]

|| **flawn,** n. (arch.). Kind of custard. [f. OF *flaon* (now *flan*) f. med. L *fladonem*]

flax, n. Blue-flowered plant cultivated for its textile fibre & its seeds called linseed; (with qualifying word prefixed or suffixed) kinds of similar plant, as *dwarf ~, toad-, ~, -lily, -dodder;* fibres of ~, dressed or undressed; cloth of ~, linen; [com.-WG; OE *fleax* cf. G *flachs,* perh. cogn. w. G *flechten,* L *plectere,* Gk *plekō,* weave]

flax'en, a. Of flax; (of hair) coloured like dressed flax, pale yellowish-brown. [-EN[5]]

flay, v.t. Strip off skin or hide of; (fig.) criticize severely; pillage, plunder, (person); peel off (skin, bark, peel); pare off (turf); ~*-flint,* extortioner, miser. [com.-Tent.; OE *flēan* cf. MDu. *vlaen,* Gk *plēssō* strike, FLAKE[2] FLAW]

flea, n. Small wingless jumping insect feeding on human & other blood (*send one away with a ~ in his ear,* discomfited by a reproof or repulse); *send ~,* small jumping crustaceans; == ~*beetle;* small or contemptible creature; ~*-bag* (sl.), sleeping-bag; ~*-bane, -wort,* kinds of plant; ~*-beetle, -bite, lit., & fig. slight inconvenience or expense, mere trifle, infesting hops; ~*-bitten,* sprinkled with these on lighter ground; also lit.); ~*-dock,* butterbur; ~*-louse,* jumping plant-louse. [com.-Tent.; OE *flēah* cf. G *floh,* prob. cogn. w. FLEE]

fleam, n. Lancet for bleeding horses. [f. OF *flieme* f. med. L *fledomum* f. LL *fle-botomum* f. Gk *phlebotomon* see PHLE-BOTOMY]

fleck (-ăsh), n. & v.t. **1.** Spot in the skin, freckle; patch of colour or light; small particle, speck; hence ~LESS a. **2.** v.t. Mark with ~s, dapple, variegate. [f. or cogn. w. ON *flekkr* blow, spot, cf. G *fleck* spot & *flicken* to patch]

flĕche (-āsh), n. Slender spire, esp. at intersection of nave & transept. [F; orig. = arrow]

flĕck′er, v.t. Dapple, variegate; scatter in patches. [prec. +-ER²]

fled. See FLEE.

flĕdge, v.t. Provide with feathers or plumage, wing for flight, deck with feathers or down. Hence ~LESS (-jl-) a. [f. obs. adj. *fledge* feathered cf. OE *unflǣge* unfledged, & G *flügge*, cogn. w. FLY¹]

flĕdg(e)′ling (-jl-), n. Young bird; inexperienced person. [as prec. +-LING¹]

flee, v.i. & t. (*fled; fly, flying*, are now usu. substituted for ~, *~ing; is fled*, see -ED¹(2), or *has fled*). Run away, seek safety in flight, (*from, before*); vanish, cease, pass away; run away from, leave abruptly; eschew, shun. [com.-Teut.; OE *flēon* cf. G *fliehen*, Goth. *thliuhan*]

fleece, n., & v.t. 1. Woolly covering of sheep or similar animal (*Golden F~*, Austrian & Spanish order of Knighthood); quantity of wool shorn from a sheep at once; rough, abundant, or woolly head of hair; thing like a ~, white cloud, falling snow, etc.; (Carding) thin sheet of cotton or wool fibre; hence (-fleecED² (-ēst), fleeˈcY² a.a. 2. v.t. Shear (sheep; rare); strip of money, property, etc. (also of), whence ~′ER n.; overspread as with ~ (*sky ~d with clouds*). [com.-WG; OE *flēos* cf. Du. *vlies*, G *fliess*, perh. cogn. w. L *pluma* feather]

fleer, v.i., & n. 1. Laugh impudently or mockingly, gibe, jeer, sneer. 2. n. Mocking look or speech. [cf. Norw. & Sw. dial. *flira* to grin]

fleet¹, n. Naval armament, number of warships under one command-in-chief (*the ~*, the navy); number of ships or boats sailing in company; group of aircraft; ~ *of cabs, taxis*, etc., those owned by one proprietor; ‖*F~ Air Arm*, aviation service of Royal Navy (now *Naval Aviation*). [OE *flēot* ship, shipping (*flēotan* FLEET⁵)]

‖ **fleet²**, n. Creek, inlet; *The F~*, stream, now covered sewer, running into Thames E. of F~ Street, also the prison that stood near it (*F~ marriage*, performed by a *F~ parson* or disreputable clergyman in & about the F~ ready to marry clandestinely; *F~ Street*, used for) the press, London journalism. [OE *flēot* cf. Du. *vliet*, G *fliess*, cogn. w. FLEET⁵]

fleet³, a. (poet. or literary). Swift, nimble. Hence ~LY² adv., ~′NESS n. [cf. ON *fliótr*, cogn. w. FLEET⁵]

‖ **fleet⁴** a. & adv. Shallow (of water); at or to no great depth (*plough or sow~*). [cf. Du. *vloot*, cogn. w. foll.]

fleet⁵, v.i. Glide away, vanish, be transitory; pass rapidly, slip away; move swiftly, fly. Hence ~ING² a., ~′ingLY² adv. [earlier senses, *float, swim, flow*; com.-Teut.; OE *flēotan* cf. G *fliessen*, cogn. w. Gk *pleō* sail, L *pluere* rain]

Flĕm′ing, n. Inhabitant of Flanders. [f. MDn. *Vlāming* (*Vlām*, whence *Flanders*, +-ING³)]

Flĕm′ish, a. & n. (Language) of Flanders; ~ BOND¹. [f. MDu. *Vlaemisch* (prec., -ISH¹)]

flĕm′ish², v.i. (Of hound) make quivering movement of tail & body while searching for trail, FEATHER². [?]

flĕnch, flinch¹, flĕnse, v.t. Cut up (whale); flay (seal). [f. Da. *flense*, cf. Norw. *flinsa* flay]

flĕsh¹, n. 1. Soft substance between the skin & the bones, esp. the muscular part of animal bodies (~ *& blood*, the body or its material, mankind, human nature with its emotions & infirmities; as adj., actually living, not supernatural or imaginary; *one's own* ~ *& blood*, near relations, descendants; ~ *& fell*, the whole body; as adv., entirely; *one* ~, united as one personality, see Gen. ii. 24; *proud* ~, overgrowth of granulations springing on wound; *make his* ~ *creep*, frighten or horrify him esp. with dread of the supernatural). 2. Pulpy substance of fruit or plant. 3. Plumpness, fat, (*lose, put on*, ~; grow thin, fat): *in* ~, fat. 4. Tissue of animal bodies (excluding fish & sometimes fowls) as meat, (~*feeding*, ~*eater*, etc.; *neither* FISH¹ ~, *nor* etc.). 5. Visible surface of human body (~*colour*, -*ed*, yellowish pink); ~ *& blood above* (*all* ~, whatever has bodily life; *in the* ~, in bodily form, in life; *after the* ~, corporeally). 6. The sensual appetites (*sins of the* ~, unchastity). 7. ~*brush, -glove*, for stimulating circulation by rubbing; ~*fly*, depositing eggs or larvae in dead ~; ~*pots* (w. ref. to *Exod.* xvi. 3), high living; ~ *side or* ~, side of a hide that adjoined the ~; ~*tints*, esp. painter's rendering of ~*colour*; ~*lights, fleshings*; ~*wound*, one not reaching bone or vital organ. Hence ~′LESS a. [com.-WG & Scand.; OE *flǣsc* cf. G *fleisch*, Da. *flesk* pork]

flĕsh², v.t. Incite (hound etc.) by taste of blood; initiate in bloodshed; inflame by foretaste of success; use *sword* etc. for first time on flesh (or fig. *pen, wit*, etc.). [f. prec.]

‖ **flĕsh′er**, n. (Sc.). Butcher. [f. FLESH +-ER¹]

flĕsh′ings (-z), n. pl. Close flesh-coloured garment etc. of silk worn on stage etc. to represent natural skin. [FLESH¹, -ING¹]

flĕsh′ly, a. Carnal, lascivious, sensual, (esp. of appetites etc., rarely of persons); mortal, material, not divine or spiritual; worldly. Hence ~iNESS n. [OE *flǣsclíc* (FLESH¹, -LIKE)]

flĕsh′ẏ, a. Plump, fat; of flesh, without bone; (of plant or fruit tissue) pulpy; like flesh. Hence ~iNESS n. [-Y²]

fleur-de-lis (flĕr′delē′ pl. *fleurs*- pr. as sing.), n. Iris flower; heraldic lily; (sing. or pl.) royal arms of France, French royal family, France. [F (first form), = lily flower (*lis* lily); the arch. E form is corrupt. of F]

fleur'ét (-oor-), n. Ornament like small flower. [f. F *fleurette (fleur* FLOWER, -ETTE)]

fleuron (flér'awn'), n. Flower-shaped ornament in architecture or printing, on coins, etc. [F]

fleur'y (-oorĭ), flŏr'ý, a. (her.). Decorated with fleurs-de-lis. [f. F *fleuré*, OF *floré* (*fleur* FLOWER.]

flew. See FLY². [f. F *fleuré*, OF *floré*

flews (-z), n. pl. Hanging lips of bloodhound etc. [?]

flex¹, v.t. Bend (in scientific use of bending limb etc. by flexor, in Geol. of distorted strata). [f. L *flectere flex-*]

flex², n. Flexible insulated wire used in electric lighting. [abbr. of foll.]

flex'ible, a. That will bend without breaking, pliable, pliant; easily led, manageable; adaptable, versatile; supple, compliant. Hence or cogn. ~BIL'ITY n., ~bly² adv. [f. f. L *flexibilis* (FLEX¹, -BLE)]

flex'ile, a. Supple, mobile; tractable; versatile. Hence **flexil'ITY** n. [f. L *flexilis* (FLEX¹, -IL)]

flex'ion (-kshn), n. Bending, curvature, bent state, (esp. of limb or joint); bent part, curve; (Gram.) = inflexion, whence ~AL, ~LESS, (-kshon-) aa. [(Math.)=flexure. [f. L *flexio* (FLEX¹, -ION)]

flex'or, n. (Also ~ *muscle, tendon*) muscle that bends a part (opp. EXTENSOR). [FLEX¹, -OR²]

flex'uóse, a. (bot.). Serpentine, undulating. Hence **flex'uós'ITY** n. [f. L *flexuosus (flexus -ūs* a bend see FLEX¹, -OSE)]

flex'uous, a. Full of bends, winding. Hence or cogn. **flex'uós'ITY** (-ōs') n., ~LY² adv. [as prec., -OUS]

flex'ure (-ksher), n. Bending, curvature, bent state; bend, curve, turn; (Math.) curving of line or surface or, in theory of elasticity, of surface or solid (~ of a curve, its bending to or from a straight line); (Geol.) bending of strata under pressure. [f. L *flexura* (FLEX¹, -URE)]

flibb'ertigibb'et, n. Gossiping, flighty, frivolous, or restless person. [imit. of chatter.]

flick, n., & v.t. **1.** Light sharp blow with whiplash etc., shot out and withdrawn, or with finger-nail; sudden movement, jerk; slight sharp cracking sound. **2.** v.t. Strike with a ~; dash or jerk (dust etc.) *away, off;* give a ~ with (whip, towel, etc.). [imit.]

flick'er, v.i. & n. **1.** Quiver, vibrate, wave to and fro, blow lightly & unsteadily, (of flags, leaves, serpents' tongues, wind, etc.); (of flame etc., & fig. of hope etc.) flash and die away by turns; hence ~ingLY² adv. **2.** n. ~ing movement or light. [OE *flicorian* imit.]

flier. See FLYER.

flight¹ (-īt), n., & v.t. **1.** Act or manner of flying through air (*take one's* or *a, wing*

one's, ~, fly), pursuit of game by hawk, migration, migrating body, flock, of birds or insects; swift movement of projectiles etc.; (of time) swift passage; soaring, excursion, sally, (of wit, fancy, ambition, etc.); distance that bird, aircraft, or missile, can fly; series (of stairs etc. mounting without change of direction, or of hurdles or rails for racing etc.); volley (of arrows etc.); in *the first* ~ *taking* a leading place; *oat-chaff:* R.A.F. unit consisting of a few machines; ~ *-deck*, for taking-off from, and landing on, an aircraft-carrier; ~-*feather, -muscle,* used in flying; ~-*lieutenant, -sergeant, see* AIR¹ *Force.* **2.** v.t. Shoot (wildfowl); also abs.). in ~; vary trajectory and pace of (cricket-ball etc.). [OE *flyht* (FLY²)]

flight² (-īt), n. Running away, hasty retreat, absconding, (*take, take to, betake oneself to,* ~; *run away; put to* ~, rout). [ME *fluht* (OTeut. *theudhan* FLEE)]

flight'ý (-ī-), a. Guided by whim or fancy, fickle; half-witted, crazy. Hence ~iLY² adv., ~iNESS n. [FLIGHT¹ +-Y²]

flim-flam, n. Trifle, nonsense, idle talk; piece of humbug, deception. [?]

flim'sy (-z), a. & n. **1.** Easily destroyed, frail, slightly put together; paltry, trivial, frivolous, superficial; hence ~iLY² adv., ~iNESS n. **2.** n. Banknote(s) (sl.); thin paper, reporter's copy. [from 18th c. prob. imit.]

flinch¹ (for *flinch¹* see FLENCH), v.i. Give way, draw back, (*from* duty, course, etc.). [f. OF *flenchir* etym. dub.]

flin'ders (-z), n. pl. Fragments, splinters, (*break, fly, in* ~). [cf. Norw. *flindra*, Du. *flender*]

fling, v.i. & (ĭ *, ((fling)* &. n. **1.** Rush, go angrily or violently (~ *out of the room* ; *flung away in a rage*); (of horse etc.) kick and plunge (often *out*), (of person) usu. *out*) break into invective; throw, hurl (often *about, aside, away, by, out, up,* at or *against* fortress or enemy); (of wrestler) reject thing, missile, flotsam, dice, throw *oneself into* person's arms, a boat, etc., *on* person's compassion etc., or *into* an enterprise (i.e. take it up with all one's might); suddenly spread out (arms), kick *up* (heels); cast (one's eyes) carelessly (*up*)on; send, emit, (sound, smell, light); put (person) suddenly or violently *into* prison; launch (troops etc.) *on* enemy or ridden horse) throw to the ground; ~ (fact etc.) *in* one's *teeth,* reproach him with it; ~ (door etc.) *open* or *to, open* or shut violently. **2.** n. Throw, cast, (*have a* ~ *at,* make an attempt at; *jeer at*); impetuous dance (esp. *Highland* ~); violent movement, plunge; spell of indulgence in impulse (*have one's* ~). [cf. ON *flengja*]

flint, n. Hard stone of nearly pure silica found in pebbly lumps steel-grey within & encrusted with white; anything hard

and unyielding; piece of ~ used with steel to produce fire (~ & steel) esp. in ~-lock gun; piece of an alloy of rare-earth metals used in automatic petrol lighters as the spark-producing element; pebble of ~ (turing water from a ~, work miracles; skin a ~, be miserly or avaricious; set one's face like a ~, be determined); ~-glass, pure lustrous kind orig. made with ~; ~-lock, (lock of) gun discharged by spark from ~. Hence **flint'Y²** a., **flin'ti-NESS** n. [OE, cf. Da. flint, perh. cogn. w. Gk plinthos brick]

flip, v.t. & i. (-pp-), & n. 1. Put (pellet, coin) in motion with a fillip; fillip (person's ear, cheek, etc.), strike lightly; make a fillip with fingers; move (fan, whip, fishing-fly) about with sudden jerk(s); strike smartly at with whip etc. 2. n. Smart light blow, fillip, flick; (colloq.) a (short) flight in an aeroplane. [imit.]

flip², n. Beer and spirit mixed, sweetened, & heated with hot iron; EGG¹-~. [perh. f. prec. in sense whip up]

flip-flap, n. Kind of somersault; kind of firework, cracker; (in places of amusement) machine with passenger cars hung at ends of long moving arms. [imit.]

flipp'ant, a. Lacking in gravity, treating serious things lightly, disrespectful. Hence **flipp'ANCY** n., ~LY² adv. [from 1605, orig. = nimble, voluble, perh. f. FLIP¹, -ANT]

flipp'er, n. Limb used to swim with, as in turtle & penguin; (sl.) hand. [FLIP¹ + -ER¹]

flipp'erty-flopp'erty, a. Loose, dangling. [FLIP¹ + -ER¹]

flirt, v.t. & i. & n. 1. Fillip, send with a jerk; wave or move briskly (fan, bird's tail); play at courtship (with), pretend to make love, whence ~A'TION n., ~a'tious (-shus) a. 2. n. Sudden jerk, quick motion quickly checked; man who pays, or usu. woman who invites or accepts, attentions merely for amusement, whence ~'ISH¹, ~Y³, aa. [imit.]

flit, v.i. (-tt-), & n. 1. Migrate, be gone, depart; change one's abode, move; pass lightly, softly, or rapidly (often about, by, to & fro); fly lightly, make short flights, (of birds & esp. bats). 2. n. Change of abode. [f. ON flytja cogn. w. FLEET⁵]

flitch, n., & v.t. 1. Side of hog salted and cured (~ of Dunmow, there given yearly to any couple proving conjugal harmony for year and day); square of blubber; steak of halibut; || slice (usu. outside one) of timber from tree-trunk; ~-beam (compound, esp. of iron plate between two slices of wood). 2. v.t. Cut (log or halibut) into ~es. [OE flicce cf. MLG vlike]

flitt'er, v.i. Flit about, flutter; ~-mouse, bat. [FLIT¹, -ER³]

***fliv'er**, n. (sl.) Cheap motor-car. [?]

flix, n. Kinds of fur; beaver's down. [?]

float¹, n. || Floating (rare; on the ~, afloat); mass of floating weeds, ice, etc.; raft; cork or quill used on fishing-line as indicator; cork supporting edge of fishing-net; inflated part supporting fish etc.; hollow ball regulating cistern tap; etc.; footnight-light; (Theatr.: sing. or pl.) footlights; (also ~-board) one of the boards of water-wheel or paddle-wheel; kind of low-bodied cart; platform on wheels with show used in processions; tool for smoothing plaster (~-stone, for smoothing curved bricks, & cf. foll.); single-cut file; passing of weft-threads over part of warp without being interwoven, thread so passed; ~-bridge, of rafts; ~-grass, kinds of sedge. [mixture of OE flot floating state, OE flota ship, fleet, FLOAT², & F flotte]

float², v.i. & t. Rest on surface of liquid; (of stranded ship) get afloat; move with moving liquid, drift; be suspended freely in liquid; move or be suspended in air as if buoyed up; hover before eye or mind; (Commerc., of acceptance) be in circulation, awaiting maturity; (Commerc.) bring (company, scheme) into favour, launch, (of scheme etc.) be launched; cover with liquid, inundate; (of water etc.) support, bear along, (buoyant object) set afloat; circulate (rumour); waft through air; ~-stone, kinds of light stone that ~ (& see prec.). [OE flotian cf. ON flota, cogn. w. FLEET⁵]

float'able, a. Capable of floating; (of stream) in which rafts etc. can float. [-ABLE]

float'age, n. Floating; || (right of appropriating) flotsam; ships etc. afloat on river; floating masses; buoyancy; part of ship above water-line. [-AGE]

floata'tion, flot-, n. Floating (centre of ~, starting of gravity in floating body); starting of company or enterprise. [flot- is attempt to disguise hybrid formation; FLOAT², -ATION]

float'er, n. In vbl senses; esp. (St. Exch.) government stock certificate, railway bond, etc., recognized as security. [-ER¹]

float'ing, a. In vbl senses; esp. (Commerc., of cargo) at sea (~ trade, rates, etc., concerned with cargoes at sea); ~ CAPITAL, DEBT, RIB; fluctuating, variable, (the ~ population); ~ anchor = DRAG²-anchor; ~ DOCK⁴; ~ bridge, kinds of bridge & ferry, also part of bridge that can be swung away on pontoon; ~ kidney, abnormal condition in which the kidneys are movable; ~ light, lightship, liebuoy with lantern. [-ING²]

||flocci-nauci-nihili-pili-fica'tion (-oks-), n. Estimating as worthless (the ~ of wealth). [four L wds = at little or nothing + -FICATION]

flocc'ose, a. (bot.). Tufted. [f. LL floccosus (L floccus FLOCK¹, -OSE¹)]

flocc'ule, n. Small portion of matter like flock of wool. [f. FLOCCULUS]

flocc'ulent, -lose, -lous, aa. Like tufts of wool; in, showing, tufts. Hence **flocc'ulence** n. [foll. -ULENT, -OSE, -OUS]

flocculus, n. (pl. -li). = FLOCCULE; (Anat.) small lobe in under surface of cerebellum. [mod. L, dim. of foll.]

floccus, n. (pl. -ci, pr. -ŏksī). Tuft of woolly hairs or filaments. [L.,=foll.]

flock¹, n. Lock, tuft, of wool, cotton, etc.; (pl.) material for quilting & stuffing made of wool-refuse or torn-up cloth; (pl. or ~s) powdered wool or cloth for making ~-paper; (Chem.; pl.) light loose masses precipitated; ~-bed, stuffed with ~s; ~-paper, wall-paper sized & then powdered with ~ either all over or in patterns. Hence ~Y² a. [prob. f. OF floc f. L floccus]

flock², n., & v.i. 1. Large number of people (chiefly in such phr. as come in ~s); number of animals of one kind, esp. birds, feeding or travelling together; number of domestic animals, usu. sheep, goats, or geese, kept together(~s & herds, sheep & cattle); the Christian body; a congregation esp. in relation to its pastor; family of children, number of pupils, etc.; ~-master, sheep-farmer. 2. v.i. Congregate, go in great numbers, troop, (often about, after, into, to, in, out, together). [OE flocc]

flōe, n. Sheet of floating ice. [perh. f. Norse flo layer]

flog, v.t.(-gg-). Beat with birch, whip, cat, etc., whence ~g'ING'(L) (-g-); (sl.) drive (learning, laziness, etc.) into or out of person; urge (horse etc.) on with whip(~ dead horse, waste energy); (sl.) defeat, excel; cast fishing-line repeatedly over (stream). [perh. imit., or school sl. f. L flagellare to whip]

|| **flōng**, n. Prepared paper for stereo-typing. [f. F flan FLAWN]

flood (flŭd), n., & v.t. & i. 1. (Also ~-tide) inflow of tide (opp. EBB); (poet.) river, stream, sea (~ & field, sea & land); irruption of water over land, inundation, (the F~, Noah's F~, that in Genesis); whence ~ŏM'ETER n.; outpouring of water, torrent, downpour, (~s of rain, a ~ of tears or words); ~-gate, opened & closed to admit or exclude water, esp. lower gate of lock, also sluice; ~-light, copious artificial light projected from many directions, eliminating all shadows in surface illuminated (so ~-lighting, ~-lit). 2. vb. Inundate, cover with a ~ (also fig., was ~ed with letters); irrigate; deluge (burning house, mine) with water; (of rain) fill (river) to overflowing; come in great quantities (usu. in); have uterine haemorrhage. [com.-Teut., OE flōd]

floor (-ōr), n., & v.t. 1. Lower surface of room, (also ~'ing) boards etc., of which it is made; bottom of sea, cave, etc.; part of House of Parliament where members sit and speak (take the ~, esp. U.S., speak in debate); set of rooms etc. on same level in house (||ground-~, on ground level, first ~, || above this), storey; level area; ~-lamp, mounted on metal etc. pillar standing on ~; ~-cloth, substitute for carpet; hence ~'LESS (-ōr-) a. 2. vb. Furnish with ~, pave; serve as ~ of; bring to the ~ or ground, knock down; confound, nonplus; ||(at school) tell (boy) to sit down as not knowing lesson; overcome, get the better of, (~ the paper, answer every question in it). Hence ~ER (-ōr-), n. Knock-down blow; dis-concerting news or argument; paper or question hard to answer. [-ER¹]

flŏp, v.i. & t. (-pp-), n., int., & adv. 1. Sway (intr.) about heavily; walk etc. in ungainly way; sit, kneel, lie, down noisily; make dull sound of soft body falling or of flat thing slapping water; (sl.) of book, play, etc.) fail, collapse; hence ~Y² a. 2. n. ~ping motion, sound made by it; (sl.) failure (of book, play, etc.). 3. int. & adv. With a ~ [= FLAP] & suddenly. [imit.]

Flora, n. (pl. -ae, -as). (List of) plants of particular region or epoch (cf. FAUNA). [L, goddess of flowers (flos -oris flower, used in titles of bot. bks)]

flŏr'al, a. Of flora(s) (~ zone, tract of earth with special vegetable charac-teristics); of flower(s). [f. L floralis of Flora (prec.)]

Flŏr'entine, a. & n. (Inhabitant) of Florence in Tuscany (~ iris, white or pale blue one); kind of twilled silk. [f. L Florentinus (Florentia Florence, -INE²)]

flōr'ĕs'cence, n. Flowering time or state. [f. L florescere (florère bloom, -ESCENT, -ENCE]

flōr'ĕt, n. (Bot.) one of small flowers making up a composite flower (~ of the disk, the ray, of the flower's centre or circumference); small flower, floweret. [f. OF florete (FLOWER, -ETTE)]

flōr'iāte, v.t. Decorate with flower-designs etc. [as foll., -ATE³]

flor'iculture, n. Cultivation of flowers. Hence floricul'tural a., floricul'turist (3) n., (-cher-). [f. L flos -oris flower + CULTURE]

flŏr'id, a. Profusely adorned as with flowers, elaborately ornate, (of literary, artistic, or musical style); ostentatious, showy; ruddy, flushed, high-coloured. Hence florid'ITY, ~NESS, nn., ~LY² adv. [f. L floridus (flos FLOWER)]

Flŏr'ida, n. State in U.S. (~ water, a per-fume; ~ wood, kind used for inlaying).

florif'erous, a. (Of seeds or plants) pro-ducing many flowers. [f. L florifer (FLOWER, -FEROUS)]

florilegium, n. (pl. -ia). Anthology. [transl. into mod. L (L flos FLOWER, legere gather) of Gk anthologion ANTHOLOGY]

flŏr'in, n. Foreign coin of gold or silver current at different times; (Hist.) English gold coin (6/8) of Edw. III; || current English coin (2/-). [F, f. It. fiorino dim.

of *flore* f. L *florem* nom. *flos* FLOWER (stamped with lily)]

flor'ist (*also* flō-), n. One who deals in, raises, or studies flowers. [L *flos -oris* flower, -IST]

flor'uit (-ōŏ-), n. Period (falling exact birth and death dates) at which a person was alive. [L, =he flourished]

flory. See FLEURY.

flos'cular, -lous, aa. Having florets, composite-flowered. [f. L *flosculus* (FLOWER, -CULE)]

flōss, n. Rough silk enveloping silk-worm's cocoon (~ *silk*, this used in cheap silk goods). Hence ~'Y² a. [perh. f. OF *flosche* down]

flotation. See FLOATATION.

flotil'la, n. Small fleet; fleet of boats or small ships. [Sp., dim. of *flota* fleet]

flōt'sam, n. Wreckage found floating (cf. JETSAM; oyster-spawn. [AF *floteson* (OF *floter*=FLOAT², -SON)]

flounce¹, v.i., & n. 1. Go with agitated or violent motion, flop, plunge, throw the body about, (*away, out, about, down, up*). 2. n. Fling, jerk, of body or limb. [cf. Norw. *flunsa* hurry (found later)]

flounce², n., & v.t. 1. Strip gathered & sewn by upper edge round woman's skirt, & with lower edge hanging, as ornament. 2. v.t. Trim with ~(s). [earlier *frounce* f. OF *fronce, froncir*, wrinkle, perh, f. L *frons -tis* brow]

floun'der¹, n. A small flat-fish. [prob. f. OF *flondre* cf. Norw. *flundra*, Da. *flynder*]

floun'der², v.i., & n. 1. Struggle & plunge (as) in mud or wading; make mistakes, manage business badly or with difficulty. 2. n. Piece of ~ing, staggering attempts to get on. [cf. Du. *flodderen*]

flour (-owr), n., & v.t. 1. Finer part of meal obtained by bolting; wheat meal; fine soft powder; ~*-box*, tin box for dredging ~; hence ~'Y² (-owr-) a. 2. v.t. Sprinkle with ~; *grind into ~. [form of FLOWER; orig. sense *finest part*]

flou'rish¹ (flŭ-), v.i. & t. Grow vigorously; thrive, prosper, be successful; be in one's prime, spend one's life, be active, *in, at, about*, etc., a certain time (cf. FLORUIT); use flourishes in handwriting or literary work or speech; show ostentatiously; wave (weapon) about; throw (limbs) about; prelude fancifully in music etc. [f. OF *florir* (-ISH²) f. L *florēre* (*flos* FLOWER)]

flou'rish² (flŭ-), n. 1. Prosperity, vigour, (rare; *in full* ~). 2. Ornament of flowing curves about letter or word in hand-writing; rhetorical embellishment, florid expression; ostentatious waving of weapon, hand, etc. 3. (Mus.) fanfare of brass instruments, florid passage, extemporized addition or prelude; hence ~'Y² a. [f. prec.]

flout, v.t. & i., & n. 1. Mock, insult, express contempt for by word or act; scoff *at*. 2. n. Mocking speech or action [from 16th c.; perh. var. of FLUTE v.]

flow (-ō), v.i., & n. 1. Glide along as a stream; (of blood) circulate; (of persons or things) come, go, in numbers; (of talk, literary style, etc.) move easily; (of garment, hair, etc.) hang easily, undulate, (Math.; of numbers) increase or diminish continuously by infinitesimal quantities; gush out, spring; (of blood) be split; result *from*; run full, be in flood (*ebb & ~*; ~*ing tide*, progressive tendency); (of wine) be poured out without stint; be plentifully supplied *with* (arch.; *land ~ing with milk & honey*). 2. n. ~ing movement in stream; amount that ~s; ~ing liquid; (of dress, figure, etc.) undulation; outpouring, stream, copious supply; rise of tide (*ebb & ~*); over-flowing of Nile etc.; ~ *of spirits*, habitual cheerfulness; ~ *of soul*, genial conversation (as complement to FEAST of *reason*). [OE *flōwan*, cf. ON *flóa*; cogn. w. FLOOD; unconnected with L *fluere*]

flow'er (*also* flowr), n., & v.i. & t. 1. (Bot.) reproductive organ in plant containing one or more pistils or stamens or both, & usu. a corolla & calyx, (pop.) coloured (i.e. not green) part of plant from which fruit or seed is later developed, whence ~AGE(1) n.; (Old Chem.; pl.) powder left after sublimation (~*s of sulphur* etc.); scum formed by fermentation (~*s of tan*); a blossom apart from the plant (No~*s*, intimation that wreaths etc. are not desired at funeral); ~*ing plant*; (pl.) ornamental phrases (usu. ~*s of speech* often iron.; *the* pick or choice *of*; *the* best part, essence; *the* choicest embodiment *of*; state of blooming (*in ~*, prime (*in the ~ of his age*); ~*de-luce*, see FLEUR-DE-LIS; ~*-girl*, who sells ~s; ~*-piece*, picture of ~s; ~*-pot*, usu. of red earthenware holding soil in which plant may be set; ~*-show*, competitive or other exhibition of ~s; hence (-)~ED² (-erd), ~LESS, aa., ~ET¹ n. 2. v.b. Produce ~s, bloom or blossom, whence ~ING² a.; (Gardening) cause or allow (plant) to ~; embellish with worked-~s or floral design. [ME f. OF *flour* f. L *florem* nom. *flos*, cogn. w. BLOW³]

flow'erer, n. Plant that flowers at specified time etc. (*late, abundant,* ~). [-ER¹]

flow'erȳ, a. Abounding in flowers; full of fine words, compliments, figures of speech, etc., whence ~INESS (-owr-) n. [-Y¹]

flow'ing (-ōi-), a. In vbl senses; also or esp.; (of style) fluent, easy; (of lines, curves, contour) smoothly continuous, not abrupt; (Naut.) *with* ~ *sheet* or *sail*, sailing with lee clews eased off when wind is nearly across course. Hence ~LY² adv. [-ING²]

flown¹ (-ōn), a. (arch.). Swollen, puffed up, (~ *with insolence and wine*). [obs. p.p. of FLOW]

flown². See FLY².

fluc·tu·āte, v.i. Move up & down like waves (rare); vary irregularly, rise & fall, be unstable; vacillate, waver. So ~ATION n. [f. L *fluctuare* (*fluctus -us* wave f. *fluere* flow), -ATE³]

flue² (flōō), n. Kind of fishing-net. [from 14th c.; cf. MDu. *vluwe*]

flue³ (flōō), n. Substance formed by loose particles of cotton etc., fluff. Hence ~Y² (-ōō¹) a. [cf. Flem. *vluwe* perh. f. F *velu* hairy]

flue¹ (flōō), n. Smoke-duct in chimney; channel for conveying heat, esp. hot-air passage in wall, tube for heating water in some kinds of boiler; ~-pipes (Mus.), organ-pipes other than reed-pipes. [perh. cogn. w. FLUE¹]

flue⁴ (flōō), n. (colloq.). (Short for IN-FLUENZA.

flu·ent, a. & n. Flowing (rare in lit. sense); ready to flow, liquid, (rare); fluid, not settled, liable to change, (rare); (of motion, curves, etc.) graceful, easy; (of speech or style) copious, coming easily, ready; expressing oneself quickly & easily; (Math., in fluxions) that flows (n., the variable quantity that flows). Hence ~LY² adv. [f. L *fluere* flow, see -ENT]

fluff, n. & v.t. 1. Light feathery stuff given off by blankets etc.; soft fur; soft downy mass or bunch; *bit of* ~ (sl.), girl, woman; soft short hair on lip or cheek; ‖ (sl.) theatrical part imperfectly known; hence ~Y² a., ~INESS n. 2. v.t. Put soft surface on (flesh side of leather); make into ~; shake (oneself, one's feathers etc.) *up* or *out into* ~y mass; ‖ (sl.) blunder in theatrical part. [perh. modification of FLUE²]

fluid (flōō-), a. & n. (Substance) consisting of particles that move freely among themselves & yield to the slightest pressure (including gases, liquids, & the assumed pervasive imponderable media of electricity etc.); moving readily, not solid or rigid, not stable; liquid constituent or secretion. Hence **fluid'**ITY v.t., **fluid'**ITY n., (flōō-). [f. F *fluide* f. L *fluidus* (*fluere* flow, -ID¹)]

flu·en·cy (flōō-), n. Smooth easy flow, esp. in speech; ready utterance. [f. L *fluentia*]

fluey. See FLUE³.

flue⁵ (flōō-), v.i. & t. Splay, make (opening) widen inwards or outwards. [f. obs. adj. *flue* shallow perh. cogn. w. FLOW]

flügel·man. See FUGLEMAN.

flummox, v.t. (sl.). Confound, bewilder, disconcert. [prob. imit.]

flump, v.i. & t., & n. Fall or move heavily, set or throw *down*, with a dull noise (n., the action or sound). [imit.]

flung. See FLING v.

flunk·ey, n. (pl. ~s). Liveried servant, footman, (usu. contempt.); toady, snob. Hence ~DOM (-kid-), ~ISM (-kizm), nn. [orig. Sc.; perh. f. FLANK, with sense *sidesman*]

fluor· (flōō-), comb. forms of *fluōroscope,* as *fluōbō'ric, fluōrhȳd'ric, fluōro-...*

fluor (flōō-), n. Kinds of gemlike readily fusible mineral containing fluorine; ~-*spar*, calcium fluoride. [L, = flow (*fluere* flow, -OR³)]

fluor·es·cence (flōō-), n. Coloured luminosity produced in certain substances by incident light or other electro-magnetic radiations of shorter wave-length, esp. violet and ultra-violet light and X-rays; property of absorbing light of short (invisible) wave-length and emitting light of longer (visible) wave-length. Hence ~ésce v.i., exhibit ~escence, Hence ~ésce'NT a., (flōō-). [prec. -ESCENT, -ENCE]

fluor·ine (flōō-), n. Non-metallic element of the HALOGEN group. Hence **fluor'**IDE [foll.]

Hence ~Y² a., ~ILY² adv., ~INESS n. (flōō-). [etym. dub.; first in billiards]

***flume** (flōōm), n.; & v.i. & t. Artificial channel conveying water for industrial use; ravine with stream; (vb) build ~s, convey down a ~. [in early use = stream; f. OF *flum* f. L *flumen* river (*fluere* flow)]

flummery, n. Food made by boiling kinds of sweet dish made with milk, flour, eggs, etc.; empty compliments, trifles, nonsense. [f. W *llymru* etym. dub.]

flurry, n., & v.t. 1. Gust, squall; commotion, excitement, nervous hurry, agitation; whale's death-throes. 2. v.t. Confuse by haste or noise, agitate. [imit.; cf. *flaw, hurry*]

flush¹, v.i. & t. & n. 1. Take wing & fly away; cause to do this, put up, (birds). 2. n. Number of birds put up at once. [perh. imit.; cf. *fly, rush*]

flush², v.i. & t. & n. 1. Spurt, rush out; cleanse (drain etc.) by flow of water; flood (meadow); (of plant) throw out fresh shoots (also causative, *rain ~es the plants*); glow with warm colour; (of blood) rush into & redden face; (of face) become red or hot, blush; cause to glow or blush, suffuse with warm colour; inflame with pride or passion, encourage, (~ed with exercise, joy, victory, insolence, etc.), [perh. = prec. influenced by *flash* & *blush*]

flush³, n. Rush of water; sudden abundance; stream from mill-wheel; rush of

flukey³ (flōōk), n. & v.i. & t. (Make) lucky accidental stroke; get, hit, etc., by ~e. [perh. f. prec.]

fluke² (flōōk), n. Broad triangular plate on arm of anchor; barbed head of lance, harpoon, etc.; (pl.) whale's tail. [perh. f. flook²]

fluke¹ (flōōk), n. Kinds of flat-fish, the flounder, (now rare); kinds of parasitic worm found in sheep's liver; ‖ kind of kidney potato. [OE *flóc* cf. ON *flóke,* cogn. w. G *flach* flat]

emotion, elation produced by it or by victory etc.; fresh growth of grass etc.; cleansing of drain by flushing; glow of light or colour; rush of blood to face, reddening caused by it; hot fit in fever; freshness, vigour. [f. prec.]

flush⁴, a., & v.t. 1. Full to overflowing, in flood; (usu. pred.) having plentiful supply of or of money etc.. (of money) abundant; even, in same plane, level *with*, without projections or raised edges. 2. v.t. Level; fill in (joint) level with surface. [prob. f. FLUSH²]

flush⁵, n. Set of cards all of one suit. [cf. F & Sp. *flux* prob. f. L FLUXUS]

flus'ter, v.t. & i., & n. 1. Confuse with drink, half-intoxicate; flurry, make nervous; be agitated, bustle. 2. n. Flurry, flutter, agitation. [cf. Icel. *flaustr* n., *flaustra* v.]

flus'tra, n. (pl. *-ae*, *-as*). Sea-mat, polyzoic species resembling sea-weed. [arbitrary mod. L coinage by Linnaeus]

flute, n., & v.i. & t. 1. Musical wind-instrument, long wooden pipe with holes along it stopped by fingers or keys, & blow-hole in side near upper end, whence **flut'IST**(3) (flōō-) n.; ~player; organ stop with ~like tone; semicylindrical vertical groove in pillar, similar groove elsewhere, e.g. in frills, whence **flut'ING¹**(6) (flōō-) n. 2. vb. Play ~; whistle, sing, or speak, in ~like tones; play (air etc.) on ~; make ~s or grooves in. [f. OF *fleüte*, *flaüte*, *flahute*, etym. dub.]

flutt'er, v.i. & t. & n. 1. Flap wings, flap (wings), without flying or in short flights; come or go with quivering motion (usu. hover; quiver, vibrate, (of pulse) beat feebly & irregularly; tremble with excitement, be agitated; move (flag etc.) irregularly, agitate, ruffle; throw (person) into confusion or agitation. 2. n. ~ing; tremulous excitement (*be, put, in a* ~); stir, sensation, (*make a* ~); vibration (*wing, tail,* ~, defects of aircraft in flight); (sl.) gambling venture, speculation. [OE *flotorian* frequent. cf. *fleotan* FLEET⁵]

flut'y (flōō-), a. Like flute in tone, soft & clear. [-Y²]

fluv'ial (flōō-), a. Of, found in, river(s). [F, f. L *fluviālis* (*fluvius* river, -AL]

fluv'iatile (flōō-), a. Of, found in, produced by, river(s). [F, f. L *fluviātilis* (prec., -ATILE]

fluv'io- (flōō-), comb. form of L *fluvius* river, as *fluvio-marine*, *fluviom'eter*.

flux, n., & v.i. & t. 1. Morbid or excessive discharge of blood, excrement, etc., (formerly) dysentery; flowing out, issue; flowing; inflow of title (usu. ~ *& reflux*, often fig.); flood of talk etc.; continuous succession of changes (*in a state of* ~); (Math.) continued motion (*time is flow of* ~ *a point*); (Physics) rate of flow of any fluid across given area, amount crossing area in given time; substance mixed with metal etc. to promote fusion. 2. vb. Issue in a ~, flow copiously; make fluid, fuse, treat with a fusing ~. [F, f. L *fluxus* (*fluere flux- flow*)]

flu'xion (-kshn), n. Flowing (rare); continuous change (rare); (Math.) rate or proportion at which a flowing or varying quantity increases its magnitude (*method of* ~s, the Newtonian calculus (*method of* ~s, aa., (-kshon-). [F, f. L *fluxionem* (*fluere flux-* flow, -ION]

fly¹, n. Two-winged insect (~ *in amber*, curious relic; ~ *on wheel*, person who over-estimates his own influence; *break* ~ *on wheel*, expend disproportionate energy; *a* ~ *in the ointment*, trifling circumstance that mars enjoyment; *no flies on him* etc., sl. praise of person's or thing's efficiency; HESSIAN, SPANISH, TSETSE, ~); kinds of plant-disease caused by various flies (*a good deal of* ~ *exists*); natural or artificial ~ used as fishing-bait; ~-*bone*, kinds of plant, esp. CATCH¹~ & Ploughman's spikenard; ~-*blow*, (n.) ~'s egg in meat etc., (v.t.) deposit eggs in, taint, (~-*blown*, tainted, lit. & fig.); ~-*book*, case for keeping fishing-flies in; ~-*catcher*, trap for flies, kinds of bird; ~-*fish* (v.i.), fish with ~; ~-*flap*, for driving away flies; ~-*net*, net or fringe protecting horse from flies; ~-*paper*, for catching or poisoning flies; ~-*trap*, for catching flies, also kinds of plant (esp. *Venus's* ~-*trap*, Dionaea; ~-*weight* (BOX⁵); ~-*whisk*, for driving away flies. [OE *fléoge*, *flýge*, cf. Du. *vlieg*, G *fliege*, cogn. w. foll.]

fly², v.i. & t. (*flew*, pr. flōō, *flown* pr. flōn; *is, has flown*, see -ED²(2); *fly* is preferred in talk & ordinary prose for *flee*, but not *flew* or *flown* for *fled*). Move through air with wings (~ *high*, be ambitious; *high-flown*, exalted, turgid, bombastic; *as the* CROW¹ *flies*; *the bird is flown*, person wanted has escaped; often *about, away, forth, off, out*) or in aircraft; direct flight of (aircraft), transport (passengers) in aircraft; make (pigeon, hawk) ~; (Hawk.) soar by way of attack at (fig., ~ *at higher game*, have nobler ambitions); pass or rise quickly through air; jump clear over or over fence etc.; make (kite) rise & stay aloft (~ *a kite*, raise money by accommodation bill, also try how the wind blows, feel one's way by ballon d'essai) (of flag, hair, garment, etc.) flutter, wave; set or keep (flag) ~ing; travel swiftly, rush along, pass rapidly; spring, start, hasten, (~ *to arms*, take up arms eagerly; ~ *in the* FACE¹ *of*; ~ *at, upon*, attack violently; ~ *into a passion, raptures*, etc.; ~ *out*, burst into violent language or action); be driven or forced off suddenly (*made sparks* ~; *send* ~*ing*; *make the money* ~, spend quickly; *door flew open*; *glass* etc. *flies*, breaks in pieces); *let* ~, discharge (missile), (abs.) shoot, hit, **or**

use strong language, &c; run away, flee, flee from (*must ~ the country*); *~away*, (of garments) streaming, loose, negligé, (of persons) flighty; *~-by-night*, one who makes night excursions or decamps by night; *~-the-garter*, kind of leap-frog. [com.-Teut.; cf. OE *flēogan*, G *fliegen*; unconnected with *flee*]

fly³, n. Flying, distance flown, (*on the ~*) on wing. In motion; *~away*, hackney-carriage; lap on garment to contain or cover buttonholes, flap at entrance of tent; part of flag farthest from staff, also its breadth from staff to end; (Theatr.; pl.) space over proscenium. *~wheel*, heavy-rimmed on revolving shaft to regulate machinery or accumulate power. [f. prec.]

fly⁴, a. (sl.). Knowing, wide awake. [?]

fly'er, fli'er, n. Bird etc. that flies (usu. *high, poor*, etc., *~*); animal, vehicle, etc., going with exceptional speed; airman; flying jump. [-ER¹]

fly'ing, a. In vbl senses; also or esp.: making movements like flight (*~ boat*, form of SEA-plane in which a boat serves as both fuselage & float; *~ bomb*, aerial torpedo, pilotless aircraft with explosive war-head; *~dog*, kind of vampire-fox; *~ fish*, kinds rising into air by wing-like pectoral fins, also nickname for native of Barbados; *~ fox*, kinds of fruit-eating bat; *~ man*, airman; *F~ Officer*, rank in AIR¹ Force; *~ squad*, police detachment with motor-cars etc. for rapid pursuit; *~ squirrel*, kinds floating in air by skin connecting fore & hind legs); hanging loose, fluttering, (*~ jib*, light sail set before jib on *~ jib-boom*; *with ~ colour's*); done or taken in passing (*~ jump*, with running start; *~ handicap, ~ start*, in which starting-post is passed at full speed); passing, hasty, (*~ visit*); movement (*~ bridge*); designed for rapid movement (*~ squadron, column*); *~ but-tress*, slanting from pier etc. to wall & so usu. carried on arch. [-ING²]

foal, n., & v.t. & i. 1. Young of horse, ass, etc., colt or filly, (*in, with, ~*, pregnant). 2. vb. Give birth to (*~*), give birth to *~*. [com.-Teut.; OE *fola*, cf. G *folien*, cogn. W. Gk *pōlos*, L *pullus*]

foam, n., & v.i. 1. Collection of small bubbles formed in liquid by agitation, fermentation, etc.; froth of saliva or perspiration; (poet.) the sea. 2. v.i. Emit *~*, froth at the mouth; (of water etc.) froth, gather *~*; run *~ing* along, down, over, etc., pass off or away in a *~*; (of cup etc.) be filled with *~ing* liquor. Hence ~'LESS, ~'Y², aa. [vb.f.n. OE *fām* cf. G *feim*]

fob¹, n., & v.t. (-bb-). Small pocket for watch etc. formerly made in waistband of breeches; (vb) put in one's *~*, pocket. (?) [from 16th c.]

fob², v.t. (-bb-). Cheat, take in; palm (something inferior) off upon (person), put (person) off with (something inferior). [from 16th c.; cf. G *foppen* befool]

fo'cal¹, a. Of, situated or collected at, a focus; (Opt.) *~ distance* or *length*, distance between centre of mirror or lens & its focus; *~-plane shutter* (Photog.), blind with (usu. adjustable) slit that moves across face of plate or film (for very short exposures). [focus v.t. Hence ~ATION n.]

fo'calize, v.t., = FOCUS v.t. Hence **focăli'za'tion** n. [focus, -IZE]

fo'c's'le. See FORECASTLE.

fō'cus, n. (pl. -ci pr. -sī, -cuses), & v.t. & i (-s-, -ss-). 1. (Plane geom.) one of points from which distances to any point of given curve are connected by linear relation. (Opt. Heat, etc.) point at which rays meet after reflection or refraction, point from which they appear to proceed, point at which object must be situated for image given by lens to be well defined (*in, out of, bring into, ~*), focal length of lens, adjustment of eye or eyeglass necessary to produce clear image; principal seat (of disease, activity, etc.). 2. vb. Converge, make converge, to a *~*; adjust *~* of (lens, eye); **bring into ~**. [L, = hearth]

fodd'er, n., & v.t. 1. Dried food, hay, straw, etc., for stall-feeding cattle; hence ~LESS a. 2. v.t. Give *~* to. [OE *fōdor*, cf. Du. *voeder*, G *futter*, f. Aryan *pat-* feed]

fōe, n. (poet. etc.). Enemy, adversary, opponent, ill-wisher; *~man* (arch.), enemy in war. [OE *fāh* adj. & *gefā* noun t. OTeut. *faiho-, gafaiho-*, cogn. W. Gk *pikros* bitter]

fœ'tus (fēt-), **fē'tus**, n. Fully developed embryo in womb or egg. Hence **f(o)et'Al** a., **f(o)et'ICIDE(2)** n. (fē-). [L *fētus -ūs* offspring]

fog¹, n., & v.t. & i. (-gg-). 1. Aftermath; long grass left standing in winter. 2. v.t. Leave (land) under *~*; feed (cattle) on *~*. [from 14th c.; etym. dub.]

fog², n., & v.t. & i. (-gg-). 1. Vapour suspended in atmosphere at or near earth's surface, obscurity caused by this (*in a ~*, puzzled, at a loss); abnormal darkened state of atmosphere. (Photog.) cloud on developed plate; *~-bow*, like rainbow produced by light on *~*; *~-horn*, sounding instrument for warning ships in *~*; *~-signal*, detonator placed on railway line in *~* to guide driver. 2. vb. Envelop (as with *~*; perplex; (Gardening) die off from damp; (Photog.) make (negative) obscure or cloudy; || (Railway) place *~-signals* on line, whence ||~'GER n. [prob. back formation f. foggy; from 16th c.]

fŏg′|y̆ (-g-), a. Thick, murky; of, like, infested with, FOG²; obscure, dull, confused, (has only a ~y idea of it); beclouded, indistinct. Hence ~INĔSS n. [earlier senses, covered with coarse grass, boggy, flabby; prob. f. FOG¹, FOG² being formed f. foggy]

fŏ′gle, n. (thieves' sl.). Silk handkerchief. [?]

fŏg′y̆, -gey, (-g-), n. (Usu. old ~) old-fashioned fellow, old man behind the times. Hence **fŏg′(e)YDOM, fŏg′YISM, nn., fŏg′YISH¹ a.,** (-g-). [perh. var. of FOGGY in obs. sense moss-grown]

Föhn (fŏrn), n. Hot southerly wind in the Alps. [G, perh. f. L Favonius]

foi′ble, n. Weak point, weakness of character, quality on which one mistakenly prides oneself; (Fenc.) part of sword-blade from middle to point (cf. FORTE). [F, obs. form of faible FEEBLE]

foil¹, n., & v.t. 1. (Archit.) arc or space between cusps of window (vb, ornament with ~s, as ~ed arch). 2. Metal hammered or rolled into thin sheet (usu. gold, tin, etc., ~); sheet of this, or now amalgam of tin & quicksilver, placed behind mirror-glass, backing; leaf of it placed under precious stone etc. to brighten or colour it or enhance its brightness by contrast (vb, supply with this). 3. Anything that sets something off by contrast (vb, set off thus). [OF, f. L folium leaf cogn. w. Gk phullon]

foil², v.t. & i., & n. 1. (Hunt.) run over or cross (scent, ground) so as to baffle hounds (also abs. of deer etc., spoil the scent thus); beat off, repulse, frustrate, parry, baffle. 2. n. Track of hunted animal (run, run upon, the ~, over same track a second time); (arch.) repulse, defeat, check. [f. OF fouler full cloth, trample, (L fullo fuller)]

foil³, n. Blunt-edged sword with button on point used in fencing. [etym. dub.; perh. f. prec. in sense parry; or f. obs. foin thrust (&=foil in 17th c.) f. OF foine f. L fuscina fish-spear]

‖ fois′on (-zn), n. (arch.). Plenty. [OF, f. L fusionem (fundere fus- pour, -ION, -SON)]

foist, v.t. Introduce surreptitiously or unwarrantably into or in (adv.); palm (off on or upon, father (composition) upon. [orig. of palming false die; prob. f. Du. dial. vuisten take in the hand (vuist fist)]

fōld¹, n., & v.t. 1. (Usu. sheep-~) enclosure for sheep; (fig.) church, body of believers. 2. v.t. Shut up (sheep etc.) in ~; place sheep in ~ or ~s on (land) to manure it. [OE fald, cf. Du. vaalt; unconnected w. foll.]

fōld², v.t. & i., & n. 1. Double (flexible thing) over upon itself (also in, over, together; ~ up, make more compact by ~ing; bend portion of (thing) back, down, become, be able to be, ~ed (~ing door(s), hung in 2 parts, often themselves ~ing, hung on 2 jambs); wind, clasp, (arms etc. about, round; lay together (arms & interlace (arms), clasp (one's hands); swathe, envelop, (~ it in paper; hills ~ed in mist). 2. n. Doubling of ~ed object; hollow between two thicknesses (carried it in a ~ of her dress), hollow or nook in mountain etc.; coil of serpent, string, etc.; ~ing (another ~ gives 32mo); line made by ~ing; (Geol.) the ~ing or curvature of strata. [comb. form ~fold as in twofold etc.] Tent.: n. f. vb, OE fealdan, cf. G falten, also Gk (di)plasios double, & Gk plekō L plicare, plait]

-fold, suf. (OE fealá; cf. Du. -voud, G -fald) cogn. w. FOLD², Gk -paltos, -plasios, & -plo- in haplós single, & prob. L -plex (simplec etc.); added to cardinals to form adji. w. sense multiplied by (orig. sense folded in ~, plaited in ~ strands). Now largely superseded by wds f. L in -ble, -ple, (treble, quadruple), but retained in the advl use (repaid tenfold), & in adji. when there is a plurality of things more or less different (a twofold charm).

fōl′der, n. In vbl senses; esp.: paper-folding instrument; folded circular etc. (pl.) folding eyeglasses. [-ER¹]

fōliā′ceous (-shus), a. Leaf-like; with organs like leaves; of leaves; laminated. [f. L foliaceus (FOLIUM leaf, -ACEOUS)]

fōl′iage, n. Leaves, leafage, (lit., or as represented in art; ~ leaf, excluding petals etc.; ~ plant, cultivated for ~, not for flowers). Hence (-)fōl′iagED²(-ĕjd) a. [F feuillage (feuille leaf f. L folia leaves, -AGE) corrected on L]

fōl′iar, a. Of leaves. [f. L folium leaf, -AR¹]

fōl′iate¹, a. Leaf-like; having leaves; having specified number of leaflets (1, 5, etc., ~); [f. L foliatus (folium leaf, -ATE²)]

fōl′iāte², v.i. & t. Split (intr.) into laminae; decorate (arch, door-head) with foils; number leaves (not pages) of (volume) consecutively. So ~A′TION n. [f. L folium leaf, -ATE³]

fōl′iō, n. (pl. -os). Leaf of paper, parchment, etc., numbered only on front; (Bookkeep.) two opposite pages of ledger etc. used concurrently, page of ledger etc. used for both sides of account; leaf-number of printed book; number of words (72 or 90) taken as unit in reckoning length of document; sheet of paper folded once (in ~, of books on such paper; volume made of such sheets, largest-sized volume, (also attrib., a ~ book, in six volumes ~). [L, abl. of folium leaf (abl.f use in reff., = on leaf 50 etc.)]

fōl′iole, n. Division of compound leaf, leaflet. [F, f. L foliolum dim. of folium leaf]

folk (fōk), n. (Arch.) a people, nation, race; (pl., the sing. being arch. or dial.) people in general, people of specified class, (now being ousted by people); ~,

of the people (chiefly in compounds imi-tated f. German, as ~-*custom*, -*song*; ~-*etymology*, perversion of word's form to make it significant; ~-*lore*, traditional beliefs etc., study of these). [OE *folc*, cf. G *volk*]

Fol'licle, n. Small sac or vesicle; cocoon. So **follic'ular**¹, **follic'ulated** [-ātĕd¹], aa. [f. L *folliculus* (*follis* bellows, -CULE)]

Foll'ow (-ō), v.t. & i. & n. **1.** Go or come after (moving thing or person; ~ *the hounds*, hunt; ~ *my leader*, game in which each player must do as leader does; ~ *one's nose*, leave one's route to chance; ~ *the plough*, be ploughman); go along (path); come after in order or time; accompany, serve; go after as admirer; result from, be the necessary consequence of, be involved in (*trade ~s the flag*); strive after, aim at; treat or take as guide or master, obey, espouse opinions or cause of; conform to (~ SUIT), act upon, take as rule; practise (profession etc.; ~ *the sea*, be sailor); keep up with mentally, grasp the meaning of, (argument, speak-er); go or come after person or thing (~ *in his steps*; ~ *in the wake of*); ~ happen after something else, ensue; result, be deducible, (*it ~s that he was not there*). **2.** ~ *after* (prep. & adv.), = ~ (in most senses, but with slightly formal effect); (Cricket, of side) ~ *on*, go in again out of turn after getting less than opponents by certain number (n., ~-*on*, doing this); ~ *out*, pursue to the end; ~ *through* (Golf), carry stroke through to fullest possible extent after striking ball (~-*through* n., this action); ~ *up*, pursue steadily, add another blow etc. to (previ-ous blow etc.), (Footb. etc.) keep near (player with) ball to support; ~-*up*, the continuation of an action, (esp.) a second advertising circular sent referring to an earlier one. **3.** n. (Billiards) stroke causing player's ball to roll on after object-ball. [OE *folgian*, cf. G *folgen* perh. cogn. w. FULL]

foll'ower (-ōer), n. In vbl senses; esp.: adherent, disciple; man courting maid-servant. [-ER¹]

foll'owing¹ (-ō-), n. In vbl senses; also, body of adherents, followers. [-ING¹]

foll'owing² (-ō-), a. In vbl senses; esp., now to be mentioned (also as pron. sing. or pl., *the ~ are noteworthy*). [-ING²]

foll'y, n. Being foolish, want of good sense, unwise conduct; foolish act, idea, or practice, ridiculous thing; costly structure (considered) useless (usu. with originator's name. —'s F~). [f. OF *folie* (*fol* mad, see FOOL¹); last sense perh. starts f. F use of *folie*=favourite abode)]

foment', v.t. Bathe with warm or medi-cated lotions, apply warmth to; foster, stimulate, or instigate (sentiment, con-duct, sedition, etc.), whence ~ER¹ n. [f. F *fomenter* f. LL *fomentare* f. L *fomentum* (*fovere* cherish, -MENT)]

fomenta'tion, n. In vbl senses; esp. (application of) warm flannels etc. for fomenting purposes. [f. LL *fomentatio* (prec., -ATION)]

fond, a. Foolishly credulous or sanguine; over-affectionate, doting; tender, loving; ~ *of*, full of love for, much inclined to. Hence ~LY² adv., ~NESS n. [p.p. of obs. *fon* become insipid]

fon'dant, n. Kind of sweetmeat. [F (*fondre* melt f. L *fundere* pour, -ANT)]

fon'dle, v.t. & i. Caress; toy amorously (*with*, together). [f. obs. *fond* vb (FOND)]

fons et or'igo, phr. The source and origin (*of*). (L)

font¹, n. Receptacle for baptismal water; receptacle for holy water; oil-reservoir of lamp. [f. L *fons -tis* fountain in eccl. L sense]

fon'tal, a. Primary, original, of the fountain-head; baptismal. [f. med. L *fontalis* (prec., -AL)]

fontanelle' (-ĕl'), n. Membranous space in infant's head at adjacent angles of parietal bones. [F (-*le*), dim. of *fontaine* FOUNTAIN]

food, n. Victuals, nourishment, provisions, (*be ~ for worms*, dead; *be ~ for fishes*, drowned; ~ *for powder*, soldiers); edibles (~ & *drink*); particular kind of ~; nutri-ment of plants; material for the mind (*mental, intellectual, ~*; ~ *for thought or meditation*); ~-*stuff*, thing used as ~. Hence ~LESS a. [OE *fóda* f. Teut. *fad-*, whence Gk *gateomai* FEED]

fool¹, n. a. & v.i. & t. **1.** Silly person, simpleton, person whose conduct one disapproves of, (*be a ~ to*, be nothing in comparison with; *play the ~*, blunder, trifle; *no ~ like an old ~*, esp. of aged lover; ~'s *bolt is soon shot*, his stock of argument is soon exhausted; *man is ~ or physician at thirty*, sensible man needs no doctor); jester, clown, in medieval great house (*play the ~*, indulge in buffoonery); take trouble to no end; *All Fools' Day*, 1st April; *April ~*, person raised in or sent on ~'s errand on that day; *send, go, on ~'s errand*, fruitless one; ~'s MATE¹; ~'s *para-dise*, illusory happiness); ~'s-*cap*, ~'s*cap*, cap with bells worn by medieval jester, dunce's conical paper cap, trademark of some 17th-c. paper, long folio writing or printing paper 15–17 × 12–13½ in.; hence ~'ERY(4, 5), ~'ĭsHLY adv., ~'ĭsHNESS n., ~'PROOF² a., ~'ĭsHRŶ². **2.** *adj.* (colloq.) ~*ish*, silly, (of rules etc. so plain as to defy misinter-pretation). **3.** vb. Play the ~, idle, trifle, (also *about* & *around); cheat (person) *out of money*

etc. or *into doing*, get (money etc.) by cajolery *out of* person; throw (time, money) *away*~ishly; make a ~ of, dupe, play tricks *on*. [f. OF *fol* f. L *follis* bellows in pop. LL sense *windbag*, *empty-headed person*]

fool[2], n. Creamy liquid of fruit stewed, crushed, & mixed with milk, cream, etc. (esp. *gooseberry*~). [prob. f. prec.]

fool'hard[1], a. Foolishly venturesome, delighting in needless risks. Hence ~i-NESS n. [f. OF *fol hardi* (FOOL[1], HARDY[1])]

foot[1], n. (pl. feet). 1. Termination of leg beginning at ankle (FIND one's feet; *have feet of clay*, be liable to overthrow, see *Dan.* ii. 33). 2. Step, pace, tread, (*swift of*~; *has a light*~). 3. Infantry (*the 4th* ~ *or regiment of*~; ~*soldier*; *a captain, of* ~; ~ *& horse*). 4. Lower end of bed, grave, couch, etc. (opp. *head*), part of stocking etc. covering ~. 5. Metrical unit with varying number of syllables one of which is accented. 6. Lineal measure of 12 in. (*10 feet long*; *a ten-*~*pole*; *six* ~ *or feet three*; see also SQUARE a., CUBIC). 7. Lower part, base. 8. (Zool.) kinds of locomotive or adhesive organ in invertebrates. 9. (Bot.) part by which petal is attached, root of hair. 10. Lowest part, bottom, of hill, ladder, wall, list, page, class, etc. 11. Dregs, oil refuse, coarse sugar, (pl. ~s). 12. Phrr.: *have one* ~ *in grave*, be near death; (*with one's*) *feet foremost*, being carried to burial; *find, know, length of one's* ~, learn his weaknesses, be able to manage him; *measure another's* ~ *by one's own last*, judge others by oneself; *set, put, have, one's* ~ *on the neck of*, utterly subdue, hold in subjection; *on one's feet*, standing, in health, with a livelihood; *carry one off his feet*, make him enthusiastic, greatly excite; FALL[1] *on one's feet*; *keep one's feet*, not fall; *put one's* ~ *down*, take up firm position (fig.); *put one's* ~ *in it*, blunder; BEST[1]~; ~*'s pace*, walk; CHANGE[2] or *feet*; *at one's feet*, as his disciple, subject, or suppliant; *have* BALL[1] *at one's feet*; *with foot at* ~, of mare that has foaled; *on*~, walking, not riding etc., also in motion (*set agitation, movement, etc., on*~, start it), busy, projected, proceeding; *tread under*~, oppress; *vet etc. under*~, on the ground. 13. ~*-&-mouth* (*disease*), kind of fever esp. in horned cattle; ~*ball*, large round or elliptical inflated ball, game played with it, ~*baller*, player at this; ~*bath*, washing of feet, small bath used for this; ~*board*, ~*man's* platform at carriage-back, board for getting in or out of carriage by, sloped board for driver's feet; ~*boy*, page, boy servant in livery; ~*bridge*, ~*path*, ~*road*, ~*way*, etc., for ~*passengers* only; ~*drill*, ~*pump*, etc., worked by or with help of ~; ~*fall*, sound of ~*step*; ~*fault*

(Lawn Tennis), fault made by overstepping the base line while serving; ~*gear*, boots, socks, etc.; || F~ *Guards*, Grenadier, Coldstream, Scots, Irish, Welsh, Guards; ~*hill*, lying at base of mountain; ~*hold*, support for feet, surface for standing on; ~*lights*, screened lights in front of stage (GET[1] *across the* ~*lights*); ~*man*, infantryman, liveried servant for carriage, door, & table, trivet to hang on grate bars; ~*mark*, ~*print*; ~*muff*, for keeping feet warm; ~*noke*, inserted at ~ of page; ~*pace*, walking pace, dais; ~*pad*, unmounted highwayman; ~*page*, boy servant; ~*pan*, for washing feet; ~*passenger*, one who walks, not rides or drives; ~*path* (for ~*passengers*); ~*plate*, driver's and fireman's platform in locomotive; ~*pound*, quantity of energy that will raise 1 lb. to height of 1 ft.; ~*print*, impression left by ~; ~*race*, running-match between persons; ~*rot*, disease of ~ in sheep & cattle; ~*rule*, rigid measure 1 ft long; ||~*slogging* n. & a.; ~*sore*, having sore feet, esp. with walking; ~*stalk*, (Bot.) stalk of leaf or peduncle of flower; ~*step*, tread, footprint, (*follow in one's* ~*steps*, do as he did); ~*stone*, foundation stone, stone at ~ of grave; ~*stool*, for resting feet on; ~*warmer*, thing to warm feet, esp. flat hot-water tin used in railway carriages; ~*wear*, = ~*gear*. Hence (-)~ED[2], ~LESS, aa. [Aryan; OE *fót*, cf. G *fuss*, Skr. *pad*, Gk *pous podos*, L *pes pedis*]

foot[2], v.i. & t. ~ *it*, dance, (rare) pace, go; set foot on, traverse on foot (rare); put new foot to (stocking); add up or *up* (account); pay (bill); (of bill, items, etc.) *mount up to*. [f. prec.]

||**foot'er**, n. (sl.). The game football [-ER[1]]

foot'ing, n. Placing of feet, foothold; surface for standing on, secure position, (lit. & fig.); conditions, relations, position, status, in which person is towards others, degree of intimacy etc.; entrance on new position, admittance to trade, society, etc., (only in *pay for* or *pay one's* ~, i.e. a customary fee for it); projecting course at foot of wall etc.; (reckoning of) sum total of column of figures etc. [FOOT[2]+-ING[1]]

foo'tle, v.i., & n. (sl.). 1. Trifle, play the fool; hence ~ING[2] n. 2. n. Twaddle, folly. [?]

foo'zle, v.t., & n. (sl., esp. golf). 1. Do clumsily, bungle, make a mess of. 2. n. Clumsy failure. [cf. G dial. *fuseln* work badly or slowly]

fop, n. Dandy, exquisite, vain man. Hence ~'LING[1](2), ~p'ERY[4], 5), nn., ~p'ISH[1] a., ~p'ishLY[2] adv., ~p'ish-NESS n. [?]

for (fôr, fĕr, *according to position or emphasis required*), prep. & conj. I. prep. Representing, in place of, in exchange against, as price or penalty of, in requital of, (*sits* ~; *member* ~; *Liverpool*; *once* ~ *all*, instead of many repetitions, finally substituted ~; *agent* ~; *got it for* 6*d.*; *thrashed* ~ *his pains*; *do you take me* ~ *a fool?*); in defence or support or favour of, on side of, (*take my word* ~ *it*, be assured, *hurrah* ~ *person or thing*; *am* ~ *tariff*-conducively) to, (*go* ~ (sl.), *a walk*; *went to be*, *soldier*; *is*, *did it*, ~ *her good*; ~ *sale*, to be sold;) to get, win, or save (*send*, *go*, ~ *a cab*; *would not do it* ~ *the world*; *not paid* ~; *play* ~ *penny points*; *was tried* ~ *his life*; *cannot do it* ~ *the life of me*; *run* ~ *it*); to reach, arrive at, be received by, or belong to (*left*, *sailed*, ~ *India*; *made* ~ *shelter*; *go* ~ (sl.), *attack*; *getting on* ~ *two o'clock*; *bought gowns* ~ *the maids*; *won a name* ~ *himself*) (after vbs, adji., nn., &c. Interjections, of emotion, faculty, or fitness; after adji. & adv. *enough*; after expressions implying fit-ness etc.) as regards, in the direction of, (*don't care* ~ *games*; *a longing* ~ *praise*; *fit* ~ *nothing*; *ready*; *dinner*; *oh* ~ *wings!*; *noun* ~ *it*; *too beautiful* ~ *words*; *good* ~ *enough* ~ *me*; *time* ~ *school*; *is not long this world, will soon die*; *nothing* ~ *it but to submit*, submission the only course open; *is the man* ~ *the job*; *it is* ~ *you to make the move*; *the motive* ~ *retreating*) with the result, at the cost, to the amount, of (*all out* ~ 44; 150 ~ 6 *wickets*; *drew on him* ~ £100); to affect, as affecting, bene-ficially or the reverse (*they live* ~ *each other*; *can shift* ~ *myself*; *things look bad* ~ *you*; *it is bad* ~ *him to smoke*; & hence ~ with noun or pron. & infin. as neutral noun-phrase = Latin acc. & inf., *it is believe it*; *did it* ~ *the second time*; *wicked* ~ *him to smoke*, *it is usual* ~ *hats to be worn* = that hats should be worn) in the character of, as being, (*hold it certain*; *mistaken* ~ *him*; *be hanged* ~ *a pirate*; *take* ~ *granted*; *I* ~ *one do not do it* ~ *my sake*; *fie* ~ *shame!*; *alas* ~ *him!*); in spite of (~ *all that*, ~ *all you say*, ~ *all he seems to dislike me*, *I still like him*); on account of the hindrance of (*were it not, but, except,* ~ *one thing I might be happy*); corresponding to, in contrast with, (~ *one enemy he has a hundred friends*; *bulk* ~ *bulk*, taking equal bulk of each; *word* ~ *word*, literally, verbatim; *so far as con-cerns*, regarding, (~ *the rest*; ~ *my part*; ~ *all, ought, I know*; *hard up* ~ *money*; *wants* ~ *nothing*) considering, making nature of (*a humane man*; *an executioner*;

very bright ~ *a winter day*); during, over, to the extent of, (*has been* ~ *months*; *walk* ~ *two miles*; *made comfortable* ~ *life*, ~ *the present*; *left him alone* ~ *once*); ~ *all the world*, exactly (*looked* ~ *all the world like a porpoise*); *be* ~ *it* (sl.), be destined for punishment. 2. conj. (Introducing new sentence or series of sentences con-taining proof of or reason for believing that, since, in order to be convinced of this observe or remember that . . . [prob. shortened f. FORE²]

for-, pref. formerly very common, but re-maining only in some dozen common words. Meanings: (1) away, off, apart, (~*by*, ~*get*, ~*give*); (2) prohibition (~*bid*, ~*fend*); (3) abstention, neglect, (~*bear*, ~*go*, ~*sake*, ~*swear*); (4) bad effect (~*do*); (5) excess, intensity (~*lorn*, ~*pine*, ~*worn*). [OE *for*, *fœr-*, cf. G *ver-*, cogn. w.

fó'rage, n., & v.t. & i. I. Food for horses & cattle, esp. for horses in army; foraging (*on the* ~ etc.); ||~*cap*, infantry undress cap. 2. vb. Collect ~ from, ravage; search for ~ or (fig.) for anything, rum-mage; supply with ~; get by foraging; so **fö'rager**(-j) [-ING¹] n. [f. OF *fourrage(r)* (œuvre f. Rom. *fodro* f. Teut. see FODDER]

foram'ĕn, n. (pl. -*mina*), Orifice, hole, passage. **fora̱m'inate¹**, **-a̱ted**, a. [L (*forare* bore, -MEN)]

forasmŭch' as (-az-; -az), conj. Seeing that, since, [= *for as much as*]

fö'ray, n., & v.i. (Go on, make) incursion, raid, inroad. [f. Rom. *fodro* (FORAGE)]

forbe'ar¹ (fŏb-, forbâr'), n. (usu. pl.) Ancestor(s). [FORE² + obs. *beer* (BE, -ER²)]

forbe'ar² (-bâr), v.t. & i. (-*bore*, -*borne*). Abstain or refrain from or from; not use or mention; be patient. Hence ~ANCE n., ~ING¹² adv., (~bâr'-). [FOR-(3), BEAR²]

forbid', v.t. (-*bad* or -*bäde*; -*bidden*). Com-mand (person etc.) not to do, (person etc.) not to go to (place), not allow (person etc. something; person or thing to exist or happen, (~ *him to go*, *him the court*, *him because not allowed*. (~ *gladiators, bullfights*; *was* ~*den wine*); (of circumstances) hinderance, etc.) exclude, prevent, make undesirable, (*God* ~!, *may it not happen!*); ~*den* DEGREES; ~*den fruit*, thing desired because not allowed. [OE *forbēodan* see FOR-(2), BID]

forbi'dding, a. Repellent, of uninviting appearance. Hence ~LY² adv., ~NESS n. [-ING²]

forby'(e²), prep. & adv. (Sc. & arch.). Besides; not to mention; in addition. [FOR-(1) + BY; cf. G *vorbei*]

fŏrce¹, n. 1. Strength, power, impetus, violence, intense effort; military strength; body of armed men, army, (pl.) troops; body of police (*the* ~, the police); strength exerted on an object, coercion, (*by* ~, by

4895

Q

compulsion), **2.** Mental or moral strength; influence, controlling power, efficacy, power to convince, vividness of effect; (*the ~ of circumstances brought it about; there is ~ in what you say; described with much ~*); (loose use) desirability, good sense, (*can't see the ~ of doing what one dislikes*). **3.** Binding power, validity, (*law remains in, comes into, ~; put in ~*, enforce); real import, precise meaning. **4.** (Phys.) measurable and determinable influence inclining body to motion, intensity of this, (formerly) kinetic energy (CONSERVATION of ~ or energy), (formerly) cause of any class of physical phenomena, e.g. of heat or motion, conceived as inherent in matter; (fig.) agency likened to these (*considers himself a ~ in the world*). **5.** *By ~ of*, by means of; (Mil.) *in ~*, in large numbers; *in great ~*, vigorous, fit, lively; *~-pump*, that forces water beyond range of atmospheric pressure. Hence ~LESS (-sl) a. [F, f. pop. L +fortia (L fortis strong)]

force², v.t. **1.** Use violence to, ravish. **2.** Constrain, compel, (*~ one's hand*, compel him to act prematurely or adopt policy unwillingly), put strained sense upon (words), (Cards) compel (player) to trump or reveal his strength, compel player to play (certain card); *~d landing*, compulsory landing of aircraft owing to damage, engine failure, etc.; compel (person) *to do, into doing*, or *into* specified action. **3.** Strain to the utmost, urge, *~ the pace* or *running*, adopt high speed in race to tire adversary out quickly; so *~ the bidding* at auction; *~ one's voice*, strain to get notes beyond usual compass or degree of loudness beyond what is easy or natural; *~d march*, requiring special effort; *~d* DRAUGHT¹; *~ the game*, run risks to score quickly; *~ an analogy, simile*, etc., apply it to death). **4.** Overpower, capture, make way through, break open, (stronghold, defences, pass, lock, door) by force. **5.** Drive, propel. **6.** Impose, press, (thing) *upon* person (*~ a card*, in conjuring, make one choose a particular card unconsciously). **7.** Effect, produce, by effort (*~ a smile*, make one self smile; *~ one's way, a passage*; take by force, extort, wring, (*~ it out of his hands*; *~d loan*; *~ tears from his eyes, the facts out of him*). **8.** Artificially hasten the maturity of (plant, scholar). Hence fo͞rˈcĕdlᴵʸ² adv. [f. F forcer (prec.)]

‖fŏrˈce³, n. (northern). Waterfall. [f. ON fors]

forceˈful (-sf-), a. (Arch. or literary or affected for) forcible. Hence ~LYᴵʸ² adv., ~NESS n. [-FUL]

force majeure (mahzhȫrˈ), n. Irresistible compulsion, coercion diplomatically recognized as irresistible; war, strike, act of God, etc., excusing fulfilment of contract. [F]

forceˈ-meat (-sm~), n. Meat chopped, spiced, & seasoned for stuffing. [f. obs. force corruption of FARCE²]

forˈceps, n. sing. & pl. Surgical pincers; (Anat., Entom., Zool.) organ resembling ~, whence forˈcipᴀᴛᴇ²a. [L (genit. -ĭpis)]

forˈcible, a. Done by, involving, force; telling, vivid, convincing, (of acts, words, style, artist, etc.); *~-feeble*, disguising feebleness under show of force. Hence ~NESS n, forˈcĭblʸ² adv. [OF (FORCE¹, -IBLE)]

ford, n., & v.t. & i. **1.** Shallow place where river etc. may be crossed by wading. **2.** vb. Cross (water), cross water, by wading. Hence ~ABLE, ~LESS, aa. [cf. G furt; cogn. w. FARE, also w. L portus PORT¹]

fordo¹(-ŏo), v.t. (arch.; -did, -done pr. dŭn). Kill, destroy, spoil; (p.p.) exhausted, tired out. [OE fordón see FOR- (4), DO¹]

fore¹, a. & n. **1.** Situated in front (opp. HIND, BACK, AFT). **2.** n. ~ part, ~ bow of ship; (Naut.) *in ~*, on the *~-royal* mast-head; *to the ~*, on the spot, ready to hand, available, alive, (recently) conspicuous (*come to the ~*, take leading part). [developed f. compounds w. FORE-]

fore², adv. & prep. **1.** adv. In front (still in *~ & aft*, at bow & stern, all over ship, backwards & forwards or lengthwise in ship; *~-&-aft rigged*, having *~-&-aft* sails, i.e. sails set lengthwise, not to yards, as chief sails; *~-&-aft cap*, with peak at each end). **2.** prep. In presence of (in adjurations), as *~ George* = by George. [com.-Teut.: OE fore, cf. G vor, cogn. w. L pro, prae, per, Gk pro, para, peri; prep. often mistakenly for as if short for before]

fore³, int. (golf), warning people in front of stroke. [prob. for BEFORE]

fore-, pref. freely used with vbs, their participial adjectives, vbl nouns, & nouns of action; also with other nouns. Meanings with vbs etc.: (1) in front (*fore-runner*); (2) beforehand, in advance, (*foreordain*). Meanings with nouns other than verbal or of action: (3) in front, front-, (*forequarter*); (4) front part of (*forearm*); (5) of, near, or towards stem of ship or connected w. foremast (*fore-castle, foreknold*); (6) anticipatory, precedent, (*foreknowledge*). [see FORE²]

foreˈarm¹ (forˈ-ŭrm), n. Arm from elbow to wrist or finger-tips; corresponding part in foreleg or wing. [FORE-(4)]

forearm²(forˈahrmˈ), v.t. Arm beforehand. [FORE-(2)]

forebodeˈ (forb-), v.t. Predict (rare; betoken, portend; have presentiment of (usu. evil) or that. Hence ~ˈingˌlʸ² adv. [FORE-(2)]

For words in fore- not given see FORE.

forebod'ing (fôrb-), n. Prediction, presage or omen, presentiment, (esp. of evil). [-ING¹]

fore'cabin (fōr'k-), n. Cabin in fore part of ship, usu. for second-class passengers. [FORE-(5)]

fore'cast¹ (fōr'kahst'), v.t. (forecast or ~ed, see in etym.). Estimate, conjecture, beforehand. [FORE-(2)+CAST¹; ~ed depends on mistaken assumption that the v.b is derived f. foll.]

fore cast² (fōr'kahst), n. Foresight, prudence, (rare); conjectural estimate of something future, esp. of coming weather. [f. prec.]

forecastle, fo'c's'le, (fōk'sl), n. (Hist.) short raised deck at bow, (in war-ship, later but now obs.) part of upper deck forward of aftermost fore-shroud; (in merchant-ship) forward part under deck where sailors live. [FORE-(5)]

foreclose¹ (fōrklōz'), v.t.& i. Bar, preclude, prevent, shut out from continuance of; (Mortgage Law) bar (person entitled to redeem) upon nonpayment of money due, bar (right of redemption), take away power of redeeming (mortgage), whence ~URE (fōrklōzher) n.; settle (arguable point etc.) by anticipation. [f. F forclore (OF for out f. L foris, CLOSE²)]

fore'court (fōr'kōrt), n. Enclosed space before building, outer court. [FORE-(3)]

fore'edge (fōr'ej), n. Front or outer edge (esp. of book); ~ painting, decoration of the front (occas. the top) edge of book with coloured design. [FORE-(3)]

fore'father (-dh-), n. (Pl.) the person, esp. in earlier generations, from whom one's father or mother is descended, (loosely) the past generations of a family or race; (sing., rare) man from whom one is descended. [FORE-(6)]

fore'finger (fōr'finggger), n. Finger next thumb (also called first or index finger). [FORE-(6)]

fore'foot (fōr't-), n. One of beast's front feet; (Naut.) foremost piece of keel, course in front of this (crossing our ~). [FORE-(3, 5)]

fore'front (fōr'frŭnt), n. Very front, foremost part, van, (in the ~ of the battle). [FORE-(3)]

foregather. See FORGATHER.

forego¹ (fōr'g-), n. See FORGO.

|| fore'gift (fōr'g-), n. (law). Premium for lease. [FORE-(6)]

forego¹ (fōr'g'), v.t.& i. (-went, -gone pr. -grawn). Precede in place or time (~ing, previously mentioned); ~ne conclusion, decision or opinion come to in advance of the evidence or necessary facts, prejudice, result that can be or could have been foreseen. [FORE-(3)]

forego². See FORGO.

forego'er (fōr'g-), n. Predecessor. [FORE-(1)]

fore'ground (fōr'g-), n. Part of view, esp. in picture, nearest observer; most conspicuous position. [FORE-(2)]

fore'hand (fōr'h-), n. & a. 1. Part of horse before rider. 2. adj. (Of stroke at tennis etc.) not backhanded. [FORE-(3)]

fore'head (fŏ'red), n. Part of face above eyebrows & between temples. [OE for-héafod see FORE-(4), HEAD¹]

fo'reign (fŏ'rin), a. Belonging to, proceeding from, other persons or things; alien from or to, irrelevant, dissimilar, or inappropriate, to; introduced from outside (esp. ~ body or substance in the tissues etc.); situated outside, coming from another district, parish, society, etc.; || (of a railway) belonging to another company; outside the country, not in one's own land; of, in, characteristic of, coming from, dealing with, some country not in the United Kingdom or English-speaking countries (~, colonial, & home trade; ~ parts, countries; F~ Office, department for ~ affairs or its building); ~ letter-paper, thin to reduce postage); Hence ~ISM2, 4) n. ~IZE(3') v.t. & i. (-rin-). [f. OF forain (L foris outside, see -(2)]

fo'reigner (-rin-), n. Person born in foreign country or speaking foreign language; foreign ship, imported animal or article. [-ER¹]

forejudge (fōrj-), v.t. Judge or determine before hearing the evidence. [FORE-(2)]

foreknow (fōrnō'), v.t. (-knew, -known). Know beforehand, have prescience of. So **foreknowledge** (fōrnŏl'ij) n. [FORE-(2)]

fo'rel, fo'rrel, n. Vellum-like parchment for covering account-books. [OF forrel]

fore'land (fōr'l-), n. Cape, promontory; strip of land in front of something. [FORE-(3)]

fore'leg (fōr'-), n. Beast's front leg. [FORE-(3)]

fore'lock¹ (fōr'l-), n. Lock of hair growing just above forehead (take time, occasion, etc., by the ~, not let chance slip). [FORE-(3)]

fore'lock² (fōr'l-), n. & v.t. Wedge put through hole in bolt to keep it in place; (v.b) secure thus. [FORE-(3), LOCK²]

fore'man (fōr'm-), n. President & spokesman of jury; principal workman superintending others (working-); one who both works & supervises). [FORE-(3)]

fore'mast (fōr'm-), n. Forward lower mast of ship (~ man, seaman, hand, sailor below rank of petty officer). [FORE-(5)]

fore'most (fōr'mōst, -ost), a. & adv. superl. 1. Most advanced in position, front, (head, end, etc. ~, with head etc. in front); most notable, best, chief. 2. adv. Before anything else in position, in the first place, (usu. first & ~). [OE formest double superl. with -m- (cf. L primus) & -EST f. st. of FORE², assimilated to most]

fore'noon (fōm-), n. The day till noon, morning. [FORE²+NOON]

foren'sic, a. Of, used in, courts of law (~ic medicine, medical jurisprudence). Hence ~ICALLY adv. [f. L forensis (FORUM)+-IC]

foreordain' (fōrōr-), v.t. Predestinate, appoint beforehand. So foreordina'TION (fōrōr-) n. [FORE-(2)]

fore'peak (fōrp-), n. (naut.). End of forehold in angle of bows. [FORE-(5)]

fore'plane (fōrp-), n. First plane used after saw or axe. [FORE-(6)]

fore'reach' (fōr-r-), v.i. &t. Shoot ahead; gain run, pass. [FORE-(3)]

fore-run' (fōr-r-), v.t. (-nn-: -ran, -run). Be precursor of, foreshadow. Hence ~n ER (1, 2) n. [FORE-(1)]

fore'sail (fōr'sl, -sāl), n. Principal sail on foremast (lowest square sail, or fore-&-aft bent on mast, or triangular before mast). [FORE-(5)]

foresee' (fōrsē'), v.t. (-saw, -seen). See that); exercise foresight (obs. exc. in ~ING² a. ~ingLY² adv.). [FORE-(2)]

foreshadow (fōrshăd'ō), v.t. Prefigure, serve as type or presage of. [FORE-(2)]

fore'sheets (fōrsh-), n. pl. Inner part of bows of boat with gratings for bowman. [FORE-(5)]

fore'shore (fōrsh-), n. Part of shore between high & low water marks, or between water & land cultivated or built on. [FORE-(4)]

foreshort'en (fōrsh-), v.t. Show, portray, (object) with the apparent shortening due to visual perspective. [FORE-(2)]

foreshow' (fōrshō'), v.t. (p.p. -~n). Foretell; foreshadow. [OE foresceawian see FORE-(1), SHOW]

fore'sight (fōr'sīt), n. Foreseeing, prevision; care for the future; front sight of gun. [FORE-(2, 3)]

fore'skin (fōrs-), n. Prepuce. [FORE-(3)]

forestall' (fōrstawl'), v.t. (Hist.) buy up (goods) in order to profit by enhanced price; be beforehand, deal with in action, anticipate and so baffle; deal with before the regular time, anticipate. [f. OE foresteall n. ambush, see FORE-(6), STALL¹]

fore'stay (fōrs-), n. Stay from foremast-head to ship's stem to support the foremast. [FORE-(5)]

fore'st, n., & v.t. 1. Large tract covered with trees & undergrowth sometimes mixed with pasture, trees growing in it (lit., & fig. as a ~ of masts); (with proper name prefixed) district formerly ~ but now cultivated, as Sherwood F~; || (Law) unenclosed woodland district kept for hunting usu. owned by sovereign; ~tree, of large growth fitted for ~. 2. v.t. Plant with trees, convert into ~. [OF, f. med. L forestis (silva wood) outside (walls of park) f. L foris outside]

fore'ster, n. Officer in charge of forest, or of growing timber; dweller in forest; (F~) member of the Ancient Order of F~s (friendly society); bird or beast of forest, e.g. New-Forest pony; kinds of moth. [f. OF forestier (FOREST, -IER)]

fore'sterie (fōr't-), n. Wooded country, forests; science & art of managing forests. [f. OF foresterie (FOREST, -ERY)]

fore'taste¹ (fōr't-), n. Partial enjoyment or suffering (of) in advance, anticipation. [FORE-(2)]

foretaste'² (fōrt-), v.t. Taste beforehand, anticipate enjoyment etc. of. [FORE-(2)]

foretell' (fōrt-), v.t. (-told). Predict, prophesy; presage, be precursor of. [FORE-(2)]

fore'thought (fōr'thawt), n. Previous contriving, deliberate intention; provident care. [FORE-(6)]

fore'time (fōrt-), n. The past, early days, old times. [FORE-(6)]

fore'token¹ (fōr't-), n. Sign of something to come, prognostic. [FORE-(6)]

foretok'en² (fōrt-), v.t. Portend, point to. [FORE-(2)]

fore'top (fōrt-), n. TOP of foremast: fore-top-gall'ant mast, mast above fore-top-mast, i.e. mast above foremast; fore-topgall'ant-sail, sail above fore-top'sail, i.e. sail above foresail. [FORE-(5)]

fore'type (fōrt-), n. Type of coming thing. [FORE-(2)]

forewarn' (fōrwôrn'), v.t. Warn beforehand (esp. in ~ed is forearmed). [FORE-(2)]

fore'woman (fōr'wooman), n. President & spokeswoman of jury of matrons; chief workwoman supervising others. [FORE-(3)]

fore'word (fōr'wěrd), n. Preface; introductory remarks, esp. by another than the author of the book etc. [from 1842; mod. formation of the anti-Latinists, cf G vorwort: FORE-(3)]

fore'yard (fōr'yărd), n. Lowest yard on FOREMAST.

forfeit (-fit), n. & a., & v.t. 1. (Thing) lost owing to crime or fault (his life was the ~ or was ~, his ~ life); penalty for breach of contract or neglect, fine; trivial fine for breach of rules in clubs etc. or in games (play ~s), article surrendered by player in game of ~s to be redeemed by performing ludicrous task; forfeiture. 2. v.t. Lose right to, be deprived of, have to pay, as penalty of crime, neglect, etc., or as necessary consequence of something; hence ~ABLE a., ~URE n., (-fit-). [f. OF forfait p.p. of forfaire t. med. L foris facere transgress (L foris outside, facere do)]

forfend', v.t. Avert, keep off, (usu. in God ~). [FOR-(2)]

for'ficate, a. (zool.). Scissor-shaped. [f. L forfex -icis scissors +-ATE²]

forgath'er (-dh-), v.i. Assemble, meet together, associate, converse. [FOR-(5)]

For words in fore- not given see FORE-.

forgave. See FORGIVE.

Forge¹, n. Smithy; blacksmith's hearth or fireplace with bellows; furnace or workshop for melting or refining metal, workshop containing it. [OF. f. L *fabrica* FABRIC]

Forge², v.t. & i. Shape by heating in fire and hammering; fabricate, invent, (tale, lie); make in fraudulent imitation, esp. write (document, signature) in order to pass off as written by another, whence **forˈgerˈy** n. Hence **forˈgerˈ¹** n. [OF *forgier* t. L *fabricare* FABRICATE]

Forge³, v.i. Make way, advance, gradually or with difficulty, esp. ~ *ahead*, take lead in race, get start. [?]

forˈgerˈy, n. Forging, counterfeiting, or falsifying, of document; spurious thing, esp. document or signature. [FORGE²; -ERY]

Forget' (-g-), v.t. & i.(-*got*, -*gotten* & poet. -*got*; -tt-). Lose remembrance of or about (noun, *that*, *how to*, or abs.); neglect (usu. *to do*), inadvertently omit to bring or mention or attend to; put out of mind, cease to think of, (esp. *forgive* & ~); disregard, slight; ~ *oneself*, neglect one's own interests, act unbecomingly or unworthily, lose consciousness; ~-*me-not*, yellow-eyed blue flowers (~-*me-not blue* as name of colour). Hence ~FUL a. (*of*), ~fulˈly² adv., ~fulNESS n., ~tˈABLE a. [OE *forgietan* cf. G *vergessen* see FOR-(1), GET]

Forgive' (-g-), v.t.(-*gave*, -*given*). Remit, let off, (debt, person debt); pardon (offence, offender, offence, or abs.). Hence ~ˈABLE a., ~eˈNESS (-givn-) n., ~ingˈly² adv. ~ingNESS n. (-g-). [OE *forgiefan* see FOR-(1), GIVE]

forgo', v.t. (-*went*, -*gone* pr. -gawn). Abstain from, go without, let go, omit to take or use, relinquish. [OE *forgán* see FOR-(3), GO]

fork, n. & v.i. & t. **1.** Pronged agricultural implement for digging, lifting, carrying, or throwing; two, three, or four-pronged instrument used in eating at table or cooking; (also *tuning*-~) steel instrument giving when struck a fixed musical note; stake with ~ed end used as prop for vines etc.; ~*ing*, bifurcation, e.g. that of human legs, of diverging roads, or of branches; flash of ~ed lightning; hence ~ˈY² a. (poet.). **2.** vb. Form ~, have or develop branches; lift, carry, dig, or throw with ~; (sl.) ~ *out* or *up*, hand over, pay. [OE *forca* f. L *furca*]

forked (-kt) a. With fork or fork-like end, branching; divergent, cleft, (*three*-~ etc., with three etc. prongs); two-legged. [-ED²]

forlorn', a. Desperate, hopeless, (cf. foll.); abandoned, forsaken, (poet.) deprived of, in pitiful condition, of wretched appearance. [p.p. of obs. *forlese*, OE *forléosan* see FOR-(1), LOSE]

forlorn' hope, n. Storming-party; desperate enterprise. [t. Du. *verloren hoop* lost troop (*hoop* = HEAP)]

form¹, n. **1.** Shape, arrangement of parts, visible aspect (esp. apart from colour), shape of body (*face* & ~). **2.** Person or animal as visible or tangible (*saw a* ~, *the* ~ *of, before me*). **3.** (Philos.) that which makes anything (*matter*) a determinate species (Scholastic); conditions of thing's existence by knowing which we can produce it (Baconian), formative principle holding together the elements of thing (Kantian). **4.** Mode in which thing exists or manifests itself (*in, under, take, the* ~ *of*); species, kind, variety. **5.** (Gram.) one of the shapes taken by a word in spelling, pronunciation, or inflexion, external characteristics of words apart from meaning. **6.** ‖ Class in most (esp. the Public) schools (usu. numbered from sixth down to first). **7.** Arrangement & style in literary or musical composition. **8.** Customary method (*in due* ~; *that is common* ~); is of no special significance, set order of words, formula, regularly drawn document, ‖ document with blanks to be filled up. **9.** Formality, mere piece of ceremony. **10.** Behaviour according to rule or custom (*good, bad,* ~); satisfying or offending current ideals). **11.** Condition of health & training (*in, out of,* ~; fit or not for racing etc., of horses or athletes; *lose one's* ~), good spirits (*was in great* ~). **12.** Long seat without back, bench. **13.** (Print.; ‖ also ~*e*) body of type secured in chase for printing at one impression. **14.** Hare's lair. [f. OF *forme* f. L *forma*]

form², v.t. & i. **1.** Fashion, mould, (*into* certain shape; *after, by, from, upon,* pattern; or abs.); assume shape, become solid. **2.** Mould by discipline, train, instruct, (person, or faculty etc.); embody, organize, (*into* a company etc. **3.** Frame, make, produce; articulate(word); conceive (idea, judgement); develop (habit); contract (alliance); be material of, make up, make one or part of. **4.** (Gram.) construct (new word) by derivation, inflexion, etc. **5.** (Mil. etc.) draw up (troops) &c.; ~ *up*, ‖ *is often up* in order, assume specified formation (~ FOURS, *line, column*). [f. OF *fourmer* f. L *formare* (prec.)]

formalde'hyde, n. comb. form of FORMIC or FORMYL, as *format'*; DEHYDE, a disinfectant & antiseptic, **form'alin,** n. solution of this.

-form', suf. (in actual use -*form*, see -(-) f-form) giving adj. (1) w. sense *having the form of* ('cruciform, cunei-form), (2) referring to number of forms (uniform, multiform, diversiform). Chloroform does not contain this suf.

form'al, a. **1.** (Metaphys.) of the essence of a thing (~ CAUSE²), essential not material; of the outward form, shape, appearance, arrangement, or external

qualities. (Log.), concerned with the form, not the matter, of reasoning. **2.** Valid in virtue of its form, explicit and definite, not merely tacit. **3.** Ceremonial, required by convention (a ~ *call*), perfunctory, having the form without the spirit; observant of forms, precise, prim, excessively regular or symmetrical, stiff, methodical, whence ~ISM(2), ~IST(2), nn., ~is'tĭc a. Hence ~LY² adv. [f. L *formalis* (FORM¹, -AL)]

formăl'ity, n. Conformity to rules, propriety; ceremony, elaborate procedure; formal or ceremonial act, requirement of etiquette or custom; being formal, precision of manners, stiffness of design. [f. L *formalitas* (prec., -TY)]

for'malize, v.t. Give definite shape or legal formality to; make ceremonious, precise, or rigid, imbue with formalism. Hence ~A'TION n. [-IZE]

for'm·at (-ah), n. Shape & size of book. [F]

forma'tion, n. Forming, being formed; thing formed; arrangement of parts, structure, (Mil.) disposition of troops; a number of aircraft engaged in an operation, whence *form'āte¹ v.i., (of aircraft) fly in(to) ~; (Geol.) assemblage of rocks or series of strata having some common characteristic. [f. L *formatio* (FORM², -ATION)]

for'mative, a. & n. Serving to fashion, of formation; (Gram., of flexional & derivative suffixes and prefixes) used in forming words, (n.) ~ element. [OF (-*if*, -*ive*) see FORM², -ATIVE]

fôrme, n. (print.). See FORM¹.

fôr'mer, a. & pron. Of the past or an earlier period (*in* ~ *times*; *more like her* ~ *self*; *our* ~ *haunts*), whence ~LY² adv.; *the* ~ (with noun, or oftener as pron. with possessive *the* ~'s), the first or first mentioned of two (opp. LATTER). [back-formation f. *formest* FOREMOST; from 12th c.]

fôr'mĭc, a. (chem.), ~*ic acid*, colourless irritant volatile acid contained in fluid emitted by ants. [f. L *formica* ant]

fôr'midable, a. To be dreaded; likely to be hard to overcome, resist, or deal with. Hence ~leNESS n., ~LY² adv. [f. F, f. L *formidabilis* (*formidare* fear, -ABLE)]

fôr'mless, a. Shapeless, without determinate or regular form. Hence ~LY² adv., ~NESS n. [-LESS]

fôrmica'tion, n. Sensation as of ants crawling over the skin. [f. L *formicatio -onis* tingling, f. *formica* ant]

fôr'mūla, n. (pl. *-ae*, *-as*). Set form of words, definition, enunciation of principle, statement prescribed for use on some occasion; rule unintelligently followed, conventional usage or belief, whence ~ISM(3), ~IST(2), nn., ~is'tĭc a.;

recipe; principle serving to accommodate differences of aim or opinion (*diplomatists seeking a* ~*a*); (Math.) rule or principle in algebraic symbols; (Chem.) expression by symbols of substance's constituents; tabulation of certain facts by symbols & figures. Hence ~arize(3) [through obs. ~*ar* a.], ~IZE(3), vv.t. =FORMULATE, ~ariz·A'TION, ~iza'TION, nn. [L, dim. of *forma* FORM¹]

fôr'mūlary, n. & a. Collection of formulas; document or book of set forms esp. for belief or ritual; (adj.) in or of formulas. [f. F *formulaire* f. neut. of L *formularius* (prec., -ARY¹)]

fôr'mūlāte, v.t. Reduce to, express in, a formula, set forth systematically. Hence ~A'TION n. [FORMULA+-ATE³]

fôr'nĭcāte, v.i. Commit fornication. So ~OR² n. [f. L *fornicari* (*fornix -icis* brothel), -ATE³]

fôrnica'tion, n. Voluntary sexual intercourse between man (occas. restricted to unmarried man) & unmarried woman (cf. *adultery*). [OF, f. LL *fornicationem* (prec., -ION)]

‖ **forpined'** (-nd), a. (arch.). Wasted by hunger, torture, etc. [p.p. of obs. *forpine* see FOR-(5)]

forrad er. See FORE¹.

forrel. See FOREL.

forsāke', v.t. (*-sook*, *-sāken*). Give up, break off from, renounce; withdraw one's help, friendship, or companionship from, desert, abandon. [earlier senses *deny*, *repudiate*, *refuse*; OE *forsacan* f. FOR-(3)+ *sacan* contend]

forsooth', adv. Truly, in truth, no doubt, (used parenthet. always in irony. [OE *forsōth* (FOR, SOOTH]

‖ **forspent'**, a. (arch.). Tired out. [p.p. of obs. *forspend* see FOR-(5), SPEND]

forswear' (-wâr'), v.t. (*-swŏre*, *-swŏrn*). Abjure, renounce on oath; ~ *oneself*, swear falsely, perjure oneself; (p.p.) perjured. [OE *forswerian*, see FOR-(3, 1), SWEAR]

forsȳth'ia, n. (Kinds of) spring-flowering ornamental shrub bearing bright-yellow flowers. [f. W. *Forsyth* (d. 1804), English botanist, +-IA¹]

fôrt, n. Fortified place (usu. single building or set of connected military buildings, cf. FORTRESS); trading-station, orig. fortified (hist.). [F, abs. use of *fort* strong f. L *fortis*]

fôrt'alice, n. (Arch. & poet.) fortress; (mod.) small outwork of fortification, small fort. [f. med.L *fortalitia* (L *fortis* strong)]

fōrte¹, n. Person's strong point; (Fenc.) sword-blade from hilt to middle (cf. FOIBLE). [f. F *fort* abs. use of adj. = strong; fem. form ignorantly adopted for masc., cf. *morale, locale*]

fōr'te², mus. direction (abbr. *f.*). Loud; ~ (abbr. *ff.*), very loud; ~ *piano* (abbr. *fp.*), loud & then immediately soft. [It.]

forth, adv. & prep. 1. Forwards (now only in back & ~, to & fro); onwards in time (now only in *from this time* ~, & in comb. as *hence*~); forward, into view, (bring, come, shoot, etc., ~); out from home etc. (sail, issue, ~); out of doors (cast ~); & so on, & the like; *so far* ~, to that extent; *so far* ~ *as*, to the like. **2. prep.** (arch.). From out of. [cf. G *fort*] [root of FORE[2]+suf.*-to-*)]

forthcom'ing (-kŭ-), a. About or likely to come forth; approaching; ready to be produced when wanted. [prec., COME, -ING[2]]

forth'right (-rīt), adv., **forth'right** (-rīt), a. & n. **1.** adv. Straight forward. **a.** & n. 1. a. Going straight; outspoken, unswerving; decisive, dextrous. **3.** n. (arch.). Straight course (~s & meanders). [FORTH+RIGHT a. & adv.]

forthwith' (-th, -dh), adv. Immediately, without delay. [for *forth with* used abs.]

fortifica'tion, n. Fortifying; strengthening of wine with alcohol: (Mil.) providing, art or science of providing, with defensive works, (usu. pl.) defensive work(s), wall(s), earthwork(s), tower(s), etc. [F, f. L *fortificationem* act of strengthening]

for'tify, v.t. & i. Strengthen structure of; impart vigour or physical strength or endurance to, strengthen mentally or morally, encourage; strengthen (liquors with alcohol; corroborate, confirm, (statement); provide (town, army, oneself) with defensive works; erect fortifications. Hence ~IABLE a. [f. F *fortifier* f. L *forti-ficāre* (*fortis* strong, -IFY)]

fortiss'imo, mus. direction (abbr. *ff.* for~, *fortiss.*). Very loud. [It.]

for'titude, n. Courage in pain or adversity. [F, f. L *fortitudo* (*fortis* strong, -TUDE)]

fort'night (-nīt), n. Period of two weeks (*to-day, this day, Monday, etc.*, ~, *a* ~ *from today* etc.; *would rather keep him* etc. *a week than a* ~, he etc. is a large eater). [OE *feowertyne niht* fourteen nights]

fort'nightly (-it-), a. & adv. (Happening, appearing) once every fortnight. [-LY[1,2]]

fort'ress, n. & v.t. Military stronghold, esp. strongly fortified town fit for large garrison; (vb, poet.) serve as ~ to, protect. [f. OF *forteresse* strength, strong place, f. *fort* see FORT]

fortu'itous, a. Due to or characterized by chance, accidental, casual. Hence ~ly[2] adv., ~NESS n. [f. L *fortuitus* (*fors -tis* chance) +-OUS]

fortu'ity, n. Fortuitousness; a chance occurrence; accident; unstudied or unintended character. [f. L as prec. (for *fortuitity*)]

fort'unate, a. Favoured by fortune, lucky, prosperous; auspicious, favourable. [f. L *fortunatus* (FORTUNE[2], -ATE[2])]

fort'unately (-tli-), adv. Luckily, successfully, (esp. as parenthesis qualifying whole sentence = it is a fortunate thing that). [-LY[2]]

fort'une[1] (-chŏŏn, -tūn), n. Chance, hap, luck, as a power in men's affairs (*F~*, this power personified as goddess; *try the* ~ *of war*, see what it will bring, risk it; SOLDIER *of* ~); luck good or bad that falls to anyone or to an enterprise etc. (in sing. or pl.; *try one's* ~, take some risky step), coming lot (*tell person his* ~, *tell* ~*s*, of gipsies etc., whence ~-téller[1] n.); good luck; prosperity, prosperous condition, wealth, (*make one's* ~, prosper; *make a* ~, become rich; *spent a small* ~ *on*; *at large sum*; *marry a* ~, heiress), whence ~LESS (-nl-) a.; ~*-hunter*, man seeking rich wife. [f. F, f. L *fortuna* cogn. w. *fors* *-tis* chance & *ferre* bring]

fort'une[2] (-chŏŏn, -tūn), v.i. (arch. & poet.). Chance, occur, (esp. impers., *it* ~*d that*); come by chance upon. [f. OF *fortuner* f. L *fortuna* make fortunate (prec.)]

fort'y, a. & n. **1.** Four times ten, 40, XL, (~*-one*, ~*-first*, etc.; ~ *winks*, short nap esp. after dinner); hence **fort'ieth** a. & n. **2.** n. Age of ~ years (*after* ~, *over* ~; *the forties*, years of life or century between 39 & 50; HUNGRY *Forties*); *roaring forties*, stormy ocean tracts between lat. 39° & 50° S.; || *the Forties*, sea area between N.E. coast of Scotland and S.W. coast of Norway (so named from its depth of ~ fathoms or more); || ~-PENNY nail; *the F~-five*, Jacobite rebellion of 1745. [OE *feowertig* cf. G *vierzig* (FOUR, -TY[2])]

for'um, n. (Rom. Ant.) public place, market-place, place of assembly for judicial & other business, esp. at Rome; place of public discussion; court, the law courts, (fig. *the* ~ *of conscience* etc.). [L]

for'ward, a. & n. **1.** (Naut.) belonging to fore part of ship; lying in one's line of motion (*the* ~ *horizon*), onward or towards the front (*the* ~ *path*; ~ *play* in cricket, see foll.; ~ *movement*, special effort at political etc. progress); ~ *party, opinions*, advanced or extreme. **2.** (Commerc.) relating to future produce (~ *contract*). **3.** Advanced, progressing to maturity or completion, (of plant, crop, season) well advanced or early; ready, prompt, eager, (often *to do*); precocious; presumptuous, pert, whence ~ly[2] adv.; hence ~NESS n. **4.** n. One of the first-line players in football, hockey, etc. [OE *foreweard* (FORE[2], -WARD), a.]

for'ward[2](s), adv. (-d is added below to senses in which the *-s* form is rare or not used). Towards the future, continuously onwards, (d: *from this time* ~; *look* ~; *date* ~, of commercial ahead; CARRIAGE ~);

orders, post-date). **2.** Towards the front in the direction one is facing. (Cricket; -d) *play*~, reach ~ to play short-pitched ball; with continuous ~ motion (*rushing* ~), (Mil., as word of command, -d, = go ~, advance). **3.** In advance, ahead, (-d; *send him* ~; *backward(s)* & ~, to & fro; to the front, into prominence, (-d; *bring* ~; draw attention to; *come* ~, offer oneself for task, post, etc.; *put or set* ~, allege, make too conspicuous). **4.** (Onward so as to make progress (-d; *go* ~, be going on, progress; *can't get any forwarder*, or usu. colloq. *forrader*, make no progress). [OE *foreweard*, prob. neut. acc. of prec.]

for'ward[3], v.t. Help forward, promote; accelerate growth of; send (letter etc.) on to further destination, (loosely) dispatch (goods etc.). [f. prec.]

∥**forwea'ried** (-id), forwŏrn', aa. (arch.). Tired out. [FOR-(5), WEARY, WEAR[2], vv.]

fosse, n. Long narrow excavation, canal, ditch, trench, esp. in fortification. (Anat.) groove, depression, also **fōsserte** n. [F, f. L *fossa* orig. fem. p.p. of *fodere* dig]

fŏss'ick, v.i. (sl.). Rummage, search about. [dial. wd current in Austral. goldmining=search in crevices or abandoned workings]

fŏss'il, a. & n. Found buried, dug up, (~ *fuel* etc.; now rare; (thing) preserved in strata of earth with more or less chemical or other change of texture & recognizable as remains of plant or animal of past (usu. prehistoric) ages (~ *bones, shells, ivory; hunting for* ~s; also fig., as *words are* ~ *thoughts*); (person or thing) belonging to the past, antiquated, incapable of further development. Hence ~ATE[3] v.t., ~IZE(3) v.t. & i., ~IZA'TION n. [F, f. L *fossilis* (*fodere* foss- dig, -IL)]

fŏssōr'ial, a. (zool.). Burrowing; used in burrowing. [f. L *fossorius* (*fossor* digger f. *fodere* see prec., -OR[2]) +AL]

fŏs'ter[1], n. Food (obs. exc. in comb., as ~-*child*, -*father*, -*mother*, -*parent*, -*son*, -*daughter*, -*brother*, -*sister*, = having the specified relationship not by blood, but in virtue of nursing or bringing up); acting or treated as — ; *~-mother*, (also) = IN-CUBATOR. [OE *fōstor* (FOOD, suf. *-tro-*)]

fŏs'ter[2], v.t. (Arch.) tend affectionately, cherish, keep warm (in bosom), promote growth of; encourage or harbour (feeling) (of circumstances) be favourable **to**. Hence ~ER[1], fŏs'tress[1], nn. [f. prec.]

fŏs'terage (-ij) n. Fostering; custom of employing foster-mothers. [-AGE]

fŏs'terling n. Foster-child, nursling, protégé. [OE *fōstorling* (FOSTER[1], -LING[1])]

fougasse (foogahs), n. Improvised mortar excavated in the ground, charged with stones, bits of iron, etc., and fired by gunpowder. [F]

fought. See FIGHT[1].

foul, a., n., adv., & v.i. & t. **1.** Offensive to the senses, loathsome, stinking, (~ *brood*, a disease of larval bees); dirty, soiled (~ *linen*), filthy; (sl.) revolting, disgusting; defaced with corrections (~ *copy*); charged with noxious matter (~ *air, water*); clogged, choked, (~ *gunbarrel*); (of ship's bottom) overgrown with weed, barnacles, etc.; morally polluted, obscene, disgustingly abusive, (*the* ~ *fiend*, the devil; ~ *deed, motive, talk*; *~-mouthed, -tongued*); (of fish at or after spawning) in bad condition; ugly (now dial. exc. in *fair or* ~), unfair, against rules of game etc., (~ *blow, stroke, riding; ~play, in games, & fig. treachery*) (of weather) wet, rough, stormy; (of wind) contrary (~ *rope is* ~), **2.** n. Something (*through* ~ *& fair*, through everything); collision, entanglement, esp. in riding, rowing, or running, irregular stroke or piece of play. **3.** adv. In irregular way (*hit him* ~; *play* one, *deal treacherously with him*). **4.** vb. Become ~, get clogged; make ~ or dirty; pollute with guilt, dishonour; cause (anchor, cable) to become entangled, jam or block (crossing, railway line, traffic); become entangled; run ~ of, collide with. [OE *fūl* cf. G *faul* f. Aryan *pu-* stink, rot, cf. Gk *puon*, L *pus*; the v.i. f. OE *fūlian*]

foul'ard (fŏŏl'ahr), n. Thin flexible material of silk or silk & cotton; handkerchief of it. [F]

foulé (fŏŏlā'), n. Light woollen dress material with glossy surface. [F, = pressed (cloth), p.p. of *fouler* FULL[2]]

foul'ly (-l-ll), adv. Abominably, cruelly, wickedly (*was* ~ *murdered*; with unmerited insult (~ *slandered*). [-LY[2]]

foul'ness, n. Foul condition; foul matter; disgusting wickedness. [-NESS]

foumart (fōō'-), n. Polecat. [ME *fulmard* (FOUL, *mard* marten)]

found[1], v.t. & i. Lay base of (building etc.); be original builder, begin building, (of town, edifice); establish (esp. with endowment), originate, initiate, (institution); construct, base, (tale, one's fortunes, classification, rule, etc.) (*up)on some ground, support, principle, etc.(also *is ~ed in justice* etc.; *well, ill,* etc., ~*ed*, reasonable, justified, baseless, etc.); rely, base oneself, (of argument etc.) be based, (*up)on*. [f. F *fonder* f. L *fundare* (*fundus* bottom)]

found[2], v.t. Melt & mould (metal), fuse (materials for glass); make (thing of molten metal, glass) by melting. So **foun'dry(3)** n. [f. F *fondre* f. L *fundere fus-* pour]

found[3]. See FIND.

founda'tion, n. Establishing, constituting on permanent basis, esp. of an endowed institution; such institution, e.g.

monastery, college, or hospital (on the ~, entitled to benefit by its funds, whence ||~ER¹ (-shon-), n.), or its revenues; solid ground or base, natural or artificial, on which building rests, lowest part of building uses, below ground-level; basis, ground-work, underlying principle, (re-port has no ~; base religion on a moral ~); body or ground on which other parts are overlaid, e.g. under-skirt, first set of stitches in crochet or knitting; ~music, & bonnets; ~school, endowed; ~stone, esp. one laid with ceremony to celebrate founding of edifice. [f. L fundatio (GROUND¹, -ATION)]

foun'der¹, n. In vbl senses of FOUND³. [-ER¹]

foun'der³, one who founds institutions (||~'s esp. heir, relatives of ~ entitled to election or preference); ~'s shares, shares issued to ~s of public company as part-considera-tion for business taken over, & separate from ordinary capital. Hence ~SHIP.

foun'der², n. In vbl senses of FOUND¹. [-ER¹]

foun'der⁴, v.i. & t. & n. 1. (Of earth, building, etc.) fall down or in, give way; (of horse; or with rider substituted as subject) fall from overwork, collapse, fall lame, stick fast in bog etc.; cause (horse) to break down by overwork; (of ship) fill with water & sink, cause (ship) to do this; (Golf) hit (ball) into ground. 2. n. In-flammation of horse's foot from over-work; (also chest, body, ~) rheumatism of chest-muscles in horses. [f. OF fondrer submerge, collapse, (L fundus bottom)]

found'ling, n. Deserted infant of un-known parents. [p.p. of FIND+-LING¹]

fount'¹, n. (poet. or rhet.). Spring, source, fountain; (shop) reservoir of oil in lamp or ink in pen. Hence ~MD² (-ind) a. [? mount: from late 16th c.]

fount'², n. (print.). Set of type of same face & size. [f. F fonte (fondre POUND²)]

foun'tain (-tin), n. Water-spring; source of river etc. (also fig., Crown is the ~ of honour; poison the ~s of trust); jet of water made to spout, structure provided for it, (also drinking~); public erection with constant supply of drinking-water; reservoir in lamp, printing-press, etc. for oil, ink, etc. (~pen, having this); ~head, original source. Hence (-)~MD² (-ind) a. [f. OF fontaine f. LL fontana f. L fons, fontanus adj. (FOUNT¹, -AN)]

four (för), a. & n. 1. One more than three, 4, IV; (~ corners of earth etc., remotest parts; ~ corners of document etc., its scope; within the ~ seas, in Gt Britain; ~ figures, some number from 1000 to 9999; twenty etc. ~ or ~-&-twenty etc.; ~-&-twentieth etc.); (ellipt.) ~ hours etc.; ~o'clock); ~ horse(carriage etc. &~); ||~-ale(Hist.), sold at 4d. a quart; ~ by two, rifle pull-through cloth; ~-coupled, with ~ coupled wheels; ~course, with fourfold rotation (of crops); ~DIMENSIONAL; *~flusher (sl.), bluffer, humbug (orig. Poker term); ~footed, quadruped (adj.); ||~foot way, space (4 ft. 8½ in.) between pair of rails; ~ FREEDOMS; ~-handed, (of monkeys) quadrumanous, (of games) for ~ persons, (of piece of music) for two players; ~horse(d), drawn by ~ horses; ~-in-hand, vehicle with ~ horses & no outrider (also adv.), ~ oars; ~ o'clock, the plant Marvel of Peru; ~-part, arranged for ~ voices to sing; ~pence, sum or coin =4d.; ~post (of bed), having ~ posts to support canopy; ~pounder, gun throwing 4 lb. shot; ~roved barley, with ~ rows of awns; ~score, eighty, age of 80 years; ~square, square-shaped, solidly based or steady; ~stroke (attrib., of internal-combustion engines), having a cycle of ~ strokes (intake, compression, combus-tion, and exhaust); ~wheel, ~-wheeled carriage; hence ~roued a. & adv., ~TEEN a., ~teenth' a. & n., (för-). 2. n. The number 4; set of persons or things, esp. ~pipped card, domino, or side of die, ~oared boat & crew (~s, races for these), hit etc. at cricket for ~ runs; on all ~s (earlier = = limbs), crawling on hands & knees, (also, fig.) completely analogous or corresponding (the cases are not on all ~s; is the simile on all ~s with the thing illustrated?). [Mil.; pl.] formation ~ deep for marching (FORM²-s); ~pennyworth of spirits (Hist.); (pl.) ~-per-cent. stock. [Aryan: OE feower, cf. Du & G vier, Gk tessares, L quatuor]

fourgon (foor'gawn), n. Luggage-van. [F]

Four'ierism (foor-), n. Fourier's system for reorganization of society (PHALAN-STERY). [Charles Fourier, French socialist, 1772-1837]

four'some (för-), n. Game of golf between two pairs. [FOUR, SOME; orig. adj.]

fourth (för-), a. & n. 1. Next after third (the, a, ~; ellipt. as n., esp. = 4th day of month; ~ part, quarter); ~ ESTATE. 2. n. Quarter; ~ part; (Mus.) interval of which the span involves four alphabetical notes, harmonic combination of notes thus separated; F~ of June, principal annual celebration at Eton College, speech-day; anniversary of declaration of Indepen-dence; ~party (Hist.), Lord R. Churchill, Sir H. D. Wolff, Sir J. Gorst, Mr Balfour, and a few other Conservatives who (1880-5) attacked impartially the Liberal Government & the Conservative front bench; (pl.) articles of ~ quality. [OE feortha cf. G vierte, Gk tetartos, L quartus]

fourth'ly (fōr-), adv. In the fourth place (in enumerations). [-LY¹]

fowl, n., & v.i. 1. Bird (rare exc. in wild-~), their flesh as food (only in fish, flesh, &~); domestic cock or hen (often qualified, as barndoor ~, game, guinea, ~; ||~-run, place where ~s may run, breeding establishment for ~s), its flesh as food. 2. v.i. Catch, hunt, shoot, or snare, wild-~, whence ~ER¹, ~ING¹ nn.; ~ing-piece, light gun used in ~ing. [com.-Teut.; OE fugel cf. G vogel perh. by dissim. f. *fluglo- (flug- FLY¹)]

fox¹, n. (fem. VIXEN, also bitch-~). Red-furred sharp-snouted bushy-tailed quadruped preserved in England as beast of chase & proverbial for cunning; crafty person; northern constellation; FLYING ~; ~& geese, game played on board; ~-brush, tail of ~; ~EARTH¹; ~glove, tall purple or white flowered plant; ~-hole (Mil.), hole in ground used as shelter against missiles or as firing-point; ~-hound, kind bred & trained to hunt ~es; ~-hunt n. & v.i., chasing of, chase, ~ with hounds, whence ~hunter¹ n.; ~hunting a. & n., (given to) this sport; ~-tail, ~'s tail, kinds of grass; ~-terrier, short-haired for unearthing ~, but kept chiefly as pet; ~-trot, an American dance. [com.-Teut.; cf. G fuchs]

fox², v.i. & t. Act craftily, dissemble; discolour (leaves of book, engraving, etc.) with brownish spots (esp. in P.P.); (sl.) deceive, trick. [f. prec.]

fox'¹y, a. Fox-like, crafty(-looking); reddish-brown, (Paint.) over-hot in colour; damaged with mildew etc. Hence ~INESS n. [-Y²]

|| **foyer** (fwah'yā), n. Large room in theatre etc. for audience's use during interval. [F]

fra'²(-ah), n. = FRATE as prefixed title. [It.]

fracas (fra'kah), n. Noisy quarrel, row. [F, f. It. fracasso uproar]

frac'tion, n. 1. Dividing of Eucharistic bread. 2. (Arith.) numerical quantity that is not an integer, one or more aliquot parts, (vulgar ~, expressed by numerator above & denominator below a line; DECIMAL~; proper, improper ~, with numerator less, greater, than denominator). 3. Small piece or amount, scrap, (esp. not a ~). Hence ~AL (al distillation, partial separation of liquids having different boiling-points by gradual heating), ~ARY¹, aa., (-shon-). [f. OF fraccion f. eccl. L fractionem (L frangere fract- break, -ION)]

frac'tionate (-shon-), v.t. Separate (mixture) into portions of different properties by distillation etc. [prec.+-ATE³]

frac'tionize (-shon-), v.t. Break up into fractions (Math.), or portions. [-IZE]

frac'tious (-shus), a. Unruly, cross, peevish. Hence ~LY² adv., ~NESS n., (-shus-). [f. FRACTION in obs. sense brawling +-OUS, after captious etc.]

frac'ture, n., & v.t. & i. 1. Breaking, breakage, esp. of bone or cartilage (COMPOUND²); surface shown by mineral when broken with hammer; substitution of diphthong, diphthong substituted, for simple vowel owing to influence of following consonant. 2. vb. Cause ~ in, break continuity of, crack (t. & i.). [F, f. L fractura (FRACTION, -URE)]

fraen'um, frē-, n. (pl. -na). Small ligament checking motion of organ. [L, = bridle]

fra'gile, a. Easily snapped or shattered, weak, perishable, of delicate frame or constitution. So **fragil'ITY** n. [F, f. L fragilis (frag- root of frangere break)]

frag'ment, n. Part broken off, detached piece; isolated or incomplete part, remainder of lost or unfinished whole, esp. extant remains or work of art. Hence ~ARY¹ a., ~A'TION n. (~ation bomb, one breaking up into small ~s when exploded). [f. L fragmentum (as prec., -MENT)]

frag'rant, a. Sweet-smelling. So **frag'RANCE** n. [f. L fragrare smell sweet, ANT]

frail¹, n. Rush basket for packing figs, raisins, etc. [f. OF frayel etym. dub.]

frail², a. Fragile; transient (~ life, bliss, etc.); in weak health; morally weak, unable to resist temptation, (euphem., of women) unchaste. [f. OF fraile FRAGILE]

frail'ty, n. Liability to err or yield to temptation; fault, weakness, foible. [f. OF frailteŧ f. L fragilitatem (FRAGILE, -TY)]

fraise¹ (-z), n. (fortif.). Horizontal or down-sloping palisade round berm. [F, orig.= mesentery of calf]

fraise² (-z), n. Tool for enlarging circular hole or cutting teeth in watch wheels. [F (fraiser enlarge hole f. fraise as prec.]

framboes'ia (-bēz-), n. Chronic contagious negro disease with raspberry-like swellings, the yaws. [mod. L, f. F framboise raspberry perh. f. Du. braambezie (BRAMBLE, BERRY)]

frame¹, v.t. & i. Shape, direct, dispose, (thoughts, acts, another person) to a purpose (for, to, to do, or with adv.); give promise of being skilful etc. (usu. well); adapt, fit, to or into; construct by combination of parts or adaptation to design, contrive, devise, invent, compose, express, (complex article, plot, rule, story, theory); articulate (words); conceive, imagine; [f. foll.] set in a frame, serve as frame for (landscape ~ed in an archway); whence ~ING⁴(3) n.; (orig., U.S. sl.) concoct false charge against, devise plot with regard to; ~e up (orig., U.S. sl.), prearrange (event) with sinister intent, fake result of (race, election, etc.). Hence ~ABLE a., ~ER¹ n. [OE framian be helpful (fram forward cf. FROM)]

frame², n. Construction, constitution, build; established order, plan, system, (the ~ of society or government); tem-

porary state (of mind); framed work or structure (*the ~ of heaven*, or *earth*, human or animal body (*sobs shook her ~*, *man of gigantic ~*); skeleton of building, of anything; case or border enclosing picture, pane of glass, etc., whence ~LESS (-ml) a.; (Gardening) glazed portable box-like structure protecting plants from cold; || (Mining) inclined board for washing ore; (Snooker) triangular ~ for setting up balls, balls so set up, round of play during which balls are pocketed; ~ *aerial*, revolving aerial composed of rectangles or loops of wire, adapted for directional reception; ~*house*, of wooden skeleton covered with boards; ~*saw*, stretched in ~ to make it rigid; *~*up*, conspiracy; ~*work*, ~, substructure, upon or into which casing or contents can be put (lit., fig.). [f. prec.]

franc, n. Standard unit of French currency, before the 1914–18 war a silver coin of about 9½d., but after depreciation stabilized 1928 at 125 to £1, 1951 at 980 to £1. [F. perh. f. *Francorum Rex* king of the FRANK's, legend on earliest coin so called (gold = 10/6)]

fran'chise (-z), n. (Chiefly hist. & U.S.) legal immunity or exemption from some burden or jurisdiction, privilege or exception, right granted to person, corporation, etc.; full membership of corporation or State, citizenship; right of voting at public elections esp. for member of Parliament, principle or qualification for this (the ~s. [f. med. L *Franciscus* Francis +

Francis'can, a. & n. (Friar) of the order founded 1209 by St Francis of Assisi; of the ~s. [f. med. L *Franciscus* Francis +

-AN]

Franc'o-, comb. form of med. L *Franci* the Franks, now used in French-&-, as ~*German.* Hence ~PHIL(E), ~PHOBE, nn.

franc'olin, n. Kind of partridge resembling pheasant. [F. f. It. *francolino*]

franc tireur (see Ap.), n. (pl. *-cs -rs*), Man of irregular light-infantry corps; a guerrilla fighter. [F]

frang'ible, a. Breakable, fragile. [ult. f. Ll *frangibilis* f. L *frangere* to break]

fran'gipane, -âni, (-)-, n. (Perfume of) red jasmine; kind of almond cream or paste. [F, prob. f. *Frangipani,* maker]

Frank¹, n. One of the Germanic nation or coalition that conquered France in 6th c.; (in Levantine use) person of Western nationality. Hence ~ISH¹ a. [f. L *Francus* f. OHG *Franko* perh. f. weapon (OE *franca* javelin)]

frank², a. Ingenuous, open, candid, outspoken; undisguised, avowed. Hence ~LY² adv., ~NESS n. [f. OF *franc* f. med. L *francus* free f. prec. (full freedom being confined to the Franks)]

frank³, v.t., & n. l. (Hist.) superscribe (letter etc.) with signature ensuring gratis conveyance; facilitate coming & going of (person); give social passport to; convey (person) gratuitously; exempt from future payment etc. (*a ~ing duty*, *imposition*). 2. n. (Hist.) ~ing signature, ~ed cover. [f. prec. in obs. sense *free of charge*]

Frank'enstein (-tin), n. ~'s *monster*, thing that becomes formidable to the person who has created it. [M. W. Shelley, *Frankenstein*]

Frank'fort bläck, n. Fine black pigment used in copperplate engraving. [German town]

***frank'furter**(-ter), n. Highly seasoned German sausage. [f. *Frankfurt* German town]

frank'incense, n. Aromatic gum resin (prop. from trees of genus *Boswellia*) used for burning as incense. [f. OF *franc encens* (FRANK² in obs. sense *luxuriant*, INCENSE²)]

frank'lin, n. (hist.). Land-owner of free but not noble birth in 14th & 15th cc. [FRANK² perh. -LING¹]

frank'-pledge, n. (hist.). System by which each member of tithing was responsible for every other (also rarely fig., e.g. of relation between members of a Government). [AF *franc plege* (FRANK², PLEDGE), perh. mistransl. of OE *frithborh* peace-pledge (not free-pledge)]

fran'tic, a. Wildly excited, beside oneself with rage, pain, grief, etc.; showing frenzy, uncontrolled. Hence ~ICALLY, ~ICLY² adv. [f. OF *frenetique* f. LL *phreneticus* f. Gk *phrenitikos* (*phrenitis* f. *phrēn -enos* brain)]

frap, v.t. (naut.). (-pp-). Bind tightly. [f. OF *fraper* bind, strike]

frappé (-âp'ā), a. (Esp. of wines) Iced, cooled. [p.p. of F *frapper* strike]

fräss, n. Excrement of larvae; refuse left by boring insects. [f. G *frass* (*fressen* devour)]

frat'e (-ântā), n. (pl. *-ti* pr. -tē), Friar. [It.]

frat'er, n. (hist.). = REFECTORY. [f. OF *fruitur* as REFECTORY]

frater'nal, a. (As) of brother(s), brotherly. [f. L *fraternus* (*frater* brother)+-AL]

frater'nity, n. Being fraternal, brotherliness; religious body; guild, company with common interests, set of men of same class etc. [f. OF *fraternité* f. L *fraternita-tem* (prec. -TY)]

frat'ernize, v.i. Associate, make friends, behave as intimates, (*with, together,* or abs.). So ~ATION n. [f. F *fraterniser*]

frat'ricide, n. Killing of one's, one who kills his, brother or sister. Hence ~AL a. [F. f. L *fratricidium, -cida,* (*frater -tris* brother, -CIDE)]

frau (frow), n. (Of German wife or widow) Mrs; German woman. [G]

fraud, n. Deceitfulness (rare); criminal deception, use of false representations (in Law, *in ~*, *to the ~*, *of*, so as to defraud); dishonest artifice or trick (*pious ~*, deception intended to benefit deceived, & esp. to strengthen religious belief); person or thing not fulfilling expectation or description. [f. OF *fraude* f. L *fraudem* nom. *fraus*]

fraud'ul|ent, a. Guilty of, of the nature of, characterized or effected by, fraud. Hence or cogn. ~ENCE n., ~ently² adv. [OF, f. L *fraudulentus* (prec., -ULENT)]

fraught (frawt), a. Stored, equipped, *with* (poet.); (fig.) *~ with*, involving, attended with, full of, threatening or promising, destined to produce, woe, danger, meaning, etc. [p.p. of obs. *fraught* v. load with cargo (obs. *fraught* cargo prob. f. MDu. *vracht* FREIGHT]

fräul'ein (froil'īn), n. (Of German spinster) Miss (with surname; also alone as voc.) German spinster; German governess. [G]

Fraun'höfer (froun'-) **lines**, n. pl. The dark lines in the solar spectrum. [J. von Fraunhofer, Bavarian optician (d. 1826)]

fraxinell'a, n. Kinds of garden dittany. [mod. L, dim. of L *fraxinus* ash]

fray¹, n. Noisy quarrel, brawl; fight, conflict, (lit. or fig.; *eager for the ~*). [for AFFRAY]

fray², v.t. & i. (Of deer) *~ head*, or *~*, rub velvet of new horns; wear through by rubbing, ravel *out* edge or end of, (usu. woven material); become ragged at edge. [f. F *frayer* f. L *fricare* rub]

frazil', n. (Canad. & U.S.). Anchor-ice, ice at bottom of stream. [perh. f. F *fraisil* cinders]

***fra'zzle**, n. Worn or exhausted state (esp. *worn*, *beaten*, *to a ~*). [perh. as FRAY²]

freak, n. Caprice, vagary; capriciousness (*out of mere~*); product of sportive fancy; (also*~of nature*) monstrosity, abnormally developed specimen. Hence ~ISH¹ a., ~'ISHLY² adv., ~'ISHNESS n. [from 16th c.; etym. dub.; cf. OE *frician* to dance]

freaked(-kt), a. Oddly flecked or streaked. [-ED²]

frec'kle, n., & v.t. & i. 1. Light brown spot on skin, (pl.) sporadic sunburn. 2. v.b. Spot, be spotted, with ~s. [earlier *frecken* f. ON *freknur* pl.]

free¹, a. (freer, freest, pr. -eer, -eest). 1. Not in bondage to another, having personal rights & social & political liberty, (*~ labour*, *~ of* men not slaves, & see 2); (of State, its citizens or institutions) subject neither to foreign domination nor to despotic government, having national & civil liberty; *~born*, inheriting citizen rights & liberty; *~hold*, (estate held by) tenure in fee simple or fee-tail or for term of life (also of corresponding tenure of office), (adj.) held by ~hold; *~holder*, possessor of ~hold estate; *~man*, person not slave or serf, citizen of ~ State (& see 4); *~mason*, member of fraternity for mutual help & brotherly feeling called *F~ & Accepted Masons* having elaborate ritual & system of secret signs (the orig. ~ masons were prob. skilled masons emancipated & allowed to move from place to place in & after 14th c., & the *accepted* may have been honorary members of the ~ masons' societies); *~masonry*, system & institutions of the ~masons, secret understanding between like characters, instinctive sympathy. 2. Loose (*~ wheel* in bicycle, driving-wheel able to revolve while pedals are at rest), unrestricted (*~ love*, sexual relations irrespective of marriage), at liberty, not confined, released from ties or duties, unimpeded (*~trade*, left to its natural course without customs duties to restrict imports or protect home industries, this principle; *~trader*, believer in ft), unfettered in action (*have or give a ~ hand*, right of acting at discretion), permitted to do, independent (*F~ Church*, unconnected with State; *F~ Churches*, nonconformists; *F~ Church of Scotland*, seceders of 1843 from Presbyterian establishment; *~ lance*, medieval mercenary, modern politician or controversialist with no party allegiance, unattached journalist; *~ labour*, of workmen not belonging to trade unions, see 1; *~thinker*, *-thinking* n. &a., *-thought*, rejector etc. of authority in religious belief, rationalist etc.), unconstrained (*~ step*, *gestures*); (of literary style) not observing strict laws of form (*~ verse*, = VERS LIBRE), (of translation) not literal; allowable (*it is ~ for or to him to do so*); open to all comers (*~ fight*, in which anyone present joins); clear of obstructions, clear of or from something undesirable, (of wind) not adverse; not fixed, not in contact, (Chem.) not combined, (of power or energy) disengaged or available; *~board*, part of ship's side between line of flotation & deck-level; *~hand*, (of drawing) done without artificial aid to the hand; *~stone*, kind of peach of which when ripe the stone is loose (& see 3); *~ will*, power of directing our own actions without constraint by necessity or fate (& see 3). 3. Spontaneous, unforced, unearned, gratuitous, willing, (*~ grace*, unmerited favour of God; *~ gift*, not in requital; *did it of my own ~will*, & so *~will* adj., voluntary; *am ~ to confess*, gratuitous entertainment; *am ~ to confess*, not unwilling); lavish, profuse, unstinted, copious, (*~ of his money*, open-handed; so *~handed*, liberal; *~ flow of water*; *~ liver*, *living*, indulger, indulgence, in pleasures esp. of the table); frank, unreserved, (*~-spoken*, blunt; *~ & easy*, unceremonious, also as n, smoking-

concert etc.), forward, familiar, impudent; (*make* or *be* ~), take liberties *with*); (of talk, stories, etc.) broad, not quite decent; ~*stone*, fine-grained easily sawn sandstone or limestone (& see 2). Released or exempt *from* (~ *from the ordinary rules, disease, difficulty,* etc.); having burgess rights (*made* ~ *of the city*); having the entrée & use of (~ *of the house*); not subject to tax, toll, duty, trade-restrictions, or fees (~ *port*, open to all traders alike; ~*list*, of persons to be admitted without fees charged; ~ *articles*, etc.; ~ *school*, with no fees charged; ~ *pass*, not paid for; also as *carriage*~, without charge for convey-ance); ~*man*, one who has the freedom of a city, company, etc. (*the* ~ *of a city*); ~*Ly*² adv. [com.-Teut.; f. *frei* 1, Aryan *pri* to love]

free², v.t. (~d). Make free, set at liberty, (~*d'man*, emancipated slave, esp. in Rom. Hist.); relieve *from*, rid or ease *of*; clear, or disengage, disentangle. [OE *frēon* (prec.)]

free'booter, n. Pirate, piratical adventurer. Hence by back formation free'boot v.i. ~ING¹ n. [f. Du. *vrij-buiter* (FREE¹, BOOTY, -ER)]

free'dom, n. Personal liberty, non-slavery; civil liberty, independence, liberty of action, right to do; power of self-determination, independence of fate or necessity; frankness, outspokenness, undue familiarity (*take* ~*s with*); facility, ease, in action; boldness of conception (Physics); capability of motion; exemption *from* duty, defect, disadvantage, burden, etc.; privilege possessed by city or corporation; participation in privileges of membership of company, etc. or citizenship of city (often given *honoris causa* to distinguished persons); unrestricted use of (*has the* ~ *of the library*); ~ *from fear and want*. [OE *frēodōm* (FREE¹, -DOM)]

free'martin, n. Hermaphrodite or imperfect female of ox kind. [?]

free'sia (-z), n. Kinds of iridaceous bulbous plant from Cape of Good Hope. [?]

freeze, v.i. & t. (froze, frozen), & n. 1. (Impers.) *it* ~*s* etc., there is etc. frost; be converted into or covered with ice; become rigid as result of cold; become fastened *to* or *together* by frost, (sl.) ~ *on to*, take or keep tight hold of; feel very cold (~ *to death*, die by frost); be chilled by fear; cause to congeal, form ice upon, (fluid or moist thing; often *in, over, up*); preserve (meat etc.) by refrigeration; make (credits, assets, etc.) temporarily or permanently unrealisable; (by exag.) ~ *one's blood*, terrify him; (sl.) ~ *out*, exclude from business, society, etc., by competition or boycotting etc.; ~*out*, variety of poker in which each player

drops out as soon as he loses his capital; ~*ing-mixture*, salt & snow or other mixture used to ~ liquids; *freezing-point*, temperature at which liquid, esp. water, ~s; *frozen limit* (colloq.), the extreme of the objectionable or unendurable. 2. n. State, coming, period, of frost. [com.-Teut.; OE *frēosan* cf. G *friesen*, also L *pruina* hoarfrost]

freez'ing, a. In vbl senses; esp.: (by exag.) very cold; (of manners) chilling, distant. Hence ~LY² adv. [-ING¹]

freight (frāt), n. & v.t. 1. Hire of ship for transporting goods; transport of goods by water (in U.S. by land also), charge for this; cargo, shipload; load, burden. 2. v.t. Load (ship) with cargo; hire or let out (ship) for carriage of goods & passengers. [prob. f. MDu. *vrecht* var. of *vracht*; see FRAUGHT]

freight'age (-āt-), n. Hire of ship, cost of, conveyance of goods; freighting or hiring of ship; cargo. [-AGE]

freight'er (-āt-), n. One who (charters &) loads ship; one who consigns goods for carriage inland; one whose business is to receive & forward freight; cargo ship. [-ER¹]

French, a. & n. 1. Of France or its people; having the qualities attributed to ~ people; || ~ *bean*, kidney or haricot bean used as vegetable both in unripe sliced pods & in ripe seeds; ~ *bread*, kind of fancy bread; ~ *chalk*, kind of steatite used for marking cloth & removing grease & as dry lubricant; ~ *drain* (of rubble, letting water soak away); ~ *grey*, tint composed of white with ivory black, Indian red, & Chinese blue; ~ *horn*; *take* ~ *leave*, depart, act, without asking leave or giving notice; || ~ *letter*, a mechanical contraceptive; ~*man*, man of ~ birth or nationality, (good etc.) ~ speaker; ~ *ship*, kind of polish for wood; ~ *polish*, kind of polish for wood; ~ *polish*, v.t., polish with this, whence ~-pol'isher¹ n.; ~ *roof*, mansard; ~ *window*, glazed folding-door serving as window & door; ~*woman*, woman of France. 2. n. The ~ language (~ *lesson, master*, etc., concerned with this); *the* ~ (pl.), the ~ people. Hence ~'NESS n., Frēn'chify¹,³ & n. [OE *frencisc* (FRANK¹, -ISH¹)]

Frēnch'ify, f-, v.t. Make French in form, character, or manners (usu. in p.p.). Hence ~FICA'TION n. [-FY]

Frēnch'less, a. Knowing no French. [-LESS]

frenum. See FRAENUM.

frĕn'zy, n. & v.t. 1. Mental derangement, temporary insanity, paroxysm of mania, (rare); delirious fury or agitation, wild folly. 2. v.t. (usu. in p.p.). Drive to ~, infuriate. (~*ied rage*, that of a ~*ied* person). [f. OF *frenesie* f. LL *phrenesis* (Gk *phrenitikos* FRANTIC)]

frēqu'ency n. Frequent occurrence, being repeated at short intervals, (of pulse) number of beats per minute; (Physics) rate of recurrence (of vibration etc.), number of repetitions in given time esp. per second (high, medium, low, ~, abbr. H.F., M.F., L.F., w. ref. to sound-waves, electro-magnetic waves, etc.); (Statistics) the ratio of the actual to the number of possible occurrences of an event. [f. L frequentia (foll., -ENCY)]

frēqu'ent¹, a. Found near together, numerous, abundant; often occurring, common, happening in close succession, (of pulse) rapid, (it is a ~ practice to), whence ~LY² adv.; (with agent-noun) habitual, constant, (a ~ caller). [f. L frequens -entis crowded cogn. w. farcire FARCE²]

frequent'², v.t. Go often or habitually to (place, meetings, company, house). Hence or cogn. frēquentā'TION, ~ER¹, nn. [f. L frequentare (prec.)]

frēquen'tative, a. & n. (gram.). (Verb or verbal form or conjugation) expressing frequent repetition or intensity of action. [f. L frequentativus (prec., -ATIVE)]

frēs'cō, n. (pl. -ōs, -oes), & v.t. Method of painting (esp. in ~), picture, in water-colour laid on wall or ceiling before plaster is dry; (vb) paint (wall etc., picture or subject) thus. [It., orig. adj. = foll.]

frēsh, a., adv., & n. 1. New, novel, not previously known, used, met with, or introduced, (break ~ ground, try something unhackneyed); additional, other, different, further, (begin a ~ chapter); recent, lately made or arrived, (~man, first-year man at University); not preserved by salting, pickling, smoking, tinning, etc. (~ herrings, meat, fruit, & see below; ~ butter, & see next sense); not salt (~ water; ~ water fish, fishing, sailor; ~ butter, not favoured with salt, & see prec. sense); not salt or bitter, drinkable, (~ water); pure, untainted, invigorating, refreshing, cool, (of air, wind, water); not stale, musty, or vapid (~ fish, mead, fruit, & see above; ~ egg); not faded (~ flowers, memories); unsullied, bright & pure in colour (a ~ complexion), looking healthy or young; not weary, brisk, vigorous, fit, (never felt ~er; as ~ as paint, quite brisk, Prob. a pun on the warning ~ paint; a ~ wind, of some strength); excited with drink; *presumptuous, forward, cheeky, amorously impudent. 2. adv. ~ly, newly, esp. in comb. as ~caught, ~coined, ~run, (of salmon) lately come up from the sea. 3. n. ~ part of day, year, etc. (in the ~ of the morning); rush of water in river, flood. Hence ~'EN¹ v.t. & i., ~'NESS n. [OE fersc cf. G frisch affected by OF freis fem. fresche from same Teut. origin]

|| frĕsh'man, = FRESHman, [-ER¹]

frĕsh'ĕt, n. Rush of fresh water flowing into sea; flood of river from heavy rain or melted snow. [FRESH n. +-ET¹]

frĕsh'lý, adv. Recently (only with participles, =fresh adv.); afresh (rare); with unabated vigour; with fresh appearance, odour, etc. [-LY²]

frĕt¹, n., & v.t. (-tt-). 1. Ornamental pattern made of continuous combinations of straight lines joined usu. at right angles (also Greek~). 2. v.t. Variegate, chequer; adorn (esp. ceiling) with carved or embossed work; ~saw, very narrow saw stretched on frame for cutting thin wood in ornamental patterns; ~work, carved work in decorative patterns esp. of straight lines, also wood cut with ~saw. [prob. f. OF frete trellis-work & freter vb]

frĕt², v.t. & i. (-tt-), & n. 1. Gnaw, wear or consume or torment by gnawing, (of moths etc., horses champing bit, action of frost, rust, corrosives, friction, etc., or the passions); make (passage etc.) by wearing away; chafe, irritate, annoy, worry, distress; distress oneself with regret or discontent (at; ~ away or out one's life etc.); ~ & fume, show angry impatience; (of stream etc.) flow or rise in little waves, chafe; ruffle (water). 2. n. Irritation, vexation, querulousness, (in a ~; in a fume; on the ~); hence ~'FUL a., ~'fully² adv., ~'fulNESS n., ~'t'Y² a. [OE fretan cf. G fressen (fra- cogn. w. FOR-, EAT]

frĕt³, n. Bar or ridge on fingerboard of some stringed instruments fixing positions of fingers to produce required notes. Hence ~'t'ED² a. [perh.f. OF frete ferrule]

Freud'ian (froid-)., a. & n. (Disciple) of Sigmund Freud or his doctrines of PSYCHO-analysis. [Sigmund Freud, psychologist, +-IAN]

fri'able, a. Easily crumbled. Hence or cogn. friabi'l'ITY, ~'NESS, nn. [f, f L friabilis (friare crumble)]

fri'ar, n. Member of certain religious orders esp. the four mendicant orders of Franciscans (Grey F~s), Augustinians (Austin F~s), Dominicans (Black F~s), & Carmelites (White F~s); ~'s balsam, tincture of benzoin. Hence~LY¹ a. [ME & OF frere f. L fratrem nom. -ter brother]

fri'arȳ, n. Convent of friars. [f. obs. frary f. OF friarie, frerie (frere see prec.) w. assim. to prec.; or f. prec. w. -y for -RY(3) by mistake of -ar for -ER¹]

frib'ble, v.i., & n. Trifle, be frivolous; (n.) trifler. [imit.; earlier senses stammer, totter]

fric'andeau (-dō), n. (pl. -z pr. -z), & v.t. (Slice of) fried or stewed meat, esp. veal, served with sauce; (vb) make into ~x. [F]

fric'assee, n., & v.t. Meat cut up, fried or stewed, & served with sauce, esp. ragout of birds or small animals cut up; (vb) make ~ of. [f. F fricassée (ricasser vb etym. dub.)]

fric'ative, a. & n. (Consonant) made by friction of breath in narrow opening, as *f, th*, Scotch *ch*. [f. L *fricare* rub + -ATIVE]

fric'tion, n. Medical chafing; rubbing of two bodies, attrition; (Phys., Mech.) resistance body meets with in moving over another (*angle of* ~), maximum angle at which one will remain on another without sliding; (fig.) clash of wills, temperaments, opinions, etc. (usu. between two persons); ~-*ball*, used in bearings to lessen ~; ~-*clutch, -cone, -coupling, -disk, -gear(ing)*, contrivances for transmitting motion by ~. Hence ~AL, ~LESS, aa., (-shon-). [f. L *frictionem* (*fricare* rub, -ION)]

Fri'day (-di), n. Sixth day of week (*Good* ~, before Easter-day, commemorating Crucifixion; *Black* ~, used as name for various disasters that fell on ~). [OE *frigedæg*; corr.-WG transl. of LL *dies Veneris* day of planet Venus, cf. G *Freitag* = day of *Frwja* wife of Odin]

friend (frend) n. & v.t. 1. One joined to another in intimacy & mutual benevolence independently of sexual or family love; person who acts for one, e.g. as second in duel; (loosely) acquaintance, stranger that one comes across or has occasion to mention anew, (*my ~ in the brown hat now left me*; used in voc. as polite form or in irony, & by Quakers as ordinary address; preceding a name, as ~ *Jones, Dick*; ‖ *my honourable* ~, of another M.P. in House of Commons; *my learned* ~, of another lawyer in court); (pl.) one's near relations, those responsible for one; sympathizer, helper, patron, (*a* ~ *of or to order, virtue*, etc.; *a* ~ *at court*, one whose influence may be made use of); helpful thing (*my shyness was here my best* ~); one who is not an enemy, who is on the same side; *be, keep, make,* ~s, be or get on good terms; (R~) Quaker (*Society of F~s*, the Quakers as a communion); hence ~'LESS a. [com.-Teut.; OE *fréond*, cf. G *freund*]. 2. v.t. Befriend, help. [p.p. of OTeut. *frijôjan* love (OE *fréon* see FREE¹,², -ND²]

friend'ly (-dli), a., n. & adv. 1. Acting, disposed to act, as friend; characteristic of friends, expressing, showing, or prompted by, kindness (‖~ *lead among London poor*, entertainment to raise funds for distressed person); not hostile, on amicable terms, (*a* ~ *nation;* ~ *action* decided; ~ *match*, played for honour at law, brought merely to get a point merely, not in competition for cup etc.); favourably disposed, ready to approve or help, (of things) serviceable, convenient, opportune; ‖ F~ *Society*, for mutual insurance against distress in sickness & old age; hence friend'LINESS n. friend'liness n. (-dli-). 2. n. (w. pl.). Native of ~ tribe. 3. adv. (rare). In ~ manner (*used, received, us* ~). [OE *fréondlíc* a., *fréondlíce* adv., see -LY²]

friend'ship (frě-), n. Being friends; friendly relation between friends; friendly disposition felt or shown. [-SHIP]

Friesian (frē'zhan), a. & n. (Of, one of) a breed of Friesland cattle. [var. of FRISIAN]

frieze¹, n. Coarse woollen cloth with nap usu. on one side only. [f. F *frise* (*friser* curl)]

frieze², n. Member of entablature coming between architrave & cornice; horizontal broad band of sculpture filling this; band of decoration elsewhere. [f. F *frise* prob. connected w. It. *fregio* frieze f. L *Phrygium* (*opus* work) of Phrygia]

frig (-j), fri(dg)e, n. (colloq.). Refrigerator. [abbr.]

frig'ate, n. (Hist.) warship next in size & equipment to ships of the line, with 28–60 guns on main deck & raised quarter-deck & forecastle; (mod., loosely for) cruiser; large corvette; (also ~-*bird*) large swift tropical bird of prey. [f. F *frégate* f. It. *fregata* etym. dub.]

fright (frīt), n. & v.t. 1. Sudden fear, violent terror, alarm; grotesque-looking person. 2. v.t. (poet.). Frighten. [OE *fryhto* metathetic form of *fyrhto* cf. OE *forht*, G *furcht*]

fright'en (-īt-), v.t. Throw into a fright, terrify, (often *out of, into, doing*); drive away, *out of* (place etc.), *into* (submission etc.), by fright; ~*ed at* or *of* (*at* w. ref. to an occasion, *of* to habitual fear). [prec. (n.) + -EN¹]

fright'ful (-it-), a. Frightening (arch.); dreadful, shocking, revolting; ugly, hideous, whence ~NESS n. (esp., as mistransl. f. G. terrorizing of civilian population as military resource); (sl.) very great, awful. Hence ~LY² adv. [-FUL]

frig'id, a. Cold (esp. of climate or air; ~ *zone*, region enclosed by either polar circle); without ardour, apathetic, formal, forced; chilling, depressing; dull, flat, insipid. Hence or cogn. frigid'ITY, ~NESS, nn., ~LY² adv. [f. L *frigidus* (*frigére* be cold f. *frigus* n. cold)]

frill, n. & v.t. & i. 1. Ornamental edging of woven material, one side of strip being gathered & the other left loose with fluted appearance; similar paper ornament on ham-knuckle etc.; natural fringe of feathers, hair, etc., on bird, animal, or plant; (pl.) airs, affectation, (*puts on* ~s), useless embellishments or accomplishments; mesentery of animal; (Photog.) puckered gelatine film at edge of plate. 2. v.t. Decorate with a ~; (esp. Photog., of gelatine film) pucker at edges of etc. Hence ~ED¹(-ld) a., ~ERY(b), ~ING¹ (3, d), nn. [?]

frill'ies (-líz), n. pl.(colloq.). Frilled petticoats etc. [f. -RY² or -Y¹]

fringe (-j), n. & v.t. & i. 1. Ornamental bordering of threads left loose or formed

into tassels or twists; such bordering made separately; border, edging, (*New-gate* ~, beard allowed to grow below shaven chin); front hair cut short & allowed to hang over forehead; natural border of hair etc. in animal or plant; hence ~'LESS (-;l-), **frin'GY²** a. **2.** v.t. Adorn or encircle with ~, serve as ~ to; hence **frin'GING'**(3) n. [ME & OF *frenge* f. L *fimbria*]

fripp'erУ, n. Finery, needless or tawdry adornment esp. in dress; empty display esp. in literary style; knick-knacks, trifles. [f. OF *freperie* (*frepe* rag, -ERY)]

*****Fris'cō**, n. San Francisco. [abbr.]

frisétte' (-z-), n. Band of small artificial curls on forehead. [F (*friser* FRIZZ)]

friseur (frēzö'r'), n. Hair-dresser. [as prec.]

Fris'ian (-zi-), a. & n. (Native, language) of Friesland. [f. L *Frisii* pl. f. OFris. *Frīse* +AN]

frisk, v.i. & t., & n. **1.** Move sportively, gambol; *feel over, search, (person) for weapon etc. (sl.) **2.** n. Gambol. Hence **fris'kr²** a., **fris'kily²** adv., **fris'kiNESS** n. [f. obs. *frisk* a. f. OF *frisque* lively perh. cogn. w. FRESH]

fris'két, n.(print.). Thin iron frame with tapes across it keeping sheet in position while printing. [f. F *frisquette* etym. dub.]

frit, n., & v.t. (-tt-). **1.** Calcined mixture of sand & fluxes as material for glass-making; vitreous composition from which soft porcelain is made. **2.** v.t. Make into ~, partially fuse, calcine. [f. It. *fritta* fem. p.p. of *friggere* FRY²]

frit'-fly, n. Small fly destructive to wheat. [?]

frith. See FIRTH.

fritill'ary (or frit-), n. Kinds of liliaceous plant, esp. Snakeshead; kinds of butterfly. [f. L *fritillus* dice-box +-ARY¹]

fritt'er¹, n. Piece of fried batter often containing slices of fruit etc. (*apple*, *oyster*, etc., ~); (pl.) =FUNKS. [f. F *friture* (L *frigere frict-* FRY² -URE), see -ER²(3)]

fritt'er², v.t. Subdivide minutely; throw (time, money, energy, etc.) *away* on divided aims. [f. obs. n. *fritter(s)* = obs. *fitters* n. pl. obs. *fitter* v. perh. cogn. w. G *fetzen* rag, scrap; or f. OF *freture* f. L *fractura* FRACTURE]

Fritz, nickname for the Germans or a German. [G, abbr. of *Friedrich* Frederick]

friv'ol, v.i. & t. (-ll-). Be a trifler, trifle; throw (money, time) *away* foolishly. [back formation f. foll.]

friv'olous, a. Paltry, trumpery, trifling, futile; given to trifling, not serious, silly. Hence or cogn. **frivol'ity**, ~NESS, nn., ~LY² adv. [f. L *frivolus* (perh. f. *fricare* rub) +-OUS]

friz(z)¹, v.t., & n. **1.** Curl, crisp, form into mass of small curls, (hair, or person etc. in regard to it); dress (wash-leather etc.) with pumice or scraping-knife. **2.** n.

Frizzed state, frizzed hair, row of curls; hence **frizz'Y²** a. [f. F *friser*]

frizz'² v.i. Make sputtering noise in frying. [f. FRY² w. imit. termin.]

friz'zle¹, v.t. & i., & n. **1.** Curl (t., & i. esp. with *up*, of hair etc.) in small crisp curls. **2.** n. ~d hair; hence **frizz'ly²** a. [etym. dub.; older than FRIZZ; cf. OFris. *frisle* head of hair]

friz'zle²·, v.i. & t. Fry, toast, or grill, with sputtering noise. [FRIZZ² +-LE(3)]

frō, adv. Away (only in *to & ~*, backwards & forwards, or of repeated journeys between two places). [f. ON *frá* prep.= OE FROM]

frôck, n., & v.t. **1.** Monk's long gown with loose sleeves, (fig.) priestly character; =SMOCK-~; sailor's woollen jersey; child's skirt & bodice as outer dress for indoor use; woman's dress; || (also ~-*coat*) man's long-skirted coat not cut away in front; military coat of like shape. **2.** v.t. Invest with priestly office, cf. UNFROCK. [f. F *froc* f. med. L *froccus, floccus*; perh. = FLOCK¹ as woollen, or f. OHG *hroch* (G *rock*) coat]

Froe'belism (frö²-), n. Education of young children on the kindergarten system. [F. W. A. *Froebel*, German educationalist (d. 1852), -ISM]

frŏg¹, n. Tailless amphibious animal developed from tadpole: (derog. for) Frenchman (as ~ *eating* ~8), whence **Frŏgg'Y²** (-g-), ~ (-g-); ~-*eater*, Frenchman; ~-*fish*, kinds of fish esp. the Angler; ~-*in-the-throat*, hoarseness; ~'s, ~, -*march*, carrying of prisoner face downwards by four men holding a limb each; ~-*spawn*, lit., & as names for kinds of freshwater algae. Hence ~**g Y²** (-g-) a. (esp. =cold as a ~). [OE *frogga*, also *froz* cf. G *frosch*]

frŏg², n. Elastic horny substance in middle of sole of horse's foot. [?]

frŏg³, n. Attachment to waistbelt to support sword, bayonet, etc.; military coat-fastening of spindle-shaped button & loop, whence ~**gED²** (-gd) a. [perh. f. Port. *froco* f. L *floccus* FLOCK¹]

frŏg⁴, n. Grooved piece of iron at place in railway where tracks cross. [?]

frŏl'ic a. (arch.), v.i. & n. **1.** Joyous, mirthful, sportive, full of pranks. **2.** v.i. (-ck-). Play pranks, gambol. **3.** n. Outburst of gaiety, prank, merriment, merry-making, gay party. Hence ~SOME a., ~somENESS n. [f. Du. *vrolijk* adj. cf. G *fröhlich* (M Du. *vrô* glad, -LIKE)]

from (from, emphatic or at end of clause frŏm), prep. expressing separation & introducing:—**1.** Person, place, etc., whence motion takes place (*comes ~ the clouds; repeated ~ mouth to mouth*). **2.** Starting-point (~ *title to colophon, throughout book; ~ 2nd July; ~ day to day, daily; ~ time to time, occasionally; ~ a child, since childhood*). **3.** Inferior

limit (saw ~ 10 to 20 boats). 4. Object etc. whence distance or remoteness is reckoned or stated (ten miles ~ Rome; am far ~ saying; ~ home, out, away; ~ home; apart ~ its moral aspect. 5. Thing or person got rid of, escaped, avoided, of which one is deprived etc., person or thing deprived etc. (look his sword ~ him; released him ~ prison; cannot refrain ~ laughing; ~ lower court, dissuade ~ folly). 6. State changed for another (~ being attacked became for the aggressor; raise penalty ~ banishment to death). 7. Thing distinguished (doesn't know black ~ white). 8. Source (dig gravel ~ pit; drew conclusion ~ premisses; quotations ~ fathers). 9. Place of vantage etc. (saw it ~ the poop; ~ his point of view, as he sees things). 10. Giver, sender, etc. (gifts ~ Providence; frocks ~ Worth's; things not required). 11. Model (painted ~ nature). 12. Reason, cause, motive, (died ~ fatigue; suffering ~ dementia; ~ his looks you might suppose). 13. Advbs or advl phr. of place or time (~ long ago, of old, above, etc.), or prepositions (~ under her spectacles, etc.) ~ out the bed). [OE from, forward cf. FRO]

frond, n. (Bot.) leaf-like organ formed by union of stem & foliage in certain flowerless plants, esp. ferns, & differing from leaf in usu. bearing fructification; (Zool.) leaf-like expansion in some animal organisms. Hence frön'dage(1) n., frön'dose(1) a. [f. L frons -dis leaf]

Fronde (-awnd), n. Party that rebelled against Mazarin & Court during minority of Louis XIV; malcontent party; violent political opposition. [F, orig. = sling]

front (-ŭnt), n. & a. & v.t. 1. Forehead (poet.; head &c.); (~ to ~; have the ~, be impudent enough usu. to do; present, show a bold ~); (Mil.) foremost line or part of army etc., line of battle, part of ground towards real or imaginary enemy, scene of actual fighting (go to the ~, join troops on campaign), direction in which formed line faces (change ~); (fig.) organized body or department of activity (home, kitchen, popular, ~); (Archit.) any face of building, esp. that of main entrance (opp. BACK); || the promenade of a seaside resort; band of false hair, set of false curls, worn over woman's forehead; breast of man's shirt, also dicky; (with prep.) forward position (in ~ of, before, in advance of, confronting; in ~; come to the ~, become conspicuous); (ellipt.) = in ~ as adv. or adj. (were beset ~ & rear; two-pair ~, second-floor room in ~); ||~'s man, salesman stationed on pavement in ~ of shop; hence ~'WARD a. & adv., ~'WARDS adv., (-un-). 2. adj. Of n, situated in, ~ (|| bench, reserved for ministers or ex-

ministers in Parliament houses; ~ door, chief entrance of house); ~ page, first page of newspaper (usu. attrib., of news of striking journalistic importance). 3. vb. Face, look to, towards, (up)on; face, stand opposite to; have ~ on side of street etc.); confront, meet, oppose; furnish with ~ (~ed with stone); (Mil.) turn (l. & t.) to the ~ (often as word of command). [n. OE f. L frons frontis; vb f. OF fronter]

fron'tage (-tin-), n. Land abutting on street or water, land between front of building & road, whence ~ER¹(4) n.; extent of front; front of building; ground occupied by troops in camp or on parade; facing a certain way, exposure, outlook. [-AGE]

fron'tal¹ (-tin-), n. Covering for front of altar; façade. [f. OF frontel f. LL frontāle]

fron'tal² (-tin-), a. Of forehead (~ bone, artery); of, on, front (~ attack, delivered direct, not on flank or rear). [-AL]

fron'tier (-tin-, -ōn-), n. Part of a country that borders on another; (attrib.) of, on, the ~; ~sman, one living on or beyond the borders of civilization (Legion of F~smen, organization enrolling men with such experience). [OF, -aria -ARY¹]

Frön'tignac (-inyǎk), n. A muscat wine. [erron. for -nan, name of French town]

fron'tispiece (-tin-), n. & v.t. (Archit.) principal face of building, decorated entrance, pediment over door etc.; illustration facing title-page of book or one of its divisions (vb, supply with as ~); face (esp. in boxing sl.). [f. F frontispice f. med. L frontispicium countenance (FRONT, -spec- specere look); w. assim. to piece]

front'less (-tin-), a. Unblushing (rare). [-LESS]

front'let (-tin-), n. Band worn on forehead; = PHYLACTERY; animal's forehead; cloth hanging over upper part of altar frontal. [f. OF frontel (FRONTAL¹ -LET)]

frön'to-, comb.form of L frons -tis = of the forehead & —, as ~nasal. [for fronti-]

fron'ton (frŭ'-), n. Pediment. [F, f. It. frontone (FRONT, -OON)]

frore, a. (poet.), Frozen, frosty. [arch. p.p. of FREEZE]

frost (-aw-, -ŏ-), n. & v.t. 1. Freezing, prevalence of temperature below freezing, point of water (|| ten etc. degrees of ~; hard, sharp, ~; white or hoar, black, ~; with, without, rime; Jack F~, ~ personified), frozen state or consistence (there is still ~ in the ground), frozen dew or vapour (windows covered with ~); influence that chills, makes grey, etc.; (sl.) failure; ~-bite, inflammation or gangrene of & below skin from severe cold, ~-bitten, affected with this; ~-work, tracery made by ~ on glass etc.; hence ~'LESS a. 2. v.t.

Nip, injure, (plants etc.) with ~; cover (as) with rime, powder with coating of sugar etc., whence ~ING¹(3) n.; give roughened or finely granulated surface to (glass, metal); turn (hair) white; arm (horse's shoes) against slipping by nails etc. [com.-Teut.; cf. G *frost*; cogn. w. FREEZE]

frost'ly (-aw-, -ö-), a. Cold with frost; cold, chilling, frigid, lacking in warmth of feeling; covered, seeming to be covered, with hoar-frost. Hence ~ILY² adv., ~I-NESS n. [-Y²]

froth (-ŏ-, -aw-), n., & v.i. & t. **1.** Collection of small bubbles, foam; impure matter on liquid, scum; worthless matter, idle talk, etc.; ‖~-*blower* (joc.), beer-drinker (esp. as designation of member of a certain charitable Order); hence ~Y² a., ~ILY² adv., ~INESS n. **2.** vb. Emit, gather, ~; cause (beer etc.) to foam. [perh. f. ON *frotha* cf. OE *á-fréothan* to ~]

frou-frou (-ōō-, -ōō), n. Rustling, esp. of dresses. [F, imit.]

frow, n. Dutchwoman. [f. Du. *vrouw* = G *frau* woman]

fro'ward, a. (arch.). Perverse, refractory. Hence ~LY² adv., ~NESS n. [FRO-, WARD]

frown, v.i. & t., & n. **1.** Knit brows esp. to express displeasure or concentrate attention; (of things) present gloomy aspect; express disapprobation (*at, on, upon*); put (interrupter, interruption, etc.) *down* with ~; hence ~ING_LY² adv. **2.** n. Vertically furrowed state of brow; look expressing severity, disapproval, or deep thought. [f. OF *froigmier* perh. f. Teut. cf. Sw. dial. *fryna*, Norw. *frȳna*, make wry face]

frowst, n., & v.i. (colloq.). Fusty heat in room (‖vb, stay in, enjoy, this). Hence ~Y²a. [?]

frowz'ly, a. Ill-smelling, fusty, musty, close; slatternly, unkempt, dingy. Hence ~INESS n. [?]

froze(n). See FREEZE.

frücťerous, a. Bearing fruit. [f. L *fructifer* (FRUIT, -FEROUS)]

frŭctifica'tion, n. (bot.). Fructifying; reproductive parts of plant, esp. of ferns & mosses. [f. L *fructificatio* (foll., -FICATION)]

frŭc'tify, v.i. & t. Bear fruit (lit. & fig.); make fruitful, impregnate. [f. F *fructifier* f. L *fructificare* (*fructus*, -FY)]

frŭc'tōse, n. Fruit sugar. [f. L *fructus* FRUIT + -OSE²]

frŭc'tuous, a. Full of, producing, fruit (lit. & fig.). [OF, f. L *fructuosus* (FRUIT)]

frug'al (frōō-), a. Careful, sparing (of), economical, esp. as regards food; sparingly used or supplied, costing little. Hence or cogn. **frugal'ITY** n., ~LY² adv., (frōō-). [f. L *frugalis* (*frugi* indecl. adj. orig. dat. of *frux* profit) + -AL]

frugiv'orous (frōō-), a. Feeding on fruit. [f. L *frux* fruit + -VOROUS]

fruit (frōōt), n., & v.i. & t. **1.** (Usu. pl.) vegetable products fit for food (usu. ~s *of the earth*), so ~AGE(1) (-ŏŏt-) n.; plant's or tree's edible product of seed with its envelope (also collect. in sing., as *feeds on* ~); vegetable seed with envelope as means of reproduction; (Bibl.) offspring (usu. ~ *of the body, loins, womb*); produce of action, (pl.) revenues produced (*the ~s of industry*); (sing. or pl.) result, issue, consequence; ~-*cake*, containing currants etc.; ~ *clipper*, fast ship carrying ~; ~-*knife*, with silver etc. blade against acid; ~-*piece*, picture of ~; ~ *salad*, of various ~s cut up & mixed in bowl often with cream etc.; ~-*sugar*, glucose, levulose, or fructose; ~-*tree*, grown for its ~; hence (-)~ED² a. **2.** vb. Bear, make bear, ~. [OF, f. L *fructus -ūs* (*frui* enjoy)]

fruita'rian (frōō-), n. Feeder on fruit. [-ARIAN]

fruit'er (frōōt-), n. Fruit-ship; tree producing fruit (*a sure* ~); ‖ fruit-grower. [FRUIT n. & v., -ER¹]
‖ **fruit'erer** (frōōt-), n. Dealer in fruit. [-ER doubled]

fruit'ful (frōōt-), a. Productive, fertile, causing fertility; productive of offspring, prolific, (lit. & fig.; *a session* ~ *in great measures*); beneficial, remunerative, whence ~LY² adv. Hence ~NESS n. [-FUL]

frui'tion (frōō-), n. Enjoyment, attainment of thing desired, realization of hopes etc. [OF, f. L *fruitionem* (*frui* fruit, enjoy, -ION)]

fruit'less (frōōt-), a. Not bearing fruit; yielding no profit, ineffectual, useless, empty, vain. Hence ~LY² adv., ~NESS n. [-LESS]

fruit'let (frōōt-), n. (bot.). = DRUPEL. [-LET]

fruit'ly (frōōt-), a. Of fruit; (of wine) tasting of the grape, whence ~INESS n.; (colloq.) suggestive, broad, full of rough humour or(usu. scandalous) interest. [-Y²]

frum'enty (frōō-), **fûrm'etý**, n. Hulled wheat boiled in milk & seasoned with cinnamon, sugar, etc. [f. OF *frumentee* (*frumente* f. L *frumentum* corn), -Y¹]

frŭmp, n. Old-fashioned dowdily-dressed woman. Hence **frŭm'pISH¹**, **frŭm'pY²**, aa. [?]

frŭs'trāte¹, a. (arch.). Frustrated. [f. L *frustratus* (foll., -ATE²)]

frŭstrāte'² (also frŭs-), v.t. Balk, baffle, neutralize, counteract, disappoint. So ~A'TION n. [f. L *frustrari* (*frustra* in vain), -ATE³]

frŭs'tûle, n. Two-valved shell of diatom. [F, f. LL *frustulum* (foll., -ULE)]

frŭs'tum, n. (pl. -ta, -tums). Remainder of regular solid whose upper part has been cut off by plane parallel to base, or part intercepted between two planes. [L, = piece broken off]

frutes'cent (frōō-), a. (bot.). Of the nature of a frutex. [for *fruticescent* (foll., -ESCENT)]

frut'ex (froo-), n. (bot.) (pl. *-icēs*). Woody-stemmed plant smaller than tree, shrub. [L genit. *-icis*]

frutĭcōse (froo-), a. (Bot.) shrubby; (of minerals, zoophytes, etc.) looking like shrub. [prec., -OSE¹]

fry¹, n. Young fishes fresh from the spawn; young of salmon in second year; young of other creatures produced in large numbers, e.g. bees or frogs; *small ~*, young or insignificant beings, children etc. [f. ON *frió* seed]

fry², v.t. & i., & n. 1. Cook (t. & i.) in boiling fat (*other* FISH *to ~*; *~ing-pan*, shallow pan used; *out of ~ing-pan into fire*, from bad to worse). 2. n. Fried meat; ||various internal parts of animals usu. fried, esp. LAMB's *~*. [f. F *frire* f. L *frigere*]

fry'er, fri'er, n. Vessel for frying fish; one who fries (fish). [-ER¹]

‖**fūb'sÿ** (-z-), a. Fat or squat. [f. obs. *fubs* small fat person]

fuchsia (fūsh'ǎ), n. Drooping-flowered shrub. [mod. L (*Fuchs* 16th-c. German botanist, -IA¹)]

fuch'sine (fook-), n. Salt of rosaniline forming deep red dye. [prec.; f. resemblance of colour to flower) +-INE¹]

fūc'us, n. (pl. *-ci* pr. *-sī*). Kinds of seaweed with flat leathery fronds. Hence **fūc'OID** a. [L, = rock-lichen, cf. Gk *phūkos*]

fŭd'dle, v.i. & t., & n. 1. Tipple, booze; intoxicate; stupefy, confuse. 2. n. Spell of drinking (*on the ~*), intoxication; confusion. [cf. Du. *vod* slack, G dial. *fuddeln* swindle]

fŭdge¹, int. & n. Nonsense!; nonsense; piece of stop-press news inserted in newspaper page at the last minute by special means; soft-grained sweetmeat made with milk, sugar, chocolate, etc. [?]

fŭdge², v.t. & i., & n. 1. Fit together, patch, make up, in a makeshift or dishonest way, cook, fake; practise such methods. 2. n. Piece of fudging. [perh. f. obs. *fadge* v.i. fit]

Fuehrer, Füh- (fūr'-), n. Leader. [G]

fū'el, n., & v.t. & i. (-ll-). 1. Material for fires, firing, coal, wood, etc.; something that feeds or inflames passion etc. 2. v.t. Supply (fire) with *~*; get *~*. [f. OF *fowaille* f. pop. L *focalia* neut. pl. of *focalis* (*focus* hearth, -AL¹)]

fŭg, n., & v.i., (colloq.: -gg-). 1. Fustiness of air in room; fluff and dust collected in corners etc. 2. v.i. Enjoy a frowsty atmosphere. Hence *~gy*² (-g-) a. [?]

fūgā'cious (-shus), a. Fleeting, evanescent, hard to capture or keep. So **fūgac'ITY** (-ăt-) n. [f. L *fugax fugac-is* (*fugere* flee, -ACIOUS)]

fū'gal, a. Of the nature of a fugue. Hence *~ly*² adv. [-AL]

-fūge, suf. in adj. & nn. f. mod. L in *-fugus*. Acc. to L anal. the sense should

be *fleeing from* (*fugere*) as in L *lucifugus*, *erĭfuga*; but in the mod. formations it is *putting to flight* (*fugare*) as in *febrifuge, vermifuge*.

fū'gitive, a. & n. 1. Flying, running away, that has taken flight; flitting, shifting; evanescent, of short duration, quickly fading; (of literature) of passing interest, ephemeral, occasional. 2. n. One who flees esp. from danger, enemy, justice, or owner; exile, refugee. [f. (-ĭv) f. L *fugitivus* (*fugere fugit-* flee, -IVE)]

fū'gleman (-gel-), n. (pl. *-men*). ||Soldier placed in front of regiment etc. while drilling to show the motions & time; leader, organizer, spokesman, etc. by back formation **fū'gle** v.i. [f. G *flügel-mann* (*flügel* wing; *mann* man)]

fugue (fūg), n., & v.i. & t. 1. Polyphonic composition in which a short melodic theme ('subject') is introduced by one of the parts and successively taken up by the others, thereafter forming the main material of the texture (*double ~*, with two such themes); hence **fū'guIST**(1) (-gĭ-) n. 2. vb. Compose or perform *~*. [F, f. It. & L *fuga* flight]

-ful, suf. orig.=FULL a. 1. Forming adji. f. nn., w. sense *full of* (*beautiful*), & sometimes *having qualities of* (*masterful*); also adji. f. adji. or f. L adji. stems (*direful, graceful, tristful*), perh. on anal. of older synonyms in *-ful*: also f. vv. (*forgetful*), *that fills a hand*. 2. Forming nn. (*helpful, & esp. thankful where the sing. n. being disused thank would naturally be taken for verb); a pass. sense is seen in *bashful*=*abashable*. 2. Forming nn., w. sense *amount required to fill* (*handful*). *Handful* is a differentiation f. *hand full*, which in the Teut. langg. had orig. besides its literal sense that of *quantity that fills a hand*. The differentiation is not carried out equally in all langg., & *handroll* etc. taking their gender f. first component, though written as single wds. In mod. E *-ful* is a living suf. freely added to nn. (*boatful, houseful, churchful*); a reminiscence of its orig. is seen in *spoonsful, cupsful*, which are ambiguous & contrary to good mod. usage.

fūl'crum, n. (pl. *-ra*). (Mech.) point against which lever is placed to get purchase or on which it turns or is supported; means by which influence etc. is brought to bear; (Bot.; usu. pl.) accessory organs, appendages, e.g. bracts, tendrils. [L, = post of couch (*fulcire* to prop)]

fulfil (fool-), v.t. (-ll-). 1. Bring to consummation, carry out, (prophecy, promise), satisfy (desire, prayer); perform, execute, do, (command, law); answer (purpose), comply with (conditions); bring to an end, finish, complete, (period,

work). Hence ~MENT (fŏŏl-) n. [OE *ful-fyllan* (FULL[1], FILL)]

ful'gent, a. [poet. & rhet.). Shining, brilliant. [f. L *fulgēre* shine, -ENT]

ful'ghrite, n. (Geol.) rocky substance fused or vitrified by lightning, tube made by passage of lightning into sand; an explosive. [f. L *fulgur* lightning +-ITE[2])

ful'ham (fŏŏl'am), n. (hist.). Loaded DIE[1]. [?]

Ful'ham Päl'ace (fŏŏl'am), n. Official residence of the Bishop of London.

fül'ginous, a. Sooty, dusky. [f. L *fuliginosus* (*fūligo -inis* soot, -OUS)]

full[1] (fŏŏl), a., v.t., & adv. **1.** Filled to utmost capacity, holding all (of, or abs.) its limits will allow, replete, (~ *to the brim, to overflowing,* & colloq. *up*); (of heart etc.) overcharged with emotion (~-*hearted,* stirred with deep feeling, also zealous, confident, courageous). **2.** Holding or having abundance of, crowded (*in a ~ house,* with a good proportion of members present), showing marked signs of (~ *of vitality*). **3.** Engrossed with the thought of (~ *of himself, of his subject;* ~ *of the news* etc., unable to keep from talking of it). **4.** Replete with food (arch. of persons; *a ~ stomach*); (chiefly Bibl.) having had one's fill of (~ *of years & honours*). **5.** Abundant, sufficient, copious, satisfactory, (*a ~ meal; turned it to ~ account; give ~ details; he is very ~ on this point*). **6.** Complete, entire, perfect, answering completely to its name, reaching the specified or usual limit, entirely visible, (~ *point* or *stop,* period in punctuation; ~ *daylight, membership;* ~ *brother, sister,* born of same father and mother; *of the ~ blood,* of pure descent, not hybrid, so ~-*blooded,* & see below; ~ *pay,* that allowed on active service; ~ *age,* after minority; ~ DRESS[2] & so ~-*dress rehearsal;* ~-*dress debate* in Parliament, prearranged on important question, not arising casually; ~ SWING n.; *at ~ length,* lying stretched out, also = *in ~* below; ~-*length portrait* etc., of whole figure; ~ *moon,* with whole disk illuminated, also the time when this comes; ~ *face,* turned straight to spectator; *waited a ~ hour; it was ~ summer*). **7.** (Of light) intense, (of colour) deep, (of motion etc.) vigorous (*a ~ pulse; gallop, speed,* etc., used adv. with *come* etc.; ~ *speed ahead;* order to pursue course with energy). **8.** Swelling, plump, protuberant, (of dress) containing superfluous material arranged in folds etc. (vb, make ~; gather, pleat). **9.** ~-*back,* football player stationed behind; ~-*blooded,* vigorous, hearty, sensual, & see above; ~-*bodied,* esp. of wine with much BODY; ~-*bottomed,* (of wig) long behind, opp. BOB[1]; ~ *house, hand,* Poker hand with three of a kind and a pair; ~-*mouthed,* (of cattle) with ~ complement of teeth, (of dogs) baying

loudly, (of oratory, style, etc.) sonorous, vigorous; ~ *pitch* (Cricket), a bowled ball pitched right up to the wicket without first touching the ground (also ~ *toss*); ~ *score* (Mus.), complete score comprising music for all performers; ~-*timer,* child who attends during all school-hours (opp. *half-timer*). **10.** (used abs. as n.). Whole (*cannot tell you the ~ of it; in ~,* without abridgement; *to the ~,* to the utmost extent, quite); height, acme, (*season, moon, 'is past the ~*); hence ~ISH[1](2) a. **11.** adv. Very (chiefly poet.; ~ *fain;* ~ *many a; know it ~ well*); quite, fully, (~ *six miles;* ~ *as useful as;* often in comb., also as ~-*blown,* of flowers, quite open, also fig. as ~-*blown dignity;* ~-*grown,* having reached maturity); exactly (*hit him ~ on the nose*); more than sufficiently (*this chair is ~ high*). [Aryan; cf. G *voll,* Skr. *purṇa,* L *plenus,* Gk *plērēs*]

ful'er[1] (fŏŏl-), n. One who fulls cloth; ~'*s earth,* hydrous silicate of alumina. [f. OF *fouler* see FOIL[2]]

ful'er[1] (fŏŏl-), n., & v.t. Grooved tool on which iron is shaped; groove made by this esp. in horse-shoes; (vb) stamp with ~. [?]

ful(l)ness (fŏŏl-), n. Being FULL[1]; esp.: (Bibl.) *the ~ of the heart,* emotion, genuine feelings, *the ~ of time,* the destined time, *the ~ of the world* etc., all that fills it; (of sound, colour, etc.) richness, volume, body. [-NESS]

fully (fŏŏl-), adv. Completely, without deficiency; quite (esp. with numbers). [-LY[2]]

ful'mar (fŏŏ-) n. Sea-bird of petrel kind & gull's size. [perh. f. ON *full* FOUL[1] + *mar* MEW[1]]

ful'minate (fŏŏl-), v.i.& t. Flash like lightning, explode, detonate, (~*ing gold, mercury*), etc., various fulminates, see FULMIN(O); thunder forth, utter or publish, (censure); issue (usu. official) censures *against* (esp. of Pope). Hence or cogn. **fülmina'TION** n., ~ORY a. [f. L *fulminare* (*fulmen* lightning), -ATE[3]]

ful'mine (fŏŏl-), v.t. & i. (poet.). Send forth (lightning, thunder); thunder (lit. & fig.). [as prec.]

fülmin'ic, a. (chem.), ~ *acid,* nitro-acetonitril, an acid forming explosive salts with some metals. Hence **fül'minäte**[2] [-ATE[2](3)] n. [f. L *fulmen -inis* lightning +-IC]

ful'ness. See FULLNESS.

ful'some (fŭ-, fŏŏl-), a. Cloying, excessive, disgusting by excess, (of flattery, servility, exaggerated affection). Hence ~LY[2](-ml-) adv., ~NESS (-mn-) n. [FULL[1], -SOME]

ful'vous, a. (nat. hist.). Reddish-yellow, tawny. So **fulves'cent** a. [f. L *fulvus* + -OUS.]

fumāde', n. Smoked pilchard. [f. Sp. *fumado* smoked.]

fum'arôle, n. Crevice in cone of volcano through which vapour issues. [f. F *fumerolle* f. L *fumariolum* dim. of *fumarium* smoke-chamber (*fumus* smoke, -ARY¹)]

fum'ble, v.i. & t., & n. 1. Use the hands awkwardly, grope about, (*at, with, for, after,* thing sought); handle or deal with awkwardly or nervously (~*e the ball,* not stop it cleanly); hence ~ER¹ n. 2. n. Bungling attempt; cf. Du. *fommelen*]. [perh. f. OE *folm* palm of hand; cf. Du. *fommelen*]

fume, n., & v.t. & i. 1. Odorous smoke, vapour, or exhalation; watery vapour; noxious vapour supposed to rise from stomach to brain (*the ~s of urine* etc.); also *fig.* of excitement, enthusiasm, etc.; fit of anger (*in a ~*); hence **fūm'y**² a. 2. vb. Perfume with incense; subject to chemical ~s esp. those of ammonia (photographic film, oak, to darken tints); emit ~s; (of vapour etc.) rise, be emitted; be peevish, chafe (*at*). [n. f. OF *fum,* vb f. F *fumer,* f. L *fumus, fumare,* smoke]

fum'igate, v.t. Apply fumes to; disinfect or purify with fumes; perfume. Hence ~ATION, ~ātOR¹(1, 2), nn. [f. L *fumigare* (*fumus* smoke), -ATE³]

fum'itory, n. Herb formerly used in medicine. [f. OF *fumeterre* f. med. L *fumus terrae* earth-smoke, W. assim. to -ORY]

fun, n., & v.i. (-nn-). 1. Sport, amusement, jocularity, drollery, (*make ~ of, poke ~ at,* ridicule; *for* or *in ~,* as a joke, not seriously; *is good, great, ~,* very amusing; *like ~,* vigorously, quickly, much; *what ~!,* how amusing!). 2. v.i. (rare). Indulge in ~, joke. [perh. f. obs. *fon* befool, etym. dub.]

fūnam'būlist, n. Rope-walker. [f. L *funambulus* (*funis* rope, *ambulare* walk), -IST]

func'tion, n., & v.i. 1. Activity proper to anything, mode of action by which it fulfils its purpose; office-holder's duty, employment, profession, calling; religious or other public ceremony or occasion; social meeting of formal or important kind; (Math.) variable quantity in relation to other(s) in terms of which it may be expressed or on which its value depends; hence ~LESS a. 2. v.i. Fulfil a ~, operate, act. [OF, f. L *functionem* (*fungi funct-* perform, -ION)]

func'tional (-shon-), a. Official, merely formal, (rare); (Physiol.) of, affecting, the functions of an organ etc. (only, not structural or organic (esp. of diseases), (of organ) having a function, not functionless or rudimentary; (Math.) of a FUNCTION. Hence ~LY² adv. [-AL]

func'tionary (-shon-), n. & a. 1. Official. 2. adj. = FUNCTION v. [-ARY¹]

func'tionāte (-shon-), v.i. = FUNCTION v. [-ATE³]

fund, n., & v.t. 1. Permanent stock of something ready to be drawn upon (*a ~ of common sense, tenderness, labour, knowledge*); stock of money, esp. one set apart for a purpose (SINK'*ing~*); (pl.) pecuniary resources (*in ~s,* having money, flush); *the ~s,* stock of national debt as mode of investment (*has £10,000 in the ~s; ~-holder,* such investor). 2. v.t. Convert (floating debt) into more or less permanent debt at fixed interest; put into a ~, collect, store, (rare); invest (money) in the ~s. [f. L *fundus* bottom]

fun'dament, n. The buttocks. [f. L *fundamentum* (FOUND¹, -MENT) founda-tion)]

fundamen'tal, a. & n. 1. Of the ground-work, going to the root of the matter, serving as base or foundation, essential, primary, original, from which others are derived, (*a ~ change; the ~ rules; the* chord in its original (uninverted) form, ~ *tone,* produced by vibration of whole sonorous body (opp. *harmonics* produced by that of its parts); hence ~ITY (-ăl-) n., ~LY² adv. 2. n. Principle, rule, article, serving as groundwork of system (usu. pl.); (Mus.) ~ note or tone. [-AL]

***fundamen'talism**, n. Maintenance, in opposition to modernism, of traditional orthodox beliefs such as the inerrancy of Scripture & literal acceptance of the creeds as fundamentals of protestant Christianity. So ~IST n. & a. [prec. + -ISM]

fūneb'rial, a. (rare). Of funeral (*custom is ~ in origin*). [f. L *funebris* (*funus* see foll.) + -AL]

fūn'eral, a. & n. 1. Of, used etc. at, burial or cremation of the dead (~ *pile, pyre,* pile of wood etc. on which corpse is burnt; ~ *oration*). 2. n. Burial of the dead with its observances, obsequies; burial pro-cession; (colloq.) unpleasant concern, lookout (*that's your~*). [early OF, f. med. L *funeralis* (L *funus -eris* funeral + -AL); n. f. OF *funeraille* f. med. L *funeralia* neut. pl. of *funeralis* -ALE²]

fūn'erary, a. = FUNEREAL. [f. LL *fune-rarius* (prec., -ARY¹)]

fūnēr'eal, a. Appropriate to funeral, gloomy, dismal, dark. Hence ~LY² adv. [f. L *funereus* (FUNERAL) + -AL]

fun'gible (-j-), a. (legal). That can serve for, or be replaced by another answering to the same definition (of goods etc. contracted for, when an individual specimen is not meant). [f. med. L *fungibilis* f. *fungi* (*vice*) serve (turn), -IBLE]

fun'gicide (-j-), n. Fungus-destroying substance. [FUNGUS, -r-, -CIDE]

fung'ous (-ngg-), a. Of fungi, having nature of a fungus; springing up like a mushroom, transitory. [f. L *fungosus* (foll., -OSE⁴)]

fung'us (-ngg-), n. (pl. ~i pr. -ji, ~uses). Mushroom, toadstool, or allied plant including moulds; (Bot.) cryptogamous plant without chlorophyll feeding on organic matter; thing of sudden growth; (Path.) spongy morbid growth or excrescence; skin-disease of fish. Hence ~AL (-ngg-), ~iFORM (-j-), ~iv'OROUS (-j-), ~OID, ~USY², (-ngg-), aa. [L, perh. cogn. w. Gk *sphoggos* SPONGE]

funic'ular, a. Of a rope or its tension (~ railway, worked by cable & stationary engine). [f. L *funiculus* (*funis* cord, -CULE)+-AR¹]

funk, n., & v.i. & t., (sl.). 1. Fear, panic, (blue ~, terror); coward; hence ~y² a.. ||~-hole, trench dug-out, employment used as pretext for evading military service. 2. vb. Flinch, shrink, show cowardice; (try to) evade (undertaking), shirk; be afraid of; inspire fear in. [called Oxford slang in 1743; etym. dub.]

funn'el, n. Diminishing tube, or truncated cone & tube, for conducting liquid, powder, etc., into small opening; ventilating or lighting shaft; metal chimney part of chimney. Hence (-)~lED² (-ld) a. [ME *fonel* perh. thr. OF (cf. Breton *founil*) f. L *infundibulum* f. IN(*fundere* pour)]

funn'iment, n. Joke, drollery. [foll., -MENT]

funn'y[¹, a. Affording fun, comical; curious, queer, perplexing, hard to account for; ~y-bone, part of elbow over which ulnar nerve passes; ~y-man, professional jester. Hence ~iLY² adv., ~iNESS n. [-Y²]

||**funn'y**², n. Narrow clinker-built boat for one sculler. [perh. f. prec.]

fur, n., & v.t. & i. (-rr-). 1. Trimming or lining made of dressed coat of certain animals, e.g. ermine, beaver; coat of such animals, as material for trimming etc. (usu. pl.) garment(s) of or having ~; short fine soft hair of certain animals distinguished from the longer hair, (pl.) skins of such animals with the ~; *make the ~ fly*, make a disturbance, stir up trouble, raise Cain; (collect.) furred animals (esp.~ & feather; hunt ~, hares); crust adhering to surface, e.g. deposit of wine; coating formed on tongue in sickness; crust of carbonate of lime in kettle etc.; hence ~r² a. 2. vb. Provide (garment, animal), clothe (person), coat (tongue, inside of kettle; also intr, become coated), with ~; clean ~ from (boiler); (Carpent.) level (floor-timbers) by inserting strips of wood. [n. f. vb, OF *forrer* (now *fourrer*) f. Rom. *fodrare* sheathe, line, f. Teut. (OE *foddor* cf. G *futter* lining)]

furb'elow (-ō), n., & v.t. 1. Flounce, pleated border of skirt or petticoat; (pl., contempt.) showy ornaments; ||kind of wrinkled seaweed. 2. v.t. Adorn with ~(s). [corrupt. of FALBALA]

furb'ish, v.t. Remove rust from, polish up, burnish; give new look to, renovate, revive, (something antiquated; usu. up). [f. OF *forbir* (-ISH²) f. OHG *forban*]

fur'cate¹ (-āt, -at), a. Forked, branched. Hence **furcat'o-** comb. form. [f. med. L *furcatus* (L *furca* fork, -ATE²)]

fur'cāte²[³, v.i. Form a fork, divide. So ~A'TION n. [f. L *furca* fork+-ATE³]

furfura'ceous (-fərāshus), a. Scurfy; (Bot.) covered with bran-like scales. [L *furfur* bran+-ACEOUS]

fur'ious, a. Full of fury, raging, frantic, violent; *fast & ~*, (of mirth etc.) eager, uproarious. Hence ~LY² adv. [f. OF *furieus* f. L *furiosus* (FURY, -OUS)]

furl, v.t. & i. Roll up & bind (sail) on yard or boom; close, fold up, draw away, relinquish, (fan, umbrella, wings, curtain, hopes); become ~ed, roll away like clouds. [prob. f. obs. *furdle* furl var. of obs. *fardel* vb (FARDEL)]

fur'long, n. Eighth of mile. [OE *furlang* (*furh* furrow, LONG adj.); orig. = length of furrow in common field, regarded as square containing ten acres]

fur'lough (-lō), n. & v.t. Leave of absence, esp. to soldier; (vb) grant ~ to. [f. Du. *verlof* cf. G *verlaub* (FOR-, LEAVE²)]

furm'ety⁴. See FRUMENTY.

furn'ace (-is), n., & v.t. 1. Apparatus including chamber for combustibles in which minerals, metals, etc., may be subjected to continuous intense heat; hot place; severe test (esp. *tried in the ~*); closed fireplace for heating building by hot pipes. 2. v.t. Heat in ~. [f. OF *fornais* f. L *fornacem* nom. -ax (*fornus* oven)]

furn'ish, v.t. Provide *with* (~ed with, having); fit up (house, room) with all necessary appliances, esp. movable furniture (~ed house, rooms, etc., esp. let with furniture); provide, afford, yield. [f. OF *furnir* (-ISH²) f. Rom. *fornire* f. Teut. (OHG *frummen* promote f. root of FROM)]

furn'iture, n. Contents of receptacle (~ of his pocket, money; ~ of my shelves, books; ~ of one's mind, knowledge & intelligence); harness etc. of horse etc. (arch.); movable contents of house or room, tables, chairs, etc. [f. F *fourniture* (*fournir* FURNISH)]

fūrō'rĕ, n. Enthusiastic admiration, rage, craze. [It., f. L *furorem* (*furere* be mad, -OR²)]

fu'rrier, n. Dealer in, dresser of, furs. [-IER]

fu̇rring, n. In vbl senses; also (Ship-build.), doubling of planks on ship's side. [-ING]

fu'rrow (-ō), n., & v.t. 1. Narrow trench made by plough; ship's track; rut, track, groove, long indentation, deep wrinkle, hollow between ridges; ∥~slice, slice of earth turned up by mould-board of plough; make ~less (-ŏl-), ~y² (-ŏi), aa.; mark with wrinkles. [com.-Teut.; OE furh cf. Du. voor, G furche]

¶ **Fu'ry Dance** (dah-), n. (dial.) Dance festival observed as part of ancient festival observed at Helston, Cornwall, on the 8th May. [etym. dub.; perh. ult. f. L feriae holidays]

fu'rther (-dh-), adv. & a. (for usage of fur-, far-, see FARTHER etym.), & v.t. 1. To or at more advanced point in space or time (unsafe to proceed ~; & then to lapse unless ~ continued); to greater extent, more, (inquire ~); (also ~more) in addition, moreover; (esp. intro-ducing fresh consideration in argument); at greater distance (I'll see you ~ first, euphem. for in hell, as strong refusal of request). 2. adj. Going beyond what exists or has been dealt with, additional, (threads of ~ punishment; till ~ notice, in announcing arrangement to continue during pleasure); more distant (on the ~ side, whence ~MOST a. 3. vb. Help on, promote, favour, (undertaking, move-ment, cause); hence ~ANCE n., ~SOME a., (-dh-). [OE furthor, fyrthra adj. (FORE²-ther), fyrthrian vb]

fu'rthest (-dh-), a. & adv. = FARTHEST. [superl. formed f. prec.]

fu'rtive, a. Done by stealth, clandestine, meant to escape notice; sly, stealthily; stolen, taken secretly; thievish, pilfering. Hence ~LY² (-vl-) adv., ~NESS (-vn-) n. [F (-if, -ive), f. L furtivus (furtum theft, -IVE)]

fu'runcle (-ŭngkl), n. Boil, tumour. Hence ~ULAR, ~ULOUS, aa., (-ŭnk⁴). [f. L furunculus (fur thief, -UNCLE)]

fu'ry, n. Fierce passion, wild anger, rage, (in a ~, fit of rage); impetuosity in battle etc. (the Spanish F~, massacre by Span-iards at Antwerp 1576); violence of weather, disease, etc. (like ~, furiously, hard); (usn. pl.) snake-haired goddess(es) of Gk myth sent from Tartarus to punish crime, (fig.) avenging spirits, remorseful pangs, (haunted by the furies of her father's blood); virago, angry or malignant woman. [f. F furie f. L furia Gnère be mad]

furze, n. Spiny yellow-flowered ever-green shrub growing on European waste lands, gorse, whin. Hence fû'rz'y² a. [OE fyrs etym. dub.]

fus'cous, a. (nat. hist.) Sombre, dark, in colour. So fûs'co- comb. form. [L fuscus, -ous]

fuse¹ (-z), v.t. & i. & n. 1. Melt (t. & i.) with intense heat; blend, amalgamate, (t. & i.) into one whole (as) by melting (of metals, living bones, institutions, motives, etc.); hence fûs'ing a., fûsībi'lity n., fūs'ible a. 2. n. (Electr.) piece of easily-fusible wire, placed in main or branch circuit, designed to melt when overloaded and thus interrupt the current and prevent the section being loaded above the safety limit. [f. L fundere fus- pour]

fuse² (-z), n., & v.t. 1. Tube, casing, cord, etc., filled or saturated with combustible matter for igniting bomb, blasting-charge, etc.; component screwed into shell, mine, etc., designed to detonate explosive charge after an interval (time-~) or on impact or when subjected to magnetic or vibratory stimulation. 2 v.t. Fit ~ to. [f. It. fuso f. L fusus spindle]

fusee' (-z), n. 1. Conical pulley or wheel esp. in watch or clock; exostosis or bony tumour on horse's cannon-bone; large-headed match for lighting cigar or pipe in wind. [f. F fusée f. med. L fusata spindleful (L fusus spindle)]

fus'elage, n. Framework of aeroplane. [F, f. fuseler cut in spindle form (fuseau spindle f. L, f. fusellus dim. of fusus). -AGE]

fus'el oil (-z), n. Mixture of several alcohols, chiefly amyl, produced, usn. in small amounts, during alcoholic fer-mentation and making alcoholic liquors harmful or poisonous. [f. G fusel bad spirit, cf. fuseln FOOZLE]

fūs'iform (-z-), a. (anat. hist.), Shaped like spindle or cigar, tapering at both ends. [f. L fusus spindle, -I-, -FORM]

fūs'il (-z), n. Obsolete light musket. [F, = It. focile (L focus hearth fire, -IL)]

fusilier' (-z-), n. (usu. pl.), (Man of) certain British regiments formerly armed with fusils. [F (prec., -IER)]

fusillade' (-z-), n., & v.t. 1. (Wholesale execution by) continuous discharge of fire-arms. 2. v.t. Assault (place), shoot down (persons), by ~. [F (fusiller shoot f. FUSIL, -ADE)]

fu'sion (-zhn), n. Fusing; fused mass; blending of different things into one; coalition, whence ~IST(2) (-zhon-) n. [f. L fusio (FUSE, -ION; cf. FOISON)]

fuss, n., & v.i. & t. 1. Bustle, excessive commotion, ostentatious or nervous activity; treatment of trifles as impor-tant; abundance of petty detail; hence ~y¹ a., ~'ily² adv., ~'iness n. 2. vb. Make ~; busy oneself restlessly with trifles; move fussily about, up & down, etc.; agitate, worry, (person). [perh. imit. f. sputtering or bubbling]

fustanella a, n. Man's white kilt in modern Greece. [It., dim. of mod. Gk phoustani perh. f. It. fustagno FUSTIAN]

fus'tian a, n. & a. 1. Thick twilled short-napped cotton cloth usn. dyed dark; turgid speech or writing; bombast. 2. adj. Made of ~, (fig.) bombastic,

worthless, sorry, pretentious. [f. OF *fustaigne* (med. L *fustaneus* adj. perh. = from Fostat suburb of Cairo)]

fūs'tic, n. Two kinds of wood yielding yellow dye (*young* ~, Venetian sumach; ~ *or old* ~, Amer. & W. Ind.) dye from these. [f. F f. Sp. *fustoc* f. Arab. *fustuq* f. Gk as PISTACHIO]

fūs'tig|āte, v.t. (joc.). Cudgel. So ~A² TION n. [L *fustigare* (*fustis* cudgel), -ATE³]

fūs'ty, a. Scale-smelling, musty, mouldy; close, stuffy; antiquated, old-fashioned. Hence ~INESS n. [f. obs. *fust* (smell of wine-cask f. OF *fust* cask f. L *fustis* cudgel]

fut. See PHUT.

fŭtch'el(l), n. One of timbers supporting shafts, pole, or axle-bar, of carriage. [1]

fŭt'ile (-īl, -ĭl), a. Useless, ineffectual, vain, frivolous. Hence or cogn. **fūtil'ITY** n., (rare) ~LY² adv. [f. L *futilis* leaky, futile, perh. f. *fud*- st. of *fundere* pour]

fŭtt'ock, n. One of ship's middle timbers between floor & top timbers; ~ *plates*, iron plates in a ship's top to which are fastened to ring on mast below) are fixed, as well as the dead-eyes of the topmast rigging. [perh. = *foot-hook*]

fū'ture, a. & n. 1. About to happen, that will be hereafter (~ *life, state, existence after death*), that will be something specified (*my* ~ *wife*), of time to come, (Gram., of tense) describing event yet to happen. 2. n. Time to come (*for the* ~, *in* ~, *from now onwards*; *past, present, &* ~); what will happen in the ~; person's, country's, etc., prospective condition; (Gram.) ~ *tense*; one's ~ betrothed; (Commerc.; pl.) goods & stocks sold for ~ delivery; contracts for these; hence ~LESS (-cherl-) a. [OF (-*ur, -ure*), f. L *futurus* fut. part. of *esse* be f. st. *fu-* BE]

fū'turist (-cher-), n. & a. 1. (Theol.) (one) believing the prophecies of the Apocalypse etc. are still to be fulfilled. 2. (Art) adherent of **fū'turISM** (-che-) n., a recent movement in (esp. Italian) art, literature, etc., marked by violent departure from traditional methods and by the use of arbitrary symbols in the expression of emotion. [-IST]

fū'turITY, n. Future time; (sing. or pl.) future events; future condition, existence after death; ~ *stakes*, stakes raced for long after entries or nominations are made. [-ITY]

fuzz, n. Loose volatile matter, fluff; fluffy or frizzed hair; ~*-ball*, a fungus, the puff-ball. [perh. imit. of blowing]

fuzz'|ly, a. Frayed, fluffy; blurred, indistinct; frizzed; *Fuzzy-wuzzy*, Soudanese warrior. Hence ~ILY² adv., ~INESS n. [-Y²]

fy, fye. = FIE.

-fy, suf. forming vbs. In the older E vbs -fy represented F -*fer*, L -*ficare*. L formed vbs in -*ficare* (with or without intervention of adji. in -*ficus*) t. nn, w, sense make, produce, (*pacificare*, orig. intr., make peace) or make into (*deificare* deify); t. adji. w. sense bring into a state (*sanctificare*); f. adji. E vb stems w. causative sense (*horrificare* horrify). In med. L -*facere* was often substituted for -*facere*; hence F & E vbs in -*fier*, -*fy*, occas. repr. L vbs in -*facere* (F *stupéfier*, but D.p. *stupefait* as well as *stupéfié*, stupefy; OF *satisfier*, but mod. F *satisfaire*; F *liquéfier* liquefy, *rubéfier* rubefy). Apart f. these in -*efy* E has always -*ify* (-i-), which is freely added to E adji. & nn. to form vbs chiefly joc. or colloq. (*speechify, Frenchify*; also, on vb, the irreg. *argufy*). Vbs formed on adji. have often intr. as well as trans. sense (*solidify* make or become solid). Vbs in -*ify* have nn. in -*fication*, those representing L vbs in -*facere* have nn. in -FACTION; but E has *petrifaction* where F has the correct *petrification*.

fyl'fot, n. Swastika, equal-armed cross of which each arm is continued rectangularly, all clockwise or counterclockwise. [name based on ancient direction for design of painted window, in which may mean either the particular pattern or something to *fill the foot of the window*] **fytte.** See FIT¹.

G

G (jē), letter (pl. *Gs, G's*). (Mus.) fifth note of diatonic scale of C major; corresponding scale or key; *G CLEF*.

găb, n. (colloq.). Talk, prattle, twaddle, (*stop your* ~, hold your tongue; *gift of the* ~, talent for speaking, also loquacity). [1]

găb'ardine (-ēn), n. Dress material of cotton or silk with wool lining; material for rain-coats. [var. of GABERDINE]

găb'ble, v.i. & t., & n. 1. Talk volubly or inarticulately, read aloud (t., often *over*, & i.) too fast; utter too fast. 2. n. Voluble confused unintelligible talk. [imit.]

găb'bro, n. A basic igneous rock of crystalline texture resembling dolerite and granite. [It.]

gabelle', n. Tax (usu. foreign tax), esp. the French pre-Revolution salt-tax. [F, f. med. L *gabella* (*gabulum* = OE *gafol* see GAVELKIND]

găb'erdine (-ēn), n. Loose long upper garment esp. of Jews & almsmen; a fine hard-laid cloth. [f. OF *gauvardine* perh. f. MHG *wallevart* pilgrimage]

găb'ion, n. Cylinder of wicker or woven metal bands to be filled with earth for use in fortification or engineering. [F, f. It. *gabbione* (*gabbia* CAGE, -OON)]

gabionade', n. Line of gabions. [-ADE(1)]

gā'ble, n. Triangular upper part of wall at end of ridged roof; ~-end, ...-topped wall; ~-shaped canopy over window or door, whence **gā'blᴇᴅ¹** a. Hence (-)**gā'blᴇᴅ²** (-ld) a. [OF, f. ON *gafl*; cf. G *gabel* fork; prob. cogn. w. OHG *gebal*, Gk *kephalē*, head]

gā'by', n. Simpleton. [?]

gad', int. of surprise, asseveration, etc. (also *by* ~, *begad*). [=GOD]

gad² v.i. (-dd-), & n. Go about idly, rove, wander, (usu. *about, abroad, out*); (of plants, esp. in part.) straggle; (*upon the* ~, going about, on the move; ~ *about*, etc. (person) given to ~-*ding*. [perh. back formation f. obs. *gadling* companion, f. OE *gædling* (*gæd* fellowship, -LING¹)]

gad³ (gŭd), n. Cushioned throne of Indian ruler; (transf.) the regal position. [Hind. *gaddī*]

gad'fly, n. Breeze, cattle-biting fly; irritating or worrying person; violent impulse, oestrum. [f. obs. *gad* spike f. ON *gaddr* cogn. w. YARD; & f. L. *hasta* spear]

gã'dget, n. (colloq.). Small fitting or contrivance in machinery etc.; (transf.) dodge, device, [first in naut. use; perh. dim. of GAUGE¹]

gadroon', n. (usu. pl. or attrib.). Convex curve(s) in series forming ornamental edge like inverted fluting. [f. F *godron* etym. dub.]

Gadhel'ic (-dĕ-), a. & n. = GAELIC in its wider sense. [literary f. Ir. *Gaedhea* Gael + -IC]

Gael (gāl), n. Scottish Celt; (rarely) Irish Celt. [f. Sc.-Gael. *Gaidheal*]

Gael'ic (gāl-, gål-), a. & n. (language) of Scottish Celts, of Scottish & Irish & Manx Celts. [-IC]

gåff'¹, n. 1. Barbed fishing-spear; stick with iron hook for landing large fish; spar extending top of fore-&-aft sail not set on stays. 2. v.t. Seize (fish) with ~. [f. F *gaffe* boat-hook]

|| **gåff²**, n. (sl.). Public place of amusement, esp. (usu. *penny*-) low theatre or music-hall. [?]

gåff', n. (sl.). *Blow the* ~, let out plot. [?]

gå'ffe, n. Blunder, indiscreet act or remark. [F]

gå'ffᴇʀ, n. Elderly rustic, old fellow, (also as prefix to name); || foreman of gang-. [contr. of *godfather* or *grandfather*; cf. GAMMER]

gåg, n., & v.t. & i. (-gg-). 1. Thing thrust into mouth to prevent speech or outcry or (Surg.) hold it open for operation, (Parl.) closure or GUILLOTINE, (vb, apply ~ to, silence, deprive of free speech). 2. Actor's interpolations in dramatic dialogue (vb, make these); (Theatr.) carefully prepared comic effect or business introduced into music-hall sketch, stage-play, etc., (vb, make these); ~-*man*, professional deviser of ~s. 3. ~-*bit*, specially powerful for horse-breaking, ~-*rein*, arranged to make bit more powerful, (*gag*, v.t.) apply ~-bit to (horse). 4. Joke, hoax; (sl.) imposture, lie, (v.t., deceive; v.i., practise deceit). [n. f. OF *gab*; b. imit. of choking sound; sl. sense perh. unrelated]

gåg'a, a. (sl.). Fatuous, senile, dotty. [F]

gage², n. & v.t. 1. Pledge, thing deposited as security; (glove thrown down as, any symbol of) challenge to fight. 2. v.t. Stake, pledge, offer as guarantee. [n. f. OF *guage* f. L. Teut. (WED); vb f. F *gager* of same orig., or for ENGAGE]

gå'ge', n. See GAUGE.

gage², n. Greengage. [abbr.]

gå'ggle, v.i. (Of geese) cackle. [imit.]

gai'ety, n. Being gay, mirth; (usu. pl.) merrymaking, festive occasion(s), amusements; bright appearance. [f. F *gaieté* (*gai* GAY, -TY)]

Gaik'war, Gaek- (gīk-), n. Ruler of Baroda. [Marathi, = cowherd]

gai'ly. See GAY.

gain¹, n. Increase of possessions etc., profit, advance, improvement; acquisition of wealth, lucre, pelf; (pl.) sums acquired by trade etc., emoluments, winnings; increase in amount. [OF]

gain² v.t. & i. 1. Obtain, secure, (desired or desirable thing; ~ *time*, obtain delay by pretexts or slow methods; ~ *the ear of*, get favourable hearing from); win (sum) as profits or as result of changed conditions, earn, whence ~*ings* (-z) [-ING¹ (2)] n. pl.; make a profit, be benefited, improve or advance in some respect, be enhanced by comparison or contrast; win (land from sea, battle, victory; ~ *the upper hand*, be victorious); bring over to one's interest or views, win over, persuade, prevail upon; reach, arrive at, (desired place); ~ *ground*, progress, advance, encroach (*up*)*on*; ~ (*ground*) (*up*)*on*, get closer to (person or thing pursued); (of sea) encroach (*up*)*on* land; ~ (*up*)*on*, win the favour of. Hence ~'ABLE a., ~'ER¹ n. [f. F *gagner* OHG (*weidemen* v. hunt. f. F *guadagnare* f. G *weide* pasturage, forage, cf. OE *widh* hunting)]

gain'ful, a. Lucrative, remunerative; bent on gain. [-FUL]

gainsay', v.t. (arch., literary; past -*said*, pr. -ād or -ĕd. Deny, contradict. Hence ~ER¹ n. [f. obs. *gain*-prep. against f. ON *gegn* cf. G *gegen* + SAY]

gainst, [poet. for) AGAINST.

gait, n. Manner of walking, bearing or carriage as one walks. [var. of GATE²]

gai'ter, n. Covering of cloth, leather, etc., for leg below knee or for ankle; ~, *for the last* ~ *button* (completely; said of French army before Franco-German war). Hence ~ED²(-₂rd) a. [f. F *guêtre* etym. dub.]

gāl′a (or gah^), n. Festive occasion, fête, (often attrib., as ~ day, dress, etc.). [F f. It.]

galac′tic, a. (astron.). Of the Galaxy. [f. Gk galaktikos (foll., -IC)]

galac′to-, comb. form of Gk gala -aktos milk, used in scientific terms as ~gogue, (substance) inducing a flow of milk.

gal′antine (-ēn), n. White meat boned, spiced, tied, boiled, & served cold. [F, altered f. galatine a fish sauce]

galan′ty show (-ŏ), n. Pantomime on screen made by shadows of puppets. [perh. f. It. galanti pl. of galante GALLANT]

galāte′a n. Superior striped cotton dress material (orig. used for children's sailor suits). [f. H.M.S. G~]

gal′axy, n. Irregular luminous band of stars indistinguishable to naked eye encircling the heavens, Milky Way; brilliant company (of beauties, talent, etc.). [f. F galaxie f. L f. Gk galaxias (gala -aktos milk)]

gal′banum, n. Gum resin from some Persian species of ferula. [L, f. Gk khalbanē prob. f. Oriental wd]

gāle[1], n. (Also Sweet~) bog-myrtle. [OE (also Du. & G) gagel]

gāle[2], n. Rather strong wind, (Naut.) storm, (poet.) gentle breeze. [perh. cogn. w. Da. gal, Norw. galen, mad, furious]

‖gāle[3], n. Periodical payment of rent (hanging ~, arrears of rent). [perh. = obs. gavel see GAVELKIND]

gāl′ēa, n. (bot., zool.). Structure like helmet in shape, function, or position. So ~ATE[2], ~ātĕd, aa. [L, = helmet]

‖galeen′ỹ, n. Guinea-fowl. [f. Sp. gallina (morisca Moorish) hen]

Gal′en, n. (joc.). Physician. [f. L f. Gk Galēnos, Pergamene 2nd-c. A.D. physician]

galē′na, n. Common lead ore, lead sulphide, lead glance. [L, = lead ore (in partly purified state), perh. conn. w. Gk galēnē a calm]

galēn′ic, a., **galēn′ical**, a. & n. Of, according to, Galen; esp. (remedy) made of vegetable, not synthetic, components. [Galen +-IC(AL)]

Galilē′an, a. Of the astronomer Galileo; ~ telescope (with bi-convex objective and bi-concave eyepiece). [-AN]

Gal′ilee, g~, n. Porch or chapel at entrance of church. [perh. as less sacred than church w. ref. to Galilee as opp. Judaea, or esp. to Matt. iv. 15 (~ of the Gentiles)]

gallēna′tias (-ăsĭah), n. Confused or meaningless talk, rigmarole. [F (formerly half naturalized, now only as foreign word)]

găl′ingāle (-ngg-), n. Aromatic root of E.-Ind. plants used in cookery & medicine; (also English ~) kind of sedge. [f. OF galingal f. Arab. khalanjan perh. f. Chin. ko-liang-kiang mild ginger from Ko]

galiot. = GALLIOT.

---

gal′ipŏt, n. Kind of hardened turpentine. [F, etym. dub.]

gall[1] (gawl), n. Secretion of liver, bile, (now only of lower animals); typical bitter substance, bitterness, (~ & wormwood); ~-bladder & its contents; asperity, rancour, (dip one's pen in ~, write violently), whence ~-LESS (gawl′i-) a.; *impudence (SL); ~-bladder, vessel containing the ~; ~-stone, calculous formation in ~-bladder. [OE gealla cf. G galle, also Gk kholē, L fel; perh. also cogn. w. YELLOW]

gall[2] (gawl), n. Painful swelling, pustule, blister, esp. in horse; sore produced by chafing; mental soreness or its cause; place rubbed bare, flaw; bare spot in field or coppice. [OE gealla sore on horse, perh. = prec.]

gall[3] (gawl), v.t. & i. Rub sore, injure by rubbing; vex, annoy, harass, humiliate, whence ~ING[2] a. [f. prec., perh. orig. as back formation f. GALLED[2]]

gall[4] (gawl), n. Excrescence produced by insect on trees, esp. on oak (also oak-~, used in making ink & tannin, & in dyeing & medicine); ~-nut, insect producing ~s; ~-nut, ~. So (in -ic acid) găll′ic[1] a. [f. F galle f. L galla]

găll′ant (also, in senses indicated below, occas. galănt′), a., n., & v.t. & i. 1. Showy, finely dressed, (arch.); grand, fine, stately, (of ship, horse, etc.); brave, chivalrous, (also Parl., as conventional epithet of a member of the services, as the honour-able & ~ member); markedly attentive to women (galănt′); concerned with love, amatory, (galănt′); hence ~LY[2] (or as above galănt′) adv. 2. n. Man of fashion, fine gentleman; ladies' man, lover, para-mour, (galănt′). 3. vb (galănt′). Play the ~, flirt with; escort, act as cavalier to, (lady). [f. F galant part. of OF galer make merry cf. GALA perh. f. OHG wallōn wander]

găll′antrỹ, n. Bravery, dashing courage; courtliness, devotion to women; a polite or amorous act or speech; conduct of a gallant, amorous intercourse or intrigue, sexual immorality. [f. F galanterie (prec., -ERY)]

găll′ēon, n. (hist.). Vessel shorter & higher than galley; ship of war (usu. Spanish); large Spanish ship used in American trade. [f. Sp. galeon, f. med. L galeonem nom. -o (GALLEY)]

găll′erỹ, n., & v.t. 1. Covered space for walking in partly open at side, portico, colonnade; balcony; long narrow passage in thickness of wall or supported on corbels, open towards interior of build-ing; platform projecting from inner wall of church, hall, etc., providing extra room for audience or reserved for musicians, reporters, strangers, etc.; (Theatr.) highest such balcony, persons there seated, least refined part of audience (play to the ~, appeal to lower taste, use

claptrap); long narrow room (e.g. *shooting~*, for indoor target practice or matches); passage, corridor; room or building used for showing works of art; chimney-holder of lamp; (Mil., Mining) underground passage; ~ *hit* (Cricket, & fig., from theatre) piece of showy play, so ~ *shot*, *stroke*; hence ~FUL(2) n. 2. v.t. Provide, pierce, etc. with ~ or galleries. [f. F *galerie* etym. dub.]

gall'ey, n. (pl. ~*s*). 1. (Chiefly hist.) low flat single-decked vessel using sails & oars, & usu. rowed by slaves or criminals; ancient Greek or Roman war-ship with one or more banks of oars; large open row-boat, e.g. that used by captain of man-of-war. 2. Ship's kitchen. 3. (Print.) oblong tray to which type is transferred from composing stick (~*proof*, in slip form, not in sheets or pages). 4. ~*slave*, person condemned to row in ~; (fig.) drudge; ~*worm*, kind of many-footed insect (from likeness of its legs to oars). [f. OF *galie*, med. L *galea*, etym. dub.]

galliam'bic, a. & n. In the metre of Catullus's *Attis* (imitated in Tennyson's *Boadicea*): (n., usu. pl.) such verse(s). [f. L *galliambus* song of Galli or priests of Cybele+-IC]

Gall'ic[2] (for *gallic* see GALL[2]), a. Of the Gauls, Gaulish; (usu. joc.) French, French-man. [f. L *Gallicus* (*Gallus* Gaul, -IC]

gall'icism(4) n, **gall'icize**(2, 3) v.t. & i. [f. L *Gallicus* (*Gallus* Gaul), -ic]

Gall'ican, a. & n. Of the ancient church of Gaul or France; (adherent) of the school of French Roman Catholics following Bossuet & claiming partial autonomy (opp. ULTRAMONTANE), whence **gall'ican-ism**(3), **gall'icanist**(2), nn. [f. L *Galli-canus* (prec., -AN]

gall'icé (-sè), adv. In French (used in giving F for English phrase etc.). [L, = in Gaulish]

galligas'kins (z), n. pl. (joc.). Breeches, trousers. (orig. wide hose of 16th & 17th cc., f. F *garguesque* for *greguesque* Greek f. It. *grechesca* fem. of *grechesco* Greek (-ESQUE]

gallimau'fry, n. Heterogeneous mixture, jumble, medley. [f. F *galimafrée* etym. dub.]

gallina'ceous (-shus), a. Of the order *Gallinae* including domestic poultry, pheasants, partridges, etc. So ~A'CEAN (-àshan) a.& n. [f. L *gallinaceus (gallina* hen, -ACEOUS]

gallina'zo (-ah-), n. (pl. ~*s*). An American vulture, the Turkey buzzard. [f. Sp. *gallinaza* (L *gallina* hen, *-aza* augment.]

Gallin'ule, n. Person, esp. official, refusing to meddle outside his province. [*Led's* xviii] *gall'iot* (-y-), n. Dutch cargo-boat or fishing-vessel; small (usu. Mediterranean) galley. [f. F *galiote* dim. of OF *galie* GALLEY]

Gallip'oli, n. ~ (*oil*), superior olive-oil [seaport in S. Italy]

gall'ipot, n. Small earthen glazed pot used for ointments etc. [prob. f. GALLEY, as brought in galleys from the Mediterranean]

gall'ium, n. Soft bluish-white metal. [f. L *gallus* cock, transl. of *Lecoq* de Bois-baudran the discoverer 1875, +-IUM]

gall'ivant', v.i. Gad about (usu. in part. or v.bl.n.). [perh. perversion of *gallant* v.l.]

Gallo-, comb. form = French-, as ~-*Briton*, ~-*German*. Hence ~*MAN'IA* n., ~*MAN'IAC* aa. & n., GALL'OPHIL, GALL'OPHOBE, nn. & aa., ~*PHOB'IA* n. [*Gallus* GAUL, -o-]

gall'on, n. A measure of capacity (|| *imperial* ~, 277¼ cubic inches; *wine* ~, 231) for liquids or corn etc. [f. ONF *galon* cf. F *jade* bowl]

gall'oon', n. Narrow close-woven braid for binding dresses etc., of gold, silver, silk, or cotton. [f. F *galon*, f. 12th-c. *galonner* tie the hair with bands, perh. cogn. w. *gallant*]

gall'op, n., & v.i. & t. 1. Horse's or other quadruped's fastest pace, with all feet off ground together in each stride (*full* ~, *at a* ~, going thus); a ride at this pace. 2. vb. (Go at a ~ (of horse, or with its rider as subj., or of other quadruped); make (horse etc.) ~; read, recite, talk, fast (often *through*, *over*); move or progress rapidly (*in a* ~*ing consumption*, dub. [f. F *galop(er)* prob. earlier *walop(er)* etym. dub.]

gal'lopade', n. Lively, orig. Hungarian, dance. [F, see GALOP, ADE(1)]

gall'oper, n. In vbl senses: esp., || (Mil.) aide-de-camp, light field gun. [-ER¹]

Gallophil etc. See GALLO-.

Gall'oviʹdian, a. & n. (Native) of Gallo-way. [f. med. L *Galloviidia* +-AN]

gall'oway (-o-), n. Horse of small strong breed from Galloway, SW. Scotland; small-sized horse; one of a breed of cattle peculiar to Galloway. [district]

gall'ows (-oz), n. pl. (usu. treated as sing.). Structure, usu. of two uprights & cross-piece, on which criminals are hanged; punishment of hanging (a ~ *look*, *have the* ~ *in one's face*, of sinister appearance); similar structure used for cookery, gymnastics, etc.; ~*bird*, person fit to be hanged; ~*ripe*, fit to be hanged. [f. OE *galga* cf. G *galgen*]

*Gall'up poll, n. Test of how representa-tive sample of public is to vote, esp. as basis of forecast. [G. H. *Gallup* (b.1901)]

galoot', n. (colloq.). Clumsy lout. [?]

gal'op, n., & v.i. 1. Lively dance in 2-4 time. 2. Dance a ~. [vb f. n., F, see GALLOP]

galore', adv. & n. (In) abundance (*with beef & ale* ~; ~ *of alcohol*; *also in* ~). [f. Ir. *go leór* to sufficiency]

galosh', **gol-**, n. Over-shoe usu. of rubber to keep shoes clean or dry; piece of

leather etc. round lower part of boot or shoe uppers, whence ~ED² (-sht) a. [f. F *galoche* perh. ult. f. Gk *kalopous* boot-last (*kāla* pl. logs, *pous* foot)]

galumph', v.i. Go prancing in triumph. [made by L. Carroll perh. on *gallop, triumph*]

galvān'ic, a. 1. hist. Of, produced by, as of, electricity (~*ic battery, pile,* former names for types of primary battery; ~*ic electricity,* electricity from a primary battery). 2. fig. (Of smile, movement, etc.) sudden & forced. Hence ~ICALLY adv. [foll., -IC]

gal'vanĭsm, n. (hist.). Electricity from a primary battery; the use of this or other direct-current electricity for medical purposes. Hence ~IST(3) n. [f. F *galvanisme* (L. *Galvani* discoverer 1792, -ISM)]

gal'vanĭze, v.t. Stimulate by or as by electricity (also fig., ~*e into life,* rouse by shock or excitement); coat with metal by electrolysis; coat (iron) with zinc (usu. without the use of electricity) to protect it from rust. Hence ~A'TION, ~ER¹, nn. [f. F *galvaniser* (prec., -IZE)]

gal'vano-, comb. form of GALVANIC, GALVANISM, as ~*graphy* (-ŏg-), method of producing copperplate engravings by ~*plasty,* metal-coating by galvanism; ~*meter* (-ŏm-), instrument for measuring electric currents; ~SCOPE.

Galwē'gian (-jn), a. & n. = GALLOVIDIAN. [f. *Galloway* on anal. of *Norwegian*]

gam'ba, n. (Also ~ *stop*) organ stop with string tone. [earlier=, & short for, VIOLA¹ da gamba]

gambāde', -ād'ō (pl. -ŏs, -oes), n. Horse's leap or bound; *fantastic* movement, freak, escapade. [-*ade* F, readopted (cf. GAMBOL) by Scott; -*ado* f. Sp. *gambada* of same orig.]

gam'bier, n. Astringent extract of oriental plant used in tanning etc. [f. Malay *gambir* the plant]

gam'bĭt, n. Kinds of opening in chess in which player sacrifices pawn or piece to secure certain ends, many ~s having special names as *King's, Queen's, Cunningham's, ~*. [ult. f. It. *gambetto* tripping up (*gamba* leg)]

gam'ble, v.i. & t., & n. 1. Play games of chance for money, esp. for high stakes ~ *away,* lose thus); take great risks to secure great results in war, finance, etc.; hence ~ER¹ n., ~ESOME (-ls-) a. 2. n. ~*ing* (esp. *on the* ~*e*); risky undertaking or attempt. [prob. f. OE *gamenian* to sport (*gamen* GAME¹)]

gambōge' (-ōōzh), n. Gum resin from Cambodian & Siamese trees used as yellow pigment. [f. mod. L *gambogium* f. *Cambodia*]

gam'bol, n., & v.i. (-ll-). Caper, frisk. [f. F *gambade* leap f. It. *gambata* (*gamba* leg)]

game¹, n. 1. Jest (*make ~ of,* ridicule);

diversion, spell of play (*a ~ of ball*). 2. Contest amusing incident (*what a ~-l*). 2. Contest played according to rules & decided by skill, strength, or luck (ROUND, SQUARE, ~; *be on, off,* one's ~, be in, out of, form; *have the ~ in* one's *hands,* be sure to win or able to direct it; *play the ~* lit. & fig., observe the rules, behave honourably; *play a good, poor,* ~, be skilful or not). (Gk & Rom. Ant.; pl. athletic, dramatic, & musical contests, gladiatorial etc. shows; scheme, undertaking, etc., followed up like a ~ (*was playing a deep, double, winning, losing,* etc., ; *the ~ is up,* success now impossible; *so that's your little* ~, *spoilt my* ~; *play* one's ~, advance his schemes unintentionally; *not worth* CANDLE). 3. pl. Dodges, tricks, (*none of your* ~*s!*). 4. Single round in some contests, e.g. whist or tennis (*set & ~,* one ~ scored to each side); (Commerc.) apparatus for a ~; winning score in (~ *and,* short for ~ *set* in tennis); state of ~ (*the ~ is four all, love three,* etc.). 5. Hunted animal, quarry, object of pursuit, (*fair* ~, legitimately to be pursued or attacked; so *forbidden* ~); ~ (collect.) wild animals, birds, etc., hunted for sport or food, flesh of these. 6. Kept flock of swans. 7. ~-*act,* -*law* (usu. pl.), regulating the killing & preservation of ~; ~-*bag,* for holding ~ killed by sportsman; ~ *ball,* state of ~ in tennis etc. at which one point may win; ~-*chicken, -cock, -egg, -fowl,* of kind bred for cockfighting; ~-*keeper,* man employed to ~ prevent poaching, etc.; ~-*licence,* to kill or deal in ~; ~-*preserver,* landowner etc. who breeds ~ & applies ~-*laws strictly; ~-tenant,* lessee of shooting or fishing. [com.-Teut.; OE *gamen* cf. OHG *gaman* joy]

game², a. Like a game-cock, spirited, (DIE³ ~); having the spirit to do, for. Hence ~LY² (-mĭ-) adv., ~'NESS (-mn-) n. [f. GAME¹-cock]

game³, v.i. & t. Play at games of chance for money, gamble; throw *away* in gambling; *gaming-house, -table,* frequented for gambling. Hence ~'STER (-ms-) n. [f. GAME¹]

game⁴, a. (Of leg, arm, etc.) lame, crippled. [?]

game'some (-ms-), a. Sportive. Hence ~LY² adv., ~NESS n. [-SOME]

gamēte', n. (biol.). Sexual protoplasmic body, which unites with another for reproduction. [f. Gk *gametē* wife, *gametēs* husband, (*gameō* marry)]

gamin, (see Ap.), n. Street Arab, neglected boy. [F]

gam'ma, n. Third letter (Γ, γ, = G) of Greek alphabet, used sometimes in enumerations to supplement 3 & c; kind of moth; ~ *rays,* X-rays of very short wave-length emitted by radio-active substances. [Gk]

gammā'dion, n. = FYLFOT. [late Gk, dim. of prec., fylfot consisting of four gammas (Γ)]

gammer, n. (Rustic name for) old woman. [f. *godmother* or *grandmother*, cf. GAFFER]

gammon¹, n., & v.t. 1. Bottom piece of flitch of bacon including hind leg (usu. ~ *of bacon*); smoked or cured ham; ~ *& spinach* (as dish &, with pun on *gammon³*; = humbug). 2. v.t. Cure (bacon). [f. ONF *gambon* (*gambe* leg, -OON)]

gammon², n. & v.t. 1. Kind of victory scoring two games at backgammon. 2. v.t. Defeat (adversary) thus. [perh.=ME *gamen* GAME¹]

gammon³, n., int., & v.i.&t. 1. Humbug, deception; (int.) nonsense! 2. v.i. Talk plausibly; feign (intr.); hoax, deceive. [perh. as prec.]

gamp, n. (colloq.). Umbrella, esp. large untidy one. [f. Mrs. G~ in *Martin Chuzzlewit*]

gamut, n. 1. hist. Lowest note in medieval scale = modern G on lowest line of bass stave; the Great Scale consisting of all notes used in medieval music (G as above the E in highest space of treble). 2. mod. Whole series of recognized notes; major diatonic scale; people's or period's recognized scale; voice's or instrument's compass; whole range or scope of anything (*the whole ~ of crime; run up & down the ~*). [f. med. L *gamma ut* (GAMMA taken as name for note one tone lower than A of classical scale+*ut* first of six arbitrary names of notes forming hexachord, being the italicized syllables of a Sapphic stanza, *Ut queant laxis resonare fibris Mira gestorum famuli tuorum, Solve polluti labii reatum, Sancte Johannes*)]

gamy, a. Abounding in game; = GAME² (rare); having flavour or scent of game kept till it is high. [-Y²]

gan, see GIN.

gander, n. Male goose (*sauce for the goose is sauce for the ~*, used in retorting an argument etc. on its first user); fool, simpleton. [OE *gan(d)ra*, -d- being prob. euphonic as in THUNDER, cf. Du. *gander*; perh. f. same st. as GOOSE, perh. orig. the f. name of another bird]

gang, n., & v.i. 1. Company of workpeople, or of slaves or prisoners; band of persons acting or going about together, esp. for criminal purpose or one disapproved by speaker (*v.i., join up, act in concert, with*); set of tools etc. arranged to work simultaneously; ~*-board*, plank usu. with cleats nailed on it for walking into or out of boat. 2. v.i. (Sc.). Go; ~ *one's ain gait* (of plan etc.) go awry; ~ *one's ain gait*, take one's own course. [earlier senses *mode of going, way*, cf. G *gang*, f. OE *gang*, & obs. & Sc. vb *gang* walk, go, f. OE *gangan*, also OHG]

gang'er, n. Foreman of gang. [-ER¹]

Gangĕt'ic, a. Of the Ganges. [f. L *Gangeticus* (L f. Gk *Gangēs*, -IC)]

gang'lion (-ngg-), n. (pl. -lia), Enlargement or knot on nerve, from which nervefibres radiate; mass of grey matter in central nervous system forming a nervenucleus (~*-on-cell*, -*corpuscule*, -*globule*, nerve-cell in this); (fig.) centre of force, activity, or interest. Hence ~**āted**, ~**ōnāted**, [-ATE³ -ED¹], ~**FORM**, ~**ōn'IC**, aa. [f. Gk *gagglion*]

gang'rēne, n., & v.t. & i. 1. Necrosis, usu. with decomposition, of part of the body (often fig.); hence **gang'renous** a. 2. vb. Become affected, affect, with mortification. [f. L f. Gk *gaggraina*]

*****gang'ster**, n. Member of a gang of violent criminals or roughs. [-STER]

gangue (gang), n. Earth etc., matrix, in which ore is found. [F, f. G *gang* lode = GANG]

gang'way, n. & int. Passage esp. between rows of seats (ǁ in House of Commons, cross-passage half-way down giving access to back benches; members *above, below*, ~ are more, less, closely associated with official policy of their party); passage etc. on ship, esp. platform connecting quarterdeck & forecastle; opening in bulwarks by which ship is entered or left, bridge laid across from this to shore etc.; (int.) make way, please! [OE *gangweg* (GANG, WAY)]

gan'net, n. A sea-bird, the solan (~*goose*). [OE *ganot* cogn. w. Du. *gent* GANDER]

gan'oid, a. & n. (Of fish-scale) enamelled, smooth & bright; (fish) having ~ scales. [f. F *ganoïde* f. Gk *ganos* brightness +-OID]

gan'try, **gaun'**, n. Four-footed wooden stand for barrels; structure supporting travelling crane; railway signals, etc. [perh. f. obs. *gawn* contr. of GALLON +*tree*, or f. OF *gauntier* var. of *chantier*]

Gan'ymēde, n. (Joc.) waiter, potboy; (Astron.) largest satellite of Jupiter. [f. L f. Gk *Ganumēdēs* cupbearer of Zeus]

gaol (jāl), **jail**, n., & v.t. (g- in official, g- & j- indifferently in literary use, j- in U.S.). 1. Public prison for detention of persons committed by process of law, (without article) confinement in this; ~*-bird*, prisoner, habitual criminal, rogue;

~*delivery*, clearing of ~ esp. at assizes by trying all prisoners awaiting trial; ~*fever*, virulent typhus formerly endemic in ~s. 2. v.t. Put in ~. [f. ONF *gaiole*, OF *jeiole*, (now *geôle*) f. Rom. dim. of L caveA CAGE]

gaol'er (jāl), **jail'er**, **jail'or**, n. (see prec.). Man in charge of gaol or prisoners in it. Hence ~NESS¹ n. [as prec.+-ER²(2)]

gāp, n. Breach in hedge or wall; gorge, pass; unfilled space or interval, blank, break in continuity, (*stop*, *fill*, *supply*, *a* ~, make up deficiency); wide divergence in views, sympathies, etc. Hence ~PED²(-pt), ~PY², aa. [ON, = chasm, cogn. w. foll.]

gāpe, v.i., & n. 1. Open mouth wide, (of mouth, oysters, wounds, chasm, etc.) open or be open wide, split, part asunder; stare, gaze curiously; *at*; yawn. 2. n. Yawn; open-mouthed stare; *the* ~s, poultry disease with gaping as symptom, (joc.) fit of yawning; expanse of open mouth or break, part of beak that opens; rent, opening; ~*seed* (joc.), staring, occasion for staring, thing stared at. [f. ON *gapa* vb cf. G *gaffen*]

gāp'er, n. In vbl senses; esp. kinds of bird, kind of mollusc. [-ER¹]

gā'rage (or garahzh'), n., & v.t. 1. Building or shed for storing or repair of horseless vehicles, esp. motor-cars. 2. v.t. Put (motor-car) in ~. [F (*garer* shunt f. Teut., cf. OE *werian* defend, -AGE)]

gârb, n., & v.t. 1. Dress, costume, esp. of distinctive kind, way one is dressed. 2. v.t. Attire, put (esp. distinctive) clothes upon (person; usu. pass. or refl.). [f. It. *garbo* elegance, f. Teut. cf. OHG *garawī* preparation cogn. w. GEAR]

gârb'age, n. Offal used for food, refuse, filth; foul or worthless reading. [perh. f. OF *garbe* sheaf, bundle, +-AGE]

gârb'le, v.t. Select best in, take pick of (rare); make (usu. unfair or malicious) selections from (facts, statements, etc.), mutilate in order to misrepresent. [f. It. *garbellare* f. Arab. *gharbala* sift cf. *kirbal* sieve]

gârb'oard (-berd), n. (Also ~ *strake*) first range of planks laid on ship's bottom next keel; corresponding plates in iron ship. [f. Du. *gaarboord* (GATHER, BOARD)]

gârçon (see Ap.), n. Waiter in French hotel etc. [F]

gârd'en, n., & v.i. 1. Piece of ground devoted to growing flowers, fruit, or vegetables (KITCHEN, || MARKET, ~); (pl.) ornamental grounds for public resort (usu. *botanical*, *zoological*, etc., ~s); specially fertile region (*the* ~ *of England*, Kent, Worcestershire, etc.); || (pl. with name prefixed as *Onslow*, *Spring*, *G~s*) set of houses in these in street, square, etc.; *the G~*, philosophy or school of Epicurus (cf. PORCH, ACADEMY); (attrib.; with or without hyphen) cultivated, not wild, (~

plants, ~*cress*:*common or* ~, sl., ordinary, living in ~s (~*spider*; ~*white*, kind of butterfly; ~*warbler*, kind of bird); = *city*, industrial or other town laid out systematically with a view to spacious and attractive surroundings; || so ~*suburb*; ~*engine*, portable force-pump for watering; ~*frame*, forcing-frame for plants; ~*glass*, bell-glass for covering plant; ~*party*, social meeting on lawn or in ~; ~*plot*, piece of ground used as ~; ~*seat*, bench etc. for use in ~, || similar seat for one or two on top of omnibus; ||~*stuff*, vegetables & fruit; (sl.) *lead up the* ~ (*path*), entice, mislead; hence ~ED²(-nd), ~ESQUE', aa., ~ING¹(1) n. 2. v.i. Cultivate a ~. [f. ONF *gardin* ult. f. Teut., cf. G *garten*, also GARTH, YARD]

gârd'ener, n. Person who gardens, esp. servant employed to tend a garden. [as prec.+-ER²(2), cf. F *jardinier*]

gârdēn'ia, n. Genus of trees & shrubs with large white or yellow flowers & usu. fragrant scent. [mod. L (Dr. A. *Garden* d. 1791, -IA²)]

Gârd'ner (gün), n. Early type of machine gun with several barrels, invented by Capt. M. W. Gardner.

gâre'fowl (-rf-), n. The great auk. [f. ON *geirfugl* (*geir* of doubtful meaning)]

gâr'fish, n. Fish with long spearlike snout & green bones. [perh. f. OE *gār* spear cogn. w. Gk *gaison*]

gârgan'tuan, a. Enormous, gigantic. [*Gargantua* giant in Rabelais+-AN]

gârg'et (-g-), n. Inflamed state of head or throat in cattle, pigs, or poultry; inflammation of cow's or ewe's udder. [perh. f. obs. *garget* throat f. OF *gargate* etym. dub.]

gârg'le, v.t. & i., & n. 1. Wash (throat), wash throat, with liquid kept in motion by breath. 2. n. Liquid used thus. [f. F *gargouiller* (foll.)]

gârg'oyle, gûr-, n. Grotesque spout usu. with human or animal mouth, head, or body, projecting from gutter of (esp. Gothic) building to carry water clear of wall. [f. OF *gargouille* throat, gargoyle]

gâribâl'di, n. Kind of woman's or child's blouse, orig. of bright red; || biscuit containing currants. [f. red shirts of *G~* (Italian patriot 1807–82) & his followers]

gâr'ish, a. ⊕brusively bright, showy, gaudy, over-decorated. Hence ~LY² adv., ~NESS n. [perh. f. obs. *gaure* to stare, etym. dub.]

gârl'and, n., & v.t. 1. Wreath of flowers, leaves, etc., worn on head or hung on something as decoration; distinction, palm, prize, for victory etc.; (arch.) anthology; miscellany; metal etc. imitation of ~. 2. v.t. Crown with ~, deck with ~s, serve as ~ to. [OF (-*e*), etym. dub.]

gârl'ic, n. Plant with bulbous strong-smelling pungent-tasting root used as

flavouring in cookery. Hence (esp. of smell) ~ky² a. [OE gārlēac, LEEK]

gärment, n. Article of dress, esp. gown or cloak, (pl.) clothes; outward and visible covering of anything; (vb. usu. in p.p.) attire. [f. OF garnement (GARNISH -MENT)]

gär'ner, n., & v.t. (poet. & rhet.). 1. Store-house for corn, granary, (also fig.). 2. v.t. Store, deposit, collect. [f. OF gernier f. L granarium GRANARY]

gär'net, n. Vitreous mineral, of which a deep transparent red kind is used as gem. [f. OF grenat f. med. L granatum POMEGRANATE (from resemblance to its seeds)]

gär'nish, v.t. & n. 1. Decorate, embellish, (esp. dish for table); (Law) serve notice on (person, called ~EE n.) for purpose of attaching money belonging to debtor, summon (person) as party to litigation started between others; hence ~ER, ~MENT, nn. 2. n. (Also ~ING² n.) things used to decorate dish for table (also fig. of literary embellishments). [f. OF garnir (-ISH²) fortify, prob. f. Teut. cogn. w. WARN]

gär'niture, n. Appurtenances, accessories; adornment, trimming esp. of dish; costume. [F (GARNISH, -URE)]

garotte. See GARROTTE.

gä'rret, n. Room on top floor, room partly or entirely in roof, attic; (sl.) head (be wrong in the ~, have one's ~ unfurnished etc.). [f. OF garite watch-tower (garir defend, f. Teut. cf. OE werian defend)]

gă'rret, v.t. (archit.), Insert small pieces of stone in joints of (coarse masonry). [?]

garrēteer', n. Dweller in garret, esp. poor literary hack. [-EER]

gä'rrison, n., & v.t. 1. Troops stationed in fortress, town, etc., to defend it (~ town, having ~). 2. v.t. Furnish with, occupy as, ~; place (troops, soldier) on ~ duty. [f. OF garison (garir see GARRET¹, -SON) defence, w. sense of F & obs. E garrison (GARNISH)]

gă'rron, n. Small inferior horse bred in Scotland & Ireland. [f. Gael. gearran]

gă'rrot, n. Kind of sea duck. [F]

gar'rŏtte, n., & v.t. 1. Spanish method of capital punishment by strangulation, apparatus used in it; highway robbery performed by throttling victim. 2. v.t. Execute by strangulation; throttle in order to rob, whence ~'ER¹ n. [f. Sp. garrote(ar), the n. (etym. dub.) meaning stick (used in twisting cord tight)]

gă'rrulous (-rŏo-), a. Given to talk, chattering, wordy; (of bird, stream, etc.) babbling. Hence or cogn. garrŭl'ity (-rŏo-), ~NESS, nn., ~LY² adv. [f. L garrulus (garrire chatter) +-OUS]

gar'ter, n., & v.t. 1. Band worn above or below knee to keep stocking up; ||the G~, (badge of) highest order of English knighthood, membership of this; (G~)= G~ King of Arms. 2. v.t. Fasten (stocking), encircle (leg), with ~. [f. OF gartier (garet, now jarret, bend of knee, perh. f. Celt., cf. Breton gar, W găr, leg-bone)]

|| **gārth**, n. (arch. & dial.). Close, yard, garden, paddock, open space within cloisters. [f. ON garthr=OE geard YARD¹]

gås, n. (pl. gåses), & v.t. & i. (-ss-). 1. Any aeriform or completely elastic fluid (used chiefly of those that do not become liquid or solid at ordinary temperatures, other ~es being usu. called vapours; such fluid, esp. COAL~ or various mixtures with carburetted hydrogen, used for lighting or heating: *(colloq.) petrol, gasoline, (step on the ~, accelerate motor engine by pressing down accelerator pedal with foot, also fig.); (Mining) explosive mixture of firedamp with air; hydrogen etc. used to fill balloon; nitrous oxide~ as anaesthetic (often laughing-~); (also poison-~) kinds used to asphyxiate enemy in war; jet of ~ used for lighting, empty talk, boasting, humbug, windbag eloquence. 2. ~-bag, bag for holding ~ (derog.) empty talker, airship's ~-container; ~-bracket, pipe with burner(s) projecting from wall; ~-coal, bituminous from which ~ can be made; ~-coke, residuum of coal when ~ has been made from it; ~-engine, ~-motor, with power obtained by production or rhythmical combustion and explosion of ~ in closed cylinder; ~-fitter, tradesman or workman providing house with ~-fittings, apparatus for heating or lighting with ~; ~-helmet, ~-mask, kinds of defence including respirator worn as appliance against poison-~; ~-light, light given by esp. coal-~; jet of burning ~ (~-light paper, plates, photographic materials that can be developed in weak artificial light); ~-main, main pipe supplying ~; ~-man, manufacturer of ~, collector of sums due for ~-supply; ~-mask (as ~-helmet); ~-meter, apparatus registering amount of ~ consumed; ~-oven (heated by ~; frequently used as a means of suicide); ~-ring, perforated with small holes & fed with ~ for cooking etc.; ~-shell (charged with poison-~, usu. in liquid form); ~-tar, COAL-tar produced in making ~; ~-works, manufactory of ~; hence gås'ēous a., gåsē'ity n., ~i-FORM, ~'LESS, aa., ~'ÏFY v.t., ~i-FICA'TION n. 3. vb. Supply (room, railway-carriage, etc.) with ~; project poison-~ upon (enemy, place), (pass.) be poisoned with ~; pass (thread, lace) through ~-flame to remove loose fibres; talk emptily or boastfully whence ~s'ER¹ n. [wd invented by Van Helmont on Gk khaos CHAOS]

Gås'con, n. Native of Gascony; braggart. [F]

gasconade', n., & v.i. Boast(ing). [f. F *gasconnade* (prec., -ADE)]

gaselier', n. Gas-lamp, usn. suspended from ceiling, with several burners often on branches. [f. GAS after CHANDELIER]

gash, n., & v.t. 1. Long & deep slash, cut, or wound; cleft such as might be made by slashing cut; act of making such cut. 2. v.t. Make ~ in, cut. [earlier *garse* v. & n. f. OF *garser* perh. f. LL *carixare* f. Gk *kharassō* incise]

gas'ket, n. Small cord for securing furled sail to yard; strip of tow etc. for packing piston or caulking joint. [?]

gasogene. See GAZOGENE.

gas'oline, -ine (-ēn), n. Volatile inflammable liquid got in distilling petroleum & used for heating & lighting; *petrol. [GAS, -OL, -ENE, -INE¹]

gasom'eter, n. (Chem.) vessel for holding gas; large reservoir in which gas is stored for distribution by pipes. [f. F *gazomètre* (*gaz* GAS, *mètre* f. Gk *metron* measure)]

gasp (gahsp), v.i. & t., & n. 1. Catch breath, strain for air or breath, with open mouth as in exhaustion or astonishment; ~ *life* etc. *away* or *out*, expire; ~ *out*, utter with ~s; hence ~ingly² adv.; ~'ER¹ n., (esp., sl.) || cheap cigarette. 2. n. Convulsive catching of breath (*at one's last~*, at point of death). [f. ON *geispa* to yawn cf. *geip* idle talk]

gass'ly, a. Of, full of, like, gas; (of talk etc.) empty, verbose. Hence ~INESS n. [-Y¹]

gas't(e)ropŏd, n. Mollusc (e.g. snail) with locomotive organ placed ventrally. So **gasterŏp'odous** a. [GASTRO-, Gk *pous podos* foot]

gastrae'a, n. (Assumed) primitive sac-like animal consisting of two layers (ectoderm & endoderm) of cells. [mod. L (GASTRO-)]

gas'tric, a. Of the stomach (~ *fever*, enteric; ~ *juice*, thin clear acid nearly colourless fluid secreted by stomach glands & effecting digestion). [f. Gk as foll. +-IC]

gastr(o)-, comb. form of Gk *gastēr -tros* stomach, as *gastro-enÆric*, of stomach & intestines, *gås'trocæle*, *gastrŏt'omy*, *gastri'tis*.

gastrŏl'ogў, n. Science of cookery. So ~ŏL'OGER, ~ŏL'OGIST, nn. [f. Gk *gastrologia* (prec. -LOGY)]

gas'tronŏme, n; Judge of cookery. [F, back formation f. *gastronomie* see foll.]

gastrŏn'omŷ, n. Art & science of good eating. So ~ER¹ n., **gåstronŏm'ic(AL)**, aa., **gåstronŏm'ically** adv., ~IST(3) n. [f. F *gastronomie* f. Gk GASTRonomia on anal. of *astronomia* ASTRONOMY]

gāte¹, n., & v.t. 1. Opening in wall of city or enclosure made for entrance & exit & capable of being closed with barrier; (Bibl.) place of judicial assembly in city; mountain pass; means of entrance or exit (~ *of ivory, horn*, by which false, true, dreams come; *Bosphorus & Hellespont are the two ~s of Constantinople*; barrier closing the opening of a wall, wooden or iron framework, solid or of bars or gratings, hung on hinges, turning on pivots, or sliding, single or double; contrivance regulating passage of water; number entering by payment at ~s to see football match etc., amount of money thus taken (also ~-*money*). 2. ||~*bill* (Oxf. & Camb.), record of undergraduate's returns to college after hours, fines imposed for these; ~*crasher* sl. (also *crasher*) uninvited intruder at ball etc., so ~-*crash* v.i. & t.; ~*house*, lodge of park etc., room over city ~ often used as prison; ~*keeper*, attendant at ~; ||kind of butterfly; ~-*legged table* (with legs in ~ like frame swinging back to allow top to fold down); ~-*meeting*, at which money is hung or against which it shuts ~ (*between you & me & the ~-post*, or *bed-post*, in close confidence); ~'*way*, = ~LESS (-tl-) a. 3. v.t. (Oxf. & Camb.). ||Confine to college entirely or after certain hours. [OE *geat* = OFris. *gat, jet, hole*]

gāte², n. (With prefixed name in North etc.) street. [f. ON *gata* cf. G *gasse* lane]

gäth'er (-dh-), v.t. & i. Bring together, cause to assemble, (*be ~ed to one's fathers*, die); acquire by collecting, amass; cull, pluck; collect (grain etc.) as harvest; receive addition of (*rolling stone ~s no moss*, change of calling does not pay; *complexion ~s colour*; *invalid ~s strength*; ~ *head*, acquire strength, swell as a festering sore; ~ *way*, begin to move, of ship); summon (energies), gain or recover (breath); infer, deduce, (*that*); draw (garment, brow) together in folds or wrinkles, esp. pucker (part of dress) by running thread through; pick *up* from ground; draw *up* (limbs, person) into smaller compass; sum *up* (scattered facts); summon *up* (thoughts, strength, etc.) for an effort; come together, congregate, form a mass; receive additions (*the tale ~ed like a snowball*); come to a head, develop purulent swelling. [OE *gaderian*, cf. Du. *gaderen* gather & OE *geador* together]

gäth'ering (-dh-), n. In vbl senses: esp.: purulent swelling; assembly, meeting; ~-*coal*, large piece to keep fire in. [-ING²]

gäth'ers (-dherz), n. pl. Part of dress that is gathered or drawn in. [f. GATHER]

Gät'ling, n. (Also ~ *gun*) machine gun with clustered barrels. [inventor's name]

gauche (gōsh), a. Tactless, without ease or grace, socially awkward. [F]

gaucherie (gōsherē'), n. Gauche manners, a gauche action. [F]

gauch'o (gow-, gaw-), n. (pl. -os). One of a mixed European & Amer.-Ind. race of mounted herdsmen. [Sp., prob. f. native S.-Amer. lang.]

gaud, n. Something gaudy, showy orna-ment, gewgaw; (pl.) showy ceremonies, galeties. [f. OF *gaudir* make merry f. L *gaudēre* rejoice]

ǁgaud'y², n. Grand entertainment, esp. annual college dinner to old members etc.; ~-day, day of rejoicing, day on which college ~ is held. [f. L *gaudium* joy]

gaud'y¹, a. Tastelessly or inappropriately fine, showy, or brilliant (of dress, deco-ration, literary style, etc.). Hence ~ILY² adv., ~INESS n. [earliest sense *luxurious*, f. GAUD +-Y¹]

gaufre. See GOFER.

gauffer. See GOFFER.

gauge¹ (gāj), gage² (in naut. sense), n. 1. Standard measure to which things must conform, esp. measure of capacity or contents of barrel, diameter of bullet, or thickness of sheet iron; capacity, extent, scope, (*take the ~ of*, estimate); distance between pair of rails (*broad, narrow, ~*, or more, less, than 4 ft. 8½ in., *standard ~*, of ...); instrument measuring force or quantity of rainfall, stream, tide, wind, etc.; contrivance attached to vessel to show height of its contents; instrument for testing and verifying dimensions of tools, wire, etc.; adjustable carpenter's tool for marking parallel lines; (Print.) strip regulating depth of margin etc.; means of estimating, criterion, test. 2. (Naut.; gage) relative position in respect to wind (*have the weather ~ of*, be to windward of, fig. have advantage of; also rarely *lee, southerly*, etc., ~). 3. Graduated instrument measuring force or ... [ONF. etym. dub.]

gauge², v.t. Measure exactly (esp. objects of standard size, as wire, bolts; fluctuating quantities or forces, as rain-fall, wind; depth of liquid content); find capacity or content of (cask etc.) by measurement & calculation (*gauging-rod*, exciseman's instrument for this); esti-mate, take measure of, (person, charac-ter); make uniform, bring to standard size or shape. Hence ~ABLE a., gau'gER¹ (1, 2) n., (gēj-) n. [f. ONF *gouger* etym. dub.]

Gaul, n. Inhabitant of ancient Gaul; (joc.) Frenchman. [f. *Gaul* the country f. F *Gaule* f. L *Gallia* (*Gallus* a Gaul)]

Gaul'ish, a. & n. (Language) of ancient Gauls; (joc.) French (adj.). [prec.+-ISH¹]

Gauleiter (gow'līter), n. Nazi district political leader. [G]

gault, n. (geol.). Series of clay and marl beds between upper & lower greensand. [?]

gaunt, a. Lean, haggard; grim or desolate looking. Hence ~NESS n. [etym. dub.;

from 1440; cf. Norw. *gand* thin stick or man]

gaunt'let¹, n. (Hist.) armoured glove; (*fling, throw, down the ~*, issue challenge; *pick, take, up the ~*, accept challenge; stout glove with long wrist for driving, fencing, wicket-keeping, etc. Hence ~ED² a. [f. F *gantelet* (*gant* glove f. OSw. *vante*, -LET)]

gaunt'let², ²gänt', n. *Run the ~*, pass between rows of men who strike one with sticks, cords, etc., as military, naval, or school punishment (also fig. of being sub-jected to criticism). [earlier *gantlope* f. Sw. *gatlopp* (GATE² *lopp* course, cf. G *gassenlaufen*) w. assim. to prec.]

gaur (gowr), n. The Indian wild ox. [Hind.]

gauss (gows), n. Unit of intensity of a magnetic field. Hence ~AGH n. [after Karl G~, German mathematician (d. 1855)]

gauze, n. Thin transparent fabric of silk, cotton, wire, etc.; slight haze. Hence ~Y² a., ~INESS n. [f. F *gaze* etym. dub.]

gave. See GIVE.

ǁgav'el, n. Auctioneer's or chairman's or judge's hammer. [?]

gavelkind, n. (legal). Land-tenure, es-pecially in Kent, involving equal division of intestate's property among all his sons. [f. obs. *gavel*, OE *gafol*, tribute, cf. med.]

gavotte, n. Slow dance of 18th c.; music for it; piece of music in common time, each phrase beginning on third beat of bar. [F f. Pr. *gavoto* (*Gavot* native of Alps)]

gawk, n. Awkward or bashful person. [?]

gawk'y, a. & n. Awkward, ungainly, bashful, (person). Hence ~INESS n. [perh. ...

gay, a. (~-er, ~-est). Full of or disposed to or indicating mirth, light-hearted, sportive; airy, off-hand; *(sl.) cheeky, imperti-nent; (euphem.) dissolute, immoral, liv-ing by prostitution; showy, brilliant, bright-coloured, finely dressed, (*with*). Hence gaï'ly² adv. [f. F *gai* perh. f. OHG *gāhi* pretty]

gaze, v.i. & n. 1. Look fixedly (*at, on, upon*); hence gāz'ER¹ n. 2. n. Intent look (*stand at ~*, looking thus). [?]

gaze'bo, n. Structure whence a view may be had, belvedere, lantern, turret, bal-cony, etc. [perh. joc. formation f. prec. on L future (cf. LAVABO), or f. some Orien-tal word]

gazelle, n. Small graceful soft-eyed kinds of antelope. [F. f. Arab. *ghazal*]

gazette, n. & v.t. 1. (Hist.) news-sheet, periodical publication giving current events; (one of three official journals (*London, Edinburgh, Belfast, G~*) issued by authority twice a week with lists of government appointments & bankrupts

& other public notices; (in newspaper titles as *Birmingham, Shields, G~*) newspaper. **2.** v.t. ||Publish in newspaper. (esp. in pass. of officials so announced). [F, f. It. *gazetta* perh. f. Venetian small coin so called]

gazetteer', n. Geographical dictionary. [so called as first provided for gazette-writers, earlier sense of ~]

gaz'ogène, gas-. n. Apparatus for making aerated waters. [f. F *gazogène* (GAS, -GEN)]

gear (gēr), n., & v.t. & i. **1.** Equipment, apparel, etc. (arch.); harness of draught animals; apparatus, appliances, tackle, tools; combination of wheels, levers, etc.; wheels working on one another by teeth etc.; arrangements connecting motor with its work (*in, out of* ~, connected or working, with connexion interrupted or not working; *high, low,* ~, by which driven part of bicycle, motor-car, etc., revolves faster, slower, relatively to driving part; similarly *top, bottom,* ~ of the available extremes), whence ~ING[1](6) (gēr-) n.; rigging; goods, household utensils; ~*box, -case*, enclosing ~ing of bicycle etc.; ~*wheel*, cog-wheel, esp. that in bicycle which transmits motion of pedals to axle; hence ~'LESS (gēr-) a. **2.** vb. Harness (draught animal; often *up*); put (machinery) in ~, provide with ~ (~ *up, down*, provide with high, low, ~); (of cog-wheel) fit exactly *into*, be in ~ *with*. [prob. f. ON *gervi* = OHG *garawī* f. OTeut. *garwi* ready]

gĕck'ō (g-), n. (pl. ~s, ~es). House lizard found in warm climates. [f. Malay *gekoq*, imit. of its cry]

||**gee**[1], **gee-gee**, n. (colloq.). Horse. [orig. child's wd, f. foll.]

gee[2], **gee-hō', gee-(h)ŭp', gee-wō'**, intt. (Words of command to horse etc.) go on, go faster, (occas.) turn to right.

*****gee**[3], int. of asseveration, etc. [abbr. of *Jesus*]

geese. See GOOSE.

geez'er (g-), n. (sl.). Old person, old creature, [var. of north. *guizer* mummer (as GUISE + -ER[1])]

Gĕhĕnn'a (g-), n. Hell; place of burning, torment, or misery. [eccl. L, f. Hellenistic Gk *geenna* f. Heb. *gēhinnom* hell, orig. valley of Hinnom where children were sacrificed]

gei'sha (gā-), n. Japanese dancing-girl. [Jap.]

Geiss'ler (gī-) **tūbe**, n. Sealed tube filled with rarefied gas that becomes incandescent when an electric current is passed through it. [H. *Geissler*, German physicist (d. 1879)]

geist (gī-), n. Intellectuality & sensibility, capacity for or tendency to mental fervour. [G, as GHOST]

gĕl, n. A semi-solid colloidal solution. [first syllable of *gelatin*]

gĕl'atin(e) (also -ēn), n. Amorphous

brittle transparent tasteless slightly yellow substance, basis of the jellies resulting from stewing skin, tendons, ligaments, bone-matrix, etc. (*vegetable* ~, constituent of gluten identical with *animal* ~; *blasting*~, an explosive nitro-glycerine compound; ~ *paper*, coated with sensitized ~ for photography). Hence **gelat'inoform** a., **gelat'imo-** comb. form. [f. F *gélatine* f. It. *gelatina* (*gelata* JELLY, -IN)]

gelat'inous, a. Jelly-like in consistence etc.; of gelatin. So ~IZE(3) v.t. & i., ~OID a. & n. [f. F *gélatineux* (prec., -OUS)]

gela'tion, n. Solidification by freezing. [f. L *gelatio* (*gelare* freeze, -ATION)]

gĕld (g-), v.t. Deprive (usu. male animal) of generative power, castrate, excise testicles or ovaries of. Hence (-)~ER[1] n. [f. ON *gelda*]

gĕl'ding (g-), n. Gelded horse or other animal. [f. ON *gelding* (prec., -ING[3])]

gĕl'id, a. Icy, ice-cold; chilly, cool. [f. L *gelidus* (*gelu* frost) cogn. w. COLD]

gĕl'ignite, n. A nitro-glycerine explosive. [f. GELATINE, L *ignis* fire, -ITE[1](2)]

gĕm, n., & v.t. (-mm-). **1.** Precious stone, esp. when cut and polished; object of great beauty or worth, choicest part of, prized thing; precious or semi-precious stone with engraved design; hence ~m'Y[2] a. **2.** v.t. Adorn (as) with ~s. [f. L *gemma* bud, jewel]

Gem'ara (g-), n. Later part of Talmud, commentary on MISHNA. [Aram., = completion]

gem'inate[1], a. (nat. hist.). Combined in pairs. [f. L *geminare* (*geminus* twin), -ATE[2]]

gem'in|ate[2], v.t. Double, repeat, arrange in pairs. So ~A'TION n. [as prec., -ATE[3]]

Gem'ini, n. & (+) int. Constellation Castor and Pollux or the Twins, third sign of Zodiac, (also as arch. or vulg. int. of surprise, pr. jīminē). [L, = twins]

gemm'a, n. (bot., zool.; pl. -ae). Leaf-bud; (in mosses etc.) small cellular body that separates from mother-plant & starts fresh one; (Zool.) bud-like growth on animal of low organization becoming detached & developing into individual. [L, see GEM]

gemm'ate[1], a. Having buds, reproducing by gemmation. [f. L *gemmatus* (prec., -ATE[2])]

gemm'ate[2], v.i. Put forth buds, propagate by gemmation. [f. L *gemmare* (GEMMA), -ATE[3]]

gemma'tion, n. Act, manner, of budding; arrangement of buds; reproduction by gemmae, formation of new individual by protrusion & separation of part of the parent. So **gemm'ATIVE** a. [F, f, L as prec., -ATION]

gemmif'erous, a. Producing precious stones; bearing buds; = foll. [f. L *gemmifer* (GEMMA, -I-, FEROUS)]

gemmip'arous, a. Of, propagating by, gemmation. Hence ~ly² adv. [GEMMA, -PAROUS (*parere* bring forth)]

gemmol'ogy, n. Science of gems. Hence ~L'OGIST n. [f. L *gemma* GEM, -O-, -LOGY]

gemm'ule, n. [f. L *gemmula*; one of the hypothetical units in Darwin's theory of pangenesis. [F. f. L *gemmula* (GEMMA, -ULE)]

gems'bŏk (gĕmz-), n. Large S.-African antelope with long slender straight horns. [Du.]

‖ gĕn, n. (R.A.F. sl.). Information etc. published for all ranks. [first syllable of *general information*]

-gĕn, suf. forming nn. in scientific use kind, (*gen-*, *gn-*, seeing-*gn-ôma*ι be born, become). (1) in *oxygen* & later chemical formations *-gen* has the sense *that which produces* (hydrogen, nitrogen, cyanogen) (2) in *endogen, exogen*, etc. (bot.) *-gen* = growth (*acrogen, thallogen*).

gĕnäppe', n. Smooth kind of worsted. [f. *Genappe* in Belgium]

gendarme (see Ap.), n. (pl. ~s). 1. Sol-dier, mounted or on foot, employed in police duties esp. in France, 2. (Moun-taineering) rock-tower occupying & blocking arête. [F]

gendarmerie (see Ap.), n. Force of gendarmes. [F]

gĕn'der¹, n. Grammatical classification (or one of the two, or three, classes) of objects roughly corresponding to the two sexes & sexlessness (MASCULINE, FEMININE, & NEUTER; see also COMMON¹, EPICENE), (of nouns & pronouns); property of belong-ing to such class, (of adji.) appropriate form for accompanying a noun of any such class; (joc.) sex. Hence ~LESS a. [f. OF *gen(d)re* f. L GENUS]

gĕn'der², v.t. (poet.). = ENGENDER. [f. OF *gendrer* f. L *generare* (prec.)]

gēne, n. (biol.). One of the factors or elements of which a germ-cell contains a pair transmitted each from one parent. [mod. formation, cf. -GEN]

gĕnéalŏg'ical, a. Of genealogy; tracing family descent; ~ *tree*, table showing descent of family or of animal species in shape of tree with branches. Hence ~ly² adv. [f. F *généalogique* f. med. L f. Gk *genealogikos* (GENEALOGY, -IC) + -AL]

gĕnéalŏg'ize, v.t. & i. Trace genealogy of; draw up genealogies. Hence ~IST(I) n. [foll.]

gĕnéal'ogy, n. Account of descent from ancestor by enumeration of intermediate persons, pedigree; investigation of pedi-grees; plant's or animal's line of develop-ment from earlier forms. [OF *-gie*) f. LL f. Gk *genealogia* (*genea* race, -LOGY)

gĕn'era. See GENUS.

gĕn'eral, a. & n. 1. Completely or approximately universal, including or affecting all or nearly all parts, not

---

partial, particular, local, or sectional, (~ *confession*, to be made by whole con-gregation; G~ *Council*, summoned by invitation to the Church at large; ~ ELECTION; G~ *Post Office*, ‖ head office in London; ~ *post*, first morning delivery, also name of indoor game); prevalent, widespread, usual, (*in a* ~ *way*, ordi-narily); not limited in application, relating to whole class of objects, occasions, etc., true of all or (opp. *universal*) nearly all cases (*as a* ~ *rule*, in most cases), including points common to individuals of a class & neglecting differences (~ *word, term, notion*); not restricted to one department, not special-ized, (‖ ~ *dealer*, trader in many articles; ~ *hospital*, large military hospital receiv-ing sick and wounded from the field cases of all kinds; ‖ ~ *practitioner*, doctor treating cases of all kinds; ‖ ~ *reader*, of miscellaneous litera-ture; ‖ ~ *servant*, maid-of-all-work; ~ *reader*, of miscellaneous litera-ture); roughly corresponding to adequate, sufficient for practical purposes, (~ *resemblance, idea*); vague, indefinite, (*spoke only in* ~ *terms*); (Mil., of officer) above rank of colonel; (appended to titles, as ADJUTANT ~, ATTORNEY ~, POST², *master* ~) chief, head, with unrestricted authority or sphere, (also joc. with other nn., as *lover* ~, one who makes love to all women); *in* ~, generally, in all ordi-nary cases, barring special exceptions, for the most part. 2. n. *The* ~ (arch.), the public; (pl.; now rare) ~ principles, notions, or rules; chief of religious order, e.g. of Jesuits, Dominicans; (Mil.) officer next below Field Marshal (also by cour-tesy of *lieutenant-* & *major-*~); com-mander of army; tactician, strategist, of specified merit (*a good, bad, great,* ~; *no* ~); ‖ = ~ servant above (colloq.). [OF, f. L *generalis* (GENUS, -AL)]

gĕneraliss'imō, n. (pl. ~s). Commander of combined military & naval & air force, or of several armies. [It., superl. of *generale* GENERAL]

gĕneral'ity, n. Being general, applica-bility to whole class of instances; vague-ness; general point, principle, law, or statement; main body, bulk, majority, of. [f. F *généralité* f. L *generalitatem* (GENERAL, -TY)]

gĕneralizā'tion, n. (Forming of) general notion or proposition obtained by in-duction (often used disparagingly, esp. *hasty* ~, one based on too few instances). [foll., -ATION]

gĕn'eralīz|e, v.t. & i. Reduce to general laws, form into a general notion, give a general character to, call by a gen-eral name; infer (law, conclusion) by induction; base general statement upon (facts etc.); (Math., Philos.) throw into general form, extend application of; form general notions by abstrac-tion; (Paint.) render only the typical

499

characteristics of; make vague, use generalities, speak vaguely; bring into general use. Hence ~ER¹ n. [-IZE]

gen'erally, adv. For the most part, extensively; in a general sense, without regard to particulars, not specially, (~ speaking, in general); as a general rule, commonly. [-LY²]

gen'eralship, n. Office of a general; strategy, military skill; skilful management, tact, diplomacy. [-SHIP]

gen'erāte, v.t. Bring into existence, produce, evolve, (plants, animals, etc., usu. in pass.; heat, force, light, friction, electricity, etc.; result, state of things, state of mind, etc.); (Math.; of point, line, surface, conceived as moving) make (line, surface, solid). [f. L generare beget (GENUS) -ATE³]

genera'tion, n. Procreation, propagation of species, begetting or being begotten, (equivocal or SPONTANEOUS ~); production by natural or artificial process; single step in descent or pedigree (have known them for three ~s; his descendant in the tenth ~); whole body of persons born about same time, average time in which children are ready to replace parents (reckoned at ⅓ of a century or at 30 years as a time-measure). [f. L generatio (prec., -ATION)]

gen'erative (-āt-, -ŏt-), a. Of procreation; able to produce, productive. [prec., -ATIVE]

gen'erātor, n. Begetter; apparatus for producing gases, steam, electricity, etc. [L (GENERATE, -OR²)]

genē'ric, a. Characteristic of a genus or class; applied to (any individual of) a large group or class; general, not specific or special. Hence ~ICALLY adv. [f. L GENUS +-IC]

gen'erous, a. Magnanimous, noble-minded, not mean or prejudiced, free in giving, munificent, so gĕneros'ITY n.; (of soil) fertile; ample, abundant, copious; (of diet, colour, wine) rich & full. Hence ~LY² adv. [f. F généreux f. L generosus (GENUS, -OUS) well-born, generous]

gen'esis, n. First book of O.T., with account of the Creation (G~); origin, mode of formation or generation, (also in comb. as abio-~ parthen-o~). [L f. Gk gen- become]

gen'et, n. (Fur of) kind of civet-cat. [f. OF genete f. Arab. jarnait]

genet'ic, a. Of in, concerning, origin; of ~ics. Hence ~ICALLY adv., ~ICS n. pl., the study of heredity & variation, including loosely the physiology of reproduction & the art of breeding. [f. GENESIS on anal. of antithesis -etic]

genē'va¹, n. Spirit distilled from grain & flavoured with juniper berries, Hollands. [f. Du. genever f. OF genevre f. L juniperus JUNIPER w. assim. to foll.]

Genē'va², a. (attrib.), & n. Of from,

Geneva (~ bands, clerical BAND's like those of Swiss Calvinists; ~ Conventions, of 1864–5 neutralizing ambulances etc. in war; ~ cross, red Greek cross on white ground distinguishing ambulances etc. in war; ~ gown, black, worn by Calvinists & low-churchmen in pulpit); (as n., used for) the ~ Conventions, the League of Nations or its proceedings. Hence **Genē'van**, **Genēvēse'**, aa. & nn.

gen'ial¹, a. Nuptial, generative, (~ bed, instinct; rare; conducive to growth, mild, warm, (of air, climate, etc.); cheering, enlivening, jovial, kindly, sociable, whence genial'ITY n., ~IZE(3) v.t.; of genius (rare). Hence ~LY² adv. [f. L geniālis (GENIUS, -AL)]

gen'ial², a. (anat.). Of the chin. [f. Gk geneion chin (genus jaw cf. L gena)+ -AL]

gēnic'ulate, -ātēd, aa. (nat. hist.). Having knee-like joints. [f. L geniculatus (geniculum f. gena knee, -CULE, -ATE³)]

gē'nie, n. (pl. usu. genii, see GENIUS). Jinnee, sprite or goblin of Arabian tales. [f. F génie f. L GENIUS]

gēn'io-, comb. form of Gk geneion chin, as ~hy'oid of chin & hyoid bone.

gēnis'ta, n. Genus of yellow-flowered shrubs (including in some classifications the common broom). [L]

gen'ital, a. & n. (pl.). 1. Of animal generation. 2. n. pl. External organs of generation. [f. L genitālis (gignere genit- beget, -AL)]

gen'itive, a. & n. ~ case or ~, grammatical form of nouns, pronouns, adjectives, & participles, corresponding in inflected languages to of, from, & other prepositions with the noun representing the source, possessor, etc. (~ ABSOLUTE, (Gk construction corresponding to Latin ablative absolute). Hence gĕnitĭv'AL a. [f. L genitīvus (casus case) of generation, mistransl. of Gk genikē (ptōsis case) of class; genitīvus as prec.+-IVE]

gen'ito-, comb. form of GENITAL, as ~urinary of the genital & urinary organs.

gēn'ius, n. (pl. -iuses, -iī). Tutelary spirit of person, place, or institution (good, evil, ~, two opposed spirits or angels working for person's salvation or damnation, also person who powerfully influences one for good or ill); (usu. pl., genii, w. sing. GENIE demon(s), supernatural being(s); nation's, age's, etc., prevalent feeling, opinions, or taste; character, spirit, drift, method, of a language, law, etc.; associations or inspirations of a place; natural ability, special mental endowments; (no pl.) exalted intellectual power, instinctive & extraordinary imaginative, creative, or inventive capacity, (pl. -iuses) person having this; ~ loci (L;16s¹), presiding deity, associations, etc., of the place. [L, in first sense, f. root of gignere beget]

Gěn'ŏa, n. Italian city (~ *cake*, rich with almonds on top). Hence **Gěnŏēse'** (-ēz) a. & n.

genre (see Ap.), n. Kind, style; (also ~-*painting*) portrayal of scenes etc. from ordinary life. [F]

Gěn'rō, n. pl. = Elder Statesmen (see STATESMAN). [Jap., = old men]

gěns (z), n. (Rom. Ant.; pl. *gentēs*). Clan, sept, among Greeks or Romans. [L, = genit. *gentis* (*gignere* beget)]

gěntēel', a. (usu. iron.; vulg. in serious use). Appropriate to, characteristic of, belonging to, the upper classes, stylish, fashionable, well-dressed, elegant. Hence ~LY (-l-li) adv. [16th-c. adoption of *genīt* (cf. 13th-c. GENTLE) see GENTILE] [short for GENTLEMAN]

gěn'tian (-shn, -tian), n. Kinds of usu. blue-flowered plant found esp. in mountain regions; ~*bitter*, tonic extracted from its root. [f. L *gentiāna* (*Gentius* king of Illyria, -AN)]

gěn'tile, a. & n. (Person) not of Jewish race, (in DŎM (-ld-) use) non-Mormon, whence ~ (a. & n. in Gram.) (word) indicating nationality; heathen, pagan. [f. F *gentil* f. L *gentīlis* (GENS, -IL)]

gěntil'ítíal (-shl), a. Of a nation, gens, or family (~ *noun*, *name*, *insignia*). [f. L *gentilítíus* (*gentilis* GENTILE) +-AL]

gěntil'íty, n. Gentle birth, status of gentleman or lady, (now rare); (usu. iron.) being genteel, social superiority, good manners, upper-class habits, (*shabby ~*, endeavour to keep up genteel appearances). [f. OF *gentilité* f. L *gentīlitātem* (GENTILE, -TY)]

gěn'tle, a. (-er, -est), n. & v.t. **1.** Well-born, (Her.) having right to bear arms, (now only in ~ & *simple*, in comb. as ~*folks*, GENTLEMAN); (of birth, blood, family, pursuits, etc.) honourable, belonging to or fit for the class of gentlemen; || (arch.) generous, noble, courteous (still playfully in ~ *reader*, author's apostrophe); tame, quiet, (*the* ~ *craft*, angling); easily managed; not stormy, rough, or violent; (of medicine) mild, not drastic; (of rule etc.) not severe; moderate (a ~ *heat*), gradual (a ~ *slope*); kind, mild, tender, (*the* ~ *sex*, women); ~*folks*), people of good position & family. **2.** n. Maggot, larva of flesh-fly or blue-bottle, used as fishing-bait (f. obs. sense *soft* of adj.); (pl., vulg.) ~*folk*. **3.** v.t. Break in (horse), handle (horse) firmly but gently. [f. OF *gentil* see GENTILE]

gěn'tlehŏŏd (-telh-), n. Position or character attaching to gentle birth. [from 1860: -HOOD]

gěn'tleman (-telm-), n. Man entitled to bear arms but not included in certain professions etc. (arch.); || man of gentle birth attached to household of sovereign or great person (~ *in waiting* etc.; ~-*at-arms*, one of sovereign's bodyguard); man of chivalrous instincts, fine feelings, & good breeding (*the* ~'s *psalm*, Ps. XV); man of good social position, man of wealth & leisure (~ *at* LARGE); (courteous synonym for) man, (pl., in voc.) male members of audience, also in letters = Sirs; || (pl. as sing. n.) men's public urinal; (joc.) *old* ~, the devil, *my* ~, the fellow I was speaking of, ~'s ~, valet; ~-*com-moner* (Hist.), privileged undergraduate at Oxf. & Camb.; || ~ FARMER; ~ *who farms*; || ~ RANKER; ~ *usher*, ~ acting as usher to great person; ~'s *agreement* (binding in honour, but not enforceable at law). Hence ~HOOD, ~SHIP(1), nn. [GENTLE + MAN after OF *gentils hom*]

gěn'tlemanlike (-telm-), a. Appropriate to, resembling, a gentleman. [-LIKE]

gěn'tlemanly (-telm-), a. Feeling, behaving, or looking, like a gentleman; befitting a gentleman. Hence ~INESS n. [-LY(1)]

gěn'tleness (-tel-), n. Kindliness, mildness; freedom from severity, suddenness, violence, steepness etc. [-NESS]

gěn'tlewoman (-telwŏŏman), n. (pl. -en, *these* ~) Woman of good birth or breeding, lady. [-NESS]

gěn'tly (-t-li), adv. As gentleman or gentlewoman (only in ~ *born*, of gentle birth); quietly, moderately, softly, slowly, (as tenderly, kindly, [-LY(1)]

gěn'try, n. People next below the nobility in position & birth; (derog., esp. *these* ~) people. [prob. f. obs. *gentrice* f. OF *genterise* var. of *gentelise* (*gentil* GENTILE)]

gěn'ūal, a. Of the knee. [L *genu* knee, -AL]

gěn'ūflěct, v.i. Bend the knee, esp. in worship. Hence or cogn. ~OR², **gěnū-flěx'ion**, -ct-n, n. [f. med. L *genū-flectere* -*flex*- (prec., *flectere* bend)]

gěn'ūine, a. Of the original stock, pure-bred; really proceeding from its reputed source or author; having the supposed character, not counterfeit, properly so called. Hence ~LY² (-n-li) adv., ~NESS (-n-n-) n. [f. L *genuinus* (cf. *ingenuus* INGENUOUS) f. Aryan *gen*- beget]

gěn'us, n. (pl. *gěn'era*). (Logic) kind of things including subordinate kinds or SPECIES (*highest* ~, not itself subordinated as species to higher ~; *subaltern* ~, so subordinated); (Zool., Bot.) group of animals or plants having common structural characteristics distinct from those of all other groups, & usu. containing several species (see CLASS; the generic

& specific names, the former with capital initial, form the proper name; *the ~ Homo*, mankind); (loosely) kind, class, order, tribe. [L, genit. *-eris* race f. Aryan as prec.]

-geny, suf. forming *mn.* indicating mode of production f. F *-génie* (-GEN), as *anthropogeny* history of human evolution, often with corresp. *nn.* in *-genesis* & adji. in *-genetic*.

geo-, comb. form of Gk *gé* earth (Gk *geo-*), as *~dynam'ic* of the latent forces of the earth, *~selen'ic* of earth & moon.

geocen'tric, *a.* Considered as viewed from the earth's centre (*~ latitude of planet*, in which it would appear to observer at earth's centre); having or representing the earth as centre, not HELIOcentric. [prec., *centric* (CENTRE1, -IC)]

geode, *n.* (Concretionary stone containing cavity lined with crystals or other mineral matter. Hence **geod'ic** *a.* [f. F *géode* f. L f. Gk *geōdes* earthy (*gé* earth, -ODE)]

geod'esy, *n.* Branch of mathematics dealing with figure & area of the earth or large portions of it. So **geodet'ic**, **geodet'ical** *aa.* (*~esia, ~etic, line*, shortest possible on surface between two points), **geodet'ically2** *adv.*, **~esist(3)** *n.* [f. F *géodésie* f. mod. L f. Gk GEO(*daisia* f. *daiō* divide)]

geog'nosy, *n.* = GEOLOGY; geology of a district; knowledge of the mineral character, grouping, & distribution, of particular rocks. So **geognos'tic(AL)** *aa.* [f. F *géognosie* (GEO-, Gk *gnōsis* knowledge, *gnostos* known]

geograph'ic, -ical, *aa.* Of geography (*~ latitude*, angle made with plane of equator by perpendicular to earth's surface at any point; *~al mile*, =1′ of longitude on equator or about 2000 yds). Hence **~ally2** *adv.* [f. F *géographique* f. L f. Gk GEO(*graphikos* -GRAPHY)]

geol'ogize, *v.i. & t.* Devote time to examining places geologically, collecting specimens, etc.; examine (place) thus. [foll. +-IZE]

geog'raphy, *n.* Science of the earth's surface, form, physical features, natural & political divisions, climate, productions, population, etc. (*mathematical, physical, & political, ~*, the science in these aspects); subject-matter of ~; features, arrangement, of place; treatise on manual of ~. So **geog'rapher** *n.* [f. F *géographie* f. L f. Gk GEO(*graphia* -GRAPHY)]

geolo'gic(AL) *aa.* (*-ic* now only of things forming part of subject-matter of ~, **geolo'gically2** *adv.*, **geo'logist** *n.* [f. med. L f. Gk GEO(*logia* -LOGY)]

geo'mancy, *n.* Divination from figure given by handful of earth thrown down, & hence from figures given by dots made at random. Hence or cogn. **~ER1** *n.*, **geoman'tic** *a.* [f. F *géomancie* f. L f. Gk GEO(*manteia* -MANCY]

geom'eter, *n.* Person skilled in geometry; kinds of caterpillar & corresp. moth (from caterpillar's seeming to measure ground by its mode of walking). [f. L f. L f. Gk *geōmetrēs* measurer]

geomet'ric, -ic|al, *aa.* Of, according to, geometry (*~al tracery*, with openings of form, as circles, trefoils, etc.; *~al proportion*, involving equal ratios in its two parts, as 1 : 3 : : 4 : 12; *~al progression*, with constant ratio between successive quantities, as 1 : 3 : 9 : 27 : 81 : *~ spider*, constructing web of ~ pattern). Hence **~ally2** *adv.* [f. L f. Gk *geōmetrikos* (prec., -IC)+-AL]

geom'etrize, *v.i. & t.* Work, form, by geometrical methods. [foll. +-IZE]

geom'etry, *n.* Science of properties & relations of magnitudes (as lines, surfaces, solids) in space. So **geom'etri'cIAN** (-ishn) *n.* [f. F *géométrie* f. L f. Gk GEO(*metria* measuring)]

geoph'ag|y, *n.* = DIRT-eating. So **~ISM(1)** *n.* [GEO-, Gk *-phagia* -eating]

geopol'itics, *n.* The politics of a country as determined by its geographical features. [GEO-]

geopon'ic, *a.* (pedantic or joc.). Agricultural. [f. Gk GEO(*ponikos* f. *ponos* toll +-IC]

|| **Geor'die** (jôr-), *n.* (Sc. & north.). =COLLIER (all senses). [*George*, -Y3]

George (jôrj), *n.* **1.** *St~*, patron saint of England from time of Edw. III who chose him as patron of Order of the Garter (*St ~'s day*, 23rd April; *St ~'s cross*, vertical & horizontal red bars crossing in centre). **2.** Jewel forming part of Garter insignia. **3.** || Automatic pilot of aircraft (sl.). **4.** *Brown ~*, vessel of brown earthenware; *by ~*, oath or exclamation; ||*~ Cross, Medal*, (abbr. *G.C., G.M.*), decorations for gallantry instituted 1940. [f. L f. Gk *Geōrgios* supposed prince of Cappadocia martyred under Diocletian]

georgette (jôr-), *n.* A thin silk dressmaterial. [f. dressmaker's name]

Geor'gian1 (jôr-), *a.* Of the time of the first four Kings George of England; of the time of George V and VI. [-IAN]

Geor'gian2 (jôr-), *a. & n.* (Inhabitant, language) of Georgia in the Caucasus; (inhabitant) of Georgia in U.S. [-IAN]

Geor'gic (jôr-), *n.* One book (*first, fourth, ~*) of the *~s*, Virgil's poem on husbandry. [f. L f. Gk *geōrgika* pl. neut. adj. (*geōrgos* husbandman f. GEO- *erg-* work, -IC)]

geostroph'ic, *a.* (meteorol.). Depending on the rotation of the earth. [GEO-+Gk *strophikos* f. *strephō* turn]

geot'ropism, *n.* Plant-growth in relation to gravity (*positive ~*, tendency of roots

to grow towards, negative ~, of stems to grow away from, centre of earth. So gĕotrŏp'ic a, gĕotrŏp'ically adv. [GEO-, Gk *tropikos* (*tropē* a turning f. *trepō* turn + -IC, -ISM)]

gĕrān'ium, n. Kinds of wild herbaceous plant bearing fruit like crane's bill, Crane's-bill; kinds of cultivated pelargonium; colour of the scarlet ~. [L, f. Gk *geranion* (*geranos* crane)]

gĕr'falcon (-awkn, -awl-), n. Any large northern falcon, esp. the Icelandic. [f. OF *gerfaucon* prob. f. OHG *gîr* vulture + ...cf. G *geier*, FALCON]

gĕrm, n. & v.i. 1. Portion of organism capable of developing into a new one (~, usu. rudiment of animal or plant; opp. *sperm-*), rudiment of animal or plant; micro-organism or microbe, esp. one of those supposed to cause disease (~ CARRIER); (fig.) that from which something may spring, elementary principle (*in ~*, not yet developed). 2. v.i. Germinate, sprout, (fig. only). [f. F *germe* f. L *germen* etym. dub.]

gĕrm'an[1], a. (Now only as appended to BROTHER, SISTER, COUSIN) in the fullest sense of relationship; =GERMANE. [f. OF *germain* f. L *germanus* of same parents cogn. w. prec.]

Gĕrm'an[2], a. & n. 1. Of, characterizing, Germany or its inhabitants or language (~ *measles*, contagious disease like mild measles; ~ *Ocean*, North Sea; ~ *sausage*, large kind stuffed with spiced partly cooked meat; ~ *text*, black letter; ~ *silver*, white alloy of nickel, zinc, & copper). 2. n. Native, language, of Germany (*High ~*, form of ~ orig. spoken in South, but now in literary use throughout Germany; *Low ~*, dialects of German that are not High ~; also, all forms of WG. including English & Dutch, except High ~). Hence ~ISM[1] a., ~ISM[2], 3, 4), ~IST(1, 3), nn., ~IZE(2, 3, 4) v.t. & i., ~iza'TION, ~IZE[1] nn., Gĕrman'ò-comb. form, Gĕrman'ophil, Gĕrman'ophobe, aa. & nn. [f. L *Germanus*, pl. *-i*, of related peoples of central & N. Europe, name perh. given by Celts to their neighbours (cf. OIr. *gair* neighbour)]

gĕrmän'der, n. Kinds of plant esp. the blue-flowered ~ *speedwell*. [f. med. L *germandra* f. late Gk *khamandrua* (*khamaidrus* f. *khamai* on the ground, *drus* oak)]

gĕrmane', a. Relevant, pertinent, to the matter or subject. [var. of GERMAN[1]]

Gĕrman'ic, a. & n. Of the Germans (chiefly hist. in ~ *Confederation*, *Empire*); of the Teutonic race or any Teutonic people (of language; =primitive Teutonic; also with limiting word: *East ~*, Gothic & some almost lost languages as Burgundian & Vandal; *North ~*, Scandinavian; *West ~*, High & Low German, English, Frisian, Dutch, etc.; see also INDO-~). [f. L *Germanicus* (GER-MAN[2]-IC)]

Gĕrman'ity, n. Characteristic German qualities. [-ITY]

gĕrm'en, n. (bot.), Rudiment of seed-vessel, ovary. [L, genit. *-inis*, =GERM]

gĕrm'icide, n. & a. (Substance) having power to destroy (esp. disease-)germs. Hence gĕrmicīd'al a. [-I-, -CIDE]

gĕrm'inal, a. Of germs, of the nature of a germ; in the earliest stage of development. Hence ~LY[2] adv. [GERMEN, -AL]

gĕrm'ināte, v.i. & t. Sprout, bud, put forth shoots, (lit. & fig.); cause to shoot, develop (trans.), produce. Hence or cogn. ~ATOR[2], nn., ~ATIVE a. [f. L *germinare* (GERMEN), -ATE[3]]

gĕrm'on, n. Long-finned tunny. [F]

gĕrŏntŏc'racy (g-, j-), n. Government by, governing body of, old men. [f. Gk *gerōn -ontos* old man, -CRACY]

-gĕrous, suf. (in use *-igerous*, see -I-) f. L *-ger* bearing (*gerere* bear) + -OUS; in some words taken f. L, & freely added to L stems, as in *frondigerous* leaf-bearing.

gĕrr'ymän'der (g-), (erron.) ‖jĕrr'y-, v.t. & n. 1. Manipulate (constituency etc.), unfairly so as to secure disproportionate influence at election for some party or class; hence ~ER[1]. 2. n. Such manipulation. [vb f. n. orig. U.S.; anecdotic; substitution of name of governor Gerry of Massachusetts for *sala-* in *salamander*]

gĕr'und, n. Forms of Latin verb *-ndum*, *-ndi*, *-ndo*) serving as cases of the infinitive in its noun use, constructed as nouns but able to govern like their verb; English verbal noun in -ING[1] when used distinctly as part of verb (*this doing this is doubtful*); ~-*grinder*, teacher of Latin. So gĕrun'dial a. [f. L *gerundium* prob. f. *gerundum* neut. gerundive & gerund of *gerere* do = thing to be done, doing]

gĕrun'dive, a. & n. Of, like, the gerund; (n.; in L Gram.) verbal adjective from gerund stem having sense *that should be done* etc. Hence gĕrundī'val a. adv., ~LY[2] *gerundivus* (prec., -IVE)]

gĕss'ō, n. Plaster of Paris, gypsum, prepared for use in painting & in sculpture. [It., f. L GYPSUM]

gĕstalt', n. (psych.). An organized whole in which each individual part affects every other, the whole being more than a sum of its parts; chiefly attrib., as ~ *psychology*, *theory*. [G, = form, shape]

Gĕsta'pō (gestah-), n. German secret state police of Nazi régime. [f. initial letters of *Geheime Staats-Polizei*]

gĕsta'tion, n. Carrying or being carried in the womb between conception & birth, this period. [f. L L *gestatio gestare* carry, -ATION]

gestatō′rial, a. ~ *chair*, for carrying the Pope on certain occasions. [f. L *gestator-ius* (*gestator* carrier as prec.+ -OR², -ORY]

gestic′ulàte, v.i. & t. Use expressive motion of limbs or body with or instead of speech; express thus. So ~A′TION, ~ātor², mn., ~ātory, aa. [f. L *gesticulari* (*gesticulus* dim. of *gestus* GESTURE), -ATE³]

ges′ture, n., & v.i. & t. **1.** Significant movement of limb or body; use of such movements as expression of feeling or rhetorical device; (transf.) step or move calculated to evoke response from another or to convey (esp. friendly) intention. **2.** vb. = GESTICULATE. [f. med. L *gestura* (L *gerere gest-* wield, -URE]

get¹ (g-), v.t. & i. (past *got*; p.p. *got*, & in comb. & arch. & U.S. *gott′en*). **1.** trans. Obtain, procure, by effort or contrivance (~ *coal*, extract it from mine), win (*cannot* ~ *a living*), gain (*got little by it*), win (~ *the upper hand, start, advantage, sun, wind, better, of a person*; ~ *the best of it*, be victorious; ~ *fame, credit, glory*, etc.; ~ *knowledge or wind of*, learn, hear rumours of); learn *by heart* or *rote*; obtain as result of calculation (*we ~ 9·5 as the average*); receive as *gift, wages*, etc.; extract by prayer, demand, inquiry, etc. (*from, out of*; *could not* ~ *leave, any supper*); come to have (desired thing, as *rest*, one's *way, speech* of someone, *a sight of, possession of*; ~ *religion*, be converted); contract (idea etc.: also ~ *it into* one's *head*, be convinced *that*; ~ *measles*; ~ *person or thing on the brain*, think of him exclusively, *on* one's *nerves*, be irritably affected by him); (of story etc.) ~ *wind*, become known; have inflicted on one, suffer, receive as one's lot or penalty, (*fall, blow, the worst of it, six months*; ~ *it*, be punished, scolded, etc.; ~ *the* BOOT¹, SACK¹, MITTEN); (with *for* or ind. obj.) procure, provide, (*got him a place*; *we can* ~ *it for you*); catch (fish etc.); bring in, carry home, (crop); (colloq.) corner, puzzle, catch in argument, (esp. in perf. & past); (colloq.) understand (person or thing); (colloq.) take, eat, (dinner etc.); (colloq., in perf.) have (*have not got a penny*; *it has got to be done*, must) (now usu. only of animals) beget; (with compl.) succeed in bringing, placing, etc. (*got it over* or *across* see below, *through door, into room*, etc.), bring into some state (~ *with child*, make pregnant; ~ *them ready*; ~ *person upon* a subject, make him talk of it; ~ *skip under way*, start her; esp. with p.p. as ~ *it done, got the laws obeyed*); suffer injury etc. to some part of one (*got my wrist dislocated*; *shall ~ my feet wet*); induce, prevail upon, (person) *to do*. **2.** intr. Succeed in coming or going *to, from, into, out of, through, over, here, there, as far as*, etc. (*where has it got to?, what has become of it?*; ~ *across* or *over* (sc.

the footlights), sl., reach audience, be effective; ~ *there*, sl., succeed); (sl.) be off, clear out; (with infin.) acquire habit (*they soon* ~ *s to like it*); come to be doing (*they got talking*); become (~ *tired, hot, excited, drunk*; ~ *well, better*, recover from illness; ~ *clear, rid, or quit, of*; *~ wise to*, become aware of; ~ *under way*, begin to sail; ~ *done with*, bring to an end; ~ *married, used to it, shelved*). **3.** (With prepp.) ~ *at*, reach (whence ~**-at-**ABLE a.), ~ *hold of, ascertain*, (sl.) tamper with, bribe, etc., (sl.) attack, banter, (*who are you ~ting at?*, often = trying to impose upon—expressing incredulity); ~ *into*, (colloq.) put on (boots, clothes), (of liquor) affect, confuse, (one's *head*); ~ *off*, dismount from, obtain release from (engagement etc.), not remain on (the grass etc.); ~ *on*, mount (horse etc.), rise on one's *feet* or *legs* to speak in public; ~ *over*, surmount (difficulty), show (evidence, argument) to be unconvincing, recover from (illness) or from surprise at, accomplish (distance, task, etc.), (sl.) circumvent; ~ *round*, cajole, evade; ~ *through*, bring to an end, (of Bill etc.) be passed by (Lords, Commons, etc.), while away (time etc.); ~ *to*, begin (business etc.); ~ *upon*, ~ *on*. **4.** (With advv.): ~ *about*, go from place to place, begin walking after illness etc., (of rumours) be circulated; ~ *abroad*, (of rumours) = ~ *about*; ~ *along*, advance, meet with success, fare ill or well etc., manage *without* something, live harmoniously *together* or *with*, (colloq.) ~ *along with you!*, be off!, nonsense!; ~ *away*, escape, start, (imperat.) be off!; ~ *away with it*, succeed in what one tries to do, escape retribution, act with impunity; ~ *back*, come home etc., recover (lost thing; ~ *back* one's or some of one's *own*, sl., have revenge); ~ *down*, dismount; ~ *in*, be elected as M.P., enter carriage, bring home (crop), collect (debts etc.), fit (work etc.) into given time, succeed in placing (blow), ~ one's *hand in*, become at home with some operation, *can't* ~ *in a word* EDGEWAYS; ~ *off*, escape (*t. & i.*), start, go to sleep, be acquitted or pardoned, be let off *with* or for specified penalty, procure acquittal or slight penalty for (person); ~ *off with*, become on friendly or amorous terms with member of opposite sex; ~ *on*, don, display (pace; ~ *a move on*, sl., make a start), advance, make progress (~ *on* or ~ *out, work* or *go*), prosper, fare, manage *without* something, agree or live socially *with*, be ~*ting on for*, approaching (an age etc.); *~ on to*, succeed in understanding; ~ *out*, (imperat.) be off!, nonsense!, transpire, elicit, ~ *out of*, escape from (*got out of bed on wrong side*, is in bad temper; ~ *out of sight*, one's *depth*, disappear, be in too deep

water to stand; ~ *out of hand*, break from control, also finish work etc.), abandon (habit) gradually, evade doing, elicit (information) or obtain (money) from (person); ~ *over*, bring (troublesome task) to an end; ~ *through*, bring to or reach destination, (of Bill) be passed in Parliament, succeed in an examination; ~ *through*, succeed in doing or enduring; ~ *together*, succeed in doing or *under*, subdue (fire); ~ *up*, rise esp. from bed, mount esp. on horseback, (of fire, wind, sea) begin to be violent, (of game) rise from cover, (of cricket-ball) rise sharply from pitch, organize, set on foot, (of laundress) dress (linen), make present-able, arrange the appearance of, (hair, print of book), make rise (*I got my, his, back up*, became, made him, angry or stubborn), produce (~ *up steam*, enough steam; self into anger or energy; ~ *the wind* emotion; subject for examination etc.). || ~ *the wind*, Hence ~'t'ABLE a. [f. ON *geta* = OE -*gietan* cf. G (*ver*)*gessen*, f. Aryan *ghed-* seize, whence L *praeda* = *prae-heda* & Gk *khandanō* hold (root *khad*)]

gew'gaw (g-), n. Gaudy plaything or ornament, bauble; paltry showy trifle. [from 13th c.; ME *giuegoue* etym. dub.]

gey (gā), adv. (Sc.), Very, considerably. (also adj. ~ *& —*, in same sense). [var. of GAY]

gey'ser (gāz, gīz-), n. Intermittent hot spring throwing up column of water; apparatus for heating water. [f. Icel. *Geysir* name of a particular specimen in Iceland (*geysa* to gush)]

gharry (gā'ri), n. (Anglo-Ind.), Indian carriage (usu. horse-drawn and plying for hire). [Hind. *gārī*]

ghast'ly (gāh-; gā-), a. & adv. Horrible, frightful, shocking; (colloq.) objection-able; deathlike, pale, wan, lurid; (of smile etc.), painfully forced; (adv., chiefly with adj. as ~ *pale*) ghastlily. Hence ~liy² adv., ~iNESS n. [f. obs. *gast*, OE *gǣstan* terrify cogn. w. GHOST]

ghaut (gawt), n. (Anglo-Ind.), Eastern, E. & W. sides of Southern Hindostan; mountain pass, defile; flight of steps leading to river landing-place; *burning-~*, level spot at the top of river ~ on which Hindus burn their dead. [Hind. *ghāt*]

Gha'zi (gah-), n. Mohammedan anti-infidel fanatic. [Arab. p.p. of *ghazī* fight]

ghee (gē), n. Indian buffalo-milk butter clarified to resemble oil. [f. Hind. *ghī*]

gher'kin (gǝr-), n. Young green, or small kind of, cucumber used for pickling. [f. Du. *gurkkein* (now *gurkje*), f. Slavonic, cf. late Gk *agguourion* etym. dub.]

ghett'ō (gē-), n. (hist.; pl. ~s), Jews' quarter in city. [It., perh. abbr. of *borghetto* (*borgo* BOROUGH)]

Ghib'ellin|e (gǐ-), n. & a. 1. One of emperor's faction (opp. GUELPH) in medieval Italian States; hence ~ism(3) n. 2. adj. Adhering to ~es. [f. It. *Ghibellino* perh. f. G *Waiblingen* estate belonging to Hohenstaufen emperors]

ghost (gō-), n. & v.t. & i. 1. Principle of life (now only in *give up the ~*, die); Spirit of God (now only in *Holy G~*; Third Person of Trinity). 2. Soul of dead person in Hades etc.; dead person appearing to the living (*raise, lay, ~*; cause it to appear or cease appearing); apparition, spectre; emaciated person; shadowy outline or semblance (*not the ~ of a chance*, none at all). 3. (Opt.) bright spot or secondary image in field of telescope due to defect of lens. 4. Artistic or literary hack doing the work for which his employer takes credit. 5. ~-*word*, one of which the existence is imaginary or based on a delusion, as GHIS² FLYLOT; *the ~ walks* (Theatr. sl.), salaries are, or will be, paid; hence ~'HOOD n., ~'LIKE a. 6. vb. (rare). Haunt, prowl, act, as a ~. [com. WG. OE *gāst* cf. G *geist*; prob. cogn. w. ON *geisa* rage & Goth. *usgaisjan* terrify]

ghost'ly (gō-), a. (Arch.) spiritual, incorporeal, concerned with sacred or ecclesiastical matters. (*our ~y enemy*, the Devil; *~y father, adviser, director, etc.*, confessor; *~y comfort, counsel, etc.*, administered by priest; *~y weapons*, religious arguments, ecclesiastical penalties, etc.; (as) of a ghost, spectral. Hence ~iNESS n. [OE *gāstlic* (prec., -LY)]

ghoul (gōōl), n. Spirit preying on corpses in Eastern tales. Hence ~ISH¹ a. [f. Arab. *ghūl* t. vb =seize]

|| ghyll, var. of GILL³

gi'antess antʻced giLLS

gi'ant, n. & a. 1. Being of human form but superhuman stature, (Gk Myth.) one of the sons of Gaea (Earth) & Uranus (Heaven) or Tartarus (Hell) who warred against the Gods; agency of enormous power; abnormally tall person, animal, or plant; person of extraordinary ability, courage, strength, etc. (*there were ~s in those days*, our fathers were superior to us); ~-*powder*, Kind of dynamite; ||~(-s)-*stride*, gymnastic apparatus of pole with revolving head & hanging ropes enabling

user to take huge strides round pole; hence ~ESS¹ n., ~ISM n., pathological condition characterized by abnormal growth, esp. of the bones, ~LIKE a. 2. adj. Of extraordinary size or force, gigantic, monstrous, (often in plant-names), [ME *geant* (afterwards affected by L) f. OF *géant* f. L f. Gk *gigant-* nom. *-as* etym. dub.]

giaour (jowr), n. (Turkish contemptuous name for) infidel, esp. Christian. [f. Pers. *gaur*]

gib (g-, j-), n. Piece of wood or metal used to keep some part of a machine etc. in place; pin or wedge. [etym. dub.]

gibb'er (j-, g-), v.i., & n. 1. Speak fast & inarticulately, chatter like an ape. 2. n. Such speed or sound. [imit.]

gibb'erish (g-), n. Unintelligible speech, meaningless sounds, jargon, blundering or ungrammatical talk. [perh. f. prec. (but found earlier) +-ISH¹ as used in names of langg.]

gibb'et, n., & v.t. 1. (Orig.) gallows; (later) upright post with arm on which bodies of executed criminals were hung up; death by hanging. 2. v.t. Put to death by hanging; expose on ~; hang up as on ~; hold up to infamy or contempt. [f. OF *gibet* gallows dim. of *gibe* club]

gibb'on (g-), n. Kinds of long-armed ape esp. of Indian archipelago. [F, etym. dub.]

gibb'ous (g-), a. Convex, protuberant; (of moon or planet) having bright part greater than semicircle & less than circle; humped, hunchbacked. Hence or cogn. gibbos'ity (-ŏs-) n., gibbōs'o- comb. form, ~IY² adv., (g-). [f. L *gibbus* hump + -OUS, cf. L *gibbosus*]

gibe, jibe, v.i., & t., & n. Flout, jeer, mock, (as vb, with *at*, or trans., or abs.). Hence gib'ER¹ n., gib'ingLY² adv. [perh. f. OF *giber* handle roughly, use horse-play, or cogn. w. ON *geip* idle talk]

gib'lets, n. pl. Parts of goose taken out or cut off before cooking, as liver, gizzard, pinions, feet; *giblet soup*, made with these. [f. OF *gibelet* ragout etym. dub.]

gib'us, n. Opera or crush hat. [G~, maker]

gidd'y (g-), a., & v.t. 1. Dizzy, disposed to fall, stagger, or spin round (*with* sickness, success, etc.); making dizzy (a ~ *precipice, maze, success*); circling with bewildering speed; mentally intoxicated, incapable of attention, excitable, frivolous (*play the ~ goat, fool*), inconstant, flighty; ~go-round, MERRY²go-round; hence gidd'ily¹ adv., gidd'iNESS n., (g-). 2. vb. Make or become ~. [OE *gydig* insane perh. cogn. w. GOD cf. Gk *entheos*]

gift (g-), n., & v.t. 1. Giving (*would not have it at a ~*, even gratis; *the living is in the ~ of*, is his to bestow; *came to me by free ~*); (Law) voluntary transference of property without consideration; thing given, present, donation; faculty, miraculously bestowed, virtue looked upon as emanation from heaven etc., (~ *of* TONGUE); natural endowment (~ *of the* GAB), talent, whence gif'tED² (g-) a.; ~*book*, one given or suitable for giving as present; ~ *coupon*, voucher issued with certain commodities, a specified number of which entitles holder to a ~; ~-HORSE, one given; hence gif'tie [-Y³] (g-) n. (Sc., *the ~ie gie us to see oursels as others see us*). 2. v.t. Endow with ~s, present with as ~; bestow as ~ (*to* person; *away*). [prob. f. ON *gift*; com.-Teut., cf. OE *gift* payment for bride, Du. & G *gift* gift, f. OTeut. *giftiz* GIVE]

gig¹ (g-), n. 1. Light two-wheeled one-horsed carriage (~*lamps*, sl., spectacles; ~*man*, person who keeps ~, member of GIGMANITY). 2. Light narrow clinker-built ship's-boat for oars or sails; rowing-boat chiefly used for racing. [f. obs. *gig* whipping-top, etym. dub.]

gig² (g-), n. Kind of fish-spear. [short for *fizgig* f. Sp. *fisga* harpoon (corrupted to *fishgig* & mistaken for compd]

gigan'tic a. Giant-like in size, stature, etc.; abnormally large, huge. Hence or cogn. ~ESQUE (-ĕsk) a., ~ICALLY adv. [f. L *gigas -antis* GIANT, -IC]

gig'gle (g-), v.i., & n. 1. Laugh like an affected, ill-bred, or undisciplined girl, titter, have small bursts of half-suppressed laughter. 2. n. Such laugh. [imit.; cf. Du. *giggelen*, G *gichelen*]

gig'let, -ot, (g-), n. Giggling girl. [orig.= lewd woman, from 14th c., etym. dub.; now associated with prec.]

gigman'ity (g-), n. The respectable unimaginative middle classes, Philistines. [*gigman* (GIG¹) +-ITY (Carlylese wds)]

gig-mill (g-), n. Machine for raising nap on cloth; building in which these stand. [f. obs. *gig* whipping-top]

gig'olo, n. (pl. ~9). Professional male dancing-partner. [F, formed as masc. of *gigole* dance-hall woman]

gig'ot, n. Leg of mutton; ~ *sleeve*=LEG-of-mutton sleeve. [F]

gila (hē'la) **mŏn'ster**, n. Large venomous lizard of Arizona, New Mexico, etc. [*Gila*, river of Southern U.S.]

Gilbert'ian (g-), a. Of the humorously topsy-turvy kind characteristic of Gilbert & Sullivan opera (a ~ *situation*). [W. S. Gilbert, librettist, d. 1911, -IAN]

gild¹ (g-), v.t. (p.p. usu. ~*ed* in the fully verbal use & in fig. use as adj., *gilt* as adj. in lit. sense). Cover with thin layer of gold laid on as gold leaf or otherwise (~*pill*, soften down unpleasant necessity), whence gil'dER¹, gil'dING¹ (2, 4), nn.; make (condition etc.) tolerable or reputable by money (or with *money* etc. as subj.); tinge, adorn, with golden colour or light; give specious brilliance to by

fair words; ||**Gilded Chamber**, House of Lords; ~ed or **gilt spurs**, emblem of knighthood; ~ed **youth**, the young men of fashion & wealth; **gill-cup**, buttercup. [f. OE (be)gyldan (GOLD)]

gild[2]. See GUILD.

gill[1] (g-), n. (usu. pl.), & v.t. 1. Respiratory organ(s) in fishes & other water-breathing animals; wattles or dewlap of fowls; vertical radiating plates on under side of mushrooms etc.; flesh below person's jaws & ears (*rosy about the* ~s, healthy-looking); ~-cover, bony case protecting fish's ~s; ~-net, for entangling fishes by the ~s; hence (-)~ED[1] (-ld) a. 2. v.t. Gut (fish); cut off ~s of (mushroom); take in ~-net. [etym. dub.; cf. Sw. *gäl*, also Gk *kheilos* lip]

gill[2], n. Quarter-pint liquid measure (in some parts half-pint). [f. OF *gille*, med. L *gillo*]

gill[3], n. Deep usu. wooded ravine; narrow mountain torrent. [f. ON *gil* glen]

Gill[4], n. *Jack &* ~, lad & lass. [abbr. of Gillian f. F *Juliane* f. L *Juliana* (Julius)]

gillaroo[1] (g-), n. Irish trout. [f. Ir. *giolla* fellow, *ruadh* red]

gillie (g-), n. 1. (Hist.) Highland chief's attendant. 2. Man or boy attending sportsman in Scotland. [f. Gael. *gille* lad, servant]

gillyflower, n. (now rare), Clove-scented pink; other similarly scented flowers, as wallflower, white stock. [f. OF *gerofle*, f. LL f. Gk *karuophullon* (*karuon* nut, *phullon* leaf) w. assim. to *flower*]

gilt[1] (g-). See GILD[1] (*cloth* ~, book-binding of cloth with ~ letters or tooling).

gilt[2] (g-), n. Gilding (*take the* ~ *off the gingerbread*, strip thing of adventitious attractions); ~-edged, strip of paper, securities, stocks, etc., such investments as trustees prefer or are restricted to. [f. prec.]

gim'bal (g-), n. (pl. exc. in comb. as ~-ring etc.). Contrivance (usu. of rings & pivots) for keeping articles (esp. compass & chronometer) horizontal at sea. [f. obs. *gimmal* dim. of the unrecorded Rom. equivalent of obs. *gemel*, f. OF *gemel* finger-ring etc. f. *gemellus* dim. of *geminus* twin]

gim'crack, n. & a. 1. Trumpery article, knick-knack, useless ornament; hence ~ERY(5) n., ~Y[2] a. 2. adj. Showy & flimsy, worthless, trumpery. [earlier *gibecrake* perh. connected w. OF *giber* shake & CRACK]

gim'let (g-), n. Kind of boring-tool (usu. semi-cylindrical with wooden crosspiece as handle & worm at pointed end). [f. OF *guimbelet* dim. of the unrecorded Rom. equivalent of obs. *wimble* boring-tool, cf. LG *wemel* boring-tool, Du. *wemelen* move about]

gimp (g-), n. Silk, worsted, or cotton twist with cord or wire running through it; fishing-line of silk etc. bound with wire; (Lacemaking) coarser thread outlining design. [etym. dub.; cf. Du. *gimp*, F *guipure*]

gin[1], n. & v.t.(-nn-). 1. Snare, net, trap, (n. & v.t.). 2. Hoisting apparatus, kinds of crane & windlass. 3. Machine for separating cotton from its seeds.(vb, remove seeds of with this). [shortened f. OF *engin* ENGINE]

gin[2], n. Spirit distilled from grain or malt, GENEVA[1]; ||~-palace, gaudily decorated public-house; ||~-shop, dramshop esp. for ~; ~-sling, American cold drink of ~ flavoured & sweetened. [short for GENEVA[1]]

gin-gall (-gawl), j-, n. Musket fired from a rest, or light swivel gun, in China & India. [f. Hind. *janjal*]

gin'ger (-j-), n., a., & v.t. 1. (Plant with) hot spicy root used in cooking & medicine & preserved in syrup or candy as sweetmeat (*black*~, unscraped, from E. Indies; *white*~, scraped, from Jamaica; ~ *shall be hot in the mouth*, the love of pleasure is immortal). 2. Mettle, spirit; stimulation (see vb; ||~ *group* in Parliament, that urges Government to more decided action). 3. (Of) light reddish-yellow colour (n. & a.). 4. ~ ale, beer, pop, kinds of aerated ~-flavoured drink; ~ brandy, a cordial; ~-bread, a cake made with treacle & flavoured with ~ (~-bread nut, small button-like cake of it; *take the gilt off the* ~-bread), also (as adj. with allusion to fancy and often gilded shapes in which it was made) gaudy, showy, tawdry, (esp. ~-bread Gothic); ~-nut, ~-bread nut; ~-race, a root of ~; ~ wine, a British wine of fermented sugar, water, & bruised ~; hence ~Y[2] a. 5. v.t. Flavour with ~; put ~ up fundament of (horse) to produce liveliness, (fig.) rouse up (person). [OE & LL *gingiber* f. L *zingiber* f. Gk *ziggiberis* f. Skr. *çrngavera* (*çrnga* horn, *vera* body)]

gingerade' (-j-), n. = GINGER beer. [prec. after LEMONADE]

gin'gerly (-j-), adv. & a. With, showing, extreme caution so as to avoid making a noise or injuring oneself or what is touched or trodden on. [perh. f. OF *gensor* compar. of *gent* graceful f. L *genitus* (well-)born]

gingham (ging'am), n. Kind of cotton or linen cloth of dyed yarn often in stripes or checks; (colloq.) umbrella. [f. F *guingan* ult. f. Malay *ginggang* (orig. adj. = striped)]

gin'gili (-j-), n. (E.-Ind. plant yielding) a sweet oil. [f. Hind. *jinjåli* f. Arab. *juljulan*]

gingiv'al, a. Of the gums. [L *gingiva* gum +-AL]

ging'ko (g-), n. (pl. ~es). Chinese & Japanese tree with fan-shaped leaves. [Jap., f. Chin. *yinking* silver apricot]

ging'lymus (g-, j-), n. (anat.). Hinge-like joint in body with motion only in two

directions (e.g. elbow). [f. Gk *gignlumos* hinge]

*gink (g-), n. (sl.). (Queer) fellow, chap. [?]

gin'sěng, n. (Root of) medicinal plant found in China, Nepaul, Canada, & Eastern U.S. [f. Chin. *jĕn shĕn* (*jĕn* man) perh. = image of man, w. allusion to forked root]

‖ **gipp'ō**, n. (army sl.). Soup, gravy, stew. [?]

‖ **gipp'y**, n. (army sl.). Egyptian soldier. [abbr.]

gip'sy, gy'psy, gy', n. Member of a wandering race (called by themselves *Romany*) of Hindu origin with dark skin and hair, fortune-telling etc., & speaking a much corrupted Hindi; (playful) mischievous or dark-complexioned woman; ~ *bonnet*, with large side flaps; ~ *moth*, European moth very destructive to foliage; ~ *rose*, scabious; ~ *table*, light round one on tripod. Hence ~DOM, ~HOOD, ~ISM(2), nn., ~ISH¹ a., ~RY (usu. in p.p. ~*fied*) v.t. [earlier *gipcyan* for *Egyptian*, the race being supposed to come from Egypt when it appeared in England in early 16th c.]

giraffe' (-ahf, -äf), n. African ruminant quadruped with spotted skin & long neck & legs, cameleopard. [ult. f. Arab. *zara-fah*.]

gi'randôle, n. Revolving firework, discharge of rockets from revolving wheel; revolving jet of water; branched candle bracket or candlestick; ear-ring or pendant with large central stone surrounded by small ones. [F., f. It. *girandola* (*girare* f. L.t. It. *girare* revolve f. L f. Gk *guros* circle)]

gi'rasôle, n. Kind of opal reflecting reddish glow, fire-opal. [It. (-e), f *girare* see prec.+ *sole* sun, orig.=sunflower]

gird¹ (g-), v.t. (poet. or rhet.; ~ed or girt). Encircle (waist, person as to waist) with belt etc. esp. to confine clothes (oneself, one's *loins*, prepare for action, often with *up*); invest *with* strength, power, etc.; equip *with* sword in belt; fasten (sword etc.) on with belt (*on* adv. or prep., *upon*, *to*); secure (clothes) on body with girdle or belt; put (cord etc.) *round*; encircle (town etc.) *with* besiegers or siege-works; (of belt, fence, etc.) encircle. [OE *gyrdan* cf. G *gürten* cogn. w. GIRTH & perh. w. GARTH, YARD², GARDEN]

gird² (g-), v.i., & n. Jeer, gibe, *at*. [?]

gĭrd'er (g-), n. Beam supporting joists of floor; iron or steel beam for like use; latticed or other compound structure of steel etc. forming span of bridge, roof, etc. [GIRD¹+ -ER¹]

gĭr'dle¹ (g-), n., & v.t. 1. Belt or (now usu.) cord used to gird waist; something that surrounds like a ~; part of cut gem dividing crown from base & embraced by the setting. (Anat.) bony supports for upper & lower limbs (*shoulder* or *pectoral*, *pelvic* or *hip*, ~); ring round tree made by removal of bark. 2. v.t. Surround with ~ (often *about*, *in*, *round*); kill (tree) or make it more fruitful by girdling. [OE *gyrdel* see GIRD¹. -LE(1), cf. G *gürtel*]

‖ **gĭr'dle²** (g-), n. (Sc. & north.). Circular iron plate hung over fire for toasting cakes; ~ *cake*, so made. [var. of GRIDDLE]

girl (g-), n. Female child, unmarried woman, (*old* ~, affectionate or disrespectful address or description for woman, mare, etc.; *the* ~*s*, daughters of family, married or not); maidservant; man's sweetheart (often *best* ~); ~ *guides*, organization parallel to boy scouts; ~ *of the period* (19th-c. nickname for one lacking demureness). Hence ~HOOD, ~'ie [-y²], nn., ~'ISH¹ a., ~'ishly² adv., ~'ishNESS n., (g-). [cf. LG *gör* child]

Girön'dist, n. & a. (Member) of moderate republican party in French assembly 1791–3; (person) of such views. [f. F *Girondiste* (*Gironde* French department from which leaders of party came]

gĭrth (g-), n., & v.t. & i. 1. Leather or cloth band tightened round body of horse etc. to secure saddle etc.; measurement round any more or less cylindrical thing; ~*web*, woven material for ~s. 2. vb. Surround; encircle (horse etc.), secure (saddle etc.), with ~; measure (so much) in ~. [f. ON *georth* cogn. w. GIRD¹]

gist (g-), n. Real ground or point, substance or pith of a matter. [OF, 3rd sing. pres. of *gésir* lie f. L *jacēre*]

gitt'ern (g-), n. Gut-stringed instrument, kind of early guitar. [f. OF *guiterne* perh. as CITHERN]

give¹ (g-), v.t. & i. (*gāve, giv'en*). (General sense) make another the recipient of something in subject's possession or at subject's disposal (with obj. of thing given, & ind. obj. usu. preceding obj. if without *to* & following it if with *to*; in pass., either obj. may become subj., the other being retained without *to* if direct, with or without *to* if indirect. Thus: *I gave him a book; I gave £50 to the R.S.P.C.A.; I gave it him; he was ~n a book; a book was ~n him; the R.S.P.C.A. was ~n £50: £50 was ~n to, or ~n, the R.S.P.C.A.* Corresponding constructions are to be assumed with the various senses unless they are inapplicable or exceptions are mentioned). 1. Bestow gratuitously, hand over as present, confer ownership of with or without actual delivery, render (benefit etc.) without payment, (abs.) bestow alms or donations (*to*); confer, grant, (favour, honour, etc.); accord

(one's heart, affection, confidence); (of God etc.) grant (faculty etc., or to be or do); ~ *me*, in imperat., I prefer or admire, as ~ *me the good old times*; bequeath; sanction marriage of (daughter etc.; usu. *in marriage*). **2.** Deliver, hand over, without reference to ownership, put (food etc.) before one, (~ MITTEN, SACK¹; cf. GIFT); administer (medicine); deliver (message, love, compliments, etc.); commit, consign, entrust, (~ *into custody* or *in* CHARGE¹); pledge, assign as guarantee, (one's *word, honour*, etc.). **3.** Make over in exchange or payment, pay, sell *for* price, (~ *as good as one gets*, retort adequately in words or blows; so ~ *a* ROLAND *for an Oliver*; ~ *one his due*, admit any merits he may have; *would* ~ *the world*, one's *ears*, make any sacrifice to secure or *for* something, or *if*). **4.** Devote, dedicate, addict, (*gave his life to* ~; *much* ~*n to these pursuits*). **5.** Put forth (some action or effort) to affect another or simply (~ *him a kick*; ~ *a jump, cry*, etc.; ~ *orders*; ~ *person one's blessing*; ~ *you joy*, prob. orig. with ellipse *of God*, now taken as = *wish* ~; *I expressed or omitted;* ~ *one his time of day*, say good morning, evening, etc.; ~ *a piece of one's mind*, scold, reproach; ~ *to the world*, publish; ~ *person to understand, know*, etc., inform, assure). ... *facts*; ~*s no sign of life*; thermometer ~*s 80° in the shade*); read, recite, sing, act, perform, (piece etc.). **7.** Make partaker of, impart, be source of, (*gave me his sore throat; gave its name to the battle*). **8.** Allot, assign, ascribe, grant, assume, (*he was* ~*n the contract*, the *name of* John, *quarters; under the* ~*n conditions*). **9.** Yield as product or result (*lamps* ~*a bad light; analysis* ~*s the following figures*). **10.** Cause or allow to have (*solitude* ~*s it its only charm; gave me much pain; this* ~*s him a right to complain*; ~ *oneself trouble*, take pains; ~ *oneself airs*, be pretentious; *gave myself an hour to get there; was* ~*n a rest*). **11.** Collapse, lose firmness, yield to pressure, become relaxed, make room, shrink. **12.** (Of window, passage, etc.) look, lead, (*up*)*on, into*. **13.** (In phr. with obj.) ~ one *best* (colloq.), admit his superiority; ~ *birth to*, bring forth (lit. & fig.); ~ *chase*, start in pursuit; ~ *ear*, listen; ~ *ground*, retreat; ~ *it him* etc., administer punishment (often *hot*); ~ *child* etc., something *to cry for, chastise for causeless crying*;

~ *one what for*, sl., punish or scold; ~ *place* (*to*), make room (for), yield precedence (to), be superseded (by); ~ *rise to*, occasion; ~ TONGUE; ~ *way*, retire, fail to resist, be superseded by (*to*), be dislodged, break down, make concessions, abandon oneself to grief etc., fall in price, begin to row or row harder. **14.** (With advv.); ~ *away*, alienate by gift, hand over (bride) to bridegroom, betray or expose to ridicule or detection (esp. sl., ~ *away the* SHOW²), distribute (prizes); ~ *back*, restore; ~ *forth*, emit, publish, report; ~ *in*, yield, cease fighting or arguing, hand in (document) to proper official, (p.p.) added as supplement; ~ *off*, emit (vapour etc.); ~ *out*, announce, emit, distribute, cease or break down from exhaustion etc., run short; ~ *over*, cease from doing, abandon (habit etc.), desist, hand over (~*n over*, abandoned to evil courses etc.); ~ *up*, resign, surrender, part with (~ *up the* GHOST), deliver (fugitive etc.) into hands of pursuers etc., abandon oneself *to* a feeling, cease to have to do with, cease from effort, (refl. & p.p.) devote or addict to, divulge (names of accomplices etc.), pronounce incurable or insoluble, relinquish hope of. Hence GIVE¹ (-ë) n. [com.-Teut.; OE *giefan* cf. Du. *geven*, G *geben*]

give² (g-), n. Yielding to pressure, elasticity, (*there is no* ~ *in a stone floor*); ~ *and take*, mutual concession, compromise, exchange of talk. [f. prec.]

giv'en (g-), a. In vbl senses; *~ name*, CHRISTIAN name. [p.p. of GIVE¹]

giz'ard (g-), n. Bird's second stomach for grinding the food mixed in the first with gastric juice; specially muscular stomach of some fish, insects, & molluscs; *fret one's* ~, worry; *sticks in one's* ~, is unpalatable (fig.). [f. OF *g(u)iser* perh. f. L *gigeria* pl. cooked entrails of fowl]

glab'rous, a. (anat. etc.). Free from hair or down, smooth-skinned. [f. L *glaber* + -OUS]

gla'cé (-ah-sā), a. (Of cloth, leather, etc.) smooth, polished; (of fruits) iced, sugared. [F]

gla'cial (-āsil, -āshal, -āsh-), a. Of ice, icy. (Chem.) crystallized; (Geol.) characterized, produced, by the presence or agency of ice (~ *epoch, era, period*, when northern hemisphere was mostly covered with ice-sheet). Hence ~ly² adv. [F, f. L *glacialis* (*glacies* ice, -AL)]

gla'ciated (-si-, -shi-), a. Marked or polished by ice-action; covered with ice formed by accumulation of snow on high ground. So **glācia'tion** n. [p.p. of *glaciate* f. L *glaciare* freeze, -ATE³]

gla'cier, n. Slowly moving river or mass of ice formed by accumulation of snow on high ground. Hence ~ED³ (-erd) a.

gla'cis (or glahs²), n. Bank sloping down from fort, on which attackers are exposed to fire. [F, orig. = slippery place (OF glacier to slip)]

glad, a., & v.t. (-d-). 1. Pleased (pred. only; I am ~, ~ of it, ~ to hear it, ~ that it is so, ~ it is so, shall be ~ to come etc.; iron., should be ~ to know); (of looks, feelings, etc.) marked by, filled with, expressing, joy; (of news or events) giving joy; (of nature etc.) bright, beautiful; the ~ eye (sl.), amorous or festive glance; ~ hand (orig., U.S), the hand of welcome; ~ rags (sl.), Sunday or dress clothes; hence ~'d'EN'⁶ v.t., ~'LY² adv., ~'NESS n., (poet.) ~'SOME a., ~'SOMELY² adv., ~'SOME-NESS n. 2. v.t. (arch.). Make ~. [OE glæd cf. Da. & Sw. glad, & G glatt smooth (the orig. sense, cf. L glaber)]

glade, n. Clear open space or passage between forest trees. [perh. cogn. w. prec.]

gla'diator, n. Man trained to fight with sword or other weapon at ancient Roman shows; political etc. champion in argument, controversialist. So glädia-tor¹IAL a. [L (gladius sword)]

gladiŏ'lus (or gladi'o-), n. (pl. -li, -luses). Iridaceous plant with sword-shaped leaves & bright flower-spikes. [L, dim. of gladius sword]

Glăd'stone, n. & a. ~ (bag), kind of light portmanteau; ~ claret, of cheap kinds that became common by Gladstone's reduction of duty 1860. [W. E. ~ statesman d. 1898]

glair, n., & v.t. 1. White of egg; kinds of adhesive preparation made from it; any similar viscid substance; hence ~'ROUS, ~'Y², aa. 2. v.t. Smear with ~. [f. 13th-c. F glaire perh. f. L clara fem. of clarus clear]

glaive, n. (arch. & poet.). Broadsword. [OF, perh. f. L gladius sword]

glăm'our (-er), n., & v.t. 1. Magic, enchantment, (cast a ~ over, enchant); delusive or alluring beauty or charm; hence glăm'orous a. 2. v.t. Affect with ~, bewitch, enchant. [corruption of GRAMMAR, cf. for sense GRAMARYE]

glance¹ (-ah-), v.i. & t., & n. 1. (Of weapon) glide off object instead of striking it full (often aside, off); (of talk or talker) pass quickly over, glide off or from, subject; ~ at, make passing & usu. sarcastic allusion to : (of bright object or light) flash, dart, gleam; (of eye) cast momentary look, flash, (~ at, give brief look ab); ~ over, read cursorily; ~ down, up, etc.; ~ one's eye, direct it at, over, etc.; hence glăn'cingLY² (-ah-) adv. 2. n. Swift oblique movement or impact, (Cricket) stroke with bat's face turned slantwise to ball; (sudden movement producing) flash or gleam; brief look (at, into, over, etc.). [perh. nasalized form of OF glaichier to slip]

glance² (-ah-), n. Lustrous ore (copper ~, native copper sulphide; lead ~, GALENA). [f. G glanz lustre]

gland¹, n. (Physiol.) simple or complex organ composed of nucleated cells secreting constituents of the blood for use or ejection; (Bot.) secreting cell or group of cells on surface of plant-structure. So (see -UL-) glăn'dULE n., glăn'dULAR, ~ULIF'EROUS, glăn'dŭlōSE¹ (Bot.), glăn'dŭlous, ~'LESS, aa. [f. F glande f. OF glandre f. L⁺glandula (glans -dis acorn, -ULE)]

gland², n. (mech.). Sleeve used to press a packing tight on a piston-rod. [perh. f. Sc. glaund iron clamp]

glăn'der|s (-z), n. pl. Contagious horse-disease with swellings below jaw & mucous discharge from nostrils; the same communicated to man. Hence ~ED⁶ (-erd), ~OUS, aa. [f. OF glandre see GLAND¹]

glăndif'erous, a. Bearing acorns. [t. L glandifer (GLAND¹, -FEROUS)]

glăn'difōrm, a. Acorn-shaped; like gland. [GLAND¹, -FORM]

glăr'|e, v.i. & t., & n. 1. Shine dazzlingly or disagreeably; be over-conspicuous or obtrusive, whence ~'ing¹LY² adv., ~'ing-NESS n.; look fixedly or fiercely (at, upon); express (hate, defiance) by look. 2. n. Strong fierce light, oppressive unrelieved sunshine; tawdry brilliance; fierce or fixed look; hence ~'Y² a. [ME, also MDu. & MLG, glaren perh. cogn. w. GLASS]

glass¹(-ah-), n. 1. Substance, usu. transparent, lustrous, hard, & brittle, made by fusing sand with soda or potash or both & other ingredients (CROWN¹, FLINT, PLATE, WATER¹, ~); substances of similar properties or composition, as ~ of antimony, vitreous oxy-sulphide fused. 2. ~ utensils, ornaments, windows, greenhouses; ~ vessel esp. for drinking, amount of liquid contained in this, drink (a friendly ~, fond of his ~; has had a ~ too much, is rather drunk); sand~, hour~; carriage window; plate of covering picture; glazed frame for plants; looking-~; eye-~, (pl.) pair of spectacles; lens; ~ disk covering watch-face; telescope, spy-~, field-~, opera-~; microscope; barometer, weather-~. 3. ~-blower, one who blows & shapes ~; ~ case, chiefly of ~ for exhibiting or protecting objects; ~-cloth, linen cloth for drying -es, cloth covered with powdered ~ like ~-paper; ~ cloth, woven fabric of fine-spun ~; ~ culture, of plants under ~; ~-dust, powdered ~ for polishing; ~ eye, false eye of kind of blindness in horses; ~-house, building where ~ is made, greenhouse, ~-roofed photographing-room, ||(sl.) military prison; ~-paper, covered with ~-dust; ~ snake, snake-like

lizard of Southern U.S., with very brittle tail; ~*ware*, articles made of ~; ~*wort*, kinds of plant formerly used in ~-making. Hence ~**FUL**(2) n., ~**LESS** a. [OE *glæs* cf. G *glas* perh. f. OTeut. *glă-*, *glō-*, shine]

glass[2] (-ah-), v.t. Fit with glass, glaze, (rare); enclose in glass (rare); make (the eye) glassy (rare); mirror, occasion reflection of (often refl., as *trees ~ themselves in the lake*); ||~*ing-jack*, machine used in dressing leather. [f. prec., cf. earlier GLAZE]

glass[2]|*y* (-ah-), a. Having properties of, resembling, glass; (of eye etc.) lacking fire, dull, fixed; (of water) lustrous & transparent, or smooth, as glass (so ~*y calm, surface*, etc.). Hence ~**ILY**[2] adv., ~**INESS** n. [-**Y**[2]]

Glăswē′gian(-z), a. & n. (Inhabitant) of Glasgow. [perh. on GALWEGIAN]

Glaub′er's salt(s) (glaw-, glow-), n. Crystalline (hydrated) sodium sulphate. [J. R. *Glauber*, German chemist]

glaucō′ma, n. An eye-disease with tension of the globe & gradual loss of sight. Hence ~**tous** a. [f. Gk *glaukōma* -*atos* (*glaukos* as foll.-M)]

glauc′ous, a. (esp. nat. hist.). Of dull greyish green or blue; (Bot.) covered with bloom as of grapes. [f. L f. Gk *glaukos*+-**ous**]

glāze, v.t. & i., & n. 1. Fit (window, picture) with glass, furnish (building) with glass windows (~ *in*, enclose thus). 2. Cover (pottery etc.) with vitreous substance fixed by fusion (n., this substance, smooth surface resulting); fix (paint) on pottery thus; overlay (cloth, leather, pastry, etc.) with smooth lustrous coating (n., this coating, surface produced). 3. Cover (eye) with a film (n., filmy look). 4. Cover (painted surface) with thin coat of different transparent colour to modify tone (n., this coat). 5. Give glassy surface to, e.g. by rubbing (n., polished look); become glassy (esp. of eyes); (of frost) =SILVER[1] *than*. Hence glāz′**ER**[1], 2) n. [ME *glasen* (GLASS[1])]

glā′zier(-zher, -zier), n. One whose trade is to glaze windows etc.; *is your father a* ~? (joc. question, = you are opaque, to person obstructing one's view). Hence **glā′zier**(2) n. [GLASS[1]+-**ER**[1] W. assim. to Rom. wds in -**IER**]

glāz′ing, n. In vbl senses; also: windows; material used to produce glaze. [-**ING**[1]]

gleam, n. & v.i. 1. Subdued or transient light; faint, temporary, or intermittent show of some quality etc. (*un occasional* ~ *of humour*; *not a* ~ *of hope*); hence ~*y*[2] a. 2. v.i. Emit ~s, shine with subdued or interrupted brightness. [OE *glǽm* gleam, GLIMMER, GLIMPSE]

glean, v.i. & t. Gather ears of corn left by reapers; gather (such remains); strip (field etc.) thus; collect in small quantities, scrape together, (news, facts, etc.). Hence ~**ER**[1], ~**ING**[1], 2), n. [f. OF *glener* etym. dub.]

glēbe, n. (Poet.) earth, land, a field; portion of land going with clergyman's benefice. [f. L *glēba* clod, soil]

glee, n. 1. Musical composition for three or more (prop. adult male) voices, one to each part, set to words grave or gay, often with contrasted movements & prop. without accompaniment. 2. Mirth, lively & manifest delight, whence ~**FUL**, ~**SOME**, aa., ~**fully**[2] adv. [OE *glēo*]

gleet, n. Thin morbid discharge from wound, ulcer, etc., (rare), or from the urethra. Hence ~*y*[2] a. [f. OF *glette* slime]

glĕn, n. Narrow valley. [f. Gael. *gleann*]

glĕn′dŏver, n. Beautiful sprite of kind represented by Southey as occurring in Hindu myths. [altered f. *grandover* in F travel-book perh. f. Skr. *gandharva* semi-divine spirit]

glĕngă′rry (-ng-), n. Kind of Highland cap. [place]

Glĕnlĭv′ĕt, n. Kind of Scotch whisky. [place]

glĕn′oid, a. (anat.), ~ *cavity, fossa, surface*, shallow cavity on bone (esp. scapula & temporal bone) receiving projection of other bone to form joint. [f. Gk *glēnoeidēs* (*glēnē* socket, -**OID**)]

glib, a. & adv.-(-bb-). 1. (Of surface etc.) smooth, offering no resistance, (of movement) unimpeded, easy, (rare); (of speaker, speech, etc.) fluent, ready, more voluble than sincere or thoughtful; hence ~**ly**[2] adv., ~**NESS** n. 2. adv. Volubly (now rare). [perh. imit., cf. GLIDE]

glīd|**e**, v.i. & t., & n. 1. Pass, change place, by smooth continuous movement (of liquid, ship, bird, carriage, snake, person skating, etc.); fly without engine (~**ER**[1](2) n., engineless aeroplane); go quietly or stealthily; (of time etc.) pass gently & imperceptibly; pass gradually, shade off insensibly, *into*; cause to ~e (*light airs* ~*ed her on her course*); hence ~**ing**[2]y[2] adv. ~**NESS** n. 2. Act of ~ing; (Mus.) succession of sounds made in passing from one note to another without silencing the voice or instrument; (Phon.) gradually changing sound made in passing from one position of speech organs to another. [com.-WG; OE *glīdan* cf. G *gleiten*]

glim, n. (sl.). Light, candle, lantern, (DOUSE *the* ~). [prob. cogn. w. GLEAM, GLIMPSE]

glĭmm′er, v.i., & n. 1. Shine faintly or intermittently. 2. n. (Also ~**ing**[1] n.) feeble or wavering light, faint gleam of hope etc., glimpse, half view, [as prec.; cf. G *glimmern*]

glimpse, n. & v.t. & i. 1. Faint & transient appearance, momentary or imperfect

view of, (the ~s of the moon, the earth by night, sublunary affairs). 2. vb. Catch ~ of, see faintly or partly; (poet.) appear faintly, dawn. [n. f. vb, ME glymsen cf. MHG glimsen & see prec.]

glint, v.i. & t., & n. Flash, glitter, sparkle, (v. & n.); make flash, reflect, (light). [n. & v.]

glissade' (-ahd), n., & v.i. (mountaineering). Slide (n. & v.) down steep slope esp. of ice or snow usu. on the feet with support of ice-axe etc. [vb f.n., F (glisser slip, -ADE²]

glis'ten (-isən), v.i., & n. Shine fitfully; glitter, sparkle, (v. & n.). [n.f. vb, OE glisnian (glisian shine, -EN⁵]

glis'ter, v.i., & n., (arch.). Sparkle, glitter. [f. OE glisian see prec. + -ER⁵]

glitt'er, v.i., (Shine with) brilliant tremulous light, gleam, sparkle; be showy or splendid (with jewels etc.). [prob. f. ON glitra cf. G glitzern f. Teut. glit- shine + -ER⁵]

gloam'ing, n. Evening twilight. [OE glōmung (glōm twilight cogn. w. GLOW, -ING⁵)]

gloat, v.i. Feast eyes or mind (usually, avariciously, malignantly, etc., (upon or over. Hence ~'ingLY² adv. [cf. G glotzen stare]

globe, n., & v.t.&i. 1. Spherical body: the earth; planet, star, sun; spherical chart of (terrestrial ~) the earth or (celestial ~) the constellations (use of the ~, arch., teaching of geography & astronomy by these); golden orb as emblem of sovereignty; (Anat.) eyeball; approximately spherical glass vessel, esp. lampshade or fishbowl; ~-fish, able to inflate itself into globular form; ~-flower, ranunculaceous plant with round yellow flowers; ~ lightning, = FIRE-ball; ~-trotter, -trotting, hurried traveller, travelling, through foreign countries for sight-seeing; so glob'AL (1) a., world-wide, embracing the totality of a group of items, categories, etc., glob'oɪD a., & n., glob'osE⁻¹ a., globos'ITY n. 2. vb. Make (usu. in pass.) or become, globular. [F, f. L globus]

glob'ular, a. Globe-shaped, spherical; composed of globules. Hence ~ITY (-æ'r-) n., ~LY² adv. [foll., -AR¹, & see -UL-]

glob'ule, n. Small globe or round particle, drop, pill. [F, f. L globulus (GLOBE, -ULE)]

glob'ulin, n. Protein found usu. associated with albumen in animal tissues. [prec., -IN]

glochid'iate (-k-), a. (bot.). Barbed at tip. [f. Gk glōkhidion (glōkhis arrowhead), -ATE²]

glock'enspiel (-pēl), n. Musical instrument consisting of a series of metal bars struck by a hammer (earlier, a kind of CARILLON). [G, = bell-play]

glom'erate, a. (bot., anat.). Compactly clustered. [L glomerare (glomus -eris ball, -ATE²]

glŏm'erule (-ōōl), n. Clustered flower-head; cluster of small organisms, tissues, blood-vessels, etc. [f. F glomérule (L glomus see prec., -ULE]

gloom, n. Darkness, obscurity; melancholy, despondency. [perh. back formation f. GLOOMY]

gloom², v.i. & t. Look sullen, frown, be melancholy; (of sky etc.) lour, be dull or threatening; appear darkly or obscurely; cover with gloom, make dark or dismal. [ME glowme cf. MG glumen be savage: cogn. w. GLUM]

gloom'|y, a. Dark, unlighted; depressed, sullen; dismal, depressing. Hence ~lɪʏ¹ adv., ~INESS n. [prec. f. prec. + -Y¹]

glor'ia, n. (Short for) G~ Patri, doxology Glory be to the Father etc., G~ tibi, response Glory be to thee etc., or G~ in excelsis, hymn Glory be to God on high; aureole, [L, = glory]

glor'ifⱼY, v.t. Make glorious, exalt to the glory of heaven; invest with radiance transform into something more splendid, invest (common or inferior thing) with charm or beauty (nothing more than a ~fied, or ~fication of a, cottage): extol, laud. Hence ~FICA'TION n. [f. F glorifier f. LL glorificare (glorificus f. L gloria glory, -FIC)]

glor'iole, n. Aureole, halo. [F, f. L gloriola dim. of gloria glory]

glor'ious, a. Possessing glory, illustrious; conferring glory, honourable; splendid, magnificent, intensely delightful, (a ~ view, day; also joc., as ~ fun; & iron., the ~ uncertainty of cricket, a ~ muddle) (colloq.) ecstatically happy with drink. Hence ~lɪʏ² adv. [AF, f. L gloriosus (foll., -OSE¹)]

glor'|y, n. Exalted renown, honourable fame; subject for boasting, special distinction, ornament, pride; adoring praise & thanksgiving (~ be! or ~!, vulgar excl. of surprise or delight); resplendent majesty, beauty, or magnificence, effulgence of heavenly light, imagined unearthly beauty; bliss & splendour of heaven (go to ~, die; send to ~, joc., kill); state of exaltation, prosperity, etc., (is in his ~); circle of light round head or figure of deity or saint, aureole, halo; ~-hole (sl.), untidy room, drawer, or receptacle. [f. OF glorie f. L gloria]

glor'|y², v.i. Exult, pride oneself, in thing or doing, to do. Hence ~ingLY² adv. [f. L gloriari boast (gloria glory]

gloss¹, n., & v.t. & i. 1. Word inserted between lines or in margin to explain word in text; comment, explanation, interpretation, paraphrase; misrepresentation of another's words; glossary, interlinear translation, or set of notes. 2. vb. Insert ~es in (text etc.); write ~es;

make comments esp. of unfavourable sort; read different sense into, explain away. [vb f.n.]

gloss², n. & v.t. 1. Superficial lustre; deceptive appearance, fair outside; hence ~Y² a., ~lY² adv., ~INESS n. 2. v.t. Make ~y; give specious appearance to (often *over*). [vb f.n.; from 16th c., cf. obs. Du. *gloos*, Icel. *glossi*, mn., glow, blaze]

gloss'al, a. (anat.). Of the tongue, lingual. [f. Gk *glōssa* tongue + -AL]

gloss'arY, n. Collection of glosses; list & explanations of abstruse, obsolete, dialectal, or technical terms, partial diction. [med. L *glossarium* f. *glossa* GLOSS¹, -ORY]

gloss(o)-, comb. form of Gk *glōssa* tongue, as *gloss'(o)-epiglott'ic* of tongue & epiglottis, *glossit'is*; also of GLOSS¹, as *glossog'rapher* commentator, *glossol'ogy* terminology.

glott'is, n. Opening at upper part of windpipe & between vocal chords, affecting modulation of voice by contracting or dilating. Hence ~AL, ~IC, aa. [Gk *glōttis* (*glōtta* var. of *glōssa* tongue)]

Gloucester (glos'ter), n. Kind of cheese (usu. *single, double,* ~), the latter of richer milk; made in ~*shire*. [place]

glove (-ŭv), n., & v.t. 1. Covering of leather, cotton, silk, wool, or formerly steel, for the hand, usu. with separated fingers (*throw down, take up, the* ~, make, accept, challenge; *fit like a* ~, exactly; HAND¹ *& or in* ~); (also *boxing-*~) padded ~ for boxing (*take off, without, etc., the* ~*s*, of arguing or contending in earnest, mercilessly, etc.); ~-*fight*, fight with boxing-~s (opp. *prize-fight* with bare fists); ~-*sponge*, in shape of ~; ~-*stretcher*, instrument for enlarging ~-*fingers*; hence ~'LESS (-ŭvl) a. 2. v.t. Provide with ~s, glo'veR¹(3)(-ŭv-) n. [OE *glōf* perh. f. OTeut. *galōfā* (*ga-*=Y, *lōf-* cogn. w. Sc. *loof* hand)]

glow (-ō), v.i., & n. 1. Be heated to incandescence, throw out light & heat without flame; shine like thing intensely heated; show warm colour; burn with bodily heat or emotional fervour (*with*); ~-*worm*, coleopterous insect with winged male & wingless female, the latter emitting green light at tail; hence ~'ingₐ¹ adv. 2. n. ~ing state (*in a* ~, *all of a* ~, hot or flushed); brightness &, warmth of colour, e.g. red of cheeks; ardour, passion; ~-*lamp*, with carbon, etc. incandescent under electric current. [OE *glōwan* cf. G *glühen*; cogn. w. GLOAM-ING & obs. or dial *gleed* ember]

glower (-owr), v.i. Stare, scowl, (usu. *at*). Hence ~'ingₐ² adv. [f.]

gloxin'ia, n. American tropical plant, with large bell flowers of various colours. [B. P. *Gloxin* botanist c. 1785 + -IA¹]

gloze, v.i. & t. ∥ Comment (*upon* arch.); palliate, explain away, extenuate, (usu. *over*); talk speciously; talk fair words, fawn. Hence glōz'ingₐ² adv. [f. F *gloser* (*glose* GLOSS¹)]

glucin'um (-ōos-), n. White metal obtained from beryl, beryllium. [f. Gk *glukus* sweet (some compds of it being sweet)]

glu'cose (glŏō-), n. (chem.). Grape-sugar or dextrose; commercially prepared from starch and other carbohydrates by hydrolysis. Hence glucos'ic a., glu'coside n., (glŏō-). [f. Gk *gleukos*, see -OSE²]

glue (-ŏō), n., & v.t. 1. Hard brittle brownish gelatin made by boiling hides & bones & used warm for uniting substances; adhesive or viscous substance got from other sources (*fish, vegetable, casein, resin,* ~); ~-*pot*, with outer coat holding water to heat ~; hence ~Y² (glŏō'i) a. 2. v.t. attach tightly or closely (*eye, ear,* ~*d to the keyhole*). [f. OF *glu* f. LL *glus glutis*]

glum, a. Sullen, looking dejected or displeased. Hence ~'lY² adv., ~'NESS n. [cogn. w. GLOOM²; cf. LG *glum* turbid]

glume (-ŏōm), n. (bot.). Chaffike bract in inflorescence of grasses & sedges; husk of grain. Hence glumₐ'CEOUS, glumOSE¹, aa., (-ŏōm-). [f. L *gluma*]

glut, v.t. (-tt-), & n. 1. Feed (person, stomach) or indulge (appetite, desire) to the full, overload with food (lit. or fig.), satiate, cloy; choke up, fill to excess; overstock (market) with goods. 2. n. Full indulgence, one's fill, surfeit; supply exceeding demand (*a* ~ *in the market*). [n. f. vb; prob. f. obs. & OF *glut* GLUTTON]

glu'ten (glŏō-), n. Sticky substance, whence ~INE(3) v.t., ~INOUS a., ~inous-lY² adv. ~inos'ITY n., (-ŏō-): viscid animal secretion; nitrogenous part of flour remaining as viscid substance when starch is washed out. [L, genit. -*inis*,

glu'tinate, v.t. Treat with glycerine (esp. vaccine lymph). [-ATE³]

gly'cerine, **-in**, n. Colourless sweet liquid got from any fatty substance, liquid or solid, by saponification, used as ointment, as vehicle for drugs, in explosives, etc. Hence glycₐ'ric a. (chem.), ~-OUSₐ¹ a. [f. Gk *glukeros* sweet, -IN¹]

gly'cerol, n. (chem.). (Name preferred in scientific use for) glycerine. [proc., -ol(1)]

glyco-, comb. form, irreg. for *glucy*, of Gk *glukus* sweet, also used in names of chem. compounds containing glycerol or other substance in *glyc-*.

glўc'ogen, n., **glўc'ogen'ic**, a., (chem.). (Substance) producing glucose in animal tissues. So **glўcogen'esis** n. [prec., -GEN(I)]

glўc'ōl, n. Any of the fatty diatomic alcohols. Hence **glўcōl(i)'ic** a. [GLYCO-, -OL(I)]

glўcon'ic, a. & n. (Gk & L pros.). (Line, metre) consisting of three trochees & dactyl, the dactyl variously placed, esp. of the catalectic form (– – | – ∪ ∪ | – ∪ ∪) used by Horace & Catullus. [*Glukōn* Gk poet, -IC]

glўcosūr'|ia, n. (path.). Diseased condition with sugar in the urine. Hence ~IO a. [F *glycose* GLUCOSE, Gk *ouron* urine, -IA¹]

glўph'ograph (-ahf), **glўphŏg'raphў**, nn. (Plate or copy, *-ph*, made by) electrotype process giving raised copy of engraved plate for use in letter-press printing (*-y*). So **glўph'ograph** (-ahf) v.t. & i., **glўphŏg'rapher** n., **glўphog'raphic** a. [f. Gk *gluphō* carving (*gluphō* carve), -GRAPHY]

glўp'tic, a. Of carving esp. on precious stones. [f. Gk *gluptikos* (*gluphō* carve, -IC)]

glўp'todŏn, n. Extinct S.-Amer. quadruped allied to armadillos with fluted teeth. [f. Gk *gluptos* carved (as prec.)+*odous -ontos* tooth]

glўptŏg'raphў, n. Art & science of gem-engraving. [as prec., -GRAPHY]

*G-man, n. (sl.). Federal criminal investigation officer. [Government]

gnarled (nahld), **gnarl'ў** (n-), aa. (Of tree; & fig.) covered with protuberances, twisted, rugged. [var. of obs. *knurled* (*knurl* knob); -ED², -Y²]

gnash (n-), v.i. & t. (Of teeth) strike together; grind the teeth, grind (the teeth). [earlier *gnast* cf. ON *gnastan* prob. imit.]

gnat (n-), n. Small two-winged fly of which female has blood-sucking proboscis; (as type) insignificant annoyance, tiny thing, (*strain at* ~, be scrupulous about trifles). [OE *gnæt*]

gnath'ic (n-), a. Of jaws. [Gk *gnathos* jaw, -IC]

gnaw (n-), v.t. & i. (p.p. ~*ed*, ~*n*). Bite persistently, wear away thus (often *away*, *off*, *in two*, etc.; also intr. with *at*, *into*); (of destructive agents, pain, etc.) corrode, waste away, consume, torture. Hence ~'ingLY² adv. [OE *gnagan*]

gneiss (gnīs, nīs), n. (geol.). Laminated rock of quartz, feldspar, & mica. Hence ~'IC, ~'OID, ~'OSE¹, ~'Y², aa. [G (OHG *gneistan* sparkle)]

gnōm'ē¹ (n-: *also* nōm), n. Maxim, aphorism. [f. Gk *gnōmē* (*gignōskō* know)

gnome² (nōm), n. Diminutive spirit of subterranean race guarding treasures of earth (cf. SYLPH, SALAMANDER, NYMPH), goblin, dwarf. Hence **gnōm'ish** (n-) a. [used by Paracelsus; perh. for *genomos* (Gk *gē* earth, *-nomos* -dwelling, or spec. use of prec.]

gnōm'ic (n-), a. Of, consisting of, using, GNOME'S, sententious; (Gram.) ~ *aorist*, used without past sense to express a general truth, e.g. *men were deceivers ever*. [f. Gk *gnōmikos* (GNOME¹, -IC)]

gnōm'on (n-), n. Pillar, rod, pin or plate of sundial, showing time by its shadow on marked surface; column etc. used in observing sun's meridian altitude; (Geom.) part of parallelogram left when similar one has been taken from its corner. Hence **gnōmŏn'ic** (n-) a. [Gk (*gnōmōn*) = inspector, ~ of dial, (*gignōskō* know)]

gnōs'is (n-), n. Knowledge of spiritual mysteries; Gnosticism. [Gk (-ŏ-), = knowledge, as prec.]

gnōs'tic (n-), a. & n. 1. Relating to knowledge, cognitive; having esoteric spiritual knowledge; of the Gnostics, occult, mystic. 2. n. (usu. pl.; *G*~) early Christian heretic(s) claiming GNOSIS, whence ~ISM(3) n., ~IZE(2, 3, 4) v.i. & t., (n-). [f. Gk *gnōstikos* (as prec.)]

gnu (nū), n. Oxlike antelope. [Hottentot]

gō¹, v.i. & t. (*wĕnt*, *gone* pr. gawn, gŏn; 2nd sing. (poet., 3rd *goes* pr. gōz & arch. *gŏeth*). 1. Start, depart, move, continue moving, with self-originated or imparted motion, from some place, position, time, etc. (often not specified because obvious, whereas the goal etc. is always specified if it matters; cf. COME). 2. Journey, travel, proceed, progress, (*going strong*, with vigour; *he will go far*, reach distinction; *go easy*, *straight*; *go used*, sl., be killed or die; *go the* RACE; *went miles round*; *go a walk*, *journey*, *voyage*; *go the same*, *the shortest*, *way*). 3. (Of line etc.) lie, point, in certain direction. 4. Be guided by, act in harmony with, judge or act upon, (*a good rule to go by*; *have nothing to go upon*; *always goes with his party*; *promotion goes by favour*; *go with tide* or *times*, do as others do). 5. Be habitually in specified state (*go hungry*, *armed*, *in rags*, *in fear of one's life*; *six months etc. gone with child*, having spent that time in gestation). 6. Be moving, acting, working, etc., (*Who goes there?*, sentry's challenge; *a going concern*, business in working order; *clock does not go*, *goes well*; *tongue goes nineteen to the* DOZEN). 7. Make specified motion (*go like this with your left foot*). 8. (Of bell, striking clock or hour, gun, etc.; also with interjections of sound as *go bang*, *crack*) sound (*go phut*, sl., collapse). 9. (Of time) pass, elapse. 10. Be current (*the sovereign went anywhere*; *the story goes*, it is said); be

known by, or under, the name of; be on the average (*is a good actor as actors go nowadays*). **11.** (Of document etc.) run, have specified tenor. **12.** (Of verse, song) be rhythmical, be adaptable to a tune. **13.** (Of events) turn out *well, ill,* HARD, etc., (of election etc.) issue for or against, (of constituency, politician, voter) take certain course or views (*Liverpool goes Labour; America went wet, adopted prohibition of intoxicants; case goes by default, dinner, play, went well, succeeded; goes without saying*). **14.** Begin motion (*Go!*, starter's word in race; *HERE goes!*). **15.** Get away free, unpunished, etc. **16.** Be sold (*go cheap, for 2/6, etc.: going!, gone!*, auctioneer's announcement that bidding is almost, quite, closed). **17.** (Of money) be spent (often *in* books etc.). **18.** Be relinquished, abolished, or lost (*Greek, the carriage, must go; my sight, our trade, is going; next wicket went for nothing*). **19.** Die (esp. in p.p.; & in many phrr.; as *go the way of all the earth* or pop. *of all flesh, to a better world, to one's account* or *own place, aloft, off the hooks*, etc.). **20.** Fall, give way, succumb, break down, crack. **21.** Make way *to, towards, into,* etc. (*go to Jericho,* || *Bath, blazes, hell,* etc., be off out of speaker's presence; *go to Canossa,* humble oneself after recalcitrance, w. ref. to Emperor Henry IV in 1077; *go to the* DEVIL; *which way goes to Bristol; go to a ball, to church, market,* etc., attend it; *go to school,* get instruction; *go on pilgrimage, an errand, the spree,* etc.; *go to sea,* become barrister, sailor; *go on the stage, the streets,* become actor, prostitute; *go to stool*). **22.** Proceed to do (*went to find him*), and do (esp. colloq. — *be so foolish as to do*; also vulg. *have been & gone & done it,* made a blunder, an error, the (a-)doing, **23.** Act as *bail* (for person; also abs. in parenthesis *I'll go bail, I assure you*). **24.** Have recourse, refer, appeal, *to* (|| *go to the* COUNTRY, test opinion by general election; *go to war, work,* etc.; vulg., *would not go to* or *for to* do it, be so inconsiderate etc. as to). **25.** Carry action to certain point (*went all lengths; will go so far as to say; will go as high as £100,* in bidding or offering price; *go halves* or *shares,* share equally *with,* or abs.; *went to great expense, trouble,* etc.; *go the whole HOG; go better* or *one better,* outbid or outdo adversary, one better. **26.** Penetrate, sink, (*ship went to the bottom; goes to one's heart,* grieves him); find room, (of number) be capable of being contained in another either without remainder or simply (*will not go into the basket; 6 into 12 goes twice, into 5 will not go, into 13 goes twice and one over; thread too thick to go through needle*). **27.** Belong *in* receptacle, *on* shelf etc. **28.** Pass, be allotted, etc., to person (of

prize, victory, inheritance, office, etc.), be applied to purpose, contribute *to* or *towards* result, amount together *to* (*12 inches go to the foot*), tend to show etc. **29.** Reach, extend, (*the difference goes deep; as, so, far as it goes,* caution against taking statement too widely; *goes a long way,* has great etc. effect *towards,* also of food, money, etc., lasts long etc., buys much etc.). **30.** Pass into certain condition (*go brown, blind, mad, to seed;* is *hot & cold,* have accesses of fever or shame; *go to pieces,* break up). **31.** v.t. Bid, declare, as *~* NAP³, *two spades.* **32.** Phr.: *~ native,* (of a white man) adopt the uncivilized mode of life of the natives among whom he lives; *go sick* (MIL.), enter oneself on the sick list; (sl.) *go it,* act vigorously, furiously, etc., indulge in dissipation; *going fifteen* etc., in one's fifteenth etc. year: *going to, about to,* intending to (used as fut. part.); *be gone,* take oneself off: *gone,* dead (often *dead & gone*), very ill, deeply entangled; *go fetch!; gone on* (sl.), infatuated with; *far* (order to dog). **33.** With prepp.: *go about,* set to work at; *go at,* attack, take in hand, energetically; *go behind* (decision etc.), re-examine grounds of; *go for,* go to fetch, pass or be accounted as nothing, little, etc., strive to attain, (sl.) attack; *go into,* enter (profession, Parliament), frequent (society), take part in, allow oneself to pass into (hysterics etc.), dress oneself in (mourning etc.), investigate; *go off one's* HEAD¹; *go on,* become chargeable to (parish, relief fund, etc.); *go over,* inspect details of, rehearse, retouch; *go over the top* or *bags* (MIL.), issue from trench to attack enemy; *go through,* discuss in detail, scrutinize, perform, (ceremony, recitation, etc.), undergo, (of book) be sold out in (so many editions); *go up the line* (MIL.), leave the base for the front; *go with,* go back from or upon one's word etc., fail to keep it; **34.** With advv.: *go about,* move from place to place, endeavour to do; *go ahead,* proceed without hesitation; *go along with,* = go with; *go back from* or *upon one's word* etc., fail to keep it: *go by,* pass; *go down,* sink (of ship), be continued to specified point, fall before conqueror, be recorded in writing, be swallowed, find acceptance, (Cricket) take the same view as, match, follow the drift of; *go in,* enter as competitor (*go in & win*), form of encouragement), (Cricket) take or begin innings, (of sun etc.) be obscured; *go in for,* take as one's object, pursuit, study, principle, etc.; *go off,* leave the stage, begin, explode, die, gradually cease to be felt, deteriorate, become unconscious in sleep, faint, etc., be got rid of by sale, succeed well, badly, etc.; *go on,* continue, persevere, (*doing, with, in,* or abs.), proceed as next step to do, conduct

oneself *shamefully* etc., rail *at* (colloq.), appear on stage, begin bowling, take one's turn to do something, (colloq. in imperat.) don't talk nonsense; *going on for*, approaching (a time, age, etc.); *go out*, leave room or house, fight duel, be extinguished, leave office (of Government), cease to be fashionable, depart *to colony* etc., (esp. of girls) leave home for employment usu. *as governess* etc., mix in society, (of workmen) strike, (of heart etc.) expand with love etc. *to person*; *go over*, change one's party or religion; *go round*, pay informal visit to, be long enough to encompass, (of food etc.) suffice for whole party; *go through with*, complete, not leave unfinished *go* in (imperat.; arch.), interjection of remonstrance, incredulity, impatience, etc.; *go together*, be concomitant, match; *go under*, sink, fail, succumb. 35. Comb.: *go-ahead*, enterprising; *go-as-you-please*, unfettered by regulations; *go-between*, intermediary; negotiator; *go-by*, passing (usu. in *give the go-by to*, outstrip, leave behind, elude, disregard, cut, slight); *go-cart*, wheeled frame for teaching child to walk, kind of perambulator, litter, palanquin, handcart; *go-off*, start (usu. *at the first go-off*); *go-to-meeting*, (of hat, clothes, etc.) fit or kept for going to church in. [com.-Teut.; OE *gān* cf. G *gehen*; past supplied f. WEND]

gŏ[2], n. (pl. *goes*). Act of going (*come-&-go*, traffic, movement to & fro); mettle, spirit, dash, animation; (colloq.) embarrassing turn of affairs (*there's, what, a go!*; *a rum go*); turn at doing something (*have a go at*); portion of liquor or food served; (Cribbage) player's inability to play, counting one to opponent; (colloq.) *it's no go*, nothing can be done; (colloq.) *all or quite the go*, in fashion; (colloq.) *near go*, close shave; (colloq.) *on the go*, in motion, also in a **state** of decline; ‖ LITTLE-GO. [f. prec.]

ǵoad, n. & v.t. 1. Spiked stick used for urging cattle; thing that torments, incites, or stimulates. 2. v.t. Urge with ~, irritate; instigate, drive, by annoyance (often *on*; also *to do*, *into doing*, *to* or *into fury* etc.). [OE *gād* cf. Lombard *gaida* arrowhead; not related to obs. *gad* in same sense]

goal, n. Point marking end of race; object of effort or ambition; destination; posts between which ball is to be driven in football etc., points so won (DROP[2] make, PLACE[2], *score*, a ~); (Rom. Ant.) pillar at turning-point in chariot race; ~*keeper*, player stationed to protect; ~*line*, line between each pair of ~posts produced as end-boundary of field of play (cf. TOUCH-*line*). Hence ~ie [-i[3]] n. (colloq.), ~*keeper*. [etym. dub.; once in 1315 = limit, then not till 1531; prob. not f. F *gaude* rod]

goat, n. Hardy lively wanton strong-smelling usu. horned & bearded ruminant quadruped (*sheep & ~s*, the good & the wicked, see *Matt*. xxv. 32, 33); (sl.) subfamily to which ~ belongs; zodiacal sign Capricorn (G~); licentious person; *get one's ~* (sl.), irritate one; *play the* GIDDY ~; ~*god*, Pan; ~*herd*, one who tends ~s; ~*'s beard* meadowsweet, also salsify; ~*skin*, (garment, bottle, made of) skin of ~; ~*sucker*, nocturnal bird resembling swift; ~*'s wool*, non-existent thing. Hence ~ISH[1], ~Y[2], aa., ~ISHLY[2] adv., ~ISHNESS n. [com.-Teut.; OE *gāt* cf. G *geiss*, cogn. w. L *haedus* kid]

goatee', n. Chin-tuft like goat's beard. [-EE]

goat'ling, n. Goat 1–2 years old. [-LING[1]]

gŏb[1], n., & v.i. (vulg.). 1. Clot of slimy substance, e.g. spittle; mouth. 2. v.i. (-bb-). Spit. [f. OF *gobe* mouthful]

*gŏb[2], n. (sl.). Sailor. [prob. abbr. of *gobby* (f. GOB[1]), sl. for coastguardsman (from a supposed addiction to spitting]

gŏbäng', n. Game played on chequerboard. [f. Jap. *goban* f. Chin. *k'i pan* chessboard, w. assim. to *go*, *bang*]

gŏb'ĕt, n. (arch.). Piece, lump, esp. of raw flesh or food; extract from a text set for translation or comment. [f. OF *gobet* (GOB[1], -ET[1])]

gŏb'ble[1], v.t. & i. Eat hurriedly & noisily; ‖ ~*stitch*, one made too long from hurry. Hence GŎB'bler[1] [-ER[1]] n. [perh. f. GOB[1]+-LE(3)]

gŏb'ble[2], n. (golf). Rapid straight putt into the hole. [perh. f. prec.]

gŏb'ble[3], v.i. (Of turkeycock) make characteristic sound in throat; make such sound when speaking, from rage etc. Hence GŎB'bler[2] n., turkeycock. [imit.]

gŏb'elin, a. G~ *tapestry*, made, or imitated from that made, at the State factory in Paris called *Gobelins* after its founders. [f. OF *gobelet* (*gobel* cup etym.

gobe'mouche (gŏb'mōōsh), n. (pl. ~s pr. like sing.). Credulous newsmonger. [f. F *gobemouches* lit. fly-catcher (*gober* swallow, *mouches* flies) mistaken by E writers for pl.]

gŏb'lĕt, n. (Arch.) Metal or glass drinking-cup, bowl-shaped & without handles, sometimes with foot & cover; (Poet.) drinking-cup; (Commerce.) glass with foot & stem. [f. OF *gobelet* (*gobel* cup etym. dub, +-ET[1])]

gŏb'lin, n. Mischievous ugly demon. [f. F *gobelin* perh. f. med. L f. Gk *Kobalos* rogue, *kobaloi* sprites invoked by rogues]

gŏb'ÿ, n. Small fish with ventral fins joined into a disk or sucker. [f. L *gobius*, co-. f. Gk *kōbios* GUDGEON]

gŏd[1], n. 1. Superhuman being worshipped as having power over nature & human fortunes, deity, (~ *of heaven*, Jupiter; ~ *of hell*, Pluto; ~ *of the sea*, Neptune; ~ *of day*, sun, Phoebus; ~ *of fire*, Vulcan; ~ *of love*, Mars; ~ *of love*, blind ~, Cupid;

~ of vine, Bacchus ; ~ of this world, the Devil ; Ye ~s !, Ye ~s & little fishes !, mock-heroic exclamations ; feast, sight, for the ~s, something exquisite etc.). 2. Image, animal, or other object, worshipped as symbolizing, being the visible habitation of, or itself possessing, divine power ; an idol. 3. Adored, admired, or influential person. 4. (Theatr., pl.) occupants of gallery. 5. (God). Supreme being, Creator & Ruler of universe, often the Lord God, Almighty God, God Almighty ; God the Father, Son, Holy Ghost, Persons of Trinity ; Act[1] of God ; with God, dead & in heaven ; God's truth, the absolute truth ; God's earth, the whole earth ; oh, my, good, etc., God!, exclamations of pain, grief, or anger ; God bless, damn, help, you!, him!, etc., God forbid, grant—!, prayers or imprecations ; God bless me!, my life!, my soul!, you!, etc., exclamations of surprise ; God willing, if circumstances allow ; under God, used to qualify attribution of full agency to man ; thank God!, parenthetic expression of pleasure at turn of events etc.; God knows, it is beyond mortal or my knowledge, I do not know ; (also) I call God to witness that ; for God's sake, with urgent petitions or imprecations ; ~speed, God's image, human body ; God's image,

by God, confirmatory oath; so HELP[1] me God.). 6. ~father, ~mother, ~parent, ~'papa, ~'mamma, sponsor at baptism, & so of the converse relation ~child, ~son, ~'daughter ; ~father (fig.), person after whom person or thing is named, (vb) be responsible for, give one's name to ; ~'fearing, sincerely religious ; ~-forsaken, devoid of all merit, dismal, (what a ~forsaken hole !); God'man, Christ ; God's-acre (imit., of German), churchyard ; God's book, Bible ; ~'send, unexpected welcome event or acquisi- tion ; God's image, human body ; ~'speed, utterance of words God speed you!, usn. in bid person ~speed, wish him success in undertaking, journey, etc. Hence ~WARDS adv. [com.-Teut.; cf. Du. god, G. gott ; perh. f. Aryan gheu invoke or gheu sacrifice]

god[2] v.t. (rare; -dd-). Deify ; ~ it, play the god. [f. prec.]

god'dess, n. Female deity in polytheism (esp. in Latin mythol.:~ of heaven, hell, love, wisdom, moon, corn, war, Juno, Pro- serpine, Venus, Minerva, Diana, Ceres, Bellona) ; woman one adores. [-ESS[1]]

go'det (-dā), n. Triangular piece of stuff inserted in a dress, glove, etc. (also attrib., as ~ skirt). [F]

gode'tia (-sha), n. Free-flowering hardy annual plant. [Godet Swiss botanist, f]

god'head (-ĕd), n. Being God or a god, di- vine nature, deity; the G~, God. [-HEAD]

god'less, a. Without a god; not recog- nizing God; impious, wicked. Hence ~NESS n. [-LESS]

god'like, a. Resembling God or a god in some quality; fit for, like that of, a god. [-LIKE]

god'ly, a. Religious, pious, devout. Hence ~INESS n. [-LY[1]]

godown' n. (Anglo-Ind.). Warehouse in parts of Asia, esp. India. [f. Malay godong w. assim. to go down]

god'wit, n. Marsh bird like curlew but with upward-curved bill. [?]

goer, n. Person, thing, that goes (good, slow, etc., ~; comers & ~s).

goethian (gö'ti·an) a. & n. (Follower) of Goethe, like Goethe, his writings, views, etc. [J. W. von Goethe, German poet 1749–1832. -IAN]

gof(f)er, goph'er, gauf'fer (gö-, gŏ-), v.t., & n. 1. Make wavy, flute, crimp, (lace edge, trimming, etc.) with heated irons ; ~ed edges of book, embossed. 2. n. Iron used for ~ing ; ornamental plaiting used for frills etc. [f. F gaufre (see prec., gaufrer stamp with patterned

*gö-gett'er, n. (colloq.). One who secures what he sets out to get; pushing person, thruster. [go[1], GET[1], -ER[1] (1)]

gog'gle, v.i. & t., a., & n. 1. Squint, roll eyes about (or with eyes as subj.), (of eyes) project ; turn (eyes) sideways or from side to side. 2. adj. (Of eyes) pro- tuberant, full & rolling ; so ~-EYED[2] (-gel-id)a. 3. n. pl. Kind of spectacles for protecting eyes from glare, dust, etc., often with coloured glasses, wire gauze, etc.; (sl.) round-lensed spectacles; sheep disease, staggers. [a. & n.f. vb; f. 14th c. etym. dub., cf. W gogi shake, Gael. gog nodding of head]

gog'let, gug'glet, n. (Anglo-Ind.). Long- necked vessel usu. of porous ware for keeping water cool. [f. Port. gorgoleta]

Goid'el, n. Member of GADHELIC races. Hence (=GADHELIC) **Goidel'ic** a. & n. [f. O.Ir. Gŏidel]

go'ing, n. In vbl senses; esp.: condition of ground for walking, riding, etc.; (for a-going, & now regarded as part.) in action (set the clock ~), existing, to be had, (one of the best fellows ~; there is cold beef ~; ~son, (usu. strange, such, etc.) behaviour. [-ING[1]]

goi'tre (-ter), n. Morbid enlargement of thyroid gland, often showing as large pendulous swelling in neck, bronchocele, dewlap. Hence **goi'trous**[2] (-terd) a. [F, back formation f. goitreux f. L guttur throat, -ous]

goi'trous, a. Affected with, like, of, (of places) characterized by prevalence of, goitre. [f. goitreux see prec.]

Golcon'da, n. Mine of wealth (lit. or fig.). [old name of Hyderabad]

gōld, n. & a. 1. Precious yellow non-rusting malleable ductile metal of high specific gravity (*as GOOD as* ~); coins made of this, money in large sums, wealth (fig.), brilliant, beautiful, or precious things, stuff, etc. (*a heart, voice, of* ~; *age of* ~, = GOLDEN *age*; *she is pure* ~; *all that glisters or glitters is not* ~); the metal used for coating surface or as pigment, gilding; the colour of the metal (*old* ~ n., dull brownish-golden yellow; *old* ~ adj., thus coloured); bull's eye of archery target (usu. gilt). 2. ~ *amalgam*, ~ combined with mercury in plastic state; ~ *beater*, one who beats ~ out into ~-*leaf*; ~-*beater's skin*, membrane used to separate leaves of ~ during beating, also as covering for slight wounds; ~ *brick* (orig. U.S. sl.), thing with only a surface appearance of value, sham, fraud; ~ *digger*, one who digs for ~, *(sl.)* coquette who wheedles money out of men; ~-*dust*, ~ in fine particles as often found; ~-*fever*, rage for going in search of ~; ~-*field*, district in which ~ is found; ~-*finch*, bright-coloured song-bird with patch of yellow on wings, (sl.) gold coin, sovereign; ~-*fish*, small red Chinese carp kept for ornament; ~-*foil*, ~-*leaf*, ~ beaten into thin sheet, *-foil* being the thicker; ~-*mine*, lit. & fig. source of wealth; ~ *plate*, vessels made of ~; ~-*rush*, a rush to new ~-*field*; ~-*smith*, worker in ~(~-*smith beetle*, with ~-coloured wing-covers); ‖ *Gold Stick*, (bearer of) gilt rod borne on State occasions by colonel of Lifeguards or captain of Gentlemen-at-arms. 3. adj. Wholly or chiefly of, coloured like, ~; (of sums in depreciated currencies) reckoned at par (~ *francs* etc., the stated amount at the nominal undepreciated value of the franc etc.). [com.-Teut.; cf. G *gold*; cogn. w. YELLOW]

gōl'den, a. Made, consisting, of gold (G~ FLEECE; ~ *key*, money used to remove obstacle; ~ *abounding* in, yielding, gold; coloured, shining, like gold; precious, excellent, important, (~ *opinions*, high respect; ~-*mouthed*, eloquent; *a ~ remedy, opportunity, saying; the ~ rule*, that in *Matt.* vii. 12: ~ *mean*, neither too much nor too little, principle of moderation; ~ *number*, year's number in Metonic lunar cycle of 19 years; ~ *age*, first of four ages, see BRAZEN), when men were happy & innocent, also most prosperous period of nation's condition or literature); ~ *balls*, = *three* BALL'S; ~-*eye*, kind of sea-duck; G~ *Horn*, curved inlet of Bosporus, the harbour of Constantinople; ‖ ~-*knop*, ladybird, ~ *rain*, kind of firework; ~-*rod*, plant with rod-like stem & spike of bright yellow flowers; ‖ ~ SYRUP; ~ *wedding*, fiftieth anniversary. [-EN'; earlier *gilden*]

gōl'dilŏcks, n. Kinds of plant, esp. a species of buttercup. [f. obs. *goldy*, LOCK[1]]

gŏlf (*also* gŏf), n., & v.i. 1. Game for two persons or couples in which a small hard ball is struck with clubs having wooden or metal heads into each of a series of (18 or 9) holes on smooth greens at varying distances apart and separated by fair-ways, rough ground, hazards, etc., the object being to hole the ball in the fewest possible strokes; ~-*club*, implement used in striking ball, (premises occupied by) association for playing ~. 2. v.i. Play ~, whence **gŏlf'ER**[1] (*also* gŏf) n. [perh. f. Du. *kolf*, cf. G *kolbe* club]

Gŏl'ath, n. Giant; ~ *beetle*, large African black white-striped beetle; ~ (*crane*), powerful travelling crane. [1 *Sam.* xvii]

gŏll'iwŏg, int. [Used, esp. by negroes, for) bugbear. [?]

gŏll'y, int. [deformation of GOD] God, *by* God. See GALOSH.

‖ **golosh**. See GALOSH.

golup'tious (-shus), **golóp'**, a. (joc.). Luscious, delightful. [perh. joc. for *voluptuous*]

-gon, suf. f. Gk -*gōnos* -angled, forming nn. as *hexagon, polygon, n-gon*, figure with six, several, *n*, angles.

gŏmbeen', n. (Anglo-Ir.). Usury (~ *man*, money-lender). [f. Ir. *gaimbín* perh. f. same OCelt. as med. L *cambium* CHANGE]

gŏm(b)rŏŏn', n. Persian pottery, imitated in Chelsea ware. [town on Persian gulf]

Gŏmŏr'rah, n. (Type of) wicked town. [*Gen.* xviii, xix]

gŏn'ad, n. (biol.). Undifferentiated germ-gland, serving both as ovary & spermary. [f. Gk *goné, gonos*, generation, seed, +-AD]

gŏn'dola, n. Light flat-bottomed boat with cabin amidships & high point at each end worked by one oar at stern, used on Venetian canals; car suspended from airship. [It. etym. dub.]

gŏndolier', n. Rower of gondola. [F, f. It. *gondoliere* (prec., -IER)]

gone (gawn, gŏn), a. In vbl senses; esp. ~ lost, hopeless, (*a ~ man*, also **gŏn'ER**[1] (*gaw-*) n., sl.; *a ~ case*, COON'); past, by-gone, (usu. *past &* ~). [p.p. of GO]

gŏn'falon, n. Banner, often with stream-ers, hung from cross-bar, esp. as standard of some Italian republics. [f. It. *gon-falone* f. OHG *gundfano* f. OTeut. *gunthjō* war, *fano* banner]

gŏnfalonier', n. Standard-bearer; chief magistrate in some Italian republics. [f. It. *gonfaloniere* (prec., -IER)]

gŏng, n., & v.t. 1. Metal disk with turned rim giving resonant note when struck; saucer-shaped bell. 2. v.t. (Of motoring traffic police) direct (motorist) to stop by striking ~. [Malay, orig. init.]

gŏn'gorism (-ngg-), n. A Spanish literary style marked by inversion, antithesis, &

classical allusion, corresponding to EUPHUISM in England. [*Góngora y Argote*, Sp. poet, 1561-1627, +-ISM]

goniom'eter, n. Instrument for measuring angles. So **goniom'etry** n., **goniomet'ric(al)** aa. [f. ~(metre), f. Gk *gōnia* angle, -METER]

gonorrhoe'a (-rēa), n. Inflammatory discharge of mucus from urethra or vagina. Hence ~AL (-rē'al) a. [med. L, f. Gk *gonorrhoia* (*gonos* seed, *rhoia* flux)]

good, a. (BETTER, BEST), & n. **1.** Having the right qualities, satisfactory, adequate, (*a ~ fire*, not too small or dull; *meat keeps ~*, untainted; *~ soil*, fertile; *not ~ enough*, collog.; not worth doing, accepting, etc.; *~ money*, genuine; as conventional epithet in *the ~ ship* —, *the town of* —; *~ law*, valid, sound; *is ~ eating* etc., attractive to eat etc.). **2.** Commendable (esp. in *~ men & true*); *~ old* —!, collog. form of approval; *that's a ~ un*, si, a lie worth telling; also in courteous, patronizing, ironically polite, or indignant address, as *my ~ friend, man, sir*, or in polite or indulgently contemptuous description, as *your ~ lady, the ~ man*; *the ~ people*, fairies; *of ~ family*, well-born; *in ~ spirits*, not depressed; *a ~ leg*, well shaped). **3.** Right, proper, *gracious!; be so ~ as, ~ enough, to*, = please to; *how ~ of you!; did me a ~ turn or office; has always been ~ to me; say a ~ word for*, commend, defend. **6.** (Esp. of child) well behaved, not giving trouble, (often *as ~ as gold*). **7.** Gratifying, agreeable, favourable, advantageous, beneficial, wholesome, (*~ news; things are in ~ train*, going well; so in forms of greeting or parting, as *~ morning*, ||*~ day, ~ night; have a ~ time*, enjoy oneself; *have a ~ night*, sleep well; *a ~ saying or story or thing, as ~ as a play*, amusing; *oh! is ~ for burns; beer is not ~ for him or his health; are acorns ~ to eat?; take in ~ part*, not be annoyed at). **8.** Adapted to an end, efficient, suitable, competent, (esp. with agent-nouns, as *a ~ driver; at describing* etc.; *has been a ~ wife to him*). **9.** Reliable, safe, sure, (*a ~ man*, financially sound, able to meet liabilities; *~ debts*, sure to be paid; *a ~ life*, likely to last long, such as insurance office will accept; *~ for an amount*, safely to be trusted to pay it, also of draft etc., drawn for so much; *~ for*, inclined for, up to, as *a ~ beating*, ample, considerable, (*gave her a ~ excuse; a ~* DEAL¹, FEW,

MANY; *have a ~ mind*, be much inclined to do; often as intensive before adj., as *went a ~ round pace, will take a ~ long time*). **11.** Not less than (*played for a ~ hour; it is three miles ~ from the station*). **12.** As *~ as*, practically (*~ as told me so; as ~ as dead; it is as ~ as done); make ~*, compensate for, pay (expense), fulfil (promise), effect (purpose), demonstrate (statement), substantiate (charge), gain & hold (position), replace or restore (thing lost or damaged), (without obj.) accomplish what one has attempted. **13.** *~ breeding*, correct or courteous manners; *~ fellow*, sociable person, agreeable companion; *~-fellowship*, conviviality, sociability; *~-for-nothing, ~-for-nought*, a. & n. worthless (person); G~ FRIDAY; *~ humour*, cheerful mood or disposition; *~-humoured*, whence *~-hum'ouredly* a. ~ *look'ing*, handsome; ~-*looking*, of virtuous appearance; *~ looks*, personal beauty; *~ luck*, being fortunate, happy chance, (often *~ luck to you!*, as wish); ||*~man* (arch.), head of household, husband, father, etc.; *~ money* (rule), high wages; *~-morrow* (arch.), = ~ morning; *~ nature*, kindly disposition, willingness to postpone one's own interests, whence *~-na'tured²* a., *~-na'turedly²* adv.; ~ -*neighbourhood, neighbourliness, ~-neighbourship*, friendly conduct; *~ sense*, soundness of judgement, practical wisdom; *~ temper*, freedom from irritability, whence *~-tem'pered²* a., *~-tem'peredly²* adv.; *~ thing*, advantageous bargain or speculation, witty saying, (pl.) dainties; *~ wife*, mistress of house (esp. Sc.). **14.** n. Virtuous persons (*the ~; & bad alike respect him*). **15.** What is ~ or beneficial, well-being, profit, benefit, advantage, (*is a power for ~; deceive him for his ~; what ~ will it do?; much ~ may it do you!*, often iron.; *do ~*, show kindness to or act philanthropically, be beneficial to or benefit; *to the ~*, as balance on right side, net profit, something extra, etc.; *come to ~*, yield ~ result; *for ~ & all*, permanently, finally, definitively; *be any, some, no, much, ~*, be of any etc. use; *what is the ~ of it?; what ~ is it?*). **16.** Desirable end or object, thing worth attaining; *no ~, some mischief* (is up to, after, no ~). **17.** pl. Movable property; *~ and chattels, wares, (piece of ~s*, joc. person); || things for transmission by rail etc. (opp. passengers; so *~s agent, station, train*, etc.; *by ~s, by ~s train*). Hence ~ISH¹(2) a. [com.-Teut.; OE *gōd* cf. G *gut*; perh. f. same root as GATHER]

good-bye', int. & n. (Saying of) farewell. [contr. of *God be with you!*, with good substituted on anal. of *good-morning* etc.]

good'ly, a. Comely, handsome; of considerable size etc.; (iron.) fine, grand. Hence ~NESS n. [OE *gódlic* (GOOD, -LY²)]

good'ness, n. Virtue; positive or comparative excellence; benevolence, kindness, generosity; (have the ~, be kind enough to); what is good in thing, its essence or strength; (in exclamations, substituted for) God (~ gracious!, excl. of surprise or indignation; ~ knows, I do not know, I appeal to Heaven to witness; I wish to~; thank~!; for ~' sake). [OE gōdnes (GOOD, -NESS)]

good'will', n. Kindly feeling to person, favour; cheerful acquiescence, heartiness, zeal; privilege granted by seller of business, of trading as recognized successor.

Good'wins, n. pl. The ~, the Goodwin sands. [place]

Good'wood, n. (Used for) race-meeting on course near ~ Park, Sussex (~ cup, chief prize at this). [place]

good'y¹, n. (arch.). Elderly woman of lower class (often as prefix to surname). [for GOODWIFE, cf. HUSSY]

good'y², n. A sweetmeat, bonbon. [-Y³]

good'y³, good'y-good'y, a. Primly, pretentiously, inopportunely, obtrusively, weakly, or sentimentally virtuous (talk ~, in ~ manner). Hence good'iness n. [-Y³]

goof, n. (sl.). Silly or stupid person. Hence ~Y² a. (sl.), silly. [cf. dial. goof doit]

goog'ly, n. (cricket). Off-break ball bowled with leg-break action. [?]

goosan'der, n. Bird allied to duck but with sharp serrated bill. [?]

goose, n. (pl. geese pr. gēs). 1. Kinds of web-footed bird between duck & swan in size, female of this (opp. GANDER), its flesh, (all his geese are swans, he over-estimates; kill the ~ that lays the golden eggs, sacrifice future profit to present necessities; COOK² person's ~; say so to ~; sauce for ~ is sauce for GANDER). 2. Simpleton, whence gōōs'ey³ n. 3. Tailor's smoothing iron (with handle like ~'s neck; pl. ~s). 4. FOX¹ & geese; ||~-club, for providing poor people with Christmas ~ paid for by small instalments; ~-flesh, rough bristling state of skin produced by cold or fright; ~-foot, kinds of plant named from shape of leaves; ~-grass, silverweed, cleavers; ~herd, one who tends geese; ~quill, quill-feather of ~ esp. used as pen; ~-skin, ~-flesh; ~-step, balancing drill taught to army recruits & much used in German army. [Aryan; OE gōs, cf. G gans, L anser, Gk khēn; gander perh. f. prec.]

¶ goose'gog gōg (-zg-), n. (colloq.). Gooseberry. [joc. corruption]

goose'berr'ly (-zb-), n. (Edible berry of) any thorny species of Ribes; wine made of ~ies; play~², act as chaperon, play propriety, for pair of lovers;~y-FOOL². [perh. f. prec.]

gopher, n. See GOFFER.

goph'er², n. American burrowing rodent; N.-American ground-squirrel; nocturnal

burrowing land-tortoise of Southern U.S. [prob. f. F gaufre honeycomb; cf. GOFFER]

goph'er³, n. Tree from wood of which Noah's ark was made; (~-wood) tree yielding yellowish timber. [Heb.]

gōr'al, n. An Indian antelope. [native name]

gōr'cock, n. Male of the red grouse. [etym. of gor dub.]

Gord'ian, a. ~ knot, intricate knot, difficult problem or task, (cut the ~ knot, solve problem by force or by evading the conditions). [f. Gordius, tier of knot cut by Alexander the Great, +-AN]

gōre¹, n. Blood shed & thickened or clotted. Hence gōr'y² a., gōr'ily² adv. [OE gor dung, dirt, cf. Du. goor mud]

gōre², n., & v.t. Wedge-shaped piece of cloth adjusting width of a garment; triangular or lune-shaped piece in umbrella, balloon, dome, globe, etc. 2. v.t. Shape, narrow, with ~. [OE gāra triangular piece of land, cogn. w. gār spear, w. ref. to shape of spearhead]

gōre³, v.t. Pierce with the horn or (rarely) tusk (also transf. of rocks piercing ship). [perh. f. OE gār a spear]

gorge, n. (Rhet.) internal throat; what has been swallowed, contents of stomach, (cast the ~ at, reject with loathing; one's ~ rises at, one is sickened or disgusted by); (Fortif.) neck of bastion or other outwork, rear entrance to a work; narrow opening, usu. with stream, between hills; solid object meant to be swallowed as bait for fish. [OF, etym. dub.]

gorge², v.i. & t., & n. 1. Feed greedily; satiate, glut; swallow, devour greedily; fill full, distend, choke up. 2. n. Act of gorging, surfeit. [f. OF gorger (prec.)]

gōr'geous (-jus), a. Richly coloured, sumptuous, magnificent; (of diction) ornate, dazzling. Hence~LY² adv.,~NESS n., (-jus-). [f. OF gorgias finely dressed, etym. dub.]

gōr'get¹, n. (Hist.) piece of armour for throat, woman's wimple; necklace; patch of colour on throat of bird etc.; ~patch, distinguishing mark on collar of military uniform. [f. OF gorgete (GORGE¹, -ET¹)]

gōr'get², n. (surg.). Channel-shaped steel instrument used in operations for stone etc. [f. F gorgeret (GORGE¹, as tubular)]

Gor'gĭō, gŏr'jĭō, n. (pl. -os). (Gipsy for) non-gipsy. [Romany]

gŏr'gon, n. (Gk Myth.) one of three snake-haired women whose looks turned any beholder to stone; terrible or ugly person, repellent woman. Hence gŏrgōn'IAN a. [f. L Gorgo -onis f. Gk Gorgō -ous (gorgos terrible)]

gŏrgō'nĭa, n. (pl. -iae, -ias). Sea-fan, kind of polyp. [prec., as hardening in air, +-IA¹]

gŏr'gŏnize, v.t. Stare at like gorgon. [-IZE]

Gorgonzol'a, n. A rich cheese. [~ in Italy]

gorill'a, n. Large powerful ferocious arboreal anthropoid ape. [Afr. for wild man in Gk account of Hanno's voyage]

gorm'andize (see Ap.), n. & v.i. & t. *gourmandise* (see Ap.), n. 1. Habits of a GOURMAND; indulgence in good eating, gluttony. 2. vb. Eat, devour, voraciously, whence **gorm'andizer[1]** n. [vb f. n., f. F gourmandise (GOURMAND, -ISE)]

gorse, n. Prickly yellow-flowered shrub, whin, furze. Hence **gors'y[2]** a. [OE gorst, cogn. w. G gerst, L hordeum, barley]

Gors'edd (-eth), n. Meeting of Welsh bards & druids (esp. as daily preliminary to the eisteddfod). [W., = session]

gosh, int. (Also by ~) by God. [for God]

gos'hawk (-s-h-), n. Kinds of large short-winged hawk. [OE gōs-hafoc (GOOSE, HAWK)]

Gōsh'en, n. Place of light or plenty. [Gen. xlv. 10 etc., Exod. viii. 22, ix. 26]

gos'ling (-z-), n. Young goose. [-LING[1]]

gos'pel, n. 1. Glad tidings preached by Christ; religious doctrine of Christ & his apostles, Christian revelation; protestant or evangelical doctrine (opp. *mass*); record of Christ's life in books of four evangelists; any of those books; portion from one of them read at Communion service. 2. Thing that may safely be believed (*takes his dreams for* ~); principle that one acts upon, believes in, or preaches (*the* ~ *of efficiency, laissez faire, soap & water*). 3. ~book, containing ~s read at Communion; ~ oath, sworn on the ~s; ||~shop, Methodist chapel; ~ side, N. side of altar, at which ~ is read; ~ truth, something as true as ~. [OE godspel, corrupted by confusion w. God f. gōd spel good tidings (GOOD, SPELL[1])]

gos'peller, n. Reader of gospel in Communion service; hot ~, zealous puritan, rabid propagandist. [-ER[1]]

Gōss, n. Kind of crest china invented by W. H. ~ of Stoke-on-Trent. [person]

göss'amer, n. & a. 1. Light filmy substance, the webs of small spiders, floating in calm air or spread over grass; a thread of this; something flimsy; delicate gauze; hence ~ED[2] (erd), ~Y[2] aa. 2. adj. Light & flimsy as ~. [ME gossomer perh. = goose-summer or St Martin's summer, i.e. early November when geese were eaten, ~ being most seen then]

göss'ip, n., & v.i. 1. || (Arch.) familiar acquaintance, friend, (esp. of women); idle talker, newsmonger, tattler, (esp. of women); idle talk, groundless rumours, tittle-tattle; easy unconstrained talk or writing esp. about persons or social incidents; hence ~ED[2], ~Y[2] aa. 2. v.i. Talk idly or tittle-tattle; write in gossipy style; hence ~ER[1] n. [earlier senses, *sponsor, fellow-sponsor, one's child's sponsor, at baptism*; OE godsibb person related to one in God (sibb, sib, akin)]

gosson', n. (Anglo-Ir.). Lad. [f. F garçon]

gōt, past & p.p. of GET. ~-up, factitious, artificially produced, adorned, etc., with a view to effect or deception.

Goth, n. One of a German tribe who invaded Eastern & Western Empires in 3rd-5th cc. & founded kingdoms in Italy, France, & Spain; rude, uncivilized, or ignorant person, esp. one who destroys works of art (cf. VANDAL), whence ~ISH[1] a. [OE Gotan pl. f. LL f. Gk Gothoi]

Goth'am (-tam), n. Typical foolish town (*wiseman of* ~, fool); "(colloq.) New York City (usu. pr. gō'tham). Hence ~ITE[1]) n. [perh. f. the village in Notts.]

Goth'ic, a. & n. 1. Of the Goths or their language. 2. (Archit.) In the pointed-arch style prevalent in Western Europe in 12th-16th cc., including in England the Early English, Decorated, & Perpendicular (orig. sense *not classical*). 3. Barbarous, rude, uncouth. 4. (Print., a. & n.) German, also black-letter, (type); hence **Goth'ically** adv., ~ISM(2,3,4) n., ~IZE(2,3) v.t. & t., 5. n. ~ language; ~ architecture; ~ type. [f. L Gothicus (GOTH, -IC)]

gött'en, p.p. (arch. & U.S.) of GET[1].

gouache (gōŏ'ahsh), n. Way of painting in opaque colours ground in water & thickened with gum & honey. [F, f. It. guazzo]

Goud'a, n. Flat round cheese made at ~ in Holland. [place]

gouge (gowj, gōō'), n., & v.t. 1. Concave-bladed chisel used in carpentry & surgery. 2. v.t. Cut with ~; cut out (a cork, a channel) (as) with ~; force (out, esp. person's eye with thumb) (as) with ~; force out eye of. [F, f. LL gubia]

Gouląd' (gōō-), n. Lotion of sub-acetate of lead in solution. [L ~, French surgeon]

goulash (gōō'lahsh), n. 1. Highly seasoned stew of steak and vegetables. 2. (Contract Bridge) re-deal of the four hands (unshuffled, but with each hand arranged in suits and order of value). [f. Magyar gulyás-hús t. gulyás herdsman + hús meat]

gourd (gōŏrd, goord), n. (Large fleshy fruit of) kinds of trailing or climbing plant; rind of the fruit emptied, dried, & used as bottle etc., whence ~FUL(2) n. [f. F gourde t. L cucurbita]

gourmand (goorm'and, & see Ap.), a. & n. 1. Gluttonous, fond of eating. 2. n. (Usu. as F) lover of delicate fare, judge of good eating; greedy feeder, glutton. Hence ~ISM(2) (goor-) n. [F, etym. dub.]

gourmandise (goorm'a). See GORMANDIZE.

gourmet (goorm'a), n. Connoisseur of table delicacies, esp. of wine. [F]

gout, n. 1. Paroxysmal disease with inflammation of smaller joints, esp. that of great toe, & chalk-stones (*rich, poor, man's* ~, ascribed to over, under, -feeding). 2. Wheat-disease caused by ~*fly*. 3. Drop, splash, or spot. Hence ~Y² a. (~*ies* as n. pl., over-shoes), ~*ily*² adv., ~*iness* n. [f. OF *goute* f. L *gutta* drop w. ref. to medieval theory of flowing down of humours]

go'vern (gŭ-), v.t. & i. 1. Rule with authority, conduct the policy, actions, & affairs, of (State, subject) despotically or constitutionally; regulate proceedings of (corporation etc.; ~*ing body*, managers of hospital, school, etc.); be in military command of (fort, town). 2. Exercise function of government in person (*king reigns but does not* ~, merely selects those who are to ~). 3. Sway, rule, influence, regulate, determine, (person, his acts, course or issue of events); be the predominating influence. 4. Conduct oneself in some way; curb, bridle, (one's passions, oneself). 5. Constitute a law, rule, standard, or principle, for; serve to decide (case). 6. (Gram., esp. of vb or prep.) have (noun, case) depending on it, require (a certain case). Hence ~ABLE a., ~ABI'LITY n. [f. OF *governer* f. L *gubernare* steer, govern, f. Gk *kubernaō* steer]

go'vernance (gŭ-), n. Act, manner, fact, or function, of governing, sway, control. [f. OF *gouvernance* (prec., -ANCE)]

go'verness (gŭ-), n. Female teacher, instructress, esp. of children in private household; ‖ ~-*cart*, light two-wheeled vehicle with side seats face to face. [earlier *governeress* f. OF *gouverneresse* (*gouverneur* GOVERNOR, -ESS²)]

go'vernment (gŭ-), n. (More modern word for) GOVERNANCE; portion of country ruled by a governor, province; system of governing, form of polity; body or successive bodies of persons governing a State, the State as an agent, an administration or ministry (‖ *form a* G~, of Prime Minister selecting colleagues); (Gram.) relation between GOVERNING & other word; ‖ G~ *house*, official residence of governor; G~ *paper, securities, bonds*, exchequer bills, etc., issued by ~. Hence **governmen'tal** a., **governmen'tally** adv., (gŭ-). [OF (-*ement*), see GOVERN, -MENT]

go'vernor (gŭ-), n. 1. One who governs, ruler; official appointed to govern province, town, etc., representative of Crown in dominion (G~ *General*) or colony; executive head of each of U.S.; officer commanding fortress or garrison; head, or one of governing body, of institution; official in charge of prison. 2. (One's employer, one's father, sir, (sl.). 3. (Mech.) automatic regulator of supply of gas, steam, water, etc., to machine, ensuring even motion. 4. Kind of fishing-fly.

5. ~ *general*, ~ *with deputy* ~ *s under him*, whence ~-**gĕn'eralship** n. Hence ~**ship¹**(2) n. [f. OF *governeur* f. L *gubernatorem* (GOVERN, -OR²)]

gow'an, n. (Sc.). Daisy. [prob. var. of obs. *golland* & connected w. obs. *gold*, OE *golde*, marigold, perh. f. GOLD]

gowk, n. (Dial.) cuckoo; awkward or half-witted person, fool. [f. ON *gaukr* cf. G *gauch*]

gown, n., & v.t. Loose flowing upper garment, esp. woman's dress (usu. of dress with pretensions to elegance, or in comb. as *tea, dinner, -*, ~); frock; ancient Roman toga (*arms, gown, war & peace*; official or uniform robe of various shapes worn by alderman, judge, lawyer, clergyman, member of university, college, or school, etc. (*town & ~*, non-members & members of university at Oxf. & Camb.); ~*s'man*, civilian, member of university; (vb, chiefly in p.p.) attire in ~. [f. OF *goune* f. med. L *gunna* fur garment (in LL=fur)]

Graa'fian (-rahf-), a. ~ *follicle, vesicle*, one of small sacs in mammal ovary in which ova are matured. [R. de *Graaf*, Dutch anatomist d. 1673, -IAN]

grab, v.t. & i. (-bb-), & n. 1. Seize suddenly; appropriate rapaciously; capture, arrest; make snatch *at*; hence (-)~**b'ER¹** n. 2. n. Sudden clutch, grasp, seizure, or attempt to seize; practice of ~bing, rapacious proceedings esp. in politics or commerce; *have the* ~ *on* (sl.), have great advantage of; (Mech.) device or implement for clutching; children's card game. [n. f. vb; cf. MDu. & MLG *grabben*, perh. modification of GRIP²]

grab'ble, v.i. Grope about, feel for something; sprawl on all fours (often *for something*). [prec.+-LE(2)]

grace, n., & v.t. 1. Pleasing quality, attractiveness, charm, esp. that belonging to elegant proportions or ease & refinement of movement, action, expression, or manner, whence ~'**FUL** a., ~'**fully**² adv., ~'**fulness** n., (-sf-). 2. Becomingness, air with which something is done, (*cannot with any* ~ *ask him; have the* ~ *to*, do something that decency requires; *with a good* ~, as if willing; *with a bad* ~, reluctantly, ungraciously). 3. Attractive feature, accomplishment, ornament, (*airs & -s*, behaviour put on with a view to effect or attraction). 4. (Mus.; also ~-*note*, -*notes*) embellishment of extra note(s) not essential to harmony or melody. 5. (Gk Myth.) the G~s, three beautiful goddess sisters, the bestowers of beauty & charm. 6. Favour, benignant regard or its manifestation, on part of superior (*be in one's good* ~s, enjoy his favour or liking). 7. Unconstrained goodwill as ground of concession (*act of* ~, privilege, concession, that cannot be claimed as right, & see below; *by the* ~ *of God*,

appended to royal titles); boon. **8.** ||(Univ.) permission of Congregation, also of College or Hall, to take degree, dispensation from statutes. **9.** (Theol.) unmerited favour of God, divine regenerating, inspiring, & strengthening influence, condition (also *state of* ~) of being so influenced, divinely given talent etc., (*the* ~*th year of* ~, usu. iron., when date =A.D.; *in this year of* ~, etc.). **10.** Favour shown by granting delay (*give a day's, year's, etc.,* ~; *days of* ~, time allowed by law for payment of bill of exchange—in Britain three days—or insurance premium after it falls due). **11.** Mercy, pardon by Act of Parliament; & see clemency (*Act of* ~, formal, esp. general, above). **12.** Short thanksgiving before or after meal (~-*cup, say or sing* ~, parting draught). **13.** ||*His, Her, Your, G*~, forms of address or description for duke, duchess, or archbishop. **14.** v.t. Add ~ *to*, adorn, set off *with*; confer honour or dignity on, honour with title etc.; do credit to. [f. F *grâce* f. L *gratia* (*gratus* pleasing, GRATEFUL)]

grace′less (-sl-), a. Unregenerate, depraved, (arch. or joc.); wanting sense of decency, unabashed; without charm or elegance (rare); ~*florin* (of 1849, on which the letters D.G. were omitted). Hence ~LY² adv., ~NESS n. [-LESS]

grā′cile, a. Slender; (erron.) slight. Hence **gracil′ITY** n., slenderness, (of literary style) unornamented simplicity. [f. L *gracilis* slender]

grā′cious (-shŭs), a. & int. **1.** Agreeable, pleasing, (arch.); kindly, benevolent, courteous, (chiefly poet.); condescending, indulgent & beneficent to inferiors, (of exalted persons, or sarcastic or joc.; esp. as polite epithet of royal or ducal persons or their acts); (of God) dispensing grace, merciful, benignant; hence ~LY² adv., ~NESS n. (-shŭs-). **2.** int. (Ellipt. for ~ *God, as*) *good* ~!, *my* ~!, excl. of surprise (also in ~ *me*!, ~ *goodness* !). Hence f. L *gratiosus* (GRACE, -OSE²)]

grac′kle, n. Kinds of bird allied to jackdaw. [alt. f. L *graculus* jackdaw]

gradate′, v.i. & t. (Cause to) pass by imperceptible degrees from one shade of colour to another; arrange in steps or grades. [back formation f. foll.]

gradā′tion, n. (Usu. pl.) stage(s) of transition or advance; series of degrees in rank, merit, intensity, divergence, etc., (pl.) such degrees; arrangement in such degrees; (fine arts) insensible passing from one shade, tone, etc., to another. Hence ~AL a., ~ally² adv. (-shon-). [f. L *gradātio* (GRADE, -OSE²)]

grade, n. & v.t. **1.** Degree in rank, proficiency, quality, value, etc., of persons or things alike in these.

2. (Cattle-breeding) variety produced by crossing native stock with superior breed. **3.** (Zool.) group supposed to have branched from parent stock at same stage of development. **4.** (Philol.) relative position in ablaut-series. **5.** Gradient, slope, rate of ascent or descent, (*on the up, down,* ~, *rising or falling,* lit. & fig.; *make the ~, *succeed*). **6.** v.t. Arrange in ~s, class, sort; blend so as to affect ~ of; colour with tints passing into each other. **7.** Reduce (road, canal, etc.) to easy gradients. **8.** (Cattle-breeding) cross with better breed (~ *up*, improve thus). **9.** (Philol., in pass.) be changed by ablaut. || **grāde′ly** [vb¹ n., F, f. L *gradus* step]

grādient, n. ||Amount of slope, inclination to the horizontal, in road, railway, etc.; proportional rise or fall of thermometer or barometer in passing from one region to another. [perh. formed on GRADE after *quotient*]

gradin(e) (also -dēn), n. One of series of low steps or tier of seats; ledge at back of altar. [f. F *gradin* f. It. *gradino* (*gradino* after *quotient*)]

grādient′ly, a. (-dli), a. (obs. exc. dial.) real, true, proper. [ME *greidhlic* (*greidh-r* = OE *gerēde* READY, -LY¹]

grād′ual¹, n. Respond sung between Epistle & Gospel in the service of Mass. [so called as sung at steps of altar or while deacon mounted ambo; f. med. L *graduale* neut. adj. as n., see foll.]

grād′ual², a. Taking place by degrees, slowly progressive, not rapid, steep, or abrupt; ~ *psalm*, ~ *song of* DEGREES. Hence ~LY² adv., ~NESS n. [f. med. L *graduale* (*gradus* -ās step, -AL²)]

grād′uate¹, n. One who holds academic degree; [f. med. L *graduatus* (foll., -ATE²)]

grad′uate², v.i. & t. Take, admit to (chiefly U.S.), academic degree; (transf.) quality or perfect oneself as; mark out in degrees or portions; arrange in gradations, apportion incidence of (tax) according to a scale; pass away by degrees, change (intr.) gradually *into*; concentrate (solution) by evaporation. Hence ~ATION, ~ATOR¹(, 2), nn. [f. med. L *graduare*]

Gr(a)e′cism (grē-), n. A Greek idiom, esp. as imitated in another language; Greek spirit, style, mode of expression, etc., imitation of these. [for ~ *ad Parnassum* step to Parnassus]

Gr(a)e′cize (grē-), v.t. & i. Give a Greek cast, character, or form, to; favour, imitate, the Greeks. [f. L *graecizare*

Gr(a)e'co- (grē-), comb. form of L *Graecus* GREEK, as ~*-Roman*. Hence ~MAN'IA(O) nn.,~PHIL a. & n.

graffi'tō (-tē-), n. (pl. *-ti*, pr. *-tē*). Drawing or writing scratched on wall etc., esp. on ancient wall as at Pompeii; decoration by scratches through plaster showing different-coloured under-surface. [It.]

graft[1] (-ah-), n., & v.t. 1. Shoot or scion inserted in slit of another stock, from which it receives sap; (Surg.) piece of transplanted living tissue; process of ~*ing*; place where ~ is inserted. 2. v.t. Insert (scion) as ~ (*in*, *into*, *on*, *upon*, *together*); (fig.) insert or fix *in* or *upon* so as to produce vital or indissoluble union; insert ~(*s*); insert ~(*s*) upon (stock) (Surg.) transplant (living tissue); (Naut.) cover (ring-bolt etc.) with weaving of small cord; ~*ing-clay*, *-wax*, composition for covering united parts of ~ & stock. [for earlier *graff* n. & v.f. OF *graffe* f. LL f. Gk *graphion* stylus (*graphō* write), named f. similarity of shape; *-t* perh. due to use of ~ as p.p. of *graff*, cf. HOIST, BASTE[3]]

‖ **graft**[2] (-ah-), n.   Depth of earth that may be thrown up at once with spade; crescent-bladed spade. [cogn. with GRAVE[2]]

*****graft**[3] (-ah-, -â-), n., & v.i. (colloq.) Illicit spoils in connexion with politics or municipal business, practices intended to secure these; (vb) seek, make, ~, whence ~ER[1] n. [?]

grail[1], n. = GRADUAL[1]. [f. OF *grael* f. eccl. L *gradale* var. of *graduale*]

grail[2], n. (Also *holy* or *saint* ~ or *sangreal*) platter used by Christ at Last Supper, & in which Joseph of Arimathea received his blood at the Cross. [f. OF *graal* f. med. L *gradalis* cup or platter, etym. dub.; *sangreal* as = *blood real* or *royal* (F *sang*) is erron. division]

grail[3], n. Comb-maker's file. [f. F *grêle* (*grêler* make thin f. *grêle* adj. f. L *gracilis*)]

grain, n., & v.t. & i. 1. A fruit or corn of a cereal; (collect. sing.) wheat or the allied food-grasses or their fruit, corn, a particular species of corn; (pl.; also ~*s* of *Paradise* or *Guinea* ~*s*) capsules of W.-Afr. plant used as spice & drug; (pl.) refuse malt after brewing or distilling. 2. Small hard particle of sand, gold, SALT, gunpowder (*large*, *small*, ~ *powder*), incense, etc. 3. Smallest unit of weight, 1/5760 of lb. Troy, 1/7000 of lb. av., smallest possible quantity (*without a* ~ *of vanity*, *love*, etc.). 4. (Hist.) Kermes, cochineal, or dye made from either of these (*dye in* ~, dye in kermes, dye in any fast colour, dye in the fibre or thoroughly; *in* ~, thorough, genuine, by nature, downright, indelible; (poet.) dye, colour. 5. Granular texture, roughness of surface, mottling; texture, arrangement & size of constituent particles, in flesh, skin, wood, stone, etc.; lines of fibre in wood giving

a pattern, lamination or planes of cleavage in coal, stone, etc.; (fig.) nature, temper, tendency; (*against the* ~, contrary to inclination). 6. ~*-leather*, dressed with the ~*-side* (on which the hair was) out; ~*-sick* n., cattle-disease, distension of rumen; hence ~'LESS, ~'Y[2], (-)~ED[3] (-rnd), aa. 7. vb. Form (t. & i.) into ~s; dye in ~; give granular surface to; remove hair from (hides); paint in imitation of ~ of wood or marble; hence ~'ER[4], 2) n. [OF, f. L *granum*, & f. OF *graine* f. pop. L *grana* collect. fem., orig. neut. pl. of L *granum*]

grains (-z), n. Forked fish-spear or harpoon. [orig. pl. of obs. *grain* fork, prong, f. ON *grein* division; now used as sing.]

grallatō'rial, a. (zool.). Of the *Grallatores* or long-legged wading birds. [f. L *grallator* stilt-walker (*grallae* stilts)]

grall'och (-ŏx, see AP.), n., & v.t. Dead deer's viscera; (vb) disembowel (deer etc.). [f. Gael. *grealach* intestines]

gräm[1], n. Chick-pea; any pulse used as horse-fodder. [f. Port. *grão* f. L *granum* grain]

gräm[2]. See GRAMME.

-gräm, suf. (chiefly) f. Gk *gramma -atos* (*graphō* write, -M) thing written, letter of alphabet, forming nn. (1) prepositional compds f. Gk (*anagram*, *diagram*, *epigram*), (2) n. compds (*chronogram*, *logogram*),(3) compds of numeral with *gramma* or with *grammé* line, where Gk would have -*grammon* neut. adj., (4) the improper compd *telegram* f. adv. *tēle*, suggested by which are (5) the hybrid formation *cablegram*, & the correctly formed *phonogram*.

gräm'a, gräm'a, n. (Also ~ *grass*) kinds of low pasture grass in W. & S.W. parts of U.S. [f. L *gramen -inis* grass, f. Sp. *grama*]

‖ **gräm'arye, n.** (arch.). Magic, necromancy. [f. OF *gramaire* learning, GRAMMAR]

gramer'cy, int. (arch.). Thank you. [f. OF *grant merci* (God give you) great reward (GRAND, MERCY)]

graminā'ceous (-shus), **graminĕ'ous,** aa. Of, like, grass, grassy. So **grämi- niv'orous** a. [f. L *gramen -inis* grass, -ACEOUS, & L *gramineus* (-EOUS)]

grämm'alogue (-ŏg), n. (shorthand). Word represented by single sign; letter or character standing for word, logogram. [irreg. f. Gk *gramma* (-GRAM), *logos* word]

grämm'ar, n. Art & science dealing with a language's inflexions or other means of showing relation between words as used in speech or writing, & its phonetic system (usu. divided into phonology, accidence, & syntax; *general*, *philosophical*, or *universal* ~, science of distinctions of thought recognized & variously expressed in the grammatical systems of actual languages; *historical* ~, study of the development of a language's

inflexions & syntax; comparative ~, study of the relation between two or more ~s); treatise or book on ~; person's manner of using grammatical forms, speech or writing regarded as good or bad by the rules of ~, what is correct according to those rules; body of forms & usages in a language; elements, rudiments, of an art or science; ~-school, school founded about 16th c. for teaching Latin, of which many a are now of public-school type. Hence ~less a. [f. OF *gramaire* irreg. f. L f. Gk *grammatikē* (*tekhnē* art) of letters (*gramma* see -GRAM)]

grammat'ical, a. Of grammar (~al sense, gender, not determined by sex; ~al sense, literal, irrespective of other considerations than the rules of grammar); conforming to the rules of grammar, or to the formal principles of an art, so (f. earlier *grammatic*) ~IZE(5) v.t. Hence ~ally¹ adv. [f. L f. Gk *grammatikos*, see GRAMMAR, -AL]

grammar'ian, n. One versed in grammar, philologist. [f. OF *gramarien* (prec., -IAN)]

gramme, gram, n. Unit of weight in metric system, weight of cubic centimetre of distilled water at maximum density, weighed in vacuo, 15·432 Troy grains; ~-centimetre, unit = work done in raising one ~ vertically one centimetre; similarly *grammetre*. [F. f. LL f. Gk *gramma* small weight, see -GRAM]

gram'ophone, n. Phonograph of the kind using flat disks for its reproduction of sound. [irreg. form perh. made by inverting PHONOGRAM]

gram'pus, n. Kinds of blowing spouting blunt-headed dolphin-like cetacean; person who breathes loud. [f. 16th-c. *grampoys* prob. f. earlier *grapeys* f. OF *grapois* f. L *crassus piscis* fat fish]

granadill'a, grē, n. Kinds of passion-flower. [Sp., dim. of *granada* pomegranate]

gran'ary, n. Storehouse for threshed grain; region producing &c. exporting much corn. [f. L *granarium* (*granum* grain, -ARY)]

grand, a. & n. 1. (In official titles) chief over others, of highest rank (G~ Almoner, Falconer, etc., holders of old offices still existing; G~ CROSS¹; G~ Duke, Duchess, ruler of some European States called G~ Duchy, also child of Tsar, whence G~ duc¹ A1 a.; ~ duke, also, Great Horned Owl; G~ Master, head of military order of knighthood, head of Freemasons or of one of their provinces, &c of Oddfellows etc.; G~ Signior, pr. sĕr-, G~ Turk, Sultan of Turkey; G~ Vizier, chief minister of Turkey). 2. (Law) great, principal, (opp. *petty, common*; ~ assize, inquest, jury). 3. Of most or great importance (*that is the ~ question; made a ~ mistake*); final, summing up minor constituents, (~ total; ~ finale; *the ~ sum or* result of his achievements). 4. (Distinguishing parts of large building) main (*the ~ staircase, entrance, etc.*). 5. (In F phrases or imitations) great (~ army, G~ Canal, G~ Hotel; G~ Fleet, main British fleet in the war of 1914–18). 6. Conducted with solemnity, splendour, etc.; fine, splendid, gorgeous. 7. Belonging to high society, distinguished, (*do the ~,* put on airs); imposing, impressive, great & handsome. 8. Dignified, lofty, in conception, treatment, or expression (~ *style,* fitted for great subjects); morally imposing, noble, admirable, (the G~ Old Man or G.O.M., W. E. Gladstone). 9. Very satisfactory (colloq.; *had a ~ run; ground was in ~ condition*). 10. (In names of relationships) in the second degree of ascent or descent (~ *son,* one's child's son; ~-nephew, one's nephew's or niece's son; ~ mother, ~aunt, one's parent's mother or aunt; so ~child, ~-daughter; ~father, ~father's clock, worked by weights in tall wooden case; ~-mamma, ~mother, whence ~motherly a., esp. of legislation etc. = excessively PATERNAL; *teach your ~mother to suck EGGS*; ~mother v.t., coddle etc., ∥~mother *the cups,* prevent their slipping by wetting the saucers; ~niece, ~papa, ~parent; ~sire, esp. of animal's sire, also = ancestor, old man, & a method of ringing changes on bells; ~uncle). 11.~ air, distinguished appearance; ~ committee, one of two standing committees of House of Commons sessionally appointed to consider Law & Trade Bills; ~ LODGE; G~ Monarch, Louis XIV of France; ∥ G~ National, annual steeplechase at Liverpool; ~ piano(forte), large horizontal piano; ~ stand, principal stand for spectators at races etc.; ~ tour (arch.), tour of chief towns etc. of Europe completing education. 12. n. ~ piano (*upright ~,* usu. a large upright piano with all improvements). 13. *A thousand dollars (sl.). Hence ~ly² adv., ~NESS n. [OF, f. L *grandis* full-grown]

gran'dam(e), n. (arch.). Grandmother; (~m only) animal's dam; ~ dam; ancestress; old woman. [f. AF *graund dame* (prec, DAM²)]

grand(d)'dad, n. (Childish or affectionate for) grandfather. [GRAND, DAD]

grande (see Ap.), fem. of GRAND (~ *toilette* pr. twahlĕt', ceremonial costume; ~ *passion* pr. păs'yawn, engrossing love affair). [F]

grandee', n. Spanish or Portuguese nobleman of highest rank; person of high rank or eminence. [f. Sp. & Port. *grande* GRAND]

grand'eur (-dyer), n. Great power, rank, or eminence; great nobility of character; sublimity, majesty, of appearance or effect; conscious dignity; splendour of living, surroundings, etc. [F (GRAND)]

Grand Guignol (grahn gēnyōl'), n. Dramatic entertainment in which short pieces often of strongly sensational type are played successively. [name (=Great Punch) of theatre in Paris; F *Guignol* perf. f. *Chignolo Po* in Italy, native place of Italian who introduced puppets at Lyons]

grandil'oquent, a. Pompous in language; given to tall talk. Hence ~ENCE n., ~ENTLY² adv. [after *eloquent* f. L L *grandiloquus* (GRAND, -*loquus* -speaking f. *loqui* speak)]

gran'diose, a. Producing, intended or trying to produce, an impression of greatness, planned on a magnificent scale, pompous. Hence grandios'ITY (-ŏs⁴) n., ~LY² (-sl-) adv. [F, f. It. *grandioso* (GRAND, -OSE⁴)]

Grandiso'nian, a. Marked by stately courtesy & chivalric magnanimity. [Sir C. *Grandison* in Richardson's novel, -IAN]

grange (-j), n. ‖ Barn (arch.); country house with farm-buildings attached. [f. AF *graunge* f. med. L *granea* (*granum* grain)]

gran'gerize (-j-), v.t. Extra-illustrate (book) by inserting prints etc. often cut from other books. Hence ~IZATION, ~IZER¹, ~ISM(1), ~TER(1), nn. [J. *Granger* published 1769 a Hist. of England with blank pages for illustrations]

granif'erous, a. Producing grain or grain-like seed. So **gran'iFORM, graniv'OROUS**, aa. [f. L *graniger* (GRAIN, -FEROUS)]

gran'ite, n. Granular crystalline rock of quartz, orthoclase feldspar, & mica, used for building (*bite on* ~, waste pains, persist in vain); ~*ware*, speckled pottery imitating ~, kind of enamelled ironware; *the* ~*city*, Aberdeen. Hence **granit'IC** a., **gran'itOID** a.&n., **granit'iFORM** a. [f. It. *granito* orig. grained (*grano* f. L *granum*)]

gran'nom, gran'am, n. Kind of water-fly; imitation of it for fly-fishing. [?]

gran'ny, n. (Fam., affectionate, or contempt. for) grandmother; (also ~*'s bend* or *knot*) reef-knot crossed the wrong way. [prob. f. obs. *grannam* for GRANDAM +-Y³]

gran'olith'iC, a. Of a kind of concrete. [L *granum* grain, Gk *lithos* stone, -IC]

grant (-ah-), v.t., & n. 1. Consent to fulfil (request etc.; in p.p. formerly common, now rare, as answer to *I beg your pardon*); concede as indulgence, allow (person) to have (thing; noun, *that, or to do*); bestow (possession, right) formally, transfer (property) legally, whence **grantEE'**, **grantOR²**, (-ah-) nn.; concede (proposition, *that*-clause, or something *to be* something; *I* ~ *you*, I admit; *take for* ~*ed*, ~ *or refusal* of): formal conferment, legal assignment; thing, esp. sum, ~ed (often *capitation* ~, ~-*in-aid*); conveyance by written instrument. [f. OF *greanter* f. pop. L ⁺*credentare* f. part. of *credere* entrust]

Granth (grŭnt), n. Sacred scriptures of the Sikhs. [Hindi, f. book, code (f. Skr. *grantha* tying, literary composition)]

gran'ular, a. Of, like, grains; with granulated surface or structure. Hence ~**ā'rITY** n., ~**ARLY²** adv., ~**O-** comb. form. (*granum*, -ULE), -AR], ~OUS a. [f. L L *granulum* small form (*granum*, -ULE), -AR]

gran'ulate, v.t. & i. Form (t. & i.) into grains; roughen surface of: (of wound etc.) form small prominences as beginning of healing or junction, heal, join. Hence or cogn. ~**āTE²**(-ăt) a., ~**A'TION**, ~**ātor²**(2), nn. [as prec., -ATE³]

gran'ule, n. Small grain. [as prec.]

grape, n. Green or purple berry growing in clusters on vine, eaten as fruit or used in making wine (*the* ~, *the juice of the* ~, wine; *the* ~*s are sour, sour* ~*s*, said when person disparages what he vainly desires); ~*shot*; diseased growth like bunch of ~*s* on pastern of horse etc., or on pleura; ~*brandy*, distilled from ~*s*, or wine, alone; ~CURE¹; ~*fruit*, kind of small shaddock; ~*house*, vinery; ~*scissors*, for thinning ~*s*bunches at early stage of growth, also for dividing bunches at table; ~*shot*, small balls put several together in bag etc. to make scattering charge for cannon; ~*stone*, one of seeds inside ~; ~*sugar*, dextrose or glucose; ~*vine*, vine, also skating figure in which both feet are on ice together & form interlacing lines. Hence **grap'ERY³** n., **grap'Y²** a., [OF, bunch of ~*s*, prob. f. *graper* gather with vine-hook (*grape* hook ult. f. Tent. cf. OHG *krapfo*)]

graph¹ (or -ahf), n. Symbolic diagram expressing system of mathematical or chemical connexion. [abbr. of *graphic formula*]

graph²(-ahf), n., & v.t. Gelatine copying apparatus; (v.t.) copy, multiply, with this. [colloq. abbr. of *chromograph*, *hectograph*, etc.]

-graph (-ahf), suf. f. Gk -*graphos*, -written, -writing, -writer, denoting (1) thing written in such a way (f. Gk, as *auto*~, *chiro*-, *hodo*~; on Gk st., as *litho*~, *photo*~; & in hybrids, as *picto*~); (2) instrument that records something or by some means (*helio*~, *seismo*~, *tele*~); (3) write in such a way (*calli*~, *hecto*~).

-grapher, suf. repr. Gk -*graphos* & forming nn. denoting one versed in -GRAPHY. [-ER]

graph'ic(al rare), a. Of drawing, painting, engraving, etching, etc.; vividly descriptive, lifelike; (of writing; (of minerals) showing marks like writing on surface or in fracture; of diagrams or symbolic curves. [f. L f. Gk *graphikos* (*graphē* writing, -IC)]

-graph'ic(al), suff. = of or by -GRAPHY.

gráph′ically, adv. As in a picture, vividly; by diagrams or graph's. [-IY²]

gráph′ite, n. PLUMBAGO. Hence **gráph′ic, gráph′iton,** aa. [f. G graphit (Gk graphō write, -ITE²)]

gráph′ure, n. S.-Afr. rodent with tail ending in pencil of hairs. [f. Gk pencil, oura tail]

gráphoï′ogy, n. Study of, art of inferring character from, handwriting; system of graphic formulae, notation for graph's. [f. Gk graphē writing, -LOGY]

gráph′otype, n. (Process for making) relief block for surface-printing. [as prec.]

-graphy, suf. f. Gk -graphia forming nn. denoting (1) styles of writing, drawing, etc.(litho~, brachy~, steno~,calli~),(2) descriptive science (geo~, biblio~, seleno~).

gráp′nel, n. Iron-clawed instrument thrown with rope to seize object, esp. enemy's ship; small anchor with several flukes used for boats & balloons. [dim. of OF grapin (GRAPE)]

gráp′ple, n. & v.t. & i. 1. Clutching-instrument, grapnel. 2. Hold or grip (as) of wrestlers, close contest. 3. vb. Seize, fasten, (as) with grapnel; take hold of, grip, with the hands, come to close quarters with; contend with, together, to overcome, accomplish, or deal with. [vb f. n. in first sense; second sense of n. vb.; f. OF dim. of grappe hook]

gráp′pling, n. In vbl senses; also, **~iron, grapnel.** [-ING¹]

grasp, (-ah-), v.t. & i. & n. 1.~at, try to seize, accept with avidity; clutch at, seize greedily, (part.) avaricious, whence **~ingly² adv., ~ingness** n.; hold firmly (~ nettle, tackle difficulty or danger boldly), grip; get mental hold of, comprehend; hence **~ABLE² a. 2.** n. Fast hold, grip, (within, beyond, one's ~, close, not close, enough to be ~ed); control, mastery; mental hold, comprehensiveness of mind. [by metath. for graspsen cogn. W. GROPE, cf. clean cleanse, & HASP]

grass (-ah-), n. & v.t. 1. Herbage of which blades or leaves & stalks are eaten by cattle, horses, sheep, etc., (not let ~ grow, ~ does not grow, under one's feet, of person who wastes no time in doing something; hear the ~ grow, be of preternatural acuteness); any species of this (including in bot. use, excluding in pop. use, the cereals, reeds, & bamboos; usu. with defining words, as bunch, spear, ~, ~ of Parnassus); (sl.) asparagus; grazing, pasture, (be at, go, put, send, turn out, to, ~; at ~, fig., out of work, making holiday; etc.; so perh. ~ widow, wife whose husband is absent); covered ground (keep off the ~); (Mining) earth's surface, pit-head; send, go, to ~,

knock (person), be knocked or fall, down; **~-cutter**, Indian domestic servant who collects fodder for horses etc.; **~-hopper**, kinds of jumping & chirping insect (~ hopper-beam, working-beam in engine pivoted at end and instead of in middle); **~-snake**, || common ringed snake; **~-tree**, kinds of Australasian tree; hence **~′LESS, ~′Y²** aa. **2.** v.t. Cover with turf; lay (flax etc.; on ~ to bleach; knock down, fell, (opponent); bring (fish) to bank, (bird by shot) to ground. [com.-Teut.; OE græs cf. G gras, cogn. W. GREEN, GROW, & w. L gramen grass]

gráte¹, n. = GRATING (rare), whence **gráted²** a.; (frame of metal bars for confining fuel in) fireplace or furnace. Hence **~′LESS (-tl-) a.** [f. med. L f. L lt. grata f. L cratis hurdle]

gráte², v.t. & i. Reduce to small particles by rubbing on rough surface, whence (-)**~′ER²(2)** n.; have irritating effect (upon; grind (teeth); rub (l. & t.) with harsh scraping noise against or (upon something else); sound harshly or discordantly (a ~ing laugh, voice); (of hinge etc.) creak. Hence **~′ingly² adv.** [f. OF grater f. Teut., cf. G kratzen scratch]

gráte′ful (-tf-), a. Acceptable, comforting, refreshing; thankful, feeling or showing gratitude (to person, for thing). Hence **~LY² adv., ~NESS n.** [f. obs. grate adj. f. L gratus + -FUL]

grat′ify, v.t. Remunerate, fee, make present (usu. of money to; bribe; please, satisfy, oblige, delight, whence **~ING² a.** (to), **~ingLY² adv.**; please by compliance, assent to wish of, give free course to or indulge (desire, feeling, impulse). So **gratifiCA′TION n.** [f. L grātificari (gratus -FY)]

grat′in (see Ap.), n. Way of cooking, dish cooked, by crumbing bread or grating cheese & cooking between two fires to produce light crust; au (ǒ) ~, so prepared. [F]

grát′ing, n. Framework of parallel or crossed wooden or metal bars; (Opt.) set of parallel wires, or surface of glass etc. ruled with parallel lines, for producing spectra by diffraction. [GRATE¹+-ING¹]

grát′is, adv. & a. Gratuitously, (given, done) for nothing, without charge, free. [L, contracted abl. pl. of gratia favour]

grát′itude, n. Being thankful, appreciation of & inclination to return kindness. [f. LL grātitūdo (gratus thankful, -TUDE)]

gratū′itous, a. Got or given free, not warranted or paid for; uncalled for, unwarranted; motiveless, done or acting without good or assignable reason (a ~ lie or liar). Hence **~LY² adv., ~NESS n.** [f. L grātuītus spontaneous, cogn. w. gratia]

gratū′ity, n. Money present of amount fixed by giver in recognition of an inferior's good offices, tip; bounty to

soldiers etc. on retirement or some other occasions. [f. med. L *gratulus* grateful, -TY]

∥grăt′ŭlāte, -ā′tion. (Arch. for) congr-.

∥grăt′ŭlātory, n. Expressing joy at another's success etc., complimentary, congratulatory. [f. L *gratulari* congratulate +-ORY]

grăvăm′ĕn, n. (pl. -*mĭna*, rare), Grievance; ∥ memorial from Lower House of Convocation to Upper on disorders or grievances of Church; essence, worst part, of accusation. [LL, inconvenience (*gravare* to load f. *gravis* heavy), -MEN]

grāve[1], v.t. Excavation to receive corpse, mound or monument over it, (*secret as the* ~, quite: *make one turn in his* ~, of act etc. that he would have been pained by while alive; *someone walking on my* ~, said when one shivers unaccountably: *one* FOOT[1] *in the* ~), whence ~LESS (-vi-) a.; being dead, death, Hades, whence ~WARD (-vw-) adv. & a.; receptacle of or for what is dead (~ *of reputations*, place where many reputations have been lost); trench for earthing up potatoes etc.; ~-*digger*, lit., also kinds of insect that bury bodies of insects etc. as food for their larvae; ~-*stone*, stone over ~; inscribed stone at head or foot of ~; ~-*yard*, burial ground. [OE *græf*, (*græfan* GRAVE[2])]

grāve[2], v.t. (p.p. ~n, ~d, as stated). (Arch.) bury (~d); (arch.) carve, sculpture, engrave, (material, representation; ~n, ~d; ~n *image*, idol); (fig.) fix indelibly (on, *in*, mind etc.; ~n, ~d). [com.-Teut., OE *grafan*, cf. Du. *graven*, G *graben*, dig; cogn. w. GROOVE]

grāve[3], a. & n. 1. Important, weighty, needing serious thought; of faults, difficulties, responsibilities, symptoms) formidable, threatening, serious; dignified, solemn, slow-moving, not gay; sombre, plain, not showy; hence ~LY[2] (-vi-) adv. 2. (Of accent) low-pitched, not acute; ~ ACCENT[1]. 3. n. ~ accent. [F, f. L *gravis* heavy, serious]

grāve[4], v.t. Clean (ship's bottom) by burning off accretions & tarring while aground or in a graving-dock. [perh. f. OF *grave*=*grève* shore]

grăv′el, n., & v.t. (-ll-), 1. Coarse sand & small water-worn or pounded stones, much used for laying paths & roads; (Geol., Mining) stratum of this, esp. one containing gold (*pay* ~, containing enough gold to yield profit); (Path.) (disease with) aggregations of visible urinary crystals; ~-*blind*, more than SAND-BLIND (Shaks., *M. of V.*, II. ii. 38); hence ~LY[2] a. 2. v.t. Lay, strew, with ~; perplex, puzzle, non-plus, (in obs. sense *run aground*): ~-*blind* in path. sense) hence ~LY[2] adv. [f. OF *gravelle* dim. of OF *grave* gravel, shore, f. Celt. cf. W *gro*]

grāv′er, n. In vbl senses; esp., burin [-ER[1]]

Graves (grahv), n. Light white wine produced in the ~ district of France. [place]

grăv′id, a. (literary). Pregnant. [f. L *gravidus* (GRAVE[3])]

grăv′ĭtāte, v.i. & t. Move or tend by force of gravity *towards* a body; sink (*aa*) down; (Diamond-digging) manipulate (gravel) so that heavy stones sink to bottom; (transf.) be strongly attracted *to(wards)* some centre of influence. Hence ~ā′TION n., ~ā′tional (-shon-), -ATL[3] aa., [f. mod.L *gravitare* (GRAVE[3], -ATE[3]]

grăv′itý, n. 1. Being grave, solemnity, importance, seriousness; staidness, sobriety, serious demeanour. 2. Weight (CENTRE[1] *of* ~; *specific* ~, relative weight of any kind of matter, expressed by ratio of given volume to same volume of a standard—usu. water for liquid or solid, & air for gas). 3. Attractive force by which bodies tend to centre of earth, degree of intensity of this measured by acceleration, degree of intensity with which any body is similarly attracted by any other. [t. L *gravitas*, -TY]

gravure′, n. (Short for) PHOTOGRAVURE.

grāv′y, n. Juices that exude from flesh during & after cooking; dressing for food made from these with other materials; ~-*boat*, boat-shaped vessel for ~; ~ *beef*, part of leg of beef cooked for its~. [etym. dub.; perh. a misreading as *gravé* of *grané* in OF cookery books, cf. OF *grain* anything used in cookery]

gray. See GREY.

grayling, n. Silver-grey freshwater fish with long high dorsal fin; butterfly with grey under-side to wings. [GREY +-LING[1]]

grāzje[1], v.i. & t. t. Feed (esp. cattle, or intr. of cattle) on growing grass etc. or ~ING[1](3) n.; feed on (grass etc., often *down*); tend ~ing cattle; pasture cattle. [OE *grasian* (GRASS n.)]

grāzje[2], v.t. & i., & n. 1. Touch lightly in passing; abrade (skin etc.) in rubbing past; suffer slight abrasion of (part of body); go with passing contact *against*, *along*, *through*, *by*, *past*, etc. 2. n. ~ing abrasion. [etym. dub.; perh. by transf. f. prec., cf. *shave*]

grā′zier (-zher), n. One who feeds cattle for market. Hence grā′ziERY(2) (-zherĭ) n. [GRASS +-IER]

grease[1] (-ēs), n. Fat of deer or other game (*in* ~, *in pride* or *prime* of ~, fit for killing, fat); melted fat of dead animals, esp. when soft; oily or fatty matter, esp. as lubricant; oily matter in wool, uncleansed wool, (*wool in the* ~, in fleeces); disease in horses' heels; ~-*box*, attached to train-wheel for lubrication; ~-*paint*, composition for painting actors' faces; ~-*trap*, appliance for catching ~ in drains. [f. OF *graisse* (L *crassus* a. fat)]

grease² (-ēz), v.t. Anoint, soil, or lubricate, with grease (~ *the wheels*, make affairs go smoothly, esp. by money; ~ *palm of*, bribe; like ~*d lightning*, sl., very fast); affect (horse) with grease. [f. prec.]

grea'ser (-z-), n. In vbl senses, esp.: head fireman on steamer; *(al.) native Mexican or Spanish-American. [-ER²]

greas'y (-z-), a. Smeared or covered with, containing, made of, like, with too much, grease; (of wool) uncleansed; (of horse) affected with the grease; slimy with mud or moisture; (of manners or expression) disagreeably unctuous; ~*y fritillary*, kind of butterfly; ~*y pole*, greased for climbing or walking on in sports. Hence ~ILY² adv., ~INESS n.(-z-). [-Y²]

great (grāt), a. & n. 1. Large, big, (usu. with implied surprise, contempt, indignation, etc., as *made a ~ blot*, *look at that ~ wasp*; often colloq. preceding other adj., *a ~ big loaf or thick stick*; as distinctive epithet of the larger species or individual as ~ *A, Z*, the capital letters, G~ *St John's wort*, also *G~er Celandine* etc., G~ *Tit-mouse*, G~ BEAR¹, *G~ Malvern* etc., G~ *Portland Street*; also in a few phrases, *G~ a*~ DEAL¹, MANY; *the ~ majority*, much the larger part; ~*est common* MEASURE, *lived to a ~ age*, *a ~ while ago*; ||~ *with child*, arch., pregnant). 2. Beyond the ordinary (*take ~ care*; *of ~ popularity*; *shows ~ ignorance*). 3. Important, elevated, distinguished, critical, the chief, pre-eminent, (*it is a ~ thing to have ~*; *a ~ occasion*; *the ~ attraction*; *the G~ Powers of Europe*, chief States; *the ~ world*, high society; in excll. as *G~ God!, Caesar!, Scott!*; *the G~*, appended in sense the best known of G~; the name, as *Alexander the G~*, or prefixed in titles, as *the G~ King*, etc., & burlesqued in *the G~ Mogul*, etc.). 4. Of remarkable ability, genius, intellectual or practical qualities, loftiness or integrity of character, (*a ~ judge, painter*, etc.; *the ~ dancer, landowner*). 7. (Prefixed once or more to *uncle, aunt, nephew, niece*, &c in kinship words compounded with GRAND) one degree further removed upwards or downwards. 8. *G~ Assize, Day*, or *Inquest*, Day of Judgement; *G~ Bible*, Coverdale's Version 1539; G~ BRITAIN, CHARTER, CIRCLE¹: ||~COAT¹, whence ~*coat'ED²*, ~*COAT¹LESS*, aa.; *the ~ COMMONER*, *G~er BRITAIN*; ~*est happiness of the ~est number*, test principle of Benthamism; ||~ *go*, final examination for B.A. at Cambridge, cf. *greats* below; ~ *gross*, twelve gross; ~ *house*, chief house in village etc.; ~ *organ*, chief manual with its related pipes and mechanism in an organ having two or more manuals; ~ PRIMER; so, now usu. BIG *toe*. G~ *WAR* (of 1914–18). Hence ~EN⁶, v.t. & i. (arch.), ~NESS n., (-āt-), 9, n. (Abs. use of adj.) *the ~*, (pl.) ~ persons (also without *the* in ~ & *small*); (sing.) what is [com.WG: OE *great* in Lit. Hum. tion, 10. ||~'s, Oxford B.A. final examination. [OE *great* cf. G *gross*, Du. *groot*]

great'ly (-āt-), adv. Much, by much, (usu. with vbs, participles, or comparatives; ~ *esteemed, superior*; *should ~ prefer*; nobly, loftily. [-LY²]

greave, n. (usu. pl.) Piece(s) of armour for shin(s). [f. OF *greve, greave*, etym. dub.]

greaves, (-vz) n. pl. Fibrous tallow refuse, used as food of dog etc. or fish-bait. [f. LG *greven* pl.]

grebe, n. Kinds of short-bodied lobe-footed almost tailless diving bird; its plumage as trimming. [f. F *grèbe* etym. dub.]

Grē'cian (-shn), a. & n. 1. Greek (rare except of architecture & facial outline; also in ||~ *bend*, affected attitude in walking prevalent c. 1870, ~ *gift*, = GREEK *gift*, ||~ *knot*, way of dressing woman's hair at back of head, ~ *nose*, straight & continuing forehead line without dip, ~ *pro-file*, with ~ *nose*, ||~ *slippers*, trade name for oriental shape). 2. n. Greek scholar; ||boy of highest class at Christ's Hospital; [f. L *Graecia* Greece + -AN]

Grecism, Grecize, Greco-. See Grae-.

greed, n. Insatiate longing esp. for wealth. [back formation f. foll.]

greed'y (-ĭ), a. Ravenous, voracious, glut-tonous, avaricious, covetous, rapacious, (often ||~ *ot*) eager, keen, intensely desirous (*to do*). Hence ~ILY² adv., ~INESS n. [OE *grēdig* cf. OHG *grātag*, cogn. w. Skr. *gṛdh* be greedy]

Greek, n. & a. 1. Native of Greece, member of ~ race, (*when ~ meets ~, then comes the tug of war*, orig. *~s joined ~s*, said of equal encounter) member of ~ Church; cunning person, sharper; the ~ language (*~ to me*, beyond my comprehension), whence ~LESS a. 2. adj. Of Greece or its people, Hellenic; of, according to, written or spoken in, (~ *Fathers*, FATHER¹s of the Church who wrote in ~); ~ *Church*, also *Orthodox* or *Eastern*, Church acknowledging Patriarch of Constantinople, divided from Rome in 9th c., & including esp. Christians of Greece, Russia, & Turkish Empire; ~ CALENDS, FIRE¹, FRET¹ or *key*¹ =; CROSS¹; ~ *gift*, one given with intent to harm (Virg. *Aen.* ii. 49). [adj. f. n.: OE *Crēcas* pl. f. L *Graecus* f. Gk *Graîkoi* prehistoric name of Hellenes]

green¹, a. & n. 1. Of the colour between blue & yellow in the spectrum, coloured like grass, sea-water, emerald, olive, etc. 2. Covered with herbage, verdant, in leaf, (a ~ Christmas, season, Yule, mild, without snow). 3. (Of complexion) pale, sickly-hued, (~ eye, jealousy, whence ~eyed² (-id) a.; ~ jaundice, kind in which patient's skin is ~); (fig.) jealous, envious. 4. Vegetable (~ food, MEAT). 5. (Of fruit etc.) unripe, young & tender, flourishing, not dried. 6. Full of vitality, not withered or worn out, (in the ~ dry, tree, under good, bad, conditions; a ~ old age). 7. Immature, undeveloped, inexperienced, gullible. 8. Not dried, seasoned, or tanned. 9. Fresh, not healed, (a ~ wound). 10. ~back, U.S. legal-tender note, note issued by any U.S. national bank; ~-blind, having retina insensitive to ~ rays; ~book, official publication of Indian Government; ~ cheese, unripened cheese, whey cheese, cheese coloured with sage; (Board of) G~ Cloth, Lord Steward's department of Royal Household; ~ crop, used for food in ~ state (opp. hay etc.); ∥ ~ drake, mayfly; ~ earth, hydrous silicate of potassium, iron, & other bases; ~ fat, of turtle, esteemed by epicures; ~finch or ~ linnet, bird with gold & ~ plumage; ∥ ~ fingers (colloq.), skill in gardening; ∥ ~ fly, kind of aphis; ~gage, roundish ~ fine-flavoured plum (Sir W. Gage c. 1725); ~ goose, killed under four months old and eaten without stuffing; ~grocer(y), (business of, things sold by) retail dealer in fruit & vegetables; ~heart, a British Guiana timber tree; ~horn, ignoramus, raw hand, simpleton; ~house, of glass for rearing delicate plants; ~man, golf-course keeper; ~ manure, growing plants ploughed into soil; ∥ ~peak, G~ Woodpecker (transl. of It. picchio verde); ~room, accommodating actors & actresses when off stage; ~sand, = earth, kind of sandstone largely of this earth, stratum largely of this sandstone; ~shank, large kind of sandpiper; ~sick(ness), (affected with) CHLOROSIS; ~stick, bone-fracture, esp. in children, in which bone is only bent; ~stone, kinds of ~ eruptive rock containing feldspar & hornblende, also kind of jade; ~ stuff, vegetation, ~vegetables; ~sward, turf; ~ table, gaming table; ~toil, granstone nom; ~ tea, made from steam-dried leaves; ~weed, kind of genista used for dyeing; ~wood, woodlands in summer, esp. as scene of outlaw life; ∥ ~yard, enclosure for stray beasts, pound; hence ~ISH¹(2), & (in comb. as ~y-yellow) ~Y², aa., ~NY² adv., ~NESS n. 11. n. What is ~, part of anything, (do you see any ~, i.e. sign of gullibility, in my eye?); ~ dye (usu. with epithet, as mineral, Paris, ~). 12. Vigour, youth, virility, (usu. in the ~). 13. Verdure, vegetation, also ~ERY n. 14. ∥ (pl.) ~ vegetables before or after cooking. 15. Piece of public or common grassy land; grass-plot used for special purpose (esp. in comb. as bleaching, bowling, putting, ~). [OE grēne cf. Du. groen, G grün, cogn. w. GROW]

green², v.i. & t. Become green, esp. with verdure; dye green, soil etc. with green; (sl.) hoax, take in. [OE grēnian (prec.)]

green'er, n. (sl.). Raw hand, esp. newly arrived foreigner seeking work. [-ER²]

green'ing, n. Kind of apple, green when ripe. [-ING³]

green'let, n. = VIREO. [GREEN¹, -LET]

greenth, n. (rare). Verdure. [-TH¹]

Greenwich (grin'ij), n. Town in Kent with State observatory (~ time, mean time for meridian of ~, standard time in Britain & some other countries); ~ Hospital, formerly used to accommodate old and disabled navy seamen (who are now out-pensioners), later occupied by the Royal Naval College for officer students.

greet¹, v.t. Accost with salutation; salute with words or gestures, receive on meeting or arrival with speech or action (friendly or not); (of cheers etc.) hail; (of sight etc.) meet (eye, ear). Hence ~ING¹ n. [com.-WG; OE grētan, cf. Du. groeten, G grüssen, etym. dub.]

greet², v.i. (Sc.). Weep. [OE grētan & grēotan]

greff'ier, n. Registrar, notary, (esp. in foreign countries & Channel Islands. [F (greffe = OF grafe GRAFT¹, -IER)]

gregãr'ious, a. Living in flocks or communities; fond of company; (Bot.) growing in clusters; of flocks, of crowds. Hence ~LY² adv., ~NESS n. [f.L gregārius (prex -egis flock, -ARY¹) +-OUS]

grege (-āzh), a. & n. (Of) colour between grey & beige. [portmanteau wd]

Gregõr'ian, a. & n. 1. Of, according to, the plain-chant or plain-song ritual music named after Pope Gregory I (n., a ~ chant); ~ tones, eight plain-song melodies prescribed for psalms in R.C. Ch. 2. Established by Pope Gregory XIII (~ CALENDAR, correction 1582 of the Julian; ~ style = new STYLE¹; ~ epoch, from 1582). [f. LL f. Gk Grēgorios Gregory + -AN]

grĕg'ory-pow'der, n. Compound powder of rhubarb, used as aperient. [J. Gregory, Scottish physician d. 1822]

grĕm'ial, n. Silk apron placed on bishop's lap at some ceremonies. [f. LL gremiālis (L gremium lap, -AL)]

∥ **grĕm'lin**, n. (R.A.F. sl.). Mischievous sprite alleged to cause mishaps. [?]

∥ **grẽnāde'**, n. Small explosive shell thrown by hand or (rifle-~) shot from rifle-barrel; glass receptacle thrown to disperse chemicals for testing drains, extinguishing fires, etc. [F, f. Sp. granada POMEGRANATE]

grenadier', n. **1.** (Orig.) soldier who threw grenades; (now) ||G~s or G~ Guards, first regiment of household infantry. **2.** S.-Afr. weaver-bird with red & black plumage. [F prec., -IER]

grenadine¹, n. Dish of veal or poultry fillets, trimmed, larded, & glazed. [f. F *grenadin* perh. f. *grain,* see GRAIN]

grenadine², n. Dress-fabric of open silk or silk & wool. [F, perh. f. *Granada* Spanish city]

grenadine³ (-ēn), n. French cordial syrup of pomegranate. [see POMEGRANATE] for walking. [f. L *gradi gress-* walk, -OR²-IAL]

gressor'ial, a. (zool.). Walking, adapted

grew¹. See GROW.

grey, **grew²,** (grū),(esp. U.S.) **gray,** a. & n., & v.i. **I.** Intermediate between black & white, coloured like ashes or lead, (~ *monk,* Cistercian; ~ *friar,* Franciscan; ~ *sister,* of third order of St Francis; ~ *eye,* with ~ iris; ~ *mare is better horse,* wife rules husband); between light & dark, dull, clouded, depressing, dismal; (of person or his hair) turning white with age etc.; ancient, immemorial; belonging to old age, experienced, mature; (~ *back,* hooded crow; ~ *beard,* old man, large stoneware jug for spirit, || kind of lichen; ||~*coat,* Cumberland yeoman; Hohen; ||~*drake,* kind of ephemera; ~ *goose,* GREYLAG; ~*-headed,* old, of long service *in,* ancient, time-worn; ~*-hen,* female of black grouse (cf. BLACK-cock); ~ *matter,* material of active part of brain; ~ *stone,* ~ volcanic rock; hence ~ISH² (2), ~LY², ~NESS n., (grī-). **2.** n. ~ clothes; cold sunless light; ~ colour; ~ pigment, (the *Greys* or *Scots Greys,* 2nd Dragoons). **3.** v.b. Become, make, ~ (Photog.) dull surface of (glass), give mezzotint effect to (photograph) by covering negative with such glass. [OE *grēg,* cf. Du. *grauw,* G *grau*]

||grey'cing (grā-), n. (colloq.). Grey-hound-racing. [abbr.]

grey'hound (grā-), n. Slender long-legged keen-sighted swift dog used in coursing hares etc. (*ocean ~,* swift ship); ~*-racing,* modern sport in which mechanical hare is coursed by ~s as opportunity for betting. [OE *grīghund* (*grīg-* etym. dub., not connected w. GREY]

grey'lag (goose) (grā-), n. Common European wild goose. [*lag* said to refer to its staying long in England for a migrant]

grey'wacke (grā'wŏke, or -ăk), n. A conglomerate rock consisting of rounded pebbles and sand cemented together. [anglicized f. G *grauwacke* (*grau* grey + WACKE)]

grid, n. Frame of spaced parallel bars, grating, (Electr.) wire network between filament and plate of valve; system of numbered squares printed on military map and forming basis of map

references; network of lines, railways, electric-power connexions, etc.; gridiron (for cooking, & docking). [back formation f. GRIDIRON]

grid'dle, n. & v.t. Circular iron plate for baking cakes on; miner's wire-bottomed screen (vb, screen with ~). [prob. f. OF *gredil* (cf. 16th-c. Norman *grédil* gridiron) perh. f. L *crāticula* (*crātis* hurdle, -CULE)]

gride, v.i., & n. Cut, scrape, (*along, through,* etc., with strident or grating sound (also sense *pierce,* prob. by metath. f. *gird¹*) [orig. sense *is way*); (n.) grating sound. [orig. *gird¹*]

grid'iron (-īrn), n. Barred metal cooking utensil for broiling; (Naut.) frame of parallel beams for supporting ship in dock; (Theatr.) plank structure over stage supporting mechanism for dropping scenes etc.; a naval evolution; (also ~ *pendulum*) compensation pendulum with parallel rods of different metals. [earlier *gredire* prob. =GRIDDLE, later confused w. iron, cf. ANDIRON]

grief, n. Deep or violent sorrow, keen regret, (*come to ~*), meet with disaster, fall, fall. [OF (*grever* GRIEVE)]

griev'ance (-ĭn), n. Real or fancied ground of complaint. [f. OF *grevance* (*grever,* -ANCE)]

grieve¹, v.t. & i. Give deep sorrow to; feel grief (*at, for, about, over*). [f. F *grever* f. L *gravāre* (*gravis* heavy)]

grieve², n. (Sc.). Farm-bailiff, overseer. [f. OE *gerēfa*; see REEVE¹]

griev'ous, a. Bringing serious trouble, injurious; (of pain etc.) severe; flagrant, heinous; exciting grief. Hence ~LY² adv.

||grif'fin¹, griff'on, n. (Anglo-Ind.). (Also **griff**) newly arrived European, novice, greenhorn. Hence ~AGE(2), ~HOOD, ~SHIP, nn. [?]

griff'in², griff'on¹, gryph'on, n. Fabulous creature with eagle's head & wings & lion's body; ||*the Griffin,* monument on site of Temple Bar, London; (~*fon*) kind of vulture (also ~*-vulture*). [f. OF *grifoun* f. L *gryphus* f. Gk *grups,* -OON]

griff'on², n. Kind of foreign, coarse-haired terrier-like dog. [F, perh.=prec.]

grig, n. || Small eel; grasshopper or cricket (*merry, lively, as a ~;* sense *cricket* doubtful, perh. invented to account for phrase). [?]

grill¹, v.t. & i., & n. **1.** Broil (t. & i.) on gridiron (also fig. of torture or great heat), whence ~'ER (1, 2) n.; *subject to severe questioning (esp. by police); scallop (oysters etc.). **2.** n. ~ed food; (also ~ *room*) room where steaks etc. are ~ed & served. [f. F *griller* (toll.)]

grill², n. Gridiron. [f. F *gril* (OF *graïl* perh. as GRIDDLE]

grill'age, n. Heavy framework of cross-timbering as foundation for building in treacherous soil. [F (toll., -AGE]

grille, grill³, n. Grating, latticed screen, esp. in door for observing callers, in

convent separating nuns from visitors, formerly in front of ladies' gallery in House of Commons, etc.; (Tennis) square opening in wall; spawn-hatching frame. Hence grilLED² (-ĭd) a. [F (-e), as GRIDDLE]

grilse, n. Young salmon that has been only once to the sea. [from 15th c.; etym. dub.]

grim, a. (-mm-). Stern, unrelenting, merciless, severe; of forbidding or harsh aspect (often of death; *hold on like ~ death, tight*); sinister, ghastly, unmirthful, (*has a ~ truth in it; a ~ smile; ~ laughter, pastime*, etc.). Hence ~ LY² adv., ~ NESS n. [cf. G *grimm*, also obs. *grame* angry]

grimace', n., & v.i. 1. Wry face expressing annoyance etc. or meant to raise a laugh; affected look; use of such looks, affectation. 2. v.i. Make wry face. Hence or cogn. grimā'CER¹, grimā'CIER, nn. [F, etym. dub.]

grimal'kin (-awl-, -ăl-), n. Old she-cat; spiteful old woman. [prob. f. grey + Malkin (Matilda, KIN)]

grime, n., & v.t. 1. Soot, dirt, ingrained in some surface, esp. the skin; hence v.t. Blacken, befoul. [cf. Flem. *grijm(en)*]

grim'Y² a., grim'INESS n. 2. v.t. Blacken, befoul.

Grimm's law. See LAW¹.

grin, v.i. & t. (-nn-), & n. 1. Show teeth in sign of pain or in forced or unrestrained or stupid smile (often at; ~ & bear'd, take pain etc. stoically; ~ like Cheshire cat, constantly & meaninglessly; ~ through horse-collar, in grimacing-match at rustic sports); express (contempt, satisfaction) by ~ning. 2. n. Act of ~ning (often on the ~ or broad ~). [OE grennian cf. OHG grennan mutter]

grind, v.t. & i. (ground), & n. 1. Reduce to small particles or powder by crushing between mill-stones, teeth, etc. (often down, small, to pieces, into dust, etc.); (quasi-pass.) admit of being ground (will not ~ fine); oppress, harass with exactions, (often down; a ~ing tyranny; also ~ the faces of the poor etc.); produce (flour) by ~ing; sharpen or smooth by friction (has an AXE to ~; ~ lenses, diamonds, etc.); work (hand-mill); turn handle of (hurdy-gurdy; also abs.); produce, bring out, (music) from hurdy-gurdy; toil monotonously, study hard; teach (subject, pupil in it) laboriously; rub (t. & i.) gratingly on, into, or against (ground his heel into it; ship was ~ing on rocks), rub (teeth) hard together (~ out an oath, utter while ~ing teeth); ~ stone, thick revolving stone disk for ~ing, sharpening, & polishing (hold, keep, one's nose to the ~stone, make him work incessantly; kind of stone used for these. 2. n. ~ing; hard monotonous work or task; walk for exercise; steeplechase; (at Cambridge) a ferry. [only in E & in Du. grenden; perh. cogn. w. L frendere gnash teeth]

grin'der, n. Molar tooth; grinding-machine; upper mill-stone; person who grinds (esp. in comb. as organ, knife, ~); crammer. [-ER¹]

grin'dery, n. Cobblers' material of all kinds. [GRIND, -ERY; perh. extended f. the cobbler's whetstone]

grin'gō (-ngg-), n. (Spanish-America; pl. -os). Foreigner (esp. an Anglo-American). [Mex. Sp.]

grip¹, n. Firm hold, tight grasp or clasp (at, come to; ~s, close combat), grasping power; way of clasping hands; way of grasping or holding (overlapping ~); control, mastery, intellectual hold; power of arresting, attention; part in machinery etc. that clips, part of weapon etc. that is held; = *grip'sack; ~brake, worked by gripping with hand. [f. OE gripe grasp & gripa handful, both f. root of GRIPE]

grip², v.t. & i. (-pp-). Seize, grasp, or hold, tightly; take firm hold; compel attention of; *~ sack, handbag. Hence ~p ER¹(2) n. [cf. MHG grippfen, cogn. w. GRIPE]

grip³, n. Small open ditch. [OE grype cogn. w. grēop burrow]

gripe, v.t. & i. & n. 1. Clutch, grip; oppress, pinch; affect with colic pains; (Naut.) secure with ~s, (of ship) come up into wind in spite of helm. 2. n. Act of griping, clutch; hold, control, (in the ~ of); (pl.) colic pains; handle of implement or weapon; (Naut., pl.) lashings securing boat in its place; ~water, horse-medicine for colic. [com.-Teut.; OE grīpan, cf. Du. grijpen, G greifen]

grippe, n. Influenza. [F]

grisaille' (-zāl, & see AP), n. Method of decorative painting, stained-glass window etc., in grey monochrome representing objects in relief. [F (gris grey f., OHG grīs)]

gris'eous (-z-), a. (bot., zool.). Bluish or pearl grey. [f. med.L griseus (prec.), -OUS]

grisette' (-z-), n. French working-class girl (formerly dressed in grey). [F (gris see GRISAILLE, -ETTE)]

gris'kin, n. Lean part of loin of bacon pig. [perh. f. obs. grice f. ON gríss young pig + -KIN]

gris'ly (-z-), a. Causing horror, terror, or superstitious dread. [OE grislic; cf. obs. grise to shudder]

grist¹, n. Corn for grinding (brings ~ to the mill, is profitable; all is ~ that comes to his mill, he utilizes everything); malt crushed for brewing. [OE grist (GRIND, cf. BLAST f. BLOW]

grist², n. Size or thickness of yarn or rope. [perh. cogn. w. GIRD¹]

gris'tle (-sl), n. Whitish tough flexible tissue in vertebrates, cartilage, (in the ~, immature—infants having ~ for bone). Hence gris'tlY² (-sli) a. [OE, cf. OFris. & MLG gristel, etym. dub.]

grit¹, n. Small particles of stone or sand, esp. as causing discomfort or clogging machinery etc., whence ~TY² a., ~TI-NESS n.; (also ~*stone*) coarse sandstone; grain or texture of stone; (colloq.) strength of character, pluck, endurance. [OE *grēot*, cf. G *griess*]

grit² v.i. & t. (-tt-). Produce, move with, grating sound; grind (teeth). [f. prec.]

grits, n. pl. Husked but unground oats; coarse oatmeal. [OE *grytte*, cf. G *grütze*; cogn. w. GROATS]

‖ **griz'zle**, v.i.(colloq.). (Esp. of children) whimper, cry fretfully. [etym. dub.]

griz'zled (-zeld), a. Grey(-haired). [f. obs. *grizzle* grey, grey hair, +-ED²]

griz'zly, a. & n. 1. Grey, greyish, grey-haired. (~ *bear*, large fierce N.-Amer. kind). [~ *king, queen*, fishing-flies. 2. n.

groan, v.i. & t. & n. (Make) deep inarticulate sound expressing pain, grief, or disapproval (~ *inwardly*, be distressed, utter with ~s (often *out*); be oppressed or loaded *under, beneath, with*, (~ *under injustice*; *shelf ~s with books*; ~*ing board*, well-loaded table); long *for*; ~ *down*, silence (speaker) with ~s. Hence ~ING-LY² adv. [OE *grānian* cogn. w. GRIN]

groat, n. (hist.). Silver coin (= 4d.; issued 1351–1662 (occasionally used of the four-penny piece 1836–56); small sum (*don't care a ~*). [f. MDu. *groot* orig. great, in sense thick; cf. GROSCHEN]

groats, n. pl. Hulled (sometimes also crushed) grain, esp. oats. [cogn. w. obs. *grout*; cf. GRITS]

Gröb'ian, n. Clownish slovenly person. [G., f. med. L *Grobianus* used as typical name]

grō'cer, n. Dealer in spices, dried fruits, sugar, & miscellaneous domestic stores (~*'s itch*, eczema, caused by handling sugar). Hence **grō'cery²**, &. usu. pl. [f. orig. one who sells in the gross, f. OF *grossier* f. med. L *grossarius* (GROSS, -ARY²)]

grog, n. & v.i. & t. 1. Drink of spirit & water; social meeting with ~; ~*blossom*, pimple or redness on nose from intemperance. 2. v.b. Drink ~; extract spirit from (empty cask) by pouring in hot water. [perh. short for GROGRAM, nickname (from his cloak) of Adm. Vernon, who first had ~ served out instead of neat rum]

grog'gily (-g-), adv. [as foll.]

grog'gy (-g-), a. Drunk(en); bibulous; (of horse) weak in forelegs, tottering; unsteady, shaky. Hence ~NESS n. [-Y¹]

grog'ram, n. Coarse fabric of silk, mohair & wool, or these mixed, often stiffened with gum. [f. F *gros grain* large grain]

groin¹, n. & v.t. 1. Depression between belly & thigh. 2. (Archit.) edge formed by intersecting vaults, fillet covering this. (vb, build with ~s, whence ~ING-I(ð) n. [earlier *grynde* etym. dub.; cf. OE *grynde* abyss, cogn. w. GROUND]

*groin². Var. of GROYNE.

Grōl'ier (-ā), n. ~ *binding* (in the highly ornate style introduced by Jean ~ de Servin, Vicomte d'Aiguisy (d. 1565), French book-collector).

"grōm(m)ét. See GRUMMET.

grom'well, n. Kinds of plant with stony seeds formerly used in medicine. [f. OF *gromil* etym. dub.]

groom, n. & v.t. 1. ‖ One of certain officers of Royal Household (~ *of the stole, in waiting*, etc.). 2. Servant having care of horses (vb, curry, feed, tend, etc.; also in p.p. of persons, as *well-~ed*, neatly got up, esp. with well-trimmed hair, beard, etc.). 3. Bridegroom; ~*s'men*, unmarried friend officially attending bridegroom at wedding. [perh. shortened f. OF *gromet* (also GOURMET) servant, etym. dub.]

groove, n. & v.t. 1. Channel or hollow, esp. one made to direct motion or receive corresponding ridge (vb, make ~ or ~s in). 2. Piece of routine, undeviating course, rut, whence **groov'y**¹ a. **groov'i-NESS** n. [f. Du. *groeve* furrow, cf. G *grube*]

grōpe, v.i. Feel about as in dark (*for, after, or* abs.), search blindly (lit. & fig.); ~ *one's way*, find it by feeling, proceed tentatively. Hence **grōp'ingLY**² adv. [OE *grāpian* (grip a grasp) cogn. w. GRIP]

grō'schen (-ōshn), n. Small obsolete silver German coin. [G]

gros de Naples (grō'denäh'pl), n. Heavy silk fabric. [F *gros GROSS, Naples*]

gross¹, n. (pl. *gross*). Twelve dozen. [f. F *grosse* orig. fem. of *gros* GROSS²]

gross², a. Luxuriant, rank; overfed, bloated, repulsively fat; flagrant, glaring; total, without deductions, not nett; dense, thick, solid; not ethereal, transparent, or impalpable; (of food) coarse, greasy, unpleasant; (of senses etc.) not delicate, dull; coarse in manners or morals, unrefined, indecent; (abs.) *in (the) ~*, a general way, apart from detail, on the whole. Hence ~LY² adv., ~NESS n. [f. F *gros grosse* big f. LL *grossus* etym. dub.]

grōt, n. (poet.). Grotto. [f. F *grotte*

grotesque' (-ēk), n. & a. 1. Decorative painting or sculpture with fantastic interweaving of human & animal forms with foliage; (pop.) comically distorted figure or design. 2. adj. (Archit.) in the above style; distorted, bizarre; ludicrous from incongruity, absurd; hence ~LY² (-ki-) adv. ~NESS (-kn-), ~NESS n. [f. F *grotesque querie* (-ski-) f.-ERY(ð)), m. F *grotesque* antique work (GROTTO, -ESQUE)]

perh. because *grotta* was used of excavated chambers with mural paintings]

grött'ö, n. (pl. ~es, ~s). Picturesque cave; artificial ornamental cave, room etc. adorned with shells etc. in imitation of cave, as cool retreat || the G~, London streetboys' celebration on 5th Aug. of end of close time for oysters]. Hence ~ED² (-öd) a. [f. It. *grotta* f. L f. Gk *kruptē* vault (*kruptō* hide) cf. CRYPT]

*grouch, v.i. & n. (colloq.). 1. Grumble. 2. n. Discontented person: fit of the sulks. [var. of *grutch*, see GRUDGE]

ground¹, n. **1.** Bottom of sea (now chiefly fig., as *touch* ~, come to something solid after vague talk etc.; of ship, *take* ~, strand); (pl.) dregs, esp. of coffee, whence ~Y² a. **2.** (Electr.)=EARTH¹. **3.** Base, foundation, motive, valid reason, (*on the* ~ *of*, by reason or under pretext of; *on public* etc. ~s), whence ~LESS a., ~²lessly² adv., ~²lessness n. **4.** Substratum, underlying part, surface worked upon in embroidery, painting, etc., undecorated part, prevailing colour or tone: (Etching) composition spread on metal & cut through with needle where acid is to act. **5.** Surface of earth (*fall, be dashed, to the* ~, be abandoned, fail, of scheme, hope; BREAK¹ ~; *down to the* ~, colloq., in all respects, thoroughly; *above* ~, alive; *cut the* ~ *from under one's feet*, anticipate & stultify his arguments or plans). **6.** pl. Enclosed land for ornament or recreation attached to house. **7.** Position, area, or distance, on earth's surface (*cover much* ~, of inquiry, report, etc., be far-reaching; *stand, shift, one's* ~, maintain, change, one's argument or intention; *gain* ~, advance; *lose, give,* ~, retreat, decline). **8.** Area of special kind or use (*fishing~s; forbidden* ~, subject that must be avoided; *classic* ~, historic place; *cricket* etc. ~). **9.** Person's property in land. **10.** (Cricket) his etc. ~, behind popping-crease (*in, out of, his* ~). || paid staff of players attached to club. **11.** (In names of beasts) terrestrial, (of plants) burrowing or lying on ~, (of plants) dwarfish or trailing. **12.** ~ash, ash & v.t., (prepare with) bait thrown to bottom of intended fishing~ to attract fish; ~ bass, short passage in bass of composition, repeated many times with upper part of music varied; ~box, small BOX¹ used to edge garden beds; ~colour, first coat of paint, prevailing colour on which design is done; ~fish, living at bottom; ~fishing, with bait near bottom; || ~floor, rooms etc. on level of outside ~ (*get in on the* ~ *floor*, be admitted to company etc. on same terms as promoters); || ~game, hares, rabbits, etc.; ~pudgeon, loach; ~hog, Amer. marmot; ~ice, formed at bottom of water, anchor-ice; ~ivy, ale-hoof, creeping herb with

bluish-purple flower & kidney-shaped leaf; || ~ landlord, owner of ~ leased for building; ~man (in charge of cricket etc. ~); ~noke, on which a common chord is built, fundamental bass; ~raut, (edible tuber of) N.-Amer. wild bean, also W.-Ind. & W.-Afr. pea with pod ripening under ~; ~pine, herb with resinous smell, also clubmoss; ~plan, plane drawing of divisions of building at ~ level, also outline or general design of anything; ~rent, that paid to ~ landlord; ~sea, heavy sea without apparent cause; ~s'man, =~man; ~ speed (Aviation), aircraft's speed relative to ~ (cf. AIR¹ speed); ~ staff, non-flying members of aerodrome staff; ~ swell, heavy sea caused by distant or past storm or earthquake; ~ torpedo, fixed to bottom of sea; ~work, foundation or basis (usu. fig.), chief ingredient, general surface of thing showing where not overlaid with embroidery or other ornament. [com. Teut.; OE & G *grund*, cf. Du. *grond*]

ground², v.t. & i. Base, establish, (institution, principle, belief) on some fact or authority (in pass. also *in*; p.p., *well, till,* etc., *founded*; = well founded, whence ~'édly² adv.); instruct thoroughly (*in* elements), whence **ground'ing¹** n.; prepare ground of (embroidery etc.); lay (esp. arms) on ground; (Electr.) connect with earth as conductor; alight on ground; run (t. & i.) ashore, strand; prevent (aircraft, airman) from flying, [f. prec.]

ground³, p.p. of GRIND. ~ *glass*, made non-transparent by grinding. [-AGE]

|| **groun'dage,** n. Duty on ship lying on beach or entering port. [-AGE]

ground'ling, n. Kinds of GROUND¹-*fish*; creeping or dwarf plant; spectator or reader of inferior taste (ref. to *Hamlet* III. ii. 12). [-LING¹]

ground'sel¹, n. Kinds of weed, of which the commonest is used as food for cage-birds. [OE *gundæswelgiæ* perh. f. *gund* pus, SWALLOW¹, =pus-absorber, as being used for poultices, later assimilated to *ground*]

ground'sel², n. (arch.). Timber serving as foundation, lowest part of wooden framework; threshold. [SILL]

group (-ōōp), n., & v.t. & i. **1.** (Fine arts) two or more figures or objects forming complete design or distinct part of one; number of persons or things standing near together, knot, cluster; number of persons or things belonging or classed together (in Pol., used of smaller unit than the party, & esp. in assemblies where the two-party system does not prevail; in scientific classification, used vaguely of cross-divisions outside the regular hierarchy of class-terms); *Oxford G~*, see BUCHMANISM; ~captain, officer of AIR¹ *Force*. **2.** vb. Form (t. & rarely i.)

into a ~, place in a ~ *with*; form (t. & i. of colours, figures, etc.), into well-arranged & harmonious whole; classify. Hence ~AGE(3) n. [f. F *groupe* f. It. *gruppo*]

group'er (~ōō-), n. Kinds of W.-Ind. & Austral. fish. [f. Port. *garupa* (prob. S.-Amer.)]

grouse¹, n. (pl. *grouse*). (Prop.) gallinaceous bird with feathered feet; (pop.) Moor Fowl or Game or Red G~, reddish game-bird of British Isles (*Black G~*, BLACK¹ *game*; *Wood* or *Great G~*, capercailzie; *White G~*, ptarmigan), its flesh. [?]

‖grouse², n., & v.i. & n. (sl.). Grumble. [?]

grout¹, n., & v.t. 1. Thin fluid mortar for filling interstices. 2. v.t. Fill up or finish with this. [cf. 16th-c. F *grouter*]

‖grout², v.i. & t. (Of pigs) turn up earth, turn up (earth etc.), with snout. [perh. f. obs. *groot* mud, cogn. w. OE *grēot* grit]

grōve, n. Small wood, group of trees, (in Bible, mistransl. of Hebrew word=pillar used as idol, or name of goddess). Hence ~ED²(vd),~e'LESS(-vl),~Y², aa. [OE *grāf*]

grŏv'el (-ŭ-), v.i. (-ll-). Lie prone, humble one-self, (often *in the dirt* or *dust*); (part.) abject, low, base, whence ~'lingLY² adv. Hence ~LER¹, n. [back formation f. obs. *grovelling* adv. (obs. *on grufe* f. ON á *grúfu* on one's face, -LING² taken as part. in *tiv* etc.]

grow (-ō), v.i. & t. (*grew* pr. grōō, *n* p.p. often as act. intr. with *is*, cf. (1)(2), & as adj.). 1. Develop or exist as living plant (also joc. of lifeless things etc., be found in some place); ~ *into one, together, yet*, coalesce, germinate, sprout, spring up, be produced, come naturally into exis-tence, arise. (~ING) *pains*, neuralgic pains in limbs of the young) quantity, degree, power, etc. (~ *downwards*, diminish; *habit, person, picture*, etc., ~s on one, becomes more in-fluential with or admired by him), whence ally (~ *rich*) ; ~ *up*, advance to maturity (*n-uy* a. & n., adult); emerge from soil, reach full size; (of custom) arise, become common. 4. Produce by cultivation, bring forth, let (beard etc.), whence coalesce, germinate, sprout, spring up, (often *up* or *over*) with some growth. [OE *grōwan* cf. Du. *groeien* f. OTeut. *grō-* cogn. w. GRASS]

grow'er (-ō'er), n. Plant that grows in specified way (*fast, free*, etc., ~); person growing produce (often in comb., as *fruit~*). [-ER¹]

growl, v.i. & t., & n. (Make) guttural sound of anger (*at*); rumble; murmur angrily, mutter with a ~ (*out*). Hence ~'ingLY² adv. [prob. imit.]

grown'er, n. In vbl senses; also : ‖four-

wheeled cab; kinds of fish; small iceberg; *(sl.)* beer-pitcher. [-ER¹]

growl'ery, n. Growling; place to growl in, private room, den. [-ERY; cf. BOUDOIR]

grown, p.p. of GROW. ~ *man* etc., mature. increase, (of foreign etc., ~, grown abroad cultivation of; size ultimately attained); or is growing. (Path.) morbid formation.

groyne, *groin, n., & v.t. 1. Timber framework or low broad wall run out to check drifting of beach & so stop en-croachment of sea. 2. v.t. Supply (beach) with ~s. [perh. f. obs. *groin* snout f. OF *groign* (L *grunnire* grunt)]

grŭb¹, n. Larva of insect, caterpillar, maggot; dull drudge, literary hack, sloven, smug; ball bowled along ground at cricket; *(sl.)* food, a feed; *~-stake* (Mining sl.), supply (prospector) with outfit, provisions, etc., in return for part of profits. (n.) outfit etc. so supplied.

grŭb², v.i. & t. (-bb-). Dig (t. & i.) super-ficially; clear (ground) of roots & stumps, clear away (roots etc.), (often *up*); fetch *up* or *out* by digging (fig., discover in books etc.); search, rummage, (intr.); plod, toil, *on, along, away*; *(sl.)* feed, provide (boarder etc., with food. [prob. f. prec.] ; *~-axe, -hoe, -hook*, for ~bing up stumps. Hence (~)~b'ER¹(1, 2) n. [prob. cogn. w. GRAVE²; cf. ON *grufa* pit]

grŭb'by², a. Of, infested with, grubs; dirty, grimy, slovenly, whence ~iNESS n. [-Y²]

Grub-street, n. & a. (Region inhabited by) the tribe of needy authors & literary hacks; (adj.) of these. [a London street (now Milton St) so inhabited in 17th c.]

grŭdge, v.t. & t. & n. 1. Be unwilling to give, grant, or allow (thing; person thing, thing to person), or to do; (part.) reluctant, whence grŭdg'ingLY² adv. 2. n. Feeling of resentment or ill will (*have a ~ against; bear, owe, one a ~*). [earlier *grutch* f. OF *groucier* etym. dub.]

grŭ'el (~ōōl), n., & v.t. (-ll-). Liquid food chiefly for invalids of oatmeal etc. boiled in milk or water (*have, get, one's ~*, be punished, severely defeated, or killed; so *give one his ~, &* ~ vb sl. in same sense; whence ~ingLY² (~ōōl-) n.]. [OF. f. med. L *+gruellum* dim. of *grutum* f. Teut., cf. OE GROATS]

grue'some (-ōōs-), a. Grisly, disgusting. Hence ~LY² adv., ~NESS n. [f. obs. *grue* to shudder, cf. G *grauen* + -SOME]

grŭff, a. Surly, laconic, rough-mannered, rough-voiced. Hence ~'LY² adv., ~'NESS n. [~'ISH²(2) a. [cf. G. *grob*]

grŭm'ble, v.i. & t. & n. (Utter) dull in-articulate sound, murmur, growl faintly; rumble; complain(t) (*at, about, over*); utter complainingly (often *out*). Hence

~ER¹ n., ~INGLY² adv. [cf. F *grommeder*. Du. *grommelen*, G *grummeln*]

grume (-ōōm), n. (med.). Clot of blood, viscous fluid. So **grum'ous** (-ōō-) a. [f. LL *grumus* small heap]

grŭmm'ĕt, ***grŏm(m)ĕt**, n. (naut.). Ring usn. of twisted rope as fastening, rowlock, wad, etc. [f. 15th-c. F *grommette* curb (*gourmer* to curb, etym. dub.)]

grŭm'plý, grŭm'pĭsh, aa. Ill-tempered, surly. Hence **~ily²** adv., **~iness** n. [f. obs. *grump* offence, snub, etym. dub.]

Grün'dyism, n. Conventional propriety, prudery. [f. 'What will Mrs Grundy (a neighbour) say?' in Morton's *Speed the Plough* 1798]

grünt, v.i. & t., & n. (Utter) low gruff sound characteristic of hogs; express discontent, dissent, fatigue, etc., by this; utter with ~ (often *out*). Hence **~'ingly²** adv. [OE *grunnettan* (cf. G *grunzen*) frequent. of *grunian* imit.]

grün'ter, n. In vbl senses; esp.: pig; kinds of fish. [-ER¹]

gru'yère (grōō'yāř), n. Swiss pale cows'-milk cheese with many cavities. [G~, Swiss town]

grỹs'bŏk, n. Small grey S.-Afr. antelope. [f. Du. *grijsbok* (*grijs* grey, BUCK¹)]

guacharo (gwăhchah'rō), n. The oil-bird of S. America. [S.-Amer. Sp.]

guacho, incorrect for GAUCHO.

guai'ăc, -acum, (gwi-), n. Genus of W.-Ind. trees & shrubs (*-um* only); brownish green wood of two kinds of these used in medicine, lignum vitae; resin from these, drug made from it. [*-um* mod. L f. Sp. *guayaco* of Haytian orig.]

guan (gwahn), n. Kinds of S.-Amer. gallinaceous bird allied to curassow. [prob. native]

gua'na (gwah-), n. Iguana; any large lizard. [var. of IGUANA]

guana'cō (gwanah-), n. (pl. -os). Wild llama with reddish-brown wool. [native S.-Amer. *huanaco*]

gua'nō (gwah-), n. (pl. -os), & v.t. Excrement of sea-fowl found esp. in islands about Peru used as manure; artificial manure esp. that made from fish; (vb) fertilize with ~. [Sp., f. native *huanu*]

guarantee' (gă-), n., & v.t. 1. Person making guaranty or giving security; thing given or existing as guaranty for fulfilment of conditions or permanence etc. of something; person to whom guaranty is given [correl. to *guarantor*; prop. a separate formation with -EE]; ~ *fund*, sum pledged as contingent indemnity for loss. 2. v.t. Be ~ for, answer for due fulfilment of (contract etc.) or genuineness etc. of; engage *that* something has happened or will happen; secure possession of *to* person; secure *against* or *from* (risk etc.), or *in* (possession etc.); hence **gua'rantŏr²** (gă-; also -ŏr')

n. [in first sense, orig. *garanti*, prob. f. Sp. *garante* = F *garant* WARRANT¹; other senses of n. by confusion w. foll. or misuse of -EE]

gua'ranty (gă-), n., & v.t. Undertaking written or other to answer for payment of debt or performance of obligation by another person liable in first instance; ground or basis of security; (vb) guarantee (now rare). [f. AF *guarantie* (*guarant* WARRANT¹)]

guard¹ (gärd), n. 1. Defensive posture or motion in fencing, boxing, etc. (in cricket, position of bat to defend wicket; *take, give,* ~, of batsman, umpire, ascertaining correct spot on ground for this). 2. Watch, vigilant state, (*keep* ~, *be on* ~, act as sentry etc.; *on, off,* one's ~, prepared, unprepared, against attack, surprise, or one's own impulses etc.). 3. Protector, defender, sentry; || official in charge of stage-coach or train; || (pl.) household troops (including *Foot-~, Horse-~, Life-~*, & by extension some orig. seven) regiments of *Dragoon G~s*). 4. Body of soldiers etc. serving as protectors of place or person, escort, separate portion of army, etc. (*advance, rear,* ~; ~ *of honour; mount, relieve,* ~, earlier *the* ~, take up, take others' place in, sentry duty). 5. Contrivance to prevent injury or accident (often in comb. as *fire, trigger,* ~). 6. ~-*boat*, boat going rounds of fleet in harbour to see that good watch is kept, also official harbour boat enforcing quarantine or customs regulations; ~-*book* (arranged for the reception of additional leaves, letters, etc.); ~-*chain*, securing watch, brooch, etc.; ~-*house*, accommodating military ~ or securing prisoners; ~-*rail*, hand or other rail to prevent falling etc.; ~-*ring*, preventing other ring from slipping off finger, keeper; ~-*room*, as ~*house* above; ~-*ship*, warship protecting harbour & receiving seamen till they can join their ships; ~*s'man*, || soldier, esp. officer, of G~s; ~-*tent*, as ~*house* above. Hence ~'LESS a. [f. F *garde* f. Teut. see WARD]

guard² (gärd), v.t. & i. Keep safe, stand guard over, keep (door etc.) so as to control passage, protect, defend (*from, against*); secure by explanations or stipulations etc. from misunderstanding or abuse, (Med.) administer correctives with (drug); keep (thoughts, speech) in check (~*ed language* etc., cautious, measured); whence ~'**edly²** adv., ~'**ednESS** n.; use a fencing guard; take precautions *against*; (Curling, Bowling) protect (stone, bowl) by placing one's own between it & later player. (Chess) protect (piece, pawn) with another. [f. prec.]

guard'ian (gä-), n. Keeper, defender, protector, (|| *G~ of the poor*, or *G~*, member of Board formerly elected to administer poor-laws in parish or district);

(Law) one having custody of person or property or both of infant, idiot, etc. (cf. ~ angel, spirit watching over person or place. [f. OF *guarden (garde GUARD).]

guard'ianship (gär-), n. Office of guardian, legal tutelage; keeping, guard, (un-der the ~ of the laws). [-SHIP]

gua'va (gwah-), n. (Tropical myrtaceous tree yielding) acid fruit used for making jelly. [f. Sp. guayaba prob. f. S.-Amer. or W.-Ind. name]

guayule (gwahyōō'lě), n. Aster-like Mexican plant the sap of which furnishes a rubber substitute. [Native name]

Guebre (gē'ber, gä-), n. Zoroastrian, fire-worshipper, Parsee. [f. F guèbre f. Pers. gabr]

guel'der rose (gě-: -z), n. Plant with round bunches of white flowers, snowball tree. [Guelders in Prussia]

Guelph, -lf, (gwě-), n. Member of medieval Italian party supporting Pope against Emperor (cf. GHIBELLINE). Hence ~'ic a. [f. It. Guelfo f. MHG Welf name (of founder of princely family of Guelphs, ancestors of British Royal Family) used as war-cry at battle of Weinsberg 1140 against Conrad III]

guerd'on (ger-), n., & v.t. (poet.). Reward, recompense. Hence ~LESS a. [OF, f. med. L widerdonum f. OHG widarlōn (widar again, LOAN) w. assim. to L donum gift]

Guern'sey (gern'zĭ), n. One of Channel Islands; (g~) also ~ shirt, coat, frock) thick knitted woollen usu. blue outer tunic or jersey worn by sailors, workmen, & children; ~ cow; ~ lily, kind of amaryllis (cf. JERSEY). [place in S. Africa.

guer(r)ill'a (ger-), n. (Usu. now ~ war) Irregular war waged by small bodies acting independently; man engaged in this. [Sp. (-rr-) dim. of guerra WAR]

guess (gěs), v.t. & i. & n. 1. Estimate without measurement or detailed calculation; think likely, think one divines nature of, form hypothesis as to, conjecture, hazard opinion about, (noun, that, how, when, whether, etc., thing to be; also intr. with at; often abs. in parenthesis: I ~, chiefly U.S., I feel sure of or know well); conjecture (answer to riddle, solution of problem) rightly, divine.

2. n. Rough estimate, conjecture, hypothesis, (by ~, at haphazard; by ~ and by God); ~-work, (procedure based on) ~ing; OTHER.~ [n. f. vb, ME guessen cf. Du. gissen: f. root of GET]

guest (gěst), n. Person entertained at another's house or table (paying ~, boarder); person lodging at hotel, board-ing-house, etc.; animal or vegetable para-site (cf. HOST²); ~-chamber, kept for ~s; ~-house, superior boarding-house; ~-night, on which ~s are entertained at club, college, mess, etc. Hence ~'SHIP n. [W.Aryan: OE giest cf. ON gestr, G gast]

guest'-rope, guess-, (gěs-), n. Second rope fastened to boat in tow to steady it; rope slung outside ship to give hold for boats coming alongside. [?]

guffaw', n., & v.i. & t. 1. Coarse or boisterous laugh. 2. vb. Make, say with, ~. [orig. Sc.: imit.]

guggle = GURGLE.

guichet (gēsh'ā), n. Grating, hatch, ticket-office window. [F]

guide (gīd), n. 1. One who shows the way; hired conductor of traveller or tourist. 2. (Mil.) one of company formed for reconnoitring etc.; the G~-s, mobile Indian frontier corps; right & left ~, subalterns of company superintending & acting as pivots etc. in evolutions; (Naut.) ship on which rest of fleet regulate their movements. 3. Adviser; directing prin-ciple or standard (the feelings are a bad ~; Scripture is our ~). 4. = GIRL ~. 5. Book of rudiments, manual, (also ~ book) book of information on a city, cathedral, museum, etc., (to). 6. (Mech.) bar, rod, etc., directing motion of some-thing, gauge etc. controlling tool. 7. Thing marking a position or guiding the eye. 8. ~-post, FINGER-post; ~-rope, GUY¹, small rope attached to load of crane to guide it, rope trailed along ground by balloon or small airship to assist in preserving altitude, one of several ropes steadying an airship before flight; ~'way, groove, track. Hence ~LESS (gīd-) a. [F, orig. fem. f. OF guie f. guier to guide prob. f. Pr. or It. guida f. guier to guide know]

guide (gīd), v.t. Act as guide to, go before, lead, direct course of; arrange course of (events); be the principle, motive, or ground, of (action, judgement, etc.); conduct affairs of (State etc.); guiding-stick, MAHLSTICK. Hence guid'ANCE n. (gī-). [f. F guider as prec.]

guid'on (gīd-), n. Pennant narrowing to point at free end (used as standard of dragoons). [F, f. It. guidone perh. f. guida GUIDE¹]

guild, gild, (gĭ-), n. Society for mutual aid or prosecution of common object; G~-hall, in which a medieval ~ met, (often, from

being used as meeting-place of Corpora-tion) town-hall; ||(the) *Guildhall*, hall of the Corporation of the City of London, used for State banquets, municipal meet-ings, etc.; ~ *socialism*, system by which the resources, methods, & profits, of each industry should be controlled by a coun-cil of its members. [OE *gild* guild, pay-ment, sacrifice, cf. Du. & G *geld* money]

guil'der (gĭ-), n. Obsolete gold coin of Netherlands etc.: Dutch silver coin=1/8. [corruption of Du. *gulden*]

guile (gīl), n. Treachery, deceit, cunning devices. Hence ~FUL a., ~FULLY² adv., ~FULNESS n., (gīlf-), ~LESS a., ~lessLY² adv., ~LESSNESS n. (gīl-l-). [OF, prob. f. Teut., cf. WILE]

guill'emot (gĭl'émot, or -tẽn²) n. Kinds of sea-bird. [F, prob. f. *Guillaume* William]

guilloche (gĭlōsh', & see Ap.), n. Architec-tural ornament imitating braided ribbons. [f. F *guillochis*, or f. F *guilloche* the tool used]

guillotine (gĭl'ŏtēn, or -tēn²) n., & v.t. 1. Machine with knife-blade sliding in grooves for beheading; surgical instru-ment for excising uvula etc., kinds of machine for cutting paper etc.; ||(Parl.) method of preventing obstruction by fixing times at which parts of Bill must be voted on. 2. v.t. Use the ~ upon. [F (Dr *Guillotin*, its proposer in 1789)]

guilt (gĭl-), n. The having committed a specified or implied offence; criminality, culpability. [excl. E; OE *gylt*]

guilt'less (gĭl-), a. Innocent (often *of* offence); not having knowledge or posses-sion of (~ *of Greek, soap, moustache, etc.*). Hence ~LY² adv., ~NESS n. [-LESS]

guil't|y (gĭl-), a. Criminal, culpable; con-scious of, prompted by, guilt (~*y con-science, behaviour, look*); having com-mitted a particular offence (*of*; ~*y, not ~y*, verdicts in criminal trials). Hence ~ILY² adv., ~INESS n. [-Y¹]

guimp. = GIMP.

Guinea, g-, (gĭn'ĭ), n. 1. (G~). Part of W. coast of Africa. 2. (g~). Former gold coin named as first coined for the African trade (1663-1717 nominally 20/- but of fluctuating value; from 1717 fixed at 21/-; last coined 1813), & now money of account 21/- used in stating professional fees, amount of subscriptions, & prices of pictures, horses, estates, etc. 3. *g~fowl, g~-hen*, gallinaceous bird with slate-coloured white-spotted plumage domesticated in Europe; *G~ grains*; *g~pig*, S.-Amer. rodent now half-domesticated in Europe etc. as pet (origin of name doubtful), person receiving ~ fees, esp. company director or deputy clergyman; *G~worm*, tropical parasite in human skin. [f. Port. *Guiné*]

Guinness (gĭn'ĭs), n. ~'s stout, bottle of this (*a small~s*). [person; P]

guipure (gēp'oor, & see Ap.), n. Kind of lace; kind of gimp. [F]

guise (gīz), n. Style of attire, garb, (arch.); external appearance; semblance, as-sumed appearance, pretence, (*under, in, the ~ of*). [F, f. Teut. WISE⁴]

guitar' (gĭ-), n., & v.i. (-rr-). 1. Six-stringed lute played with hand with fretted finger-board; hence ~ıst(8) n. Gk 2. v.i. Play ~. [f. Sp. *guitarra* f. Gk *kithara*; cf. CITHER, GITTERN]

gulch, n. Ravine, esp. one with gold deposit. [perh. f. obs. *gulch* to swallow]

gul'den (goō-), n. Dutch & Austro-Hung. silver coin 1/8. [Du. & G, = golden (orig. name of various gold coins)]

gules (-lz), n., & a. (usu. after noun), (her.) Red. [f. OF *goules* pl. ermine dyed red]

gulf, n., & v.t. 1. (Geog.) portion of sea, proportionally narrower at mouth than bay, partly surrounded by coast; deep hollow, chasm, abyss, (poet.) profound depth or the sea; whirlpool, what-swallows up anything; impassable divid-ing line (*Luke* xvi. 26); ||(Univ. sl.) degree allowed to honour-candidate who falls but deserves pass; *G~stream*, oceanic warm current issuing from *G~* of Mexico. 2. v.t. Engulf, swallow up; ||(Univ.) give ~ *to*. [f. F *golfe* f. Pr. *golfo* f. late Gk *kolpikos* (Gk *kolpos*)]

gull¹, n. Kinds of long-winged web-footed mostly marine bird, usu. white with mantle varying from pearl-grey to black, & bright bill. Hence ~ERY(3) n. [perh. f. W *gwylan*]

gull², n., & v.t. Dupe, fool. So ~IBLE a., ~IBIL'ITY n., ~ISH¹ a., [perh. vb f. n. in fig. sense of prec.; perh. n. f. vb in fig. sense of obs. *gull* to gorge, cf. *cram & stuff* = take in]

gull'et, n. Food-passage from mouth to stomach, oesophagus; throat; water-channel, strait, defile, (arch. & dial.). [f. OF dim. of *gole* (now *gueule*) f. L *gula*]

gull'y¹, n., & v.t. 1. Water-worn ravine; deep artificial channel, gutter, drain, sink; (Cricket) fielding position between point & the slips; ~*drain*, to sewer from ~*hole*, opening in street for drainage; ~*trap*, anti-gas TRAP¹ in ~*drains*. 2. v.t. Make gullies in, form (channels) by water action. [prob. f. prec.]

gull'y², n. Large knife. [perh. orig. butcher's for cutting *gullet*]

gulō'sĭty, n. (rare). Gluttony. [f. LL *gulo-sitas* (L *gulosus* gluttonous f. *gula* GULLET)]

gulp, v.t. & i., & n. 1. Swallow (usu. *down*) hastily, greedily, with effort (~*down sobs, tears*, suppress them); perform act of swallowing with difficulty, gasp, choke; hence ~ingLY¹ adv. 2. n. Act of ~ing (*drained it at one ~*): effort to swallow; large mouthful; hence ~Y² a. [imit., cf. Du. *gulpen*]

gum¹, n. (usu. pl.) Firm flesh in which the teeth stand; ~*boil*, small abscess on ~s. [OE *gōma* orig. G *gaumen*]

gŭm², n. & v.t. & i. (-mm-). 1. Viscid secretion of some trees & shrubs that hardens in drying but is soluble in water (cf. RESIN), used to stick paper etc. together & stiffen linen etc.; secretion collecting in inner corner of eye; hard transparent sweet made of gelatine etc.; (also ~-tree) any tree exuding ~, esp. kinds of euca-lyptus (up a ~-tree, in a fix, at end of one's resources); ~ ARABIC; ~ juniper, sandarac; ~ disease of fruit-trees: *~dragon, traga-canth; ~ as gamboge; ~ senegal, kind of ~, as gamboge; ~ arabic from Senegal. 2. vb. Stiffen, smear, with ~; fasten down, together, up, on, etc., with ~; exude ~. [f. OF gomme f. L

||gŭm³, n. (vulg.). God (in oaths, as my, by, ~!). [deformation of God]

***gŭm'bō**, n. =OKRA; soup thickened with okra, pods. [negro patois]

gŭm'lah, n. Large Indian earthenware water-jar. [Hind. gamlā]

gŭm'ma, n. (path.; pl. -s, -ta). Syphilitic tumour. Hence ~tous a. [mod. L, f. L gummi GUM² from nature of contents]

gŭm'my¹ a. Viscid, sticky; abounding in, exuding, gum; (of ankles & legs) puffy, swollen. Hence ~INESS n. [-Y¹]

gump'tion, n. (colloq.). Resource, enter-prising spirit, go, ready practical sense; (Painting) vehicle for colour. [Sc, etym. dub.]

gŭn, n. 1. Metal tube for throwing missiles with gunpowder or some explosive force, piece of ordnance, cannon, musket, fowling-piece, rifle, carbine, (sure as a ~, certainly, beyond question; stand, stick, to one's ~s, maintain position; son of a ~, contemptible fellow; blow great ~s, violently, a gale); *(sl.) revolver. 2. Member of shooting-party. 3. ~-BARREL¹, ~boot, small war-ship carrying heavy ~; ~-CARRIAGE; ~-case, case for sporting ~, || also judge's tippet; ~-cotton, explosive made by steeping cotton in nitric & sulphuric acids used for blasting; ~-fire, firing of ~, esp. (Mil. Naut.) of morning or evening ~ to show time; ~-harpoon, propelled from ~, not by hand; ~-house, shelter for ~ & gunner in action; ~-lock, mechanism by which charge of ~ is exploded; ~man, (esp. U.S. sl.) armed robber; ~-metal, alloy of copper & tin or zinc (formerly used for ~s); ~-pit, to protect ~s from enemy's fire; ~powder, explosive of saltpetre, sulphur, & charcoal, for use in 1605 to blow up Parliament), fine green tea of granular appearance, white ~powder, kinds of modern explosive; ||~-room, compartment in warship fitted up for junior officers or as lieutenants' mess-room (orig. for gunner & his mates); ~-runner, -running, (person engaged in illegal introduction of fire-arms into dependent country; ~-shot, ~-shy, frightened at report of ~ (esp. of sporting dog); ~-smith, maker and repairer of small fire-arms; ~-stock, wooden mounting of ~-barrel. Hence (heavily etc.) ~NED² (-nd), ~'LESS, aa. [perh. f. Gunna pet-form of Scand. woman's name used as personal name (as with ships, & cf. Mons Meg cannon kept at Edinburgh) for ballistae & cannon (una magna batista de cornu quae vocatur Domina Gunilda, 1330)]

gŭn'el¹, n. A small eel-shaped sea-fish, the butter-fish. [?]

gŭn'el², n. See GUNWALE.

gŭn'er, n. || Officer or man of artillery (as official term, private); Master G~, R.A. warrant officer in charge of equip-ment etc. in a fort, or similarly employed; (Naut.) warrant officer in charge of battery, magazine, etc., (~'s daughter, gun to which sailors were lashed for flogging; kiss, marry, the ~'s daughter, be flogged); game-shooter. [-ER² (2)]

gŭn'era, n. The prickly rhubarb, an ornamental foliage plant with gigantic leaves. [f. J. E. Gunnerus, naturalist; see -A(1)]

gŭn'ery, n. Construction & management of large guns (~-lieutenant, || (sl.) ~-jack, with warrant of competence to supervise scale); G~'s chain, 66-ft surveying CHAIN, of guns. [-ERY]

gŭn'ing, n. Shooting, esp. of game (usu. go ~). [-ING¹]

gŭn'ny, n. Coarse sacking, sack, usu. of jute fibre. [f. Hind. goṇī, Skr. goṇī sack]

gŭn'ter, n. (Also G~'s scale) flat 2-ft rule with scales, logarithmic lines, etc., used for solving mechanically problems in surveying & navigation; topmast, or its sail, sliding up & down lower mast on rings (from resemblance to sliding G~'s scale); G~'s chain, 66-ft surveying CHAIN. [E. G~, mathematician d. 1626]

gŭn'wale (-nl), **gŭnn'el²**, n. Upper edge of ship's or boat's side (~ to, under, level with, below, water). [GUN + WALE (former)]

gŭn'yah, n. Native Australian hut. [native]

gŭp, n. (Anglo-Ind.). Gossip. [Hind.]

gŭrgita'tion, n. Surging, bubbling motion or sound. [f. L gurgitare to surge (gurges -itis whirlpool) + -ATION]

gŭr'gle, n., v.i. & t., & n. (Make) bubbling sound as of water from bottle or among stones; utter with such sounds. [imit., or f. Du. gorgelen, G gurgeln, or It. gorgo-gliare, f. L (gurguio gullet); cf. GARGLE, GUGGLE]

gŭr'jun, n. E.Ind. tree yielding ~ bal-sam or oil, used medicinally. [native]

Gurkha (goork'a), n. Member of ruling Hindu race in Nepal (~ *regiments, of* ~s in British army). [native]

gūrn'ard, gūrn'ĕt, n. Kinds of sea-fish with large head, mailed cheeks, & three free pectoral rays. [prob. f. F *grognard* grumbler (*grogner* grunt, -ARD)]

gū'rrah, n. Common Indian earthen jar. [native name]

gū'rry, n. Small Indian fort. [Hind. *garhī*]

gūru (gōō'rōō), n. Hindu spiritual teacher. [Skr., = grave, dignified]

gūsh, v.i. & t., & n. (Issue fn, send forth) sudden or copious stream (often fig. of speech, tenderness, etc.); emit (water copiously); (speak, behave, with) effusiveness, sentimental affectation, whence ~ER[1] n., (also) oil-well from which the oil flows without pumping, ~ing[2] a., ~Y[2] a. [ME *gosshe* perh. imit.]

gūss'ĕt, n. Triangular piece let into garment to strengthen or enlarge some part; iron bracket strengthening angle of structure. Hence ~ED[2] a. [f. OF *goussed* (*gousse* nut-shell) flexible piece filling up joint in mall-coat]

gūst[1], n. Sudden violent rush of wind; burst of rain, fire, smoke, sound, or passion. Hence **gūs'ty**[2] a., **gūs'tily**[2] adv. [prob. f. ON *gustr*, cf. *giósa* gush]

gūst[2], n. (arch. & poet.). Sense of taste; keen relish (*have a* ~ *of*, appreciate); flavour. [f. L *gustus* taste]

gūstā'tion, n. Tasting. So **gūs'tative, gūs'tatory**, aa. [f. L *gustatio* (*gustare* f. *gustus* taste, -ATION)]

gūs'tō, n. Special flavour (arch.; *enjoy the full* ~ *of*); zest, enjoyment with which something is done. [It., as GUST[2]]

gūt, n., & v.t. & i. (-tt-). 1. (Pl.) bowels or entrails (esp. of animals), contents of anything (*has no* ~*s in it*, is of no real value or force); particular part of lower alimentary canal, intestine, (*blind* ~, caecum). 2. (Usu. pl.) belly as seat of appetite (vulg.); (pl. sl.) pluck, force of character, staying power. 3. Material for violin strings made from intestines of animals; material for fishing-lines made from intestines of silkworm. 4. Narrow water-passage, sound, straits, || (Oxf. & Camb.) bend of rivers in racing-course; defile, narrow lane or part of street. 5. vb. Take out ~s of, clean, (fish); remove or destroy internal fittings of (house etc.); extract essence of (book etc.); eat greedily (vulg.). [OE *guttas* pl., prob. cogn. w. *géotan* pour]

gūtt'ae, n.pl. Drops in a row as ornament esp. in Doric architecture. [pl. of L *gutta* drop]

gūtta-pěrch'a, n. Greyish horny substance flexible when thin, of inspissated juice of various Malayan trees. [f. Malay *getah* gum, *percha* name of tree]

gūtt'ate, a. (nat. hist.). Speckled. [f. L *guttatus* (*gutta* drop, -ATE[2])]

gūtt'er, n., & v.t. & i. 1. Track made by running water (rare); shallow trough below eaves, or channel at side of street, carrying off rain-water (~-*child*, street arab; *take child etc. out of* ~, remove from poor surroundings); open conduit for outflow of fluid; groove; ~-*man*, cheap street-vendor of trifles; ~ *press, journalism* (catering for depraved or vulgar tastes); ~-*snipe*, street arab. 2. v.b. Furrow, channel; flow in streams; (of candle) melt away by becoming channelled so that wax etc. runs down. [f. OF *gutiere* (*goutte* drop f. L *gutta*]

gūt'tle, v.i. & t. Eat gluttonously. Hence **gūtt'lER**[1] n. [prob. f. GUT after GUZZLE]

gūtt'ural, a. & n. Of the throat; (of sounds) produced in throat or by back of tongue & palate (n. ~ sound or letter, as **k, g**). Hence ~IZE(3) v.t., ~ISM(1) n., ~LY[2] adv. [f. L *guttur* throat +-AL]

gūtt'uro-, comb. form of L *guttur* throat (see -O-), as ~*maxill'ary* of throat & jaws.

gūtt'y, n. (golf sl.). Gutta-percha ball. [-Y[3]]

guy[1] (gī), n., & v.t. 1. Rope, chain, etc., to steady load of crane etc. or hold tent etc. in place. 2. v.t. Secure with ~(s). [f. OF *guis* cf. GUIDE]

guy[2] (gī), n., & v.t. & i. 1. Effigy of Guy Fawkes burnt on 5th Nov.; || grotesquely dressed person, fright; *(sl.) man, fellow; || (sl.) act of decamping (*give the* ~ *to*, escape from; *do a* ~, disappear). 2. v.b. Exhibit in effigy; ridicule; (sl.) run away. [person]

Guy's (gīz), n. (Used for) Guy's Hospital in London. [person]

gŭz'zle, v.i. & t. Drink, eat, greedily (i. & t.); consume (money etc.) in guzzling (often *away*). Hence **gŭzz'lER**[1] n. [perh. f. OF *gosiller* vomit (*gosier* throat)]

gwȳn'iăd, n. White-fleshed lake fish of salmon kind. [W (*gwyn* white)]

gȳbe, *jibe, v.i. & t., & n. (Of fore-&-aft sail or boom) swing across, make (sail) do this, in wearing or running before wind; (of ship, crew, etc.) change course so that this happens. [prob. f. Du. *gijben*]

gȳle (g-), n. Quantity of beer brewed at once; fermenting wort; fermenting-tun. [f. Du. *gijl* (*gijlen* to ferment)]

gȳm, n. (sl.). Gymnasium, gymnastics. [abbr.]

gȳmkha'na (-kah-), n. (orig. Anglo-Ind.). Public place with facilities for athletics; athletic-sports display. [mixture of *gym*(*nastics*) & Hind. (*gend*-)*khana* ball-house, racquet court]

gȳmnā'sium (-z-), n. (pl. -*ums*, -*a*). 1. Place, room, or building, with appliances for practice in gymnastics. 2. Continental, esp. German, school of highest grade preparing for universities (*often pr.* gimnah-); pl. sometimes -*ien*, whence **gȳmnā'siAL** a. [L, f. Gk *gymnasion* (*gumnazō* exercise f. *gumnos* naked)]

gym'nast, n. Expert in gymnastics. [f. Gk gumnastēs (gumnazō see prec.)]

gymnas'tic, a. & n. 1. Of gymnastics, involving bodily or (rarely) mental exercise, discipline, effort, or activity; hence ~ICALLY adv. 2. n. Course of instruction ~ic(s)(pl.) exercises developing the muscles, (also in same sense as sing.). [f. L f. Gk gumnastikos (prec., -IC)]

gymno-, comb. form of Gk gumnos naked, bare, used in many bot., zool., & biol. terms, as ~sperm'ous having seeds unprotected by seed-vessels.

gymnos'ophist, n. One of ancient Hindu philosophic sect going nearly naked & given up to contemplation; mystic, ascetic. So ~Y[?] n. [f. L f. Gk gumnosophistai pl. (prec., SOPHIST)]

gymnot'us, n. The electric eel. [f. Gk gumnos naked +notion back (from absence of dorsal fins)]

gynaec'ium (g-, j-), n. (Gk & Rom. Ant.) women's apartments in house; (Bot.; often incorrectly -oec'ium) female organs of flower. [L, f. Gk gunaikeion (gunē -aikos woman): -oecium from confusion with Gk oikion house]

gynaeco- (g-, j-), comb. form of Gk gunē -aikos woman, as ~logy (-ŏl-), science of diseases of women. Hence ~L'OGY n.

gynan'drous (g-, j-), a. (bot.). With stamens & pistil united in one column as in orchids. [f. Gk gunandros (gunē woman, anēr andros man) of doubtful sex +-OUS]

gyn(o)- (g-, j-), shortened form of GYNAECO-, esp. in Bot. = pistil-, ovary-, as gyn'obase, enlargement of receptacle supporting gynaeceum, gyn'ophore, pedicel supporting ovary, also (Zool.) bud-bearing branch in hydrozoa; also = woman-, whence gynōc'RACY n.

gy'nous (g-, j-), suf. f. Gk -gunos (gunē woman) +-OUS, forming adji. = having specified female organs or pistils, as mono-, tetra-, andro-.

‖ **gyp'**[1], n. College servant at Cambridge & Durham (cf. scout¹); ~-room, pantry. [perh. for obs. gippo scullion]

gyp'sum, n. Hydrated calcium sulphate, mineral from which plaster of Paris is made, whence ~um v.t.; this used as manure, whence ~um v.t. Hence ~EOUS, ~IFEROUS, ~OUS, aa. [f. L f. Gk gupsos]

gyp'sy. See GIPSY.

gy'rate[1], a. (bot.). Arranged in rings or convolutions. [f. L gyratus (GYRE, -ATE²)]

gy'rate[2], v.i. Go in circle or spiral, revolve, whirl. Hence gyra'TION n., gyr'atory a. [f. L gyrare (foll.) -ATE²]

gyre, v.i. & n. (poet.). = prec.; (n.) gyration. [vb as prec.; n. f. L f. Gk gūros ring]

gyr'o, n. (pl. -os). Gyroscope (see foll.); ~-compass, gyroscope arranged to serve as compass when magnetic compass cannot be used. [abbr. of foll.]

gyro-, comb. form of Gk gūros ring, as ~graph (-ahf), instrument recording revolutions; ~plane, form of aircraft deriving its lift mainly from freely rotating overhead vanes; ~scope, ~stat, instruments illustrating dynamics of rotating bodies, also (~scope) rapidly spinning wheel fixed in something, e.g. car on single rail, to keep it in equilibrium, & having, by the independent stability of its axis, great value in mechanics.

gyr'ose, a. (bot.). Folded & waved, marked with wavy lines. [GYRE, -OSE]

gyve, n. (usu. pl.) & v.t. (poet.). Shackle, fetter. [ME give (pr. g-), etym. dub.]

H

H, h, (āch), letter (pl. Hs, H's). DROP² one's he; H-iron, girder of H-shaped section.

ha[1] (hah). Int. expr. surprise, joy, suspicion, triumph, etc.

ha[2] (hah). See HUM v.

haaf (hahf), n. (In Shetland & Orkney) deep-sea fishing ground. [f. ON haf high sea]

hab'eas corp'us, n. Writ requiring body of person to be brought before judge or into court, esp. to investigate lawfulness of his restraint; Habeas Corpus Act (of Charles II, 1679, facilitating use of this). [L, = you must have the body]

hab'erdash'er, n. Dealer in small articles of dress etc. Hence ~ERY[?] n. [conn. w. obs. haberdash small wares, prob. f. AF hapertas, etym. dub.]

hab'ergeon (-jon), n. (hist.) Sleeveless coat of mail. [f. F haubergeon (HAUBERK, -OON)]

hab'ile, a. (literary). Skilful, dextrous. [var. of ABLE]

hab'iliment, n. (pl.) dress suited to any office or occasion (joc. of ordinary clothes); (sing) equipment, attire, (rare). [f. OF habillement (habiller fit out f. habile ABLE, see -MENT)]

habil'itate, v.t. & i. Furnish (mine) with working capital; (intr.) qualify for office (esp. in German Univ.). So ~A'TION n. [f. L habilitare (as ABILITY), see -ATE³]

hab'it[1], n. Settled tendency or practice, as he is in, has (fallen into), the or a ~ of contradiction; mental constitution, as a man of corpulent ~; (Bot., Zool.) mode of

growth; (arch.) dress, esp. of religious order; (also *riding-~*) lady's riding-dress. [OF, f. L *habitus -ūs* f. *habēre habit-* have, (refl.) be]

hab'it, v.t. Clothe; || (arch.) inhabit. [f. F *habiter* f. L *habitare* inhabit, as prec.]

hab'itable, a. That can be inhabited. Hence ~ABILITY, ~ableNESS, nn., ~ablY² adv. [F, f. L *habitabilis* (as prec., see -ABLE)]

hab'itant, n. Inhabitant; (pr. ahbētahnî) Canadian of French descent. [F (HABIT² -ANT)]

hab'itat, n. Natural home of plant or animal; habitation. [L, 3rd sing. pres. as HABIT²]

habita'tion, n. Inhabiting; as *fit for human* ~; place of abode; branch of Primrose League. [F, f. L *habitationem* (as HABIT² -ATION)]

habit'ual, a. Customary; constant, continual; given to (specified) habit, as *a ~ drunkard.* Hence ~LY² adv., ~NESS n. [f. med. L *habitualis* (as HABIT², -AL)]

habit'uate, v.t. Accustom (*to* thing, *to* doing). So ~ATION n. [f. L *habituare* (as HABIT²), see -ATE³]

hab'itude, n. Mental or bodily constitution; custom, tendency. [F, f. L *habitudo* (*habēre* have, see -TUDE)]

habit'ué (-ā), n. Habitual visitor or resident. [F, p.p. of *habituer* (as HABITU-ATE)]

hachures (hăshū'r), n. pl. Lines used in hill-shading on maps to indicate slope. [F]

hacien'da (ăs-, ah-), n. Estate, plantation, with dwelling-house (in Spain or Sp. colonies). [Sp., f. L *facienda* neut. pl. gerund. of *facere* to]

hack¹, n. Mattock; miner's pick; gash, wound, esp. from kick with toe of boot. [prob. cogn. w. G *hacke*, Da. *hakke*, mattock]

hack², v.t. & i. Cut, notch, mangle; kick shin of (opponent at football); deal cutting blows (*at*); emit short dry coughs; *a ~ing* (short dry frequent) *cough*; *~saw* (for metal-cutting). [ME *hacken* f. com.-WG *hakkōn*, cf. G *hacken*, Du. *hakken*; conn. w. prec.]

hack³, n. Board on which hawk's meat is laid; (of eyas hawk) *be at* ~ (not allowed to prey for itself); frame for drying bricks. [var. of HATCH¹]

hack⁴, n. Horse let out for hire; jade; horse for ordinary riding; common drudge (also attrib., as *~ writer*); *~ *stand*, cabstand. [abbr. of HACKNEY]

hack⁵, v.t. & i. Make common, hackney; ride (horse), ride on horseback, on road at ordinary pace; use hired horses. [f. prec.]

hack'ery, n. Indian bullock-cart. [?]

hac'kle¹, n., & v.t. 1. Steel flax-comb; long feathers on neck of domestic cock & other birds; *with his ~s up*, (of cock, dog, man) angry, ready to fight; artificial fly dressed with ~. 2. v.t. Dress (flax, fly) with ~. [vb f. n.; MHG has *hachele*, perh. f. *hak-* root of OHG **hakjan* prick]

hăc'kle², v.t. Hack, mangle. [HACK² +-LE(3)]

hack'ly, a. Rough, jagged. [as prec.]

hack'matack, n. Amer. Larch. [native]

hack'ney, n., & v.t. 1. Horse of middle size & quality for ordinary riding; drudge, hireling; *~ carriage*, *~ coach* (kept for hire). 2. v.t. (Esp. in p.p. *~ed*) make common or trite. [vb f. n.] f. OF *haquenée* ambling horse, etym. dub.]

had. See HAVE.

hădd'ock, n. Fish allied to cod. [?]

hāde, v.i. (geol., mining). Incline from the vertical. [?]

Hād'es (-z), n. (Gk Myth.). Lower world, abode of departed spirits. [Gk, orig. a name of Pluto]

Hādj'i, Hājj'i, n. (Title of) Mohammedan pilgrim who has been to MECCA. [f. Arab. *ḥaǧ'i*]

haec'ceity (hēks-), n. (philos.). Thisness; individuality. [f. med. L *haecceitas* (*haec* fem. of *hīc* this, see -TY)]

haem'al, a. (anat.). Of the blood; situated on same side of body as the heart & great blood-vessels. [f. Gk *haima* blood + -AL]

haemat'ic, a. & n. Of or containing blood; (n.) medicine acting on the blood. [f. Gk *haimatikos* as foll., see -IC]

haem'atin, n. (chem.). Bluish-black amorphous substance, constituent of haemoglobin. [f. Gk *haima -matos* blood +-IN]

haem'atite, hēm', n. A red, brown, or blackish, iron oxide ore. [f. L f. Gk *haimatitēs* (*lithos*) blood-like stone (as prec., see -ITE)]

haem'ato-, hēm'ato-, in comb.= Gk *haima-matos* blood, as *~cele*, tumour containing extravasated blood.

haematū'ria, n. (path.). Presence of blood in the urine. [f. prec.+Gk *ouron* urine]

haemoglob'in, n. Colouring matter of the red corpuscles of the blood. [f. HAEMATIN+GLOBULIN]

haemophil'ia, n. (med.). (Hereditary) tendency to bleeding from even a slight injury. [f. Gk *haima* blood, -o-, *philia* affection]

haem'orrhage, hem', (hĕm'orij), n. Escape of blood from blood-vessels, bleeding. [f. F *emorragie* f. L f. Gk *haimorrhagia* (*haima* blood + st. of *rhēgnumi* break)]

haem'orrhoids, hem', (hĕm'oroidz), n. pl. Piles. [f. OF *emoroyde* (cf. EMERODS) f. L f. Gk *haimorrhoides* (*phlebes*) (veins) (*haima* blood +-*rhoos* flowing)]

haffe (hah-), n. Mohammedan who knows Koran by heart (used as title). [Arab.]

haf'nium, n. (chem.). Metallic element discovered in 1923. [Da. (*Kjōbenhaven* Copenhagen +-IUM]

haft (haft-), n., & v.t. Handle (of dagger, knife, etc.); (v.t.) furnish (knife etc.) with ~. [(vb f.n.) OE hæft(e) f. OTeut. haftjom f. root haf- HEAVE]

hăg¹, n. Ugly old woman; witch; (formerly) evil spirit in female form; (also ~ fish) a parasite fish allied to lamprey; ~ridden, afflicted by night-mare. Hence ~GISH¹(-g-) a. [?]

‖**hăg²**, n. Soft place in moor; firm place in bog. [cf. ON hǫgg ravine]

haggadah (-gah-), n. Legendary part of the Talmud. [Heb., = tale, f. higgid tell]

hăg'gard, a. & n. 1. Wild-looking (esp. as a result of fatigue, privation, worry, etc.). 2. (Of hawk) caught in her adult plumage, untamed; (n.) such a hawk. Hence ~NESS n. [cf. F hagard, etym. dub.]

‖**hăg'gis** (-g-), n. Minced heart, lungs, & liver, of sheep etc., boiled in maw with suet, oatmeal, etc. [?]

hăg'gle, v.i. & n. Dispute, wrangle, (about, over). [f. dial. hag chop f. ON hǫggva +-LE(3)]

hăg'iarchy (-gi-: -ki), n. Rule, order, of saints. [f. foll.+Gk arkhō rule]

hăgio- (-g-) in comb.=Gk hagios saint(ly), as: ~cracy (-ŏk-²), government of holy persons; ~grapha (-ŏg-²), books of the Hebrew Scriptures not included under Law & Prophets; ~grapher (-ŏg-²), (writer) of any of these, or ~graphic, ~al (-ăf-), writing of saints' lives; ~latry (-ŏl-), worship of saints; ~logy (-ŏl-), literature treating of lives & legends of saints; ~scope (-g-y-l), ... [f. Gk HAGIO-]

hah, int. & v.i. ... repr. [com.-Teut.=HA¹,²]

ha ha (hah hah), int. repr. laughter.

ha-ha (hah'hah), n. Sunk fence bounding park or garden. [F, etym. dub.]

haic|k (hah'ik, hāk), n. Arabian outer wrapper for head & body. [Arab. ḥayk]

hail¹, n. Pellets of frozen vapour falling in shower, as ~storm; shower of missiles, curses, questions, etc.; ~stone, pellet of ~. Hence ~Y² a. [com.-Teut. hagol, Du. & G hagel]

hail², v.i. & t. It ~s, hail falls; (fig.) pour down (blows, words, etc.), come down, violently. [OE hagalian f. OTeut. haga-lojan (cf. prec.)]

hail³, int. of greeting: ~fellow, ~fellow-well-met, intimate, too intimate, with. [ellipt. use of obs. adj. hail f. ON heill sound, HALE]

hail⁴, v.t. & i. & n. 1. Salute; greet (person etc. as king etc., also ~ him king); call to (ship, person) to attract attention; (of ship, person) be come from (place). 2. n. Salutation, esp. within ~, near enough to be ~ed. [f. prec.]

hair, n. 1. One or (collect. sing) all of the fine filaments growing from skin of animals, esp. from human head (pl. ~s in collect, sense is arch.); (of plants) elon-gated cell growing from epidermis; ~like a., ... thing; jot, tittle; against the ~, against the grain; to a ~, exactly; a ~ of the DOG that bit you; (sl.) keep your ~ on, keep cool; get person by the short ~s (sl.), have complete control over, have at one's mercy; (of girl) put up, turn up, her ~, dress it in woman's fashion; do or put up, let down, her ~ (in the toilet); not turn a ~, show no sign of exhaustion or discomposure; ~ stands on end (with fright or horror). 2. ~'s breadth, a ~'s breadth, minute distance (~breadth escape, very narrow); ~brush, toilet brush for ~; ~cloth (made of ~, for various purposes); ~dresser, one whose business is to dress and cut ~; ~line, line, rope, made of ~; (also) up-stroke in writing; ~net, ~oil (used for the ~); ~pin (for fastening the ~; ~pin bend, doubling back of road); ~powder, scented powder for ~, now used by men-servants; ~shirt (of ~cloth, for ascetics); ~slide, horn or tortoise-shell clip for keeping ~ in position; ~space (Typ.), very thin space; ~splitting a. & n., over-subtle(ty); ~spring, fine spring in watch, regulating balance-wheel; ~stroke, fine up-stroke in writing; ~trigger, secondary trigger releasing main one by slight pressure. Hence ~INESS n, (-)~ED²(-rd), ~LESS, ~LIKE, ~Y², aa. [com.-Teut.: OE hær, hēr, Du. ...]

hāke¹, n. Fish like cod. [?]

hāke², n. haik. [?]

hāke³, n. Wooden framework for drying bricks & other purposes. [prob.=HACK³]

hakeem', ~**kim¹** (-ēm, -), n. (In India &c.) Mohammedan physician. [Arab. ḥakīm wise, physician]

ha'kim² (hah-), n. (As prec.) Judge, ruler, governor. [Arab. ḥākim]

halā'tion, n. (photog.). Spreading of light beyond its proper boundary in a negative (and consequent forging) caused by in-ternal reflection in the support of the emulsion. [irreg. f. HALO+-ATION]

hăl'berd, ~**t**, n. (hist.). Combined spear & battle-axe. [f. OF hallebarde f. MHG helmbarde (helm helmet or helm handle +barta broad-axe f. OTeut. bardō beard)]

hăl'berdier (-ēr), n. Man armed with hal-berd. [f. OF halleberdier (as prec., see -IER)]

hăl'cyon, n. & a. 1. Bird fabled by the ancients to breed in floating nest on sea at winter solstice, & to charm wind & waves into calm for the purpose; (Zool.) Australasian kingfisher. 2. adj. Calm, esp. ~ days (orig. 14 days about winter sol-stice). [f. L halcyon f. Gk alkuōn king-fisher.]

hāle¹, a. Robust, vigorous, (esp. of old persons). Hence ~NESS(-in-) n. [north. repr. of OE hāl WHOLE]

hāle², v.t. (arch.). Drag, draw, forcibly

half (lit. & fig.) [f. OF *haler* t. OHG *halōn* (G *holen* fetch)]

half (hahf), n. (pl. halves), a., & adv. **1.** One of two equal or corresponding parts into which a thing is divided, as *the ~ of 10 is 5, cut it in ~* (into halves), *your ~ is bigger than mine, two pounds & a ~* (pound) *or two & a ~ pounds, ~ of it is* (but *of them are*) *rotten*; (colloq.) =~*pint, -mile, -back, -holiday*; || school term (the school year being formerly divided into two portions); *better ~*, wife; *do a thing by halves* (imperfectly); *too clever by ~* (far); *go halves*, share equally (*with* person *in* thing); *cry halves*, claim equal share. **2.** adj. Forming a ~, as *a ~ length, a ~ share*; (adj. now viewed as = *the ~ of*) *the men, ~ your time, ~ a crown* (2/6), *~ a pound* (is ~ *the battle*, goes a long way towards success). **3.** adv. To the extent of ~, (loosely) to a considerable extent, as *it is ~ cooked, a ~-cooked potato, ~ dead, I ~ wish, not ~* (nearly) *long enough*, (colloq.) *not ~* (not at all) *bad, not ~ a bad fellow*; || *not ~* (sl.), to the greatest possible extent, as *he didn't ~ swear* (swore violently); (adv.) half-, prob. orig. adj.) *~* (an hour) *past two* (o'clock); (Naut.) *~ three*, 3½ (fathoms), *east ~-south* (5¼° south of east). **4.** *~-d~*, (what is) ~ one thing & ~ another, esp. mixture of ale & porter; *~ as much as many again*, 1½ times the amount; *~-back*, (Footb.) position, player, immediately behind forwards; *~-baked*, (fig.) not thorough, not earnest, *~-witted*; *~-ball* (Billiards etc.), with moving ball directed at edge of object ball; *~ binding* of book, leather back & corners, cloth or paper sides (similarly *~-bound, ~-calf, ~-morocco*, etc.); *~-blood*, person having one parent in common with another, this relationship, (also) person of mixed nationality; *~-blooded*, born of different races; *~-blue*, badge or colours (see BLUE) awarded to second string or to representative in minor sports; *~-boot* (reaching up to the calf); *~-bred*, of mixed breed, mongrel; *~-breed, ~-blooded* person; *~-brother, -sister* (by one parent only); *~ butt*, one of length between ordinary one & long butt; *~-caste* a. & n., *~-bre(e)d*, (child) of European father & Indian mother; *~ cock* ½(2); || *~-crown*, (n.) silver coin of 2/6, (usu. *~ a crown*, see above) amount of 2/6, (adj.) priced at or worth 2/6; *~-deck*, (esp.) quarters of cadets & apprentices on a merchant vessel; *~-fifteen, -thirty, -forty* (Lawn Tennis), handicap (in strokes allowed in certain games of each set) given to a weaker player; *~-hearted*, lacking courage or zeal, so *~-heartedly, ~ness*; *~ HITCH*; *~ holiday*, day of which (the latter) is taken as holiday; *~-length*, portrait of upper ~ of person; *~-mast high*, (of flag) lowered to ~ height of mast as mark of respect for the dead; *~ measures*, com-promise, *~-&~ policy* etc.; *~ moon*, moon of which only ~ is illuminated, crescent, crescent-shaped thing; *~ mourning*, black relieved by grey etc.; *~(-)nelson*, a hold in wrestling (*get a ~ nelson on*, hold in a crippling position, gain complete mastery over); *~ pay*, reduced allowance to army etc. officer when neither retired nor in actual service; *~-seas-over, ~ drunk*; ||*~-timer*, child attending school for ~ usual time, earning money in other ~; *~-title*, title or short title of a book, printed on recto of leaf preceding the title-leaf; also title of section of a book printed on recto of leaf preceding it; *~-tone*, illustration printed from a block (produced by photographic agency) in which the lights & shades of the original are represented by small or large dots (*~-tone block, process*); *~-truth*, statement that conveys only part of the truth; *~ VOLLEY*; *~-way house*, inn midway between two towns etc. (fig.) compromise; *~-witted*, imbecile, so *~-wit* n.; *~-yearly* a. & adv., (occurring) every year. [com.-Teut.: OE *h(e)alf*, G *halb*]

|| **halfpenny** (hāp'ni), n. (pl. as PENNY). Bronze coin worth half a penny (*turn up again like a bad ~*, persistently, (unfailingly); *three halfpence* (hāp'ens), (usu. for) *a penny ~*, 1½d.; *~worth* (usu. pron. hāp'əth), *ha'p'orth*, as much as a ~ will buy.

hal'ibut, hōl', n. Large flat fish used for food. [prob. f. *haly* HOLY + *butt* flat fish, because eaten on holy-days]

hal'idom, n. (arch.). Holy thing, esp. (as oath) *by my ~*. [OE *hāligdōm* (HOLY, -DOM]

halieut'ic, a. & n. Of fishing; (n. pl.) art of fishing. [f. L f. Gk *halieutikos* (*halieuō* fish f. *hals* sea, see -IC]

halito'sis, n. (med.). Abnormally foul breath. [f. L *halitus* breath + -OSIS]

hall (hawl), n. Large public room in palace etc.; *servants' ~*, room in which servants dine; || (Univ.) residence of landed proprietor; || (Univ.) institution governed by a head without fellows, (also) building for students having or not having Univ. privileges; || (in Eng. colleges etc.) common dining-room, dinner in this; building of guild, as *Saddlers' H~*; large room for public business; entrance-passage of house; *Liberty H~*, place where one may do as one likes; *~mark*, mark used at *Goldsmiths' H~* (& by Government assay offices) for marking standard of gold & silver, (v.t.) stamp with this (often fig.). [com.-Teut.: OE *heall*, Du. & Da. *hal*]

hallelujah, -luiah. See ALLELUIA.

halliard. See HALYARD.

hallo', -loa' (-lō), int., n., & v.i. Int. calling attention or expr. surprise; (n., & v.i.)(the) cry ~. [perh. var. of HOLLO]

halloo', int. inciting dogs to the chase, calling attention, or expressing surprise (also as n., theory~). [perh. var. of HOLLO]

halloo²ˀ³, v.i. & t. Cry 'halloo!', esp. to dogs; urge on (dogs etc.) with ~, shout (t. & i.) to attract attention; (prov.) *do not ~ until you are out of the wood.* [f. prec.; or = HALLOW³]

hallow¹(-ō), v.t. Make holy; (now only in *all~s*, *~mas*, feast of All-hallows, = *All Saints' Day*; *Hallowe'en*, Sc., U.S., eve of this). [OE *hālga*, form of *hālig* holy]

hallow²(-ō), v.t. Make holy; honour as holy. [com.-Teut.: f. OE *hālgian*, G. *heiligen*, f. *hailag-* HOLY]

hallow³(-ō), v.t. & i. Chase with shouts; incite with shouts; shout to incite dogs etc. [ME *halowen* prob. f. OF *halloer*]

Hallstatt (hahl'shtaht), a. (Used attrib.) relating to the civilization of a phase of the early iron age. [~, village in Upper Austria, where remains of this period were discovered]

halm. See HAULM.

hal'o, n. (pl. ~es), & v.t. **1.** Circle of light round luminous body, esp. sun or moon; circle, ring; disk of light surrounding head of saint, nimbus; (fig.) ideal glory investing person etc. **2.** v.t. Surround with ~. [(vb f. n.) F., f. L f. Gk *halōs* threshing-floor, disk of sun or moon]

hal'ogen, n. (chem.). Any of the group of elements fluorine, chlorine, bromine, & iodine, which form haloids by simple union with a metal (e.g. sodium chloride or common salt). [f. Gk *hals* salt + -GEN]

hal'oid, a. & n. (chem.). (Salt) having a composition like that of common salt. [f. Gk *hals* salt +-OID]

halt¹ (hawlt), n. & v.i. & t. **1.** Temporary stoppage on march or journey; [] railway stopping-place used for local services only and without regular station buildings etc. **2.** v.i. Make a ~. **3.** v.t. Cause (troops etc.) to ~. [(vb f. n.) orig. in phr. *make halt* f. G *halt machen* (*halt* hold)]

halt² (hawlt), a. (arch.), Lame; crippled. [com.-Teut.: OE & Da. *halt*]

halt³ (hawlt), v.i., & n. Walk hesitatingly; hesitate, as ~ *between two opinions*; (of argument, verse, etc.) be defective; (arch.) be lame; (n., arch.) limp. Hence ~ingly² adv. [(n. f. vb) OE *healtian*, f. prec.]

hal'ter (hawl'-), n., & v.t. **1.** Rope, strap, with noose or headstall for horses or cattle; rope with noose for hanging person; death by hanging; ~-*break* v.t., accustom (horse) to ~. **2.** v.t. Fasten (often *up*) with ~; hang (person) with ~. [(vb f. n.) OE *hælftre* f. root *halb*, whence HELVE]

halve (hahv), v.t. Divide into halves; share equally; reduce to half; (Golf) ~ *a hole with*, reach it in same number of strokes as (other player); ~ *a match*, win same number of holes; fit (crossing timbers) together by cutting out half thickness of each. [ME HALF(N)]

hal'yard, hall'yard, haul'yard, (naut.), Rope, tackle, for raising or lowering sail, yard, etc. [HALE v., -YER]

ham¹, n. Back of thigh, thigh & buttock; (formerly) bend of the knee; thigh of hog salted & dried in smoke or otherwise for food; *(sl.) inexperienced or ineffective actor (also attrib.). [OE, prob. f. OTeut. *ham-* be crooked]

ham², n. (hist.). Town, village. [OE *hām* HOME; seen in *Oakham* etc.]

hamadry'ad, n. (Gk Myth.) nymph living & dying with the tree she inhabited; venomous Indian serpent; Abyssinian baboon. [f. L f. Gk *hamadruas* (*hama* with + *drus* tree)]

Ham'burgh (-berg, -buro), n. Black variety of grape; small variety of domestic fowl. [Hamburg in Germany]

hames, n. pl. Two curved pieces of wood or metal forming (part of) collar of draught horse. [cf. Du. *haam*]

Ham'ite¹, n. (Supposed) descendant of Ham, member of Egyptian or other African race. Hence Hamīt'ic a. [-ITE]

ham'ite², n. Fossil cephalopod with hook-shaped shell. [f. L *hamus* hook, see -ITE]

ham'let, n. Small village, esp. one without church. [f. OF *hamelet* dim. of *hamel* dim. f. Teut. (OE *hām* HOME)]

hammam (hamam', ham'um), n. Turkish bath or bathing establishment. [Arab.]

hammer, n. Instrument for beating, breaking, driving nails, etc., with solid (usu. metal) head at right angles to handle; machine with metal block serving same purpose; similar contrivance, as for exploding charge in gun (whence ~LESS a.), striking string of piano, etc.; auctioneer's mallet indicating by rap that article is sold; *come under the* ~, be sold by auction; *knight of the* ~, blacksmith; *throwing the* ~, athletic contest with heavy ~; ~ *& tongs*, with might & main; ~-*beam* (projecting from wall at foot of principal rafter); ~-*cloth* (covering driver's seat in coach; hist. unexpl.); ~-*head*, head of ~; kind of shark, African bird; ~-*lock*, hold in which a wrestler's arm is bent behind his back; ~-*man*, smith, smith who works with ~; ~-*toe* (permanently bent upwards). [com.-Teut.: OE & Du. *hamer*, G *hammer*]

hăm'mer², v.t. & i. Strike, beat, drive, (as) with hammer; (colloq) inflict heavy defeat(s) on in war or games; ~ *out*, devise; ~ (force) *idea into* person's *head*; work hard *at*; ∥ (St. Exch.) declare (person) a defaulter with three taps of hammer. [f. prec.]

hăm'mock, n. Hanging bed of canvas or netting suspended by cords at ends, used esp. on board ship; ~ *chair* (made of canvas suspended on adjustable framework). [f. Sp. *hamaca* of Carib. orig.]

hăm'per¹, n. Basketwork packing-case; consignment of eatables, wines, etc., however packed (usu. as a present; *Christmas* ~). [f. obs. *hanaper* f. OF *hanapier* case for goblet (*hanap* f. OFrank. +*knapp*)]

hăm'per², v.t., & n. **1.** Obstruct movement of (person etc.) with material obstacles; (fig.) impede, hinder. **2.** n.(naut.). Necessary but cumbrous part of equipment of vessel. [?]

Hămp'ton Court (kōrt), n. (Used for) ~ Palace, now partly occupied by persons of rank in reduced circumstances, partly open to the public. [place]

hăm'shăckle, v.t. Shackle (horse etc.) with rope connecting head and foreleg. [?]

hăm'ster, n. Rodent like large rat, with cheek-pouches for carrying grain to its winter store. [G]

hăm'string, n., & v.t. (-inged or -ung). **1.** (In man) one of five tendons at back of knee; (in quadrupeds) great tendon at back of knee in hind leg. **2.** v.t. Cripple (person, animal) by cutting the ~s. [HAM¹]

hăm'ŭlus, n., (anat., zool., bot.; pl. -lī). Hook-like process. [L, dim. of *hamus* hook]

hănd¹, n. **1.** Terminal part of human arm beyond wrist; similar member of all four limbs of monkey; forefoot of quadruped. **2.** Authority, disposal, as *in the* ~s *of*; agency, as *by the* ~s *of, pass through many* ~s; share in action, as *have a* ~ *in it*. **3.** Pledge of marriage, as *give one's* ~. **4.** (Usu. pl.) manual worker(s) of factory etc. **5.** Person who does something, as a *picture by the same* ~; *all* ~s, the whole crew; *a good* ~ (skilful) *at singlestick or acrostics, an old parliamentary* ~, *an old* ~ *at test matches*; person, source, from which thing comes, as *first*, SECOND, ~ (*at 1st etc.* ~, directly, more or less indirectly; *first etc.* ~, of hearsay); COOL ~. **6.** Skill, as *a* ~ *for pastry*; style of workmanship; turn, innings, at cricket, billiards, etc. **7.** Style of writing, as *a legible* ~; signature, as *witness the* ~ *of A.B.* **8.** ~-like thing, esp. pointer of clock or watch (~ of BANANAS). **9.** Fixed quantity of various commodities, e.g., bundle of tobacco leaves. **10.** A lineal measure of horse's height, = 4 in. **11.** (Cards) cards dealt to a player, player holding these, as *first*, *third*, ~. **12.** (Theatr. sl.) applause.

13. *At* ~, close by, about to happen soon; *by* ~, by manual labour (*brought up by* ~, of child fed from bottle); *for one's own* ~, on one's own account; (*tee*) *from* ~ *to mouth*, improvidently; *in* ~, held in the ~, at one's disposal, under control, receiving attention; *off* ~, without preparation, then & there; *on* ~, in one's possession, *on one's* ~, resting on one as a responsibility; *on all* ~s, *to, from, all quarters; on the one* ~, *on the other*~, (of contrasted points of view etc.); *out of* ~, at once, extempore, (also) out of control; *to* ~, within reach; *to one's* ~, ready for one without exertion on one's own part; *bear a* ~, take part *in*; *come to* ~, turn up, be received; *do a* ~'*s turn*, make the slightest effort; *lay* ~s *on*, touch, seize; *take in* ~, undertake *change* ~s, (of property) pass from one person to another; *clean* ~s, (fig.) innocence; *with a heavy* ~, oppressively; *have*, *keep, one's* ~ *in*, be in practice; *his* ~ *is out*, he is out of practice; (*win*) ~s *down*, easily; ~s *off!*, do not touch; ~s *up!* (direction to persons to hold up their ~s as a sign of assent etc., or to preclude resistance); *go* ~ *in* ~ *with*, keep step with, lit. & fig.; ~ *over* ~ *or fist*, with each ~ successively passing over the other, as in climbing rope, (fig.) with steady or rapid progress (in overtaking etc.); ~ *to* ~, (of conflict etc.) at close quarters; *bind one* ~ *&* foot (completely), *serve* (person) ~ *&* foot (assiduously); *be* ~ *in* (or *&*) *glove* (intimate) *with*; ~ (opp. *machine-*, as ~-*knitted*, -*sewn*, -*painted*). **14.** ~*bag* (small, for carrying about); ~*ball*, ball for throwing with ~, game played with this between two goals; ~-*barrow* (carried by ~); ~*bell*, bell rung by ~, esp. one of a set for musical performance; ~*bill*, printed notice circulated by ~; ~*book*, short treatise, manual, guide-book; ~-*canter*, gentle canter; ~*cart* (pushed or drawn by ~); ~*cuff* v.t. secure with ~-*cuffs* (pair of metal rings joined by short chain, for securing prisoner's ~s); ∥~*fast(ing)* (Sc.), betrothal; ~-*gallop*, easy gallop; ~*glass*, magnifying glass held in ~, small mirror with handle; ~*grip*, grasp, seizure with the ~ (friendly or hostile); ~*hold*, something for the ~s to grip on (in climbing etc.); ~*line*, fishing-line worked without rod; ~*made*, made by ~ (esp. opp. to *machine-made*); ∥~'*maid(en)*, female servant (arch., exc. fig.); ~ *of glory*, charm made from mandrake root or embalmed ~ of executed felon (transl. of F *main de gloire*, corrupted f. *mandragore* mandrake); ~-*organ*, portable barrel-organ with crank turned by ~; ~-*rail*, railing along edge of stairs etc.; ~*shake*, shake of person's ~ with one's

own, as greeting; ~spike, wooden lever shod with iron, used on shipboard & by artillery; ~writing, writing with the ~, esp. of particular person. Hence (-)~ED², often (-)~ED². [com.-Teut.: OE hand, ho-, OHG hant] ~LESS, aa.

hand, v.t. Help (person) with the hand (into, out of, carriage etc.); (Naut.) take in (sail); deliver, transfer, by hand or other-wise (over to person, down to succeeding generations, in at office, on, up, etc.); ~-off (Rugby football), push off opponent with hand (also as v.t. and as n.); *~-out, food or money given to beggar at the door. [f. prec.]

hand'ful, n. (pl. ~s), Quantity that fills the hand; small number (of men etc.); (colloq.) troublesome person or task. [OE handfull (HAND¹, see -FUL)]

hän'dicap, n., & v.t. (-pp-). I. Race, com-petition, in which chances of competitors are equalized by start, difference in weight to be carried (in horse-races), etc., extra weight or other condition imposed on competitor; (fig.) hindrance. 2. v.t. Im-pose ~ on (competitor); (fig., of circum-stances) place (person) at disadvantage. Hence ~PER¹ n. [?]

hän'dicraft (-ahft), n. Manual skill; manual art or trade; ~sman, man who exercises a ~. [earlier handcraft]

hän'diwork (-wêrk), n. Work done, thing made, by the hands or by anyone's personal agency. [OE handgeweorc (HAND¹ +collect. form of weorc WORK)]

handkerchief (häng'kerchif), n. Square of linen, silk, etc., carried in pocket (pocket-~) for wiping nose etc. or worn about neck (also neck~, neckerchief); throw the ~ to (person, in certain games, also, express condescending preference for (person). [HAND¹+KERCHIEF]

hän'dle, n. That part of a thing which is made to hold it by; ~-bar of bicycle etc., steering-bar with ~ at each end; ~ of the face, (joc.) nose; ~ to one's name, title; fact that may be taken advantage of. [OE handle (HAND¹), cf. G handeln]

hän'dle², v.t. Touch, feel, with the hands; manipulate; manage (thing, person); treat (person roughly, kindly, etc.); treat of (subject); deal in (goods). [OE hand-lian (HAND¹), cf. G handeln]

hän'dsel (-ns-), n., & v.t. (-ll-), 1. Gift at beginning of New Year, or on entering on new circumstances; earnest-money; foretaste. 2. v.t. Give ~ to, inaugurate, be the first to try. [vb f. n.]; OE has handselen giving into a person's hands; Da. has handsel earnest-money]

hän'dsome (-ns-), a. Of fine form or figure; (of conduct etc.) generous, as a ~ present, ~ treatment; (prov.) ~ is that does; (of price, fortune, etc.) considerable. Hence ~LY² (-ml-) adv., ~NESS (-mi-) n. [HAND¹, -SOME]

hän'd(y)², a. Ready to hand; convenient to handle; clever with the hands; ~y-dandy, child's game in which one player guesses which of other player's hands conceals some object; ~y man (useful for odd jobs, often of sailors). Hence ~ILY² adv., ~INESS n. [-Y¹]

hăng¹, v.t. & i. (hăng, exc. as below). 1. Suspend, attach loosely, (from, to, hook or other object above); suspend (meat, game) to dry (hung beef, so cured or be-come tender or high. 2. Place (pictures) on wall (hung on the line, at best height for seeing; HANGING committee of Royal Academy etc.). 3. Attach (wall-paper); fit up (bells in house). 4. Suspend floating in space. 5. Rest (door on hinges, coach on springs) in free swinging position. 6. (past & p.p. ~ed). Suspend on gibbet as capital punishment; (as imprecation) ~!, ~it, ~ you, I'll be ~ed if —. 7. Let droop, as ~ the head (from shame etc.). 8. Remain, be, suspended, lit. & fig., as rogue shall ~ for it; ~s in the balance, is undecided; curtain ~s loose, in folds, etc. 9. Decorate with (things suspended). 10. ~ (loiter) about; ~ fire, (of firearm) be slow in going off (also fig.); ~ heavy, (of time) pass slowly; ~ on, depend, rely, on, attend carefully to (& see below); ~ back, show reluctance to act or move; ~ (lag) behind; ~ off, ~ back; ~ on, stick closely (to; & see above); ~ out, suspend from window etc., (intr.) protrude downwards, (sl.) reside; ~ together, be coherent, be associated; ~ up, suspend, (fig.) put aside, postpone indefinitely; ~ dog n. & a., base & sneaking (fellow); ~ over n. (sl.), un-pleasant after-effects of (esp. alcoholic) dissipation. [(1) OE hōn trans., cf. OHG hāhan, MDu., haen; (2) OE hangian intr. cf. OFris. hangia; (3) ON hengia causal,

hăng², n. Downward droop or bend; the way a thing hangs; get the ~ of, get the knack of, understand; (colloq.) not a ~, not at all. [f. prec.]

hăng'ar (or -nggr), n. Shed for housing aeroplane etc. [F, = shed for carriages etc., etym. dub.]

|| hăng'er², n. In vbl senses, esp.: bell, paper, ~; loop etc. by which thing is hung; chain, rod, to which pot is hung in fireplace by pot-hook; stroke with double curve in writing (ℓ), cf. POT-hook; short sword, orig. hung from belt; ~-on, follower, dependant. [-ER¹]

hăng'ing, n. In vbl senses, esp.: drapery with which walls etc. are hung; || com-mittee (deciding on ~ of pictures in exhibition); a ~ matter (resulting in capital punishment). [-ING¹]

hănk, n. Circular loop or coil, esp.

definite length of cotton yarn (840 yds.) worsted (560 yds.), etc.; (Naut.) ring of rope, iron, etc., for securing staysails to stays. [14th c., cf. ON *hönk* hank, Swed. *hank* string, Da. *hank* handle]

hank′er, v.i. Crave, long, *after*. Hence ~ING[1] n. [etym. dub.; Du. has *hankeren*]

hank′y, n. (colloq.). Handkerchief. [abbr.: see -Y[3]]

hank′y-pank′y, n. Jugglery; underhand dealing. [arbitrary, perh. on *hocus-pocus*]

Han′over, n. *House of* ~, British sovereigns from George I to Victoria. [place]

Hans (-z), n. (Nickname for) German or Dutchman. [G & Du. f. L *Johannes* John]

‖**Hän′sardize**, v.t. Confront (M.P.) with his former utterances recorded in Hansard (official report of proceedings in Parliament). [-IZE]

Hänse, n. (hist.). Guild of merchants; political and commercial league of Germanic towns, whence **Hänseat′ic** a.; entrance-fee of guild. [OF. f. OHG *hansa* company]

hän′som (cab), n. Two-wheeled cabriolet for two inside, with driver mounted behind and reins going over roof. [*Hansom, patentee*, 1834]

Han′well, n. (Used for) ~ Lunatic Asylum for county of London. [place]

häp[1], n. (arch.). Chance, luck, lot; (w. pl.) chance occurrence. [ME, f. ON *happ*]

häp[2], v.t. (arch.: -pp-). Come about by chance; happen (*to* do). [ME *happe(n)*, f. prec.]

häp′tä **legön′enon**, n. (pl. *-ena*). Word of which only one use is recorded. [Gk. = once said]

haphäz′ard (-p-h-), n., a., & adv. Mere chance, esp. *at, by,* ~; casual(ly). [HAP[1] + HAZARD]

häp′less, a. Unlucky. Hence ~LY[2] adv. [-LESS]

häplŏg′raphy, n. The mistake of writing once what should be written twice (e.g. *philoy* for *philology*), cf. DITTOGRAPHY. [f. Gk *haplous* single + -GRAPHY]

häp′ly, adv. (arch.). By chance; perhaps. [HAP[1], -LY[2]]

‖ **ha′p′orth**. See HALFPENNY.

häpp′en, v.i. Come to pass (by chance or otherwise), whence ~ING[1] n. (usu. pl.); chance. have the fortune, *to* (do); come *upon* (person, thing) by chance; (euphem., of death) *if anything should* ~ *to me*, if I die. [ME (HAP[1] + -EN[6])]

häpp′y, a. (Of person or circumstance) lucky, fortunate; contented with one's lot; *I shall be* ~ (pleased) *to assist*; ~ *dispatch,* = foll.; ~ FAMILY; apt, felicitous (of language or conduct); (sl.) dazed (*bomb, shell,* ~); ~-*go-lucky,* haphazard (adj.). Hence **häpp′ily**[2] adv., **häpp′iNESS** n. [f. HAP[1] + -Y[2]]

härä-ki′ri, n. Suicide by disembowelment, as practised by higher classes in

Japan when in disgrace or sentenced to death, happy dispatch. [Jap. (vulg.), f. *hara* belly + *kiri* cut]

harängue′ (-ng), n. & v.i. & t. Speech to an assembly; loud or vehement address.; (v.i.) make ~; (v.t.) make ~ to. [(vb f. F *haranguer*) f. OF *arenge* f. med. L *harenga* (lt. *aringa*, cf. *aringo* arena)]

hä′ras (or *ahrah*°), n. Breeding station for horses. [f. OF *haras*, etym. dub.; now usu. treated as F]

hä′rass, v.t. Vex by repeated attacks; trouble, worry. Hence ~MENT n. [f. F *harasser*, perh. f. OF *harer* set a dog on]

härb′inger (-j-), n., & v.t. One who announces another's approach, forerunner; (formerly) one sent to purvey lodgings for army, royal train, etc.; (v.t.) announce approach of. [(vb f. n.) f. OF *herbergere* f. *herberge* lodging f. OHG *heriberga* (*hari +berga* shelter f. *bergan* protect)]

härb′our (-ber), n., & v.t. & i. 1. Place of shelter for ships; shelter; ~ *master,* officer in charge of ~. 2. v.t. Give shelter to (esp. vermin, criminal, evil thoughts); (v.i.) come to anchor in ~. Hence ~LESS (-berl-) a. [(vb f. n.) ME *herebeorge* (*here* army + *beorg* shelter)]

härb′ourage (-ber-), n. (Place of) shelter. [-AGE]

härd, a., n., & adv. 1. Firm, unyielding to touch, solid; ~ *cash,* specie, as opp. to paper currency; ~ *facts* (not disputable like opinions etc.); difficult (*to* do; ~ *nut to crack,* ~ problem, person ~ to make out or influence); ~ *of hearing,* somewhat deaf; difficult to understand or explain, as ~ *words, question;* (of person or conduct) unfeeling, harsh; involving or unfair suffering (~ *cases make bad law*); stingy; difficult to bear, as ~ *life, times,* LINF's; (severe) *winter;* a ~ *bargain* (without concession); harsh, unpleasant, to eye or ear; *(of liquor) intoxicating, spirituous; ~ *water* (unfit for washing owing to its mineral salts) (of markets and prices) high, unyielding (Phonetics) k, t, and p, are ~ as opposed to g, d, & b, c is ~ in *cat,* g is ~ in *go;* strenuous, as ~ *fight,* ~ *labour* (imposed on some criminals), ~ *row to hoe* (difficult task), ~ *worker;* ~ *swearing,* (euphem. for) unabashed perjury. 2. n. ‖ Sloping roadway across foreshore.; (sl.) = ~ *labour* (*got 2 years* ~). 3. adv. Strenuously, severely, as *try* ~, *raining* ~, *freezing* ~, ~ *pressed* (closely pursued); with difficulty, as ~-*earned* (cf. HARDLY), ~-*baked, boiled* (so as to be ~); ~-*boiled,* (also, orig. U.S. colloq.) callous, ~-*headed, tough; be* ~ *put to it,* be in difficulties; *die* ~ (only after ~ struggle); *it will go* ~ *with him* (prove to his disadvantage); *it shall go* ~ *but* (short of overpowering difficulties) *I will find them;* ~ *by,* close by; ~ (*upon,* too severe in criticism or treatment (*don.° be too* ~ *on him*), (of circumstances) bearing

with undue severity on; ~ *upon*, close
to; ~ *run* (person) ~, pursue him closely.
4. ~ & *fast*, (of rules) strict; ||~*bake*,
almond toffee; ~*bitten*, tough in fight;
||~ *core*, heavy material forming founda-
tion of road; ~ *court*, lawn tennis court
made of asphalt, concrete, etc. (opp.
grass court); ~ *currency*, one not likely to
depreciate suddenly or fluctuate greatly
in value, e.g. U.S. dollar; ~*favoured*,
-*featured*, of harsh or ugly features; ~
fisted, stingy; ~*headed*, practical, not
sentimental; ~*hearted*, unfeeling, so ~
heartedly-*ness*; ~ *hit*, severely troubled;
~*laid*, (of string, fabric, etc.) tightly
twisted or woven; (of person) hungry; ~
pay, granted to officers & men while
serving in torpedo boats & other small
craft; ~*mouthed*, (of horse) not easily
controlled by bit (also *fig.*); ~ *set*, set so as
to be ~, (of egg) that has been subjected
to incubation, (of person) hungry; ~*shell*,
having a ~ shell, (fig.) rigid, uncompromising, esp. *Hardshell Baptists*; ~
tack, ship-biscuit; ~*up*, in want (esp. of
money), at a loss *for*, (Naut., adv. of
tiller) as far as possible to windward;
~*ware*, ironmongery; ~*warenam*, dealer
in this; ~*wood*, wood of deciduous trees
as opposed to pines and firs. Hence
~NESS n [com.-Teut. adj.: OE *heard*,
Du. *hard*, G *hart*, cf. Gk *kratus* strong]

hard'en, v.t. & i. Make or become hard,
callous (esp. in p.p.), or robust. [-EN⁴]
HARDI'HOOD. *see* HARDY.

hard'ihood, n. Boldness, audacity. [f.
HARDY & +-HOOD]

hard'ly, adv. In a hard manner; with
difficulty; harshly; scarcely; ~*earned*,
earned with difficulty or(joc.)ease. [-LY²]

hard'ship, n. Hardness of fate or circumstance; severe suffering or privation.
[-SHIP]

hard'y¹, a. Bold, audacious, whence
~iry²*adv.*; robust, capable of endurance;
(Hort., of plants) able to grow in the
open air all the year; *half* ~*y*, requiring
shelter in winter only; ~*y annual*, one that
may be sown, or sows itself, in the open.
(fig.) subject that comes up yearly. Hence
~INESS n. [f. F *hardi* p.p. of *hardir* f. WG
hardjan make HARD]

HARDY², n. Blacksmith's bar of hard iron
for cutting metal on etc. [prob. f. prec.
or HARD]

hare, n. || Rodent quadruped with long
ears, short tail, & divided upper lip; *mad
as a March* ~ (~ in breeding season);
(prov.) *first catch your* ~ (*then cook him*);
hold (or *run*) *with the* ~ & *run* (or *hunt*)
with the hounds, keep in with both sides;
& *hounds*, paper-chase; ~*bell* (-ărĕ¹-),
round-leaved bell-flower, also (see BLUE¹,
bell) wild hyacinth; ~*brained*, rash, wild;
~*lip* (-ărĭ̄-), fissure of upper lip; ~*s-foot*,
species of clover, (also) corkwood tree,
(also) ~'s foot used for applying rouge

etc. to face. [com.-Teut.: OE *hara*, Du.
haas, G *hase*]

ha'rem, -am, n. Women's part of
Mohammedan dwelling-house; its occupants; (usu.-*em*) Mohammedan sacred
place. [f. Arab. *haram*, -*im*, prohibited f.
harama prohibit; also *hareem* -*im* (-ēm)
f. *harīm* Ragout(usu. of mutton) as
~ (*toon*), French bean. [F, etym. dub.]

hark, v.i. & t. Listen (usu. *to*, rarely
trans.; also abs. in imper.); (as call to
hounds) go *forward*, *away*, *off*, etc.; ~
back, (of hounds) retrace course to find
scent, (fig.) revert (*to* subject), (trans.)
recall (hounds). [ME *herkien*, cf. MDu.
horken, G *horchen*]

hari'cot, n. 1. Ragout(usu. of mutton)
as ~ (*toon*), French bean. [F, etym. dub.]
= M.f.G *herle, harle*, fibre of flax or hemp]
-[EAN]

Harle'ian (-lē-), a. Of (the library of)
Robert Harley Earl of Oxford, d. 1724.

harl'equin, n. 1. Character in Italian
comedy; mute character in English
pantomime, invisible to clown & pantaloon, usu. wearing particoloured tights;
buffoon. 2. (Also ~ *duck*) northern duck
with variegated plumage. [F, f. It. *ar-
lecchino*, etym. dub.]

harl'equinade', n. Part of pantomime in
which harlequin plays chief part. [f. F
arlequinade (as prec., see -ADE)]

Harl'ey Street, n. London street associated with fashionable physicians.

harl'ot, n., & v.i. Prostitute; (v.i.) play
the ~. Hence ~RY(4) n. [vrb f. n.) orig.
masc.~ vagabond, knave, f. OF (*h)erlot,
herlot*, lad, knave, vagabond, = It. *arlotto* hedge-
priest; etym. dub.]

harm, n., & v.t. Damage, hurt, (*out of* ~*'s
way*, in safety). Hence ~ FUL, ~ LESS
(doing no ~), aa., ~*fully*², ~*lessly*²
advv., ~*fulness*, ~*lessness*, nn. [vrb f.
OE *hearm(an* f. n.) com.-Teut. n.: OE *hearm*,
G *harm*, Da. *harme*]

harm'attan, n. Parching land-wind on
coast of Upper Guinea in Dec., Jan., &
Feb. [f. W.-Afric. *haramata*]

harmon'ic, a. & n. 1. Harmonious, concordant; relating to harmony; ~ *tones*
(produced by vibration of aliquot parts
of strings etc.); ~ *quantities* (whose
reciprocals are in arithmetical progression, as ⅓, ⅓, ⅓, or as 12, 15, 20, ~ *progression*, series of these. 2. n. ~ *tone*.
Hence **harmon'ically** adv. [f. L f. Gk
harmonikos (as HARMONY, see -IC)]

harmon'ica, n. Name of several musical
instruments; *mouth organ*.

harmon'ious, a. Concordant, forming a
consistent or agreeable whole; free from
dissent; sweet-sounding; singing, playing, tunefully. Hence ~iry² adv. [f. F
harmonieux (as HARMONY)]

harm'onist, n. Person skilled in harmony; musician; collator of parallel narratives, whence ~**is'tic a.**; harmonizer. [f. L, HARMONIZE, see -IST]

harmón'ium, n. Keyboard instrument in which notes are produced by air blown through reeds. [F, as HARMONY]

harm'oniz|**e**, v.t. & i. Bring into, be in, harmony (*with*); make, be, agreeable in artistic effect; add notes to (melody) to form chords. Hence ~**A'TION n**. [f. F *harmoniser* (as HARMONY, see -IZE)]

harm'ony, n. Agreement; *pre-established* ~ (between body & soul before their creation); agreeable effect of apt arrangement of parts; combination of simultaneous notes to form chords (cf. MELODY); sweet or melodious sound; collation of parallel narratives etc., esp. of the four Gospels. [f. F *harmonie* f. L f. Gk *harmonia* (*harmo-* join)]

harn'ess, n., & v.t. **1.** Gear of draught horse or other animal; (fig.) working equipment; *in* ~, in the routine of daily work; apparatus in loom for shifting warp-threads; (Hist.) defensive armour; ~*cask* (with rimmed cover, for keeping salt meat on board ship). **2.** v.t. Put ~ on (horse etc.); (fig.) utilize (river, waterfall, natural forces) for motive power. [(vb f. OF *harneschier*) f. OF *harneis* (It. *arnese*), etym. dub.]

harp[1], n. Stringed musical instrument, roughly triangular, played with the fingers. [com.-Teut.: OE *hearpe*, Du. *harp*, G *harfe*]

harp[2], v.i. Play on harp, whence ~**ER[1]**, ~**IST, nn.**; dwell tediously *on* (subject). [OE *hearpian* as prec.)]

harpoon', n., & v.t. **1.** Spear-like missile with rope attached, for catching whales etc.; ~*gun* (for firing this). **2.** v.t. Strike, spear, with ~. [(vb f. n.) f. F *harpon* (*harpe* clamp f. L f. Gk *harpe* sickle)]

harp'sichord (-k-), n. Keyboard instrument with strings plucked by quill or leather points, used 16th–18th c. [f. obs. F *harpechorde* (LL *harpa* harp + *chorda* string)]

harp'y, n. (Gk & L Myth.) rapacious monster with woman's face & body & bird's wings & claws; rapacious person; ~*eagle*, S.-Amer. bird of prey. [f. L f. Gk *harpuiai* pl. (cf. *harpazō* snatch)]

harq'uebus, ăr-, n. (hist.). Early type of portable gun, supported on tripod by hook or on forked rest. So ~**IER' n.** [f. F *harquebuse* f. It. *arcobugio* corrupt. (as it = *arco* bow + *bugio* hollow) of MHG *hakenbühse* (*haken* hook + *bühse* gun)]

hă'rridan, n. Haggard old woman, vixen. [perh. f. F *haridelle* old jade]

hă'rrier[1], n. One who harries. [-ER[1]]

hă'rrier[2], n. Hound used for hunting hare; (pl.) pack of these with huntsmen (also as name of hare-&-hounds club); kind of falcon. [perh. = prec.]

Hă'rris tweed, n. Kind made in Harris in the Hebrides.

Harrŏv'ian, n. (Member) of Harrow school; (inhabitant) of Harrow. [-IAN]

hă'rrow[1] (-ō), n. Heavy frame with iron teeth for breaking clods on ploughed land, covering seed, etc.; *under the* ~, in distress. [ME *harwe*, etym. dub.]

hă'rrow[2] (-ō), v.t. Draw harrow over (land); lacerate, wound, (lit., & fig. the feelings etc.), whence ~**ING[2]** (-ōi-) a. [f. prec.]

hă'rrow[3] (-ō), v.t. Harry, spoil, (chiefly in phr. ~ *hell*, of Christ). [var. of foll.]

hă'rrÿ, v.t. Ravage, waste, spoil, (land, or abs.); despoil (person); harass, worry. [OE *hergian* f. OTeut. *harjōjan* (*harjo-* army)]

hărsh, a. Rough to the touch, taste, eye, or ear; repugnant to feelings or judgement; cruel, unfeeling. Hence ~**LY[2]** adv., ~**'NESS n.** [ME *harsk*, cf. Swed. *hårsk*, Da. *harsk*, rank, G *harsch* harsh]

hărt, n. Male of (esp. red) deer, esp. after fifth year; ~ *of ten* (branches on horns); ~'*s-tongue*, fern with slender undivided fronds. [OE *heort* f. OTeut. *herut-* perh. conn. w. Gk *kerat-* horn]

hăr'tal, n. Closing of Indian shops as political gesture or mark of sorrow. [Hindi]

hăr'l'(ë)beest, n. S.-African kind of antelope. [S.-Afr. Du.]

hăr'ts'horn (-s-h-), n. Substance got from horns of hart, formerly chief source of ammonia; (spirit of) ~, aqueous solution of ammonia; *salt of* ~, smelling-salts.

hăr'um-scăr'um, adv., a. & n. Reckless (person, conduct). [arbitrary]

hăr'vest, n., & v.t. **1.** (Season for) reaping & gathering in of grain or other products; corncrop; season's yield of any natural product; (fig.) product of any action; ~*-bug*, mite troublesome during ~; ~*festival*, thanksgiving service for ~; ~ *home*, close of ~ing, festival of this; ~ *moon* (full within fortnight of Sep. 22 or 23); ~ *mouse*, small species, nesting in stalks of growing grain. **2.** v.t. Reap & gather in (crop, or abs.), lay up, husband. [(vb f. n.) OE *hærfest* f. OTeut. *harbistoz* (*harb-* = L *carpere* pluck)]

hăr'vĕster, n. Reaper; reaping-machine (esp. sheaf-binding); harvest-bug. [-ER[1]]

has. See HAVE[1].

hăs'been (-z-), n. (colloq.). Person who, thing which, has lost a quality or proficiency formerly possessed, a back number. [HAVE[1]]

hăsh[1], v.t. (Also ~ *up*) cut (meat, also fig.) in small pieces. [f. F *hacher* (*hache* HATCHET)]

hăsh[2], n. Dish of hashed meat; old matter served up in new form; medley;

make a ~ of, spoil in dealing with; settle person's ~, make an end of, do for, him. chewing, in Arabia, Egypt, Turkey, etc. (cf. BHANG). [Arab. *hashīsh* dry herb]

hās'let, hārs', n. Piece of meat to be roasted, esp. pig's fry. [f. OF *haslet* (*haste* spit f. L *hasta* spear, -LET)]

hasp (hahsp), n., & v.t. Fastening contrivance, esp. clasp passing over staple & secured by padlock; hank, skein, of yarn. (v.t.) fasten with ~. [vb f. OE *hæpsian* (n. f. OE *hæpse*, cf. OHG *haspa* hinge]

hass'ock, n. Cushion for kneeling; tuft of matted grass etc.; || (in Kent) soft calcareous sandstone. [OE *hassuc*, etym. dub.]

hās'tāte, a. Spear-shaped. [f. L *hastatus* (*hasta* spear, see -ATE²)]

haste, n. & v.i. 1. Urgency of movement; hurry; precipitancy, as *more ~, less speed*; *make ~*, be quick (*to do*, & do). 2. v.i. Make ~ (*to do*, or abs.). [vb f. OF *haster*) f. OF *haste* f. WG †*haisti*-violence]

hā'sten (-sn), v.t. & i. Cause (person) to make haste; accelerate (work etc.); make haste; come or go in haste (*to* etc.). [-EN⁶]

hās'tily, a. Hurried; speedy; rash, inconsiderate; quick-tempered; || *~y pudding* (of flour stirred to thick batter in boiling milk or water). Hence ~iLY² adv., ~iNESS n. [f. OF *haste*, for -*if* (as HASTE¹, see -IVE)]

hăt, n. & v.t. (-tt-). 1. Man's, woman's, outdoor head-covering, usu. with brim (cf. BONNET, CAP); *top, high, chimney-pot, ~, cylindrical silk ~; opera ~* (cylindrical compressible); *cardinal's* or *red ~*, (fig.) office of cardinal; *~ in hand*, servilely; *send round the ~*, solicit contributions; *talk through one's ~* (sl.), boast or bluff or exaggerate; *as black as my ~*, quite black; *~'band* (put round ~); *~-trick*, (Cricket) taking 3 wickets by successive balls, (transf.) scoring of 3 goals by same player, winning of 3 races, etc. [OE *hæt* f. OTeut. *hattu-*, *hód-*, whence HOOD)]

hătch¹, n. Lower half of divided door; aperture in door, wall, floor, or deck; (Naut.) *~way*, trap-door covering this; *under ~es*, below deck, (fig.) down out of sight, brought low, dead; floodgate; *~way*, opening in ship's deck for lowering cargo. [OE *hæc, heca*, cf. Du. *hek*, Da. *hække*]

hătch², v.t. & i. & n. 1. Bring forth (young birds etc., or abs.) from eggs; incubate (eggs); emerge from eggs; (of egg) produce young; contrive & develop (plot etc.). 2. n. ~ing, brood ~ed, (~es, catches

hătch³, v.t. & n. 1. Engrave (usu. parallel) lines on (surface); (Archit.) ~ed moulding (with two crossing sets of parallel lines). 2. n. Engraved line. [(n. f, vb) ME *hacchen* (as HATCHET)]

hătch'ery, n. Place for hatching fish & chickens. [-ERY]

hătch'et, n. Light short-handled axe; ~ (narrow, sharp) *face*; BURY *the ~*, *throw the ~*, exaggerate; *throw the helve after the ~*, add new loss to that already incurred. [f. F *hachette* dim. of *hache* f. OHG †*happja* sickle]

hătch'ment, n. Escutcheon; tablet with deceased person's armorial bearings, affixed to front of his house. [corrupt. of ACHIEVEMENT]

hāte¹, n. (chiefly poet.), *morning* etc. ~, enemy bombardment (army sl.) *morning* etc. ~, customary at dawn etc. [OE *hete* f. OTeut. *hatoz*]

hāte², v.t. Have strong dislike of; bear malice to. Hence hāt'ABLE a. [OE *hatian* (root *hat-*, whence prec.)]

hāte'ful (-tf-), a. Exciting hatred. Hence ~LY² adv., ~NESS n. [-FUL]

hăth. Arch. 3rd sing. pres. of HAVE¹.

hăt'red, n. Active dislike; enmity, ill-will. [ME (HATE¹ + -*red* = OE *rǣden* condition)]

hătt'i, n. Turkish edict made irrevocable by Sultan's mark. [in full *hattisherif* (-ēf), *hăttheumáyun* (-hoŏmah'ūn), f. Pers. *khattfsheri-f, -humayun*, sacred writing]

haube'rk, n. Coat of mail. [f. OF *hauberc* f. OHG *halsberg* (*hals* neck + -*bergan* cover)]

haugh (hahx, hahf), n. Piece of flat alluvial land by river. [perh. f. OE *healh*]

haught'ly (-awt-), a. Proud, arrogant; dignified. Hence ~iLY² adv., ~iNESS n. [extension of older *haught* a. f. F *haut* f. L *altus* high, -γ¹]

haul, v.t. & i. & n. 1. Pull, drag, forcibly; transport by cart or other conveyance; *pull at, upon,* (rope etc.); (Naut.) turn ship's course; *~ upon the wind*, bring ship round to sail closer to wind; (of wind) shift. 2. n. ~ing, (fig.) amount gained, acquisition. Hence ~AGE(3) n. [(n. f, vb) var. of HALE v.]

haul'ier, n. One who hauls (esp. tubs in coal-mine to bottom of shaft); jobbing carter. [f. prec., see -IER]

|| **ha(u)lm** (hawm, hahm), n. Stalk, stem; (collect. sing.) stems, stalks, of peas, beans, potatoes, etc., without the pods etc. [OE *healm*, cf. G & Da. *halm*, Gk *kalamos* reed]

|| **haunch** (hawn-, hah-), n. Part of body (of men & quadrupeds) between last ribs & thigh; leg & loin of deer etc. as food; side

of arch between crown & piers. [f. OF *hanche*=med. L *hancha* prob. of G orig., cf. OHG *ancha* joint, leg]

haunt, v.t. & i., & n. 1. Frequent (place); frequent company of (person): (of thoughts etc.) visit (person) frequently; (p.p.) visited, frequented, by ghosts; stay habitually (*in, about, place, with person*). 2. n. Place of frequent resort, usual feeding-place of animals, den frequented by criminals. [n. f. vb) f. F *hanter*, etym. dub.]

haut'boy (hō̄b-), **hō̄'boy**, **ōb'oe** (-bō), n. Wood-wind double-reed instrument of treble pitch; reed-stop on organ imitating this; tall species of strawberry. [f. F *hautbois* (*haut* high + *bois* wood)]

haute école (ōt'ākōl), n. The more difficult feats of horsemanship. [F, = high school]

hauteur (hōtĕr', & see Ap.), n. Haughtiness of manner. [F]

haut goût (hōgoo̅'), n. Taint, high flavour. [F, = seasoning, lit. high flavour]

Havàn'a, n. Cigar made at Havana or in Cuba. [place]

have [or hav], v.t. & i. & auxil. (Pres.: *I have*, arch. *thou hast*, *he has*, pr. *hăz*, *haz*, arch. *he hăth*, *we*, *you*, *they*, *have*; past *had*, pr. *hăd*, *had*, arch. 2nd sing. *hădst*, p.p. *had*; abbr. *I've*, *we've*, etc., *I'd*, *we'd*, etc., *'s*=*has*; colloq. neg. *haven't*, *hasn't*, *hadn't*). Hold in possession; experience the existence of (persons etc. in various relations), as *I* ~ *two sons, no uncle, no equals*; possess, contain, as appendage, part, quality, etc., as *June has 30 days*, *trees* ~ *leaves, it has its advantages*; enjoy, suffer, as *I had that pleasure, a toothache*, *no fear*; permit (person) to, as *I will not* ~ *you say such things*; know, as *he has no Greek*; be burdened with, as *I had my work to do*; be obliged, as *I had to do my work*; retain, as ~ *this in mind*; entertain, as ~ *no doubt*; show by action etc. that one possesses, as ~ *the impudence to say*; engage in, carry on, as *had some conversation*, as ~ *a try* (make an attempt); he will ~ *it* (maintains) *that*; *as Plato has* (expresses) *it*; obtain, receive, take (food), as *we had news*, ~ *an egg*; *the Ayes* ~ *it* (~ the advantage); *let him* ~ *it*, punish or reprimand him; *I had him there* (gained advantage over him); ||(sl.) *you* ~ *been had* (cheated); ~ *him* (cause him to be) *shot*; ~ *him up*, cause him to be brought before court of justice; *I had my leg broken* (experienced such breakage); ~ *it your own way* (form of refusal to argue further); *he has had it* (sl.), he is a fatal casualty, (also) he is now a back number; ~ *at*, make attack upon; ~ *done*, stop; ~ *on*, be wearing (clothes); ~ *it out*, settle dispute (*with person*) by discussion etc., (also) get tooth extracted; ~ *nothing on* (person), ~ *no advantage over*; (in past subj., =

would ~) *had rather* (would prefer to) *go*, *had better go*, would act more wisely in going; (auxiliary) *I* ~, *had*, *shall* ~ *packed*, my packing is, was, will be, complete, *had I* (if I had) *known* etc. [com.-Teut.: OE *habban*, Du. *hebben*, G *haben*, perh. conn. w. L *habēre*]

hāve², n. ~*s* & ~*nots*, rich & poor; ||(sL.) a swindle, take-in. [f. prec.]

hāv'en, n. Harbour, port; (fig., often ~ *of rest*) refuge. [OE *hæfen*, cf. Du. *haven*, G *hafen*; perh. f. root of **HAVE** or **HEAVE**]

hāv'ersack, n. (Soldier's) stout canvas bag for provisions. [f. F *havresac* f. G *habersack* (*haber* oats + **SACK¹**)]

hāv'ildar, n. Sepoy officer corresponding to sergeant. [f. Pers. *bawáldár* (Arab. *bawálah* charge + Pers. *dār* holder)]

hāv'ing, n. In vbl senses; also, property, belongings, (often pl.). [-ING¹]

hāv'oc, n., & v.t. (~*king*, ~*ked*). Devastation, destruction, as *make* ~ *of*, *play* ~ *among*; *cry* ~, give signal to army to seize spoil (now fig.); (v.t.) devastate (often abs.). [(vb f. n.) f. AF *havok* f. OF *havot*, prob. of Teut. orig.]

haw¹, n. (Fruit of) hawthorn. [Hist.) hedge, enclosure; OE *haga*, country bumpkin; ~*finch*, common grosbeak. [OE *haga*, cf. Du. *haag* hedge, G *hag* hedge, bush]

haw², n. Third eyelid of horse, dog, etc., cartilage within inner corner of eye. [?]

haw-haw¹, int. & n. Boisterous laugh. Hence *haw-haw* v.i. [imit.]

haw-haw². = **HA-HA**.

hawk¹, n., & v.i. & t. 1. Bird of prey used in falconry, with rounded wings shorter than falcon's; *know a* ~ *from a handsaw* (perh. corrupt of HERNSHAW), have ordinary discernment (see *Haml.* II. ii. 397); rapacious person; ~*eyed*, keen-sighted; ~*moth*, sphinx-moth; ~*nosed*, with aquiline nose; ~*s-bill*, kind of turtle. 2. v.i. Hunt game with ~ (v.i. & t.) ~ *(at)*, attack as ~ does, (of swallows etc.) hunt insects. Hence ~**ISH¹**, ~**LIKE**, aa. [v.b f. n.) OE *hafoc*, cf. Du. *havik*, G *habicht*, perh. f. root *haf-* seize]

hawk², v.t. Carry (goods) about for sale (often fig.). [prob. f. **HAWKER**]

hawk³, v.i. & t. Clear the throat noisily, bring (phlegm etc.) *up* from throat. [prob. imit.]

hawk⁴, n. Plasterer's square board with handle. [?]

hawk'er, n. One who hawks goods about. [prob. f. MLG *hoker* (G *hoker*, Du. *heuker*) perh. f. *hocken* carry on one's back]

hawse (-z), n. Part of ship's bows in which ~*holes* are cut for cables; space between head of anchored vessel & anchors: situation of cables before ship's stem when moored with two anchors out from forward, one on starboard, other

on port bow. [16th c. *hau(s)se*, prob. f. ON *hals* neck.]

haw'ser, n. [-s-, -z-), n. (naut.). Large rope, small cable, now often of steel. [prob. f. OF *haucier* hoist f. LL *altiare* (*altus* high)]

haw'thorn, n. Thorny shrub, with white, red, or pink blossom & small dark red berry, the HAW[1]. [OE *hagathorn* (as HAW[1], see THORN)]

hay, n., & v.t. & i. 1. Grass mown & dried for fodder; *Burgundian* ~, Lucerne; *took* ~; *make* ~, turn it over for exposure to sun; *make* ~ *of*, throw into confusion; *make* ~ *while the sun shines*, seize opportunities. 2. ~'*box* (stuffed with ~, in which heated food is left to continue cooking); ~'*cock*, conical heap of ~; ~'*fever*, summer disorder usu. with asthmatic symptoms, caused by pollen or dust; ~'*fork* (for turning over or loading ~); ~'*maker*, one who lifts, tosses, & spreads ~ after mowing, instrument for shaking & drying ~, (sl.) swinging blow; ~'*rick*, ~'*stack*, regular pile of ~ with pointed or ridged top; ~'*seed* (colloq.), a rustic, hick; ~'*wire*, anything tangled (*go* ~*wire*, become excited or distracted). 3. v.t. Put (land) under ~; (v.i.) make ~. [OE *hēg*, Du. *hooi*, G *heu*, f. st. of HEW]

hay'ward (-ôrd), n. Officer of parish etc. in charge of fences & enclosures. [obs. *hay* hedge (as HAW[1]) + WARD]

haz'ard, n., & v.t. 1. Game at dice, with complicated chances; chance; danger; *at all* ~s (risks); each of winning openings in tennis-court; ||(Billiards) *winning* ~, striking object ball into pocket, *losing* ~, pocketing own ball of another; (Golf) any kind of bad ground, e.g. bunker; ||(in Ireland) cab-stand. 2. v.t. Expose to ~, run the ~ of; venture on (action, statement, guess). [kyb f. F *hasard* [?] f. OF *hasard*, prob. of Arab. orig.]

haz'ardous, a. Risky; dependent on chance. Hence ~LY[2] adv., ~NESS n. [-OUS]

hāze[1], n., & v.t. 1. Obscuration of atmosphere near earth, often arising from heat; (fig.) mental obscurity or confusion. 2. v.t. Make hazy. [?]

hāze[2], v.t. (naut.). Harass with overwork, *bully. [cf. OF *haser* harass, worry]

hāze[1], n. Bush whose fruit is the ~'*nut*; (stick of) its wood; reddish-brown colour (esp. of eyes); WYCH-~. Hence ~LY[2] a. [OE *hæsel*, cf. Du. *hazel*, G *hasel*]

hāz'el[?], a. Misty; vague; indistinct; slightly drunk. Hence ~ILY[2] adv., ~INESS n. [etym. dub.; known earlier than HAZE[1]]

hē[1], pron. (obj. *him*, poss. *his*, pl. *they*, obj. *them*, poss. *their*) & n. (pl. *hes*). 1. The male person in question. 2. n. (attrib.; esp. of animals) *he-goat* etc.; ~ *he-man*, masterful or virile man. [OE, cogn. w. OFris. *hi*, *he*; High G & Goth. use st. *i-*]

head[1] (hĕd), n. 1. Anterior part of body of animal, upper part of man's body, containing mouth, sense-organs, and brain; (as measure) *taller by a* ~, (Horse-racing) *won by a* ~; *cannot make* ~ *or tail of* (understand). 2. Seat of intellect or imagination; natural aptitude or talent (a *good* ~ *for business*). 3. ~*ache*, esp. as result of overnight intoxication (colloq.). 4. Life, as *it cost him his* ~. 5. Image of head, esp. on one side of coin (opp. to *tail*), as ~s *I win, tails you lose*. 6. Antlers of deer, as *deer of the first* ~ (when antlers are first developed). 7. Person, as *crowned* ~, *some hot* ~ (hasty person); individual, as *twopence a* ~ per ~, esp. of cattle, as *every* ~ *of cattle, twenty* ~; *large* ~ (number) of game; *good* ~ (stock) of shell. 8. Thing like ~ in form or position, e.g. cutting or striking part of tool, knobbed end of nail etc.; (of plants) compact mass of leaves or flowers at top of stem. 9. Foam on top of liquor; || cream on top of milk. 10. Top (of mast, staircase, page, etc.). 11. Maturated part of boil etc. 12. Upper end; end of lake at which river enters it; end of bed at which one's ~ rests; FOUNTAIN-~. 13. Body of water kept at height for mill etc.; pressure (per unit of area) of confined body of steam etc. 14. Front (of procession, army, etc.); front part of plough, holding ~ the share; bows of ship, as *by the* ~, with ~ lower in water than stern, (fig.) slightly drunk. 15. Promontory, as *Beachy H~*. 16. Underground passage for working coal mine. 17. Ruler, chief, (often attrib.); master of college; ~*master* of school. 18. Position of command; *at the* ~ *of*. 19. Main division in discourse; category. 20. Culmination, crisis, as *come to a* ~. 21. (Naut.) seamen's latrine in ship's bows. 22. Phrases: *old* ~ *on young shoulders*, wisdom in the young; *put thing out of one's* ~, cease to think of it, give up the idea of it; *put thing out of person's* ~, make him forget it (*something put it out of my* ~); *off one's* ~, crazy; *on one's* ~ (of vengeance falling, guilt resting, on person); (*stand* etc.) *on one's* ~, with feet in air (*could do it on my* ~, sl., find it quite easy); *out of one's own* ~, from one's own invention; *over* ~, above one, esp. fig. of danger impend-ing etc., (also) beyond one's comprehen-sion, as *he talks over our* ~s, (also) *person is promoted over another's* ~, (who has prior claim); *by the* ~ & *ears*, forcibly (esp. of dragging in a story); *over* ~ & EARS; *from* ~ *to foot*, all over the person; ~ *of hair*, the hair on the ~, esp. when copious;

~ *over heels,* topsy-turvy; *by ~ & shoulders,* = *by ~ & ears,* (also) considerably (*taller,* & fig. of mental or moral stature); *keep one's ~,* keep calm; *keep one's ~ above water,* (fig.) keep out of debt; *lose one's ~,* be beheaded, (also) become confused; *make ~,* press forward; *make ~ against,* resist successfully; *put* (thing) *into person's ~,* suggest it to him; ~ *first* or *foremost,* with the ~ foremost (of plunge etc.), (fig.) precipitately; *give* (horse) *his ~,* (fig.) let him go freely; *lay* (*our* etc.) ~*s together,* consult together; *talk person's ~ off,* weary him with talk; *beat person's ~ off,* outdo him thoroughly; (prov.) *two ~s* (*minds*) *are better than one.* **23.** Comb.: ~*ache,* continuous pain in ~, (colloq.) troublesome problem; ~*'achy*(-ĭ), suffering from, producing, this; ~ *& ~ front,* essence (of offence etc.; but cf. *Oth.* I. iii 80), (pop.) leader, ringleader; ~*'band,* band worn round ~; ~*'borough* (hist.), petty constable; ~*'dress,* covering (esp. woman's ornamental attire) for the ~; ~*'fast,* rope at ~ of vessel to make her fast to wharf etc.; ~*'gear,* hat, cap, dress; ~*'hunter,* savage who collects ~s of his enemies as trophies; ~*'land,* promontory, (also) strip left unploughed at end of field; ~*'light,* powerful light carried on front of locomotive, car, or aeroplane, or at mast-head of ship; ~*'line,* line at top of page containing title etc., title or sub-title in newspaper, (pl., also) ||summary at beginning of BBC news bulletin; ~*'man,* chief man, chief of tribe etc.; ||~*'master, mistress,* principal master, mistress, of school; ~*'money* (paid for or by each person); ~*'on* (adj.), involving the meeting ~ *to* ~ of two vehicles (*a ~ on collision*), or of the ~ of a vehicle with stationary object; ~*'on'* (adv.), with the ~ pointed directly towards some object; ~*'phone,* (in wireless and other telephony) telephone receiver fitting over ~; ~*'piece,* helmet, (also) intellect, man of intellect, (also) ornamental engraving at ~ of chapter etc. in book; ~*'quart'ers,* (Mil.) commander-in-chief's residence, (gen.) centre of operations; ~*'spring,* main source of stream (also fig.); ~*'stall,* part of bridle or halter that fits round ~; ~*'stock,* bearings of revolving parts in machine; ~*'stone,* gravestone; ~ *stone,* chief stone in foundation (also fig.); ~*'voice,* one of higher registers of voice in singing or speaking; ~*'way,* progress, (of ship) rate of progress, (Archit.) height of arch etc.; ~*'wind* (meeting one directly in front); ~*'work,* mental work. Hence (-)~'ED², ~'LESS, aa. [OE *hēafod,* Du. *hoofd,* G *haupt;* connexion w. L *caput* doubtful]

head² (hĕd), v.t. & i. Furnish with head; (also ~ *down*) lop off head of (plant, tree) be, form, the head of; place name etc., be (of name etc.) be placed, at the head of (chapter, list, etc.); come to a head, develop; be, put oneself, at the head of (a company etc.); lead; excel; oppose; go round the head of (lake etc.); (Footb.) strike (ball) with head; ~ *back, off,* get ahead of so as to turn back, aside; (intr.) front (in named direction); (of ship) make for (place, point). [f. prec.]

-head, -hood, suff. forming nn. of condition or quality on nn. & aa. An independent noun appearing in Goth. as *haiduz* manner, way, gives OHG *-heit, -hēd,* the E suff. (1) *-head,* ME *-hēde, -hǒd,* first joined to aa. but extended to nn. & finally giving place to *-hood* exc. in a few wds such as *godhead, maidenhead,* (distinct in meaning f. *godhood, maidenhood*). (2) *-hood,* ME *-hod,* OE *-hād,* orig. noun= person, personality, condition, quality; then as suff. to nn. & later to adj., both in new formations & to replace *-head.*

head'er (hĕd-), n. One who puts heads on casks etc.; brick, stone, laid at right angle to face of wall (cf. STRETCHER); plunge head first. [-ER¹]

head'ing (hĕd-), n. In vbl senses; also or esp.: (Footb.) striking ball with head; title etc. at head of page etc.; horizontal passage in preparation for tunnel. [-ING¹]

head'long (hĕd-), adv. & a. Head foremost (in falling etc.); precipitate(ly); impetuous(ly). [earlier *headling* (HEAD¹+ -LING²), assim. to -LONG]

head'most (hĕd-), a. Foremost.

heads'man (hĕd-), n. One who beheads; man in command of whaling boat. [HEAD¹+-ES+MAN]

head'strong (hĕd-), a. Violently self-willed. Hence ~NESS n. [=strong in head]

head'y (hĕd-), a. (Of person, thing, action) impetuous, violent; (of liquor etc.) apt to intoxicate. Hence ~ILY² adv., ~iNESS n. [-Y²]

heal, v.t. & i. Restore (person, wound) to health (lit. & fig.); cure (person of disease); (of wound) become sound or whole; ~*all,* universal remedy (pop. name of various plants). Hence ~ER¹ n. (*time is a great ~er*). [com.-Teut. n.; OE *hǣlan,* Du. *heelen,* G *heilen,* cogn. w. HALE, WHOLE]

health (hĕl-), n. Soundness of body (also fig.); condition of body, as *good, bad, ~;* ~*-officer, officer of ~,* (charged with administering ~ laws etc.); toast drunk in person's honour; BILL⁴ of ~. [OE *hǣlth,* cogn. w. HALE, see -TH¹]

health'ful (hĕl-), a. Health-giving; conducive to moral or spiritual welfare. Hence ~LY² adv., ~NESS n. [-FUL]

health'y (hĕl-), a. Having good health (lit. & fig.); conducive to good health. Hence ~ILY² adv., ~iNESS n. [HEALTH +-Y²]

heap¹, n. Group of things lying one on another; (colloq.) large number, as *a ~*

of people, ~s of times, (adv.) *he is ~s better*; (colloq) *struck all of a ~*, mentally prostrated. [OE *héap*, cf. Du. *hoop*, G. *haufe*; also L. *cumbere, cubare, lie*] **heap**[2], v.t. Pile (things *up, together*, etc.) in a ~; load (cart, person, etc. *with* goods, benefits, etc.); accumulate (insults etc. *upon*. [OE *héapian*, as prec.]

hear, v.t. & i. (*heard* pr. hĕrd). Perceive (sound etc.) or (intr.) with the ear, *as I ~'d a groan, I ~ him groaning, I ~'d him groan* (but *he was ~'d to groan*); listen, give audience, to, as *give a fair ~*, listen to him, *his lesson, ~ a sermon*; listen judicially to (case, plaintiff, etc.); grant (prayer); *he will not ~* (entertain the notion) *of it; you will ~ of this* (be reprimanded for it); be informed (*that, of, about*); ~ *from*, receive letter or message from; ~ *tell of* (arch.), be told about; || (as form of cheering, often *hear*,) ~! ~!. Hence ~ABLE a., ~ER[1] n. [OE *híeran*, Du. *hooren*, G *hören*]

hear'ing, n. In vbl senses, esp.: perception by ear, as *hard of ~*, deaf; *within ~*, near enough, too far off, to be heard; *give him a fair ~*, listen impartially to him. [-ING[1]]

hear'k'en (hä-), v.l. Listen (*to*). [OE *heorcnian* (as HARK, w. suf. *-n*)]

hear'say, n. What one hears (but does not know to be true), gossip, (often attrib., as ~ *evidence*).

hearse (hĕrs), n. Car for carrying coffin at funeral; (formerly) framework supporting pall at funeral, often adapted for carrying tapers. [F. *herse*, f. L *hirpicem* (nom. *-ex*) rake, harrow]

heart (härt), n. 1. Hollow organ keeping up circulation of blood by contracting & dilating; *right, left,* ~ (side of ~); *smoker's ~* = disorder due to smoking. 2. Breast; mind; soul (~ *to* ~), with candour; so ~-*to*-~*talks*; *after one's (own)* ~ (desire). 3. Seat of the emotions, esp. of love, as *give, lose, one's ~ to, win the ~ of*, (person); *union of* ~s (depending on affection, not constraint). 4. Sensibility, as *he has no ~*; *courage, as pluck up or take, lose,* ~. 5. (As term of endearment to person) *dear, sweet,* ~; (Naut.) *my ~s* (brave fellows). 6. Central part, esp. of tree, as (fig.) ~ *of oak*, courageous man; vital part, essence, (*the ~ of the matter*). 7. (Of land) fertility, as *out of* ~, in poor condition. 8. ~-shaped thing. 9. *At* ~, in one's (pl.) suit marked with ~s. 9. *At* ~, in one's inmost feelings; *by* ~, in, from, memory, as *learn, say, by* ~; *from one's* ~, sincerely; *in* one's ~, secretly; *in* ~, in good spirits; *near(est)* one's ~, dear(est) to one; *out of* ~, in low spirits; *with all one's* ~, sincerely, with the utmost goodwill; *find in* one's ~, (esp. w. neg.) prevail on oneself (*to do*); *have* thing *at* ~, be deeply interested in it; *lay* thing *to* ~, think it over seriously; *searchings of* ~,

misgivings; *take* thing *to* ~, be much affected by it; *break* person's ~, overwhelm him with sorrow; *cry one's* ~ *out*, cry violently; *eat one's* ~ *out*, pine away from vexation etc.; *have a* ~ (sl.), be merciful; *have the* ~, (esp. w. neg.) be hard-hearted enough (*to do*); ~ *& hand*, enthusiastically; *in one's* ~ *of* ~s (inmost feelings); ~ *& soul*, with all one's energy; *have one's* ~ *in one's mouth*, be violently alarmed or startled; *his* ~ *is in the right place*, he means well; *take* ~ *of grace*, pluck up courage; *lose one's* ~ *upon one's sleeve*, lack proper reserve; *it does my* ~ *good*, it rejoices me. 10. ~ *of ~s* (inmost good, it rejoices me. 10. ~-*ache*, mental anguish; ~-*beat*, pulsation of ~; ~-*blood*, life-blood, life; (fig.) emotion; ~-*(s)-blood*, life-blood, life; ~-*break*, overwhelming distress; ~-*breaking*, ~-*broken*, causing, crushed by, this; ~-*burn*, burning sensation in lower part of chest; ~-*burning*, jealousy, grudge; ~-*disease*; ~-*(of)-~*; ~-*felt*, sincere (emotion etc.); ~-*rending*, distressing; ~-*sick*, despondent; ~-*sore*, grieved at ~-*strings*, (fig.) ~; deepest affections; ~-*whole*, undismayed, with the ~ unengaged, sincere. Hence ~'ED[2] (här-) a. [com.-Teut.: OE *heorte*, Du. *hart*, G *herz*; cf. L *cor-dis*, Gk *kardia*]

heart'en (här-), v.t. & i. Inspirit, cheer (often *up*, also *on*); (intr.) cheer *up*. [-EN[6]]

hearth (härth), n. Floor of fireplace; ~-*rug* (laid before fireplace); ~-*stone*, stone forming ~, (also) stone etc. for whitening ~s. [OE *heorth*, cf. Du. *haard*, G *herd*]

heart'ily (här-), adv. With goodwill, courage, or appetite; very, as ~ *sick of it*. [HEARTY, -LY[2]]

heart'less (här-), a. Unfeeling, pitiless, cruel. Hence ~LY[2] adv., ~NESS n. [-LESS]

heart'y (här-), a. & n. 1. Cordial, genial, (of feelings) sincere; vigorous; (of meals) abundant. 2. n. (As address to sailors) *my ~ies*; || (in English university use) outdoor man, athlete (opp. AESTHETE). Hence ~INESS n. [-Y[1]]

heat[1], n. 1. Hotness; sensation, perception, of this; *red, white,* etc., ~, at which metals etc. are red, white, etc. 2. (Physics) kinetic & potential energy of the invisible molecules of bodies, capable of transmission by conduction or radiation (formerly held an elastic material fluid); *latent* ~, ~ required to convert a solid into liquid or vapour, or a liquid into vapour; *specific* ~, ~ required to raise temperature of a given substance to given extent (usn. one degree), usn. calculated relatively to water. 3. Hot weather. 4. Inflamed state of body. 5. Pungency of flavour. 6. *Prickly* ~, skin disease common in hot climates. 7. Single effort, esp. *at a* ~; (*trial*) ~s, races, contests, the winners of which compete in *final* (~),

8. Warmth of feeling, anger; violent stage (of debate etc.). 9. Sexual excitement of animals during breeding season (*on, at, ~, of females*). 10. ~*-spot*, freckle, (also) point of the skin at which ~ can be felt; ~*-stroke*, prostration by excessive ~; ~*-wave*, wave of radiant ~ (also) access of great ~ in atmosphere regarded as passing from place to place. [OE *hātu*, cf. MDu. *heete*; also G *hitze*, Du. *hitte*] **heat²** v.t. & i. Make hot; inflame (blood etc.), inflame with passion, whence ~'edly² adv.; (intr.) become hot (lit. & fig.). Hence ~ER²(2) n. [com.-Teut. OE *hātian*, Du. *heten*, G *heizen*; cogn. w. HOT]

heath, n. ‖ Bare flat waste tract of land, esp. if covered with shrubs; plant of such shrubs, esp. of genus *Erica*; ~*-bell*, flower of ~ & other plants; ~*-berry*, bilberry, crowberry, & other berries ~*-cock*, blackcock. Hence ~Y² a. [OE *hǽđh*, cf. Du. & G. *heide*]

heath'en (-dh-), a. & n. (One who is) neither Christian, Jewish, nor Mohammedan; (in. pl. collect.) *the* ~; unenlightened person; *the* CHINEE. Hence ~DOM, ~ISM(2), ~ishNESS, ~RY, nn., ~ISH¹ a., ~ishLY² adv., ~IZE(3) v.t. & i., (-dh-). [OE *hǽđhen*, cf. Du. *heiden*, G *heide*, Goth. has *haiđhnō* heathen woman, perh. f. *haiđhi* heath]

heath'er (hĕdh-), n. Various species of genus *Erica* (called in the North Ling); ‖ *take to the* ~ (Sc.), become an outlaw; ~*-bell*, (flower of) species of *Erica*; ~*-mixture*, (fabric) of mixed hues supposed to resemble ~. Hence ~Y² a. [ME *hathir* etym. dnb, now assim. to *heath*]

heave¹, v.t. & i. (past & p.p. ~d or *hóve*). Lift (heavy thing); (of vein or stratum) displace (another); utter (groan, sigh) with effort; (Naut. & colloq.) throw; (Naut.) haul up, haul, by rope; rise, swell up; rise with alternate falls, as waves; pant; retch; pull (*at* rope etc.); ~ *down*, turn (ship) over on one side for cleaning etc.; ~ *to*, bring (sailing-ship, or abs.) to a standstill without anchoring or making fast; ~ *in sight*, become visible; ~ *ho* (cry of sailors in heaving anchor up). [com.-Teut.: OE *hebban*, Du. *heffen*, G *heben*, cf. L *capere* take]

heave², n. Heaving; ~ *of the sea*, force exerted by swell of sea on ship's course; a recognized chip in wrestling (*Cornwall* ~); horizontal displacement of vein or stratum; (pl.) disease of horses, broken wind. [f. prec.]

heav'en (hĕv-), n. Sky, firmament, (in prose now usu. pl.); region of the atmosphere in which clouds float, winds blow, & birds fly; (formerly) each of the heavenly SPHERES; habitation of God & his angels, usually placed beyond sky (cf. HELL); *seventh* ~, ~ *of* ~s, highest of seven ~s recognized by Jews, abode of God; God, Providence, as *it is* H~'s *will*; (in asseverations & exclamations) *by* ~!, *good* ~s!; place, state, of supreme bliss; ~*-born*, of divine origin. Hence ~WARD a., ~WARD(s) adv. [OE *hefen*, later *heofone*, cf. LG *heben*; etym. dub.]

hea'venly (hĕ-), a. Of heaven, divine, (*the* H~ *City*, Paradise); of the sky, as ~ *bodies*; *the* H~ *Twins*, =GEMINI; of superhuman excellence; (colloq.) *what* (excellent) *figs!*; ~*-minded*, holy, devout. Hence **hea'venliNESS** (hĕ-) n. [OE *heofonlic* (as prec., see -LY¹)]

Hea'viside (hĕ-) **lay'er**, n. Layer of the atmosphere that reflects wireless waves back & causes them to follow the contour of the earth. [Oliver Heaviside, English physicist (d. 1925)]

heav'y¹ (hĕ-), a., n., & adv. **1.** Of great weight (of great specific gravity; weighty because abundant, as *a* ~ *crop*; laden *with*; (of ordinance of the larger kind) ~ *metal*, *guns*, *metal*, *artillery*; (fig.) *metal*, formidable opponent(s); (Mil.) carrying ~ *arms*. **2.** Striking, falling, with force, as ~ *storm*, *sea*. **3.** (Of ground) clinging, difficult to travel over. **4.** (Of bread etc.) dense from not having risen; (of food) hard to digest. **5.** (Of horse) ~ *in* or *on hand*, bearing or hanging on bit, (fig.) dull, hard to entertain. **6.** (Of sky) overcast, gloomy. **7.** Clumsy in appearance or effect; (of persons) intellectually slow; unwieldy; (of artistic or literary productions) dull, tedious; (Theatr.) serious, sombre, as ~ *father*. **8.** Oppressive, grievous, as *a* ~ *fate*; sad, as ~ *news*; despondent; doleful; drowsy; *it lies* ~ (makes its weight felt); *time hangs* ~ (passes slowly). **9.** n. pl. ‖ *The Heavies*, Dragoon Guards, (also) ~ artillery. **10.** adv. Heavily (now chiefly in compounds; as ~*-buying*, *-laden*, *-pulling*). **11.** ~*armed*, bearing ~ arms or armour; CHEMICALS; ~*-hearted*, melancholy, doleful; ~ *oil*, a heavier-than-water oil obtained from coal-tar by distillation; ~ *spar*, barytes; ~ *swell* (colloq.), man who emphasizes his real or imagined importance by overdressing etc.; ~ *water*, water with a density about 10 per cent. greater than that of ordinary water, the oxide of DEUTERIUM or ~ *hydrogen*; ~*-weight*, jockey etc. of more than average weight, boxer over 12st. 10. Hence **hea'viLy²** adv., **hea'viNESS** n., ~ISH¹ a., (hĕ-). [OE *hefig* (*hefe* weight, cogn. w. HEAVE), cf. Du. *hevig*]

hĕb'domăd, n. Week (esp. in reference to *Dan.* ix. 27). [f. L f. Gk *hebdomas -ados* (*hepta* seven, see -AD)]

hĕbdŏm'adăl, a. Weekly; ‖ (Oxf. Univ.) H~ *Council*, board meeting weekly. [f. L *hebdomadalis* (as prec., see -AL)]

Hēb'ē, n. (Gk Myth.) goddess of youth, cupbearer of Olympus; (joc.) waitress, barmaid. [Gk]

hĕb'ĕtāte, v.t. & i. Make, become, dull. [f. L *hebetare* (*hebes -etis* blunt), see -ATE³]

hĕb'ĕtŭde, n. Stupidity. [f. LL *hebetudo* (*hebes*, see prec., -ATE³)]

Hēbrā'ĭc, a. Of Hebrew or the Hebrews. Hence ~ICALLY adv. [f. LL f. Gk *Hebraïkos* (as HEBREW, see -IC)]

Hēbrā'ĭsm, n. Attribute of the Hebrews; Hebrew system of thought or expression. So ~IZE(3) v.t. & i., ~IS'TIC a. [f. prec., see -ISM]

Hēbrā'ĭst, n. Hebrew scholar; adherent of Hebrew thought or religion. [as prec. -IST]

Hē'brew (-ōō), n. & a. 1. Israelite, Jew; *Epistle to the* ~s, book in N.T.; language of the ancient ~s; *modern* ~, as now used by Jews; (colloq.) unintelligible speech (cf. GREEK). 2. adj. Of ~, of the Jews. [f. OF *Ebreu* f. med. L f. Gk *Hebraios* f. Aram. *ëbrai* = Heb. '*ibri* one from the other side ('*abar* cross over)]

Hĕc'atomb (-ŏm, -ōŏm), n. (Gk Ant.) Great public sacrifice (prop. 100 oxen); ... [f. L f. Gk *hekatombē* (*hekaton* hundred + *bous* ox)]

hĕck, n. Frame obstructing passage of fish in river. [OE *hec*, see HATCH¹]

hĕc'kle, v.t. & n. (Dress flax, hemp, with) HACKLE; catechize (esp. election candidate) severely. [= HACKLE¹]

hĕc'tare, n. (In metric system) superficial measure of 100 ares (2·471 acres). [f. HECTO- + ARE¹]

hĕc'tic, a. & n. 1. ~ *fever*, that which accompanies consumption and similar diseases, attended with flushed cheeks and hot skin; consumptive; morbidly flushed (lit. & fig.); (sl.) exciting, wild, impassioned, (*for a* ~ *moment*). 2. n. ~ fever, patient, flush, hectic, (*hec's* habit of body, f. habitual, hectic, flush; see -IC]

hĕc'to- in comb.= Gk *hekaton* hundred, as: ~*graph*, apparatus for multiplying copies, (v.t.) multiply with this; ~*gram(me)*, weight of 100 grammes (3·52 oz), ~*litre*, ~*liter*, (-lēter), 100 litres (3·52), ~*metre* (-ter), -*meter*, 100 metres (328·089 ft); cf. CENTI-.

hĕc'tor, n. & v.t. & i. Bluster(er), bully, (vb f. n.) f. Gk *Hektōr*, son of Priam and Hecuba, Trojan hero in *Iliad*]

hĕd'dles, n. pl. Small cords or wires through which warp is passed in loom before going through the reed. [?]

hedge, n. Fence of bushes or low trees, living (*quickset* ~) or dead (*dead* ~), of turf, stone, etc. (*doesn't grow on every* ~, *is rare*); line of things or persons forming barrier; (fig.) barrier; (Betting) act, means, of hedging; ~-*priest*, illiterate priest of low status; ~-*row*, row of bushes forming ~; ||~-*school*, low-class school, (formerly) open-air school esp. in Ireland; ~-*sparrow*, common British and Euro-

pean bird, one of the Warblers. [OE *hecg*, cf. Du. *hegge*, G *hecke*; cogn. w. HAW¹]

hedge², v.t. & i. Surround with hedge (lit. & fig.); fence off; hem in; make, trim, hedges, whence hedg'ER¹ n.; secure oneself against loss on (bet, speculation, or also) by compensating transactions on the other side; (intr.) avoid committing oneself. [f. prec.]

hedge'hŏg, (-jh-), n. Spiny insectivorous quadruped, rolling itself up into ball for defence; name of various animals armed with spines; (Mil.) small self-contained defensive position bristling with fortifications on all sides; prickly seed-vessel of some plants; person hard to get on with, whence ~gy¹ (-g-) a. [HEDGE (from its habits) + HOG (from its snout)]

hēdŏn'ĭc, a. & n. Of pleasure; (n. pl.) doctrine of pleasure. [f. Gk *hēdonikos* (foll., -IC)]

hēd'onĭsm, n. Doctrine that pleasure is the chief good. So ~IST n., ~IS'TIC a. [f. Gk *hēdonē* pleasure + -ISM]

heed, v.t. (Sc. & literary) & n. 1. Concern oneself about, take notice of. 2. n. Careful attention, as *take* ~, *pay* or *give* ~ *to*. Hence ~'FUL, ~'LESS, aa., ~'FULLY, ~'LESSNESS, nn. [n. prob. f. vb) OE *hēdan*, cf. Du. *hoeden*, G *hüten* (*hut* guard)]

hee'haw, n. Ass's bray; loud laugh. [imit.]

heel¹, n. 1. Hinder part of human foot below ankle (~ *of Achilles*, only vulnerable spot, weak point); (Anat.) corresponding part of hind limb in quadruped, often raised above ground; (pop., of quadruped) hinder part of hoof, (pl.) hind feet. 2. Part of stocking that covers ~; part of boot that supports ~. 3. Thing like ~ in shape or position, as handle end of violin bow, crook in head of golf club, after end of ship's keel. 4. *Cad, low-down person (sl.). 5. *At* ~, *on*, *upon*, *one's* ~s, close behind one; *down at* ~, (of shoes) with ~ part crushed down, (of person) wearing such shoes, slovenly; *to* ~, (of dog) close behind, under control; ~-*a-toe* WALK'*ing*; ~s *over head*, (usu.) *head over* ~s, upside down, in a somersault; *kick one's* ~s, stand waiting; *cool one's* ~s; *lag, clap, by the* ~s, imprison; *shoot a clean pair of* ~s, *take to one's* ~s, run away; *have the* ~s *of*, outrun; *turn on one's* ~s, turn sharply round; *be carried with the* ~s *foremost* (as a corpse); (Cribbage) *his* ~s, knave if turned up by dealer, scoring two (cf. NOB); ~-*ball*, shoemaker's polishing mixture of hard wax and lamp-black; ~-*tap*, a thickness of leather in ~, liquor left at bottom of glass. [OE *hēla*, cf. Du. *hiel*]

heel², v.i. & t. Touch ground with heel, e.g. in dancing; furnish (boot etc.) with

heel; chase or follow closely; (Football) pass ball *out* at back of scrummage with the heels; (Golf) strike (ball) with heel of club. Hence *~ED² (-id) a. (colloq.), armed with revolver, supplied with money. [f. prec.]

heel³, v.i. & t. (Of ship etc.) lean over owing to pressure of wind or uneven load; cause (ship) to do this. [corrupt. of obs. *heeld*, OE *hieldan* (*heald* sloping), cf. Du. *hellen*]

heel⁴, n. (naut.). Inclination of heeling ship (of. LIST³). [f. prec.]

heft, n., & v.t. (dial., U.S.). Weight; (dial.) lift, push, (v.t.) lift, esp. to judge weight. [(vrb prob. f. n.) 16th c., f. HEAVE v., cf. *weave weft*]

heft'y, a. Sturdy, stalwart, (*a battalion of ~ fellows*). [prec., -Y²]

hegemon'ic (hēji-, hēgi-), a. Ruling, supreme. [f. Gk *hēgemonikos* (as foll., see -IC)]

hegem'ony (-g-, -j-; *also* hēgˀ), n. Leadership, esp. of one State of a confederacy. [f. Gk *hēgemonia* (*hēgemōn* leader)]

hē'gira, -jira, n. Mohammed's flight from Mecca to Medina; Mohammedan era reckoned from this (622 A.D.). [med. L. f. Arab. *hijrah* departure from one's country (*hajara* separate)]

heif'er (hef'-), n. Young cow that has not had calf. [OE *heahfore*, etym. dub.]

heigh (hā), int. expr. encouragement or inquiry; *~-ho*, int. expr. boredom, disappointment, etc.

height (hīt), n. Measurement from base to top; (esp. sea) level; considerable elevation, as *situated at a ~*; high point; top; *the ~* (utmost degree) *of folly* etc.; rising ground; *at its ~* (highest degree). [OE *hiehtho* (as HIGH, see -TH¹)]

height'en (hīt-), v.t. & i. Make high(er); intensify; inflate (description, story). [prec. +-EN⁶]

hei'nous (hān-), a. (Of crime or criminal) odious, atrocious. Hence *~LY²* adv., *~NESS* n. [f. F *haineux* (*haine* hatred f. *haïr* hate, f. Goth. *hatjan*; see -OUS]

heir (ār), n. Person receiving or entitled to receive property or rank as legal representative of former owner; (fig.) one to whom something (joy, punishment, etc.) is morally due; *~ APPARENT; ~-at-law* (by right of blood); *~ in tail* (to entailed estate); *~ male*, male *~* tracing descent wholly through males; *~ PRESUMPTIVE*. Hence *~DOM, ~ESS¹, ~SHIP*, nn., *~LESS* a., (ār-). [OF. f. LL *herem* = L *heredem* (nom. *heres*)]

heir'loom (ār-), n. Chattel that follows devolution of real estate; piece of personal property that has been in family for generations (also fig. of qualities). [prec. +LOOM¹]

hejira. See HEGIRA.
held. See HOLD¹.

hel'iacal, a. (Astron.) relating to, near, the sun; *~ rising, setting*, first rising of a star after, last setting before, a period of invisibility due to conjunction with the sun. [f. Gk *hēliakos* (*hēlios* sun, see -AC) +-AL]

hēliăn'thus, n. Genus including common sunflower. [f. Gk *hēlios* sun +*anthos* flower]

hel'ical, a. Spiral. Hence or cogn. *~ally²* adv., *~OID, ~oid'AL, aa.* [as HELIX +-AL]

Hĕl'icon, n. Bootian mountain, sacred to Muses; source of poetic inspiration. So **Hĕlicōn'IAN** a. [L, f. Gk *Helikōn*]

hel'icopter, n. Flying-machine deriving both its lift and its propulsive power from horizontally revolving blades or rotors, and capable of ascending and descending vertically. [f. Gk *helix -ikos* screw, *pteron* wing]

hēl'iō, n. (colloq.). Abbr. of HELIOgram, *-graph*.

hēl'io- in comb.=Gk *hēlios* sun, as: *~cĕn'tric*, as viewed from centre of sun, taking sun as centre; *~chrōma*, photographic representation in natural colours; *~gram*, message by *~graph* (3); *~graph*, n., (1) engraving obtained by exposure to light, (2) apparatus for photographing sun, (3) signalling apparatus reflecting flashes of sunlight; *~graph*, v.t., send (message) by *~graph*, photograph by *~graphy*; *~graph'ic*, of *~graphy*; *~graphy* (-ŏgˀ-), description of the sun, engraving process, signalling by *~graph*; *~gravure*, photogravure; *~meter* (-ŏmˀ-), instrument for finding angular distance between two stars (orig. for measuring diameter of sun); *~scope*, apparatus for observing sun without injury to eye; *~thĕ'rapy*, use of sun-baths in treating disease; *~trōp'ic, ~tropism* (-ŏtˀ-), (of plants) turning, property of turning, in particular way under influence of light; *~type*, picture obtained from gelatine film exposed to light.

hēliolith'ic, a. Of the civilization characterized by megaliths & sun-worship. [f. HELIO-, after *eolithic* etc.]

hēliŏs'is, n. (Bot.) spots on leaves caused by concentration of sun's rays through glass etc.; sunstroke. [Gk *hēliōsis* (*hēlios* sun, see -OSIS]

hēl'iotrōpe, n. Plant with fragrant purple flowers; colour, scent, of these; bloodstone. [f. L. f. Gk *hēliotropion* plant turning flowers to the sun (*hēlios* sun +*tropos* f. *trepō* turn)]

hēl'ium, n. A colourless gas, inferred as existing in sun's atmosphere in 1868, first obtained in 1895. [f. Gk *hēlios* sun]

hēl'ix, n. (pl. *-cēs*). Spiral (like corkscrew, in one plane like watch-spring); (Archit.) spiral ornament; rim of external ear; genus including common snail. [Gk *helix*]

hell, n. Abode of the dead; abode of condemned spirits; place, state, of wicked-

ness or misery; *a* ~ *of a* (considerable) noise; den for captives in Prisoner's Base & other games; gaming-house; (in imprecations) ~*!, what the* ~ *do you want?*; *give* (a person) ~, make things hot for him; ~ *on*, desperately, extremely (often as mere intensive); ~*box* (printer's sl.), receptacle for refuse type; ~*cat*, spiteful or furious woman; ~*for leather*, at top riding-speed (usu. *ride* ~ *for leather*); ~*hound*, fiend; ~*weed*, name of various plants. Hence ~*ISH*¹ a., ~*ish=x*¹ adv., & ~*ishNESS* n. [OE *hell*(cf. Du. *hel*, G *hölle*, f. root *hel-* hide]

hel'lebore, n. Ancient name of various plants supposed to cure madness; (Bot.) species including Christmas Rose. [f. L f. Gk *helleboros*]

Hel'lene, n. Ancient Greek of genuine Greek race; subject of modern kingdom of Greece. So **Hellen'ic** a. [f. Gk *Hellēn*]

Hell'enism, n. Greek idiom or construction; imitation of the Greeks; Grecian culture; Greek nationality. So ~**IZE**(3) v.t. & i. [f. Gk *Hellēnismos* (as prec., see -ISM]

Hell'enist, n. One who used the Greek language but was not a Greek, whence ~**is'tic** a.; Greek scholar. [f. Gk *Hellēn-istēs* (as prec., see -IST]

hello, n. & v. = HALLO.

helm¹, n. (Arch.) helmet; (also ~*cloud*) cloud forming over mountain before or during storm. Hence ~**ED**² (-md) a. [com.-Teut.: OE, Du., G; f. *hel-* cover]

helm², n. & v.t. 1. Tiller, wheel, by which rudder is managed; space through which the ~ is turned, as *more, little,* ~; *down* (*with the*) ~, *up* (*with the*) ~, place ~ so as to bring rudder to windward, to leeward; *weather, lee,* ~, ~ put up, down; (fig.) government, guidance, (*take the* ~, assume control);~*s'man,* steersman. 2. v.t. Steer (usu. fig.). [vb 1 f. n.] OE *helma*, cf. ON *hjálm*]

hel'met, n. Defensive head-cover of soldiers, firemen, etc.; felt or pith hat for hot climates; upper part of retort; (Bot.) arched upper part of corolla in some flowers; shell of a genus of molluscs. Hence ~**ED**² a. [obs. F, dim. of *helme* HELM¹]

hel'minth, n. Worm (usu. intestinal), presence of ~s in the body, **hel'min'thic,** aa. ~**oi'ogy** n. [f. Gk *helmins -inthos* maw-worm]

he'lot, n. (*H*~) one of a class of serfs in ancient Sparta; serf; (fig.) drunken man as warning to Spartan youth); serf. Hence ~**ISM**(2), ~**RY**(1, 2), nn. ~**IZE**(3) v.t., taken as = inhabitant of *Helos, Heilōtēs* (pl. of *Heilōs,* Laconian town)]

help,¹ v.t. (~*ed*: arch. past *halp* & p.p. *holpen*). Aid, assist, as ~ *me, ~ me to lift it,*

~ *me to an answer, ~ the work on* or *forward, ~ me over the stile, ~ me out* (of a difficulty); ~ *person on, off, with coat* etc., ~ *him to put it on, take it off*; ~ (person) *to*, serve him with (food); distribute (food at meal); remedy, prevent, (*as it can't be ~ed,* I *can't ~ that, don't be longer than you can* (cannot); (w. neg.) *hoping that* ~; (in invocation or oath) *so ~ me God* (as I keep my word, as I speak the truth, etc.). [com.-Teut.: OE *helpan,* Du. *helpen,* G *helfen*]

help,² n. Assistance, as *we need your* ~, *she, it, is a great* ~, *by* ~ *of*; *domestic servant;* ‖ *lady* ~, assistant & companion to mistress of house; *mother's* ~, superior nursemaid; remedy or escape, as *there is no* ~ *for it*; helping (of food). Hence **help'ful,** a. (Of person or thing) useful, serviceable. Hence ~**LY**² adv., ~**NESS** n. [-FUL]

help'ing, n. In vbl senses, esp. portion of food served. [-ING¹]

help'less, a. Lacking help; unable to help oneself. Hence ~**LY**² adv., ~**NESS** n. [-LESS]

help'mate, n. Helpful companion or partner (usu. husband or wife). [HELP + MATE]

help'meet, n. = prec. [formed by misunderstanding of *Gen.* ii. 18, 20]

hel'ter-skel'ter, adv., a., & n. (In) disordered haste. [imit.]

helve, n. Handle of weapon or tool; *throw the* ~ *after the* HATCHET. [OE *hielfe,* cf. MDu. *helf, helve;* f. same root as HALTER]

Helve'tian (-shn), a. & n. Swiss. [f. L *Helvetius* + -AN]

hem,¹ n. Border, edge, of cloth etc., esp. border made by turning in edge & sewing it down. [OE, cf. NFris. *heam*]

hem,¹ v.t. (-mm-). Turn down & sew in edge of (cloth etc., or abs.); ~ *in, about, round,* enclose, confine. [f. prec.]

hem,² int., n., & v.i. 1. (Also *h'm*) int. calling attention or expressing hesitation. 2. n. Utterance of this. 3. v.i. (-mm-). Utter sound ~; clear throat, hesitate in speech. [imit.]

hematic etc. See **haem-.**

hemi-, pref. in wds f. Gk or in Gk elements, = half, affecting one half, etc., as ~*anō'psia,* half-blindness, *hem'icycle,* half-moon figure, ‖ ~*dēmisemiquaver,* half a demisemiquaver, ~*hed'ral* (Cryst.), having half proper number of planes, ~*metāb'ola,* insects undergoing incomplete metamorphosis, ~*plē'gia,* paralysis of one side. [Gk *hēmi-* = L *semi-*]

hem'isphere, n. Half sphere; half the celestial sphere, esp. as divided by the equinoctial or by the ecliptic; half the earth, containing (*Eastern* ~) Europe, Asia, & Africa, or (*Western* ~) America; half of brain. Hence **hemispher'ic,** **~al,** aa. [f. OF *emisphere* f. L f. Gk *hēmisphairion* (HEMI-, SPHERE]

earth as divided by equator; *Magdeburg* ~s, pair of brass ~s exhausted of air to show atmospheric pressure by their cohesion. Hence **hēmisphē′rĭc**(AL) a. [f. OF *emispere* f. Gk HEMI(*sphaira* SPHERE)]

hĕm′istich (-k), n. Half of line of verse. [f. LL f. Gk HEMI(*stikhion* f. *stikhos* verse)]

hĕm′lŏck, n. Poisonous umbelliferous plant, used as powerful sedative; poisonous potion got from this. [OE *hymlic(e)*, etym. dub.]

hemorrhage etc. See **haem~**.

hĕmp, n. Annual herbaceous plant, native of India; its cortical fibre, used for rope & stout fabrics; (joc.) rope for hanging; =BHANG, HASHISH; name of various other plants yielding fibre. Hence **hĕm′pen** a. [OE *henep*, cf. Du. *hennep*, G *hanf*; cogn. w. Gk *kannabis*]

hĕm′-stitch, v.t., & n. (Hem cloth etc. with) kind of ornamental stitch.

hen, n. Female of common domestic fowl (cf. COCK[1]); second element in name of other female birds, as *guinea-*~, *pea-*~; *like a* ~ *with one chicken*, absurdly fussy; ~ *& chickens*, name of a compound daisy & other plants; ~*bane*, narcotic & poisonous plant, drug got from this; ~*coop* (for keeping poultry in); ~ *crab*, *lobster*, female; ~*harrier*, blue hawk, a bird of prey (of women only); ~*pecked*, ~*party* (of women only); ~*roost*, place where fowls roost at night. [OE *henn* (fem. of *hana* cock), cf. Du. *hen*, G *henne*]

hence, adv. (Arch.) from here, from this, (often pleonast. *from* ~); (poet., rhet.) ~! go away, ~ *with*, away with, take away, *go* ~, die; ~*forth*, ~*forward*, from this time forward; *five years* ~, in five years' time from now; as a result from this; as an inference from this (~ *it appears that*), therefore. [ME *hennes*, *henne* adv. f. root of HE+-ES]

hench′man, n. 1. (Hist.) squire, page of Highland chief; attendant of Highland honour. 2. Chief attendant of Highland chief; trusty follower; political supporter. [14th c.; OE *heng(e)st* male horse, cf. Du. & G *hengst*, +MAN]

hĕn′dĕca- in comb. = Gk *hendeka* eleven, as *hendĕc′agon*, plane rectilineal figure of eleven sides; ~*syllăb′ic* a. & n., (verse) of eleven syllables; ~*syllăb′able*, such a verse (esp., in Latin: ─ (or ─) ─ ─ ─ ─ ─). [med.L, f. Gk *hen dia duoin* one thing by two]

Hĕn′don, n. Town in Middlesex associated with aviation. [place]

Hĕn′ley, n. (Used for) annual regatta at ~-on-Thames. [place]

hĕn′na, n. Egyptian privet; its shoots & leaves used as a dye for the body. [Arab. *hanna′*]

hĕnn′ỹ, a. & n. Hen-like; (n.) hen-like cock. [HEN+-Y[2]]

hĕn′othēïsm, n. Belief in one God without asserting that he is the only God (cf. MONOTHEISM). [f. Gk *heis henos* one +*theos* god +-ISM]

hĕpăt′ĭc, a. Of, good for, the liver; liver-hued. [f. L f. Gk *hēpatikos* (HEPATO-, -IC)]

hĕpatī′tis, n. Inflammation of the liver. [f. Gk *hēpatitis* (HEPATO-, -ITIS)]

hĕp′ato- in comb. = Gk *hēpar -atos* liver, as ~*genous* (-ŏj-), originating in the liver. [G. ~, d. 1786]

Hĕp′plewhite (-elwīt), n. A delicate style of furniture.

hĕp′ta- in comb. = Gk *hepta* seven, as: ~*chord*, 7-stringed instrument, 7-note scale; ~*glot* a. & n., (book) in seven languages; ~*gon*, plane rectilineal figure of seven sides, so ~*gonal* (-âg-) a.; ~*hĕd′ron* (-a-h-), solid of seven faces; ~*syllăb′ic*, of seven syllables; ~*teuch* (-k), first seven books of Bible.

hĕp′tad, n. Set, group, of seven. [f. Gk *heptas -ados* set of seven (*hepta*)]

hĕp′tárchy (-k-), n. Government by seven rulers; seven kingdoms of Angles & Saxons in Britain. So **hĕp′tarch′ĭc**(AL) (-k-) aa. [f. HEPTA- + Gk *-arkhia* government]

her[1], pron. Objective case of SHE: colloq. also subjective, as *Was that* ~? [OE *hire*, dat. of *hēo*, *heo*, SHE]

her[2], pron. & a. Possessive case of, & adj. correspg. to, SHE, with absolute form ~*s*, as *it is* ~*s*, *hat, it is* ~*s*, ~*s is best*, *my father & my* ~*s* *suffer*(*e*)*s for it*, ~ (vulg. ~*e*) *& my* (common) *father*, ~ (vulg. ~*s*) *& my* (respective) *father*(*s*). [OE *hĕ*(*e*)*re*, genitive as prec.]

hĕr′ald[1], n. 1. Officer who made State proclamations, bore messages between princes, officiated in the tourney, arranged various State ceremonials, regulated use of armorial bearings, settled questions of precedence, & recorded names & pedigrees of those entitled to armorial bearings; ||*H*~*s' College*, corporation (now) recording pedigrees & granting bearings. 2. Messenger (often as title of newspaper); forerunner. [f. OF *heraut*, prob. of Teut. orig.]

hĕr′ald[2], v.t. Proclaim the approach of; usher in. [f. OF *herauder* (as prec.)]

hĕrăl′dĭc, a. Of heraldry. [-IC]

hĕr′aldry, n. Science of a herald; CANT[3]. *ing* ~; armorial bearings; heraldic pomp. [-RY]

hĕrb, n. Plant whose stem is not woody or persistent; plant of which leaves etc. are used for food, medicine, scent, flavour, etc.; ~ *beer*, drink made from ~s; ~ *bennet*, yellow-flowered species of Avens [prob. f. OF *herbe beneïte*=L *herba bene-dicta* blessed herb]; ~*tea*, ~*water*, medi-

cinal infusion of herbs. So ~ACEOUS (-āshus; ~aceous border in gardens, one devoted to perennial flowering plants), ~IF'EROUS, ~IV'OROUS, ~LESS, aa. [f. OF erbe f. L herba grass]

herb'age, n. Herbs collectively; succulent parts of herbs; (Law) right of pasture on another's ground. [OF, f. med. L herbaticum (as prec., see -AGE)]

herb'al, a. & n. (Book with descriptions of herbs. [f. L herbalis (as prec., see -AL)]

herb'alist, n. One skilled in herbs (now of early botanical writers); dealer in medicinal herbs. [prec. +-IST]

herbā'rium, n. (Book, case, room, for) collection of dried plants. [LL (HERB, -ARIUM)]

herb'orize, v.i. Gather herbs, botanize. So ~IZA'TION, ~IST, nn. [f. F herboriser (herbe HERB, confused w. L arbor tree); correct forms herbalize, -arize, are arch.]

herb'y, a. Abounding in herbs; of the nature of a herb. [-Y²]

Hercū'lean (also -ū'ri̯an), a. Of Hercules; difficult as his labours. [f. L Herculeus (as foll.) +-AN]

Her'cŭlēs (-z), n. (Gk & Rom. Myth.) hero of prodigious strength, who performed 12 immense labours; Pillars of ~, rocks on either side of Strait of Gibraltar, (fig.) ultimate limit; strong man; ~ beetle (S. Amer. 5 in. long); a northern constellation; ~ powder, explosive used in mining. [L, f. Gk Hēraklēs]

herd¹, n. Company of animals, esp. cattle, feeding or travelling together; large number of people (derog.), esp. the, the common, the vulgar, ~; the ~ instinct, gregariousness & mutual influence as a psychological factor; ~-book, pedigree-book of cattle or pigs; ~s'man, keeper of ~s. [com.-Teut.: OE heord, G herde, Da. hjord]

herd², n. Keeper of herds, herdsman, esp. w. word prefixed, as cow~, swine~. [com.-Teut.: OE hirde, G hirte, Da. hyrde]

herd³, v.i. & t. Go in a herd (together, with others; esp. fig. of persons); tend (sheep, cattle). [f. HERD¹,²]

here, adv. & n. 1. In this place; (answering roll-call) ~, I am present; (calling attention to person's presence) may son ~ will show you; (in drinking healths) ~'s (a health) to; in this life (esp. ~ below) ~'s to this point (in discourse etc.); at this point (in discourse etc.); in this matter; to this place; look ~ (in this direction; esp. in bespeaking attention or making protest); I don't belong ~ (to this place); ~ & there, in various places; ~, there, & everywhere, all about; neither ~ nor there, not to the point, of no importance; (colloq., to announce commencement of bold act) ~ goes! 2. n. This place or point, as from, near ~, near, ~; 3. ~ (about's?), somewhere near ~; ~after, in future, later on, in the

4895

world to come, (n.) the future, the world to come; ~dit (arch.), at this; ~by', by this means, as a result; ~in', in this point, book, etc.; ~inaf'ter, below (in document etc.); ~inbefore', in a preceding part (of this document etc.); ~of' (arch.), of this; ~to' (arch.), to this matter; ~tofore', formerly; ~un'der, below (in book etc.); ~upon', after this, in consequence of this; ~with', with this (esp. of enclosure in letter etc.). [com.-Teut.: OE hér, cf. Du. & G hier; prob. f. HE]

here'dit'able, a. That may be inherited. So ~BIL'ITY n. [f. obs. F hereditable f. L hereditāre inherit (heres -edis heir), see -ABLE]

here'dit'ament (or hĭrěd'-), n. Property that can be inherited; real property; inheritance. [f. med. L hereditamentum (as prec., see -MENT)]

heredita'rian, n. One who holds the doctrine of heredity. [-ARIAN]

heredit'arily, a. Descending by inheritance; (of diseases, instincts, etc.) transmitted from one generation to another; like, in the same as, that one's parents had, as ~y creed, hatred; of, holding position by, inheritance. Hence ~Ly² adv., ~INESS n. [f. L hereditarius (as HEREDITY, see -ARY²)]

hered'ity, n. Tendency of like to beget like. Hence ~ISM(3) n. [f. F hérédité f. L hereditatem heirship (as HEIR, see -TY)]

Her'eford, n. (Used for) a breed of cattle originating in Herefordshire, England. [place]

her'esy, n. Opinion contrary to the orthodox doctrine of the Christian Church, or to the accepted doctrine on any subject. Hence heresiol'ogist, heresiol'ogy, nn. [f. OF eresie f. L +heresis f. Gk hairesis choice, sect (haireomai choose)]

her'etic, n. Holder of an unorthodox opinion (orig. in the matter of religion). So heret'ical a. [f. F hérétique f. eccl. L f. Gk hairetikos (as prec., see -IC)]

heret'rix. See HEIR.

her'iot, n. (law). Render of best live beast or dead chattel, or money payment, to lord on decease of tenant (now only of manorial tenures). [OE heregeatu (here army +geatwa trappings)]

her'itage, n. What is or may be inherited; (fig.) portion allotted to any one; (Bibl.) the ancient Israelites, the Church; inherited lot. [OF (as prec., see -AGE)]

her'itable, a. That passes to heirs-at-law (opp. to movable property); transmissible from parent to child; capable of inheriting. Hence ~LY² adv. [f. F héritable (hériter, see HEREDITARY)]

her'itor, n. One who inherits. [f. OF heritier (as HEREDITARY), assim. to wds in -OR]

herl, n. Var. of HARL(E)².

T

hermaph'rodite, n. & a. **1.** Human being, animal, combining characteristics of both sexes; (Zool.) animal having normally both male & female sexual organs, e.g. earth-worm; (Bot.) plant in which same flower has stamens & pistils; person, thing, combining opposite qualities; ship having characters of two kinds of craft. **2.** adj. Combining both sexes or opposite characteristics. Hence~it'ic(AL) aa., ~itism n. [f. L f. Gk *Hermaphroditos*, who became one with the nymph *Salmacis*]

hermēneu'tic, a. & n. Of interpretation: (n. pl.) interpretation, esp. of Scripture. So~AL a. [f. Gk *hermēneutikos* (*hermēneuō* interpret, see -IC)]

Hēr'mēs (-z), n. (Gk Myth.) son of Zeus & Maia, messenger of the gods, god of science, eloquence, etc.; ~ *Trismegistus* (Thrice-Great), Neo-platonist name of Egyptian god Thoth, as author of mysterious doctrines, secrets of alchemy, etc. [L f. Gk *Hermēs*]

hermet'ic, a. Of alchemy, as ~*ic art*; ~*ic seal*, air-tight closure by fusion etc. (also fig.), whence ~ICALLY adv. [f. med. L *hermeticus* irreg. f. HERMES *Trismegistus*]

herm'it, n. Early Christian recluse; person living in solitude; ~*crab*, kind that lives in mollusc's cast-off shell to protect its shell-less hinder parts. [f. OF *ermite* f. L (-*ta*) f. Gk *erēmitēs* (*erēmia* desert, see -TE¹)]

herm'itage, n. Hermit's abode; solitary abode; French wine from hill near Valence (with ruined ~ on top). [OF (as prec., see -AGE)]

hern. See HERON.

hern'ia, n. (path.). Rupture. Hence ~AL, ~ARY¹ aa., ~OT'OMY n. [L]

hern'shaw. See HERON (etym.).

hēr'ō, n. (pl. ~es). (Gk Ant.) man of superhuman qualities favoured by the gods, demigod; illustrious warrior, (rhet.) one who has fought for his country (*homes for ~es*, housing for ex-service men); man admired for achievements & noble qualities; chief man in poem, play, or story; ~*worship(per)*, worship(per) of the ancient ~es or of some great man or men. [f. L f. Gk *hērōs*]

hēro'ic, a. & n. **1.** (Of acts or qualities) of, fit for, a hero; (of persons) having the qualities of a hero; *the ~ age* (of Greece, before return from Troy); (of poetry) dealing with heroes; ~ *verse*, that used in ~ poetry (Gk & L hexameter, E five-foot iambic, F Alexandrine); (of language) grand, high-flown; bold, attempting great things. **2.** n. ~ verse; (n. pl.) high-flown language or sentiments. Hence hēro'ic-ALLY adv. [f. L f. Gk *hērōikos* (as prec., see -IC)]

hēro'i-cŏm'ic, a. Combining the heroic with the comic. [HERO+-I-+COMIC]

hēro'ify, v.t. Make a hero of. [as prec. + -FY]

hĕ'rŏin (or hirō'ĭn), n. A sedative drug prepared from morphine. [?]

hĕ'rŏine, n. Demigoddess; heroic woman; chief woman in poem, novel, etc. [f. L f. Gk *hērōinē*, fem. of *hērōs* HERO]

hĕ'rŏism, n. Heroic conduct or qualities. [f. F *héroïsme* (*héros* HERO, see -ISM)]

hĕ'rŏize, v.t. & i. Make a hero of; make heroic; play the hero. [-IZE]

hĕ'rŏn, hērn (poet. etc.), n. Long-legged wading bird. [f. OF *hairon* f. pop. L *hagironem* (nom. -*ro*) f. OHG *heiger*; OF dim. *heronceau* gives *heronsew*, -*shew*, -*shaw, hernshaw*, now dial.]

hĕ'rŏnry (-z), n. Place where herons breed. [-RY]

hĕr'pēs (-z), n. Skin disease, with patches of distinct vesicles. Hence **hĕrpĕt'ic** a. [L, f. Gk *herpēs, -ētos* shingles (*herpō* creep)]

hĕrpĕt(ŏl')ogў, n. Zoology of reptiles. So ~OL'OGIST n. [f. Gk *herpeton* reptile (*herpō* creep) + -LOGY]

Herr (här), n. (pl. *Herren*). German equivalent of *Mr*; German gentleman.

hē'rring, n. North Atlantic fish, much used for food, coming near coast in large shoals to spawn; *kippered ~*, = KIPPER, RED~; ~*bone*, stitch resembling bones of ~, (Archit.) zigzag arrangement of stones or tiles, (v.t.) work with ~*bone* stitch, mark with ~*bone* pattern; ~*pond*, (joc.) North Atlantic. [OE *hæring*, cf. Du. *haring*, G *hering*]

Herrn'huter (hărn'hŏō-), n. One of the sect of Moravians. [f. *Herrnhut*, their first German settlement]

hers. See HER.

hĕrsĕlf', pron. Emphatic & reflexive form corr. to SHE, as *she said it~, she has hurt ~, ask the woman ~; she is not ~* (in her normal state of body or mind). [OE *hire self*]

Hĕrt'zian, a. ~ *waves*, electric waves (so called from the discoveries of H. R. Hertz, German physicist, d. 1894); ~ *telegraphy*, wireless. [-IAN]

hĕs'itant (-z-), a. Hesitating; irresolute. So~ANCE, ~ANCY nn. [as foll., see -ANT]

hĕs'itāte (-z-), v.i. Show, speak with, indecision; scruple; be reluctant, (to do). Hence or cogn. ~ingLY² adv., hĕsitā'TION n., ~IVE a. (-z-). [f. L *haesitare* frequent. of *haerēre* haes- stick fast, see -ATE³]

Hĕspē'rian, a. (poet.). Western. [f. L f. Gk *Hesperios* (as HESPERUS)+-AN]

hĕs'peris, n. Genus including ROCKET¹ & Dame's Violet. [L, f. Gk *Hesperis* of evening, (of the West (as foll.)]

hĕsperŏrn'is, n. American genus of fossil birds. [as foll. + Gk *ornis* bird]

Hĕs'perus, n. Evening star. [L, f. Gk *hesperos* a. & n., western, evening (star)]

Hĕs'sian (-shn), a. & n. **1.** Of Hesse in Germany; ~ (*boot*), high boot first worn by ~ troops; ~ *fly*, fly whose larva de-

stro'ys wheat. 2. n. Strong coarse cloth of hemp or jute. [-IAN]

hest n. (arch.). Behest. [OE hǣs (hātan, see HIGHT), assim. to OE hn in -t]

hetae'ra (-tēra), **-ai'ra** (-īra), n. (pl. -rae, -rai). Courtesan, mistress. [Gk hetaira, fem. of hetairos companion]

hetae'rism(-ēr-), **-air'ism**(-īr-), n. Open concubinage; communal marriage in a tribe. [f.Gk hetairismos (as prec., see -ISM)]

he'tero- in comb. (before vowel heter-)= Gk heteros other, different, as: ~chōrī́mous, a. of different colours; ~gamous (-ŏg^h), irregular as regards stamens & pistils; ~graphy (-ŏg^h), incorrect or inconsistent spelling; ~morph'ism, diversity of form; ~morph'ic, ~morph'ous, of dissimilar form; etc.), subject to different laws (of growth etc.), subject to an external law (cf. AUTONOMOUS); ~nomous (-ŏn^), presence of a different law, subjection to external law; ~path'ic, = ALLOPATHIC, (also) differing in effect; ~phÿll'ous, bearing leaves of different forms on same plant; ~sexual a., relating to or characterized by the normal relation of the sexes (also as n.; opp. HOMOSEXUAL); ~taxy, abnormal disposition of organs or parts.

het'eroclite, a. & n. Irregularly declined; (n.) ~ noun. [f. F hétéroclite f. L f. Gk HETERO(klitos f. klinō inflect)]

het'erodox, a. (Of person or opinion) not orthodox. So ~y¹ n. [f. Gk HETERO(doxos (doxa opinion)]

het'erodyne, **-dÿning**, nn. Apparatus for, process of, converting a high-frequency wireless wave to one of an audible frequency by superposing another high-frequency wave of nearly the same period and so producing a pulsation. [HETERO-, Gk dunamis force]

heterogene'ous, a. Diverse in character; composed of diverse elements; (Math.) incommensurable because of different kinds. Hence or cogn. **heterogene'ITY**, ~NESS, nn. ~LY² adv. [f. scholastic L heterogeneus f. Gk HETERO(genēs f. genos kind)+-OUS]

heterogen'esis, n. Birth of a living being otherwise than from parent of same kind, esp. spontaneous generation from inorganic matter. So **heterogen'ETIC** a. [HETERO-]

heterozÿg'ote, n. (Mendelism). Zygote resulting from fusion of unlike gametes. So ~ous a. [HETERO-]

hett'man, n. Polish military commander (retained as title among Cossacks). [Polish]

heuris'tic (hūr-), a. & n. Serving to discover; ~ method, system of education under which the pupil is trained to find out things for himself, so ~s n. pl. [irreg. f. Gk heuriskō find, see -IC]

hew, v.t. & i. (p.p.~n or-ed). Chop, cut, (thing down, away, off, asunder, to pieces, etc.) with axe, sword, etc.; cut into shape; ~ one's way, make a way for oneself by ~ing; deal cutting blows at, among, etc. [com.-Teut.: OE hēawan, Du. houwen, G hauen]

hew'er, n. One who hews; man who cuts coal from seam; ~s of wood & drawers of water, drudges (Joshua ix. 21). [-ER¹]

hex'a- in comb. (before vowel, & in some mod. words before consonant, hex-)= Gk hex six, as: ~chord (-k-), diatonic series of six notes with semitone between third & fourth; ~gon, ~gonal (-ăg^h), (figure) having six sides; ~gram, figure formed by two intersecting equilateral triangles (the angular points coinciding with those of a ~gon), figure of six lines; ~hēd'ral (-a-h) a., ~hēd'ron (-a-h) n., (figure) having six faces; ~pod n. & a., (animal) with six feet; ~pody (-ăp^), line of verse of six feet; ~style & n., (portico) of six columns; ~syllab'ic; ~teuch (-k), first six books of Bible.

hex'ad, n. A six (uses as PENTAD). [f. Gk hexas -ados (hex six, -AD)]

hexam'eter, n. Line of six metrical feet, esp. dactylic ~ (five dactyls & trochee or spondee, any of first four feet, & rarely the fifth, being replaced by spondee). Hence **hexamĕt'ric** a., **hexam'etrist** n. [L, f. Gk HEXA(metros f. metron measure)]

hex'apla, n. Six-fold text in parallel columns, esp. of Old or New Testament. [Gk, neut. pl. of HEXA(ploos -fold)]

hey (hā), int. calling attention, or of joy, surprise, or interrogation; ~ for —! (expr. applause or exultant appreciation); ~ presto (conjuror's phrase of command, hence used to announce surprising transformation etc.). [ME, Du. G]

hey-day¹ (hā-), int. expr. joy, surprise, etc. [hey prob.: day unexpl.]

hey'day² (hā-), n. Full bloom, flush, (of youth, vigour, prosperity, etc.), [?]

hey'duck (hīˈdook), n. Hungarian of an ennobled military class; Polish liveried retainer. [f. Pol. hajduk: brigand]

hi, int. calling attention. [parallel form to HEY]

hiā'tus, n. (pl. ~es). Break, gap, esp. in a series, account, or chain of proof; break between two vowels coming together not in the same syllable. [L, vbl n. f. hiāre gape]

hib'ernāte, v.i. Spend the winter (of animals) in torpid state, (of persons) in mild climate; (fig.) remain inactive. So ~ANT a., ~ATION n. [f. L hibernāre (hibernus wintry), see -ATE³]

Hibēr'nian, a. & n. (Native) of Ireland. [f. L Hibernia Ireland, corrupt. of Iverna f. Gk Iernē f. OCelt. +Iverĭu, whence Erin: see -AN]

Hibēr'nicism, n. Irish idiom, expression, or bull. [as prec., on Anglicism etc.]

hibis'cus, n. Cultivated malvaceous plant or shrub; rose-mallow. [L f. Gk hibiskos marsh mallow]

hicc'up, n., & v.i. & t. Involuntary spasm of respiratory organs, with sudden closure of glottis & characteristic sound; (v.i.) make ~; (v.t.) say, bring out, with ~(s). [[vb f. n.) earlier *hicked*, imit.; *hiccough* due to pop. etym.]

hĭc jă'cĕt, n. Epitaph. [L, = here lies]

'hick, H~, n. (colloq.). Countryman, farmer, provincial. [?]

hick'ory, n. N.-Amer. tree allied to walnut, with tough heavy wood; wood, stick, of this. [f. native Virginian *pohickery*]

hid, hidden. See HIDE².

hĭdăl'gō, n. (pl. ~s). Spanish gentleman. [Sp., f. *hijo dalgo* (L *filius de aliquo*) son of something]

hide¹, n., & v.t. 1. Animal's skin, raw or dressed; (joc.) human skin, as *to save his own* ~; *~'bound*, (of cattle) with skin clinging close as result of bad feeding, (fig.) narrow-minded. 2. v.t. (colloq.). Flog. Hence (-)**hid'ED²** a. [OE *hȳd*, cf. Du. *huid*, G *haut*, & L *cutis*, Gk *kutos*]

hide², v.t. & i. (past *hĭd*, p.p. *hĭdden*, *hĭd*), & n. 1. Put, keep, out of sight (~ *one's light under a* BUSHEL); keep (fact) secret (*from*); keep (thing) from view without that intention; ~ *one's head*, keep out of sight from shame etc.; (intr.) conceal oneself; *~-&-seek*, children's game (also fig. of dealings with evasive person or thing). 2. n. Place of concealment used in observation of wild animals; *~-out* (colloq.), hiding-place. [OE *hȳdan*, cf. MDu. *hūden*; cogn. w. Gk *keuthō*]

hide³, n. (hist.). Measure of land, as much as would support one free family & dependants (perh. about 120 acres). [OE *hīd*, *hīgid* (*hīw-* household)]

hid'eous, a. Frightful, repulsive, revolting, to senses or mind, as ~ *crime, noise, pattern*. Hence ~**LY²** adv., ~**NESS** n. [f. OF *hidos* (*hisde* fear, etym. dub., -OUS]

hid'ing¹, n. Thrashing. [f. HIDE² +-ING¹]

hid'ing², n. In vbl senses of HIDE², esp.: *be in* ~, remain hidden; *~-place*, place of concealment. [-ING¹]

hie, v.i. (poet.). Go quickly (*to* etc.); (with pers. pron. used reflexively, orig. dat.) ~ *thee, he ~d him*. [OE *hīgian* strive, pant, cf. Du. *hijgen*, G *heichen*]

hi'erarch (-k), n. Chief priest; archbishop. [f. med. L (-*cha*) f. Gk *hierarkhēs* (*hieros* sacred +*arkhēs* ruler)]

hi'erarchy (-k), n. Each of three divisions of angels; the angels; priestly government; organized priesthood in successive grades; any graded organization. Hence **hierãrch'IC(AL)** aa., **hi'erãrchISM**(3) n. (-k-). [f. OF *ierarchie* f. LL (*ier-*) f. Gk *hierarkhia* (as prec.)]

hierăt'ic, a. Of the priests (esp. of ancient Egyptian writing, & of Egyptian & Greek traditional styles of art); priestly. [f. L f. Gk *hieratikos* f. *hieraomai* be a priest (*hiereus*). -IC]

hiero- in comb.= Gk *hieros* sacred, holy, as: ~*cracy* (-ŏk-), priestly rule; ~*gram*, ~*graph*, (hi²) sacred inscription or symbol; ~*latry* (-ŏl-), worship of saints; ~*logy* (-ŏl-), sacred literature or lore.

hi'eroglyph, n. Figure of an object standing for a word, syllable, or sound, as used in ancient Egyptian & other writing; writing of this kind; secret symbol; writing difficult to make out. [f. foll.]

hieroglyph'ic, a. & n. 1. Of, written in, hieroglyphs; symbolical. 2. n. pl. Hieroglyphs. Hence ~**AL²a.**, ~**ALLY²adv.** [f. LL f. Gk HIERO(*gluphikos* f. *gluphē* carving, see -IC)]

hi'erophant, n. (Gk Ant.) initiating priest; expounder of sacred mysteries. Hence **hierophăn'tic** a. [f. LL f. Gk HIERO(*phantēs* f. *phainō* show)]

hig'gle, v.i. Dispute about terms; chaffer. [prob. conn. w. HAGGLE]

high (hi), a., n., & adv. 1. Of great or specified upward extent, as *a* ~ *hill, one inch* ~; situated far above ground, sea level, etc.; upper, inland, as *H~ Asia, H~ Dutch, German*; (of physical actions) extending to or from, performed at, a height, as ~ *jump*, ~ *flying*; of exalted rank; *the Most H~*, God; of exalted quality, as ~ *art*, ~ *minds*; *spirit* (courageous, enterprising; *a* ~ (very favourable) *opinion of*; ~ *life*, that of the upper classes); (luxurious) *feeding*; (of meat or game) slightly tainted; great, intense, extreme, as *in* ~ *favour*, ~ *pressure*, ~ *temperature*; *how is that for* ~? (sl. appeal to wonder); ~ *latitude* (far from equator); ~ *colour*, (esp.) red complexion, flush, blush; (angry) words; extreme in pitch, shrill; ~ (angry) *words*; extreme in opinion, as *a* ~ *Tory*; ~ (elated, hilarious) *spirits*; ~ *& dry*, (of ship) out of the water, (fig.) out of the current of events, of the old High Church before the Oxford movement; (of officers etc.) chief, as *H~ Admiral, Chancellor*; *with a* ~ HAND; *on the* ~ HORSE; ~ *& low*, (people) of all conditions, (adv.) everywhere (esp. *search* ~ *& low*); ~ *& mighty*, arrogant; *on the* ~ *ropes*, (colloq.) elated, disdainful, enraged. **2.** n. A ~ level or figure; the *~est card dealt or drawn*; *from on* ~, from heaven or *a* ~ *place*; *on* ~, in or to heaven or *a* ~ *place*; *the H~* (colloq.), H~ Street, esp. at Oxford. **3.** adv. Far up, aloft; in, to, *a* ~ *degree*; *at a* ~ *price*; (of sounds) at, to, *a* ~ *pitch*; *play* ~, *play for* ~ stakes, play card of ~ value; *run* ~, (of sea) have strong current with ~ tide; (also fig. of feelings). **4.** ~ (chief) *altar*; *~'ball*, a whisky-and-soda served in a tall glass; *~-blower*, horse that flaps nostrils noisily; *~'brow*, & n. (colloq.), (person) of detached intellectual

or cultural interests (~-*browed*, *of ~-brow kind*); **H~ Church** n. & a. (party, principles) giving a ~ place to authority of Episcopate and priesthood, saving grace of sacraments, etc.; **H~-Churchman** holder of these principles; **~(er) command**, the commander-in-chief of an army and his staff; ‖ **H~ Court**, supreme court (usu. has ~*flown notions*); **~flying**, (fig.) ambitious; **~ FREQUENCY**; **~-handed**, overbearing, arbitrary; **~-hat**, (n.) person affecting superiority, (v.t.) treat superciliously, (v.i.) assume a superior attitude; **~ JINKS**; **~lands**, mountainous or elevated country, esp. (Sc. pron. hēī'ǎnts) N. part of Scotland; **High'lander**, inhabitant of the (Scottish) ~lands; **~ light**, (of paintings etc.) any of the brightest parts of the subject or its representation (often pl.); **~-lows** (arch.), boots reaching over ankles; **~ MASS**; **~-minded**, of morally lofty character, (arch.) proud (*Lord, I am not ~-minded*); **~-mindedness**, one of these qualities; **~-pitched**, (of sound) acute in pitch, (of roof etc.) steep, (fig.) of lofty character; **~ priest**, chief priest, esp. of the Jews; **~ priori road**, resort to assumption (see A PRIORI) in preference to reasoning; **~ road**, main road; **~ school** (for secondary education); **~ SEAS**; **~-spirited**, of lofty or courageous spirit, in ~ state of vigour or sensitiveness; ‖ **H~ Street**, (often proper name of) principal street in town, at Oxford usu. *the H~*); **~ table** (for the fellows of college, colloq. *the ~ table*); **~ tea**, tea at which meat is served; **~ TIDE**; **~ TREASON**; **~ water**, state of tide when water is ~est, time when tide is at the full; **~-water mark**, level reached at fluctuation; **~ways**, public road (often *the king's ~way*), main route by land or water, (fig.) ordinary direct course of action etc.; **~-wayman**, man (usu. mounted, cf. FOOTpad) who robs passengers on ~way; **~WING** [com.-Teut.: OE *hēah*, Du. *hoog*, G *hoch*]

high'ly (hīl-), adv. In a high degree, as ~ *amusing*, ~*polished*, *command*, *esteem*, *favourably*, as *think*, *speak*, *of*; ~*-descended* (of noble parentage). [OE *héahlíce* (as prec., see -LY[2])]

high'ness (hin-), n. Title of various British and other princes etc., as *His* & *Her*, (*Royal*, *Serene*, *Imperial*) *H~*; (used where height is not idiomatic) *the ~ of his character*, *of taxation*, *fell from sheer ~ of* (but *reached the height of his*) *ambition*. [OE *héhnes* (as HIGH, see -NESS)]

hight (hīt), p.p. (arch., poet., joc.), Called, named. [Ireg. p.p. of OE *hātan*, com.-Teut., cf. Du. *heeten*, G *heissen*]

hijra. = HEGIRA.

'hi'jacker, etc. (sl.). Person who preys on bootleggers, appropriating & profiting by their illicit liquor. [?]

hike, n., & v.i. & t. (colloq.). 1. Long tramp in the country undertaken for pleasure or exercise. 2. v. Walk vigorously or laboriously; go for long tramp; hoist, shove, force to move. Hence **hīk'ER[1]** n. [etym. dub.]

hilar'ious, a. Mirthful, joyous. Hence or cogn. ~LY[2] adv., ~NESS, **hilă'rı̆TY**, nn. [f. L *hilaris* + -OUS]

‖ **Hil'ary,** n. ~ term, legal or university term beginning in Jan. [*Hilarius*, d. 367, w. festival 13 Jan.]

hill, n., & v.t. Natural elevation of earth's surface, small mountain; *the ~s* (Anglo-Ind.), a ~-*station* as health-resort etc.; heap, mound, however raised, as *ant-*, *dung-*, *mole-*, ~; (v.t.) form into ~, bank up (plants) with soil. Hence ~y[3] a., ~iNESS n. [(vrb f. n.) OE *hyll*, cf. MDu. ~, *hil*, *hil*; also L *collis* hill, *celsus* high, *culmen* top]

hill'ŏck, n. Small hill or mound. [-OCK]

hilt, n., & v.t. Handle of sword or dagger; *up to the ~*, completely; (v.t.) furnish with ~. [(vrb f. n.) OE & MDu.]

hil'um, n. (bot.; pl. -la). Point of attachment of seed to seed-vessel. [L, = little thing, trifle]

him, pron. Objective case of HE; colloq. also subjective, esp. after *than*, as *that's ~, you are worse than ~*. [OE, dat. of HE & M]

himself', pron. Emphatic & reflexive form corr. to HE, as *he did it*, ~ *I saw the man* ~; *he is not* ~ (not in his normal state of body or mind). [HIM + SELF]

hind[1], n. Female of (esp. red) deer, esp. in pairs, front & back, as ~ *leg*, *quarters*, and after third year. [OE, cf. Du. & G *hinde*]

hind[2], n. Farm servant, esp. (in Scotland & northern England) married & skilled farm-workman, having charge of two horses, & provided with cottage on the farm; steward; rustic, boor. [ME *hine*, prob. f. OE *hīna*, *hīgna*, genit. pl. of *hīgan*, *hīwan*, domestics]

hind[3], a. Situated at the back, posterior, (less usn. than *hinder* exc. of things in *wheel*). [ME, perh. back formation f. OE *hinder* adv.; = Goth. *hindar*, back formation of *behindan* BEHIND]

hind'er[1], a. See prec.

hin'der[2], v.t. Impede, obstruct, prevent, as *you will ~ him*, ~ *his work*, ~ *me*

completion, ~ *him from working* (or abs.). [OE *hindrian*, cf. G *hindern*; f. *hindar* adv., see HIND³]

Hin′di (-ē), a. & n. (Aryan vernacular language) of N. India. [Hind. (*hind* India)]

hind′most, a. Furthest behind; most remote. [HIND³]

hin′drance, n. Obstruction, prevention; obstacle. [f. HINDER² + -ANCE]

Hindu′ (-dōō), **-dŏŏ′**, (or hǐ⁴), n. & a. **1.** Aryan of N. India who (also, any one who) professes Hinduism. **2.** adj. Of the ~s, that is a ~; (loosely) Indian. [Pers., f. *hind* India = Skr. *Sindhu* river (esp. the Indus)]

Hin′duism (-ōō-), **-dŏŏism**, n. Polytheistic religion of the Hindus. [-ISM]

Hin′duize (-ōō-), **-dŏŏize**, v.t. Render Hindu in religion, customs, etc. [-IZE]

Hindusta′ni, **-doosta′nee**, (-ōŏstahnē) a. & n. **1.** Of Hindustan. **2.** n. Hindu, Mohammedan, of Upper India; language of Mohammedan conquerors of Hindustan, Urdu (Hindi mixed with Arabic, Persian, etc.). [Pers. (-ĭ), = of *Hindustan* country of the Hindus (HINDU + *stan* place)]

hinge (-j), n., & v.t. & i. **1.** Movable joint or mechanism like that by which door is hung on side post; natural joint doing similar work, as that of bivalve shell; *off the* ~*s*, in disordered state of body or mind; (fig.) central principle, critical point, on which all turns. **2.** v.t. Attach (as) with ~. **3.** v.i. ~ *on* (post, principle, etc.), hang & turn *on* (post, principle, etc.). Hence **hinge**D² (-jd), ~′LESS (-jl-), aa. [(vb f. n.) ME *henge*, cf. Du. *henghe*, conn. w. HANG]

hinn′y¹, n. Offspring of she-ass by stallion, cf. MULE¹. [f. L *hinnus*, cf. Gk *hinnos, ginnos*]

‖ hinn′y², **-nie**. See HONEY.

hint, n., & v.t. & i. **1.** Slight indication, covert or indirect suggestion. **2.** v.t. Suggest slightly (thing, *that*). **3.** v.i. ~ *at*, give a ~ of. [(vb f. n.) prob. f. obs. *hent* lay hold of, etym. dub.]

hin′terland, n. District behind coast or river's banks. [G]

hip¹, n. Projection of pelvis & upper part of thigh-bone, in men & quadrupeds; *have* (person) *on the* ~ (at a disadvantage); *smite* ~ *& thigh* (unsparingly); (Archit.) arris of roof from ridge to eaves; ~*-bath* (in which one sits immersed to the ~s); ~*-disease* (of ~*-joint*, with fungous growth); ~*-roof* (with ends as well as sides inclined). Hence (-)**hip**PED² (-pt) a. [OE *hype, hēpe*, n. Fruit of (esp. wild) rose. [OE *hēope, hīope*, cf. OHG *hiufo, hiafo*]

hip³, **hўp**, n. Morbid depression, the blues. [= *hyp*(*ochondria*)]

hip⁴, v.t. (-pp-). Make low-spirited. [f. prec.]

hip⁵, int. introducing united cheer, as ~, ~, *hurrah*.

hipe, v.t., & n. Throw (antagonist in wrestling) in a particular manner; (n.) such throw. [?]

hipp′o, n. (colloq.; pl. ~**s**). Hippopotamus. [abbr.]

hippo- in comb. = Gk *hippos* horse, as: ~*cen′taur*, = CENTAUR; ~*phagy* (-ŏf-), practice of eating horse-flesh; ~PHIL (hĭ⁴) ~PHOB′IA.

hippocăm′pus, n. (pl. **-pī**). Genus of small fishes, sea-horse; (Anat.) ~ *major*, ~ *minor*, eminences on floor of each lateral ventricle of brain. [f. LL f. Gk HIPPO-(*kampos* sea-monster)]

hippo′cras, n. (hist.). Wine flavoured with spices. [f. OF *ipocras* f. *Hippokratēs* Gk physician of 5th c. B.C., prob. because strained through filter called *Hippocrates's sleeve*]

Hipp′ocrēne, n. Fountain on Mount Helicon sacred to the Muses. [L f. Gk (*hippos* horse, *krēnē* fountain, as having been produced by stroke of Pegasus's hoof)]

hipp′odrome, n. (Gk & Rom., Ant.) course for chariot races etc.; circus; (*H*~) theatre for various stage entertainments. [F, f. L f. Gk HIPPO(*dromos* race, course)]

hipp′ogriph, -grўph, n. Fabulous griffin-like creature with body of horse. [f. F *hippogriffe* f. It. *ippogrifo* (HIPPO- + *grifo* GRIFFIN)]

hippopot′amus, n. (pl. **-muses, -mī**). Large African pachydermatous quadruped inhabiting rivers etc. [f. LL f. Gk HIPPO(*potamos* river)]

hīr′cine, a. Goat-like. [f. L *hircīnus* (*hircus* goat, see -INE¹)]

hīre¹, n. Payment by contract for use of thing or for personal service; engagement on these terms; (fig.) reward; ‖ ~*-purchase*, ~ *system*, (by which hired thing becomes hirer's after certain number of payments); *on* ~, ready to be hired. [OE *hўr*, cf. Du. *huur*, G *heuer*]

hīre², v.t. Employ (person) for wages; procure, grant (also ~ *out*), temporary use of (thing) for stipulated payment. Hence **hīr**′ABLE a., **hīr**′ER¹, nn. [OE *hўrian*, cf. Du. *huren*, G *heuern*]

hīre′ling (hīrl-), n. One who serves for hire (usu. derog.). [OE *hўrling* (as HIRE¹, see -LING¹)]

hīrs′ūte, a. Hairy, shaggy; untrimmed. Hence ~NESS (-tn-) n. [f. L *hirsūtus*, cf. *hirtus* shaggy]

his (hiz), a. & pron. Possessive case of, & adj. corr. to, HE, also in absolute use, as ~ *hat, it is* ~. [OE, genit. of HE & IT]

his′pid, a. (bot., zool.). Shaggy; bristly. [f. L *hispidus*]

hiss, v.i. & t., & n. (Of person, snake, goose, liquid poured on fire, etc.) (make) sharp spirant sound of s, esp. as sign of

disapproval or derision; express disapproval of (person etc.); thus; ~ off (the stage) angrily, away, down, etc., drive off etc. by ~es; utter (quoted words) with angry ~. [imit.]

hist, int. used to call attention, enjoin silence, or incite dog etc.

histo- in comb. = Gk *histos* web, tissue, in biol. wds, as; ~*gen*esis, ~*gen*y (-ŏj·), production of organic tissues; ~*gen*ĕt·ic, science of organic tissues, whence ~*lŏgy* (-ŏl·), ~*lŏgist* (-ŏl·).

histō'rian, n. Writer of history (esp. in higher sense, as opp. to mere annalist or compiler). [f. F *historien* f. L as HISTORY]

histō'ric, a. Noted in history; (Lat. & Gk Gram.) ~ *tenses*, those normally used of past events (cf. PRIMARY), ~ *present* (used for past), ~ *infinitive* (used for indicative); = foll. [f. L f. Gk *historikos* (as HISTORY, see -ATE²]

histō'riated, a. (Of ornamental letters etc.) decorated with figures of men or animals. [f. med. L *historiare*(as HISTORY, see -ATE²]

histō'rical, a. Of history, as ~ *evidence*, *legend*; ~ *method* (of investigation), that based on history's in connexion with history, from the historian's point of view (of *purely* ~ *interest*); belonging to the past, not of the present; (of novel, picture, etc.) dealing with ~ *events*; = prec. Hence ~LY² adv. [-AL]

historī'city, n. Historical character, genuineness, of alleged event etc. [-ITY]

historiŏg'rapher, n. Writer of history, esp. official historian of a court etc. [f. L & n. [-ER¹]

historiŏg'raphy, n. Writing of history. Hence **historiŏgrăph'ic**(AL) aa. [f. Gk *historiographia* (as foll. See -GRAPHY]

his'tory, n. Continuous methodical record of public events; (no pl.) study of growth of nations; whole train of events connected with nation, person, thing, etc.; eventful past career, as *this knife has a* ~; (no pl.) aggregate of past events, course of human affairs; *ancient* ~ (usu. to A.D. 476), (joc.) thing that is out of date; *mediÆval*, *modern*, ~ (to, from, 15th c.); systematic account of natural phenomena etc., esp. NATURAL¹ ~; *historical play*. [f. L f. Gk *historia* inquiry, ~, (*histŏr* learned man f. id- know]

his'trion, n. Stage-player (usu. derog.). [f. F, f. L *histrionem* (nom. -io)]

histriŏn'ic, a. & n. 1. Of actors or acting; stagy, hypocritical. [f. L *histrionicus*, (-ion.; n. 2. n. pl. Theatricals, theatrical art, pretence. Hence ~ICALLY adv. [f. L *histrionicus* (as prec., see -IC)]

hit, v.t. & i. (*hit*). Strike with blow or

missile; direct blow *at*; (of moving body) strike; (intr.) strike *against*, *upon*; de-liver (blow, person etc. a blow); (fig.) affect sensibly, wound, as *hard* ~ (e.g. by money losses); (also ~ *upon*) light upon, get at, (thing aimed at); (also ~ *off*) imitate to a nicety; fall in with, suit; ~ *below the belt*, play foul in boxing & fig.; ~ *the* (*right*) *nail on the head*, guess right, express the exact truth; ~ *it off*, agree (*with*, *together*); ~ *out*, deal vigorous blows; ~ *up* (Cricket), score, make (runs). [OE *hyttan*, cf. Sw. *hitta*, Da. *hitte*]

hit², n. Blow, stroke; stroke of sarcasm etc. (*at*); stroke of good luck; successful attempt. [f. prec.]

hitch¹, v.t. & i. 1. Move (thing) with jerk; ~ *up*, lift with jerk; contrive to bring (thing *into* story etc.); fasten with loop, hook, etc.; become so fastened (*in*, *on to*, etc.); ~ *one's WAGGON to a star*; ~ *hike* v.i., & n., travel by begging lifts from passing motor vehicles. [?]

hitch², n. Jerk, abrupt pull or push; (Naut.) noose, knot, of various kinds, as *half* ~ (formed by passing end of rope round its standing part & then through the bight); temporary stoppage; impediment. [f. prec.]

hith'er (-dh-), adv. & a. 1. To, towards, this place (now usu. *here*); ~ *& thither*, in various directions, here & there. 2. adj. Situated on this side, *the nearer* (of two). 3. ~*to* (-tŏŏ), up to this time; ~*ward* (arch.), in this direction. [OE *hider*, f. stem of HE, HERE, +suf. seen in L *citra* on this side)

Hit'lerism, n. The political system, aims, or methods of the German Fuehrer, Adolf Hitler (1889–1945). So ~ITE¹(I) a.

hive, n. & v.t. & i. 1.(Also *bee*~)artificial habitation for bees; (fig.) busy swarming place; ~*ful* of bees; swarming multitude; ~-shaped thing. 2. v.t. Place (bees) in ~, house (persons etc.) snugly, hoard up; (v.i.) enter ~, live together like bees. [OE *hÿf*, prob. conn. w. ON *hÿfr* hull & L *cupa* tub]

hives (-vz), n. pl. Skin eruption; inflammation of bowels, larynx, etc. [?]

h'm, int. [HEM³ HUM²]

hō, int. expr. surprise, admiration, triumph, derision; calling attention; added to other intt. as *heigh-ho*, *what ho*, or *westward ho*. [Nat.) to name of destination etc., as *westward ho*. [not in OE]

hoar, (hôr), a. & n. 1. Grey-haired with age; greyish white; ~*frost*, white frost, frozen dew; (of things) grey with age; ||~*stone*, ancient boundary stone. 2. n. Hoariness, ~frost. [OE *hár*, cf. OHG *hêr* old, G *hehr* august]

hoard (hôrd), n. & v.t. & i. 1. Stock, store, (esp. of money) laid by; amassed stock of facts etc. 2. v.t. Amass (money etc. or abs.) & put away, store up; treasure up

in the heart; (v.i.) overstock oneself with food etc. in war-time. [(vb OE *hordian*) OE *hord*, cf. OS *hord*, Goth. *huzd*, treasure]

‖ **hoard'ing** (hōr-), n. Fence of boards round building during erection or repairs, often used for posting bills. [f. obs. *hoard* ult. f. OF *hurt* f. OHG *hurt* hurdle, +-ING²]

hoarhound. See HOREHOUND.

hoarse (hōrs), a. (Of voice) rough, husky, croaking; having such a voice. Hence ~LY² (-sl-) adv., hoars EN⁶ v.t. & i., ~NESS(-sn-) n. [OE *hās*, +*hārs*, ME *hōrs*, cf. MDu. *hees*]

hoar'|y̆ (hōr-), a. (Of hair) grey, white, with age; having such air, venerable; (Bot., Entom.) covered with short white hairs. Hence ~INESS n. [-Y²]

hoax, v.t., & n. 1. Deceive, take in, (person) by way of joke. 2. n. Humorous or mischievous deception. [f. 18th c.; perh. conn. w. HOCUS]

hŏb, n. Side casting of fireplace, having surface level with top of grate; peg, pin, as mark in quoits etc.; ‖ shoe of sledge; = HOBNAIL. [?]

hŏb'ble¹, v.i. & t. Walk lamely, limp; (fig.) proceed haltingly in action or speech; (of verse) have halting rhythm; cause to ~; tie together legs of (horse etc.) to prevent it from straying etc.; the (legs) thus. [14th c.; prob. cogn. w. Du. *hobbelen* rock from side to side, stammer]

hŏb'ble², n. Uneven or infirm gait; awkward situation; rope, clog, etc., for hobbling horse etc.; ~ *skirt* (so narrow at foot as to impede wearer in walking). [f. prec.]

hŏb'bledĕ|**hoy'** (-bĕldĭ-), **hŏbbăd-, hŏb-bĕd-,** n. Awkward youth, between boyhood & manhood. Hence ~hoy'HOOD, ~hoy'ISM, nn., ~hoy'ISH¹ a., (-bĕldĭ-). [?]

hŏb'b|**y̆¹,** n. Favourite subject or occupation that is not one's main business; (arch.) small horse; (hist.) early type of velocipede. [f. OF *hobin, hobi*, prob. var. of name *Robin*]

hŏb'b|**y̆²,** n. A small falcon. [f. OF *hobel*]

hŏb'b|**y̆-hôrse,** n. Wicker horse used in morris-dance etc.; child's stick with horse's head; rocking-horse; horse on merry-go-round; (now rare) =HOBBY¹.

hŏb'gŏblin, n. Mischievous imp; bogy; bugbear. [f. *hob* for *Rob(in)*+GOBLIN]

hŏb'nail, n. Heavy-headed nail for boot-soles. [HOB]

hŏb'nailed (-ld), a. Furnished or set with hobnails; ~ *liver* (studded with projections like nail-heads). [-ED²]

hŏb'|**nŏb,** (-bb-). Drink together; hold familiar intercourse (with). [f. *hob* or *nob*=give & take, earlier *hab nab*, perh. =have or not have]

*hŏb'ō, n. (pl. ~s). Wandering workman or tramp. [?]

Hŏb'son's choice. See CHOICE¹. [person]

hŏck¹, n. Joint of quadruped's hind-leg between true knee & fetlock. [southern by-form of HOUGH]

hŏck², n. German white wine (prop. that of Hochheim). [earlier *hockamore* f. G *Hochheimer*]

hŏck³, v.t., & n. (sl.). Pawn, pledge; *in* ~, in pawn, in prison, or in debt. [f. Du. *hok* in sl. sense of debt]

hŏck'ey, n. Game played with ball (or puck in *ice* ~) & curved clubs between goals. [?]

Hŏck'-tide, n. (hist.). Old festival kept on second Monday and Tuesday after Easter. [etym. of first element dub.]

hŏc'us, v.t. (-ss-). Take in, hoax; stupefy (person) with drugs; drug (liquor). [f. obs. n. *hocus*=foll.]

hŏc'us-pŏc'us, n., & v.i. & t. (-ss-). Jugglery, deception; typical conjuring formula; (v.i.) juggle; (v.t.) play tricks on. [17th-c. sham L]

hŏd, n. Builder's light open trough on staff for carrying mortar etc.; ~'*man*, labourer who carries ~, (fig.) mechanical worker, literary hack. [prob.=obs. *hot* f. OF *hotte* panier, f. G orig.]

‖ **hŏdd'en,** n. (Sc.). Coarse woollen cloth; ~ *grey*, grey ~, typical rustic garb. [?]

‖ **Hŏdge,** n. Typical English agricultural labourer. [changed from *Roger*]

hŏdge-pŏdge, n. = HOTCH-POTCH. [assim. to prec.]

hŏdiĕrn'al, a. Of the present day. [f. L *hodiernus (hodie* to-day) +-AL]

hŏdŏm'ĕter, ŏd-, n. Instrument for measuring distance travelled by wheeled vehicle. [f. Gk *hodos* way, see -METER]

hŏe, n., & v.t. & 1. 1. Tool for loosening soil, scraping up weeds, etc.; *Dutch* ~, kind pushed forward by user. 2. v.t. Weed (crops), loosen (ground), dig *up*, cut *down*, with ~; (v.i.) use ~. [f. OF *houe* f. OHG *houwâ (houwan* HEW)]

hŏg¹, n. Swine, esp. castrated male reared for slaughter; ‖ (dial.) young sheep before first shearing; (fig.) coarse, gluttonous, or filthy person; =ROAD¹-~; *go the whole* ~, do the thing thoroughly; ~'*back, ~'s-back,* crested hill-ridge; ~-*fish,* fish with bristles on head; ~ *in armour,* stiff clumsy person; ~ *mane,* horse's mane cut short; ~'s *pudding,* ~'s entrail variously stuffed; ~-*wash,* kitchen swill etc. for ~s. Hence ~g'ISH¹ (-g-), ~'LIKE, aa., ~'g'ish-IY² adv., ~g'ishNESS, ~'LING¹, nn. [ME, etym. dub.]

hŏg², v.t. & i. (-gg-). Raise (back etc.), rise, archwise in the centre; cut (mane) short; (colloq.) behave like a road-hog. [f. prec.]

‖ **hŏgg'ĕt (-g-),** n. Yearling sheep. [HOG¹ +-ET¹]

‖ **hŏg'manay,** n. (Sc.). Last day of year; gift of cake etc. demanded by children on that day. [f. OF *aguillanneuf* (mod. Norman *hoguinettes,* Guernsey *hoginano*)

etym. dub., prob. containing *l'am neuf* the new year]

hogs'head (-z-hĕd), n. Large cask; liquid measure, 52½ imperial gallons (abbr. *hhd*). [f. HOG¹ (unexpl.) + HEAD]

hoic(k, v.t. & i. Force (aeroplane) to turn abruptly upwards; ~ aeroplane. [cf. dial. *hike* swing, toss]

hoick(s), int. used to incite hounds (also *yoicks*). [?]

hoi polloi. See POLLOI.

hoist¹, v.t., & n. 1. Raise aloft (esp. flags); raise by means of tackle etc. 2. n. ~ing, shove up; elevator, lift. [f. (n.t. vb) corrupt. of obs. *hoise*, earlier *hysse*, cf. Du. *hisse*, Du. *hijschen*, F. *hisser*, etym. dub.]

hoist², p.p. ~ *with his own petard*, blown up by his own bomb, ruined by his own devices against others. [p.p. of *hoise*, see prec.]

hoit'y-toit'y, n., a., & int. 1. n. (now rare). Riotous or giddy conduct. 2. adj. Frolicsome; haughty; petulant. 3. int. expr. surprised protest at undue assumption etc. [prob. f. obs. *hoit* v. romp, etym. dub.]

hok'ey-pok'ey, n. = HOCUS-POCUS; cheap ice-cream sold by street vendors. [f. HOCUS-POCUS; second sense perh. of diff. orig.]

hok'um, n. (orig. U.S., sl.) Theatrical plot or business, (now esp.) film scenario, designed to appeal to the uncritical. [perh. portmanteau of HOCUS-POCUS and BUNKUM]

hold¹, v.t. & i. (*held*; also arch. p.p. ~*en* in formal reports of meetings etc.). 1. Keep fast, grasp (*held!* at Rugby foot-ball, claim that ball being held by oppo-nent as well as runner must be put down); keep (oneself), one's head, etc, in particular attitude; (of vessel) contain; possess, be the owner or holder or tenant of, (property, stocks, land); (Mil.) keep possession of (place); occupy (place, person's thoughts, etc.); engross (person, person's attention); keep (person etc.) in speci-fied place, condition, etc., as ~ *him at bay, in suspense*; *detain in custody; ~ *thing over* one, threaten him constantly with it; make (person) adhere to (terms, promise); observe, celebrate, conduct, (festival, meeting, conversation); use (insolent etc. language); ~ *to* (bind by) *bail*; restrain, refrain from punishing or other action; keep (person etc.) in; keep (person's attention); keep (person etc.) in special place, condition, etc., ~ *him in* bay, ... make (person) adhere to (terms, promise); observe, celebrate, conduct, (festival, meeting, conversation); use (insolent etc. language); ~ *your noise, tongue,* ~ *one's hand,* refrain from punishing or other action; *there is no* ~*ing him* etc., he etc. is restive or in high spirits or determined; think, believe, (thing, that, person etc. to be; *it good,* think it advisable to do); (of judge or court) lay down, decide (*that*); enter-tain specified feeling towards, as ~ *him in esteem, contempt*; ~ *thing cheap* (not value it); ~ *dear* (regard with affection). 2. intr. Remain unbroken, not give way; as ~ *by, to,* adhere to (choice, purpose, etc.); ~ *with,* approve of; (of laws etc, also ~

hold², n. Grasp (lit. & fig.), esp. *take, get, keep,* ~; ~ *of,* opportunity of holding, thing to hold by; (fig.) ~ (*on*), influence (over). [f. prec.]

hold³¹, n. Cavity in ship below deck, where cargo is stowed. [corrupt. of HOLE]

hold'er, n. In vbl senses, esp.: tenure of land; land held; stocks etc. held; ~ *com-pany,* one created to hold the shares of subsidiaries. [-ING¹]

hole¹, n. Hollow place in solid body; deep place in stream etc.; animal's burrow; small mean abode; cavity into which ball etc. must be got in various games; (Golf) point scored by player who gets ball from one ~ to another with fewest strokes; perforation; (sl.) awk-ward situation (*am in rather, a devil of, a hole*); ~ *pick,* ~*s in,* find fault with; *make a ~ in,* use large amount of; *round* (*square*) *peg in square* (*round*) ~, person not fitted for his place; ~*-and-corner,* secret, underhand. Hence **hōl'ey²** a. [OE *hol,* orig. neut. adj.]

hole², v.t. & i. Make holes in; (Naut.) pierce side of (ship); make (shaft, tunnel) (Mining, intr.) dig through from one working to another; put into hole; (also ~ *out*) put (golf-ball, or abs.) into hole. [OE *holian,* as prec.]

hol'iday (-i- *or* -dā), n. Day of cessation from work or of recreation; (usu. pl.) period of this, vacation; ~ || BANK²; ~

good, true) be valid, apply; keep going, esp. ~ *on one's way*; (arch.) ~, stop, wait. 3. ~ *one's hand,* forbear; ~ *one's head high,* behave proudly; ~ *up one's head,* not be downcast; ~ *one's ground,* or *one's own,* not give way; ~ *the BABY*; ~ *aloof,* avoid communication with persons etc.; ~ *back,* (trans.) restrain, (intr.) hesitate, refrain *from*; *~ *down,* restrain; ~ *forth,* speak publicly (usu. de-rog.); ~ *hard,* stop (imperative); ~ *in,* confine, restrain; ~ *in check*; ~ *off,* (intr.) delay; ~ *on,* keep one's grasp on some-thing, (colloq. imper.) stop; ~ *out,* (trans.) stretch forth, offer (inducement etc.), (intr.) endure, persist; ~ *over,* postpone; ~ *together* (t. & i., (cause to) cohere; ~ *up,* support, sustain, (lit. & fig.), exhibit, display, (stop to derision etc.), arrest, pro-gress of, obstruct, stop & rob on high-way, (of horse) keep up, not fall; ~*-up,* detention by force (of person, vehicle, train, etc.) for purposes of robbery (also attrib.). 5. ~ *all,* portable case for clothes etc.; ~ *back,* hindrance; ~ *fast,* firm grasp, staple or clamp securing object to wall etc. [com.-Teut.: OE *haldan,* MDu. *houden,* G *halten*]

hold'ing, n. In vbl senses, esp.: tenure of land; land held; stocks etc. held; ~ *com-pany,* one created to hold the shares of subsidiaries. [-ING²]

BLIND¹ man's ~; make ~; take a ~, cease from work; ~ (gay) clothes; || ~ task (to be done by schoolboy during ~s); ~=HOLY-day. [OE hāligdæg, see HOLY & DAY]

hōl'ily, adv. In a holy manner. [-LY²]

hōl'iness, n. Sanctity; H~, his H~, title of Pope. [OE hālignes (HOLY, -NESS)]

hōl'ism, n. (philos.). Tendency in nature to form wholes that are more than the sum of the parts by creative evolution. [as HOLO- +-ISM]

hōll'a, int. See HOLLO. [f. F holà]

Hōll'and, n. Province of northern Netherlands, kingdom of the Netherlands, whence ~ER'(4) n.; a linen fabric; brown ~, this unbleached. [Du., f. holt wood +-lant land]

Hōll'ands (-z), n. A grain spirit. [f. Du. hollandsch genever, Holland gin]

hōll'ō¹, int. calling attention; (n.) the cry ~. [conn. w. HOLLA]

hōll'ō², -low¹ (-ō), -la, -loa (-ō), v.i. & t. Shout (i. & t.); call to hounds. [as prec.]

hōll'ow²(-ō), a., n., & adv. Having a hole, not solid; ~ SQUARE; empty, hungry; (of sound) not full-toned; (fig.) empty, insincere, false; (n.) ~ place, hole, valley, basin; (adv.) beaten ~ (completely); ~-eyed, with eyes deep sunk; ~-hearted, insincere; ~ race etc., feebly contested. Hence ~LY²(-ōli) adv., ~NESS (-ōn-) n. [ME holg, holeh, holu, a., OE holh n., prob.=hol HOLE]

hōll'ow³ (-ō), v.t. (Also ~ out) excavate; bend into hollow shape. [f. prec.]

|| Hōll'oway (-o-w-), n. (Used for)~ prison (for women awaiting trial & convicted debtors). [place]

hōll'y, n. Evergreen shrub with prickly leaves, small green flowers, & red berries. [OE hole(g)n, cf. Du. & G huls]

hōll'yhock, n. Tall plant with large flowers of many varieties of colour. [f. HOLY+obs. hock mallow, OE hoc, etym. dub.]

Hōll'ywood, n. (Used for) moving pictures of American type, chiefly made at ~ in California. [place]

hōlm¹, -me, (hōm), n. Islet, esp. in river or near mainland; || flat ground by river, submerged in time of flood. [f. ON holmr]

hōlm² (hōm), n. (Usu. ~-oak) evergreen oak, ilex. [corrupt. of OE holen HOLLY (from resemblance in foliage)+OAK]

hōl'o- in comb.=Gk holos whole, as: ~graph a. & n., (document) wholly in handwriting of person in whose name it appears; ~hēd'ral, (of crystal) having full number of planes for perfect symmetry; ~metăb-ola in. pl., insects undergoing complete metamorphosis; ~phōte, apparatus for making available all the light of a lamp (in lighthouse etc.).

hōl'ocaust, n. Whole burnt-offering; wholesale sacrifice (fig.) or destruction. [f. F holocauste f. LL f. Gk HOLO(kauston burnt f. kaiō)]

hŏlothūr'ian, a. & n. (Animal) of the genus Holothuria, sea-slug. [f. mod. L Holothuria, n. pl. f. Gk holothourion, a zoophyte]

hŏlpen. See HELP¹.

hŏl'ster, n. Leather case for pistol, fixed to saddle or worn on belt. [17th-c. E & Du., cf. Icel. hulstr case, Sw. holster]

|| hōlt¹ (hōlt), n. (Poet.) wood, copse; wooded hill. [OE, cf. Du. hout timber, G holz wood, a wood]

hōlt², n. Animal's (esp. otter's) lair. [var. of HOLD²]

hōl'y, a. & n. 1. Consecrated, sacred; morally & spiritually perfect; belonging to, commissioned by, devoted to, God; of high moral excellence. 2. n. ~ of holies, inner chamber of sanctuary in Jewish temple, separated by veil from ~ place or outer chamber, (fig.) innermost shrine. 3. H~ Alliance, covenant formed in 1815-16 between the sovereigns of Russia, Prussia, and Austria, by which they bound themselves to be guided by Christian principles in domestic and foreign policy; H~ CITY; ~ cross (of Christ); H~ Cross day, festival of Exaltation of the Cross, Sep. 14; ~ day, religious festival; H~ FAMILY; H~ Ghost, Spirit, third person of the Godhead; H~ GRAIL; ~ Joe (naut. sl.), pious person; H~ Land, W. Palestine, esp. Judaea; H~ OFFICE; ~ ORDERS; H~ ROMAN Empire; ~ terror (sl.), formidable person, embarrassing child, bore; H~ Thursday, (prop.) Ascension Day, (pop.) Thursday in H~ Week; H~ Saturday (in H~ Week); ~ water, water dedicated to ~ uses, or blessed by a priest; H~ Week (before Easter Sunday); H~ Writ, ~ writings collectively, the Bible. [OE hālig (hāl whole, see -Y²), cf. Du. & G heilig]

hōl'ystōne, n., & v.t. (Scour with) soft sandstone used for scouring decks. [?]

hōm'age, n. (Feud.) formal public acknowledgement of allegiance; acknowledgement of superiority, dutiful reverence, as pay, do, ~ to (person, his qualities). [f. OF ommage f. LL hominaticum (homo -minis man, see -AGE]

Hōm'bŭrg, n. (Used for) soft felt hat with narrow brim and dent in top of crown, trilby. [~ in Prussia, where first worn]

hōme¹, n., a., & adv. 1. Dwelling-place; fixed residence of family or household; native land; long or last ~, the grave; place where thing is native or most common; institution of refuge or rest for destitute or infirm persons; (in games) goal; at ~, in one's own house or native land, at one's ease, familiar with or on or in (subject etc.), accessible to callers (esp. not at ~), (n.) see AT-HOME. 2. adj. Of, connected with, ~; carried on at ~; proceeding from ~; in the neighbourhood

of ~; ||H~ *Counties*, those nearest to London (Middlesex, Surrey, Kent, Essex, & occas. Hertford & Sussex); carried on, produced, in one's own country, as ~ *industries*, *products*; *the* ~ *trade or market* (inland); opp. *foreign*; treating of domestic affairs; ||H~ *Office*, department of Secretary of State for H~ Affairs, building used for this; *that comes* ~ *to one*, as ~ *question*, *truth*, *thrust*. **3.** *adv*. To one's ~ or country, as *come*, *go*, ~; arrived *at* ~, as *he is* ~; to the point aimed at, as *the thrust went* ~; *as far as possible*, as *drive a nail* ~; *bring charge* ~ *to person*, convict him of it; *come* ~ *to*, affect intimately; *nothing* ~ *to write* ~ *about* (colloq.), unexciting, trivial. **4.** ~*born*, native; ~*bred*, bred *at* ~; ~*brewed* **a.** & n. (beer etc.) brewed *at* ~; ~*coming*, arrival at home; ~*felt*, felt intimately; H~ *Guard*, (member of) British citizen army formed in 1940 (orig. called *Local Defence Volunteers*); ~*keeping* a., stay-at-home; H~ *Rule*, government of a country (ll esp. Ireland) by its own citizens; ~*sick(ness)*, ~*made*, made *at* ~ or for ~ consumption; H~ *Counties*, ~ (*-ml-*). [com.-Teut.: OE *hám*, Du. *heem*, G *heim*; (adv.) accus. case of this]

hōme', **v.i.** & **t.** Go home (esp. of pigeons); send or guide homewards; furnish (person etc.) with a home. [f. prec.]

hōme'ly (*-ml-*), a. Simple, plain; primitive; unpretending; (of persons or features) uncomely, plain. Hence ~INESS n. [-LY¹]

homoeo-. See homoeo-.

hōm'er, n. Homing pigeon. [-ER¹]

Homē'ric, a. Of, in the style of, Homer or the poems ascribed to him; ~ *laughter* (like that of Homer's gods as they watched lame Hephaestus hobbling). [f. L f. Gk *homērikos* (*Homēros*, see -IC)]

hōme'spun (*-ns-*), a. & n. (Cloth made of yarn) spun at home; (anything) plain, homely.

hōme'stead (*-nstd*), n. House with outbuildings; farm. [OE *hāmstede* (HOME, STEAD)]

hōme'ward (*-mw-*), adv. & a., ~**wards** (*-z*), adv. (Going, leading) towards home; ~*bound*⁵ (esp. of ship) preparing to go, or on the way, home. [-WARD(S)]

hōm'icide, n. **1.** One who kills a human being. **2.** Killing of a human being. Hence **homici'dal**(*-sī-*) a. [F, f. L (1) *homicīda*, (2) *homicīdium* (*homo* man, see -CIDE)]

hōmilē'tic, a. & n. Of homiletics; (n. pl.) art of preaching. [f. Gk *homilētikos* (*homileō* hold converse, consort, as foll.: see -ETIC)]

hōm'ily, n. Sermon (*Books of H~ies*, for use in parish churches of the Ch. of England, published in 1547 & 1563); tedious

moralizing discourse. [f. F *omelie* f. eccl. L f. Gk *homīlia* f. *homilos* crowd (*homos* together+*īlē* crowd)]

hōm'ing, a. That goes home; (of pigeons) trained to fly home. [part. of HOME²]

hōm'iny, n. Coarsely ground maize boiled with water or milk. [of Amer.-Ind. orig.]

hōm'ō, n. (zool.). Man; H~ *sāp'iēns* (*-z* wise), modern man regarded as a species. [L]

hōm'ō- in comb. =Gk *homos* same, as: ~*cen'tric*, having same centre; ~*gamous* (*-ŏg-*), (Bot.) having all florets hermaphrodite or of same sex; ~*genē'ic*, having common descent or origin; ~*geny* (*-ŏj'-*), similarity due to common descent; ~*morph'ic*, ~*morph'ous*, of same or similar form; ~*nomous* (*-ŏn*), having same law of growth; ~*phone*, word having same sound as another, but of different meaning or origin (e.g. *gait*, *gate*), (also) symbol denoting same sound; ~*phony* (*-ŏf*), (Mus.) of same pitch, in unison; ~*phonous* (*-ŏf-*), (of music) in unison, (of symbols) denoting same sound; ~*plas'tic*, similar in structure; ~*type*, part, organ, like another in structure; ~*zȳg'ōte* (Mendelism), zygote of like gametes (cf. HETEROZYGOTE), & so ~*zȳg'ous* a.

hōm'oeopath (*-mǐ-*), n. One who practises homoeopathy. [f. foll.]

hōmoeŏp'athy (*-mǐ-*), n. Hahnemann's treatment of disease by drugs (usu. in minute doses) that in healthy person would produce symptoms like those of the disease. So ~*path'ic* a. (often *joc.*, ~*path'ically* adv.), ~*path'ist* n. [f. Gk *homoio-* (*homoios* like + -IST n. [f. Gk *homoios* like + *patheia* f. *pathos* suffering; first used by Hahnemann (G *homoöpathie*)]

hōmoge'nēous, a. Of the same kind; consisting of parts all of the same kind, uniform. Hence or cogn. *homoge'nēITY*, ~*NESS*, nn. ~LY² adv. [f. schol. L *homogeneus* f. Gk HOMO*genēs* f. *genos* kind) +-OUS]

hōm'ograph (*-ahf*), n. Word spelt like another, but with different meaning. [HOMO-+-GRAPH]

homoiousi'an (*-ows-*), a. & n. (One who held that Father & Son in the Godhead were) of like substance (cf. HOMOOUSIAN). [f. Gk *homoioŭsios* (*homoios* like +*ousia* essence) +-IAN]

||homŏl'ogāte, v.t. (Sc.). Acknowledge, admit; confirm. So ~A'TION n. [f. med. L *homologare* f. Gk HOMO(*logeō* f. *logos* word), see -ATE³]

homŏl'ogize, v.i. & t. Be homologous, correspond; make homologous. [as foll. +-IZE]

homŏl'ogous, a. Having the same relation, relative position, etc.; corresponding. [f. med. L f. Gk HOMO(*logos* ratio)]

hŏm'ologue (*-ŏg*), n. Homologous thing. [F, f. Gk (neut. adj.) as prec.]

homol'ogy, n. Correspondence, sameness of relation. Hence **homolo'gical** a., **homolo'gically²** adv. [f. LL f. Gk *homologia* (as prec.)]

hom'onym, n. Word of same form as another but different sense (e.g. POLE¹, POLE²); namesake. So **homonym'ic, homon'ymous,** aa. [f. LL f. Gk *homōnumon,* neut. adj. (HOMO-+*onoma* name)]

homöous'ian, homöous-, (-ow-), a. & n. (One who held the persons of the Trinity to be) of the same substance (cf. HOMOIOUSIAN). [f. med. L f. Gk HOMO(*ousios t. ousia* essence)+-AN]

homosex'ual, a. & n. Having a sexual propensity for persons of one's own sex; (n.) ~ person. [irreg. f. HOMO-+SEXUAL]

homunc'ule, -cle, n. Little man, manikin. [f. L *homunculus* (*homo -minis* man, see -CULE)]

hom'y, a. Suggesting home, home-like. [-Y²]

hone, n. & v.t. 1. Whetstone, esp. for razors; various stones as material for this. 2. v.t. Sharpen on ~. [(vb f. n.) OE *hān,* cf. ON *hein,* Da. *heen*]

hon'est (ŏ-), a. Fair & upright in speech & act, not lying, cheating, or stealing; sincere: (of act or feeling) showing uprightness; (of gain etc.) gained by fair means, as *turn, earn, an ~ penny*; (of things) unadulterated, unsophisticated: (arch., of woman) chaste, virtuous; *make an ~ woman of,* marry (seduced woman); ~ (patronizing or joc.) good, worthy; ~ *Injun* (=Indian), sl. phr. questioning (*Injun?*) or confirming statement. Hence ~LY² adv. [f. OF *honeste* f. L *honestus* honourable, handsome (*homos* HONOUR]

hon'esty (ŏ-), n. Uprightness; truthfulness; ~ *is the best policy* (maxim of self-interested morality); plant with purple flowers & semi-transparent pods. [f. OF *oneste* f. L *honestātem* (prec., -TY)]

ho'ney (hŭ-), n. (pl. ~s). Sweet viscid yellow fluid, the nectar of flowers collected by bees & other insects; (fig.) sweetness (also Sc. & North. *hinnie,* -*ny*) sweetheart, darling; ~*bee,* common hive-bee; ~*buzzard,* bird of prey feeding on larvae of bees & wasps; ~ *dew,* sweet sticky substance found on leaves & stems, held to be excreted by aphides, ideally sweet substance, tobacco sweetened with molasses; ~*suckle,* woodbine, climbing shrub with fragrant yellow flowers; ~*sweet,* sweet as ~. Hence ~ED², **honied,** (hŭn'ĭd), a. [OE *hunig,* cf. Du., G, *honig*]

ho'neycomb (hŭ-; -m), n., & v.t. 1. Bees' wax structure of hexagonal cells for honey & eggs; cavernous flaw in metal, esp. guns; ornamental or other work hexagonally arranged. 2. v.t. Fill with cavities, undermine, mark with ~ pattern. [(vb f. n.) OE *hunigcamb,* see prec. & COMB]

ho'neymoon (hŭ-), n., & v.i. 1. Holiday spent together by newly married couple. 2. v.i. Spend ~ (*in, at,* place). [(vb f. n.) HONEY+MOON, reference being orig. **to** waning affection, not to period of **a** month]

hong, n. (In China) set of buildings used as factory etc.; foreign trading establishment in China or Japan. [f. Chin. *hang* row, rank]

honk, n. & v.i. 1. Wild goose's cry; sound of motor horn. 2. v.i. Emit or give ~. [imit.]

honorār'ium (hŏ-, ō-), n. (pl. -*ums, -a*). (Voluntary) fee esp. for professional services. [LL as foll.]

hon'orary (ŏ-), a. Conferred as an honour (without the usual requirements, functions, etc.); holding ~ title or position; ~ *secretary, treasurer,* etc., serving without pay (abbr. *hon.*); (of obligations) depending on honour, not legally enforceable. [f. L *honorārius* (as HONOUR, see -ARY²)]

honorif'ic (ŏ-), a. & n. (Expression) implying respect (esp. of Oriental forms of speech). [f. L *honorificus* (as HONOUR¹, see -FIC)]

hon'oris caus'a, adv. phr. As a mark of honour. [L, =for the sake of honour]

hon'our¹ (ŏ-), n. 1. High respect; glory; reputation, good name; nobleness of mind. 2. Allegiance to what is right or **to** conventional standard of conduct; (of woman) chastity, reputation for this. 3. Exalted position (*your, his, H~,* said to or of County-Court judge, & in rustic speech to or of any person of rank). 4. Thing conferred as distinction; (Golf) right of driving off first as having won last hole (*it is my* ~); (pl.) civilities rendered to guests etc., esp. *do the* ~*s* of (the table, a house, the town, etc.); *last, funeral,* ~*s,* observances of respect at burial of soldier, to royalty, etc.; ~*s of war,* privileges granted to capitulating force, as that of marching out with colours flying etc. 5. (Univ., pl.) special distinction for proficiency beyond that required to pass examination. 6. Person, thing, that reflects ~ on (to) another, as *he is an* ~ *to his profession.* 7. (In Whist) ace, king, queen, knave, of trumps (in Bridge the ten also). 8. (Commerc.) acceptance (of protested bill by third party) *for the* ~ *of* (to save the credit of) drawer or indorser. 9. *in* ~ (celebration) of; *bound in* ~ (as a moral duty) to (do); *be on one's* ~ (under moral obligation) to (do); (forms of asseveration) *upon my* ~, (colloq.) ~ *bright*; *code, law, of* ~, rules forming conventional standard of conduct; AFFAIR, DEBT, LEGION, MAID, POINT¹, WORD¹, *of* ~. [f. OF *onor* f. L *honorem* (nom. -*or*) repute, office, beauty]

hon'our² (-ŏ-), v.t. Respect highly; confer dignity upon; (Commerc.) accept, pay, (bill) when due. [f. OF *honorer* f. L *honorare* (as prec.)]

hon'ourable (-ŏner-), a. Worthy of and consistent with honour; upright; person's *intentions* (in courting woman) *are* ~, he has marriage in view; title (abbr. *Hon.*) || of younger sons of Earls and of children of peers below rank of Marquis, Maids of Honour, Justices of High Court, Lords of Session, members of Government or Executive Councils in Dominions & Colonies; || *Most H~*, title of members of Order of Bath, & Privy Council; || *Right H~*, title of peers below rank of Marquis, Privy Councillors, & others. Hence **hon'ourabl·y²** (-ŏner-) adv. [f. OF *honorable* (as prec., see -BLE)]

*hooch, n. (sl.). Alcoholic liquor. [abbr. of *hoochinoo* an Amer.-Ind. name for spirit]

hood, n., & v.t. 1. Covering for head & neck, whether part of cloak etc. or separate; (Univ.) badge worn over gown etc. to indicate degree; leather covering for hawk's head; thing like ~ in shape or use. 2. v.t. Cover with ~. Hence ~ED² a. [(vb f. n.) OE *hōd*, cf. Du. *hoed*, G *hut* hat]

-hood. See -HEAD.

hood'ie, -dy, n. (Also ~ *crow*) Hooded or Royston Crow. [HOOD + -Y³]

*hood'lum, n. Street rowdy, young ruffian. [?]

hood'man-blind, n. Old name for BLIND-MAN'S-BUFF.

hoo'doo, n. & v.t.(chiefly U.S.), Bad luck; (vb) render unlucky. [var. of VOODOO]

hood'wink, v.t. Deceive, humbug; blindfold. [HOOD + WINK v.]

hoo'ey, n. & int. (sl.). Nonsense, humbug. [?]

hoof, n. (pl. -fs, -ves), & v.t. & i. 1. Horny casing of foot of horse & other animals; CLOVEN ~; (joc.) human foot; ~-*pad*, pad to prevent one foot from striking the other; ~-*pick* (for removing stones from ~). 2. v.t. Strike with ~; (sl., of person) kick (another) *out* etc.; (v.i.) go on foot. Hence (-)~ED²(-f-) a. [(vb f. n.) com.-Teut.: OE *hōf*, Du. *hoef*, G *huf*]

hook¹, n. Piece of metal or other material bent back or having sharp angle, for catching hold or for hanging things upon; (also *fish-~*) bent piece of wire, usu. barbed, for catching fish; ~, *line, & sinker*, (fig.) entire(ly); (fig.) trap, snare; stroke (see foll.) in cricket or golf; (Box-ing) short swinging blow with elbow bent; curved cutting instrument, esp. *reaping-~*; ~ & *eye*, small metal ~ & loop as dress-fastening; sharp bend, e.g. *H~ of Holland*; =POT-~; *by ~ or by crook*, by fair means or foul; *drop off the ~s*, (sl.) die; (sl.) *on one's own ~* (account); *take one's ~* (sl.), = *hook it* (see foll.); ~*nosed*, (having aquiline nose; ~*worm*, kind of nematoid worm infesting men and animals, male of which has ~-like spines. [OE *hōc*, cf. Du. *hoek* corner, point of land]

hook², v.t. & i. 1. Grasp with hook; secure with hook(s); ~ *on, in, up*, etc., attach with hook; ~ *on* intr., take person's arm; steal; catch (fish) with hook (also fig., of husband); (Golf) drive (ball) widely to left; (Cricket) play (ball) round from off to on side without hitting it at the leg; (Rugby football) secure and pass (ball) backward with foot in scrummage; (Boxing) strike (opponent) with elbow bent; ~ *it* (sl.), make off, run away; ~-*up* (orig. U.S.), interconnexion of broad-casting stations for special transmissions. [f. prec.]

hook'ah (-kə), n. Smoking-pipe with long flexible tube, smoke being drawn through water in vase to which tube and bowl are attached. [f. Arab. *ḥuqqah*, casket, hookah-bottle]

hooked (-kt), a. Hook-shaped; furnished with hook(s). [-ED¹·²]

hook'er¹, n. In vbl senses, esp. (Rugby football) each of the two players in front row of scrummage who try to get the ball by hooking it. [-ER¹]

hook'er², n. Kinds of small Dutch & Irish sailing ship (*the old* ~, said scorn-fully or fondly of any ship). [prob. f. Du. *hoeker* (*hoek* hook)]

hook'ey, -ky, n. **Play* ~ (sl.), play truant; *blind* ~, gambling game at cards. [f. HOOK¹·²]

|| hooli'gan, n. One of gang of young street roughs. Hence ~ISM(3) n. [name]

hoop¹, n., & v.t. 1. Circular band of metal, wood, etc., esp. for binding staves of casks etc.; wooden or iron circle trundled along by child; circle of elastic material for expanding woman's skirt; iron arch used in croquet; large ring with paper stretched over it through which circus-riders jump (*go through the* ~ *or* ~s, undergo an ordeal); kind of finger-ring; ~-*iron* (in long thin strips for binding purposes); ~ *petticoat* (expanded by ~s). 2. v.t. Bind with ~s, surround as ~ does. [(vb f. n.) OE *hōp*, cf. Du. *hoep*]

hoop², v.i., & n. 1. Utter the cry ~; ~*ing-cough*, contagious disease, esp. of children, with short violent cough followed by long sonorous inspiration. 2. n. The cry ~, sound heard in ~*ing-cough*. [(n. f. v.) f. F *houper* (*houp*, limit.); *whoop* is late spelling]

hoop'la (-äh), n. Game played at fairs etc., in which rings are thrown at objects that are won if encircled. [HOOP + -*la* (int.)]

hoo'poe (-ōō), n. A S.-European bird with variegated plumage & large erectile crest. [earlier *hoop* t., F *huppe* tuft, crest, bird, f. pop. L *ūpūpa*=L *ūpūpa* hoopoe]

hōōsh, n. (sl.). Hotchpotch or stew in Arctic travel. [?]

hōōt, v.i. & t., & n. 1. Make loud sounds, esp. of disapproval (*at* or abs.); assail (person etc.) with derisive shouts; drive (person) *out, away*, etc. by ~*ing*; (of owl) utter cry; (of steam whistle or motor car or driver) sound (intr.). 2. n. Inarticulate shout, esp. of derision or disapprobation; owl's cry; *not care, not worth*, a ~ *or two* ~*s* (sl., = anything at all). [(n. f. vb) ME *huten*, perh. imit.]

‖ **hōōt(s)**, int. (Sc. & north.) expr. dissatisfaction or impatience. [cf. Sw. *hut* begone, W *hwt* away, Ir. *ut* out, all in similar sense]

hōōt'er, n. In vbl senses, esp. siren, steam whistle, etc. as signal for work to begin or cease. [-ER¹]

hōōve, n. Disease of cattle, with inflation of stomach, usu. caused by green fodder. [f. OE *hóf-*, a stem of HEAVE]

Hōōv'er, n., & v.t. Make of vacuum cleaner; (v.t.) clean (carpet etc.) with ~. [P]

hōp¹, n., & v.t. & i. (-pp-). 1. Climbing perennial plant, cultivated for the cones borne by the female; (pl.) ripe cones of this, used for giving bitter flavour to malt liquor etc.; ~-*bind, -bine*, climbing stem of ~; ~-*fly*, aphis destructive to ~s: ‖~-*garden*, field for cultivation of ~s; ~-*picker*, labourer, machine, employed to pick ~s; ~-*pillow* (stuffed with ~s, to produce sleep); ~POCKET; ~-*pole* (on which ~ plant is trained). 2. v.t. Flavour with ~s; (v.i.) bear, gather, ~s. [vb f. n.) earlier *hoppe*, MDu., etym. dub.]

hōp², v.i. & t. (-pp-). Spring (of person) on one foot, (of animals) with all feet at once; (trans.) ~ *over* (ditch etc.); (sl.) ~ *the twig* or *stick*), depart suddenly; die, ~ (*it*), go away, ~ *off*, (of aircraft) start; *cloud*~*ping*, (of aircraft) flying from cloud to cloud esp. to gain cover; *hedge, wave,* ~*ping*, flying very low over land, over water;‖~-*to'-my-thumb*, dwarf, pygmy; ~ *scotch*, child's game of ~*ping* on one foot & with it pushing flat stone etc., over *scotches* (lines) marked on ground. [OE *hoppian*, cf. Sw. *hoppa*, Da. *hoppe*, G *hopfen*]

hōp³, n. Hopping (*on the* ~, colloq., bustling about): spring; (colloq.) dance; (Aviation) one of the stages of a long-distance flight; ~, *skip* (or *step*), *& jump*, exercise consisting of these three movements in sequence. [f. prec.]

hōpe¹, n. Expectation & desire combined (*of thing, of doing, that*); feeling of trust; ground of ~, probability, (*hoping against* ~, clinging to a mere possibility); person, thing, that ~ centres in; FORLORN HOPE. [OE *hopa*, cf. Du. *hoop*, G *hoffe*]

hōpe², v.i. & t. Look with expectation & desire (*for* thing or abs.); expect & desire (thing, *that, to do*.) [OE *hopian*, cf. Du. *hopen*]

hōpe'ful (-pf-), a. & n. Feeling hope; inspiring hope, promising, often iron. as (n.) *young* ~ (of boy or girl). Hence ~LY² adv., ~NESS n. [HOPE¹+-FUL]

hōpe'less (-pl-), a. Feeling no hope; admitting no hope, as a ~ *case*. Hence ~LY² adv., ~NESS n. [-LESS]

hōp'lite, n. Heavy-armed foot-soldier of ancient Greece. [f. Gk *hoplités* (*hoplon* weapon, see -ITE³)]

hōpp'er¹, n. One who hops; hopping insect, esp. flea or cheese-maggot; inverted pyramid or cone (orig. with hopping motion) through which grain passes in mill; similar contrivance in various machines; barge carrying away mud etc. from dredging-machine & discharging it; ~-*light* or -*casement* (hinged below with opening at top for ventilation). [HOP²+-ER¹]

hōpp'er², n. Hop-picker. [HOP¹+-ER¹]

hōp'ple, v.t., & n. Fasten together legs of (horse etc.); (n.) apparatus for this. [(n. f. vb) etym. dub.; earlier than *hobble* in this sense]

hōr'arý, a. Of the hours; occurring every hour. [f. med. L *horarius* (*hora* hour, see -ARY¹)]

Horā'tian (-shn), a. Of, like, (the poems of) Horace (Q. Horatius Flaccus, d. B.C. 8). [f. L *Horatianus* (*Horatius*, see -AN)]

hōrde, n. Troop of Tartar or other nomads; gang, troop, (usu. in contempt). [ult. f. Turki *orda*, see URDU]

hore'hound, hoar-, (hōr-), n. Herb with bitter aromatic juice used for coughs etc. (also *common, white*, ~); other allied herbs. [OE *hāre hūne* (*hár* hoar+*hūne*, a plant)]

hori'zon, n. Line at which earth & sky appear to meet; *apparent, sensible, visible,* ~, circle of contact with earth's surface of a cone whose vertex is at observer's eye; *celestial, rational, true,* ~, great circle of the celestial sphere, plane of which passes through centre of earth & is parallel to that of sensible ~ of a place; (fig.) limit of mental perception, experience, interest, etc. [f. OF *orizonte* f. LL *horizontem* (nom. -*on*) f. Gk *horizōn* (*kuklos*) bounding (circle), part. of *horizō* (*horos* boundary, -IZE)]

horizon'tal, a. & n. 1. Of, at, the horizon; parallel to the plane of this, at right angles to the vertical; level, flat; (of machinery etc.) having its parts working in ~ plane. 2. n. ~ line, bar, etc. Hence ~ITY (-ǎl-) n., ~LY² adv. [f. L as prec.+-AL]

hor'mōne, n. (physiol.). Kinds of internal secretion that pass into the blood & stimulate organs to action. [f. Gk hor-

mōn part, of hornǎ impel, with -e to mark sound of ŏ]

hôrn¹, n. **1.** Non-deciduous excrescence, often curved & pointed, on head of cattle, sheep, goats, & other mammals, found in pairs, single, or one in front of another; *take the* BULL¹ *by the* ~s; each of two decidious branched appendages on head of deer; projection on head of other animals, as snail's tentacles, insect's antennae, crest of horned owl; *draw in one's* ~s, restrain one's ardour; draw back; substance of which ~s consist; ~-*shavings* (used as manure); thing made of ~, as SHOE-~; drinking-vessel, powder-flask, made of ~; ~ *of plenty*, = CORNUCOPIA; wind instru-ment (not now made of ~, but of brass), as *hunting*-~, *French*-~ (of trumpet class, used in orchestra), *English* ~ (kind of oboe); ~-*shaped* projection; extremity of moon or other crescent; arm, branch, of bay, river, etc.; either alternative of a dilemma; *the* Hŏ~, *Cape* H~. **2.** ~-*bar*, cross-bar of carriage; ~*beam*, tree of beech kind with hard tough wood; ~*bill*, bird with ~-*like* excrescence on bill; ~*book* (hist.), paper containing alphabet, Lord's Prayer, etc., mounted on wooden tablet with handle, & protected by thin plate of ~; ~*mad* (arch.), stark mad (orig. of horned beasts); ~-*plate*, axle-guard of railway carriage; ~*rimmed* (of spectacles or their wearers); ~-*stone*, brittle siliceous rock; ~*work* (Fortif.), outwork consisting of two demi-bastions joined by a curtain. Hence ~'FUL n., ~'LESS a. [com.-Teut.; OE & ON *horn*, Goth. *haurn*, cogn. w. L *cornu*, Gk *keras*]

hôrn², v.t. & i. Furnish with horns (esp. in p.p.); gore with the horns; adjust (frame of ship) at right angles to line of keel; *~ in*, intrude, interfere. [f. prec.]

hôrn'blende, n. Dark-brown, black, or green mineral, a constituent of granite & many rocks, composed chiefly of silica, magnesia, & lime. [G (*horn* + BLENDE)]

hôrn'er, n. Maker of horn spoons, combs, etc.; one who blows a horn. [HORN¹ + -ER¹]

hôrn'et, n. Large insect of wasp family, inflicting serious sting; *bring* ~s' *nest about one's ears*, stir up host of enemies. [OE *hyrnet(u)*, cf. MDu. *hornete*, LG *hornte*, G *hornisse*]

hôrn'pipe, n. Obsolete wind instrument; (music for) lively dance, usu. of single person (esp. associated with merry-making of sailors).

hôrn'y², a. Of, like, horn; abounding in horns; hard as horn, callous, as ~y *handed*. Hence ~NESS n. [-Y²]

hŏrŏl'oge, n. Time-piece, dial, clock. So **horŏl'oger¹**(3), **horŏl'ogist**(3), nn. [f. OF *orloge* f. L f. Gk *hōrologion* (*hōra* time + -*logos* -telling)]

horŏl'ogy, n. Art of measuring time or making clocks. So **hŏrŏl'ogĭc(Al)** aa. [f. Gk *hōra* time + -o- + -LOGY]

horŏp'ter, n. Aggregate of points seen single in any given position of eyes. [f. Gk *horos* limit + *optēr* one who looks]

hŏ'roscōpe, n. (astrol.). Observation of sky & planets at certain moment, esp. at person's birth; scheme showing dis-position of the heavens at particular moment; *cast a* ~, erect such scheme by calculating degree of ecliptic on eastern horizon at person's birth etc. So **hŏro-scŏp'ic(Al)** aa., **horŏs'copy¹** n. [f. f. Gk *hōroscopos* (*hōra* time + *skopos* observer)]

hŏ'rrent, a. (poet.). Bristling. [f. L *horrēre* bristle, shudder at, see -ENT]

hŏr'rible, a. Exciting, fit to excite, horror; hideous, shocking; (colloq.) ex-cessive, unpleasant, as ~*le noise*, *bore*, *weather*. Hence ~*ness* (-beln-) n., ~**ly²** adv. [OF. f. L *horribilis* (as prec., see -BLE)]

hŏ'rrid, a. Terrible, frightful; (poet., arch.) rough, bristling; (colloq.) as prec. Hence ~**ly²** adv., ~*ness* n. [f. L *horridus* (as prec., see -ID)]

hŏr'rify, v.t. Excite horror in; shock, scandalize. So **horrific** a., **hŏrrĭfĭc-A'TION** n. (joc.). [f. L *horrificare* (as prec., see -FY)]

hŏrrĭpĭlā'tion, n. Goose-flesh; bristling of the skin caused by chill, fright, etc. [f. LL *horripilatio*, ult. f. L *horrēre* to bristle + *pilus* hair]

hŏr'ror, n. Terrified shuddering; intense dislike (*of*); (Med.) shuddering, as symptom of disease; *the* ~s, out of ~ or depression of disease; esp. as in delirium tremens; ~-*struck* or -*stricken*, shocked; horrifying thing; *Chamber of* H~s, place full of ~s (orig. room of criminals etc. in Tussaud's waxwork exhibition). [f. OF *orror* f. L *horrorem* (as prec., see -OR²)]

horse, n. (See Ap.), adv. & prep. Outside, as ~ *concours*, (of exhibit) not competing for prize; ~ *de combat*, out of fight, disabled; ~*d'œuvre* (pl. usu. -s), extra dish served as relish at beginning or in interval of meal. [F wds]

horse, n. **1.** Solid-hoofed quadruped with flowing mane & tail, used as beast of burden & draught, & for riding on (*you may take a* ~ *to the water, but you can't make him drink*, prov.; (esp.) adult male ~, stallion or gelding; (cf. MARE, COLT); (collect. sing.) cavalry; *light* ~, lightly armed mounted soldiers; SEA-~. **2.** Vaulting-block in gymnasium; frame (often with legs) on which something is supported, as *clothes*-~; (Naut.) rope, bar, in various uses; (Mining) obstruction in vein. **3.** *To* ~, (as command) mount your ~s; FLOG *a dead* ~; *grin through a* ~ *collar*, practise elementary humour; *look a gift* ~ *in the mouth*, find fault with a ~; *mount, ride, the high* ~, put on airs;

DARK, WILLING, ~; *eat, work, like a* ~ (much); *on* ~*back*, mounted on a ~. **4.** = artillery (the light mobile type); ~*-block*, small platform of stone or wood for mounting ~; ‖~*-box*, closed vehicle for taking ~ by rail or for slinging ~ into ship, (joc.) large pew; ~*-breaker*, large tree with conical clusters of white or pink flower, fruit of this (like edible chestnut, but of coarse bitter taste); ~*-cloth* (used to cover ~, or as part of trappings); ~*-*COPER; ~*'flesh*, flesh of ~, esp. as food; ~s collectively; ~*-fly*, inseet (of various kinds) troublesome to ~s; ‖H~ *Guards*, cavalry brigade of English Household troops, esp. (*Royal H.G.*) second regiment of it, (also) headquarters of such cavalry, esp. a building opposite Whitehall, (also) military authorities at head of army; ~*'hair*, hair from mane or tail of ~ (often attrib.); ~ *latitudes*, belt of calms at northern edge of N.E. trade-winds; ~*-laugh*, loud coarse laugh; ~ *leech*, large kind of leech, insatiable person, (*daughters of the* ~*leech, Prov.* xxx. 15); ~*-mackerel*, (kinds of) large fish of the mackerel type, cavally, scad, tunny, etc.; ~*'man*, (skilled) rider on ~back; ~*'manship*, art of riding, skill in riding, on ~back; ~*-marines*, imaginary corps of mounted marines, as type of men out of their element, (prov.) *tell that* (nonsense) *to the* ~*-marines*; ~*-mastership*, skill in managing ~s; ~*-mushroom*, coarse but edible variety with hollow stem; ~*opera* (sl.), western film; ~*'play*, boisterous play; ~*-pond* (for watering & washing ~s, prov. as ducking-place for obnoxious persons); ~*-power*, machine by which work of ~ is made to drive other machinery, (Mech.) unit of rate of doing work, =550 foot-pounds per second (abbr. *h.p.*); ~*-race* (between ~s with riders); ~*-radish*, plant whose pungent root is scraped or grated as condiment; ~ *sense* (colloq.), plain rough sagacity; ~ *shoe*, iron shoe for ~, thing of this shape (often attrib., as ~*shoe table*); ~*-tail*, tail of ~ (used in Turkey as standard, or as ensign denoting rank of pasha), genus of cryptogamous plants like ~*'s tail*; ~*-whip*, whip for ~, (v.t.) chastise (person) with this; ~*'woman*, woman who rides on ~back. Hence ~LESS (-sl-) a. [com.-Teut.: OE *hors*, OHG *hros*, Du. *ros*, G *ross*]

hŏrse², v.t. & i. Provide (person, vehicle) with horse(s); carry (person) on one's back; place (person) on man's back to be flogged; (intr.) mount, go, on horseback. [f. prec.]

hŏrs'ly̆, a. Concerned with, addicted to, horses or horse-racing; affecting dress & language of groom or jockey. Hence ~LĬNESS n. [f. HORSE¹+-Y²]

hŏrt'ătive, a. Tending, serving, to exhort. So ~ORY a. [f. L *hortātīvus* (*hortāri* exhort, see -IVE)]

hŏrt'iculture, n. Art of garden cultivation. Hence **hŏrticŭl'turăl** a., **hŏrticŭl'turist** n...(-cher). [f. L *hortus* garden +CULTURE]

hŏrt'us sicc'us, n. Arranged collection of dried plants. [L, =dry garden]

hŏsănn'a (-z-), n. Cry of ~, shout of adoration (*Matt.* xxi. 9, 15, etc.). [LL f. Gk *hōsanna* f. Heb. *hoshā'na* for *hoshī'ahnna* save, pray!]

hose (hōz), n., & v.t. **1.** (Collect. as pl.) stockings, *half-*~, socks, (now chiefly shop); (w. pl. ~s) flexible tube for watering plants etc.; ‖~*-tops* (Sc. pron. *hŏt'ŏps*), footless stockings. **2.** v.t. Provide with ~, drench or water with ~ [(vb f. n.) OE *hosa*, cf. Du. *hoos*, G *hose*] frame-knitted or woven undercothing. Hence **hŏ'sier(1)** (-zher) n. [f. HOSE+-IER]

hŏ'sier (-zher), n. Dealer in hose &

hŏs'pice, n. House of rest for travellers, esp. one kept by religious order; ‖ home for the destitute or sick. [F, f. L *hospitium* (as HOSP²)]

hŏs'pitable, a. Giving, disposed to give, welcome & entertainment to strangers or guests. Hence ~LY¹ adv. [f. f. med. L *hospitāre* entertain, as prec., -ABLE]

hŏs'pital, n. Institution for care of the sick or wounded; charitable institution (in proper names, as *Christ's H~*, public school formerly in London); (Hist.) hospice, establishment of Knights Hospitallers; ~*fever*, kind of typhus formerly prevalent in crowded ~s; *H~ Saturday, Sunday*, days for collecting money in streets etc. (*Saturday*), in churches (*Sunday*), for the local ~s. [OF, f. med L *hospitāle* neut. adj. place for guests (as HOSP² see -AL)]

hŏs'pitalism, n. (Hygienic imperfections of) the hospital system. [-ISM]

hŏspităl'ity, n. Friendly & liberal reception of guests or strangers; *afford me the* ~ *of your columns*, put my letter in. [f. OF *hospitalité* f. L *hospitālitātem* (as HOSPITAL, see -TY)]

hŏs'pital(l)er, n. Member of charitable religious order; ‖ (in some London hospitals) chaplain; *Knights H~s*, order of military monks founded c. 1048. [f. OF *hospitalier* f. med. L *hospitālārius* (as prec., see -ARY²)]

hŏs'podăr, n. Lord (formerly title of governors of Wallachia & Moldavia), [Roumanian, of Slav. orig.]

hŏst¹, n. Large number (*of*; *person is a* ~ *in himself*, can do as much as a number of ordinary persons); (arch.) army; (Bibl.) *Lord* (*God*) *of* ~s (armies), ~(s) *of heaven*, sun, moon, & stars, (also) angels. [OF, f. L *hostis* stranger, enemy]

hŏst², n. One who lodges another; landlord of inn; *reckon without one's* ~, overlook difficulty, opposition, etc.; (Biol.) animal, plant, having parasite or

host¹, n. commensal. [f. OF *oste* f. L *hospitem* (nom. *-pes*) host, guest]

host², n. Bread consecrated in the Eucharist. [f. OF *oiste* f. L *hostia* victim]

hŏs'tage, n. Person given to another as pledge; pledge, security; ~ *to fortune*, person, thing, that one may lose. Hence ~SHIP (-ĭjsh-) n. [OF, f. L obes *-tidis* hostage, see -AGE]

‖ **hŏs'tel,** n. (Arch.) Inn; house of residence for students or other special class. [OF (as HOSPITAL)]

hŏs'telry, n. (arch.) Inn. [f. OF *ostelerie* (ostelier innkeeper, f. med. L as HOSPITALIER, see -ERY)]

hŏs'tess, n. Woman who entertains guests; mistress of inn. [f. OF *ostesse* (HOST¹, -ESS¹)]

hŏs'tile, a. Of an enemy; unfriendly; opposed. Hence ~LY² (-l-li) adv. [f. L *hostilis* (as HOST¹, see -IL)]

hŏsti'lity, n. Enmity; state of warfare; (pl.) acts of warfare; opposition (in thought etc.). [f. Ll *hostilitas* (as prec., see -TY)]

hŏs'tler (ŏs'ler), n. = OSTLER.

hŏt¹, a. & adv. (-tt-). 1. Of a high temperature; very warm; communicating or feeling heat; producing the sensation of heat, as ~ *fever, blush*; (of pepper etc.) pungent, biting; excited; exciting; (Hunt., of scent) strong; (fig., of news etc.) fresh, recent; ‖(colloq., of Treasury bills) newly issued; (of a hit, return, etc., in ball-games) difficult for opponent to deal with; (of competitor in race or other sporting event) strongly fancied to win (a ~ *favourite*); (of dance music) highly elaborated & florid, fast & with great emphasis on rhythm; BLOW¹ ~ *& cold*; *give it him* ~, chastise, reprimand, him severely; *make it, the place, too* ~ (uncomfortable, for, to hold, him. **2.** adv. Hotly, eagerly, angrily. **3.** ~ *air* (sl.), excited or boastful talk; ~ *& strong*, vehement(ly); ~ *bed*, bed of earth heated by fermenting manure, (fig.) place favourable to growth of (vice etc.); ~ *blast* (of heated air forced into furnace); ~-*blooded*, ardent, passionate; ~-*brained*, -*headed*, excitable; ~-*cockles* (hist.), rustic game in which blindfolded person guessed who struck him; *~ dog* (colloq.), ~ sausage sandwiched in roll of bread; ~-*foot*, in haste; impetuous person; ~-*house*, heated building with glass roof & sides for growing plants out of season or in colder climate; ~-*pot*, mutton, beef, with potatoes etc. cooked in oven in tight-lidded pot; ~-*press*, press of glazed boards & ~ metal plates for smoothing paper or cloth, (v.t.) press (paper etc.) in this; ~-*short*, (of iron) brittle in its state; ~-*spur*, rash person (surname

‖ **hôtel'** (also hō-, ō-), n. House for accommodation of travellers etc.; (usu. large) inn. [F *hôtel*, later form of HOSTEL]

Hŏt'tentŏt, n. Member of S.-African race formerly occupying region near the Cape; (fig.) person of inferior intellect or culture. [Du., perh. = stammerer]

‖ **hough** (hŏk), n., & v.t. 1. Joint of quadruped's hind leg between knee & fetlock. **2.** v.t. Hamstring. [OE *hōh* heel, cogn. w. HEEL¹]

hound, n. Dog for the chase, esp. one hunting by scent; *the* ~, pack of fox-~s; MASTER *of* ~s; despicable man; player who follows scent in HARE *& ~s*; *~ *, *tongue*, genus of plants of the borage family. Hence ~'ISH¹ a. [com.-Teut.; OE & G *hund*, Du. *hond*, perh. cogn. w. Gk *kuōn kunos*, L *canis*]

hound², v.t. Chase (as) with hound; set (person, or fig. person) *at* (quarry etc.); urge (person) *on*. [f. prec.]

hour (owr), n. Twenty-fourth part of day, 60 minutes; short time; *the* time o'clock; (pl.) fixed time for daily work etc., as *office* ~*s are* 10 *to* 5; *at the eleventh* ~, at a late stage (*Matt.* xx); *small* ~*s*, 1, 2, etc., a.m.; *a good or early bad or late, regular*, ~*s*, (time for getting up & going to bed); *the question of the* ~ (present time); *in a good, evil*, ~, (unluckily); (prayers to be said at) seven stated times of day appointed for prayer; (Astron.) 15° of longitude; ~-*circle*, meridian (24 of which are usu. marked on globe); ~-*glass*, sand-glass running for an ~; ~-*hand* (showing ~ on clock etc.). [f. OF *ure* f. L f. Gk *hōra* season, hour]

hour'i (owr'), n. Nymph of Mohammedan Paradise; voluptuously beautiful woman. [F, f. Pers. *hurī* f. Arab. *haurā* (*hawira* have eyes like gazelle's)]

hour'ly (owr-), a. & adv. (Occurring, done, reckoned) every hour; continual-(ly), frequent(ly). [HOUR-+-LY¹,²]

house¹ (hows), n. (pl. pron. -zĭz). 1.

hŏt², v.t. (colloq.; -tt-). Heat, warm up. [f. prec.]

Hŏtch'kiss, n. A kind of machine-gun. [inventor's name]

hŏtch'pŏtch, -pŏt, n. Dish of many mixed ingredients, esp. mutton broth with vegetables; (Law) blending of properties for purpose of securing equal division of property of intestate parent; mixture, medley. [f. F *hochepot* (*hocher* shake+*pot*); *-potch* by assim.]

Building for human habitation or (usu. w. defining prefix) occupation, as ALMS~, BAKE~, LIGHT¹~, SUMMER~; ~ of God, church, place of worship; inn (a drink on the ~, at innkeeper's expense); bow down in the ~ of Rimmon, sacrifice one's principles for the sake of conformity (2 Kings v. 18); ALE, COFFEE, EATING, ~; PUBLIC, TIED, ~. 2. Building for keeping animals or goods, as hen~, STORE~, WARE¹~. 3. ||(Oxf. Univ.) the H~ = Christ Church. 5. =(boys in) BOARDING-~. 6. (Building used by) an assembly, as H~ of COMMONS, LORDS, H~s of PARLIA-MENT; make a H~, secure presence of 40 members in H~ of Commons; || the H~, (colloq.) Stock Exchange, (euphem.) work~, (Pol.) H~ of Commons or Lords; CLEARING, CUSTOM, ~; || COUNTING-HOUSE. 7. (Audience in) theatre (full ~, with all seats engaged; performance in theatre etc. (second ~ starts at 9 o'clock). 8. Household, family, dynasty (the H~ of Windsor, British Royal family); ~ mercantile firm. 9. (Astrol.) twelfth part of the heavens. 10. A game of chance playable by large numbers with no apparatus but pencil & paper; (Army sl.) gambling form of lotto. 11. attrib. (Of animals) kept in, frequenting, infesting, the ~, as ~-cat, -fly, etc. 12. ~ of call, ~ where carriers call for commissions, ~ where person may be heard of, etc.; ~ of cards (built by child out of playing-cards; often fig. of insecure scheme etc.); ~ of ill fame, brothel; || H~ of Keys, branch of Manx legislature; ~ & home, (empha-tic) home; ~-to-~, carried on from ~ to ~; BRING down the ~; keep ~, maintain, provide for, a household; keep open ~, provide general hospitality; keep the ~, not go outdoors; like a ~ on fire, vigo-rously, fast. 13. ||~-agent (for sale & letting of ~s); ~-boat, boat fitted up for living in; ~-breaker, person entering another's ~ by day (cf. BURGLAR) with felonious intent, man employed in demolishing old ~s; ~-dinner, (at clubs) specially appointed dinner for mem-bers & guests; ~-dog (kept to guard ~); ~-flag, that flown by a firm's ship; ~-flannel (coarse, for cleaning floor etc.); ~-keeper, woman managing affairs of household, (also) person in charge of ~, office, etc.; ~-keeping, (good, bad, liberal, etc.) domestic economy; ~-leek, plant with pink flowers growing on walls & roofs; ~-maid, female servant in charge of reception & bed rooms; ~-maid's knee, inflammation of knee-cap due to kneel-ing; ~-master (of school boarding-~); ~-party (of guests staying at country ~ etc.); ||~-place, living-room in farm-~ etc.; ~-proud, preoccupied with the care & beautification of the home; ~-room, accommodation in ~ (would not

give it ~-room, take it as a gift); ~-surgeon, -physician, residing in the hospital; ~-top, esp. proclaim from the ~-tops, publicly; ~-warming, celebration of en-trance into new ~; ~-work, cleaning, cooking, etc. Hence ~'FUL(2) (-sf-) n. ~'LESS (-sl-) a. [com.-Teut.: OE hūs, Du. huis, G haus]

house²(-z), v.t. & i. Receive (person etc.), store (goods), in house or as house does; (Naut.) place (gun etc.) in secure position, (lower (upper masts); take shelter (as) in house; provide houses for (population); esp. the housing problem); (Carpentry) fix in a socket, mortise, etc. [OE hūsian (as prec.), cf. Du. huizen, G hausen]

house'hold (-s-h-), n. Inmates of house; domestic establishment; (pl.) second quality of flour; ||~ troops (employed to guard sovereign's person); ~ gods, (Rom. Ant.) Lares & Penates, (fig.) essentials of home life; ~ word, familiar saying or name. [HOUSE¹+HOLD²]

house'holder(-s-h-), n. One who occupies house as his own dwelling (esp. formerly as entitled to franchise); head of house-hold. [HOUSE¹+HOLDER]

housewife, n. 1. (hows'wif). Mistress of family; (good, bad) domestic economist. 2. (hŭz'if). Case for needles, thread, etc. Hence house'wifely¹ (-fli) a. [ME hus(e)wif (HOUSE¹, WIFE)]

house'wifery (-swifri), n. Domestic eco-nomy, housekeeping. [prec.+-RY]

hous'ing (-z-), n. Horse's cloth covering, for protection or ornament. [obs. house f. OF huche housing, etym. dub., +-ING¹]

Houyhnhnm (hwi'nim), n. Horse with human characteristics (Gulliver's Travels). [imit. of horse's neigh; made by Swift]

Hō'va, n. One of ruling tribe in Mada-gascar. [native]

hove. See HEAVE.

hov'el (or hŭ-), n. Open shed, out-house; mean dwelling; conical building enclosing kiln. [?]

hov'eller (or hŭ-), n. Unlicensed pilot or boatman, one who goes out to wrecks. [?]

hov'er (or hŭ-), v.i., & n. (Of bird etc.), hang in the air (over, about, spot); loiter about (person, place). (n.) ~ing, state of suspense. [n. f. vb] perh. f. obs. hove, etym. dub.]

how, adv. & n. 1. (In direct or indirect question) in what way, as ~ does he do it?, ask him ~ he does it, tell him ~ to do it, (with intensive addition) ~ the deuce, devil, dickens, ever, ~ on earth; ~ are you?, ~ do you do?, what is your state of health?; ~ is that for high, queer, etc.? (colloq. invitation to wonder); (colloq.)~ d'ye-do, embarrassing situation; (Crick.) ~'s that?, is he out or not?; ~ now?, what is the meaning of this? ; (can you show that to be) so?; ~ (at what price) is corn?; (in indirect statement, rhet. for)

that (told us ~ **God was almighty**); (in question or exclamation) to what extent, as ~ *far is it?*, ~ *far it is!*, ~ *many are there?*, ~ *many there are!*, ~ *would you like it?*, ~ *he snores!*; (in relative clause) in whatever way, as, (do it ~ *you can*); *& ~! (sl.), = & a good deal more (chiefly used ironically or intensively); *here's ~!* = here's your good health (drinking formula). 2. n. The way a thing is done (the ~ *of it*). 3. ~be'it (arch.), nevertheless; ~ever, in whatever way, to whatever extent, nevertheless, (arch.) in any case; ~EVER; ~soer'er, *how — soever*, in whatsoever manner, to what extent soever; ~much?, (sl.) what? (as request to repeat what was said); ~ *much?*, (sl.) what? (as request to person to repeat his remark or a particular word; *he plays the ~ much?*). [OE hú, cf. Du. hoe; f. stem of WHO]

howd'ah (-a), n. Seat for two or more, usu. with canopy, on elephant's back. [f. Pers. *haudah* f. Arab. *haudaj* litter].

how'itzer, n. Short piece of ordnance for high-angle firing of shells at lower velocities than a gun. [earlier *howitz* f. G. *haubitze* f. Boh. *houfnice* catapult]

howl[1], v.i. & t. (of animals) utter long loud doleful cry; (of persons) utter long cry of pain, derision, etc.; utter (words) with ~ing. [ME *houlen*, cf. Du. *huilen*, G *heulen*, also Gk *kaláō*, L *ululare*]

howl[2], n. Long doleful cry of dog, wolf, etc.; loud cry of pain; yell of derision; (Wireless) whining noise in receiver during tuning-in, often affecting other listeners. [f. prec.]

howl'er, n. In vbl senses; esp.: S.-Amer. monkey; (sl.) glaring blunder; (sl.) come a ~, come to grief. [-ER[2]]

‖ howl'et, n. (dial.). Owl. [prob. f. F *hulotte* (as OWL)]

howl'ing, a. That howls; ~ DERVISH; glaring, as a ~ *shame*. [-ING[2]]

hoy[1], n. Small vessel, usu. rigged as sloop, carrying passengers & goods esp. for short distances. [prob. f. MDu. *hoei*, etym. dub.]

hoy[2], int. used to call attention, drive beasts, & (Naut.) hail or call aloft. [natural cry]

hoy'a, n. Genus of climbing plants with pink, white, or yellow flowers, known as *wax-flowers*. [f. *Hoy*, gardener, d. 1821]

hoyd'en, n. Boisterous girl. Hence ~HOOD, ~ISM, nn., ~ISH[1] a. [?]

hub[1], n. Central part of wheel, rotating on or with axle, & from which spokes radiate; nave; (fig.) central point of interest etc. (esp. ~ *of the universe*). [?]

hub[2], hubb'y[2], n. (colloq.). Husband. [abbr.]

hub'ble-bubble, n. Form of hookah; bubbling noise; confused talk. [limit.]

hubb'ub, n. Confused din; disturbance, riot; confused yelling of war-cry. [of Ir. orig.; cf. Gael. *ubub* int. of contempt. Ir. *abu*, a war-cry]

hub'ris, n. Insolent pride or security. So hubris'tic a. [Gk: prop. *hy-*]

huck'aback, n. Stout linen fabric with rough surface, for towels etc. [?]

huc'kle, n. Hip; haunch; ~back(ed), hump-backed(); ~-bone, hip, haunch, -bone, (also) knuckle-bone of quadruped, [dim. of obs. *huck* hip, etym. dub.]

huc'kleberry (-kelb-), n. (Fruit of) low berry-bearing shrub common in N. Amer. [perh. corrupt. of *hurtleberry* WHORTLE-BERRY]

huck'ster[1], n. Pedlar, hawker; mercenary person. Hence ~ERY(2) n. [earlier than obs. *huck* v. higgle; see -STER]

huck'ster[2], v.i. & t. Bargain, haggle; carry on petty traffic in (lit. & fig.); adulterate. Hence ~ER[1], ~ESS[1], nn. [f. prec.]

hüd'dle, v.t. & i., & n. 1. Heap together confusedly; crowd (things etc.) promiscuously together, *up, into, out of*, etc.; coil oneself *up*; hurry *over, through*, botch *up*, (work etc.); (intr.) nestle closely together. 2. n. Confused mass; confusion, bustle; *(secret) conference, esp. *go into a ~ (with)* (sl.). [(n. f. & vb) perh. f. Teut. root *hud*- cover +-le[3]]

Hud'ibras'tic, a. In the metre or manner of Butler's *Hudibras*, mock-heroic poem of 1663-78. [after *fantastic* etc.]

hue[1], n. Colour, tint; variety of colour caused by admixture of another. Hence ~(huED) (hūd) a. [OE *híw*, cf. Goth. *hiwi* form, also Skr. *chavi*]

hue[2], n. & cry; clamour of pursuit or assault; outcry (*against*); proclamation for capture of criminal; (formerly) police gazette with particulars of offenders wanted etc. [f. OF *hu, huё*, outcry, f. *huer* shout, imit.]

huff, v.t. & i. Bully, storm at; bully (person *into, out of*, thing or doing); offend; take offence; (Draughts) remove (opponent's man) from board as forfeit (orig. after blowing on the piece). [limit. f. sound of blowing; v. & n. f. 16th c.]

huff[2], n. Fit of petulance, esp. *in a ~, take ~*; (Draughts) act of huffing. Hence ~'ISH[1], ~'Y[1] aa., ~ily[2], ~ishness nn. [see prec.]

hug, v.t. (-gg-), & n. 1. Squeeze tightly in one's arms, usu. with affection; (of bear) squeeze (man etc.) between its forelegs; delight in, cling to, (prejudices etc.); exhibit fondness for (person); congratulate oneself (*on, for*); keep close to (shore etc.). 2. n. Strong clasp; grip in wrestling, esp. Cornish—. [?]

huge, a. Very large; enormous; (of immaterial things) great. Hence ~NESS n., ~(-in-)n, [prob. f. OF *ahuge*, etym. dub.]

huge'ly (-jli), adv. Enormously, very much.

hu'geous (-jus), a. (usu. joc.). Huge. Hence ~LY² adv., ~NESS n., (-jus~). [-OUS; f. 1529]

hugg'er-mugg'er (-g-), n., a., adv., & v.t. & i. Secrecy; secret(ly); confusion; confused(ly); (v.t.) conceal, hush up; (v.i.) proceed in secret or muddled fashion. [?] || **hugg'ery** (-g-), n. Practice (on part of barrister etc.) of courting attorney etc. for employment. [f. HUG¹ + -ERY]

hug'uenot (-ge-), n. (hist.). French Protestant. [F, perh. assim. of G *eidgenosz* confederate to F pers. name *Hugues*]

hul'a (-ōō-), n. Hawaiian woman's dance. [native word]

hulk, n. Body of dismantled ship, used as store vessel etc. or (pl., hist.) as prison; unwieldy vessel; (fig.) big person or mass. [OE *hulc*, cf. OF *hulke*, Du. *hulk*, perh. f. Gk *holkas* towed ship, ship of burden (*helkō* draw)]

hul'king, a. Bulky; clumsy. [prec. + -ING²]

hull¹, n., & v.t. 1. Outer covering of fruit, esp. pod of peas & beans; (fig.) covering. 2. v.t. Remove ~ of. [OE *hulu* (*helan* cover), cf. G *hülle* covering]

hull², n., & v.t. 1. Frame of ship; ~*down*, far away, so that ~ is invisible. 2. v.t. Strike (ship) in ~ with shot torpedo, etc. [perh.=prec.]

hullabaloo', n. Uproar. [prob. redupl. f. HULLO; f. 18th c.]

hullo', **-loa** (-lō), int. used to call attention, express surprise, or answer call, esp. on telephone. [cf. HALLO]

hum¹, v.i. & t. (-mm-). Make continuous murmuring sound, as of bee, spinning top, etc.; make low inarticulate vocal sound, esp. (usu. ~ *& ha*) of hesitation; sing with closed lips; (colloq.) be in state of activity, as *make things* ~; (sl.) smell unpleasantly; (v.t.) utter, sing, with closed lips. [imit.]

hum², n. Humming sound esp. of hesitation (usu. ~*s & ha's*), applause, surprise, etc.; (sl.) bad smell. [imit.]

hum³, int. expr. hesitation, dissent, etc. [= HUMBUG]

hum', n. (sl.). Sham, hoax. [=HUMBUG]

hum'an, a. & n. Of, belonging to, man, as ~ *nature*; that is a man or consists of men, as ~ *race, creature*; of man as opp. to God, as ~ *affairs*; having, showing, the qualities distinctive of man, as *more,* ~NESS, *than* ~; (n., joc.) ~ *being*. Hence ~NESS (-n-n-) n. [f, F *humain* (12th c.) f. L *humanus* (*homo* man, see -AN²)]

hum'ane, a. Benevolent, compassionate; ||H~ *Society* (for rescue of drowning persons); ~ *killer*, instrument for painless slaughter of cattle; (of branches of study) tending to refinement, elegant. Hence ~LY² (-nl-) adv., ~NESS (-n-n-) n. [differentiated f. prec. after 1700]

hum'anism, n. Devotion to human interests; system concerned with human (not divine) interests, or with the human race (not the individual); Religion of HUMANITY; literary culture, esp. that of the humanists. [-ISM]

hum'anist, n. Student of human nature or human affairs; student (esp. in 14th-16th cc.) of Roman & Greek literature & antiquities, whence **hūmanis'tic** a. [f. F *humaniste* (as HUMAN, see -IST)]

hūmanitā'rian, n. & a. 1. One who professes humanism (Religion of Humanity); visionary philanthropist. 2. adj. Holding, concerned with, the views of ~s. Hence ~ISM n. [f. foll. + -ARIAN]

hūmăn'itў, n. Human nature; (pl.) human attributes; the human race; humaneness, benevolence; (pl.) benevolent acts; *Religion of H~y* (rejecting the supernatural & concerned chiefly or wholly with the advancement of man's welfare; *the* ~*ies*, polite scholarship, esp. of Latin & Greek classics; || (Sc. Univv.; H~y) study of Latin. [f. F *humanité* f. L *humanitatem* (as HUMAN, see -TY)]

hūman'ize, v.t. & i. Make human, give human character to (~*ed milk*, cow's milk prepared to resemble human milk); make, become, humane. Hence ~A'TION n. [f. F *humaniser* (as HUMAN, see HZE)]

hūm'ankind, n. Mankind.

hūm'anlỹ, adv. In a human manner; by human means; from human point of view; with human feelings. [-LY²]

hūm'ble, a. (comp. & sup. pron. -bler, -blist), & v.t. 1. Having, showing, low estimate of one's own importance; (formerly, esp. in subscribing letter) *your* ~ *servant*; of lowly condition; (of things) of modest pretensions, dimensions, etc.; *eat* ~ *pie*, make ~ apology, submit to humiliation; *H~ Plant*, common sensitive plant. 2. v.t. Make~, bring low, abase (oneself etc.). Hence ~NESS (-bel-) n., **hūm'blŷ²** adv. [(vb f. a.) OF f. L *humilis* lowly (*humus* ground, -IL)]

hūm'ble-bee (-bel-), n. Bumble-bee. [f. 15th c.; cf. G *hummel* large wild bee, Du. *hommel* drone bee]

hūm'bug, n., & v.t. & i. (-gg-). 1. Fraud, sham; deception; (as int.) nonsense!; impostor; kind of hard boiled sweet usu. flavoured with peppermint. 2. v.t. Delude (person *into, out of*, thing or *doing*); (v.i.) be, behave like, a ~. Hence **hūmbŭg'gERY** (-g-) n. [(vb f. n.) f. 1750, etym. dub.]

hūm'drum, a. & n., & v.i. (-mm-). Commonplace(ness), dull(ness); (v.i.) proceed in ~ way. Hence ~NESS n. [f. 1550; prob. redupl. f. HUM v.]

hūm'er|us, n. (anat.). Bone of the upper arm in man; corresponding bone in other vertebrates. Hence ~AL a. (also n., ~*al veil*, oblong silk scarf worn round priest's shoulders during parts of the Mass etc.). [L, =shoulder]

hūm'id, a. Moist, damp. So **hūmid'ifY**

v.t., **húmíd'ity** n. [f. L (ūmēre be moist, see -ID)]

húmíl'iate, v.t. Lower the dignity or self-respect of; mortify. Hence or cogn. ~**āting**[2] a., ~**ā'tion** n. [f. LL *humiliare*]

húmíl'ity, n. Humbleness; meekness; humble condition. [f. F *humilité* f. L *humilitatem* (as HUMBLE, see -TY)]

|| hümm'el, a. (Sc.). (Of cattle and stags) hornless. [cf. LG *hommel* hornless beast]

hümm'ing, a. In vbl senses; also or esp. (colloq.) Vigorous, energetic, as a ~ knock on the head; ~**bird** (of several species that make ~ sound by vibration of wings); ~**top** (~ when it spins). [f. HUM v. +-ING[1]]

hümm'ock, n. Hillock; rising ground, esp. in marsh; hump or ridge in icefield. Hence ~**y**[1] a. [orig. dub.]

húm'oral, a. (med.). Of the bodily humours; ~ *pathology*, doctrine referring all disease to state of the humours. [f. F, f. LL, f. L as HUMOUR, see -AL]

húm'orist, n. Facetious person; humorous talker, actor or writer. Hence **húm'oríst'ic** a. [f. F *humoriste* f. med. L *humorista* (as prec., see -IST)]

húm'orous, a. Full of humour; facetious, funny. Hence ~**LY**[2] adv., ~**NESS** n. [-OUS]

húm'our[1] (-mer; also ū-), n. State of mind, mood; inclination, as *in the ~ for fighting*; facetiousness, comicality; faculty of perceiving this; jocose imagination (less intellectual & more sympathetic than wit), whence ~**LESS** a; *out of the* ~, displeased; *good, ill,* ~ (temper), whence ~**ED**[2] (-erd) a.; *cardinal* ~**s** (hist.), four chief fluids of the body (blood, phlegm, choler, melancholy), determining person's physical & mental qualities; *aqueous, vitreous,* ~, transparent fluid parts of the eye. [AF, f. L (*humorem* moisture)]

húm'our[2] (-mer; also ū-), v.t. Gratify, indulge, (person, taste, temper, etc.); adapt oneself to, make concessions to. [f. prec.]

húm'oursome (-mer-), a. Capricious; peevish. Hence ~**NESS** n. [-SOME]

húmp, n., & v.t. I. Protuberance, esp. on the back, as deformity or (in camel etc.) as normal feature; rounded boss of earth etc.; || (sl.) fit of depression or vexation, as *it gives me the* ~; ~**back**, (person having) back with a ~; ~**backed**, having such a back. 2. v.t. Make ~-**shaped**; annoy, depress; (Austral.) hoist up, shoulder, (one's pack, swag, or bluey). Hence ~**ED**[2] (-pt), ~**LESS**, ~**y**[2], aa. [f. 1680, ~**backed** replacing *crump-backed*. Du. *homp*=thick piece (cut off)]

humph (hmf), int. & v.i. Int. expr. doubt or dissatisfaction; (v.i.) utter this. [So.]

húmp'ty-dúmp'ty, n. Short dumpy person; (from nursery rhyme in which H~ is taken to mean an egg) person, thing, that once thrown down cannot be restored. [for *humpy-dumpy*]

húm'pý, n. Australian hut. [native compd.]

Hún, n. One of an Asiatic nomad race who invaded & ravaged Europe in 4th & 5th cc.; (derog.) German (esp. Prussian). Hence ~**n'ish** a. [OE *Hūne* f. med.L *Hunni*]

húm'us, n. Vegetable mould. [L,=ground]

hunch[1], v.t. Bend, arch, convexly; thrust out, up, to form a hump. [?]

hunch[2], n. Hump; thick piece; *(sl.) have a ~ that*, conceive the idea, suspect, rather think, that. Hence ~**y**[2] a. [?]

hún'dred, n. & a. (Cardinal number) ten times ten (100, C), as *a, one, six, several, ~s of men, ~s of them or of my friends, men, a, one, six~ of them, some, several, ~s of* etc.; (ordinal, in compds) *the ~-&-first, six~-&-ninth*; (also ~ *& one*) large number; *not a ~ miles from* (joc.), at or close to; *a ~ per cent efficient*, doing the utmost in practice that it theoretically should; ~ *pounds* (of money); || (chiefly hist.) subdivision of county or shire, having its own court; CHILTERN HUN-DREDS; *great, long,* ~ 120; ~ *of* BRICK's; ~**weight**, 112lb. avoirdupois (abbr. cwt, *100lb.; ~s *& thousands*, sweets like small shot used chiefly for decorating cakes etc. Hence ~**FOLD** n., ~**TH**[2] a. & n. [OE *hundred*, hym 'All people that ~', version of Ps. C, or its tune). [OE (*hund* hundred +-*red* = Goth. -*rath* number]

hung. See HANG v.

húng'er[1] (-ngg-), n. Uneasy sensation, exhausted condition, caused by want of food; (fig.) strong desire (*for, after,* etc.); ~-**march** (undertaken by body of unemployed to call attention to their condition; so ~-**marcher**); ~-**strike**, prisoner's refusal to take food in order to procure release. [OE *hungor*, cf. Du. *honger*, G *hunger*]

húng'er[2] (-ngg-), v.i. & t. Feel hunger; have craving (*for, after*); (p.p., arch.) hungry; (trans.) starve (*into* submission. [OE *hyngran*, f. prec.]

húng'rý (-ngg-), a. Feeling hunger (~ *as a hunter*); showing hunger, as *a ~ look*; inducing hunger, as *a ~ air*; ~ *rice*, W.-African grain allied to millet; (fig.) eager, greedy; (of soil) poor, barren; || *H~ Forties* (hist.), the decade 1840–9 in England, a period of great distress among the poor. Hence **hún gril'y**[2] adv., **hún'griness** n. [OE *hungrig* (as HUNGER]

hunk, n. Large piece cut off; clumsy piece; hunch. [19th c.; cf. WFlem *hunke*]

|| hunk'ers, n. pl. The hams (esp. in phr. *on one's* ~, in a squatting position). [Sc., f. *hunker* to squat]

hunks, n. Close-fisted man, miser. [?]

•**hunky-dory**, a. (sl.). Excellent, top-hole. [f. U.S. *hunky*, f. *hunk* a, right]

Hunnish. See HUN.

hunt¹, v.i. & t. Pursue wild animals or game; (trans.) chase (these) for food or sport; seek *after, for*; drive *away, out*; scour (district) in pursuit of game; use (horse, hounds) in ~*ing*; ~ *down*, bring to bay; ~ *out*, track out, find by search; ~ *up*, search for; ~ *in* COUPLES; ~ *the hare, slipper, squirrel*, games. [OE *huntian* f. *hunta* hunter, cogn. w. Goth. *hinthan* seize]

hunt², n. Hunting (lit. & fig.); persons hunting with a pack; hunting district; ~ *ball* (given by members of ~, men wearing pink). [f. prec.]

hun'ter, n. One who hunts; (fig.) *fortune, place*, etc., ~; horse for hunting; watch with hinged cover protecting glass or (*half*-~) outer part of it; ~'s *moon*, full moon after harvest moon. Hence **hün'tress¹** n. [-ER¹]

hun'ting, n. In vbl senses; ~-*box*, small house for use during ~-season; ~ cog¹, ~-CROP; ~-*ground*, place where one hunts (often fig.) *happy* ~-*ground(s)*, the future state (prop. as expected by Amer. Indians), good place for ~ (fig.); ~-*horn*, horn used in ~, second pommel on near side of side-saddle. [-ING¹]

hunts'man, n. Hunter; man in charge of (esp. fox-) hounds.

hur'dle, n., & v.t. Portable rectangular frame strengthened with withes or wooden bars, for temporary fence etc.; ~ *race*, (hist.) frame on which traitors were dragged to execution; (v.t.) fence off etc. with ~s. [(vb f. n.) OE *hyrdel*; cf. Du. *horde*, G *hürde*, also L *cratis* hurdle, Gk *kurtia* wickerwork]

hurd'ler, n. One who makes hurdles, or runs in hurdle-races. [-ER¹]

hurd'y-gurdy, n. Musical instrument with droning sound, played by turning handle, orig. one with rosined wheel turned by right hand & played by left; (colloq.) barrel organ & street piano. [prob. imit.]

hurl, v.t., & n. 1. Throw violently from some position (lit. & fig.); throw (missile etc., also fig.); ||(Sc.) convey in a wheeled vehicle. 2. n. ~*ing*, violent throw; ||(Sc.) a ride in a wheeled vehicle. [cf. LG *hurreln*; prob. imit.]

hūr'ley, n. (Ir.) Hockey; hockey-stick. [as prec.]

Hur'lingham (-ngam), n. (Used for ~ Park, Fulham, headquarters of ~ Polo Club.

hūr'ly, n. (arch.). Commotion. [as HURL]

hūr'ly-būr'ly, n. Commotion, tumult. [f. 1540; redupl. f. HURL v.]

hurrah' (hu-, hoo-), **-ray'**, int., n., & v.i. Int. expr. exultation or approbation; (n.) this cry; (v.i.) shout ~. [replaces *huzza*; cf. Swed. & Da. *hurra*, Du. *hoera*]

hū'rricane, n. Storm with violent wind with velocity of 75 miles an hour or over, esp. W.-Indian cyclone (also fig.); ~-*bird*, frigate-bird; ~ *deck*, light upper deck; ~ *lamp* (designed to resist wind). [f. Sp. *huracan*, of Carib orig.]

hū'rry¹, n. Undue haste; eagerness (*to do*, a thing) done quickly; eagerness (*to do*, *for* thing); (w. neg. or interrog.) need for haste; (colloq.) *you will not beat that in a* ~ (easily), *shall not ask again in a* ~ (willingly); ~-*scurry* adv., adj., & n. (in) disorderly haste, (v.i.) proceed thus. [f. 16th c.; imit., cf. HURL]

hū'rry², v.t. & i. Carry, drive, (person etc. *away, along, into, into doing*, etc.) with undue haste; move, act, with great or undue haste; ~y *up*, make haste. Hence ~**iedly²** adv., ~**iedness** n., (-id-). [as prec.]

hurst, n. Hillock; sandbank in sea or river; wooded eminence; wood. [OE *hyrst*, cf. G dial. *horst* sandbank, MDu. *horst* thicket]

hurt¹, n. Wound, material injury; harm, wrong. Hence ~'**FUL**, ~'**LESS**, aa., ~'**fulIY²** adv., ~'**fulness** n. [prob. f. OF *hurte*, as foll.]

hurt², v.t. & i. (*hurt*). Cause bodily injury or pain to; damage; inflict injury upon; distress, wound, (person, his feelings etc.); (colloq.) suffer injury or pain. [prob. f. OF *hurter* (mod. *heurter*) knock, etym. dub.]

hūr'tle, v.t. & i., & n. (arch.). Strike against; hurl swiftly; strike *against*; move with clattering sound; come with a crash; (n.) hurtling, clashing sound. [(n. f. vb) prob. f. HURT² +-LE(3)]

hus'band¹ (-z-), n. Man joined to woman by marriage; ~'s *tea*, weak & cold; ||(arch.) *good, bad*, ~ (economist). Hence ~**HOOD**, ~**SHIP**, nn., ~**LIKE** a. [OE *hūsbonda* master of house (*hūs* house + *bónda* f. ON *bóndi* freeholder f. *būa* dwell)]

hus'band² (-z-), v.t. Manage thriftily; economize; ||(arch.) till (ground), cultivate (plants); (poet., joc.) provide with husband; (rare) marry (woman). [f. prec.]

hus'bandman (-z-), n. Farmer.

hus'bandry (-z-), n. Farming; (*good, bad*) economy; careful management. [-RY]

hush¹, n. Stillness; silence; ~-*money*, paid to prevent exposure. [f. foll.]

hush², v.t. & i. Silence, quiet; ~ *up*, suppress (affair); be silent, esp. (as int.) ~!; ~'*abỹ* int. used to lull child; ~-*ed* adj. phr., to be kept specially secret; ~-*ship* (of great length, speed, & gun-power, secretly built; cf. Q-ship). [back formation f. obs. adj. *husht* f. *husht, hast*, intt. (imit.)]

husk, n., & v.t. 1. Dry outer covering of some fruits or seeds; (fig.) worthless

husky outside part of anything; disease of cattle. 2. n. t. Remove ~ from. [late ME *huske*, etym. dub.]

hus'ky[1], a. Of, full of, husks; dry as a husk; (of voice or person) dry, hoarse, whence ~LILY[2] adv., ~NESS[1] n.; (colloq.) tough, strong, hefty (& as n., ~y person). [-Y[2]]

hus'ky[2], n. Eskimo dog; (*Hu~*) Eskimo person or language. [prob. = ESKIMO]

hussar' (-z-), n. Soldier of light cavalry regiment (orig. Hungarian light horseman of 15th c.). [f. Hung. *huszár* f. OSerb. *husar* f. It. *corsaro* CORSAIR]

Huss'ite, n. Follower of John Huss, Bohemian religious reformer of 15th c. [-ITE[1]]

huss'y, -zzy, n. Woman of light or worthless character; pert girl. [f. HOUSEWIFE]

hus'tings (-z), n. Platform from which (before 1872) candidates for Parliament were nominated; election proceedings; court (now rarely) held in Guildhall of London. [OE *hūsting* house-assembly]

hus'tle (-sl), v.t. & i., & n. 1. Push roughly, jostle; thrust (person etc. *into*, *out of*, etc.); impel unceremoniously (*into* thing or *doing*); (v.i.) push roughly *against*; push one's way; hurry, bustle. 2. n. ~ing. [(n. f. vb) f. Du. *husselen* shake, toss]

hut, n., & v.t. & i.(-tt-). 1. Small mean house of rude construction; (Mil.) temporary wooden house for troops; ~*circle* (Archaeol.), ring of stones or earth indicating site of prehistoric ~. 2. v.t. Place (troops etc.) in ~s; (v.i.) lodge in ~. Hence ~MENT n., ~ encampment. [(vb. f. F *hutte*) f. F *hutte* f. G *hütte*]

hutch, n. Box-like pen for rabbits etc.; hut, cabin, small house; truck used in mining etc. [ME & F *huche* f. med. L *hutica*, etym. dub.]

huzoor', n. Title of respect used by Indians in addressing superiors. [Arab. *hadūr* the presence]

huzza' (-ah), int., n., & v.i. & t. Int. of exultation, encouragement, or applause; (make, greet with) the cry ~. [imit.]

hy'acinth, n. Genus of bulbous plants with bell-shaped flowers of various colours, esp. purplish blue, so (esp. as Homeric epithet of doubtful sense for *locks*, *hair*) ~INE[1] (-in) a.; this colour; precious stone, orange variety of zircon. [earlier *jacynth*, ult. f. L f. Gk *huakinthos*, flower & gem, also name of youth loved by Apollo]

Hy'adēs (-z), n.pl. Group of stars near Pleiades. [f. Gk *Huades* (acc. to pop. etym., f. *huō* rain, but perh. f. *hus* swine)]

hyaena. See HYENA.

hy'aline, a. & n. Glass-like, vitreous (chiefly techn.); (n., poet.) smooth sea, clear sky, etc. [f. L f. Gk *hualinos* (*hualos* glass, see -INE[2])]

hy'alite, n. Colourless variety of opal. [f. Gk *hualos* glass, see -ITE[1]]

hy'aloid, a. & n. (anat.). Glassy; ~ (*membrane*), thin transparent membrane enveloping vitreous humour of eye. [f. F *hyaloïde* f. L f. Gk *hualoeidēs* (as prec., -OID)]

hy'brid, n. & a. 1. Offspring of two animals or plants of different species or varieties; person of mixed nationality; (fig.) thing, word, composed of incongruous elements. 2. adj. Crossbred, mongrel; heterogeneous; ~ *bill* in Parliament, one combining characteristics of public & private bill; referred to a ~ *committee*. Hence ~ITY (-id·) n. [f. L *hybrida* offspring of tame sow & wild boar; etym. dub.]

hy'bridism, n. Fact, condition, of being hybrid; cross-breeding. [prec. + -ISM]

hy'bridīze, v.t. & i. 1. Subject (species etc.) to cross-breeding; produce hybrids; (of animal or plant) interbreed. Hence ~ABLE a., ~A'TION n. [HYBRID + -IZE]

Hyde Park, n. A London park, a fashionable resort, & of late years the scene of many political and other demonstrations.

hy'dra, n. (Gk Myth.) snake whose many heads grew again when cut off; (fig.) thing hard to extirpate; water-snake; a fresh-water polyp. [L, f. Gk *hudra* watersnake]

hydrān'gea (-jə), n. Genus of shrubs with globular clusters of white, blue, or pink flowers. [L f. Gk *hudōr* water + *aggos* vessel]

hy'drant, n. Pipe (esp. in street) with nozzle to which hose can be attached, for drawing water from main. [U.S. (HYDRO-, -ANT)]

hy'drate[1], n. (chem.). Compound of water with another compound or an element. [f. Gk *hudōr* water, see -ATE[1]]

hy'drāte[2], v.t. (chem.). Combine with water. Hence ~A'TION n. [f. prec.]

hydraul'ic, a. & n. 1. Of water conveyed through pipes or channels; operated by water-power, as ~ *lift*, ~ *ram*, automatic pump in which kinetic energy of descending column of water raises some of the water above its original level; hardens under water, as ~ *cement*; ~ *press*, hydrostatic press. 2. n. pl. Science of conveyance of liquids through pipes etc., esp. as motive power. Hence or cogn. **hydraul'ically** adv., **hydraul'icon** (-ikon) n. [f. L f. Gk *hudraulikos* (*hudōr* water + *aulos* pipe, see -IC)]

hy'drō, n. (pl. ~s). = HYDROPATHIC. [colloq. abbr.]

hy'dro-, comb. form of Gk *hudōr* water. 1. (chem.) containing hydrogen. So ~DEN n. [f. HYDROGEN + -IC]

hydro- in comb. = Gk *hudro-* comb. form of *hudōr* water, (1) in miscell. terms. w. sense 'having to do with water', (2) in names of diseases, w. sense 'dropsical' or 'affected with accumulation of serous fluid', (3) in chem. terms, usu. w. sense ' combined with hydrogen '; as:—*carb'on*, compound of hydrogen & carbon;—*céphá'ie*, —*céph'alous*, affected with this:—*chlor'ic*, containing hydrogen & chlorine:—*cyáni'ic*, containing hydrogen & cyanogen, esp. —*cyanic acid*, prussic acid;—*dynám'ic(al)*, of the forces acting on or exerted by liquids;—*dynám'ics*, science of these forces;—*elec'tric*, developing electricity by utilization of water power, (of electricity) produced by utilization of water power;—*grapher* (-ŏg⁻), person skilled in, —*graph'ic(al)* having to do with, —*graphy*; —*graphy* (-ŏg⁻), scientific description of the waters of the earth; —*kinĕt'ic(s)*, (science) of the motion of liquids:—*logy* (-ŏl⁻), science of the properties, laws, etc., of water; —*lysis* (-ŏlĭ⁻), decomposition of a compound by reaction with water, the water also being decomposed; —*mánĭa*, craving for water;—*mechăn'ics*(of liquids); —*meter* (-ŏm⁻), instrument for finding specific gravity of liquids (occas. also of solids);—*met'ric*, —*metry* (-ŏm⁻), concerned with, determination of, specific gravity of liquids; hўd'rophane, opal that absorbs water & becomes transparent on immersion; hўd'rophone, instrument for detection of sound-waves in water; hўd'rophĭte, aquatic plant; hўd'roplane, fin-like device enabling submarine to rise or fall, light fast motor-boat designed to skim over surface, seaplane;—*pneumăt'ic*, involving combined action of water & air;—*quin'one*, preparation from quinone, used (Phot.) as developer; hўd'rosphere, waters of the earth's surface; hўd'rostat, electrical device for detecting presence of water;—*therapeut'ic*, —*the'rapy*, hydropathic, hydropathy;—*therm'al*, of the action of heated water on earth's crust; —*thor'ax*, dropsy of the chest;—*tropism* (-ŏĭ⁻), (of plants) tendency to turn to or from moisture;—*zō'a* n. pl., class of coelenterate animals chiefly marine, including jelly-fish & fresh-water hydra. **hўd'rogen**, n. Colourless invisible odourless gas, an element, the lightest substance known, forming two-thirds in volume of water. Hence hўdrō'gĕn-ous a. [f. F HYDRO(*gène* -GEN)] **hўdrō'gĕnĭāte**, v.t. Charge, cause to combine, with hydrogen. So —IZE v.t. [prec. +-ATE³]

hўd'roid, a. & n. (zool.). (Animal) like, allied to, the hydra (polyp). [-OID]

hўd'romĕl, n. Mixture of honey & water; *vinous*;—(also *mead*), this fermented. [L, f. Gk *hudromĕli* (*meli* honey, see HYDRO-)]

hўdropăth'ic, a. & n. 1. Of, concerned with, hydropathy. 2. n.—establishment. [f. foll. +-IC]

hўdrŏp'ath)ў, n. Medical treatment by external & internal application of water. So—IST n. [HYDRO-+-PATHY]

hўdrophōb'ĭa, n. Aversion to water, esp. as symptom of rabies in man; rabies, esp. in man; (joc.) dread of water. So —IC a. [L, f. Gk *hudrophobia*, see HYDRO-]

hўdrŏp'ĭc, a. Dropsical. [ME, f. OF *ydropique* f. L f. Gk *hudrōpikos* (as HYDROPSY, see -IC)]

hўdropŏn'ics, n. Soilless culture, art of growing plants without soil, in water impregnated with chemicals. [HYDRO-, Gk *ponos* labour]

hўd'rŏpsў, n. (arch. or med.). Dropsy. [ME, f. OF *ydropisie* f. med. L *hydropisia* (for L -*sis*) f. Gk *hudrōps* (*hudor* water)]

hўdrostăt'ic, a. & n. 1. Of the equilibrium of liquids & the pressure exerted by liquids at rest; ~ *paradox*, principle that any quantity of a perfect liquid, however small, may be made to balance any other quantity; ~ *press* (also *hydraulic*, *Bramah's*, *press*), machine in which pressure of a body of water is multiplied by transmission from small to larger cylinder. 2. n. pl. Branch of mechanics concerned with the pressure & equilibrium of liquids at rest. Hence —AL a., —ALLY adv. [HYDRO-+STATIC; Gk had *hudrostatēs* ~ balance]

hўd'rous, a. (chem., mineral.). Containing water. [Gk *hudōr* water+-OUS]

hўēn'a, hўaen'a, n. Carnivorous quadruped allied to dog tribe; *striped* ~, variety whose howl is compared to fiendish laughter; cruel, treacherous, or rapacious person; Tasmanian tiger;—*dog*, S.-African canine quadruped like ~. [L (-*ae*-) f. Gk *huaina* fem. f. *hus* pig]

hўēto- in comb. = Gk *huetos* rain, as ~*graphy* (-ŏg-), mapping of rainfall, ~*meter* (-ŏm-), rain-gauge.

Hygēi'a (-jē'a), n. Goddess of health; health personified. Hence hўgēi'AN (-jē'an) a. [f. Gk *Hugeia* late for *Hugieia* (*hugiēs* healthy)]

hў'giēne (or -jēn), n. Principles of health; sanitary science. Hence ~ēn'ic(al) aa., ~ēn'ically adv.—ēn'ics, ~enist, nn., (or -jēn⁻). [f. F *hygiène* f. Gk *hugieinē* (*tekhnē* art) of health, f. *hugiēs* healthy]

hўgro- in comb. = Gk *hugros* wet, fluid, as: hўg'rodeik (-dik), form of ~*meter*; ~*logy* (-ŏl-), study of the humidity of atmosphere etc.; ~*meter* (-ŏm-), instrument for measuring humidity of air or gas; ~*met'ric*, ~*metry* (-ŏm-), concerned with, measurement of, humidity; hўg'roscōpe, instrument indicating humidity of air; ~*scōp'ic*, of the ~*scope*, (of bodies) tending to absorb moisture.

Hўk'sōs (-x), n. pl. The shepherd kings of Egypt (about 2000 B.C.). [Gk *Huksōs*]

hȳlic, a. Of matter, material. [f. med. L, f. Gk *hulikos* (*hulē* matter, see -IC)]

hylo- in comb. = Gk *hulē* matter, see -O-; **~morph'ism**, doctrine that primordial matter is first cause of the universe; **~zō'ism**, doctrine that God & matter are identical; **~zō'ist(ic)**, **~zō'ism**, f. Gk *hulozōos*.

Hȳmen¹, n. (Gk & Rom. Myth.) God of marriage. So **hȳmenē'al** a. LY² adv. [L, f. Gk *Humēn*]

hȳmen², n.² (anat.) Virginal membrane, stretched across external orifice of vagina. [f. Gk *humēn* membrane]

hȳmen|o- in comb. = Gk *humēn* membrane, as **~op'tera** n. pl., large order of insects with four membranous wings, so **~op'teral**, **~op'terous**, aa.

hymn (him), n., & v.t. & i. 1. Song of praise to God, esp. metrical composition sung in religious service; song of praise in honour of a god or other exalted being; **~-book** (of **~s**). 2. v.t. Praise (God etc.) in **~s**, express (praise etc.) in **~**; (v.i.) sing **~s**. Hence **hym'nic** a., **hym'nist** n. [(vb f. n.) f. L f. Gk *humnos*]

hym'n|al, a. & n. Of hymns; (n.) hymn-book, so **~ARY¹** n. [HYMN+-AL]

hym'nody, n. Singing of hymns; composition of hymns, whence **~IST** n.; hymns collectively. [f. L f. Gk *humnōdia* (*humnos* hymn+*ōdē* song, ODE)]

hym'nog'rapher, n. Composer of hymns. [f. Gk *humnographos* (as prec., see -GRAPHER)]

hymnol'ogy, n. Composition, study, of hymns; hymns collectively. So **hymno-log'ic** a., **~IST** n. [HYMN+-O-+-LOGY]

hy'oid a., & n. (anat.) 1. **~ bone**, tongue-bone between chin & thyroid cartilage; pertaining to this. 2. n. **~ bone**. [f. F *hyoïde* f. Gk *huoeidēs* shaped like letter U]

hyoscy'amine, **hy'oscine**, nn. Alkaloids contained in henbane & used in medicine. [f. Gk *huoskuamos* henbane (*hus huos* pig, *kuamos* bean), -INE⁵]

hyp. See HIP³.

hypæthral, **-pēthral**, a. Open to the sky, roofless; open-air. [f. L f. Gk *hupaithros* (*aithēr* air, see HYPO-)]

hyp'allage, n. (gram.) Reversal of natural relations of two elements in a proposition (e.g. *apply the wound to water* for *apply water to the wound*). [L, f. Gk *hupallagē* (*allassō* exchange, see HYPO-)]

hy'per-, pref. = Gk *huper* in senses 'over', 'above', 'exceeding', 'excessive'.

hyperæsthē'sia, n. (Path.) morbid sensitiveness of nerves; excessive sensibility. So **~ET'IC** (-ĕt-) a. [HYPER-+Gk *-aisthēsia* f. *aisthanomai* perceive]

hyperb'aton, n. Inversion of normal order of words, esp. for sake of emphasis. [L, f. Gk *huperbaton* (*bainō* step, see HYPER-)]

hyperb'ola, n. (geom.). Curve produced when cone is cut by plane making larger angle with base than side of cone means (cf. ELLIPSE). [mod. L, f. Gk *huperbolē* f. *huperballō* (*ballō* throw, see HYPER-)]

hyperb'olē, n. (rhet.). Exaggerated statement not meant to be taken literally. Hence **hyperbol'ical** a., **hyperbol'ical-**LY² adv. [L, f. Gk, as prec.]

hyperbor'ean, a. & n. (Inhabitant) of the extreme north of the earth or (colloq.) of a country; (Gk Myth.) one of a race living in land of sunshine & plenty beyond north wind. [f. LL *hyperboreanus* (-*i* -*boreus*) f. Gk *huperboreos* (*Boreas* north wind, see HYPER-)]

hypercatalec'tic, a. (pros.). (Of verse) having extra syllable after last complete dipody. [f. LL HYPER(*catalecticus* CATA-LECTIC)]

hypercrit'ic|al, a. Too critical, esp. of small faults. Hence **~ALly²** adv., **~ISM** n., **~IZE** v.t. & i. [HYPER-+CRITICAL]

hypermet'ric|al, aa. (Of verse) having a redundant syllable; (of syllable) redundant. [f. Gk *hupermetros* (*metron* metre, HYPER-)]

hypermetrōp'ia, n. Morbidly long sight. Hence **~ōp'ic** a. [as prec.+Gk *ōps* eye HYPER-]

hyperphys'ical (-z-), a. Supernatural. [HYPER-]

hyp'ersthēne, n. Greenish mineral allied to hornblende. [f. F *hypersthène* f. Gk *sthenos* strength, from its hardness]

hypert'rophy, n. Enlargement (of organ etc.) due to excessive nutrition. Hence or eogn. **hypertroph'ic**, **~iED²** (-id), aa. [HYPER-+Gk *-trophia* nourishment f. *trephō*]

hypethral. See HYPÆTHRAL.

hy'ph|en, n., & v.t. 1. Sign (-) used to join two words together, to join separated syllables of word broken at end of line, or to divide word into parts; short pause between syllables in speaking. 2. v.t. Join (words) with **~**, write (compound word) with **~**. [(vb f. n.) LL, f. Gk *huphen* together (*hupo* under+*hen* one)]

hyph'enate, v.t. = prec. vb [**~d** Americans, German-Americans, Irish-Americans, etc.]. [prec., -ATE³]

hypno- in comb. (before vowel hypn-)= Gk *hupnos* sleep, as **~gen'esis**, **~genēt'ic**, induction of, inducing, the hypnotic state; **~logy** (-ŏi-), science of the phenomena of sleep.

hypnōs'is, n. (pl. -ōsēs). Artificially produced sleep; hypnotic state. [f. Gk *hupnoō* make sleep, -OSIS]

hypnot'ic, a. & n. 1. Of, producing, hypnotism. 2. Thing that produces sleep; person under influence of hypnotism. [f. F *hypnotique* f. LL f. Gk *hupnōtikos* (as prec., see -OTIC)]

hyp'notism, n. (Artificial production of) a state resembling deep sleep, in which

the subject acts only on external suggestion. So ~IST n., ~IZE v.t. [f. prec. +-ISM]

hy̆p'ŏ, n. (photog.). Hyposulphite (or thiosulphate) of soda, used in fixing. [abbr.]

hy̆po- in comb. (before vowel *hyp-*) = Gk *hupo* under, below, slightly; (Chem.) forming names of oxygen compounds lower in the series than those with the simple name. Exx.: *hy̆p'oblast*, inner layer of cells in blastoderm; *~brăn'chial* (-ngk-), situated under the gills; *~cŏc'loid*, curve traced by point in circumference of circle rolling round interior circumference of another circle; *~găs'trium*, lowest region of abdomen; *~pĕ'al, ~pĕ'an, aa,* underground; *hy̆p'ogēne,* (of rocks) formed under the surface; *~ge'um,* pl. *~gea,* underground chamber; *~gloss'al (nerve),* motor nerve of tongue; *~gynous (-ŏjĭ²) (Bot.), situated below pistils or ovary; *hy̆p'onăsty* (Bot.), tendency in plant-organs to grow more rapidly on under side; *~phŏs'phĭte,* salt of hypophosphorous acid; *hy̆p'ostĭle,* (hall etc.) with roof supported on pillars; *~trach'el'ium (-kē-),* lower part of capital of column.

hy̆p'ocaust, n. (Rom. Ant.). Hollow space under floor in which heat from furnace was accumulated for heating house or bath. [f. Ll f. Gk *hupokauston* place heated from below (*kaiō, kau-,* burn, see prec.)]

hy̆pochŏn'drĭa (-k-), n. Morbid depression either apparently causeless or due to (unnecessary) anxiety about health. So **~'ĭĂSĬS** n. [f. Ll f. Gk (*ta) hupokhondria* soft parts of body below costal cartilages (*khondros* cartilage, see HYPO-)]

hy̆pochŏn'drĭăc (-k-), a. & n. **1.** Of, affected by, hypochondria. **2.** n. *~'ĭăc* person. Hence *~'ĭaCAL* a., *~'ĭacALY²* adv. [f. F *hypochondriaque* f. med.L f. Gk *hupokhondriakos* (as prec., see -AC)]

hy̆pocŏrĭs'tĭc, a. (gram.). Of the nature of a pet-name. [f. Gk *hupokoristikos* (*hupokorizomai* play the child)]

hy̆pŏc'rĭsy, n. Simulation of virtue or goodness; dissimulation, pretence. [f. OF *ypocrisie* f. eccl. L f. Gk *hupokrisis* lit. acting of a part f. *hupokrinomai* (*hupo-* +*krinō* decide, judge)]

hy̆p'ocrĭte, n. Person guilty of hypocrisy; dissembler, pretender. So **hy̆pocrĭt'ĬCAL** a., **hy̆pocrĭt'ĭcALY²** adv. [f. OF *ypocrite* f. eccl. L (*-ta*) f. Gk *hupokritēs* actor (as prec.)]

hy̆podĕrm'ĭc, a. (Med., of drugs etc.) introduced beneath the skin, as *~io ĭn-jection*; (Anat.) lying under the skin. Hence *~ICALY* adv. [f. HYPO- +Gk *derma* skin +-IC]

hy̆pŏs'tasĭs, n. (pl. *~es,* pr. -ēz). **1.** (Med.) excess of blood in organs of body. **2.** (Metaphys.) underlying substance, opp. to attributes or to what is unsubstantial.

3. (Theol.) personality (of Christ), person (of the Godhead). So **hy̆pŏstăt'ĬC**(AL) aa., **hy̆pŏstăt'ĭcalY²** adv., ~IZE(3), **hy̆pŏs'tatĬZE**(3), vv.t. (metaphys.). [f. Ll f. Gk *hupostasis* (*hupo-* HYPO- +*stasis* standing, state)]

hy̆pŏt'enŭse, n. Side opposite right angle of triangle. [f. Ll f. Gk *hupoteinousa* (*grammē*) subtending line (*hupo-* HYPO- +*teinō* stretch); also (improp.) *-thenuse*]

hy̆p'othec, n. (Rom. & Sc. Law). Security established by law over thing belonging to debtor. So **hy̆pŏth'ĕcarY¹** a. [f. Ll f. Gk *hupothēkē* f.*hupotithēmi* place under, deposit as pledge (*hupo-* HYPO- +*tithēmi* place)]

hy̆pŏth'ĕcāte, v.t. Pledge, mortgage. Hence ~A'TION n. [f. Ll *hypothecare* (as prec.), see -ATE³]

hy̆pŏth'ĕsis, n. (pl. *-thesēs*). Supposition made as basis for reasoning, without reference to its truth, or as starting-point for investigation; groundless assumption. So **hy̆pŏthĕt'ĭcALX²** aa., **hy̆pŏthĕt'ĭcalY²** adv. [f. Gk *hupothesis* foundation (as HYPOTHE0)]

hy̆pŏth'ĕsīze, v.i. & t. Frame a hypothesis; (trans.) assume. [f. prec. +-IZE]

hy̆pso- in comb. = Gk *hupsos* height, as: *~graphy (-ŏgĭ²),* department of geography dealing with altitudes; *~meter (-ŏmĕ-), ~mĕt'rĭc(al), ~mĕtry (-ŏmĕ-),* instrument for, concerned with, science of, measuring altitudes.

hy̆r'ăx, n. Genus of small rabbit-like quadrupeds, including Syrian rock-rabbit and S.-Afr. rock-badger. [f. Gk *hurax* shrew-mouse]

hy̆s'on, n. Kind of green tea from China. [f. Chin. *hsĭ-ch'un* lit. bright spring]

‖ **hy̆'-spy̆, I spy̆,** n. Kind of hide-&-seek.

hy̆ss'op, n. Small bushy aromatic herb, formerly used medicinally; (Bibl.) plant whose twigs were used for sprinkling in Jewish rites, bunch of this used in purification. [f. L f. Gk *hussōpos,* prob. of eastern orig.]

hystere'sis, n. (physics). Lagging of magnetic induction behind the magnetizing force. [f. Gk *husterēsis (husteros* coming after)]

hysté'rĭa, n. Functional disturbance of nervous system (esp. of women), characterized by anaesthesia, convulsions, etc., & usu. attended with disturbance of moral & intellectual faculties (formerly thought to be due to disturbance of womb); morbid excitement. [mod. medical L, on foll.]

hysté'rĭc, a. & n. **1.** = foll. **2.** n. pl. Hysterical fits or convulsions. [f. L f. Gk *husterikos* of the womb (*hustera,* see -IC)]

hysté'rĭcAL, a. Of, affected with, hysteria; morbidly emotional. Hence ~LY² adv. [prec. +-AL]

hystero- in comb.=Gk *hustera* womb, as: *~gĕn'ic, ~gĕny (-ŏjĭ²),* productive, produc-

tion, of HYSTERIA; ~*logy* (-ŏ́-), treatise on the uterus; ~*tomy* (-ŏ́t-), operation of cutting into the uterus. [f. Gr. *hustéra* womb]

hysterŏn protʹerŏn, n. (Gram.) figure of speech in which what should come last is put first; inversion of natural order. [L., f. Gk *husteron proteron* latter (put in place of) former]

I

I, i, (ī), letter (pl. **Is, I's**). As Roman numeral I or i = 1, as i 1, ii 2, iii 3, iv (rarely iiii) 4, vi 6, viii 8, ix (rarely viiii) 9, xi 11, xiv 14, li 51, cii 102, miv 1,004.

I¹ (ī), pron. & n. Subjective case of 1st pers. pron. (objective *me*, poss. *my*; pl. *we*, obj. *us*, poss. *our*); (n., metaphys.) the *I*, the ego, subject or object of self-consciousness. [OE *ic*, cf. Du. *ik*, G *ich*, also L *ego*, Gk *egō*]

-i, suf. forming pl. of L nn. in -*us* & -*er* of 2nd decl. & of Ital. nn. in -*o*, -*e*; retained in E in wds of scientific or learned use, as *cirri*, *foci*, *dilettanti*, *literati*; also freq. in mod. L names of groups or orders in Nat. Hist., as *acanthopterygii*, *acrocarpi*.

-i-, connecting vowel in L, being stem-vowel, as in *omnivorus*, weakened representative of this, as in *herbivorus* (*herba-*), or merely connective, as *Cryptogamia*, & personal names, as *dahlia*, *fuchsia*); in names of countries, as *Australia*; & in names of alkaloids, as *morphia*, *strychnia*, (in more recent nomenclature -*ine*). F· -*i-e* f. -*ia* gives -*y*¹.

-ia¹, suf. forming pl. of Gk nn. in -*ion* & -*ma*, as *paraphernalia*, *regalia*; freq. in mod. L names of classes etc. in Zool., as *mammalia*, *reptilia*.

-ial, suf. repr. L -*ialis*, in adji. f. n.-stems in -*io*-, -*ia*-, as *curialis*, *tibialis*; much used in med. L, F, & E, to form adji. f. L adji. in -*is* & -*ius*, as *celestial*, *dictatorial* (L -*tis*, -*rius*).

I̥ǎnb, n. = IAMBUS.

ĭǎmʹbic, a. & n. (pros.). Of, containing, based on, iambuses; (n.) ~ verse. [f. F *iambique* f. L f. Gk *iambikos* (as foll., see -IC)]

ĭǎmʹbus, n. (pl. -*buses*, -*bī*). The metrical foot ˘ˉ. [L, f. Gk *iambos* iambus, lampoon (*iaptō* assail)]

-ian, suf. of aa. & nn. = L -*ianus*, f. -*ius* & -*anus*. In adji. & nn., connective -*i*-, as *Italian*, *Virgilian*, or with connective -*i*- & -*c*-*us*, as *Christian*; esp. forming adji. on proper names, as *Addisonian*, *Bostonian*, (varying in place-names with -

-er, as *Londoner*, & often added to Latinized stems, as *Mancunian*, *Glasuegian*, *Oxonian*, *Liverpudlian*).

Ibērʹian (ī-), a. & n. 1. Of ancient Iberia, of Spain & Portugal as one country. 2. n. Inhabitant, language, of ancient Iberia. [f. L *Ibēria* f. Gk *Ibēres* Spaniards + -AN]

ī′bex, n. (pl. ~*es*). Wild goat of Alps & Apennines, with large recurved horns. [L]

ib′idem, adv. In the same book, chapter, passage, etc. (abbr. *ib.*, *ibid.*). [L., = in the same place (*ibi* there + demonstr. suf. -*dem*)]

ĭ′bis, n. (pl. ~*es*). Stork-like bird found in lakes & swamps of warm climates; *Sacred I*~, kind venerated by ancient Egyptians. [L f. Gk]

-ible, suf. f. L -*ibilis*, i.e. -*bilis* -BLE as appended to p.p. stems, 3rd conj. vbs, & some 2nd conj. (*terrible*), or f. L -*ibilis* (-*bilis* with 4th conj.); also in mod. formns many wds taken thr. F or formed really or apparently on E vbs. Meaning: 'that can be -d'.

-ic, suf. 1. Forming adji. (often thr. F -*ique*) f. L -*icus*, occas. f. L -*icus*, as in *classicus*, *publicus*, *domesticus*, but usu. f. Gk -*ikos*, as in *grammaticus*, *poëticus*, E adji. in -*ic* are direct f. Gk, or on Gk elements, or (esp scientific terms) on wds f. L or other langs, as *carbonic*, *Byronic*. (Chem.) -*ic* in names of oxygen acids etc. indicates higher degree of oxidation than -*ous*, as in *chloric*, *sulphuric*. 2. Gk adji. in -*ikos* were used as nn. in 3 ways: in masc. sing. for names of arts & sciences, as *kritikos* man able to discern, critic; in fem. sing., as *mousikē* (*tekhnē*) art of the muses, music; in neut. pl., as *ta oikonomika* things pertaining to management, economics. In L the last two both became -*ica*, whence much fluctuation in med. L as to grammatical treatment. The Rom. langs usu. had fem. sing. for names of arts & sciences, but F occas. had pl., as *les mathématiques*. E wds before 15th c. were sing., as still *arithmetic*, *music*, *magic*, *logic*, *rhetoric*, later, -*ics* became usu. form for names of sciences, as *acoustics*, *comics*, *dynamics* (treated as sing.), & of practical matters, as *athletics*, *politics*, *tactics*, (pl.). Besides this spec. use, other adji. in -*ic* become nn. as *epic*, *emetic*, *cosmetic*, *rustic*, *mechanic*.

-ical, suf. (-*ic*+-*al*) forming adji. f. nn. as *musical*, or more commonly secondary adji. f. adji. as *comical*, *historical*. Many adji. have both the -*ic* & -*ical* form, often with distinction in meaning (see -AL).

-ically, suf. (-*ical*+-LY) forming advv. corr. to adji. in -*ic*, -*ical*, advv. in -*icly*, as *publicly*, *politicly*, being rare.

ice¹, n. 1. Frozen water; *break the* ~, (fig.) make a beginning, break through reserve or stiffness; *cut¹ no* ~; (w. pl.) frozen

confection, ~-cream, water-~. 2. ~-age, glacial period; ~-axe (used by Alpine climbers for cutting steps); ~'blink, luminous appearance on horizon, caused by reflexion from ~; ~-boat, boat mounted on runners for travelling on ~, (also ~-breaker) boat used for breaking ~ in river etc.; ~-cream, flavoured cream or custard congealed in freezing-mixture; coco-nut etc. ~, slabs of sugar flavoured with coco-nut etc.; ~-fall, steep part of glacier like frozen waterfall; ~-field, expanse of ~, esp. in Polar regions; ~-foot, belt of ~ along coast in Arctic regions; ~-house, building often partly or wholly underground for storing ~; ~'man, man skilled in traversing ~, (also) maker of ~s; (~'PACK¹; ~'pick, stiletto for splitting up table ~; ~-plant (with leaves covered with watery vesicles looking like ~ specks); ~-pudding, a frozen confection; ~-run, artificial tobogganing track of ~; ~-wool (glossy kind used in crochet etc.). [com.-Teut.: OE ís, Du. ijs, G eis]

ice², v.t. Freeze; cover (as) with ice; cool (wine) in ice; cover (cake etc.) with concretion of sugar. [f. prec.]

-ice, suf., OF, f. L -itia in abstract nn. (justice, avarice, malice, notice, & F formations cowardice, jaundice) & f. L -itius, -itium, (novice, precipice, service). But E -ice has freq. diff. orig., as in apprentice, bodice, practice, where -ice is partly due to assim.

ice'berg (ís'b⁻), n. Huge floating mass of ice, detached portion of glacier carried out to sea; (fig.) unemotional or cold-blooded person. [prob. f. Du. ijsberg (ijs ice + berg hill)]

Ice'land (ís'l⁻), n. Large island between Norway and Greenland; ~ lichen, moss, edible species; ~ poppy, yellow Arctic poppy; ~ spar, transparent variety of calcite. Hence ~ER'⁴(4) n. [f. ON Island (íss ice + LAND')]

Icelan'dic (ísl-), a. & n. (Language) of Iceland. [-IC]

ich'abod (ík⁻), n. (As exclamation of regret=) the glory has departed. [Heb., see 1 Sam. iv. 21]

ichneu'mon (ík⁻), n. 1. Small brown weasel-like quadruped allied to mongoose, noted for destroying crocodiles' eggs. 2. (Also ~-fly) small parasitic hymenopterous insect depositing eggs in or on larva of another insect. [L, f. Gk ikhneumōn spider-hunting wasp f. ikhneuō track (ikhnos)]

ichno- (ík⁻) in comb. = Gk ikhnos track, trace, as: ~graph'ic(al), ~graphy (-òg⁻), (of the drawing of ground-plans; ~lite (ík⁻), fossil footprint (also ichnite, pr. ik'nit); ~logy (-òl⁻), study of fossil footprints.

ich'ör (ík⁻), n. (Gk Myth.) fluid flowing like blood in veins of gods; (Path.) watery acrid discharge from wounds etc. Hence ~ous (ík'or⁻) a. [Gk ikhōr]

ichthy̆o- (ík⁻) in comb. (before vowel ichthy-) = Gk ikhthus fish, as: ~grapher, ~graphy, (-òg⁻), writer on, description of, fishes; ~latry (-òl⁻), worship of a fish-god; ~lite (ík⁻), fossil fish'; ~logy (-òl⁻), natural history of fishes, whence ~lo'gical, ~logist (-òl⁻); ~phagi, ~phagist, (-òf⁻), fish-eater(s); ~phagous (-òf⁻), fish-eating; ichthyor'nis, extinct genus of toothed birds.

ich'thyoid (-k⁻), a. & n. Fish-like; (n.) vertebrate of fish type. [as prec.+ -OID]

ichthyosaur'us (-k⁻), n. Extinct marine animal with huge head, tapering body, four paddles, & long tail. [ICHTHYO-+Gk sauros lizard]

ichthy̆ōs'is (-k⁻), n. Disease in which epidermis becomes dry & horny. So ~òt'IC (-òt⁻) a. [f. Gk ikhthus fish+ -osis]

-ician, suf. (-ʃ⁻ + -ician), spec. form of -IAN added to names of arts or sciences in -ic(s) to form personal designations (= one skilled in or concerned with), as arithmetician, logician, ophician, politician; occas. used when there is no corresp. n. (& even no adj.) in -ic, as academician, algebrician.

i'cicle, n. Tapering ice-formation, produced by freezing of successive drops trickling from the point of attachment. [OE has íses gicel (is ICE + gicel, cogn. w ON jokull icicle, glacier]

i'cing, n. Icing sugar. [-ING¹]

ic'kle, a. (nursery). Little. [corrupt.]

ic'ŏn, n. Image, statue; (Eastern Church) painting, mosaic, etc., of sacred personage, itself regarded as sacred. [LL, f. Gk eikōn image (*eikō be like)]

icŏn'ic, a. Of (the nature of) an image or portrait; (of statues) following a conventional type. [f. LL f. Gk eikonikos (as prec., see -IC)]

icono- in comb.= Gk eikōn image, as: ~graphy (-òg⁻), illustration of subject by drawings or figures, book whose essence is pictures, treatise on pictures or statuary, so ~grapher (-òg⁻), ~graph'ic; ~later, ~latry, (-òl⁻), worshipper, worship, of images; ~logy (-òl⁻), study of icons (in any sense); ~machy (-òm'akì), war against use of images in connexion with worship; ~stasis (-òs⁻), (Eastern Church) screen separating sanctuary from main body of church, & on which icons are placed.

icŏn'oclăsm, n. Breaking of images (lit. & fig.). [prec.+ Gk klasma (klaō break, -M]

icŏn'oclăst, n. Breaker of images, esp. one who took part in movement in 8th & 9th cc. against use of images in religious worship in churches of the East; (fig.) one who assails cherished beliefs. Hence ~ro (-ăs⁻) a. [f. LL f. Gk eikonoklastēs (eikōn ICON + klastēs f. klaō break)]

iconom'eter, n. (Photog.) direct-vision view-finder (either fixed to camera, or detached & adjustable for various lenses & sizes of plate). (Surveying) optical instrument for ascertaining size or distance of an object. [ICONO- + -METER]

ic'osahed'ron (-a-h-), n. Solid contained by twenty plane faces. [f. Gk *eikosaedron* (*eikosi* twenty + *hedra* base)]

-ics. See -IC(2).

ic'tus, n. (pros.). Rhythmical or metrical stress. [L, = blow, f. *icere* strike]

I'cy, a. Abounding in, covered with, ice; very cold (lit. & fig. as ~ *manners*). Hence **I'cILY²** adv., **I'cINESS** n. [-Y¹]

id, n. (Biol.) a unit of germ-plasm or idioplasm; (Psycho-anal.) *the* instinctive impulses of the individual. [first sense, abbr. IDIOPLASM; second, f. L *id* that]

-id¹, suf. f. F-*ide* f. L L-*idus*, which forms adj; chiefly f. vbs w. -ē- stems, as *acidus* acid f. *acere*, but also f. vbs w. -ē- or consonant stem, as *fluidus* fluid f. *fuēre*, & f. nn., as *morbidus* morbid f. *morbus*. Earlier E vds come thr. F; others f. L direct.

-id², suf. of nn. (= F-*ide*) f. L L f. Gk -*id*- (nom. -*is*), as *chrysalid*, *pyramid*. In bot., *amaryllid*, *orchid*, etc., should denote plants *amaryllis*, *orchis*, etc., but in fact denote members of the family of which these are typical genera (*amaryllidaceae*, *orchidaceae*).

-id³, suf. of nn. & aa. (zool.). **1.** Through -*ites* f. L L names of families in -*idae* pl. of -*ites* f. Gk -*idēs* son of, as *Aramid*, member of the family *Aramidae*. **2.** f. L L names of classes in -*ida* taken as neut. pl. of -*ides* (= Gk -*idēs*), as *Arachnid*, member of the class *Arachnida*.

-id⁴, suf. Early spelling of -IDE, now chiefly U.S.

ide, n. Fish allied to carp. [f. Swed. *id*]

-ide, suf. (chem.) forming names of simple compounds of an element with another element or radical, the suf. -*ide* being added to the name (usu. abbrev.) of the more electro-negative element, as *bromine chloride, sulphur bromide, carbon sulphide, boron carbide*; first used in *oxide* from oxygen.

idē'a (or -iə), n. **1.** Archetype, pattern, as distinguished from its realization in individuals; (Platonic) eternally existing pattern of which individual things in any class are imperfect copies. **2.** Conception, plan, of thing to be aimed at, created, etc.; plan of action. **3.** Notion conceived by the mind; vague belief, fancy, as *the ~ of his doing such a thing, I had no ~ you were there*. **4.** (Descartes, Locke) immediate object of thought or mental perception; (Kant) conception of reason transcending all experience. **5.** *Man of ~s*, resourceful person; **the big ~*, scheme, proposal (usu. ironical: *what's the big ~?*, what folly have you in

mind?). Hence ~'d, ~ED² (i'ad), ~LESS (-val-), aa. [f. L L f. Gk, = form, kind, f. *id*- see]

idē'al, a. & n. **1.** Answering to one's highest conception; embodying an idea; existing only in idea; visionary; relating to, consisting of, (Platonic) ideas. **2.** n. Perfect type; actual thing as standard for imitation. Hence ~'ıv² adv. [f. F *idéal* f. LL *ideālis* (as prec., see -AL)]

idē'alism, n. Representation of things in ideal form, imaginative treatment, (cf. REALISM), so ~IZA'TION n., ~IZE v.t. & i.; (Philos.) system of thought in which the object of external perception is held to consist of ideas (cf. REALISM). So ~IST n., ~is'rıc a. [-ISM]

idē'ality, n. Quality of being ideal; imaginative faculty. [-ITY]

idē'āte, v.t. & i. Imagine, conceive, form ideas. Hence **idēā'TION** n., **idēā'tional** (-shon-) a. [f. med. L *ideātus* p.p. of *ideāre* (as prec.)]

idée fixe (ēdāfēks') n. Idea that dominates the mind, monomania. [F, fixed idea]

id'em, n. or adv. (abbr. *id.*), (In) the same author (*i-*); the same word (*i-*); *idem quod*, the same as. [L *idem* same, *idem* neut., same]

idēn'tic, a. (Diplom.) ~ *note*, simultaneous & uniformly worded expression of opinion from several powers to another; = foll. [f. schol. L *identicus* (cf. IDENTITY)]

idēn'tical, a. (Of one thing viewed at different times) the very same; (of different things) agreeing in every detail (*with*); (of twins), developed from a single fertilized ovum; (Logic, Math.) expressing an identity (~ *proposition*, of the type *Man is man*). Hence ~LY² adv. [-AL]

idēn'tify, v.t. Treat (thing) as identical (*with*), associate oneself inseparably *with* (party, policy, etc.); establish identity of. Hence ~FIABLE a., ~FICA'TION n. (~*fication* or ~*fy*) (of rubber or metal worn by soldier etc. on active service & bearing his name etc.). [f. LL *identificare* (as foll.: see -FY)]

idēn'tity, n. Absolute sameness; individuality, personality, (~ *disk*, see prec.); (Alg.) equality of two expressions for all values of the literal quantities, equation expressing this, e.g. $(x+1)^2=x^2+2x+1$. [f. F *identité* f. L L *identitas*, irreg. f. *idem* same (see -ITY)]

id'eo- in comb. = IDEA, as ~*gram*, ~*graph*, character symbolizing the idea of a thing without expressing its name (e.g. Chinese characters), whence ~*graph'ic(al)*, ~*graphy* (-ŏgr-).

ideŏl'ogy, n. Science of ideas; visionary speculation; manner of thinking characteristic of a class or individual, ideas at the basis of some economic or political theory or system, as *Fascist, Nazi, ~*. So **ideŏlo'gical** a., **ideŏl'ogist** n., **id'eo-LOGUE** (-lŏg) n., theorist, visionary.

ides (īdz), n. pl. (Rom. Ant.). Eighth day after nones (15th of March, May, July, October, 13th of other months). [F, f. L *Īdūs*]

id'est (abbr. *i.e.*). That is to say. [L]

id'iocy, n. Extreme mental imbecility. [f. Gk *idiōteia* (as IDIOT) or f. *idiot*+-CY; *idiotcy* is irreg. form]

id'iom, n. Language of a people or country; specific character of this; form of expression peculiar to a language. [f. L f. Gk *idiōma -matos* (*idiōomai* make one's own f. *idios*, see -M)]

idioma'tic, a. Characteristic of a particular language; relating to or conforming to idiom. Hence ~ICALLY adv. [f. Gk *idiōmatikos* (prec.,-IC)]

idiop'athy, n. (path.). Disease not preceded or occasioned by another. Hence **idiopath'ic** a., **idiopath'ICALLY** adv. [f. Gk *idiopatheia* (*idios* own, see -PATHY)]

id'ioplasm, n. (biol.). Portion of PLASM that determines an organism's nature. [Gk *idios* own, PLASM]

idiosync'rasy, n. Mental constitution, view, feeling, peculiar to a person; mode of expression peculiar to an author; (Med.) physical constitution peculiar to a person. So **idiosyncrat'ic** a. [f. Gk *idiosugkrasia* (*idios* own+*sun* together+*krasis* mixture f. *kerannumi* mix)]

id'iot, n. Person so deficient in mind as to be permanently incapable of rational conduct; utter fool; ~stitch, TRICOT-stitch (the easiest in crochet work). So **idiot'ic** a., **idiot'ICALLY** adv. [(*-ta*) f. OE *idiōtēs* private person, 'layman', ignorant person, f. *idios* own, private]

i'dle, a.(-er,-est), & v.i. & t. 1. (Of action, thought, word) ineffective, worthless, vain; groundless; useless; unoccupied; lazy, indolent; ~ wheel or ~r, safety wheel coming into operation in case of breakdown, (also) intermediate wheel between two geared wheels. 2. v.i. Be ~; (v.t.) pass (time etc.) away in ~ness. Hence ~NESS (i'dln-), **id'lER**[1], nn., **id'lY**[2] adv. [(vb f. a.) OE *idel*, cf. Du. *ijdel*, G *eitel*; orig. sense prob. 'empty']

Ido (ēd'ō), n. An artificial universal language based on Esperanto. [= offspring (in Ido)]

id'leness, n. Idleness. [sham arch., -NESS[1]]

id'ol, n. Image of deity used as object of worship; false god; person, thing, that is the object of excessive devotion; phantom; (Logic) false mental conception; ~s of the tribe, cave, market, theatre, (L. *idola tribus, specus, fori, theatri*), four classes of fallacies (Bacon, *Nov. Org.* I. xxxix) referable respectively to limitations of human mind, prejudices of idiosyncrasy, influence of words, philosophical & logical prepossessions. [f. OF *idole* f. L f. Gk *eidōlon* phantom (*eidos* form), de-

voted admirer (*of*). So ~ress[1], ~ry[1] (*honour one on this side* ~ry, short of making a god of him), nn., ~rous a., ~rousLY[2] adv. [f. OF *idolatre* shortened f. eccl. L f. Gk *eidōlolatrēs* (IDOL, -LATRY). F had also *idolâtre* by confus. w. suf. -âtre -ASTER, whence earlier E *idolatrer*]

id'olize, v.t. & i. Make an idol of; venerate, love, to excess; practise idolatry. Hence ~A'TION n. [-IZE]

idol'um, n. (pl. *-la*), Mental image, idea.; (Logic) fallacy (see IDOL). [L, as IDOL]

id'yll, -īl, n. Short description in verse or (*prose* ~) in prose of picturesque scene or incident, esp. in rustic life; episode suitable for such treatment. Hence **idyll'ic** a., **idyll'ICALLY** adv., ~IST n. The latter & perh. usu. a., **idyll'ra** ... [f. L f. Gk *eidullion* (*eidos* form)]

if, conj. & n. 1. On the condition or supposition that, as *if you are* (now) *tired we will sit down, if you* (hereafter) *see him give him the message, if he has found it he will send it, if he had fair warning he has nothing to complain of, if he had been warned he has* (or *had*) *nothing to complain of*, (w. past tense implying that condition is not fulfilled) *if I knew what to do I should do it, if he had been warned he would have* (or *would have had*) *nothing to complain of*; whenever, as *if I feel any doubt I inquire, if I felt any doubt I inquired, if I had been badly treated I complained*; whether, as *ask, see, try, if you can turn the handle*; (when *if* is omitted, order of verb & subject is inverted, as) *were I* (if I were) *in your place, would, could, should, might, had, he* (if he would, could, etc.), (poet.) *loved I not honour more*; (without apodosis) *if I only knew!, I wish I knew, if I haven't lost my watch!* (I have, to my surprise or disgust); *as if*, as the case would be if, *as if seems as if he meant* (vulg. *means*) *to compromise, he talks as* (he would) *if he were drunk*; *as if you didn't know*, you know quite well. 2. n. Condition, supposition, as *if ifs & ans were pots & pans*. [OE *ġif*, cf. Du. *of*, G *ob* whether; perh. cases of a noun (OHG *iba*) meaning 'doubt']

ig'loo, n. Eskimo dome-shaped hut. [native, = house]

ig'neous, a. Of fire, fiery; produced by volcanic agency. [f. L *igneus* (*ignis* fire) +-OUS]

ig'nis fat'uus, n. Will-o'-the-wisp, phosphorescent light (now rarely) seen on marshy ground, supposed due to spontaneous combustion of gas from decaying organic matter; delusive hope or gain. [med. or mod. L, = foolish fire]

ignite', v.t. & i. Make intensely hot; (Chem.) heat to the point of combustion, or chemical change; set fire to; take fire. Hence or cogn. ~'ABLE a., **igni'tion** n., (also) mechanism for, act of, starting combustion of the mixture in cylinder of internal-combustion engine. [f. L ignire -it- (ignis fire)]

igno'ble, a. (-er, -est). Of low position, or reputation; mean, base, dishonourable. Hence ~ness (-n-) n., ~LY² adv. [F, f. L ignobilis NOBLE]

ig'nominy, n. Dishonour, infamy; infamous conduct. So **ignomin'ious** a. (now usu. in less damnatory sense, = humiliating), **ignomin'iously¹** adv. [f. F ignominie f., L ignominia (in- not + (g)nomen name)]

ignoram'us, n. (pl. ~es). Ignorant person. [L, = we do not know, (legal) we take no notice of (bill): mod. sense perh. f. Ruggle's Ignoramus (1615) exposing lawyers' ignorance]

ig'norance, n. Want of knowledge (of thing, or in general; where ~ is bliss, 'tis folly to be wise). [F, f. L ignorantia (as foll., see -ANCE)]

ig'norant, a. Lacking knowledge; uninformed (of, in, subject, of fact). Hence ~LY² adv. [F, f. L, as IGNORE, see -ANT]

ignora'tio (-shiō) **elen'chi** (-ki), n. (logic). Argument that appears to refute opponent while actually disproving something not advanced by him. [L]

ignore', v.t. Refuse to take notice of; (of Grand Jury) reject (bill) as unfounded. [f. F ignorer f. L ignorare not know, ignore (in- not + gno- know)]

ignō'tum per igno'tius, = the explanation of a thing more obscure than the thing it is meant to explain. [L, = the unknown by the still less known]

igua'na (-gwah-), n. Large W.-Ind. & S.-Amer. arboreal lizard. [Sp., f. Carib iwana]

iguan'odon (-gw-), n. Huge herbivorous lizard, found fossil. [f. prec. + Gk odous odontos tooth, after mastodon etc.]

IHS, abbr. repr. Gk Iēsous Jesus (Gk cap. ε being like H); often taken to mean Jesus Hominum Salvator (Saviour of men), In Hoc Signo (vinces) in this sign (thou shalt conquer), In Hac (cruce) Salus in this (cross) is salvation.

il-, pref. = IN¹,² before l.

-il, -ile, suf. of adj. & sometimes nn., repr. -ilis or when added to -c- stems -tlis (civilis). In OF -ilis appeared as -il, but -tlis lost l, tonic accent falling on prec. syllable (humble L humilem, frêle L fragilem). L wds adopted early in OF took -il masc. -ile fem. (civil, -ile); later wds have -ile for both genders (agile, facile). Few E wds have -ile (not in U.S.) is to pronounce -ile of either origin with i.

Il'ex, n. (pl. ~es). Holm-oak; (Bot., genus including common holly. [L]

Il'iac, a. Of the flank(-bone), as ~ artery; ~ passion, painful affection due to intestinal obstruction. [f. F iliaque f. L iliacus (ilium, class. L only in pl. ilia flanks; but orig. the adj. corr. to L ileus f. Gk eileos colic)]

Il'iad (i-), n. Epic poem attributed to Homer & describing siege of Troy; (fig.) ~ (long series) of woes. [f. L f. Gk Ilias (poietis) (poem) of Ilium or Troy]

il'ium, n. (pl. -ia). Hip-bone. [L; see ILIAC]

ilk, a. (Sc.) Of that ~, of the same, as Guthrie of that ~, Guthrie of Guthrie; (vulg.) that ~, that family, class, or set. [OE ilca same, prob. f. pronominal st. i- (cf. Goth. is he) + -lic LIKE]

ill, a., n., & adv. 1. Out of health, sick, as he is ~, was taken ~, (of or with disease, with anxiety etc.); (of health) unsound, disordered; morally bad, as ~ fame, disrepute, ~ blood, ~ will, animosity, strife, ~ nature, churlishness, ~ (morose) humour, temper; harmful, as (prov.) ~ weeds grow apace; do an ~ turn to person, harm him or his interests; wretched, disastrous, as (prov.) it's an ~ wind that blows nobody good; (arch.) difficult, as ~ to please; manners or conduct) Improper; (imperfect) success. 2. n. Evil, the opposite of good; harm, injury; speak ~ (some thing unfavourable) of; (pl.) misfortunes. 3. adv. Badly, as beloved ~; take (thing) ~, take offence at it; unfavourably, as it would have gone ~ with him; imperfectly, scarcely, as ~ provided, it ~ became him to speak; ~ at ease, embarrassed, uneasy. 4. ~ advised', -advis'edly, imprudent(ly); ~ affect'ed, not well disposed; ~ bred, badly brought up, rude; ~ breed'ing, bad manners; ~ condi'tioned, of evil disposition, (also) in bad condition; ~ dis- posed, disposed to evil, malevolent; (also) unfavourably disposed (towards); ~ fat'ed, destined to, bringing, bad fortune; ~ fav'oured, uncomely, (also) displeasing; objectionable; ~ gott'en, gained by evil means; ~ judged, unwise; ~ mann'- ered, unmannerly, rude; ~ na'tured(ly), churlish(ly); ~ om'ened, attended by bad omens; ~ starred', born under an evil star, unlucky; ~ tem'pered, morose, peevish; ~ timed, unseasonable; ~ treat', -use', treat badly. [early ME, f. ON illr, etym dub.]

illa'tion, n. Deduction, conclusion; thing deduced. [f. L L illatio (as INFER, see -ION)]

illa'tive, a. (Of words) stating, introducing, an inference, as ~ particles; inferential. Hence ~LY² (-vl-) adv. [f. L L illativus (as prec., see -IVE)]

ille'gal, a. Not legal; contrary to law. Hence or cogn. **illega'lity** n., ~LY² adv [f. med. L L (illegalis LEGAL)]

illeg′ible, a. Not legible. Hence ~IBILⁱTY n., ~ibly² adv. [IL-]

illegit′imate², a. & n. Not authorized by law; improper; not born in lawful wedlock, bastard; wrongly inferred; abnormal; (n.) one whose position is ~ate, esp. bastard. Hence ~ACY n., ~ately² adv. [IL-]

illegit′imāte³, v.t. Declare illegitimate. Hence A°TION n. [f. prec.]

illib′eral, a. Not befitting a free man; without liberal culture; vulgar, sordid; narrow-minded; stingy. Hence or cogn. ~ITY (-ǎl¹) n., ~LY² adv. [f. F illibéral f. L Il(liberalis LIBERAL)]

illic′it, a. Unlawful, forbidden. Hence ~LY² adv. [f. F illicite f. L Il(licitus p.p. of licēre be allowed)]

illim′it|able, a. Boundless. Hence ~ABILⁱTY, ~ableNESS, nn., ~ably² adv. [IL-]

illit′er|ate,a. & n. Ignorant of letters; unlearned; unable to read; (n.) ~ate person. Hence ~ACY, ~ateNESS, nn. (f. L Il(litteratus LITERATE]

ill′ness, n. Unhealthy condition of body, sickness. [-NESS]

illō′gical, n. Devoid of, contrary to, logic. Hence ~ITY (-ǎl²) n., ~LY² adv. [IL-]

illth, n. (rare). Evil state. [-TH¹]

illume′ (-lōō-, -lū-), v.t. (poet.). Light up, make bright, (lit. & fig.). [for ILLUMINE, cf. F allumer]

illum′in|āte (-ōō-, -ū-), v.t. Light up, whence ~ANT a. & n.; give spiritual or intellectual light to; throw light upon (subject); shed lustre upon; decorate (buildings etc.) profusely with lights as sign of festivity; decorate (initial letter in manuscript etc.) with gold, silver, & brilliant colours. So A°TION, ~ātor², nn., ~ātive a., (-ōō-, -ū-). [f. L Il(luminare f. lumen -minis light), see -ATE²]

illūminăt′i (-ōō-, -ū-; also -aḣ′tē), n. pl. Secret society founded by Weishaupt in 1776, holding deistic & republican principles, & organized like freemasons; persons claiming to possess special enlightenment. So **illum′inism**(3), **illum′-inist**(2), nn., (-ōō-, -ū-). IL(as prec., -ato ¬ATE²·³) or IT, whence occasional sing., -ato]

illum′ine (-ōō-, -ū-), v.t. Light up; enlighten spiritually; brighten. [f. F illuminer (as ILLUMINATE]

illu′sion (-lōōzhn), n. Deception, delusion; sensuous perception of an external object involving a false belief; a transparent tulle. [f. f. L illusionem f. Il(ludere lus- play), see -ION]

illu′sion|ist (-lōōzhon-), n. One who disbelieves in objective existence, so ~ISM n.; one who produces illusions, esp. conjurer. [-IST]

illus′ive (-lōō-), a. Deceptive. Hence or cogn. ~iveLY², ~oriLY², advv., ~ive-NESS, ~oriNESS, nn., ~ORY a. [as ILLUSION, see -IVE]

ill′ustrāte, v.t. Make clear, explain; make clear by examples; elucidate (description etc.) by drawings; ornament (book, newspaper, etc.) with designs. Hence ~OR² n. [f. L Il(lustrare light up, prob. f. st. of lumen light)]

illustrā′tion, n. Illustrating; example; drawing etc. illustrating book or article in paper, [F, f. L illustrationem (prec., -ATION]

illus′trative, a. Serving as explanation or example (of). Hence ~LY² (-vī-) adv. [as ILLUSTRATE, see -IVE]

illūs′trious, a. Distinguished, renowned. Hence ~LY² adv., ~NESS n. [f. L Il(lustris see ILLUSTRATE) +-OUS]

im-.¹,², pref. = IN-¹,¹² before b, m, p.

im′age², n. Artificial imitation of the external form of an object, e.g. statue (esp. of saint etc. as object of veneration); optical counterpart produced by rays of light reflected from mirror, refracted through lens, etc.; form, semblance; counterpart, as he is the very ~ of his father; type; simile, metaphor; idea, conception. Hence ~LESS (-ijī-) a. [F, f. L imaginem (nom. -go) prob. f. same root as IMITATE]

im′age², v.t. Make an image of, portray; reflect, mirror; picture (thing to oneself); describe vividly; typify. Hence ~ABLE (-ija-) a. [f. prec.]

im′agery (-ij-), n. Images; statuary, carving; figurative illustration. [f. OF imagerie (as IMAGE¹, see -ERY]

ima′ginable, a. That can be imagined, as the greatest difficulty ~le, took all the trouble ~le. Hence ~LY² adv. [f. LL imaginabilis (as IMAGINE, see -BLE)]

ima′ginal, a. (entom.). Of an insect imago. [f. L as IMAGE³ +-AL]

ima′ginar|y, a. Existing only in imagination; (Math.) having no real existence, but assumed to exist for a special purpose (e.g. square root of negative quantity). Hence ~iLY² adv. [f.L imaginarius (as prec., see -ARY¹]

imaginā′tion, n. Imagining; mental faculty forming images of external objects not present to the senses; fancy; creative faculty of the mind. [F, f. L imaginationem (as IMAGINE, see -ATION]

ima′ginative (or -ātiv-), a. Of, given to using, having or showing in a high degree, the faculty of imagination. Hence ~LY² (-vī-) adv., ~NESS (-vn-) n. [OF (-if, -ive), f. LL imaginatif (as prec., see -ATIVE]

ima′gine, v.t. Form mental image of; conceive (thing, thing to be or do, that it is, how, what, etc.); guess, as cannot ~ what he is doing; suppose, be of opinion, (that); take into one's head (idea, that). [f. F imaginer f. L imaginari (as IMAGE³]

im′agist, n. One of a group of early 20th-c. poets who, in revolt against romanticism, seek clarity of expression through the use of precise images. [IMAGE¹+ -IST(2)]

imāg'ō, n. (pl. ...). Final & perfect stage of insect after all metamorphoses, e.g. butterfly. [mod. L sense of *imago* IMAGE]

imâm', imaum', (-ahm), n. Officiating priest of mosque; title of various Mohammedan leaders. Hence **imam ATE**[1] (-ahm-) n. [Arab, (*am-i ammago* before)]

imbēc'ile, a. & n. 1. Mentally weak, stupid, idiotic; physically weak. 2. n. Person of weak intellect. Hence or cogn. **~LY**[2] (-l-) adv., **imbēcil'ITY** n. [f. F *imbécile* (now -*ile*) f. L *imbecillus* etym. dub.]

imbĭbe', v.t. Drink in, assimilate, (ideas etc.); drink (liquid); inhale (air etc.); ab-(partly thr. F *imbiber*) f. L IM(*bibi-* drink) conceive (opinions), drink]

im'bricāte, v.t. & i. Arrange (leaves, scales of fish, etc.), be arranged, so as to overlap like tiles. So **~ATE**[1](-ŏt), **~ATIVE** aa... **~A'TION** n. [f. L *imbricare* form like a tile (*imbrex-icis* f. *imber* shower), **~ATE**[3]]

imbrō'glio (-ōlyō), n. (pl. **~s**). Confused heap; complicated (esp. political or dramatic) situation. [It., f. *broglio*, cf. BROIL[2]]

imbrue' (-ōō), v.t. Stain (one's hand, sword, etc, *in, with*, blood, slaughter, etc.). [f. OF *embruver* moisten for EM-(*beuvre* f.) +*biberare* f. *bibere* drink]

imbrute', ēm-, (-ōōt), v.t. Brutalize. [IM-[1]]

imbūe', v.t. Saturate (*with*); dye (*with*); permeate, inspire, (*with* feelings etc.); = IMBRUE. [f. L IM(*buere* cogn. w. *bibere* drink)]

im'itāte, v.t. Follow example of; mimic; be (consciously or not) like. So **~ABLE** a. **IMITÂtor**[2], nn., **~ātor**[2] m., **~ATRIX** a. ... see **~ATOR**[2] see -ARY[3]]

imitā'tion, n. Imitating (~ *is the sincerest flattery*); copy; counterfeit (often attrib. as **~** *leather*); (Mus.) repetition of melody etc, usu. at different pitch, in another part or voice. [f. L *imitatio* (prec., -ION)]

im'itative, a. Following model or example (of); **~** *arts*, painting & sculpture; **~** *word*, one that reproduces a natural sound (e.g. *fizz*) or whose sound is thought to correspond to appearances etc. of object described; counterfeit. Hence **~LY**[2] adv., **~NESS** n. [f. LL *imitativus* (as IMITATE, see -ATIVE)]

immac'ūlate, a. Pure, spotless; faultless (often iron.); **I~** *Conception* (of Virgin Mary, as conceived free from taint of original sin); (Nat. Hist.) not spotted. Hence **immac'ULACY**, **~NESS**, nn., **~LY**[2] adv. [f. L IM(*maculata* f. *macula* spot)]

imm'anent, a. Indwelling, inherent, (often) (of God) permanently pervading the universe. Hence **~ENCE**, **~ENCY**, nn. [f. LL IM(*manere* remain), see -ENT]

immatēr'ial, a. Not material, incor-

immatēr'ial...poreal; unimportant. Hence **~ITY** (-ăl-) n., **~IZE**(3) v.t. [f. med. L IM(*materialis* MATERIAL)]

immatēr'ialįism, n. Doctrine that matter does not exist in itself apart from perception. So **~IST** n. [-ISM]

immatūr'e, a. Not mature. So **~ITY** n., **~ableNESS**, nn., **~abLY**[2] adv., Hence **~abIL'ITY**, MATURE]

immē'diate (-dyǎt), a. (Of person or thing in its relation to another) not separated by any intervening medium; (of relation or action) direct, without intervening medium; (Logic) **~** *inference* (from single premiss, without intervention of middle term); nearest, next, as *my* = *neighbour*; occurring at once, without delay, as an **~** *reply*. Hence **immēd'IACY**, **~NESS** nn., **~LY**[2](-tl-) adv. [f. med. L IM(*mediatus* MEDIATE)]

immemor'ial, a. Ancient beyond memory; very old. Hence **~LY**[2] adv. [f. med. L IM(*memorialis* MEMORIAL)]

immēnse', a. Vast, huge; (sl.) very good. Hence or cogn. **~NESS**(-sn-), **immēns'ITY**, nn. [F, f. L IM(*mensus* p.p. of *metiri* measure; immeasurable)]

immense'ly (-slī), adv. In an immense degree; (colloq.) very much. [-LY[2]]

immers'e, v.t. Dip, plunge, (in liquid); put overhead in water, esp. baptize thus; bury, imbed, (*in*); involve deeply, absorb, (in debt, difficulties, thought, etc.). [f. L IM(*mergere mers-* dip)]

immers'ion (-shn), n. Immersing; baptism by plunging whole person in water (cf. AFFUSION); (Astron.) disappearance of celestial body behind another in its shadow; **~** *heater*, electric water-heater placed in hot-water tank. [f. LL *immersio* (prec., -ION)]

imm'igrate, v.i. & t. Come as settler (*into* foreign country); bring in (person) as settler. So **~ANT** a. & n., **~A'TION** n. [f. L IM(*migrare* MIGRATE)]

imm'inent, a. (Of events, esp. dangers) impending, soon to happen. Hence or cogn. **~ENCE** n., **~entLY**[2] adv. [f. L IM(*minere* overhang, see -ENT)]

immis'cible, a. That cannot be mixed. Hence **~IBIL'ITY** n., **~ibLY**[2] adv. [f. IM-[2]+L *miscēre* mix, see -BLE]

immit'igable, a. That cannot be softened or toned down. Hence **~LY**[2] adv. [f. L IM(*mitigabilis*, see MITIGATE)]

immix'ture, n. Mixing up; being involved (in). [IM-[1]+MIXTURE]

immō'bile, a. Immovable; not mobile; motionless. So **immobIL'ITY** n. [f. L IM(*mobilis* MOBILE)]

immō'bilīze, v.t. Fix immovably; make (troops, vehicle) incapable of being shifted; withdraw (specie) from

circulation. Hence ~A'TION n. [f. F *immobiliser* (as prec., see -IZE)]

immod'erate, a. Excessive; wanting in moderation. Hence ~LY² (-tli-) adv. [f. L im²(*moderatus* MODERATE)]

immod'est, a. Indecent, indelicate; forward, impudent. Hence ~LY² adv., ~Y¹ n. [f. L im²(*modestus* MODEST)]

immo'late, v.t. Kill (victim) as sacrifice; (fig.) sacrifice (thing etc. *to* another). So ~A'TION, ~ātor², nn. [f. L im²*molare* sprinkle with meal (*mola*), sacrifice, -ATE³]

immo'ral, a. Opposed to morality; morally evil; vicious, dissolute. Hence immoral'ITY n., ~LY² adv. [IM-²]

immort'al, a. & n. 1. Undying; divine; unfading, incorruptible; famous for all time; (colloq.) constant, long-lasting. 2. n. ~ being, esp. (pl.) gods of antiquity; person esp. author of enduring fame, member of French Academy; (pl.) royal bodyguard of ancient Persia. So ~ITY (-ǎl-) n. [f. L im²(*mortalis* MORTAL)]

immort'alize, v.t. Confer enduring fame upon; endow with endless life; perpetuate. Hence ~A'TION n. [-IZE]

immort'ally, adv. Eternally; (colloq.) infinitely, very. [-LY²]

immortelle', n. Composite flower of papery texture retaining colour after being dried, often used to adorn graves. [F, fem. of *immortel* IMMORTAL]

immo'vable (-moo-), a. & n. That cannot be moved; motionless; not subject to change; ~able FEAST; firm, steadfast, unyielding; emotionless; (Law, of property) consisting of land, houses, etc. (also as n. pl.). Hence ~ABIL'ITY n., ~ableNESS, nn., ~ably³ adv. [IM-²]

immune', a. & n. Having immunity (*from, against, to,* poison, contagion, etc.); (n.) ~ person. [f. L im²*munis* exempt from public burden (*munus*)]

immu'nity, n. Exemption (*from* taxation, jurisdiction, etc.); freedom (*from*); being proof against contagion etc. [f. L *immunitas* (as prec., see -TY)]

immu'nize, v.t. Render immune (*against* contagion). Hence ~A'TION n. [-IZE]

immure', v.t. Imprison; shut oneself up. Hence ~MENT (-ûr-) n. [f. med. L im²(*murare* f. *murus* wall)]

immu'table, a. Unchangeable; not subject to variation in different cases. Hence ~ABIL'ITY n., ~ably³ adv. [f. L im²*mutabilis* MUTABLE]

imp¹, n. Child of the devil; little devil; mischievous child; ‖ (arch.) child. [OE *impa* young shoot, scion, conn. w. foll.]

imp², v.t. ~ *the wings of* (bird), strengthen its flight; (rare) enlarge, eke out. [OE *impian* graft, prob. f. Gk *emphuō*, cf. F *enter* (for †*emper*)]

im'pact¹, n. Striking (*on, against*), collision. [f. L *impingere*-pact- IMPINGE]

impăct², v.t. Press, fix, firmly (*into, in*). So impăc'TION n. [prob. back formation f. *impacted* n. L p.p. as prec. +-ED¹]

impair', v.t. Damage; weaken. So ~MENT n. [f. OF *empeirer* f. L im²(*pejorare* f. *pejor* worse) make worse]

impale', v.t. Transfix (body etc. *upon, with*, stake etc., esp. as form of capital punishment); (Her.) combine (two coats of arms) by placing side by side on one shield separated by vertical line down middle; ‖ (rare) fence in with stakes. So ~MENT (-lm-) n. [f. F *empaler* f. med. L im¹(*palare* f. *palus* stake)]

impal'pable, a. Imperceptible to the touch; not easily grasped by the mind, intangible. Hence ~ABIL'ITY n., ~ably³ adv. [f. med. L im²(*palpabilis* PALPABLE)]

impalu'dism, n. Morbid state, with tendency to intermittent fevers & enlargement of spleen, found in dwellers in marshes. [f. im-¹ + L *palus -udis* marsh +-ISM]

impăn'ate (or im'pa-), a. (Of the body of Christ) contained in the bread after consecration. So impana'TION n. [f. med. L im¹(*panare* f. *panis* bread), see -ATE²]

impanel. See EMPANEL.

impă'radise, ém., v.t. Bring into state of supreme happiness; ravish; make a paradise of (place, state). [IM-¹]

imparisyllăb'ic, a. & n. (Gk & Lat. Gram.). (Noun) that has more syllables in genitive than in nominative. [f. L im²(*par* equal) +SYLLABIC]

impărk', v.t. Enclose (beasts) in park; enclose (land) for park. Hence ~A'TION n. [f. OF EM(*parquer* f. *parc* PARK]

impart', v.t. Give share of (thing *to* person etc.); communicate (news etc. *to*). Hence ~A'TION, ~MENT, nn. [f. OF *empartir* f. L im¹(*partire* PART²)]

impar'tial (-shal), a. Not partial, unprejudiced, fair. Hence ~ITY (-shiǎl⁵) n., ~LY² (-shal-) adv. [IM-²]

impart'ible, a. (Of estate) not divisible. [f. LL im²(*partibilis* PARTIBLE]

impass'able (-pah-), a. That cannot be traversed. Hence ~ABIL'ITY, ~ableNESS, nn. [IM-²]

impasse' (-ahs; or ăñpahs°), n. Blind alley; position from which there is no escape. [F (im-² +*passer* PASS¹)]

impass'ible, a. Incapable of feeling or emotion; incapable of suffering injury; not subject to suffering. Hence ~BIL'ITY, ~ibleNESS, nn., ~iblY³ adv. [f. eccl. L im²(*passibilis* PASSIBLE]

impa'ssion (-shn), v.t. Stir the passions of, excite strongly, (chiefly in p.p.). [f. It. im²(*passionare* f. *passione* PASSION)]

impass'ive, a. Deficient in feeling or emotion; serene; without sensation; not subject to suffering. Hence ~LY² adv., ~NESS, impăssiv'ITY, nn. [IM-²]

impaste', v.t. Enclose (as) with paste; make into a paste; paint by laying on

colours thickly. [f. It. *impasto* f. *pasta* PASTE]

Impas'to, n. (paint.), Laying on of colour thickly. [It., as prec.]

Impa'tient (-shent), a. Not enduring with composure; intolerant of; restlessly desirous (*for* thing). Hence or cogn. ~NESS (-shens) n., ~ently² (-shent-) adv. [OF, f. L IM²(*patientem* part. of *pati* suffer)]

Impawn', v.t. Put in pawn; (fig.) pledge, plight. [IM-²]

impay'able (or ãpãyah'bl), a. Beyond price; (colloq.) going beyond ordinary limits. [F IM-²]

Impeach', v.t. Call in question, disparage, (character etc.); accuse (person) *of*, charge (*with*); find fault with (thing); accuse of treason or other high crime before competent tribunal. [f. OF *empecher* impede f. LL IM²(*pedicare* f. *pes pedis* foot) entangle f. *pedica* fetter, f. *pes pedis* foot]

Impeach'ment, n. Calling in question, accusation, esp. (joc.) *the soft* ~ (Sheridan, *Rivals* v. iii); accusation & prosecution for treason etc. [f. OF *empechement* (as prec., see -MENT)]

Impecc'able, a. Not liable to sin; (of things) faultless. Hence or cogn. ~ABIL·ITY n., ~ably² adv., ~ANT a. [f. LL IM²(*peccabilis* f. *peccare* sin, see -BLE)]

Impecu'nious, a. Having little or no money. Hence ~OS'ITY n. [f. IM-² +obs. *pecunious* f. L *pecuniosus* (*pecunia* money f. *pecu* cattle, see -OUS)]

Imped'ance, n. (electr.). Total virtual resistance of electric circuit to alternating current, arising from the resistance & the reactance of the conductor. [f. foll. +-ANCE]

Impede', v.t. Retard, hinder. [f. L IM-²(*pedire* f. *pes* foot) lit. shackle the feet of]

Imped'iment, n. Hindrance, obstruction; ~ (in one's speech), stammer; (pl., also L *impedimenta*) baggage, esp. of army. Hence ~AL (-en'-) a. [f. L *impedimentum* (as prec., see -MENT)]

Impel', v.t. (-ll-). Drive, force, (person etc. *to* action, *to do*); drive forward, propel. So ~LENT a. & n. [f. L IM²(*pellere puls-* drive)]

Impend', v.i. Hang, be suspended, (*over*); (fig., of danger) hang threateningly (*over*), be imminent. So impen'dENCE, -ENCY, nn., impen'dENT a. [f. L IM²(*pendēre* hang)]

Impen'etrable, a. That cannot be penetrated; inscrutable, unfathomable; impervious (*to, by* ideas etc.); (Nat. Phil.) having that property in virtue of which two bodies cannot occupy same place at same time. So ~ABIL'ITY, ~ableNESS, nn., ~ably² adv. [f. F *impénétrable* f. L IM²(*penetrabilis* PENETRABLE)]

Impen'itent, a. Not penitent. Hence or cogn. ~ENCE, ~ENCY, nn., ~ently² adv. [f. L IM²(*pænitens* PENITENT)]

Imper'ative, a. & n. 1. (Gram.) expressing command; commanding, peremptory; urgent; obligatory. 2. n. ~ mood, whence imperativ'AL a. Hence ~LY² (-vl-) adv., ~NESS (-vn-) n. [f. LL *imperativus* f. IM²(*perare* = *parare* make ready) command. -IVE]

imperãtor', n. (Rom. Hist.). Commander (title conferred by salutation of soldiers on victorious general, under the Republic); emperor. So imperatōr'IAL a. [L (as prec., see -OR²)]

Impercep'tible, a. That cannot be perceived; very slight, gradual, or subtle. Hence ~LY² adv. [F, f. med. L IM²(*perceptibilis* PERCEPTIBLE)]

imper'cipient, a. Lacking perception. [IM-²]

im'perence, n. (Form, ascribed to illiterate speakers, of) impudence, [corrupt.]

imper'fect, a. & n. 1. Not fully formed or done, incomplete; faulty; (Gram.) ~ tenses, those that denote action going on but not completed (e.g. *he is, he will be, he was singing,* but usu. of past time, as *he was singing*). 2. n. ~ tense. Hence ~LY² adv. [f. *imparfait* f. L IM²(*perfectus* PERFECT), refash. on L]

imperfec'tion, n. Incompleteness; faultiness; fault, blemish. [f. L *imperfectio* prec., see -ION]

imper'forate, a. Not perforated, esp. (Anat.) lacking the normal opening (also of sheet of postage-stamps or single stamp). [IM-²]

imper'ial, a. & n. 1. Of an empire or sovereign state ranking with an empire. 2. Of Great Britain, as dist. from its constituent kingdoms etc.; ~ *federation*, proposed adjustment of British Empire, giving colonies share in control & cost of measures taken for joint interest; *I~ Institute*, building in London devoted to promoting trade between parts of the Empire; ~ *preference*, taxing of imports from parts of the Empire at lower rates than those from foreign countries. 3. Of an emperor; supreme in authority; majestic, august; magnificent. 4. (Of weights & measures used by statute in U.K.) ~ *gallon, acre,* etc.; (of paper) 22 × 32 in. 5. n. Small part of beard left growing beneath lower lip (from Napoleon III); trunk for luggage, adapted for root of coach; Russian tsarist gold coin = 15 silver roubles. Hence ~LY² adv. [OF, f. L *imperialis* (IMPERIUM, see -AL)]

imper'ialism, n. Rule of an emperor; extension of British Empire where trade requires protection of the flag; union of different parts of British Empire for purposes of warlike defence, internal commerce, etc.; belief in value of colonies & dependencies (cf. LITTLE *Englandism*). So ~IST'IC a., ~IZE(3) v.t. [-ISM]

impe'rialist, n. Adherent of an emperor, esp. (1600-1800) of German Emperor; advocate of imperial rule, esp. adherent of Bonaparte family; advocate of (British) imperialism. [-IST]

impe'ril, v.t. (-ll-). Bring into danger. [IM-¹]

impe'rious, a. Overbearing, domineering; urgent, imperative. Hence ~LY² adv., ~NESS n. [f. L *imperiosus* (as IMPERIUM, see -OUS)]

impe'rishable, a. That cannot perish. Hence ~ABIL'ITY, ~ableness, nn., ~ably² adv. [IM-²]

impē'rium (or -pēr-), n. Absolute power; empire: ~ *in imperio*, supreme authority within jurisdiction of another authority. [L, = command, dominion]

imperm'anent, a. Not permanent. Hence ~ENCE, ~ENCY, nn. [IM-²]

imperm'éable, a. That cannot be passed through; (Physics) that does not permit passage of fluids. Hence ~A'TION, ~ITY n. [f. LL IM²(*permeabilis* PERMEABLE)]

impermiss'ible, a. Not permissible. [IM-²]

imperscript'ible, a. Not backed by written authority. [f. IM-²+L PER- (*scribere script-* write) register, see -BLE]

impers'onal, a. (Gram.) ~ verb, one used only in 3rd sing. (e.g. *it rains*); having no personality or personal reference or tone. Hence ~ITY (-ăl-) n., ~LY² adv. [f. LL IM²(*personalis* PERSONAL)]

impers'onate, v.t. Represent in bodily form, personify; play the part of, personate; act (character). Hence ~A'TION, ~ATOR² nn., ~ATIVE a. [f. IM-¹+L *persona* PERSON + -ATE³]

imperson'ify, v.t. Personify. [IM-¹]

impert'inent, a. Insolent, saucy; intrusive; out of place, absurd; not to the point. Hence or cogn. ~ENCE n., ~ently² adv. [f. L IM²(*pertinens* PERTINENT)]

imperturb'able, a. Not excitable, calm. Hence ~ABIL'ITY, ~ableness, nn., ~ably² adv. [IM-²]

imperv'ious, a. Not affording passage (*to*); (fig.) ~ (dead) *to argument* etc. Hence ~LY² adv., ~NESS n. [f. L IM²(*pervius* PERVIOUS)]

impetī'go, n. Contagious pustular disease of skin. So impeti'ginous a. [L, gen. *-ginis*, f. IM²(*petere* seek) assail, cf. *vertigo*]

im'petrate, v.t. (Theol.) obtain by request; (rare) ask for. So ~A'TION n., ~ATORy a. [f. L IM²(*petrare=patrare* bring to pass), see -ATE³]

impe'tuous, a. Moving violently or rapidly; acting with rash or sudden energy. Hence or cogn. impetūos'ITY, ~NESS, nn., ~LY² adv. [f. F *impétueux* f. L *impetuosus* (as foll.)]

im'petus, n. (pl. ~es). Force with which a body moves; (fig.) moving force, impulse. [L, = assault, force, f. IM²(*petere* seek) assail]

im'peyan(-piăn), a. ~ *pheasant*, E.-Indian pheasant, with crested head & brilliant plumage. [Sir Elijah *Impey*, 1787]

im'pi, n. Body of Kafir warriors. [Zulu]

impī'ety, n. Ungodliness; want of dutifulness or reverence. [f. L IM²(*pietas* PIETY)]

impinge' (-j), v.i. & t. Make impact (*on, upon*); (trans.: arch.) make (thing) do this. Hence ~MENT (-jm-) n. [f. L IM²(*pingere* = *pangere* fix, drive) drive (thing) at]

im'pious, a. Not pious, wicked, profane. Hence ~LY² adv. [f. L IM²(*pius* PIOUS)]

im'pish, a. Of, like, an imp. Hence ~LY¹ adv., ~NESS n. [-ISH¹]

impla'cable (or -lăk-), a. That cannot be appeased. Hence or cogn. ~ABIL'ITY n., ~ably² adv. [F, f. L IM²(*placabilis* PLACABLE)]

impla'cental, a. With no placenta. [IM-²]

im'plant (-ahnt), v.t. Insert, infix, (*in*); instil (principle, idea, etc., *in* mind etc.). Hence ~A'TION n. [f. IM²(*planter* PLANT)]

impledge', v.t. Put in pledge, pawn. [IM-¹]

im'plement¹, n. Article of furniture, dress, etc., (pl.) equipment of these; tool, instrument, (esp. in pl.); || (Sc. Law) full performance. [prob. f. L *implementum*, in sense 'that which serves to stock a house etc.' f. IM²(*plēre* fill), see -MENT]

im'plement², v.t. Complete (contract etc.); fulfil (engagement); fill up, supplement.

imple'tion, n. Filling; fullness. [f. LL *templetio* f. IM²(*plēre plet-* fill), see -ION]

im'plicate¹, n. Thing implied. [f. L IM²(*plicare plicat-* or *plicit-* fold), see -ATE²]

im'plicate², v.t. Entwine, entangle; involve, imply, as inference, so ~ātive a.; involve (person *in* charge, crime, etc.); (pass.) be affected in (a thing's operation). So ~A'TION n. [as prec., see -ATE³]

im'plicit, a. Implied though not plainly expressed; virtually contained (*in*); ~ *faith* (not independently reached by the individual, but involved in general belief of Church), absolute, unreserved, cf. EXPLICIT). Hence ~LY² adv., ~NESS n. [(perh. thr. F) as IMPLICATE¹]

implore', v.t. Beg earnestly for; entreat (*person to do*). Hence ~ingly² adv., ~ingNESS n. [f. L IM²(*plorare* weep)]

implu'vium (-ploo-), n. (Rom. Ant.). Square basin in middle of atrium receiving rain-water from open space in roof. [L, f. IM²(*pluere* rain)]

imply', v.t. Involve the truth of (thing not expressly asserted, *that*); mean; insinuate, hint. Hence impli'edly¹ adv. [f. OF *emplier* (as IMPLICATE, cf. EMPLOY)]

||impōld'er, v.t. Make a POLDER of; reclaim from sea. [IM-¹+POLDER]

impol'icy, n. Bad policy; inexpediency. [IM-²]

impolite', a. (-est). Uncivil, rude. Hence ~ly² (-tl-) adv., ~NESS (-tl-) n. [f. L IM²(politus POLITE)]

impol'itic, a. Not politic; inexpedient. Hence ~ly² adv. [IM-²]

impon'derable, a. & n. 1 (Physics) having no weight; very light; (fig.) that cannot be estimated. 2. n. ~ thing (esp. fig.; pl., of qualities, emotions, etc.). [IM-²]

impon'ent, a. & n. 1 (Person) that imposes a duty etc. [f. L IM¹(ponere lay on, see -ENT]

import¹, v.t. Bring, introduce, (things, esp. goods from foreign country, (into), whence ~ABLE a., ~ABIL¹ITY, ~A¹TION n.; imply, indicate, mean, (thing, that); express, make known, (that); be of consequence to, as questions that ~ us nearly, it ~s us to know; (f. L IM¹(portare carry) bring in, in med. L=be of consequence]

im'port², n. What is implied, meaning; importance; (usu. pl.) commodity imported; importation. [f. prec.]

import'ance, n. Being important; weight, significance; personal consequence, dignity; pompousness (usu. self-~). [f. f. med. L importantia (as IMPORT¹, see -ANCE)]

import'ant, a. Carrying with it great consequence (to person concerned or purpose etc.), weighty, momentous; consequential, pompous. Hence ~ly² adv. [F, f. med. L as IMPORT¹, -ANT]

importa'tion. See IMPORT¹.

import'unate, a. Persistent, pressing, in solicitation; (of affairs) urgent. Hence or cogn. ~ly² adv., importū'nity n. [f. L IM¹(portunus f. portus port) inconvenient, -ATE²]

importune' (or impôr'-), v.t. Solicit pressingly (person or abs.). [f. F im-portuner f. med. L importunari (as prec.) take f. L prehendere) as prec.]

impose' (-z), v.t. & i. (Arch.) place (thing) upon; (Print.) lay (pages of type) in proper order & secure them in a chase; lay (tax, duty, charge, obligation, upon); palm off (thing upon person); exert influence (on person) by striking character or appearance, whence ~ingly² adv.; ~ingnEss n., (-z-); ~e upon, take advantage of (person); practise deception (upon). [f. F IM¹(poser, cf. COMPOSE)]

imposi'tion (-z-), n. In vbl senses of IMPOSE; also or esp.: laying on of hands (in ordination etc.); impost, tax, duty; piece of deception or overcharge; || work set as punishment at school (colloq. abbr. impo, impos). [f. L impositio f. IM¹(ponere)]

impòss'ible, a. Not possible (often w. tò as subj., as it is ~ible to alter them); (loosely) not easy, not convenient; (colloq.) outrageous, intolerable, as an ~ible hat, person. Hence or cogn.

~ibil'ITY n., ~ibly² adv. [f. L IM²(possi-bilis POSSIBLE)]

im'post¹, n. (Hist.) tax, duty, tribute; (Racing sl.) weight horse carries in handicap. [OF, f. L med. L IM¹(ponere post(i)t-place)]

impost'or, n. One who assumes a false character or passes himself off for some-one else; swindler. Hence ~FOUS a. [f. F imposteur f. LL impostor (as IMPOST¹, see place)]

impos'ture, n. Fraudulent deception. [F, f. LL impostura (IMPOST¹, -URE)]

im'potent, a. Powerless; helpless, de-crepit; (of males) wholly lacking in sexual power. Hence or cogn. ~ENCE, ~ENCY nn., ~ently² adv. [F, f. L IM²(potens POTENT)]

impound', v.t. Shut up (cattle) in pound; shut up (person, thing) as in pound; take legal possession of; confiscate. [IM-¹]

impov'erish, v.t. Make poor; exhaust strength of. So ~MENT n. [f. OF EM-]

imprac'ticable, a. Impossible in practice; (of persons or things) unmanageable; (of roads etc.) impassable. Hence ~ABIL-ITY, ~ableNESS nn., ~ably² adv. [IM-²]

im'precate, v.t. Invoke, call down, (evil upon person etc.). So ~A¹TION n. (esp. spoken curse), ~ātory a. [f. L IM¹(precari pray)]

impreg'nable, a. (Of fortress etc.) that cannot be taken by arms; (fig.) proof against attack. Hence ~abil'ITY n., ~ably² adv. [f. F IM²(prenable f. prendre take f. L prehendere); -g- in imit. of reign, deign, etc.]

impreg'nate, v.t. Make (female) preg-nant; (Biol.) fecundate (female reproduc-tive cell or ovum); fill, saturate, (with); imbue, fill, (with feelings, moral qualities, etc.). Hence ~A¹TION n. [as prec., see -ATE³]

imprē'sa, n. (pl. ~s). Organizer of public entertainments, esp. manager of operatic or concert company. [It. (im-presa undertaking, as EMPRISE, see -ARY²)]

imprescrip'tible, a. Not subject to pre-scription, that cannot be legally taken away, esp. ~ right. [F (IM-²)]

im'press¹, n. Stamping; mark made by seal, stamp, etc.; (fig.) characteristic mark. [f. foll.]

impress², v.t. Apply (mark etc.) with pressure, imprint, stamp, (on); imprint,

enforce, (idea etc., *that, what,* etc., *on* person, his mind); mark (thing *with* stamp etc. lit. & fig.); affect, influence, deeply, whence ~IBLE a., ~IBILITY n.; affect (person) strongly (*with* idea etc.). [f. L IM²(*primere* = *premere* PRESS²)]

impréss'[3], v.t. Force (men) to serve in army or navy; seize (goods etc.) for public service; enlist, make use of, (thing) in argument etc. Hence ~MENT n. [IM⁻¹ + PRESS³]

impréss'ion (-shn), n. Impressing (of mark); mark impressed; print taken from type or engraving; (printing of) number of copies forming one issue of book, edition, (also, unaltered reprint from standing type or plates, as opp. to *edition*); effect produced (esp. on mind or feelings); notion, (vague) belief, impressed on the mind, as *that is my ~, I was under the ~ that.* [f., f. L *impressio* (as IMPRESS², see -ION)]

impré'ssionable a. Susceptible of impressions, easily influenced. Hence ~ABILITY n. [f (*impressionner*, as prec., see -ABLE]

impré'ssionism (-shon-), n. Method of painting or writing so as to give general tone & effect without elaborate detail, or (in painting, opp. *pre-Raphaelitism*) with details so treated as to be apprehended simultaneously, & not successively with changes of focus. So ~ARY¹, ~is'tic, aa., ~IST n. [-ISM]

impréss'ive, a. (Of language, scenes, etc.) able to excite deep feeling. Hence ~LY²(-vi-) adv., ~NESS (-vn-) n. [-IVE]

im'prést[1], n. Money advanced to person to be used in State business. [earlier *prest* & v.; it. has IM²(*praestare* = L *praestare* be surety for, fulfil) lend, *impresto* loan]

imprimā'tūr, n. Official licence to print (now usu. of works sanctioned by R.-C. Church); (fig.) sanction. [mod. L, = let it be printed]

imprī'mis, adv. In the first place. [L, = *in primis* among the first things]

im'print[1], n. Impression, stamp, (lit. & fig.); *publisher's, printer's, ~* (name, place etc., on title-page or at end of book. [f. F *empreinte* stamp (as foll.)]

imprint'[2], v.t. Stamp (figure etc. *on*); impress (idea etc. *on, in,* mind etc.); impress (quality etc. *on, in,*) stamp (thing *with* figure). [f. OF *empreinter* f. *em-preindre* f. pop. L IM²(*premere* press]

impris'on (-z-), v.t. Put into prison; (fig.) confine, shut up. So ~MENT (-z-) n. [f. OF EM(*prisoner* f. PRISON]

improb'able, a. Not likely to be true or to happen. Hence ~ABILITY n., ~ably² adv. [f. L IM²(*probabilis* PROBABLE]

improb'ity, n. Wickedness; dishonesty. [f. L *improbitas* f. IM²(*probus* honest), see -TY]

imprómp'tū, adv., n., & a. Extempore (performance, composition); musical com-position having character of improvisa- tion. [= L *in promptu* in readiness (*promere,* see PROMPT)]

impróp'er, a. Inaccurate, wrong; ~ *frac-tion* (greater than 1, with numerator greater than denominator); unseemly, indecent. Hence ~LY² adv. [IM⁻²]

‖ **impróp'rïāte**, v.t. Annex (ecclesiastical benefice) to corporation or person as property; place (tithes, ecclesiastical property) in lay hands. So ~ATE²(-ǎt) a., ~A'TION n. [f. med. or mod. L IM²(*pro-priare* f. *proprius* own), see -ATE²]

‖ **impróp'rïātor**, n. One to whom bene- fice is impropriated. [as prec., see -OR³]

imprópri'ety, n. Incorrectness; unfit- ness; indecency. [f. L IM²(*proprietas* PROPRIETY]

impróv'|able (-ōōv-), a. That can be im- proved; adapted for cultivation. Hence ~ABILITY, ~ableness, nn. [-ABLE]

impróve' (-ōōv-), v.t. & i. Make, become, better; ~ *away,* get rid of by improve- ments; make good use of (*the occasion, the opportunity);* ~ *upon,* produce some- thing better than ; preach on (*the occasion*) with a view to edification. So ~MENT (-ōōvm-) n., (also) addition, alteration, etc., that adds to the value (of lands, houses, etc.). [f. AF EM(*prouer* f. OF *prou* profit, = L *pro* prep. used as n.)]

impróv'er (-ōōv-), n. In vbl senses; also or esp.: one who works at trade for low wage or none to improve his skill; = DRESS~. [-ER¹]

impróv'ident, a. Unforeseeing; heed- less; thriftless. Hence or cogn. ~ENCE n., ~entry² adv. [IM⁻²]

impróv'isātor (-z-), **imprō(v)visātor'e** (-vēzahtōrě), n. (It. pl. *-ori,* pron. -ōrē). One who improvises or composes extem- pore. So **impróv(v)issātric'e** (-vēzah- trēch'ǎ) [-TRIX] n. [It. (-*e*), as IMPROVISE, see -OR²]

improvise' (-z; *also* im⁴), v.t. Compose, utter, (verse, music, etc., or abs.) extem- pore; provide, provide, get up, extempore. Hence **improvis'a'TION** n., **improvisātōr'IAL, improvis'atory,** aa., (-z-). [f. F *im-proviser* f. It. *improv(v)isare* f. *improv(v)iso* f. L IM²(*provisus* p.p. as PROVIDE]

imprud'|ent (-rōō-), a. Rash, indiscreet. Hence or cogn. ~ENCE n., ~entry² adv. [f. L IM²(*prudens* PRUDENT]

im'pūd|ent, a. Shamelessly forward; un- blushing; insolently disrespectful. Hence ~ENCE n., ~entry² adv. [f. L IM²(*pudens* = *pudere* be ashamed, -ENT]

impūdi'city, n. Shamelessness, im- modesty. [f. F *impudicité* f. L IM²(*pudicus* as prec.), -TY]

impūgn' (-ūn), v.t. Assail by word, call in question, (statement, action). Hence ~ABLE a., ~MENT n., (-ūn-). [f. F *impugner* f. L IM²(*pugnare* fight) assail]

impū'iss|ant, a. Impotent, weak. So ~ANCE n. [F(IM⁻²+PUISSANT]

im'pulse, n. Impelling, push; (Dynam.) indefinitely large force enduring in-appreciably short time but producing finite momentum, e.g. blow of hammer; (also) product of average value of force multiplied by time during which it acts; mental incitement; sudden tendency to act without reflection; impetus. [f. L *impulsus -ūs* (as IMPEL)]

impul'sion (-shn), n. Impelling, push; mental impulse; impetus. [f. L *impulsio* (as IMPEL, see -ION)]

impul'sive, a. Tending to impel; (of per-sons, conduct, etc.) apt to be moved, prompted, by sudden impulse. Hence ~LY² (-vl-) adv., ~NESS (-vn-) n. [f. med. L *impulsivus* (as prec., see -IVE)]

impu'nity, n. Exemption from punish-ment, esp. *with ~*; exemption from injury as consequence of act. [f. L *impunitas* (*impunis* f. *poena* penalty), see -TY]

impure', a. Dirty; unchaste; mixed with foreign matter, adulterated, (lit. & fig.); (of colour) mixed with another colour. Hence or cogn. ~LY² (-rl-) adv., **impur'-ITY** n. [f. L IM(*purus* PURE)]

impute', v.t. Attribute, ascribe, (fault etc.); (Theol.) ascribe (righteousness, guilt, *to* person) by vicarious substitu-tion. So ~ABIL'ITY, ~A'TION, nn., ~ATIVE a., ~'ATIVELY² adv. [f. F *im-puter* f. L IM(*putāre* reckon) enter in the account]

in¹, prep. expr. inclusion or position with-in limits of space, time, circumstance, etc., as: *in Europe, England, London* (so of any large city or of town etc. in which speaker lives, cf. AT¹), *in the house, a box, a cab, a pond, a crowd*; (of dress etc.) *in muslin, mourning,* CALF, *in* (supplied with) *cash, in* (under influence of) *liquor*; (of occupation) *in search of, in pursuance of, in* (while) *crossing the river*; (of form or arrangement) *packed in dozens, sold in building-plots, falling in folds, in* ORDER¹ (2) *to* or *that*; (of instrument or material) *drank his health in a cup of ale, the coat was in green velvet*; (of purpose) *in reply to, in quest of, in honour of*; (of time) *in* (during) *the day, in* (within the space of) *three months, in* (at the end of) *five minutes; in itself*, apart from all else, absolutely; (colloq.) *the latest thing in* (within the sphere of) *telephones*; (of person's capa-city etc.) *as far as in me lies, did not think he had it in him* (was capable of it); *not in it, not in the running*, not a serious competitor; *nothing, little, not much, in it*, (Racing sl.) no decided advantage as yet gained by any competitor, no guessing who will win; (with vbs of motion or change) *put it in your pocket, cut it in half, throw it in the fire*; (expr. relation of vb to indirect object), *believe in, trust in, share in, engage in, rejoice in*; (so with adj. & nn.) *weak in* (as regards) *algebra, wanting in courage, your trust in him, a change in the constitution*, (of number or dimension) *seven in number, four feet in width*; (form-ing adv. phr.) *in fact, in truth, in honour, in any case; in so* (or *as*) *far as, in such measure as; in that*, since, because. [com.-Teut.: OE, OSax., OHG, Goth., *in*, Swed., Da., *i*; cogn. w. L *in*, Gk *en*]

in², adv. expr. position bounded by certain limits or motion to a point enclosed by them, as: *come in, send him in, walk in*, (into house, enclosed ground, etc.), *put a notice in* (into a paper), *lock him in, he is in* (the house etc., esp.=at home); *with it, put, take, it in; throw in the harness* (to the bargain, in addition); *a coat with the woolly side in* (nearest the body); *the Liberals were in* (office); *short skirts, oysters are in* (in fashion or season); (Crick.) *before he had been in* (batting) *five minutes; keep the fire in* (burning); *breed in & in* (repeatedly within same stock); *in & out*, now in, now out, *in & to & fro*, with alternation or oscillation. [com.-Teut.:

in³, a. Internal, living etc. inside, as *in patient, in-patient*, one who remains in hospital while under treatment. [prec.

in⁴, n. (Pl.) political party in office; *ins & outs*, turnings to & fro (usu. fig.), details (of procedure etc.). [f. IN²]

in⁵, prep. (L). *In absen'tia*, in (his or her) absence; *in artic'ulo mort'is*, in the in-stant of death; *in* CAMERA¹, *in commen-dam*, as a charge or trust (of benefice pending appointment of regular incum-bent, or of its revenue enjoyed by layman etc.); *in contumā'ciam* (-shi-), in contempt of court; *in ess'e*, in actual existence, cf. *in posse; in exten'sō*, at full length; *in extrem'is*, at the point of death; *in flagran'tē delic'tō*, in the very act of com-mitting an offence; *in form'ā paup'eris*, as poor person not liable to costs; *in loc'ō paren'tis*, in place of a parent; *in med'iā res*, into the thick of it; *in memōr'iam*, in memory of; *in neb'ibus*, in the clouds, vague, speculative; *in part'ibus (in-fidel'ium)*, (of Rom. Cath. titular bishop)

in a heretical country; *in pŏss'é*, poten-tially, opp. to *in esse*; *in prŏp'riă pĕr-sōn'ā*, in his (her) own person; *in pūr'is nătŭrāl'ĭbus*, stark naked; *in* RE²; *in sĭt'ū*, in its (original) place; *in stāt'ŭ pŭpĭllār'ī*, under guardianship; *in stāt'ŭ quō*, in the same state (as formerly); *in tĕrrŏr'ĕm*, as a warning; *in tŏt'ō*, completely; *in vĭt'rō*, (in laboratory use) in a test-tube etc. (lit. in glass).

in-¹, pref. = L *in* in, on, into, towards, against (becoming *il-* before *l*, *im-* before *b, m, p, ir-* before *r*). In OF *in-, im-*, be-came *en-, em-*; E has usu. *in-, im-*, in wds obviously of L orig., whether thr. F or otherwise. Words that still retain both forms are given in this dictionary under the more usual form.

in-², pref. = L *in-* (*il-* etc. as prec.), cogn. w. Gk *a, an-*, com.-Teut. *un-*; prefixed to adj. & their derivatives to express nega-tive changes with *un-*, which is preferred in wds not obviously answering to L types (*unavailing, uncertain, undevout*).

-in, suf. (chem.) forming names of neutral substances such as glycerides, glucosides, proteins, etc. (*albumin, casein, fibrin, gelatin*) to distinguish them from names of alkaloids & basic substances in -INE⁵. Some wds of this class were formerly spelt *-ine*, & are still so spelt in pop. use [IN-²]

-ina¹, L fem. suf. found in *regina*, ex-tended in It. or Sp. & used in E to form fem. titles (*czarina*) & proper names (*Georgina*); occuring also in names of musical instruments (*concertina, sera-phina*).

-ina², suf., neut. pl. of (often mod.) L adji., used, in agreement with *animalia* animals understood, to form names of groups of animals related to some typical genus, as *Bombycina* (genus *Bombyx*).

inabil'ity, n. Being unable; lack of power or means. [IN-²]

inăccĕss'ible (-ks-), a. That cannot be reached; (of persons) not open to ad-vances, unapproachable. Hence ~IBIL'ITY n., ~iblY² adv. [F, f. LL IN²(*accessibilis* ACCESSIBLE)]

inăcc'ūrate, a. Not accurate. Hence ~ACY n., ~atelY² adv. [IN-²]

inăc'tion, n. Absence of action; sluggish-ness, inertness. So ~IVE a., ~ivelY² adv., ~iv'ITY n. [IN-²]

inădăptăbil'ity, n. Want of adaptability. [IN-²]

inăd'ĕquate, a. Not adequate (*to pur-pose, to do*); insufficient. Hence ~ACY n., ~atelY² adv. [IN-²]

inadhēs'ive (-h-), a. Not adhesive. [IN-²]

inadmiss'ible, a. That cannot be ad-mitted or allowed. Hence ~IBIL'ITY n. [IN-²]

inadvert'ent, a. Not properly attentive; negligent; (of actions) unintentional.

Hence or cogn. ~ENCE, ~ENCY, nn., ~entlY² adv. [IN-²+obs. *advert*ENT AD-VERT]

inăl'ienable, a. Not alienable. Hence ~ABIL'ITY n., ~ablY² adv. [IN-²]

inăl'terable, a. Unalterable. [IN-²]
Hence ~ABIL'ITY n., ~ablY² adv. [IN-²]

inamŏrā'tō (-rah-), n. (fem. *-ta*). Lover. [It. (now *inn-*) f. IN²(*amorare* f. *amore* f. L *amor* love) enamour]

ināne', a. & n. Empty, void, silly; sense-less; (n.) *the ~*, vacuity, infinite space. Hence or cogn. ~LY²(-nl-) adv., inăn'ITY n. [f. L *inanis* empty, vain]

inăn'imate, a. Destitute of life; not endowed with animal life, as ~ *nature* (outside the animal world); spiritless, dull. Hence or cogn. ~LY² adv., inănimā'-TION n. [f. LL IN²(*animātus* ANIMATE¹)]

inani'tion, n. Emptiness, esp. from want of nourishment. [f. L *inanīto* f. *inanīre* make empty (as INANE, see -ION]

inappeas'able (-z-), a. Not appeasable. [IN-²]

inappell'able, a. Not to be appealed against. [f. IN-²+L *appellare* APPEAL+ -BLE]

inăpp'etence, n. Want of appetence. [IN-²]

inăpp'licable, a. Not applicable, unsuit-able, (*to case, purpose*). Hence ~ABIL'ITY n., ~ablY² adv. [IN-²]

inăpp'osite, a. Not apposite, out of place. Hence ~LY² adv. [IN-²]

inapprē'ciable (-sha-), a. Imperceptible, not worth reckoning; that cannot be appreciated. Hence ~LY² adv. [IN-²]

inapprēciā'tion, n. Failure to appreciate. So **inapprē'ciative** (-sha-) a. [IN-²]

inapprēhĕn'sible, a. That cannot be grasped by senses or intellect. [IN-³]

inapproach'able, a. Unapproachable. [IN-²]

inapprŏp'riate, a. Not appropriate. Hence ~LY² adv., ~NESS n. [IN-³]

inăpt', a. Unfit, unskilful. Hence in-ăp'TITUDE, ~NESS, nn., ~LY² adv. [IN-²]

inărch', v.t. Graft by connecting growing branch without separation from parent stock. [IN-¹+ARCH v.]

inārm', v.t. (poet.) Embrace. Hence ~ARM¹+

inartic'ūlate, a. Not jointed; (of speech) not articulate; unable to speak dis-tinctly; dumb. Hence ~LY² adv., ~NESS n. [f. LL IN²(*articulatus* ARTICULATE)]

inartific'ial (-shal), a. Lacking in art, inartistic; artless, natural. Hence ~LY² adv. [f. L IN²(*artificialis* ARTIFICIAL)]

inartis'tic, a. Not following the prin-ciples of art; unskilled in art. Hence ~ICALLY adv. [IN-²]

inasmŭch' (-az-), adv. ~ *as*, since, be-cause; (arch.) in so far as. [orig. three wds]

inattĕn'tion, n. Want of attention, heed-lessness; neglect to show courtesy. So ~IVE a., ~ivelY² adv., ~iveNESS n. [IN-²]

inaud'ible, a. That cannot be heard. Hence ~ibil'ity n., ~ibly² adv. [f. L IN²(audibilis AUDIBLE)]

inaug'ural, a. & n. Of inauguration; *(n.) ~ speech or address. [F, f. inaugurer (as foll.)]

inaug'urate, v.t. Admit (person) to office etc. with ceremony; enter with ceremony upon (undertaking etc.); initiate public use of (building etc.). Hence or cogn. ~A'TION, ~ātor² nn., ~atory a. [f. L IN¹(augurare take omens, f. augur), see -ATE³]

inauspi'cious (-shus), a. Not of good omen; unlucky. Hence ~LY² adv., ~NESS n. [IN-²]

in'board (-ŏrd), adv. & a. (naut.). (Situated) within sides of or towards centre of ship. [IN¹]

in'born, a. Implanted by nature. [IN¹]

inbreathe' (-dh), v.t. Breathe (thing) in (lit. & fig.). [IN¹]

in'bred, a. Innate, inherent by nature; bred in and in. [IN¹]

in'breeding, n. Breeding in & in, breeding from animals closely related. [IN¹]

Inc-a (t-), n. Emperor or king of Peru before Spanish conquest; one of royal race of Peru. [Peruv.]

incal'culable, a. Too great for calculation; that cannot be reckoned beforehand; (of person, character, etc.) uncertain. Hence ~abil'ity n., ~ably² adv. [IN-²]

incande'sce', v.i. & t. Glow, cause to glow, with heat. Hence f. L IN¹(candescere incept. of candēre be white)]

incande'scent, a. Glowing with heat; shining brightly; (of electric & other light) produced by glowing of filament etc. Hence ~ENCE n. [as prec., see -ENT]

incanta'tion, n. (Use of) magical formula; spell, charm. [F, f. L incantationem f. IN¹(cantare chant) bewitch, see -ION]

incap'able, a. Not capable (of conduct etc., of doing; often in good sense, = too honest etc. to do); not susceptible (of improvement etc.); lacking in ordinary powers, as drunk & ~able. Hence ~ABIL'ITY n., ~ably¹ adv. [f. med. L IN²(capabilis CAPABLE)]

incapa'citate, v.t. Render incapable or unfit (for work etc., for, from, doing). Hence ~A'TION n. [f. foll. + -ATE³]

incapa'city, n. Inability (for doing, for work etc., to do, or abs.); legal disqualification. [f. F IN²(capacité CAPACITY)]

incar'cerate, v.t. Imprison (lit. & fig.). Hence or cogn. ~A'TION, ~ātor² nn. [f. med. L IN¹(carcerare f. carcer prison), see -ATE¹]

incar'nadine, a. & v.t (poet.), (Dye) flesh-coloured, crimson, red. [f. F -in, -ine) f. It. incarnadino (for -tino) f. in-carnato INCARNATE¹]

incarn'ate¹, a. (Of person, spirit, quality, etc.) embodied in flesh, esp. in human form, as he is an ~ (in flesh, Liberty ~; (as p.p. of Christ) was ~ by the Holy Ghost. [f. L IN¹(carnare f. caro carnis flesh), see -ATE¹]

incarn'ate² (or in⁴k-), v.t. Embody in flesh; put (idea etc.) into concrete form, realize; (of person etc.) be living embodiment (of quality). [as prec., see -ATE³]

incarna'tion, n. Embodiment in (esp. human) flesh, esp. the I~ (of Christ); impersonation, living type, (of quality etc.). [F, f. LL incarnationem (as prec., see -ION)]

incau'tious (-shus), a. Rash. Hence ~LY² adv., ~NESS n. [IN-²]

incen'diar'y, a. & n. 1. Of, guilty of, the malicious setting on fire of property (~ bomb, filled with inflammatory substance(s) for causing fires); (fig.) tending to stir up strife, inflammatory. 2. n. ~y person (lit. & fig.); ~y bomb. Hence ~ISM n. [f. L incendiarius f. incendium conflagration f. IN¹(cendere cens-=+candēre cause to glow, cf. candēre glow), see -ARY¹]

in'cense¹, n. Gum, spice, producing sweet smell when burned, smoke of this, esp. in religious ceremonial; (fig.) praise, flattery. [f. OF encens f. eccl. L incensum thing burnt, incense, neut. p.p. as prec.]

in'cense², v.t. Fumigate (person, thing) with incense; burn incense to (deity etc.); suffuse with fragrance. Hence ~A'TION n. [f. L incendere cens-]

incense³, v.t. Enrage, make angry (~d against, with, at, by). [f. OF incenser f. L IN¹(censer (as prec.)]

in'censory, n. Vessel for burning incense, censer. [f. med. L incensorium (INCENSE¹, -ORY)]

incen'tive, a. & n. 1. Tending to incite. 2. n. Incitement (to action, to do, to doing), provocation, motive. [f. L incentivus setting the tune f. IN¹(cinere cent- canere sing) sing to, blow on instrument = -IVE]

in'cept, v.i. & t. ||(Formerly at Camb. Univ.), commence the taking of Master's or Doctor's degree, so incep'tor² n.; (Biol.) take in. [f. L IN¹(cipere cept- capere take) begin]

incep'tion, n. Beginning. [f. L inceptio (as prec., see -ION)]

incep'tive, a. & n. Beginning; initial; (Gram.) ~ verb, one that denotes the beginning of an action; (n.) ~ verb. [obs. F (-if, -ive), as INCEPT, see -IVE]

incer'titude, n. Uncertainty. [F, f. L IN²(certus CERTAIN), see -TUDE]

incess'ant, a. Unceasing, continual, repeated. Hence incess'ANCY, ~NESS nn., ~ly² adv. [f. f. LL IN²(cessantem part. of cessare cease)]

In wds from *incalculable* to *incautious* pronounce In-k-, not Ingk-.

in'cēst, n. Sexual commerce of near kindred. [f. L *incestus -ūs* or IN²(*cestum* neut. adj.=*castum* chaste)]

incēs'tŭous, a. Involving, guilty of, incest. Hence ~LY² adv. [f. L *incestuosus* (as prec., see -OUS)]

inch¹, n., & v.t. & i. **1.** Twelfth part of (linear) foot; *square, cubic*, ~, area equal to square, content equal to cube, whose side is an ~; (as unit of rainfall) quantity that would cover surface to depth of an ~; (of atmospheric or other pressure) amount that balances weight of column of mercury 1 in. high in mercurial barometer; *small amount; by* ~*es, bit by bit; every* ~, entirely; (pl.) stature (*a man of your* ~*es*); *give him an* ~ *& he'll take an* ELL; *flog person within an* ~ *of his life*, almost to death; *an* ~ *of cold iron*, stab with a dagger etc. **2.** v.t. & i. Move by ~es, *edge in, forward*, etc. [(vb f. n.) OE *gnce* f. L *uncia* twelfth part, inch]

‖ **inch²**, n. Small (esp. Scottish) island. [f. Gael. *innis*]

-in'cher, n. *Six* etc. ~, thing of six inches in length, diameter, etc. [-ER¹]

in'choāte¹ (in-kō-), a. Just begun; undeveloped. [f. L IN¹(*cohare, choare*), see -ATE²]

in'choāte² (in-kō-), v.t. Begin; originate. So ~A'TION n., ~ātĭvE (*or*-kō'a-) a. [prec., -ATE³]

in'cidence, n. Falling on, contact with, a thing; *what's the* ~ *of the tax?*, on whom will it fall? ; (Physics) falling of line, or of thing moving in a line, upon a surface; *angle of* ~, that which the incident line, ray, etc., makes with the perpendicular to the surface at point of ~; range, scope, extent, of influence. [F (as INCIDENT², see -ENCE)]

in'cident¹, n. Subordinate or accessory event, occurrence; detached event attracting general attention; distinct piece of action in play or poem; (Law) privilege, burden, etc., attaching to estate etc. [F (as foll.)]

in'cident², a. Apt to occur, naturally attaching, (*to*); (Law) attaching *to* (cf. prec.); (of light etc.) falling, striking, (*upon*). [F, f. L IN¹(*cidere*=*cadere* fall), see -ENT]

incidén'tal, a. Casual, not essential; liable to happen *to*; ~ *images, colours* (perceived as consequence of impressions no longer present); ~ *music* (introduced during the action of a play). Hence ~LY² adv. [INCIDENT¹+-AL]

incin'erāte, v.t. Reduce to ashes; consume (body etc.) by fire. Hence *or* cogn. ~A'TION, ~ātor²(-ĕ-), nn. [f. med. L IN¹-(*cinerare* f. *cinis -eris* ashes), see -ATE³]

incip'ient, a. Beginning; in an initial stage. Hence ~ENCE, ~ENCY, nn., ~ent-LY² adv. [f. L as INCEPT, see -ENT]

in'cīpĭt, sent. n. (Here) begins (book etc. [L]

incīse' (-z), v.t. Make a cut in; engrave. [f. F *inciser* f. L IN¹(*cīdere cīs-* = *caedere* cut)]

incī'sion (-zhn), n. Cutting into a thing; cut, gash, notch. [F, f. L *incisionem* (prec., -ION)]

incī'sive, a. Cutting, penetrating; (fig.) mentally sharp; acute, trenchant. Hence ~LY² (-vl-) adv., ~NESS (-vn-) n. [f. med. L *incisivus* (as INCISE, see -IVE)]

incī'sor (-z-), n. Any tooth between the canine teeth in either jaw. [med. L, = cutter (as INCISE, see -OR²)]

incīte', v.t. Urge, stir up, (person etc. *to* action, *to* do). Hence *or* cogn. **incitā'TION**, ~MENT (-tm-), nn. [f. F *inciter* f. L IN¹-(*citare* rouse frequent. of *cière cit-*)]

incivil'itý, n. Rudeness, discourtesy. [f. F *incivilité* f. LL IN²(*civilitatem* CIVILITY)]

in civism, n. Want of good citizenship, esp. of loyalty to French Revolution principles. [f. F IN²(*civisme* f. L *civis* citizen)]

‖ **in-clearing**, n. The cheques etc. collectively payable by a bank & received through clearing-house for settlement. [IN adv.]

inclēm'ent, a. (Of weather or climate) severe, esp. cold or stormy. So ~ENCY n. [f. L IN¹(*clemens* CLEMENT)]

inclī'nable, a. Inclined, disposed, (*to* thing, *to* do); favourable (*to*). [f. OF *enclinable* (as INCLINE¹, see -ABLE)]

inclinā'tion, n. Leaning, slope, slant; difference of direction of two lines, esp. as measured by angle between them; disposition, propensity, (*to, for*; thing, *to* do); liking, affection, (*for*). [F, f. L *inclinationem* (foll., -ATION)]

inclīne'¹, v.t. & i. Bend (head, body, one-*self*) forward or downward; ~ *one's ear*, listen favourably (*to* person, prayer, etc.); dispose (mind, heart, person, *to* do), as ~ *our hearts to keep this law, I am* ~*d to think*; be disposed, as *I* ~ *to think*; lean, cause to lean, from the vertical etc.; ~*d* (sloping) *plane*, one of the MECHANICAL *powers*; tend (*to* corpulence etc.). [f. OF *encliner* f. L IN¹(*clinare* bend)]

in'clīne'² (*or* in'-), n. Inclined plane; slope. [f. prec.]

inclinŏm'ēter, n. Instrument measuring vertical intensity of earth's magnetic force as shown by dip of magnetic needle, or for measuring slope. [INCLINE + -O- + -METER]

includle' (-lōō-), v.t. Comprise, embrace, (thing etc.) as part of a whole; (part. in abs. constr.) if we ~*e*, as *seven were killed,* ~*ing the guard*; treat, regard, as so comprised; (D.D.) shut in. [f. L IN¹(*cludere clus-* = *claudere* shut)]

inclū'sive (-lōō-), a. Including, compris-

In wds from *in-clearing* to *incurve*, pronounce In-k-, not Ingk-.

incóg, (of, or abbr.); (abbr. incl.) pages 7 to 26 ~ (including pages 7 & 26); including much or all, as ~ terms (at hotel etc.). Hence or cogn. inclu'sion (-lōzhn) n. ~ly² adv., -NESS n. [f. med. L inclusīvus (as prec., see -IVE)]

incóg', a., n., & adv. Colloq. abbr. of foll.

incóg'nitŏ, a. & n. (pl. -tos). (as pron. -ta, pl. -te pron. -tā), & adv. [f. It., = unknown, f. L IN²(cognitus good, ~. [It., = unknown, f. L IN²(cognitus P.p. of cognoscere get to know)]

incog'nizable (-kŏgn-, -kŏn-), a. That cannot be apprehended by senses or intellect. [IN²]

incog'nizant (as prec.), a. Unaware, un-conscious of. So ~ANCE n. [IN²]

incoher'ent, a. Not coherent (lit. & fig.). So ~ENCE n., ~ENCY n. [IN²]

incohe'sive, a. Not cohesive. Hence ~NESS n. [IN²]

incombus'tible, a. That cannot be con-sumed by fire. Hence ~IBIL'ITY n. [f. med. L IN²(combustibilis COMBUSTIBLE)]

in'come, n. Periodical (usu. annual) receipts from one's business, lands, work, investments, etc.; ~-tax (levied on this). [IN adv.]

in'comer (-kŭ), n. One who comes in; immigrant; intruder; successor. [IN adv.]

in'coming¹ (-kŭ-), n. Entrance, arrival; (usu. pl.) revenue, income. [IN adv.]

in'coming² (-kŭ-), a. Succeeding; immi-grant; (of profit) accruing. [IN adv.]

incommen'surable (-sher-), a. (Of magnitudes) having no common measure (with another); not comparable in respect of magnitude; not worthy to be measured with. Hence ~ABIL'ITY n., ~abIY² adv. [f. med. L IN²(commensura-bilis COMMENSURABLE)]

incommen'surate (-sher-), a. Out of pro-portion, inadequate, (with, to); = prec. Hence ~NESS n. [IN²]

incommōde', v.t. Trouble, annoy; hinder. [f. F incommoder f. L IN²(commo-dare f. commodus COMMODIOUS)]

incommō'dious, a. Not affording good accommodation, uncomfortable. Hence ~NESS n. [IN²]

incommu'nicable, a. That cannot be shared; that cannot be told. Hence ~ABIL'ITY, ~ableNESS, nn., ~abIY² adv. [IN²]

incommu'nicative, a. Not communica-tive. Hence ~IY² adv., ~NESS n. [IN²]

incommū'table, a. Unchangeable; not commutable. Hence ~IY² adv. [f. L IN²(commutabilis COMMUTABLE)]

incompa'ct, a. Not compact (esp. fig.). [IN²]

incom'parable, a. Matchless; not to be compared (with, to). Hence ~NESS n.,

~IY² adv. [F. f. L IN²(comparabilis COM-PARABLE)]

incompat'ible, a. Opposed in character, discordant; inconsistent (with). So ~I-BIL'ITY n. [f. med. L IN²(compatibilis COMPATIBLE)]

incom'petent, a. Not qualified or able (to do); not legally qualified. Hence or cogn. ~ENCE n., ~ENCY n., ~ly² adv. [f. F incompétent f. L IN²(competentem COMPETENT)]

incomplēte', a. Not complete. Hence ~ly² adv., ~NESS n. [f. L IN²(completus COMPLETE)]

incomprehen'sible, a. That cannot be understood (Athanas. Creed) boundless (also as n. three ~ibles). Hence ~IBIL'ITY, ~ibleNESS, nn., ~IbIY² adv. [f. L IN²(comprehensibilis COMPREHENSIBLE)]

incomprehen'sion (-shn), n. Failure to understand. [IN²]

incompress'ible, a. That cannot be compressed. Hence ~IBIL'ITY n. [IN²]

incom'putable, a. That cannot be com-puted. [IN²]

inconceiv'able (-sēv-), a. That cannot be imagined; (pop.) very remarkable. Hence ~ABIL'ITY n., ~abIY² adv. [IN²]

inconclu'sive, a. (Of argu-ment, evidence, action) not decisive or convincing. Hence ~IY² adv., ~NESS n. [IN²]

inconden'sable, a. That cannot be con-densed, esp. that cannot be reduced to liquid or solid condition. [IN²]

incon'dite, a. (Of literary composition etc.) ill constructed; crude, unpolished. [f. L IN²(conditus p.p. of condere put to-gether)]

inconfŏrm'ity, n. Dissimilarity, want of conformity, (to, with); = NONCONFORMITY. [IN²]

incon'gruous (-konggrōō-), a. Disagree-ing, out of keeping, (with); out of place, absurd. Hence or cogn. incongru'ity (-grōō-), ~NESS, nn., ~ly² adv. [f. L IN²(congruus CONGRUOUS)]

inconse'quent, a. Not following natu-rally, irrelevant; wanting in logical se-quence; disconnected. Hence or cogn. ~ENCE n., ~ĕn'tial (-shal), a., ~ĕn'tially² adv. [f. L IN²(con-sequens CONSEQUENT)]

inconse'quential (-shal), a. Not following; of small size, value, etc. Inconsequent. Hence ~IY² adv. [f. L IN²(consequens CONSEQUENT)]

inconsi'derable, a. Not worth consider-ing; of small size, value, etc. [f. F IN²(considérable CONSIDERABLE)]

inconsi'derate, a. (Of person or action) thoughtless, rash; lacking in regard for feelings etc. of others. Hence or cogn. ~ately² adv., ~ateNESS, ~A'TION, nn. [f. L IN²(consideratus CONSIDERATE)]

inconsi'stent, a. Not in keeping, dis-cordant, incompatible, (with); (of single thing) having ~ent parts; acting at

inconsól'able, a. (Of person, his grief, etc.) that cannot be consoled. Hence ~LY² adv. [f. L IN²(consolabilis CONSOLABLE]

incón'sonant, a. Not harmonizing (with, to). Hence ~ANCE n. [IN-²]

incónspic'uous, a. Not conspicuous; (Bot., of flowers) small, pale, or green. Hence ~NESS n. [f. LL IN²(conspicuus CONSPICUOUS)]

incón'stant, a. (Of person) fickle, changeable; variable, irregular. Hence or cogn. ~ancy n., ~antLY² adv. [F, f. L IN²(constantem CONSTANT)]

inconsúm'able, a. That cannot be consumed by fire etc.; (Pol. Econ.) not meant to be consumed in use. [IN-²]

incontés'table, a. That cannot be disputed. Hence ~LY² adv. [F (IN-²)]

incón'tinent, a. Wanting in self-restraint (esp. in regard to sexual appetite); unable to hold in something (of secrets, tongue, urine, etc.). So ~ENCE n. [F, f. L IN²(continentem CONTINENT)]

incón'tinently, adv. (literary). At once, immediately. [arch. incontinent (tempore) in continuous time, +-LY²]

incontrovér'tible, a. Not to be disputed. Hence ~LY² adv. [IN-²]

inconvén'ience, n., & v.t. Want of adaptation to personal requirement or ease; instance of this; (v.t.) put (person etc.) to ~, incommode. [(vb f. n.) OF, f. LL inconvenientia (as foll., see -ENCE)]

inconvén'ient, a. Unfavourable to ease or comfort, awkward, troublesome. Hence ~LY² adv. [f. 18th-c. F inconvénient f. L IN²(convenientem CONVENIENT)]

inconvèr'tible, a. Not convertible (esp. of currency). Hence ~IBILITY n., ~ibLY² adv. [IN-²]

inconvín'cible, a. Not to be convinced. [IN-²]

incoördiná'tion, n. Want of coordination. [IN-²]

incórp'orate¹, a. (Of company etc.) formed into a corporation; (of persons) united in a corporation. [as foll., see -ATE²]

incórp'orate², v.t. & i. Unite (in one body, with another thing); combine (ingredients) into one substance; constitute as a legal corporation; become ~ated (with). Hence or cogn. ~ATION, ~ATOR², nn. [f. LL IN²(corporare f. corpus -oris body), -ATE³]

incórpór'eal, a. Not composed of matter; of immaterial beings; (Law) having no material existence, esp. ~ hereditament. Hence ~LY² adv., incórpóré'ITY n. [f. L IN²(corporeus f. corpus -oris body)+-AL]

incorréct', a. Not in accordance with fact; (of style etc.) improper, faulty; (of book) not properly corrected for press. Hence ~LY² adv., ~NESS n. [f. L IN²(correctus CORRECT)]

incorrígible, a. (Of person or habit) incurably bad or depraved. Hence ~IBILITY n., ~ibLY² adv. [F, f. L IN²(corrigibilis CORRIGIBLE]

incorrúp'tible, a. That cannot decay, so ~ION n. (Bibl.) eternal; that cannot be corrupted, esp. bribed. Hence or cogn. ~IBILITY n., ~ibLY² adv. [f. LL IN²(corruptibilis CORRUPTIBLE)]

incráss'ate, a. (Bot, zool.) Of thick or swollen form. [f. L IN²(crassare f. crassus thick), see -ATE²]

increase'¹, v.i. & t. Become greater; grow in numbers, esp. by propagation; advance (in quality, attainment, etc.); make greater or more numerous; intensify (quality). Hence ~ingLY² adv. [f. OF encreistre (st. -eiss-) f. L IN²(crescere grow)]

in'crease², n. Growth, enlargement; growth in numbers, multiplication (of men, animals, or plants); on the ~, increasing; increased amount; (arch.) crops. [f. prec.]

incréd'ible, a. That cannot be believed; (colloq.) hard to believe, surprising. So ~IBILITY n., ~ibLY² adv. [f. L IN²(credibilis CREDIBLE)]

incréd'ulous, a. Unbelieving (of or abs.). Hence or cogn. incrédúl'ITY n., ~LY² adv. [f. L IN²(credulus CREDULOUS)]

in'crement, n. Increase; amount of this; profit; UNEARNED ~, see UN-²(1): (Math.) small amount by which variable quantity increases. [f. L incrementum (as INCREASE, see -MENT)]

incrim'inate, v.t. Charge with crime; involve in an accusation. Hence ~atory a. [f. med. L IN²(criminare CRIMINATE)]

incrústá'tion, n. Encrusting; crust, hard coating; facing of marble etc. on building; (fig.) accretion of habit; scab. [f. LL incrustatio (as ENCRUST, see -ATION)]

in'cubate, v.t. & i. Hatch (eggs) by sitting on them or otherwise; sit on eggs, brood. [f. L IN²(cubare cubit- or cubat-lie), see -ATE³]

incubá'tion, n. Hatching; artificial ~ (by artificial heat); (of the Holy Ghost) brooding; (Path.) phase through which germs of disease pass before development of first symptoms. So in'cubátive, in? cúbátory, aa. [f. L incubatio (as prec., see -ATION)]

in'cubator, n. Apparatus for hatching birds, rearing children born prematurely, or developing bacteria. [L (as prec., see -OR²)]

in'cubus, n. Evil spirit supposed to descend on sleeping persons; nightmare;

In wds from in-clearing to incurve, pronounce in-k-, not ingk-.

person, thing, that oppresses like night-mare. [LL., = L *incubare* (as INCUBATE)]

In·cul·cate, v.t. Urge, impress, (fact, habit, idea) persistently (*upon*, or *in* person, mind). So ~A'TION, ~ātor², nn. [f. L IN¹(*culcare*=*calcare* tread f. *calc -cis* heel), -ATE³]

in·cul·pate, v.t. Accuse, blame; involve in charge. Hence **incul·pA'TION** n, **in·cul'-patory** a. [f. LL IN¹(*culpare* f. *culpa* fault), -ATE³]

incult', a. (rare). Untilled; unpolished, rude; (of person or manners) coarse. [f. L IN¹(*cultus* p.p. of *colere* till)]

in·cum'bency, n. Office, tenure, sphere, of an incumbent. [f. foll., see -ENCY]

in·cum'bent², n. Holder of ecclesiastical benefice or (rare) of any office. [as foll.]

in·cum'bent², a. Lying, pressing, (*on*); resting (*upon* person) as duty, as *it is ~ on you to warn them*. [f. L IN¹(*cumbere* lie), -ENT]

incunā'b·ula, n. pl. Early stages of thing; (w. sing. *-um*) books printed early, esp. before 1501. [L.]

incŭr', v.t. (-rr-). Fall into, bring on one-self, (danger, blame, punishment, etc.). [f. L IN¹(*currere curs-* run)]

incŭr'able, & n. (Person) that cannot be cured. Hence ~ABIL'ITY, ~ableNESS, nn., ~ably² adv. [OF, f. L IN¹(*curabilis* CURABLE)]

incŭr'ious, a. Devoid of curiosity; heed-less, careless; uninteresting (usu. *not ~*). Hence **incūrios'ITY** n, ~LY² adv. [f. L IN¹(*curiosus* CURIOUS)]

incŭr'sion (-shn), n. Hostile invasion; sudden attack. So ~IVE a. [f. L *incursio* (as INCUR, see -ION)]

incŭr've, v.t. Bend into a curve; curve inwards (esp. in p.p.). So ~A'TION n. [f. L IN¹(*curvare* CURVE)]

in'cus, n. Bone of ear receiving vibra-tions from MALLEUS. [L., = anvil (as foll.)]

incūse'¹ (-kūz), a. & n. (Of impression on coin etc.) hammered or stamped in; (n.) such impression. [f. L IN¹(*cudere cus-* forge)]

incūse'² (-kūz), v.t. (esp. in p.p.). Im-press (figure etc.) by stamping; mark (coin etc.) with such figure. [as prec.]

Ind (i-), n. (arch. or poet.). India. [f. F *Inde*]

in·da'ba (-ah-), n. A conference between or with S-African natives. [Zulu, = business]

indēbt'ed (-dět-), a. Owing money (*to*); owing gratitude (*to* person, or fig. *to* thing, *for* benefit etc.). Hence ~NESS n. [f. OF *endetté* p.p. of ENdetter f. *dette* DEBT]

indē'cent, a. Unbecoming; immodest, obscene. Hence or cogn. **indē'cenCY** n, ~LY² adv. [f. L IN¹(*decens* DECENT)]

indēcīd'ūous, a. Not deciduous. [IN-¹]

indēcīph'erable, a. That cannot be de-ciphered. [IN-²]

indēcī'sion (-zhn), n. Want of decision, hesitation. [f. F IN¹(*décision* DECISION)]

indēcī'sive, a. Not decisive; undecided, irresolute. Hence ~LY² adv., ~NESS n. [IN-²]

indēclī'nable, a. That cannot be de-clined, having no inflexions. [f. F IN¹(*déclinable* DECLINABLE)]

indēcompōs'able (-z-), a. That cannot be decomposed or resolved into constituents. [IN-²]

indēcor'ous (or -děk'o-), a. Improper; in bad taste. Hence ~LY² adv., ~NESS n. [f. L IN¹(*decorus* DECOROUS)]

indēcō'rum, n. Lack of decorum; im-proper proceeding. [L, neut. adj. as prec.]

indeed', adv. In truth, really, as *he was, ~ a remarkable man*; (intensifying) *I shall be very glad ~, this is quick work ~; yes, ~! no, ~!*; (echoing last speaker's words with approval or irony), *is this Mr Smith?—who is he, ~!* (= you may well ask, or, can you ask?); (concessively) *there are ~ exceptions*; (interrog.) *really? is it so?*; as int., expr. irony, contempt, in-credulity, etc. [IN prep. + DEED]

indēfat'igable, a. (Of persons, qualities, etc.) that cannot be tired out, unremit-ting. Hence ~ABIL'ITY n, ~abLY² adv. [f. obs. F *indéfatigable* f. L IN¹(*defatigabilis*)]

indēfeas'ible (-z-), a. That cannot be forfeited or done away with, esp. *~ible right*. Hence ~IBIL'ITY n, ~ibLY² adv. [IN-²]

indēfec'tible, a. Unfailing; not liable to defect or decay; faultless. [IN-² + DEFECT + IBLE]

indēfen'sible, a. Admitting of no defence (by force of arms or by argument). Hence ~IBIL'ITY n, ~ibLY² adv. [IN-²]

indēfin'able, a. That cannot be defined. Hence ~ibLY² adv. [IN-²]

indéf'inite, a. Vague, undefined; un-limited; (Gram., of adj., pronouns, etc.) not determining the person, thing, time, etc., to which they refer, esp. *~ article* (a, an); (of tenses) denoting an action with-out specifying whether it is continuous or complete (e.g. Greek aorist, English past). Hence ~LY² adv., ~NESS (-tn-), nn. [f. L IN¹(*definitus* DEFINITE)]

indēhis'cent, a. (bot.). Not dehiscent. [IN-²]

indel'ible, a. (Of mark, stain, ink, etc., or fig. of disgrace etc.) that cannot be blotted out. Hence ~IBIL'ITY n, ~ibLY² adv. [f. L IN¹(*delebilis* f. *delere* blot out, see -BLE)]

indel'icate, a. Coarse, unrefined; im-modest; tactless. Hence ~NESS n, ~ately² adv. [IN-²]

indemˈniˌfy, v.t. Protect, secure, (person *from, against,* harm or loss); secure (person) against legal responsibility (*for actions*); compensate (person *for* loss, expenses incurred, etc.). Hence ~FICAˈTION n. [f. L IN²*demnis* f. *damnum* loss), see -FY]

indemˈniˌty, n. Security against damage or loss; legal exemption from penalties etc. incurred; compensation for loss incurred; sum paid for this, esp. sum exacted by victorious belligerent as one condition of peace. [f. F *indemnité* f. LL *indemnitas* as prec., see -TY]

indemonˈstrable, a. That cannot be proved (esp. of primary truths). [IN-²]

indentˈ, v.t. & i. **1**. Make tooth-like notches in; form deep recesses in (coast-line etc.). **2**. Divide (document drawn in duplicate) into two halves with zig-zag line, draw up (document) in exact duplicate. **3**. (Print.) set back (beginning of line) farther from margin to mark new paragraph. **4**. Make requisition (prop. written order with duplicate) *upon* (person *for* thing); order (goods) by an indent. [f. F *endenter* f. L IN¹*dentare* f. *dens -ntis* tooth]

indentˈ² (or inˈ²), n. Indentation; indenture; || official requisition for stores; order (esp. from abroad) for goods. [f. prec.]

indentˈ³, v.t. Make a dent in; impress (mark etc.). [IN-¹]

inˈdentˈ⁴, n. Dent, depression. [f. prec.]

inˈdentaˈtion, n. Indenting; cut, notch; zigzag; deep recess in coast-line etc. [IN-DENT¹ + -ATION]

indentˈtion, n. Indenting of line in printing; = prec. [irreg. f. INDENT¹ + -ION]

indentˈure, n., & v.t. **1**. Indented document (see INDENT²); any sealed agreement or contract, esp. that which binds apprentice to master; *take up* one's ~s, receive them back on completion of service; formal list, certificate, etc.; indentation. **2**. v.t. Bind (person) by ~s esp. as apprentice. [(vb f. n.) f. OF *endenture* (as INDENT¹, see -URE)]

indepenˈdenˌce, -enˌcy, nn. **1**. (~ce). Being independent (*on, of,* or *abs.*); independent income; *~I~ce Day,* July 4 (on which, in 1776, the DECLARATION of I~ce was made). **2**. (~cy). = CONGREGA-TIONALISM; independent State. [f. foll., see -ENCE, -ENCY]

indepenˈdent, a. & n. **1**. Not depending on authority (*of,* or *abs.*); (I~) = CONGREGA-TIONAL; not depending on something else for its validity, efficiency, etc., as ~ *proof, research, observer;* not needing to earn one's livelihood; ~ *income* (dispensing one under obligation to others. **2**. (~*cy*). = Person who acts (in politics etc.). ~*ly of any party;* Congregationalist. Hence ~LY² adv. [IN-²]

indescribˈ/able, a. Vague, indefinite; too great, beautiful, bad, etc., to be described. Hence ~ABLˈITY n., ~ABLY² adv. [IN-²]

indestrucˈt/ible, a. That cannot be destroyed. Hence ~IBILˈITY n., ~IBLY² adv. [IN-²]

indetermˈinable, a. That cannot be ascertained; (of disputes etc.) that cannot be settled. [f. L IN²*determinabilis* DETERMINABLE]

indetermˈinate, a. Not fixed in extent, character, etc.; vague; left doubtful; ~ *sentence,* one that leaves prisoner's release dependent on his conduct & on probability of amendment; ~ *vowel,* sound in *ago, moment, cousin, opine, support, certain;* (Math., of quantity) not limited to fixed value(s). Hence ~LY² (-tl-) adv., ~NESS (-tn-) n. [f. L IN²*determinatus* DETERMINATE]

indetermiˈnaˈtion, n. Want of determination; being indeterminate. [IN-²]

indetermˈinˌism, n. Theory that human action is not wholly determined by motives. So ~IST n. [IN-²]

inˈdex, n. (pl. ~es, *in'dĭcĕs*), & v.t. **1**. Forefinger; (on instruments) pointer showing measurements etc.; ~ *number* (indicating the relative level of prices or wages at a particular date compared with the figure (100) ruling at a period taken as standard); *I~ librōr'um prohibitōr'um;* ~ *expŭrga-tōr'ius,* list of passages to be expunged in books otherwise permitted (in fig. use often confused with last); (Alg.) exponent. **2**. v.t. Furnish (book) with ~ (esp. in p.p.), enter (word etc.) in ~ Hence ~LESS a. [(vb f. n.) L (gen. *-icis*), = forefinger, informer, sign, f. IN-¹ + *dic-* point out]

Inˈdia (-ĭ-), n. Country of S. Asia east of river Indus & south of Himalayas; *Further ~,* country between this & China; *~man,* ship engaged in Indian trade; *~ Office,* former department of British Government dealing with Indian affairs; *~ paper,* soft absorbent kind imported from China, used for proofs of engravings (*Oxford ~ paper,* thin tough opaque printing-paper); ~ *proof* (on ~ paper); *~rubber, India-rubber,* coagulated juice of certain plants, used for tires, rubbing out pencil marks, etc. [L, f. Gk (*Indos* Indus, f. Pers. *hind* = Skr. *sindhu* river, -IA¹]

Inˈdian (-ĭ-), a. & n. (Native) of India; (one) of the original inhabitants of America & W. Indies; European, esp. Englishman, formerly resident in India; *Red ~,* one of aboriginal race of N. America; || ~ *civilism,* member of ~ Civil Service; ~ *club* (bottle-shaped, for use in gymnas-

ties; || ~ *corn*, maize, N. American graminaceous plant; ~ *file*, single file; *India(n)* ink, black pigment made in China & Japan; ~ *med* (made from corn); ~ *summer*, period of calm dry hazy weather in late autumn in North. U.S.; ~ *weed*, tobacco. Hence ~IZE(3) v.t., ~IZA'TION n., process or policy of mak-~ in character or composition, etc.; see -ATE[3]]

indic'ate, v.t. (Med.) suggest, call for, (treatment); state briefly; be a sign of, betoken, (thing, that, etc.); ~*ated horse-power* (shown by ~*ator*; abbr. *i.h.p.*). So ~A'TION n. [f. L IN[2](*dicare* make known), see -ATE[3]]

indic'ative, a. & n. 1. (Gram.) stating a thing as a fact, not as conception, wish, etc., of speaker; (*also in dicative*) suggestive, giving indications *of*, 2. n. ~ mood. Hence ~IY[2](-vi) adv. [F (-*if*, -*ive*), f. L *indicativus* (prec., -IVE)]

indica'tor, n. Person, thing, that points out, esp. recording instrument attached to apparatus etc. Hence ~ORY a. [L (as prec., see -OR[2])]

indic'ium (-shi-), n. (pl. -*ia*), Indication, sign, (now rare). [L (as INDEX)]

indict' (-It), v.t. Accuse (person *for* riot etc. *as* a rioter, *on* charge), esp. by legal process. [f. AF *enditer* indict f. LL [1]IN[2](*dictare* DICTATE)]

indict'able (-It-), a. Liable, (of action) rendering one liable, to be indicted. [-ABLE]

indic'tion, n. Fiscal period of 15 years instituted by Constantine & reckoned from Sep. 1st, 312; assessment of property tax by Roman Emperors at beginning of each 15 years; this tax; proclamation. [f. L *indictio* f. IN[2](*dicere dict-* say), see -ION]

indict'ment (-It-), n. Formal accusation; legal process in which this is preferred to & presented by Grand Jury; document containing charge; *bill of* ~, written accusation as preferred to Grand Jury. [f. AF *enditement* (as INDICT, see -MENT)]

In'dies (in'diz), n. pl. (Also *East* ~) India, Further India, & the islands beyond; *West* ~, group of islands lying at mouth of Gulf of Mexico. [pl. of *Indy* f. L *India*]

indiff'erence, n. Absence of interest or attention (*to, towards*, or abs.); neutrality; unimportance, esp. *a matter of* ~*ence*, see -ENCE).]

indiff'erent, a. & n. 1. Impartial, neutral; having no inclination for or against (*to*); neither good nor bad; rather bad, esp. *very* ~; neutral in chemical, electrical, or magnetic quality; unimportant (*to*). 2. n. Neutral person, esp. in religion or politics. Hence ~IY[2] adv. [f. L *indifferens* (as foll., see -ENT)]

indiff'erentism, n. Spirit of indifference, professed or practised, esp. in religious matters. So ~IST n. [-ISM]

in'digène, n. Native. [f. F *indigène* f. L *indigena* (*indu-* = IN-[1] + *gen-* be born)]

indi'genous, a. Native, belonging naturally (*to* soil etc., also fig.). Hence ~IY[2] adv. [f. L *indigenus* (as prec.)]

in'digent, a. Needy, poor. So ~ENCE n. [F, f. L L *indigère* (*indu-*=IN-[1] + *egère* want), see -ENT]

indiges'tible, a. Not digestible (lit. & fig.). Hence ~BIL'ITY n. [f. L IN[2](*digesti-bilis* DIGESTIBLE)]

indiges'tion (-schon), n. Difficulty in digesting food, dyspepsia; undigested condition (lit. & fig.). [F, f. LL *indigestio* f. L IN[2](*digestus* p.p. as DIGEST[2], +-ED[1])]

indiges'tive, a. Suffering from, tending to, indigestion. [IN[2]]

|| **indign'** (-in), a. (arch.) Unworthy. [f. F *indigne* f. L *indignus* worthy]

indig'nant, a. Moved by mingled anger & scorn or feeling of injured innocence (*at* thing, *with* person, or abs.). Hence ~IY[2] adv. [f. L *indignari* (as prec.), see -ANT]

indigna'tion, n. Anger excited by meanness, injustice, wickedness, or misconduct (*at* thing, *against, with*, person); ~ *meeting* (to express public ~). [f. L *indigna-tio* (prec., -ATION)]

indig'nity, n. Unworthy treatment; slight, insult. [f. L *indignitas* (as INDIGN, see -TY)]

in'digo, n. (pl. ~s), Blue powder from plants of genus *Indigofera*, used as dye; ~ *blue*, blue-violet (often attrib.); ~-*bird*, N.-Amer. species of painted finch; ~ *white*, reduced or deoxidized ~, a white crystalline powder. Hence indigot'ic [-t- euphon.] a. [f. I.f. Gk *indikon* Indian (dye)]

indirect', a. 1. (Of road etc.) not straight; not going straight to the point. 2. (Pol. Econ., of taxes) not direct, paid by consumer in the form of increased price for the taxed goods. 3. (gram.,) ~ *speech*, reported speech, with necessary changes of pronouns, tenses, etc., (e.g. *I will help you, he said he would help me*); ~ *object*, person, thing, affected by verbal action but not primarily acted on (e.g. *him* in *give him the book*); ~ *passive*, passive having for subject the ~ object of the active (e.g. *I* in *I was told to*). 4. Not directly aimed at, as *an* ~ *result*. Hence ~IY[2] adv., ~NESS n. [f. L IN[2](*directus* DIRECT[2])]

indirec'tion, n. Round-about means, esp. *by* ~ (after Shak. *Ham.* II. i. 66); deceit, trickery. [prec.,+-ION]

indiscern'ible, a. & n. [Thing] that cannot be discerned or distinguished from another; *identity of* ~*les*, doctrine that things cannot exist together as

separate entities unless they have different attributes. Hence ~LY² adv. [IN-²]

indiscerp'tible, a. Incapable of, not destructible by, dissolution of parts. Hence ~IBIL'ITY n. [IN-²]

indis'ciplinle, n. Want of discipline. So ~ABLE a. [IN-²]

indiscreet', a. Injudicious, unwary. Hence ~LY² adv. [f. L IN²(*discretus* DISCREET)]

indis'crète, a. Not divided into distinct parts. [IN-²]

indiscrè'tion, n. Injudicious conduct; accidental or (*calculated* ~) supposed accidental revelation of official secret etc.; imprudence; transgression of social morality. [f. F *indiscretion* f. LL IN²(*discretionem* DISCRETION)]

indiscrim'inlate, a. Confused, promiscuous; making no distinctions. Hence ~ATELY² adv., ~ATENESS, ~A'TION, nn., ~ATIVE a. [IN-²]

indispen'slable, a. That cannot be dispensed with, necessary, (of law, duty, etc.) that cannot be set aside. Hence ~ABIL'ITY, ~ABLENESS, nn., ~ABLY² adv. [f. med. L IN²(*dispensabilis* DISPENSABLE)]

indispose' (-z), v.t. Render unfit or unable (*for* thing, *to* do); make averse (*towards, from*, thing, *to* do); (esp. in p.p.) put out of health. [IN-²]

indisposi'tion (-zi-), n. Ill health, alllment, (esp. of passing kind); disinclination (*to* thing, *to* do); aversion (*to, towards*). [IN-²]

indis'pūt|able, a. That cannot be disputed. Hence ~ABIL'ITY, ~ABLENESS, nn., ~ABLY² adv. [f. LL IN²(*disputabilis* DISPUTABLE)]

indiss'ollulable (-lōō-; or indiso̅l-), a. Lasting, stable, as *an ~uble bond*; that cannot be dissolved or decomposed. Hence ~UBIL'ITY n., ~UBLY² adv. [f. L IN²(*dissolubilis* DISSOLUBLE)]

indistinct', a. Not distinct; confused, obscure. Hence ~LY² adv., ~NESS n. [f. L IN²(*distinctus* DISTINCT)]

indistinc'tive, a. Not distinctive. Hence ~LY² adv. [IN-²]

indisting'uishable (-nggw-), a. Not distinguishable. Hence ~LY² adv. [IN-²]

indistrib'ūtable, a. That cannot be distributed. [IN-²]

indĭte', v.t. Put into words, compose, (poem, speech, etc.); (usu. joc.) write (letter etc.). [f. OF EN(*diter* f. L *dictare* DICTATE)]

indivért'ible, a. That cannot be turned aside. Hence ~LY² adv. [IN-²+DIVERT +-IBLE]

indivíd'ual, a. & n. 1. Single; particular, special, opp. to *general*; having distinct character; characteristic of particular person. 2. a. Single member of class; single human being, opp. to *society, family*, etc.; (vulg.) person, as *an ~ of somewhat prepossessing appearance*. [f. med. L *indi-vidualis* f. IN²(*dividuus* f. *dividĕre* DIVIDE), see -AL]

indivíd'ualism, n. Self-centred feeling or conduct, egoism; social theory favouring free action of individuals (cf. SOCIALISM). So ~IST n., ~IS'TIC a. [-ISM]

indivíd'uál'itỹ, n. Separate existence; individual character, esp. when strongly marked; (pl.) individual tastes etc. [-ITY]

indivíd'ūaliz|e, v.t. Give individual character to; specify. Hence ~A'TION n. [-IZE]

indivíd'uallỹ adv. Personally, in a distinctive individual capacity; in a distinctive manner; one by one, not collectively; ~ *different,* different as individuals though perhaps identical in species. [-LY²]

indivíd'ūāte, v.t. Individualize, form into an individual. So ~A'TION n. [f. med. L *indivíduare* (as INDIVIDUAL), see -ATE²]

indivís'|ible (-z-), a. & n. Not divisible. (n.) Infinitely small particle or quantity. Hence ~IBIL'ITY n., ~IBLY² adv. [f. LL IN²(*divisibilis* DIVISIBLE)]

In'dō- (-ī-) in comb.=Indian, as: ~*Ar'yan,* Aryan of or in India; ~*Chinese',* of Further India; ~*Europe'an,* ~*German'ic,* of the family of languages spoken over greater part of Europe & Asia as far as N. India; ~*Irān'ian,* of the subfamily of ~European languages spoken chiefly in India & Persia; ~*nes'ian,* of the East Indian islands. [f. L, f. Gk *Indos*]

indō'cile (or -dōsil), a. Not docile. Hence indō'ci'lity n. [f. L IN²(*docilis* DOCILE)]

indō'lent, a. Slothful, lazy; (Med.) causing no pain, as ~*ent tumour.* Hence or cogn. ~ENCE n., ~ently² adv. [f. LL *indolens* (IN-²+*dolere* grieve, see -ENT]

indōm'itable, a. Unyielding; stubbornly persistent. Hence ~LY² adv. [f. LL IN²(*domitabilis* f. *domitare* tame, see -BLE)]

in'door (-dōr), a. Situated, carried on, within doors or under cover, as ~*games*; within workhouse, as ~*relief.* [IN prep.]

indoors' (-ōrz), adv. Within a house; under cover. [earlier *within doors*]

indōrsā'tion, n. Endorsement. [f. *indorse* var. of ENDORSE+ATION]

indōrsee', n. One in whose favour note or bill is endorsed. [as prec., see -EE]

in'draught (-ahft), **-draft** (-ah-), n. Drawing in; inward flow or current. [IN adv.]

in'dri, n. Babacoote, lemurine animal of Madagascar. [f. Malagasy *indry* behold, mistaken for its name]

indū'bitable, a. That cannot be doubted. Hence ~LY² adv. [f. L IN²(*dubitabilis* f. *dubitare* doubt, see -BLE)]

indūce', v.t. Prevail on, persuade, (*to* do, now rarely *to* action etc.; *nothing shall ~ me to,* I will never); bring about, give rise to; (Electr.) produce (current) by induction; infer, derive as an induction. [f. L IN²(*ducere duct-* lead)]

indūce'ment (-sm-), n. What induces; attraction that leads one on (*to*). [-MENT]

Induce', v.t. Introduce formally into possession (*to* benefice); install (*into* seat, room, etc.); introduce, initiate, (*to, into*). [as INDUCT]

Induc'tile, a. Not ductile. [IN-²]

Induc'tion, n. Inducting; ||(arch.) preamble, prologue, introduction; producing (of facts) to prove general statement; inferring of general law from particular instances (cf. DEDUCTION); *mathematical* ~, proving universal truth of theorem by showing (1) that if true of any particular case it is true of the next case in a series, (2) that it is true of a particular case; (Electr., Magnet.) bringing about of electric or magnetic state in a body by proximity (without contact) of electrified or magnetized body; ~-*coil* (for converting direct current to alternating one by ~), *coefficient of self*-~; So **induc'tance** n., capacity for magnetic ~, *coefficient of self*-~. [f. L *inductio* (as INDUCT, -ION²]

Induc'tive, a. (Of reasoning etc.) of, based on, induction; of electric or magnetic induction. Hence ~LY² (vi•) adv., ~NESS (-v-) n. [f. L *inductivus* (as INDUCE, see -IVE]

Induc'tor, n. One who inducts clergyman; any part of electric induction apparatus. [L, as INDUCE, see -OR²]

Indulge' (-j), v.t.&i. Gratify (person, oneself, *in* wish, matter, etc.); gratify (person *with* thing given); give free course to, entertain, (desire etc.); (intr.) take one's pleasure freely *in* (strong language, cycling, a cigar); (colloq.) partake (too freely) of intoxicants. Hence **indul'gENT** gENT² adv. [f. L *indulgēre*, -dult, etym. dub.]

Indul'gence, n. Indulging (*in*, t. & i.) (also *self*-~); habitual indulging of one's desires; privilege granted; *Declaration of* ~, proclamation of religious liberties, esp. those of Charles II in 1672 & of James II in 1687; (R.-C.Ch.) remission of punishment still due to sin after sacramental absolution. [f. L *indulgentia* (as prec.)

Indul'genced (-nst), a. (R.-C. Ch.) (Of prayers, material objects, etc.) procuring Indulgence to the user. [-ED²]

Indult', n. Pope's licence for thing not sanctioned by common law of Church. [f. L L *indultum*, neut. p.p. as INDULGE]

Indun'a (-ŏŏ-), n. (S. Afr.). Native headman. [Zulu]

In'durate, v.t. & i. Make, become, hard; make callous or unfeeling; become inveterate. Hence or cogn. ~ATION n., ~ATIVE² a. [f. L IN(*durare* f. *durus* hard), see -ATE³]

Indu'sium (-z-), n. (pl. -ia). Membranous shield covering fruit-cluster of fern; collection of hairs enclosing stigma of some flowers; case of larva. [L, = tunic, f. *induere* ENDUE]

Indus'trial, a. & n. 1. Of industries (~ *seat*, benefice); industry, system by which each in industry should provide for its own unemployed; *the* ~ *revolution*, changes in the relation between employers & employed in the late 18th & early 19th cc. esp. by mechanical inventions; designed, or only fit, for ~ use (~ *alcohol*); ~ *school*, one where neglected children are taught a trade besides ordinary subjects. 2. n. One engaged in ~ pursuits; (pl.) shares in joint-stock enterprise. Hence ~ISM(3), n., ~IZE(3) v.t., ~LY² adv. [as INDUSTRY, see -AL]

Indus'trious, a. Diligent, hard-working. Hence ~LY² adv. [f. L *industriosus* (as foll., see -OUS)]

In'dustry, n. Diligence; branch of trade or manufacture. [f. L *industria*, etym. dub.]

indwell', v.t. & i. (indwelt). (Usu. fig.) (intr.) be permanently present *in*. Hence **indwell'er**

-ine¹, suf. [IN prep.]

-ine², suf. of adjj., repr. L *-inus*, w. sense 'pertaining to, of the nature of'; appearing in F as *-in* masc., *-ine* fem., in E formerly as *-in*, now usu. as *-ine* (*asinine*, *divine*, *marine*, *supine*); a previous suf. is sometimes blended, as in *clandestine*, *vespertine*. On model of proper names f. L, adjj. like *Florentine*, *Caroline*, are formed in E. Nat. Hist. forms adjj. on names of genera (*bovine*, *equine*, *cyprine*, *feline*); these have (-īn) unstressed; others have (-in) stressed or not (*divine'*, *Al'pine*), or (-ĕn)

-ine³, suf. forming fem. nn., repr. F *-ine* f. L *-īna* f. Gk *-īnē* (*heroine*). E represents in same way *-in* in G *markgräfin* etc. (*margravine*).

-ine⁴, suf. of adjj., repr. L *-inus*, orig.=-INE¹ used in L to form abstract nn.; F agent nouns (*discipline*, *doctrine*, *ruin*), & f. other sources (*resina*, *medicine*), L adjj. in *-inus*, *-ina*, were also used as nn. (*concubina*, *turpinus*), esp. in prop. names (*Aridentinus*, *Augippina*). For *-ina*, E has *-ine*, sometimes *-in* (*resin*); for *-ine*, E has *-in* (*Crispin*), E further forms (thir. F) names of derivative products (*dentina*, *brilliantine*, *nectarine*). Fem. names of Rom. orig. also often take *-ine* (-in), as *Caroline*, *Catherine*, *Justine* (or *-ine* (*lupine*, *Constantine*). E names of derivative substances, orig. used unsystematically, & interchangeable with -IN; now confined to alkaloids & basic

substances (*aconitine, cocaine, nicotine* & (less freq.) Hofmann's names of hydrocarbons; also retained in the four elements *chlorine, fluorine, iodine, bromine*. ~ person, esp. habitual drunkard. [f. L IN²(*ēbriāre* f. *ēbrius* drunk), see -ATE²]

inēb'riāte¹, a. & n. 1. Drunken. 2. n. inēb'riāte², v.t. Make drunk, intoxicate (lit. & fig.). So ~A'TION n. [as prec., -ATE³]

inēbri'ety, n. (Habit of) drunkenness. [IN-¹]

ined'ible, a. Not edible. Hence ~IBIL'ITY n. [IN-²]

ined'ited, a. Not published; published without editorial alterations. [IN-²]

ineff'able, a. Unutterable, too great for words. Hence ~LY² adv. [F, f. L IN²(*effābilis* f. *effāri* speak, utter, see -BLE)]

inefface'able (-sabl), a. That cannot be effaced. Hence ~ABIL'ITY n., ~ably² adv. [IN-²]

ineffec'tive, a. Not producing the desired effect; (of person) inefficient; lacking artistic effect. Hence ~LY² adv., ~NESS n. [IN-²]

ineffec'tual, a. Without effect, fruitless. Hence ~LY² adv., ~NESS n. [IN-²]

ineffica'cious (-shus), a. (Of remedy etc.) not efficacious. [IN-²]

ineff'icient (-shent), a. (Of person) not fully capable, not well qualified; ineffective. Hence ~ENCY n., ~ently² adv., (-shen-). [IN-²]

inelas'tic, a. Not elastic; unadaptable, unyielding. Hence inēlāsti'cITY n. [IN-²]

inel'egant, a. Ungraceful; unrefined; (of style) unpolished. Hence ~ANCE n., ~antly² adv. [f. F IN²(*élégant* ELEGANT]

inel'igible, a. Not eligible (esp. of men unfit for military service). Hence ~i-BIL'ITY n., ~IBLY² adv. [IN-²]

inelūc'table, a. That cannot be escaped from. [f. L IN²(*ēluctābilis* f. *ēluctārī* struggle out, see -BLE]

inept', a. Out of place; absurd, silly. Hence or cogn. inep'tITUDE, ~NESS, nn., ~LY² adv. [f. L IN²(*ēptus=aptus* APT]

inequal'ity, n. Want of equality in magnitude, quality, rank, circumstances, etc.; variableness; (of surface) irregularity; (Astron.) deviation from uniformity in motion of heavenly body. [f. OF *ínequalité* f. med. L IN²(*aequalitātem* EQUALITY]

inequilat'eral, a. Of unequal sides. [IN-²]

inĕq'uitable, a. Unfair, unjust. Hence ~LY² adv. [IN-²]

inĕq'uity, n. Unfairness. [IN-²]

inerad'icable, a. That cannot be rooted out. Hence ~LY² adv. [IN-²]

inĕ'rrable, a. Not liable to err. Hence or cogn. ~ABIL'ITY, ~ANCY, nn., ~ably² adv., ~ANT a. [f. L IN²(*errābilis* f. *errāre* ERR, see -BLE]

inert', a. Without inherent power of action, motion, or resistance; without active chemical or other properties; sluggish, slow. Hence ~LY² adv., ~NESS n. [f. L IN²(*ers -ertis* f. *ars* ART]

inertia (-shia), n. (Physics) property of matter by which it continues in its existing state of rest or uniform motion in straight line, unless that state is changed by external force (also *vis inertiae* force of ~); inertness, sloth. [L, as prec.]

inescap'able, a. Not to be escaped. [IN-²]

inessen'tial (-shal), a. Not indispensable. [IN-²]

inēs'timable, a. Too great, intense, precious, etc., to be estimated. Hence ~LY² adv. [f. F IN²(ESTIMABLE]

inev'itable, a. Unavoidable, sure to happen, esp. the ~able: (colloq.) tiresomely familiar (the ~able Derby dog); (Critics' sl., of character-drawing, development of plot, etc.) so true to nature etc. as to preclude alternative treatment or solution, convincing. Hence ~ABIL'ITY, ~ableNESS, nn., ~ably² adv. [f. L IN-²(*ēvītābilis* f. *ēvītāre* avoid, see -BLE]

inexact' (-gz-), a. Not exact. Hence inexac'tITUDE, ~NESS, nn., ~LY² adv. [IN-²]

inexcūs'able (-za), a. (Of person, action, etc.) that cannot be justified. Hence ~LY² adv. [f. L IN²(*excūsābilis* EXCUSABLE]

inexec'ūtable (-gz-), a. That cannot be carried out. [IN-²]

inexhaus'tible (-igzaw-), a. That cannot be exhausted. Hence ~IBIL'ITY n., ~ibly² adv. [IN-²]

inex'or'able, a. Relentless. Hence ~a-BIL'ITY n., ~ably² adv. [f. L IN²(*exorabilis* f. EXorāre entreat, -ABLE]

inexpec'tant, a. Not expectant. [IN-²]

inexpē'dient, a. Not expedient. Hence ~ENCY n. [IN-²]

inexpen'sive, a. Cheap. Hence ~LY² adv., ~NESS n. [IN-²]

inexpē'rience, n. Want of experience. So ~ED² (-st) a. [f. F IN²(*expérience* EXPERIENCE]

inexpert', a. Unskilled. Hence ~LY² adv. [OF, f. L IN²(*expertus* EXPERT]

inex'piable, a. (Of offence) that cannot be expiated; (of resentment etc.) implacable. Hence ~LY² adv. [f. L IN²(*expiābilis* EXPIABLE]

inex'plic'able, a. That cannot be explained or accounted for. Hence ~ABIL'ITY n., ~ably² adv. [F, f. L IN²(*explicabilis* EXPLICABLE]

inexplic'it, a. Not definitely or clearly expressed. Hence ~LY² adv., ~NESS n. [IN-²]

inexplos'ive, a. Not explosive. [IN-²]

inexpress'ible, a. & n. That cannot be expressed in words; (n. pl., joc.) trousers. Hence ~LY² adv. [IN-²]

inexpress'ive, a. Not expressive; (arch.) inexpressible. Hence ~LY² adv., ~NESS n. [IN-²]

inexpug′nable, a. Impregnable, in-vincible, (lit. & fig.). [F, f, L L IN²(*ex*-*pugnabilis* f. *expugnare* storm, see -BLE)]

inexten′sible, a. Not extensible. [IN.²]

inexting′uishable, a. (-ngsw-), a. Un-quenchable (lit. & fig.). [IN-²]

inex′tricable, a. (Of place, state, etc.) that cannot be escaped from; (of knot, problem, etc.) that cannot be unravelled or solved. Hence ~LY² adv. So ~BI′LITY, **inex′tricableness**, nn. [f. L L IN²(*extricabilis* EXTRICABLE)]

infall′ible, a. Incapable of erring; (of method, test, proof, etc.) unfailing. Hence ~IBI′LITY n. (esp. as attribute of the Pope speaking *ex cathedrâ*, defined 1870 by the Vatican Council), ~ibly² adv. [f. med. L IN²(*fallibilis* FALLIBLE)]

infall′ibilism, n. Principle of the Pope's Infallibility. So ~IST n. [-ISM]

in′famous, a. Of ill fame, notoriously vile; abominable; (Law) deprived of all or some rights of citizen on account of ~crime. Hence or cogn. ~LY² adv., **in′famy¹** n. [f. med. L *infamosus* = L *infamis* (see prec.)]

in′fancy, n. Early childhood, babyhood; (Law) minority (to end of one's 21st ~year); early stage of development. [f. L *infantia* (foll. -ANCY)]

in′fant, n. Babe; child under 7 years of age; minor (under 21); ~-*school* (for children, usu. under 7). [f. OF *enfant* f. L IN²(*fans -ntis* part. of *fari* speak)]

in′fan′ta, n. Daughter of king & queen of Spain or Portugal (usu. eldest daughter who is not heir to throne). So **infan′te** (-tā) n. (second son). [Sp., Port., f. L as prec.]

in′fan′ticide, n. Murder of infant after birth, esp. with mother's consent; cus-tom of killing new-born infants. Hence ~CIDE(1) n., ~CID′AL a. [f. L L *infanticidium* (as INFANT, see -CIDE(2))]

in′fantile, a. Of, as of, infants (~*tile paralysis*, a form of spinal meningitis); in its infancy. So ~INE¹ a. [f. L L *infantilis* (INFANT. -IL)]

in′fantilism, n. (med.), State of being mentally or physically undeveloped. [prec., -ISM]

in′fantry, n. Foot-soldiers; *mounted* ~ (mounted for transit but fighting on foot); ~*man* (-măn), soldier of ~ regiment, [f. F *infanterie* f. It. *infanteria* (*infante* youth, foot-soldier, as INFANT, see -ERY)]

infat′uate, v.t. Affect (person) with ex-treme folly; inspire with extravagant passion. Hence ~*edly*² adv., ~A′TION n. [f. L *infatuare* f. *fatuus* foolish), see -ATE²]

infect′, v.t. Fill (air etc.) with noxious corruption or germs; affect (person, body, mind, *with* disease etc.). lit. & fig.);

(person *with* opinion etc.). So **infec′tive** a., **infec′tiveness**, **infectiv′ity**, nn. [f. L IN²(*ficere fect-=facere* make) taint]

infec′tion, n. Communication of disease, esp. by agency of atmosphere or water (cf. CONTAGION); moral contamination or diffusive influence of example, sympathy, etc. [F, f. L L *infectionem* (as INFECT, see -ION)]

infec′tious (-shŭs), a. Infecting with disease, pestilential; (of disease) liable to be transmitted by air or water (cf. CONTAGIOUS); (of emotions etc.) apt to spread, catching. Hence ~LY² adv., ~NESS n. [prec., -IOUS]

infelic′itous, a. Not felicitous. [IN-²]

infelic′ity, n. Unhappiness; misfortune; inaptness of expression etc. [f. L IN²(*felicitas* FELICITY)]

infer′, v.t. (-rr-), Deduce, conclude, imply, (*thing, that, when,* etc.; *from* fact etc.). Hence **in′ference** n. [f. L IN²(*ferre* bring)]

in′ferential (-shl), a. That is inferred, (of poor quality; (of planets) whose orbit lies within that of the earth; (Bot, of calyx) below ovary, (of ovary) below calyx; (Print) placed at bottom of ordi-nary letters (e.g. H₂ C₂). 2. n. Person to another esp. in rank (*kind* *to* ~*s*). Hence **inferio′rity** n. (~*ity complex*, ab-normal mental reactions, such as assertiveness or megalomania, from suppressed sense of ~*ity*, (pop) sense of ~*ity*). ~LY² adv. [L, comp. of *inferus* low]

infer′nal, a. Of hell; hellish, fiendish; (colloq) abominable, confounded; ~*machine*, apparatus (usu. disguised) for producing explosion destructive of life or property. Hence ~LY (-ăl-) adv., ~IZE² v.t. [f. L L IN²(*infernalis* (*infernus* situated below, see -AL)]

infer′nō, n. (pl.-*s*). Hell(esp. w. reference to Dante's *Divine Comedy*); scene of horror. [It., f. L *infernus*, see prec.]

infer′tile, a. Not fertile. So **infertil′ity** n. [F, f. L L IN²(*fertilis* FERTILE)]

infest′, v.t. (Of vermin, pirates, diseases, etc.) haunt, swarm in or about, (place). So ~A′TION n. [f. L *infestare* assail (*infestus* hostile)]

∥ **infeuda′tion**, n. Enfeoffment; ~ *of tithes*, granting of tithes to laymen. [f. med. L IN²(*feudatio* f. *feudare* f. *feudum* fee, see -ATION)]

infibula′tion, n. Fastening of sexual or-gans with clasp to prevent copulation. [f. rare *infibulate* v. f. L IN²(*fibulare* f. FIBULA), -ATION]

in'fidel, n. & a. **1.** Disbeliever in religion; (Hist.) adherent of religion opposed to Christianity; (from Jewish or Mohammedan point of view) disbeliever in the true religion; (gen.) unbeliever. **2.** adj. Unbelieving, of unbelievers. Hence ~IZE(3) v.t. & i. [f. OF *infidèle* f. L IN²*fidelis* faithful f. *fides* faith]

infidel'ity, n. Disbelief in Christianity; disloyalty, esp. (also *conjugal* ~) to husband or wife. [f. L *infidelitas* (as prec., see -TY)]

in'field, n. Farm land around or near homestead; arable land; land regularly manured & cropped; (Cricket) part of the ground near the wicket, or fieldsmen stationed there (opp. OUTFIELD). [IN³]

in'fight'ing (-fīt-), n. Boxing at closer quarters than arm's length. [IN²]

infil'tr|āte, v.t. & i. Introduce (fluid) by filtration (*into*, *through*); permeate (t. & i.) by filtration. Hence ~A'TION n. (esp. Mil. & Pol.; gradual unobserved occupation of ground or territory by detached parties or settlers). [IN-¹]

in'finite, a. & n. Boundless, endless; very great; (w. pl. noun) innumerable, very many; (Gram., of verb parts) not limited by person or number, e.g. infinitive, gerund, supine (cf. FINITE); (n.) *the* I~, God; *the* ~, space. Hence ~LY² (-tĭ-) adv. [f. L IN²*finitus* FINITE]

infinites'imal, a. & n. Infinitely or very small (amount); ~ *calculus*, the differential & integral calculuses conceived as one. Hence ~LY² adv. [as prec. on CENTESIMAL etc.]

infin'itive, a. & n. (gram.). (Verb-form) that expresses the verbal notion without predicating it of any subject (e.g. *see*, *to see*). Hence **infinīti'val** a. [f. L IN-² *finitivus* f. *finire* -īt- define, see -IVE]

infin'itūde, n. Boundlessness; boundless number or extent (*of*). [as INFINITE, -TUDE]

infin'ity, n. =prec.; (Math.) quantity (symbol: ∞). [f. F *infinité* f. L *infinitas* (as INFINITE, see -TY)]

infirm', a. Physically weak, esp. through age; (of person, mind, judgement, etc.) weak, irresolute (often ~ *of purpose*). Hence ~ITY n., ~LY² adv. [f. L IN²*firmus* FIRM²]

infir'mary, n. Hospital; sick-quarters in school, workhouse, etc. [f. med. L *infirmaria* (as prec., see -ARY⁴)]

infix', v.t. Fix (thing *in* another); impress (fact etc. *in* mind); (Gram.) insert (formative element) in body of word. [IN adv.]

in'fix, n. (gram.). Modifying element infixed in word. [IN-¹, after *prefix*, *suffix*]

inflame', v.t. & i. Set ablaze; light up (as with flame); excite passionately (~*d with*, *by*); raise (body, blood, etc.) to morbid heat; aggravate; catch fire; become excited; become morbidly ~d. [f. OF

enflammer f. L IN²*flammare* f. *flamma* flame)]

inflamm'|able, a. & n. Easily set on fire; easily excited; (n.) ~able substance. Hence ~ABIL'ITY, ~ableness, nn. [f. L as prec., see -BLE]

inflammā'tion, n. Inflaming (lit. & fig.); morbid process affecting a part of the body with heat, swelling, pain, & redness. [f. L *inflammatio* (as prec., see -ATION]

inflamm'atory, a. Tending to inflame with desire or passion (usu. in bad sense); of, tending to, inflammation of the body. [f. L as INFLAME, see -ORY]

inflāte', v.t. Distend with air or gas; puff up (person *with* pride etc.); (Finance) resort to inflation of ((the currency), or abs.). [f. L *inflatus* f. *flare* blow), see -ATE³]

inflā'tion, n. (in vbl senses, & esp.) abnormal increase of the currency, e.g. by the issue of inconvertible legal-tender notes, **inflā'tion**² n. [f. L IN²*flare* blow), see -ATE³]

inflect', v.t. Bend inwards, curve; (Gram.) vary grammatical relation of (word) to express grammatical relation; (Mus.) flatten, sharpen, (note). [f. L IN²*flectere flex-* bend]

inflec'tion, = INFLEXION.

inflec'tive, a. (gram.). Of inflexion. [-IVE]

inflex'|ible, a. Unbendable; (fig.) unbending, rigid. Hence ~IBIL'ITY n., ~ibly² adv. [f. L IN²*flexibilis* FLEXIBLE]

inflex'ion (-kshon), n. Inflecting; inflected form of word; suffix etc. used to inflect; modulation of voice; (Geom.) change of curve from convex to concave. Hence ~AL, ~LESS, aa., (-kshon-). [f. L *inflexio* (as INFLECT, see -ION]

inflict', v.t. Lay on (stroke, wound, *upon*); impose (suffering, penalty, oneself, one's company, etc., *upon*). Hence or cogn. ~ABLE a., **inflic'tion** n. (esp., trouble-some or boring experience), ~OR² n. [f. L IN²*fligere flict-* dash)]

inflor'escence n. (bot.). Arrangement of flowers of plant in relation to axis & to each other; collective flower of plant; flowering (also fig.). [f. L IN²*florescere* come into flower f. *flos floris*), see -ESCENT, -ENCE]

in'flow (-ō), n. Flowing in. So ~ING¹,² (-ōing) n. & a. [IN adv.]

in'fluence (-ōö-), n., & v.t. **1.** (Astrol.) flowing from stars of ethereal fluid affecting character & destiny of man (also exercised of personal power); action insensibly exercised *upon*; UNDUE ~, see UN-²(1); ascendancy, moral power, (*over*, *with*, person etc.); thing, person, (Electr.=INDUCTION. **2.** v.t. Exert ~ upon, have effect upon. [(vrb f.n.) f. LL *influentia* f. L IN²*fluere* flow), see -ENCE]

in'fluent (-ōö-), a. & n. Flowing in (lit. & fig.); (n.) tributary stream. [f. L as prec., see -ENT]

influen'tial (-ŏŏĕnshal), a. Having great power (of body) f. IN¹+fundere pour)].
Influence. Hence ~LY² adv. [INFLUENCE,
-AL]

influen'za (-lŏŏ-), n. Infectious febrile
disorder, usu. with rapid prostration &
severe catarrh; (also ~ cold) severe
catarrh; (fig.) mental or commercial
epidemic. [It., as INFLUENCE]

in'flux, n. Flowing in, esp. of stream etc.
(into river etc.), or of persons or things
(into place etc.). [f. LL IN¹fluxus FLUX)]

inform', v.t. & i. Inspire, imbue, (person,
heart, thing, with feeling, principle, life,
quality, etc.); tell (person of thing, that,
how, etc.), so ~ANT n.; bring charge
(against person). [f. OF enfourmer f. L
IN¹formare f. forma form) give shape to f.
fashion]

inform'al, a. Not according to due form;
without formality. Hence ~ITY² n.,
~LY² adv. [IN-²]

inform'ation, n. Informing, telling;
thing told, knowledge, items of knowledge, news, (on, about); (Law) charge,
complaint, lodged with court or magistrate (against). Hence ~AL a. [f. OF,
enformacion f. L informationem (as INFORM,
see -ATION)]

inform'at¦ive, a. Giving information, in-
structive. So ~ORY a. [-ATIVE]
informed' (-md), a. Instructed, knowing
the facts, educated, intelligent, esp. well,
ill-, ~. [-ED¹]

inform'er, n. One who informs against
another, esp. (also common ~) one who
makes it his business to detect offenders & lay information against them.
[-ER¹]

in'fra, adv. (abbr. inf.), Below, lower
down, further on, (in book), as vide ~, see
below. [L., = below]

infra- in comb.=L infra below; used esp.
in anat. terms in sense ' below, under,
lower part ', as ~ren'al, ~scap'ular,
~stern'al, beneath the kidneys, shoulder-
blade, breast-bone; ~red', of invisible
rays beyond red end of spectrum.

infrac'tion, n. Violation, infringement.
[f. L infractio (as INFRINGE, see -ION)]

in'fra dig', pred. a. Beneath one's dignity,
unbecoming. [abbr. L infra dignitatem]

in'fralapsar'ian, n. & a. Calvinist who
held that God's election of some was
consequent to his prescience of the Fall,
or that it contemplated man as already
fallen (cf. SUBLAPSARIAN, SUPRALAPSARIAN);
(adj.) of these views. [f. INFRA-+L lapsus
fall+-ARIAN]

infre'quent, a. Not frequent. Hence or
cogn. ~ENCY n., ~ently² adv. [f. L
IN²(frequens FREQUENT)]

infringe', v.t. Transgress, violate,
(law, oath, etc.). Hence ~MENT (-jm-) n.
[f. L IN¹fringere fract-=frangere break)]

infrac'tious, a. Unfruitful; (fig.) fruitless. [IN-²+FRUCTUOUS]

infundib'ular, a. Funnel-shaped. [f. L

infundibulum funnel (used in E of parts
of body) f. IN¹fundere pour)]

infur'iate, v.t. Fill with fury, enrage. [f.
med. L IN¹(furiare f. furia FURY), see
-ATE³]

infuse' (-z), v.t. & i. Pour (thing into);
(-z-), (v.t.) undergo infusion (let it ~
for five minutes). [f. L IN¹fundere fus-
pour)]

infus¦'ible (-z-), a. That cannot be fused
or melted. Hence ~IBIL'ITY n., ~IAN,
~IST. [f. L IN¹infusio (as INFUSE,
med. L IN¹(furiare fundere fus-]

infu'sion (-zhn), n. Infusing (lit. & fig.);
liquid extract thus obtained; infused element, admixture. [f. L infusio (as INFUSE,
see -ION)]

-ing¹, suf. forming vbl nn., OE -ung, -ing.
n. OfTent. -unga. -ing orig. formed mere
nn. of action (asking), but came in ME to
acquire partly vbl (gerundial) character,
being qualified by adv. (the habit of speaking loosely) or governing an object (the
idea of building him a house. This use,
peculiar to E, led to introduction of perf.,
fut., & pass. forms (having killed, being
killed). The substantival nature of -ing
is marked by the possess., case or adj.
that often precedes it (after John's behaving so badly, upon my granting the
request); but med. tendency is to drop the
possess. sign exc. with pron. or single
noun. Meanings: (1) vbl action (bicycling,
forebodings), esp. as occupation (banking)
or as inflicted (thrashing); also perh. f. nn.
action (soldiering); (2) thing produced by vbl
action (carving, filings, building); (3)
material for (sacking), whether f. n. or vb
(fencing=what fences or serves as fence);
(4) what is used to do vbl action (binding,
dentist's filling); (5) what is to be operated
on (washing, darning); (6) set or arrangement of (colourings, featherings).

-ing², suf. of pres. part. (often used as
adj., as charming, sometimes as prep. or
adv., as during). OE -ende (cf. OHG
-anti, L -ent-, Gk -ont-, Skr -ant-) was
weakened to -inde & thus confused with
-inge -ING¹, which became the regular
form in 14th c. As result of the confusion,
some constructions gerundial in orig. now
appear participial, as he went hunting
(i.e. on hunting, vbl n.), the ark was
building (on building). On the other hand,
some wds in -ing that might be explained
as attrib. nouns in -ING¹ are perh. better
regarded as quasi-pass. participles (washing tub, cooking apple, breech-loading gun).
Compds are formed with advb. & adji.
(well-meaning, fair-seeming; for stress cf.
-ED²), & with objective nn. (cheese-paring,

heart-breaking; stressed on first component.

-ing³, suf. (*-ing*, *-ung*, in other Teut. langg.) forming m. w. sense 'one belonging to', 'one having the quality of'; also used as patronymic & dim. Exx.: *Atheling, king, shilling, farthing, Riding, gelding, herring, whiting*.

in'gathering (in-gădh-), n. Gathering in, harvest.

ingem'inate (-j-), v.t. Repeat, reiterate, (esp. ~ *peace*, constantly urge it). [f. L IN¹(*geminare* f. *geminus* twin)]

ingen'ious (-j-), a. Clever at contriving; cleverly contrived. Hence ~LY² adv. [f.L *ingeniosus* (*ingenium* cleverness, see -OUS)]

ingénue (see Ap.), n. Artless girl, esp. as stage type. [F]

ingěnu'ity (-j-), n. Skill in contriving. [f. L *ingenuitas* ingenuousness (as foll., see -TY); E meaning by confusion of IN-GENIOUS w. foll.]

ingěn'uous (-j-), a. Open, frank; innocent, artless. Hence ~LY² adv.,~NESS n. [f. L IN¹(*genuus* f. *gen-* beget) free-born, frank]

ingěst' (-j-), v.t. Take in (food) to the stomach. So **ingěs'tion** (-schon) n., **ingěs'tīve** a. [f. L IN¹(*gerere gest-* carry)]

ingle (ing'gl), n. Fire burning on hearth; ~-*nook*, chimney-corner. [Sc.; etym. dub.]

inglō'rious (in-g-), a. Shameful, ignominious; obscure. Hence ~LY² adv. [f. L IN²(*gloriosus* GLORIOUS)]

in'gōing (in-g-), a. & n. Going in; sum paid for fixtures, improvements, etc., by incoming tenant of business or other premises.

ing'ot (-ngg-), n. Mass (usu. oblong) of cast metal, esp. of gold, silver, or steel. [perh. f. IN adv. + *goten* p.p. of OE *gēotan* cast]

ingrain (in-grān before noun, in-grān' after n. or in pred.), a. Dyed in grain; inherent, inveterate, ingrained. [orig. two wds]

ingrained (in-grānd before noun, -and' elsewhere), a. Deeply rooted, inveterate; thorough. Hence **ingrain'ĕdLY²** (in-g-) adv. [prob. var. of *engrained*]

∥**ingrāte'** (in-g-), a. & n. (arch.). Ungrateful; (n.) ungrateful person. [f. L IN²(*gratus* grateful)]

ingrā'tiāte (in-grāshi-), v.t. Bring oneself into favour with. Hence ~ingLY² adv. [prob. f. 16th-c. It. *ingratiare* f. L *in gratiam* into favour, see -ATE³]

ingrāt'itūde (in-g-), n. Want of gratitude. [F. f. LL *ingratitudo* (as INGRATE, see -TUDE)]

ingrāvěs'cent (in-g-), a. (med.). (Of disease etc.) growing worse. So ~ENCE n. [f. L IN²(*gravescere* f. *gravis* heavy), see -ENT]

ingrēd'ient (in-g-), n. Component part, element, in a mixture. [f. L IN¹(*gredi gress-*=*gradi* step) enter, see -ENT]

in'grĕss (in-g-), n. Going in; right of entrance. [f. L *ingressus -ūs* (as prec.)]

in'growing (-n-grōi-), a. Growing inwards, esp. (of nail) growing into the flesh. So **in'growth** (in-grōth) n. [IN adv.]

ing'uinal (-nggw-), a. Of the groin. [f. L *inguinalis* (*inguen -inis* groin, see -AL)]

ingur'gitāte (-n-g-), v.t. Swallow greedily; (fig.) engulf. So ~A'TION n. [f. L IN¹(*gurgitare* f. *gurges -itis* whirlpool), see -ATE³]

inhǎb'it, v.t. (Of men or animals) dwell in, occupy, (region, town, house; also fig.). Hence or cogn. ~ABLE³ a., ~ANT, ~A'TION, nn. [f. OF *enhabiter*, f. L IN(*habitare* dwell, see HABIT)]

inhǎb'itancy, n. Residence as inhabitant, esp. during specified period, so as to acquire rights etc. [-ANCY]

inhāle', v.t. Breathe in (air, gas, etc., or abs.), take (esp. tobacco-smoke or abs. of this) into the lungs (also fig.). So **inhala'tion**, **inhāl'er²**(2), nn. [f. L IN¹(*halare* breathe)]

inharmŏn'ic, a. Not harmonious. [IN-²]

inharmŏn'ious, a. Not harmonious. Hence ~LY² adv. [IN-²]

inhēre', v.i. (Of qualities etc.) exist, abide, *in*; (of rights etc.) be vested *in* (person etc.). So ~ENCE n., ~ENT a., ~ENTLY² adv. [f. L IN¹(*haerere haes-* stick)]

inhěr'it, v.t. Receive (property, rank, title) by legal descent or succession; derive (quality, character) from one's progenitors; (abs.) succeed as heir. Hence ~OR², ~RESS¹, **inhěr'ITRIX**, nn. [f. OF EN(*heriter* put in possession as heir f. LL *hereditare* f. *heres -edis* heir]

inhěr'itable, a. Capable of inheriting or of being inherited (lit. & fig.). Hence ~ABIL'ITY n. [AF (as prec., see -ABLE]

inhěr'itance, n. Inheriting; what is inherited (lit. & fig.). [f. AF *enheritance* (as prec., see -ANCE]

inhē'sion (-zhn), n. Inheriting. [f. LL *inhaesio* (as INHERE, see -ION]

inhǐb'it, v.t. Forbid, prohibit, (person etc. *from doing*; esp. in Eccl. Law); forbid (ecclesiastic) to exercise clerical functions; hinder, restrain, (action, process). So **inhibi'tion** n. (in vbl senses, & esp. Psych.) instinctive or induced habitual shrinking from some impulse or action as a thing forbidden, ~ORY a. [f. L IN¹(*hibere hibit-*=*habere* hold)]

inhŏs'pitable, a. Not hospitable; (of region, coast, etc.) not affording shelter etc. Hence ~leness n.,~LY² adv. [OF (IN-²)]

inhŏspital'itý, n. Being inhospitable. [f. L IN²(*hospitalitas* HOSPITALITY]

inhūm'an, a. (Of person or conduct) brutal, unfeeling, barbarous, so ~ITY (-ăn-) n., ~LY² adv.; not of the ordinary human type. [f. L IN²(*humanus* HUMAN)]

inhūm'e, v.t. Bury. Hence ~A'TION n. [f. L IN²(*humare* f. *humus* ground)]

inim'ical (to), a. Hostile (to); harmful (to). Hence ~LY² adv. [f. LL inimicalis f. IN²(inimicus=amicus friend), see -AL]

inim'itable, a. That defies imitation. Hence ~LY² adv. [f. L IN²(imitabilis IMITABLE)]

iniq'uity, n. Unrighteousness, wicked-ness; gross injustice. Hence ~OUS a. ~OUSLY² adv. [f. OF iniquité f. L iniquitatem f. IN²(iquus just), see -TY]

ini'tial (-shal), a. & n. & v.t. (-ll-). 1. Of, existing or occurring at, the beginning, as ~ stage, expenses, difficulties; ~ letter (standing at beginning of word). 2. n. ~ letter, esp. (pl.) first letters of person's name & surname. 3. v.t. Mark, sign, with ~s. Hence ~LY² adv. [(vb)f.n.f.LL initialis f. initium (f. IN¹(ire=go), see -AL)]

ini'tiate¹ (-shi'-), v.t. Begin, set going, originate; admit (person), esp. with intro-ductory rites or forms, (into society, office, secret, in mysteries, science, etc.). So ~A'TION, ~ATOR, ~ATRIX, nn., ~ATORY (-shya-) a. [f. L initiare (as INITIAL, see -ATE³]

ini'tiate² (-shi'-), a. & n. (Person) who has been initiated. [as prec., see -ATE²]

ini'tiative (-shya-) n. & a. 1. First step, origination; take the initiative, take the lead (in doing); have the (power, right, to take the). 2. (Mil.) be able to make enemy conform to one's movements; right of citizen(s) outside legislature to originate legislation (as in Switzerland). 2. adj. Be-ginning, originating. [as noun, f. F) as prec., see -IVE]

ta'tio (-shio), n. At the beginning (in reference to passage in book etc.; abbr. init.). [L]

inject', v.t. Drive, force, (fluid, medicine, into cavity etc.) as by syringe; fill (cavity etc. with) by ~ing. Hence inject'or² n. [f. L IN²(jicere ject-=jacere throw)]

injec'tion, n. Injecting (as prec., see -ION); liquid or solution injected.

injudi'cious, a. Unwise, ill-judged. Hence ~LY² adv. ~NESS n. [IN²]

injunc'tion, n. Authoritative admonition or order; judicial process restraining per-son from wrongful act or compelling restitution etc. to injured party, whence injunct' v.t. (colloq.). [f. LL injunctio f. injungere ENJOIN, see -ION]

injure (-jer), v.t. Do wrong to; hurt, harm, impair. [back formation f. INJURY]

injured (-jerd), a. Wronged; showing sense of wrong, offended, as in an ~ voice. [p.p. of prec.]

injur'ious (-oor-), a. Wrongful; insulting; (of language) insulting, calumnious; hurtful. Hence ~LY² adv., ~NESS n. [f.F injurieux f. L injuriosus (as foll., see -OUS)]

in'jury, n. Wrongful action or treatment; harm, damage. [f. L L IN²(juris f. jus juris right) wrong]

injus'tice, n. Want of equity, unfairness; unjust act; you do him an ~ (judge him unfairly). [F. f. L IN²(justitia JUSTICE)]

ink, n. & v.t. 1. Fluid (black, red, etc.) for writing with pen; MARKING~; (printer's ~) viscous paste similarly used in print-ing; black liquid ejected by cuttle-fish etc. from bladder (~bag) to assist its escape; ~bottle, ~pot, (for holding ~); ~stand, stand for one or more ~bottles, often with pen-tray etc.; ~well (pot fitted into hole in desk). 2. v.t. Mark (in, over, etc.) with ~; cover (types etc.) with ~ so as to print from them. Hence ~INESS n., ~Y² aa. [(vb f.) f. AF enque f. LL encaustum f. Gk egkauston (as ENCAUSTIC) purple ~ used by Roman emperors for signature; It. inchiostro follows L accent]

ink'er, n. Telegraph instrument recording message in ink; (Print. etc.) inking-roller.

ink'ling, n. Hint, slight knowledge or suspicion, (of). [f. obs. or dial. inkle hint, get a notion of, etym. dub.]

in'land, a., n., & adv. 1. Interior of country. 2. adj. Placed in this, remote from sea or border; carried on within limits of a country, as ~ trade, ~ duty (on ~ trade), ~ revenue (consist-ing of taxes & ~ duties). 3. adv. In, towards, the interior. Hence ~ER¹(4) n. [IN¹ a., IN³]

in'law, n. (colloq.). (Usu. pl.) relative by marriage. [IN prep.]

inlay¹, v.t. (inlaid). Embed (thing in another) so that their surfaces are even; ornament (thing with another inlaid) by insert (page, plate, cut) in space out in larger stouter page. [IN²]

in'lay² (or inla'), n. Inlaid work. [f. prec.]

in'let, n. Small arm of sea, creek; piece inserted. [IN adv. + LET² v.]

in'lier, n. (geol.). Space occupied by one formation & completely surrounded by later formation. [IN adv.]

in'ly, adv. (poet.). Inwardly, in the heart; intimately. [OE inlice (IN¹, see -LY²)]

in'lying, a. Lying inside. [IN adv.]

in'mate, n. Occupant (of house etc.), esp. one of several. [IN adv.]

in'most (or -ost), a. Most inward; deepest, most intimate. [OE innemest (IN adv., see -MOST)]

inn, n. Public house for lodging etc. of travellers; ~keeper, one who keeps an ~; || Inns of Court, (buildings in London belonging to) four legal societies having exclusive right of admitting persons to practise at bar (Inner Temple, Middle Temple, Lincoln's Inn, Gray's Inn); || Inns of Chancery, buildings in London formerly used for residence of law stu-dents, societies occupying these. [OE, f. IN adv.]

innate (or in[5]), a. Inborn, natural. Hence ~LY[2](-tl-) adv., ~NESS(-tn-) n. [f. L L IN[1](natus p.p. of nasci be born)]

innavigable, a. Not navigable. [f. L IN[2](navigabilis NAVIGABLE)]

inner, a. & n. 1. Interior, internal; ~ tube, separate inflatable tube inside cover of pneumatic tire; the ~ man, man's soul or mind, (joc.) stomach, as refreshed his ~ man. 2. n. Division of target next outside bull's-eye, shot that strikes this. Hence ~MOST a. [OE innera a., compar. of IN[2]]

innerv[5]|ate, v.t. Supply (organ etc.) with nerve-force or nerves. Hence ~A[5]TION n. [f. IN-[1]+NERVE+-ATE[3]]

innings (-z), n. (pl. same, colloq. ~es). 1. (Cricket etc.) portion of game played by either side while in or batting, play of one batsman during his turn. 2. (fig.). Tenure of office, dominance, of political party, cause, etc. [orig. pl.: in sense 1 sing. inning is usu. in U.S.; f. IN adv.+-ING[1]]

inn[5]ocent, a. & n. 1. Free from moral wrong, sinless; not guilty (of crime etc.); (colloq.) windows ~ of (without) glass; simple, guileless; harmless. 2. n. ~ person, esp. young child; I~s' Day, Dec. 28, festival of the slaughter of children by Herod (Matt. ii. 16); ||(Parl. sl.) massacre of the ~s, sacrifice of measures at end of session for want of time; simple person; idiot. Hence or cogn. inn[5]OCENCE, -ENCY (rare), nn., ~LY[2] adv., ~NESS n. [f. L L IN[2](nocentem part. of nocēre hurt)]

innoc[5]uous, a. Not injurious, harmless (esp. of snakes). Hence innocu[5]ITY, ~NESS, nn., ~LY[2] adv. [f. L L IN[2](nocuus as prec.)+-OUS]

innom[5]inate, a. Unnamed; (Anat.) ~ bone, hip-bone (made up of three original bones). [f. L IN[2](nominatus, as NOMINATE)]

inn[5]ovate, v.i. Bring in novelties; make changes in. Hence or cogn. ~A[5]TION, ~ATOR[2], nn., ~ATORY a. [f. L L IN[1](novare make new f. novus), see -ATE[3]]

innox[5]ious, a. Harmless. Hence ~LY[2] adv., ~NESS n. [f. L IN[2](noxius NOXIOUS)]

innuen[5]do, n. (pl. ~es), & v.i. Oblique hint, allusive remark (usu. depreciatory); (v.i.) make ~es. [(vb f. n.) L, gerund of IN[1](nuere nod), = by nodding, i.e. by way of explanation, as 'he, innuendo the plaintiff']

innum[5]erable, a. Countless. [f. L IN[2](numerabilis NUMERABLE)]

innutri[5]tion, n. Lack of nutrition. [IN-[2]]

innutri[5]tious (-shus), a. Not nourishing. [IN-[2]]

inobserv[5]ance (-z-), n. Inattention; non-observance (of law etc.). [f. f. L IN[2](observantia OBSERVANCE)]

inoccupa[5]tion, n. Want of occupation. [IN-[2]]

Inoc[5]ul|ate, v.t. Impregnate (person, animal, with virus or germs of disease) to induce milder form of it & so safeguard person against its attacks; implant (disease etc.) thus (into, on, person etc.); insert (bud, scion) in plant, treat (plant) thus. Hence or cogn. ~A[5]TION, ~ATOR[2], nn., ~ATIVE a. [f. L L IN[1](oculare f. oculus eye, bud) engraft, see -ATE[3]]

inod[5]orous, a. Having no odour. [f. L IN[2](otorus ODOROUS)]

inoffen[5]sive, a. Unoffending; not objectionable. Hence ~LY[2] adv., ~NESS n. [IN-[2]]

inoffi[5]cious, a. Without office or function; (Law) not in accordance with moral duty. [f. L IN[2](officiosus dutiful, see OFFICIOUS)]

inop[5]erable, a. (Of tumours etc.) that cannot be operated on. [IN-[2]]

inop[5]erative, a. Not working or taking effect. [IN-[2]]

inopp[5]ortune, a. Unseasonable. Hence ~LY[2] adv.,~NESS n. [f. L L IN[2](opportunus +OPPORTUNE]

inor[5]dinate, a. Immoderate, excessive; intemperate; disorderly. Hence ~LY[2] adv. [f. L IN[2](ordinatus p.p. of ordinare f. ordo -dinis order)]

inorgan[5]ic, a. Having no organized physical structure; (Chem., of compounds etc.) of mineral origin, not ORGANIC; ~ chemistry, that of ~ substances; not arising by natural growth, extraneous. [IN-[2]]

inorganiza[5]tion, n. Lack of organization. [IN-[2]]

inor[5]nate, a. Not ornate. [IN-[2]]

inos[5]cul|ate, v.i. & t. (Of blood-vessels etc.) join, have terminal connexion, (with); (of fibres etc.) unite (fibres etc.), interwoven; (trans.) unite closely, be closely. Hence ~A[5]TION n. [f. IN-[1]+L osculare furnish with mouth (osculum dim. of os mouth), -ATE[3]]

inpour[5]ing (-pôr-), a. & n. Pouring in. [IN-[2]]

inqu[5]est (-kw-), n. Legal or judicial inquiry to ascertain matter of fact; =CORONER's ~; great, last, ~, last Judgement; coroner's jury; grand ~, grand jury (grand ~ of the nation, House of Commons). [f. OF enqueste f. med. L inquesta as INQUIRE]

inqui[5]etude (in-kw-), n. Uneasiness of mind or body. [f. L L (-do) f. IN[2](quietus QUIET), -TUDE]

inquire[5], en-, (in-kw-), v.i. & t. Make search (into matter); seek information (of person, about, after, thing etc.); ~e after, for, him (how he is); ask for (goods in shop etc.); ask to be told (person's name, business, etc., whether, how, etc.). Hence ~ingLY[2] adv. [ME enquere f. OF enquerre f. com.-Rom. inquerere -quest = L IN[1](quirere quisit- = quaerere seek); wholly (in-) or partly (en-) refash. on L]

inquir[5]|y, en-, (in-kw-), n. Asking; question; investigation; make ~ies, ask (about etc.); court of ~y investigating

charge against person or soldier). [f. prec. +-Y¹]

inquisi'tion (in-kwiz-), n. Investigation; judicial or official inquiry; (Rom. Cath.), the I~, ecclesiastical tribunal for suppression of heresy, the Holy Office. Hence ~AL (in-kwizish-) a. [OF. f. L *inquisitionem* (as INQUIRE, see -TION)]

inqui'sitive (in-kwiz-), a. Inquiring, curious; prying. Hence ~LY² adv., ~NESS n. [OF (-*if*, -*ive*), f. LL *inquisitivus* (as prec., see -IVE)]

inqui'sitor (in-kwiz-), n. Official investigator; officer of the Inquisition. *Grand I~*, director of court of Inquisition in some countries; *I~ General*, head of this in Spain. [f. OF *inquisiteur* f. L *inquisitorem* (as INQUIRE, see -OR²)]

inquisito'rial (in-kwiz-), a. Of, like, an inquisitor; offensively prying. Hence ~LY² adv. [f. med. L *inquisitorius* (as prec., see -OR) +-AL]

in'road, n. Hostile incursion, raid; (fig.) forcible encroachment. [IN adv. + ROAD¹ n. in sense 'riding']

in'rush, n. Rushing in. [IN adv.]

insa'livate, v.t. Mix (food) with saliva. Hence ~A'TION n. [f. IN-¹ + SALIVA + -ATE³]

insalu'brious (-loo-), a. (Of climate or place) unhealthy. So ~ITY n. [f. L IN¹(*salubris* SALUBRIOUS]

insane', a. Mad; senseless; ~ *asylum* (for ~ persons). Hence or cogn. ~ITY⁴ (-ti-) adv., **insa'nity** n. [f. L IN¹(*sanus* SANE)]

insa'nitary, a. Not sanitary. [IN-²]

insa'tiable (-sha-), a. That cannot be satisfied; inordinately greedy (*of*). Hence ~ABILITY n., ~abLY² adv. (-sha-). [f. L IN²(*satiabilis*, as SATIATE, see -BLE)]

insa'tiate (-shyat), a. Never satisfied. [f. L IN²(*satiatus*, as prec.]

inscribe', v.t. Write (words etc. *in*, *on*, stone, metal, paper, etc.); enter name of (person) on list; (esp. in p.p.) issue (loan) in form of shares with registered holders, as ~*ed stock*; mark (sheet, tablet, etc. with characters); (Geom.) trace (figure) within another so that some particular points of it lie in the boundary of that other, whence ~ABLE a. [f. L IN¹(*scribere script-* write)]

inscrip'tion, n. Words inscribed, esp. on monument, coin, etc., so ~AL (-shon-), **inscrip'tive**, aa.; inscribing (of loan). [f. L *inscriptio* (as prec., see -ION)]

inscru'table (-rōō-), a. That cannot be penetrated (fig.), wholly mysterious. Hence ~ably (fig.), ~abLY² adv. [f. LL IN¹(*scrutabilis* f. *scrutari* search, see -BLE)]

in'sect, n. Small invertebrate animal, usu. with body divided into segments & several pairs of legs, esp. (Zool.) one with body divided into three regions (head, thorax, abdomen), six legs upon thorax, & (usu.) two or four wings; (fig.) insignificant person or creature; ~*powder* (for killing or driving away ~s). Hence ~IVORA n. pl., **insec'tIVORE** n., ~IVOROUS a. [f. L *insectum* (*animal*) notched animal, f. IN¹(*secare sect-* cut)]

insec'tarium, n. Place for keeping insects. [-ARIUM]

insec'ticide, n. Insect-killer, esp. preparation used for killing insects. Hence ~cidAL a. [-CIDE]

insectol'ogy, n. Science of insects, esp. in their economic relations to man. [f. F *insectologie* (as INSECT, see -o- & -LOGY)]

insécure', a. Unsafe; (of ice, ground, etc.) liable to give way. Hence or cogn. ~LY²(-rl) adv., ~ITY n. [f. L IN¹(*securus* SECURE)]

insem'inate, v.t. Sow (seed etc, lit. & fig., *in*). Hence ~A'TION n. [f. L IN¹(*seminare* t. *semen -minis* seed)]

insen'sate, a. Without physical sensation. Hence ~LY²(-tl-) adv. [f. LL IN²(*sensatus* f. *sensus* SENSE, see -ATE²)]

insensibi'lity, n. Lack of mental feeling or emotion; indifference (*to*); unconsciousness, swoon. [f. LL *insensibilitas* (as foll., see -TY)]

insen'sible, a. Too small or gradual to be perceived, imperceptible, whence ~LY¹ adv.; unconscious, as *he fell down & was long ~le*; unaware (*of*, *to*, *how*, etc.); emotionless, callous. [f. L IN¹(*sensibilis* SENSIBLE]

insen'sitive, a. Not sensitive (*to* touch, sight, light, mental or moral impressions). Hence ~NESS n. [IN-²]

insen'tient (-shi-), a. Inanimate. [IN-²]

insep'arable, a. & n. That cannot be separated; (Gram.)~*able prefix*, one that cannot be used as separate word (e.g. *dis-*, *mis-*, *un-*); (n., usu. pl.)~able person or thing, esp. friend. Hence ~ABILITY n., ~abLY² adv. [f. L IN¹(*separabilis* SEPARABLE)]

insert', v.t. Place, fit, thrust, (thing *in*, *into*, another, *between* edges etc.); introduce (letter, word, article, *in*, *into*, written matter, newspaper, etc.). [f. L IN¹(*serere sert-* join)]

inser'tion, n. Inserting; thing inserted, esp. in writing or print; ornamental needlework etc. inserted into plain material, as *lace* ~; (Anat.) mode of attachment of muscle, organ, etc. [f. L *insertio* (as prec., see -ION)]

in'set¹, n. Extra page(s) inserted in sheet or book; small map etc. inserted within border of larger; piece let into dress; pair of white slips worn as edging to waistcoat opening. [IN adv. + SET n.]

inset², v.t. ~ or ~(ed), Put in as an inset. [IN adv. + SET u.]

in'shore', adv. & a. Close to shore; ~ *of*, nearer to shore than. [IN¹]

inside, n., a., adv. & prep. **1.** n. (In'sīd), Inner side or surface, (of path) side next

to wall or away from road; inner part, interior; (insid') stomach & bowels (colloq.); ‖ *the in'side'* (middle part) *of a week*; (insid') passenger travelling *'n'side out*, so that inner side becomes outer. **2.** adj. (in'sid). Situated on or in, derived from, the ~ (~ *information*, not accessible to outsiders). **3.** adv. (insid'). On or in the ~; (colloq.) ~ *of* (in less than) *a week*. **4.** prep. (insid'). On the inner side of, within. [IN a.+SIDE]

insid'er, n. One who is in some society, organization, etc. (cf. OUTSIDER); one who is in the secret. [f. prec.+-ER¹]

insid'ious, a. Treacherous, crafty; proceeding secretly or subtly, as ~ *disease*. Hence ~LY² adv., ~NESS n. [f. L *insidiosus* cunning f. IN¹(*sidiae* f. *sedēre* sit) ambush, see -OUS]

in'sight (- īt), n. Penetration (*into* character, circumstances, etc.) with the understanding. [IN adv.+SIGHT]

insig'nia, n. pl. Badges, distinguishing marks, (*of* office, honour, etc.). [L, neut. pl. of IN¹(*signis* f. *signum* SIGN¹) distinguished

insignif'icant, a. Unimportant, trifling; contemptible; meaningless. Hence ~ANCE, ~ANCY, nn., ~antLY² adv. [IN-²]

insincere', a. Not sincere, disingenuous. Hence ~LY² (-rī-) adv., **insince'rity** n. [f. L IN²(*sincere* SINCERE)]

insin'uäte, v.t. Introduce (thing, oneself, *into* place; oneself, person, *into* favour, office, etc.) gradually or subtly; convey indirectly, hint obliquely, (idea, *that*). Hence **~ātingLY²** adv., **~A'TION, ~ātor²**, nn., **~ātīve** a. [f. L IN²(*sinuare* f. *sinus* -*ūs* curve), see -ATE³]

insip'id, a. Tasteless; wanting in flavour; lifeless, dull, uninteresting. Hence ~ITY (-id-), ~NESS, nn., ~LY² adv. [f. LL IN²(*sipidus=sapidus* well-tasting, f. *sapere* taste, be wise, see -ID-)]

insist', v.i. & t. Dwell long or emphatically (*on*), as ~ *on this point, on his unpunctuality*; maintain positively, as ~ *on his innocence*, ~ (*on it*) *that he is innocent*; make a stand on as essential (I ~ *on your presence, on it that you shall be present*). Hence ~ENCE, ~ENCY, nn., ~ENT a., ~entLY² adv. [f. L IN¹(*sistere* stand)]

insob'rïety, n. Intemperance, esp. in drinking. [IN-²]

insola'tion, n. Exposure to sun's rays, for purposes of bleaching etc., as medical treatment, or as cause of disease. [f. L *insolatio* f. IN¹(*solare* f. *sol* sun), see -ATION]

in'solent, a. Offensively contemptuous, insulting. Hence or cogn. ~ENCE n., ~entLY² adv. [f. L IN²(*solens* part. of *solēre* be accustomed), see -ENT]

insol'üble (or in-), a. That cannot be solved; that cannot be dissolved. Hence ~ūbil'ITY, ~übleNESS, nn., ~übly² adv. [f. L IN²(*sotubilis* SOLUBLE)]

insöl'vent, a. & n. (Debtor) unable to pay debts; relating to ~s, as ~ *laws*. Hence **insöl'vENCY** n. [IN-²]

insöm'nia, n. Sleeplessness. [L, f. IN²(*somnis* f. *somnus* sleep) sleepless]

insomüch', adv. To such an extent *that*. [see AP.), a. Careless, unconcerned. So ~ANCE n. [F (IN-²+*souciant* part. of *soucier* care f. L *sollicitare* disturb)]

inspän', v.t. (S.-Afr.; -nn-). Yoke (oxen etc.) in team to vehicle; harness (wagon). [f. Du. IN¹(*spannen* SPAN²)]

inspect', v.t. Look closely into; examine officially. So **inspec'tion, inspec'tor²** (esp., police officer below superintendent & above sergeant), **inspec'torshIP**, nn., **inspec'toral**, ~ō'RIAL, aa. [f. L IN¹-(*spicere spect*- look)]

inspec'torate, n. Office of inspector; body of inspectors; district under inspector, esp. in Greenland. [-ATE¹]

inspira'tion, n. Drawing in of breath; inspiring; divine influence, esp. that under which books of Scripture are held to have been written, whether *verbal* ~ (dictating every word), *plenary* ~ (covering all subjects treated), or *moral* ~ (confined to moral & religious teaching), whence ~ISM(3), ~IST(2), nn.; thought etc. inspired, prompting; sudden happy idea; inspiring principle. Hence ~AL a. [OF, f. L *inspirationem* (as INSPIRE, see -ATION)]

in'spirātor, n. Apparatus for drawing in air or vapour. [L (as foll., see -OR²)]

inspire', v.t. Breathe in, inhale, (air etc. or abs.), whence ~**atory** a.; infuse thought or feeling into (person; esp. of divine or supernatural agency; often in p.p.); animate (person etc. *with* feeling); infuse (feeling *into* person etc.), create (feeling *in* person); *an* ~*ed article* (in journal), one secretly suggested by or emanating from influential person etc. [f. OF *enspirer* f. L IN¹(*spirare* breathe)]

inspi'rit, v.t. Put life into, animate; encourage (person *to* action, *to* do). Hence ~ING² a. [IN-¹+SPIRIT n.]

inspiss'äte (or in-), v.t. Thicken, condense. So ~A'TION n. [f. LL IN²(*spissare* f. *spissus* thick), see -ATE³]

instabil'ity, n. Lack of stability (usu. fig. of moral qualities etc.). [f. F *instabilité* f. L *instabilitatem* f. IN²(*stabilis* STABLE¹), see -TY]

install' (-awl), v.t. Place (person *in* office or dignity) with ceremonies, whence ~ANT (-awl-) a. & n.; establish (person, oneself, *in* place, condition, etc.); place (heating or lighting apparatus etc.) in position for use. So ~A'TION n. [f. med.L IN¹(*stallare* f. *stallum* STALL¹)]

instal'ment (-awl-), n. Each of several parts, successively falling due, of a sum payable; each of several parts supplied etc. at different times. [f. obs. IN¹(*stall* v. arrange, fix)+-MENT]

in'stance¹, n. Fact illustrating a general truth, example; particular case (*in your, this, ~*); *for ~*, as an example (*in the ~, in the first place, at the first place, stage of a proceeding. [F. f. L *instantia* presence, urgency, pleading, objection to general statement, rel. to *instant*¹; see -ANCE] (as INSTANT¹; see -ANCE]

in'stance², v.t. Cite (fact, case) as an instance; (usu. pass.) exemplify. [f. prec.]

in'stancy, n. Urgency.

in'stant¹, a. Urgent, pressing; (abbr. *inst.*) (of the current month, as *the 6th inst.*; (cf. PROXIMO, ULTIMO); immediate. [F. f. L *instare* stand) be present, press upon, see -ANT]

in'stant², n. Precise (esp. the present) point of time, moment, as *come this ~; I went that ~ or on the ~; I told you the ~ (as soon as) I knew*; short space of time, moment. [prec. as n.]

instantané'ous, a. Occurring, done, in an instant; (Dynam.) existing at a particular instant. Hence ~LY² adv., ~NESS n. [INSTANT² + -ANEOUS, after *momentaneous*]

instantané (see Ap.), n. Snap-shot, (fig.) short sketch in a few sentences. [F]

in'stanter, adv. Immediately, at once, (now usu. joc.). [L, f. *instans* INSTANT¹+ -LY²]

in'stantly, adv. At once. [-LY²]

instaura'tion, n. Restoration, renewal. [f. L *instauratio* f.]

So **in'staurā'tor² n.** [f. L *instaurare*, see RESTORE & -ATION]

instead', (-ĕd), adv. As a substitute or alternative; in place of, as *~ of this, ~ of going, you should be out ~ of (sitting) in on this fine day*, (also *in his, my, our,* STEAD). [IN² prep.+STEAD n.]

in'step, n. Upper surface of foot between toes & ankle; part of shoe etc. fitting this; ~-shaped thing. [f. 16th c.; etym. dub.]

in'stigate, v.t. Urge on, incite, (person to action, to do usu. something evil); bring about (revolt, murder, etc.) by persuasion. So ~A'TION, ~ātor², n. [f. L IN¹(stigare, cf. Gk *stizō* prick, root *stig-*), see -ATE³]

instil(l)', v.t. (-ll-). Put in (liquid *into* thing) by drops; infuse (feeling, ideas, etc. *into* person, mind, etc.) gradually. Hence or cogn. instilla'TION, instil'MENT, nn. [f. L IN¹(*stillare* drop)]

in'stinct¹, n. Innate propensity, esp. in lower animals, to certain seemingly rational acts performed without conscious design; innate impulse; intuition, unconscious skill. Hence **instinc'TIVE² a.,** cf. Gk *stizō* prick, root *stig-*).

instinc'tivery² (-vi) adv. [f. L *instinctus -ūs f.* IN¹(*stinguere stinct-* prick) incite]

in'stinct², pred. a. Imbued, charged, (*with* life, beauty, force, etc.). [f. L p.p. as prec.]

in'stitute¹, n. 1. Society, organization, for promotion of scientific or other object; building used by this. **2. pl.** Digest of ele-

ments of a subject, esp. of jurisprudence, as *I~s of Justinian*. [f. L neut. p.p. as foll.]

in'stitute², v.t. Establish, found; set on foot (inquiry etc.); appoint (person *to*, *into*, benefice). [f. L IN¹(*stituere -tut-= statuere* set up)]

institu'tion, n. Instituting; establishment (of person) in cure of souls; established law, custom, or practice; (colloq.) of person etc., familiar object; organization for promotion of some public object; building used by this. Hence ~AL (-shon-) a², (also, of religion) organized into or finding expression through ~s (churches, priests, ritual, etc.). [OF, f. L *institutio* (as prec., see -ION]

in'strict¹, v.t. Teach (person etc. *in* subject); inform (person *that, when,* etc.); (of client, solicitor) give information to (solicitor, counsel); direct, command, (person *to do*). Hence or cogn. **instrúc**tor², **instrúc'tress¹** nn. [f. L IN¹(*struere struct-* pile up) build, teach]

instrúc'tion, n. Teaching; (pl.) directions, orders; (pl.) directions to solicitor or counsel. Hence ~AL (-shon-) a. [OF, f. L *instructionem* (as prec., see -ION]

instrúc'tive, a. Tending to instruct, conveying a lesson. Hence ~LY² adv., ~NESS n. [-IVE]

in'strument (-ŏo-), n. & v.t. 1. Thing used in performing an action; person so made use of; tool, implement, esp. for contrivance for producing musical sounds by vibration of strings etc. (*stringed* etc. ~*s*) or of body of air in pipe etc. (*wind* ~*s*); formal, esp. legal, document. **2. v.t.** Arrange (music) for ~s. [vb I. n.) F, f. L *instrumentum* (as IN¹ STRUCT, see -MENT]

in'strumental (-ŏo-), a. Serving as instrument or means (*to* purpose, *in* work, *in doing*); (of music) performed on instruments (cf. VOCAL), whence ~IST(3) n.; (Gram.) ~ *case* (denoting the instrument). Hence ~LY² adv. [F. f. med. L *instrumentalis* (as INSTRUMENT, see -AL)]

instrumentálity (-ŏo-), n. Agency, means, esp. *by the ~ of.* [-ITY]

instrumentā'tion (-ŏo-), n. Arrangement of music for instruments; study of character, power, pitch, etc., of musical instruments; operation with surgical or other instrument; instrumentality, [F, *instrumenter*] (as INSTRUMENT, see -ATION)

insubōrd'in̄ate, a. Disobedient, rebellious. Hence ~A'TION n. [IN-³]

insubstán'tial (-shl), a. Not real; lacking solidity or substance. Hence ~ITY (-shiăl) n. [f. LL IN³(*substantialis* SUBSTANTIAL)]

insuff'erable, a. Unbearable, intolerable. Hence ~LY adv. [IN-³]

insuffi′cient (-shent), a. Not sufficient, inadequate. Hence **or** cogn. **~ENCY** n., **~ently²** adv., (-shen-). [OF, f. L IN²(*sufficientem* SUFFICIENT)]

in′sufflate, v.t. Blow, breathe, (air, gas, nose etc.) into cavity of the body etc.; treat (nose etc.) thus. Hence **~OR²(2)** n., (also) device for blowing powder on to surface of object in order to make latent finger-prints visible. [f. L IN²(SUF*flare* blow upon), see -ATE³]

insuffla′tion, n. Blowing on **or** into; breathing on person as rite of exorcism. [f. L *insufflātiō* (as prec., see -ION)]

in′sular, a. Of (the nature of) an island; applied to a development of Latin hand-writing current in the British Isles in the early Middle Ages; of, like, islanders, esp. narrow-minded, whence **~ISM** n. Hence **insulā′RITY** n., **~LY²** adv. [f. L *insulāris* (as foll., see -AR²)]

in′sulate, v.t. Make (land) into an island; detach (person, thing) from surroundings, isolate; isolate (thing) by interposition of non-conductors, to prevent passage of electricity **or** heat. Hence **~A′TION, ~A′TOR²(2)**, nn. [f. L *insula* island +-ATE³]

in′sulin, n. A specific for diabetes extracted from the islets of Langerhans in the pancreas of animals. [f. L *insula* island +-IN¹]

in′sult¹, n. Insulting speech **or** action, affront. [f. LL IN²(*saltus=saltus* leap, as foll.)]

insult′², v.t. Treat with scornful abuse, offer indignity to; (of person **or** thing) ∥ (rare) unsurpass-able. Hence **~ingLY²** adv. [f. L IN²(*saltare=saltare* frequent. of *salire* salt- leap)]

insup′erable, a. (Of barriers etc. & fig. of difficulties etc.) that cannot be surmounted **or** overcome; ∥ (rare) unsurpassable. Hence **~ABIL′ITY** n., **~ably²** adv. [f. L IN²(*superabilis* f. *superare* overcome, -BLE)]

insuppôrt′able, a. Unbearable. Hence **~LY²** adv. [F (IN-⁵)]

insur′ance (-shoor-), n. Insuring; sum paid for this, premium; *National I~ Act*, that of 1911 requiring wage-earners to make weekly payments supplemented by their employers in return for which they receive State assistance in sickness, unemployment, etc., (earlier *en*-, f. OF *en-seurance* (as ENSURE, see -ANCE)]

insur′ant (-shoor-), n. Person to whom insurance policy is issued. [f. foll. +-ANT]

insure′ (-shoor), v.t. Secure payment of sum of money in event of loss of **or** damage to (property, life; cf. ASSURANCE) by payment of premium; secure payment of (sum of money) thus (said of owner of the property **or** of insurance company); *the~ed*, the person to whom such payment is secured. Hence **~ABLE** (-shoor-) a. [earlier ENSURE]

insur′er (-shoor-), n. One who insures

property in consideration of premium, underwriter. [-ER¹]

insur′gent, a. & n. **1.** Rising in active revolt; (of sea etc.) rushing in. **2.** n. Rebel. Hence **~ENCY** n. [f. L IN²(*surgere surrect*- rise), see -ENT]

insurmount′able (-ser-), a. Not to be surmounted. Hence **~LY²** adv. [IN-²]

insurrec′tion (-su-), n. Rising in open resistance to established authority; incipient rebellion. Hence **~AL, ~ARY¹, aa., ~IST(3)** n., (-rĕkshǝ-). [F, f. *insurrectionem* (as INSURGENT, see -ION)]

insuscep′tible, a. Not susceptible (of treatment, *to* agency etc.). Hence **~IBIL′ITY** n. [IN-²]

intact′, a. Untouched; entire; unimpaired. [f. L IN²(*tactus* P.P. of *tangere* touch)]

inta′gliated (-tal-), a. Carved on the surface. [f. It. *intagliato* P.P. of IN²(*tagliare* cut f. LL *taleare* f. *talea* twig) +-ED¹]

inta′glio (-tal-), n. (pl. **~s**), & v.t. Engraved design; carving in hard material; gem with incised design (cf. CAMEO); (v.t.) engrave (material, design) thus. [(vb f. n.) It. (as prec.)]

in′take, n. Place where water is taken into channel **or** pipe from river etc.; air-way in mine; abrupt narrowing in pipe, stocking, etc.; person(s) **or** thing(s) taken in **or** received; land reclaimed from moor. [IN adv. +TAKE v.]

intăn′gible (-j-), a. That cannot be touched; impalpable; that cannot be grasped mentally. Hence **~IBIL′ITY** n., **~ibLY²** adv. [f. med. L IN²(*tangibilis* TANGIBLE)]

in′teger, n. Whole number, undivided quantity, (cf. FRACTION); thing complete in itself. [L, adj. = untouched, whole (IN-²+ *tag-* root of *tangere* touch)]

in′tegral, a. & n. **1.** Of, necessary to the completeness of, a whole; whole, complete; (Math.) of, denoted by, an integer, involving only integers; **~** *calculus* (dealing with finding & properties of **~**s of functions, cf. DIFFERENTIAL. **2.** n. Quantity of which a given function is the differential coefficient. Hence **or** cogn. **~TY** (-ăl-) n., **~LY²** adv. [f. LL *integralis* (as prec., see -AL)]

in′tegrant, a. (Of parts) component, making up a whole. [as foll., see -ANT]

in′tegrate², v.t. Complete (imperfect thing) by addition of parts; combine (parts) into a whole; (Math.) find the integral of; indicate mean value **or** total sum of (area, temperature, etc.), whence **~ātor²(2)** n. Hence **or** cogn. **~A′TION** n., **~ātive** a. [f. L *integrare* make whole (INTEGER), see -ATE³]

integ′rity, n. Wholeness; soundness; uprightness, honesty. [f. L *integritās* wholeness, purity, (INTEGER, see -TY)]

intég'ument, n. Skin, husk, rind, or other (usu. natural) covering. Hence ~ARY¹ (-ĕn) a. [f. L *integumentum* f. *tegere* cover].

in'tellect, n. Faculty of knowing & reasoning; understanding; person, persons collectively; of good understanding. [f. L *intellectus* -ūs (as INTELLIGENT)]

intellec'tion, n. Action, process, of understanding, esp. as opp. to *imagination*. So ~IVE a. [f. LL *intellectio* (as IN-TELLIGENT, see -ION)]

intellec'tual, a. & n. 1. Of, appealing to, requiring the exercise of, intellect. **2.** (Person) possessing a good understanding, enlightened person, esp. the ~s (of a country etc.). Hence or cogn. ~ITY (-ăl-), ~IZATION, nn., ~IZE(2) v.t. & i., ~LY² adv. [f. L *intellectualis* (as INTELLECT, see -AL)]

intellec'tualism, n. Doctrine that knowledge is wholly or mainly derived from pure reason. So ~IST(2) n. [-ISM]

intel'ligence, n. Intellect, understanding; quickness of understanding, sagacity, (of person or animal; ~ test; ~ quotient, abbr. I.Q., a number denoting the ratio of a given person's ~ to the normal or average); rational being; information, news, (~ Department, engaged in collecting information esp. for mil. purposes). [F, f. L *intelligentia* (as INTELLIGENT)]

intel'ligencer, n. Bringer of news, spy. [-ER¹]

intel'ligent, a. Having or showing (usu. a high degree of) understanding. Hence ~LY² adv. [f. L *intelligere* understand (INTER-+*legere* gather, pick out, read). -ENT]

intelligen'tsia, -zia, n. The part of a nation that aspires to independent thinking. [Russ. *intelligentsiya* f. It. *intelligenza* f. L as INTELLIGENCE]

intel'ligible, a. That can be understood, comprehensible to; (Philos.) that can be apprehended only by the intellect, not by the senses. Hence ~IBIL'ITY n., ~IBLY² adv. [f. L *intelligibilis* (as prec., see -BLE)]

in'tem'perate, a. (Of person or conduct) immoderate, unbridled, violent; excessive in the indulgence of an appetite; addicted to drinking. Hence or cogn. ~ANCE n., ~ATELY² adv. [f. LL²*temperatus,* as TEMPER v.)]

intend', v.t. Purpose, design, as ve ~ to go, ve ~ no harm, ve ~ that it shall be done today, vas this ~ed (done on purpose)?; design, destine, (person, thing) for a purpose, as ve ~ our son for the bar, ~ him to you; ~ it as a stop-gap, this bun is ~ed for you (to eat), this daub is ~ed (or meant) to represent me; mean, as what exactly do you ~ by the word?. [f. F *entendre* f. L IN²*tendere tent-* or *tens-* strain, direct, tend]

inten'dant, n. Superintendent, manager,

of public business etc. (chiefly as foreign title). Hence ~CY n. [F, f. L as prec., -ANT]

intend'ed, n. (colloq.). Affianced lover, as *your, his, her,* ~. [p.p. of INTEND as n.]

intend'ment, n. True meaning as fixed by law. [f. F *entendement* (as IN-TEND, see -MENT)]

intense', a. (-er, -est). (Of quality etc.) existing in a high degree, violent, vehement; having some quality in high degree; (of feeling or action) eager, ardent; feeling, apt to feel, ~ emotion. Hence ~LY² (-sl-) adv., ~NESS (-sn-) n. [f. OF, f. L *intensus* (as INTEND)]

inten'sify, v.t. & i., (also, Photog.) increase the opacity of the deposit in a negative by chemical or other means. [f. as INTENT² + -FY]

inten'sion (-shn), n. Intensity, high degree, of a quality, opp. to *extension*; strenuous exertion of mind or will. [f. L *intensio* (INTEND, -ION)]

inten'sive, a. Of, relating to, intensity, as opp. to extent; producing intensity, (Gram.) expressing intensity; giving force; concentrated, directed to a single point or area or subject, (~ *bombardment,* ~ *study*); (Econ.) serving to increase production of given area, as ~ *methods,* *agriculture;* (Med.) ~ *inoculation* (in which intensity of matter introduced is increased in successive operations). Hence ~LY² (-vl-) adv. [f. (-if, -ive), f. L as INTEND, see -IVE]

intent'¹, n. Intention, purpose, esp. *with* ~ *to* (defraud etc.), *with malicious, good,* etc., ~; (pl.) *to all* ~*s & purposes,* practically, virtually; [ME & OF (1) *entent* f. L *intentus -ūs,* (2) *entente* f. pop. L *intenta* fem. p.p., both as INTEND]

intent'², a. Resolved, bent, (on doing, on object); sedulously occupied (on); (of faculties, looks, etc.) earnest, eager. Hence ~LY² adv., ~NESS n. [f. L as INTEND; doublet of *intense,* L *-tens-* having chiefly the physical, *-tent-* the mental sense)]

inten'tion, n. Intending; thing intended, purpose, whence (-)~ED² (-shnd) a.; ultimate aim; (pl., colloq.) purposes in respect of proposal of marriage; (Med.) *second* ~, healing of wound by granulation, *first* ~, healing without its by immediate re-union of parts; (Logic) conception, as *first* ~s, primary conceptions of things (e.g. a tree, an oak), *second* ~s, secondary conceptions (e.g. difference, identity, species); (Theol.) *special, parti-cular,* ~, special object for which mass is celebrated etc. [OF, f. L *intentionem* (as INTEND, see -ION)]

inten'tional (-shon-), a. Done on purpose. Hence ~LY² adv. [f. med. L *intentionalis* (as prec., see -AL)]

inter', v.t. & i., (-rr-). Deposit (corpse etc.) in earth, tomb, etc.; bury. [f. OF *enterer* f. pop. L IN²(*terrare* f. *terra* earth)]

in'ter[2], prep. (L). Between, among, as ~ al'ia, amongst other things; ~ nos, sē, between ourselves, themselves; ~ vīv'ōs, between the living (esp. of gift as opp. legacy).

inter-, pref. = prec. Besides wds given in their alphab. place, inter- is used freely to form (1) vbs, nn., & aa., expr. mutual or reciprocal action or relation, or with sense 'among', 'between', as: ~bed', embed (thing) between others; ~cen'sal, carried on etc. between two censuses; ~collē'giate, carried on etc. between colleges; ~colum'nar, placed, existing, between two columns; ~columnia'tion, placing of columns at intervals, such interval; ~connect', connect by reciprocal links; ~convert'ible, interchangeable; ~cross', t. & i., lay, lie, across each other, (cause to) propagate with each other; ~flow, n. & v.i., flow into each other; ~grada'tion, gradual approximation; ~grade, (v.i.) pass into another form by intervening grades, (n.) such grade; ~growth', growing of things into each other; ~jac'ulatory, expressed in parenthetical ejaculations; ~knit', intertwine; ~lap', overlap; ~link', link together (things, one with another); ~ocean'ic, between, connecting, two oceans; ~plait', plait together; ~provin'cial, situated, carried on, between provinces; ~punc'tuate, punctuation; ~ra'cial, existing between different races; ~shoot', shoot or glance (t. & i.) at intervals, variegate (thing with colours etc., esp. in p.p. ~shot); in'terspace, interval of space or time; ~tan'gle, tangle together; whence ~tan'glement n.; ~tex'ture, interweaving; ~trib'al, existing between different tribes; ~twist', twist together; ~vein', intersect (as) with veins; ~work', (trans.) interweave lit. & fig.; (intr.) work upon each other; ~wreathe', wreathe together. (2) Scientific, esp. anat., wds w. sense 'between', chiefly adjj., as: ~artic'ular, between contiguous surfaces of a joint; ~cos'tal, between the ribs (of body or ship), (n. pl.) ~costal parts; ~di'gital, between fingers or toes; ~di'gitate, interlock like fingers of clasped hands, so ~digita'tion n.; ~fa'cial, included between two faces of crystal or other solid; ~fem'oral, between the thighs; ~folia'ceous, placed alternately between a pair of opposite leaves; ~gla'cial, between glacial periods; ~lob'ular, between lobes; ~node', (Bot.) part of stem between two of the knots from which leaves arise, (Anat.) slender part between two joints, esp. bone of finger or toe; ~oss'eous, between bones; ~pari'etal, between right & left parietal bones of skull; ~sep'tal, between partitions; ~spin'al, ~spin'ous, between spines or spinous processes; ~stell'ar, between stars; ~stratifica'tion, ~strat'ified, interspersion, interspersed, (with strata).

in'teract[1], n. Interval between two acts of play; interlude. [INTER-, after F ENTR'ACTE]

interāct'[2], v.i. Act reciprocally, act on each other. Hence interāc'tion n., interāc'tive a. [INTER-]

interblend', v.t. & i. Mingle (things, one with another); (intr.) blend with each other. [INTER-]

interbreed', v.t. & i. Cross-breed; (intr., of animals of different race or species) breed with each other. [INTER-]

intēr'calary, a. (Of day or month) inserted in calendar to harmonize calendar with solar year; (of year) having such additions; interpolated, intervening. [f. L intercalarius (as foll., see -ARY[1])

intēr'calate, v.t. Insert (intercalary day etc., or abs.); interpose (anything out of ordinary course, esp. in p.p. of strata). So ~a'tion n. [f. L intercalare proclaim), see -ATE[3]]

intercēde', v.i. Interpose on behalf of another, plead (with one person for another). [f. L INTER(cedere cess- go)]

intercept', v.t. Seize, catch, (person etc.) on the way from place to place; cut off (light etc. from); check, stop; (Math.) mark off (space) between two points etc. Hence or cogn. ~cep'tion, ~cep'tor[2], nn., ~cep'tive a. [f. L INTER(cipere cept- = capere take)]

intercē'ssion (-shn), n. Interceding, esp. by prayer. So ~cēss'or[2] n., ~cess'oriaL, ~cēss'ory, aa. [f. L intercessio (as INTERCEDE, cess- -ION)]

in'terchange[1] (-j), n. Reciprocal exchange (of things) between two persons etc.; alternation. [f. OF entrechange (as foll.)]

interchānge'[2] (-j), v.t. (Of two persons) exchange (things) with each other; put each of (two things) in the other's place; alternate. Hence or cogn. ~abil'ity, ~ableness, nn., ~able a., ~ably adv., (-jab-). [f. OF entrechangier (entre- INTER- + changier CHANGE)]

intercolō'nial, a. Existing, carried on, between different colonies. [INTER-]

in'tercom, n. System of intercommunication esp. in aircraft. [abbr.]

intercommū'nicate, v.i. Have mutual intercourse; have free passage to each other. So ~a'tion n. [INTER-]

intercommū'nion (-yon), n. Intimate intercourse; mutual action or relation. [INTER-]

intercommū'nity, n. Being common to various parties; having things in common. [INTER-]

in'tercourse (-ōrs), n. Social communication, dealings, between individuals; com-

For other words in *inter-* see INTER-.

-munion between man & God; communication for trade purposes etc., between
different countries etc.; sexual connexion.
[f. OF *entrecours* & *entrecorre* run between f. L INTER(*currere curs-* run)]

intercu'rrent, a. (Of time or event)
intervening; (of disease) occurring during
progress of another, (also) recurring at
intervals. Hence ~ENCE n. [f. L as prec.
-ENT]

interde'pend', v.i. Depend on each other.
So ~'ENCE, ~ENCY, nn.; ~'pen'dent a.
[f. DE(pen'dent)]

in'terdict', n. Authoritative prohibition;
(Sc. Law)=INJUNCTION; (R.-C. Ch.) sentence debarring person or place from ecclesiastical functions etc. [f. OF *entredit*
f. *entredire* f. L INTER(*dicere dict-* say)]

interdic't, v.t. Prohibit (action); forbid
use of; restrain (person *from doing*); forbid (thing to person). So interdic'TION n.,
interdic'TORY a. [ME *entredite* (as prec.,
refash. on L)]

in'terest[1], n. 1. Legal concern, title, right,
(*in* property); pecuniary stake (*in* commercial undertaking etc.); VESTED ~s.
2. Advantage, profit, as *it is* (&c) *your*
interest; *I do it in your* ~, *in the* ~ (or ~s) *of*
truth. 3. Thing in which one is concerned;
principle in which a party is concerned;
party having a common ~, *as the brewing*
~. 4. Selfish pursuit of one's own welfare; *make* ~, bring personal ~ to bear
(*with* person). 5. Concern, curiosity, or
quality exciting them (*take an* ~, *no* ~,
in; this has no ~ *for me*). 6. Money paid
for use of money lent or for forbearance of
debt (*with* ~, transf., with increased force
etc., *as returned the blow, his kindness,*
with ~); *simple* ~ (reckoned on principal
only, & paid at fixed intervals); *com-*
pound ~ (reckoned on principal & on
accumulations of ~). [~, =ft matters,
3rd sing. pres. of INTER(*esse* be); earlier
interess f. L inf. in sense compensatory
payment]

in'terest[2], v.t. Cause (person) to take
personal interest or share (*in*; (p.p.)
having a private interest, not impartial
or disinterested, as *~ed parties, motives*);
excite curiosity or attention of, whence
~ING[2] a. (*ll in an* ~*ing condition*, pregnant),
~ING[2] adv. Hence ~ED[2]*ly* adv. [earlier
s'entrefre & *interess* vbs]

interfere', v.i. (Of things) come into
collision or opposition (*with*); (of person)
meddle (*with* or *abs.*), whence ~'FER'ING[2]
a.; intervene, take part, (*in*); (Physics, of
waves of light etc.), strike against each
other; (of horse) knock one leg against
another. Hence ~'fer'ENCE n. [f. OF
s'entreferir strike each other (*entre-* INTER-
+*ferir* f. L *ferire* strike)]

interfe'rom'eter, n. Instrument for measuring the length of light-waves by means
of interference phenomena. [prec. +
-METER]

---

in'terflu'ent (-ōō-), a. Flowing into each
other. [f. L INTER(*fluere* flow), see -ENT]

interfu'se (-z), v.t. & i. Interspere, mix,
(thing *with*); blend (things) together;
(of two things) blend with each other.
So interfu'SION (-zhn) n. [f. L INTER(*fun-*
dere fus- pour)]

in'terim, adv., n., & a. 1. adv. (arch.)
Meanwhile. 2. n. Intervening time;
the I~ (Eccl.), truce pending a General
Council between German Protestants &
the Papacy in 16th c. 3. adj. Intervening;
provisional, temporary; ~ *dividend* (paid
between two annual etc. balances & not
in pursuance of a published balance
sheet). [L (INTER-+adv. suf.-*im*)]

inte'rior, a. & n. 1. Situated within;
inland, remote from coast or frontier;
internal, domestic, opp. to *foreign*; existing in the mind or soul, inward. 2. n. ~ part,
inside; inland region; internal of building or
room, picture of this; inner nature, soul
(department dealing with) home affairs of
a country, *as Minister of the* I~. Hence
inte'rior'LY[2] adv. [L, compar. adj. f. INTER-]

interja'cent, a. Lying between. Intermediate. [f. L INTER(*jacēre* lie), see -ENT]

interje'ct, v.t. Throw in, interpose, (remark etc.) abruptly; remark parenthetí-
cally. [f. L INTER(*jicere ject-* = *jacere*
throw)]

interje'ction, n. Ejaculation, exclamation; natural ejaculation viewed as part
of speech (e.g. *ah!, whew?*). Hence or
cogn. ~AL(-shon-), interje'ctORY, aa.,
~aliy[2] adv. [F, f. L INTER(*jicere ject-*
-ION)]

**in'terla'ce', v.t. & i. Bind together intri-
cately, entangle; interweave (often fig.);
mingle (two things, one *with* another);
(intr.) cross each other intricately. Hence
~MENT (-sm-) n. [f. F *entrelacer* (*entre-*
prec.)]

interli'ne', v.t. Insert words between lines
of (document etc.); insert (words) thus.
So interlinea'TION n. [prob. f. med. L
INTER(*lineare*, f. *linea* LINE[1])]

interlin'ear, a. Written, printed, between
the lines. [f. med. L INTER(*linearis*
LINEAR)]

interleave', v.t. Insert (usu. blank) leaves
between leaves of (book), (also fig.). [f.
prec.]

interleaf', n. (pl. *-ves*). Extra leaf (usu.
blank) between leaves of book. [INTER-]

in'terlock', v.i. & t. (intr.) engage with
each other by overlapping etc.; (trans.,
usu. pass.) lock, clasp, within each other
(Italways); connect (levers for signals
etc.) by bolts etc. to ensure uniformity of
movement. [INTER-]

in'terlo'cutor, n. One who takes part in
dialogue or conversation; compere of
nigger minstrel troupe; *my* ~*tor*, the

person in conversation with me. Hence or cogn. **interlocu′tion**, ~**TRESS**[1], ~**TRIX**, nn., ~**TORY** a., (also) pronounced during course of a legal action (*an* ~*tory decree*). [f. L INTER(*loqui locut-* talk), see -ION]

in′terloper, n. Intruder, one who (esp. for profit) thrusts himself into others' affairs; (Hist.) unauthorized trader. So **interlõpe′** v.i. [INTER- + *loper* f. *lope* dial. form of LEAP]

in′terlude (-lōõd), n. Pause between acts of play; what fills this up; (Mus.) instrumental piece played between verses of psalm or hymn etc.; intervening time or space of different character; event, amusing incident, etc., interposed; (Hist.) dramatic or mimic representation between acts of mystery-plays or moralities. [f. med. L INTER(*ludium* f. *ludus* play)]

intermã′rriage (-rij), n. Marriage between members of different families, castes, tribes, etc., or (loosely) between near relations. [INTER-]

intermã′rry, v.i. (Of tribes, nations, families, etc.) become connected by marriage (*with* others or *with* each other tribes etc.). [INTER-]

intermêd′dle, v.i. Concern oneself (*with*, *in*, esp. what is not one's business). [f. OF *entremesler* (*entre-* INTER- + *mesler* MEDDLE)]

intermêd′iary, a. & n. 1. Acting between parties, mediatory; intermediate. 2. n. ~ person, thing, esp. mediator. [L, next. adj. as INTERMEDIATE[1]]

intermêd′iate[1], a. & n. Coming *between* two things, as regards time, place, or order; (n.) ~ thing. Hence ~**LY**[2] (-tī-) adv. [f. med. L *intermediatus* f. L INTER-(*medius* middle) -ATE[2]]

intermêd′iate[2], v.i. Act between others, mediate, (*between*). Hence ~**A′TION**, ~**ã-tor**[2], nn. [INTER-]

intermê′dium, n. (pl. ~*ia*, -*iums*). Intermediate thing, medium, esp. one serving to transmit energy through space. [L, next. adj. as INTERMEDIATE[1]]

inter′ment, n. Burial. [INTER[1] + -MENT]

intermê′zzo (-dzõ), n. (pl. -*zi*, -*zos*). Short light dramatic or other performance between acts of drama or opera, short movement connecting main divisions of large musical work. [It., pop. form of *intermedio* (as INTERMEDIATE[1])]

intermigrã′tion, n. Reciprocal migration. [INTER-]

inter′minable, a. Endless; tediously long. Hence ~**lENESS** n., ~**LY**[2] adv. [f. LL IN-[2](*terminabilis* f. *terminare* TERMINATE, see -BLE)]

intermingle, -(mĭng′gl), v.t. & i. Mix together (two things, one *with* another); (intr.) mingle (*with*). [INTER-]

intermi′ssion (-shn), n. Pause, cessation, esp. *without* ~. [f. L *intermissio* (as foll., see -ION)]

intermi′t, v.t. & i. (-*tt*-). Suspend, discontinue; stop for a time (esp. of fever, pain, etc., or of pulse). Hence or cogn. ~**TENCE** n., ~**t′ENT** a., ~**t′ENTLY**[2] adv. [f. L INTER(*mittere miss-* send)]

intermi′x, v.t. & i. Mix together. So ~**TURE** n. [first in p.p., see MIX]

intêrn′[1], v.t. Oblige to reside within limits of country etc. Hence ~**EE′** n., ~**MENT** n. (~*ment camp*, for prisoners of war & aliens). [f. F *interner* f. L *internus* internal (*in-* + suf. *-ternus*)]

•**in′tern**[2], n. Advanced student or recent graduate residing in hospital & acting as assistant physician or surgeon. [after F *interne*]

intêrn′al, a. & n. 1. Of, situated in, the inside of a thing; of the inner nature of a thing, intrinsic; ~ *evidence*, derived from what is contained in the thing itself (cf. EXTERNAL); ~*combustion engine* (in which motive power is derived from explosion of mixture of gas, or vaporized oil or petrol, & air in the cylinder); of the domestic affairs of a country; of the mind or soul, inward, subjective. 2. n. pl. Intrinsic qualities. Hence ~**TY** (-ăl-) n., ~**LY**[2] adv. [f. late med. L *internalis* (as INTERN[1], see -AL)]

internã′tional (-shon-), a. & n. 1. Existing, carried on, between different nations; the I~ Working Men's Associations (for promoting joint political action of working classes in all countries). 2. n. One who takes part in ~ (usu. athletic) contests; ~ contest; *first, second, third, I*~, three Associations as above (1st, Marxist, 1862-73; 2nd, French socialist, 1889 — ; 3rd, Russian communist, abbr. *Comintern*, 1919-43); member of any of these. Hence ~**TY** (-shonăl-) n., ~**LY**[2] adv. [INTER-]

Internã′tionale′ (-shonähl), n. *The* ~ (orig. French) communist song sung at demonstrations; = *International Association* (see prec.). [F]

internã′tionalist (-shon-), n. One who advocates community of interests between nations, esp. supporter of Association named in prec., so ~**ISM** n.; one versed in international law. [-IST]

internã′tionalize (-shon-), v.t. Make international, esp. bring (territory etc.) under combined protection etc. of different nations. Hence ~**A′TION** n. [-IZE]

internê′cine, a. Mutually destructive; (erron.) deadly, as ~ *war*. [f. L *internecinus* f. INTER(*necare* kill) destroy, see -INE[1]]

internûn′cial (-shal), a. (Of nerves) communicating between different parts of the system. [f. L as foll. + -AL]

internûn′cio (-shō), n. Ambassador of Pope when or where no nuncio is employed; (Hist.) minister representing (esp. Austrian) government at Ottoman Porte.

For other words in *inter-* see INTER-.

[f. It. *intermezzo* f. L INTER(*medius* messenger)]

interos'culate, v.i. Intermingle with each other ; form connecting link. Hence **~A'TION** n. [INTER-]

interpage', v.t. Print, insert, on intermediate pages. [INTER-]

interpel'läte, v.t. (In foreign, esp. French, Chamber) interrupt order of day by demanding explanation from (Minister concerned). So **~A'TION**, **~A'T(OR**)³ nn., L INTER(*pellare* var. of *pellere* drive, see -ATE³]

interpen'eträte, v.t. & i. Penetrate thoroughly, pervade ; penetrate reciprocally. (intr. ; of two) penetrate each other. So **~A'TION** n., **~A'TIVE** a. [INTER-]

in'terplay, n. Reciprocal play ; operation of two things on each other. [INTER-]

interplead', v.i. Litigate with each other in order to settle a point in which a third party is concerned. [INTER-]

interpo'läte, v.t. Make insertions in (book etc.), esp. so as to give false impressions as to date etc. ; introduce (words) thus ; (Math.) insert (intermediate term) in series. So **~A'TION**, **~A'TOR**³ nn. [f. L INTER(*polare* cogn. w. *polīre* POLISH¹) furbish up. -ATE³]

interpōṣe' (-z), v.t. & i. Insert, make (veto, objection, authority, etc.) by way of interference ; intervene (*between* disputants etc.) ; say (quoted words) as an interruption ; make an interruption. Hence **~AL** (-z-) n. [f. F INTER(*poser*, see COMPOSE)]

interpoṣi'tion (-z-), n. Interposing ; thing interposed ; interference. [F, f. L *interpositionem* f. INTER(*ponere* posit- place)]

interprèt, v.t. & i. Expound the meaning of (abstruse words, writings, etc.) ; make out the meaning of ; bring out the meaning of, render, by artistic representation or performance ; explain, understand, in specified manner, *as this we ~ as a threat* ; act as interpreter. Hence or **COMPOSE**. [f. OF *interpreter* f. L *interpretārī*]

interpretā'tion, n. (as prec., see INTERPRET)

interprè'ter, n. One who interprets ; one whose office it is to translate orally in their presence the words of persons speaking different languages. Hence **~ERSHIP**, **~RESS¹**, nn. [f. OF *interpreteor* (as prec., see INTERPRET)]

interreg'num, n. (pl. *-na, -nums*). Period during which State has no normal ruler, esp. between end of King's reign & accession of successor ; interval, pause. [L INTER(*regnum* REIGN)]

interrelā'tion, n. Mutual relation. [INTER-]

interrelā'tionship (-shon-), n. Mutual relationship. [INTER-]

4895

---

inter'rogate, v.t. Ask questions of (person etc.), esp. closely or formally. So **~OR²** n. [f. L INTER(*rogare* ask), see -ATE³]

interrogā'tion, n. Asking questions ; question ; point, mark, note, of (used to express) **~** (?). [F, f. L *interrogationem* (as prec., see -ATION)]

interrog'ative, a. & n. 1. Of, having the form or force of, a question ; of inquiry, as *an ~ tone* ; (Gram., of words) used in asking question, as *~ pronouns (who?, which?, etc.)*. 2. n.*~* word, esp. pronoun. Hence **~LY²** (-vl-) adv. [f. LL *interrogativus* as prec., see -IVE]

interrog'atory, a. & n. 1. Of inquiry, as *an ~ tone*. 2. n. Question, set of questions, esp. (Law) one formally put to accused person etc. [f. LL *interrogatorius* (as prec., see -ORY)]

interrupt', v.t. Break in upon (action, process, speech, person speaking, etc., or abs.) ; obstruct (view etc.) ; break the continuity of. Hence or cogn. **~rup'-tedly²** adv., **~rup'ter, ~rup'tion**, **~rup'tory** a. [f. L INTER(*rumpere rupt-* break)]

intersect', v.t. & i. Divide (thing) by passing or lying across it ; (of lines etc.) cross, cut, each other. [f. L INTER(*secare sect-* cut)]

intersec'tion, n. Intersecting ; point, line, common to intersecting lines, planes. Hence **~AL** (-sho-) a. [f. L *intersectio* (as prec., see -ION)]

intersperse', v.t. Scatter, place here & there (*between, among*) ; diversify (thing) *with* (others so scattered). So **inter-spers'ion** (-shn) n. [f. L INTER(*spergere* = *spargere* scatter)]

in'terstate, a. Existing, carried on, between States. [INTER-]

inter'stice (or *in'ter-*), n. Intervening space ; chink, crevice. [f. L *interstitium* f. INTER(*sistere* stit- stand)]

interstï'tial (-shl), a. Of, forming, occupying, interstice(s). [as prec. + -AL]

intertwine', v.t. & i. Entwine (things, one *with* another) ; become entwined. Hence **~MENT** (-nm-) n. [INTER-]

in'terval, n. Intervening time or space ; pause ; break, gap ; *at ~s*, here & there, now & then ; (Mus.) difference of pitch between two sounds, in melody or harmony ; distance between persons or things ; (in respect of qualities). Hence **interval'ic** a. [f. L INTER(*vallum* rampart), interval]

intervene', v.i. Come in as something extraneous ; occur in the meantime ; (of person or thing) come between, interfere, so as to prevent or modify result etc. (*between* persons, *in* affair) ; (Law) interpose in lawsuit to which one was not an original party (||esp. of King's Proctor in divorce cases), whence **~ER¹** n.; be situated, *between*. So **inter-vēn'tion** n. [f. L INTER(*venire vent-* come)]

4895

In'terview (-vū), n., & v.t. 1. Meeting of persons face to face, esp. for purpose of conference; meeting between person employed by newspaper & someone from whom he seeks to get statements for publication. 2. v.t. Have an ~ with (person), esp. with a view to publication of his statements. Hence ~ER¹ (-vūer) n. [(vb f. n.) f. F entrevue f. s'entrevoir (entre-INTER- + voir f. L vidēre see)]

Interwove', v.t. Wind, roll up, (things) within each other. [f. INTER- + L volvere roll

Interweave', v.t. Weave together, interlace, (things, one with another); blend (things) intimately. [INTER-]

Interwind', v.t. & i. Wind together. [INTER-]

Intes'tate, a. & n. 1. (Of person) not having made a will, as he died ~. 2. n. ~ person. Hence intes'tacy n. [f. L IN²(testātus p.p. of testāri make will f. testis witness)]

Intes'tine¹, n. (Usn. pl.) lower part of alimentary canal from pyloric end of stomach to anus; small, large, ~e, parts of this, So ~AL(or -īn-) a. [f. L neut. adj. as foll.]

Intes'tine², a. (Of wars etc.) internal, domestic, civil; ~ motion (entirely within a body). [f. L intestīnus internal (intus within)]

In'timate¹, a. & n. 1. Close in acquaintance, familiar, as ~ friend(ship); ~ (close) connexion; ~ knowledge (resulting from familiarity); essential, intrinsic; (of diary) recording emotions etc. 2. n. ~ friend. Hence in'timacy n., (also, enphem.) illicit sexual relations, ~LY² (-tl-) adv. [foll., -ATE²]

In'timate², v.t. Make known, state, (fact, wish, that); imply, hint. So ~A'TION n. [f. LL intimāre (intimus inmost), -ATE³]

Intim'idate, v.t. Inspire with fear, cow, esp. in order to influence conduct. Hence ~A'TION, ~ātor¹ nn. [f. med. L IN¹(timidāre f. timidus TIMID), see -ATE³]

Intim'ity, n. Inwardness; privacy. [f. L intimus inmost, see -TY]

Intinc'tion, n. Dipping of the Eucharistic bread in the wine, to enable the communicant to receive both kinds. [f. LL intinctio f. IN¹(tingere tinct- TINGE)]

Intit'ule, v.t. Entitle (Act of Parliament, usn. p.p.). [f. OF intituler f. LL IN¹(titulāre f. titulus TITLE)]

In'to (-tŏŏ, before consonant -tŏ), prep. 1. Expr. motion or direction to a point within a thing, lit. & fig., as come ~ the garden, throw it ~ the fire, look ~ the box, the matter, inquire ~ it, get ~ trouble, come ~ (acquire) property, watching far on ~ the night. 2. Expr. change, condition, result, as turn stones ~ gold, collect them ~ heaps, divide them ~ three classes, flogged ~ submission. [IN + TO]

In'toed (-ōd), a. Having the toes turned inwards. [IN adv. + TOE + -ED²]

Intŏl'erable, a. That cannot be endured. Hence ~leNESS n., ~LY² adv. [f. L IN²(tolerābilis TOLERABLE)]

Intŏl'er¡ant, a. Not tolerant (of, esp. religious opinions differing from one's own). Hence or cogn. ~ANCE n., ~antLY² adv. [f. L IN²(tolerans TOLERANT)]

Intŏnate, v.t. = INTONE. [-ATE³]

Intona'tion, n. Reciting in singing voice; (Church Mus.) opening phrase of plainsong melody; utterance, production, of musical tones; modulation of voice, accent. [as foll, see -ATION]

Intŏne', v.t. Recite (psalm, prayer, etc., or als.) in singing voice; utter with particular tone. [f. L IN¹(tonāre f. tonus TONE)]

Intŏx'icant, a. & n. Intoxicating (liquor). [as foll., see -ANT]

Intŏx'icate, v.t. Make drunk; excite, exhilarate, beyond self-control (~ated with, byp.). Hence ~ātING²a., ~A'TION n. [f. med. L IN¹(toxicāre smear with poison f. toxicum f. Gk toxikon f. toxa arrows), see -ATE³]

Intra-, in comb. = L intra on the inside, within, as: ~cra'nial, within the skull; ~mu'ral, existing, done, within walls; ~na'tional, (not inter)national.

Intrac'table, a. Not docile, refractory; (of things) not easily dealt with. Hence ~ABIL'ITY, ~ableNESS, nn., ~abLY² adv. [f. L IN²(tractābilis TRACTABLE)]

Intrad'os, n. (archit.). Lower or interior ourve of arch (cf. EXTRADOS). [F (INTRA- + dos back)]

Intran'sigent (-z-), a. & n. 1. Uncompromising in politics. 2. n. An irreconcilable (in politics). So ~ENCE n. [f. F intransigeant f. Sp. los intransigentes extreme republicans f. IN²+L TRANSIGERE (igere=agere act) come to an understanding, see -ENT]

Intran'sitive (-ahns-), a. & n. (Verb) that does not take a direct object (cf. TRANSITIVE). Hence ~LY² adv. [f. L IN²(transitīvus TRANSITIVE)]

In'trant, n. One who enters a college, association, etc. [f. L intrāre enter, see -ANT]

Intrĕp'id, a. Fearless, brave. Hence intrĕpid'ITY n., ~LY² adv. [f. L IN²(trepidus alarmed)]

In'tric¡ate, a. Perplexingly entangled; involved; obscure. Hence ~ACY n., ~ateLY² adv. [f. L IN²(tricare f. tricae tricks), see -ATE²]

In'trig(u)ant (-gant; or äntregahn'), n. (fem. ~e, pr. äntregahnt'). Intriguer. [F (-guant), part. as foll.]

Intrigue'¹ (-ēg), v.i. & t. Carry on underhand plot; employ secret influence (with); have a liaison (with); (as journalistic gallicism, v.t.) rouse the interest or curiosity of. [f. F intriguer (as INTRIGUE)]

For other words in inter- see INTER-.

Intrigue² (-ēg), n. Underhand plotting or plot; secret amour, liaison. [F., f. It. *intrigo* f. *intrigare* (as INTRIGUE¹)]

intrin'sic, a. Belonging naturally, inherent, essential, esp. ~*ic value* (cf. EXTRINSIC). Hence ~ICALLY adv. [f. F (-IQUE), f. L *intrinsecus* f. med. L *intrinsecus* (adj. f. L adv., cf. EXTRINSIC]

Intro- in comb.=L *intro* to the inside, as: ~*flexion*, inward bending; ~*gression*, going or coming in; ~*susception* (Physiol., Biol.)=INTUSSUSCEPTION.

Introduce', v.t. Bring in; place in, insert; bring into use (custom, idea, improvement, etc., *into* place, system, etc.); usher in, bring forward, (matter etc.); (of conjunctions etc.) open (sentence etc.); make known, esp. in formal manner (person to another); bring (young lady) out, into society; draw attention of (person *to* subject etc.); bring (bill etc.) before Parliament. So **introduc'tory** a. [f. L INTRO(*ducere duct-* lead)]

Introduc'tion, n. Introducing; preliminary matter prefixed to book; (as title) introductory treatise; formal presentation of one person to another; *letter of* ~ (given by one person to another) introducing him to a third. [F., f. L *introductionem* (as prec., see -ION)]

Intrō'it, n. (eccl.). Psalm, antiphon, sung while priest approaches altar to celebrate mass or Holy Communion. [F. *introït*-us f. L INTRO(*ire it-* go)]

Intromit', v.t. (arch.; -tt-). Let in, admit, (into); insert. So **intromi'ssion** (-shn) n., ~**t**ENT aa. [f. L INTRO(*mittere miss-* send)]

intro spect', v.i. Examine one's own thoughts & feelings. Hence ~spec'tion, ~spec'tionist n., ~spec'tiveness, nn., ~spec'tive a., ~spec'tively² adv. [f. L INTRO(*spicere spect-* look)]

introvert', v.t. Turn (mind, thought) inwards upon itself; (esp. Zool.) withdraw (organ etc.) within its own tube or base, as finger of glove, whence ~ver'sible a. Hence ~ver'sion (-shn) n., in'trovert n., person given to ~version, ~ver'sive, ~ver'tive, aa. [f. L INTRO(*vertere vers-* turn)]

Intrude' (-rŏŏd), v.t. & i. Thrust, force, (thing *into*); force (thing *upon* person); come uninvited, thrust oneself in, (*into* place, company, etc., *upon* person, his privacy, etc.). Hence ~**ER**¹ (-dər) n. (also, raiding aircraft). [f. L IN²(*trudere trus-* thrust)]

intru'sion (-rŏŏzhn), n. Intruding; forcing in; forcing oneself in (*into*, *upon*); (Geol.) influx of rock in state of fusion between strata etc.; settlement of minister of Church of Scotland without consent of congregation, whence ~IST(2) n. So **intru'sive** a., ~**IVE**¹ a., **intru'sively²** adv., **intru'siveness** n. [OF. f. med. L *intrusionem* (as prec., see -ION)]

in'tubate, v.t. (med.). Insert tube into (larynx etc.) to keep it open. Hence ~ATION n. [f. IN.¹+L *tuba* tube+-ATE³]

in'tuit, v.t. & i. Know by intuition; receive knowledge by direct perception. [f. L IN²(*tuēri tuit-* look)]

intui'tion, n. Immediate apprehension by the mind without reasoning; immediate apprehension by sense; immediate insight. Hence ~AL (-shon-) a. [F., f. med. L *intuitionem* (as prec., see -ION)]

intui'tionism (-shon-), n. Doctrine that the perception of truth is by intuition. So ~IST n. [-ISM]

intui'tive, a. Of, possessing, perceived by, intuition. Hence ~LY² (-vl-) adv., ~NESS n. [f. med. L *intuitivus* (INTUIT, -IVE)]

intui'tivism, n. Doctrine that ethical principles are matters of intuition. So ~IST n. [-ISM]

intumesce' (-tū-), a. Swelling up. So ~ENCE incept. of *tumēre* swell), see -ENT]

in'tussuscep'tion, n. (Physiol.) taking in of foreign matter by living organism, & its conversion into organic tissue; taking in (of ideas etc.); withdrawal of one portion of intestine within another. [f. L *intus* within + *suscipere*, SUS(*cipere* take) take up, see -ION]

inurbane', a. Not urbane, discourteous. Hence **inurban'ity** n. [f. L IN¹(*urbanus* URBANE]

inure', ĕn-, v.t. & i. Accustom, habituate, (person etc. *to* thing, *to* do), whence ~MENT (-ūr-) n.; (intr., chiefly Law; *en-*) come into operation, take effect. [IN-¹+obs. *ure* work f. F *œuvre* f. L *opera*]

inurn', v.t. Put (ashes of cremated body) in an urn. [IN-¹]

invag'inate, v.t. Put in a sheath; introvert (tubular sheath). Hence ~ATION n. [f. IN.¹+L *vagina* sheath + -ATE³]

invade', v.t. Make hostile inroad into (country etc.); (fig. of sounds, diseases, feelings, etc.) assail; encroach upon (rights etc.). Hence ~ER¹ n. [f. L IN²(*vadere vas-* go)]

in'valid¹ (-ēd), a. & n. (Person) enfeebled or disabled by illness or injury. Hence ~HOOD, ~ISM(3), nn., ~(-ēd-), v.t. & n. [F. *invalide*, pronunc. after F *invalidé*]

invalid'² (-ēd; *also* in-²), v.t. & i. **1.** Lay up, disable, (person) by illness (usu. pass.); treat as an invalid; remove from active service, send *home* etc., as an invalid; (intr.) become an invalid, go on the sick-list. [f. prec.]

invāl'id³, a. Not valid, esp. having no legal force. Hence ~LY² adv. [as INVALID¹, without assim. to F]

invāl'idāte, v.t. Make INVALID³. Hence ~A'TION n. [prec. + -ATE³]

invalid'ify, n. Want of validity; bodily infirmity. [INVALID³,¹ + -ITY]

invāl'uable, a. Above price, priceless. [IN-²]

invâr, n. Alloy of nickel & steel with negligible coefficient of expansion, used in manufacture of clocks and scientific instruments. [abbr. of foll.; P]

invâr'iable, a. Unchangeable; always the same; (Math.) constant, fixed. Hence ~ABIL'ITY, ~ableNESS, nn., ~abLY² adv. [IN-²]

invā'sion (-zhn), n. Invading; encroachment. So **invās'IVE** a. [F, f. L *invasionem* (as INVADE, see -ION)]

invec'tive, n. Violent attack in words; abusive oratory. [F, f. med. L *invectiva* (*oratio*) f. LL *invectivus* (as foll., see -IVE)]

inveigh' (-vā), v.i. Speak violently, rail loudly, *against*. [f. L IN¹(*vehi* pass. of *vehere ved-* carry) go into, assail]

inveig'le (-vē-, -vā-), v.t. Entice, seduce, (*into* place, conduct, etc., *into doing*). Hence ~MENT (-vēgelm-, -vā-) n. [16th-c. *enveigle* prob. f. F *aveugler* blind f. *aveugle* adj. f. pop. L AB(*oculus* eye) taken as *a-vegle*, & so changed to *enveigle*]

invēn'it, **invēn'unt**, (abbr. *inv.*), v. sing. & pl. 3rd pers. (So-&-so) designed this work (used with artist's signature). [L, perf. of *invenio*, see foll.]

invent', v.t. Devise, originate, (new method, instrument, etc.); fabricate (false story etc.). Hence or cogn. **inven'tIVE** a., **inven'tIVEly²** adv., **inven'tiveNESS**, **inven'tor²**, (esp. in Law, patentee of INVENTION), **inven'tRESS¹**, nn. [f. L IN¹(*venire vent-* come) find, contrive]

inven'tion, n. Inventing; thing invented, contrivance, (Law) any new manufacture the subject of letters patent; fictitious story; inventiveness; *I~ of the Cross*, (festival, May 3, commemorating) finding of the Cross by Helena mother of Constantine, A.D. 326. [OF, f. L *inventionem* (as prec., see -ION)]

inven'tory, n., & v.t. **1.** Detailed list (of goods, furniture, etc.); stock of goods in this. **2.** v.t. Enter (goods etc.) in ~, make ~ of. [(vb f. n.) f. med. L *inventorium* (as INVENT, see -ORY)]

inverā'city, n. Untruthfulness. [IN-²]

Invernesś (-ř), n. Town in Scotland; ~ *cloak, coat*, or ~, as n., man's sleeveless cloak with removable cape.

inverse' (or in-²), a. & n. **1.** Inverted in position, order, or relations; ~ *ratio, proportion*, (between two quantities one of which increases in proportion as the other decreases). **2.** n. Inverted state, thing that is the direct opposite (*of* another). Hence **inverse'LY²** (-sl-) adv. [f. L as INVERT]

inver'sion (-shn), n. Turning upside down; reversal of position, order, or relation, esp. (Gram.) of order of words; reversal of a ratio; (Mus.) process or result of inverting (see foll.). So **inverś-IVE** a. [f. L *inversio* (as foll., see -ION)]

invert', v.t. Turn upside down (~*ed commas*, those above the line before & after quotations, the first single or double comma being ~*ed*, as *what is a 'German peace' or "German peace"?*): reverse position, order, or relation, of; (Mus.) change relative position of notes of (chord, interval) by placing lowest note higher. [f. L IN¹(*vertere vers-* turn)]

in'vert², n. Inverted arch, as at bottom of sewer; (Psych.) person whose sex instincts are inverted. [f. prec.]

inver'tebrate, a. & n. **1.** Not having backbone or spinal column; (fig.) wanting in firmness. **2.** n. ~ animal or (fig.) person. [f. IN-²+L *vertebra* joint of spine + -ATE²]

invest', v.t. & i. **1.** Clothe (person etc. *in, with*); cover as garment; clothe, endue, (person etc. *with* qualities, insignia of office, rank, etc.). **2.** Lay siege to. **3.** Employ (money *in* stocks etc.); (intr.) ~ *in*, put money into (stocks), (colloq.) lay out money on, as ~ *in a bun*. Hence **invés'tor²** n. [f. L IN¹(*vestire* clothe)]

inves'tigāte, v.t. Examine, inquire into. Hence or cogn. ~A'TION, ~ātoR² nn., ~ātIVE, ~ātORY, aa. [f. L IN¹(*vestigare* track), see -ATE³]

inves'titure, n. Formal investing of person (*with* office); enduring (*with* attributes). [f. med. L *investitura* (as INVEST, see -URE)]

invest'ment, n. Investing of money; money invested; property in which money is invested; investiture; clothing; (Mil.) act of besieging, blockade. [-MENT]

invet'erᵃte, a. Long-established; (of disease, habit, prejudice, etc.) deep-rooted, obstinate. Hence ~ACY n., ~atelY² (-tl-) adv. [f. L IN¹(*veterare* make old f. *vetus -eris* old), see -ATE²]

invid'ious, a. (Of conduct etc.) giving offence, esp. by real or seeming injustice etc.; (of thing) likely to excite ill feeling against the possessor. Hence ~LY² adv., ~NESS n. [f. L *invidiosus* (*invidia* ENVY, see -OUS)]

invig'illāte, v.i. || Watch over students at examination. Hence ~A'TION, ~ātoR², nn. [f. L IN¹(*vigilare* watch), -ATE³]

invig'orāte, v.t. Make vigorous; animate. Hence ~atIVE a., ~ātoR² n. [f. IN-¹+L *vigor* VIGOUR +-ATE³]

invin'c|ible, a. Unconquerable (lit. & fig.). Hence ~IBIL'ITY n., ~ibly² adv. [F., f. L IN²+vincibilis f. vincere conquer, -BLE]

invi'olable, a. Not to be violated; (of laws, persons, places, etc.) to be kept sacred from infraction, profanation, etc. Hence ~ABIL'ITY n., ~ably² adv. [f. L IN²violabilis, as foll., see -BLE]

invi'olate, a. (Of laws, places, etc.) not violated; unbroken; unprofaned. Hence invi'olacy, ~NESS, nn., ~ly² adv. [f. L IN²violatus p.p. as VIOLATE]

invis'ible (-z-), a. & n. That cannot be seen; not to be seen at particular time, as when I called she was ~; ~le exports, shipping services, foreign investments, & other items that account for the apparent excess of a country's imports over exports; ~le ink (visible only after heating etc.); (n.) the ~le, the unseen world, God. Hence or cogn. invisibil'ity, ~NESS, nn., ~ly² adv., (-z-). [F., f. L IN²visibilis VISIBLE]

invite', v.t. & n. 1. Request courteously (to come (to dinner, to one's house, etc.); request courteously (to do what is presumably agreeable); solicit courteously (suggestions, opinion, confidence); bring on, tend to bring on, (thing) unintentionally; (of thing) present inducements, attract, whence ~ingly² adv., ~'ingNESS n. 2. n. (colloq.) Invitation. So invi'tATION n., ~'atory a. [n.f.vb] f. F inviter f. L invitare]

invoca'tion, n. Invoking, calling upon God etc. in prayer; the ~ (esp.) the words 'In the name of the Father' etc. as used by preacher before sermon (cf. ASCRIPTION); appeal to Muse for inspiration or assistance in poem. So invoc'atory (or in'vokā-) a. [OF, f. L invocationem (as INVOKE, see -ATION)]

in'voice, n. & v.t. 1. List of goods shipped or sent, with prices & charges. 2. v.t. Make an ~ of (goods). [vb f.n.; orig. invoyes pl. of invey as ENVOY¹]

invoke', v.t. Call on (God etc.) in prayer or as witness; summon (spirit) by charms; ask earnestly for (vengeance, help, etc.). [f. F invoquer f. L IN²voco (voco call)]

in'volucre (-lōōker), n. Covering, envelope, (esp. Anat.); (Bot.) whorl of bracts surrounding inflorescence. [F, f. L involucrum (as INVOLVE)]

invōl'untar|y, a. Done without exercise of the will, unintentional. Hence ~iLY² adv., ~iNESS n. [f. L IN²voluntarius VOLUNTARY]

in'volute (-lōōt), a. & n. 1. Involved, intricate; curled spirally; (Bot.) rolled inwards at edges. 2. n. (geom.). Locus of point in a straight line that rolls without sliding on a curve in the plane of that curve (cf. EVOLUTE). [as INVOLVE]

invōlu'tion (-lōō-), n. Involving; entanglement; intricacy; curling inwards; part so curled; (Math.) raising of quantity to any power. [f. L involutio (as foll., see -TION)]

invōlve', v.t. Wrap (thing in another); wind spirally; entangle (person, thing, in difficulties, mystery, etc.); implicate (person in charge, crime); include (in); imply, entail; (p.p.) complicated in thought or form (an ~d sentence). Hence ~MENT n. [f. L involvo (volvo roll)]

invōlve'ment (-vm-), n. Involving; financial embarrassment; complicated affair. [-MENT]

invul'nerable, a. That cannot be wounded or hurt, (esp. fig.). Hence ~ABIL'ITY n., ~ably² adv. [f. L IN²nerabilis VULNERABLE]

in'ward, a. & n. 1. Situated within; mental, spiritual; directed towards the inside. 2. n. pl. Entrails, etc. [OE innweard (innan in adv., see -WARD)]

in'ward(s) (-z), adv. (Of motion or position) towards the inside; within mind or soul. [prec.]

in'wardly², adv. On the inside; (of speaking) not aloud; in mind or spirit. [-LY²]

in'wardness, n. Inner nature, essence; quality of being inward; spirituality. [-NESS]

inweave', en-, v.t. Weave in (thing with another, into another, lit. & fig.). [IN-¹]

inwrought (inrawt', before noun in-¹), a. (Of fabric) decorated (with pattern); (of pattern) wrought (in, on, fabric); (fig.) intimately blended (with). [IN-¹+wrought p.p. of WORK]

i'odine, n. Non-metallic element resembling chlorine & bromine in chemical properties, used in medicine & photography. Hence iŏd'ic a., ~IDE n. [f. Gk iōdēs violet-like (ion violet, see -OID]

i'odoform (or ĭŏ-), n. Compound of iodine analogous to chloroform, used as antiseptic etc. [f. prec.+-o-, see CHLOROFORM]

i'olite, n. Silicate of aluminium, iron, & magnesium, of blue or violet colour. [f. Gk ion violet, see -LITE]

i'on, n. One of the electrically charged particles into which the atoms or molecules of certain chemicals (esp. salts, acids, & bases) are dissociated by solution in water, and which make such a solution a conductor of electricity; a similarly charged molecule of gas occurring e.g. in air. Hence ~IZE v.t., convert into ~s, ~iza'TION n. [Gk ion neut. part.]

-ion, suf. mainly thr. F -ion f. L -ionem (nom. -io) forming nouns of condition or action f. adji. & nn. (communio, f. vb

stems (*legio*), but esp. **f.** p.p. stems, producing the compd suffs. **-tion, -sion, -cion, -ation, -ation, -son.**

Ion'ian (i-), a. & n. **1.** Of Ionia; (Mus.) ~ *mode*: ancient Greek MODE; eleventh of eccl. modes, with C as final & G as dominant, corresp. to modern major key of C. **2. n.** Member of part of the Hellenic race which occupied Attica, western Asia Minor, etc. [f. L f. Gk *Iōnios* +-AN]

Ion'ic (i-), a. Of Ionia, as ~ *dialect*, that of which Attica was a development; ~ ORDER (characterized by two lateral volutes of the capital); (Pros.) *i-~ ā major e*, metrical foot --ˇˇ, *i-~ ā minor e*, ˇˇ--. [f. L f. Gk *Iōnikos*]

Ion'ium, n. Radioactive element obtained from uranium. [f. ION +-IUM]

Ion'osphere, n. = HEAVISIDE LAYER. [f. ION, -O-, SPHERE]

-ior¹, suf., later spelling of -IOUR, as in *warrior*.

-ior², suf. = L. *-ior* of comparatives, as in *senior, ulterior.*

iōt'a, n. Greek letter (I, ι,=I); atom, jot, (after *Matt.* v. 18). [Gk *iōta*]

iōt'acism, n. Excessive use of iota; pronunciation of other Greek vowels like iota (θ), of, ITACISM. [f. L f. Gk *iōtakismos*]

I O U (ī ō ū'), n. Signed document bearing these letters followed by specified sum, constituting formal acknowledgement of debt. [=I owe you]

-iour, suf.=-i- representing some formative or stem element **-our** -OR², as *saviour* f. *salvatorem* thr. OF *salve(d)or*, AF *sauveour.*

-ious, suf. repr. L *-iosus*, F *-ieux*, = -i-(part of another suf.)+-OUS, w. sense 'characterized by, full of'. L has *-iosus* (1) in adjj. f. derivative nn. in *-ia, -ies, -ius, -ium*, (*invidiosus, perniciosus, odiosus*, & by false anal. *curiosus* f. *cura*), (2) in adjj. f. nn. in *-ion-* (nom. *-io*), as *ambitiosus, captiosus, religiosus.* E tends to use *-ious* for any noun in *-ion* (*rebellious, cautious, contradictious*). E also forms adjj. in *-ious* by adding -OUS to stem of L adjj. in *-ius* (*various*); see also -ITIOUS & -OUS.

ipecacuan'ha (-na), n. Root of a S.-Amer. shrub, used as emetic & purgative. [Port., f. native *ipekaaguene*]

ip'se dix'it, n. Dogmatic statement resting on bare authority. [L,=he himself (the master) said it]

ipsiss'ima verb'a, n. pl. The precise words. [L]

ip'so fac'tō, adv. By that very fact. [L]

ir-¹,² (i-r), pref. =IN-¹,² before r.

ira'dé (-ah-), n. Written decree of Sultan of Turkey. [Turk., f. Arab. *iradah* will]

Irak', 'Iraq' (irahk'), n. Arab kingdom including Mesopotamia, formerly administered by British Empire as mandatary. So **Ira'ki, -qi,** (-ahki) a.

Irān'ian (i-), a. & n. **1.** Persian; (of languages) of the Asiatic family comprising Zend, Old Persian, & their modern descendants. **2. n.** Member of ~ race. [Pers. *irān* Persia, -IAN]

irās'cible (or ir-), a. Irritable, hot-tempered. Hence ~**ibil'ity** n. [F, f. L *irascibilis* (*irasci* grow angry, see -BLE]

īrāte' i, a. Angry. [f. L *īrātus* p.p. as prec.]

īre, n. (poet.). Anger. Hence ~**ful** a., ~**fully²** adv., (inf-). [OF, f. L *īra*]

īrēn'ic(al), aa. Aiming or aimed at peace. [f. Gk *eirēnikos* (*eirēnē* peace) +-AL]

irenicon. See EIRENICON.

īridā'ceous (-shus), a. Of the iris kind. [-ACEOUS]

irides'c|ent, a. Showing colours like those of rainbow; changing colour with position. Hence ~ENCE n. [as IRIS +-ESCENT]

īrid'ium, n. White metallic element of the platinum group. [as IRIS +-IUM]

īrid'ō'mine (or ir-), n. Native alloy or mixture of osmium & iridium, used in pointing gold pens. [IRID(IUM) + OSM-(IUM) +-INE²]

īr'is, n. **1.** Flat circular coloured membrane in aqueous humour of eye, with circular opening (PUPIL) in centre. **2.** Gems of plants, chiefly with tuberous roots, sword-shaped leaves, & showy flowers. **3.** Kind of rock-crystal reflecting prismatic colours. **4.** ~ *diaphragm* (Opt.), contractile diaphragm of thin overlapping plates for regulating the admission of light to a lens or lens system. [Gk *īris -idos* (goddess of) rainbow, iris]

Īr'ish (ī-), a. & n. **1.** Of Ireland; || ~ *bridge*, open stone drain carrying water across road; ~ BULL; ~ *Free State*, part of Ireland separated from the U.K. & established as a British Dominion 1922; ~ STEW. **2. n.** ~ language; (as pl.) the ~ (people); ~*man*, ~*woman*, native of Ireland. Hence ~**ism**(4) n., ~**ize**(3) v.t. [f. Ir- st. of OE *Iras* n. pl. +-ISH¹]

īrit'is, n. Inflammation of the iris. [-ITIS]

īrk, v.t. (arch.). Disgust, tire, bore, esp. *it ~s* (me, him, etc.). [ME *irken*, etym. dub.]

īrk'some, a. Tedious, tiresome. Hence ~**ly²**(-ml-) adv., ~NESS (-mn-) n. [-SOME]

īr'on¹ (ī'ern), n. & a. **1.** Metal largely used for tools etc. (*wrought ~, cast ~*, STEEL), often fig. as type of hardness, as *a man of ~, rod of ~*; preparation of ~ as tonic; tool made of ~; as curling, grappling, ~; branding tool; golf-club with ~ head; ~ tool for smoothing out linen etc.; (usu. pl.) fetters (esp. *in ~s*, handcuffed); (esp. in pl.) stirrup; (pl.) leg-supports to correct malformations etc.; *the ~ entered into his soul* (Ps. cv. 18, L mistranslation of Heb. 'his person entered into the iron', i.e. fetters); (Provv.) *strike while the ~ is hot* (at a good opportunity), *have (too) many ~s in the fire* (many undertakings. also,

many expedients). **2. adj.** Of ~ very robust, firm, unyielding, merciless. **3.** ~ *age*, age of cruelty, oppression, etc. (cf. BRAZEN¹), (also, cf. BRONZE, STONE, *age*) era of ~ implements; ~*bark*, species of eucalyptus with solid bark; ~*-bound*, bound with ~, (of coast) rock-bound, (fig.) rigorous, hard & fast; ~*-clad*, clad in plates of ~; ~ *I~ Cross*, Prussian and Austrian war decoration; ~ *curtain* (fig.), impenetrable veil of secrecy; *I~ Duke*, Duke of Wellington; ~*-grey* a. & n., (of) the colour of freshly broken ~; ~ *horse*, locomotive steam-engine, also, bicycle or tricycle; ~ *lung*, = case fitted over artificial respiration by means of mechanical pumps; ~*master*, manufacturer of ~; ~*-mould*, spot caused by ~-rust or ink-stain, (v.t. & i.) stain, be stained, with this; ~ *rations*, soldier's modicum of food to be touched only in emergency; *I~sides*, man of great bravery, esp. (pl.) Cromwell's troopers; ~*-stone*, name of various hard ~-ores; ~*-work*, work in ~, things made of ~; ~*-works* (sing. or pl.) place where ~ is smelted or ~ goods are made. [OE (1) *īsern, īsen*, n. & a., cf. Du. *ijzer*, G *eisen*, (2) OE *īren* n., not paralleled in other langg.]

iron² (ī'ern), v.t. Furnish, cover with iron; shackle with irons; smooth (linen etc.) with flat-iron etc. [f. prec.]

īron'ic(al), aa. Of, using, said in, addicted to, irony. Hence ~**ally²** adv. [f. L f. Gk *eirōnikos* (as IRONY¹, see -IC)]

ī'ronist, n. One who uses irony. [f. Gk *eirōn* dissembler + -IST]

||ir'onmonger (īrŭnmŭng-'), n. Dealer in ... Hence ~ERY(1, 2, 3) n.

ī'rony¹, n. Expression of one's meaning by language of opposite or different tendency, esp. simulated adoption of another's point of view for purpose of ridicule; ill-timed or perverse arrival of event or circumstance in itself desirable, due to the feigned good will & actual malice of (Fate, circumstance, etc.); use of language that has an inner meaning for a privileged audience & an outer meaning for the persons addressed or concerned (occas. including speaker, cf. TRAGIC ~); *Socratic* ~, simulation of ignorance as means of confuting adversary. [f. L f. Gk *eirōneia* simulated ignorance]

ī'rony², (īrŭ'n-y), a. Of, like, iron. [-Y²]

irra'diant, a. Shining brightly. So ~ANCE n. [as foll., see -ANT]

irra'diate, v.t. Shine upon; (fig.) throw light on (subject); make bright. (fig.) throw joy etc.). Hence ~IVE a., [f. L IR (*radiare*, f. *radius* RAY¹), see -ATE³]

irradia'tion, n. Shining, Illumination, (lit. & fig.); apparent extension of edges of illuminated object seen against dark ground. [f (as prec, see -ATION)]

irra'tional (-shon-), a. & n. **1.** Unreasonable, illogical, absurd; not endowed with reason; (Math., of roots etc.) not rational, not commensurate with the natural numbers (e.g. non-terminating decimal). **2. n.** ~ *number*, surd. Hence ~IrY (-shonăl'-), ~IZE(3) v.t., ~IY² adv. [f. L IR²(*rationālis* RATIONAL)]

irreclaim'able, a. Not to be reclaimed or reformed. Hence ~IY² adv. [IR²]

irrec'ognizable, a. Unrecognizable. [IR²]

irrec'oncilable, a. & n. **1.** Implacably hostile; (of ideas etc.) incompatible. **2. n.** Implacable opponent of political measure etc. Hence ~ABIL'IrY, ~ableNESS, nn., ~abIY² adv. [IR²]

irrecov'erable (-kŭv-), a. That cannot be recovered or remedied. Hence ~IY² adv. [IR²]

irrecus'able (-z-), a. That must be accepted. [f. LL IR²(*recūsābilis* f. *recūsāre* refuse, see -BLE)]

irredeem'able, a. (Of government annuities) not terminable by repayment; (of paper currency) for which issuing authority does not undertake to pay coin; irreclaimable, hopeless, whence ~IY² adv. [IR²]

irreden't|ist, n. (It. politics) advocate of recovery to Italy of all Italian-speaking districts; Greek, Pole, etc., of similar views. So ~ISM n. [f. It. *irredentista* f. (*Italia*) *irredenta* unredeemed (Italy)]

irredu'c|ible, a. That cannot be brought (to desired condition); that cannot be reduced, as ~*ible minimum*; that cannot be simplified. Hence ~ibIl'IrY n. [IR²]

irref'ragable, a. (Of statement, argument, person) indisputable, unanswerable. Hence ~IY² adv. [f. LL IR²(*refragābilis* f. *refragari*)]

irrefran'gible, a. Inviolable; (Opt.) incapable of being refracted. [IR²]

irrefu'table, a. Not to be refuted. Hence ~ABIL'IrY n., ~abIY² adv. [IR²(*refūtābilis* REFUTABLE)]

irreg'ular, a. & n. **1.** Not regular, contrary to rule; abnormal; not of symmetrical form; (of surface) uneven; disorderly; uneven in duration, order, etc.; (Gram., of part of speech) not normally inflected; (of troops) not in regular service. **2. n.** pl. ~ troops. Hence or cogn. ~IrY (-ăr'-) ..., ~IY² adv. [f. OF *irreguler* f. med.L IR²(*regulāris* REGULAR)]

irrel'ative, a. Unconnected, unrelated, (to); having no relations, absolute. Hence ~ANCE, ~ANCY, nn., ~antIY² adv. [IR²]

irrel'evant, a. Not to the point; that does not apply (to matter in hand). Hence ~ANCE, ~ANCY, nn., ~antIY² adv. [IR²]

irreli'gion (-jn), n. Hostility to, disregard of, religion. Hence or cogn. ~ionIST(2) ..., ~ioUS (-jus) a., ~iousIY² adv. [f. L IR²(*religiō* RELIGION)]

Irremed'iable, a. That cannot be remedied. Hence ~LY² adv. [f. L IR². (remediabilis REMEDIABLE)]

Irremiss'ible, a. Unpardonable; unalterably binding. Hence ~LY² adv. [f. F irrémissible f. L IR²(remissibilis, as REMIT, see -BLE)]

Irremo'v(i)able (-mōō-), a. That cannot be removed, esp. from office. Hence ~ABIL'-ITY n., ~ABLY² adv. [IR².]

Irrep'arable, a. (Of injury, loss, etc.) that cannot be rectified or made good. Hence ~leNESS n., ~LY² adv. [f. F irréparable f. L IR²(reparabilis REPARABLE)]

Irreplace'able (-sa-), a. Of which the loss cannot be supplied. [IR².]

Irrepress'ible, a. & n. Not to be repressed or restrained; (n., colloq.) ~le person. Hence ~LY² adv. [IR².², REPRESS, -IBLE]

Irreproach'|able, a. Free from blame, faultless. Hence ~ABIL'ITY n., ~ABLY² adv. [f. F IR²(irréprochable, as REPROACH v., see -ABLE]

Irresis'tible (-zis-), a. Too strong, convincing, charming, etc., to be resisted. Hence ~ABIL'ITY n., ~ibLY² adv. [f. LL IR²(resistibilis, as RESIST, see -BLE]

Irres'olute (-zolōōt), a. Undecided, hesitating; wanting in resolution. Hence or cogn. ~LY² adv., ~NESS, irrésolu'tion (-zolōō-), nn. [f. L IR²(resolutus RESOLUTE]

Irresol'vable (-zòl-), a. That cannot be resolved into parts; (of problem) that cannot be solved. [IR².²]

Irrespec'tive, a. ~ of, not taking into account, without reference to, (often quasi-adv., as the posts were filled ~ of nationality). Hence ~LY² adv. [IR².²]

Irrespon'sible, a. Not responsible for conduct; acting, done, without due sense of responsibility. Hence ~iBIL'ITY n., ~ibLY² adv. [IR².²]

Irrespon'sive, a. Not responsive (to). Hence ~NESS n. [IR².²]

Irreten'tion, n. Failure to retain (esp. the urine). [IR².²]

Irreten'tive, a. Not retentive. Hence ~NESS n. [IR².²]

Irretriev'|able, a. That cannot be retrieved. Hence ~ABIL'ITY n., ~ABLY² adv. [IR².²]

Irrev'erent, a. Wanting in reverence. Hence or cogn. ~ENCE n., ~ĕn'TIAL (-shl) a., ~entLY² adv. [f. L IR²(reverens REVERENT]

Irrevers'|ible, a. Unalterable; not reversible. Hence ~iBIL'ITY n., ~ibLY² adv. [IR².²]

Irrev'ocable, a. Unalterable; gone beyond recall. Hence ~ABIL'ITY n., ~ABLY² adv. [f. L IR²(revocabilis REVOCABLE)]

I'rrigate, v.t. (Of streams etc.) supply (land) with water; water (land) with channels etc.; (Med.) supply (wound etc.) with constant flow of liquid; (fig.) refresh as with moisture. Hence or cogn. ~ABLE, ~ATIVE, aa., ~A'TION, ~ātor²(1, 2), nn. [f. L IR²(rigare moisten), see -ATE³]

I'rritable, a. Quick to anger, touchy; (of organ etc.) very sensitive to contact etc.; (Physiol. of muscles & nerves) capable of being excited to vital action by physical stimulus. So ~ABIL'ITY n. [f. L irritabilis (as IRRITATE², see -BLE]

I'rritancy¹, n. Irritation, annoyance. [as IRRITANT, see -BLE]

I'rritancy², n. (law). Making, being, null & void. [as IRRITATE³, see -ANCY]

I'rritant, a. & n. 1. Causing (usu. physical) irritation. 2. n. ~ substance or agency (also fig.). [as foll., see -ANT]

I'rritate¹, v.t. Excite to anger, annoy, vex, (~ed at, by, with, against); whence ~ingLY² adv.; excite, produce uneasy sensation in (bodily organ etc.); (Physiol.) stimulate (organ) to vital action. Hence or cogn. irrita'tion n., ~IVE a. [f. L irritare, see -ATE³]

I'rritate², v.t. (law). Make null & void. [f. L irritare f. IR²(ritus=ratus established) invalid, see -ATE³]

Irrup'tion, n. Invasion; violent entry. [f. L IR²(ruptio f. IR²(rumpere rupt- break), see -ION]

Irv'ingite (ûrv-), n. Member of a religious body called by its members the Catholic Apostolic Church. [E. Irving, minister of Ch. of Scotland, d. 1834]

is. See BE.

Isabell'a, Is'abĕl, (iz-), a. & n. Greyish yellow. Hence Isabĕll'INE (-z-) a. [female name; history unknown]

isagō'gic, a. Introductory; (n. pl.) study of literary & external history of Bible. [f. L f. Gk eisagōgikos f. eisagōgē introduction (eis into + agōgē leading f. agō), see -IC]

Is'atin, n. (chem.) Crystalline reddish substance got from indigo by oxidation. [f. L f. Gk isatis woad + -IN]

ischiat'ic, -dic, (-k-), a. Of the hip, sciatic. [ff. med. L ischiaticus f. L f. Gk iskhiadikos f. iskhias -ados pain in hip (iskhion), see -IC]

-ise, suf. of nn. = OF -ise, prop. f. L -ītia, but also (in learned formations) f. L -īcia, -itia, -icium, -itium (OF justise, juise, servise, f. L justitia, judicium, servitium). In wds f. L, later F changed -ise to -ice, which E adopted; but in native wds F & E retain -ise (franchise, merchandise; E also has exercise, f. -ice).

-ish, suf. of adjj. = OE -isc of com.-Tent. orig. (cf. Dn. & G -isch), cogn. w. Gk -iskos dim. suf. of nn. In old formations, prec. vowel was modified, as still in English, French, Welsh. 1. OE chiefly formed aa. f. national names (British, Danish), with a few in sense 'belonging to, of the nature of' (heathenish, outlandish); later aa. have usu. not the neutral sense (boyish, girlish), but that of 'having

-ish[1] the bad qualities of' (*foppish, monkish, swinish, hellish*, &c.); names of things (*bookish, snappish, skendoffish, uppish*). 2. Sense peculiar to E is 'somewhat' (*selfish*). 3. Added to names of hours of the day or numbers of years to denote 'round about, somewhere near' (*eightish, fortyish*).

-ish[2], suf. of vb repr. F -iss- seen in some parts of some vbs in -ir (*perissant, finissais*), f. L inceptive suf. -isc- used in It. & F to form vbs without incep. sense to correspond to L vbs in -ire, -ére. In a few wds F -iss- became in E -ise (*chastise, advertise*), but in many others F -iss- endings have become -ish (ADMONISH, LAVISH, RELISH).

Ish'mael (-āl), n. Outcast, one at war with society. Hence ~ITE[1] n. [*Gen.* xvi. 12]

is'inglass (izingglahs), n. Whitish semitransparent substance, a form of gelatin, got from some fresh-water fish, esp. sturgeon, & used in making jellies, glue, etc. [perh. corrupt. of obs. Du. *huisenblas* sturgeon's bladder]

Is'lam (iz-; or -ahm'), n. Mohammedan faith; the Mohammedan world. Hence **Islam'ic**, ~ITE'ic, aa., ~ISM(3), ~ITE'(1), nn., (iz-). [Arab., = surrender, f. *aslama* he surrendered f. *salama* he became safe, whence also *salaam, Moslem, Mussulman*]

isl'and (ī-), n., & v.t. 1. Piece of land surrounded by water; (fig.) anything detached or isolated, surrounded by prairie, street REFUGE; (Naut.) ship's superstructure, bridge, etc.; (Physiol.) detached portion of tissue or group of cells. 2. v.t. Make into an ~, isolate: dot as with ~s. Hence ~ER[1](4) n. [vb f. n.) OE *īgland* (*īeg* isle, f. ON & OFris. *ey*+LAND); -s- by confus. w. *isle*]

isle (īl), n. Island (in prose form, only with proper name, as *Isle of Wight, British Isles*, & usu. of small islands). [ME & OF *isle* f. L *insula* island (IN-, see CONSUL)]

isl'et (īl-), n. Little island; isolated tract or spot. [f. F *islette* (as prec., see -ET2)]

-ism (izm) n. Any distinctive doctrine or practice. [foll. used as n.]

-ism, suf. forming abstract. nn.: (1) of action on vbs in -IZE, as *baptism*; (2) of typical conduct or condition on class nouns, as *heroism, barbarism*; (3) of system or principle on name of subject or founder or connected catchword, as *conservatism, Arianism, jingoism*; (4) of peculiarity in manner or language, as *Gallicism, archaism*; (5) of morbid condition induced by excessive use of drug, as *alcoholism*. [=F -isme f. L f. Gk -ismos or -isma f. -izō -IZE]

iso- in comb. =Gk *isos* equal, as: **is'obār** n., **~bār'ic** a., (line on map) connecting places at which barometric pressure is the same; (at given time or on the average); **is'o**-**chein** (-kīm) n., **~cheim'al**, **~chim'enal**, (-k-), aa., & nn., (line on map) places of same mean winter temperature; **~chromat'ic**, of same colour; **~chromous** (-ōk-), occupying equal time, vibrating uniformly, as pendulum; **~clĩn'al**, **~clĩn'ic**, showing equalmagneticinclination (~clĩnic lines, lines joining, on a map or chart, points at which the magnetic dip is the same); **~cracy** (-ŏk-) n., **~crăt'ic** a., (polity) in which all have equal political power; **~dynam'ic**, indicating equal magnetic force; **~gĕ'othĕrm**, line connecting points in interior of earth having same temperature; **~gon'ic**, indicating equal angles (of magnetic variation); **~mĕt'ric**, composed of same elements in same proportions, & having same molecular weight, but differently grouped; **~met'ric(al)**, of equal measure; **~mŏrph'ism**, **~mŏrph'ous**, (property of) crystallizing in same or closely related geometric forms; **~nomy** (-ŏn-), equality of political rights; **~perimĕt'rical**, having equal perimeters; **~seis'mal**(-sīz-),connecting places at which earthquake-shock is of same intensity; **~therald** (-bk-) a. & n., (line) connecting places of same mean summer temperature; **~thĕrm'al** a. & n. (line) connecting places of same mean annual temperature.

is'olate, v.t. Place apart or alone; (Chem.) free (substance) from its combinations; (Electr.) =INSULATE; subject (person etc.) to quarantine. Hence ~OR[1](2) n. [orig. in p.p., f. F *isolé* f. It. *isolato* f. L INSULATE]

isola'tion, n. Isolating or being isolated; ~ *hospital* or *ward* (for patients with infectious diseases). Hence ~ISM(3) n., policy of holding aloof from affairs of other countries, ~IST n., advocate of this policy (also attrib.), [prec., -ATION]

-ison, suf. of nn., f. OF -aison, -eison, -ison, f. L -ationem, -etionem, -itionem; later formations took -ATION, -ITION. For exx. see -SON.

is'opŏd, n. Crustacean with seven pairs of equal & similarly placed thoracic legs. [ISO-+Gk *pous podos* foot]

isos'celes (-selēz), a. (Of triangle) having two sides equal. [LL, f. Gk *isoskelēs* f. *skelos* leg]

is'otope, n. One of two or more forms of an element differing from each other in weight of atoms. Hence **isotŏp'ic** a., **isotŏp'y** n. [f. ISO-+Gk *topos* place]

Is'raĕl (iz-), n. The Jewish people, whence ~ITE[1](1) n., ~ISH[1] a.; (fig.) God's elect, [L, f. Gk *Israēl* f. Heb. *yisrael* striver with God (*Gen.* xxxii. 28)]

iss'ue, n. 1. Outgoing; outflow; termination (of matter etc.); discharge of blood etc, incision to procure this. 2. Way out, outlet; mouth of river. 3. Progeny, children, as *without male* ~. 4. Result, outcome; *in the* ~, as things turn out.

5. Point in question, esp. (Law) between contending parties in action, as ~ *of fact* (when fact is denied), ~ *of law* (when application of the law is contested). **6.** *At* ~, (of persons) at variance, (of things) in dispute; *join* ~, proceed to argue (*with* person *on* point agreed upon as basis of dispute); (Law) submit an ~ jointly for decision, (of one party) accept the ~ tendered by the other. **7.** Giving out, issuing, (of bills of exchange, notes, stamps, etc.); number of coins, notes, copies of newspaper, etc., issued at one time. Hence ~LESS (-ŭl-) a. [OF, f. pop. L *exīta=L exĭtus -ūs f. EX(ĭre it- go), whence OF issĭr]

iss'ūe², v.i. & t. Go or come out (often *out, forth*); emerge from a condition; be derived, spring, (*from*); result (*from*); end, result, (*in*); come out, be published; send forth; publish, put into circulation, (notes, newspaper), whence **iss'ŪABLE** a., **iss'ŪANCE** n.; (Mil.) supply (soldier) *with* article of equipment. [f. prec.]

-ist, suf. forming personal, nn.: (1) of agent, corresp. to Gk vbs in -izō or possible E vbs in -IZE, as *antagonist, plagiarist*; (2) of adherent of creed etc. in -ISM, as *atheist, ventriloquist, Darwinist, fatalist*; (3) of one concerned with any subject (apart from -ism, -ize), as *dentist, tobacconist, balloonist*, esp. as player of musical instrument (*violinist*). [=F -iste, It. & Sp. -ista, f. L -ista f. Gk -istēs (izō -IZE + -tēs agent-suf.); *tobacconist, accompanist* are formed irreg.]

-ister, suf. of nn., f. OF -istre, by-form of -iste -IST, perh. by false anal. f. *ministre* (L *minister*) etc.: in E prob. associated with -ER¹. Exx.: *chorister, palmister, sophister*.

isth'mus (or is'mus), n. (pl. ~uses). Neck of land; (Anat., Bot.) narrow part connecting two larger parts. Hence ~IAN a. [L, f. Gk *isthmos*]

is'tle (-tlĭ), n. Fibre used for cord, nets, etc., got from species of agave etc. [f. Mex. *ĭxtli*]

it¹, pron. (poss. *its*; pl. *they*, obj. *them*, poss. *their*). **1.** The thing in question; the person in question, as *who is* it (that knocks)?, *it* (the person that knocks) *is I*, (arch. poet.) *it* (what occupies my mind) *is the miller's daughter, & she is grown so dear*, (nursery sympathetic) *has* it *lost its rattle then?* (have you, your). **2.** (As subject of impers. vb) *it rains, it is cold*; *it* (the season) *is winter, it* (the day) *is Ash Wednesday, it is Ash Wednesday today, it* (the distance) *is 6 miles to Oxford*; *it says in the Bible* (the Bible says) *that all men are liars*; *I would go if it were not* (would go but) *for the expense*. **3.** (As subject, anticipating deferred virtual subject in more or less conscious apposition) *it is absurd talking* (or *to talk*) *like that, it is incredible that he should refuse, it is a dirty business,*

this meat-canning. **4.** (Anticipating deferred subject introduced by *that* conj., separated from *it* by adv. predicate) *it is seldom that he fails, it is in vain that you quibble, it is to him that you must apply.* **5.** (As antecedent to relative of either number & any gender, separated by predicate) *it was a purse that he dropped, it was the Russians that began it.* **6.** (As indef. obj. w. trans. or intr. vb) *face it out, carry it with a high hand, deuce take it, run for it, lord it over him, cab it* (go habitually or on the particular occasion in cab), *give it him* (hot), *have done it* (blundered). **7.** The ne plus ultra (colloq.; *for barefaced lying you really are it*). **8.** Sex appeal (colloq.). [OE hit nom. & acc. f. (orig. demonstr.) stem hĭ- (nom. masc. HE); OE gen. his, dat. him; OE hit corresponds to Du. het & its equivalent in Goth. hĭta this]

|| **it²**, n. (colloq.). Short for Italian vermouth (in *gin & ~*). [abbr.]

it'acism (ē-), n. Pronunciation of Greek ē like English ē, cf. ETACISM; substitution in MS. of Greek iota for other vowels. [f. Gk *ēta* the letter ē, spelt *ĭta* to indicate the pronunc. (ēta)]

Ital'ian (ĭtăl'yan), a. & n. **1.** Of Italy; ~ *cloth*, satin-faced linen cloth for linings; ~ *handwriting*, that now current in Britain, France, etc., opp. to Gothic; ~ *iron* (cylindrical, with rounded end, for crimping lace etc.); || ~ *warehouse(man)*, for supply of ~ groceries, fruits, olive oil, etc. **2.** n. Language, native, of Italy. Hence ~ISM(2, 4) n., ~IZE(3) v.t. & i. [f. L *Italianus* (Italia Italy, see -AN)]

ital'ic, a. & n. **1.** (I~) of ancient Italy, as apart from Rome; ~ *type*, sloping type introduced by Aldus Manutius of Venice (c. 1500). **2.** n. pl. Letters thus sloping, now used for emphasis or distinction, e.g. to indicate foreign word (cf. ROMAN). [f. L f. Gk *Italikos* (Italia Italy, see -IC)]

ital'icize, v.t. Print (words) in italics, usu. for emphasis or distinction. [-IZE]

Ital'iot (i-), **-ōte**, n. & a. (Inhabitant) of ancient-Greek colonies in S. Italy. [f. Gk *Italiōtēs* (Italia Italy, see -OT²)]

itch, n. **1.** Contagious skin-disease accompanied by this & caused by the ~-*mite*, which burrows in the skin; restless desire, hankering, (*for* thing, *to* do). Hence ~INESS n., ~Y² a. [OE *gicce*, as foll.]

itch¹, v.i. Feel irritation in skin; *scratch where it ~es* (where there is an ~*ing*); (of person or his fingers) crave uneasily (*for* thing, *to* do). [OE *gicc(e)an*, cf. Du. *jeuken*, G *jucken*]

-ite¹, suf. of adj. & nn. =F -ite f. L -īta f. Gk -itēs (also used in E, as *pyrites*), w. sense ' (one) belonging to or connected with '; (1) in names of persons, in mod. formation often derog. (*Stagirite, Sybarite,*

-ite¹, ... Parnellite, Shelleyite, Pre-raphaelite); (2) in names of fossil organisms (ammonite, belemnite; of mineral species, often superseding -ine, -in, etc. (anthracite, haematite, graphite, dynamite); of constituent parts of body or organ (somite, cerite, segment of body, of horn); of some saccharine substances, glucoses, etc. (dulcite, pinite); of explosives (cordite, dynamite); of commercial products (ebonite, vulcanite); of salts of acids denominated by aa. in -ous (nitrite, sulphite).

-ite², suf. formed in adjj. f. L p.p. in -ītus (erudite, composite) & similar vbl nn. (appetite), & in vbs formed on L p.p. stem in -īt- (expedite, unite); but vbs f. L p.p. st. in -īt- usu. end in -it (deposit, merit).

i'tem, n. & adv. 1. Article, unit, included in enumeration; entry of this in account etc.; detail of news etc. in newspaper etc.; hence *~ɪ(E)D v.t., state by ~s. 2. adv. Likewise, also, (introducing mention of he +-tem adv. suf.]

it'erate, v.t. Repeat (quoted words etc.); make (change, assertion, objection, etc.), repeatedly. Hence or cogn. ~ANCE, iterative (iterum again), see -ITE.]

-ites. See -ITE¹.

Ithu'riel's spear (i-), n. Infallible test of genuineness. [Milt. Par. Lost, iv. 810]

ithyphall'ic, a. & n. Of the phallus carried in Bacchic festivals; in the metre used for Bacchic hymns; (n.) poem in this metre, licentious poem. [f. LL f. Gk ithuphallikos (ithus straight+phallos PHALLUS, see -IC)]

itin'erant, a. Travelling from place to place; (of justices) travelling on circuit; (of Methodist ministry) removing from circuit to circuit. Hence ~ANCY, ~ncy nn. [as ITINERATE, see -ANT]

itin'erary, n. & a. Route; record of travel; guide-book; (adj.) of travelling, of roads. [f. LL itinerarius a., -um n. (also used in E), f. iter itineris journey, see -ARY¹]

itin'erate, v.i. Travel from place to place; (of Methodist minister) remove from circuit to circuit. Hence ~A'TION n. [f. L itinerari (as prec.), see -ATE¹]

-ition, suf. = -ION appended to L 3rd or 4th conj. p.p. stems (perdition, sortition), -itious¹, suf. of adjj. f. L -icius (+-ous (+-itious¹, suf. of c & t in LL MSS.), formed usu. on L p.p. stems (factitious); E wds in -icious, on the other hand, often repr. L stems with -iti- +-IOUS (suspicious) as well as those in -ic- +-IOUS (avaricious) as -itious², suf. (in appearance compd) in which -ious is appended to L stems in -it- (ambitious, nutritious, cf. suppositious, surreptitious), occas. also disguised as -icious (malicious).

-itis, suf. forming esp. names of inflammatory diseases (appendicitis, bronchitis, f. Gk -ītis adj., fem. of -ītēs, w. nosos disease understood.

-itous, suf. of adjj. = -ITY(+-OUS corresp. to L -itosus (calamitosus calamitous).

its, poss. a. See IT. [replaces HIS in 16th c.]

itself', pron. Emphatic & reflexive form corresp. to IT; by ~, automatically, apart from its surroundings; in ~, apart from its surroundings, viewed in its essential qualities etc. [IT+SELF, cf. its own self]

-ity. See -TY.

-ium, suf. forming names of elements, after sodium (soda), potassium (potass) aluminium is changed to -minum to conform to the type, but some later metals have names in -um, the L termination for metals.

-ive, suf. forming adjj. w. sense 'tending to, having the nature of', f. F -if (fem. -ive) f. L -īvus added to p.p. stem (activus, passivus), pres. stem (cadivus), or noun (tempestivus). Most E wds are of mod. formation, chiefly in -sive, -tive, & esp. -ative, which tends to become living suf. Some are formed instead, on vb stems (esp. in -s, -c, -t), as amusive, coercive. COSTIVE is not an ex.

i'vory, n. Hard white substance composing main part of tusks of elephant, hippopotamus, walrus, narwhal, & (fossil ~) mammoth; vegetable ~, hard albumen of seed of S.-Amer. palm (~ nut); black ~, African negro slaves; colour of ~; (al., pl.) dice, billiard-balls, piano-keys; (sl., sing. or pl.) teeth; (pl.) articles made of ~; ~ black, black pigment from calcined ~; ~ TOWER. [f. OE ifor f. L eboreus a. (ebur -oris)]

i'vy, n. Climbing evergreen shrub, with dark-green shining leaves, usu. five-angled; ~ geranium, ~-leaved pelargonium. Hence iv'iED² (-id) a. [OE īfig, etym. dub.]

Ixi'on, n. Genus of S.-Afr. iridaceous plants, with large showy flowers. [Gk]

Ixi'on's wheel (i-), n. (Gk Myth.) Wheel on which Ixion was condemned to revolve eternally in Hades.

iz'ard, n. Capriform antelope of Pyrenees, allied to chamois. [f. F isard, etym. dub.]

-ize, -ise, suf. of vbs (= F -iser f. L -izāre f. Gk -izō; in Gk either intr., as like ; as hellenizō, speak, act as a, Greek, or trans., as katharizō clean; Christian Gk vbs, as euangelizō evangelize, were first Latinized, & -izare so established as L for Gk vbs (cf. G -iren for Rom. vbs); F extended -iser to form vbs from names etc., whence the mod. use. -ize is the better spelling for all wds, mod. or f. Gk, that contain the Gk suf. Meanings: (1) intr., follow, have, such a way (catechize, tyrannize, sympathize); (3) t. & i., bring,

come, into such a state (*pulverize, anglicize, cicatrice*); (4) t. & i., act like, treat on system of, (*Calvinize, Bowdlerize*); (5) trans, impregnate etc. with (*oxidize*). Nn. are formed in *-izer, -ization*, as well as -IST, -ISM.

izz'ard, n. (arch.). The letter z (from *A to I~*). [var. of ZED]

izz'at, n. (Anglo-Ind. and Eastern). Honour, reputation, self-respect (occas. self-importance). [Arab.]

J

J, j, (jā), letter (pl. *Js, J's, J'e*), J (pen), broad-pointed pen stamped with J.

jā'al-goat (or yah), n. Wild goat of Sinai, Upper Egypt, etc. [f. Heb. *ya'ēl* wild goat]

jāb, v.t. (-bb-) & n. **1.** Poke roughly; stab; thrust (thing) abruptly (*into*). **2.** n. Abrupt blow with pointed thing or fist; (Mil.) supplementary bayonet thrust delivered without full withdrawal from previous one. [prob. imit.]

jabb'er, v.i. & t. & n. **1.** Speak volubly & with little sense; utter (words) rapidly & indistinctly; chatter, as monkeys etc. **2.** n. ~ing, gabble, gibberish. [(n. f. vb) prob. imit., with -ER⁵]

jab'iru (-ōō), n. Tropical American bird of stork family. [native]

jāborān'di, n. Dried leaflets of Brazilian plant with diuretic & sudorific properties. [f. native *jaburandi*]

jab'ot (zhàbō'), n. Ornamental frill on woman's bodice; (Hist.) frill on man's shirt-front. [F. etym. dub.]

jac'ana (-ah), n. Small tropical wading bird with disproportionately large straight claws, enabling it to walk on floating leaves. [corrupt. f. native name]

jac'inth, n. Reddish-orange gem, variety of zircon. [f. OF *iacinte*, as HYACINTH]

jack¹, n. (|| familiar form of name *John*, esp. as type of the common people, as *J~ & Gill; every man~,* every individual; = ~ tar; || labourer, man who does odd jobs, etc.; CHEAP *J~*; STEEPLE-~; (Cards) knave; machine for turning spit in roasting meat; machine for lifting heavy weights; (also *carriage-~*) machine for lifting axle off ground while cleaning wheel; BOOT⁻~; parts of various machines etc.; pike, esp. young or small one; (Bowls) ball for players to aim at; *J~ Frost,* frost personified; *before you could say J~ Robinson,* very quickly or suddenly; *J~-a-dandy,* dandy; ~ass, male ass, dolt, blockhead; *laughing-~ass,* Giant Kingfisher of Australia; ~boot, large boot coming above knee; ~daw, thievish small crow haunting church towers; *J~ in office,* fussy official; ~-*in-the-box,* toy figure that springs out of box when opened, (also) kind of firework; *J~-in-the-green,* man or boy enclosed in framework covered with leaves in May-day sports; *J~-Ketch,* common hangman; ~-knife, large clasp-knife for the pocket; *J~ of all trades,* one who can turn his hand to anything; ~-o'-lantern, will-o'-the-wisp (often fig.); ~-plane (for coarse work); ~-pot (Poker), accumulating pool that can only be opened by player holding two ~s or better; ~-pudding, buffoon, clown; ~-rafter, short rafter in hip-roof; ~-snipe (small species); ~-tar, common sailor; ~-towel (endless, hung from roller). [prob. conn. w. *John,* but perh. f. F *Jacques* James f. L f. Gk *Iakōbos* Jacob]

jack², v.t. Hoist with jack; ~ *up,* abandon (attempt etc., or abs.). [first sense t. prec.; for second cf. *chuck*]

jack³, n. Ship's flag, smaller than ensign, esp. one flown from ~-*staff* at bow, indicating nationality, as *British, French, ~*; single flag flown on foremast as signal for pilot (Brit. pilot's ~, union w. white border); UNION *J~*; ~-*staff*, (also) stick on which flag is bent that is to show above mast-head. [prob. = JACK¹]

jack⁴, n. (arch.). Foot-soldier's sleeveless tunic; (also *black~*) vessel for liquor, usu. of waxed leather coated with tar etc. [f. F *jaque,* etym. dub.]

jack⁵, n. E.-Ind. fruit, like bread-fruit but coarser. [f. Port. *jaca* f. Malayalam *chakka*]

jack'al (-awl), n., & v.i. (-ll-). Animal of dog kind, of size of fox, formerly supposed to hunt up lion's prey for him; (fig.) person who does preparatory drudgery etc.; (vb) act as ~ (*for*). [f. Turk. *chakal* f. Pers. *shaqal,* cogn. w. Skr. *s'ṛgāla*]

jack'anapes (-ps), n. || (Arch.) monkey; pert fellow; coxcomb; pert child. [earlier *Jack Napes,* first found of William de la Pole, Duke of Suffolk (d. 1450), whose badge was a clog & chain, such as was used for tame ape]

jack'aroo, n. (Austral. sl.). New chum, novice. [perh. portmanteau of *Jack* and *kangaroo*]

jack'et, n., & v.t. **1.** Sleeved outer garment for man or woman; NORFOLK, ETON, || DINNER, ~; *dust his ~,* beat him; outer covering round boiler etc. for protection, keeping in heat, etc.; paper wrapper, freq. coloured & artistically designed, in which a bound book is issued; animal's coat; *potatoes boiled in their ~s* (skins). **2.** v.t. Cover with ~. [(vb f. n.) f. OF *jaquet,* dim. as JACK¹]

Jāc'ob, n. ~'s *ladder,* plant with corymbs of blue or white flowers, & leaves suggesting ladder, (Naut.) rope ladder with wooden rungs, esp. one slung from a boom to the water; ~'s *staff,* surveyor's iron-shod rod used instead of tripod, (also) instrument for measuring distances & heights. [f. L f. Gk *Iakōbos* f. Heb. *ya'aqob*]

Jăcobē'an, a. Of the reign of James I; of St James the Less; (in furniture trade) of the colour of dark oak. [f. LL *Jaco-baeus* (*Jacobus* as prec., whence *James*), see -AN]

Jăcobin¹, n. Dominican friar [from convent near to church of S. Jacques]; member of extreme democratic club established in Paris in old ~ convent (1789), sympathizer with its principles, extreme radical; whence **Jăcobin'ĭc**(AL) aa., ~ISM(3) n., ~IZE(3) v.t. [F. f. med. L *Jacobīnus* (JACOB, -INE¹)]

jăcobin², n. Pigeon with reversed feathers on back of neck, suggesting cowl. [f. F *jacobine*, fem. as prec.]

Jăcobīte, n. Adherent of James II after his abdication, of his descendants. Hence ~ĭcAL a., ~ĭtĭsm(3) n. [f. L *Jacobus* James + -ITE¹]

jăc'onet, n. Cotton cloth of medium thickness, esp. dyed waterproofed kind for poulticing etc. [f. Hind. *Jagannāthī*]

Jăcquerie (zhäkĕrē'), n. peasantry, esp. that of 1357–8 in France. [F *Jacques* James, peasant, see -ERY]

jăctĭtā'tion, n. ∥(Law) ~ *of marriage*, offence of falsely claiming to be a person's wife or husband; (Med.) restless tossing of body in illness; twitching of limb or muscle. [f. med. L *jactitātio* f. L *jactitāre* toss, boast, (*jactre* *jact*-throw), see -ATION]

jāde¹, n., & v.t. Inferior, wearied, or worn-out horse; (in reprobation, usu. playful) woman; (v.t., esp. in p.p.) wear out with hard work. [?]

jāde², n. A silicate of lime & magnesia, a hard green, blue, or white stone, a variant of hornblende; (also ~'īte, pr. -īt) silicate of sodium & aluminium like this in appearance. [f. F *le jade* for *l'ejade* f. Sp. *(piedra de) ijada* (stone of) the colic, f. L *ilia* pl. flank]

j'adoube (zhädōōb'), phr. Expression used by a chess-player touching a piece he does not propose to move (= I adjust). [F]

Jaeg'er, n. (Used for) kind of woollen clothing-material from which vegetable fibres are excluded as unwholesome. [person ; P]

∥ Jăff'a, n. (Used for) kind of dessert orange. [~ in Palestine, the bibl. *Joppa*]

jăg¹, n. Sharp projection, e.g. point of rock. Hence ~gy²(-g-) a. [prob. imit.]

jăg², v.t. (-gg-). Cut, tear, in uneven manner; make indentations in, whence ~gedness n. [f. prec.]

jăg³, n. (dial). Drinking bout, [dial. = load for one horse, etym. dub.]

jăg'gery (-g-), n. Coarse brown Indian sugar made from palm-sap; other crude sugar. [f. Indo-Port. *jágara* (cf. Hind.)]

jăghir'(e)²(jăgir'), n. (India). Assignment by the State of a district & its revenue to an individual or body, with power to administer; tract so assigned. Hence ~'dār (-ērd-) n., holder of a ~e. [Pers. jā'dār holder]. [f. Pers. *jā place* + *gīr* holding]

Jăg'uar(-war, -ūer), n. Large carnivorous spotted quadruped of cat kind, in some wooded parts of America. [f. native *yaguara*]

Jah, n. Jehovah. [repr. Heb. *Y*ah shortened form of *Yahweh* JEHOVAH]

Jail etc. See GAOL etc.

Jain (jin), n. & a. (Member) of a non-Brahminical E.-Ind. sect, with doctrines like those of Buddhism. Hence ~ISM n. [f. Hind. f. Skr. *jaina* f. *ji* conquer]

jăl'ap, n. Purgative drug got esp. from tuberous roots of a Mexican climbing plant. [F, f. Sp. *jalapa* f. *Xalapa*, *Ja-*, Mexican city, f. Aztec *Xalapan* (*xalli* sand + *atl* water + *pan* upon)]

jălousie (zhäl'ōōzē), n. Blind, shutter, with slats sloping upwards from without. [F, as JEALOUSY]

jăm¹, v.t. & i. (-mm-), & n. 1. Squeeze (thing) between two surfaces; cause (part of machine) to be fixed so that it cannot work; squeeze (things) together in compact mass; thrust (thing) violently (*into space*); block, fill up, (passage etc.) by crowding into it; become tightly wedged; (Wireless) make (message, instrument) unintelligible by operating elsewhere. 2. n. Crush, squeeze, stoppage (of machine etc.) due to this; crowded mass; (sl.) fix, awkward position; ~-*stroke*, = PENDULUM stroke. [prob. imit.]

jăm², n. Conserve of fruit, made by boiling it with sugar to a thick consistency; (sl.) *real* ~, a real treat. [perh. f. prec.]

Jamai'ca, n. ~ (*rum*), rum made in ~. [sl.] *real* ~, a real treat. [perh. f. prec.]

jamb (jăm), n. Side post of doorway, window, etc., esp. (pl.) stone sides or cheeks of fireplace. [f. F *jambe* leg f. LL *gamba* hoof, perh. f. Celt. *camb*-crooked]

jămboree', n. (sl.). Celebration, merry-making; large rally of boy scouts. [U.-S.]

jăn'e(')īte, n. Admirer of Jane Austen's novels. [-ITE¹(1)]

jăngle (jăng'gl), v.i. & t., & n. (Make) harsh noise; cause (bell etc.) to do this; speak, utter, in discordant or noisy way; (arch.) dispute, wrangle, (n. & vb.) vb) f. OF *jangler*, etym. dub.]

jăn'itor, n. Doorkeeper. [L, f. *janua* door]

jăn'izarỹ, -nissarỹ, (jă-, yă-), n. (Hist.) one of body of Turkish infantry forming Sultan's guard (abolished in 1826); Turkish soldier; (fig.) personal instrument of tyranny. [ult. f. Turk. *yeñi-tsheri* (*yeñi* new + *tsheri* soldiery)]

jăn'ock, a. (dial., esp. Lancs. & Yorks.). Straightforward, honest, genuine. [?]

Jăn'senist, n. Member of party in Rom. Cath. Church holding with Cornelius Jansen (d. 1638) the perverseness & inability for good of the natural human will. So ~ISM n., ~ĭs'tic a. [-IST]

Jăn'uarỹ, n. (abbr. *Jan.*). First month of year. [f. L *Januarius (mensis* month) of JANUS, see -ARY[1]]

Jăn'us, n. Ancient Italian god, guardian of doors & gates, represented with faces on front & back of head. [L]

Jăp, a. & n. (colloq.). Japanese. [abbr.]

japăn'[1], n. 1. (J~) island group on east of Asia, whence **Japanese'** (-ēz) a. & n., **Japanesque'** (-ēsk) a. **2.** Hard varnish, esp. kind brought orig. from J~; work in Japanese style. [prob. f. Malay *Japung* f. Chin. *Jih-pun* sunrise (*jih* sun + *pun* origin)]

japăn'[2], v.t. (-nn-). Lacquer with japan; make black & glossy as with japan. [f. prec.]

jāpe, v.i., & n. (literary). Jest. [f. 14th c.; etym. dub.]

Jăphĕt'ic, a. Of, descended from, Japheth son of Noah; Indo-European. [-IC]

japŏn'ic, a. Japanese. [F *Japon* JAPAN. -IC]

japŏn'ica, n. Kinds of Japanese plant, esp. ornamental variety of pear or quince. [mod. L fem. adj. as prec.]

jăr'[1], n. Sound, vibration, esp. harsh one; thrill of nerves or feelings; shock; want of harmony, disagreement; quarrel. [asfoll.]

jăr'[2], v.i. & t. (-rr-). Sound discordantly, make grating impression (*upon* person, his ear, nerves, etc.); strike with grating sound (*upon, against,* object); (of body affected) vibrate, resound, discordantly (of opinion, statement, action) be at variance, disagree, (*with*); dispute, wrangle; cause (thing) to ~; send shock through (nerves). Hence ~r'ingLY[2] adv. [prob. imit.]

jăr'[3], n. Earthenware, stoneware, or glass vessel with or without handle(s), usu. cylindrical; LEYDEN ~. Hence ~'FUL(2) n. [f. F *jarre* f. Arab. *jarrah*]

jăr'[4], n. (colloq.). *On the, on a, on, ~, ajar.* [corrupt. of AJAR]

jardinière (zhă:dĭnyăr'), n. Ornamental pot or stand for display of growing flowers in room, on window-sill, etc. [F]

jŏrg'on[1], n. Unintelligible words, gibberish; barbarous or debased language; mode of speech full of unfamiliar terms, as *critics'* ~, *metaphysical* ~; twittering of birds. Hence ~IZE(2, 3) v.t. & L [OF, etym. dub.]

jărg'on[2], jărgŏŏn', n. Translucent, colourless, or smoky variety of zircon found in Ceylon. [F, perh. ult. f. ZIRCON: see that for ZIRC]

jărgŏnĕlle', n. Kind of pear that ripens early. [F, dim. of prec.]

jărl (y-), n. (hist.). Old Norse or Danish chief. [ON, orig. man of noble birth; = EARL]

jăr'rah, n. (Durable timber of) W. Austral. mahogany gum-tree. [f. native *jerryhyl*]

‖ **jăr'vey, n.** (pl. ~s). Hackney-coachman; driver of Irish car. [by-form of surname *Jarvis*]

‖ **jăs'ey, n.** (old sl.). Wig, esp. of worsted. [?]

jăs'min(e), jĕss'amin(e), n. Genus of shrubs with white or yellow salver-shaped flowers, esp. *common* or *white* ~, climbing shrub with fragrant flowers. [f. Arab. f. Pers. *yasmīn*; F has *jasmin, jessemin*]

jas'per (-ah-), n. Opaque variety of quartz, usu. red, yellow, or brown. [f. OF *jaspre* f. L f. Gk *iaspis*, of oriental orig.; ~ any bright chalcedony except carnelian; cf. Heb. *yashpeh*]

Jat (jaht), n. Member of a people widely distributed in N.W. India & varying in religion & occupation.

jaun'dice (jawn-, jah-), n., & v.t. **1.** Morbid state caused by obstruction of bile, & marked by yellowness of skin, fluids, & tissues, constipation, & loss of appetite; disordered vision (usu. fig.), as characteristic of this. **2. v.t.** Affect with ~; (fig. esp. in p.p.) affect (person, his judgement etc.) with envy or jealousy. [vb prob. back formation f. jaundiced[b] f. F *jaunice (jaune* yellow f. L *galbinus* f. *galbus*, -ICE)]

jaunt (jawn-, jah-), v.i., & n. (Take) excursion, journey, esp. for pleasure; *~ing-car,* light two-wheeled vehicle popular in Ireland. [?]

jaun'tỹ (jaw-, jah-), a., & n. **1.** Having or affecting easy sprightliness, airy self-satisfaction. **2.** n. (naut. sl.). Head of ship's police. Hence ~ILY[2] adv., ~INESS n. [earlier *jantee* f. F *gentil* GENTEEL]

Ja'van, Javanese' (-z), (jah-), aa. & nn. (Native) of Java; (-*ese*) language of central Java. [-AN, -ESE; the needless -*ese* prob. on false anal. of *Japanese*]

jăv'elin (-vl-), n. Light spear, dart. [f. F *javeline,* perh. f. Celt. orig.]

jaw, n., & v.i. & t. **1.** *Lower, upper,* ~, two bones or sets of bones forming framework of mouth & masticating apparatus in vertebrates; ~*bone,* each of the two bones forming lower ~ in most mammals, these two combined into one in others; (pl.) bones of mouth including teeth, mouth; (pl.) narrow mouth of valley, channel, etc.; (pl.) seizing members of machine, e.g. vice; (colloq.) loquacity, as *hold your* ~, stop talking, (also) sermonizing talk; lecture; ~*-breaker* (colloq.) word hard to pronounce. **2. vb.** (sl.). Speak

esp. at tedious length; lecture (person). [(vb.f.n.) perh. cogn. w. CHEW]

jay, n. Noisy chattering European bird of brilliant plumage; (fig.) impertinent chatterer; ~*-walker*, pedestrian who crosses, or walks in, a street or road without due care or regard for traffic regulations. [OF. perh. f. OHG *gâhi* quick]

jazz, n., a., & v.i. & t. 1. Music & dance of U.S. negro origin with characteristic harmony & ragtime rhythm; noisy or grotesque proceedings. 2. adj. Discordant, loud in colour etc., rude, burlesque; ~ *band* (of such combinations as piano, trumpet, saxophone, banjo, & drums). 3. vb. Play, dance, indulge in, ~ ; transform into, arrange as, ~. [?]

jea'lous (jěl), a. Solicitous for preservation of (rights etc.); apprehensive of being displaced in the love or good-will of (wife, husband, lover, friend; also of the supposed rival); envious (of person, his advantages, etc.); (Bibl.) (of God) intolerant of unfaithfulness; (of inquiry, supervision, etc.) suspiciously vigilant. Hence ~LY² adv. [f. OF *gelos* f. LL. *zelosus* (as ZEAL, see -OUS)]

jea'lousy (jěl-), n. Quality, state, of being jealous. [f. OF *gelosi* (as prec., see -Y)]

jean (jān or jēn), n. Twilled cotton cloth; (pl.) garment of this, short slacks. [prob. =ME *Gene* f. med. L *Janua* Genoa]

***jeep**, n. Small utility motor vehicle. [f. G P, pr. jē pē, initials of *general purposes*]

jeer¹, n. (naut.). (Usu. pl.) tackle for hoisting & lowering lower yards. [?]

jeer², v.i. & t., & n. 1. Scoff derisively (*at*); deride. 2. n. Gibe, taunt. [?]

jehad. See JIHAD.

Jehō'vah (-ǎ), n. Principal name of God in O.T. [repr. Heb. *yĕhāveh*, perh. f. *hāvāh* be, exist]

Jehō'vist, n. Author(s) of those parts of the Hexateuch in which God is called Jehovah (cf. ELOHIST). Hence **Jehōvis'tic** a. [-IST]

Jě'hu, n. (joc.). Furious driver; driver. [2 *Kings* ix. 20]

jějune', (-ōōn), a. Meagre, scanty; (of land) barren; unsatisfying to the mind. Hence ~LY² adv., ~NESS n. [f. L *jējunus* fasting]

Jěk'yll and Hýde, n. Single person in whom two personalities alternate. [*Dr J. & Mr H.*, by Stevenson]

jěll'ý, n., & v.i. & t. 1. Soft stiff semi-transparent food, consisting chiefly of gelatin, got from skin, bones, etc., by boiling & cooling; similar preparation of juice of fruit etc.; ~*-bag* (for straining nettle; ~*-fish*, pop. name of medusa or sea-); ||~*graph*, copying apparatus employing sheet of ~ in tray. 2. vb. (Cause to) set as ~, congeal. [(vb.f.n.) f F *gelée* frost f. L *gelata* (*gelare* freeze, see -Y)]

jēm'adár, n. Junior native officer of Indian army; Indian police-officer; head servant; (Anglo-Ind. colloq.) sweeper (domestic scavenger). [Urdu, f. Pers. *dār* holder]

||jěmm'ian as (-z), n. pl. (colloq.). Elastic-sided boots; goloshed cloth over-boots. [f. female personal name]

jěmm'ý², n. Crowbar used by burglars, usu. made in sections; ||sheep's head as a dish. [fam. form of *James*]

je ne sais quoi (zhenēsākwah'), n. An indescribable something. [F. = I know not what]

jěnn'ět, n. Small Spanish horse. [f. F *genet* f. Sp. *jinete* light horseman, etym. dub.]

jěnn'ěting, n. Kind of early apple. [prob. f. F *Jeannet* +-ING³]

jěnn'ý, n. Locomotive crane; = SPINNING ~ ; a stroke at billiards; ~ *wren*, (pop. & nursery name for) wren. [fam. form of *Janet*]

jěo'pardize (jěp-), v.t. Endanger. [foll., -IZE]

jěo'pardy (jěp-), n. Danger. [ME *iupardi* f. OF *iu* (or *ieu*) *parti* divided (i.e. even) game, f. L *jocus* game + *partitus* p.p. of *partīri*, divide f. *pars -rtis* part]

jěqui'rity, n. Indian twining shrub with parti-coloured seeds used for ornament & in medicine. [f. F *jequirity* f. native *jekirikti*]

jěrbō'a (or jěrbō), n. Small rodent of African deserts, with long hind legs & flesh of loins, jerboa]. [f. Arab. *yarbū*]

jěrěmī'ad, n. Lamentation, doleful complaint. [f. F *jérémiade* f. *Jérémie* f. L *Jeremias* Jeremiah, see -AD]

Jěrěmī'ah, n. Doleful prophet or denouncer of the times. [*Lamentations of ~*, O.T. bk]

Jě'richo (-kō), n. Town in Palestine; *go to ~* (to the devil).

jěrid' (-ēd), n. Javelin used by Persian, Turkish, & Arabian horsemen; game in which this is used. [f. Arab. *jarīd*]

jěrk¹, v.t. & i. Pull, thrust, twist, etc., with a jerk; throw with suddenly arrested motion; (intr.) move with a jerk. [as prec.]

jěrk², n. Sharp sudden pull, twist, etc.; involuntary spasmodic contraction of muscle; (pl.) spasmodic movements of limbs or face, esp. in religious excitement; PHYSICAL ~s. Hence ~ILY² adv., ~INESS n., ~Y² a. [prob. imit.]

jěrk³, v.t. Cure (esp. beef) by cutting in long slices & drying in sun. [f. Amer. Sp. *charquear* (*charqui* f. Peruv. *echarqui* dried flesh)]

jěr'kin, n. (hist.). Man's close-fitting jacket, often of leather. [?]

Jěrobō'am, n. Wine-bottle of 8-12 times ordinary size. ['A mighty man of valour']

' who made Israel to sin '—1 *Kings* xi. 28, xiv. 16]

jě'rry, n. ~-*builder*, -*building*, builder, building, of unsubstantial houses with bad materials; ~-*built*, so built; ‖ (also ~-*shop*) low beer-shop; ‖ (sl.) chamber-pot; (army sl., J~) German soldier, the Germans. [prob. fam. form of *Jeremiah*]

jerrymander. Erron. var. of GERRY-MANDER.

Jěrs'ey (-zǐ), n. (pl. ~s). **1.** (J~). One of the Channel Islands (often attrib.); J~ cow. **2.** Close-fitting woollen knitted tunic, esp. as worn in athletic exercises; similar garment worn as undervest; woman's close-fitting knitted jacket.

Jerus'alem (-rōō-), n. City in Palestine; ~ (*pony*, donkey; ~ ARTICHOKE.

jess'amine. See JASMINE.

jess'é, n. ~ *window* (with Christ's descent from ~ represented). [*Is.* xi. 1, *Matt.* i. 6, 16]

jěss, n., & v.t. Short strap of leather, silk, etc., round legs of hawk used in falconry. **2.** v.t. Put ~es on (hawk). [(vb f. n.) f. OF *ges* nom. of *get* f. L *jacius -ūs* throw f. *jacēre jact-*]

jest¹, n. Piece of raillery or banter; taunt, jeer; joke; fun, esp. *in* ~, not seriously; object of derision, as *a standing* ~; ~ *book*, book of ~s. [orig.=exploit, f. OF *geste* f. L *gesta*, neut. pl. p.p. of *gerere* do]

jest², v.i. Joke; jeer; speak, act, in trifling manner, whence ~'ing.ly² adv. [f. prec.]

jěs'ter, n. One who jests, esp. professed maker of amusement maintained in court or noble household. [-ER¹]

Jěs'ūit (-z-), n. Member of Society of Jesus, R.-C. order founded by Ignatius Loyola (1533); (fig., hist.) dissembling person, prevaricator; ~s² (Peruvian) bark. Hence Jěsūit'ICAL a., Jěsūit'icaLLY² adv., ~ISM²(2),~RY(4),nn.,~IZE(3) v.t. & i., (-z-). [f. mod. L *Jesuita* (*Jesus*, see -ITE¹)]

jět¹, n. & a. Hard black lignite taking brilliant polish; (of) colour of this, deep glossy black, (also ~-*black*). [f. OF *jaiet* f. L f. Gk *gagatēs*, acc. to Pliny f. *Gagae* town in Lycia]

jět², n. Stream of water, steam, gas, etc., shot forward or upwards esp. from small opening; spout, nozzle, for emitting water etc. thus; ~-*propelled*, (esp. of aircraft) deriving propulsive power from the backward thrust of high-velocity ~s of gas discharged through nozzles in the rear of the wings, fuselage, etc.; so *jet* attrib., as ~ *engine, plane.* [f. foll. & f. F *jet* as foll.]

jět³, v.t. & i.(-tt-). Spurt forth in jets. [f. F *jeter* throw f LL *jectare*=L *jactare* frequent. of *jacĕre jact-* throw]

jět'sam, n. Goods thrown overboard from ship to lighten it, & (in mod. use) washed ashore (cf. FLOTSAM). [=foll.]

jět'tison, n., & v.t. **1.** Throwing of goods overboard, esp. to lighten ship in distress. **2.** Throw (goods) overboard thus. [(vb f. n.) f. AF *getteson* (OF *getaison*) f. L *jactatio-nem jactare* throw, see JET³ & -ATION]

jětt'on, n. Counter with stamped or engraved device. [F *jeton* (*jeter*, see JET³)]

jětt'y¹, n. Mole running out to defend harbour or coast; landing-pier. [f. OF *jetee* (mole) thrown out, fem. p.p. as JET³]

jětt'y², a. Jet-black. [JET¹, -Y²]

jeu (see Ap.), n. (pl. ~x, pr. zhėr). ~ *de mots* (dėmō), play on words, pun; ~ *d'es-prit* (dėsprē), witty or humorous (usu. literary) trifle. [F]

jeune premier (zhŏrn prėmyā'), n. (Theatr.) juvenile lead. [F]

jeunesse dorée (see Ap.), n. The gilded youth, young swells. [F]

Jew¹ (jŏō), n. Person of Hebrew race (transf., colloq.) extortionate usurer, driver of hard bargains; *rich as a* ~; ~*baitering* ~, incredulous person; *tell that* (an unlikely tale) *to the* ~s; ~-*baiting*, persecution of ~s; ~'s-*ear*, edible cup-shaped fungus; ~'s-*harp*, small lyre-shaped musical instrument, played by holding frame between teeth & striking metal tongue. Hence ~'ESS¹ n., ~'ISH¹ a., (jŏō-). [f. OF *giu* f. L f. Gk *Ioudaios* f. Aramaic *y'hudai*=Heb. *y'hudi* f. *y'hudah* Judah]

Jew² (jŏō), v.t. (colloq.). Cheat, overreach. [prec.]

jew'el (jŏō-), n., & v.t. (-ll-). **1.** Ornament containing precious stone(s), worn for personal adornment; precious stone; highly prized person or thing; *the* ~*house*, room in Tower of London in which crown ~s are kept; hence or cogn.~JER¹, ~LERY(1), ~RY, nn., ~IY²a. **2.** v.t. Adorn, furnish, with ~s; fit (watch) with ~s for the pivot-holes. [(vb f. n.) f. AF *juel*=OF *joel*, perh. ult. f. L *gaudium* joy, or cogn. w. F *jeu* play f. L *jocus*]

jew'ing (jŏō-), n. Wattles at base of beak in some domestic pigeons. [*Jew* (from resemblance to hooked nose) + -ING¹]

Jewry (jŏŏr'ǐ), n. The Jews; (Hist.) Jews' quarter in town etc. [f. OF *juerie* (JEW, -ERY)]

jezail' (-zīl), n. Long Afghan musket. [Pers. *jazā'il*]

Jěz'ebel, n. Impudent or abandoned woman; woman who paints her face. [~, wife of Ahab]

jib¹, n. Triangular stay-sail from outer end of ~-*boom* to fore-topmast head in large ships, from bowsprit to masthead in smaller ones; *cut of his* ~, his personal appearance; ~-*boom*, spar run out from end of bowsprit; projecting arm of crane. [perh. abbr. of GIBBET]

jib², v.t. & i. (naut.; -bb-). Pull (sail, yard) round from one side of ship to the other; (intr., of sail etc.) swing round thus. [Da. has *gibbe* (hard *g*) in same sense]

jib³, v.t. (Of horse etc.) stop & refuse to go on, move backwards or sideways instead of going on, whence **~b'ER¹** n.; (fig.) refuse to proceed in some action; **~ at**, show repugnance to (course, person). [?]

jibb'ah(¹), **jib-** (or jūb-), **djĭ**, n. Mohammedan's long cloth coat. [Arab. (jŭ-)]

jib door (dōō), n. Door flush with wall in which it stands, usu. painted etc. so as to be indistinguishable. See GIBE.

jibe. See GIBE.

jiff(y), n. (colloq.). Very short time, as *in* a **~**, (*wait*) *half a* **~**. [?]

jig¹, n. Lively dance; music for this, usu. in three-four or six-eight time; appliance that holds a piece of work & guides the tools operating upon it. [etym. dub.; mod. F *gigue*, kind of fiddle; this, not F. OF *gigue*, is prob. f.]

jig², v.i. & t. (-gg-). Dance a jig; move(t, &c.) up & down rapidly & jerkily; separate coarser & finer portions of (ore) by shaking it under water in box with perforated bottom; **~saw**, machine fretsaw (**~saw puzzle**, picture pasted on board & cut in irregular pieces with **~saw**). [as prec.]

jigg'er¹(-g-), n. (Naut.) small tackle consisting of a double & single block with rope; small sail, small smack with this; (Billiards) rest for cue (sl.); (Golf) iron club with narrow face; one who jigs ore; **~mast**, aftermost mast in four-master. [partly f. prec.; +-ER¹]

jigg'er²(-g-), n. CHIGOE. [corrupt.]

jigg'er³(-g-), v.t. (only in pass.). (As substitute for a oath) *I'm* **~ed** etc. [?]

jigg'ery-pok'ery(-g-), n. (colloq.). Underhand scheming; hocus-pocus, humbug. [etym. dub., cf. Sc. *jouk* to dodge]

jig'gle, v.t. Rock or jerk lightly. [f. JIG² +-LE³]

jihad', **je-**, (-ahd), n. Religious war of Mohammedans against unbelievers; (fig.) crusade for or against a doctrine etc. [Arab. (ji-)]

Jill. See GILL⁴.

jilt, v.t. & n. 1. Woman who capriciously casts off lover after giving him encouragement; (rarely) man who treats woman thus. 2. v.t. Play the **~** towards, be faithless to. [vb f. n.) prob. f. obs. *gillot*, prob. dim. of name GILL]

*Jim Crow (-ō), n. Negro (**~ car**, to which Negroes are restricted on railroads); implement for straightening iron bars or rails by screw pressure. [nickname]

jim'iny, int. (arch.). = GEMINI.

jim-jams, n. pl. (sl.). Delirium tremens; fit of the creeps. [whimsical reduplication]

‖jimp, a. (Sc.). Slender, graceful; scanty. [?]

jingle (jing'gl), n. & v.i. & t. 1. Mingled noise like that of small bells, links of chain, etc.; repetition of same or similar sounds in words, esp. if designed to catch the attention; **~ing verse**; Irish & Australian covered two-wheeled car. 2. vb. Make, cause (keys etc.) to make, sound; **~s** (of writing) be full of alliterations, rhymes, etc. [imit.]

jing'o (-nggō), int., n. (pl. **~es**) & a. 1.(In asseveration) *by (the living)* **~!**; supporter of bellicose policy, blustering patriot (esp. supporter of Lord Beaconsfield's policy in 1878, f. use of *by* **~** in popular song). 2. adj. Vulgarly dashing. Hence **~ISM(2)**, **~ISM(2)**, nn., **~IS'TIC** a. [orig. conjurer's gibberish]

jink, v.i. & t., & n. 1. Move elusively, dodge, elude by dodging; (sl.) manoeuvre aircraft, be manoeuvred, jerkily to avoid anti-aircraft fire etc. 2. n. Act of **~ing**; *high* **~s**, boisterous sport, merrymaking. [orig. Sc.; prob. imit. of nimble motion]

jinnee', n. (pl. *jinn*, often used as sing.; fem. **~yeh** pr. -yǎ). (In Mohammedan demonology) spirit, lower than angels, able to appear in human & animal forms, & having supernatural power over men (also GENIE). [f. Arab. *jinnī*]

jinrik'sha, **-rik'isha**, n. Light two-wheeled hooded vehicle drawn by man or men, first used in Japan c. 1870. [Jap. (-kisha), f. *jin* man + *riki* power + *sha* vehicle]

*jinx, n. (sl.). Person or thing that brings bad luck. [?]

jīrg'a, n. Assembly of Afghan headmen. [Pushtu]

*jit'ney, n. (sl.). Five cents; motor-bus carrying passengers at low rates. [?]

jitt'er, v.i., & n. (sl., orig. U.S.). 1. Be nervous, act nervously; **~bug** n. person addicted to dancing to 'hot' music, nervous person. 2. n. pl. Extreme nervousness, 'nerves', (*have the* **~s**, be in a blue funk). Hence **~Y²** a. (sl.), nervy, jumpy. [?]

jiu-jitsu. See JU-JUTSU.

job¹, n. Piece of work, esp. one done for hire or profit; (colloq.) employment, post; transaction in which duty is sacrificed to private advantage; anything one has to do (*on the* **~**, sl., in action, alert); *do person's* **~**, ruin him; *bad* **~**, thing on which labour is wasted, failure; *good, bad,* **~** (state of affairs); **~ lot**, lot of goods bought as speculation; ‖**~master**, one who lets out horses & carriages by the **~**; **~~work**, done & paid for by the **~**. [?]

job², v.i. & t. (-bb-). Do jobs; ‖hire (horse, carriage) for definite time or job, let out on hire thus; buy & sell (stock, goods) as broker; deal in stocks; turn position of trust to private advantage; deal corruptly with (matter), whence **~b'ERY(4)** n. Hence **~b'ER¹** n. [f. prec.]

job³, v.t. & i. (-bb-), & n. 1. Prod, stab slightly; hurt (horse) with bit; (intr.) thrust at (thing). 2. n. Prod, thrust, jerk at bit. [prob. imit.]

Jŏb⁴, n. Patriarch whose story forms *Book of Job* in O.T. (*would try the patience of ~*, is vexatious); *~'s comforter*, one who under guise of comforter aggravates distress; *~'s tears*, seeds of a grass used as beads.

jŏbā'tion, n. (colloq.). Reprimand, esp. lengthy one. [f. obs. *jobe* reprove f. prec. +-ATION]

jŏbb'ernowl (-ōl), n. (colloq.). Stupid head; stupid person. [prob. f. obs. (& F) *jobard* fool (*jobe* silly) +NOLL]

Jŏck, n. (army sl.). Scottish esp. Highland] soldier. [=Jack]

jŏck'ey¹, n. (pl.~s). Professional rider in horse-races (also colloq. *jock*); *J~ Club*, club established at Newmarket, the body controlling horse-racing; ∥ lad, understrapper. Hence ~DOM, ~SHIP(3), nn. [f. Sc. *Jock* Jack +-Y³]

jŏck'ey², v.t. & i. Outwit, cheat; get (person etc.) *away, out, in*, etc., by trickery; cheat (person *into, out of, doing*) (intr.) cheat. [f. prec. in obs. sense 'cheat.']

jŏck'ō, n. (pl.~s). Chimpanzee. [F. made by Buffon f. Gaboon *engeco* (prop. *ncheko*)]

jŏcōse', a. Playful; waggish. Hence ~LY² adv., ~NESS, jocōs'ITY, nn. [f. L *jocosus* (*jocus* jest, see -OSE¹)]

jŏc'ular, a. Mirthful; humorous. Hence or cogn. ~ITY (-ă'r-) n., ~LY² adv. [f. L *jocularis* (*joculus* dim. of *jocus* jest, -AR³)]

jŏc'und, a. Merry, sprightly; pleasant. Hence or cogn. jocun'dITY n., ~LY² adv. [OF. f. LL *jocundus* f. L *jucundus* (*juvare* please), influenced by assoc. w. *jocus* jest]

jŏdhpurs' (jŏdpoorz), n. pl. Long breeches for riding etc., tight from knee to ankle. [*Jodhpur* in India]

∥ **Jŏe**, n. *Not for ~* (i.e. me)!, sl. refusal. [*Joseph Miller*, comedian, d. 1738]

jŏ'ey, n. (pl.~s). Young kangaroo; young animal. [f. native Austral. *joe*]

jŏg, v.t. & i. (-gg-), & n. 1. Shake with push or jerk; nudge (person), esp. to arouse attention; stimulate (person's, one's own, memory); move up & down with unsteady motion; proceed laboriously, trudge, (often *on, along*) go on one's way, depart, *as we must be ~ging*; proceed, get through the time, *as we must ~ on somehow*, *matters ~ along*; ~*'trot*, slow regular trot, (fig.) monotonous progression (often attrib.). 2. n. Shake, push, nudge, slow walk or trot. [prob. init.]

jŏg'gle¹, v.t. & i., & n. 1. Shake, move, (as) by repeated jerks. 2. n. Slight shake. [prob. f. prec. +-LE³]

jŏg'gle², n. & v.t. 1. Joint of two pieces of stone or timber, contrived to prevent their sliding on one another; notch in one of two pieces, projection in the other, or small piece let in between both, for this purpose. 2. v.t. Join by means of a ~. [(vb f.n.) perh. cogn. w. JAG]

Jŏhänn'ine, a. Of the apostle John. [f. L as JOHN, see -INE¹]

Jŏhänn'isbẽrger(-g-), n. Fine white wine from Johannisberg in the Rheingau. [G]

John (jŏn), n. Masculine Christian name; ~ BARLEYcorn; ~ *Bull*, English nation, typical Englishman; ~ *Chinaman*, typical Chinese; ~ COMPANY; ~ *Doe*, fictitious character in law; ~ DORY¹; ~*o'-Groat's* (*-House*), north of Scotland (*from ~'o-Groat's to Land's End*, through Gt Britain). [=OF *Jehan* f. L f. Gk *Iōannēs* f. Heb. *Yokhanan*]

John'ian (jŏn-), a. & n. (Member) of St John's College, Cambridge. [-IAN]

john'ny (jŏn-), n. ∥ Fellow, esp. fashionable idler; ∥ *J~ Armstrong* (naut. sl.), hand-power; *J~ Raw*, novice; ~*-cake*, cake of (U.S.) maize-meal or (Austral.) wheat-meal. [f. JOHN, -Y³]

Johnsōn'ian (jŏn-), a. Of, like, Samuel Johnson, man of letters & lexicographer (d. 1784), esp., abounding in Latin-derived polysyllables. So **Johnson**ESE' (jŏnsonēz') n. [-IAN]

joie de vivre (zhwah de vē'vr), n. Feeling of healthy enjoyment of life. [F. = joy of living]

join, v.t. & i., & n. 1. Put together, fasten, unite, (things, one *to* another); connect (two points) by straight line; unite (persons, one *with* or *to* another) in marriage, friendship, alliance, etc.; (intr.) come together, be united, (*with, to*, or abs.); take part with others (*in doing*); come into the company of (person); become member of (club etc.); take, resume, one's place in (regiment, ship, company, etc.); come into connexion with, *as the Cherwell ~s the Thames below Oxford*; ~ *battle*, begin fighting; ~*hands*, clasp one's hands together, clasp each other's hands, (fig.) combine in action or enterprise; ~ ISSUE¹; ~ *up* (intr.), enlist in the army. 2. n. Point, line, of junction. [(n. f. vb) f. OF *joindre* (st. *joign-*) f. L *jungere junctum*]

join'der, n. (rare exc. law). Joining, union. [f. F *joindre* JOIN taken as noun, cf. -ER⁴]

join'er, n. In vbl senses, esp. one who makes furniture, house fittings, & other woodwork lighter than carpenter's, whence ~ERY(1, 2) n. [f. OF *joigneor* (*joigner* JOIN)]

joint¹, n. Place at which two things are joined together; structure in animal body by which two bones are fitted together; *out of ~*, (of bone) dislocated, (fig.) out of order; *put* (person's) NOSE *out of ~*; part of stem from which leaf or branch grows; point at which, contrivance by which, two parts of artificial structure are joined, rigidly or so as to allow of movement; (Geol.) fissure in mass of rock; one of the parts of which a body is made up; ∥ one of the parts into which butcher

divides carcass, esp. as served at table; ~ (sl. esp. U.S.) a place of meeting or resort; ~stool (orig. made of parts fitted by a joiner. Hence ~'LESS a. [OF. p.p. as JOIN]

joint² a. Held or done by, belonging to, two or more persons etc. in conjunction; as ~ *action, opinion, estate*; (of persons sharing (*with* others in possession, action, state, etc.), as ~ *owners; during their* ~ *lives*, while they are all alive; ~ *stock*, capital divided into shares, common fund, (attrib.) holding, formed on basis of, a ~ stock, as ~*-stock bank, company.* Hence ~'LY² adv. [F. as prec.]

joint³, v.t. Connect by joints; fill up joints of (masonry etc.) with mortar etc.; prepare (board etc.) for being joined to another by planing its edge; divide (body, member) at a joint or into joints. [f. JOINT¹]

join'ter, n. In vbl senses, esp.: plane for jointing; mason's tool for pointing; workman employed in jointing esp. electric wire. [-ER¹]

join'tress, n. Widow who holds a join-ture. [f. obs. *jointer* + -ESS¹]

join'ture, n. & v.t. 1. Estate settled on a wife, to be enjoyed by her after her husband's death. 2. v.t. Provide (wife) with ~. [(vrb f. n.) F. f. L *junctura* (as JOIN, see -URE)]

joist, n. One of parallel timbers stretched on edge from wall to wall for ceiling laths or floor boards to be nailed to. Hence **jois'ted²** a. [f. OF. *giste* lie f. L *jacēre*]

joke¹, n. Thing said or done to excite laughter; witticism, jest; ridiculous circumstance; *practical* ~, trick played on person in order to have laugh at his expense; *it is no* ~ (a serious matter). Hence **jok'Y²** a. [f. 17th c., prob. f. L *jocus* jest]

joke², v.i. & t. Make jokes; poke fun at, banter. Hence **jok'ingLY²** adv. [f. prec.]

jok'er, n. One who jokes; (sl.) fellow, chap; (Cards) odd (often blank) card in some games, counting as (highest) trump.

jol'ly, n. Merrymaking, festivity. [f. OF *jolivete* (as JOLLY, see -TY]

jol'ly¹, a., adv., n., & v.t. 1. Joyful; slightly drunk; festive, jovial; (of god, Bacchus) (colloq., of person or thing) very pleasant, delightful, (often iron, as *he must be a* ~ *fool to do it*), whence **jol'liLY²** adv. 2. adv. (colloq.) Very, as *he will be* ~ *savage, you will* ~ *well have to.* 3. n. (sl.) ¶ Royal Marine. 4. v.t.

jokul, jökull, (yō'kŏŏl, yŏ-), n. Snow-mountain in Iceland. [Icel. (jö-), = icicle, glacier, dim. of *jaki* piece of ice]

jole, ... Make merry, esp. tipple?

joll'ify, v.i.& t. Hence ~FICA'TION n. [-FY]

joll'ity, n. ...

jör'um, n. Large drinking-bowl; its contents, esp. punch. [?]

jos'eph (-z-), n. (J~) chaste man; woman's long riding-cloak of 18th c. [see *Gen.* xxxix, xxxvii. 3]

*josh, n., & v.t. & i. (sl.). 1. Good-natured joke, leg-pull. 2. vb. Hoax, banter; indulge in ridicule. Hence ~ER¹ n. [?]

jos'kin, n. (sl.). Country bumpkin, dolt. [cf. dial. *joss* bump, -KIN]

joss, n. Chinese idol; ~*-house*, Chinese temple; ~*-stick* (of fragrant tinder mixed with clay, as incense). [prob. f. Port. *deos* f. L *deus* god]

||joss'er, n. (sl.). Fool; fellow. [?]

jo'stle (-sl), v.t. & i. & n. 1. Knock, push, *against*; struggle *with* (person *for* thing); push against, elbow; push (person *away*) *from*, etc.). 2. n. Jostling encounter. [(n. f. vb) earlier *justle*, f. *just* JOUST +-LE(3)]

jot¹, n. (Usu. w. negative expressed or implied) small amount, whit. [f. L f. Gk *iota* letter *i*]

jot², v.t. (-tt-). Write (usu. *down*) briefly or hastily. [prob. f. prec.]

joule (jōōl), n. (electr.). Unit of work or energy. [Dr. J. P. Joule, Eng. physicist (d. 1889)]

journal (jer-), n. 1. [in bookkeeping by double entry] book in which each transaction is entered, with statement of accounts to which it is to be debited & credited. 2. Daily record of events; (Parl.) *the* ~*s*, record of daily proceedings;

(colloq.). Flatter, cajole (usu. ~ *along*); chaff, banter. [ME & OF *jolif*) gay, etym. dub.]

joll'y-boat, n. (Also *jolly*) clinker-built ship's boat, smaller than cutter. [?]

jolt, v.t. & i., & n. 1. Shake (person etc.) with jerk from seat etc., esp. in locomotion; (of vehicle) move along with jerks, as on rough road. 2. n. Such jerk. Hence **jol'ty²** a. [?]

jol'terhead, [-hèd], n. Clumsy head; stupid person. [extension of obs. *jolt-head*, etym. dub.]

Jon'ah (-a), n. Person who brings, or is sacrificed lest he bring, ill luck. [see *Jonah*, O.T. book]

Jon'athan, n. 1. (*Brother*) ~, personified people of, typical citizen of, United States. 2. Kind of dessert apple. [pern. f. ~ *Trumbull*, governor of Connecticut]

jong'leur (see Ap.), n. (hist.). Itinerant minstrel. [F. var. of *jingleur* JUGGLER]

jonq'uil (or jü-), n. Species of narcissus, rush-leaved daffodil; ~ *colour*, pale yellow. [ult. dim. of L *juncus* rush; F]

jörd'an, n. (not in polite use). Chamber-pot. [?]

jörd'an alm'ond (ahm-), n. Fine almond from Malaga. [prob. f. F *jardin* garden]

(Naut.) log-book; daily newspaper, other periodical. 3. Part of shaft or axle that rests on bearings (hist. unexpl.); ~box (enclosing ~ & bearings). [OF as DIURNAL]

journ'alist (jĕr-), n. One whose business it is to edit or write for a public journal. Hence or cogn. ~ESE (-ēz) n., style of language characteristic of (hasty or inferior) newspaper writing, ~ISM n., ~IS'TIC a. [-IST]

journ'alize (jĕr-), v.t. & i. 1. (Bookk.) enter in journal; record in, keep, private journal. [-IZE]

journ'ey (jĕr-), n. (pl. ~s), & v.i. 1. Distance travelled in specified time, as a day's, 4 days'; expedition to some distance, round of travel (usu. by land, cf. VOYAGE), as take, undertake, perform, a ~; ~man, qualified mechanic or artisan who works for another; (fig.) mere hireling; (Astron.) ~man (clock), secondary clock in observatory; ~work, work of a ~man (esp. fig.). 2. v.i. Make a ~. [(vb f. ~ OF journée) n. OF jornee day, day's work or journey, f. pop. L diurnata (diurnus DIURNAL, see -ADE)]

joust (jŏŏst), jūst, v.i., & n. (Engage in) combat between two knights etc. on horseback with lances. [(n. f. OF jouste) t. OF juster f. pop. L juxtare approach (juxta near)]

Jōve, n. Jupiter, esp. || by ~! [f. L Jovem (nom. Jupiter)]

jō'vial, a. Merry; convivial. Hence or cogn. ~ITY (-ăl') n., ~LY² adv. [F, f. L Jovialis of Jupiter (Jupiter Jovis, see -AL)]
Jō'vian, a. Of, like, Jove; of the planet Jupiter.

jowl, n. Jawbone, jaw; cheek, esp. cheek by ~; external throat or neck when prominent, dewlap of cattle, crop of bird; head & shoulders of salmon & other fish. [(1) OE ceafl jaw; (2) ~ cf. Du. kevel gum; (2) the ME forms (1) jowle (2) cholle, both of unexplained development, were ult. confused]

joy, n. Vivid emotion of pleasure, gladness; thing that causes delight; ~-bells (rung on festive occasions); ~-ride (sl.), stolen or other pleasure-ride in motor etc.; ~stick (sl.), control lever of aeroplane. Hence or cogn. ~FUL, ~LESS, ~OUS, aa., ~fully², ~lessly², ~ously², adv., ~fulNESS, ~lessNESS, ~ousNESS, nn. [f. OF joie f. pop. L¹ gaudia fem.f.L gaudia pl. of gaudium]

joy², v.i. & t. (chiefly poet.). Rejoice; gladden. [f. OF joir rejoice ult. f. L gaudēre rejoice]

jub'ilate¹ (jōō-), v.i. Exult, make demonstrations of joy. Hence or cogn. ~ANCE, ~A'TION, nn., ~ANT a., ~antly² adv. [f. L jubilare (jubilum shout), see -ATE³]
Jubilat'e² (jōō- or yŏŏbilāt'i), n. Hundredth psalm as canticle in Anglican service; outburst of triumph. [L, = shout ye (its first word)]

jub'ilee (jōō-), n. 1. (Jewish Hist.) year of emancipation & restoration, kept every 50 years, acc. to Lev. xxv.; (R.-C. Ch.) year of remission from penal consequences of sin, granted formerly at various intervals, now at any time. 2. Fiftieth anniversary; silver ~, twenty-fifth anniversary; Diamond J~, sixtieth year of reign of Queen Victoria. 3. Season of rejoicing; exultant joy. [f. F jubilé f. LL jubilaeus year of jubilee f. Gk Iōbēlaios (iōbēlos f. Heb. yobel ram, ram's-horn trumpet, jubilee) by assoc. w. native L jubilum shout]

Juda'ic (jōō-), a. Jewish. [f. L f. Gk Ioudaikos (Ioudaios JEW, see -IC)]
Jud'aïze (jōō-), v.i. & t. Follow Jewish customs or rites; make Jewish. So ~ISM, ~IST, nn. [f. LL judaizare f. Gk ioudaizō (as prec., see -IZE)]

jud'as (jōō-), n. (J~) disciple who betrayed Christ, infamous traitor; peephole in door; (of beard etc.) J~-coloured), red; J~-kiss (see Matt. xxvi. 48); J~-tree (with purple flowers appearing before the leaves).

Jud'enhetze (yōōdenhĕtze), n. Systematic persecution of Jews. [G]

judge¹, n. Public officer appointed to hear & try causes in court of justice; (of God) supreme arbiter; (Heb. Hist.) officer having temporary authority in Israel in period between Joshua & the kings; (pl., abbr. Judg.) book of O.T.; person appointed to decide dispute or contest; person who decides a question; person who is qualified to decide on merits of thing or question, as am no ~ of that, good~ of claret; J~ Advocate General, civil officer in supreme control of courts martial; ~-made law, principles based on ~s' decisions. Hence~'SHIP(1, 2) n.[f.OF fuge f. L judicem (nom. -dex) f. jus right + -dicus speaking]

judge², v.t. & i. Pronounce sentence on (person) in court of justice; try (cause); decide (question); decide, decree, (that etc.); form opinion about, estimate, (person etc. by his deeds etc.); criticize, censure; conclude, consider, suppose, (thing to be, that, etc., from or by data); act as judge; form a judgement (of thing etc.). [f. OF jugier f. L judicare (as prec.)]

judgemat'ic(al) (-jm-), aa. (colloq.). Judicious, discerning. Hence~ally² adv. [f. JUDGE, on dogmatic etc.]

judge'ment (-jm-, -gment, n. Sentence of court of justice; the last ~ (by God at end of world); misfortune viewed as sign of divine displeasure, as it is a ~ on you for getting up late; criticism; opinion, estimate, as in my ~; critical faculty, discernment; good sense; ~-day (of God's final ~); ~ debt (for payment of which a ~ has been given); ~ creditor, debtor

(for, against, whom ~ has been given): ~ summons (for failure to pay ~ debt); ~seat, judge's seat, tribunal. [f. F juge-ment (as prec., see -MENT)]

judicature (jōō-; also -kū-), n. Adminis-tration of justice; Supreme Court of J~ in England (consisting of the Court of Appeal & the High Court of Justice; the latter is composed of the King's Bench, the Chancery, & the Probate, Divorce, & Admiralty divisions, & the Court of Criminal Appeal); judge's (term of) office; body of judges; court of justice. [f. med. L judicatura (as JUDGE, -URE)]

judicial (jōōdish'al), a. Of, done by, proper to, a court of law; ~ murder, legal but unjust death sentence; inflicted as a divine infatuation; (esp. ~ blindness, punitive infatuation), as a ~ assembly; of, proper to, a judge; expressing a judge-ment, critical; impartial. Hence ~ly² adv. [f. L judicialis (as foll., -AL)]

judiciary (jōōdish'ari), n. The judges of a State collectively. [f. L judiciarius (med. L -aria fem. as n.) of judgement (as JUDGE²), see foll.]

judicious (jōōdish'us), a. Sensible, pru-dent; sound in discernment. Hence ~ly² adv., ~NESS n. [f. F judicieux f. L L judicium (as JUDGE²), see -OUS]

jug¹, n. Deep vessel for holding liquids, with handle & often with spout, whence ~FUL(2) n.; (sl., also stone-~) prison. [?]

jug², v.t. (-gg-). Stew, boil, (hare, rabbit) in jug or jar (usu. in p.p.); (sl.) imprison. [f. prec.]

jug³, v.i. (-gg-). (Of nightingale or other bird) utter sound jug. So ~, ~~, nn. [imit.]

jug'ate (jōō-), a. (bot.). Having leaflets in pairs. [f. L jugare join (jugum yoke), see -ATE²]

Jugg'ernaut (-g-), n. (Hind. Myth.) Krishna, eighth avatar of Vishnu, his idol at Puri, annually dragged in proces-sion on huge car, under wheels of which devotees are said to have formerly thrown themselves; (fig., also ~ car) institution, notion, to which persons blindly sacrifice themselves or others. [f. Hind. Jagannāth f. Skr. Jagannātha (jagat world+nātha lord)]

jugg'ins (-ginz), n. (sl.). Simpleton. [?]

jug'gle, v.i. & t., & n. 1. Play conjuring tricks; ~with, deceive (person), misrepre-sent (facts); cheat (person etc. out of thing); bring, get, change, (away, into, etc.) by trickery. 2. n. Piece of juggling, fraud. [(n. f. vb) f. OF jogler f. LL jocu-lare (L -ri) jest (joculus dim. of jocus jest)]

jugg'ler, n. Conjurer; trickster, im-postor. So ~ERY(2, 4) n. [f. OF jogler, jogleour (whence var. JONGLEUR), f. L L joculatorem (as JUGGLE, see -OR²)]

Jugoslav (ūg'oslahv), a. & n. (Inhabitant) of the State, including Serbia, Monte-negro, & parts of the former Austrian Empire, called Jugoslavia. [Serb. = south Slav]

jug'ular (or jōō-), a. & n. 1. Of the neck or throat; ~ veins, great veins of neck, conveying blood (external ~) from super-ficial parts of head, (internal ~) from in-side of skull; (of fish) having the ventral fins in front of the pectoral. 2. n. ~ vein. [f. L jugulum collar-bone, see -AR¹]

jug'ulate (or jōō-), v.t. Kill, esp. (fig.) arrest course of (disease etc.) by powerful remedy etc. [f. L jugulare (as prec.), see -ATE³]

juice (jōōs), n. Liquid part of vegetables or fruits; fluid part of animal body or sub-stance, esp. the ~s, the bodily humours, gastric ~; (fig.) essence, spirit, of any-thing; (sl.) petrol or electricity used in engine etc. Hence ~LESS (-sl-) a. [f. F jus f. L jus broth, juice]

ju'icy (jōō-), a. Full of juice, succulent; (of weather) wet; (colloq.) of rich intel-lectual quality, interesting; (Art sl.) of rich colouring suggestive of moisture. Hence ~INESS n. [-Y²]

ju-ju (jōō/jōō), n. (W.-Afr.). Charm or fetish; ban effected by this. [perh. f. F jou-jou toy]

ju'jube (jōō'jōōb), n. Edible berry-like drupe of certain plants; lozenge of gelatin etc. flavoured with or imitating this. [F, f. med. L jujuba f. Gk zizyphon]

ju-jutsu, jiu-jitsu, (jōō'jutsoō'), n. Japan-ese art of wrestling etc. [Jap. (in.)]

jul'ep (jōō-), n. Sweet drink, esp. as ve-hicle for medicine; medicated drink as stimulant etc.; *iced or spiced spirit & water, esp. mint ~. [F, f. Arab, julab f. Pers. gulab (gul rose+ab water)]

Jul'ian (jōō-), a. Of Julius Caesar; ~ calendar (introduced by him, cf. GREGOR-IAN). [f. L Julianus (Julius, see -AN)]

julienne (see Ap.), n. Soup of vegetables cooked in meat broth. [F]

July' (jōō-), n. Seventh month of year, called after Julius Caesar. [ME & OF Jule f. L Julius; 18th-c. pron. jōō'li, mod. pron. irreg. & unexpl.]

jum'bal, ~ble¹, n. Kinds of crisp thin sweet cake. [?]

jum'ble², v.t. & t. Move (t. & i.) about in disorder; mix up, confuse. [prob. imit.]

jum'ble³, n. Confused assemblage; muddle; jolting; ||~-sale (of miscellane-ous cheap articles at bazaar etc.); ~-shop (where miscellaneous goods are sold). Hence jūmb'ly² a. [f. prec.]

jum'bo, n. (pl. ~s). Big clumsy person, animal, or thing; (J~) famous ele-phant in London Zool. Gardens; notably successful person. [?]

jump¹, n. Leap, bound, spring from ground; long, high, ~, athletic competi-tions; start caused by shock or excite-ment, esp. (sl.) the ~s, delirium tremens;

abrupt rise in amount, price, value, etc.; sudden transition, gap in series, argument, etc. Hence **jŭm′py** **pĭɴᴇss** n., **jŭm′pỿ²** a. [f. foll.]

jŭmp², v.i. & t. 1. Spring from ground etc. by flexion & sudden muscular extension of legs or (of fish) tail; move suddenly with leap or (of fish) tail; move suddenly *out*, etc.); ~ *in*, get quickly into carriage etc.; start with sudden jerk from excitement, shock, etc., esp. ~ *for joy*. 2. Rise suddenly in price etc. 3. Come to, arrive *at*, (conclusion) hastily. 4. ~ *at*, (fig.) accept (offer, bargain) eagerly; ~ (*up*)*on*, attack (offender etc.) crushingly with word or act. 5. Agree, coincide, (*together*, one *with* another). 6. Pass over (gate etc.) by leap; (of railway carriage) leave (line). 7. Help (child etc.) to ~ *down* etc.; cause (thing) to ~; startle (person, nerves). 8. Cook (potatoes etc.) in frying-pan, occasionally shaking them (usu. in p.p.). 9. Pounce upon (thing); steal a march upon (Colon.) take summary possession of (claim abandoned or forfeited by former occupant). 10. Skip over (subject, part of book, etc.). 11. Drill (rock, hole in rock) with jumper. 12. ~ *down* person's *throat*, answer, interrupt, him violently; ~ *out of* one's *skin*, with surprise; ~ *over the* ʙʀᴏᴏᴍsᴛɪᴄᴋ. Hence ~ᴀʙʟᴇ a. [f. 1500; prob. imit.]

jŭm′per¹, n. In vbl senses, esp.: member of Welsh Methodist body (or later sects) who jump(ed) as part of worship; jumping insect, e.g. flea; rope made fast to keep yard, mast, etc., from jumping; heavy chisel-ended iron bar for drilling blasting-holes. [-ᴇʀ¹]

jŭm′per², n. Loose outer jacket of canvas etc. worn by sailors etc.; woman's loose outer garment of any material slipped on over head & reaching hips. [prob. f. obs. *jump* short coat perh. f. F *juppe*]

jŭnc′tion, n. Joining; joint, meeting-place; station where railway lines meet & unite (often in proper names, as *Clapham J.~*). [f. L *junctio* (as ᴊᴏɪɴ, see -ɪᴏɴ)]

jŭnc′ture, n. Joining; place where things join; concurrence of events, state of affairs, as *at this ~*. [f. L *junctura* (ᴊᴏɪɴ, -ᴜʀᴇ)]

June (jᴏᴏɴ), n. Sixth month of year. [(partly thr. F *juin*) f. L *Junius*]

jungle (jŭng′gl), n. Land overgrown with underwood or tangled vegetation, esp. in India (often attrib. of animals inhabiting ~, as ~*-bear*, *-cat*, *-fowl*); wild tangled mass; ~ *fever*, kind of severe malaria. Hence **jŭng′ʟᴇᴅ²**, **jŭng′ʟỿ²**, (-ngɡ-), aa. [f. Hind. *jangal* desert, forest]

jun′ior (jᴏᴏ-), a. & n. 1. The younger (esp.

of son having same name as father, as *John Smith ~*, or of younger of two boys of same surname in school; abbr. *jun.*, *jr*) of less standing, of lower position, as ~ *partner*. 2. n. ~ person, as *the ~s*, *is my ~*. Cf. sᴇɴɪᴏʀ. Hence ~ɪᴛỿ (-ŏ′ᴛĭ-) n. [L, compar. of *juvenis* young]

jun′iorate (jᴏᴏ-), n. (In Society of Jesus) two-years' course attended by junior members before entering priesthood. [-ᴀᴛᴇ¹]

jun′iper (jᴏᴏ-), n. Genus of coniferous evergreen shrubs, esp. *common ~*, shrub with prickly leaves & dark berries yielding *oil of ~* used in medicine & in making gin. [f. L *juniperus*]

jŭnk¹, n., & v.t. Old cable cut up for oakum etc.; discarded material, rubbish; lump, chunk; (Naut.) salt meat; lump of tissue in sperm-whale, containing spermaceti; ~*-shop*, marine store; (v.t.) divide into ~s. [?]

jŭnk², n. Flat-bottomed sailing vessel used in Chinese seas. [prob. f. Javanese *djong*]

junker (yŏŏng′ker), n. Young German noble; member of exclusive aristocratic party in Prussia. [G, earlier *junkher* (ʏᴏᴜɴɢ, ʜᴇʀʀ]

jŭnk′et, n., & v.i. 1. Dish of sweetened curds & whey, usu. with scalded cream on top; feast. 2. v.i. Feast, picnic. Hence ~ɪɴɢ¹ n. [vb f. n.) prob. f. ONF *jonquette* rush-basket (for making ~) f. *jonc* rush f. L *juncus*]

Jun′ō (jᴏᴏ-), n. (pl. ~*s*). Wife of Jupiter; woman of stately beauty; third of the asteroids. [L]

jun′ta, n. Deliberative or administrative council in Spain or Italy; =foll. [Sp., f. L *juncta*, fem. p.p. as ᴊᴏɪɴ]

jun′tō, n. (pl.~*s*). Clique, faction, political or other combination of persons. [erroneous f. prec.]

jupe (jᴏᴏp), n. Woman's skirt. [F]

Ju′piter (jᴏᴏ-), n. (Rom. Myth.) king of gods; ~ *Plu′vius* (plᴏᴏ-), god of rain; largest planet of solar system. [L]

jur′al (jᴏᴏr-), a. Of law, of (moral) rights & obligations. [f. L *jus juris* right + -ᴀʟ]

Jurăs′sic (jᴏᴏr-), a. Of the Jura mountains between France & Switzerland; marked like these by prevalence of oolitic limestone. [f. F *jurassique* after *triassic*, *triassic*]

‖**jur′at** (jᴏᴏr-), n. Municipal officer like alderman; life magistrate in Channel Is. [f. med. L *juratus* (*jurare* swear)]

jurid′ical (jᴏᴏr-), a. Of judicial proceedings; legal. [f. L *juridicus* (*jus juris* right +-*dicus* f. *dicere* sᴀʏ) +-ᴀʟ]

jur′isconsult (jᴏᴏr-), n. One learned in law, jurist. [f. L *jurisconsultus* (*jus juris* law- + p.p. as ᴄᴏɴsᴜʟᴛ)]

jurisdic′tion (jᴏᴏr-), n. Administration of justice; legal or other authority; extent of this, territory it extends over. Hence

~AL (joorisdik'shon) a. [f. L *jurisdictio*]

jurisprud'ence (jjoorisproo-), n. Science, philosophy of human law, whence ~**en'tial** (joorisproodën'shal) a.; skill in law, so ~ENT (joorisproo-) a. & n. [f. L *jurisprudentia* (as prec., see PRUDENCE)]

jurist (joor-), n. One versed in law; legal writer; student of, graduate in, law. Hence **jurist'ic(AL)** aa., **jurist'ically** adv. (joor-). [f. F *juriste* f. med. L *jurista* (as *juris* law, see -IST)]

jur'or (joor-), n. Member of jury; one who takes an oath (cf. NON-juror). [f. OF *jurour* f. L *juratorem* (*jurare* swear, see -OR)]

jur'y (joor-), n. Body of persons sworn to render verdict on question submitted to them in court of justice; *grand* ~ (of from 12 to 23 persons appointed to inquire into indictments before they are submitted to trial ~); *trial, common, petty, ~* (of 12 persons who try final issue of fact in civil or criminal cases & pronounce unanimous verdict); *special* ~ (of persons of certain station in society); CORONER'S ~; ~ *of matrons* (in case where pregnancy is pleaded in stay of execution); body of persons selected to award prizes in competition; ~-*box*, enclosure for ~ in court; ~*man*, ~*woman*, member of ~. [f. OF *jurée* oath, inquiry, f. med. L *jurata* (*jurare* swear, cf. -Y]]

jur'y-mast (joor'imahst), n. Temporary mast in place of broken or lost one. [?]

juss'ive, a. (gram.). Expressing a command. [f. L *jubēre juss-* command]

just[1], a. (Of person or conduct) equitable, fair, (to person etc.); (of treatment etc.) deserved, (as a ~ *reward*); (of feelings, opinions, etc.) well-grounded, as ~ *resentment, fear*; right in amount etc., proper. Hence ~'LY² adv., ~'NESS n. [f. L *justus* (*jus* right)]

just², adv. Exactly, as ~ *at that spot*, ~ *there*, ~ *then*, ~ *three o'clock*, ~ *as you say*, ~ *so, that is* ~ *it* (precisely the point in question); barely, as *I* ~ *managed it*; exactly at that moment, (loosely) not long before, as *I have* ~ (a moment, or not long, ago) *seen him pass*; ~ *now*, at this moment, (also) a little time ago; (colloq) positively, quite, as *it is* ~ *splendid, not* ~ *yet*; (as sl, emphasizer) *Won't I* ~ *give it him!*, *Did he swear? Didn't he,* ~!' [f. JUST¹]

just³. See JOUST.

justice, n. Just conduct; fairness; exercise of authority in maintenance of right; judicial proceedings, as *Court of J~*; magistrate; judge, esp. (in England) of Supreme Court of Judicature, whence ~SHIP n.; *J~ of the Peace*, lay magistrate appointed to preserve peace in county, town, etc.; *do* ~ *to*, treat fairly, show due appreciation of; *do oneself* ~, perform worthily of one's abilities. [OF (-ice, -ise), f. L *justitia* (as JUST¹, see -ICE)]

justi'ciable (-shya-), a. Subject to jurisdiction. [(n.; person subject to jurisdiction) [OF, f. *justicier* (as prec.), see -ABLE]

justi'ciar (-shyar), n. Chief political & judicial officer under Norman & early Plantagenet kings. [as foll., see -AR¹]

justi'ciary (-shya-), n. & a. **1.** Administration of justice; = prec. **2.** adj. Of the administration of justice. [f. med. L *justitiarius* (JUSTICE, -ARY¹]

jus'tify, v.t. Show the justice or rightness of (person, act, etc.); vindicate, (of circumstances) be such as to ~*fy*; (Theol.) declare (person) free from penalty of sin on ground of Christ's righteousness or (Rom. Cath.) of the infusion of grace; (Printing) adjust (line of type) to fill a space neatly; make good (statement etc.); adduce adequate grounds for (conduct, claim, etc.); ~*fy bail*, show by oath of person furnishing bail that he is pecuniarily qualified. Hence or cogn. ~**fiant**-ry, ~FICATION, nn., ~**fiable**² adj., ~**fiably**² adv. [f. F *justifier* f. LL *justificare* (as JUST¹, see -FY)]

jut, n., & v.i. (-tt-). **1.** Projection; protruding point. **2.** v.i. Project (often *out, forth*). [var. of JET¹²³]

jute¹ (joot), n. Fibre from certain plants, chiefly imported from Bengal, used for sacking, mats, etc. [f. Bengali *jhoto* f. Skr. *jūta*=*jata* braid of hair]

Jute² (joot), n. One of Low German tribe invading Britain in 5th & 6th cc. [Baeda has *Jutae* pl., OE *Eotas* = Icel. *Iotar* people of Jutland]

juvenes'cence (joo-), n. (Transition from infancy to) youth. So ~ENT a. [f. L *juvenescere* reach age of youth (*juvenis* young, see -ENCE]

juv'enile (joo-), a. & n. **1.** Young, youthful; suited to, characteristic of, young. **2.** n. Young person; (pl.) books meant for children. Hence or cogn ~LY² adv., **juvenil'ITY** (joo-) n. [f. L *juvenilis* (as prec., -IL)]

juvenil'ia (joo-), n. pl. Works produced in author's youth (often as title of collection of such writings). [L, neut. pl. of *juvenilis* JUVENILE]

juxtapose' (-z), v.t. Place (things) side by side. [f. F *juxtaposer* (L *juxta* next + *poser*, see COMPOSE)]

juxtaposi'tion (-zi-), n. Placing, being placed, side by side. [f. (L *juxta* next + POSITION)]

K

K, k, (kā), letter (pl. *Ks, K's*).

kaama (kah'mo), n. Hartebeest. [S. Afr.]

kabbalah. = CABBALA.

Kabyle′, n. A Berber of Algeria or Tunis; Berber dialect spoken by the ~s. [f. Arab. *qabāïl* tribes]

kāddī′sh, n. Jewish mourner's prayer; the *Magnificat* in the synagogue service. [f. Aram. *qaddīsh* holy]

kadi. See CADI.

Kāf′(f)ir, Căf′fre, (-fer), n. Member of a S.-Afr. race of Bantu family; native of Kafiristan in Asia; (pl.) S.-Afr. mine shares. [Arab. *kafir* infidel]

Ka′gō (kah-), n. Japanese basket-work palanquin slung on pole. [f. Jap. *kango* of Chin. orig.]

kail(yard). See KALE.

kain′it(e) (kīn-), n. Hydrous chlorosulphate of magnesium & potassium, used as fertilizer. [G (-ē), f. Gk *kainos* new, see -TE²]

kai′ser(kīz-), n. (hist.). Emperor; German Emperor; Emperor of Austria; head of Holy Roman Empire. Hence ~SHIP n. [ult. f. L *Caesar*]

baja′wah (-jahwa), n. Camel-litter for women. [Hind. & Pers.]

ka′ka (kah-), n. New Zealand parrot. So ~pō (kah-), n. New Zealand owl-like nocturnal parrot. [Maori (*po*=night)]

Kăkemōn′o, n. Japanese wall-picture (usu. painted on silk & mounted on rollers) [f. Jap. *kake-hang*+*mono* thing]

kala-azar (kahlah-ahzăr′), n. Virulent infectious malarial disease of oriental tropics. [Assamese: a=black disease]

kāle, kail, n. Kinds of cole or cabbage, esp. borecole, kind with wrinkled leaves; *Scotch* ~, kind with purplish leaves; broth made of this or other vegetables; ~*yard*, kitchen-garden; ~*yard school*, writers of fiction describing, with unsparing use of the vernacular, common life in Scotland. [northern form of COLE]

kaleid′o′scōpe (-līd-), n. Tube through which are seen symmetrical figures, produced by reflections of pieces of coloured glass, & varied by rotation of the tube; (fig.) constantly changing group of bright objects. Hence ~SCŎP′IC(AL) aa., ~scŏp′-icALLY² adv. [f. Gk *kalos* beautiful+*eidos* form+-SCOPE]

kalends. See CALENDS.

Kăl′i, n. Prickly saltwort, from which soda-ash was obtained. [f. Arab. *qalī* ALKALI]

Kalian, -lioun, (kahlyahn′, -yōon), n. Persian form of hookah. [Pers. (-*an*), f. Arab. *qalyan, -un*]

Kăl′mŭck, -mўk, a. & n. (Member, language) of a Mongolian race living on the Caspian.

ka′lŏng (kah-), n. Malay frugivorous fox-bat, largest known bat. [Malay]

kăl′pa, n. Great age of the world, day of Brahma, (4,320,000,000 years). [Skr.]

kămerad′ (-ahd′), int. of German soldier offering to surrender. [G, f. f. *as* COMRADE]

ka′mi (kah-), n. Japanese title of gover-

nors etc.; divinity, god, in Japanese native religion.

kămpти′icon, n. Floor-cloth of mixed rubber, gutta-percha, & cork, mounted on canvas. [f. Gk *kamptos* flexible + *oulos* thick + -kon -IC]

kăn′aka, n. South Sea Islander, esp. one formerly employed in Queensland on sugar plantations. [Hawaiian, = man]

Kănarēse′ (-z), n. (Member of) Dravidian race living in western India; language of the ~. [f. N. & S. *Kanara* in India]

kăngarōō′ (-ngg-), n. Marsupial mammal with strongly developed hindquarters & great leaping-power, native of Australia, Tasmania, etc.; ~ *rat*, small Australian marsupial; (sl., pl.) W.-Australian mining shares, dealers in these; ~ *bicycle,* one with sloping back, early form of safety; ∥ ~ *closure* (when chairman in committee selects some amendments for discussion and excludes others). [perh. native Austral.]

kănoon′, n. Kind of harp with fifty to sixty strings. [f. Pers. or Arab. *qanun*]

Kănt′ian, a. Of Immanuel Kant, German philosopher, d. 1804. So ~ISM n. [-IAN]

ka′olin (kah-, ka-), n. Fine white clay produced by decomposition of feldspar, used in making porcelain. Hence ~IZE(3) v.t. [F, f. Chin. *kao-ling,* name of mountain (*kao* high+*ling* hill)]

kăpell′meister (-mī-), n. Conductor of orchestra, opera, choir, etc.; ~ *music,* uninspired music in routine style. [G]

ka′pŏk (kah-), n. Fine cotton wool surrounding seeds of certain tree, used for stuffing cushions etc. [f. Malay *kapoq*]

kăpp′a, n. Greek letter k (K, κ).

kăput′ (-ōŏt), a. (sl.). Done for, smashed (in pred. use only). [G]

Kar′aite, n. Member of Jewish sect that rejects Rabbinical tradition & interprets scriptures literally, found chiefly in Crimea. [f. Heb. *q'raïm* (*qara* read)+-ITE¹]

kăr′ma, n. (Buddh.). Sum of person's actions in one of his successive states of existence, viewed as deciding his fate in the next; destiny. [Skr., = action, fate]

kar(r)ōō′, n. Elevated plateau of clayey soil in S. Africa, waterless in dry season; *the Great* ~ (in Cape Colony). [of Hottentot orig.]

karōss′, n. Mantle of animals' skins with the hair on, used by S.-African natives. [f. S.-Afr. *karos,* perh. of Du. orig.]

kăr′tel, n. Wooden bed in S.-African ox-wagon. [S.-Afr. Du., prob. f. Port. *cated* catel]

kartĕll′. See CARTEL.

kătabăt′ic, a. (meteorol.). (Of winds) caused by air flowing downward (cf. ANABATIC). [f. Gk *katabatikos* f. *katabainō* go down]

katăb′olism, cata-, n. (biol.). Destructive METABOLISM. [f. Gk *katabolē* throwing down (*kataballō* throw down)+-ISM]

kathode. Var. of CATHODE.

kation. Var. of CATION.

kät'ydïd, n. Large green orthopterous insect abounding in America. [imit. of the sound the insect produces]

kauri (kowr'ï), n. Coniferous tree of New Zealand, furnishing valuable timber & a resin, ~ -gum. [Maori]

ka'va (kah-), n. (Diuretic beverage from roots of) a Polynesian shrub. [native]

kavass', n. Armed constable, servant, or courier, in Turkey. [f. Turk. qawwas]

kay'ak (kï-), n. Eskimo canoe of light wooden framework covered with sealskins. [Eskimo]

kea (kā'ä), n. Green Alpine parrot of New Zealand which destroys sheep for their kidney-fat. [Maori, imit.]

kêck, v.i. Make sound as if about to vomit; ~ at, reject (food etc.) with loathing. [imit.]

kêdge, v.i. & t. & n. 1. Change position of ship by winding in hawser attached to small anchor at some distance; (of ship) move thus; move (ship) thus. 2. n. (Also ~ -anchor) small anchor for this purpose. [perh. var. of CADGE]

kêd'geree, n. Indian dish of rice, split pulse, onions, eggs, etc.; European dish of fish, rice, eggs, etc. [f. Hind. khichŗī, Skr. kṛṣara]

‖**keek,** v.i. & v.t. (Sc.), Peep. [ME kīkel]

keel[1], n., & v.t. 1. Lowest longitudinal timber of vessel, on which framework of the whole is built up; combination of iron plates serving same purpose in iron vessel; (poet.) ship; false ~ (attached to bottom of true ~ to protect it); ~ blocks (on which ~ rests in building etc.); ~ haul, haul (person) under ~ as punishment. 2. v.t. Turn (ship) ~ upwards; ~ over, upset, capsize, (person etc.). Hence ~LESS (1-1-) a. [(vb f. n.) prob. f. ON kjǫlr, cf. Sw. kɵl]

keel[2], n. Flat-bottomed vessel, esp. of kind used on Tyne etc. for loading colliers; amount carried by this. [prob. f. MDu. kēle, cogn. w. OE cēol]

keelson. See KELSON.

keen[1], n. Irish funeral song accompanied with wailing. [f. Ir. caoine, as foll.]

keen[2], v.i. & t. Utter the keen; bewail (person) thus; utter in wailing tone. [f. Ir. caoinim wail]

keen[3], a. Having sharp edge or point; (of edge etc.) sharp; (of sound, light, etc.) penetrating, vivid, strong; (of cold) intense; (of pain etc.) acute, bitter; (of person, desire, interest) eager, ardent, (colloq. on thing, on doing, ~ as mustard, enthusiastic, w. pun on Keene's mustard); (of eyes, sight, smell) sharp, highly sensitive; intellectually acute; ~ -set, hungry, eager. (for). Hence ~ly² adv., ~NESS n. [comm.-Teut. (for): OE cēne, Du. koen, G kühn, bold]

keep[1], v.t. & i. (kĕpt). 1. Pay due regard to, observe, stand by, (law, promise, faith, treaty, appointment; ~ the PEACE). 2. Celebrate (feast, ceremony, etc.). 3. Guard, protect, (person, as God ~ you!, fortress, town, etc.; goal at football etc.), not lose. 5. Maintain (house etc.) in proper order (~ open house, entertain all comers), carry on (shop etc.); maintain (diary, accounts, books) by making requisite entries. 6. Provide for sustenance of (family, oneself, etc.); own & manage (cows, bees, etc.); maintain (woman) as mistress. 7. Have (commodity) habitually on sale. 8. ~ COMPANY, ~ PACE, STEP, LOOK out, time, WATCH, WICKET (also abs., act as wicket-keeper). 9. Maintain in proper or specified condition (often in spec. senses, as ~ the BALL rolling, ~ one's HAIR on, one's HEAD[1], ~ one's balance, not lose lit., fig.). 10. Detain (person in prison, in custody, etc.); restrain (person, thing, oneself, from doing, from thing); refrain from. 11. Reserve (thing for future time etc.). 12. Conceal (~ one's COUNSEL, a secret). 13. Continue to follow (way, course; ~ track of, follow the course or development of). 14. Remain in (one's bed, room, house); retain one's place in (the saddle, the field, the stage, one's ground, etc.) against opposition; ~ one's feet, not fall; ~ HOUSE; remain (indoors etc.). ‖(colloq., esp. Camb. Univ.) reside, as where do you ~? 15. Remain in specified condition, as ~ cool, ~ in good health, ~ in TOUCH with, ~ cool, ~ friends. 16. Continue in specified direction, course, or action, as ~ straight on for two miles; he ~s giggling. 17. (Of food etc.) remain in good condition; (fig., of news etc.) admit of being reserved for later occasion. 18. ~ at, (abstain) from; ~, cause to work, persistently at; ~ (abstain) from; ~ to, adhere to (course, promise), confine oneself to; ~ (thing etc.) to oneself, refuse to share it with others; ~ HOUSE; remain indoors, remain on good terms with; ~ one's HAND in; ~ off, avert, (intr.) stay at a distance; ~ on, continue to hold, use, show, etc. (intr.) continue (doing); ~ out, not let enter; ~ together, remain, cause to remain, together; ~ under, hold in subjection; ~ up, prevent (one's spirits, prices, etc.) from sinking, maintain (~ one's END! up: ~ it up, not slacken), (intr.) remain in repair, (~ up your Greek), carry on

(correspondence etc.), cause (person) to sit up at night, (intr.) bear up, not break down, proceed at equal pace with. [late OE *cēpan*, etym. dub.]

keep², n. (Hist.) tower, stronghold; maintenance, food required for this, as *you don't earn your ~* *for ~s* (sl.), in permanence. [f. prec.]

keep'er, n. In vbl senses, esp.: ||=GAME¹-~; lunatic's attendant; ring that keeps another, esp. wedding-ring, on the finger. [-ER¹]

keep'ing, n. In vbl senses, also or esp.: custody, charge, as *in safe ~*, *in his ~*; agreement, harmony, as *in, out of, ~ (with)*: (attrib., or intr. part.) fit for ~, as *~ apples*; *~-room*, sitting-room usually occupied. [-ING¹]

keep'sake, n. Thing kept for sake, or in remembrance, of giver; (attrib.) namby-pamby, like certain literary annuals of 19th c. called ~s. [KEEP¹+SAKE]

keeshond (kās'hŏnd), n. Breed of Dutch dogs resembling the chow. [Du.]

kef, kief (kif), **kief**, n. Drowsy state produced by bhang etc.; enjoyment of idleness; Indian hemp etc. smoked to produce ~. [f. Arab. *kaif*, colloq. *kef*, well-being]

keffi'yeh (-fēyā), n. Bedouin Arab's kerchief worn as head-dress. [f. Arab. *kaffiyah, kuffiyah*, perh. f. LL *cofea* COIF]

keg (-er), n. Small barrel, usu. of less than 10 gals. [earlier *cag*, cf. Icel. *kaggi*, Sw. *kagge*]

kelp, n. Large kinds of seaweed used for the sake of carbonate of soda, iodine, etc. contained, formerly used in making soap & glass. [ME *culp*, etym. dub.]

kel'pie, -py, n. (Sc.). Water-spirit, usu. in form of horse, reputed to delight in the drowning of travellers etc. [?]

kel'son, keel'son, n. Line of timber fastening ship's floor-timbers to keel. [f. KEEL; -son unexpl., cf. Du. *kolzwijn*, G *kielschwein*]

Kelt¹ etc. See CELT etc.

kelt², n. Salmon or sea trout after spawning. [?]

kemp, n. Coarse hair in wool. Hence **kem'py²** a. [prob. f. ON *kampr* beard, whisker, etc.]

ken¹, n. Range of sight or knowledge, esp. *in, out of, beyond, one's ~*. [f. foll.]

|| **ken²**, v.t. (now Sc. or north.; *kent*). Recognize at sight: know (person, thing, fact, *that* etc.). [com.-Teut.: OE *cennan*, Du. & G *kennen*]

ken³, n. **1.** House for shelter of house-dog or hounds; mean dwelling. **2.** v.i. Live in, go to, ~; (v.t.) put into, keep in, ~. [(vb f. n.) prob. f. ONF *kenil* (F *chenil*) f. pop. L *canile* (*canis* dog)]

kěnn'el², n. Gutter. [earlier *cannel* f. OF *canel* CHANNEL]

kěnō'sis, n. (theol.). Renunciation of divine nature, at least in part, by Christ in the incarnation. So **kěnŏt'ic** (-ŏt-) a., **kěnŏt'icĭsm**(3) n. [Gk *kenōsis* (*kenoō* vb empty) f. *kenos*, see -OSIS]

Ken'tish, a. Of Kent; || ~ *fire*, prolonged volley of applause or demonstration of dissent; ~ *man* (born W. of Medway, opp. *man of Kent* born E.); ~ *rag*, hard limestone found in Kent. [OE *Centisc* (*Cent* f. L *Cantium*, see -ISH¹)]

Kent'ledge, n. (naut.). Pig-iron used as permanent ballast. [?]

kěp'i, n. French military cap with horizontal peak. [f. F *képi* f. G-Swiss *käppi* dim. of *kappe* cap]

kept. See KEEP¹.

kě'ratin, n. Nitrogenous substance forming the basis of horns, claws, nails, etc. [as foll.+-IN]

kě'ratōse, a. & n. **1.** Of horny substance. **2.** n. Horn-like substance forming part of some sponges. [f. Gk *keras -atos* horn +-OSE¹]

|| **kěrb, *cŭrb**, n. **1.** Stone edging to pavement or raised path; ~-*stone*, one of stones forming this. **2.** (St. Exch. sl.). The STREET; ~-*stone broker* (not a member of the Stock Exchange); ~ *market*, (place for) sale of securities after hours or of shares not dealt with on the Stock Exchange). [var. of CURB n.]

kěrch'ief (-if), n. Cloth used to cover head; (poet.) handkerchief. Hence ~ED¹ (-ift) a. [ME *curchef, ker-*, f. OF *couvrechef, cuevre-*, (*couvrir* COVER+*chief* head f. L *caput*)]

kerf, n. Slit made by cutting, esp. with saw; cut end of felled tree. [OE *cyrf*, f. st. of CARVE]

kěrm'es (-iz), n. Pregnant female of an insect, formerly taken for a berry, feeding on ~ *oak*, an evergreen oak of S. Europe & N. Africa; red dye-stuff consisting of dried bodies of these; amorphous trisulphide of antimony, of brilliant red. [f. Arab. & Pers. *qirmiz*]

kěrm'is, n. Periodical fair in Holland etc., with much noisy merrymaking. [Du., orig.=mass on anniversary of dedication of church, when yearly fair was held (KIRK+*mis* MASS¹)]

kern¹(e), n. (hist.). Light-armed Irish foot-soldier; peasant, boor. [f. Ir. *ceithern*]

kern'el, n. Softer (usu. edible) part within hard shell of nut or stone fruit; body of seed within husk etc., e.g. grain of wheat; nucleus, centre of formation (often fig.). [OE *cyrnel*, dim. of CORN]

kě'rosēne, n. Lamp-oil obtained by distillation of petroleum & from coal & bituminous shale, paraffin. [irreg. f. Gk *kēros* wax+-ENE]

Kě'rry, n. attrib. ~ *blue*, a breed of terrier. [place]

kers'ey (-zi), n. Kind of coarse narrow cloth woven from long wool, usu. ribbed. [perh. f. K~ in Suffolk]

kers'eymere (-zi-), n. Twilled fine woollen cloth; (pl.) trousers of this. [corrupt. of *cassimere*, var. of CASHMERE, assim. to prec.]

kes'trel, n. Species of small hawk. [ME *castrel*, prob. =OF *cresserelle*, etym. dub.]

ketch, n. Two-masted vessel with mizzen-mast stepped forward of rudder. [earlier *cache*, *catch*, f. CATCH v.]

ketch'up, n. Sauce made from juice of mushrooms, tomatoes, etc. [prob. f. Chin. *kôe-chiap* brine of pickled fish]

ket'one, n. One of a class of organic compounds allied to the aldehydes of which acetone is the simplest. [f. G *keton* var. of *acetone*]

kett'le, n. Vessel, usu. of metal with spout & handle, for boiling water; FISH~; *a pretty ~ of fish*, awkward state of affairs; ~*drum(mer)*, (player of) hollow brass or copper hemisphere, over edge of which parchment is stretched & tuned to definite note; ~*drum*, (also) large afternoon tea-party; ~*holder*, piece of cloth etc. to protect hand from heat of ~ handle. Hence ~FUL(2) n. [com.-Teut.: OE *cetel*, Du. *ketel*, G *kessel*]

kev'el, n. (naut.). Peg, cleat, usu. fixed in pairs, to which certain ropes are belayed. [f. ONF *keville* (F *cheville*) f. L *clavicula* dim. of *clavis* key]

Kew Gard'ens, n. pl. National botanical gardens at Kew, London.

key (kē), n. 1. Instrument, usu. of iron, for moving bolt of lock forwards or backwards; *get*, *have*, *the ~ of the street*, be shut out for the night, homeless; MASTER ~. 2. *House of Keys*, elective branch of legislature of I. of Man; *St Peter's ~s*, cross ~s borne in Papal arms. 3. What gives or precludes opportunity for or access to something; *golden*, *silver*, ~, money used as bribe. 4. (pl.), Ecclesiastical authority as transmitted to the Pope, esp. *power of the ~s*. 5. Place that from its position gives control of sea, territory, etc. 6. Solution, explanation, translation of foreign book; book of solutions of mathematical problems etc. 7. (Mus.) system of notes definitely related to each other & based on particular note; (fig.) tone, style, of thought or expression; ~*note*, note on which a ~ is based, (fig.) prevailing tone or idea. 8. Piece of wood or metal inserted between others to secure them. 9. Part of first coat of wall plaster passing between laths & so securing the rest. 10. Lever pressed by finger in playing organ, piano, flute, concertina, etc.; similar lever in typewriter etc. 11. Instrument for grasping screws, pegs, nuts, etc., esp. one for winding clock or watch. 12. ~*board*, set of ~s on piano etc.; ~*bugle* (fitted with ~s to increase number of sounds); ~*hole* (by which ~ is put into lock); ~ *industry*, one essential to the carrying on of others, e.g. coal-mining, dyeing; ~ *map* (in bare outline, to simplify use of full map); ~ (move), (Chess) first move in solution of a problem; ~*ring* (for keeping ~s on); ~*stone*, stone at summit of arch locking the whole together, (fig.) central principle etc. on which all depends. Hence ~LESS (kē-) a. [OE *cǣg*, etym. dub.]

key² (kē), v.t. Fasten (often *in*, *on*, etc.) with pin, wedge, bolt, etc.; regulate pitch of strings of (piano etc.); word (an advertisement in a particular periodical) so that answers to it can be identified (usu. by varying the form of address given); (fig.) ~ *up*, stimulate (person to do, to condition etc.), raise the tone or standard of, brace up, raise (offer, demand, endeavour). [f. prec.]

key³ (kē), n. Low island or reef. [f. Sp. *cayo*, see QUAY]

khadd'ar (kä-), n. Indian homespun cloth. [Hindi]

khakham (kahkahm'), n. = KHAN¹. [f. Hindi]

kha'ki (kah-), a. & n. 1. Dust-coloured, dull-yellow. 2. n. ~ fabric of twilled cotton or wool, used in Brit. army; || ~ *election* (so timed as to exploit war-enthusiasm & secure majority for general purposes). [Hind.,=dusty (*khak* dust)]

khalī'fa, **khal'ifat**, (kā-), nn. =CALIPH-

kham'sīn (kā-), n. Hot S. or S.E. wind in Egypt for about 50 days in March, April, & May. [Arab. (*khamsun* fifty)]

khan¹ (kän, kahn), n. Title of rulers & officials in Central Asia, Afghanistan, etc.: (Hist.) supreme ruler of Turkish, Tartar, & Mongol tribes, & emperor of China, in middle ages. Hence ~ATE'(1) n. [Turk., perh. as KHAKAN]

khan² (kän, kahn), n. Caravanserai. [Arab.,=inn]

khe'da (kā-), *kheddah*, (kā-), n. Enclosure used in Bengal etc. to catch elephants. [Hind. (-dā)]

Khedive' (kidēv'), n. Title of viceroy of Egypt, accorded to Ismail Pasha by Turkish Government in 1867; abolished in 1914. Hence **Khedi'v**(1)AL aa. [f. F *khédive* f. Turk.]

khi (kī), n. Greek letter (X, χ)=ch. [Gk]

khid'mutgar (ki'-), n. Male servant who waits at table (in India). [f. Hind. *khidmatgar* (*khidmat* service + *-gar* suf.)]

khil'afat, n. =KHALIFA'; ~ *agitation*, anti-British movement in India based on Moslem resentment of the loss of power by Islam in & after the 1914-18 war, & contemporary Hindu discontents.

|| kib'ble, n. Iron hoisting-bucket used in mines. [prob. f. G *kübel*]

kibe, n. Ulcerated chilblain, esp. on heel; *tread on one's ~s*, hurt his feelings. [?]

kibit'ka, n. Tartar's circular tent covered with felt; Tartar household; Russian hooded sledge. [Russ.]

kib'lah, n. Point to which Mohammedans turn at prayer, i.e. temple at Mecca. [f. Arab. *qiblah* (*qabala* be opposite)]

kib'ōsh (or kibŏsh'), n. (sl.). Nonsense, humbug; *put the ~ on*, do for, knock on the head. [?]

kick[1], n. Act of kicking; (colloq.) reacting-power, resilience; (*has no ~ left*; (colloq.) sharp stimulant effect, pleasurable thrill; DROP[1], PLACE~, ~; *more ~s* (harshness) *than halfpence* (kindness); recoil of gun when discharged; (Footb.) *good, bad*, etc. ~ (kicker); ~-*off*, ~ with which game is started; ~-*starter*, lever on motor-cycle by which it can be started. [f. foll.]

kick[2], v.i. & t. 1. Strike out with the foot; ~ *against the pricks*, resist to one's own hurt. 2. Show annoyance, dislike, etc. (*against, at*, proposal, treatment). 3. Strike with foot; (sl.) ~ *the bucket*, die; ~ *one's* HEELS. 4. Drive, move, (thing) by ~ing, 5. (Footb.) score (goal) by a kick. 6. Drive forcibly & contemptuously (*out, downstairs*, etc.; ~ *one upstairs*, fig., shelve him by giving him peerage or titular promotion). 7. ~ *off*, throw off (shoes) by ~ing, (Footb.) give first kick; ~ *up*, raise (dust), create (fuss, noise), ~ *up its heels* (of horse in play); ~*ing-strap* (arranged to prevent carriage-horse from ~ing. [ME *kike*, etym. dub.]

kick[3], n. Indentation in bottom of glass bottle. [?]

kick'er, n. In vbl senses, esp. horse given to kicking. [-ER[1]]

kick'shaw, n. Fancy dish in cookery (usu.derog.);toy, trifle. [f. F *quelque chose* something]

kid[1], n., & v.t. & i. (-dd-). 1. Young of goat; leather from skin of this, used for gloves & boots; *the Kids* or *Kid*, three small stars in Auriga; (sl.) child, whence ~d'y[3] n.; ~-*glove* (adj.), over-dainty, avoiding everyday work etc. 2. v.t. Give birth to (~); (v.i.) give birth to ~. [(vb f. n.) ME *kide*, cf. ON *kidh*, G *kitz*]

kid[2], v.t. (-dd-), & n. (sl.). Hoax, humbug, (vb often abs.). [perh. f. prec.]

kid[3], n. Small wooden tub, esp. sailor's mess-tub. [perh. var. of KIT[1]]

Kidd'erminster, n. Town in Worcestershire; ~ *carpet* (with pattern formed by intersection of two cloths of different colours).

kid'dle, n. Barrier in river with opening fitted with nets etc. to catch fish; arrangement of stake-nets on sea-beach. [f. OF *quidel, qu-*]

kid'nap, v.t. (-pp-). Steal (child); carry off (person) by illegal force. Hence ~per[1] n. [KID[1] + obs. *nap* seize, cf. NAB]

kid'ney, n. (pl.~s). One pair of glandular organs in abdominal cavity of mammals, birds, & reptiles, serving to excrete urine & so remove effete nitrogenous matter from blood; ~ of sheep, cattle, & pigs, as food; temperament, nature, as *a man of that ~, of the right ~*; (also *potato*) oval kind of potato; || ~ *bean*, (1) dwarf French bean, (2) scarlet-runner. [?]

kief. See KEF.

kie-kie k(ē'kē), n. New Zealand climbing plant with leaves used for baskets etc. [Maori]

kier, n. Vat in which cloth is boiled for bleaching etc. [cf. ON *ker*, Da. etc. *kar*]

kieselguhr (kē'zĕlgoor), n. Diatomaceous earth used for polishing & as absorbent of nitro-glycerine in manufacture of dynamite. [G *kiesel* gravel + *guhr* sediment]

Kikuyu' (-ōoyoō), n. (Used for) the controversy in the Anglican Church on the admissibility to Holy Communion of members of other Christian Churches. [~ in Brit. E. Africa (now Kenya), a conference at which in 1913 gave rise to the controversy]

kil'derkin, n. Cask for liquids etc., containing 16 or 18 gal.; this as measure. [corrupt. of Du. *kindeken* (*kind* child, see -KIN)]

kill[1], v.t. & i. 1. Put to death, slay (~ *two birds with one stone*, effect two purposes at once); (of disease, grief, shock, drink, poison, etc.) cause the death of; ~ *off*, get rid of (number of persons etc.) by ~ing. 2. (Abs., esp. Sport.) perform act of ~ing, do execution. 3. (Intr., quasi-pass.) yield good or much meat when ~ed, as *pigs do not ~ well at that age*. 4. Represent in fiction etc. as dead, as ~ *your villain in the last chapter*. 5. Destroy vitality of (plant, disease, etc.); destroy, put an end to, (feelings etc.). 6. Neutralize (colour etc.) by contrast. 7. Consume (time) for the sake of doing so. 8. Overwhelm (person) with admiration, amusement, etc. (*got up to ~*, fascinatingly dressed), whence ~ing[3] a., ~'ingly[3] adv. 9, (Lawn Tennis) strike (ball) so that it cannot be returned; (Footb.) stop (ball) dead. 10. Totally defeat (bill in Parliament). 11. ~ (fatally harm) *with* (mistaken) *kindness*; ~*devil*, artificial bait made to spin in water; ~*joy*, one who throws gloom over social enjoyment; ~*time*, & a., (occupation intended to ~ time. [?]

kill[2], n. Act of killing; animal killed, esp. by sportsman. [f. prec.]

kill'er, n. One who, that which, kills; murderous ruffian; HUMANE ~; ~ *whale*, voracious cetacean (esp. the grampus). [-ER[1]]

kill'ick, -ock, n. Heavy stone used by small craft as anchor; small anchor. [?]

kiln (or kil), n. Furnace, oven, for burning, baking, or drying, esp. (*lime~*) for calcining lime, or (*brick~*) baking bricks;

~dry v.t., dry in ~. [OE *cylene* f. L *culīna* kitchen]

kilo- in comb., arbitrary representative (f. F) of Gk *khīlioi* 1,000, as: ~*cycle*, unit of frequency of vibration (1,000 oscillations per second) used esp. of wireless waves; ~*gram(me)*, weight of 1,000 grammes (2·205 lb. avoirdupois); ~(*-ter*), energy that will raise one kilogramme to the height of one metre; ~*litre*, ~*liter*, (*-lēter*), measure of 1,000 litres (35·31 cub. ft.); ~*mètre*, measure of 1,000 metres, whence ~*mĕtrĭc(al)* aa.; ~*watt*, 1,000 watts.

kilt[1], v.t. Tuck up (skirts) round body; gather in vertical pleats (esp. in p.p.). [prob. of Scand. orig., cf. Da. *kilte*]

kilt[2], n. Skirt, usu. of tartan cloth, reaching from waist to knee, part of Highland male dress; hence **kil'tie** [-i'] n., Highland soldier. [f. prec.]

•kil'ter, kĕ'-, n. Good working order (*out of ~*, not working properly). [Eng. dial.]

kīmŏ'nō, n. (pl.~s), Long loose Japanese robe with wide short sleeves, held together by a sash; European dressinggown or wrap modelled on this. [Jap.]

kin, n. & a. Ancestral stock, family, as *comes of good ~*; one's relatives; KITH & ~; (pred. adj.) related, *as we are, he is ~ to me*; (of) ~, akin, related by blood ties or (fig.) in character; NEXT OF ~, closely related; NEAREST OF ~. Hence ~'LESS a. [com.-Teut.: OE *cyn(n)*. Du. *kunne*, Da. & Sw. *kön*, f. root *ken, kan, kun*: cogn. w. Gk *genos* race, L *genus* kind]

-kin, suf. form. dimin., corresp. to MDu. *-kĕn, -ken*, G. *-chen*; chiefly in wds f. Du. or of doubtful orig., *lambkin* being the only E formation of real currency: ME had proper names, as *Malkin, Perkin, Simkin*.

kin'chin, n. (cant.). Child: ~ *lay*, practice of stealing money from children sent on errands. [prob. f. G *kindchen* child, see prec.]

kin'cŏb (·ngkŏ-), n. Rich Indian stuff embroidered with gold or silver. [f. Hind. *kimkhāb*]

kind[1], n. 1. Race, natural group, of animals, plants, etc., as *human ~, the rabbit ~*. 2. Class, sort, variety, as *of what is it?, of a different ~; something of the ~*, something like the thing in question; *nothing of the ~*, not at all like it; *we had coffee of a ~* (that scarcely deserved the name). 3. (Eccl.) each of the two elements in the Eucharist. 4. (In transposed constr.) *what ~ of tree is this?, this is the ~ of what ~ is this tree? this is the ~ of thing I meant*; (colloq.) *these ~ of men (men of this ~) annoy me*. 5. (Implying looseness, vagueness) *he is a ~ of stockbroker, of millionaire, felt a ~ of compunction*; (colloq.) *I ~ of (to some extent) expected it*. ‖ 6. (arch.).

Nature in general, as *the law of ~*; way, fashion, natural to person etc., as *they act after their ~*. 7. Character, quality, as *they differ in ~* (not merely in degree). 8. *In ~*, (of payment) in goods or natural produce, not in money, (of repayment, esp. fig.) *repay his insolence in ~* (with insolence). [OE *gecynde* (ge- Y- +*cynde* f. root *kun*- see KIN)]

kind[2], a. Of gentle or benevolent nature; friendly in one's conduct to (person etc.); (arch.) affectionate: *~-hearted*, having a ~ heart. Hence ~*ly*[1], ~*[-i*²] adv. (often politely in requests, or ironically in commands), ~'NESS n. [OE *gecynde* (as prec.)]

kin'dergärten, n. School for developing minds of children by object-lessons, toys, games, etc. Hence ~*ism* n. [G.= children's garden]

kin'dle, v.t. & i. Set on fire, light, (flame, fire, substance); (fig.) inflame, inspire, (passion etc.), stir up (person *to* emotion etc., *to do*); (intr.) catch fire, burst into flame; (fig.) become animated, glow with passion etc.; make, become, bright, (cause *to*) glow (often *up*); hence **kind'-lING**[1] n. (esp., sing. or pl.) small wood for lighting fires. [prob. f. ON *kynda* kindle +-LE(3)]

kindl[y]² (tor ~*y*[1] see KIND[2]), a. Kind; (of climate etc.) pleasant, genial; ‖ (of native-born, as *a ~ Scot*. Hence ~*ix*² adv., ~'INESS n. [OE *gecyndelic* (as KIND², see -LY[1])]

kin'dred, n. & a. 1. Blood relationship; (fig.) resemblance in character; one's relatives. 2. adj. Related by blood; (fig.) allied, connected, similar, as *frost & ~ phenomena*. [f. KIN+-red, OE *rēden* condition, reckoning]

kine. See cow[1].

kinēmăt'ic, a. & n. 1. Of motion considered abstractly without reference to force or mass. 2. n. pl. Science of this, of particles). 2. n. pl. Science of the relations between the motions of bodies & the forces acting on them. [f. Gk *kinēma -matos* (*kineō* move, see -MA) +-IC]

kinēmat'ograph, -ic, -y. = CINEMATOGRAPH etc.

kinĕt'ic, a. & n. 1. Of, due to, motion; ~ ENERGY; ~ *theory of heat*, of gases (that heat, the gaseous state, is due to motion of particles). 2. n. pl. = CINEMATOGRAPHY etc. Hence ~*AL* a. [f. Gk *kinētikos* (*kineō* move, see -M) +-IC]

king, n. 1. Male sovereign (esp. hereditary) ruler of independent state (~ *sends*, *his carriage*, i.e. BLACK[1] *Maria*). 2. K~ (*of*) U.K. & India; hist.) *Baby*, baby as household idol; K~ *Emperor* (of U.K. & India; hist.) K~ *Log*, K~ *Stork*, rulers going to extremes of laissezfaire, oppression (w. ref. to fable of the frogs); K~ *of ~s*, God, (also) title assumed by many Eastern ~s; K~ *Charles's SPANIEL*; K~ *of Terrors*, Death; K~ *Charles's* SPANIEL; K~'s

BENCH, BOUNTY, COLOUR¹, COUNSEL¹, ENGLISH, EVIDENCE¹, HEAD¹, HIGHWAY, PIPE¹, SHILLING, WEATHER; K~ of the Castle, child's game. 3. Great merchant etc., as fur, railway, ~. 4. ~ of beasts, birds, lion, eagle. 5. Best kind (of fruits, plants, etc.). 6. (Chess) piece that has to be protected from checkmate, ~'s bishop, knight, rook (placed on ~'s side of board at beginning); (Draughts) piece that, having traversed the board & reached opponent's base-line, is crowned; (Cards) card bearing representation of ~, & usu. ranking next below ace. 7. ~'bird, kind of bird of paradise, (also) American tyrant flycatcher; ~'bolt, main or large bolt; ~-crab, large arachnid or crustacean animal with horseshoe-shaped carapace; ~'craft, skilful exercise of royalty; ~'cup, buttercup, ||(also) marsh marigold; ~'fisher, small bird with long cleft beak & brilliant plumage, feeding on fish it captures by diving; ~'maker, one who sets up ~s, esp. Earl of Warwick in reign of Henry VI; || K~ of Arms, any of five chief heralds of College of Arms, Garter, Clarenc(h)eux, Norroy, (Scotland) Lyon, (Ireland) Ulster; ~'pin, = ~bolt, also fig.; ~'post, upright post from tie-beam to rafter-top; ~'s evil, scrofula, formerly held to be curable by ~'s touch; ~'s peg, drink of champagne & brandy; || K~'s Roll (of employers pledged to employ at least a fixed proportion of ex-service men). Hence ~'LESS, ~'LIKE, ~'LY¹ aa., ~'liNESS, ~'SHIP(1), nn. [com.-Teut.: OE cyni(n)g, Du. koning, G könig, f. same root as KIN]

king², v.i. & t. Act the king, govern, esp. ~ it; make (person) a king.

king'dom, n. Monarchical State; United K~, Great Britain & (Northern) Ireland; territory subject to king; spiritual reign of God, sphere of this, esp. the ~ of heaven; domain; province of nature, esp. animal, vegetable, mineral, ~; (sl.) ~ come, the next world (echo of thy ~ come in Lord's Prayer). Hence ~ED² (-omd) a. [OE cyningdóm (as KING¹, see -DOM]

king'let, n. Petty king (usu. derog.), so ~LING¹ n.; golden-crested wren. [-LET]

kink, n. & v.i. & t. 1. Back-twist in wire or chain or rope such as may cause obstruction or a break; (fig.) mental twist, crotchet. 2. v.i. (Of rope etc.) form a ~; (v.t.) cause (rope) to do this. Hence ~Y² a. [(vb) prob. f. Du. kinken; (n.) Du., G, Da., Sw., f. root †kék bend]

kink'ajou (-ōō), n. Animal allied to racoon, with prehensile tail & nocturnal habits. [f. F quincajou f. N. Amer. Ind.]

kinn'ikinic', n. Mixture of dried sumach-leaves, bark of willow, etc., as substitute for tobacco, or mixed with it; any plant used for this. [Algonquin]

ki'nō (kē-), n. Gum of various trees, resembling catechu. & used in medicine & tanning as astringent. [prob. of W.-Afr. orig.]

kins'folk (-ōk), n. pl. (literary), Relations by blood. So ~MAN, ~WOMAN, nn. [f. KIN+FOLK]

kin'ship, n. Blood relationship; similarity, alliance, in character. [-SHIP]

kin'tal, early form of QUINTAL.

kiōsk', n. Light open pavilion in Turkey & Persia; Y'ŭdiz K~, Turkish Sultan's palace; light out-of-door structure for sale of newspapers, bandstand, etc. [f. Turk. kiushk]

kip¹, n. Hide of young or small beast as used for leather. [?]

kip², n., & v.i. (-pp-; sl.). Common lodging-house; lodging; bed; (v.i.) sleep. [cf. Da. kippe mean hut or alehouse]

kipp'er¹, n. Male salmon in spawning season; kippered fish, esp. herring. [?]

kipp'er², n. Cure (salmon, herring, etc.) by splitting open, cleaning, rubbing with salt, pepper, etc., & drying in open air or smoke. [perh. f. prec.]

Kirghiz (kēñgēz'), a. & n. (Member, language) of a Mongolian race living on the Caspian, N.E. of the Kalmucks.

|| kīrk, n. (Sc. & north.) church: (in E use) K~ of Scotland, Church of Scotland as opp. to Church of England or to Episcopal Church in Scotland; ~'man, member of K~ of Scotland; ~ session, lowest court in K~ of Scotland & other Presbyterian Churches, composed of ministers & elders. [north, form of CHURCH]

kirsch(wasser) (kēñsh'vahser), n. Spirit distilled from fermented liquor of wild cherries. [G (kirsche cherry+wasser water)]

|| kir'tle, n. (arch.). Woman's gown or outer petticoat; man's tunic or coat. [OE cyrtel, cf. Da. & Sw. kjortel, perh. f. L curtus short]

kis'met, n. Destiny. [Turk., f. Arab. qismat(t) f. qasama divide]

kiss¹, n. Caress given with lips; (Billiards) impact between moving balls; kind of sugar-plum. [OE coss, cf. Du. kus, G kuss]

kiss², v.t. Touch with the lips, esp. as sign of affection, greeting, or reverence: (abs., of two persons) ~ & be friends, etc.: (Billiards, of ball) touch (ball) with KISS (also abs., of two balls); ~ away, remove (tears etc.) with kisses; ~ the book (Bible, in taking oath); ~ the dust, yield abject submission, (also) be slain; ~ the ground, prostrate oneself in token of homage, (fig.) be brought low; ~ one's hand to, wave a kiss to; ~ hands or the hand (of sovereign etc. as ceremonial salutation or on appointment to office); ~ the rod, accept chastisement submissively; ~-in-the-ring, game for young people in which one pursues & ~es another of opposite sex; ~-me-quick, kinds of plant, small bonnet standing far back on head, curl

worn on forehead. Hence ~ABLE a. [OE cyssan, cf. Du. kussen, G küssen.]

kiss'ing, a. & n. In vbl senses; ~crust, soft crust where loaf has touched another in baking; ~gate (hung in U or V shaped enclosure); ~ kind, on affectionate terms. [-ING¹, ²]

kit¹, n., & v.t. & i. (-tt-). 1. || Wooden tub for various purposes; (articles carried in) soldier's etc. pack etc.; personal equipment, esp. as packed for travelling; workman's outfit; ~bag (for carrying soldier's or traveller's ~). 2. vb. Fit out, be fitted out, with ~ (freq. up). [prob. f. MDu. kitte wooden bowl, etym. dub.]

kit², n. Abbr. of KITTEN.

kit³, n. (now rare). Small fiddle used by dancing-master. [perh. ult. as CITHERN]

kit-cat, n. K~ Club, club of Whig politicians founded under James II; member of this; ~(portrait), portrait of less than half-length, but including hands. [f. Christopher(or Kit) Cat, keeper of pie-house where club met]

kitch'en, n. Part of house where food is cooked; ~garden (for fruit & vegetables); ~-maid, servant employed in ~, usu. under cook; ~MIDDEN; ~physic, good & plentiful food; ~-stuff, ~ requisites, esp. vegetables. [OE cycene, cf. Du. keuken, G küche f. vulg. L cucina var. of coquina (coquere cook)]

kitch'ener, n. || Cooking-range; person in charge of monastery kitchen. [-ER¹]

kitchenette', n. Small room, alcove, etc., fitted up as miniature kitchen & scullery (esp. in modern flat). [-ETTE]

kite, n., & v.i. & t. 1. Bird of prey of same family as falcon, with long wings, usn. forked tail, & no tooth in bill; rapacious person, sharper; toy consisting of light wooden frame, usu. in form of isosceles triangle with circular arc as base, with paper stretched over it, flown in strong wind by string; fly a ~, (fig.) make experiment to gauge public opinion etc.; (sl.) aeroplane; (Commerc. sl.) accommodation bill (fly a ~, raise money by this); (pl.) highest sails of ship, set only in light wind; ~ balloon, sausage-shaped captive balloon for military observation. 2. v.i. Soar like ~; (v.t.) cause to do this, (Commerc.) convert into ~. [vb f. n.]

kith, n. ~ & kin, acquaintance & kinsfolk. [OE cȳthth, orig. = knowledge, known country, cogn. w. cunnan CAN¹]

kitt'en, n., & v.t. & i. 1. Young of cat; skittish young girl. 2. v.t. Bring forth (~s, or of cat) kittens. Hence ~ISH¹ a. [vb f. n.; prob. f. OF chitoun var. of chaton kitten, see CAT]

kitt'ereen', n. W.-Ind. one-horse chaise. [?]

kitt'iwake, n. Kind of sea-gull. [imit.]

kit'tle, v.t. & a. Tickle, difficult to deal with, esp. ~ cattle (usu. fig. of persons or things). [f. ME vb kytyle tickle, puzzle; prob. imit.]

kittul' (-ool), **kĭtōōl'**, n. Kind of palm; strong black fibre from leaf-stalks of this. [f. Cingalese kitul]

kitt'y¹, n. Pet name for kitten. [f. KIT² + -Y³]

kitt'y², n. Pool in some card games; joint fund; (Bowls) jack. [?]

kī'wī (kē'wē), n. =APTERYX; ||(sl.) non-flying member of Air Force. [Maori]

klax'on, n. Powerful electric motor-horn. [P: f. Gk klazō shriek]

klepht, n. One of the Greeks who after Turkish conquest of Greece in 15th c. maintained independence in mountains; brigand. [f. mod. Gk klephtēs f. Gk kleptēs thief]

kleptomā'nia, n. Irresistible tendency to theft in persons not tempted to it by needy circumstances. Hence ~MAN'IAC n. [f. Gk kleptēs thief + -o- + -MANIA]

klip'springer, n. Small S.-Afr. antelope. [S.-Afr. Du. (klip rock + springer springer)]

kloof, n. Ravine, valley, in S. Africa. [Du., =cleft]

knack, n. Acquired faculty of doing a thing adroitly; ingenious device; trick, habit, of action, speech, etc. Hence ~'Y² a. [?]

knack'er, n. || One who buys & slaughters useless horses, whence ~ERY(3) n.; one who buys old houses, ships, etc., for the materials. [?]

knag, n. Knot in wood, base of a branch. Hence ~'G'Y²(-g-) a. [ME, =G knagge]

knap¹, n. (dial.). Crest of hill, rising ground. [OE cnæp(p), perh. cogn. w. KNOP]

knap², v.t. (-pp-). Break (flints for roads) with hammer, whence ~p'ER(1, 2) n.; (Bibl., dial.) knock, rap, snap asunder. [imit.]

knap'sack, n. Soldier's or traveller's canvas or leather bag, strapped to back & used for carrying necessaries. [LG, prob. f. knappen bite + SACK¹]

knap'weed, n. Common weed with hard stem & light purple flowers on dark globular head. [earlier knopweed(KNOP + WEED)]

knar, n. Knot in wood, esp. protuberance covered with bark on trunk or at root of tree. [ME knarre = LG knarre(n).]

knāve, n. Unprincipled man, rogue, whence ~ERY(4), ~'ISHNESS nn., ~'ISH¹ a., ~'ishly² adv.; (Cards) lowest court card of each suit. [OE cnafa boy, servant, knave, cf. G knabe]

knead, v.t. Work up (moist flour or clay) into dough or paste; make (bread...

pottery; thus; (fig.) blend, weld together; operate on (muscles etc.) as if ~ing, massage. Hence ~ABLE a., ~ER¹(1, 2) n. [OE *cnedan*, cf. Du. *kneden*, G *kneten*]

knead'ing, n. In vbl senses; ~-*trough*, wooden trough in which dough is kneaded. [-ING¹]

knee¹, n. 1. Joint between thigh & lower leg in man, corresponding joint in animals; *give a ~ to*, support (pugilist) on one's ~ between rounds, act as second to; *on one's ~s*, kneeling, esp. in supplication, worship, or submission; *bring* (person) *to his ~s*, reduce him to submission; *is on the ~s of the gods*, is yet uncertain. 2. Part of garment covering the ~. 3. Thing like ~ in shape or position, esp. piece of wood or iron with angular bend. 4. ~ *breeches* (reaching down to or just below ~); ~-*cap*, convex bone in front of ~ joint, (also) protective covering for ~; ~-*deep*, so deep as to reach the ~s; ~-*hole* (*table*), (writing-table with) hole between drawer pedestals to admit ~s; ~-*joint*, joint of ~, joint of two pieces hinged together; ~-*pan*, ~-*cap*; ~-*swell*, (in Amer. organ etc.) lever worked by ~, for producing crescendo & diminuendo effects. [com.-Teut.: OE *cnéow*, Du. & G *knie*, cf. L *genu*, Gk *gonu*, Skr. *janu*]

knee², v.t. Touch with the knee; fasten (framework etc.) with knees; (colloq.) cause (trousers) to bulge at knees. [f. prec.]

kneel, v.i. (*knelt*). Fall, rest, on the knee(s) esp. in prayer or reverence (*to* person). [ME *cneolen* f. OE *cnéowlian* (as KNEE¹)]

knell¹, n. Sound of bell, esp. of one rung solemnly after death or at funeral; (fig.) announcement, event, etc., regarded as an omen of death or extinction. [OE *cnyll* (as foll.)]

knell², v.i. & t. (arch.). (Of bell) ring, esp. at death or funeral; give forth doleful sound; (fig.) sound ominously; (v.t.) proclaim as by a knell. [OE *cnyllan*, cf. MHG *erknellen*]

knelt. See KNEEL.

knew. See KNOW¹.

knick'erböcker, n. (K~) New Yorker; (pl.) loose-fitting breeches gathered in at knee. [K~, pretended author of W. Irving's *History of New York*]

knick'ers, n. pl. Knickerbockers (colloq.); woman's drawers of knickerbocker shape. [abbr. of prec.]

knick'-knack, nick-nack, n. Light dainty article of furniture, dress, or food; trinket, gimcrack. Hence ~ERY(2, 5) n., ~ISH¹ a. [redupl. of KNACK in obs. sense "trinket"]

knife, n. (pl. *knives* pr. nīvz), & v.t. (-*fed*). 1. Blade with sharpened longitudinal edge fixed in handle either rigidly, as in *table, carving,* ~, or with hinge, as in *pocket*-~, used as cutting instrument or as

weapon; (of malicious or vindictive person) *get a ~ into* (person); *war to the* ~, relentless war; blade forming part of machine, as in turnip-cutter etc.; *the* ~, surgical operations, as *have a horror of the* ~; *before you can say* ~, very quickly or suddenly; *play a good* ~ *& fork*, eat heartily. 2. ~-*board* (on which knives are cleaned), (transf.) ‖ double bench placed lengthways on the top of omnibus; ~-*boy* (employed to clean table-knives); ~-*edge*, edge of ~, steel wedge on which pendulum etc. oscillates; = ARÊTE; ~-*grinder*, itinerant sharpener of knives etc., one who grinds knives etc. in process of making; ~-*machine* (for cleaning knives); ~-*rest*, metal or glass support for carving ~ or fork at table. 3. v.t. Cut, stab, with ~. [vb f. n.) late OE *cníf*, cf. Du. *kníjf*, G *kneif*]

knight (nīt), n. & v.t. 1. Military follower, esp. one devoted to service of (lady) as attendant or champion in war or tournament. 2. Person, usu. one of noble birth who had served as page & squire, raised to honourable military rank by king or qualified person. 3. One on whom corresponding rank is conferred as reward for personal merit or services to crown or country. 4. (Hist., also ~*of the shire*) person representing shire or county in parliament. 5. (Rom. Ant.) one of the class of equites, orig. the cavalry of Roman army; (Gk Ant.) citizen of second class at Athens. 6. Piece in game of chess, usu. with horse's head. 7. ~ BACHELOR, COMMANDER, COMPANION¹, HOSPITALLER, TEMPLAR; ~ *errant*, medieval ~ wandering in search of chivalrous adventures, (fig.) person of chivalrous or of quixotic spirit; ~-*errantry*, practice, conduct, of a ~ errant (lit. & fig.); ~-*heads*, two vertical timbers supporting bowsprit; ~ *of the post*, one who got his living by giving false evidence; ~-*service* (hist.), tenure of land by military service. 8. v.t. Confer ~hood on. Hence ~HOOD n., ~LIKE, ~LY¹, aa., ~LY² adv. (poet.), (nit-). [com.-WG.: OE *cniht*, Du. & G *knecht* lad, servant, soldier]

knight'age (nit-), n. Whole body of knights; list & account of knights. [-AGE]

knit, v.t. & i. (~*ted* or *knit*). Form (close texture, garments etc. of this) of interlooping yarn or thread; contract (brow) in wrinkles; make, become, close or compact (esp. in p.p., as *a well-~ frame*); (fig.) unite (t. & i.) intimately by means of common interests, marriage, etc., (often *together*); ~ *up*, repair by ~ing, (fig.) close up, conclude, (argument etc.). [OE *cnyttan*, cf. MDu. *knutten*, G *knütten*]

knit'ting, n. In vbl senses, esp. work in process of ~; ~-*needle*, slender rod of steel, wood, ivory, etc., two or more of

kn: pronounce n-

knit'tle, n. (naut.). Small line made of yarn. [f. KNIT + -LE]

knob, n. & v.t. & i. (-bb-). 1. Rounded protuberance, esp. at end or on surface of thing; handle of door (often door-~) or drawer; small lump (of sugar, coal, etc.). Du. knop(korel), short stick with ~ (bed-head used (aust. nob); ~'kerrie [after Cape Du. knoplorie], short stick with ~bed head as weapon of S.-Afr. tribes; ~'stick, knobbed stick, esp. as weapon; (also) workman who works during strike; with ~s on (sl.), = that, & more (phr. indicating ironic or emphatic agreement). 2. v.t. Furnish with ~s; (v.i.) bulge out. Hence ~'by[1] a., ~b'iness n. [vb f. n.] ME, cf. G knobbe]

knob'ble, n. Small knob. Hence ~y[2] a. [f. KNOB + -LE]

knock[1], v.t. & i. 1. Strike with hard blow; strike door, strike at the door, to gain admittance; (of motor or other engine) make thumping or rattling noise as result of loose bearing or other mechanical defect; *(sl.) criticize; ||(sl.) make strong impression on, as what ~s me is his impudence; ~ (person etc.) on the head, stun, kill, him by blow on head, (fig.) put an end to (scheme etc.); ~ one's head against, (fig.) come into unpleasant collision with (unfavourable facts or conditions); ~ head, vb, kotow; drive (thing) in, out, off, etc., by striking (see also below); ~ into a cock'ed hat; ~ one into the middle of next week, send him flying; ~ the bottom out of, render (argument etc.) invalid. 2. ~ about, strike repeatedly, treat roughly, (intr.) wander, lead irregular life; ~ against, collide with, come across casually; ~ down, strike (person etc.) to ground with blow, (fig.) cause to succumb, (at auction) dispose of (article to bidder) by knock for a song etc.), (colloq.) lower (prices), take (machinery etc.) to pieces to save space in transport; ~ off, strike off with blow, leave off work, (colloq.) dispatch (business) or rapidly compose (verses etc.), deduct (sum from price, bill, etc.), ~ person's head off, (fig.) surpass him easily; ~ out, empty (one's pipe) by tapping, disable (pugilist) so that he cannot respond to call of 'Time', (fig.) vanquish, (colloq.) make (plan etc.) hastily; ~ together, put hastily together; ~ under, submit, knuckle under; ~ up, drive upwards with blow, make or arrange hastily, score (runs) at cricket, arouse (person) by ~ing at cricket, become exhausted, (performance in music-hall etc.), noisy rough use; ~-down a. & n. (of blow, lit. & fig.) overwhelming, (of price at auction) reserve, minimum, (n.) free fight; ~-

knees (that ~ together in walking; ~-kneed, having ~-knees; ~-out, (blow) that ~s boxer out, (n.) ||one of gang who join at auction to buy goods at low price, afterwards reselling among themselves, this practice, such sale, (sl.) outstanding person or thing. [late OE cnocian, cf. ON knoka, prob. imit.]

knock[2], n. Blow; rap esp. at door; sound of knocking in motor etc. engine (see prec.); (sl.) innings at cricket; ~-up, practice or casual game at cricket, fives, etc.; take the ~ (sl.), be hard hit financially. [f. prec.]

knock'er, n. In vbl senses, esp.; appendage, usu. of iron or brass, so hinged to door that it may be struck against metal plate to call attention (up to the ~, sl., to perfection); goblin held to dwell in mines & indicate presence of ore by knocking. [-ER[1]]

knoll[1], n. Small hill, mound. [OE cnoll, cf. Du. knol clod, ball, MHG knolle clod]

||knoll[2], v.t. & i. (arch.). Ring (bell); (of bell) sound; toll out (hours); summon by sound of bell. [var. of KNELL]

knop, n. (arch.). Knob; bud of flower. [ME & Du., cf. G knopf]

knot[1], n. 1. Intertwining of parts of one or more ropes, strings, etc., to fasten them together; GRANNY'S, REEF[1], SLIP-, WEAVER'S, ~; ribbon etc. so tied as ornament or adjunct to dress, as SHOULDER, SWORD, TOP, TRUE-love, ~. 2. (Naut.) division marked by ~s on log-line, as measure of speed; (loosely) nautical mile (6,080 ft). 3. Difficulty, problem; GORDIAN ~; central point in problem or plot of story etc.; marriage, wedding, ~ (bond). 4. Hard lump in animal body; excrescence in stem, branch, or part of plant; (hard) mass formed in trunk at insertion of branch, causing round cross-grained piece in board; node on stem of plant. 5. Group, cluster, of persons or things. 6. ||(Usu. collect.) double shoulder-pad used for carrying loads. 7. ~-grass, common weed with intricate creeping stems & pale pink flowers; ~-work, ornamental work representing or consisting of intertwined cords, (also) kind of fancy needlework. Hence ~LESS a. [OE cnotta, cf. Du. knot, G knoten]

knot[2], v.t. & i. (-tt-). Tie (string etc.) in knot; make knots for fringes, (trans.) make (fringe) thus, whence ~TING[1] n.; knit (one's brows); unite closely or intricately; entangle. [f. prec.]

knot[3]y, a. Full of knots; (fig.) puzzling, hard to explain, as ~y subject, question, point. Hence ~INESS n. [f. KNOT[1]+-Y[2]]

knout (or noot), n., & v.t. (Flog with) scourge formerly used in Russia, often fatal in its effects. [vb f. n.] F, f. Russ.

know[1] (nō), v.t. & i. (knew (nū). 1. Recognize, identify, as I knew

him at once, knew him for an American, shall you ~ him again?; be able to distinguish (don't ~ him from Adam; ~ one from another, a HAWK[1] from a handsaw). **2.** Be acquainted with (thing, place, person) by sight, to speak to, etc. (~ by name, have heard the name of, be able to give the name of); have personal experience of (fear, pain, etc.); be on intimate terms with. **3.** Be aware of (fact), be aware (that, how, what, etc.); ~ (person etc.) to be (that he is). **4.** Be versed in (language, science, etc.). **5.** He would do it if he knew how (knew the way); all one ~s, all one can, (adv.) to the utmost of one's power: ~ better (than that), I am too well informed of the facts to believe that; ~ better than, be too discreet to do; ~ of, be aware of: not that I ~ of, not so far as I ~; ~ one's own mind, not vacillate: ~ what's what, have proper knowledge of the world & of things in general; don't you ~ (esp. as parenthetic expletive in various contexts; it's such a bore, don't you ~); ~ the ROPES. **6.** ~-all, one who ~s or professes to ~ everything; ~-how, faculty of ~ing how; ~-nothing, ignorant person, (also) agnostic, whence ~-nothingism. Hence ~ABILITY, ~ableness, nn., ~'ABLE a., (n6a.). [com.-Teut. (retained only in E) & Aryan: OE (ge)cnāwan, OHG -cnāan, L & Gk gnō, Skr. jnā-]

know[2] (nō), n. (colloq.). In the ~, knowing (about) the thing in question or what is not generally known. [f. prec.]

know'ing (nōi-), a. In vbl senses, esp.: cunning, wide-awake; (colloq.) stylish, smart, as a ~ hat. Hence ~NESS n. [-ING[2]]

know'ingly (nōi-), adv. In a knowing manner; consciously, intentionally, as I have never ~ injured him. [-LY[2]]

know'ledge (nŏl-), n. Knowing, familiarity gained by experience, (of person, thing, fact); person's range of information, as it came to my ~ (became known to me), not to my ~, not so far as I know, he had to my (certain) ~ been bribed (I know he had); theoretical or practical understanding (of subject, language, etc.); the sum of what is known, as every branch of ~. Hence ~ABLE (nŏlĭja-) a. (colloq.), well-informed, intelligent. [ME knowlage, century later than obs. vb knowledge confess (KNOW, -ledge unexpl.)]

knuc'kle, n., & v.t. & i. **1.** Bone at finger-joint, esp. at root of finger; projection of carpal or tarsal joint of quadruped; joint of meat consisting of this with parts of meat above & below it; a RAP[1] on the ~s; near the ~ (colloq.), verging on the indecent; ~bone, bone forming ~, esp. of sheep or the like, (pl.) game played with such bones; || ~duster, metal instrument protecting ~s from injury in striking. **2.** v.t. Strike, press, rub, with ~s, (v.i.) place ~s on ground in playing at marbles; ~ down, under, give in, submit (to). [(vb f. n.) ME knokel, cf. Du. kneukel, G knöchel, prob. dim. of wd appearing in MLG as knoke bone]

knūr(r), n. Hard excrescence on trunk of tree; hard concretion; wooden ball in north-country game like trap-ball. [ME knorre, cf. Du. knor, G knorre(n)]

knŭrl, n. Knot, knob (esp., that by which typewriter platen is turned); bead or ridge in metal work, whence ~ED[2] (-ĭd) a. [prob. f. prec.]

knŭt, joc. spelling of NUT used of youths.

kŏ'a'la, n. An acacia in Sandwich Is. [native]

koa'la (-ah-), **koō'lah** (-lä), n. Arboreal mammal of Australia, like sloth in form. [native]

kŏb'ŏld, n. (Germ. Myth.). Familiar spirit, brownie; underground spirit in mines etc. [G, etym. dub.]

kŏd'ăk, n. & v.t. **1.** Kind of photographic camera with continuous roll of sensitized film. **2.** v.t. Photograph with ~, (fig.) seize quickly, describe vividly, (scene, view). [P]

kŏ'el, n. Indian & Australian kinds of cuckoo. [f. Hind. kōīl f. Skr. kōkila]

koh-i-noor (kōī-), n. Famous Indian diamond, property of British Crown since 1849; anything superb (of its class). [f. Pers. kohi nur (koh mountain + nur light)]

kohl (kōl), n. Powder, usu. antimony, used in East to darken eyelids etc. [f. Arab. koh'l, see ALCOHOL]

kohlra'bi (kōlrah-), n. Cabbage with turnip-shaped stem, used in England as food for cattle. [G, f. It. cavoli rape pl. (see COLE & RAPE[3])]

kola. See COLA.

Kola'rian, a. & n. Of various primitive non-Aryan tribes in the forests & hill districts of Bengal; (n.) ~ native. [?]

kolin'sky, n. Fur of the Siberian mink. [Russ. (-ski) f. Kola, district in N.-W. Russia]

komita(d)ji. Var. of COMITADJI.

koō'doō, kudu (koō'dōō), n. Large white-striped spiral-horned S.-Afr. antelope. [native]

koolah. See KOALA.

kopec(k), ~peek, ~pek, =COPECK.

kŏpp'ie, kop'je (-pĭ), n. (S.-Afr.). Small hill. [Du. dim. of kop head]

Kŏr'an (or korahn'), n. Sacred book of the Mohammedans, collection of Mohammed's oral revelations, written in Arabic. Hence koran'ĭc a. [f. Arab. qoran recitation (qara'a read)]

kŏsh'er, a. & n. **1.** (Of food or shop where food is sold or shop) fulfilling requirements of Jewish law. **2.** n. ~ food or shop. [f. Heb. kasher right]

km.: pronounce n-.

kōtow', n., & v.i. 1. Chinese custom of touching ground with forehead as sign of worship or absolute submission. 2. v.i. Perform the ~, act obsequiously (*to* person etc.). [(vb f.) f. Chin. *k'o-t'ou* (*k'o* knock + *t'ou* head)]

kŏt'wal (-ahl), n. Chief constable of Indian town; magistrate. [Hind.]

koum'iss (kōō-), n. Fermented liquor pre-pared from mare's milk. [f. Tartar *kumiz*]

kourb'ash (koor-), **koor-**, n. Hide whip as instrument of punishment in Turkey & Egypt. [f. Arab. *qurbash* f. Turk. *qirbach*]

kowtow. Var. of kotow.

kraal (krahl), n. S.-African village of huts enclosed by fence; enclosure for cattle or sheep. [colon. Du., f. Port. *corral*]

krait (krīt), n. Peculiarly venomous snake common in Bengal. [Hind., *karáit*]

kra'ken (-ah-, -ä-), n. Mythical sea-monster appearing off coast of Norway. [Norw.]

krans (-ah-), n. (S.-Afr.). Precipitous or overhanging wall of rocks. [Du. *krans* coronet]

krem'lin, n. Citadel within Russian town, esp. that of Moscow. [F, f. Russ. *kreml*]

kreu'tzer (kroit-), n. Small silver & cop-per coin formerly current in Germany & Austria. [f. G *kreuzer* (*kreuz* cross)]

krieg'spiel, n. War-game in which blocks representing troops etc. are moved about on maps. [G]

kris. See CREESE.

Krish'naism, n. Worship of Krishna, great deity of later Hinduism, wor-shipped as incarnation of Vishnu. [-ISM]

kromes'ky, n. Minced chicken etc. rolled in bacon & fried. [f. Russ.]

krōn'e (-ĕ), n. Silver coin of Denmark, Norway, & Sweden, worth about 1s. at par; former Austrian silver coin (10d.); former German 10-mark gold piece. [G & Da. *krone*, Sw. *krona*, crown]

Krōō, Krou, Kru, (-ōō), n. & a. (Member) of negro race on coast of Liberia, skilful as seamen (often, for the n., ~-*boy*, ~-*man*). [W.-Afr.]

kryp'tŏn, n. (chem.). A rare inert gaseous element discovered by Ramsay in 1898. [f. Gk *krupton* hidden, neut. adj. f. *kruptō* hide]

ksha'triya (-ah-), n. Member of the second or military caste of the Hindus. [Skr. f. *kshatra* rule]

kūd'ōs, n. (sl.). Glory, renown. [Gk]

Kūfic. See CUFIC.

***Kū-klux-Klan)**, n. Secret society hostile to Negroes formed in southern States after civil war; similar organiza-tion throughout U.S. to combat alien influences after 1914–18 war. [arbitrary]

kŭlăk' (kōō-), n. (Russ. pl. ~i). Well-to-do Russian peasant (-proprietor). [Russ., = tight-fisted person]

kultur (kooltoor'), n. Civilization as con-ceived by the Germans. [G, =culture]

kultur'kampf (kooltoor'kahmpf), n. Con-flict between German imperial govern-ment and Pope for control of schools and church appointments (1872–87). [G]

kümm'el (see AP.), n. Cumin-flavoured liqueur. [G]

Kuo'mintang' (kōō-), n. Nationalist radical (or revolutionary) party in China (founded in 1912). [Chin., lit. ' people's national party ']

Kurd (koord), n. Native of Kurdistan.

kŭrsaal (koor'zahl), n. Building for use of visitors esp. at German health resort. [G, =cure-room]

kvass, n. Russian rye-beer. [f. Russ. *kvas*]

ky'anize, v.t. Treat (wood) with solution of corrosive sublimate to prevent decay. [f. J. H. *Kyan*, inventor + -IZE]

kyl'in (kē-), n. Fabulous composite ani-mal figured on Chinese & Japanese pot-tery. [f. Chin. *ch'i-lin* (*ch'i* male + *lin* female)]

|| **kyl'ōe**, n. One of small breed of long-horned Scotch cattle. [?]

kym'ograph (-ahf), n. Instrument record-ing variations in pressure, e.g. in blood-waves. [Gk *kuma* wave + -o- + -GRAPH(2)]

Kyrie eleison (kēr'ǐǐ ǐlā'ǐson), n. Words of short petition used in Eastern & Roman Churches, esp. at beginning of Mass, musical setting of these; response to commandments in Anglican Service in Communion Service. [f. Gk *Kurie eleēson* Lord, have mercy]

L

L, (ĕl), letter (pl. Ls, L's). Thing shaped like L (L-*iron*, = ANGLE[1]-*iron*); rectangu-lar joint of pipes etc.; Roman numeral = 50, as CL 150, XL 40, lx 60, lv 55, (LXX, the Septuagint).

la (lah), n. (mus.). Sixth note of octave. [first syl. of L *labii*, see GAMUT]

laag'er (lahg'-), n., & v.t. & i. 1. Camp, en-campment, esp. in circle of wagons; (Mil.) park for armoured vehicles. 2. vb. Form (vehicles) into ~; encamp (persons) in ~; encamp. [S.-Afr. Du., & G. *lager*, Du. *leger*, see LEAGUER[1]]

lā'barum, n. Constantine the Great's imperial standard with Christian added to Roman-military symbols; symbolic banner. [L, f. Gk *labaron* etym. dub.]

labefac'tion, n. Shaking, weakening, downfall. [f. L *labefacere* (*labare* totter, *facere* make), see -FACTION.]

labda'cism. See LAMBDACISM.

lā'bel, n., & v.t. (-ll-). I. Slip of paper, card, linen, metal, etc., for attaching to object & indicating its nature, owner, name, destination, etc.; (fig.) short classifying

phrase or name applied to persons etc.; adhesive stamp; (Archit.) dripstone. **2.** v.t. Attach ~ to; assign to a category (as, obj. & compl., or abs.). [OF, = ribbon, fillet, etym. dub.]

lāb'ial, a. & n. Of the lips; (Anat., Zool.) of, like, serving as, a lip, lip-like part, or labium; (Mus.) ~ *pipe,* in organ, one furnished with lips, flue-pipe; (Phonet.) (so&nd) requiring closure or approximation of lips (*p, b, m, f, v, w,* & vowels in which lips are rounded, as *o*), whence ~ISM(1), ~IZA'TION, nn., ~IZE(3) v.t. [f. med.L *labialis* (LABIUM, -AL)]

lāb'iate, a. & n. (Bot.) with corolla or calyx divided into two parts suggesting lips (in, such plant); (Bot., Zool.) like lip or labium. [LABIUM + -ATE²]

lāb'ile, a. (physics, chem.). Unstable, liable to displacement or change. [f. L *labilis* (*labi* to LAPSE², -IL)]

lāb'io-, comb. form of foll.=of the lip(s) & ~, as ~*dental,* made with lip & teeth.

lāb'ium, n. (pl. *-ia*). (Anat.; usu. pl.) lip(s) of female pudendum; floor of mouth of insects, crustaceans, etc.; inner lip of univalve shell; lip, esp. the lower, of labiate corolla. [L, = lip]

lāb'oratory (or labŏ-), n. Room or building used for experiments in natural science, esp. chemistry, or for manufacturing chemicals etc.(also fig., ~ *of the mind, of ideas,* etc.). Hence lāboratŏ'rī-AL a. [f. med. L *laboratorium* (*laborare* LABOUR², -ORY)]

labŏ'rious, a. Hard-working; toilsome; (of style etc.) showing signs of toil, not facile or fluent. Hence ~LY² adv., ~NESS n. [f. L *laboriosus* (foll., -IOUS)]

lāb'our¹ (-ber), n. **1.** Bodily or mental toil, exertion, (HARD ~; *lost* ~, fruitless efforts; ~ *of love,* task one delights in); toil tending to supply wants of community; body of those who contribute by toil to production, labourers; (opp. CAPITAL², usu. L~) the working classes as a political force. **2.** Task (~ *of Hercules, Herculean* ~, one needing enormous strength etc.). **3.** Pains of childbirth, travail, (*in* ~). **4.** || *L~ Exchange,* local office under State for directing ~ to places requiring it; *L~ leader,* (esp.) trade-union official; ~*market,* supply of unemployed ~ with reference to demand on it; *L~ Party,* that claiming to represent wage-earners, M.P.s elected by it. [f. OF *labor* f. L *laborem* nom. *-or*]

lāb'our² (-ber), v.i. & t. Use labour, exert oneself, work hard; strive for end or *to* do; advance with difficulty (*wheels* ~ *in the sand*); be troubled (*her* ~*ing heart*) or impeded; suffer *under* mistake etc.; (of ship) roll or pitch heavily; (arch. or poet.) till (ground); elaborate, work out in detail, treat at length, (*I will not* ~ *the point;* ~*ed,* much elaborated, showing signs of labour, not spontaneous); ~*ing*

man, labourer. [f. F *labourer* f. L *laborare* (*labor* LABOUR¹)]

lāb'ourer (-ber), n. In vbl senses; esp., man doing for wages work that requires strength or patience rather than skill or training. [-ER¹]

lāb'ourite (-ber), n. Member, adherent, of Labour Party. [-ITE⁴(1)]

Lab'radŏr, n. attrib. ~ *dog, retriever,* breed of retriever. [place]

lāb'rēt, n. Piece of shell, bone, etc., inserted in lip as ornament. [L *labrum* lip, -ET¹]

labûrn'um, n. Small tree with racemes of bright yellow flowers. [L]

lăb'yrinth, n. Complicated irregular structure with many passages hard to find way through or about without guidance, maze; intricate or tortuous arrangement; (Anat.) complex cavity of internal ear; entangled state of affairs. Hence ~INE² (-in'thin) a. [f. L f. Gk *laburinthos* etym. dub.]

lăbyrin'thodŏn, n., **-dŏnt,** n. & a. (Kinds of large fossil amphibian) with labyrinthine teeth. [-*dont* f. -*don* mod. L, f. Gk as prec. +*odous -ontos* tooth]

lăc¹, n. A resinous substance secreted by the lac insect as a protective covering. [f. Hind. *lakh* f. Skr. *laksha*]

lăc², lākh(-k), n. (Anglo-Ind.). A hundred thousand (usu. ~ *of rupees*). [Hind. (-*kh*) f. Skr. *laksha*]

lāce¹, n. Cord or leather strip for fastening or tightening opposite edges of boot-uppers, stays, etc., by help of eyelets or hooks; braid for trimming men's coats etc.(usu. *gold or silver* ~); fine open fabric of linen, cotton, silk, woollen, or metal threads usu. with inwrought or applied patterns; ~*glass,* Venetian with ~-like designs; ~-*pillow,* laid on lap of woman making ~. Hence lā'cy² a. [f. OF *las, las,* f. L *laqueus* noose]

lāce², v.t. & i. Fasten or tighten (boot, stays, etc.) with lace(s); compress waist of by drawing stay-laces tight, (intr.) compress one's waist; interlace or embroider (fabric) with thread etc.; pass (cord etc.) *through;* trim with lace; diversify (flower *with* streaks of colour); lash, beat, (also intr. as ~ *into* person); flavour, fortify, (milk, beer, etc.) *with* spirit. Hence lā'cING¹(1, 3, 6) n. [f. OF *lacier* as prec.]

lā'cerāte, v.t. Mangle, tear, (esp. flesh or tissues); afflict, distress, (heart, feelings). Hence or cogn.~ATION, ~ATE²(-ăt), ~ATIVE, aa., ~A'TION n. [f. L *lacerare* (*lacer* torn), -ATE³]

lăcĕrt'ian, -tine, aa. Of lizards; lizard-like. [f. L *lacerta* lizard +-IAN, -INE¹]

lăcĕt', n. Work made of braid or tape shaped into a design with lace stitches. [-ET¹]

lăch'es (-iz), n. (Law) negligence in performing a legal duty, delay in asserting

lachryma Christi (~ vase, or ~ as n., to hold tears; ~ canal, duct, gland, sac, in Anat.; also ~'s as n., these organs), cf. Gk dakru]

lach'ryma tear, cf. Gk dakru]

lach'rymal (-k-), a. & n. Of, for, tears [med. L (-alis), f. L lacrima tear. L, = Christ's sweet red S.-Ital. wine. [L, = Christ's tear]

lachryma'tion (lacrimare as prec., -ATION) n. Flow of tears. [f. L lacrimatio (lacrimare as prec., -ATION)]

lach'rymatory (-k-), a. & n. 1. Of, causing, (~ bomb, emitting gas that disables by making eyes water). 2. n. Phial of kind found in anc.-Roman tombs & conjectured to be tear-bottles. [f. lacrimare see prec. +-ORY]

lach'rymose (-k-), a. Tearful, given to weeping. Hence ~IY² adv. [f. L lacrimosus (lacrima tear, -OSE¹)]

laci'niate, -āted, aa. (bot., zool.). Cut into deep irregular segments, slashed, jagged, fringed. [f. L lacinia lappet, -ATE²]

lack, n., & v.i. & t. 1. Deficiency, want, need, of (no ~, plenty of; for ~, owing to want or absence of). 2. vb. Be wanting (only in part. forms, as money was ~ing, is ~ing in courage); be without, not have, be deficient in; ~'land, (person) having no land; ~'lustre, (of eye etc.), dull. [cf. MLG lak, MDu. lac, deficiency, blame, fault]

lackadais'ical (-z-), a. Languishing, affected, given to airs & graces, feebly sentimental. Hence ~IY² adv., ~NESS n. [f. arch. lackaday, -daisy, int. (ALACK) +-ICAL]

lacker. See LACQUER.

lack'ey, lacq'uey (-ki), n. (pl. ~s), & v.t. 1. Footman, man-servant (usu. liveried); obsequious person, parasite. 2. v.t. Dance attendance on, behave servilely to. [f. F laquais (in OF also alacays pl.), etym. dub.]

lacon'ic, a. Brief, concise, sententious; given to such speech or style. Hence ~ICALLY adv., ~ICISM(2) n. [f. Gk lakōnikos (Lakōn Spartan, -IC)]

lac'onism, n. Brevity of speech; short pithy saying. [f. Gk lakōnismos (lakōnizō behave like Spartan or Lakōn, -ISM)]

lacq'uer (-ker), **lack'er**, n., & v.t. 1. Gold-coloured varnish of shellac dissolved in alcohol used esp. as coating for brass; ~) taking hard polish & used for wood etc., articles so coated. 2. v.t. Coat with ~. [f. obs. F lacre sealing-wax perh. f. Port. lacca LAC¹]

lacquey. See LACKEY.

lacrim-, lacrym-. See LACHRYM-.

lacrosse (lakhraws', -ŏs), n. N.-Amer. game like hockey, but with ball driven by & carried in CROSSE. [F la the +CROSSE]

lactā'tion, n. Suckling; secreting of milk. [f. L lactare suckle (lac -tis milk) +-ATION]

lac'teal, a. & n. 1. Of milk; conveying chyle or other milky fluid. 2. n. pl. Vessels of mesentery doing this. [f. L lacteus lac -ENCE, -ENT]

lac'tic, a. (chem.). Of milk; ~ic acid, formed in sour milk, whence ~ATE(3) n. [f. L lac -tis milk +-IC]

lactif'erous, a. Yielding milk or milky fluid. [f. L lactifer (prec., -FEROUS)]

lac'to-, comb. form (f-, -o) of L as prec.; ~profein, albuminous constituent of milk; ~METER(-ŏm²), ~SCOPE, instruments for testing purity of milk.

lactose, n. Milk sugar, less sweet than cane sugar. [as prec. +-OSE²]

lacū'na, n. (pl. ~ae, ~as). Hiatus, blank, missing portion, empty part; cavity in bone, tissue, etc. Hence ~AL, ~AR, ~ARY, ~OSE¹, aa. [L (lacus LAKE¹)]

lacus'trine, a. Of, dwelling or growing in, lake(s); ~ age, of LAKE¹-dwellings. [f. L lacus -tris LAKE¹ on anal. of L palustr- f. palus -udis marsh +-INE¹]

lacy. See LACE¹.

lad, n. Boy, youth, young fellow; fellow. Hence ~d'ie [-z³] n. [ME ladde; earlier sense servimg-man; perh. orig. p.p. of LEAD²]

ladd'er, n., & v.i. Set of steps (called rungs) inserted usu. in two uprights of wood or metal or in two cords to serve as (usu. portable) means of ascending building etc.; || (transf.) vertical flaw in stocking caused by stitch(es) becoming undone through several rows (v.i., develop ~, whence ~PROOF² a.; (fig.) means of rising in the world or attaining object (kick down ~, abandon friends or occupation that have helped one to rise); ~dredge, with buckets carried round on ~like chain; ~-stitch, crossbar stitch in embroidery. [OE hlǣder, cf. G leiter cogn. W. LEAN² & Gk lēkmaz CLIMAX]

lade, v.t. (p.p. ~n). Put cargo on board (ship); ship (goods) as cargo (BILL⁴ of lading), whence lād'ing(3) n.; (p.p., of vehicle, beast of burden, person, tree, branch, table, etc.) loaded (with); (p.p.) painfully burdened with sin, sorrow, etc. [com.-Teut.; OE hladan, cf. Du. & G laden]

la-di-da' (lah-, -ah), a. & n. (Person given to) swagger or pretension in manners & pronunciation; pretentious in this way. [limit. of pronunciation used]

Ladin' (-ēn), n. RHAETO-ROMANIC of the Engadine. [f. L. Ladino f. L LATINUS]

la'dle, n., & v.t. 1. Large spoon with cup bowl & long handle for transferring liquids; hence ~FUL(2) (-dfool) n. 2. v.t. Transfer (liquid) with ~ from one

receptacle to another. [OE *hlædel* f. *hlædan* LADE in obs. sense to bale + -LE(1)] **lad'y**, n. **1.** Ruling woman (poet. exc. in ~ *of the manor, our sovereign* ~). **2.** Woman to whom man is devoted, mistress, love. **3.** *Our* L~, Virgin Mary. **4.** Woman belonging to, or fitted by manners, habits, & sentiments, for, the upper classes (corresp. to GENTLEMAN; ‖ ~*of bedchamber*, ~*-in-waiting*, ~ *attending sovereign*; FINE³ ~). **5.** (Courteously for) woman (as voc. only poet. or vulg. in sing., but usu. form of address in pl.). **6.** ‖ (Title used as less formal prefix for) Marchioness, Countess, Viscountess, Baroness, (also prefixed to Christian name of) daughter of duke, marquis, or earl, (or to husband's Christian name of) wife of holder of courtesy title *lord William* etc., (or to surname of) wife of baronet or knight, (also in the compound title) L~ *Mayoress*, wife of Lord Mayor. **7.** *My* ~, form of address used chiefly by servants etc. to holders of title ~; *my dear* or *good* ~ (address in ord. use). **8.** Wife (arch. or vulg., exc. of those who hold the title ~); *your good* ~, your wife. **9.** *Ladies & gentlemen* (voc. in addressing company of both sexes). **10.** (With *clerk, doctor, president, dog*, etc.) female: ‖ (with *cook, parlourmaid, help*, etc.) claiming to be treated as ~. **11.** *Ladies* (as sing. n.) women's public lavatory etc.; *Ladies' chain*, figure in quadrille; *Ladies' gallery*, in House of Commons reserved for ladies. **12.** ~ *of* EASY *virtue*; *painted* ~, kind of butterfly. **13.** L~*-altar* (in L~*-chapel*); ~*bird*, coleopterous insect, usu. reddish-brown with black spots; L~ *Bountiful*, ~ playing the part of Providence in a village etc. (character in Farquhar's *Beaux's Stratagem*); ~*chair*, made by two persons' interlaced hands to carry wounded man etc.; L~*-chapel*, in large church usu. east of high altar & dedicated to Virgin; ~*clock, -cow*, bird; L~ *Day*, Feast of the Annunciation, 25th March, ‖ one of the quarter-days; ~*fern*, tall slender kind; ‖ ~ *help*, ~, employed as domestic; ~*-killer*, man devoting himself to making conquests of ladies; ~*love*, sweetheart; L~*'s* BED¹*straw*; ~*'s companion*, roll containing cottons etc.; ‖ L~*'s cushion*, mossy saxifrage; ‖ L~*'s finger*, kidney vetch; L~*'s laces*, kind of striped grass; ~*'s-maid*, in charge of ~*'s* toilet; ~*'s man, ladies' man*, (fond of female society); L~*'s mantle*, rosaceous herb; L~*-smock*, cuckoo flower; L~*'s slipper*, orchidaceous wild & garden plant with usu. yellow bag- or slipper-shaped flowers, calceolaria; L~*'s tresses*, kind of orchis. Hence ~HOOD n. [OE *hlǽfdige* (*hláf* loaf, *dige-* knead cf. DOUGH); in ~*-altar, -bird, -chapel, -clock, -cow, -day, -smock*, ~ is old genit.=(Our Lady's]

lād'yfy, -ify, v.t. Make lady of; call lady; (p.p.) having the airs of a fine lady. [-FY] **lād'ylike**, a. With manners etc. of a lady; (of man) effeminate; befitting a lady. [-LIKE]

lād'yship, n. Being a lady; *her, your,* ~, *their* ~*s*, she, you, they (in respectful mention of or address to titular lady). [-SHIP]

l(a)ae'vo- (lēv'o), comb. form of L *laevus* left, esp. in terms concerned with chem. property of causing plane of polarized light ray to rotate to left (opp. DEXTRO-); so ~*gyrous*,~*rotatory*, of substances having this; ~*com'pound*, chemical compound having it.

l(a)ae'vŭlōse (lēv-), n. (chem.). Laevo-rotatory sugar of fruit & honey, fruit-sugar. [prec., -UL-, -OSE²]

lăg¹, v.i. (-gg-), & n. **1.** Go too slow, not keep pace, fall behind (often *behind* abs. & prep.). **2.** n. (phys.). (Amount of retardation in current or movement (~ *of tide*, interval by which it falls behind mean time in 1st & 3rd quarters of moon, cf. PRIMING²). Hence ~g'ARD n. & a., ~g'ER¹ n., ~g'ING² a., (-g-). [n. f. vb; vb perh. f. obs. n.=hindmost person, which is perh. corruption of *last* in children's games (*fog, seg,* ~, =1st, 2nd, last, in diall.]

lăg², v.t. (-gg-), & n. (sl.). **1.** Send to penal servitude; apprehend, arrest. **2.** n. Convict. [?]

lăg³, n., & v.t. (-gg-). **1.** (Piece of the) non-conducting cover of boiler etc. **2.** v.t. Case with ~s, whence ~g'ING¹(³) (g-) n. [f. ON *logg* barrel-rim]

lăg'an, n. (legal). Goods or wreckage lying on bed of sea. [OF, perh. f. Teut. LIE³, LAY³]

la'ger (beer) (lahg-), n. Light kind of (orig. German) beer. [f. G *lager-bier* (*lager* store)]

lagōon', -une (-ōōn), n. Stretch of salt water parted from sea by low sand-bank; enclosed water of atoll. [F (-*une*), f. It. & Sp. *laguna* f. L LACUNA]

lā'ic, a. & n. Non-cleric(al), lay(man), secular, temporal. So ~AL a.,~alLY² adv. [f. LL f. Gk *laikos* (*laos* people, -IC)]

lā'icize, v.t. Make lay; commit (school etc.) throw open (office), to laymen. Hence ~A'TION n. [prec., -IZE]

laid. See LAY³.

lain. See LIE³.

lair, n., & v.i. & t. **1.** Place where animals lie down; ‖ shed or enclosure for cattle on way to market, whence ~AGE(1, 3) n.; wild beast's lying-place. **2.** vb. Go to, rest or place in, ~. [OE *leger* bed, also Du., cf. G *lager*; cogn. w. LIE³]

‖ **laird**, n. (Sc.). Landed proprietor in Scotland. Hence ~SHIP n. [Sc. form of LORD w. changed sense]

Lā'is, n. Accomplished or beautiful courtesan. [name of two celebrated Greek hetaerae]

laissez-aller (lĕs'ā ăl'ā), n. Unconstrained freedom, absence of constraint. [F,=let go]

laisser-faire (-sā-), n. Government abstention from interference with individual action esp. in commerce. [F,=let act]

la'ity, n. Being a layman; laymen; unprofessional people, those outside any particular learned profession. [f. F laï-]

lake¹, n. Large body of water entirely surrounded by land; the Great L~s, Atlantic ocean; the Great L~s, Superior, Huron, Michigan, Erie, & Ontario, forming boundary of U.S. & Canada; ~country, ~land, the L~s, region of England in Westmorland, Cumberland, & Lancs.; ~dweller, prehistoric inhabitant of ~dwelling, built on piles driven into bed of ~; ~poets, Coleridge, Southey, & Wordsworth, who lived in ~-land. Hence ~LESS a., ~LET n., (-kl-). [f. OF lac f. L lacus]

lake², n. Pigment, orig. made from lac, now formed by dye & mordant. [var. of LAC¹]

lakh. See LAC².

Lalla'tion, n. LAMBDACISM. [f. L lallare sing lullaby +-ATION]

lam, v.t. & i. (sl.; -mm-). Thrash, hit (t. & i. with into) hard with cane etc. [perh. cogn. w. LAME]

la'ma¹ (lah-), n. Tibetan or Mongolian Buddhist monk; (Dalaï (pr. dä'ï) L~, (obs.) Grand L~), head of ~ist church & ruler of Tibet. Hence ~ISM n., ~IST n. & a. [Tibetan blama superior]

lama². See LLAMA.

Lamarck'ian, a. & n. (Follower) of Lamarck or his theory of organic evolution by inheritable modifications produced in the individual by habit etc. [Lamarck, F botanist & zoologist, d. 1829, +-IAN]

lama'sery (-mah-), n. Monastery of lamas. [f. F lamaserie irreg. f. LAMA¹]

lamb (-m), n. & v.t. & i. 1. Young of sheep (as well be hanged for a sheep as for a ~, sin boldly, go the whole hog; like a ~, unresistingly; wolf, fox, in ~'s skin, hypocrite); its flesh as food; young member of church flock; innocent, weak, or dear person; The L~ (of God), Christ; ~'s-fry, product of ~'s castration; ~skin, with wool on, or as leather; ~'s-tails, || hazel catkins; ~'s-wool, used in hosiery; hence ~HOOD (-mh-), ~KIN (-mk-), nn., ~LIKE (-ml) a. 2. vb. (Pass.; of ~s) be brought forth; bring forth ~, yean; tend (~ing ewes), whence ~ER¹ (-mer) n. [OE]

lambaste', v.t. (jüal.). Thrash, beat. [perh.=LAM+BASTE³]

lamb'da, n. Greek letter L (Λ); ~ moth, with ~ on wings. [Gk; also labda]

la(m)b'dacism, n. Pronunciation of r as l. [prec.,-ISM]

lamé, n. Thin plate, scale, layer, or film, esp. of bone or tissue. Hence ~AR¹, lăm'ĕllATE², -ātĕd, ~OSE¹, aa., ~ı-comb. form. [L, dim. of LAMINA]

lament', n. & v.t. & i. 1. Passionate expression of grief; elegy, dirge. 2. vb. Express or feel grief for or about, be distressed at, regret, (also intr. with for or over, or abs.); (p.p.) mourned for (esp. conventionally of the dead, as the late ~ed —). [f. L tn. lamentum & vb lamentari]

lam'entable, a. Mournful (arch.); (of events, fate, condition, character, etc.), deplorable, regrettable. Hence ~LY² adv. [f. L lamentabilis (prec., -ABLE)]

lamenta'tion, n. Lamenting, lament; L~s (of Jeremiah), O.-T. book (abbr. Lam.). [f. L lamentatio (LAMENT, -ATION)]

lam'ia, n. Monster in woman's shape preying on human beings & sucking children's blood. [L f. Gk]

lam'ina, n. (pl. -ae). Thin plate, scale, layer, or flake, of metal, bone, membrane, stratified rock, vegetable tissue, etc. Hence ~AR¹, ~OSE¹, aa., ~ı- comb. form. [L]

lam'inate, v.t. & i. Beat or roll (metal) into thin plates; split (t. & i.) into layers or leaves; overlay with metal plates; manufacture by placing layer on layer. Hence or cogn. ~ATE² (-àt) a., ~A'TION n. [prec. +-ATE³]

Lăm'mas, n. First of August, formerly observed as harvest festival (latter ~, non-existent date, day that will never come; cf. Greek CALENDS). [OE hlāfmæsse (LOAF, MASS¹)]

lamb'doid, lambdoid'al, aa. Lambda-shaped (~ suture, connecting two parietal bones with occipital). [f. F lambdoïde f. Gk lambdoeides (LAMBDA, -OID)+-AL]

lamb'ient, a. (Of flame or light) playing on surface without burning it, with soft radiance; (of eyes, sky, etc.) softly radiant; (of wit etc.) gently brilliant. Hence ~ENCY n., ~ently² adv. [f. L lambere lick, -ENT]

Lăm'beth, n. (Used for) Archbishop of Canterbury's palace at ~, the Archbishop as representing the Church, etc.

lăm'brequin (-kĭn), n. Short piece of drapery over top of door or window, or hung from mantelpiece. [F; etym. dub.; orig. scarf worn over helmet]

lame, a., & v.t. 1. Crippled by injury or defect in a limb, esp. foot or leg, limping or unable to walk, (of person, limb, steps, etc.; ~ of or in a leg etc.); (of argument, story, excuse) imperfect, unsatisfactory; (of metre) halting; ~ DUCK¹; hence ~NESS n. 2. v.t. Make ~, cripple, (lit. & fig.). [OE lama, cf. Du. lam, G lahm]

lamé (lahmā'), a. & n. (Material) with gold or silver thread inwoven. [F]

lammergeyer (-gī-), n. Bearded Vulture, largest European bird of prey. [f. G

lämmergeier (*lümmer-* lambs, *geier* vulture)]

lămp, n., & v.i. & t. **1.** Vessel with oil & wick for giving light; glass vessel enclosing candle, gas-jet, incandescent wire, or other illuminant (*smell of the ~*, betray nocturnal study, be laborious in style etc.; with allusion to ancient-Greek torch-race, *pass, hand, on the ~*, do one's part in advancing knowledge, a cause, etc.); SAFETY ~; SPIRIT-~; (fig.) sun, moon, star; source of spiritual or intellectual light, hope, etc.; ~*black*, pigment made from soot; ~*chimney*, glass cylinder making draught for ~-flame; ~*light*, given by ~ or ~s; ~*lighter*, man who lights street ~s (*like a ~lighter*, with speed); ~*post*, usu. of iron supporting street ~; hence ~LESS a. **2.** vb. Shine: supply with ~s: illuminate: *(sl.) look at. [f. F *lampe* f. L, f. Gk *lampas* (*lampō* shine)]

lăm'pas¹, n. Horse-disease with swelling in roof of mouth. [F, earlier=disease proticing thirst, etym. dub.]

lăm'pas², n. Kind of flowered silk orig. from China. [F, etym. dub.]

lăm'pion, n. Pot of usu. coloured glass with oil & wick used in illuminations. [F, f. It. *lampione* (*lampa* LAMP, -OON]

lampoon', n., & v.t. **1.** Virulent or scurrilous piece of satire; hence ~IST (1) n. **2.** v.t. Write ~ or ~s against, whence ~ER¹ n. [f. F *lampon* perh. f. *lampons* let us drink]

lăm'prey, n. (pl. ~s). Eel-like pseudo-fish with sucker mouth, pouch gills, & seven spiracles on each side, & fistula on top of head. [f. OF *lampreie* f. med. L *lampreda* perh.=*lampetra* taken as f. L *lambere* lick, *petra* stone w. ref. to use of sucker]

Lăncas'trian, a. & n. (Inhabitant) of Lancashire or Lancaster: (adherent) of family descended from John of Gaunt Duke of Lancaster, or of the Red-rose party fighting for it in Wars of the Roses. [Lancaster, -IAN]

lance¹ (-ah-), n. Weapon with long wooden shaft & pointed steel head used by horseman in charging: similar implement for spearing fish or killing harpooned whale; (pl., w. numbers)=lancers: ~*corporal* (&, sl. ~*jack*), N.C.O. below corporal: ~*sergeant*, corporal acting as sergeant; ~*fish*, launce; ~*snake*, venomous Amer. kind: ~*wood*, tough elastic W.-Ind. kind used for carriage-shafts, fishing-rods, etc. [F, f. L *lancea*; ~*corporal* on anal. of obs. *lancepesade* f. It. *lancia spezzata* broken lance.]

lance² (-ah-), v.t. Fling, launch, (poet.); (Surg.) prick or cut open with lancet; pierce with lance. [poet. sense f. OF *lancier* f. L *lanceare* (*lancea* LANCE¹); other senses f. prec.]

lance'let (-ahnsl-), n. A fish, the lowest true vertebrate. [LANCE¹, -LET]

lăn'ceolate, a. Shaped like spear-head, tapering to each end. [f. L *lanceolatus* (*lanceola* dim. of *lancea* lance, -ATE²]

la'ncer (-ah-), n. Soldier of cavalry regiment orig. armed with lances; (pl.) kind of quadrille, music for it. [f. F *lancier* (LANCE¹, -IER)]

la'ncet (-ah-), n. **1.** Surgical instrument usu. with two edges & point for bleeding or lancing. **2.** (Also ~*arch, light, window,* etc.) arch or window with pointed head, whence ~ED² a. [f. OF *lancette* (LANCE¹, -ETTE)]

la'ncinating (lah-), a. (Of pain) acute, shooting. [part. of rare *lancinate* f. L, *lancinare* rend]

land¹, n. **1.** Solid part of earth's surface (opp. sea, water; *travel by ~; how the ~ lies*, what is the state of affairs); ground, soil, expanse of country; nation, State (~ *of promise*, Canaan; ~ *of* CAKE¹s; ~ *of the leal*, heaven; ~ *of the living*, present life); landed property, (pl.) estates; (S. Afr.) ground fenced off for tillage; strip of plough or pasture parted from others by water furrows. **2.** Any of the divisions between the rifling-grooves in guns. **3.** ~*-agent, -agency,* ||steward(ship) of estate, agency, agent, for sale etc. of estates; ~*bank*, ||issuing notes on security of landed property; ~*breeze*, blowing seaward from ~; ~*carriage*, transport by ~; ~*crab*, kinds that live on ~ but breed in sea; ~*fall* (Naut.), approach to ~ esp. for first time on voyage (*good, bad, ~fall*, according, not a:cording, to calculation); ~*force(s)*, military, not naval: ||~*girl* (doing farmwork, esp. in wartime): ~*grabber*, (esp.) man who takes Irish farm after eviction of tenant; ~*holder*, proprietor or (usu.) tenant of ~; ~*hunger, hungry*, eagerness to acquire ~; ||~*jobber*, speculator in ~; ~*lady*, woman keeping inn, boarding-house, or lodgings, also woman having tenants; ~*law* (usu. pl.), law(s) of landed property; L~ *League*, Irish association 1879–81 for reducing rents, introducing peasant-proprietorship, etc.; ~*locked*, almost or quite enclosed by ~; ~*lord*, person of whom another holds any tenement (opp. tenant), keeper of inn, lodgings, etc.; ~*lubber* (Naut.), person ignorant of the sea & ships; ~*mark*, object marking boundary of country, estate, etc., conspicuous object in district etc., object or event or change marking stage in process or turning-point in history; ~*mine*, explosive mine laid in or on ground, parachnte mine; ~*owner*, owner of ~; ~*rail*, corncrake; (see JOHN-o'-*Groat's*); ~*service*, military; ~*shark*, one who lives by preying on seamen ashore; ~*sick* (Naut.; of ship), impeded in movement by nearness of ~; ~*slide* (orig. U.S.), overwhelming majority of votes for one side, esp. in an election; ||~*slip*, sliding down of mass

of ~ on cliff or mountain; ~s'man, non-sailor; ~swell, roll of water near shore; ~tax, assessed on landed property; ~tie, rod, beam, or piece of masonry, securing or supporting wall etc. by connecting some part of it with the ground; ~wind, = ~breeze. Hence ~¹ to damage rigging. [1] LESS a., ~WARD a. & adv., ~WARDS adv. [com.-Teut.; OE, Du., G, Sw., & Da., land]

land², v.t. & i. Set or go ashore (p.p. = having come ashore, see -ED*(2), esp. in comb. as newly-~ed, disembark; bring to, reach or find oneself in, a certain place, stage, or position; deal (person blow etc.; ~ed him one in the eye); bring (fish) to land, (fig.) win (prize etc.); (trans. of jockey, intr. of horse) bring or come in (first etc., or abs. =first); alight after jump etc. [f. prec.]

lan'dau, n. Four-wheeled carriage with top of which front & back halves can be independently raised & lowered. [i~ in Germany]

landaulet(te), n. Coupé with landau top. [-LET]

lä'nd·drŏst, n. (hist.). Magistrate in S. Africa. [Du.,=sheriff]

land'ed, a. Possessed of land (the ~ interest, owners & holders of land); consisting of land (~ estate, property). [LAND¹ +-ED²]

land'grave, n. (fem. ·gravine, pr. -grāvēn). Title of certain German potentates. [f. MHG landgrâve (LAND¹, G graf count)]

lăn'ding, n. In vbl senses; also; (also ~-place) place for disembarking; platform between two flights of stairs; ~net, for landing large fish when hooked; ~stage, platform, often floating, on which passengers & goods are disembarked. [-ING¹]

lä'ndlŏ'rdĭsm, n. System by which land is owned by landlords receiving fixed rents from tenants (esp. deprecatively of Irish system). [-ISM]

lă'ndŏc'răcy̆, n. (joc.). The landed class. So **lă'ndŏcrat** n. [-CRACY]

lă'nd'scape (or -ns-), n. || ~-gardening, -gardener, senting art reproducing, or actual piece of inland scenery; laying, layer, out of grounds in imitation of natural scenery; ~-painter, who paints treelike markings; ~-marble, kind with ~s, also länd'scäpist(1) n. [f. Du. landschap (LAND¹, -SHIP)]

land'sturm (lah-, -oorm), n. (Hist., in Germany etc.), general levy in war, of men outside army, navy, & Landwehr. [G]

land'tag (lah-, -ahg), n. Legislative body, diet, of a German State. [G]

Land'wehr (lah-, -vâr), n. (In Germany etc.) militia serving during war. [G]

lane, n. Narrow road usn. between hedges (it is a long ~ that has no turning, change is sure to come), narrow street; passage made or left between rows of persons; course prescribed for ocean steamers; ~red ~, throat; ||the ~, Drury L~ (theatre). [OE; cf. OFris. lana, Du. laan]

läng'rage, -ridge, (-grij-), n. Case-shot with irregular pieces of iron formerly used

|| **lang syne**, adv. & n. (In) the old days. [Sc., = long since]

läng'uage (-nggw-), n. A vocabulary & way of using it prevalent in one or more countries (DEAD ~); (transf.) method of expression (finger~); ~ of flowers, symbolic signs with meanings attached to various kinds); words & their use; faculty of speech; person's style of expressing himself (bad ~, or || vile ~, oaths & abusive talk; strong ~, expressing vehement feelings); professional or sectional vocabulary; literary style, wording; ~-master, teacher of (usu. mod. foreign) ~, or ~s. [f. F langage (L lingua tongue, -AGE)]

tongue d'oc, tongue d'oïl, nn. (see Ap.). Medieval French as spoken south, north, of the Loire, the latter the staple of modern French. [OF, f. L lingua tongue, de oïl, hoc this, hoc illud this (is) that (oc & oïl being the respective forms for yes)]

läng'uid, a. Inert, lacking vigour, indisposed to exertion, spiritless, apathetic, not vivid, dull, uninteresting; sluggish, slow-moving, faint, weak. Hence ~LY² adv., ~NESS n. [f. L languidus (foll.; -ID¹)]

läng'uish (-nggw-), v.i. Grow or be feeble, lose or lack vitality; live under enfeebling or depressing conditions; grow slack, lose intensity; droop, pine (for); put on languid look, affect sentimental tenderness, whence ~ingly² adv. Hence ~MENT n. [f. F languir (-guïr-) f. L languére cf. LANGUID]

läng'uor (-nggor), n. Faintness, fatigue; lassitude, inertia, want of alertness; soft or tender mood or effect; slackness, dullness, drooping state; (of sky etc.) oppressive stillness. So ~OUS a., ~OUSLY² adv. [OF f. L languorem nom. -or (prec., -OR²)]

langur (lŭngeoor'), n. (Kinds of) common Indian long-tailed monkey. [Hind.]

län'iary, a. & n. (Tooth) adapted for tearing, canine. [f. L laniarius (lanius butcher f. laniare tear, -ARY¹)]

läni'ferous, -i'gerous, aa. Wool-bearing (of limbs, person). Hence ~INESS n. [-FEROUS f. L lana wool, -GEROUS]

länk, a. Shrunken, spare; tall & lean; (of grass etc.) long & flaccid; (of hair) straight & limp, not wavy. [OE hlanc; exc. E; perh. cogn. w. G lenken to bend]

länk'y̆, a. Ungracefully lean & long or tall. Hence ~INESS n. [-Y²]

län'ner, län'erĕt, nn. Kind of falcon, female of it (-er); (-el) male of it. [f. F lanier prob. f. OF lanier cowardly]

lan'olin, n. Extract from sheep's wool as basis of ointments. [f. L *lana* wool + -OL(2)+-IN²]

läns quenê (-kî-), n. Card-game of German origin. [F, f. G *landsknecht* 17th-c. mercenary (lit, servant of country)]

län'tern, n. Transparent case protecting flame of candle etc. (BULL'S-eye, CHINESE, DARK¹, MAGIC, ~); || *parish* ~, the moon; = magic ~, whence ~-IST(3) n.; lightchamber of lighthouse; erection on top of dome or room with glazed sides to admit light; luminous proboscis of ~-*fly*; ~*jaws*, long & thin, giving hollow look to face, whence ~-jaweD² a. [f. F *lanterne* f. L *lanterna* perh. f. Gk *lamptēr* (*lampō* shine) w. assim. to L *lucerna*]

lan'thanum, n. (chem.). Rare element belonging to aluminium group, discovered 1839–41. [f. Gk *lanthanō* lurk (w. ref. to lateness of discovery)+-UM]

|| **län'thorn** (-tern), n. Lantern. [pop. assim. of *lantern* to *horn*, common former material]

lan'yard, n. (naut.). Short rope or line attached to something to secure it or serve as handle. [f. F *lanière*, w. assim. to *yard*]

Laodicê'an, a. & n. (Person) lukewarm esp. in religion or politics. [*Rev.* iii. 15, 16]

läp¹, n. Hanging part or flap of garment, saddle, etc.; lobe of ear; front part of skirt held up to contain something; waist to knees of one sitting, as place on which child is nursed or object held (*in Fortune's* ~, *in the* ~ *of luxury*, etc.), whence ~'FUL(2) n.; hollow among hills; ~-*dog*, small pet dog; ~'*stone*, shoemaker's stone held in ~ to beat leather on. [OE *lappa*, cf. G *lappen*]

läp², v.t. & i. (-pp-). Coil, fold, wrap, (garment etc. *about*, *round*, advv. *over* or prepp.): enfold, swathe, *in* wraps etc.; (of influences etc.) surround, encircle, (often *round*), enfold caressingly (esp. pass., ~*ped in luxury*); make (valve, roof-slate, etc.) overlap; project *over* something (also ~ *over* adv. = *overlap* intr.); (Racing) pass (competitor) by one or more laps. [prob. f. prec.]

läp³, n. Amount of overlapping, overlapping part (*half-*~, joining of rails, shafts, etc., by halving thickness of each at end); layer or sheet of cotton etc. being made) wound on roller; single turn of rope, silk, thread, etc., round drum or reel; one circuit of race-track; ~-*joint*, = *half-*~, whence ~-*streak*, clinker-built boat. [f. prec.]

läp⁴, n., & v.t. (-pp-). 1. Rotating disk for polishing gem or metal. 2. v.t. Polish with ~. [perh. f. prec.]

läp⁵, v.i. drink (up liquid), by scooping with tongue; consume (liquid) greedily (usu. *up* or *down*); (of water) move, beat upon (shore), with sound of ~ping. 2. n. Liquid food for dogs; (sl.) weak beverage, also alcoholic liquor; single act of ~ping, amount taken up by it; sound of wavelets on beach etc. [OE *lapian* cf. OHG *laffan*; cf. G *löffel* spoon, L *lambere*, Gk *laptō*, lick]

lä'par|(o)-, comb. form of Gk *lapara* flank, in anat. & surg. ~*ectomy*, excision of part of intestine at side; ~*ot'omy*, cutting of abdominal walls.

lapĕl', n. Part of coat-breast folded back. Hence ~leD²(-ld) a. [LAP¹, -EL]

läp'icide, n. Cutter of stones or inscriptions on stone. [f. L *lapicida* for *lapidicida* (*lapis -idis* stone + *caedere* cut, kill, cf. -CIDE]

läp'idary, a. & n. 1. Concerned with stones (esp. ~ *bee*, building in stone walls etc.); engraved on stone, (of style) suitable for inscriptions, monumental. 2. n. Cutter, polisher, or engraver, of gems. [f. L *lapidarius* (*lapis -idis* stone, -ARY¹)]

läp'idāte, v.t. Stone, stone to death. So ~A'TION n. [f. L *lapidare* (prec.), -ATE³]

lapid'ify, v.t. Make into stone. Hence ~FICA'TION n. [f. F *lapidifier* f. med. L *lapidificare* (prec., -FY)]

läp'is läz'ûli, n. A silicate containing sulphur; bright blue pigment from it; its colour. [L, = stone of AZURE]

Läpp, n. & a. 1. One of dwarfish race of northern Scandinavia; (also ~'ISH¹ n.) their language; *Läp'land*, their country, whence **Läp'lander**(4) n. 2. adj. (Also ~'ISH¹ a.) of the ~s or their language. [f. Sw. *Lapp*, perh. term of contempt, cf. MHG *lappe* simpleton]

läpp'et, n. Flap, fold, loose or overlapping piece of garment, flesh, membrane, etc.; lobe of ear etc.; = lapel; streamer of lady's head-dress. Hence ~ED² a. [LAP¹ +-ET¹]

Läppon'ian, a. & n. =LAPP. [f. med. L *Lappo -onis*+-IAN]

läpse¹, n. Slip of memory, tongue, or pen, slight mistake; weak or careless deviation from right, moral slip; falling away from faith or into heresy; decline to lower state; termination of right or privilege through disuse; (of water) gentle flow; passage or interval of time; ~ *rate* (Meteor.), rate of fall of temperature with height. [f. L *lapsus -ūs* (*labi laps-* glide)]

läpse², v.i. Fail to maintain position or state for want of effort or vigour; fall back or away (often *into* inferior or previous state); (of benefice, estate, right, etc.) fall in, pass away, become void, revert to someone, by failure of conditions, heirs, etc.; glide, flow, subside, pass away; (p.p.) that has lapsed, see ·ED²(2). [f. L *lapsare* frequent. (prec.)]

läp'sus, n. (pl. -ūs). Slip (usu. in ~ *linguae*, pr. -gwē, of the tongue, ~ *cäl'ämi* of the pen). [L]

Lapú'tan, a. & n. (Inhabitant) of Laputa; chimerical, visionary, absurd. [*Laputa* in Gulliver's *Travels* + -AN]

lap'wing, n. Bird of plover family, peewit. [OE *hléapwince* (*hléapan* LEAP¹, WINK, w. ref. to manner of flight) assim. to LAP, WING]

lär, n. 1. (pl. *lār'es*, pr. -ēz). Ancient-Roman household deity (usu. pl.; *Lares, Lares & Penates*, the home). 2. (pl. -s, pr. -z). White-handed Burmese gibbon. [L]

lar'board (-berd), n. & a. (naut.). (Older term now replaced, to save confusion with *starboard*, by) PORT⁵. [ME *lade-, bortde*; *lade-* (etym. dub.) changed to *lar-* by assim. to STARBOARD]

lar'cen|y, n. (Law) felonious taking away of another's personal goods with intent to convert them to one's own use (*petty* ~y, formerly, of property below value of 12*d*.); theft. Hence ~ER¹ (n.), ~OUS a., ~OUSLY² adv. [f. F *larcin* f. L *latrocinium* (*latro* robber) +-Y¹]

larch, n. Bright-foliaged coniferous tree yielding Venetian turpentine, & bark used in tanning; its wood, timber, & bark used in tanning; its wood. [f. G *lärche* f. L *larix -icis*]

lärd¹, n. Internal fat of abdomen of pigs esp. when rendered & clarified for use in cooking & pharmacy. Hence ~Y² a. [OF. = bacon, f. L *lardum* perh. cogn. w. Gk *laros* fat, *laros* pleasant to taste]

lärd², v.t. Insert strips of bacon in (meat etc.) before cooking (~*ing-needle, -pin*, etc.); (fig.) garnish (talk, writing) *with* metaphors, technical terms, foreign words, etc. [f. F *larder* (prec.)]

lär'daceous (-shus), a. (med.). Lardlike (esp. of degeneration of tissue or of patient suffering from it). [-ACEOUS]

lär'der, n. Room or closet for meat etc. [f. OF *lardier* f. med. L *lardarium* (LARD¹)-ARY¹)]

lärd'on, lärdoon', n. Strip of bacon or pork used to lard meat. [F(-*on*); LARD¹, -OON]

lär'dy-dárd'y a. (sl.), Affected, languidly foppish. [cf. LA-DI-DA]

large, a., n. & adv. 1. (Arch.)liberal, generous, kindly, munificent, unprejudiced, (still in ~ *views, charity, tolerance, ~minded*, whence ~-*mind'edness* n., ~-*hearted*, whence ~-*heart'edness* (-hār-) n., etc.) of wide range, comprehensive, (~ *powers, discretion*); (of artistic treatment) free, sweeping, broad; of considerable or relatively great magnitude (less collog. than *big*, & without emotional implications of *great*; seldom used of persons except as in ~ *of limb* =with ~ limbs etc.); (with agent nouns) on a ~ *scale* (~ & small farmers); hence **lär'gish**(2) a., ~-NESS (-jn-) n., **lär'gen** v.i. & t. (poet.), 2. n. (now only with *at, in, At* ~: at liberty, free; (of narration etc.) at full length, with details; as a body or whole

(popular with the people *at*~); without particularizing, without definite aim, (*scatters imputations at* ~; *gentleman at* ~, gentleman attached to the court without special duties, person who has no occupation; *in* ~, *on*~ *scale* (opp. *in little*). 3. adv. *by*& ~, [F, f. fem. of L *largus* copious]

large'ly (-jl-), adv. In adj. senses; also, to a great or to a preponderating extent (*is* ~ *due to*). [-LY²]

lar'gess(e), n. (arch.). Money or gifts freely bestowed esp. by great person on occasion of rejoicing; generous or plentiful bestowal. [F (-*e*), f. L *largus* copious]

lär'gō, adv. & n. (mus.). (Movement) in slow time with broad dignified treatment. [It., = broad]

lä'riat, n. Rope for picketing horses etc., lasso. [f. Sp. *la reata* f. *reatar* tie again (RE-, L *aptare* fit)]

lärk¹, n., **lär'erock** (-vr-; poet.), n. Kinds of small bird with sandy-brown plumage & long hind-claws, esp. the SKYLARK (*Crested, Horned, Red, Shore, L~*), other kinds; *rise with the* ~, get up early; *if the sky fall, we shall catch* ~s (comfort for alarmists); ~-*heel*, ~-*spur*, also Indian cress or garden nasturtium; ~-*spur*, plant with spur-shaped calyx. [OE *láferce*, cf. Du. *leeuwerik*, G *lerche*, etym.

lärk², n. & v.i. 1. Frolic, spree, amusing incident (*what a* ~!, how amusing!); hence ~Y² a. 2. v.i. Play tricks, frolic. [f. 1811: etym. dub.]

lär'rikin, n. (Usu. young) street rowdy, hooligan. [orig. Australian; etym. dub.]

lä'rrup, v.t. (colloq.). Thrash. [?]

lär'um, n. (pl.~ne). (Now rare for) ALARUM.

lär'va, n. (pl.~ee). Insect from time of leaving egg till transformation into pupa, grub; immature form of other animals that undergo some metamorphosis. Hence ~AL a., ~I- comb. form. [L, = ghost, mask]

lar'ynge'oscope (-ngg-), n. Mirror apparatus for examining larynx. [LARYNX, -SCOPE]

laryngö'tom|y (-ngg-), n. Cutting into larynx from without, esp. to provide breathing-channel, [foll., -TOMY]

lä'rynx, n. Cavity in throat holding vocal cords. Hence **laryn'geäl, laryn'gic**, a. (-j-), **laryn'go-** comb. form, **läryngö'logy** (-ngg-). [f. Gk *larungx -ggos*]

Läs'car (or -ār), n. E.-Indian sailor. [perh. incorrect use of Hind. *lashkar* army]

lasci'vious, a. Lustful, wanton; inciting to lust. Hence ~LY² adv., ~NESS n. [f. LL *lasciviosus* (L *lascivia* f. *lascivus* sportive, -OSE¹)]

lash, v.t.& i. 1. Make sudden movement of limb, tail, etc.; pour, rush, vehemently, whence ~ings n. pl. (sl.),

plenty (of); strike violently *at*; hit or (of horse) kick *out*; break *out* into excess, strong (language), etc. **2.** Beat with lash, flog; (of waves) beat upon; castigate in words, rebuke, satirize; urge as with lashes (~ *oneself into a fury*, work up a rage); hence ~ING¹(1) n. **3.** Fasten (*down*, *on*, *together*, *to* something) with cord, twine, etc., whence ~ING¹(4) n. [sense 1 perh. imit.; sense 2 f. foll.; sense 3 prob. separate wd, etym. dub.]

lash², n. Stroke with thong, whip, etc.; flexible part of whip (*the* ~, punishment of flogging); = EYE—~, whence ~LESS a.; goading influence. [f. prec. in sense 1]

lash'er, n. In vbl senses; || esp. (water rushing over) weir, pool below weir. [-ER¹]

lash'kar, n. Body of armed Indian tribesmen. [Hind.,=army]

|| **läs'pring**, n. Young salmon. [perh. corruption of obs. *lax-pink* (obs. *lax*, OE *leax*, see LAX²; cf. G *lachs*, salmon)]

lasque (lahsk), n. Flat, ill-formed, or veiny diamond. [perh. f. Pers. *lashk* piece]

lass, n. Girl (north., poet., etc.); sweetheart. Hence ~'ie [-Y¹] n. [ME *lasce*, cf. MSw. *lösk (kona)* unmarried (woman), dis-

lass'itude, n. Weariness, languor, disinclination to exert or interest oneself. [F, f. L *lassitudo* (*lassus* tired, -TUDE)]

lass'o (or lasoo'), n. (pl. ~s), & v.t. **1.** Sp. Amer. noosed rope of untanned hide for catching cattle etc. **2.** v.t. Catch with ~. [f. Sp. *lazo* LACE¹]

last¹ (-ah-), n. Shoemaker's wooden model for shaping shoe etc. on (*stick to one's* ~, not meddle with things one does not understand, w. ref. to L prov. *ne sutor supra crepidam*). [OE *lǽst* footstep, *lǽst* boot, cf. G *leisten* last, *geleise* track, perh. cogn. w. L *līra* furrow]

last² (-ah-), n. Commercial measure of weight, capacity, or quantity, varying with place & goods (~ *of wool*, 12 sacks or 4,368 lb.; ~ *of malt*, 10 qrs or 80 bushels). [OE *hlæst*, cf. G *last*, load]

last³ (-ah-), a., n., & adv. **1.** After all others, coming at the end, (*the* ~ *two* etc. = *the* ~ *& ~ but one* etc., *the two* etc. being now usu. held incorrect in this sense; ~ *but not least*, ~ in order of mention or occurrence but not of importance); belonging to the end, esp. of life or the world (*the four* ~ *things*, death, judgement, heaven, hell; ~ *day*, Day of Judgement; *on one's* ~ LEGS); next before expressed or implied point of time, latest up to date, most recent, (*in the* ~ *fortnight*, ~ *Christmas*, ~ *Tuesday* or *Tuesday* or ~ *evening* or *night* or *week* or *month* or *year* used as adverbs, but not ~ *morning*, *day*, or *afternoon*; also ellipt, as n. for ~ *letter*, *joke*, *baby*, etc., *as I said in my* ~, *have you heard* ~'*s* ~?, *Mrs* —'*s* ~); lowest, of least rank or estimation; only remaining (~ *crust*, *resource*); latest to be (*was the* ~

to be consulted); least likely, willing, suitable, etc. *to* or *to be* (*should be the* ~ *to do it*; *is the* ~ *thing to try*); conclusive, definitive, (*has said the* ~ *word on the matter*); utmost, extreme, (*is of the* ~ *importance*). **2.** n.—mentioned person or thing (*the*, *this*, *which*, ~); ~ *day* or *moments*, death, (*the* or *his* etc. ~); ~ performance of certain acts (*breathe*, *look*, *one's* ~); ~ mention (*shall never hear the* ~ *of it*; *at* ~, (also) *at long* ~, in the end, after much delay; *to*, *till*, *the* ~, to the end, esp. till death. **3.** adv. After all others (often in comb., as ~-*made*, ~-*mentioned*); on the ~ occasion before the present (*when did you see him* ~?); (in enumerations) in the ~ place, finally, also ~LY² adv.; cf. G *letz*, & for dropping of -t- BEST]

last⁴ (-ah-), v.i. & t., & n. **1.** Go on, remain unexhausted or adequate or alive; suffice (*will* ~ *me eight months*); ~ *out*, continue esp. in vigour or use at least as long as. **2.** n. Staying power, stamina. [OE *lǽstan* fulfil, cf. G *leisten*]

last'ing (-ah-), a. & n. **1.** Enduring, permanent (*no* ~ *benefit*); durable; hence ~LY² adv., ~NESS n. **2.** n. Kind of durable cloth. [-ING²]

lăt, n. Latvian unit of gold currency (par value about 10d.). [first syllable of *Latvija* Latvia]

Lātaki'a (-ĕa), n. Kind of Turkish tobacco chiefly used in mixtures. [~ (anc. *Laodicea*), a Syrian port]

lătch, n., & v.t. **1.** Door or gate fastening made of small bar falling into catch & lifted by lever etc. from outside; small spring-lock of outer door catching when door is closed & worked by ~'key from outside (|| ~*key vote*, LODGER franchise as tested by possession of ~key); *on the* ~, fastened by ~ only. **2.** v.t. Fasten with ~. [perh. f. OF *lache* LACE¹; or f. obs. *latch*, OE *læccan*, to grasp]

|| **lătch'et**, n. (arch.). Thong for fastening shoe. [f. OF *lachet* (LACE¹, -ET¹)]

lāte¹, a. (comp. ~r, LATTER; superl. ~st, LAST³), & n. After the due or usual time (*was* ~ *for dinner*; *it is too* ~ *to go*; with agent nouns, as ~-*comer*=one who comes ~); backward in flowering, ripening, etc.; far on in day or night (~ *dinner*, in evening; ~ *hours*, after usual time for rising or going to bed), or in time (*on Wednesday at* ~*st*, then if not before); far on in a period, development, etc. (~ *stained glass*, ~ LATIN); no longer alive, no longer having specified status etc., that was recently so-&-so, (*the* ~ *prime minister*, dead or resigned; *my* ~ *husband*, *the* ~ *floods*, *war*; *of* ~ *years*, in the last few; also as n. in *of* ~, recently); || ~ *fee*, on letter posted after ordinary collection time. Hence lāt'EN⁵ v.t. & i., ~NESS (-tn-) n., lāt'ISH¹

(2)a. & adv. [com.-Teut.; cf. Du. *laat*, G *lass*, sluggish, cogn. w. L *lassus* tired.]

late², adv. (~r, ~st, LAST⁹). After proper time (*better* ~ *than never*), far on in time (*this happened* ~r *on*; *soon or* ~r, early or ~ till late hour (*we sat* ~); (poet.) recently, lately, (*I sent thee* ~ *his own room*, ~ *the chaplain* 8); at late stage of development etc. (*races remained as* ~ *as the Stuart times*); ~ *in the day*, (colloq.) at a late stage, esp. unreasonably ~ *in the proceedings* etc. [OE, f. LATE see prec.]

lateen', a. ~ *sail*, triangular on long yard at angle of 45° to mast; (of ship etc.) so rigged. [f. F (*voile*) *latine* (sail)]

late'ly (-t-), adv. Not long ago, recently, in recent times. [OE *lætlice* (LATE, -LIKE)]

lat'ent, a. Hidden, concealed; existing but not developed or manifest; dormant; ~ HEAT. Hence lāt'ENCY n., ~ly² adv. [f. L *latere* be hidden, -ENT]

-later, suf. See -LATRY.

lāt'eral, a. & n. 1. Of, at, towards, from, the side, side-, (~ *branch* of family, descended from brother or sister of person in direct line). 2. n. Side part, member, or object, esp. ~ shoot or branch. Hence ~ly² adv. [f. L *lateralis* (*latus -eris* side, -AL)]

Lāt'eran, n. & a. The ~, St John ~, cathedral church of St John ~ (*Sancti Joannis in ~o*) in Rome; ~ *Council*, one of five general councils of Western Church there held. [f. L ~*a*, ~*um*, named f. ancient-Roman family of Plautii ~*i*]

lat'erite, n. Red friable ferruginous surface clay much used for roadmaking in tropics. [f. L *later* brick+-ITE¹(2)]

lat'ex, n. (bot.). Milky fluid of (esp. rubber) plant. [L.]

lath (-ȧth-), n. (pl. pr. -dhz), & v.t. 1. Thin narrow strip of wood esp. for use as support for slates or plaster or as material for trellis or Venetian blind (*as thin as a* ~, of persons, whence **lath'y¹**(-ah-) a.; & *plaster*, material for interior wall-faces, ceilings, partitions, etc.), 2. v.t. Provide (wall, ceiling) with ~s, whence **la'thing**(3) (-ah-) n. [ME *laththe*, cf. G *latte*, perh. cogn. w. G *laden* shop-counter]

la'the¹ (-dh-), n. One of (now five) administrative districts of Kent. [OE *læth*]

‖**lāthe²** (-dh), n. (Also *turning-*~) machine for turning wood, metal, ivory, etc., by rotating article against tools used; (also *potter's* ~) machine with horizontal revolving disk for throwing & turning pottery; ~-*bearer*, -*carrier*, -*dog*, appliance connecting object with ~ centres or holders; ~-*bed*, lower framework of ~ with slot from one end to end for adjustment.

[prob. cogn. w. Da. -*lad* structure, frame, & LADE; or perh. modification of LATH]

lāth'er (-dh-), n., & v.t. & i. 1. Froth of soap & water; frothy sweat of horse; hence ~r² a. 2. v.b. Cover (esp. chin etc. for shaving) with ~; (of horse) become covered with ~; (of soap) form ~; beat, thrash, whence ~ING¹(1) n. [n. f. OE *leathor* washing soda cogn. w. Gk *loetron* bath, L *lavare* wash; vb f. OE *lēthren*, f. same root]

lathi (laht'i), n. Long heavy iron-bound stick used as weapon by Indian natives & police. [Hind.]

lāt'ifun'dia, n. pl. Large estates, esp. as characterizing a country's social system. [L (sing. -*ium*), f. *latus* broad, *fundus* farm]

Lāt'in, a. & n. 1. Of Latium or ancient ~s or Romans; of, like, in, the language of the ancient Romans, whence ~ISM(4) n.; of the Roman Catholic Church; ~ (see WESTERN) *Church*; (of peoples) inheriting Roman customs etc., speaking one of the languages descended from ~ Romance, (*the* ~ *peoples*, France, Spain, Portugal, Italy, etc.). 2. n. The ~ language (*old* ~, before about 75 B.C., preclassical; *classical* ~, that of great writers of late republican & early imperial Rome, about 75 B.C. to A.D. 175; *late* ~, about A.D. 175 to 600; *medieval* ~, about A.D. 600 to 1500; *modern* ~, since A.D. 1500; *low* ~, =medieval, or late & medieval; SILVER¹ ~; *thieves'* ~, secret language of thieves etc.; DOG ~), whence ~LESS a., ~IST(3) n.; inhabitant of Latium, (Rom. Ant.) Italian with special franchise, [f. L *Latinus* (*Latium* Roman district, -INE¹)]

Lati'n², adv. In Latin (giving Latin equivalent of word etc.). [L]

Lati'nity, n. Way person writes Latin, quality of Latin style or grammar. [f. L *Latinitas* (prec., -TY)]

lāt'inize, v.t. & i. Give Latin form to (word), put into Latin; make conformable to ideas, customs, etc., of the ancient Romans, Latin peoples, or Latin Church; use Latin forms, idioms, etc. Hence ~A'TION, ~ER¹ nn. [f. L *latinizare* (LATIN, -IZE)]

lat'itude, n. 1. (Joc.) breadth (*hat with great* ~ *e of brim*); (rare) scope, full extent, (*understood, taken, in its proper* ~*e*). 2. Freedom from narrowness, liberality of interpretation, tolerated variety of action or opinion, whence (esp. of religious matters) ~inAR'IAN a. & n., ~inAR'ianISM(3) n. 3. (geog.). Angular distance on a meridian (*degree, minute, etc., of* ~); place's angular distance on its meridian N. or S. of equator (*in* ~ 40° *N.* etc.); (usu. pl.) regions, climes, esp. w. ref. to temperature (*high* ~es, far N. or S.; *low* ~es, near equator). 4. (Astron.) angular distance of heavenly body from ecliptic.

So ~inal (-ŭd⁴) a. (Geog.). [f. L latitudo -inis (latus broad, -TUDE)]

latrine' (-ēn), n. Place for evacuation of bowels or bladder, esp. in camp, barracks, hospital, etc. [F, f. L latrina for lavatrina (lavare wash, -INE⁴)]

-latry, suf. f. Gk latreia worship, in wds f. an existing Gk original (idolatry), & mod. formations on same model (angelolatry, Mariolatry). In (humorous) hybrid formations -o- is added to the initial component as lordolatry, babyolatry. Corresponding personal nn. (-worshipper) are formed in -o)later f. Gk -latrēs.

lătt'en, n. & a. (Of) a mixed yellow metal like (or the same as) brass. [f. OF laton perh. f. Teut. (LATH)]

lătt'er, a. (Arch.) later, second, (~ grass, aftermath); belonging to end of period, world, etc. (in these ~ days, at this late period of the world's history; ~ end, death; second-mentioned (opp. former; also the ~ ellipt. = second-mentioned thing or person); ~day, modern (~day saints, Mormons). [OE lætra comp. of læt LATE¹, later being a new formation]

lătt'erly, adv. Towards the end of life or some period; nowadays, of late. [f. prec.]

lătt'ice, n. Structure of cross laths with interstices serving as screen, door, etc.; (also ~work) laths so arranged; ~ bridge, made with ~ girders; ~ frame or girder, girder made of two flanges connected by iron ~work; ~ window, one having ~, also one with small panes set in diagonal lead-work. Hence lătt'iceD² (-st) a., lătt'iciNG¹(6) n. [f. OF lattis (latte LATH)]

Lăt'vian, a. & n. (Inhabitant) of the Republic of Latvia, the country of the Letts, on the Gulf of Riga in the Baltic. [f. Latvi see LETTISH +-AN]

laud, n., & v.t. 1. Praise (rare exc. in hymns); (pl.) first of day-hours of church; hymn of praise. 2. v.t. Praise, celebrate; so ~ATION, ~ăt'OR² nn., ~'ATIVE, ~'ATORY, aa. [n. f. OF laude, vb f. L laudare, f. L laudem nom. laus praise]

laud'able, a. Commendable, praiseworthy; (Med., of secretions) healthy, sound. Hence or cogn. ~ABIL'ITY n., ~ABLY² adv. [f. L laudabilis (prec., -ABLE)]

laudanum (lŏd'nŭm), n. Alcoholic tincture of opium. [name given by Paracelsus to a costly panacea or elixir, later transferred to preparations containing opium; perh. var. of L ladanum or med. L labdanum f. a gum-resin, or f. L laudare praise]

laudat'or témpóris ăc'tī, n. One who prefers the good old days. [L, =praiser of time past]

laugh (lahf, -ăf), v.i. & t., & n. 1. Make the sounds & movements of face & sides by which lively amusement, sense of the ludicrous, exultation, & scorn, are instinctively expressed, have these emo-

tions, (~ in one's sleeve, be secretly amused; ~ing HYENA, JACKASS; ~ on wrong side of mouth, have revulsion from joy or amusement to tears or vexation; he ~s best who ~s last, warning against premature exultation); (of water, landscape, corn, etc.) be lively with play of movement or light; utter ~ingly; hold up to scorn; ~ at, make fun of, ridicule, also look pleasantly or smile at; get (person) out of habit, belief, etc., by ridicule (~ person, opinion, etc., out of court, deprive of a hearing by ridicule) ~ away, dismiss (subject) with a ~, while away (time) with jests; ~ down, silence with laughter; ~ off (embarrassment etc.), get rid of with a jest; ~ over, discuss with laughter; hence ~ER¹ n., ~ING² a., ~ingly² adv., (~ahf-, -ăf-). 2. n. Sound made in, act of, ~ing (join in the ~, esp. of person taking banter good-humouredly; have, get, the ~ of, turn the tables on assailant, also have the ~ on one's side; person's manner of ~ing. [com.-Teut. OE hlehhan, cf. Du. & G lachen; prob. imit.]

laugh'able (-ahf-, -ăf-), a. Exciting laughter, amusing. Hence ~LY² adv. [prec., n. or v.+-ABLE]

laugh'ing (-ahf-, -ăf-). In vbl senses; esp.: no ~ matter, serious thing, not a fit subject for ~; ~gas, nitrous oxide, with intoxicating effect when inhaled, used as anaesthetic; ~stock, person or thing generally ridiculed. [-ING¹]

laugh'ter (-ahf-, -ăf-), n. Laughing (Homeric ~, loud & general, such as Homer attributes to spectators of ludicrous incident). [OE hleahtor, cf. G geléchter (lachen LAUGH)]

launce (lahns, lăns), n. Sand-eel. [perh. var. of LANCE¹]

launch (lawn-, lah-), v.t. & i., & n. 1. Hurl, discharge, send forth, (missile, blow, censure, threat, decree); burst (usu. out) into expense, strong language, etc., (also ~ out, abs., spend money freely, expatiate in words); set (vessel) afloat; send off, start, (person, enterprise) on a course; go forth, out, on an enterprise. 2. n. Process of ~ing ship. [f. ONF lancher = OF lancier LANCE²]

launch² (law-, lah-), n. Man-of-war's largest boat, rather flat-bottomed & usu. sloop-rigged; large boat driven by steam, petrol, etc. for passengers, pleasure trips, etc. [f. Sp. lancha pinnace perh. f. Malay lancharan (lanchar swift)]

laun'der, v.t. & i. (Chiefly as p.p.) wash & get up (linen); (of fabric, with adv.) admit of being ~ed. [f. obs. launder n. washer of linen f. OF lavandier f. LL lavandarius (lavanda neut. pl. gerundive of L lavare wash, -ARY¹)]

laun'dress, n. Woman who washes & gets up linen; [caretaker of chambers in Inns of Court. [f. prec.+-ESS¹]

laun'dry, n. Establishment for washing linen; batch of clothes sent to or from ~. [as prec., -RY]

laur'eate, a. & n. Wreathed with, (of wreath) consisting of, laurel; worthy of receiving stipend as writer of Court odes, etc. ~SHIP (t-sh-) n.), or for eloquence whence ~ (poet ~, or ~ as n., poet laureled as poet, laureate). [f. L laureatus (laurea laurel-wreath f. laurus laurel, -ATE²)]

laur'el (lŏ-), n. & v.t. (-ll-). 1. Kinds of glossy-leaved shrub; foliage of bay-tree as emblem of victory or distinction in poetry (collect. sing. or pl.; recp. win, ~s; rest on one's ~s, cease to strive for further glory; look to one's ~s, beware of losing pre-eminence); ~-bottle, filled with ~ leaves for killing insects. 2. v.t. Wreathe with ~. [f. F laurier f. L laurus; -l by dissim.]

laurustin'us, **-res-** (lŏ-), n. Evergreen flowering shrub. [mod. L, prop. two wds (L laurus laurel, tinus a plant, perh. the ~)]

la'va (lah-), n. Matter flowing from volcano, solid substance it cools into; (w. pl.) kind, bed, of ~. [It. (lavare It. & L wash)]

lavăb'ō, n. (pl. ~s). Ritual washing of celebrant's hands at offertory, towel or basin used for this; monastery washing-trough; wash-basin, (pl.) lavatory, (after F). [L.=I willwash, first wd of Ps. xxvi.6]

lava'tion, n. Washing. [f. L lavatio]

lav'atory, n. Vessel for washing (arch.); room etc. for washing hands & face; (euphem.) water-closet(s) and urinal. [f. L lavatorium f. lavare wash, -ORY(2)]

lāve, v.t. (poet.). Wash, bathe; (of stream etc.) wash against, flow along; [repr. both OE lafian pour (water) cf. G laben refresh, & F laver f. L lavare = Gk louō wash, cf. LATHER]

lāve'ment (-vm-), n. (med.). Injection, enema. [f (spec., -MENT)]

lăv'ender, n. & v.t. 1. Small lilac-flowered narrow-leaved shrub cultivated for perfume; its flowers & stalks laid among linen etc. (lay up in ~, often fig., put aside for future use); pale blue colour distilled ~, alcohol, & ambergris. 2. v.t. Put ~ among (linen). [f. AF lavendre f. med.L lavendula, livendula, perh. f. L LIVID(us)]

lav'er, n. Kinds of marine algae, esp. the edible species. [L]

lā'ver, n. (Bibl.) large brazen vessel for Jewish priests' ablutions; (arch.) washing or fountain basin, font. [f. OF laveir LAVATORY]

laverock. See LARK¹.

lăv'ish, a. & v.t. 1. Giving or producing without stint, profuse, prodigal, (of money etc., in giving); very or over abundant; hence ~LY² adv., ~NESS n.

2. v.t. Bestow or spend (money, effort, blood, admiration, etc.) profusely; hence ~MENT n. [f. obs. lavish profusion f. OF lavache deluge of rain]

law¹, n. 1. Body of enacted or customary rules recognized by a community as binding, this personified, (the ~ forbids, allows; often the ~ of the land; the ~ of the Medes & Persians, unalterable, see Dan. vi. 12; lay down the ~, talk authoritatively, hector). 2. One of these rules. 3. Their controlling influence, ~-abiding state of society, (often ~ & order; necessity knows no ~, over-rides its sanctity; be a ~ unto oneself, take one's own line, disregard convention; the ~s as a system (court of ~; so son-in-~ etc.) or science (learned in the ~; read ~, study the ~s), jurisprudence. 4. Binding injunctions (give the ~ to, impose one's will upon). 5. (With defining word) one of the branches of the study of ~, the ~s concerning specified department, (commercial ~; the ~ of evidence; CANON, CIVIL, COMMON¹, MARTIAL, ~; international ~, ~ of nations, regulating relations between States). 6. The statute & common ~ (opp. EQUITY). 7. (In pred. use, of decisions, opinions, etc.; also good, bad, etc., ~) borne out, or not, by the relevant ~s (it may be common sense, but it is not ~). 8. The legal profession (usu. the ~; bred to the ~); legal knowledge. 9. Judicial remedy; ~-courts as providing it, litigation, (go to ~; have, take, the ~ of person; take the ~ into one's own hands, redress one's wrong by force); the Law Courts, ||(esp.) the ROYAL Courts of Justice. 10. (Also ~ of Moses) precepts of Pentateuch, Mosaic dispensation. 11. Rule of action or procedure, esp. in an art, department of life, or game. 12. (Also ~ of nature or natural ~) correct statement of invariable sequence between specified conditions & specified phenomenon (~s of motion, three propositions formulated by Newton; Gresham's ~, that bad money drives out good; Kepler's ~s, three propositions on planetary motions; Grimm's ~, Verner's ~, on consonant changes in Germanic languages). 13. ~s of nature, regularity in nature (where they saw chance, we see ~); Law of Nature (see also above) or Reason, principles of conduct recognized as pleasing to God or as intrinsically reasonable. 14. (Sport) allowance, start, given to hunted animal or competitor in race, (whence gen.) time of grace, respite. 15. ~-abiding(ness), obedient, obedience, to ~; ~-calf, unstained used for binding ~-books; ~-COURT¹; ~-French, the Anglo-Norman terms used in ~-books & ~; ~-giver, one who makes (esp. code of) ~s; ||~-hand, handwriting used in legal documents; ||~-Latin, barbarous Latin of early English statutes; ||~-lord, member of House of Lords qualified to assist in its

legal work; ~'maker, legislator; ~ mer-chant, ~s regulating trade & commerce, differing in some respects from Common Law; ~-officer, legal functionary, || esp. Attorney or Solicitor General; ~-stationer, selling stationery needed by lawyers || & taking in documents to be engrossed; ~'suit, prosecution of claim in ~-court; ~-term, word or expression used in ~, also period appointed for sitting of ~-courts; ~-writer, writer on ~, || also engrosser of legal documents. [OE lagu f. ON, orig. sense thing laid, cogn. w. LAY³]

|| law², laws, int. (vulg.) expressing aston-ishment. [var. of LO, or earlier la, or lor for Lord]

law'ful, a. Permitted, appointed, quali-fied, or recognized, by law, not illegal or (of child) illegitimate. Hence ~LY² adv., ~NESS n. [-FUL]

lawk(s), int. (vulg.) expressing astonish-ment; lawk-a-mussy (vulg.), =Lord have mercy. [for ALACK or Lord]

law'less, a. (Of country etc.) where law is non-existent or inoperative; regardless of, disobedient to, uncontrolled by, law, unbridled, licentious. Hence ~NESS n. [-LESS]

lawn¹, n. Kind of fine linen used esp. for bishop's sleeves; ~ sieve, fine sieve of ~ or silk. Hence ~Y² a. [prob. f. Laon in France]

lawn², n. || Glade (arch.); (extent of) grass-covered land; close-mown turf-covered piece of pleasure-ground or garden, whence ~Y² a.; ~-mower, machine with revolving spiral knives for mowing ~s; ~-sprinkler, machine with revolving pipe-end for watering ~s; ~ tennis, modification of tennis played by two persons (single) or four (double) on a level court ('grass' or 'hard') without walls. [earlier laund f. OF launde f. OCelt. (W llan, cogn. w. LAND¹]

law'yer (or loi'er), n. Member of legal profession, esp. attorney, solicitor; person versed in law (good, no, etc., ~); Penang ~, walking-stick of Penang palm (perh. f. native tree-name). [-YER]

lax¹, a. Loose, relaxed, not compact, porous, (rare); negligent, careless, not strict, vague. Hence or cogn. ~ITY n., ~LY² adv. [f. L laxus cogn. w. languēre LANGUISH]

lax², n. Swedish or Norwegian salmon. [OE leax salmon, cf. Da., Swed., etc., lax: now only as an alien word]

lax'ative, a. & n. (Medicine) (tending to) loosen the bowels. [F {-if, -ive}, t. L laxativus (lazare, see LAX¹, -ATIVE]

lay¹, n. Short lyric or narrative poem meant to be sung; (loosely) song, poem, song of birds. [f. OF lai perh. f. Teut. (OHG leich melody); not cogn. w. G lied]

lay², a. Non-clerical, not in orders; of, done by, ~man or laity; non-professional, not expert, (esp. w. ref. to law or medi-cine); ~ brother, sister, person who has taken habit & vows of religious order but is employed in manual labour & ex-cused other duties; ~ clerk, singing man in cathedral or collegiate church, parish clerk; ~ communion, membership of church as ~man, also communicating of laity in eucharist; ~ deacon, man in deacon's orders but also following secular employment; || ~ lord, peer who is not LAW¹-lord; ~'man, one of the laity, non-expert in regard to some profession, art, or science (esp. law or medicine); ~ reader, ~man licensed to conduct reli-gious services. [f. F lai f. eccl. L, f. Gk laïkos LAIC]

lay³, v.t. & i. (laid), & n. 1. Prostrate (~ low, bring down, humble); (of wind or rain) beat down (crops); cause (sea, wind, dust, misgivings, ghost) to subside. 2. Deposit; place in recumbent posture (~ to sleep or rest, lit., & fig.=bury; ~ one's bones, be buried in specified place); (of hen) produce (egg, or abs.); put down (amount, one's head or life, etc.) as wager, stake, (abs.) announce readiness to bet (that ~). 3. Place, set, apply, (~ to HEART; ~ heads together, confer; laid a spark to the train; ~ hounds on scent; ~ hold on or of, seize, grasp, & fig. make capital of opponent's weak point etc.; ~ one's hopes on; ~ great store upon, value highly; ~ snare, trap, ambush; = WAR²; ~ siege to, besiege, importune; locate (scene; scene of tale is laid in London); put (limb etc.) in certain position (horse laid his ears back; ~ hands on, seize, appropriate, also do violence to, esp. oneself = commit suicide, also find, as cannot ~ my hands upon it, also confirm or ordain by imposition of hands); aim (big gun); (with compl.) put into specified state (~ land fallow, under water; ~ person under obligation, oblige him, under ne-cessity, compel him, under contribution, make him contribute; ~ bare, denude, reveal; ~ waste, ravage; ~ open, reveal, explain, also break skin of; ~ fast, by the heels, confine or imprison; ~ ABOARD). 4. Present, put forward, (esp. claim to something; ~ an information, bring indictment in legal form); place (facts, question) for consideration before person; (Parl.) Foreign Secretary etc. will ~ papers (i.e. on the table, to give information to the House of Commons); (of suitor) fix (damages) at certain sum; (arch.) impute (fault) to person or (mod.) to his charge, at or to his door; represent (evil) as conse-quent on some cause. 5. Impose (penalty, command, obligation, burden, tax; place (blame), (upon ~ stress, weight, emphasis, on, emphasize, treat as important; bring (stick etc.) down on (also ~ blows or it on adv.; & abs. ~ into, sl., belabour; ~ about one, hit out on all sides). 6. Dispose, arrange, esp. horizontally (foundation,

floor, bricks, submarine cable; ~ *table, cloth, or breakfast* etc., prepare table for meal; ~ *the fire,* put fuel ready for lighting; ~ *(naut.)* make (strand, rope) by twisting yarn or strands; fix outlines of, devise workman is temporarily discharged; (plan, plot); ~ one's ACCOUNT); put (colour etc.) on a surface in layers; cover, coat, strew, (surface) *with* carpet, metal, straw, etc.; ~ *laid paper* (having ribbed surface owing to wires used in making). **7.** v.i. (vulg.) put away, cease to use or practise or think of, abandon, save (money etc.) for future needs; ~ *down,* put on the ground etc. (~ *down one's arms, surrender*); relinquish (office, hopes), pay or wager (money), sacrifice (one's life), (begin to) construct (ship, railway), formulate (rule, principle, course; ~ *down the LAW*), set down (chart etc.) on paper, convert (land) into pasture (*in, to, under, with, grass, clover,* etc.), store (wine) in cellar; ~ *in,* provide oneself with stock of, (also, colloq.) shower blows; ~ *on,* impose (tax, command, penalty), deal blows, inflict (blows), ply (lash etc.), apply coat of (paint etc.; ~ *it on thick or with a trowel,* use obvious flattery), put (hounds) on scent, provide pipes etc. for supplying (gas, water, electricity); ~ *out,* spread, expose to view etc., prepare (body) for burial, (sl.) kill, (colloq.) put (person) out of action temporarily at football etc., expend (money), (refl.) take pains to do, dispose (grounds, garden) according to a plan; ~ *up,* store, put by, put (ship) out of commission, save (money, or ~* out*), (pass.) be confined to bed or house. **9.** n. Line of business, job, pursuit, (sl.); direction or amount of twist in rope-strands; way, position, or direction, in which something (esp. country) lies, lie; disposing or arrangement of ground etc.; ~ *shaft,* secondary shaft of a machine, not forming part of main system of power-transmission. [OE *lecgan,* cf. Du. *leggen,* G *legen,* & see LIE³]

lay.⁴ See LIE³.

lay.⁵ n. & v.t. & i. In vbl senses; also: stratum, thickness of matter (esp. one of several) spread over surface; (Gardening) shoot fastened into earth to strike root while attached to parent plant (v.t., propagate thus); (pl.) patches of laid corn (v.i., of corn, be laid flat by weakness of growth); oyster-bed; mare, cow, etc., ~ (of hens) [*good, bad,* etc., ~ (of hens); ~s & *backers,* persons betting against, on, individual horse etc.]. Hence ~ED² (*-erd*) a. [LAY³,-ER²]

layer. n. Clothes, toilet articles, & bedding, needed for newborn child. [F]

lay fig′ure (*-ger*), n. Jointed wooden figure of human body used by artists for arranging drapery on etc.; unimportant person, nonentity; unreal character in

novel etc., (lay f. obs. *layman* lay figure f. Du. *leeman* (led joint))

lay′lock, n. (Dial. for) LILAC.

lay-off (-awf), n. Period during which a workman is temporarily discharged; slack season. [LAY³]

∥ **lay′stall** (-awl), n. Refuse heap. [LAY³, STALL]

lāz′ar (-), n. (arch.) Poor & diseased person, esp. leper; ~*house,* = foll. [f. med. L *lazarus* f. proper name (*Luke* xvi. 20)]

lāz′arět, **-ětt′ō** (pl. -os), n. Hospital (chiefly in foreign countries) for diseased poor, esp. lepers; building or ship for performing quarantine in; after part of ship's hold used for stores. [F (*-et*), & It. *lazzaretto* (lazzaro LAZAR)]

Lăz′arus, n. Beggar, poor man, (esp. in contrasts, ~ & *Dives* etc.). [see LAZAR]

lāze, v.i. & t., & n. (colloq.) **1.** Be lazy; pass (time) *away* in laziness. **2.** n. Lazy time. [back formation f. LAZY]

lāz′ūli, n. = LAPIS LAZULI.

lāz′ȳ, a. & v.i. & t. **1.** Averse to labour, indolent, slothful; appropriate to or inducing indolence; ~*bed,* bed for potato-growing about 6 ft wide with trench on each side; ~*bones,* ~ person; ~ *pinion,* serving as transmitter of motion between other pinions or wheels; ~*tongs,* arrange-ment of zigzag levers for picking up distant objects; hence **lāz′ily²** adv., **lāz′inĕss** n. **2.** vb.= LAZE [earlier *laysi,* perh. f. LAY² + -sy as in *tipsy, tricksy*]

lăzzarō′nē, n. (pl. *-ni,* pr. -nē). Neapoli-tan street-lounger living by odd jobs & begging. [It. (LAZAR, -OON)]

′ld, abbr. of *would* (now rare, cf. 'd).

-le, -el, suf. **1.** f. ME -el, -le, f. OE -el, -ela, (-el)e in nn. *-ol, -al, -el,* in adji.; after ch, soft g, n, r, sh, th, v, -le is retained, & after m the suf. becomes -*ble.* Nn. formed on n. stems have dim. sense (*bramble,* or that of tool, appliance, (*bittmble, handle,* or that of woould now rare, cf. 'd). nn. formed on vb stems express agent (*beadle*), instrument (*bridle, girdle*), or less definite relations (*brindle*); adji. formed on vb stems have the sense *apt or liable to the vbl action* (*brittle, nimble*). **2.** f. ME -el, -elle in nn. f. F -el f. L -*ellum* (*castle, mantle*) or L -*ale* (*battle,* or F -*elle* f. L -*ella* -*alia* see -AL (*bottle*), or F -*elle* f. L -*tenda* (*bottle*); f. L -*ulus, -ula, -ulum,* (*angle*; -*el* in some med. scientific. wds on L anal. (*carpel*). **3.** Verbal, f. ME -(*e*)*len* f. OE -*lian* f. OTeut. -*ilôjan,* w. frequent. or dim. sense (*nestle, twinkle, wrestle, crumple, dazzle.*)

lea.¹ n. (poet.). Tract of open ground, esp. grass land. [OE *lēah,* cf. OHG *lôh* grove]

lea.² n. Measure of yarn (300, 200, 120, & 80 yds in different districts etc.). [perh. f. *lier* f. L *ligare* to bind]

leach, v.t. Make (liquid) percolate through some material; subject (bark, ore) to action of percolating fluid; purge (soluble

matter) *away* etc. by such means. [prob. f. OE *leccan* to water]

lead¹ (lĕd), n., & v.t. & i. **1.** Heavy easily fusible soft malleable base metal of dull pale bluish grey colour (*red* ~, red oxide of ~ used as pigment, minium; *white* ~, mixture of ~ carbonate & hydrated ~ oxide used as pigment, ceruse; =BLACK-~, whence ~ is used, w. pl., for the small stick of graphite in pencil or pencil-case; *ounce of* ~, bullet). **2.** Lump of ~ used in sounding water (*cast, heave, the* ~; *arm the* ~, fill hollow in it with tallow, to learn nature of bottom; ‖ *swing the* ~, Nav. & Mil. sl., malinger or scrimshank). **3.** ‖ pl. Strips of ~ used to cover roof, piece of (esp. horizontal) ~-covered roof; ~ frames or canes holding glass of lattice or painted window. **4.** (Print.) metal strip for widening space between lines. **5.** ~-*comb*, made of ~ & used to darken hair; ~ *pencil*, of graphite usu. enclosed in cedar; ~-*poisoning*, acute or chronic poisoning by taking of ~ into system; ~'*s'man*, sailor who heaves the ~; ~ *wool*, ~ in a fibrous state, used for jointing water-pipes; ~-*work*, plumber's or glazier's work; ~-*works*, place where ~-ore is smelted; hence ~LESS a. **6.** vb. Cover, weight, frame, (printed matter) with ~s; (of gun-barrel) become foul with coating of ~. [OE *lēad*, cf. Du. *lood*, G *lot*]

lead² (lēd), v.t. & i. & n. **1.** Force to go with one (~ *captive*, take away as prisoner). **2.** Conduct, guide, esp. by going in front (of person, also of motive, circumstance, etc.; *curiosity, chance, led him to Rome*; ~ *one a dance*, give him much trouble to secure his end; ~ *one a life*, worry him constantly; ~ *the way*, go first, take the lead in course lit. or fig.). **3.** (Of commander) direct movements of. **4.** Conduct (person) by the hand or contact, (animal) by halter etc., (*led horse*, spare horse led by groom etc.; *led captain*, hanger-on, toady, parasite; ~ *woman to altar*, marry); guide by persuasion (*is easier led than driven*; ~ *astray*, esp. tempt to sin etc.; ~ *by the nose*, induce to do unconsciously all one wishes). **5.** Guide actions or opinions of, bring by argument etc. to conclusion, induce to do (~ *one to suppose* etc., deceive him into thinking); ply (witness) with leading questions. **6.** (Of road etc.) conduct (person, or usu. abs.) to place (*all roads* ~ *to Rome*; also fig.= have as result, *this led to confusion*). **7.** Make (rope, water, etc.) go through, pulley, channel, etc. **8.** Pass, go through, spend, (life etc., esp. w. epithet as ~ *a miserable existence, a double life*). **9.** Have first place in (~ *the dance, van*); (abs.) go first (~ *off*, begin intr.), be first at some point in race. **10.** Direct by example (~ *orchestra, band, chorus,* etc.); also abs.; be official director or spokesman of (party, esp. in Houses of Parliament), ‖ act as leading counsel in (case, or usu. abs.). **11.** (Cards) play as first card, be first player, in trick (~ *up to*, play so as to elicit specified card), play one of (suit when ~*ing*, **12.** ~ *away*, (usu. in pass.) induce to follow unthinkingly; ~ *off*, begin (dance, conversation, or abs.); ~ *on*, entice into going further than was intended; ~ *up the* GARDEN (*path*); ~ *up to*, form preparation for, serve to introduce, direct conversation towards, (subject). Hence ~ABLE a. [com.-Teut.; OE *lǣdan*, cf. Du. *leiden*, G *leiten*, cogn. w. LOAD, LODE]

lead³ (lēd), n. Direction given by going in front, example, (*follow the* ~ *of*; *give one a* ~, encourage him by doing thing, esp. leaping fence in hunting, first); leading place, leadership, (*take the* ~); artificial water-course, esp. leading to mill; (Electr.) conductor conveying current from source to place of use, (~-*in*, conducting wire joining wireless receiver with external aerial); channel in ice-field; string etc. for leading dog; (Cards) act or right of playing first (*return* ~, lead from suit already led by partner); (Theatr.) (player of) chief part; ~-*off*, commencement. [f. prec.]

lea'den (lĕd-), a. (As) of lead (*sleep's* ~ *sceptre*, stupefying power; ~ *sword*, useless); heavy, slow, burdensome, (~ *limbs*); inert, deadening, (~ *rule*); lead-coloured. [-EN¹]

Leadenhall (lĕd'enhawl'), n. (Used for) ~ meat and poultry market in London.

lead'er (lĕd-), n. In vbl senses of LEAD² (*follow my* ~); also or esp.~ *of House of Commons*, member of Government with official initiative in business; ‖ counsel who leads in case, also K.C., also senior counsel of circuit; front horse in team or tandem (opp. WHEELER); shoot growing at apex of stem or principal branch; tendon; ‖ =LEADING² *article*; (Print.) line of dots or dashes to guide eye. Hence ~LESS a., ~SHIP(1, 3) n. [-ER¹]

‖ **leaderétte'** (lĕd-), n. Short editorial paragraph in same type as leading article. [prec., -ETTE]

lead'ing¹ (lĕd-), n. In vbl senses; esp.: ~ *men of light &* ~, of deserved influence; ~-*business*, parts usu. taken by ~ actor; ~-*rein*, to lead horse with; ~-*staff*, attached to ring in bull's nose; ~-*strings*, with which children were formerly taught to walk (*in* ~-*strings*, in state of pupilage). [-ING¹]

lead'ing² (lĕd-), a. In vbl senses: ‖ ~-*article*, editorial expression of opinion at full length in newspaper, (Commerce). article of trade sold at low price to attract custom for other things; ~ *case* (Law), serving as precedent for deciding others; ~ *edge*, foremost edge of aircraft's wing, opp. *trailing edge*; ~ *lady, man,*

leaf¹, n. (pl. *leaves*), & v.i. **1.** Expanded organ (usu. green) of plant springing from side of stem or branch or direct from root; (pop.) petal (esp. *rose*~); foliage (*fall of the* ~, autumn; *in* ~, with leaves out); leaves of tobacco or tea. **2.** Single thickness of folded paper, esp. (= 2 pages) in book (*take* ~ *out of person's book*; *turn over new* ~, mend one's ways). **3.** Very thin sheet of metal esp. gold or silver, or horn, marble, talc, etc. **4.** Hinged part or flap of door, shutter, table (also used of extra section inserted in expansible table), bridge (= bascule), or rifle-sight. **5.** Tooth of pinion. **6.** ~ *brass*, brass foil; ~ *insect* (having wings resembling ~ of plant); ~-*lard* (made from layers of fat round pig's kidneys); ~-*mould*, soil composed chiefly of decaying leaves; hence ~'AGE(1) n., (-)~ED² (tħ), ~'LESS, aa., ~'LESSNESS n. ~'Y² a., ~'INESS n. **7.** v.i. Put forth leaves. [OE *leaf*, cf. Du. *loof*, G *laub*]

‖**leaf²**, n. (nav. & mil. sl.). Leave of absence, furlough. [= LEAVE¹]

leaf'let, n. (Bot.) one division of compound leaf; young leaf; small leaf of paper, or sheet folded but not stitched, with printed matter, esp. for gratuitous distribution. [-LET]

league¹ (-g), n. Varying measure of road-distance, usu. about three miles. [f. LL *lĕuga* perh. f. Gaulish]

league² (-g), n., & v.t. & i. **1.** Compact for mutual protection & assistance or prosecution of common interests, parties (whether States or individuals) to such compact, (*Solemn L*~ & *COVENANT*; *PRIMROSE L*~; *in* ~ *with*, allied with); ‖ *L*~ *football* (in which clubs forming a ~ play each other for championship); *L*~ *of Nations* (established by the treaty of peace 1919 to try to prevent war). **2.** v.b. Join (t. & i.) in (esp. in p.p. ~*d together* or *with*). [f. F *ligue* f. It. *liga, lega*, (L *ligare* bind)]

leak, n. & v.i. **1.** Hole caused by injury, wear, etc., through which fluid makes way into or out of vessel that is immersed in or contains it (*spring a* ~, be found to have one). **2.** v.i. Let fluid, (of fluid) pass, out or in through ~; (of secrets etc.) transpire, come out gradually; hence ~'AGE(3) n., what ~s out or in, transpiring of secrets, unexplained disappearance of money pointing to embezzlement etc. [vb prob. f. ON *leka* drip; relation of n. doubtful]

leak'y, a. Having leak(s); incontinent of urine; given to letting out secrets. Hence ~INESS n. [-Y²]

leag'uer¹ (-ger), n. Member of LEAGUE². [-ER¹]

‖**leag'uer²** (-ger), n. [f. Du. *leger*, see LAIR]

‖**leal**, a. (Sc. & literary). Loyal, honest, (*LAND o' the* ~). [f. OF *leel* (cf. LOYAL) f. L *legalis* lawful (*lex lēgis* law, -AL)]

lean¹, a. & n. **1.** (Of persons) thin, not plump; meagre, of poor quality, innutritious, (~ *crops, diet*; ~ *years*, of scarcity); unremunerative; (of meat) consisting chiefly of muscular tissue, not of fat. **2.** n. ~ part of meat. Hence ~NESS n. [OE *hlǣne* etym. dub.]

lean², v.i. & t. (past & p.p. ~ed, or ~t pr. lĕnt), & n. **1.** Incline one's body against something for support, support oneself (of thing, be supported in sloping position) *against* or *on* (Mil., ~ *upon*, have as protection on flank); rely or depend (*upon*; incline body *back, forward, over, towards*, etc.; stand obliquely, out of the perpendicular; have tendency to mercy etc., be partial to cause, opinion, or person, whence ~ING(1) n.: place (thing) in ~ing position; ~-*to*, building with rafters resting against side of another, pent-house. **2.** n. Inclination, slope, (*has a decided* ~ *to the right*). [OE *hleonian*, w. LADDER; & w. CLIMAX & Gk *klīmō* bend, & L *inclīnare*]

leap¹, v.i. & t. (past & p.p. ~t pr. lĕpt, or ~ed). = JUMP (still in poet., literary, & dignified use; *LOOK¹ before you* ~); ~-*frog*, (n.) game in which players vault with parted legs over others bending down, (vb) perform such vault (*over*). Hence ~ER¹ n. [com.-Teut.; OE *hleapan*, cf. Du. *loopen*, G *laufen* run]

leap², n. Jump (by which wd it is now replaced in ordinary use; ~ *in the dark*, hazardous attempt of doubtful issue; *by* ~s & *bounds*, with startlingly rapid progress); thing to be jumped; ~-*day* (perh. Feb.) ~-*year*, with intercalary day (perh. because fixed festivals after February in ~-*year* fall two weekdays, instead of as usual one, later than in the preceding year), ~-*year proposal* (of woman to man, allowable only in ~-*year*). [OE *hlīp* f. root of prec.]

learn (lĕrn), v.t. & i. (past & p.p. ~t, ~ed pr.-nd). Get knowledge of (subject) or skill in (art etc.) by study, experience, or being taught (*from, of*); commit to memory *that, how*, etc., (*I am* or *have yet to* ~, do not know, usu. with implication of disbelief, be informed of, ascertain; receive instruction; (arch., joc., or vulg.) teach. Hence ~ABLE a., ~ER¹ n., (lĕr-).

learnèd (lĕr-), a. Deeply read, erudite; showing profound knowledge; ‖(in conventionally courteous mention of lawyer in the law (esp. *my* ~ *friend* or *brother*); (of language, profession, etc.) pursued or

studied by, (of words in a language) introduced by, ~ men. Hence ~LY² adv. [f. prec. in obs. sense (still in vulg. use) teach, +-ED¹]

learn'ing (lẽr-), n. In vbl senses: esp. (possession of) knowledge got by study, esp. of language or literary or historical science (*the new* ~, studies, esp. of Greek, introduced into England in 16th c., renaissance). [-ING¹]

lease¹, n., & v.t. 1. Contract by which lessor, usu. in consideration of rent, conveys land or tenement to lessee for specified time (*put out to* ~; *by or on* ~; *a new* ~ *of life*, prospect of living due to recovered health or removal of anxiety etc.); ~*hold(er)*, (person having) tenure, real property held, by ~; L~-*Lend* (later *Lend-L*~), applied orig. in 1941 to an arrangement whereby sites in British oversea possessions were ~d to the United States as bases in exchange for the loan of destroyers, later extended to the pooling of the resources & output of the United Nations, also attrib. & as v.t. 2. v.t. Grant or take ~ of. [f. AF *les(ser)*, cf. F *laisser*, f. L *laxare* (LAX) to loose]

lease², n. Crossing of warp-threads in loom; = foll. (weaving). [prob. var. of foll.]

leash, n., & v.t. 1. Thong in which hounds or coursing-dogs are held (*hold in a* ~, control); set of three hounds, hares, etc.; (Weaving) cord with eye to receive warp-thread extending between parallel laths of loom-heddle. 2. v.t. Connect, hold in, with ~. [f. OF *lesse* perh. f. fem. of L LAXus]

leas'ing (-z-), n. (bibl.). Lying, lie. [OE *léasung* (*léasian* f. *léas* false, destitute of, =-LESS)]

least, a., n., & adv. 1. Smallest, slightest; (*the* ~, esp. after neg., any however small; ~ *common* MULTIPLE; *line of* ~ RESISTANCE). 2. n. ~ amount (*to say the* ~ *of it*, to put the case moderately; ~ *said soonest mended*, discussion will only make things worse); *at* ~, at all events, even if a wider statement is disputable, (also *at the* ~) at the lowest computation; (*in*) *the* ~, in the smallest degree, at all. 3. adv. In the ~ degree. [OE *lǣst* superl. of LESS]

least'ways (-z; vulg.), **least'wise** (-z; rare), advv. Or at least, or rather, [-WAYS, -WISE]

leat, n. Open water-course conducting water to mill etc. [OE *-gelǣt* (Y-+root of LET²)]

lea'ther (lĕdh-), n., & v.t. 1. Skin prepared for use by tanning or similar process (*patent* ~, with fine black varnished surface; || *American* ~, kind of oilcloth; ~ & *prunella*, a difference in clothes only, see Pope, *Essay*, iv. 204; *nothing like* ~, one's own goods will serve all purposes; vb, cover or arm with ~). 2. Article, or part of one, made of ~, piece of ~ for polishing;

thong (esp. *stirrup*~; vb, beat with strap, ~*hunting*, ~ING¹(1) n.); (sl.) cricket-ball (~*branding*, fielding or football); (pl.) leggings or breeches. 3. (sl.) One's skin (*lose*~, suffer abrasion). 4. ~*back*, kind of turtle; ~*head*, blockhead; ~*jacket*, kinds of fish, || crane-fly grub; ~*neck*, (sailor's name, w. ref. to ~ stook formerly worn, for) soldier; ~*wood*, kinds of tough-barked tree. Hence ~ETTE²(2) n., ~n [-EN¹), ~Y² (esp. of meat etc., tough), aa. [OE *lether*, cf. Du. & G *leder*]

lea'theroid (lĕdh-), n. Cotton paper chemically treated & resembling raw hide. [-OID]

leave¹, n. Permission (*to do*; *by your* ~, apology, often iron., for taking liberty, making unwelcome statement, etc., esp. as porter's formula for asking person to make way for him & his load; *without a 'with your* ~' *or* '*by your* ~', colloq., without even asking ~); (in Services, offices, schools) ~ (*of absence*), permission to be absent from duty, period for which this lasts, (*on* ~, absent thus; ~*breaker*, person remaining away beyond the period; || TICKET *of* ~); *take* (one's) ~ (*of*), bid farewell (to; *take* ~ *of one's senses*, go mad), whence ~*taking*¹(2) n.; FRENCH ~. [OE *léaf* prob. = orig. pleasure or approval, cogn. w. LOVE, LIEF]

leave², v.t. (*left*), & n. 1. Cause to or let remain, depart without taking, (~*s a wife & three sons*; *six from seven* ~*s one*; ~*s much etc. to be desired*, is unsatisfactory; *has left a soreness behind*); bequeath. 2. Abstain from consuming or dealing with; (pass.) remain over. 3. Let remain in specified state (*this* ~*s me cool, cold*, does not excite me; ~ *it at that*, colloq., abstain from comment or further action; *be well* etc. *left*, provided for by legacy etc.; ~ *undone, unsaid*, etc.). 4. Commit, refer, to another agent etc. than oneself (~ *it to you, sir*, fix my pay yourself; *nothing was left to accident*; ~ *him to himself*, do not try to control). 5. Allow (person, thing) to do something without interference. 6. Deposit, entrust, (thing, instructions, message), station (person), to be seen to, delivered, etc., or to discharge function, in one's absence (~ *card on* person, as equivalent of formal call). 7. Quit, go away from, (*left him quite well an hour ago*; ~ *this or here*; ~ *the track, room*); (abs.) depart (*we* ~ *to-morrow*, often *for* destination). 8. Pass (object) so as to put it in specified relative direction (~ *the church on the left*). 9. Cease to reside at (place), belong to (school, society), or serve (employer), (also abs., as *I am leaving at Christmas*). 10. Abandon, forsake (esp. ~ *in the lurch*; *get left*, colloq, be deserted or worsted). 11. ~ *alone*, not interfere with; ~ *behind*, go away without, ~ as consequence or trace, pass; ~ *go* (vulg.), relax one's hold; ~

hold of, cease holding; ~ off, cease to
wear, discontinue (habit, doing, work),
come to or make an end; ~ out, omit; ~
over, let stand over for the time. 12. n.
(Billiards) position in which player ~s
the balls. Hence (usu. pl.) leav'ing'(²)n.
[OE læfan, cf. MHG leiben; cogn. w. obs.
leave remainder, & w. G bleiben (MHG
belîben) remain]

(~)leaved (-vd), a. Having leaves (rare);
having ~ leaves (one~ table; red~). [f.
LEAF + -ED²]

lea'ven (lĕ-), n., & v.t. 1. Substance added
to dough to produce fermentation, esp.
fermenting dough reserved for purpose;
(fig.) spreading & transforming influence
(Matt. xiii. 33), tinge or admixture of
some quality; the old ~, traces of unregenerate state (1 Cor. v. 6, 7). 2. v.t.
Ferment (dough) with ~; permeate &
transform, modify with ~ tempering element. [f. F levain f. L levāmen (levāre
lift, -MEN)]

leaves. See LEAF.

lebensraum (lāb'ĕnsrowm), n. Territory
which a State believes is needed for its
natural development. [G.=living-space]

lĕch'er, n. (arch.). Fornicator, debauchee.
So ~ous a., ~ously adv., lĕch'erY(⁴) n.
[f. OF lecheor (lechier live in debauchery
or gluttony f. OHG lecôn LICK)]

lĕc'tern, n. Reading or singing desk in
church, esp. that for the lessons. [ME &
OF lettrun f. LL lectrum (legere lect- read)]

lĕc'tionary(⁴) n. Book containing
list of, portions of Scripture appointed
to be read at divine service. [f. eccl. L
lectionarium (lectio reading, see prec.,
-ARY¹)]

lĕc'ture, n., & v.i. & t. 1. Discourse
before audience or class on given subject,
usu. by way of instruction; admonition,
reproof, (read one a ~e, reprove him).
2. vb. Deliver ~e or ~es (on subject);
instruct or entertain (class etc.) by
~e; admonish, reprimand; hence ~ER¹
(~-kche) n. [vb f. Fr. f. L lectura (legere
lect- read, -URE)]

lĕc'tureship (-kcher-), (rare)~urership,
n. Office of lecturer. [prec. + SHIP unusual
formation]

led. See LEAD².

lĕdge, n. Narrow horizontal surface projecting from wall etc.; shelf-like projection on side of rock or mountain; ridge of
rocks, esp. below water; (Mining) stratum
of metal-bearing rock. Hence lĕdg'Y(²)
a. [ME legge LAY]

lĕdg'er, n. & a. 1. Principal book of the
set used for recording trade transactions,
containing debtor-&-creditor accounts;
horizontal timber in scaffolding, parallel
to face of building; flat grave-stone;
~-bait bait fixed in one place (so
~-hook, -line); ~-blade, stationary blade
in cloth-shearing machine acting with
revolving spiral blade. 2. adj. (mus.)

lĕe, n. Shelter given by neighbouring
object (under the ~ of); (also ~ side)
sheltered side, side away from wind, (opp.
windward, weather side; often attrib., ~
or ~, = belonging to ship's ~ side, or to
leeward of other object, whence ~MOST
a.; ~-board, plank frame fixed to side
of flat-bottomed vessel & let down into
water to diminish ~way; ~ shore, shore
to leeward of ship; ~way, lateral drift of
ship to leeward of course (make up ~way,
fig., struggle out of bad position, often
much ~way to make up). [OE hlēo, cogn.
w. Ofris. hlī, ON hlý shelter, warmth]

leech¹, n. Kinds of aquatic bloodsucking
worm, esp. that used medicinally for
bleeding (stick like a ~, persistently);
person who sucks profit out of others,
parasite; (arch.) physician or surgeon (now
only fig.). [OE lǣce, cf. MDu. lake]

||leech², n. Perpendicular or sloping side
of sail. [cf. Du. lĳk, G liek]

leek, n. Culinary herb like onion, but with
cylindrical bulb, this as Welsh national
emblem (cf. ROSE; eat the ~). [OE lēac,
cf. Du. look, G lauch]

leer¹, v.i., & n. Glance (esp. sideways)
with sly, lascivious, or malign expression.
Hence ~'ingLY² adv. [n. f. vb, perh.
f. obs. leer cheek (= look over one's
cheek), cf. MDu. liere]

leer², n. Annealing-furnace for glass. [?]

leer³, a. (sl.). Knowing, sly. [perh. f.
LEER¹ n. + -Y¹]

lees (-z), n. pl. Sediment of wine etc.
(drink, drain, to the ~, lit. & fig.); basest
part, refuse. [earlier lee sing. also, f. F
lie f. Gaulish L lia]

leet¹, n. (hist.). Yearly or half-yearly
court of record (also court-~) holdable by
lords of certain manors; its jurisdiction,
its district. [perh. f. OE lǣth LATHE¹]

||leet², n. (Sc.). Selected list of candidates
for some office. [f. ME élite election]

lee'ward (or, esp. Naut., lit'ard) a. adv.
& n. On, towards, the sheltered side (opp.
windward); (n.) this direction (to~, on the
~ of). Hence ~MOST a. [LEE + -WARD]

lee'wardly (see prec.), a. (of ship) apt to
fall to leeward (opp. weatherly). [-LY¹]

left¹, a., adv., & n. 1. Belonging to the
side of a person's body that is westward
when he faces N, or that has normally the
less-used hand, having corresponding
relation to front of any object (~ wing or
flank of army; ~ bank of river, assuming
it to face the way it flows); situated
nearer to or more directly in front of
observer's or speaker's ~ hand than his

~ (or layer) line, short line added above
or below stave for outside notes (perh.
attrib, and of n. in scaffolding sense),
[perh. f. LIE³, LAY³, +-ER¹ in imit. of Du.
ligger, legger]

right; ~ **hand**, lit., &=region or direction nearer the ~ hand, (on the ~ hand of, in that direction relatively to: *marry with the ~ hand*, morganatically; *~-hand blow*, delivered with it; *~-hand man*, standing next one on ~; *~-hand rope*, twisted counter-clockwise); *over the ~* (shoulder now rare), sl. phr. denoting that what is said is to be interpreted by contraries; *~ turn*, that brings one's front to face as one's ~ side did before; hence ~MOST &., ~WARD a. & adv., ~'WARDS adv. **2.** adv. On or to the ~ side. **3.** n. ~ hand (lit. in pugilism, as *got in one with his ~*; *cannon to ~ of them*); ~ wing of army; (Pol., L~, orig., of continental legislatures) more radical section of legislative chamber seated on president's ~; advanced or innovating section of philosophical school, religious sect, etc. [OE, orig. sense *weak, worthless*, cf. EFris. *luf*]

left³. See LEAVE³.

left'-hand'ed, a. Having left hand more serviceable than right, using it by preference; awkward, clumsy; ambiguous, double-edged, of doubtful sincerity or validity, (esp. ~ *compliment*; also sometimes of marriage=fictitious, cf. correct sense below); (arch.) ill-omened, sinister; (of marriage) morganatic (from German custom by which bridegroom gave left hand in such marriages; adapted for use of, (of blow) delivered with, left hand. Hence ~LY² adv., ~NESS n. [-ED²]

left'hand'er, n. Left-handed person or blow. [-ER¹]

leg, n., &v.i.&t.(-gg-). **1.** Organ of support & locomotion in animal, esp. human, body, part of this from hip to ankle, (*all ~s*, overgrown; BOOT² *is on other ~*; *pull one's ~*, colloq., befool him; *give one a ~ up*, help him to mount or get over obstacle material or other; BONE *in one's ~*; *have the ~s of*, be able to go faster than; *put* BEST¹ ~ *foremost*; *shake a ~*, dance; *show a ~*, get out of bed; *stretch one's ~s*, take walking exercise; *take to one's ~s*, run away; *on one's ~s*, also joc. *hind ~s*, standing esp. to make speech, also well enough to go about, also in prosperous or established state, esp. *set one on his ~s*; *stand on one's own ~s*, be self-reliant or independent; FALL¹ *on one's ~s*; *has not a ~ to stand on*, cannot support thesis by any facts or sound reasons; *on one's last ~s*, near death or end; *walk* etc. *one off his ~s*, tire him out in walking etc.; *feed, find, one's ~s*, get power of standing or walking; *keep one's ~s*, not fall; *~ before wicket*, abbr. *l.b.w.*, illegal stopping of cricket ball by batsman's ~; SEA~s). **2.** ~ of animal as food (*~ of mutton*; *~-of-mutton sail, sleeve*, so shaped). **3.** Obeisance made by drawing back one ~ (usu. *make a ~*, arch.). **4.** ‖Swindler (for BLACK L~). **5.** (Cricket) part of field to right rear of batsman in position (~

stump, stump nearest this; *long, short, square*, ~, fielders variously posted in it; *hit to ~*), **6.** Artificial ~ (*cork, wooden*, etc., ~). **7.** Part of garment covering ~. **8.** Support, pole, prop, of machine etc.; support of chair, table, bed, etc.; one branch of forked object; side of triangle other than base. **9.** (Naut.) run made on single tack (usu. *long, short*, ~). **10.** *Give ~-bail*, decamp; ~-BYE; *~-guard*, pad for ankle, shin, & knee, in cricket; *~-pull* (colloq.), an attempt to befool a person; *~-rest*, support for seated invalid's ~; *~ theory* (Cricket), bowling to ~ with fieldsmen massed on that side. Hence (-)~GED² (-gd), ~LESS, aa. **11.** v.i. ~ *it*, walk or run hard; (v.t.) propel (boat) through canal-tunnel by pushing with ~s against tunnel-sides, whence ~g'ER¹ (-g-) n. [f. ON *leggr* limb, perh. cogn. w. Gk *laktizō* kick, L *lacertus* arm]

leg'acy, n. Sum of money or article given by will; material or immaterial thing handed down by predecessor; *~-hunter*, person who pays court to another to secure ~. [f. OF *legacie* legatoship (LEGATE, -ACY)]

leg'al, a. Of, based on, falling within province of, occupied with, law; required or appointed by law (*~ tender*, money that creditor is bound to accept in payment); recognized by law as distinguished from equity; lawful, whence ~IZE(3) v.t., ~IZA'TION n.; (Theol.) of the Mosaic law, of salvation by works not faith. Hence ~LY² adv. [f. L *legalis* (*lex legis* law, -AL), cf. LEAL, LOYAL]

leg'alism, n. (Theol.) preference of the Law to the Gospel, doctrine of justification by works; exaltation of law or formula, red tape. So ~IST(2) n. [-ISM]

legal'ity, n. Legalism; lawfulness. [f. F *légalité* (LEGAL, -ITY]

leg'ate¹, n. Ecclesiastic deputed to represent Pope (~ *à latere*, one of highest class & full powers), whence leg'atINE¹ (-in) a.; (arch.) ambassador, delegate. Hence ~SHIP (-tship) n. [f. OF *legat* f. L *legatus* p.p. of *legare* commission]

legāte'² v.t. Bequeath (often *give &~e*). So ~OR² n. [f. L *legare* (prec.), -ATE³]

legatee', n. Recipient of legacy. [prec., -EE]

legā'tion, n. Sending of legate or deputy; body of deputies; diplomatic minister & his suite (esp. when he does not rank as ambassador), his official residence; legateship. [f. L *legatio* (LEGATE¹, -ION)]

legā'tō (-ah-), mus. direction. Smoothly, without breaks. [It., =bound (L *ligare* bind)]

le'gend, n. Collection of lives of saints or similar stories, esp. the (Golden) L~, particular 13th-c. collection (hist.); traditional story popularly regarded as historical, myth, such literature or tradition (so '*in ~*), whence ~ARY¹ a.,

inscription or motto, esp. on coin or medal. Hence ~RY(4) n. [f. F *légende* f. med. L *legenda* what is read (L *legere* read)]

lē′ger. Var. of LEDGER a.

lĕg′erdemain′, n. Sleight of hand, conjuring tricks, juggling; trickery, sophistry. [f. F *léger de main* light of hand]

lĕg′ging (-g-), n. (usu. pl.). Outer covering of leather etc. for leg usu. up to knee. [-ING]

lĕg′gy (l̶y̶-g-), a. Lanky-legged (esp. of boy, colt, puppy). Hence ~INESS n.

lĕg′horn (-gôrn), n. Kind of straw plait for hats etc.; kind of domestic fowl. [*Leghorn* (now *Livorno*) in Italy]

lĕg′ible, a. (Of handwriting or print) clear, easily read. Hence ~ibil′ITY n., ~ibly² adv. [f. LL *legibilis* (*legere* read), -IBLE]

lē′gion (-jn), n. Division of 3,000–6,000 men, including complement of cavalry, in ancient Roman army; || *British L~,* national association of ex-service men formed 1921 & incorporated 1925 by Royal Charter; *foreign ~,* body of foreign volunteers in modern, esp. French, army; vast host, multitude, or number (*their name is L~,* they are numberless, see *Mark* v. 9; *L~ of Honour,* French order of distinction. [OF, f. L *legionem* nom. -o (*legere* choose)]

lē′gionary (-jo-), a. & n. (Soldier) of (a) legion(s). [f. L *legionarius* (prec., -ARY¹)]

lē′gioned (-jond), a. (poet.). In legions. [-ED]

legisla′tion, n. (Enacting of) laws. Hence **lē′gislative** a., **lē′gislatively²** adv. [f. LL *legislatio* (*lex legis* law, *latio* proposing f. *lat-* part. st. of *ferre* bring, -ION)]

lē′gislātor, n. Lawgiver, member of legislative body. Hence ~ate (by back formation) v.i., ~atōr′IAL a. (rare), ~ātress¹ n. [L (as prec., -OR³)]

lē′gislature, n. Legislative body of a State. [after prec., -URE]

lē′gist, n. Person versed in law. [f. F *légiste* f. med. L *legista* (*lex legis* law, -IST)]

legĭt′imate¹, a. Born in lawful wedlock (also said of parent, birth, descent, etc.); lawful, proper, regular, conforming to standard type (*the ~ate drama,* body of plays, Shakesperian or other, of recognized merit, also ellipt., sl., *the ~ate*); (of sovereign's title) based on strict hereditary right; logically admissible. Hence ~ACY(1) n., ~ately²(-tl-) adv., ~ateness(3) n. [as foll., -ATE²]

legĭt′im|ate², v.t. Make legitimate by decree, enactment, or proof; justify, serve as justification for. Hence ~A′TION n. [f. med. L *legitimāre* (L *legitimus* lawful, -ATE³]

legĭt′imism, n. Adherence to sovereign or pretender whose claim is based on direct descent (esp. in Spanish & French

legĭt′imist, n. [f. mod. L *legitimāre* (L *legitimus* lawful n. [f. mod. L *legitimāre* ...

politian). So ~ISM(2) n. & a. [f. F *légitimisme* (*légitime* f. I see prec., -ISM)]

legĭt′imize, v.t. Legitimatize (see LEGITMATE¹). Hence ~A′TION n. [as LEGITIMATE² -IZE]

lēg′um, n. genit. pl. (*abbr.* LL.). Of laws (in titles of academic degrees). [L (*lex* law)]

légŭme, legŭm′en, n. Fruit, edible part, pod, of leguminous plant; vegetable used for food. [F (*légume*), f. L (-en) f. L *legere* pick]

legūm′inous, a. Of, like, of the botanical family of, pulse, LEGUMEN (-mina -OUS]

Leibnĭtz′ian (līb-), a. (Follower of) G. W. Leibnitz (d. 1716) or his philosophy. [-AN]

leis′ter (lēs-), n. & v.t. Pronged salmon-spear; (vb) spear with this. [f. ON *ljóstr* (*ljósta* to strike)]

leis′ure (lĕzh′er), n. (Opportunity to do, for, afforded by) free time, time at one's own disposal (*wait* etc. *one's ~e,* wait till he has ~e; *at ~e,* not occupied, also deliberately, without hurry; *at one's ~e,* when one has time). Hence ~ED² (lezh′erd), ~eLESS(-erl-), aa. [f. OF *leisir* n. use of infin., f. L *licēre* be allowed: see -URE]

leis′urely (lĕzh′er-), a. & adv. Having, acting, or done at, leisure, deliberate; hence ~INESS n.; (adv.) deliberately, without haste. [-LY¹,²]

leit-motiv, -if (līt′mōtēf′), n. (mus.). Theme associated throughout piece with some person, situation, or sentiment. [G (LEAD² MOTIVE]

|| lēm′an, n. (arch.). Lover, sweetheart; unlawful lover or (usu. in mod. archaistic use) mistress. [ME *leofman* (LIEF, MAN)]

lĕmm′a, n. (pl. ~ās, ~æ). Assumed or demonstrated proposition used in argument or proof; argument or subject of literary composition, dictionary article, annotation, etc., prefixed as heading; motto appended to picture etc. [Gk (-ē-) f. *lambanō* take, see -M]

lĕmm′ing, n. Small arctic rodent resembling field-mouse. [Norw.]

lĕm′on¹, n. Pale-yellow oval acid-juiced fruit used for flavouring & for making the beverage ~ADE(1) (-ād′) n.; SAIR of ~, an oxalate used in removing ink-stains (tree bearing ~s; pale-yellow colour; (sl.) unattractive girl (cf. PEACH¹); ~-drop, sugar-plum flavoured with ~; ~ kali, effervescing drink of tartaric acid, soda bicarbonate, & water; ~-plant, ~-scented verbena; ~ pudding (flavoured with ~); || ~ squash, drink of ~-juice & soda-water; ~-squeezer, instrument for pressing juice out. Hence ~y² a. [f. F *limon* f. Oriental source (Arab. *laimun,* Pers. *līmun*), cf. LIME²]

lĕm′on², n. (Usu. ~ *dab,* ~ *sole*) kind of plaice resembling sole. [f. F *limande*]

lĕm′ur, n. Kinds of nocturnal mammals esp. of Madagascar, allied to monkeys but with pointed muzzle. Hence **lĕm′ur**INE¹ a.

lĕm'ūrǒid a. & n. [f. L *lemures* pl. spirits of the dead]

lend, v.t.(*lent*). Grant (person) use of (thing) on understanding that it or its equivalent shall be returned; let out (money) at interest, (books etc.; so *~ing-library*) for hire; bestow, contribute, (something of temporary service or effect, as *enchantment, aid, dignity*; *~ ear, an ear, one's ears*, listen; *~ a hand* or *helping hand*, help; arch., *~ person a box on the ear*); accommodate oneself to some policy or purpose (thing *~s itself to*, is serviceable for); *Lend-Lease*, (later form of) LEASE¹-*Lend*. Hence ~'ABLE a., **lĕn'dᴇʀ**¹, **lĕn'dɪɴɢ**¹(1, 4), nn. [earlier *len*, OE *lǣnan* (cf. Du. *leenen*, G *lehnen*) f. *lǣn* LOAN]

length, n. **1.** Thing's measurement from end to end, greatest of body's three dimensions (*know ~ of person's FOOT*). **2.** Extent in, of, or with regard to, time (*a stay of some ~; the ~ of a book, speech*, etc.). **3.** Distance thing extends (*at arm's ~*, as far away as an arm can reach; *keep one at arm's ~*, avoid intimacy with him; *ships a cable's ~ apart*; *horse, boad, wins by three* etc. *~s*, i.e. of itself). **4.** (With *go*) degree of thoroughness in action (*prepared to go all ~s, went to great ~s, will not go the ~ of asserting*). **5.**(Pros.) vowel's or syllable's quantity. **6.**(Cricket) distance from wicket at which ball pitches (*bowler keeps a good ~*; or *good-~ ball*, that pitches at right*~*). **7.** Long stretch or extent; piece of cloth etc. of certain length (also *at full, great, some,~*), at last or after a long time; *at full ~* (see above; also) lying with body fully extended. Hence ~'WAYS(-āz) adv., ~'WISE(-ɪz) adv. & a. [OE *lengthu*, cf. Du. *lengte*, (LONG)]

lĕng'then, v.t. & i. Make or become longer; (Pros.) make (vowel) long. [-ᴇɴ⁶]

lĕng'thȳ, a. (Of speech, writing, style, speaker, etc.) of unusual length, prolix, tedious. Hence ~ɪʟʏ² adv., ~ɪɴᴇss n. [-Y²; orig. an Americanism]

lēn'ient, (-nyᴇ-), a. Emollient (arch.); tolerant, gentle, indisposed to severity; (of punishment etc.) mild. Hence ~ᴇɴᴄᴇ, ~ᴇɴᴄʏ, nn., ~ᴇɴᴛʟʏ² adv., (-nyᴇ-). [f. L *lenire* soothe (*lenis* gentle), -ᴇɴᴛ]

Lĕn'inism, n. Policy & economic principles of Lenin (assumed name of V. I. Ulianov (d. 1924), leader of the Russian Revolution of 1917). [-ɪsᴍ]

lēn'itive, a. & n. Soothing (drug, appliance), palliative. [f. med. L *lenitivus* LENIENT, -ɪᴠᴇ]

lĕn'itȳ, n. Mercifulness; mercy shown. [f. L *lenitas* (*lenis* gentle, -ᴛʏ]

lĕn'ō, n. Kind of cotton gauze for caps, veils, curtains, etc. [perh. f. F *linon*]

lĕns (-z), n. (pl. ~es). Lentil-shaped glass with both sides (or one only) curved for concentrating or dispersing light-rays; combination of ~es in photography; (Anat.)=CRYSTALLINE ~, also one facet of compound eye. Hence ~ᴇᴅ²(-zd), ~'LESS (-z), aa. [L *lens* lentil]

Lĕnt, n. Period from Ash Wednesday to Easter Eve of which the 40 week-days are devoted to fasting & penitence in commemoration of Christ in the wilderness; || (pl., at Cambridge) ~ *term boat-races*; || ~ *lily*, daffodil; || ~ *term*, university term in which ~ falls. [f. LENTEN]

lent². See LEND.

-lent, suf. in adjj. f. L, =-FUL; the L suf. is normally preceded by *-u-* (*turbulentus*): but *pestilentus, violentus*.

Lĕn'ten, 1-, a. Of, in, or appropriate to, Lent (*~ fare*, without meat;*~ face*, dismal look). [prop. n., of which the attrib. use is now regarded as adj.=LENT¹+-ᴇɴ⁴; orig. sense *spring*, now obs. in E, but the only sense in cogn. Teut. wds; OE *lencten*, cf. G *lenz*, prob. f. same root as LONG perh. w. ref. to lengthening of day in spring]

lĕntĭc'ular, a. Shaped like lentil or lens, double-convex; of the lens of the eye. [f. LL *lenticularis* (foll., -ᴀʀ³)]

lĕn'til, n. (Seed of) leguminous plant grown for food. [F (*-lle*), f. L *lenticula* (LENS, -CULE)]

lĕn'tĭsk, n. The mastic tree. [f. L *lentiscus*]

lĕn'titūde, n. Sluggishness. [f. L *lentitūdo* (*lentus* slow, -TUDE]

lĕn'tǒ, adv. & mus. direction. Slow(ly). [It.]

lĕn'tǒid, a. Lens-shaped. [LENS, -OID]

Lē'ō, n. Zodiacal constellation the Lion; fifth sign of the zodiac. [L,=LION]

Lē'ǒnĭd, n. One of the meteors that seem to radiate from Leo. [f. L *Leo -ōnis*, -ɪᴅ³]

lē'ǒnine¹, a. Lionlike, of lions. [f. L *leoninus* (prec., -INE³)]

Lē'ǒnine², a. & n. Of, made or invented by, person (esp. one of the Popes) called Leo; ~ *City*, part of Rome round Vatican fortified by Leo IV; ~ *verse*, line (also ~ as n.) or lines of medieval Latin verse in hexameter or elegiac metre with internal rhyme (e.g. *Daemon languebat, monachus tunc esse volebat*). [as prec., inventor of ~ verse unknown]

leo'pard (lĕp'-), n. Large African & S.-Asiatic carnivorous quadruped with dark-spotted yellowish-fawn coat, panther, (*black-, black-coated kind*; *American ~*, jaguar; *hunting~*, cheetah; *snow ~*, ounce; *can the ~ change his spots?*, character persists); (Her.) lion passant guardant as in arms of England; (in names of animals etc.)*~*, spotted like*~*. Hence ~ᴇss¹ n. [OF, f. LL, f. late Gk *leopardos* (LION, PARD)]

lĕp'cha, n. One of a race of people inhabiting Sikkim & parts of Tibet.

lĕp'er, n. Person with leprosy. [perh. attrib. use of obs. *leper* leprosy f. OF *lepre* f. L f. Gk *lepra* fem. of *lepros* scaly (*lepos* scale)]

lĕpidŏp'ter|ous, a. Of the *Lepidoptera*, order of insects with four membranous scale-covered wings including butterflies & moths. So ~IST(3) n. [often *doubtless*] f. nn. f. Gk *lepis -idos* scale, *pteron* wing, -OUS]

lep'orine, a. Of the hare kind. [f. L *leporinus* (*lepus -oris* hare, -INE1)]

lep'rechaun' (-x: see Ap.), n. (Irish). Sprite. [perh. f. OIr. *luchorpán* (*lu* small, *corp* body)]

lep'rosy, n. (In mod. Path.) an endemic chronic constitutional disease, *Elephantiasis Graecorum*, varying in manifestations as the skin, nerves, or other tissues are affected; (pop., partly by confusion with PSORIASIS, formerly *Lepra Graecorum*) loathsome disease eating body slowly away & forming silvery scales on skin; (fig.) moral corruption or contagion. [foll. -Y1]

lep'rous, a. Having, like, (as) of, leprosy. [OF, f. LL *leprosus* (*lepra* see LEPER, -OSE+]

lept|o-, comb. form of Gk *leptos* fine, small, thin, delicate, in zool. & bot. terms, as ~cephal'ic narrow-skulled; ~dac'tyl n. & a. (bird) with long slender toes.

Lĕs'bian (-z-), a. Of Lesbos (~ *vice*, SAP-PHISM]. [L f. Gk *Lesbios* (*Lesbos*), -AN]

lese-majesté (läz mäzh'festy), n. = foll. (in frequent use about foreign States, part of inferiors etc.). [F]

lese-maj'esty (lèz-), n. (civil law). Treason. [f. F *lèse-majesté* f. L *laesa majestas* injured majesty (of the sovereign people)]

lé'sion (-zhn), n. Damage, injury, esp. (Path.) morbid change in functioning or texture of organs. [f. F *lésion* f. L *laesionem* nom. -o (*laedere laes-* injure, -ION)]

lĕss, a., prep., n., & adv. **1.** adj. (Of abstracts expressing measurement, as size, degree, duration, number) smaller (opp. *greater*; *in a ~ degree, of ~ magnitude or importance*): of smaller quantity, not so much, not so much of, (opp. *more*; *find ~ difficulty*; *eat ~ meat*; *of two evils choose the ~*; *it may your shadow never be ~*, may you not grow too ~ etc. of lower rank etc. (rare; *no ~ a person than*; *James the L~*). **2.** prep. Minus, deducting, (*a year ~ three days*). **3.** n. Smaller amount, quantity, or number (*cannot take ~*; *in ~ than no time*, joc., very quickly or soon; often *far, little, much, nothing ~ than an attack*, expected an attack & no milder procedure, but see under the adv.). **4.** adv. To smaller extent, in lower degree, (often *none the, no, not the, ~*; *~ known* etc. or *~-known* etc.; *do not suspect him of equivocation, still ~* or *much ~ of lying*; *nothing ~*; anything rather; *expected nothing ~ than an attack*, did not expect attack at all, but see the now usu. sense under n.), [OE *lǽs* adv., *lǽssa* adj., cf. OFris. *lès* & *lèssa*]

-less, suf. f. OE *lĕas* (used both as separate adj. in sense *free from, devoid of*, & as suf.) forming adjj. (*priceless, homeless*) & advv. (*doubtless*) f. nn. On anal. of compds in which the component n. was of same form as the corr. vb (*countless, dauntless, numberless*) & the sense was *unable*, *-less* has been appended to vbs (*resistless, dauntless, tireless*).

lĕssee', n. Holder of, tenant (of house, theatre, etc.) under, lease. Hence ~SHIP n. [f. OF *lessé* (LEASE1, -EE)]

lĕss'en, v.i. & t. Decrease, diminish. [-EN6]

lĕss'er, a. (attrib. only). Not so great as the other or the rest, minor, (*the L~ Bear*; *the ~ evils of life*). [double compar.; LESS + -ER3]

lĕss'on, n. **1.** One of two readings from O.T. (*first ~*) & N.T. (*second ~*) at morning & evening prayer (PROPER ~); thing to be learnt by pupil; amount of teaching given at one time, time assigned to it, (pl.) systematic instruction in subject (*give, take, ~s in*); occurrence, example, rebuke, or punishment, that serves as encouragement or warning. **2.** v.t. Admonish, rebuke, discipline. [f. OF *lecon* (now *leçon*) f. L *lectionem* (*legere lect-* read, -ION)]

lĕss'or, n. Person who lets on lease. [AF (LEASE1, -OR2)]

lĕst, conj. In order that ― not, for fear that; (after *fear* vb or n., & similar words) that. [OE *thý lǽs the* whereby less; *thý* was dropped in ME, & *lǽs the* became *le te* by normal change]

lĕt,1 v.t. (arch.; *lĕtted* or *lĕt*, & n. **1** Hinder, obstruct. **2.** n. Stoppage, hindrance, (arch.): (Rackets, Lawn Tennis, etc.) obstruction of ball or player in certain ways, requiring round to be played again. [OE *lĕttan*, cf. OHG *lezzan*]

lĕt,2 v.t. & aux. (*lĕt*,2 & n. **1.** v.t. Allow or enable (liquid, air) to escape (*~ BLOOD*); grant use of for rent or hire (also intr. in pass. sense, as *the rooms ~ well*; *to ~*, offered for rent; || n. *~ting*, as *cannot get a ~ for the rooms*); allow to, suffer to, (*we ~ them go*; *I was ~ see him*; pass. now rare, & occas. followed by *to*); cause to (only in *~ one know*, inform him). **2.** *~ alone*, not interfere with, attend to, or do (*~ WELL3 alone*; *~ one alone to do*, he may be trusted to do; *~ alone* imperat., not to mention, far less or more); *~ be*, not interfere with, attend to, or do; *~ down*, lower, fail (friend) at need, disappoint (*~ him down gently*, avoid humiliating abruptly), (n.) disappointment; *~ drop*, *~ fall*, drop (lit., & fig. hint, significant word) intentionally or by accident, (Geom.) draw (perpendicular) from outside point (*w/m line*; *~ FLY3*; *~ go*, release, set at liberty, lose hold of, lose or relinquish hold of, dismiss from thought, cease to restrain(*~ oneself go*.

give way to enthusiasm, impulse, etc.); ~ *in*, admit or open door to (~ *in a flood of light*; *this would* ~ *in all sorts of evils*); insert into surface of something, involve in loss or difficulty (often *for*); ~ (trans.) *into*, admit to, insert into surface of, make acquainted with (secret etc.); ~ (intr. or abs.) *into*, assail with blows or words; ~ *loose*, release or unchain (dog, fury, maniac, etc.); ~ *off* adv., discharge (gun, & fig. joke etc.), not punish or compel, punish *with* light penalty, allow or cause (fluid etc.) to pass away, (n., ~-*off*) being allowed to escape something (esp. in cricket, not being caught etc. when there is a chance); ~ *off* prep., excuse (person penalty); ~ *on*, sl., peach, reveal secret, betray fact; ~ (trans.) *out*, open door for exit to, allow (person etc., secret) to escape (~ *cat out of* BAG¹), make (garment) looser, put out to hire esp. to several tenants, divulge (often *that*); ~ (intr. or abs.) *out*, strike out with fist, lash out with heels, use strong language; ~ *slip*, loose from leash, miss (opportunity); ~ *up* (colloq.), become less severe, diminish; ~-*up* n., cessation, diminution. **3.** v. aux. supplying 1st & 3rd persons of imperat. in exhortations (~ *us pray*; ~ *you & me try now*), commands (~ *it be done*, ~ *him do it, at once*), assumptions (~ *AB be equal to CD*), & permissions (~ *him do his worst*). [com.-Teut.; OE *lǣtan*, cf. G *lassen*, cogn. w. LATE & L *lassus* tired]

-let, suf, forming nn. usu. dim. (*ringlet, streamlet*), but occas. denoting articles of attire or ornament (*armlet, frontlet*); *-let* appears to come f. wrong division of wds taken f. OF diminutives in which *-et(e)* is added to nn. in *-el* (f. L *-ellus, -ella, -ellum,* dim. suff., or L *-ale* neut. adj. used as n.), as *chaplet, hamlet,* f. OF *chapelet, hamelet,* dimm. of *chapel, hamel,* mod. F *chapeau, hameau*.

lēth'al, a. Causing, sufficient or designed to cause, death (~ *chamber*, for killing animals painlessly). [f. L *let(h)alis* (*letum* death, -AL)]

lēth'argy, n. Morbid drowsiness, prolonged & unnatural sleep; torpid, inert, or apathetic state, want of interest & energy. So **lēthar'gic** a., **lēthar'gically** adv., ~IZE(3) v.t. [f. L f. Gk *lēthargia* (*lēthargos* forgetful f. *lēth-, lanthanō* forget), -Y¹]

Lēth'ē, n. (River in Hades producing) forgetfulness of the past. So **Lēthe'AN** a. [L, use of Gk *lēthē* forgetfulness, see prec.]

Lett, n. Member of a people living about the Baltic; = LETTISH n. [see LETTISH]

lett'er, n., & v.t. **1.** Character representing one or more of the simple or compound sounds used in speech, one of the alphabetic symbols, (*capital* ~, of the large form A, B, etc., opp. *small*, a, b, etc.; ROMAN, ITALIC, ~); (Print.) type, fount of type; (pl.) ~*ing*, inscription, (now only in PROOF¹ before ~*s*). **2.** Missive, epistle, (~ *of advice*, notifying dispatch of goods, drawing of bill, etc.; ~ *of attorney*, = POWER *of attorney*); (pl.) epistle of legal or formal kind for various purposes (~*s of* PATENT, *of* ADMINISTRATION, etc.; ‖=*s of business*, royal authority to Convocation to deal with a matter). **3.** Precise terms of statement (*to the* ~, with adherence to every detail), strict verbal interpretation (opp. SPIRIT; esp. *in* ~ & *in spirit*, in form & substance). **4.** pl. Literature, acquaintance with books, erudition, (*man of* ~*s*, scholar, author; *commonwealth* or *republic of* ~*s*, authors as a body; *the profession of* ~*s*, authorship), whence ~ED² (-erd) a. **5.** ~-*balance*, for ascertaining postage of ~*s*; ~-*book*, in which copies of correspondence are kept; ~-*bound*, too subservient to the ~; ‖~-*box*, in which ~*s* are posted; ‖~-*card*, folded card with gummed edge for use as postal missive; ~-*case*, pocket-book for holding ~*s*; ~-*lock*, kind of padlock opened by making out of certain ~*s* on it a word known to owner; ~-*paper*, quarto-sized paper for ~*s*; ~-*perfect* (Theatr.), knowing one's part perfectly; ~-*press*, contents of illustrated book other than the illustrations, printed matter relating to illustration; ~-*weight*, = ~-*balance*, also thing used to keep papers still on table; ~-*worship*, undue devotion to the ~; ~-*writer*, lit., also as title for manuals of ~-*writing*; hence ~LESS a. **6.** v.t. Impress title etc. on (book-cover); classify with ~*s*; hence ~ING¹(1, 6) n. [f. OF *lettre* f, L *littera* ~ of alphabet, (pl.) epistle]

Lett'ic, a. & n. =foll.; (of) the group of languages comprising Lettish, Lithuanian, & Old Prussian; of these peoples. [as foll., -IC]

Lett'ish, a. & n. (Language) of the Letts. [*Lett* f. G *Lette* f. native *Latvi*+-ISH¹]

lett'uce (-tis), n. Garden herb with crisp leaves much used as salad (*cabbage, cos,* ~, kinds of it). [f. L *lactuca* (*lac lactis* milk, w. ref. to milky juice of root)]

leuc'o-, comb. form of Gk *leukos* white, as ~*cyte*, colourless corpuscle of blood or found in lymph etc.; ~*pathy* (-op-), albinism; ~*rrhoe'a*, mucous discharge from female genitals, the whites. So **leukaem'ia**, n. (med.). Disease in which there is an excess of white corpuscles in the blood. [f. Gk *leukos* white, *haima* blood]

lēv, n. (pl. ~*a*). Bulgarian monetary unit, formerly equivalent to the franc. [Bulg., = lion]

Levant¹, n. Eastern part of Mediterranean with its islands & neighbouring countries; ~ MOROCCO. [F, part., of *lever* rise, used as n. = sunrise, east, f. L *levare* lift (*lēvis* light)]

‖ **levant'**[1,2], v.i. Abscond, bolt, esp. with betting or gaming losses unpaid. Hence **levan'ter**[1-ER1] n. [perh. f. Sp. *levantar el campo* break up camp (*levar* f. L *levare* lift)]

Levant'[2] n. (L~) inhabitant of Levant; strong Mediterranean easterly wind. [LEVANT[1], -ER1]

Levan'tine, a. & n. Of, inhabitant of, the Levant. [-INE[1]]

levat'or, n. (Also ~*muscle*) muscle that raises organ. [LL (L *levare* lift, -OR[2])]

lev'ee[1] (-vi), n. (Formerly) reception of visitors on rising from bed; assembly held by sovereign or his representative at which men only are received; assembly of visitors. [F *levé* var. of *lever*, see LEVANT[1]]

•**levee**[2] (-vi), n. Embankment against river floods. [f. F *levée* fem. p.p. of *lever* raise, see LEVANT[1]]

lev'el, n., a., & v.t. (-ll-). **1.** Instrument giving line parallel to plane of horizon for testing whether things are horizontal; horizontal line or plane (*on a ~ with, in same horizontal plane as; find one's ~, reach right place with regard to others; water finds its ~*), its surface in communicating receptacles will be at same ~ unless they have no common ~; plane or ~less surface; flat country; *on the ~* (colloq.), truthful(ly), honest(ly). **2.** adj. Horizontal, perpendicular to the plumb-line; on a ~ or equality (*with*, or abs.; ~ *race*, in which leading competitors are close together; ‖~ CROSSING); even, equable, uniform, well-balanced, in quality, style, temper, judgement, etc. (~*-headed; do one's ~ best*, not be remiss, take all possible pains); hence ~LY[2] adv. (rare), ~NESS n. **3.** v.t. Make ~, bring up or down to a standard; raze, lay low, (*to or with the ground; in the dust*, or abs.); (rarely) knock (person down); abolish (distinctions); aim (missile, or abs.), lay (gun), direct (satire, accusation, or abs.), (*at or against*); ~*ing-screw*, for adjusting parts of machine etc. to exact ~. [f. OF *livel* (now *niveau*) f. L *libella* dim. of *libra* balance]

lev'eller, n. In vbl senses; esp. person who would abolish social distinctions, advocate of equality. [-ER1]

lev'er, n., & v.t. & i. **1.** Bar used to prize up heavy or fixed object; (Mech.) straight bar or other rigid structure of which one point (*fulcrum*) is fixed, another is connected with the force (*weight*) to be resisted or acted upon, & a third is connected with the force (*power*) applied (~ *of first order* with fulcrum, *of second order* with weight, *of third order* two); piece by which barrel or breechloader is opened; = ~ *watch*; ~, *acting as or worked by ~;* ~ *escapement*, with connexion between pallet & balance made by two ~s; ~ *watch*, with ~ escapement. **2.** vb. Use ~; lift, move, act on, with ~ (*often along, away, out, over, up, etc.*). [f. OF *leveour* (*lever* see LEVANT[1]), -OR2]

lev'erage, n. Action of, way of applying, lever; set or system of levers; power, mechanical advantage gained by use, of lever; means of accomplishing a purpose, power, influence. [-AGE]

lev'eret, n. Young (esp. first-year) hare. [f. OF *levrete* (*lievre* f. L *leporem* nom. *-us* hare, -ET2)]

levi'athan, n. Sea monster (Bibl.); huge ship; anything very large of its kind; person of formidable ability, power, or wealth. [f. Heb. *liwyāthān* etym. dub.]

lev'igate, v.t. Reduce to fine smooth powder; make smooth paste of. Hence ~A'TION n. [f. L *levigare* (*levis* smooth), -ATE[3]]

lev'in, n. (poet.). (Flash of) lightning. [ME *levene*, etym. dub.]

lev'irate, n. Jewish etc. custom by which dead man's brother or next of kin had to marry his widow. Hence ~at'ic(al) aa. [f. L *levir* brother-in-law + -ATE[3]]

lev'itate, v.i. & t. (Make) rise & float in air (w. ref. to spiritualism). Hence ~A'TION n. [f. L *levis* light, after GRAVITATION]

Lev'ite, n. One of tribe of Levi, esp. of those in lower grade of Jewish ministers, that part of it which provided assistants to priests in worship of Jewish temple. [f. LL Gk *leuitēs* (*Leui* f. Heb. *Lewi*)]

Levit'ical, a. Of Levites or the tribe of Levi; of Levites' ritual; of Leviticus. So ~ISM(3) n. [f. LL f. Gk *leuitikos* (prec., -IC) + -AL]

Levit'icus, n. (abbr. *Lev.*). Third book of Pentateuch with Levitical law & ritual. [prec.]

lev'ity, n. Lightness of weight (rare); want of thought, frivolity, unseasonable jocularity, inconstancy; light behaviour. [f. OF *levité* f. L *levitatem* (*levis* light, -TY)]

levulose. See LAEVULOSE.

lev'y, n., & v.t. **1.** Collecting of assessment, tax, etc. (*capital ~*, appropriation by the State of a fixed proportion of all the wealth in the country); enrolling of men for war etc. (~ *in mass*, of all able-bodied men); amount or number levied, body of men enrolled (also pl.). **2.** v.t. Raise (contribution, taxes), impose (rate, toll), whence lev'IABLE a.; raise (sum) by legal execution or process on person's goods; extort (~ *blackmail*); enlist, enrol, (soldiers, army); collect men & munitions for, proceed to make, (*war; usu. upon, against*). [f. F *levée* (*lever* see LEVANT[1], -Y[4])]

lewd, a. Base, worthless, (Bibl.); lascivious, unchaste, indecent, whence ~LY[2] adv., ~NESS n. [OE *læwede*; earlier senses *lay, unlearned*; perh. as LAY[2] + -ED[3]]

lew'is (lōō-), n. Iron contrivance for gripping heavy blocks of stone for lifting; son of a freemason. [?]

Lew'is gŭn (lōō-), n. Kind of light machine gun. [I. N. *Lewis*, inventor]

lew'isite (lōō-), n. A blister gas used in chemical warfare. [W. L. *Lewis*, -ITE²(2)]

lĕx'ical, a. Of the words of a language (opp. *grammatical*); (as) of a lexicon. Hence ~LY² adv. [f. Gk *lexikos*, & LEXI-CON, +-AL]

lĕxicŏg'raphy, n. Dictionary-making. So **lĕxicŏg'RAPHER** n., **lĕxicOGRAPH'ICAL** a. [foll., -GRAPHY]

lĕx'icon, n. Dictionary, esp. of Greek, Hebrew, Syriac, or Arabic. [Gk (-kon) neut. of *lexikos* (*lexis* word f. *legō* speak, -IO)]

lĕxig'raphy, n. System of writing in which each character represents a word. [*lexis*, see prec., -GRAPHY]

lĕx tālion'is, n. The law of retaliation, an eye for an eye. [L]

ley (lā), n. Land temporarily under grass. [var. of LEA¹]

Ley'den (lī-), n. Dutch city (~ *jar*, kind of electrical condenser invented 1745 at ~; battery, of several ~ jars).

li (lē), n. Chinese mile (about 633 yds); Chinese weight (about ⅓ gr.). [Chin.]

liabil'ity, n. Being liable ‖ (*limited* ~, being responsible only to limited amount for debts of trading company; *so limited* ~ *company*, or *ellipt. limited company*); what one is liable for, (pl.) debts or pecuniary obligations. [foll., -BILITY]

li'able, a. Legally bound, answerable *for*, subject or amenable *to* tax or penalty, under obligation *to* do; exposed or open *to*, apt *to* do or suffer, something undesirable (*difficulties are* ~ *to occur*). [perh. f. L *ligabilis* (*ligare* bind, -ABLE]

liais'on (-zn), n. 1. Illicit intimacy between a man & a woman. 2. Sounding of ordinarily silent final consonant before vowel or mute *h* in French. 3. (Mil.) connexion, touch, (~ *officer*, acting as go-between for allied forces). [F, f. L *ligationem* (*ligare* bind, -ATION)]

li'ana (-ah-), **liane'** (-ahn), n. Kinds of climbing & twining tropical-forest plant. [F (-e), perh. f. *lier* bind f. L as prec.; -a form a Latinization of -e]

li'ar, n. Teller (esp. habitual) of lie(s). [OE *léogere* (LIE², -AR³]

li'as, n. Blue limestone rock of some S.-W. counties; (Geol.) lower strata of Jurassic series; blue argillaceous limestone rich in fossils. Hence **liass'ıc** a. [f. OF *liois* etym. dub.]

liba'tion, n. (Pouring of) drink-offering to god; (joc.) potation. [f. L *tibatio* (*libare* pour a little of, -ATION)]

li'bel, n., & v.t. (-ll-). 1. (Civil & Eccl. Law) plaintiff's written declaration; (Law) published statement damaging to; person's reputation, act of publishing it (*the greater the truth, the greater the* ~); (pop.) false & defamatory statement, (transf.) thing that brings discredit *on* by unsuccessful portrayal etc. (*the portrait is a* ~ *on him; the book, play, is a* ~ *on human nature*); hence ~LIST(1) n., ~LOUS a., ~LOUSLY² adv. 2. v.t. Defame by ~lous statements, accuse falsely & maliciously, (Law) publish ~ against, whence ~LER¹ n.; (Eccl. & Admiralty Law) bring suit against, whence ~LANT(1), ~LEE', nn. [vb.f. n., OF, f. L *libellus* dim. of *liber* book]

lib'eral, a. & n. 1. Fit for a gentleman (now rare exc. in ~ *education*, i.e. directed to general enlargement of mind, not professional or technical); generous, open-handed, not sparing of; ample, abundant, not rigorous or literal; open-minded, candid, unprejudiced; (Pol.) favourable to democratic reforms & abolition of privilege (esp. *L*~ *party*; cf. CONSER-VATIVE; *L*~ *Conservative*, member of Conservative party not ill disposed to reforms; *L*~ *Unionist*, member of section that seceded from L~ party in 1886 on Home Rule), whence ~ISM(3) n., ~IST(2) n. & a., ~ıze(3) v.t. & (rarely) i., ~ıza'TION n.; hence ~LY² adv. 2. n. (L~) member of (esp. the British) L~ party. [OF, f. L *liberalis* (*liber* free, -AL)]

liberăl'itý, n. Free giving, munificence; freedom from prejudice, breadth of mind. [f. OF *liberalité* f. L *liberalitatem* (prec., -TY)]

lib'erāte, v.t. Set at liberty, release *from* (in Chem., from combination). Hence ~OR² n. [f. L *liberare* (*liber* free), -ATE³]

libera'tion, n. Releasing, release; ‖*L*~ *Society*, advocating church disestablishment, whence ~ISM(3) n., ~IST(2) n. & a., (-sho-). [f. L *liberatio* (prec., -ATION)]

libertā'rian, n. & a. Believer, believing, in free will (opp. *necessitarian*): advocate of liberty. Hence ~ISM(3) n. [-ARIAN]

lib'erticide, n. & a. Destroyer, destructive, of liberty. [f. (LIBERTY, -CIDE)]

lib'ertine, n. & a. Free-thinker on religion; licentious (man); free-thinking, antinomian; *chartered* ~*e*, person allowed to do as he pleases (Shak. *Hen. V*, i. i. 48). Hence ~ISM(3) & (in same sense) ~AGE, nn. [f. L *libertinus freedman* (*libertus* made free, cogn. w. *liber* free)]

lib'erty, n. 1. Being free from captivity, imprisonment, slavery, or despotic control (CAP.¹ of ~; *natural* ~, state in which there are no laws; *civil* ~, natural ~ limited only by laws established on behalf of community; ~ *of conscience*, system allowing all members of State to follow what form of religion seems good to them; ~ *of the press*, system by which anyone may print & publish what he pleases without previous permission, but not without liability to penalties for publishing libellous or criminal matter). 2. Right or power to do as one pleases or

to do something; (Philos.) freedom from control of fate or necessity. **3.** A setting aside of rules, licence, (*take the ~ to do, of doing*, presume or venture to; *take liberties*, be unduly familiar *with* person or abs., deal freely *with* rules or facts). **5.** pl. Privileges, immunities, or rights, enjoyed by prescription or grant. **6.** *At ~*, free (*set at ~*, liberate); having the right to do, disengaged; *~ HALL*; *~ man*, sailor with leave to go ashore. [f. F *liberté* f. L *libertatem* (*liber* free, -TY)]

Libi'dinous a. Lustful. Hence ~LY² adv. [f. L *libidinosus* (*libido -inis* lust, see prec.)]

Libi'do, n. (psych.) Emotional craving prompting any specific human (esp. sexual) activity. [L, = lust]

Li'bra, n. (pl. *-ae*). **1.** Pound weight (used only in abbr. *lb.*, as 1 *lb.*, 10 *lb.*); pound sterling (used only in abbr. *£ s. d.*, & *l.* ~). **2.** (Astron.; *L~*) zodiacal constellation the Scales, seventh sign of zodiac. [L]

Libra'rian, n. Custodian of library. Hence ~SHIP(1) n. [f. L as foll. + -AN]

Li'brary, n. Room or building containing books for reading or reference; writing & reading room in house; collection of books for use by the public, some part of it, or members of some society; public institution charged with care of such collection, (*lending ~*, from which books may be taken away with or without payment; *reference ~*, in which books may be consulted; *free~*, used by public without payment & ~, letting out use of books for profit); person's book-collection; series of books issued by publisher in similar bindings as connected in some way; books used by or familiar to an author; (*walking ~*, person of erudition; ~ *edition*, of good size & print. [f. F *librairie* book-shop (L *librarius* of books f. *liber -bri* book, orig. bark, -ARY¹, + -Y³)]

li'brate, v.i. Oscillate, be poised, balance, sway, quiver. Hence **libra'tion** a. [f. L *libro* balance), -ATE³]

libra'tion, n. Librating (~ *of moon*, apparent oscillation by which parts near edge of disk are alternately visible & invisible). [f. L *librātio* (prec., -ATION)]

libre'tto, n. (pl. *-ti, -tos*). Book or words of an opera or long musical work. Hence ~IST(1) n. [It., dim. of *libro* book f. L *liber -bri*]

Li'bya, a. & n. (Inhabitant) of ancient Libya; (poet.) African; (of) the Berber language or the group of mod. Hamitic languages to which it belongs. [f. L f. Gk *Libua* + -AN]

lice. See LOUSE.

Li'cence, n. **1.** Leave, permission, (*have I your~ to remove the fence?*); permit from government etc. to marry, print something, preach, carry on some trade (esp.

that in alcoholic liquor, etc. **2.** University certificate of competence in some faculty. **3.** Liberty of action esp. when excessive, abuse of freedom, disregard of law or propriety; licentiousness. **4.** Writer's or artist's irregularity in grammar, metre, or perspective, etc. (usu. *poetic ~*). [F, f. L *licentia* (*licēre* be lawful, -ENCE)]

li'cense, -ce², v.t. Allow (person to do, thing to be done; rare); (in p.p.) allow complete freedom to (*a ~d satirist*); VICTUALLER); authorize use of (premises for certain purpose); authorize publication of (book etc.) or performance of (play). Hence **licensee'** n. [f. prec., -se on anal. of *practise, prophesy*, vv., cf. *advice, advise*, where the sound differs]

li'censer, n. In vbl senses: esp. ~ *of the press*, ~ *of plays*, officials licensing publication or performance when satisfied that law, morals, & decency are not outraged. [-ER¹]

licen'tiate(-shiat), n. Holder of university licence or attestation of competence from collegiate or examining body (chiefly in abbr. L. as part of title); licensed preacher not yet having appointment esp. in Presbyterian Church. [f. med. L *licentiatus* (LICENCE¹), -ATE³)]

licen'tious (-shus), a. Disregarding accepted rules esp. of grammar or style (rare); lascivious, libertine, lewd. Hence ~LY² adv.,~NESS n. [f. L *licentiosus* (LICENCE¹, -OSE²)]

lich, lych, lyke, n. (obs.). ‖ Corpse; *~ch-gate*, roofed gateway of churchyard where coffin awaits clergyman's arrival; *~ch-house*, mortuary; ‖ *~ch-owl*, (boding death); *~ch-stone*, to place coffin on at *~gate*; ‖ *lyke-wake*, watch kept at night over corpse. [OE *līc*, cf. G *leiche*; orig. sense prob. *form*, cf. LIKE]

li'chen (-k-, li-), n. Kinds of cellular cryptogamic plant (prob. fungus parasitic on alga) usu. of green, grey, or yellow tint growing on & colouring rocks, tree-trunks, etc., whence ~ED² (-kend) a.; ‖ ~ŌU'GY n.; skin-disease with reddish eruption. Hence ~OUS a. [f. L f. Gk *leikhēn*]

li'cit, a. Not illicit. Hence ~LY² adv. [f. L *licitus* (*licēre* be lawful)]

lick, v.t. & i., & n. **1.** Pass tongue over to taste, moisten, clean, etc. (*~ one's chops* or *lips*, in relish or anticipation of food; *~ into shape*, mould, make presentable or efficient; *~ one's shoes*, show servility to him; *~ the dust*, fall, be vanquished); take *up* or *off*, make clean, by ~ing; (of waves, flame, etc.) play lightly over; (of flame) swallow *up* in passing; (sl.) thrash (person, fault *out of* person), beat, in fight or competition, excel, (*~s creation*,

is beyond everything), whence ~ING¹(1) n.; (sl.) surpass comprehension of (*this ~s me*); (sl.) go, hasten, (*as hard as he could* ~); ~*spittle*, toady. **2.** In Act of ~ing with tongue; (also *salt*-~) spot to which animals resort for salt; smart blow with stick etc.; (sl.) pace (*at a great* ~; *full or at full* ~). [OE *liccian*, cf. G *lecken*: cogn. w. Gk *leikhō*, L *linguere*]

lick'erish, liq'uorish (-ker-), a. Fond of dainty fare; greedy, longing; lecherous. [earlier *lickerous* var. through ONF of *lecherous* (see LECHER) & retaining its obs. orig. sense]

licorice. See LIQUORICE.

licorous. Var. of *lickerous*, LICKERISH.

lic'tor, n. Officer attending ancient-Roman consul (12 ~s) & dictator (24 ~s), bearing fasces, & executing sentence on offenders. [L, perh. f. st. of *ligare* bind]

lid, n. Hinged or detached cover for aperture, esp. for opening at top of vessel; *with the* ~ *off*, with all horrors etc. exposed to view; ‖ *put the* ~ *on* (sl.), be the culmination (of), surpass all; = EYE¹-lid; (Bot., Conch.) operculum. Hence (-)~d'ED², ~'LESS, aa. [OE *hlid*, cf. Du. *lid*, G (*augen*)*lid*]

*lid'ō (lē-), n. Public open-air swimming pool. [L~, bathing beach in Venice]

lie¹, n. Intentional false statement (*tell a* ~, make this; *act a* ~, deceive without verbal lying; *white* ~, excused or justified by its motive; *give one the* ~, accuse him of lying; *give the* ~ *to* supposition etc., serve to show its falsity); belie it); imposture, false belief, mistaken convention, (*worship, maintain, a* ~). [OE *lyge*, cf. G *lug* & see foll.]

lie², v.i. & t. (*ly'ing*). Speak falsely, tell lie(s), (*you* ~ *in your teeth, throat*, arch. or joc, forms of accusation); *take away* (repu-tation etc.), get (oneself, person) *into, out of*, by lying; (of things) deceive (part, deceptive). [com.-Teut.; OE *lēogan*, cf. Du. *liegen*, G *lügen*, as prec.]

lie³, v.i. (*ly'ing*; past *lay*; p.p. *lain* & bibl. *li'en*). **1.** Of persons or animals: Have one's body in more or less horizontal position along ground or surface (often *asleep, sick*, etc.; ~ DOGGO; *let sleeping dogs* ~, avoid mooting debatable ques-tions; ~ *on the bed one has made*, endure consequences of past acts); have sexual intercourse *with*; (of the dead) be in the grave *at* or *in*, ~ *in* STATE; assume lying position (usu. *down, back*, etc.); be kept or remain in specified state (~ *in prison*, *at the mercy of, helpless, idle*, CLOSE¹, LOW¹, PERDU, *in ambush, in* WAIT²; ~ *out of one's money*, remain unpaid); (of game-birds) not rise; (of troops) be en-camped *at, in, near*; a place. **2.** Of things: Be at rest, usu. more or less horizontally; on surface (~ *in ruins or the dust*, be fallen; ~ *heavy*, be a weight on one's *stomach* or *conscience*); be stored up in

specified place (*money lying at the bank*); remain in specified state esp. *vaste, hid, barren*; be situated (*land lying high, to the east, round*; *find out how the land* ~s, fig., how affairs stand); be spread out to view (~*s on the surface, before us, open*); (of road) lead through, *by, along, among*, etc.; (of ship) float in berth or at anchor; (of abstracts) exist, be to be found, reside, be arranged or related, in some position or manner (*the choice* ~*s between* —; *his acquaintance lay among* —; *knows where his interest* ~s; *how do they* ~ *to each other*?; *as far as in me* ~*s*, to best of my power; ~*s with you to do*, is your business or right; *the remedy* ~*s in education*; *her strength lay in her weakness*; ~*s in a NUTSHELL*); (Law) be admissible or sustain-able (*action, appeal, objection, will not* ~). **3.** With adv.: ~ *by*, be unused, keep quiet or retired; ~ *down* in part, behav-ing in abject manner, not standing up to opponent etc., (*take defeat, chastisement*, & esp. *it, lying down*); ~ *in*, be brought to bed in childbirth (*lying-in hospital*); ~ *off* (Naut.), stand some distance from shore or other ship; ~ *over*, be deferred; ~ *to* (Naut.), come almost to a stop with head near wind by backing or shortening sail; ~ *up*, go into or be in retirement, take to one's bed or room, (of ship) go into dock or be out of commission. **4.** ~*abed*, late riser. [com.-Teut.; OE *licgan*, cf. Du. *liggen*, G *liegen*, cogn. w. Gk *leikhos*, L *lectus*, bed]

lie⁴, n. Way, direction, or position, in which thing lies; ~ *of the land*, (fig.) posture of affairs; place where beast, bird, or fish, is accustomed to lie. [f. prec.]

Lie'big('s extract of beef (lē-), n. Con-centrated preparation of beef without albumen, gelatin, or fat. [Baron von Liebig, d. 1873, inventor]

lied (lēd), n. (pl. ~*er*). German song or poem of ballad kind. [G]

lief, adv. (poet. ~*er*, rare). Gladly, willingly, (usu. *I would as* ~ *do* something out of the question *as*). [prop. adj. (earlier construction being *I had as* ~, i.e. should find it as pleasant, now cor-rupted *to would*); OE *lēof* dear, cf. G *lieb*, cogn. w. LOVE]

liege, a. & n. **1.** (Of superior) entitled to receive, (of vassal) bound to give, feudal service or allegiance (~ *lord*, feudal superior, sovereign; ~ *man*, sworn vas-sal, faithful follower). **2.** n. ~ lord (esp. *my* ~ voc.); vassal, subject, (usu. *the* ~s). [f. OF *lige*, perh. f. OHG *lēdig* free]

li'en² (lē'en), n. Right to keep possession of property till debt due in respect of it is discharged (usu. *a* ~ *on* or *upon*). [F, f. L *ligamen* (*ligare* bind), -MEN]

lien². See LIE³.

lierne', n. Short rib connecting bosses & intersections of vaulting-ribs. [F, etym. dub.]

lieu (lū), n. In ~, in the place, instead of. [F, f. L *locus* place]

lieuten·ant (leftén·ant, *in navy* let-), n. (abbr. Lieut. & *in comb.* Lt-). Deputy, substitute, vicegerent, acting for a superior (still as formal title in *L~ of the Tower*, acting commandant of Tower of London; & see LORD L~); *~-colonel, ~-commander, ~-general*, OFFICERS of navy & army; *~-governor(ship)*, (position of) actual governor of district etc. in subordination to governor general. Hence **lieuten·ANCY** n. [F (prec., TENANT)]

life, n. (pl. *lives*). **1.** State of ceaseless change & functional activity peculiar to organized matter, & esp. to the portion of it constituting an animal or plant before death, animate existence, being alive, (*a matter of ~ & death*, something on which it depends whether one shall live or die; NECESSARY, STAFF, *of ~*; *come, bring, to ~*, recover (i. & t.) from swoon; *lose, save, lay down, one's ~*; *safe in, escape with, ~ & limb*; SELL *one's ~ dear*; (lit.) *great sacrifice of ~*, many killed; *have no regard for human ~*, kill men or let them die recklessly; *for one's ~, for dear, ~*, to escape death; *cannot for my ~*; *depended on it*; *'pon my ~*, asseveration). **2.** Energy, liveliness, vivacity, animation; vivifying influence (*was the ~*, or *~ & soul, of the party*; *my ~*, voc. of affection). **3.** Living things & their motions (*very little ~ to be seen*); the living form or model, *~size* or figure etc. (*taken from the ~*; *as large as ~*, *~size*, also joc. *as here he is as large as ~*, i.e. in person; *portray etc. to the ~*, with fidelity to the original), whence **~LIKE** (-lī-) a. **4.** Period from birth to death, birth to present time, or present time to death (*have done it all my ~*; *have the time of one's ~*, sl., enjoy oneself as never before; *~ sentence, rent, annuity*, to continue for rest of person's ~; *lease for three etc. lives*, to terminate with last of three etc. named persons' lives; *~*ASSURANCE; INSURE *one's ~*; *expectation of ~* average period that person at specified age may expect to live; *a good, bad, ~*, person likely to pass, fall short of, this. **5.** Fresh start after narrowly escaped lit. or metaph. death (*cat has nine lives*, is hard to kill; *batsman was given a chance*; *pool-player has three* average successive chances). **6.** Individual's actions & fortunes, manner of existence, (*with all the pleasure in ~*, greatest possible; *nothing in ~*, at all; *this ~*, that on earth; *the other, future, eternal, everlasting, ~*, state of existence after death; *the* SIMPLE *~*; *has led a good etc. ~*, written story of these, biography. **7.** Active part of existence, business & pleasures of the world, (see *~*, mix freely with others; *high, low, ~*, social customs of upper, lower,

classes). **8.** (Theol.) salvation, regenerate condition, (also *eternal, everlasting, ~*, see above also). **9.** *~belt*, of buoyant material to support body in water; *~blood*, blood necessary to ~, vitalizing influence, in voluntary twitching of lip or eyelid; *~boat*, of special construction for saving ~ in storms; *~breath*, inspiring influence, sustaining principle; *~buoy*, *~ estate*, property that one holds for ~ but cannot dispose of further; *~giving*, that gives or restores, physical or spiritual sustains, or restores; *~guard*, body-guard of soldiers; ‖ L~ *Guards*, regiment of household cavalry; ‖ L~-*Guardsman*, soldier of L~ Guards; *~interest*, right to ~ estate; *~jacket*, as *~belt*; *~line*, rope used for ~-saving, e.g. that attached to ~buoy, diver's signalling line, (Palmistry) = line of ~; *~long*, continued for a ~time; *~office*, for *~assurance*; *~peer(age)*, with title lapsing at death; *~preserver*, short stick with heavily loaded end; *~spring*, source of;~strings, hold on ~; *~strings are cut* or broken, person dies); *~table*, statistics of expectation of ~; *~time*, duration of person's ~; *~work*, task pursued through person's ~. Hence **~LESS** a., **~LESS²** adv., **~lessness** n. [OE *līf*, cf. OFris. *lif* life, body, Du. *lijf* & G *leib* body, cogn. w. LIVE & LEAVE²; f. Aryan *leip- loip-*, endure, cf. Gk *liparēs* persistent]

lifer (-f-), (sl.) One sentenced to, sentence of, penal servitude for life. [-ER¹]

lift, v.t. & i. & n. **1.** Raise to higher position, take up, hoist, (often *up, off, out*), elevate to higher plane of thought or feeling, give upward direction to (eyes, face), (*~ up* or *~ one's hands* or *heart*, in prayer etc.; *~ one's hand*, to take oath; *~ a hand*, make the slightest effort, usu. to do; *never ~ed a hand against* one, struck him; *~ up one's head*, recover vigour after prostration, *~ up another's head*, Bibl., restore to liberty or dignity; *~ up one's heel*, kick; *~ up one's horn*, be ambitious or proud; *~ up a cry, one's voice*, cry out); hold or have on high (*church ~s its spire*); steal (esp. cattle), take (passage, information) in the way of plagiarism; remove (tents etc.); dig up (potatoes); lift (cricket-ball) into air; (of ship afloat) rise on wave; yield to a ~ (*window will not ~*); (of cloud, fog, darkness) rise, disperse; (of floor) swell upwards, bulge. **2.** n. ~ing (DRAG ~); *give* one *a ~*, take him up into vehicle for part of way, also fig. give him helping hand); one layer of leather in boot-heel; apparatus for raising & lowering people or things to other floor of house, elevator, hoist; rise in to the ground; vertical component of the air pressure on an aeroplane, counteracting the force of gravity. [f. ON *lypta* (*lopt* air, sky; cf. G *luft*, obs. E *lift*, & LOFT)]

lig'ament, n. Tie, bond of union, (rare); (Anat.) short band of tough flexible fibrous tissue binding bones together, (loosely) any membranous fold keeping organ in position, similar part in lower organisms. Hence ~AL, ~ARY[1], ~OUS, aa., (-mĕn⁴). [f. L *ligamentum* (ligare bind, -MENT)]

lig'ate, v.t. (surg.). Tie up (bleeding artery etc.). Hence ~A'TION n. [f. L *ligare*, -ATE³]

lig'ature, n. & v.t. Thing used in tying, esp. band or cord used to tie up bleeding artery, strangulate tumour, etc. (vb, bind with ~); thing that unites, bond; tying, ligation; (Mus.) slur, tie; (Print.) two or more letters joined (fi etc.). [f. L *ligatura* (prec., -URE)]

light¹ (līt), n. 1. The natural agent that stimulates the sense of sight. 2. Medium or condition of space in which sight is possible (opp. *darkness*). 3. Appearance of brightness (NORTHERN ~s; ZODIACAL ~; *saw a distant ~*). 4. Sensation peculiar to optic nerve. 5. Amount of illumination in place (*in a good ~*, easily visible); one's fair or ordinary share of this (*stand in one's ~*, deprive him of this, (fig.) prejudice his chances). 6. Vivacity in person's eyes. 7. Favouring aspect (~ of one's *countenance*, his favour, approving presence, or sanction, often iron.). 8. Sun's direct or diffused or reflected rays, daylight, (*see the ~*, be born). 9. Being visible or exposed (*come, bring, to ~*, be revealed, reveal). 10. (Poet.) eyesight; (sl., pl.) eyes. 11. Object from which brightness emanates (~ *of one's eyes*, beloved person), sun or other heavenly body, ignited candle or lamp or the like; (collect.) lamps etc. illuminating place; beacon lamp esp. of ship or ~house, ~house; (fig.) eminent person or luminary (often *shining* ~). 12. Mental illumination, elucidation (*throw, shed, ~ upon*, help to explain), enlightenment (*by the ~ of nature*, without aid of revelation or teaching; *men of ~ & LEADING*); (pl.) facts or discoveries serving to explain subject (*we have many new ~s upon it since then*); (pl.) one's natural or acquired mental powers (usu. *do one's best etc. according to* one's ~s); (sing.) aspect in which thing is viewed (*in the ~ of these facts*, with the help given by them; *appeared in the ~ of a scoundrel*, seemed to be one; *place thing in a good ~*, represent it favourably); (in acrostic puzzles) one of the words whose initial & final letters make up the answer. 13. (Theol.) brightness of heaven, illumination of soul by divine truth. 14. Window or opening in wall for admission of ~, perpendicular division of mullioned window, glazed compartment of side or roof in greenhouse. 15. (Paint.) Illuminated surface, part of picture represented as lighted up.

16. (Law) ~ *falling on windows*, the obstruction of which by neighbour is illegal (*Ancient L~s*, inscription giving notice of this). 17. Flame or spark serving to ignite (*strike a ~*, produce this with match etc.); thing used for igniting, spill, taper, match. 18. ~ *due, duty*, toll on ships for maintenance of ~*houses* (tower or other structure) & ~*ships* (moored or anchored) containing beacon ~s for warning or guiding ships at sea. Hence ~'LESS a. [OE *lēoht*, cf. Du. & G *licht*, f. Aryan *leuk-* whence Gk *leukos* white, L *lux* light]

light² (līt), a. Well provided with light, not dark; pale-coloured (often prefixed to adjj. & nn. of colour, as *a ~blue ribbon*, *I prefer ~ blue*; *the ~ BLUE²s*). [as prec.]

light³ (līt), v.t. & i. (*lit* or ~*ed*; as attrib. adj., ~*ed* is usu.). Set (lamp etc., fire, combustible) burning (often *up*; ~ *up*, abs., begin to smoke pipe etc., also kindle the lights in street or room at dusk), (of fuel, lamp, etc.) take fire, begin to burn; give light to (room, street, etc.; ~ *up*, brightly or make conspicuous by light); brighten (t. & i., with *eyes, face*, etc., as obj. or subj.) with animation; show (person his) way or surroundings with a light. Hence (-)~**er¹** (līt'), (exc.) for ~*ing* cigarette etc. [OE *lihtan* (LIGHT¹,²)]

light⁴ (līt), a. & adv. 1. Of little weight, not heavy, (~*armed*, with ~ equipment & weapons); deficient in weight (~ *coin, gold*, etc.). 2. Of small specific gravity. 3. Having or affording a small load (~ *ship*, unladen; ~ *watertime* etc., that of ship when ~; ~ *engine*, with no train attached; ~ *railway*, for ~ traffic; ~ *porter*; ~ *horse*, ~armed cavalry, & so ~ *horseman*, ~*infantry*; ~*marching order*, in which only arms & ammunition are taken); (of ship, cart, etc.) made ~ly for small loads & quick movement. 4. (Of building) not looking heavy, graceful, elegant. 5. Acting gently, applied delicately, not violent, (~ *hand*, lit., & fig. = tactful management, whence ~-**hand**'ED² a., ~**hand**'EDLY² adv., ~-**hand**'EDNESS n.; ~ *touch, blow, wind, step*, etc.). 6. Not dense or tenacious; porous, friable, (~ *soil, bread*). 7. Easy of digestion; (of wine or beer) not strong. 8. (Of syllable) unemphatic. 9. Not important (*make ~ of*, treat as of no consequence); slight, trivial, venial, not grave, jesting, thoughtless, frivolous (whence ~-**mind**'ED² a., ~-**mind**'EDNESS n.). 10. Wanton, unchaste, (esp. of women or their conduct). 11. Nimble, quick-moving, (~ *of foot*; ~ *heels*, whence ~-**heel**ED² a.; ~ *movements*; ~ *rhythm*; ~ *fingers*, good at stealing, whence ~-**fing**'ERED² a.). 12. Fickle, inconstant. 13. Easily borne (~ *punishment, taxation, rule, expense*) or done (~ *work, task*).

14. Aimed or aiming at entertainment merely (~ *literature, writer, comedy, comedian, programme*). **15.** (Of sleep) easily disturbed, not profound, (so ~ *sleeper*). **16.** Free from sorrow, cheerful, sanguine, (now only in ~ *heart*; *did it with a ~ heart*, ~**heart′edly**, rashly; so ~**′heart**′ed[2] a., ~**′heart′edly** adv.; so n.). **17.** Delirious (now only in ~**′head**′ed, ~**′head**′edness n.). **18.** ||~**′heav**′**y** a. (Of plants) woody (opp. ~ *heavy* (BOX[2]); ~ *skirts*, harlot; ~ *heart*, below average weight, esp. in boxing 9 st. 9 to 9 st., hence—′LY[2] adv.,~′NESS n. (lit-), **19.** adv. *go, what is easily grained is soon lost*). In ~ *manner*(esp. *tread, sleep,* ~) *come* (prec.).

[OE *lēoht*, cf. Du. *licht*, G *leicht*, also Skr. *laghu*, Gk *elaphros* light & *elakhus* small]

light[5] (līt), v.t. & i. (*lit* or ~*ed*). **1.** (Naut.) hauling ropes etc.; (arch.) alight, descend, come down; chance, come by chance, (*up)on. (orig., sense make light, or lit. meanings coming from idea of relieving horse etc. of weight; OE *lihtan*)

light′en[1] (līt-), v.t. & i. Reduce load of (ship etc.), (of ship) have her load reduced; relieve (heart etc.), (of heart etc.) feel relief; reduce weight of, (fig.) mitigate; grow lighter. [LIGHT[4]+-EN[6]]

light′en[2] (līt-), v.t. & i. Shed light upon, make bright; (of face, eyes, sky, etc.) grow bright, shine, flash; (of sky, clouds, or it) emit lightning (also fig.of scorn etc.). [LIGHT[1]+-EN[6]]

light′er[1] (līt-; for *lighter*[1] see LIGHT[3]), n. & v.t. **1.** Boat, usu. flat-bottomed, for unloading & loading ships not brought to wharf & for transporting goods in harbour. **2.** v.t. Remove (goods) in ~. Hence ~AGE (4) n. [LIGHT[4]+-ER[1]]

light′ish[1,3] (līt-), aa. Somewhat LIGHT[4]. [-ISH[1](2)]

light′ning (līt-), n. Visible electric discharge between clouds or cloud & ground (*forked, chain*, or *chained* ~, ~-*flash* in form of zigzag or divided line; *sheet* ~, flash of diffused brightness; *summer, heat,* ~ *sheet* ~ without audible thunder, result of distant storm; *like* ~, with greatest conceivable speed; *with* ~ *speed*;) ~-*rod*, ~-*conductor*, metal rod or wire fixed to exposed part of building or to mast to divert ~ into earth or sea, ~-*strike*, labour strike at short notice by way of surprise. [differentiated form of *lightning* vbl n. of LIGHTEN[2]]

lights (līts), n. pl. Lungs of sheep, pigs, bullocks, etc., used as food esp. for cats & dogs. [n. use of LIGHT[4], cf. LUNG]

light′some[1] (līt-), a. Light, graceful, elegant, in appearance; light-hearted, merry; nimble. Hence ~LY[2] adv., ~NESS n. [LIGHT[1], -SOME]

4895

light′some[2] (līt-), a. (rare). Light-giving, luminous; well lighted, bright. [LIGHT[1], -SOME]

light′wood (līt-), n. Kinds of tree with light wood; kinds of tree with wood that burns with bright flame. [LIGHT[1], ~ WOOD]

lign-aloes (līnăl′ōz), n. The drug aloes-wood, an aromatic Mexican wood. [f. Ll *lignum aloes* wood of the ALOE]

lig′neous, a. (Of plants) woody (opp. *herbaceous*). [f. Ll *ligneus* (foll.) +-OUS]

lig′ni-, comb. form of L *lignum* wood. Hence ~FICA′TION n.

lig′nite, n. Brown coal showing trace of ligneous structure. [F; see prec.]

lig′num vit′ae, n. Guaiacum. [L, = wood of life]

lig′ulate, a. (bot.). With strap-shaped fillet(s). [f. L *ligula* strap (*lingua* tongue, -ULE), -ATE[2]]

like[1], a. (often governing noun like trans. part.; *more, most*, rarely or poet. ~*r*, ~*st*), prep., adv. (arch.), conj. (vulg.), & n. **1.** adj. Similar, resembling something or each other or the original, (*in* ~ *manner* or *wise*; *on this & the* ~ *subjects*; *the two letters are very* ~; *as* ~ *as two peas*; ~ *father* ~ *son*, ~ *master* ~ *man*, as the one is so will the other be; *the picture is not* ~ *you*, of the class that you exemplify; in Alg. ~ *signs*, both positive or both negative, ~ *quantities* expressed by same letters; occas. with *with*, as *beings of* ~ *passions with us*; now rarely, & chiefly in comp., with *to*, as ~*r to God than man*); resembling, such as, (*nothing* ~ *LEATHER*, as good as; *what is he, it,* ~?, what sort of person or thing is he or it?; *look* ~, have appearance of; *that*, or *the* ~, of the class that you exemplify; *something* ~ £1,000, nearly, about; *something* ~ *a day*, with stress on ~, remarkably fine or otherwise satisfactory; so abs., *this is something* ~; *nothing* ~ *good*, not nearly); characteristic of (*that's* ~ *your impudence; it was* ~ *him to think of himself last*); in promising state or right mood for doing (*looks* ~ *lasting; feel* ~ *working* or *stopping work*; also *looks* ~ with n.=promises the finding or suggests the agency of, as *looks* ~ *rabbits*); (arch.) likely, (arch. & colloq.) likely to (*had*, =*was*, ~ *to have done*, narrowly escaped doing); ~-*minded*, having same tastes, views, etc. **2.** prep. In the manner of, to the same degree as, (*cannot do it* ~ *you; do not talk* ~ *that*; ~ *a shot*, ~ *one o'clock*, ~ *anything*, MAD, etc., vigorously); (in proverbial or joc. pseudo-proverbial phr.; ~ *a fish, fit* ~ *a glove, get on* ~ *a house on fire, smoke* ~ *a chimney, swim* ~ *a fish, drink* ~ *a fish; spread* ~ *wildfire, swear* ~ *a trooper, swim*...

~ a duck; less usu. w. noun in objective relation, hate person etc. ~ poison, scatter them ~ chaff.). **3.** adv. In the same manner as (arch.); Probably (now only in very ~ enough, usu. parenthetic; (vulg.) so to speak (by way of argument ~). **4.** conj. (for arch. ~ as; vulg. & colloq.). As (cannot do it ~ you do; snow is falling ~ in January). **5.** n. Counterpart, equal, (a thing or person, (mix with your ~s); shall not see his ~ again; did you ever see the ~ of it?; ~ cures ~; the ~s of me, colloq., persons so humble as I; the ~s of you, colloq. persons so distinguished as you); (Golf) stroke that equalizes number of strokes played by each side; (ellipt. use of adj. with pl. ~) thing(s) of the same kind (will never do the ~ again; & the ~ often as pl.=etcetera, as music, painting, & the ~; or the ~, or other thing(s) of the kind). [ME lich f. OE gelíc, ON glíkr & see ALIKE, f. OTeut. galíko- (ga- with, líko- body, cf. LICH]

like², v.t. & i., & n. **1.** Be pleasing to (arch. or joc.; chiefly impers., it ~s me not, well, etc.); thrive (obs. exc. in well-liking); find agreeable, congenial, or satisfactory, feel attracted by, wish for, (I ~ you, the offer, his visits, (iron.) his impudence, her to be within reach, to see them now & then; do not ~ such subjects discussed; should much ~ to come; should ~ to know or see (iron.), think you will find it hard to tell me, am not likely to see; should ~ time to consider it; how do you ~ it?; do you ~ it much or little or dislike it?), whence lik'ABLE a., lik'ableNESS n.; if you ~ (expr. consent to request, as you will come if you ~, or limited assent, as I am shy if you ~, i.e. but not misanthropic, or emphatic selection, as I am shy if you ~, i.e. but someone else is not); suit (only in I ~ it, i.e. kind of food, but it does not ~ me). **2.** n. (Usu. pl.) liking(s), predilection(s) (esp. ~s & dislikes). [OE lícian cf. Du. lijken (prec.)]

-like, suf. (i.e. LIKE a. & adv. in comp.). **1.** Appended to nn.=forms adj. (god-~, woman~, plumbago~); adverb. of similar form are perh. arch., & in mod. use possible adverb. can usu. be explained as adj. (he, coward~, refused). **2.** Appended to adjj. it forms adjj. chiefly Sc. (human~, auld~) & Sc. advv.

like'lihood (-kl-), n. Being likely, probability, (esp. in all ~, probably). [-HOOD]

like'ly (-kl-), a. & adv. (more, most, -ier, -iest) **1.** Probable, such as might well happen, or be or prove true, or turn out to be the thing specified, (a ~ story, often iron.; it is not ~ he will come; his most ~ hatling-place is —); to be expected to (he, this, is or was not ~ to come, happen); promising, apparently suitable for purpose or to do or be, capable-looking, (called at every ~ house; six ~ young fellows; the likeliest place for smugglers

or to find him in). **2.** adv. Probably (usu. most or very ~). [f. ON líklígr (LIKE¹, -LY²)]

lik'en, v.t. Find or point out resemblance in (thing) to; (rare) make like to (its arbitrary character ~s it to a despotism). [-EN⁶]

like'ness (-kn-), n. Being like, resemblance (between, to); semblance (enemy in ~ of friend); representation, copy, portrait (take one's ~, portray him); person or thing having the exact appearance of another. [-NESS]

like'wise (-kwiz), adv. & conj. Similarly (Bibl.); also, moreover, too. [for in like wise]

lik'ing, n. What one likes, one's taste (is it to your ~?); regard, fondness, taste, fancy, for (have a ~ for him, for precise statement; no ~ for flattery). [OE lícung (LIKE², -ING⁴)]

***lil.** Dial. var. of LITTLE.

lil'ac, n. & a. Shrub with fragrant pale pinkish violet, or white, blossoms; (of) pale pinkish violet colour. [F f. Sp., f. Pers. līlak var. of nīlak (nīl blue)]

liliā'ceous (-shus), a. Of the lily kind. [f. L liliaceus (LILY, -ACEOUS]

Lilliburlē'ō, n. Song popular at end of 17th c., often referred to by writers. [part of refrain]

Lillipu'tian (-shn), a. & n. Native of Lilliput, diminutive (person or thing). [Lilliput in Gulliver's Travels, -IAN]

lilt, v.t. & i., & n. **1.** Sing melodiously or rhythmically. **2.** n. (Song with) marked rhythmical cadence or swing. [n. f. vb, ME lulte etym. dub.]

lil'y, n. (Flower of) kinds of bulbous plant bearing large showy white or reddish or purplish flowers on tall slender stem, esp. the White or Madonna L~ (orange, tiger, turk's cap, etc., ~); kinds of plant allied to these (belladonna, calla, Guernsey, Lent, water, etc., ~); ~ of the valley, spring flower with two large leaves & racemes of white bell-shaped fragrant flowers; person or thing of special whiteness or purity (lilies & roses, fair complexion); heraldic fleur-de-lis (the lilies, arms of old French monarchy, Bourbon dynasty); (attrib.) delicately white (~ maid, hand, etc.), pallid; ~-iron, harpoon with detachable head for killing swordfish; ~-liv'ered, cowardly; ~-white, as a ~. Hence lil'iED²(-lid) a. [OE líe f. L lilium f. Gk leirion]

limb¹ (-m), n., & v.t. **1.** Leg, arm, or wing (escape with life & ~, without grave injury); (orig. ~ of the devil or Satan) mischievous child, so ~ of the law, lawyer, policeman, etc.; main branch of tree, one of four branches of cross, clause of sentence, spur of mountain; hence (-)~ED² (-md), ~'LESS (-ml-), aa. **2.** v.t. Disable

of (person or animal), dismember (body). [OE *lim*, cf. ON *limr*]

limb² (-m), n. (sclent.). Edge of surface; graduated edge of quadrant etc.; edge (*eastern, lower*, etc., ~) of sun, moon, etc.; expanded part of petal, sepal, or leaf. [f. L *limbus* hem]

limb'ate, a. (biol., bot.). Having distinct or different-coloured border. [f. LL *limbātus* (prec.), -ATE²]

limb'ec, n. (arch.). = ALEMBIC.

limb'er¹, n. & v.t. **1.** Detachable front of gun-carriage (two wheels, axle, pole, & ammunition-box). **2.** v.t. Attach ~ to (gun); fasten together two parts of (gun-carriage; also abs.), (usu. ~ *up*). [earlier *lymor*, perh. f. F *limonière* shafts & frame-work (*limon* shaft)]

limb'er², n. (naut.). One of the holes cut in floor-timbers for drainage to pump-well. [perh. f. F *lumière* light, so used]

limb'er³, a. & v.t. **1.** Flexible; lithe, nimble. **2.** v.t. Make ~; also abs.; usu. ~ *up*. [?]

limb'o, n. (pl. ~s). Region on border of hell where pre-Christian just men & un-baptized infants are confined; prison, durance; condition of neglect or oblivion. [f. L phr. *in limbo* (LIMB²)]

lime¹, n., & v.t. **1.** Sticky substance made from holly bark for catching small birds (usu. *bird~*). **2.** White caustic alkaline earth (calcium oxide) got by burning ~-stone, kinds of rock chiefly carbonate of ~, & used for making mortar, as manure, etc. (also *quick~*; this after combination with water, hydrate of ~), whence ~'LESS (-ml-), lim'Y², aa. **3.** ~-burner, maker of ~; ~-cast, outer layer of ~ on building; ~'light, intense white light got by heating cylinder of ~ in oxyhydrogen flame (*the ~light*, fig., w. ref. to use in theatre, full glare of publicity); ~'pit, for steeping hides to remove hair; ~-twig, smeared with bird~. **4.** v.t. Smear (twigs), catch (bird), with bird~ (also fig.); treat, dress (land), with ~; steep (skins) in ~ & water. [OE *līm*, cf. Du. *lijm*, G *leim*, cogn. w. L *līmus* mud, *linere* smear, & w. LOAM]

lime², n. Round fruit smaller & more acid than lemon; ~-*juice*, used as drink & esp. as antiscorbutic; *~-juicer* (Naut. sl.), British sailor (also* *lim'ey*) or ship (because use of ~-juice was enforced on board). [F, f. Arab. as LEMON]

lime³, n. Ornamental tree with heart-shaped leaves & small fragrant yellowish blossom (often *~-tree*). [prob. var. of *lind* LINDEN]

lim'en, n. (psych.). Limit below which given stimulus ceases to be perceptible, minimum of nerve-excitation required to produce sensation. Hence **lim'inal** a. [L (*genit. -inis*), =thre..hold, representing G *schwelle*]

lim'erick, n. Kind of nonsense verse (now usu. applied to the five-line form based on Lear's nursery rhymes). [said to be f. chorus 'Will you come up to L~?' sung after extempore verses contributed each by member of party]

||**lime·wort** (-ôrt), **limp**, n. =BROOK¹.

lim'it¹, n. Bounding line, terminal point (*superior, inferior*, ~, earliest & latest possible date, largest & smallest possible or permissible amount), bound that may not or cannot be passed, (*without ~*, un-limited; *is the ~*, sl., is the last straw, intolerable etc.; ~ *man*, receiving longest start allowed in handicap, opp. *scratch*). Hence ~'LESS a. [f. F *limite* f. L *līmitem* nom. *-mes*]

lim'it², v.t. Confine within limits, set bounds to (usu. immaterial) bounds to, restrict to; serve as limit to; (n.p.) scanty; ||*~ed mail*, taking only *~ed* number of passengers; *~ed monarchy* etc., subject to constitutional restrictions (opp. *absolute*). So ~ATIVE a. [f. F *limiter* f. L *līmitāre* (prec.)]

lim'itary, a. Subject to restriction; of, on, serving as, limit. [f. L *līmitāri-* -ARIAN]

limitā'tion, n. Limiting; limited condition, disability or inability (*has his ~s*, is not talented in all directions); limiting rule or circumstance; legally specified period beyond which action cannot be brought, estate or law is not to continue, etc. (*statute of ~s*, any that fixes such period). [f. L *limitātio* (LIMIT², -ATION²)]

lim'iter, a. (Of district etc.) on frontier, adjacent to. [f. L *limes* LIMIT¹, Gk *trophos* -feeding, orig. of lands set apart for support of frontier troops]

||**limn** (-m), v.t. (arch.). Paint (picture); depict, portray. Hence **lim'ner¹** n. [f. obs. *lumine* Illuminate (MSS.) f. OF *luminer* (L *lumen -inis* light)]

limnol'ogy, n. Study of physical phenomena of lakes; study of pond-life. [Gk *limné* lake, -o-, -LOGY²]

lim'ousine (-ōozēn), n. Motor-car with permanently enclosed body (cf. *cabriolet*). [F, fem. adj. of *Limoges*]

limp¹, v.i., & n. **1.** Walk lamely, (of verse) halt; (of damaged ship, aircraft, etc.) proceed slowly or with difficulty. **2.** n. Lame walk. Hence ~'ing² adv. [cf. MHG *limphin*]

limp², a. Not stiff, flexible, (of book-bindings) not stiffened with mill-board; (fig.) wanting in energy. Hence ~'LY² adv.; ~'NESS n. [f. 18th c.; etym. dub.]

lim'pet, n. Gasteropod mollusc with tent-shaped shell sticking tightly to rocks; (fig.) person, esp. State employee, who clings to office; ~ *mine* (attached to

ship's bottom). [OE *lempreda* f. LL *lampreda* limpet, LAMPREY]

lim'pid, a. Pellucid, clear, not turbid, (of liquids, atmosphere, eyes, literary style). Hence ~ly adv. ~-ITY (-id⁴), ~NESS, nn. [f. L *limpidus* prob. cogn. w. *lympha* LYMPH]

limp'kin, n. Kinds of bird between cranes & rails. [LIMP¹, -KIN, from their movements]

‖[limp-wort. See LIME-WORT.

lin'age, n. Number of lines in printed matter; payment according to this. [-AGE]

linch'pin, n. Pin passed through axle-end to keep wheel on. [OE *lynis*, cf. G *lünse*, PIN]

Lin'coln green (-ngkon), n. Bright green stuff made at Lincoln.

lin'den, n. Lime-tree. [orig. adj. (obs. *lind* line, cf. G *linde* cogn. w. Gk *elatē* fir +-EN⁵)]

line¹, n. Fine long flax separated from the tow. [OE *līn* flax, cf. G *lein-* perh. cogn. w. L *linum* & Gk *linon*]

line², n. (Order of main senses) 1. Cord; 2. Long narrow mark; 3. Row; 4. Series; 5. Direction. 1. Piece of rope (esp. Naut. e.g. for sounding; so prob. *hard* ~s, bad luck, hardship; also=CLOTHES-~); wire or cable for telegraph or telephone (~*man*, charged with keeping wire etc. in repair); route traversed by this; cord bearing fish-hook(s) (~-*fishing*, opp. *net-fishing*; HOOK¹, ~, *& sinker*; *give one* ~ *enough*, let him go his own way for a time in order to secure or detect him later); cord for measuring, levelling, etc. (PLUMB-~; *by rule & ~*, with precision); (pl.) one's lot in life (*Ps*. xvi. 6, w. ref. to marking out land); rule or canon (obs. exc. in ~ *upon* ~, see Is. xxviii. 10, with slow & regular progress). 2. Long narrow mark traced on surface; use of these in draughtsmanship (*boldness, purity, of* ~; *translate life* etc. *into & colour*; ~-*drawing*, done with pen or pencil; ~-*engraving*, done with incised ~s, as opp. *etching & mezzotint*; ~-*work*, with pen or pencil not wash etc.; ~ *of beauty*, ~ with two opposite curves like elongated S); (Games) mark limiting court or ground or special parts of them; thing resembling traced mark, band of colour, seam, furrow, wrinkle (~ *of life, fortune*, etc., folds in palm of hand significant in palmistry); (Math.) straight or curved continuous extent of length without breadth, track of moving point, (with defining word, as *isothermal* ~) curve connecting all points having specified common property; *the L~, equator: straight* (~ *of* FIRE¹, *force*, etc.; *picture hung on the* ~, exhibited with its centre about level of spectator's eye; *go as straight as a* ~; *contour, outline, lineament* (*the savage* ~s *of his mouth*, (pl.) plan or draft (esp. of ship in hori-

zontal, vertical, & oblique sections) or manner of procedure (*on conservative, political, the same*, etc., ~s; *on the* ~s *laid down by someone*); (as measure) 1/12 inch; limit, boundary, (DRAW¹ *the* ~; *so dividing* ~; *on the* ~, not clearly one thing or the other). 3. Row of persons or things (*come, bring, into* ~, agree or co-operate, induce to do so; *toe the* ~, fig., accept party programme etc.): (Mil., pl.) connected series of field-works (*go¹ up the* ~), also row of tents or huts in camp; (Naut.) ~ *abreast*, number of parallel ships ranged on ~ crossing keels at right angles, ~ *ahead*, ships following in a string, ~ *of* BATTLE¹, *ship of the* ~ or ~-*of-*BATTLE¹ *ship*; (Mil.) double row (front & rear ranks) of men ranged side by side, also arrangement of companies side by side (opp. COLUMN; *drawn up in, form, wheel into*, ~; *all along the* ~, at every point, often fig. of success etc.; ~-*firing*, by body of men in ~; (Army) *the* ~, regular & numbered regiments (not Guards, Engineers, or Artillery, & occas. understood to exclude Cavalry); row of words in page or newspaper column (*read between the* ~s, detect hidden meaning in document, speech, etc.; ~-*filling*, flourish or ornament in blank space at end of ~ in MS.); (by exag.) short letter (*just a* ~ *to tell you that* ~); single verse of poetry, (pl.) piece of poetry (often *upon* subject or *to* person); ‖ (pl.) specified amount (*100* etc. ~s) of usu. Latin verse to be written out as school punishment; (pl., also *marriage* ~s) certificate of marriage; (pl.) words of actor's part. 4. Series or regular succession of steamers, omnibuses, etc., plying between certain places; connected series of persons or things following one another in time (*can show a long* ~ *of heroes*), esp. several generations of family (*male, female, direct*, etc., ~), family, lineage, stock (*comes of a good* ~). 5. Direction, course, track, (~ *of march, communication*, etc.); (Railways) single track of rails (*up, down*, ~, to, from, chief terminus esp. London); one branch of traffic under one management (*Southern* etc. ~); course followed in riding to hounds (*take, keep to*, one's *own* ~, often also fig.); course of procedure, conduct, thought, etc.; department of activity, province, branch of business, (*something in, out of*, one's ~, *that interests or concerns one, or not; in the banking, oil-&-colour*, etc., ~); (Commerc.) class of goods, order for or stock of this. [partly thr. OE *line*, cf. G *leine* cord, partly thr. F *ligne*, f. L *linea* line orig. fem. of *lineus* of linen (*linum* flax)]

line³, v.t. & i. Mark *in, off, out*, with lines on paper etc.; cover with lines (*a face* ~*d with pain*); ~ *through*, cross out; draw (men or objects) *up* in line; come *up* or spread (t. & i.) *out* in line: post troops etc.

line (road, hedge, etc; (of troops) form open or close line along (pass one), (of things) stand at intervals along (wall etc). [f. prec.]

line⁴, v.t. Apply layer of (usu. different material to inside of (garment, box, vessel, bag, etc.); fill (purse, pocket, stomach, etc.); serve as lining for. Hence lin′er¹[-ər¹] n., (esp.) removable metal lining saving wear & tear (in heavy guns & machinery). lin′ing¹(4) n. (every cloud has a silver lining, there is good in every evil). [f. LINE¹, w. ref. to use of linen for linings]

line⁵, v.t. Copulate with, cover, (bitch). [f. ligne¹]

lin′eage, n. Lineal descent, ancestry, pedigree. [f. OF lignage (L linea LINE²; -AGE]

lin′eal, a. In the direct line of descent or ancestry (opp. collateral); (rare) of, in, line(s), linear. Hence ~ly² adv. [f. F linéal f. LL lineālis (LINE², -AL)]

lin′eament f. L lineamentum (lineare in unrecorded sense draw lines f. linea LINE²)]

lin′ear, a. Of, in, line(s) (~ PERSPECTIVE); (Math., Physics) involving measurement in one dimension only (~ equation, of first degree); long, narrow, & of uniform breadth. Hence ~ly² adv. [f. L lineāris (LINE² -AR¹)]

lineā′tion, n. Drawing of, marking with, arrangement of, lines. [f. L lineatio (LINEAMENT, -ATION)]

lin′en, a. & n. 1. Made of flax (~ cloth). 2. n. Cloth woven from flax, (with pl.) particular kind of this; (collect.) shirts, sheets, cloths, etc., of ~, calico, etc. (wash one's dirty ~ at home, in public, keep, not keep, quiet about domestic quarrels etc.); ∥ ~-draper, dealer in ~, calico, etc.; ~fold, carved or moulded ornament representing a fold or scroll of ~; hence ~ETTE′(2) n. [OE linen (LINE¹, -EN⁵)]

lin′er² (for liner¹ see LINE⁴), n. Ship, usu. steamer, belonging to line of passenger ships; aircraft belonging to a regular line, used esp. for passenger transport. [-ER¹]

lines′man (-nz-), n. 1. Soldier of line regiment; (Lawn tennis, Football) official assisting umpire or referee by deciding whether or where ball touches or crosses line. [LINE's LINE²]

ling¹, n. Long slender N.-Europ. sea-fish used (usu. cured) for food. [cf. Du. & G leng prob. cogn. w. LONG¹]

ling², n. Kinds of heather. [ME f. ON lyng]

-ling¹, suf. forming nn.: com.-Teut., arising f. addition of - inges -ING³ to n. stems w. suf. -elo- -LE¹. 1. In OE, ME, mod. E, ~ is added to n. to form nn. denoting person or thing connected w.

primary n. (hire~, nurs~, sap~), & to adj. to form nn. (grey~, dar~, young~); so also, f. adv., under~. On anal. of nurs~ etc., where first component is ambiguous, share~, share~, are formed on vv. 2. In ON ~ had dim. force; instances of this appear in E in 14th & 15th cc. (cod~, gos~, duck~); in this use alone (esp. in formation of contemptuous dimm., as lord~, prince~) the suf. is a living one.

-ling², -lings, suf. forming advv.; Teut. ~ling, -land, -lang, (+-ES) used in OE added to nn. to form advv. of direction as backling, andlang, grund-tunga to ground; in other wds the suf forms advv. of condition or situation (darkling), usu. now dial. only.

ling a(m) (-ngg-), n. The phallus (esp. as symbol of Siva). [Skr. linga]

ling′er (-ngg-), v.i. & t. Put off departure, esp from reluctance to go; stay about, not depart or arrive at expected or right time; daily round place or over (upon subject; drag on a feeble existence (of invalids & moribund customs); be pro-tracted (~throw (time) away in delay). Hence ~ER¹ n., ~ingly² adv. [f. obs. leng OE lengan lengthen, linger, cf. G lingen, (LONG¹)+-ER⁵]

lingerie (see Ap.), n. (Stock of) linen articles, women's underwear. [F]

ling′ō (-ngg-), n. (pl. ~es). (Derog. for) foreign language, vocabulary of special subject or class of people. [prob. corrupt. of LINGUA (FRANCA)]

-lings. See -LING².

ling′ua fránc′a (-nggwə), n. Mixture of Italian, French, Greek, & Spanish, used in the Levant; any language serving as medium between different peoples (also fig. of common ideas etc). [It., = Frank-ish tongue]

ling′ual (-nggw-), a. & n. (Anat.) of the tongue; (Phonet.) formed by the tongue (n., ~ sound; both a. & n. now rare), whence ~IZE(3) v.t.; of speech or lan-guages (~ studies). [f. med. L linguālis (L lingua tongue, -AL)]

linguis′tic (-nggw-), a. & n. 1. Of the study of languages; of language, lingual. 2. n. pl. ~ic science. Hence ~ICALLY adv. [prec.]

ling′uist (-nggw-), n. Person skilled in foreign languages (good, bad, no, ~). [as prec., -IST]

ling′uiform (-nggw-), a. (bot., anat., zool.). Tongue-shaped. [prec. -i-, -FORM]

ling′uo- (-nggw-), comb. form of L lingua tongue (-o-), as ~dent′al made with tongue & teeth (of sounds).

∥ lin′hay, linn′(e)y, (lin′i), n. (S.-W. Eng. dial.), Farm-shed or outbuilding open in front. [perh. f. LEAN²+hay (dial.) fence]

lin'iment, n. Liquid usu. made with oil used in rubbing body for rheumatism etc., embrocation. [f. L *linimentum* (*linire* smear, -MENT)]

lin'ing, See LINE⁴.

link¹, n., & v.t. & i. **1.** One ring or loop of chain (as measure, 1/100 of surveying chain or 7.92 in.); =SLEEVE-~; loop in knitting etc.; connecting part, thing or person that unites others, filler of gap, member of series (MISSING ~). **2.** vb. Connect, join, (things, persons) *together* or (thing, person) *to*; clasp (hands); hook (arm *in* or *through* another's, arms); attach oneself *on* or *in to* system, company, etc.; ||~*ed battalions*, two, of which one at home supplies drafts for other on foreign service. Hence ~'AGE(1, 3) n. [f. ON (Icel. *hlekkr*, Sw. *länk*) cogn. w. G *gelenk* joint, & w. FLANK]

link², n. Torch of pitch & tow formerly used for lighting people along streets; ~-*bon*, ~'*man*, employed to carry ~s. [perh. f. prec. in sense *segment of the material*]

links, n. pl. Level or undulating sandy ground near sea-shore, with turf & coarse grass (Sc.); ground on which golf is played, often resembling that of prec. sense (also *a* ~ as sing.). [OE *hlinc* perh. cogn. w. LEAN²]

|| linn, n. (chiefly Sc.). Waterfall; pool below this; precipice, ravine. [perh. mixture of OE *hlynn* torrent & Gael. *linne*]

Linn(a)e'an (-nēan), a. & n. (Follower of) Linnaeus or his system of classifying plants & animals. [*Linnaeus* latinized name of C. Linné, Swedish naturalist (d. 1778), +-AN]

linn'et, n. Common brown or warm-grey song-bird. [f. OF *linette* (*lin* flax, f. its food)]

linn(e)y. See LINHAY.

lin'ocut, n. Design cut in relief on block of linoleum; print obtained from this. [LINO]

linol'eum, n. (also **lin'ō** abbr.). Floor-cloth or canvas with thick coat of oxidized linseed oil etc. Hence ~ED¹ (-ōd) a. [L *linum* flax, *oleum* oil]

lin'otype, n. Machine for producing stereotyped lines of words as substitute for type-setting, much used in printing newspapers. [=*line o' type*]

lin'säng, n. Civet cat of Borneo & Java. [Javanese]

lin'seed, n. Seed of flax; ~ *cake*, ~ (with the ~ *oil* pressed out) as cattle-food; ~ *meal*, ground ~; ~ *poultice*, of ~ or ~ meal. [LINE¹]

lin'sey-wool'sey (-z-, -z-), n. Dress material of coarse inferior wool woven on cotton warp (orig. of wool & flax). (from 1483; *linsey*, perh. a coarse linen (LINE¹ perh.+obs. *say* silk); *woolsey*=wool w. jingling termination]

lin'stock, n. (hist.). Match-holder used in old gunnery. [f. Du. *lontstok*(*lont* match)

lint, n. Soft material for dressing wounds made by scraping linen cloth on one side. [cogn. w. LINE¹; perh. f. F *linette* linseed (*lin* linen)]

lin'tel, n. Horizontal timber or stone over door or window. Hence ~LED² (-ld) a. [OF=threshold, f. pop. L *limitale* or *limitellum* see LIMIT¹, -LE(2)]

lin'y, a. Marked with lines; wrinkled; (Art) using line too much. Hence **lin'i-NESS.** [-Y²]

li'on, n. **1.** Large powerful tawny African & S.-Asiatic carnivorous quadruped with tufted tail & (in the male) flowing shaggy mane (~ *in the way* or *path*, obstacle, esp. imaginary; ~'*s mouth*, perilous position; ~ *& uni-corn*, supporters of royal arms; ~'*s skin*, false assumption of courage; *twist* ~'*s tail*, of foreign, esp. U.-S., journalists or orators defying or insulting Great Britain. **2.** Courageous person, so ~-**hearted²** a. **3.** pl. || Sights worth seeing in town etc. (from custom of showing country visitors the ~s formerly kept in Tower of London; *see, show, the ~s*). **4.** || Person of literary or other celebrity sought after to be shown off at social gatherings (~-*hunter*, host or hostess depending much on ~s), whence ~HOOD, ~SHIP, nn. **5.** National emblem of Great Britain (*the British L~*, the nation personified). **6.** (L~) constellation & zodiacal sign LEO. Hence ~LIKE, a., ~ESS¹, ~ET¹, nn. [f. AF *leun* f. L *leonem* nom. *leo* f. Gk *leōn leontos*]

li'onize, v.t. & i. See or show the sights (see prec.) of (place); show these to (visitor); see the sights; treat (person) as celebrity, make a lion (see prec.) of, whence ~ISM(1) n. [-IZE]

lip, n., & v.t. & v.t. (-pp-). **1.** One of the fleshy edges of the opening of the mouth (*upper, lower* or *under*, ~; *bite* one's ~, in vexation or to repress emotion, stifle laugh, etc.; *stiff upper* ~, fortitude or obstinacy; *curl* one's ~, in scorn; *hang* one's ~, in humiliation; *lick, smack,* one's ~*s*, in enjoyment or anticipation of food or fig.; *hang on* one's ~*s*, listen to his every word in reverence; *word* etc. *escapes* one's ~*s*, is uttered thoughtlessly). **2.** Saucy talk, impudence, (sl., esp. *none of your* ~!). **3.** Edge of cup, vessel, cavity, wound, etc. **4.** ~, *from the* ~*s only*, professed, not heartfelt or sincere, (~-*homage*, -*religion*, -*Christian*, -*service*, -*worship*); ~-*deep*, superficial, insincere; ~-*language*, -*reading*, -*speaking*, use & interpretation of silent motions of ~s by & with the deaf or dumb; ~-*salve*, ointment for sore ~s, (fig.) flattery; ~-*stick*, stick of cosmetic for rouging ~s; whence ~PED³ (-pt), ~'LESS, aa. **5.** v.t. Touch with ~s, apply ~s to; (of water) just touch, lap; (Golf) hit ball just to edge of (hole), (of ball) reach edge of (hole) but fail to drop in;

murmur, utter softly. [OE *lippa*, cf. Du.
lippe, G *lippe*, cogn. w. L *labium, labrum*]

lipog'raphy, n. = HAPLOGRAPHY. [f. Gk
lip- st. of *leipo* omit, -GRAPHY]

lipp'er, n. (naut.). Rippling or ruffled
motion, surface roughness, of sea. [prob.
cogn. w. LAP[3] + -ER[1]]

liquate', v.t. Separate or purify (metals)
by liquefying. Hence **liqua'tion** n. [f. L
liquare (*liquat-*) melt, cogn. w. LIQUOR, -ATE[3]]

liq'uefy, v.t. & i. Bring (solid or gas) or
come into liquid condition. Hence or
cogn. ~**FA'CIENT**(-ǎshent) a. & n., ~**FAC-
TION** n., ~**FA'CTIVE**, ~**FIABLE** aa., ~**FIER'**(I,
2) n. [f. F *liquéfier* f. L *liquefacere* (*liquēre*
be LIQUID, -FY)]

liquesʹcent, a. Becoming, apt to become,
liquid. [f. L *liquescere* (prec., -ESCENT)]

liqueur' (-kūr), n. Strong alcoholic liquor
sweetened & flavoured with aromatic
substances & usu. drunk in small quantities; mixture of sugar & alcohol or
wines used to flavour champagne, whence
~ v.t. ~ *brandy*, of special quality for
drinking as ~; ~*-glass*, very small for ~s.
[F., = LIQUOR]

liq'uid, a. & n. **1.** (Substance that is) in-
compressible but offering no resistance
to change of shape, neither solid nor
gaseous, resembling water or oil in
normal state, in fluid but not gaseous
condition (~ *air*, reduced to ~ state by
intense cold; ~ *fire*, projected from flame-
thrower); watery. **2.** Having the transparence, translucence, or brightness, of
water or wine (~ *lustre, eyes, sky, air,
blue*). **3.** (Of sounds) flowing clear, fluent,
pure, not grating or discordant, not
guttural, vowel-like, (*blackbird's ~ notes;
in his ~ Italian*; one of the letters *l, r,*
& occas. *m, n*). **4.** Not fixed, unstable,
(*has very ~ convictions or principles*).
5. (Of assets, securities, etc.) easily convertible into cash. Hence or cogn. ~**IFY**
(-idʒ-), n., ~**IZE**(3) v.t., ~**Iʒ** adv.,
~**LY**, ~**NESS**, nn. [f. OF *liquide* f. L *liquidus*
(*liquēre* be liquid f. LIQUATE, LIQUOR]

liq'uidate, v.t. & i. Pay, clear off, (debt);
put an end to, suppress, get rid of, (often
by violent means); wind up, ascertain
liabilities & apportion assets of, (company, firm), whence ~**A'TION** n.; (intr., of
company) have this done. Hence ~**A'TION**
n. (*go into ~ation*, of company, have its
affairs wound up, become bankrupt). [f.
LL *liquidare* make LIQUID, -ATE[3]]

liq'uor (-ker), n. Liquid part
of secretion or product (of operation);
liquid used as wash etc.; water used in
brewing; liquid (usu. fermented or distilled) for drinking (*malt ~, ale, beer,
porter*, etc.; *spirituous ~, spirits; disguised with ~; in ~, the worse for ~*, more
or less drunk; *a ~* or *~-up*, sl., taking
of ~ as refreshment); water in which food
has been boiled; (Pharmacy, pr. lik'wor)

solution of specified drug in water (~ *am-
moniae* etc.). **2.** vb. Dress (leather, shoes)
with grease or oil; steep (malt etc.) in
water; (sl.) ~ *up* or ~, have a drink of
alcoholic ~. [earlier & OF *licur* (now *liqueur*) f. L *liquor* (*liquēre* see LIQUID, -OR[2])
to which spelling has been assimilated]

liq'uorice (-ko-), n. (Black
substance used in medicine & as sweetmeat made from) root of *Glycyrrhiza
glabra*; the plant. [f. AF *lycorys* s. LL
liquiritia f. Gk *glukurrhiza* (*glukus* sweet,
rhiza root)]

liq'uorish (-ko-), a. Fond of, indicating
fondness for, liquor. Hence ~**LY**[2] adv.
[NESS n.: misuse of LICKERISH]

lira (lēr'ȧ), n. (pl. *lire* pr. -ā, ~s; abbr. L.).
Italian monetary unit. [It., f. L LIBRA]

lisle thread (līl thrĕd), n. Fine hard-
twisted thread made orig. at Lisle (now
Lille) in France.

lisp, v.i. & t., & n. **1.** Substitute one of the
sounds of *th* for sibilants in speaking; (of
child) speak with imperfect pronunciation; say with a ~ (often *out*); hence
~**ingLY**[2] adv. **2.** n. ~ing pronunciation,
rippling of waters, rustling of leaves. [f.
OE *wlisp* a. lisping, cf. Du. *lispen*, G
lispeln, to lisp]

list[1], n. **1.** Selvage or edge of
cloth, usu. of different material, whence
~**ING**[1](3) n.; such edges torn off & used
as a material (~ *slippers*; *line edges of
door with ~*, to keep out draughts; vb.
fasten ~ round edges of, as *have ~ed my
ground*). **2.** pl. Palisades enclosing tilting-
ground; (fig.) scene of contest (*enter the
~s against*, challenge or accept challenge
to controversy). **3.** Roll or catalogue of names, of persons or things belonging to a class, of articles with prices,
of things to be done, etc. (*active ~*, of
officers in army or navy or air force
liable to be called on for service; *free ~*,
of persons to be admitted free to theatre
etc., also of duty-free articles; ARMY,
CIVIL, SICK, ~); (vb) enter in a ~,
rare or vulg.; go as soldier, enlist. [senses
1 & 2 f. OF *liste*, cf. Du. *lijst*, G *leiste*;
sense 3 f. F *liste* f. Teut. as in 1]

list[3], v.t. (arch.; 3 sing. pres. ~ or ~*eth*,
past ~ or ~*ed*). Be pleasing to (*shall do
what him ~eth*; *did as him ~*); desire,
choose, (to do or abs.; *ye who ~ to hear;
wind bloweth where it ~eth*). [OE *lystan*,
cf. Du. *lusten*, G *lüsten*, cogn. w. LUST]

list[4], v.i. & t. (arch.). Listen. Listen to.
[OE *hlystan* (*hlyst* sense of hearing), cf.
G *lüstern & lauschen* f. Aryan *klus-* (*klu-*
see LOUD)]

lis'ten (-sn), v.i. & t. Make effort to hear something, hear person speaking with attention; give ear to or now usu. *to* (person or sound or story); yield *to* temptation or request; ~ *in*, tap telephonic communication, use wireless receiving set; ~*ing-post*, point near enemy's lines for detecting his movements by sound. Hence ~ER¹ (-sn-) n. (*good* ~*er*, one who habitually ~s with interest or sympathy), (also) person receiving broadcast wireless programmes. [ONorthumb. *lysna*, cf. OE *hlosnian* & *hlyst*, see prec.]

lis'terine, n. An antiseptic solution. [*Lord Lister* (d. 1912), -INE⁴; **P**]

lis'terize, v.t. Treat (wound) on the antiseptic methods introduced by Lord Lister. So **lis'ter′IAN** a. [-IZE]

list'less, a. Languid, indifferent, uninterested, disinclined for exertion. Hence ~LY² adv., ~NESS n. [f. obs. *list* inclination (LIST²) + -LESS]

lit. See LIGHT³,⁵.; ~ *up* (sl.), drunk.

lit′any, n. Series of petitions for use in church services or processions recited by clergy & responded to by usu. in repeated formula(s) by people (*the L*~, that contained in the Book of Common Prayer); ~*desk, -stool*, at which reciter of ~ kneels. [f. med.L f. Gk *litaneia* prayer (*litaneuō* pray f. *litanos* suppliant f. *litē* prayer)]

li′tchi (lēchē′), n. Fruit(-tree) orig. from China, grown in Bengal. [f. Chin. *li-chi*]

lit′eracy, n. Ability to read & write. [LITERATE, -CY]

li′terae hūmāniōr′es (-z), n. (abbr. *Lit. Hum.*). Polite letters, esp. as name of classical school or examination for B.A. degree at Oxford. [L]

lit′eral, a. & n. **1.** Of, in, expressed by, letter(s) of alphabet (~ *error*, also ~ as n., misprint). **2.** Following the letter, text, or exact or original words (~ *translation, transcript*, etc.), whence ~ISM(4) n. **3.** Taking words in their usual or primary sense & applying the ordinary rules of grammar, without mysticism or allegory or metaphor, (~ *interpretation*; *I hear nothing in the* ~ *sense of the word*, with the ears as opp. other means of getting news), whence ~ISM(3), ~IST(2), nn.; (of persons) prosaic, matter-of-fact. **4.** So called without exaggeration (~ *decimation*; often incorrectly used, as *a* ~ *flood of pamphlets*). Hence ~LY²(-āl·), ~NESS, nn., ~LY² adv. [OF, f. L *litteralis* (LETTER, -AL)]

lit′eralize, v.t. Take (metaphor etc.) in literal sense. [-IZE]

lit′erā′tim dŏc′tŏr, n. Doctor of literature (as University degree). [L]

lit′erary, a. Of, constituting, occupied with, literature, polite learning, or books & written composition esp. of the kind valued for form (~*y history of a thing*, of its treatment in literature; ~*y property*, ex-

clusive right of publication, books etc. subject *to* this; ~*y man*, man of LETTERS; (of word or idiom) uncolloquial, affected by writers. Hence ~LY² adv., ~NESS n. [f. L *litterarius* (LETTER, -ARY¹)]

lit′erate, a. & n. (Person) having some acquaintance with literature or (now usu.) able to read & write; || man admitted to Anglican orders without university degree. [f. L *litteratus* (LETTER, -ATE²)]

literāt′i, n. pl. Men of letters, the learned class. [L, as prec.]

literā′tim, adv. Letter for letter, texturally, literally. [L]

lit′erātor, n. Literary man. [L (LITERATE, -OR²) elementary teacher, grammarian, sciolist]

lit′erature, n. Literary culture (arch.); literary production (*engaged in* ~), the literary profession (~ *was represented by* ~); realm of letters, writings of country or period; writings whose value lies in beauty of form or emotional effect (LIGHT⁴ ~); *the* books treating of a subject; (colloq.) printed matter. [f. L *litteratura* (LITERATE, -URE)]

-lith, suf. repr. Gk *lithos* stone (*aerolith, monolith*); cf. -LITE.

lith′ărge (-j), n. Lead monoxide. [f. OF *litarge* f. Gk *litharguros* (*lithos* stone, *arguros* silver) so called as by-product in separation of silver from lead]

lithe (-dh), a. Flexible, supple. Hence ~NESS (-dhn-) n., ~SOME (-dhs-) a. [OE *lithe* soft, cf. G *lind*, cogn. w. L *lentus*]

lith′ia, n. Oxide of lithium; ~-*water*, used for gout. [changed f. earlier *lithion* f. Gk neut. of *litheios* (*lithos* stone) after *soda* etc.]

lith′ic¹, a. Of the stone or calculus; of stone. [f. Gk *lithikos* (prec., -IC)]

lith′ic² a. (chem.). Of lithium. [foll., IC]

lith′ium, n. Metallic element resembling sodium. [LITHIA, -UM]

lith(**o**)-, comb. form of Gk *lithos* stone, esp. in wds having ref. either to the treatment of stone in the bladder or kidneys, or to the use of stone in printing.

lith′ograph (-ahf), n., & v.t. **1.** Lithographic print. **2.** v.t. Print by lithography; write or engrave on stone. [prec., -GRAPH]

lithŏg′raphy, n. Drawing or writing on kind of yellow slaty limestone (*lithographic stone*) so that impressions in ink can be taken. So **lithŏg′RAPHER** n., **lithō-**GRAPH′IC a. [LITHO-, -GRAPHY]

lithŏl′ogy, n. Science of the nature & composition of stones & rocks, whence **lithŏl′ŏ**GICAL a.; department of medical science dealing with calculus. [LITHO-, -LOGY]

lithŏntrip′tic, a. & n. (Medicine) that breaks up stone in bladder. [f. F *lithontriptique* f. Gk *lithon thruptika* (drugs) comminutive of stones]

lith'ophyte, n. (Zool.) polyp whose substance is calcareous, as some corals; (Bot.) plant that grows on stone. [litho-, Gk *phuton* plant (*phuō* grow)]

lithot'omy, n. Operation of cutting for stone in bladder. Hence or cogn. litho-tōm'ic(al) aa., ~ist(1) n., ~ize(1) v.t. [f. Ll.f. Gk *lithotomia* (litho-, -tomy)]

lithot'rity, n. Operation of crushing stone in bladder into small particles that can be passed through urethra. Hence ~ist(1) n., ~ize(1) v.t. [f. lithotriptic, earlier lithontriptic, by change of *lithon* to litho- & confusion of -tript- (already transferred f. Gk *thruptō* wear) with Lithuan-; -ite]

Lithuā'nian, a. & n. (Language or native) of Lithuania. [-AN]

lit'igate, v.i.& t. Go to law, be party to lawsuit; contest (point) at law, whence ~ABLE a. Hence ~ANT(2) n. & a., ~A'TION n. [f. Ll *litigare* (*lis litis* lawsuit), -ATE³]

litig'ious (-jus), a. Given to litigation, fond of going to law; disputable at law, offering matter for lawsuit; of lawsuits. Hence ~IY² adv., ~NESS n. [f. F *litigieux* f. L *litigiosus* (*litigium* litigation, cf. prec.)]

lit'mus, n. Blue colouring-matter got from lichens that is turned red by acid & restored to blue by alkali; ~-paper, unsized & stained with ~ as test for acids. [f. MDu. *leecmos* (luc¹, *moes* pulp)]

litō'tes (-z), n. Understatement often ironical (as ' scoundrel ' is rather a rude word), esp. the expressing of an affirmative by the negative of its contrary, as *no small* for *great*. [Gk (-ēs) f. *litos* plain, meagre]

litre (lē'ter), n. Unit of capacity in metric system, = cube of 1/10 metre, about 1¾ pints. [F, from 1793, prob. f. Ll.f. Gk *litra* pound]

lit'ter, n., & v.t. & i. 1. Vehicle containing couch shut in by curtains & carried on men's shoulders or by beasts; framework with couch for transporting sick & wounded; straw, rushes, etc., as bedding esp. for animals; straw & dung of farm-yard; odds & ends, leavings, state of untidiness, disorderly accumulation of papers etc., whence ~y² a.; the young brought forth at a birth. 2. vb. Provide (horse etc.) with ~ as bed (usn. *down*); spread ~ or straw on (floor, stable; usn. *down*); make (place) untidy (of objects lying about, or of person *with* these or simply); scatter & leave lying; bring forth (whelps etc., or abs.). [f. OF *litiere* f. med. L *lectaria* (L *lectus* bed, -ARY¹)]

lit'térateur (see Ap.), n. Literary man. [F]

lit'tle, a. (less, lesser, least; also smaller, smallest), n., & adv. (less, least). 1. Small (often with emotional implications not given by *small*, cf. *great*), not great or big (the idiomatic antitheses are *great* & ~, *big* & ~, *great & small*, *large & small*, *not large* & ~, *nor big* & *small*); (as distinctive epithet) of smaller or smallest size etc. (the L~ Ack, the L~ Malvern, the L~ Bear); the ~ finger or toe). 2. Young (the ~ Joneses, Jones's children; ~ men or woman, boy or girl, esp. as voc.; his, her, its, our, ~ ones, children or cubs etc.). 3. As of a child, evoking tenderness, patronage, amusement, etc., (her poor efforts to please; we know his ~ ways; so that is your ~ game, what you are hoping to do undetected). 4. Short in stature, distance, or time (a ~ man; the ~ people, fairies; will go a ~ way with you; wait a ~ while). 5. Trivial, unimportant, (every little difficulty); mean, paltry, contemptible, (with the ~ cunning of ~ minds). 6. Not much (gained ~ advantage from it; often but or very ~). 7. A ~, some though not much, even a small amount of, (prob. f. the n. use with ellipse of of; give me a ~ butter; a ~ care would have prevented it); (absl.) the ~, persons of ~ power or importance, what is ~; in ~, on a small scale; ~-ease (hist.), prison-cell too small to stand or lie full-length in; ~-Englander, -ism, (holder of) principle that Great Britain should contract her responsibilities for colonies & dependencies (opp. IM-PERIALIST, -ISM); ||~-go (colloq.), first examination for B.A. degree at Cambridge; ||~ Mary (colloq.), the stomach; L~ Masters, group of 16th-c. German engravers, followers of Dürer, named from size of their prints; hence ~NESS (-ln-) n. 8. n. Not much, only a small amount, a mere trifle, [~ or nothing, hardly anything; did not a ~ for the cause, much; got but, every, rather, ~ out of it; a ~ makes us laugh; gives me ~ of his company; did what ~ he could; the ~ of his work that remains; in certain but no great amount (knows a ~ of everything; a ~, rather, somewhat not a ~, extremely); (for a) short time or distance (after, for, a ~; leave me here a ~; by ~, by degrees). 9. adv. To a small extent only (I like him ~; ~-known authors; is ~ more than a cento); not at all (the ~ knows, dreams, etc.). [OE *lytel*, *lytel*, prob. cogn. w. *litan* bow down]

lit'oral, a. & n. 1. Of, on the shore. 2. n. Region lying along the shore. [f. L *littoralis* (*litus -oris* shore, -AL)]

lit'urgy (-ter-), n. Communion office of Eastern Church; form of public worship, set of formularies for this; the Book of Common Prayer; (Gk Ant.) public office or duty performed gratuitously by rich Athenian. Hence litur'gical a., litur'gi-cally¹ adv. [f. med. L f. Gk *leiturgia* (*leitourgos* public servant prob. f. *leōs* people, *-ergos* -working)]

liv'able, a. (Of house, room, climate, etc.) fit to live in; (of life) worth living; companionable, easy to live with. Hence ~NESS n. [LIVE², -ABLE²; cf. RELIABLE]

live¹, a. (attrib.). That is alive, living; (joc.) actual, not pretended or pictured or toy (*a real ~ burglar, steam-engine, mountain*); full of power, energy, or importance, not obsolete or exhausted, (*make the question a ~ issue*; glowing (*~ embers*) (of shell, match, wire) unexploded, unkindled, charged with electricity; (of rock) not detached, seeming to form part of the earth's frame; (of wheels etc. in machinery) moving or imparting motion; *~ bait*, living fish or worm as fishing-bait; *~ load*, stress resulting from transverse motion of weights (as of locomotive crossing bridge); *~ oak*, American evergreen tree; *~ stock*, animals kept or dealt in for use or profit; *~ wire* (fig.), highly energetic forceful person. [= ALIVE used attrib.]

live², v.i. & t. 1. Be alive, have animal or vegetable life. 2. Subsist (*up*)*on* (*~ on fruit*), depend (*up*)*on* for subsistence (*~s upon his wife, wife's earnings*, etc.; *living WAGE¹*); (fig.) sustain one's position or repute (*up*)*on* (*~s on his name*), get livelihood *by* one's wits etc. or *by doing*, (*~ & let ~*, wink at others' incompetence or deficiencies to secure the same treatment for oneself; *~ from HAND¹ to mouth*). 3. Conduct oneself honestly, viciously, like *a saint*, etc. (*~ up to one's principles, faith*, etc., put them in practice). 4. Arrange one's habits, expenditure, feeding, etc. (*~ FAST⁴, in CLOVER*; *~ well*, on dainty food; *~ on air*, (appear to) take no food; *~ in a small way, cheaply & quietly*; *~ close, stingily*; *~ a double life*, (esp.) sustain two different characters, act two different parts, in life; *~ to oneself*, in isolation). 5. (With cogn. obj.) spend, pass, experience, (*~ a virtuous life*; *he ~d what he narrated*). 6. Wear down (scandal, prejudice, effect of past guilt) by blameless course of life. 7. Express in one's life (*~ a lie*). 8. Enjoy life intensely. 9. Continue alive, have one's life prolonged, (*patient cannot ~*; *~d to see his children's children*; *& learn!*, way of greeting new fact; *~ out the night*, remain alive through it) (of things) survive (*his memory ~s*), (of ship) escape destruction (*nothing could ~ afloat*); dwell (|| *~ in, out*, of shop-assistants residing on premises or not), spend daytime *in* room (*room does not seem to be ~d in*). [com.-Teut.; OE *libban* cf. Du. *leven*, G *leben*, cogn. w. LIFE]

live'lihŏŏd (-vl-), n. Means of living, sustenance. [OE *līflād* (LIFE, *lād* course, see LOAD¹) gradually assimilated to obs. *livelihood* liveliness]

live'lŏng (-vl-), a. (poet., rhet.). Whole length of (*the ~ day, night, summer*, with implication of weariness or delight). [earlier *lefe lŏng* (LIEF)]

live'ly (-vl-), a. Lifelike, realistic, (*a ~y description*; *give a ~y idea of*); full of life,

vigorous, energetic, brisk, vivid, interesting; (joc.) exciting, dangerous, difficult, (*police had a ~y time*; *press is making it or things ~y for ~*); (of colour) bright; gay, vivacious; (of boat etc.) rising lightly to waves. Hence *~LI·Y* adv., *~NESS* n. (*a certain ~ness*, sl., some heavy gunfire). [OE *līflīc* (LIFE, -LY¹)]

liv'en, v.t. & i. Brighten, cheer, (usu. *up*). [LIFE, -EN⁶]

liv'er¹, n. Large glandular organ in vertebrates secreting bile & purifying venous blood; (also *~complaint*) diseased state of *~*, whence *~ISH¹* a.; (also *~colour*) dark reddish brown; flesh of some animals' *~* used as food; (arch.) *~* as seat of emotion (*hot ~*, passionate or amorous temperament; *white* or *lily ~*, cowardice, whence *~ED²* a.); *~-line*, one of lines of palm significant in palmistry; *~ wing*, right wing of cooked fowl, under which *~* is tucked, (joc.) right arm; *~wort*, kinds of plant with *~*-shaped parts or used in *~* disease. Hence *~LESS* a. [OE *lifer* cf. Du. *lever*, G *leber*]

liv'er², n. One who lives in specified way (*clean, loose, ~*; *good ~*, virtuous person, also one given to *good LIVING*). [-ER¹]

Liverpud'lian, a. & n. (Inhabitant) of Liverpool. [joc. formation]

liv'ery, n. 1. Provision of food or clothing served out to retainers etc. (hist.); allowance of provender for horses (*at ~*, of horse, kept for owner & fed & groomed for fixed charge). 2. Distinctive clothes worn by member of city company or person's servant (*in, out of ~*, of servant, so attired or in plain clothes); also fig., *birds in their winter ~*, the *~ of grief*, *of other men's opinions*, etc.), whence **liv'erIED²** (-rīd) a. 3. Membership of city company (*take up one's ~*, become *~-man*). 4. (Law) legal delivery of property (|| *sue one's ~*, bring suit as heir in court of wards to get possession), writ allowing this. 5. || *~ company*, one of London City companies that had formerly distinctive costume; || *~ fine*, payment for becoming member of *~ company*; *~man*, member of *~ company*, keeper of or attendant in *~ stable*; *~ servant*, wearing *~*; *~ stable*, where horses are kept at *~* or let out for hire. [f. F *livrée* (*livrer* see DELIVER, *-Y⁴*)]

liv'ery², a. Of the consistence or colour of liver; (of soil) tenacious; having a disordered liver, feeling out of sorts, irritable. [-Y²]

liv'id, a. Of bluish leaden colour; discoloured as by bruise; || (colloq.) furiously angry. Hence or cogn. **liv'idITY n.**, *~LY¹* adv. [f. L *lividus*]

liv'ing, n. In vbl senses; also or esp.: livelihood, maintenance, (*make one's ~*; || (Eccl.) benefice; *good ~*, luxurious feeding; *plain ~ & high thinking*, frugal & philosophic life; *~-room* (for general day use); *~-space*, transl. of LEBENSRAUM; *~*

usage, on which it is possible for worker to live. [-ING¹]

liv'ing², a. In vbl senses: esp.: contemporary, now existent, (*no man ~ could do better; the greatest ~ master of irony; the first of ~ artists*; those now alive; *in the land of the ~*, alive); whence ~LY² adv.; ~ *water*, perennially flowing; ~ *rock, cod.*; ~ *death*, state of persons still ~; *within* ~ *memory*, that of persons still ~. [-ING²]

livre (lēˈvr), n. Old French money of account (20 sous). [F, f. L LIBRA]

lixiv'iāte, v.t. Separate (substance) into soluble & insoluble constituents by percolation of water. Hence ~ATION n. [f. L *lixivius* made into lye (*lix*), -ATE³]

lizard, n. Kinds of reptile having usn. long body & tail, four legs, & scaly or granulated hide; fancy variety of canary. [f. OF *lesard* f. L *lacertus* w. assim. to -ARD]

'll, contr. of WILL in *I'll, he'll, that'll*, etc.

lla'ma (lah-, lyah-), n. S.-Amer. ruminant allied to camel but smaller, humpless, & woolly-haired, used as beast of burden; (material made of) its wool. [Sp., prob. f. Peruvian]

lla'nō (lah-, lyah-), n. S.-Amer. treeless plain or steppe. Hence **llanero** (lyah-nārˈō) n., inhabitant of the ~s. [Sp., f. L *planus -wm* PLAIN¹]

Lloyd's (loidz), n. Incorporated society of marine underwriters in London; ~ *list*, newspaper devoted to maritime intelligence; ~ *register*, annual alphabetic list of ships assigned to various classes. [orig. 17th-c. coffee-house established by *Edvard Lloyd*]

lō, int. (arch.) Look!, see!, behold! (usn. *lo and behold!*, as joc. introduction of surprising fact). [mixture of OE *lā* int. & ME *lo*=*loke*, LOOK¹]

loach, n. Small edible freshwater fish. [f. F *loche*]

load¹, n. What is (to be) carried, burden, amount usn. carried (*cart ~* etc.), recognized unit in measure or weight of certain substances; material object or force acting as weight or clog, resistance of machinery worked to motive power, pressure of superstructure on arch etc.; (Electr.) amount of current supplied by a dynamo or generating station at any given time (see PEAK¹); burden of responsibility, care, grief, etc. (*take a ~ off one's mind*, relieve him of anxiety); (pl., colloq.) plenty, superabundance, heaps, lots, *of*; ~*displacement*, -*draught*, of ship when laden; ~'*stone*, lodestone, magnetic oxide of iron, piece of it used as magnet, thing that attracts, (=way stone, see etym.); ~(*water*)*line*, ship's flotation line when laden, Plimsoll's mark. [OE *hlād* way, journey, conveyance, cf. G *leite*, cogn. w. LEAD²]

load², v.t. & i. Put load on or aboard (person, vehicle, ship, etc.), (of ship, vehicle, person responsible for these, or person) take load aboard etc. (often *up*); place (load, cargo) aboard ship, on vehicle, etc.; add weight to, be burden upon, oppress *with* (*stomach ~ed with food*), weight with lead (*a ~ed cane; ~ed dice*, so weighted as to fall with a certain face up), strain bearing-capacity of (*table ~ed with food*); adulterate with something to increase weight or (of wines) strength; supply or assail overwhelmingly *with* (*~ed her with gifts, praise, abuse; air ~ed with food*); charge (fire-arms; *am ~ed*, have my gun etc. charged); (Stock-Exch.) buy heavily of stock (*~ed up with*, having large amounts of in hand as security); (Life-insurance) add extra charge or [~ING¹ n. to (premium) for special reasons. [f. prec.]

load'er, n. In vbl senses: esp.: attendant loading sportsman's guns; loading-machine; ~, gun loaded in specified way (*breech, muzzle, single, ~*), so -load ING²

loaf¹, n. (pl. *loaves* pr. lōvz). Piece of bread baked alone or as separate or separable part of batch, usn. of some standard weight as 1lb., 2lb., or 4lb. (COTTAGE, *household, tinned*, ~, various shapes; QUARTERN ~; *brown* ~, of BROWN bread; *white* ~, of FESTS; *loaves & fishes*, personal profit as inducement to religious profession or public service, see *John* vi. 26; *half a ~ is better than no bread*, motto of compromise, opp. *all or nothing*); (also *sugar~*) conical moulded mass of sugar (~ *sugar*; this as whole or cut into lumps); || solid roundish head of cabbage or lettuce, whence **loaved²** (-vd) a. [com-Teut.; OE *hlāf*, cf. G *laib*, etym. dub.] || **loaf²**, **loave**, v.i. (Of cabbage etc.) form a loaf or head. [f. prec.]

loaf³, v.i. & t., & n. 1. Spend time idly; saunter; ~ (time) *away*, spend in ~ing; hence ~'ER¹ n. 2. n. ~ing (*going to have a, on the, ~*). [etym. dub.; ~ may be back-form. f. *loafer*]

loam, n. Paste of clay & water, composition of moistened clay & sand with chopped straw etc. used in making bricks, plastering, etc.; fertile soil chiefly of clay & sand with admixture of decayed vegetable matter, whence ~Y² a. [OE *lām*, cf. Du. *leem*, G *lehm*, cogn. w. LIME¹]

loan, n., & v.t. 1. Thing, esp. sum of money, lent to be returned with or without interest; word, custom, etc., adopted by one people from another (so ~*god, -myth, -word*); lending or being lent (*on ~; may I have the ~ of ~?*, may I borrow it?); money contribution from individuals or public bodies to State expenses acknowledged as debt; arrangement or contract by which a government receives advances of money usn. for stipulated

interest. **2.** ~ *collection*, of pictures etc. lent by owners for exhibition; ~*holder*, person holding debentures or other acknowledgements of ~, mortgagee; ~*office*, for lending money to private borrowers, also for receiving subscriptions to government ~; ~*society*, of periodical subscribers to fund from which members may have ~s. **3.** v.t. (now chiefly U.S.). Grant ~ of, whence ~ABLE a., ~EE¹, ~ER¹, nn. [OE *lǣn*, cf. Du. *leen*, G *lehn*, cogn. w. Gk *leipō* leave, & OE *lēon* lend]

loath, lōth, a. (pred. only). Disinclined, reluctant, unwilling, (usu. *to do* or abs.; also *for person to do*, or *that*; *nothing ~*, quite willing or willingly); ~*-to-depart*, tune played as farewell. [OE *lāth*, cf. Du. *leed*, also G *leid* sorrow, f. OTeut. *laitho-* whence F *laid* ugly]

loathe (-dh), v.t. Regard with disgust, abominate, detest. Hence ~ING¹(1) n., ~ingly¹ adv., (-dh-). [OE *lāthian* (prec.)]

loath'ly¹ (-dh-), a. (Arch. & literary for) loathsome. Hence ~INESS n. [OE *lāthlic* (LOATH, -LY¹)]

loath'some (-th-, -dh-), a. Exciting nausea or disgust, offensive to the senses, sickening, repulsive, odious. Hence ~LY² adv., ~NESS n. [LOATH, -SOME]

loaves. See LOAF¹.

lob, v.i. & t. (-bb-), & n. **1.** Walk, run, or move, heavily or clumsily or slowly (often *along*); toss, bowl, or send, (ball) with slow or high-pitched motion. **2.** n. Ball bowled underhand at cricket or sent high in air at lawn tennis. [f. obs. *lob* n. fowl's wattle etc.]

Hence ~ATION n. (nat. hist.). Having lobe(s).

lob'by, n., & v.t. & i. **1.** Porch, anteroom, entrance-hall, corridor; (in House of Commons etc.) large hall open to public used esp. for interviews between members & outsiders, (also *division ~*) one of two corridors to which members retire to vote. **2.** vb (chiefly U.S.). Influence (members of legislature), get (bill etc.) through, by interviews etc.; frequent ~ of legislature, solicit members' votes, whence ~IST(1) n. [f. med. L *lobia* LODGE¹]

lobe, n. Roundish & flattish projecting or pendulous part, often one of two or more such parts divided by fissure (so ~ *of liver* or *lungs*; ~*s of brain*; ~ *of ear*, lower soft pendulous external part). Hence lōb'AR¹ a. (esp. of the lungs, as *lobar pneumonia*), lōbED² (-bd), ~LESS (-bl-), aa. [f. LL f. Gk *lobos* lobe, pod, cogn. w. LEGUME]

lobē'lia, n. Kinds of herbaceous plant with blue, scarlet, or purple flowers having deeply cleft corolla without spur. [M. de *Lobel*, -IA¹]

lōbloll'y mǎn, boy, nn. (naut.). Surgeon's mate, attendant. [f. obs. *loblolly* gruel, prob. imit. of bubbling]

lŏb'scouse (-ows), n. Sailor's dish of meat stewed with vegetables & ship's biscuit. [?]

lŏb'ster, n. Large marine stalk-eyed ten-footed long-tailed edible crustacean with large claws formed by first pair of feet, bluish black before & scarlet after boiling; its flesh as food; (derog.) British soldier; ~*-eyed*, with protruding eyes; ~*-joint* (adaptable kind in pipe or tube); ~*-pot*, basket in which ~s are trapped. [OE *loppestre* corrupt. of L *locusta* LOCUST, (orig.) lobster, cf. F *langouste*; ending assim. to -STER]

lŏb'üle, n. Small lobe. Hence ~AR¹ a. [LOBE, -ULE]

lŏb'worm (-wěrm), n. Large earthworm used as fishing-bait; marine worm (also *lug*) similarly used. [f. obs. *lob* n., see LOB]

lō'cal¹², lōcale' (-ahl), n. Scene or locality of operations or events. [F(-*l*), abs. use of adj.=foll.: -*e* is E respelling to indicate stress, cf. MORALE]

lō'cal¹², a. & adv. & n. **1.** In regard to place (~ *habitation*, position in space as test of thing's material existence; *London is a ~ name*; ~ *adverb*). **2.** Belonging to, existing in, or peculiar to certain place(s) (~ *time*, reckoned from sun's transit over place's meridian; *the ~ lawyer*; *globe-flower is very ~*, not generally distributed; ~ *government*, administration of town etc. by inhabitants' representatives, || *L~ Government Board*, State department later absorbed by MINISTRY *of Health*; || ~ *examination*, held in various places under university board & giving certificates to boys & girls; ~ *preacher*, Methodist layman authorized to preach in his own circuit; ~ *option, veto*, system by which inhabitants of district may prohibit sale of liquor in it; ~ *colour*, details characteristic of the scene or time represented in novel or other literary work inserted to give actuality, & see below). **3.** Affecting, of, a part & not the whole (~ *disease, pain, remedy*; ~ *colour* in picture, that of separate objects apart from general colour-scheme, & see above). **4.** (Math.) of a locus. **5.** || (Post.; written on cover of letter as warning to P.O. officials) for delivery in this town or district; hence ~LY² adv. **6.** n. Inhabitant of, professional man practising in, particular district; ~ *preacher*; (item of) ~ *news* in newspaper; postage-stamp current in limited district; train serving stations of district; || (collog.) *the ~* public house; || (pl.) ~ *examination(s)*. [F, f. L *localis* (*locus* place, -AL)]

lō'calism, n. Attachment to a place; limitation of ideas etc. resulting; favouring of what is local; a local idiom, custom, etc. [-ISM]

local'ity, n. Thing's position, place where it is; site or scene of something; faculty of remembering & recognizing places,

finding one's way, etc. [f. F localité f.
LL localitātem (LOCAL², -TY)]

lō'calize, v.t. Invest with the characteristics of a particular place; restrict to
particular place; attach to districts, decentralize; concentrate (attention) upon;
(rare) = LOCATE. Hence ~ABLE a., ~ATION
n. [-IZE]

lōcǎrn'ō, n. *Pact of* ~, set of treaties
concluded at ~ in 1925, with France,
Germany, & Belgium as chief parties,
& Great Britain & Italy as guarantors,
intended to secure inviolability of the
frontiers & other safeguards of peace;
the spirit of ~, renunciation of ancient
enmities, esp. of that between France &
Germany. [~ in Switzerland]

lō'cative, a. & n. (gram.). (Case) denoting
place where. [prec., -IVE]

loch (lǒχ), n. Scottish lake; an arm of
the sea, esp. when narrow or partially
landlocked. [Gael.]

lŏck¹, n. Portion of hair that hangs together, tress, (pl.) hair of head; tuft of
wool or cotton. [OE *locc*, cf. Du. *lok*, G *locke*, prob. cogn.
w. Gk *lugos* withy]

lŏck², n. 1. Appliance for fastening door,
lid, etc., with bolt that requires key of
particular shape to work it (*under* ~ *&
key*, locked up); appliance to keep wheel
from revolving or slewing. 2. Mechanism
for exploding charge of gun (~, *stock, &
barrel*, whole of thing, completely). 3.
Confined section of canal at point where
level changes for raising & lowering boats
by use of sluiced gates. 4. Ante-chamber
to chamber in which engineering work is
done in compressed air. 5. Interlocking,
e.g. block or jam of vehicles in street.
6. Extent to which fore-wheel's can be
made to cross hind-wheel's plane. 7. (Also
L~) *Hospital*] hospital for venereal
disease. 8. ~*fast*, secured with ~; ~-
keeper, ~*sman*; ~*man*, coroner's summoner in I. of Man; ~*smith*, maker &
mender of canal ~; ~*smith*, maker & mender of
~s. Hence ~'LESS a. [OE *loc* neut., cf. G
loch hole, Da. *laag* lid]

lŏck³, v.t. & i. 1. Fasten (door, box, etc.)
with lock, shut up (house etc.) by fastening doors thus, (of door etc.) admit of
being so fastened, have a lock; shut (person, thing) up, in, or out (~ *the stable
door after the horse has been stolen*, take
precautions too late. 2. (Of land, hills,
etc.) hem in (usu. in pass.). 3. fig. Store
(*up* or *away*) inaccessibly (*facts* ~*ed up in
hieroglyphics; capital* ~*ed up in land*);
imprison (*senses* ~*ed in sleep*). 4. Keep

(person) *out* by ~*ing door* (esp. of employer coercing workmen by refusing
them work; ~-*out* n., this procedure, cf.
STRIKE). 5. Bring or come into rigidly
fixed position, engage, (make) catch,
fasten by interlacing or fitting of corresponding parts, entangle; (p.p.) joined in
hostile or other embrace. 6. (Mil., of rear
rank) march so close to front rank that
feet overlap. 7. (Of vehicle or wheels)
(have fore-wheels that) admit of being
slewed into different planes from those
of hind-wheels. 8. Provide (canal etc.)
with locks; convey (boat) *up* or *down*
through lock; go through lock. 9. ~-*chain*,
for ~*ing* wheels of vehicle; ~-*jaw*, ~*ed-
jaw*, (pop. name for) trismus, variety of
tetanus, tonic spasm of muscles of mastication causing jaws to remain rigidly closed;
~-*nut*, extra nut screwed over another
to prevent its starting; ~-*spring*, closing
watch-case; ~-*stitch*, sewing-machine
stitch by which two threads are firmly
~*ed together*; ~-*up*, (time of) ~*ing* up
school etc. for night, unrealizable state
of invested capital or amount of capital
~*ed up*, house or room for temporary
detention of prisoners; (attrib.) that can
be ~*ed up* (~-*up garage*). [f. prec.]

lŏck'age, n. Amount of rise or fall effected
by canal locks; toll for use of lock; use
or number of locks. [-AGE]

lŏck'er, n. In vbl senses; also : small cupboard, esp. one of many reserved each
for individual's use in public room, e.g.
cricket pavilion or schoolroom; (Naut.)
chest or compartment for clothes, stores,
ammunition, etc. (*not a shot in the* ~, no
money in one's pocket; DAVY JONES'S
LOCKER). [-ER¹]

lŏck'ĕt, n. Metal plate or band on scabbard; small gold or silver case holding
portrait, lock of hair, etc., & usu. hung
from neck. [f. OF *locquet* (*loc* latch f.
Teut. cogn. w. LOCK², -ET²)]

Lŏck'ian, a. Of John Locke or his philosophy or followers. So ~IST(2 n. [-IAN]

lŏck'ō¹, n. Locomotive engine. [abbr.]

lŏck'ō², n. Poisonous leguminous plant
found in U.S. (~-*disease*, brain disease
affecting cattle eating ~). Hence *~,
lŏc'ō cĭtā'tō, adv. (abbr. *loc. cit.* or *l.c.*).
In the passage already quoted. [L]

lŏc'omōte, v.i. (biol.). Move from place
to place. [back formation f. foll.]

lōcomō'tion, n. (Power of) motion from
place to place; travel, way (esp. artificial)
of travelling. [f. L *loco* see foll., *motio*
MOTION]

lŏc'omŏtive, a. & n. 1. Of locomotion (~
faculty, power), (joc.) of travel (*in these
days*); having power of or given to locomotion, not stationary, (*the* ~ *bivedives;
a* ~ *person*, joc., constantly travelling;
~ *engine*, that goes from place to place
by its own power, esp. steam-engine for

drawing train along rails); effecting locomotion (the ~ organs). **2.** n. ~ engine; (sl., pl.) legs (use your ~s); ~ animal. [f. L loco abl. of LOCUS, MOTIVE a.; suggested by scholastic phr. *in loco moveri* move in space]

lŏc'omōtŏr, n. & a. **1.** Locomotive person or thing. **2.** adj. Of locomotion (~ ATAXY). [as prec., MOTOR]

lŏc'omōtŏry̆, a. Of, having, locomotion. [as prec., MOTORY]

lŏc'ŭlus, n. (zool., anat., bot.; pl. **-ī**). One of a number of small separate cavities. Hence ~AR¹ a. [L, dim. of LOCUS]

lŏc'um tĕn'ens (-z; also colloq. **lŏc'um**), n. Deputy acting esp. for clergyman or doctor. Hence **lŏc'um-tĕn'ency** n. [med. L, (one) holding place TENANT, (foll.)]

lŏc'us, n. (pl. **-cī** pr. -sī). Locality or exact place of something; (Math.) curve etc. made by all points satisfying particular equation of relation between co-ordinates, or by point, line, or surface, moving according to mathematically defined conditions; ~ **class'icus**, best known or most authoritative passage on a subject; ~ **in quō**, scene of event; ~ **poenitĕn'tiae** (-shiō), opportunity allowed for receding until decisive step has been taken; ~ **stān'dī**, recognized position, right to intervene, appear in court, etc. [L, = place]

locū'tion, n. Style of speech; word or phrase considered in regard to style, idiom, (*a barbarous* ~; *to use the Greek* ~). [f. L *locutio* (*loqui locut-* speak, -ION¹)]

lŏc'ūtŏry̆, n. Parlour or conversation room in monastery; grille for interviews between inmates of monastery & outsiders. [f. med. L *locutorium* (prec., -ORY)]

lōde, n. ‖ Watercourse, open drain in fens; vein of metal ore; ~'**star**, loadstar, star that is steered by, esp. the pole-star, (fig.) guiding principle, object of pursuit; ~'**stone**, see LOAD¹stone. [var. of LOAD¹]

lōdge¹, n. **1.** Small house (arch.). **2.** Cottage at gates of park or grounds of large house, occupied by gardener or other servant; house (e.g. in Scottish Highlands) occupied in the hunting or shooting season. **3.** Porter's room at gate of college, factory, or house of chambers or flats. **4.** (Freemasonry etc.) (place of meeting for) members of branch; *grand* ~, governing body of freemasons & societies imitating them. **5.** ‖ Residence of head of college at Cambridge.

6. Beaver's or otter's lair. **7.** N.-Amer. Indian's tent or wigwam. [f. OF *loge* f. med. L *lobia* (LOBBY) f. Teut. (G *laube* arbour, prob. cogn. w. LEAF¹)]

lōdge¹, v.t. & i. **1.** Provide with sleeping-quarters; receive as guest or inmate; establish as resident in house or room(s), (pass.) be *well, ill,* etc., accommodated in regard to house-room. **2.** Serve as habitation for, contain, (pass.) be contained in. **3.** Leave *in* place or *with* person for security. **4.** Deposit in court or with official a formal statement of (complaint, information); (pop.) allege (objection etc.). **5.** Place (power etc.) *in, with, in the hands of,* (person). **6.** (Of wind) lay (crops) flat. **7.** (Make, let) stick or remain in place without falling or going further (~*d bullet, bullet* ~*d, in his brain; tide* ~*s mud in the cavities*). **8.** Reside, be situated; ‖ be inmate paying for accommodation in another's house, whence **lōdg'ER¹** n. (~*r franchise,* right to vote at election of M.P. enjoyed by a class of ~s before the 1918 extension). [f. OF *logier* (prec.)]

lŏdg'ing, n. In vbl senses; esp.: accommodation in hired rooms; dwelling-place, abode, (pl.) room(s) hired elsewhere than in hotel for residing in; ~-**house**, in which ~s are let (‖ *common* ~-*house,* usu. one with dormitory in which bed can be had for the night). [-ING¹]

lŏdge'ment, -gment, (-jm-), n. (Mil.) temporary defensive work on captured part of enemy's works; stable position gained, foothold, (*make, effect, a* ~; (Law) deposit(ing) of money; accumulation of matter intercepted in fall or transit. [f. F *logement* (prec., -MENT)]

lō'ĕss, n. Deposit of fine yellowish-grey loam in Rhine & other river valleys. [G *löss*]

loft (law-, lō-), n., & v.t. **1.** Attic; room over stable; pigeon-house; flock of pigeons; gallery in church or hall; (Golf) backward slope in club-head, ~ing stroke. **2.** v.t. Hit (golf-ball) high up, clear (obstacle) thus; keep (pigeons) in ~. [ON, = sky, air, loft, cf. G *luft*]

lof'ter (law-, lō-), n. Golf-club for lofting. [-ER¹]

lof'ty̆ (law-, lō-), a. Of imposing height, towering, soaring, (~*y mountain, flight, stature;* not of persons); haughty, consciously superior or dignified, (~*y contempt, good humour);* exalted, distinguished, high-flying, high-flown, elevated, sublime, grandiose. Hence ~ilY¹ adv., ~iNESS n. [-Y²]

lŏg¹, n., & v.t. (-gg-). **1.** Unhewn piece of felled tree or similar rough mass of wood (*in the* ~, unhewn; *float, lie, fall, like a* ~, in helpless or stunned state; *roll my* ~ & *I'll roll yours,* applied to mutual help, esp. to unprincipled political combinations & puffing of each other's works by author-

reviewers, whence ~-TROLL v.i., ~TROLL
w. ref. to fable of *King Log*. [It.]
STORE.] **2.** Float attached to line wound
on reel for gauging speed of ship, other
apparatus for same purpose, (*heave*,
throw, the ~, use this; *heel by the* ~, calculate ship's position by it); = ~-*book*,
daily made of all events occurring in
ship's voyage including rate of progress
shown by ~, (also) traveller's diary etc.;
~ *cabin*, hut built of ~-*line*, to which
float of ship's ~ is attached); ~-*wood*,
(wood of) Amer. tree used in dyeing.
5. v.t. Cut into ~s; enter (distance made
etc.) in ship's ~-*book*, (of ship) make (distance); enter (seaman's name with offence
committed) in ~-*book*, fine (offender).
[ME *logge*, etym. dub.; cf. CLOG]

log² n. = LOGARITHM of (prefixed to number
or algebraic symbol).

lóg'anberry, n. Fruit got by cross between raspberry & blackberry. [*Logan*,
surname]

lóg'an(-stóne), n. Poised heavy stone
rocking at a touch. [= *logging* (dial. *log*
to rock)]

logaoed'ic (-*ēē*-), a. & n. (Line) in metre
composed of dactyls & trochees. [f. LL
f. Gk *logaoidikós* combining prose &
poetry (*logos* speech, *aoidē* song, -IC)]

lóg'arithm, n. One of a class of arithmetical functions tabulated for use in
abridging calculation & enabling computer to substitute addition & subtraction for multiplication & division, &
the latter two for involution & evolution;
index of power to which fixed number
(the *base*) must be raised to produce
given number (*the* ~ *of 1,000 is* 3 *if common*
~s, *whose base is* 10). Hence **lógarith'-
mic** a., **lógarith'mically** adv. [f. Gk
logos reckoning, ratio, *arithmos* number]

loge (lŏzh), n. Box in theatre etc. [F]

lóg'gerhead (-gerhĕd), n. **1.** Blockhead,
fool, (arch.: *We three* ~*s be*, inscription
under two wooden heads on inn-sign).
2. Iron instrument with ball at end heated
for melting pitch etc.; post built into boat
for catching turn of rope to; kinds of
large-headed turtle & bird. **3.** *At* ~*s (with)*,
disagreeing or disputing (with) (prob. f.
notion of trying whose head is harder).
[f. dial. *logger* block of wood for hobbling
horse]

lóg'gia (-jya), n. (pl. ~s or *loggie* pr. -ā).
Open-sided gallery or arcade. [It.]

lö'gic, n. Science of reasoning, proof,
thinking, or inference; particular scheme
of or treatise on this; chain of reasoning,
correct or incorrect use of argument,
ability in argument, arguments (CHOP
~), (*argues with great learning &* ~ *is not
governed by* ~); (with purposely perverted
sense) converting-power, compulsion, (*the*
~ *of events, facts, necessity, grape-shot,
war,* etc.). So **lŏgi'cian** (-ĭshn) n. [f. F
logique f. med. L f. Gk *logikē* (*tekhnē* art)
of reason f. LOGOS, -IC(2)]

-logic, -logical. See -LOGY.

lö'gical, a. Of logic or formal argument;
not contravening the laws of thought,
correctly reasoned; deducible, defensible,
on ground of consistency, reasonably to
be believed or done; capable of correct
reasoning. Hence ~ITY (-ăl²) n., ~LY²
adv. [-AL]

lō'gie (-gi), n. Zinc ornament looking
like jewel used in theatres. [perh. inventor's name]

lö'gion (-g-), n. (pl.-*ia*). Saying of Christ,
not recorded in Gospels but preserved
elsewhere. [Gk.= oracle (LOGOS)]

-logist, suf. forming nn. meaning *one
versed in* -*logy*. f. -LOGY, -IST.

lögis'tics, n. pl. Art of moving & quartering troops (cf. STRATEGY, TACTICS), *&*
supplying & maintaining a fleet. [f. F
logistique (*loger* LODGE², -IC)]

lö'gogram, n. Sign or character representing a word in shorthand. [LOGOS,
-GRAM]

lö'gograph (-ahf), n. = prec.; = LOGOTYPE.
[LOGOS, -GRAPH]

lögŏ'grapher, n. (Gk Ant.). One of the
Greek prose historians before Herodotus;
ancient-Greek professional speech-writer.
[f. Gk *logográphos* (LOGOS, -GRAPHER)]

lö'gogriph, n. Kind of anagrammatic
word-puzzle. [f. F *logogriphe* (LOGOS, Gk
griphos riddle)]

lögŏm'achy (-k-), n. (literary). Dispute
about words, controversy turning on
merely verbal points. [f. Gk *logomakhia*
(LOGOS, *makhia* -fighting)]

lŏ'gŏs, n. (no pl.). "The Word or Second
Person of the Trinity. [Gk, = word,
reason, f. *legō* speak, used in mystic sense
by Hellenistic & Neo-Platonist philosophers & in St John]

lö'gotype, n. Word, or more letters than
one, cast in one piece but not as ligature,
for use in printing. [prec., TYPE]

-logue, suf. repr. Gk -*logos*, -*logon*,
chiefly in wds f. F (*cata*~, *dia*~). Personal
nn.= *one skilled in* -LOGY (*ideo*~) are now
rare. -LOGER or -LOGIST being usu. preferred.

-logy, suf. f. Gk -*logia* (in early instances,
thr. F *-logie* f. med. L -*logiā*). **1.** In most
wds -*log*- is the *o* form of Gk *leg*- speak-
logia indicating the character, action, or

branch of knowledge, of a person (Gk -logos n. or a.) who speaks in a certain way (brachy~, tauto~, eu~) or treats of a certain subject (theo~, astro~). E compounds of the latter kind, in which first component is genea~, minera~. Socio~, termino~, are hybrids. **2.** In a few wds -log- is the Gk logos discourse (tri~, tetra~).—Mod. formations in ~y may alw. have correl. adj. in -logical (rarely -logic); & nn. in logist (occas. -LOGER).

loin, n. (Pl.) part of body on both sides of spine between false ribs & hip-bones (gird up one's ~s, prepare for journey or effort; fruit, child, etc., of, spring from, etc., one's ~s, one's begotten offspring; joint of meat that includes the ~ vertebrae; ~-cloth, worn for decency & fastened round ~s. Hence ~ED[2] (-nd) a. [f. OF loigne (L lumbus) cogn. w. Du. lende]

loir (loi'er), n. The Fat Dormouse. [F, f. L glirem nom. glis]

loi'ter, v.i. & t. Linger on the way, hang about; travel indolently & with frequent pauses; pass (time etc.) away in ~ing. Hence ~ER[1] n., ~ingly[2] adv. [f. MDu. loteren wag about]

loll, v.t. & i. Hang (one's tongue) out, (of tongue) hang (usu. out); stand, sit, or recline, in lazy attitude; let (one's head or limbs) rest lazily on something. Hence ~ingly[2] adv. [prob. imit.; cf. LULL]

Loll'ard, n. One of the 14th-c. heretics who followed Wyclif or held opinions like his. Hence ~ISM(3) n. [f. MDu. lollaerd (lollen mumble, -ARD)]

loll'ipop, n. (usu. pl.). Sweetmeat(s), sugar-plum(s). [?]

loll'op, v.i. (colloq.). Flop about; move or proceed in a lounging or ungainly way. [extension of LOLL]

Lom'bard (lŭ-, lō-), n. & a. **1.** One of the Germanic 6th-c. conquerors of Italy; native of Lombardy. **2.** adj. Of the ~s or Lombardy, Lombardic; ~ street, a London street formerly occupied by ~ bankers, & still containing many of chief London banks, (transf.) the money market, virtual certainty, long odds. [F, f. It. Lombardo f. LL Longobardus (LONG[1], L Bardi name of the people]

Lombardic, a. Of the Lombards or Lombardy (esp. of N.-Ital. 7th–13th-c. architecture & 15th–16th-c. painting). [f. med. L Lombardicus (prec., -IC)]

lom'ent, n. (bot.). Kind of pod that breaks up when mature into one-seeded joints. Hence ~A'CEOUS (-āshus) a. [f. L lomentum bean-meal (orig. cosmetic) f. lo-, lavare, wash, -MENT]

Lo'ndon (lŭ-), attrib. a. ~ clay, geological formation in lower division of eocene tertiary in S.-E. England; ~ ivy, fog or smoke of ~; ~ particular, colloq. kind of fog peculiar to ~; ~ pride, kind of saxifrage; ~ smoke, dull grey colour. So ~ER[2](4), ~ISM(4), nn., ~IZE(3) v.t.

lone, attrib. a. Solitary, companionless, unfrequented, uninhabited, lonely, (poet. or rhet., exc. in ~ hand, hand played or player playing against the rest at quadrille & euchre, also fig.; feeling or making feel lonely, whence ~SOME (-ns-) a., ~somely[2] adv., ~someness n.; (of woman) single or widowed. [attrib. form of ALONE, cf. LIVE[1]]

lone'ly, a. Solitary, companionless, isolated; unfrequented. Hence ~INESS n. [-LY[1]]

long[1], a. & n. **1.** Measuring much from end to end in space or time (~ lines, distance, journey; ~ life, whence ~-lIVED[2] (-vd) a.; make a ~ arm, reach out for something esp. at table; has a ~ arm, can make his power felt far; ~ face, dismal; ~ head, of more than average length, (fig.) shrewdness or foresight, whence ~head[1] ED[2] a., ~head'edness n., (-hĕd-), lit. & fig.; make a ~ nose, cock a SNOOK; ~ tongue, loquacity; two etc. ~ miles etc., more than that; by a ~ CHALK[1]; grievances etc. of ~ standing, not recent); (prefixed to name; colloq.) tall (L~ Tom, gun of great length or range). **2.** Far-reaching, acting at a distance, involving great interval or difference, (~ sight, that sees distant objects, (fig.) penetration, whence ~-sight'ED[2] a., ~sight'edness n., (-sīt-), lit. & fig.; little PITCHERS have ~ ears; take ~ views, consider remote effects; ~ odds in betting, very uneven; ~ bowls, fighting at ~ range, opp. close quarters; ~ date, distant date for maturing of bill etc.; ~ waist in dress, made far down). **3.** (Usu. appended to measurement) having specified length or duration (tail 6 in. ~; vacation is two months ~; as BROAD as it is ~). **4.** Of elongated shape; remarkable for or distinguished by or concerned with length or duration (~ clay, churchwarden pipe; ~ DIVISION; ~ drink, one served in tall glass; ~ ears, stupidity as of ass, whence ~-eared[2] (-ĕrd) a.; ~ finger, the second; ~ jump, measured along ground, opp. high jump; ~ measure, miles, yards, inches, etc.; ~ metre, hymn-stanza of four eight-syllable lines; L~ Parliament, that elected 1640 & dissolved 1660; ~ PRIMER; ~ robe, legal attire, esp. gentlemen of the ~ robe, lawyers; in the ~ run, in the end after vicissitudes; || ~ service, system of military enlistment for many e.g. 12 years; || ~ vacation, summer vacation of law-courts & universities; ~ WHIST[3]; ~ wind, capacity for running far without rest, or fig. for talking or writing at tedious length, whence ~-wind'ED[2] a., ~wind'edness n.). **5.** Expressed by many ciphers or consisting of many individuals (~ figure or price, heavy cost; ~ family, of many children; ~ bill, of many items; ~ suit, many cards of one

lŏng¹ ... suit in a, hand, also, colloq., thing at which one excels). **6.** Lengthy, prolix, tedious. **7.** Of more than the usual numerical amount (~ DOZEN, HUNDRED, &c). **8.** Lasting, going far back or forward, (a ~ custom, memory, farewell). **9.** (Phonet., Pros., of vowel or syllable) (prop.) having the greater of the two recognized durations, (pop.) stressed, (also, of vowel) having the pronunciation shown in its name (e.g. ~ a; ~ pate & tacre have ~; pad & pad short a & u). **10.** ~bill, kinds of bird, esp. snipe; ~boat, sailing-ship's largest boat (cf. LAUNCH¹); ~bow, bow by hand & discharging ~bow, drawn by hand & discharging ~feathered arrow (cf. CROSS-BOW), draw the ~bow, tell exaggerated or invented stories; ~butt, cue for reaching billiard-ball beyond range of ~tail-butt; ~cloth, kind of calico made in ~ pieces; ~clothes, & arch. ~coats, clothes of baby in arms; ~field, ~ off or on (see below), also part of ground behind bowler; ~firm¹; ~hand, ordinary writing (opp. SHORTHAND); ~hop, short-pitched ball in cricket; ~off, on, man fielding at bowler's left, right, rear; ~pig, sailors' transl. of cannibals' name for human flesh; ~pull, over-measure given by public-houses to attract custom; ~shanks, stilt or ~legged plover; ~stop, man fielding straight behind wicket-keeper, (vb) field there; ~wave (Wireless), having a wave-length of (about) 800 metres or more; hence ~-ISH¹(2) a., ~WAYS, ~WISE, (z), advv. **11.** n. ~ interval or period (shall see you before ~; it is ~ since I saw him; so of ~est, to mention the most distant date possible); recital at length (the ~ & the short of it, all that can or need be said, the total upshot); ~ syllable (~s & shorts, verse esp. Latin); (Archit.) ~s & shorts, ~ & short blocks placed alternately; || = ~ vacation. [comn. -Teut.; OE & Du. & G lang, cogn. w. L longus & perh. Gk dolikhos]

lŏng², adv. (~er, ~est, pr. -ŋg-). For a long time (have ~ thought so; nor wants that tittle; ~ so or as~as, transf., provided that, if only; be ~ doing, &c, prob. by confusion of the adv. w. the adj., in doing, take a long time, be slow, to do, as he was ~ finding it out, the chance was ~ in coming; not be ~ for this world, have short time to live; ~liver, one who lives ~); by a long time (~before, after, since, ago); (appended to nn. of duration) throughout specified time (all day ~; his life ~); (comp. with no, any, much, etc.) after implied point of time (shall not wait any ~er; no ~er, not henceforth as formerly); ~ago (belonging to) the distant past; ~drawn(-out), unduly prolonged; ~stand-ing, that has ~ existed; ~suffering n. & a., bearing provocation patiently. [OE lange (prec.)]

lŏng³, v.i. Yearn, wish vehemently, for thing or to do. Hence ~ING¹(1), ~ING²] [OE langian]

-long, suf., f. LONG¹ in side~, head~, End~ f. ON endlangr adj. orig. meaning extending from end to end was used in E as adv. meaning endwise, & ~ thus came to be regarded as var. of -ling.

lŏngan'imĭtÿ (-ngg-), n. (rare). Long-suffering, forbearance. [f. LL longani-mitas (longanimus f. longus long, animus spirit, -TY)]

lŏn'geron (-j-), n. (usu. in pl.), dinal member of aeroplane's fuselage or nacelle. [F, =girder]

lŏngē'val, -gae-, (-j-), a. Long-lived. [f. L longaevus (longus long, aevum age, -AL)]

lŏngē'vĭtÿ (-j-), n. Long life. [f. L longaevitas (prec., -TY)]

lŏn'gi- (-ji-), comb. form of L longus long in scientific terms, as ~caud'ate long-tailed, ~corn kinds of beetle with long threadlike antennae.

lŏn'gĭtūde (-j-), n. Length (now joc.); (Geog.) angular distance east or west from a standard meridian, as that of Greenwich, to the meridian of any place, reckoned to 180° E. or W. (abbr. long.); (Astron.) angular distance eastward on ecliptic from vernal equinoctial point to foot of body's or point's circle of latitude. [f. L longitudo -inis (prec. -TUDE)]

lŏngĭtūd'ĭnal (-ji-), a. Of or in length; running lengthwise; of longitude. Hence ~LY² adv. [-AL]

Lŏng'obård, n. =LOMBARD (1st sense).

lŏngueur (lawnggŏr'), n. Tedious passage in book, film, or play (usu. pl.). [F]

lŏn'gue hâleine (lawnggahlān'), n. Work etc. of (or de) ~ (requiring long persistent effort; esp. of books). [F, =long wind]

100, n. & v.t. Round card-game with penalties paid to the pool; (having to pay) this penalty; unlimited ~, in which penalty is =amount already in pool; (vb) subject to the penalty. [abbr. of obs. lanteloo f. F lanterlu refrain of a song]

100b'y, n. Silly fellow. [cf. LUBBER]

100f'ah (-a), n. Pod of luffa Aegyptiaca used as flesh-brush. [f. Arab. lufah the plant]

look, v.i. & t. & n. **1.** Use one's sight, turn eyes in some direction, direct eyes at, (fair etc. to ~ at, in outward appearance; ~ before you leap, avoid precipitate action; to ~ at him etc., judging by his etc. ~s; will not ~ at, refuses to take, rejects, scorns); stare, show surprise, (~ daggers, &c); ~ through (of eyes) penetrate; ~ in the face, face him etc.

boldly or at close quarters). **3.** Express, threaten, show, by one's ~s (~ *compassion, death, daggers*, etc.). **4.** Ascertain or observe by sight (*who, how, whether*, etc. **5.** (fig.). Make mental search (*let him ~ at home*), inquire (*when one ~s deeper*), aim one's attention at & consider (*way of ~ing at things; what I ~ at is the comfort of it*), take care or make sure that, expect (~ *to do*, ~ *you!*, observe, mind; ~ *here!*, formula for demanding attention or expostulating ~ *sharp*, orig., keep strict watch, now, lose no time, bestir oneself, ~ *well* or *ill*, in good or bad health, also of things, seem to be going so; ~*s to be*, seems; ~ *as if*, suggest by appearance the belief that; ~ *like*, seem to be, also threaten or promise, as *it ~s like rain, he ~s like biting* or *winning*); seem to be (~*s his age*, seems as old as he really is; ~ *oneself again*, seem recovered). **8.** ~ **in'**, informal call or visit, (Sport) *will have a ~in*, come near winning & perhaps win; ~**ing-glass**, mirror, quicksilvered glass for mirrors; ~**'out'**, watch, ~**ing out**, (*keep a good ~out; on the ~out for* or *to do*), post of observation, man or party or boat stationed to ~ out, view over landscape, prospect of luck (*it's a bad ~out for him*), person's own concern (*that is his ~out, he must see to that himself*); ||~**see** (sl.), a survey, inspection. **9.** (With prepn.). ~ **about** one, examine one's surroundings, take time to form plans; ~ **after**, follow with the eye, seek for, attend to, take care of; ~ **down** one's *nose at* (colloq.), regard with covert displeasure; ~ **for**, expect, hope or be on the watch for, search for (~ *for* TROUBLE); ~ **into**, examine the inside of (box etc.), dip into (book), investigate; ~ **on**, regard as, regard with distrust etc.; ~ **over**, inspect, overlook or pardon; ~ **through**, direct eyes through (window etc.), penetrate (veil etc.) with sight or (pretence or pretender) with insight, be visible through (*his greed ~s through his eyes*), glance through (book etc.); ~ **to**, consider, take care of, be careful about (~ *to your manners*; ~ *to it that*), keep watch over, rely on (person or thing) for, expect, count upon, aim at; ~ **towards** (colloq.), drink health of; ~ **upon**, regard with specified feeling (also with adv., as *favourably*), regard as. **10.** (With adv.). ~ **about**, be on the watch, be in search for, let one's eyes rove; ~ **ahead**, (of rower) turn round to see where he is going (esp. imperat.); ~ **back**, be half-hearted about enterprise one has begun, turn one's thoughts upon

or to something past, cease to progress (usu. w. neg.), ~ **in** again, call back; ~ **down**, subdue with a, ~, (Commerce.) sink in price, ~ **down** (*upon*, consider oneself superior to; ~ **forward** to, anticipate (usu. with pleasure); ~ **in**, make short visit or call; ~ **on**, be mere spectator, whence ~**ER¹-ON¹** n.; ~ **on** *with*, read from book etc. at same time as (another person); ~ **out**, direct eyes or put head out of window etc., be vigilant, keep one's eyes open *for* expected person, be prepared *for* squalls etc., have or afford outlook *on, over*, etc., select by inspection; ~ **over**, inspect, one by one or part by part; ~ **round**, esp. examine the possibilities etc. with a view to deciding on a course; ~ **through**, survey with searching glance (~*ed him through*), inspect exhaustively or successively; ~ **up**, (esp. Commerce.) improve in price or prosperity, search for (esp. word in dictionary or facts in book of reference), call on (person), raise eyes (~ *up to*, respect, venerate), one *up & down*, scrutinize him keenly or contemptuously; hence ~**ER¹** n, (esp.) *handsome person (colloq.; also *good~er*). **11.** n. Act of ~ing, direction of eyes, glance (*a kind, scornful*, ~); (sing. or pl.) appearance of face, expression, personal aspect, (*good ~s*, beauty; (of things) appearance (*the place has a European ~*). [OE *lōcian*]

lōom¹, n. Machine for weaving yarn or thread into fabric; (inboard part of) shaft of oar. [earlier sense *tool*, OE *gelōma* (y- +*lōma* as in *andlōman* pl. apparatus)]

lōom², v.i., & n. **1.** Appear indistinctly, be seen in vague & often magnified or threatening shape, (lit. & fig.: often ~ *large* etc.). **2.** n. Vague first appearance of land at sea etc. [cf. EFris. *lōmen* move slowly, MHG *luomen* be weary]

lōom³, n. Kinds of guillemot & diver.

lōon¹, n. Kinds of guillemot & diver. Hence ~**'ERY(3)** n. [f. ON *lōmr*]

lōon², n. (Sc. & arch.). Scamp, idler, boor; lad. [earlier *lowne*; etym. dub.]

lōon³, n. Kinds of water-bird, esp. of diver & grebe. [perh.=LOOM³ w. assim. to prec.]

lōon¹y, lu~, n. & a. (sl.). Lunatic. [-Y³]

lōop¹, n., & v.t. & i. **1.** Figure produced by a curve, or bent string or withe, that crosses itself; attachment or ornament formed of cord, thread, etc.. so crossed & fastened at crossing; ring or curved piece of metal as handle etc.; (also ~*line*) railway or telegraph line that diverges from main line & joins it again; circuit in centrifugal railway along top of which passenger travels head downwards (~*ing the ~*, bicyclist's or airman's similar feat); (Skating) curve crossing itself made on single edge; hence ||~**'Y²** a. (sl.), crazy. **2.** vb. Form (string etc.) into ~(s): form ~ (esp. of LOOPER larvae); enclose (as) with ~; fasten (*up, back*) or join (*together*) with ~. [cf. Ir. & Gael. *lub*]

lŏŏp², n. (rare). = LOOP-HOLE. [prob. cogn. w. MDu. *lūpen* to peer.]

lŏŏp'er, n. Caterpillar of geometer moths, progressing by arching itself into loops; making loops. [-ER¹]

lŏŏp'hōle, n. & v.t. 1. Narrow vertical slit in wall for shooting or looking through or to admit light or air; outlet, means of evading rule etc. 2. v.t. Make ~s in (wall etc.). [LOOP²]

loose, a. 1. Released from bonds or restraint. 2. Detached or detachable from its place (*come, get,* ~; *play* FAST² *&* ~). (Chem.) free, uncombined; hanging partly free (esp. ~ *end*; *at a* ~ *end*, without definite occupation); not rigidly fixed, apt to shift, (*have a* SCREW ~). 3. Slack, relaxed, not tense or tight, (*with* ~ *rein*, lit. of riding, & fig. indulgently; ~ *tongue*, given to blabbing; ~ *bowels*, tending to diarrhoea; ~ *clothes*; ~ *build or make*, ungainly figure). 4. Not compact, dense, or serried (~ *soil, fabric*; ~ *order*, military arrangement with wide intervals; ~ *handwriting*, straggling; ∥ ~ *play or game* in football in which players do not lock together). 5. (Of statements, ideas, etc.) inexact, indefinite, vague, incorrect; (of translation) not close or (of agent) doing the act ~ly (~ *thinker*). 6. (Cricket) ~ *bowling*, inaccurately pitched, ~ *fielding*, careless or bungling. 7. Morally lax, dissolute, wanton in speech or act, (~ *fish*, dissolute person; *on the* ~, having a spree). 8. ~ BOX²; ~*leaf* (of ledgers, note-books, etc.) with each leaf separate & detachable. Hence ~·ly², ~·NESS nn. [-sl-] adv., ~NESS (-sn-) n., **lŏŏs'ISH**(²) a. OE *lēas*, cf. G *los*, cogn. w. Gk *lúō*]

loose, v.t. & n. 1. Release, set free, free from constraint (*wine ~d his tongue*); untie, undo, (knot, fetters, seal, hair of head); detach from moorings; discharge (arrow), (abs.) discharge gun (*at*); relax (now only in ~ *hold*). 2. n. Vent, free expression, (*give* ~ *or a* ~ *to one's feelings* etc.); ∥ loose play (see prec.). [f. prec.]

loos'en, v.t. & i. Loose (person's tongue); make or become less tight or compact or firm; relieve (bowels) from costiveness or (cough) from dryness; relax (discipline etc.). [-EN⁶]

loose'strife (-s-s-), n. Two kinds of herbaceous plant (*Golden* or *Yellow*, & *Red* or *Purple* or *Spiked*, L~). [mistransl. of Ll.f. Gk *lusimachion* (Gk pers. name *Lusimakhos*) as if directly f. *luō* undo, *makhe* battle]

loot, n. & v.t. & i. 1. Goods taken from enemy, spoil; booty, illicit gains made by official. 2. vb. Plunder, sack, (city etc., or abs.); carry off as booty. Hence ~ER¹ n. [f. Hind. *lūt*]

lŏp¹, n., & v.t. & i. (-pp-). 1. Smaller branches & twigs of trees (~ *& top*, ~ *& crop*, trimmings of trees). 2. vb. Cut off branches & twigs & rarely top of (tree); strip tree of (branches etc.; often *off*, *away*), whence ~PINGS [-ING¹] n. pl.; cut off (person's limb or head); make ~ping strokes at. [vb prob. f. n.; etym. dub.]

lŏp², v.i. & t. (-pp-), & n. 1. Hang limply; let (ears) hang; slouch, dawdle, hang about; = LOPE; ~-*ears*, drooping ears, whence ~-EARED²(-ērd) a.; ~-*ear*, kind of rabbit; hence **lŏp'Y²** a. 2. n. ~-eared rabbit. [prob. init.]

lŏp³, v.i. (-pp-), & n. 1. (Of water) break in short lumpy waves. 2. n. Such motion of water. [imit.]

lōpe, v.i. & n. (Run with) long bounding stride (esp. of animals). [f. ON *hloupa* cogn. w. LEAP]

lŏph'o-, comb. form of Gk *lophos* crest, in scientific wds as: ~*dŏnt*, (animal) with transverse ridges on crowns of molars; ~*brin'chiāte*, (fish) with gills disposed in tufts.

lŏp-sid'ĕd, a. With one side lower or smaller than the other, unevenly balanced. Hence ~LY² adv., ~NESS n.

loquā'cious (-shus), a. Talkative; (of birds, water) chattering, babbling. Hence or cogn. ~LY² adv., ~NESS, **loquā'CITY** (-ăs-), nn. [f. L *loquax* (*loqui* talk)..-ACIOUS]

lŏq'uat (-ŏt), n. Chinese & Japanese fruit (-tree) naturalized in S. Europe, Australia, etc. [f. Chin. *luh kwat* rush orange]

lŏq'uitur, v.i. 3 sing. pres. (abbr. *loq.*). Speaks (with speaker's name added, as stage-direction or notice to reader). [L]

lor', int. form of LORD used (vulg.) as int.

lor'al, a. Of the LORE². [-AL]

∥ **lor'cha**, n. Ship with hull of European shape but Chinese rig. [Port., etym. dub.]

lord, n. & int. & v.i. & t. 1. Master, ruler, chief, prince, sovereign, (*our sovereign the King*; ~*s of creation*, mankind, also joc. men as opp. women); (poet.) owner (~ *of ten acres*; cf. landlord); magnate in some trade (*the cotton* ~*s*; cf. *king*). 2. Feudal superior (MESNE ~; ~ *of the* MANOR; ~ PARAMOUNT). 3. (Poet. & joc.) husband (also ~ *& master*). 4. (Astrol.) dominant planet. 5. (Usu. *the* L~ exc. in voc.; also with *God*) God (L~ *knows who, how,* etc.; *I cannot guess who* etc., *some one* etc. or *other*; L~ *have mercy*, L~ *bless me* or *us* or *my soul* or *you*, excll. of surprise etc.; also L~! alone as excl.); Christ (*our* L~; *in the year of our* L~, *anno domini*; L~*'s day*, Sunday); L~*'s prayer*, the *Our Father*; L~*'s supper*, Eucharist, *the* L~*'s table*, Christian altar, Eucharist. 6. Nobleman, peer of the realm or person entitled by courtesy to the prefix L~ (see below) as part of his ordinary style (*live, treat, like a* ~, *fare,*

entertain, sumptuously; drunk as, swear like, a ~, excessively; L~ in waiting, of the Bedchamber, nobleman attending sovereign, called by former title if queen is reigning, by latter if king): (pl. the L~s) temporal & spiritual peers of Parliament (*House of L~s*, upper legislative chamber of United Kingdom, also committee of specially qualified members of this appointed as ultimate judicial appeal court), **7.** pl. (Also in full *L~s Commissioners*) members of board performing duties of high State office put in commission (*L~s of the Admiralty, Treasury,* etc.; *First L~*, president of such board; *Civil L~*, civilian member of Admiralty board, opp. *Sea L~s*); *L~s of Session*, judges of Scottish *Court of* session. **8.** First word of many official titles (*L~ CHAMBERLAIN, CHANCELLOR, Chief Justice, High Commissioner; L~ Justice General, L~ Justice Clerk*, president, vice-president, of Scottish Court of Justiciary; *L~ Lieutenant*, viceroy of Ireland till 1922, chief executive authority & head of magistracy in each county; *L~ Rector*, triennially elected honorary head of a Scottish university court; *L~ Mayor*, mayor of London, York, Dublin, & some great towns; *L~ Bishop*, any bishop in ceremonious mention). **9.** (Prefixed as part of personal designation) marquis, earl, viscount, or baron (whether peer, or peer's eldest son holding his second title by courtesy; with suppression of *of*, e.g. *Earl of,* or *L~ Derby; ~* is invariable instead of *baron*, which is used as prefix only in foreign titles); (followed by Christian & family name) younger son of duke or marquis. **10.** *My ~* (voc.), respectful or polite formula for addressing nobleman below duke, bishop, *~ mayor*, or judge of supreme court; *~s & ladies*, wild arum; hence ~'NESS a., ~'LING¹(2), ~ÓI'ATRY, nn. **11.** vb. Play the *~ over* (usu. in pass., *will not be ~ed over*; or with *it*, as *~ing it over his household*); ennoble, confer title of *~* upon. [OE *hláford* orig.= bread-keeper (LOAF¹, WARD)]

lord'ly, a. Haughty, imperious, lofty, disdainful; grand, magnificent, fit for or belonging to a lord. Hence ~iNESS n. [OE *hláfordlíc* (prec., -LY¹)]

Lord's (-z), n. (Used for) ~ cricket ground in London, headquarters of the M.C.C. and English cricket. [Thomas Lord (d. 1832), maker of successive grounds named after him]

lord'ship, n. Dominion, rule, ownership of or over; dominion, estate, manor; lord's personality (*your ~, his ~*, you, he, in speaking deferentially to or of a lord, also joc. to or of other persons or animals). [-SHIP]

lore, n. **1.** (arch.). Doctrine; erudition, scholarship. **2.** Body of traditions & facts on a subject (*ghost, bird, animal, fairy,* etc., *~*). [OE *lár* cf. Du. *leer,* G *Lehre*, cogn. w. LEARN]

lore², n. (nat. hist.). Strap-like surface, in birds between eye & upper mandible, in snakes between eye & nostril. [f. L *lorum* strap]

Lorett'ian, a. & n. (Member) of Loretto School in Scotland.

lorgnette (lôrnyét'), n. Pair of eye-glasses usu. held by long handle; opera-glass. [F]

lo'ricate, a. (zool.). Having defensive armour of bone, plates, scales, etc. [f. L *loricatus* (*lorica* cuirass f. *lorum* strap, -ATE²)]

lo'rikeet (or -eet'), n. Small brightly-coloured Polynesian parrot allied to the lory. [dim. of LORY, after *parakeet*]

lo'riner, n. (hist.). Bit-maker, spurrier, (now only in title of a livery company). [f. OF *lorenier* (*lorain* harness-strap f. L *lorum* thong)]

lo'ris, n. Small slender tailless nocturnal climbing quadrumanous Cingalese mammal; kinds of lemur. [F]

lorn, a. (poet. & joc.). Desolate, forlorn, (often *lone ~*). [p.p. of obs. *leese* LOSE, OE *lěosam* cf. G *verlieren*]

lo'rry, n. Long low flat sideless wagon; truck used on railways & tramways; motor truck for transporting troops etc. [?]

lo'ry, n. Kinds of bright-plumaged parrot-like bird. [f. Malay *luri*]

lose (looz), v.t. & i. (*lost* pr. law- or lŏ-). **1.** Be deprived of, cease by negligence, misadventure, separation, death, etc., to possess or have (property, life, quality, limb, father, friend, etc.; *doctor~s patient*, fails to keep him alive, also is left by him for another doctor; *~ patience*, one's *temper*, become impatient, angry; *~ one's* HEAD¹; *~ one's* HEART; *~* HEART; *~ ground*, fail to keep position, recede, decline; *have lost my cold*, got rid of it; *~ interest*, of person, cease to be interested, of thing, cease to interest); (pass.) disappear, perish, die or be dead, (*letter-writing is a lost art; the ship & all hands were lost; lost to sense of duty, shame,* etc., no longer affected by them; *lost soul*, damned). **2.** Suffer loss or detriment, incur disadvantage, be the worse off in money or otherwise by transaction etc. (*the publisher lost by it; the army lost heavily; story does not ~ in the telling*, is if anything exaggerated). **3.** Become unable to find, fail to keep in sight or follow or mentally grasp. (*~ a document, one's way, the thread of a discourse, a person etc. under observation*). **4.** Spend (time, opportunities, pains) to no purpose, waste, (pass., *be lost upon*, fail to influence or draw the attention of). **5.** Fail to obtain, catch, see, or hear (*~ one's train, a legacy, a word or remark, a fox*). **6.** Forfeit (stake), be defeated in (*game, battle, lawsuit,* or

abs.: *losing game*, in which defeat seems inevitable; *cannot play a losing game*, (motion). **7.** Cause person the loss of (refl. & pass.); go astray, become merged or engrossed (*in*), be observed (*in*); ‖ *losing* HAZARD. Hence **los'ABLE** (-ooz-) a. [OE *losian* (*los* LOSS) intr. the trans. senses being f. the cogn. obs. *leese*]

‖ **lös'el** (-z-), n. (arch.), Profligate, rake, ne'er-do-well. [prob. f. base of obs. *leese* LOSE]

los'er (-ooz-), n. In vbl senses; esp.: *be a ~ by*, suffer loss by; *good ~*, person not dejected or angered by losing game etc.; person, horse, etc., that loses race etc.; ‖ (Billiards) *losing* HAZARD. [-ER¹]

loss, n. Losing or being lost (see LOSE); person, thing, or amount lost (OUT² a or *the~*); detriment, disadvantage, resulting from ~ (*person etc. is a great, no, little, etc.,~, the ~ of him is a serious etc. blow*); *at a ~* (*for, to discover, etc.*), puzzled, at fault. [prob. partly f. OE *los* (cf. ON *los*) dispersion, rout, & partly back formation f. *lost* p.p. of LOSE]

‖ **löss** (G), n. =LOESS.

lost, See LOSE.

löt¹, n., & v.t. (-tt-). **1.** One of a set of objects used to secure a chance decision in dividing goods, selecting officials, etc. (now only in *draw, cast, ~s*, usu. *between, for, who*, etc., & in *throw* or *cast in one's ~ with*, share fortunes of); this method of deciding (*the ~; by ~*); choice resulting from (*the ~ fell upon me*). **2.** What falls to person by ~, share (*have no part nor ~ in*); person's destiny, fortune, condition, (*the ~ falls to me, it falls to my ~, it falls to me as my ~, to do*). **3.** ‖ Tax, duc, (Scot. & ~). **4.** Plot or allotment of land. **5.** Article or set of articles offered separately at sale, item at auction, (*bad ~*, disreputable or vicious person). **6.** Number or quantity of persons or things of same kind or somehow associated (*the ~*, the whole number or quantity); (colloq.) considerable number or amount, a good or great deal,(also in pl., as *has~s of friends*); **7.** v.t. Divide (land, usu. *out*, or goods for sale) into ~s. [OE *hlot*, cf. Du. *lot*, cogn. w. G *loos*]

loth, See LOATH.

Lothar'io, n. (pl. ~s). Libertine, rake. [character in Rowe's *Fair Penitent*]

lö'tion, n. Liquid preparation used externally to heal wound, cure skin-disease, clear complexion, etc. [f. L *lotio* (*lavare lot-* wash, -TION)]

löt'ery, n. Arrangement for distributing prizes by chance among purchasers of tickets; ~wheel, wheel with box used for shuffling numbers corresponding to those on tickets; (fig.) thing that defies calculation. [f. It. *lotteria* (*lot*, LOTTO)]

löt'o, n. Game of chance with drawing of numbers as in lottery. [It. f. Teut. (*lot*)]

löt'us, n. Plant represented in ancient Greek legend as inducing luxurious dreaminess & distaste for active life (~-*eater*, person given to indolent enjoyment; so ~-*eating* a. & n.); Egyptian & Asiatic water-lily; kinds of plant, esp. Bird's-foot Trefoil; ~-*land*, place of indolent enjoyment. [L, f. Gk *lōtos*]

loud, a. & adv. **1.** Strongly audible, sonorous (~ *speaker*, apparatus that converts electrical impulses into sounds ~ enough to be heard at some distance); clamorous, noisy; (of colour, dress, pattern, manners) obtrusive, conspicuous, flashy; hence ~EN¹ v.t., ~ISH¹ a., ~LY² adv., ~NESS n. **2.** adv. ~ly (*don't talk so ~; laughed ~ & long*). [OE *hlūd*; comb. -WG; OE *hlūd*, cf. Du. *luid*; G *laut*; cogn. w. Gk *klutos* hear, L *clēre* be famed]

lough (see Ap.), n. (Anglo-Ir.). Lake, arm of sea. [perh. f. O Northumb. *luh* f. Gael. & Ir. LOCH]

Louis (loo'ē), n. (pl. Louis pr. -z). Name of many French kings; *louis* or *louis-d'or* (-dōr'), French gold coin of about 20 fr. from ~ XIII to ~ XVI; ~ *Treize* (trāz), *Quatorze* (kătôrz'), *Quinze* (kănz), *Seize* (sāz), used adj.; of furniture etc. in styles prevalent in those reigns.

lounge (-j), v.i. & n. **1.** Go lazily, saunter; loll, recline; idle (intr. & ~ *away time* etc.); hence ~ER¹ n., ~ing² -ly adv. **2.** n. Spell of ~ing, saunter, stroll; place where one can ~e, esp. entrance-hall or gallery furnished for the purpose (~e-*lizard*, sl., professional dance-partner at hotel; ~e-*dance*); sitting-room in house; sofa or deep chair; ‖ ~e (*suit*), man's suit for day wear, with tailless jacket. [?]

lour, lower, (lowr), v.i., & n. **1.** Frown, scowl, look sullen, (*on, upon, at*); (of clouds, sky, storm) look dark & threatening; hence ~ing¹y² adv. **2.** n. Scowl; gloominess of sky etc., whence ~Y² a. [ME *louren*, cf. Du. *loeren* frown, G *lauern* watch; spelling *lower* prob. due to confusion w. LOWER¹]

louse, n. (pl. *lice*). Parasitic insect infesting human hair & skin; kinds of parasite of mammals, birds, fish, & plants. Hence **lous'Y²** (-z-) a., (also, sl.) supplied with money etc., **lous'INESS** (-z-) n. [common Teut.; OE *lūs*, cf. Du. *luis*, G *laus*]

lout¹, n. Awkward fellow, bumpkin, clown. Hence ~ISH¹ a., ~ISH¹Y² adv., ~ISHNESS n. [?]

lout², v.i. (arch.). Bow, make obeisance. [OE *lūtan*, cf. ON *lūta*]

louver, -vre, (loo'ver), n. Domed turret-like erection on medieval hall-roof etc. with side openings to let smoke out or air in; (pl., also ~-*boards*) arrangement of overlapping boards or slips of glass to

admit air but exclude rain. Hence **louvered²** (-erd) a. [f. OF *lover*, cf. med. L *lodium*]

Louvre (lo̅o̅vr), n. *The* ~, former royal palace, now art museum, in Paris. [F]

lo'vable (lŭ-), a. Deserving love, amiable. Hence ~LY² adv., **~leness** n. [LOVE², -ABLE]

lo'vage (lŭ-), n. Kinds of herb. [ME *loveache* f. OF *levesche* f. LL *levisticum* perh. f. L *ligusticum* Ligurian; assim. to *love, ache*]

love¹ (lŭv), n. **1.** Warm affection, attachment, liking, or fondness, paternal benevolence, affectionate devotion, (*of*, *for*, *to*, or *towards* person, *for* or *to* thing; *give* ~ *to*, convey affectionate message to; *send* one's ~ *to*, get this done; *for the* ~ *of*, for sake or in name of; in adjurations; *for* ~ *or money*, by any means; *labour of* ~, that one delights in, or that one does for ~ of someone; *there's no* ~ *lost between them*, they dislike each other; *play for* ~, for the pleasure of it, not for stakes). **2.** Sexual affection or passion or desire, relation between sweethearts, this feeling as a literary subject, a personified influence, or a god (also representation of Cupid, or of naked winged child, or in pl. children, symbolizing); (*in* ~, possessed by this; *in* ~ *with*, enamoured of, also transf. fond of a pursuit, thing, etc.; *fall in* ~, become enamoured; *all's* FAIR² *in* ~ *& war*; ~ *in a cottage*, marriage on insufficient means; *make* ~, pay amorous attentions *to* or abs., whence ~-MAKING¹ n.). **3.** Beloved one, sweetheart, (esp. of woman, cf. LOVER; hence ~Y³ n.; *my* ~, common form of address between husband & wife); (colloq.) delightful person or pretty thing (*he is an old* ~; *what* ~ *of teacups!*). **4.** (Games) no score, nothing, nil, (~ *all*, neither side has yet scored); ~ *game*, in which loser has not scored). **5.** ~-*affair*, ~-*apple*, (old name for) tomato; ~-*begotten*, illegitimate; ~-*bird*, small bird of parrot kind said to pine away at death of its mate; ~-*child*, illegitimate ~-*feast*, meal in token of brotherly ~ among early Christians, religious service among Methodists etc. imitating this; ~-*in-a-mist*, Fennel-flower; ~-*in-idleness*, Heart's-ease; ~-*knot*, peculiarly interlaced bow of ribbon; ~-*letter*, between sweethearts & concerned with ~'s *business*; ~-*lies-bleeding*, garden plant with long drooping spike of purple-red bloom; ~-*lock*, tress or curl worn on temple or forehead; ~-*lorn*, pining with ~, deserted by one's love(r); ~-*match*, marriage made for ~'s sake only; ~-*philtre*, philtre; ~-*sick*, languishing with ~; ~-*song*, about or expressing ~; ~-*story*, novel etc. of which main theme is ~'s facts of a wooing etc.; ~-*token*, thing given in sign of ~. Hence ~WORTHY a., **~worthiness** n. [OE

lufu, cogn. w. G *liebe*, Du. *lieven*, to love; also w. LIEF, LEAVE¹, BELIEVE]

love² (lŭv), v.t. & i. **1.** Hold dear, bear love to, be in love with, be fond of, (~ *me*, ~ *my* DOG¹; *Lord* ~ *you!*, excl. of surprise at person's mistake etc.; ~ one's *love with an A, a B*, etc, formula in game of forfeits); be in love; cling to, delight in, enjoy having, be addicted to, admire or be glad of the existence of, (life, honour, comfort, golf, doing, virtue, man who knows his own mind, etc.; (w. inf.) be (habitually) inclined (*children* ~ *to ape their elders*); (colloq.) like, be delighted, (*he simply* ~*s to find mistakes*; *Will you come?—I should* ~ *to*). [OE *lufian* (prec.)]

Love'lace (lŭvl-), n. Libertine, accomplished rake. [character in *Clarissa Harlowe*]

love'less (lŭvl-), a. Unloving; unloved. Hence ~LY² adv., **~NESS** n. [-LESS]

love'ly (lŭvl-), a. Attractively or admirably beautiful; (colloq.) delightful, very pleasing, intensely amusing. Hence ~LY² adv. (rare), **~iness** n. [OE *luflic* (LOVE¹, -LY¹)]

lo'ver (lŭ-), n. Woman's sweetheart or suitor, (pl.) pair in love; paramour, gallant; admirer, devotee, of, thing, action, or idea; ~*s' knot*, LOVE¹-knot. Hence ~LESS a., ~LIKE, ~LY¹,², aa. & adv. [-ER¹]

lo'ving (lŭ-), a. That loves, affectionate, (*our* ~ *subjects*, formula in royal proclamation; *your* ~ *friend* etc., formula in concluding letter); manifesting or proceeding from love (~-*cup*, large drinking-vessel passed round at banquet; ~-*kindness*, tender consideration). Hence ~LY² adv., **~NESS** n. [-ING²]

low¹ (lō), a. & adv. (~*er*, ~*est*, as aa. & advv.), & n. **1.** Not reaching far up, not high or tall, (~ *house*, *forehead*, *stature*; not used of persons: ~ *dress*, leaving neck & part of shoulders & breast exposed, so ~ *neck*; ~ *relief*, bas-relief). **2.** Not elevated in geographical etc. position (*Low Countries*, Netherlands; *Low* GERMAN², DUTCH; *Lower Egypt* etc.; ~ *moon* etc., near horizon; ~ *tide* or *water*, level of ebbed sea, time of extreme ebb; ~ *water mark*, ~est point reached by ebbtide, & fig.; *in* ~ *water*, out of funds etc.). **3.** Of or in humble rank or position (*the* ~ *er orders* or *classes*; ~ *birth*; *high &* ~, every one). **4.** Not exalted or sublime, commonplace, undignified, little civilized, not highly organized; abject, mean, degraded, coarse, vulgar, (~ *cunning*). **5.** Ill-nourished, not nourishing, indicative of ill nutrition, wanting in vigour, depressed, not intense, (~ *condition*, *diet*, *fever*; ~ *spirits*, whence ~-**spi'rited³** a.). **6.** Of small amount as measured by a scale or degrees (~ *price*, *wages*, *rates*, *temperature*, *power*; *have* ~ *opinion of*, do not estimate highly; *at* ~*est*, to mention

the least possible amount etc.; ~ *latitudes*, near equator). **7.** (Of sounds) not shrill or high up, produced by slow vibrations, (also) not loud. **8.** (Of liquid, receptacle, supply of anything, esp. fig. of purse or money) nearly exhausted or empty (often *run* ~). **9.** Recent (*belongs to a* ~*er date*). **10.** (Also ~*-church*) giving ~ place to authority of bishops & priests, inherent grace of sacraments, ecclesiastical organization, & ritual, not sacerdotal, approximating to protestant non-conformity, thus minded; ~ *Churchman*, member of it). **11.** Bring ~, depress, reduce, in health, wealth, or position; *lay* ~, overthrow; *lie* ~, crouch, be prostrate or dead or abased, (sl.) keep quiet or out of the way, say nothing, bide one's time; BURN[2] ~. **12.** ~*brow* (colloq.) (one who is) not highly intellectual or cultured (opp. HIGHBROW); ~*browed*, lit., also (of rocks) beetling, (of building etc.) with ~ entrance, gloomy; ~ *celebration* of Eucharist, without choir or assistant ministers; ~ *comedian*, actor in ~ *comedy*, in which subject & treatment border on farce; *~-down*, abject, mean, dishonourable; *~-down* n. (sl.) true facts, inside information; ||~*er boy*, in ~*er school* at public schools; ~*er CASE*[2]; ~*er chamber*, = *~er House*; *~er critic(ism)*, of the verbal or textual kind; ~*er deck*, immediately over hold (||*the ~er deck*, petty officers & men of the Navy or of a ship); *~er Empire*, later Roman Empire, usu. from Constantine; *~er House*, ~*er branch* of legislative assembly, e.g. House of Commons; ~*er school* in public schools, usu. forms below fifth; *~er world*, the earth, (also) hell; *~land*, (usu. pl.) ~*lying country*, (adj.) of or in this; *Low*/*lands* (-*mdz*), SE. part of Scotland, whence *Low*/*lander*[4](-) n.; *Lowland* (adj.), of or in this; ~ LATIN; ~ *life*, that of the ~er classes, whence ~*-lived*[3] (-*vd*') a.; ~ *MASS*[1]; ~ *pitch*, ~ *key* or note, also slight angular elevation of roof, whence *low-pitched*[2] a.; ~ PRESSURE; *Low Sunday*, *Week*, after Easter Day & Week; ~*WING*[1]; hence ~' *ermost* (*lo''er-*), ~*ISH*[2] (*lo''i-*), aa., ~'*NESS* (*lo''n-*) n. **13.** adv. In or at ~ or mean position (*hangs* ~; *aim* or *shoot* ~; ~*er* : *collar* ~ in football, catch at or below waist; *bowed* ~; *never fell so* ~ *as that*); on poor diet (*live* ~ *for a time*); for small stakes (*play* ~); in ~ tone, on or to ~ note, (*talk* ~ ; *cannot get so* ~); (of date) late (*find it as* ~ *as the 18th century*); ~*born*, of humble birth; ~*-bred*, of vulgar manners; ~*down*, far down, also in mean or ungenerous way (esp. *play it* ~ *down or* ~, *upon*, treat scurvily). **14.** n. What is ~; an area of ~ barometric pressure. [ME *lah* f. ON *lāgr* cogn. w. LIE[3]]

low[2](lō), v.i. & t., & n. **1.** Utter cry (as) of

cow, moo; *say*, utter *forth*, with ~*ing sound*. **2.** n. Cow's cry. [com.-Teut.; OE *hlōwan*, cf. OHG *hluojen*, Du. *loeien*, cogn. w. L *clāmare*]

low'er[1](lō'er), v.t. & i. & t. Let or haul down; (Naut., abs.) let down boat, haul down; sail, etc.; diminish height of; sink, descend, slope downwards; diminish (price etc.), (of price etc.) come down; diminish (t. & i.) in intensity or pitch; degrade, disgrace; reduce bodily condition of (*a ~ing diet*). [f. *lower* comp. of LOW[1]]

low'er[2]. See LOUR.

low'ly(lō-), a. & adv. **1.** Humble in feeling, behaviour, or condition, modest, unpretending. **2.** adv. In ~*y manner*. Hence ~*ily*[2] adv., ~*iNESS* n. [LOW[1], -LY[1, 2]]

lŏxŏdrŏm'ic, a. & n. Of oblique sailing or sailing by the RHUMB; (n.) ~*ic line* or table. Hence ~*ICS* n. [f. Gk *loxos* oblique, *dromos* course, -IC]

loy'al, a. & n. **1.** True, faithful, to duty, love, or obligation (*to*); faithful in allegiance to sovereign, government, or mother-country; enthusiastically devoted to sovereign's person & family; exhibiting loyalty; hence ~*iSM*(3), n., ~*IZE*(3) v.t., ~*iz*[2] adv. **2.** n. Person **who** remains ~ in time of disaffection. [F, f. L *legālis* LEGAL]

loy'alty, n. Loyal temper or conduct. [f. OF *loialté* (prec., -TY)]

lŏz'enge (-j), n. RHOMB, diamond figure, esp. as bearing in heraldry; ~-shaped shield for spinster's or widow's arms; ~-shaped facet of cut gem; small tablet (orig. ~-shaped) of flavoured sugar, medicine, meat essence, etc., to be dissolved in mouth; ~-shaped pane in casement. [f. OF *losenge*, cf. Pr. *lausa* tombstone perh. ult. f. L *lapis* stone]

'lŏz'enged (-jd), a. With lozenges or alternate colours; with lozenge panes. [-ED[2]]

£.s.d. (ĕl'ĕsdē'), n. Pounds, shillings, & pence: money, riches; L.S.D.é'tsm (loc., money-worship. [L *lībrae, solidī, denariī*, pounds, shillings, pence]

'it. See WILL[1].

lŭbb'er, n. Big clumsy stupid fellow, lout; clumsy seaman; ~'*s hole* (Naut.), hole in platform of ship's top (saving climbing by FUTTOCK shrouds). Hence ~*LIKE* a., ~*LY*[1, 2] & adv., ~*iNESS* n. [prob. f. or cogn w. LOB]

lub'ricate (loo-, lū-), v.t. Make slippery or smooth by applying fluid or unguent; minimize friction of (machinery) with grease etc. (also fig.). Hence ~*ANT* (2) a. & n. ~*ATOR*(1, 2), ~*ATION*, nn. ~*lubricāre* (*lubricus* slippery cogn. w. SLIP), -ATE[3]]

lubri'city (loo-, lū-), n. Slipperiness, smoothness, oiliness, (lit. & fig.); lewdness, wantonness. So ~*ous* (-shus), ~*lub'ricous* aa. [f. L *lubrĭcĭtas* (prec., -TY)]

Lūc'an (loo-, lū-), a. Of St Luke. [f. L *Lūcas* Luke, -AN]

Lucca (lŏŏk'a, lŭk'a), n. ~ *oil*, superior quality of olive oil. [~ in N. Italy]

luce (lōōs, lūs), n. Pike fish, esp. when full-grown. [f. OF *lus* f. LL *lucius*]

lu'cent (lōō-, lū-), a. Shining, luminous; translucent. Hence **lu'cency** n. [-ENT]

¶**lucern(e)** (lōō-, lū-), n. Cloverlike plant used for fodder. [f.F *luzerne* from F. dub.]

Lucian'ic (lōōsi-), a. After the manner of Lucian, witty & scoffing. [f. L f. Gk *Loukianos*, writer of Greek dialogues c. A.D. 160.-IC]

lu'cid (lōō-, lū-), a. Bright (poet.); (Entom., Bot.) with smooth shining surface; clear, pellucid, (usu. fig. of reasoning, literary style, etc.); ~ *interval*, period of quiet between attacks of madness, or sanity between disturbances. Hence or cogn. **lucid'ITY** n., **~LY²** adv. [f. L *lucidus* (LUCENT)]

Lu'cifer (lōō-, lū-), n. **1.** (Planet Venus as) morning star. **2.** (Supposed name as A.V. & R.V. of *Isa.* xiv. 12, of) the chief rebel angel, Satan, the devil, (*as proud as* ~). **3.** l~ (*match*), friction match (now rare). [L, light-bringing, morning star, (*lux lucis* light, *-fer* f. *ferre* bring)]

lucif'ugous (lōō-, lū-), a. (nat. hist.). Shunning daylight. [f. L *lucifugus* (prec., *fugere* flee), -OUS]

luck, n. **1.** (Chance as bestower of good or ill fortune, fortuitous events affecting one's interests, person's apparent tendency to be (un)fortunate, supposed tendency of chance to bring a succession of (un)favourable events, (*bad* ~ *to him* etc.!, form of imprecation; *as* ~ *would have it*, fortunately or unfortunately; *down on one's* ~, dispirited by misfortune, temporarily unfortunate; *try one's* ~, make a venture at gaming-table or in anything; *just my* ~, usu.=I am unlucky as usual; *worse* ~, parenth. more's the pity, unfortunately for me or us). **2.** Good fortune, success due to chance, (*have the* ~, be fortunate enough to; *for* ~, to bring good ~; *in, out of,* ~; *have no* ~), whence **~LESS** a., **~'lessness** n. **3.** ~-*money*, -*penny*, piece of money kept for ~, also sum returned by seller to buyer esp. in livestock sale. [f. LG *luk*, short for *geluk*. dub.]

luck'ily, adv. (As ordinary adv.) by luck (rare); (as qualification of sentence or clause) which is etc. a fortunate thing; thank goodness, (~ *for me I was wrong*; *on a snow-slope which was* ~ *in good order*).

luck'y¹, a. Constantly attended by good luck, enjoying it on a particular occasion, having as much success or happiness as one deserves & more, (*you're a* ~ *dog*, lover; ~ *beggar!*, ~ *bargee!*, of or to person in luck; right by luck, of the nature of a fluke, (~ *guess, hit, shot*); coming in the nick of time; presaging, bringing, worn etc, for, good luck, well-omened, (~ *penny, stone, day*); ~*bag*, -*tub*, at bazaars etc, containing articles of more or less value for one of which payer of small sum may dip. Hence **luck'iness** n. [-Y²]

luck'y², n. (Sl.), ~. Cut one's ~, decamp, make off. [?]

luc'rative (lōō-, lū-), a. Yielding gain, profitable. Hence **~LY²** adv.,**~NESS** n. [f. L *lucrativus* (*lucrari* to gain, see foll. -ATIVE)]

lucre (lōōk'er, lū-), n. Pecuniary profit as motive; FILTHY ~. [f. L *lucrum*, cogn. w. Gk *apolauō* enjoy, G *lohn* reward]

Lucretia (lōōkrēsh'a), n. Model of chastity, woman preferring honour to life. [see Livy I. 57-8]

luc'ubrate (lōō-, lū-), v.i. Express one's meditations in writing; produce lucubrations. Hence **~or²** n. [f. L *lucubrare* work by lamplight (*lux lucis* light). -ATE³]

lucubra'tion (lōō-, lū-), n. Nocturnal study or meditation; literary work esp. of pedantic or elaborate character. [f. L *lucubratio* (prec., -ATION)]

luc'ulent (lōō-, lū-), a. (rare). Clear, convincing, lucid, (~ *proof, instance, explanation*). Hence **~LY²** adv. [f. L *luculentus* (*lux lucis* light. -LENT)]

luc'us à non lucen'dō (lōō-, lū-), n. Paradoxical derivation; (transf.) reference of effect to paradoxical cause, explanation by contraries. [L,=*lucus* (grove) is derived from *lucere* (shine) because it does not shine there]

¶ **lūd.** *My* ~,=my lord in representations of counsel's pronunciation in addressing judge.

Lüd'dīte, n. & a. (Member) of band of mechanics (1811-16) who raised riots for destruction of machinery. [origin doubtful; leaders were called *Captain Ludd*]

lud'icrous (lōō-, lū-), a. Absurd, ridiculous, exciting or deserving derision. Hence **~LY²** adv., **~NESS** n., **lud'icro-** comb. form. [f. L *ludicrus* prob. f. *ludicrum* stage-play (*ludere* play)]

lüd'ō, (or lū-), n. Simple game played with dice & counters on special board. [L, = I play]

lues (lū'ēz), n. Plague, contagious disease, contagion, (~ *Boswelliana*, biographer's tendency to magnify his subject, see BOSWELL); (also ~ *venerea*) syphilis, whence (irreg.) **luET'IC** (lōōēt'-) a. [L, genit. *luis*]

luff, n. & v.i. & t. (naut.). **1.** Side of fore- & -aft sail next mast or stay; || broadest part of ship's bow where sides begin to curve in. **2.** vb. Bring ship's head, (helm) up so as to secure this; (Yacht-racing) get windward side of (opponent; ~*ing-match*, struggle for this). [prob. f.F *lof* of some contrivance for altering ship's course, cf. Du. *loef*]

Lufewaffe (lŏŏft'vahfe), n. German Air Force. [G]

lug¹, n. [perh. cogn. w. LOG¹]

lug², n. = LUG-SAIL.

lug³, v.t. & i. (-gg-), & n. 1. Drag or tug (heavy object) with effort or violence; (intr.) pull hard at; bring (subject etc.) irrelevantly in into; force (person) along. 2. n. Hard or rough pull. (cf. Sw. lugga pull person's hair (lugg forelock))

lug⁴, n. ||(Sc.) ear; (Mech.) projection from a casting etc. by which it may be fixed in place. [?]

Large marine worm used as bait. [?]

luge (lŏŏzh), n. Toboggan used in Switzerland. [Swiss dial. wd]

luggage, n. ||Traveller's baggage, portmanteaus, boxes, etc. [LUG³, -AGE]

lugger (-g-), n. Small ship with four-cornered sails set fore & aft. [prob. f. foll.]

lug'sail (-sl), n. Four-cornered sail bent on yard slung at a third or quarter of its length from one end. [?]

lugu'brious (loo-, lū-), a. Doleful, dismal, mournful. Hence ~LY² adv., ~NESS n. [f. L lugubris (lugēre mourn)]

lukewarm (look'worm, lū-), a. & n. Moderately warm, tepid; not zealous, indifferent. (n., ~ person). Hence ~NESS n., ~LY² adv. [f. obs. luke tepid, cf. obs. lew, & ON hlýr warm]

lull, v.t. & i. & n. 1. Soothe or send to sleep by sounds or caresses, quiet (suspicion etc.) usu. by deception; (of storm or noise) lessen, find quiet; hence ~ingLY² adv. 2. n. Intermission in storm lit. or fig., limit. of sounds used in lullaby]

lull'aby, n., & v.t. Soothing refrain or song to put child to sleep; (vb) sing to sleep. [prec., -by as in BYE-BYE]

lumbago, n. (pl. ~s). Rheumatic affection in loins. Hence **lumbaginous** a. [L lumbus loin]

lum'bar, a. & n. (Artery, vein, nerve, or vertebra) of or in loin. [prec., -AR¹]

lum'ber¹, v.i. Move in clumsy blundering noisy way (along, past, by, etc.). Hence ~ING² a., ~ingLY² adv., ~SOME a. [ME lomere perh. f. LAME]

lum'ber², n. & v.t. & i. 1. Disused articles of furniture etc. taking up room (~-room, in which such things are kept), useless or cumbrous material; superfluous fat; roughly prepared timber (~-carrier, boat in ~-trade; ~jack, ~man; ~-mill, conveyer of ~; ~man, feller, dresser, or measures of ~; ~-scaler, one who measures ~). 2. vb. Fill up inconveniently, obstruct, (room, place; often up, over); heap together, treat, as ~; cut & prepare forest timber, whence ~ER¹ n. [prob. f. prec.; or f. obs. lumber pawnbroker's shop (LOMBARD)]

lumbo-, comb. form of L lumbus loin, as ~-abdominal, combination of loins & abdomen.

lum'brical, a. & n. ~ muscle or ~, one of the muscles flexing fingers or toes. [f. L lumbricus earthworm, w. ref. to the shape]

Lumière (loom'iār), a. ~ process, a colour-photography method; so ~ plate. [Brothers ~, inventors]

lum'inary (loo-, lū-), n. Natural light-giving body, esp. sun or moon; person of intellectual, moral, or spiritual eminence, person of light & leading. [f. F luminaire f. med. L luminarium (L lumen -inis light, -ARY¹)]

lumin'iferous (loo-, lū-), a. Producing or transmitting light. [prec., -FEROUS]

lum'inous (loo-, lū-), a. Emitting or full of light, bright, shining, (~ paint, phosphorescent kind making thing conspicuous at night), whence **luminOS'ITY** n.; (of writers etc.) throwing light upon subject. Hence ~NESS n., ~LY² adv. [f. L luminosus (lumen -inis light, -OUS)]

lum'iné, int. (vulg.) of surprise or emphasis. [=(Lord) love me]

lump¹, n. & v.t. & i. 1. Compact shapeless or unshapely mass (~ in throat, feeling of pressure caused by emotion; is a ~ of selfishness, is selfish through & through); great quantity, lot, heap; mass of clay or dough ready for moulding or baking; protuberance, excrescence, swelling, bruise; heavy dull person; in the ~, taking things as a whole, in gross, wholesale; ~ sugar, loaf sugar broken or cut into ~s or cubes; ~ sum, covering number of items, also paid down at once (opp. instalments). 2. vb. Put together in one mass together, treat as all alike, disregard differences between or among, (together, with, in with, under title etc.; lay whole of (sum) on horse, event, etc.; rise or collect (intr.) into ~s; go heavily along, sit heavily down. [cf. Du. lomp rag]

lump², v.i. Uncouth spiny-thinned leaden-blue fish clinging tightly to objects by sucking-disk on belly. [cf. MLG lumpen, MDu. lompe; perh. f. prec., but the G & Du. forms are found earlier]

lump³, v.t. Be displeased at, put up with ungraciously, (now only in if you don't like it you may ~ it). [earlier=sulk; prob. imit.]

lump'er, n. Labourer employed in (un)loading cargoes; ||small contractor taking work in the lump & giving it out in the piece; classifier who avoids minute subdivision. [LUMP¹, -ER¹]

lump'ing, a. (colloq.). Big, plentiful, (~ weight, good weight). [LUMP¹, -ING²]

lump'ish, a. Heavy & clumsy; stupid, lethargic. Hence ~LY² adv., ~NESS n. [LUMP¹, -ISH¹]

lump'y, a. Full of or covered with lumps; (of water) cut up by wind into small waves. Hence ~ILY² adv., ~INESS n. [-Y²]

lun'acy (loo-, lū-), n. Being a lunatic, (formerly of the intermittent kind attributed to changes of moon). [Law]

such mental unsoundness as interferes with civil rights or transactions || (*Commission of* ~, authorization of inquiry into person's sanity; *Commissioner in* ~, member of board of ten for inspecting asylums etc.; *Master in* ~, officer investigating cases of alleged ~); great folly. [LUNATIO, -ACY]

lun'ar (lōō-, lū-), a. & n. **1.** Of, in, as of, the moon (~ CYCLE; ~ *distance*, of moon from sun, planet, or star, used in finding longitude at sea; ~ *month*, interval between new moons, about 29½ days, (pop.) period of four weeks; ~ *nodes*, at which moon's orbit cuts ecliptic; ~ *observation*, finding of longitude by ~ *distance*; ~ *politics*, unpractical questions; ~ *rainbow*, made by moon's rays; (of light, glory, etc.) pale, feeble; crescent-shaped, lunate, (esp. ~ *bone* in wrist); of or containing silver (from alchemists' use of *luna* moon for silver; ~ *caustic*, nitrate of silver fused). **2.** n. ~ distance or observation; ~ bone. [f. L *lunaris* (*luna* moon, -AR¹)]

lunar'ian (lōō-, lū-), n. Inhabitant of moon; astronomer or navigator with special knowledge of the moon. [prec., -IAN]

lun'āte (lōō-, lū-), a. (nat. hist.). Crescent-shaped. [f. L *lunatus* (*luna* moon, -ATE²)]

lun'atic (lōō-, lū-), a. & n. Insane (person; see LUNACY), mad(man); (of actions etc.) outrageously foolish, frantic, mad; eccentric, foolish, (person; ~ *asylum*, hospital for reception & treatment of ~s. [f. LL *lunaticus* (*luna* moon, -ATIC)]

luna'tion (lōō-, lū-), n. Time from one new moon to next. [f. med. L *lunatio* (prec., -ATION)]

lunch, n., & v.i. & t., **lun'cheon** (-ohn), n., (-ch now usu. exc. in formal or ceremonious use), **1.** (With late diners) midday meal; (with midday diners) light refreshment taken between breakfast & dinner. **2.** vb (-ch). Take ~; provide ~ for. [etym. & relation between forms, doubtful; both had earlier sense *lump* (of bread, meat, etc.), & *lunch* may be related to it as *hunch*, *bunch*, to *hump*, *bump*]

lune (lōōn, lūn), n. (geom.). Figure formed on sphere or plane by two arcs enclosing space. [F, f. L *luna* moon]

lunette' (lōō-, lū-), n. Arched aperture in concave ceiling to admit light; crescent-shaped or semicircular space in dome or ceiling decorated with painting etc.; (Fortif.) work larger than redan, with two faces & two flanks; watch-glass of flattened shape; hole for neck in guillotine. [F (prec., -ETTE)]

lung, n. Either of the pair of breathing-organs in man & most vertebrates (*good* ~s, strong voice); IRON¹~; ~s *of London* etc., open spaces in or close to great city; ~s *of oak*, ~wort; ~-*fish*, having ~s as well as gills; ~-*power*, power of voice; ~-*wort*, plant of borage kind with white-

spotted leaves likened to diseased ~, (|| also ~s *of oak*) kind of lichen supposed to be good for ~-disease. Hence ~-ED² (-gd), ~'LESS, aa. [OE *lungen*, cf. Du. *long*, G *lunge*, cogn. w. Gk *elaphros* LIGHT⁴ (named from lightness of substance), & see LIGHTS]

lunge¹ (-j), **lounge** (-ounj), n. & v.t. **1.** Long rope with which horse-breaker holds horse while he makes it canter in circle; circular exercise-ground for training horses. **2.** v.t. Exercise (horse) with or in ~. [F *longe* halter (L *longus* long)]

lunge² (-j), n., & v.i. & t. **1.** Thrust with sword etc. esp. in fencing; sudden forward movement, plunge, rush. **2.** vb. Make ~ in fencing, deliver blow from shoulder in boxing, (*at*, *out*); (of horse) kick *out*; drive (weapon, sting, etc.) violently in some direction; rush, make sudden start in some direction. [f. earlier *allonge*, F, f. *allonger* lengthen (*à* to, L *longus* long)]

lunisōl'ar (lōō-, lū-), a. Of sun & moon (~ *period*, of 532 years between agreements of solar & lunar cycles; ~ *year*, with divisions regulated by changes of moon, & average length made to agree with sun's revolution). [f. L *sol* sun, -AR¹]

lunk'ah (-a), n. Kind of strong Indian cheroot. [f. Hind. *lanka* islands (of delta where the tobacco is grown)]

luny. See LOONY.

lup'in(e¹) (lōō-, lū-), n. Kinds of garden & fodder plant with long tapering spikes of blue, purple, white, or yellow flowers; (usu. pl.) seed of these. [f. L *lupinus*]

lup'ine² (lōō-, lū-), a. Of wolf or wolves, wolf-like. [f. L *lupinus* (*lupus* wolf, -INE²)]

lup'us (lōō-, lū-), n. Ulcerous disease of skin. Hence ~OID, ~OUS, aa. [L, =wolf]

lurch¹, n. *Leave in the* ~, desert (friend, ally) in difficulties. [formerly=state of score in some games in which winner was far ahead of loser, f. F *lourche* game like backgammon, also bad defeat in this]

lurch², n., & v.i. **1.** Sudden lean to one side, stagger. **2.** v.i. Make ~(es), stagger. [?]

lurch'er, n. Petty thief, swindler; spy; || cross-bred dog between collie or sheep-dog & greyhound, used esp. by poachers. [f. obs. *lurch* vb var. of LURK]

lūre, n., & v.t. **1.** Falconer's apparatus for recalling hawk (bunch of feathers, within which it finds its food while being trained, attached to thong); something used to entice; enticing quality of a pursuit etc. **2.** v.t. Recall (hawk) with ~; entice (person, animal; usu. *away* or *into*). [f. OF *leurre*, cf. It. *logoro* bait, prob. f. Teut. (G *luder* bait)]

lūr'id, a. Ghastly, wan, glaring, unnatural, stormy, terrible, in colour or combination of colours or lights (of complexion, landscape, sky, lightning, thunder-clouds,

smoky flame, glance, etc.; *casts a ~ light on* facts or character, explains or reveals them in a tragic or terrible way).(Bot. etc.) of dingy yellowish brown. Hence ~IY² adv. ~NESS n. [f. L *luridus* pale-yellow]

lirk, v.i. & n. Be hidden *in*, *under*, *about*, etc.; escape notice, exist unobserved, be latent; (n.) *on the ~*, spying; ~*ing-place*, hiding-place. [perh. cogn. w. LOUR; cf. LG *lurken* shuffle along, Norw. *lurka* loiter in work]

lus'cious (-shus), a. Richly sweet, cloying; (of taste or smell) sickly sweet, cloying; (of language or literary style) over-rich in sound, imagery, or voluptuous suggestion. Hence ~IY² adv., ~NESS n. [ME *lucious*, perh. = DELICIOUS]

lush¹ n. & a. Luxuriant & succulent (of plants, esp. grass). [?]

lush² n. & v.t. & i. (sl.). 1. Liquor, drink. 2. v.t. Ply with liquor; drink. [?]

lust, n., & v.i. 1. (Bibl., Theol.) sensuous appetite regarded as sinful; animal desire for sexual indulgence, lascivious passion, whence ~FUL a.; passionate enjoyment or desire of (~ *of battle*, *conquest*, *accumulation*, *applause*). 2. v.i. Have strong or excessive desire (*usu. after* or *for*). [com.-Teut.: so Du. & G]

lus'tral, a. Of, used in, ceremonial purification. [f. L *lustralis* (LUSTRUM, -AL)]

lus'trate, v.t. Purify by expiatory sacrifice, ceremonial washing, or other such rite. So ~A'TION n. [f. L *lustrare* (LUSTRUM, -ATE³)]

lus'tre (-ter), n. & v.t. 1. Gloss, refulgence, shining surface, brilliance, bright light, radiant beauty, whence ~LESS (-terl-).] **lus'trous**, aa., **lus'trously²** adv.; splendour, glory, distinction, (*add ~ to*, *throw* or *shed ~ on*). 2. (Prismatic glass pendant of) chandelier. 3. Thin dress-material with cotton warp, woollen woof, & lustrous surface; kind of wool with lustrous surface. 4. v.t. Put ~ on (cloth, pottery, etc.). [F (L *lustrare* illumine, prob. f. *lux lucis* light)]

lus'tre² (-ter), n. = LUSTRUM.

lus'trine, **lus'tring**, nn. Glossy silk fabric. [LUSTRE¹]

lus'trum, n. (pl. ~*a*, ~*ums*). Period of five years. [L, orig. purificatory sacrifice after quinquennial census, prob. f. *luere* wash]

lus'ty, a. Healthy & strong; vigorous, lively. Hence ~HOOD, ~NESS, nn., ~IY² adv. [-Y¹]

lu'sus natūr'ae (lōō-, lū-), n. Freak of nature, strikingly abnormal natural production, sport. [L]

lu'tanist (lōō-, lū-), n. Lute-player. [f. med. L *lutanista* (*utana* LUTE¹, -IST)]

lute¹ (lōōt, lūt), n. Guitar-like stringed instrument (RIFT *within the ~*). [f. F *luth* f. Arab. *al'ud* (al the, *ud*, lute, orig. wood)]

---

lute² (lōōt, lūt), n., & v.t. 1. Clay or cement used to stop hole, make joint airtight, coat crucible, protect graft, etc. 2. v.t. Apply ~ to. Hence **lu'ting** (³) n. [f. OF *lut* f. L *lutum* mud]

lute'string (lōōts-, lūts-), n. Glossy silk fabric. [perh. assim. of *lustring* var. of *lustrine* to *lute*, *string*]

lu'teous (lōō-, lū-), a. (nat. hist.). Of deep orange yellow. [prec., -OUS]

lu'teo- (lōō-, lū-), comb. form of L *luteus* orange-coloured (*lutum* weld), as ~*ful'vous* orange-tawny, ~*ful'vous* orange-yellow.

Lutetian (lōōtē'shn, lū-), a. Parisian. [f. L *Lutetia* ancient name of Paris, -AN]

Lu'theran (lōō-, lū-), a. & n. (Follower) of Martin Luther, (member) of Church accepting the Augsburg confession. Hence ~ISM(3) n., ~IZE(2) v.i., (3) v.t. [-AN]

luxe (lōōks, lūks), n. Disloca(te)d. Hence ~A'TION n. [f. L *luxare* dislocate f. Gk *loxos*, -ATE³]

luxe (lōōks), n. *De* ~, of unusual sumptuousness (*édition de* ~) or comfort (*train de* ~), see Ap. [F]

luxur'iant, a. Prolific (lit. & of imagination etc.); profuse of growth, exuberant, rank; (of literary or artistic style) florid, richly ornamented. Hence ~ANCE n., ~*antly²* adv. [f. L *luxuriare* grow rank (*luxuria* LUXURY), -ANT]

luxur'iate, v.i. Revel, enjoy oneself, *in* or *on*; take one's ease, be luxurious. [prec., -ATE³]

luxur'ious, a. Given, contributing, to luxury, self-indulgent, voluptuous, very comfortable. Hence ~IY² adv., ~NESS n. [f. OF *luxurious* f. L *luxuriosus*(foll., -OUS)]

lux'ury (-ksheri), n. (Habitual use of) choice or costly food, dress, furniture, etc.; thing that one enjoys; thing desirable but not indispensable; luxurious-ness. [f. OF *luxurie* f. L *luxuria* (*luxus* abundance)]

-ly¹, suf. f. OE *-lic*, cf. OHG *-lih*, G *-lich*, f. OTeut. *-liko-* (*likom* form). The suf. forms adjj. f. nn. w. sense *having the qualities of* (*kindly*, *scholarly*, *soldierly*).

-ly², suf. forming advv., f. OE *-lice* (prec.)+adv. suf. *-e*. In OTeut. an adv. in *-ly* implies the existence of an adj. in *-ly*¹; but even in OE the suf. (in the form *-lice*) was added to other adjj., & later became the usu. ending for adv. Down to 17th c. adv. *-ly* was added even to adjj. in *-ly*, the orig. *-lic̄ó* being thus doubly represented; these advv. in *-lily* are now avoided as awkward, & as the adv. use of the adj. (*to live godly*) is also avoided, adjj. in *-ly* have in ordinary use no corr. adv. *Partly* is a solitary formation on n. Wds in *-le* have *-ly* for *-lely* (*feebly*, *supply*, not *feebely*, *supplely*).

lycan'thropy, n. Transformation of witch into a wolf; form of madness in which

patient imagines himself some beast & exhibits depraved appetites, change of voice, etc. [f. Gk *lukanthrōpia* (*lukos* wolf, *anthrōpos* man, -Y²)]

lycée (lēsʹā), n. State secondary school in France. [F]

Lycēʹum, n. Garden at Athens in which Aristotle taught, his philosophy & followers (usu. ACADEMY, GARDEN, PORCH); literary institution, lecture-hall, teaching-place. [L, f. Gk *Lukeion* neut. of *Lukeios* epithet of Apollo (from whose neighbouring temple the ~ was named)]

lych. See LICH.

lychʹnis (-k-), n. Genus of plants including Campion & Ragged Robin. [L, f. Gk *lukhnis* red flower (*lukhnos* lamp)]

lycʹopōd, -pōdʹium, n. Clubmoss; (·*ium* only) fine powder from kind of ~ used as absorbent in surgery, & in making stage-lightning. [-d anglicized f. -*ium* mod. L (Gk *lukos* wolf, *pous podos* foot)]

lyddʹite, n. High explosive chiefly of picric acid used in shells. [*Lydd* in Kent, -ITE¹]

Lydʹian, a. & n. (Language, inhabitant) of Lydia, ancient division of Asia Minor; ~ **mode**: ancient Greek MODE, reputedly effeminate in character; fifth of eccl. modes, with F as final & C as dominant. [f. L f. Gk *Ludios*, -AN]

lye, n. Water alkalized by lixiviation of vegetable ashes, any strong alkaline solution esp. for washing, any detergent. [OE *lēag* cf. Du. *loog*, G *lauge*, prob. cogn. w. LATHER]

lȳʹing¹, n. In vbl senses of LIE²,³; also: place to lie (*soft, dry,* ~); ~ *in*, being in childbirth (also *attrib.*, as ~*in hospital*). [-ING¹]

lȳʹing², a. In vbl senses of LIE²,³; esp.: deceitful, false; whence ~lȳ² *adv.*; ~ placed, as *low—land.* [-ING²]

‖ **lȳkeʹ-wāke**, n. Watch kept at night over dead body. [LICH, WAKE²]

lyme-ʹgrass (-ahs), n. Kind of grass planted on sand to keep it from shifting. [perh. f. LIME¹ w. ref. to its binding effect]

lymph, n. Pure water (poet.); (Physiol.) colourless alkaline fluid from tissues or organs of body, like blood but without red corpuscles; exudation from sore etc., (also *vaccine* ~) matter taken from cowpox vesicles & used in vaccination, other morbid matter used for similar purposes. Hence ~**ous** a. [f. L *lympha* water prob. cogn. w. LIMPIDUS]

lymphatʹic, a. & n. **1.** Of, secreting, conveying, lymph, (~ *gland, vessel*; ~ *system*, these glands & vessels); (of persons or temperament) flabby-muscled, pale-skinned, sluggish, (qualities formerly attributed to excess of lymph). **2.** n. Veinlike vessel conveying lymph. [f. L *lymphaticus* mad (*lympha* see prec.; the L sense perh. due to supposed connexion

w. Gk *numphē* nymph, which affected spelling of *lympha*) as though = of water]

lynceʹan, a. Lynx-eyed, keen-sighted. [f. L f. Gk *lugkeios* (*lugx* lynx), -AN; often also w. ref. to *Lynceus* the keen-sighted Argonaut]

lynch, n., & v.t. **1.** ~ (or L~) *law*, procedure of self-constituted illegal court that summarily executes person charged with flagrant offence: *Judge L~*, imaginary authority to whom sentences are attributed. **2.** v.t. Execute (person) thus. [orig. U.S., earlier *Lynch's law,* doubtfully referred to Charles L~, J.P. in Virginia, indemnified 1782 for illegally punishing persons]

lynx, n. Kinds of animal of the cat tribe with tufted ear-tips, short tail, spotted fur, & proverbially keen sight; ~ *fur*; ~*eyed,* sharp-sighted. [L, f. Gk *lugx*, cf. G *luchs,* prob. cogn. w. Gk *leussō* see]

Lȳʹon, n. (Also ~ *King of Arms*) chief herald of Scotland. [arch. for *lion*; named f. lion on royal shield]

Lȳʹra, n. Northern constellation. [L, f. Gk *lura* LYRE]

Lȳrʹaid, Lȳrʹid, n. (usu. pl.). Meteor(s) radiating from Lyra about 20 Apr. [-ID²] [-ATE²]

lȳrʹate, a. (nat. hist.). Lyre-shaped. [-ATE²]

lyre (līr), n. Obsolete instrument of harp kind but of size fit for holding up in left hand, & with strings supported by two symmetrically curved horns, chiefly used for accompanying voice; ~*bird,* Australian bird with ~-shaped tail. So **lȳrʹ·ist**(3) n. [f. L f. Gk *lura*]

lȳrʹic, a. & n. **1.** Of or for the lyre, meant to be sung; of the nature of, expressed or fit to be expressed in, song (~ *drama, the* ~ *stage, opera*); (of poet) expressing writer's own thoughts & sentiments usu. at no great length & in stanzas or strophes, (of poet) writing in this manner. **2.** n. ~ poem, (pl.) ~ verses. Hence ~**o-** comb. form. [f. L f. Gk *lurikos* (prec., -IC)]

lȳrʹical, a. = prec. (now rare); resembling, couched in or using language appropriate to, lyric poetry. Hence ~lȳ² *adv.* [-AL]

lȳʹricism, n. Lyric character or (w. pl.) expression; high-flown sentiments. [-ISM]

lȳsʹol, n. Saponified mixture of cresol (see CREOSOTE) & oil, soluble in water, used as disinfectant. [P; f. Gk *lusis* (*luō* loosen) +-OL]

M

M, m, (ĕm), letter (pl. *Ms, M's*). (As numeral) 1,000, as MMCI 2,101, MCMLI 1,951; (Print., m), = EM.

-m, -ma, -me, suf. in nn. taken f. Gk (-*ma -matos*), usu. expr. result of verbal action; as *phlegm, poem, comma, coma, scheme, theme.* Adj. formed on these

na. (rŭlg.), *=* MAMMA[1].

ma'am (mahm, mäm, m'm), n. Madam (esp. used at Court in addressing Queen or royal princess, pr. mäm, or by servants, pr. m'm).

ma'bre (-ahbr), a. *Danse* ~, dance of death; grim, gruesome. [F, perh. corrupt. of OF *Macabé* Maccabee.]

maca·cō[2], n. Monkey of genus Macacus. [Port.]

macā'cŏ[1], n. Kinds of lemur. [?]

macad'am, a. & n. 1. (Of roads) made in the manner & with the materials advocated by J. L. McAdam (d. 1836), i.e. with successive layers of broken stone of nearly uniform size, each subjected to pressure before next is laid. 2. n. Such material. Hence ~IZE v.t., ~IZA'TION n.

mácarō'ni[1], n. 1. Wheaten paste formed into long tubes, used as food; ~i cheese, savoury pudding of ~i & cheese baked. 2. (hist.), 18th-c. exquisite affecting continental tastes, whence ~ISM n. [It. *maccaroni*, etym. dub.]

mácarŏn'ic, a. & n. pl. (Verses) of burlesque form containing Latin (or other foreign) words & vernacular words with Latin etc. terminations; medley. [f. prec., +-IC]

mácaroon', n. Small cake or biscuit of ground almonds, white of egg, sugar, etc. [F *macaron* (as MACARONI)]

macăr'ney, n. Kind of pheasant. [George, Earl M~, d. 1806]

macăss'ar, n. & n. ~ (*oil*), kind of hair oil. [f. *Mangkasara*, n island of Celebes]

macaw'[1], n. Kinds of parrot. [f. Port. *macao*, etym. dub.]

macaw'[2], n. Kinds of palm. [prob. Carib]

Maccabē'an, a. Of the *Maccabees*, Jewish princes who freed Judæa from tyranny of Antiochus Epiphanes, c. 166 B.C. [f. L, f. Gk *Makkabaios*]

macc'aboy, -baw, n. Kind of snuff, usu. scented with attar of roses. [f. *Macouba*, district in Martinique]

māce'[1], n. (Hist.) heavy usu. metal-headed & spiked club; staff of office resembling this; ~-*bearer*, official carrying this staff; stick used in bagatelle. [OF, f. L *mattea* whence *matteola* (prob.)=mallet]

māce'[2], n. Dried outer covering of nutmeg, as spice. [f. F *macis*, etym. dub.]

năc'edoine (-edwahn), n. Fruit or vegetables in jelly as a dish or as cook's material. [F]

mă'cerāte, v.t. & i. Soften by soaking; waste away by fasting. So ~A'TION n. [f. L *macerare*, cogn. w. Gk *massō* knead, see -ATE[3]]

măchan' (-ahn), n. (Anglo-Ind.), Elevated platform used in tiger-shooting etc. [Hind.]

machete (-ăt'ă), n. See MATCHET.

Măchiavĕll'i (-ki-), n. Unscrupulous schemer; one who practises duplicity in statecraft, whence ~IAN a., ~ISM n. [f. Niccolò *Machiavelli*, Florentine states-man, author of work *del Principe*, in which unscrupulous statecraft is advocated]

machicŏllāte, v.t. Furnish (parapet etc.) with openings between supporting corbels for dropping stones etc. on assailants. Hence ~A'TION n. [f. med. L *machicollare*, conn. w. foll.]

machicoulis (mahshikoo'i), n. Machicolation. [f. F *machicoulis*]

măch'inate (-k-), v.t. Lay plots, intrigue. So ~A'TION, ~ātor[2] nn. [f. L *machinari*]

machine' (-shēn), n., & v.t. & i. 1. Apparatus for applying mechanical power, having several parts each with definite function (the kind often being specified, as *sewing*, *printing*, ~); bicycle, tricycle; mechanically & without intelligence, or with unfailing regularity; (Mech.) instrument that transmits force or directs its application, as *simple* ~, one without organization (esp. in U.S.); ~-*gun*, mounted gun mechanically loaded & fired, delivering continuous fire, (v.t.) shoot at with ~-gun; ~-*made*, made by ~; ~-*tool*, tool worked by machinery, not by hand. 2. vb. Make or operate on with ~ (esp. of sewing & printing); use ~. [F, f. L *machina* f. Gk *mēkhanē* f. *mēkhos*]

machi'nery (-shē-), n. Machines; work of a machine, mechanism; contrivances, esp. supernatural persons & incidents, used in literary work. [f. prec. + -ERY]

machi'nist (-shē-), n. One who makes or controls machinery; one who works (esp. sewing-) machine. [f. prec. + -IST]

machom'ēter (-k-), n. Instrument giving air speed as a fraction of the local speed of sound in air. [f. *Mach* inventor, -O-, -METER]

măć(k), n. (colloq.) Mackintosh. [abbr.]

măck'erel, n. Sea-fish used as food & approaching shore in shoals in summer to spawn; ~ *breeze*, *gale* (strong, & so favourable to ~-catching); ~ *sky* (dappled with small white fleecy clouds). [f. OF *maquerel*, etym. dub.]

măć(k)'intosh, n. Waterproof material of rubber & cloth for garments, esp. that patented by C. Macintosh (d. 1843); cloak, coat, of this.

mā'cle, n. Twin crystal; dark spot in mineral. [F, f. MACULA]

Mâcon (mahkawn'), n. Wine produced in the neighbourhood of ~ in France. [place]

‖ **măcon'ochie** (-ki), n. Tinned stew as part of army rations. [M~, maker]

măcra'mé (-rahm), n. Fringe, trimming, of knotted thread or cord. [prob. f. Turk. *magrama* towel]

măc'ro- in comb. = Gk makros long, large, as: ~cephal'ic, long, large, -headed; ~cosm, the great world, the universe, (cf. MICROCOSM), any great whole; ~meter (-ŏmĕ-), instrument for measuring distant objects; ~scop'ic, visible to naked eye.

măc'rŏn, n. Mark placed over vowel (ā) to show that it is long. [Gk, neut. adj. as prec.]

măc'ŭla, n. (pl. ~æ). Dark spot in sun; spot in mineral; spot, esp. permanent one, in skin, whence ~AR¹ a., ~A'TION n. [L macula]

măd', a. (-dd-). Out of one's mind, insane; (of person or conduct) wildly foolish; ~, furiously, violently, as I ran like like ~; wildly excited, infatuated, (after, about, for, on, thing, subject, etc.); (colloq.) annoyed, as I was rather ~ at missing my train; (of animals) rabid; (prov.) ~ as a March HARE, as a hatter; extravagant, wild, in gaiety; ~cap, wildly impulsive person; ~-doctor (treating the ~); ~house, lunatic asylum; ~'man, ~'woman, ~ person; ~ minute (army sl.), rapid fire in class-firing. Hence ~'LY² adv., ~NESS n. [OE gemǣd(e)d, p.p. of gemǣdan make mad (gemǣd mad, cf. OS gimēd foolish, OHG gameit, & L mūtare change)]

măd², v.t. & i. (-dd-: rare). Make mad; be mad, act madly, as the ~ding crowd (as quot. from Gray's Elegy, now often taken as =distracting). [f. prec.]

măd'am, n. Polite formal address to woman. [f. OF ma DAME my lady]

madame (mădahm', mă'dăm; pl. mesdames pr. mādahm'). F form of prec. as title or form of address: M~ Tussaud's (tōōsōz'), show in London of waxwork figures of celebrated & notorious persons (often w. ref. to the chamber of HORRORS in it). [as prec.]

mădapŏl'am, n. A cotton cloth, orig. of Indian make. [f. M~ in Madras]

mădd'en, v.t. & i. Make, become, mad; irritate. Hence ~ingly¹ adv. [f. MAD¹+ -EN⁶]

mădd'er, n. Herbaceous climbing plant with yellowish flowers; dye got from this. [OE mǣdere, cf. Sw. madra, Norw. modra]

māde, a. P.p. of MAKE. Special uses:- ~ dish (of several ingredients); ~ gravy (artificially compounded); a ~ man, one whose success in life is assured; (of person etc.) well, stoutly, loosely, powerfully, ~ (built, formed).

Madeir'a (-ēra), n. Island in Atlantic Ocean; white wine there produced; ~ cake, kind of sponge-cake. [Port., f. L materia MATTER, timber from its thick woods]

mademoiselle (mădmwazĕl', & see Ap.), n. (pl. mesdemoiselles, pr. mādmwazĕl'). Unmarried Frenchwoman; French governess. [F]

măd'ia, n. Plant allied to Sunflower; ~ oil (got from its seed, & made into cake for cattle). [f. Chil. madi]

mădŏn'a, n. (Picture, statue, of) Virgin Mary; ~ lily (white, as in pictures of M~). [It. (ma=mia my +donna lady f. L domina)]

mădrăs'ah (-ă), **mădrăss'eh** (-ĕ), n. Mohammedan college. [Arab. (-sah) t. darasa v. study]

măd'rĭpŏre, n. Genus of perforate corals; animal producing these. Hence ~pŏr'ic, ~pŏr'IFORM, aa. [f. It. madrepora (madre mother + poro, coral-like but porous substance)]

măd'rĭgal, n. Short amatory poem; part-song for several voices, prop. with elaborate contrapuntal imitation & without instrumental accompaniment. Hence ~al'IAN a. [f. It. madrigale, etym. dub.]

maduro (mahdoor'ō), a. (Of cigars) full-flavoured. [Sp., = matured]

Maecēnas, n. Generous patron of literature or art. [~, patron of Horace & Virgil]

mael'strom (māl-), n. Whirlpool (lit. & fig.). [Du. (malen grind + stroom stream)]

maen'ad, n. Bacchante. [f. L f. Gk mainas -ados f. mainomai rave]

maestōs'ō (mah-), adv. (mus.). Majestically. [It.]

maes'trō (mah-), n. (pl. -rī, pr. -ē). Great musical composer, teacher, or conductor. [It.]

Mae' West (mā), n. (sl.), Airman's life-jacket. [person]

măff'ick, v.i. Exult riotously. [back formation f. Mafeking (relief of which in 1900 was celebrated extravagantly in London etc.), treated as gerund]

mafi'a (mahfē'a), n. Hostility to law & its ministers among Sicilian population, often shown in crimes; those who share in this. [Sicil.]

‖ măg¹, n. (sl.). Halfpenny. [?]

măg², n. (Short for) MAGNETO (esp. in comb., as ~-generator).

măga'zine (-zēn), n. 1. Store for arms, ammunition, & provisions, in time of war; store for gunpowder or other explosives; ~ gun (with chamber containing supply of cartridges fed automatically to the breech). 2. Periodical publication containing articles by various writers. [f. F magasin f. Arab. makhazin pl. of makhzan storehouse (khazana store up)]

Măg'dalen, **-lene**, n. Reformed prostitute. [Mary Magdalene of Magdala (Luke viii. 2) identified with the sinner of Luke vii. 37. Magdalen College, Oxford, & Magdalene College, Cambridge, are pr. mawd'lin]

Măgdalēn'ian, a. (archaeol.). Of the (latest) palaeolithic period represented by remains found at La Madeleine, Dordogne, France. [-IAN]

māge, n. (arch.). Magician; learned person. [f. MAGUS]

magěn'ta, n. & a. 1. Brilliant crimson aniline dye, discovered soon after battle at

M~ in N. Italy (1869). **2.** adj. Coloured with or like ~.

maggot, n. Larva, esp. of cheese-fly & bluebottle; red~, larva of wheat-midge; whimsical fancy, esp. ~ *in one's head*. Hence ~Y² a. [prob. conn. w. ME *madhek* in same sense]

Ma'gi. See MAGUS.

Ma'gian, a. & n. (One) of the Magi; magician. Hence ~ISM(3) n. [-IAN]

má'gic, a. & n. (Of the pretended art of influencing course of events by occult control of nature or of spirits; witchcraft; *black, white, natural,* ~ (involving invocation of devils, angels, no personal spirit); inexplicable or remarkable influence producing surprising results; ~ *square*, one divided into smaller squares containing each a number, so arranged that sum of a row, vertical, horizontal, or diagonal, is always same; ~ *lantern*, optical instrument throwing magnified image of glass picture on white screen in dark room; ~ *mirror* (in which future or distant scenes are presented to spectator). Hence~ALLa.,~ALLY²adv. [f. F *magique* a. & n. f. L f. Gk *magikos* (as MAGUS, see -IC)]

magi'cian (-shn), n. One skilled in magic, wizard. [f. F *magicien*(as prec., see -ICIAN)]

magilp'. See MEGILP.

Maginot line (mah'zhēnō), n. French fortified line on Franco-German frontier. [person]

magiste'rial, a. Of, conducted by, a magistrate; invested with authority; dictatorial; (of opinions) authoritative. Hence ~LY² adv. [f. med. L *magisterialis* f. LL *magisterius* (as MASTER)]

ma'gistral, a. Of a master or masters, as *the* ~ *staff* (of a school); (Pharm., of particular case, not included in the pharmacopoeia (cf. OFFICINAL). [f. L *magistralis* (as MASTER, see -AL)]

ma'gistrate, n. Civil officer administering law; JUSTICE of the peace. Hence or cogn. ~ACY, ~ateship, ~ature, nn. [f. L *magistratus -ūs* (orig. office of) magistrate (as prec., see -ATE¹)]

Māglemō'sian (-z-), a. Of the early European culture illustrated by articles found at Maglemose in Denmark. [-IAN]

mág'ma, n. (pl. ~ta, ~s). Crude pasty mixture of mineral or organic matters; one of supposed fluid strata under solid crust of earth. [f. Gk (*massō* knead, root *mag-*, see -M)]

Mag'na Chārt'a (k-), n. Great charter of English personal & political liberty obtained from John in 1215. [med. L]

magná'nium, n. Light tough alloy of aluminium & magnesium. [MAGN(ESIUM) +AL(UMINIUM)+IUM]

magnán'imous, a. High-souled, above petty feelings. Hence or cogn. **magna'ni-**nim'ITY n. ~LY² adv. [f. L *magnanimus* (*magnus* great+*animus* soul)+-OUS]

mág'nate, n. Great man; wealthy or eminent man. [f. LL *magnas -ātis* (*mag-nus* great)]

magné'sia (-sha), n. Oxide of magne-sium; (pop.) hydrated magnesium car-bonate, white powder used as antacid & cathartic. Hence ~AN (-shn) a. [med. L f. Gk *magnēsia* (*lithos* stone) of Mag-nesia, (1) loadstone, (2) perh. talc]

magné'sium (or -zhyum), n. Metallic element, present in magnesia; ~ *light*, blinding light got by burning ~ wire. [f. prec., see -IUM]

mág'net, n. Piece of iron or ore having the properties of attracting iron & of pointing north & south when suspended; natural (as in loadstone) or induced by contact with a ~, by induction, or by electric current; *horse-shoe* ~ (in shape of bar bent till ends nearly meet); = LOAD)*stone*; (fig.) thing that attracts. [f. L f. Gk *Magnēs -ētos* (*lithos* stone) of Magnesia]

magné'tic, a. & n. **1.** Having properties of magnet; producing, produced by, act-ing by, magnetism; ~ *equator*, ACLINO line; ~ *mine*, submarine mine detonated by approach of large mass of ~ material, e.g. ship; ~ NEEDLE, NORTH; capable of receiving properties of, or being attracted by, loadstone; (fig.) very attractive; mesmeric. **2.** n. pl. Science of magnetism. Hence **magnét'**ICALLY adv. [-IC]

magnet'ite, n. Magnetic iron oxide. [-ITE]

mág'netize, v.t. Give magnetic proper-ties to; attract (lit. & fig.) as magnet does; mesmerize. Hence~ATION n. [-IZE]

magnēt'ō, n. (pl. ~s). An electric genera-tor using magnets which are independent of the current produced (esp. type of igniting-apparatus of internal-combus-tion engines producing the required intermittent high-tension current inde-pendently of a battery). [abbr. of *magneto-electric*]

magnēt'o-, in comb. = magnetic, as: ~*-electric*, (of electric generators) using magnets which are independent of the current produced, so ~*-electricity*; ~*-graph*, instrument recording movements of ~*meter* (-ōm?) (instrument measuring of magnetic forces, esp. terrestrial magne-tism).

magni'fic(al), aa. (arch.) Magnificent, sublime. [f. F *magnifique* f. L *magnificus* (*magnus* great, see -FIC) +-AL]

magni'ficat, n. Hymn of Virgin Mary in *Luke* i. 46-55, used as canticle, & begin-ning thus. [L, 3rd sing. of *magnificare* MAGNIFY]

măgnĭf′ĭcent, a. Splendid, stately; sumptuously constructed or adorned; splendidly lavish; (colloq.) fine, excellent. Hence or cogn. ~ENCE n., ~ENTLY adv. [OF, f. L *magnĭficent-* stem seen in comp. & sup of *magnĭficus* MAGNIFIC]

măgnĭf′ĭcō, n. (pl. ~es). Venetian magnate; grandee. [It., as MAGNIFIC]

măg′nĭfy, v.t. Increase apparent size of (thing), as with lens or microscope; exaggerate; (rare) increase; (arch.) extol. Hence or cogn. ~FICA′TION, ~FIER¹(2), nn. [f. L *magnĭficare* (*magnus* great, see -FY)]

măgnĭl′oquent, a. Lofty in expression; boastful. Hence ~ENCE n., ~ENTLY² adv. [f. L *magnĭloquus* (*magnus* great +-*loquus* -speaking) +-ENT]

măg′nĭtūde, n. Largeness; size; importance; *first, seventh, etc.,* ~, classes or fixed stars arranged according to degree of brilliancy, (fig.) *of the first* ~ (importance). [f. L *magnitūdo* (*magnus* great, see -TUDE)]

măgnōl′ia, n. Genus of trees or shrubs cultivated for foliage & flower. [f. P. *Magnol,* botanist (d. 1715)]

măg′num, n. (Bottle containing) two quarts (of wine or spirits). [L, neut. of *magnus* great]

măg′num bŏn′um, n. Large yellow cooking plum; kind of potato. [L wds= large good]

magnum opus. See OPUS.

măg′pie, n. 1. European bird with long pointed tail & black-&-white plumage; idle chatterer; variety of pigeon. 2. (Rifle shot that strikes) outermost division but one of target. [f. *mag* abbr. of *Margaret* +PIE¹]

măg′us, n. (pl. -*gī,* pr. -jī). Member of ancient Persian priestly caste; sorcerer; *the (three) Magi,* the 'wise men' from the East who brought offerings to the infant Christ. [L, f. Gk *magos* f. OPers. *magus*]

Magyar, n. & a. 1. (mŏd′yar). (Member, language) of the Mongoloid race now predominant in Hungary. 2. (mag′yar). (*blouse*), blouse with sleeves cut in one piece with main part of garment. [native]

Mahābharata (mahhābhah′rata), n. An ancient Hindu epic. [Skr.]

maharaja(h) (mah-harahj′a), n. Title of some Indian princes. [Hind. (*maha* great +RAJAH)]

maharanee (mah-harahn′ĭ), n. Maharajah's wife. [Hind. (*maha* great, *rani* queen)]

mahāt′ma (ma-h-), n. (esoteric Buddhism). One of a class of persons with preternatural powers, supposed to exist in India & Tibet. [f. Skr. *mahatman* (*maha* great+*atman* soul)]

Mahd′ī, n. Spiritual & temporal leader expected by Mohammedans (often applied to leaders of insurrection in Sou-

dan), whence **Mahd′i**(ī)ĭsm(3) n. [f. Arab. *mahdīy* he who is guided right, p.p. of *hada* guide]

mah-jŏng(g)′, n. A Chinese game for four played with 144 pieces called tiles, adopted in Europe & America c. 1923. [Chin., = sparrows]

mahlstick. See MAULSTICK.

mahŏg′any, (ma-h-). n. Wood of a tropical American tree, much used for furniture, & taking high polish; the tree; dining-table (*have one's knees under person's* ~, be dining with him); the colour of ~, reddish-brown, (often attrib.). [?]

Mahŏm′ĕtan (ma-h-). See MOHAMMEDAN.

Mahound′ (ma-hoōnd), n. (arch., joc.). Mohammed. [f. OF *Mahun* short for *Mahomet*]

mahout′ (ma-howt), n. Elephant-driver. [f. Hind. *mahaut*]

Mahrătt′a (ma-ră-), n. Member of a war-like Indian race. [Hind. *Mariattā*]

mah′seer, n. Large Indian freshwater game fish. [Hind. *mahāsir*]

maid, n. Girl; young unmarried woman; spinster; *old* ~, elderly spinster, (also) round game at cards; (also ~′*servant*) female servant, as *house-, nurse-, lady's-,* ~, ~*-of-all-work*; ~ *of honour,* unmarried lady attending on queen or princess, (also) kind of cheesecake. Hence ~′ISH¹ a., ~′Y³ n. [f. MAIDEN; not same as OE *mægeth,* G *magd*]

maidan (mīdahn′), n. (Anglo-Ind.). Parade-ground. [Pers.]

maid′en, n. & a. 1. Girl; spinster; (Hist.) kind of guillotine used at Edinburgh; = ~ *over.* **2.** adj. Unmarried; ~ *name* (before marriage); (of female animals) uncoupled; (of horse) that has never won prize, (of race) open to such horses; (of plant) grown from seed; (of soldier, sword, etc.) untried; ‖ = *assize,* one *at* which there are no cases for trial; (Crick,) ~ *over* (in which no runs are scored); ~ *speech,* M.P.'s first speech in the House; ~*hair,* kinds of fern with fine hairlike stalks & delicate fronds (~*head* (-hĕd), virginity. Hence ~HOOD n., ~ISH¹, ~LIKE, ~LY¹, aa. [OE *mægden,* dim. corresp. to OE *mægeth,* Du. *maagd,* G *magd,* see -EN²]

maleut′ic (māū-), a. (Of Socratic mode of inquiry) obstetric, serving to bring out a person's latent ideas into clear consciousness. [f. Gk *maieutikos* f. *maieomai* act as midwife (*maia*), see -IC]

mail¹, n. Armour composed of rings or chain-work, defensive armour for the body, as *chain-, plate-, ring-,* ~. [f. F *maille* f. L *macula* spot, mesh]

mail¹, v.t. Clothe (as) with mail; *the* ~*ed fist,* (fig.) physical force. [f. prec.]

mail³, n., & v.t. **1.** Bag of letters for conveyance by post; this system of conveyance, the post, (esp. for foreign letters); *the* ~, all that is so conveyed on one occasion; ~ (*train*), train carrying this;

|| ~-cart, cart for carrying ~ by road, (also) light vehicle for carrying children; ~-coach, (now) = ~-cart, (formerly) stage-coach for entire conveyance of ~; ~ order, order for goods sent by post (~ system). 2. v.t. Send (letters etc.) by post. [(vb f. n.), f. OF *male bag, of Teut. orig.]

maim, v.t. Mutilate, cripple, (lit. & fig.). [ME *mayme f. OF *maignier, etym. dub.]

main[1], n. (In game of hazard) number (5, 6, 7, 8, or 9) called by caster before dice are thrown; match between cocks. [?]

main[2], a. Physical force (only in *with might & ~*); for the most part; principal channel, duct, etc., for water, sewage, etc. [OE *mægen*, see MAY v.]

main[3], a. 1. Exerted to the full, as *by ~ force*; chief in size or extent, as *the ~ body* (of army etc.); principal, most important, as *the ~ point* (in argument), || ~*land* (of railway), whence ~*ly* adv.; *have an eye to the ~ chance* (one's own interests). 2 (naut.), ~ *brace* (attached to ~ *yard*, *splice the ~ brace*, serve extra rum ration); ~ *deck*, (in man-of-war) deck next below spar deck, (in merchantman) upper deck between poop & forecastle; ~*sail* (-sāl, -sl), (in square-rigged vessel) sail that is bent to the ~ yard, (in fore-&-aft rigged vessel) sail set on after part of ~*mast*; ~*stay*, stay from ~*top to foot of foremast*, (fig.) chief support; ~*top*, platform above head of lower ~*mast*; ~ *guard*, *yard on which ~sail is extended*.
3. ~*land*, extent of land excluding the neighbouring islands; ~ *spring*, principal spring of watch, clock, etc.; *M~ Street*, principal street of a town (esp. attrib., as *M~-street ideals*). [prob. partly as prec., partly f. cogn. ON *megenn* strong]

maintain' (or měn-), v.t. Carry on, keep up, (war, contest, action at law, condition, position, attitude, relations, correspondence); cause (person etc.) to continue in (condition, possession of thing, etc.); support (life, one's state in life) by nourishment, expenditure, etc.; furnish (oneself, children) with means of subsistence; keep (road etc.) in repair; back up (cause, party); assert as true (opinion, statement, that). Hence ~ABLE a. [f. F *maintenir* f. L *manū tenēre* hold in the hand]

main'tenance, n. Maintaining; enough to support life; *cap of* ~, cap, hat, worn as symbol of official dignity or carried before sovereign etc.; (Law) offence of aiding a party in litigation without lawful cause. [F (as prec., see -ANCE)]

maison(n)ette (-z-), n. Small house; part of a house let separately (not necessarily all on one floor). [F (*-ett*), dim. of *maison* house]

|| ~-*cart*, ... maître d'hôtel (mātr dōtěl'), n. Major-domo; hotel manager. [F; = house-master]

|| maize, n. Indian corn, its grain. [f. Sp. *maiz*, of Cuban orig.]

|| maizen'a, n. Maize starch prepared for use as food. [f. prec.; P]

majes'tic, a. Possessing grandeur, imposing. Hence ~ICALLY adv. [f. foll.+-IC]

maj'esty, n. Impressive stateliness of aspect, bearing, language, etc.; sovereign power; (in speaking to or of sovereign) *Your, His, Her, M~*, you, he, she, as sovereign; *Your M~ forgets that with the best of intentions it is scarcely in your M~'s (or your) power to do this*; representation of God (the Father or Son) enthroned within aureole. [f. F *majesté* f. L *majestātem* (as MAJOR, see -TY)]

Majlis', n. Persian parliament. [Pers.]

majol'ica, maio- (-yō-), n. Kinds of glazed & ornamented Italian ware; modern imitation of these. [It. (*mai̇̀-*), perh. f. *Majorca* (earlier *Majolica*)]

maj'or[1], n. Officer next below lieutenant-colonel & above captain (also in army sl. for *sergeant-*~). Hence ~SHIP n. [f. foll.+-OR]

maj'or[2], a. & n. 1. Greater (not foll. by *than*) of two things, classes, etc.; ~ PROPHET; ~ *epilepsy*, epilepsy proper; ~ *suit* (Bridge), spades or hearts; (Log.) ~ *term* (that enters into predicate or conclusion of syllogism); ~ *premiss* (containing ~ term); ~ *axis* of conic section (passing through by chromatic semitone than minor intervals, as ~ *third*, (of keys) in which scale has a ~ third; ~ *part*, majority (*of*); (Mil.) ~-*general* (see OFFICER), SERGEANT-~; *bugle, drum, pipe, trumpet*, ~ (head bugler etc. of unit); || (in schools) *Brown, Smith*, ~ (the elder or first to enter school); of full age. 2. n. Person of full age; (Log., ellipt. for) ~ *dōm* & (pl. -*os*), chief official of Italian or Spanish princely household, (loosely) house-steward. [L, compar. of *magnus* great]

major'ity, n. 1. Greater number or part (*of*); *the* ~, the dead, esp. *join the* ~, die; *absolute* ~ of votes, more than half number of electors or actual voters; number by which votes cast on one side exceed those on other. 2. Full age, as *attained his* ~. 3. Office of MAJOR[1]. [f. F *majorité* f. med. L *majoritātem* (as prec., see -TY)]

majus'cule, a. & n. (palaeogr.). Large (letter), whether capital or uncial. Hence ~AR[1] a. [F f. L *majuscula* (*littera* letter, dim. of MAJOR)]

make[1], v.t. & i. (*made*). 1. Construct, frame, (as *God made man* (*a rational creature*), *bees* = *cells of wax*, *you were made for this work*; *pipes are made* (consist)

of clay. **2.** ~ GOOD, SURE. **3.** Compose, draw up, (book, will, document). **4.** Prepare (tea, coffee, beds); ~ HAY¹; (arrange & light materials for) a fire. **5.** Cause to exist, bring about, (disturbance, sport, noise, one's mark in the world, a corner in wheat); ~ no BONES; ~ *fun, game, of,* trifle with, treat with ridicule; ~ (conclude treaty of) *peace;* ~ (give) *place, room, way* (for others); ~ *way,* progress. **6.** Result in, as *it ~s a difference;* 'find' ~s (becomes) in the past tense 'found'. **7.** Establish, enact, (distinctions, rules, laws); ~ FRIENDS. **8.** Get together (a HOUSE¹, quorum); ~ *a bag,* kill number of game; ~ *a book,* arrange series of bets on some event; ~ WATER¹. **9.** ~ *a habit of it,* cause it to become one, so ~ *an* EXAMPLE¹, *exhibition, fool, beast* (of oneself, person); ~ *a night of it,* carry it (festivity etc.) on through the night. **10.** ~ *of,* conclude to be the meaning or character of (*can you ~ anything of it?; what am I to ~ of your behaviour?*); ~ *much, little, the best,* etc., *of,* derive much etc. importance from, (also) attach much etc. importance to, so ~ LIGHT⁴ *of;* ~ *a* HASH². **11.** Entertain, feel, (doubt, scruple, *of, about*); ~ HEAD¹ *or tail of.* **12.** (Naut.) discern, come in sight of, (also) arrive at; (sl.) catch (a train etc.); ~ *it,* succeed in traversing a certain distance, (fig.) be successful. **13.** Amount to, as *2 & 2 ~ 4;* constitute, as *one swallow does not ~ a summer;* form, be counted as, (*this ~s the tenth time; will you ~ one of the party?*); serve for, as *this ~s pleasant reading.* **14.** Become, turn out to be, as *she will ~ a good wife.* **15.** Gain, acquire, (money, a living, one's fortune); (Cards) win (trick), play (card) to advantage, (also) shuffle (cards, or abs.). **16.** Proceed (*towards* etc.). **17.** ~ *sail,* set sail, (also) spread additional sail. **18.** Secure the advancement of, cf. MADE; ~ *or mar,* cause success or ruin of. **19.** Cause to be, as ~ *it* HOT, ~ *oneself a martyr,* ~ *oneself* SCARCE, ~ *him a duke;* convert *into.* **20.** Consider to be, (*what do you ~ the time?; I ~ it 5 miles*). **21.** Cause, compel, (without *to* in act.), as ~ *him repeat it,* but *he was made to repeat it.* **22.** ~ *believe,* pretend (to do, that); ~ *do,* manage with (something) as an inferior or temporary substitute; *what bird do you ~* (consider) *that to be?; he ~s Richard die* (represents him as having died) *in 1026.* **23.** Wage (war). **24.** Execute (bodily movement, bow, FACE¹, LEG). **25.** Perform (journey etc., & with many nn. expr. vbl action, as acquisition, attempt, blunder, start, venture); ~ (eat) *a good breakfast;* ~ HEAD¹, LOVE. **26.** Accomplish (distance, knots, etc.). **27.** ~ *as if one had,* pretend one has; ~ BOLD, FREE¹, MERRY. **28.** (Of flood or ebb tide) begin to flow or ebb. **29.** ~ *after* (arch.), pursue; ~ *against,* be unfavourable to; ~ (hasten) *away;* ~ *away with,* get rid of, kill, squander; ~ *for,* conduce to (happiness etc.), confirm (view), proceed towards, assail; ~ *off,* run away, decamp, (often with stolen goods etc.); ~ *out,* draw up, write out, (list, document, cheque), get together with difficulty, as *articles put in to ~ out a volume,* (try to) prove, as *how do you ~ that out?, you ~ me out (to be) a hypocrite,* understand, as *I can't ~ him out, can't ~ out what he wants,* decipher (handwriting etc.), distinguish by sight, as *I made out a figure in the distance;* ~ *over,* transfer possession of (thing to person), esp. by formal agreement; ~ *up,* supply (deficiency), complete (amount, party), compensate, as ~ *up lost ground,* ~ *up for lost time, we must ~ it up to* (compensate) *him somehow,* compound, put together, (medicine, hay into bundles, butter, etc.), sew together (coat etc.), get together (company, sum of money), arrange (type) in pages, compile (list, account, document), concoct (story), (of parts) compose (whole), prepare (actor) for his part by dressing, false hair, etc., apply cosmetics (to), arrange (marriage etc.), settle (dispute), ~ *it up,* be reconciled, ~ *up one's mind to,* decide to (do), resolve upon (course); ~ *up to,* court, curry favour with. **30.** ‖ ~*bate* (arch.), breeder of strife; ~*believe,* pretence; ~*peace,* peacemaker; ~*shift,* temporary substitute or device; ~*up,* disguise of actor, cosmetics etc. used for this, making up of type, type made up; ~*weight,* small quantity added to ~ up weight, (also fig. of persons), (fig.) unimportant point added to ~ case seem stronger. [com.-WG: OE *macian,* Du. *maken,* G *machen*]

māke², n. (Of natural or manufactured thing) style of structure or composition; mental or moral disposition; *American ~,* made in America; *is this your own ~* (made by you)?; *on the ~* (sl.), intent on gain; (Electr.) making of contact, position in which this is made, esp. *at ~;* ‖ *~ & mend* (Naut.), a period of leisure or no fixed duties for the hands (orig. for work on their clothes). [f. prec.]

māk'er, n. In vbl senses, esp. *the, our,* etc., *M~,* the Creator. [-ER¹]

māk'ing, n. In vbl senses, esp.: *be the ~ of,* ensure success or favourable development of; (pl.) earnings, profits; (pl.) essential qualities, as *he has the ~s of a general;* *(pl.) paper & tobacco for rolling a cigarette. [-ING¹]

māl- pref. =F *mal¹.* L *male* badly, in sense (1) bad(ly), as *maltreat,* (2) un-, as *maladroit.*

Malacc'a, n. Town & district on Malay peninsula; ~ *cane,* rich-brown walking-cane, from stem of a palm.

māl'achite (-kīt), n. Hydrous carbonate of copper, green mineral taking high polish. [f. OF *melochite* (Gk *malakhē* mallow, see -ITE¹]

mǎl'aco- in comb. = Gk *malakos* soft, as : ~*derm*, soft-skinned animal (esp. of sea-anemones & of one division of reptiles); ~*logist*, ~*logy* (-ŏl-), student, science, of molluscs; ~*straca* (-ŏs-), member of one order of crustaceans. [MAL-]

mǎladjust'ment, n. Faulty adjustment. [MAL-]

mǎladministrā'tion, n. Faulty administration. [MAL-]

mǎl'adrŏit, a. Clumsy, bungling. Hence ~'LY[2] adv., ~'NESS n. [F (MAL-+ADROIT)]

mǎl'ady, n. Ailment, disease, (lit. & fig.). [F *maladie* f. *malade* sick f. LL *male habitus* (*male* ill+*habitus* p.p. of *habēre* have)]

mǎl à fidé, adv. & a. (Acting, done) in bad faith. [L]

Mǎl'aga, n. Seaport in S. Spain; white wine from this.

Mǎlagǎs'y, a. & n. (Language, inhabitant) of Madagascar. [used in native lang., but prob. of foreign orig.]

mǎl'aise (-z), n. Bodily discomfort, esp. without development of specific disease. [F (OF *mal* bad+*aise* EASE)]

mǎl'amūte, mǎl'e-, n. An Eskimo dog. [name of Alaskan Eskimo tribe]

mǎl'anders, mǎl'en-, n. pl. Scabby eruption behind knee in horses. [f. F *malandre* f. L *malandria*]

mǎl'apĕrt, a. & n. (arch.). Impudent, saucy, (person). [OF (MAL-+*appert*= *espert* EXPERT)]

mǎl'aprop(ism), n. Ludicrous misuse of word, esp. in mistake for one resembling it (e.g. *a nice derangement of epitaphs* for *arrangement of epithets*). Hence **mǎla-prŏp'IAN** a. [f. Mrs *Malaprop* in Sheridan's *Rivals*]

mǎlaprŏpos' (-pō), adv., a., & n. (Thing) inopportunely (said, done, or happening). [f. F *mal à propos* (mal ill, see APROPOS)]

mǎl'ar, a. & n. (Bone) of the cheek. [f. L *mala* jaw, see -AR[1]]

malār'ia, n. Kinds of intermittent & remittent fever caused by bite of mosquito, which conveys the germs; unwholesome atmosphere caused by exhalations of marshes, to which these fevers were formerly referred. Hence ~IAL, ~IAN, ~IOUS, aa. [f. It. *mal' aria* bad air]

Malay', a. & n. (Language, member) of race predominating in Malaya & Eastern Archipelago; ~ *fowl*, large domestic variety. Hence ~AN a. & n. [f. native *malāyu*]

Mǎlaya'lam (-yah-), n. Language of Malabar. [native]

mǎl'contĕnt, a. & n. Discontented (person), (one) inclined to rebellion. [OF (MAL-)]

māle, a. & n. 1. Of the sex that begets offspring or performs the fecundating function (used of persons or animals, & of plants whose flowers contain only fecun-

dating organs, also of plants to which sex was once attributed on account of colour etc., as ~ *fern*); of men or ~ animals; (of parts of machinery etc.) designed to enter or fill the corresponding FEMALE part, as ~ *screw*; ~ (masculine) *rhyme*. 2. n. ~ person or animal. [OF, f. L *masculus* (*mas* male, see -CULE)]

mǎlé- in comb. = L *male* ill.

mǎledǐc'tion, n. Curse. So ~ORY a. [f. L *maledictio* f. MALE(*dīcĕre dict-* speak), see -ION]

mǎl'efǎctor, n. Criminal; evil-doer, esp. opp. to *benefactor*. So **mǎléfǎc'TION** n. [L, f. MALE(*facĕre fact-* do), see -OR[1]]

mǎléf'ic, a. (Of magical arts etc.), harmful, baleful. [f. L MALE(*ficus* -FIC)]

mǎléf'icent, a. Hurtful (to); criminal. So ~CENCE n. [f. L *male-* altered stem of *male-ficus* MALEFIC]

mǎlĕv'olent, a. Desirous of evil to others. Hence or cogn. ~ENCE n., ~*ently* adv. [f. L MALE(*volens* part. of *velle* wish)]

mǎlfeas'ance (-ēz-), n. (law). Evil-doing, esp. official misconduct. So ~ANT a. & n. [f. OF *malfaisant* part. of *faire* do f. L *facere*]

mǎlformā'tion, n. Faulty formation. So ~ED[1] (-md-) a. [MAL-]

mǎl'ic, a. (chem.). ~ *acid* (derived from apple & other fruits). [f. F *malique* f. L *mālum* apple, see -IC]

mǎl'ice (-is), n. Active ill-will; desire to tease; bear ~ (*to*), cherish vindictive feelings (against); (Law) wrongful intention, esp. as increasing guilt of certain offences; ~ *prepense*, ~ *aforethought*. So **malǐ'cious** (-shǔs), a., **malǐ'ciousLY[2]** adv. [F, f. L *malitia* (*malus* bad, see -ICE)]

malǐgn' (-īn), a. (Of things) injurious; (of diseases) malignant; (rare) malevolent. Hence ~LY[2] adv. [f. OF *maligne* f. L MALIGN(*us* (*malus* bad, cf. BENIGN)]

malǐgn'[2] (-īn), v.t. Speak ill of, slander. [f. OF *maligner* f. L *malignāre* contrive malciously, as prec.]

malǐg'nant, a. & n. 1. (Of disease) very virulent or infectious (now usu. denoting definite variety of disease, as ~ *and cholera*); harmful; feeling or showing intense ill-will. 2. (hist.). Supporter of, supporting, Charles I against Parliament. Hence ~ANCY n., ~*antly*[2] adv. [f. LL *malignānt-* part. as prec.]

malǐg'nity, n. Deep-rooted ill-will; (of diseases) malignant character. [f. OF *malignité* f. L *malignitātem* (as MALIGN, see -TY)]

maling'er (-ngg-), v.i. Pretend, produce, or protract, illness in order to escape duty (esp. of soldiers & sailors). Hence ~ER[1] n. [f. F *malingre* sickly, etym. dub.]

māl'ism, n. Doctrine that it is a bad world. [f. L *malus* bad +-ISM]

mǎl'ison (-sn, -zn), n. (arch.). Curse. [f. OF *maleison* MALEDICTION]

mall (mawl), n. Sheltered walk as promenade, || esp. *the M~* (mǎl) in St James's Park, London, orig. alley for game of PALL-MALL; (Hist.) this game, alley for it, mallet for it. [= MAUL¹]

mall'ard, n. Wild drake or duck; its flesh. [f. OF *mall(l)art*, etym. dub.]

mall'eable, a. (Of metals etc.) that can be hammered or pressed out of form without tendency to return to it or to fracture; (fig.) adaptable, pliable. Hence **mälleabil'ity** n. [OF, f. L *malleare* hammer (*malleus*), see -BLE]

mäll'emuck, möll'ymawk, n. Fulmar, petrel, or similar bird. [f. Du. *mallemok* (*mal* foolish +*mok* gull)]

mäll'ét, n. Hammer, usu. of wood; implement for striking croquet or polo ball. [f. F *maillet*, dim. as MAUL¹]

mäll'éus, n. Bone of ear transmitting vibrations of tympanum to incus. [LL = hammer]

mäll'ow (-ō), n. Wild plant with hairy stems & leaves & purple flowers; garden varieties of this. [OE *mealuwe* f. L *malva*, prob. conn. w. Gk *malakhē*]

malm (mahm), n. Soft chalky rock; loamy soil from disintegration of this; fine-quality brick made originally from ~, marl, or similar chalky clay. [OE *mealm*, cf. Icel. *mālmr*, Da. *malm*, f. *mal-* grind]

malmaī'son (-z-), n. Kind of carnation. [*M~*, palace of empress Josephine]

malmsey (mahm'zĭ), n. Strong sweet wine from Greece, Spain, etc. [f. med. L *malmasia* corrupt. of Gk *Monembasia*, Napoli di Monemvasia, in the Morea]

malnutri'tion, n. Insufficient nutrition. [MAL-]

mälod'orous, a. Evil-smelling. [MAL-]

mälprāc'tice, n. Wrong-doing; (Law) physician's improper or negligent treatment of patient; (Law) illegal action for one's own benefit while in position of trust. [MAL-]

malt¹ (mawlt), n. Barley or other grain prepared for brewing or distilling; *extract of ~* (as food for invalids); *~ liquor* (made from ~ by fermentation, not distillation, e.g. beer, stout); *~-house* (for preparing & storing ~); *~-worm*, (fig.) toper. [com.-Teut.: OE *mealt*, Du. *mout*, G *malz*, cogn. w. OHG *malt* soft]

malt² (mawlt), v.t. & i. Convert (grain) into malt; (of seeds) come to condition of malt from germination's being checked by drought. [f. prec.]

Mal'ta (maw-), n. Island in Mediterranean; *~ fever*, complicated fever common in ~. **Maltese'** (mawltēz), a. & n. (pl. same). (Language, native) of Malta; *~ cat, dog*, fancy kinds; *~ CROSS¹*. [-ESE]

mal'tha, n. Cement of pitch & wax or other ingredients. [L f. Gk]

Mäl'thūs'ian (-z-), a. & n. (Follower) of T. R. Malthus (d. 1835) who advocated moral restraint (pop. understood as

abstention from marriage) as means of checking increase of population. Hence **~ISM** (-zhan-) n. [-IAN]

mal'ting (maw-), n. In vbl senses; also, malt-house. [-ING¹]

mal'tōse (maw-), n. (chem.). Sugar produced from starch-paste by action of malt. [F (MALT +-OSE²)]

mältreat', v.t. Ill-treat. So **~MENT** n. [f. F MAL(*traiter* TREAT)]

maltster (mawl(t)'ster), n. One who makes malt. [-STER]

mälvā'ceous (-shus), a. Of the genus Mallow. [f. LL *malvaceus* (as MALLOW, -ACEOUS)]

mälversā'tion, n. Corrupt behaviour in position of trust; corrupt administration (*of public money* etc.). [F, f. *malverser* f. L *male* badly + *versari* behave frequent. of *vertere* vers- turn, see -ATION]

mäm'ba, n. (Kinds of) venomous African tree snake. [f. Kaffir *m'namba*]

mäm'elon, n. Rounded eminence. [F, = nipple f. *mamelle* breast f. MAMILLA]

Mäm'eluke (-ōōk), n. (hist.). Member of military body (orig. Caucasian slaves) that seized throne of Egypt in 1254; (in Mohammedan countries) slave. [ult. f. Arab. *mamluk* slave (*malaka* possess)]

mamil'la, n. Nipple of female breast; nipple-shaped organ etc. So **mäm'il-lARY¹**, **mäm'illāte²**(2), **mäm'illāted¹**, ~iFORM, aa. [L, dim. of MAMMA²]

mam(m)a'¹ (-ah), n. Mother (used esp. by children). [instinctive]

mämm'a² n. (pl. *~ae*). Milk-secreting organ of female in mammals; corresponding structure in males. Hence ~ARY¹, **mämm'IFEROUS**, ~iFORM, aa. [L]

mämm'al, n. One of foll. class. [f. foll.] *mammā'lĭa*, n. pl. Class of animals having mammae for nourishment of young. Hence **mämmā'lIAN** a. & n., **mammā'o̱IST**, **mammäl'oGY**, nn. [neut. pl. of LL *mammalis* (as MAMMA², see -AL)]

mämmalif'erous, a. (geol.). Containing mammalian remains. [f. prec. +-FEROUS]

mämmee', n. Tropical American tree with large yellow-pulped fruit. [f. Sp. *mamey* f. Haytian]

mäm'mon, n. Wealth regarded as idol or evil influence; the worldly rich; *the ~ of unrighteousness*, wealth ill used or ill gotten. Hence ~ISH¹ a., ~ISM, ~IST, ~ITE, nn. [f. LL *mammona* f. Gk *mamōnas* f. Aram. *mamon* riches; see *Matt.* vi. 24, *Luke* xvi. 9–13]

mäm'moth, n. & a. 1. Large extinct elephant. 2. adj. Huge. [f. Russ. *mamoð*, etym. dub.]

mämm'ý, n. Child's word for mother; *coloured woman in charge of white children. [f. *mam* (instinctive) +-Y³]

män¹, n. (pl. *mĕn*). 1. Human being (*a ~ & a brother*, fellow ~); (in indefinite or general application) person, as *any, no, ~, some, few, men; (all) to a ~*, all without

exception. **2.** The human race, as ~ *wants but little here below*; ~ *is* (joc.) *spiritual, material, parts of* ~; *interior, esp. stomach, exterior, of* ~; NEW, OLD, ~. **4.** Adult male, opp. to *woman, boy, or both*; ~ *& boy* (adv.), from boyhood upwards. **5.** (As impatient or lively vocative) *nonsense*, ~! *hurry up*, ~ (*alive!*); (joc. or endearing) *little* ~, *young boy*. **6.** One, as *what can a* ~ *do in such a case?* **7.** Individual (male) person, as ~ *for* ~, *between* ~ *& ~, &-per* ~; *as a* ~, viewed simply in regard to his personal character; *if you want noise, he is your* ~ (can supply you); *I'm your* ~ (accept your offer etc.); *be one's own* ~, be free to act, (also) be in full possession of one's faculties, senses, etc.; *every* ~ JACK[1]. **8.** (In comb., denoting one who follows profession, uses implement, trades in article, etc.) *clergy*~, *post*~, *brake*~, *per*~, *rag-&-bone*~; BEST[1], HANDY, ~. **9.** ~ eminently endowed with manly qualities, as *be a* ~, *play the* ~, ~. INDIA~, MERCHANT~. **16.** ~ *of the WORLD*; ~ *Friday*, servile follower, factotum. (name given by Robinson Crusoe to his servant); ~ *about town*. ||London society idler; ~-*at-arms*, soldier, esp. heavy-armed & mounted; ~ (male) *child*; ~-*eater*, cannibal, biting horse, ~-eating shark or tiger; ~ *handle*, move by force of ~ alone, (sl.) handle roughly; ~ *hole*, opening in floor, sewer, etc., for ~ to pass through; ~ *in the moon*, semblance of ~ in moon, esp. as type of imaginary person; *the* ~ *in* (*or on*) *the street*, the ordinary ~ (esp. as expert on the matter in question); ~-MILLINER; ~ *of* Kent (see KENTISH); ~ *of LETTERS*; ~ *power*, amount of men available for military or other service; ~ *servant*, male servant; ~ *slaughter*, slaughter of human beings, (Law) criminal homicide without malice aforethought; ~*trap* (for catching men, esp. trespassers). Hence ~*LESS* a. [com-Tent.: cf. OE & Du. *man*, G *mann*] mān[2], v.t. (-nn-). Furnish (fort, ship, etc.) with men for service or defence; (Naut.) place men at (part of ship); fill (post), fortify spirits or courage of (esp. oneself). [OE *mannian*, as prec.] mān'acle, n. (usu. pl.), & v.t. **1.** Fetter (prop. for the hand; also fig.). **2.** v.t. Fetter with ~s. [f. OF *manicle* handcuff f. L *manicula* dim. of *manus* hand] mān'age[1], n. (arch.). Training of horse; trained movements of horse, esp. short gallop; riding-school. [f. It. *maneggio*, as foll.]

mān'age[2], v.t. & i. Handle, wield, (tool etc.); conduct (undertaking etc.); control (household, institution, State); take charge of (cattle etc.); subject (person, animal) to one's control; gain one's ends with (person etc.) by flattery etc., whence mān'aging[1] (-nij-) a.; contrive (*to do*, often intr., as *he* ~*d to muddle it*); succeed in one's aim (often *with* inadequate material etc.); (with *can* or *be able to*) cope with, make proper use of, as *can you* ~ *another slice?* Hence ~*abl*y[2] adv., ~*able-*NESS, nn. ~*ABLE* a., ~*ABIL'ITY*, ~*able-*[f. It. *maneggiare* f. vulg. L *manidiare* (*manus* hand)]

mān'agement (-ijm-), n. In vbl senses; also or esp.: trickery, deceitful contrivance; *the* ~, governing body, board of directors, etc. [-MENT]

mān'ager (-nij-), n. Person conducting a business, institution, etc.; || member of either House of Parliament appointed with others for some duty in which both Houses are concerned; *good, bad*, etc., ~ (of money, household affairs, etc.). || (Law) person appointed, usu. by Court & Chancery, to manage a business for benefit of creditors etc. Hence ~*SHIP*, nn., mān'ager[IAL] a. [-ER[1]]

mān'akin. (Kinds of) brightly-coloured small tropical American bird. [var. of MANIKIN]

mān'atee[3], n. Large aquatic herbivorous mammal, sea-cow. [f. Sp. *manati* f.Carib *manattoua*]

Man'chester, n. || ~ *goods*, cotton textiles (sold in ~ *department* of a shop); ~ *School*, adherents of the doctrines of free trade & laissez-faire (name given by Disraeli to Cobden & Bright & their followers). [place]

mānchineel', n. W.-Ind. tree with poisonous milky sap & acrid fruit. [f. F *mancenille* f. Sp. *manzanilla* f. L *mattiana*]

mān'ciple, n. Officer who buys provisions for college, inn of court, etc. [OF, f. L *mancipium*=(in med. L) office of *manceps* buyer (*manus* hand + *capere* take)]

Mancū'nian, a. & n. (Inhabitant) of Manchester; (member) of Manchester Grammar School. [f. L *Mancunium* Manchester, -AN]

-mancy, suf. f. OF *-mancie* f. LL f. Gk *-manteia* divination by —.

Man'dae'an, a. & n. (Member, language) of agnostic sect surviving in Mesopotamia. [f. Aram. *mandā* knowledge]

mandā'mus, n. || Judicial writ issued from King's Bench Division as command to inferior court. [L, = we command]

man'darin[1], n. Chinese official in any of 9 grades; standard spoken Chinese; party leader who lags behind the times; nodding toy figure in Chinese costume; ~ *duck*, small Chinese duck noted for its bright plumage. [f. Port. *mandarim* f. Malay f. Hind. *mantri* f. Skr. *mantrin* counsellor]

măn´darin², **-ine** (-ēn), n. Small flat deep-coloured orange; colour of this (got from coal-tar); a liqueur. [F (-ine): perh. f. prec. w. ref. to his yellow robes]

măn´datary, n. (law). One to whom a mandate is given (for spec. sense see foll.). [f. L mandatarius (foll., -ARY¹)]

măn´date¹, n. Judicial or legal command from superior; commission to act for another, esp. one from League of Nations to a State (the *mandatory*) to govern a people not qualified for independence; (poet.) command; papal rescript; (Law) contract by which mandatary undertakes to perform gratuitously some service in respect of thing committed to him; (after F *mandat*) political authority supposed to be given by electors to (party in) parliament. [f. L *mandatum*, neut. p.p. of *mandare* command (*manus* hand +*dare* give)]

măndāte², v.t. Commit (State etc. *to* mandatary). [back formation f. MANDATARY]

măn´datory, a. & n. 1. Of, conveying, a command. 2. n. = MANDATARY. [f. LL *mandatorius* (as prec., see -ORY)]

măn´dible, n. Jaw, esp. lower jaw in mammals & fishes; upper or lower part of bird's beak; (in insects) either half of upper pair of jaws. So **măndib´ular¹**, **măndib´ulate²**(2), aa. [f. LL *mandibula* (*mandere* masticate)]

măndŏl´a, -ōr´a, n. Kind of mandolin or lute. [It., var. of PANDORA]

măn´dolin(e), n. Musical instrument of lute kind with paired metal strings, played with plectrum. [F (-ine), f. It. *mandolino* dim. of prec.]

măndrăg´ora, n. = foll., esp. as type of narcotic (Shak. *Othello* III. iii. 330). [LL, f. Gk *mandragoras*]

măn´drake, n. Poisonous plant with emetic & narcotic properties, with root thought to resemble human form & to shriek when plucked. [ME *mandra(o)e*, shortened f. prec.]

măn´drel, -il, n. (In lathe) axis to which work is fixed while turned; cylindrical rod round which metal or other material is forged or shaped; (dial.) miner's pick. [?]

măn´drill, n. Large, hideous, & ferocious baboon. [prob. MAN¹+DRILL³]

mane, n. Long hair on neck of horse, lion, etc. (also fig. of person). Hence (-)mānED² (-nd), ~LESS (-nl-), aa. [OE *manu*, cf. Du. *mane*, G *mähne*, f. OTeut. *manō* neck]

manège´, -ege, (manäzh´), n. Riding-school; movements of trained horse; horsemanship. [F (-ège), as MANAGE¹]

măn´ēs (-z), n. pl. Deified souls of departed ancestors; shade of departed person, as object of reverence. [L]

măn´ful, a. Brave, resolute. Hence ~LY² adv., ~NESS n. [MAN¹+FUL]

măn´gabey (-ā), n. African genus of monkey. [M~, region of Madagascar]

măng´anese (-nganēz), n. Black mineral used in glass-making etc.; metallic element of which this is the oxide. Hence **măngane´sian** (-ngganēz-), **măngān´ic** (-ngg-), aa. [f. F *manganèse*, corrupt. of MAGNESIA]

mange (-j), n. Skin disease in hairy & woolly animals, caused by an arachnidan parasite; (loosely) dirty condition of skin. [ME *manjewe* f. OF *manjue* itch f. *manjuer* (mod. *manger*) eat (as MANDUCATE)]

‖ **măng´el(-wǔrz´el), măng´old (-wǔrz´el),** (-ngg-), n. Large kind of beet, used as cattle food. [G (-gold, corrupt. -geld), f. *mangold* beet+*wurzel* root]

măn´ger (-j-), n. Box, trough, in stable etc. for horses or cattle to eat from; Dog in the ~. [f. F *mangeoire* f. vulg. L *manducatoria (as MANDUCATE, see -ORY)]

mangle¹ (mäng´gl), n. & v.t. 1. Machine of two or more cylinders for rolling & pressing washed clothes. 2. v.t. Press (clothes) in ~. [(vb f. n.) f. Du. *mangel* f. Gk as MANGONEL]

mangle² (mäng´gl), v.t. Hack, lacerate, by blows; cut roughly so as to disfigure; spoil (quotation, text, etc.) by gross blunders, disguise (words) by mispronouncing. [f. AF *mahangler*, prob. frequent. of *mahaignier* MAIM]

măng´o (-nggō), n. (pl. ~es). (Indian tree bearing) fleshy fruit yellowish-red in colour, eaten ripe or green for pickles etc.; ~-*fish*, golden-coloured Indian fish; ~ *trick* (in which ~-tree appears to spring up & bear fruit in few hours). [f. Port. *manga* f. Tamil *mankay* (*man* ~-tree+*kay* fruit)]

mangold (-wurzel). See MANGEL.

măng´onel (-ngg-), n. (hist.). Military engine for casting stones etc. [OF, dim. f. LL *mango -onis* f. Gk *magganon*]

măng´osteen (-ngg-), n. (E.-Indian tree bearing) fruit with thick red rind & white juicy pulp. [f. Malay *mangustan*]

măng´rōve (-ngg-), n. Tropical tree or shrub, bark of which is used in medicine & tanning. [?]

măng´y (-jĭ), a. Having the mange; squalid, shabby. Hence ~ĭLY² adv., ~ĭNESS n. [MANGE+Y¹]

mănhătt´an, n. Cocktail made of vermouth, whisky etc. [f. *Manhattan* in N. York]

măn´hŏŏd, n. State of being a man (in any sense); ~ *suffrage* (granted to all male citizens of lawful age not disqualified by crime, insanity, etc.); manliness, courage; the men of a country. [MAN¹+HOOD]

mān´ia, n. Mental derangement marked by excitement, hallucination, & violence; great enthusiasm (*for* thing, *doing*). [L f. Gk.=madness (*mainomai* be mad, st. *man-*)]

-mania, suf. denoting scientifically a special type of madness (*klepto-*, *megalo-*

~, *wamano*~); also (pop.) eager pursuit (*biblio*~) or admiration (*Anglo*~). Hence personal suf. **-maniac** (cf. -PHOBE, -PHOBIA). [as prec.]

mán'iac, a. & n. (Person) affected with mania, raving mad(man). Hence **maní'acal** a., **maní'acally²** adv. [f. LL *maniacus* (as MANIA, see -AC)]

-mániac, suf. See -MANIA.

Mánichee (-k-), n. Adherent of religious system (3rd to 5th c.) that represented Satan as coeternal with God. Hence **Mánichae'an** n. & a., **Mánich(a)e'ism** n. (-kē-). [f. LL f. Gk *Manikhaios*, founder of sect, living in Persia]

mán'icure, n. & v.t. 1. (One who under-takes) treatment of hands & finger-nails as profession. 2. v.t. Apply ~e treatment to (hands, person). Hence **mán'icurist** (t. n.) f. [f. L *manus* hand + *cura* care])

mán'ifest¹, a. Clear, obvious, to eye or mind. Hence ~**ly²** adv. [f. L *manifestus*, perh. f. *manus* hand, +*festus* struck f. root of DEFEND]

mán'ifest², v.t. & i. Show plainly to eye or mind; be evidence of, prove; display, evince, (quality, feeling) by one's acts etc.; (of thing) reveal *itself*; record in ship's manifest; (of government or political party) take measures, hold public meeting, etc., as public expression of opinion; (of ghost) appear. So ~**A'TION** n., ~**ATIVE** (-ēs-) a. [f. F *manifester* f. L *manifestare* (as prec.)]

mánifes'to, n. (pl.~s). Public declaration by sovereign, State, or body of indivi-duals, making known past actions & motives of actions announced as forth-coming. [It. as MANIFEST²]

mán'ifold¹, a. & n. 1. Having various forms, applications, etc.; performing several functions at once; many & various, as ~ *vexations*; ... 2. n. (mech.). Pipe or chamber with several openings. Hence ~**IY²** adv., ~**NESS** n. [com.-Teut.: OE *manigfeald*, MDu. *menichvout*, G *man-nigfalt*: (MANY + FOLD)]

mán'ifold², v.t. Multiply (letters etc.) as by MANIFOLD¹ writer. [OE *manigfealdian* multiply, as prec.]

mán'ikin, n. Little man, dwarf; artist's lay figure; anatomical model of the body; small tropical American bird. [f. Du. *manneken*, dim. of MAN¹]

manill'a¹, n. Metal bracelet used by African tribes as medium of exchange. [Sp.; dim. of L *manus* hand or f. L *monilla* ring]

Manill'a², **-ll'a**, n. Capital of Philippine islands; (also ~ *hemp*) fibrous material for ropes, matting, etc.; cheroot made in ~; ~ *paper*, brown wrapping-paper made from ~ hemp etc. [native(-*ila*)]

manille', n. Second best trump or honour in quadrille & ombre. [corrupt. of Sp. *malilla* dim. of *mala* bad f. L *malus*]

mán'ioc, n. Plant cassava; meal made from it. [f. Tupi *mandioca*]

mán'iple, n. 1. (Rom. Ant.) subdivision of legion, containing 120 or 60 men. 2. Eucharistic vestment, strip about 3 feet long hanging from left arm. [OF, f. L *manipulus* (*manus* hand + *pl-* weak form of root *plē-* fill)]

manip'ulate, v.t. Handle, treat, esp. with skill (material thing, question); manage (person) by dextrous (esp. un-fair) use of influence etc. Hence or cogn. ~**A'TION**, ~**ator²**(1, 2) nn., ~**ATIVE**, ~**ATORY**, aa. [prob. back formation f. manipulation (F, f. *manipuler* f. L as prec.)]

mán'itou (-ō̄), n. (Amer. Ind.). Good or evil spirit; thing having supernatural power. [f. Algonquin *manito, -tu*]

mankind', n. 1.(-kīnd'). Human species, all men. 2. (mán-). Male sex. [MAN¹+KIND n.]

mán'like, a. Having good or bad qualities of a man; (of woman) mannish. [-LIKE]

mán'ly², a. Having a man's virtues, courage, frankness, etc.; (of woman) having a man's qualities; (of things, qualities, etc.) befitting a man. Hence ~**NESS** n. [-LY¹]

mán'na, n. Substance supplied as food to Israelites (*Exod.* xvi); spiritual nourish-ment, esp. the Eucharist; sweet juice from ~-*ash* & other plants, used as gentle laxative (~ *in tears, in sorts,* superior, in-ferior, kinds of this); ~-*croup*, coarse gra-nular wheat meal [Russ., *krupa* groats]. [LL f. Gk. f. Heb. *man*, explained as = *man hu?* what is it, but perh. = Arab. *mann* exudation of *Tamarix gallica*]

mán'nequin (or -kin), n. Person, usu. woman, employed by dressmakers etc. to wear & show off costumes. [F, = lay figure, f. Du. as MANIKIN]

mán'ner, n. Way a thing is done or happens, as *in, after, this* ~; (arch.) *in a* ~ *of speaking,* so to speak; (Gram.) *adverb of* ~, one that asks or tells how; *to the* ~ *born,* (Shak. *Ham.* I. iv. 15) destined by birth to be subject to the position etc.; (pl.) modes of life, condi-tions of society; outward bearing; *the grand* ~, old-fashioned dignity; (pl.) good, bad, etc. behaviour in social inter-course, habits indicating good breeding, as *he has no* ~*s*, whence ~**LESS** a.; style in literature or art; mannerism; (arch.) kind, sort, as *what* ~ *of man is he?*; *all* ~ *of*, every kind of; *no* ~ *of right*, no right at all; *in a* ~, in some sense, to some extent. [f. OF *manière* f. pop. L *man(u)-aria* fem. adj. as n. = mode of handling (*manus* hand.)]

mánn'ered (-erd), a. *IU, well, rough,* ~, having bad etc. manners; (of style, artist, writer) showing mannerism. [-ED²]

mănn'er|ism, n. Excessive addiction to a distinctive manner in art or literature; a trick of style; trick of gesture or speech (esp. of an actor). Hence ~IST n., ~IST|ĬC(AL) aa. [-ISM]
Hence ~iNESS n. [-LY¹]

mănn'ish, a. (Of woman) masculine; characteristic of man as opp. to woman, as *what a ~ way to thread a needle!* Hence ~NESS n. [-ISH¹]

mănn'ite, n. (Also ~-*sugar*) substance obtained from manna. Hence **mănn'i-tōSE²** n. [f. MANNA + -ITE¹]

mănœu'vre¹, *-euver, (-nŏŏver, -nū-), n. Planned movement of troops or ships of war; deceptive or elusive movement; skilful plan; MASS² of ~. [F. f. LL *manopera*, see foll.]

mănœu'vre¹, *-euver, (as prec.), v.i.&t. Perform, cause (troops) to perform, manœuvres; employ artifice: force, drive (person, thing, *into, out, away,* etc.) by contrivance; manipulate adroitly. Hence ~ER¹ n. [f. F *manœuvrer* f. LL *manoperare* = L *manū operārī* work by hand (*opus -eris* work)]

mănŏm'ĕter, n. Pressure gauge for gases & vapours. Hence **mănŏmĕt'rĬo** a. [f. F *manomètre* (Gk *manos* thin, see -METER)]

ma nŏn trŏpp'ō, mus. direction appended to another. But not to excess. [It.]

măn'or, n. English territorial unit, orig. of nature of feudal lordship, now consisting of lord's demesne & of lands from whose holders he can exact certain fees etc.; *lord of the ~,* person, corporation, having rights of this; ~-*house,* his mansion. Hence **manŏr'IAL** a. [f. OF *manoir* (vb as n.) f. L *manēre* remain]

măn'sard, n. (Usu. ~ *roof*) curb roof in which each face has two slopes, lower one steeper than upper. [f. F *mansarde* (F. M~, architect, d. 1666)]

mănse, n. Ecclesiastical residence, esp. Scottish Presbyterian minister's house. [f. med. L *mansus, -sa, -sum,* house (*manēre mans-* remain)]

măn'sion (-shn), n. Large residence (|| in pl. often of large buildings divided into flats); ||~-*house,* house of lord of manor or landed proprietor, official residence, esp. (*the M~-house*) of Lord Mayor of London. [OF, f. L *mansionem* (as prec., see -ION)]

măn'suetūde (-swi-), n. (rare). Meekness, docility. [f. L *mansuētūdo* (*mansuetus* tame f. *manus* hand, *suesco* be used)]

măn'tel, n. (Now usu. ~-*piece*) structure of wood, marble, etc., above & around fireplace; (usu. ~-*shelf*) shelf projecting from wall above fireplace; ~-*board,* wooden shelf (usu. draped) fixed upon this; ~-*tree,* beam across opening of fireplace. [var. of MANTLE¹]

mantl(e)'lĕt, n. Kinds of short mantle; bullet-proof screen for gunners. [OF (*-et-*), dim. as MANTLE¹]

măn'tĬc, a. Of divination. [f. Gk *mantikos* (*mantis* prophet, see -IC)]

măntill'a, n. Large veil covering woman's hair & shoulders; small cape. [Sp., dim. of *manta* MANTLE¹]

măn'tĬs, n. Orthopterous insect; *praying ~,* kind that holds forelegs in position suggesting hands folded in prayer. [Gk, =prophet]

măntĭss'a, n. Decimal part of logarithm. [L]

măn'tle¹, n. Woman's loose sleeveless cloak; (fig.) covering; fragile lace-like tube fixed round gas-jet to give incandescent light; outer fold of skin enclosing mollusc's viscera. [(1) OE *mentel*, (2) f. OF *mantel,* both f. L *mantellum* cloak]

măn'tle², v.t. & i. Clothe (as) in mantle; cover, conceal, envelop; (of liquids) become covered with coating or scum; (of blood) suffuse cheeks, (of face) glow, with blush. [f. prec.]

mantlet. See MANTLET.

măn'tūa, n. Woman's loose gown in 17th-18th cc.; ~-*maker,* dressmaker. [corrupt. of *manteau* (F, as MANTLE¹)]

măn'ŭal, a. & n. 1. Of, done with, the hands, as ~ *labour;* (Mil.) ~ (*exercise*), drill in handling rifle; ~ *fire-engine* (worked by hand, not steam); ~ (*finger*) *alphabet;* SIGN¹ ~. 2. n. Small book for handy use, handbook; organ keyboard played with hands; (Hist.) book of the forms to be used by priests in the administration of the Sacraments. Hence ~LY² adv. [f. L *manualis* (*manus* hand, see -AL)]

mănŭfac'torў n. Factory, workshop. [f. L as foll, see -ORY]

mănŭfac'tūre, n. Making of articles by physical labour or machinery, esp. on large scale; branch of such industry, as *woollen ~; of home, English,* etc., ~, made at home etc.; (derog.) mechanical production (of literature etc.). [F. f. L *manu* by hand + *facere fact-* make, see -URE]

mănŭfac'tŭre², v.t. Work up (material) for use; produce (articles) by labour, esp. on large scale (derog. of literary work etc.); invent, fabricate, (story). Hence ~ER¹ n. [f. prec.]

mănŭmit', v.t. (hist.: -tt-). Set (slave) free. So **mănŭmĭs'sion** n. [f. L *manumittere* (*manus* hand + *mittere miss-* send)]

manūre¹, n. Dung, compost, spread over or mixed with soil to fertilize it. Hence **manūr'IAL** a. [f. foll.]

manūre², v.t. Apply manure to (land, or abs., also *fig.*). [f. AF *maynoeuver,* as MANŒUVRE²]

măn'ūscript, a. & n. (abbr. *MS.* pr. émés', pl. *MSS.* pr. émés'iz). (Book, document) written by hand, not printed;

author's copy for printer. [f. med. L *manuscriptus* (*manu* by hand + *scriptus* write]

man·ward, a. Tending, directed, towards man. [-WARD]

Mānx, a. & n. 1. Of the Isle of Man, as ~ *cat*, tailless variety; ~*man*, inhabitant of I. of Man. 2. n. ~ *cat*, language; (as pl., *Manx*) ~ people. [f. ON *mansk* of...*manx*]

ma·ny (mĕ-), a. & n. Numerous, as ~ *times*, (poet., rhet.) ~ *a time* (dē-of), ~ *& ~ a time*; ~ *people wish*, ~ *of us wish*, *how* ~ (of them) *can I have?*, *as as you like*, (pred., rare) *his reasons were as* ~ *and good*, *six mistakes in as* ~ *lines*; ~ '*s the*, *there are* ~ *that* (~ '*s the tale he has told us*), ~ '*s the time*, often the multitude; *one too* ~, not wanted, in the way; *he was* (*one*) *too* ~ *for us* (out-witted, baffled, us); *a good, great,* ~, *fair, large, number*; ~*-headed beast, monster*, the populace; ~*-sided*, having ~ sides, aspects, capabilities, etc., so ~*-sidedness*. [com.-Teut.: OE *manig*, G *manch*]

Maori (mowr'ĭ), n. Member, language, of brown race in New Zealand. [native]

map[1], n. Representation on paper etc. of (part of) earth's surface, showing physical & political features etc., or of the heavens; *off the* ~ (colloq.), of no account, obsolete; *on the* ~ (colloq.), to be reckoned with, of importance. Hence ~LESS a. [f. L *mappa* napkin; med. L has *mappa mundi* map of world]

map[2], v.t. (-pp-). Represent on map; ~ *out*, plan out, arrange in detail (course of conduct, one's time, etc.). [f. prec.]

ma·ple, n. Genus of trees & shrubs grown for shade, ornament, wood, or sugar; wood of these; ~*-leaf*, emblem of Canada. [OE has *mapulder*, MLG *mapeldorn*]

Maquis (mahkē'), n. Secret force of patriots in France in 1939-45 war. [F, = brushwood, f. Corsican It. *macchia*]

mar, v.t. (-rr-). Impair fatally, ruin, esp. *make* (or *mend*) *or* ~; ~*-plot*, one who hinders undertaking by officiousness. [com.-Teut.: OE *merran*, OFris. *meria* hinder, MDu. *merren* hinder]

ma·rabou (-bŏŏ), n. Large W.-Afr. stork; tuft of down from its wings or tail as trimming for hat etc. [F, prob. f. vulg. Arab. use of foll.]

ma·rabout (-bŏŏt), n. Mohammedan hermit or monk, esp. in N. Africa; shrine marking ~s burial-place. [f. Arab. *marabit*]

ma·raschi·no (-kē-), n. (pl. ~s). Liqueur from a small black cherry. [It. (*marasca* small black cherry, for *amarasca* f. *amaro* bitter f. L *amarus*)]

ma·ra·s·mus (-z-), n. Wasting away of body. Hence ~ic a. [f. Gk *marasmos* (*marainō* wither]

Mā·rathon, n. ~ (*race*) a race of abnormal length (w. ref. to Phidippides, who ran 150 miles to secure Spartan aid in the battle of ~ in 490 B.C.); (attrib.) requiring extreme endurance (applied to competitions of various kinds).

maraud', v.i. & t. Make plundering raid (on); go about pilfering; (trans.) plunder. Hence ~ER[1] n. [f. F *marauder* (*maraud* rogue)]

ma·rave·di (-vā-), n. (hist.). Spanish coins, gold worth 14s., copper ½d. [Sp. f. Arab. *Murābitīn* MARABOUTS, Moorish dynasty at Cordova]

ma·rble, n., & v.t. 1. Limestone in crystalline (also, in granular) state & capable of taking polish, used in sculpture & architecture; this as type of hardness or smoothness (often attrib.); (pl.) collection of sculptures, as *Elgin* ~s; small ball of ~, clay, glass, etc., as toy. 2. v.t. Stain, colour, (paper, edges of book, soap) to look like variegated ~ (esp. in p.p.). Hence **ma·rb'ly**[2] a. [vb f. n.; f. F *marbre* f. L *marmor*, cogn. w. Gk *mar-maros* (*marmairō* sparkle)]

marc, n. Refuse from pressed fruit. [F, f. *marcher* MARCH[3] in sense 'crush']

mar·casite, n. (Usu. white iron) pyrites. [f. med. L *marcasita*, etym. dub.]

mar·cel', n., & v.t. (-ll-). 1. ~ (*wave*), kind of artificial wave in hair. 2. v.t. Wave (hair) thus. [M~, inventor of method]

mar·cescent, a. (Of parts of plants) withering but not falling. Hence ~ENCE n. [f. L *marcescere* frequent. of *marcēre*, see -ENT]

March[1], n. (abbr. *Mar.*). Third month of year; ~ *brown*, fly used in angling; ~ HARE. [OF, f. L *Martius* (*mensis* month) of Mars]

march[2], n. (hist.). Boundary, frontiers, (often pl., esp. of borderland between England & Scotland or Wales); tract of (often debatable) land between two countries. [f. F *marche* f. Teut. *markā* MARK[1]]

march[3], v.i. (Of countries, estates, etc.) border *upon*, have common frontier *with*. [f. OF *marchir* (as prec.)]

march[4], n. (Mil.) marching of troops; distance covered by troops in a day; progress (*of events, time, intellect, mind*); *forced* ~; uniform step of troops etc., as *quick, slow*, ~; ~ *past*, of troops in quick time saluting-point at review; (Mus.) composition meant to accompany ~, as *dead* ~. [f. F *marche* (as foll.)]

march[5], v.i. & t. Walk *away, forth, past* (reviewing officer or sovereign), *out*, etc., in military manner with regular and measured tread; walk, proceed, steadily, ~*ing orders*, direction for troops to depart for war etc.; (as gallicism) make progress;

(trans.) cause to go on, off, etc. [f. F marcher, etym. dub.]

mar'chioness (-sho-), n. Wife, widow, of marquis; lady holding in her own right position equal to that of marquis. [f. med. L marchionissa f. marchio -ōnis MARCH² captain (marca)]

mar'ch'pane, marz'ipan, n. Paste of pounded almonds, sugar, etc., made up into small cakes etc.; such cake. [cf. F massepain, G marzipan, etc., etym. dub.]

mar'con'i'gram, n. Message sent by Marconi's system of wireless telegraphy. Send ~, send (message) thus. [see foll.] [-GRAM]

Mardi gras (mahd'ē'grah), n. Shrove Tuesday; last day of carnival. [F, = fat Tuesday]

mar'e¹, n. ~ claus'um, sea under jurisdiction of particular country; ~ lib'erum, sea open to all nations. [L]

mare², n. Female of equine animal, esp. horse; GREY¹ ~; SHANKS's ~; ~'s-nest, illusory discovery; ~'s-tail, kinds of aquatic plant, long straight streaks of cirrus. [OE mere, cf. Du. merrie, G mähre jade]

Maréchal Niel (usu. pr. mahsh'al nēl), n. Kind of climbing rose. [after AdolpheNiel, Marshal of France (d. 1869)]

marémm'a, n. Low marshy unhealthy country by seashore. [It.]

mar'garine (-g-, -j-; also -ēn), n. Legal name for all materials made in imitation of butter. [F, misapplication of a chem. term, f. Gk margaron pearl, see -IN]

mar'g'ay, n. S.-Amer. tiger-cat. [F, f. native mbaracaia]

mar'ge, (poet.) =foll. [F, as foll.]

mar'gin, n., & v.t. 1. Edge, border, of surface, whence ~ATE²(2), ~āted, aa.; condition near the limit below or beyond which a thing ceases to be possible etc.; extra amount of time, money, etc.) over & above the necessary; (Commerc.) sum deposited with stockbroker to cover risk of loss on transaction of account; space round main body of printed matter on page. 2. v.t. Furnish with ~ or marginal notes; deposit ~ on (stock). [(vb f. n.) f. L margo -ĭnis]

mar'ginal, a. Of, written in, the margin; having ~ notes; of, at, the edge; close to the limit. Hence ~LY² adv. [-AL]

margina'l'ia, n. pl. Marginal notes. [mod. L neut. pl., as MARGIN, see -AL]

mar'g'rāve, n. (hist.). German title of some princes of Holy Roman Empire, orig. of military governor of border province. [f. MDu. markgrave border count [MARK² + grave count)]

mar'g'ravine, n. Margrave's wife. [f. Du. markgravin (as prec., see -INE²)]

mar'g'uerite (-gerēt), n. Ox-eye daisy. [F, f. LL (-ta) f. Gk margarītēs (margaron pearl, see -ITE¹)]

mariage de convenance (see Ap.], n. Marriage contracted from prudential motives. [F]

Mar'ian, a. & n. 1. Of the Virgin Mary, Mary Queen of England, or Mary Queen of Scots. 2. n. Adherent of the last. [f. L Maria Mary + -AN]

ma'ri'd, n. Jinn of most powerful class. [Arab., part. of marada rebel]

ma'rigold, n. Kinds of plant with golden or yellow flowers; MARSH ~. [f. Mary (prob. the Virgin) + gold]

marin'āde', n., & (also -te) v.t. Pickle of wine, vinegar, & spices; fish, meat, thus pickled; (v.t.) pickle with ~. [(vb f. n.) F, f. Sp. marinada (marinar pickle in brine, as foll. -ADE]

marine' (-ēn), a. & n. 1. Of, found in, produced by, the sea; of shipping or naval matters, as ~ insurance; || ~ stores, old ships' materials & similar odds & ends as merchandise; for use at sea; (of soldiers) serving on board ship. 2. n. Country's shipping, fleet, or navy, esp. mercantile ~; soldier on warship (blue, red, ~s, hist., artillery, light infantry); tell that to the (HORSE¹) ~s. [f. F marin (fem. -ine) f. L marinus (mare sea, -INE¹)]

mar'iner, n. Sailor, seaman; master ~, captain of merchant ship. [AF, f. med. L marinarius (as prec., see -ARY¹)]

Marin'ism (-ēn), n. Affected style of It. poet Marini (d. 1625). So ~IST n. [-ISM]

Mariol'atry, n. (derog.). Worship of the Virgin Mary. [f. Gk Maria Mary + -LATRY]

mariōnětte', n. Puppet worked by strings, representing person etc. [f. F marionnette (Marion dim. of Marie Mary, -ETTE)]

ma'rish, n. & a. (poet.). Marsh(y). [ME & OF mareis f. med. L mariscus MARSH]

Mar'ist, n. Member of Rom. Cath. Society of Mary. [f. F Mariste (Marie Mary, see -IST)]

ma'rital (or marit'), a. Of a husband; of marriage. Hence ~LY² adv. [f. L marītālis (marītus husband, see -AL)]

ma'ritime, a. Living, found, near the sea; connected with the sea, as ~ insurance. [f. L marītimus (mare sea; for suf. cf. ultimus)]

mar'joram, n. Genus including Sweet M~, aromatic herb used in cookery. [f. OF majorane f. med. L majorana, etym. dub.]

mark¹, n. 1. Target or other object to be aimed at; beside, wide of, the ~, not hitting it, (fig.) not to the point. 2. (Boxing) pit of stomach. 3. Desired object, as hit, miss, the ~. 4. Sign, indication, (of quality, character, etc.), esp. ~ of mouth, depression in horse's tooth indicating age. 5. Affixed or impressed sign, seal, etc.;

EAR¹, HALL, TRADE, ~. **6.** Cross etc. made in place of signature by illiterate person. **7.** Written symbol; this as sign of *good* or *bad* conduct. **8.** Unit of numerical award of merit in examination, as *he gained 46 ~s*. **9.** Line etc. serving to indicate position; *Plimsoll's ~*; line showing how far ship may legally be submerged when loaded; *below, up to,* etc., *the ~*; (Footb.) *heel~* on ground made by player who has obtained fair catch. **11.** Stain, scar, etc. **12.** *Make one's ~,* attain distinction; *of ~,* noteworthy. **13.** (As apology for mentioning anything horrible etc.) *(God) save the ~*. **14.** (Hist.) tract of land held by Teutonic village community. **15.** (Athletics) line indicating the starting-point (*get off the ~,* start). **16.** *Easy ~* (orig. U.S., sl.), person easily gulled. [OE *mearc*, cf. Du. & G *mark*, f. OTeut. *marka*]

mark², v.t. 1. Make a mark on (thing) by stamping, cutting, writing, etc.; put identifying mark or name on (linen); attach figures indicating prices to (goods); (pass.) have natural marks, as *~ed with silver spots*. **2.** *~ out,* trace out boundaries for (ground), plan (course), destine, as *~ed out for slaughter;* *~ off,* separate (thing from another, lit. & fig.) by boundary. **3.** Indicate (place on map, length of syllable) by signs or marks. **4.** Record (points gained in games). **5.** Manifest (one's displeasure etc. *by*); (pass.) *this tendency is strongly ~ed* (noticeable), *a ~ed difference,* whence **~'ed·ly** [-idli] adv., **~'edness** n., of, as *no triumph ~s her manner*. **7.** *~ time,* move feet as in marching, but without advancing (often fig.). **8.** See, notice; observe mentally, as *~ my words; a ~ed man,* one whose conduct is watched with suspicion or hostility. **9.** (Also *~ down*) note & remember spot to which (grouse etc.) has retired. **10.** ||(Footb.) keep close to (opponent) so as to hamper him if he receives ball. **11.** *~ down,* (also) *~ at a lower price;* *~ up,* *~ at a higher price.* [OE *mearcian,* cf. Du. & G *merken,* (as prec.)]

mark³, n. Denomination of weight for gold & silver, usu. 8 oz (now only of continental weights); German coin (formerly about 1/-); (Hist.) English money of account, 13/4. [com.-Teut. & Rom. etym. dub.]

mark'er, n. In vbl senses, esp.: one who marks down game; one who records score, esp. in billiards; flare etc. to assist bombers in air-raid; = BOOK¹-~. [MARK¹ +-ER¹.]

mark'et¹, n. Gathering of people for purchase & sale of provisions, livestock, etc.; time of this; *bring one's eggs or hogs to a bad ~,* fail in one's schemes; open space or covered building in which cattle etc. are exposed for sale; *make a ~*

of, (fig.) barter away; demand (for commodity); *the corn ~,* the trade in corn; *come into the ~,* be offered for sale; *put on the ~,* offer for sale; BLACK¹~; MONEY-~; rate of purchase & sale, value, as *the ~ fell;* seat of trade; *~ cross* (erected in ||-place); *~-day* (on which ~ is held); ||*~-garden* (in which vegetables are grown for ~); *~-place, square,* open space, where ~ is held; *~-town* (where ~ is held). [ONF. f. L *mercatus* (*mercari* trade, see MERCANTILE)]

mark'et², v.i. & t. Buy or sell in market; sell (goods) in market; *~ing* n. [MARK² +-ING¹]

mark'hor (-kôr), n. Large spiral-horned wild goat of N. India. [Pushtu, = snake-eater]

mark'ing, n. In vbl senses, esp. colouring of feathers, skin, etc.; *~-ink* (indelible, for marking linen). [MARK² +-ING¹]

marks'man, n. (pl. -men). One skilled or practised in aiming at mark, esp. one who attains certain standard of proficiency in rifle practice. Hence **~SHIP** (1, 3) n. [MARK¹ + -ES + MAN]

Mark Tap'ley, n. Invincibly cheery person. [character in Dickens's *Martin Chuzzlewit*]

marl, n., & v.t. **1.** Soil consisting of clay and carbonate of lime, a valuable fertilizer. **2.** v.t. Apply ~ to (ground). Hence **~'y²** a. [(vbl.n.) f. OF *marle* f. LL *margila* dim. of L *marga*]

Marl'borough House, n. (maw¹bro), n. Royal Palace used as a London residence. [f. Marlborough College. [-IAN] **Marlbur'ian** (mawl-), n. & a. (Member) of Marlborough College. [-IAN]

marl'ine, n. (naut.). Small line of two strands; *~-spike, marlinspike,* pointed hard-wood or iron tool for separating strands of rope in splicing. [f. Du. *mar-lijn* (*marren* bind+*lijn* LINE²)]

marl'ite, n. Kind of marl that resists action of air. [-ITE¹]

marm'alade, n. Preserve of oranges or specified fruit. [f. F *marmelade* f. Port. *marmelada* f. *marmelo* quince f. L f. Gk *melimēlon* (*meli* honey+*mēlon* apple) see -ADE]

marm'ite, n. Extract made from fresh brewer's yeast. [P ; F.=stockpot]

marm'olite, n. Laminated serpentine of pale green colour. [irreg. f. Gk *marmairō* shine, see -LITE]

marm'o~real, a. (poet.). Of, like, marble. [f. L *marmoreus* (as MARBLE) +-AL]

marm'oset (-z-), n. Small tropical American monkey with bushy tail. [f. OF *marmouset* grotesque image, etym.]

marm'ot, n. Rodent of squirrel family; kind of bathing-cap. [f. F *marmotte* prob. f. Roumansch *murmont* f. L *murem* (nom. *mus*) *montis* mouse of the mountain]

marocain, n. A dress-fabric made in silk (or other materials). [F,=Moroccan]

Mā'ronite, n. One of a sect of Syrian Christians dwelling in Lebanon. [f. LL *Maronīta* (*Maron* founder, see -ITE[1])]

maroon'[1], n. & a. **1.** (Of) brownish-crimson colour. **2.** Firework exploding with loud report. [f. F *marron* chestnut f. It. *marrone*]

maroon'[2], n. One of class of negroes, orig. fugitive slaves, in mountains & forests of Dutch Guiana & W. Indies; marooned person. [f. F *marron* perh. corrupt. of Sp. *cimarron* wild (*cima* mountain-top perh. ult. f. Gk *kuma* wave)]

maroon'[3], v.t. & i. Put (person) ashore & leave him on desolate island or coast as punishment; idle, hang about. [f. prec.]

mā'rque (-k), n. (hist.). *Letter(s) of* ~ (& *reprisal*), licence to fit out armed vessel & employ it in capture of enemy's merchant shipping; (sing.) ship carrying such licence. [F., f. Prov. *marca* f. *marcar* seize as pledge, perh. conn. w. MARK[1]]

mā'rquee' (-kē), n. Large tent. [f. MAR-QUISE taken as pl. n.]

mā'rquetry, -terie, (-kē-), n. Inlaid work. [F (*-erie*), f. *marqueter* variegate (MARK[1])]

mā'rquis, -quess, n. Noble ranking between duke & earl or (in foreign countries) count. Hence **mā'rq'uis**ATE[1](1) n. [f. OF *marchis*=It. *marchese* ruler of MARCH[2], -ESE]

mā'rquise' (-kēz), n. **1.** (Of foreign nobility) marchioness. **2.** Finger-ring set with oval pointed cluster of gems. **3.** (arch.). Tent. [F, fem. of *marquis*]

mā'rq'uois (-kwoiz), n. ~ *scale*, apparatus for drawing equidistant parallel lines. [prob. blunder for F *marquoir* marker (MARK[1])]

mā'rram, n. A shore grass that binds sand. [f. ON *maralm-r* (*mar-r* sea, HAULM)]

mā'rriage (-rĭj), n. Relation between married persons; wedlock; *give, take, in* ~ (as husband or wife); *communal* ~, system by which all the men in small community are married to all the women; *companionate* ~, see COMPANION[1]; act, ceremony of marrying; *civil* ~ (performed by civil official without religious ceremony); (fig.) intimate union; (Cards) declaration of king & queen of same suit; ~ *articles*, antenuptial agreement respecting rights of property & succession; ~ *LICENCE*[1], ~ *bed*, (fig.) marital intercourse; ~ *LICENCE*[1]; ~ *lines*, certificate of marriage; ~ *market*, supply & demand of eligible partners for ~; ~ *settlement*, arrangement securing property to wife & sometimes to children. [f. F *marriage* f. pop. L †*marita-ticum* (*maritus* husband, see -AGE)]

mā'rriageable (-rĭja-), a. Of an age to marry; (of age) fit for marriage. [-ABLE]

mā'rried (-ĭd), a. United in wedlock; of person(s) so united, as ~ *life*. [p.p. of MARRY[1]]

marron glacé (see Ap.), n. Chestnut iced with sugar as sweetmeat. [F]

mā'rrow[1] (-ŏ), n. Soft fatty substance in cavities of bones, often a type of rich food or of vitality (*chilled to the* ~, right through); *spinal* ~, substance forming spinal cord; essential part, as *pith & ~*; *vegetable* ~, kind of gourd; *bone, bone containing, edible* ~, (pl. joc.) knees; ~*(fat)*, kind of large pea; ~*-spoon* (for getting ~ from bones). Hence ~LESS (-ŏl-), ~Y[2] (-ŏĭ), aa. [com.-Teut.: OE *mearg*, Du. *merg*, G *mark*]

mā'rrow[2] (-ŏ), n. (dial.). Mate, consort, match, very image of. [?]

‖ **mā'rry[1]**, v.t. & i. (Of priest etc.) join (persons, one to another) in wedlock; (of parent or guardian) give (son, daughter, etc.) in marriage; (of either contracting party) take in marriage; (fig.) unite intimately; (Naut.) splice (rope-ends) together without increasing girth; (intr.) take husband or wife. [f. F *marier* f. L *maritare* f. *maritus* husband (*mas maris* male)]

mā'rry[2], int. (arch.) expr. surprise, asseveration, indignation, etc.; ~ *come up* expr. indignant or contemptuous surprise. [=(the Virgin) *Mary*]

Mārs (-z), n. Roman god of war; warfare; planet fourth in order of distance from sun. [L]

Marsā'la (-sah-), n. White wine like light sherry, from ~ in Sicily.

Marseillaise' (-selāz, & see Ap.), n. National song of French Republic, first sung by Marseilles patriots. [F, fem. adj. f. *Marseille*, -ESE]

Mārseilles' (-sālz), n. Seaport in S. France; stiff cotton fabric like piqué.

mā'rsh, n. Low land flooded in winter & usu. watery at all times; ~ *gas*, light carburetted hydrogen; ~ *mallow*, (confection made from root of) shrubby herb growing near salt ~es; ~ *marigold*, golden-flowered ranunculaceous plant growing in moist meadows. Hence ~INESS n., ~Y[2] a. [OE *merse* f. WG *+marisk-* (whence med. L *mariscus*) f. OTeut. *mari-* sea, see -ISH[1]]

mā'rsh'al[1], n. ‖ EARL~, officer of highest rank in former armies; PROVOST~; FIELD~; ~ *of the Royal* AIR[1] *Force*, AIR[1]~; (Hist.) *knight* ~, officer of royal household with judicial functions; ‖ (*judge's*) ~, official accompanying judge on circuit, with secretarial duties; officer arranging ceremonies etc. Hence ~SHIP n. [f. OF *mareschal* f. Frank. L *mariscalcus* f. OHG *marahscalh* (OTeut. *marhoz* horse + *skalkoz* servant)]

mā'rsh'al[2], v.t. & i. (-ll-). Arrange in due order (persons at feast etc., soldiers, facts, etc.); (Her.) combine (coat of arms); conduct (person) ceremoniously (*into* etc.); ~*ling yard*, railway yard in which goods trains etc. are assembled. [f. prec.]

Marsh'alsea, n. (hist.). Court held, by knight marshal, &c. [f. obs. *marshalsey* (MAR-SHAL'+-CY)]

marsh'ial, a. & n. (anat. zool.). 1. Of, like, a pouch, as ~ *muscle.* 2. (Animal) of the class or mammals characterized by having a pouch in which to carry their young, born imperfect. [f. L f. Gk *marsupion,* dim. of *marsupos* purse +-AL]

mart, n. (Poet.). market-place; auction room : trade centre. [f. Du. *markt,* f. L as MARKET]

martell'o, n. (pl. ~s), ~ (*tower*), small circular fort, usu. on coast to prevent hostile landing. [corrupt. of Cape *Mor-tella* in Corsica.]

mar'ten, n. Animal like weasel, with valuable fur. [f. OF (*peau skin*) *martrine* of the marten (*martre* f. OTeut. *martrine*)]

mar'tial (-shl), a. Of, suitable for, appro-priate to, warfare, whence ~IZE (+-shr)- v.t.; ~ *law,* military government, by which ordinary law is suspended ; brave; fond of fighting ; (M~) of the planet Mars. Hence ~IY[2] adv. [F, f. L *martialis* of MARS, see -AL]

Mar'tian (-shn), n. Inhabitant of Mars. [f. L *Martius* of MARS (+-AN]

mar'tin, n. 1. *St M~,* bishop of Tours in 4th c. ; *M~-mas, St M~'s day,* Nov. 11; || *St M~'s summer,* fine season about this family, building mud nest on house walls etc. [f. f. L *Martinus*]

martinet', n. Strict (esp. military or naval) disciplinarian. Hence ~t'ISM n., ~t'ISH[1] a. [M~, French drill-master in reign of Louis XIV.]

mar'tingale (-ngg-), n. 1. Strap, set of straps, fastened at one end to nose-band, at other end to girth, of horse to prevent rearing etc. ; (Naut.) rope for guying down jibboom. 2. Gambling system of doubling stakes in hope of eventual turn of luck. [F, etym. dub.]

mar'tini[1], n. The M~-Henry rifle. [M~, inventor of its breech action]

martin'i[2] (-ēnē), n. Cocktail made of gin, vermouth, orange bitters, etc. [M~, inventor]

mar'tlet, n. (Her.) footless bird. [f. F *martelet* prob. f. *martlet* dim. f. MARTIN]

mar'tyr (-er), n. & v.t. 1. One who undergoes penalty of death for persistence in Christian faith or obedience to law of Church, or undergoes death or suffering for any great cause; ~ *to* (constant sufferer from) *gout* etc.; *make a* ~ *of* (one-self,* (pretend to) sacrifice one's inclina-tions, for sake of credit thus gained. 2. v.t. Put to death as ~, torment. [(vb f. n.) eccl. L f. late Gk *martur*=Gk *martus* *-uros* witness]

mar'tyrdom (-ter-), n. Sufferings & death of martyr; torment. [-DOM]

mar'yrize, v.t. Make a martyr of (one-self, person). [f. med. L *martyrizare* (MARTYR, -IZE)]

mar'tyr|o- in comb. = of martyrs, as : ~*ól'ogy,* worship of martyrs ; ~*ól'ogy,* list, register, history of martyrs, whence ~*ol'ogical.*

mar'tyry, n. Shrine, church, erected in honour of martyr. [f. med. L f. Gk *marturion* (as MARTYR)]

mar'vel, n. Wonderful thing ; wonderful example of (quality) ; (arch.) astonish-ment. [f. OF *merveille* f. L *mirabilia* neut. pl. of *mirabilis* (*mirari* wonder at, see -BLE)]

mar'vel, v.i.(literary ; -ll-). Be surprised (*at, that*) ; wonder (*how, why,* etc.). [f. OF *merveillier* (as prec.)]

mar'vellous, a. Astonishing ; extrava-gantly improbable, esp. *the* ~. Hence ~LY[2] adv., ~NESS n. [f. OF *merveillos* (as prec.)]

Marx'ian, a. & n. (Adherent) of the doctrines of the German socialist Karl Marx (1818-83). So ~ISM(3) n., ~IST(2) n. [-IAN]

marzipan. See MARCHPANE.

mas'cara, n. Preparation for dyeing eyelashes etc. [?]

más'cot, n. Person, thing, that brings luck. [f. provincial F *mascotte,* perh. cogn. w. Pr. *masco* witch]

ma'sculine (má-, mah-), a. & n. 1. Of the gender to which names of males normally belong ; ~ *rhyme* (in French verse, between words ending in stressed syllables, not, e mute), ~ *ending,* ending of line with stressed syllable ; of the male sex ; manly, vigorous ; (of woman) having qualities appropriate to man. 2. n. ~ gender, word. Hence ~NESS, masculin'ity, nn. [f. F *masculin* (fem. *-ine*) f. L *masculinus* (as MALE, see -INE[1])]

mash[1], n. Malt mixed with hot water to form wort ; mixture of boiled grain, bran, etc., given warm to horses etc.; soft pulp made by crushing, mixing with water, etc.; (sl.) mashed potatoes (*sausage &* ~); confused mixture; ~*tub* (in which malt is mashed). [OE *mäsc-,* cf. G *meisch* crushed grapes, malt, Da. *mask* grains for pigs, perh. cogn. w. MIX]

mash[2], v.t. Mix (malt) with hot water; crush, pound, to pulp; reduce (potatoes etc.) to uniform mass by crushing. [f. prec.]

mash[3], v.t., & n. (sl.). 1. Excite senti-mental admiration in (one of opposite sex); *be* ~*ed on,* have such admiration for. 2. n. Person on whom one of opposite sex is ~ed. [?]

mash'er, n. Fop posing as lady-killer. [f.]

mash'ie, -y, n. Iron golf club used for lofting or for medium distances; ~ *niblick,* club intermediate between ~ & niblick. [perh. corrupt. of F *massue* club]

ma'sjid (mŭ-), n. Mosque. [Arab.]

mask¹ (mah-), n. Covering, usu. of velvet or silk, for concealing face at balls etc., or of wire, gauze, etc., for protection; hollow figure of human head worn by ancient Greek & Roman actors; clay or wax likeness of person's face, esp. (also *death*~) one made by taking mould from face; (fig.) disguise, as *throw off the* ~; masked person; face, head, of fox. [f. F *masque* f. Sp. *máscara*, or f. med. L *mascus*, etym. dub.]

mask² (mah-), v.t. Cover (face) with mask; (pass.) be disguised with mask; (Mil.) conceal (force etc.) from enemy's view, hinder (army etc.) from action by watching with adequate force, hinder (friendly force) by standing in line of its fire; disguise (feelings etc.); ~*ed ball* (at which masks are worn). [f. prec.]

ma'sker, -quer, (mah-), n. One who takes part in masquerade or masque. [prec.+-ER¹]

mâskinŏn'ge (-j, -jĭ), n. Large pike in great lakes of N. America. [Odjibwa]

masochism (măz'ŏkĭzm), n. Form of (esp. sexual) perversion in which a sufferer derives pleasure from pain or humiliation (opp. SADISM). [f. L. von Sacher *Masoch* (d. 1895), Austrian novelist who described a case of ~]

mãs'on, n., & v.t. 1. Worker in stone; freemason, whence **mãsŏn'ic** a. 2. v.t. Build, strengthen, with masonry. [vb f. F *maçonner*; med. OF *maçon*; etym. dub.]

mãs'onry̆, n. Mason's work, stonework. [f. F *maçonnerie* (as MASON, see -ERY)]

Măs(s)ōr'a(h) (-ŏ-*ra*), n. Body of traditional information on text of Hebrew Bible. [f. Heb. *masoreth* perh.= bond]

Măs(s)ōrēte, -ite, n. Jewish scholar contributing to the Masora. Hence **măs(s)ŏrĕt'ic** a. [(-*ēte*) corrupt. of Heb. as prec.; (-*ite*) prec.+-ITE¹]

mâsque (mahsk), n. Amateur histrionic & musical entertainment, orig. in dumb show, later with metrical dialogue; dramatic composition for this. [as MASK¹]

masquerade'¹ (mahske-), n. Masked ball; false show, pretence. [f. Sp. *mascarada* (*máscara* mask, see -ADE¹]

masquerade'² (mahske-), v.i. Appear in disguise; assume false appearance. [f. prec.]

mãssĭ¹, n. (A) celebration (now usu. Rom. Cath.) of the Eucharist, as *was said, we attend, go to, hear,* ~, ~*es were said for his soul*; liturgy used in this; musical setting of parts of this; *high* ~ (with incense, music, & assistance of deacon & subdeacon; *low* ~ (with no music & minimum of ceremony). [OE *mæsse* f. vulg. L *messa* f. eccl. L *missa* (*mittere miss-* send); sense history doubtful]

mãss², n, & v.t. & i. 1. Coherent body of matter of indefinite shape; dense aggregation of objects, as *a* ~ *of fibres*; large number (*of*); *he is a* ~ *of* (covered with) *bruises*; unbroken expanse (of light etc.); *the (great)* ~, the majority (*of*); *the* ~*es*, the lower orders, cf. CLASSES; *in the* ~, in the aggregate; (Physics) quantity of matter a body contains; ~ ENERGY; ~ *meeting*, large (usu. political) assembly of people; ~ *observation*, study & reporting of social customs etc, of ordinary people; ~ *of manœuvre*, body of troops kept free for strategic needs; ~ *production* (of large quantities of a standardized article by standardized mechanical processes). 2. vb. Gather (t. & i.) into ~; (Mil.) concentrate (troops). [(vb f. F *masser*) f. F *masse* f. L *massa* prob. f. Gk *maza* barley-cake (*massō* knead)]

mãss'acre (-ker), n., & v.t. 1. General slaughter, carnage, (of persons, occas. of animals). 2. v.t. Make a ~ of, murder cruelly or violently. [vb f. F *massacrer* F; OF *macacre*, etym. dub.]

massage (-ahzh), n., & v.t. 1. Rubbing, kneading, etc., of muscles & joints of the body with the hands, to stimulate their action, etc. 2. v.t. Treat (part, person) thus. [(vb f. n.) F (*masser* treat with massage, perh. f. Port. *amassar* knead, f. *massâ* dough, see -AGE)]

massé (măs'ā), n. (billiards). Stroke made with cue held perpendicular. [F, p.p. of *masser* make such stroke (as MACE¹)]

mãsseur', mãsseuse', (-ĕr, -ĕrz, & see Ap.), nn. Man, woman, who practises massage. So **mãss'ER¹, mãss'OR²**, nn. [F (as MASSAGE, see -OR²)]

mãss'if, n. Mountain heights forming a compact group. [F (see MASSIVE) in n. use]

mãss'ive, a. Large & heavy or solid; (of features, head, etc.) largely moulded; (fig.) solid, substantial; impressive, imposing; (Psych.) of sensation etc.) having large volume or magnitude. Hence ~LY² adv., ~NESS n. [F (-*ĭf, -ĭve*), as MASS², see -IVE]

mãss'y̆, a. Solid; weighty. Hence ~IVESS n. [MASS²+-Y²]

mast¹ (-ah-), n. 1. Long pole of timber, iron, etc., set up on ship's keel to support sails; BEFORE *the* ~; HALF-~*high*; hence (of ship) ~*ED²* a., ~*ER*¹ n.; ~*head*, highest part of ~, esp. of lower ~ as place of observation or punishment, (v.t.) send (sailor) to this, raise (sail) to its position. 2. Post, or lattice-work upright, for supporting a wireless aerial; (also *mooring-*~) strong steel tower to top of which an airship can be moored. [com.-Teut.: OE *mæst*, Du. & G *mast*]

mast² (-ah-), n. Fruit of beech, oak, & other forest-trees, esp. as food for swine. [com.-WG: OE *mæst*, G *mast*]

mãs'taba, n. (archaeol.). Ancient Egyptian tomb with sloping sides & flat roof. [Arab. *maṣṭaba* bench]

ma'ster[1] (mah-), n. **1.** Person having control; (Naut.) captain of merchant vessel; employer; owner of dog, horse, etc.; male head of household, as ~ *of the house*; *be* ~ *of*, have at one's disposal; *be one's own* ~, be independent or free to do as one will; *make oneself* ~ *of*, acquire thorough knowledge of or facility in using; one who has or gets the upper hand, as *we will see which is* ~. **2.** Teacher, tutor, esp. (also *school-*~) in school; HOUSE~; teacher in philosophy etc. **3.** *The M*~, Christ; *M*~ *of Arts* (abbr. *M.A.*), holder of university degree giving authority to teach in university. **4.** Skilled workman, or one in business on his own account, as ~ *carpenter.* **5.** Great artist, esp. *old* ~ (esp. of painters of 13th-17th cc.), picture etc. by a ~. **6.** Head of some colleges. **7.** (As title of legal functionaries) *M*~ *in Chancery* etc.; *M*~ *of Ceremonies* (see CEREMONY), MISRULE, ROLLS; *M*~ (organizer, leader, esp. in Royal Household & Inns of Court) *of the revels; M*~ *of the Horse*, official in English royal household; *M*~ (*M.F.H.*), *beagles*, etc. **8.** (Prefixed, esp. to name of young gentleman) *M*~ *Tom, M*~ *Jones.* **9.** attrib. Commanding, superior, (*a* ~ *mind*). **10.** ~-*at-arms*, police officer on man-of-war; ~-*key* (opening many locks, each also opened by separate key); ~ *mason*, (as above, also) freemason who has passed third degree; ~-*piece*, consummate piece of workmanship; ~-*stroke*, surpassingly skilful act (of policy etc.). Hence ~DOM, ~HOOD, nn., ~LESS a. [OE *mægester* cogn. w. also f. OF *maistre*) f. L *magister* cogn. w. *magis* more]

ma'ster[2] (mah-), v.t. Overcome, defeat; reduce to subjection; acquire complete knowledge of (subject) or facility in using (instrument etc.); rule as a master. [f. prec.]

ma'sterful (mah-), a. Self-willed, imperious. Hence ~LY[2] adv., ~NESS n. [-FUL]

ma'sterly (mah-), a. Worthy of a master, very skilful. Hence ~iNESS n. [-LY[1]]

ma'stership (mah-), n. Dominion, control; office, function, of master, esp. in school. [-SHIP]

ma'stery (mah-), n. Sway, dominion; the upper hand; masterly skill; masterly use or knowledge (of instrument, subject). [f. OF *maistrie* (as MASTER[1], see -Y[1])]

ma'stic, n. Gum or resin exuding from bark of certain trees, used in making varnish; trees yielding this; kinds of cement; liquor flavoured with ~, used in Turkey & Greece; ~ *colour*, pale yellow. Hence **mâsti'cic** a. (chem.). [F, f. LL *mastichum* f. L f. Gk *mastíkhē*, etym. dub.]

mâ'sticàte, v.t. Grind (food) with teeth, chew. Hence or cogn. ~ABI'LITY, ~A'TION, nn., ~ATORY a. [f. LL *masticare* (perh. as prec.), -ATE[3]]

mâ'stiff (mah-), n. Large strong dog with drooping ears & pendulous lips. [f. OF *mastin* f. pop. L *mansuetinus* (*mansuetus* tame f. *manus* hand + *suescere suet-* grow accustomed, see -INE[1])]

mâsti'tis, n. Inflammation of female breast. [f. Gk *mastos* breast, see -ITIS]

mâs'todon, n. Large extinct mammal like elephant, with nipple-shaped tubercles on crowns of molar teeth. Hence **mâstodôn'tic** a. [f. Gk *mastos* breast + *odous odontos* tooth]

mâs'toid, a. & n. (anat.). **1.** Shaped like female breast; ~ *process*, conical prominence in the temporal bone to which muscles are attached. **2.** n. ~ process. (colloq.) abscess on ~. [f. Gk *mastoeides* breast, see -OID]

mâs'turbàte (-ter-), v.i. Practise self-abuse. Hence ~A'TION n. [f. L *masturbari*, etym. dub., see -ATE[3]]

mât[1], n. Coarse fabric of plaited rushes, straw, etc., for lying upon, packing furniture, etc.; piece of this for wiping shoes upon, esp. *door-*~; *on the* ~ (Army sl.), in trouble (i.e. on the orderly room ~ before the C.O.). [OE *matt* f. LL *matta*]

mât[2], v.t. & i. (-tt-). Cover, furnish, with mats; entangle (often *together*) in thick mass (esp. in p.p., as ~*ted hair*); become ~ted. [f. prec.]

mât[3], a., n., & v.t. (-tt-). **1.** (Of colours, surfaces, etc.) dull, without lustre. **2.** n. Border of dead gold round framed picture; appearance of unburnished gold; roughened or frosted groundwork. **3.** v.t. Make (gilding etc.) dull; frost (glass). [vrb f. F *mater*) F f. med. L *mattus* t.]

mât'adôr, n. Man appointed to kill bull in bull-fight; principal card in some games. [Sp., f. L *mactator(em* (*mactare* kill, -OR[2])]

mâtch[1], n. **1.** Person able to contend with another as an equal, as *find, meet,* one's ~; *be (more than) a* ~ *for*; person equal to another in some quality, as *we shall never see his* ~; person, thing, exactly like or corresponding to another. **2.** Contest of skill etc. in which persons are matched against each other, as *cricket-*~. **3.** Matrimonial alliance; *make a* ~, bring this about; person viewed in regard to his or her eligibility for marriage, esp. as to rank or fortune, as *he is an excellent* ~. **4.** ~-*board*, one with tongue cut along one edge & groove along another, so as to fit into similar boards; ~-*maker*, one fond of scheming to bring about marriages; ~-*point(s)*, state of a game when one side needs only one more point to win the ~ (occas. ~-*ball*). [OE *gemæcca*, cogn. w. MAKE]

mâtch[2], v.t. & i. Join (person *with* another) in marriage; prove a match for;

place (person etc.). **In conflict** *against* another; *well ~ed,* fit to contend with each other, live together, etc., on equal terms; place (person, thing) in competition *with*; be equal, correspond in quantity, quality, colour, etc., to, (thing etc.; also intr. *with*) as *the carpets ~ the wall-paper, these ribbons do not ~, do not ~ with your hat, trimmed with velvet to ~;* find material etc. that *~es* with (another), as *can you ~ me this silk?* [f. prec.]

match³, n. Short piece of wood, wax taper, etc., tipped with composition that bursts into flame when rubbed on rough or (*safety ~*) specially prepared surface; piece of wick, cord, etc., designed to burn at uniform rate, for firing cannon etc.; *~-box* (for holding *~es*); *~'lock,* (gun with) lock in which *~* is placed for igniting powder; *~'wood,* wood suitable for *~es,* minute splinters, (*make ~wood of,* utterly smash). [f. OF *mesche* (F *mèche* wick), etym. dub.]

match'et (*or -ĕt'*), n. Broad heavy knife used in America etc. as tool & weapon. [f. Sp. *machete*]

match'less, a. Without an equal, peerless. Hence *~LY*² adv. [MATCH¹+-LESS]

mate¹, n., & v.t. (chess). = CHECKMATE; *fool's ~* (in which first player is *~d* at opponent's second move); STALE¹-. [see CHECKMATE]

mate², n. 1. (In working-classes) companion, fellow worker, (also as general form of address). 2. One of a pair, esp. of birds; fitting partner in marriage. 3. (Naut.) officer on merchant ship who sees to execution of master's commands & takes command in his absence, (also) assistant to some functionary, as *cook's, gunner's, surgeon's, ~.* Hence *~LESS* (-tl-) a., *mat'*(e)y² a., sociable, familiar (*with*). [prob. f. MLG *made* for *gemate* f. OTeut. *gamaton* messmate (*ga-Y- + -mat- MEAT*)]

mate³, v.t. & i. Join (two persons, one *with* another) in marriage; marry (*with,* or abs.); pair (birds), (of birds) pair; keep company (*with*). [f. prec.]

ma'té (-ā), n. (Vessel for) infusion of leaves of a shrub, Paraguay tea; the shrub, || *maté* f. Sp. *mate* f. native *mati*]

matelot, || māt'lō(w), (māt'lō), n. (naut. sl.), Sailor. [F (*-elot*)]

mat'elote (-ŏt), n. Dish of fish etc. with sauce of wine, onions, etc. [F, f. *matelot* sailor]

māt'er, n. || (School sl.) mother; DURA MATER, PIA MATER; *~famil'ias,* mother of household. [L]

material, a. & n. 1. Concerned with the matter, not the form, of reasoning; of matter, corporeal; *~ theory* of heat (that it is a *~* substance); (of conduct, point of view, etc.) unspiritual; concerned with bodily comfort etc., as (*to,* or abs.), 2. n. Matter from which thing is made, as *raw*

(unmanufactured) *~;* elements, constituent parts, (of substance, *for* historical composition etc.); stuff, fabric; *writing-~s* (requisites). Hence *~ITY* (-āl-) n., *~LY*² adv. [f. LL *materiālis* (as MATTER, see -AL)]

mate'rialism, n. Opinion that nothing exists but matter & its movements & modifications, also, that consciousness & will are wholly due to material agency; (Art) tendency to lay stress on material aspect of objects. So *~IST* n., *~ISTIC* a., *~ISTICALLY* adv. [-ISM]

materia'lize, v.t. & i. Make, represent as, material; cause (spirit) to appear, (of spirit) appear, in bodily form; (chiefly U.S.) become actual fact; make materialistic. Hence *~A'TION* n. [-IZE]

mate'ria mĕd'ica (*-sha*), n. Remedial substances used in practice of medicine. [med. L]

mate'riel (*matārĭĕl'*), n. Stock-in-trade, available means (opp. *personnel*). [F, as MATERIAL]

matern'al, a. Of mothers; motherly; related on the mother's side, as *~ uncle,* mother's brother; (joc.) one's mother's. Hence *~LY*² adv. [f. F *maternel* f. L *maternus* (*mater* mother), see -AL]

matern'ity, n. Motherhood; motherliness; *~ hospital, nurse, ward,* (for women during confinement); *~ robe, skirt,* (suitable for wear by pregnant woman). [f. F *maternité* f. L *maternitatem* (prec., -TY)]

mathema't'ical, a. Of mathematics; (of proofs etc.) rigorously precise. Hence *~LY*² adv. [f. L L f. Gk *mathēmatikos* (*mathēma* science f. *manthanō,* root *math-,* learn, see -IC)]

mathema't'ics, n. pl. (usu. treated as sing.). (Also *pure ~*) abstract science of space & number; (also *mixed, applied, ~*) this applied to branches of physical research, e.g. astronomy. So **mathé-matic'ian** (-ĭshn) n. [as prec., see -ICS]

mat'ico (-tē-), n. Peruvian shrub; its leaves used as styptic. [Sp., dim of *Mateo* Matthew]

mat'in, n. (PL) one of canonical hours of breviary, prop. a midnight office, but also recited at daybreak; (pl.) morning prayer in Church of England (often *mattins*); (poet., sing. or pl.) morning song of birds. [f. F *matines* f. eccl. L *matutinas,* acc. fem. pl. adj. as n. (*Matuta* goddess of morning, see -INE¹)]

matinée (măt'ĭnā), n. Afternoon theatrical or musical performance (*the ~ hat,* lady's hat obstructing, also hat designed not to obstruct, view of stage). [F; =what occupies a morning (*matin* morning, -ADE)]

māt'lō, -low (-lō). See MATELOT.

mat'rass, n. Long-necked glass vessel with round or oval body, used for distilling etc. [f. F *matras,* etym. dub.]

mat'riarch (-k), n. Woman corresponding in status to patriarch (usu. joc.). [f. L *mater* mother on false anal. of *patriarch*]

mātriärchy (-k-), n. Social organization in which mother is head of family. So **mātriärch¹** a. (-k-) a. [prec. + -Y¹]

mātricide, n. One who kills his, killing of one's, own mother. So ~AL a. [f. L *matricida* (MATER, see -CIDE)]

matric'ūlāte, v.t. & i. Admit (student) to privileges of university; (intr.) be thus admitted. Hence ~A'TION n., ~ATORY a. [f. LL *matricula* register, dim. of MATRIX, + -ATE³]

mat'rimony, n. **1.** Rite of marriage; state of being married. **2.** A card game; combination of king & queen of trumps in some card games. So **mātrimon'IAL** a., **mātrimon'ialy²** adv. [f. OF *matremoine* f. L *matrimonium* (*mater* mother, see -MONY)]

mā'trix, n. (pl. -*ices* pr. -*isēz*, -*ices*). Womb; place in which thing is developed; formative part of animal organ; mass of rock etc. enclosing gems etc.; (Biol.) substance between cells; mould in which type etc. is cast or shaped. [L, prob. f. *mater* mother]

mā'tron, n. Married woman; woman managing domestic affairs of hospital, school, etc. Hence ~AGE(L, 2), ~HOOD, ~SHIP, nn., ~AL, ~LY¹ aa. [f. F *matrone* f. L *matrona* (*mader* mother)]

mātt. Var. of MAT³ (esp. Photogr.).

mātt amore, n. Subterranean dwelling or storehouse. [f. F *madmara* store up)]

mǎtt'er, n. **1.** Substance(s) of which a physical thing is made. **2.** Purulent discharge, whence ~Y² a., purulent, fester-ing. **3.** Physical substance in general, as opp. to spirit, mind, etc. **4.** (Logic) particular content of proposition, distinguished from its form. **5.** Material for thought or expression; substance of book, speech, etc. (often opp. to manner). **6.** Occasion (of, for, complaint, regret, etc.). **7.** Thing(s), as *printed* ~; *postal* ~, all that may be sent by post; *no* ~, it is of no importance (*when, how, etc., or* abs.); *what* ~*s*, that need not disquiet us. **8.** Affair; thing (of a kind specified esp. by vbl n.), as *a hanging* ~, *no laughing* ~, *money* ~*s*; *that is a* ~ (case, question) *of habit etc.; for that* ~, so far as that is concerned; *a* ~ *of* (about) *40 years; what is the* ~*?, what is amiss (with)? (what is the* ~ *with)* —, sl., surely — will do); *the* ~ *of*, as regards. **9.** ~ *of course* (also as adj., w. hyphens), thing to be expected in natural course; ~ *of fact*, what pertains to the sphere of fact (opp. to *opinion* etc.), esp. *as a* ~ *of fact*, (Law) part of judicial inquiry concerned with truth of alleged facts (opp. to ~ *of law*), (adj., with hyphens) unimaginative, prosaic. [f. OF *matere* f. L *materia* timber, stuff]

mǎtt'er, v.i. **1.** Be of importance, signify, (to person etc., *how, when, etc.*, or *neg.*). **2.** Secrete or discharge pus.[f. prec.]

mǎtt'ing, n. In vbl senses (MAT³), esp. fabric of hemp, bast, grass, etc. as covering etc., as *coco-nut* ~. [-ING¹]

matins, n. See MATIN.

mǎtt'ock, n. Tool of PICK¹ shape, with an adze & a chisel edge as ends of head. [OE *mattuc*, etym. dub.]

mǎtt'oid, n. Person of erratic mind, compound of genius & fool. [f. It. *mattoide* (*matto* mad)]

mǎtt'ress, n. Canvas case stuffed with hair, straw, etc., as bed or support for bed; (usu. *spring* ~) similar appliance of springs stretched in frame. [f. OF *materas* f. It. *materasso* prob. f. Arab. *almatrah* place, cushion (*taraha* throw)]

mātūrāte, v.i. come to maturation. [f. L *maturare* (as MATURE²)]

mātūrā'tion, n. Ripening of morbific matter; causing of this, whence **matūrā'ti-vE** a.; ripening of fruit; maturing, development. [f. f. L *maturationem* (as MATURE², see -ATION)]

matūre¹ a., Complete in natural development; with fully developed powers of body & mind; ~ (careful) *deliberation*, ~ *plans* (formed after this); (of bill) due. So ~LY² (-l-) adv., ~NESS (-rn-), **matū'rity** n. [f. L *maturus* ripe]

matūre², v.t. & i. Develop fully; ripen; perfect (plan etc.); come to maturity; (of bill) become due. [f. obs. F *maturer* f. L *maturare* (as prec.); & f. prec.]

mātū'tin'al (or *matūt'inal*), a. Of, occurring in, the morning; early. So **mǎt'ūtine** a. [f. L *matutinalis* (*matutinus* f. *Matuta* goddess of dawn)]

maud, n. Scots shepherd's grey striped plaid; travelling-rug like this. [?]

maud'lin, a. & n. Mawkishly sentimental, esp. of tearful stage of drunkenness; (n.) mawkish sentiment. [adj. f. n., f. OF *Madeleine* MAGDALEN]

‖ **mau'gre** (-ger), prep. (arch.), in spite of. [f. OF *maugré* (*mal* bad f. L *malus* + *gré* f. L *gratus* pleasing)]

maul¹, mall (mawl), n. Kinds of special hammer, commonly of wood. [f. F *mail* f. L *malleus* hammer]

maul², v.t. Beat & bruise; handle (material thing, subject, quotation) roughly or carelessly; damage by criticism. [f. prec.]

maul'ey, n. (sl.), Fist, hand. [prob. f. prec.]

maul stick, mahl', n. Light stick held by painter in left hand as support for right, with padded leather ball at one end. [f. Du. *maalstok* (*malen* paint + *stok* stick)]

maund, n. Asiatic measure of weight of varying value (Indian standard ~ = 82⅟₇ lb.). [Hind. & Pers. *man*, cogn. w. Gk *mna* & L *mina*]

maun'der, v.i. Move, act, listlessly; talk in dreamy or rambling manner. [?]

maun'dy, n. (In R.-C. countries) ceremony of washing the feet of poor people

(*John* xiii. 14); (in English use) distribution of ~ *money* by royal almoner to the poor on *M~ Thursday* (next before Easter). [f. OF *mandé* f. L *mandatum* MANDATE]

Mau'ser (mowz-), n. Kind of magazine rifle or pistol. [inventor's name]

mausolē'um, n. Magnificent tomb, orig. that of Mausolus king of Caria erected by his queen Artemisia in 4th c. B.C. [L, f. Gk *Mausōleion* (*Mausōlos*)]

mauvais (mō'vā, & see Ap.), a. ~ *sujet* (see Ap.), black sheep, rogue; ~ *quart d'heure* (kârdɛ̄r, & see Ap.), short but unpleasant experience, interview, etc. [F] **mauvaise honte** (mōvāz'awnt, & see Ap.), n. False shame; painful diffidence. [F; =ill shame]

mauve (mōv), n.&a. **1.** Bright but delicate purple dye from coal-tar aniline. **2.** adj. Of the colour of this. [F, f. L *malva* MALLOW]

•măv'erick, n., & v.i. Unbranded calf or yearling; (transf.) masterless person, rover; (v.i.) stray. [f. S. A. *M~*, Texas engineer who owned unbranded cattle c. 1850]

măv'is, n. (poet.). Song-thrush. [f. F *mauvis*= Sp. *malviz*, etym. dub.] **mavour'neen** (-oor-), n. & int. My darling. [Ir. *mo mhuirnín*]

maw, n. Stomach (only joc. of men), esp. last of ruminant's four stomachs; ~*worm*, intestinal worm, also [f. *Maw-worm*, character in Bickerstaffe's play *The Hypocrite*] hypocrite. [com.-Teut.: OE *maga*, Du. *maag*, G *magen*]

mawk'ish, a. Of faint sickly flavour; feebly sentimental. Hence ~LY² adv., ~NESS n. [f. obs. *mawk* maggot f. ON *maðkr* + -ISH²]

maw'seed, n. Seed of opium poppy. [f. G (dial.) *mohsamen* (G *mohn* poppy)]

maxill'|a, n. (pl. ~*ae*). Jaw(bone), esp. upper jaw in animals & most vertebrates. Hence ~ARY¹, ~IFORM, aa. [L]

Măx'im¹, n. A general truth drawn from science or experience; principle, rule of conduct. [f. F *maxime* f. L *maxima*, fem. adj., greatest]

Măx'im², n. Single-barrelled quick-firing machine gun, with water-casing to keep parts cool. [Sir Hiram S.~, inventor]

măx'imalist, n. Person who holds out for the maximum of his demands & rejects compromises, [*maximum*, -AL, -IST]

măx'imi|ze, v.t. Increase, magnify, to the utmost; interpret (doctrine etc.) vigorously. Hence ~A'TION n. [f. L *maximus* greatest+-IZE]

‖ **măx'imum**, n. (pl. usu. -*ima*). Highest possible magnitude or quantity (often attrib.); ~ *price* (that may not be exceeded); ~*thermometer* (recording highest temperature within given period). [L, neut. as prec.]

---

may¹, v. auxil. (3rd sing. *may*; past *might*, pr. mít; no infin. or part. or gerund). **1.** Expr. possibility, as *it ~ be true* (neg. *it cannot be*), *it ~ not be* (= perhaps is not true, *you ~ walk miles without seeing one*, *he ~ or might* (perhaps will) *lose his way*, *I was afraid he might* (perhaps would) *lose his way*, *afraid he might have* (perhaps had) *lost it*. **2.** Expr. permission, as *you ~* (neg. MUST⁴ *not* or *cannot*) *go*, *I wish I might* (I request you to) *call at the baker's*; *you might* (ought to, yet do not) *offer to help*, *you might* (ought to) *have offered*. **3.** (In final clauses, & after *wish*, *fear*, etc.) *take*, *took*, *such a course as ~*, *might*, *avert the danger*; *I hope he ~*, *hoped he might*, *succeed*. **4.** (Expr. wish) *~ you live to repent it!* **5.** (In questions, emphasizing uncertainty) *who ~ you be?* **6.** *~ be* (also arch. *~háp*), perhaps; *might-have-been*, a past possibility. [com.-Teut.: OE *mæg*, past *meahte*, Du. *mag*, *mocht*, G *mag*, *mochte*]

may², n. (poet.). Maiden. [OE has *mæg* kinswoman]

May³, n. **1.** Fifth month of year; (fig.) bloom, prime; *Queen of* (*the*) *~*, girl chosen to be queen of games on ~ Day. **2.** (*may*). Hawthorn (blossom). **3.** ‖(Camb. Univ., pl.) ~ examination, ~ boat-races held during ~ *Week* (late in m. or early in June). **4.** ~ *Day*, May 1 (*maying* ⁴, keeping this, picking may); ‖ *May'fair*, fashionable London district enclosed by Park Lane, Oxford Street, Regent Street, & Piccadilly (named from fair formerly held in ~); *may'fly*, an ephemeral insect; ~*games*, on ~ Day; *may'pole*, pole painted & decked with flowers, for dancing round on ~ Day; ‖~ *meetings* (of religious & philanthropic societies held during ~ in London). [f. F *mai* f. L *Maius*]

ma'ya (mah-), n. (Hind. philos.) Illusion. [Skr.]

Ma'yan (mah-), a. Of the ancient culture of the Mayas before their conquest by the TOLTECS.

may'hém, n. (hist.). Crime of maiming a person so as to render him partly or wholly defenceless. [f. AF *mahaym*, cf. MAIM]

mayonnaise (-āz), n. (*Salmon*, *chicken*, etc., ~, dish with) dressing of eggs, oil, cream, vinegar, etc. [F]

mayor (mâr), n. Head of municipal corporation of city or borough; LORD ~; ~ *of the palace*, nominal subordinate to whom the power of his titular superior has passed (see ROI *fainéant*). Hence may'ORAL a. [f. F *maire*, as MAJOR²]

may'oralty, n. Mayor's (period of) office. [f. OF *mairalté* (as prec., see -AL & -TY)]

may'oréss, n. Mayor's wife; female mayor; lady fulfilling ceremonial duties of ~. [-ESS¹]

măz'ard, n. (arch.). Head, face; [perh. different wd] small black cherry. [prob. f. obs. *mazer* f. OF *masere* of Teut. orig.]

mazarine' (-ēn), n. & a. Deep rich blue. [?]

Măz'daism, n. Zoroastrianism. [f. Aves-tic *mazda*, good principle in Persian theology]

maze, n., & v.t. 1. Complex network of paths, labyrinth; confused mass etc. 2. v.t. Bewilder, confuse, (esp. in p.p.). Hence **maz'ily²** adv., **maz'iness** n.

māz'y² a. [?]

māz'er, n. (hist.) Hard-wood drinking-bowl, usu. silver-mounted. [as MAZARD; cf. MHG *maser* maple]

mazŭŕk'a, n. Lively Polish dance like polka; music for this in triple time. [Polish,=woman of province Mazovia]

me (mē, mǐ), pron., objective case of I (& colloq. subjective, as *it's only me*); (arch. & poet., reflexive) myself, *I laid me down*; (in intt.) *ah me!*, *dear me!* [OE had (1) *me*, cf. Du. *mǐj*, L *me*, Gk (e)*me*; (2) *mec* (lost in ME), cf. Du. *mǐch*, Gk *emege* me at least]

mead¹, n. Alcoholic liquor of fermented honey & water. [com.-Teut. & Aryan; OE *meodu*, Du. *mede*, G *met*; cf. Skr. *madhu* honey, Du. *mede*, sweet drink, Gk *methu* wine]

mead², n. (poet.). =foll. [see foll.]

meadow (měd'ō), n. Piece of grass land, esp. one used for hay; low well-watered ground, esp. near river; ~ pipit, titlark; ~-sweet, rosaceous plant common in moist ~s, with creamy-white heads & fragrant flowers. Hence ~y² (měd'ōï) a. [OE *mǣdwe* oblique case of *mǣd* (whence prec.), f. Teut. root *me-*, whence MOW¹]

mea'gre (-ger), a. (Of persons etc.) lean, thin; poor, scanty; (of literary composition, ideas, etc.) wanting in fullness. Hence ~LY² adv., ~NESS n. (-ger-). [OF *maigre* f. L *macer -cri*, cogn. w. Gk *makros* long]

meal¹, n. Edible part of any grain or pulse (usu. exc. FLOUR) ground to powder; ~ WHOLE ~. [com.-Teut.: OE *melu*, Du. *meel*, G *mehl*, f. Teut. root *mel-*, cogn. w. L *molere* grind]

meal¹, n. & v.t. Customary (also, any) occasion of taking food; food so taken (make a ~ of, consume); || quantity of milk given by cow at a milking; ~'time, usual time of eating; (v.i.) eat a ~. [vb f. n.] com.-Teut.: OE *mǣl* mark, fixed time, meal, Du. *maal*, G *mal* time, *mahl*]

meal'ie, n. (S.-Afr.). Maize (usu. pl.), f. Cape Du. *milie* f. Port. *milho* MILLET]

meal'y, a. Of, like, containing, meal; (of boiled potatoes) dry & powdery; ~ bug, insect infesting vines etc.; ~ prim-rose (mauve-flowered with powdery stem); (usu. ~-mouthed) apt to mince matters, soft-spoken. Hence **meal'iNESS** n. [MEAL¹+-Y²]

mean¹, n. 1. Condition, quality, course, equally removed from two opposite (usu. blamable) extremes, esp. the golden, happy, ~. 2. (Math.) term between first & last terms of arithmetical, geometrical, etc., progression. 3. pl. (Often treated as sing., as a ~s) that by which a result is brought about, as *it has been the ~s of extending our trade*, *by fair ~s*, WAYS & ~s, ~s of grace (sacraments etc.). 4. Pecuniary resources, means (as *he lives beyond his, on his own, ~s* (also attrib., as ~s *test*); wealth, as *a man of ~s*. 5. By all (manner of) ~s, in every possible way, at any cost, certainly; by no (manner of) ~s, not at all, certainly not; by-~s (the instrumentality) of (person, thing, doing). [f. foll.]

mean², a. (Math.) equally far from two extremes, as *5 is the ~ quantity between 2 & 8*; ~ sea level (half-way between those of high and low water); ~ sun, fictitious sun moving in celestial equator at ~ rate of real sun; ~ proportional, second of three quantities of which first is to it as it to third; *in the ~ (intervening) time, while*; ~'time, ~'while, adv., in the ~ time. [f. OF *mëen*, *mëien*, f. LL *mëdïanus* (*medius* mid, see -AN)]

mean³, a. (Of capacity, understanding, etc.) inferior, poor; (Hist.) ~ white, land-less white man in S. United States; not imposing in appearance, shabby; *he is no ~ (a good) scholar*; ignoble, small-minded; stingy; *(colloq.) secretly ashamed (feel ~). Hence ~NESS n. [OE *gemǣne* common, cf. Du. *gemeen*, G *gemein*, cogn. w. L *communis* COMMON]

mean⁴, v.t. (~t, pr. mĕnt). Purpose, have in mind, (mischief, business, to do); design, destine, for an object etc., as *it to be used, ~ it for a stopgap, he was ~t (by person) be or (specified) importance to (another); (of words) signify, import, (thing, that); what do you ~ by (how do you justify) it?* [com.-WG: OE *mǣnan*, Du. *meenen*, G *meinen*]

mëan'der, n., & v.i. 1. (Pl.) sinuous wind-ings of river; (pl.) winding paths; (usu. pl.) circuitous journey; ornamental pat-tern of lines winding in & out. 2. v.i. Wander at random, (of stream) wind about. [vb f. n.] L, f. Gk *Maiandros*, river in Phrygia]

mëan'drine, a. Full of windings (esp. of genus of corals with surface like human brain). [MEANDER+-INE¹]

meaning¹, n. What is meant; *with ~*, significantly. Hence ~LESS a. [-ING¹]

meaning'¹, a. Expressive, significant, whence ~LY² adv.; well-~, having good intention. [-ING²]

mea'sles (-zlz), n. pl. Infectious disease

of man, marked by red spots on skin; such spots; disease in swine; GERMAN² ~. [ME *maseles*, cf. Du. *mazelen*, cogn. w. OHG *masala* blood-blister]

meas·ly (-z:), a. Of, affected with, measles; (sl.) contemptible, worthless. [f. prec. +-Y¹]

measure¹ (mězh'er), n. 1. Size, quantity, found by measuring, whence ~LESS a., beyond ~, infinite; *short*, *full*, ~, less, not less, than professed amount; ∥ *clothes made to* ~ (in accordance with measurements taken); *take* (person's) ~, measure him for clothes etc., (fig.) gauge his character, abilities, etc. 2. Degree or extent or amount (esp. *in a* or *some* ~, partly). 3. Vessel of standard capacity for dealing out liquids etc., as *pint* ~. 4. Rod, tape, etc., for measuring, as *tape*~, *yard*~. 5. Unit of capacity, e.g. bushel, as 20 ~*s of wheat*. 6. System of measuring, as *liquid*, *linear*, ~. 7. That by which a thing is computed; *as a chain's greatest link is the* ~ *of its strength*. 8. Quantity contained in another an exact number of times; *greatest common* ~ (greatest that divides each of given quantities). 9. Prescribed extent or quantity, as *set* ~*s to*, limit, *beyond* ~, excessively. 10. Poetical rhythm, metre; time of piece of music; (Mus.) bar; (arch.) dance, as *tread a* ~. 11. Suitable action, as *take* ~s. 12. Legislative enactment. [f. F *mesure* f. L *mensura (metiri mens-*ure, -URE)]

measure² (mězh'er), v.t. 1. Ascertain extent or quantity of (thing) by comparison with fixed unit or with object of known size; ascertain size & proportions of (person) for clothes. 2. Look (person) up & down *with one's eye*. 3. Mark off or *off* (line etc. of given length). 4. ~*e* one's *length*, fall prostrate; ~*e swords*, (of duellists) see that swords are of equal length, (fig.) try one's strength *with* (person); *it* ~*es 7 inches* (is 7 inches long). 5. Estimate (immaterial thing, person's character, etc.) by some standard or rule. 6. Deal *out* (thing to person). 7. Bring (one's strength etc.) into competition *with* (another's). 8. Traverse (distance). Hence ~ABLE (mězh'er-) a. (*within* ~*able distance of* ruin etc., getting near it), ~ABLY² adv., ~EMENT(mězh'erm-) n., (esp., pl., detailed dimensions). [f. F *mesurer* (as prec.)]

mea·sured (mězh'erd), a. In vbl senses, also: rhythmical, regular in movement, as ~ *tread*; (of language) carefully weighed. [p.p. of prec.]

meat, n. Animal flesh as food, usu. (also *butcher's* ~) excluding fish & poultry; *green* ~, grass, green vegetables, as food; (arch.) food of any kind (*as full as an egg is of* ~, quite full; *one man's* ~ *is another man's poison; this was* ~ *& drink* (a great pleasure) *to him;* (arch.) meal, as

before, *after*, ~; ~*-safe*, cupboard for storing ~, usu. of wire gauze etc.; (Bibl.) ~*-offering* (R.V. *meat-*), sacrifice of flour & oil. Hence ~LESS a. [OE *meta*, cf. Sw. *mat*, Da. *mad*]

meāt·us, n. (anat.; pl. -*ūs*, -*uses*), Channel, passage, in the body, as *auditory* ~, channel of the ear. [L, f. *meare* flow, run]

meat·y, a. Full of meat, fleshy; (fig.) full of substance; or of like meat. [-Y¹]

Mec·ca, n. Mohammed's birthplace; (fig.) place one aspires to visit, (also) birthplace of a faith, policy, pursuit, etc. [f. Arab. *makkah*]

mec·ca·nō (-ah-), n. Set of miniature parts from which engineering models can be constructed. [P]

mechan·ic (-k-), n. 1. Handicraftsman; skilled workman, esp. one who makes or uses machinery. 2. pl. Branch of applied mathematics treating of motion & tendencies to motion, (also) science of machinery. [f. L f. Gk *mēkhanikos* (as MACHINE, see -IC)]

mechan·ical (-k-), a. Of machines or mechanism; *the* ~ *powers*, lever, wheel & axle, pulley, inclined plane, wedge, screw; of the nature of handicraft; working, produced, by machinery; ~ *drawing* (done with compasses etc.); ~ *transport* (abbr. M.T.), motor branch of R.A.S.C.; (of persons or actions) like machines, automatic, lacking originality; (of agencies, principles, etc.) belonging to mechanics, often opp. to *chemical*, as *air* is *a* ~ *mixture, not a chemical compound;* (of theories etc.) explaining phenomena by assumption of ~ action, whence ~ISM n.; of mechanics as a science. Hence ~LY² adv., ~NESS a. [as prec. see -AL]

mechani·cian (-kanishn), n. One skilled in constructing machinery. [MECHANIC +-IAN]

mech·anism (-k-), n. Structure, adaptation of parts, of machine (lit. & fig.); system of mutually adapted parts working together (as) in machine; (Art) mechanical execution, technique. [f. MECHANIC +-ISM]

mech·anist (-k-), n. Machinist (now rare); mechanician, expert in mechanics; (Philos.) one who holds that all natural phenomena admit of mechanical explanation (opp. VITALIST), whence ~IS'TIC a. [as prec. +-IST]

mech·anize (-k-), v.t. Give mechanical character to. Hence ~A'TION n., (esp.) substitution of motor transport for horse-drawn vehicles, replacement of cavalry by tanks & armoured cars, etc. [-IZE]

Mēch·lin (-k-), n. (Also ~ *lace*) lace made at ~ in Belgium.

mēcon·ic, a. ~ *acid*, white crystalline acid obtained from opium. [f. Gk *mēkōn* poppy +-IC]

med·al, n. Piece of metal, usu. in form of coin, struck or cast with inscription & device to commemorate event etc., also

awarded as distinction to soldier, scholar, etc., for services rendered, proficiency, etc.; *the reverse of the* ~, other side of question; ~ *play* (Golf), play in which the score is reckoned by counting the number of strokes taken for the round. Hence ~IND² (id), méDALL²IO, méDALL²IST, etc. t. pop. L †*metallea* (as METAL)]

médáLL²ion (-yon), n. Large medal; thing so shaped, e.g. decorative panel or tablet, portrait, etc. [f. F *médaillon* (as prec., see -OON)]

médáLL²ist, n. Engraver, designer, of medals; recipient of medal, as ~. [-IST]

méd'dle, v.i. Busy oneself unduly *with*, Interfere *in*. Hence ~ER¹, ~esomeNESS nn., ~esome (-dls-), a. [f. OF *medler* = *mesler* t. pop. L †*misculāre* (*miscēre* mixt)=] Voiced or soft mute

médiæv'al, -diev'al, a. Of, imitating, the middle ages. Hence ~ISM(2), ~IST(3). ~IZE(2, 3) v.t. & i., ~IY² adv. [f. L *medius* middle + *aevum* age + -AL]

méd'ial, a. Situated in the middle; of average dimensions. Hence ~IY² adv. [f. LL *mediālis* (as prec., see -AL)]

méd'ian, a. & n. Situated in the middle; (b, d, ∅), cf. TENUIS; middle membrane of artery or vessel. LL, fem. of *medius* middle]

méd'iant, n. (mus.). Third of any scale. [f. L *mediānte* (as prec., see -ANT)]

médiastin'um, n. (anat.). Membranous middle septum, esp. between lungs. Hence ~AL¹ a. [med. L, neut. adj. = middle, f. L *medius*]

méd'iate¹, a. Connected not directly but through some other person or thing; involving intermediate agency. Hence ~LY² adv. [as foll., see -ATE²]

méd'iate², v.i. & t. Form connecting link between; Intervene (*between* two persons) for purpose of reconciling them; be the medium for bringing about (result) or conveying (gift etc.). So ~A²TION n. [f. LL *mediāre* (*mediātus* middle), see -ATE²]

méd'iatize, v.t. Annex (principality) to another State, leaving former sovereign his title & some rights of government. Hence ~A²TION n. [f. F *médiatiser* (*médiat*,

méd'iator, n. One who mediates, esp. (M-) Christ. Hence or cogn. médiató²RIAL, médiáTORY aa., médiáTRIX n. [f. F *médiateur* (as MEDIATE²), see -OR³]

méd'icable, a. Admitting of remedial treatment. [f. L *medicābilis* (as MEDICATE, see -BLE)]

méd'ical, & n. 1. Of the healing art; ~ *man*, physician or surgeon; of medicine as opp. to surgery, obstetrics, etc.; re-quiring ~, not surgical, treatment; ~ *jurisprudence*, the legal knowledge re-quired of a doctor. 2. n. (colloq.) ~ stu-dent. Hence ~LY² adv. [f. F *médical* f. LL *medicālis* (*medicus* physician, see -AL)]

méd'icament (or méd'-), n. Substance used in curative treatment. [f. F *médica-ment* f. L *medicāmentum* (as MEDICATE, see -MENT)]

méd'icaster, n. Quack. [f. L *medicus* physician, see -ASTER]

méd'icate, v.t. Treat medically; impreg-nate with medicinal substance. Hence or cogn. ~A²TION n., ~ative a. [f. L *medicārī* (as prec.), see -ATE³]

médicʹan, a. Of the Medici family, rulers of Florence in 15th c. [f. med. L *Mediceus* + -AN]

méd'icinal, a. Of medicine; having heal-ing properties. Hence ~LY² adv. [f. L *medicinālis* (as foll., see -AL)]

méd'icine (méd'sn), n., & v.t. 1. Art of restoring & preserving health, esp. by means of remedial substances & regula-tion of diet etc., as opp. to surgery & ob-stetrics; substance, esp. one taken in-ternally, used in this; (among savages) spell, charm, fetish, as ~*man*, magician; *take one's* ~, submit to the disagreeable; ~ *ball*, stuffed leather ball thrown & caught as means of exercise. 2. v.t. (arch.). *Give* ~ *to, cure with* ~. [(vb f. OF *mede-ciner*) f. OF *medecine* f. L *medicīna* (as MEDIC)]

méd'ico-, in comb. = L *medicus* physician, medical; as ~*botán'ical*, ~*judi'cial*.

medieval. See MEDIÆVAL.

méd'iocre (-ker), a. Of middling quality, indifferent, neither good nor bad. So médióc'rity n. (in adj. senses & esp. ~ person). [f. F *médiocre* f. L *mediocris* of middle degree (*medius* middle)]

méd'itate, v.t. & i. Plan mentally, de-sign; (intr.) exercise the mind in (esp. religious) contemplation (*on, upon, sub-ject*). Hence or cogn. médita²TION, ~IVE a., ~IVENESS nn., ~IVELY² adv. [f. L *meditāri*, f. root *med-*, cf. Gk *medomai* think about.]

méditerrán'ean, a. & n. (Of land) remote from coast; (of water surfaces) land-locked; M~ (*Sea*), that which separates Europe from Africa. [f. L *mediterrāneus* (*medius* middle + *terra* land) + -AN]

méd'ium, n. & a. (pl. -*a*, -*ums*). 1. Middle quality, degree, etc. (between extremes, or abs.); intervening substance through which impressions are conveyed to senses etc., e.g. air; (fig.) conditions of life; ~ *of circulation*, what serves as instru-ment of commercial transactions, e.g. coin; liquid vehicle with which pigments are mixed, e.g. oil, water; person claiming ultraphysical perception and revealing its results to others, whence ~ISM n., ~is²TIC a. 2. adj. Inter-

mediate between two degrees or amounts; average, moderate; **~ wave** (Wireless), having a wave-length between 100 & 800 metres. [L, neut. of *medius* middle]

méd'lar, n. (Tree with) fruit like small brown apple, eaten when decayed. [f. OF *medler* f. L f. Gk *mespilē*]

méd'ley, n. (pl. ~s), a., & v.t. Heterogeneous mixture; mixed company; literary miscellany; (adj.) mixed, motley; (v.t.) make a ~ of, intermix. [vb & a.f. n.], f. OF *medlee* (as MEDDLE)]

Médoc' (mā-), n. Red wine from ~, district in S.W. France.

médŭll'a, n. Marrow of bones; spinal marrow; **~ (oblongāt'a** prolonged) hindmost segment of brain; central parts of some organs, esp. kidney; pith of mammalian hair, soft internal tissue of plants. So **médŭll'ARY² a.** [L,= pith, marrow, prob. cogn. w. *medius* middle]

mēdūs'a, n. (pl. ~ae, ~as). 1. (Gk Myth.; M~a) one of the three Gorgons, with snakes for hair. 2. (Zool.) jelly-fish, whence ~AL, ~AN, aa., ~OID a. & n. [L, f. Gk *Medousa*]

meed, n. (poet.). Reward; merited portion (of praise etc.). [OE *mēd*, cf. MDu. *miede*, G *miete*, cogn. w. Gk *misthos* reward, Skr. *mīdha* prize]

meek, a. Piously humble & submissive; submitting tamely to injury etc.; (provv.) *as ~ as a lamb, as Moses*. Hence ~'LY² adv., ~'NESS n. [ME *meoc* f. ON *miukr* soft, gentle]

meer'kăt, n. Small S.-Afr. mammal like an ichneumon. [Du.]

meer'schaum (-shm), n. Hydrous silicate of magnesium, found in soft white masses; tobacco-pipe with ~ bowl. [G,= sea-foam (*meer* sea + *schaum* foam)]

meet¹, n. Meeting of hounds & men for hunt of or cyclists etc. [f. foll.]

meet², v.t. & i. (mét). 1. Come face to face with (person coming from opposite direction) go to or place to receive (person, train, etc.) on arrival; make the acquaintance of (imperat., U.-S; form of introduction, as ~ *Dr Smith*); ~ (person) *half-way*, respond to friendly advances of, come to compromise with. 2. (Of line, road, etc.) reach point of contact with (another line etc.). 3. ~ *the eye, ear*, be visible, audible; ~ person's *eye*, see he is looking at one, (also) return his gaze. 4. Oppose in battle or duel; grapple with (evils etc.). 5. Come by accident or design into the company of. 6. Come into conformity with (person, his wishes). 7. Satisfy (demand; ~ *the case*, be adequate); pay (bill) at maturity. 8. (Of two or more persons) come face to face; come *together*, as *they had* or *were met together*. 9. Come into contact (*waistcoat won't ~*, is too small); (of qualities) unite in same person. 10. ~ *with*, come across (person, obstacle,

etc.), experience (treatment etc.). [OE *mētan*, cf. Du. *moeten*, Da. *möde*, cogn. w. MOOT n.]

meet³, a. (arch.). Suitable, fit, proper, (for thing, *to do, to be done*); *it is ~* (proper) *that*. Hence ~'LY² adv., ~'NESS n. [ME *mēte* prob. repr. OE †ᵹemǣte f. OTeut. *gamǣtje* (ga- Y- + *mæta* measure)]

meet'ing, n. In vbl senses, esp.: duel; race~; assembly of people for entertainment etc.; assembly for worship; persons assembled, as *address the ~*; **~house**, place of worship (usu. disparaging exc. of Quakers); **~-place** (appointed for ~). [MEET² + -ING¹]

mēg'a- in comb.= Gk *megas* great, as: ~cephăl'ic, large-headed; ~lith, large stone, esp. as monument; ~lith'ic, made of, marked by use of, large stones; ~phōne, instrument for carrying sound a long distance, large speaking-trumpet (v.t., announce with ~phone); ~pōde, ~pŏd, genus of mound-building birds (lit. large-footed); ~scope, kind of magic lantern; ~scŏp'ic, visible to naked eye; ~thēr'ium, extinct genus of huge herbivorous sloth-like animals; ~watt, 1,000 kilowatts.

mēg'alo- in comb.= Gk *megas* (fem. *megalē*) great, as: ~mān'ĭa, insanity of self-exaltation, passion for big things; ~saur'us, extinct genus of huge carnivorous lizards.

mēgăss(e)'r, n. Fibrous residue after expression of sugar from cane. [?]

mĕgg'er (-g-), n. (electr.). Apparatus for measuring insulation resistance. [P; cf. MEGOHM]

mēgilp' (-g-), n. Vehicle (usu. linseed oil & turpentine) for oil colours. [?]

mĕg'ohm (-ōm), n. (electr.). Unit of resistance (one million ohms). [MEGA- + OHM]

mēg'rim¹, n. Severe headache usu. on one side only; whim, fancy; (pl.) low spirits, vapours; (pl.) staggers, vertigo, in horses etc. [f. F *migraine* f. L f. Gk HEMI(*kranĭa* f. *kranion* skull)]

mēg'rim², n. (Local name for) the smooth sole or similar flat fish. [?]

meios'is (mīŏ-), n. = LITOTES. [Gk *meiōsis* (*meioō* lessen, f. *meiōn* less, see -OSIS]

meis'tersinger (mīs-), n. pl. & sing. German lyric poets & musicians of 14th-16th cc. organized in guilds & having elaborate technique; (sing.) member of such guild. [G (*master*)]

mĕkŏm'ĕter, n. Portable military rangefinder. [f. Gk *mēkos* length + -METER]

mĕlanchŏl'ĭa (-k-), n. Emotional mental disease marked by depression & illgrounded fears. [LL, see MELANCHOLY]

mĕlanchŏl'ĭc (-k-), a. Melancholy; liable to melancholy. [f. LL f. Gk *melankholikos* (as foll.)]

mĕl'anchŏly (-k-), n. & a. 1. (Habitual or constitutional tendency to) sadness &

mélange (see Ap.), n. Mixture, medley. [F (*mêler* mix, as MEDDLE)]

mel'anism, n. Darkness of colour resulting from abnormal development of black pigment in epidermis, hair, etc. [f. Gk *melas -anos* black +-ISM]

mélanch'roi (-k-), n. pl. (anthrop.). Smooth-haired class of men with dark hair & pale complexion. [f. Gk *khroos* (*melas* black + *khroa* skin)]

melanos'is, n. Morbid deposit, abnormal development, of black pigment in tissue; black cancer. Hence **~or'ic** (-ot-) a. [Gk *melanōsis* f. *melanoō* blacken (*melas* black), see -OSIS]

mêtée (mel'ā), n. Mixed fight, skirmish; lively debate. [F, as MEDLEY]

mel'ic, a. (Of poem, esp. Gk lyric) meant to be sung. [f. Gk *melikos* (*melos* song, -IC)]

mel'inite, n. An explosive of French invention. [f. F *mélinite* f. Gk *mēlinos* (*mēlon* apple), see -ITE¹]

mel'iorate, v.t. & i. Improve. Hence **mel'iorative** a. [f. LL *meliorare* (as foll.), -ATE³]

mel'iorism, n. Doctrine that the world may be made better by human effort. So **mel'iorist** n. [f. L *melior* better +-ISM]

mel'lay, n. (arch.). = MÊLÉE.

mellif'erous, a. Yielding, producing, honey. [f. L *mellifer* (*mel* honey, see -FEROUS)]

mellif'luous (-lōō-), a. (Of voice, words) sweet as honey. So **~ENCE** n., **~ENT** a., (-lōō-). [f. L *mellifluus* (*mel* honey, *fluere* flow) +-OUS]

mel'low (-ō), a. (-er, -est) & v.t. & i. **1.** (Of fruit) soft, sweet, & juicy; (of wine) well-matured; (of earth) rich, loamy; (of character) softened by age or experience; (of sound, colour, light) full & pure without harshness; genial, jovial; partly intoxicated. **2.** v.b. Make, become, ~. Hence **~LY¹** (-ōli) adv., **~NESS** (-ōn-) n. [vbl f. adj.; perh. f. OE *melo* MEAL¹]

melo'deon, -dion, -dium, n. Small organ with suction-operated reeds; kind of accordion. [f. MELODY]

melo'dious, a. Of, producing, melody; sweet-sounding. Hence **~LY¹** adv., **~NESS** n. [f. OF *melodieus* (as MELODY, see -OUS)]

mel'odist, n. Singer; composer of melodies. [f. MELODY+-IST]

mel'odize, v.i. & t. Make melody; make melodious. [f. MELODY+-IZE]

melodra'ma (-rah-), n. Sensational dramatic piece with violent appeals to emotions & happy ending; language, behaviour, suggestive of this; (formerly) play with songs interspersed & with orchestral music accompanying the action. Hence **melodramat'ic** a., **mélodramat'ically** adv., **mélodram'atist** n., **melodram'atize** v.t. [earlier *drame* f. F *mélodrame* (Gk *melos* music + F *drame* DRAMA)]

mel'ody, n. Sweet music; musical arrangement of words; arrangement of single notes in musically expressive succession; principal part in harmonized music, air. [f. OF *melodie* f. LL f. Gk *melōidia* f. *melōidos* musical (*melos* song +-*aoidos* singing f. *aeidō* sing)]

mel'on, n. Kinds of gourd, some ~; ~-*cutting* (sl.), sharing of spoils or profits, WATER ~; [f. LL *melonem* (nom. -*lo*), prob. shortened f. L (-*lo*) f. Gk *mēlopepōn* (*mēlon* apple + *pepōn* gourd f. *pepōn* ripe)]

melt, n. Melted metal; amount melted at a time. [f. foll.]

melt, v.i. & t. (p.p. ~ed &, as adj. of metal, *molten*). Become liquefied by heat; (of person) suffer extreme heat; (of tender food) *it* ~*s* (is easily dissolved) *in the mouth*; (of clouds) break *into* rain; (of person, heart, feelings) be softened by or *with* pity or love, dissolve *into* tears, esp. *the* ~*ing mood*, whence **mel'tingly²** adv.; dwindle *away*; (of sound) be soft & liquid; pass imperceptibly *into* (another form); reduce (metal, etc.) to liquid condition by heat; ~ *down* (plate etc., to use the metal as raw material); *go into the* ~*ing-pot* (fig.), be revolutionized; soften (person, feelings). [OE (1) *meltan* intr., (2) *mieltan* trans.; cf. ON *melta* digest]

mem'ber, n. Part, organ, of body, esp. limb; *unruly* ~ tongue; (fig.) ~ *of Christ*, Christian; constituent portion of complex structure; person belonging to a society etc.; M~ (one formally elected to take part in proceedings) *of Parliament* (abbr. M.P.; pl. MM.P. or M.P.s); part, branch, of political body; division, clause, of sentence; group of figures, part, of numerical expression. Hence (-)**~ED²** (-erd), **~LESS** aa. [f. F *membre* f. L *membrum* limb]

mem'bership, n. Being a member; number of members. [-SHIP]

mem'brane, n. Pliable sheet-like connective tissue or lining in animal or vegetable body; morbid formation in some diseases; skin of parchment, forming part of a roll. So **mêmbra'neous** (-āshus), **mêmbran'ous**, **mêm'branous** aa. [f. L *membrana*, parchment, as MEMBER]

mem'brum viri'le, n. =PENIS. [L,=male member]

mêmen'to, n. (pl. ~*es*, ~*s*). Object serving as reminder or warning, or kept as memorial of person or event; ~ *mo'ri* (=remember you must die), warning or

reminder of death (e.g. skull). [L, imperat. of *meminisse* remember]

mem'oir (-wǎr), n. Record of events, history written from personal knowledge or special sources of information; (auto)biography; essay on learned subject specially studied by the writer. [f. F *mémoire* masc, spec. use of *mémoire* fem. MEMORY]

mem'orabil'ia, n. pl. Memorable things. [L, neut. pl. as foll.]

mem'or|able, a. Worth remembering, not to be forgotten. Hence ~**ABIL'ITY** n., ~**ably**[2] adv. [f. L *memorabilis* (*memorare* bring to mind f. *memor* mindful, -BLE)]

memoran'dum, n. (pl. *-da*, *-dums*; abbr. *mem.*, *memo.*). Note to help the memory; record of events etc. for future use; (Law) document recording terms of contract etc.; informal letter without signature etc., usu. on paper headed M~. [L, neut. sing. gerundive as prec.]

memor'ial, a. & n. 1. (Of statue, festival, etc.) serving to commemorate; of memory. 2. n. ~ object, custom, etc.; record, chronicle, (usu. pl.); statement of facts as basis of petition etc. Hence ~**IST** n. [OF, f. L *memorialis* (as MEMORY, see -AL)]

memor'ialize, v.t. Commemorate; address memorial to (person). [prec. + -IZE]

memor'ia tech'nica (těk-), n. System, contrivance, used to assist memory. [L, = artificial memory]

mem'orize, v.t. Put on record; commit to memory. [f. foll. +-IZE]

mem'ory, n. Faculty of remembering; this in an individual, as *a good, bad,* ~ (*convenient* or *accommodating* ~, that retains only what it is to one's interest to remember); recollection; *in* ~ *of*, as a record of, to keep alive the ~ *of*; posthumous repute, as *his* ~ *has been censured, of blessed, happy,* etc., ~ (used esp. of deceased princes etc.); length of time over which ~ extends, as *beyond, within, the* ~ *of men, within living* ~. [f. OF *memoire* f. L *memoria* (*memor* mindful f. root *mer-* remember)]

mem|sah'ib, n. (In India) European married lady. [f. MA'AM +SAHIB]

-men, suf. in L wds, often side by side with L *-mentum*-MENT & w. same meaning, as *fundamen-tum*. Many wds of slightly technical or learned use, as *acumen, stamen, gravamen, albumen, cognomen, regimen, specimen*; cf. *crimen*, shortened in F f, L *crimen*.

men'ace[1], n. (literary). Threat. [OF, f. L *minacia* (*minax-acis* f. *minari* threaten)]

men'ace[2], v.t. Threaten. Hence ~**ingly**[2] adv. [f. F *menacer* f. pop. L [+] *minaciare* (as prec.)]

ménage (mānahzh'), n. Household management; domestic establishment. [f. OF *mesnage* f. pop. L [+] *mansionaticum* (as MANSION, see -AGE)]

ména'gerie, n. Collection of wild animals in cages etc. [f. F *ménagerie* (as prec.. see -ERY)]

mend[1], n. Repaired hole in material etc.; *on the* ~, improving in health or (of affairs etc.) condition. [f. foll.]

mend[2], v.t. & i. 1. Restore to sound condition, repair, (broken articles, clothes, roads, etc.); ~ (correct) one's *ways*; *least said soonest* ~*ed* (rectified); ~ (add fuel to) *fire*; cut to required shape (quill pen); (intr.) regain health; ~ (improve state of) *matters*; ~ (quicken) one's *pace*; ~ *or end*, improve or abolish. Hence ~**ABLE** a. [f. AMEND, but found earlier.]

menda'cious (-shus), a. Lying, untruthful. Hence or cogn. ~**LY**[2] adv., **menda'CITY** n. [f. L *mendax* f. root of *mentiri* lie, see -ACIOUS]

Men'delism, n. A theory of heredity tending to reduce to numerical law the recurrence of inherited characters. So **Mendē'lian** a. & n. [G. J. *Mendel*, 1822-84]

men'di|cant, a. & n. 1. Begging; ~*ant friars* (living solely on alms). 2. n. Beggar. Hence or cogn. ~**ANCY**, **mendi'cITY**, nn. [f. L *mendicare* (*mendicus* beggar), see -ANT]

menhad'en, n. Fish of herring family, used for manure, & yielding valuable oil [Amer. Ind. *munnawhatteaug*]

men'hir (-ēr), n. (archaeol.). Tall upright monumental stone found in Europe, Africa, & Asia. [f. Breton *men hir* long stone]

men'ial, a. & n. 1. (Of service) servile; (of servant, usu. derog.) domestic. 2. n. ~ servant. Hence ~**LY**[2] adv. [AF, f. OF *mesnie* household (obs. E *meinie*) f. pop. L [+] *mansionata* (as MANSION, see -ADE)]

men'inx, n. (usu. in pl. *menin'ges*). Any of three membranes enveloping brain & spinal cord (*dura mater, arachnoid, pia mater*). Hence **menin'gEAL** a., **menin'git'is** (-jīt-), **menin'gocELE**, nn. [Gk *mēninx*]

menis'cus, n. (pl. *-ci*). Lens convex on one side, concave on the other; (Math.) figure of crescent form; (Phys.) curved upper surface of liquid in tube. [f. Gk *mēniskos* crescent (*mēnē* moon)]

Menn'onite, n. Member of a Protestant sect that arose in Switzerland c. 1625, with tenets resembling those of Quakers & Baptists. [f. *Menno* Simons founder]

men'o- in comb. Of the menses, as: ~*pause,* final cessation, ~*rrhoe'a,* ordinary flow, of the menses. [f. Gk *mēn* month]

menol'ogy, n. Calendar, esp. that of Greek Church, with biographies of saints. [f. late Gk *mēnologion* (*mēn* month +*logos* account)]

mēns (-nz) **cŏn'scia** (-shia) **rěc'ti**, L phr. = a clear conscience.

men'ses (-z), n. pl. Flow of blood from

mucous coat of uterus of female, occurring on the average at intervals of lunar month. [L, pl. of *mensis* month]

Men'shevik, n. Russian socialist of the more moderate party (cf. BOLSHEVIK). [Russ, = minority party, cf. BOLSHEVIK]

mēns (-nz) **sāna in corp'orĕ sān'ō**, [L] phr. = sound mind in sound body, used esp. as expressing the ideal of education.

men'strual (-oo-), a. Of the menses, so **~OUS** a.; (Astron.) monthly. [f. F *men-strual* f. L *menstrualis* (as MENSTRUUM, see -AL)]

mēn'strulāte (-oo-), v.i. Discharge the menses. Hence **~A°TION** n. [f. L *men-struāre* (as foll.)]

mēn'struum (-oo-), n. (pl. *-rua*). Solvent (lit. & fig.) [neut. of L *menstruus* monthly (*mensis* month), named as analogue of *menses*]

mēn'surable, a. Measurable, having fixed limits; (Mus.) having fixed rhythm. [F, f. L L *mensurābilis* (as *mensurare* f. *mensura* MEASURE, see -BLE)]

mēn'sural, a. Of measure; (Mus.)=prec. [f. med. L *mensurālis* (as MEASURE, see -AL)]

mēnsurā'tion, n. Measuring; (Math.) rules for finding lengths, areas, & volumes. [f. L L *mensurātio* (as MENSURABLE, see -ATION)]

-ment, suf. forming nn. expr. result or means of vbl action (*atone~*); some formed in L(*frag~*), some in F (*abridge~*), some in E on L, F, or E vbs; a few are on adji. (*odd~*; *funny~*, perh. on anal. of *merri~*, which is really f. obs. vb *merry*); *-y* of first element is changed to *-i-*. [OF, f. L *-mentum*]

mĕn'tal[1], a. & n. Of the mind; done by the mind, as **~ arithmetic** (performed without use of written figures); **~ patient** (under care for disordered mind); **~ case** or **patient**. Hence **~LY**[2] adv. [F, f. L L *mentālis* (*mens -ntis* mind, see -AL]

mĕn'tal[2], a. Of the chin. [F, f. L *mentum* chin, see -AL]

mĕntăl'ity, n. The being mental or in or of the mind; (degree of) intellectual power; (loosely) mind, disposition, char-acter. [f. MENTAL[1]+-ITY]

mĕntā'tion, n. Mental action; state of mind. [f. L *mens -ntis* mind, see -ATION]

mĕn'thol, n. Camphor-like substance got from oil of peppermint etc., used to relieve neuralgia etc. [G, f. L *mentha* mint, see -OL[2]]

mĕn'tion[1], n. Mentioning, naming, (of thing); **honourable ~**, award of merit to candidate in examination, work of art, etc., not entitled to prize. [F, f. L *men-tionem* (*mens-* root of *mens* mind, see -ION)]

mĕn'tion[2], v.t. Refer to, remark upon, specify by name, (esp. thing not ob-viously essential to context, as *this was expressly ~ed*; *that*); (in deprecation of apology or thanks) *don't ~ it*; (introduc-ing fact or thing of secondary or, as rhet. artifice, of primary importance) *not to ~*. [f. F *mentionner* (as prec.)]

mĕn'tor, n. Experienced & trusted ad-viser. [F, f. Gk *Mentōr* adviser of Tele-machus (not *men-* think)]

mĕn'ū (-oo, & see Ap.), n. Bill of fare. [F adj., = small, n. = detailed list]

Mĕphistŏph'elēs (-z), n. Evil spirit to whom Faust, in German legend, sold his soul; fiendish person. Hence **~ŏphĕlē'AN**, **~ŏphĕlī'AN**, aa. [G, etym. dub.]

mĕphī'tis, n. Noxious emanation, esp. from the earth; noisome or poisonous stench. So **mĕphĭt'ic** a. [L]

mĕr'cantĭle, a. Of trade, commercial; **~e theory** (that money is the only wealth); **~e marine**, shipping employed in com-merce; mercenary, fond of bargaining. Hence **~ISM**, **~IST**, nn. [F, f. It. *mercantil* (as MERCHANT)]

Mĕr'cātor. See PROJECTION.

mĕr'cenary, a. & n. 1. Working merely for money or other reward; hired. 2. n Hired soldier in foreign service. Hence **~NESS** n. [f. L *mercenārius* (*merces -ēdis* reward, see -ARY[2])]

|| **mĕr'cer**, n. Dealer in textile fabrics, esp. silks & other costly materials. Hence **~ERY**(1) n. [f. F *mercier* f. pop. L [+*mer-ciārius* (*merx mercis* goods, -ARY[1])]

mĕr'cerize, v.t. Treat (cotton fabrics & thread) with caustic alkali under tension to give greater strength and impart lustre. [J. Mercer, patentee, +-IZE]

mĕr'chandise (-z), n. Commodities of commerce, goods for sale. [f. F *mar-chandise* (as MERCHANT)]

mĕr'chant, n. & a. Wholesale trader, esp. with foreign countries; **~ prince**, wealthy merchant; **~ ship**, **~-man**, (ship convey-ing merchandise); **~** (mercantile marine) **service**; **~** (sl.), one given to **~** (*speed~*, speed-loving motorist; *slow bow-ler*). [f. OF *marchant* f. pop. L *mercātāre* frequent. of *mercāri* trade (*merx mercis* merchandise), see -ANT]

mĕr'chantable, a. Salable, marketable. [f. *marchand* v. (now rare) f. OF *mar-chander* (as prec.)+-ABLE]

mĕr'ciful, a. Having, showing, or feeling mercy. Hence **~LY**[2] adv., **~NESS** n. So **mĕr'ciless**, a. Pitiless, showing no mercy. Hence **~LY**[2] adv., **~NESS** n. [-LESS]

mĕrcū'rial, a. & n. 1. Sprightly, ready-witted, & volatile, whence **~ITY** (-ăl·i) n.; of, containing, mercury; (M~) of the planet Mercury. 2. n. **~ drug**, whence [f. L *mercuriālis* (as MERCURY, see -AL)]

Mĕr'cury, n. 1. (M~) Roman god of elo-quence, skill thieving, etc., & messenger of gods, messenger (joc., & often in news-paper titles). 2. (M~) planet nearest to sun. 3. A white normally liquid metal

mercy (cont.) usu. got from cinnabar & used in barometers, thermometers, amalgams, & mirrors (*the ~ is rising*, weather or temper is improving), quicksilver, whence **mercū′rĭc, mĕrc′ŭrous**, aa. (chem.); (fig.) liveliness (*has no ~ in him*). [f. L *Mercurius*, prob. f. *merx -rcis* merchandise]

mĕr′cў, n. Compassion shown by one to another who is in his power & has no claim to kindness (*have ~ on* or *upon, show ~ to; ~! , ~ on* or *upon us!*, appeals, or excll. usu. playful of terror or surprise); compassionateness; *at the ~ of*, wholly in the power of, (blessing, thing to be thankful for); (joc.) *left to the tender mercies of*, exposed to probable rough handling by; *~-seat*, golden covering of Ark of Covenant, throne of God. [f. F *merci* f. L *mercedem* (nom. *-ces*) reward, (LL) pity]

mēre¹, n. Lake, pond. [OE, cf. Du. & G *meer* sea, cogn. w. L *mare* sea]

mēre², a. That is solely what the noun implies, as *a ~ swindler, the ~st buffoonery*; (Law) *~ right* (without possession). Hence **~lў²** (mḗrĭ) adv. [f. L *merus* unmixed]

mĕretrĭ′cious (-shus), a. Of, befitting, a harlot; (of ornament, literary style, etc.) showily attractive. Hence **~lў²** adv., **~NESS** n. [f. L *meretricius* f. *meretrix* harlot (*mereri* earn, see -TRIX) +-OUS]

mĕrgăn′ser, n. Diving fish-eating duck. [f. L *mergus* diver+*anser* goose]

mĕrge, v.t. & i. Lose, cause (thing) to lose, character or identity *in* (another), esp. sink (title, estate, *in* greater one). Hence **mĕr′gENCE** n. [f. law F *merger* f. L *mergere mers-* dip]

mĕr′ger, n. Merging; combine. [-ER⁴]

merĭd′ian, n., & a. 1. Circle passing through celestial poles & zenith of any place on earth's surface; circle lying in the plane of this & passing through the place & the poles, as *~ of Greenwich* (of longitude 0° in British maps); point at which sun or star attains highest altitude; *~* (to suit the tastes etc.) of (place, people). 2. adj. Of noon; (fig.) of the period of greatest splendour, vigour, etc. [(n. f. adj.) f. OF *meridien* f. L *meridianus* (*meridies* midday f. *medius* middle +*dies* day, see -AN)]

merĭd′ional, a. & n. Of (the inhabitants of) the south of Europe; of a meridian; (n.) inhabitant of the south (esp. of France). [f. F *méridional* f. LL *meridionalis* (irreg. as prec., -AL)]

meringue′ (-ăng), n. Confection of sugar, white of eggs, etc., small cake of this. [F]

merĭ′nō (-rē-), n. (pl. *~s*). (Also *~ sheep*) kind of sheep with fine wool; soft woollen or wool-&-cotton material like French cashmere, orig. of *~ wool*; fine woollen yarn. [Sp., prob. f. L *majorinus* of a larger kind (*major* greater, see -INE¹)]

mĕr′it, n., & v.t. 1. Quality of deserving well; excellence, worth; (usu. pl.) thing that entitles to reward or gratitude (often *a ~ of*, view, represent, (one's own conduct) as meritorious; *the ~s*, intrinsic rights & wrongs (of case etc., esp. Law); *judge* (proposal etc.) *on its ~s* (with only its intrinsic excellences etc. in view). 2. v.t. Deserve (reward, punishment). [(vb f. F *mériter*) f. OF *merite* f. L *meritum* neut. p.p. of *mereri* earn, deserve]

meritō′rious, a. (Of person or act) deserving reward, praise, or gratitude (often as term of limited praise, =well-meant, well-meaning). Hence **~lў²** adv., **~NESS** n. [f. L *meritorius* (*mereri merit-* earn, see -ORY)+-OUS]

mĕrle, n. (arch., Sc.). Blackbird. [F, f. L *merulus, -la*]

mĕr′lin, n. Kind of falcon. [f. AF *merlun* f. OF *esmerillon* f. com.-Rom. ⁸*smerillo* (med. L *smerillus*), perh. of Teut. orig.]

mĕr′lon, n. Part of embattled parapet between two embrasures. [F, f. It. *merlone* (*merlo* battlement, perh. f. med. L *mergola* dim. f. L *mergae* pitchfork; see -OON]

mĕr′maid, n. Half-human being, with head & trunk of woman & tail of fish. So **mĕr′man** n. [f. MERE¹+MAID]

mē′ro- in comb. = Gk *meros* part, **in** senses 'partly', 'partial', as: *~blast*, ovum that is only partly germinal; *~hĕd′rad*, (of crystal) having less than full number of faces admissible.

-merous, suf. (bot.) = having so many parts, as *dimerous, 5-merous*. [f. Gk as prec.+-OUS]

Mĕrovĭn′gian (-j-), a. & n. (King) of the Frankish line founded by Clovis & reigning in Gaul & Germany c. 500-750. [f. F *Mérovingien* f. med. L *Merowingi* of Germanic orig.]

mĕr′riment, n. Hilarious enjoyment, mirth, fun. [f. obs. vb *merry* be merry+-MENT]

mĕr′rў¹, n. Kind of black cherry. [f. F *merise* etym. dub., prob. taken as pl.]

mĕr′rў², a. Joyous, mirthful; *~* (pleasant) *England, the ~ monarch*, Charles II; slightly tipsy; *make ~*, be festive; *make ~ over*, make fun of; *~ andrew*, mountebank's assistant, clown, buffoon, (also fig.); *~ DANCERS; ~-go-round*, revolving machine with wooden horses or cars; *~-making*, festivity; *~thought*, forked bone between neck & breast of bird. Hence **mĕr′rĭlў²** adv., **mĕr′rĭNESS** n. (rare). [OE *myr(i)ge*, whence *myrgth* MIRTH, cf. MDu. *merchte* mirth; perh. f. OTeut. *murgjo-* short, prob. cogn. w. Gk *brakhus*]

***mē′sa** (mā-), n. High rocky tableland with precipitous sides. [Sp., =table, f. L *mensa*]

mésalliance (see AP.), n. Marriage with person of inferior social position. [F]

mesdames, mesdemoiselles. See MADAME, MADEMOISELLE.

mëseems' (-z), v.i. (arch.). It seems to me. [*me* dat. +SEEMS]

mësembrïan'themum, -brý-, n. Fig-marigold. [f. Gk *mesembria* noon +*anthemon* flower]

mës'entery, n. Fold of peritoneum attaching some part of intestinal canal to posterior wall of abdomen. Hence mës-enter'ic a., mës'enterïtis n. [f. med. L f. Gk *mesenterion* (MESO-+*enteron* intestine)]

mes'merism (mëz-), n. Open space, interstice, of net; usu. involving insensibility to pain & musuclar rigidity, produced on patient by operator's influence over will & nervous system; doctrine concerning, influence producing, this. Hence mës-mër'ic a., ~ISM, ~iz,'TION, nn., ~izE(4) v.t., (mëz-). [f. A. *Mesmer*, Austrian physician, d. 1815, +-ISM]

mesne (mën), a. Intermediate, as ~ profits (received from estate by wrongful tenant between two dates); ~ process, proceedings in suit intervening between primary & final process; (Feud.) ~ lord (holding of superior lord). [law F, =MEAN²]

Mës'o- in comb. = Gk *mesos* middle, intermediate, as: ~*gas'ter*, membrane attaching stomach to dorsal wall of abdomen; ~*lith'ic*, of stone age between palaeolithic & neolithic; ~*phyll*, inner tissue of leaf; ~*thron*, sub-atomic positive or negative particle having a mass about 200 times that of an electron; ~*zō'ic*, of second geological period (cf. CAINOZOIC, PALAEOZOIC).

Mës'pot, n. (sl.). Mesopotamia. [abbr.]

mës'quite(e) (-kēt), n. N.-Amer. leguminous tree; (also ~*grass*) kinds of grass growing near this. [f. Mex. Sp. *mezquite*]

mess¹, n. 1. Portion of liquid or pulpy food; ~ *of pottage*, material comfort etc. for which something higher is sacrificed (Gen. XXV. 29–34); liquid or mixed food for hounds etc.; concoction, medley. 2. Dirty or untidy state of things; *make a* ~ *of*, bungle (undertaking). 3. Company of persons who take meals together, esp. (Navy etc.) each of several parties into which ship's company etc. is divided; meal so taken, as *at* ~, *go to* ~; attrib., as ~*jacket*, coat worn at ~; Hence ~'Y².a.(~*y floor*, *food*, *job*), ~IY² adv., ~'iness n. [f. OF *mes* f. LL *missum*, p.p. of *mittere* send]

mess², v.t. & i. Make a mess of, dirty (thing); muddle (business); potter *about*; take one's meals (*with* or abs.). [f. prec.]

mess'age¹, n. Oral or written communication, sent by one person to another; prophet's, writer's, preacher's, inspired communication. [F. f. pop. L f. *missum*: see -AGE]

mess'age², v.t. Send as a message; transmit (plan etc.) by signalling etc. [f. prec.]

mess'enger, n. One who carries a message; paper sent up string from flier to kite; endless rope passing from capstan to cable to haul it in. [f. F *messager* (as prec., see -ER¹); for *-n-* cf. *passenger*]

Messïah' (-ə), n. 1. Promised deliverer of Jews; Christ as this; liberator of oppressed people or country. Hence ~SHIP n. [f. F *Messie* f. L f. Gk *Messias* f. Heb. *mashiah*, anointed (*mashah* anoint)] Messïan'ic a. Of the, inspired by hope of or belief in a, Messiah.

messïeurs' (mĕsyœr'), n. pl. Pl. of MON-SIEUR or (in abbr. form *Messrs*, pron. mes'erz) of Mr, used esp. as prefix to simpler substances (*destructive* ~).
L *mĕschĕus* (*miscēre* MIX)]

mess'uage (-swij), n. (law). Dwelling-house with outbuildings & land assigned to its use. [AF. prob. corrupt. of *mesnage* MENAGE]

mestï'zo (-tē-), n. (pl. ~s). Spanish or Portuguese half-caste, esp. child of ~) or protoplasm is broken down into simpler substances (*destructive* ~). So **mëtabō'lō a., mëtab**OLIZE(3) v.t. [f. Gk *metabolē* change f. META(*ballō* throw)]

mët'age, n. Official measuring of load of coal etc.; duty paid for this. [f. MÈTE² + -AGE]

mëtag'énesis, n. Alternation between sexual & asexual reproduction. So mëta-genet'ic a. [META-+GENESIS]

mēt'al, n. & v.t.(-ll-). 1. Any of a class of substances represented by gold, silver, copper, iron, lead, & tin, but containing many substances that have few of the characteristics of these; BELL¹, BRITANNIA, GUN, WHITE, YELLOW, ~; HEAVY ~; (Mil.) tanks, armoured vehicles, etc.; material used for making glass, in molten state; (also *road*—) broken stone for macadam roads or railway; || (pl.) rails of a railway line (*train leaves the* ~*s*, is derailed).

mēta- in comb. (before vowel *met*-, before aspirate *meth*-) = Gk *meta* with, after; occas. w. sense 'change'.

mëtab'olism, n. Process, in organism or single cell, by which nutritive material is built up into living matter (*constructive*

mëtacarp'us, n. Part of hand between wrist & fingers. So mëtacarp'al a. wrist & fingers. [f. META-+Gk *karpos* wrist]

2. v.t. Furnish, fit, with ~; mend (road) with ~. [(vb f.n.) OF, f. L f. Gk *metallon* mine, perh. cogn. w. *metallaō* seek after]

metăll′ic, a. Of metal(s); of ~ *currency*, gold, silver, copper, etc., cf. PAPER; characteristic of metals, as ~ *lustre* (peculiar sheen of metals), ~ *sound*. So **mĕt′alline**[1] a. [f. L f. Gk *metallikos* (as METAL, see -IC)]

mĕt′alliz|**e,** v.t. Render metallic; vulcanize (rubber). Hence ~**A′TION** n. [f. METAL +-IZE]

mĕtallŏg′raphy, n. Descriptive science of internal structure of metals. [f. Gk *metallographia* (as METAL, see -GRAPHY)]

mĕt′alloid, a. & n. **1.** Having form or appearance of metal. **2.** n. Element with characteristics both of metals and non-metals. [-OID]

mĕt′allurgy (-ler-), n. Art of working metals, esp. of extracting metals from their ores. Hence **mĕtallŭr′gic**(AL) aa., **mĕt′allurgist** (-ler-) n. [f. Gk *metallourgos* metal-worker (*metallon* METAL +-ergos -worker), see -Y[1]]

mĕt′amere, n. (zool.). One of several similar segments of a body. [f. META-+ Gk *meros* part]

mĕtamĕr′ic, a. (Chem.) having same composition & molecular weight, but different chemical properties; (Zool.) of metameres. So **mĕtăm′erism** n. (chem., zool.). [as prec.+-IC]

mĕtamŏrph′ic, a. Of, marked by, metamorphosis; (Geol., of rock) that has undergone transformation by natural agencies, whence ~**ISM** n. [irreg. f. META- + Gk *morphē* form +-IC]

mĕtamŏrph′ose (-z), v.t. Change in form, turn (*to, into, new form*); change nature of. [f. F *métamorphoser* (*métamorphose*, as foll.)]

mĕtamŏrph′osis, n. (pl. -oses, pr. -ēz). Change of form (by magic or by natural development etc.); changed form; change of character, conditions, etc. [L, f. Gk *metamorphōsis* f. META(*morphoō* f. *morphē* form)]

mĕt′aphor, n. Application of name or descriptive term to an object to which it is not literally applicable (e.g. *a glaring error*); instance of this; *mixed* ~, combination of inconsistent ~s. Hence **mĕtapho′rical**[2] a., **mĕtapho′rically** adv. [f. F *métaphore* f. L f. Gk *metaphora* f. META(*pherō* bear) transfer]

mĕt′aphrase (-z), n., & v.t. Translation, esp. word-for-word; (v.t.) put into other words. So **mĕtaphrăs′IC**[0] a. [(vb f.n.) f. Gk *metaphrasis* f. META(*phrazō* show) translate]

mĕtaphys′ical (-z-), a. Of metaphysics; based on abstract general reasoning; over-subtle; incorporeal; supernatural; visionary. Hence ~**LY**[2] adv. [-AL]

mĕtaphys′ics (-z-), n. pl. (often treated as sing.). Theoretical philosophy of being

& knowing; philosophy of mind; (pop.) abstract or subtle talk, mere theory. So ~**I′CIAN** (-ĭshn) n., ~**ICIZE**(2) v.i. [earlier ~*ic*; med. L as *metaphysica* fem. sing. & neut. pl., f. med. Gk *metaphysika* f. Gk *ta meta ta phusika* the works (of Aristotle) placed after the PHYSICS]

mĕt′aplăsm (-z-), n. (biol.). Part of protoplasm that contains formative material. [META-+-*plasm* as in PROTOPLASM]

mĕtapŏl′itics, n. pl. Abstract political science (often derog.). Hence **mĕtapolit′ical** a., **mĕtapolĭti′cIAN** (-ĭshn) n. [META-, after METAPHYSICS]

mĕtapsych′ics (-sīk-), n. pl. Psychical research. [META-+PSYCHICS, after *metaphysics*]

mĕtas′tasis, n. (pl. -ses, pr. -sēz). Transference of bodily function, disease, etc., from one part or organ to another: transformation of chemical compounds into others in process of assimilation by an organism. So **mĕthistĕmi** remove (META-+ *histēmi* place)]

mĕtatăr′s|us, n. (anat.). Group of five long bones of foot between tarsus & toes. Hence ~**AL** a. [META-]

mĕtath′esis, n. (pl. -ses, pr. -sēz). (Gram.) transposition of sounds or letters in word; (Chem.) interchange of atoms between two molecules. [LL f. Gk META(*tithēmi* place) transpose]

mĕtayage (mĕt′āyahzh), n. Land tenure in which farmer pays part (usu. half) of produce as rent to owner, who furnishes stock & seed. [F, irreg. as foll., see -AGE]

mĕtayer (mĕt′āyā), n. Holder of land on prec. system. [F, f. med. L *medietārius* (*medietas* MOIETY, see -ARY[1])]

mēte[1], n. Boundary, boundary stone, esp. (Law) ~*s & bounds*. [OF, f. L *meta* goal]

mēte[2], v.t. (literary). (Poet.)measure; portion *out, allot*; (punishment, reward); ‖~*scand, yard*, (fig.) standard of estimation. [com.-Teut.: OE *metan*, Du. *meten*, G *messen*]

mĕtĕmpī′ric, n. (Also ~s) philosophy of things outside the sphere of experience; believer in this. Hence ~**AL** a., ~**IST** n. [f. META-+EMPIRIC, after *metaphysics*]

mĕtĕmpsychō′sis (-k-), n. (pl. -es, pr. -ēz). Transmigration of soul of human being or animal at death into new body of same or different species. Hence ~**IST**(2) n. [LL f. Gk META-+*en* in+ *psudhē* soul +-OSIS]

mĕt′eor, n. (Any atmospheric phenomenon, esp.) shooting star, small mass of matter from celestial space rendered luminous by collision with earth's atmosphere. [f. Gk *meteōros* lofty, (neut. pl.) atmospheric phenomena (META-+*aeirō* raise).]

mĕteŏr′ic, a. Of the atmosphere; dependent on atmospheric conditions; of

měteorʹic, a. ...of meteors; (fig.) dazzling, rapid. [prec.+-ic].

mě'teor|ite, n. Fallen meteor, meteoric stone. So ~OLITE n. [METEOR+-ITE¹]

mě'teorograph, n. Apparatus recording meteorological phenomena. [METEOR,-GRAPH]

mě'teor|oid, n. Body moving through space, of same nature as those which by passing through atmosphere become visible as meteors. Hence ~oidʹAL a. [-OID]

meteor|olʹogy, n. Study of notions & phenomena of atmosphere, esp. for changes of weather; atmospheric character (of region). Hence or cogn. ~oloʹgicALLY adv., ~olʹogisT n. [f. Gk meteorologia (as METEOR,-LOGY)]

mē'ter, n. Person, thing, that measures, esp. gas, water, etc.; ~, instruments for recording volume of gas etc. supplied. [f. METE²+-ER¹; prob. after wds w. foll. suf., as gasometer]

-meter, suf. in names of measuring instruments on Gk nn. (but not on Gk anal.), as barometer, L nn., as calorimeter, mod. wds as if Gk or L, as gasometer, or without assim. to Gk or L, as ammeter. [f. Gk metron measure]

mē'thāne, n. (chem.). Odourless colourless inflammable gaseous hydrocarbon, marsh gas, fire-damp. [f. METH(YL)+-ANE]

mēthě'glin, n. (hist., dial.). Spiced kind of mead. [f. W meddyglyn (medig heal-ing f. L medicus+llyn liquor)]

měthi'nks, v.i. (arch.; past methought pr. -awt). It seems to me. [ME dat.+THINKS]

mē'thod, n. Special form of procedure esp. in any branch of mental activity; whence ~ōlʹOGY n.; orderly arrangement of ideas; orderliness, regular habits; there's ~ in his etc. madness, (joc.) his conduct or proposal is not so mad as it seems; (Nat. Hist.) scheme of classification. Hence or cogn. mēthō'dicAL a., mēthō'dicALLY² adv. [f. L f. Gk methodos (META-+hodos WAY)]

mē'thodist, n. 1. (M-) member of any of several religious bodies (now united) originating in the evangelistic movement of Charles & John Wesley & George Whitefield, whence mē'thodisM n. [as aa., mē'thodisTIC(AL)³ aa., mē'thodis'ticALLY² adv. 2. (derog.) Person of strict religious views. 3. One who follows a method, esp. in Nat. Hist. Hence Mē'thodisE n. [-IST]

mē'thodize, v.t. Reduce to order, arrange in orderly manner. [-IZE]

mē'thought. See METHINKS.

Mēthu'selah (-z-), n. A pre-Noachian patriarch who is stated to have lived 969 years (hence as type of longevity). [Heb.]

mē'thyl, n. Radical of ~ alcohol (wood spirit), present in many organic compounds. Hence mēthy'lIC a. [f. F méthyle (Gk methu wine+hulē wood)]

mē'thylāte, v.t. Mix, impregnate, (esp. spirit of wine, to make it unfit for drinking, so as to exempt it from duties) with methyl alcohol, as ~d spirit. [-ATE³]

mēti'culous, a. Over-scrupulous about minute details. Hence -LY² adv. [f. L meticulosus (metus fear, see -CULE,-OUS)]

mět'ier (mět'yā), n. One's trade, profession, or line. [F]

mět'is, n. Offspring of white & American Indian, esp. in Canada. [f. F métis (as MESTIZO)]

mēto'nic, a. ~ cycle, period of 19 years (235 lunar months), covering all the changes of the moon. [Meton, Athenian astronomer of 5th c. B.C.]

mětŏ'nymy, n. Substitution of the name of an attribute for that of the thing meant (e.g. crown for king). Hence mětŏny'micAL a., mětŏny'micALLY² adv. [f. LL f. Gk metōnumia (META-+onoma name)]

mět'ope (-opi, -ōp), n. (archit.). Square space between triglyphs in Doric frieze. [f. L f. Gk metopē (META-+opē hole for beam)]

mētre' (-ter), n. Any form of poetic rhythm, determined by character & number of feet; metrical group, esp. pair of feet in iambic & other rhythms. Hence mět'ricAL (-ishn), mět'rics, mět'risT, nn. [f. L f. Gk metron measure]

mētre'² (-ter), n. Unit of length in metric system (39·37 in.). [f. F mètre (as prec.)]

mět'ric, a. Of the METRE²; ~ system, decimal measuring-system with the metre & the litre & gramme determined by it, as units of length, capacity & weight (the prefixing to metre etc. of the Greek-derived deca-, hecto-, kilo-, denotes multiplication by 10, 100, 1,000, as kilo-metre 1,000 metres; that of the Latin-derived deci-, centi-, milli-, division by 10, 100, 1,000, as decilitre tenth of a litre). [-IC]

mět'rical, a. Of, composed in, metre; of, involving, measurement, as ~ geometry. Hence ~LY² adv., METRI|CIAN. [as METRE¹+-AL]

mētrŏ'logy, n. Science, system, of weights & measures. Hence mětrolŏ'gicAL a. [as METRE¹+-LOGY]

mět'ronōme, n. (mus.). Instrument marking time by means of pendulum, beating rod, etc. Hence mětronŏ'mic a. [as METRE¹+Gk nomos law]

mētro'polis, n. Chief city of a country; capital; || the ~, London; metropolitan bishop's see; centre of activity. [L, f. Gk mētropolis parent State (mētēr -tros mother+polis city)]

mětropŏ'litan, a. & n. Of a or the metropolis; belonging to, forming (part of), mother country as dist. from its colonies etc.; of an ecclesiastical metropolis; ~ (bishop), bishop having authority over bishops of a province, in the West equivalent to archbishop, in Greek church

ranking above archbishop & below patriarch, whence ~ATE¹(-ət) n.; inhabitant of
a metropolis. [f. LL *metropolitanus* f. Gk
mētropolitēs (as prec., -ITE¹), as -AN¹]

-metry, suf. in names of systems corresp.
to instruments in -METER on anal. of Gk
geōmetria GEOMETRY, but also in hybrids,
as *alkalimetry*. [f. Gk *-metria* (*-metrēs*
measurer, as METRE¹)]

met'tle, n. Quality of disposition; natural
ardour; spirit, courage; *be on one's ~e*
(incited to do one's best). Hence (-)~ED²
(-ld), ~ESOME (-tĭs), aa. [var. of METAL n.]

mē'um, n. ~ *& tū'um*, mine & thine
(used to express rights of property). [L,
neut. of *meus*]

mew¹, n. (Also *sea-~*) gull, esp. common
gull. [OE *mǣw*, cf. Du. *meeuw*, G *mōwe*]

mew², n., & v.t. 1. Cage for hawks, esp.
while moulting. 2. v.t. Put (hawk) in ~;
(fig.) shut up, confine. [(vb f. n.), f. F
mue (as foll.)]

mew³, v.t.(arch.) (Of hawk) moult, shed,
(feathers). [f. F *muer* f. L *mutare* change]

mew⁴, v.i., & n. 1. (Of cat, sea-birds) utter
sound mew. 2. n. This sound, esp. of cat.
[imit.]

mewl, mule, v.i. Cry feebly, whimper;
mew like cat. [imit., cf. MIAUL]

mews, n. Set of stabling round open
yard. [pl. (now used as sing.) of MEW²,
orig. of royal stables on site of hawks'
mews]

mě'zzanine (-ēn), n. Low storey between
two higher ones (usu. between ground &
first floors). (Theatr.) floor beneath stage.
[F, f. It. *mezzanino* dim. of *mezzano* f. L
medianus (*medius* middle, see -AN¹)]

mě'zzo (-dzō), adv. (Mus.) half, moderately, as ~FORTE², PIANO¹; ~-*rĭlǐe'vo*
(-lyāvō), half-relief, in which figures
project half their true proportions; ~
sopra'no, (person with, part for) voice between soprano & contralto. [It., f. L
medius middle]

mě'zzotint (-dz-), n., & v.t. 1. Method of
engraving in which plate is roughened
uniformly, lights & half-lights being
given by scraping away the nap thus
produced, deep shadows by leaving it;
2. v.t. Engrave
in ~. [(vb f. n.) f. It. *mezzotinto* (also used
in E) f. *mezzo* half + *tinto* TINT]

mi (mē), n. (mus.). Third note of octave.
[first syllable of L *mira*, see GAMUT]

miaow (miow²), n., & v.i. (Make) cry of
cat. [imit.]

mias'ma (-z-), n. (pl. ~ata, ~as). Infectious or noxious emanation, esp. malaria.
Hence ~AL, ~ăt'ic, aa., (-z-). [Gk (*miainō*
pollute, see -M)]

miaul', v.i. Cry like cat. [f. F *miauler*,
imit.]

mic'a, n. Any of several minerals composed of silicate of aluminium with other
silicates, found in small glittering scales in
granite etc., or in crystals; ~*schist*, -*slate*,

slaty rock of quartz & ~. Hence mica'ceous (-āshus) a. [L, =crumb]

Micaw'ber, n. ~, *Mr ~, Wilkins ~*,
sanguine idler trusting that something
good will turn up. Hence ~ISM(3) n.
[person in Dickens's *David Copperfield*]

mice. See MOUSE¹.]

Mich'ael (-kel), n. An archangel; *Order of
St ~ & St George*, English civil & military order of knighthood; ~*mas* (mĭk'ĕl-),
feast of St ~, Sep. 29, || a quarter-day.
[f. Heb. *mikhael* who is like God?]

Mick'ey Mouse, n. (R.A.F. sl.), Electrical distributor which releases bombs
from aircraft. [character in film cartoons]

|| mic'kle, mŭc', a. & n. (arch., Sc.).
Much, great; (n.) a large amount (in prov.
many a little, or pickle, makes a ~). [com-
Teut.: OE *micel*, Sw. *mycken*, Da. *megen*,
cogn. w. Gk *megas* great]

mic'ro-¹ in comb.=Gk *mikros* small, as:
~*cephal'ic* & n., (person) with abnormally small head, so ~*cĕph'alous* a.;
~*film* n. P, (photographic reproduction
on) a very small film; ~*lith'ic*, constructed
of small stones, marked by monuments so
constructed; ~*logy* (-ŏl-), hair-splitting;
~*meter* (-ŏm²), instruments for measuring
small objects or (Astron.) distances, so
~*met'rical*, ~*metry* (-ŏm²); ~*phŏt'ograph*
(of microscopic object on magnified scale);
~*phile*, microscopic plant, esp. bacterium; ~*seism* (-sīzm), faint earthquake
tremor, whence ~*seis'mic*, ~*seis'mograph*,
~*seismŏl'ogy*; ~*spore*, parasitic fungus
with small spores, small spore; ~*tome*,
instrument for cutting thin sections for
microscope; ~*tŏne*, mus. interval smaller
than semitone; ~*zȳme*, zymotic microbe.

mic'ro-² (etym. as prec.) prefixed in
Physics to unit-names = the millionth
part of the unit; ~*ampere*, ~*coulomb*,
~*farad*, ~*gramme*, ~*litre*, ~*metre*, mic'rohm,
~*volt*.

mic'robe, n. Minute living being, plant or
animal (esp. of bacteria causing diseases
& fermentation). Hence microb'IAL a.,
microbiŏl'ogy n. [F (MICRO-¹+ Gk *bios*
life)]

mic'rocosm (-zm), n. Man viewed as
epitome of the universe; any community
or complex unity so viewed; miniature
representation (*of*). Hence microcŏs'-
MIC (-z-) a. [f. F *microcosme* f. med. L
MICRO(*cosmus* f. Gk *kosmos* world)]

mic'rŏn, n. The millionth of a metre. [f.
Gk neut. of *mikros* small]

mic'rophŏne, n. Instrument for intensifying small sounds or converting sound
waves into electrical energy which may
be reconverted into sound after transmission by wire or wireless, as the transmitter of a telephone or (colloq. abbr.
mike) the mouthpiece for broadcasting.
[f. MICRO-¹+Gk *phōnē* sound]

mic'roscōpe, n. Instrument magnifying
objects by means of lens(es) so as to

reveal details invisible to naked eye. [MICRO-.] ~ally² adv. [-IC]

microscopy, n. Use of the microscope. So ~IST n. [-Y²]

mictur'ition, n. Morbidly frequent desire to make water; (improp.) making water. [f. L *micturīre* -īt-, desiderative f. *mingere*]

mid¹, a. (sup. ~most). The middle of (usu. after *in*, as *in* ~ *air, career, Channel, course, stream, winter*; also with *from, to*, etc., as *from* ~ *June to* ~ *August*; & in attrib. compounds, as *a* ~*winter day*); that is in the middle, medium, half, (~ *iron*, golf iron with medium loft; ~ *off*, ~ *on*, = ~*wicket off, on*; ~'rib, central rib of leaf; ~*way* adv., in middle of distance between places; ~*wicket off* or *on*, fielder near bowler on off or on, side); ~WING. [com.-Teut.; cogn. w. Gk *mesos*, L *medius*]

mid², prep. (poet.). = AMID.

mid'day, n. Noon (often attrib.). [OE *middæg*, see MID¹ & DAY]

mid'den, n. (dial.). Dunghill; kitchen ~, prehistoric refuse-heap, chiefly of shells & bones. [of Scand. orig.]

mid'dle¹, a. (not pred.; rare sup. ~most) & n. 1. (Of member or group) so placed as to have same number of members on each side; equidistant from extremities; intermediate in rank, quality, etc.; ~ *course, way*, compromise between two extremes; (Gram.) applied to a voice in form (esp. Greek) verbs that is passive in form but reflexive or active in sense, cf. DEPONENT; M~ ENGLISH; ~ *age*, between youth & old age; ~*aged*, of such age; *the M~ Ages* (about 1000-1400, or in a wider sense 600-1500); || ~ *article*, brief essay of literary kind in weekly or other journal often placed between political articles & book-reviews; ~ *class*, class of society between upper & lower (often attrib., ~*class*); M~ EAST; ~ (second) *finger*; M~ *Kingdom*, China (orig. of Honan as central & sovereign State); ~ *life*, ~ *age*; *in the* ~ *of*, while (doing), during (process); (Log.) ~ (*term*), term common to both premisses, *principle of excluded* ~ (that anything must be included either under a given term or under its negative); ~*man*, any of the traders through whose hands commodity passes from producer to consumer; ~ *passage*, sea journey between W. Africa & W. Indies (with ref. to the slave trade); ~ *watch* (from midnight to 4 a.m.); ~*weight* (Boxing), position or part (of), waist. 2. n. ~ point or part (of). [OE *middel*, G *mittel*, f. OTeut. *midjo*- MD]

mid'dle², v.t. (Footb.) return (ball or abs.) from wing to mid field in front of goal; (techn.) place in the middle. [f. prec.]

mid'dling, a. & adv. 1. (Commerce, of goods) of the second of three grades, so ~s n. pl. (also in spec. senses, flour of medium fineness, & comminuted bran); moderately good; second-rate; (colloq.) fairly well (in health), as *I am only* ~. 2. adv. Fairly or moderately, as ~ *good, fast*. Hence ~LY² adv. [prob. of Sc. orig. f. MID¹ + -LING¹ & ² (confused)]

mid'dy, n. See MIDSHIP.

midge, n. Kinds of gnat-like insect; small person. [OE *mycg*, cf. Du. *mug*, G *mücke*]

mid'get, n. Extremely small person, esp. when exhibited as curiosity; very small thing (also attrib.). [f. prec. + -ET¹]

midinette (médē-), n. Parisian shop-girl (esp. milliner's assistant). [F, perh. f. *midi* noon + *dînette* light dinner, because those girls are usually seen about the streets at lunch-time]

mid'land, n. & a. 1. Middle part of country; (pl.) *the middle counties of England*). 2. a. Of, in, the ~ or ~s. [MID¹ + LAND]

mid'night, n. The middle of the night, 12 o'clock; intense darkness (often attrib.). [OE *midniht* (MID¹ + NIGHT)]

mid'riff, n. Diaphragm. [OE *midhrif* f. MID¹ + *hrif* belly]

mid'rash, n. (pl. ~im, pr. -ăsh'ĕm). Ancient Jewish commentary on part of Hebrew Scriptures. [Heb.]

mid'ship, n. Middle part of ship or boat; ~*man* (abbr. *middy*—not used by Royal Navy), rank between naval cadet & sub-lieutenant; ~s, = AMIDSHIPS. [MID¹ + SHIP]

midst, n., adv., & prep. *In the* ~ *of*, among; *in our, your,* ~, among us, you; (poet.) *in the* ~ *of*. [(1) MID¹ + -ST, see -ES. (2) sup. of MID]

mid'summer, n. Period of summer solstice, about June 21; M~ *day*, June 24; || a quarter-day; ~ (the height of) *madness*. [MD]

mid'wife, n. (pl. -wives). Woman who assists other women in childbirth. Hence **mid'wifery**(-), (-wīfri, *-wǐ-) n., obstetrics. [MID¹ (or obs. prep. *mid* with, cf. G *mit*) + WIFE]

mien (mēn), n. (literary). Air, bearing, of person, as showing character or mood. [prob. shortened f. *demean* n., assim. to F *mine* expression, etym. dub.]

miff, n., & v.i. & t. (colloq.). Petty quarrel; huff; (v.i.) take offence *with* or *at*; (v.t.) put out of humour. [perh. imit.; cf. G *muff*, exclamation of disgust]

might¹ (mīt), n. Great (bodily or mental) strength; power to enforce one's will (opp. *right*); *with* ~ *&* MAIN². [OE *miht*, cf. Du. & G *macht*, f. OTeut. *mag*- MAY¹]

might². See MAY¹.

might'y, a. & adv. 1. Powerful,

strong, in body or mind; (Bibl.) ~y works, miracles; massive, bulky; (colloq.) great, considerable; HIGH & ~y. 2. adv. (colloq.). Very, as that 'is ~y easy. Hence ~ILY² adv., ~INESS n. (esp. in your etc. high ~iness as burlesque title). [OE mihtig (as MIGHT¹, see -Y²)]

mignon (see Ap.), a. Small & delicately formed. [F]

mignonette (minyo-), n. 1. Plant with fragrant flowers; colour of these, greyish green. 2. Kinds of lace & fine net. [f. F (-onn-), dim. of prec.]

migraine (mē-), n. = MEGRIM (first sense). [as MEGRIM]

migrate (or mī-), v.i. Move from one place (country, town, college, house) to another; (of birds & fishes) come & go with the seasons. Hence or cogn. mig'RANT a. & n., migRA'TION, migRA'TORY a. [f. L migrare, see -ATE³]

nika'dō (-kah-), n. (pl. ~s). Emperor of Japan. [Jap. mi august +kado door]

mike¹, v.i., & n. (sl.). Shirk work; idle; (n.) idling (on the ~). [cf. dial. miche app. f. OF muchier to skulk]

mike², n. (colloq.). Microphone. [abbr.]

mil, n. A thousand (per ~, as per cent); (Pharm., short for) MILLILITRE; unit measure for diameter of wire etc., = 1000 in. [f. L mille thousand, millesimum thousandth]

mil'age, n. Miles travelled, used, etc.; expenses per mile. [-AGE]

Milanese' (-z), a. & n. (pl. same). (Native) (n.) a. & n. of Lombardy; the ~, the territory of old duchy of Milan. [It. (Milano Milan), -ESE]

milch, a. (Of domestic mammals) giving, kept for, milk; ~ cow, (fig.) source of profit, esp. person from whom money is easily drawn. [ME mielch, f. OTeut. melukjo- (meluk- milk)]

mild, a. Gentle & conciliatory (of rule, punishment, etc.) not severe; (of weather) calm & warm; (of medicine) operating gently; (of food, tobacco, etc.) not sharp or strong in taste etc.; (of beer) not strongly flavoured with hops, opp. to bitter; tame, feeble, lacking in energy or vivacity; ~ steel, containing small percentage of carbon, strong & tough, but not readily tempered. Hence ~EN⁶ v.t. & i., ~LY² adv., ~NESS n. [com-Teut.: OE milde, Du. & G mild]

mil'dew, n., & v.t. & i. 1. Destructive growth of minute fungi on plants; similar growth on paper, leather, etc., exposed to damp. 2. vb. Taint, be tainted, with ~. Hence ~Y² a. [(vb f. n.) OE meledēaw, f. OTeut. +melith honey +daewo- DEW]

mile, n. Unit of lineal measure, in England now 1,760 yards (orig. Roman measure of 1,000 paces, about 1,618 yards); geographical, nautical, ~, one minute of great circle of earth, fixed by

British Admiralty at 6,080 feet; race extending over a ~; not 100 ~s from, in or at or close to (as sham-mysterious indication); ~stone, pillar set up on road to mark ~s, (fig.) stage, event, in life. [OE mīl, ult. f. L mīl(l)ia pl. of mille thousand]

mil'er, n. (colloq.). Man, horse, qualified or trained specially to run a mile; also in comb., as two-~s. [-ER¹]

Milē'sian (-shn), a. & n. Irish(man). [f. Milesius fabulous Spanish king whose sons are said to have conquered Ireland c. 1300 B.C., +-AN]

mil'foil, n. Common yarrow & other plants, [ME & OF f. L millefolium (mille thousand +folium leaf)]

mil'iary, a. (path.). Like millet-seed in size or form, as ~ gland, tubercle; ~ fever (marked by rash like measles, with vesicles of form of millet-seed). [f. L miliarius (as MILLET, -ARY¹)]

milieu (see Ap.), n. Environment, state of life, social surroundings. [F]

mil'itant, a. Engaged in (esp. spiritual) warfare, as the Church ~; combative. Hence mil'itANCY n., ~LY² adv. [F, as MILITATE, see -ANT]

mil'itarism, n. Spirit, tendencies, of the professional soldier; undue prevalence of military spirit or ideals. So ~izA'TION n., ~IZE(3) v.t. [f. F militarisme (as MILITARY, see -ISM)]

mil'itarist, n. Student of military science; one dominated by military ideas. [-IST]

mil'itary, a. & n. 1. Of, done by, befitting, soldiers; ~ band, wood-wind, brass, & percussion combination; ~ chest, treasury of army; ~ fever, enteric; ~ testament, soldier's nuncupative will. 2. n. (Usu. the ~) soldiery, troops, the army. Hence mil'itarILY² adv. [f. F militaire f. L militaris (miles -itis soldier, see -ARY²)]

mil'itate, v.i. Take part in warfare (usu. fig.); (of facts, evidence) have force, tell, (against, rarely in favour of, conclusion etc.). [f. L militare (miles -itis soldier), see -ATE³]

militia (-sha), n. Military force, esp. citizen force; branch of British military service formerly raised by the several counties, usn. by voluntary enlistment; || British conscript army formed 1939; ~man, member of the ~. [L (as prec.)]

milk¹, n. 1. Opaque white fluid secreted by female mammals for nourishment of their young; (fig.) ~ for babes, simple forms of literature, doctrine, etc., opp. to strong meat; CONDENSED ~; ~ & honey, abundant means of enjoyment; ~ of human kindness, kindness natural to humanity; no use crying over spilt ~ (irremediable loss or error); ~-like juice of plants; ~-like preparation of herbs, drugs, etc., as ~ of almonds. 2. ~ & water, feeble or mawkish discourse or sentiment

(attrib. ~-&-water); ~-bar (for sale of beverages made from ~, other non-alcoholic drinks, ice cream, etc.); ~-crust, skin-eruption in infants; ~-fever (occurring to women shortly after childbirth); ~-legs, swelling, esp. of legs, after childbirth; ||~-float, light low vehicle used in delivering ~; ~-maid, woman who sells ~; ~-powder, ~ dehydrated by evaporation, etc.; ~-pudding (of rice, sago, tapioca, etc., baked with ~ in dish); ~-punch, drink made of spirits & ~; ~-SHAKE²; ~-sop, spiritless man or youth; ~-tooth, temporary tooth in young mammals, ~-walk, man's round; ~-weed, kinds of wild plant with milky juice; ~-white (as ~); ~-wort, kinds of plant. [com.-Teut.: OMercian *milc*, Du. *melk*, G *milch*, f. OTeut. *meluks* (mlk vb, cogn. w. Gk *amelgō*, L *mulgere* to milk)]

milk². v.t. Draw milk from (cow, ewe, goat); ~ *the ram or bull*, engage in hopeless enterprise; get money out of, exploit, (person); (sl.) steal message from (telegraph or telephone wire); extract juice, virus, etc., from (snake etc.). [OE *melcan* (as prec.)]

milk'y, a. Of, like, mixed with, milk; (of liquid) cloudy, not clear; effeminate, weakly amiable; M~y Way, luminous band of countless stars encircling the heavens. Hence ~INESS n. [-Y²]

mill¹, n. 1. Building fitted with machinery for grinding corn (often *under~, wind~; pot, go, through the ~*, subject to, undergo, training or experience; *the ~s of God grind slowly*, retribution is often delayed). 2. Any mechanical apparatus for grinding corn; apparatus for grinding any solid substance to powder or pulp, as *coffee, pepper, paper, ~*. 3. Any machine, or building fitted with machinery, for manufacturing processes etc., as *saw-, cotton, silk.. ~ (~-hand*, factory worker). 4. Pugilistic encounter. 5. ~-board, stout pasteboard for bookbinding etc.; ~-dam, put across stream to make it available for ~; ~-pond, water retained by this (*like a ~-pond*, said of calm sea); (joc.) = HERRING-pond; ~-race, current of water that drives ~-wheel; ~-stone, one of pair of circular stones for grinding corn, as NETHER ~stone, *see far into a ~stone*, (usu. iron.) be extraordinarily acute, *between upper & nether~-stone*, subject to irresistible pressure; ~-stone, a hard siliceous rock; ~-wheel, one (esp. water-wheel) used to drive ~; ~-wright, one who designs or erects ~s. [OE *mylen* f. LL *molīnum, -na (mola* mill f. root of *molere* grind)]

mill². v.t. & i. Thicken (cloth etc.) by fulling; grind (corn), produce (flour), in mill; produce regular markings on edge of (coin, esp. in p.p.); beat (chocolate) to froth; beat, strike, fight, (person); (of

cattle or persons) move round & round in a mass. [f. prec.]

*mill³, n. One-thousandth of a dollar, money of account. [f. L *millesimum* thousandth part, on anal. of CENT]

millenar'ian, a. & n. Of the millennium; (person) believing in this. Hence ~ISM n. [as foll. +-AN]

mill'enary, a. & n. (Period) of 1,000 years; of, (person) believing in, the millennium. [f. L *millenarius* consisting of a thousand, f. *milleni* a thousand each f. *mille* thousand, -ARY¹)]

millenn'i|um, n. Period of a thousand years, esp. that of Christ's reign in person on earth (*Rev.* xx. 1-5); (fig.) period of good government, great happiness, & prosperity. Hence ~AL a. [f. L *mille* thousand +*annus* year, on anal. of *biennium* two years' space]

mill'epede, mill'i-, n. Kinds of myriapods, with numerous legs usu. placed on each segment in double pairs; kinds of terrestrial crustacean, esp. common woodlouse & armadillo. [f. L *millepeda* woodlouse (*mille* thousand + *pes pedis* foot)]

mill'er, n. Proprietor, tenant, of corn-mill; one who works any mill; kinds of white or white-powdered insect; cock-chafer; ~'s thumb, bull-head & other fishes. [MILL¹+-ER¹]

milles'imal, a. & n. Thousandth (part); consisting of thousandths. [f. L *mille-simus (mille* thousand +-AL)]

mill'et, n. Gramineous plant, native of India, bearing large crop of small nutritious seeds; its seed; ~-grass, a tall handsome grass. [F, dim. of *mil* f. L *milium*]

mill'i- in comb. = one-thousandth of a — (in metric system), as ~gramme (·0154 of English grain); ~litre (·0·61 cub. in.); ~mètre (·ter: ·0394 in.). [L *mille* thousand -i-]

||mill'iard (-yard), n. A thousand millions. [F (*mille* thousand)]

mill'in|er, n. Person (usu. woman) who makes up hats & other female headgear; man ~er, (fig.) man busied in trifling occupations. Hence ~ERY(1) n. [f. *Milan* +-ER¹; orig. =vendor of Milan goods]

mill'ion (-yon), n. & a. A thousand thousand (things, of things, or abs.); a ~ population. Hence ~FOLD a. & adv. [f. F *million* f. Rom. *millione (mille* thousand +*-one* -oon)]

millionaire (-yon-), n. Person possessing a million pounds, dollars, francs, etc.; person of great wealth. [f. F *millionnaire* (prec., -ARY¹)]

millipede. See MILLEPEDE.

Mills bomb, n. Oval hand-grenade. [inventor]

milord', n. French word for English lord or wealthy Englishman. [f. E *my lord*]

mil′reis (-āis), n. Former Portuguese gold coin worth 4s. 5¼d. [Port. (mil thousand + REIS)]

milt, n., & v.t. 1. Spleen in mammals; analogous organ in other vertebrates; roe of male fish. 2. v.t. Impregnate (roe of female). [(vb f. n.) OE milte, cf. Du. milt, G milz, perh. cogn. w. MELT]

mil′ter, n. Male fish in spawning time. [-ER¹]

Milton′ic, a. Of, in the style of, Milton. So **Mil′ton′IAN** a. [-IC]

mime, n., & v.i. 1. (Gk or Rom. Ant.) simple farcical drama marked by mimicry; performer in this; pantomimist, buffoon. 2. v.i. Act with mimic gesture, usu. without words. [(vb f. n.) f. L f. Gk mimos]

mim′eograph (-ahf), n., & v.t. Apparatus for making stencils of written pages, from which many copies may be taken; (v.t.) reproduce by means of ~. [irreg. f. Gk mimeomai imitate, see -GRAPH]

mimē′sis, n. (biol.). Close external resemblance between animal & another animal or inanimate object. [Gk, =imitation (as prec.)]

mimet′ic, a. Of, addicted to, imitation, mimicry, or mimesis. Hence ~ICALLY adv. [f. Gk mimētikos (as prec., see -ETIC)]

mim′ic¹, a. & n. 1. Apt to imitate; imitative as opp. to real. 2. n. Person skilled in ludicrous imitation. [f. L f. Gk mimikos (as MIME, see -IC)]

mim′ic², v.t. (~ked, ~king). Ridicule by imitating (person, manner, etc.); copy minutely or servilely; (of things) resemble closely. [f. prec.]

mim′icry, n. Mimicking; thing that mimics another; (Zool.) =MIMESIS. [MIMIC¹+-RY]

mim′iný-pim′iný, a. Over-refined, finicking. [imit.]

mimō′sa (or -z-), n. Genus of leguminous shrubs, including common Sensitive Plant. [f. L as MIME+-osa fem. suf., see -OSE¹]

min′ūlus, n. Genus of flowering plants, incl. monkey-flower. [prob. dim. as prec.]

min′a¹, n. (pl. -ae). Ancient-Greek denomination of money, about £4; ancient unit of weight in Greece, Egypt, etc., about 1 lb. [L, f. Gk mna]

min′a², n. Kinds of eastern passerine bird. [f. Hind. mainā]

mina′cious (-shus), a. Threatening. Hence ~ITY² adv., **mina′CITY** n. [f. L minax (minari threaten), see -ACIOUS]

∥mina′r, n. Lighthouse; turret. [f. Arab. manar f. root of nar fire]

min′aret, n. Slender turret connected with mosque, from which muezzin calls people to prayer. [f. Arab. manarat (as prec.)]

min′atory, a. Threatening. [f. OF minatoire f. LL minatorius (minari threaten, -ORY)]

mince¹, n. Minced meat; ~′meat, mixture of currants, raisins, sugar, apples, candied-peel, etc., for ~ pie (small round pie containing this); make ~meat of, destroy (person, argument, etc.). [f. foll.]

mince², v.t. & i. Cut (meat etc.) small; (usu. w. negative) ~ matters, express oneself politely in condemnation; restrain (one's words) within bounds of politeness; utter (words), walk, with affected delicacy, whence **min′cing**LY² adv. [f. OF mincier f. pop. L +minutiare (as MINUTIA)]

Min′cing Lāne, n. (Used for) the wholesale trade in tea & similar imports. [London street]

mind¹, n. 1. Remembrance, as have or keep in ~, bring or call to ~, remember, go or pass out of ~, be forgotten; TIME¹ out of ~. 2. Candid opinion, as speak one's ~, tell (person) one's ~, give him a piece of one's ~. 3. Be of (person's) ~, agree in opinion with him; to my ~, as I think; be of a or one ~, agree; know one's own ~, form & adhere to decision; make up one's ~, resolve (to do, to a course etc., or abs.), reconcile oneself to fact as inevitable (the crop is ruined, we must make up our ~s to that); change one's ~, alter one's purpose; have a good or great ~, half a ~, be strongly, somewhat, disposed (to do); be in two ~s, vacillate, be irresolute; MONTH'S ~. 4. Direction of thoughts or desires, as set one's ~ on, desire to attain, give one's ~ (attention) to; to one's ~, as one would have it. 5. Way of thinking & feeling, as frame, state, of ~. 6. Seat of consciousness, thought, volition, & feeling. 7. Soul, opp. to body; ~'s eye, mental view. 8. Person, as embodying mental qualities. 9. Intellectual powers, opp. to will & emotions, whence ~LESS a. 10. ABSENCE, PRESENCE, of ~; ~-stuff (Philos.), supposed rudimentary form of psychical existence regarded as the reality of which matter is an aspect. [ME mynd, of. OHG gemund f. OTeut. gamundiz (ga- Y-+ mun- think, mind, cogn. w. L mens mind, Gk menos rage)]

mind², v.t. & i. 1. Bear in mind (chiefly in imperat.); give heed to, as never ~ the expense. 2. Concern oneself (never ~ if imperat., take comfort, also as refusal to answer question). 3. Apply oneself to (business etc.; ~ your own business, leave other people's alone). 4. (Chiefly in neg. or quasi-neg. sentences) object to, as would you ~ ringing?, I should not ~ (should like) a cup of tea, if you don't ~ (have no objection). 5. Remember & take care (that thing is done, or omit that). 6. ~ you or ~ (parenth. imperat.), please to observe (but I have no objection, ~ you; now ~, not a word till I give the signal); (sl.) ~ your eye, be on the lookout; ~ one's P's & Q's, be careful as to one's words or behaviour. 7. Be on one's guard against

or about, as ~ *the ship* (remember there is one). **8.** Have charge of. Hence ~'ER¹ n.² [f. prec.]

mind'ed, a. Disposed (*to do*); having (specified) mind, as *high, small*, ~. [-ED¹]

mind'ful, a. Taking thought of or care (of, or abs.). Hence ~LY² adv., ~NESS n. [MIND¹+-FUL]

mine, n. **1.** Excavation in earth for metal, coal, salt, etc.; (fig.) abundant source (*of information* etc.). **2.** (Mil. etc.) subterranean gallery in which explosive is placed to blow up fortifications, (formerly) subterranean passage under wall of besieged fortress; receptacle filled with explosive placed in or on ground for destroying enemy personnel or material, one of number floating on or near surface of water for destroying or impeding enemy ships; ~s; ~*thrower* [tr. of G *minenwerfer*], trench mortar. [f. F *mine* (prec.)]

mine², v.t. & i. Burrow in (earth); make (hole) underground; make subterranean passages under; (fig.) undermine (Mil. etc.) lay mines under or in; obtain (metal etc.) from mine; dig in (earth etc.) for ore etc. [f. F *miner* (prec.)]

mine³, poss. pron. & a. corresponding in pred. & elliptical uses to MY, as *it is* ~, *I have lost* ~, *me & ~* (my relations), *is a friend of* ~; also used (arch., poet.) as ~ *eyes*. [com.-Teut.: OE *mīn*, Du. *mijn*, G *mein*]

min'er, n. One who works in a mine; soldier whose duty it is to lay mines; SAPPERS *&* ~s. [f. OF *minour* (as MINE²), see -OR²]

min'eral, a. & n. (Substance) obtained by mining; (belonging to) any of the species into which inorganic substances are classified; ~ KINGDOM; ~ *water*, water found in nature impregnated with ~ substance, artificial imitation of this, esp. soda-water, also, other effervescent drink, e.g. ginger-beer; || (esp. in pl.) artificial ~ *water*; ~ *jelly*, vaseline; ~ WOOL. Hence ~IZA'TION n., ~IZE(3) v.t. & i. [f. F *minéral* f. med. L *mineralis* (*minera* mine f. com.-Rom. +*mina*, see -AL)]

miner'alo̅gy n. Science of minerals. Hence ~alo̅'gical a., ~alo̅'gically² adv., ~alo̅'gist n. [f. prec. +-LOGY]

Minēr'va, n. Roman goddess of wisdom; ~ *press*, printing-press in London, ultra-sentimental novels issued from it c. 1800. [L.]

min'ever, -iver, n. Kind of fur used in ceremonial costume. [f. F *menu vair* (*menu* small, as MINUTE²; VAIR kind of fur, as VARIOUS)]

mingle (ming'gl), v.t. & i. Mix, blend; ~ *their* etc. *tears*, weep together; ~ *with*, go about among. [ME *mengel* f. obs. *meng* f. OE *mengan*, cf. Du. & G *mengen*, see -LE(3)]

|| **min'gy** (-ji), a. (colloq.). Mean, stingy. [prob. portmanteau of MEAN³ and STINGY]

min'iate, v.t. Paint with vermilion; illuminate (manuscript). [f. L *miniare* (*miniūm* native cinnabar, red lead), see -ATE³]

min'iature, n. & a. & v.t. **1.** Picture in illuminated manuscript; small-scale minutely finished portrait, usu. on ivory or vellum; this branch of painting, as *portrait in* ~; reduced image; *in* ~, on a small scale, small-scale. **2.** adj. Represented on small scale, small-scale. **3.** v.t. Represent in ~. Hence **min'iatur**IST (-ya-) n. [vb f. n.) f. It. f. med. L *miniatūra* (as prec., see -URE)]

min'ify, v.t. Represent as smaller or less important than it is; lessen in size or importance. [irreg. f. L *minor* less, see -FY]

min'ikin, n. & a. Diminutive (creature); affected, mincing. [f. Du. *minneken* (*minne* love + *kijn* -KIN)]

min'im, n. (Mus.) note half the value of SEMIBREVE; single down-stroke of pen; creature of the smallest size or importance; sixtieth part of fluid drachm. [f. L *minimus* smallest]

min'imal, a. Very minute; the least possible, of minimum. [as prec., see -AL]

min'imalist, n. Person ready to accept a minimum provisionally (opp. MAXIMAL-IST). [prec., -IST]

min'imize, v.t. Reduce to, estimate at, smallest possible amount or degree. Hence ~A'TION n. [as prec., see -IZE]

min'imum, n. (pl. -*ima*). Least amount attainable, usual, etc.; ~ *thermometer* (automatically recording lowest temperature within period); ~ *wage* (than which, by law or agreement, less is not to be offered). [L, neut. as foll.]

|| **min'imus,** a. (In schools) youngest of the name, as *Jones* ~. [L.,=least]

min'ion (-yon), n. Favourite child, servant, animal, etc. (derog.); slave; ~s *of the law*, gaolers, police, etc.; (Print.) size of TYPE. [f. F *mignon*, etym. dub.]

min'ish, v.t. & i. (arch.). Diminish (t. & i.); reduce in power etc. [f. OF *menisier* f. vulg. L +*minūtiare* (as MINUTE²)]

min'ister, n. Person employed in execution (of purpose, will, etc.); person administering department of State; PRIME ~; political agent accredited by one State to another; clergyman esp. in Presbyterian and Nonconformist Churches; (also ~ *general*) superior of some religious orders. [f. OF *menestre* f. L *minister* servant (*minus* less)]

min'ister², v.i. & t. Render aid or service (to person, cause, etc.; ~*ing angel*, w. ref. to *Mark* i. 13, esp. of sick-nurse)

etc.); be helpful, contribute, (to result); (arch.) furnish, supply, (help etc.). [f. OF *ministrer* f. L *ministrare* (prec.)]

minister'ial, a. Concerned with the execution of law; subsidiary, instrumental; of a minister of religion or his office; of a minister of State; siding with the Ministry against Opposition, whence ~ISM(2) n. Hence ~LY² adv. [f. F *ministériel* t. L *ministerialis* (as MINISTER, see -AL)]

ministra'tion, n. Ministering, esp. in religious matters; supplying (of). So **min'istrant** a. & n., **min'istrative** a. [f. L *ministratio* (as MINISTER² see -ATION)]

min'istry, n. Ministering; the body of ministers of State or of religion; State department, as *Air M~, M~ of Agriculture & Fisheries, of Education, of Food, of Fuel & Power, of Health, of Labour, of Transport.* [f. L *ministerium* (as MINISTER²)]

min'ium, n. Red oxide of lead; cinnabar. [L]

min'iver. See MINEVER.

mink, n. Small semi-aquatic stoat-like animal; its fur. [Sw. has *menk*]

minn'esinger, n. German lyrical poet & singer in 12–14th cc. [G (*minne* love)]

Minn'ie, n. (army sl.). Trench mortar. [abbr. of G *minenwerfer* minethrower]

minn'ow (-ō), n. Small freshwater fish (loosely used of several kinds, esp. stickleback); *Triton among the ~s*, one who seems great from insignificance of others. [prob.=OHG *munewa*; OE has *myne*]

Mino'an, a. (archaeol.). Of the Cretan civilization (3000–1500 B.C.) named from king Minos. [f. Gk *Minōs*+-AN]

min'or, a. & n. 1. Lesser [not followed by *than*), as ~ PROPHETS; ~ *canon*, clergyman assisting in daily cathedral service, not member of chapter; comparatively *in*-important, as ~ *poet*; (Log.) ~ *term*, subject of conclusion of categorical syllogism, ~ *premiss* (containing this); (Mus.) ~ *interval*, see MAJOR²; ~ *key* (in which scale has ~ third), (fig.) *conversation in a ~ key* (doleful); ~ *suit* (Bridge), diamonds or clubs; (in schools) *Jones* ~ (the younger). 2. n. Franciscan friar; ~ term or premiss; person under age. [L, =less]

Minorc'a, n. One of the Balearic Isles: ~ (*fowl*), black variety brought from Spain. [f. Sp. *Menorca*]

mino'rity, n. State of being under age, period of this; smaller number or part, esp. smaller party voting together against majority; number of votes cast for this. [f. med. L *minoritas* (as MINOR, see -TY)]

Min'otaur (-tōr), n. *The* ~, fabulous monster, half bull half man, fed with human flesh. [f. Gk *Minōtauros* (*Minōs*, king of Crete, husband of ~'s mother, + *tauros* bull)]

min'ster, n. Church of a monastery; large or important church, cathedral. [OE *mynster* (as MONASTERY)]

min'strel, n. Mediaeval singer or musician, who sang or recited (often his own) poetry; (hist.) person who entertained his patrons with singing, buffoonery, etc.; (pl.) band of public entertainers, with blacked faces etc., performing songs & music ostensibly of negro origin. [f. OF *menestral* (as MINISTERIAL)]

min'strelsy, n. Minstrel's art; minstrels; minstrel poetry. [f. OF *menestralsie*, as prec.]

mint¹, n. Place where money is coined, usu. under State authority; (fig.) source of invention etc.; (transf.) ~ *state*, *condition*, (of books, prints, postage-stamps, etc.) fresh, unsoiled, perfect; vast sum of money; ~*mark*, mark placed on coin to show at what ~ it was struck (also fig.); ~*master*, superintendent of coinage at ~. [OE *mynet* f. L *moneta* MONEY]

mint², v.t. Make (coin) by stamping metal; invent, coin, (word, phrase, etc.). Hence **mint'age(3, 4)** n. [f. prec.]

mint³, n. Aromatic plant, much used in cookery; ~ *sauce* (of finely chopped ~ with vinegar & sugar, eaten with roast lamb), ||also, with pun on *mint¹*, money. [OE *minte*=OHG *minza* f. L *menta* f. Gk *minthē*]

minuet', n. Slow stately dance for two in triple measure; music for this, music in same rhythm & style. [f. F *menuet*, dim. of *menu* (as MINUTE a.)]

min'us, quasi-prep. & a. With the deduction of (symbol –), as *7 ~ 4 is equal to 3*; (colloq.) deprived of, as *he came back* ~ *an arm*; *a* ~ (negative) *quantity*. [L, neut. of MINOR]

minus'cule, a. & n. (Of kind of cursive script developed in 7th c.) small; (n.) small letter. [F, f. L *minusculus* dim. of MINOR]

min'ute¹ (-it), n. 1. Sixtieth part of hour; short time, instant; exact point of time, as *the* ~ (*that*), as soon as. 2. Sixtieth part of degree (in angles). 3. Rough draft, memorandum; (pl.) brief summary of proceedings of assembly, committee, etc.; official memorandum authorizing or recommending a course, as *a Treasury* ~. 4. ~*book* (for writing ~s in); ~*gun* (fired at intervals of a ~); ~*hand* (indicating ~s on watch or clock); *~man* (hist.), American militiaman of revolutionary period (because ready to march at a ~'s notice); ~*mark* (', cf. SECOND-*mark*). [F, f. L *minuta* fem. as MINUTE³]

min'ute² (-it), v.t. Find the exact time of; draft (document, scheme); record in minutes; ~ *down*, make a note of. [f. prec.]

minute'³, a. Very small; trifling, petty; (of inquiry, inquirer, etc.) accurate, precise. Hence ~**ly¹** (-ūt-li) adv., ~**NESS** (-ūt'n-) n. [f. L *minūtus*, p.p. of *minuere* lessen]

min'utely² (-nitli), a. Occurring every

minute. So ~LY² (-nitli) adv., [MINUTE¹ +-LY¹]

minu'tia (-shio), n. (usu. in pl. -æ). Precise or trivial detail. [L (as MINUTE²)]

minx, n. Pert girl, hussy, flirt. [16th c.]

mi'ocene, a. & n. (geol.). (Of) a division of the Tertiary preceding the Pliocene. [irreg. f. Gk meiōn less + kainos new]

mir (mēr), n. Russian village community. [Russ.]

mi'racle, n. Marvellous event due to some supernatural agency; remarkable occurrence; remarkable specimen (of ingenuity, impudence, etc.); to a ~, surprisingly well; (also ~ play) dramatic representation in Middle Ages, based on life of Christ or saints. [OF, f. L miraculum (mirari look at, f. mirus wonderful)]

mira'culous, a. Supernatural; surprising. Hence ~LY² adv., ~NESS n. [f. F miraculeux f. med. L miraculosus (as prec., see -OUS)]

mirage' (-ahzh), n. Optical illusion, esp. illusive appearance of sheet of water in desert, etc. (also fig.). [F, f. (se) mirer look at oneself in mirror, be reflected, f. L mirari wonder at]

mire¹, n. Swampy ground, bog; stick, find oneself, in the ~ (in difficulties); mud, dirt. [ME, f. ON myrr, cogn. with MOSS]

mire², v.t. Plunge in mire; (fig.) involve in difficulties; defile, bespatter. [f. prec.]

mi'rror, n. & v.t. 1. Polished usu. glass surface reflecting image, looking-glass; (fig.) what gives faithful reflection or true description of thing. 2. v.t. Reflect as in ~. [(vb f. n.) f. OF mirour f. pop. L *miratorium (mirare look at, f. L mirari wonder at, see -ORY)]

mfrth, n. Merriment. Hence ~FUL, ~LESS, aa., ~'fully² adv., ~'fulNESS n. [OE, cf. Du. mirth, cogn. w. MERRY]

mir'y, a. Muddy; vile. [f. MIRE¹ +-Y¹]

mir'za (mēr'zah), n. (In Persia) title added to name of prince or prefixed to that of official or man of learning. [Pers.]

mis-¹, pref., added freely to vbs & vbl nn. w. sense 'amiss', 'badly', 'wrongly', 'unfavourably', or intensifying unfavourable meaning contained in vb (misdoubt). [OE, cf. Du. mis-, G miss-¹. O'Teut. misso- (1) divergent (2) mutual]

mis-², pref. to vbs, adjj., & nn., derived f. F, in same sense as prec. [f. OF mes-. f. MINUS, used in comb.-Rom. as pref.]

misadven'ture, n. (Piece of) bad luck; (Law) homicide by ~ (accident). [f. OF (as MIS-² & ADVENTURE)]

misalli'ance, n. Unsuitable alliance, esp. marriage. [MIS-¹, after MÉSALLIANCE]

mis'anthrope, n. Hater of mankind; one who avoids human society. Hence ~, misanthrop'IC(AL) aa., misan'thropist, misan'thropy¹, nn., misan-

For words in mis- not given see MIS-¹.

thropize(2) v.i. [f. Gk misanthrōpos (misos hate + anthrōpos man)

misa'pplica'tion, n. Wrong application, wrong use (esp. of funds). [MIS-¹]

misapply', v.t. Apply wrongly. [MIS-¹]

misapprehend', v.t. Misunderstand (words, person). So ~ên'sion (-shn) n. [MIS-¹]

misappro'priate, v.t. Apply (usu. another's money) to wrong (esp. one's own) use. So ~â'tion n. [MIS-¹]

misbecome' (-kŭm), v.t. Suit ill, be unbecoming to. [MIS-¹]

misbegott'en, a. Illegitimate, bastard, (often as general term of opprobrium). [MIS-¹+begotten p.p. of BEGET]

misbehave', v.t. Behave (oneself, or abs.) improperly. So misbehav'iour (-yer) n. [MIS-¹]

misbelief', n. Wrong religious belief; false opinion. So~iev'er n., ~iev'ing a. [MIS-¹]

misbeseem', v.t. Misbecome. [MIS-¹]

miscal'culate, v.t. & i. Calculate (amount, results, etc., or abs.) wrongly. So ~â'tion n. [MIS-¹]

miscall' (-awl), v.t. Call by a wrong name; ‖(dial.) call (person) names. [MIS-¹]

miscă'rriage (-rij), n. Failure (of letter etc.) to reach destination; ~ (failure of count to attain the ends) of justice; untimely delivery (of woman), abortion; failure (of scheme etc.). [MIS-¹]

miscă'rry, v.i. (Of person or business) fail, be unsuccessful; (of woman) be delivered prematurely (of child); (of letter) fail to reach destination. [MIS-¹]

miscast', v.t. ~, n. Wrong addition (of accounts); unsuitable casting (of actors). [MIS-¹]

miscëgëna'tion, n. Mixture of races, esp. sexual union of whites with negroes. [irreg. f. L misceo mix + genus race + -ATION]

miscella'nea, n. Literary miscellany. [L, neut. pl. as foll.]

miscella'neous, a. Of mixed composition or character; (w. pl. noun) of various kinds; (of persons) many-sided. Hence ~LY² adv., ~NESS n. [f. L miscellaneus (miscellus mixed f. miscere mix, see -ANEOUS)]

mis'cellany (or miselă'ny), n. Mixture, medley; collection of treatises etc. in one volume; such volume. Hence miscell'anIST(3) n. [prob. f. F miscellanées fem. pl. (as MISCELLANEA)]

mischance' (-ahns), n. (Piece of) bad luck, esp. by ~. [f. OF mesch(e)ance (as CHANCE n.)]

mis'chief (-chif), n. Harm, injury, wrought by person or other agent (do one a ~, vulg., wound or kill him); make ~, create discord, so ~-maker, -making; the ~ (annoying part) of it is that etc.;

worker, source, of harm or annoyance: vexatious conduct, esp. of children: pranks, scrapes, (*get into, keep out of,* ~); playful malice, archness, satire, (*eyes full of* ~); *where the* ~ (devil) *have you been?* [f. OF *meschief* (MIS-², *chief* end, CHIEF)]
mis'chievous (-chĭv-), a. (Of things) having harmful effects; (of persons, conduct, etc.) disposed to acts of playful malice or annoyance. Hence ~LY² adv., ~NESS n. [f. AF *meschevous* (prec., -OUS)]
mis'cible (-sĭ-), a. That can be mixed (*with*). Hence ~BIL'ITY n. [f. L *miscēre* (with), mix, -BLE]

misconceive' (-sēv), v.i. & t. Have a wrong conception (*of*, or abs.); misunderstand (word, person). So **misconcep'tion** n. [MIS-¹]
miscon'duct, n. Improper conduct, esp. adultery; bad management. So **miscon-duct'** v.t. & refl. [MIS-¹]
miscon'strue (-ōō; *or* -kŏnstrōō'), v.t. Put wrong construction on (word, action); mistake meaning of (person). So **misconstruc'tion** n. [MIS-¹]
miscount', n., & v.t. & i. (Make) wrong count, esp. of votes; count (things) wrongly. [MIS-¹]
mis'creant, a. & n. 1. (Arch.) heretical; depraved. 2. n. (arch.). Heretic; vile wretch. [f. OF *mescreant* (MIS-² + *creant* f. L *credere* believe, see -ANT)]
miscrēā'ted, a. Ill-formed (often as abusive epithet). So ~ā'tion n. [MIS-¹]
mis-cue', n., & v.i. (billiards). 1. Failure to strike ball properly with cue. 2. v.i. Make a ~. [MIS-¹ or MISS v.)]
misdāte', v.t. Date wrong. [MIS-¹]
misdeal', v.t. & i., & n. 1. Make mistake in dealing (cards, but usu. abs.). 2. n. Such mistake. [MIS-¹]
misdeed', n. Evil deed; crime. [OE *misdǣd* (see MIS-¹ & DEED)]
misdeem', v.t. & i. (arch., poet.). Have wrong opinion of; mistake (person, thing for another); form wrong judgement (*of*). [MIS-¹]
misdemean'ant, n. Person convicted of misdemeanour or guilty of misconduct; *first, second, -class* ~ (to be treated with more, less, indulgence). [f. arch. *misdemean* (MIS-¹+DEMEAN)+-ANT]
misdemean'our (-nor), n. (Law) indictable offence less heinous than felony; offence, misdeed. [MIS-¹]
misdirect', v.t. Direct (person, blow, etc.) wrongly. So **misdirec'tion** n. [MIS-¹]
misdo'ing (-dōō-), n. Misdeed. [MIS-¹]
misdoubt' (-owt), v.t. (arch.). Have doubts as to the truth or existence of; have misgivings, be suspicious, about; suspect (*that*). [MIS-¹]
mise (mēz, mǐz), n. (Hist.) settlement by agreement, as *M~ of Lewes* (between Henry III & barons, 1264); ~ *en scène*

(F, see AP,), scenery & properties of acted play, (fig.) surroundings of an event. [OF fem. p.p. of *mettre* put f. L *mittere* miss- send, used as n.]
mis'er¹ (-z-), n. One who hoards wealth & lives miserably; avaricious person. [L, = wretched]
mis'er² (-z-), n. Boring instrument for well-sinking. [?]
mis'erable (-z-), a. Wretchedly unhappy; (of events etc.) causing wretchedness; contemptible, mean, as *a* ~*le hovel*. Hence ~LY² adv. [f. F *misérable* f. L *miserabilis* (*miserārī* pity f. *miser* wretched, -BLE]
miserē're (-z-), n. Fifty-first psalm (*M~ mei Deus*); cry for mercy; (improp.) =foll. (last sense). [L, = have mercy (*miserērī* as MISER¹)]
mis'ricord (-z-), n. 1. Apartment in monastery in which some indulgences were permitted. 2. Dagger for giving the *coup de grâce*. 3. Shelving projection on under side of hinged seat in choir stall, serving when seat was turned up to support person standing. [f. OF *misericorde* f. L *misericordia* f. *misericors* compassionate (stem of *miserērī* pity+*cors -rdis* heart)]
mis'erly (-z-), a. Like a miser, stingy. Hence ~INESS a. [-LY¹]
mis'ery (-z-), n. Wretched state of mind or of outward circumstances; (Cards, colloq. for F *misère*) declaration by which caller undertakes not to take any tricks. [f. OF *miserie* f. L *miseria* (as MISER¹)]
misfeas'ance (-z-), n. (Law) transgression, esp. wrongful exercise of lawful authority (also gen., esp. joc.). [f. OF *mesfaisance* f. *mesfaire* misdo (MIS-² *faire* do f. L *facere*), -ANCE]
misfire', v.i., & n. (Of gun, motor engine, etc.) fail(ing) to go off or start action. [prob. for MISS²*fire*]
misfit', n. Garment etc. that does not fit the person it is meant for. [MIS-¹]
misfor'tune (-chn, -tyōōn), n. Bad luck (*more his* ~ *than his fault*). [MIS-¹]
misgive', v.t. (Person's) *mind* ~*s him*, fills him with suspicion or foreboding (*about thing, that*). [MIS-¹]
misgiv'ing, n. Feeling of mistrust or apprehension. [f. prec.+-ING¹]
misgo'vern (-gŭ-), v.t. Govern (State etc.) badly. So ~ment n. [MIS-¹]
misguide' (-gīd), v.t. (chiefly in p.p.). Mislead, cause to err in thought or action. Hence ~'ēdly² adv. [MIS-¹]
mishan'dle (-s-h-), v.t. Handle (person, thing) roughly or rudely, ill-treat. [MIS-¹]
mishap' (-s-h-), n. Unlucky accident. [MIS-¹]
mishear' (-s-h-), v.t. Hear amiss or imperfectly. [MIS-¹]
mis'hit, n., & v.t. 1. Faulty or bad hit.

For words in **mis-** not given see **MIS-¹**.

mis- **2.** v.t. (pr. mis-hit'), Hit (a ball) faultily. [MIS-¹]

mish'mash, n. Confused mixture. [re-dupl. f. MASH n.]

mish'n|a(h) (-na), n. Collection of precepts forming basis of Talmud. Hence ~IC a. [post-bibl. Heb.,=repetition, instruction. (shanah repeat)]

misinform', v.t. Give wrong information to. [MIS-¹]

misinterp'ret, v.t. Give wrong interpretation to, mislead. So ~forma'tion n. [MIS-¹]

misjudge', v.t. & i. Judge wrongly (person etc., or abs.); have wrong opinion of. So ~ã'tion n. [MIS-¹]

mislay', v.t. Put (thing) by accident where it cannot readily be found. [MIS-¹]

mislead' (-lēd), v.t. Lead astray, cause to go wrong, in conduct; give wrong impression to. [OE *mislǣdan*, see MIS-¹ & LEAD²]

mislike', v.t. (arch.). Dislike. [OE *mislician*, see MIS-¹ & LIKE v.]

misman'age, v.t. Manage badly or wrongly. So ~ment (-ijm-) n. [MIS-¹]

misname', v.t. Call by wrong name. [MIS-¹]

misnom'er, n. Use of wrong name, wrong use of term. [f. OF *mesnommer* (mes- MIS-²+*nommer* vb name f. L *nominare*)]

miso- in comb.=Gk miso- comb. form of ~**logist**, ~**logy**, (-ŏl-), hate,=; ~**neism**, *mē'ism*, ~**nē'ist**, hatred, hater, of novelty.

miso'g|amy, n. Hatred of marriage. So ~IST n. [f. Gk MISO(gamos marriage), -Y¹]

miso'g|ynist (j-, -g̱-), n. Hater of women. So **misogy'nŏus** a. [f. Gk MISO(*gunēs* f. *gunē* woman)+-IST]

mis'pickel, n. Arsenical pyrites. [G]

misplace', v.t. Put in wrong place or hands; set (affections) on wrong object; place (confidence) amiss; time (words, action) badly. So ~MENT(-smŭ-) n. [MIS-¹]

misprint', n., & v.t. **1.** Mistake in printing. **2.** v.t. Print wrongly. [MIS-¹]

mispri'sion¹ (-zhn), n. (law). Wrong action or omission, esp. ~ *of treason or felony*, (now restricted to) concealment of one's knowledge of treasonable designs etc. [f. OF *mesprision* mistake (see MIS-² & PRISON)]

|| **mispri'sion²** (-zhn), n. (arch.). Contempt; failure to appreciate the value (of). [f. foll., after prec.]

misprize', v.t. Despise; fail to appreciate. [f. OF *mespriser* (see MIS-² & PRIZE¹)]

mispro'nounce', v.t. Pronounce wrongly. So ~**nuncia'tion** n. [MIS-¹]

misquote', v.t. Quote wrongly. So **mis-quota'tion** n. [MIS-¹]

misread', v.t. (-read, pr. -rĕd). Read or interpret wrongly. [MIS-¹]

misrepresent' (-z-), v.t. Represent wrongly, give false account of. So ~a'tion n. [MIS-¹]

misrule' (-ool), n. Bad government; [MIS-¹]

miss¹, n. Failure to hit or attain; *a ~ is as good as a mile*, however narrow the margin; NEAR²; (Billiards) *give a ~*, avoid hitting object ball so as to leave one's own in safe position; *give* (something) *a ~*, (also, transf.) avoid, leave alone (*I shall give the party, the prunes, a ~*). [f. foll.]

miss², v.t. & i. (Of person or missile) fail to hit (mark etc., or abs.); fail to find, get, or meet; let slip (opportunity); fail to catch (train); ~ *the* BUS; fail to hear or understand (remark etc.); (also ~ *out*) leave out (words etc. in reading, writing, etc.); fail to keep (appointment) or perform; notice esp. with regret the absence of, feel the want of; (ellipt., of internal-combustion engines) misfire; ~ *fire*, (of gun) fail to go off, (fig.) fail in one's object; (Naut.) ~ *stays*, fail in attempt to go about from one tack to another. [OE *missan*, cf. Du. & G *missen*]

miss³, n. (As title of unmarried woman or girl) *M~ Smith*, (pl. *the M~ Smiths, the Misses Smith*; *M~ 1948* or current year, *the modern girl*); (usu. derog. or playful) girl, esp. schoolgirl; *as a pert ~*, whence ~ISH¹ a., ~'ISHNESS n.; (voc. in servants' or trade use) young lady. [abbr. of MISTRESS]

miss'al, n. Book containing service of Mass for whole year; (loosely) Rom. Cath. book of prayers, esp. illuminated one. [f. eccl. L *missale* (as MASS¹, see -AL)]

miss'el, n. (Usu. ~*thrush*) kind of thrush that feeds on mistletoe berries. [OE *mistel* basil, mistletoe, cf. Du. & G *mistel*]

mis-shāp'en, a. Ill-shaped, deformed. [MIS-¹+*shapen* p.p. of SHAPE]

miss'ile, & n. (Object, weapon) suitable for throwing or for discharge from machine or engine (or, rarely, gun). [f. L *missilis* (*mittere miss-* send, see -IL)]

miss'ing, a. In vbl senses; also: wanting, not in its place, as *there is a page ~, a page is ~*; *the ~*, soldiers neither present after battle etc. nor known to have been killed or wounded; ~ *link*, thing lacking to complete series, (Zool.) hypothetical intermediate type, esp. between man & anthropoid apes. [MIS²+-ING²]

mi'ssion (-shn), n. **1.** Body of persons sent to foreign country to conduct negotiations etc. **2.** Body sent by religious community to convert heathen; field of missionary activity; missionary post; organization in a district for conversion of the people; course of religious services etc. for this purpose. **3.** Errand of political or other ~. **4.** Person's vocation or divinely appointed work in life. [f. L *missio* (*mittere miss-* send, -ION)]

mi'ssionary (-sho-), a. & n. 1. Of, concerned with, religious missions; ~-*box* (for contributions to ~ work). 2. n. Person who goes on ~ work; ‖ person attached to police-court for help or help offenders or applicants. [-ARY¹]

mi'ssioner (-sho-), n. Missionary; person in charge of parochial mission. [-ER¹]

miss'is, -us, n. (As used by servants) the mistress; (vulg., joc.) the ~, one's own or another's wife. [corrupt. of MISTRESS]

miss'ive, a. & n. 1. *Letter*(s)~, letter from sovereign to dean & chapter nominating person to be elected bishop. 2. n. Letter, esp. official one. [F. f. med. L *missivus* (as MISSION, -IVE)]

mis-spell', v.t. (-*spelt*). Spell wrongly. [MIS-¹]

mis-spend', v.t. (-*spend*). Spend amiss or wastefully (esp. in p.p.). [MIS-¹]

mis-state', v.t. State wrongly. Hence ~MENT (-tm-) n. [MIS-¹]

miss'y̆, n. (Affectionate, playful, or derog.) = MISS³ (not followed by name). [-Y³]

mist, n., & v.i. & t. 1. Water vapour descending in fine drops smaller than raindrops; *Scotch* ~, ‖ like the rain frequent on Scottish hills; filmy appearance before eyes caused by disorders of body or by tears. 2. vb. Cover, be covered, as with ~. Hence ~FUL a., ~LIKE a. & adv. [vb 1. f. OE *mistian*) OE & Du., cogn. w. Gk *omikhlē*]

mistake'¹, n. Misunderstanding of a thing's meaning; error, fault, in thought or action; (emphasizing preceding statement) *and, or make, no ~, undoubtedly. [f. foll.]

mistake'², v.t. & i. Misunderstand meaning or intention of (person, statement, purpose); err in opinion; (p.p.) wrong in opinion, (of action etc.) ill-judged, *as you are ~en, ~en kindness, whence ~'enLY² adv., ~'enNESS (-n-n-) n.; ~*e A for* (think he is) *B*; *there is no ~ing*, no one can help recognizing (person, fact). Hence ~'ABLE a. [f. ON *mistaka* (MIS-¹+taka TAKE)]

mis'ter, n., & v.t. 1. Title prefixed to man's name or to designation of office etc. (written Mr), as *Mr Jones, Mr Secretary, Mr Speaker; Mr Right*, destined husband; (alone as voc., vulg.)=*sir*; the word ~ (*think ~ A for* (alone as voc., vulg.)=*sir*; the word ~ (*please don't call me ~*; untitled person, as *be he prince or mere ~*. as title, as *please don't call me ~*; 2. v.t. Address as Mr, as *don't ~ me*. [vb f. n.) weakened form of MASTER]

mis'tigris, n. (cards). (Blank card in) a variety of poker. [f. F *mistigri* knave of spades]

mistime', v.t. Say, do, (thing) out of season (esp. in p.p.). [MIS-¹]

mis'tletoe (-zltŏ, -sltŏ), n. Parasitic plant growing on apple & other trees, & bearing glutinous fruit used in making birdlime;

kiss under the ~ (w. ref. to the custom permitting a girl standing below ~ used as Christmas decoration to be kissed by the finder). [OE *mistiltan* (as MISSEL+*tān* twig)]

mis'tral (or -trahl'), n. Cold NW. wind in Mediterranean provinces of France etc. [F. & Pr., f. L as MAGISTRAL]

mistransla'te (-z), v.t. Translate incorrectly. So ~la'tion n. [MIS-¹]

mis'tress, n. 1. Woman in authority over servants; female head of household. 2. Woman who has power to control or dispose of, *as you are ~ of the situation, you are your own ~*, (fig. of countries) ~ *of the world etc. 3. Woman who has thorough knowledge (*of* subject). 4. Woman loved & courted by a man; woman illicitly occupying place of wife. 5. Female teacher in school or of special subject, as *music-~*. 6. ‖ *M~ of The Robes*, lady charged with care of Queen's wardrobe. 7. (As title) see MRS. Hence ~SHIP n. [f. OF *maistresse (maistre MASTER², see -ESS¹)]

mis'tri̇̆al, n. Trial vitiated by error. [MIS-¹]

mistrust', v.t., & n. 1. Feel no confidence in (person, oneself, one's powers etc.). 2. n. Lack of confidence, whence ~FUL a., ~FULLY² adv., ~FULNESS n. [MIS-¹]

mis'ty̆, a. Of, covered with, mist; indistinct in form; (fig.) obscure, vague, *as a ~y idea*. Hence ~ILY² adv., ~INESS n. [OE *mistig* (as MIST, see -Y²)]

misunderstand', v.t. (-*stood*). Take (words etc., or abs.) in wrong sense; misinterpret words or actions of (person, esp. in p.p.). So ~ing n. [MIS-¹]

misuse' (-z), v.t. Use wrongly, apply to wrong purpose; ill-treat. So misuse'(-s) n. [MIS-¹]

mite¹, n. (Orig.) Flemish copper coin of small value; (pop.) half-farthing (as in *Mark* xii. 42); modest contribution; the best one can do, as *let me offer my ~ of comfort*; (colloq.) *not a ~*, not at all; small object, esp. child; *a ~ of a* (a tiny) *child* etc.; [OE *mīte*, perh. different wd f. kinds of arachnid, esp. *cheese~* (found in cheese), whence mit'y² a. [f. MDu. *mīte*, cf. G *meite* small thing]

Mith'ras, -ra, n. Persian god identified with sun. Hence ~ra'ic a., ~raIsm, ~raIST(2), nn. [L f. Gk (-as) f. OPers. (-a)]

mith'ridat'ize, v.t. Render proof against poison by gradually increasing doses of it. So mith'ridat'ic a., ~ISM n. [f. *Mithridates* VI, king of Pontus, +-IZE]

mit'igate, v.t. Appease (anger etc.); alleviate (pain, grief); reduce severity of (punishment), moderate (heat, cold, severity, etc.). So ~A'TION n., ~ātORY a. [f. L *mitigare* (*mītis* mild), see -ATE³]

mitō'sis, n. (biol.; pl. -*oses* pr. -ōs'ēz). Process of division of a cell into minute

For words in *mis-* not given see MIS-¹.

threads. Hence **mitōr'o** a. [f. Gk *mitos* thread +-OSIS]

mitrailleuse (-trahyöz, & see Ap.), n. Many-barrelled breech-loading machine-gun discharging small missiles simultaneously or in rapid succession. [F, fem. agent.-n. f. *mitrailler* (*mitraille* small missiles, OF small money, f. *mite* MITE)]

mi'tral, a. & n. Of, like, a mitre; ~ (valve &c.), a valve of the heart. [f. as foll., see -AL)]

mi'tre¹(-ter), n. Bishop's tall cap, deeply cleft at top, esp. as symbol of episcopal office, whence **mi'tred²**(-terd) a.; [perh. different wd] joint of two pieces of wood etc. at angle of 90°, such that line of junction bisects this angle; angle of 45°; ~-block, -board, -box, guide for saw in cutting ~-joints; ~-wheels, pair of bevelled cog-wheels with teeth set at 45° & axes at right angles. [F, f. L f. Gk *mitra* girdle, turban]

mi'tre²(-ter), v.t. Bestow mitre on; join with mitre; shape off (end of wood etc.) to a mitre; *mitring-machine* (for doing this). [f. prec.]

mitt, mitt, n. (*Mitten*) kind of glove with thumb but no fingers, for warmth or protection in hedgers' work etc.; (sl.) boxing-gloves; (now usu. *mitt*) woman's lace or knitted glove covering forearm & part of hand, but not fingers; *give, get, the mitten*, dismiss (lover), be dismissed. Hence **mitt'ened²**(-nd) a. [f. F *mitaine*, etym. dub.]

mitt'imus, n. Warrant committing person to prison; (colloq.) dismissal from office, as *get one's* ~. [L, = we send]

mix, v.t. & i. Put together (two or more substances or groups, one *with* another) so that the particles or members of each are diffused among those of the others (also of immaterial things); prepare (compound) by ~ing ingredients; (intr.) join, be ~ed, as *oil will not* ~ *with water, they* (persons) *do not* ~ *well* (get on to-gether); have intercourse *with*; ~ *up*, thoroughly, also, confuse esp. in thought; *be* ~*ed up*, be involved (*in, with*, shady dealings etc.). Hence ~ER¹ n. one who, that which, ~es (esp. apparatus control-ling the combination of various sounds in preparation of talking films & in dramatic broadcasting); (orig. U.S. colloq.) *good, bad,* ~*er*, one who gets on well, badly, with other people (esp. those of a different social class). [back formation f. foll. taken as E p.p.]

mixed (-kst), a. In vbl senses, esp.: of diverse qualities or elements: (of com-pany) not select, containing persons of doubtful status; (colloq.) mentally con-fused, muddled; for persons of both sexes as ~ *school, bathing*; ~ MATHEMATICS. Hence **mix'edNESS** n. [earlier *mixt* f. F *mixte* f. L *mixtus* p.p. of *miscēre* mix]

‖**mix'en**, n. (dial.). Dung-hill. [OE *mixen*]

mix'ture, n. Mixing; what is mixed, mechanical mixing of two substances, involving no change in their character, opp. to chemical combination; gas or vaporized oil mixed with air, forming explosive change in internal-combustion engine. [f. L *mixtura* (as MIXED, see -URE)]

Miz'pah, n. ~ *ring*, one inscribed ~ w. ref. to *Gen.* XXXI. 49 & given as love-token.

miz'z(l)en, n. (naut.). (Also ~-*sail*) lowest fore-&-aft sail (rarely set, SPANKER being usual) of full-rigged ship's ~-*mast* (after-most mast of three-masted ship); ~ *yard* (on which ~ is extended). [f. F *misaine* perh. f. It. *mezzana* ~-sail, fem. adj. see MEZZANINE]

‖**miz'zle¹**, v.i. (sl.). Decamp. [?]

Hence **miz'zly¹** a. [cogn. w. Du. dial. *miezelen* & LG *misig* drizzly]

miz'zle²(-l) v.i. (sl.). Go, decamp. [?]

mnemon'ic(n-), a. & n. Of, designed to aid, the memory. 2. n. pl. Art of, system for, improving memory. Hence **mnēm'o-nist** (n-) n. [f. Gk *mnēmonikos* (*mnēmōn* mindful f. *mnē-* remember, see -IC)]

mnemotech'n|y (n-, -tēk-), n. = prec. [memory +*technē* art]

mō, mōa, abbr. (vulg. & joc.) for *moment* (esp. *wait, in, half a mo*).

moa¹, n. n.=DINORNIS. [Maori]

moan¹, n. Long low murmur of physical or mental suffering; (arch.) *make* (one's) ~, complain. Hence ~FUL a. [cogn. w. OE *mǣnan*, obs. *mean*, vb, replaced by foll.]

moan², v.i. & t. Make moan(s); utter (specified words) with moans; lament for, (misfortune etc.); lament for (dead per-son etc.). [f. prec.]

moat, n., & v.t. Deep wide ditch sur-rounding town, castle, etc. usu. filled with water; (v.t.) surround (as) with ~. [vb f. n.] ME & OF *mote* mound prob. of Teut. orig.]

mob¹, n. The lower orders; rabble, tu-multuous crowd; promiscuous assem-blage of persons; ~ *law* (imposed, en-forced, by ~); *swell* ~, class of stylishly dressed pickpockets. Hence ~b'ISH a., ~öc'RACY n. [earlier *mobile vulgus*, L, = excitable crowd (MOBILE)]

mob², v.t. & i. (-bb-). (Of mob) attack, molest; assemble in a mob. [f. prec.]

mob-cap, n. Woman's indoor cap cover-ing whole head, worn in 18th & early 19th cc. [f. obs. *mob* in same sense, cf. Du. *mop* woman's coif, *mopmuts* woman's nightcap]

mob'ile, a. Movable, not fixed, free to move; (of person or mind) easily, too easily, changing; (of troops) that may be easily moved from place to place. So

mobil'ity n. [F, f. L *mobilis* (*movère* move, see -BLE)]

mōb'iliz|e, v.t. Render movable, bring into circulation; prepare (forces) for active service (also quasi-pass. of forces). So ~**ABLE** a., ~**A'TION** n. [f. F *mobiliser*, as prec.]

mŏcc'asin, n. Foot-gear of deerskin etc. worn by N.-Amer. Indians, trappers, etc. [f. native *mockasin*]

mō'cha¹(-k-), n. Kind of chalcedony. [f]

mō'cha²(-k-), n. [Also *M~ coffee*) fine quality of coffee, orig. from *M~*, Arabian port at entrance of Red Sea.

mŏck¹, n. (arch.). Derision; thing deserving scorn; imitation, counterfeit. [f. MOCK³]

mŏck², a. (not pred.). Sham; ~ *sun, moon,* = PARHELION, PARASELENE; ~ *duck, goose,* pork with duck stuffing; ~-*turtle soup* (usu. of calf's head; to imitate turtle); ~-*heroic* a. & n., burlesquely imitating, burlesque imitation of, heroic style. [prec. & foll.]

mŏck³, v.t. & i. Hold up to ridicule; defy contemptuously; impose upon; ridicule by imitation; mimic, counterfeit; scoff at; ~*ing-bird,* American song-bird that mimics notes of other birds, other birds that do this; ~*up* n., special model showing appearance of (part of) proposed machine. Hence ~'**ingly²** adv. [f. OF *mocquer*, etym. dub.]

mŏck'ery, n. Derision; subject, occasion, of this; counterfeit representation (*of*); ludicrously or insultingly futile action etc. [f. F *moquerie* (as prec., see -ERY)]

mŏd'al, a. Of mode or form as opp. to substance; ~ *legacy* (with directions as to mode in which it is to be applied); (of Gram.) of the mood of a verb, (of particle) denoting manner; (Logic) ~ *proposition,* one in which predicate is affirmed of subject under some qualification, (also) one that involves affirmation of possibility, impossibility, necessity, or contingency. Hence or cogn. **modāl'ITY** n. (esp. in pl. = method laid down for discharge of obligation etc.), ~**LY²** adv. [f. med. L *modalis* (as foll., see -AL)]

mōde, n. **1.** Way, manner, in which thing is done; prevailing fashion or custom; (arch.) *the ~,* the fashion in dress etc. **2.** (Mus.) ancient Greek scale system, as DORIAN, LYDIAN, PHRYGIAN, ~; used similarly in mediaeval music; in either music, each of the two chief scale systems (MAJOR², MINOR², ~). **3.** (Logic) character of modal proposition. [(partly F) f. L *modus* measure, manner]

mŏd'el, n. Representation in three dimensions of proposed structure etc.; (imitating movements of) *working ~* machine that it represents); figure in clay, wax, etc., to be reproduced in other material; design, style of structure; person, thing, proposed for imitation; person who poses for artists; woman in draper's shop wearing clothes etc. to show their effect to customers; *The New M~,* plan for reorganization of Parliamentary army 1644-5; (attrib.) exemplary, ideally perfect. [f. OF *modelle* f. It. *modello* dim. of *modo* (as MODE)]

mŏd'el, v.t. (-ll-), Fashion, shape, (figure) in clay, wax, etc.; give shape to (document, argument, etc.) form (thing) *after, on, upon,* a model. [f. prec.]

mŏd'ena, n. Deep purple. [*M~,* Italian city]

mŏd'erat|e¹, a. & n. **1.** Avoiding extremes, temperate in conduct or expression; fairly large or good; ~*e prices,* low (in advertisements etc., as *prices strictly ~e*). **2.** n. One who holds ~*e* opinions in politics etc., whence ~**ISM** n. Hence ~**ELY²** adv., ~**ENESS** n. [f. L *moderari* f. st. *modes-* (cf. MODEST) cogn. w. *modus* MODE, -ATE²]

mŏd'erat|e² v.t. & i. Render less violent, intense, vigorous, etc.; (of fury, storm, etc.) become less vehement; act as moderator. [as prec., see -ATE³]

mŏderā'tion, n. Moderating; moderateness; *in ~,* in a moderate manner or degree; || (Oxf. Univ., pl.) first public examination for degree of B.A. (abbr. *mods*). [f. F *modération* f. L *moderationem* (as MODERATE¹, see -ATION)]

mŏd'erātor, n. Arbitrator; mediator; presiding officer; || one of two officers presiding over mathematical tripos at Cambridge; || examiner for moderations; Presbyterian minister presiding over any ecclesiastical body; ~ *lamp* (with contrivance for regulating flow of oil). Hence ~**SHIP** n. [f. F *modérateur* f. L *moderator* (as prec., see -OR²)]

mŏd'ern, a. & n. **1.** Of the present & recent times; || ~ *school, side,* in schools, division in which subjects other than ancient languages are taught; newfashioned, not antiquated. **2.** n. Person living in ~ times. Hence or cogn. **modern'ITY, ~NESS,** nn., ~**IZA'TION,** nn., ~**IZE**(3) v.t. & i., ~**LY²** adv. [f. LL *modernus* (*modo* just now)]

mŏd'ern|ism, n. Modern view(s) or method(s), esp. tendency in matters of religious belief to subordinate tradition to harmony with modern thought; so ~**IST**(2) n.; modern term or expression. [-ISM]

mŏd'est, a. Having a humble estimate of one's own merits; retiring, bashful; (of women) decorous in manner & conduct, scrupulously chaste; (of demands, statements, etc.) not excessive; (of things) unpretentious in appearance, amount, etc. Hence or cogn. ~**LY²** adv., ~**y¹** n. (~*y* or ~*y vest,* lace slip worn above point of corsage). [f. F *modeste* f. L *modestus* (see MODERATE¹)]

mŏd'icum, n. Small quantity (*of food*

etc.), [L., neut. of *modicus* moderate (*modus* measure)]

mŏd'ĭfӯ, v.t. Make less severe or decided, tone down; quality sense of (word etc.) (Gram.) qualify sense of (word etc.); change (vowel) by umlaut. Hence or cogn. ~fīabĭl'ĭtӯ, ~fīca'tion, nn., ~fī'ABLE, ~fĭc'atory, aa. [f. F *modifier* f. L *modificare* (as MODE, see -FY)]

mŏdĭl'ion (-yon), n. (archit.). Projecting bracket under corona of cornice in Corinthian & other orders. [f. It. *modiglione*, etym. dub.]

mŏd'ish, a. Fashionable. Hence ~LY² adv., ~NESS n. [f. MODE +-ISH¹]

mŏdiste' (-ēst), n. Milliner, dressmaker. [F (as MODE, see -IST)]

mŏd'ūlāte, v.t. & i. Regulate, adjust; vary (thing) conformably to; adjust or vary tone or pitch of (speaking voice); (Mus.) pass (*from one key to another*); So ~A'TION n., ~ātor² n., chart, used in tonic solfa system for exercise in sight-singing. [f. L *modulari*, measure, adjust, (as foll.), see -ATE³]

mŏd'ūle, n. Standard, unit, for measuring; (archit.) unit of length for expressing proportions, usu. semidiameter of column at base. [F, as foll.]

mŏd'ūlus, n. (pl. -lī). Constant multiplier esp. for converting Napierian into common logarithms; constant indicating relation between amount of physical effect & that of force producing it. [L,=measure, dim. of foll.]

mō'dus, n. ~ *ŏperăn'dī*, way a person goes to work, way a thing operates; ~ *vīvĕn'dī*, mode of living, i.e. arrangement between disputants pending settlement of debate; money payment in lieu of tithe (orig. ~ *děcĭmăn'dī*). [L,=MODE]

moÿĕtte', n. [Fissure in earth from which issues] exhalation of nephitic gas. [F]

moÿiss'ŭt, n. (Anglo-Ind.). Rural localities as opp. to chief station. [f. Hind. *mauſaçÿĭl* f. Arab. *mufaçÿĭl* p.p. of *façÿala* divide]

Mogul', n. & a. Mongolian; *the* (*Great* or *Grand*) ~, emperor of Delhi. [f. Pers. *mugul* f. MONGOL]

mō'hair, n. (Fine camlet, yarn, from) hair of Angora goat. [ult. f. Arab. *mukhayyar* (*khayyara* choose)]

Mŏhămm'ĕdan, n. & a. (Follower) of Mohammed, founder of the Moslem religion. Hence ~ISM(3) n., ~IZE(3) v.t. [*Mohammed* f. Arab. *Muhammad* +-AN]

Moha'rram (-hŭr-), **Mu-**, n. First month of Mohammedan year; great Shiite fast during first ten days of this month. [Arab. (Mu-),=sacred]

Mŏ'hawk, n. One of a tribe of N.-Amer. Indians; their language; (Skating) step from either edge in one direction to same edge on other foot in opposite direction (cf. CHOCTAW). [native]

Mŏ'hŏck, n. (hist.). One of a class of aristocratic ruffians infesting London streets at night in 18th c. [f. prec.]

mŏ'hŭr (-hōō), n. (Also *gold* ~) gold coin of British India, worth 15 rupees. [f. Pers. *muhr* seal]

‖ **moid'ŏre**, v.t. (dial.). To perplex, confuse, worry (esp. in p.p.). [?]

moid'ŏre, n. Former Portuguese gold coin worth, sum of, 27s. [f. Port. *moeda d'ouro* (*moeda* MONEY + *ouro* f. L *aurum* gold)]

moi'ety, n. Half, esp. in legal use; (loosely) one of two parts into which thing is divided. [f. OF *moit(i)é* f. L *medietatem* middle point (as MEDIUM, see -TY)]

moil, v.i. Drudge, esp. *toil & ~*. [f. OF *moillier* moisten, paddle in mud, f. L *mollis* soft]

moire (mwăhr), n. (Also ~ *antique*, see Ap.) watered fabric, usu. silk, orig. mohair. [F; perh. f. MOHAIR]

moiré (mwah'rā), a. & n. (Of silk) watered; (of metals) having clouded appearance like watered silk; (n.) this appearance. [F, p.p. of *moirer* give moiré appearance to]

moist, a. Slightly wet, damp; (of season etc.) rainy; (of disease) marked by discharge of matter etc. Hence ~'NESS n. [f. OF *moiste*, etym. dub.]

moi'sten (-sn), v.t. & i. Make moist; become moist. [-EN⁵]

mois'ture, n. Water or other liquid diffused in small quantity as vapour, condensed on surface, etc. Hence ~NESS a. [f. OF *moisture* (as MOIST, see -OR⁸)]

mōke, n. (sl.). Donkey. [?]

mŏk'ō, n. Maori system of tattooing. [Maori]

mōl'ar¹, a. (Usu. of mammal's back teeth) serving to grind. 2. n. ~ tooth. [f. L *molaris* (*mola* millstone, see -AR¹)]

mōl'ar², a. Of mass; acting on or by means of large masses. [f. L *moles* mass, see -AR¹]

molass'ēs (-z), n. pl. (treated as sing.). Uncrystallized syrup drained from raw sugar; syrup got from sugar in process of refining, treacle. [f. Port. *melaço* f. LL *melacceum* must (*mel mellis* honey, see -ACEOUS)]

mōle¹, n. [OE *māl*, cf. OHG *meil*]

mōle², n. Spot, blemish, on human skin. [OE *māl*, cf. OHG *meil*]

mōle², n. Small burrowing animal with (usu. blackish) velvety fur & very small eyes; other mammals of same family; *blind as a* ~ (quite); ~'hĭll, small mound thrown up by ~ in burrowing (*make mountains out of ~hills*, exaggerate obstacles etc.; ~'skin, skin of ~ as fur, kind of cotton fustian with surface shaved before dyeing, (pl.) clothes, esp. trousers, of this. [ME *mŏlle*, *molle*, cf. M.Du. *mol*]

mōle⁴, n. Massive structure, usu. of stone, as pier, breakwater, or junction between places separated by water; artificial harbour. [f. F *môle* f. L *moles* mass]

molec'ular, a. Of, relating to, consisting of, molecules; ~ *weight* or *weight of substance* (of one of its molecules relatively to the weight of one atom of hydrogen). Hence ~ITY (-ǎ'r-) n., ~LY² adv. [-AR¹]

mol'ecule, n. (Physics, Chem.) one of the minute groups of atoms (in some elements. esp. the inert gases, one of the single atoms) of which material substances consist, the smallest portion to which a substance can be reduced by subdivision without losing its chemical identity; (loosely) small particle. [f. F *molécule* dim. of L *moles* mass]

molest', v.t. (Usu. after neg.) meddle hostilely or injuriously with (person). So **moleSTA'TION** n. [f. OF *molester* f. L *molestare* (*molestus* troublesome, perh. cogn. w. *moles* mass)]

Mol'inism, n. Doctrine of Luis Molina (d. 1600), that efficacy of grace depends on the will that freely accepts it; doctrine of Miguel de Molinos (d. 1696), quietism. Hence ~IST n. [f. *Molina, Molinos,* +-ISM]

moll'ify, v.t. Appease, soften. So ~FICA'TION n. [f. F *mollifier* f. L *mollificare* (*mollis* soft, see -FY)]

moll'usc, n. Animal belonging to the *Mollusca*, sub-kingdom of soft-bodied & usu. hard-shelled animals, including limpets, snails, cuttle-fish, oyster, mussel, etc. Hence **mollus'can**, **mollus'cous**, aa., **mollus'coid** a. & n. [f. L *molluscus* (*mollis* soft)]

moll'y, n. Effeminate man or boy; milksop; ~*-coddle*, (n.) milksop, (v.t.) coddle, cocker up. [pet form of *Mary*]

Mol'och (-k), n. Canaanite idol to whom children were sacrificed (often fig.); thorn-lizard, a hideous Australian reptile. [f. Gk *molokh* f. Heb. *molek*]

molos'sus, n. Metrical foot - - -. [Gk *molossos*]

Mol'otov. Name of Soviet commissar used attrib.; ~ *cocktail* (sl.), anti-tank inflammatory hand-grenade used in 1939-45 war.

mol'ten. See MELT.

mol'to, adv. Very (preceding mus. direction, as ~ *espressivo*). [It., f. L *multus* much]

mol'y, n. Fabulous herb with white flower & black root, endowed with magic properties; wild garlic & other plants. [L, f. Gk *mōlu*]

molyb'denum, n. Silvery-white brittle metallic element with which steel is alloyed for making high-speed tools. [f. Gk *molubdaina* f. *molubdos* lead or plumbago]

mo'ment, n. 1. Minute point of time, instant: *one* ~, *half a* ~, (ellipt.) *wait a* ~; *come here this* ~ (at once); *came the very* ~ (as soon as) *I heard of it; timed to the* ~ (with absolute accuracy); *the* ~ (time that affords an opportunity); *am, was, busy at the* ~ (just now, then), so *men of*

(important *at*) *the* ~. 2. (Mech.) ~ *of a force about a point*, measure of its power in causing rotation. 3. Importance, as of *great, little, no,* ~, whence **momen'tous** a., **momen'tously¹** adv., **momen'tous-NESS** n. [f. MOMENTUM]

mo'mentarily, a. Lasting only a moment; short-lived, transitory. Hence ~ILY¹ adv., ~INESS n. [f. L *momentarius* (as prec., see -ARY¹)]

mo'mently, adv. From moment to moment; every moment; for a moment. [-LY²]

momen'tum, n.(pl. *-ta*). (Mech.) quantity of motion of moving body, product of its mass by its velocity; (pop.) impetus gained by movement (lit. & fig.). [L (as MOVE, see -MENT)]

Mo'mus, n. Greek god of ridicule; faultfinder. [L, f. Gk *Mōmos*]

mon'achal (-k-), a. Monastic. So **mon'achism** (-k-) n. [f. eccl. L *monachalis* (MONK, -AL)]

mon'ad, n. The number one, unit; ultimate unit of being (e.g. a soul, an atom, a person, God), esp. in philosophy of Leibnitz, whence ~ISM(3) n.; (Biol.) simple organism assumed as first term in genealogy of living beings; (Chem.) element, radical, with combining power of one atom of hydrogen. Hence **monad'ıc** a. [f. L f. Gk *monas -ados* unit (*monos* alone)]

monadelph'ous, a. (bot.). (Of stamens) having filaments united into one bundle; (of plants) with ~ *stamens*. [f. Gk *monos* one +*adelphos*, brother+-OUS]

monan'drous, a. (bot.). Having a single stamen. [f. Gk *monandros* (*monos* one+ *anēr andros* male)+-OUS]

monan'dry, n. Custom of having only one husband at a time. [as prec.+-Y¹]

mon'arch (-k), n. 1. Sovereign with title of king, queen, emperor, empress, or equivalent; supreme ruler (often fig.). 2. Large red & black butterfly. Hence **monarch'AL, monarch'ıc(AL)**, aa., **mo-narch'ALLY, monarch'ICALLY**, advv., (-k-). [f. L (*-cha*) f. Gk *monarkhēs* (*monos* alone+*arkhō* rule)]

monarch'ism (-k-), n. Principles of, attachment to, monarchy. So ~IST (-k-) n. [-ISM]

mon'archy (-k-), n. (State under) monarchical government; *constitutional, limited,* ~ (subject to constitutional restrictions). [f. F *monarchie* f. L f. Gk *monarkhia* (MONARCH, -Y¹)]

mon'astery (-k-), n. Residence of community (usu. of monks) living secluded under religious vows. [f. eccl. L f. late Gk *monastērion* (*monazō* live alone f. *monos*)]

monas'tic, a. Of monks or monasteries; ~ (Bookbind.) finished by tooling without gold (also *antique*). Hence ~TICALLY adv., ~ICISM(3) n., ~ICISM(3) v.t. [f. med. L f. late Gk *monastikos* (as prec., see -IC)]

mondaine (mawndǎn'), n. Woman of the fashionable world; worldly woman. [F]

Mon'day (mǔn'dǐ), n. Second day of week; Black ~ (school sl.), first day of term; ||St~, ~'s day of little work (w. ref. to Saint's-day holidays). [OE *Mōnan dæg* (*mōna* moon +*dæg* DAY)]

Mon'dayish (mǔn'dǐ-), a. (Of clergy) indisposed as result of Sunday work; (of others) slack as result of Sunday holiday. [-ISH1]

monde (mawnd), n. The fashionable world, society; the set in which one moves. [F]

mon'dial, a. World-wide. [F, f. LL *mundiālis* f. L *mundus* world.]

mo'netary (mǔ-, mǒ-), a. Of the coinage; of money. [f. L *monetārius* (as MONEY, see -ARY1)]

mo'netize (mǔ-, mǒ-), v.t. Put (metal) into circulation as money. Hence ~A'TION n. [f. L *monēta* MONEY +-IZE]

mo'ney (mǔ-), n. (pl. ~s). 1. Current coin; coin & promissory documents representing it (*paper* ~), esp. government & bank notes; (w. pl.) particular kind; (pl. arch., legal) sums of ~; ~ *of* ACCOUNT2; CONSCIENCE ~; property viewed as convertible into ~; coin in reference to its purchasing power, as (prov.) ~ *makes the mare to go*, *time is*~, *for* LOVE1 *or* ~; *make* ~, acquire wealth, *coin*~, do this rapidly; ||~ *for jam* (sl.), a profitable return for little or no trouble; *have one's* ~'s~, not worth its price to every one. 2. ~-*bag*, *beg for*~, (pl.) wealth; ~-*bags*, wealthy or avaricious person; ~-*box*, closed box into which savings or contributions are dropped through slit; ~-*changer*, one whose business it is to change~ at fixed rate; ~-*grubber*, person sordidly intent on amassing ~, ~-*grubbing*; ~-*lender*, one whose business it is to lend ~ at interest; ~-*market*, sphere of operation of dealers in stocks etc.; ~ORDER2(3); ~-*spinner*, small spider thought to bring good luck; ~-*wort*, plant with round glossy leaves; ~'s-*worth*, anything recognized as equivalent to ~. Hence ~LESS (mǔn'lǐ) a. [f. OF *moneie* f. L *monēta* mint, money, orig. goddess in whose temple at Rome ~ was coined]

moneyed (mǔn'ǐd), a. Rich; consisting of money, as ~ *resources, assistance*; *interest*, the class concerned in money as a possession. [-ED2]

mo'nger (mǔng-), n. Dealer, trader, (chiefly in comb., as *cheese*~, *fish*~, *iron*~, *costers*~, & fig. *scandal*~ etc.; mango dealer). [OE *mangere* (*mangian* to traffic f. L *mango* dealer)]

Mōngo'l (-ngg-), n. & a. (Member) of Asiatic race now inhabiting Mongolia, between China & Siberia. Hence ~OID a., of Mongolian type (also, n. = MONGO-LIAN). [native, perh. f. *mong* brave]

Mōngō'lian (-ngg-), a. & n. = prec.; (Anthrop.) of the yellow-skinned straight-haired type of mankind; of a class of idiots like ~s. [-IAN]

mŏng'oose, mŭng'oose, (-ngg-), n. An ichneumon, common in India, & able to kill venomous snakes unharmed; kind of lemur. [f. native *maṅgūs*]

mŏn'grel (mŭngg-), n. & a. 1. Dog of no definable breed; animal, plant, resulting from crossing of different breeds or kinds; person not of pure race. 2. adj. Of mixed origin, nature, or character. Hence ~ISM(2) n., ~IZE(3) v.t., ~LY1 a. [prob. f. root *mang-, mong-*, mix, +-REL]

mōnĭl'ĭform, a. Suggesting necklace or string of beads. [f. L *monīle* necklace, -FORM]

mŏn'ĭsm, n. Doctrine that only one being exists; any of the theories that deny the duality of matter & mind. Hence ~IST n., monĭs'tĭc a. [f. Gk *monos* one, -ISM]

mŏnĭ'tion, n. Warning (of danger); formal notice from bishop or ecclesiastical court admonishing person to refrain from some offence; (in courts that use civil law process) summons. [f. L *monĭtĭo* (*monēre monĭt-* warn, -TON)]

mŏn'itor, n., & v.t. & i. 1. (Arch.) one who admonishes. 2. Senior pupil in school with duties of keeping order etc., whence ~IAL a., ~SHIP n. 3. Lizard supposed to give warning of approach of crocodiles. 4. Shallow-draught warship. 5. One who listens to & reports on foreign broadcasts, misuse of official telephones, etc. 6. vb. Act as ~ (sense 5), act as ~ of. Hence mŏn'itress1 n. [L (as prec., -OR2)]

mŏn'itory, a. & n. 1. Warning, admonitory. 2. n. Bishop's or pope's letter of admonition. [f. L *monitorius* (as prec., see -ORY)]

mŏnk (mŭnk), n. Member of community of men living apart under vows of poverty, chastity, & obedience; ~'s-*hood*, kinds of plant. Hence ~HOOD, ~SHIP, nn. [OE *munuc* f. pop. L *monicus* = L f. Gk *mona-khos* solitary (*monos* alone)]

mŏnk'ery (mŭnk-), n. Monastic life; monastery; monks; monkish practices. So ~DOM n. [-ERY]

mŏn'key (mŭnk-), n. (pl. ~s), & v.t. & i. 1. Mammal of a group closely allied to & resembling man, ranging from anthropoid apes to marmosets; (as term of playful contempt, to or of person) *young* ~ etc. 2. Machine hammer for pile-driving etc.; globular earthenware water-vessel with straight upright neck. 3. (sl.) ||*Put his* ~ *up*, enrage him; *get one's* ~ *up*, become angry. 4. ||£500 (sl.). 5. ~-*bread*, fruit of baobab tree; ~-*cup*, pitcher-plant; ~-*jacket*, short close-fitting one worn by sailors etc.; ||~-*nut*, peanut; ~-*puzzle*, Chile pine, prickly tree of genus

Araucaria; ~*wrench*, one with movable jaw. **6.** v.t. Mimic, mock; (v.i.) play mischievous tricks (*with*), fool *about*. Hence ~ISH¹ a., ~ISHNESS n., (mŭng'kĭ-). [?]

monk'ish (mŭ-), a. Of monks, monastic; characteristic of monks (usu. in bad sense). [-ISH¹]

mon'o- in comb. (before vowels *mon-*) =Gk *monos* alone, sole, single; as: (1) ~*bāsĭc* (Chem.), having one base or atom of a base; ~*carp'ic*, ~*carp'ous*, bearing fruit only once; ~*cĕph'alous* (Bot.), having only one head; ~*clīn'al*, (of strata) dipping in one & the same direction; ~*cotylē-dŏn'ous*, (plant with) single cotyledon; *monŏc'racy*, government by single person; *monŏc'ūlar*, with, adapted to, one eye; ~*cycle*, velocipede with one wheel; ~*dac'tylous*, having one finger, toe, or claw; ~*drama*, piece for one performer; *monoē'cious* (-nēshus), (Bot.) with male & female organs on same plant, (Zool.) hermaphrodite; ~*genĕsis*, development of all beings from single cell, so ~*genĕt'ic* a.; *monŏg'eny*, descent of mankind from one pair of ancestors; ~*glŏt* a. & n., (one who uses only one language; *monŏ'glŏtous*, with only one pistil or stigma; *monŏ'gȳny*, usage of mating with only one female; ~*īdĕ'ism*, concentration on single idea, esp. as form of monomania; *monŏl'atry*, worship of one god without denying that others may exist; ~*mān'ia*, insanity on one subject only, so ~*mān'iăc* n., ~*mani'acal* a.; ~*mer*, one of the units forming a polymer molecule, (also) a compound which can undergo polymerization; ~*mĕt'allism*, standard of currency based on one metal, so ~*mĕtăll'ic* a.; ~*morph'ic*, ~*morph'ous*, not changing form during development; ~*pĕt'alous*, having corolla in one piece, or petals united into tube; ~*phthŏng*, single vowel sound; ~*plane*, aeroplane with one plane; ~*psy'chism* (-sĭk-), theory that all souls are one; ~*rail*, railway of one rail; ~*rhyme*, poem in which all lines have same rhyme; ~*sperm'ous* (Bot.), having one seed; *monos'tichous* (-k-) (Bot., Zool.), arranged in, consisting of, one layer or row; ~*strŏph'ic*, consisting of repetitions of one scrophic arrangement; ~*tint*, representation, picture, in only one colour; ~*trēme*, member of lowest order of mammals with one vent for urinary, genital, & digestive organs; ~*type*, composing-machine that casts & sets up single types; ~*tȳp'ic*, representing one type, (2) chem. wds denoting presence of a single atom or combining equivalent, as ~*brōm'ide*, ~*carb'on*, ~*chlor'ide*, *monŏx'ide*.

mŏn'ochŏrd (-k-), n. Instrument for determination of musical intervals. [f. F *monocorde* f. L f. Gk MONO(*khordon* f. *khordē* CHORD)]

mŏnochrŏmăt'ic (-k-), a. (Of light) presenting one colour only; executed in monochrome. [MONO-+CHROMATIC]

mŏn'ochrome (-k-), n. & a. **1.** Painting executed in different tints of one colour; representation in one colour. **2.** adj. Having only one colour. [ult. f. Gk MONO-(*khrōmatos* f. *khrōma* colour)]

mŏn'ocle, n. Single eye-glass. [F. f. LL *monoculus* one-eyed being MONO-+*oculus* eye]

mŏn'odȳ, n. Ode sung by single actor in Greek tragedy; poem in which mourner bewails someone's death. Hence or cogn. **monŏd'ic** a.~IST n. [f. Lf. Gk *monōdia* f. *monōidos* singing alone (MONO-+ōid-, *aoid-*, f. *aeidō* sing)]

monŏg'amȳ, n. Practice, circumstance, of being married to one at a time; (rare) practice of marrying only once; (Zool.) habit of having only one mate. Hence or cogn. ~IST n., ~OUS a. [f. F *monogamie* f. Lf. Gk MONO(*gamia* f. *gamos* marriage)]

mŏn'ogram, n. Two or more letters, esp. person's initials, interwoven. So **mŏno-grammăt'ic** a. [f. LL *monogramma* f. late Gk MONO(*grammon*, neut. adj. **as** -GRAM)]

mŏn'ograph (-ahf), n., & v.t. Separate treatise on single object or class of objects; (v.t.) write a ~ on. Hence **monŏg'raphER¹**, **monŏg'raphIST**, nn., **mŏnŏgrăph'IC** a., **mŏnŏgrăph'ICALLY** adv. [MONO-+-GRAPH]

mŏn'olith, n. Single block of stone, esp. shaped into pillar or monument. Hence **mŏnolith'IC** a. [f. Lf. Gk MONO(*lithos* stone)]

mŏn'ologue (-ŏg), n. Scene in drama in which one person speaks by himself; dramatic composition for single performer; long speech by one person in a company; soliloquy. Hence **mŏnŏlŏ'gIST** n., **monŏl'ogIST**, **mŏn'olŏgUIST** (-gĭst), nn., **monŏl'ogIZE**(2) v.i. [F., =one who loves to hear himself talk, f. Gk MONO(*logos* -LOGUE)]

|| **mŏn'omark**, n. Combination of letters and/or figures registered as identification mark for goods, articles, addresses, etc. [MONO-]

monōm'ial, n. & a. (alg.). (Expression) consisting of one term. [MONO-, on *binomial*]

Monŏph'ysite, n. One who holds that Christ is only one nature in the person of Christ. [f. eccl. L (-*ta*) f. eccl. Gk MONO(*phusitēs* f. *phusis* nature, see -ITE²)]

monŏp'olist, n. One who favours monopoly; one who assumes monopoly (*of*). [-IST]

monŏp'olIZ|e, v.t. Obtain exclusive possession or control of (trade, commodity, the conversation, person's attention, etc.). Hence ~A'TION n. [f. foll.+-IZE]

monŏp'olȳ, n. Exclusive possession of the trade in some commodity; this con-

ferred as privilege by State; exclusive possession, control, or exercise (of); thing that is monopolized. [f. LL f. Gk *(pōlion* f. *pōleō* sell)]

monopŏl′ylogue (-og), n. Entertainment in which sole performer plays many parts. [MONO- + POLY- + -LOGUE]

monosyll′able, n. Word of one syllable; *speak in ~ables*, answer little but Yes or No, with intentional curtness. Hence or cogn. **~ăb′ic** a., **~ăb′ICALLY** adv. **~abISM**(2) n., **~abIZE**(3) v.t. [f. LL MONO(*syllabus* SYLLABLE)]

monŏthe′ism, n. Doctrine that there is only one God. Hence **~IST** n., **~IS′TIC** a. [f. MONO- + Gk *theos* god + -ISM]

monŏt′onē, a. & n. & v.t. 1. (Utterance of) successive syllables) without change of pitch, whence **monŏton′IC** a. (mus.); sameness of style in writing. 2. v.i. Recite, speak, sing, in unvaried tone. [(vb f. n.) f. late Gk MONO(*tonos* TONE)]

monŏt′onous, a. (Of sound or utterance) without variation in tone or cadence; lacking in variety, wearisome through sameness. Hence or cogn. **~OUSNESS**, **~Y**[1], nn. **~OUSLY**[2] adv., **~OUSNESS**, **~Y**[1], nn. [as prec. + -OUS]

Monrōe′ism (-ōi-), n. Monroe DOCTRINE. So **~ISM** n. [-ISM]

monseigneur′ (see Ap.), n. (pl. *nosseigneurs* pr. nosānyŏr′). French title given to eminent persons, esp. princes, cardinals, archbishops, & bishops. [F]

monsieur(mŭsyŏr′, & see Ap.), n. (pl. *messieurs* pr. mĕsyŏr′), French equivalent of MR, but also used by itself as substitute for name, as *did M~ ring?*; Frenchman; brother of French king. [F]

monsignore′ (mŏnsēnyŏr′, -i; pl. -ori), n. Title of prelates, officers of Papal court, & others. [It., after MONSEIGNEUR]

monsōōn′, n. Wind in S. Asia, esp. in Indian Ocean, blowing from SW. in summer (*wet ~*) & NE. in winter (*dry ~*); rainy season; other winds with periodic alternations. [f. Du. *monssoen* f. Port. *monção* perh. f. Arab. *mausim*, lit. season. (*mausema* mark)]

mŏn′ster, n. & a. 1. Mis-shapen animal or plant; abortion; imaginary animal compounded of incongruous elements, e.g. centaur, sphinx, griffin; inhumanly wicked person. inhuman example of (cruelty etc.); animal, thing, of huge size, ~); huge. [f. OF *monstre* f. L *monstrum* portent, monster (*monēre* warn)]

mŏn′strance, n. (R.-C. Ch.). Open or transparent vessel of gold or silver in which the host is exposed. [OF. f. med. L *monstrantia* (*monstrare* show, see -ANCE)]

mŏnstrŏs′itÿ, n. Monstrousness; abortion, imaginary monster, outrageous thing. [f. LL *monstrositas* (as foll., see -TY)]

mŏn′strous, a. & adv. 1. Abnormally

formed, of the nature of a monster; huge; outrageously wrong or absurd; atrocious. 2. adv. (arch.). Extremely, as *~ good friends*. Hence **~LY**[2] adv., **~NESS** n. [f. OF *monstreux* f. LL *monstrosus* (MONSTER, -OUS)]

mŏn′tage (-ahzh), n. (cinemat.). Selection, cutting, & piecing together as a consecutive whole of the separate shots taken in the making of a film. [F, f. *monter* to mount]

mŏn′tāne, a. Of, inhabiting, mountainous country. [f. L *montanus* (as MOUNT, see -ANE)]

mŏntbrē′tia (-sha), n. Iridaceous plant with bright orange-coloured flowers. [after A. F. E. C. de *Montbret*, French botanist (d. 1801)]

mŏn′tē, n. Spanish game of chance, played with 45 cards; *three-card ~*, game of Mexican origin. [Sp.— mountain, heap of cards]

Mŏntenēg′rin, n. & a. (Inhabitant) of Montenegro (now in Jugoslavia). [-INE[1]

Montessōr′i sys′tem, n. Method of educating very young children, both normal & defective, initiated by Dr Maria Montessori of Rome (by direction of natural activities rather than strict control).

month (mŭ-), n. Any of the twelve portions into which the year is divided (also *calendar ~*); *lunar ~*, period in which moon makes complete revolution; space of time from a day in one ~ to corresponding day in next; space of 28 days; *~ of Sundays*, indefinite period; *this day ~*, a ~ from today; *~'s mind*, mass etc. in commemoration of deceased person a ~ after death. [(also) incli- nation, liking. [com.-Teut.: OE *mōnadh*, cogn. w. MOON]

mŏn′thly (mŭn-), a. & n. 1. Done, recurring, payable, etc., once a month; *~ nurse* (attending woman during first month after childbirth); *~ rose*, China rose, supposed to flower monthly. 2. n. Magazine etc. published each month; (pl.) menses. So **mo′nthly**[2] (mŭn-) adv. [-LY[1]]

mŏn′ticle, n. Small mound; small mound caused by volcanic eruption; minute eminence on surface of animal etc. [F, f. LL *monticulus* (*mons* MOUNT, see -CULE)]

mŏn′ument, n. Written record; anything that serves to commemorate, esp. structure, building; || *the M~*, column in London commemorating fire of London in 1666; stone or other structure placed over grave or in church etc. in memory of the dead. [f. L *monumentum* (*monēre* remind, see -MENT)]

mŏnūmĕn′tal, a. Of, serving as a monu- ment; *~ mason*, tombstone maker; (of literary works) massive & permanent; stupendous, as *~ ignorance*. Hence **~LY**[2] adv. [f. LL *monumentalis* (as prec., see -AL)]

monūmen'talize, v.t. Record, commemorate, as by monument. [prec. + -IZE]

-mony, suf.=L. -monia, -monium, which formed nn. f. aa. (acrimonia), nn. (patrimonium), & vbs (alimonium), adopted in E thr. F or direct; in E the -a & -um forms are alike; in F -um gave -moine, -a -monie, (patrimoine, parcimonie).

moo, v.i., & n. (Of cow or ox) low, make the sound moo; (n.) this sound. [imit.]

mooch, mouch (mōō-), v.i. & t. (sl.). Loiter about, slouch along; (trans.) steal [perh. f. OF muchier hide, skulk]

mood¹, n. State of mind or feeling; in the ~, in no ~, inclined, disinclined, (for thing, to do). [com.-Teut.: OE mōd, Du. moed, G mut]

mood², n. (Gram.) any of the groups of forms in conjugation of verb that serve to indicate its function, as indicative, imperative, subjunctive, ~; (Mus.)=MODE; (Log.) any of the classes into which each of the figures of valid categorical syllogism is subdivided. [var. of MODE, by assoc. w. prec.]

mood'|y̆, a. Gloomy, sullen. Hence ~ILY² adv., ~INESS n. [OE mōdig (see MOOD¹ & -Y²]

moollah. See MULLAH.

mool'vi(e), mou-, n. Mohammedan doctor of the law; learned person, teacher (esp. as term of respect among Indian Moslems). [Hind. mulvī f. Arab. maulawiyy=judicial]

moon¹, n. 1. Satellite of the earth, revolving round it monthly, & deriving light from sun & reflecting it to earth; this in particular month, regarded as a distinct object from that visible in other months, as age of the ~, new ~ (at beginning of revolution), full ~ (with disk entirely illuminated); HARVEST, HUNTER'S, ~; (poet.) month (where summer is but three ~s long); once in a BLUE¹ ~; old ~ in new ~'s arms, ~ during first quarter, when dark part of orb is made faintly luminous by earth-light. 2. (~flower, ray of ~light; ~calf, born fool; ~flower, ox-eye daisy; ~light, light of ~ (often attrib.); ~light fitting, removal of household goods by night to avoid paying rent; ~lighter, one who in Ireland perpetrated outrages by night on tenants who incurred hostility of Land League; ~ful, lit up by ~; ~shine, visionary talk or ideas, (also) smuggled spirits; *~shiner (sl.), illicit distiller, spirit-smuggler; ~ shiny, lighted by ~, (also) visionary; ~stone, feldspar of pearly appearance; ~struck, deranged in mind. Hence ~LESS a. [com.-Teut.: OE mōna, Du. maan, G mond, cogn. w. L mensis, Gk mēn, month]

moon², v.i. & t. Move, look, listlessly (about, around, etc.); pass away (time) in listless manner. [f. prec.]

moon'shee, n. Native secretary or language-teacher in India. [f. Hind. munshī f. Arab, munshī' (ansha'a compose]

moon'y, a. Of, like, the moon; listless, stupidly dreamy. [MOON¹,² + -Y²]

moor¹, n. Tract of open waste ground, esp. if covered with heather; (in Cornwall) waste land where tin is found; ~ game, red (rarely, black) grouse; ~cock, male of this; ~hen, female of this, (also) water-hen; ~land, country abounding in heather; ~stone, kind of granite. Hence ~ISH¹, ~Y², aa. [OE mōr, cf. Du. moer, G moor]

moor², v.t. Attach (boat or other floating thing) to moorings; ~ing-MAST. Hence ~AGE(3, 4) n. [OE has mǣréls mooring rope (cf. MDu. māren moor)]

moor'ing, n. (Usu. pl.) permanent anchors & chains laid down for ships to be moored to, what a floating object is moored to; (pl.) place where vessel is moored. [-ING¹]

moose, n. N.-Amer. animal closely allied to or same as European elk. [f. native moos]

moot, n., a., & v.t. 1. (Hist.) assembly; (Law) students' discussion of hypothetical case for practice. 2. adj. Debatable. 3. v.t. Raise (question) for discussion. [(vb f. OE mōtian, adj. f. n.) OE (ge)mōt, cf. Du. gemoet, cogn. w. MEET v.]

mop¹, n. Bundle of coarse yarn or cloth fastened at end of stick, for cleaning floors etc.; similar instruments for various purposes; ~head, (fig.) thick head of hair like ~, person with this. Hence ~p'Y² a. [15th c. mappe ult. f. L mappa napkin]

mop², v.t. (-pp-). Wipe, clean, (as) with mop; wipe tears, sweat, etc., from (brow etc.); (sl.)~ the floor with, have & use overwhelming advantage of (combatant); ~ up, wipe up (as) with mop; (sl.) absorb (profits etc.), dispatch, make an end of, (Mil.) complete the occupation of (district etc.) by capturing or killing troops left there, capture or kill (stragglers). [f. prec.]

mop³, v.i. (-pp-), & n. ~ & mow, make grimaces; ~s & mows, grimaces. [perh. imit.; cf. Du. moppen pout]

|| mop'⁴, n. A fair or gathering in the autumn at which farm hands & servants were hired. [etym. dub.]

mōpe, v.i. & t., & n. 1. Abandon oneself to listless condition; (refl. or pass.) make oneself, be, the victim of ennui. 2. n. One who ~s; the ~s, depression of spirits. Hence mōp'ISH¹ a., mōp'ishLY² adv., mōp'ishNESS n. [?]

Moor³, n. One of a Mohammedan race, mixed Berber & Arab, inhabiting NW. Africa. Hence ~'ISH¹ a. [f. F More f. L f. Gk Mauros inhabitant of Mauretania, region of N. Africa]

mō'poke, more'poke (mōrp-), n. In New Zealand, an owl; in Tasmania, nightjar; in Australia, various birds. [imit. of bird's note]

moquette (-kĕt), n. Material of wool & hemp or linen, used for carpets & up-holstery. [F; etym. dub.]

mó'ra, -rra, n. Italian game in which player guesses number of fingers held up simultaneously by another. [It. *mora*, etym. dub.]

moraine', n. Debris carried down & de-posited by glacier. [F]

mó'ral, a. & n. 1. Concerned with charac-ter or disposition, or with the distinction between right & wrong, in the matter of distinguishing right & wrong; (of literary work etc.) dealing with regulation of con-duct, as ~ *science*; ~ *philosophy*, ethics; ~ *law*, the requirements to which right action must conform; (of rights etc.) founded on ~ law; capable of ~ action; ~ *victory, defeat*, indecisive result, that eventually produces the ~ effects of victory; ~ *courage*, courage to encounter odium, contempt, etc., rather than aban-don right course; ~*ly good*, conform-ing to rules of morality; virtuous as regards general conduct; ~ *certainty*, probability so great as to admit of no reasonable doubt. 2. n. The ~ teaching of a fable, story, event, etc. (*draw the* ~, show what it is); ~ maxim or prin-ciple (*point a* ~, illustrate or apply it); (vulg.) *the very* ~ (exact likeness) of; (pl.) ~ habits, esp. sexual conduct; =foll. Hence ~ly² adv. [f. L *moralis* (*mos moris* morals, -AL¹)]

morale' (-ahl), n. Moral condition, esp. (of troops) as regards discipline & con-fidence. [f. F *moral* respelt to preserve pronunciation, cf. LOCALE, CHORALE]

mó'ralism, n. Natural system of moral-ity, religion reduced to moral practice. [-ISM]

mó'ralist, n. One who practises or teaches morality; man who is merely moral. Hence ~is'tic a. [MORAL+-IST]

morál'ity, n. Moral science; (pl.) moral principles, points of ethics; particular system of morals, as *commercial* ~; moral conduct (esp. good); moralizing; (Hist.) kind of drama inculcating moral lesson, popular in 16th c. [f. F *moralité* f. L *moralitatem* (MORAL, -TY)]

mó'ralize, v.i. & t. Indulge in moral re-flection or talk (*on* subject); interpret morally, point the moral of; improve the morals of. So ~A'TION n. [f. F *moraliser* f. LL *moralizare* (as MORAL, see -IZE)]

mó'rass, n. (literary). Bog, marsh. [f. Du. *moeras* f. MDu. *maersch* f. OF as MARISH]

mó'rat, n. (hist.). Drink made of honey flavoured with mulberries. [f. med. L *moratum* (*morus* mulberry, see -ATE)]

mörator'ium, n. Legal authorization to debtors to postpone payment. [neut. of LL *moratorius* (L *morari* delay, -TORY)]

Morä'vian, a. & n. (inhabitant) of Mo-ravia; (one) of Protestant sect holding Hussite doctrines, founded in Saxony by ~ emigrants. [f. Moravia, now part of Czechoslovakia, -AN]

morb'id, a. (Of mind, ideas, etc.) un-wholesome, sickly; given to ~ feelings; disease; ~ *anatomy* (of diseased organs etc.). Hence ~ly² adv., ~NESS n. [f. L *morbidus* (*morbus* disease f. root of *mori* die)]

morbid'ezza (-dtso), n. (painting). Life-like delicacy in flesh-tints. [It. (*morbido* soft)]

morbid'ity, n. Morbidness; prevalence of disease (in a district). [-ITY]

morbif'ic, a. Causing disease. [f. F *mor-bifique* (L *morbus* disease, see -FIC)]

mor'ceau (-sō), n. Short literary or musi-cal composition. [F (as MORSEL)]

mord'ant, a. & n. 1. (Of sarcasm etc.) caustic, biting; so ~A'CITY n. 2. n. (Of acids) corrosive or cleansing (n. such acid). 3. (Substance) serving to fix colouring-matter or gold-leaf. [f. F, part. of *mordre* bite f. L *mordere*]

mord'ent, n. (mus.). Grace consisting in rapid alternation of written note with one immediately below it. [G, f. It. part, of *mordere* bite, as prec.]

more, a. & adv. 1. Existing in greater quantity, amount, or degree, as *there is more truth in it than you think, 10 is 2 ~ than 8, bring some ~ water*; (abs.) greater quan-tity, as ~ *is meant than meets the ear, hope to see ~ of you; what is ~* (important); *it so*. 2. adv. In greater degree, as *you must attend ~ to details, ~ in sorrow than in anger, ~ frightened than hurt*; (forming compar. of most adj. of more than one syllable & most adv.), ~ *absurd(ly)*, ~ *curious*, ~ *easily*, ~ *truly*; ~ *& ~*, in an increasing degree; ~ *or less*, in greater or less degree, or thereabouts; THE ~; *be no ~*, be dead; *again*, as *once, twice, never,* ~; *neither ~ nor less than* (simply literally absurd etc. [com.-Teut. adj.: OE *māra*, MDu. *mēre*, f. OTeut. *maizon-* f. *maiz* adv. whence obs. *mo* more (OE *mā*) adv.]

moreen', n. Stout woollen or woollen & cotton material for curtains etc. [?]

morel¹, n. Kinds of nightshade. [f. OF *morele* prob. fem. f. It. *morello* dark-coloured perh. f. L *morum* mulberry]

morel², n. An edible fungus. [f. F *morille*, etym. dub.]

morell'ö, n. Bitter kind of cherry. [?]

moreov'er (mōrōv-), adv. Further, be-sides, (introducing new statement). [MORE+OVER]

morepork. See MOPOKE.

Moresque (-k), a. Moorish in style or design. [F, f. It. *moresco*]

morganat'ic, a. ~*ic marriage*, one be-tween man of exalted rank & woman of

lower rank, who remains in her former station, the issue having no claim to succeed to possessions or title of father; ~ic wife (so married). Hence ~ICALLY adv. [f. med. L phr. matrimonium ad morganaticam prob. f. morganaticum f. OHG +morgangeba morning gift from husband to wife the morning gift from husband to wife the morning after consummation of marriage (the ~ic wife's only claim on husband's possessions)]

mö'rgue¹ (-g), n. Building (esp. one formerly in Paris) in which bodies of persons found dead are exposed for identification. [F]

mö'rgue² (-g), n. Haughty demeanour, esp. (~ anglaise, see Ap.) as English characteristic. [F]

mö'ribund, a. At the point of death (lit. & fig.). [f. L moribundus (mori die)]

mö'rion, n. (hist.). Helmet without beaver or visor. [F; etym. dub.]

Moris'cö, a. & n. 1. Moorish. 2. n. Moor, esp. in Spain; morris dance. [Sp. (Moro MOOR²)]

Mö'rmon, n. Member of religious body founded in 1830 by Joseph Smith in New York on basis of supposed Divine revelations in Book of ~ (imaginary author); person who practises polygamy (formerly regarded as chief feature of the sect). Hence ~ISM n.

mörn, n. (poet.). Morning. [OE morgen, myrgen, margen, cf. Du. & G morgen, perh. f. root +mergh- twinkle]

mö'rn'ing, n. Early part of day-time, ending at noon, or at hour of midday meal; good ~, form of salutation; (poet.) dawn; (attrib. of clothes) meant to be worn in the ~, as ~ coat, tail-coat with front sloped away; ~ call, visit paid during afternoon; ~ draught, liquor taken before breakfast; ~ gift (see MORGANATIC, etym.); ~ glory, kind of convolvulus; ~ performance, matinée; ~ prayer, Anglican service of matins; ~ room, sitting-room for the ~; ~ star, Venus (or other planet or bright star) seen in E. before sunrise; ~ watch (Naut.), 4–8 A.M. [ME morwening (morwen MORN, +-ING³)]

morocc'ö, n. (pl.~s). Leather made (orig. in Morocco, now also in Europe) from goatskins tanned with sumac; French ~, inferior small-grained kind; Levant ~, high-grade large-grained kind. [f. native Marrakesh]

mö'ron, n. Adult whose mental development is arrested at the stage normal in a. child of 9–12 years; (pop.) degenerate brute, fool. [neut. of Gk möros dull]

moröse', a. Sullen, gloomy; & unsocial. Hence ~LY² adv.,~NESS n. [f. L morosus (mos moris manner, see -OSE¹)]

Mörph'eus, n. God of dreams or sleep; in the arms of ~, asleep. [L]

mörph'ia, mörph'ine, nn. Alkaloid narcotic principle of opium, largely used to alleviate pain. Hence mörph'inism(5) n. [(-ine f. G morphin, dim. see -INE⁵) f. next.]

mörphöl'ogy, n. (Biol.) study of the form of animals & plants; (Philol.) study of the form of words. Hence mörphölo'gical a., mörphölo'gically² adv. ~ISTN. (biol.), [f. Gk morphē form + -LOGY]

mö'rris, n. (in full ~ dance), grotesque dance by persons in fancy costume, usu. as characters in Robin Hood legend (medieval, & as modern revival); ~ pike (hist.), form of pike supposed to be of Moorish origin. [f. morys, var. of MOORISH]

∥Mö'rrison shel'ter, n. Indoor steel table-like shelter for protection in air raids. [H. Morrison, Home Secretary]

mö'rris tübe, n. Small-bore rifle barrel insertable in rifle for practice on miniature range. [R. Morris, inventor]

mö'rrow (-ō), n. (literary). The ~, the following day; (fig.) on the ~ of (time following on) a long war etc. [ME morwe, shortened f. morwen MORN]

mörse¹, n. Walrus. [f. Lapp. morsa]

Mörse², n.&a. (Of) the recording telegraph invented by S. F. B. Morse (d. 1872), as ~ alphabet, code (in which letters are represented by variations on two signs, e.g. dot & dash, long & short flash, etc.).

mörse³, n. Clasp, often jewelled etc., of cope. [f. OF+mors f. L morsus bite, catch]

mör'sel, n. Mouthful, small piece, (of food etc.); fragment. [OF, dim. of mors a bite f. L mordēre mors- bite]

mört¹, n. Note sounded on horn at death of deer. [F, f. L mortem (nom. mors) death]

mört², n. Salmon in third year. [?]

mört³, n. (dial.). A great amount or number of (a ~ of). [?]

mört'al, a. & n. 1. Subject to death; causing death, fatal, (to, often fig.); (of battle) fought to the death; (of enemy) implacable; (of pain, fear, etc.) deadly; (of sin) entailing spiritual death, deadly; accompanying death, as ~ agony; (sl.) very great, as in a ~ hurry; (sl.) long & tedious, as for two ~ hours. 2. n. ~, a esp. human, being; (joc.) person, as a thirsty ~. Hence ~LY² adv. [f. OF mortel f. L mortalis (mors -rtis death, see -AL)]

mörtäl'ity, n. Mortal nature; loss of life on large scale; number of deaths in given period etc.; death-rate; BILL's of ~; ~ tables (showing expectation of life at various ages etc.). [f. F mortalité f. L mortalitatem (as prec., see -TY)]

mört'ar, n., & v.t. 1. Vessel of hard material, e.g. marble, in which ingredients are pounded with pestle. 2. Short piece of ordnance for throwing shells at high angles; contrivance for firing shells in pyrotechnic displays. 3. Mixture of lime, sand, & water, for joining stones or bricks, whence ~LESS, ~² aa.; ~-board, board for holding ~, (pop.) square college cap. 4. v.t. Plaster, join, with ~; attack,

bombard, with ~s. [(vb f. n.) f. F mortier f. L mortarium, etym. dub.]

mortgage¹ (mŏ'gīj), n. Conveyance of property by debtor (mortgager, -or) to creditor (mortgagee) as security for debt, with proviso that it shall be reconveyed on payment of debt within certain period; deed effecting this. [OF.=dead pledge (mort f. L mortuus dead +GAGE¹)]

mortgage², v.t. (mŏ'gīj). Make over (property) by mortgage; pledge (oneself, one's powers etc., to object etc.). Hence **mortgagee** (mŏ'-), **mortgagor²** (mŏ'gĭjŏ'), **mortgager¹** (mŏ'gijĕr), nn.

mortician (-shn), n. Undertaker. [f. L mors -tis death +-ICIAN]

mortify, v.t. & i. Bring (body, passions, etc.) into subjection by self-denial or discipline; cause (person) to feel humiliated, wound (feelings), whence ~**fying²** a.; (vb intr., of flesh) be affected by gangrene or necrosis. So ~FICA'TION n. [f. F mortifier f. L mortificare (mors -tis death, see -FY)]

mortise, -ice, n., & v.t. 1. Hole in a framework designed to receive the end of some other part esp. a TENON; ~ chisel (with stout blade, for cutting ~s). 2. v.t. Join (things together, one to or into another) securely, esp. by tenon & ~. [(vb t., n.) f. F mortaise, etym. dub.]

mortmain, n. (law). (Condition of) lands or tenements held inalienably by ecclesiastical or other corporation. [f. OF mortemain med. L mortua manus dead hand, prob. in allusion to impersonal ownership]

mortuary, a. & n. 1. Of death or burial. 2. n. Building in which dead bodies are kept for a time. [f. L mortuarius (mortuus dead, see -ARY¹)]

mosaic¹ (-z-), a., n., & v.t. (~king, ~ked). 1. (Form or work of art) in which pictures etc. are produced by joining together minute pieces of glass, stone, etc. of different colours (also fig. of any diversified whole); ~ disease (in plants, esp. tobacco, maize, & sugar-cane); ~ wood (producing effect like that of ~); ~ gold, a disulphide of tin, also alloy of copper & zinc used in cheap jewellery etc. 2. v.t. Adorn with ~s; combine (as) into ~. Hence ~IST(3) n. [(vb t. f., n.) f. F mosaïque f. med. L mosaicus, mus-, as if f. a Gk mousaïkos of the Muses (mousa MUSE), see -IC]

Mosaic² (-z-), a. Of Moses, esp. ~ Law (in Pentateuch). [f. L Moses +-IC]

mosasaur'us (-ŏ'-), n. (pl. -rī). Large extinct marine reptile, first found near Maestricht on Meuse. [L Mosa Meuse + Gk sauros lizard]

moschatel' (-k-), n. Small plant with pale-green flowers & musky smell. [f. F moscatelle f. It. moscatella (moscato MUSK)]

moselle' (-z-), n. Dry white wine produced near the river M~.

Mos'es (-ziz), n. (Nickname for) Jewish moneylender.

Mōs'lem, Mŭs'lim, (-z-, -s-), a. & n. (pl. -ms, -min), Mohammedan. Hence **Mōs'lemism** n. [Arab. (-im), part. of aslama whence ISLAM]

mosque (-k), n. Mohammedan place of worship. [16th-c. mosquée f. F mosquée f. It. moschea f. Arab. masjid (sagada vb worship)]

mosqui'tō (-kē-), n. (pl. ~es). Kinds of gnat, female of which punctures skins of animals with long proboscis & sucks their blood; ~net, -curtain (to keep off ~es); ~croft, small light vessels for rapid manœuvring. [Sp. dim. of mosca f. L musca fly]

moss, n., & v.t. 1. Wet spongy soil; peatbog; kinds of small herbaceous cryptogamous plant, some growing in bogs, others on surface of ground, trees, stones, etc., in crowded masses, whence ~INESS n., ~'y² a.; rolling stone gathers no ~, one who constantly changes his place or employment will not grow rich. 2. ~booter of 17th c. 3. v.t. Cover with ~. [(vb f. n.) OE mos, cf. Du. mos, G moos]

most, a. & adv. 1. Existing in greatest quantity or degree, as you have made ~ mistakes, see who can make ~ noise, (abs. quasi-noun) this is the ~ I can do; make the ~ of it, employ it to the best advantage, (also) represent it at the best or worst; the majority, as ~ people think so, (quasi-n.) ~ of them are broken; for the ~ part, in the main, usually, whence ~'LY² adv. 2. adv. In the highest degree, as what ~ annoys me, (forming superl. of most adj.) of more than one syllable &, most adv.) ~ ludicrous(ly), ~ certain(ly), ~ callous(ly); ten at ~, not more than ten; this is as ~ (is no more than) a makeshift. [com.-Teut.: OE mǣst, prob. for *mā-ist-: cf. Du. meest, G meist, see -EST]

-most, suf. forming superl. adjj. formed not on adj. but on prep. or demonstr. stems (after~, fore~, in~, ut~) & later on wds indicating position in place, time, or order, (back~, top~, centre~, & the like in better~); altered form of OE -mest, combining two superl. suff. -mo- & -isto- -EST: in late OE -mest was confused with MOST (see prec.), whence subst. mod. pron. -most.

mot (mō), n. (pl. ~s pr. mōz). Witty saying; ~ juste (here Ap), the expression that conveys a desired shade of meaning with more precision than any other. [F, =word, f. pop. L *mottum =L muttum (muttire murmur)]

mote, n. Particle of dust; ~ in (another's)

eye, trifling fault if compared to one's own (see *Matt.* vii. 3). [OE *mod*, perh. cogn. w. Du. *moed*, G *mut*; see MOOD².]

motet, n. (mus.). Anthem (usu. unaccompanied) in R.C. or Lutheran Church; non-ecclesiastical work on similar lines. [F, dim. of MOT]

moth, n. (Also *clothes~*) small nocturnal lepidopterous insect breeding in cloth etc., on which its larva feeds (*~, the ~*, collect., *~s*), whence *~*Y² a.; one of two great divisions of Lepidoptera including this, distinguished from butterflies by not having clubbed antennae, & apt to scorch themselves by fluttering about light; (fig.) person hovering around temptation; *~-ball* (of chemical preventive for keeping *~s* from clothes); *~-eaten*, destroyed by *~s*, (fig.) antiquated, time-worn. [OE *moththe* cf. MDu. & G *motte*]

mo'ther¹ (mŭdh-), n. 1. Female parent. 2. Quality, condition, etc., that gives rise to another, as *necessity is the ~ of invention*. 3. Head of female religious community (often *M~ Superior*). 4. (Term of address for) elderly woman of lower class. 5. (Also *artificial ~*) apparatus for rearing chickens. 6. (Arch., f. obs. sense *womb*) hysteria. 7. *M~ Carey's* CHICKEN; *M~ Church* (as of maternal authority); *M~-Church* (whence others have sprung); *~ country*, country in relation to its colonies; *~-craft*, skill in treatment of offspring; *~ earth*, earth as *~* of its inhabitants etc., (joc.) the ground; *M~ Hubbard*, person in nursery rhyme, kind of cloak or overall; *~-in-law*, one's wife's or husband's *~*; *~land*, one's native land; *~ lodge* (Freemasonry), masonic lodge in which one was initiated; *~ of pearl*, smooth shining iridescent substance forming inner layer of some shells (often attrib, w. hyphens); *~ of thousands* or *millions*, Ivy-leaved toad-flax; *~ship* (in charge of torpedo-boats, submarines, etc.); *~'s son*, man, esp. *every ~'s son of* (you etc.); *~ tongue*, one's native tongue, (also) tongue from which others spring; *~ wit*, native wit, common sense. Hence ~HOOD n., ~LESS, ~LY, aa. [com.-Teut.: OE *mōdor*, Du. *moeder*, G *mutter*, cogn. w. Gk *mētēr*, L *mater*]

mo'ther² (mŭdh-), v.t. Give birth to (usu. fig.); protect as a mother; acknowledge or profess oneself the mother of (child, lit. & fig.); ||*~ing Sunday*, Mid-lent Sunday, with old custom of visiting parents with gifts. [f. prec.]

mo'ther³ (mŭdh-), n. (Also *~ of vinegar*) mucilaginous substance produced in vinegar during fermentation by mould-fungus. Hence ~Y² a. [prob.=MOTHER¹; cf. MDu. *moeder*, G *mutter*]

mo'therlỹ (mŭdh-), a. Having, showing, the good qualities of a mother. Hence ~INESS n. [OE *mōdorlic* (see MOTHER¹ & -LY¹)]

motif' (-ēf), n. Constituent feature, dominant idea, in artistic composition; ornament of lace etc. sewn separately on dress. [F, as MOTIVE a.]

mo'tile, a. (zool., bot.). Capable of motion. Hence moti'lITY n. [as MOVE, see -IL]

mo'tion¹, n. 1. Moving, change of place; manner of moving the body in walking etc.; change of posture; gesture; *in ~*, moving, not at rest; *put in ~*, set going or working; *~ picture*, cinematographic film. 2. Formal proposal in deliberative assembly; (Law) application by party etc. for rule or order of court. 3. Evacuation of bowels. 4. Piece of moving mechanism. Hence ~AL, ~LESS, aa., (-shon-). [F, f. L *motionem* (as MOVE, -ION)]

mo'tion², v.t. & i. Direct (person *to, towards, away*, etc., *to do*) by sign or gesture; make gesture (to person) directing him (*to do*). [f. prec.]

mo'tive¹, a. & n. 1. Tending to initiate movement, whence MŌTIV'ITY n.; *~ power*, moving or impelling power, esp. form of mechanical energy used to drive machinery, e.g. steam, electricity; concerned with movement. 2. n. What induces a person to act, e.g. desire, fear, circumstance, whence ~LESS a.; =MOTIF. [f. F *motif* f. med. L *motivus* (MOVE, -IVE)]

mo'tive², **mō'tivāte**, vv.t. Supply a motive to, be the motive or motif of. Hence MŌTIVA'TION n. [f. prec. n.]

mo'tley, a. & n. 1. Diversified in colour; of varied character, as *~ assembly*. 2. n. Incongruous mixture; (Hist.) fool's particoloured dress, esp. *wear ~*, play the fool. [f. 14th c., etym. dub.]

mo'tor, n., a., & v.i. & t. 1. What imparts motion; machine supplying motive power for carriage or vessel, esp. internal-combustion engine, as (attrib.) *~ bicycle, cab, (omni)bus, boat, ship; ~car; ~ bandit*, thief who uses a *~-car* in his depredations; || *~-car*, carriage propelled by *~* for use on ordinary roads, whence ~IST(3) n.; *~ cycle*, bicycle etc. worked by *~* engine. 2. (anat.). Muscle designed to move a part of the body; (nerve) designed to excite muscular activity, whence MŌTŌR'IAL, mō'tORY, aa. 3. vb. Go or convey in *~-car*. [L, (MOVE, -OR²]

mo'torīze, v.t. Equip (troops etc.) with motor transport. Hence ~A'TION n. [-IZE]

mo'ttle, n. & v.t. 1. Arrangement of colour; such spot or confluent blotches of colour; such spot; variegated woollen yarn. 2. v.t. Mark (esp. soap) with ~s (esp. in p.p.). [prob. f. MOTLEY]

motto, n. (pl. ~es). Sentence inscribed on some object & expressing appropriate sentiment; maxim adopted as rule of conduct; verses etc. in paper cracker; quotation prefixed to book or chapter; (Mus.) recurrent phrase having some symbolical significance. [It., as MOT]

moue (mōō), n. POUT². [F; cf. MOW²]

mouflon (mōō-), n. Wild mountain sheep of S. Europe. [F. f. It. *muflone*]

moujik, muzhik (mōō'zhik), n. Russian peasant; lady's loose fur cape. [f. Russ. *muzhik* peasant]

mould¹ (mōld), n. Loose earth; upper soil of cultivated land; ~ man of ~, mere mortal; ~-board, board in plough that turns over the furrow-slice. [OE *molde*; cf. Du. *moude*, G dial. *molt*, f. OTeut. *mal-*; grind, cf. MEAL¹]

mould² (mōld), n. Pattern, templet, used by masons, bricklayers, etc., as guide in shaping mouldings; hollow form into which molten metal etc. is cast to cool in required shape; metal or earthen-ware vessel used to give shape to puddings etc., pudding etc. so shaped; (fig.) cast in *heroic* etc., of such character; form, shape, of animal body; (Archit.) group of mouldings; (Archit.) form, ~); ~-loft, room on floor of which plans of ship are drawn full size. [ME *moulde* prob. f. OF *modle* f. MODULUS]

mould³ (mōld), v.t. Produce (object) in certain shape, out of (elements), or upon (pattern), lit. & fig.; bring into certain shape (bread) into loaves. [f. prec.]

mould⁴ (mōld), n. Woolly or furry growth of minute fungi on things that lie for some time in moist warm air. [prob. f. obs. *mould* a., p.p. of *mould* grow mouldy, cf. Swed. *mögla*]

moul'der¹ (mōl-), n. One who moulds, esp. workman making moulds for casting. [-ER¹]

moul'der² (mōl-), v.i. Decay to dust, *rot away*, (often fig.). [perh. MOULD¹+-ER⁵]

mould'ing (mōl-), n. In vbl senses, esp. moulded object, esp. ornamental variety of outline in cornices etc. of building, woodwork, etc.; ~-board (on which dough is kneaded). [MOULD³+-ING¹]

moul'dy (mōl-), a. Overgrown with mould; (fig.) stale, out-of-date; (sl.) dull, tiresome, boring. Hence ~iness n. [MOULD¹+-Y²]

moul'dy² (mōl-), n. (naut. sl.). Torpedo. [?]

moulin (mōō'lăn'), n. Nearly vertical shaft in glacier, formed by surface water falling through crack in ice. [F, lit. = mill]

moult (mōlt), v.t. & i. & n. 1. (Of birds) shed (feathers), shed feathers, in changing plumage (also fig.). 2. n. ~ing. [(n. & v.) ME *mouten* f. OE **mūtian* f. L *mutare* change; -t- on false anal. of *fault* etc.]

mound¹, n. Ball of gold etc. representing earth, surmounting crown etc., & used in heraldry. [f. F *monde* f. L *mundus* world]

mound², n., & v.t. Elevation of earth or stones, esp. of earth heaped on grave; hillock; ~-builder, one of prehistoric Indian race in N. America who erected ~s, (also) kinds of bird depositing eggs in a heap; (v.t.) enclose with, heap up in, ~s. [?]

mount¹, n. Mountain, hill, (abbr. Mt. preceding name, as *Mt Ephraim*); (Palm-istry) fleshy prominence on palm of hand. [OE *munt* f. L *mons -ntis*]

mount², v.i. & t. 1. Ascend (hill etc. or abs.); proceed upwards; (of blood) rise into cheeks. 2. Rise to higher level of rank, power, intensity, etc.; (also ~ up) rise in amount. 3. Get on horse etc. for purpose of riding; get on (horse etc., or abs.); put (person) on horse etc.; furnish (person) with horse. 4. Raise (guns) into position; put (loom etc.) in working order; put (picture etc.) in a MOUNT³; fit (gems etc.) in gold etc.; fix (object) on microscope slide. 5. Put (play) on stage; display (article of costume). 6. ~ an offensive (Mil.), act on, take, the offensive; ~ (go on duty as) *guard* (over thing or abs.). [f. OF *munter* f. pop. L **montare* (as prec.)]

mount³, n. Margin surrounding picture, card on which drawing is mounted; ornamental metal parts of thing; horse for person's riding; chance of riding, esp. as jockey. [f. prec.]

mountain (-tin), n. Natural elevation of earth's surface, large or high hill; *Ma-homet & the ~, Mahomet will go to the ~*, phrases applied to the pretender who is not abashed under exposure (w. ref. to the story told in Bacon's Essay on Bold-ness); *waves ran ~s (very) high*, ~-high; large heap or pile; (also ~ *wine*) Malaga wine from ~ grapes; *the M~*, extreme party in first French Revolution, occupy-ing elevated position in chamber of assembly; ~ *ash*, tree with delicate pin-nate leaves & scarlet berries; ~ *chain*, series of ~s; ~ *dew* (colloq.), Scotch whisky; ~ *sickness*, malady caused by rarefied ~ air. [f. OF *montaigne* f. pop. L *montanea* f. **montaneus*=L *montanus* (*mons -ntis* mountain; -AIN)]

mountaineer' (-tin-), n. Dweller amongst mountains; one skilled in mountain climbing, whence ~ING¹ n. [-EER]

moun'tainous (-tin-), a. Abounding in mountains; huge. [f. OF *montaignous* (MOUNTAIN; -OUS)]

moun'tebank (mountĭbănk), n. Itinerant quack who held forth to audience from platform; charlatan. Hence ~ERY⁴ n. [f. It. *montambanco*=*monta in banco* mount on bench]

mourn (môrn), v.i. & t. Feel sorrow or regret (for, over, dead person, lost thing, loss, misfortune, etc.); show conventional signs of grief for period after person's death; sorrow for (dead person, thing), (esp. ~ one's death); be anxious (lest). [OE *murnan*, OHG *mornén* be anxious, ON *morna* pine]

mourn'er (môr-), n. One who mourns, esp. who attends funeral of friend or

relation; person hired to attend funeral. [-ER¹]

mourn′ful (mộr-), a. Doleful, sad, sorrowful. Hence ~LY² adv., ~NESS n. [MOURN]

mourn′ing (mộr-), n. In vbl senses, also or esp.: (wearing of) black clothes as sign of ~; DEEP¹, HALF, ~; complimentary~ (worn as tribute to unrelated dead); in ~, wearing such garments, (of the eye) blacked in fighting etc., (of finger-nails) dirty; ~-coach (attending funeral); ~paper, notepaper with black edge; ~ring (worn as memorial of deceased person). [-ING¹]

mouse¹ (mows), n. (pl. mice). Animal of any of the smaller species of a genus of rodents, esp. house, field-, harvest-, ~; timid, shy, retiring person; weight & cord for passing sash-lines over pulleys etc.; (sl.) black eye; ~-colour, dark grey with yellow tinge; ~-ear, hawkweed & other plants; ~-trap (for catching mice). Hence **mous′Y²** a. [com.-Teut.: OE mūs, Du. muis, G maus, cf. L & Gk mus]

mouse² (-z), v.i. & t. (Of cat or owl) hunt for or catch mice, whence **mous′ER¹** (-z-) n.; search industriously; prowl about in search of something; (Naut.) put some turns of spunyarn round (point & shank of a hook). [f. prec.]

mousse (mōos), n. Dish of flavoured cream whipped & frozen (chestnut, chocolate, etc.). [F, =froth]

mousseline (mōoslēn′), n. French muslin; ~-de-laine, dress material of wool & cotton; ~-de-soie (swah), thin silk fabric of muslin-like texture. [F, see MUSLIN]

moustache, ˙mus-, (mustahsh′), n. Hair on either side or both sides of a man's upper lip; similar hair round mouths of some animals; ~-cup (with partial cover to protect ~ when drinking). [F, f. It. mostaccio f. Gk mustax -akos]

Mouster′ian (mōo-), a. (archaeol.). Of the palaeolithic epoch represented by remains found in the Moustier cave in France. [-IAN]

mouth¹ (mowth), n. (pl. pr. -dhz). 1. External orifice in head, with cavity behind it containing apparatus of mastication & organs of vocal utterance; (sl.) impudent talk, check; (of horse, with reference to his readiness to feel & obey pressure of bit) good, bad, hard, ~; ~ waters at (food; referring to flow of saliva caused by anticipation); useless ~, one who does no work but must be fed; this sounds strange in your ~ (when said by you); put words into his ~, tell him what to say; put (speech) into person's ~, represent him as having made it; take the words out of person's ~, say what he was about to say; (of dog) give ~, bark, bay; down in the ~, dejected; laugh on wrong side of one's ~, lament; make a wry ~, grimace in sign of disapproval etc.

2. Opening of bag, cave, furnace, etc.; outfall of river. 3. ~filling, bombastic, inflated; ~organ, thin rectangular box containing metal reeds, each tuned to a note, moved before ~ to play tunes; ~piece, part of pipe, musical instrument, etc., placed between lips, (also) one who speaks for others. Hence (~)-ED²(-dhd), ~′LESS, aa., ~′FUL n. [com.-Teut.: OE mūth, Du. mond, G mund, cogn. w. L mentum chin]

mouth² (mowdh), v.t. & i. Utter (words or abs.) pompously or very distinctly; take (food) in, touch with, the mouth; train mouth of (horse); grimace. [f. prec.]

mouth′y (-dhĭ), a. Railing, ranting; bombastic. [MOUTH¹ + -Y²]

mo′vable (mōo-), a. & n. 1. That can be moved; (of property) that can be removed, personal as opp. to real; ~ feast, one that varies its date, (joc.) meal taken at no regular time. 2. n. Article of furniture that may be removed from the house, opp. to fixture; (pl.) personal property. Hence **movaBIL′ITY**, ~NESS, nn., **mo′vabLY** adv. [OF (as MOVE², see -ABLE)]

move¹ (mōov), n. Moving of a piece in chess & other games; player's turn to do this; device, step taken to secure object; on the ~, moving about; make a ~, go, esp. rise & go from dinner-table etc.; get a ~ on (sl.), hurry up, bestir oneself. [f. foll.]

move² (mōov), v.t. & i. 1. Change position of, change position of (piece) in chess etc.; put, keep, in motion, shake, stir; heaven & earth, make every effort (to do); change posture of (one's body, limbs, etc.). 2. Cause (bowels) to act. 3. Provoke (laughter, anger, etc., in person, person to those); affect (person) with (usu. tender) emotion, whence **mo′vING³** a., **mo′vING-** LY² adv., (mōo-). 4. Prompt, incline, (person to action, to do); the spirit (orig. in Quaker use,=Holy Spirit) ~s me, I feel inclined (to do). 5. Make formal application to (court etc. for); propose (question, resolution, that thing be done) in deliberative assembly. 6. Go, pass, (about, away, etc.) from place to place; make progress, as the work ~s slowly; make a move at chess etc. 7. Change one's abode; ~ about, do this often; ~ in, take possession of new abode. 8. ~ on (policeman's order to person who stands too long in one place), (trans.) cause person to ~ on by giving this order. 9. (Of person or part of body) change posture; (of inanimate things) suffer change of position; moving staircase, one made on principle of endless chain, with steps moving up or down continuously, escalator. 10. (Of bowels) be ~d. 11. Make request or application (for); take action, proceed, (in matter). Hence ~′LESS a. (rare). [f. OF movoir f. L movēre mot-]

move′ment (mōovm-), n. Moving; military evolution; moving parts of machine,

particular group of these; mental impulse; development of poem, story, etc.: (Mus.) principal division of a musical work (e.g. suite, sonata, symphony); having a distinctive structure of its own; series of actions & endeavours of a body of persons for special object, as *the* OXFORD ~; activity in market for some commodity. [OF, f. med. L *movimentum* (as prec., see -MENT)]

mo'ver (mōō-), n. In vbl senses, esp.: one who moves proposal; *prime* ~, initial source (natural or mechanical) of motive power, (also) author of fruitful idea. [-ER¹]

mo'vies (mōōviz), n., pl. (sl.). Cinema pictures. [=*moving pictures*]

mow¹, n. Stack of hay, corn, peas, etc.; place in barn where hay etc. is heaped; ~*burnt*, spoilt by becoming overheated in the ~. [OE *mūga*, cf. ON *mūge*, Sw. & Norw. *muga*.]

mow² (mō, mow), n., & v.i. See MOP³. [vb f. n.] f. OF *moue* mouth, lip, pout, etym. dub.]

mow³ (mō), v.t. (~*ed* pr. mōd, ~*n*), Cut down (grass etc. or abs.) with scythe or machine; cut down produce of (field) thus; destroy sweepingly, *cut off* or *down* in great numbers. Hence ~ER¹(1, 2) (mō'er) n. [com.-WG: OE *māwan*, Du. *maaien*, G *mähen*]

mox'a, n. Down from dried leaves of a plant, used for burning on skin as counter-irritant for gout; anything so used. [f. Jap. *mokusa* (*moe kusa* burning herb)]

Moza'rab, n. (hist.). Christian owning allegiance to Moorish king but allowed his own religion. Hence ~IC a. [f. Sp. *Mozárabe* f. Arab. *mustá'rib* would-be Arab (*'arab*)]

Mpret, n. Albanian ruler. [f. L *imperator* emperor]

Mr (mis'ter). See MISTER.

Mrs (mis'iz), n. Title prefixed to surname of married woman who has no superior title; *Mrs Grundy* (see GRUNDYISM). [abbr. of MISTRESS]

mu, n. Greek letter M (M, μ). [Gk]

much, a. & adv. **1.** Existing in great quantity, as ~ *trouble*, *too* ~ *noise*, *not* ~ *rain*, (abs., quasi-n.) *I have stood* ~, ~ *of what you say is true; too* ~ (more than a match) *for*; THINK, MAKE, ~ *of; he is not* ~ *of a* (not a good) *scholar*. **2.** adv. In a great degree (qualifying vb or p.p., cf. VERY), as *I* ~ *regret the mistake, was* ~ *annoyed*; (qualifying compar. or superl. adj.) ~ *better*, ~ *the most likely*; pretty nearly, as ~ *of a size*, about the same size. Hence ~LY² adv. (joc.). [f. OE *micel* MICKLE]

much'ness, n. Greatness in quantity or degree; *much of a* ~, very nearly the same or alike. [prec. +-NESS]

mu'cilage, n. Viscous substance from various plants; gum; viscous fluid in animal bodies, e.g. mucus. So **muci-**la'ginous a. [F, f. LL *mucilago* -*ginis* (MUCUS)]

muck¹, n. Farmyard manure; dirt; (colloq.) anything disgusting; (colloq.) untidy state; ~-*rake* (for collecting ~, usu. fig.); ~'*worm*, worm that lives in ~, (fig.) money-grubber, street arab. Hence ~Y² a. [ME *muk*, prob. of Scand. orig.]

muck² v.t. & i. Make dirty; (sl.) bungle (job); (sl.) go aimlessly *about*. [f. prec.]

|| **muck'er**, n. (sl.). Heavy fall (lit. & fig.); *come a* ~, experience this; *go a* ~, plunge into extravagance (*on, over, pur-chase*). [-ER¹]

mic'kle. See MICKLE.

muc'ous, a. Of, covered with, mucus, as ~ *membrane*, internal prolongation of the skin so covered. So **mucos'ITY** n. [f. L *mucosus* (as MUCUS, see -OUS)]

muc'ro, n. (bot., zool.; pl. ~*nes* pr. -ōn'ēz). Pointed part or organ. Hence **muc'ron**-ATE²(2) a. [L =point]

mucus, n. Slimy substance secreted by mucous membrane; gummy substance found in all plants; slimy substance exuded by some animals, esp. fishes [L, cogn. w. *emungere* blow the nose, & Gk *mussomai*]

mud, n. Wet soft earthy matter, mire; (fig.) what is worthless or polluting; *fling, throw,* ~, make disgraceful imputations; STICK *in the* ~; ~-*bath* (in ~ of mineral springs, for rheumatism etc.); ~*guard*, piece of metal attached to wheel of cycle etc. to protect rider from ~; ~'*lark*, one who dabbles, works, or lives, in ~, esp. street arab; ~'*pie*, ~ shaped like pie by child; ~ *volcano* (discharging ~). [ME *mode*, cf. Du. *modden* dabble in ~, G dial. *mott* bog]

mudar', ma-, n. E.-Ind. shrub, of which root-bark is used in medicine & inner bark yields silky fibre (*yercum*). [Hind. (ma-)]

mud'dle¹, n. Disorder; *make a* ~ *of* bungle; ~-*headed(ness)*, stupid(ity). [f. foll.]

mud'dle² v.t. & i. **1.** Bewilder, esp. with drink; mix (*things up, together*) blunder-ingly; bungle (affair); busy oneself in confused & ineffective way; ~ *on*, get on in haphazard way; ~ *through*, attain one's end by tenacity not skill. [f. MUD +-LE(3)]

mud'dy, a., & v.t. **1.** Like, abounding in, covered with, mud; (of light) dull; (of voice) thick; mentally confused; obscure. **2.** v.t. Make ~y. Hence ~ILY² adv., ~INESS n. [-Y²]

Mud'ie's (-diz), n. (Used for a circulat-ing library. [name of London firm]

mudir' (mōdēr'), n. Governor of Turkish village or of Egyptian province. [Turk. f. Arab., part. of *adara* govern]

muezz'in (mōō-), n. Mohammedan crier who proclaims hours of prayer from

minaret. [f. Arab. *ma'adhdhin* (*adhana* proclaim)]

muff[1], n. Woman's fur or other covering (usu. cylindrical) into which both hands are thrust from opposite ends to keep them warm; *food-~*, contrivance serving same purpose for feet. [prob. f. Du. *mof* f. F as MUFFLE[2]]

muff[2], n., & v.t. 1. Person who is awkward or stupid, esp. in some athletic sport; failure, esp. to catch ball at cricket etc. 2. v.t. Bungle, miss (catch, ball, etc.). Hence ~ISH[1] a. [?]

muffetee', n. Worsted cuff worn on wrist. [prob. irreg. f. MUFF[1]]

muff'in, n. ‖ Light flat round spongy cake, eaten toasted & buttered; ‖ ~-*bell* (rung by ~-*man*, seller of ~s). [?]

muffineer', n. Small castor for sprinkling salt or sugar on muffins. [-EER]

muff'le[1], n. Thick part of upper lip & nose of ruminants & rodents. [f. F *musfle*, etym. dub.]

muff'le[2], n. 1. Leather glove for lunatics who tear clothes etc.; mitten. 2. Receptacle within furnace, in which substances may be heated without contact with products of combustion; chamber in kiln for baking pottery. [f. F *moufle* mitten f. med. L *muffula*]

muff'le[3], v.t. Wrap, cover *up*, (oneself, one's throat etc., or abs.) for warmth; wrap up head of (person) to prevent his speaking; wrap up (oars, bell, drum, horse's hoofs) to deaden sound; repress, deaden, sound of (curse etc., usu. in p.p.). [prob. as prec.]

muff'ler, n. Wrap, scarf, worn for warmth; boxing-glove; thick glove; thing used to deaden sound, esp. felt pad between hammer & string of piano. [f. prec. +-ER[1]]

muf'ti, n. 1. Mohammedan priest or expounder of law, esp. official head of religion in Turkey. 2. ‖ Plain clothes worn by one who has right to wear uniform, esp. in ~. [Arab., part. of *afta* decide point of law]

mug[1], n. Drinking-vessel, usu. cylindrical, with or without handle; its contents; a cooling drink; [perh. diff. wd] (sl.) face, mouth. [?]

mug[2], n. (sl.). Simpleton, muff. [?]

mug[3], v.i. & t. (-gg-), & n. (sl.). 1. Study hard (*at* subject or abs.); (also ~ *up*) get up (subject). 2. n. One who studies hard; examination. [?]

mugg'er[1] (-g-), n. Broad-nosed Indian crocodile. [f. Hind. *magar*]

mugg'ins (-g-), n. Simpleton; children's game of cards; game of dominoes. [perh. the surname M~, w. allusion to MUG[2]]

Muggleton'ian (-gel-), a. & n. (Member) of sect founded by, & believing in personal inspiration of, L. Muggleton & John Reeve, c. 1650. [-IAN]

mugg'ly[ÿ] (-g-), a. (Of weather, day, etc.) damp & warm; stifling, close. Hence ~INESS n. [f. dial. *mug* drizzle, cf. ON *mugga*, +-Y[1]]

*****mug'wump**, n. Great man, boss; one who holds aloof from party politics. [f. native *mugquomp* great chief]

Muhammadan. See MOHAMMEDAN.

mulatt'o, n. (pl. ~s), & a. 1. Offspring of European & Negro. 2. adj. Of ~ colour, tawny. [f. Sp. *mulato* young mule, mulatto, irreg. f. *mulo* MULE[1]]

mul'berry, n. 1. Genus of tree, leaves of which are much used for feeding silkworms: its fruit; ~ *bush*, children's game with ditty *Here we go round the ~ bush*. 2. (M~) code name of prefabricated harbour used in the invasion on D-DAY and subsequently. [ult. f. OHG *mûlberi* (*mûr* f. L *morum* mulberry + *beri* berry)]

mulch, n., & v.t. 1. Mixture of wet straw, leaves, etc., spread to protect roots of newly planted trees. 2. v.t. Treat with ~. [prob. f. obs. adj. *mulch* soft, cf. dial. *melch* (OE *melsc*) & G dial. *molsch* soft]

mulct, n., & v.t. 1. Fine imposed for offence. 2. v.t. Punish (person) by fine (*in* amount, or with amount as second object), deprive (person etc. *of*). [vb f. L *mulctare*) f. L *mul(c)ta*]

mule[1], n. 1. Offspring of he-ass & mare, or (pop.) of she-ass & stallion (prop. *hinny*), used as beast of draught & burden & noted for obstinacy; stupid or obstinate person; hybrid plant or animal; ~ *canary*, cross between canary & other finch. 2. Kind of spinning-machine. Hence **mul'ISH**[1] a., **mul'ISHLY** adv., **mul'ISHNESS** n. [f. OE *mûl*, & f. OF *mul(e)*, f. L *mulus*, -*la*]

mule[2], v.i. =MEWL.

mule[3], n. Heelless slipper. [F]

muleteer', n. Mule-driver. [f. F *muletier* (*mulet* dim. of OF *mul* mule, see -EER)]

mulieb'rity, n. Womanhood; the normal characteristics of a woman (opp. VIRILITY); softness, effeminacy. [f. L *muliebritas* (*mulier* woman)]

mull[1], n. Thin variety of plain muslin. [shortened f. *mulmull* f. Hind. *malmal*]

‖ **mull**[2], n., & v.t. & i. 1. Muddle, mess, esp. *make a ~ of.* 2. v.t. Make a ~ of (catch etc.); *(v.i.) ponder over.* [?]

mull[3], v.t. Make (wine, beer) into a hot drink with sugar, spices, yolk of egg, etc. [?]

‖ **mull**[4], n. (Sc.). Promontory (*M~ of Cantyre*). [Icelandic *múli*]

‖ **mull**[5], n. (Sc.). Snuffbox. [var. of MILL[1], box orig. having a grinder]

mull'ah, **mooll'ah**, n. Mohammedan learned in theology & sacred law. [f. Pers., Turk., Hind., *mulla* f. Arab. *maula*]

mull'ein (-lin), n. Kinds of herbaceous plant with woolly leaves & yellow flowers. [f. AF *moleine*, perh. f. F *mol* soft f. L *mollis*]

müll'er, n. Stone used for grinding powders etc. on slab. [perh. f. OF *moldre* grind.]

müll'et, n. Two genera of fishes of which *Red & Grey M~* are the types. [f. OF *mulet* dim. f. L *mullus* red ~]

mülligatawn'y, n. (Also ~ *soup*) highly seasoned soup; ~ *paste*, curry paste used for this. [f. Tamil *milagu-tannīr* pepper-water]

müll'igrübs (-z), n. pl. Depression of spirits; stomach-ache. [arbitrary]

müll'ion (-yon), n. Vertical bar dividing lights in window. Hence ~ED² (-yond) a. [prob. var. of MONIAL]

müll'ock, n. (Austral.) rock containing no gold, also, refuse from which gold has been extracted; (dial.) rubbish. [f. dial. *mull* dust, rubbish, f. Teut. root *mul-*]

müll'ti-, in comb. (before vowel occas. *mult-*) = L *multus* many, as ~*coloured(-ed)*, of many colours; ~*fid* (Bot., Zool.), cleft into many parts; ~*flor'ous*, (of stalk) bearing more than three flowers; ~*foil* (Archit.), ornament consisting of more than 5 foils; ~*form*, having many forms, of many kinds, so ~*fōrm'ity* n.; ~*lāt'eral*, having many sides; ~*millionaire* (-yon-), person with fortune of several millions; ~*nōm'ial* a. & n. (Alg.), (expression) of more than two terms; ~*par'ous*, bringing forth many young at a birth, (of woman) who has borne more than one child; ~*part'ite*, divided into many parts; ~*valve* a. & n. (shell, animal with shell) of many valves; *multic'ocal* a. & n. (word) susceptible of many meanings; *multic'ular*, having many eyes; *multung'ulate* a. & n. (animal) with more than two functional hoofs.

multifā'rious, a. Having great variety; (w. pl. n.) many & various. Hence ~LY² adv., ~NESS n. [f. LL *multifarius* f. L *-fariam* adv.) & +OUS]

müll'tiple, a. & n. 1. Of many parts, elements, or individual components (~ *shop*, with branches in various places); (w. pl. n.) many & various; ~PERSONALITY. 2. n. Quantity that contains another some number of times without remainder, as *14 is a ~ of 7*; *least common ~*, (abbr. L.C.M.) least quantity that contains two or more given quantities exactly. [F. f. LL *multiplus* =foll.]

müll'tiplex, a. Manifold, of many elements. [L (MULTI-+*plex* -fold)]

müll'tiplicable, a. Multipliable. [f. L *multiplicāre* (as MULTIPLY, see -ABLE)]

müll'tiplicand, n. Quantity to be multiplied, cf. MULTIPLIER. [f. L as MULTIPLY, see -ND¹]

müll'tiplicā'tion, n. Multiplying, esp. the arithmetical process (*symbol of ~*, as in 2×3); ~ *table*, table of products of factors taken in pairs. So **müll'tiplica-TIVE** a. [F, f. L *multiplicātiōnem* (as MULTIPLY, see -ATION)]

müll'tiplic'ity, n. Manifold variety; *a, the, ~* (*great number*) of. [f. L *multiplicitās* (as MULTIPLEX, see -TY]

müll'tiplier, n. In vbl senses, esp.: quantity by which MULTIPLICAND is multiplied; (Econ.) factor by which an increment of income exceeds the resulting increment of saving over or investment; (Electr., Magn.) instrument for multiplying intensity of force, current, etc., so as to make it appreciable. [f. foll. +-ER¹]

müll'tiply, v.t. & i. Produce large number of (instances etc.); breed (animals), propagate (plants); (intr.) increase in number by procreation; (Math.) substitute for (given number, the ~*icand*) a number (the ~*ier*) of times its value, as ~*y 6 by 4 & the product is 24*, or *6 ~ted by 4 is 24*. Hence ~TABLE a. [f. OF *multiplier* f. L *multiplicāre* (MULTIPLEX)]

müll'titude, n. Numerousness; great number (*of*); large gathering of people, crowd; *the ~tude*, the common people. Hence ~TUD'INOUS a., ~TUD'INOUSLY² adv. [f. OF *multitude* f. L *multitūdinem* (*multus* many, see -TUDE)]

müll'titū'dinism, n. Principle that prefers interests of multitudes to those of individuals. So ~IST n. [as prec. +-ISM]

müll'ture, n. Toll of grain or flour paid to miller. [f. OF *molture* f. med. L *molitūra* (*molere -it-* grind, see -URE)]

mūm¹, int. & a. 1. Silence!, esp. ~'s *the word*. 2. adj. Silent. [imit., cf. G *mumm*]

mūm², v.i. (-mm-), Act in dumb show; ~ *chance* (arch.), silent, tongue-tied. [prec.]

mūm³, n. (hist.). Kind of beer orig. brewed in Brunswick. [f. G *mumme*]

|| **mūm'⁴**, n. (nursery). =MUMMY²

mŭm'ble, v.i. & t., & n. 1. Speak indistinctly; utter indistinctly; bite, chew, (as) with toothless gums. 2. n. Indistinct utterance. [(n. f. vb) ME *momele*, as MUM¹, -LE(3)]

Mŭm'bō Jŭm'bō, n. (pl. ~s). Grotesque idol said to have been worshipped by some tribes; (fig.) object of senseless veneration. [?]

mŭm'mer, n. Play-actor (derog.); actor in dumb show (hist.). [f. OF *momeur* (*momer* MUM²)]

mŭm'mery, n. Performance of mummers; ridiculous (esp. religious) ceremonial. [f. OF *mommerie* (as prec, -ERY)]

mŭm'mify, v.t. Preserve (body) by embalming & drying; shrivel, dry up,

(tissues etc., esp. in p.p.). Hence ~FICA-
TION n. [f. F *momifier* (as foll., see -FY)]

mum'my¹, n. 1. Body of human being or animal embalmed for burial; dried-up body. 2. Pulpy substance or mass, esp. *beat (thing) to a ~*. 3. Rich brown pigment. [f. F *momie* f. med. L *mumia* f. Arab. *mumaya* (*mum* wax]

|| **mum'my²**, n. Mother. [nursery form of MAMMA¹]

mump¹, v.i. Be silent & sullen; assume demure expression, whence ~ING² a. [conn. w. MUMPS]

mump², v.i. Beg, go about begging. [prob. f. Du. *mompen* cheat]

mumps, n. pl. (treated as sing.). Contagious disease with swelling of parotid & salivary glands; sulks, whence **mump'**ISH¹ a. [imit.]

munch, v.t. & i. Eat (food, or abs.) with much action of jaws, as cattle chew fodder. [prob. imit.]

Munchausen (-zn), n. *Baron ~*, hero of extravagant book of adventures written in English by R. E. Raspe, a German (1785); extravagantly mendacious story.

mun'dane, a. Of this world; of the universe. Hence ~LY² adv., ~NESS n. [f. F *mondain* f. L *mundanus* (*mundus* world, see -AN)]

|| **mŭnding'us** (-ngg-), n. (arch.). Badsmelling tobacco. [f. Sp. *mondongo* tripe]

mŭng'ō (-ngg-), n. Woollen fibre like SHODDY, but of better quality. [?]

muni'cipal, a. Of, under, local self-government or corporate government of city or town, whence ~ISM(2), 3), nn. ~IZE(3) v.t.; carried on etc. by a municipality (*~ debt, kitchen, trading, undertaking*); *~ law*, that of particular State, opp. to *law of nations*. Hence ~LY² adv. [f. L *municipalis* f. *municeps -cipis* citizen of city that had privileges of Roman citizens (*munia* civic offices + root of *capere* take), see -AL]

municipăl'ity, n. Town, district, having local self-government; governing body of this. [f. F *municipalité* (as prec., see -TY)]

munĭf'icent, a. Splendidly generous, bountiful. Hence or cogn. ~ENCE n., ~ENTLY² adv. [f. L *munificent-*, var. stem of *munificus* (*munus* gift, see -FIC)]

mŭn'iment, n. (usu. pl.). Document kept as evidence of rights or privileges. [OF, f. L *munimentum* defence (*munire* fortify, -MENT)]

muni'tion, n., & v.t. 1. (Pl. exc. in comb.) military weapons, ammunition, equipment, & stores (*Ministry* etc. *of ~s*; *~ factory*); (arch.) *~, or ~s, of war*; hence ~ER¹ (-sho-) n. (usu. *worker in ~-factory*) 2. v.t. Supply with ~s. [(vb f. n.-factory), f. L *munitionem* fortification (as prec., see -ION)]

munnion. = MULLION.

mŭnt'jăk, n. Small Asiatic deer. [f. native *minchek*]

Mŭntz, n. (Also *~ metal*, alloy (60% copper, 40% zinc) used for sheathing ships etc. [G. F. ~, inventor]

mŭr'age, n. (hist.). Tax levied for building or repairing walls of town. [OF, f. med. L *muragium* (*murus* wall, see -AGE]

mur'al, a. & n. 1. Of, like, on, a wall, as *paintings*; (Rom. Ant.) *~ crown*, garland (given to soldiers who first scaled wall of besieged town). 2. n. *~ painting* etc. [F, f. L *muralis* (*murus* wall, see AL]

Mŭrato'rian, a. Of Muratori, Italian scholar, d. 1750; *~ fragment or canon*, earliest Western canon of N.T. [-AN]

mūrd'er, n. Unlawful killing of human being with malice aforethought; JUDICIAL *~*; (prov.) *~ will out* (cannot be hidden); *the ~ is out*, the secret is revealed or mystery explained; (as int. of alarm) *~!*; *cry blue ~*, make extravagant outcry. [OE *morthor*, cf. Goth. *maurthr*, cogn. w. L *mori* die, Gk *brolos* mortal]

mūrd'er², v.t. Kill (human being) unlawfully with malice aforethought; kill wickedly or inhumanly; spoil by bad execution, mispronunciation, etc. Hence ~ER¹, ~ESS¹, nn. [OE *mýrdhrian*, & see prec.]

mūrd'erous, a. (Of person, weapon, action, etc.) capable of, bent on, involving, murder. Hence ~LY² adv. [-OUS]

mūre, v.t. Confine as in prison; shut up. [f. F *murer* f. L *murare*, see IMMURE]

mŭr'ex, n. (pl. -ices, -exes). Shell-fish yielding purple dye. [L, prob. cogn. w. Gk *muax* sea mussel]

mūr'iate, n. (now commerc.). Chloride. [F, f. *muriatique*, as foll.]

mūriăt'ic, a. (now commerc.). *~ (hydrochloric) acid*. [f. L *muriaticus* (*muria* brine, see -ATIC]

mŭrk, mĭrk, a. (arch., poet.). (Of night, day, place, etc.) dark; misty, dense. [OE *mirce* cf. Sw. *mörk*]

mŭrk'y, a. Dark, gloomy; (of darkness) thick. Hence ~LY² adv., ~INESS n. [f. *mark* n. darkness, cogn. w. prec., +-Y²]

mŭrm'ur¹ (-er), n. Subdued continuous sound, as of waves, brook, etc.; subdued expression of discontent; softly spoken word or speech. Hence ~OUS a., ~OUSLY² adv. [f. F *murmure* (as to'l.)]

mŭrm'ur² (-er), v.i. & t. Make low continuous sound; complain in low tones, grumble, (*at, against*); utter (words) in low voice. [f. F *murmurer* f. L *murmurare* (*murmur*)]

mŭrph'y, n. (sl.). Potato. [Irish surname]

mŭr'rain (-rin), n. Infectious disease in cattle; (arch.) *a ~* (plague) *on you!* [f. F *morine*, cf. Sp. *morriña*, perh. f. L *mori* die]

mŭr'rey, a. & n. (arch.). (Of) the colour of a mulberry, purple-red. [f. OF *moré* f. med. L *moratus* (*morum* mulberry]

mu'rrhine (-rīn, -rĭn), a. ~ *glass*, modern delicate ware from the East, made of fluor-spar. [f. L *murr(h)inus* (*murra*, substance of which precious vases etc. were made, see -INE¹)]

mus'cadine, n. Musk-flavoured kinds of grape. [prob. f. Pr. as MUSCAT]

mus'cardine, n. Disease of silkworms caused by vegetable parasite. [F, f. It. *moscad(r)ino* musk-lozenge (ult. as MUSK)]

mus'cat, muscatel', -dĕl', n. Muscadine; strong sweet wine from muscadines; (-*tel*) raisin from muscadine. [Pr., f. It. *moscato* musk-flavoured f. L *muscus* MUSK; (-*tel*, -*dĕl*) OF, dim.]

mu'scle (-sl), n. (-*tel, del*) **1.** Any of the contractile fibrous bands or bundles that produce movement in animal body; *not move a* ~, be perfectly motionless; that part of a ~ the animal body which is composed of ~s, the chief constituent of flesh; ~-*bound*, with ~s stiff & inelastic through over-exercise or over-training; hence ~LESS a. **2.** v.i. ~ *in*, intrude by violent means (as of one racketeer poaching on another's preserves). [f. L *musculus* dim. of *mus* mouse]

musc'ology, n. Study of mosses. So ~OL'OGIST n. [f. L *muscus* moss, -LOGY]

muscova'dō (-vah-), n. Unrefined sugar got from juice of sugar-cane by evaporation & draining off molasses. [f. Sp. *mascabado* of lowest quality]

mus'covite¹, n. Common mica (earlier *Muscovy glass*). [as foll.]

Mus'covite², n. & a. Russian; citizen of Moscow... [f. foll.+-ITE¹]

Mus'covy, n. (Arch.) Russia; ~ *duck*, MUSK-duck. [f. F *Muscovie* f. Russ. *Moskova* Moscow]

mus'cular, a. Of, affecting, the muscles; having well-developed muscles; ~ *Christianity*, ideal of religious character exhibited in writings of C. Kingsley. Hence musculā'RITY n. [as MUSCLE, see -AR¹]

mus'culature n. Muscular system of body or organ. [F, as MUSCLE, see -URE]

muse¹ (-z), n. *The* ~, nine goddesses, daughters of Zeus & Mnemosyne, inspirers of poetry, music, etc. (*Calliope, Clio, Erato, Euterpe, Melpomene, Polyhymnia, Terpsichore, Thalia, Urania*, Muse of epic poetry, history, lyric poetry, comedy, tragedy, sacred song, dancing, astronomy); *the* ~, poet's inspiring goddess, poet's genius; (poet.) poet. [F, f. L f. Gk *Mousa* f. root *men-, mon-*, think, remember]

muse² (-z), v.i. & n. **1.** Ponder, reflect, (*on, upon*); graze meditatively (*on scene* etc.). **2.** n. (arch.) Fit of abstraction. [f. F *muser*, prob. f. OF *muse* MUZZLE², orig. w. sense 'sniff the air when in doubt about scent']

musette' (-z-), n. Kind of bagpipe; soft pastoral air imitating bagpipe's sound; dance for which this served; reed stop on organ. [F, dim. of OF *muse* bagpipe]

muséum (-z-), n. Building used for storing & exhibition of objects illustrative of antiquities, natural history, art, etc.; ~ *piece*, specimen of art, manufacture, etc., fit for a ~ (also derog. of old-fashioned person, machine, etc.). [L, f. Gk *mouseion* seat of the Muses (*Mousa*)]

mush¹, n. Soft pulp; (N.-Amer.) kind of porridge. Hence ~INESS n., ~Y² a. [prob. var. of MASH¹]

‖ **mush²**, n. (sl.) Umbrella; small cab-proprietor. [shortened f. foll.]

mush'room, n., & v.i. **1.** Edible kind of fungus, proverbial for rapid growth (~ *growth* etc., sudden development or thing suddenly developed); (fig.) upstart; (colloq.) lady's straw hat with down-curved brim. **2.** v.i. Gather ~s; (of bullet) expand & flatten. [xvi f. n., f. F *mousseron*, perh. f. *mousse* moss]

mus'ic (-z-), n. Art of combining sounds with a view to beauty of form & expression of emotion; sounds so produced; pleasant sound, e.g. song of bird, murmur of brook, cry of hounds; *set* (poem etc.) *to* ~, provide it with ~ to which it may be sung; written or printed score of musical composition; *face the* ~, face one's critics etc., not shirk; *rough* ~, noisy uproar, esp. with vexations intention; ~ *box*, =MUSICAL *box*; ~-*hall* ‖(used for singing, dancing, & other entertainments); ~-*stool* (with adjustable seat, for piano-player). [f. F *musique* f. L f. Gk *mousikē* (*teknē* art) of the Muses (*Mousa* Muse, see -IC)]

mus'ical (-z-), a. & n. **1.** Of music; (of sounds, voice, etc.) melodious, harmonious; fond of, skilled in, music; set to, accompanied by, music; ~ *box*, mechanical instrument played by causing toothed cylinder to work in comb-like metal plate; ~ *chairs*, drawing-room game in which *n* players circulate round *n*-1 chairs till piano ceases, when the one who finds no seat is eliminated, and a chair is removed before the next round; ~ *comedy*, light dramatic entertainment of songs, dialogue, & dancing connected by a slender plot; ~ *film* (in which music is an important feature); ~ *glasses*, kinds of ~ instrument in which notes are produced by graduated glass bowls or tubes; ~ *ride*, military equestrian dance-like exercise performed to ~ accompaniment. **2.** n. (colloq.) ~ film; *MUSICALE. Hence musicAL'ITY, ~NESS, nn., ~LY² adv. [f. med. L *musicalis* (*musica* MUSIC, see -AL¹)]

*musicale' (-zĭkahl), n. Musical party. [F, for *soirée* or *matinée* ~]

musi'cian (-zĭshn), n. Person skilled in science or practice of music. [f. F *musicien* (as MUSIC, see -CIAN)]

musk, n. Odoriferous reddish-brown substance secreted in gland by male deer, used for perfumes & as stimulant etc.; kinds of plant with ~y smell; ~deer, small hornless ruminant of Central Asia; ~duck (also *Muscovy duck*), tropical American variety, (also) Australian variety male of which has ~y smell; ~ox, ruminant found in Arctic America, with strong ~y smell; ~rat (also *musquash*), large N.Amer. aquatic rodent, its fur; ~rose, rambling rose with large fragrant white flowers; ~tree, ~wood, trees with ~y smell. Hence **músk'y²** a. [f. F *musc* f. LL *muscus* f. late Gk *mosk(h)os* perh. ult. f. Skr. *muska* scrotum]

muskèteer', n. (hist.). Soldier armed with musket. [-EER]

mús'kètrý² n. Muskets; art of using, troops armed with, muskets; (Mil., in mod. use) instruction, practice, in rifle-shooting. [f. F *mousqueterie* (as MUSKET, see -ERY)]

Muslim. See MOSLEM.

mús'lin (-z-), n. Kinds of delicately woven cotton fabric for ladies' dresses, curtains, etc.; (colloq.) *bit of ~*, woman, girl; ~-de-laine, (as MOUSSELINE f. It. ~ED² (-nd) a. [f. F *mousseline* f. It. *mussolina* (*Mussolo*, town in Mesopotamia whence ~ came, see -INE¹)]

múslinét' (-z-), n. Thick kind of muslin. [-ET¹]

mús'mon, n. = MOUFFLON. [f. L *musimo*(n) f. late Gk *mousmōn*]

mús'quash (-ŏsh), n. (Fur of) MUSK-rat. [f. Algonkin *muskwessu*]

múss¹, v.t., & n. (colloq.). **1.** Disarrange, throw into disorder (*up*). **2.** n. State of confusion, untidiness, mess. Hence ~Y² a. [prob. var. of MESS]

múss², n. (Anglo-Ind.). Leather water-bag. [Hind. *masak*]

Mússulman, n. & a. (pl. ~s). Mohammedan. [f. Pers. *musulmān* (as MOSLEM)]

múss'el, n. Kinds (*Sea*, *Fresh-water*, *M~*) of bivalve mollusc; ~ *plum*, dark purple plum. [OE *muscle* f. LL *muscula*, fem. as MUSCLE]

múst¹, n. New wine; grape-juice before fermentation is complete. [f. L *mustum* neut. of *mustus* new]

múst² n. Mustiness, mould. [prob. back formation f. MUSTY]

múst³, a. & n. **1.** (Of male elephants & camels) in state of frenzy. **2.** n. This state. [f. Hind. f. Pers. *mast* intoxicated]

múst, v. auxil. (3rd sing. *must*; past *must*, only as below; no infin. or part. or gerund). Be obliged to (do), as *you* ~ (neg. *need not*, see below & cf. MAY¹) *find it*, ~ *it* ~ *be found*, (w. necessity less emphasized) *we* ~ *see what can be done*, I ~ *ask you to retract that*, *you* ~ *know* (I now tell you); be certain to (do), as *you* ~ *lose*, *whichever happens*; *you* ~ *be* (surely are) *aware of this*; *he* ~ *be* (clearly is) *mad*; (as past tense, reporting reflection made at the time) *it was too late now to retreat*, *he* ~ *make good his word or incur lasting disgrace*; (past or historic present, w. reference to perverse destiny) *just as I was getting better*, *what* ~ *I do but break my leg!*, *just as I was busied*, *he* ~ *come worrying*; ~ *have done*, (1) surely did, as *you* ~ *have known quite well what I meant*, (2) necessarily would have done, as *you* ~ *have caught it if you had run*; (w. negative belonging in sense to dependent vb., cf. MAY¹) *you* ~ *not infer* (~ avoid the inference), *you* ~ *never contradicted*. [OE *mōste*, past of *mōt* (later *mote*) may, be permitted to, cf. Du. *moet*, G *muss*]

mustache. See MOUSTACHE.

*músta'chio (-ahsho), n. (arch.; pl. ~s). Moustache. [(partly f. Sp. *mostacho*) f. It. as MOUSTACHE]

mús'táng, n. Wild horse of Mexico & California; ~ (small red Texas) grape. [f. Sp. *mestengo*, perh. f. *mesta* company of *graziers*]

mús'tard, n. Kinds of plant, esp. *black & white*, ~ seeds of which are ground, made into paste, & used as condiment or for poultice or ~ *plaster*; (fig.) *zestful thing or person* (sl.); *grain of* ~ *seed*, small thing capable of vast development (*Matt.* xiii. 31); || ~ & *cress* (used in seed-leaf for salad); *French* ~ (mixed with vinegar); ~ *gas*, kind of liquid poison gas, a powerful irritant & vesicant; ~*-pot* (for table ~), [orig. of the condiment; f. OF *moustarde* f. com.-Rom. *mosto* MUST¹]

mús'ter¹, n. Assembling of men for inspection etc. (*pass* ~, be accepted as adequate), assembly, collection; ~*-book*, (for registering military forces); ~*-roll*, official list of officers & men in army or ship's company (also fig.). [f. OF *mostre* f. L *monstrare show*]

mús'ter², v.t. & i. Collect (orig. soldiers) for inspection, to check numbers, etc.; collect, get together, (t. & i.); summon (courage, strength, etc.; often *up*). [f. OF *mostrer* f. L as prec.]

mús't[y, a. Mouldy; of mouldy or stale smell or taste; (fig.) stale, antiquated. Hence ~INESS n. [?]

mút'able, a. Liable to change; fickle. Hence **mútabil'ïty** n. [f. L *mutabilis* (*mutare* change, see -BLE)]

mútā'tion, n. Change, alteration; (Biol.) change resulting in production of new species; (Mus.) ~ *stop*, organ stop in

which notes produced are not at normal pitch but at that of some harmonic (other than mere octaves). [F. f. L *mutationem* (as prec., see -ATION)]

mutā'tis mutā'ndis, adv. With due alteration of details (in comparing cases). [L.]

‖ **mŭtch**, n. (Sc.) Woman's or child's linen cap. [f. MDu. *mutse*, cf. G *mütze*]

mūte[1], a. & n. 1. Silent; not emitting articulate sound; (Law) *stand ~ of malice*, refuse deliberately to plead; (of person or animal) dumb; (of hounds) not giving tongue; not expressed in speech, as ~ *appeal*, *adoration*; temporarily bereft of speech; (of consonant) produced by entire interruption of passage of breath or complete closure of organs of mouth, stopped, (usu. applied to *b p ph d t th k g*); (of letter) not pronounced, as the *e* in *late* is ~. 2. n. ~ consonant; dumb person; actor whose part is in dumb show; dumb servant in Oriental countries; hired mourner; clip for deadening resonance of strings of violin etc., pad for deadening sound of wind instrument. Hence ~LY[2] adv., ~NESS n. [f. F *muet* f. pop. L *mutitus* dim. of L *mudus*]

mūte[2], v.t. Deaden, muffle, the sound of (esp. musical instrument). [f. prec.]

mūte[3], v.i. & t. (Of birds) void the faeces, discharge thus. [f. OF *mutir* etym. dub.]

mŭt'ilāte, v.t. Deprive (person etc.) of limb or organ; cut off, destroy the use of, (limb etc.); render (book etc.) imperfect by excision etc. So ~ATION, ~ātor[2] nn. [f. L *mutilare* (*mutilus* maimed), see -ATE[3]]

mūtineer', n. One who mutinies. [f. F *mutinier* (*mutin* rebellious, ult. f. L as MOVE)]

mū'tinous, a. Rebellious. Hence ~LY[2] +-OUS]

mū'tiny, n. & v.i. 1. Open revolt against constituted authority, esp. of soldiers etc. against officers; *Indian M~*, revolt of Bengal native troops, 1857-8; *M~ Act* (dealing with offences against military & naval discipline, now embodied in Army Act, 1881). 2. v.i. Revolt (*against* or abs.). [vb f. n. as prec. +-Y[1]]

mū'tism, n. Muteness; silence; dumbness. [f. F *mutisme* f. L as MUTE[1], see -ISM]

mūt'ō-, comb. form (irreg.) of L *mutare* change, as: ~*graph*, apparatus for taking series of photographs of moving objects, etc. (v.t.) portray with this; ~*scope*, apparatus for exhibiting scene recorded by ~*graph*, so ~*scopic* a.

mŭtt, n. (sl.). Ignorant blunderer, dunderhead; small dog (derog.). [perh. abbr. of *mutton-head*]

mŭtt'er, v.i. & t., & n. 1. Speak low in barely audible manner; murmur, grumble, (*against*, *at*); utter (words etc.) in low

tone; (fig.) say in secret. 2. n. ~ing; ~ed words. [prob. imit. w. suf. -ER[5]]

mŭtt'on, n. Flesh of sheep as food; (joc.) *sheep* (*to our ~s*, gallicism=let us come back to our subject); *dead as ~*, quite dead; *eat one's ~*, dine *with*; ~ *chop*, piece of ~ (usu. rib & half vertebra to which it is attached) for frying etc., side whisker shaped like this; ~ *dressed like lamb* (colloq.), elderly woman got up to look young; ~*head* (colloq.), dull, stupid person. Hence ~Y[2] a. [f. OF *moton* f. med. L *mutonem* nom. -to, cf. Olr. *molt* ram.]

mūt'ūal, a. (Of feelings, actions, etc.) felt, done, by each to(wards) the other, as ~ *affection*, *benefit*, *suspicion*; standing in (specified) ~ *relation*, as ~ *well-wishers*; (*admiration society*, set of persons who overestimate each other's merits; ~ *insurance company* (in which some or all of the profits are divided among the policy-holders); (Commerce) ~ *terms* (by which exchange of services takes the place of money payments); (improp.) common to two or more persons, as *our* ~ *friend*. Hence **mūtŭǎl'ITY** n., ~LY[2] adv. [f. F *mutuel* f. L *mutuus* borrowed (cf. *mutare* change), see -AL]

mūt'ūalism, n. Doctrine that mutual dependence is necessary to well-being. So ~IST n. [-ISM]

mūt'ūle, n. (archit.), Modillion proper to cornice in Doric order. [F, f. L *mutulus*]

‖ **mŭzhik**, n. See MUJIK.

‖ **mŭzz**, v.t. (sl.). Make muzzy. [?]

mŭz'zle, n. Projecting part of animal's head including nose & mouth; open end of fire-arm; contrivance of strap or wire put over animal's head to prevent its biting, eating, etc.; ~*loader*, gun that is loaded at the ~. [f. OF *musel* f. med. L *musellum* dim. of *musus*]

mŭz'zle[2], v.t. Put muzzle on (animal, its mouth, &, fig., a person); impose silence upon; take in (sail). [f. prec.]

mŭzz'y, a. Dull, spiritless; stupid from drinking. Hence ~ILY[2] adv., ~INESS n. [?]

my (mī, mǐ), poss. adj. of 1st pers. sing. (with abs. form MINE); (prefixed to some terms of address) *my boy*, *friend*, *man*, *son*, *daughter*, (not colloq. w. other terms of relationship), *dear*, *darling*, *love*; *my* (vulg. *mine*) & *her* (common) *father*, *my* (vulg. *mine*) & *her* (respective) *father*(s); *mi*, reduced f. OE *mīn* MINE[1])

myǎl'gia, n. (path.). Muscular rheumatism. [Gk *mus* muscle, *algos* pain, -IA[2]]

my'alism, n. Kind of sorcery practised esp. in W. Indies. [prob. of W.-Afr. orig.]

my'all, n. (Austral.). Acacia, with scented wood used for pipes. [f. native *maial*]

mȳcēl'ium, n. (bot.). Spawn of fungi. Hence ~AL a. [f. Gk *mukēs* mushroom +]

Mycenae'an, a. (archaeol.). Of the prehellenic or Achaean culture illustrated by remains at Mycenae in Greece, & by Homer. [f. L f. Gk *Mukēnaios* +-AN]

mycetō'ma, n. Fungoid disease of foot or hand. [as MYCELIUM, see -M]

mycōl'ogȳ, n. Study of fungi. So ~IST n. [irreg. f. Gk as prec, see -LOGY]

mycō'sis, n. Presence of, disease caused by, parasitic fungi. [as prec, see -OSIS]

myelit'is, n. Inflammation of spinal cord. [f. Gk *muelos* marrow, see -ITIS]

my̆'lodŏn, n. Extinct genus of gigantic sloths with cylindrical teeth. [f. Gk *mulē* mill + *odous -ontos* tooth]

myna. = MINA².

my̆nheer', n. Dutchman. [f. Du. *mijn-heer* Mr, sir, (*mijn* my + *heer* master)]

my̆o- in comb. = Gk *mus muos* muscle, as: ~*cardium*, muscular substance of heart, whence ~cardiT'IS; *my̆ŏl'ogy*, science of muscles.

my̆'ŏpe, n. Short-sighted person. Hence or cogn. my̆ŏp'IA¹, my̆'ŏpY¹, nn., my̆ŏp² IC a. [f. f. LL f. Gk *muōps (muō* shut + *ōps* eye)]

my̆ŏs'is, n. Contraction of pupil of eye. So MYʹOT'IC a. [f. Gk *muō* shut, see -OSIS]

my̆'osŏte, n. Forget-me-not. [f. foll.]

my̆osŏt'is, n. Genus of small plants with blue, pink, or white flowers. [f. L f. Gk *muosōtis (mus muos* mouse + *ous ōtos* ear)]

my̆'riad, a. & n. 1. n. (poet., rhet.). Ten thousand ; (of) indefinitely great number. [f. LL f. Gk *murias -ados (murioi* 10,000)]

my̆'riapŏd, a. & n. (Animal) with many legs, of the class comprising centipedes & millepedes. [as prec. + Gk *pous podos* foot]

my̆riora'ma (-rah-, -rä-), n. Entertainment consisting of series of views. [f. Gk *murios* countless + *horama* view (*horaō* see)]

myrm'idon (mẽr-), n. (M~) any of a warlike Thessalian race who followed Achilles ; hired ruffian ; base servant, as ~ *of the law*, policeman, bailiff, etc. [f. L f. Gk *Murmidones* pl.]

my̆rŏb'alan, n. Astringent plum-like fruit used in dyeing, tanning, etc. [f. L *myrobalanum* f. Gk *myrobalanos (muron* unguent + *balanos* acorn)]

myrrh¹ (mẽr), n. Gum resin used in perfumery & medicine. [f. OE *myrra*, f. L f. Gk *murra*]

myrrh² (mẽr), n. Sweet Cicely, an aromatic plant. [f. LL f. Gk *murris*]

myr'tle (mẽr-), n. Genus of plants, esp. *Common M~*, shrub with shiny evergreen leaves & white scented flowers, sacred to Venus. So **myrta'CEOUS** (mẽrtā'shus) a., of family *Myrtaceae* (~ etc.). [f. OF *myrtille*, dim. f. L f. Gk *murtos* marra]

myself', pron. Emphatic & reflexive form corresp. to I, as *I saw it* ~, *I* ~ (for my part), *am doubtful, I have hurt* ~; *I am not* ~ (in my normal state of body or

mind). [f. ME + SELF ; *my-* perh. on anal. of *herself*]

my̆s'tagogue (-ŏg), n. Teacher of mystical doctrines, esp. (Gk Ant.) to candidates for initiation in Eleusinian & other mysteries. So **my̆stagŏ'gIC**(AL) aa. [f. L f. Gk *mustagōgos (mustēs* one initiated into mysteries, f. *muō* close eyes or lips, + *agōgos* -leading f. *agō* lead)]

my̆ster'ious, a. Full of, wrapt in, mystery ; (of persons) delighting in mystery. Hence ~LY² adv., ~NESS n. [f. foll. + -OUS]

my̆s'tery¹, n. Hidden or inexplicable matter ; *make a* ~ *of*, treat as a secret ; secrecy, obscurity, as *is wrapt in* ~; (practice of) making a secret of (unimportant) things ; religious truth divinely revealed, esp. one beyond human reason ; religious rite, esp. (pl.) Eucharist ; (pl.) secret religious rites of Greeks, Romans, etc. ; miracle-play ; ~*ship*, warship disguised as tramp steamer etc. to decoy submarines in the 1914-18 war. [f. OF *mistere* f. L f. Gk *mustērion (muō* close lips or eyes)]

∥**my̆s'tery²**, n. (arch.). Handicraft, trade, esp. (in indentures) *art &* ~. [f. med. L *mi(ni)sterium* (MINISTER), confused w. prec.]

my̆s'tic, a. & n. 1. Spiritually allegorical ; occult, esoteric ; of hidden meaning, mysterious ; mysterious & awe-inspiring. 2. n. One who seeks by contemplation & self-surrender to obtain union with or absorption into the Deity, or who believes in spiritual apprehension of truths beyond the understanding, whence ~ISM n. (often derog.). Hence ~AL a., ~alLY² adv., ~IZE(3) v.t. [f. OF *mystique* f. L f. Gk *mustikos* (as MYSTERY¹, -IC)]

my̆s'tify, v.t. Hoax, play on credulity of ; bewilder ; wrap up in mystery. So ~FICA² TION n. [f. F *mystifier* (irreg. as prec, -FY)]

my̆th (or mĭ-), n. Purely fictitious narrative usu. involving supernatural persons etc. & embodying popular ideas on natural phenomena, etc. ; fictitious person or thing. Hence **my̆th'IC**(AL) aa., **my̆th'i-calLY²** adv. [f. Gk *muthos*]

my̆th'iclize, v.t. Treat (story etc.) as a myth, interpret mythically. So ~ISM, ~IST, nn. [MYTHO¹ + -IZE]

my̆tho- in comb. = Gk *muthos* myth, as: ~*grapher* (-ŏg²), writer of myths ; *my̆'thŏȳ* (-ŏg²), representation of myths in plastic art ; ~*poeic* (-pē'ĭk), ~*poet'ic*, making, productive of, myths ; ~*po'et*, ~*po'etry*, poetical writer, writing, of myths.

mythŏl'ogȳ (or mĭ-), n. Body of myths, esp. relating to particular person or subject ; study of myths. Hence or cogn. ~ER², -IST, nn., **my̆thŏlŏ'gIC**(AL) aa., **my̆thŏlŏ'gicalLY²** adv., ~IZE(2, 3) v.t. & i. [f. Gk *muthologia* (see prec. & -LOGY)]

my̆th'us, n. Myth. [mod. L, as MYTH]

myxoedēm'a (-ēd-), n. A metabolic disease caused by sluggish working or atrophy of the thyroid gland, & characterized by thickening of the subcutaneous tissues & loss of physical & mental energy. [f. Gk *muxa* mucus + OEDEMA]

N

N (en), letter (pl. *Ns, N's*), (Print.) n (also *en*) unit of measurement; (Math.) indefinite number (*to the nth*, to any required degree; also fig., to any extent, to the utmost); *N-rays, N¹-rays*, forms of radiation. [=

nāb, v.t. (sl.; -bb-). Apprehend, arrest; catch in wrong-doing. [?]

nā̆b'ŏb, n. (Hist.) Mohammedan official or governor under Mogul empire; (arch.) wealthy luxurious person, esp. one returned from India with fortune. [= NAWAB]

Nāb'ŏth's vine'yard (-ny-), n. Possession that one will stick at nothing to secure. [see 1 Kings xxi]

nā̆c'arăt, n. Bright orange-red colour. [F, perh. f. Sp. & Port. *nacarado* (NACRE)]

nacelle', n. Outer casing of aeroplane's engine; car of airship. [F, f. LL *navicella* dim. of L *navis* ship]

nā̆'cre (-ker), n. Pinna or sea-pen; (shell-fish yielding) mother of pearl. Hence **nā̆c'reous, nā̆c'rous**, aa. [F, = Sp. & Port. *nacar*, etym. dub.]

nā̆'dir, n. Point of heavens directly under observer (opp. ZENITH); (transf.) lowest point, place or time of greatest depression etc. [f. Arab. *nazir* (*as-samt*) opposite to (zenith)]

nā̆g¹, n. Small riding horse or pony; horse (colloq.). [?]

nă̆g², v.i. & t. (-gg-). Find fault or scold (at person); annoy thus. Hence ~**g'ing¹** (-g-) n. [cf. Norw. & Sw. *nagga* gnaw]

naga'na (-ahnə), n. (S. Africa). Tsetse-fly disease. [Zulu *nakane*]

năg'ôr, n. Senegal antelope. [wd made by Button]

nai'ad (nī-), n. (pl. ~s, ~es pr. -ēz). Water-nymph. [f. L f. Gk *naias -ados* (*naō* flow)]

nail¹, n. 1. Horny covering of outer tip of finger & upper tip of toe (~-*brush*, -*scissors*, for cleaning & paring ~s; TOOTH &~), whence ~-ED²(-ld) a.; claw, talon; hard excrescence on some soft-billed birds' upper mandible. 2. Small metal spike usu. with point & broadened head driven in with hammer to hold things together or as peg or ornament (*hit* ~, or *right* ~, *on head*, give true explanation, propose or do right thing, hit the mark; ~ *in one's COFFIN*; *on the* ~, without delay, esp. of payment; *right as* ~s, in fine training); *right as* ~s, quite right); ~

head, architectural ornament. 3. An old measure of length (2¼ in.). Hence ~**LESS** a. [OE *nægel* cf. Du. & G *nagel*, cogn. w. L *unguis*, Gk *onux*]

nail², v.t. Fasten with nails (*on, to, together, down, in*, etc.; ~ *colours to mast*, persist; ~ *to counter, barndoor*, expose as spurious, vile; ~ *up*, close, affix at height, with nails; ~*ed-up drama*, ill-constructed, loosely put together); fix or keep fixed (person, attention, etc.); secure, catch, engage, succeed in getting hold of, (person or thing). [OE *næglan* cf. prec.]

nail'er, n. Nail-maker, whence **nail'ERY**(3) n.; (sl.) excellent specimen, person very skilful at. [-ER¹]

nail'ing, a. In vbl senses; also (sl.) splendid, excellent (*it a* ~, or ~ *good, race*). [-ING²]

nain'sook, n. Fine cotton fabric, orig. Indian. [f. Hind. *nainsukh* (*nain* eye, *sukh* pleasure)]

nā̆'ive (nah-ēv), a. Artless, unaffected; amusingly simple. Hence **naïve'ry¹, naïve'ly** (-vl-), adv., **naïveté** (naïve-ēv'tā), **naïvery** (nah-ēv'ri), **naïve'ety**, n. [F, fem. of *naïf* f. L *nativus* NATIVE]

nā̆k'ed, a. Unclothed, nude, (*as* ~ *as my mother bore me*); defenceless; unsheathed; plain, undisguised, (*the* ~ *truth*; ~ *facts*; *in its* ~ *absurdity*), exposed for examination (*his* ~ *heart*); devoid of; treeless, leafless, barren; (of rock) exposed; (of rooms) unfurnished; without ornament; (of candles etc.) exposed to air; without pericarp, leaves, hairs, scales, shell, etc.; without addition, comment, support, evidence, etc. (~ *faith, quotations, word, assertion*); unassisted (~ *eye*, without telescope etc.); ~ LADY, ~ BOYS, meadow saffron. Hence ~**ly²** adv., ~**NESS** n. (*the* ~*ness of the land*, person's or institution's or State's lack of resources or openness to attack; see Gen. xliii. 9). [OE *nacod, næced*, cf. Du. *naakt*, G *nackt*, cogn. w. L *nudus*]

nā̆k'er, n. (hist.). Kettledrum. [f. OF *nacre*, f. Arab. & Pers. *naqārā(h)*]

nă̆m'by-păm'bŷ, a. & n. 1. Insipidly pretty, mildly sentimental. 2. n. Talk of this kind. [formed on name of Ambrose Philips, pastoral writer, d. 1749]

nāme, n. 1. Word by which individual person, animal, place, or thing is spoken of or to (*mention person by* ~, *by* ~, *by* ~ *Tom*, called; *know by* ~; *Tom by* ~, also by hearsay only; *of or by the* ~ *of*, called; *put one's* ~ *down for*, apply as candidate etc.; *keep one's* ~ *on, take one's* ~ *off, the books*, remain, cease to be, member of college, club, etc.). 2. Word denoting any object of thought, esp. one applicable to many individuals (*call person* ~s, describe him by uncomplimentary ~s; *give it a* ~, mention the drink, present, etc., that you wish). 3. Person as known, famed, or spoken of (*adore the* ~ *of God*; *Nelson himself &*

many great ~s were there. **4.** All who go under one ~, family, clan, people. **5.** Reputation (*has an ill, a good,* ~; *has a ~ for honesty, the ~ of being honest; win oneself a ~; bequeath a great ~; persons of ~; one's good ~*). **6.** Merely nominal existence, practically non-existent thing, (opp. *fact, reality, deed; virtuous in ~; honour had become a ~*). **7.** In person's ~, in the ~ of, invoking, relying upon, calling to witness, (*in God's ~; in the ~ of goodness, fortune, common sense*), acting as deputy for or in the interest of (*in one's own ~*, independently, without authority); ~-*child*, one named after another (*my* etc. ~-*child*); ~-*day*, day of saint after whom person is named (esp. of continental sovereigns); ~-*part*, that after which play is named, title-role; ~-*sake* (-ms-), person or thing with same ~ as another (*his* etc. ~*sake*) [prob. f. phr. *for the ~'s sake*]. [Aryan; OE *nama*, cf. Du. *naam*, G *name*, Skr. *naman*, L *nomen*, Gk *onoma*]

name², v.t. Give name to (*after, from*); call so-&-so; call (person, thing) by right name; nominate, appoint (*to office* etc.); mention, specify, (*not to be ~d on* or *in same day with*, quite inferior to; ~ *your price*); ∥ (of Speaker) mention (M.P.) as disobedient to Chair (~!, vb or n., appeal to do this, or to give name of some person alluded to in speech); cite as instance; specify as something desired (~ *the day*, of woman fixing date for wedding). Hence **nām´ABLE** a. [OE (*ge*)*namian* as prec.]

name´less (-ml-), a. Obscure, inglorious; not mentioned by name, left unnamed on purpose (esp. *who shall be* ~); anonymous, unknown; having no name, bearing no name-inscription; inexpressible, indefinable; too bad to be named, abominable, loathsome, (esp. ~ *vices*). [-LESS]
name´ly (-ml-), adv. That is to say, viz. [NAME¹, -LY²]
∥ **narmnet.** Var. of NUMMET.
nan´cy, n. & a. (sl.). Effeminate (man or boy); homosexual. [pet-form of female name *Ann*]
∥ **nankeen´**, n. Kind of cotton cloth orig. made of naturally yellow cotton; (pl.) trousers of this; yellow or pale buff colour. [f. *Nankin(g)* in China]
nann´y, n. ~(-*goat*), she-goat (cf. BILLY); child's nurse. [f. the female name]
∥ **Nāntz**, n. (arch.). Brandy (often *right* ~). [f. *Nantes* in France]
nap¹, v.i. (-pp-), & n. **1.** Sleep lightly or briefly (*catch ~ping*, find asleep, take unawares, detect in negligence or error). **2.** n. Short sleep, doze, esp. by day (often *take a* ~). [n. f. vb, OE *hnappian*, cf. OHG (*h*)*naffez*]
nap², n., & v.t. (-pp-). **1.** Surface given to cloth by raising & then cutting & smoothing the short fibres, pile, whence ~LESS a.; soft or downy surface. **2.** v.t. Raise ~ on (cloth). [f. MDu. or MLG *noppe(n)*]
nap³, n. A card-game (~ *hand*, fig., position that justifies confident expectation of winning if one takes a risk: *go* ~, also fig.); (Betting) the putting of all one's money on one chance, a tipster's choice for this. [abbr. of *Napoleon*]
nāpe, n. Back of or usu. of neck. [?]
nap´ery, n. (Sc. & arch.). Household, esp. table, linen. [f. obs. F *naperie* (NAPKIN, -ERY)]
nāph´tha, n. Kinds of inflammable oil got by dry distillation of organic substances, as coal, shale, or petroleum. [L, f. Gk, = inflammable volatile liquid issuing from earth]
nāph´thal¦ene, -ine, n. White crystalline substance got in distilling coal-tar & used in manufacture of dyes etc. Hence ~IZE(5) v.t. [prec. + -L + -ENE, -INE⁵]
nap´kin, n. (Also *table-*~) square piece of linen for wiping lips or fingers with at meals, or serving fish etc. on; small towel esp. for nursery purposes, baby's diaper; ~*ring*, to distinguish person's table-~. [prob. f. F *nappe* f. L *mappa* table-cloth + -KIN]
napōl´eon, n. French gold twenty-franc piece of Napoleon I (*double* ~, forty-franc piece); kind of top-boot; the game NAP³. [f. name of French emperor]
Napōlēon´lic, a. Of, like, etc., Napoleon I. Hence or cogn. ~ICALLY² adv., **Napōlēonism**(3), **Napōl´ēonist**(2), nn., **Napōl´ēonize**(4) v.t. & i. [as prec., -IC]
∥ **napōō** (nah-). int. (obs. army sl.). Vanished!, lost!, done!, finished!, no go! [f. F (*il n'y en a plus* there is no more of it)]
nāpp´y¹, a. (arch.). (Of ale etc.) foaming, heady, strong. [perh. f. NAP², -Y²]
∥ **nāpp´y²**, n. (colloq.). Baby's napkin. [abbr.; see -Y³]
napu (nah´pōō), n. Musk-deer of Java & Sumatra. [Malay]
nar´cēīne, n. Alkaloid got from opium occas. used instead of morphine. [f. Gk *narkē* numbness + -INE⁵]
nārcīss´¦ism, n. (psycho-anal.). Tendency to self-worship, absorption in one's own personal perfections. Hence ~īs´tᵒ a. [Gk *Narkissos* youth who fell in love with his reflection in water, -ISM]
nārcīss´us, n. (pl. ~uses, ~ī). Kinds of bulbous plant, esp. one bearing heavily scented single white flower with undivided corona edged with crimson & yellow. [L, f. Gk *narkissos* perh. as NARCINE w. ref. to narcotic effect]
nārc´olepsy, n. Disease with fits of somnolence. [f. Gk *narkē* numbness + (EP)ILEPSY]
nārcōs´is, n. Operation or effects of narcotics; state of insensibility. [f. Gk *narkōsis* (*narkoō* benumb)]

nar cot´ic, a. & n. (Substance) inducing drowsiness, sleep, stupor, or insensibility; soporific (a. & n.); of narcosis. Hence ~ICALLY adv., narcotiza´TION n. [f. Gk *narkōtikos* (prec., -IC)]

nar´cotize(2), v.t. [f. Gk *narkōtikos* ...]

nard, n. (Plant yielding) aromatic balsam of ancients. [f. L f. Gk *nardos* f. Oriental wd]

nar´ghile (-gīlē), n. Oriental tobacco-pipe with smoke passed through water, hookah. [f. Pers. *nargīleh* (*nargīl* coco-nut)]

nark, n. (sl.) Police decoy or spy. [Romany *nāk* nose]

narr´ate, v.t. Relate, recount, give continuous account of, (abs.) utter or write narrative. Hence or cogn. ~A´TION, ~āt´or,² ~āt´ress,¹ nn. [f. L *narrare* (-*rat*-), f. *gnarus* aware, cogn. w. KNOW, -ATE³]

narr´ative, n. & a. 1. Tale, story, recital of facts; kind of composition or talk that confines itself to these. 2. adj. In the form of, concerned with, narration, whence ~LY² adv. [f. L *narrativus* a. (prec., -IVE)]

narr´ow (-ō), a. (~er, ~est) & n. & v.i. & t. 1. Of small width in proportion to length, wanting in breadth, constricted, (the ~ *way*, righteousness, see Matt. vii. 14; ~ *vowels*, made with tongue & uvula tense;) ~ *sense*; ~ *circumstances*, (*after a* poverty); with little margin (*a ~ major-ity, escape*); lacking in breadth of view or sympathy, illiberal, prejudiced, exclusive, self-centred, whence ~mind´ED² a., ~mind´edly² adv., ~mind´edNESS n.; searching, precise, exact, (*after a examination*); ~ *cloth*, under 52 in., of single width; ~ *goods*, ribbons, braid, etc.; ~ GAUGE on railway; any of less than 4ft 8½in. (formerly, the gauge of 4ft 8¼in.); ||~ *seas*, English & Irish channels; hence ~² (-ōl) n. 2. n. (usn. pl.,) ~ part of a sound, strait, river, pass, or street. 3. vb. Make or become ~er, diminish, lessen, contract. [OE *nearu*, cf. Du. *naar* dismal]

nā´thex, n. Railed-off western portico or ante-nave in early Christian churches for women, penitents, & catechumens. [Gk (-ēx), orig. name of a plant=FERULA]

nā´whal(-wəl), n. Arctic delphinoid cetacean with straight horn(s) developed from one or both of its two teeth. [f. Da. *narhval* cf. ON *náhvalr* (perh. *nár* corpse w. allusion to its colour, WHALE)]

nās´al(-z-), a. & n. 1. Of the nose (~ *organ*, joo, nose). 2. (Of letters or sounds) requiring the nose passage to be open (n, such a letter etc., e.g. *m, n, ng*), of voice or speech) having the twang described as speaking through the nose, whence ~IZE(2, 3) v.i. & t., ~IZA´TION n., (-z-). Hence nasal´ITY n., ~LY² adv., (-z-). [f. med. L *nasalis* (L *nasus* nose, -AL)]

nas´cent, a. In the act of being born, just beginning to be, not yet mature. So **nás´CENCY** n. [f. L *nasci* be born -ENT]

nāse´berry (-zb-), n. W.-Ind. tree yielding Sapodilla plum. [f. Sp., Port., *néspera* -ENT]

nās´o- (-z-), comb. form of L *nasus* nose, as ~*from/tal* of nose & forehead.

nastúr´tium (-shm), n. (Bot.) genus of pungent-tasted cruciferous plants including watercress; trailing garden plant with bright orange flowers, Indian cress. [L, derived by Pliny f. *nasus* nose, *torquēre tort-* pain]

nas´ty, (nah-), a. Disgustingly dirty, filthy; obscene, delighting in obscenity; disagreeable to smell or taste, unpalatable lit. & fig., annoying, objectionable, (of weather etc.) foul, wet, stormy; hard to deal with or get rid of, serious, (*a ~y sea, fence, blow, illness; a ~y one*, rebuff, snub, disabling blow, etc.); ill-natured, spiteful *to*. Hence ~INESS n. [from 1400; etym. dub.; cf. Du. *nestig* dirty]

na´tal, a. Of, from, one's birth. [f. L *natalis* (NATION, -AL)]

natá´tion, n. Swimming. [f. L *natatio* (*natare* swim, -ATION)]

natatór´ial, **natat´ory**, aa. Swimming, of swimming. [LL *natatorius* (prec.), -ORY, -AL]

nat´es (-z), n. pl. (anat.) Buttocks; anterior pair of optic lobes in brain. [L]

nāthe´less(-thi-), adv. (arch.). Nevertheless. [f. OE *nā* (*ne* not, *ā* ever)+THE+LESS]

nā´tion, n. Distinct race or people having common descent, language, history, or political institutions (*most favoured ~*, to which State accords lowest scale of import duties); ||(in medieval & some Scots univv.) body of students from particular country or district; LAW of ~s; LEAGUE² of N~s; UNITED N~s. Hence ~HOOD n. [F, f. L *nationem* nom. -o (*nasci nat-* be born, -ION)]

nā´tional(-she-), a. & n. 1. Of a or the nation, common to the whole nation; peculiar to or characteristic of a particular nation; ~ *anthem*, 'God save the King' & corresponding hymns of other peoples; ~ DEBT; ||N~ *Gallery*, buildings in London in which pictures, portraits, owned by the nation are permanently exhibited; N~ INSURANCE; ||N~ *Liberal Club*, club in close connexion with the Liberal party (cf. national); N~ *Socialist*, NAZI; ||N~ *Society*, founded 1811 to promote education of the poor; ||*Grand N~* (steeple-chase), chief steeplechase of year, at

Aintree in March. **2.** n. pl. (diplom.). One's fellow countrymen (*consul's powers over his own ~s*). Hence ~LY² adv. [F (prec., -AL)]

nā'tional**ism** (-sho-), n. Patriotic feeling, principles, or efforts; policy of national independence; policy of nationalizing industry. So ~IST(2) n. [-ISM]

nā'tionǎl'ĭtў (-sho-), n. Being national; national quality; patriotic sentiment; one's nation (*what is his ~y?*); a nation (*men of all ~ies*); existence as a nation; race forming part of one or more political nations. [-ITY]

nā'tionaliz̧e (-sho-), v.t. Make national; make into a nation; naturalize (foreigner); convert (land, railways, coal-mines, etc.) into national property or undertakings. Hence ~A'TION n. [-IZE]

nā'tive¹, n. **1.** One born, or whose parents are domiciled, in a place (*of*); (Austral.) white born in Australia. **2.** Member of non-European or uncivilized race. **3.** Indigenous animal or plant; oyster reared wholly or partly in British waters, esp. in artificial beds. [f. med. L *nativus* a., see foll.]

nā'tive², a. **1.** Belonging to a person or thing by nature, innate, inherent, natural *to*, whence ~LY² adv. **2.** Unadorned, simple, artless. **3.** Of one's birth, where one was born; belonging to one by right of birth. **4.** (Of metals etc.) found in pure or uncombined state (*~ rock*, in its original place). **5.** Born in a place (esp. of non-Europeans), indigenous, not exotic; of the natives of a place; *the N~ States*, territories ruled by the Indian Princes. [f. L *nativus* (NATION, -IVE)]

nā'tiv**ism**, n. (philos.). Doctrine of innate ideas. So ~IST(2) n. [-ISM]

nativ'**itў**, n. Birth of Christ, the Virgin, or St John Baptist; picture of the N~ of Christ; festival of Christ's N~, Christmas, or of birth of Virgin (8 Sept.) or St John (24 June); birth; (Astrol.) horoscope. [f. F *nativité* f. L *nativitatem* (NATIVE, -TY)]

nā'tron, n. Native sesquicarbonate of soda. [F f. Sp., f. Arab. *natrun* f. Gk *nitron* NITRE]

‖nǎtt'erjǎck, n. British species of toad with yellow stripe down back. [?]

nǎtt'ier blue (-ōō), n. Soft shade of blue, much used by the French painter J. M. Nattier (d. 1766).

nǎtt'ў, a. Spruce, trim, daintily tidy, deft-handed; showing deftness. Hence ~LY² adv., ~INESS n. [?]

nā'tural (-cher-), a. & n. **1.** Based on the innate moral sense, instinctive; (*~ law, justice*). **2.** Constituted by nature (*~ DAY, year*). **3.** (mus.) *~ note* or *key*, not sharp or flat, so *B ~, F ~*, etc.; *~ scale*, having no sharps or flats, i.e. C major. **4.** (sci.) *~ classification*, (now obs.) *orders* with abbr. N.O., etc., esp. in Bot. of Jussieu's arrangement of species according to likeness as opp. Linnaeus's sexual system. **5.** Normal, conformable to the ordinary course of nature, not exceptional or miraculous or irregular, (*~ magic; ~ death*, by age or disease, not accident, poison, or violence). **6.** Not enlightened or communicated by revelation (*the ~ man; ~ religion, theology*). **7.** Physically existing, not spiritual or intellectual or fictitious, concerned with physical things, (*the ~ world; one's ~ life*, duration of one's life on earth; *~ law*). **8.** Existing in or by nature, not artificial, innate, inherent, self-sown, uncultivated. **9.** Lifelike; unaffected, easy-mannered, not disfigured or disguised. **10.** Not surprising, to be expected. **11.** Consonant or easy to (*comes ~ to him*). **12.** Destined to be such by nature only, (*~ enemies, antithesis*). **13.** So related by nature only, illegitimate, (*~ son, child, brother*, etc.). **14.** Dealing with nature as a study (*~ history*, study of animal life, esp. as set forth for popular use, also aggregate of facts about the ~ objects or the characteristics of a place or class; *~ historian*, writer on ~ history; *~ philosophy*, physics; *~ philosopher*, physicist; *~ SCIENCE*). **15.** *~-born*, having the character or position by birth. Hence ~NESS n. **16.** n. Person half-witted from birth. **17.** (mus.) *~ note*, white key in piano. **18.** Hand making 21 as first dealt in vingt-et-un. [f. L *naturalis* (NATURE, -AL)]

nā'tural**ism** (-cher-), n. Action based on natural instincts; moral or religious system on purely natural basis; (Philos.) view of the world that excludes the supernatural or spiritual; realistic method, adherence to nature, in literature & art; indifference to conventions. [prec., -ISM]

nā'tural**ist** (-cher-), n. & a. **1.** One who believes in or practises naturalism; student of animals or plants; ‖(shop) dealer in cage animals, dogs, etc.; ‖(shop) taxidermist. **2.** adj. =foll. [-IST]

nā'turalis'**tic** (-cher-), a. Of, according to, naturalism; of natural history. Hence ~ICALLY adv. [-IC]

nā'turaliz̧e (-cher-), v.t. & i. Admit (alien) to citizenship; adopt (foreign word, custom, etc.); introduce (animal, plant) into another country; become ~ed; free from conventions, make natural; free from the miraculous, place on naturalistic basis; pursue natural history. Hence ~A'TION n. [f. F *naturaliser* (NATURAL, -IZE)]

nā'tural**ly** (-cher-), adv. In adj. senses; esp., as might be expected, of course. [-LY¹]

nā'ture, n. **1.** Thing's essential qualities, (*in* or *by* or *from the ~ of the case* or *of things*, inevitably considering these qualities); person's or animal's innate character (whence ~nā'tured² (-cherd) a.; *by ~*, innately; GOOD, ILL, SECOND, ~);

general characteristics & feelings of man-kind (often *human* ~; TOUCH² of ~) speci-fied element of human character (the *rational, animal, moral,* ~); person or specified character (*sanguine* ~s *do not feel this; there are* ~s *who can never*~).
2. Kind, sort, class, (*things of this* ~; *is in* or *of the* ~ *of a command*); (of guns or shot) size (100 *of each* ~ *of case-shot*). 3. In-herent impulses determining character or action (*against* ~, unnatural, immoral).
4. Vital force or functions or needs (~ *is exhausted; such a diet will not support* ~; *ease* ~, evacuate bowels or bladder).
5. Resin or sap in wood (esp. *full of* ~, still resinous). 6. Physical power causing phenomena of material world, these phenomena as a whole, (*N*~, these per-sonified; *N*~'s *engineering; all* ~ *looks gay; N*~ *is the best physician;* LAW¹ of ~; *in the course of* ~, in the ordinary course; *debt of* ~, death; *in* ~, actually existing, also anywhere, at all; *against* ~ or *contrary to* ~, miraculous, miracu-lously). 7. Naturalness or fidelity in art.
8. *State of* ~, unregenerate condition (opp. *state of* GRACE¹), condition of man before society is organized, uncultivated or un-domesticated state of plants or animals, bodily nakedness. 9. ~*printing,* method of producing print of leaves etc. by press-ing them on prepared plate; ~ *study* (as school subject), practical study of plant & animal life, physical phenomena, etc. [F, f. L *natura* (*nasci nat-* be born, -URE)]

naught (nawt), n. & pred. a. (arch.).
1. Nothing, nought, (*set at* ~, or NOUGHT); (Arith.) cipher, nought. 2. adj. Worthless, useless. [OE *nāwuht* (*nā* see NATHLESS, WIGHT)]

naught'ly (nawt-), a. (used of, to, or by children, or in imit. of childish speech), Wayward, disobedient, badly behaved; wicked, blameworthy, indecent. Hence ~ily² adv., ~INESS n. [prec., -Y¹]

naus'ea, n. Feeling of sickness; sea-sick-ness; loathing. [L, f. Gk *nausia* (*naus* ship)]

naus'eāte, v.t. & i. Reject (food, or fig.) with loathing; affect with nausea, whence ~ING² a.; feel sick (*at*), loathe food, occupation, etc. [f. L *nauseare* (prec.), -ATE³]

naus'eous, a. Causing nausea; offensive to taste or smell, nasty; disgusting, loathsome. Hence ~LY² adv., ~NESS n. [NAUSEA, -OUS]

nautch, n. E.-Indian exhibition of pro-fessional dancing-girls (~-*girl*, one of these). [f. Hind. *nach*]

naut'ical, a. Of sailors or navigation, naval, maritime; ~ *almanac*, year-book containing astronomical & tidal informa-tion for navigators etc. Hence ~LY² adv. [f. L Gk *nautikos* (*nautēs* sailor f. *naus* ship), -AL]

naut'ilus, n. (pl. -luses, -lī), *Paper* ~, small cephalopod of which the female has very thin shell & webbed sail-like arms; *pearly* ~, cephalopod with chambered shell having nacreous septa. [f. L f. Gk *nautilos* sailor (prec.)]

nāv'al, a. Of, in, for, etc., ships or (usu.) the or a navy (~ *stores*, all materials used in shipping; ~ *officer*, in navy); fought, won, etc., by or consisting of or based on ships or ships of war; ||N~ *Aviation*, aviation service of Royal Navy. Hence ~rY² adv. [f. L *navalis* (*navis* ship), -AL)]

nāve¹, n. Central block of wheel holding axle & spokes, hub. [OE *nafu*, cf. Du. *naaf*, G *nabe*, & see NAVEL]

nāve², n. Body of church from inner door to chancel or choir, usu. separated by pillars from aisles. [f. L *navis* ship]

nāv'el, n. Depression in front of belly left by severance of umbilical cord; central point of anything; ~ *orange*, large orange with ~-*like* formation at top; ~-*string*, structure connecting foetus & placenta, umbilical cord; ~-*wort*, kinds of plant. [OE *nafela*, cf. Du. *navel*, G *nabel*, de-rivatives of st. of NAVE¹, cogn. w. Skr. *nabhīla*, Gk *omphalos*]

nāv'icert, n. Certificate that ship's cargo does not contravene war contraband regulations; commercial passport for a particular consignment. [f. L *navis* ship +CERT(IFICATE)]

nāv'icūlar, a. & n. Boat-shaped (of shrines, &c of parts of plants or body; esp. ~ *bone* in hand or usu. foot; ~ *disease*, esp. as noun, disease in horse's ~ bone). [f. LL *navicularis* (L *navicula* dim. of *navis* ship, -AR¹)]

nāv'igable, a. (Of river, sea, etc.) afford-ing passage for ships; seaworthy (*in* ~*ble condition*); (of balloon) steerable, diri-gible. Hence ~BIL'ITY n. [f. L *navigabilis* (foll. -ABLE)]

nāv'igāte, v.i. & t. Voyage, sail ship; sail over or up or down (sea, river); manage, direct course of, (ship or aircraft). [f. L *navigare* (*navis* ship, *agere* drive), -ATE³]

nāvigā'tion, n. Navigating (*inland* ~, communication by canals & rivers; *aerial* ~, of airship or aeroplane); methods of determining ship's or aircraft's posi-tion & course by geometry & nautical astronomy, seamanship; voyage; ~-*coal*, steam-coal. [f. L *navigatio* (prec., -ATION)]

nāv'igātor, n. One charged with or skilled in navigation; sea explorer; ||(now rare) navvy. [L (NAVIGATE, -OR²)]

nāv'vy, n. Labourer employed in ex-cavating etc. for canals, railways, roads, etc.; (also *steam-*~) mechanical excavator. [abbr. of prec.]

nāv'y, n. Fleet (poet.); whole of State's ships of war with their crews & all the organization for their maintenance; offi-cers & men of ~; ~ *bill*, issued by Ad-miralty in lieu of cash payment; ~ *blue*

n., ~blue a., (of) the dark blue used in naval uniform; ‖ ~ cut, cake tobacco finely sliced; ~ league, association founded to rouse national interest in ~; ~ list, official book with all naval officers' names & other information. [f. OF navie fleet (L navis ship, -Y¹)]

nawab (-wawb), n. Native governor or nobleman in India; (rare) rich retired Anglo-Indian, nabob. [f. Hind. nawwab, orig. pl. f. Arab. nā'ib deputy]

nay, particle equivalent to negative sentence, & n. 1. =NO⁴ (arch.): why, well, (vaguely introducing comment on another's statement etc.; arch.); or rather, & even, & more than that, (weighty), ~ unanswerable). 2. n. The word ~ (will not take ~, disregards refusals; yea & ~, shilly-shally; say ~, utter denial or usu. refusal; ~ refuse or contradict, as cannot say him ~). [f. ON nei (ne not, ei ever)]

Nazarēne¹, n. & a. Native of Nazareth; (in Jewish, Mohamm., use) Christian; member of early Jewish-Christian sect (adj. of this sect). [f. L f. Gk Nazarēnos (Nazaret Nazareth)]

Naz'arite¹, n. Native of Nazareth. [f. L Nazaraeus f. Gk Nazōraios +-ITE¹(1)]

Naz'arite², -zir-, n. Hebrew who had taken certain vows of abstinence (Numb. vi). [f. L Nazaraeus f. Heb. nazir (nazar separate oneself) +-ITE²(2)]

nāze, n. Promontory, headland, ness. [=NESS]

Nazi (naht'si, nah'zi), n. & a. (Member) of the German National Socialist party; (loosely) German. Hence ~DOM, Na'zi(i)ISM, nn., ~FY v.t. [abbr. of G National-sozialist]

-nd¹, suf. of nn. & adjj. formed f. L gerundive (-andus, -endus, -undus) to be treated in such a way, as deodand, reverend, dividend; also in the full L form, as memorandum, agenda; & an element in -band (moribund), -cund (fecund, rubicund). **-nd²,** suf. forming nn. as fiend (hating), friend (loving)=the old part. termination -and.

neap, a. & n., & v.t. & i. 1. ~'tide' or ~, tide soon after moon's first & third quarters in which high-water level is at lowest. 2. v.b. (Of tides) tend towards ~ (of tide) reach highest point of ~tide; (pass., of ship) be prevented from getting off by ~ing of tides. [OE nēpflōd etym. dub.]

Neapol'itan, a. & n. (Inhabitant) of Naples (~ ice, ice-cream made in strata of different colours & flavours, sweetmeat of similar appearance; ~ violet, double sweet-scented kind of viola). [f. L.Neapolitanus (Neapolites f. L f. Gk Neapolis f. neos new, polis city, -AN)]

near¹, adv. & prep. (~er, ~est, also as advv. & prepp.) 1. To, at, a short distance, in(to) proximity in space or time, (far & ~, everywhere; ~ at hand, within easy reach. not far in the future; ~ by, not far off; ~ upon, not far in time from;) almost, nearly, not nearly or anything like, (now usu. nearly; was ~ dead with fright; lasted ~ a century; so ~ upon, not ~ so numerous); closely (as ~ as one can guess; the ~er it resembles him the less I like it); parsimoniously (lives very ~); go ~ to do, come or go ~ doing, nearly do etc. 2. prep. ~ in space, time, condition, or resemblance, to (comes no ~er the end; lies ~ his heart, affects him deeply; the time draws ~ Christmas; sun is ~ setting; hope came ~ fulfilment; who comes ~est him in wit?); (in comb.) resembling, intended as a substitute for, as ~-beer. [f. ON nǣr orig. comp. of nāh =OE nēah NIGH]

near², a. (often governing n. in pred. use; so also in comp. & superl). Closely related (~ relation; is ~ akin to; is ~ me in blood; ~ & dear), intimate (a ~ friend); (of parts of animals or vehicles, or horses etc. in team) left (opp. off; the ~ fore leg, wheel; the ~ wheeler); close at hand, close to, in place or time (also, now U.S., ~ by; the ~est mam; on a ~ day; the man ~ or ~est you; is ~er to, or ~er, us; ~ work, that must be done with the eye close to it; the ~ distance, part of scene between background & foreground; the ~ prospect of reward); (of road or way) direct; close, narrow, (a ~ guess, resemblance, translation, race, escape); niggardly; ~ miss, not a hit, but ~ enough to damage target, esp. in bombing; ~-sighted, short-sighted. Hence ~ISH(2) a., ~NESS n. [f. prec.]

near³, v.i. & t. Draw near (to), approach. [f. NEAR¹,²]

Nēarc'tic, a.(zool.). Of arctic & temperate parts of N. America. [f. Gk neos new (w. ref. to the New World), ARCTIC]

near'ly, adv. Closely (examine it ~; ~ related; concerns me ~; approached the place ~; correspond, resemble, ~); almost; not ~, nothing like, far from. [NEAR², -LY¹]

neat¹, n. (sing. & (collect. as pl.), Any animal of ox kind; (collect.) cattle; ~ herd, cowherd; ~-house, cattle-shed; ~'s-foot, ~'s-tongue, used as food; ~'s-leather, ox-hide. [OE nēat, cf. ON naut, cogn. w. OE nēotan possess]

neat², a. (Of liquor, esp. alcoholic) undiluted; (of elegant simplicity in form or arrangement, nicely made or proportioned; (of language, style, sayings) brief, clear, & pointed, cleverly phrased, epigrammatic; deft, dextrous, cleverly done; tidy, methodical; ~-handed, dextrous. Hence ~LY² adv., ~NESS n. [AF neit=F net f. L nitidus shining (nitēre shine)]

‖**neath,** prep. (poet.). Beneath. [f. BE-NEATH]

neb, n. (Sc.). Beak or bill; nose; snout; tip, spout, point. [OE nebb, cf. Du. nebbe]

nebula, n. (pl. **~lae**). Clouded speck on cornea causing defective sight; (Astron.) luminous patch made by cluster of distant stars or by gaseous or stellar matter outside solar system. [L., =mist, vapour, f. Gk *nephelē*, G *nebel*.]

neb'ular, a. Of nebula(e); ~ *theory* or *hypothesis*, that solar & stellar systems were developed from nebulae. [-AR¹]

nebū'lium, n. Element formerly assumed to exist in gaseous nebulae as cause of bright lines in green part of spectrum. (These lines are now believed to be due to one of the known terrestrial elements in a more rarefied gaseous state than has yet been produced on earth.) [-IUM]

neb'ulous, a. (Astron.; of, like, nebula(e); = star, small cluster of indistinct stars, or star in luminous haze; cloud-like; hazy, vague, indistinct, formless; clouded, turbid. So **nebūlŏ'sity** n. [f. L *nebulosus* (NEBULA, -OUS)]

necessā'rian, n. & a. = NECESSITARIAN. Hence **~ISM(3)** n. [L *necesse* NECESSARY, -ARIAN]

nĕ'cessarily, [-ILY²] adv. As a necessary result, inevitably.

nĕ'cessary, a. & n. 1. Indispensable, requisite, (*to* or *for* person etc.; *it is ~ that, to do*); requiring to, that must, be done; determined by predestination or natural laws, not by free will, happening or existing by necessity; (of concept or mental process) inevitably resulting from nature of things or the mind, inevitably produced by previous state of things; (of agent) having no independent volition. 2. n. Thing without which life cannot be maintained (often the ~*ies of life*); (loosely) desirable thing not generally regarded as a luxury; (abs. use of adj.) the ~*y* (sl.), money or action needed for a purpose (*provide, find, do, the ~y*). [f. L *necessarius* (*necesse* needful), -ARY²]

necessitā'rian, n. & a. (Person) denying free will & maintaining that all action is determined by antecedent causes. Hence **~ISM(3)** n. [NECESSITY, -ARIAN]

necĕ'ssitāte, v.t. Force, compel, (person) to do (now rare); render necessary, involve as condition or accompaniment or result. [f. med. L *necessitare* (NECESSITY, -ATE³)]

necĕ'ssitous, a. Poor, needy, [foll., -OUS]

necĕ'ssity, n. Constraint or compulsion regarded as a law prevailing through the material universe & governing all human action (often *physical ~, logical ~*), compulsion to believe that of which the opposite is inconceivable; *absolute, moral, natural*, etc., ~); constraining power of circumstances, state of things compelling to certain course, (*of ~, unavoidably; make a virtue of ~,* claim credit for doing what one cannot help doing, do thing with a good grace; *am under the ~ of doing; ~ knows no law,* absolves from any

offence); imperative need (*for; ~ is the mother of invention*); indispensability (*the ~ of protecting life & property*)); indispensable thing, necessary, (usu. pl.). want, poverty, hardship, pressing need. [f. F *nécessité* f. L *necessitatem* (*necesse* needful, -TY)]

nĕck, n., & v.i. & t. 1. Part of body that connects head with shoulders (*break one's ~;* dislocate vertebrae of this, be killed so; *break ~ of task* etc., get hardest part of it over; *save one's ~,* escape hanging; *& crop,* headlong; *get it in the ~,* sl., suffer fatal or severe blow; *~ or nothing,* desperately, staking all on success, *it is a case for desperate attempts; ~ & ~,* running even in race); flesh of animal's ~ as food (esp. *~ of mutton*); part of shirt etc. that touches ~. 2. Narrow part of vessel, esp. of bottle near mouth, or of passage, pass, or channel; narrow channel, isthmus; narrow connecting part between two parts of thing; (Archit.) lower part of capital. 3. ~*cloth,* cravat; ~*erchief* (-chif), kerchief worn round ~; ~*lace* (-lis), ornament of precious stones or metal, or beads etc, worn round ~; ~*tie,* band of silk etc. securing or seeming to secure shirt-collar; ~*verse,* Latin verse (usu. beginning of Ps. li) printed in black letter by reading which person claiming benefit of clergy might save his ~; ~*wear* (shop), collars & ties; hence (-)~ED² (-t) a. 4. v¹b. *(sl.), (Of couples) clasp one another round the ~; hug, embrace, (person). [OE *hnecca,* cf. Du. *nek,* G *nacken*]

‖ **nĕck²**, n. Last sheaf of corn cut. [?]

nĕck'ing, n. (archit.,). Part of column between shaft & capital. [NECK¹, -ING¹]

nĕck'let, n. Ornament or fur protector for neck. [-LET]

nĕc'rō-, comb. form of Gk *nekros* corpse, dead body, as ~*gen'ic* produced by contact with dead bodies, ~*phore* burying beetle, ~*biō'sis* decay in tissues of body, ~LATRY (-ŏl-), ~*logy* (-ŏl-) death-roll or obituary notice, ~*phagous* (-ŏf-) feeding on carrion, ~*polis* (-ŏp-) cemetery, *nĕc'romancy* or ~*scopy* (-ŏs-), post-mortem examination.

nĕc'romăncy, n. Art of predicting by means of communication with the dead; magic, enchantment. So **~ER¹** n., **nĕcrōmăn'tic** a. [f. OF *nigromancie* f. med. L *nigromantia* changed by assoc. w. L *niger* black f. L f. Gk *nekromanteia* (prec., -MANCY)]

nĕcrō'sis, n. (path.; pl. -ōsēs). Death of circumscribed piece of tissue, esp. mortification of bodies. Hence **nĕcrō'tic(3)** a. [f. Gk *nekrōsis* (*nekroō* kill, see NECRO-)]

nĕc'tar, n. (Gk Myth.) drink of the gods (cf. AMBROSIA); any delicious drink; sweet fluid or honey produced by plants; kind

of aerated water. Hence or cogn. **néc-**
tar̆'ᴇᴀɴ, néc̆tar̆'ᴇᴏᴜs,~ᴏᴜs, aa. [f. Gk *nektar* etym. dub.]

néc̆'tarine, n. Kind of peach with thin downless skin & firm flesh. [n. use of obs. or rare adj. (NECTAR, -INE¹)]

néc̆'tarȳ, n. Flower's or plant's honey-secreting organ. [f. NECTAR, prob. on false anal. of *ovary* (-ARY¹) for *nectarary*]

Nĕd'dȳ, n. Donkey. [dim. of Edward; -Y³]

née (nā), a. Born (used in adding woman's maiden name, as *Mrs Smith,* ~*Jones*). [F]

need¹, n. Circumstances requiring some course (*if* ~ *be* or *were, there is no* etc. ~, *to do* or abs.; *have* ~, require to; *had* ~, ought to, as *had* ~ *remember*); imperative demand for presence or possession of (*the* ~ *of further securities; have* ~ *of,* require, want); emergency, crisis, time of difficulty, (*a friend in* ~ *is a friend indeed; good at* ~; *failed him in his* ~); destitution, lack of necessaries, poverty, whence ~Y² a., ~'ɴᴇss n.: thing wanted, respect in which want is felt, requirement, (*my* ~*s are few*); (pl.) offices of nature (*do one's* ~*s*); ~'*fire,* fire got from dry wood by friction, [com.-Teut.: OE *nied, nĕod,* cf. Du. *nood,* G *not*]

need², v.i. & t. (3 sing. pres. ~s, & ~ as specified below). Be necessary (arch.; *it* ~*s not,* it is needless; *there* ~*s, so-&-so* is required; *more than* ~*s,* than is necessary; *what* ~ or ~*s?,* why should one?); stand in need of, require, (intr.) be needy; be under necessity or obligation to (do etc.) or to do (3 sing. ~, & *to* omitted, in neg. & interrog. forms; *he* ~ *not trouble himself; it* ~*s to be done with care; why have we come tonight?;* ~ *not have done* etc., usu. form=*did not* ~ *to do* etc.; often ellipt., as *don't be longer away than you* ~). [OE *nĕodian* (prec.)]

need'ful, a. Requisite, necessary, in-dispensable, (*to, for,* or abs.; *it is* ~ *to do,* or *that; the* ~, what is necessary, esp. sl., the money required, also *do the* ~ in football, convert try into goal). Hence ~ɴᴇss n. [-FUL]

need'le, n. & v.t. & i. **1.** Thin round long piece of steel pointed at one end & with eye for thread at other used in sewing (*knitting, darning, packing, crochet,* etc., ~, shapes or modifications of it for different purposes; *sharp as a* ~, lit., & fig. acute, observant; *look for* ~ *in* BOTTLE³ etc. *of hay;* PINS & ~s; ~*'s eye,* least possible aperture, esp. w. ref. to *Matt.* xix. 24). **2.** Piece of magnetized steel used as indicator on dial of compass & magnetic & electric apparatus, esp. in telegraphy; strip of standard gold or silver used for comparison in assaying with touchstone. **3.** Pointed etching instrument; pointed surgical instrument used in soft cataract; end of hypodermic syringe; thin pointed piece of metal,

wood, or fibre, or long thorn, that receives & transmits the vibrations set up by a revolving gramophone record; steel pin exploding cartridge of breechloader. **4.** Obelisk; sharp rock, peak. **5.** Beam or pin used as temporary support during under-pinning. **6.** ~-shaped crystal. **7.** Leaf of fir or pine. **8.** ‖ *The* ~ (sl.), fit of nervous-ness. **9.** ~-*bath,* shower-bath with fine spray discharged horizontally from ver-tical pipes surrounding bather; ~-*book,* book-shaped case for ~s; ~-*fish,* kinds of fish, garfish; ~'*ful,* length of cotton etc. put into ~ at once; ~-*game, match,* etc., one closely contested & arousing personal feeling or animosity; ~-*gun,* in which cartridge is exploded by impact of ~;~-*lace,* made with ~s not bobbins; ~-*point,* fine sharp point, also point-lace made with ~s; ~-*woman,* sempstress, also *good* or *bad user of* ~; ~-*work,* sewing or embroidery. **10.** vb. Sew, pierce, or operate on, with ~; thread (one's way) between or through things; under-pin with ~-beams; form ~-shaped crystals; thread one's way. [OE *nǣdl,* cf. G *nadel,* Da. *naal,* prob. cogn. w. L *nĕre* spin, Gk *nēsis* spinning & *nēma* thread]

need'less, a. Unnecessary, uncalled for, (~ *to say* used parenth., as I need not tell you). Hence ~lY² adv., ~ɴᴇss n. [-LESS]

need'ments, n. pl. Things needed, esp. personal necessaries carried on journey. [NEED n. or v., -MENT]

needs (z), adv. Of necessity (now only after or before *must;* ~ *must do,* cannot help or avoid or get out of doing; *must,*~ *do, occas.* ~ *must do,* usu. foolishly in-sists or ~ insisted on doing). [OE *nēdes* (NEED¹, -ES¹)]

ne'er (nâr), adv. (Poet.) never (not used ellipt. for sentence like *never*); ~ *a,* not a single; ~-*do-well, -weel,* good-for-nothing (person). [contr. of NEVER]

nefār'ious, a. Wicked, iniquitous. Hence ~lY² adv., ~ɴᴇss n. [f. L *nefarius* (*nefas* wrong), -OUS]

negāte', v.t. Nullify, deny existence of, imply or involve non-existence of, be the negation of. [from 1835 only, f. L *negare* deny, -ATE³]

negā'tion, n. Denying; negative state-ment or doctrine; refusal, contradiction, denial *of;* (Log.) affirmation of difference or exclusion; absence or opposite of something actual or positive; negative or unreal thing, nonentity. So **nĕg'atorʏ** a. [f. L *negatio* (prec.-, -ATION)]

negā'tionist (-sho-), n. One who denies accepted beliefs without proposing sub-stitutes. [-IST]

nĕg'ative, a. **1.** Expressing or implying denial, prohibition, or refusal (~ *pro-position* in logic, asserting difference or discrepancy; ~ *statute, vote, answer;* ~ *voice,* right of veto). **2.** Wanting, consist-ing in the want of, positive attributes (~

virtue, abstention from wrongdoing; ~ instance, evidence, of non-occurrence of, something; ~ causes of dissatisfaction, sins of omission). **3.** (Alg.) denoting quantities to be subtracted from others or from zero (~ sign, —); (colloq, joc.) ~ quantity, nothing. **4.** (Electr.) of the kind produced by friction on resin etc. (opp. positive, on glass), containing or producing such electricity. **5.** Of opposite nature to thing regarded as positive (debt is a ~ capital, & capital a ~ debt). **6.** (Photog.) having lights & shadows of the actual object or scene reversed. Hence ~LY² adv. ~NESS, negativ'ITY, nn. [f. LL negativus (NEGATE, -IVE)]

nĕg'ative³, v.t. Veto, reject, refuse to accept or countenance; disprove (inference, hypothesis); contradict (statement); neutralize (effect). [as prec.]

nĕg'ativism, n. Attitude of NEGATIONIST. So ~IST(2) n. [-ISM]

nĕglĕct', v.t., & n. **1.** Slight, not pay attentions to; leave uncared-for; leave undone, be remiss about; omit to do or doing; hence ~ABLE a. (rare). **2.** n. ~ing or being ~ed: disregard of; negligence; hence ~FUL a., ~fully² adv., ~fulNESS n. [(n. f. L neglectus -ûs) f. L neglegere -lect- (neg- not, legere pick up)]

négligé (neg'lizhā), n. Free & easy or unceremonious attire. [F, p.p. of négliger (prec.)]

nĕg'ligeable, a. (rare), Negligible. [f. F négligeable (prec., -ABLE)]

nĕg'ligence, n. Want of proper care or attention. (piece of) carelessness; contributory ~ence, ~ence on a person's part that has helped to bring about the injury that he has suffered; freedom from restraint or artificiality in literature or art. So ~ENT a. (of duty etc.), ~ently² adv. [f. L negligentia (NEGLECT, -ENCE)]

nĕg'ligible, a. That need not be regarded (esp. ~ quantity). [as prec., -IBLE]

reply, or word (it is hard to prove a ~; returned a ~, answered 'no' etc.; two ~s make an affirmative); right of veto; in the ~, negatively) (esp. in Parliament, the answers in ministerial answers ~ no); it was decided in the ~, proposal was rejected). **3.** Negative quality, want of something. (his character is made up of ~s). **3.** (Alg.) negative or minus quantity. **4.** (Photog.) Image on glass etc. with reversed lights & shadows from which positive pictures are taken. **5.** Negative plate or metal in voltaic battery. [f. prec.]

neigh (nā), v.i., & n. (Utter) cry (as) of horse. [OE hnǣgan, cf. MHG nēgen, imit.]

neighbour (nāb'er), n., & v.i. & t. **1.** Dweller next door, near, in same street or village or district, or in adjacent country (my ~ Jones; as next-door ~s; his nearest ~ is 12 miles off; our ~s across the Channel), esp. regarded as one who should be friendly (good, bad, ~s; ~LY¹ a., ~LINESS n.) or as having claim on others' friendliness (duty to one's ~, to any fellow man); person or thing near or next another (my ~ at dinner; falling tree brought down its ~); (attrib.) ~ing tree ~LESS a., ~SHIP n. **2.** vb. Adjoin, border upon, (chiefly now in ~ING² a.). [OE néahgebúr (NIGH, BOOR), cf. G nachbar]

neighboured (nāb'erd), a. Having neighbours or surroundings of specified kind (ill-~; a beautifully ~ town). [-ED²·¹]

neighbourhood (nāb'er-), n. Neighbourly feeling or conduct (usu. good~); nearness, vicinity of (in the ~ of £100, about); neighbours, people of a district, district. [-HOOD]

neither (nīdh'-, nēdh-), adv., conj., a., & pron. **1.** adv. (Introducing word, clause, etc., that is to be negatived equally with a following one or added to it by nor) not either, not on the one hand, (~ knowing nor caring; ~ you nor I know, he ~ know, ~ I nor he knows); also often irreg. ~ he nor she knows'; does cowardice ensure nor courage preclude defeat; ~ HERE nor there). **2.** (placed at end to emphasize preceding negative) either, any more

négrill'o, n. (pl. ~s), Small Negro; one of dwarf negro race in Central & S. Africa. [Sp., dim. of NEGRO]

négri'to (-rē-), n. (pl. ~s), One of small negroid race in the Malayo-Polynesian region. [as prec.]

Neg'ro, n. (pl. ~es; fem. *Negress*) & a.
1. Member, esp. male, of black-skinned woolly-haired flat-nosed thick-lipped African race. **2.** adj. Of this race, black-skinned, (n~ minstrels, troupe of real or sham ~es performing ~ songs & dances); occupied by, connected with, ~es; black or dark (n~ ant, bot, monkey, dark species). **3.** n~-head, strong black plug tobacco, also inferior indiarubber; ~land, part of Africa inhabited by ~es. Hence neg'roID a. & n., négroph'ILISM n., negro-PHIL a. & n., négroph'ILISM n., negro-PHOB'IA n. [Sp., f. L nigrum nom. niger black]

Neg'us¹, n. Ruler of Abyssinia. [native]

neg'us², n. Hot sweetened wine & water. [Col. F. N~, d. 1732]

than something else, (*I don't know that
~*); (in apodosis after negative protasis)
not either (*if you do not go*, ~ *shall I*);
(Bibl.) not even (*but ~ so did their witness
agree*). **2.** conj. (arch.). Nor, nor yet, (*I
know not*, ~ *can I guess*). **3.** adj. & pron.
Not either, not the one nor the other, (~
accusation, ~ *of the accusations, is true*; ~
of them knows, often also irreg. *know*);
(loosely) none of any number of specified
things. [ME *naither*, *neyther*, assim. of
OE *nawther* contr. of *nahwæther* (*nā* not,
WHETHER) to EITHER]

nek, n. (S.-Afr.). =COL. [Du., = NECK[1]]

nek'ton, n. (biol.). The forms of free-
swimming organic life found at various
depths in the ocean & in lakes, taken
collectively. [G, f. Gk *nēktos* swimming
(*nēkhō* swim)]

nell'y, n. Largest kind of petrel. [perh.
the feminine name]

nem'at-o-, comb. form of Gk *nēma -atos*
thread in scientific terms (=filamentous,
having filament, thread-like), as ~*ocyst*,
cell in jelly-fish etc. containing coiled
thread that can be projected as sting,
~*ode* & ~*oid*, aa. & nn., (worm) of slender
cylindrical shape.

Nem'esis, n. Goddess of retribution; retributive justice, downfall that satisfies
this. [Gk (*nemō* give what is due)]

nem'ine, abl. of L *nemo* no one; ~ *contra-
dicente* or *dissentiente* (pr. kŏntradīsen'tī,
dīsentĭen'tī; abbr. *nēm. con.* or *diss.*)
unanimously (or without a dissenting
vote).

nen'uphar, n. Water-lily. [med. L, ult. f.
Skr. *nīlotpala* (*nīl* blue, *utpala* lotus)]

neo-, comb. form of Gk *neos* new, used as
living pref. to adj. & nn., & adding the
notions *new*, *modern*, *later*, *recast*, *lately
found* or *invented* (~*Cath'olic*, ~*pāg'anism*; ~*Cām'brian*, Geol., of the later
Cambrian period; ~*Hell'enism*, revival
of Greek ideals; ~*Maltha'sianism* (-zhə-),
use of preventives against conception; ~
Plat'onism, 3rd-cent. mixture of Platonic ideas with Oriental mysticism;
nē'odoxy, new doctrine or view; *nēōn-
tŏl'ogy*, study of extant animals; ~*zō'ic*,
Geol., of later period of geological history,
post-palaeozoic).

neolith'ic, a. Of the later stone age, when
ground or polished stone weapons & implements prevailed. [prec., Gk *lithos*
stone, -IC]

neolo'gian, a. & n. **1.** Of, inclined to,
marked by, neologism in theology. **2.** n.
Neologist in theology. [NEOLOGY, -AN]

neol'ogism, **neol'ogy**, nn. Coining or
using of new words, new-coined word;
tendency to or adoption of novel or
rationalistic religious views. So ~*IST*(1)
n., ~*IZE*(2) v.i. [f. F *néologie*, *néologisme*]

ne'on, n. (chem.). Inert gaseous element
occurring in the atmosphere; used in

Illuminated signs (~ *lights*), giving a
coloured glow when electricity is passed
through it in a sealed low-pressure tube.
[neut. of Gk *neos* new; discovered in
1898]

ne'ophrōn, n. White Egyptian vulture &
allied birds. [name of man turned to
vulture in *Metamorphoses* of Antoninus
Liberalis]

ne'ophyte, n. New convert esp. among
primitive Christians or Roman Catholics;
newly ordained R.-C. priest; novice of
religious order; beginner, novice, tiro.
[f. eccl. L f. Gk *neophutos* newly planted
(NEO-, *phuō* plant)]

neote'ric, a. Recent, newfangled, modern. [f. LL f. Gk *neōterikos* (*neōteros* comp.
of *neos* new, -IC)]

neotrop'ical, a. Of, found in, tropical &
S. America. [NEO-, TROPICAL]

nepen'the(s) (-ĭ, -ēz), n. Drug producing
forgetfulness of grief (poet.); (-ēs) genus of
plants with pitcher-shaped leaves, Pitcher-
plant. [(-ē) L f. Gk, neut. of *nēpenthēs*
griefless (*nē-* not, *penthos* grief)]

ne'phew (-v-), n. Brother's or sister's son.
~*pos* f. OF *neveu* f. L *nepotem* nom. -*pos*
grandson, nephew, cogn. w. OE *nefa*,
G *neffe*]

nephol'ogy, n. Study of the clouds. [f.
Gk *nephos* cloud, -LOGY]

nephrit'ic, a. Of or in the kidneys, renal.
[f. LL f. Gk *nephritikos* (foll., -IC)]

nephri'tis, n. Inflammation of the kidneys. [LL f. Gk (*nephros* kidney, -ITIS)]

nephr'(o)-, comb. form (prec.)=kidney-,
~*ec'tomy* excision of kidney, ~*ŏi'ocy*,
~*ŏt'omy*.

ne' plus ul'tra, n. Prohibition of advance,
impassable obstacle; furthest point attained or attainable; highest pitch or
form of, acme, culmination. [L, = not
more beyond, supposed inscription on
Pillars of Hercules]

nep'otism, n. Undue favour from holder
of patronage to relatives (orig. from Pope
to illegitimate sons called nephews). So
~*IST*(1) n. [f. It. *nepotismo* (*nepote* NEPHEW,
-ISM)]

Nep'tune, n. **1.** (God of) the sea (~*'s cup*,
kinds of coral). **2.** One of the farthest
planets of solar system. [f. L *Neptūnus*]

Neptūn'ian, a. & n. (Geol.) produced by
water action; (person) maintaining aqueous origin of certain rocks, so **Nep'tūn-
ism**(2) n. (opp. *Vulcanist*); of planet Neptune. [f. L*Neptūnius* (prec.), -AN]

neptūn'ium, n. Unstable element produced when uranium atoms absorb
neutrons, & changing to plutonium. [as
NEPTUNE, -IUM]

nēr'eid, n. Sea-nymph; (Zool.) long sea-
worm or centipede. [f. L f. Gk *Nērĕis
-idos* daughter of sea-god Nereus]

ner'ō ànti'cō (nāĭ'-, -tē-), n. Kind of black
marble found in Roman ruins. [It.]

nēr'oli, n. Essential oil from orange-

flowers used in perfumery. [F (né-), f. name of Italian princess]

Nero'nian, a. Of, as of, the emperor Nero or his times, cruel, licentious, tyrannical. [f. L *Neronianus* (*Nero -onis*, -IAN)]

Nér'vate, a. (bot.), (Of leaves) having ribs.

nerve, n., & v.t. 1. Sinew, tendon, (now poet. exc. in *strain every ~*, make all possible efforts; also in pl. fig., as *good laws are the ~s of a State*). 2. Vigour, energy, well-strung state (A, 3. (Bot.) rib, esp. midrib, of leaf. 4. (Anat.) fibre or bundle of fibres connecting & conveying impulses of sensation & motion between brain or spinal cord or ganglionic organ & some part of body. 5. pl. Bodily state in regard to physical sensitiveness & interaction between brain & other parts, disordered state in these respects, exaggerated sensitiveness, nervousness, (*does not know what ~s are*, of equable temper; *a fit of ~s*, nervous state; *get on one's ~s*, be a worry or annoyance to him; *has iron ~s*, ~*s of steel*, etc., is not easily upset or frightened; *war of ~s*, neuron). 6. Nervous fibre. 7. Coolness in danger, boldness, assurance, (*lose one's ~*, become timid or irresolute). 8. ~-*centre*, group of closely connected ganglion-cells; ~-*knot*, gang-lion; hence (-)**nerved²** (-vd) a., **nérv-6-**comb.form. 9. v.t. Give strength, vigour, or courage, to; collect oneself to face danger or suffering. [f. L *nervus*, cf. Gk *neuron*]

nerve'less (-vl-), a. Inert, wanting in vigour or spirit, listless; (of style) flabby, diffuse; (Bot., Entom.) without nervures; (Anat., Zool.) without nerves. Hence ~LY² adv., ~NESS n. [-LESS]

ner'vine, a. & n. (med.), (Medicine) relieving nerve-disorders. [NERVE, -INE¹]

ner'vous, a. Sinewy, muscular; (of literary style) vigorous, terse; full of nerves; of the nerves (~ *system*, nerves & nerve-centres as a whole); acting on the nerves; having disordered or delicate nerves, excitable, highly strung, easily agitated, timid. Hence ~LY² adv., ~NESS n. [f. L *nervosus* (NERVE, -OSE¹)]

ner'vure (-yer), n. One of the tubes forming insect's wing; principal vein of leaf. [F (NERVE, -URE)]

ner'vy, a. Sinewy, strong, (poet.); (sl.) cool, confident, impudent; jerky, nervous; (sl.) trying to the nerves. [-Y²]

nescience (nèsĭ'yens), n. Not knowing, absence or knowledge of. [f. LL *nescientia* f. L *nescire* not know (*ne-* not, *scire* know), -ENCE]

nescient (nèsĭ'yent), a. & n. Ignorant (of); agnostic (a. & n.). [prec., -ENT]

ness, n. Promontory, headland, cape. [OE *næs* cf. *nasu* nose]

-ness, sui. appended freely to adji. (*bitter~*), participles (*loving~*, *tired~*), compl-adj. (*tongue-tied~*), & adj. phr. (*up-to-date~*) to form nn. expressing state or condition. [OE *-nes(s)*, *-nis(s)*, *-nys(s)*, cf. Du. *-nis*, G *-niss*; not orig. part of suf. (*-assus*, *-assi*, f. vbs in *-atian*) but an accretion f. stem]

nest, n., & v.t. & i. 1. Structure or place made or chosen by bird for laying eggs & sheltering young (*it's an ill bird that fouls its own ~*, one should not speak ill of home etc.; FEATHER² *one's ~*; animal's or insect's abode or spawning or breeding place; snug or secluded retreat, lodging, shelter, bed, receptacle; haunt of robbers etc.; fostering-place of vice etc.; brood, swarm; collection, series, of similar objects; small chest *of drawers*; ~*egg*, real or imitation egg left in ~ to induce hen to go on laying there, sum of money kept as reserve or nucleus; hence ~FUL(2) n. ~LIKE a. 2. vb. Make ~, (of boxes etc.) be packed one inside another; take bird's ~s. [OE, Du., & G, cogn. w. L *nidus* (*ni-* down), cf. NETHER, *sed-* sit)]

né'stling (-sl-, -stl-), n. Bird too young to leave nest. [NEST n. + -LING¹, or prec. + -ING²]

Nès'tor, n. Wise old man, senior of company etc. [name of character in Homer]

Nestor'ian, a. & n. (Adherent) of doctrine of Nestorius patriarch of Constantinople A.D. 428 asserting that Christ had distinct divine & human persons. Hence ~ISM(3) n. [f. L *Nestorianus* (-AN)]

nét¹, n. & v.t. & i.(-tt-). 1. Meshed fabric of twine, cord, hair, etc.; piece of this used for catching fish etc. (*beach*, *casting*, *trawl*, *herring*, *tuck*, *clap*, etc., ~), or for covering, confining, protecting, carrying, etc. (*fruit*, *hair*, *tennis*, *cricket*, etc., ~); moral or mental snare; spider's web; reticulation; ~*work*; ~*ball*, girls' game in which a ball has to be thrown so as to fall through an elevated horizontal ring from which a ~ depends; ~*work*, arrangement with intersecting lines & interstices recalling those of ~, complex system of ~, railways, rivers, canals, etc., ramification; hence ~FUL(2) n. 2. vb. Cover, confine, catch, with ~(6); fish (river etc.) with ~s, set ~s in (river); make netting; make (purse, hammock, etc.) by ~ting; (usu. in p.p.) mark with ~ting pattern, reticulate. [com.-Teut., OE, Du., Da., *net*, cf. G *netz*]

net², a., & v.t. (-tt-). **1.** Free from deduction, remaining after necessary deductions, (~ *profit*, true profit, actual gain after working expenses have been paid, opp. GROSS; ~ *price*, real price off which discount is not allowed, opp. *nominal, publisher's, price*). **2.** v.t. Gain or yield (sum) as ~ profit. [F. see NEAT²]

nē tēm'erē, n. The papal decree of 1907 under which marriages between Roman Catholics and others are not valid unless solemnized by R.-C. bishop or his deputy. [initial L words, =lest at random]

neth'er (-dh-), a. (arch. or joc.). Lower (~ *lip* or *jaw*; ~ *garments* etc., trousers; ~ *man* or *person*, legs etc.; ~ *millstone*, simile for hard heart etc.; ~ *world*, rarely the earth, usu. hell, also ~ *regions*). Hence ~MOST a. [com.-Teut.; cf. Du. *neder-*, G *nieder*]

Neth'erlander, n., **Neth'erlandish**, a., (-dh-). (Native) of the Netherlands. [f. Du. *Nederlander, -landsch*, (*Nederland*, -ER¹, -ISH¹)]

net'suke (-sŏŏkā), n. Carved buttonlike ornament worn by Japanese. [Jap.]

nett'ing, n. In vbl senses; also: netted string, thread, or wire; piece of this used for various purposes. [-ING¹]

net'tle, n. & v.t. **1.** Genus of plants including *Great* or *Common N~* & *Small N~*, two species growing profusely on waste land & covered with stinging hairs; other plants resembling these, esp. DEAD~; ~-*rash*, eruption on skin in patches like those made by ~ stings. **2.** v.t. Beat with ~s; get *oneself* stung with ~s; Irritate, provoke, annoy. [com.-Teut.; OE *netele*, cf. Du. *netel*, G *nessel*]

neume (nūm), n. (mus.). Sign in plainsong indicating note or group of notes to be sung to a syllable. [F (-e), f. med. L *neuma* f. Gk *pneuma* breath (*pneō* breathe, -M)]

neur'al (nūr-), a. Of the nerves, of the central nervous system. [f. Gk *neuron* nerve, -AL]

neura'tion (nūr-), n. Distribution of nervures. [irreg. f. foll., -ATION]

neur(o)- (nūr-), comb. form of Gk *neuron* nerve; ~al'gia (-ja), affection of nerve(s) usu. of head or face causing intense intermittent pain, so ~al'gic a.; ~asthēn'ia, nervous debility, so ~asthēn'ic a.; ~ĕc'tomy, excision of nerve; ~'ine, nerve-tissue; ~ĭt'is n.; ~ŏl'ogy, ~ŏl'ogist, ~ŏlŏ'gical; ~o-mūs'cular, of nerves & muscles; ~opath, person of abnormal nervous sensibility or affected by nervous disease, so ~opath'ic a., ~opathŏl'ogy, ~ŏp'athy¹; ~ŏp'athist, specialist in ~opathy; ~o-physiŏl'ogy, physiology of nervous system; ~o-psych'ic (-sik-), of nervous & psychic functions; ~ŏp'terous, of the *Neuroptera*, order of insects having four naked membranous transparent wings with reticulate neuration; ~ŏt'omy,

cutting of nerve to produce sensory paralysis; ~hypnŏl'ogy, science of hypnotism. [Gk *neuron*]

neurŏm'a (nūr-), n. (pl. ~ta). Tumour on nerve or in nerve-tissue. [f. Gk *neuron* nerve, -M]

neurŏs'is (nūr-), n. (pl. -ōsēs). Functional derangement due to disorders of nervous system; change in nerve-cells of brain prior to psychic activity. [as prec., -OSIS]

neurŏt'ic (nūr-), a. & n. (Drug) affecting nervous system; (person) affected with nervous disorder, of abnormal sensibility. [as prec., -OTIC]

neut'er, a. & n. **1.** (Gram.) neither masculine nor feminine (cf. COMMON¹, EPICENE), (of verb) intransitive; neutral, not taking or assisting either side, in war, argument, opinion, etc. (esp. *stand ~*, remain neutral, declare neutrality); (Bot.) without pistils & stamens, asexual; (Entom.) sexually undeveloped, sterile. **2.** n. noun, adjective, verb, or gender; person standing ~; sexually undeveloped female insect, esp. bee or ant; castrated animal. [L, =neither (*ne-* not, *uter* either)]

neut'ral, a. & n. **1.** Not assisting either of two belligerent States, belonging to a State that thus stands aloof, exempted or excluded from active or passive hostilities, taking neither side in dispute or difference of opinion, indifferent, impartial. **2.** Not distinctly marked or coloured, indefinite, vague, indeterminate, (~ *tint*, grey or slate-colour, whence ~-tint²ᴱᴰ² a. lit. & fig.). **3.** (Chem.) neither acid nor alkaline; (Electr.) neither positive nor negative; (Entom., Bot.) sexually undeveloped, asexual; hence or cogn. **neutral'ity** n., ~LY² adv. **4.** n. State or person; subject of ~ State. **5.** Position of the parts in a gear mechanism in which no power is transmitted. [f. L *neutralis* of neuter gender (prec., -AL)]

neut'ralize, v.t. Counterbalance, render ineffective by opposite force or effect; exempt or exclude (place) from sphere of hostilities. Hence ~A'TION n. [f. med. L *neutralisare* (prec., -IZE)]

neut'ron, n. Electrically neutral particle of about the same mass as a proton and probably consisting of an electron & a proton in close association. [f. NEUTRAL after *electron*]

névé (nāv'ā), n. Expanse of granular snow not yet compressed into ice at head of glacier. [F (L *nix nivis* snow, -ATE²)]

nev'er, adv. At no time, on no occasion, not ever, (often ~ *before, since, after, yet*; also repeated for emphasis; NOW *or* ~; ~ *is a long word or day*, comment on rash renunciation or despair or negative prophecy; *it is ~ too late to mend*, reformation is always possible); (colloq. expressing surprise or incredulity in sentence or elliptcally) surely not, you do not mean it, (*you ~ left the key in the lock!*; *He ate the whole turkey.*—'*Never!*'; *I ~ did!*,

new, a. **1.** Not existing before, now first made, brought into existence, invented, introduced, known or heard of, experienced, or discovered. (*New TESTAMENT*;) unfamiliar to. **2.** Renewed, fresh, further, additional; different, changed, (*a ~ mo-rality*; ~ *man*, Theol., one converted to Christianity, *put on the ~ man*, show con-version by amendment; *a ~ fashion*, ... whence *~fa'shioned* (-shond) a.; *may ~* **3.** (With the, as distinctive epithet implying difference of character) later, modern, ~*fangled*, (the ~ LEARNING, MODEL, COMEDY; *the ~ diplomacy, journal-ism, theology*, etc., advanced in method or doctrine, usu. derog.; *the ~ poor, rich, the ~ woman*, women who aspire to free-dom & independence & reject convention (the New World, America). **4.** Of recent origin, growth, arrival, or manufacture, now first used, not worn or exhausted, (~ *red sandstone*; ~ *potatoes, wine, cheese*; ~ *furniture, clothes, ever* ~; ~ OHUM; ~ *heart, pleasures, ever* ~; ~ *members of Parliament* etc.); not yet accustomed to, fresh from. **5.** (Of family or person) lately risen in position. **6.** ~ *comer*, person lately arrived; ~ DEAL²; New Englander, inhabitant of New Eng-land, six NE. States of U.S.A.; ~*fang'led* (-ngld) f. obs. ~*fangle* a. in same sense (-fangel inclined to take f. OE st. fang-, infin. fón takel). fond of novelty (now rare), different from the good old fashion, objectionably novel; ~ *moon*, moon when first seen as crescent after conjunction with sun, time of such appearance, (Bibl.) Hebrew festival; ~*year*, coming or lately begun year, first few days of year (~ *year's gift, wishes, etc.; ~year's eve, 31 Dec.*); *New year's day*, 1 Jan.; ~*year's eve, 31 Dec.*); New Zea-lander, Maori, also European settler in New Zealand. Hence (-)NESS n. [Aryan; OE níwe, cf. G neu, Gk neos, L novus]

new, adv. (preceding, & now usu. hy-phened with, qualified word), **1.** Newly, recently, just, (~*blown*, having just come into bloom, lit. & fig.; ~*born, & see below; ~built, & see below; ~coined*, esp. of words; ~*come*, lately ar-rived; ~*fallen snow; ~fledged; ~come, lately ar-rived; ~fallen snow; ~fledged; ~found*;

~*laid eggs; ~made; ~mown hay or lawn.* **2.** Anew, afresh, re-, (~*born*, re-generated, & see above; ~*build*, rebuild, & see above; ~*create*; ~*front*, put new front to; ~*furnish*; ~*model*, recast). [f. prec.]

new'el, n. Centre pillar of winding stair (open or hollow ~, central well of winding stair); post supporting stair-handrail at top or bottom. [f. OF nouel (L nux nucis nut, -AL)]

Newfound'land (or -fn̄dlănd'), n. Island at mouth of St Lawrence (~ *dog* or ~, also ~*er*, large breed of spaniel kind noted for swimming powers). Hence ~ER⁴(4) n.

Newg'ate, n. Celebrated London prison (~ *Calendar*, publication with accounts of ~ *prisoners*; ~ *fringe, frill*, beard grown below chin while face is shaven; || ~ knocker, curl worn by costermongers etc.). [place]

new'ish, adv. Recently (usu. with p.p. =NEW in sense 1 & often now preferred; hyphened w. attrib. part.; *the ~dis-covered country*; *a guest ~ arrived*; in new manner. [-IY³]

Newm'an, n. Town noted for horse-races (~ *coat* or ~, close-fitting overcoat for men or women); a card-game.

news (-z), n. pl. (usu. followed by sing. vb). **1.** Tidings, new information, fresh events reported, (have you heard the, this, or rarely these, ~?; *ill ~ flies apace*; *no ~ is good ~*; *that is too ~* already well known; *is there any, what is the, ~?*); (N~) part of newspaper title, as Evening N~. **2.** || ~ *agent*, dealer in ~papers etc.; ~*boy*, ~*man*, selling ~papers in streets; ~*letter*, letter sent out periodically with the ~ to country towns etc.; ~*monger*, gossip; ~*paper*, printed publication usu. daily or weekly containing the ~, advertise-ments, & literary matter; ~*print*, paper for printing ~papers on; ~*reel*, cinema film giving the ~ of the day; ~*room*, || reserved for ~paper-reading; ~*sheet*, simple form of ~paper; ~*stand*, stall for sale of ~papers; ~*vendor*, ~paper-seller. Hence ~*LESS*, ~*y²*, aa., ~*iNESS n.*(-z-), [pl. of NEW¹ after med. L nova neut. pl. of L novus new]

newt, n. Small tailed amphibian allied to salamander, eft. [for ewt (a newt=an ewt, cf. NICKNAME) var. of evet EFT]

Newt'on'ian, a. & n. **1.** Of Newton or his theory of the universe; devised eto. by Newton. **2.** n. Follower of Newton; ~ telescope or reflector. [Sir Isaac Newton (1642-1727). -IAN]

next, a. (occas. governing noun), adv., prep., & n. **1** adj. Lying, living, being, nearest or nearest to or nearest to (in the ~ *house*; *my ~ neighbour*; *lives ~ door*, in the ~ house; ~*-door neighbours*; ~ to felony, to blasphemous, almost; ~ to nothing, none, impossible, almost; ~ the fire; the skin with the flesh ~

ti; the shop ~ *to the corner*); soonest come to, first ensuing, immediately following, coming nearest in order etc. to, immediately before, (*will ask the ~ man I see, the ~ policeman; shall return ~ year, ~ Friday, on Friday ~; what is the ~ article?*, shopman's formula; *the Sunday ~ before Easter; what is true one day may be false the ~; not till ~ time*, joc. addition to promise of abstention; *the ~ town to London in size*; ~-*best*, second-best; *the person ~ him*, or ~ *to him*, in rank). 2. adv. (Often indistinguishable f. pred. use of adj.) In the ~ place or degree, on the ~ occasion, (*in the week ~ ensuing; what ~ came a strange figure; what ~?*, can anything follow to beat this for absurdity etc.; *placed his chair~ to hers; New York is the largest city ~ to London; when I ~ saw him he was lame*). 3. prep. (Often indistinguishable f. pred. adj. governing noun) In or into the ~ place, on the ~ occasion, in the ~ degree, to (*I was standing ~ him; placed his chair ~ hers; loves him ~ her own child; wear flannel ~ your skin*). 4. n. (or ellipt. use of adj.). ~ person or thing (~ *of kin*, person nearest of kin to someone; *will tell you in my ~*, i.e. letter; *to be continued in our ~*, i.e. issue of magazine etc.; *her ~*, i.e. husband, *was a greengrocer*, i.e. child, *was a girl; please, ask your ~ question, let the ~ man come*, etc.). [OE *nēahst* (NIGH, -EST)]

nex'us, n. Bond, link, connexion, (fig.) *the cash ~* (consisting in money payments). [L (*nectere nex-* bind)]

Niăg'ara, n. Cataract, torrent, din, (*shoot ~*, run fearful risks). [N.-Amer. waterfall]

nib, n., & v.t. (-bb-). 1. Point of quill pen; metal or quill pen-point for insertion in penholder; point of tool etc. 2. pl. Fragments of crushed cocoa-beans. 3. v.t. Make, mend, insert ~ of, (pen). [=Sc. *neb* nose, OE *nebb*, cf. ON *nef*, Du. *neb*]

nib'ble, v.t. & i., & n. 1. Take small bites at; bite (t. & i.) gently or cautiously or playfully (esp. of fish with bait, or rabbits; often ~ *at*, lit., & fig. of dallying with temptation, bargain, etc.); carp at, make trifling criticisms. 2. n. Act of nibbling, esp. of fish at bait; enough (grass etc.) to ~ at. [cf. LG *nibbelen*]

nib'lick, n. Golf-club with large round heavy head, used esp. for playing out of bunkers. [?]

nibs (-z), n. (sl.). *His* etc. ~, burlesque title after *His Grace* etc. [?]

nice, a. & adv. 1. Fastidious, dainty, hard to please, of refined or critical tastes; precise, punctilious, scrupulous, particular, (*must not be too ~ about the means*). 2. Requiring precision, care, tact, or discrimination (*a ~ experiment, question, point, negotiation*). 3. Minute, subtle, (*a ~ distinction, shade of meaning*). 4. Attentive, close, (*a ~ inquiry, observer*). 5. Delicately sensitive, discriminative, or deft (*a ~ ear, judgement, hand; weighed in the ~st scales*, lit. or fig.). 6. (colloq.). Agreeable, attractive, delightful, well-flavoured, satisfactory, kind, friendly, considerate, generally commendable (often iron., as *here is a ~ mess*). 7. ~ (*and*), satisfactorily, as *the house stands ~ & high, car is going ~ & fast, this is a ~ long one*; ~-*looking*, pretty or of engaging appearance. Hence ~'LY[2] (-sl-) adv., ~'NESS (-sn-) n., ni'cish[1][2] a. [earlier senses, stupid, wanton; OF f. L *nescius* ignorant (NESCIENCE)]

Nicene' (or ni²), a. Of Nicaea (*first & second ~ councils*, held A.D. 325, 787, to settle the Arian controversy & the question of images; ~ *Creed*, formal statement of Christian belief based on that adopted at first ~ council). [f. LL *Nicenus* (L f. Gk *Nikaia*)]

ni'cety, n. Punctiliousness; precision, accuracy, (*to a ~*, exactly); intricate or subtle quality (*a point of great ~*); minute distinction, subtle or unimportant detail, (pl.) minutiae. [f. OF *niceté* (NICE, -TY)]

niche, n., & v.t. 1. Shallow recess in wall to contain statue, vase, etc.; (fig.) place destined for person's occupation, esp. ~ *in the temple of fame*, right to be remembered for one's achievements. 2. v.t. Place (statue etc.) in ~ (usu. in p.p.); ensconce, settle, (esp. oneself, or in p.p.) in some hollow or corner. [F, f. It. *nicchia* etym. dub.]

nick¹, n. Notch serving as catch, guide, mark, etc.; certain throws in hazard; *in the ~ (of time)*, just at the right moment. [?]

nick², v.t. & i. 1. Make nick(s) in, indent; make incision at root of (horse's tail; also with *horse* etc. as obj.) to make him carry it higher; hit upon, guess rightly, (~ *it, the truth*, etc.); just catch (the time, a train, etc.); catch, nab, (criminals etc.); make (certain winning throws) at hazard; cut *in* by short cut, at corner, etc., in hunting or racing; (of breeding stocks) mingle *well* etc. with others. [?]

nick'el, n., & v.t. (-ll-). 1. Hard silvery-white lustrous ductile metallic element much used esp. in alloys; U.S. five-cent piece or kinds of Continental coin corresponding to English & French coppers; ~ *silver*, alloy like German silver; ~ *steel*, alloy of iron with ~. 2. v.t. Coat with ~. [abbr. of G *kupfernickel* copper-coloured ore f., which ~ was first got (*kupfer* copper, *nickel* demon, w. ref. to disappointing nature of ore, which yielded no copper]

nick-nack. See KNICK-KNACK.

nick'name, n., & v.t. 1. Name added to or substituted for person's, place's, or thing's proper name; abbreviation or familiar form of Christian name. 2. v.t. Call (person or thing a ~), give ~ to, (*some people are never ~d; they ~ patience*

courandice; Cumberland, ~d. Butcher), [NEWT]

nicō'tian (-shi-), a. & n. Of tobacco; (n.) smoker. [foll., -IAN]

nic'otin|e (-tēn), n. Poisonous alkaloid extracted as oily liquid from tobacco. Hence ~ISM(3) n., ~ĪZE(3) v.t. [F (Nicot, introducer of tobacco into France. -INE3)]

nic'tāte, nic'titate, v.i. Close & open the eyes, wink, chiefly in nict(it)ating membrane, third or inner eyelid of many animals. Hence nicta'TION, nictita'TION, nn. [f. (med.) L nictitare frequent. of L nictāre, -ATE3]

nī'cy, n. (nursery). Sweet, lollipop. [NICE, -Y3]

nidamen'tal, a. Serving as receptacle for ova in molluscs etc. (~ gland, capsule, ribbon). [f. L nidamentum (NIDUS, -MENT]

nid(d)'ering, n. & a. (pseudo-arch.). Base or cowardly (person), [misreading (in early printed text of William of Malmesbury) of obs. nithing f. ON nithing (with satire, cf. L neid envy); given currency by Scott]

nid'dle-nod'dle, a., & v.i. & t. 1. Nodding, quivering, unsteady. 2. v.b. Keep nodding (head, or intr.), totter, sway. [redupl. f. NOD, -LE(3)]

nī'de, n. Brood of pheasants. [f. L NIDUS]

nid'ificate, nid'ify, vv.i. Build nest(s). Hence nidifica'TION n. [f. L nidificare]

nid'us, n. (pl. -dī, -duses). Place in which insects etc. deposit eggs; place in which spores or seeds develop; place of origin or development for disease, or for some quality, doctrine, etc.; natural receptacle; collection of eggs, tubercles, etc. [L, see NEST]

niece, n. One's brother's or sister's daughter. [f. F nièce (L neptis cogn. w. NEPHEW]

Nietzsch'ean (nēch4-), a. & n. (Admirer, follower) of the German philosopher F. Nietzsche (d. 1900); (supporter) of his principles (see ÜBERMAN). [-AN]

Nier'steiner (nēist4-), n. A white hock. [G]

*****nif'ty**, a. (sl.). Spruce, smart, stylish; smelly. [?]

nigg'ard, n. & a. Stingy person, grudging giver of; (adj., rhet. & poet.)=foll. [etym. dub.; cf. obs. nig, nigon; prob. of F orig.]

nigg'ardly, a. & adv. Parsimonious, stingy, sparing, scanty, giving or given grudgingly or in small amounts; hence ~INESS n.; (adv.) in ~y manner. [-LY1,2]

nigg'er (-g-), n. Negro (usu. derog.; ~ in the woodpile or fence, sl., suspicious circumstance, something that spoils a good thing); (loosely) member of any dark-skinned race, e.g. E.-Indian, native Australian; black turnip caterpillar; ~(-brown), dark shade of brown.; ~head, see NEGRO; ~ melody, song, etc., such as prevail among American Negroes; ~head, = NEGRO-head. Hence ~DOM n. [earlier neger f. F nègre f. Sp. NEGRO]

nigg'le, v.i. Spend time, be over-elaborate on petty details. [cf. Norw. nigla]

nigg'ling, a. Trifling, petty, lacking in breadth, largeness, or boldness of effect; (of handwriting) cramped. [-ING2]

night (nit), n. 1. Dark period between day & day, time from 6 p.m. to 6 a.m. or from sunset to sunrise, darkness then prevailing, the dark, (also ~fall) end of daylight, weather or experiences or occupation of a ~; (black, dark, as ~) went forth into the ~; the ~ of ignorance or barbarism; stormy or rainy ~s with them; a dirty ~, cf. GOOD-~; make a ~ of it, spend ~ in festivity; ~ out, festive evening, also evening on which servant is allowed out; ~ & day, always, without cessation; all ~, long, for the whole ~; by ~, during the ~; at ~, at hours from 6 p.m. to midnight, cf. in the morning for the hours 1-6 a.m.; cannot sleep o' ~s for thinking of); ~-cellar, underground drinkshop of low class; ~-chair, =~-stool; ~-clothes, worn in bed; ~-club (open to members for dancing, supper, etc.); ~-dress, ~-gown (also ~'y'n, pr. nit'i), woman's or child's ~attire; ~-flower, that opens at ~ & closes in the day; ~-glass, short telescope for ~ use at sea; ~-hag, female demon riding the ~ air at ~; ~mare; ~-hawk, thieving or other nocturnal prowler; ~-jar, the goatsucker; ~-light, short thick candle giving dim light through ~ for invalids etc.; ~-time, left with baited hooks to catch fish by ~; ~-long, lasting

through the ~; ~'man, employed to remove ~soil; ~'mare, female monster sitting upon & seeming to suffocate sleeper, incubus, oppressive or paralysing or terrifying or fantastically horrible dream (whence ~'mārīsh¹ a.), also haunting fear or thing vaguely dreaded; ~'piece, (painting of) ~ scene or landscape; ~'school, providing instruction for workmen after day's work; ~ season, =~'time (poet., rhet.); ~'shirt, boy's or man's long shirt for sleeping in; ~'soil, contents of cesspools etc. removed at ~; ~'stool, closestool or commode for use at ~; ~'suit, set of pyjamas; ~'time, ~ as a state of things or opportunity (in the ~time, by ~); ~'watch, (person or party keeping) watch by ~, Hebrew or Roman division (one of three or four) of the ~ (in the ~watches, during the anxious, wearisome, wakeful, etc., ~); ~'work, done, that must be done, by ~. Hence ~'LESS (nit-)a. [Aryan; OE niht, cf. G nacht, L nox-ctis, Gk nux-ktos, Skr. nakta]

night'ingāle (nitinggr-), n. Small reddish-brown migratory bird singing melodiously & powerfully both by night & in the day. [OE nihtegale (NIGHT, galan sing), cf. G nachtigall]

night'ly¹ (nit-), a. Happening, done, existing, etc., in the night; happening every night; (poet.) of or suiting night. [OE nihtlic (NIGHT, -LY¹)]

night'ly² (nit-), adv. Every night. [-LY²]

night'shāde (nit-), n. Kinds of plants, esp. Black N~ with white flowers & black poisonous berries, Woody N~ with purple flowers & bright red berries, & Deadly N~ or belladonna. [OE nihtscada, cf. Du. nachtschade, G nachtschatten, probably f. NIGHT, SHADE, w. ref. to its poison]

nigrēs'c|ent, a. Blackish. So ~ENCE n. [f. L nigrescere (niger black), -ENT]

nig'ritūde, n. Blackness (lit. & fig.). [f. L nigritudo (prec., -TUDE)]

nī'hil dă rēm, pred. a. Irrelevant. [L]

nī'hilism (nī'il, nī'hil-), n. Negative doctrines, total rejection of current beliefs, in religion or morals: (Philos.) scepticism that denies all existence; doctrines of extreme revolutionary party in 19th-c. Russia finding nothing to approve of in the constituted order of things. Hence ~IST(2) n., ~IS'TIC a. [f. L nihil nothing, -ISM]

nihil'ity, n. Non-existence, nothingness; mere nothing, trifle, nullity. [f. med. L nihilitas (prec., -TY)]

nil, n. Nothing, no number or amount, (esp. in scoring at games etc., as three goals to ~); no number. [L]

nī'l'gai (-gī), n. Var. of NYLGHAU.

||nill, v.i., 3rd sing. pres. condit. Will he~ he, whether he likes it or not (now usu. willy-nilly). [obs. ne not, WILL¹]

Nilōm'ēter, n. Graduated pillar etc. showing height to which Nile rises. [f. Gk Neilometrion (-METER)]

Nilŏt'ic, a. Of the Nile or Nile region or its inhabitants. [f. L f. Gk Neilōtikos (Neilos Nile, -OT², -IC)]

nim'ble, a. Quick in movement, agile, swift, (the ~ shilling, or ninepence arch., circulating quickly); (of the mind etc.) versatile, clever, quick to apprehend, dextrous. Hence ~NESS n., nim'bLY² adv. [f. OE numol f. niman take, -LE(1)]

nim'bus, n. (pl. -bī, -buses). Bright cloud or halo investing deity or person or thing; bright disk or aureole round or over head of saint etc. in picture; (Meteorol.) raincloud. Hence ~RD² (-st) a. [L, = cloud]

nimī'etý, n. (rare). Excess, too much. [f. LL nimietas (L nimius excessive f. nimis too much, -TY)]

nim'inÿ-pim'inÿ, a. Affected, mincing, prim. [imit.]

Nim'rŏd, n. Great hunter or sportsman. [see Gen. x. 8, 9]

ninc'ompŏŏp, n. Simpleton, person without sense or character, ninny. [?]

nine, a. & n. 1. One more than eight, 9, IX, (often agreeing with understood noun, as ~ of the men, ~ of them, ~ o'clock or ~, cost ~ & six, will be ~ next birthday; ~o'clock wind, blowing from rifleman's left hand; twenty~ etc. or, not beyond ~ & ninety, ~ & twenty etc.; the N~, the Muses; ~ days' wonder, novelty that attracts much attention but is soon forgotten; ~ times out of ten, generally; possession is ~ POINTS of the law; cat has ~ lives, see LIFE; ||~'pins, kind of skittles; ~ tenths, nearly the whole; hence ~'FOLD (-nf-) a. & adv. 2. n. The number ~; card of ~ pips; to the ~s, to perfection (esp. dressed up to the ~s, elaborately). [Aryan; OE nigon, cf. G neun, Skr. năvan, Gk ennea, L novem]

nine'teen' (-nt-), a. & n. One more than eighteen, 19, XIX, (is nearly~, years old; twice ~ is 38; a ~&-sixpenny pair of shoes~, to the DOZEN). Hence ~TH² a. (~th hole, joc., golf-club's bar) & n. [-TEEN]

nine'tiÿ (-nt-), a. & n. 1. Nine times ten, 90, XC, (~y-one etc., or one etc. &~y; ~y-first etc.; ~y-nine out of a hundred, nearly all); hence~IETH² a. & n. 2. n. The number ~y; (pl.) the ~ies, degrees on thermometer etc., years of century or life, between 89 & 100. [-TY²]

Nin'evite, n. Inhabitant of Nineveh. [f. L Ninivita (Ninive, -ITE¹)]

ninn'ÿ, n. Simpleton, fool, person of weak character or mind. [perh. for INNOCENT]

ninon (nē'nawn), n. Light-weight silk dress fabric. [F]

ninth, a. & n. 1. Next after eighth (on the ~, day of month); ~ part, one of nine equal parts into which thing may be divided; ~ part of a man, tailor). 2. n.

~ part; (Mus.) interval of octave & second. [NINE, -TH¹]

ninth'ly, adv. In the ninth place (in enumerations). [-LY²]

Ni'obe, n. Inconsolable bereaved woman. Hence **Niōbē'an** a. [Gk (-ē), name of) turned to stone while weeping for slain children]

niŏb'ium, n. (chem.). A rare metallic element usn. found associated with tantalum. Hence ~**ic** (chem.). aa. [prec., -IUM: named 1845]

nip¹, v.t. & i. (-pp-), & n. 1. Pinch, squeeze sharply, bite; pinch off (bud etc.); check growth of (esp. ~ *in the bud*); (lit. & fig.); (of cold) affect injuriously; pain, whence ~**p'ing**² a., ~**p'ingly**² adv.; take *up, out*, etc., hurriedly or unobserved; (sl.) step in, nimbly *in(to), out, up*, whence ~**p'y**² a. ||(also as n., colloq. P, waitress in a restaurant of Messrs J. Lyons & Co., Ltd.). 2. n. Pinch, sharp squeeze, bite; sharp saying, sarcasm; (check to vegetation caused by) coldness of air. [cf. Du. *nijpen* nip, Du. & G *nippen* sip, Du. & G *nippen* wrangle]

nip², n., & v.i. & t. (-pp-). Small quantity of spirits etc. as pick-me-up; (vb) take ~s, take ~s of. [prob. for obs. *nipperkin* small measure of ale etc., etym. dub., prob. f. Du. orig.]

ni'pa (nē-, nĭ-), n. Kind of E.-Indian palm. [f. Malay *nīpah*]

nip'per, n. In vbl senses of NIP¹,²; also or esp.: kinds of fish; || boy, lad, esp. coster-monger's assistant or street arab; (pl.) implement with jaws for gripping or cutting, forceps, pincers, pliers, (often *pair of* ~s); (pl.) pince-nez; horse's incisor tooth; perforated projection of musket-lock on which percussion-cap was placed; ||~**swort**, yellow-flowered weed. [?]

nip'ple, n. Small projection in which mammary ducts terminate in mammal of either sex, teat, esp. on woman's breast; cover for protecting woman's teat while child sucks; teat of nursing-bottle; ~ etc.; small rounded elevation on mountain; perforated projection of musket-etc. the protuberance on skin, glass, metal,

Nipp'on, n. Japan. Hence **Nippon'ian** a. [f. Dai ~, native name of Japan (lit. 'Great land of the rising sun')]

nīrva'na (-vah-), n. Buddhist beatitude, i.e. extinction of individuality & absorption into the supreme spirit. [Skr. f. *nirvāṇa* (*nir, vās*, out + *vā* to blow)]

nis'i, conj. (legal). Unless (*decree, order, rule*, etc., ~, decree etc. valid unless cause is shown for rescinding it before absolute pointed time at which it is 'made absolute'; ||~ *prius*, hearing of civil causes by judges of assize, court-business of this kind). [L; ~ *prius*, unless before that, words from writ directing sheriff to provide jury on certain day unless judges come sooner]

Niss'en hut, n. Tunnel-shaped hut of corrugated iron with cement floor. [named after inventor]

nit¹, n. Egg of louse or other parasitic insect. [OE *hnitu*, cf. Du. *neet*, G *niss*]

nit'ōn, n. (Orig. name of) RADON. [f. L *nitēre* to shine, after *argon* etc.]

ni'trate¹, n. Salt given by combination of nitric acid with base, or compound made by interaction of nitric acid & alcohol; (short for) *potassium* or *sodium* ~. **nitrāte²'**, v.t. Treat, combine, or impregnate, with nitric acid. Hence ~**A'TION** n. [NITRE, -ATE¹(3)]

ni'tre (-er), n. Saltpetre, potassium nitrate; *cubic* ~, sodium nitrate. [F, f. L *nitrum* perh. of Oriental orig.]

ni'tric, a. Of, containing, nitrogen; ~ *acid*, clear colourless pungent highly corrosive & caustic liquid, aquafortis. [f. F *nitrique* (prec., -IC)]

ni'trify, v.t. Impregnate with nitrogen, turn into nitrous or nitric acid. So ~**FICA'-TION** n. [f. F *nitrifier* (NITRE, -FY)]

ni'trite, n. Compound of base or alcohol with nitrous acid. [NITRE, -ITE¹(2)]

nitro-, comb. form of Gk *nitron* NITRE, = of, containing, made with or by use of, nitric acid or nitroxyl or nitre or nitrogen; ~*a'cid*, compound of nitric with organic acid; ~*com'pound* (made by action of nitric acid); ~*explos'ive* (prepared by means of nitric acid); ~*gly'cerine*, yellowish oily violently explosive liquid made by adding glycerine to mixture of nitric & sulphuric acids; ~*pow'der*, gunpowder made with nitric acid; ~*sulphur'ic*, formed by mixture of nitric & sulphuric acids; *nitrox'yl*, chemical grouping of nitrogen & oxygen.

nit'rogen, n. Colourless tasteless scentless gas forming four-fifths of atmosphere. Hence **nitrŏ'genous** a. [f. F *nitrogène*, see NITRE, -GEN(1)]

nit'rous a. Of, like, impregnated with, nitre (~ *acid*, containing less oxygen than nitric acid; ~ *oxide*, gas used as anaesthetic, laughing-gas). [f. L *nitrosus* (NITRE, -OUS)]

nix¹, n. (fem. ~*ie*). Water-elf. [G (fem. cogn. ~*ie*), cf. OE *nicor*, Du. *nikker*, perh. cogn. w. Gk *nizō* wash]

nix², int. (sl.). Nothing. [f. G *nichts*]

Nizam' (-ahm), n. Ruler of Hyderabad; (man, men, of) Turkish regular army. [Hind. & Turk. f. Arab. *nidām* order, arrangement]

nō², a. 1. Not any (*no circumstances could justify it; no date*, abbr. n.d., = undated, in library lists etc.; *no song no supper,*

you must sing first; no END¹; by no MEAN¹s). **2.** Not a, quite other than a, (service of no honourable kind; is no part of my plan; is no genius); hardly any (is no distance; did it in no time); there is etc. no —ing, none is etc. possible (there's no ac- counting for tastes; there was no mistaking what he meant). **3.** Imperfect substitute for, absence of, (often *no-*: these opinions or rather no opinions; his faith or no-faith). **4.** (In ellipt. sentences) we will not have any, let there not be any, there is not any, (no Popery, surrender, etc., whence no-Popery riots, a no-confidence vote, etc.; now no mistake, understand me clearly; & no MISTAKE¹; no cards, no flowers, invitations to funeral are not being sent out, floral tributes are not desired; no DOUBT¹; no FEAR¹; no WONDER¹). **5.** No ball, unlawfully delivered ball in cricket, umpire's announcement of this, (vb, no-ball) pronounce (bowler) to have bowled no ball; no-being, non-existence *is nobody's business*; *nobody ever did his*, or irreg, *their*, *work better*), (w. pl.) person of no importance, authority, or position; no bon (army sl.), no good; no GO²; no'how, In no way, by no means, (now chiefly dial.), be, feel, look, etc., nohow, out of order, out of sorts; no mam, no person (no man's land, piece of waste, unowned, or debatable ground, esp. Mil. the space between opposed trenches); no meaning, nonsense; no one, no person, (also, as adj.) no single (no one man could lift it); no side (Football), (referee's announcement of the) end of the game; no thoroughfare, notice that path, street, etc., is closed at other end, or that entrance is not per- mitted, (also) such path; no trump(s) (Bridge), declaration, bid, involving playing without a trump suit; no-trumper, hand on which a no-trump bid can be, or has been, made; no'way(s), no'wise, in no manner, not at all; no-whence, no'whither, from, to, no place; no whit, not at all (usu. w. compar.). [for NONE, orig. only before consonants]

nō², adv. **1.** (Alw. with compar.) by no amount, not at all, (no better than before; is no better than she should be, is not quite respectable; no sooner had he said it than, as soon as he had said it; no LONG¹er). **2.** No less (than) as much (n., a., adv.) or many (as)(have me £50, no less, no less than £50; no less than ten people have told me; did it no less for my warning; is no less than a scandal; a no less fatal victory). **3.** No more, (n.) nothing further (have no more to say; want no more of it; often ellipt. for say no more or let us have no more of it); (adj.) not any more (no more wine?); (adv.) no longer (is no more, is dead or passed away), never again, to no greater extent (is no more a lord than I am; could no more help laughing than I could fib), just as little, neither, (you did not come, no more did he). [OE nā, see NATHLESS]

nō⁴, particle equivalent to negative sen- tence, & n. (pl. noes). **1.** The answer to your question is negative, your request or command will not be complied with, the statement made or course intended or conclusion arrived at is not correct or satisfactory, (no, nor, form for substitut- ing stronger phrase, as a man could not lift it, no, nor half a dozen). **2.** n. The word no, a denial or refusal, (two noes make a yes; will not take no for an answer; persists in spite of refusals); (pl.) voters against a motion (the noes have it, are in a majority). [as prec.]

Nōach'ian, Nōach'ic, (-k-), aa. Of Noah or his time. [Noah= Noah, -IAN]

Nō'ah (-ǝ), n. Hebrew patriarch; ~'s ark, in which ~, his family, & animals were saved (Gen. vi), imitation of it as a child's plaything, large or cumbrous or old- fashioned trunk or vehicle, small bivalve, detached fragment of flying cloud; ~'s nightcap, the plant eschscholtzia (w. ref. to conical head-sheaths).

nŏb¹, n., & v.t. (sl.; -bb-). Head: (Crib- bage) knave of same suit as turn-up (one for his ~, point scored by holder of this); (vb, Boxing) hit on the head. [perh. var. of KNOB]

nŏb², n. (sl.). Member of upper classes. [perh. for nobleman, but Sc. form is knabb]

‖ nŏb'le, v.t. (sl.). Tamper with (race- horse) to prevent its winning; secure par- tiality of by underhand means; get hold of (money etc.) dishonestly; catch (crimi- nal). [?]

nŏbb'y, a. (sl.). Smart, elegant. [-Y²]

nōbil'iary (-lyǝ-), a. Of (the) nobility (~ particle, preposition, as French de, Ger- man von, prefixed to title; ~ pride, rank, etc.). [f. F nobiliaire (NOBLE, -ARY]

nōbil'ity, n. Noble character, mind, birth, or rank; the or a class of nobles. [f. L nobilitas (foll. -TY]

nō'ble, a. & n. **1.** Illustrious by rank, title, or birth, belonging to the nobility (~ of lofty character or ideals (so ~-mindED² a., ~-mind'edness n.); showing great- ness of character, magnanimous, morally elevated; splendid, magnificent, stately, imposing, impressive, in appearance; excellent, admirable, (a ~ horse, cellar, etc.); (of metals such as gold, silver, platinum) resisting chemical action, not corroding or tarnishing in air or water, not easily attacked by acids; ~man,

peer; **~woman**, woman of ~ birth or rank; hence **~NESS** n. [L,=man: cf. ~man: obsolete coin, usu. 6/8. [F, f. L *nobilis* (*noscere* KNOW,-BLE)]

noblesse', n. The class of nobles (esp. of a foreign country); ~ *oblige* (ŏblēzh'), privilege entails responsibility. [F]

nock¹, n. & v.t. **1.** Notch at ends of bow for holding string; notched horn tip of arrow for receiving bowstring. **2.** v.t. Set (arrow) on string. [perh.=foll.: prob. not conn. w. NOTCH]

nock², n. Forward upper corner of some sails. [f. Du. *nok*]

noct(i)-, comb. form of L *nox noctis* night ~*ámb'ulant* night-walking, ~*iva'gous* night-wandering.

noct'ûíne, n. [F.f. It. *nottola* bat]

noctûrn'al, a. Of, in, done by, active in, the night. [f. LL (-*tis*) f. L *nocturnus* (NOCT-),-AL]

noctûrne, n. Dreamy musical piece; night-scene. [F; cf. prec.]

nod, v.i. & t. (-dd-), & n. **1.** Incline head slightly & quickly in salutation (~*ding acquaintance*, very slight one with person or subject), assent, or command; let head fall forward in drowsiness, be drowsy, make sleepy mistake (*Homer sometimes* ~*s*, the best of us may be dull or make a slip); (of buildings etc., also fig.) incline from perpendicular (esp. ~*s to its fall*); (of plumes) dance up & down; incline (head); signify (assent etc.) by ~. **2.** ~*ding* of the head; this as sign of absolute power (*the empire was at or dependent on his* ~); *land of Nod*, sleep (with ref. to phr. in *Gen.* iv. 16). [exal. E; from 14th c.; etym. dub.]

nod'dle¹, n. (colloq.). Head, pate. [?]

nod'dle², v.t. Nod or wag (head). [NOD,-LE(3)]

nodd'ÿ, n. Simpleton, noodle; tropical sea-bird. [perh. f. obs. *noddy* foolish (perh. NOD,-Y²)]

node, n. Knob on root or branch; point at which leaves spring; hard tumour esp. on gouty or rheumatic joint; intersecting point of planet's orbit & ecliptic or of two great circles of celestial sphere, whence **nod'ICAL** a.; point or line of rest in vibrating body; central point in system; point at which curve crosses itself. Hence **nodose'**, a. Knotty, knobbed. [f. L NODUS]

nod'ÿ a. [f. L NODUS]

nodôs'itÿ, n. Knottiness (proc.,-ITY)]

nodôs'ÿ, a. Knottiness (proc.,-TY)]

nod'ûle, n. Small rounded lump of anything; small node in plant; small knotty tumour, ganglion. Hence **~ated** [-ATE²], ~OSE¹, ~OUS, aa.,~A'TION n. [f. L *nodulus* (foll.,-ULE)]

nôd'us, n. (pl. -dï).

culty, complication in plot of story etc. [L,=knot, w. spec. ref. to *dignus vindice nodus* complication requiring divine intervention]

Noël, =NOWEL.

noét'ic, a. & n. **1.** Of the intellect; purely intellectual or abstract; given to intellectual speculation. **2.** n. (Sing. or pl.) science of the intellect. [f. Gk *noētikos* (*noeō* apprehend,-IC]

nog¹, n., & v.t. (-gg-). **1.** Pin, peg, small block, of wood; snag or stump on tree. **2.** v.t. Secure with ~s; build in form of (*brick-*, *concrete-*, *stone-*) ~. [?]

nog², n. Kind of strong beer brewed in E. Anglia. [?]

nogg'in, n. Small mug; small measure, usu. ¼ pint, of liquor. [?]

noil, n. (Sing. or pl.) short wool-combings. [?]

noise (-z), n., & v.t. & i. **1.** Loud outcry, clamour, shouting, din of voices & movements; any sound, esp. loud or harsh or undesired one, whence ~*LESS* a., ~*less-ly* adv., ~*LESSNESS* n., (-z¹-); *big* ~ (colloq., orig. U.S.), person of importance; *make a* ~, lit., also talk or complain much about, also be much talked of, attain notoriety in the world. **2.** vb. Make public, spread abroad, (person's fame, fact; *it was* ~*d abroad that*—); (rare) make ~. [F, cf. Pr. *noysa*, *nosa*, *nausa*, etym. dub.]

noisette' (nwahzět'), n. Kind of rose, cross between China & musk. [N~, grower, 1817]

noisette² (as prec.), n. (Usu. pl.) small piece(s) of meat cooked in certain way. [F]

nois'ome, a. Harmful, noxious; ill-smelling; objectionable, offensive. Hence ~*NESS* n. [obs. *noy* for ANNOY n.,-SOME]

nois'ÿ (-z-), a. Clamorous, turbulent; full of, making much, noise; (of colour, costume, literary style) loud, conspicuous, violent, gaudy. Hence ~*LY*² adv., ~*NESS* n. [-Y¹]

nol'ens vol'ens (-z), adv. Willy-nilly, perforce. [L partic.=unwilling, willing]

nōl'ī mē tān'gere (-j-), n. Erosive ulcer(s), lupus; warning against meddling or approach (*carries a* ~ *in his face*; ~ *manner*); picture of Christ as he appeared to Magdalen at sepulchre (*John* xx. 17). [L,=touch me not]

‖ nōll, n. (now dial.). (Crown of) head. [OE *hnol*, cf. OHG *hnol*]

nōl'ē prōs'equī, n. (legal). Relinquishment by plaintiff or prosecutor of (part of) his suit, stay of proceedings, entry of it on record. [L,=to refuse to pursue]

nôt'ē ēpiscopā'rī, n. (Formula expressing avoidance of responsible office. [L,=I do not wish to be a bishop]

nōm'ad (*also* nō'-), n. & a. (Member of tribe) roaming from place to place for pasture; wanderer; wandering. Hence or

cogn. **nomād'ic** a., **nomād'ically** adv., ~**ISM**(2) n., ~**IZE**(2) v.i. [f. L f. Gk *nomas -ados* (*nemō* to pasture)]

nŏm'āde. Var. (now rare) of prec.

nom de guerre (see Ap.), n. Pseudonym, assumed name under which person fights, plays, writes, etc. [F, = war-name]

nom de plume (see Ap.), n. Writer's pseudonym, title or initials or borrowed name under which he writes. [formed in E of F words=pen-name on anal. of prec.]

nŏm'enclātor, n. Slave or client in ancient Rome charged with naming persons met, usher assigning places at banquet, (also in mod. use with ref. to these senses): giver or inventor of names, esp. in nat.-hist. classification. [L (*nomen*, *calare* call, -OR²)]

nŏm'enclāture, n. Catalogue, register, (now rare): person's or community's system of names for things; terminology of a science etc.: systematic naming. So ~**ATIVE** a. [f. L *nomenclatura* (prec., -URE)]

nŏm'inal, a. Of, as, like, a noun (~ *& verbal roots*); of, in, names (~ *& essential distinctions*): ~ *definition*, statement of all marks connoted in name of concept); existing in name only, not real or actual, (~ *& real price, ruler*; ~ *sum, rent*, etc., virtually nothing), whence ~**LY²** adv.; ~ consisting of, giving, the names (~ *list of officers* etc.; ~ *roll*). [f. L *nominalis* (*nomen -inis* name f. *noscere* KNOW, -MEN)]

nŏm'inalism, n. (philos.). Doctrine that universals or abstract concepts are mere names (opp. *realism*). So ~**ist** n., ~**is'**tic a. [f. F *nominalisme* (prec., -ISM)]

nŏm'ināte, v.t. Call by the name of, mention by name, name or appoint (date, place), (now rare): appoint, propose for election, to office (*a board of six* ~*ed & six elected members*; *the candidates were* ~*ed today*), whence or cogn. ~**OR²**, **nŏminēE'**, nn. [f. L *nominare* (NOMINAL, -ATE³)]

nŏminā'tion, n. In vbl senses: also, right of nominating for appointment (*have a* ~ *at your service*). [f. L *nominatio* (prec., -ATION)]

nŏm'inative, a. & n. 1. (Case) used as or in agreement with subject of verb, (~ *absolute*, construction like Latin ablative absolute, *as this being so, I did* (*now&then*): word in this case (~ *ending, form*): word in this case, (loosely) subject (of verb); hence **nŏm'inatīv'AL** a. 2. (*pr. -ātiv*). Of, appointed by, nomination (*the* ~ *& the elective principles, members*). [f. L *nominativus* (NOMINATE, -IVE)]

nŏn-, Latin adv. = not, forming part of phrases: ~ *assūmp'sit* (he did not undertake), plea that defendant made no promise: ~ *cŏm'pŏs* (*mĕn'tis*), (not master of his mind), hnmatic, mad, (legal, & in gen. use): ~ *ĕss'e* (not to be), non-existence; ~ *ĕst ĭnvĕn'tus* (he has not been found),

~ *ĕst*, or ~ *ĭnvĕn'tus*, sheriff's statement, in returning writ, that defendant is not to be found in his bailiwick (legal, & transf. in gen. use): ~ *liq'uĕt* (it is not clear), jury's verdict in doubtful case deferring matter to another day: ~ *nŏb'īs* (not unto us: *Ps.* cxv), formula attributing victory etc. not to oneself but to God, song of rejoicing: ~ *plā'cet* (it does not please), negative vote in ecclesiastical or university assemblies (also as v.t., throw out): ~ *plūs ūl'tra*, = NE PLUS ULTRA: ~ *pŏss'ūmus* (we cannot), statement of inability, refusal to act or move: ~ *sĕq'uĭtur* (it does not follow), illogical inference, paradoxical result.

nŏn-, pref. (AF *noun-* f. OF *non-*, *nom-*, *num-*, *num-*, f. prec.) now freely prefixed: 1. Usu. to vbl n. giving neg. vbl n. corresp. to *not* w. parent vb., = failure to do, abstention from doing, or rarely to other n. giving neg. abstract n. corresp. to *not* w. connected adj.: ~*accept'ance*: ~*ac'cess*, impossibility of access for sexual intercourse (in questions of paternity): ~*acquain'tance*: ~*appear'ance* (esp. in court as party or witness): ~*atten'dance*: ~*claim*, failure to make claim within legal time: ~*committ'al*, avoidance of committing oneself to definite course or either side (usu. attrib., as ~*committal answer*): ~*compli'ance*: ~*co-opera'tion* (Indian pol.), refusal or failure to co-operate (with the British): ~*feas'ance* (-z-: legal), omission of act that ought to have been done: ~*inter-fēr'ence*, ~*interven'tion*, principle or practice, esp. in politics & international affairs, of keeping aloof from others' disputes: ~*intru'sion* (Church of Scotland), principle that patron shall not thrust unacceptable minister on congregation: ~*join'der* (legal), omission of partner etc. to join another as party to suit: ~*pay'ment*: ~*percep'tion*: ~*perform'ance*: ~*resis'tance* (hist.), 17th-c. principle that authority must not be resisted even if unjustly exercised: ~*success*: ~*us'age*: ~*use*, ~*us'er* (legal), neglect to use a right, by which it may become void. 2. To n. of designation, giving n. (occas. w. derivatives)=person, thing, or all, that is not the thing specified: ~*abstain'er*, one who does not abstain (esp. from liquor): ~*eg'o* (metaphys.), all that is not the conscious self, the object as opposed to the subject: ~*mem'ber* (so ~*mem'bership*): ~*met'al* (esp. chem.=element that is not a metal: so ~*metall'ic*). 3. To attrib. n., giving adj. (occas. w. derivatives) that can only be used attributively, = unconnected with, not involving: ~*jur'y*, tried without jury: ~*part'y*, that may be dealt with irrespective of political partisanship: ~*skid'*, (of tires) safe against skidding: ~*soci'ety*, ~*ăn'ion* (also ~*ăn'ionist*), not belonging to a workman's society or trade

union; **~-stop**, (of trains, buses, etc.) not stopping at intermediate stations, halts, etc., (of journey) made without a stop, (n.) ~-stop train, bus, or run, (adv.) without a stop. **4.** To adj. (usn. participial in *-ant*, *-ent*, *-ing*, *-ate*, *-ed*), giving adj. (& occas. n. or derivatives) = not; **~-belli'gerent** a. & n., (country) taking no active part in war; **~-colle'giate**, (student) not belonging to a college, (of universities) without colleges; **~-com'batant**, (person, esp. in the fighting services, e.g. surgeon, chaplain, ambulance man) who has not to fight, civilian; **~-commi'ssioned**, not holding commission (esp. of army officers such as sergeant, corporal, abbr. N.C.O. or non-com.); **~-comman'dant**, (person) who does not attend the communion service; **~-conducting**, that will not conduct heat or electricity (so ~-conduc'tor, ~-conducting medium or substance; ~-conductiv'ity); **~-content**, voter against motion in House of Lords; **~-essen'tial** a. & n.; **~-Eucli'dean**, denying or dispensing with any of the assumptions of Euclid's geometry; **~-exis'tent**, ~-exis'tence; **~-flamm'able**, (of flannelette etc.) not inflammable; **~-ju'ring**, -jur'or, (joor-; hist.), (beneficed clergyman) who refused oath of allegiance to William & Mary; **~-provi'ded**, (of schools) other than PROVIDED. **5.** To adj. requiring a neutral negative form free from some special sense, usn. of condemnation, attached to the compd in *in-*, *un-* = not coming under the description of, not; **~-effec'tive**, ~-effi'cient a. & n.; **~-off'ice-holding** etc.; (soldier, sailor) not qualified for active service (cf. INEFFECTIVE); **~-hūm'an**, not belonging to human race (cf. INHUMAN); **~-lo'gical**, proceeding by other means than logic (cf. ILLOGICAL); **~-mo'ral**, unconcerned with morality (cf. IMMORAL); **~-na'tural**, deviating from the natural order (cf. UNNATURAL). **6.** To adv., as ~contentiously.

non'age, n. Being under age, minority; immaturity, early stage. [OF (prec., AGE)]

nonagenar'ian, a. & n. (Person) between 89 & 100 years old. [f. L *nonagenarius* (*monagem* 90 each, -ARY[1]), -IAN]

non'ary a. & n. (Arith.) (of SCALE[2] of notation) having nine as basis; (n.) group of nine. [f. L *nonarius* (*nonus* ninth, -ARY[1])]

nonce, n. Time being, present occasion, (only in *for the ~*); **~-word**, coined for one occasion. [ME *to*, +*for*, *than ones* = (for) the ONCE, cf. NEWT]

non'chalant (-sh-), a. Unexcited, unmoved, cool, indifferent. Hence ~ANCE (-NON-, ~anty[2] adv. [F, part. of *nonchaloir* (NON-, L *calēre* be warm)]

nonconform'ist, n. One who does not conform to doctrine or discipline of an established Church, esp. member of sect dissenting from Anglican Church (usn. not including Roman Catholics), protestant dissenter (the ~ *conscience*, opinions as to right & wrong prevalent among ~s esp. as affecting their political attitude). [NON-(2)]

nonconform'ity, n. Principles, practice, the body, of nonconformists, protestant dissent; failure to conform (to rule etc.); want of correspondence between things. [NON-(2)]

non'descript, a. & n. (Person, thing) not easily classified, neither one thing nor another, hybrid. [NON-(4), l. *descriptus* (DESCRIBE)]

none (nŭn), pron., a., & adv. **1.** Not any of (~ *of them came*; ~ *of them is*, or *are*, acc. to sense required; ~ *of this concerns me*; (now rare; ~ *can tell*; no persons, no one, *fools have ever believed it*). **2.** adj. (rarely with noun; usn. ellipt. ~ no with reference defined by noun previously used or shortly to follow). No, not any, not to be counted in specified class, (*make of ~ effect*, arch.; *you have money & I have ~*; *he is ~ of my friends*, *you of your canting clearest*; *this is ~ other but the house of God*; *seeking rest & finding ~*; *if a linguist is wanted, I am ~*; *would rather have a bad reputation than ~ at all*; *poetry we have almost ~*). **3.** adv. By no amount, not at all, (w. *the* & comparat., *so*, or *too*; *am ~ the better for it*; ~ *the less*, = NEVERthe-less; *we ~ so fond of him*; *the pay is ~ too high*). [OE *nān* (*ne* not, ONE)]

nonen'tity, n. **1.** (tōn-). Non-existence, non-existent thing, figment. **2.** (non-). Person or thing of no importance, cipher. [NON-(2)]

nonesuch. See NONSUCH.

nonet' (-ā), n. (mus.). Composition for nine instruments or voices. [f. It. *nonetto* (*nono* ninth f. L *nonus*)]

nonill'ion (-yon), n. ‖ Ninth power of million, 1 with 54 ciphers. [see NONARY, BILLION]

non'ius, n. Contrivance for graduating mathematical instruments, of which the VERNIER is an improved form. [latinized from *Nunes*, Portuguese inventor]

nonpareil' (-rěl), a. & n. Unrivalled or unique (person, thing); (Print.) size of TYPE; kinds of comfit, apple, bird, wheat, moth, etc. [F (NON-, L *par* equal, -eil-dim.)]

nonplus', n., & v.t. (-ss-). **1.** State of perplexity, standstill, (usn. *at a ~*, perplexed, *reduce etc. to a ~*). **2.** v.t. Reduce to hopeless perplexity. [f. L *non plus* not more]

nŏn-rĕs'ident (-zĕ-), a. & n. (Clergyman) not residing where his duties require him, absentee (incumbent); (person) sojourning in place only for short time or residing elsewhere. So ~ENCE n. [NON-(2)]

nŏn'sense, n. & int. 1. Absurd or meaningless words or ideas, foolish or extravagant conduct; arrangement etc. that one disapproves of. 2. int. You are talking or proposing ~, it surely cannot be true, etc. 3. ~book, meant to amuse by absurdity; ~ verses, having no sense or an absurd one. Hence **nŏnsĕn'sical**¹ a., **nŏnsĕn'sically**² adv. [NON-(2)]

nŏn sŭch, nōne'sŭch (nŭns-), n. Person or thing that is unrivalled, paragon; kind of lucerne. [NONE, SUCH, usu. now assim. to NON-]

nŏn'suit (-sūt), n., & v.t. 1. Stoppage of suit by judge when plaintiff fails to make out legal case or bring sufficient evidence. 2. v.t. Subject (plaintiff) to ~. [NON-(2)]

nŏn'us. See PRIMUS¹.

nŏo'dle¹, n. Simpleton. Hence ~DOM n. [?]

nŏo'dle², n. Strip of dough made of flour & eggs, dried & used in soups. [f. G *nudel* vermicelli]

nook, n. Out-of-the-way corner, recess, secluded place. [?]

noon, n. Twelve o'clock in the day, midday; ~*day*, ~*tide*, midday. [OE *nōn* f. L *nona* (*hora*) ninth hour; orig.=3 p.m.]

nōose, n., & v.t. 1. Loop with running knot, tightening as string is pulled, esp. in snare, lasso, or hangman's halter; the marriage tie; snare or bond. 2. v.t. Capture with ~, ensnare; make ~ on (cord); arrange (cord) in ~ round neck etc. [cf. OF *nous* f. L *nodus* knot]

nŏp'al, n. American cactus grown in plantations for breeding cochineal. Hence ~RY(3) n. [Sp., f. Mex. *nopalli* cactus]

nor (nôr, nŏr), adv. & conj. 1. (arch.). Neither (as the first *nor* in ~*gold* ~*silver*). 2. conj. And not, & no more, neither, & not either, (*had neither arms* ~ *provisions*; *not a man* ~ *a child was to be seen*; *I said I had not seen it*, ~ *had I*; *all that is true*, ~ *must we forget*; also poet. & arch. w. omission of preceding *neither* or ~, *as thou* ~ *I have made the world*). [prob. f. obs. *nother* (OE *nā* see NATHLESS, WHETHER)]

nor'-. Shortened form of NORTH.

Nŏrd'enfĕlt, n. Kind of machine-gun. [Swedish inventor]

Nŏrd'ic, a. (ethnol.). Of the tall blond dolichocephalic race found in northern Europe esp. in Scandinavia (of more limited application than *Teutonic*). [G *nord* north+-IC]

Nŏr'folk (-ŏk), n. English county (||~ *capon*, red herring; ||~ *dumpling*, *turkey*; inhabitant or native of ~; ||~ *Howard*, sl., bed-bug; ~ *jacket*, man's loose jacket with waistband; ~ *plover*, stone-curlew). || **nŏr'land**, n. Northern region. [for *north*.]

nŏrm, n. Standard, pattern, type. [f. L *norma* carpenter's square]

nŏrm'al, a. & n. 1. (Geom.) standing at right angles, perpendicular; conforming to standard, regular, usual, typical; ~ *school*, for training teachers; hence **nŏrmāl'ITY** (also irreg. ~CY) n., ~IZE(3) v.t., ~ĪZA'TION n., ~LY² adv. 2. n. (Geom.) line; (Physics) average or mean of observed quantities; usual state, level, etc., ~ *temperature* (98.4°) of human body. [f. L *normalis* (prec., -AL]

Nŏr'man, n. & a. 1. Inhabitant or native of Normandy, descendant of mixed Scandinavian & Frankish race there established; ~ *French* below; = ~ *style* below. 2. adj. Of the ~s (~ *Conquest*, of England by ~s 1066; ~ *English*, *French*, French as spoken by ~s or later in English law-courts; ~ STYLE in architecture, whence ~ESQUE', pr. -ĕsk, a.); hence ~ISM(2,4) n., ~IZE(3, 4) v.t. & i., ~ĪZA'TION n. [f. OF *Normans* pl. f. Teut. NORTH+MAN]

Nŏrn, n. One of the female fates of Scandinavian mythology. [ON, etym. dub.]

Nŏr'roy, n. Third KING of Arms, with jurisdiction north of the Trent. [f. AF *nor-* NORTH, *roy* king]

Nŏrse, n. & a. 1. The Norwegian language (*Old* ~, language of Norway & its colonies down to 14th c.). 2. adj. Norwegian, of Norway, so ~*land*, ~*man*. [prob. f. Du. *noorsch* (*noord* NORTH, -ISH¹)]

Nŏrth, adv., n., & a., (abbr. N.; in compp. & deriv. often shortened to *nor'-*). 1. Towards or in the region lying to right of observer on equator at equinox who faces setting sun (~ BY *east* etc.; ~ *of*, further ~ than; DUE¹; *lies* etc. ~ *& south*, lengthwise along line running between ~ & south); ~*-east*, ~*-west*, (abbr. NE., NW.), advv., nn., & aa., (regions) midway between ~ & east, west, ~~*east*, ~*west*, (abbr. NNE., NNW.), advv., nn., & aa., (regions) midway between ~ & ~ east, ~*west*, (with uses & derivatives corresponding to those of *north*; so esp. ~*-east'erly*, ~*west'erly*, ~*east'ern*, ~*west'ern*, ~*east'ward*, ~*west'ward*, ~*east'wardly*, ~*west'wardly*, see NORTHERLY etc.; ~*-east*, ~*-west*, *passage*, passages for ships along northern coasts of Europe & Asia, northern coast of America, formerly thought of as possible routes to E. & from Atlantic to Pacific; *the N~-west*, = NW. territories of Canada); hence ~*WARD adv.*, n., & a., ~*WARDS advv.*. &c. 2. n. Cardinal point lying ~ (*magnetic* ~, point indicated by ~ end of compass-needle); northern part of England (beyond Humber); Great Britain, Scotland, Ireland, or Europe; *northern* States in which slavery did not exist; northern part of any country; ~ *wind*. 3. adj. Situated, dwelling, in or more towards the ~ (*N~ Germany*, *Wales*,

America; the N~ Germans; ~ latitude; ~ POLE² whence ~-pŎ'LAR a.; ~ transept); facing the ~ (~ window, aspect); coming from the ~ (~ wind; ~ light, esp., as described by painters); N~ Britain, Scotland; Scot; ||N~ Country, ~ part of England or Great Britain (N~-coun'tryman, native or characteristic of N~ Country); N~'land (poet.,) northern part of a country; ~ light, Aurora Borealis; N~'man, native of Norway or Scandinavia; N~ Sea, between Britain, Netherlands, Germany, & Scandinavia; N~'star, POLE²-star. [com.-Teut.; OE north, f. Du. noord, G nord]

north-east'er, n. NE. wind. [-ER¹]

*north'er, n. Strong cold north wind blowing in autumn & winter over Texas, Florida, & Gulf of Mexico. [-ER¹]

north'erly (-dh-), a. & adv. =foll. (rare); (of direction) towards the north; (of wind) blowing from the north or thereabouts. [f. NORTH as EASTERLY]

north'ern (-dh-), a. & n. 1. Living or situated in, coming from, the north esp. of England or Europe; *of the NORTH; (of wind) northerly (rare); characteristic of the north (a pallid ~ day); ~ lights, Aurora Borealis; hence ~ER·¹⁴) n., ~MOST a. 2. n. ~er. [-EN¹]

north'ing, n. Northward progress or deviation in sailing or travelling (two miles ~; have made very little ~). [-ING¹]

North'um'brian, a. & n. (Native, dialect) of ancient Northumbria (England N. of Humber) or modern Northumberland. [Northumber, person living beyond Humber, +-IAN]

north'wardly, adv. & a. Northwards; (of wind) northerly. [-LY²]

north-west'er, n. NW. wind. [-ER¹]

nor'ward(s) (-z). =NORTHWARD(s).

Norwe'gian (-jn), a. & n. (Native, language) of Norway. [f. medL Norvegia +-AN, w. assim. to Norway]

nor'-west'er, n. North-wester; glass of strong liquor; oilskin hat, sou'-wester. [NOR·¹]

nose (nōz), n., & v.t. & i. 1. Member of face or head placed above mouth containing the nostrils & serving as organ of smell (as plain as the ~'in your face, easily seen; bite or snap one's ~ off, answer him snappishly; count or tell ~s, count supporters etc., decide question by mere numbers; cut off one's ~ to spite one's face, indulge pique at one's own expense; follow one's ~, go straight forward, be guided by instinct; keep ~ to GRINDstone; LEAD¹ by the ~; make LONG¹ ~; ~ of wax, person or thing easily influenced or moulded; parson's ~, rump of cooked fowl; pay through the ~, be overcharged, have to pay exorbitant prices; poke, thrust, etc., one's ~, pry or intrude into something; put

one's ~ out of joint, supplant or discomfit or frustrate him; speak through one's ~, pronounce with nasal twang; turn up one's ~ at, show disdain for; under one's ~, straight before him, regardless of his displeasure). 2. Sense of smell (has a good ~; ~ of dogs, & fig. of detectives etc.). 3. || N~ Country, ~ part of England. 4. Open end or nozzle of pipe, tube, bellows, retort, etc. 5. Prow; projecting part. 6. ~-ape, proboscis-monkey; ~bag, containing fodder for hanging to horse's head; ~band, lower band of bridle passing over ~ & attached to check-straps; ~'dive, aeroplane's downward plunge (v.i., make this); ~flute, musical instrument blown with ~ among Siamese, Fijians, etc.; ~'gay [GAY in obs. n. use =toy], bunch of (esp. sweet-scented) flowers; ~'monkey, proboscis-monkey; ~'piece, =band, also part of microscope to which object-glass is attached; ~'pipe, piece of piping used as nozzle; ~'rag (sl.), pocket-handkerchief; ~'ring, fixed in ~ of bull etc. for leading, also ornament worn by savages; ~'warmer (sl.), short pipe; hence (-)nŌSED² (zd), ~'LESS (-zl-), aa. 7. v.b. Perceive smell of, detect by smell, (fig.) detect (~s a job in everything), smell out; rub with the ~, thrust ~ against or into; sniff (at, about, for) push one's way, push (one's way), with ~ [OE nosu, cf. MLG nose, Du.

nose'er (-z), n. Strong head wind (esp. moulding, etc., or metal shield for it. [NOSE, -ING¹]

noso-, comb. form of Gk nosos disease, as noso'GRAPHY, systematic description of diseases; nosŎ'lOGY, (branch of medical science dealing with) classification of diseases (so nosŏ'lŎGICAL, nosŎ'lOGIST).

nostal'gia, n. Home-sickness as a disease. Hence ~IC a. [f. Gk nostos return home, Gk algos pain, -IA¹]

nos'toc, n. Kinds of gelatinous blue-green algae. [name invented by Paracelsus]

Nostrada'mus, n. Prediction-monger, professed seer. [Latinized f. M. de Nostredame, French physician who made prophecies 1555]

nos'tril, n. Either opening in nose admitting air to lungs & smells to olfactory nerves (stink in one's ~s, be offensive to him). Hence (~)LED²(-l̩d)a. [OE nosthyrl (NOSE, obs. thirl f. OE thyrel hole, cf. THRILL)]

nos'trum, n. Medicine prepared by person recommending it, quack remedy; patent medicine; pet scheme for political or social reform, special device. [L, neut. of noster our, my]

nos'y (-z), a. & n. Large-nosed (person;

esp. of Duke of Wellington); ill-smelling (esp. of heated corn, mouldy hay, etc.); fragrant (of tea); sensitive to bad smells; (sl.) inquisitive (‖ esp. N~ *Parker*, busybody). [-Y²]

not, **n't** (see below), adv. **1.** Negativing & following ordinary verbs (arch. for usu. neg. with do; *I know* ~; *I doubt* ~; *say* ~ *so*; *fear* ~; *saidst thou* ~?). **2.** (Often *n't* joined to word) negativing auxiliaries having *not* in full) their subjects (*I cannot or can't say*; *he will* ~ or *won't*, or arch. *he'll* ~, *come*; *she is* ~, *isn't*, or vulg. *ain't*, *here*; *do* ~, or usu. *don't*, *stir*; *didn't you*, or formally *did you* ~, *tell me*?; *am I* ~, or *ain't I*, *aren't we*, *smart*?). **3.** Negativing & preceding participles & infinitives (~ *knowing*, *I cannot say*; *begged him* ~ *to move*). **4.** Used elliptically for negative sentence or verb or phrase (*Are you ill? Not at all. Not so. If it clears we will go out*; *if* ~, ~. *Popular or* ~, *it is right. I would us soon do it as* ~); preceding that with sense *it is* ~ *to be inferred, however, that*, or *but what* or (formal) *but that* or (arch.) *but* with sense *all the same or nevertheless* (*If he said so—that he ever did—he lied. I cannot do it*; ~ *but what etc. a stronger man might*). **5.** Preceding word etc. that is to be rejected for one that follows with *but* or to emphasize by contrast one already used (*He is* ~ *my son, but yours, or but my nephew. He's your son*, ~ *or &* ~ *mine*). [contr. of NOUGHT]

not·a bén'é, vb imperat. (abbr. N.B.). Observe what follows, take notice, (usu. drawing attention to a qualification of what has preceded). [L, = note well]

notabil'ity, n. **1.** Worthy of note, remarkable, striking, eminent; (Chem.) perceptible (*a* ~ *quantity of*); (of women: *occas. pr.* nŏt-) capable, bustling, housewifely; hence **nŏt'abĭy²** adv. **2.** n. Eminent person (esp. *Assembly of N*~s, irregular council serving as temporary parliament in emergencies). [F, f. L *notabilis* (NOTE², -ABLE]

nŏt'arў, n. Person publicly authorized to draw up or attest contracts etc., protest bills of exchange etc., & perform other formalities (chiefly used about foreign countries; also ~ *public*). Hence **nŏtar'ial a., nŏtar'ially² adv.** [f. L *notarius* secretary (NOTE¹, ², -ARY¹]

nota'tion, n. Representing of numbers, quantities, pitch and duration of sound, etc., by symbols; any set of symbols used for this, esp. in Arith., Alg., & Mus.; SCALE² of ~. [f. L *notatio* (NOTE², -ATION)]

nŏtch, n., & v.t. **1.** V-shaped indentation in edge or on convex surface; nick made on stick etc. by way of keeping count, (now rare) run scored at cricket; *defile, pass*; ~*wing*, kinds of moth; hence ~Y², ~ED² (-cht; Bot., Zool.), aa. **2.** v.t. Make ~es in; make into saw etc. by ~ing; score (steps etc.; often *up, down*) by ~es; make (number of runs) at cricket; secure or insert (steps in staircase etc.) by ~es. [f. F *hoche* with (a)n prefixed, cf. NEWT]

nŏte¹, n. **1.** Written sign representing pitch & duration of a musical sound; key of pianoforte etc.; single tone of definite pitch made by musical instrument, voice, etc.; (single tone in) bird's song or call; significant sound or way of expressing oneself (*there is a* ~ *of self-complacency in his voice*; *sound the* ~ *of war*; *change one's* ~, become suddenly more, or less, aggressive, humble, etc.). **2.** Sign, token, characteristic, distinguishing feature, proof of genuineness, guarantee consisting of, (*these are the* ~*s of Neo-paganism*; *catholicity is one* ~ *of the true Church*; *has the* ~ *of catholicity*); stigma, mark of censure, (*on which the law has set a* ~ *of infamy*); mark of exclamation or admiration, interrogation. **3.** Brief record of facts, impressions, or topics for speech or article (usu. pl.; *make or take a* ~ *of*, ~*s*; COMPARE ~*s*; *preaches from* ~*s*; *spoke for an hour without a* ~); annotation appended to passage in book etc.; short or informal letter; formal diplomatic communication; (usu. ~ *of hand*) written promise to pay sum by certain time; ‖ BANK³~; CIRCULAR ~. **4.** Eminence (*critic, philosopher, person, of* ~, distinguished) notice, attention, (*worthy of* ~; *take of*), whence ~WORTHY -twêrdhi) a. **5.** ~*book*, kinds for entering memoranda in; ~*paper*, kinds used for (esp. private) correspondence. Hence ~'LESS a., ~'LET n., (-ĭt-). [OF, f. L *nota* mark]

nŏte², v.t. Observe, notice, give attention to; set down, set *down*, as thing to be remembered or observed; annotate (book etc.); (p.p.) celebrated, well known for, whence ~WORTHY -twêrdhi) a. [f. OF *noter* f. L *notare* (prec.)]

no'thing (nŭ-), n. & adv. **1.** No thing (with adj. following, as ~ *great is easy*). **2.** Not anything, nought, (*has* ~ *in him*, is insignificant or without individuality; *there is* ~ *in it*, it is untrue or unimportant,

& see IN¹; ~ *doing* sl. announcement of failure or refusal of request; ~ *venture* ~ *have*, excuse for or encouragement to bold action; ~ *like* LEATHER; NECK *or* ~, *dance on* ~, be hanged; *fade away* etc. *to* ~ disappear gradually; ~ *no* ~, colloq. conclusion of negative list, as *no bread, no butter, no cheese, no* ~; ~ *else than* or force etc. alone, unmistakable force etc., *there is* ~ *for it but to*, no alternative; ~ *if not critical* as leading, critical as leading; characteristic; *get thing for* ~, gratis; *have endured it for* ~, to no purpose; *so it was not for* ~ *that he read Plato; that is* ~ *to you*, not your concern; *make* ~ *of*, treat as trifle; *make* ~ *of doing*, do without hesitation or as ordinary matter; *can make* ~ *of*, cannot understand, find solution of, use, develop, or deal with; *come to* ~, turn out useless, fall, not amount to anything; *have* ~ *to do with*, not be concerned with, avoid dealing with or society of; *all to* ~, longest odds). **3.** Trifle, very inferior thing, (*that is* ~, i.e. in comparison with what I am going to tell you; *he is* ~ *without his money*; (*that is*~,) *learning is* ~ *compared with*, genius). **4.** (Arith.) no amount, nought, (*multiply 6 by* ~, & *the result is* ~). **5.** Non-existence, what does not exist. **6.** (With a & pl.) trifling thing, event, remark, or person (*the little* ~*s of life; whisper soft* ~*s; the new commander-in-chief was a* ~). **7.** (Of religious belief) *be* ~; belong to no denomination, be an atheist or agnostic, whence ~ARIAN n. **8.** adv. Not at all, in no way, (*differs from* ~ *less than monstrous*, positively; *helps us* ~; *avails* ~; *is* ~ *like* as or so good etc.; *is* ~ *near so extensive*; *is* ~ to(A)YH) *as int., colloq.) not at all (*is it gold? Gold* ~; *it's pinchbeck*).

no'thingness (mǐ-), n. Non-existence, the non-existent, worthlessness, triviality, unimportance, insignificance, trifles. [-NESS]

nő'tice, n., & v.t. **1.** Intimation, intelligence, warning, (*give, have*, ~; *at short, ten minutes', etc.*, ~, with such time for preparation); placard etc. conveying information or directions. **2.** Formal intimation of something or instructions to do something (~ *to* QUIT; *till* FURTHER¹ ~); announcement by party to agreement that it is to terminate at specified time (esp. between landlord & tenant or employer & employed; *give a week's etc.* ~). **3.** Heed, attention, cognizance, observation, (*come into* ~, attract attention; *takes no* ~ *of it*, does not observe it, or takes no ~ action in consequence of it; *brought it to his* ~; *take* ~ *that*, I warn you that; *baby takes* ~, shows signs of intelligence). **4.** Paragraph or article upon something in newspaper, esp. review of book, play, etc. **5.** ~-*board*, bearing ~ or provided for ~s to be posted on. **6.** v.t. Remark upon, speak of. **7.** Perceive, take ~ of; treat with politeness or condescension. **8.** Serve with ~, give ~ to, (*was* ~*d to quit*); hence nótíCE'-a-BLY² adv. [F., f. L *notitia* (*notus* p.p. of *noscere* know, -ICE)]

nőt'ifiable, a. (Of diseases) that must be notified to public-health authorities. [-ABLE]

nőt'íFY, v.t. Make known, announce, report; inform, give notice to, (person *of, that*, or abs.). Hence nōtifiCá'TION n. [f. F *notifier* f. L *notificare* (NOTICE, -FY)]

nő'tion, n. **1.** General concept under which particular thing may be classed (in Philos., *first, second*, ~; = first, second, INTENTION). **2.** Idea, conception, (*the* ~ *of my doing it is absurd; what he means I have not the haziest* ~); view, opinion, theory, (*has a* ~ *that; such is the common* ~). **3.** Faculty, capability, or intention of (*has no* ~ *of obeying, obedience, discipline, letting himself be made a fool of*). **4.** *Something in the way of miscellaneous wares, esp. cheap useful ingenious article. **5.** pl. || Traditional special vocabulary of Winchester College. [f. L *notio* (NOTICE, -ION)]

nő'tional (-sho-), a. (Of knowledge etc.) speculative, not based on experiment or demonstration, whence ~ISM2 n., ~IST2 adv.; (of things, relations, etc.) existing only in thought, imaginary; (of persons) fanciful. [f. med. L *notionalis* (prec., -AL)]

nōto-, comb. form of Gk *nōton* back, in scientific terms, as ~*branch'iate* (-ngk-), having dorsal gills; nōt'*ochord*, cartilaginous band forming basis of spinal column; ~*nec'ta* [Gk *nēktēs* swimmer], waterbeetle swimming on back, the boat-fly.

Nōtogæ'a (-jēa), n. Zoological region comprising Australian, New-Zealand, & neotropical regions. [f. Gk *notos* south, *gaia* land]

notō'rious, a. (Of facts) well or commonly known (esp. *it is* ~ *that*); (with designations of persons, conduct, etc., that imply condemnation) undisguised, talked of, (~ *smuggler, offender, vice*); unfavourably known (*for* some quality or conduct, or abs.; *a ship* ~ *for ill-luck; the* ~ *Titus Oates*). Hence or cogn. nōtōri'ety n., ~LY² adv. [f. med. L *notorius* (NOTICE, -ORY), -OUS]

Notre-Dame (nŏtr dahm'), n. The Cathedral of Paris. [F., = Our Lady]

nōtwithstand'ing, prep., adv., & conj. **1.** In spite of, not the less for; (~ *his resistance; this* ~. The second order is the orig., the prep. having been developed f. a part. abs.). **2.** adv. Nevertheless, all the same. **3.** conj. (arch.). (Developed from prep. or part. abs. with *that*, still occas. retained) although, in spite of the fact (*that*). [NOT, WITHSTAND, -ING²]

nou'gat (nōō'gah, -t), n. Sweetmeat of sugar, nuts, etc. [F (L *nux nucis* nut, -ATE²)]

nought (nawt), n. Nothing (poet., arch., & Arith.; *come, bring, to ~*, be ruined or fall, ruin or baffle; *set at ~*, disregard, ridicule); figure 0, cipher; (~*s & crosses*, child's game). [OE *nōwiht* (*ne* not, see AUGHT, NAUGHT)]

noum'en|ŏn, n. (pl. ~*a*), Object of intellectual intuition devoid of all phenomenal attributes. Hence ~AL a., ~ALLY² adv. [f. Gk *nooumenon* neut. pres. part. pass. of *noeō* apprehend, taken by Kant as antithesis to *phenomenon*]

noun, n. (gram.). Word used as name of person or thing, substantive; (formerly) substantive or adjective (~ *substantive*, ~ *adjective*, adjective). Hence ~AL a. [AF, f. OF *num, nom*, f. L *nomen* name (*noscere* KNOW, -MEN)]

nou'rish (nŭ-), v.t. Sustain with food (lit. & fig.), whence ~ING² a.; foster, cherish, nurse, (feeling, hope, etc.) in one's heart. [f. OF *norir* (-ISH²) f. L *nutrire*]

nou'rishment (nŭ-), n. Sustenance, food; nourishing. [f. OF *nourissement* (prec., -MENT)]

nous, n. (Gk philos.) mind, intellect; (colloq.) common sense, gumption. [Gk]

nouveau riche (nŏŏvō'rēsh'), n. Wealthy parvenu. [AF =new rich]

nov'el¹, a. Of new kind or nature, strange, hitherto unknown. [OF, f. L *novellus* dim. of *novus* new]

nov'el², n. **1.** One of the tales in such a collection as Boccaccio's *Decameron*. **2.** Fictitious prose narrative of sufficient length to fill one or more volumes portraying characters & actions representative of real life in continuous plot; *the ~*, this type of literature; whence ~ESE' (-ēz) n. **3.** (Rom. law) new decree supplementary to the Codex. [f. It. *novella* f. L *nent.* pl. as foll.]

nov'elette', n. Short novel, story of moderate length; (Mus.) piano piece of free form with several themes. [-ETTE]

nov'elist, n. Novel-writer. Hence ~is'-tic a. [-IST]

nov'elize, v.t. Convert (drama, facts) into a novel. Hence ~A'TION n. [-IZE]

nov'elty, n. New or unusual thing or occurrence; novel character of something. [f. OF *novelté* (NOVEL², -TY)]

Novem'ber, n. Eleventh month. [L (*novem* nine); cf. DECEMBER]

novér'c|al, a. Stepmotherly. [f. L *noverca(lis* (*noverca* stepmother, -AL)]

nov'ice, n. Person received in religious house on probation before taking the vows; new convert; inexperienced person, beginner, tiro. [OF, f. L *novicius* (*novus* new, -ITIOUS)]

novi'ciate, -tiate, (-shi-), n. Novice's probationary period or initiation or apprenticeship; novice; quarters assigned to novices. [f. F *noviciat* f. med. L *noviatus* (prec., -ATE²)]

nov'ocaine, n. (pharm.). A regional anaesthetic. [P: f. L *novus* new +(CO)-CAINE]

now, adv., conj., & n. **1.** adv. At the present time; by this time; under the present circumstances (*I cannot ~ ever believe you again*; ~ *that I know you, it is different*); immediately (*must go~*); in the immediate past (*just ~*, & arch. *even, but*, ~); (in narrative) then, next, by that time, (*Caesar ~ marched east; it was ~ clear*); (*every*) ~ *& then* or *again*, from time to time, intermittently; ~*...*, ~ *...then*, ~ *...& again*, at one moment —at another; ~ *or never*, this is the nick of time. **2.** (Without temporal force, giving various tones, soothing, reproving, explanatory, threatening, etc., to sentence) pray, I beg, I insist, I warn you, & yet, you must know, it must be admitted, surely, (*Now what do you mean by it?. Oh, come ~!. No nonsense ~!. You have revealed the secret; ~ you were paid to keep it. Now Barabbas was a robber. Now this was bad enough, but ~. Now then, what mischief are you at?. You don't mean it, ~*). **3.** conj. (Orig., as often still, *now* adv. followed by *that*) consequently upon or simultaneously with the fact that (*Now I am a man I think otherwise. Now you mention it, I do remember*). **4.** n. This time, the present, (chiefly after prepp.; *is there by, ere, till, ~, from ~ till, etc.; read the future by, ere, till, ~*). [Aryan; OE *nu*, also in all older Teut. langg., cf. Skr. *nu*, Gk *nun*, L *nunc*]

now'aday, a. Of nowadays. [f. foll.]

now'adays (-z), adv. & n. (At) the present day, (in) these advanced or newfangled times. [NOW adv., A², DAY, -ES]

Nowel (nōĕl'), int. expr. joy in Christmas carols. [f. OF *noel* f. L NATALIS]

nō'where (-hwâr, -wâr), adv. In, at, to, no place (~ *near*, not nearly; *be, come in*, ~, not be placed in race or competition), [NO¹ WHERE]

nō'xious (-kshus), a. Harmful, unwholesome. Hence ~LY² adv., ~NESS n. [f. L *noxius* (*noxa* harm), -OUS]

noyade (nwahyahd'), n. Execution by drowning, esp. wholesale as in France in 1794. [F]

noyau (nwahyō'), n. Liqueur of brandy flavoured with fruit-kernels. [F (L *nux nucis* nut, -AU)]

nŏz'zle, n. Spout, mouthpiece, end fitted to hose etc. [NOSE, -LE(1)]

n't. See NOT.

nū, n. Greek letter (N, ν)=n. [Gk]

nuance (see Ap.), n. Delicate difference in or shade of meaning, feeling, opinion, colour, etc. [F, f. *nuer* to shade, ult. f. L *nubes* cloud]

nŭb, nŭb'ble, nn. Small knob or lump, esp. of coal. Hence **nŭbb'ly² a.** [=KNOB]

nŭb'ile, a. Marriageable (esp. of woman). Hence **nūbil'ITY n.** [f. L *nubilis* (*nubere* become wife)]

nū'chal (-kl), a. Of nape of neck. [f. med. L *nucha* spinal cord, f. Arab. orig.]

nūci-, comb. form of L *nux nucis* nut, as **nuci'ferous**, **nū'cIFORM**, **nuci'vorous**, adjs.

nū'cle|ŏle, n. (biol.). Nucleus of or within a nucleus. Hence ~OLAR¹, ~OLATʹed [-ATE²], aa., ~olo- comb. form. [f. L *nucleolus* dim. of foll.]

nū'cleus, n. (pl. ~ī), (Astron.) condensed part of comet's head; (Phys.) positively charged central portion constituting main mass of atom; central part or thing round which others are collected, kernel of aggregate or mass, beginning meant to receive additions, central part of ovule, seed, plant-cell, animal cell, etc., portion of medullary matter from which nerves spring. (*the ~s of a sun-spot, community, library, story, empire, etc.*). Hence ~AL, ~AR¹ (*esp. of atomic ~i*), ~ARY, aa., ~o- comb. form. [L. f. *nucula* dim. of *nux nucis* nut]

nūde, a. & n. 1. Naked, bare, unclothed, undraped, (~ *contract* in law, lacking a consideration & therefore void unless under seal); so **nūd'i-** comb. form (zool.), **nūd'ITY** n.; (as colour adj., esp. of stockings) flesh-coloured. 2. n. figure in painting or sculpture; *the ~*, the undraped figure, undraped state. Hence (also attrib., as *nudist colony*). [f. L *nudus*]

nūdge, v.t., & n. 1. Push slightly with elbow to draw attention privately, (fig.) draw attention of. 2. n. Such push. [?]

nū'gae (-gē, -jē), n. pl. Trifles, learned triflings, profitless minutiae. [L]

nū'gatory, a. Trifling, worthless, futile; inoperative, not valid. [f. L *nugatorius* (*nugae* trifle f. prec., -ORY)]

nūgg'ar, n. Large broad-beamed boat used on upper Nile. [native]

nūgg'et (-g-), n. Rough lump of native gold. [?]

nuis'ance (nūs-), n. Anything injurious or obnoxious to the community or member of it for which legal remedy may be had (l *commit no ~*, notice to public not to defile place); obnoxious person, offensive object, annoying action, anything disagreeable. [OF (*nuire* nuis- f. L *nocēre* hurt, -ANCE)]

null, a. & n. Not binding, invalid, (often ~ *& void*); without character or expression; non-existent, amounting to nothing, (rare); || (n.) dummy letter in a cipher. [f. L *nullus* (*ne* not, *ullus* any)]

null'a(h), n. (Anglo-Ind.). Stream, watercourse, ravine. [f. Hind. *nala*]

null'IFY, v.t. Cancel, neutralize. So ~FICA'TION n. [f. LL *nullificare* (NULL, -FY)]

null'ipore, n. Kind of marine vegetation. [L *nullus* no +PORE¹]

null'ity, n. Being null, invalidity, (esp. *of marriage*; ~ *suit*, for this); act, document, etc., that is null; nothingness; a mere nothing; a nonentity. [f. med. L *nullitas* (NULL, -ITY)]

numb (-m), a., & v.t. 1. Deprived of feeling or power of motion (~ *with cold* etc.; ~ *fish*, the Electric Ray or Torpedo; ~ *skull*, NUMSKULL; hence ~'ly (-mli) adv.; ~'NESS (-mn-) n. 2. v.t. Make ~, (fig.) stupefy, paralyse. [earlier *num* p.p. of obs. *nim* take, com.-Teut., cf. G *nehmen*, prob. cogn. w. Gk *nemō* occupy]

num'ber¹, n. (written N°, for *numero*=in ~, with pl. N°s before distinguishing figure, as *bedrooms N° 15, N°s 1–10*). 1. Tale, count, sum, company, or aggregate, of persons (also *of*) or things (also *of*) or abstract units, symbol or figure representing such aggregate, ticket etc. bearing such figure, person or thing (esp. single issue of magazine, or part of opera etc.) whose place in series is indicated by such figure, (*the ~ of fools is infinite*; N~s, abbr. *Num.*, O.T. book containing census; *the greatest ~ on record is 59 persons*; *to the ~ of 80, as many as*; GOLDEN ~; *science sleeps in N° 5*; *N° 9 (pill)*, army doctor's reputed panacea; *N° 10 Downing Street*, *N° 10*, (used for) Prime Minister's official residence (when he is also First Lord of the Treasury); *lose the ~ of one's mess*, die; *one's ~ goes up, he dies*; *one, one-self, esp. in take care of ~ one*, also || (Nav., sl.) first lieutenant; *story issued in parts successively published bearing N~s; back ~*, earlier issue of magazine, (fig.) anything out of date; *is not of our ~*, included among us; *is now added to the ~ of my enemies*; (sing. or pl.) large, small, etc., or large, collection or company of or abs. (*were present in great, only in small or in, ~s*; *saw a great*, or *a*, ~ *of birds*; *a small ~ came; there are ~s who live by begging*). 2. pl. Numerical preponderance (*won by ~s or force of ~s*). 3. Numerical reckoning (*the laws of ~ & proportion pervade Nature; without ~*, innumerable, also ~LESS a.; *in ~*, when counted or estimated, numerically, as *one people exceeds another in ~*). 4. (Gram.) class of word-forms including all singular, all plural, or all dual etc. words (*Greek has three ~s*; *things ~ is of the plural ~*). 5. Rhythm; (pl.) groups of musical notes, metrical feet, verses. [f. OF *nombre* f. L *numerus*]

num'ber², v.t. Count, ascertain number of; (pass.) be restricted in number (*his years are ~ed*, he has not long to live); include, regard as, among, in, or with some class; assign a number to, distinguish with a number; have lived, live, (so many years); be able to show (so many inhabitants etc.); amount to (specified

number). [f. OF *nombrer* f. L *numerare* (prec.)]

‖ **num'bles** (-blz), n. pl. (arch.). Deer's entrails. [OF, cogn. w. L *lumbus* loin; later *umbles* whence HUMBLE pie]

num'erable, a. That can be numbered. [f. L *numerabilis* (NUMBER², -ABLE)]

num'eral, a. & n. (Word, figure, group of figures) denoting a number; of number. [f. LL *numeralis* (NUMBER², -AL)]

numera'tion, n. Method or process of numbering or computing; calculation; assigning of numbers; (Arith.) expression in words of number written in figures; ∼ *table*, showing value of figures according to their place in system of notation. [f. L *numeratio* (NUMBER², -ATION)]

num'erator, n. Number above line in vulgar fraction showing how many of the parts indicated by the denominator are taken; person who numbers. [LL (NUMBER², -OR³)]

nume′ric, n. What is either a number, a proper or improper fraction, or an incommensurable ratio. [f. L *numerus* number, -IC]

nume′rical, a. Of, in, denoting, etc. number. Hence ∼LY² adv. [-AL]

num'erous, a. Comprising many units (*a* ∼ *acquaintance, library, family, army, class*); coming from many individuals (*the* ∼ *voice of the people*; *a* ∼ *hum*); (arch.) thronged (*a* ∼ *country*); (with pl. noun) many (*received* ∼ *gifts*); (of verse or prose) rhythmic, harmonious. Hence ∼LY² adv. [f. L *numerosus* (NUMBER¹, -OUS)]

num'inous, n. The ∼, the combined feeling of attraction & awe characteristic of man's sense of communion with God & religion. [in recent use; f. L *numen -inis* divine will, divinity]

numismat'ic (-z-), a. Of coins or coinage. So ∼ICALLY adv., ∼ICS, **numis'matəs**(3), **numismatol'ogy**, nn. [F (-*ique*), f. L *num-* f. Gk *nomisma -atos* coin (*nomizō* use currently f. *nomos* custom), -IC]

numm'ary, numm'ulary, aa. Of, in, coin. [f. L *nummarius* (*nummus* coin, -ARY¹), & *nummulus* dim. +-ARY¹]

‖ **numm'et,** n. (dial.). Lunch. [=*noon meat*]

numm'ulite, n. Disk-like fossil shell of Tertiary strata. [*nummulus* (see NUMMARY), -ITE²(2)]

num'nah (-*a*), n. Saddle-cloth, pad placed under saddle. [Anglo-Ind. *numdah* felt f. Hind. *namda* f. Pers. *namad* carpet]

num'skull, n. Dolt or his head. [NUMB]

nun, n. Woman living in convent usu. under vow of poverty, chastity, & obedience; kinds of bird & moth; ∼*'s cloth,* thin woollen stuff; ∼*'s thread,* fine white sewing cotton; ∼*'s veiling,* thin dress-stuff. Hence ∼'HOOD, ∼n'ERY(3), ∼'SHIP, nn., ∼'LIKE, ∼n'ISH¹, aa. [OE *nunne* f. eccl. L *nonna* fem. of *nonnus* monk, orig. =old man, gaffer]

nun-buoy (-boi), n. Buoy circular in middle & tapering to each end. [f. obs. *nun* spinning-top, perh. f. prec.]

nunc dimit'tis, n. The canticle *Lord, now lettest thou* (*sing* ∼, be willing to depart from life etc.). [L, = now lettest thou go]

nun'ciature (-shətūr), n. (Tenure of) office of papal nuncio. [f. It. *nunziatura* (foll.)]

nun′cio (-shiō), n. (pl. ∼s). Pope's ambassador at foreign court. [It., f. L *nuncius* messenger]

nunc'upate, v.t. Declare (will, testament) orally, not in writing. So ∼A'TION n., ∼ATIVE a. [f. L *nuncupare* name, capere take). -ATE³]

nunna'tion, n. Addition of final *n* in declension of (orig. Arabic) nouns. [f. Arab. *nun* the letter *n* +-ATION]

nuph'ar, n. Yellow water-lily. [for NENUPHAR]

nup'tial (-shl), a. & n. **1.** Of marriage or wedding. **2.** n. (usu. pl.). Wedding. [f. L *nuptialis* (*nuptiae* wedding f. *nubere nupt-* become wife)]

nurse¹, n. 1. Woman employed to suckle & take charge of infant (usu. *wet*-∼), or having charge of young children (also *dry*-∼). **2.** Country etc. that fosters some quality etc. (*the* ∼ *of liberty*). **3.** Nursing or being nursed (*at* ∼, *put out or put to* ∼, of child, & fig. of estate). **4.** Person, usu. woman, charged with or trained for care of the sick or decrepit. **5.** (Forestry) tree planted as shelter to others; (Entom.) sexually imperfect bee, ant, etc., caring for the young brood, worker; (Zool.) individual in asexual stage of metagenesis. **6.** ∼*-child, foster-child;* ∼*-frog,* kind of which male carries eggs till hatched; ∼*-maid, girl* having charge of child(ren); ∼ *ship* (Nav.). = MOTHER¹ ship. Hence **nūrs′ey¹** n. (earlier & OF *norice* f. LL *nutricia* fem. of *nutricius* f. L *nutrix -icis* (*nutrire* nourish)]

nūrse², v.t. & i. **1.** Suckle (child), give suck, act as wet-nurse; act as nursemaid to, have charge of; (pass.) be brought up (*in luxury, certain place, etc.*). **2.** Foster, tend, promote development of, (the arts, hatred, etc.); manage (plants, estate) with solicitude; cherish (grievance etc.). **3.** Wait upon (sick person), try to cure (sickness), be sick-nurse. **4.** Hold or clasp (baby, one's knees or foot) caressingly; sit close over (fire). **5.** ‖Keep(constituency) in good humour by attentions. **6.** (Billiards) keep (balls) together for series of cannons. **7.** Keep close to (rival omnibus to interfere with its custom, or horse in race to impede it). **8.** ‖*Nursing home,* house for surgical operations, reception of invalids, etc.; *nursing father, mother, foster-.* [earlier *nursh* f. NOURISH]

nūrse³, n. Kinds of dog-fish or shark. [prob. f. obs. *huss* dog-fish etym. dub., w. adherent (*a*)n, cf. NEWT, & assim. to prec.]

nūrs′ery, n. **1.** Room assigned to children & their nurses (~ *governess*, one combining duties of nurse & governess). **2.** (*fig.*) Practice, institution, sphere, place, in or by which qualities or classes of people are fostered or bred. **3.** Plot of ground in which young plants are reared for transplantation (~*man*, owner of this); fish-rearing pond; place where animal life is developed. **4.** (Billiards) grouped balls (see NURSE[2]; esp. in ~ *cannon*). [-ERY(3)]

nūrs(e)′ling (-sl-), n. Infant, esp. in relation to its nurse; ~ *of*, person or thing bred in or fostered by. [NURSE[1], -LING[1]]

nŭr′ture, n., & v.t. **1.** Bringing up, training, fostering care; nourishment, food. **2.** v.t. Nourish, rear, foster, train, educate. [f. OF *nourture* f. L *nutrire* nourish, -URE]

nŭt, n., & v.i. (-tt-). **1.** Fruit consisting of hard or leathery shell enclosing edible kernel (see also EARTH~, PEA~); DEAF~; *can′t shoot* etc. *for* ~s, sl., do thing even tolerably well; *hard* ~ *to crack*, difficult problem, person or thing hard to deal with or get the better of; *be* ~*s* or *dead* ~*s on*, sl., delight in, be skilful at). **2.** (sl.) Showy young man (now rare); head (*off one's* ~, insane, mad); (pl.) crazy (also *merts*). **3.** Small toothed projection on spindle engaging with cog-wheel, small spur-wheel. **4.** Small block usu. of metal pierced with female screw for securing or adjusting bolt. **5.** Holder that tightens or relaxes horse-hair of fiddle-bow etc. **6.** pl. Small lumps of coal. **7.** ~*brown*, coloured like ripe hazel~ (esp. of girl's complexion, & of ale); ~*cracker*, (usu. pl.) instrument for cracking ~s, promi-nent chin & nose with points naturally, or by loss of teeth, near each other (also used attrib. in sing., as *a* ~*cracker face*), (sing.) common European but rare British bird; ~*gall*, gall found on dyer's oak used as dye-stuff; ~*hatch*, small creeping bird feeding on ~s [HATCH[2]]; ~*oil*, got esp. from hazel~s & wal~s, & used in paints & varnishes; ~*shell*, hard exterior covering of ~, tiny receptacle or dwelling, briefest possible way of expressing; epitome, (*can give it you in a* ~*shell*); ~*tree*, bearing ~s, esp. hazel; ~*sweet*, beetle laying eggs in green hazel & filbert ~s. **8.** v.i. Seek or gather ~s (usu. in gerund, *vent* ~*ting* etc.). [com. Teut.; OE *hnutu*, cf. Du. *noot*, G *nuss*]

nŭt′āte, v.i. (bot.). Nod, droop. So~ANT a. [f. L *nutare* frequent. of *nuere* nod]

nūtā′tion, n. Nodding; (Astron.) oscilla-tion of earth's axis making motion of pole of equator round pole of ecliptic wavy; oscillation of spinning top; curvature in stem of growing plant. [f. L *nutatio* (prec., -ATE[3]), -ION]

nŭt′mĕg, n. Hard aromatic spheroidal seed got from fruit of evergreen E.-Indian tree (~*apple*, used as spice & in medicine; ~*s*; ~*liver*, diseased state of liver, red atrophy. [partial transl. of OF *nois mugede*, = med. L *nux muscata* musky nut]

nŭt′ria, n. Skin or fur of the S.-Amer. coypu, an aquatic rodent. [Sp., = otter f. L *lutra*]

nū′trient, a. Serving as or providing nourishment. [f. L *nutrire* nourish, -ENT]

nŭt′riment, n. Nourishing food (lit. & fig.). L *nutrimentum* (prec., -MENT)]

nūtri′tion, n. (Supplying or receiving of) nourishment, food. [as NUTRIENT, -ION]

nūtri′tious (-shŭs), a. Nourishing, effi-cient as food. Hence ~LY[2] adv., ~NESS n. [f. L *nutritius* (NURSE[1], -ITIOUS[2])]

nū′tritive, a. & n. Serving as food; con-cerned in nutrition; (n.) article of food. [F (-*if*, -*ive*) f. med. L *nutritivus* (NU-TRIENT, -IVE)]

nŭt′ty, a. Abounding in nuts; tasting like nuts, of rich mellow flavour; (sl.) amorous or enthusiastic (*upon*); *(sl.)* crazy.

nŭx vŏm′ica, n. Seed of E.-Ind. tree yielding the poison strychnine. [med. L (L *nux* nut, *vomere* vomit, -IC)]

nŭz′zle, v.i. & t. Nose, burrow or press or rub or sniff with the nose, press nose or press (nose) *into* or *against*; nestle, lie snug. (also refl.). [NOSE[1], -LE(3)]

nyctalō′pia, n. Night-blindness or re-current loss of vision after sunset; in-ability to see clearly except at night. [f. (Gk *nuktalōps* f. *nukt*- night, *alaos* blind, *ōps* eye, -IA[1]); incorrect second sense due to overlooking of -*al*-]

nyctitrŏp′ic, a. (bot.). Turning in certain direction at night. [f. Gk *nux nuktos* night, -TROP, -IC]

nylghau (-gaw), n. Short-horned Indian antelope. [f. Pers. *nilgaw* (nīl blue, *gaw* ox)]

nylŏn, n. Synthetic plastic material of great toughness, tensile strength, & elas-ticity, widely used in industry & as a dress fabric; (pl., colloq.) garments, esp. women's stockings, made of ~. [?]

nymph, n. **1.** One of class of mythologi-cal semi-divine maidens inhabiting sea, rivers, fountains, hills, woods, or trees, or attending superior deities, whence of cogn. ~*ēan*, ~*ish*, ~*like*, aa. **2.** (poet.) Young & beautiful woman. **3.** Pupa. [f. F *nymphe* f. L f. Gk *numphē*]

nymphŏlĕpsy, n. Ecstasy or frenzy caused by desire of the unattainable. [foll., *epilepsy*]

nym′pholĕpt, n. Person inspired by vio-lent enthusiasm esp. for an ideal. Hence ~ĕp′tic a. [f. Gk *numpholēptos* nymph-caught (NYMPH, *lambanō* take)]

nymphomān'ia, n. (path.). Morbid & uncontrollable sexual desire in women. [f. Gk *numphē* bride, -o- -MANIA]

nystag'mus, n. Eye-disease common among miners, with continual oscillation of eyeballs. [f. Gk *nustagmos* nodding (*nustazō* nod)]

O

O¹ (ō), letter (pl. Os, O's, Oes). O-shaped mark, circle, (esp. *round* O).

O², oh, (ō), int. prefixed to vocative name (O), or expressing various emotions (usu. *oh* if separated by punctuation, otherwise *O. O dear me!; O for a breathing-space!; Oh, what a lie!; Oh, is that so?); O yes!; O yes!* = OYEZ. [ME. prob. f. L]

O'¹ (ō), pref. of Irish names, as *O'Connor*. [Ir. *ō*, *ua*, descendant]

O'² (ō), prep. short for *of, on*, still in some phrases, as (= *of*) *o'clock, Jack-o'-lantern, Will-o'-the-wisp, man-o'-war*, (colloq.) *cup o' tea*, (= *on*) *cannot sleep o' nights*. **-o-**, letter used to adapt first part of double-barrelled word for connexion with second; prop. used in Gk compounds, *-i-* being usu. in L, but now extended to many scientific & other terms made of non-Gk wds (*occipito-frontal, joco-serious*; &, in meaning, expressing not merely modification of second element but being a product of both, as *Franco-German war, Franco-German characteristics*, but equal or any other relations (*Franco-German war*; used also in forming true derivatives w. Gk endings as *-cracy, -logy, & perh. taken for part of the suf., whence 'ologies' etc.

oaf, n. (pl. *~s, oaves*). Elf's child, change-ling, (arch.): misbegotten, deformed, or idiot child; awkward lout. Hence ~ISH¹ a. [var. of obs. *auf* f. ON ĀLFR]

oak, n. 1. Kinds of tree & shrub, of which the best known is a forest tree yielding hard timber & acorns & having jagged leaves (*Dyer's, Holm, Scarlet*, etc., ~, other species; *Dwarf, Ground*, etc., ~; wood of the ~ (HEART *of* ~), (poet.) wooden ships; || (Univ.), outer door of set of rooms (*sport* one's ~, shut this to exclude visitors); leaves *of* ~ (~ *is still worn on 29th May*); colour of young ~ leaves; the *Oaks*, race at Epsom for three-year-old fillies [f. name of estate]; (attrib., =, but now more usual than)~en. 2. *~-apple, -fig, -gall, -plum, -potato, -spangle, -wart*, kinds of excrescence produced on ~s by gall-flies; ||*~apple day*, 29th May (Charles II restored 1660) on which ~apples are worn in memory of the ROYAL~ incident; *~-beauty, -eager, -hook-tip, -moth*, kinds of moth bred on or resembling leaf etc. of ~; *~-fern*, smooth three-branched Polypody; ~-

tree, ~; ~-wood, forest, copse, etc., *of* ~s, also ~ timber. Hence ~EN⁵ a., ~'LET, ~'LING¹(2), nn. [com.-Teut.; OE *āc*, cf. Du. *eik*, G *eiche*]

oak'um, n. Loose fibre got by picking old rope to pieces & used esp. in caulking (*pick* ~, make this, esp. as formerly common task of convicts & paupers). [OE *ācumbe* lit. off-combings (*ā-* off, *cemban* cf. G *kämmen* COMB²)]

oar (ōr), n., & v.t. & i. 1. Pole with blade used (usu. in even numbers) to propel boat by leverage, esp. one worked by single rower (cf. SWEEP) with both hands (cf. SCULL), or to steer (*chained to the* ~, constrained to work hard & long, with allusion to galley-slaves; *pair* ~, *four* ~, etc., boat with two, four, etc., ~s; *pulls a good* ~, is good ~sman; *put in one's* ~, interfere; *have an* ~ *in every man's boat*, be a meddler; *rest on* one's ~s, cease work for a time); *good, bad, young, practised*, etc., ~sman; (fig.) wing, fin, arm used in swimming, etc.; ~*s'man*, ~*s'woman*, rower, whence ~*s'manSHIP*(3) n.; hence ~*AGE*(1) n. (poet.), (~)ED² (3rd), ~LESS, ~*y²* (poet.), aa., (*ōr*-). 2. vb. Row (t. & i.; (poet.) *boat, water, air*, obs.) *way*; ~ one's *arms* or *hands*, move them as in swimming. [OE (& ON) *ār*, perh. cogn. w. Gk *eretēs* rower]

ōā'sis, n. (pl. *oasēs*). Fertile spot in desert (lit. & fig.). [L f. Gk, prob. of Egypt. orig.]

oast, n. Hop-drying kiln; ~-*house*, building containing this. [OE *āst*, cf. Du. *eest*, cogn. w. L *aedes* house, *aestus* heat, *aestas* summer, Gk *aithos* heat]

oat, n. (Pl.) (grain yielded by) hardy cereal grown in cool climates as food for men & horses; (sing., rare exc. in comb.) ~-plant, variety of ~; *Wild Oat*, tall grass resembling ~s (*sow* one's *wild* ~s, indulge in youthful follies before becoming steady); (poet.) ~-stem used as musical pipe by shepherds etc., pastoral or bucolic poetry; *~cake*, thin unleavened cake made of ~meal, esp. in Scotland & N.; *~meal*, meal from ~s used esp. in *~cake* & *porridge*; *feel* one's ~s (colloq.), feel important, display self-importance. Hence ~EN⁵ a. [OE *āte*, excl. E, etym. dub.]

oath, n. (pl. *pr. ōdhz*). 1. Solemn appeal to God or revered or dreaded person or object in witness that statement is true or promise shall be kept (*take an, make, swear an*, ~, bind oneself thus; *on* ~, having thus sworn, made or stated or given by sworn person; BIBLE, CORPORAL,¹ ~); (form of words containing) statement or promise so corroborated (~ *of allegiance, office, supremacy*, etc.). 2. Name of God etc. used as expletive to give emphasis or express anger etc., piece of profanity in speech, curse. [com.-Teut.; OE *āth*, cf. Du. *eed*, G *eid*]

ob- (before *c*) **oc-**, (before *f*) **of-**, (before *p-*) **op-**; pref. f. L *ob* in the way of, occurring chiefly in wds already compounded in L, w. senses: **1.** Exposure, openness, (*object, obnoxious, obtrude, obverse*). **2.** Meeting (*occasion, occur, offend*), facing (*observe, obstetric, obviate, oblique, obtune*), direction (*oblation, oblique, obing*), observance, obeis, offer), spontaneity or friendliness (*obey, obsequious, office*). **3.** Opposition or hostility (*objurgate, obloquy*), or resistance (*obdurate, obmutes- cent, obstinate, obtuse*) **4.** Hindrance, blocking, veiling, (*obbligato, obese, obfus- cate, oblige, obliterate, obscure, obsess, obstacle, obstruct, obturate, occlude, occult, oppilate*). **5.** Finality or completeness (*obit, oblivion, obsolete, obtain, obtruncate, occident, occupy*). **6.** (In mod. sci. wds) inversely, in direction or manner contrary to the usual (*obconical, obcordate, obovate, obovoid*), shaped like cone, heart, spike, egg, with thick end presented.)

obbligā'tō (-ah-), a. & n. (mus.). **1.** (Of accompaniment or part) inseparable, forming integral part of the composition, (opp. *ad libitum*). **2.** n. (pl. -os). Such part or accompaniment. [It. f. L *obligatus* (OBLIGE)]

ob'durate (or -ūr'-), a. Hardened, impenitent, stubborn. Hence **obdū'racy** n., ~LY² adv., (or- -ūr'-). [f. L OB(*durare* harden f. *durus* hard). -ATE²]

ōb'eah (-a), **ōb'i**, n. Kind of sorcery practised by Negroes. [W. Afr.]

obēd'ience, n. Obeying as act or practice or quality, submission to another's rule, compliance with law or command, (in ~ *to*, actuated by or in accordance with; *passive* ~, surrender of one's will to another's without co-operation, also compliance with commands irrespective of their nature); (Eccl. esp. R.-C.) being obeyed, (sphere of) authority, district or body of persons bound to ~; (*return to the ~ of the Pope; not belonging to either the Roman or the Byzantine ~*). [f. F *obédience*]

obēd'ient, a. Submissive to or complying with superior's will, dutiful, (ll *your ~ servant*, phrase spoken formerly in courtesy, now only ironically, in taking leave, & written as concluding formula in letters of official or public character). Hence ~LY² adv. [f. OF *obedient* (OBEY, -ENT)]

obedien'tial (-sha-), a. Of or pertaining to obedience. [f. med. L *obedientialis*]

obedien'tiary (-sha-), n. Holder of any office under superior in monastery or convent. [f. med. L *obedientiarius*]

obēi'sance (-bās'-), n. Gesture, esp. bow or curtsy, expressing submission, respect, deference, homage, submission, (*do, make, pay, ~*). [f. F *obéissance* (OBEY, -ANCE)]

ōb'elisk, n. **1.** Tapering usu. monolithic shaft of stone square or rectangular in section with pyramidal apex; ~-shaped mountain, tree, etc. **2.** (Also *obelos*) mark used in ancient MSS. to indicate ÷); (also *obelus*) mark of reference to note in margin etc. (†: *double* ~, ‡). [f. L f. Gk *obeliskos* dim. of *obelos* spit]

ōb'elīze, v.t. Mark with the obelisk as spurious etc. [f. Gk *obelizō* (*obelos* see prec.,-IZE)]

ōb'elus, n. (pl. -lī). See OBELISK.

obēse', a. Corpulent. So **obēs'ITY** n. [f. L *obesus* p.p.,-having eaten, (f. *edere* eat)]

obey' (-bā), v.t. & i. Perform bidding of, be obedient to; execute (command); be actuated by (force, impulse); do what one is bidden. [f. F *obéir* f. L OB(*edire=audīre* hear)]

ōb'fuscāte, v.t. Darken, obscure, (mind etc.); stupefy, bewilder. So ~A'TION n. [f. L OB(*fuscare* f. *fuscus* dark), -ATE³]

ōb'i¹. See OBEAH.

ōb'i², n. Bright broad sash worn by Japanese women & children. [Jap.]

ōb'it, n. (arch.). Memorial service esp. in institution on anniversary of founder's or benefactor's death. [f. L *obitus* death, as prec.]

ōb'iter, adv. By the way, in passing, (usu. ~ *dic'tum*, pl. -*ta*, judge's expression of opinion uttered in arguing point or giving judgement but not essential to his decision & therefore without binding authority; also gen., incidental remark). [L, =*ob iter* by the way]

obit'uary, n. & a. **1.** Notice of death(s) esp. in newspaper, brief biography of deceased person; hence ~ISM(1) n. **2.** adj. Recording a death, concerning deceased person. [f. med. L *obituarius* =L *obitus* death, see OBIT, -ARY¹]

ōb'ject¹, n. & a. **1.** Thing placed before eyes or presented to sense, material thing, thing observed with optical instrument or represented in picture. **2.** Person or thing presented to sight, material thing. **3.** Person or thing to which action or feeling is directed, subject of or for, (*the Bible had been the ~ of his study; he is a proper ~ of or for charity*). **4.** Thing aimed at, end, purpose; *no* ~, formula in advertisements make its own terms in the specified respect. **5.** (Metaphys.) thing thought of or apprehended as correlative to the thinking mind or subject, external thing, the non-ego. **6.** (Gram.) noun or noun-equivalent governed by active transitive verb or by preposition (*direct, indirect, ~, that*

For words in *ob-* not given see OB-.

primarily, secondarily, affected by action, as *shilling*, *him*, in *I gave him a shilling*). **7.** ~*-ball*, at which player aims his in billiards etc.; ~*-finder*, contrivance for registering position of ~ on mounted microscopic slide so as to find it again; ~*-glass* or *-lens*, lens in telescope etc. nearest the ~; ~*-lesson*, instruction about a material ~ that is present for inspection. (fig.) striking practical illustration of some principle; ~*-plate*, **on which** ~ is placed for microscopic examination. Hence ~*-staff*, surveyor's levelling staff. Hence ~LESS a. [f. med.L *objectum* thing presented to the mind, neut. p.p. of L OB(*jicere jact-* throw)]

object², v.t. & i. Adduce (quality, fact) as objection (to theory etc.); state (usu. *that*-clause) as damaging fact to or against person etc.; state objection, feel or express disapproval, have objection or dislike *to* (*I* ~ *to being*, & incorrectly *to be*, *treated like this*; ‖*I* ~, words used in tion to oppose a motion etc. & so shelve it as not unopposed business). Hence **objec'tor²** n. (*conscientious* ~*or*, excused compulsory service, vaccination, etc., on pleading conscience). [f. L *object-* (prec.)]

objec'tify, v.t. Present as object of sense, make objective, express in concrete form, embody. Hence ~FICA'TION n. [OBJECT¹, -I-, -FY]

objec'tion, n. Objecting, thing objected, adverse reason or statement; expression or feeling of disapproval or dislike. [F, f. L *objectio* (OBJECT¹, -ION)]

objec'tionable (-sho-), a. Open to objection; undesirable, unpleasant, offensive, disapproved of. Hence ~LY² adv. [prec., -ABLE]

objec'tive, a. & n. **1.** (Philos.) belonging not to the consciousness or the perceiving or thinking subject but to what is presented to this or the non-ego, external to the mind, real. **2.** (Of person, writing, picture, etc.) dealing with outward things & not with thoughts or feelings, exhibiting actual facts uncoloured by exhibitor's feelings or opinions; (Med., of symptoms) observed by another & not only felt by patient, whence ~NESS, **objectiv'ITY**, nn. **3.** (Gram.) constructed as, appropriate to, the object (~ *case* in English, that governed by transitive verb or preposition, distinguished in form from the subjective only in some personal pronouns, as *him*, cf. *he*; ~ *genitive*, as in '*the fear of God*', cf. SUBJECTIVE *genitive*). **4.** (Mil.) ~ *point*, towards which advance of troops is directed, (transf.) point aimed at; hence ~LY² adv. **5.** n. (=OBJECT¹-*glass*; (Gram.) ~ *case*; (Mil. & transf.) ~ *point*. [f. med. L *objectivus* (OBJECT¹, -IVE)]

objec'tivism, n. Tendency to lay stress on the objective; doctrine that knowledge

of non-ego is prior & superior to that of ego. [-ISM]

ŏb'jŭrˌgāte, v.t. Chide, scold. Hence ~A'TION n., ~ȦTORY (or -ŏ̄rg'a-) a. [f. L OB(*jurgare* quarrel), -ATE³]

ŏb'lāte¹, n. Person dedicated to monastic or religious life or work. [f. (med. L sense of) L OB(*latus* p.p. of *ferre* bring)]

ŏblāte² (or ŏb'-), a. (geom.). (Of spheroid) flattened at poles (cf. PROLATE). [as prec.; sense of *ob-* doubtful]

oblā'tion, n. (Presenting of bread & wine to God in) Eucharist; thing offered to God, sacrifice, victim; donation for pious uses. Hence ~AL (-sho-), **ŏb'lȧtory**, aa. [OF, f. LL *oblationem* (OBLATE², -ION)]

ŏb'lȧgāte, v.t. Bind (person, esp. legally) *to* do (chiefly in p.p.). [f. L (OBLIGE, -ATE³)]

ŏblȧgā'tion, n. Binding agreement esp. one enforceable under legal penalty, written contract or bond; constraining power of a law, precept, duty, contract, etc. (*of* ~, obligatory); one's bounden duty, a duty, burdensome task; (indebtedness for) service or benefit (*be, put, under an* ~; *repay an* ~). [OF, f. L *obligationem* (OBLIGE, -ATION)]

oblig'atory (or ŏb'lȧgȧ-), a. Legally or morally binding, imperative & not merely permissive; constituting an obligation. [f. LL *obligatorius* (foll., -TORY)]

oblige', v.t. Bind (person, oneself) by oath, promise, contract, etc., *to* person or *to* do (arch., legal; also with *oath* etc. as subj.); be binding on; make (person) do (*by doing*) by conferring favour, gratify (*by doing* or *with*; (colloq.) make contribution to entertainment (*with* song etc., or abs.); (pass.) be bound (*to* person) by gratitude (*for* small service); constrain, compel, *to* do. [f. OF *obliger* f. L(*ligare* bind)]

ŏbligee', n. (Law) person to whom another is bound by contract or to whom bond is given (cf. OBLIGOR); (rare) person who has received a favour. [prec., -EE]

obli'ging, a. Courteous, accommodating, ready to do kindness, complaisant. Hence ~LY² adv., ~NESS n. [-ING²]

ŏb'ligōr, n. (legal). One who binds himself to another or gives bond. [OBLIGE, -OR²]

oblique' (-ēk), a., a. & v.i. **1.** Slanting, declining from the vertical or horizontal, diverging from straight line or course. **2.** (Geom.) (of line, plane figure, surface) inclined at other than right angle, (of angle) acute or obtuse, (of cone, cylinder, etc.) with axis not perpendicular to plane of base; (Anat.) neither parallel nor perpendicular to body's or limb's long axis; (Bot., of leaf) with unequal sides. **3.** Not going straight to the point, roundabout, indirect. **4.** (Gram.) ~ *case*, other than nominative or vocative; ~ *oration* or *nar-*

For words in *ob-* not given see OB-.

-ration or speech, speaker's words with the changes of person, tense, etc., usual in reports, indirect speech; hence or cogn. ~LY² (-ĕkl-) adv., **obliq'uitry** n. 5. v.i. (esp. mil.). Advance ~ly. [f. L *obliquus*, cf. *licinus* bent upward)]

oblit'erate, v.t. Blot out, efface, erase, destroy, leave no clear traces of. So ~ATION n. [f. L *oblitterare* (*littera* letter)]

obliv'ion, n. Having or being forgotten; disregard, unregarded state, (Act, Bill, of O~, amnesty; *fall into* ~, be forgotten or disused). [OF. f. L *oblivionem* f. OB(*liviscī*...

obliv'ious, a. Forgetful, unmindful, (*of*); (poet.) f ... ~LY² adv. ~NESS n. [f. L *obliviosus*]

ob'long, a. & n. 1. Deviating from square or circular form by having one long axis, (of spheroid) prolate; (Geom.) rectangular with adjacent sides unequal; (of paper, book, rectangular postage stamp or panel, etc.) greater in breadth than height; hence **oblong'o-** (-ngg) comb. form. (bot.). 2. n. ~ figure or object. [f. L OB(*longus* long); sense of *ob-* doubtful]

ob'loquy, n. Abuse, detraction; being generally ill spoken of. [f. LL *obloquium* f. L OB(*loqui* speak) gainsay)]

obmutes'cence, n. Obstinate silence. So ~ENT a. [f. L OB(*mutescere* f. *mutus* dumb)]

obnox'ious (-kshus), a. Liable to harm or evil or attack (now rare); offensive, objectionable, disliked, whence ~LY² adv. ~NESS n. [f. L *obnoxius* (*ob* in the way of, *noxa* harm)]

ob'ōe, n. Wood-wind double-reed instrument of treble pitch & plaintive incisive tone; organ reed-stop imitating this. Hence **ob'ōist(3)** n. [It., f. F as HAUTBOY]

ob'ol, n. Ancient-Greek silver coin = about 1¼d. [f. L f. Gk *obolos*]

obscēne', a. Repulsive, filthy, loathsome, (arch.); indecent, lewd. Hence or cogn. ~LY² adv., **obscēn'ITY** n. [f. L *obsc(a)enus* etym. dub.]

obscūr'ant, n. Opponent of inquiry, enlightenment, & reform. Hence ~ISM(3) n. ~IST(2) n. & a. [G. f. L (OBSCURE. -ANT)]

obscūre', a. & n. & v.t. 1. Dark, dim, (~ *rays*), invisible heat-rays of solar spectrum; (of colour) dingy, dull, indefinite; indistinct, not clear; hidden, remote from observation; unnoticed; unknown to fame, humble; unexplained, doubtful; not perspicuous or clearly expressed; hence or cogn. ~LY² adv., **obscūr'ITY** n. 2. n. Obscurity, indistinctness. 3. v.t. Make ~, dark, indistinct, or unintelligible; dim glory of, outshine; conceal from sight; so OBSCURA'TION n. [adj. f. OF *obscur* f. L OB(*scurus* f. *scu-* cover, cf. *scutum* shield, Gk *skeuê* attire); vb f. adj. f. L *obscurare*]

obsecra'tion, n. Earnest entreaty; Li-

-tany petition beginning with *By*, [f. L *obsecratio* f. OB(*secrare* = *sacrare* f. *sacer* sacred) entreat]

ob'sequies (-iz), n. pl. Funeral rites, a funeral. Hence **obsēq'uIAL** a. [pl. of obs. *obsequy* f. OF *obseque* f. med. L *obsequiae* = L *exsequiae* funeral with *obsequium* see foll.]

obsēq'uious (-z-), a. Obedient, dutiful, (arch.); servile, fawning. Hence ~LY² adv., ~NESS n. [f. L *obsequiosus* f. OB(*sequium* f. *sequi* follow) compliance]

obsēr'vance, n. Keeping or performance of (also *of*) law, duty, custom, ritual, etc.; act of religious or ceremonial character, customary rite; the rule of a religious order; ‖ paying of deference or respect (arch.), also ~ANCY n. [F. f. L *observantia* (OBSERVE, -ANCE)]

obsēr'vant, a. & n. 1. Attentive in observance; acute or diligent in taking notice; hence ~LY² adv. 2. n. Member of branch of Franciscan order that observes the strict rule. [F (OBSERVE. -ANT)]

obsērva'tion (-z-), n. 1. Noticing or being noticed, perception, faculty of taking notice; *post, attitude*, ‖ ~ *car*, in train esp. watching for ... 3. Accurate watching & noting (of phenomena as they occur in nature (cf. *experiment*) with regard to cause & effect or mutual relations. 4. Taking of sun's or other heavenly body's altitude to find latitude or longitude. 5. Remark or statement, esp. one of the nature of comment. Hence ~AL a., ~ALLY² adv., (-zervāsho-), [f. L *observatio* (OBSERVE, -ATION)]

obsēr'vatory (-z-), n. Building etc. whence natural, esp. astronomical, phenomena may be observed. [f. L *observatory* (OBSERVE. -TORY]

obsērve' (-z-), v.t. & i. 1. Keep, follow, adhere to, perform duty, (law, command, appointed time, method, principle, silence, rite, anniversary, etc.). 2. Perceive, mark, watch, take notice of, become conscious of, (*the* ~*ed of all* ~*ers*, person etc. on whom etc. attention is concentrated). 3. Examine & note (phenomena) without aid of experiment. 4. Say, esp. by way of comment; make remark(s) on. Hence ~ABLE a., ~'ER¹ n. (esp., interested spectator, person carried in aeroplane to note enemy's position etc., person trained to watch for & identify aircraft; *O~er*, newspaper title), ~ingLY² adv. [f. L *observare* (-ATION keep)]

obsess' (-z-), v.t. (Of evil spirit, delusion, or fixed idea) haunt, harass, preoccupy, fill mind of, (~*ed by, with*). So **obsĕs'sion** (-shn) n. [f. L OB(*sidēre sess-* = *sedēre* sit)]

obsid′ian, n. Dark vitreous lava or volcanic rock like bottle-glass. [f. L *obsidiānus*, erron. for *Obsiānus* (*Obsius* personal name, -AN)]

obsoles′c(ent, a. Becoming obsolete, going out of use or date; (Biol., of organ once developed more fully) gradually disappearing. So ~ENCE n. [f. L (*obsolescere* f. *solēre* be accustomed, see -ESCENT), -ENT]

ob′solēte, a. & n. 1. Disused, discarded, antiquated; (Biol.) less developed than formerly or in cognate species, rudimentary; hence ~NESS, **ob′solētism**(3, 4), nn. 2. n. ~ person or thing. [f. L *obsolētus* p.p. as prec.]

ob′stacle, n. Hindrance, impediment, (~ *race*, in which artificial ~s of natural ~s have to be passed). [OF, f. L *obstāculum* f. OB(*stāre* stand) impede]

obstet′ric(al), a.a. Of midwifery, of childbirth & its antecedents & sequels, as branch of medicine & surgery. Hence **obstet′rics, obstetri′cian** (-ĭshn), nn. [irreg. by confusion with -ıc f. L *obstetricius* f. *obstetrix* midwife f. OB(*stāre* or *sistere* stand), -TRIX]

ob′stinate, a. Stubborn, inflexible, self-willed, refractory. Hence or cogn. ~ACY n., ~ately[1] adv. [f. L *obstinātus* p.p. of OB(*stināre* deriv. form of *stāre* stand) persist]

obstrep′erous, a. Noisy, vociferous; turbulent, unruly, noisily resisting control. Hence ~LY[2] adv., ~NESS n. [f. L *obstreperus* f. OB(*strepere* make noise), -OUS]

obstruct′, v.t. & i. Block up, fill with impediments, make impassable or difficult of passage; prevent or retard progress of, impede; practise (esp. Parliamentary) obstruction. [f. L OB(*struere struct*-build)]

obstruc′tion, n. Blocking or being blocked, making or becoming more or less impassable; hindering, esp. of Parliamentary business by talking against time, whence ~ISM(3), ~IST(2), (-sho-), nn.; obstacle (~*guard*, bar fixed before locomotive to remove ~s from rails). [f. L *obstructio* (prec., -ION]

obstruct′ive, a. & n. 1. Causing, intended to produce, obstruction; hence ~LY[2] adv., ~NESS n. 2. n. ~ person, esp. in House of Commons. [OBSTRUCT, -IVE]

obtain′, v.t. & i. 1. Acquire, have granted one, get, whence ~MENT n. (rare), ~ABLE a.; be prevalent or established or in vogue. [f. F *obtenir* f. L OB(*tinēre = tenēre* hold) keep]

obtec′ted, a. (entom.). (Of the pupae of certain insects) enclosed in an outer chitinous case. [f. L OB(*tegere tect*- cover)]

obtest′, v.t. & i. (arch.). Adjure, supplicate, call to witness; protest. So **obtesta′tion** n. [f. L OB(*testārī* f. *testis* witness)]

obtrude′ (-ŏŏd), v.t. Thrust forward(*upon* or *on* person or his attention) importunately. So **obtru′sion** (-ŏŏzhn) n., **obtru′sive** a., **obtru′sively**[2] adv., **obtru′siveness** n., (-ŏŏ-). [f. L OB(*trudere trus*- push]

obtrunc′āte, v.t. Cut off head of, top. [f. L OB(*truncare* f. *truncus* maimed), -ATE[3]]

obtund′, v.t. (med.). Blunt, deaden, (sense or faculty). [f. L OB(*tundere tus*-beat]

ob′tūrāte, v.t. Stop up, close, seal, (orifice in body, breech of gun, etc.). Hence or cogn. ~A′TION, ~ātor[2](2), nn. [f. L *obtūrare*, -ATE[3]]

obtūse′, a. Of blunt form, not sharp-pointed or sharp-edged; (Geom., of angle) greater than one & less than two right angles; (of pain, the senses) dull, not acute; stupid, slow of perception. Hence ~LY[2] adv., ~NESS n., **obtūs′i**-comb. form. [f. L p.p. of OBTUNDE]

ob′verse, a. & n. 1. Narrower at base or point of attachment than at apex (esp. in Nat. Hist, including as general term *obovate, obovate, obovate-lanceolate*, etc.); answering as counterpart to something else; hence ~LY[2] adv. 2. n. Side of coin or medal bearing the head or principal design (cf. REVERSE); face of anything meant to be presented; front; counterpart of a fact or truth. [f. L *obversus* p.p. (foll.)]

obvert′, v.t. (log.). Infer another proposition with contradictory predicate by changing quality of (proposition). So **obver′sion** (-shn) n. [f. L OB(*vertere vers*-turn)]

ob′viāte, v.t. Clear away, get rid of, get round, neutralize (danger, inconvenience, etc.). [f. L OB(*viāre* f. *via* way) withstand]

ob′vious, a. Open to eye or mind, clearly perceptible, palpable, indubitable. Hence ~LY[2] adv., ~NESS n. [f. L *obvius* (*ob viam* in the way), -OUS]

oc-, pref. See OB-.

ocari′na (-rē-), n. Small egg-shaped porcelain or metal musical wind-instrument. [It. (*oca* goose, -INA[1])]

occā′sion (-zhn), n., & v.t. 1. Juncture suitable for doing something, opportunity, (*take ~*, avail oneself of opportunity *to do*; *take ~ by the* FORELOCK[1]). 2. Reason, ground, justification, incitement, need, (*there is no ~ to be angry*; *avoid all ~s of quarrel*; *King has no ~ for services of* officer, formula of dismissal; *gave ~ to a burst of laughter*). 3. Subsidiary, incidental, or immediate cause (*the cause of a revolution may be obscure while its ~ is obvious*). 4. pl. Affairs, business, (esp. *go about one's lawful ~s*). 5. (Particular time marked by) special occurrence (*on this festive ~*; *on the ~ of his marriage*; *celebrate the ~*; *rise to the ~*, show requisite energy etc.; *this 'is a great ~*; (*upon ~*,

For words in **ob-** not given see OB-.

whenever need arises, now & then. **6,** v.t. Be the ~ or cause of, bring about esp. incidentally, cause (action etc., or person or thing to do). [f. L *occásio* f. *occídere* *cas-=cadere* fall). [f. L *occásio* f. *occídere* -TON]

occá'sional (-zho-), a. Arising out of, made or meant for, adapted for use on, acting on, special occasion(s); happening irregularly as occasion presents itself; coming, now & then, not regular or frequent; ~ *cause*, secondary cause, occasion, also apparent cause (see foll.); ||~ *licence* (to sell liquor only at specified times & places). Hence ~**ITY** (-ǎl-) n., ~**LY**[2] adv. [-AL]

occá'sionalism (-zho-), n. Doctrine of some Cartesians that volition & sensation are connected with the following & preceding material phenomena not causally but as separate productions of God on the same occasion. So ~**IST**(2) n.

Ŏc'cident (ǒks-), n. Back of head. Hence **ŏccíp'ital** a., **ŏccíp'ito-** comb. form, (-ks-). [L oc(*ciput -itis=caput* head)]

Ŏc'cident (ǒks-), n. (poet., rhet.), The west; western Europe; Europe; America; America; European as opposed to Oriental civilization, whence **ŏccidén'talism**(3) n. **ŏccidén'talize**(3) v.t. **ŏccidén'talist**(2,3) n., (-ks-), Hence **ŏccidén'tal** a., **ŏccidén'tally**[2] adv., (-ks-). [F, f. L *occident-* setting (OCCASION, -ENT)]

occult'[1], a. Kept secret, esoteric; recondite, mysterious, beyond the range of ordinary knowledge; involving the supernatural, mystical, magical, whence ~**ISM**(3), ~**IST**(2, 3), nn. Hence ~**LY**[2] adv., ~**NESS** n. [f. L oc(*culere -cult-* cf. *celare* hide)]

occult'[2], v.t. & i. Conceal, cut off from view by passing in front, (usu. Astron., & applied only when concealing body is of much greater apparent size than concealed); ~*ing light* in lighthouses, one that is cut off at regular intervals. Hence **ŏcculTA'TION** n. [f. L *occultare* frequent. as prec.]

ŏc'cupant, n. Person holding property, esp. land, in actual possession; one who occupies, or resides or is in, a place; one who establishes title to unowned thing by taking possession. Hence ~**ANCY** n. [f. L as OCCUPY, -ANT]

ŏccupá'tion, n. Occupying or being occupied; taking or holding possession, esp. of country or district by military force (*army of* ~, left to hold occupied region till regular government is set up); tenure, occupancy; what occupies one, means of filling one's time, temporary or regular employment, business, calling, pursuit;

||~ *franchise,* right to vote as tenant; ~ *bridge, road,* etc., private for use of occupiers of land. Hence ~**AL**(-sho-) a., (esp.) incident to or arising from a person's ~ (~*al disease*), based on or utilizing esp. light employment (~*al therapy*). [F, f. L *occupationem* (OCCUPY, -ATION)]

ŏc'cupier, n. Person in (esp. temporary or subordinate) possession of land or house, holder, occupant. [foll., -ER[1]]

ŏc'cupy, v.t. Take possession of (country, region, town, strategic position) by military force or settlement; hold (office, residence, tenant: take up or fill (space, time), reside or be in (place, position); busy, keep engaged, (esp. in pass, & refl.; *occupied* ~ *oneself, with* or *in*). [irreg. f. F *occuper* f. L oc(*cupare* cf. *capere* take; seize; ~ & *obtain,* as compared w. 1 origins, have exchanged senses; in 17th & 18th cc., ~ almost disappeared, being avoided owing to now obs. sense *cohabit*]

occur', v.i. (-rr-), Be met with, be found, exist, in some place or conditions; come into one's mind (esp. *it* ~s or ~*red to me that* --); take place, befall, happen. [f. L oc(*currere* run) go to meet]

occú'rrence, n. Happening (*is of frequent* ~, *often occurs*); incident, event. [f. obs. or rare *occurrent* (prec., -ENT), -ENCE]

ocean (ō'shn), n. Great body of water surrounding the land of the globe; one of the main areas into which geographers divide this (usu. reckoned as five, the *Atlantic, Pacific, Indian, Arctic, & Antarctic, O~s; German~, =* NORTH Sea); immense expanse or quantity of anything (often ~s *of*); ~ *greyhound,* swift ship, esp. passenger liner; ~ *lane, track* prescribed for steamers; ~ *tramp,* cargo-carrying steamer not engaged in single trade. Hence ~**ōG'RAPHY** (ōshŏ-) n., ~**OGRAPH'IC**(AL) (osēŏ-, ōshŏ-)aa., ~**WARD**(s) adv. [f. L f. Gk *ōkeanos* stream encircling earth's disk, Atlantic]

Oceán'ia (ōshi-, ōsi-), n. Islands of Pacific & adjacent seas. [f. F *Océanie* (prec., -IA[1])]

Oceán'ian (ōshǎn'yǎn, ōsi-), a. & n. (Native) of Oceania. [-AN]

oceán'ic, O~, (ōshi-, ōsi-), a. Of, like, etc., the ocean; of Oceania. [-IC]

Océ'anid (os-), n. (pl.~s, ~es pr. -ǎn'idēz). Ocean nymph of Greek mythology. [f. Gk *Ōkeanis -idos* daughter of Ocean]

oc'elot (os-), n. Feline quadruped of S. & Central America, resembling leopard. [F, abridged by Buffon f. Mex. *tlalocelotl* jaguar) of the field, & applied to different animal]

||**och** (see Ap.), int. =*oh, ah,* used in Scotland & Ireland.

ocelli, pl. of OCELLUS.

océll'us (os-), n. (pl. *-lī*). One of simple as opposed to compound eyes of insects; facet of compound eye; spot of colour surrounded by ring of other colour, whence **ō'cellāte**[2], **-āted,** aa. [L, dim. of *oculus* eye]

ŏchlŏc′racy (-kl-), n. Mob-rule. Hence ŏch′locRATn, ŏchlocRAT′ic▲..(-kl-). [f. F ochlocratie f. Gk okhlokratia (okhlos mob, -CRACY)]

ochre (ōk′er), n. Kinds of native earth consisting of clay & hydrated oxide of iron used as pigments varying from light yellow to brown; pale brownish yellow. Hence ~ISH (ōk′er-), ochRA′CEOUS (-krā-shus), ~OUS (ōk′ri-), ŏch′rous, ŏch′ry², (-kr-), aa., ~o- (ōk′ri-) comb. form. [f. F ocre f. L f. Gk ōkhra yellow ochre fem. of ōkhros yellow]

-ock, suf. forming nn. orig. w. dim. sense (hill~, bitt~, bull~, perh. padd~), which many of them have lost (padd~, bull~, poll~); hass~, bann~, matt~, are prob. of different orig.

o′clock. See CLOCK¹.

oct-, = OCTA-, OCTO-, before vowel.

ŏc′ta-, comb. form of Gk oktō eight. Hence OCTĀM′EROUS (4-).

ŏc′tachŏrd (-k-), a. & n. Eight-stringed (musical instrument); series of eight notes, e.g. the diatonic scale. Hence ~AL (-kŏrd¹-) a. [f. LL f. Gk oktakhordos (prec., CHORD)]

ŏc′tad, n. Group of eight. [f. L f. Gk oktas f. októ eight, -AD(1)]

ŏc′tagon, n. & a. Plane figure with eight angles & sides, object or building of such section; hence ŏctăg′onAL a., ŏctăg′o-nALLY² adv.; (adj.) ~al. [f. L f. Gk oktagōnos (OCTA-, gōnia angle)]

ŏctahĕd′ron, n. Solid figure contained by eight plane faces, & usu. by eight tri-angles (regular~on, by equal & equilateral triangles); body, esp. crystal, of regular ~al form. So ~AL a. [f. Gk oktaedron (OCTA-, hedra seat)]

ŏc′tane, n. Hydrocarbon of the paraffin series; high~, (of fuels used in internal-combustion engines) having good anti-knock properties, not detonating readily during the power stroke. [OCT-, -ANE(2)]

ŏc′tant, n. 1. Arc of circle=1/8 of circum-ference; 1/8 of circular area, contained within two radii & arc; one of eight parts into which three planes intersecting at right angles) at point divide space round it. 2. (Astron.) point in planet's apparent course 45° distant from given point, esp. point at which moon is 45° from conjunction or opposition with sun. 3. Instrument in form of graduated eighth of circle used in astronomy & navigation. [f. LL octans (L octo eight, cf. QUADRANT]

ŏc′tarchy (-kl), n. Aggregate of eight petty kingdoms (substituted by some historians for HEPTARCHY). [OCTA-, cf. HEPTARCHY]

octaroon. See OCTOROON.

ŏc′tastyle, a. & n. (Portico or building) with eight columns at end or in front. [f. LL f. Gk oktastulos (OCTA-, stulos pillar)]

ŏc′tateuch (-k), n. First 8 O.T. books. [f. LL f. Gk OCTAteukhos, cf. PENTATEUCH]

ŏc′tave (-iv), n. 1. The day week of a festival, eight days including festival & its day week. 2. Group or stanza of eight lines, octet. 3.(mus.) Note produced by twice or half the vibration-rate of given note & eight diatonic degrees above or below it (second ~, ~ of the ~ in same direction; so third etc. ~); interval be-tween note & its ~; series of notes filling this; note & its ~ sounding together. 4. Group of eight. 5. A fencing position. 6. ‖ Wine-cask holding 13½ gal. 7. ~ coupler, device connecting organ-keys an ~ apart; ~flute, piccolo, also organ flute-stop an ~ higher than the ordinary. [F, f. L octava dies eighth day by inclusive reckoning (octavus f. octo eight)]

ŏctāv′ō, n. (abbr. 8vo, oct.; pl. ~8). (Size of) book or page given by folding sheets three times or into eight leaves. [f. L IN⁸ octavo (form prec.)]

ŏctāv′us. See PRIMUS¹.

ŏctĕnn′ial, a. Lasting, recurring every, eight years. [f. L OCT(ennium f. annus year) period of eight years, -AL]

ŏctĕt(te)′, n. (Composition for) eight singers or players; group of eight lines, esp. the first eight of sonnet. [f. L octo eight, after DUET]

ŏctĭll′ion (-lyon), n. ‖ Eighth power of million (1 followed by 48 ciphers). Hence ~TH² a. & n. [F (now=ninth power of thousand) as prec. after MILLION]

‖ ŏctĭngĕntĕn′arỹ (-j-), n. 800th anniver-sary. [f. L octingenti 800, after CENTENARY]

octo-, oct-, comb. form of L octo, & occas. (=OCTA-) of Gk oktō, eight.

Octŏb′er (ō-), n. Tenth month; beer brewed in ~ (arch.). [L (prec.), cf. DECEMBER]

Octŏb′rist (ō-), n. & a. (Member) of moderate party in Russian Duma. [Oct. 30, 1905, date of Imperial Constitutional Manifesto]

ŏctŏcĕntĕn′arỹ (or -sĕn′tĕn-), ŏctŏcĕn-tĕnn′ial, nn. (Irreg. for) OCTINGENTENARY.

ŏctŏdē′cimō, n. (abbr. 18mo; pl.~8). (Size of) book or page given by folding sheets into eighteen leaves. [for IN⁵ ~ f. L OCTO-(decimus tenth) eighteenth, cf. OCTAVO]

ŏctŏgēnār′ian, a. & n. Eighty-year-old (person); of such person. [f. L octogena-rius (octogeni eighty each, -ARY¹), -AN]

ŏc′tonal, a. Proceeding by eights (of coinage, numeral system, etc.). [f. L octoni, see foll., -AL]

ŏctonār′ian, a. & n. (pros.). Eight-foot (line). [f. L octonarius versus eight-foot line (octoni eight each f. octo eight, -ARY¹), -AN]

ŏc′tonarỹ, a. & n. = OCTONAL (n.) group of eight, eight-line stanza (esp. of divi-sions of Ps. 119). [see prec.]

ŏc′topus, n. (pl.~es). (Genus of) cephalo-pod mollusc with eight suckered arms

ŏc'tuple, a., n., & v.t. Eightfold; (a.) pro-duct after multiplication by eight of; (vb) multiply by eight. [see prec.]

ŏc'troi (-rwah), n. Duty levied in some continental countries on goods entering town; place where, officials by whom, it is levied. [F (octroyer grant, as AUTHOR-IZE)]

ŏc'ular, a, & n. Of, for, by, with, etc., the eye(s) or sight, visual, (~ demonstration, proof appealing to the eyes); (n.) eye-piece of optical instrument. Hence ~LY² adv. [f. L ocularis (oculus eye, -AR¹)]

ŏc'ularist, n. Maker of artificial eyes. [f. oculist]

ŏc'ulate, -āted, aa. =OCELLATE. [f. L oculus eye, -ATE²]

ŏc'ulist, n. Specialist in eye-diseases. Hence ~ĭc a. [f. L oculus, -IST]

ŏc'ulo-, comb. form of L oculus eye, as ~nāsäl of eye & nose.

ŏd, n. Power assumed to pervade nature & account for magnetism, crystallization, chemical action, mesmerism, etc. [arbi-trary formation of Baron v. Reichenbach 1788–1869]

ŏd'alisque (-k), n. Eastern female slave or concubine, esp. in Turkish Sultan's seraglio. [f. Turk. odaliq (odah chamber].

ŏdd, a. & n. 1. Left over when the rest have been divided into two numerically equal sets (the ~ man, to whom casting-vote falls in uneven-numbered committee etc.; the ~ trick in whist, thirteenth when each side has won six; ~ man out, way of selecting one of three persons by tossing coins till only two agree). 2. (Of number) not divisible by two (~ & even, a game of chance); (of things or persons numbered consecutively) bearing such number. 3. (Appended to number, sum, weight, etc.) with something over of lower denomination (forty ~, between 40 & 50; sixty thousand ~, with some extra hundreds, tens, or units; sixty~thousand, between 60 & 70 thousand; ~ money, what shall we do with the ~ six?). 5. Additional, casual, unoccupied, incalculable, (picks

round mouth; organized & usu. harmful ramified power or influence. [f. Gk oktō-eight-footed (pous foot)]

ŏctŏroon, -ta-, n. Offspring of quadroon & white, person of one-eighth negro blood. [irreg. f. OCTO- after QUADROON]

ŏctŏsyllăb'ic, a. & n. Eight-syllable (verse). [f. LL OCTOsyllabus f. syllaba SYLLABLE), -IC]

ŏctŏsyll'able, n. & a. = prec.; word of eight syllables. [see prec.]

up ~ jobs; do it at ~ moments; in some corner~; ~ numbers, volumes, belonging to incomplete sets of magazines etc.). 6. Extraordinary, strange, queer, remarkable, eccentric, whence ~ISH'(2) a., ~LY² adv. 7. ~come-short, remnant, (pl.) odds & ends; ~come-short, some near day (see); one of these ~come-shortlies, before long); ~fellow, member of friendly society of Oddfellows with rites imitative of freemasonry; hence ~NESS n. 8. n. (golf). The ~, the stroke which one player has played more than his opponent (opp. the like). [f. ON odda in odda-(mathr man) with casting-vote (oddi angle, triangle, cogn. w. OE ord tip)]

ŏd'dǐty, n. Strangeness; peculiar trait; queer person; fantastic object, strange event. [-ITY]

ŏd'dments, n. pl. Odds & ends. [-MENT]

ŏdds, n. pl. (formerly always, & still in phrases as below, treated as sing.). In-equalities (make ~ even, do away with these); difference (what's the ~?, what does it matter?); variance, strife, (are at ~ with fate); balance of advantage (the ~ are in our favour; have fought against longer~); equalizing allowance to weaker competitor (give, receive, ~; ratio be-tween amounts staked by parties to bet (lay, give, ~ of three to one, said of party offering the advantage; take ~, accept the advantage); chances or balance of probability in favour of some result (it is ~ that or but, the ~ are that, he will do th); ~ & ends, remnants, stray articles, (perh. alteration of earlier odd ends). [prob. pl. of ODD used as n.]

ōde, n. (Orig.) poem meant to be sung (choral, song of chorus in Greek play etc.); (mod.) rhymed or rarely unrhymed lyric often in form of address, often in ex-alted style and enthusiastic tone, often in varied or irregular metre, & usu. between 50 & 200 lines in length. [F, f. LL oda f. Gk ōidē contr. of aoidē (aeidō sing)]

-ode, suf, forming nn. w. sense thing of the nature of (geode, phyllode); anode, cathode, electrode, are not examples. [f. Gk -ōdēs]

ōdĕ'um, n. (pl. -s, -ĕa). Building for musi-cal performances, esp. among ancient Greeks & Romans. [f. Gk ōideion ODE]

ōd'ious, a. Hateful, repulsive. Hence ~LY² adv, ~NESS n. [f. OF odieus f. L odiosus (ODIUM, -OSE¹)]

ŏd'ium, n. General or widespread dislike or reprobation incurred by person or at-taching to action (exposed me to ~; the ~ of the transaction); ~ theol'ogicum, bitter-ness notoriously characterizing theolo-gians who disagree. [L, = hatred]

odŏm'eter. See hod-.

odŏn't(o)-, comb. form of Gk odous odontos tooth, as ~orhing'enous, having

toothlike serrations in the bill; ~ogloss²um, genus of orchids with large beautifully coloured flowers; **~OID; ~õdoufi²ocy. ~õdorif²erous**, a. Diffusing (usu. agreeable) scent, fragrant. Hence **~LY²** adv. [f. L *odorifer* (chiefly poet.). = prec. Hence **~LY²** adv. [foll. -OUS]

õd²orous, a. Pleasant or unpleasant smell, whence ~LESS a.; fragrance; (arch. usu. pl.) substance(s) emitting sweet scent, perfume(s); (fig.) savour, trace, (no ~ of intolerance attaches to it); *good or bad or ill repute or favour* (*is in bad ~ with the nonconformists*); ~ *of sanctity*, reputation for holiness (orig. lit., sweet ~ exhaled by dying or exhumed saint). [f. OF *odor* f. L *odorem* (-OR*¹*)]

õd²yl, n. = OD. [-YL]

Od²yssey (ŏ-), n. (pl. ~s). One of two great ancient-Greek national epics (cf. ILIAD) describing adventures of Odysseus or Ulysses returning from siege of Troy; any of the 24 books of this (*in the fourth etc.* ~); series of wanderings, long adventurous journey. [f. L f. Gk *Odusseia* (*Odusseus*, -IA*¹*)]

œ²cist (ēs-), n. Founder of (esp. ancient-Greek) colony. [f. Gk *oikistēs* (*oikizō* settle f. *oikos* house, -IST)]

œcŏl²ogy (ēk-), n. Var. of ECOLOGY.

œcumēn²ical (ēk-), a. Of or representing the whole Christian world or universal church, general, universal, catholic, (of general councils of early, & of mod. R.-C., Church); world-wide. So **œcŭmēn²cITY** (ēk-) n. [f. L f. Gk *oikoumenicos* f. *hē oikoumenē* the inhabited (earth) f. *oikeō* inhabit, -AL]

œdēm²a (ēd-), n. (path.; no pl.). Swollen state of tissue etc. with serous fluid, local dropsy. Hence ~TOSE¹, ~TOUS, aa., ~-TOUSLY² adv., (ēdēm-² or ēdēm⁴). [f. Gk *oidēma -atos* (*oideō* swell, -M)]

Œd²ipus (ēd-), n. Solver of riddles; ~ *complex*, a sexual complex held by psychoanalysis of the Freudian school to influence the child in regard to the parent of opposite sex. [f. Gk *Oidipous*, who guessed the Sphinx's riddle, & in ignorance married his mother]

o²er (ōr), adv. & prep. = OVER (poet.).

œsŏph²agus (ēs-), n. (pl. ~i pr.-jī, ~uses). Canal from mouth to stomach, gullet. Hence **œsophâg²ĕal** (-j-) a., ~o- comb. form. [f. Gk *oisophagos* etym. dub.]

œs²trum, -us, (ēs-), n. Gadfly; stimulus, vehement impulse, frenzy. [f. Gk *oistros*]

of (ŏv, ŏv), prep. connecting its noun with preceding n., adj., adv., or vb, & indicating the relations roughly classified as follows: **1.** Removal, separation, point of departure, privation, (*north, within a mile, upwards, have the advantage, of; *back of, cured, brought to BED¹, of; destitute, rid, ease, brought to BED¹, of; destitute, empty, free, bare, of; take LEAVE¹ of; balk,**

---

cheat, defraud, deprive, disappoint, of; independently, guiltless, irrespective, of). **2.** Origin, derivation, cause, agency, authorship, (*be, come, descend, spring, of; borrow, buy, win, receive, hire, of; TAKE it ill of; have comfort, wish one joy, of; ask, demand, learn, expect, of; of one's own ACCORD², of COURSE¹, of RIGHT, of NECESSITY.* of oneself, spontaneously; *die of; smell, savour, smack, of; tired, ashamed, afraid, glad, proud, of; sick of measles, laid up with, sick of delays, disgusted by; warned of God, forsaken of God & man, by; it was kind, foolish, naughty, clever, cruel, well done, of you to say so; has the approval of his master; the works of Shakspere, Iliad of Homer*). **3.** Material, substance, closer definition, identity, (*house of cards; built of brick; make a FOOL¹, the BEST¹, of; MAKE¹ much of; a family of eight; the name of Jones; the class of idiots; city of Rome, vice of drunkenness; a fool of a man, her scamp of a husband, the worst liar of any man I know; had a bad time, troublesome journey, of it*). **4.** Concern, reference, direction, respect, (*think well of him; never heard of it; was informed of the fact; is true of every case; repent, beware, of; cannot conceive, accept, approve, THINK, of; does not admit or allow of; accuse, convict, suspect, of; acquit, bethink, oneself of; SHORT, guilty, certain, sure, confident, fond, of; swift of foot, blind of an eye, hard of heart, HARD of hearing; at 30 years of age*). **5.** Objective relation (the *levying of taxes; love of virtue; in search of knowledge; great eaters of pork; redolent, productive, fruitful, lavish, prodigal, sparing, capable, sensible, careful, observant, desirous, impatient, characteristic, destructive, indicative, of*). **6.** Description, quality, condition, (*man of tact, person of consequence, farm of 100 acres, the hour of prayer, potatoes of our own growing; girl of ten years old, with mixed construction, of ten years old*). **7.** Partition, classification, inclusion, selection, (*no more of that; some, five, of us, = a, a portion, or five, of us who are more numerous, or by extension b. we, being several or five persons; so any part, or the whole, of it; the most dangerous of enemies; he of all men, he most or least of all; is the one thing of all others that, illog.; for of all that; song of songs, holy of holies, those best deserving the name; is one of a, ten, thousand, such as occurs only in one among 1,000, 10,000 cases; a friend of mine, of the vicar's, i.e. orig. in the number of my, the vicar's, friends, but extended to illog. contexts, as that long nose of his, this only son of the vicar's; drink deep of flattery, partake of food; was sworn of the Council, admitted as member; his temper is of the quickest, belongs to the quickest class; a sort of thud; comes in of an evening, at some time in the evenings; of old, yore,*

late years, late, somewhere in the specified periods). **8.** Belonging, connexion, possession, (we of the middle class; companions of today; a thing of the past; the master of the house; the widow of the man who was killed; a topic of conversation; esp. with words that naturally require supplement, as the cause, result, counterpart, opposite, image, of). **9.** BECAUSE, by MEAN's, for FEAR, for the SAKE, in BEHALF, in CASE, in FACE, in RESPECT, in SPITE, INSTEAD, on ACCOUNT, on BEHALF, on the POINT, of. [OE. ab off adv., cf. Du. af & G ab; off are one word, differentiated in 14th–16th cc.]

of-, pref. See OB-.

off (awf, ŏf), adv., prep., a., n., & v.t. **1.** adv. Away, at or to a distance, (rode ~; beat ~ the attack; keep assailant ~; ward ~ disaster: take oneself, be, make, ~; depart; ~ with you!, go, ~ with his head!, behead him!; full, go, ~, deteriorate; of ship, fall ~, become less close to wind; the bullet glanced ~; go ~, fall asleep; is far, three miles, two years, ~; (so as to be) out of position, not on or touching or dependent or attached, loose, separate, gone, (my hat is ~; take his clothes ~; cut, break, shake, etc., ~; throw ~ reserve, become open or candid; be ~ with the old love, have severed connexion; get one's daughters, stock, ~, disposed of by marriage, sale; the gilt is ~, disillusionment has come; we are ~ now, just started, starting, or about to start); so as to break continuity or continuance, discontinued, stopped, not obtainable, (broke ~; ceased to speak; leave ~ work; the engagement, bargain, negotiation, is ~; declare ~, refuse or rescind engagement; cut ~ supplies; the gas, asparagus, is ~, no longer to be got); to the end, entirely, so as to be clear, (clear, drink, pay, polish, work, ~); BUY, COME, DASH¹, GET, MAKE², PALM, PASS, RATTLE, SHOW, TAKE, ~; RIGHT, STRAIGHT, ~; well, badly, comfortably, etc., ~, so circumstanced or supplied with money; ~ & on, intermittently, waveringly, now & again; ~loud, ~ saddle, S-Afr. for un-.
2. prep. From, away or down or up from, disengaged or distant from, (so as to be) no longer on, (drove them ~ the seas; is ~ dish; eats ~ silver plate; take thing, matter, ~ one's hands, relieve him of it; had borrowed £20 ~ plaintiff vulg.; ~ one's HEAD¹, FEED²; ~ colour, out of condition, indisposed; ~ smoking, not indulging in it, disinclined for it; took something ~ the price; is ~ duty or work; cut a slice ~, dine ~, the joint; was only a yard ~ me; keep ship two points ~ the wind; ~ the point, irrelevant(ly); ~ the map, sl., vanished, no longer existing; in a street ~ the Strand, turning out of it;

from ~, arch., poet., or vulg., = ~; ~ hand, extempore, without premeditation, unceremoniously, whence ~ hand', ~ hand'EDNESS n.; ~ shore, a short way out to sea; so ~ shore fisheries; ~ shore wind, blowing seawards; anchored ~ the point, cape, etc., opposite & a short way from it; ~ side in football, between ball & opponents' goal, so ~ side play, rule). **3.** adj. Farther, far, (on the ~ side of the road); (of horses etc. or vehicles) right (opp. NEAR¹; w. ref. to side at which rider usu. mounts; the ~ leader, front wheel, hind leg, side); (Cricket) towards, in, or coming from, that half of the field as divided by line through two middle stumps in which playing batsman does not stand (opp. ON, LEG¹; an ~ drive, whence ~ drive v.t., ~ stump; LONG¹, ~; an ~ break); subordinate, divergent, (in is an ~ street; is an ~ issue); contingent, improbable, (there is an ~ chance that); disengaged (will do it on my next ~ day); ~-licence, to sell beer etc. for consumption ~ the premises; ~-print, separation, printed copy of article etc. that was orig. part of larger publication. **4.** n. (Cricket) The ~ side. **5.** v.t. (colloq.) Announce intention of abandoning or annulling (negotiation, agreement, undertaking); withdraw from negotiation or engagement with (person). [see OF]

ŏff'al, n. Refuse, waste stuff, scraps, garbage; parts cut off as waste from carcass meant for food, esp. entrails, also head, tail, kidneys, heart, tongue, liver, etc.; carrion, putrid flesh; low-priced fish (e.g. plaice as opp. sole or other prime fish); bran or other by-product of grain (often pl.); offscourings, dregs; ~ wood, etc., inferior. [=off-fall or what falls off]

offence', *offense', n. Stumbling-block, occasion of unbelief etc., (now rare); attacking, aggressive action, taking the offensive, (the most effective defence is ~); wounding of the feelings, wounded feeling, annoyance, umbrage, (no ~ was meant; too quick to take ~; give ~ to; cannot be done without ~); transgression, misdemeanour, illegal act, (esp. commit an ~ against). Hence ~LESS (sf-) a. [ME & OF offens f. L offensus -ūs annoyance, & ME & F offense f. L offensa a striking against, both f. OF(fendere fens- strike)]

offend', v.i. & t. Stumble morally, do amiss, transgress, (against law, decency, person, etc.), whence ~ING¹ n. (esp. FIRST ~er), ~ING² a.; wound feelings of, anger, cause resentment or disgust in, outrage, (am sorry you are ~ed; ~ed at or by thing, with or by person; ~ her delicacy, my sense of justice), whence ~edly² adv. [f. OF offendre f. L as prec.]

offen'sive, a. & n. **1.** Aggressive, intended

for or used in attack, (~ *arms, movement*; opp. DEFENSIVE); meant to give offence, insulting, (~ *language*); disgusting, illsmelling, nauseous, repulsive; hence ~LY² adv., ~NESS n. **2.** n. Attitude of assailant, aggressive action, (*take, act on, abandon, the* ~); an attack, ~ *campaign or stroke*, (*the long-expected German* ~); movement, as *peace* ~. [f. med. L *offensivus* (OFFENCE, -IVE)]

off'er¹, v.t. & i. **1.** Present (victim, firstfruits, prayer) to deity, revered person, etc., by way of sacrifice, give in worship or devotion, whence ~ING¹(4) n. **2.** Hold out in hand, or tender in words or otherwise, for acceptance or refusal (~*ed me his hymn-book to look over*; TAKEN & ~*ed*; *was* ~*ed a free pardon*; ~ *an opinion, a few remarks*, etc.; ~ *no apology*). **3.** Make proposal of marriage. **4.** Show for sale. **5.** Give opportunity to enemy for *battle*. **6.** Express readiness *to do* if desired; essay, try to show, (violence, resistance, etc., often *to*); show an intention to do (~*ed to strike me*). **7.** (Of things) present to sight or notice (*each age* ~*s its characteristic riddles*); present itself, occur, (as *opportunity* ~*s; the first path that* ~*ed*). [OE. *offrian* in religious sense f. L OR(*ferre* bring); other senses f. F *offrir* of same orig.]

off'er², n. Expression of readiness to give or do if desired, or to sell on terms (*on* ~, for sale at certain price), proposal esp. of marriage; bid. [f. F *offre* (prec.)]

off'ertory, n. Part of mass or communion service at which offerings are made, the offering of these, the gifts offered; collection of money at religious service. [f. eccl. L *offertorium* (LL *offert-* for L *oblat-* p.p. st. of *offerre* OFFER¹, -ORY) offering]

off'ice, n. **1.** Piece of kindness, attention, service, (*ill* ~) disservice, (*owing to, by, the good* or *ill* ~*s of*). **2.** Duty attaching to one's position, task, function, (*it is my* ~, *the* ~ *of the arteries, to*). **3.** Position with duties attached to it, place of authority or trust or service esp. of public kind (*was given an* ~ *under Government*), tenure of official position esp. that of minister of State (*take, enter upon, hold, leave, resign,* ~; JACK¹ *in* ~). **4.** Ceremonial duty (esp. *perform the last* ~*s to*, rites due to the dead). **5.** (Eccl.) authorized form of worship, daily service of R.-C. breviary (also *divine* ~; *say* ~, recite this), Anglican morning & evening prayer, (introit at beginning of) mass or communion service, any occasional service such as the *O~ for the Dead*. **6.** Place for transacting business (*goes down to the* ~ *at 9 a.m.*); room etc. in which the clerks of an establishment work, counting-house; (with qualification) room etc. set apart for business of particular department of large concern (|| *booking, inquiry, goods, lost-property,* ~ in railway station) or local branch of dispersed organization (*our Manchester* ~; *a post, telegraph,* ~) or company for specified purpose (*insurance, fire or fire-insurance,* ~). **7.** (O~) quarters or staff or collective authority of a Government department (*the* FOREIGN, WAR¹, POST², O~). **8.** pl. Parts of house devoted to household work, storage, etc. **9.** || (sl.) Hint, signal, as *give, take, the* ~. **10.** *Holy O~*, the inquisition; ~-*bearer*, official or officer. [OF. f. L OR(*ficium* f. *facere* do) service]

off'icer, n., & v.t. **1.** Holder of public, civil, or ecclesiastical office, king's servant or minister, appointed or elected functionary, (usu. with qualification, as ~ *of* HEALTH, *of the Household*, or *public, medical,* ~; || *relieving* ~, see RELIEVE), **2.** President, treasurer, secretary, etc., of society. **3.** Bailiff, catchpole, constable. **4.** Person holding authority in navy, army, air force, or mercantile marine, esp. with commission in army or navy (GENERAL, STAFF, COMMISSION¹ed, FIELD¹, COMPANY¹, BREVET, WARRANT¹, NON-COMmissioned, ~ in army; FLAG⁴, COMMISSION¹ed, WARRANT¹, PETTY, ~ in navy; *Naval* ~s: Admiral of the Fleet, Admiral, Vice-Adm., Rear-Adm., Commodore, Captain, Commander, Lieut.-Commander, Lieutenant, Sub-lieut., Midshipman; *Army* ~s: Field Marshal, General, Lieut.-Gen., Major-Gen., BRIGADIER (formerly *Brigadier-Gen.*), Colonel, Lieut.-Col., Major, Captain, Lieutenant, Second Lieut.; AIR¹ *Force* ~s); || *Officers' Training Corps* (abbr. O.T.C.; orig. for the Territorial Force, & multiplied for the 1914–18 war). **5.** v.t. (usu. in p.p.). Provide with ~s, act as commander of. [f. OF *officier* f. med. L *officiarius* (prec., -ARY¹)]

offi'cial (-shl), a. & n. **1.** Of an office, the discharge of duties, or the tenure of an office; holding office, employed in public capacity; derived from or vouched for by person(s) in office, properly authorized; (Med.) according to the pharmacopoeia, officinal; usual with persons in office (~ *solemnity, red tape*, etc.); hence ~LY² adv. ~IZE(3) v.t., (-sha~). **2.** n. Presiding officer or judge of archbishop's, bishop's, or esp. archdeacon's court (usu. ~ *principal*); person holding public office or engaged in ~ duties, whence ~DOM, ~ISM(2), nn., (-sha~). [f. L *officialis* (OFFICE, -AL)]

offi'ciate (-shi-), v.i. Discharge priestly office, perform divine service, so ~ANT(1) n.; act in some official capacity, esp. on particular occasion (usu. *as host, best man*, etc.). [f. med. L *officiare* perform divine service (OFFICE, -ATE³]

offi'cinal, a. (Of herb or drug) used in medicine or the arts; (of medical preparation) kept ready at druggist's, made from pharmacopoeia recipe (now usu. OFFICIAL, (of name) adopted in pharmacopoeia.

officious (-shus), a. (Given to) offering service that is not wanted, doing or undertaking more than is required, in- trusive, meddlesome, whence ~NESS n.; (Diplom., opp. official) informal, un- officially friendly or candid, not binding. Hence ~LY² adv. [f. L officiosus obliging (OFFICE, -OUS)]

offing (or aw-), n. Part of visible sea distant from shore or beyond anchoring ground (was seen in the ~); position at distance from shore (gain, keep, etc., an ~). [OFF, -ING¹]

offish (aw-, o-), a. (colloq.) Inclined to aloofness, distant or stiff in manner. Hence ~NESS n. [OFF, -ISH¹; cf. UPPISH]

off scourings n. pl. Refuse, filth, dregs, (usu. of; lit. & fig. of persons as the ~ of humanity). [OFF, SCOUR, -ING¹(2)]

off set (aw-, o-), n. Start, set-off, outset, (rare); short side shoot from stem or root serving for propagation, (transf. & fig.) offshoot, scion, mountain-spur; compen- sation, set-off, consideration or amount diminishing or neutralizing effect of con- trary one; (Surv.) short distance meas- ured perpendicularly from main line of measurement; (Archit.) sloping ledge in wall etc. where thickness of part above is diminished; bend made in pipe to carry it past obstacle; (Typ.) smudging of clean sheet through being laid on freshly- printed surface; ~ process, method of printing in which ink is first transferred from a plate to a uniform rubber surface and then to the paper etc. [OFF, SET¹]

off shoot (aw-, o-), n. Side shoot or branch (lit. & fig.), derivative. [OFF, SHOOT]

off spring (or aw-), n. Progeny, issue, (fig.) result. [OE ofspring (OF, OFF, SPRING)]

Of ting (o-), n. German prison camp for officers. [G]

oft (av-, o-), adv. Often (arch. except in comb. with p.p. or part., as ~told, ~- recurring; many a time & ~, often); ~- times, often (arch.). [com.-Teut.: OE & ON, cf. G, oft]

often (aw'fn, o'fn; occas. -ten), adv. & a. (~er, ~est). Frequently, many times, at short intervals, (with singular generalized subject) in a considerable proportion of the instances (the victim ~ dies of it); ~ & ~, emphatic form; ~times, ~ (arch.); frequent (by ~ study of it). [extended f. prec.]

og'doad, n. The number, a set of, eight. [f. LL f. Gk ogdoas (oktō eight, -AD)]

og'ee, n. & a. (Moulding) showing in section a double continuous curve, con- cave below passing into convex above; S-shaped (line); ~ arch, doorway, window, with two ~ curves meeting at apex,

---

Hence ~'d' [-ED²] a. [prob. f. F OGIVE, L officina contr. of officinalis f. officina workshop

ogham (og'am), n. Ancient British and Irish alphabet of twenty characters; inscription in this; one of the characters. [Olr. ogam, referred to Ogma supposed inventor]

ogive (ŏji'v, ōji'v), n. Diagonal groin or rib of vault; pointed or Gothic arch, whence ogiv'AL a. [F, etym. dub.]

ō'gle, v.t. & i., & n. 1. Cast amorous glances; eye amorously; hence ŏg'l'ER¹ n. 2 n. Amorous glance. [prob. f. LG oegeln or G äugeln dim. of augen look about (auge eye]

Og'pu (ŏg'poŏ), n. Former organization for combating counter-revolutionary acti- vities in Soviet Russia. [Initial letters of Obedinennoe Gosudarstvennoe Politiches- koe Upravlenie, United State Political Administration]

ō'gre (-ger), n. Man-eating giant. Hence or cogm. ~ISH¹ (-ger-), ōg'rish¹ aa., ŏg'ress¹ n. [F, first used by Perrault 1697, etym. dub.]

Ogyg'ian (o-), a. Of obscure antiquity, prehistoric. [f. L f. Gk Ōgugos of Ōgugēs mythical king of Attica or Boeotia]

oh (ō), int. See o².

ohm (ōm), n. Unit of electrical resistance; ~ammeter, instrument measuring electri- cal current & resistance. Hence ~'METER n. [G. S. Ohm, German physicist 1787- 1854]

ohó', int. expressing surprise or exulta- tion. [o² HO]

oh yes. See OYEZ.

-oid, suf. forming adji. & nn. w. sense (something) having the form of, resembling, chiefly on Gk (rhomboid), rarely L (fucoid), or other (alkaloid) stems; adji. as thyroid, lable, subdivided into drying ~s, which by exposure harden into varnish, & non- drying ~s, which by exposure ferment, the latter used as lubricants, illuminants, soap constituents, etc.; essential or volatile ~s chiefly of vegetable origin, acrid, lim- pid, & distillable, giving plants etc. their scent, used in medicine & perfumery; mineral ~s used as illuminants. Particu- lar kinds are named from source or use as ~ of almonds, or with source or use preceding, as cod-liver, olive, salad, hair, ~); pour ~ on the flame etc., aggravate passion etc.; pour ~ on the waters, smooth matters over; smell of ~, bear marks of study; burn the midnight ~, read or work

oh (ō), int. See o².

-oid, suf. forming adji. & nn. w. sense (something) having the form of, resembling, chiefly on Gk (rhomboid), rarely L (fucoid), or other (alkaloid) stems; adji. as thyroid, sinoid, nn. as asteroid, amygdaloid; from the nn. an adj. in -oidal is formed as cycloidal. If. mod. L -oides f. Gk -oeidēs (-o- + -eidēs like) f. which also -ODE]

oil, n. 1. (Kinds of) liquid viscid unctuous inflammable chemically neutral sub- stance lighter than & insoluble in water & soluble in alcohol & ether (there are three classes: fatty or fixed ~s of animal or vegetable origin, greasy & non-distil-

far into the night; strike ~, lit., find petroleum by sinking shaft, fig., attain prosperity or success; ~ & vinegar, type of dissimilar or irreconcilable things; strap etc. ~, flogging with strap etc. 2. = ~colour (often pl.). 3. = ~skin (usu. pl.). 4. ~bird, nut, palm, plant, seed, ~tree, kinds of bird etc. from which ~ is got; ~bush, ~-filled socket for upright spindle [BUSH³]; ~cake, mass of compressed linseed etc. left when ~ has been expressed, used as cattle food or manure; ~can, containing ~, esp. long-nozzled for oiling machinery; ~cloth, fabric waterproofed with ~; ~skin, canvas coated with drying ~ & used to cover table or floor; ~coat, of ~skin; ~colour, paint made by grinding pigment in ~ (usu. pl.); ~(-)engine (driven by the explosion of vaporized ~ mixed with air); ~field, district yielding mineral ~; ~gauge, hydrometer measuring specific gravity of ~s; ~gilding, ~gold, goldleaf laid on linseed-~ mixed with yellow pigment; ~-gland, secreting ~-hole, in machinery to receive lubricating ~; ~man, maker or seller of ~s; ~meal, ground linseed cake; ~paint, = ~-colour; ~-painting, art of painting, picture painted, in ~-colours; ~-paper, made transparent or waterproof by soaking in ~; ~-press, apparatus for pressing ~ from seeds etc.; ~skin, cloth waterproofed with ~, garment or (pl.) suit of this; ~-spring, yielding mineral ~; ~stone, (fine-grained stone used with ~ as) whetstone; ~-TANKER. Hence ~'LESS a. [f. ONF *oile* f. L *oleum* (*olea* olive)]

oil'er, n. In vbl senses; esp. oilcan for oiling machinery, (sl.) unctuous person. [-ER¹]

oil'y, a. Of, like, covered or soaked with, oil; (of manner etc.) fawning, insinuating, unctuous. Hence ~ILY² adv., ~INESS n. [-Y²]

oint'ment, n. Unctuous preparation applied to skin to heal or beautify, unguent. [f. OF *oignement* (L UNGUENTUM, -MENT]

Oireachtas (ĕr′axthəs), n. Legislature of Eire, the President & two Houses, Dail Eireann (Chamber of Deputies) & Seanad Eireann (Senate). [Ir.]

oka'pi (-ah-), n. Bright-coloured partially striped Central-Afr. ruminant discovered 1900 with likeness to giraffe, deer, & zebra. [native]

ŏk′ra, n. Tall malvaceous plant bearing mucilaginous seed-pods used as a vege-

table & for thickening soups. [W.-Afr. native name]

-ol, chem. suf. 1. Termination of alcohol used in names of alcohols in the wider sense or analogous compounds (*methol, phenol*). 2. = L *oleum* oil (*benzol*).

ōld, a., (ELDER¹, eldest, in particular uses; ordinarily ~er, ~est), & n. 1. Advanced in age, far on in natural period of existence, not young or near its beginning, (*the ~, aged people; young & ~, every one; ~ age,* later part of life; ~-*age pensions,* ‖ weekly payments under Acts of 1908-1936 to ~ persons on account of their age; ‖ *Old Lady of Threadneedle Street,* Bank of England; ~ *man of the sea,* person who cannot be shaken off; ~ *man, woman, party,* etc.; ~ *man,* also as name for southernwood, & naut. sl. for ship's captain; *my* etc. ~ *man,* colloq., husband; ~ *man's beard,* kind of moss, also TRAVELLER'S JOY; *my* etc. ~ *woman,* colloq., wife; ~ *woman,* fussy or timid man, whence ~-**wo'manish**¹, ~-**wo'manly,** aa., ~-**wo'manish**NESS, ~-**wo'manli**NESS, nn.; (~wōō-) *my* etc. ~ *bones,* I or me etc. *who am* ~; *the century grows* ~). 2. Having characteristics, experience, feebleness, etc., of age (~ *head on young shoulders,* wisdom beyond one's years; *child has an* ~ *face; ~ buffer, fogy,* etc.; *a man is as ~ as he feels*); worn, dilapidated, shabby, (~ *clothes* etc.). 3. (Appended to period of time) of age (*is ten years ~, a ten-year-~ boy, a boy or ten years ~, could read Greek at ten years ~;* also ellipt. *four* etc. ~-*year-~,* person or animal, esp. racehorse, of that age, w. pl. ~). 4. Practised or inveterate *in action* or quality or as agent etc. (~ *in crime, folly, cunning, diplomacy; an ~ campaigner, offender; ~ bird,* person on his guard against snares; ~ *hand,* practised workman, person of experience in something, *at doing;* ~ STAGER; ~ *bachelor,* man confirmed in bachelorhood; ~ *maid,* elderly spinster, whence ~-**maid'**ISH¹ a., also precise & tidy & fidgety man, also a round card game). 5. Dating from far back, made long ago, long established or known or familiar or dear, ancient, not new or recent, primeval, (~ *Ocean, Night,* etc.; ~*red* SANDstone; ~ *standing,* long established; so ~-*established;* ~ *as the hills;* ~ *countries,* long inhabited or civilized; ~ *friends;* ~ *debt, grudge,* SCORES; *an ~ name, family;* ~ *wine,* matured with keeping; so *Old Tom,* kind of gin; ~ *gold,* colour of tarnished gold; ~ CATHOLIC; *the ~,* what is not new; ~ TESTAMENT; ~ *boy, chap, fellow, man,* esp. in voc., intimate or person treated as such, also in mod. sl. ~ *bean, egg, fruit, thing, top; Old England; Old Glory,* the Stars & Stripes; *the ~ one or gentleman, Old Harry, Nick, Scratch,* etc., the devil; *good ~* with name, sl. exclamation in real

or ironical commendation of person's or thing's performance; *have a fine, good, high*, etc., ~ *time* etc., sl., be well amused or entertained; *any* ~ *thing*, sl., anything no matter what). **6.** Belonging only or chiefly to the past, obsolete or obsolescent, out of date, antiquated, antique, concerned with antiquity, not modern, by-gone, only lingering on, former, quondam, (*the good* ~ *times*, customs etc. of earlier generations; ~ *annals*; ~ *fashions*, that have gone or are going out, whence ~-*fâ´shioned² a., ~-fâ´shionedness n.* (-shond²), opp. *newfangled* etc.; *am-fashioned enough to think*, used in ironical self-depreciation; *of the* ~ *school*, ~ *fashioned*; *the* ~ *country, home*, etc., used by colonists or colonials of mother-country; *call up* ~ *memories; the* ~ *order changeth; have lost my* ~ *beliefs; the* ~ *boy, fellow, man*, as term of address etc.; ~ School¹ *tie; the Old Comedy*, etc.: ~ *masters*, great painters of earlier times, pictures by these; ~ *London, Paris, England*, etc., London etc. as it once was, or the extant relics of its former state; *the* ~ *man*, one's unregenerate self; *the Old World*, Eastern hemisphere; ~-*world*, not American, also belonging to ~ times, & so ~-*time attrib.; Old Style*, abbr. O.S.; *the* ~ *year*, just ended or about to end; ~ *clothes*, discarded; ~-*clothesman*, dealer in these; hence ~'ish¹(²) a., ~'NESS n. (rare), ~ *time* (only in *of* ~ adj. & adv., as the *men of* ~, or *of* ~ *there were giants; have heard it of* ~, from long ago). [com.-Teut.: OE *ald*, cf. Du. *oud*, G *alt*, f. OTeut. *al*-grow, nourish, cf. L *alere* feed]

öld'en¹, a. (arch. & literary). Old-time, of a former age, (esp. *the* ~ *time*). [-EN⁵]

öld'en², v.t. & i. Make or grow feeble etc. as with age. [-EN⁶]

öld'ster, n. One who is no longer a young-ster (usu. antithetically to *youngster*). [-STER]

öldeã'ginous, a. Having properties of or producing oil, oily, fatty, greasy. [f. F *oléagineux* f. L *oleagineus* (*olea* olive)]

öleã'nder, n. Evergreen poisonous Levantine shrub with leathery lanceolate leaves & fine red & white flowers. [med. L, etym. dub.]

öleã'ster, n. The wild olive; small yellow-flowered tree like it. [L (*olea* olive, -ASTER)]

öl'éo-, comb. form of L *oleum* oil, as ~graph, picture printed in oils, so ~GRAPHY (-ogy); ~margarine, fatty substance extracted from beef fat & serving as constituent of margarine; ~meter (-om²), instrument determining density of volatile oils; ~res'in, natural mixture of volatile oil & resin, balsam, also artificial mixture of fixed or volatile oil & resin etc.

olfac'tion, n. Smelling, sense of smell.

So ~-IVE a. [f. L *olefacere* (*olēre* v.i. smell, *facere fact-* make)]

ölfac'tory, a. & n. Concerned with smelling (~ *organ, nose; ~ nerves*); (n., usu. pl.) ~ organ. [prec., -ORY]

olib'anum, n. Aromatic gum resin used as incense. [med. L, f. Gk *libanos* frank-incense (o- perh. f. L *oleum* oil, Gk *ho* the, or Arab. *al* the)]

öl'id, a. Rank-smelling, fetid. [f. L *olidus* (*olēre* smell, -ID)]

öl'igarch (-k), n. Member of oligarchy, [f. Gk *oligarkhēs* (*oligoi* few, *arkhō* rule)]

öl'igarchy (-ki), n. Government, State governed, by the few; members of such government. So **öligârch'ic(al)** aa., **öligârch'ically** adv., (-ki-). [f. Gk *oligarkhia* (prec., -Y¹)]

olig(o)-, comb. form of Gk *oligos* small, *oligoi* few, as ~*carp'ous*, having few fruits; ~*ocène*, Geol., between MIOCENE & EOCENE.

öl'iö, n. (pl. ~s). Mixed dish, hotchpotch, stew of various meats & vegetables; medley, farrago, miscellany. [f. Sp. *olla* stew f. L *olla* jar]

öliva'ceous (-shus), a. (nat. hist.). Olive-green, of dusky yellowish green. [L *oliva* olive, -ACEOUS]

öl'ivary, a. (anat.). Olive-shaped, oval. [f. L *olivarius* (foll., -ARY¹)]

öl'ive, n. & a. **1.** (Also ~-*tree*, evergreen tree with narrow leaves hoary below & axillary clusters of small white flowers, & bitter pulp, of dusky yellowish green when unripe & bluish black when ripe, yielding oil, & pickled unripe for eating as relish; leaf, branch, or wreath of ~ as emblem of peace (also ~-*branch*, often fig.; *hold out the* ~-*branch*, make over-tures, show disposition, for reconcilia-tion); *wood of the* ~ (also ~-*wood*). **2.** ~-shaped kinds of gasteropod mollusc. **3.** pl. Slices of beef or veal rolled up with herbs & stewed (usu. *beef, veal*, ~s). **4.** ~-shaped bar or button for fastening gar-ment by insertion in corresponding loop, whence öl'iver¹, or öliverTte' n. **5.** ~-colour. **6.** ~ *crown*, garland of ~ as sign of victory; ~-*branch*, see above, also (usu. pl., w. ref. to Ps. cxxviii. 3) children; ~ *oil*, extracted from ~s. **7.** adj. Coloured like the unripe ~ (also ~-*green*) (of com-plexion) yellowish-brown. [F, f. L *oliva*]

öl'iver¹, n. Tilt-hammer attached to axle & worked by treadle for shaping nails etc. [?]

Öl'iver² (ö-), n. See ROLAND.

öliv'ine, -in, n. Kind of chrysolite, chiefly olive-green. [L *oliva* olive, -INE⁴]

öll'a podri'da (-rē-), rarely öll'a, n. = OLIO. [Sp. = lit. rotten pot (OLIO, L PUTRIDUS)]

-ology (-)ŏl'ogy) suf. = -o- + -LOGY, & n. used joc. = any science, w. pl. = the sciences, mere theory.

olym'piad, n. Period of four years between celebrations of Olympic games, used by ancient Greeks in dating events (abbr. Ol.), 776 B.C. being first year of first O~. [f. F *olympiade* f. L f. Gk *Olumpias -ad-* (Olumpios see foll. -AD)]

Olym'pian, a. & n. **1.** Of Olympus; celestial; (of manners etc.) magnificent, condescending, superior; = foll. **2.** n. Dweller in Olympus, one of the greater ancient-Greek gods; person of superhuman calmness & detachment. [f. LL *Olympianus* (L.f. Gk *Olumpios* f. *Olumpos*, -AN)]

Olym'pic, a. Of or at Olympia (~ *games*, held there every four years by ancient Greeks with athletic, literary, & musical competitions; also, modern quadrennial international athletic meeting at various places, the first at Athens 1896). [f. L f. Gk *Olumpikos* of Olympus (*Olumpia* being named from the games in honour of Zeus of Olympus)]

Olym'pus, n. Thessalian mountain on which dwelt the chief Greek gods, divine abode, heaven. [L. f. Gk *Olumpos*]

ŏm'bre (-ber, & see Ap.), n. Card-game popular in 17th–18th cc. [f. Sp. *hombre* f. L *hominem* nom. *homo* man, perh. thr. F (*h)ombre*]

ŏmbro-, comb. form of Gk *ombros* rain, as ~LOGY (-ŏl²), ~METER (-ŏm²).

ŏm'ĕga, n. Last letter (Ω, ω) of Greek alphabet, long o; last of series; final development etc. (ALPHA *&* ~). [Gk, = great o]

ŏm'elĕt(te) (-ml-), n. Whipped eggs fried & folded & often flavoured with or containing herbs, cheese, chopped ham, jam, etc. (*savoury* ~, with herbs etc.; *sweet* ~, with sugar or jam; *cannot make an* ~ *without breaking eggs*, end necessitates means). [f. F(-te), earlier *amelette* for metath. f. *alemette* var. of *alemelle* thin plate prob. f. L LAMELLA]

ŏm'ĕn, n. & v.t. Occurrence or object portending good or evil, prognostic, presage; prophetic signification (*is of good* etc.~); (vb) foreshow, give presage of. [L, earlier *osmen* perh. f. *audire* hear, -MEN]

omĕn'tum, n. (anat.; pl. ~*a*). Fold of peritoneum connecting stomach with other viscera, caul. Hence ~AL a. [L]

omĭc'ron, n. Greek letter (O, o)=ŏ. [Gk, = small o]

ŏm'inous, a. Giving or being an omen (of good or evil, or abs.), portentous, (rare) of evil omen, inauspicious, foreshowing disaster, threatening. Hence ~LY² adv. [f. L *ominosus* (OMEN *-ōsus -OUS*]

omĭ'ssion (-shn), n. Omitting, non-inclusion; non-performance, neglect, duty not done, (*sins of* ~ *&* commission, negative & positive). So **omĭss'IVE** a. [f. L *omissio* (foll. -ION²]

omĭt', v.t. (-tt-). Leave out, not insert or include; leave undone, neglect doing, fail

to do. So **omĭss'IBLE** a. [f. L *omittere -iss-* (o- for OB-, *mittere* send]

ŏmni-, comb. form of L *omnis* all, in compounds taken f. L or formed chiefly in L elements, w. sense *all-, of all things, in all ways or places*, as ~*com'petent*, having jurisdiction in all cases; ~*far'ious*, of all sorts; *ŏmnif'ic*, all-creating; *ŏmni'genous*, of all kinds; *ŏmnip'otence*, infinite power, also God, also great influence; so *ŏmnip'o-tent* a. (*the Omnipotent*, God), *~p'otentLY²* adv.; ~*pres'ence*, ubiquity, also being widespread or constantly met with; so ~*pres'ent* a.; *ŏmni'science* (-shns), infinite knowledge, also God, also wide information or the affectation of it; so *ŏmni'scient* (-shyent) a. (*the Omniscient*, God), ~*scientLY²* adv.; *ŏmniv'orous*, feeding on anything that offers (esp. fig. of reading); so ~*v'orousLY²* adv., ~*v'orousNESS* n.

ŏm'nĭbus, n. (pl. ~*es*) & a. **1.** (Now usu. *bus*) large wheeled public vehicle plying on fixed route & taking up & setting down passengers at fixed, or at any, points in this; (also *hotel* ~) vehicle conveying guests between hotel & railway station; (also *private* or *family* ~) vehicle provided by railway company for conveying party & luggage to or from station; ~ *book*. **2.** adj. Serving several objects at once, comprising several items, (*an* ~ *bill, resolution, clause,* etc.; ~ *book*, volume containing several stories, plays, etc. (freq. by a single author), published at a low price to be within the reach of all; ~ *box* in theatre, box on pit tier appropriated to number of subscribers;||~*train*, stopping at all stations; ~ *bar, wire,* etc. in electricity, through which whole current passes). [f. L dat. pl. of *omnis*=for all

ŏm'nium găth'erum (-dh-), n. Miscellaneous assemblage of persons or things, queer mixture, party to which everyone is invited. [mock L (L *omnium* of all, GATHER]

ŏm'oplate, n. Shoulder-blade, scapula. [f. Gk *ōmoplatē* (*ōmos* shoulder, *plate* blade]

ŏm'phalo-, comb. form of Gk *omphalos* NAVEL, chiefly in surg. & med. wds as ~CELE, ~TOMY (-ŏt²), dividing of umbilical cord.

ŏm'phalŏs, n. (Gk Ant.) boss on shield, conical stone at Delphi supposed to be central point of earth; centre, hub, (*the centre & ~ of a world-wide empire*). [see prec.]

on¹ (ŏn, on), prep. **1.** (So as to be) supported by or attached to or covering or enclosing (*sat on the table; floats on the water; is on the horns of a dilemma; lives on the continent, on an annuity; have you a match on you?, about your person; is, gets, falls, on his* LEGS, *knees,* etc.; *travels on foot, wheels, the wing, the wings of the wind; tread on air, one's toes; dropped it, threw him, on the floor; had, put, a ring,*

gloves, on his finger, hands; put a notice on the board; hangs on the wall; walks on the ceiling; has a blister on the sole of his foot; a scholar on the foundation; a colonel on half-pay; went on board; is on the jury, committee, general staff; a writer on the press; dog is on the chain; on the BENCH, BOARD¹s, CARD²s, FENCE¹, MARKET¹, NAIL¹, PARISH⁴s, RACK³, SHELF, SPOT¹, STREETS, STUMP, TURF, WAY¹; on CHANGE¹, HAND¹, one's HAND⁴s, one's own HOOK¹, one's KNEE²s, HANDEN; TENTERhooks; on a LEVEL¹, an EQUALITY, a PAR). **2.** With axis, pivot, basis, motive, standard, confirmation, or guarantee, consisting in (turn in one's heel; works on a peg; based on fact; imprisonment on suspicion; on my conscience; swear on the Bible; had it on good authority; decided on no evidence; did it on purpose, deliberation; got it on good terms; on account of; on the average, whole; on penalty of death; charged him on his life to do it; a tax on paper; borrowed money on his jewels; interest on one's capital; profit on sales). **3.** (So as to be) close to, in the direction of, touching, against, just at, of; Clacton-North, far side, both sides, of; Clacton-on-sea; marched on London; hit him on the head; serve a notice, writ, on; lay hold, seize, on; bouting is on the wicket, straight; drew his knife on me; smile, frown, turn one's back, on; make an attack on; put one on inquiring or inquiry, induce him to inquire; curse, plague, etc., on him, it; rose on their oppressors; on HIGH; on side in football, not off side; skip is driving on shore; an on-shore wind). **4.** (Of time) during, exactly at, contemporaneously with, immediately after, as a result of, (happened on the morning etc. of 29 Feb., on Christmas eve, on the next day; on the instant, punctually; on time, the minute, etc., punctually; on arriving, my return, analysis, examination, I found). **5.** In manner specified by adj. (on the cheap, sly, SQUARE) or state or action specified by noun (on fire, TAP, loan, lease, sale, strike, guard; on the look-out, move, run, wane, watch; on one's best behaviour). **6.** Concerning, about, while engaged with, so as to affect, (keen, mad, bent, determined, set, on; gone on, sl., enamoured of; court martial was held on him; my opinion on free trade; writes, speeches, lectures, on finance; a book, an essay, on grammar; meditating on vanity; take vengeance on person; did it on my way; was, went, on an errand; is not binding on us; work tells severely on him; title was conferred on him; drew cheque on bank; condoled with him on his loss). **7.** Added to (ruin on ruin, heaps on heaps). [OE on, on, cf. Du. aan, G an, Gk ana²]

ōn², adv., a., & n. **1.** (So as to be) supported by, attached to, covering, enclosing, or touching, something (has, drew, his boots on; put the tablecloth on; keep your HAIR on; on with your coat, put it on). **2.** In some direction, towards something, farther forward, towards point of contact, in advanced position or state, with continued movement or action, in operation or activity (LOOK¹, LOOK¹-er, on; getting on for two o'clock; broadside, stem, ends, on, with that part forward; ellipt. for imperat. of go or come on, as on, Stanley, on!; send on, in front of oneself; MOVE on; happened later on; from that day on; was well on in the day; is rather on, sl., half-drunk; speak, work, wait, etc., on, continue to do; so struggle on to the end, ct. on to below; slow bowler is, went, on, is began, bowling; Macbeth is on, being performed; gas, water, is on, lit, running, or procurable by turning tap; get, be, on, make, have made, bet; drove Jones on for 4 in cricket, to 10; on). **3.** CARRY¹, CATCH¹, COME¹, GET¹, GO¹, HOLD¹, KEEP¹, PUT¹, TAKE¹, TRY, on. **4.** Be on (colloq.), be in favour of, willing to be a party to, something (There's a show tonight; are you on?); be on to (person), be aware of his intentions etc., find fault with, nag (he's always on to me). ōn & off, = OFF ᵈᵉ on; on to, compound prep. (corresponding to on as into to in, but usu. written as two words, & avoided in writing though common in speech; to be distinguished from the use in which each word has independent force as in went on to (the next), to a position on (jumped on to the landing-stage). **5.** adj. Towards or in part of field to left front of playing batsman's wicket (cf. OFF, LEG; MID¹ on; an on drive, whence ōn-drive; v.t.); || on licence, for selling beer etc. to be drunk on premises. **6.** n. The on side in cricket (a fine drive to the on). [f. prec.]

on-, pref. used with attrib. participles, gerunds, verbal nouns, agent-nouns in -ER², & other derivative nn., f. vv. followed idiomatically by ON² (occas. alternatively with the reverse order) oncoming n. & a., approaching; on-fall n., assault; on-flow, onward flow; on-goings or goings-on², (usu. strange or improper) proceedings; on-hanger, HANGER-on²; on-looker or LOOK¹-er-on²; on-rush n., on-rushing a.; ONSET.

ōn-ager, n. (pl. -s, -grī). Kinds of wild ass. [L, f. Gk onagros (onos ass, agrios wild)]

ōn'anism, n. Uncompleted coition; masturbation. [Onan (Gen. xxxviii. 9) -ISM]

once (wŭns), adv., conj., & n. **1.** For one time or on one occasion only, multiplied by one, by one degree, (have read it more than ~; shall die ~; or twice, ~ & again, a few times; ~ more, again, another time; ~ for all, in final manner, definitively; ~ in a while or way, very rarely; ~ & away, = ~ for all, ~ in a way; ~ bit twice shy, pain, loss, etc., teaches caution; ~

nought is nought; second cousin ~ RE-MOVED). **2.** (In negative or conditional or indefinite clause etc.) ever, at all, even for one or the first time, (*if we ~ lose sight of him; when ~ he understands; have not seen him ~; within call, we are safe*). **3.** On a certain but unspecified past occasion (also *~ upon a time*), at some period in the past, former(ly), (*~ there was a giant; a ~-famous doctrine, ~-loved friend; my ~ master, ally*). **4.** At ~, immediately, without delay, at the same time, (*do it at ~, please; don't all speak at ~*, lit., & as iron. deprecation inviting offers etc. from reluctant party; *at ~ stern & tender*) for this, or that, ~, on one occasion by way of exception; *~-over* n. (colloq.) preliminary inspection (often with additional sense of cursoriness). **5.** conj. As soon as, if ~, when ~, (*he hesitates, we have him*). **6.** n. One time, performance, etc. (~, -ES) [ME *ánes*, *ónes*, (ONE, -ES)]

‖ **oncer** (wün'ser), n. (colloq.). One who attends church only once on a Sunday. [ONCE+-ER¹]

on dit (see Ap.), n. Piece of hearsay. [F]
one (wün), a., n., & pron. **1.** numeral adj. Single & integral, neither none nor fractional nor plural, numbered by the first or lowest integer, half of two, a, (*~ man ~ vote*, principle of equality in voting; *~ vote = value*, principle of equal constituencies; *~-&-twenty* etc., or usu. *twenty* etc. ~ *dozen, hundred,* etc., precise or formal for *a; ~ man in ten, a thousand,* etc., relatively few; *some ~ man must direct; for ~ thing, he drinks; ~ or two people,* a few; *God is ~*). **2.** adj. with secondary senses developed from the numeral. The only, single, forming a unity, united, identical, the same, unchanging, a particular but undefined, to be contrasted with another, (*the ~ way to do it; no ~ man is equal to it; is ~-&-undivided; cried out with ~ voice; were made ~,* married; *become ~,* coalesce; *remains for ever ~,* always the same; *all in ~ direction; met him ~ night; will take you there ~ day; ~ man's mead is another man's poison*). **3.** numeral noun. (With *a* & pl.; often used as substitute for repetition of previously expressed or implied noun) the number, thing numbered with it, written symbol for it, a unit, unity, a single thing or person or example, (*~ is half of two; in the year ~,* long ago; *Aeneid, book ~,* first book of; *number ~,* oneself, esp. as centre of selfish care; *write down a ~, three ~s; came by ~s & twos; sell scores where they sold ~s; never a ~,* none; *will you make ~?,* arch., join the party; *ten* etc. *to ~,* long odds, high probability; *all in ~,* combined; *the all & the ~,* totality & unity; *at ~,* reconciled, in agreement; *I lose a neighbour & you*

gain ~; pick me out a good ~, some good ~s; which, what kind of, ~ or ~s do you like; that ~, the ~ in the window, will do). **4.** adj. used ellipt. for itself or a with noun elsewhere expressed or customarily omitted & to be supplied with more or less of certainty. Single person or thing of the kind implied (*~ of them lost his or her hat; ~ of the richest men in England; shall see you again ~ of these fine days; at ~ o'clock or ~,* i.e. hour; *~ sixpence,* i.e. shilling; *gave him ~ in the eye, ove him ~ that was a nasty ~,* blow lit. or fig.; *at ~-&-twenty years of age; I for ~ do not believe it; go ~ better, bid, offer, risk,* more by ~ point; *is ~ too many for him,* too hard etc. for him to deal with *by ~ degree; it is all ~ to me,* the same thing, indifferent; *& all,* all jointly & severally; *~ by ~, ~ after another,* singly, successively; *with another,* on the average; *~ or the other,* formula distinguishing members of pair, as *~ is immoral, the other nom-moral,* also with pl. constr., as *sheep & goats,* of which *the ~ are the good* etc.; *~ another,* formula of reciprocity with orig. subjective & another objective or possessive, as *struck ~ another, write to ~ another, buy ~ another's goods*). **5.** pron. A particular but unspecified person (arch., *~ came running; said it pleased him not*); a person of specified kind (ANY, EVERY, SOME, NO¹, SUCH a, ~; *many a ~,* rhet., many people; LITTLE, *dear, loved, ~s; the Holy One, One above,* God; *the Evil One,* the devil; *behaves like ~ frenzied; what a ~ he is to make excuses!* colloq.; *bought it from ~ Stephens*); any person, esp. the speaker, spoken of as representing people in general (possessive *~'s,* objective *~,* reference-form *~,* refl. *~self,* formerly *his, him, he & him, himself,* or ungrammatically *their, them, they & them, themselves; if ~ cuts off ~'s nose, ~ hurts only ~self; it offends ~; to be told ~ is not wanted;* also incorrectly for I, as *~ let it pass,* for *~ did not want to seem mean*). **6.** *~-eyed,* having only, blind of, eye; *~-handed,* having, done etc. with, ~ hand only; *~-horse,* drawn or worked by single horse, (fig., sl.) petty, poorly equipped; *~-idea'd, ~-idea'd,* possessed by single idea, narrow-minded; *~-legged,* having only ~ leg, (fig.) *~-sided,* unequal; *~-man,* requiring, consisting of, done or managed by, ~ man; *~-pair,* ‖ room or set of rooms on first floor (above ~ pair or flight of stairs; *~-pair back, front,* ‖ such room in back or front of house); *~-self,* reflexive, & emphatic appositional, form of ~ as generalizing pronoun (*to starve ~self is suicide; to do right ~self is the great thing*); *~-sided,* having, occurring on, ~ side only (*a ~-sided street,* with houses on ~ side only; *a ~-sided plank,* with leaves or flowers all on ~ side of stem), larger etc, *on ~ side,* partial, unfair, prejudiced; *so*

~sid'edly² adv.; ~sid'edness n.; ~step, vigorous kind of foxtrot in duple time; ~way street (in which traffic may pass in ~ direction only). Hence ~FOLD a. [com.-Teut.; f. OE ān, cf. Du. een, G ein, cogn. w. Gk oinos, oinē, L ūnus one; -one, a, are weakened forms]

-one, comb. suf. (1) used unsystematically as in OZONE; (2) in names of hydrocarbons (see -ANE). [f. Gk -ōnē fem. patronymic]

oneir'o- (-nīr-), comb. form of Gk oneiros dream; ~MANCY; so ~crit'ical a., ~crit'icism n.

one'ness (wŭn-n-), n. Being one, single-ness; singularity; uniqueness; wholeness, unity, union, agreement, concord; iden-tity, sameness, changelessness. [-NESS]

on'er (wŭ-), n. Remarkable or pre-eminent person or thing (sl.; a ~ at, on); gave him a ~, severe blow; (colloq.) stroke etc. counting one, esp. one-run hit at cricket; ...he. [-ER¹]

ŏn'erous, a. Burdensome, causing or requiring trouble, (~ properly in law, accompanied with obligations). Hence ~LY² adv., ~NESS n. [f. OF onereus f. L onerosus (onus, oneris burden, -OUS)]

one'self, pron. (One's) self; so **on'e's**,

onion (ŭn'yon), n. & v.t. 1. (Plant with) edible rounded bulb of many concentric coats & pungent smell & flavour, much used in cooking or eaten pickled; (sl.) off one's ~ (sl.), off one's head; ~couch or ~grass or ~twitch, kind of wild oat; ~shell, kinds of mollusc; hence ~Y² (ŭn'yo-) a. 2. v.t. Rub (eyes) with ~ to make them o large pearl, onion]

on'ly, a. That is (or are) the one (or all the) specimen(s) of the class, sole, (the ~ way is to die; the ~ child of his parents; the ~ instances known; was an ~ son; one mother's the ~ wear, best or ~ one worth considering). [OE ānlic]

on'ly, adv. & conj. I. Solely, merely, ex-clusively, & no one or nothing more or besides or else, & that is all, (is right be-cause it is customary ~, is right because it is customary; ~ you can ~ guess or you can guess, no one else can; can do no more; I ~ thought I would do it, or did it without external instigation; I ~ heard it, but saw it; if ~, assuming merely that, also as wishing formula, as if ~ someone would leave me a legacy!; ~ not, all but; has ~ just come, came ~ yesterday, no longer ago; ~ too glad, true, etc., glad etc. & not, as might be expected, the opposite). 2. conj. It must however be added that, but then, (he makes good resolutions, ~ he never keeps them); with the exception, were it not, that (he does well, ~ that he is nervous at the start; ~

that you would be bored, I should—). [ONE, -LY²]

on'omatŏp, n. Onomatopoeic word. [shortened f. foll.]

onomatopoe'ia (-pē'a, -pēya), n. Forma-tion of names or words from sounds that resemble those associated with the object or action to be named, or that seem natu-rally suggestive of its qualities; word so formed (e.g. cuckoo). So ~poe'ic (-pē-), ~poet'ic aa., ~poe'ically (-pē-), ~poet'ically adv. [f. L f. Gk onomatopoiia poet-making (onoma -atos name, poiĕo make)]

on'set, n. Attack, assault, Impetuous be-ginning, (esp. at the first ~). [f. to SET on]

on'slaught (-awt), n. Onset, fierce attack. [perh. f. Du. aanslag or G anschlag (an on, schlagen strike) w. assim. to draught etc.]

on'to, prep. See on² to.

ontŏ-, comb. form of part. of Gk ĕmi be: ~gĕn'esis, origin & development of the individual being (cf. PHYLOGENESIS), whence ~genĕt'ic a, ~genĕt'ically adv.; ontŏl'ogy, department of metaphysics concerned with the essence of things or being in the abstract, so ~lŏ'gical a, ~lo'gically adv., ontŏl'ogist n. [L]

on'us, n. (no pl.) Burden, duty, responsi-bility; ~probŏn'di, = BURDEN¹ of proof. [L]

on'ward, adv. & a., **ôn'wards** (-z), adv. Further on, towards the front, with advancing motion; (adj.) directed ~. [on² -WARD(S)]

ôn'ymous, a. Not anonymous. [f. Gk ōnuma name + -OUS after anonymous]

ô'olite, n. Granular limestone, each grain being a calcareous particle in carbonate of lime, roe-stone; (Geol.) series of fossili-ferous rocks of this formation lying be-tween Chalk, or Wealden, & Lias. Hence oōlit'ic a. [f. F oölithe (oo-, -LITE)]

oolŏng, n. A dark kind of cured Chinese tea. [Chin. wulung, = black dragon]

oom, n. (S.-Afr.) Uncle (esp. *Oom Paul* = President Kruger). [Du.]

oomph, n. (sl.). Sex appeal. [?]

-oon, suf. formerly used in borrowing F wds in -*on* (*drag*~) except when the final syl. was not accented (*baron*); esp. for F ~*on* f. It. ~*one* f. L ~*onem* nom. ~*o* (*ball*~, *carl*~); rarely in native wds (*spit-toon*~); F wds now taken have ~*on* in E (*chignon*); the L expresses humorous or contemptuous description (*Naso Nosey*), the It. bigness or coarseness, the F (exc. in It. borrowings) small size; in E the suf. has no definite meaning.

oont, n. (Anglo-Ind.). Camel. [Hind.]

ooze[1], n. 1. Wet mud, slime, esp. in river-bed or estuary or on ocean bottom. 2. Tanning liquor, infusion of oak-bark etc.; ~-*calf*, calf-skin through which dye has been forced. 3. Exudation, sluggish flow, something that oozes. Hence **ōoz**'Y[2] a., **ōoz**'ILY[2] adv., **ōoz**'INESS n. [f. OE *wāse* cogn. w. ON *veisa* puddle; 2 f. OE *wōs* juice, sap; 3 f. foll.]

ooze[2], v.i. & t. (Of moisture) pass slowly through the pores of a body, exude, perco-late; (of substance) exude moisture; (fig.) leak out or away (*the secret ~d out; my courage is oozing away*); emit (moisture, information, encouragement). [f. prec. 2]

op-. See OB-.

opa'**city**, n. Being opaque, quality of not allowing passage to or (rarely) of not re-flecting light, non-transparency, obscur-ity; obscurity of meaning, obtuseness of understanding. [f. F *opacité* f. L *opacita-tem* (OPAQUE, -TY)]

opah, (-*o*), n. Rare brilliant-coloured large N.-Atlantic fish of mackerel family, king-fish, moon-fish. [W.-Afr. name]

opal, n. Amorphous quartz-like form of hydrous silica some kinds of which show changing colours (e.g. *common* ~, milk-white or bluish with green, yellow, & red reflexions), whence ~ES'CENT, ~ESQUE' (-ĕsk), aa., ~ES'CENCE n.; (Commerc.) semi-translucent white glass. [f. L *opalus* f. Skr. *upala* gem]

opal'**ine**, a. & n. 1. Opal-like, opalescent, iridescent. 2. n. Semi-translucent white glass. So ~IZE(3) v.t. [prec., -INE[1]]

opaque' (-k), a. (~*er*, ~*est*), & n. Not re-flecting (rare) or transmitting light, not shining (rare), impenetrable to sight; not lucid, obscure; dull-witted; (n.) *the* ~, darkness. Hence ~LY[2] (-kl-) adv., ~NESS (-kn-) n. [f. L *opācus* shaded; earlier *opake*, now assim. to F]

ope, v.t. & i. (Poet. for) OPEN[2]. [after obs. adj. *ope* reduced f. *open* on anal. of p.p. (cf. *awake, woke, ↓est*, *woven*)]

ōp'en[1], a. (~*er*, ~*est*), & n. 1. Not closed or blocked up, allowing of entrance or passage or access, having gate or door or lid or part of boundary withdrawn, unenclosed, unconfined, uncovered, bare, exposed, undisguised, public, manifest, not exclusive or limited, (~ *gate, passage, church, drawer, box, field, grave, carriage, hostilities, scandal, contempt*; ~ *air, out-door*; *door flew* ~; ~ *boat*, undecked; *lay* ~, expose esp. by cutting skin etc. of; ~ *ears*, eagerly attentive, whence ~-*eared*[2] a.; ~ *mouth*, in voracity, frank-ness, etc., & esp. in gaping stupidity or surprise, whence ~-*mouthed*[2], pr. -dhd, a.; ~ *mind*, accessibility to new ideas, unprejudiced or undecided state, whence ~-*minded*[2] a., ~-*mind'edly*[2] adv.; ~-*mind'edness* n.; *ts* ~ *to* conviction, offers, etc.; *keep* ~ *doors* or *house*, entertain all comers, be hospitable; *the* ~ *door*, free admission of foreign nations to country for trade; *force an* ~ *door*, demand from willing giver; *the exhibition is now* ~, admitting visitors; *shop, show, court, is* ~ *at such hours*; ~ *heart*, frankness, un-suspiciousness, kindliness, cordiality, whence ~-*hearted*[2] a., ~-*heart'edly*[1] adv., ~-*heart'edness* n.; ~ *champion*, ‖ *scholarship*, successful, won, after un-restricted competition; *race is* ~ *to all*; *position is* ~ *to attack*; O~ *Brethren*, less exclusive section of the Plymouth Brethren; ~*cast* (surface) *coal*; ~ *hearth process* (of steel-making in shallow rever-beratory furnace); ~ *time*, what is not close[1] time; *river, harbour, is* ~, free of ice; ~ *weather, winter*, not frosty; *bowels are* ~, not constipated; ~ *country*, free of fences; *there are three courses* ~ *to us*; ~ *question*, matter on which differences of opinion are legitimate; ~ *verdict*). 2. Ex-panded, unfolded, outspread, spread out, not close, with intervals, porous, com-municative, frank, (~ *book, flower*; ~ *letter*, esp. protest etc. printed in news-paper etc. but addressing individual; ~ *country*, affording wide views; ~ *order*, Mil. & Nav., formation with wide spaces between men or ships; ~ *harmony*, of chord with wide intervals; ~ *ice*, through which navigation is possible; *receive with* ~ *arms*, heartily, whence ~-*armed* a.; *with* ~ *eyes*, not unconsciously or under misapprehension, in eager attention or surprise, whence ~-*eyed*[2] (-īd) a.; *has* ~ *hand*, gives freely, whence ~-*hand'-ed*[2] a., ~-*hand'edly*[2] adv., ~-*hand'ed-ness* n.; ~ *face*, ingenuous-looking, whence ~-*faced*[2] a.; ~ *work* or ~-*work*, pattern with interstices in metal, lace, etc.; *will be* ~ *with you*, speak frankly). 3. (mus.). (Of note) produced from un-stopped pipe or string or without slide, key, or piston. 4. (phonet.). (Of vowel) produced with relatively wide opening of mouth (cf. close[1]); (of syllable) ending in vowel; hence ~NESS n. 5. *The* ~, space or country or air, public view. [com.-Teut., cf. Du. *open*, G *offen*; f. root of UP]

ōp'en[2], v.t.&i. 1. Make or become OPEN[1] or more open (~ SESAME; *shops* ~ *at 9.0 a.m.*;

~ a business, shop, account, campaign, etc., start or establish it or set it going; ~ fire, begin shooting; abs. for ~ book, as ~ed at p. 12; ~ ground, break up with plough etc.; ~ bowels, cause evacuation of the BALL²; ~ PARLIAMENT; ~ the case, (of counsel in lawcourt) make preliminary statement before calling witnesses; ~ the debate, begin it, be first speaker; ~ the door to, give opportunity for; ~s one's eyes, reveal or communicate to them; ~ one's eyes, show surprise; ~ another's eyes, undeceive or enlighten him; ~ the mind, heart, etc., expand or enlarge it; not ~ lips, remain silent; ~ one's designs, reveal or communicate. 2. Commence speaking (~ed upon the fiscal question, with a compliment, etc.). 3. Make a start (lard ~ed active, was in demand at once; session ~ed yesterday). 4. (Of hounds, & deriv. of men) begin to give tongue. 5. (naut.). Get view of by change of position, come into full view (take care not to ~ the obelisk; the harbour had ~ed). 6. ~ out, unfold, develop, expand, (t. & i.), accelerate, become communicative; ~ up, make accessible, bring to notice, reveal. Hence~ABLE a.,(~)ER¹ (1, 2) n. [f. prec.]

ō̌p'ening¹ (-pn-), n. In vbl senses: also or esp.: gap, passage, aperture; commencement, initial part; counsel's preliminary statement of case; (Chess) recognized sequence of moves for beginning game; opportunity, favourable conjuncture for. [-ING¹]

ō̌p'ening² (-pn-), a. In vbl senses; esp., initial, first, (his ~ remarks). [-ING¹]

ō̌p'enly, adv. Without concealment, publicly, frankly. [-LY²]

ŏp'era, n. Dramatic performance or composition of which music is an essential part, branch of art concerned with these, (grand ~, without spoken dialogue; comic ~, with spoken dialogue, not necessarily humorous; ~ bouffe pr. boof, of farcical character); ~ -cloak, -hood, lady's for wearing at ~ or going to evening parties; ~ -glass(es), small binocular for use at ~ or theatre; ~ -hat, man's tall collapsible hat; ~ -house, theatre for performance of ~s. [It. f. L,=labour, work]

ŏp'erate, v.i. & t. 1. Be in action, produce an effect, exercise influence, (the tax ~s to our disadvantage); play (upon person's fears etc., try to act (upon) medicines etc.) have desired effect, act. 2. Perform surgical or other operation (whence, of cases, ŏp'erable a.); (try to) execute purpose; (Mil.) carry on strategic movements; (of stockbroker etc.) buy & sell esp. with view of influencing prices.

3. Bring about, accomplish, (energy ~es changes); manage, work, conduct, (chiefly U.S.). **4.** ~ing-room, -table, for use in surgery; ~ing-theatre, room for surgical operations done before students. So ~OR² n. [f. L operārī work (opus -eris work)]

ŏperāt'ic, a. Of, like, opera. Hence ~ALLY adv. [as OPERATE, DRAMATIC]

operā'tion, n. 1. Working, action, way in which works, efficacy, validity, scope, (is in, comes into, ~; its ~ is easily explained; must extend its ~, make it valid for longer time or in wider sphere). **2.** Active process, activity, performance, discharge of function, (the ~ of breathing, thinking, pruning, etc.). **3.** Financial transaction. **4.** (surg.). Thing done with hand or instrument to some part of body to remedy deformity, injury, disease, pain, etc. **5.** Strategic movement of troops, ships, etc. (COMBINED ~). **6.** (math.). Subjection of number or quantity to process affecting its value or form, e.g. multiplication. Hence ~AL (-sho-) a., (esp.) engaged in or on, used for, (warlike) ~s. [OF, f. L operātiōnem (OPERATE, -ION)]

ŏp'erative, a. & n. 1. Having effect, in operation, efficacious; practical, not theoretical or contemplative, (the ~ part of work); of surgical operations; hence ~LY² adv. **2.** n. Worker, artisan, mechanic, workman, mill-hand. [f. LL operātīvus (OPERATE, -IVE)]

ŏp'eratōr, n. Put into operative form. [irreg. after DRAMATIZE, cf. OPERATIC]

ŏpe'rōse, a. (pedant.). Requiring or showing or taking great pains, laborious. Hence ~LY² adv., ~NESS n. [f. L operōsus (opus -eris work, -OSE¹)]

ō̌ph'iclēide (-īd), n. Keyed wind-instrument consisting of tapering brass tube bent double serving as bass or alto to key-bugle; (also tuba) powerful organ reed-pipe. [f. F ophicléide (Gk ophis ser-pent, kleis -dos key)]

ophid'ian, a. & n. (Member) of the Ophi-dia or order of reptiles including snakes. [mod. L ophidia pl., prob. irreg. f. Gk ophis snake, -AN]

ō̌ph'io-, comb. form of Gk ophis snake, as ~LATER, ~LATRY, (-ŏl-), serpent-wor-ship(per), ~LOGY (-ŏl-), serpent-wor... Hence ophit'ic a. [f. L f. Gk ophités marble, ophios snake]

ophthal'mia, n. Inflammation of the eye. [L f. Gk (ophthalmos eye)]

ophthal'mic, a. & n. Of the eye; affected

with ophthalmia; (remedy) good for eye-disease. [f. L f. Gk ophthalmikos (prec., -IC)]

ophthalm(o)-, comb. form of Gk *ophthalmos* eye, as ~ITIS, ~OLOGY, ~OLOGIST, ~OTOMY; *ophthal'moscope*, instrument for inspecting retina.

o'piate¹, a. (arch.), & n. **1.** Containing opium, narcotic, soporific. **2.** n. Drug containing opium & easing pain or inducing sleep. [f. med. L *opiatus* (OPIUM, -ATE²)]

o'piate², v.t. Mix with opium. [prob. f. med. L *opiare* (OPIUM, -ATE³)]

opine', v.t. Express or hold the opinion (*that*, or abs. in parenthesis). [f. L *opinari*]

opin'ion (-yon), n. **1.** Judgement or belief based on grounds short of proof, provisional conviction, view held as probable, (*in my ~*, as it seems to me; *am of ~ that*, believe; *a matter of ~*, disputable point); (also *public ~*) views or sentiment, esp. on moral questions, prevalent among people in general. **2.** What one thinks on or on a particular question, a belief, a conviction, (*the* COURAGE *of, act up to,* one's *~*). **3.** Formal statement by expert when consulted of what he holds to be the fact or the right course, professional advice, (*you had better have another ~*). **4.** Estimate (*have, formed, a very high, low, favourable, ~ of him*); (with neg.) favourable estimate (*have no ~ of Frenchmen*). [F, f. L *opinionem* (OPINE, -ION)]

opin'ionated (-nyo-), a. Obstinate in opinion, dogmatic; self-willed. Hence ~NESS n. [f. obs. *opinionate* in same sense, perh. latinized form of obs. *opinioned*²]

opin'ionative (-nyo-), a. = prec. [OPINION +-ATIVE, cf. TALKATIVE]

o. pip. See OBSERVATION, PIP.⁵

opisom'eter, n. Instrument for measuring curved lines as on map, made of wheel running on screw. [f. Gk *opisō* backwards, -METER]

opis'thograph (-ahf), n. (Gk & Rom. Ant.). Parchment or slab with writing on both sides. [f. Gk *opisthographos* f. *opisthen* behind +-GRAPH]

o'pium, n., & v.t. **1.** Reddish-brown heavy-scented bitter drug prepared from juice of kind of poppy, smoked or eaten as stimulant, intoxicant, or narcotic, & used as sedative (LAUDANUM) in medicine; ~ den, haunt of ~-smokers; ~ habit, ~ taking; hence ~ISM(5) n., ~IZE(5) v.t. **2.** v.t. Drug or treat with ~. [L, f. Gk *opion* poppy-juice (*opos* juice)]

o'podel'doc, n. Kinds of soap liniment. [wd used & prob. made by Paracelsus for kinds of medical plaster]

opo'panax, n. A fetid gum resin formerly used in medicine; a gum resin used in perfumery. [L f. Gk, f. *opos* juice, *panax* (*pas panto* all, *akos* cure) name of plant]

opos'sum, n. Kinds of American small arboreal or aquatic nocturnal marsupial mammal with thumbed hind-foot (see also POSSUM); (Austral.) = PHALANGER. [Amer.-Ind.]

∥ **opp'idan**, a. & n. (Inhabitant) of a town (now rare); (at Eton) non-colleger, boy in boarding-house in town. [f. L *oppidanus* (*oppidum* town, -AN)]

Hence ~A'TION n. [f. L OP(*pilare* ram)]

oppon'ency, n. (rare). Antagonism, opposition. [foll., -ENCY]

oppon'ent, a. & n. **1.** Opposing, contrary, opposed, (now rare; ~ *muscle*, opposing thumb or lateral digit to other digit). **2.** n. Adversary, antagonist. [f. L OP(*ponere* place), -ENT]

opp'ortune (also -tūn'), a. (Of time) suitable, well-selected or as favourable as if chosen; (of action or event) well-timed, done or occurring by design or chance at favourable conjuncture. Hence ~LY² adv., ~NESS n., (also -tūn²). [f. F *opportun* f. L OP(*portunus* f. *portus* -*us* harbour)]

opportun'ism, n. Allowing of time or undue weight to circumstances of the moment in determining policy; preference of what can to what should be done, compromise, practical politics, adaptation to circumstances; putting of expediency before principle or place before power, political time-serving. So ~IST (2) n. [f. prec. after It. (-ismo) & F (-isme)]

opportun'ity, n. Opportuneness (rare); favourable juncture, good chance, opening, (*of doing, to do, for action,* or abs.; *find, make, get, seize, give, afford, an ~, take ~*). [f. F *opportunité* f. L *opportunitatem* (OP-PORTUNE, -TY)]

oppose' (-z), v.t. **1.** Place or produce or cite (thing, person) as obstacle, antagonist, counterpoise, or contrast, to, (*to fury let us ~e patience; you are ~ing things that are practically identical; to Plato I ~s Aristotle; ~ed himself to it with all his power; the thumb can be ~ed to any of the fingers*, placed against it front to front, whence ~'ABLE-(-z-)a., ~ABIL'ITY n.). **2.** Set oneself against (person, thing); withstand, resist, obstruct, propose the rejection of (resolution, motion, etc.); (abs.) act as opponent or check (*it is the duty of an opposition to ~e*). **3.** p.p. Contrary, opposite, contrasted, (*characters strongly ~ed; black is ~ed to white*); (of persons) hostile, adverse, (*is firmly ~ed to protection*). [f. F OP(*poser* POSE³)]

oppo'seless (-zɪ-), a. (poet.). Irresistible. [-LESS]

opp'osite (-zɪ-), a. (often governing n. by ellipse *of to*), n., adv., & prep. **1.** Contrary in position (to), facing, front to front or back to back (with); (*on ~ sides of the square; came from, went in, ~ directions; the tree ~ to or ~ the house; ~ leaves* etc. in Bot., placed at same height on ~ sides of stem, or placed straight in front of other

organ, opp. *alternate*; ~ *number*, person or thing similarly placed in another set etc. ~NESS n. (-z-). 2. n. ~ thing or term (*you are cold-blooded, she is the ~; the most extreme ~s have some qualities in common*). 3. adv. & prep. In ~ place, position, or direction (to) (*there was an explosion ~, in the house across the street*; ~ *prompter*, in theatre, abbr. *o.p.*, usu. to actor's right; *happened ~ the Mansion House*); *play ~*, (of leads in stage-play or film) have (specified actor or actress) as one's leading man, lady. [f. f. L op(*positus* p.p. of *ponere* place).]

opposit- (-z-), comb. form f. L as prec. In bot. wds. as ~*folious*, opposite-leaved; ~*sepalous*, (of stamen) placed straight in front of sepal.

opposition (-z-), n. 1. Placing opposite (~ *of the thumb*, cf. OPPOSE); diametrically opposite position (esp. Astron., of two heavenly bodies when their longitude differs by 180°, opp. CONJUNCTION; *planet is in ~* opposite sun); contrast, antithesis. 2. (log.). Relation between two propositions with same subject & predicate but differing in quantity or quality or both. 3. Antagonism, resistance, being hostile, (*offer a determined ~; did it in ~ to public opinion; was in ~ at the time*, belonging to the ~ in next sense). 4. || *The O~, His Majesty's O~*, chief parliamentary party opposed to that in office (*the leader of the O~; the O~ whips, benches*, etc.). 5. Any party opposed to some proposal. Hence ~AL a. (rare), ~IST(2) n. & a. (rare) (-isto-.) [f. L OP(*positio* POSITION)]

oppositive (-z-), a. (rare). Adversative, antithetic; fond of opposing. [prec., -IVE]

oppress', v.t. Overwhelm with superior weight or numbers or irresistible power; lie heavy on, weigh down, (spirits, imagination, etc.); govern tyrannically, keep under by coercion, subject to continual cruelty or injustice. So **oppre'ssion** (-shn), ~OR2, nn., ~IVE a., ~IVE'LY2 adv., ~IVENESS n. [f. OF *oppresser* f. med. L OP(*pressare* frequent. of L *premere* press) -IVE]

oppro'brious, a. Conveying reproach, abusive, vituperative. Hence ~LY2 adv. [f. OF *opprobrieux* (foll., -OUS)]

oppro'brium, n. Disgrace attaching to some act or conduct, infamy, crying of shame. [L. f. OP(*probrum* f. *probrum* disgraceful act)]

oppugn' (-ūn), v.t. Controvert, call in question, whence ~ER1 (-ūn-) n.; (rare) attack, resist, be in conflict with, (so **oppugn'ant** a. & n., **oppugn'ance, oppug'nancy** (-nans-), **oppugn'ation** nn. all rare). [f. L op(*pugnare* fight) attack, besiege]

op'simath, n. (rare). One who learns late in life. So **opsim'athy**1 n. [f. Gk *opsimathēs* (*opse* late, *manthanō* learn)]

opson'ic, a. Having the effect on bacteria of making them easier of consumption by phagocytes (~ *action, power*; ~ *index*, numerical expression of the phagocytic power of the serum of a patient under anti-bacterial injections as below). So **op'sonin** n., the substance produced in patient's blood by injection of dead cultures of the bacteria of his disease. [f. Gk *opsonion* provisions (*opson* cooked meat). -IC]

op'tative, v.i. Exercise an option, make choice, of alternatives or for alternative. Hence ~ANT n. [f. F *opter* f. L *optare* choose, wish]

op'tative (or ŏptā'-), a. & n. (gram.). 1. Expressing wish (~ *mood*, set of verbal forms of this kind, distinct chiefly in Greek and Sanskrit; ~ *use of subjunctive*); hence ~LY2 adv. 2. n. ~ mood, verbal form belonging to. [f. (-if, -ive), f. LL *optativus* (prec., -ATIVE)]

op'tic, a. & n. (anat.). Of the eye or sense of sight (~ *nerve, neuritis*, etc.; ~ *angle*, between lines from extremities of object to eye, or from two eyes to one point). 2. n. Eye (now usu. joc.); (pl., with sing. constr.) science of sight & esp. of the laws of its medium, light. [f. F *optique* f. med. L f. Gk *optikos* (*optos* seen f. op-, cf. *opsomai* fut. of *horaō* see, -IC)]

op'tical, a. Visual, ocular, (~ *illusion*, produced by too implicit confidence in the evidence of sight); of sight or light in relation to each other, belonging to optics, constructed to assist sight or on the principles of optics. Hence ~LY2 adv. [prec., -AL]

|| **optic'ian** (-shn), n. Maker or seller of optical instruments esp. spectacles. [f. F *opticien* (OPTIC, -CIAN)]

op'time. See WRANGLER.

op'timism, n. Doctrine, esp. as set forth by Leibnitz, that the actual world is the best of all possible worlds; view that good must ultimately prevail over evil in the universe; sanguine disposition, inclination to take bright views. So ~IST(2) n. & a., ~IS'TIC a., ~IS'TICALLY adv., ~ISM n. [f. F *optimisme* (L *optimus* best, -ISM)]

op'timum, n. (chiefly biol.). Most favourable (natural) conditions (for growth, reproduction, etc.); (attrib.), best or most favourable (~ *temperature*). [L, neut. of *optimus* best]

op'tion, n. Choice, choosing, thing that is or may be chosen, (*make one's ~; none of the ~s is satisfactory*); liberty of choosing, freedom of choice, (LOCAL2 ~; *imprisonment without the ~ of a fine; have no ~ but to*, must); (Stock Exch. etc.) purchased right to call for or make delivery within specified time of specified stocks etc. at

specified rate. [F, f. L *optionem* (st. of *optare* choose, -TION)]

ŏp'tional (-sho-), a. Not obligatory. [prec., -AL]

ŏptŏm'eter, n. Instrument for testing the refractive power & visual range of the eye. [f. Gk *optos* seen + -METER]

ŏp'tophōne, n. Instrument converting light into sound, & so enabling the blind to read print etc. by ear. [f. OPTIC, -o-, + Gk *phōnē* sound]

ŏp'ŭlent, a. Rich, wealthy; abounding, abundant, well stored. Hence or cogn. ŏp'ŭlENCE n., ~LY² adv. [f. L *opulens* or *-lentus* (*opem* accus. quantity, -ULENT)]

ŏp'ŭs, n. (no pl.). Musician's separate composition of any kind (used esp. in citing it from among his works by a number; abbr. *op.*; *Beethoven op. 15*); *măg'num ~, ~ măg'num*, or ~, great literary undertaking, writer's or other artist's chief production. [L, = work]

ŏpŭs'cūle, ŏpŭs'cŭlum (pl. *-la*), n. Minor musical or literary composition. [(-ule F¹) f. L (-um) dim. of prec. (-CULE)]

‖ ŏr¹, n. (her.), Gold or yellow in armorial bearings. [F, f. L *aurum* gold]

ŏr², prep. & conj. (arch.). Before, ere, (chiefly now in *or ever, or e'er*, poet.). [OE *ǣr* adv. early, w. sense of its compar. *ǣr* ERE]

ŏr³ (ôr, or), conj. introducing second of two alternatives (*white or black*), all but the first (*white or grey or black*) or only the last (*white, grey, or black*) of any number, the second of each of several pairs (*white or black, red or yellow, blue or green*), or (poet.) each of two (*or in the heart or in the head*). An alternative introduced by *or* may be (1) on equal footing with preceding (*shall you be there or not?; any Tom, Dick, or Harry*); (2) as true as the preceding (*ripe tomatoes are red or yellow*); (3) mere synonym (*common or garden*); (4) indication that preceding is doubtfully accurate (*one or two, five or six*, etc., *a few*); (5) explanation of preceding (*saw a dug-out or hollowed-tree boat*); (6) statement of only remaining possibility after choice given (often after *either*; *a thing must surely be or not be; for goodness' sake either take it or leave it*); (7) statement of result of rejection etc. of preceding (often with *else; she must weep or she must die; make haste, or else you will be late*); (8) second etc. member of indirect question or conditional protasis after *whether* (*ask him whether he was there or not; must do it whether I like or dislike it*). In syntax, a set of alternatives with *or* is sing. if each member is sing. (*man or woman, boy or girl, goes unmolested; not go*); if the nearest prevails (*were you or he, was he or you, there; either he or you were, either you or he was*), but some forms (e.g., *was I or you on duty?*) are avoided; forms in which difference of gender in the members causes difficulty with pronouns (*a landlord or landlady expects their, his or her, his, rent*) are usually avoided, *their rent or the rent due to them* being ungrammatical, *his or her rent or the rent due to him or her* clumsy, & *his rent or the rent due to him* slovenly. [f. obs. *other* conj., prob. modif. of OE *ohthe* or (cf. G *oder*, earlier *eddo, ode*, etc.) on anal. of alternative etc. wds in -THER]

-or¹, suf. varying with *-our* (ME), f. AF *-our* f. OF *-or, -ur*, F *-eur*, in wds f. L nn. of condition in *-or -oris* mostly f. vbs in *-ēre*, as *liquor* (ME *licour*), *ardour*; all changed in U.S. to *-or*; in Britain many retain *-our*.

-or², suf. (varying with *-er*, see below) in nn. expressing (1) personal agent (*possessor*), (2) thing that acts, instrument, machine, etc., (*extensor*), f. L *-or -oris* appended to p.p. stems. L *-or* was always preceded by *-t-* or *-s-*, which remains in all E recent adoptions (mis-spelt in *author* f. *auctor*) taken direct or thr. F *-teur, -seur*; but L wds in *-ator, -itor*, taken f. OF have lost *-t-* & usu. the preceding vowel; thus L *donador(em)*, OF *doneor, doneur*, AF *donour*, E *donor*; *saviour* retains trace of *-at-* (see -IOUR) in *-t-*; some E agent nn. were formed orig. in F on this anal., as *surveyor, warrior*. In E, *-or*, pronounced like -ER¹,², has been displaced by it in some wds, as *barber* (ME & AF *barbour* f. L *barbatorem*), & has displaced it in others, as *sailor* (perh. on anal. of *tailor*), *chancellor*. When *-er* & *-or* coexist, *-or* has occas. a more legal or professional sense.

ŏr'ach, n. Kitchen-garden plant, Mountain Spinach. [earlier *arache* f. F *arroche* f. L *atriplicem* nom. *-ex* f. Gk *atraphaxus*]

ŏr'acle, n. 1. Place at which ancient Greeks etc. were accustomed to consult their deities for advice or prophecy (*work the ~*, secure desired answer by tampering with priests etc., also fig. bring secret influence to bear in one's favour); response, often ambiguous or obscure, given at such place. 2. Holy of holies or mercy-seat in Jewish temple. 3. (Vehicle, personal or other, of) divine inspiration or revelation. 4. Person or thing serving as infallible guide, test, or indicator; authoritative, profoundly wise, or mysterious adviser or advice, judge or judgement, prophet or prophecy. Hence (esp. w. ref. to obscurity) ŏrăc'ŭlar¹ a., ŏrăc'ŭlarILY¹ adv., ŏrăcŭlä'rITY n. [f. L *oraculum* (*orare* speak, *-culo-* instr. suf.]

ŏr'al, a. & n. 1. Spoken, verbal, by word of mouth. 2. (Anat.) of the mouth. 2. n. (colloq.). ~ examination etc. Hence ~LY² adv. [f. L *os oris* mouth, -AL]

ŏr'ange¹(-inj), n. & a. 1. (Evergreen tree bearing) large roundish many-celled juicy acid or sweet fruit enclosed in bright

reddish-yellow tough rind (*squeeze the* ~,
take all the good from anything; *squeezed*
~, thing from which no more good can be
got; *China* ~, former name of common
~; *mock* ~, the shrub Syringa; ~*s &
lemons*, nursery game, also kind of toad-
flax; *Blenheim* ~, kind of apple); (also
~-*colour*) reddish-yellow. Hence **ŏ'rangery(3)**
(-inj-) n. [OF, ult. f. Arab. *nāranj*]

Orange² (ŏ'rinj), n. Town on Rhône from
which *Princes of* ~ took title (*William
III*), King William from ~ in Eng. hist.;
ŏ'rangism(3) (-inj-) n. [F, f. L *Arau-
sionem* nom.-o.]

ŏrangeade' (-injād), n. Effervescent or
still drink of orange juice etc. [-ADE]

orang-outang (-ŏŏt-, -ŏōt-), **ŏr'ang-ut'an**
(-ŏŏt-), n. Large long-armed arboreal
anthropoid ape of Borneo & Sumatra.
[Malay (-ūtan)=man of the woods]

ŏrāte', v.i. (joc.). Make speech, hold forth,
play the orator. [back form. f. foll.]

ŏrā'tion, n. Formal address or harangue
or discourse esp. of ceremonial kind;
(Gram.) language, way of speaking (*direct,
indirect* or *oblique*, ~, person's words as
actually spoken, or with the changes of
person, tense, etc., usual in reporting).
[f. L *ōrātio* (*orare* speak, -ATION)]

ŏr'ator, n. Maker of a speech; eloquent
public speaker; || *Public O~*, official at
Oxford & Cambridge speaking for university on State occasions. Hence
ŏr'atress¹ n. [f. OF *orateur* f. L *oratorem*]

ŏr'atorize, v.i. [-IZE]

ŏr'atory¹, n. Small chapel, place for private worship; (*O~*) R.-C. religious society
of simple priests without vows founded
in Rome 1564 to give plain preaching &
popular services, also any branch of this
in England etc., whence **ŏratō'rian** a. &
n. [f. L *oratorium* neut. of *oratorius* (*orare*
pray, speak, -TORY)]

ŏr'atory², n. (Art of making) speeches,
rhetoric; highly coloured presentment of,
eloquent or exaggerating language.
Hence **ŏratō'rical** a., **ŏratō'rically²**
adv. [f. L *oratoria* (*ars* art) of speaking,
fem. as prec.]

ŏr'atŏr'iō, n. (pl. ~s). Semi-dramatic
musical composition usu. on sacred
theme performed by soloists, chorus, &
orchestra, without action, scenery, or
costume. [It., orig. of musical services at
oratory of St Philip Neri]

ŏrb, n., & v.t. & i. Circle, circular disk,
ring, (now rare); sphere, globe; heavenly
body; eyeball, eye, (poet.); globe surmounted by cross as part of regalia; organized or collective whole; hence ~*LESS*
a., 2. vb. Enclose in, gather (t. & i.) into,
~. [f. L *orbis* ring]

ŏr'bic'ūlar, a. Circular, discoid, ring-
shaped (*-ar muscle*, sphincter); spherical;
globular, rounded, (fig.) forming complete whole. Hence or compn., **ŏrbic'ū-
~ariy¹** adv., ~*ATE²* a. (nat. hist.), f. L
moon (*orbis* ring)]

ŏrc, **ŏr'ca**, n. Kinds of cetacean; sea or
other monster. [f. F *orque* f. L *orca* kind
of whale]

Orcā'dian (ŏr-), a. & n. (Native) of Orkney. [f. L *Orcades* Orkney Islands, -IAN]

ŏrch'ard, n. Enclosure with fruit-trees;
~*man*, fruit-grower, also ~IST(3) n. [OE
ortgeard prob. f. L *hortus* garden, YARD²]

ŏrchĕs'tic (-k-), a. Of dancing. Hence
~*ICS* n. [f. Gk *orchēstikos* (*orchēstēs*
dancer, see foll.)]

ŏr'chestra (-k-), n. 1. Semicircular space
in front of ancient-Greek theatre-stage
where chorus danced & sang. 2. Part of
modern theatre or concert-room assigned
to band or chorus. 3. Body of instrumental performers, or combination of
bowed, wood-wind, brass, & percussion
instruments, in theatre or concert-room,
whence **ŏrchĕs'tral** (-k-) a. [L, f. Gk
orchēstra (*orkhēomai* dance)]

ŏr'chestrāte (-k-), v.t. & i. Compose (t. &
i.), arrange, or score, for orchestral performance. Hence ~A'TION n. [-ATE³]

ŏrchĕstri'na (-kĭstrē-), **ŏrchĕs'trion**
(-k-), nn. Elaborate kind of barrel-organ
meant to give orchestra-like effect.
[-INA³]

ŏr'chid (-k-), n. Member of
large family of monocotyledonous herb-
(*-is* is usu. of wild English kinds, *-id* of
exotics or in bot. use), of which English
kinds are terrestrial with tuberous root &
erect fleshy stem with spike of usu. red or
purple flowers, & many exotic kinds have
flowers of fantastic shapes & brilliant
colours. Hence **ŏrchid'ACEOUS** (-kidáceous)
a., **ŏr'chidist(3)** (-k-) n. [*-id* made 1845
by Lindley, see -ID²; f. L f. Gk *orkhis -ios*
testicle, orchis, (w. ref. to shape of tuber)]

ŏr'chido- (-k-), comb. form of prec., as
~MANĬA, ~IOĞY (-ŏlŏ-), llrreg. for *orchio-* f.
Gk as prec.]

ŏr'chil, n. Red or violet dye from lichen.
[f. OF *orcheil* etym. dub.]

ŏr'chis (-k-), n. Inflammation of the
testicles. [f. Gk *orkhis* testicle + -ITIS]

ŏr'cin, n. (chem.). Colourless crystalline

substance extracted from lichens & yielding various dyes when compounded. [f. mod. L *orcina* (ORCHIL, -IN)]

Ordain', v.t. (Eccl.) appoint ceremonially to Christian ministry, confer holy orders (esp. those of deacon, or priest) on (*was ~ed priest, elder, etc., or abs.*); (of God, fate, etc.) destine, appoint, (*has ~ed the time, death as our lot, us mortal, us to die, that we should live*); appoint authoritatively, decree, enact, (*what the laws ~; ~ that . . .*). [f. OF *ordener* f. L *ordinare* (*ordo -inis* order)]

Ordain'/ment, n. (rare). Decree(ing). [-MENT]

Ordeal' (or *ōrd'ēl*), n. Ancient Teutonic mode of deciding suspected person's guilt or innocence by subjecting him to physical test such as plunging of hand in boiling water, taken as divine acquittal; experience that tests character or endurance, severe trial. [com.-Teut.; OE *ordāl -āl*, cf. Du. *oordeel*, G *urteil*, judgement; n. f. compd vb (OHG *ar-tailan*, OE *ā-dēlan*, deal out)]

Ord'er[1], n. (Main senses) 1. Rank, row, class. 2. Sequence, arrangement. 3. Mandate. **1**. Tier (now rare; ~ *on* ~ *of sculptured figures*); social class or rank, separate & homogeneous set of persons, (esp. *the* ~ *of the baronets; the clerical, military,* ~); kind, sort, (*talents of a high, considerations of quite another,* ~); any of the nine grades of angels (seraphim, cherubim, thrones, dominations, principalities, powers, virtues, archangels, angels); grade of Christian ministry (*holy* ~s in Anglican church, those of bishop, priest, & deacon, in R.-C., these & subdeacon; *minor* ~s in R.-C. Church, those of acolyte, exorcist, reader, & doorkeeper); (pl.) status of clergyman (*take* ~s, be ordained; *in* ~s, ordained; often in these phrr., & always elsewhere, *holy* ~s); fraternity of monks or friars, or formerly of knights, bound by common rule of life (the *Franciscan* ~; the *Teutonic* ~; the ~ *of Templars*); || company usu. instituted by sovereign to which distinguished persons are admitted by way of honour or reward (~ *of the Garter, the Bath, Merit, etc.*), insignia worn by members of this (*sent him, wears, the* ~ *of the Golden Fleece*); (Archit.) mode of treatment with established proportions between parts (esp. one of the five *classical* ~s, Tuscan, Doric, Ionic, Corinthian, & Composite, each of which is superior to the preceding in height, lightness, & decoration, of pillar & capital; Tuscan & Composite were Roman developments of the others, which were Greek; (Math.) degree of complexity (*line, equation, fluxion, of the first etc.* ~), (also ~ *of magnitude*) class in a system of classification determined by size (*measurements of the* ~ *of one in a million*); (Nat.

Hist.) classification-group below CLASS[1] & above family (*natural* ~ in bot., abbr. N.O., of plants allied in general structure, not merely agreeing in single characteristic as in Linnaean system). **2**. Sequence, succession, manner of following, (*in alphabetical, chronological, etc.,* ~; *out of* ~, not systematically arranged; *follow the* ~ *of events: inverts the natural* ~; *take them in* ~, one after another according to some principle); regular array, condition in which every part or unit is in its right place, tidiness, normal or healthy or efficient state, (*drew them up in* ~; *are scattered without any; love of* ~; *is in bad, out of,* ~, not working rightly; *is in* ~ *or good* ~, fit for use); || (arch.) suitable action, measures, (*take* ~ *to do; take* ~ *with*, arrange, dispose of); constitution of the world, way things normally happen, collective manifestations of natural forces or laws, natural or moral or spiritual system with definite tendencies, (esp. *the* ~ *of nature or things or the world; the old* ~ *changeth; whether there is a moral* ~ *or not*); stated form of divine service (the ~ *of confirmation*); principles of decorum & rules of procedure accepted by legislative assembly or public meeting, or enforced by its president (*Speaker called him to* ~; *O~!* *O~!*, protest against interruption of it; *rise to* ~ *or a point of* ~, interrupt debate etc. with inquiry whether something being said or done is *in* or *out of* ~; ~ *of the day*, programme, business set down for treatment, whence, in gen. use, prevailing state of things, as '*industry, thunder, cricket, is the* ~ *of the day*; || ~-*paper*, written or printed ~ of the day; || ~-*book*, in which motions to be submitted to the House of Commons must be entered); prevalence of constituted authority, law-abiding state, absence of riot, turbulence, & violent crime, (often *law & ~; was restored; keep* ~, enforce it); *close, open,* ~ (Mil. etc.), formation with narrow, wide, spaces between men or ships; *marching, review, etc.,* ~ (Mil.), the regulation uniform & equipment carried by the soldier in marching, at review, etc. (cf. MARCH'*ing* ~s; (Mil.) *the* ~, position of company etc. with arms ordered (see foll.); *in* ~ *to do*, with a view to, for the purpose of, doing; *in* ~ *that*, with the intention or to the end that. **3**. Mandate, injunction, authoritative direction or instruction, (often pl.; *gave* ~s, *an* ~, *the* ~, *for something to be done, that it should be done, etc.*; *is obedient to* ~s; || *O~ in Council*, sovereign ~ on some administrative matter given by advice of Privy Council; *by* ~, according to direction of the proper authority; *judge gave, made, refused, an* or *the* ~); (Banking etc.) instruction to pay money or deliver property signed by owner or responsible agent (~ *cheque,*

cheque to person's ~, one requiring payee's endorsement before being cashed; postal, money or pop. post-office, ~, kinds of Post-Office cheque for remitting money; the latter non-transferable; (Commerc.) direction to manufacturer, tradesman, etc., to supply something (made to ~, according to special directions, to suit individual measurements, etc., opp. *ready-made*; *grocer has sent for ~'s as on ~*, has been ordered but not yet supplied; *a large ~*, colloq. difficult job; *~-book*, in which tradesman enters ~s; *~-clerk*, with duty of entering ~s; *~-form*, skeleton ~ to be filled in by customer); pass admitting bearer gratis, cheap, or as privilege, to theatre, museum, private house, etc. [f. OF *ordre* f. L *ordinem* nom. -o]

Ord'er², v.t. Put in order, array, regulate, (arch.; *~ed his troops*); ~ one's affairs; *has ~ed his life well*); (Mil.) *~ arms*, stand rifles butt on ground & hold them close to right side; (of God, fate, etc.) ordain (*so we hoped, but it was otherwise ~ed*); command, bid, prescribe, (*~ a retreat*, thing to be done, person to do, that person or thing should; *~ed him a mustard plaster*); command or direct (person etc.) to go to, away, home, etc. (*was ~ed to Egypt*; ~ *about*, send hither & thither, domineer over); direct tradesman, servant, etc., to supply (*~ dinner*; settle what it shall consist of). [f. prec.]

Ord'erly², a. & n. 1. Methodically arranged or inclined, regular, obedient to discipline, not unruly, well-behaved, (of troops etc.) *~ room*; (Mil.) of, charged with conveyance or execution of, orders (*~y book*, regimental or company book for entry of orders; *~y officer*, officer of the day; *~y-room*, in barracks for company's business); ||*~y bin*, street box for refuse. 2. n. Soldier in attendance on officer to carry orders etc.; attendant in (esp. military) hospital. [-LY¹]

Ord'inal, a. & n. 1. (Number) defining thing's position in series (*first, twentieth,* etc., are ~s or ~ *numbers*; cf. CARDINAL). 2. Of a nat.-hist. order. 3. n. Service-book used at ordinations. [f. LL *ordinalis* (ORDER¹, -AL¹)]

Ord'inand, n. Candidate for ordination. [f. L *ordinandus* (*ordinare* ORDAIN)]

Ord'inary, a. & n. 1. Regular, normal, customary, usual, commonplace, (*in ~* ordinary; not temporary or extra-ordinary; *in an ~ way I should refuse, if the circumstances were not exceptional; something out of the ~*; *~ seaman*, abbr.

O.S., lower rating than *able*; *in ~*, of ships laid up, not in commission. ~, **Ord'inarily²** adv. **Ord'inariness** n. 2. ||(Authority) having immediate or *ex officio* & not deputed jurisdiction (*the O~*, archbishop in province, bishop in diocese; *O~* or *Lord O~* in Scotland, one of five judges of Court of Session constituting Outer House). 3. Rule or book laying down order of divine service. 4. || Public meal provided at fixed time & price in inn etc. 5. (her.) Charge of earliest, simplest, & commonest kind (esp. chief, pale, bend, fess, bar, chevron, cross, saltire). 6. Early type of bicycle, with one large & one very small wheel (opp. *safety*). [f. L *ordinarius* (ORDER¹, -ARY²)]

Ord'inate, n. (geom.) Any of series of parallel chords of conic section in relation to bisecting diameter (esp. used of straight line from any point drawn parallel to one co-ordinate axis & meeting the other. [f. L (*linea*) *ordinate* (*applicata*) parallel]

Ord'inā'tion, n. Arrangement in ranks, classification; conferring of holy orders, admission to church ministry; decreeing, ordainment. [f. L *ordinationem* (ORDAIN, -ATION)]

Ord'inee', n. Newly ordained deacon [ORDAIN, -EE]

Ord'nance, n. Mounted guns, cannon; ||branch of public service dealing esp. with military stores & materials (*Royal Army O~ Corps*, formerly with wider powers *Board of O~*; ||*~ survey*, Government survey of Great Britain & Ireland; ||*~ datum*, mean sea level as defined for ~ survey). [var. of ORDINANCE]

Ord'ure, n. Excrement; dung; obscenity, foul language. [F (*ord* foul f. L HORRIDUS, -URE)]

Ore¹, n. Native mineral from which precious or useful metal may be profitably extracted; (poet.) metal, esp. gold. [prob. f. OE *ōr* brass (cf. L *aes aeris*, Skr. *ayas* metal) with sense changed to that of OE *ōra* unwrought metal (cf. Du. *oer*), which would itself have given a mod. form, not *ore*]

Ore², n. (L & Gk Myth.), Mountain nymph. [f. L *oreas -ados* f. Gk *oreias* f. *oros* mountain. -AD(1)]

ŏrĕc'tic, a. (philos., med.), Of desire or appetite, appetitive. [f. Gk *orektikos* (*orego* stretch out, -IC)]

Ore'ide, n. Kind of brass resembling gold, used in imitation jewellery. [f. F *oréide* (*or* f. L *aurum* gold)]

Orfe, n. Kind of goldfish. [G & F, f. Gk *orphos* sea perch]

Org'an, n. 1. Musical instrument of pipes supplied with wind by bellows, sounded by keys, & distributed into sets or stops having special tone, which in turn form groups or partial ~s (*great, choir, swell,*

solo, pedal, ~) each with separate keyboard, whence ~IST(3) n.; =BARREL 1.~ (~grinder, player of this); Keyboard wind-instrument with metal reeds, harmonium; AMERICAN ~; *mouth* ~, child's toy reed-instrument. **2.** Part of animal or vegetable body adapted for special vital function (~*s of speech, perception, digestion, generation,* etc.; NASAL ~). **3.** Person's voice with reference to its quality or power (*has a magnificent* ~). **4.** Medium of communication, mouthpiece of opinion, esp. newspaper or magazine or review representing a party, cause, sect, pursuit, etc. **5.** ~-*blower*, person or mechanism working; ~*bellows*; ~*builder*, of musical ~s; ~-*loft*, gallery in church or concert-room for ~; ~ *piano*, with mechanism giving sustained tones as in ~; ~-*screen*, ornamental screen often between choir & nave on which ~ is placed in cathedral etc.; ~-*stop*, set of pipes of similar tone in ~; handle of mechanism that brings it into action. Hence ~LESS a. [f. L f. Gk *organon* tool (*erg*- WORK)]

org'andie, n. Kind of very fine translucent muslin. [f. F *organdi* etym. dub.]

org'anic, a. **1.** (Physiol.) of the bodily organs, vital; (Path., of disease) affecting structure of an organ (opp. *functional*). **2.** Having organs or organized physical structure, of animals or plants, (opp. *inorganic*). **3.** (Chem., of compound substances etc.) existing as constituent of organized bodies or formed from bodies so existing, containing carbon in its molecule (~ *chemistry*, that of carbon compounds). **4.** Constitutional, inherent, fundamental, structural. **5.** Organized or systematic or co-ordinated (~ *unity*; *an* ~ *whole*). Hence org'anICALLY adv. [f. L f. Gk *organikos* (ORGAN, -IC)]

org'anism, n. Organized body with connected interdependent parts sharing common life, (material structure of) individual animal or plant; whole with interdependent parts compared to living being. [ORGANIZE, -ISM]

organiza'tion, n. In vbl senses of foll.; also, organized body or system or society. [f. med. L *organizatio* (foll., -ATION)]

org'aniz|e, v.t. & i. Furnish with organs, make organic, make into living being or tissue, (usu. in p.p.); (intr.) become organic; form into an organic whole (with constituents or resulting whole as obj.); give orderly structure to, frame & put into working order, make arrangements for or get up (undertaking involving co-operation). Hence ~ABLE a., ~ER¹ n. [f. med. L *organizare* (ORGAN, -IZE)]

org'anon, -anum, n. Instrument of thought, system of or treatise on logic. [Gk (-*on*), & L (-*um*), see ORGAN; -*on* was title of Aristotle's logical writings, & *novum* (new) *organum* that of Bacon's]

org'anothe'rapy, n. Treatment of disease with organic extracts. [f. Gk ORGANON + -THERAPY]

org'anzine (-ēn), n. Silk thread in which the main twist is in contrary direction to that of the strands. [f. F *organsin* f. It. *organzino*]

org'asm, n. Violent excitement, rage, paroxysm; height of venereal excitement in coition. So org̃as'tic a. [f. Gk *orgaō* swell. -*sm* as in SPASM, -ISM]

or'geat (or -zhah), n. Cooling drink made from barley or almonds & orange-flower water. [F(*orge* f. L *hordeum* barley, -ADE)]

orgias'tic, a. Of the nature of an orgy. [f. Gk *orgiastikos* (*orgiastēs* agent n. f. *orgiazō* celebrate ORGY)]

or'gy, n. (Gk & Rom. Ant.; usu. pl.) secret rites in worship of various gods, esp. in that of Bacchus celebrated with wild dancing, drinking, and singing; drunken or licentious revel, (pl.) revelry or debauchery. [earlier pl. only, f. F *orgies* f. L f. Gk *orgia* pl.]

or'iel, n. Large windowed polygonal recess projecting usu. from upper storey & supported from ground or on corbels; (also ~ *window*) window of ~, projecting window of upper storey. [f. OF *oriol*, etym. dub.]

or'ient, n. & a. **1.** *The* eastward part of sky or earth (poet.); *the* East or countries E. of Mediterranean & S. Europe; ~ *pearl*; peculiar lustre of pearl of best quality. **2.** adj. Oriental (poet.); (of precious stones and pearls, of finest kinds, as coming anciently from the East) lustrous, sparkling, precious; (of sun, daylight, etc., or fig.) rising, nascent. [F, f. L *orientem* nom. -*ens* rising sun, east, (*oriri* rise, -ENT)]

ori'ent², **o'rientāte**, (or ōr-), v.t. & i. Place (building etc.) so as to face E., build (church) with chancel end due E., bury with feet eastward; place or exactly determine position of with regard to points of compass, settle or find bearings of, (fig.) bring into clearly understood relations (~ *oneself*, determine how one stands); (intr.) turn eastward or in specified direction. Hence orienta'TION n. [f. F *orienter* (prec.)]

orien'tal (or ōr-), a. & n. Easterly (arch.); (inhabitant) of the East or countries E. of Mediterranean & S. Europe, esp. Asiatic, occurring in or coming from or characteristic of the civilization etc. of the East, whence ~ISM(2, 4), ~IST(3), nn., ~IZE(2, 3) v.i. & t.; (of pearls etc.) orient; ~ *stitch*, close kind of herringbone stitch. Hence ~LY² adv. [F, f. L *orientalis* (ORIENT¹, -AL)]

o'rifice, n. Aperture, mouth of cavity, perforation, vent. [F, f. LL *orificium* (*os oris* mouth, *ficere*=*facere* maker)]

o'riflamme, n. Sacred banner of St Denis, banderole of red silk on lance re-

ceived by early French kings from abbot of St. Denis on starting for war; (fig.) anything material or ideal serving as rallying-point in struggle; bright conspicuous object, blaze of colour, etc. [F (L *aurum* gold, *flamma* flame)]

ŏ'rigan, orig'anum, n. Wild Marjoram, & kinds of allied plant. [L (-um), f. Gk *origanon*]

ŏ'rigin, n. Derivation, beginning or rising from something, person's extraction, source, starting-point, (*a word of Latin, a* man of humble, ~). [f. F *origine* f. L *originem* nom. -go (*oriri* rise)]

orig'inal, a. & n. 1. Existent from the first, primitive, innate, initial, earliest, (~ *sin*, innate depravity common to all human beings in consequence of the fall); that has served as pattern, of which copy or translation has been made, not derivative or dependent, first-hand, not imitative, novel in character or style, inventive, creative, thinking or acting for oneself, (*where is the ~ picture?; what does the ~ Greek say?; where is the ~; is* an ~ *drawing or a woodcut?; made a* very ~ *remark; has an ~ mind; ~ people do ~ things*); hence or cogn. orig'inal'ITY n., ~LY² adv. 2. n. Derivation, descent, origin, (rare); pattern, archetype, thing from which another is copied or translated, (*several transcripts of the same* ~; *reads Don Quixote in the* ~); eccentric person. [F, f. L *originalis* (prec., -AL)]

orig'inate, v.t. & i. Give origin to, initiate, cause to begin, whence ~ATIVE a.; have origin, take rise, (usu. *from* or *in* thing or place, *with* or *from* person). So ~A'TION, ~ĀTOR², nn. [ORIGIN, -ATE³]

ŏrinas'al (-zl), a. & n. Of, sounded with, both mouth & nose (esp. of French nasalized vowels); (n.) ~ vowel. [L *os oris* mouth, -i-, L *nasus* nose, -AL]

ŏ'riōle, n. (Also Golden ~) bird with black & yellow plumage visiting British Isles in summer; other old-world birds of same genus; kinds of bird of similarly coloured American genus. [f. med. L *oriolus* f. L *aureolus* dim. of *aureus* golden (*aurum* gold)]

Orī'on, n. (astron.). Brilliant constellation S. of zodiac, figured as hunter with belt & sword (~'s *belt*, three bright stars in short line across ~; ~'s *hound*, Sirius). [L, f. Gk *Ōriōn*]

Orī'ond, n. (astron.). One of meteor-system with radiant point in Orion. [prec., Gk -is -idos fem. patronymic]

ŏ'rison (-zn), n. (arch.). A prayer (usu. in pl.). [F, f. L *orationem* speech (*orare* speak, pray. -ATION, -SON)]

Orlé'ans (ŏ-), n. Kind of plum; fabric of cotton warp & worsted weft. [name of French city]

ŏrl'op, n. Lowest deck of ship with three or more decks. [f. Du. *overloop* covering (*overloopen* run over, see OVER, LEAP)]

Ŏrm'er, n. Edible univalve mollusc, the Sea-ear. [Channel-I.F.f.F *ormier* contr. of *oreille de mer* ear of sea]

Ŏrm'olu (-ōō), n. Gilded bronze used in decorating furniture; gold-coloured alloy of copper, zinc, & tin; articles made or decorated with these. [f. F *or moulu* ground gold (for use in gilding)]

Ŏrn'ament¹, n. (Eccl., usu. pl.) what is necessary for worship (e.g. altar, chalice, sacred vessels, service books); ~ *rubric*, that immediately before Order for Morning & Evening Prayer in prayer-book); thing used or serving to adorn, quality or person whose existence or presence confers grace or honour, (*mantel-piece was crowded with* ~s; *the* ~ *of a quiet spirit*; *was an* ~ *to his country or age*); (pl., Mus.) grace notes; (sing. only) adorning, being adorned, embellishment, features or work added for decorative purposes, (*a tower rich in* ~; *by way of* ~). Hence ~AL a., ~ally adv., ~alism(3), ~ALIST(3), nn., (all -ěn²). [f. OF *ornement* f. L *ornamentum* equipment (*ornare* equip, -MENT)]

Ŏrn'amĕnt² (or -ĕnt'), v.t. Adorn, beautify. Hence ~A'TION n. [f. prec.]

Ŏrnāte', a. Elaborately adorned, (of literary style) embellished with flowers of rhetoric etc. Hence ~LY² adv., ~NESS n. [f. L *ornatus* p.p. (prec.)]

Ŏrnith(o)-, comb. form of Gk *ornis -ithos* bird, in many scientific wds, as orn'ithoID, approaching birds in structure (of some reptiles); ~ŏl'ogy, ~ŏlo'gicAL, ~ŏl'ogIST n., ornith'omANCY; ~orh'ýnc'us (-ri-), Australian duck-billed platypus, an aquatic mammal with dark-brown fur, webbed feet, & duck's bill, & laying eggs; ~ŏs-

Ŏrog'raphy, ŏrĕŏ-, n. Branch of physical geography dealing with mountains; hence orogra'phicAL aa. So ŏr(e)ŏŏGy n., ŏr(e)ŏŏGICAL a., ŏr(e)ŏŏL'ogIST n. [Gk *oros -eos* mountain, -GRAPHY]

Ŏrŏhipp'us, n. Fossil quadruped held to be ancestral form of horse. [Gk *oros* mountain, *hippos* horse]

Ŏr'oide, n. Gold-coloured alloy of copper & zinc. [F *or* gold f. L *aurum*, Gk *eidos* form]

Ŏrŏtŭnd, a. (Of utterance or phrasing) swelling, mouth-filling, imposing, dignified, pompous, magniloquent, pretentious. [f. L *ore rotundo* (Hor. A.P. 323) with round mouth]

Ŏrph'an, n. & a., & v.t. 1. (Child) bereaved of parent(s); hence ~HOOD n., ~IZE(3) v.t. 2. v.t. Bereave of parent(s). [f. L.L.f.Gk *orphanos* orphan]

Ŏrph'anage, n. Orphanhood; institution for orphans' education etc. [-AGE]

Ŏrph'ic, Orphé'an, (ŏ-), aa. Of Orpheus or the mysteries or doctrines associated with his name, oracular, mysterious, (usu. -ic); like Orpheus's music, melodious.

entrancing, (usu. -ean). [f. Gk *Orphikos* (Orpheus, -IC)]

Orph'rey, Orf'ray, n. Ornamental often richly embroidered border of ecclesiastical vestment. [earlier sense *embroidery,* f. OF *orfreis* f. L *auriphrygium* gold embroidery (*aurum* gold, *Phrygian*; -s dropped as though pl. sign, cf. PEA)]

Orp'iment, n. A mineral, trisulphide of arsenic, used as yellow dye. [OF, f. L *auripigmentum* (*aurum* gold, PIGMENT)]

Orp'in(e), n. Succulent herbaceous fleshy-leaved purple-flowered plant common in cottage gardens. [F (-*n*), prob. corrupt. of prec., orig. of yellow-flowered species of same genus]

Orp'ington (ŏr-), n. A breed of poultry. [village in Kent]

O'rrery, n. Clockwork model of the planetary system. [named after Earl of O~ c. 1700]

O'rris¹, n. Kind of Iris, flower-de-luce, (now rare); ~-*root,* fragrant root of three species of Iris used in perfumery & medicine; ~-*powder,* powdered ~-root. [prob. corrupt. of IRIS]

O'rris², n. Kinds of gold or silver lace or embroidery. [prob. cogn. w. ORPHREY]

Ors'on (ŏr-), n. Rough valiant person. [tale of *Valentine &* ~]

Ort, n. (dial. & arch.; usu. pl.). Refuse scrap(s), leavings. [15th-c. *ortus* pl., cf. Du. *oor-aete* remains of food (*oor-* not, *etan* eat)]

Orth(o)-, comb. form of Gk *orthos* straight, in many scientific wds w. senses *straight, rectangular, upright, right, correct:* ~-*cephal'ic,* with breadth of skull from ⅘ to ⅘ of length, between brachycephalic & dolichocephalic; ~*ochromat'ic,* giving correct relative intensity to colours in photography; *orth'oclase,* common feldspar in crystals with two cleavages at right angles; ~*o'epy,* science of correct pronunciation, whence ~*oep'ic,* ~*o'epist*(s); ~*ogen'esis,* a view of evolution according to which variations follow a defined direction & are not merely sporadic & fortuitous; ~*og'nathous,* upright-jawed, not prognathous; ~*og'onad,* of or involving right angles; ~*op'terous,* of the insect order *Orthoptera* with straight narrow forewings including cockroaches, crickets, grasshoppers, etc.; ~*op'tic,* of straight or correct seeing, esp. used as n. or a. of opaque perforated eyeglass assisting aim in rifle-shooting; *orth'otone,* (word) having independent accent, not enclitic or proclitic.

Orth'odox, a. Holding correct or the currently accepted opinions esp. on religious doctrine, not heretical or independent-minded or original; generally accepted as right or true esp. in theology, in harmony with what is authoritatively established, approved, conventional; *the O~ Church,* the Eastern or Greek recognizing Patriarch of Constantinople as head & the national Churches of Russia, Rumania, etc., in communion with it. Hence ~LY² adv. [f. Gk ORTHO(*doxos* f. *doxa* opinion)]

Orth'odoxy (-ks-), n. Being orthodox. [f. Gk *orthodoxia* (prec.; -Y²]

Orthog'raphy, n. **1.** Correct or conventional spelling; spelling with reference to its correctness (*his* ~ *is shocking*). **2.** Perspective projection used in maps & elevations in which the point of sight is supposed infinitely distant so that the rays are parallel, map etc. so projected. So **Orthograph'ic**(AL), aa., **Orthograph'ically²** adv. [f. OF *ortografie* f. L f. Gk ORTHO(*graphia* -GRAPHY)]

Orth'opaed(y, n. The curing of deformities in children or others, surgery directed to this. So **Orthopaed'ic** a. [f. F *orthopédie* f. Gk *paideia* rearing of children f. *paideō* train f. *pais* child)]

Ort'olan, n. The garden bunting, small bird esteemed as table delicacy. [F, f. It. *ortolano* orig. gardener f. L *hortulanus* (*hortulus* dim. of *hortus* garden, -AN)]

-ory, suf. (1) of adjj., originating in O.Norm. F *-ori* masc., *-orie* fem., & repr. (occas. thr. F *-oir, -oire*) L in *-orius, -oria, -orium;* = agent termination -OR² added to p.p. stems + *-tus* adj. suf. As every L vb could form agent n. in -OR, E has adjj. in -ory corr. to L vbs even when L has neither adj. in *-orius* nor agent n. in -OR (*compuls~, dispensat~, illus~*), or when the L vb is not itself represented in E (*amat~, perfunct~*). As alternatives to -ory, E often has *-orial* (~ +AL), *-orious* (~ +-OUS). (2) of nn., chiefly f. L neut. adjj. in *-orium* (*dormit~, fact~, lavator~*). In a few wds ~ is -Y¹ added to agent-termination -OR² (*rect~, ord~*). In some technical wds L *-orium* is preserved, as *auditorium, crematorium, sensorium,* (also *-ory*).

O'ryx, n. (Genus of) large straight-horned African antelope. [L, f. Gk *oryx*]

Os'can (-ŏ-), a. & n. (Of, in) the language, allied to Latin, of the *Osci, Osci,* or *Opici,* a primitive people of Campania. [L *Osci,* -AN]

Os'cillate, v.i. & t. Swing (i., rarely t.) like pendulum, move to & fro between two points; vacillate, vary between extremes of opinion, action, condition, etc.; (Electr., of current) undergo high-frequency alternations as across spark-gap or in valve-transmitter circuit; (of wireless receivers) radiate electromagnetic waves owing to faulty operation. Hence or cogn. ~A'TION, ~ātor²(1, 2), nn., ~atory² a. [f. L *oscillare,* -ATION]

Oscita'tion (ŏsĭ-), n. (rare). Yawning, inattention, negligence. [f. L *oscitatio* (*oscitare* gape f. *os* mouth, *citare* move, -ATION)]

Os'cular, a. Of the mouth, of kissing

osculate (joc.); (Math.) that osculates. [f. L *osculari* mouth, kiss, (*os* mouth, -CULE)]

ôs'cūlāte, v.i. & t. **1.** Kiss (i. & t., rare, usu. joc.). **2.** (Nat. Hist., of species etc. have contact through intermediate species etc.), have common characters with another or with each other; (Math., of curve or surface) have contact of higher order with, coincide in three or more points. Hence or cogn. ~ANT a. (esp. math.), ~ATION n., ~ATORY a. (esp. math.). [f. L *osculari* kiss (prec.), -ATE³]

-ōse¹, suf. f. L *-osus* abounding in; chiefly in adj. of a technical kind, adji. in ordinary use having -ous; but there are *belli-cose, jocose, grandiose,* & a few others. Nn. are formed from them usu. in *-osity,* also in *-oseness.*

-ōse² suf. in chem. wds formed on *glucose* (mod. F adoption of Gk *gleukos* must) giving names for the related carbohydrates *saccharose* & *cellulose* & isomeric substances, as *dextrose, laevulose.*

ō'sier (-zher), n. (Shoot of) species of willow used in basket-work; ~-BED¹; (attrib.) of ~, s. [F, cf. LL *auseria, os-,* willow-bed]

-ōsis, suf. forming nn. of process or condition on Gk & occas. L stems; names of diseases or pathological states (*amaur~, trichin~*); a few rhetorical terms (*metei~*); & some in gen. use (*metamorph~, apothe~*). [f. Gk *-ōsis* n. suf. usu. f. vbs in -oō]

-ōsity, suf. See -OSE¹, -OUS.

Osman'li (òs-), a. & n. =OTTOMAN¹. [Turk. native wd for which *Ottoman* is the usu. E form]

ôs'mium (òs-, òz-), n. A metal of the platinum group, the heaviest substance known. [f. Gk *osmē* smell, -IUM, named from pungent smell of volatile acid formed by it with oxygen]

ôs'mōse, ôsmōs'is (òs-, òz-), n.(physics). (Tendency to) percolation & intermixture of fluids separated by porous septa. Hence **ôsmô'ic** a., **ôsmô'ically** a. [irreg. f. Gk *ôsmos* push (*ōtheō* push) + -OSIS]

ôs'mund (òz-, òs-), n. The Flowering Fern; any fern of genus *Osmunda.* [?]

ôs'prey (-ā, ǐ), n. (pl. -s). **1.** Large bird preying on fish, the sea-eagle, fishing eagle, or sea-hawk. **2.** (Milliner's name for) egret-plume on hat or bonnet. [prob., f. L *ossifraga* (*os ossis* bone, *frangere* break) perh. the lammergeyer]

ôss'eous, a. Consisting of bone, ossified; having bony skeleton (~ & cartilaginous fishes); abounding in fossil bones. [f. L *osseus* (*os ossis* bone) +-OUS]

ôss'icle, n. (anat.). Small bone, small piece of bony or chitinous or calcareous substance in animal framework. [f. L *ossiculum* (prec., -CULE)]

ôss'ifrage, n. =OSPREY. [OSPREY]

ôss'ify, v.i. & t. Turn (i. & t.) into bone,

harden, make or become rigid or callous or unprogressive. Hence **ôssific** a., **ôssiFICA'TION** n. [L *os ossis* bone, -FY]

ôss'uary, n. Receptacle for bones of dead, charnel-house, bone-urn; cave in which ancient bones are found. [f. LL *ossu-arium* (irreg. f. *os* see prec., -ARY²)]

ôsten'sible, a. Professed, for show, put forward to conceal the real (*this ~e errand was to —*). Hence ~LY² adv. [f. F f. med. L *ostendere -ens- -ibile)*]

ôsten'sorý, n. Receptacle for displaying Host to congregation, monstrance. [f. med. L *ostensorium* as prec., +-OR¹(2)]

ôstentā'tion, n. Pretentious display esp. of wealth or luxury, showing off, attempt or intention to attract notice. Hence ~IOUS (-shus) a., ~IOUSLY² adv. [F, f. L *ostentationem* (*ostentare* frequent. of *ostendere -tent-* show, -ATION)]

ôs'tler (-sl-), n. Stableman at inn. [earlier *hostler* (HOSTEL, -ER¹)]

ôs'tracīze, v.t. **1.** (Gk Ant.; at Athens) banish (dangerously powerful or unpopular citizen) for ten or five years by means of voting-system, name of person to be ~ized being written on potsherd. **2.** Exclude from society, favour or common privileges, send to Coventry, etc. Hence ~ISM(3) n. [f. Gk *ostrakizō* (*ostrakon* potsherd)]

ôs'trei-, ôs'treo-, comb. forms of L *ostreon, ostreum,* & Gk *ostreon,* oyster, as *ostreiculture,* oyster-breeding; *ostreopha-gous,* eating oysters.

ôs'trich, n. Large swift-running African & Arabian bird with wing & tail feathers valued as ornaments, swallowing hard substances to assist working of gizzard, & reputed to bury its head in sand when pursued in the belief that it cannot be seen (*has the digestion of an ~; ~ policy, belief,* etc., depending on self-delusion); ~-*farm,* breeding ~es for feathers; ~-*plume,* feather, or bunched feathers, of ~; ~-*fern,* tip of ~-feather. [f. OF *ostruce* f. pop. L *avis struthio* (*avis* bird, LL f. Gk *strouthiōn* ostrich f. *strouthos* sparrow, ostrich)]

-ot¹, suf. =F *-ot,* orig. dim., but often not so now; *ballot, chariot, parrot.*

-ot², suf. giving nativity in ancient Gk names, as *Epirot,* & in mod. names from places near Greece, as *Cypriot;* also in a few Gk derivatives of other meanings

(idiot, helot, patriot, zealot). [=F -ote f. L -ota f. Gk -ōtēs]

o'ther (ŭdh-), a., n. or pron., & adv. **1.** Not the same as one or more or some already mentioned or implied, separate in identity, distinct in kind, alternative or further or additional, the etc. only remaining, (or *very second, different than or from*, (for sing. use with *an*, see ANOTHER; *we have ~ evidence; ~ people think otherwise; it must be decided by quite ~ considerations; have no ~ place to go to; ~ things being equal*, if the conditions are or were, in everything but the point in question, alike, as *~ things being equal, I should prefer you to him, but he is rich & you are poor; a few ~ examples would be useful; give me some ~ ones; now open the, your, ~ eye; ~ happens every ~ day*, on alternate days, as often as not; *any person ~ than yourself; do not wish him, them, ~ than he is, they are; a world far ~ from ours; on the ~ hand*, used to introduce fact or argument making against or contrasted with previous one; *the ~ day* adv., a few days ago; *some time or ~* adv., one day etc.; *someone or ~*, a person unknown; *some idiots or ~ have been shouting all night; it was none ~ than Jones*, = no ~ one or person; *the ~ world*, future life, *~-world*, concerned with or thinking of this only, whence **~-wor'ldly**¹ (-wēr-) a., **~-wor'ldliness** n.; often ellipt. with numerals, as another, *the ~ two*, i.e. person or persons, thing or things, of kind not needing specification);**~guess** a. [corrupt. of *~gates* adv. (GATE². ES) in another way], of very different kind (arch. & colloq.); **~whence**, from elsewhere, **~where(s)**, elsewhere (poet.); **~while(s)**, at other times. **2.** n. or pron. (orig. elliptic use of adj., & often indistinguishable from this in sing., but now distinguished in pl. by *~-s*, cf. *the ~ six, the six ~s*). ~ person, thing, specimen, etc. (*give me another, some ~s; do good to ~s; if this soap is, these candles are, too soft, have you any ~, ~s?; one or ~ of us will be there; let ~s talk, I act; I can do no ~*, arch., nothing else; *you are the man of all ~s for the work; one neutralizes the ~; they neutralize* EACH ~ or ONE another; *in ~s of his sermons*), **3.** adv. Otherwise (*~ than cursorily*). [Aryan; OE ŏther, cf. Du. & G ander, Skr. ántaras, L alter; see -THER]

o'therness (ŭdh-), n. (rare). Being other, diversity, difference; thing or existence that is not the thing mentioned or the thinking subject. [-NESS]

o'therwise (ŭdh'erwīz), adv. In a different way (*could not have acted ~; Judas, ~ called, or ~, Iscariot*; occas. preceded by any, no, with reminiscence of its etym., as *could do it no ~, does not influence him any ~ than by example*); if circumstances are or were different, else, or (*seize the chance, ~ you will regret it*); in other

respects (*he is unruly, but not ~ blame-worthy*; also qualifying the adj. sense in n., as *his ~ dullness*); in different state (*how can it be ~ than fatal?; should not wish it ~*); *& ~, & ~, or ~*, followed by the negation or opposite of a noun or adj. or by other (*the merits or ~ of the Bill*, i.e. or demerits usu. omissible; *additions automatic & ~*, i.e. & other); **~minded**, having different, or jarring, inclinations or views, averse to current opinions. [OE *on ōthre wīsan* (OTHER, WISE²)]

-ŏtic, suf. forming adji. corr. to nn. in -osis, in sense affected with or producing or resembling -osis, so *near~, hypn~, narc~*; *Quix~, ex~, er~* are not exx. [f. Gk -ōtikos †. nn. in -ōēs formed on same stems as -OSIS]

otiose (ōshĭŏs, also ō-), a. At leisure, lazy, unoccupied, (rare); sterile, futile, (rare); not required, serving no practical purpose, functionless. Hence **~LY²** adv., **~NESS** n. [f. L ōtiōsus (ōtium leisure, -OSE¹)]

o'tium cŭm dignitāt'e (ōshĭ-), n. Dignified ease. [L]

ōt(o)-, comb. form of Gk ous ōtos ear, as ŏtŏL'OGY, science of ear diseases, anatomy, etc.; ŏt'oscope, instrument for examining cavity of ear, or for auscultation of sounds in it.

otta'va rī'ma (-tah, rē-), n. Stanza of eight lines, 11-syllabled in Italian, 10-syllabled in English, with rhymes as ababacbcc (as in Byron's *Don Juan*). [It.]

ŏtt'er, n. Furred aquatic fish-eating mammal with fin-like legs, webbed feet, & long flattened tail; its fur; kinds of fishing-tackle (also as name for the paravane when used on non-naval craft); *~dog, -hound*, breed used in *~-hunting*; *~spear*, used in *~-hunting*. [com.-Teut.; OE otr, cf. Du. & G otter, also Skr. udrís; cogn. w. Gk hudōr water, & w. WATER]

ŏtt'ō (ō-), n. *~ of roses*, = ATTAR. [f. attar]

Ŏtt'oman¹ (ŏ-), a. & n. **1.** Of the dynasty of Othman I, his branch of the Turks, or the empire ruled by his descendants, Turkish. **2.** n. (pl. *~s*). ~ person, Turk. [F. f. Arab. name of Othman (pronounced in Turk. ŏsman, whence OSMANLI)]

ŏtt'oman², n. Cushioned seat like sofa or chair without back or arms, often a box with cushioned top. [f. prec. (cf. DIVAN)]

ou'bit (ōō-), n. = WOOBUT.

oubliette' (ōō-), n. Secret dungeon with entrance only by trapdoor. [F (oublier forget)]

‖ **ouch**, n. (arch.). Clasp or buckle often jewelled; setting of precious stone. [f. OF nouche (cf. ADDER) f. LL nusca f. OHG nuscha prob. f. Celt.]

ought¹ (awt), n. (vulg.). Figure denoting nothing, nought. [perh. f. *an ought* for a *nought*, cf. ADDER]

ought² (awt), v. aux. (the only form in

ought, use, except arch., ~*est* or ~*st*, ~ serving as present or past finite) expressing duty, rightness, shortcoming, advisability, or strong probability; the past sense (except when merely due to sequence of tenses in reporting etc.) is indicated by a following perf. infin. Exx.: *it* ~ *we* ~ *to love our neigh-bours*; *it* ~ *not to be allowed*; *you* ~ *to know better*; *you* ~ *to go to Pinafore*; *Eclipse* ~ *to win*; *it* ~ *to be done at once, have been done long ago*; *I told you it* ~ *to be, have been, done*; *I said it, & still think I* ~ *to have said it*. [OE *áhte* past of *águn* owe; the mod. uses represent the impert. subj.=would owe]

ought[2], var. of AUGHT.

ouija (wē'jah, -yah), n. (Also ~-*board*) board lettered with alphabet & other signs, used with movable pointer to ob-tain messages in spiritualistic séances. [f. F *oui* and G *ja*.=yes]

ounce[1], n. (abbr. oz). Unit of weight, 1/12 lb. in Troy weight, 1/16 lb. in avoir-dupois (also fig., as *an* ~ *of practice* etc. *is worth a pound of theory* etc.). [f. OF *unce* f. L *uncia* twelfth of pound or foot (cf. INCH[1])]

ounce[2], n. (Poet., etc.) lynx or other vaguely identified medium-sized feline beast; (Zool.) the mountain panther or snow leopard smaller than leopard but marked like it. [f. OF *once*, cf. It. *lonza*, f. L *lyncea* (LYNX); for *once* f. *l'once* by mistake for *lonce* cf. ADDER]

our (owr), a. Of or belonging to us (see WE), that we are concerned with or speak-ing or thinking of, (*is in* ~ *midst*; *acting on* ~ *behalf*; *have done* ~ *share*; *Our Saviour, Lady*, of us Christians, Christ, the Virgin; *given under Our seal*, of Us the king or queen, emperor or empress; *a worthless book in* ~ *opinion*, of us the present spokesman of a newspaper etc.). [com.-Teut.; OE *úre* orig. genit. pl. of first pers. pron.=of us, afterwards in-flected as adj.; cf. G *unser*, OSax. *úser*]

-our[1], suf. in *colour* etc.; see -OR[1].

-ours (owrz), pron. & pred.a. 1. The one(s) belonging to us (~ *is a large family*; *I like* ~ *better*; *let me give you one of* ~; *look at this garden of* ~, this our garden); [OURS our regiment or corps (*Jones of* ~). 2. pred. adj. Belonging to us (*became* ~ *by pur-chase*). [OUR, -ES; double possessive for the emphatic abs. use]

ourself (owr-), pron. (pl. ~*ves*, which is the usn. form, the sing. being used simi-larly when *We* represents a sovereign, & alternatively with the pl. when *we* represents a newspaper writer or the average man). 1. (emphat.: usn. pl.), We or us in person, in particular, in our normal condition, & not others, or alone, (usn. in apposition with *we*, & either next after it or later, rarely substituted for it; usn. substituted for *us*, rarely after it in apposition; *we* ~*ves will see to it*; *we will see to it* ~*ves are first to be thought of*; *it was good for the others, if not for* ~*ves*; *we were not* ~*ves for some time*; *what touches us*~f *shall be last served*; *can we imagine a world in which* ~f *does not exist?*). 2. (refl.: usn. pl., always in objective case). The person(s) previously described as *we* (*we shall only harm, do harm to,* ~*ves*; *we cannot persuade* ~f *or* ~*ves that the Government is in earnest*; *we shall give* ~*ves the pleasure of calling*. [OUR, SELF]

-ous, suf. forming adj.: f. L -*osus*, cf. -OSE[1], abounding in, thr. OF -*os*, -*us*, & OE -*ús*, written after 1300 -*ous* (ôus) & gradually weakened in sound to (ūs); familiarized in L & F wds f. OF, -*ous* has now become the established anglicizer for many L adj., esp. in -*eus*, -*ius*, -*er*, -*ax* -*acis*, -*oz* -*ocis*, -*endus*, -*ulus*, & -*orus* (*igne*~, *dubi*~, *adulter*~, *cupaci*~, *feroci*~, *tremend*~, *bibul*~, *herbivor*~); *righte*~, *courte*~, *gorge*~, are by false anal.; (Chem., of acids etc.) with larger proportion of the element indicated by the stem than those in -*ic* (*chlor*~ *acid*). Nn. f. adji. in ~ have usn. -*ousness*, sometimes -*osity* (*curiosity*), cf. -OSE[1].

ousel. See OUZEL.

oust, v.t. Put out of possession, eject, deprive *of*, expel *from*, drive out, force oneself or be put into the place of. Hence **ous'ter** n. (legal). [f. OF *oster* (now *ôter*) take away, etym. dub.]

out, adv., prep., n., a., int., & v.t., (for spec. uses of the adv. in comb. with vbs see the vb). 1. adv. Away from or not in or at a place, the right or normal state, the fashion, etc., (*is* ~, not at home; *keep him* ~; *go* ~ *for a walk*; *has her Sundays* ~; *arm is* ~, dislocated; *Tories are* ~, not in office; *her son is* ~ *in Canada*; *anchored some way* ~; *on the voyage* ~; *batsman is* ~, no longer in possession of wicket; *all* ~, *side's innings over*; ~, *not* ~, umpire's decision against, for, batsman in answer to claim of opponents; *miners are* ~, not at work, on strike; *candle, fire, is* ~, not burning; *crinolines are* ~, not in fashion; *was* ~ *in my calculations*, incorrect; *was with, no longer on friendly terms with*; also as interj., ~ *with him* etc., turn him ~!; in(to) the open, publicity, existence, notice, hearing, sight, clearness, etc. (*book, rose, chicken, secret, girl, is* ~, published, open, hatched, revealed, intro-duced to society; *is the best game* ~; *tell him right* ~; *the eruption is* ~ *all over him*; ~ *for*, ~ *to do*, colloq., engaged in seeking, *as is* ~ *for kudos*, ~ *to capture the market*; *all* ~, sl., showing one's utmost pace or effort; ~ *at* ELBOW's; ~ *& about*, able to leave bed or house & appear; also ellipt. for *come* ~, *as murder will* ~); to or at an end, completely, (*she had her cry* ~; *tired* ~; *before the week is* ~; ~ *& away, by far*;

~ &, thorough, **-ly,** surpassing, **-ly,** whence **out-&-out**ᴱᴿ¹ n. sl.); **~** of compd prep., from within, not within, from among, beyond range of, (so as to be) without, from, owing to, by use of (material), at specified distance from (town etc.), beyond, transgressing rules of (*come ~ of he house; happened ~ of England; ~ of doors,* in or into the open air, so *~of-door* as adj.; *must choose ~ of these; is ~ of sight; was swindled ~ of his money; is ~ of breath, his mind, work, brown sugar,* etc.; *get money ~ of him; a filly got by Persimmon ~ of Lutetia: asked ~ of curiosity; what did you make it ~ of?; is seven miles ~ of Liverpool; ~ of wedlock,* without marriage; *times ~ of number,* beyond counting; *~ of doubt,* undoubtedly; *is ~ of drawing,* incorrectly drawn; *~ of it,* not included, forlorn, at a loss, wrongly informed or mistaken; *~ of* DATE², CHA-RACTER¹, HAND¹, one's own HEAD¹, KEEP-ING, TEMPER, the WOOD, SORTS, *the* WAY). **2,** prep. **~** of (only now in *from ~,* as *from ~ the dungeon came a groan*). **3, n.** The ~s, the party ~ of office; *the* IN's & ~s. **4, adj.** *An~match,* played away from home ground; *~ size,* (of) exceptionally large size (in garments etc.). **5,** int. (arch.). Expr. abhorrence, reproach, etc. (*Out upon you!*). **6, v.t.** (sl. or colloq.). Eject forcibly; (Boxing) knock ~. [com.-Teut.; OE *ūt,* cf. Du. *uit,* G *aus*]

out-, pref.= prec. prefixed adverbially or adjectivally or prepositionally to vbs or nn. **1.** To any vb followed by *out*; chiefly in poet. & rhet. use. So *~blaze', ~branch', ~speak', ~spread'.*

2. Vbs that are followed in other parts by *out* often form partt. & gerunds with prefixed *out*; the meaning is often a specialized one. So *~'cast* a. & n., (person) cast out from home & friends, homeless & friendless (vagabond); ‖*~'clearing* n., sending out of bills & cheques to Clearing-house for settlement; *~'fighting,* boxing at arm's length, opp. *infighting; ~'lying* a., situated far from a centre, remote; *~mōd'ed* a., out of fashion; *~'spoken* (or *-ōk-*) a., frank, given to plain speaking, whence *~spok'enNESS* n.; *~spok'enNESS* n.; *~'spread, ~'standing* a., prominent, still unsettled; *~'stretched; ~'worn,* worn out (poet.), (fig.) out of date, obsolete, exhausted.

3. Nn. are formed f. vbs that can be followed by *out,* either with the simple vb form or with a derivative n.; the meaning, which is often specialized, may be:—

a. the verbal action or its occurrence. So *~'break,* a breaking out of emotion esp. anger, hostilities, disease, volcanic energy, etc., *~'crop,* an insurrection;

~'burst, explosion of feeling esp. expressed by vehement words, volcanic eruption, *~'crop; ~'crop,* emergence of stratum, vein, or rock, at surface (also b.); *~'cry* (also c.); *~'flow; ~'going* (also b.); *~'look* (also c.); *~'rush* (also b.); *~'sight,* perception of external things (only as antithesis to *insight*); *~'thrust,* outward pressure of some part in architecture.

b. that which does the action. So *~'come,* issue, result; *~'crop* (also a.); *~'fit,* complete equipment material or mental, (colloq.) group of persons regarded as a unit, gang, (v.t.; *-tt-*) provide (person) with, *~'fitter,* supplier of equipment; *~'flow* (also a.); *~'go, ~'goings* (also a. in sing.), expenditure, *~'lay; ~'growth,* offshoot, natural product; *~'lier, ~'lying* part or member, (Geol.) minor part of formation separated from main body by denudation; *~'pour; ~'rush* (also a.).

c. that which is made or done by or suffers the action. So *~'cry* (also a.), clamour, uproar; *~'lay,* what one spends, expenses; *~'look,* what one sees on looking out, view, prospect, esp. fig. of what seems likely to happen; *~'pouring,* effusion, verbal or literary expression of emotion; *~'put, ~'turn,* amount produced by manufacture, mining, labour, etc.; *~'throw,* amount ejected.

d. the place or time of occurrence. So *~'fall, ~'let* of river etc.; *~'let,* means of exit or escape, vent, way out; *~'set, start,* commencement, (usu. *at or from the ~set*).

4. *out-* is prefixed w. adj. force to nn., meaning:—

a. external. So *~'back* a. & n. (Austral.), (of) the more remote settlements; *out-LINE, OUTSIDE.*

b. connected but separate, subordinate & detached, not at the centre, some way off. So *~'building, ~'house; ~'field,* ‖*~'lying land* of farm, *~'lying region* of thought etc. (Cricket) part remote from wickets; *~'house,* house or building or shed belonging to & near or built against main house; *~'land'ish* a. [f. obs. *~'land* foreign countries], foreign looking or sounding, unfamiliar, bizarre, uncouth; *~'patient, ~'pensioner,* receiving aid from institution etc. without being lodged in it; *~'post,* detachment on guard at some distance from army to prevent surprise; ‖*~'relief, ~'door relief* (5); *~'rider,* mounted attendant riding before, behind, or with carriage, also commercial traveller; OUTRIGGER; *~'runner,* running attendant on carriage, horse in traces outside shafts, dog acting as guide to sledge-team; *~'sentry,* man stationed as ~'post; *~'skirts,* outer border, fringe, of city, district, etc., or subject; *~'station,* at distance from headquarters; ‖*~'voter,*

For words in *out-* not given see OUT-.

non-resident parliamentary elector; ~´work, advanced or detached part of fortification, also work done outside shop or house; ~´worker, one who does ~work.

5. out- is prefixed in vbs & governs nn. with the force of *out of*, forming adjj. or advv., f. which vbs or nn. may be secondary formations. So ~´board a. & adv. (Naut.) on or towards or nearer than something else to ship's outside; (of a motor-boat) having the engine & driving apparatus attached outside the boat; ~´caste a. & n. (person) having lost or been expelled from his or not belonging to a caste; ~´caste¹ v.t., expel from caste; to person not resident in workhouse or institution; ~´door agitation etc., conducted outside Parliament; ~´doors adv., in the open air; ~´law n. & v.t. [OE *ūtlagu* n. f. *ūtlag* a. outlawed], person deprived of the protection of the law, banished or exiled person, (vb) proscribe, declare ~law, whence ~´lawry, condition of or condemnation of or con-

6. out- with general sense of excess is prefixed

a. to simple vbs capable of taking the same object, adding the idea of more than, or successively, doing the action. So ~bal´ance, weigh down; ~brave´, defy; ~face´, look out of countenance; ~fight´; ~hec´tor; ~last´ (*will out-last six months*; also b.); ~match´; ~meas´ure; ~ri´val; ~scold´); ~trump´, at cards.

b. to any vb, in such as *general* used for the nonce as vb, enabling it to take an obj., a person or thing that the subj. surpasses or defeats by doing the action more, better, or longer. So ~act´, ~arg´ue, ~bell´ow; ~bid´, bid higher than at auction, promise more than, surpass in exaggeration or anecdote; ~blaze´, ~brag´, ~dance, ~dare´; ~do´; surpass; ~eat´; ~fight´, fight better than (also a.); ~fly´; ~gen´eral, defeat by superior generalship; ~go´, go faster than, (fig.) surpass; ~grow´, grow faster or get taller than (also c.); ~hec´tor, be more formidable at hectoring than (also a.); ~jock´ey, overreach ~jug´gle; ~jump´; ~lab´our; ~last´, last longer than (another; also a.); ~live (also c.); ~manoeu´vre, ~march, ~point´, ~preach ~reach, ~reas´on, ~ride´, ~run´ (b)· ~run (*~run the* CONSTABLE; also c.); ~scold (also a.); ~shine´ lit. & fig.; ~shoot´; ~sing´; ~sit´, stay longer than (other guests); ~spar´kle, ~spend´; ~stare´; ~stay´ (also c.); ~stink´, ~swim´, ~talk´, ~think´ -than´der, -toil, -trade, -trav´el; ~vie´ ~watch; Keep awake longer than (also c.); surpass in competition; ~weigh´, exceed in importance, or influence; ~work´; ~well´. c. to vb, enabling it to take as obj.

something in the nature of a limit or amount that is exceeded. So ~grow´, get too big for (clothes); get rid of (childish habit or ailment or taste) with advancing age, (also b.); ~live, live beyond (a century, the ordinary span, etc.), come safely through (accident etc.), get over effect of (disrepute etc.), (also b.); ~ride´, (of ship) keep afloat through (storm; also b.); ~run´, pass the limit of (*his imagination ~runs the facts*; also b.); ~stay (*never ~stay your welcome*; also b.); ~step, pass limit of (*~steps the truth*); also ~watch´, keep awake beyond the end of (the night etc.; also b.); ~wear´, pass away (time) by endurance.

d. to n., forming vb expressing that subj. surpasses obj. in this respect. So ~class´, belong to higher class than; ~dis´tance, get far ahead of; ~flank´; ~num´ber; ~pace´, go faster than; ~range´, (of gun or its user) have longer range than; ~speed´; ~val´ue; ~voice´, speak louder or more effectively or persuasively than; ~wit´, prove too clever for, overreach, take in.

e. to name of person noted for some quality, forming vb (w. the name usu. repeated as obj.) indicating that subj. surpasses even him in it. So ~he´rod, Herod, ~zol´a Zola, be more blustering, realistic, than Herod or Zola.

out´back, a. & n., see OUT- 4 a.; out´bal´ance v.t., OUT- 6 a.; out´bid´ v.t. (-dd-), OUT- 6 b; out´board a. & adv., OUT- 5; out´brave´ v.t., OUT- 6 a; out´break n., OUT- 3 a; out´building n., OUT- 4 b; out´burst n., OUT- 3 a; out´cast a. & n., OUT- 5; out´caste a. & n., outcaste v.t., OUT- 5; out´class´ v.t., OUT- 6 d; out´clearing n., OUT- 2; out´college a., OUT- 5; out´come n., OUT- 3 b; out´crop n., OUT- 3 a b; out´cry n., OUT- 3 a c; out-dis´tance v.t., OUT- 6 d; out´do´ v.t., OUT- 6 b; out´door a., out´doors´ adv., OUT- 5.

out´er, a. & n. **1.** Farther from centre or inside, relatively far out, external, of the outside; objective, physical, not subjective or psychical; *the ~ man*, personal appearance, dress; *the ~ world*, people outside one's own circle; hence ~ MOST a. **2.** n. Circle of rifle-target farthest from the bull's-eye, hit on this. [14th-c. formation substituted for & differentiated f. UTTER as compar. of OUT]

out´face, v.t., see OUT- 6 a; out´fall n., OUT- 3 d; out´field n., OUT- 4 b; out´fighting, OUT- 2; out´fit n., out´fitter, nn., OUT- 3 b; outflank´ v.t., OUT- 6 d; out´flow n., OUT- 3 a; outgen´eral v.t., OUT- 6 b; outgo´ n., OUT- 3 b, vb, OUT- 6 b; out´going(s) n., OUT- 3 a b; outgrow´ v.t., OUT- 6 c; out´growth n., OUT- 3 b; out-he´rod v.t., OUT- 6 e; out´house n., OUT- 4 b.

out'ing, n. Pleasure-trip, holiday away from home. [f. obs. *out* vb put or go out, -ING¹]

out-jock'ey, v.t., see OUT- 6 b; outland'ish a., OUT- 4 b; outlast' v.t., OUT- 6 a b; out'law n. & v.t., out'lawry n., OUT- 5; out'lay n., OUT- 3 c; out'let n., OUT- 3 d; out'lier n., OUT- 3 b.

out'line n., & v.t. 1. (Sing. or pl.) lines enclosing the apparently plane figure presented by any object to sight, contour, external boundary; sketch containing only contour lines & no shading (*in ~*, so sketched); rough draught, verbal description of essential parts only, summary, (pl.) main features, general principles. 2. v.t. Draw or describe in ~, mark ~ of in decorating etc. [OUT- 4 a]

out'live, v.t., see OUT- 6 b c; out'look n., OUT- 3 c; out'lying a., OUT- 2; outmanœu'vre v.t., OUT- 6 b; outmarch' v.t., OUT- 6 b; outmatch' v.t., OUT- 6 a; out-mod'ed a., OUT- 2.

out'most, a. =OUTERMOST.

out'ness, n. Externality, objectivity. [-NESS]

outnum'ber, v.t., see OUT- 6 d; outpace' v.t., OUT- 6 d; out'patient n., OUT- 4 b; out'post n., OUT- 4 b; out'pouring n., OUT- 3 c; out'put n., OUT- 3 c.

out'rage, n. (-ij), & v.t. (-āj). 1. Forcible violation of others' rights, sentiments, etc. (*never safe from ~*); deed of violence, gross or wanton offence or indignity (*an ~ upon decency, justice, etc.*). 2. v.t. Do violence to, subject to ~, injure, insult, violate, ravish; infringe (law, morality, etc.) flagrantly. [f. OF *ultrage* (L *ultra* beyond, -AGE)]

outra'geous (-jus), a. Immoderate, extravagant, extraordinary; violent, furious, grossly cruel, immoral, offensive, or abusive. Hence ~LY² adv., ~NESS n. [f. OF *outrageus* (prec., -OUS)]

outrange', v.t. See OUT- 6 d.

outré (ōŏtrā), a. Outside the bounds of propriety, eccentric, outraging decorum. [F]

out-relief', n., see OUT- 4 b; outride' v.t., OUT- 6 b c; outrid'er n., OUT- 4 b.

out'rigged (-gd), a. (Of boat etc.) having outriggers. [f. OUT-, RIG, -ED¹, after foll.]

out'rigger (-g-), n. Beam, spar, framework, rigged out & projecting from or over ship's side for various purposes; similar projecting beam etc. in building; extension of splinter-bar enabling extra horse to be harnessed outside shafts, such horse; iron bracket bearing rowlock attached horizontally to boat's side to increase leverage of oar, boat with these. [OUT-, RIG, -ER¹]

outright' (-rīt), adv. & a. 1. Altogether, entirely, once for all, not by degrees or instalments or half & half, (*kill, buy, ~*);

without reservation, openly. 2. adj. Downright, direct, thorough, whence ~ NESS (-rīt-) n. [OUT, RIGHT]

outri'val, v.t. (-ll-), see OUT- 6 a; outrun' v.t., OUT- 6 b c; out'runner n., OUT- 4 b; out'set n., OUT- 3 d; outshine' v.t. OUT- 6 b.

out'side', n., adj., adv., & prep. 1. External surface, outer parts, (*knows only the ~s of books*; *ride on the ~ of an omnibus*); external appearance, outward aspect; all that is without, the world as distinguished from the thinking subject, (*impressions from the ~*); position without (*open the door from the ~*); highest computation (*there were a hundred, it is a mile, at the ~*); (pl.) outer sheets of ream of paper; || ~ passenger on coach etc.; ~ *in*, =INSIDE *out*. 2. adj. Of, on, nearer, the ~, outer, (~ *edge* in skating, progression on outer edge of one skate; ~ *seat*, nearer the end; ~ *work*, done of the premises; || ~ *porter*, conveying luggage from station); || ~ *broker*, not member of Stock Exchange; greatest existent or possible or probable (*quote the ~ prices*). 3. adv. On or to the ~, the open air, open sea, etc., not within or enclosed or included, (*come ~*, out from room or house, esp. as challenge to fight; *is black ~ & in*; ~ *of*, = prep.; *~ of a horse*, sl., mounted; *get ~ of*, sl., eat or drink; ~ *his own family no one will speak to him*). 4. prep. External to, not included in, beyond the limits of, not in, to the ~ of, at or to the exterior of, (*natural forces are ~ morality*; *cannot go ~ the evidence*). [OUT- 4 a, SIDE¹]

outsid'er, n. Non-member of some circle, party, profession, etc., uninitiated person, layman; person without special knowledge, breeding, etc., or not fit to mix with good society; competitor not known to have a chance in race or competition. [-ER¹]

out'sight, n., see OUT- 3 a; outsit' v.t., OUT- 6 b; out'skirts n. pl., OUT- 3 b.

out'span, v.i. & t. (-nn-), & n. (S. Afr.). 1. Unyoke, unharness. 2. n. Act, time, or place of ~ning. [f. Du. *uitspannen* (OUT, SPAN)]

out'spok'en a., see OUT- 2; out'spread a., OUT- 2; out'standing a., OUT- 2; outstay' v.t., OUT- 6 b c; outstep' v.t., OUT- 6 c; out'stretched a., OUT- 2.

outstrip' v.t. (-pp-). Pass in running etc., surpass in competition or relative progress or ability. [OUT- 6 b, STRIP in obs. sense *run fast*]

out'thrust, n., see OUT- 3 a; out'turn n., OUT- 3 c; outval'ue v.t., OUT- 6 d; outvie' v.t., OUT- 6b; outvoice' v.t., OUT- 6 d; outvote' v.t., OUT- 6 b; out'voter n., OUT- 4 b.

For words in *out-* not given see OUT-.

out'ward, a., adv., & n. 1. Outer (arch.); directed towards the outside; bodily, external, material, visible, apparent, superficial, (*the ~ eye*, opp. *mind's eye*; *~ form*, appearance; *~ man* in Theol., body, opp. *soul*, also joc. = clothing etc.; *to ~ seeming*, apparently); hence ~LY² adv. 2. adv. =OUTWARDS (*~-bound*, of ship or passenger, going away from home). 3. n. *~ things*, the world around us.; hence ~LY² adv. 2. adv. =OUTWARDS (OUT-, -WARD]

out'wardness, n. External existence, objectivity; interest or belief in outward things, objective-mindedness. [-NESS]

out'wards (-z), adv. In an outward direction, towards what is outside. [-WARDS]

outwatch', v.t., see OUT- 6 b c; **outweigh'** v.t., OUT- 6 b; **outwit'** v.t. (-tt-), OUT- 6 d.

|| **out'with** (-dh), prep. (Sc.), Outside of. [f. OUT & WITH]

out'work n., see OUT- 4 b; **outworker** n., OUT- 4 b; **out'worn** (-), see OUT- 2.

ouzel, -sel, (ōō'zl), n. Kinds of small bird (*Ring, Water, Brook, ~*). [OE *ōsle*, cf. G *amsel*]

ova. See OVUM.

ov'al, a. & n. 1. Egg-shaped or ellipsoidal; having the outline of an egg or elliptical; hence ~LY² adv. ~NESS n. 2. n. Closed curve with one axis considerably longer than the other, like ellipse or outline of egg; thing with ~ outline; || *the O~*, the Surrey County cricket ground, Kennington O~ in S. London. [OVUM, -AL]

ov'ary, n. Either of two reproductive organs in which ova are produced in female animals, whence ovār̆ŏt'omy, ovărr'is, nn.; lower part of pistil, consisting of one or more carpels, seed-vessel, germen. Hence ovā'rīaN a., ovā'rio- comb. form.

ov'ate, a. (nat. hist.). Egg-shaped as solid or in outline, oval. Hence ovāt'o- comb. form. [f. L *ovātus* (OVUM, -ATE²)]

ovā'tion, n. (Rom. Ant.) lesser triumph; enthusiastic reception, spontaneous applause. [f. L *ovātio* (*ovāre* exult, -ATION)]

ov'en (ŭ-), n. Brick or stone or iron receptacle for baking bread or other food in (*Dutch ~*, metal box of which open side is turned towards ordinary fire); small furnace or kiln used in chemistry, metallurgy, etc.; *~-bird*, kinds making domed nests. [com.-Teut.; OE *ofn*, cf. Du. *oven*, G *ofen*, Gk *ipnos*]

ov'er, adv., n., a. & prep., **o'er** (ōr), adv. & prep. (poet.). 1. Outward & downward from brink or from erect position (*lean, fall, jump, knock, give, ~*). 2. So as to cover or touch whole surface (*brush, paint, it ~*). 3. With motion above something, so as to pass across something (*climb, look, boil, ~*). 4. So as to produce fold or reverse position, upside down, (*bend it ~*; *turn ~*, turn other side of leaf up; *turn him ~ on his face*; *roll ~ &.*, so that same point comes uppermost repeatedly); (Cricket, as umpire's direction) change ends for bowling etc. 5. Across a street or other space or distance (*take this ~ to the post-office*; *asked him to come* as visitor from some place not far off; *is ~ in, am going ~ to, America*; *~ against*, in opposite situation to, in contrast with). 6. With transference or change from one hand, party, etc., to another (*malcontents went ~ to the enemy*; *handed ~, the seals*; *made ~, the balance to a charity*; GIVE¹ ~). 7. Too, in excess, in addition, besides, more, apart, (*~ anxious* etc., more than is right, see OVER- ; not be dealt with now; *~ & above*, moreover, into the bargain). 8. From beginning to end, with repetition, in detailed consideration, (*read, count, ~*; *did it six times ~, & ~ again, ~ & ~ again*; *talk, think, the matter ~*). 9. At an end, done with, settled, (*the struggle is ~*). 10. *All ~*, in characteristic attitude, behaviour, etc. (*that is Jones all ~*, that is what one would expect of Jones). 11. n. (cricket). Number of balls (orig. 4 or 5, later 6 or 8) allowed between two calls of (sense 4); the play that results : MAIDEN ~. 12. adj. Upper, outer, superior, excessive, (usu. written as one word with ~, see OVER-). 13. prep. Above, on, at all or various points upon, to & fro upon, all through, round about, concerning, engaged with, (*an umbrella ~ his head*; *projects ~ the street*; *doubt hangs ~ the question*; *~ our heads*, beyond our comprehension, also without consulting us; HAND¹ ~ hand; *writing ~ the signature X...*; *~ head & ears*, completely immersed lit. & fig.; *~ shoes ~ boots*, no half measures; *with his hat ~ his eyes*; *drew a veil ~ it*; *a change came ~ him*; *blush spread ~ his face*; *rice is grown all ~ India*; *you may travel ~ Europe or Europe ~*; *all the world ~*, in all countries etc.; *went ~ his notes*; *sitting ~ the fire, a cheerful glass*, etc.; *pause ~ the details*; *laugh ~ one's work*); *all ~* (sl.), infatuated with (a person); *~ all*, from end to end (in attrib. use *~-all*; *an ~-all length of 200 ft*); see also OVERALL. 14. With or so as to get or give superiority to, beyond, more than, (*is king, reigns, has jurisdiction, ~ twenty millions*; *was victor, won the victory, was victorious, ~*; *set him ~ the rest*; *has no command ~ herself*; *give me the preference ~ him*; *cost ~ £50*; *~ & above*, besides, not to mention). 15. Out & down from, down from edge of, so as to clear, across, on or to the other side of, throughout, through duration of, till end of, (*fell ~ the

edge, precipice; *stumble* ~, be tripped up by; *jumped* ~ *the brook*; ~ *the bags or top*, of troops emerging from trench to attack; *looking* ~ *the hedge*; *spoke* ~ *her shoulder*; *coursing* ~ *the plain*; *a pass* ~ *the company's line*; *the house* ~ *the way*, opposite; *the King* ~ *the water*, Jacobite phr. for exiled king; *if we can tide* ~ *the next month*; *payments spread* ~ *a series of years*; *will not live* ~ *today*; *can you stay* ~ *Wednesday?*). [Aryan; OE *ofer*, cf. Du. *over*, G *über*, *ober*, Gk *huper*, Skr. *upari*; cogn. w. ABOVE, & having compar. termin.]

o'ver-, pref. = prec. Unless otherwise shown stress is on first part of compound.

1. Used as adj, in agreement with second part of compound, = upper, outer, of higher kind, upside down, extra, to or in higher position. So ~**arm** a. & adv., = ~**hand**; ~**coat**, worn outside another; ~**dress**, outer part of gown made to resemble one dress worn over & showing parts of another of different colour etc.; ~**fault** (Geol.), reverse fault with inclination towards upthrow side; ~**fold** (Geol.), fold of strata so complete that middle part is upside down; ~**hand** a. & adv., with hand above object held, with hand above shoulder (~*hand bowling*; *bowls* ~*hand*), out of water (~*hand stroke* in swimming), etc.; ~**lord**, supreme lord, suzerain, whence ~lord'SHIP n.; ~**man** (Philos.), also superman, the ideal man, beyond good & evil, or superior to moral restrictions, of Nietzsche's philosophy; ||~**shoe**, of rubber or felt worn outside another; ~**sleeve**, for pulling on over sleeve to protect it; ~**soul**, God as animating the universe & including all human souls; ~**thrust** (Geol.), thrust of strata on one side over those of other side of fault; ~**time**, during which workmen works beyond regular hours; ~**tone** n. (Mus.), upper PARTIALS; ~**weight**, preponderance, excessive weight.

2. As prep. governing second component & making with it n. a., or adv. So ~**all** n., woman's loose work-garment, (pl.) outer trousers or leggings or combination suit for dirty work, ||(Mil., pl.) officer's full-dress tight trousers; ~**board** adv., from within ship into water (usu. *fall, throw,* ~*board*; *throw* ~*board*, fig., abandon, discard); ~**door** n., ornamental woodwork above door; ~**front** n., armflap of Inverness cape etc.; ~**ground** a., raised above ground, not underground; ~**head**' adv., on high, in the sky, in the storey above; ~**head** a., placed ~head (esp. ~*head wires*; ~*head charges* etc., Commerce, those due to office expenses, management, interest on capital, & other general needs of a business); ~**house** a., (of wires) supported on housetops instead of poles; ~**knee** a., reaching above knee; ~**land** adv., by land & not sea; ~**land** a., entirely

or partly by land (esp. of route by Mediterranean to India, or from Atlantic to Pacific across continent); ~**leaf**' adv., on other side of leaf (of book); ~**mantel** n., ornamental shelves etc. over mantelpiece; ~**night**' adv., on the preceding evening with a view to, or as regarded from, the next day; ~**night** a., done etc. ~night; ~**proof** a., containing more alcohol than proof spirit; ~**sea(s)** adv., ~**sea(s)** a., across or beyond sea; ~**side**' adv., ~**side** a., (of loading & unloading ship) over the side into or out of lighters; ~**time**' adv., beyond regular hours of work; ~**weight** a., beyond weight allowed (esp. ~*weight luggage*).

3. As prep. prefixed to vbs, but itself governing case independently, often with specialized sense; also in abs. uses of, or in derivatives from, such vbs. So ~**brim**' v.t. & i. (*water* ~*brimmed the cup*); also said of the vessel); ~**come**' v.t. & i., prevail over, master, get the better of, be victorious, (p.p.) exhausted, made helpless, deprived of self-possession, (*with* or *by* emotion etc.; ~*come with liquor*, drunk); ~**crow**' v.t., exult or triumph over (rival), outswagger; ~**flow** n., what ~flows or is superfluous (~*flow meeting*, of kindness, harvest, etc.) be very abundant, whence ~**flow-ING**¹ a. & n. (esp. *full to* ~*flowing*), ~**flow'ING**¹·² adv.; ~**grow**' v.t. (of creeping plants); ~**growth** n., plants that have grown over anything, (fig.) accretion; ~**hang**' v.t. & i (-*hung*), jut out over, jut out, (fig.) impend over, impend; so ~**hang** n., fact or amount of ~hanging; ~**lap**' v.t., partly cover, cover & extend beyond, (reciprocally of pl. subj.) partly coincide (*the great difficulty in classification is the* ~*lapping of species*); ~**lap** n., fact or process of ~lapping, ~lapping part; ~**leap**' v.t., leap over, surmount, omit, ignore; ~**lie**' v.t., lie on top of, smother (child) thus; ~**look**' v.t., have prospect of or over from above, be higher than, fail to observe, take no notice of, condone, superintend, ~see, bewitch with the evil eye; ~**pass**' v.t. & i., pass over, across, beyond, etc., get to the end of, surmount, surpass; ~**ride**' v.t., ride over (enemy's country) with armed force, trample (person) under one's horse's hoofs, (fig.) trample under foot, set aside, refuse to comply with, have or claim superior authority to, (Surg., of fractured bone) ~lap; ~**run**' v.t., flood, harry & spoil (enemy's country), (of vermin, weeds, etc.) swarm over or spread over, exceed (limit); ~**sail'ing**, (of masonry course etc,) projecting beyond the one below; ~**see**' v.t.

look at from above (rare), superintend or look after (workmen, execution of work, etc.), whence ~seer (-sēr) n. (||~seer of the poor, parish officer charged with relief & other duties); ~shoot' v.t., send missile, go, beyond (mark etc. lit. & fig.; ~shoot oneself), go too far, exaggerate, also ~shoot the mark; ~wheel, turned by water flowing above it; ~sight n., supervision (rare), omission to notice, mistake of inadvertence; ~spread' v.t., become diffused over, cover or occupy surface of; ~step v.t., pass beyond (boundary lit. or fig.).

4. As adverb in local senses (above, by way of cover down from above or from erectness, past, beyond, in addition, modifying vb or derived n. without itself governing object. So ~arch' v.t. & i.; ~bal'ance v.i. & t., lose balance & fall, cause to do this; ~bear' v.t., bear down or upset by weight or force, put down or repress by power or authority, surpass in importance etc., outweigh; ~bear'ing a., domineering, masterful, whence ~bear'ingly² adv., ~bear'ingNESS n.; ~bloom' p.p., (of storm etc.) passed; ~can'opy v.t.; ~cloud' v.t.; ~crust' v.t.; ~fall n., turbulent stretch of sea etc. caused by set of tide or current over submarine ledge or meeting of currents, ~flow openning to keep water of lock or canal up or down to required level; ~film' v.t.; ~gild v.t.; ~haul' v.t., pull to pieces for purposes of examining, examine condition of, (esp. Naut.) catch up, come up with; ~haul n., thorough examination, esp. with a view to repairs; ~hear' v.t., hear as an eavesdropper or as an unpereceived or unintended listener; ~lay' v.t., cover surface of with coating etc., (incorrectly) ~lie; ~lay n., thing laid over, small tablecloth etc.; ~passed', ~past', a., gone by, past; ~sew v.t., sew (two edges) with every stitch passing in same direction through both, the inter-stitch parts of thread lying across & outside united edge; ~shad'ow v.t., shelter from sun, protect from attack (rare), cast into the shade, diminish conspicuousness of by outshining; ~spill v.t.; ~spread v.t., cover with (chiefly pass.; heaven was ~spread with clouds); ~strung a., (of piano) with strings in sets crossing each other obliquely; ~take v.t., come up with, catch up, (person etc. who has start, or arrears of work), (of storm, misfortune, etc.) come suddenly upon, ~taken in drink, drunk); ~throw' v.t., upset, knock down, cast out from power, vanquish, subvert, put an end to (institution etc.); ~throw n., defeat, subversion, (Cricket) fielder's return not stopped near wicket & so allowing further run(s); ~turn v.t. & i., upset, (cause to) fall down or over, ~throw, subvert, abolish;

~turn n., upsetting, revolution; ~whelm' v.t., bury beneath superincumbent mass, submerge utterly, crush, bring to sudden ruin, overpower with emotion etc., deluge with inquiries etc.; ~whel'ming a., irresistible by numbers, amount, etc., whence ~whel'mingly² adv.

5. As adv. with trans. vb, adding sense of effectually, completely, into submission. So ~awe' v.t.; ~cloy' v.t.; ~joyed' p.p., transported with joy (at); ~mas'ter v.t.; ~persuade' v.t., persuade in spite of reluctance.

6. As adv. or adj. prefixed to vb, adj, adv., or n, adding notion of excess over the desirable, the truth, or a definite limit. So ~abound' v.i.; ~abun'dant a.; ~abun'dantly adv.; ~abun'dance n.; ~act' v.t. & i., act (part, emotion, etc.), act part, with exaggeration; ~ac'tive a.; ~anx'ious a.; ~anx'iously adv.; ~ac'tiv'ity n.; ~anx'ious a.; ~bid' v.t. (Bridge); ~bid n.; ~call n.; ~cap'italize v.t., fix or estimate capital of (company etc.) too high; ~care' n.; ~care'ful a.; ~care'fully adv.; ~cau'tious a.; ~cau'tiously adv.; ~charge' v.t., put too much explosive or electricity or the like into, put exaggerated details or too much detail into (description, picture, etc.), charge too high a price for (thing) or to (person), charge (specified sum) beyond right price; ~charge n., excessive charge (of explosive, or in money, see prec.); ~col'our v.t., exaggerate (details of descripton etc.); ~con'fident a.; ~con'fidently adv.; ~con'fidence n.; ~cred'ulous a.; ~cred'ulity n.; ~crop' v.t., exhaust (land) by continuous cropping; ~crowd' v.t.; ~cun'ning n., cunning that reaches itself; ~cur'ious a., too inquistive, too careful or precise or fastidious; ~cur'iously adv.; ~curios'ity n.; ~del'icacy n.; ~del'icate a.; ~devel'op v.t. (photog.); ~do' v.t., carry to excess, go too far in, cook too much (esp. in p.p.), overtax strength of (esp. in p.p.); ~dose n.; ~draft n., drawing of bank account, amount by which draft exceeds balance; ~draw' v.t. & i., draw cheque in excess of (one's account) or in excess of one's account, exaggerate in describing; ~dress' v.t. & i.; ~drive' v.t., drive (horse etc.), work (person), to exhaustion; ~eag'er a.; ~eag'erly adv.; ~eag'erness n.; ~eat' v.t.; ~eat'ing, ~earn'est a.; ~es'timate v.t., put value or amount of too high;

~estimate (-āt) n.; ~excite' v.t.; ~exer'tion n.; ~expose' v.t., ~expo'sure n., (photog.); ~fatigue' v.t., & n.; ~fish' v.t., fish (stream etc.) to depletion; ~fond' a.; ~go'vern v.t., subject to needless restrictions & regulations; ~go'vernment n.; ~growth' growth too great for health etc.; ~haste' n.; ~has'ty a.; ~has'tily adv.; ~heat' v.t.; ~housed' (-zd) a., living in too large a house; ~indulge' v.t. & i.; ~indul'gence n.; ~is'sue v.t., issue (notes, shares, etc.) beyond authorized amount or ability to pay; ~is'sue n., things or amount so issued; ~lad'en a.; ~large' a.; ~load' v.t., ~load n.; ~long' a.; ~ma'ny a.; ~mast'ed a., with too tall or heavy masts; ~meas'ure n., amount beyond the due or sufficient; ~mod'est a. ~much' a., n., & adv. (be not righteous ~much); ~nice' a., too fastidious; ~nice'ness, ~ni'cely, nn.; ~pay' v.t., recompense (person, service) too highly; ~peo'pled a., ~stocked with people; ~pitch' v.t., bowl (cricket ball) so that it pitches too near wicket; ~popu-lated a., too thickly populated; ~popu-la'tion n.; ~populated condition; ~pot' v.t., plant to too large a pot; ~praise' v.t., & n.; ~pre'ssure n., pressing or being pressed too hard, esp. ~work; ~print' v.t. (photog.), also, print additional matter on (an already printed surface, esp. of postage stamps); ~produce' v.i. & t., produce too much of (commodity, or usu. abs.) for the demand; ~produc'tion n.; ~pun'ish v.t.; ~rate' v.t., have too high an opinion of, assess too high for rating purposes; ~read' v.i. do too much reading; ~refine' v.t., make too subtle distinctions; ~ride' v.t., exhaust (horse) by riding; ~ripe a.; ~scrup'ulous a.; ~sell' v.t. & i., sell more of (commodity, stock, or abs.) than one can deliver; ~sen'sitive a.; ~sen'sitiveness n.; ~soli'citous a.; ~soli'citude n.; ~state' v.t., state too strongly, exaggerate; ~state'ment n.; ~stock' v.t.; ~stock n.; ~strain' v.t., damage by exertion, make too much of (scruples etc.; esp. in p.p.); ~strain n., ~straining or being ~strained; ~strung' a., (of person, his nerves, etc.) intensely strained or wound up; ~stud'y v.i., & n.; ~su'btle a.; ~supply' n.; ~swoll'en a.; ~tax' v.t., give or be too heavy a task to or for; ~tax' v.t., make excessive demand on (person's strength etc.), burden with excessive taxes; ~tire' v.t.; ~toil' n.; ~tone' v.t. (photog.); ~train' v.t. & i., subject to or undergo too much athletic training, with injury to condition; ~use' v.t., ~use n.; ~val'ue v.t.; ~ween'ing a., arrogant, presumptuous, conceited, self-confident; ~weight'ed a., unduly loaded with; ~wind' v.t., wind (watch etc.) beyond proper stopping-point; ~work' v.t. & i., (cause to) work too hard, weary or exhaust with work; ~work' n., excessive work; ~wrought' a., ~excited, suffering reaction from excitement, too elaborate; ~zeal' n.; ~zea'lous a.; ~zea'lously adv.

7. Prefixed to vb & enabling it to take *self* as obj. or be used in p.p. with sense *damage oneself by doing action to excess*; many of these compounds can also be used abs. in same sense. So ~drink', ~eat', ~feed' (also trans.), ~grow' (in p.p., *that has ~grown himself* etc.); ~jump' oneself, strain sinew etc. in jumping; ~preach', ~reach' oneself, strain oneself by reaching too far, (of horse) injure forefoot by striking it with hind-hoof; ~run', ~sleep' oneself, miss intended hour of rising by sleeping too long; ~smoke', ~spend' (oneself or abs.), spend money beyond one's means; ~toiled' p.p. ~walk', ~watched' p.p., exhausted by keeping awake; ~write' oneself, damage one's style by writing too much.

8. Prefixed to vb or deriv., or adj., with added sense of *more than*. So ~bal'ance v.t., outweigh lit. & fig.; ~balance n., (amount of) excess; ~due' a.; ~fill' v.t.; ~full' a.; ~match' v.t., be too strong etc. for, defeat; ~match n.; ~poise' v.t., outweigh; ~subscribe v.t., subscribe more than amount of (loan etc.; usu. in p.p.).

9. As prefix making trans. vb out of intr. vb, or vb not taking same obj., or n. usu. with sense of *exceeding*. So ~build', built too closely on (land); ~cast', cover (sky etc.) with clouds or darkness (usu. p.p.), stitch over (edge) to prevent unravelling, esp. with blanket or button-hole stitch; ~live', live beyond (income etc.) be too intense for, ~whelm; ~pow'ering a., irresistible; ~pow'eringly adv.; ~reach', circumvent, outwit, get the better of by cunning or artifice; ~rend', charge too high a rent for (land etc.) or to (farmer etc.); ~rule', set aside (decision, argument, proposed course) by superior authority, annul decision or reject proposal of (person); ~stay', stay beyond (one's welcome etc.); ~top', be or become higher than; ~trump', play higher trump than.

overact', v.t. & i., see OVER- 6; **overall** n., OVER- 2; **overarch** v.t. & i., OVER- 4; **overarm** a. & adv., OVER- 1; **overawe** v.t., OVER- 5; **overbalance** v.i. & t., & n., OVER- 4, 8; **overbear** v.t., **overbearing** a., OVER- 4; **overbid** v.t., & n., **overblow** v.t., OVER- 6; **overblown** a., OVER- 4, 6; **overboard** adv., OVER- 2; **overbrim** v.t. & i., OVER- 3; **overbuild** v.t., OVER- 9; **overburden** v.t., **overbusy** a., **overbuy** v.i., **overcall** v.t., & n., OVER- 6; over-

canopy v.t., OVER- 4; over-capitalize v.t., OVER- 6; overcare n., OVER- 9; OVER- 9; over-caution n., overcharge v.t., & n., OVER- 6; overcloud v.t., OVER- 4; overcloy v.t., OVER- 5; overcoat n., OVER- 1; over-colour v.t., OVER- 6; over-come v.t., OVER- 3; over-confidence n., over-credulity n., OVER- 6; overcrow v.t., OVER- 3; overcrowd v.t., OVER- 6; overcrust v.t., OVER- 4; overcunning a., overcurrent n., over-delicacy n., over-curious a., overdo v.t., OVER- 6; over-develop v.t., 2; overdose v.t., & n., overdraft n., overdraw v.t., & i., OVER- 6; overdress & i., OVER- 7, v.i. OVER- 6; overdrink v. refl. overdue a., OVER- 8; overeat v. refl. & i., OVER- 7; over-estimate v.t., OVER- 6; expose v.t., over-exposure n., OVER- 6; overfall n., over-fatigue v.t., & n. OVER- 6; overfault n., OVER- 1; overfeed v.t. & i., OVER- 7; overfill v.t., OVER- 8; overfilm v.t., OVER- 4; overfish v.t., OVER- 3; overflow v.t. & i., & n., overflowing n. & a., OVER- 3; overfold full a., OVER- 1; overfront n., OVER- 2; over-overhoused a., OVER- 8; overgild v.t., OVER- 4; over-govern v.t., over-government n., overground a., overground a., OVER- 2; overgrow v.t., OVER- 3, v. refl. & i. OVER- 7; overgrowth n., OVER- 3, 6; overhand adv. & a., OVER- 3, 6; overhang v.t. & i., & n., OVER- 3; overhaul v.t., & n., OVER- 4; overhead adv. & a., OVER- 2; overhear v.t., OVER- 4; overhouse a., OVER- 2; overhoused a., over-indulgence n., over-issue v.t., & n., OVER- 6; overjoyed a., OVER- 5; overjump v. refl., overknee a., OVER- 2; overlabour v.t., overladen a., OVER- 2; overland adv. & a., OVER- 3; overlap v.t. & i., & n., OVER- 4; 3; overlay v.t., & n., OVER- 4; overleaf adv., OVER- 4; overleap v.t., overlie v.t., OVER- 3; overlive v.t., OVER- 9; overload v.t., & n., OVER- 6; overlook v.t., OVER- 3; overlord, overlordship, overman, nn., OVER- 1; overmantel n., OVER- 2; over-many, overmasted, aa., OVER- 2; overmaster v.t., OVER- 5; over-match v.t., & n., OVER- 8; over-measure n., OVER- 3; over-much a., adv., & n., overnice a., over-niceness, over-nicety, nn., 6; overnight adv. & a., OVER- 2; over-pass v.t., OVER- 3; overpassed, -past, a., OVER- 6; overpay v.t., overpeopled a., OVER- 4; over-persuade v.t., OVER- 5; overpitch v.t., OVER- 6; overplus n., OVER- 1; overpoise v.t., OVER- 8; over-population n., overpot v.t., OVER- 6; overpower v.t., overpowering a., OVER- 9; overpraise v.t., & n., OVER- 6; over-preach v. refl. & i., OVER- 7; overpres-sure n., overprint v.t., over-produce v.t. & i., over-production n., OVER- 6; overproof a., OVER- 2; overrate v.t., OVER- 7; OVER- 6; overreach v. refl. & i., OVER- 7;

v.t., OVER- 9; over-read v.i., over-refine v.t., OVER- 6; over-rent v.t., OVER- 9; override v.t., OVER- 3, 6; overripe a., OVER- 6; overrule v.t., OVER- 9; overrun v.t., OVER- 3, 7; oversailing a. & adv. OVER- 3; oversea a. & adv., overseas a. & adv., OVER- 2; oversee v.t., overseer n., OVER- 3; oversell v.i. & v.t., OVER- 6; oversew v.t., OVER- 4; overshadow v.t., OVER- 4; overshoe n., OVER- 1; overshoot v.t., a., OVER- 2; oversight n., OVER- 3.

|| ōv'erslaugh (-aw), n. (mil.). Passing over of one's turn of duty in consideration of another duty that takes precedence of it. [f. Du. *overslag* (*overslaan* omit f. OVER, *slaan* strike)]

oversleep, v.t. refl. & i., see OVER- 7; over-sleeve n., OVER- 1; oversmoke v.t. & i., i., OVER- 7; oversoul n., OVER- 1; over-spend v. refl. & i., OVER- 7; overspill n., overspread v.t., OVER- 3, 4; overstate v.t., overstatement n., OVER- 6; overstay v.t., OVER- 3, 4; overstep v.t., overstock v.t. & n., overstrain v.t., & n., OVER- 6; overstrung a., OVER- 4, 6; overstudy v.i. & n., OVER- 8; over-subscribe v.t., OVER- 8; over-supply n., overswollen a., OVER- 6.

ōv'ert, a. Openly done, unconcealed, patent; market ~, open displaying of goods for sale to all comers. Hence ~ly² adv. [OF, p.p. of *ovrir*, now *ouvrir*, open, f. L *aperire*]

overtake v.t., see OVER- 4; overtask v.t., overtax v.t., OVER- 6; overthrow v.t., & n., OVER- 4; overthrust n., OVER- 1; overtime adv. OVER- 2, n. OVER- 1; overtire v.t., OVER- 6; overtoil v.t., OVER- 6; overtoiled a., OVER- 7; overtone v.t., OVER- 6; overtone n., OVER- 1; overtop v.t., & n., OVER- 6; overtrain v.t. & i., OVER- 6; v.t., OVER- 9; overtrump v.t., OVER- 9.

ōverture, n. Opening of negotiations with another, formal proposal or offer, (usu. pl., esp. make ~s to); (Mus.) orches-tral piece opening opera, oratorio, etc. (*concert* ~), one-movement composition in same style); beginning of poem etc. [OF (OVERT, -URE)]

overturn, v.t. & i., & n., see OVER- 4; over-use v.t., & n., overvalue v.t., OVER- 6; overwalk v. refl. & i., over-watched a., OVER- 7; overweening a., OVER- 6; overweight n. OVER- 1, adj. OVER- 2; overweighted a., OVER- 6; overwhelm v.t., overwhelming a., OVER- 4; overwind v.t., overwork v.t., & i., & n., OVER- 6; overwrite v. refl. & i., OVER- 7; overwrought a., OVER- 6.

ōvi-¹, ōvo-, comb. forms of OVUM; ovi-duct n., canal through which ova pass from ovary esp. in oviparous animals; ovi'form a., egg-shaped; ovip'arous a., producing young by means of eggs ex-pelled from body before being hatched (opp. VIVIPAROUS); ovipos'it (-z-) v.i., lay

egg(s), esp. with *ovipos'itor* n., pointed tubular organ with which female insect deposits eggs; *ovorhomboid'al* etc., between rhomboid etc. & oval; *ovol'ogy* n., science of the formation of animals' ova; *ovovivip'arous* a., producing young by eggs hatched within body.

ōvi-[2], comb. form of L *ovis* sheep; ~ *bō'vine* a. & n., (animal) having characters intermediate between sheep & ox, musk-ox; *ov'icide* n. (joc.), sheep-killing. Ovid'ian, a. (As) of Ovid or his poetry. [L *Ovidius* Ovid, -IAN]

ōv'ine, a. Of, like, sheep. [f. L *ovinus* (*ovis* sheep, -INE[1])]

ōv'oid, a. & n. 1. Solidly or superficially egg-shaped, oval with one end more pointed. 2. n. ~ body or surface. [OVUM, -OID]

ōv'olō, n. (pl. *-lī* pr. -lē). Convex moulding of quarter-circle or quarter-ellipse section, receding downwards. [It. (now *uovolo*), dim. of *uovo* egg f. L OVUM]

ōv'ūle, n. Rudimentary seed, female germ-cell, unfertilized ovum. Hence *ov'ular*[1] a. [F (foll., -ULE[1])]

ōv'um, n. (pl. *ova*). Female germ in animals, capable of developing into new individual when fertilized by male sperm, egg esp. of mammals, fish, or insects. [L, = egg]

owe (ō), v.t. & i. (*owing*). Be under obligation to (re)pay (person money, money to person) or render (person honour etc., gratitude etc. to person), be in debt (for thing, with creditor in dat.; *he ~s not any mam; I ~ you for your services, ~d for all my clothes*); ~ one a grudge, cherish resentment against him; be indebted for to person (or with dat.; *we ~ to Newton the principle of gravitation; I ~ him much*). [com.-Teut.; OE *āgan*, cf. OHG *eigan*, Da. *eie* own; earlier past tense, OUGHT[2], OE *āhte*]

Ow'enism (ō-), n. Communistic co-operation advocated by Robert Owen (d. 1858). [-ISM]

ow'ing (ōi-), pred. a. Yet to be paid, owed, due, (*paid all that was ~*); ~ *to*, attributable to, caused by, (*all this was ~ merely to ill luck*), (as prep.) on account of (~ *to the drought, crops are short*). [OWE, -ING[2]]

owl, n. Kinds of large-headed small-faced hook-beaked large-eyed soft-plumaged nocturnal bird of prey (esp. *Barn Owl, Tawny Owl, & Long-eared or Horned Owl*, each with other names, as *Church, Screech, Hooting*, etc., *Owl*; *fly with the ~, have nocturnal habits*; ~*s to Athens*, = COAL[1]*s to Newcastle*); solemn person, wise-looking dullard, whence ~'*ISH*[1] a., ~'*ISHLY*[2] adv.; (also ~ *pigeon*) fancy variety of pigeon; ~*light*, dusk, twilight. Hence ~'ERY[2] n. [com.-Teut.; OE *ūle*, cf. G *eule*; prob. imit., cf. L *ulula* owl, *ululare* HOWL[1]]

owl'et, n. Owl, young owl. [earlier HOWLET]

own[1] (ōn), a. 1. (Appended to possessive adj. or case) in full ownership, proper, peculiar, individual, & not another's, (*saw it with my ~ eyes; has a value all its ~; let them STEW*[2] *in their ~ juice; loves truth for its ~ sake; be one's ~ man*, independent, free; *God's ~ heaven; may I have it for my ~ or may very ~?; my ~ sweetheart* etc., or abs. *my ~*), esp. in voc. expressing affection; often also used to emphasize not the ownership, but the personality of the subject etc., as *cooks her ~ meals, every man his ~ lawyer, am my ~ master*; also used abs. = private property, kindred, etc., as *may I not do what I will with my ~?, the DEVIL's* ~ *; of one's ~*, belonging to one, as *I have nothing of my ~, will give you one of my ~; get one's ~ back*, colloq., get even with, revenge oneself (*on*); *hold one's ~*, maintain position, not be defeated; *on one's ~*, sl., independently, on one's ~ account or responsibility or resources). 2. (Without preceding possessive) ~ *brother, sister*, with both parents the same; ~ *cousin*, first. [OE *āgen, āgen*, p.p. of OWE (in obs. sense *possess*); cf. Du. & G *eigen*]

own[2] (ōn), v.t. & i. Have as property, possess, whence OW'NER[1], OW'NERSHIP(1), nn., OW'NERLESS a., (ōn-); acknowledge authorship, paternity, or possession, of (*child, pamphlet, hat, that nobody will ~*); admit as existent, valid, true, etc. (~*s his deficiencies, himself indebted, he or that he did not know*); confess to (~*s to a sense of shame, to having done*); ~ *up*, colloq., make frank confession; submit to (*person's sway* etc.) without protest; *the ~er* (Nav. sl.), captain of the ship. [OE *āgnian* (*āgen* OWN[1])]

ōx, n. (pl. *oxen*). 1. Any bovine animal, individual of kinds of large usu. horned cloven-footed ruminant quadruped used when domesticated for draught, for supplying milk, and for eating as meat, (esp. the *black ox has trod on one's foot*, misfortune or old age has come upon him); *ox-bird*, kinds of small bird, esp. the dunlin. 2. *Ox-eye*, large human eye, whence ŏx-eyed[2] (*-id*) a., kinds of plant esp. (*Yellow Ox-eye*) Corn Marigold, (*White Ox-eye*) Ox-eyed Daisy; *ox-fence* or ŏX'EN[1] n., strong cattle-fence of railing & hedge & occas. ditch; *ox-gall* (used for cleansing, & in painting & pharmacy); *ox'herd*, cowherd; *ox'hide; ox'lip*, primula rare in Britain, (pop.) hybrid of primrose & cowslip; *ox'tail*, tail of ox, much used for soup-making. [com.-Teut.; OE *oxa*, cf. Du. *os*, G *ochse*, also W *ych*, Skr. *ukshān* pl.]

ŏx-, comb. form (chem.)=OXY-, as *oxacet'ic* or *oxyacet'ic*, or=OXAL-, as *oxam'ic*.

ŏxal(o)-, comb. form of *oxalic acid*, whence ŏx'alATE[3](3) n.; *oxalo-nit'rate* etc.

ŏxăl'ic a. (chem.). Derived from wood-sorrel (~ *acid*, a highly poisonous & sour

acid found in wood-sorrel & other plants). [f. F *oxalique* (L f. Gk *oxalís* kinds of plant including wood-sorrel, -IC)]

Ox'ford (ŏ-), n. University town in England; || ~ *bags*, very wide trousers; ~ *blue* (dark with purple tinge); ~ *clay*, deposit of stiff blue clay underlying coral rag in midland counties; ~ *frame*, picture-frame of which sides cross each other at corners & project; ~ *Group* (*Movement*), see BUCHMANISM; ~ *man*, educated at ~ Univ.; ~ *mixture*, dark-grey cloth; ~ *movement*, for revival in Church of England & observance in Catholic doctrine c. 1833; ~ *shoes*, low shoes lacing over instep; ~ *shirting*, kind of shirt or dress material; ~ *Tracts*, the 'TRACT's for the Times'.

ŏx'ide, n. Compound of oxygen with another element or with organic radical. [F after *acide* acid (OX-+OXY'-IDE)]

ŏx'idize, v.t. & i. Cause to combine with oxygen; cover (metal) with coating of oxide, make rusty; take up or enter into combination with oxygen, rust; ~*ed silver*, (incorrect name for) silver with dark coat of silver sulphide. Hence ~ABLE a., ~A'TION, ~ER'(2), nn. [prec., -IZE]

Oxō'nian (ŏ-), a. & n. (Past or present member) of University of Oxford. [*Oxonia* latinized name of Oxen(ford), -AN]

ŏxy-, comb. form of Gk *oxus* sharp: (1) in gen. senses, as ~*oxy'tos*, abnormal acidity; OXYGEN; OXYMORON; OXYTONE: (2) in chem. was as comb. form of oxygen, denoting presence or admixture of oxygen; ~*acet'ylene*, consisting of, involving use of, a mixture of oxygen & acetylene (~*acetylene blowpipe*, for producing intensely hot flame for welding etc.); ~*house-gas*, ~*-par'affin*, etc., used attrib. of flame produced by mixing the vapour of the gas etc. with oxygen; ~*calcium light*, limelight; ~*-hyd'rogen blowpipe, flame, light*, etc.; ~*a'cid* (& see b.); *oxy'gsalt*, containing oxygen:(b)loosely used for *hydroxy-*, denoting compound of organic substance having atom of hydroxyl substituted for one of hydrogen, as ~*ac'id* (& see a.).

ŏx'ygen, n. Colourless tasteless scentless gas, one of the non-metallic elements, existing in air & combined in water & most minerals & organic substances, & being essential to animal & vegetable life. Hence **ŏxy'genous** a. [f. F *oxygène* acidifying principle, see OXY-(1), -GEN; it was at first held to be the essential principle in formation of acids]

ŏx'ygenate (or ŏksǐ-), v.t. Supply, treat, or mix, with oxygen, oxidize; charge (blood) with oxygen by respiration. Hence ~A'TION, nn. [f. F *oxygener* (prec.), -ATE²]

ŏx'ygenize (or ŏksǐ-), v.t. = prec. [-IZE]

ŏx'ymel, n. Syrup of honey & vinegar. [L f. Gk *oxumeli* (OXY-, *meli* honey)]

ŏxymŏr'on, n. (rhet.). Figure of speech with pointed conjunction of seeming contradictories (e.g. *faith unfaithful kept him falsely true*). [Gk (~mó-) f. OXY-(1), *mōros* foolish]

ŏx'ytone, a. & n. (Gk gram.). (Word) with acute accent on last syllable. [f. Gk *oxutonos* f. OXY-(1), *tonos* TONE]

oy'er, n. Criminal trial under the writ of ~ & *terminer* or commission to judges on circuit to hold courts. [f. AF *oyer ed terminer* (L *audīre* hear, *termināre*, determine), -ER¹]

oyez, oyes, o yes (ōyěs'), int. uttered, usu. thrice, by public crier or court officer to bespeak silence & attention. [OF (-e), imperat. of *oïr* hear = L *audītis* (*audīre* hear]

oys'ter, n. Kinds of edible bivalve mollusc usu. eaten alive; ~-shaped morsel of meat in fowl's back; ~*-bank, -bed*, part of sea-bottom where ~s breed or are bred; ~*-bar*, counter in restaurant etc. where ~s are served; ~*-catcher*, wading seabird; ~*-farm*, sea bottom used for breeding ~s; ~*-knife*, of shape adapted for opening ~s; ~*-patty*, piece of pastry containing cooked ~s. [f. OF *oistre* f. L *ostrea* f. Gk *ostreon*]

ŏzŏ cerite, ŏzŏk'erit, n. Wax-like fossil resin used for candles, insulating, etc. [G (~kerît), irreg. f. Gk *ozō* smell, *kēros* wax]

ōzō'ne, n. Condensed form of oxygen with three atoms to molecule having pungent refreshing odour, (fig.) exhilarating influence. Hence **ŏzŏn'IC**, ~IFEROUS, aa., ~IZE(3, 5) v.t., ~IZER'(2), ~ON'ETER, nn. [f. Gk *ozō* smell, -ONE]

P

P, p, (pē), letter (pl, Ps, P's), *Mind one's P's & Q's*, be careful of propriety.

pa (pah), n. (colloq.). = PAPA. [abbr.]

pab'ulum, n. Food (often fig., as *mental* ~). [L (*pascere* feed)]

pac'a, n. Genus of large rodents in Central & South America. [native]

pace', n. Single step in walking or running; space traversed in this (about 30 in.); space between successive stationary positions of same foot in walking (about 60 in.); mode of walking or running gait; any of various gaits of (esp. trained) horse, mule, etc.; ~AMBLE; *put person through his* ~s, test his qualities in action etc.; speed in walking or running; rate of progression (often fig.); *keep* ~, advance at equal rate *with*; *go the* ~, go at great speed, (fig.) indulge in dissipation; ~*-maker, rider, runner*, etc., who sets ~ for another in race etc.; ~*-stick*, drill-sergeant's adjustable two-legged appliance for measuring length of ~.

Hence **-pācĕd²** (-st) a. [ME, f. OF *past.* L
passus (*pandere* pass- stretch)]
pace², v.i. & t. Walk with slow or regular
pace; traverse thus; measure (distance)
by pacing; (of horse) amble; set pace for
(rider, runner, etc.). [f. prec.]
pā'cĕ³, prep. ~ *tū'ā,* ~ *Smith,* (in announcing contrary opinion) with all deference
to you, to Smith. [L, abl. of PAX]
pā'cer, n. In vbl senses, esp. horse that
paces. [-ER¹]
pacha etc. See PASHA etc.
pachi'sī (-chē³), n. Four-handed Indian
game with cowries for dice. [Hind.,=of
25]
pach'ydĕrm (-k-), n. Thick-skinned
quadruped, esp. one of Cuvier's (now
discarded) group *Pachydermata* (hoofed
quadrupeds that do not chew cud, e.g.
elephant, horse, etc.); (fig.) thick-skinned
person. So **pachydĕrm'atous** (-k-) a. [f.
F *pachyderme* f. Gk *pakhudermos* (*pakhus*
thick +*derma -matos* skin)]
pacifi'c, a. & n. Tending to peace; of
peaceful disposition; the P~ (Ocean), that
between America & Asia. Hence **pacifi'-
cally** adv. [f. L *pacificus* (*pax pacis*
peace, see -FIC)]
pacifica'tion, n. Pacifying; treaty of
peace. So **pacifi'cātŏry** a. [F, f, L *paci-
ficātiōnem* (as PACIFY, see -FICATION)]
pacifi'cism, pā'cifism, n. The doctrine
that the abolition of war is both desirable
& possible. Hence **pacifi'cisr, pā'cifisr**,
n. [PACIFIC, -ISM; the -*fism*, -*fist* forms are
barbarous but usual]
pā'cifȳ, v.t. Appease (person, anger, excitement, etc.); reduce (country etc.) to
state of peace. [f. F *pacifier* f. L *pacificare* (as PACIFIC, see -FY)]
pack¹, n. 1. Bundle of things wrapped up
or tied together for carrying, parcel, esp.
pedlar's bundle or soldier's knapsack.
2. A measure of various goods. 3. Lot,
set, (~ *of fools, lies, nonsense,* etc.). 4.
Number of hounds kept together for
hunting, or of beasts (esp. wolves) or
birds (esp. grouse) naturally associating;
organized group of U-boats. 5. (Rugby
footb.) a side's forwards. 6. Set of playing-cards. 7. Large area of large pieces
of floating ice in polar sea. 8. Quantity
of fish, fruit, etc., packed in a season etc.;
(Commerce.) method of packing for the
market. 9. ~*drill*, military punishment
of walking up and down in full *marching*
ORDER(2); ~*-horse* (for carrying ~s);
~*man*, pedlar; ~*-saddle* (adapted for
supporting ~s); ~*-thread*, stout thread for
sewing or tying up ~s. [ME *packe*, cf.
Du. *pak*, G *pack*]
pack², v.t. & i. 1. Put (things) together
into bundle, box, bag, etc., for transport
or storing (often ~ *up*, esp. abs.); (of
things) admit of being ~ed *well, easily,*
etc. 2. Prepare & put up (meat, fruit,
etc.) in this etc. for preservation. 3. Put

closely together; (Naut.) ~ (put) *on a
sail*; form (hounds) into pack; place
(cards) together in pack; (intr.) crowd
together, (of animals) form into pack.
4. Cover (thing) with something pressed
tightly round; (Med.) wrap (body etc.) in
wet cloth. 5. (Boxing sl.) be capable of
delivering (a punch) with skill or force.
6. Fill (bag, box, etc.) with clothes etc.;
cram (space etc. *with*); load (beast) with
pack. 7. Depart with one's belongings;
send (person) ~*ing*, dismiss him summarily; ~ (person) *off*, send him away.
8. [prob. diff. wd]. Select (jury etc.) so
as to secure partial decision. 9. ~ *up* (sl.),
(of an engine) peter out, go out of action.
[f. prec.]
pack'age, n. & v.t. 1. Bundle of things
packed, parcel; box etc. in which goods
are packed. 2. v.t. Make up into, enclose
in, a ~. [-AGE]
pack'er, n. In vbl senses, esp.: one who
packs meat, fruit, etc., for market; machine for packing. [-ER¹]
pack'ĕt, n. Small package; ||(sl.) con-
siderable sum won or lost in betting,
speculation, etc.; || *catch, stop, a ~* (sl.),
be (severely) wounded by bullet etc.;
~(-*boat*), mail-boat. [PACK¹+-ET¹]
pack'ing, n. In vbl senses; also (of-
absorbing) material closing a joint or
assisting in lubrication of a JOURNAL; ~
box, = STUFFING-*box*; ~-*needle*, large
needle for sewing up packages; ~-*sheet*,
(1) sheet for packing goods in, (2) wet
sheet used in hydropathy. [-ING¹]
pact, n. Compact; P~ of LOCARNO, PEACE
P~. [OF, f. L *pactum*, neut. p.p. of
paciscere agree]
pad¹, n. 1. (sl.), Road, esp. *gentleman,
knight, squire, of the ~*, highwayman.
2. (Also ~-*nag*) easy-paced horse. [Du.,
cogn. w. PATH]
pad², v.t. & i. (-dd-). Tramp along (road
etc.) on foot; travel on foot; ~ *it*, ~ *the
hoof*, (sl.), go on foot. [cogn. w. prec.]
pad³, n. 1. Soft stuffed saddle without
tree; part of double harness to which
girths are attached. 2. Cushion, stuffing,
used to diminish jarring, fill out hollows,
etc.; guard for parts of body in cricket
etc. 3. Number of sheets of blotting-,
writing-, or drawing-paper fastened together at edge. 4. Fleshy cushion forming
sole of foot in some quadrupeds; paw of
fox, hare, etc. 5. Socket of brace, tool-
handle. [?]
pad⁴, v.t. (-dd-). Furnish with a pad,
stuff; fill out (sentence etc.) with superfluous words; ~*ded cell*, room in lunatic asylum with ~*ded walls*. Hence
~d'ING⁴(4) n. [f. prec.]
pad⁵, n. Open pannier used as measure of
fruit etc. [?]
pad'dle¹, n. Small spade-like implement
with long handle; short broad-bladed oar
used without rowlock; *double* ~ (with

blade at each end); one of the boards fitted round circumference of ~-wheel; ~-shaped instrument; (Zool.) fin or flipper; ~-wheel, wheel for propelling ship, with boards round circumference so as to press backward against water; ~-door, casing over upper part of this. [?]

pad'dle², v.i. & t. & n. 1. Move on water, propel canoe, by means of paddles; ~ one's own canoe, (fig.) depend on oneself alone; row gently. 2. n. Action, spell, of paddling. [f. prec.]

pad'dle³, v.i. Dabble with the feet in shallow water; toy with the fingers (in, on, about, thing); (of child) toddle. [?]

pad'dock¹, n. Small field, esp. one for stud farm; turf enclosure near racecourse, where horses are assembled before race. [prob. var. of parrock, OE pearroc, cf. G pferch fold, Du. perk pen, PARK]

pad'dock², n. (arch., dial.), Frog or toad. [f. OE pade, cf. Du. pad, toad + -OCK]

Pad'dy¹, n. (Nickname for) Irishman. [pet-form of Padraig, Patrick]

pad'dy², n. Rice in the straw or in the husk. [f. Malay padi]

||**pad'dy³**, **pad'dywhack**, nn. (colloq.). A rage, fit of temper. [PADDY¹; -whack unexpl.]

pa'dishah, **pa'dshah**, (pah-), n. Title in Persia of shah, in Europe formerly of Sultan of Turkey, in India, of British sovereign. [Pers. (padi master + shah)]

pad'lock, n., & v.t. 1. Detachable lock hanging by pivoted hoop on object fastened. 2. v.t. Secure with this. [ped, etym. dub.; +LOCK²]

padouk (pădowk'), n. Burmese timber-tree; its wood, resembling rosewood. [native name]

padre (pähd'rā), n. (colloq.). Chaplain. [Port. etc., = father, priest]

padrone (pahdrō'nā), n. Master of Mediterranean trading-vessel; Italian employer of street musicians; begging-children, etc.; proprietor of Italian inn. [It.]

pad'uasoy, n. Strong corded silk fabric much worn in 18th c. (cf. POULT-DE-SOIE). [corrupt. f. F pou-de-soie, etym. dub., by assoc. with Padua]

pae'an, n. Chant of thanksgiving for deliverance (orig.) addressed to Apollo or Artemis; song of praise or triumph. [L, f. Gk paian hymn to Apollo under name of Paian]

paed-, **paedo-**, in comb. = Gk pais paidos child, as ~bāp'tist, adherent of this. [Gk]

paed'erïasty, **pēd'-**, n. Sodomy. So ~äst n., sodomite. [f. Gk paiderastia (pais paidos boy + erastēs lover)]

pae'on, n. Metrical foot of one long syllable placed first, second, third, or fourth (first, etc. ~) & three short. Hence paeon'ic a. [L, f. Gk paiōn, Attic form of paiān PAEAN]

pāg'an, n. & a. Heathen; unenlightened (person). Hence ~ISM(2), n., ~ISH¹ a., ~IZE(3) v.t. & i. [f. L paganus (pagus country district, the ~)]

pāge¹, n. & v.t. 1. Boy, usu. in livery, employed to attend to door, go on errands, etc.; ||~ of honour, one of various officers of royal household, boy employed as personal attendant of person of rank; boy in training for knighthood & attached to knight's service. (hist.); hence ~HOOD, ~SHIP, nn. 2. v.t. *Summon by means of a ~ (who calls out the name of person wanted until found). [OF, etym. dub., cf. It. paggio]

pāge², n. One side of leaf of book etc.; (fig.) episode fit to fill a ~ in history etc. [F, f. L pagina (pangere fasten)]

pāge³, v.t. Put consecutive numbers on pages of (book etc.). [f. prec.]

pā'geant (-jnt; also pă-), n. Brilliant spectacle, esp. procession, arranged for effect; spectacular procession, or play performed in the open, illustrating the history of a place; tableau, allegorical device, etc., on fixed stage or moving car; (fig.) empty or specious show. [etym. dub., perh. f. pagina PAGE²]

pā'geantry (-jn-), n. Splendid display; empty show. [prec.+-RY]

||**Pă'gĕt, M.P.**, n. Traveller who expects to know all there is to know of a country in a few months. [character in Kipling's the ~-tree, make rapid fortune in India.]

pā'gin|al, a. Of pages; page for page. So ~ARY¹ a., [f. LL paginalis (PAGE²; -AN)]

pā'gin|āte, v.t. Page (book etc.). Hence ~A'TION n. [f. L pagina PAGE²+-ATE³]

pagō'd|a, n. 1. Sacred building, esp. tower usu. of pyramidal form, in India, China, etc.; ornamental imitation of this. 2. Gold coin once current in S. India; ~tree, fabled to produce ~s (coin), esp. shake the ~-tree, make rapid fortune in India. [f. Port. pagode of Ind. orig.]

pagū'r|ian, a. & n. (Of) the hermit-crab. [f. L f. Gk pagouros, kind of crab.+-IAN]

pah¹, int. expr. disgust. [natural]

pah², n. Native fort in New Zealand. [f. Maori pā (pā vb, block up)]

paid. See PAY².

pail, n. Vessel, usu. round, of wood or metal for carrying liquids etc.; amount contained in this, as ~ful a ~ of milk. Hence ~FUL n. [OE has pægel gill; OF paelle frying-pan, bath, etc., f. L patella dim. of patina dish]

paillasse, **palliasse** (pălyăs' or păl'yăs), n. Straw mattress. [F (paille), f. paille straw f. L palea]

paillette (pălyĕt'), n. Piece of bright metal used in enamel painting; spangle. [F (dim. as prec.)]

pain, n. Suffering, distress, of body or mind, whence ~FUL, ~LESS, aa., ~FULLY² adv., ~FULNESS², ~LESSNESS², nn.; (pl.) throes of childbirth; (pl.) trouble

taken, esp. *take* ~s, *be at the* ~*s of* (*doing*), *get* (a thrashing etc.) *for* one's ~s ; punishment, now only in ~*s & penalties*, *on* or *under* ~ *of* (death or other punishment to be incurred); ~-*killer*, medicine for alleviating ~ ; ~-*s'taking*, careful, industrious. [f. OF *peine* f. L *poena* penalty]

pain[2], v.t. & i. Inflict pain upon; give rise to pain, ache (*my arm is* ~*ing*). [f. OF *pener* f. med. L *poenare* (as prec.)]

paint[1], n. Solid colouring-matter, suspended in liquid vehicle so as to impart colour to a surface; LUMINOUS ~ ; colouring-matter for face etc, rouge etc. [f. foll.]

paint[2], v.t. Portray, represent, (object, or ~ing) in colours; adorn (wall etc.) with ~ing; (fig.) represent (incident etc.) in words vividly as by ~ing; *not so black as he is* ~*ed* (represented); cover surface of (object) with paint; apply paint of specified colour to, as ~ *the door green*; (sl.) ~ *the town red*, cause commotion by riotous spree etc. ; apply rouge to (face, often abs.); ~ *out*, efface with paint; *P*~*ed Lady*, butterfly of orange-red colour with black & white spots. Hence ~ING[1] (1, 2) n. [f. OF *peindre* f. L *pingere pict*-]

paint'er[1], n. One who paints pictures; workman who colours woodwork etc. with paint; ~*'s colic*, form of colic to which ~s who work with lead are liable. So **paint'RESS**[1] n. [f. AF *peintour* f. com.-Rom. *pinctorem* = L *pictorem* (as prec., see -OR[2])]

paint'er[2], n. Rope attached to bow of boat for making it fast to ship, stake, etc. ; *cut the* ~, (fig., usu. of colony) effect a separation. [?]

paint'y, a. Of paint ; (of picture) overcharged with paint. [-Y[2]]

pair[1], n. Set of two, couple, (esp. of things that usu. exist or are used in couples, as gloves, shoes, sculls, heels, eyes); ~ *royal*, set of three cards of same denomination or of three dice turning up same number; article consisting of two corresponding parts not used separately, as ~ *of scissors*, *tongs*, *trousers*; engaged or married couple; mated couple of animals; ~ (*of horses*), two horses harnessed together; (Parl.) two voters on opposite sides absenting themselves from division by mutual agreement, person willing to act thus (*cannot find a* ~); the other member of a ~ (*where 'is the* ~ *to this sock?*); ~ (*flight*) *of stairs*, *of steps* (one, two, three, ~ *front* or *back*, room on the first etc. floor or its occupant); *another* ~ *of* SHOES; ~*horse* a., for a ~ of horses ; ~*oar*, boat rowed by ~ of oars. [f. F *faire* f. L *paria* neut. pl. of *par* equal]

pair[2], v.t. & i. Arrange (persons, things), be arranged, in couples; unite (t. & i.) in love or marriage; (of animals) mate; unite (*with one of opposite sex*); ~ *off*,

put two by two, (intr.) go off in pairs, (Parl.) make a pair, (colloq.) marry (*with*). [f. prec.]

pajamas. See PYJAMAS.

Pakistan' (pah-, -ahn), n. **1.** Idea of Muslim autonomy: proposed separate Muslim State. **2.** Since 1947 an independent State in Asia: since 1956 an independent Republic.

pal, n., & v.i. (sl. ; -ll-). **1.** Comrade, mate. **2.** v.i. (Usu. ~ *up*) associate (*with*). [E Gipsy]

pal'ace, n. Official residence of sovereign, archbishop, or bishop; stately mansion; spacious building for entertainment, refreshment, etc. ; || GIN[2] ~ ; || ~ *car*, luxurious railway-carriage. [f. OF *palais* f. L *Palatium*, hill in Rome, house of Augustus built on this]

pal'adin, n. Any of the Twelve Peers of Charlemagne's court, of whom the Count Palatine was the chief; knight errant. [F, as PALATINE[1]]

palaeo-, **palaeio-** (before vowel *palae*-) = Gk *palaios* ancient (cf. NEO-), as: ~*oarc'tic*, of northern part of Old World; ~*ocrys'tic*, of ancient ice, frozen from remote ages; ~*og'raphy*, study of ancient writing & inscriptions, so ~*og'rapher*, ~*ograph'ic*; ~*olith'ic*, marked by use of primitive stone implements; ~*ontol'ogy*, study of extinct organized beings, so ~*ontolo'gical*, ~*ontol'ogist*; *pāl'aeothere*, extinct genus of tapir-like mammal; ~*ozo'ic*, of, containing, ancient forms of life, of the first geological period (cf. CAINOZOIC, MESO-zoic).

palaes'tra, **palēs-**, n. Wrestling-school, gymnasium. [L, f. Gk *palaistra* (*palaiō* wrestle)]

pal'affite, n. Prehistoric hut on piles over lake in Switzerland or N. Italy. [F, f. It. *palafitta* pile-fence (*palo* stake + *fitto* fixed)]

palanquin', **-nkeen'**, (-kēn), n. Covered litter for one, in India & the East, carried usu. by four or six men; (loosely) closed carriage in the East. [f. Port. *palanquin*, cf. Malay *palangki*, Hind. *palki*]

pal'atable, a. Pleasant to the taste; (fig.) agreeable to the mind. Hence ~LY[2] adv. [f. PALATE + -ABLE]

pal'atal, a. & n. Of the palate; (sound) made by placing tongue against (usu. hard) palate, whence ~IZE(3) v.t. [F (foll., -AL)]

pal'ate, n. **1.** Roof of the mouth in vertebrates; *bony* or *hard*, *soft*, ~, its front, back part; *cleft* ~ (see CLEAVE[1]). **2.** Sense of taste; mental taste, liking. [f. L *palatum*]

pal'atial (-shl), a. Like a palace; splendid. [f. L as PALACE + -AL]

pal'atinate, n. **1.** Territory under a count palatine; *the* (*Rhine*) *P*~, State of old

German Empire, under rule of the Count Palatine of the Rhine. 2. ||(In Durham Univ.) light shade of purple or lavender, blazer of this colour as sports distinction. [f. foll. +-ATE¹]

pā'latine¹, a. & n. 1. (Count) P~, count having within the territory jurisdiction such as elsewhere belongs only to sovereign (in Eng. Hist. also Earl P~); County P~, his territory (still in England of Lancashire and Cheshire). 2. n. Woman's fur tippet. [f. (n. pl.) palatinus, a. & n. Of the palace, whence also ~ bones) two bones forming hard palate. [F (-in, -ine), as PALATE, see -INE¹]

pā'latine², a. & n. Of the palate, see -INE¹]

pa'latogram, n. Record of the use made of the palate in producing a sound. [f. L palatum palate +-GRAM]

palā'ver (-lah-), n., & v.i. & t. 1. Conference, (prolonged) discussion, esp. between African or other natives and traders etc.; profuse or idle talk; cajolery; (sl.) affair, business. 2. vb. Talk profusely; flatter, wheedle. [f. Port. palavra word f. L as PARABLE]

pale¹, n. Pointed piece of wood for fence etc., stake; boundary, esp. (fig.) within, beyond, etc., the ~; (Hist.) the (English P~, part of Ireland under English rule; (Her.) vertical stripe in middle of shield. [f. OF pal f. L palus]

pale², a. (Of person or complexion) whitish or ashen appearance; (of colours) faint; faintly coloured; of faint lustre, dim.; ~-face, supposed N.-Amer. Ind. name for white man. Hence ~LY² adv., ~NESS n. [f. OF pale f. L pallidus]

pale³, v.i. & t. Grow pale; (fig.) become pale in comparison (usu. before or beside); make pale. [f. OF palir (as prec.)]

paled (-ld), a. Having palings. [PALE¹, -ED²]

pālæ'stra. See PALAESTRA.

pā'letot (-ētō), n. Loose cloak for man or woman. [F, etym. dub.]

pā'lette, n. Artist's flat tablet for mixing colours on; colours used by particular artist or on particular occasion; ~-knife, thin steel blade with handle for mixing colours. [F, dim. of pale shovel f. L pala]

pā'lfrey (paw-), n. (arch., poet.) Saddle-horse for ordinary riding, esp. for ladies. [f. OF palefrei f. LL palafredus, paraveredus (Gk para beside, extra, +veredus light horse, whence G pferd)]

Pa'li (pah-), n. Language used in canonical books of Buddhists. [for palibhasa (pali canon +bhasa language)]

pā'likar (pǎl-), n. Member of band of Greek or Albanian military chief, esp. during War of Independence. [f. mod. Gk palikari lad (Gk pallax -akos youth)]

pā'limpsest, n. & a. Writing-material, manuscript, the original writing on which has been effaced to make room for a second; (adj.) so treated. [f. L Gk palimpsestos (palin again + psao rub smooth)]

pā'lindrome, n. & a. (Word, verse, etc.) that reads the same backwards as forwards (e.g. madam). Hence pālindrōm'ic a. [f. Gk palindromos running back again (palin again + drom- run)]

pā'ling, n. (Fence of) pales. [PALE¹, -ING¹]

pālingĕn'ĕsis (-nj-), n. Regeneration (lit. & fig.); revival; (Biol.) exact reproduction of ancestral character, whence ~gĕnĕt'ĭc a. [f. Gk palin again + GENESIS]

pā'linōde, n. Poem in which author retracts thing said in former poem; recantation. [f. L f. Gk palinōidia (palin again + ōidē song)]

pālisade', n., & v.t. 1. Fence of pales or of iron railings; (Mil.) strong wooden stake. 2. v.t. Furnish, enclose, with ~. [f. F palissade (palisser enclose with pales, as PALE¹, see -ADE¹)]

pā'lish, a. Somewhat pale. [-ISH¹]

pall¹ (pawl), n. Cloth, usu. of black or purple or white velvet, spread over coffin, hearse, or tomb; woollen vestment worn by Pope & some metropolitans or archbishops; (fig.) mantle, cloak; ~bearer, person holding up corner of ~ at funeral. [OE pæll f. L pallium cloak]

pall² (pawl), v.i. & t. Become insipid (now only fig.), esp. ~ on (person, mind, taste); satiate, cloy. [prob. aphetic f. APPAL]

Palla'dian, a. (archit.). In the pseudoclassical style of the 16th-c. Italian Palladio. [-AN]

palla'dium¹, n. (pl. -ia). Image of Pallas on which safety of Troy was held to depend; safeguard. [L, f. Gk palladion]

palla'dium², n. Rare hard white metallic element of platinum group. [f. Pallas, an asteroid +-IUM]

pallet¹ (-ēt), n. Straw bed; mattress. [ME & dial. f. paillet (paille straw f. L palea)]

pallet² n. Flat wooden blade with handle, used by potters etc.; artist's PALETTE; projection on a part of a machine, serving to change mode or motion of wheel; valve under each pipe in wind-chest of organ. [f. PALETTE]

palliasse. See PAILLASSE.

pā'lliāte, v.t. Alleviate (disease) without curing; extenuate, excuse. So ~A'TION n. [f. L palliare cloak (PALLIUM), see -ATE³]

palliative, a. & n. (Thing) that serves to palliate. [F (-if, -ive), as prec., see -IVE]

pā'llid, a. Pale. Hence ~LY² adv., ~NESS n. [f. L as PALE¹]

pā'llium, n. Man's large rectangular cloak, esp. among the Greeks; archbishop's PALL¹; integumental fold of mollusc, whence ~A1 a. [L]

pall-mall (pĕl'mĕl'), n. Game in which ball was driven through iron ring suspended in long alley; (Pall-Mall, street

in London developed from such an alley, & noted for clubs. [f. obs. F pallemaille f. It. pallamaglio (palla ball+maglio mallet f. L malleus)]

pâll'or, n. Paleness. [L (pallēre be pale, see -OR²)]

pâll'ý, a. (colloq.). Friendly. [PAL, -Y²]

palm¹ (pahm), n. Large family of trees, chiefly tropical, usu. with upright un-branched stem & head of large pinnate or fan-shaped leaves; branch of ~tree as symbol of victory; supreme excellence, prize for this, esp. *bear*, *yield*, *the ~*; branch of various trees substituted for ~ in northern countries, esp. in celebrating *P~ Sunday*; *~oil* (got from various ~s; also, with pun on palm², bribe-money); *P~ Sunday*, Sunday before Easter, on which Christ's entry into Jerusalem is celebrated by processions, in which branches of ~ are carried. Hence **pâlm·ā'ceous** (-āshus) a. [OE, f. L *palma*]

palm² (pahm), n. Part of hand between wrist & fingers, esp. its inner surface; breadth of glove that covers this; breadth (about 4 in.), length (about 8 in.), of hand as measure; *grease person's ~*, bribe him; *sailmaker's ~*, lead boss mounted in leather straps fastened round ~, used as thimble. Hence (-)~ED² (pahmd) a., ~FUL n. [ME & F *paume* f. L *palma*]

palm³ (pahm), v.t. Impose fraudulently, pass off (thing on person); conceal (cards, dice, etc.) in hand; touch with palm~. bribe. [prec.]

Pâl'ma Chris'tī (k-), n. Castor-oil plant. [med. L, = palm of Christ, from handlike shape of leaves]

pâl'mar, a. Of, in, the palm of the hand. [f. L *palmāris* (as PALM², see -AR¹)]

pâl'mary, a. Bearing the palm, pre-eminent. [f. L *palmārius* (as PALM¹, see -ARY¹)]

pâl'mate, -āted, aa, PALM²-shaped. [f. L *palmātus* (as PALM¹, see -ATE²)]

pa'lmer (pahm-), n. **1.** Pilgrim returning from Holy Land with palm branch or leaf; itinerant monk under vow of poverty. **2.** (Also ~worm) destructive hairy caterpillar. **3.** Hairy artificial fly. [AF (as PALMARY)]

palmett'ō, n. (pl. ~s). Kinds of small palm, esp. dwarf fan-palm. [f. Sp. *palmito* dim. of *palma* PALM¹, refash. on It. wds in -etto]

pâl'mipěd, -pēde, a. & n. Web-footed (bird). [f. L *palmipēs -pedis* (as PALM²+*pes pedis* foot)]

pa'lmistrý (pahm-), n. Divination from palm of hand. So **pa'lmist**(3) (pahm-) n. [ME (PALM²+-istry, -istry, unexpl.)]

pa'lmý (pahm-), a. Of, like, abounding in, palms; triumphant, flourishing, esp. *days, ~*. [PALM¹+-Y²]

pâlmyr'a, n. Kind of palm grown in India & Ceylon, with fan-shaped leaves used for matting etc. [f. Port. *palmeira*

organ in insects etc., feeler. Hence **pâl'PAL** a. [L (-pus)]

pâl'pable, a. That can be touched or felt; readily perceived by senses or mind. Hence ~ABIL'ITY n., ~ABLY² adv. [f. LL *palpabilis* (as foll., see -BLE)]

pâl'pāte, v.t. Handle, esp. in medical examination. So ~A'TION n. [f. L *palpāre*, -ATE³]

pâl'pēbral, a. Of the eyelids. [f. L *palpebralis* (*palpebra* eyelid, see -AL)]

pâl'pitāte, v.i. Pulsate, throb; tremble (with fear, pleasure, etc.). [f. L *palpitāre* frequent. as PALPATE, see -ATE³]

pâlpitā'tion, n. Throbbing; increased activity of heart due to exertion, agitation, or disease. [f. L *palpitātio* (as prec., see -ATION)]

pa'lsgrāve (pawl-), n. Count palatine. [f. Du. *paltsgrave*=G *pfalzgraf* (*pfalenza* palace+*grāvo* count)]

pa'lstāve (pawl-), n. Celt of bronze etc. shaped to fit into split handle. [f. Da. *paalstav* f. Icel. *pálstafr* (*páll* hoe)]

palsy (pawl'zi), n. & v.t. **1.** Paralysis; (fig.) cause, condition, of utter helplessness. **2.** v.t. Paralyse (usu. fig.). [ME, f. OF *paralisie* as PARALYSIS]

pa'lter (pawl-), v.i. Shuffle, equivocate, (with person) haggle (with person about thing); trifle (with subject). [?]

pa'ltrÿ (pawl-), a. Worthless, petty, contemptible. Hence ~INESS n. [perh. attrib. use of dial. *paltry* rubbish (Fris., MDu., & E dial. *palt* rubbish +-RY²)]

palūd'al (or pālū), a. Of a marsh; malarial. [f. L *palūs -ūdis* marsh +-AL]

pâl'ÿ, a. (poet.). Somewhat pale. [-Y²]

pam, n. Knave of clubs, esp. in five-card loo. [Sc. has *Pamphie*, F *Pamphile*, prob. f. Gk name *Pamphilos*]

pâm'pa, n. (usu. pl., pr. -az, -as). Large treeless plain in S. America south of the Amazon; *~-grass*, gigantic grass introduced into Europe from S. America. [Sp., f. Peruv. *bamba* steppe, flat]

pâm'per, v.t. Over-indulge (person, tastes, etc.); *~ed menial*, flunkey. [prob. frequent. of obs. *pamp* cram, cf. G *pampen*; see -ER⁵]

pâmper'o (-âr'ō), n. (pl. ~s). Cold wind blowing from Andes to Atlantic. [Sp. as PAMPA]

pâmph'let, n. Small usu. unbound treatise, esp. on subject of current interest. [prob. f. *Pamphilet*, familiar name of 12th-c. Latin amatory poem *Pamphilus seu de Amore*, see -ET¹]

pâmphlèteer', n. & v.i. Writer of pamphlets. [-EER]

pân¹, n. Metal or earthenware vessel, usu. shallow, for domestic purposes; STEW, WARM²*ing, ~*; *~like* vessel in which substances are heated etc.; part of lock that held the priming in obsolete types of gun; hollow in ground, as SALT~; (also

hard(-~) hard substratum of soil; BRAIN-
~, esp. flat as a ~cake, quite flat (v.i., sl.,
position). Hence ~FUL n. [OE *panne*,
cf. Du. *pan*, G *pfanne*]
pān², v.t. & i. (-nn-). ~ **off**, **out**, wash
(gold-bearing gravel) in pan; (intr.) ~**out**,
yield gold, (fig.) succeed, work, (well etc.).
[f. prec.]
Pān³, n. Greek rural god: the spirit of
nature, paganism, the pre-Christian or
the non-moral world. [Gk]
‖ **pan⁴** (pahn), n. Leaf of the BETEL; (used
for) the mixture of ~, lime, & areca-nut
parings chewed by Asiatics as a mastica-
tory. [Hind.]
pān-¹ in comb.=Gk *pas pantos* all, as
~-**Af'rican**, of, for, all Africans; as
Ang'lican, of the Anglican Church & its
branches (*~-Anglican conference*); ~-
cos'mism, doctrine that material universe
is all that exists; ~-**gen'esis**, theory that
each unit of an organism reproduces
itself; ~-**Germ'an**, of all the Germans in
political union; ~-**Hell'enism**, political
union of all Greeks, so ~-**Hell'en'ic** a.;
~-**Is'lam**, union of Mohammedan world,
so ~-**Islām'ic** a.; ~**logis'tic**, (of Hegel's
philosophy) treating only the rational as
real, so ~'**logism**; ~-**Sla'vism**, (-lah-),
movement for political union of all Slavs;
~**sperm'atism**, ~**sperm'ism**, theory that the
atmosphere is full of minute germs that
develop in favourable environment.

pānace'ā, n. Universal remedy. [L, f.
Gk *panakeia* f. PAN(*akēs* f. *akos* remedy)]
panache' (-ahsh, -āsh), n. Tuft, plume, of
feathers esp. as head-dress or on helmet;
(fig.) display, swagger. [F. f. It. *pen-
nacchio* (*penna* feather)]
pana'da (-nah-), n. Bread boiled to pulp
& flavoured. [Sp. = It. *panata* (*pane*
bread f. L *panis*, see -ADE)]
Pānamā' (-ah), n. ~ **(hat)**, hat of fine
pliant strawlike material made (orig. in
Ecuador) from leaves of the screw-pine.
[place]
‖ **pān'arōpe**, n. Electrical apparatus for
reproduction of gramophone records
through a loud-speaker. [perh. f. PAN+
Gk *tropos* turn, after *tropē*]
panchayat (pūnchā'yat), n. (India). Village council. [Tamil *panchāyattu* f. Skr.
pancha five]
panchromat'ic(-k-), a. (photog.). Equally
sensitive to all spectrum colours. [PAN-]
pānc'rĕ'ac, a. Of the pancreatum; (Opt.,
of eyepiece) extensively adjustable. [f.
foll.+-IC]
pānc'rĕ'atium (-shi-), n. (Gk Ant.). Athletic contest combining wrestling & boxing. So ~AST, **pānc'rĕatist**, n. [L, f.
Gk *pagkration* (PAN-+*kratos* strength)]
pānc'rĕ'as, n. Gland near stomach dis-

charging a digestive secretion (~**atic
juice**) into duodenum, sweetbread. So
~**at'ic** a., ~**atin** n., one of the active
principles of~, descend vertically in level
prepared from the ~ases of animals. [f.
Gk *pagkreas* (PAN-+*kreas* flesh)]
pān'da, n. Indian racoon-like animal, red
bear-cat. [native]
Pānde'an, -aean, a. Of PAN³; ~ **pipe**,
PAN-PIPE. [irreg. f. PAN]
pān'dĕct, n. (usu. pl.). Compendium in 50
books of Roman civil law made by order
of Justinian in 6th c.; complete body of
laws. [f. F *pandecte* f. L f. Gk PAN(*dektēs*
f. *dekhomai* receive) all-receiver]
pāndĕm'ic (-di-), & n. (Disease) prevalent
over the whole of a country or over the
world; ~, or *pandēm'ian*, VENUS. [f. Gk
PAN(*dēmos* people)+-IC]
pāndēmōn'ium, n. Abode of all demons;
place of lawless violence or uproar; utter
confusion. [mod. L (Milton) f. PAN-+
DEMON]
pān'der, n., & v.i. & t. 1. Go-between in
clandestine amours, procurer; one who
ministers to evil designs. 2. v.i. Minister
(to base passions, evil designs); (v.t.) act
as ~ to (person's lust). [vb f. n. f. *Pandare*,
character in Chaucer's *Troilus & Criseyde*
& in Boccaccio, f. L f. Gk *Pandaros*]
pandit. See PUNDIT.
pāndŏ'rā, -dō're', n. Stringed instrument of either type. [It. f. L f. Gk
pandoura, prob. of foreign orig.]
Pāndō'rā's bōx, n. The box in which
Hope alone remained when by its rash
opening all objects of desire were dispersed to play havoc among mankind.
[Gk Myth., see Hesiod, *Op.*, 50-105]
pān'dour (-oor), n. (Pl.) force of
rapacious & brutal soldiers raised by
Baron Trenck in 1741 & afterwards enrolled in Austrian army. [f. Serbo-
Croatian *pandūr* f. med. L *banderius*
follower of a BANNER]
pāne¹, n. Single sheet of glass in compartment of window; rectangular division of
chequered pattern etc. Hence~LESS (-nl-)
a. [f. F *pan* f. L *pannus* piece of cloth]
pāne², v.t. Make up (garment etc.) of
strips of different colours (chiefly in p.p.).
[f. prec.]
pānĕg'yric, n. & a. Laudatory discourse
(upon); (adj.) laudatory. Hence ~AL a.
[f. F *panégyrique* f. L f. Gk *panēgurikos* f.
PAN(*agurís*=*agora* assembly), see -IC]
pān'ĕgÿrize, v.t. Speak, write, in praise
of, eulogize. So **pānĕg'ÿrist** n. [f. Gk
panēgurizō (as prec., see -IZE)]
pān'el¹, n. 1. Stuffed lining of saddle;
kind of saddle. 2. Slip of parchment;
list of jury; jury; (Sc. Law) person(s) on
trial, the accused; ‖ list of the doctors
registered in a district as accepting
Insurance-Act patients (on the ~, so

For words in *pan-* not given see PAN-.

registered). **3.** Distinct compartment of surface, esp. of wainscot, door, etc., often sunk below or raised above general level. **4.** Piece of stuff of different kind or colour inserted in woman's dress. **5.** Large size of photograph, with height much greater than width. [ME & OF, f. med. L *pannellus* dim. as PANE¹]

păn'el², v.t. (-ll-). Saddle (beast) with panel; fit (wall, door, etc.) with panels; ornament (dress etc.) with panel(s). Hence ~lInG¹(²) n. [f. prec.]

păng, n. Shooting pain; sudden sharp mental pain. [?]

păngōl'in (-ngg-), n. Scaly ant-eater. [f. Malay *peng-goling* roller (from habit of rolling itself up)]

*****păn'handle**, n. Narrow strip of one political division of a country extending between two others. [PAN-¹]

păn'ic¹, n. Genus of grasses including Italian millet. [f. L *panicum*]

păn'ic², a., n., & v.t. & i. **1.** (Of terror) unreasoning, excessive. **2.** n. Infectious fright, sudden alarm (e.g., in commerce) leading to hasty measures; ~monger, one who fosters a ~. **3.** vb. Affect, be affected, with ~. Hence ~kY² a. (colloq.). [f. F *panique* f. Gk *panikos* of god Pan, reputed to cause ~]

păn'icle, n. (bot.). Loose irregular type of compound inflorescence, as in oats. [f. L *paxicula*, dim. of *panus* swelling, ear of millet]

pănifica'tion, n. Bread-making. [F, f. L *panis* bread, see -FICATION]

pănjan'drum, n. Mock title of exalted personage; pompous official or pretender. [arbitrary]

‖ **pănn'age**, n. (Right of, payment for) pasturage of swine; acorns, beech-mast, etc., as food for swine. [f. OF *pasnage* f. LL *pastionaticum* (*pastio* pasture f. *pascere past-*, -AGE]

‖ **pănne**, n. A soft long-napped cloth used as dress-material. [F, etym. dub.]

pănn'ier¹ (-nyer), n. **1.** Basket, esp. one of those carried, usu. in pairs, by beast of burden or on the shoulders; covered basket for surgical instruments & medicines for ambulance. **2.** Part of skirt looped up round hips. [f. F *panier* f. L *panarium* bread-basket (*panis* bread, see -ARY¹)]

‖ **pănn'ier²** (-nyer), n. (colloq.). Robed waiter in Inner Temple. [?]

pănn'ikin, n. Small metal drinking-vessel; its contents. [f. PAN-¹+-KIN]

păn'oplÿ, n. Complete suit of armour (often fig.). Hence ~iED² (-lid) a. [f. Gk PAN(*oplia* f. *hopla* arms)]

pănŏp'ticon, n. Bentham's proposed circular prison with cells round warders' well in centre. [f. PAN-¹+Gk *optikos* of sight (opt- see)]

pănŏra'ma (-rah-, -rä-), n. Picture of landscape etc. arranged on inside of cylindrical surface or successively rolled out before spectator; continuous passing scene; unbroken view of surrounding region (often fig.). Hence **pănŏrăm'Ic** a., **pănŏrăm'ICALLY** adv. [f. PAN-+Gk *horama* view (*horaō* see)]

păn'pipe(s), n. Musical instrument made of series of reeds. [Pan, Greek rural god, +PIPE]

păn'sÿ (-zi), n. **1.** Wild & garden plant with flowers of various colours, heartsease. **2.** (colloq.). (Also ~ boy) effeminate youth, homosexual. [f. F *pensée* thought, pansy, f. *penser* think f. L *pensare* frequent. of *pendere pens-* weigh]

pănt, v.i. & t. & n. **1.** Gasp for breath; (fig.) yearn (*for, after*, thing, *to do*); throb violently; utter gaspingly. **2.** n. Gasp, throb. [n. f. vb, prob. cogn. w. OF *pantoisier* pant f. pop. L *phantasiare* be oppressed with nightmare (as PHANTASY)]

pant- in comb.=PANTO- before vowels.

păntagru'ellism (-ōō-), n. Extravagant coarse humour like that of Pantagruel, a character in Rabelais. So **pănta-gruël'IAN** (-ōō-) a., ~IST n. [-ISM]

pantalĕt(te)s' (-ts), n. pl. Woman's drawers, cycling knickerbockers, etc. [f. foll., see -ETTE]

pantalōon', n. **1.** (P~). Character in Italian comedy wearing ~s; (now) clown's butt & abettor in pantomime. **2.** (hist.; pl. or sing.). Garment of breeches & stockings in one piece, close-fitting breeches down to ankle as transition from knee-breeches to trousers. **3.** (pl.; chiefly U.S., & being ousted by *pants*). Trousers. [f. F *pantalon* f. It. *pantalone*, Venetian character in Italian comedy, perh. f. *San Pantaleone*, favourite Venetian saint]

‖ **păntĕch'nicon** (-kn-), n. Furniture warehouse (orig. name of a bazaar); ~ van (for removing furniture). [f. PAN-+Gk *tekhnikon* of art (*tekhnē*, see -IC)]

păn'thĕïsm, n. Doctrine that God is everything & everything God; heathen worship of all gods. So ~IST n., ~-is¹¹c(AL) ea., [f. PAN-+Gk *theos* god+-ISM]

păn'thĕon (or -ē'on), n. Temple dedicated to all the gods, esp. circular one at Rome; deities of a people collectively; building in which illustrious dead are buried or have memorials; building in London opened for public entertainment in 1772. [L, f. Gk PAN(*theion* holy f. *theos* god)]

păn'ther, n. Leopard; American ~, puma or cougar. Hence ~ESS¹ n. [f. OF *pantère* f. L *panthera* f. Gk *panthēr* etym. dub.]

păn'ties (-tēz), n. pl. (colloq.). Pants worn by children; close-fitting knickers worn by women. [dim. of PANTS; see -Y²]

For words in *pan-* not given see PAN-.

pan'tile, n. Roof tile transversely curved to ogee shape, one curve being much larger than the other. [PAN¹+TILE]

pāntisoc'racy, n. Community in which all are equal & all rule. [PANT-+ISO-+ -CRACY]

panto- in comb. (before vowels **pant-**) = Gk *pas pantos* all, as ~*lo'gic*, *pantōl'ogy*, (of) universal knowledge; ~*morph'ic*, (taking all shapes); ~*pragmat'ic* a. & b., (person) meddling in everything; ~*scop'ic*, with much range or vision. [Gk]

pan'to|graph (-ahf), n. Instrument for copying plan etc. on any scale. Hence ~**graph'ic** a. [f. PANTO-+Gk *-graphos* writing]

pan'tomime, n., & v.t. & i. 1. (hist.), Roman actor performing in dumb show, mimic actor. 2. ‖ English dramatic performance ending with transformation scene followed by broad comedy of clown & pantaloon & dancing of harlequin & columbine. 3. Dumb show. 4. vb. Express oneself, express (thing), by dumb show. Hence or cogn. **pāntomim'ic** a, f. med. L *panetaria* bread-shop (*panis* bread, see -ARY¹)]

pants, n. pl. (colloq.). ‖ (Shop) long trousers; ‖ (Chiefly U.S.) trousers. [abbr. of PANTALOON]

pän'zer (-tser), a. & n. Armoured (~ *division*, *troops*); (n.pl., colloq.) ~ *troops*. [G., = small coat]

pap¹, n. (arch.). Nipple of woman's breast; corresponding part of man; (pl.) conical hilltops side by side. [limit. of sound made by infant in feeding]

pap², n. Soft or semi-liquid food for infants or invalids; mash, pulp. Hence ~**'py²** a. [limit., cf. prec.]

papa', n. Father (used chiefly by children). [F f. L limit.]

pāp'acy, n. Pope's (tenure of) office; papal system. [f. med. L *papatia* (*papa* pope, -ACY)]

pāp'al, a. Of the pope or his office. Hence ~**ISM**(2), ~**ISM**(2), nn., ~**IZE**(2) v.t. & i., ~**LY³** adv. [F f. eccl. L *papalis* (as prec, see -AL)]

papāv'erous, a. Like, allied to, the poppy. So **papāvera'ceous** (-āshus) a. [f. L *papaver* poppy +-OUS]

papaw', n. (Fruit of) palm-like S.-Amer. tree of which stems, leaves, & fruit contain a milky juice that makes meat tender; *N.-Amer. tree with purple flowers & oblong edible fruit. [f. Sp. *papaya*, of Carib orig.]

pāp'er, n. 1. Substance used for writing, printing, drawing, wrapping up parcels, etc., made of interlaced fibres of rags, straw, wood, etc.; *commit to* ~, *write down*; *put, pen to* ~, *begin writing*; negotiable documents, e.g. bills of exchange; (also ~ *money*) bank-notes etc. used as currency, opp. to coin, so ~ *currency* (cf. METALLIC); (pl.) free passes to theatre etc.; (pl.) documents proving person's or ship's identity, standing, etc.; *send in one's* ~s, resign; set of questions in examination; = NEWS~; essay, dissertation, esp. one read to learned society; ~ *war(fare)* (carried on in books or newspapers); *on* ~, hypothetically, to judge from statistics, etc., *as on* ~ *he is the better man*, so (attrib.) ~ *profits* (hypothetical). 2. ~ *bag cookery*), method of cooking food of various kinds by enclosing it in buttered ~-*bag* before putting it in moderately hot oven; ~-*chase*, cross-country run in which a trail of torn-up ~ is laid by one or more runners to set a course for the rest; ~-*hangings*, *wall-*~, ~ for covering walls of room etc.; ~-*hanger*, one who covers walls with these; ~-*knife* (of ivory, wood, etc., for cutting open leaves of book etc.); ~-*mill* (in which ~ is made); ~-*stainer*, one who stains ~ or makes ~ *hangings*; ~-*weight*, small heavy object for securing loose ~s from being displaced. Hence ~**Y²** a. [f. OF *papier* f. PAPYRUS]

pā'per, v.t. Enclose in paper; decorate (wall etc.) with paper; furnish with paper; (sl.) fill (theatre etc.) by means of free passes. [f. prec.]

papier mâché (păp'yā māshā'), n. Moulded paper pulp used for boxes, trays, etc. [F., = chewed paper]

papiliona'ceous (-yonāshus), a. (bot.) With corolla like a butterfly. [f. L *papilio -onis* butterfly, see -ACEOUS]

papill'a, n. (pl. -ae). Small nipple-like protuberance in a part or organ of the body; (Bot.) small fleshy projection on plant. Hence or cogn. **pāp'illary¹**, **pāp'illate¹**(2), **pāp'illose¹**, aa. [L,]

pāp'ist, n. Advocate of papal supremacy; Roman Catholic (usu. in hostile sense). Hence **papis'tic(al)** aa., **papis'tically²** adv. [f. mod. L *papista*, f. eccl. L *papa* pope, see -IST]

papoose', n. N.-Amer.-Indian young child. [native]

papoose', n. =BAROUCHE. [f. Pers. *paposh* (*pā* foot+*posh* covering)]

pāp'us, n. (bot.). Downy appendage on fruit of thistles, dandelions, etc. Hence **pāp'pose¹** a. [mod. L f. Gk *pappos*]

pāp'rika (-ē-), n. Hungarian red pepper. [Hungarian]

pap'ula, -ule, nn. (pl. ~*ae*,~*es*). Pimple; small fleshy projection on plant. Hence **pāp'ula'ceous** (-shus), aa. [L (-la)]

papyra'ceous (-shus), a. (nat. hist.). Of the nature of, thin as, paper. [f. PAPYRUS, see -ACEOUS]

papyro- in comb. = Gk *papyros* usu. in

sense 'paper', as: ~graph, apparatus for copying documents by means of paper-stencil; ~graphy (-ŏgˀ-), ~type, copying processes in which picture etc. is trans-ferred from paper to zinc plate etc.

papy̆r'us, n. (pl. -ri). Aquatic plant of sedge family, paper reed; ancient writing-material prepared by Egyptians etc. from stem of this; (with pl.) MS. written on this. [L, f. Gk papuros]

pa̅r¹, n. Equality, equal footing, esp. on a ~ (with); ~ of exchange, recognized value of one country's currency in terms of another's; (of stocks, shares, etc.) at face value, above ~, at a premium, below ~, at a discount; average or nor-mal amount, degree, or condition, as on a ~, on an average, above, below, up to, ~; (Golf) the number of strokes a scratch player should require for a hole or course (calculated according to a formula & usu. less than the BOGEY figures). [L, a. & n., = equal(ity)]

pa̅r², n. (colloq.). Paragraph.

par'a-¹ in comb. = Gk para in senses 'be-side', 'beyond', 'wrong, irregular'; ~mil'itary a., having a status or function ancillary to that of military forces.

par'a-² in comb. = It. para imperat. of parare ward off, shelter, as parasol.

parab'asis, n. (pl. -bases). Part sung by chorus in Greek comedy, addressed to audience in the poet's name. [Gk, f. PARA¹(bainō go) go aside, step forward]

par'able, n. Fictitious narrative used to typify moral or spiritual relations; alle-gory; (arch.)enigmatical saying, proverb; (arch.) take up one's ~, begin to discourse. [f. F parabole, as foll.]

parab'ola, n. Plane curve formed by in-tersection of cone with plane parallel to its side. [f. L f. Gk PARA¹(bolē throw, f. ballō) placing side by side, comparison, parable, etc.]

parab'olˀic(al, aa. 1. (Usu. -ical of), expressed in, a parable, whence -ICALLY adv. 2. (Usu.-ic) of, like, a parabola. [f. LL f. late Gk parabolikos (as prec., see -IC)]

parab'oloid, n. Solid some of whose plane sections are parabolas, esp. (also ~ of revolution) that generated by revolution of parabola about its axis. [-OID]

parach'ronism (-k-), n. Error in chrono-logy. [f. PARA-¹+Gk khronos time+-ISM]

par'achute (-shoot), n., & v.t. & i. 1. Umbrella-like apparatus for descending safely from a height, esp. from aircraft, (~ flare, one dropped by ~ to illuminate target area; ~ mine, large case containing explosive dropped from aircraft by ~; ~ troops (airborne troops landing by ~); natural or artificial contrivance serving this purpose. 2. vb. Convey, descend, (as if) by means of ~. Hence pă'rachutˀist (-shoot-) n., user of ~, (pl.) ~ troops. [F (PARA-²+chute fall)]

pa̅'raclēte, n. Advocate (as title of the Holy Spirit, see John xiv. 16, 26, etc.). [f. F paraclet f. L f. Gk PARA-¹(kletos f. kaleō call)]

parā̆de¹, n. 1. Display, ostentation, esp. make a ~ of (one's virtues etc.). 2. Muster of troops for inspection, esp. one held regularly at set hours; ground used for this. 3. Public square or promenade (often as name of street). [F, = show, f. It. para-ta f. L parare prepare, furnish, see -ADE]

parā̆de², v.t. & i. Assemble (troops) for review or other purpose; display ostenta-tiously; march through (streets etc.) with display; (intr.) march in procession with display. [f. prec.]

pa̅'radigm (-ĭm), n. Example, pattern, esp. of inflexion of noun, verb, etc. So **păradigmăt'ic** (+ĭg-) a. [f. F paradigme f. L f. Gk paradeigma f. PARA¹(deiknumi show), see -M]

pa̅'radise, n. (Also earthly ~) garden of Eden; heaven; region, state, of su-preme bliss; FOOL's ~; park in which animals are kept; BIRD of ~. Hence or cogn. **păradisā'ic(al)** (irreg. so in Mosaic etc.], **păradis'ĕan**, **pă̆radis'ıac**(AL), **pă-radis'ıAL**, **păradis'ıAN**, **pă̆radis'ıc**(AL, aa. [f. F paradis f. L f. Gk paradeisos f. OPers. pairidaeza park (pairi around + diz mould)]

pa̅'radŏs (or -dō), n. Elevation of earth behind fortified place to secure from reverse attack or fire, esp. the mound along back of trench. [F (PARA-¹+dos back f. L dorsum)]

pa̅'radŏx, n. Statement contrary to re-ceived opinion; seemingly absurd though perhaps really well-founded statement; self-contradictory, essentially absurd, statement; person, thing, conflicting with preconceived notions of what is reasonable or possible; HYDROSTATIC ~. Hence or cogn. ~ER¹(3), ~ıST(3), ~ıcal'ıTY, ~y¹, nn., **pă̆radŏx'ıcAL** a., **păradŏx'ıcALˀLY²** adv. [f. L f. Gk paradoxon neut. adj. (PARA-¹+doxa opinion)]

pa̅radŏx'ure, n. Palm-cat, animal with remarkably long curving tail. [f. Gk paradoxos (see prec.)+oura tail]

pa̅'raffin (-ĭn), n., & v.t. Colourless tasteless inodorous oily & waxy substance got by distillation from petroleum & shale & used for making candles etc. (~ wax, solid ~ obtained by distillation from petro-leum: liquid ~, odourless tasteless mild laxative); ‖(also ~ oil) oil so obtained & used as illuminant or lubricant; (v.t., treat with ~. [f. L parum little+affinis, from small AFFINITY it has for other bodies]

pa̅rago̅'ge (-jĭ), n. (gram.). Addition of letter or syllable to a word. Hence **pă̆rago̅j'gıc** a. [L, f. Gk paragōgē leading past (PARA-¹+agō f. agō lead)]

pa̅'ragon, n., & v.t. Model of excellence; supremely excellent person or thing, model (of virtue etc.); perfect diamond of

paragraph (-ahf, -åf), n., & v.t. **1.** Distinct passage or section in book etc., marked by indentation of first line; symbol (usu. ¶) formerly used to mark new ~, now as REFERENCE mark; detached item of news etc. in newspaper, without heading, whence ~ER(3), ~Y(1) nn. **2.** v.t. Write ~ about (person, thing); arrange (article etc.) in ~s. Hence **pāragraph'ic** a., **paragraph'ically** adv. [f. F paragraphe f. LL f. Gk para(graphos f. graphō write) short stroke marking break in sense]

Pār'aguay (-gwā, -gwī), n. = MATÉ. [name of S. Amer. river & republic]

pāralleī'ot'ropism, n. Tendency in plants to turn leaves parallel to incidence of light-rays. So ~otrōp'ic a. [PARA-¹+HELIOTROPISM]

pār'akite, n. **1.** Kite acting like parachute. **2.** Tailless kite for scientific purposes. [f. PARACHUTE+KITE]

pār'akeet, pār'roquet (-kēt), n. Small (esp. long-tailed) kinds of parrot. [f. OF paroquet prob. f. It. parrochetto dim. of parroco parson, or f. It. parrucchetto dim. of parrucca peruke]

pāralip'sis, -leip'sis (-li-), n. Trick of securing emphasis by professing to omit all mention of subject, e.g., I say nothing of his antecedents, how from youth upwards etc. [f. Gk PARA(leipsis f. leipō leave) passing over]

pār'allax, n. (Angular amount of) apparent displacement of object, caused by actual change of point of observation. So **~ac'tic** a. [f. F parallaxe f. Gk parallaxis change f. parallassō (PARA-¹+allassō)]

pār'allel¹, a. & n. **1.** (Of lines etc.) continuously equidistant, (of line) having this relation to; ~ bars, pair of ~ bars supported on posts for gymnastic exercises; ~ ruler, two rulers connected by pivoted cross-pieces, for drawing ~ lines; (fig.) precisely similar, analogous, or corresponding. **2.** n. ~ (of latitude), each of the ~ circles marking degrees of latitude on earth's surface in map, as the 49th ~; (Mil.) trench ~ to general face of works attacked; person, thing, precisely analogous to another; ~ position; comparison, as draw a ~ between (two things); two ~ lines (||) as REFERENCE mark. [f. F parallèle f. L f. Gk parallēlos (PARA-¹+allēlous one another)]

pār'allel², v.t. (-l-). Represent as similar, compare, (things, one with another); find, mention, something parallel or corresponding to; be parallel, correspond to. [f. prec.]

pārallelē'pipēd (or -epip'id), n. Solid contained by parallelograms. [f. Gk parallēlepipedon, as PARALLEL¹+EPI(pedon plane surface)]

pā'rallelism, n. Being parallel (lit. or fig.); comparison or correspondence of successive passages, esp. in Hebrew poetry. [f. Gk parallelismos (parallel-, see -ISM)]

pārallēl'ogram, n. Four-sided rectilineal figure whose opposite sides are parallel; ~ of forces, (~ illustrating) theorem that if two forces acting at a point be represented in magnitude & direction by two sides of a ~, their resultant is represented by a diagonal drawn from that point. [f. F parallélogramme f. Gk parallélogrammon (as PARALLEL¹+gramme line)]

pāralog'ism, n. Illogical reasoning (esp. of which reasoner is unconscious, cf. SOPHISM); fallacy. So **~IZE(2)** v.i. [f. F paralogisme f. LL f. Gk paralogismos f. paralogizomai f. para(logos reason)]

pāralȳs'e (-z), v.t. Affect with paralysis; (fig.) render powerless, cripple. Hence **~ATION** n. [prob. f. F paralyser, as foll.]

pāral'ysis, n. Nervous affection marked by impairment or loss of motor or sensory function of nerves; (fig.) state of utter powerlessness. [L, f. Gk para(lusis f. luō loose) disable]

pāralyt'ic, a. & n. (Person) affected with paralysis (lit. or fig.). Hence **~ICALLY** adv. [f. F paralytique f. L f. Gk para(lutikos (as prec., see -IC)]

pāra'magnēt'ic, a. Capable of being attracted by poles of magnet (cf. DIAMAGNETIC). So **~mag'netĭsm** n. [PARA-¹+MAGNETIC]

pāramätt'a, n. Light dress fabric of merino wool & silk or cotton. [f. Parra(matta, town in New S. Wales]

pāram'ēter, n. (math.). Quantity constant in case considered, but varying in different cases. [f. PARA-¹+Gk metron measure]

pāramō', n. (pl. ~s). High treeless plateau in tropical parts of S. America. [f. Sp. paramo, prob. of native orig.]

pār'amount, a. Supreme; lord, lady, ~ (in supreme authority); pre-eminent, as of ~ importance; superior (to). Hence **~CY** n., **~LY²** adv. [f. AF paramont f. OF par amont above f. L ad montem to the hill]

pār'amour (-oor), n. (rhet.). Illicit partner of married man or woman. [f. OF par amour by love]

pār'ang (pahr-), n. Malay heavy sheath-knife. [Malay]

pāranoi'a, -noe'a (-nēə), n. Mental derangement, esp. when marked by delusions of grandeur etc. [Gk (~noia) f. PARA-¹(noos mind) distracted]

pār'apet, n. Low wall at edge of balcony, roof, etc., or along sides of bridge etc.; (Mil.) defence of earth or stone to conceal & protect troops, esp. mound along front of trench (cf. parados). Hence **~ED²** a. [f. It. parapetto (petto breast f. L pectus)]

pā'raph, n. Flourish after a signature, orig. as precaution against forgery. [f. F *paraphe* f. med. L *paraphus* for *paragraphus* PARAGRAPH]

paraphernā'lia, n. pl. Personal belongings; mechanical accessories, appointments, etc.; (formerly) articles of personal property that law allowed married woman to keep & treat as her own. [L, neut. pl. adj. f. L f. Gk PARA¹(*pherna* f. *phernē* dower), see -AL]

pā'raphrāse(-z), n., & v.t. 1. Free rendering or amplification of a passage, expression of its sense in other words; any of a collection of metrical ~s of passages of Scripture used in Church of Scotland etc. 2. v.t. Express meaning of (passage) in other words. So **pā'raphrās'tic** a., **pā'raphras'tically** adv. [(n.) F, f. L f. Gk *paraphrasis* f. PARA¹(*pharazō* tell); (vb) f. F *paraphraser*]

pāraplē'gia, n. Paralysis of lower limbs & part or whole of trunk. So ~IC a. [Gk (-ē-) f. PARA¹(*plēssō* strike)]

pā'rasāng, n. Ancient-Persian measure of length, about 3½ miles. [f. L (-ga) f. Gk *parasangēs*, of Pers. orig.]

pārasēlē'nē, n. (pl. -ae). Bright spot on lunar halo, mock-moon. [PARA-¹+Gk *selēnē* moon]

pā'rasīte, n. Interested hanger-on, toady; animal, plant, living in or upon another & drawing nutriment directly from it (cf. COMMENSAL); (loosely) plant that climbs about another plant, wall, etc. Hence or cogn. **pārasīt'ic**(Ai) a&., ~ISM(2),~OL'OGY, nn. [f. L f. Gk PARA¹(*sītos* food)]

pārasīt'icīde, n. Agent that destroys parasites. [as prec.+-CIDE]

pā'rasītīze, v.t. Infest as a parasite (chiefly in p.p.). [as prec.+-IZE]

pārasōl'(*or* pā'r-), n. Sunshade. [F, f. It. PARA²(*sole* sun f. L *sol*)]

pārasȳn'thēsis, n. (philol.). Derivation from a compound. So **pārasȳnthēt'ic** a. [PARA-¹+SYNTHESIS]

pāratāx'is, n (gram.). Placing of clauses etc. one after another, without words to indicate co-ordination or subordination. So **pāratāc'tic** a., **pāratāc'tically** adv. [f. Gk PARA¹(*taxis* arrangement f. *tassō*)]

pā'ratroōp/s, n. pl. Airborne troops landing by parachute (~*er*, one of these). [PARA(CHUTE)TROOP]

pā'ratyph'oīd, n. Kinds of fever resembling typhoid, but caused by different bacteria. [PARA-¹]

pā'ravāne, n. Torpedo-shaped device towed at a depth regulated by its vanes or planes to cut the moorings of submerged mines. [PARA-²]

pā'rb'oīl, v.t. Boil partially; (fig.) overheat. [f. OF *parbouillir* f. LL PER(*bullire* boil) boil thoroughly, by confus. w. *part*]

pā'rb'uckle, n., & v.t. 1. Rope for raising or lowering casks & cylindrical objects, the middle being secured at the upper level, & both ends passed under & round the object & then hauled or let slowly out. 2. v.t. Raise (*up*) or lower (*down*) thus. [?]

pā'cel¹, n. & adv. 1. (Arch.) part, esp. PART¹ & ~; piece of land, esp. as part of estate; goods etc. wrapped up in single package; ~ *post*, branch of postal service concerned with ~s; (Commerce.) quantity dealt with in one transaction. 2. adv. (arch.). Partly, as ~ *blind*, *drunk*; ~ *gilt*, partly gilded, esp. (of cup etc.) with inner surface gilt. [f. F *parcelle* f. L +*particella*, dim. as PARTICLE]

pā'cel², v.t. (-ll-). Divide (usu. *out*) into portions; (Naut.) cover (canlked seam) with canvas strips & pitch, wrap (rope) with canvas strips. [f. prec.]

pā'celling, n. In v.bl senses, esp. (Naut.) strip of canvas, usu. tarred, for binding round rope. [-ING¹]

pā'cēnary, n. Joint heirship. [f. AF *parcenarie* = OF *parçonerie* (as foll., see -ERY]

pā'cēner, n. Coheir. [AF, = OF *parçoner* f. med. L *parti(tionarius* (PARTITION, -ER²)]

pā'ch, v.t. & i. Roast (pease etc.) slightly; (of sun, thirst, etc.) make (person etc.) hot & dry; become hot & dry. [?]

pā'ch'ment, n. Skin, esp. of sheep or goat, prepared for writing, painting, etc.; manuscript on this; ~like skin, esp. husk of coffee-bean. Hence ~v² a. [f. F *parchemin* f. L *pergamena* (*charta* paper) of *Pergamum*, city in Asia Minor]

∥ **pā'rd**¹, n. (arch.). Leopard. [OF, f. L f. Gk *pardos*]

∗**pā'rd'on**¹, n. (sl.). Partner. [abbr.]

pā'rd'on², n. Forgiveness; (Eccl.) = INDULGENCE, festival at which this is granted; (Law) remission of legal consequences of crime; *general* ~ (for offences generally, or to number of persons not named individually); courteous forbearance, esp. *I beg your* ~ (apology for thing done, for dissent or contradiction, or for not hearing or understanding what was said). [f. OF *perdun*, as foll.]

pā'rd'on², v.t. Forgive (person, offence, person his offence); make allowance for, excuse, (person, fault, person *for doing*). So ~ABLE a., ~ABLENESS n., ~ably² adv. [f. OF *pardoner* f. LL PER(*donare* give)]

pā'rd'oner, n. (hist.). Person licensed to sell papal pardons or indulgences. [PARDON¹+-ER²]

pāre, v.t. Trim (thing) by cutting away irregular parts etc.; cut away skin, rind, etc. of (fruit etc.); ~ (nails etc.) *to the quick* (so deep as to reach sensitive parts); (fig.) diminish little by little (often *away*, *down*); shave, cut, *off*, *away*, (edges etc.). Hence **pā'rER¹**(2), **pā'rING¹**(1, 2), nn. [f. F *parer* f. L *parare* prepare]

paregŏr'ic, a. & n. ~ (elixir), camphor-ated tincture of opium flavoured with aniseed & benzoic acid. [f. LL f. Gk *parēgorikos* soothing (PARA-¹ + *agoros* speaking f. *agora* public assembly)]

pareir'a (-āˈa), n. Drug from root of Brazilian shrub, used in urinary dis-orders. [f. Port. *parreira* vine trained against wall]

parĕn'chyma (-ngkˈ-), n. (Anat.) proper substance of gland, organ, etc., as dis-tinguished from flesh & connective tissue; (Bot.) tissue of cells of about equal length & breadth placed side by side (cf. PROS-ENCHYMA), usu. soft & succulent, found esp. in softer parts of leaves, pulp of fruits, etc. Hence ~AL, **parĕnchym'a-tous**, aa., (-ngkˈ-), **parĕnchym'a-** some-thing poured in beside (PARA-¹ + *enchuma* f. *enchéō* pour in f. *en* in + *khéō* pour)]

pā'rent, n. Father or mother; forefather, esp. *our first ~s*, Adam & Eve; animal, plant, from which others are derived (often attrib., as the ~ *bird, tree*); (fig.) source, origin, (of evils etc.). So **parĕn'-tal**, a., **parĕn'taly²** adv., ~hood (t-h-) n. [OF, f. L *parens* (*parent-* *parere* beget, see -ENT)]

parĕn'tage, n. Descent from parents, lineage, as *his ~ is unknown*. [F, as prec., see -AGE]

parĕn'thesis, n. (pl. *-theses*). Word, clause, sentence, inserted into a passage to which it is not grammatically essen-tial, marked off by brackets, dashes, or commas; (sing. or pl.) round brackets ( ) used for this; (fig.) interlude, interval. [med. L, f. Gk *parenthesis* f. *parentithēmi* put in beside (PARA-¹ + EN-(2) + *tithēmi* place)]

parĕn'thesize, v.t. Insert (words etc., or abs.) as parenthesis; put between marks of parenthesis. [f. prec., see -IZE]

parĕnthĕt'ic, a. Of, inserted as a, paren-thesis; (fig.) interposed. Hence ~AL a., ~ally² adv. [f. med. L *parentheticus* (as PARENTHESIS, see -ETIC)]

parĕrg'on, n. (pl. *-erga*). By-work, work apart from one's main employment. [L, f. Gk *parergon* (PARA-¹ + *ergon* work)]

pā'resis, n. (med.). Partial paralysis, affecting muscular motion but not sensa-tion. So **parĕt'ic** a. [f. Gk *paresis* f. *pariēmi* let go]

par excellence (see Ap.) adv. By virtue of special excellence, above all others that may be so called, as *Mayfair was the fashionable quarter ~*. [F]

pār'get (-j-), v.t. & n. 1. Plaster (wall etc.). 2. n. Plaster. [prob. f. OF *pargeter*, *por-*, f. L PROJ*ectare*=*jactare* frequent. of *jacĕre* ject- throw)]

parhēl'ion (-lyon), n. (pl. *-ia*). Spot on solar halo at which light is intensified, mock sun. Hence ~l'ACAL, ~ic, aa. [f. L f. Gk *parēlion* (PARA-¹ + *hēlios* sun)]

in S. India; member of low or no caste; (fig.) social outcast; ~-*dog*, yellow vaga-bond dog of low breed in India etc. [f. Tamil *paraiyan* pl. of *paraiyan* drummer (*parai* drum)]

Pār'ian, a. & n. 1. Of the island of Paros, famed for white marble. 2. n. Fine white kind of porcelain. [+AN]

pari'etal, a. Of the wall of the body or of any of its cavities; ~ *bones*, pair forming part of sides & top of skull; (Bot.) of the wall of a hollow structure etc. [f. F *pariétal* f. L *parietalis* (*paries -etis* wall, see -AL]

parĭ mutŭ'el, n. Form of betting in which winners divide losers' stakes (less a percentage for management). [F] = mutual stake]

Pā'ris, n. Capital of France; ~ *blue*, kinds of pigment; ~ *doll*, dressmaker's lay figure; ~ *green*, poisonous chemical used as pigment & insecticide; ~ *white*, fine whiting used in polishing. [F]

pā'rish, n. Subdivision of county, having its own church & clergyman; || (also civil ~) district constituted for administration of Poor law etc., as *go on the ~*, *receive parochial relief*; the inhabitants of a ~; ~ *clerk*, official performing various duties connected with the church, esp. (formerly) leading responses; || ~ *council*, local ad-ministrative body in rural civil ~; ~ LANTERN; ~ *register*, book recording christenings, marriages, & burials, at ~ church. [f. OF *paroche* f. LL *parochia* f. Gk *paroikía* district round (a church) f. *paroikos* (PARA-¹ + *oikos* dwelling)]

parish'ioner (-sho-), n. Inhabitant of parish. [f. OF *paroissien* (*paroisse* f. pop. L **parocia* as prec., see -AN) + -ER¹]

Parī'sian (-zhyan), a. & n. Of, native, inhabitant of Paris. [f. F *parisien* f. med. L *parisianus* (*Parisii* Paris, see -AN)]

parīsyllăb'ic, a. (Of Gk & L nouns) having same number of syllables in nomi-native as in oblique cases of singular. [f. L *par* equal + SYLLABIC]

pā'rity, n. Equality, esp. among mem-bers or ministers of church; parallelism, analogy, as ~ *of reasoning*; (Commerce) equivalence in another currency, being at par. [f. L *paritas* (as prec., see -ITY)]

pārk, n. 1. Large enclosed piece of ground, usu. with woodland & pasture, attached to country house etc.; enclosure in town ornamentally laid out for public recreation; || *the P~*, (now) Hyde P~, (formerly) St James's P~; large tract of land kept in natural state for public benefit. 2. (Space occupied by) artillery, stores, etc., in encampment; area as-signed for motor-cars etc. to wait in. 3. *Oyster-~*, enclosed area for oyster-

breeding, overflowed by sea at high tide. Hence ~ISH¹ a. [ME, f. OF parc f. WG †parruk, whence OE pearroc, dial. parrock, PADDOCK¹]

park², v.t. Enclose (ground) in or as park; (Mil.) arrange (artillery etc.) compactly in a park; leave (car etc.) in park. [f. prec.]

park'a, n. Skin jacket with hood attached, worn by Eskimos. [Aleutian]

∥ **Park'hurst**, n. ~ (prison), a convict prison. [place]

∥ **park'in**, n. (dial.), Cake of oatmeal & treacle. [?]

∥ **park'y**, a. (sl.). Chilly (of air, morning, etc.). [?]

parl'ance, n. Way of speaking, as in common, legal, etc., ~. [OF (parler speak f. LL parabolare talk, as PARABLE, see -ANCE)]

parl'ement (-mahn), n. (hist.), French judicial court (abolished 1792). [F']

parlementaire' (-mahntār), n. Bearer of a flag of truce. [F']

parl'ey¹, n.(pl.~s). Conference for debating of points in dispute, esp. (Mil.) discussion of terms, as beat, sound, a ~, call for it by drum or trumpet. [f. F parler, see PARLANCE²]

parl'ey², v.i. & t. Discuss terms (with enemy etc.); speak (esp. foreign language). [f, or as prec.]

parleyvoo' (-liv-), n., & v.i. (joc.). **1.** French; Frenchman. **2.** v.i. Speak French. [f. F parlez-vous (français)? do you speak (French)?]

parl'iament (-lmn-), n. **1.** Council forming the supreme legislature of United Kingdom, consisting of House of Lords (Spiritual & Temporal) & House of Commons (representatives of counties, cities, etc.), (of King) open P~, declare it open with ceremonial; corresponding legislative assembly in other countries; the P~ Act, that of 1911 depriving the Lords of their veto on money bills & making their veto on other bills merely suspensory; Long¹ P~ (met. Nov. 3rd, 1640, dissolved March 1660); Short P~ (sat from Apr. 13 to May 5, 1640). **2.** (Also ~-cake) thin crisp cake of gingerbread. [f. OF parlement speaking (as PARLANCE, see -MENT)]

parliamentar'ian (-lam-), n. & a. **1.** Skilled debater in parliament; adherent of Parliament in Civil War of 17th c. **2.** adj. =foll. [foll., -AN]

parliamen'tary (-lam-), a. Of parliament (old ~ HAND¹); ∥~ agent (charged with interests of party concerned in private legislation of Parliament); enacted, established, by Parliament; ∥~ train (formerly carrying passengers at rate not above 1d. per mile); (of language) admissible in Parliament, (colloq.) civil. [-ARY¹]

parl'our (-ler), n. Ordinary sitting-room of family in private house; room in inn for private conversation; ~ boarder, boarding-school pupil living in principal's family; *~ car, luxuriously fitted railway carriage; ∥~maid, maid who waits at table. [f. OF parleor f. med. L parlatorium (parlare talk, see PARLANCE & -ORY)]

parl'ous, a. & adv. (arch., joc.). Perilous; hard to deal with; surprisingly clever etc.; (adv.) extremely. [=PERILOUS]

Parmesan' (-z-), a. & n. ~ (cheese), kind of cheese made at Parma & elsewhere. [F, f. It. parmegiano of Parma]

Parnass'us, n. Mountain in central Greece, anciently sacred to Muses. So ~IAN a. & n. (esp., member) of a later 19th-c. school of French poets. [L, f. Gk Parnas(s)os]

Parn'ellism, n. Policy of Irish Home-Rule party led by C. S. Parnell from 1880 to 1891. So ~ITE¹ n. [-ISM]

paroch'ial (-k-), a. Of a parish; (fig., of affairs etc.) confined to narrow area. Hence ~ISM, paroch'ialˡTY, ~IZE(3) v.t., ~LY² adv., (-k-). [OF, f. LL parochialis (as PARISH, see -AL)]

pa'rodly, n., & v.t. **1.** Composition in which an author's characteristics are ridiculed by imitation; feeble imitation, travesty. **2.** v.t. Make (literary work, manner, etc.) ridiculous by imitation. So ~IST(3) n. [(vb f. n.)f. Gk parōidia (PARA-¹+ōidē song, ODE)]

parole', n., & v.t. **1.** (Also ~ of honour, F~ d'honneur pr. dŏnĕr') word of honour, esp. (Mil.) prisoner's promise that he will not attempt escape, or will return to custody if liberated, or will refrain from taking up arms against captors for stated period; on ~, (liberated) on this understanding; (Mil.) password used only by officers or inspectors of guard (cf. COUNTERSIGN). **2.** v.t. Put (prisoner) on ~. [(vb f. n.) F~ = word, as PARABLE]

paronomas'ia (-zyɑ, -siɑ), n. Word-play, pun. [L, f. Gk paronomasia (PARA-¹+ onomasia f. onomazō f. onoma name)]

paroquet. See PARAKEET.

parot'id, a. & n. **1.** Situated near the ear, esp. ~ gland (in front of ear), with ~ duct, opening into mouth). **2.** n. ~ gland. [f. F parotide f. L f. Gk parōtis, -idos (PARA-¹+ ous ōtos ear)]

parotit'is, n. Mumps. [f. prec. +-ITIS]

pa'roxysm, n. Fit of disease; fit (of rage, laughter, etc.). Hence paroxys'MAL (-zm-) a. [f. F paroxysme f. L f. Gk paroxusmos f. paroxunō exasperate (PARA-¹+oxunō sharpen f. oxus sharp)]

parox'ytone, a. & n. (Gk gram.). (Word) with acute accent on last syllable but one. [f. Gk paroxutonos (PARA-¹+OXYTONE)]

pārp'en, n. Stone passing through wall from side to side, with two smooth vertical faces. [f. OF parpain, etym. dub.]

parq'uet (-kit), n., & v.t. 1. Wooden flooring of pieces of wood, often of different kinds, arranged in pattern. 2. v.t. Floor (room) thus. So ~RY(1) n. [F., = small compartment, floor, dim. of *parc* PARK]

pär, pärr, n. Young salmon. [?]

pä'rricide, n. 1. One who murders his father or near relative or one whose person is held sacred; person guilty of treason against his country. So ~CID'AL a. [F. f. L (1) *parri-cida* (2) *-cidium,* etym. dub., see -CIDE]

pä'rrot, n., & v.t. Genus of birds, of which some can be taught to repeat words; person who repeats another's words or imitates his actions unintelligently; (v.t.) repeat (words, or abs.) mechanically, drill (person etc.) to do this, whence ~RY(4) n.; ~*fish,* kinds with brilliant colouring or mouth like ~'s bill. [?]

pä'rry, v.t., & n. 1. Ward off, avert, (weapon, blow, awkward question). 2. n. Warding off. [f. F *parer* f. It. & L *parare* prepare]

parse (-z, -s), v.t. Describe (word) grammatically, stating inflexion, relation to sentence, etc.; resolve (sentence) into its component parts & describe them. [prob. f. L *pars* part]

pär'sec, n. Unit of stellar distances, the distance at which a star would have a parallax of one second of arc, i.e. at which the mean radius of the earth's orbit subtends this angle. [f. PARALLAX +SEC(OND)]

Pärsee', n. 1. Adherent of ZOROASTRIAN-ism, descendant of Persians who fled to India from Mohammedan persecution in 7th & 8th cc. whence ~ISM(3) n. 2. Language of Persia under Sassanian kings. [f. Pers. *Pärsi* Persian (*Pars* Persia)]

pär'simony, n. Carefulness in employ-ment of money etc. or (fig.) of immaterial things; stinginess; *law of* ~ony (that no more causes or forces should be assumed than are necessary to account for facts). So ~ÔN'IOUS a., whence ~ÔN'IOUSLY adv., ~ÔN'IOUSNESS n. [f. L *parsimonia, parci-* (*parcere pars-* spare, see -MONY)]

pärs'ley, n. Biennial umbelliferous plant with white flowers & aromatic leaves, used for seasoning & garnishing dishes. [(partly thr. OF *peresil*) f. LL *petroselinum* f. L f. Gk *petroselinon* (*petra* rock +*selinon* parsley)]

pärs'nip, n. (Plant with yellow flowers &) pale yellow root used as culinary vege-table; *fine words* BUTTER[2] *no* ~*s*. [ME *passenep,* ult. f. L *pastinaca* (*pastinum* digging-fork)]

pärs'on, n. Rector; vicar or any bene-ficed clergyman; (colloq.) any clergyman; ~*bird,* New Zealand bird with dark plumage & white neck; ~*'s nose,* rump of fowl etc. Hence **pärson'ic a.** [ME & OF *persone* f. L *persona* PERSON, (med. L) rector]

pärs'onage, n. Rector's or other in-cumbent's house. [var. of PERSONAGE]

pärt[1], n. & adv. 1. Some but not all of a thing or number of things, as (*a*) ~ *of it was spoilt,* (*a*) ~ *of them have arrived,* (*a*) *great part of this is true, the majority of them failed.* 2. Division of books etc., esp. as much as is issued at one time. 3. Portion of animal body; the (*privy*) ~*s.* 4. Each of several equal portions of a whole, as *three ~s* (*twentieths*), *take a ~s of sugar, 5 of flour, 2 of ground rice,* etc. 5. Portion allotted, share, esp. *have neither ~ nor lot* (no concern) *in;* ART[2] *& ~;* person's share in action, his duty, *as I have done my ~, it was not my ~ to interfere.* 6. Character by actor on stage; copy of these, (fig.) *play a noble, an unworthy, ~, behave nobly etc.; play a ~, act deceitfully.* 7. (mus.) Melody assigned to particular voice or instrument, 8, pl. (arch.) Abili-ties, *as a man of (good) ~s.* 9, pl. Region (*a stranger in these ~s*). 10. Side in dispute. 11. ~ *& parcel,* essential ~; *of speech,* each of the grammatical classes of words (noun, adjective, pro-noun, verb, adverb, preposition, conjunc-tion, interjection); *for the most* ~, in most cases, mostly; *take* ~, assist (*in doing in* discussion etc.); *take the* ~ *of,* support, back up; *for my* ~, as far as I am con-cerned; *in* ~, partly; *take* (words, action) *in good* ~, not be offended at; *on the* ~ *of,* proceeding from, done etc. by, as there *was no objection on my* ~; ~*-owner,* one who owns in common with others; ~*-song,* song with three or more voice-~s, freq. without accompaniment, & harmonic rather than contrapuntal in character. 12. adv. In ~, partly (*made ~ of iron & ~ of wood; a lie that is ~ truth*). [OE, f. L *pars partis*]

pärt[2], v.t. & i. 1. Divide (t. & i.) into parts, as *the crowd* ~*ed & let him through, an islet* ~ *the stream, the cord* ~*ed* (broke). 2. Separate (hair of head) with comb; separate (combatants, friends, etc.); company, dissolve companionship (*with*); ~ BRASS RAGS *with.* 3. Quit one another's company, as *let us* ~ *friends, the best of friends must* ~; ~ *from* or *with, say good-bye to;* ~ *with,* give up, surrender, (property etc.). 4. (colloq.) ~ *with one's money,* pay, (*if I know him, he won't* ~). 5. (arch.) Distribute (thing) in shares. [f. F *partir* f. L *partīrī* (prec.)]

pärtake', v.t. & i. (-*took, -taken*). Take a share in; take a share (*in of* thing, *with* person); take, esp. eat or drink some or (colloq.) all of, *as he partook of our lowly fare, partook of a bun;* have some (*of quality* etc.), *as his manner* ~*s of insolence.* [back formation f. *partaker*=part-taker]

‖ **part'an**, n. (Sc.) Crab. [Celt.]

parterre' (-tār'), n. Level space in garden occupied by flower-beds; part of ground-floor of auditorium of theatre, behind orchestra. [F; = *par terre* on the ground]

parthenogen'esis, n. (biol.) Reproduction without sexual union. So ~**genet'ic** a. [f. Gk *parthenos* virgin]

Parth'ian, a. Of Parthia, ancient kingdom of W. Asia; ~ *shaft, glance,* etc., remark, glance, etc., reserved for the moment of departure, like missile shot backwards by flying ~ horseman. [-AN]

parti (pàrtē'), n. Person regarded as eligible etc. in the marriage market (*is quite* a, *a desirable, an unsuitable,* ~); ~ *pris* (prē), preconceived view, bias. [F]

par'tial (-shl), a. & n. 1. Biased, unfair; ~ *to,* having a liking for (person, thing); forming only a part, not complete, as a ~ *success;* ~ *eclipse* (in which part only of the luminary is covered or darkened). 2. n. (mus.) A ~ note; *upper* ~*s,* higher notes more faintly heard than main note produced from string, pipe, etc. Hence ~LY² (-sha-) adv. [f. OF *parcial* f. LL *partialis* (as PART¹, see -AL)]

partial'ity (-shi-), n. Bias, favouritism; fondness (*for*). [f. OF *parcialité* f. med. L *partialitas* (as prec., see -TY)]

par'tible, a. That can or must be divided (*among,* esp. of heritable property). [f. LL *partibilis* f. L as PART¹, -IBLE]

parti'cipate, v.t. & i. 1. Have share in (thing *with* person); have share (*in* thing *with* person); have something of, as *his poems* ~ *ate of the nature of satire.* So ~ANT, **partic'ipa'tion,** ~**ātor**², nn. [f. L *participare* (as PART¹ + *cip-* = *cap-* st. of *capere* take)]

par'ticiple, n. Verbal adjective qualifying noun but retaining some properties of verb, e.g. tense & government of object. So ~**d** (-id) a.; (sl. substitute for *damned* etc.), **partic'ip'ial,** a., **partic'ip'ially**² adv. [OF, f. L *participium* sharing, participle, (as prec.)]

par'ticle, n. Minute portion of matter; smallest possible amount, as *has not a* ~ *of sense;* minor part of speech, esp. short indeclinable one; common prefix or suffix such as *un-, out-, -ness, -ship.* [f. L *particula* (PART¹, -CULE)]

par'ti-coloured, par'ty-, (-tilerd), a. Partly of one colour, partly of another. [prob. f. PARTY²]

partic'ular, a. & n. 1. Relating to one as distinguished from others, special; *P~ Baptists,* body holding doctrines of ~ *election* & ~ *redemption* (i.e. of only some of the human race); (Log., of a proposition) in which something is predicated of some, not all, of a class (opp. *universal*); one considered apart from others, individual, as *this* ~ *tax is no worse than others;* worth notice, special, as *took* ~ *trouble, for no* ~ *reason;* minute, as *full &*

~ *account;* scrupulously exact; fastidious (*about, what* or *as to what* one eats etc.); in ~, especially, *as mentioned one case in* ~. 2. n. Detail, item; (pl.) detailed account. Hence or cogn. ~**ITY** (-ǎ'r-) n., ~**LY²** adv. [f. OF *particuler* f. L *particularis* (as PARTICLE, see -AR¹)]

particula'risa'tion, n. Doctrine of PARTICULAR election or redemption; exclusive devotion to a party, sect, etc.; principle of leaving political independence to each State in an empire etc. So ~IST n. [-ISM]

partic'ularise, v.t. Name specially or one by one, specify, (often abs.). Hence ~**A'TION** n. [f. F *particulariser* (as PARTICULAR, see -IZE)]

part'ing, n. In vbl senses, esp.: leave-taking (often attrib., as ~ *injunctions*); dividing line of combed hair; ~ *of the ways,* point at which road divides into two or more (often fig. of choice between courses). [-ING¹]

partisan'¹ (-z-), -**zǎn,** (or part²), n. 1. Adherent of party, cause, etc., esp. unreasoning one (often attrib., as *in a* ~ *spirit*). 2. (mil.) Member of light irregular troops employed in special enterprises (hist.); (in recent use) a guerrilla (applied orig. to Russians resisting in parts of their country occupied by the enemy). Hence ~SHIP n. [F, f. It. *partigiano* (*pars* PART, PARTI, see -AN)]

partisan'² (-z-), -zǎn, n. (hist.). Long-handled spear like halberd. [f. F *partizane* f. It. *partesana,* etym. dub.]

part'ite, a. (bot., entom.). Divided (nearly) to the base. [f. L *partiri -īt-* PART²]

parti'tion, n. & v.t. 1. Division into parts; such part; structure separating two such parts, esp. slight wall, whence ~ED² (-shond) a.; (Law) division of real property between joint tenants etc. 2. v.t. Divide into parts; ~ *off,* separate (part of room etc.) by a ~. [(vb f. n.) F, f. L *partitionem* (as prec., see -ION)]

part'itive, a. & n. (Word) denoting part of a collective whole (e.g. *some, any*); ~ *genitive,* that used to indicate a whole divided into parts, expressed in English by *of.* Hence ~LY² adv. [f. L *partitivus* (PARTITE, -IVE)]

Part'let, n. (arch.). Used as proper name for a hen, esp. *Dame* ~, also applied to women. [f. OF *Pertelote,* female proper name]

part'ly, adv. With respect to a part; in some degree. [-LY²]

part'ner, n., & v.t. 1. Sharer (*with* person, *in* or *of* thing); person associated with others in business of which he shares risks & profits; ‖ SLEEP²*ing* ~; ~ *pre-dominant,* England (among constituents of United Kingdom); wife, husband; companion in dance; player associated with another in bridge, tennis, etc.;

(Naut., pl.) timber framework round hole in deck through which mast, pump, etc., passes. **2. v.t.** Associate (persons, one *with* another) ~s, (also) be ~ of. Hence ~LESS a., ~SHIP n. [prob. var. of *parcener*; see CO-PARCENER.]

par′tridge, n. Kinds of game-bird, esp. *Common* or *Grey P~*; ~*wood*, hard red speckled effect produced on wood by certain fungus. [ME *pertrich*, uk. f. L f. Gk *perdix* -*dikos*]

par′turi̇ent, a. About to give birth (often fig. of the mind etc.). [f. L *parturire* be in labour (*partu-* bear; see -ENT)]

par′turi̇tion, n. Childbirth (also fig.). [f. L *parturitio*, as prec., see -ION]

par′ve̅nu̇ mon′tés (-z) (. *na̅scĕt′ur̄ ri̅dic′u̅lus mūs*), sent. (As comment on fiasco; the mountains are in labour (, the product a poor mouse). [Hor., *A.P.* 139]

par′ty[1], n. **1.** Body of persons united in a cause, opinion, etc.; system of taking sides on public questions; ~ *spirit*, zeal for a ~, so ~*spirited*; body of persons travelling or engaged together, as *fishing*, *reading*, ~; social gathering, esp. of invited guests at private house, as *dinner*, *tea*, ~. **2.** Each of the two or more persons making the two sides in legal action, contract, marriage, etc.; accessory (*to action*) (now vulg. or joc.) person, as *an old* ~ *with spectacles*. **3.** ~*coloured*, see PARTI-COLOURED; ~*wall*, wall shared by each of the occupiers of the two buildings etc. that it separates. [f. F *partie* (*partir* f. L as PART[2])]

par′ty[2], a. (her.). Divided into parts of different tinctures. [f. F *parti*, as prec.]

parve̅nu̇ (-o̅o̅), n. (-ti f. & see AP.), n. Person of obscure origin who has gained wealth or position, upstart, (often attrib.). [F, p.p. of *parvenir* arrive f. L PER(*venire* come)]

parvis, n. Enclosed area in front of cathedral, church, etc. [f. F OF *pare-* (*vis* f. L *paradisus* PARADISE court in front of St Peter's, Rome]

pas (pah), n. Precedence, esp. *give*, *take*, *the* ~; step in dancing, as ~ *seul* (su̅l, & see Ap.) ~ *de deux* (de̅dö′, & see Ap.) dance for one, two. [F= step]

pasch′a(-k-), n. Of the Jewish Passover; Of Easter. [f. F *pascal* f. L.L *paschalis* f. Heb. *pesakh* Pass-over f. *pasakh* pass over, see -AL]

pa̅sha̅, -cha, (pah′sha̅, pä′sha̅, pa̅shah′)*n.* Turkish officer of high rank, e.g. military commander, governor of province, etc.; ~ *of three, two, tails*, of one tail, (of first, second, third, grade; from number of horse-tails displayed as symbol in war). [Turk.-(sha)]

pa′shalic, **-ch-**, (pah-; *also pashahk′*), n. Jurisdiction of pasha. [f. Turk. *pashalik*]

pa̅sh′m, n. Under-fur of hairy quadrupeds in Tibet etc., esp. that of goats as used for Cashmere shawls. [Pers.,= wool]

pasque̅flower (-skˈ-), n. Anemone with bell-shaped purple flowers. [orig. *passe-flower*, f. F *passefleur* (surpassing flower) w. assim. to obs. *Pasque* Easter (PASCHAL)]

pasquinade′, n. Lampoon, satire, orig. one affixed to public place. [f. It. *pas-quinada* (*Pasquino*, statue at Rome on which Latin verses were annually posted, see -ADE)]

pass[1](-ah-), v.i. & t. (p.p. ~*ed* or as adj. *past*). **1.** intr. Move onward, proceed, (*along*, *down*, *over*, *on*, etc.); circulate, be current; ~ *for*, be accepted as; ~ (be currently known) *by the name of*; be trans-ported from one place to place; change (*into* something, *from* one state to another); die (now usu. ~ *hence*, ~ *from among us*, etc.); go by, as *saw the procession* ~, *time* ~*es rapidly*, *remarks* ~ *unnoticed*; come to an end, as *kingdoms & nations* ~; get through, effect a passage; go uncensured, be accepted as adequate; (of bill in Parliament, proposal, etc.) be sanctioned; (of candidate) satisfy examiner; happen, be done or said, as *I saw* or *heard what was* ~*ing*; adjudicate (*upon*); (of judgement) be given (*for* plaintiff etc.); forgo one's opportunity, e.g. of making a bid, (also) throw up one's hand; *~ed pawn* (Chess), pawn with no opposing pawn on its own or adjoining files. **2.** trans. Leave (thing etc.) on one side or behind as one goes (*has* ~*ed the chair*, been chairman, president, mayor, etc.); be examined & approved by (House of Commons etc.); reach standard required by (examiner, examination); ~ MUSTER[1]; outstrip; surpass; be too great for, as *it ~es my comprehension*; transport (usu. w. prep. or adv.); move, cause to go, as *pass his hand across his forehead*; *your eye* (glance) *over this letter*; *~ a rope round it*, ~(=hand) *in* one's CHECK[1]s; (Football, Hockey, etc.) kick or hand or hit (ball) to player of one's own side (also abs.); cause to go by, as ~ (troops) *in review*; cause, allow, (measure in Parliament, candidate for examination, etc.) to proceed after scrutiny; spend (*time*, *the winter*, etc.); hand round, transfer, as *read this* & ~ *it on*; give currency to (coin, esp. base coin); pledge (one's word, oath, etc.); utter (criticism, judicial sentence, *upon*; *the* TIME[1] *of day*; ~ *water*, void urine. **3.** Spec. senses w. adv. fade away, die, come to an end; ~ *by* (adv. or prep.), omit, disregard; walk etc. past; ~ *off*, (of sensations etc.) fade away, (of proceedings) be carried through (*without a hitch* etc.); palm off (*thing upon* person *for* or *as* what it is not), distract attention from (awkward situation or allusion); ~ *out* (colloq.), die, become insensible as a result of drinking; ~ *over* (adv. or prep.),

omit, make no remark upon, as ~ *over his subsequent conduct*, ~ *it over in silence*; ~ *through*, experience; ~ *up*, refuse to have further dealings with, renounce. [f. F *passer* f. L *passus* PACE¹]

pass² (-ah-), n. **1.** Passing, esp. of examination; ‖(Univv.) attainment of standard that satisfies examiners but does not entitle to honours. **2.** *Bring to* ~, accomplish, carry out; *come to* ~, happen. **3.** Critical position, as *things have come to a (strange)* ~ **4.** Written permission to pass into or out of a place, or to be absent from quarters (*on* ~, *away thus*); (usu. *free* ~) ticket authorizing holder to travel free on railway etc. **5.** Thrust in fencing; juggling trick; passing of hands over anything, esp. in mesmerism; *make a* ~ *at* (sl.), make amatory advances to. **6.** (Football etc.) transference of ball to another player of one's own side. **7.** ~*book*, book supplied by bank to person having current or deposit account, showing all sums deposited & drawn; ~*key*, private key to gate etc. for special purposes, (also) master-key; ‖~*man*, one who takes ~ degree at university; ~*word*, selected word or phrase distinguishing friend from enemy. [partly f. prec., partly f. F *passe* as prec.]

pass³ (-ah-), n. Narrow passage through mountains; (Mil.) such passage viewed as key to a country (*sell the* ~, fig., betray a cause); navigable channel, esp. at river's mouth; passage for fish over weir. [f. F *pas* f. L *passus* PACE¹]

pa'ssable (-ah-), a. In vbl senses, esp. that can pass muster, fairly good, whence ~LY² adv. [-ABLE]

pass'age¹, n. Passing, transit (BIRD of ~); transition from one state to another; liberty, right, to pass through; voyage, crossing, from port to port; right of conveyance as passenger by sea; passing of a measure into law; way by which one passes; corridor etc. giving communication between different rooms in house; (pl.) what passes between two persons mutually, interchange of confidences etc.; ~ (*of* or *at arms*), fight (often fig.); part of a speech or literary work taken for quotation etc. [F (as PASS¹, see -AGE)]

pass'age², v.i. & t. (Of horse or rider) move sideways, by pressure of rein on horse's neck & of rider's leg on opposite side; make (horse) do this. [f. F *passager*, earlier *passéger* f. It. *passeggiare* (*passeggio* walk f. L *passus* PACE¹)]

passé (pás'ā, & see Ap.), a. (fem. ~e). Past the prime, esp. (of woman) past the period of greatest beauty; behind the times. [F, p.p. as PASS¹]

pásse'menterie (-smentri, & see Ap.), n.

Trimming of gold or silver lace, braid, beads, etc. [F (*passement* gold lace etc. as PASS¹, see -MENT & -ERY]

pass'enger (-j-), n. Traveller in public conveyance by land or water or air; (colloq.) member of team, crew, etc., who does, or can do, no effective work; *foot*-~, traveller on foot; ~*pigeon*, wild pigeon of N. America, capable of long flight (now rare or extinct). [ME & F (n. & a.) *passager* (see PASSAGE, see -ER)]

pa'sser (-ah-), n. In vbl senses; ~*by*, one who passes, esp. casually. [-ER¹]

pass'erine, a. & n. (Bird) of the order of *Passeres* or Perchers; of the size of a sparrow. [f. L *passer* sparrow +-INE¹]

pass'ible, a. (theol.) Capable of feeling or suffering. So ~IBI'LITY n. [OF, f. LL *passibilis* (*pati* pass- suffer, see -BLE)]

páss'im, adv. (Of allusions, phrases, etc., to be found in specified author or book) in every part, as *this occurs in Milton* ~. [L, = scatteredly (*pandere pass-* spread)]

‖ **pássim'eter**, n. Automatic railway ticket-booking machine. [f. PASS¹ (or PASSENGER) + -METER]

pa'ssing¹ (-ah-), n. In vbl senses; ~*bell* (rung in moment of person's death); ~*note* (not belonging to the harmony but interposed to secure smooth transition). [-ING¹]

pa'ssing² (-ah-), a. & adv. In vbl senses, esp.: transient, fleeting; cursory, incidental; (adv., arch.) very (esp. ~ *rich*). [-ING²]

pa'ssion¹ (-shn), n. **1.** Strong emotion; outburst of anger; sexual love; strong enthusiasm (*for thing, for doing*). **2.** (*The P*~) sufferings of Christ on cross, (musical setting of) narrative of this from Gospels; ~*play*, mystery-play representing Christ's P~; ~*flower*, kinds of (chiefly climbing) plants, flower of which was supposed to suggest instruments of Christ's P~; P~ *Sunday*, fifth Sunday in Lent; P~ *Week*, week between P~ *Sunday* and PALM *Sunday*, (also)=HOLY *Week*. Hence ~LESS a., ~'LESSLY² adv., ~LESS-NESS n., (-sho-). [OF, f. L *passionem* (*pati* pass- suffer, see -ION)]

pá'ssion² (-shn), v.t. (poet.). Feel or express passion. [f. OF *passionner*, as prec.]

pá'ssional (-'sho-), n. Book of the sufferings of saints & martyrs. [f. med. L *passionale* neut. adj. as n. (as foll.)]

pá'ssional² (-'sho-), a. Of, marked by, passion. [f. LL *passionalis* (as PASSION¹, see -AL)]

pá'ssionate (-sho-), a. Easily moved to anger; dominated by, easily moved to, strong feeling; due to, (of language etc.)

~showing, passion. Hence ~ɪsᴛ[2] n. [f. med. PASSION[1], see -ɪsᴛ[2]]

Pa'ssionist (-sho-), n. Member of an order pledged to do their utmost to keep alive the memory of Christ's Passion. [-ɪsᴛ]

pa'ssive, a. & n. **1.** Suffering action, acted upon; (Gram.) ~ *voice* (comprising those forms of transitive verbs that attribute the verbal action to the person etc. to whom it is directed, cf. ACTIVE); offering no opposition, submissive; ~ RESISTANCE; not active, inert; ~ *debt* (on which no interest is paid). **2.** n. (gram.), ~ voice or form of verb. Hence ~ɪʏ[2] adv., ~ɴᴇss, **passɪv'ɪᴛʏ**, nn. [f. L *passivus* (*pati pass-* suffer, see -ɪᴠᴇ]

pa'ssover (-ah-), n. (P~) Jewish festival commemorating liberation of Israelites from Egyptian bondage (*Exod.* xiii), held from 14th to 21st day of month Nisan; Paschal lamb, (fig.) Christ (1 *Cor.* v. 7). [f. *pass over*]

pa'ssport (-ah-), n. Document issued by competent authority permitting person specified in it to travel in the country & entitling him to to protection; (fig.) thing that ensures admission, as *flattery is the sole ~ to his favour*. [f. F *passeport* (*passer* PASS[1]+PORT[3])]

past[1] (-ah-), a. & n. **1.** As p.p. or adj. in vbl senses of PASS[1], esp.: gone by in time, as *his prime is ~, our ~ years*; just gone by, as *the ~ month, for some time ~*;(Gram.) expressing ~ action or state, as ~ *tense*, ~ *particible*; ~ *master*, one who has been master in guild, freemasons' lodge, etc., (also) thorough master (*in, of,* a subject). **2.** n. ~ time, esp. *the ~*; what has happened in ~ time, as *cannot undo the ~*; person's ~ life or career, esp. one that will not bear inquiry, as *a woman with a ~*.

past[1] (-ah-), prep. & adv. **1.** Beyond in time or place, as *stayed till ~ two o'clock, half ~ three, old man ~ seventy, run ~ the house*; beyond the range or compass of, as ~ *endurance, bearing, praying for*. **2.** adv. So as to pass by, as *hastens ~*. [prob. f. misuse of *am past* with object, *past* being then mistaken for prep., e.g. *I was noun ~ the house*]

paste[1], n. Flour moistened & kneaded, with butter, suet, etc., as cooking material; kinds of sweet confection; relish of pounded fish, as *anchovy ~*; cement of flour & water; any soft plastic mixture; hard vitreous composition used in making imitation gems; ~*board*, stiff substance made by pasting together sheets of paper, (attrib., fig.) unsubstantial, flimsy, (sl.) visiting-card, railway-ticket. [OF, f. com.-Rom. *pasta* perh. f. Gk *pastē* (*passō* sprinkled)]

paste[2], v.t. Fasten with paste; stick up (playbill etc.) on wall with paste; cover (thing *with* paper etc.) by pasting; (sl.) beat, thrash. [f. prec.]

pãs'tel, n. Woad; blue dye from this; dry paste made by compounding pigments with gum-water, used for crayons; drawing in ~, whence ~(l)ɪsᴛ n. [F, f. It. *pastello* woad, dim. of *pasta* PASTE[1]]

pãs'tern, n. Part of horse's foot between fetlock & hoof. [f. OF *pasturon*, f. OF *pasture* (perh. as PASTURE)]

pãs'teurism (-ter-), n. Prevention or cure of diseases esp. hydrophobia by successive inoculations. [f. L. *Pasteur*, French scientist (1822–1895) +-ɪsᴍ]

pãs'teurize (-ter-), v.t. Subject (milk etc.) to Pasteur's method of partial sterilization; treat by pasteurism. Hence PAS'TION n. [-ɪᴢᴇ]

pãsti'ccio (-ichō), **pãstiche'** (-ēsh), nn. Medley, esp. musical composition, picture, made up from various sources; (usu. -*iche*) literary or other work of art composed in the style of a known author. [f. (-iche) f. It. (-iccio), f. *pasta* PASTE[1]]

pãs'til, **pãstille'** (-tēl), n. Small roll of aromatic paste burnt as fumigator etc.; lozenge. [F (-le), f. L *pastillus* small roll, etym. dub.]

pas'time (-ah-), n. Recreation; game, sport. [f. PASS[1]+TIME]

pa'stor (-ah-), n. **1.** Minister in charge of church or congregation, whence ~SHIP n.; person exercising spiritual guidance. **2.** Kind of starling. [OF, f. L *pastorem* shepherd (*pascere past-* feed, see -OR[2])]

pa'storal (-ah-), a. & n. **1.** Of shepherds; (of land) used for pasture; (of poems etc.) portraying country life, whence ~ɪsᴍ n.; of a pastor, as ~ *epistles* (of Paul to Timothy & Titus, dealing with pastor's work). **2.** n. ~ play, poem, poetry, or picture; letter from pastor, esp. bishop, to clergy or people. Hence ~ɪᴛʏ (-ali) n., ~ɪᴢᴇ[2] adv. [f. L *pastoralis* (as prec., see -AL)]

pastora'le (paelstoraeh-), n. (pl. -*ali* pr. -lē, or -*ales*). Simple opera etc. with rural subject; slow quiet instrumental composition with notes flowing in groups of three & usu. with drone notes in bass suggesting bagpipes. [It., as prec.]

pa'storate (-ah-), n. Pastor's (tenure of) office; body of pastors. [f. med. L *pastoratus* (as PASTOR, see -ATE[2])]

pa'sturage (-ah-), n. Pasturing; herbage for cattle etc.; pasture-land. [OF, as foll., see -AGE]

pa'sture (-ah-), n. & v.t. & i. **1.** Herbage for cattle; (piece of) land covered with this. **2.** v.t. Lead, put, (cattle) to ~; (of sheep etc.) eat down (grass-land); (of person) put sheep etc. on (land) to graze, whence **pa'sturable** (-abscher-) a. **3.** v.i. Graze. [f. LL *pastura* (as PASTOR, see -URE)]

pa'sty¹ (pah-, pā-), n. Pie of meat, fruit, jam, etc. enclosed in paste & baked without dish. [f. OF *pastée* f. com.-Rom. *pasta* PASTE, cf. -ADE]

pās'ty², a. Of, like, paste; (also ~*faced*) of pale complexion. [-Y²]

pat¹, n. Stroke, tap, esp. with hand as caress etc.; small mass (esp. of butter) formed by patting; sound made by striking lightly with something flat. [prob. imit.]

pat², v.t. & i. (-tt-). Strike (thing) gently with flat surface (~*ball*, ‖ poor or feeble lawn tennis); flatten thus; ~*a-cake*, first words of nursery rhyme, connected child's game; strike gently with inner surface of fingers, esp. to mark sympathy, approbation, etc.; (fig.) ~ (person, one*self*) *on the back*, express approbation of; beat lightly *upon*. [as prec.]

pat³, adv. & a. Apposite(ly), opportune(ly), as *story came* ~ *to his purpose*; ready for any occasion, as *has the story* ~; *stand* ~, (Poker) abide by hand dealt to one, not draw other cards, (fig.) refuse to change, stick to one's decision etc. [prob. as PAT¹]

Pat⁴, n. (Nickname for) Irishman. [abbr. of *Patrick*]

pâtâg'ium, n. (zool.; pl. -*ia*). Wing-membrane of bat or similar animal. [L, f. Gk *patagēion* gold edging on gown, etym. dub.]

pátavin'ity, n. Dialectal characteristics of Patavium (Padua) as seen in Livy's Latin; provincialism. [f. L *patavinitas* (*Patavinus* of Padua, see -INE¹ & -ITY)]

patch¹, n. 1. Piece of cloth, metal, etc., put on to mend hole or rent; piece of plaster etc. put over wound; pad worn to protect injured eye; *not a* ~ *on*, not comparable to, nothing to. 2. Small piece of black silk or plaster worn esp. in 17th & 18th cc. to show off complexion. 3. Large or irregular spot on surface. 4. Piece of ground; number of plants growing on this, as *a* ~ *of beans*. 5. Scrap, remnant. 6. *Strike a bad* ~, go through a period of bad luck; ~*pocket* (consisting of a piece of cloth sewn on garment); ~*work*, work made up of fragments of different kinds & colours (often fig. & attrib.). Hence ~'ERY(1), ~'INESS, nn., ~'IER² adv., ~'Y² a. [ME, etym. dub.]

patch², v.t. Put patch(es) on; ~ *up*, repair with patches; (of material) serve as patch to; (fig., usu. ~ *up*) repair, set to rights (matter, trouble, quarrel); (usu. ~ *up*) put together hastily; piece (things) together (lit. or fig.); appear as patches (on surface). [f. prec.]

pátch'ouli (-ōōl-; *also* pacho̅o̅4-), n. Odoriferous Indian plant; perfume got from it. [native]

pāte, n. (now colloq.). Head, often as seat of intellect. Hence ~-PĀ'TED² a. [?]

pâté (păt'ā, & see AP.), n. Pie, patty; ~ *de*

foie gras (de fwah grah), pie etc. of fatted goose liver. [F, f. OF *pasté*, cf. PASTY]

patel'la, n. (pl. -*ae*). Knee-cap, whence patel'LAR¹, patel'LATE²(2), aa.; [Rom. Ant., small pan. [L, dim. as foll.]

pât'en, n. Shallow dish used for bread at eucharist; thin circular plate of metal. [f. OF *patene* f. L *patena, -ina*]

pât'ent¹ (or pā-) a. ‖ *Letters* ~, open letter from sovereign etc. conferring right, title, etc., esp. sole right for a term to make, use, or sell, some invention; conferred, protected, by this; ~ LEATHER; ~ *log*, elaborated rotary form of ship's log, recording speed on dial fixed on taffrail; (fig.) to which one has proprietary claim; (colloq.) such as might be patented, ingenious, well-contrived; (of door etc.) open, (fig.) plain, obvious, whence pāt'-ENCY n., ~-LY² adv. [partly thr. F) f. L *patēre* lie open, see -ENT]

pât'ent² (or pā-), n. ‖ = *letters* PATENT¹; government grant of exclusive privilege of making or selling new invention, invention, process, so protected; (fig.) sign that one is entitled to something, possesses a quality, etc., as *a* ~ *of gentility*; ~*roll* (containing ~s are issued) ‖~-*office* (from which ~s are issued) in Great Britain in a year). [short for *letters patent*]

pât'ent³ (or pā-), v.t. Obtain patent for (invention). [f. prec.]

pâtentee', n. Taker-out or holder of a patent, person for the time being entitled to the benefit of a patent. [-EE]

pât'er, n. (sl.). Father; P-~, *peccavī*, = PECCAVI. [L, = father]

pâterfamil'iās, n. (Rom. Law & joc.), head of family. [L]

pater'nal, a. Of a father; fatherly; related through the father, as ~ *grand-mother*, father's mother; ~ *government*, *legislation*, etc. (that limits the freedom of the subject by well-meant needless regulations). Hence ~LY² adv. [f. L *paternus* (*pater* father), + -AL]

pater'nity, n. Fatherhood; one's paternal origin; (fig.) authorship, source. [f. F *paternité* f. L *paternitatem* (as prec., see -TY)]

pât'ernos'ter, n. The Lord's Prayer, esp. in Latin; *black, white,* ~, forms of words said as charms etc.; *devil's* ~, muttered imprecation; bead in rosary indicating that ~ is to be said; ~ *line*, weighted fishing-line with hooks at intervals. [f. L *pater noster* our father]

path, n. (paîth, *pl. pr.* pahdhz). Footway, esp. one merely beaten by feet, not specially constructed (also ~'*way*); track laid for foot or cycle racing, esp. *cinder*-~; line along which person or thing moves; ~*finder*, explorer, aircraft (or its pilot) sent ahead of bombers to guide them to their objective & mark out their targets. Hence ~'LESS (-ah-) a. [com.-WG.: OE *pæth*, Du. *pad*, G *pfad*]

Pathan' (-tahn), n. Member of the Afghan tribes settled in India or on its NW. frontier. [f. PUSHTOO]

pathet'ic, a. & n. Exciting pity or sadness; of the emotions (~*ic fallacy*, crediting nature with human emotion); (n. pl.) these. Hence ~ICALLY adv. [f. LL f. Gk *pathētikos* (*path*-, root of *paskhō* suffer; see -ETIC)]

path'ic, n. = CATAMITE. [f. Lf. Gk *pathikos* passive (PATHOS, -IC)]

patho- in comb. =Gk *pathos* suffering, disease, passion, as: ~*genesis*, ~*geny* (-ŏj-), production of disease, so ~*genĕt'ic*, ~*gĕn'ic*, ~*genous* (-ŏj-), aa.; ~*gnomon'ic*, characteristic of particular disease; ~*gnomy* (-ŏg-), study of the emotions, so ~*gnom'ic* a.; *pathol'ogy*, science of (usu. bodily) diseases, so ~*lo'gical* a.,~*lo'gically* adv., *pathol'ogist* n.

path'os (or pā-), n. Quality in speech, writing, events, etc., that excites pity or sadness. [f. Gk *pathos* suffering, see PATHETIC]

-pathy, suf. repr. Gk -*patheia* suffering, feeling, in *homœopatheia* suffering or feeling alike, extended to ALLOPATHY & (w. sense curative treatment) to other compds. as *hydro*~, *kinesi*~, *electro*~.

pā'tience (-shns), n. 1. Calm endurance of pain or any provocation; perseverance; *have no* ~ *with*, be irritated by, be unable to endure, (person, his conduct, etc.); *out of* ~ *with*, no longer able to endure; *the* ~ *of Job*, the utmost limits of ~ (*would try the* ~ *of Job*). 2. Game of cards, usu. for one. 3. ~*dock*, kinds of plant. [OF, f. L *patientia* (as foll., see -ENCE)]

pā'tient (-shnt), a. & n. 1. Having, showing, patience; ~ *of*, enduring with patience, (also) admitting of or compatible with (*the facts are* ~ *of two interpretations*). 2. n. Person under medical treatment, see -ENT]. Hence ~LY² adv. [OF, f. L *pati* suffer,

pat'in, a, n. Incrustation, usu. green, on surface of old bronze, esteemed as ornament; gloss produced by age on woodwork. Hence ~*āted* [-ATE¹], ~OUS, aa. ~A'TION n. [f. F *patine* etym. dub.; L has *patina* dish]

pŭt'iō (pah-), n. (pl.~s). Inner court open to sky in Spanish or Span.-Amer. house. [Sp.]

păt'ois (-twah, & see AP.), n. Dialect of common people in a district, differing materially from the literary language. [F etym. dub.]

pā'triärch (-k), n. 1. Father & ruler of family or tribe; (pl.) sons of Jacob, (also) Abraham, Isaac, & Jacob, & their forefathers. 2. (In early & Eastern Churches) bishop, esp. of Antioch, Alexandria, Constantinople, Jerusalem, or Rome; (in R.-C. Church) bishop ranking next above primates & metropolitans. 3. Founder of

an order, science, etc.; venerable old man; *the* oldest living representative (*of* a class etc.). Hence **patriärch'al**¹ (-k-) a. [f. OF *patriarche* f. L (*-cha*) f. Gk *patriarkhēs* (*patriā* family f. *patēr* father+*arkhēs* ruler)]

pā'triärchate (-k-), n. Office, see, residence, of ecclesiastical patriarch; rank of tribal patriarch. [f. med. L PATRIARCH-*ātus* (-ATE¹)]

pā'triärchy (-k-), n. Patriarchal system of society, government, etc. So ~ISM n. [f. Gk *patriarkhia* (as PATRIARCH, see -Y¹)]

patri'cian (-shn), a. & n. 1. Ancient Roman noble (cf. PLEBEIAN); member of a noble order in later Roman Empire; officer representing provinces of Italy & Africa; nobleman of the ancient Roman nobility. Hence ~SHIP n. [f. L *patricius* (*pater -tris* father +-AN)]

patri'ciate (-shi-), n. Patrician order, aristocracy; rank of patrician. [f. med. L *patriciātus* (as prec., see -ATE¹)]

pat'ricide, n. Parricide (less correct & less usual than *parricide*, but occas. preferred of one's father). Hence **pătri-cid'al** a. [PATER, -CIDE]

pat'rimony, n. Property inherited from one's father or ancestors; heritage (often fig.); endowment of church etc. So **pātri-mon'ial** a. [f. F *patrimoine* f. L *patri-monium* (*pater -tris* father, see -MONY)]

pā'triot, n. One who defends or is zealous for his country's freedom or rights. Hence or cogn. **patriot'ic** a., **patriot'-ICALLY** adv., ~ISM n. [f. F *patriote* f. LL (-ŏt-) f. Gk *patriōtēs* (*patrios* of one's fathers f. *pater -tris* father, see -OT²)]

patris'tic, a. Of the Fathers of the Church. [f. L *pater -tris* father, see -IC]

patrōl', n. & v.i. & t. (-ll-). 1. Going the rounds of garrison, camp, etc.; perambulation of town etc. by police; detachment of guard, police constable(s), told off for this; detachment of troops sent out to reconnoitre; routine operational flight of aircraft. 2. vb. Act as ~; go round (camp, town, etc.) as ~. [n. (thr. F *patrouille*) & vb f. F *patrouiller*, orig. = paddle in mud, earlier *patouiller*, cf. OF *patouil* pool]

pā'tron, n. One who countenances, protects, or gives influential support to (person, cause, art, etc.); (Shop) regular customer; (also ~ *saint*) tutelary saint; (Rom. Ant.) former owner of manumitted slave, (also) protector of a CLIENT; || one who has right of presentation to benefice. So **pā'troness¹** n. [OF, = patron, PATRON, f. L *patronus* (*pater -tris* father) given by patron; ||right of presentation

to benefice or office, as *has a great deal of ~ in his hands*, (attrib.). P~ *Secretary* (of the Treasury), *patronizing airs*; customer's support. [F (as prec., see -AGE)]

pā'tronal, a. Of a patron saint (*the ~ festival* etc.). [-AL]

pā'troniz|e(, v.t. Act as patron towards, support, encourage, (person, practice, etc.); treat condescendingly, whence ~ing$_{\text{LY}}$[1] adv. [-IZE]

patronym'ic, a. & n. (Name) derived from that of a father or ancestor. [f. L.f. Gk *patrōnumikos* f. *patrōnumos* (*patēr -tros* father + *onoma* name), see -IC]

*patrōōn', n. (hist.). Possessor of landed estate with manorial privileges (abolished c. 1850) under Dutch governments of New York & New Jersey. [var. of PATRON]

patt'en, n. Overshoe with wooden sole on iron ring etc., for raising wearer's shoes out of mud etc. [ME, f. F *patin*, etym. dub.]

patt'er[1], n. Lingo of a profession or class; speechifying; rapid speech introduced into song; words of song, comedy, etc. [f. foll.]

patt'er[2], v.t. & i. Repeat (prayers etc.) in rapid mechanical way; talk glibly. [f. PATERNOSTER]

patt'er[3], v.i. & t. & n. 1. Make rapid succession of taps, as rain on window-pane; run with short quick steps; cause (water etc.) to ~. 2. n. Succession of taps. [f. PAT[2]+-ER[5]]

patt'ern, n., & v.t. 1. Excellent example, as *she is a ~ of domestic virtues*; (attrib.) perfect, ideal, model, (esp. of persons, as *~ wife, father*); model from which thing is to be made; sample (of tailor's cloth etc.); decorative design as executed on carpet, wall-paper, cloth, etc.; marks made by shot from gun on target; *~ room, -shop*, part of foundry etc. in which ~s are prepared. 2. v.t. Model (thing *after, upon*, design etc.), decorate with ~. [(vb f. n.) f. ME PATRON]

patt'y, n. Little pie or pasty; ~pan (for baking ~ in). [f. F *pâté* PASTY[1]]

pat'ulous, a. Open, expanded; (of boughs etc.) spreading. Hence ~$_{\text{LY}}$[2] adv., ~NESS n. [f. L *patulus* (*patēre* be open)+-OUS]

pau'city, n. Smallness of number or quantity. [f. L *paucitas* (*paucus* few, see -TY)]

Paul, n. *Rob* PETER[1] *to pay ~*; ~ *Pry*, inquisitive person (character in comedy by J. Poole 1825).

Paul'ine[1], a. & n. 1. Of St Paul, as *the ~ epistles*. 2. n. || Member of St Paul's School in London. [-INE[1]]

paulo-pōst-fū'ture, n. (Gk Gram.) tense expressing state resulting from future act, future-perfect; (joc.) immediate future. [L,=future a little after]

paunch, n., & v.t. 1. Belly, stomach; ruminant's first stomach; (Naut., perh.

diff. wd) thick strong mat, (*rubbing ~*) wooden shield on mast, to prevent chafing. 2. v.t. Disembowel. [f. ONF *panche* f. L *pantex -icis*]

paup'er, n. Person without means of livelihood, beggar; recipient of poor-law relief; person who may sue IN[5] *forma pauperis*. Hence ~DOM, ~ISM(2). ~izA[4]TION, nn., ~IZE(3) v.t. [L,=poor]

pause (-z), n., & v.i. 1. Interval of inaction or silence, esp. from hesitation; *give ~ to*, cause (person) to hesitate; break made in speaking or reading; (Mus.) mark (⌢ or ⌣) over or under note or rest that is to be lengthened indefinitely. 2. v.i. Make a ~, wait; linger *upon* (word etc.). [(vb f. n.) F, f. L *pausa* f. Gk *pausis* (*pauō* stop)]

pāv'age, n. Paving; tax, toll, towards paving of streets. [f (as PAVE, see -AGE)]

pāv'an, n. Stately dance in which dancers were elaborately dressed. [f. F *pavane* f. It. or Sp. *pavana*, etym. dub.]

pāve, v.t. Cover (street, floor, etc.) with or as with pavement (often fig., as *~d with flowers, with good intentions*); (fig.) ~ (prepare) *the way* (*for, to*, reform etc.). Hence pāv'ER[1], pāv[4]OUR (-vyer) [perh. after *saviour*], nn. [f. F *paver* f. L *pavire* beat, ram]

pavé (pāv'ā), n. Pavement; setting of jewels placed close together. [F, p.p. as prec.]

pāve'ment (-vm-), n. Covering of street, floor, etc., made of stones, tiles, wooden blocks, asphalt, etc., || esp. paved footway at side of road (*crazy ~*, of irregular flat stones for garden paths etc.); ||~*artist*, one who draws coloured figures on ~ to get money from passers-by; (Zool.) ~like formation of close-set teeth etc. [OF, f. L *pavimentum* (as PAVE, see -MENT)]

pavil'ion (-lyon), n., & v.t. 1. Tent, esp. large peaked one; light ornamental building, esp. one attached to cricket or other ground for spectators & players; projecting (usu. highly decorated) subdivision of building; part of cut gemstone below girdle. 2. v.t. Enclose in, furnish with, ~. [f. F *pavillon* f. L *papilionem* (nom. *-io*) butterfly, tent]

pavonā'zzo (pah-, -dtsō), a. & n. (Marble) with peacock-coloured markings. [It.]

pāv'onine, a. Of, like, a peacock. [f. L *pavoninus* (*pavo -onis* peacock, see -INE[1])]

paw[1], n. Foot of beast having claws or nails, opp. to HOOF; (colloq.) hand, person's handwriting. [f. OF *poue*, prob. of Frank. orig.]

paw[2], v.t. & i. Strike with paw; (of horse) strike (ground), strike ground, with hoofs; (colloq.) handle awkwardly or rudely. [f. prec.]

|| **pawk**[1], n. [y̆, a. (Sc., dial.). Sly, arch. Hence ~$_{\text{LY}}$[2] adv., ~INESS n. [*pawk* trick, etym. dub., +-Y[2]]

pawl, n., & v.t. 1. Lever with catch for teeth of wheel or bar; (Naut.) short bar

used to prevent capstan, windlass, etc., from recoiling. **2.** v.t. Secure (capstan etc.) with ~. [!]

pawn¹, n. Piece of smallest size & value in chess (often fig. of persons). [f. AF *poun* f. L *pedonem* (nom. -o) foot-soldier (*pes pedis* foot)]

pawn², n. Thing, person, left in another's keeping as security, pledge, (now chiefly fig.); state of being pledged, esp. *in, at,* ~; ~*broker*, one who lends money upon interest on security of personal property pawned; ~*broking*, his occupation; ~*shop*, his place of business. [f. OF]

pawn³, v.t. Deposit (thing) as security for payment of money or performance of action; (fig.) pledge (one's life, honour, word). [f. prec.]

pawnee', n. Person with whom pawn is deposited. [-EE]

pax, n. **1.** Tablet with representation of Crucifixion etc. kissed at Mass by priests & congregation, osculatory; the kiss of peace as liturgical form at High Mass. **2.** ~ *Rōmā'na, Brītān'ĭca,* abstention from war enforced on States subject to the Roman, British, empire; ~ *vōb'is, vōbīscum,* peace be to, with, you (esp. as priestly blessing). **3.** || (school sl., as int.) Peace!, truce! [L, = peace]

pax'wax, n. (dial., colloq.). Stout tendon extending from dorsal vertebræ to occiput in man & other mammals. [earlier *faxwax*, prob. f. OE *feax* hair + *weax* growth]

pay¹, n. Payment; *in the* ~ (employment) of; ~*days,* day on which payment is (to be) made, || (Stock Exch.) day on which transfer of stock has to be paid for; ~*load*, part of aircraft's load which produces revenue; ~*master*, official who pays troops, workmen, etc. (often fig.); ~*master general*, || officer at head of a department of Treasury. [f. OF]

pay², v.t. & i.(*paid*). **1.** Give (person) what is due in discharge of debt or for services done or goods received; ~ *off,* ~ *in full* & discharge or be quit of (ship's crew, creditor, etc.); (fig.) reward, recompense; ~ (person) *out*, punish him; ~ *him in his own coin*; (colloq.) *that has put paid to his* (settled) *him*. **2.** Recompense (work). **3.** Hand over (money owed to person, or & double object); hand over the amount of (debt, wages, ransom, tithes). **4.** ~ *in,* ~ *to* one's own or another's banking account; ~ *one's way*, not get into debt; ~ *through the* NOSE, ~ *the* PIPER; ~ *up,* ~ *down,* **5.** Render, bestow, (attention, respect, court, compliment, *to*). **6.** (Of business etc.) yield adequate return, yield adequate return to (person). **7.** ~ *for,* hand over the price of, bear the cost of (~ *for one's* WHISTLE), (fig.) be punished for(fault etc.);

~ *off,* (of ship) fall off to leeward when helm is put up; (Naut.) ~ *out, away,* let out (rope) by slackening it. **8.** ||~*-as-you-earn* (abbr. *P.A.Y.E.*), method of collecting income-tax by deducting at source as income is earned. Hence ~EE, ~'ER¹, n. [f. F *payer* f. L *pacare* appease (*pax pacis* peace)]

|| **pay³**, v.t.(Naut.). Smear with pitch, tar, etc., as defence against wet. [f. ONF *peier* f. L *picare* (*pix picis* pitch)]

pay'able, a. That must be paid; due; that may be paid; (of mine etc.) profitable. [-ABLE]

pay'ment, n. Paying; amount paid; (fig.) recompense. [f. F *paiement* f. *payer*]

paynim, n. (arch.). Pagan, esp. Mohammedan (often attrib.). [f. OF *paienime* f. LL *pāganismus* (PAGAN, see -ISM)]

payn'ize, v.t. Impregnate (wood) with certain preservatives. [*Payne*, inventor, -IZE]

paysage' (-zahzh), n. Rural scene, land-scape; landscape painting; so **pays'agist** (-zh-), n. [F]

pea, n. **1.** Leguminous plant whose seeds are used for food; its seed, as *green* ~s (gathered unripe for food); SWEET ~; *as like as two* ~s, undistinguishable. **2.** ~'*nut*, (plant whose fruit is a pod containing) seed used as food & yielding oil; ~'*shooter*, tube from which dried ~s are shot; ~'*soup* (made from esp. dried ~s); ~-*soupy*, (of fog) thick & yellow. [back formation f. PEASE taken as pl.]

peace, n. **1.** Freedom from, cessation of, war, as ~ *with honour; at any price, make* (bring about) ~; *a treaty of* ~ between two powers at war. **2.** Freedom from civil disorder; *the (king's)* ~, general ~ of the realm as secured by law, as *commission,* JUSTICE, *of the* ~, *be sworn of the*~ (made a magistrate). **3.** Quiet, tranquility; (in & after bibl. use) ~ *be with you,* ~ *to his ashes!*; mental calm, as ~ *of mind, conscience*. **4.** *At* ~, in state of friendliness, not at strife (*with*); *hold one's* ~, keep silence; *keep the* ~, prevent, refrain from, strife; *make* (person's, one's) ~, bring person, oneself, back into friendly relations (*with*); ~ (joc.) revolver, war-ship, etc.; ~*offering*, propitiatory gift, (Bibl.) offering presented as thanks-giving to God; ~*pipe*, tobacco-pipe as token of ~ among N.Amer. Indians. [f. OF *pais* f. L *pacem* (nom. *pac-*)]

peaceable (-sa-), a. Disposed, tending, to peace; free from disturbance, peaceful. Hence ~NESS n., ~LY² adv. [f. OF *paisible* (as prec., see -BLE)]

peace'ful (-sf-), a. Characterized by, belonging to a state of, peace. Hence ~LY² adv., ~NESS n. [-FUL]

peach¹, n. Large fruit, usu. round, with downy white or yellow skin flushed with

red, highly flavoured sweet pulp, & rough stone; (also ~-tree) tree bearing this; (sl.) person or thing of superlative merit, specially attractive girl; ~-blow, (glaze of) delicate purplish-pink colour; ~ juice; ~ spirituous liquor from ~ juice; ~ colour(ed), (of) soft pale red. [f. OF pesche f. LL persica f. L persicum (malum), lit. Persian apple]

peach², v.i. (now sl.). Turn informer; inform (against, upon, accomplice). [earlier appeach f. OF empechier IMPEACH]

pea-chick, n. Young pea-fowl.

peach'[y̆], a. Like a peach, esp. (of cheeks) in colour & softness. Hence ~INESS n. [-Y²]

pea'cock, n., & v.t. & i. **1.** Bird with splendid plumage & tail that can be expanded erect like fan (often as type of ostentatious display; *proud as a* ~); ~ *blue*, lustrous blue of ~'s neck; ~ *butterfly*, European butterfly with ocellated wings; ‖ ~ *coal* (iridescent); ~-*fish*, fish with brilliant green, blue, red, & white colouring. **2.** vb. Plume oneself, make display; strut about ostentatiously; whence ~ERY (4) n. Hence ~ISH¹, ~LIKE, aa. [(vb f. n.) f. OE péo, pawa, f. L pavo, + COCK¹]

pea'fowl, n. Peacock or peahen. [see prec.]

pea'hen, n. Female of the peacock. [see PEACOCK]

pea-jacket, n. Sailor's short overcoat of coarse woollen cloth. [f. obs. *pee* f. MDu. *pije* (now *pij*) pea-jacket + JACKET]

peak¹, n. **1.** Projecting part of brim of cap. **2.** (naut.). Narrow part of ship's hold esp. (also *fore-*, *after-*) at bow or stern; upper outer corner of sail extended by gaff. **3.** Pointed top, esp. of mountain; point e.g. of beard. **4.** Highest point in curve or record of fluctuations (~-*load*, maximum of electric power, traffic, etc.). Hence ~ED² (-kt), ~Y², aa. [f. 16th c., var. of PIKE¹]

peak², v.i. Waste away, esp. (Shakspere) ~ *& pine*; (p.p.) sharp-featured, pinched. So ~Y² a., sickly, puny. [?]

peak³, v.t. & i. (naut.). Tilt (yard) vertically; place (oars) APEAK; (of whale) raise (tail, flukes), raise tail or flukes, straight up in diving vertically. [f. APEAK]

peaky. See PEAK¹, PEAK².

peal, n., & v.i. & t. **1.** Loud ringing of bell(s), esp. series of changes on set of bells; set of bells; loud volley of sound, esp. of thunder or laughter. **2.** v.i. Sound forth in a ~. **3.** v.t. Utter sonorously; ~ *bells*, ring them in ~s. [(vb f. n.) perh. short for APPEAL]

pear (pār), n. A fleshy fruit, tapering towards stalk; ~-*shaped*; ~-*tree*; PRICKLY ~. [OE *pere* f. LL *pira* f. L *pirum*]

pearl¹ (pĕrl), n. Concretion, usu. white or bluish-grey, formed within shell of ~ *oyster* & other bivalve molluscs, having beautiful lustre & highly prized as gem;

MOTHER¹-*of-* ~; SEED ~. **2.** Precious thing, finest example (*of its kind*); *cast* ~*s before swine*, offer good thing to one incapable of appreciating it. **3.** ~-*like thing*, e.g. dewdrop, tear, tooth. **4.** Size of TYPE. **5.** Small fragment of various substances. **6.** ~-*ash*, potassium carbonate; ~-*barley*, -*sago*, etc. (reduced to small rounded grains); ~-*diver*, one who dives for ~-oysters; ~-*fisher*, one who fishes for ~s; ~-*fishery*, his occupation, place of this; ~-*powder*, -*white*, cosmetic used to whiten skin; mother-of-~ as naturally found. Hence ~ED² (-ld), ~Y², aa., ~INESS n., (pĕr-). [f. F *perle*, med. L *perla*, etym. dub.]

pearl² (pĕrl), v.t. & i. Sprinkle with pearly drops; make pearly in colour etc.; reduce (barley etc.) to small pearls; form pearl-like drops; fish for pearls. [f. prec.]

pearl³ (pĕrl), n. One of a row of fine loops forming decorative edging on pillow-lace etc. [prob. var. of PURL¹]

‖ **pear'lies** (pĕr'liz), n. pl. Costermongers' dress with many pearl buttons.

pear'main (pār-), n. Kind of apple. [f. OF *permain* prob. f. L †*parmanus* of Parma]

pea'sant (pĕz-), n. Countryman, rustic, worker on the land. [AF *paisant* f. L *pagensis* of a canton (*pagus*)]

pea'santry (pĕz-), n. (Body of) peasants. [-RY]

pease (z), n. Peas, esp. in ~-*pudding*. (arch.) ~*cod*. pea-pod. [OE *pise* pea, pl. *pisan*, f. LL *pisa* f. L *pisum* f. Gk *pison*; cf. PEA]

peat¹, n. (Cut piece of) vegetable matter decomposed by water & partly carbonized, used for fuel; ~*bog*, ~*moss*, bog composed of ~; ~*reek*, smoke of, whisky distilled over, ~-fire. Hence ~ERY(3) n., ~Y² a. [13th c. *pete*, etym. dub.]

peat², n. (arch.). Girl, belle, (esp. *proud* ~). [?]

pĕb'ble, n. Small stone worn & rounded by action of water; colourless transparent rock-crystal used for spectacles, lens of this; kinds of agate or other gem. Hence **pĕbb'ly²** a. [?]

pébrine (pābrēn'), n. Epidemic disease of silkworms characterized by black spots. [F, f. Pr. *pebrino* (*pebre* PEPPER)]

pecan, n. Kind of hickory of the Mississippi region; its nut. [Algonkin *pakan*]

pĕcc'|able, a. Liable to sin. Hence ~ABIL'ITY n. [f. med. L *peccabilis* (*peccare* sin, see -BLE)]

pĕccadill'ŏ, n. (pl. ~es). Trifling offence, [f. Sp. *pecadillo*, dim. of *pecado* sin, as foll.]

pĕcc'|ant, a. Sinning; (Med.) morbid, inducing disease. So ~ANCY n. [f. L *peccare* sin, see -ANT]

pĕcc'ary, n. American gregarious quadruped allied to swine. [f. native *pakira*]

peccāv'ĭ, sent. & n. I have sinned, esp. *cry* ~; (n.) this confession. [L]

pêche Mël'ba (päsh), n. Confection of ice-cream & peaches flavoured with liqueurs etc. [F, after Dame Nellie *Melba*, Australian prima donna (d. 1931)]

pêck[1], n. Measure of capacity for dry goods, = 2 gallons; vessel used for this; *a ~* (large number, amount) *of troubles, of dirt.* [ME & OF *pek*, etym. dub.]

pêck[2], v.t. & i. & n. **1.** Strike (thing) with beak; *~ out*, pluck out thus; make (hole etc.) thus; kiss (person's cheek etc.) perfunctorily; aim at (thing) with beak, (fig.) carp at; (colloq.) eat (food, or absol.), esp. in nibbling fashion; break (ground, wall, etc. *up, down,* etc.) with pointed tool. **2.** n. Stroke with beak, mark made with this; hasty kiss; (sl.) victuals. [prob. var. of PICK[2]]

pêck[3], v.t. & i. (sl.). Throw (stone), throw stones (at). [dial. var. of PITCH[2]]

pêck'er, n. Bird that pecks (chiefly in comb., esp. *woon~*); kind of hoe; (sl.) *keep your ~ up.* [-ER[1]]

pêck'ish, a. (colloq.). Hungry. [-ISH[1]]

Pêck'sniff, n. Unctuous hypocrite prating of benevolence etc. [in *Martin Chuzzlewit*]

pêc'tën, n. (zool.). pl. *~ines* pr. -ēz). Comb-like structure of various kinds in animal bodies, so *~inate*, aa. *~ina'tion* n.; scallop. [L, gen. *-tinis*, = comb]

pêc'tin, n. (chem.). Soluble gum-like carbohydrate, the setting agent in jams & jellies, formed in fruits from pectose by ripening or (in fruits & fruit-juice) by heating. So *~ic* a. [f. Gk *pēktos* congealed (*pēgumi* make solid)+-IN]

pêc'toral, n. & a. **1.** Ornamental breast-plate, esp. that of Jewish high priest; *~ fin, muscle*, etc. **2.** adj. Of, for, good for diseases of the breast or chest; worn on the breast (*~ cross*, by bishops); [(partly thr. F) f. L *pectoralis* a. *-le* n. (*pectus -oris* breast, see -AL)]

pêc'tose, n. (chem.). Insoluble substance related to cellulose & found with it in unripe fruits etc. [as PECTIN, see -OSE[2]]

pêc'ulate, v.t. & i. Embezzle (money, or absol.). So *~ATION, ~ātor²*, nn. [f. L *peculari* (as foll.)]

pecü'liar (as foll.), a. & n. **1.** Belonging exclusively *to*; belonging to the individual, esp. one's own~ (character etc.); particular, special, *as a point of ~ interest*; strange, odd, *as a ~ flavour, he has always been a little ~; ~ people*, the Jews, (in wider sense) God's elect, (*P~ People*) evangelical Christian denomination founded 1838 relying on divine healing for cure of disease. **2.** n. ~ property, privilege, etc.; parish, church, exempt from jurisdiction of diocese, in which it lies (hist.); (*P~*) one of the P~ People. [f. L *peculiaris* of private property (*peculium* f. *pecu* cattle, see -AR)]

pecülia'rity, n. Being peculiar; characteristic; oddity. [-ITY]

pecü'liarly, adv. As regards oneself alone, individually, *as does not affect him ~*; especially, more than usually, *as ~ annoying*; oddly, *as they dress ~*. [-LY²]

pecü'niar'y, a. (Consisting) of money, as *~y aid, considerations*; (of offence) having *~y penalty*. Hence *~iry²* adv. [f. L *pecuniarius* (*pecunia* money f. *pecu* cattle, see -ARY²)]

pěd'agōgue (-g), n. Schoolmaster, teacher, (usu. derog., implying pedantry). Hence or cogn. **pědagōg'ic(al)** (-ǒg-, -ōj-) aa., **pědagōg'ically²** adv., **pěd'agōg(u)ism**(l)(-gizm) n. [OF, f. L f. Gk *paidagōgos* (*pais paidos* boy + *agōgos* f. *agō* lead)]

pěd'agōgy (-gi, -ji), n. Science of teaching. So *~ics* (-gǒg-, -gōj-) n. [f. F *pédagogie* f. Gk *paidagōgia*, as prec.]

pěd'al[1], n. & a. & v.t. & i. (-ll-). **1.** (In organ) each of the wooden keys played upon by the feet, (also) foot-lever for drawing out several stops at once or other purposes; (in piano) foot-lever for making the tone fuller (*loud ~*) or softer (*soft ~*); foot-lever in various machines, esp. bicycle or tricycle; (Mus.) note sustained in one part, usu. bass, through successive harmonies some of which are independent of it. **2.** vb. Play on organ *~s*, work bicycle *~s*; work (bicycle) thus. [prob. f. F *pédale* f. It. *pedale* f. L as foll.]

pěd'ant, n. One who overrates or parades book-learning or technical knowledge or insists on strict adherence to formal rules; one who is possessed by a theory, doctrinaire. Hence or cogn. **pědan'tic** a., *~ically* adv., *~ISM*(2,4,5), nn. [(perh. thr. F *pédant*) f. It. *pedante*, perh. cogn. w. PEDAGOGUE]

pěd'ate, a. (Zool.) footed; (Bot., of leaf) having divisions like toes or bird's claws. [f. L *pedatus* (*pes pedis* foot, see -ATE²]

pěd'dle, v.i. & t. Follow occupation of pedlar; busy oneself with trifles; deal out in small quantities, retail, (usu. fig.). [?]

pěd'erasty. See PAEDERASTY.

pěd'estal, n. & v.t. (-ll-). Base supporting column in construction; base of statue etc.; each of two supports of knee-hole table; foundation (lit. & fig.); movable cupboard for chamber-pots; (v.t.) set, support, on ~. [f. F *piédestal* f. It. *piedestallo* foot of stall (*piè* foot f. L *pes pedis* + *di* of + *stallo* STALL²]

pědes'trian, a. & n. **1.** Going, performed, on foot; of walking; prosaic, dull, un-inspired. **2.** n. One who walks, esp. as athletic performance, whence *~ISM(2)* n., (esp.

péd'icel, péd'icle, nn. (bot., zool.). Small (esp. subordinate, cf. PEDUNCLE) stalk-like

structure in plant or animal. Hence **ped'icellate²**, **pedic'ulate²**, aa. [f. L (-cel) *pediccllus* double dim., (-cle) *pedi-culus* dim., f. *pes pedis* foot, see -CULE]

pedic'ular, -lous, aa. Lousy. So **pedi-culo'sis** n. [f. L *pedicularis*, *-losus* (*pedi-culus* louse, see -AR¹, -OUS]

ped'igree, n. Genealogical table: ancestral line (of man or animal); derivation (of word); ancient descent; (attrib.) having known line of descent, as ~ *cattle*. Hence **ped'igreed²** a. [earlier *pedegreed* prob. f. F *pié de grue* crane's foot, mark denoting succession in ~s (*pied* foot f. L *pes pedis* + *de* of + *grue* crane f. L *grus*)]

ped'iment, n. Triangular part crowning front of building in Grecian style, esp. over portico; similarly placed member of same or other form in Roman & Renaissance styles. Hence **pedimen'tal**, ~ED², aa. [earlier *peremind*, perh. corrupt. of PYRAMID]

pedo-. See PAEDO-.

ped'lar, n. Travelling vendor of small wares usu. carried in pack; (fig.) retailer (of gossip etc.); ~'s *French*, thieves' cant. Hence **ped'lary** n. [prob. f. Sc. *pedder* prob. f. *ped* basket, etym. dub.; found long before PEDDLE]

pedom'eter, n. Instrument for estimating distance travelled on foot by recording number of steps taken. [f. F *pédomètre* f. L *pes pedis* foot +-o- + -METER]

ped'rail, n. Device for facilitating progress of heavy vehicles over rough ground by attachment of broad footlike supporting surfaces to wheel-rims. [f. L *pes pedis* foot + RAIL¹]

pedunc'le, (-ting'kl), n. (Bot.) stalk of flower, fruit, or cluster, esp. main stalk bearing solitary flower; or subordinate stalks (pedicels); (Zool.) stalklike process in animal body. Hence ~**ular¹**, ~**ulate²** (-at), aa. [f. L *pes pedis* foot + -UNCLE]

peek, v.i. Peep, peer, (*in, out,* etc.); ~*a-boo* (now U.S.), =BO-PEEP. [ME *pike*, etym. dub.]

peel¹, n. (hist.). Small square tower built in 16th c. in border counties of England & Scotland. [earlier=palisade, ult. f. L *palus* stake]

peel², n. Shovel, esp. baker's for thrusting loaves etc. into oven. [f. OF *pele* f. L *pala*]

peel³, v.t. & i., & n. **1.** Strip the ~, rind, bark, etc., from (orange, potato, tree, etc.); take *off* (skin, ~, etc.); (arch., from *Isa.* xviii. 2, perh. mistransl.) *scattered & ~ed* (pillaged); (intr., of tree, animal body, etc.) become bare of bark, skin, etc., (of bark, surface, etc.) come off or off like ~, (of person, now sl.) strip for exercise etc. **2.** n. Rind, outer coating, of fruit; *candied ~* (usu. of citron). Hence ~**er¹** [-ER¹(1, 2)] n., ~**ING²**(2) n. (esp. *potato~ings*), [=PILL², orig. in all senses

peel'er², n. || Policeman (sl.); member of Irish constabulary, founded under Peel's secretaryship (hist.). [Robert *Peel*, cf. BOBBY, +-ER¹]

Peel'ite, n. Conservative siding with Sir R. Peel when he introduced measure for repeal of Corn-laws in 1846. [-ITE¹]

peen, n. Wedge-shaped or thin end of a hammer-head (opp. *face*). [etym. dub.; cf. G *pinne* in same sense]

peep¹, v.i. & n. (Make) feeble shrill sound of young birds, mice, etc., chirp, squeak. [(n., f. vb) var. of PIPE²]

peep², v.i. Look through narrow aperture (*at, into,* etc.); look furtively (~*ing Tom*, type of prurient curiosity, in tale of Godiva); (of daylight, flower, distant object) come cautiously or partly into view, emerge, (often *out*); (fig., of qualities etc.) show itself unconsciously. [f. 15th c., cf. PEEK]

peep³, n. Furtive or peering glance; first appearance, esp. of dawn, of day; ~*of-day boys*, Protestant organization in Ireland (1784–95) searching opponents' houses at day-break for arms; ~*-hole*, small hole to peep through; ~*-show*, small exhibition of pictures etc. viewed through lens in small orifice (also fig.); ~ *sight*, aperture sight of some rifles. [f. prec.]

peep'er, n. One who peeps; (sl.) eye. [PEEP²+-ER¹]

peep'ul, pi'pal (pē-), n. Large Indian fig-tree allied to banyan, bo-tree. [Hind. *pipal*]

peer¹, n. **1.** An equal in civil standing or rank; equal in any respect, as *you will not easily find his* ~, whence ~'**LESS** a., ~'**lessly²** adv., ~'**lessness** n. **2.** Member of one of the degrees (duke, marquis, earl, viscount, baron) of nobility in United Kingdom, whence ~'**ESS¹** n.; ~*s of the realm* or *United Kingdom* (all of whom may sit in House of Lords); ~*s of Scotland*, *of Ireland*, (represented in H. of Lords by 16 elected to each parliament, by 28 elected for life); noble (of any country). [ME & OF *per* f. L *par* equal]

peer², v.t. & i. Rank *with*, equal; rank as equal *with*; make (man) a peer. [f. OF *perer* f. L *pariare* (*par* equal)]

peer³, v.i. Look narrowly (*into, at,* etc.); appear, peep out; come in sight. [?]

peer'age n. The peers: nobility, aristocracy; rank of peer; book containing list of peers with genealogy etc. [-AGE]

peev'ed (-vd), a. (sl.). Irritated. [PEEVE(ISH), -ED¹]

peev'ish, a. Querulous, irritable. Hence ~**LY²** adv., ~**NESS** n. [?]

peewit. See PEWIT.

peg¹, n. Pin, bolt, of wood, metal, etc., usu. round & slightly tapering, for holding together parts of framework etc., stopping up vent of cask, hanging hats etc. on, holding ropes of tent, tightening or loosening strings of violin etc, marking

peg[1], n. cribbage score, etc.; *round ~ in square* HOLE[1]; CLOTHES-~; (fig.) *a ~ to hang* (discourse etc.) *on*, (occasion, pretext, theme); ~, a drink, esp. of spirits; *off the ~*, (of clothes) ready-made; [] *put* (a man) *on the ~* (Army sl.), bring before the C.O. for an offence; *take* (person) *down a ~ or two*, humble him; ~*top*, pear-shaped spinning-top with metal ~, ~*top trousers* (wide at hips, narrow at ankles). [prob. of LG orig.; cf. dial. Du. *peg*]

peg[2], v.t. & i. (-gg-). Fix (thing *down*, *out*, etc.) with peg; (Stock Exch.) prevent price of (stock etc.) from falling (rising) by freely buying (selling) at given price; strike, pierce, aim at, with peg; (sl.) throw (stone), throw stones etc., (*at*); mark (score) with pegs on cribbage-board; mark out boundaries of (mining claim etc.); ~ (*away*), work persistently (*at*); drive pegs into (cricket-bat); ~ *out*, (Croquet) hit peg with ball as final stroke in game; (sl.) die, be ruined. [f. prec.]

peg'amoid, n. Kind of imitation leather used in coach-building etc. [?]

Peg'asus, n. Winged horse that, with stroke of hoof caused fountain Hippocrene to flow on Mt Helicon, (fig.) poetic genius. [L, f. Gk *Pēgasos* (*pēgē* fount)]

peignoir (pān'wahr, pĕn'-), n. Woman's loose dressing-gown worn while hair is combed or on coming out of bath. [F (*peigner* comb)]

peine forte et dure (pān fŏrtā dūr'), n. Severe & hard punishment, i.e. pressing to death, inflicted on person charged with felony who refused to plead. [F]

pej'orative (or pǐjŏ'r-), a. & n. Deprecatory (word), as the ~ *suffix* -aster. [f. L *pejorare* make worse (*pejor*), see -ATIVE]

pek'an, n. N.-Amer. carnivorous beast of weasel family, valued for fur. [f. native *pékané*]

pēke, n. PEKINESE dog. [abbr.]

pēk'in (or -ēng'), n. Kind of silk stuff; [f. F *pékin* as used by Napoleon I's soldiers] civilian. [f. F *pékin* f. Chin. *Pe-king* northern capital]

Pēking')ēse' (-z), n. & a. (Inhabitant) of Peking[1]; small short-legged snub-nosed dog with long silky hair. [-ESE]

Pēking màn, n. Prehistoric type of man represented by remains first found in 1929 at Peking.

pēk'ŏe, n. Superior kind of black tea. [f. Chin. *pek-ho* (*pek* white+*ho* down), leaves being picked young with down on them]

pelf'age, n. Fur, hair, wool, etc., of quadruped. [F (OF *pel* hair +-AGE)]

Pelā'gian[1], a. & n. (Follower) of the monk Pelagius (4th-5th c.), who denied doctrine of original sin. Hence ~ISM n. [-AN]

pelā'gian[2], a. & n. Of, inhabiting, inhabitant of, the open sea. [f. Gk *pelagios* (*pelagus* sea f. Gk *pelagos*)+-AN]

pelā'gic, a. Of, performed on, the open sea, esp. ~ *sealing*. [f. L *pelagicus* (as prec., -IC)]

pelargō'nium, n. Genus of plants with showy flowers & fragrant leaves. [f. Gk *pelargos* stork]

Pelas'gic (-zj- or -zg'-), a. Of the Pelasgians, an ancient race on coasts & islands of Eastern Mediterranean & Aegean; ~ *architecture*, oldest form of masonry found in Greece. [f. L *Pelasgicus* (*Pelasgi* f. Gk *Pelasgoi*), see -IC]

pelerine' (or -ēn'), n. Woman's long narrow cape or tippet. [f. F *pélerine*, fem. of *pèlerin* PILGRIM]

pelf, n. Money, wealth, (usu. derog.). [f. OF *pelfre*, etym. dub.]

pel'ican, n. Large water-fowl with pouch for storing fish, fabled to feed its young with its own blood. [f. LL *pelicanus* f. Gk *pelekan*, cf. *pelekas* woodpecker perh.]

pelisse' (-ēs), n. Woman's mantle with armholes or sleeves, reaching to ankles; child's outdoor garment worn over other clothes; hussar officer's fur-trimmed undress jacket. [F, f. L *pellicia* (*vestis* garment) of fur (*pellis* skin)]

pellag'ra, n. Deficiency disease characterized by cracking of skin & often ending in insanity. So ~ous a. [perh. f. It. *pelle agra* rough skin]

pel'let, n. & v.t. Small ball of paper, bread, etc.; small shot; circular boss ~s, (in coins etc.; (vb) hit with (esp. paper) ~s. [f. OF *pelote* f. med. L *pelota* f. L *pila* ball]

pel'licle, n. Thin skin; membrane; film of *pellis* skin]. Hence **pellic'ular** a. [f. L *pellicula*, dim of *pellis* skin]

pell'itory, n. 1. (~ *of Spain*) plant with pungent-flavoured root, used as local irritant etc. 2. (~ *of the wall*) low bushy plant with greenish flowers growing on or at foot of walls. [1. earlier *pelleter* f. L f. Gk *pyrethron* feverfew, cf. *puretos* fever. 2. f. L *parietaria* (*paries -etis* wall)]

pell-mell' adv., a., & n. 1. In disorder, promiscuously; headlong, recklessly. 2. adj. Confused; tumultuous. 3. n. Confusion, medley, mêlée. [f. F *pêle-mêle* (*pêle* etym. dub.+*mêle* prob. f. *mêler* mix f. L *misculere* f. L *misceēre*)]

pellū'cid, a. Transparent, clear; clear in style or expression; mentally clear. Hence or cogn. **pellucid'ity** n., ~LY[2] adv. [f. L *pellucidus* f. PER(*lucēre* shine), see -ID[1]]

Pel'manism, n. A 20th-c. memory-training system. [?]

pel'met, n. Valance or narrow pendant border (esp. over window or door to conceal curtain rods). [prob. f. F *palmette* conventional palm-leaf design used on cornices]

pelō'ta, n. Basque game like tennis, played with ball & wicker racket. [Sp., = ball, f. *pella* f. L *pila* ball]

pelt[1], n. Skin of sheep or goat with short wool on; undressed skin of fur-bearing animal; raw skin of sheep etc. stripped of wool or fur, so **pel'try**(1) n. [cogn. w. obs. *pell* skin f. OF *pel* f. L *pellis*]

pelt[2], v.t. & i. & n. 1. Assail with missiles (also fig.); (intr. of rain etc.) beat with violence; strike repeatedly with missiles, go on firing *at*. 2. n. ~*ing*; (*at*) full ~ (speed). [?]

pel'ta, n. (pl. ~*ae*), Small light shield of ancient Greeks, Romans, etc.; (Bot.) shield-like structure, so ~ATE[2](2) a. [L, f. Gk *peltē*]

pel'vis, n. (anat.). Basin-shaped cavity formed in most vertebrates by haunch-bones with sacrum & other vertebrae, whence ~IC a.; ~ basin-like cavity of kidney. [L, = basin]

Pem'broke, n. Town in Wales; ~ *table*, p~, table on four fixed legs with hinged flaps that can be spread out & supported on other legs.

pěm'mican, n. N.-Amer.-Ind. cake of dried & pounded meat mixed with melted fat; beef so treated & flavoured with currants etc. for travellers; (fig.) condensed literary matter. [f. native *pime-can* (*pime* fat)]

pem'phig'us, n. (path.). Formation of watery vesicles or eruptions on skin of body. Hence ~OID, ~OUS, aa. [f. Gk *pemphix-igos* babble]

pen[1], n. Small enclosure for cows, sheep, poultry, etc., or for other purposes; (W.-Ind.) farm, plantation; *submarine* ~, enclosure (often with concrete roof) for sheltering submarines. [OE *penn*, etym. dub.]

pen[2], v.t. (-nn-). Enclose, shut up, shut in; shut up (cattle etc.) in pen. [prob. f. prec.]

pen[3], n., & v.t. (-nn-). 1. Quill-feather with quill pointed & split into two sections, for writing with ink; similar instrument of steel, gold, etc., fitted into rod of wood etc. (~*holder*); writing, style of this, *as made a living with his* ~, *wields a formidable* ~, FOUNTAIN-~. 2. ~ *& ink*, -&-*ink* a., drawn, written, with these; ~-*feather*, quill-feather of bird's wing; ~*knife*, small knife usu. carried in pocket; ~*man* (-măn), one who writes a (*good, bad,* etc.) hand, author; ~*manship*, skill in writing, style of handwriting, action or style of literary composition; ~-*name*, literary pseudonym; ~*wiper*, appliance usu. of small pieces of cloth for wiping ~ after use. 3. v.t. Write, compose & write, (letter etc.). Hence ~FUL n. [(vb f. n.) f. OF *penne* f. L *penna* feather]

Pen[4], n. Female swan. [?]

pen'al, a. Of punishment; concerned with inflicting this, as ~ *laws*; (of offence) punishable, esp. by law; inflicted as punishment, as ~ *servitude, imprisonment with hard labour*; used as place of punishment, as *a* ~ *colony*. Hence ~LY[2] adv. [f. F *pénal* f. L *penalis* (*poena* penalty f. Gk *poinē* fine, see -AL)]

pen'alize, v.t. Make, declare, (action) penal; (Sport.) subject (competitor, also fig.) to penalty or comparative disadvantage. [-IZE]

pen'alty, n. Punishment, esp. (payment of) sum of money, for breach of law, rule, or contract; *the* ~ *of*, disadvantage resulting from (quality etc.); (Sport.) disadvantage imposed on competitor for breaking rule or winning previous contest; (Bridge) points added to player's score under the laws of the game; (Football) ~ *area*, part of ground in front of goal in which a breach of the rules by defenders involves award of a ~ *kick* (at goal). [ult. f. med. L *poenalitas* (as PENAL, see -TY)]

pen'ance, n., & v.t. (In theological use) a sacrament including contrition, confession, satisfaction, & absolution; act of self-mortification as expression of penitence, esp. one imposed by priest; *do* ~, perform such act; (v.t.) impose ~ on. [f. OF *penance* f. L *paenitentia* (as PENITENT, see -ANCE)]

Penat'es (-z), n. pl. (Rom. myth.). Household gods. [L, perh. f. *penus* sanctuary]

pence. See PENNY.

penchant (see Ap.), n. Inclination, liking, (*for*). [F, part. of *pencher* slope f. L †*pendicare* (*pendere* hang)]

pen'cil, n. (Arch.). artist's paint-brush (still tech. of small brushes, esp. in comb., as *sable-, camelhair,* ~); (fig.) painter's art or style; instrument for drawing or writing, esp. of black lead enclosed in cylinder of wood or in metal case with tapering end; (Optics) set of rays meeting at a point; (Geom.) figure formed by set of straight lines meeting at a point; ~-shaped object; ~-*case, holder,* usu. of metal, for ~ or ~-*lead*. [f. OF *pincel* ult. f. L *penicillum* dim. of *peniculus* brush dim. of PENIS]

pen'cil[2], v.t. (-ll-). Tint or mark (as) with lead pencil; jot down with pencil; enter (horse's name) in betting-book, whence ~**ler**[1] n. (Racing sl.), bookmaker or his clerk; (esp. in p.p.) mark delicately with thin concentric lines of colour or shading. [f. prec.]

pen'dant, n., **-ent**[1]. 1. Hanging ornament, esp. one attached to necklace, bracelet, etc. 2. (Naut., also *pennant*) short rope hanging from head of mast etc. with eye at lower end for receiving hooks of tackles, (also) tapering flag, esp. that flown at mast-head of vessel in commission; *broad* ~, short swallow-tailed ~ distinguishing commodore's ship in squadron; shank & ring of watch by which it is suspended. 3. (*Also gr. pahni* (*dahni*) match, parallel, companion, complement,

(to.) [F (-ant), f. pendre hang f. L pendēre, see -ANT]

pěn'dent², -ant², a. Hanging; overhang-ing; undecided, pending, whence pěn'd-ENCY n.; (Gram.) of which the construc-tion is incomplete. [as prec.]

pěndente lī'tě, adv. Pending the suit. [L]

pend'ing, a. & prep. 1. Undecided, awaiting decision or settlement, as a suit, a treaty; vos then ~. 2. prep. During, as ~ these negotiations (orig.=while these negotiations are~); until, as ~ his return. [after F pendant²: see -ANT]

pěndrag'on, n. Ancient British or Welsh prince. [W,=chief leader (pen head + DRAGON standard)]

pěn'dūlāte, v.i. Swing like a pendulum; (fig.) be undecided. [as foll.+-ATE³]

pěn'dūline, a. (Of nest) suspended; (of bird) building such nest. [f. as foll.+ -INE²)]

pěn'dūlous, a. Suspended, hanging down, (esp. of bird's nest, flower, etc.); oscil-lating. Hence ~LY² adv. [f. L pendulus (pendēre hang)+-OUS]

pěn'dūlum, n. Body suspended so as to be free to swing, esp. rod with weighted end regulating movement of clock's works; swing of the ~, alternation of power between political parties; COMPEN-SATION ~; person, thing, that oscillates (lit. & fig.). [f. L neut. adj. as prec.]

Pēněl'opē, n. Chaste wife. [f. Gk Pēnelopē, -peia, wife of Odysseus]

pēn'ēplain, n. (geol.). A region that is almost a plain. [f. L paene almost, PLAIN¹]

pěnětrā'lia, n. pl. Innermost shrine or recesses. [L, pl. of penetral, cogn. w. foll.]

pěn'ētrāte, v.t. & i. Find access into or through, pass through; (of sight) pierce through (darkness, thicket, etc.); per-meate; imbue (person, thing, with); (fig.) see into, find out, discern, (person's mind, meaning, design, the truth); (intr.) make a way (into, through, to); (part.) gifted etc.) easily heard through or above other sounds. Hence or cogn. ~ẠBIL'ĪTY, ~-TION, ~ĀTOR², nn., ~ĀBLE, ~ĀTIVE, aa., ~ātingLY², ~ātively² advv. [f. L pene-trāre, cogn. w. penitus interior, see -ATE³]

pěng'uin (-ngw-), n. Sea-fowl of south-ern hemisphere with wings represented by scaly paddles with which it swims under water. [?]

pěn'ial, a. Of the penis. [-AL]

pěn'icillate, a. (nat. hist.). Furnished with, forming, small (tufts); marked with streaks as of pencil or brush. [as PENCIL, -ATE²]

pěnicill'in, n. Therapeutic drug (first discovered in mould) for preventing the growth of certain disease bacteria. [f. L penicillium mould (L penicillus PEN-CIL¹,)+-IN]

pěnin'sūla, n. Piece of land almost sur-rounded by water or projecting far into the sea; the P~, Spain & Portugal, into 1914-18 war) Gallipoli. [f. L paeninsula (paene almost+insula island)]

pěnin'sūlar, a. & n. 1. Of (the nature of) a peninsula; of the Peninsula or of the war there carried on between French & English etc. (1808-14). 2. n. Inhabitant of a peninsula; (P~) soldier of the P~ war. [-AR¹]

pěnin'sūlāte, v.t. Make (land) into a peninsula. [-ATE³]

pěn'is, n. (pl. -nēs). Copulatory organ of male animal. [L,=tail, penis]

pěn'itent, a. & n. 1. That repents, contrite. 2. n. Repentant sinner, person doing penance under direction of con-fessor; (pl.) various R.-C. orders asso-ciated for mutual discipline etc. Hence or cogn. ~ENCE n., ~entry² adv. [f. F pénitent f. L paenitēre repent, -ENT]

pěnitěn'tial (-nshl), a. Of penitence or penance; the ~ psalms (vi, xxxii, xxxviii, li, cii, cxxx, cxliii). Hence ~LY² adv. [f. med. L paenitentialis (paenitentia penitence, as prec., see -ENCE & -AL)]

pěnitěn'tiary (-sha-), n. & a. 1. Office in papal court deciding questions of pen-ance, dispensations, etc.; Grand P~, cardinal presiding over this; [] asylum for prostitutes resolving on amendment; reformatory prison. 2. adj. Of penance, of reformatory treatment. [PENITENCE, -ARY]

pěnn'ant, n. [compromise between pendant & pennon]=PENDANT¹ (naut.); =PEN-NON.

pěnn'iform, a. (nat. hist.). Having the form or appearance of a feather. So pěnnif'ẹrous a. [f. L penna feather, see -FORM]

pěnn'iless, a. Having no money; poor, destitute. [f. PENNY+-LESS]

pěnn'ill, n. (pl. ~ion pr. -il'yon). (Stanza of) improvised verse sung to harp at Eisteddfod etc. [Welsh, f. penn head]

pěnn'on, n. Long narrow flag, triangular or swallow-tailed, esp. as military en-sign of lancer regiments; long pointed streamer of ship; flag. Hence ~ED² (-nd), a. [f. OF penon prob. f. L penna feather, see -OON]

pěnn'y, n. (pl. pence exc. as below). 1. English bronze coin worth 1/12 of shilling (in pl. pence combined with numbers from 2 to 11 & 20, pr. without stress, as six-pence but eighteen pence'; after numeral written d.=DENARIUS, as 6d.; pl. pennies of individual coins as such, as gave me my

change in pennies, doled it out in single pennies); *(colloq.). **pen′ny** n. a cent; (Bibl.) = DENARIUS. **2.** *A pretty* ~, a good sum of money; PETER's ~, *pence*; *a* ~ *for your thoughts* (said to person absorbed in thought); *in for a* ~, *in for a pound*, thing once begun must be concluded at all costs; *take care of the pence*, be sparing in small outlays; *turn an honest* ~, make something by an odd job; *a* ~ *plain & twopence coloured* (jeer at cheap showiness). **3.** ~*-a-line* a., (of writing) cheap, superficial; ~*-a-liner*, hack writer; ||~ *blood* (sl.), = ~ DREADFUL; ||~ *farthing* (colloq.), old type of high bicycle; ~*-in-the-SLOT*; |~*post* (for conveyance of letters at former ordinary charge of 1d.); ~ *weight* (abbr. *dwt*), measure of weight, 24 grains, 1/20 of an ounce Troy; ~ *wise*, (over-)careful in small expenditures, esp. ~ *wise & pound foolish*, careful in small, wasteful in large matters; ~*wort* (-wĕrt), (also *wall* ~*wort*) plant with rounded concave leaves growing in crevices of rocks & walls, (*marsh* or *water* ~*wort*) small herb with rounded leaves growing in marshy places; ~*worth*, *penn′orth*, (pĕn′twĕrth, pĕn′ĕrth), as much as can be bought for a ~, *not a* ~*worth*, not the least bit, *a good, bad,* ~*worth* (bargain); ||~ *fiver* ~, *ten* ~, etc., *nail*, sizes of nail orig. costing 5d. etc. per 100. [OE *penning*, cf. Du. *penning*, G *pfennig*]

pennyroy′al, n. Kind of mint cultivated for supposed medicinal virtues. [prob. f. L *pensilis* (*pendēre pens-* hang, see -IL) earlier *pulyole ryale* f. OF *poliol* thyme f. L *pulegiolum* dim. of *pulegium* + ROYAL]

penol′og|ȳ, n. Study of punishment & of prison management. Hence **penōlo̅′gi-CAL** a., ~IST n. [f. Gk *poinē* fine + -o- + -LOGY]

pen′sile, a. Hanging down, pendulous; (of bird etc.) that constructs ~ nest. [f. L *pensilis* (*pendēre pens-* hang, see -IL)]

pen′sion (-shn), n., & v.t. **1.** Periodical (usu. annual) payment made esp. by government, company, or employer, in consideration of past services or of relinquishment of rights etc. (|| *Ministry of P*~*s*, department instituted in 1914-18 war); such payment to person who is not a professed servant for good will, secret service, etc., or to artists, scientists, etc., to enable them to carry on work of public interest; *old-age* ~, weekly or monthly payment by government to workmen, poor persons, or every one, after specified age. **2.** || Consultative assembly of members of Gray's Inn. **3.** (*pr. pahn′si-awn*). Boarding-house at fixed rate; *live en* ~ (as boarder). **4.** v.t. Grant ~ to, buy over with ~; ~ *off*, dismiss with ~. Hence ~LESS (-sho-) a., ||(vb f. n.) F, f. L *pensionem* payment (*pendēre pens-* pay, -ION)]

pen′sionable (-sho-), a. Entitled, (of

services etc.) entitling person, to pension. [-ABLE]

pen′sionary (-sho-), a. & n. (Recipient) of a pension; creature, hireling; *Grand P*~ (hist.), first minister of Holland & Zealand (1619-1794). [f. med. L *pensionarius* (as PENSION, see -ARY[1])]

pen′sioner (-sho-), n. Recipient of pension; hireling, creature (obs.); ||(Camb. Univ.) undergraduate who is not a scholar on the foundation or a sizar but pays for his own commons etc. (=COM-MONER at Oxf. Univ.). [f. OF *pensionnier* (as prec.)]

pen′sive, a. Plunged in thought; melancholy. Hence ~LY[2] adv., ~NESS n. [F (-*if*, -*ive*), f. *penser* think f. L *pensare* frequent. of *pendēre pens-* weigh]

pen stŏck, n. Sluice, flood-gate. [PEN[1] in sense 'mill-dam' + STOCK]

pent, a. Closely confined, shut *in* or *up*. [p.p. of *pend* var. of PEN[2]]

penta-, in comb. (before vowel *pent-*)=Gk *pente* five, as: *pen′tachord* (-k-), musical instrument of 5 strings, series of 5 notes; ~*dactyl* a. & n., (person, animal) with 5 toes or fingers on each limb, so ~*dactyl′ic* a., ~*dac′tylism* n.; ~*d′gynous*, with 5 pistils; ~*ahēd′ron* (-a·h-), solid figure of 5 faces, so ~*ahēd′ral* a.; ~*am′erous*, (Bot., also written 5-*merous*) having parts of flower-whorl 5 in number, (Zool.) consisting of 5 joints; ~*an′drous*, with 5 free stamens; ~*apet′alous*, with 5 petals; ~*ap′ody*, verse, sequence in verse, of 5 feet; *pen′tastich* (-k), group of 5 lines in verse; ~*atom′ic*, having 5 atoms of some substance in the molecule; ~*atôm′ic*, of 5 notes; ~*āv′alent*, with combining power of 5 atoms of hydrogen etc.

pen′tacle, n. Figure used as symbol, esp. in magic, prob.=PENTAGRAM. [f. med. L *pentaculum*, prob.=PENTA- +-CULE]

pen′tăd, n. The number, group of, five; five-day period; (Chem.) element, radical, with combining power of five. [f. Gk *pentas -ados* (*pente* five, -AD)]

pen′tagon, n. Five-sided (usu. plane rectilineal) figure. Hence **pentăg′onAL** a. [f. L f. Gk PENTA(*gōnon* f. *gōnia* angle)]

pen′tagram, n. Five-pointed star formed by producing sides of pentagon both ways till they intersect, formerly used as mystic symbol. [f. Gk PENTA(*grammon* f. *gramme̅* line)]

pentam′eter, n. (Gk & Lat. Pros.) form of dactylic verse composed of two halves each of two feet (dactyls in second half, dactyls or spondees in first) & long syllable, chiefly used alternately with hexameters to form elegiac verse; English iambic verse of ten syllables. [L, f. Gk PENTA(*metros* f. *metron* measure)]

pen′tāne, n. Paraffin hydrocarbon having five carbon atoms in the molecule occurring as a colourless fluid in petroleum etc. [f. Gk *pente* five + -ANE(2)]

Pĕn'tateuch (-k), n. First five books of O.T. traditionally ascribed to Moses. Hence **pĕntateuch'al** (-k'-), a. [f. L f. Gk PENTA(teuchos implement, in late Gk book) of five books]

pĕntath'lon, n. (Gk Ant.) athletic contest of five events in each of which all competitors took part; similar contest in modern Olympic Games. [Gk, f. PENTA-+ athlon contest]

Pĕn'tecŏst, n. Jewish harvest festival, on fiftieth day after the second day of Passover (Levit. xxiii. 15, 16), (later) anniversary of giving of Law on Sinai; (arch.) Whit Sunday. Hence **pĕntecŏs'-tal** a. [f. eccl. L f. Gk pentēkostē (hēmera) fiftieth (day), f. pentēkonta fifty]

pĕnt'house, n. (-t-h-), (arch.) **pĕn'tice**, n. Sloping roof, esp. as subsidiary structure attached to wall of main building; awning, canopy, or the like. [ME pentis, prob. f. OF apentis -diz, f. L'L appendi-cium appendage (APPEND)]

∥**Pĕn'tonville**, n. London prison associated with the principle of confinement in separate cells, to suit which and to serve as a model it was designed.

pĕntstē'mon, n. Bright-flowered garden plant. [irreg. f. PENTA-+Gk stēmōn warp (cf. STAMEN)]

pĕnŭlt' (or pē'-), **pĕnŭl'tĭmate**, aa. & nn. Last but one; (n.) last syllable but one. [(-ult abbr.) f. L paene almost+ULTIMATE after L paenultimus]

penŭm'brĭa, n. Partly shaded region around shadow of opaque body, esp. round total shadow of moon or earth in eclipse; lighter outer part of sun-spot; partial shadow. Hence **~al**, a. [f. L paene almost+umbra shadow]

penŭr'ious, a. Poor, scanty; stingy, grudging; whence **~LY²** adv., **~NESS** n. [f. med. L penuriosus (foll., -OUS)]

pĕn'ūry, n. Destitution, poverty; lack, scarcity, (of). [f. L penuria, cogn. w. Gk peina hunger, penia poverty, spaniswant]

pĕ'on (or pūn), n. (In India) office-messenger, attendant, orderly; (Amer.) day-labourer; (Mex.) enslaved debtor. [OF, Sp., f. L as PAWN¹]

pĕ'onage, n. Employment, service, of peons. [-AGE]

pĕ'ony, n. Plant with large globular red or white flowers, in cultivation often double. [OE peonie f. L f. Gk paiōnia (Paiōn, physician of the gods)]

people (pē'pl), n. & v.t. 1 Persons composing community, race, or nation, as the English ~, English-speaking ~s, a warlike ~, (treated as sing.); the persons belonging to a place or forming a company or class etc. (the ~ of the western counties were in revolt, the ~ here are furious), subjects of king etc., congregation of

parish priest etc., (as pl.); armed followers, retinue, workpeople, etc., (as pl.); one's parents or other relatives, as his ~ are sure to hear of it; the commonalty (as pl.); the body of the entranchised or qualified citizens (as sing. or pl.); persons in general, as ~ don't like to be kept waiting; (with library, entertainments, educational classes, etc., for the use of the working class. 2 v.t. Fill with ~, populate, fill (place with animals etc.); (of persons, animals, etc.) inhabit, occupy, fill, esp. in p.p. as a thickly ~d country. [f. OF poeple, peuple, etc., f. L populus]

*pĕp, n. (sl.). Vigour, go, spirit. Hence ***~'pȳ²** a. (sl.), full of ~. [abbr. pepper]

pepĕri'nō (-rē-), n. Light porous (usu. brown) volcanic rock formed of sand, cinders, etc. [It., f. pepere PEPPER, see -INE¹]

pĕpp'er, n. 1 Pungent aromatic condiment got from dried berries of certain plants used whole (~corns) or ground into powder; Black P~, plant chiefly used for this; black, white, ~ (from unripe, ripe berries); CAYENNE ~; (fig.) anything pungent. 2. ~-&-salt, cloth of dark & light wools woven together, showing small dots of dark & light intermingled; ~box, small usu. round box with perforated lid for sprinkling ~; ~-castor, -er, =~box; Eton fives-court; ~ ||irregular buttress in (1st sense); ~corn, dried berry of Black P~, esp. as nominal rent; ~mint, kind of mint grown for its essential oil, this oil, lozenge flavoured with ~mint; ~pot, etc. stewed with red ~ etc. (also, as nickname) Jamaican. [OE pipor, f. L piper = Gk peperi of oriental orig.]

pĕpp'er², v.t. Sprinkle, treat, with pep-per; besprinkle as with pepper; pelt with missiles (lit. or fig.); punish severely. [f. prec.]

pĕpp'erȳ, a. Of, like, abounding in, pepper; (fig.) pungent, stinging, hot-tempered. [-Y¹]

pĕp'sĭn, n. A ferment contained in gastric juice, converting proteins into peptones in presence of weak acid. [f. Gk pepsis digestion (pep- cook)+-IN¹]

pĕp'tĭc, a. & n. Digestive; ~ glands (secreting gastric juice); (n. pl. joc.) digestive organs. [f. Gk peptikos (as prec., see -IC)]

pĕp'tōne, n. Class of albuminoid substances soluble in water & non-coagulable by heat into which proteins are converted by the action of pepsin in the process of digestion. Hence **~OMIZE(3) v.t. [f. G peptōn f. Gk peptōn cooked]

pĕr, prep. Through, by, by means of. 1. In L phr. (usu. ital.): ~ annum, (so much) by the year, yearly; ~ cap'ut (& erron. ~ cap'ita), a head, each; ~ con'tra adv. & n. (on) the opposite side (of an

account etc.); ~*dī'ĕm, mĕn'sĕm*, (so much) by the day, month; ~*mill'e*, in or to the thousand; ~*procurātiōn'em* (abbr. ~*proc.*, ~*pro., p.p.*), by proxy, by the action of (person signing document); ~*ed'tum*, without intermediate steps, all at once; ~*sē*, by or in itself, intrinsically. **2.** As E prep.: by, by means or instrumentality of, as ~*post, rail, steamer, bearer*; (joc.) *as* ~*usual*, as usual; for each, as *a shilling* ~*man, 5* ~*cent.*; ~*second* ~*second*, ~second every second (of rate of acceleration over indefinite period). [L]

per- in comb. = prec. **1.** In L senses; through, all over, (~*forāde, ~vade*); completely, very (~*turb*); to destruction, to the bad. (~*vert, ~dition*). **2.** Chem. denoting maximum of some element in combination; in names of binary compounds in *-ide* (formerly *-uret*), as ~*chloride, ~iodide, ~oxide, ~sulphide*; in adjj. in *-ic* naming oxides, acids, etc., as ~*chloric, ~iodic, ~manganic*; in names of salts of these etc., as ~*chlorate, ~iodate, ~manganate, ~sulphate*.

peradven'ture, adv. & n. (arch.). **1.** Perhaps; *if, lest,* ~, if, lest, it chance thus. **2.** n. Uncertainty, chance, conjecture; *beyond, without, (all)* ~ (doubt). [f. OF *per* or *par aventure* by chance (PER + *aventure* ADVENTURE)]

pérai' (-rahi, -rī), **pira'ya** (-rahyo), n. Voracious Amer. freshwater fish. [native (-*ya*)]

péram'bŭlāte, v.t. Walk through, over, or about; travel through & inspect (territory); formally establish boundaries of (parish etc.) by walking round them. Hence or cogn. ~A'TION n., ~ātORY a. [f. L PER(*ambulare* walk), see -ATE²]

‖**péram'bŭlātor**, n. Hand carriage for one or two children, with three or four wheels, pushed from behind (colloq. abbr. *prám*). [f. prec.+-OR²]

percāle' (or -ahl), n. A closely woven cotton fabric. [F, etym. dub.]

perceive' (-sēv), v.t. Apprehend with the mind, observe, understand, (circumstance, *that, how,* etc.); apprehend through one of the senses, esp. sight. [f. OF *perçoivre*, +-*ceivre*, f. L PER(*cipere cepd-=capere* take) seize thoroughly]

percén'tage, n. Rate, proportion, per cent; (loosely) proportion, as *only a small* ~ *of books are worth reading*. [-AGE]

pér-cépt, n. (philos.). Object of perception; mental product, as opp. to action, of perceiving. [as PERCEIVE]

percép'tible, a. That can be perceived by senses or intellect. Hence ~IBIL'ITY n., ~IBLY² adv. [f. LL *perceptibilis* (as prec., see -BLE)]

percép'tion, n. Act, faculty, of perceiving; intuitive recognition (of truth, aesthetic quality, etc.); (Philos.) action by which the mind refers its sensations to

external object as cause; (Law) collection (of rents etc.). Hence ~ional (-sho-), ~IVE, aa., ~ively² adv., ~iveness, pércéptiv'ITY, nn. [OF, f. L *perceptionem* (as PERCEIVE, see -ION)]

pérch¹, n. European spiny-finned freshwater fish, used as food. [f. F *perche* f. L f. Gk *perkē*]

pérch², n. **1.** Horizontal bar for bird to rest upon; anything serving for this, as *bird takes its* ~ (alights); (fig.) elevated or secure position; *hop the* ~, die, *knock* (person) *off his* ~, vanquish, destroy, him; centre pole of some four-wheeled vehicles. **2.** (Also *pole, rod*) measure of length esp. for land, 5½ yds; *square* ~, 30¼ sq. yds. [f. F *perche* f. L *pertica* pole]

pérch³, v.i. & t. Alight, rest, alight (*upon bough* etc.); (of person etc.) settle, alight, (*upon*); place (as) upon perch (esp. in p.p., as *town* ~*ed on a hill*). Hence ~ER¹ n., (one of) a large class of passerine birds with feet adapted for ~ing. [f. F *percher*, as prec.]

perchance' (-ah-), adv. (arch.). By chance; possibly, maybe. [f. AF *par chance* (*par* by + CHANCE)]

percheron (pār'sherawn), n. Strong & swift horse bred in le Perche, district of France. [F]

percip'ient, a. & n. **1.** Perceiving, conscious. **2.** n. One who perceives esp. (Telepathy) something outside range of senses. Hence ~ENCE n. [f. L as PERCIPE, see -ENT]

pérc'olāte, v.i. & t. (Of liquid) filter, ooze, through (also fig.); (trans.) ooze through, permeate; (of person or strainer) strain (liquid, powder) through pores etc. Hence or cogn. ~A'TION, ~ātOR²(2), nn. [f. L PER(*colare* strain f. *colum* strainer), -ATE³]

percuss', v.t. (med.). Tap gently with finger or instrument for purposes of diagnosis etc. [f. L PER(*cutere cuss-=quatere* shake) strike]

percú'ssion (-shn), n. Forcible striking of one (usu. solid) body against another; (Med.) percussing; (Mus.) *instrument of* (played by) ~; ~*cap*, small copper cap or cylinder in fire-arm, containing fulminating powder and exploded by ~ of a hammer. So percuss'IVE a. [f. L *percussio* (as prec., see -ION)]

percútán'éous (-shn), a. Made, done, through the skin. [PER-+CUTANEOUS]

perdi'tion, n. Eternal death, damnation. [f. OF *perdiciun* f. L *perditionem* f. PER(*dere dit-=dare* give) destroy, see -ION]

pérdū(e)', a. (Mil.) placed as an outpost in hiding, esp. *lie* ~; (often as F, with fem. *due*) hidden. [F, p.p. of *perdre* lose, as prec.]

perdū'rable, a. Permanent; eternal; durable. Hence or cogn. ~ABIL'ITY n., ~ABLY² adv. [OF, f. L PER(*durabilis* DURABLE)]

père (pār, & see Ap.), n. Father(appended to surname to distinguish father from son, cf. FILS). [F]

pè'regrïnäte, v.i. (now joc.). Travel, journey. So ~ATION, ~ATOR³ m. [f. L peregrinari (as foll.), see -ATE³]

pè'regrïne(r), a. & n. 1. (arch.), Foreign, imported from abroad, outlandish. 2. ~ (falcon), kind esteemed for hawking. [f. L peregrinus (peregre abroad, f. PER + ager field, see -INE¹)]

pě'remptory (or peremp'·), a. Final, esp. (Law) ~y mandamus (in which the command is absolute), ~y writ (enforcing defendant's appearance without option), (of statement or command) admitting no denial or refusal; absolutely fixed, essential; (of person etc.) dogmatic, imperious, dictatorial. Hence ~ily² adv., ~iness n. [f. L peremptorius destructive f. PER(imere empt-=emere take, buy) destroy, see off, see -ORY]

perě'nnial (-nyǎl), a. & n. 1. Lasting through, (of stream) flowing through all seasons of, the year; lasting long or for ever; (of plant) living several years (cf. ANNUAL). 2. n. ~ plant. Hence perě'nnially² adv. [f. L PER(ennis f. annus year) + -AL]

pě'rfèct, a. & n. 1. Complete, not deficient; faultless; (of lesson) thoroughly learned; thoroughly trained or skilled (in duties etc.); exact, precise, as a ~ square, circle; entire, unqualified, as a ~ stranger, ~ nonsense; (Gram., of tense) denoting completed event or action viewed in relation to the present (future ~), giving four whorls of the flower; (Bot.) having all four whorls & fifth as they would occur in the major or minor scale starting upon the lower note of the interval, also the octave. 2. n. ~ tense. Hence ~ly² adv., (esp.) quite, quite well, completely. ~NESS n. [f. OF parfit f. L PER(ficere fect-=facere do) complete]

perfè'ct², (or pě'rfĭkt), v.t. Complete, carry through; make perfect; improve. Hence ~ibi'lity n, perfè'ctible a. [f. prec.]

perfě'ction, n. Completion; making perfect; full development; faultlessness; (loosely) comparative excellence; perfect person or thing; highest pitch, extreme, perfect specimen or manifestation, (of quality etc.); (w. pl.) accomplishment. [OF, f. L perfectionem (as PERFECT, see -ION)]

perfě'ctionist (-sho¬), n. One who holds that religious or moral perfection may be attained; (P~ist) member of communistic community of Oneida Creek, N.Y. So ~ISM n. [-IST]

pě'rfërvĭd, a. Very fervid. [PER-]

pě'rfĭdy, n. Breach of faith, treachery. Hence or cogn. perfĭd'ious a., perfĭd'iously² adv., perfĭd'iousness n. [f. F or L perfidia f. PER(fidus f. fides faith) treacherous]

perfoliate, a. (bot.). Having the stalk apparently passing through the leaf. [f. PER-² + L folium leaf + -ATE²]

perfo'räte, v.t. & i. Make hole(s) through, pierce, esp. make rows of holes in (sheet of stamps etc.); make rows of holes in, an opening into; pass, extend, through; (intr.) penetrate (into, through, etc.). Hence or cogn. ~A'TION, ~ATOR³(2), nn., -ATE³]

perfo'rce', adv. & n. Of necessity; (n. rare) necessity, esp. of, by, ~. [f. OF par force by FORCE]

perfo'rm, v.t. & i. Carry into effect (command, promise, task, operation, etc.); go through, execute, (public function, play, piece of music, etc.); (intr.) act in play, sing, etc.; (of trained animals) execute tricks etc. at public show etc., whence ~ING³ a. Hence ~ABLE a., ~ER¹ n. [f. OF par- PER-+former FORM, or perh. corrupt. of parfournir f. fournir FURNISH]

perfo'rmance, n. Execution (of command etc.); carrying out, doing; notable feat; performing of play or public exhibition, as there are too ~s a day, the afternoon ~. [-ANCE]

pě'rfume¹, n. Odorous fumes of burning substance; sweet smell; smell; fluid containing essence of flowers etc., scent. Hence ~LESS a. [f. F parfum, as foll.]

perfume'², v.t. Impart sweet scent to, impregnate with sweet smell, (esp. in p.p.). [f. F parfumer (PER-+ L fumare smoke)]

perfum'er, n. Maker, seller, of perfumes. Hence ~Y³(1, 2, 3) n. [-ER¹]

perfu'nctory a. Done merely for sake of getting through a duty; acting thus, superficial, mechanical, as a ~y inspection, inquirer, in a ~y manner. Hence ~ily² adv., ~iness n. [f. LL perfunctorius f. PER(fungi funct- perform), see -ORY]

perfuse' (-z), v.t. Besprinkle (with water etc.); cover, suffuse, (with radiance etc.); pour (water etc.) through or over. Hence or cogn. perfu'sion (-zhn) n., perfu's've a. [f. L PER(fundere fus- pour)]

pergamen'eous, a. Of or like parchment. [f. L as PARCHMENT + -EOUS]

pě'rgola, n. Arbour, covered walk, formed of growing plants trained over trellis-work. [It., f. L pergula projecting roof (pergere proceed)]

pergŭnn'ah (¬ä), ~ga'na (-gŭ¬), n. Division of territory in India, group of villages. [f. Pers. & Hind. parganah district]

perhaps' (colloq. prăps), adv. It may be, possibly, as ~ he has lost it, he has ~ lost it, ~ you would like to see it? [PER+HAPS (pl.)]

pě'ri¹, n. (Pers. Myth.) fairy, good (orig. evil) genius; beautiful or graceful being. [Pers.]

pe'ri- in comb. = Gk peri round, about,

as; *pĕ'rianth*, floral envelope; ~*cardi'is* n., inflammation of the ~*cardium*; ~*cardi'um*, membranous sac enclosing the heart, so ~*cardi'ac*, ~*cardi'al*, aa.; *pĕ'ricarp*, seed-vessel, wall of ripened ovary of plant; ~*chon'drium* (-k-), membrane enveloping cartilages (except at joints); ~*cli'nal* (Geol.), sloping in all directions from central point; ~*gy'noous* (*peri*⁴-), (of stamen) situated around pistil or ovary; ~*os'teum*, membrane enveloping the bones, so ~*os'tial* a., ~*ostri'tis* n.; ~*pteral* (*perip*²-), (of temple) surrounded by single row of pillars; *pĕ'risperm*, mass of albumen outside embryo-sac in some seeds; *pĕ'ristōme*, (Bot.) fringe of small teeth around mouth of capsule in mosses, (Zool.) parts around mouth in various invertebrates; ~*typhli'tis*, inflammation of some part around the caecum, **e.g.** appendicitis.

pĕ'riapt, n. Thing worn about the person as charm, amulet. [f. F *pĕriaple* f. Gk PERI(*aptos* f. *haptō* fasten)]

pĕ'riclase, n. Mineral consisting of magnesia & protoxide of iron, found esp. at Vesuvius. [f. PERI- (in sense 'very') + Gk *klasis* breaking, from its perfect cleavage]

peric'opē, n. Short passage, paragraph; portion of Scripture read in public worship. [f. LL f. Gk PERI(*kopē* cutting f. *koptō* cut)]

pericrā'nium, n. Membrane enveloping skull; (joc.) skull, brain, intellect. [f. PERI(*kranion* CRANIUM)]

pĕ'ridot, n. (Jeweller's name for) olivine, kind of chrysolite. [f. F *pĕridot*, etym. dub.]

pĕ'rigee, n. That point in planet's (esp. moon's) orbit at which it is nearest to earth (cf. APOGEE). Hence **pĕrigē'AN** a. [f. F *pĕrigée* f. LL f. late Gk PERI(*geion* f. *gē* earth)]

perihē'lion (-lyon), n. That point in planet's orbit at which it is nearest to sun (cf. APHELION). [f. PERI-+Gk *hēlios* sun]

pĕ'ril, n., & v.t. (-ll-). **1.** Danger; *in* ~ *of* (*in danger of losing*) *one's life* etc.; *you do it at your* ~, *you take the risk*; *keep off at your* ~ (take the risk if you do not). **2.** v.t. Expose to danger, imperil. Hence or cogn. ~*OUS* a., ~*OUSLY* adv., ~*OUSNESS* n. [(vb f. n.) f. F *pĕril* f. L *periculum* (-*peri*᷾i try)]

perim'eter, n. Circumference, outline, of closed figure; length of this; instrument for measuring the field of vision. [f. L f. Gk PERI(*metros* f. *metron* measure)]

perinē'um, n.(anat.). Region of the body between anus & scrotum or vulva. Hence ~*AL* a. [LL, f. Gk *pĕrinaios*, cf. *pĕris* -*inos* scrotum]

pĕ'riod, n. & a. **1.** Round of time marked

by recurrence of astronomical coincidences; time of planet's revolution. **2.** Time during which disease runs its course; (pl.) menses. **3.** Indefinite portion of history, life, etc.; any portion of time; *the* ~, the present day (*the girl, costume, catchwords, etc., of the* ~). **4.** Complete sentence, esp. one of several clauses; (pl.) rhetorical language. **5.** Full pause at end of sentence, full stop (.) marking this, (*put a* ~ *to*, bring to an end). **6.** Set of figures marked off in large number, as in numeration, recurring decimals, etc. **7.** adj. Belonging to, characteristic of, a particular (past) ~ (esp. of furniture, dress, & architecture). [f. F *pĕriode* f. L f. Gk PERI(*odos* = *hodos* way)]

pĕriod'ic, a. Of revolution of heavenly body, as ~ *motion*; recurring at regular intervals, so **pĕriodi'city** n.; recurring at intervals; ~ *table* (Chem.), arrangement of elements in order of atomic numbers & in which elements of similar chemical properties appear periodically & fall into definite groups; expressed in (rhetorical) periods. [f. F *pĕriodique* f. L f. Gk *periodikos* (as prec., see -IC)]

pĕriod'ical, a. & n. 1. = prec. (not in last sense). **2.** (Magazine, miscellany) published at regular intervals, e.g. monthly. Hence ~LY² adv. [-AL]

pĕripatĕ'tic, a. & n. 1. (*P*~*ic*). Aristotelian (a. & n.; so called from Aristotle's custom of walking in Lyceum while teaching). **2.** Walking from place to place on one's business, itinerant, whence ~ICALLY adv. **3.** n. (chiefly joc.). Itinerant dealer. Hence ~ICISM(2, 3) n. [f. F *pĕripatĕtique* f. L f. Gk *peripatētikos* f. PERI(*pateō* walk), see -IC]

pĕripetei'a (-ia), -**tia,** n. Sudden change of fortune in drama or in life. [Gk PERI(*peteia* f. *pet*- fall)]

periph'ery, n. Bounding line esp. of round surface; external boundary or surface. Hence ~AL a., ~alLY² adv. [f. OF *pĕriferie* f. LL f. Gk PERI(*phereia* f. *pherō* bear) circumference]

periph'rasis, n. (pl. ~*ēs*). Roundabout way of speaking, circumlocution; roundabout phrase. Hence or cogn. **pĕriphrās'tIC** a. (~*tic conjugation, genitive*, one formed ANALYTICALLY w. aux. vb, w. preposition, instead of by inflexion, as *did go*=went, *of Caesar*=Caesar's), **pĕriphrās'tICALLY** adv. [L f. Gk, f. PERI(*phrazō* declare, vbl adj. -*phrastos*); also anglicized *pĕ'riphrase* (pl. pron. -iz)]

perique' (-ēk), n. Dark Louisiana tobacco of a choice kind. [?]

pĕ'riscōpe, n. Kinds of tube-&-mirror apparatus by which an observer in a trench or in a submarine submerged to a small depth can see things above the parapet or water; kind of photographic

For other words in *peri*- see PERI-.

object-glass. Hence **pĕriscŏp'ic** a., enabling one to see distinctly for some distance round axis of vision. [PERI-, -SCOPE]

pĕr'ish, v.i. & t. Suffer destruction, lose life, come to untimely end (by the sword etc.); (of cold or exposure) reduce to distress or inefficiency (usu. in pass.; *we were ~ed with cold; in ~ing cold; the heat had ~ed us all; ~ed all vegetation*, whence ~ingly² adv.; *we were ~ed (much incommoded) with cold, hunger,* etc. Hence ~ING² a., blighter. ||~ING² a., (sl.), beastly, bloody. [f. OF *perir* (see -ISH²) f. L PER(*ire* go) perish]

pĕr'ishable, a. & n. 1. Liable to perish; subject to speedy decay. 2. n. pl. Things (esp. foodstuffs) in transit; subject to this. Hence ~NESS n. [-ABLE]

pĕris'sŏ- in comb. = Gk *perissos*, uneven, odd, redundant, as *~dáctýlate* (Zool.), having an odd number of toes on each foot.

peris'talith, n. (archaeol.). Ring of standing stones round burial-mound etc. [f. reg. f. Gk PERI(*statos* standing) + -LITH]

pĕristal'sis, n. (physiol.). Automatic muscular movement consisting of wavelike contractions in successive circles, by which contents of alimentary canal etc. are propelled along it. Hence or cogn. ~TIC a., ~TICALLY adv. [Gk, f. PERI(*stellō* send)]

pĕristĕrŏn'ic, a. Of pigeons. [prob. f. Gk *peristerōn* dovecot (*peristera* dove)]

pĕr'istyle, n. Row of columns surrounding temple, court, cloister, etc.; space so surrounded. [f. F *péristyle* f. L f. Gk PERI(*stulos* f. *stulos* pillar)]

pĕrĭtŏnē'um, n. (anat.), **-nae'um**, n. Double serous membrane lining cavity of abdomen. Hence ~ē'AL a., ~IT'IS n. [L, f. Gk PERI(*tonaion* f. *ton-* stem of *teinō* stretch)]

pĕr'iwig n. Wig. Hence ~ged² (-gd) a. [earlier *peruyke* f. F as PERUKE]

pĕr'iwinkle¹, n. Kinds of plants, esp. *Lesser & Greater P~*, evergreen trailing plants with light-blue flowers; ~ (blue), colour of ~s. [OE *pervince* f. L *pervinca*]

pĕr'iwinkle², n. Gastropod mollusc much used for food. [OE has *pinewincla*, wine-]

pĕr'jure (-jer), v. refl. *~e oneself, forswear oneself* (p.p.) guilty of perjury. So ~ER¹ (-er) n. [f. OF *parjurer* f. L]

pĕr'jury (-eri), n. Swearing to statement known to be false; wilful utterance of false evidence while on oath; breach of oath. So **perjur'ious** (-joor-) a., **perjur'iously²**

adv. [f. AF *perjurie* f. L *perjurium* as prec.]

pĕrk¹, v.i. & t., & a. (Also ~ *up*) lift one's head, thrust oneself forward, briskly or impudently; (trans.) smarten *up*; hold *up* (head, tail) self-assertively; ~ (adj., rare)

pĕrk² n. [sl.] (Usu. pl.) perquisite. [abbr.]

pĕrk'ȳ, a. Self-assertive, saucy; pert. Hence ~ily² adv., ~NESS n. [PERK¹+-Y²]

pĕrm, n. (colloq.). Permanent wave. [abbr.]

pĕrm'alloy, n. Alloy of nickel & iron of great sensitiveness to magnetic forces, used for cores of telegraphic cables. [f. PERM(EABLE)+ALLOY]

pĕrm'anent, a. Lasting, intended to last, indefinitely (cf. TEMPORARY); ~ *set*, condition of metal after being subjected to the strain of use: ~ *wave*, lasting artificial wave in the hair produced by one of several processes (colloq. abbr. *perm*); *~ way*, finished road-bed of railway. Hence or cogn. **pĕrm'anence**, **pĕrm'anency** (-si) n., ~LY² adv. [f. L PER(*manère* remain), -ENT]

pĕrmang'anate (-ngg-), n. (chem.). Salt of permanganic acid, esp. *potassium ~* ~ *of potash*, used as disinfectant & oxidizer when dissolved in water. [f. foll. +-ATE(3)]

pĕrmangan'ic (-ngg-), a. (chem.). ~ *acid*, acid obtained from manganese. [PER-, MANGAN(ESE), -IC]

pĕrm'ĕate, v.t. & i. Penetrate, pervade, saturate; diffuse itself *through, among,* etc. Hence or cogn. ~ABIL'ITY, ~ANCE, ~A'TION, nn., ~ABLE, ~ANT, aa. [f. L PER(*meare* run), see -ATE³]

pĕrmiss'ible, a. Allowable. Hence ~IY² adv. [OF, prob. f. med. L *permissibilis* (as PERMIT¹, see -BLE)]

pĕrmiss'ion (-shn), n. Leave, licence, (*to do*). [f. L *permissio* (as PERMIT, see -ION)]

pĕrmiss'ive, a. Giving permission; ~ *legislation* (giving powers, but not enjoining their use). Hence ~IY² adv., ~NESS n. [OF (-*if, -ive*), as foll., see -IVE]

pĕrmit'¹, v.t. & i. (-tt-). Allow, *as ~ me to remark, appeals are ~ed, ~ it to be altered, weather ~ing*; (intr.) admit of (*alteration* etc.). [f. L PER(*mittere miss-* let go)]

pĕrmit'², n. Written order giving permission esp. for landing or removal of dutiable goods etc.; (*also permit'*) permission. [f. prec.]

pĕrmutā'tion, n. (Math.) variation of the

order of a set of things lineally arranged, any one such arrangement; (rare) alternation. [f. OF *permutacion* f. L *permutationem* (foll., -ION)]

permūte, v.t. Alter the order of. [f. L PER(*mutare* change)]

pern, n. HONEY-buzzard. [irreg. f. Gk *pternis*, kind of hawk]

perni'cious (-shus), a. Destructive, ruinous, fatal; ~ *anaemia*, severe freq.-fatal kind. Hence ~LY² adv., ~NESS n. [f. F *pernicieux* f. L *perniciosus* (*pernicies* ruin f. PER-+*nex necis* death, see -OUS)]

pernick'ety, a. (colloq.). Fastidious; ticklish, requiring careful handling. [?]

pernocta'tion, n. Passing the night; (Eccl.) all-night vigil. [f. L *pernoctatio* f. PER(*noctare* f. *nox noctis* night), see -ATION]

pé'ror|āte, v.i. Sum up & conclude speech, whence ~A'TION n., ~ATOR. [f. L PER(*orare* speak)]

perox'ide, n. & v.t. 1. (Chem.) compound of oxygen with another element containing the greatest possible proportion of oxygen; (pop.) ~ *of hydrogen*, a colourless viscid liquid used as an antiseptic, and (esp.) to bleach hair. 2. v.t. Bleach (hair) with this. [PER-2+OXIDE]

perpend'¹, v.t. (arch.). Ponder, consider, (matter, or abs.). [f. L PER(*pendere* weigh)]

pe'rpend², n. Var. of PARPEN.

perpendic'ular, a. & n. 1. At right angles to plane of horizon; (loosely, of ascent etc.) very steep; erect, upright; (joc.) in standing position; (Geom.) at right angles (*to* given line, plane, or surface); ~STYLE. 2. n. Plumb-rule or other instrument for showing ~ line; (pl.) two plumb-lines used in designing ship & fixing its nominal length (*between* ~s); ~ line; *the* ~, ~ line or direction (*is out of* ~ *or the* ~, not straight up and down); ||(sl.) meal etc. at which guests stand. Hence ~ITY² (-ǎ'r-) n., ~LY² adv. [f. OF *perpendiculer* f. L *perpendicularis* (*perpendiculum* plumb-line, see -AR¹)]

perp'etrāte, v.t. Perform, commit, (crime, blunder, pun or other thing viewed as outrageous). So ~A'TION, ~ATOR², nn. [f. L PER(*petrare* = *patrare* effect), -ATE³]

perpet'ūal, a. Eternal; permanent during life; applicable, valid, for ever or for indefinite time; ~ *motion* (of machine that should go on for ever unless stopped by external force or worn out); continuous; (colloq.) frequent, repeated, as *this* ~ *nagging*. Hence ~LY² adv. [f. F ~*pétuel* f. L *perpetualis* f. *perpetuus* (perf. f. PER-+*petere* seek), see -AL]

perpet'ūāte, v.t. Make perpetual; preserve from oblivion. Hence or cogn. ~ANCE, ~A'TION, ~ATOR², nn. [f. L *perpetuare* (as prec.,) see -ATE³]

perpetū'ity, n. Quality of being perpetual; *in, to, for,* ~, for ever; perpetual

possession or position; perpetual annuity. [f. F *perpétuité* f. L *perpetuitatem* (as PERPETUAL, see -TY)]

perplex', v.t. Bewilder, puzzle, (person, his mind); complicate, confuse, (matter); entangle, intertwine, (esp. in p.p.). Hence ~EDLY², ~ING1LY² advv. [f. obs. *perplex* a. f. L PER(*plexus* p.p. of *plectere* plait)]

perplex'ity, n. Bewilderment; what causes this; entangled state. [f. LL *perplexitas* (as prec., see -TY)]

perq'uisite (-z-), n. (sl. abbr. *perk*). Casual profit, esp. ||(Law) that coming to lord of manor beyond regular revenue; thing that has served its primary use and to which subordinate or servant has then a customary right, as *remains of the daily commons are among the* ~s *of college scouts*; customary gratuity. [f. L PER(*quirere quisit.,* = *quaerere* seek) search narrowly for]

pe'rron, n. Platform in front of door of church or other large building, ascended by steps. [F, f. L *petra* stone, see -OON]

pe'rry, n. Drink from juice of pears fermented. [f. OF *peré* f. LL *pera*=L *pirum* pear]

perse, a. & n. (arch.). Bluish-grey, bluish grey. [ME, f. OF *pers* f. LL *persus* etym. dub.]

pers'ecūte, v.t. Pursue with enmity and injury (esp. holder of opinion held to be heretical); harass, worry; importune (person *with* questions etc.). So ~ū'tion n. (~*ution mania*, insane delusion that one is ~uted), ~ūtor² n. [f. F *persécuter* f. L PER(*sequi secut-* follow) pursue]

persevēr'|ance, n. Steadfast pursuit of an aim, constant persistence, so ~ANT a. (rare); (Theol.) continuance in state of grace, (f. F *persévérance* f. L *perseverantia* (as foll., see -ANCE]

persevēr'e, v.i. Continue steadfastly, persist, (*in course, in doing, with* task, or abs.). Hence ~ing1LY² adv. [f. F *persévérer* f. L *perseverare* f. PER(*severus* SEVERE)]

Per'sian (-shn), a. & n. (Inhabitant, language) of Persia, as ~ *carpet, cat* (with long silky hair & thick tail). [-AN]

persiennes' (-nz), n. pl. Outside window blinds of light, horizontal laths. [F, = Persian (fem. pl. adj.)]

pers'iflage (-ahzh), n. Light raillery, banter. [F, f. PER(*siffler*=*siffler* f. L *sibilare* whistle), see -AGE]

persimm'on, n. American date-plum, yellow fruit becoming sweet when softened by frost. [corrupt. of native name]

persist', v.i. Continue firmly or obstinately (*in* opinion, course, *doing*) esp. against remonstrance etc.; continue in existence, survive. Hence or cogn. ~ENCE, ~ENCY, nn., ~ENT a. (esp., in Zool. & Bot., of horns, hair, leaves, etc.) permanent (opp. DECIDUOUS), ~ently² adv. [f. L PER(*sistere* stand)]

pĕrs'on, n. **1.** Individual human being; (derog.) who is this ~?; young ~, young man or (usu.) woman; living body of human being, as he had a fine ~, by her fortune not her ~; acting, appearing, in his own (proper) ~ or in ~ (himself, personally); found a friend in (the ~ of) his landlord; (~ of) ... ~) or body corporate (artificial ~) with recognized rights & duties; character in play or story. **2.** The three ~s (modes of being) of the Godhead, Father, Son, Holy Spirit. **3.** (gram.) Each of the three classes of personal pronouns etc. de-noting respectively the ~ etc. speaking (first ~), spoken to (second ~), & spoken of (third ~). **4.** (zool.) Individual of a compound or colonial organism. [f. OF persone f. L persona player's mask, charac-ter in play, (LL) human being, perh. cogn. w. PERSONARE sound)]

pĕrsōn'a, n. Person, as:~ grāt'a, accept-able person; in⁵ prŏp'riā.~. [L]

pĕrs'onable, a. Handsome, comely. [-ABLE]

pĕrs'onage, n. Person of rank or impor-tance; person; character in play etc. [OF, = med. L personaticum (as PERSON, see -AGE)]

pĕrs'onal, a. & n. **1.** One's own, indivi-dual, private, (as to suit his ~ convenience, this is ~ to myself); done, made, etc., in person, as ~ service, acquaintance, inter-view; directed, referring, (esp. hostilely) to an individual, as ~ abuse, remarks; ~ column, part of a newspaper devoted to short advertisements of a ~ or semi-~ nature; making, given to making, ~ remarks, as do not let us become ~; (Law) ~ property, estate, chattels or chattel interests in land, all property except land and those interests in land that pass to one's heir, (cf. REAL); (Gram.) of, denoting, one of the three persons, esp. ~ pronouns. **2.** n. (usu. pl.) *Newspaper paragraph relating to individual person(s). [OF, f. L personālis (PERSON, -AL)]

pĕrsonal'ity, n. Being a person; personal existence or identity; distinctive personal character; person; (of remarks) fact of being aimed at an individual, (usu. pl.) such remark(s); (rare)=PERSONALTY; multiple ~y (Psych.), the apparent exist-ence of two or more distinct and alternat-ing ~ies in a single individual. [f. OF personalité f. med. L personālitātem (as prec., see -TY)]

pĕrs'onalize, v.t. Personify. Hence **pĕrs'onall̆y̆**, adv. In person, in one's own person, as he conducted them ~, a ~ conducted tour (conducted by someone in person), writ was served on them ~; a God existing ~ (as a person); for one's own part, as ~ I see no objection. So **pĕrs'onal̆ty**, n. Personal estate. [f. AF personaltie PERSONALITY]

pĕrs'onate, v.t. Play the part of (charac-ter in drama, also fig.); pretend to be (person) esp. for fraudulent purpose. Hence ~ATION, ~ATOR², nn. [f. L personāre (as PERSON, see -ATE²)]

pĕrsonif'ication, n. Personifying; per-son, thing, viewed as striking example or embodiment of (quality etc.). [f. foll., see -ATION]

pĕrson'if̆y̆, v.t. Attribute personal nature to (abstraction); symbolize (quality) by figure in human form; embody (quality) in one's own person, exemplify typically, as in one's own person. [prob. f. F personnifier, see PERSON & -FY]

pĕrsonnel', n. Body of persons engaged in some public service or in a factory, office, etc. (opp. MATERIEL). [F, = PERSON]

pĕrs'onate², a. (bot.). Having the open-ing of the lips closed by upward pro-jection of the lower, as in snapdragon. [f. L personātus masked (as foll., see -ATE²)]

pĕrspĕc'tive, n. & a. **1.** Art of delineating solid objects on plane surface so as to give same impression of relative posi-tions, magnitudes etc., as the actual ob-jects do when viewed from particular point; picture so drawn; apparent rela-tion between visible objects as to posi-tion, distance, etc.; linear ~ (concerned with apparent form, magnitude, & posi-tion, of objects); (fig.) relation in which parts of subject are viewed by the mind; view, prospect, (lit. & fig.); in (drawn according to rules of)~. **2.** adj. Of, in, ~. whence ~LY² adv. [f. med. L perspectīva (ars art)]

pĕrs'pex, n. Tough unsplinterable plastic material, much lighter than glass, widely used for transparent parts of aircraft. [P; f. L PER(spicere spect- look)]

pĕrspĭcā'cious (-shǔs), a. Having mental penetration or discernment. Hence or cogn. ~LY² adv., perspicā'cĭty n. [f. L perspicax (spicere spect- look)]

pĕrspĭc'ūous, a. Easily understood, clearly expressed; (of person) clear in ex-pression. Hence or cogn. perspicū'ity, ~NESS, nn., ~LY² adv. [f. L perspicuus (as prec.), + -OUS]

pĕrspīr'able, a. Allowing the passage of perspiration; that can be thrown off in perspiration. [f. PERSPIRE + -ABLE]

pĕrspīrā'tion, n. Sweating; sweat. [f. OF (as foll., see -ATION)]

pĕrspīr'atory a. [F as foll.]

pĕrspīre', v.i. & t. Sweat; (trans.) give off (liquid) through pores in form of vapour or moisture. [f. L PERspīrāre breathe; breathe, (of wind) blow]

pĕrsuāde' (-swā-), v.t. Convince (per-son, oneself, of fact, that thing is so); in-duce (person to do, into action); (p.p. convinced of thing, that). Hence or cogn. ~ABLE, persuās'ı̆BLE, aa., persuāsı̆-BĬL'ITY n. (-sw-), [f. L PERsuādēre suās-advise)]

persuadˈer (-sw-), n. Person or thing that persuades, esp. (pl., sl.) spurs (clap in the ~s, spur horse). [-ER¹]

persuaˈsion (-swāzhn), n. Persuading; persuasiveness; conviction, as *it is my private ~ that he is mad*; religious belief; sect holding this, as *he is of the Roman Catholic ~*; (joc.) race, kind, sort, as *a man of the Jewish ~* (Jew), *no one of the male ~ was there*. [f. L *persuasio* (as prec. see -ION)]

persuaˈsive (-sw-), a. & n. Able to persuade, winning; (n.) motive, inducement. Hence ~LY² adv., ~NESS n. [f. med. L *persuasivus* (as PERSUADE, see -IVE)]

pert, a. Forward, saucy, in speech or conduct. Hence ~LY² adv., ~NESS n. [earlier (& OF) *apert* f. L (1) *apertus* p.p. of *aperire* open (2) *expertus* EXPERT]

pertainˈ, v.i. Belong as part, appendage, or accessory, *to*; be appropriate *to*; have reference, relate, *to*. [f. OF *partenir* f. L *pertinēre* = *tenēre* hold]

pertinaˈcious (-shus), a. Stubborn, persistent, obstinate. Hence or cogn. ~LY² adv., ~NESS, pertinaˈcity, nn. [f. L *pertinax*=*tenax* TENACIOUS]

pertˈinent, a. & n. Pertaining, relevant, apposite, (to matter in hand etc.); to the point; ||(n., usu. pl.) appurtenance(s). Hence or cogn. ~ENCE, ~ENCY, nn., ~entlyˈ adv. [f. L as PERTAIN, see -ENT]

perturbˈ, v.t. Throw into (physical) confusion; disturb mentally, agitate. So perturbaˈTION (-ter-) n., ~ativE (or pertˈerbāt-) a. [f. L PER(*burbare* disturb)]

peruke (-ōōk), n. Wig. [f. F *perruque* f. It. *perruca*, *parruca*, perh. ult. f. L *pilus* hair]

peruseˈ (-ōōz), v.t. Read thoroughly or carefully; read; (fig.) examine (person's face etc.). Hence peruˈSAL (-ōōzl) n. [(In earlier sense 'use up') PER-+USE]

Peruˈvian (-ōō-), a. & n. 1. Of Peru; ~ bark (of CINCHONA tree). 2. n. Native of Peru. [f. mod. L *Peruvia* Peru +-AN]

pervadeˈ, v.t. Spread through, permeate, saturate, (often fig. of influences etc.). Hence or cogn. pervaˈSION (-zhn), pervaˈsivENESS, nn., pervaˈsivE a., pervaˈsivELYˈ adv. [f. L PER(*vadere* vas- go)]

perverseˈ, a. Persistent in error; different from what is reasonable or required; wayward; peevish; perverted, wicked; (of verdict) against weight of evidence or judge's direction. Hence or cogn. ~LY² adv., ~NESS, perverˈsITY, nn. [F (-rs, -rse), f. L as foll.]

pervertˈ¹, v.t. Turn aside (thing) from its proper use; misconstrue, misapply, (words etc.); lead astray (person, mind) from right opinion or conduct or esp. religious belief. Hence or cogn. perverˈSION (-shn) n., perverˈsivE a. [f. F *pervertir* f. L PER(*vertere* vers- turn)]

perˈvert², n. Perverted person, apostate. [f. prec. cf. CONVERT²]

pervˈious, a. Affording passage (to); permeable; (fig.) accessible (to reason etc.). Hence ~NESS n. [f. L PER(*vius* f. *via* way) +-OUS]

peseˈta (-sā-), n. Spanish silver coin nominally worth about 10d. [Sp.]

Peshiˈtō, -itta, (-shē-), n. Principal ancient Syriac version of O. & N.T. [f. Syriac *p'shiṭō*(ṭā, -ō, simple)]

peshwa (pāsh'wah), n. (hist.). Hereditary sovereign (earlier, chief minister) of the Mahratta State. [Pers., = chief]

pesˈky, a. (colloq.). Troublesome, confounded, annoying, plaguy. [?]

peˈsō (pā-), n. Silver coin worth about 4s., used in most S.-Amer. republics. [Sp.]

pessˈary, n. (med.). Instrument worn in the vagina to prevent uterine displacements; vaginal suppository. [f. med. L *pessarium* f. L f. Gk *pessos* oval stone used in game like draughts]

pessˈimism, n. Tendency to look at the worst aspect of things (cf. OPTIMISM); doctrine that this world is the worst possible, or that all things tend to evil. So ~IST n., ~isˈtIC a., ~isˈtICALLY adv. [f. L *pessimus* worst +-ISM]

pest, n. Troublesome or destructive person, animal, or thing; (now rare) pestilence; ~-house, hospital for plague etc. [f. F *peste* f. L *pestis* plague]

pesˈter, v.t. Trouble, plague. [perh. f. F EM(*pestrer* f. L *pastorium* tether, as PASTOR)]

pestifˈerous, a. Noxious, pestilential; (fig.) bearing moral contagion, pernicious. [f. L *pestifer* (as PEST, see -FEROUS)]

pesˈtilence, n. Any fatal epidemic disease, esp. bubonic plague. So pestilenˈtial (-shl) a. [F, f. L *pestilentia* (as foll., see -ENCE)]

pesˈtilent, a. Destructive to life, deadly; (fig.) injurious to morals etc.; (colloq.) troublesome, plaguy. Hence ~LY² adv. [f. L *pestilens* (also -lentus) f. *pestis* plague]

pesˈtle (-sl), n. & v.t. (-t-). Club-shaped instrument for pounding substances in a mortar; kinds of appliance for pounding etc.; (v.t.) pound (as) with ~; (v.i.) use ~. [f. OF *pestel* f. L *pistillum* (*pinsere* pist- pound)]

pestolˈogy, n. Scientific study of pests (esp. harmful insects) & the methods of dealing with them. [f. L *pestis* PEST + -o-+-LOGY]

pet¹, n. & v.t. (-tt-). 1. Animal tamed & kept as favourite or treated with fondness; darling, favourite, (often attrib.); one's ~ aversion, what one specially dislikes; ~-cock, small stop-cock for draining, letting out steam, etc.; ~-name, one expressing fondness or familiarity. 2. v.t. Treat as a ~, fondle; *~-ting party (colloq.) social gathering of young people at which hugging, kissing, etc., are indulged in. [?]

pet², n. Offence at being slighted, ill-

humour, esp. take (usu. the) ~, be in a ~.

pet²al, n. Each of the divisions of the corolla of a flower. Hence ~INE⁴ (-in), (-)(-)ED² (-ld), ~OID, aa. [f. Gk *petalon* thin plate, leaf, (*pet-* spread)]

pet²alon, n. Gold plate on mitre of Jewish high priest. [as PETAL]

petard´, n. Small engine of war formerly used to blow in door etc.; kind of fire-work, cracker; HOIST² *with his own* ~. [f. F *pétard* (*péter* break wind ult. f. L *pedere*, see -ARD)]

pét´asus, n. Ancient Greek low-crowned broad-brimmed hat, esp. as worn by Hermes; winged hat of Hermes. [L, f. Gk *petasos*]

pétaur´ist (pé-tŏr-), n. Marsupial of the genus *Petaurista* with a patagium enabling it to take flying leaps. [f. Gk *petauristēs* performer on spring-board (*petauron*)]

Pe´ter¹ (-tŏr), n. A male Christian name; *Si*~, one of Christ's disciples; *rob* ~ *to pay Paul*, take away from one to give to another; discharge one debt by incurring another; BLUE ~; ~*'s fish*, haddock or other fish with marks supposed to have been made by St ~'s thumb & finger; ~-*penny*, ~*'s-penny* or *pence*, (Hist.) annual tax of penny paid to papal see, (since 1860) voluntary payments to papal treasury. [f. L f. Gk *Petros* stone] [?]

pe´ter², v.i. (sl.). (Of stream, vein of ore, & fig.) ~ *out*, give out, come to an end.

pet´ersham, n. Thick ribbed or corded silk ribbon; heavy overcoat or breeches formerly worn; cloth for these. [Viscount P~, c. 1812]

pét´iôle, n. (bot.). Leaf-stalk. Hence ~AR¹, ~ATE²(2), aa. [f. L *petiolus* little foot, stalk]

petit (petĕ´), a. (pl. ~*s* pr. petĕ´). ~*cheroux* (shĕvŏ´), a gambling game; ~*maître* (mā´tr), dandy, coxcomb; ~*mal* (māl), mild form of epilepsy; ~*souper* (soŏp´ā), informal supper for a few intimates; ~*s soins* (see Ap.), small attentions; ~*s verre* (vār), glass of liqueur. [F. = little]

petite (petē´), a. (Of woman) of small dainty make. [F fem. of prec.]

petĭ´tĭo (-tishiō, -tĭttiō), n. ~ *principi´i*, begging the question. [L, as foll.]

petĭ´tion, n. & v.t. & i. 1. Asking, supplication, request; formal written supplication from one or more persons to sovereign etc.; P~ & *Advice* (hist.), Parliament's remonstrance to Cromwell 1657; P~ *of Right* (hist.), parliamentary declaration of rights & liberties of the people assented to by Charles I in 1628; (Law) kinds of formal written application to a court. 2. v.t. Make ~ to (sovereign etc. for thing, to do). 3. v.i. Ask humbly (for thing, to be allowed to do etc.). So ~ARY¹ (-sho-) a., ~ER¹ (-sho-) n. (esp., plaintiff in divorce suit). [f. F *pétition* f. L *petitionem* (*petere* -tit- seek, see -ION)]

pet´rel, n. (Also *storm*~, *stormy* ~) small sea-bird with black & white plumage & long wings. [perh. f. St Peter+-REL]

petrĭfac´tion, n. Petrifying; petrified substance or mass. [irreg. f. foll., see -FACTION; the reg. *petrification* is now rare]

pet´rify, v.t. & i. Convert into stone; (fig.) paralyse, stupefy, with astonishment, terror, etc. (~*ied with fear* etc.); deprive (mind, doctrine, etc.) of vitality; stiffen; (intr.) turn into stone (lit. & fig.). [f. F *pétrifier* f. L f. Gk *petra* rock, see -FY]

pet´ro-, in comb.=Gk *petra* rock, as: ~*glyph*, rock-carving; ~*graphy*, rock-inscription; ~*graphy* (petrog´-), scientific description of formation & composition of rocks, so ~*grapher* (-trog´-) n., ~*graphic(al)* aa., ~*logy* (pĕtrŏl´-), study of origin, structure, etc., of rocks, so ~*lo´gic(al)* aa., ~*lo´gically* adv., ~*logist* (pĕtrŏl´-) n.

pét´rol, n. Refined petroleum as used in motor-cars, aircraft, etc. [f. F *pétrole* f.]

petrol´eum, n. Mineral oil found in upper strata of earth, used as fuel for heating & in internal-combustion engines. [med. L (L & Gk *petra* rock + L *oleum* oil)]

petro´leur (pătrŏlĕr´), n. (fem. -euse pr. -ōz) Incendiary who uses petroleum. [F f. *pétrole* petroleum]

pét´ronel, n. (hist.). Large pistol used esp. by horse-soldiers in 16–17th cc. [f. F *petrinal* (*poitrine* chest, ult. f. L *pectus*)]

pét´rous, a. Of, like, rock, esp. (Anat.) applied to hard part of the temporal bone. [f. L *petrosus* (L & Gk *petra* rock, see -OUS)]

pett´icoat, n. Woman's (under-)garment fastened round waist & hanging loose usn. inside a skirt (*have known him since he was in* ~*s*, a small child); *she is a Cromwell in* ~*s* (in all but sex); woman, girl, (pl.) female sex; (attrib.) feminine, esp. ~ *government*, predominance of woman in the home or in politics. Hence ~ED²

pett´ifŏg, v.i.(-gg-). Practise legal chicanery; quibble, wrangle, about petty points. [prob. back formation f. foll.]

pett´ifŏgger (-g-), n. Inferior legal practitioner; rascally attorney; petty practitioner in any department. Hence ~ERY(4), ~ING² a., (-g-). [f. PETTY; -fogger uncertain]

pett´ish, a. Peevish, petulant, easily put out. Hence ~LY² adv., ~NESS n. [f. PET²+-ISH¹]

pett´itoes (-ōz), n. pl. Pig's trotters. [?]

pet´tö, n. *In* ~, in one's own breast, in secret. [It., f. L *pectus*]

pett´y, a. Unimportant, trivial; little-minded; minor, inferior, on a small scale,

as ~y princes, farmers; ~y cash, small cash items of receipt or expenditure; ~y officer, in navy corresponding in rank to N.C.O.; ~y JURY, LARCENY, ‖ SESSION. Hence ~ILY² adv., ~INESS n. [earlier petit f. F petit etym. dub.]

pet′ulant, a. Peevishly impatient or irritable. Hence or cogn. ~ANCE n., ~antLY² adv. [f. F pétulant f. L petulantem (+petulare dim. of petere seek, see -ANT)]

petun′ia, n. Plant with white, purple, or violet flowers of funnel shape; dark violet, purple, (esp. attrib.). [f. F pétun f. S.-Amer. pety tobacco]

pétun′tse (-ōon-, -ïn-), n. White earth used in China for making porcelain. [f. Chin. pai-tun-tze (pai white+tun stone+suf. -tze)]

pew, n., & v.t. Place (often enclosed & raised) in church appropriated to a family (~) or others; fixed bench with back in church; (colloq.) seat, as find, take, a ~; ~-rent (for ~ in church); (v.t.) furnish with ~s, enclose in ~. Hence ~AGE(4) n., ~LESS a. [ME puwe prob. f. OF puye balcony f. L podia pl. of podium f. Gk podion pedestal (pous podos foot]

pewit, peewit, (pē′wĭt, pū′ĭt), n. Lapwing; its cry; ~ (gull), black-headed gull. [imit.]

pew′er, n. Grey alloy of tin & lead or other metal; utensils of this; ~ pot; ~ (sl.) prize-money. [ME & OF peutre, It. peltro, etym. dub.]

pfenn′ig, -ing, n. Small German copper coin 1/100 of a mark. [G, cogn. w. PENNY]

pha′éton (or fā′tn), n. Light four-wheeled open carriage usu. drawn by pair of horses. [f. Gk Phaethōn, son of Helios (Sun-god) and famous for bad driving of sun chariot]

phāgedaen′a, -dien′a (-j-, -g-), n. Spreading ulcer. So ~aenIC, ~enIC, a. [L, f. Gk phagedaina (phag- eat)]

phăg′ocyte, n. Leucocyte capable of guarding the system against infection by absorbing microbes. [f. Gk phag- eat+-O-+-CYTE]

-phagous in comb.=Gk -phagos -eating +-OUS.

phal′ange (-j), n. See PHALANX.

phalăn′ǵeal (-j-), a. (anat.). Of a phalanx. [-AL]

phalăn′ger (-j-), n. Kinds of Australian marsupial of arboreal habits, e.g. flying squirrel or opossum. [f. Gk phalangion spider's web (PHALANX), from webbed toes of hind feet]

phal′anstĕry, n. (Buildings of) socialistic PHALANX. Hence ~ĒR′IAN a. & n. [f. F phalanstère f. foll. after monastère]

phal′an|x, n. (pl. ~xes, ~ges pr. -jēz), 1. (Gk Ant.) line of battle, esp. body of Macedonian infantry drawn up in close

order. 2. Set of persons banded together for common purpose; socialistic community of about 1800 persons as proposed by Fourier. 3. (Anat., also ~ge) each bone of finger or toe; (Bot.) bundle of stamens united by filaments. [L, f. Gk phalagx -ggos]

phal′arōpe, n. Kinds of small wading and swimming bird allied to snipe. [F, irreg. f. Gk phalaris coot+pous foot]

phăll′|us, n. (pl.~ī). Image of the penis, venerated in religious systems as symbolizing generative power in nature. Hence or cogn. ~IC a., ~(IC)ISM(3) nn. [L, f. Gk phallos]

phană′riŏt, n. Resident in the Phanar quarter of Constantinople; member of the Greek official class under the Turks. [f. mod. Gk phanariōtēs (phanari lighthouse f. Gk phanarion, see -OT³)]

phăn′er|ogăm, n. (bot.). Plant that has stamens & pistils, flowering plant, (cf. CRYPTOGAM). So ~ogām′IC, ~ŏg′amous, aa. [f. F phanérogame f. Gk phaneros visible+-gamos -married]

phăn′sĭgar, n. Thug. [Hind. (phansĕ noose)]

phăn′tăsm, n. Illusion, phantom; illusive likeness (of); (Psychics) supposed vision of absent (living or dead) person. Hence phantăs′mAL, phăntăs′mIC, aa., phăntăs′malLY² adv., (-z-). [f. F fantasma f. L f. Gk phantasma (phantazō make visible f. phan- stem of phainō show, see -M)]

phăntăsmăgŏr′ia (-z-), n. Exhibition of optical illusions in London in 1802; shifting scene of real or imagined figures. Hence ~ŏ′rIC a. [f. prec. + Gk agora assembly]

phăn′tasy. See FANTASY (the ph- form is used esp. for the first sense there given).

phăn′tom, n. Apparition, spectre; image (of); vain show, form without substance or reality; mental illusion; (attrib.) apparent, illusive, as ~ tumour, temporary swelling. [ME & OF fantosme PHANTASM]

Phăr′aoh (-rō), n. Generic name of ancient Egyptian kings; ~'s serpent, chemical toy fusing in serpentine form. [f. L f. Gk Pharaō ult. f. Egypt. pr'o great house]

Phă′risee, n. One of ancient Jewish sect distinguished by strict observance of traditional & written law & pretensions to sanctity; self-righteous person, formalist, hypocrite. Hence or cogn. **Phărisā′ic(AL)** aa.. **Phărisā′icalLY²** adv., **Phă′risāism** n. [f. L f. Gk Pharisaios ult. f. Heb. parush separated]

phărmăceu′t|ical (-sū-, -kū-), a. Of, engaged in, pharmacy; of the use or sale of medicinal drugs. Hence or cogn. ~′icalLY² adv., ~ICS n. [f. L f. Gk pharmakeutikos (pharmakeutēs druggist f. pharmakon drug)+-AL]

phărmăcŏl′og|y, n. Theory of pharmacy.

pharmacopoe'ia (-pēa), n. Book (esp. one officially published) containing list of drugs with directions for use; stock of drugs. Hence ~IAL (-pēal) a. [f. Gk *pharmakopoiia* (as prec. + *-poiia* making)]

pharm'acy, n. Preparation & (esp. medicinal) dispensing of drugs; drug-store, dispensary. [f. OF *farmacie* f. Ll f. Gk *pharmakeia* practice of the druggist (*pharmakeuō* f. *pharmakon* drug)]

phar'os, n. Lighthouse or beacon to guide mariners. [Ll f. Gk *Pharos*, island off Alexandria, lighthouse on this]

pharyng'o- (-ngg-) in comb. = foll., as: ~*cele*, abnormal enlargement at base of pharynx; ~*tomy* (-ŏt-), incision into pharynx.

pharynx, n. Cavity, with enclosing muscles & mucous membrane, behind & communicating with nose, mouth, & larynx. Hence **pharyng'AL**, **pharyng'geal** (-j-), aa.; **pharyng'Gr's** (-j-) n. [f. Gk *pharunx -ggos*]

phase (-z), n. Aspect of moon or planet, according to amount of illumination (esp. applied to new moon, first quarter, full moon, last quarter); stage of change or development; (Physics) particular stage in recurring sequence of movements or changes (esp. of alternating electric currents), usu. expressed in degrees, the complete sequence or period being 360°; (of electric generators, motors, etc.), designed to supply or use simultaneously three separate alternating currents of the same voltage, but having their periods 120° apart. Hence **phas'ic** (-z-) a. [f. Gk *phasis* appearance (*phan*-show), also in E.w. pl. *phases*]

phea'sant (fez-), n. A game-bird naturalized in Britain & other parts of Europe; ~*-eyed*, (of flowers) marked like ~'s eye. [AF *fesant*, L f. L f. Gk *Phasianus* (bird) of the river *Phasis*]

phen(o)- in comb. = Gk *phainos* shining (*phan*-show), in chem. names of substances derived from coal-tar (orig. in manufacture of illuminating gas), as: *phenö'cetin*, an anti-pyretic; *phen'ol*, carbolic acid; *phen'yl*, radical found in benzene, phenol, etc.

phenŏl'ogy, n. Study of the times of recurring natural phenomena esp. in relation to climatic conditions. So **pheno-lŏ'gICAL** a. [f. PHENOMENON + -LOGY]

phenŏm'enal, a. Of the nature of a phenomenon; cognizable by, evidenced only by, the senses; concerned with phenomena; remarkable, prodigious. Hence ~LY² adv., ~IZE v.t, make, or represent as ~, [-AL]

phenŏm'en(a)lism, n. Doctrine that phenomena are the only objects of knowledge. So ~IST n., ~IS'TIC a. [prec. + -ISM]

phenŏm'énon, n. (pl. -ena). Thing that appears or is perceived, esp. thing the cause of which is in question; (Philos.) that of which a sense or the mind directly takes note, immediate object of perception; remarkable person, thing, occurrence, etc. [f. Ll f. Gk *phainomenon* neut. part. of *phainomai* appear]

phew, int. expr. impatience or disgust.

phi, n. Greek letter (Φ, φ) = ph. [Gk]

phi'al, n. Small glass bottle, esp. for liquid medicine. [f. F *fiole* f. L f. Gk *phialē* broad flat vessel]

phil- in comb. = PHILO- before vowel or h.

-phil, -phile, etc. in comb., forming nn. w. sense 'lover of' and adjj. = '-loving', as *biblio-phil*(e), *Russophil*(e), *gastrophil*(e); repr. Gk *philos* dear, in Gk found as suf. only in personal names w. sense 'dear to,' (*Diphilos* dear to Zeus), the sense 'lov-' being given in Gk by PHILO-. Hence **-philous** adj. suf.

philän'der, v.i. Make love esp. in trifling manner, dangle after woman. Hence ~ER¹ n. [f. *philander* n. f. Gk *philandros* f. *anēr* man) prop. = fond of men, taken in sense 'lover']

phil'anthrŏpe, n. = PHILANTHROPIST. [f. Gk *philanthrōpos* man)]

philanthrŏp'ic, a. Loving one's fellow men, benevolent, humane. Hence ~ALLY adv. [f. *philanthropique* (as prec., see -IC)]

philăn'thropist, n. Lover of mankind; one who exerts himself for the well-being of his fellow men. So ~ISM n. [f. PHILAN-THROPY + -IST]

philăn'thropize, v.i. & t. Practise philanthropy; make (persons) objects of this; make philanthropic. [-IZE]

philän'thropy, n. Love, practical benevolence, towards mankind. [f. Ll f. Gk *philanthrōpia* (as philanthrope)]

philatély, n. Stamp-collecting. Hence **philatel'IC** a., ~IST n. [f. F *philatélie* f. Gk *ateleia* exemption from payment f. *a*- not + *telos* toll, tax)]

philharmŏn'ic (-lär-), a. & n. (Person) fond of music. [f. F *philharmonique* HARMONIC)]

phil'hellēne (-lel-), a. & n. (Person) loving or friendly to the Greeks or supporting the cause of Greek independence. So **phil-hellēn'ic** (-lel-) a., **philhell'enism**, **philhell'enist**, nn. [f. Gk PHILhellēn f. *Hellēn* Greek)]

Philipp'i. *Thou shalt see me at* ~, meet at ~. [battle ref. to Shaksp., *J.C.*, IV. iii. 283).

philipp'ic, n. (pl.) orations of Demosthenes against Philip of Macedon, Cicero's orations against Antony; bitter invective. [f. L f. Gk *philippikos* (*Philippos* Philip, see -IC)]

philipp'ina (-pē-), **philo-poen'a** (-pē-), *-open'a, n. Almond or

other nut with double kernel, the finding of which at dessert etc. & sharing it with another person involves the giving or receiving of a present at next meeting; the present; the custom. [perh. f. G *vielliebchen* darling (*viel* much + *liebchen* dim. of *lieb* dear)]

Phil'istine, n. & a. **1.** One of an alien war-like people in S. Palestine who harassed the Israelites; (joc.) enemy into whose hands one may fall, e.g. bailiff, critic, etc.; (in German univ., after G *philister*) non-student, outsider; uncultured person, one whose interests are material & commonplace, whence **phil'istinism n. 2.** adj. Uncultured, commonplace, prosaic. [f. F *Philistin* f. LL f. Gk *Philistinos=Palaistinos* f. ASSYR. *Palastu, Pilistu*]

philo- in comb. (before vowel or *h, phil-*) = Gk *philos*, lover of, friend of, in wds f. Gk & mod. formations, as: *~bib'lic*, fond of books; *~gÿnist* (-ǒj-), lover of women; *phil'omath*, lover of learning, esp. of mathematics; *~progen'itive*, prolific, (Phrenol.) loving one's offspring, whence *~progen'itiveness*; *~tech'nic* (-těk-), fond of (esp. the industrial) arts.

philŏl'ogÿ, n. Science of language: (now rare) love of learning & literature. Hence **philo-lŏ'gian, philolŏ'gical**ly adv. [f. F f. L f. Gk PHILO(*logia* f. *logos* word, speech) love of learning]

Phil'omēl, Philomēl'a, nn. (poet.). The nightingale. [f. F *philomèle* f. L f. Gk PHILO(*mēla* f. *melos* song or *mēlon* apple), cap. *P* in reference to myth of *~* transformed into nightingale]

philo(o)en'a. See PHILIPPINA

philos'opher, n. Lover of wisdom; *natural, moral, ~*, student of natural, moral, philosophy; one who regulates his life by the light of philosophy; one who shows philosophic calmness in trying circumstances; *~s'* (not *~'s*) *stone*, supreme object of alchemy, substance supposed to change other metals into gold or silver. [var. of OF *filosofe* f. L f. Gk *philosophos* (as PHILOSOPHY)]

philosŏph'ic(al), aa. Of, consonant with, philosophy; skilled in, devoted to, philosophy (often in titles of societies); wise; calm; temperate. Hence *~al*ly² adv. [f. LL *philosophicus* f. Gk as prec., see -IC]

philos'ophism, n. Philosophizing system (usu. derog., esp. of the French Encyclopaedists). So *~IST* n. [f. F *philosophisme* (as PHILOSOPHER, see -ISM)]

philos'ophize, v.i. & t. Play the philosopher; speculate, theorize; moralize; render philosophic. [as PHILOSOPHER + -IZE]

philos'ophÿ, n. Love of wisdom or knowledge, esp. that which deals with ultimate reality, or with the most general causes & principles of things; *natural ~*, study of natural objects & phenomena; *moral*

~, study of principles of human action or conduct; (w. pl.) philosophical system; system for conduct of life; serenity, resignation. [f. OF *filosofie* f. L f. Gk PHILO(*sophia* wisdom) f. *sophos* wise]

phil'tre (-ter), -**ter**, n. Love-potion. [F (*-tre*) f. L f. Gk *philtron* (*philĕo* love + *-tron* suf. of instrument)]

phiz, n. (colloq.). Face; expression of face. [abbr. of PHYSIOGNOMY]

phlebi'tis, n. Inflammation of walls of vein. Hence *~it'*ıc a. [f. Gk as foll. + -ITIS]

phlĕb'o- in comb. = Gk *phleps phlebos* vein, as: *~tite, ~tith*, morbid calcareous concretion in vein, so *~litⁱ(h)'ĭc* a. **phlĕbŏt'omize, v.i. & t.** Practise phlebotomy; bleed (person, part of body). So *~IST* n. [f. F *phlébotomiser* (foll., -IZE)] **phlĕbŏt'omÿ,** n. Blood-letting as medical operation. [f. OF *flebothomie* f. L f. Gk *phlebotomia* f. PHLEBO(*tomos* -cutter f. *temnō* cut)]

phlegm (flĕm), n. **1.** Thick viscid (semi-) fluid substance secreted by mucous membranes (formerly regarded as one of the four HUMOURS) esp. when morbid or excessive & discharged by cough etc., whence *~*y³ (flĕm'ĭ) a. **2.** Coolness, sluggishness, apathy, (supposed to result from predominance of *~* in constitution), so **phlĕgmăt'ıc a., phlĕgmăt'**ıcal**ly adv.** [f. OF *fleume* f. LL f. Gk *phlegma -matos* inflammation, phlegm (*phlegō* burn, see -M)]

phlĕg'mon, n. Inflammatory tumour, boil. Hence **phlĕgmŏn'ıc, ~ous,** aa. [ME f. L f. Gk *phlegmonē* (*phlegō* burn)]

phlō'ĕm, n. (bot.). Bast with associated tissues. [f. Gk *phloos* bark + *ēma* (see -M)]

phlogis'tic (-j-, -g-), a. Of phlogiston; (Med.) inflammatory. [-IC]

phlŏgis'ton (-j-, -g-), n. Principle of inflammability formerly supposed to exist in combustible bodies. [Gk, f. *phlogizō* set on fire (*phlox phlogos* flame, see -IZE)]

phlŏriz'in (or flō'rĭ-), n. (chem.). Bitter substance got from bark of root of apple & other trees. [f. Gk *phloos* bark + *rhiza* root + -IN]

phlŏx, n. Genus of plants with clusters of salver-shaped flowers of various colours. [L f. Gk *phlox* (lit. flame), a plant]

-phōbe, suf. forming aa. & nn. = -fearing, -fearer, f. F *-phobe* f. L f. Gk *-phobos*, adj. suf. f. *phobos* fear, as in *hydro~, Anglo~, Russo~*.

phō'bia, n. (Morbid) fear or aversion. [foll. used as a separate wd]

-phōb'ia, suf. f. L f. Gk *-phobia*, forming abstract nn. f. adjj. in -PHOBE, as *hydro~, Anglo~, xeno~*.

Phoeb'us (fēb-), n. The Greek sun-god; (poet.) the sun. [L, f. Gk *Phoibos*]

Phoenician (fēnish'n), a. & n. (Inhabitant) of Phoenicia (ancient name for part

of coast of Syria)or its colonies; Carthaginian. [f. F *Phénicien* f. L *Phoenicia* f. Gk
Phoinīkē+-AN]

phoe'nix (fē-), phē-, n. (Myth.) bird, the
only one of its kind, that after living
five or six centuries in Arabian desert,
burnt itself on funeral pile & rose from
the ashes with renewed youth to live
through another cycle; paragon. [L, f.
Gk *phoinix* Phoenician, purple, phoenix]

phon, n. (physics). Unit of loudness used
in measuring intensity of sounds. [f. Gk
phōnē voice]

phōn'āte, v.i. Utter vocal sound (usu.
opp. to *articulate*). Hence **phona'TION** n.

phonaut'ograph (-ahf), n. Apparatus for
automatically recording vibrations of
sound. [as prec.+AUTO-+GRAPH]

phone[1], n., & v.i. & t. (colloq.). Telephone.

phone[2], n. Simple vowel or consonant
sound. [f. Gk *phōnē* voice]

phonen'doscope, n. Apparatus for making small sounds (esp. in human body)
distinctly audible. [as prec.+Gk *endon*
within+-SCOPE]

phonet'ic, a. & n. 1. Representing vocal
sounds, esp. (of systems of spelling) using
always same symbol for same sound,
whence ~ISM, ~IST, nn., ~IZE(3) v.t.; of
vocal sounds. 2. n. pl. (Study of)
phenomena of a language. Hence **pho-
nět'ICALLY** adv., **phonetI'CIAN** (-ĭshn) n.
[f. Gk *phōnētikos* (*phōneō* speak, see -ETIC)]

phon'etist, n. Person versed in phonetics;
advocate of phonetic spelling. [-IST]

*****phon'ey**, -nȳ, a. (sl.). Sham, counter-
feit, fictitious. [?]

phon'ic, a. Of sound, acoustic; of vocal
sounds. [f. Gk *phōnē* voice+-IC]

phon'o- in comb.=Gk *phōnē* sound, as:
~lite, kinds of volcanic rock ringing when
struck; *phonŏl'ogy*, science of vocal
sounds, system of sounds in a language,
so ~lo'gica(al) aa., ~lo'gically adv., *phonol'-
ogist* n.; *phonŏm'eter*, instrument recording number or force of sound-waves;
~pore, apparatus for transmitting telephone messages along telegraph wire
without interfering with the current
transmitting telegraph messages [Gk
poros passage], so ~pŏ'ric a.; ~scope,
apparatus for testing musical strings,
(also) instrument for representing sound-
vibrations in visible form; ~type, phonetic
print, character used in this, so ~tȳp'ic-
(al) aa., ~typist, ~typy, nn.

phŏn'ograph, n. Symbol representing
spoken sound, esp. in Pitman's phono-
graphy; sound-record made by phonograph. [PHONO-+GRAPH]

phŏn'ograph (-ahf), n., & v.t. ‖Earlier
form of gramophone using cylinders;
*gramophone; (v.t.) record, reproduce,
by ~. [PHONO-+GRAPH]

phonŏg'raphý, n. Pitman's phonetic
shorthand, whence ~ER[1], ~IST, nn.;
automatic recording of sounds, as by
phonograph. Hence **phŏnŏgräph'ic** a.,
phŏnŏgräph'ICALLY adv. [PHONO-+
-GRAPHY]

-phŏre, suf.=bearer, f. F *-phore* f. Gk
-phoros (*pherō* bear), used to form technical wds, as *carpophore, semaphore*. Hence
-phorous, adj. suf.,= -phore +-OUS,
SYNONYMOUS w. -FEROUS, but prop. used
only in wds f. Gk as *carpophorous*.

phŏrm'ium, n. (Kinds of) liliaceous plant
whose fibre is used commercially; New
Zeeland flax. [f. Gk *phormion* (*phormos*
wicker basket)]

phŏs'gene, n. A poison gas, carbon oxy-
chloride, used in the 1914–18 war. [f. Gk
phōs light+-GEN(1), w. ref. to its orig.
production by action of sunlight on
chlorine & carbonic oxide]

phŏs'phate, n. A salt of phosphoric
acid, esp. (pl.) of lime or iron & alumina
as constituents of cereals etc. Hence
phŏs'phāt(e) a. [F (PHOSPHO-+-ATE[3])]

phŏs'phēne, n. Appearance of rings of
light produced by pressure on eyeball,
due to irritation of retina. [irreg. f. Gk
phōs light+*phainō* show]

phŏs'phide, n. (chem.). Combination of
phosphorus with other element or radical.
[f. PHOSPHO- +-IDE]

phŏs'phĭte, n. (chem.). A salt of phos-
phorous acid. [F (PHOSPHO-+-ITE[3])]

phŏs'phō(o)- in comb.=PHOSPHORUS.

phŏs'phorate, v.t. Combine, impregnate,
with phosphorus. [-ATE[3]]

phŏs'phor-brŏnze, n. Tough hard bronze
alloy containing a small proportion of
phosphorus, used (esp.) for bearings.
[PHOSPHORUS]

phŏsphorĕs'ce', v.i. Emit luminosity
without combustion, or by gentle combustion without sensible heat. So
~es'CENCE n., ~ĕs'CENT a. [f. PHOS-
PHOR(US)+L -esce or inceptive vbs]

phŏs'phorĭte, n. A non-crystallized variety of phosphate of lime. [f. PHOSPHORUS
+-ITE[1]]

phŏs'phorio- in comb.=phosphorus, as:
~ogŕăph'y, causing ~escence; ~ogŕăph,
a yellowish wax-like substance undergoing slow combustion at ordinary temperatures & hence appearing luminous in
the dark; ~es' nervȯ'is (colloq. phossy
jaw), gangrene of jawbone due to ~.
eogn. **phŏsphŏ'ric**, ~OUS, aa., whence or
(path.). [L, = morning star, f. Gk *phŏs-
phoros* (*phōs* light+*-phoros* -bringing f.
pherō)]

phŏs'phorus, n. A non-metallic element,

phŏs'phŭrĕt(t)ĕd, a. Combined chemically with phosphorus. [f. obs. *phosphuret* phosphide +-ED²]

phŏs'phў . See PHOSPHORUS.

phŏt'ĭsm, n. Hallucinatory sensation or vision of light. [f. Gk *phōtismos* (*phōtizō* shine f. *phōs phōtos* light, see -ISM)]

phŏt'ŏ, n. (pl. ~s), & v.t. = PHOTOGRAPH.

phŏt'o- in comb. = Gk *phōs phōtos* light (oocas. = photographic), as: ~*chromy* (-krō-), colour-photography; ~*gen*, kind of paraffin oil; ~*gēn'ĭc*, producing or emitting light, (also) suitable for being photographed; ~*glyph*, ~*glyphy*, engraved plate produced by action of light, art of producing such plates; *photŏm'ĕter*, instrument for measuring intensity of light, so ~*mĕt'rĭc*, *photŏm'ĕtry*; ~*mĭc'rograph*, photograph of object as enlarged under the microscope; ~*phŏb'ia* (Path.), dread of light; ~*phone*, apparatus in which sounds are transmitted by light; ~*sphere*, luminous envelope of sun or star from which its light & heat radiate, so ~*sphĕr'ĭc* a.; ~*stăt* (P), apparatus for making direct facsimile reproductions of documents, drawings, etc., a reproduction so made; ~*tĕlĕg'raphy*, electric reproduction of pictures, writing, etc., at a distance (cf. TELEPHOTOGRAPHY); ~*type*, plate for printing from produced by photographic process, picture etc. printed from this; ~*zincŏg'raphy*, photographic production of design on zinc plate.

phŏt'ograph (-ahf), n. & v.t. 1. Picture, likeness, taken by means of chemical action of light on sensitive film on basis of glass, paper, metal, etc. 2. v.t. Take ~ of (person etc., or abs.); (quasi-pass.) *I always ~ badly* (come out badly in ~). Hence *photŏg'rapher*, *photŏg'raphy²*, nn., *photŏgraph'ĭc* a., *photŏgraph'ĭcally* adv. [(vb f. n.) PHOTO-+-GRAPH]

photogravure (-z), n., & v.t. 1. Picture produced from photographic negative transferred to metal plate & etched in; this process. 2. v.t. Reproduce thus. [F (PHOTO-+*gravure* engraving)]

phrase (-z), n., & v.t. 1. Mode of expression, diction, as *in simple ~*, *felicity of ~*; an idiomatic expression; small group of words usu. without predicate, esp. preposition with the word(s) it governs, equivalent to adjective, adverb, or noun (e.g. *the house on the hill*, *I refuse to do it*); short pithy expression; (pl.) mere words, as *we have had enough of ~s*; (Mus.) short & more or less independent passage forming part of longer passage or of whole piece; ~*monger*, person addicted to fine-sounding~s. 2. v.t. Express in words, as *thus he ~d it*. [vb f. n. f. LL f. Gk *phrasis* (*phrazō* tell)]

phrǎs'ĕogrăm, n. Written symbol representing a phrase esp. in shorthand. [as prec. +-o-+-GRAM]

phrǎs'ĕograph (-ahf), n. Phrase for which there is a phraseogram. [as PHRASE+-o-+-GRAPH]

phrǎs'ĕol'ŏġy, n. Choice or arrangement of words; mode of expression. Hence ~*olŏ'ġĭcal* a., ~*olŏ'ġĭcally²* adv. [as PHRASE+-o-+-LOGY]

phrāt'rў, n. (Gk Hist.), a kinship unit, esp. (in Athens) each of three sub-divisions of the (*phȳle* or) tribe; tribal division among primitive races. [f. Gk *phratria* (*phrātēr, -tŏr*, clansman, cogn. w. BROTHER)]

phrĕnĕt'ĭc, a. Frantic; fanatic. [f. OF *frenetike* f. L f. late Gk *phrenētikos* = Gk *phrenitikos* (*phrenitis* delirium, as foll., see -ITIS & -IC)]

phrĕn'ĭc, a. (anat.). Of the diaphragm. [f. Gk *phrēn phrenos* diaphragm, mind, see -IC]

phrēnŏl'ŏġў, n. Study of external conformation of cranium as index to development & position of organs belonging to the various mental faculties. Hence *phrēnŏlŏ'ġĭcal* a., *phrēnŏlŏ'ġĭcally²* adv., ~IST n. [as prec. +-LOGY]

phrŏn'tĭstĕrĭŏn, n. (joc.). Place for thinking in, thinkery. [f. Gk *phrontistērion* (*phrontizō* think f. *phrontis* thought)]

Phrÿ'ġian, a. Of Phrygia, ancient country in Asia Minor; (Mus.) ~ *mode*, ancient Greek MODE reputedly warlike in character, third of eccl. modes with E as final & C as dominant; ~ *cap*, ancient conical peaked cap now identified with cap of liberty. [f. L *Phrygianus* (*Phrygia*, see -AN)]

phthĭs'ĭs (th-, fth-), n. Progressive wasting disease, esp. pulmonary consumption. So (through OF *tisike*) **phthĭs'ĭcal** (tĭz-, fthĭz-) a., of *tisike*, ~. [Gk (*phthinō* decay)]

phthĭt, n. & adv. The sound of a bladder collapsing, a bullet passing, etc.; (adv., esp.) *go ~*, collapse (also fig. of scheme etc.). [f. Hind. *phatna* to burst]

phylǎc'tĕrў, n. Small leather box containing Hebrew texts on vellum, worn by Jews to remind them to keep the law (*make broad one's ~y* or *~ies*, make a display of righteousness); (usu. ostentatious) religious observance; amulet, charm. [f. L f. Gk *phulaktērion* amulet (*phulassō* guard)]

phylĕt'ĭc, a. (biol.). Of a phylum, racial. [f. Gk *phuletikos* (*phuletēs* tribesman f. *phulē* tribe, see -IC)]

phȳllo- in comb. = Gk *phullon* leaf, as: ~*ŏph'agous* a.; ~*'ŏpŏd* a. & n., leaf-footed (crustacean); ~*'ostome*, leaf-nosed bat; ~*otax'is*, arrangement of leaves on axis or stem; ~*oxēr'a* [f. Gk *xēros* dry], genus of plant-lice, vine-pest.

phȳlo- in comb. = Gk *phulon* race, tribe, in biol. wds., as: ~*gĕn'esis*, ~*geny* (-jĕ-), racial evolution of animal or plant type, history of this, so ~*genĕt'ĭc*, ~*gĕn'ĭc*, aa., ~*genĕt'ĭcally* adv.

phy'lum, n. (biol.; pl. **-la**). Race of organisms descended from common ancestral form. [mod. L f. Gk *phŭlon* race]

phys'ic (-z-), n., & v.t. (-ck-). **1.** Art of healing; medical profession; (colloq.) medicine, as *a dose of* ~. **2.** pl. Sciences treating of properties of matter & energy or of action of different forms of energy on matter in general (excluding chemistry & biology). **3.** v.t. Dose with ~ (lit. & fig.). [(vb f. n.) f. OF *fisique* f. L f. Gk *phusikē* (*epistēmē* knowledge) of nature

phys'ical (-z-), a. ... Of matter, material, as ~ *force* (opp. to *moral*); of, according to laws of, natural philosophy, as ~ *explanation of miracles*, a ~ *impossibility*; belonging to physics; bodily, as ~ *exercise, strength, beauty, drill* (also sl. ~ *jerks*); ~ *geography* (dealing with natural features). Hence ~LY² adv., **phys'ico-** comb. form. [f. med. L *physicalis* (as prec., see -AL)]

phys'ician (-zishn), n. One who practises the healing art including medicine & surgery; one legally qualified in medicine as well as in surgery; (fig.) healer. [f. OF *fisicien* (as PHYSIC, see -ICIAN)]

phys'icist (-z-), n. Student of physics or of natural science in general; believer in the material origin of vital phenomena (cf. VITALIST), so ~ISM n. [PHYSIC + -IST]

phys'icky (-z-), a. Suggestive of physic. [-Y²]

physio-(-z-) in comb. = Gk *phusis* nature, as: ~*ŏ'cracy*, government according to natural order; **phys'iocrat**, advocate of this, esp. member of Quesnay's school in France in 18th c.; ~*ŏ'geny*, genesis of vital functions; ~*ŏ'latry*, nature-worship; ~*ŏthĕrapy*, electrical treatment & massage; ~*ŏthĕrapist*, person skilled in this.

physiogn'omy (-zion-, -ziŏgn-), n. Art of judging character from features of face or form of body, whence ~IST(3) n.; cast or form of features, type of face; (vulg.) face; external features of country etc.; characteristic (of natural or other) aspect. Hence cogn. **physiognom'ic(al)** aa., **physiognom'ically²** adv., (-zion-, -ziŏgn-). [ME *fisnomye* f. med. L f. Gk *phusiognōmonia* judging of a man's nature (by his features) f. *phusis* nature + *gnōmōn* judge f. *gnō* know]

physiog'raphy (-z-), n. Description of nature, of natural phenomena, or of a class of objects; physical geography. Hence ~ER¹ n., **physiograph'ic(al)** aa. [PHYSIO- + -GRAPHY]

physiol'ogy (-z-), n. Science of normal functions & phenomena of living things (comprising *animal & vegetable* ~). Hence or cogn. **physiolŏ'gic(al)** aa., **physiolŏ'gically²** adv., ~IST n. [f. L f. Gk *phusiologia*, see PHYSIO- & -LOGY]

physique¹ (-zēk), n. Bodily structure, organization, & development. [F, n. f. -physique, suf. repr. Gk physico]

phyto- in comb. = Gk *phuton* plant, denoting a vegetable organism, as *proto*~, *sapro*~. See also ZOOPHYTE.

phyto- in comb. = Gk *phuton* plant, as: ~*ogen'esis*, ~*ŏ'geny*, generation or evolution of plants; ~*ŏ'graphy*, descriptive botany; ~*ŏ'tomer*, plant unit; ~*ŏph'agous*, feeding on plants; ~*ŏl'omy*, dissection of plants; ~*ozŏ'on* (pl. *-zŏ'a*), plant-like animal or zoophyte.

pi¹, n. Greek letter p (Π, π), esp. (Math., π) as symbol of ratio of circumference of circle to diameter (3·14159).

pi²², a. (school sl.) ... [= PIOUS; *pi' jaw*, sermonizing, moral lecture. [abbr.]

piac'ular (-z-), a. Expiatory. [f. L *piacularis* (*piaculum* expiation f. *piare* appease, see -AR¹)]

piaffe', v.i. (Of horse etc.) move as in trot, but slower. [f. F *piaffer*, etym. dub.]

piaff'er, n. Movement of piaffing. [as prec.]

pi'a mat'er, n. (anat.). Innermost MENINX. [med. L transl. of Arab. *umm raqīqah* tender mother]

pianette' (pēa-), n. Low pianino. [PIANO², -ETTE]

piani'no (-ēnō-), n. (pl. ~s). Small upright piano. [It., dim. of PIANO²]

pianiss'imo (pēa-), adv. & n. (mus.). (Passage to be played) very softly. [It., superl. of PIANO¹]

pi'anist (pēa-), n. Player on piano. [f. F *pianiste* (also in E, usu. as fem.), see -IST]

pian'o¹ (-ah-), adv. & n. (mus.). (Passage to be played) softly. [It., f. L *planus* flat, (LL) soft]

pian'o² (-ah-), n. (pl. ~s). Musical instrument with metal strings struck by hammers worked by levers from a keyboard (vibration being stopped by dampers), & with pedals regulating character of tone; *grand* ~, large horizontal ~ of full tone; *upright* ~, vertical ~; *cottage* ~, small upright ~; ~ *organ*, mechanical ~ constructed like barrel-organ; ~*player*, contrivance for playing ~ mechanically. [It., earlier *piano e forte* soft & strong]

pianofort'e (or piăn'ofŏ̄rt), n. [Full name, now in formal use only, for] PIANO²

pian'ola (pēa-), n. Kind of mechanical piano-player. [P]

pias'tre (-ter), **-ter**, n. Spanish silver coin; small Turkish & Egyptian coin. [F (-tre), f. It. *piastra*, ult. as PLASTER]

piăzz'a (-tsa), n. Public square or market-place esp. in Italian town; *veranda of house. [It., ult. f. L *platea* f. Gk *plateia* (*hodos*) broad (street)]

pibroch (pēbrŏk, & see Ap.), n. Series of variations for bagpipe, chiefly martial. [f. Gael. *piobaireachd* (*piobair* piper f. *piob*, f. E PIPE)]

pic'a, n. Size of TYPE¹. [earlier sense, collection of rules about Easter and other

movable feasts, f. med. L *pica* magpie, hist. unexpl.]

pic'ador, n. Mounted man with lance in bull-fight. [Sp. (*picar* prick)]

pic'amar, n. Bitter oil got from wood-tar. [f. L *piz picis* pitch + *amarus* bitter]

picaresque'(-k), a. (Of a style of fiction) dealing with adventures of rogues. [f. Sp. *picaresco* (*picaro* rogue, etym. dub., -ESQUE)]

picaroon', n., & v.i. Rogue; thief; pirate; pirate ship; (v.i.) play the pirate or brigand. [f. Sp. *picaron* (as prec., see -OON)]

*****picayune'**(-yōōn), n. & a. 1. Small coin, esp. 5-cent piece; (colloq.) insignificant person or thing. 2. adj. Mean, contemptible. [prob. f. F *picaillon* farthing]

picc'alilli, n. Pickle of chopped vegetables & hot spices. [?]

picc'aninny, pick', n. & a. Child, esp. of Negroes or S.-African or Australian natives; (adj.) very small, baby. [f. Sp. *pequeño* or Port. *pequeno*, dim. -*nino*, small]

picc'olō, n. (pl. ~s). Small flute, octave higher than the ordinary. [It., = small (flute)

pice, n. E.-Ind. copper coin, ¼ of anna. [f. Hind. *paisa*]

pichiciā'gō, n. Small burrowing animal of Chili, allied to armadillos. [f. Sp. *pichiciego* perh. f. native *pichey* + Sp. *ciego* blind f. L *caecus*]

pick[1], n. Tool consisting of iron bar usu. curved with point at one end & point or chisel-edge at other, with wooden handle passing through middle perpendicularly, used for breaking up hard ground etc.; instrument for picking; TOOTH~. [prob. = PIKE[1]]

pick[2], v.t. & i. 1. Break surface of (ground etc.) with or as with pick; make (hole etc.) thus; (fig.) ~ HOLES in. 2. Probe (teeth etc.) with pointed instrument to remove extraneous matter. 3. Clear(bone, carcass) of adherent flesh; pluck, gather, (flower, fruit, etc.) from stalk etc. 4. (Of birds) take up (grains etc.) in bill; (of persons) eat (food, or meal, or abs.) in small bits, (colloq.) eat (t. & i.). 5. Select carefully, as ~ one's *words, way, steps*; ~ *& choose*, select fastidiously; ~ (contrive) *a quarrel with*. 6. ~ (person's) *pocket*, steal its contents; (intr.) ~ *& steal*, pilfer; ~ *a lock*, open it (esp. with intent to rob) with pointed instrument, skeleton key, etc. 7. Pull asunder, esp. ~*oakum*; ~*to pieces*, pull asunder, (fig.) criticize (person etc.) hostilely. 8. ~ *at*, nag at, gird at; ~ *off*, pluck off, (also) shoot (persons etc.) deliberately one by one; *~ *on*, = ~ *at*; ~ *out*, select, distinguish from surrounding objects, relieve (ground colour *with* another), make out (meaning of passage etc.), play (tune) by ear on piano etc.; ~ *up*, break up (ground etc.) with pick,

lay hold of & take up, (Golf, ellipt.) ~ up one's ball, raise *oneself* from a fall etc., gain, acquire (livelihood, profit, tricks, information), succeed in seeing or hearing with searchlight, radio, etc., take (person, or thing overtaken) along with one, esp. *train stops to ~ up passengers*, make acquaintance of (person) casually (~*up* n., such person), regain (lost path etc., flesh, spirit), (intr.) recover health, make acquaintance *with*, (Games) select sides by alternate choosing (~*up* n., game between such sides). 9. ~'*lock*, person who ~s locks, instrument used for this; ~'*-me-up*, stimulating drink (also fig.); ~'*pocket*, one who steals from pockets; ‖~'*thank* (arch.), sycophant; ~-*up*, ~*ing-up* (esp. of ball in cricket), device replacing sound-box in a gramophone & enabling a record to be heard through a loud-speaker. [OE has *piken, pikken*, hist. dub., cf. prec. & F *piquer* prick]

pick[3], n. Picking; selection; *the* best part of (*the ~ of the bunch*, best of the lot). [f. prec.]

pick-a-back, adv. On shoulders or back like a bundle (of the way person or thing is carried). [?]

pick'ax(e), n., & v.t. & i. = PICK[1]; (v.t.) work (ground etc.) with ~; (v.i.) work with ~. [ME & OF *picois* cogn. w. OF *pic* PIKE[1], assim. to AXE]

pick'elhaube (-howbe), n. German spiked helmet. [G., = spike cap]

pick'er, n. One who picks, gathers, or collects, as *hop, rag,* ~; kinds of instrument for picking (in var. senses). [-ER[1]]

pick'erel, n. Young pike. [PIKE[1], -REL]

pick'et, n., & v.t. & i. 1. Pointed stake or peg driven into ground to form palisade, tether horse, etc.; (stake with pointed top on which person stood as) form of military punishment (hist.). 2. (mil.). (Also *piquet, picquet*) small body of troops sent out (*outlying* ~) held ready for enemy, or (*inlying* ~) in quarters, party of sentries, outpost; (in mod. use, chiefly camp-guard doing police duty in garrison town etc. 3. (Usu. pl.) men stationed in a body or singly by trade union to dissuade men from work during strike etc. 4. vb. Secure (place) with stakes, tether; post (men) as ~; beset (workmen) with ~s; act as ~, [(vb f. n.)] f. F *piquet* pointed stake f. *piquer* prick]

pick'ing, n. In vbl senses, esp.:~ *& stealing*; (pl.) gleanings, remaining scraps; (pl.) perquisites, pilferings. [-ING[1]]

pic'kle, n., & v.t. 1. Brine, vinegar, or similar liquor in which flesh, vegetables, etc., are preserved (ROD *in.* ~; food, esp. (pl.) vegetables preserved in ~; acid solution for cleaning purposes etc.; *sad, sorry, nice,* etc. ~ (plight); mischievous child. 2. v.t. Preserve in ~ (esp. in p.p.), treat with ~; (Naut.) rub salt or vinegar

on (person's back) after flogging; ~'d (sl.), drunk. [prob. f. MDu. *pekel* etym. dub.]

||pick'some, a. Fastidious. [PICK²+-SOME]

||pick'wick, n. Cheap kind of cigar. [f. Mr ~ in Dickens]

Pickwick'ian, a. (joc.). (Of words) used in a ~ (technical, constructive, or eso- teric) sense. [see Dickens *Pickwick* ch. 1]

pic'nic, n. & v.i. (-ck-). 1. Pleasure party including meal out of doors; (colloq.) something specially agreeable or easily accomplished (*no* ~, not an easy job). 2. v.i. Take part in ~. Hence ~KER² n., ~KY² a. (colloq.). [(vb f. n.) f. F *pique- nique* etym. dub.]

picot' (·kō), n. Small loop of twisted thread in edging to lace etc. [F, dim. of *pic* peak, point]

picotee', n. Carnation of which flowers have light ground with darker edging to petals. [f. F *picoté* p.p. of *picoter* prick, as prec.]

picquet. See PICKET.

pic'ric, a. ~ *acid*, yellow very bitter sub- stance used in dyeing & surgery, & in explosives. [f. Gk *pikros* bitter+-IC]

Pict, n. One of an ancient people in N. Britain. Hence Pic'tish¹ a. [LL has *Picti* perh. f. *pingere pict-* paint]

pic'tograph (-ahf), n. Pictorial symbol; primitive record consisting of these. Hence pictograph'ic a., pictog'raphy¹ n. [f. L *pingere pict-* paint+-GRAPH]

pictor'ial, a. & n. 1. Of, expressed in, pic- ture(s); illustrated; picturesque. 2. n. Journal of which pictures are main feature. Hence~LY² adv. [f. LL *pictorius* (*pictor* painter, as foll.)+-AL]

pic'ture, n. & v.t. 1. Painting, drawing, etc. of objects esp. as work of art; portrait; beautiful object, as *her hat is a* ~; scene; total visual impression produced, (fig.) conjecture or affair (*out of, come into, the* ~, irrelevant, become interesting, etc.); *she looks the very* ~ (a perfect type) *of health*. 2. ~-*book* (for children, con- sisting chiefly or wholly of ~s); ~-*card*, court-card; ~-*gallery*, (hall etc. con- taining) collection of ~s; ~ *hat*, lady's wide-brimmed hat usn. black with ostrich feathers as in ~s of Reynolds & Gains- borough. 3. v.t. ~ *postcard* (with ~ on back); Represent in ~, describe graphically, imagine (*to oneself*). Hence pic'turIZE (-kcher-) v.t., ~*ing* n. [ME *picture*, *-theatre, -drome*, building etc. in which moving ~s are shown. [ME *pictura* (*pingere pict-* paint, see -URE)]

picturesque' (-kcheresk), a. Like, fit to be the subject of a striking picture; (of lan- guage etc.) strikingly graphic, vivid. Hence ~LY² adv., ~NESS n. [f. F pit- toresque f. It. *pittoresco* (*pittore* painter, as PICTORIAL, see -ESQUE)]

pic'ul, n. Chinese weight (133⅓ lb.); ~-*stick* (for carrying weights across shoul- ders). [Malay]

pidd'le, v.i. (Arch.) work, act, in trifling way; (colloq. or childish) make water. [?]

pidd'ock, n. Bivalve mollusc used for bait. [?]

pidg'in, pig'eon (-jin), a. & n. 1. (~ *Eng- lish*, jargon chiefly of English words used between Chinese & Europeans. 2. n. ||(colloq.). (A person's) business, job. [corrupt. of *business*]

pie¹, n. = MAGPIE; French, rain-~, wood-~, kinds of woodpecker; SEA-~. [OF, f. L *pica*]

pie², n. Dish of meat, fruit, etc., enclosed in or covered with paste & baked; APPLE- ~ (fig.); *have a finger in the* ~, be (esp. officiously) concerned in the matter; ~ *bran*, tub of bran with toys etc. hidden in it to be drawn at random at Christmas festivities etc.; MUD ~; ~*crust*, baked paste of ~; (prov.) *promises are like* ~*crust, made to be broken*; ~*man* (-an), vendor of ~s. [perh. = prec., f. miscel- laneous contents compared to piebald appearance of magpie]

pie³, n. & v.t. (print.). (Also *printers'* ~), confused mass of type; (fig.) chaos; (v.t.) mix (type). [perh. as prec.]

pie⁴, n. [Anglo-Ind.]. Copper coin, twelfth part of anna. [f. Hind. *pā'ī* f. Skr. *pad*]

piebald (pib'awld), a. Of two colours irregularly arranged, esp. black & white (usu. of animal, esp. horse); (fig.) motley, mongrel. [PIE¹+BALD]

piece, n. 1. One of the distinct portions of which thing is composed (*in* ~s, broken; *break to* ~s (fragments); *pick up the* ~s (said to fallen child etc.). 2. Enclosed portion (of land). 3. Detached portion (of a substance); a ~ *of one's mind*, one's candid opinion, rebuke. 4. Definite quantity (*of* wallpaper=12 yds. of muslin =10 yds, etc.) in which thing is made up. 5. Cask (*of wine* etc.), varying in capacity. 6. ~ (product) *of work*; example, speci- men, as a ~ *of impudence, fine* ~ *of paint- ing, cricket, etc.; ~ *of goods*. 7. Fire-arm, (barrel of) artillery weapon. 8. Man at chess, draughts, etc. 9. Coin, as *crown, penny, ~; ~ of eight* (i.e. REAL¹ 8.), Spanish dollar. 10. Picture; literary or musical composition, usu. short; drama. 11. *Paid by the* ~ (according to amount done); *of a* ~ (*with*); uniform, consistent, in keeping (*with*); ~*goods*, textile fabrics (esp. Lan- cashire cotton goods) woven in recognized lengths; ~*work* (paid for by the ~). [ME & OF *pece*, cf. It. *pezza, -zo*, etc., etym. dub.]

pie'cer¹ n. Put together, form into a whole; join threads in spinning, whence out; make out (story, theory, chain of evidence) by combination of parts; join together; patch up. [f. prec.]

pièce de résistance (see Ap.), n. Most substantial dish at meal (also fig.). [F]

piece'meal (-sm-), adv., a., & n. (Also *by* ~) piece by piece, part at a time; (adj.) done etc. ~. [ME (PIECE, OE *-mǣlum* suf. f. instr. pl. of *mǣl* MEAL²)]

pied (pīd), a. Particoloured. [PIE¹ -ED²]

pied à terre (pyăd'ahtār'), n. Rest for the sole of one's foot, somewhere to stay. [F]

pie(e)-dog̣. See PYE-DOG.

pier, n. Breakwater, mole; structure of iron or wood open below running out into sea & used as promenade & landing-stage, whence ~'AGE(4) n.; support of spans of bridge; pillar; solid masonry between windows etc.; ~-*glass*, large mirror orig. used to fill up this. [12th c. *per* f. med. L *pera* etym. dub.]

pierce, v.t. & i. (Of sharp instrument etc., also fig. of cold, pain, grief, glance, discernment, discerning person, shriek, etc.) penetrate; prick (substance *with* pin etc.); make hole in (cask etc.); force one's way through or into; penetrate *through*, *into*, etc. Hence **pier'cingly²** adv. [f. OF *percer* etym. dub.]

Pier̄'ian (or -ĕ'ri), a. Of Pieria in N. Thessaly, reputed home of Muses. [f. L *Pierius* +-AN¹]

pierrot (pē'erō, pyĕ'rō), n. (fem. *pierrette*). French pantomime character; itinerant minstrel with whitened face & loose white dress. [F, dim. of *Pierre* PETER¹]

pieta (pyĕt'ah), n. Picture, sculpture, of Virgin Mary holding dead body of Christ on her lap. [It. f. L as PIETY]

pi'etism, n. Spener's movement for revival of piety in Lutheran Church in 17th c.; pious sentiment, exaggeration or affectation of this. So ~IST n., ~IS'TIC(AL) aa. [f. G *pietismus* (as PIETY, see -ISM)]

pi'ety, n. Quality of being pious. [f. OF *piete* f. L *pietatem* (as PIOUS, see -TY)]

piezom'eter, n. Kinds of instrument for measuring pressure or the sense of it. [f. Gk *piezō* press +-O-+-METER]

pif'fle, v.i. & n. (sl.). 1. Talk or act feebly, trifle. 2. n. Twaddle. Hence ~ER¹ n., ~ing a., trivial, worthless. [?]

pig, n., & v.i. & t. (-gg-). 1. Swine, hog; flesh of (usu. young or sucking) ~ as meat, esp. *roast* ~; GUINEA-~ (lit. & fig.). 2. (colloq.). Greedy, dirty, sulky, obstinate, or annoying person, whence ~g'ISH¹ a., ~g'ishly² adv., ~g'ISHNESS n., (-g-). 3. Oblong mass of metal (usu. iron) from smelting-furnace, esp. ~-*iron*. 4. Segment of orange. 5. *Buy a* ~ *in a poke*, buy thing without seeing it or knowing its value; *bring one's* ~*s to a fine, a pretty, the wrong, market*, fail in a venture; ~*s might fly*, wonders might happen; *please the* ~*s*, joc. substitute for *please God*. 6. ~-*headed, obstinate, stupid, whence* ~-*headedly* adv., ~*headedness* n.; ~-*jump*, (of horse) jump sportively from all four legs not brought together as in buck-

jumping; ~-*nut*, a tuber, kind of EARTH-*nut*; ~-*skin*, (leather made of) ~'s skin, (sl.) saddle; ~-*sticking*, hunting of wild boar with spear, butchering of swine, so ~-*sticker* n. (also, long-bladed pocket-knife); ~-*sty*, sty for ~s, (fig.) dirty hovel; ~'s *wash*, ~-*wash*, swill of brewery or kitchen given to ~s; ~-*weed*, kinds of herb eaten by ~s. 7. v.t. & i. Bring forth (~s, or abs.). 8. v.i. Herd together like ~s (also ~ *it*). Hence ~'LET, ~'LING¹, nn., ~'LIKE a. [ME *pigge*, etym. dub.]

pi'geon (-jn), n., & v.t. 1. Bird with many varieties, wild, domesticated, produced by fancy breeding, trained to carry missives, etc., the dove, (now preferred to *dove* exc. in poet. & rhet. contexts, or of the turtle-dove): *carrier-~*, *homing ~*, (trained to carry home messages tied to its neck etc.). 2. Simpleton, gull, as PLUCK² *a* ~. 3. *Clay* ~, clay saucer thrown into air from trap as mark for shooting; ~-*breast*, deformed human chest laterally constricted, so ~-*breasted*; ~ *English*, see PIDGIN; ~-*gram*, message carried by ~; ~-*hole*, small recess for~ to nest in, one of a set of compartments for papers etc. in cabinet etc., (v.t.) deposit (document) in this, put aside (matter) for future consideration, assign (thing) to definite place in memory; ~ *pair*, boy & girl twins, or boy & girl as sole children; ~'s *milk*, partly-digested food with which ~s feed their young, || imaginary article for which children are sent on fool's errand; ~-*toed*, having the toes turned inwards. 4. v.t. Cheat (person of thing). [f. OF *pijon* f. LL (*pipiomem* (nom. -*io*) young cheeping bird (*pipire* cheep)]

pi'geonry (-jn-), n. Pigeon-house. [-RY]

pigg'ery (-g-), n. Pig-breeding establishment; pigsty; dirty place; piggishness. [-ERY]

pigg'y (-g-), n. Little pig; (nursery) ~ *wiggy*, little pig, dirty child; || game of tip-cat. [-Y³]

pig'ment, n. Colouring-matter used as paint or dye; natural colouring-matter of a tissue. Hence ~AL (-ĕn¹), ~ARY¹, aa. [f. L *pigmentum* (*pig-* root of *pingere* paint, -MENT)]

pig'my. See PYGMY.

pig'tail, n. Tobacco twisted into thin roll; plait of hair hanging from back of head, esp. as worn by Chinese under the Manchus, by young girls, & formerly by soldiers & sailors. Hence ~ED² (-ld) a.

pike[1], n., & v.t. 1. Long wooden shaft with steel or iron head, infantry weapon superseded by the bayonet; || (dial.) pickaxe, spike; ~'*man*, miner who uses pickaxe. 2. [perh. diff. wd of Norse orig.] || Peaked top of hill (in names of hills in Lake district). 3. [prob. abbr. of ~*-fish*, from its pointed snout]. Large voracious freshwater fish, jack. 4. v.t. Thrust through, kill, with ~. [(in first sense f.

F *pique*, cf. F *piquer* prick, *pic* pickaxe, *pié* pickaxe, cogn. w.) OE *píc*, etym. dub.]

pike², n. Toll-bar; toll; turnpike road; [abbr. of TURNPIKE]

pike³ (-ēk-), n. Kind of teacake. [f. W (*bara*) *pyglyd* pitchy (bread)]

*pik'er, n. (colloq.). Cautious or timid gambler, a poor sport. [?]

pike'staff (-kstahf), n. Wooden shaft of pike; *plain as a* ~ [orig. *packstaff*, smooth staff used by pedlar], quite plain. [PIKE¹ +STAFF]

pilas'ter, n. Rectangular column, esp. one engaged in wall. [f. F *pilastre* f. med. It. *pilastro* f. med. L *pila* pillar, see -ASTER]

pilau', -aw, -âf, n. Oriental dish of rice with meat, spices, etc. [Pers. (-au)]

pilch, n. Infant's wrapper worn over diaper. [OE *pylece*, as PELISSE]

pil'chard, n. Small sea-fish allied to herring. [?]

pil'corn, n. Kind of oat in which husk does not adhere to grain. [=pilled corn]

pile¹, n., & v.t. **1.** Pointed stake or post; heavy beam driven vertically into bed of river etc. as support for bridge etc.; ~*driver*, machine for driving ~s. **2.** v.t. Furnish with ~s, drive ~s into. [OE *píl* f. L *pilum* javelin]

pile², n. **1.** Heap of things laid more or less regularly upon one another; (*funeral*) ~, heap of combustibles on which corpse is burnt; (colloq.) heap of money, fortune, as *make a* ~, *make one's* ~ (as much as one wants). **2.** Lofty mass of buildings. **3.** Series of plates of dissimilar metals laid one upon another alternately for producing electric current; (also *atomic* ~) apparatus designed to contain uranium & a moderating agent for the study or utilization of atomic energy. [F, f. L *pila* pillar]

pile³, v.t. Heap up (often *up, on*); ~ *arms*, place (usu. four) rifles with butts on ground & muzzles interlocked; ~ *up* (Naut.), run (ship) on rocks or aground; (colloq.) ~ *up* (or *on*) *the agony*, intensify painful description etc., ~ *it on*, exaggerate; load (table etc. *with*). [f. prec.]

‖pile⁴, n. (arch.). Reverse of coin; *cross or* ~, heads or tails. [as PILE², orig. = un-der iron of minting apparatus]

pile⁵, n. Soft hair, down, wool of sheep; nap on cloth, esp. on velvet, plush, etc., or on carpet, as *fine, three,* ~ *carpet*. Hence **pile'y²** a. [f. L *pilus* hair]

pile⁶, n. (pl.) haemorrhoids, disease marked by tumours of veins of lower rectum; (sing.) such tumour. [f. L *pila* ball]

pil'fer, v.t. & i. Steal (thing, or abs.), esp. in small quantities. Hence ~AGE(3), **pil'garlic**, n. (arch.). Bald head; bald-headed man; poor creature. [=pilled or peeled garlic]

pil'grim, n., & v.i. One who journeys to sacred place as act of religious devotion; person regarded as as journeying to a future life (*The P~'s Progress*); traveller; *The P~s of Gt Britain, of the U.S.*, societies fostering Anglo-American friendship by mutual hospitality etc.; *P~ Fathers*, English Puritans who founded colony of Plymouth, Massachusetts, in 1620; (v.i.) wander like a ~. Hence ~IZE(2) v.i. [ME *pelegrim* f. OF †*peregrin* f. L *peregrinus* stranger f. *peregre* (= *per ager* field) abroad, -INE¹]

pil'grimage, n., & v.i. Pilgrim's journey, esp. a journey; (v.i.) *go on a* ~. [f. OF *pelerinage* f. *pelerin* see prec.)]

pil'iferous, a. Having hair (esp. in Bot.), So **pil'iform** a. [f. L *pilus* hair, see -FEROUS]

pill¹, n., & v.t. **1.** Small ball of medicinal substance for swallowing whole (*a ~ to cure an earthquake*, half measures); (fig.) something that has to be done, a humilia-tion etc., (*swallow the ~, a bitter ~*, etc.); ~*'box*, shallow cylindrical box for holding ~s, (joc.) small vehicle or building. (Mil.) small isolated chiefly underground con-crete fort; *gun) the* ~; (sl. or joc.) ball, e.g. cannon-ball, tennis-ball, ‖(pl.) bill-ards; ~*'wort*, kinds of plant with small globular involucres. **2.** v.t. (sl.). Blackball, defeat. [f. L *pilula* dim. of *pila* ball]

‖pill², v.t. (arch.). Pillage, plunder; (dial.) ~. [PEEL³. [prob. f. L *pilāre* make bare of hair (*pilus*)]

pill'age, n., & v.t. **1.** Plunder, esp. as practised in war. **2.** v.t. Sack, plunder, (place, person, or abs.). Hence ~ER¹ n. [vb.f. n.) F, f. *piller* as prec., see -AGE]

pill'ar, n., & v.t. **1.** Vertical structure of stone, wood, metal, etc., slender in pro-portion to height, used as support or ornament; post, pedestal; (fig.) person who is a main supporter, as *a ~ of the faith*; upright mass of air, water, etc.; (Mining) solid mass of coal etc. left to support roof of the working; *driven from ~ to post* (to & fro, from one resource to another); ‖~*box*, hollow ~ about 5 ft high in which letters may be posted. **2.** v.t. Support (as) with ~s. Hence ~ED¹ a. [f. OF *piler* f. late pop. L *pilare* (*pila* ball)]

pill'ion (-lyon), n. (Hist.) woman's light saddle, cushion attached to hinder part of saddle for second rider, usu. woman; (mod.) seating for passenger behind motor-cyclist etc. [prob. of Celt. orig., ult. f. L *pellis* skin]

pill'iwinks, n. (hist.). Instrument of tor-ture for squeezing fingers. [?]

pill'ory, n., & v.t. **1.** Wooden framework with holes for head & hands of offender

exposed to public ridicule etc. **2. v.t.** Put in the ~, (fig.) expose to ridicule. [f. OF *pelori*, etym. dub.]

pill′ow (-ō), n., & v.t. & i. **1.** Cushion of linen etc. stuffed with feathers etc. as support for head in reclining esp. in bed; *take counsel of one's* ~, take a night to reflect; (techn.) ~-shaped block or support; ~*-case*, *-slip*, washable case of linen etc. for ~; ~*-fight*, = BOLSTER²*-fight*. **2. vb.** Rest, prop up, on ~; rest on ~. Hence ~Y² (-ō) a. [OE *pyle*, *pylu*, cf. Du. *peluw*, G *pfühl*]

pil′ōse, **-ous**, aa. Covered with hair. Hence **pilōs′ITY** n. [f. L *pilosus* (*pilus* hair, -OSE²)]

pil′ot, n., & v.t. **1.** Person qualified to take charge of ships entering or leaving a harbour (*drop the* ~, abandon trusted adviser); steersman (arch.); (Aeronaut.) person navigating aircraft or qualified to do so, (now) one who operates the flying controls of an aircraft (*P~ Officer*, rank in air Force); (fig.) guide, esp. in hunting field. **2.** ~*-cloth*, blue woollen cloth for greatcoat etc., ~ *engine* (clearing the way for another); ~*-jacket*, = PEA-JACKET; ~ *fish*, small fish said to act as ~ to shark. **3. v.t.** Conduct as ~ (lit. & fig.); act as ~ on (way, piece of water); act as ~ of (aircraft). Hence or cogn. ~LESS a. [f. F *pillote*, f. It. *pilota* perh. f. It. *pedota*, cf. It. *pedota* rudder perh. f. Gk *pēdon* oar, (pl.) rudder]

Pilt′down, n. A Sussex hamlet; ~ *skull* (found at ~, & until 1953 believed to belong to a prehistoric type of man).

pil′ule, **pill-**, n. Pill; small pill. Hence **pil′ular¹**, **pil′ulous**, aa. [F, as PILL¹]

I pim′eldde, n. Cat-fish. [f. Gk *pimelōdēs* fatty (*pimelē* fat, see -ODE)]

pimen′tō, n. Dried aromatic berries of a certain tree, Jamaica pepper; the tree. [f. Sp. *pimienta* f. L *pigmentum* PIGMENT, med. L) spice]

pimp, n., & v.i. Pander. [etym. dub.]

pim′pernel, n. Small annual found in cornfields & waste ground, with scarlet (also blue or white) flowers closing in cloudy or rainy weather. [f. OF *pimprenele* f. med. L *pipinella* perh. corrupt. of *bipinnella* double dim. of bi(*pennis* f. *penna* feather) two-winged]

pim′ping, a. Small, mean; sickly. [?]

pim′ple, n. Small solid round tumour of the skin, usu. inflammatory. Hence ~ED²(-ld), ~Y² aa. [?]

pin¹, n. **1.** Thin piece of (usu. tinned brass or iron) wire with sharp point & round flattened head for fastening together parts of dress, papers, etc. **2.** Peg of wood or metal for various purposes (*split* ~, metal cotter to be passed through hole & held there by the gaping of its split end); each of the pegs round which strings of musical instrument are fast-

---

ened; THOLE², BELAYING, DRAWING, ~, HAIR-, || NINEPIN; *don't care a* ~ (at all). **3.** pl. (colloq.). Legs, as *quick on his* ~s. **4.** ~*s & needles*, tingling sensation in limb recovering from numbness. **5.** Small cask of 4½ gal. **6.** ~*-cushion*, small cushion for sticking ~s in to keep them ready for use; ~*-feather*, ingrown feather; ~*-fire cartridge* (exploded by means of ~); ~*-head*, (fig.) minute thing; ~*-hole* (made by ~ or into which peg fits); ~*-money*, annual allowance to woman for dress expenses etc., allowance settled on wife for private expenditure; ~*-point*, point of ~, (fig.) something very small, (attrib., of targets) small & requiring very accurate & precise bombing & shelling, (v.t.) locate or bomb (such target) with the requisite accuracy & precision; ~*-prick*, (fig.) trifling irritation; ~*-table*, kinds of mechanical amusement & gambling device; ~*-tail*, kinds of duck & grouse with pointed tail; ~*-tuck*, very narrow ornamental tuck; ~*-wheel*, small Catherine-wheel. [com-LG: OE *pinn*, Du. *pin*, G *pin(ne)*; perh. f. L *pinna* point]

pin², v.t. (-nn-). Fasten (thing to another, *up*, etc., things *together*) with pin(s); ~ *up* (Archit.), = UNDERPIN; transfix with pin, lance, etc.; ~ *one's faith* (rely implicitly) *on* (person etc.); seize & hold fast (*against* wall etc.); bind (person etc., often *down*) *to* (promise, arrangement); enclose by bars etc.; ~*-up* n. picture of some favourite or famous person ~ned up on wall etc. (also attrib., esp. ~*-up girl*). [f. prec.]

pin′afōr′e, n. Child's washable covering worn over frock to protect it from dirt. Hence ~ED²(-ōrd) a. [PIN²+AFORE]

pinās′ter, n. A pine indigenous to SW. Europe. [L, = wild pine (*pinus*, -ASTER)]

pince-nez (see Ap.), n. Pair of eyeglasses with spring to clip nose. [F, lit.=pinch-nose]

pin′cers (-z), n. pl. (Also *a pair of* ~) gripping tool made of two limbs pivoted together forming pair of jaws with pair of handles to press them together with; similar organ of crustaceans etc.; ~ *movement*, (Mil.) converging movement (also *pincer movement*, *attack*, etc.). [ME *pinsours* (as PINCH v., see -OR²)]

pincette (pănsĕt′), n. Small pincers, tweezers. [F]

pinch¹, n. Nip, squeeze; (fig.) stress (of poverty etc.); *at a* ~(critical juncture); as much as can be taken up with tips of finger and thumb, as *a* ~ *of snuff*, *salt*. [f. foll.]

pinch², v.t. & i. Nip, squeeze, esp. between tips of finger & thumb (also fig. of cold, hunger, etc., esp. ~*ed with cold*); *that is where the shoe* ~s, that is the difficulty or trouble; extort (money etc. *from*, *out of*, person etc.); stint (person etc. *in*, *of*,

pink¹, n. & a. 1. Garden plant with sweet-smelling white, ~, crimson, or varie- [continued in column]

for, food, etc.); be niggardly; ||urge (horse esp. in race); sail (purposely or not) too close to wind; (sl.) steal (thing), rob (person), arrest, take into custody. [f. ONF +*pinchier* (F *pincer*), etym. dub.]

pinch'beck, n. & a. 1. Gold-like alloy of copper & zinc used in cheap jewellery etc. 2. adj. Counterfeit, sham. [f. C.P~, watchmaker, d. 1732]

Pinda'ri (-ahre), n. Mounted marauder in India in 17th & 18th cc. [f. Hind. *pin-dari*]

Pinda'ric, a. & n. 1. Of, like, the Greek poet Pindar. 2. n. (usu. pl.) ~ ode(s), metre, verse(s). [f. L f. Gk *Pindarikos* (*Pindaros*, see -IC)]

pine¹, n. Genus of trees with evergreen needle-shaped leaves growing in sheathed clusters of two or more (cf. FIR); many species of which afford timber, tar, & turpentine; ~apple; ~apple, large collective fruit of the ananas, so called from resemblance to ~-cone, (sl.) hand-grenade; ~-beauty, ~ carpet, moths whose larvae feed on ~-trees; ~-cone, fruit of the ~; ~ marten, dark-brown British marten. [OE *pīn* f. L *pinus*]

pine², v.i. Languish, waste away, from grief, disease, etc.; long eagerly (*for, after, to do*). [OE *pīnian* f. obs. *pīn* pain f. L *poena* punishment, pain]

pin'eal, a. (anat.). Shaped like a pine-cone; ~ gland, gland of unknown func-tion behind third ventricle of brain. [f. F *pinéal* f. L *pinea* PINE¹-cone, see -AL]

pin'ery, n. Place in which pineapples are grown; plantation of pines. [-ERY]

pin'fold, n. & v.t. Pound for stray cattle (~, v.t.), confine in this. [OE *pundfald* (+pound POUND²+fold FOLD¹)]

ping, n. & v.i. 1. Abrupt ringing sound as of rifle bullet flying through air. 2. v.i. Make, fly with, this. [imit.]

ping-pong', n. Table-tennis, game like lawn-tennis played on table with celluloid balls & (usu.) parchment or wooden bats. [imit.]

pin'guid, a. (usu. joc.). Fat, oily, greasy. [f. L *pinguis* fat+-ID¹]

ping'uin, (-nggw-), n. W.-Ind. plant allied to pineapple; its fruit. [?]

pin'ion¹ (-nyon), n. Terminal segment of bird's wing; (poet.) wing; any flight-feather of wing; (in carving) part of wing corresponding to forearm. [f. OF *pignon* corresponding to forearm. f. L *penna* feather. -OON]

pin'ion² (-nyon), v.t. Cut off pinion of (wing, bird) to prevent flight; bind the arms of (person), bind (arms); bind (person etc.) fast to (thing). [f. prec.]

pin'ion³ (-nyon), n. Small cog-wheel engaging with larger one; cogged spindle engaging with wheel. [f. F *pignon* f. OF *peignon* battlement f. L *pinna* battlement, see -OON]

gated flowers. 2. The ~ (embodied per-fection) *of elegance* etc.; the ~ (most per-fect condition) *of health*, etc. (also sl., *in the ~*, abs., quite well). 3. (Of a) pale red slightly inclining to purple. 4. Fox-hunter's red coat, cloth of this; fox-hunter. 5. adj. Of pale red colour of various kinds, as *rose, salmon*, ~, whence ~ISH¹, ~Y² aa., ~NESS n.; (Pol.) verging on red; ~-eye, contagious fever of horse, contagious ophthalmia in man. [?]

pink⁴, n. Yellowish pigment made by combining vegetable colouring matter with some white base (*Brown, French, Dutch*, etc., ~). [?]

pink⁵, n. (hist.). Sailing-vessel esp. with narrow stern (orig. small & flat-bottomed).

pink⁶, v.t. Pierce with sword etc.; (also ~ *out*) ornament (leather etc.) with per-forations; adorn, deck. [cf. LG *pinken* strike, peck, perh. var. of *picken* PICK¹]

|| **pink⁷**, n. Young salmon; (dial.) minnow. [also in dial. G]

pink⁸, v.i. (Of a motor-engine) emit series of high-pitched explosive sounds caused by detonation of mixture following partial combustion. [imit.]

*'**Pink'ster**, n. Whitsuntide; P~ *flower*, pink azalea. [Du.; = Pentecost]

pinn'a, n. (pl. -ae). Broad upper part of external ear; primary division of pinnate leaf; fin, fin-like structure. [L, = *penna*]

pinn'ace, n. Warship's double-banked (usu. eight-oared) boat now usu. driven by steam or petrol. [f. F *pinasse* prob. f. L *pinus* PINE¹]

pinn'acle, n. & v.t. Small ornamental turret usu. ending in pyramid or cone, crowning a buttress, roof, etc.; natural peak; (fig.) culmination, climax; (v.t.) set (as) on ~, form the ~ of, furnish with ~s. [ME & OF *pinacle* f. LL *pinnaculum* (*pinna* wing, see -CULE¹)]

pinn'ate, a. (Bot. of compound leaf) with series of leaflets on each side of com-mon petiole; (Zool.) with branches, ten-tacles, etc., on each side of an axis. Hence **pinn'ātěd** [-ATE²] a., ~ly² adv. [f. L *pinnatus* feathered (PINNA, see -ATE²)]

pinn'er, n. In v.bi senses; also, coif with two long side-flaps pinned on. [f. PIN v. +-ER¹]

pinn'i- in comb.=PINNA fin, as: ~grade, ~ped. aa. & nn., fin-footed (animal).

pinn'othēre, -tēr, n. Genus of small crabs commensally inhabiting shells of oyster, mussel, etc. [f. L f. Gk *pinno-tērēs* (*pinna* bivalve mollusc, +*tēreō* guard)]

pinn'ūle, n. (Bot.) secondary division of pinnate leaf; (Zool.) part, organ, like small wing or fin; sight at end of index of astrolabe etc. Hence ~AR¹ a. [f. L *pinnula* dim. of PINNA]

pinn'y, n. Childish abbr. of PINAFORE.

*'**pin'ŏchle** (-ŏkl; or pē-), n. Game like bezique. [?]

•pinōl'e, n. Meal made from parched corn-flour mixed with sweet flour, sugar, etc. [Amer.-Sp., f. Aztec pinolli]

pint, n. Measure of capacity for liquids etc., ⅛th of gallon. [f. F pinte, etym. dub.]

pinta'dŏ (-ah-), n. (pl. ~s), (Now usu. ~ bird, petrel) kind of petrel; guinea-fowl. [f. Port. pintado painted, p.p. of pintar f. L pingere +pinct- for pict-]

pin'tle, n. Kinds of pin or bolt, esp. one on which some other part turns. [OE pintel penis, etym. dub, cf. Du. & G pint penis]

•pin'tō (or pē-), a. & n. Piebald (horse). [Sp.]

pinx'it, pinze—tint, v.t. (So-&-so) painted it (in signature to picture, as FECIT). [L]

pin'y, a. Of, like, abounding in, pines. [-Y²]

piolet (pyōlā'), n. Alpinist's ice-axe. [F]

pioneer', n., & v.i. & t. 1. (Mil.) one of body of foot-soldiers marching in advance with spades etc. to prepare road for main body; beginner of enterprise, original explorer, etc. 2. v.i. Act as ~. 3. v.t. Open up (road etc.) as ~; act as ~ to, conduct. [(vb f. n.) f. F pionnier foot-soldier, pioneer, (pion, f. L as PAWN¹, -IER)]

piou-pion (pyōō-pyōō'), n. (Pop.) typical French private soldier. [F]

pi'ous, a. Devout, religious; ~ founder (of college etc. for glory of God & good of man); (arch.) dutiful; ~ FRAUD. Hence ~NY² adv. [f. L pius dutiful, pious, -OUS]

pip¹, n. Disease of poultry, hawks, etc., marked by thick mucus in throat & often by white scale on tip of tongue; ||(sl.) fit of depression, bad temper, (he has, gives me, the ~). [prob. f. MDu. pippe f. pop. L pipita corrupt. of pituita phlegm]

pip², n. Each spot on playing-cards, dice, or dominoes; star (1–3 acc. to rank) on army officer's shoulder; single blossom of clustered inflorescence; rhomboidal segment of surface of pineapple. [earlier peep, etym. dub.]

|| pip³, v.t. (colloq.; -pp-). Blackball; defeat; hit with shot. [f. prec. or foll.]

pip⁴, n. Seed of apple, pear, orange, etc. ~LESS a. [prob. abbr. of PIPPIN]

|| pip⁵, signallers' letter P, as in ~ emma, o.~.

|| pip⁶, n. Short high-pitched sound, usu. mechanically produced (the six ~s of the time-signal). [imit.]

pipal, n. See PEEPUL.

pipe¹, n. 1. Tube of wood, metal, etc., esp. for conveying water, gas, etc. 2. Musical wind-instrument consisting of single tube; each of the tubes by which sound is produced in organ; (pl.)=BAG¹~s; 3. Voice, esp. in singing; song, note, of bird. 4. Tubular organ, vessel, etc., in animal body. 5. Cylindrical vein of ore. 6. Channel of decoy for wild fowl. 7. (Also tobacco-~) narrow tube of clay, wood, etc., with bowl at one end for drawing in smoke of tobacco, quantity of tobacco held by this, as light, smoke, a ~; PEACE-~; ||King's or Queen's; furnace at London Docks used formerly for burning contraband tobacco; put that in your ~ & smoke it, digest that fact etc. if you can. 8. Cask for wine, esp. as measure usu.=105 gal. 9. ~clay, fine white clay used for tobacco-~s & (esp. by soldiers) for cleaning white breeches, belts, etc., (fig.) excessive attention to minutiae of dress etc. in regiment, (v.t.) whiten with ~clay; *~ dream, a notion as fantastic as a dream produced by opium-smoking; ~-fish, (kinds of) long slender fish with elongated snout; ~-light, spill for lighting ~; ~line (esp. for conveying petroleum to a distance); ~ major, N.C.O. commanding regimental pipers; ~-rack (for tobacco-~s); ~-rolls (hist.), records of the old national Exchequer offices (prob. because subsidiary documents were rolled in ~ form); ~-stone, hard red clay used by Amer. Indians for tobacco-~s. Hence ~FUL(-pfŏŏl) n., ~LESS (-pl-), pip'Y² aa. [OE pīpe, cf. Du. pijp, G pfeife, ult. f. L as foll.]

pipe², v.i. & t. 1. Play (tune etc. or abs.) on pipe; lead, bring, (person etc.) by sound of pipe; summon (crew up, to meal, work, etc.) by sounding whistle (~ away, give signal for boat to start); whistle; utter in shrill voice; ~ down, (Naut.) dismiss from duty, (sl.) be less noisy or cocksure; ~ up, begin to play or sing; ~ one's eye(s), weep. 2. Propagate (pinks etc.) by cuttings taken off at joint of stem. 3. Trim (dress), ornament (cake etc.), with PIPING¹. 4. Furnish with pipes; convey (oil, water, gas, etc.) by pipes. [OE pīpian f. L pīpare pipe, chirp]

|| pip êmm'a, adv. (sl.). Post meridiem. [signallers' names for letters P, M]

pip'er, n. One who plays on pipe, esp. strolling musician; bagpipe-player; pay the ~ (& call the tune), bear the cost (& have control) of a proceeding etc.; kinds of fish; broken-winded horse; || decoy-dog. [OE pīpere (PIPE¹+-ER¹)]

pipêtte'(le)', n. Slender tube for transferring etc. small quantities, esp. in chemistry. [F, dim. of PIPE¹]

pip'ing¹, n. In vbl senses, also: ornamentation of dress by means of cord enclosed in pipe-like fold; ornamental cord-like lines of sugar on cake. [f. PIPE²+-ING¹]

pip'ing², a. In vbl senses; the ~ time(s) of peace (marked by piping as opp. to martial music); ~ (hissing) hot. [f. PIPE²+-ING²]

pipistrel(le)', n. Small kind of bat. [F (-le), f. It. pipistrello, vip-, f. L vespertilio bat (vesper evening)]

pip'it, n. Bird like lark. [prob. imit.]

pip'kin, n. Small earthenware pot or pan. [?]

pipp'in, n. Kinds of apple. [ME & OF *pepin* seed, etym. dub.]

pip'-squeak, n. (sl.), Shell that emits sound so described; insignificant or contemptible person or thing. [imit.]

piquant (pēk'ant), a. Agreeably pungent, sharp, appetizing; (fig.) pleasantly stimulating or disturbing to the mind. Hence **piquancy** (pēk'an-), n. **~iy²** adv. [F (as *piqué*, see -ANT)]

pique¹ (pēk), v.t. & n. 1. Irritate, wound the pride of; arouse (curiosity, interest); plume oneself on. 2. n. Ill-feeling, enmity, resentment; *in a fit of* ~; *took a* ~ *against me.* [f. F *piquer* vb prick, irritate, pique²; cf. PIKE²]

pique² (pēk), n., & v.t. & i. Winning of 30 points in cards and play at piquet before opponent begins to count; (v.t.) score a ~ against; (v.i.) score a ~. [f. F *pic* etym. dub.]

piqué (pēk'ā), n. Stiff ribbed cotton fabric. [F p.p. of *piquer*, see PIQUE¹]

piquet¹ (-kēt; or pīk'), n. Card game for two players with pack of 32 cards. [F, etym. dub.]

piquet². See PICKET.

pirā'gua, pērī'gua, (-gwa), n. Long narrow canoe made from single tree-trunk; two-masted sailing-barge. [Sp., f. Carib., = dug-out]

pīr'ate, n., & v.t. & i. 1. (Ship used by) sea-robber; marauder; one who infringes another's copyright; ||boats that encroaches on recognized routes or overcharges or preys on passengers. 2. v.t. Plunder; reproduce (book etc.) without leave for one's own profit. 3. v.i. Play the ~. Hence or cogn. **pīr'ACY** n., **pīr'atICAL** a.,(v.t.f. n.) f. L (-t.) f. Gk *peirātēs* (*peirō* attempt, assault)]

pirogue (-ōg), n. = PIRAGUA. [F]

pirouette (-ōo-), n., & v.i. 1. Ballet-dancer's spin round on one foot or on point of toe. 2. v.i. Dance thus. [(n.) F, = top, cf. It. *piruolo* top, *pirone* iron peg; vb f. F *pirouetter*]

pis aller (pēzäl'ā, & see Ap.), n. Course taken for want of a better. [F (*pis* worse+*aller* go)]

pis'cary, n. *Common of* ~, right of fishing in another's water in common with owner (& others). [f. med. L *piscaria* fishing (*piscis* fish), neut. pl. of *piscarius*]

pis'catory, a. Of fishers or fishing; whence **piscatōr'IAL** a.; addicted to fishing. [f. L *piscator* (*piscador* fisher f. *piscis* fish)]

Pis'ces (-ēz), n. pl. The Fishes, 12th zodiacal constellation; 12th sign of zodiac. [L, pl. of *piscis* fish]

pis'ciculture, n. Artificial rearing of fish. Hence **pisciCUL'tural** a., **pisciCUL'turist** n. (-cher-). [f. L *piscis* fish+CULTURE]

pis'cina (-sī-, -sē-) n. (pl. -ae, -as). Fish-pond; ancient-Roman bathing-pond; (Eccl.) perforated stone basin for carrying away water used in rinsing chalice etc. [L, f. *piscis* fish]

pis'cine¹ (or -ēn), n. Bathing-pool. [F, f. prec.]

pis'cine², a. Of fish. [f. L *piscis* fish, **piscīv'orous,** a. Fish-eating. [as prec. + -VOROUS]

pisé (pēz'ā), n. Rammed clay or earth (& gravel) as building-material. [F, p.p. of *piser* pound f. L *pĭnsĕre* pound]

Pis'gah (-zgə), n. Mountain whence Moses viewed the Promised Land (*Deut.* iii. 27); (fig.) ~ *glance*, *prospect*, etc. [Heb.]

pish, int. expr. contempt, impatience, or disgust; (v.i.) say ~. [natural]

||pishogue (-ōg), n.(Ir.). Sorcery; charm, spell. [f. Ir. *pisiceog*]

pis'iform (pis-, piz-), a. Pea-shaped; ~ *bone*, small bone of upper row of carpus. [f. L *pīsum* pea+-FORM]

pis'mire, n. Ant. [f. foll. (from smell of anthill) +obs. *mire* ant, cf. Du. *mier*]

piss, v.i. & t., & n. (not now in polite use). 1. Make water; discharge (blood etc.) with the urine; wet with urine; (p.p., sl.) drunk 2. n. Urine. [(n. f. vb) f. OF *pisser*]

pista'chio (-ästō, -ächō, n. (pl. -s). (Tree yielding) nut with greenish edible kernel; colour of this. [f. It. *pistacchio* & Sp. *pistacho* f. L f. Gk etym. dub.]

pis'til, n. Female organ of flower, comprising ovary, style, & stigma. Hence **~LARY, ~LATE², ~LIFEROUS, ~LINE¹,** aa. [as PESTLE]

pis'tol, n., & v.t. (-ll-). 1. Small fire-arm held & fired by one hand; *within, beyond,* ~-*shot* (range of ~); ~-*grip*, handhold of ~-*butt* shape below gunstock. 2. v.t. Shoot with ~. [f. obs. F *pistole* prob. shortened f. *pistolet* dagger, pistol, dim.

pis'tole, n. (hist.) Foreign gold coin, esp. Spanish coin worth about 16s. [F, prob. shortened f. *pistolet*, etym. dub., perh. as prec.]

pis'tolgraph (-ahf), n. Early apparatus for instantaneous photography. [-GRAPH]

pis'ton, n. Disk or short cylinder of wood, metal, etc., fitting closely within tube in which it moves up & down, used in steam-engine, pump, etc., to impart or receive motion by means of ~-*rod*; sliding valve in cornet etc. [F, f. It. *pistone* valve of

pit¹, n. 1. Natural hole in ground; hole made in digging for mineral, etc. or for industrial purposes, as *chalk, clay, gravel, coal, saw, tan,* ~; covered hole as trap for wild beasts or (esp. Bibl.) for enemies

(dig a ~ *for*, fig., try to ensnare); *the* ~ (*of hell*), hell; COCKPIT. **2.** Hollow in animal or plant body or on any surface; ~ *of the stomach*, depression between cartilages of false ribs; depressed scar, as after smallpox. **3.** ‖ That part of auditorium of theatre which is on floor of house, now usu. the part of this behind stalls; ‖ people occupying this. **4.** (Motor-racing) place at which cars are refuelled, re-tired, etc. **5.** *Part of floor of an exchange allotted to special trading (wheat~). **6.** ~*fall*, covered ~ as trap for animals etc., (fig.) unsuspected snare or danger; ~*man*, collier, *connecting rod in machinery; ‖ ~ *pony* (kept underground in coal-mines). [OE *pytt*, cf. Du. *put*, G *pfütze*, f. L *puteus* well]

pit¹, v.t. & i. (-tt-). Put into a pit (esp. vegetables etc. for storage); set (cock, dog, etc.) to fight in pit (*against* another), (fig.) match (person *against*); make pits, esp. scars, in (esp. in p.p.); (Path., of flesh etc.) retain impression of finger etc. when touched. [f. prec.]

pit²(-a~)**pǎt**, adv. & n. With the sound ~, palpitatingly, falteringly, as *his heart, feet, went* ~; (n.) the sound ~. [imit.]

pitch¹, n., & v.t. **1.** Black or dark-brown tenacious resinous substance, semi-liquid when hot, hard when cold, got from distillation of tar or turpentine, used for caulking seams of ships etc. (~ *black*, ~ *darkness*, with no light at all; ~-*like* masses, important source of radium; ~-*cap*, cap lined with ~, used as instrument of torture; ~-*pine*, specially resinous kinds of pine; ~*stone*, old volcanic rock looking like ~. **2.** v.t. Cover, coat, smear, with ~. [(OE *pician* vb f.) OE *pic* f L *pix picis*]

pitch², v.t. & i. **1.** Fix & erect (tent, camp); **2.** (Crick.) *wickets*, fix stumps in ground & place balls; fix, plant, (thing) in definite position; expose (wares) for sale in market etc. **3.** Pave (road) with set stones. **4.** ~*ed battle* (of set kind, not casual). **5.** (Mus.) set at particular pitch, (fig.) express in particular style. **6.** Throw, fling; (in games) throw (flat object) towards a mark; (sl.) tell (tale, yarn). **7.** (Golf) play (ball) with pitch shot (see foll.). **8.** Fall heavily (*on* one's head, *into*, etc.); (of ship) plunge in longitudinal direction (cf. ROLL²). **9.** ~ *in* (colloq.), set to work vigorously; ~ *into* (colloq.), assail forcibly with blows, words, etc., make vigorous attack on, (person, food, etc.); ~ *upon*, happen to select; ~-*&-toss*, game of skill & chance in which coins are ~ed at a mark; ~-*farthing*,=CHUCK³-*farthing*. [ME *pichen*, etym. dub., perh. cogn. w. PICK²]

pitch³, n. **1.** Pitching (e.g. of ship). **2.** Mode of delivering cricket-ball in bowling; (Golf, also ~ *shot*) lofted approach shot with little run to ball after alighting. **3.** Quantity of commodity pitched in market. **4.** ‖ Place at which one (e.g. street performer, bookmaker) is stationed; (Crick.) place between & about wickets. **5.** Height to which falcon etc. soars before swooping on prey, as *fly a high etc.* ~ (also fig.). **6.** Height, degree, intensity, (of quality etc.); (Mus.) degree of acuteness or graveness of tone. **7.** Degree of slope; steepness of roof's slope; (Mech.) distance between successive points or lines, e.g. between successive teeth of cog-wheel. **8.** ~-*pipe*, small pipe blown by mouth to set ~ for singing or tuning; ~-*wheel*, toothed wheel engaging with another. [f. prec.]

pitch'er¹, n. Large usu. earthenware vessel with handle or two ears & usu. a lip, for holding liquids; *little ~s have long ears*, children are apt to overhear; (Bot.) modified leaf in ~ form. ~-*plant* (with such leaves). Hence ~FUL(2) n. [f. OF *pichier* f. med. L *picarium, bic.*, BEAKER]

pitch'er², n. In vbl senses of PITCH²; esp. player who delivers ball, esp. in baseball; ‖ street vendor who pitches stall in fixed place; stone used for paving. [-ER¹]

pitch'fork, n., & v.t. **1.** Long-handled fork with two sharp prongs for pitching hay etc.; tuning-fork. **2.** v.t. Cast (as with ~, (fig.) thrust (person) forcibly (*into* position, office, etc.). [earlier *pickfork*, prob. f. PICK² + FORK, assoc. w. PITCH²]

pitch'y, a. Of, like, dark etc. as, pitch. [-Y²]

pit'eous, a. Calling for pity, deplorable. Hence ~LY² adv., ~NESS n. [ME *pitous* f. OF *pitos* f. L *pietosus* (as PIETY, see -ITOUS)]

pith, n., & v.t. Spongy cellular tissue in stems & branches of dicotyledonous plants; similar tissue lining rind of orange etc.; spinal cord; (fig.) essential part, quintessence, (often ~ *& marrow of*); physical strength, vigour; force, energy, *of ~* (importance) *& moment* (Shaks. *Ham.* III. i. 86); (v.t.) slaughter (animal) by severing spinal cord. Hence ~LESS a. [(ph f. n.) OE *pitha*, cf. MDu. *pitte*, Da. *pit*]

pithĕcan'thrōpe, n. Ape-man, hypothetical link between ape & man. [f. Gk *pithēkos* ape + *anthrōpos* man]

pithĕc'oid, a. Ape-like. [as prec., see -OID]

pith'y, a. Of, like, abounding in, pith; condensed & forcible, terse. Hence ~LY² adv., ~INESS n. [-Y²]

pit'iable, a. Calling for pity or contempt. Hence ~LENESS n., ~LY² adv. [OF (as PITY, see -ABLE]

pit'iful, a. Compassionate; (of things) calling for pity; contemptible. Hence ~LY² adv., ~NESS n. [-FUL]

pit'iless, a. Showing no pity. Hence ~LY² adv., ~NESS n. [-LESS]

pit′pan, n. Central American dug-out boat. [peruv. native]

pit′tance, n. (Hist.) pious bequest to religious house for extra food etc.; allowance, remuneration, esp. scanty one, as *a mere* ~; small number or amount. [f. OF *pitance*; OF has also *pitance pity* (as PIETY +-ANCE)]

‖ **pitt′ite,** n. Person occupying seat in pit of theatre. [-ITE¹]

pitu′itary, a. Of or secreting phlegm; mucous; ~ *gland, body,* a small ductless gland at the base of the brain believed to have an important influence over the growth of the body. So **pitu′itous** a., **pitu′itrin** n. hormone produced by ~ body, solution containing this used medicinally. [f. L *pituitarius* (*pituita* phlegm, see -ARY¹)]

pit′y, n., & v.t. **1.** Feeling of tenderness aroused by person's distress or suffering; *as cannot help feeling a* ~ *for him, felt no* ~ *for him, in* ~ *of his fate; take a* ~ *on, feel or act compassionately towards; (as form of entreaty) for* ~*'s sake; regrettable fact, ground for regret, as what a* ~*, 'more's the* ~ (so much the worse), *it is a thousand pities you did not mention it; (arch.) it is or was a* ~ *of them,* one feels sorry for them. **2.** v.t. Feel (often contemptuous) ~ for, *as he is much to be pitied, I* ~ *you if you think that.* Hence ~**ingly²** adv. [vb f. n.] [f. OF *pité* f. L as PIETY]

pityri′asis, n. (path.). Skin disease characterized by the shedding of branlike scales. [f. Gk *pituríasis (pituron* bran, -ASIS)]

piv′ot, n., & v.t. & i. **1.** Short shaft or pin on which something turns or oscillates; (fig.) cardinal or crucial point, *as on* ~; man on whom body of troops wheels; (fig.) cardinal or crucial point, *as on* ~; man on whom body of troops wheels. **2.** vb. Furnish with, attach by, ~; turn as on ~, hinge *(upon,* often fig.). Hence ~**AL** a. [F, etym. dub.]

pix′y, -xie, n. Being akin to fairy. Hence **pix′y-ish** a. [f. -xie, n.) (now vulg.). Penis of animal esp. that of bull formerly used as flogging instrument. [16th c.; cf. Du. *pees*]

plac′able, a. Easily appeased, mild, forgiving. Hence or cogn. ~**ABIL′ITY** n., **~ABLY²** adv. [OF, f. L *placabilis (placare* appease, see -BLE)]

plac′ard, n., & v.t. **1.** Document printed on one side of single sheet for posting up, poster. **2.** v.t. *(also* plăckård′). Set up ~s (wall etc.), advertise (wares etc.) by ~s, display (poster etc.) as ~. [OF, f. *plaquier* vb plaster (OF, f. Du. *plakken* glue, prob. imit., see -ARD)]

plac′ate *(or* plăc′āt), v.t. Pacify, conciliate, (now chiefly U.S. of purchasing the

connivance etc. of opponents). [f. L *placare, placere,* see -ATE³]

plăce¹, n. **1.** Particular part of space; part of space occupied by person or thing, *as it has changed its* ~. **2.** City, town, village, etc.; (in names of groups of buildings) *Ely* etc. *P*~; residence, dwelling; country-house with surroundings. **3.** Building, spot, devoted to specified purpose, as ~ *of amusement, worship, bathing*~; as ~ *(H. of Commons) another* ~, H. of Lords. **4.** Particular spot on surface etc., as *a sore* ~ *on his wrist.* **5.** Passage of book etc. **6.** Rank, station, as servants *must know their* ~, *keep him in his* ~. **7.** (Racing) position among placed competitors. **8.** Position of figure in series as indicating its value in decimal or similar notation, *as calculated to 50 decimal* ~s. **9.** Step in progression of argument, statement, etc., *as in the first, second,* ~. **10.** Proper or natural position, *as take your* ~s, *there is no* ~ *for doubt, is in or out of (its, his)* ~; space, seat, accommodation, for person etc. at table, in conveyance, etc., *as take two* ~*s in the coach, always a* ~ *for you at our table; in* ~ *of,* instead of; *take the* ~ *of,* be substituted for. **11.** Office, employment, esp. government appointment; duties of office etc., *as it is not my* ~ *to inquire into that.* **12.** *In, out of,* ~, (un)suitable, (in)appropriate; *give* ~ *to,* make room for, be succeeded by; *take* ~, happen. **13.** ~*-brick*(imperfectly burnt ~, from being on windward side of kiln; ~(*-kick)* (Footb.), kick made when ball is previously placed by another player for that purpose on ground; ~*man,* holder of public office, esp. one appointed from motives of interest. [F, f. L f. Gk *plateia (hodos)* broad (way)]

plăce², v.t. **1.** Put(thing etc.)in particular place; arrange (set of things) in their proper places. **2.** Appoint (person, esp. clergyman) to post; find situation, living, etc., for. **3.** Invest (money); dispose of (goods) to customer; put (order for goods etc.) into hands of firm etc. **4.** Repose (confidence etc. *in, on).* **5.** Assign rank to; locate; fully identify, remember circumstances of previous meeting with, assign to a class *(I know that man's face but I can't* ~ *him).* **6.** State position of (usu. any of first 3 horses or runners) in race; *be* ~*d,* be among first three. **7.** Get (goal) by PLACE¹-*kick.* [prec.]

placeb′o, n. (pl. ~s, ~es). (Eccl.) opening antiphon of the vespers for the dead; (Med.) medicine given to humour, rather than cure, the patient. [L,=I shall be acceptable *(placēre* please), first word of Ps. cxvi. 9 (Vulg.)]

placen′ta, n. (pl. ~ae). Flattened circular spongy vascular organ in higher mammals, expelled in parturition after nourishing foetus, which is attached to it by umbilical cord; (Bot.) part of carpel to

which ovules are attached. Hence **~AL** a. [f. L placenta=Gk plakoeis -entos flat cake f. root of plaz plakos flat plate]

plā'cer, n. Deposit of sand, gravel, etc., in bed of stream etc. containing valuable minerals in particles. [Amer. Sp., cogn. w. *placel* sandbank f. *plaza* PLACE¹.]

∥ **plā'cēt**, sentence & n. (Univ v.). = ~ *non* ~, it pleases me (not) (forms used in voting for or against measure); (n.) such vote. [L]

plā'cid, a. Mild; peaceful; serene. Hence or cogn. **placīd'ITY** n., **~LY²** adv. [f. L *placidus* (*placēre* please, see -ID¹)]

plack'ēt, n. Pocket, esp. in woman's skirt; **~hole**, opening in outer skirt giving access to this. [perh. var. of PLACARD]

plăc'oid, a. (Of scales) plate-shaped; (of fish) with ~ scales. [f. Gk *plax plakos* plate, -OID¹]

plafond (plafawn'), n. Ceiling, esp. one enriched with paintings; such painting. [F]

plăg'al, a. (mus.). (Of ecclesiastical modes) having their sounds comprised between the dominant & its octave; ~ *cadence* (in which chord of subdominant immediately precedes that of the tonic). Cf. AUTHENTIC. [f. med. L *plagalis* f. *plaga*=mode, prob. f. L f. Gk *plagios* oblique, (med. Gk plagal, f. *plagos* side]

plage (plahzh), n. Sea beach (esp. at fashionable resort). [F]

plā'giarize, v.t. Take and use another person's (thoughts, writings, inventions, etc.) as one's own. So **~ISM**, **~IST**, nn. [f. foll. +-IZE]

plā'giary, n. (arch.). = PLAGIARISM; = PLAGIARIST. [f. L *plagiarius* kidnapper (*plagiare* kidnap)]

plăg'io- in comb. = Gk *plagios* oblique, as: **~cephăl'ic**, having anterior part of skull more developed on one side, posterior on the other; **~clas'tic** (Min.), having oblique cleavage; **~stōme**, fish with mouth placed transversely beneath snout, as sharks & rays.

plăgue (-g), n., & v.t. 1. Affliction, esp. as divine punishment; (colloq.) nuisance, trouble; pestilence, esp. *the* (oriental or bubonic) ~; (as imprecation) ~ *on it!* etc.; **~-spot**, spot on skin characteristic of ~, locality infected with ~, (fig.) source of symptom of moral corruption. 2. v.t. Afflict with ~; (colloq.) annoy, bother, whence **~'SOME** (-gs-) a. (colloq.). [ME & OF *plāge* f. L *plaga* stroke (*plag-* root of *plangere* beat breast, cf. Gk *plēgē* stroke, *plēssō* strike)]

plăg'uily (-gi), a. & adv. (colloq.). Annoyingly; exceedingly(ly), as *'twas ~ glad to get back again*. Hence **~iLY²** (-gi-) adv. [f. prec. +-Y³]

plaice, n. European flat-fish much used as food. [f. OF *plaïz* f. LL *platessa* perh. f. Gk *platus* broad]

plaid (plăd, Sc. plād), n. Long piece of twilled woollen cloth, usu. with chequered or tartan pattern, outer article of Highland costume; cloth used for this. Hence **~ED²** a. [cf. Gael. *plaide*, Ir. *ploid*, etym. dub.]

plain¹, a., adv., & n. **1.** Clear, evident; simple, readily understood, as ~ *words, English*; not intricate, as ~ *sewing*; unembellished, (of drawings etc.) not coloured; (of food) not rich or highly seasoned; not luxurious, as ~ *living*; outspoken, straightforward, (esp. *be ~ with*, tell home truths to); unsophisticated, as *I am a ~ man*; of homely manners, dress, or appearance; ugly, as *a pity the poor girl is so ~*; ~ *as a* PIKESTAFF. **2.** adv. Clearly, as *learn to speak ~*. **3.** ~ *cards* (not court-cards); **~chant**, = ~-*song*; **~clothes**, unofficial dress; ~ *dealing*, candour, straightforwardness; ~ *sailing*, sailing in a ~ *course*, (fig.) simple course of action; **~-song**, vocal music composed in medieval modes & in free rhythm depending on accentuation of the words, and sung in unison; **~-spoken**, outspoken; ~ *suit* (not trumps); ~ *tile*, flat roofing-tile. **4.** n. Level tract of country; **~s'man**, inhabitant of a ~. Hence **~'LY²** adv., **~'NESS¹** (-n-n-) n. [OF, f. L *plānus* a., *~um* neut. adj. as n.]

∥ **plaint²**, v.i. (arch., poet.). Mourn; complain; emit plaintive sound. [f. OF *plaindre* (st. *plaign-*) f. L *plangere planct-* beat breast]

plaint, n. ∥ (Law) accusation, charge; (poet.) lamentation, complaint. [ME & OF (1) *plaint* f. L *planctus -ūs*, (2) *plainte* f. med. L *plancta* fem. p.p. as n.; both as prec.]

plain'tiff, n. Party who brings suit into court of law, prosecutor. [OF, as foll.]

plain'tive, a. Expressive of sorrow, mournful. Hence **~LY²** adv., **~NESS** n. [OF (-*if*, -*ive*), f. L as PLAIN². see -IVE]

plait (plăt), n., & v.t. **1.** (Now usu. PLEAT) fold, crease, esp. flattened fold in cloth made by doubling it upon itself; (v.t.) fold (cloth etc.) thus. **2.** (Now rarely PLAT²) contexture of three or more interlaced strands of hair, ribbon, straw, etc.; (v.t.) form (hair, straw, etc.) into ~. [vb f. n.] f. OF *pleit*, *ploit*, f. L *plicare plicitum* fold]

plăn, n., & v.t. (-nn-). **1.** Drawing, diagram, made by projection on flat surface (cf. ELEVATION), esp. one showing relative position of parts of (one floor of) a building; large-scale detailed map of town or district; table indicating times, places, etc., of intended proceedings etc.; scheme of arrangement; project, design; way of proceeding, as *the better ~ is to peel them after boiling*; ~ *of* CAMPAIGN; (Perspective) any of the imaginary planes, perpendicular to line of vision, passing through objects shown in picture. **2.** vb. Make a ~ of (ground, existing building);

design (building to be constructed etc.); scheme, arrange beforehand. (procedure etc.); ~s make ~s. Hence ~LESS a. [vb f. n.] F.f. L as PLAN¹]

‖**planch** (-sh), n. F.f. L as PLAN¹) [f. F *planche* PLANK¹]

plan'chet (-sh-), n. Plain disk of metal of which coin is made. [prec.+-ET¹]

planchette' (-sh-, & see Ap.), n. Small heart-shaped board supported by two castors & pencil, which when person's fingers rest lightly on board is said to trace letters etc. without conscious direc- tion. [F, dim. of *planche* PLANK¹]

plane¹, n. Tall spreading tree of genus *Platanus* with broad angular palmately- lobed leaves; ~*tree* (of this genus). [F, f. L f. Gk *platanos* (*platus* broad)]

plane², n., & v.t. 1. Tool for smoothing surface of woodwork by paring shavings from it, consisting of wooden or metal stock from smooth bottom of which pro- jects a steel blade; similar tool for smoothing metal; *smoothing*~ (used to finish surface, cf. JACK¹ & TRYING~); *moulding*~ (for making mouldings). 2. v.t. Smooth (wood, metal etc.) with ~, pare *away* or *down* (irregularities) with ~. (arch.) level, esp. ~ *the way*. [(n.) F, f. LL *plana*, (vb) f. F *planer*; both f. L *plānāre* (as PLANE⁴)]

plane³, n., & v.i. 1. Surface such that the straight line joining any two points in it lies wholly in it; imaginary surface of this kind in which points or lines in material bodies lie; level surface; flat thin object such as table-top, supporting part of aeroplane; (colloq.) aeroplane; INCLINE'd~; each of the natural faces of a crystal. 2. Main road in mine. 3. (fig.), Travel, glide (*down* etc.), in aeroplane. [f. L *plānum* neut. as foll.]

plane⁴ a. Perfectly level, as a PLANE³; (of angle, figure, etc.) lying in a plane; ~ *chart* (on which meridians & parallels of latitude are represented by equidistant straight lines, used in PLANE³ *sailing*); ~ *table*, surveying instrument used for direct plotting in the field. (v.t.) survey (area) with this. [f. L *plānus* flat, level, refash. f. PLAIN a.]

plan'et¹, n. (Hist.) heavenly body distin- guished from fixed stars by having appar- ent motion of its own (Moon, Mercury, Venus, Sun, Mars, Jupiter, Saturn, esp. (Astrol.) with reference to its supposed influence on persons & events; (Astron) *primary* ~*s*, heavenly bodies revolving in approximately circular orbits round sun (*major* ~*s*, Mercury, Venus, Earth, Mars, Jupiter, Saturn, Uranus, Neptune, Pluto; *minor* ~*s*, the asteroids, whose orbits lie between those of Mars & Jupi- ter; *secondary* ~*s* (also *satellites*), those that revolve round primary; SUN & ~; ~-*struck*, -*stricken*, bewildered, terrified. [ME & OF *planete* f. LL f. Gk *planētēs* wanderer, planet, f. *planaomai* wander]

plan'et², n. Chasuble. [f. med. L *planeta* perh. as prec.]

planeta'rium, n. Orrery, model of planet- ary system. [as foll.]

plan'etary, a. Of planets, as ~ *influence*; *motions* ; ~ *hour*, twelfth part of natural day or night; ~ (*solar*) *system* ; terrestrial, mundane ; wandering, erratic. [f. LL *planetarius* (as PLANET, see -ARY¹]

plan'etoid, n. Minor PLANET¹. [-OID]

planetēs'imal, n. One of a vast number of minute planetoids which, according to the ~ *hypothesis*, formed the bodies of the planets by accretion in a cold state. [f. PLANET¹ after *infinitesimal*]

plan g,ent (-j-), a. (Of sound) thrilling, vibrating, moaning, insistent. Hence ~ENCY n. [f. L *plangere* beat the breast, see -ENT]

plani- in comb. = L *plānus* level, smooth, plane, as: ~*im'eter*, instrument for me- chanically measuring area of irregular plane figure; ~*im'etry*, measurement of plane surfaces, so *planimet'ric(al)* aa.; *planipel'dlous*, with flat petals; *plăn'i- sphere*, map formed by projection of ~*isphere*, device for showing the part of the heavens visible at given time & place), so *plănisphĕr'ic* a.

plan'ish, v.t. Flatten (sheet metal etc.) with smooth-faced hammer or otherwise; flatten out (coining-metal) between rollers; polish (photograph etc.) with roller etc. Hence ~ER¹ (1, 2) n. [f. obs. F *planir* smooth (*plan* a. as PLANE⁴), see -ISH²]

plank¹, n. Long flat piece of timber, 2 to 6 in. thick, 9 or more in. wide (cf. BOARD¹); item of political or other pro- gramme (cf. PLATFORM); *walk the* ~, (of pirates' captive etc.) walk blindfold into sea along ~ laid over side of ship ; ~ *bed* (of boards, without mattress, used as prison discipline etc.). [f. ONF *planke* f. LL *planca* prob. f. root of Gk *plax placos* flat plate]

plank², v.t. Furnish, cover, floor, with planks, whence ~ING¹ (2, 3) n.; (sl.) put *down*, esp. pay (money, or abs.) *down* on the spot. [f. prec.]

plank'ton, n. (biol.). The (chiefly micro- scopic) forms of drifting or floating organic life found at various depths in seas, lakes, rivers, etc., taken collectively (cf. BENTHOS & NEKTON). [G, f. Gk *plagktos* wandering (*plazomai*)]

plano- in comb. = L *plānus* level, flat, as: ~*conc'ave*, -*con'vex*, (of lens etc.) with one

surface plane & the other concave, convex; *plănŏm'ĕter*, flat plate, usu. of cast iron, as gauge for plane surfaces.

plant¹ (-ah-), n. 1. Living organism capable of living wholly on inorganic substances & having neither power of locomotion nor special organs of sensation or digestion, member of the vegetable kingdom (often restricted to the smaller ~s, excluding trees and shrubs). 2. Crop; growth, as *in* ~, growing, *lose* ~, die off. *miss* ~, fail to spring from seed. 3. Mode of planting oneself, pose. 4. Fixtures, implements, machinery, etc., used in industrial process; (fig.) machinery of intellectual work etc. 5. (sl.) Planned swindle or burglary, hoax. 6. ~*louse*, kinds of insect that infest ~s, esp. aphis. Hence ~LET n., ~'LIKE a. [OE *plante* f. L *planta* slip, cutting; partly also f. foll.]

plant² (-ah-), v.t. 1. Place (tree, shoot, bulb, seed, crop, etc.) in ground (that it may take root & grow; deposit (young fish, spawn, oysters) in river etc.; ~ *out*, transfer (plant) from pot or frame to open ground, set out (seedlings) at intervals. 2. Fix firmly (*in, on*, ground etc.); station (person), esp. as spy; ~ *oneself*, take up a position. 3. Establish, found, (community, city, church); settle (person) in a place as colonist etc.; cause (idea etc.) to take root *in* (mind); furnish (land *with* plants, district *with* settlers, etc.). 4. Deliver (blow, thrust) with definite aim. 5. (sl.) Conceal (stolen goods etc.); bury; place (gold-dust, ore) in mining claim to encourage prospective buyer, cf. SALT v.; devise (fraudulent scheme). 6. Abandon, as *there I was, fairly ~ed*. Hence ~ABLE a. [OE *plantian* f. L *plantare*, cf. prec.]

Plantă'genet, n. & a. (Member of the family founded by Geoffrey of Anjou, esp. any of the English kings from Henry II to Richard III. [surname, f. sprig of broom (L *planta* plant, *genesta* broom) worn as cognizance]

plăn'tain¹ (-tin), n. Genus of plants, esp. *Greater P*~, low herb with broad flat leaves spread out close to ground & seeds much used for cage-birds. [ME & OF, f. L *plantaginem* (nom. -*go*) prob. f. *planta* sole of foot, from its prostrate leaves]

plăn'tain² (-tin). n. Tree-like tropical herbaceous plant allied to banana and bearing similar fruit; its fruit. [16th-c. *plă(n)tan* f. Sp. *plá(n)tano*; Sp. has also *plá(n)tano* PLANE¹-tree (obs. E *plantain*)] [f. L *plantaris* (*planta* sole, see -AR¹)]

plănta'tion, n. Assemblage of planted growing plants, esp. trees; estate on which cotton, tobacco, etc., are cultivated (formerly by servile labour); ~ *song* (of the kind sung by Negroes on American ~s); (Hist.) colonization, colony. [f. L *plantatio* (as PLANT² see -ATION)]

plă'nter (-ah-), n. Cultivator of soil; (in Ireland) English settler on forfeited lands in 17th c., (19th c.) person settled in evicted tenant's holding; occupier of plantation, esp. in (sub-)tropical countries, as *coffee, cotton, sugar, tobacco, ~*; machine for planting, as *corn, potato, ~*. Hence ~SHIP n.

plănt'igrāde, a. & n. (Animal) that walks on its soles (cf. DIGITIGRADE); (of human being) placing whole sole on ground at once in walking. [F, f. L *planta* sole + *-gradus* -walking]

plāntŏc'racy̆, n. Dominant class of planters in W. Indies etc. [irreg. f. PLANTER + -o- + -CRACY]

plăn'ty̆, n. (Ir. mus.). Animated harp-tune moving in triplets. [f]

plaque (plahk), n. Ornamental tablet of metal, porcelain, etc., plain or decorated; small tablet as badge of rank in honorary order; (Path.) patch of eruption etc. So **plaquĕtte'** (-ăkĕt) n. [F, f. Flem. *placke*, small coin, whence Sc. *placke*]

plăsh¹, n. Marshy pool; puddle. Hence ~*y²*, a. [OE *plæsc*, cf. Du. *plas*, prob. imit.]

plăsh², v.t. & i., & n. 1. Strike surface of (water) so as to break it up; splash (t. & i.). 2. n. Splash, plunge. Hence ~*y²* a. [cf. Du *plassen*, G *platschen*, prob. imit.]

plăsh³, v.t. Bend down and interweave (branches, twigs) to form hedge; make, renew, (hedge) thus. [f. OF *plaissier* ult. f. L *plectere* plait; cf. PLEACH]

plăsm, n. Living matter of a cell, protoplasm, esp. general body of this as distinct from nucleus. [f. foll.]

plăs'ma (-z-), n. 1. Green variety of quartz. 2. Colourless coagulable part of blood, lymph, or milk, in which the corpuscles or oil-globules float, so ~*ăt'ic* a. 3. = prec., whence ~IC (-z-) a. [LL & Gk (gen. *-matos*) = thing moulded (*plasma* mould, see -M]

plăsmŏd'ium (-z-), n. (biol.; pl. *-ia*). Mass of naked protoplasm formed by fusion or aggregation of amoeboid bodies without fusion of their nuclei; generic name of microscopic parasitic organism whose presence & rapid multiplication in the blood of man constitute malaria. [mod. L, f. PLASMA + *-odium*, see -ODE]

plăsmŏl'ysis (-zm-), n. Loss of water from, & consequent contraction of, protoplasm of vegetable cell due to immersion in a solution stronger than the cell fluid. So **plăs'molyse** (-zm-) v.t., subject to ~. [f. PLASM, -O-, Gk *lusis* loosing f. *luō* to loose]

plă'ster¹ (-ah-), n. 1. Curative application consisting of some substance spread upon muslin etc. & capable of adhering at the temperature of the body, as COURT¹, MUSTARD, *sticking-*, ~. 2. Soft plastic mixture, esp. of lime, sand, & hair, for spreading on walls etc. to form smooth surface; ~ *of Paris*, fine white ~ of gypsum used for making moulds & as

cement etc. [prepared from gypsum of Montmartre, Paris]. Hence ~Y² a. [OE, f. pop. L plastrum f. L f. Gk emplastron for emplaston thing daubed on f. EM(plasso mould)]

pla'ster² (-ah-), v.t. **1.** Cover (wall etc.) with plaster or the like, whence ~ER¹ n.; coat, bedaub; (fig.) load to excess (with praise etc.). **2.** Apply medical plaster to, (joc.) give compensation for (blow, wound); stick, fix, (thing) like plaster upon surface. **3.** Treat (wine) with gypsum etc. to neutralize acidity. [f. prec.]

plas'tic, a. Moulding, giving form to clay, wax, etc.; ~ arts, those concerned with modelling, e.g. sculpture, ceramics; ~ surgery (repairing deficiency of structure); causing growth of natural forms, forma-tive of immaterial things; produced by moulding; capable of being (easily) moulded; (Geol.), middle group of Eocene beds; (fig.) pliant, supple; (Biol.) capable of forming living tissue, (also) accompanied by this process, as ~ bronchitis. Hence plas'tically adv., plasti'cITY n., plas'tics n. pl., group of synthetic resinous or other substances that can be moulded into any form. [f. L f. Gk plastikos (plasso mould, see -IC)]

plas'ticine, n. Plastic substance used esp. in schools as substitute for modelling clay. [P; -INE¹]

plas'tron, n. Fencer's leather-covered breast-plate; breast-covering of facings; cloth worn by lancers; ornamental front of woman's bodice; man's starched shirt-front; ventral part of shell of tortoise or turtle, corresponding part in other animals; (Hist.) steel breast-plate. [F, f. It. piastrone (piastra breast-plate, as PLASTER; see -OON]

plat¹, n. Patch, plot, of ground, as grass-~. [collat. form of PLOT]

plat² n. & v.t. (-tt-). =PLAIT (2nd sense), **plat³** (plah), n. Dish of food. [F, see PLATE¹]

plat'an, n. Plane-tree. [f. L platanus plane-tree]

plate, n. **1.** Flat thin usu. rigid sheet of metal etc. of even surface and more or less uniform thickness; this as part of mechanism. **2.** Smooth piece of metal etc. for engraving; impression from this; = BOOK ~. **3.** Piece of metal with name or inscription for affixing to something, as coffin, door, name, ~. **4.** Thin sheet of metal, glass, etc., coated with sensitive film for photograph (whole~, 8½ × 6½ in., half-~, 6½ × 4¾, quarter-~, 4¼ × 3¼). **5.** Stereotype or electrotype cast of page of composed movable types, from which sheets are printed. **6.** Horizontal timber laid along top of wall to support ends of joists or rafters, or at top or bottom of a framing, as roof, wall, window, ~. **7.** (Also ~-rail) early form of railroad. **8.** (collect.

sing.). ||Table & domestic utensils of silver, gold, or other metal, as pewter ~, electro-~. **9.** Silver or gold cup as prize for (orig. horse-) race, such race; selling ~, horse-race winner of which must be sold at fixed price. **10.** Shallow usu. circular vessel, now usu. of earthenware or china, from which food is eaten, as this, as a ~ of strawberries; similar vessel used for collection in churches etc., as put a shilling in the ~. **11.** Thin piece of plastic material, moulded to shape of gums etc., to which artificial teeth are attached. **12.** *Home, pitcher's, ~, stations of batter, pitcher, in baseball. **13.** ||~-basket (for spoons, forks, etc.); ~ glass, thick glass of fine quality cast in ~s for shop windows etc.; ||~-layer, man employed in fixing & repairing railway; ~-mark, =HALL-mark, (also) impression left on margin of engraving by pressure of the ~ (hence ~-marked mount for photographs); ~-powder (for cleaning silver); ||~-rack (in which ~s are kept or placed to drain). Hence ~'FUL(2) (-tfool) n., ~'LESS a. [ME & OF, fem. of plat flat, perh. ult. f. Gk platus broad]

plate², v.t. Cover (esp. ship) with plates of metal for protection, ornament, etc.; cover (other metal) with thin coat of silver, gold, or tin; make a plate (of type) for printing. [f. prec.]

plateau' (-tō), n. (pl. ~s, pr. -z). Tableland; ornamented tray or dish; decorative plaque; woman's hat with level top. [F. f. OF platel dim. of PLAT³]

plat'en, -tt-, n. Plate in printing-press by which paper is pressed against type; corresponding part in typewriters etc. [f. OF platine flat piece (plat, see PLATE¹)]

plat'er, n. One who plates with silver etc.; one who makes or applies plates in ship-building; inferior race-horse, competing chiefly for plates. [-ER¹]

plat'form, n. & v.t. & i. **1.** Raised level surface, natural or artificial terrace; ||raised surface of planks etc. along side of line at railway station; raised flooring in hall or open air from which speaker addresses audience, (fig.) the~, ~oratory; *declaration issued by representatives of party assembled to nominate candidates for election. **2.** v.b. Place (as) on ~; speak on ~. [f. F plateforme ground-plan, lit. flat form (as PLATE¹+ forme FORM)]

plat'ing, n. In vbl senses; coating of gold, silver, etc.; plate-racing. [f. PLATE¹,²+-ING¹]

plat'inize, v.t. Coat with platinum. [-IZE]

plat'inoid, n. Alloy of copper, zinc, nickel, & tungsten; kind(s) of metal found associated with platinum. [-OID]

plat'inotype, n. Process of photographic printing in platinum black. [f. foll. +-o- +TYPE]

plat'inum, n. White heavy ductile malleable metallic element unaffected by simple acids & fusible only at very high temperature; ~*um black*, ~*um in form* of powder like lamp-black; ~*um blonde* (colloq., orig. U.S.), woman with gold-grey hair; ~*um metals*, platinoids. Hence **platin'ic**, ~**iferous**, ~**ous**, aa. [f. Sp. & earlier E) *platina* dim. of *plata* silver, see PLATE¹]

plat'itude, n. Commonplaceness; commonplace remark, esp. one solemnly delivered. Hence ~**ud'inize**(2) v.i., ~**ud'inous** a., ~**ud'inously²** adv. [F, f. *plat* (see PLATE¹) after *latitude* etc.]

platitudinar'ian, n. & a. Dealer in platitudes; (adj.) of the nature of platitude. [-ARIAN]

Platon'ic, a. Of Plato the Greek philosopher (died c. 347 B.C.) or his doctrines; ~ *love*, purely spiritual love for one of opposite sex (p~s, ~ *lovers' talk or relation*); (pop.) confined to words or theory, not issuing in action, harmless; ~ *year*, cycle in which heavenly bodies were supposed to go through all their possible movements & return to original positions. So **Platon'ically** adv. **Plat'onism**, **Plat'onist**, nn., **Plat'onize**(2, 3) v.i. & t. [f. L f. Gk *Platōnikos* (*Platōn* Plato, see -IC)]

platoon', n. (Hist.) small infantry detachment, esp. a unit for volley-firing etc., volley fired by it; (in mod. use) subdivision of a company, a tactical unit commanded by a lieutenant & usu. divided into three sections. [f. F *peloton* small ball (as PELLET, see -OON)]

platt'er, n. (chiefly arch. exc. U.S.). Flat dish or plate, often of wood. [ME & OF *plater* (PLAT³)]

plat'y-, in comb.=Gk *platus* broad, flat, as:~*pus*, Australian duck-mole, ornithorhynchus; ~*rrhine* (-rrīn), (of monkeys) with nostrils far apart & directed forwards or sideways.

plaud'it, n. (usu. in pl.). Round of applause; emphatic expression of approval. [shortened f. L *plaudite* applaud (also as E noun) pl. imperat. of *plaudere plaus-* applaud, said by Roman actors at end of play]

plaus'|ible (-z-), a. (Of arguments, statements, etc.) specious, seeming reasonable or probable; (of persons) fair-spoken (usu. implying deceit). Hence or cogn. ~**IBILITY** n., ~**ibly²** adv. [f. L *plausibilis* as prec., see -BLE)]

play¹, v.i. & t. 1. Move about in lively or capricious manner, frisk, flit, flutter, pass gently (*around, about*, etc.), strike lightly (*upon* etc.), alternate rapidly, as *bees ~ about flowers, tresses ~ on her neck, his fancy ~ed round the idea*. 2. (Of part of mechanism etc.) have free movement. 3. Wield freely, as ~ *a good knife & fork*, eat heartily; ~ *a good stick*, fence well 4. Allow (fish) to exhaust itself by pulling against line. 5. Discharge (guns etc. *on*), discharge guns (*on*), (intr., of guns) be fired (*on*). 6. Direct (light *on, over, along*, etc.), (intr., of light) pass (*over, along*, etc.) 7. Perform, execute, (trick, prank, joke, *on* person, or with double object). 8. Amuse oneself, sport, frolic; ~*boy*, one living for pleasure; ~ *with*, amuse oneself with, trifle with, treat lightly; ~ *upon words*, pun. 9. (dial.). (Esp. of workmen on strike) abstain from work. 10. Employ oneself in the game of (cricket, whist, etc., or abs.). 11. ~*ed out*, exhausted of energy or vitality or usefulness (*our horses were, I felt, Free Trade is ~ed out*); ~ *up*, put all one's energy into the game etc.; ~ DUCK's & *drakes*; ~ FAST³ & *loose*. 12. (In cricket, lawn tennis, etc., as bowler's warning to batsman etc.) ~! 13. Pretend for fun (*that we are gipsies* etc.). 14. (crick.). (Of ground) ~ *well* etc., be in good etc. condition for play. 15. ~*-or-pay bet* (holding good whether horse runs or not). 16. Game, gamble. 17. ~ *fair, foul*, ~ or (fig.) act (un)fairly; ~ (observe the rules of) *the game* (also fig. of keeping to code of honour); ~ *into the hands of*, act so as to give advantage to (opponent or partner); (sl.) ~ *it on*, ~ *it low on*, (*low*) *down on*, take mean advantage of (person); ~ *upon the* SQUARE; ~ *at*, engage in (game), (fig.) engage in (fighting etc.) in trivial or half-hearted way. 18. Contend against (person) in game; employ (person) to ~ in game, include in team. 19. Move (piece in chess etc.); take (playing-card) from one's hand & lay it face upwards on table in one's turn; (fig.) ~ *one's cards well*, make good use of opportunities. 20. (Crick. etc.) strike (ball) in specified esp. defensive manner; (Crick.) ~ *on* (abs.), ~ *the ball on* to one's own wicket and so put oneself out. 21. ~ *off*, oppose (person *against* another) esp. for one's own advantage; cause (person) to exhibit himself disadvantageously; pass (thing) off as something else; ~*off* n., additional match to decide a draw or tie. 22. Perform on (musical instrument, or abs.); perform (on instrument); ~ *by ear*, perform on an instrument without technical knowledge of music; perform (music *on* instrument). 23. (congregation etc.) ~ *in, out*, ~ on organ etc. as they come in, go out; ~ (*up*)*on*, make use of (person's fears, credulity, etc.); ~ *first, second*, FIDDLE. 24. Perform (drama, or abs.) on stage; act (*in* drama); act (part) in drama, as ~ *Shylock*, (fig.) act in real life the part of (the DEUCE² or *devil, the fool, the man, truant*, etc., also ~ *one's part well* etc.); ~ *up to*, act in drama so as to support (another actor), (fig.) back up, flatter, toady. Hence ~**ABLE** a. [OE *plegan*,

plagian, plaegian, cf. M.Du. plegen dance, cogn. w. Du. plegen, G pflegen, be glad, cogn. w. Du. plegen, G pflegen, be wont, take charge of]

play², n. 1. Brisk, light, or fitful movement. 2. Activity, operation, as lively ~ of fancy, other forces come into ~; are in full ~, are brought or called into ~; make ~, act effectively, esp. (Racing, Hunting) exercise pursuers or followers. 3. Freedom of movement, space for this, scope for activity, as bolts should have half an inch of ~, allow full ~ to curiosity. 4. Amusement, as at ~, engaged in playing; said it only in ~ (not seriously); ~ of words, trifling with words. 6. on words, pun. 5. Playing of game; manner, style, (of this; (Chick., Footb., etc.) ball is in ~ (being used in ordinary course of ~, according to rules); so ~ part of ground within definite boundaries. 6. CHILD's~; FAIR², FOUL ~. 7. Cessation from work (of workmen on strike etc.). 8. Dramatic piece, drama. 9. Gaming, gambling. [OE plega as prec.]

play'er, n. In vbl senses, esp.: person engaged at the time, person skilful, in a game; performer on musical instrument; || professional ~ at cricket etc.; actor; (Pool, Croquet) ball that after present ~ has finished break etc. will play on him; ~-piano (fitted with apparatus enabling it to be played automatically). [-ER²]

play'ful, a. Frolicsome, sportive; humorous, jocular. Hence ~lY² adv., ~NESS n. [-FUL]

play'ing, n. In vbl senses; ~-cards, set or pack of cards used in games. [-ING¹]

pla'za (-ah-), n. Market-place, open square (esp. in Spanish town). [Sp. = place]

plea, n. Pleading, argument, excuse; (Law) formal statement by or on behalf of defendant, defence, special ~ (alleging new fact); || Court of COMMON¹ P~s; f. L placitum decree, neut. p.p. of placēre please]

pleach, v.t. Entwine, interlace; esp. = PLASH³. [ME plechè, as PLASH]

plead, v.i. & t. Address court as advocate on behalf of either party, so ~'ER¹ n.; maintain (cause) in court;

4895

G g

allege formally as plea, (fig.) allege as excuse etc., as I can only ~ inexperience, so ~ABLE a., ~ (not) guilty, deny, confess, liability or guilt; ~ with, make earnest appeal to (person for person, for, against, thing, decision, etc.), whence ~'ing² adv. [f. OF plaidier (as PLEA)]

plead'ing, n. In vbl senses, esp: formal (now usu. written) statement of cause of action or defence; ~ SPECIAL ~, [ING¹]

plea'sance (-lěz-), n. (arch.). Pleasure, enjoyment; pleasure-ground, esp. one attached to mansion (now chiefly surviving in proper names). [f. OF plaisance

plea'sant (-lěz-), a. Agreeable to mind, feelings, or senses, as a ~ breeze, flavour, spend a ~ evening; || (arch.) jocular, facetious. Hence ~lY² adv., ~NESS n. [f. OF plaisant (as PLEASE see -ANT)]

plea'santry (-lěz-), n. Jocularity; humorous speech, jest. [f. F plaisanterie (prec., -ERY)]

please (-z), v.t. & i. 1. Be agreeable to, as meant only to ~ you; his last book will ~ you; ~ yourself, do as you like; be ~d with, derive pleasure from; I shall (vulg. will) be ~d (glad) to (do, esp. as polite form of consent or offer). 2. Think fit, as take as many as you ~. 3. (In formal or iron. deference) His Majesty has been graciously ~d to confer etc., your lordship was ~d to doubt my veracity. 4. (With it as subject, expressed or omitted, representing a prec. or foll. infinitive, clause, or sentence, now chiefly as in last use) it has never ~d him to explain; (may it) your honour, there was no moon that night!; the matter will be cleared up some day,~God (or, joc., ~ the pigs). 5. Give pleasure, as he was anxious to ~. 6. (As polite form of request esp. for trifling services) I will take another cup, if you ~; (with iron. implication that nothing could be more reasonable) & now, if you ~, he expects me to pay for it!; (imperat., orig.=may it ~ you) ring the bell, ~; may I come in, ~?, coffee for two, ~; ~ (to) return it soon, ~ don't (or ~ not to) forget the key. Hence PLEASED¹ (-zd), pleas'ing²a., pleas'ingly²adv. (-zg.) [ME plaise f. OF plaisir (F plaire) f. L placēre]

plea'surable (plězh'er-), a. Affording pleasure. Hence ~leNESS n., ~lY² adv. [f. foll. + -ABLE]

pleasure (plězh'er), n. & v.t. & i. 1. Enjoyment, delight; sensuous enjoyment as chief object of life, as a life given up to ~, man of ~, profligate; will, desire, as shall not consult his ~, can be postponed during our ~, can be altered at ~; (royal formula) it is our ~ to, we are graciously pleased to; (vulg.) it is our ~ to submit (we have ~ in submitting) balance sheet etc.; to converse with him is a (source of)

~ ; do me the ~ of (gratify me by) *dining with me*; he takes (a) ~ in (likes) *contradicting their* ~ (enjoying themselves) *at Bath*; ~*-boad* (used for ~, not business); ~*-ground* (laid out for ~). **2.** vb. Give ~ to; take ~ (*in thing, in doing*). [(vb f. n.) ME & OF *plesir, plaisir*, PLEASE used as n.]

pleat, n., & v.t. =PLAIT (1st sense). [collateral form of PLAIT]

pleb, n. (sl.) Plebeian, person of lower classes. [abbr.]

***plebe,** n. (colloq.) Member of lowest class at U.S. Naval or Military Academy. [shortened f. PLEBEIAN]

plebei'an (-bēan), n. & a. **1.** Commoner in ancient Rome (cf. PATRICIAN); commoner. **2.** adj. Of low birth, of the common people, coarse, base, ignoble. Hence ~NESS n. ~IZE(3) v.t. [f. L *plebeius* (*plebs* common people) + -AN]

pleb'iscite (-sit), n. (Rom. Hist.) law enacted by commonalty in *comitia tributa*; (mod.) direct vote of all electors of State on important public question; public expression of community's opinion, vote without binding force. So **plebis'citary** a. [f. F *plébiscite* f. L *plebiscitum* (*plebs* commons + *scitum* decree f. *sciscere* vote for)]

plec'trum, n. (pl. -ra). Small instrument of ivory, quill, etc., for plucking strings of zither etc. [L, f. Gk *plēktron* (*plēssō* strike)]

pledge¹, n. Thing handed over to person as security (cf. REPLEVIN) for fulfilment of contract, payment of debt, etc., & liable to forfeiture in case of failure; thing put in pawn; (fig.) one's child; thing given as token of favour etc. or of something to come; drinking of a health, toast; promise, as *under* ~ *of secrecy*; solemn engagement to abstain from intoxicants, as *take, sign, keep, the* ~; (Pol.) leader's public promise (not) to adopt some course; state of being pledged, as *goods lying in* ~, *taken out of* ~. [ME & OF *plege* etc., prob. f. med. L *plevire* warrant, engage, of G orig., cf. PLIGHT¹]

pledge², v.t. Deposit as security, pawn; (fig.) plight (one's honour, word, etc.); drink to the health of. Hence ~'ABLE a. [f. prec.]

pledgee', n. One with whom pledge is deposited, pawnee. So **pledg'ER¹** n. [-EE]

pledg'et, n. Small wad of lint etc. [?]

Plei'ad (plī-), n. (pl. ~s pr. -dz, ~es pr. -dēz), (Pl.) cluster of small stars in Taurus, usu. spoken of as 7; (fig., sing.) brilliant group of (usu. 7) persons or things. [f. L *Plēias* f. Gk *Pleias -ados*]

pleis'tocēne (-lis-), a. & n. (geol.). (Of) the division immediately overlying the pliocene formation. [f. Gk *pleistos* most + *kainos* new]

fied; (of assembly) fully attended; ~y INSPIRATION. Hence ~ILY² adv. [f. LL *plenarius* (*plenus* full, see -ARY¹)]

plenipoten'tiary (-sha-), a. & n. (Person) invested with full power, esp. as ambassador deputed to act at discretion; (of power) absolute. [f. med. L *plenipoten-tiarius* f. LL *plenipotens* (*plenus* full + *potens* POTENT), see -ARY¹]

plen'itude, n. Fulness, completeness; abundance. [OF, f. L *plenitudo* (*plenus* full, see -TUDE)]

plen'teous, a. (chiefly poet.). Plentiful. Hence ~LY² adv., ~NESS n. [ME & OF *plentivous* (PLENTY, -IVE, -EOUS)]

plen'tiful, a. Abundant, copious. Hence ~LY² adv., ~NESS n. [f. foll. + -FUL]

plen'ty, n. & adv. **1.** Abundance, as much as one could desire, (of thing, or abs.), as ~ *of cake, here is cake in* ~, *we are in* ~ (colloq.). **2.** adv., *time*; *horn of* ~, cornucopia. **2.** adv. (colloq.). Quite, as *it is* ~ *large enough*. [f. OF *plentet* f. L *plenitatem* (*plenus* full, see -TY]

plen'um, n. Space filled with matter (~ *system*, of ventilation by forcing air in); full assembly. [L, neut. of *plenus* full]

ple'onasm, n. (gram.). Redundancy of expression, e.g. *hear with one's ears, a false lie*. So ~as'tic a., ~as'tically adv. [f. L f. Gk *pleonasmos* (*pleonazō* add superfluously f. *pleon* more)]

plesiosaur'us, n. (pl. -rī, -ruses). Extinct marine reptile with long neck, short tail, & two large paddles. [f. Gk *plēsios* near + *sauros* lizard]

plēth'ora (or plethō'ra), n. Morbid condition marked by excess of red corpuscles in the blood; (fig.) unhealthy repletion. Hence or cogn. **plēthō'ric** a., **plēthō'rically** adv. [med. L, f. Gk *plēthōrē* (*plēthō* become full)]

pleur'a (ploor'a), n. Either of the two serous membranes lining the thorax & enveloping the lungs in mammals; part of the body-wall in invertebrates. Hence ~AL a. [Gk.=side of body, rib]

pleur'isy (ploor-), n. Inflammation of the pleura, usu. caused by chill, & marked by pain in chest or side, fever, etc. So ~IT'IC (ploor-) a. [f. OF *pleurisie* f. LL *pleurisis* altered f. Gk *pleuritis* (as prec., see -ITIS), also used in E]

pleuro- (ploor-) in comb. (before vowel pleur-)=Gk *pleura*, side, *pleura*, rib, as: *pleur~~dyn'ia*, pain in side caused by rheumatism in muscles of chest; ~*pneumōn'ia*, pneumonia complicated with pleurisy, esp. as contagious disease of horned cattle.

plexim'ēter, n. (med.). Thin plate of ivory etc. placed on part of the body & struck with plexor in medical percussion. [f. Gk *plēxis* stroke (*plēssō* strike) + -METER]

plex'or, n. (med.). Small hammer used with pleximeter. [irreg. as prec. + -OR²]

plex'us, n. (Anat.) network of fibres or vessels in animal body, as gastric, pulmonary, SOLAR, ~; network, complication. Hence **plex'iform** a. [L, gen. -ūs, f. plectere plex- plait]

pli'able, a. = foll. Hence pliABIL'ITY n.

pli'ant, a. [F] **pli'abLY²** adv. [F [plier bend f. L plicare] Bending, supple; (fig.) yielding, compliant. Hence **pli'ANCY** n., ~**LY²** adv. [F (as prec., see -ANT)]

plic'a, n. (pl. -ae). Fold, as of skin or membrane; ~ (polōn'ica Polish), matted filthy condition of hair due to disease. [med. L, as foll.]

plic'ate, a. (bot., zool., geol.). Folded. So **plica'ted¹** a. [f. L plicare fold, -ATE²]

plica'tion, n. Folding; fold; folded condition. [OF (as prec., see -ATION)]

pli'ers (-z), n. pl. Pincers having long jaws with parallel surfaces, for bending wire etc. [f. (dial.) ply bend (see PLIABLE) + -ER¹]

plight¹ (plīt), v.t., & n. **1.** Pledge (one's troth, faith, promise, esp. in p.p.); engage oneself (to person, esp. in p.p.; as ~ed lovers). **2.** n. Engagement. [OE plihtan danger, cf. Du. plicht, G pflicht, perh. cogn. w. PLUMP¹]

plight² (plīt), n. Condition, state, esp. a sorry, evil, hopeless, etc., ~. [ME plit, doublet of PLAIT]

plim, v.t. & i (dial.; -mm-), Swell, fill out, make or grow plump. [also plim, perh. cogn. w. PLUMP¹]

Plim'soll, a. & n. ~ line, ~'s MARK¹; || (n. pl.; p~s) cheap rubber-soled canvas shoes. [S. ~, agitator for Merchant Shipping Act of 1876]

plinth, n. Lower square member of base of column; projecting part of wall immediately above ground. [f. Gk plinthos tile, brick]

plin'thite, n. Kind of brick-red clay. [as prec.+-ITE¹]

Pli'ocene, a. & n.(geol.). (Of) the newest division of Tertiary formation. [f. Gk pleiōn more+kainos new]

plod, v.i. & t.(-dd-), n. **1.** Walk laboriously, trudge, (on, along, etc.); drudge, slave, (at etc.); make (one's way) laboriously. **2.** n. Laborious walk or work. Hence ~**d'ER¹** n., ~**d'ingLY²** adv. [prob. imit.]

plom'bé, a. Officially lead-sealed. [F]

plop, n. & adv., & v.t. & i.(-pp-). **1.** Sound as of smooth object dropping into water without splash; act of falling with this. **2.** adv. With a ~. **3.** vb. (Cause to) fall thus. [imit.]

plot¹, n. Piece (usu. small) of ground; plan of play's, poem, novel, etc., whence ~'**LESS** a.; conspiracy; sly plan. [?]

plot², v.t. (-tt-). Make plan or map of (existing object, place or thing to be laid out, constructed, etc.); plan, contrive, (evil object, or abs.). Hence ~**t'ER¹** n. [f. prec.]

plough¹ (plow), n. **1.** Implement for cutting furrows in soil & turning it up, consisting of cutting blade (~share) fixed in frame drawn by horses etc. & guided by man (~man); put one's hand to the ~, undertake task (Luke ix. 62); ploughed land; kinds of instrument resembling ~ as ice-~ (for clearing away snow); the P~s, CHARLES'S WAIN; || [f. foll.] rejection of candidate in examination. **2.** ~-beam, central beam of ~; ~-boy, boy who leads ~horses etc.; ~-land (hist.), as much land as could be ploughed by one team of 8 oxen in the year, unit of assessment labour etc.; ~-tail, rear of ~, (fig.) farm labour, as at the ~-tail. [late OE plōh, cf. Du. ploeg, G pflug]

plough² (plow), v.t. & i. Turn up (earth, or abs.) with plough, esp. before sowing (~ the sand or sands, labour uselessly), (~ back (grass, clover, etc.) into soil to enrich it, (fig.) reinvest (profits) in business etc.; root out, cast up, thrust down, (roots, weeds) with plough); furrow, scratch (surface) as with plough; produce (furrow, line) thus; produce wrinkles in (brow etc.); advance laboriously (through snow etc., through book etc.); (of ship etc.) cleave (surface of water, its way, etc.); || (sl.) reject (candidate) in examination [f. prec.]

plo'ver (-ŭ-), n. Kinds of gregarious grallatorial bird, esp. Golden, Grey, P~, & (pop.) lapwing (whose eggs are sold as ~'s); ~-page, ~'s-page, dunlin & other birds said to follow golden ~. [f. OF plovier f. LL *plovarius (pluvia rain, reference unexpl., see -ARY³]

ploy, n. (north.). Expedition, undertaking, occupation, job. [perh. f. employ]

pluck¹, v.t. & i. **1.** Pull off, pick, (flower, feather, hair); (arch.) pull, drag, snatch, (away, off, etc.); pull at, twitch; tug, snatch, at; strip (bird) of feathers; CROW¹ to ~; plunder, swindle, as ~ a PIGEON; || reject (candidate) in examination; ~ up one's heart, spirits, courage, take courage. [com.-WG; OE pluccian, Du. & MG plocken]

pluck², n. Plucking, twitch; || rejection, failure, in examination; heart, liver, & lungs, as of beast as food; courage, spirit, whence (-y²)~**ED²** (-kt), ~'**LESS**, ~'**Y²**, adj.; ~'**ILY²** adv., boldness of effect. [f. foll.]

plug¹, n. Piece of wood etc. fitting tightly into hole, used to fill gap or act as wedge (in various techn. uses); natural or moral bid concretion acting thus; kinds of

stopper for vessel or pipe; (pop.) release-mechanism of water-closet flushing apparatus; FIRE¹~; ~; tobacco pressed into cake or stick, piece of this cut off for chewing; *~ugly (sl.) street rowdy. [prob. f. MDu. plugge, etym. dub.]

plug², v.t. & i. (-gg-). Stop (hole etc., often up) with plug; (sl.) shoot; (sl.) strike with fist; (colloq.) plod (away at work etc.); (colloq.) endeavour to popularize (a song, theory, policy, etc.) by dinning it into the public ear. [f. prec.]

plum, n. 1. Roundish fleshy fruit with sweet pulp & flattish pointed stone; (also ~ tree) tree bearing this; dried grape or raisin as used for cakes etc.; SUGAR~; [French~, fine the kind of prune; (fig.) good thing, best of a collection, prize in life etc.; || (sl.) £100,000. 2. ~ cake (contain-ing raisins, currants, etc.); ~ duff, plain flour pudding with raisins or currants; ~ pudding, boiled pudding of flour, bread-crumbs, suet, raisins, currants, eggs, spices, etc., eaten at Christmas, (also) ordinary suet-pudding with raisins; ~-pudding (Dalmatian or Spotted Coach) dog; ~-pudding stone (Geol.), conglome-rate of flint or other pebbles. [OE plûme, cf. G pflaume, Du. pruim, f. LL pruna (L prunum) f. late Gk prounon (Gk prounon)]

plu'mag|e (-ōō-), n. A bird's feathers. Hence (-)~ED²(-ijd) a. [OF (PLUME, -AGE)]

plumassier (plōōmaseŕ'), n. One who trades or works in ornamental feathers. [F (plumasse augment. of PLUME, see -IER)]

plumb¹(-m), n., a., & adv. 1. Ball of lead, esp. that attached to mason's ~-line (string for testing perpendicularity of wall etc., also fig.); out of ~, not vertical; sounding-lead, plummet; ~-rule, mason's ~-line attached to board. 2. adj. Vertical; (fig.) downright, sheer, as ~ nonsense; (Crick., of wicket) level, true. 3. adv. Vertically; (fig.) exactly, as points ~ in the same direction; *(sl.) quite, utterly, as ~ crazy, clean mad). [adj. & adv. f. n.] f. F plomb f. L plumbum lead]

plumb²(-m), v.t. & i. Sound (sea), measure (depth, lit. & fig.), with plummet, whence ~ING (-m¹-) a.; make vertical; (intr.) work as plumber. [f. prec.]

plumbāg'ō, n. Black lead, graphite, a form of carbon used for pencils etc. & mixed with clay for making crucibles; leadword, plant with ~-coloured flowers. Hence plumbā'ginous a. [L, gen. -ginis, f. plumbum lead]

plumb'beous, a. Of, like, lead; lead-glazed. [f. L plumbeus (as prec.)+-ous]

plumb'er (-mer), n. Artisan who fits & repairs pipes, cisterns, etc., with lead, zinc, or tin. So ~ERY(2, 3)(-mer-) n. [f. OF plumaber f. L plumbarius (as prec., see -ARY²)]

plumb'blic, a. (Chem.) combined with lead, so ~ir'EROUS a.; (Path.) due to presence of lead, so ~ISM(5) n. [f. L plumbum lead +-IC]

plume¹(-ōō-), n. Feather, esp. large one used for ornament; (fig.) borrowed ~s (referring to fable of jackdaw in pea-cock's ~s); ornamental feather or bunch of feathers or horsehair, esp. as attached to helmet or hat, or worn in hair, as court ~ (of ostrich feathers); (Zool.) feather-like part or formation. Hence ~TESS, ~LIKE, aa., ~LET n., (-ōōml-). [OF, f. L pluma down]

plume²(-ōō-), v.t. Furnish with plume(s); dress oneself with borrowed plumes; pride oneself (on esp. something trivial or to which one has no claim); (of bird) trim, dress, (feathers). [f. prec.]

plumm'er-block, n. (mech.). Metal case for supporting revolving shaft, with movable cover giving access to bearings. [?]

plumm'et, n. plumb-line; sounding-lead; (fig.) oppres-sive or obstructive weight; weight attached to fishing-line to keep float upright. [ME & OF plommet dim. as PLUMB¹]

plumm'y, a. Of, abounding in, plums; (colloq.) rich, good, desirable. [-Y²]

plump¹, a., & v.t. & i. 1. (Esp. of person or parts of body) full, rounded, fleshy, filled out. 2. vb. Make ~, fatten up; become ~, swell out or up. Hence ~LY² adv., ~NESS n., ~Y² a. [cf. Du. plomp blunt]

plump², v.i. & t., n., adv., & a. 1. Drop or plunge (t. & i.) with abrupt descent (down upon etc.); || vote for(one candidate alone, when one might vote for two). 2. n. Abrupt plunge, heavy fall. 3. adv. With sudden or heavy fall, as came ~ into the river; flatly, bluntly, as I told him ~, I lied ~. 4. adj. Direct, unqualified, as answer with a ~ No. [com.-LG: Du. plompen, G plumpen. prob. imit.]

|| plump³, n. (arch.). Company, troop, esp.~ of spears (spearmen); cluster. [?]

plum'per¹, n. Ball, disk, carried in mouth to fill out hollow cheeks. [PLUMP¹ +-ER¹]

plum'per², n. ||(vote of) one who plumps for candidate; down-right lie. [PLUMP²+-ER¹]

plu'mule (plōō-), n. Rudimentary stem of embryo plant, whence ~AR¹ a.; little feather of down, whence ~A'CEOUS (-āshus) a. [f. L plumula, dim. as PLUME¹]

plu'my (-ōō-), a. Plume-like; feathery; adorned with plumes. [-Y²]

plun'der, v.t., & n. 1. Rob (place, person) forcibly of goods, etc. as in war; rob systematically; steal, embezzle, (goods, or abs.). 2. n. Violent or dishonest ac-quisition of property; property so acquired; (sl.) profit, gain. Hence ~ER¹

n. [(n. f. vb) f. G *plündern* (plunder, *bl.*, bed-clothes etc.]

plun′derage, n. Plundering, esp. embezzling of goods on shipboard; spoil thus obtained. [-AGE]

plunge (-j), v.t. & i. & n. 1. Thrust violently (*into* liquid, cavity, etc.); (fig.) thrust (person etc. *into*, *in*, condition, action, etc.); sink (pot containing plant) **in** ground; throw oneself, dive, (*into* water, difficulty, discussion, etc.); enter impetuously (*into* room, *up*, *down*, stairs, etc.); (of ship) pitch; (sl.) gamble deeply, run into debt; *plunging fire* (from guns at higher level). 2. n. Plunging, dive, (~*bath*, large enough to dive into); (fig.) critical step, as *take the* ~. [f. OF *plungier* f. LL *plumbicare* heave the lead (*plumbum*)]

plun′ger (-j-), n. In vbl senses, esp.: parts of mechanism that work with plunging motion; (sl.) cavalryman; (sl.) gambler, speculator. [-ER¹]

plunk, v.t. & i. & n. 1. Throw or fall heavily or suddenly; *hit unexpectedly. 2. n. Sound made by plucking strings of musical instrument (v.i., make such sound). 3. *(colloq.). Heavy blow; dollar. [imit.]

plu′perfect (-ōō-), a. & n. (Tense) expressing action completed prior to some past point of time specified or implied (expr. in E by *had* with p.p. as *he had called*). [f. L *plus quam perfectum* more than perfect]

plur′al (-ŏŏr-), a. & n. (Form of noun, verb, etc.) denoting more than one (or, in languages with dual, more than two); more than one in number; ~*vote*, *voter*, *voting* (of one person in more than one constituency). Hence ~ITY² adv. [f. L *pluralis* (*plus* *pluris* more, see -AL)]

plur′alism (-ŏŏr-), n. Holding of more than one office, esp. benefice, at a time; (Philos.) system that recognizes more than one ultimate principle (cf. MONISM). So ~IST n., ~IS′TIC a. [-ISM]

plural′ity (-ŏŏr-), n. State of being plural; large number, multitude; holding of two or more benefices or offices; benefice, office, held with another; majority (of votes etc.). [f. OF *pluralite* f. LL *pluralitas* (as PLURAL, see -TY)]

plur′alize (-ŏŏr-), v.t. & i. Make plural, express in the plural; hold more than one benefice. [f. F *pluraliser* (as PLURAL, see -IZE]

pluri- (-ŏŏr-) in comb. = L *plus pluris* more, as: ~*lit′eral* (Heb. Gram.), having more than 3 letters in the root; ~*pres′ence*, presence in more than one place at same time; ~*ser′ial*, ~*ser′iate*, consisting of several series.

plus, prep., a., & n. 1. (As oral rendering of symbol +) with the addition of, as 3 ~ 4 (cf. MINUS); ~ 1 etc., golfer's handi-

cap; ~*fours*, long wide knickerbockers (so named because, to produce the overhang, the length is normally increased by four inches). 2. adj. Additional, extra; (Math.) positive; (Electr.) positive, positively electrified. 3. n. The symbol (+); additional quantity, positive quantity. [L.=more]

plush, n. Kind of cloth of silk, cotton, etc., with nap longer & softer than that of velvet; ~(pl.) footman's ~ breeches. Hence ~′Y² a. [f. F *pluche* *peluche* f. LL *pilucces* (cf. OSp. *peluza*) f. *pilus* hair]

plu′tarchy (plōō-, -kĭ), n. Plutocracy. [f. Gk *ploutos* wealth + -ARCHY -rule]

Plu′tō (-ō-), n. A more remote planet than Neptune (discovered 1930). [f. Gk *Ploutōn* ~, god of internal regions]

plutoc′racy (-ōō-), n. Rule of the wealthy; ruling class of wealthy persons. So **plu′tocrat** n. **plutocrat′ic** a. (~ōō-), **plu′tocrati̇cally** adv. (-CRACY)

plut′olatry (-ōō-), n. Worship of wealth. [f. Gk *ploutos* wealth, see -LATRY]

Plutō′nic (-ōō-), a. & n. Of Pluto, infernal; (Geol.) igneous, as ~ *rocks*, ~ *theory* (attributing most geological phenomena to action of internal heat, whence **Plu′tonism**(3), **Plu′tonist**(2), nn.); (n.) ~ rock. So **Plutō′nian** (-ōō-), a. [as PLUTO, -IC]

plutō′nium (-ōō-), n. Element arising from NEPTUNIUM. [f. PLUTO + -IUM]

plutoc′ratyly (-ōō-), n. Political economy. Hence **plutonom′ic** a. (-ōō-). [f.]

plu′vial (-ōō-), a. & n. Of rain, rainy, so ~OUS a.; (Geol.) caused by rain; (n., Eccl. Hist.) long cloak as ceremonial vestment. [(adj.) f. L *pluvialis* (*pluvia* rain, see -AL); (n.) f. med. L *pluviale* rain-cloak]

pluviom′eter (-ōō-), n. Rain-gauge. Hence ~OMET′RIC(AL) aa. [f. L *pluvia* rain + -0- + -METER]

ply¹, n. Fold, thickness, layer, of cloth etc.; strand of rope etc.; *two, 3, ~, having 2 etc. thicknesses or strands; (fig.) turn, tendency, esp. *take a ~* (*wood, windward*; (of vessel or its master, coach, etc.) go to & fro *between* (places); ∥(of boatman, porter, cabman) attend regularly for custom (*at* place). [aphetic form of APPLY]

ply², v.t. & i. Use, wield vigorously, (tool, weapon); *work at (one's business, task); supply (person etc.) persistently *with* (food etc.); assail vigorously (person *with* questions, arguments); (Naut.) work to windward; (of vessel or its master, coach, etc.) go to & fro *between* (places); ∥(of boatman, porter, cabman) attend regularly for custom (*at* place). [aphetic form of APPLY]

Plym′outh (-mŭth), n. ~ *Brethren*, religious body that arose at ~ c. 1830, with no formal creed & no official order of ministers, whence ~ISM(3), ~IST(2), ~ITE¹,(-mŭth-), nn.; ~ *Rock*, large breed

of domestic fowl of Amer. origin. [port in England]

pneumat'ic (-ū-), a. & n. **1.** Of, acting by means of, wind or air; ~ *tire* (inflated with air); ~ *dispatch*, conveyance of parcels etc. along tubes by compression or exhaustion of air; ~ *trough* (for collecting gases in jars over surface of water or mercury); containing, connected with, air-cavities esp. in bones of birds; spiritual. **2.** n. ~ tire, cycle with such tires; (pl.) science of mechanical properties of air or other elastic fluids or gases. Hence **pneumat'ic**ALLY adv., **pneumati'city** n. (-nĭ-). [f. L f. Gk *pneumatikos* (*pneuma* wind f. *pneō* breathe. see -IC)]

pneum'at|o- (n-) in comb. = Gk *pneuma -matos* air, breath, spirit, as: ~*ocyst*, air-sac in body of bird etc.; ~*ol'ogy*, theory of spiritual beings, doctrine of the Holy Spirit, psychology, so ~*olo'gical* a.; ~*om'eter*, instrument for measuring amount of air breathed at each inspiration; ~*ophore*, part of some compound hydrozoa containing air-cavity.

pneumogās'tric (n-), a. Of lungs & stomach; ~ *nerves*, tenth pair of cerebral nerves. [irreg. f. Gk *pneumon -monos* lung + GASTRIC]

pneumon'ia (n-), n. Inflammation of the substance of one (*single* ~) or both (*double* ~) lungs. So **pneumon'ic** a., **pneumoni'tis** n. (-nī-). [f. Gk *pneumonia* (*pneumōn -monos* lung f. *pneō* breathe)]

pō (pō), n. (pl. ~s). See POT 1.

poach 1, v.t. Cook (egg) by dropping it without shell into boiling water. Hence ~ER(2) n. [f. OF *pochier* (*poche* POKE 1)]

poach 2, v.t. & i. Thrust (stick, finger, etc. into etc.); trample, cut up (turf etc.) with hoofs; (of land) become sodden by being trampled; encroach, trespass, (*on person's preserves* often fig., lands, etc.), whence ~ER 1 n.; trespass on (land etc.), capture (game, fish) by illicit or unsportsmanlike methods; obtain (advantage, start, in race) by unfair means; (Lawn Tennis) strike (ball, or abs.) in partner's court. [prob.=POKE v.]

pŏch'ard (*also* -k-), n. European diving-bird with bright reddish-brown head & neck. [?]

pŏck, n. Eruptive spot esp. in smallpox. [OE *poc*, cf Du. *pok*, G *pocke*; see also POX]

pŏck'et 1, n. **1** Bag, sack, esp. as measure of hops (168 lb.) or wool (= half sack); small bag inserted in garment for carrying purse etc., as *coat, waistcoat, trouser, watch, ticket, ~*; (fig.) pecuniary resources, as *he will suffer in his ~*; *empty ~*, person without money; *be prepared to put your hand in your ~* (spend some money); *put one's pride in one's ~*, submit to doing something that mortifies it; *out-of-~ expenses*, actual outlay incurred; *am 5s. in ~*, have 5s. available; *am 5s. in ~, out*

of ~, *by the transaction* (have gained. lost); *has him in her ~* (completely under control); pouch at each corner & on each side of billiard-table into which balls are driven; cavity in earth filled with gold or other ore, whence ~Y 2 a.; cavity in rock esp. (Geol.) filled with foreign matter; (Mil.) isolated area occupied by enemy, forces occupying this, (*mopping up enemy ~s* or *~s of resistance*); = AIR 1 ~; (attrib.) of suitable size or shape for carrying in ~. **2.** ~ *battleship*, a ship armoured & equipped like, but smaller than, a battleship; ~-*book*, notebook. book-like case for papers etc. carried in ~; ||— *borough* (under control of one person or family); ~ *expenses* ~ *handkerchief* (carried in ~). ~-*money* (for occasional expenses, esp. that allowed to children); ~-*piece*, lucky coin carried in ~ as charm; ~-*pistol*, (joc.) ~ spirit-flask. Hence ~FUL n., ~LESS a. [ME *poket* f. Anglo-Norman *pokete* dim. f. F *poche* POKE 1]

pŏck'et 2, v.t. Put into one's pocket; confine as in pocket; hem in (competitor) in race; appropriate, usu. dishonestly; submit to (affront, injury); conceal, suppress, (feelings); (Billiards) drive (ball) into pocket. Hence ~ABLE a. [f. prec.]

pock-pudding. See POKE 1.

pŏcŏcuran'te (-koorahntā, -kūrănti), a. & n. Indifferent (person). Hence ~(e)ISM n. [It., = caring little]

pŏd 1, n. Socket of brace & bit. [?]

pŏd 2, n., & v.i. & t. (-dd-). **1** Long seed-vessel esp. of leguminous plants; cocoon of silkworm; case of locust's eggs; narrow-necked eel-net. **2.** vb. Bear ~s; shell (peas etc.). [?]

pŏd 3, n. & v.t. (-dd-). Small herd of seals or whales; (v.t.) drive (seals) into a ~. [?]

pŏd'agra (or podăg-), n. (med.). Gout, esp. in feet. Hence or cogn. **pŏd'agRAL, podăg'ric, pŏd'agrous**, aa. [L, f. Gk *podagra* (*pous podos* foot + *agra* catching)].

pŏdd'ed, a. Bearing pods; growing in pod.; (fig.) well-off, smug. [-ED 2]

pŏdĕstà (-tah'), n. Magistrate in Italian municipalities; (Hist.) chief magistrate in medieval Italian towns. [It., f. L *potestatem* power (*potis* able, see -TY]

pŏdge, n. (colloq.). Short fat person. Hence **pŏdg'Y** 2 a. [var. of PUDGE]

pŏd'ium, n. (pl. -*ia*). Continuous projecting base or pedestal; raised platform round arena of amphitheatre; continuous bench round room. [L, f. Gk *podiom* (*pous podos* foot)]

podophyll'in, n. (chem.). Yellow bitter resin of cathartic properties got from root of wild mandrake. [f. bot. L *podophyllum*, may-apple, wild mandrake, (Gk *pous podos* foot + *phullon* leaf)+-IN]

pō'ē-bīrd, n. =PARSON-bird. [f. Otaheitan wd for 'ear-rings', from tufts under throat]

po'em, n. A metrical composition, esp. of elevated character; elevated composition in prose or verse, as *prose* ~; (fig.) something (other than a composition of words) akin or compared to a ~, as *their lives are a* ~. [f. F *poème* f. L f. Gk *poiēma*=*poiēma* (*poieō* make)]

po'esy, n. (arch.). Art, composition, of poems; poems collectively. [f. OF *poesie* f. L f. Gk *poēsis* as prec.)]

po'et, n. Writer of poems; writer in verse, esp. one possessing high powers of imagination, expression, etc.; *Poets' Corner*, part of Westminster Abbey containing graves & monuments of several ~s, (joc.) part of newspaper devoted to poetry. Hence ~ESS¹ n. [f. OF *poete* f. L (-*ta*) prec.]

po'etas'ter, n. [-ASTER]

po'et'ical(l), aa. Of, proper to, poets or poetry; (usu. ~*ic*) having the good quality of poetry; (usu. ~*ical*) written in verse, as *~ical works*; *~ic* JUSTICE, LICENCE¹. Hence ~ICALLY adv., ~ICS n. [f. F *poetique* f. L f. Gk *po(i)ētikos* (as POET, see -IC & -AL)]

po'etry, n. Art, work, of the poet; elevated expression of elevated thought or feeling in metrical form; poems; quality (in any thing) that calls for poetical expression; *prose* ~, prose having all the qualities of poetry except metre. [f. OF *poetrie* f. LL *poetria* (as POET)]

po'etize, v.i. & t. Play the poet, compose poetry; treat poetically; celebrate in poetry. [f. F *poetiser* (as POET, see -IZE)]

po'go, n. (pl. ~s). Toy like stilt with spring, used to jump on. [?]

pogro'm, n. Organized massacre orig. or esp. of Jews in Russia. [Russ.]

poig'nant (poin-), a. Sharp, pungent, in taste or smell; painfully sharp, as *~ hunger, regret, sarcasm*; pleasantly piquant. Hence **poign'ancy** n., ~ly² adv., (poin-). [OF, part. of *poindre* prick f. L *pungere*]

poilu (see Ap.), n. (sl.). French soldier (nickname, cf. TOMMY). [F, lit. hairy, unshaven]

poinsett'ia, n. Plant with large scarlet floral leaves & small yellowish flowers. [f. J. R. *Poinsett*, discoverer]

point, n. **1.** Small dot on a surface. **2.** Stop or punctuation-mark (chiefly now in full *~*, full stop); dot, small stroke, used in Semitic languages to indicate vowels or distinguish consonants; dot separating integral from fractional parts in decimals, as *four ~ six* (4·6). **3.** Single item, detail, particular, as *we differ on these ~s, it is a ~ of conscience*, STRETCH a ~. **4.** *~ of war* (arch.), short phrase sounded on instrument as signal; *possession is nine ~s of the law* (nine-tenths, almost the whole); *give ~s* (odds) *to* (opponent in game); be superior to. **5.** Unit in appraising qualities of exhibit in show; unit of value in rationing (*on ~s*, rationed on a basis of such units); unit (of varying value) in quoting price of stocks etc. **6.** (print.). Unit of measurement for type bodies (British & U.S.A. 0·0138 in.). **7.** (geom.). That which has position but not magnitude, e.g. *~ of intersection of two lines*. **8.** Precise place or spot, as *~ of contact*; (Hunt.) spot to which straight run is made, such run, *~-to-~ race* (over course defined only by certain landmarks); (Her.) any of nine particular spots on shield used for determining position. **9.** Stage, degree, in progress or increase, esp. of temperature, as *boiling-, freezing-, ~* (at which thing boils etc.). **10.** Precise moment for action etc., as *when it came to the ~, he declined*; exact moment (of death etc.). **11.** Distinctive trait, characteristic, as *singing is not his strong ~*; the essential thing, the thing under discussion, as *that is just the ~, come to the ~*; *to the ~*, relevant(ly) to the purpose; *make a ~ of*, regard, treat, as essential; *carry one's ~*, secure one's object; *make a ~*, establish proposition, prove contention. **12.** (Also *~ lace*) thread lace made wholly with needle; (improp.) pillow lace imitating this. **13.** Sharp end of tool, weapon, pin, pen, etc. (*not to put too fine a ~ upon it*, to speak bluntly). **14.** Tip (*the ~ of the jaw* or *the ~*, in boxing, tip of chin as spot for knock-out blow); promontory, esp. in names, as *Start P~*; (Mil.) small leading party of advanced guard; (pl.) extremities of horse, as *bay with black ~s*. **15.** Sharp-pointed tool, esp. (; etching-needle; tine of deer's horn. **16.** || (On railway) tapering movable rail by which train is directed from one line to another; tapered division on backgammon board. **17.** (hist.). Tagged lace for lacing bodice, attaching hose to doublet, etc. **18.** (naut.). Short piece of cord at lower edge of sail for tying up a reel. **19.** *~s of the compass*, 32 equidistant ~s on compass (N, N by E, NNE, NE by N, NNE, NE by E, ENE, E by N, E by E, E by S, ESE, SE by E, SE by S, SSE, S by E, S by S, SSW, SW by S, SW, SW by W, WSW, W by S, W, W by N, WNW, NW by W, NW, NW by N, NNW, N by W), at angular intervals of 11° 15′. **20.** Salient feature of story, joke, etc., as *don't see the ~*; pungency, effectiveness, as *his remarks lack ~*. **21.** (crick.). (Position of) fieldsman placed more or less in line with popping-crease a short distance on off-side of batsman. **22.** (Of dog) act of pointing; esp. *make, come to, a ~*; *potatoes &c. to ~*, eat & bacon etc. to look at. **23.** *At all ~s*, in every part; *at the ~* (on the verge) of

death etc.; *in* ~, *apposite, as the case you take is not in* ~; *in* ~ (as a matter) *of fact*; (*upon the* ~, *on the very verge of* (action, doing); ~ *of* (thing that vitally affects one's) *honour*, esp. *the* ~ *of honour* (obligation to demand satisfaction, esp. by duel); ~ *of view*, position from which thing is viewed, (fig.) way of looking at a matter; ||~*-duty* (of constable stationed at particular ~ to regulate traffic etc.); ||~*-s'man*, man in charge of railway ~s, constable on ~-duty. [[partly thr. F *point, pointe*, & f. foll.] f. L *punctum*, neut. p.p. of *pungere* prick]

point[2], v.t. & i. **1.** Sharpen (pencil etc.). **2.** Punctuate (now rare); mark (Psalms etc.) with signs for chanting. **3.** Give point to (words, actions), as ~*ing his remarks with apt illustrations, to* ~ *a moral.* **4.** Fill in joints of (brickwork etc.) with mortar or cement smoothed with trowel. **5.** Prick in (manure), turn over (soil), with point of spade. **6.** Direct attention (*to, at,* lit. & fig.); ~ *out,* indicate, show, (thing, fact, *that* etc.); (of hound) indicate presence of (game, or abs.) by standing looking rigidly towards it; direct (finger, weapon, etc., *at*); direct attention of (person *to*); aim *at,* tend *towards.* [f. OF *pointer,* as prec.]

point'blank, a. & adv. **1.** (Of shot) fired horizontally, level; ~ *distance* (within which gun may be fired horizontally). **2.** adv. With direct aim, horizontally, in direct line; (fig.) directly, flatly, *as told him* ~ *it would not do*; offhand, *as refused it* ~. [prob. f. prec. + BLANK, i.e. white spot in centre of target]

point d'appui (pwăn dăpwē'), n. (mil.) Point of support, base, rallying-place. [F]

point'-device, a. & adv. (arch.). Perfectly correct, extremely neat or precise; (adv.) in ~ manner. [ME *at point devis* prob. f. OF *à point devis* to the point arranged, or arranged to the proper point (see POINT[1] & DEVICE)]

point'er, n. In vbl senses, esp.: index hand of clock, balance, etc.; rod used for pointing to words etc. on blackboard, map, etc.; (colloq.) hint; dog that on scenting game stands rigidly, with muzzle stretched towards it & usu. one foot raised; (pl.) two stars in Great Bear, straight line through which points nearly to pole-star. [-ER[1]]

point'ed, a. Having, sharpened to, a point; (of remark etc.) having point, penetrating, cutting; emphasized, made evident. Hence ~LY[2] adv., ~NESS n. [-ED[1,2]]

point'ing, n. In vbl senses, esp.: punctuation; filling up joints of brickwork etc. with cement, facing thus given to the joints; (Psalms etc.) system of signs for Anglican chanting. [-ING[1]]

point'less, a. Without a point, blunt; without point, meaningless; not having

scored a point. Hence ~LY[2] adv., ~NESS n. [-LESS]

poise (-z), v.t. & i., & n. **1.** Balance; hold suspended or supported; carry (one's head etc. in specified way); be balanced; hover in air etc. **2.** n. Equilibrium (lit. & fig.), carriage (of head etc.); state of indecision, suspense. [(vb) f. OF *peser* (st. *pois-*) f. LL *pesare* f. L *pensare* frequent. of *pendĕre pens-* weigh; (n.) f. OF *pois* f. pop. L *pesum* f. L *pensum* weight]

pois'on (-zn), n., & v.t. **1.** Substance that when introduced into or absorbed by a living organism destroys life or injures health, esp. (pop.) one that destroys life by rapid action & when taken in small quantity; *slow* ~ (of which repeated doses are injurious); *hate each other like* ~ (bitterly); *what's your* ~? (colloq.), *what will you have to drink*?; (fig.) baneful principle, doctrine, etc.; ~ *pen,* anonymous writer of libellous or scurrilous letter(s) to a private individual; ~ *tree, -wood,* kinds of tree or plant with ~*ous* properties. **2.** v.t. Administer ~ to (man, animal), kill or injure thus, whence ~ER[1] (-z-) n.; produce morbid effects in (blood etc.), whence (-)~ING[1] (-z-) n.; infect (air, water, etc.) with ~, smear (weapon) with ~ (esp. in p.p.); corrupt, pervert, (person, mind); destroy, spoil, (person's pleasure etc.); render (land, furnace, etc.) foul & unfit for its purpose by noxious application etc. Hence ~OUS a., ~OUSLY[2] adv., (-z-). (n.) [(vb) f. OF *poisoner* (as POTION, see -SON)]

poissarde (pwŏs'ärd), n. Parisian market-woman leading riots during first revolution; French fishwife. [F]

poke[1], v.t. & i. Thrust, push, (thing *in, up, down,* etc.) with hand, arm, point of stick, etc.; stir (fire) with poker; (colloq.) shut (oneself etc.) *up* in poky place; produce (hole etc. *in* thing) by poking; make thrusts with stick etc. (*at* etc.); thrust forward, esp. obtrusively, as (fig.) *don't* ~ *your nose into my affairs*; ~ *about, & pry,* be inquisitive; ~ *one in the ribs,* nudge him with finger or elbows; ~ *fun at,* assail with ridicule; *pry* (*into*); one's *head,* carry head thrust forward, stoop. [ME & Du. *poken,* cf. Du. *pook* dagger, & POACH[2]]

poke[2], n. Poking; thrust, nudge; device fastened on cattle etc. to prevent their breaking through fences; projecting brim or front of woman's bonnet or hat; ~ (*-bonnet*), bonnet with this, esp. as worn by Salvation Army women. [f. prec.]

pok'er[1], n., & v.t. **1.** Stiff metal rod with handle, for poking fire; (of person's car-

riage or manner) *as stiff as a* ~; ||(Oxt. & Camb.) hedel carrying mace or stave before Vice-Chancellor; kinds of instrument used in ~*-work*; *red-hot*, spikes of scarlet or yellow flowers; (joc. asseveration) *by the holy* ~; ~*-work*, burning of designs on white wood with heated implement. **2.** v.t. Execute (design) in, adorn (thing) with, ~*-work*. [-ER[1]]

pok'er[2], a. American card-game for two or more persons, each of whom if not bluffed into declaring his hand bets on its value; ~*-face*, impassive countenance appropriate to a ~*-player*; so ~*-faced*. [?]

pok'y, a. (Of place, room, etc.) confined, mean, shabby; (of occupation etc.) pottering, petty. [f. POKE[2]+-Y[2]]

pola'cre(=-aker), **-âcc'a**, n. Three-masted Mediterranean merchant vessel. [f. F *polacre -acque*, Polish, Pole, hist, unexpl.]

pōlar, a. & n. **1.** Of, near, either pole of the earth or of the celestial sphere; ~ (*white*) *bear*, *hare*; ~ *circles* (parallel to equator at distance of 23° 28' from the poles); ~ *distance*, angular distance of point on sphere from nearer pole. **2.** Having polarity, magnetic; having positive & negative electricity; (of molecules) symmetrically arranged in definite direction. **3.** (geom.). Relating to a pole; ~ *curve* (related in particular way to given curve & to fixed point called pole). **4.** (fig.). Analogous to the pole of the earth or to the pole-star; directly opposite in character. **5.** n. ~ *curve*. Hence ~ITY... adv. [f. med. L *polaris*(as POLE[3], see -AR[1])]

polari- in comb.=prec., as: *polarim'eter, polar'iscope*, instruments for showing polarization of light, so *polarimēt'ric, polariscop'ic*, &c., *polarim'etry* n.

pola'rity, n. Tendency of lodestone, magnetized bar, etc., to point with its extremities to the magnetic poles of earth; tendency of a body to place its mathematical axis in particular direction; possession of two poles having contrary qualities (also fig.); electrical condition of body as positive or negative; (fig.) magnetic attraction towards an object. [-ITY]

po'larize, v.t. & i. Modify the vibrations of (light, radiant heat, etc.) so that the ray exhibits different properties on different sides, opposite sides being alike & those at right angles showing maximum difference; (Magn., Electr.) give polarity to (bar, coil); (fig.) give arbitrary direction, special meaning, etc., to (word etc.); (also) give unity of direction to. Hence or cogn. ~ABLE a., ~A'TION, ~ER(2), nn. [-IZE]

po'latouche' (-ōōch), n. Small flying squirrel. [F., f. Russ. *poletuchii* flying]

pol'der, n. Piece of low-lying land reclaimed from sea or river in Netherlands. [Du.]

pōle[1], n., & v.t. **1.** Long slender rounded tapering piece of wood or (rarely) metal esp. as support for tent, telegraph wires, etc., as support for tent, telegraph wires, etc.; wooden shaft fitted to fore-carriage of vehicle & attached to yokes or collars of the horses etc.; *under bare* ~*s* (Naut.), with no sail set; *up the* ~ (sl.), in a fix (as measure); rod, perch, 5½ yds; ~*-jump-ing* (and (with help of ~) held in hands). **2.** v.t. Furnish with ~s; push, move, (off etc.) with ~. [(vb f. n.) OE *pāl*, cf. Du. *paal*, G *pfahl*, f. L *palus* stake]

pōle[2], n. *North*, *South*, ~, the two points in the celestial sphere about which the stars appear to revolve, (also) N. & S. extremities of earth's axis; *magnetic* ~, *points*, N. & S., in these extremitie where the magnetic needle dips vertically (Geom.)~*s of a circle of a sphere*, the two points in which axis of that circle cuts surface of sphere; (Geom.) fixed point to which others are referred; each of the two opposite points on surface of magnet at which magnetic forces are manifested, each of two terminal points (*positive, negative*,) of electric cell, battery, etc.; (Biol.) extremity of main axis of any spherical or oval organ; (fig.) each of two opposed principles etc.; ~*-star*, a star of Ursa Minor, now about 1° distant from N. ~ of heavens, (fig.) thing serving as guide, lodestar, centre of attraction. Hence ~WARD a., ~WARD(S) adv. [f. L f Gk *polos* pivot, axis, sky]

Pōle[3], n. Native of Poland. [G, f. Pol. *Polane*, f. *pole* field]

pol'e-axe(-ks), n., & v.t. Battle-axe, formerly used in naval warfare as weapon & for cutting ropes etc.; halbert; butch-(beast) with this. [ME *pollax*(POLL[1]+AXE)]

pōle'cat (-k-), n. ||Small dark-brown fetid carnivorous quadruped of weasel family, native of Europe. [ME *polcat* (*pol*-etym. dub.+CAT)]

Pol'emarch (-k), n. (Gk Hist.), Military commander-in-chief with varying civil functions; (in Athens) third archon orig with military functions. [f. Gk *polemarchos* (*polemos* war+-*archos* -ruler)]

polem'ic, a. & n. **1.** Controversial, disputatious. **2.** n. Controversial discussion; (pl.) practice of this, esp. in theology; controversialist. Hence ~AL a., ~ally[2] adv., *pōl'emize*(2) v.i. [f. Gk *polemikos* (*polemos* war, see -IC)]

pōlen'ta, n. Italian porridge made of barley, chestnut meal, etc. [It.]

police'(-ēs), n., & v.t. **1.** Civil administration, public order; department of government concerned with this; civil force responsible for maintaining public order; (as pl.) members of this, as *the* ~ *are on his track*; ~*-court* (of summary jurisdiction, dealing with charges preferred by the ~); ~*-magistrate* (presiding in ~*-court*); ~*-man*, member of ~ force; ||~*-office*,

headquarters of ~ in city or town; ~officer, ~man; ~ State, totalitarian one controlled by political ~; ~-station, office of local ~ force. **2.** v.t. Control (country etc.) by means of ~, furnish with ~; (fig.) keep order in, control. [F, f. med. L politia=L polītīa POLICY¹]

políclin'ic, n. Clinic in private houses, not in hospital; out-patients' department of hospital. [f. G políklinik (Gk polis city, CLINIC)]

pŏl'icy¹, n. Political sagacity; statecraft; prudent conduct, sagacity; craftiness; course of action adopted by government, party, etc.; || (Sc.) park round country seat etc.; Court of P~, legislative council in British Guiana. [f. OF policie f. L f. Gk politeia citizenship, polity f. polītēs citizen f. polis city); in Sc. sense (earlier=improvement of estate) confused w. L polītus polished]

pŏl'icy², n. (In full, ~ of assurance, insurance~) document containing contract of assurance or insurance, prob. f. med. L apodissa f. L f. Gk apodeixis demonstration, proof, f. APO(deiknumi show)]

pŏl'ygar, n. Feudal chief in S. India; predatory follower of such chief; ~-dog (variety from the ~ country). [ult. f. Tamil palaiyakkaran (palaiyam feudal estate)]

pŏl'iomyelit'is, n. (path.). Inflammation of the grey matter of the spinal cord; infantile paralysis. [f. Gk polios grey + MYELITIS]

pŏl'ish¹, v.t. & i. Make, become, smooth & glossy by friction; (fig.) make elegant or cultured, refine, (esp. in p.p.); smarten up; ~ off, finish off quickly. Hence ~ABLE a., ~ER¹ (l, 2) n. [f. F polir (see -ISH³) f. L polīre -īt-]

pŏl'ish², n. Smoothness, glossiness, produced by friction; such friction; substance used to produce smooth surface; (fig.) refinement. [f. prec.]

Pŏl'ish³, a. & n. **1.** Of Poland or the Poles. **2.** n. The language of Poland. [-ISH¹]

polite', a. Of refined manners, courteous; cultivated, cultured; well-bred; (of literature etc.) refined, elegant, as ~ letters. Hence ~LY² (-tl-) adv., ~NESS (-tn-) n. [f. L as POLISH¹]

pŏl'itic, a. & n. **1.** (Of person) sagacious, prudent, (of actions etc.) judicious, expedient; scheming, crafty; BODY¹ ~. **2.** n. pl. Science & art of government, political affairs or life, political principles, as what are his ~s?, talk ~s, is not practical ~s (is too remote to be worth discussing). Hence ~LY² adv. [f. F politique f. L f. Gk politikos (as POLICY¹, see -IC)]

polĭt'ical, a. & n. **1.** Of the State or its government; of public affairs; of politics; (of person) engaged in civil administration, as ~ agent, resident, (in India) government official advising ruler of native State; having an organized polity; belonging to, taking, a side in politics; ~ ECONOMY; ~ geography (dealing with boundaries & possessions of States); ~ verse, modern Greek verse composed by accent, not quantity, with accent on last syllable but one. **2.** n. ~ agent. Hence ~LY² adv. [-AL]

polĭti'cian (-shn), n. One skilled in politics, statesman; one interested or engaged in politics, esp. as profession; one who makes a trade of politics. [f. POLITIC, see -CIAN]

polĭt'icize, v.i. & t. Act the politician; engage in, talk, politics; give political character to. [-IZE]

polĭt'ico- in comb.=politically, political & ~, as ~economical, ~geographical, ~moral, ~social; ~religious, (usu.) pertaining to politics as influenced by religion. [as POLITIC]

pŏl'ity, n. Condition of civil order; form, process, of civil government; organized society, state. [f. obs. F politie, as POLICY¹]

pŏlk, v.i. Dance polka. [f. F polker as foll.]

pŏl'ka, n. **1.** Lively dance of Bohemian origin in binary time; music for this, usu. knitted. [F & G, etym. dub.] **2.** Woman's tight-fitting jacket,

pŏll¹, n. (Now dial. or joc.) human head; part of this on which hair grows, as grey, flaxen, ~; counting of voters esp. at parliamentary or other election; voting at election, as exclusion of women from the ~; number of votes recorded, as heavy, light, ~; ~-tax (levied on every person). [ME & obs. Du. polle top of head, cf. Da. puld, Sw. dial. pull]

pŏll², v.t. & i. **1.** (Arch.) crop the hair of; cut off top of (tree, plant), esp. make a pollard of; cut off horns of (cattle, esp. in p.p.); take the votes of, (pass.) have one's vote taken; (of candidate) receive (so many votes); give (vote); give one's vote. Hence ~ABLE a. [f. prec.]

pŏll³, a. & n. Polled, cut evenly; (in comb.) hornless, as ~beast, ~ox; (n.) ~ beast, esp. one of a breed of hornless oxen. [short for p.p. of prec.]

pŏll⁴, n. (P~) conventional proper name of parrot; ~ parrot, parrot, user of conventional phrases & arguments. [altered f. Moll familiar equivalent of Mary]

|| **pŏll⁵,** n. (Camb. Univ. sl.), The P~, the passmen; go out in the P~, take pass degree; (attrib.) ~ degree, man. [perh. f. POLLOI]

pŏll'ack, -ock, n. Sea-fish allied to cod. [?]

pŏll'am, n. Feudal estate of polīgar. [f. Tamil palaiyam]

pollan, n. Irish freshwater fish. [cf. Gael. *pollag*, Ir. *pollóg*, perh. f. Ir. *poll* in-land lake)]

poll'ard, n., & v.t. 1. Animal that has cast or lost its horns; ox, sheep, goat, of hornless variety; tree polled so as to produce close rounded head of young branches; bran sifted from flour, (techn.) fine bran sifted from flour. 2. v.t. Make a ~ of (tree), [POLL¹+-ARD]

poll'en, n., & v.t. 1. Fine powdery substance discharged from anther of flower, male element that fertilizes ovules. 2. v.t. Convey ~ to, cover with ~. Hence ~LESS, **pollin'ic**, **pollinif'erous**, aa. [L, gen. *-inis* = fine flour, dust]

pollicita'tion, n. (civil law). Promise not yet formally accepted, & therefore revocable. [f. L *pollicitatio* (*pollicitari* frequent. of *polliceri* promise, see -ATION)]

poll'inate, v.t. Besprinkle with pollen, shed pollen upon. Hence ~A'TION n. [-ATE³]

poll'oi, n. pl. Hoi ~, most people, the majority, the rabble. [Gk, lit. the many]

pollute' (-ōōt), v.t. Destroy the purity or sanctity of; make (water etc.) foul or filthy. So **pollu'tion** (-ōō-) n. [f. L *polluere -lut-* (*pol-* = *pro* forth + *luere* wash)]

pol'o, n. (Also P~). Game of Eastern origin like hockey played on horseback; ~-stick, long-handled mallet used; WATER-~. [native]

polonaise' (-āz), n. 1. Woman's dress consisting of bodice with skirt open from waist downwards. 2. (Music for) slow processional dance of Polish origin with three beats in bar. [F, fem. (as n.) of *polonais* Polish]

polo'nium, n. A radio-active metallic element forming the last stage before lead in the radio-active disintegration of radium. [f. med. L *Polonia* Poland, discoverer's country, -IUM]

polo'ny, n. (Also P~ sausage) sausage of partly cooked pork. [perh. f. med. L *Polonia* Poland, or f. *Bologna*]

pol'tergeist (-gīst), n. (Folklore & Spiritualism) noisy mischievous spirit. [G]

pol'tfoot, n. & a. (arch.), Club-foot(ed). [*poll* pestle, club, etym. du.², + FOOT]

poltroon', n. Spiritless coward. So ~ERY(4) n. [f. F *poltron* f. It. *poltrone* (*poltro* sluggard, lazy, f. obs. *poltro* bed perh. f. OHG *polstar* bolster, see -OON)]

poly-, in comb.=Gk *polus* many, as: ~adel'phous, with stamens united in 3 or more bundles; ~án'drian, woman with several husbands; ~án'dry, (Bot.) with numerous stamens; **pol'yandry**, plurality of husbands; ~atóm'ic, containing many (esp. replaceable hydrogen) atoms; ~autog'-raphy, lithography; ~bās'ic, (Chem.), having more than two bases or atoms of a base; ~carp'ellary, ~carp'ous, having several carpels; ~chaete (-kēt) a. & n., ~chaet'an, ~chaet'ous (-kēt-), aa. (worm) with many bristles on the foot-stumps; ~chroïte (-kr-), colouring-matter of saffron, exhibiting various colours under various reagents; ~dac'tyl a. & n., (animal) with more than normal number of fingers or toes; ~daem'onism, belief in many natural powers; ~gas'tric, with many stomachs; ~gen'esis, origination of a race or species from several independent ancestors or germs, so ~genĕt'ic, ~gen'ic, (Chem.) forming more than one compound with hydrogen etc. (Geol.)=~genous; **pol'ygenism**, theory of ~geny; **pol'ygenist**, holder of this, so ~genĭs'tic a.; **polyg'enous**, (Geol.) composed of various kinds of rock,(Chem.)=~genic; **pol'ygeny**, origination of mankind from several independent pairs of ancestors; **pol'ygram**, many-lined figure or design; **pol'ygraph**, kinds of copying apparatus, (also) writer of many or various works, so ~graph'ic a., **polyg'raphy** n.; **polyg'ynous** (-g-), of, practising, ~gyny, (Bot.) with many pistils, styles, or stigmas; **polyg'yny** (-g-), plurality of wives; **polyg'ynry** n. (usu. more than six)-sided solid, so ~hēd'ral, ~hēd'ric, aa.; **pol'ymer**, compound formed by simple chemical addition from a number of identical molecules each of which consists of a number of identical units; ~mēr'ic, (of compounds) composed of, differing in molecular weight; **polym'erism**, condition of being ~meric or ~merous; ~meriza'tion, formation of a ~mer by simple chemical addition of a number of identical smaller molecules; **pol'ymerize**, render ~meric or ~merous; **polym'erous** (Nat. Hist.), composed of many parts; ~morph'ic, ~morph'ous, ing in individuals, passing through successive variations, so ~morph'ism n.; ~nōm'ĭd a. & n. (Alg.), = MULTINOMIAL; ~ōn'ymous, called by several different names; ~ōn'ymy, use of different names for same thing; ~ŏp'ia, affection of the eyes in which one object appears as two or more; ~pet'alous, having separate petals; **polĭpĕt'agous**, voracious, (Zool.) feeding on various kinds of food; **pol'y-phone**, letter, symbol, standing for different sounds; ~phŏn'ĭc, (Philol.) standing for many-voiced, (Mus.) contrapuntal; **polĭphŏn'ous**, quality of being ~phonic, ~phony, (Mus.) counterpoint; ~phylĕt'ĭc, = ~genetic; **polĭphĭl'ous**, ~sĕp'alous, having separate perianth-leaves, sepals; **pol'y-stome** a. & n., (animal) with many mouths or suckers; ~syllăb'ĭc, (of languages) combining several words of a sentence into one; ~thăl'amous

(Nat. Hist.), many-chambered; *pol'ytype*, kind of stereotype, copy of engraving etc. made from this; ~ *zo'a*, class of compound invertebrates, so ~ *zō'ic* a.; ~ *zōn'al*, (of lighthouse lens) composed of several annular segments.

pŏlyăn'thus, n. Kinds of cultivated primula. [f. POLY- + Gk *anthos* flower]

pŏlychrōmăt'ic (-kr-), a. Many-coloured. [POLY-]

pŏl'ychrōme (-kr-), a. & n. 1. Painted, printed, decorated, in many colours. 2. n. Work of art in several colours, esp. coloured statue; varied colouring. Hence **pŏlychrōm'ic, pŏl'ychrōmous,** aa. [F, f. Gk *polukhrōmos* (POLY-, *khrōma* colour)]

pŏl'ychrŏmy (-kr-), n. Art of painting in several colours, esp. as applied to ancient pottery etc. [f. F *polychromie* (as prec., see -Y[1])]

pŏlyclin'ic, n. Clinic devoted to various diseases, general hospital. [POLY-; altered in sense & form f. POLICLINIC]

pŏlyg'amous, a. Having more than once, so **pŏlygăm'ic** a., ~IST, ~Y, nn.; (Zool.) having more than one mate; (Bot.) bearing some flowers with stamens only, some with pistils only, some with both, on same or on different plants. [f. late Gk *polugamos* (POLY- + *gamos* marrying)]

pŏl'yglŏt, a. & n. Of many languages; (person) speaking or writing several languages; (book, esp. Bible) written in several languages. Hence **pŏlyglŏtt'AL, pŏlyglŏtt'IC,** aa., ~ISM n. [f. Gk *poluglōttos (polu-* POLY- + *glōtta* tongue)]

pŏl'ygon, n. Figure (usu. plane rectilineal) with many (usu. more than four) angles or sides; ~ of forces, ~ illustrating theorem relating to number of forces acting at a point. Hence **pŏlyg'onAL** a., **pŏlyg'onALLY** adv. [f. L. f. Gk *polugōnon* neut. adj. as n. (*polu-* POLY- + *-gōnos* angled)]

pŏlyg'onum, n. Genus of plants including knotgrass, smakeweed, etc. [f. Gk *poluzonon (polu-* POLY- + *gonu* knee)]

pŏl'yhis'tor, n. Man of varied learning, great scholar. [f. Gk *poluistōr (polu-* POLY- + *histōr,* see HISTORY)]

pŏl'ymăth, n. = prec. So **pŏlym'athy**[1] n. [f. Gk *polumathēs (polu-* POLY- + *math-* st. of *manthanō* learn)]

Pŏlynē'sia (-sha), n. Small islands in Pacific Ocean east of Australia. Hence **~IAN** (-shn) a. [f. POLY- + Gk *nēsos* island]

pŏlyn'ia, n. Space of open water in midst of ice, esp. in arctic seas. [f. Russ. *polwinya (pole* field)]

pŏl'ype, n. Kinds of animal of low organization, e.g. hydra; individual of some compound organisms. [F (-pe), as POLY-PUS]

pŏl'ypary, n. Common stem or supporting structure of a colony of polyps. [-ary = -ARIUM]

pŏlyp'idom (or pŏl̄), n. = prec. [f. POLY-PUS + L *domus* house]

pŏl'ypīte, n. Individual polyp. [-TE[1]]

pŏl'ypŏd, a. & n. (Animal) with many feet. [f. F *polypode* f. Gk as POLYPUS]

pŏl'ypŏdy, n. Genus of ferns, esp. (common ~) species growing on moist rocks, walls, etc. [f. L f. Gk *polupodion,* as POLYPUS]

pŏl'ypoid, a. Of, like, a polyp or a polypus. So ~ous a. [-OID]

pŏl'ypus, n. (pl. -*pi*). Kinds of tumour, usu. with ramifications like tentacles. [L, f. Gk *polupous* cuttle-fish, polypus in nose (*polu-* POLY- + *pous -podos* footed)]

pŏlysyllăb'ic, a. (Of word) having many syllables; marked by polysyllables. Hence ~ICALLY adv. [f. med. L f. Gk *polusullabos* (as foll.) +-IC]

pŏlysyll'able, n. Polysyllabic word. [f. med. L *polysyllaba (vox word),* see POLY- & SYLLABLE]

pŏlytech'nic (-k-), a. & n. Dealing with, devoted to, various arts, as ~ *school; P~ (Institution),* technical school, esp. one in London orig. opened 1838. [f. F *polytechnique* f. Gk *polutekhnos (polu-* POLY- + *tekhnē* art), see -IC]

pŏl'ytheïsm, n. Belief in, worship of, many gods or more than one god. So ~IST n., ~is'TIC a. [f. F *polythéisme* f. Gk *polutheos* of many gods (*polu-* POLY- + *theos* god), see -ISM]

pŏm, n. Pomeranian dog. [abbr.]

pomace (pǔm'is), n. Mass of crushed apples in cider-making before or after juice is pressed out; any pulp; refuse of fish etc. after oil has been extracted, used as fertilizer. [ult. f. L *pomum* apple]

pomade (-ahd, -ăd), n. & v.t. 1. Scented ointment (perh. orig. from apples) for hair & skin of head. 2. v.t. Anoint with ~. [f. F *pommade* (*pomme* apple, POME, + -ADE]

Pŏm'ander (or pomăn[2]), n. (hist.). Ball of mixed aromatic substances carried in box, bag, etc., as preservative against infection; ball of gold, silver, etc., in which ~ was carried. [earlier *pomamber* f. OF *pomme d'ambre (pomme* apple, see prec., + *ambre* AMBER)]

Pomard', Pomm-, (-ahr), n. A red Burgundy wine. [~, village in France]

pomăt'um, n., & v.t. = POMADE. [f. L *pomum* apple +-*atum-* ATE[1]]

pŏm'bé, n. Intoxicating drink from various kinds of grain & fruit in Africa. [native]

pōme, n. (Bot.) succulent INFERIOR fruit with firm fleshy body enclosing carpels forming the core, e.g., apple, pear, quince, so *pomif'EROUS* a.; (poet.) apple; metal

For other words in *poly-* see POLY-.

ball. [OF, f. L *poma* pl. of *pomum* fruit, apple]

pŏme'grănăte (-ng-; *also* pŭm-), n. Fruit of a tree native to N. Africa & W. Asia, a large red berry about size of orange with tough golden or orange rind & acid reddish pulp enveloping seeds; the tree. [f. OF *pome grenade* f. L *granata* seeded (GRAIN, -ATE?)]

pŏm'elō (pŭm-), n. (pl. ~s), Small shad-dock or grape-fruit. [etym. dub.]

Pŏmerā'nian, a. & n. (Dog) of Pomerania on S. coast of Baltic; ~ (*dog*), small dog with long silky hair, pointed muzzle, & pricked ears. [-AN]

pŏm'fret, n. Fish found in Indian & Pacific Oceans, used as food. [prob. ult. f. Port. *pampo*]

|| **pŏm'fret-căke**, n. Liquorice cake made at Pontefract (earlier Pomfret) in Yorks. [f. place]

pŏm'iculture, n. Fruit-growing. [f. L *pomum* fruit + CULTURE]

Pommard. See POMARD.

pomm'el (pŭm-), n., & v.t. (-ll-). **1.** Rounded knob esp. at end of sword-hilt; upward projecting front part of saddle. **2.** v.t. Strike or beat (as) with ~; beat with fists. [(vb f. n.) f. OF *pomel* f. LL *pomellum* dim. as POME]

pŏmŏl'ŏgÿ, n. Science of fruit-growing. Hence **pŏmŏlo'gICAL** a., **~IST** n. [as POME + -LOGY]

Pŏmō'na, n. (Rom. Myth.) goddess of fruits; ~ *green* (in which yellow pre-dominates). [L]

pŏmp, n. Splendid display, splendour; (pl.) *the ~s & vanity of this wicked world*. [f. F *pompe* f. L f. Gk *pompē* pomp, procession.]

Pŏm'padour (-ōōr), n. Marquise de ~, mistress of Louis XV; (attrib., designat-ing) style of hair-dressing, cut of bodice, etc.

pŏm'panŏ, n. (pl. ~s), Kinds of W.-Ind. & N.-Amer. fish esteemed for food. [f. Sp. *pámpano*]

|| **Pŏm'pey**, n. (sl.) Portsmouth. [?]

pŏm'pier, a. ~ *ladder*, fireman's scaling ladder. [F, = fireman (as PUMP, see -IER)]

pŏm-pŏm, n. Long-range Maxim automa-tic quick-firing gun. [initial.]

pŏm'pon (& see Ap.), n. Ornamental tuft or bunch of ribbon, flowers, etc., on women's & children's hats & shoes; round tuft on soldier's cap, front of shako, etc. [F, etym. dub.]

pŏm'pous, a. Magnificent, splendid; self-important, consequential, (of language) inflated, so **pŏmpos'ITY** n. Hence **~LY²** adv., **~NESS** n. [F]

pŏn'ceau (-sō), n. Poppy colour; bright red. [F]

pŏn'chō, n. (pl. ~s), S.-Amer. cloak, ob-long piece of cloth with slit in middle for head; cape for bicycling etc. on same plan. [native]

pŏnd, n., & v.t. & i. **1.** Small body of still water artificially formed by hollowing or embanking; (joc.) the sea; cf. HERRING-~; ~-*life*, animals esp. invertebrates that live in ~s; ~*weed*, kinds of aquatic herb growing in still water. **2.** v.t. Hold back, dam up, (stream); (v.i., of water) form a pool or ~. [prob. var. of POUND²]

pŏn'dage, n. Capacity of pond; storage of water. [-AGE]

pŏn'der, v.t. & i. Weigh mentally, think over, (matter, how, etc.); think on, muse over. Hence **~ingLY²** adv. [f. OF *pon-derer* f. L *ponderare* (*pondus -eris* weight)]

pŏn'derable, a. Having appreciable weight (lit. & fig.). Hence **~ABIL'ITY** n. [f. LL *ponderabilis* (as prec., see -BLE)]

pŏnderā'tion, n. Weighing, balancing. (lit. & fig.). [f. L *ponderatio* (as prec., see -ATION)]

pŏn'derous, a. Heavy; unwieldy; labori-ous; (of style) dull, tedious. Hence or cogn. **pŏnderos'ITY**, **~NESS**, nn., **~LY²** adv. [f. F *pondéreux* f. L *ponderosus* (*pondus -eris* weight)]

pŏn'ĕ², n. (In Leader('s partner) in some card games. [L, 2nd sing. imperat. of *ponere* place]

pōne¹, n. Maize bread, esp. as made by N.-Amer. Indians; fine light bread made with milk, eggs, etc.; cake, loaf, of this. [native]

pŏngee (pŭnjē'), n. Soft unbleached kind of Chinese silk. [perh. f. Chin. *pun-chi* own loom]

pŏn gō (-ggō), n. (Early name for) a large anthropoid African ape; (improp.) orang-outang. [native]

pŏn'iard (-yard), n., & v.t. Dagger; (v.t.) stab with ~. [f. F *poignard* (*poing* fist f. L *pugnus*, -ARD)]

pŏns (-nz), n. ~ *āsinō'rum*, bridge of asses, i.e. 5th proposition of 1st book of Euclid, hence, anything found difficult by begin-ners; ~ (*Varō'lĭĭ*), band of nerve-fibres in brain [f. *Varolĭ*, Italian anatomist]. [L, = bridge]

pŏn'tĭfex, n. (pl. -*tĭfĭces* pr. -ēz), (Rom. Ant.) member of principal college of priests in Rome, P~ *maximus*, head of this; = foll. [L, f. *pons -ntis* bridge or Osc.-Umbr. *puntis* sacrifice + -*fex -ficis* f. *facere* make]

pŏn'tĭff, n. (Also *sovereign* ~) the Pope; bishop; chief priest. [f. F *pontife* f. prec.]

pŏntĭf'ical, n. (pl. -*tĭfĭces*) a. & n. **1.** Of, befitting, a pon-tiff. **2.** n. Office-book of Western Church containing forms for rites to be performed by bishops; (pl.) vestments & insignia of bishop. Hence **~LY²** adv. [f. L *ponti-ficalis* (as PONTIFEX, see -AL)]

pŏntĭf'icate, n. Office of pontifex, bishop,

or pope; period of this. [f. L pontificatus (as PONTIFEX, see -ATE¹)]

pon'tify, v.i. Play the pontiff, assume airs of infallibility. [f. F pontifier f. L pontificare (as PONTIFEX), see -FY]

pont-levé'is (or pawn levē'), n. Draw-bridge. [F]

pontoneer', -nier (-nē'), n. One who has charge of pontoons or of construction of a pontoon-bridge. [f. F pontonnier f. med. L pontonarius (as foll., see -EER)]

pontoon'¹, n., & v.t. Flat-bottomed boat used as ferry-boat etc.; one of several boats, hollow metal cylinders, etc. used to support temporary bridge; = CAISSON (not in first sense); (v.t.) cross (river) by means of ~s. [f. F ponton f. L ponto -onis (pons -ntis bridge, see -OON]

|| **pontoon'²,** n.=VINGT(ET)-UN. [prob. corruption]

pon'y, n. Horse of any small breed, esp. not more than 13 or (pop.) 14 hands; || (sl.) £25. [f. Sc. powney prob. f. OF poulenet little foal dim. of poulain f. LL pullanus (pullus foal)]

pood, n. Russian weight, 36 lb. avoirdupois. [f. Russ. pudu f. Norse pund POUND]

poo'dle, n., & v.t. Kinds of pet dog with long curling hair often clipped & shaved fantastically; (v.t.) clip & shave (dog) thus. [f. G pudel(hund) f. pudeln splash in water, cf. pudel PUDDLE]

poo'dle-fāk'er, n. (sl.) Youth too much given to tea-parties and ladies' society generally. So ~ing vbl. n. [?]

pooh (pōō, pōōh), int. expr. impatience or contempt. [imit. f. sound of blowing a thing away]

Pooh-Bah' (pōō'b-), n. Holder of many offices at once. [person in W. S. Gilbert's *The Mikado*]

pooh-pooh' (pōōpōō'), v.t. Express contempt for, make light of, as he ~ed the idea. [see POOH]

poo'ja, Var. of PUJA.

poo'ka, n. Hobgoblin. [Ir. púca]

poo'kroo, puku (pōō'krōō), n. Red antelope of S. Central Africa. [f. Zulu mpuku]

pool¹, n., & v.t. 1. Small body of still water, usu. of natural formation; puddle of any liquid; deep still place in river. 2. v.t. Make (hole) for insertion of wedge in quarrying, undermine (coal). [(vb f. n.) OE pōl, cf. Du. poel]

pool², n., & v.t. 1. (Cards) collective amount of players' stake & fines; receptacle for these. 2. || Game on billiard-table in which each player has ball of different colour with which he tries to pocket the others in fixed order, winner taking the whole stakes. 3. (Collective stakes in) a joint gambling venture. 4. Arrangement between competing parties by which prices are fixed & business divided to do away with competition. 5. Common fund, e.g. of the profits of separate firms; common supply of persons, commodities, etc. (also attrib., as ~ petrol). 6. v.t. Throw into common fund, share in common; (of transport organizations etc.) share (traffic, receipts). [(vb f. n.) prob. f. F poule hen (perh. in sense 'booty'), in E early assoc. with prec.]

poon, n. E.-Indian tree; ~-oil, oil from seeds of this, used in medicine & for lamps. [f. Cingalese puna]

poon'ah (-ă), n. ~ painting (on rice or other thin paper in imitation of oriental work); ~ brush, paper(used for this). [P~, Indian city]

poop¹, n., & v.t. 1. Stern of ship; aftermost & highest deck. 2. v.t. (Of wave) break over stern of (ship); (of ship) receive (wave) over stern. Hence (-)~ED² (-pt) a. [f. OF pupe f. LL puppa f. L puppis]

poop². See POPE³.

|| **poop³,** n. (sl.), Foolish insignificant person. [abbr. NINCOMPOOP]

poor, a. 1. Wanting means to procure comforts or necessaries of life, needy, indigent; ill supplied, deficient, (in a possession or quality); (of soil) unproductive; scanty, inadequate, less than is expected, as the crop was ~, a three weeks' holiday; paltry, sorry, as that is a ~ consolation; spiritless, despicable, as he is a ~ creature; humble, insignificant, (often iron. or joc., as in my ~ opinion); (expr. pity or sympathy) unfortunate, hapless, as ~ fellow!, the ~ child is incomsolable; the ~, (esp.) those dependent on charitable or parochial relief. 2. ~-box, money-box esp. in church for relief of the ~; ~-house, workhouse; ~-law (relating to support of paupers); ~-rate, rate, assessment, for relief or support of the ~; ~-spirited, timid, cowardly. [ME & OF povr(e)re, poure, f. L pauper]

poor'ly, adv. & pred. a. 1. Scantily, defectively; with no great success; meanly, contemptibly. 2. adj. Unwell, as he is (looking) very ~. [prec. + -LY¹; pred. a. prob. orig. adv.]

poor'ness, n. Defectiveness; lack of some good quality or constituent. [POOR + -NESS]

|| **poort** (pōōt), n. (S. Afr.). Pass, narrower than a nek. [Du., =gate(way)]

pop¹, v.i. & t. (-pp-). Make small quick explosive sound as of cork when drawn; let off (fire-arm etc.); fire gun (at bird etc.); put (thing in, out, down, etc.) quickly or suddenly; move, go, come, (in etc.) thus; put (question) abruptly, esp. (colloq.) ~ the question, propose marriage; (sl.) pawn; (sl.) ~ off (the hooks), die; *parch (maize) till it bursts open, ~ corn, maize so parched; ~ gun, child's toy gun shooting pellets by compression of air with piston, (derog.) inefficient fire-arm; ||~ shop, pawnbroker's shop. [imit.]

pop², n., adv., & int. 1. Abrupt explosive

sound; dot, spot, esp. in marking sheep etc.; (colloq.) effervescing drink, esp. ginger-beer or champagne; ||(sl.) pawn-ing, esp. *in* ~, in pawn. **2.** *int.* or *adv.* *Heard it go* (make the sound) ~; ~ *goes the weasel*, country dance in which dancer darted under arms of others to his part-ner. [as prec.]

pŏp³, n. (colloq.). Popular concert, as *Saturday* ~s. [abbr.]

||Pŏp⁴, n. Social & debating club (orig. meeting-place]

pŏp⁵. See POPPA.

pŏpe¹, n. **1.** Bishop of Rome as head of Roman Catholic Church; (fig.) person assuming or accredited with infallibility etc. **2.** P~ *Joan*, fabulous female ~, a card-game; ~'s *eye*, lymphatic gland surrounded with fat in middle of leg of mutton; ~'s *head*, round long-handled broom; ~'s *nose*, = PARSON'S *nose*. Hence ~DOM(-pd-) n., ~'LESS(-pl-) a. [OE papa f. eccl. L *papa* f. late Gk *papas*=Gk *pappas* father, cf. PAPA]

pŏpe², n. Parish priest of Greek Church in Russia, etc. [f. Russ. *popŭ* f. Gk as prec.]

pŏpe³, pŏp, n., & v.t. Place in thigh on which blow is painful or paralysing, esp. *take person's* ~, strike this; (v.t.) *take the* ~ *of*. [?]

pŏp'ery, n. Papal system, Roman Catho-lic religion. (in hostile use). [f. POPE¹ + -ERY]

*pŏp'-eyed (-id), a. (colloq.). Having bulging eyes; open-eyed (with surprise etc.). [pop¹]

pŏp'injay, n. (Arch.) parrot; (Hist.) figure of parrot on pole as mark to shoot at; conceited person; ||(dial.) green wood-pecker. [f. OF *papingay* etc., cf. med. Gk *papagas*, Arab. *babaghā*, prob. imit. & of Afr. orig.]

pŏp'ish, a. Of popery, papistical. Hence ~LY² adv. [f. POPE¹+-ISH¹]

pŏp'lar, n. Genus of large trees of rapid growth (often w. allusion to straightness of trunk); *trembling* ~, aspen. [f. OF *poplier* f. L *pōpulus*+-ER]

||Pŏp'larism, n. Policy of giving extra-vagant out-relief (as practised by the Poplar Board of Guardians c. 1920); any similar policy tending to raise the rates. [-ISM]

pŏp'lin, n. (Formerly) woven fabric of silk warp & worsted weft with corded surface; (now usu.) fabric of mercerized cotton. [f. F *popeline* f. It. *papalina*, from the papal town Avignon where it was made]

pŏplit'eal, a. Of the ham, of the hollow at back of knee, as ~ *artery*, ~ *tendons* (ham-strings). [f. L *poples -itis* ham, see -AL]

*pŏpp'a, *pŏp, n. Papa. [f. papa]

pŏpp'ĕt, n. ||(Now dial.) small person, esp. as term of endearment; lathe-head; (Naut.) short piece of wood for various purposes; ~*head*, lathe-head, ||(Mining) frame at top of shaft supporting pulleys for ropes used in hoisting. [earlier form of PUPPET]

pŏpp'ing, n. In vbl senses; (Crick.) ~-*crease* [pron.=striking-crease], line 4 feet in front of & parallel to wicket within which batsman must stand. [-ING¹]

pŏp'ple, v.i., & n. (Of water) tumble about, toss to & fro; (n.) rolling, tossing, ripple. Hence **pŏpp'ly²** a. [prob. imit.]

pŏpp'y, n. Genus of herbs having milky juice with narcotic properties & showy flowers of scarlet or other colour; *opium* ~, species from which opium is obtained; *Flanders poppies* (sacred to dead of 1914–18 war; also as name of those made for & sold on *P~ Day*, Saturday nearest 11 Nov.); ~-*head*, seed capsule of ~, (Archit.) ornamental top to end of church seat; *Shirley* ~, cultivated variety of common corn ~. [f. Shirley Vicarage, Croydon, where first produced]. Hence **pŏpp'ied²** (-pid) a. [OE *popæg*, *papopg*, ult. f. L *papaver*]

*pŏpp'ycŏck, n. (sl.). Nonsense. [f. Du. *pappekak*]

pŏp'sy-wŏpsy, n. An endearing appel-lation for a girl. [prob. f. *pop* abbr. of POPPET, with dim. suf.]

pŏp'ulace, n. The common people; the rabble. [F. f. It. *popolaccio* (*popolo* PEOPLE + -*accio* pejorative suf.)]

pŏp'ular, a. Of, carried on by, the people, as ~ *election, meetings, tumult*; adapted to the understanding, taste, or means, of the people, as *in* ~ *language*, ~ *science*, ~ (low) *prices*; liked, admired, by the people or by people generally or with specified class, as ~ *teachers, the* ~ *hero, is* ~ *with his men*, so **pŏpŭlā'rity** n.; prevalent among the people, as ~ *falla-cies*; ~ *front* (Pol.), party representing Left elements. Hence ~LY² adv. [f. L POPULAR+-AR²]

pŏp'ularize, v.t. Make popular, cause (person, principle, etc.) to be generally known or liked; extend (suffrage etc.) to the common people; present (technical subject etc.) in popular form. Hence ~A'TION n. [-IZE]

pŏp'ulate, v.t. Inhabit, form the popula-tion of, (country, town, etc.); supply with inhabitants, as *a densely* ~d *district*. [f. LL *populare* (as PEOPLE)]

pŏpŭlā'tion, n. Degree in which place is populated; total number of inhabitants, the people of a country etc. (*an A1, a C3,* ~, of highest, lowest efficiency, w. ref. to military classification of men in cate-gories ranging from A1 to C3); the in-habitants of a place (*the* ~ *turned out to welcome him*). [f. LL *populatio* (as prec., see -ATION)]

pŏp'ulist, n. Adherent of U.S. political party aiming at public control of rail-ways, graduated income-tax, etc., formed 1892; adherent of Russian political party

advocating collectivism. So ~ism n., ~is'tic a. [f. L *populus* PEOPLE + -IST]

pop'ulous, a. Thickly inhabited. Hence ~NESS n. [f. L *populōsus* as PEOPLE, see -OUS)]

por'beagle, n. Mackerel-shark. [Cornish dial., etym. dub.]

por'celain (-slin), n. Fine kind of earthenware with translucent body & transparent glaze; thing made of this; (fig., attrib.) delicate, fragile; ~ *shell*, cowrie; ~ *clay*, kaolin. Hence or cogn. ~OUS (-slin-), **por'cellāin'ous**, **por'cellān'ic**, **por'cel'lanous**, aa. [f. F *porcelaine* Venus shell, porcelain, f. It. *porcellana* (*porcella* dim. of *porco* hog f. L *porcus*, from resemblance of the shell to hog's back)]

por'celainize (-slin-), v.t. Convert (clay, shale, etc.) into porcelain or similar substance. [-IZE]

porch n. Covered approach to entrance of building; *the P*~, colonnade at Athens to which Zeno & his disciples resorted, (hence) Stoic school or philosophy (cf. ACADEMY, GARDEN, LYCEUM). Hence ~ED² (-cht), ~LESS, aa. [f. F *porche* f. L f. Gk *porticus*]

por'cine, a. Of or like swine. [F (-*ia*, -*ine*), f. L *porcinus* (*porcus* hog, see -INE¹)]

por'cupine, n. ‖ Rodent quadruped with body & tail covered with erectile spines: kinds of machine with many spikes or teeth, e.g. for heckling flax etc.; (attrib., applied to animals with spines etc.) ~ *ant-eater, crab, fish, grass*. Hence ~ISH¹, ~Y², aa. [f. OF *porc espin* ult. f. L *porcus* hog + *spina* thorn; earlier also *porkenpick* f. F *porc-épic* (L *spicus=spica* spike) & *porpentine*]

pore¹, n. Minute opening (esp. in skin of animal body) through which fluids may pass. [F, f. L f. Gk *poros* passage, pore]

pore², v.i. & t. ~ *over*, be absorbed in studying (book etc.), (fig.) meditate think intently upon, (subject); (arch.) look intently *at, on, over*; ~ *one's eyes out*, tire them by close reading. [ME *puren*, etym. dub.]

porge, v.t. (Jew. ritual). Make (slaughtered beast) ceremonially clean by removing sinews etc. Hence **por'ger¹** n. [prob. f. L as PURGE]

*****porg'y** (-g-), n. Perch-like salt-water fish; sea-bream (applied also, esp. locally, to many other fish). [perh. corruption of Amer.-Ind. wd, but cf. L *pagrus* bream]

por'ism (or pōr'-), n. (math.). Proposition concerned with the conditions that will render a given problem capable of innumerable solutions; corollary. So **por'ismat'ic**, **pōris'tic**, aa. [f. L f. Gk *porisma -matos* (*poriō* deduce f. *poros* way, see -M]

pork, n. Flesh (esp. fresh) of swine used as food; ~ *butcher*, one who slaughters pigs for sale; ~ *pie* (of minced etc. ~); ‖ ~ *pie hat* (with flat crown & brim turned

up all round). [f. F *porc* f. L *porcus* hog]

pork'er, n. Pig raised for food; young fattened hog, so **pork'et¹** n. [prec. + -ER¹]

pork'ling, n. Young or small pig. [-LING¹]

pork'y¹, a. Of, like, pork, esp. (colloq.) fleshy, fat. [-Y²]

porn'o- in comb. =Gk *pornē* harlot, as: ~*oc'racy*, dominant influence of harlots, esp. in government of Rome in 10th c.; ~*og'raphy*, description of manners etc. of harlots, treatment of obscene subjects in literature, such literature, so ~*og'rapher* n., ~*ograph'ic* a.

por'oplas'tic (or pōr'-), a. (surg.). (Of felt) both porous & plastic. [as PORE¹ + PLASTIC]

por'ous, a. Full of pores (lit. & fig.). Hence or cogn. **poros'ity**, ~NESS, nn. [-OUS]

por'phyry, n. Hard rock anciently quarried in Egypt, composed of crystals of white or red feldspar in red ground-mass; (Geol.) unstratified or igneous rock having homogeneous base in which crystals of one or more minerals are disseminated. [ult. f. Gk *porphuros* purple]

por'poise (-pus), n. Cetaceous mammal five feet long with blunt rounded snout. [f. OF *porpeis* f. L *porcus* hog + *piscis* fish]

por'ridge, n. Soft food made by stirring oatmeal or other meal or cereal in boiling water or milk; *keep one's breath to cool one's* ~, keep one's advice etc. for one's own use. [altered f. POTTAGE]

por'ringer (-j-), n. Small basin from which soup etc. is eaten esp. by children. [earlier *potager* (as PORRIDGE, see -ER¹); for -n- cf. *passenger, messenger*]

por'ra'ceous (-shus), a. Leek-green. [f. L *porraceus* (*porrum* leek, see -ACEOUS)]

porrect', v.t. (Nat. Hist.) stretch out (part of body); (Eccl. Law) tender, submit, (document). [f. L *porrigere -rect-* (*por-* PRO-+*regere* direct)]

por'rigin'ous a. [L, gen.-*g'inis*]

‖ **port¹**, n. Harbour (lit. & fig.); town, place, possessing harbour, esp. one where customs officers are stationed; (in proper names) *P~ Arthur, Said*, etc.; *P~ of London Authority*, corporate body set up by P~ of-London Act 1908 for control of ~ & docks; *free*~, one open for merchants of all nations to load & unload in, (also) exemption for imports or exports; *close* ~ (lying up river); CINQUE PORTS; ~ *admiral* (in command of naval ~). [OE, f. L *portus*]

port², n. ‖ Gate, gateway, esp. of walled town (chiefly Sc.); (Naut.) opening in side of ship for entrance, loading, etc., (also)~*hole*; (Mech.) aperture for passage of steam, water, etc.; curved mouthpiece of some bridle-bits; ~*hole*, aperture in ship's side for admission of light & air,

or (formerly) for pointing cannon through. [f. F *porte* f. L *porta* gate]

pôrt³, n. External deportment, carriage, bearing; (MIL.) position taken in porting arms. [F, as foll.]

pôrt⁴, v.t. (mil.). Carry (rifle, or other weapon) diagonally across & close to the body, with barrel etc., opposite middle of left shoulder, esp. *~ arms!* [f. F *porter*]

pôrt⁵, n. (naut.). **1.** (Also formerly *larboard*) left-hand side of ship looking forward (cf. STARBOARD), as *put the helm to ~* or *a~*; (attrib.) *on your ~* (left) *bow* etc. **2.** v.t. Turn (helm, or abs.) to left side of ship; (v.i., of ship) turn to her *~ side.* [etym. dub.; perh. f. PORT¹, vb earlier than n.]

pôrt⁶, n. Strong sweet dark-red (occas. white) wine of Portugal. [shortened f. *Oporto*, city of Portugal]

pôrtable, a. & n. Movable (article), convenient for carrying; (as n. ~) furnace, radio, etc. Hence **pôrtabĭl´itȳ** n. [f. F, f. L *portabilis*]

pôrtage, n. & v.t. **1.** Carrying; carriage; cost of this; *mariner's ~*, space allowed by him for own venture or to be let for freight in lieu of wages; carrying of boats or goods between two navigable waters, place at which this is necessary. **2.** v.t. Convey (boat, goods) over a ~. [F, as PORT¹, see -AGE]

pôrtal¹, n. Door(way), gate(way), esp. elaborate one. [obs. F, f. med. L *portale* neut. adj. as n. (*porta* gate, see -AL)]

pôrtal², a. (anat.). Of the *porta* or transverse fissure of the liver, as *~ vein* (conveying blood to liver). [f. med. L *porta-lis* as prec.]

pôrtamē´nto, n. (mus.). Gliding continuously from one pitch to another. [It.]

pôrtative, a. Serving to carry or support. [F (*-if, -ive*), f. L *portare* carry, see -IVE]

pôrtcŭll´is, n. Strong heavy grating sliding up & down in vertical grooves at sides of gateway in fortress etc. Hence **~ED²** (-ĭst) a. [f. OF *porte coleïce* sliding door (*porte* door f. L *porta*, see COULISSE)]

Pôrte, n. *The* (*Sublime* or *Ottoman*) ~ (hist.), Ottoman court at Constantinople, Turkish government to 1923. [F (*la Sublime ~*), transl. of Turk. title of central office of Ottoman government]

pôrte- in comb. = F *porte-* imperat. of *porter* carry in wds meaning '-case', '-holder', as : *porte(-crey)on*, metal tube or other holder for crayon; *~feuille* (-fû´y'e), portfolio; *~monnaie* (-mŏné'), flat leathern purse or pocket-book. [F]

porte-cochère (pŏrtkŏshâr'), n. Gateway & passage for vehicles through house into courtyard. [F]

pŏrtend´, v.t. Foreshow, foreshadow, as an omen; give warning of, as *this ~s a renewal of the conflict*. [f. L *portendere* (*por-* PRO-+*tendere* stretch)]

-tent- (por-

gy, marvellous thing. So **pŏrtĕn´tous** a., **pŏrtĕn´tously** adv. [f. L *portentum* as -TENT]

pŏrt´er¹, n. Gate-keeper, door-keeper. [ME & AF, f. LL *portarius* (*porta* door, see -ER²)]

pŏrt´er², n. **1.** Person employed to carry burdens, esp. servant of railway company who handles luggage, whence ~AGE (4) n. **2.** Dark-brown bitter beer brewed from charred or browned malt [perh. orig. made esp. for ~s]. **3.** **~-house*, house at which ~ etc. were retailed, (also) one where steaks, chops, etc. were served (~*house steak*, choice cut of beef from region of undercut); ||~*'s knot*, pad resting on shoulders & secured to fore-head used by ~s in carrying loads. [f. OF *porteour* f. L *portatorem* (*portare* carry, see -OR²)]

pŏrt´fire, n. Device for firing rockets, igniting explosives in mining, etc. [f. PORTE-+FIRE]

pŏrtfō´lĭō, n. (pl. ~s). Case for keeping loose sheets of paper, drawings, etc.; (fig.) office of minister of State. [f. It. *porta-foglio* (*porta* imperat. of *portare* carry + *foglio* leaf f. L *folium*)]

pŏrt´icō, n. (pl. ~s). Colonnade, roof supported by columns at regular intervals, usu. attached as porch to a building. [It., f. L *porticus* (*porta* door)]

pŏrtière (pŏrtyâr'), n. Curtain hung over door(way). [F, f. med. L *portaria* fem. adj. as n. (*porta* door, see -ARY²)]

pŏrt´ion, n., & v.t. **1.** Part, share; (in restaurants) amount of a dish served to a customer; dowry, whence ~LESS (-sho-) a.; one's destiny, one's lot; *a~*, some (of anything). **2.** v.t. Divide (thing) into shares, distribute out, assign (thing *to* person) as share; give dowry to. [vb f. F *portionner*; n. f. OF *porcion* f. L *por-tionem* (nom. *-io*) cogn. w. *pars* PART]

Pŏrt´land, n. (Used for) ~ *cement*, artificial cement manufactured from chalk and clay, in colour rather like ~ *stone*, a valuable building limestone obtained from the Isle of ~. [Dorsetshire peninsula]

pŏrt´ly, a. Bulky, corpulent; of stately appearance. Hence ~INESS n. [PORT³-LY¹]

pŏrtman´teau (-tō), n. (pl. ~s, -z, pr. -z). ||Leather trunk for clothes etc. opening into two equal parts; (fig.) factitious word blending the sounds & combining the meanings of two others (e.g. *slithy*=lithe & slimy). [f. F PORTE-(*manteau* MANTLE)]

pŏrtolā´nō (-lah-), n. (hist.). Book of sailing directions with description of harbours etc. [f. It. (*porto* PORT¹)]

pŏrt´rait (-rĭt), n. Likeness of person or animal, made by drawing, painting, photography, etc.; (fig.) type, similitude; verbal picture, graphic description. [F, p.p. as PORTRAY]

port′raitist (-rit-), n. One who paints or takes portraits. [-IST]

port′raiture (-richer), n. Portraying; portrait; graphic description. [OF (PORTRAIT+-URE)]

portray′, v.t. Make likeness of; describe graphically. Hence ~AL(2) n. [f. OF pourtraire f. L PRO(trahere tract- draw)]

port′reeve, n. (Hist.) chief officer of town or borough; (now) officer inferior to mayor in some towns. [OE port-gerēfa (port town. = PORT¹ or ²+-REEVE¹]

Port′uguese (-gēz), a. & n. (pl. same). (Native, language) of Portugal. [f. Port. portugués f. med. L portugalensis (see -ESE)]

pōse¹ (-z), v.t. & i., & n. 1. Lay down (assertion, claim, etc.); propound (question); place (artist's model etc.) in certain attitude; assume an attitude, esp. for artistic purposes; set up, give oneself out, as (connoisseur etc.); (Dominoes) place first domino on table. 2. n. Attitude of body or mind, esp. one assumed for effect, as his philanthropy is a mere ~; (Dominoes) posing, right to ~. [n. f. F pose; f. F poser f. L pausare PAUSE; some senses by confus. w. L ponere place, cf. COMPOSE]

pōse² (-z), v.t. Puzzle (person) with question or problem. [short for OPPOSE]

pōs′er (-z), n. In vbl senses of prec., esp. puzzling question or problem. [-ER¹]

pōseur′ (-zĕr, & see Ap.), n. Affected person. [F]

posh, a. (sl.). Smart, tiptop. [?]

pos′it (-z) v.t. Assume as fact, postulate; put in position, place, as ~ed by natural agency. [f. L ponere posit- place]

position (-z), n. & v.t. 1. Proposition, laying down of this. 2. Bodily posture; eastward (of priest at eucharist standing in front of altar & facing east). 3. Mental attitude, way of looking at question. 4. Place occupied by a thing; in, out of, ~ (proper place); (Mil.) place where troops are posted for strategical purposes (the ~ was stormed), the being advantageously placed (manoeuvring for ~); in a ~ to do, state, etc., enabled by circumstances or resources or information to. 5. Situation or vowel in syllable, esp. (Gk & L Pros.) of short vowel before two consonants, making the vowel metrically long. 6. (fig.). Situation in relation to other persons or things, as difficult (people of ~, esp. upper & upper-middle classes); official employment. 8. v.t. Place in ~, determine ~ of. [f. L positionem (as prec., see -ION)]

pos′itive (-z), a. & n. 1. Formally laid down, artificially instituted, (opp. to natural), as ~ laws. 2. Explicitly laid down, definite, admitting no question, as ~ assertion, have no ~ proof, here is proof

~. 3. (Of person) convinced, confident in opinion, cocksure. 4. (Gram.) ~(degree of) adjective, primary form expressing simple quality without comparison (cf. COMPARATIVE, SUPERLATIVE). 5. Absolute, not relative; (colloq.) downright, out-&-out, as he is a ~ nuisance. 6. Dealing only with matters of fact, practical, as ~ philosophy. 7. Marked by presence, not absence, of qualities (cf. NEGATIVE). 8. (Alg., of quantity) greater than zero (cf. NEGATIVE), ~ sign (+); tending in the direction naturally or arbitrarily taken as that of increase or progress, as clockwise rotation is ~. 9. ~ electricity (of the kind produced by rubbing glass with silk, vitreous); ~ pole, (of magnet) north-seeking pole, (of earth) south pole. 10. (Photog.) showing lights & shades as seen in nature. 11. ~ organ, small (orig. portable) organ used to supplement large one in church. 12. n. ~ degree, adjective, quantity, etc. Hence ~LY² adv., ~NESS, positiv′ITY, nn., (-z-). [F (-if, -ive), f. L positivus (as POSIT, see -IVE)]

pos′itiv|ism (-z-), n. Philosophical system of Auguste Comte, recognizing only positive facts & observable phenomena; religious system founded on this. So ~IST n., ~is′tic a. [f. F positivisme (as prec., see -ISM)]

pos′itron (-z-), n. A positive electron. [POSI(TIVE ELECTRON]

posol′ogy, n. Study of the quantities in which drugs should be administered. (Bentham's word for) mathematics. Hence posol′ogi′cal a. [f. F posologie f. Gk posos how great, see -LOGY]

poss′e, n. Body (of constables); strong force or company; ~ comitat′us, body of men above age of 15 in a county, whom sheriff may summon to repress riot etc.; in ~. [L, = to be able, (med. L power]

possess′ (-z), v.t. Hold as property, own; have (faculty, quality, etc.), as they ~ a special value for us; maintain (oneself, one's mind, soul, in patience etc.); (of demon or spirit) occupy, dominate, (person etc.), as ~ed by a devil, you are surely ~ed, (fig.) he is ~ed by or with this idea, what ~es you to think of such a thing?; like all ~ed, with the utmost vehemence or energy; ~ oneself of, take, get for one's own; be ~ed of, own, have. So ~OR² n., ~ORY a., (-zĕs-). [f. OF possess(i)er f. L possidēre -sess- (+sedēre sit]

posse′ssion (-zĕshn), n. Possessing; actual holding or occupancy; (Law) visible power of exercising such control as attaches to (but may exist apart from) lawful ownership; in ~, (of thing) possessed, (of person) possessing; ~ is nine points of the law; in ~ of, having in one's ~ (am in ~ of a fine specimen); in the ~ of, held by (the specimen is in the ~ of the present writer); rejoice in the ~ of, be so

fortunate as to possess; thing possessed; (pl.) property, wealth; subject territory, esp. foreign dominions; SELF-~. [OF. f. L *possessionem* (as prec., see -ION)]

possess'ive (poz-), a. & n. 1. Of possession; (Gram.) indicating possession, as ~ *pronoun* (e.g. *my, mine, his, ours*), ~ *case* (e.g. *John's, the baker's*). 2. n. ~ case or word. Hence ~**ly**² adv., ~**NESS** n. [f. L *possessivus* (as POSSESS, see -IVE)]

poss'et, n. Drink made of hot milk curdled with ale, wine, etc., often flavoured with spices etc., formerly much used as remedy for colds etc. [ME *poshote*, etym. dub.]

possib'ilist, n. Member of (esp. Spanish republican or French socialist) political party aiming at being at reforms only that are immediately practicable. [f. F *possibiliste* (as POSSIBLE, see -IST)]

possib'ility¹, n. State, fact, of being possible, as *the ~y of miracles, cannot by any ~y be in time, there is no ~y of his coming, it is within the range of ~y*; thing that may exist or happen, as *what are the ~ies?, there are three ~ies*. [f. F *possibilité* (as POSSIBLE, see -ITY)]

poss'ible, a. & n. 1. That can exist, be done, or happen, as *that is quite ~, it is scarcely ~ to say, it is ~ (that) he knows or may know, there are three ~ excuses (that may be made), provide against a ~ loss of men (that may occur), get all the assistance ~; come if (it is) ~, come as early as ~ (as you can)*; tolerable to deal with, reasonable, intelligible, etc., as *only one ~ man among them*. 2. n. Highest ~ score esp. in rifle practice, member of team, etc. (as in *P~s v. Probables*, teams for football etc. trial match); *do one's ~*, do all one can (imit. of F *faire son ~*). [F, f. L *possibilis* (*posse* be able, -BLE)]

poss'ibly, adv. In accordance with possibility, as *cannot ~ do it, how can I ~?*; perhaps, maybe, for all one knows to the contrary. [f. prec. + -LY²]

poss'um, n. (colloq.) = OPOSSUM; *play ~*, pretend to be ill (from ~'s habit of feigning death when attacked). [abbr.]

post¹, n., & v.t. 1. Stout piece of timber usu. cylindrical or square & of considerable length placed vertically as supportin building; stake, stout pole, for various purposes; BED¹, DOOR, GOAL, KING¹, LAMP, SIGN¹, ~; *starting, winning, ~*, ~ that marks starting, finishing, point in race. 2. Thick compact stratum of sandstone etc.; vertical mass of coal left as support in mine. 3. v.t. Stick (paper etc., usu. *up*) to~ or in prominent place, advertise (fact, thing, person) by placard; ~ (in colleges) place in list that is ~ed up the names of (unsuccessful students); publish name of (ship) as overdue or missing; placard (wall etc.) with bills. [(vb f. n.) OE, f. L *postis*]

post², n. & adv. 1. (hist.). One of a series of men stationed with horses along roads at intervals, the duty of each being to ride forward with letters to next stage; courier, letter-carrier, mail-cart. 2. ‖ A single dispatch of letters, letters so dispatched; letters taken from ~-office or pillar-box on one occasion, as *I missed the morning ~*: ‖ letters delivered at one house on one occasion, as *the ~ has come, had a heavy ~ today*; ‖ official conveyance of letters, parcels, etc., as *send it by ~*; GENERAL, PARCEL, PENNY, ~; ~-office or postal letter-box, as *take it to the ~; by return of ~*, (orig.) by same courier who brought the dispatch, (now) by next mail in opposite direction. 3. (As title of newspaper) *Evening P~* etc. 4. Sizes (about 20×16 in.) & kinds of writing-paper, as *ride ~*. With ~ express, with haste, as *ride ~*. 6. ‖ ~-*bag*, mail-bag; ‖ ~-*boat*, mail-boat, (also) boat conveying travellers between certain points; ‖ ~-*boy*, letter-carrier, (also) postilion; ‖ ~-*card*, card of regulation size for conveyance by ~; ~-*chaise* (-shy-), (Hist.) travelling carriage hired from stage to stage or drawn by horses so hired; ‖ ~-*free*, carried free of charge by ~, or with postage prepaid; ~-*haste*¹, n. (arch.) & adv. (with) great expedition; ~-*horse* &c. (with) great expedition; ~-*horse* letters etc.; ~-*man*, one who delivers or collects letters etc.; ~-*mark*, (n.) official mark stamped on letter, esp. one giving place, date, & hour, of dispatch or arrival, & serving to cancel stamp, (v.t.) mark (envelope etc.) with this; ~-*master*¹, official in charge of a ~-office, *P~-master General*, minister at head of the postal service; ~-*mastership*, office of ~-master; ~-*mistress*, woman in charge of a ~-office; ~-*office*, public department for conveyance of letters etc. by ~, house or shop where postal business is carried on (GENERAL *P~-Office*; ~-office ORDER, *savings-bank*, see SAVE¹); ~-*paid*, on which postage has been paid; ~-*town* (with ~-office, esp. one that is not sub-office of another). [f. F *poste* fem. f. It. f. L LL *posta=posita* fem. p.p. of *ponere posit-* place]

post³, v.i. & t. ‖ Travel with relays of horses; travel with haste, hurry; ‖ put (letter etc.) into post-office or letter-box for transmission; (Book-keep.) carry (entry) from auxiliary book to more formal one, esp. from day-book or journal to ledger, (also ~ up) complete (ledger etc.), thus, (fig., also ~ up) supply (person) with full information. [f. prec.]

post⁴, n. & v.t. 1. Place where soldier is stationed, (fig.) place of duty; position taken by body of soldiers, force occupying this; fort. 2. (Also *trading-~*) place occupied for purposes of trade esp. in uncivilized country. 3. Situation, employment. 4. (Naval, hist.) commission as

officer in command of vessel of 20 guns or more; ‖~ captain, holder of such commission (not of courtesy title or inferior command). **5.** (Mil.) first, last, ~, bugle-call giving notice of hour of retiring for night (last ~ also blown at mil. funerals). **6.** v.t. Place, station, (soldiers etc.); ‖(Mil., Nav.) appoint to a ~ or command. [(v b f. n.) f. F poste masc. f. It. posto f. L neut. p.p. as POST²]

pōst- in comb. = L post after, behind, in wds f. L; & as living E prefix, as: ~-class'ical, occurring later than the classical period of (esp. Greek & Roman) language, literature, or art; ~-commun'ion, part of eucharistic office following act of communion; ~-os'tal, behind a rib; ~-date', (v.t.) affix, assign, a later than the actual date to (document, event, etc.), (n., ~-date) such date; ~-diluv'ian, a. & n., (person) existing, occurring, after the Flood; ~-en'try, late or subsequent entry (for race, in book-keeping, etc.); ~-exil'ian, ~-exil'ic, subsequent to the Babylonian exile; ~-fix', (v.t.) append (letters at end of word, (n., ~fix) suffix; ~-glā'cial, subsequent to the glacial period; ~-grād'uate, (of course of study) carried on after graduation; ~-impre'ssionism, ~-impre'ssionism, artistic aims & methods (so named as a reaction from IMPRESSIONISM) directed to expressing rather the individual artist's than the ordinary observer's presumable conception of the objects represented; ~-lūde, concluding voluntary [after PRELUDE]; ~-millenn'ial, of the period following the millennium; ~-millenn'ialism, doctrine that second Advent will follow the millennium, so ~-millenn'ialist n.; ~-nā'tal, occurring after birth; ~-nup'tial, subsequent to marriage; ~-or'al, situated behind the mouth; ~-pli'ocene, of the formation immediately overlying the pliocene; ~-ter'tiary, of the formations subsequent to the tertiary.

pōs'tage, n. Amount charged for carriage of letter etc. by post, now usu. prepaid by ~ stamp, adhesive label to be affixed, or stamp embossed or impressed on envelope etc., having specified value. [-AGE]

pōs'tal, a. Of the POST² ; ~ ORDER²(3); ~ union, union of governments of various countries for regulation of international postage. [F (poste POST², see -AL)]

pōsteen', n. Afghan sheepskin greatcoat. [Pers. postīn]

pōs'ter, n. (Also bill-~) one who posts bills; placard displayed in public place; (Rugby ftb.) attempt at goal that passes straight over a post. [POST¹, ER¹]

pōste rēstante' (-tah-, & see Ap.), n. Department in post-office in which letters are kept till applied for. [F, prop.=remaining post]

pōstē'rior, a. & n. **1.** Later, coming after in series, order, or time, so ~ITY (-ŏ'r-) n.;

hinder, whence ~LY¹ adv., as viewed from behind. **2.** n. (in sing., or arch. in pl.). The buttocks. [L, compar. of posterus (post after)]

pōstē'rity, n. The descendants of any person; all succeeding generations, as deserves the gratitude of ~. [f. F postérité f. L posteritātem (as prec., see -TY)]

pōs'tern, n. (arch.). Back door; side way or entrance; (attrib.) ~ door, gate. [f. OF posterne, -rle, f. LL posterula dim. f. posterus coming after (post)]

pōst hōc ērg'ō prōp'ter hōc, L phr. (after this, therefore on account of this) ridiculing the tendency to confuse sequence with consequence.

pōst'humous (-tū-), a. (Of child) born after death of its father; (of book etc.) published after author's death; occurring after death. Hence ~LY¹ adv. [f. L postumus last (post after), in LL posth- by assoc. w. humus ground, +-OUS]

pōstiche' (-ēsh), n. & a. **1.** Something added after the completion of a work (esp. a superfluous or unsuitable addition to sculpture or architectural work); (shop) coil of false hair, false front. **2.** adj. Counterfeit, artificial. [F, = false f. It. posticcio]

pōstīc'ous, a. (bot.). Posterior, hinder. [f. L posticus (post behind) +-OUS]

pōs'til, n. (hist.). Marginal note, commentary, esp. on text of Scripture; commentary. [f. F postille f. med. L postilla etym. dub.]

pōstil'ion, -llion, (-lyon), n. One who rides the near horse of the leaders, or near horse when one pair only is used & there is no driver on box. [f. F postillon f. It. postiglione (posta POST² + compd suf.)]

pōstlim'inÿ, n. (Rom. Law) right of banished person or captive to resume civic privileges on return; (Internat. Law) restoration to their former state of persons & things taken in war, when they come again into the power of the nation they belonged to. [f. L POST(limīnium f. līmen -minis threshold]

pōst'master² (-mah-), n. See POST².
‖**pōst'master²** (-mah-), n. Scholar of Merton College, Oxford. Hence ~SHIP n. [?]

pōst merid'iem, adv. (usu. abbr. p.m., pr. pē ēm). After midday, as 3.30 p.m. [L]

pōst mōrt'em, adv., pōst-mōrt'em, a. & n. After death; (examination) made after death. [L]

pōst-ōb'it, a. & n. **1.** Taking effect after death. **2.** n. Bond securing to lender a sum to be paid on death of specified person from whom borrower has expectations. Hence ~LY¹ adv. [f. L post after + obitus -ūs decease f. OB(īre go) die]

pōstpōne' (or po-), v.t. & l. Put off, defer; treat (thing) as inferior in importance (to

another); (intr., Path., of ague etc.) be later in coming on. Hence ~MENT (-ni-) n. [f. L POST (ponere posit-place)]

postposi'tion (-z-), n. Particle, word, placed after another, usu. as enclitic, (e.g. -wards). Hence ~AL, **postpos'itive**, aa. (-z-). [as prec., see -ION]

postprăn'dial, a. (usu. joc.), After-dinner, as ~ oratory, eloquence. [f. POST- + L prandium lunch + -AL]

post'script, n. (or posk-), n. (abbr. P.S.), Additional paragraph esp. at end of letter after signature; || talk at the end of some B.B.C. news bulletins. [f. L postscriptum, neut. p.p. of POST(scribere write)]

pos'tulant, n. Candidate esp. for admission into religious order. [f (as foll., see -ANT]

pŏs'tulāte¹, n. Thing claimed or assumed as basis of reasoning, fundamental condition; pre-requisite; (Geom.) claim to take for granted the possibility of simple operation, e.g. of drawing straight line between any two points. [as foll., see -ATE²]

pŏs'tulāte², v.t. & i. Demand, require, claim, take for granted (thing, that, to do); stipulate for; (Eccl. Law) nominate or elect subject to superior sanction. So ~A'TION, ~ātŏr², n. [f. L postulare]

pŏs'tūre, n. & v.t. & i. 1. Carriage, attitude of body or mind; condition, state, (of affairs etc.); ~e-maker, acrobat, contortionist; ~e-master, teacher of calisthenics. 2. vb. Dispose the limbs of (person) in particular way; assume ~e (lit. & fig.). Hence ~AL, ~ER¹ n. [vb see -URE]

pos'y (-z-), n. (arch.). Short motto, line of verse etc., inscribed within ring (~ring) (also ~ nosegay. [= POESY]

pŏt, n. 1. Rounded vessel of earthenware, metal, or glass, for holding liquids or solids, as GLUE, ink, jam, WATER²ing, ~; such vessel for cooking; drinking-vessel of pewter etc.; contents of ~, as a ~ of porter, honey); COFFEE-~; TEA-~; (also, childish, pō)=CHAMBER-~; = FLOWER-~; vessel, usu. of silver, as prize in athletic sports, (sl.) any prize in these. 2. ~ paper or ~ (also poth), writing or printing paper 15½ in. × 12½, named from the orig. water-mark of a ~. 3. LOBSTER-~; CHIMNEY-~; mark of a ~. 4. Large sum, as made a ~ or ~s of money; (Racing sl.) large sum staked or betted, as put the ~ on, || (also) favourite. 5. Big ~ important person; the ~ calls the kettle black, person blames another for fault he too has; go to ~ (vulg.), be ruined or destroyed; make the ~ boil, make a living; keep the ~ boiling, make a living, keep anything going briskly; watched ~ never boils (proverb against worrying). 6. ~-ale, completely fermented wash in distillation; ~-belly, (person with) protuberant belly; ~-boiler, work of literature or art done merely to make a living; writer or artist who does this; ~-bound, (of plant) whose roots fill flower-~ & want room to expand (also fig.); ~-boy, ~-man, publican's assistant; ~ hat, bowler; ~-herb, any of those grown in kitchen-garden; ~-hole, (Geol.), deep cylindrical hole worn in rock, depression in road surface caused by traffic etc.; ~-hook, hook over fireplace for hanging ~ etc. on or for lifting hot ~, curved stroke in handwriting esp. as made in learning to write (cf. HANGER²); ~-house, ale-house; ~-hunter, sportsman who shoots anything he comes across, || person who takes part in contest merely for sake of prize, so ~-hunting n. & a.; ~ lead, black-lead esp. as used for hull of racing-yacht; ~ luck, whatever is to be had for a meal, as come & take ~ luck with us; ~-metal, stained glass coloured in melting ~ so that the colour pervades the whole; ~-shot, shot taken at game merely to provide a meal, shot aimed at animal etc. within easy reach; ~-still, kind of still; ~(opp. patent still) in which heat is applied directly & not by steam; ~-stone, granular variety of soapstone; ~-valiant, valiant because drunk, so ~ valour's ~val(i)or; householder voter (before 1832). [Naut., ~-walloper) cook's assistant [f. vval(l)op]

pŏt², v.t. & i. (-tt-). Place (butter, fish, minced meat, etc., usu. salted or seasoned) in pot or other vessel to preserve it (esp. in p.p., as ~ted ham); plant (plant) in pot; (Billiards) pocket; bag (game), kill (animal) by pot-shot; (intr.) shoot (at, or abs.); seize, secure. [f. prec.]

pŏt'able, a. & n. (usu. joc.). Drinkable; (n. pl.) drinkables. [F, f. LL potābilis (potare drink, see -BLE)]

pŏtamŏl'ogy n. [f. Gk potamos river + -rc] Of rivers. So **pŏtamŏl'ogy**

pŏt'ăsh, (arch.) **potăss'** (or pŏtä'), n. An alkaline substance, crude form of potassium carbonate, orig. got by lixiviating vegetable ashes & evaporating the solution in iron pots; caustic ~, hydroxide of potassium; PERMANGANATE of ~; ~-water, an aerated drink. [early mod. E pot-ashes, prob. f. Du. pot-asschen]

pŏtăss'ium, n. Soft white metallic element, one of the alkali metals, used mainly in compounds; ~ cyanide, white soluble crystalline salt, extremely poisonous; ~ PERMANGANATE. Hence **potăss'ic** a. [-IUM]

pŏtā'tion, n. Drinking; (usu. pl.) tippling; draught. So **pŏt'atory** a. [OF, f. L potātiōnem (potare drink, see -ATION)]

pŏtā'tō, n. (pl. ~-es). Plant with farinaceous tubers used for food; its tuber; sweet, Spanish, ~, tropical plant with

tuberous roots used for food; ~es & POINT¹; (sl.) *quite the* ~ (proper thing); (sl.) ~*boz*, ~*ring*, mouth; ~*ring*, Irish (usu. silver) ring used as stand for bowl etc. [f. Sp. *patata* var. of native Amer. *batata*]

poteen', -theen', n. Irish whiskey from illicit still. [f. Ir. *poitín* dim. of *pota* pot]

pot'ent, a. (Chiefly poet. or rhet.) powerful, mighty; (of reasons etc.) cogent: (of drugs etc.) strong. Hence or cogn.~ENCE, ~ENCY, nn., ~ently² adv. [f. L *potens* part. of *posse* be able]

pot'entate, n. Monarch, ruler. [f. L *potentatus -ūs* (as prec., see -ATE²)]

poten'tial (-shl), a. & n. 1. Capable of coming into being or action, latent; (Med.) ~ *cautery*, *corrosive* (agent producing same effect on skin as an actual one); (Gram.) ~ *mood*, subjunctive expressing possibility; (Electr.) ~ *difference*, difference in electric ~, usu. expressed in volts, between two separate bodies or points on a conductor, being properly the work done when a unit charge is moved from one to the other; ~ *energy* (existing in form, not as motion); (rare) powerful. 2. n.~ mood; (Electr.) degree of electrification, electrical pressure; possibility, as *reached its highest* ~; possible resources. Hence or cogn. ~ITY (-shiǎl´-) n., ~LY¹ (-shǎ-) adv. [f. LL *potentialis* (*potentia*, as POTENT, see -AL)]

poten'tialize (-sha-), v.t. Make potential; convert (energy) into potential condition. [-IZE]

poten'tiate (-shi-), v.t. Endow with power; make possible. [f. L as foll. +-ATE³]

potentiom'eter (-shi-), n. Instrument for measuring or adjusting electrical potential. [f. L *potentia* power (POTENT) +-o-+-METER]

potheen. See POTEEN.

poth'er (pŏdh-, pŭdh-), n., & v.t. & i. Choking smoke or cloud of dust; noise, din; verbal commotion, as *made a* ~ *about it*; display of sorrow; (v.t.) fluster, worry; (v.i.) make a fuss. [etym. dub.; prob. not connected w. *powder*]

pŏtichomān'ia (-sh-), n. (Craze for) imitation of Japanese porcelain by covering inner surface of glass vessels with designs on paper etc. [f. F *potichomanie* (*potiche* oriental porcelain, see -MANIA)]

pō'tion, n. Dose, draught, of liquid medicine or of poison. [OF, f. L *potionem* (*potus* drunk, see -ION)]

pot'latch, -lâtch(e), n. Tribal feast of N.-Amer. Indians given by aspirant to chiefship. [native]

pot-pourri (pōpŏorē´), n. Mixture of dried petals & spices kept in jar for its perfume; musical or literary medley. [F, lit. rotten pot]

∥ pŏt'shĕrd, n. (arch.). Broken piece of earthenware. [POT¹+SHERD]

pŏtt, n. Var. of POT¹ as applied to paper.

∥ pŏtt'age, n. (arch.). Soup, stew; (fig.) MESS¹ *of*~. [f. F *potage* (POT¹+-AGE)]

pŏtt'er¹, n. Maker of earthenware vessels; ~'s *wheel*, horizontal revolving disk in ~'s *lathe* (machine for moulding clay); ~'s *asthma*, *bronchitis*, etc. (caused by dust in the pottery industry). [OE *pottere* (-ER¹)]

pŏtt'er², v.i. & t. Work in feeble or desultory manner (*at*, *in*, subject or occupation): dawdle, loiter, (*about* etc.): trifle *away* (one's time etc.). [prob. f. obs. *pote* push, OE *potian*, etym. dub., +-ER⁵]

pŏtt'erý, n. Earthenware; potter's work or workshop; ∥ *the* P~*ies*, district in N. Staffordshire, seat of ~y industry. [f. F *poterie* (POT¹, -ERY)]

pŏt'tle, n. ∥(Arch.) measure for liquids, half gallon, pot etc. containing this; small wicker or chip basket for strawberries etc. [ME & OF *potel* (POT¹, see -LE)]

pŏtt'ō, n. (pl.~s). W.-Afr. lemur; kinkajou. [native]

pŏtt'ý, a. (sl.). Insignificant, trivial, (often ~ *little*; ~ *little State*, *details*; ~ *questions* in examination paper, easy to answer); foolish, crazy, mad *about* (someone or something). [?]

pouch¹, n. Small bag or detachable outside pocket; (arch.) purse; soldier's leathern ammunition bag; bag-like receptacle of marsupials etc.; bag-like cavity, esp. seed-vessel, in plant. Hence ~ED² (-ntd), ~Y² aa. [f. ONF *pouche* =OF *poche* POKE¹]

pouch², v.t. & i. Put into pouch; take possession of, pocket; ∥(sl.) give money to, tip; make (part of dress) hang like pouch, (intr., of such part) hang thus. [f. prec.]

poudrette' (pōō-), n. Manure of night-soil mixed with charcoal etc. [F, dim. of *poudre* POWDER]

pouf(fe) (pōōf), n. Woman's high roll or pad of hair; large cushion used as low seat; soft stuffed couch. [F]

poulpe (pōō-), n. Octopus or other cephalopod. [F (-*pe*), as POLYPUS]

poult (pōlt), n. Young of domestic fowl, turkey, pheasant, etc. [as PULLET]

poult-de-soie (pōōdeswah´), n. Fine corded (now usu. coloured) silk. [F, etym. dub.]

poul'terer (pōl-), n. Dealer in poultry. [f. earlier *poulter* (still in City Company's name) f. OF *pouletier* (as PULLET, see -ER²) +-ER¹]

poul'tice (pōl-), n., & v.t. 1. Soft mass of bread, linseed, etc., usu. made with boiling water & spread on muslin etc. & applied ~ *to*, or inflamed part. 2. v.t. Apply ~ to. [ult. f. L *puls* (also L *pult*-) thick pap etc.]

poul'trý (pōl-), n. Domestic fowls, e.g. barn-door fowls, ducks, geese, turkeys. [f. OF *pouletrie* (as PULLET, see -ERY)]

pounce¹, n., & v.t. & i. 1. Claw, talon, of bird of prey; pouncing, sudden swoop,

esp. *make a* ~. **2.** v.t. Swoop down upon, (fig.) seize eagerly *upon* (blunder etc.). [?]

pounce², n. & v.t. **1.** Fine powder used to prevent ink from spreading on unsized paper etc.; powdered charcoal etc. dusted over perforated pattern to transfer design to object beneath. **2.** v.t. Smooth (paper, surface of hat, etc.) with pumice or ~, transfer (design) by use of ~, dust (pattern) with ~. [vb f. F *poncer*) f. F *ponce* PUMICE]

poun′cet-box, n. (arch.). Small box with perforated lid for perfumes. [in Shak-spere: f. prec. hist. unexpl.]

pound¹, n., & v.i. **1.** (Abbr. *lb.*=L *libra*) measure of weight, 16 oz avoirdupois, 12 oz Troy; ~ *of flesh* (see Shak. *Merchant of Venice*, IV. 1); (also ~ *sterling*) a money of account, 20 shillings, formerly represented by gold sovereign, as *five* ~*s* (written £5 or 5*l.*), *five* ~ *ten* (shillings); (Hist.) ~ *Scots*, 1*s.* 8*d.*; *pay* 5*s. in the* ~ (for each ~ owing); PENNY *wise &* ~ *foolish*; ~, *five* ~, *note*, bank-note for one ~, five ~s; ~*cake*, rich cake containing a ~ (or equal weight) of each of chief ingredients; ~*-day* (on which a charity etc. receives contributions from all comers of a ~ of anything, e.g. £1, 1lb. of tea, etc.). **2.** v.i. ‖ Test the weight of coins by weighing the number that ought to weigh a ~. [vb f. n.) OE *pund*, cf. Du. &c. ab. of "*pondus*-di=*pondus*-*eris* weight]

pound², n., & v.t. **1.** Enclosure for detention of stray cattle or of distrained cattle or goods till redeemed; enclosure for animals; (fig.) place of confinement, (Hunt.) difficult position; ~*-lock* (with two gates, opp. *flash-lock* with one). **2.** v.t. Shut (cattle etc., often *up*) in ~; (Hunt.) ~ *the field*, (of barrier) be impassable, (of rider) clear fence that others cannot. [(vb f. n.) OE *pund(fald)*, etym. dub.]

pound³, v.t. & i. Crush, bruise, as with pestle; thump, pummel, with fists etc.; knock, beat, (thing *to pieces*, into a *jelly*, etc.); deliver heavy blows, fire heavy shot, (*at, on, away at*); walk, run, ride, make one's way, heavily (*along* etc.). [OE *pūnian*, cf. LG *pūn* chips of stone, Du. *puin* rubbish]

pound′age, n. Commission, fee, of so much per pound sterling; percentage of total earnings of a business, paid as wages; payment of so much per pound weight; TONNAGE *&* ~. [-AGE]

pound′er¹, n. In vbl senses, esp. instrument for pounding with or in, pestle, mortar. [POUND³+-ER¹]

pound′er², n. Thing that, gun carrying shot that, weighs a pound or(~) so many pounds, as *a three-*~; (~) thing worth, person possessing, so many pounds sterling. [POUND¹,-ER¹]

---

pour (pôr), v.t. & i. & n. **1.** Cause (liquid, (fig.) granular substance, light, etc.) to flow, discharge copiously, as ~ *hot water over it*, ~ *out the tea*, *rivers* ~*s itself into the sea*; ~ *oil upon troubled waters*, (fig.) calm disturbance with soothing words etc.; ~ *cold water on*, (fig.) discourage (person, zeal, plan); discharge (missiles, crowd from building, etc., often *forth*, *out*) copiously or in rapid succession; *send forth* or *out* (words, music, etc.); (intr. of liquids etc.) flow (usu. *forth*, *out*, *down*) in stream, (of rain) descend heavily, whence (fig.) events esp. misfortunes always come together; (fig.) come *in*, *out*, etc. abundantly, as *letters* ~ *in from all quarters*. **2.** n. Heavy fall of rain, downpour. [etym. dub.]

pour·boire (poorbwahr′), n. Gratuity, tip. [F, =*pour boire* (money) for drinking]

pour·parler (poor′pahlā′), n. (usn. in pl.). Informal discussion preliminary to negotiation. [F]

pour·point (poor-), n. (hist.). Stuffed & quilted doublet. [OF (*pour*-, p.p. of *pourpoindre* perforate (*pour* PRO-substituted for *par* PER-+*poindre* prick f. L *pungere*)]

poussette′ (pōō-), v.i., v.i., & n. Dance round one another with hands joined, as two couples in country dance; (n.) this action. [(vb f. n.) F, dim. of *pousse* PUSH]

pou·sto (poō-), n. Standing-place, basis of operation. [Gk *pou stō* where I may stand]

pout¹, n. Kinds of fish, as *whiting*, *eel*, *horn-*, ~. [OE -*pūta*, cf. Du. *puit*, G -*putte*]

pout², v.t., v.i., & n. **1.** Protrude (lips), protrude lips, (of lips) protrude, esp. as sign of displeasure, whence ~*ing·ly²* adv. **2.** n. Such protrusion; *in the* ~*s*, sulky. [n. f. vb) perh. cogn. w. prec., cf. Da. *pude* cushion, Sw. *puta* pad, dial. *puta* inflated]

pout′er, n. In vbl senses, esp.; kind of pigeon with great power of inflating crop; (also *whiting-pout*) kind of fish. [-ER¹]

pov′erty, n. Indigence, want; scarcity, deficiency, (*of*); deficiency *in* (a property); inferiority, (*of*), poorness, meanness; ~*-stricken*, poor, esp. fig., as *a* ~*-stricken language*. [f. OF *poverté* f. L *paupertatem* (as PAUPER, see -TY)]

pow′der, n., & v.t. **1.** Mass of dry particles or granules, dust; medicine in the form of ~; cosmetic ~ applied to face, skin, or hair; =GUN~, *as smell of* ~, experience of fighting, *food for* ~; *not worth* ~ *and shot*, not worth shooting, or fighting or striving for; (Games etc.) force put-into a blow or stroke (*no* ~ *behind the ball*; *put more* ~ *into it*). **2.** v.t. Sprinkle ~ on, cover (with ~ etc.); apply ~ to (hair,

or abs. in same sense); decorate (surface) with spots or small figures; (esp. in p.p.) reduce to ~(-ed sugar). **3.** ~ blue, ~ed smalt esp. for use in laundry, deep blue colour of this (also attrib.); ~down, down-feathers found in definite patches on some birds; ~flask, case for carrying gun~; ~horn, ~-flask orig. & esp. of horn; ~magazine, place where gun~ is stored; ~monkey (hist.), boy employed on board ship to carry ~ to guns; ~puff, soft pad usu. of down for applying ~ to skin. Hence ~iness n., ~y² a. [vb f. F poudrer f. F poudre f. L pulvis -eris]

pow'er, n. **1.** Ability to do or act, as will do all in my ~, has the ~ of changing its colour; particular faculty of body or mind, ~s. **2.** Vigour, energy, as more ~ to your elbow! (formula of encouragement or approval). **3.** Active property, as has a high heating~. **4.** Government, influence, authority, (over); in one's ~, under one's control; personal ascendancy (over); political ascendancy as the party now in ~. **5.** Authorization, delegated authority, as a bill to extend & define their ~s; ~ of ATTORNEY². **6.** Influential person, body, or thing; as the ~s that be, constituted authorities; State having international influence. **7.** Deity, as merciful~s!; sixth ORDER¹ of angels. **8.** (vulg.). Large number or amount, as saw a ~ of people, did a ~ of work. **9.** (Math.) third, tenth, etc., of a number, product obtained by multiplying the number into itself three, ten, etc., times, as the third ~ of 2 is 8. Instrument for applying energy to mechanical purposes, esp. the MECHANICAL~s, the simple MACHINES. **11.** Mechanical energy as opp. to hand-labour, esp. attrib., as ~lathe, -loom, -mill; ~-station (in which electric ~ is generated for distribution). **12.** Capacity for exerting mechanical force, esp. HORSE¹~, whence (-)~ED² (-erl) a. **13.** Magnifying capacity of lens. **14.** ~dive n. & v.i. (of aircraft) dive without shutting off engine(s); ~politics, diplomacy backed by the threat of force. [ME & OF poer (vb inf. as n.) f. LL potere = L posse be able (potis)]

pow'erful, a. Having great (physical or other) power or influence as ~ grasp, horse, mind, ally, book, speech, odour. Hence ~LY² adv. [-FUL]

pow'erless, a. Without power; wholly unable (to help etc.). Hence ~LY² adv., ~NESS n. [-LESS]

pow'wow, pawaw', n., **powwow',** v.i. & t. **1.** N.-Amer.-Indian medicine-man or sorcerer; magic ceremonial, conference, of N.-Amer. Indians; *political or other meeting; ||(sl.) conference of officers during army manoeuvres etc. **2.** v.i. Practise medicine or sorcery, hold a ~, *confer, discuss, (about etc.); (v.t.) doctor, treat with magic. [f. native powwaw, powah]

pox, n. Syphilis (colloq.); CHICKEN~, COWPOX; SMALL~. [= POCKs]

poz²(z)olana (pótsolahl'na, -tswo-), n. Volcanio ash found near Pozzuoli, much used for hydraulic cement. [It.]

praam. See PRAM¹.

prac'ticable, a. That can be done, feasible; (of road, passage, ford) that can be used or traversed; (Theatr., of window etc.) real, that can be used as such. Hence ~ABILITY, ~ABLENESS, nn., ~ably² adv. [f. F praticable (pratiquer PRACTISE, -ABLE)]

prac'tical, a. Of, concerned with, shown in, practice (cf. THEORETICAL), as ~ agriculture, philosophy; ~ JOKE; available useful, in practice; engaged in practice rather than speculation, as does not appeal to minds; that is such in effect though not nominally, virtual, as a ~ atheist, has ~ control. Hence ~ITY (-ăl'-), ~NESS, nn. [f. obs. practic n. & a. f. obs. F practique f LL f. Gk praktikos (prassō do, see -IC) + -AL]

prac'tically, adv. In a practical manner, virtually, almost, (~ nothing). [-LY²]

prac'tice, n. **1.** Habitual action or carrying on, as naval ~, the ~ of advertising, makes a ~ of cheating; method of legal procedure; habit, custom, (has been the regular ~). **2.** Repeated exercise in an art, handicraft, etc., as ~ makes perfect, in, out of, ~ (lately, not lately, practised in thing); is good ~ (improves skill); spell of this (ball, target, ~). **3.** Professiona work, business, or connexion, of lawyer or doctor, as has a large ~, sold his ~. **4.** (arch.). Scheming, (usu. underhand contrivance, artifice, (esp. in pl., & ef SHARP¹~). **5.** (Arith.) mode of finding value of given number of articles, or of quantity of commodity at given price when quantity or price or both are in several denominations. **6.** In ~, in the realm of action, as quite useless, would never work, in ~; put (plan, method in(to) ~, carry it out. [earlier practiz prob. f. PRACTISE, replacing earlier practiz as PRACTICAL]

prac'tician (-shn), n. Worker, practitioner. [f. obs. F practicien (as PRACTICAL see -ICIAN]

prac'tise, v.t. & i. Perform habitually, carry out in action, as ~e the same method, ~e what you preach; exercise, pursue, (profession; ~ing doctor, barrister, etc., engaged in actual practice, not retired not merely qualified); exercise oneself in or on (art, instrument, or abs.), as ~e the flute, the piano, music, running; exercise (person, oneself, in action or subject), whence ~ED¹ (-st) a.; (arch.) scheme, contrive, as when first we ~e to deceive; ~e (up)on, impose upon, take advantage of, (person, his credulity etc.). [f. OF

prac(ti)ser, -tiquer, f. med. L *practicare* (as PRACTICAL).]

practi'tioner (-sho-), n. Professional or practical worker, esp. in medicine & surgery; general ~ (in both medicine & surgery; abbr. G.P.). [erron. f. PRACTICIAN + -ER]

prae-, pref., the L form of PRE-, kept only in a few wds.

praeco'cial (shăl), a. (Of birds) whose young can feed themselves as soon as hatched. [as PRECOCIOUS, see -AL]

praemuni're, n. (law). Writ charging sheriff to summon person accused of asserting or maintaining papal jurisdiction in England; *Statute of* ~ (of 16th Richard II, on which the writ is based). [med. L, = L PRAEMONERE warn), the wds ~ *facias* warn (so-&-so to appear) occurring in the writ]

praenŏm'ĕn, n. (Rom. ant.) First or personal name (e.g. *Marcus Tullius Cicero*). [PRAE-, cf. COGNOMEN]

∥**praepŏs'tor, pre-**, (prtp-), n. (pub. school). = PREFECT, MONITOR. [syncop. f. *praepositor* f. L PRAE(*ponere posit-* place) set over, see -OR²; irreg. altered f. L p.p. -*tus*]

praet'or, n. (Rom. hist.) (Orig.) Roman general or emperor. [L, f. PRAE(*ire it-* go)]

praetor'ian, pre-, (prit-), a. & n. 1. Of a praetor; of the bodyguard of Roman general or emperor. 2. n. Man of ~ rank, soldier of ~ guard. [L L *praetorianus* (as prec., see -AN)]

prag'matism, n. Officiousness; pedantry; matter-of-fact treatment of things; (Philos.) doctrine that estimates any assertion solely by its practical bearing upon human interests. So ~IST n.

prag'matize, v.t. Represent as real; rationalize (myth). [as prec., see -IZE]

prair'ie, n. Large treeless tract of level or undulating grass-land; ~-*chicken*, -*hen*, N.-Amer. kind of grouse; ~-*dog*, N.-Amer. rodent with bark like dog's; ~-*oyster*, raw egg swallowed whole; ~-*schooner*, early emigrant's white-tilted wagon used in crossing the ~s. [F, f. Rom. +*pratāria* (L *pratum* meadow, see -ARY²)]

praise (-z), v.t. & n. 1. Express warm approbation of, commend the merits of, (person, thing); glorify, extol the attributes of, (God etc.). 2. n. Praising, commendation, as *won high* ~; *was loud in his* ~s. Hence ~FUL a., ~worthy a. [(n. f. vb) f. OF *preiser* price, prize, praise, f. L L *preciare, pret-*, (*pretium* price)]

praise'worthy (prāz'wēdhi), a. Worthy of praise, commendable, (often patronizing). Hence ~ILY² adv., ~INESS n.

Pra'krit (prah-), n. Any of the dialects of N. & Central India existing alongside of *prakṛta* unrefined). [f. Skr.

pra'line (prah-), n. Sweetmeat made by browning nuts in boiling sugar. [F (*Praslin*, surname)]

pram¹, pram, (prahm), n. Flat-bottomed boat used in Baltic etc. for shipping cargo etc.; flat-bottomed boat mounted with guns; Scandinavian ship's boat corresp. to dinghy. [Du.-(-*am*)]

pram², n. (colloq.) = Perambulator; milkman's handcart. [abbr. of PERAMBULATOR]

pran'cle (-ah-), v.i. & n. 1. (Of horse) rise by springing from hind legs; cause (horse) to do this; (fig.) walk, behave, in elated or arrogant manner (esp. ~*ing proconsuls*). 2. n. ~ing, ~ing movement. [?]

prān'dial, a. (joc.) Of dinner. [f. L *prandium* lunch, see -AL]

∥**prang**, v.t. (R.A.F sl.). Bomb (target) successfully. [?]

prank¹, n. Mad frolic, practical joke; (fig. of machinery etc.), erratic action. Hence ~FUL, ~ISH, aa., ~ishNESS n. [?]

prank², v.t. & i. Dress, deck, (person, oneself, thing, often *out*); adorn, spangle, (field *with* flowers etc.); (v.i.) show oneself off. [cf. Du. *pronken*, G *prunken*, show

prase (-z), n. Kind of leek-green translucent quartz. [F f. L f. Gk *prasios* leek-green (*prason* leek)]

prate, v.i. & t., & n. 1. Chatter; talk too much; blab; tell, say, (thing) in ~ing manner. 2. n. ~ing, idle talk. Hence ~ER¹ n., ~ingLY² a. [(n. f. vb) f. 15th c., cf. Du. *praten*, Sw. *prata*, Da. *prate*]

∥**prāt'incōle** (-ngk-), n. Bird like swallow in appearance & habits, & allied to plover. [f. L *pratum* meadow+*incola* inhabitant]

prăt'ique (-ēk, or pratēk-), n. Licence to hold intercourse with port, granted to ship after quarantine or on showing clean bill of health. [F, = PRACTICE, intercourse]

prăt'tle, v.i. & t., & n. 1. Talk in childish or artless fashion; say (thing) thus. 2. n. Childish chatter, small talk. Hence ~R¹ n., prătt'ling² a. [dim. f. PRATE+-LE(3)]

prăv'ity, n. (rare). Depravity; ∥badness, corruptness, (of food etc.). [f. L *pravitas* (*pravus* crooked, bad, see -TY]

prawn, n., & v.i. Crustacean like large

shrimp; (v.i.) fish for ~s, so ~ING[1] n. [ME *pra(y)ne*, etym. dub.]

prax'is, n. Accepted practice, custom; (Gram.) set of examples for practice. [Gk. = doing, f. *prassō* do]

pray, v.t. & i. Make devout supplication to (God, object of worship); beseech earnestly (God, person, for thing, to do, *that*); ask earnestly for (permission etc.); engage in prayer, make entreaty, (*to God, to person, for thing, for or on behalf of person, to do, that*); ~ (I beg you to) consider etc.; *what is the use of that*, (tell me)?; ~ *in aid of* (arch.; *in adv.*, not prep.), summon to one's support. [f. OF *preier* f. LL *precare* (L ~*ri*)]

prayer[1] (prâr), n. Solemn request to God or object of worship; formula used in praying, e.g. LORD'S ~; form of divine service consisting largely of ~s, as *morning* ~, *evening* ~, *family* ~s; action, practice, of praying; entreaty to a person; thing prayed for; ~*book*, book of forms of ~, esp. Book of Common P.~, public liturgy of Church of England; ~*meeting*, religious meeting at which several persons offer ~; ~*wheel*, revolving cylindrical box inscribed with or containing ~s, used esp. by Buddhists of Tibet. Hence ~FUL (âr-), ~LESS (âr-), aa., ~'fully[2], ~'lessly[2] advv., ~'fulness, ~'lessness, nn. [ME & OF *preiere* f. med. L *precaria* fem. sing. (orig. neut. pl.) adj. as n. (as PRECARIOUS)]

pray'er[2], n. One who prays. [-ER[1]]

prē-, pref., = med. L *pre-*, L *prae-*. Deliver sermon or L *prae-* (in time, place, order, degree, or importance). Besides wds of L orig. *pre-* as living E pref. forms unlimited vbs & vbl nn., only the more important of which are given in their alphabetical place. In secondary wds such as those here classified, the pron. is (prē-) & the hyphen is usu. written. 1. Vbs & vbl nn. w. sense 'do, doing, thing done, beforehand', as: ~*acquaint'*; ~*admin'ister*; ~*admon'ish*, ~*acquaint'ance*; ~*admi'ssion*; ~*admoni'tion*; ~*announce*; ~*admoni'tion*; ~*advise'*; ~*arrange*; ~*advise'ment*; ~*appoint'(ment)*; ~*arrange'(ment)*; ‖ ~*aud'ience*, right of (lawyer at Bar) to be heard before another'; ~*cal'culate*, ~*calcula'tion*; ~*cal'culable*, ~*calcula'tion*; ~*concert'*; ~*condemn'*; ~*compose'*; ~*concert'*; ~*condemn'*; ~*condi'tion*, prior condition, one that must be fulfilled beforehand; ~*consid'er*, ~*considera'tion*; ~*contract'* v.i., ~*con'tract* n.; ~*decease'*, ~*con'tract* (n.) such death; ~*define'*; (person), (n.) such death; ~*define'*; ~*digest'*, render food easily digestible before introduction into stomach (also fig.), ~*dige'stion*, this process; ~*doom'* v.t., ~*elect'*, ~*elec'tion* (see also in 2); ~*engage'(ment)*; ~*estab'lish*; ~*exist'* v.t., ~*es'timate* n.; ~*exist'* v.t., ~*es'timate* v.t., ~*es'timate* a.; ~*exist'ence* n., so ~*exist'ent* a.; ~*in'dicate*; ~*in'timate* v.t.; ~*kim'it* v.t.; ~*mo'tion*, (as

motion given beforehand, esp. divine act as determining the will of the creature; ~*ordain'*, appoint beforehand, fore-ordain; ~*percep'tion*. 2. Adj. & nn. w. sense '(person etc.) existing, dating from, before the time of—', as: ~*adam'ic* a., ~*ad'amite* n. & a., (one of supposed race) existing before the time of Adam; ~*Chris'tian*, before Christ(ianity); ~*class'ical*, before the classical age (usu. of Greek & Roman literature); ~*con'queror*, ~*con'quest*, before the Norman conquest; ~*con'scious*, antecedent to consciousness; ~*elec'tion*, (of acts, promises) done, given, before election; ~*exil'ian*, ~*exil'ic*, before (usu. the Babylonian) exile; ~*gla'cial*, before the glacial period; ~*hum'an*, existing before man existed; ~*millenn'ial(ism)*, (belief that Christ's Second Advent will occur) before the millennium, so ~*millenn'ium*, ~*millenn'ialist*; ~*nat'al*, existing, occurring, before birth; ~*pran'dial*, before-dinner; ~*scientif'ic*, before the rise of modern science; ~*war'* adj. (as ~*war prices*) & (vulg.) adv. (as *that happened* ~*war*) before the war. 3. Adj., chiefly anat. & zool., w. sense 'situated in front of', as: ~*cord'ial*, in front of or about the heart; ~*cos'tal*, in front of the ribs; ~*dors'al*, anterior to the dorsal region; ~*fron'tal*, in front of frontal bone of skull, in fore part of frontal lobe of brain; ~*maxill'ary*, in front of the upper jaw; ~*oc'ular*, in front of the eye.

preach, v.i. & t. & n. Deliver sermon or religious address, deliver (sermon); give moral advice in obtrusive way; proclaim, expound, (the Gospel, Christ, *that*, etc.) in public discourse; advocate, inculcate, (quality, conduct, principle, etc.) thus; ~*up*, extol, commend; ~*down*, disparage, put down by ~ing or speaking; (n., colloq.) ~ing, sermon, lecture. Hence or cogn. ~'ABLE a., ~'ER, ~'ership, ~'MENT (usu. derog.), nn. [f. OF *prechier* f. L PRAE(*dicare* proclaim)]

preach'ify, v.i. Preach, moralize, hold forth, tediously. [-FY]

preach'i|ly, a. (colloq.). Fond of preaching or holding forth. Hence ~ness n. [-Y[2]]

preăm'ble, n., & v.i. Preliminary statement in speech or writing; introductory part of statute, deed, etc.; (v.i.) make ~. [(vb f. n.) f. F *préambule* f. med. L *prae-ambulum* f. L *praeambulus* going before f. PRAE(*ambulare* walk)]

prĕb'end, n. Part of revenue of cathedral or collegiate church granted to canon or member of chapter as stipend; portion of land or tithe from which this stipend is drawn; =foll. So ~AL a. [f. OF *prebende*, f. med. L *praebenda* pension, neut. pl. gerund. of L *praebēre* grant, =PRAE(*hibēre* =*habēre* have, hold)]

For other words in *pre-* see PRE-.

preb'endary, n. Holder of prebend; ~ *stall*, ~'s stall in cathedral. Hence ~SHIP n. [f. med. L *praebendarius* (as prec., see -ARY¹)]

precā'rious, a. Held during the pleasure of another, as ~ *tenure*; question-begging, taken for granted, as a ~ *assumption*; dependent on chance, uncertain, as *makes a* ~ *living*; perilous, as *the* ~ *life of a fisherman*. Hence ~LY² adv., ~NESS n. [f. L *precarius* obtained by entreaty (*precem* prayer, see -ARY¹)+-OUS]

prec'atory, a. (Gram., of word or form) expressing entreaty; (in wills) ~ *trust* (requesting that a thing be done), ~ *words* (words that are held to be binding. So **prec'ative** a. [f. LL *precatorius* (*precari* pray, see -ORY)]

precau'tion, n. Prudent foresight, measure taken beforehand to ward off evil or ensure good result. Hence ~ARY¹ (-sho'-) a. [f. F *précaution* f. med. L *praecautionem* f. L PRAE(*cavēre caut-* beware of), med. L *caut-*]

precēde', v.t. & i. (Of person or thing) go before in rank or importance, as *such duties* ~ *all others, sons of barons & baronets*; come before (thing etc., or abs.) in order, as *the words that* ~ (*this paragraph*); walk in front of, as ~*d by your guide*; come before in time, as *in the years preceding his accession*; cause (thing) to be ~*d by*, as *must* ~ *this measure by milder ones*. [f. F *précéder* f. L PRAE(*cedere cess-* go)]

prec'edence (or prēsēd-), (rarely) -**cy**, n. Priority in time or succession; superiority, higher position, as *takes* ~ *of* (is recognized as superior to) *all others*; right of preceding others in ceremonies & social formalities. [prob. f. PRECEDENT², see -ENCE, -ENCY]

prec'edent¹, n. Previous case taken as example for subsequent ~*es* or as justification, as *there is no* ~ *for this, it is without* ~, *do not take this as a* ~; (Law) decision, procedure, etc., serving as rule or pattern. [as foll.]

precē'dent² (or prēs'i-), a. (now rare). Preceding in time, order, rank, etc., as *condition* ~. Hence ~LY² adv. [f. F *précédent* á. & n. f. L as PRECEDE, see -ENT]

precē'dented, a. Having, supported by, precedent. [-ED²]

prec'entor, v.t. & t. Act as precentor; lead (psalm etc.) in singing. [back form. f. foll.]

precen'tor, n. (In some Presbyterian churches etc.) one who leads singing of congregation (in English cathedrals) member of clergy in general control of musical arrangements, in old foundations ranking next to dean and having succentor as his deputy, and in new foundations being a minor canon. Hence or cogn. ~SHIP, **precen'TRIX**, nn. [f. LL *praecentor* f. L PRAE(*cinere cent-*=*canere* sing)]

prē'cept, n. Command, maxim, so **prē-cep'tIVE** a.; moral instruction, as *example is better than* ~; divine command; writ, warrant; written order to arrange for & hold election; order for collection or payment of money under a rate. [f. L *praeceptum* neut. p.p. of PRAE(*cipere cept-*=*capere* take) instruct]

precep'tor, n. Teacher, instructor. Hence or cogn. **precep'tORIAL** a., ~*or-*SHIP, ~TRESS¹, nn. [f. L *praeceptor* (as prec., see -OR²)]

precep'tory, n. (hist.). Subordinate community of Knights Templars; estate, buildings, of this. [f. med. L *praeceptoria* fem. adj. as n. (as prec., see -ORY)]

precē'ssion (-shn), n. (astron.) ~ *of the equinoxes* (earlier occurrence ~ of the equinoxes, in each successive sidereal year, due to retrograde motion of equinoctial points along ecliptic. Hence ~AL (-sho'-) a. [f. LL *praecessio* (as PRECEDE, see -ION)]

prē'cinct, n. Space enclosed by walls or other boundaries of a place or building, esp. of place of worship; (pl.) the environs of; boundary; *subdivision of county or city or ward for election and police purposes. [f. med. L *praecinctum* neut. p.p. of PRAE(*cingere* gird)]

prē'cious (-shus), a. & adv. **1.** Of great price, costly; ~ *metals*, gold, silver, (ocas.) platinum; ~ *stone, gem*; of great, non-material worth, as ~ *words, privilege, knowledge, blood of Christ*; affectedly refined in language, workmanship, etc., so **prē'cioSITY** (-shiōsi-) n.; (colloq., as intensive) *made a* ~ *mess of it, a* ~ *sight more than you think*; (ellipt.) *my* ~ (dear etc.). **2.** adv. (colloq.). Uncommonly, as *took* ~ *good care of that,* ~ *little of it*. Hence ~LY² adv., ~NESS n. [ME & OF *precios* f. L *pretiosus* (*pretium* price, see -OUS]

prē'cipice, n. Vertical or steep face of rock, cliff, mountain, etc. [f. L *prae-cipitium* falling headlong, precipice (as PRECIPITOUS)]

precip'itate¹, n. (Chem.) body precipitated from solution, so ~ANT(2), nn. ~ABLE a.; (Physics) moisture condensed from vapour by cooling & deposited, e.g. rain, dew. [as foll.]

precip'itate², a. Headlong. Violently hurried, as ~*ate flight*; (of person or act) hasty, rash, inconsiderate. Hence or cogn. ~ANCE, ~ANCY, ~*ateness*, nn. ~*ate*LY² adv. [as foll., see -ATE²]

precip'itate³, v.t. Throw down headlong; (fig.) hurl, fling, (person etc. into condition etc.); hurry, urge on, (course of events etc.); hasten the occurrence of, as *served to* ~ *his ruin*; (Chem.) cause (substance in solution) to be deposited in solid form; condense (vapour) into drops & so deposit. So **precipitā'TION** (esp. Meteorol., fall of rain, sleet, snow, or

ball),~OR², nn. [f. L *praecipitare*(as foll.), -ATE²]

precip'itous, a. Of, like, a precipice; steep; (rare)=PRECIPITATE². Hence ~LY² adv., ~NESS n. [f. obs. F *precipiteux* f. L PRAE(*ceps -cipitis* f. *caput* head) head-long, see -OUS]

précis (prās'ē), n., & v.t. **1.** Summary, abstract. **2.** v.t. Make a ~ of. [F.=foll.]

precise', a. Accurately expressed, definite, exact; punctilious, scrupulous in observance of rules etc.; *the* ~ (exact, identical)*moment* etc. Hence ~NESS (-sn-) n. [f. F *précis, -ise,* f. L PRAE(*cidere cis-=caedere* cut) cut short]

precise'ly (-sl-), adv. In precise manner; (in emphatic or formal assent) quite so. [-LY²]

preci'sian (-zhn), n. One who is rigidly precise or punctilious, esp. in religious observance. Hence ~ISM (-zha-) n. [-IAN]

preci'sion (-zhn), n. Accuracy; *arm of* ~, fire-arm fitted with sights or other mechanical aids; (attrib.) marked by, adapted for, ~ (*bombing, instruments, tools*). Hence ~IST (-zho-) n. [f. L *prae-cisio* (as PRECISE, see -ION²)]

preclude' (-ōōd), v.t. Exclude, prevent, make impracticable, *as so as to* ~ *all doubt*. So **preclu'sive** (-lōō-) a. [f. L PRAE(*cludere clus-=claudere* shut)]

preco'cious (-shus), a. (Of plant) flowering or fruiting early; (of person) prematurely developed in some faculty; (of actions etc.)indicating such development. Hence or cogn. ~LY² adv., ~NESS, **preco'CITY**, nn. [f. L *praecox -cocis* f. PRAE(*coquere* cook)+-OUS]

preconceive' (-sēv'), v.t. Conceive beforehand, anticipate in thought. So **preconcep'tion** n. (esp.=*prejudice*). [PRE-]

prec'onize, v.t. Proclaim publicly; commend publicly; summon by name; (Rom. Cath., of pope) approve publicly the appointment of (bishop). So ~A'TION n. [f. med. L *praeconizare* (L *praeco -onis* herald, see -IZE)]

precur'sor, n. Forerunner, harbinger, esp. John the Baptist; one who precedes in office etc. [f. L *praecursor* f. PRAE(*currere curs-* run), see -OR²]

precur'sory, a. Preliminary, introductory, serving as harbinger (*of*). So ~IVE a. [f. L *praecursorius* (as prec; see -ORY)]

preda'cious (-shus), a. (Of animals) naturally preying on others, predatory; pertaining to such animals, as ~ *instincts*. So **preda'CITY** n. [as PREDATORY, see -ACIOUS]

predāte, v.t. Antedate. [PRE-]

pred'atory, a. Of, addicted to, plunder or robbery; (of animals) preying upon others. [f. L *praedatorius* (*praedari* plunder f. *praeda* booty, see -ORY)]

pred'ecessor, n. Former holder of any office or position, as *my, William's,* ~*s, his immediate* ~; that to which another has succeeded, as *will share the fate of its* ~; forefather. [f. LL PRAE(*decessor,* see DECEASE, -OR²)]

predell'a, n. (Painting on vertical face of) altar-step; (painting, sculpture, on) raised shelf at back of altar. [It., =stool, prob. f. OHG *pret* board +-*ella* dim. suf.]

predes'tinar'ian, n. & a. (Holder of the doctrine) of predestination. [-ARIAN]

predes'tināte, v.t. (Of God) foreordain (person) to salvation or *to* (any fate), *to* (do); determine beforehand. So ~ATE² (-at) a. [f. L PRAE(*destinare* DESTINE), see -ATE³]

predestina'tion, n. God's appointment from eternity of some of mankind to salvation & eternal life; God's fore-ordaining of all that comes to pass; fate, destiny. [f. LL *praedestinatio* (as prec., see -ION)]

predes'tine, v.t. Determine beforehand, appoint as if by fate; (Theol.)=PRE-DESTINATE. [as PREDESTINATE]

predeterm'ine, v.t. Decree beforehand, predestine, so ~ATE² (-at) a.; (of motive etc.) impel (person etc. *to* thing, *to* do) beforehand. Hence ~A'TION n. [f. LL PRAE(*determinare* DETERMINE)]

pred'ial, a. & n. **1.** Of land or farms; rural, agrarian; (of slaves) attached to the land. **2.** n. ~ slave. [f. med. L *praedialis* (L *praedium* farm, see -AL)]

pred'icable, a. & n. **1.** That may be predicated or affirmed; so ~ABILITY n. **2.** n. ~able thing, esp. (pl.) Aristotle's classes of predicates viewed relatively to their subjects (viz., genus, species, difference, property, accident). [f. F *prédicable* (as PREDICATE², see -BLE)]

predic'ament, n. Thing predicated, esp. (pl.) Aristotle's ten categories, whence **predicamen'tAL** a.; unpleasant, trying, or dangerous situation. [f. LL *praedica-mentum* (as foll., see -MENT)]

pred'icant, a. & n. **1.** (Of religious order, esp. Dominicans) engaged in preaching. **2.** n.=PREDIKANT. [as foll., see -ANT]

pred'icate¹, n. (Logic) what is predicated, what is affirmed or denied of the subject by means of the copula (e.g. *a fool in he is a fool*); (Gram.) what is said of the subject, including the copula (e.g. *is a fool in prec. ex.*); quality, attribute. [as foll., see -ATE²]

pred'icate², v.t. Assert, affirm, as true or existent, as *many truths may be* ~*d about humanity*; *we* ~ *goodness or badness of a*

For other words in *pre-* see PRE-.

motive; **~ of a motive** that it is good or
bad; (Logic) assert (thing) about subject.
So **prĕdĭcā´tĭon** n. [f. LL
dēclārĕ) prōclaim, see -ATE³]

prĕdĭc´ătĭve, a. Making a predication;
(Gram.) of adj. or n., opp. *attributive*;
forming part or the whole of the predicate,
as in 'This is *absurd*', cf. 'an *absurd*
notion'. Hence **~ly²** adv. [as prec., see
-IVE]

prĕdĭc´ătŏry, a. Of, given to, marked by,
preaching. [f. LL *praedicatorius* (prec.,
-ORY)]

prĕdĭct´, v.t. Foretell, prophesy, (thing,
that, who, etc.). Hence or cogn. **~ABIL´-
ITY, prĕdĭct´ion,** nn. **~ABLE** a., **~IVE** aa.,
~IVELY² adv. [f. LL PRAE(*dicere dict-* say)]

prĕdĭc´tor, n. In vbl senses; also instrument for determining the height, direction,
speed, and range of aircraft and the fuse-
setting etc., required in engaging hostile
aircraft with anti-aircraft fire. [-OR²]

prĕdikant´ (also ´-), n. Minister of Dutch
Protestant church, esp. in S. Africa.
[Du., as PREDICANT]

prĕdĭlĕc´tion, n. Mental preference, partiality, (*for*). [f. F *prédilection* f. med. L
PRAE(*diligere*), see DILIGENT & -ION]

prĕdĭspōse´ (-z), v.t. Render liable, subject, or inclined (*to* feeling, disease, etc.,
to do). [PRE-]

prĕdĭspŏsĭ´tĭon (-zĭ-), n. State of mind
or body favourable *to* (mercy, malaria,
etc.). [PRE-]

prĕdŏm´ĭnāte, v.i. Have or exert control
(*over* person etc.), be superior; be the
stronger or main element, preponderate,
as *garden in which dahlias ~ate.*
or cogn. **~ANCE** n., **~ANT** a., **~antly²
~atingly²** advs. [f. med. L †PRAE-
(*dominare* DOMINATE)]

prĕ-ĕm´ĭnent, a. Excelling others; distinguished beyond others in some quality.
Hence or cogn. **~ENCE** n., **~ently²** adv.
[f. L PRAE(*eminens* EMINENT)]

prĕ-ĕmpt´, v.t. & i. Obtain by pre-
emption; *occupy (public land) so as to
have right of pre-emption; (fig.) appropriate beforehand; (Bridge) make pre-
emptive bid. [back formation f. foll.]

prĕ-ĕmp´tĭon, n. Purchase by one
person etc. before opportunity is offered
to others; right so to purchase. So **~IVE**
a. (*~ive bid,* bid at Bridge intended to be
high enough to prevent further bidding).
[f. med. L PRAE(*emere empt-* buy), -ION]

prēen, v.t. Trim (feathers) with beak; (of
person) trim oneself. [prob. var. of
PRUNE², assoc. w. Sc. & obs. E *preen* prick,
pin]

prē´fäce, n. & v.t. 1. Introduction to
book stating subject, scope, etc.; preliminary part of a speech; introduction

to central part of eucharistic service.
2. v.t. Furnish (book etc.) with ~; introduce (as a snort; (of event etc.) lead up to
(another); (v.i.) make preliminary remarks. So **prē´fătōr´ĭal, prē´fătŏry,** aa.
[f. F *préface* prob. f. med. L *prefatia* for
L *praefatio* f. PRAE(*fari* speak), see -ION]

prē´fĕct, n. (Rom. Ant.) title of various
officers, civil & military; chief administrative officer of French department; ~
of police, head of Paris police; (in some
public schools) senior pupil authorized to
maintain discipline. So **prēfĕc´tŏral,**
~ōr´ĭal, aa. [OF., f. L *praefectus* f. PRAE-
(*ficere fect-=facere* make) set over]

prē´fĕctŭre, n. (Period of) office, official
residence, district under government, of
a prefect. Hence **prēfĕc´tŭral**(-cher-) a.
[f. L *praefectura* (as prec., see -URE)]

prĕfer´, v.t. (-rr-). Promote (*person to
office*), whence **~MENT** n.; bring forward,
submit, (statement, information, etc., *to*
person in authority etc., *against* offender
etc.); choose rather, like better, as *gentlemen ~ blondes, ~ water to wine, ~ to leave
it alone, ~ that it should be left* (than is
unidiomatic after ~ unless *rather* is
inserted, as *~red to die rather than pay*),
so **prĕf´ĕrable** a., **prĕf´ĕrăbly²** adv.
[f. F *préférer* f. L PRAE(*ferre lat-* bear)]

prĕf´ĕrence, n. Liking of one thing better
than another (*of* A *to* or *over* B); thing
one prefers; prior right esp. to payment
of debts; || *~ bond, share, stock,* (on which
dividend is paid before any is paid on
ordinary stock); favouring of one person
or country before others in business
relations, esp. favouring of a country by
admitting its products at lower import
duty. [f. F *préférence* f. med. L *praefer-
entia* (prec., -ENCE)]

prĕfĕrĕn´tial (-shl), a. Of, giving, receiving, preference; (of duties etc.) favouring
particular countries, || esp. favouring
trade between Great Britain & her
colonies, whence **~ISM,** nn., (-sher-).
Hence **~ly²** adv. [as prec. + -AL]

prĕfer´red (-ĕrd), a. In vbl senses; *~
shares, stock,* etc., preference shares etc.
[-ED¹]

prēfĭg´ure (-ger), v.t. Represent beforehand by figure or type, picture to oneself
beforehand. Hence or cogn. **prēfĭgŭr-
ā´TĬVE** a. [f. LL PRAE (*figurare* FIGURE)]

prē´fĭx¹, n. Verbal element placed at
beginning of word to qualify meaning or
(in some languages) as inflexional formative; title placed before name, e.g. *Mr,
Mrs, Sir, Dr.* [f. L PRAE(*figere* FIX)]

prēfĭx², v.t. Add (chapter, paragraph,
etc., *to* book etc.) as introduction; join
(word, verbal element) as prefix (*to* word),
so **prēfĭx´ĭon, prēfĭx´tŭre,** nn. [f. OF
PRAE(*figere* FIX¹)]

prēform´, v.t. Form beforehand. [PRE-]

preförmā'tion, n. Previous formation; (Biol.) theory of ~ (that all parts of the perfect organism exist in the germ & are merely developed). [PRE-]

preförm'ative, a., & n. Forming beforehand; (syllable, letter) prefixed as formative element. [PRE-]

preg'nable, a. Not impregnable. [ME & F prenable, see IMPREGNABLE]

preg'nant, a. (Of woman or female animal) with child, gravid; teeming with ideas, imaginative, inventive; fruitful in results, big with (consequences etc.); (of words or acts) having a hidden meaning, significant, suggestive, whence~LY² adv.; (Gram.) ~ construction (in which more is implied than the words express). Hence preg'NANCY n. [f. L praegnans -ntis pref. f. PRAE-+gna- root of (g)nasci be born; but older L has praegnas -atis]

prehen'sile, a. (zool.). (Of tail or limb) capable of grasping. Hence prehēnsil²ITY n. [f. F préhensile f. L PRAE(hendere -hens- cogn. w. Gk khandanō grasp), see -ILE]

prehen'sion (-shn), n. Grasping; seizing; mental apprehension. [f. L prehensio (prec.,-ION)]

prēhistō'ric, a. Of the period antecedent to history. Hence ~ICALLY adv. [PRE-]

prēhis'tory, n. Prehistoric matters or times. [PRE-, after prec.]

prē-igni'tion, n. Premature firing of explosive mixture in internal-combustion engine. [PRE-]

prējudge', v.t. Pass judgement on (person) before trial or proper inquiry; form premature judgement upon (person, cause, action, etc.). So ~MENT (-jm-), prejudicATION (-jōō-), nn. [f. F préjuger f. L PRAE(judicare JUDGE]

prej'udice (-jōō-), n., & v.t. 1. Preconceived opinion, bias; (as divest your mind of, person or thing), as divest your mind of,~, has a ~ against foreigners, has a ~ in our favour, this is mere ~; injury that results or may result from some action or judgement, as to the ~ of; without ~, without detriment to existing right or claim. 2. v.t. Impair the validity of (right, claim, statement, etc.); cause (person) to have a ~ (against, in favour of), esp. in p.p. [(vb f. F préjudicier) f. F préjudice f. L PRAE(judicium judgement f. judex JUDGE) preceding judgement, precedent, damage]

prējudi'cial (-jōōdishl), a. Causing prejudice, detrimental, (to rights, interests, etc.). Hence ~LY² adv. [f. L as prec., see -AL]

prel'acy, n. Office, rank, see, of a prelate; the prelates; church government by prelates (usu. hostile for EPISCOPACY). [f. AF prelacie f. med. L praelatia (as foll., see -ACY)]

prel'ate, n. High ecclesiastical dignitary, e.g.(arch)bishop, metropolitan, patriarch, (hist.) abbot or prior. Hence prēlāt²IC(AL) aa., prēlāt'ICALLY² adv. [f. OF prēlat f. L praelatus (as PREFER]

prel'atess, n. Abbess, prioress; (joc.) prelate's wife. [-ESS¹]

prel'atize, v.t. Bring (church) under prelatical government. [f. PRELATE +-IZE]

prel'ature, n. Office of prelate; the prelates. [f. F prélature f. med. L praelatura (as PRELATE, see -URE)]

prēlect', v.i. Discourse, lecture, (to audience on subject, esp. in univ.). So prēlēc'TION, prēlēc'TOR², nn. [f. L PRAE(legere lect- read)]

prēlibā'tion, n. Foretaste (usu. fig.). [f. LL PRAE(libatio LIBATION)]

prēlim', n. (colloq.). Preliminary examination. [abbr.]

prēlim'inarLY, a. & n. 1. Introductory, preparatory. 2. In ~y arrangement (usu. in pl.). Hence ~LY² adv. [f. L PRAE-+ līmen -minis threshold, see -ARY¹]

prel'ūde¹, n. Performance, action, event, condition, serving as introduction (to another); (Mus.) introductory movement esp. one preceding fugue or forming first piece of suite. Hence prēlūd'IAL a., prēlū'dize(2) v.i. [f. F prélude f. LL praeludium, as foll.]

prel'ūde² (or prēlūd'), v.t. & i. Serve as prelude to, introduce, foreshadow; introduce with a prelude; be, give, a prelude to; (Mus.) play a prelude. So prēlū'sION (-zhn) n., prēlū'sIVE a. [f. L PRAE(ludere lus- play]

prēmatūre' (also prēm²), a. Occurring, done, before the usual or proper time, too early, hasty, as ~ decision, decay. Hence or cogn.~LY² adv.,~NESS, prēmatūr'ITY, nn. [f. L PRAE(maturus MATURE]

prēmed'itāte, v.t. Think out, design, (action etc.) beforehand (esp. in p.p.). Hence or cogn.~ātedLY² adv.,~ATION n. [f. L PRAE(meditari MEDITATE)]

prem'ier (or prē-), a. & n. 1. (Now chiefly sl.) first in position, importance, order, or rime, as secured ~ place (in race). 2. n. Prime Minister in Great Britain or some British dominions. Hence ~SHIP n. [F, =first, f. L as PRIMARY]

premiere' (prīmyār'), n. First performance of play. [F, fem. adj. as prec.]

prēm'ise', ~-ss (as below), n. 1. (Logic, often -ss) previous statement from which another is inferred, esp. MAJOR², MINOR, ~ in syllogism. 2. (pl.). The aforesaid, the foregoing, esp. (Law) the aforesaid houses, lands, or tenements. 3. (pl.). House, building, with grounds & appurtenances, as to be drunk on the ~s. [f. F prémisse f. med. L praemissa (propositio proposition) set in front f. L PRAE(mittere miss- send)]

For other words in pre- see PRE-.

premise² (-z), v.t. Say, write, (thing, that) by way of introduction. [f. prec.]

prem'ium, n. Reward, prize, (chiefly now in *put a* ~ *on*, provide or act as incentive to, as *you, this, will put a* ~ *on fraud*); amount to be paid in consideration of contract of insurance; sum additional to interest, wages, etc.; bonus; fee for instruction in profession etc.; charge for changing one currency into another of greater value, agio; *at a* ~, at more than nominal value (cf. DISCOUNT), (fig.) in high esteem. [f. L *praemium* booty, reward, f. PRAE- + *emere* buy, take]

prémôľar, n. Tooth in front of true molars (in man, BICUSPID). [PRE-]

prémôni′tion, n. Forewarning. So **prémôn′itor** n., **prémôn′itory** a. [f. obs. F *premonicion*, f. LL *praemonitio* f. L PRAE(*monère -it-* warn). -ION]

Prémônstratēn′sian, a. & n. (Member) of order of regular canons founded at Prémontré in 1119, or of corresponding order of nuns. [f. med. L *Praemonstratensis* (*Praemonstratus* Prémontré, see -ESE) + -AN]

prémôrse′, a. (bot., entom.), With the end abruptly truncate. [f. L PRAE-(*mordère mors-* bite) bite off in front]

prén′tice, n., & v.t. (arch.). = APPRENTICE, esp. ~ (*tiro's*) *hand*. [aphetic]

prëôccupā′tion, n. Prepossession, prejudice; occupation of a place beforehand; occupation, business, that takes precedence of all others; mental absorption. [f. L *praeoccupatio* (foll. -ATION)]

prëôcc′up̄ỹ, v.t. Engage beforehand, engross (mind etc.); (p.p., esp.) distrait, with thoughts elsewhere, whence ~iedly² adv. (-pid-) adv.; = appropriate beforehand. [f. L PRAE(*occupare* OCCUPY)]

prep. (in school sl.). ‖Preparation. [abbr.]

prépaȧ′tion, n. Preparing; (usu. pl.) thing(s) done to make ready (*for*); *make* ~s, prepare (*for*); ‖(abbr. *prep.*) ~ *of* (abbr. *prep.*) of lessons as part of school routine; substance, e.g. food or medicine, specially prepared; (Mus.) preparing of a discord. [f. F *préparation* f. L *praeparationem* (as PREPARE, see -TION)]

prépar′ative, a. & n. Preparatory; (n.) ~ act, (Mil., Naut.) signal on drum, bugle, etc., as order to make ready. Hence ~ly² adv. [F (-*if -ive*), f. med. L *prae-parativus* (as PREPARE, see -IVE)]

prépar′atory, a. & n. Serving to prepare, introductory (*to*); ~y (*school*), ‖where pupils are prepared for higher school; (quasi-adv.) *am packing it up* ~y *to sending it by post*. Hence ~ily² adv. [f. med. L *praeparatorius* (as foll., see -ORY)]

prépare′, v.t. & i. Make (person, thing) ready (*for*); make ready (food, meal) for eating; make (person) mentally ready for

fit (*for news, to hear*, etc.); get (lesson, speech, sermon) ready by previous study; get (person) ready by teaching (*for college, examination, the army*, etc.); make preparations (*for, to do*, etc.); *be* ~d, be ready or willing (*to do*); make (chemical product etc.) by regular process; (Mus.) lead up to (discord) by sounding the dissonant note in it as consonant note in preceding chord. Hence **prepaŕ′edness** n., readiness (esp. of nav. and mil. preparations for possible hostilities). [f. F *préparer* f. L PRAE(*parare* make ready)]

prepay′, v.t. Pay (charge) beforehand; pay (cost of telegram), pay (cost of parcel), beforehand. Hence ~ABLE a., ~MENT n. [PRE-]

prepénse′, a. Deliberate, intentional, chiefly in *malice* ~, with intent to injure, of *malice* ~, with intent to injure. Hence ~ly² adv. [earlier *prepensed* p.p. of obs. *prepense* altered f. earlier *purpense* f. OF PUR(*penser*); see PENSIVE]

prepôn′derāte, v.i. Weigh more, be heavier; ~*ate over*, exceed in number, quantity, etc.; be of greater moral or intellectual weight; be the chief element, predominate; (of scale of balance) sink. So ~ANCE n., ~ANT a., ~antly² adv. [f. L PRAE(*ponderare* PONDER), -ATE³]

prepôsi′tion (-z-), n. Indeclinable word serving to mark relation between the noun or pronoun it governs & another word (as *in*, the italic wds in: *found him at home, wait in the hall, what did you do it for?, the bed (that) he slept on, won by waiting, came through the roof*, that is what I was thinking *of*). Hence ~AL a., ~ally² adv., (-zisho-). [f. L PRAE(*ponere posit-* place)]

prepôs′itive (-z-), a. (gram.). (Of word, particle, etc.) proper to be placed before or prefixed. [f. LL *praepositivus* (as prec., see -IVE)]

prepôs′itor (-z-). See PRAEPOSTOR.

prepôssĕss′ (-z-), v.t. Imbue, inspire, (person *with* notion, feeling, etc.); (of idea etc.) take possession of (person, usu. pass.); prejudice, usu. favourably, whence ~ING² a., ~ingly² adv., ~ingness, prépossĕss′ion (-zĕshn), n. [PRE-]

prepôss′terous, a. Contrary to nature, reason, or common sense; perverse, foolish; absurd. Hence ~ly² adv., ~NESS n. [f. L PRAE(*posterus* coming after reversed, absurd]

prepô′tent, a. Very powerful; more powerful than others; (Biol.) having stronger fertilizing influence or power of transmitting hereditary qualities. So ~ENCE, ~ENCY, nn. [f. L PRAE(*potens* part. of PRAE(*posse* be able)]

prépūce, n. Foreskin, loose integument covering end of penis. So **prepū′tial**

(-shl) a. [f. L PRAE(*postium* perh.=Gk *posthion* penis)]

Pre-Raph'aelite, n. Artist who aims at producing work in the spirit that prevailed before the time of Raphael; ~ *Brotherhood* (abbr. *P.R.B.*), group of English artists including Holman Hunt, Millais, D. G. Rossetti. So **pre-Raph'aël** a., **Pre-Raph'aël(it)ism** n. [PRE-+*Raphael*+-ITE¹]

prēréq'uisite (-z-), a. & n. (Thing) required as previous condition. [PRE-]

prērog'ative, n. & a. **1.** (Also *royal* ~) right of the sovereign, theoretically subject to no restriction; peculiar right or privilege, as *it is our* ~ *to* (do), *we have the* ~ *of* (doing), *the* ~ *of* (right to show) *mercy*; natural or divinely-given advantage, privilege, or faculty, as *it is the* ~ *of man to drink without thirst*; ||(pedantio) right of giving first vote and thus influencing those that follow; (Hist.) ~ *court*, archbishop's court for probate of wills etc. **2.** adj. Privileged, enjoyed by privilege; (Rom. Hist.) having the right to vote first. [adj. f. L PRAE(*rogativus* f. *rogare* ask, see -IVE) asked first; n. f. F *prérogative* f. L *praerogativa* previous choice, prognostic, privilege, fem. adj. as n.]

prēs'age¹, n. Omen, portent; presentiment, foreboding. Hence **prēsāge'FUL** (-jf-) a. [f. F *présage* f. L *praesagium* f. PRAE(*sagus* predicting)]

prēsāge'², v.t. Portend, foreshadow; give warning of (event etc.) by natural means, as *such ideas are held to* ~*insanity*; (of person) predict, (also) have presentiment of. [f. F *présager*, as prec.]

prēsby'ōp'ia (-s-, -z-), n. Form of longsightedness incident to old age. Hence **-ōp'ic** a. [f. Gk *presbus* old man +*ōps ōpos* eye]

prēs'byter (-s-, -z-), n. (In early Church) one of several officers managing affairs of local church; (in Episcopal church) minister of second order, priest; (in Presbyterian church) elder. Hence or cogn. **prēsbyt'erAL**, **prēsbyt'erᴵAL** aa., **prēsbyt'erᴀᴛᴇ¹**(-at), **~SHIP**, nn. [LL, f. Gk *presbuteros* elder]

Presbytēr'ian (-s-, -z-), a. & n. **1.** *church*, one governed by elders, all (including ministers) of equal rank; *United* ~ *church*, that formed in 1847 by union of United Secession & Relief churches, later embodied in the United Free church of Scotland. **2.** n. Adherent of ~ system, member of ~ church. Hence **~ᴵsᴍ** n., **~ᴵᴢᴇ**(3) v.t. [f. L as foll. +-AN]

prēs'bytery (-s-, -z-), n. Eastern part of chancel beyond choir, sanctuary; body of presbyters, esp. court next above KIRK-session, district represented by this; (R.-C. Ch.) priest's house. [f. OF *presbiterie* f. LL f. Gk *presbuterion* (as PRESBYTER)]

prē'scient (-shyent), a. Having foreknowledge or foresight. Hence or cogn. **prē'scᴵᴇɴᴄᴇ** (-shyens) n., **~LY²** adv. [F, f. L PRAE(*scire* know), see ENT¹]

prescind', v.t. & i. Cut off (part from whole) esp. prematurely or abruptly; ~ *from*, leave out of consideration. [f. L PRAE(*scindere* cut)]

prescribe', v.t. & i. Lay down or impose authoritatively, as *do not* ~ *to me what I am to do or how to do it, the statutes*~*the practice*; (Med.) advise use of (medicine etc., or abs.; *to* or *for* patient, *for* complaint; also *fig.*); assert prescriptive right or claim (*to, for*, thing). [f. L PRAE-(*scribere script*- write) direct in writing, (Law) bring exception against]

prēs'cript, n. Ordinance, law, command. [as prec.]

prescrip'tion, n. Prescribing; physician's (usu. written) direction for composition & use of medicine; (Law) (*positive*) uninterrupted use or possession from time immemorial or for period fixed by law as giving title or right, such title or right, *negative* ~, limitation of the time within which action or claim can be raised; (fig.) ancient custom viewed as authoritative, claim founded on long use. [f. L *praescriptio* (as prec., see -ION)]

prescrip'tive, a. Prescribing; based on prescription, as ~ *right*; prescribed by custom. Hence **~LY²** adv. [f. LL *praescriptivus* (as PRESCRIBE, see -IVE)]

prēsēlēc'tive, a. (Of motor-car gears) that can be selected and set in advance. [PRE-]

prēs'ence (-z-), n. Being present, as *your* ~*is requested, in the* ~ *of a large company*; REAL²; place where person is, as *admitted to, banished from, his* ~, *in this* (august etc.), *in the* ~ *of this* (etc.) person; || *the* ~, ceremonial attendance on person of high esp. royal rank, as *remained in, retired from, the* ~; carriage, bearing, as *a man of* (a) *noble* ~; ~ *of mind*, calmness & self-command in sudden emergencies; ~*chamber* (in which great personage receives guests etc.). [OF, f. L *praesentia* (as foll., see -ENCE)]

prēs'ent¹ (-z-), a. Being in the place in question (chiefly pred.), as *no one else was* ~ (in place, *at* proceedings etc.); being dealt with, discussed, etc., as *no excuse in the* ~ *case, the* ~ *volume* (the book you are reading or I am reviewing), *the* ~ *writer* (I) *could not verify this*; ~ *to* (felt, remembered, by) *the mind, the imagination*; ||(arch.) ready at hand, ready with assistance, as *a very* ~ *help in trouble*; existing, occurring, being such, now, as *the* ~ *Duke of York, in the* ~ *fashion*; *the* ~ *worth of* (sum that with compound interest dating from now will amount to £100 in 12 years; (Gram.) ~

For other words in *pre-* see **PRE-**.

present tense (denoting action etc. now going on), of OF. f. L præsens -ntis part. of PRÆ(esse be) be at hand]

présent² (-z-), n. The present time, time now passing; *at ~, now, as do not want any more at ~, is ad ~ in Egypt; for the ~*, just now, as far as the ~ is concerned, *as that will do for the ~*; = ~ *tense*; (*imæ all men etc.*) *by these ~s*, by this document (now legal or joc.). [prec.]

présent³ (-z-), n. Gift; *make a ~ of*, present (thing to person). [OF (as prec., orig. in phr. *mettre une chose en ~ à quelqu'un*, put a thing into the presence of a person]

présent⁴ (-z-), v.t. & i. & n. **1.** Introduce (person to another); introduce (person) to sovereign at court; ~ *oneself*, appear esp. as candidate for examination etc. **2.** (Of theatr. manager) cause (actor) to take part in play, produce (play). **3.** Recommend (clergyman) to bishop for institution (to benefice). **4.** Exhibit (thing to person etc.), as ~ *a ragged appearance, ~ed its front to me*; show (quality etc.), as *cases that ~ some difficulty*. **5.** (mil.). Hold (fire-arm) in position for taking aim; (also ~ *arms*) hold fire-arm etc. in deferential position in saluting. **6.** (Of idea etc.) offer, suggest itself. **7.** (Law) bring formally under notice, submit, (complaint, offence, to authority). **8.** Aim (weapon *at*), hold out (weapon) in position for aiming (also abs., ~! as word of command). **9.** Offer, give, (thing to person *to*); deliver (bill etc. to person etc.) for acceptance etc.; ~ *person with thing*, offer (compliments, regards, etc.). **10.** n. Act of aiming weapon, position of 'P~ arms' in salute. [n. f. vb] f. OF *presenter* f. L *præsentare* (as PRESENT¹)]

présent'able (-z-), a. Of decent appearance, fit to be introduced or go into company; suitable for presentation as a gift etc. Hence ~ant'ITY n., ~ably² adv. [-ABLE]

présentā'tion (-z-), n. Presenting; ~(*gratis*) *copy of book* etc.; exhibition; theatrical representation, etc.; formal introduction esp. at court; (Metaphys.) all the modification of consciousness directly involved in the knowing or being aware of an object in a single moment of thought, whence ~AL (-sho-) a. [f. LL *præsentatio* (as PRESENT⁴, see -ATION)]

présentā'tionism (-z-, -sho-), n. (metaphys.). Doctrine that in perception the mind has immediate cognition of the object. So ~(al)IST m. [prec.+-ISM]

présent'ative (-z-), a. (Of benefice) to which patron has right of presentation; serving to present an idea to the mind; (Metaphys.) of (the nature of) presentation. [-ATIVE]

présentee² (-z-), n. Clergyman presented.

to benefice; person recommended for office; person presented at court; recipient of present. [AF (as PRESENT⁴, see -EE)]

présent'ient (-shi-), a. Having a presentiment of event etc., or abs.). [f. L PRAE-(*sentiens* SENTIENT)]

présent'iment (-z-, -s-), n. Vague expectation, foreboding, (of coming event esp. evil). [f. obs. F PRESSENTIMENT)]

présent'ive (-z-), a. (Of word) presenting an object or conception directly to the mind (opp. to *symbolic*). [-IVE]

présent'ly (-z-), adv. Soon, after a short time; (arch.) as direct result, necessarily, as *it does not ~ follow that he knew*.

présent'ment (-z-), n. (Law) statement or oath (by jury) of fact within their knowledge; formal complaint of offence made by parish authorities to bishop or archdeacon at his visitation; theatrical representation; delineation, portrait, statement, description, (of); act, mode, of presenting to the mind. [f. OF *presentement* (as PRESENT⁴, see -MENT)]

préserva'tion (-z-), n. Preserving, being preserved, from injury or destruction; *an excellent state of ~, in (a state of) fair ~*, [f. F *préservation* f. med. L *præservatio*]

préserv'ative (-z-), a. & n. (Drug, measure, etc.) tending to preserve; chemical substance for preserving perishable foodstuffs, whence ~IZE(5) v.t. [f. F *préservatif* f. med. L *præservativus* (as PRESERVE, see -ATIVE)]

préserve'¹ (-z-), n. Jam; ground set apart for protection of game (often fig.); piece of water for fish; (pl.) goggles used as protection from dust etc. [f. foll.]

préserve'² (-z-), v.t. Keep safe (*from* harm etc.); keep alive (name, memory, etc.); maintain (state of things); retain (quality, condition); prepare (fruit, meat, etc.) by boiling with sugar, pickling, etc.; keep (game, game-run, river, or abs.) undisturbed for private use; *well ~ed*, (of elderly person) showing little sign of age. Hence ~ABLE a., ~ER n. [f. F *préserver* f. LL *præservare* (*serve* keep)]

préside' (-z-), v.i. Occupy chair of authority at meeting of society or company (often *over*); sit at head of table; exercise control, sit or reign supreme, (often fig.); ~ *at the organ, piano*, etc., act as organist etc. [f. F *présider* f. L *præsidere* (*sedere* sit)]

prés'idency (-z-), n. Office of president; period of this; district administered by president, esp. (formerly) division of E. India Company's territory (*Bengal, Madras, Bombay, P~*). [f. med. L *præsidentia* (prec. -ENCY)]

prĕs'ident (-z-), n. Head of temporary or permanent body of persons, presiding over their meetings & proceedings; presiding over some colleges; person presiding over meetings of academy, literary or scientific society, etc.; *person presiding over proceedings of bank or company; head of advisory council, board, etc., as P~ *of the Board of Trade*; *Lord P~ of the Council*, English crown officer presiding at meetings of Privy Council; elected head of government in U.S. & other modern republics; (Hist.) governor of province, colony, etc. Hence or cogn. **prĕsĭdĕn'tial** adv. [-z-, -shl] a., **prĕsĭdĕn'tĭalĭty²** adv.,~**SHIP** n. [f. F *président* f. L as PRESIDE, see-ENT]

prĕs'identĕss (-z-), n. Female president; wife of president. [-ESS²]

prĕsĭd'iary, a. Of, having, serving as, a garrison. [f. L *praesidiarius* (*praesidium* garrison, as PRESIDE, see -ARY¹)]

prĕsĭd'ĭo, n. (pl. ~s). (In Spain & Sp. America) fort, garrison town. [Sp., as prec.]

prĕsĭd'ium, n. Standing committee in various Communistic organizations. [L (*praesidium*, = garrison]

press³, n. **1.** Crowding; crowd (*of* people etc.); throng, crush, in battle; pressure, hurry, of affairs, as *the ~ of modern life*. **2.** Pressing, as *give it a slight* ~. **3.** (Naut.) ~ *of sail, canvas* (as much as wind etc. will allow). **4.** Kinds of instrument for compressing, flattening, or shaping, or for extracting juice etc. **5.** (Also *printing-*~) machine for printing; printing-house or establishment; the art, practice, of printing; *in the* ~, being printed, send, *go, come, to* (*the*) ~ (to be printed), *correct the* ~ (errors in printing); *freedom of the* ~, right to print & publish anything without censorship; *the newspapers generally*, as *favourably noticed by the* ~ (*have a good* ~, *receive such notice*); *the* GUTTER, YELLOW, ~; ~ *campaign* or *stunt*, prosecution of political or other aims by newspaper letters & articles; (as name of newspaper) *Aberdeen P*~ *and Journal*. **6.** Large usu. shelved cupboard for clothes, books, etc., esp. in recess in wall. **7.** ~ *agent*, person employed by theatre, actor, etc., to attend to advertising and ~ *publicity*; ~*-box*, shelter for newspaper reporter at cricket match etc.; ||~ CUTTING, ~*-gallery* (for reporters esp. in House of Commons); ~*man*, journalist, operator of printing-~; ~*mark*, mark, number, in book showing its place in library. [ME & F *presse*, as foll.]

press², v.t. & i. **1.** Exert steady force against (thing in contact), as *let a heavy weight* ~ *it*, ~ *it under* or *with a stone*, *the two plates together*; ~ *the button*, set electric machinery in motion, (fig.) take decisive initial step; (as sign of affection

etc.) *he* ~*ed my hand*, ~*ed her to his side*; move (thing *up, down, against*, etc.) by ~*ing*. **2.** Exert pressure, bear with weight or force, (*on, against*, etc.). **3.** Squeeze (juice etc. *out of, from*, etc.); compress, squeeze, (thing) to flatten or shape or smooth it, or to extract juice etc., as ~*ed beef*. **4.** (Of enemy, attacking force, etc.) bear heavily on, esp. in p.p. *hard* ~*ed*; weigh down, oppress, (feelings, mind, spirits); (pass.) *am* ~*ed for* (have barely enough) *space, time, funds*, etc. **5.** Produce strong mental or moral impression, esp. weigh heavily, (*up*)*on* (mind, person). **6.** Be urgent, demand immediate action, as *time* ~*es, nothing remains that* ~*es*. **7.** Urge, entreat, (person to do, person or without object for answer etc.). **8.** Insist on strict interpretation *of* (words, metaphor). **9.** Urge (course, opinion, *upon* person); force (offer, gift, etc. *upon*). **10.** Crowd, throng, (*up, round*, etc.); hasten, urge one's way, *on, forward*, etc. [f. OF *presser* f. L *pressare* frequent. of *premere* press-]

press³, v.t. & n. Force (man, or abs.) to serve in army or navy (also fig., esp. ~ *thing into the service of*); take (horses, boats, etc.) for royal or public use; (m., Hist.) compulsory enlistment in navy or (less usu.) army; ~*-gang*, body of men employed to ~ men. [earlier *prest* f. OF *prest* loan, advance, f. *prester* lend f. L PRAE(*stare* stand) vouch for, furnish]

press'ing, a. In vbl senses, esp.: urgent, as ~ *need, danger*; importunate, persistent, as *a* ~ *invitation, since you are so* ~. Hence ~**LY²** adv. [PRESS² + -ING²]

prĕ'ssure (-sher), n. **1.** Exertion of continuous force, force so exerted, upon or against a body by another in contact with it; amount of this, expressed by the weight upon a unit area. **2.** *Atmospheric*~ (of the ATMOSPHERE; *high, low*, ~, local atmospheric condition sending barometer up, down); *blood*~, varying tension, now measured for diagnosis etc., of blood-vessels. **3.** Affliction, oppression; trouble, embarrassment, as *financial* ~. **4.** Urgency, as *wrote hastily & under* ~; constraining influence, as ~ *must be brought to bear upon him*. **5.** *High* ~, (orig.) ~ higher than atmospheric (now indefinite, used esp. of compound engines in which steam is used at different ~s in different cylinders, so *low* ~), (fig.) high degree of activity, speed, etc., as *working at high* ~, *high-* ~ *work*. Hence **prĕ'ssurize** (-sher-), v.t., ~ (esp. in p.p.) construct (aircraft, cabin) so that air~, temperature, etc. can be controlled in such a way that high-altitude flying is possible without discomfort and without the use of oxygen apparatus. [obs. F, f. L *pressura* (as PRESS², see -URE)]

For other words in *pre-* **see** PRE-.

Pres'ter John (jŏn), n. Alleged Christian priest & king in Abyssinia or some eastern country in Middle Ages. [f. OF prestre (as PRESBYTER) Jehan priest John]

prestidi'gitator, n. Juggler, conjurer. So **prestidigita'tion** n. [f. F prestidigitateur (preste, as PRESTO + L digitus finger. see -OR²)]

prestige' (-ēzh, or prĕs'tĭj), n. Influence, reputation, derived from past achievements, associations, etc. [F, = illusion, glamour, f. L praestigium (for -strig-) f. PRAE(stringere bind) blindfold, dazzle)]

prestis'simo¹, a., adv., & n. (mus.). Quick (piece, movement). [It., f. LL praestus]

prestis'simo², a., adv., & n. (mus.). Very quick (piece, movement). [It., superl. as foll.]

prĕs'to¹, a., adv., & n. [f. L praesto ready]

prĕs'to² adv. & n. (In conjurer's formula) quickly, as hey ~ pass! ; (adj) rapid, juggling. [= prec.]

presume' (-z-), v.t. & i. Take the liberty, venture, (to do) : assume, take for granted, as I ~e that he has seen them, I ~e this decision to be final, you had better ~e no such thing, whence ~ABLE a., ~e me, ~ably², ~'edly² adv.,(-z-);~e(up)on, take advantage of, make unscrupulous use of, (person's good nature, one's acquaintance with him, etc.), whence ~ingly² (-z-) adv. [f. L PRAE(sumere stimpt take)]

presump'tion (-z-), n. Arrogance, assurance ; taking for granted, thing taken for granted, as this was a mere ~ ; the (only natural) ~ is that he had lost it ; ground for presuming, as there is a strong ~ against its truth ; (Law) ~ of fact, interence of fact from known facts, ~ of law, (1) assumption of truth of thing until the contrary is proved, (2) inference established by law as universally applicable to certain circumstances. [f. OF presumpcion f. L praesumptionem (as prec.; see -ION)]

presump'tive (-z-), a. Giving grounds for presumption, as ~ evidence, whence ~LY² adv. ; heir ~ (whose right of inheritance is liable to be defeated by birth of nearer heir; cf. APPARENT). [f. LL praesumptivus f. LL praesumptiosus = L praesumptivus (as prec.; see -IVE)]

presump'tuous (-z-), a. Unduly confident, arrogant, forward. Hence ~LY² adv., ~NESS n. [f. OF presumptueux f. LL praesumptiosus (as SUPPOSE.)]

presuppose' (-z-), v.t. Assume beforehand (thing, that) ; involve, imply, as effects ~ causes. [f. F présupposer (see PRE- & SUPPOSE)]

presupposi'tion (-zĭ-), n. Presupposing ; thing assumed beforehand, as basis of argument etc. [f. med. L praesuppositio (as SUPPOSITION)]

pretence', n. Claim (to merit etc.) ; ostentation, display, as devoid of all ~ ; false profession of purpose, pretext, as under the ~ of helping, on the slightest ~ ; pretending, make-believe. [f. late AF pretensse, as foll.]

pretend', v.t. & i. Feign, give oneself out, (to be or do), as does not ~ to be a scholar ; make believe (to do, that) in play ; profess falsely to have, as you should ~ illness ; allege falsely (that) ; venture, aspire, presume, (to do) ; lay claim to (right, title, etc.); ~ to, try to win (person, person's hand) in marriage ; ~ to, profess to have (quality etc.). Hence ~EDLY² adv. [f. L PRAE(tendere tent- later tens- stretch)]

preten'der, n. One who makes baseless pretensions (to title etc., or abs.) ; Old Pretender, P~ son, grandson, of James II as claimants to British throne. Hence ~SHIP n. [-ER²]

preten'sion (-shn), n. Assertion of a claim (to thing, or abs.) ; justifiable claim (to thing, to be or do), as he has no ~s to the name, has some ~s to be chosen as the site, f. med. L praetensio, -tio, (as PRETEND, see -ION)]

preten'tious (-shus), a. (Of person, book, speech, etc.) making ostentation to great merit or importance; ostentatious. Hence ~LY² adv., ~NESS n. [f. F prétentieux f. L+ praetentiosus (as prec., see -OUS)]

prěter-, pref. = L praeter past, beyond, in senses ~ beyond, outside the range of, more than ; as ~cani'ne, more than canine; ~hu'man, beyond what is human, superhuman : ~na'tural, outside the ordinary course of nature, (also) supernatural, whence ~na'turally adv.; ~na'turalism, system, doctrine, of the natural ; ~sen'sual, beyond the domain of the senses.

prě'terite, -it, a. & n. (Gram.) ~ (tense), one expressing past action or state, ~ present (tense), one originally ~ but now used as present (tense), (e.g. can, may, shall) (joc.) past, bygone, whence ~NESS n. [f. L praeteritus p.p. of praeterire pass (treit- go, see preo.)]

prěteri'tion (-shn), n. Omission, disregard, (of); (Theol.) passing over of the non-elect. [f. LL praeteritio (as prec. see -ION)]

preter'mit, v.t.(-tt-). Omit to mention (fact etc.) ; omit to do or perform, neglect ; leave off (custom, continuous action) for a time ; (improp.) leave off. So ~mi'ssion (-shn) n. [f. L PRAE(termittere (mittere miss- let go, see PRETER-)]

prě'text¹, n. Ostensible reason, excuse; on or under, or upon, the ~ of or that, professing as one's object etc. [f. L PRAE-(texere text- weave)]

prětext'², v.t. Allege (thing, that) as pretext. [f. L prétexter, as prec.]

prě'tone, n. Syllable, vowel, preceding the stressed syllable. So **prěton'ic** a. [PRE-]

pretor etc. See PRAETOR etc.

Pre'ttify (pri-), v.t. Make pretty, represent with finicking prettiness. [-FY]

pre'ttily (pri-), adv. In a way that pleases the eye, ear, or aesthetic sense, as *dressed*; (Nursery) *eat, ask, behave,* ~ (in the approved manner). [f. PRETTY + -LY²]

pre'ttiness (pri-), n. Beauty of a dainty or childish kind; pretty thing, ornament, etc.; affected or trivial beauty of style in literature or art, so **pre'ttyism** (pri-) n. [-NESS]

pre'tty (pri-), a., adv., & n. 1. (Of woman or child) beautiful in dainty or diminutive way; attractive to eye, ear, or aesthetic sense, as ~ *cottage, song, scene, story*; fine, good of its kind, as *has a ~ wit, very* ||(arch.) *fine, stout, as a ~ fellow*; ||(arch.) considerable in amount or extent, as *earned a ~ sum*; (ellipt.) *my ~* (one, child). 2. adv. Fairly, moderately, as *am ~ well, find it ~ difficult, that is ~ much* (very nearly) *the same thing.* 3. n. ||Fluted or cut part of wine-glass or tumbler, as *fill it up to the ~*; (Golf) fairway (colloq.). 4. ~~, overdoing the ~, aiming too much at prettiness, (n. pl.) *~pretties,* ornaments, knick-knacks. Hence ~ISH¹ a. [OE *prættig* (*prætt* trick, cf. Du. *part, pred,* Norw. *pretta,* see -Y²)]

pret'zel, b~, n. Crisp knot-shaped biscuit flavoured with salt, used esp. by Germans as relish with beer. [G]

preux chevalier (prē' shŭvalyā'), n. Gallant knight. [F]

prevail', v.i. Gain the mastery, be victorious, (*against, over*); ~ (*upon,* persuade (*to* do); be the more usual or prominent, predominate; exist, occur, in general use or experience, be current, whence or cogn. ~ingly², **prev'alently²** advv., **prev'alence** n. [f. L PRAE(*valēre* have power]

prevā'ricate, v.i. Speak, act, evasively; quibble, equivocate. So ~A'TION, ~ātor², nn. [f. L PRAE(*varicari* straddle f. *varicus* straddling f. *varus* bent) walk crookedly, deviate, practise collusion]

preven'ient, a. Preceding, previous; having in view the prevention (*of*); (Theol.) ~ *grace* (preceding repentance & predisposing the heart to seek God). [as foll., see -ENT]

prevent', v.t. Hinder, stop, as *this may ~ him from writing, ~ his* (pop. *him*) *writing, wish to ~ all dispute*; ||(arch.) meet, deal with, (wish, question, etc.) before it is expressed etc.; (Theol.) *God* ~ *grace.* Hence or cogn. ~ABLE, ~IBLE, aa., **preven'tion** n. [f. L PRAE(*venire vent-* come) come before, hinder]

preven'ter, n. In vbl senses, also; (Naut.) rope, chain, bolt, etc., used to supplement another. [-ER¹]

preven'tive, a. & n. 1. Serving to prevent, esp. (Med.) to keep off disease; ||P~ (Coastguard) *Service.* 2. n. ~ agent, measure, drug, etc. Hence or cogn. **preven'tively** a. & n., ~LY² adv. [-IVE]

pre'view (-vū), n., & v.t. View or examination of a film, play, book, etc., before it is submitted to the general public; (v.t.) view in advance of public presentation. [PRE-]

prev'ious, a. & adv. 1. Coming before in time or order; prior *to*; (sl.) done or acting hastily, as *you have been a little too ~,* whence ~NESS n.; (Parl.) ~ *question,* question whether vote shall be taken on main question (put to avoid putting of main question); || P~ *Examination,* = LITTLE-go. 2. adv. ~ *to,* before, as *had called ~ to writing.* Hence ~LY² adv. [f. L PRAE(*vius* f. *via* way) +-OUS]

previse' (-z), v.t. Foresee, forecast, (event etc., or abs.). So **prevī'sion** (-zhn) n., **prevī'sional** a., **prevī'sionally²** adv., (-zho-). [f. L PRAE(*vidēre vis-* see)]

prey¹ (prā), n. Animal hunted or killed by carnivorous animal for food (also fig.); *beast, bird, fish, of ~,* kinds that kill & devour other animals; (Bibl.) what one brings away safe from contest etc. (*Jer.* xxi. 9); person, thing, that falls a victim (*to* enemy, disease, fear, etc.). [f. OF *preie, proie,* f. L *praeda*]

prey² (prā), v.i. ~ *upon,* seek, take, (animal etc.) as prey, plunder (persons); (of disease, emotion, etc.) exert baneful or wasteful influence *upon.* [f. OF *preer* f. LL *praedare* as prec.]

pri'apism, n. Licentiousness; (Path.) persistent erection of penis. [f. LL f. Gk *priapismos* (*Priapos,* god of procreation, see -ISM)]

price, n., & v.t. 1. Money for which thing is bought or sold, as *what is the ~ of this?, try our superb tea, ~ 3/6 per lb., offered at reduced ~s; ~ current, ~-list,* list of current ~s of commodities; LONG¹, COST¹, ~; *above, beyond, without, ~,* so valuable that no ~ can be stated; *set ~ on* person's *head,* offer reward for his capture or death; (Betting) odds, as *the starting ~ of a horse*; (fig.) what must be given, done, sacrificed, etc., to obtain a thing, as *must be done at any ~; every man has his ~* (can be won over by some inducement; *would not have it,* do it, etc., *at any ~,* on any terms, for any consideration; || *what ~ the Concert of Europe* etc.? (sl.), taunting allusion to the failure of something vaunted; ||(arch.) preciousness, value. 2. v.t. Fix, inquire, the ~ of (thing for sale); (fig.) estimate the value of. [(n.) f. OF *pris* f. L *pretium*; ME *pris* became *prise* to secure i, and *price* to avoid z

For other words in *pre-* see PRE-.

sound of *s* between vowels; (vb) earlier
prise PRIZE[1]; *price*, *prize*, *praise*, are all
variants of same wd.]

priced (-ĭst), *a.* **To which a price is as-**
signed, esp. in comb., as *high*, *low*, ~;
~ *catalogue* etc. (in which prices are
named). [-ED[1,2]]

price'less (-sl-), *a.* Invaluable; (sl.) most
amusing; incredibly absurd. Hence~NESS
n. [-LESS]

prick[1], *n.* Pricking, puncture; (fig.) ~*s*
(stinging reflections) *of conscience*; mark
made by pricking; ||(arch.) goad for
oxen, esp. (fig.) *kick against the* ~*s*, hurt
oneself by useless resistance (*Acts* ix. 5);
(vulg.) penis; ~*ears*, erect pointed ears
(of some dogs etc., conspicuous ears of
person, esp. ~*of* Roundheads, ~*eared*,
having such ears. [OE *prica*, Sw. *prick*,
& Da. *prik*, Sw. *prick*, cogn. w. foll.]

prick[2], *v.t. & i.* **1.** Pierce slightly, make
minute hole in; ~ *a* or *the bladder* or
bubble, show the emptiness of a person or
thing that has passed for important;
(fig.)*cause sharp pain to, as my conscience*
~*ed me*. **2.** Make a thrust (*at*, *into*, etc.).
3. (arch.). Spur, urge on, (horse); (intr.)
advance on horseback. **4.** Mark off (name
etc. in list) with a prick, ||select (sheriff)
thus; mark (pattern *off*, *out*) with dots.
5. ~ *in*, *out*, *off*, plant (seedlings etc.) in
small holes ~*ed in earth*; ~ *up one's ears*
(of dog) erect the ears when on the alert,
(fig., of person) become suddenly attentive. [late OE *prician*, cf. Du. *prikken*,
Da. *prikke*]

prick'er, *n.* In vbl senses, esp. pricking
instrument, e.g. awl. [-ER[1]]

prick'et, *n.* ||Buck in second year, with
straight unbranched horns; ||~*'s sister*,
female fallow deer in second year; spike
to stick candle on. [prob. f. med. L
pricketus f. PRICK, see -ET]

prick'le, *n. & v.t. & i.* **1.** Thorn-like process developed from, & capable of being
peeled off with, epidermis of plant; (pop.)
small thorn; hard-pointed spine of hedgehog etc. **2.** *vb.* Affect, be affected, with
sensation of pricks, whence **prick'ling**
n., **prick'ling**[2] *a.* [OE *pricel* f. stem of
PRICK, cf. Du. *prikkel*]

prick'ling *n.* [-Y[2]]

pride, *n. & v.t. refl.* **1.** Overweening opinion of one's own qualities, merits, etc., a
deadly SIN, often personified, as *I*~ *will
have a fall*; arrogant bearing or conduct;
~ *of place*, exalted position, consciousness of this, arrogance; (also *proper* ~)
sense of what befits one's position, pre-

||pric'kle[2], *n.* Kinds of wicker basket or
measure. [?]

prick'ly, *a.* Armed with prickles (esp. in
names of plants & animals); tingling; ~
heat, inflammation of sweat glands with
eruption of vesicles & ~ sensation, common in hot countries; ~ *pear*, (~ plant
bearing) pear-shaped edible fruit. Hence
prick'liness *n.* [-Y[1]]

venting one from doing unworthy thing;
false ~, mistaken feeling of this kind;
feeling of elation & pleasure, as *take a* ~
in, be proud of (person, thing, doing);
object of this feeling, as *he is his mo her's*
~; esp. in names of plants, as LONDON ~;
(Her.) *peacock in his* ~ (with tail expanded and wings drooping); company
(of lions); best condition, esp. ~ *of
the morning*, mist or shower
at sunrise. **2.** *v. refl.* ~ *oneself* (*up*)*on*, be
proud of (thing, quality, doing). Hence
~'FUL (chiefly Sc.), ~'LESS, aa., ~'fully[2]
adv. [(vb) ME *priden*, (n.) OE *prȳto*, *-te*,
-te (*prūt* PROUD]

prie-dieu (prēdyö', & see Ap.), *n.* Kneel-
ing-desk; (also ~ *chair*) chair with tall
sloping back for use in praying. [F., lit.
pray God]

priest, *n. & v.t.* **1.** (Now usu. *clergyman*,
exc. in official use) clergyman, esp. one
above deacon & below bishop with authority to administer sacraments & pronounce
absolution; (fig.) ~ *of nature*, *science*, etc.,
minister of the altar, esp. officiant at
Eucharist; HIGH ~; official minister of
non-Christian religion, whence ~'ESS[1] *n.
2. ||Mallet used to kill fish when spent
(chiefly in Ireland). **3.** ~'*croft*, ambitious
or worldly policy of ~*s*; ~'*s hood*, ~*-in-
the-pulpit*, wild arum; ~'*s hood*, (person)
subjection by ~*s*; ||~ *vicar*, minor canon
in some cathedrals. **4.** *v.t.* Make (person)
a ~. Hence ~'HOOD (-t-h-), ~'LING[1] *nn.*,
~'LIKE, ~'LIKE, aa. [vb f. n.) OE *prēost*,

f. L *presbyter*]

priest'ly, *a.* Of, like, befitting, a priest;
(O. T. criticism) ~*y code*, one of the constituent elements in the Hexateuch. ~*y
writer* (of this). Hence ~INESS *n.* [-LY[1]]

prig, *n. & v.t.* (-gg-). **1.** Precisian in
speech or manners, conceited or didactic
person, whence ~g'ISM, nn., ~g'GERY[2]),
(-g'-); (sl.) thief. **2.** *v.t.* (sl.), Steal. [orig.
cant, etym. dub.]

prim, *a. & v.i. & t.* (-mm-). (Of persons,
manner, speech, etc.) formal, demure;
(v.i.) assume prim air; (v.t.) form (face, lips,
etc.) into ~ expression. Hence~ly[2] *adv.,*
~'NESS *n.* [f. 17th c., orig. cant]

pri'ma (prē-), *a.* First, chief; as ~ *buff'a
(-boŏ-), chief female comic singer or actress; ~ *donn'a*, (pl. ~ *donnas*, *prime
donne* pr. prēm'ā don'ā), chief female
singer in opera, (transf.) temperamental
person. [It., fem. adj.]

prim'acy, *n.* Office of a primate; pre-
eminence. [f. OF *primacie* f. med. L *pri-
matia* (as PRIMATE, see -ACY]

prim'a fā'cie (-shiē), *adv.* & *a.* (Arising)
at first sight, (based) on the first impression, *as has* ~ *a good case, see a* ~
reason for it. [L]

prim'age[1], *n.* Percentage addition to
freight, paid to owners or freighters of
vessels. [med. L *primagium*, etym. dub.]

prim'age², n. Amount of water carried off suspended in steam from boiler. [f. PRIME v. +-AGE]

prim'al, a. Primitive, primeval; chief, fundamental. Hence ~ly² adv. [f. med. L *primalis* (as PRIME a., see -AL)]

prim'ary, a. & n. 1. Earliest, original; of the first rank in a series, not derived, as *the ~ vowel sounds, ~ meaning of a word*; of the first importance, chief; (Geol.) of the lowest series of strata; (Biol.) belonging to first stage of development; ~ *amputation* (performed before inflammation supervenes); ~ *education*, that which begins with the rudiments of knowledge, esp. that provided for children liable to compulsory attendance, so ~ *school, scholar* (cf. SECONDARY); (Gram.) ~ *tenses*, present, future, perfect, & future perfect, (cf. HISTORIC); ~ *assembly, meeting* (for selection of candidates for election); ~ COLOUR; ~ *planets* (revolving directly round sun as centre); ~ *battery* (in which current is produced). 2. n. ~ planet, meeting, etc. Hence **prim'arily²** adv. [f. L *primarius* (as PRIME a., see -ARY¹)]

prim'ate, n. Archbishop; P~ of England, Archbishop of York, P~ of all England, Archbishop of Canterbury; (Zool.) sing. of foll. Hence **prima'tial** (-āshl) a. [f. LL *primas -ātis* (as PRIME a.)]

primat'es (-z), n. pl. (Zool.; for sing., see prec.). Highest order of mammals, including man, monkeys, lemurs, & (in Linnaean order) bats. [as prec.]

prime¹, n. State of highest perfection, as *in the ~ of life, manhood,* etc.; the best part (of thing); beginning, first age, of anything; a canonical hour of the divine office, appointed for first hour of day (i.e. 6 a.m. or sunrise), (arch.) this time; (arch.) GOLDEN number; prime number; (Chem.) single atom as unit in combination; a position in fencing. [partly abs. use of foll.; OE has *prím*, the canonical hour, f. L *prima (hora)* first (hour)]

prime², a. Chief, most important, as *~ agent, motive*; first-rate (esp. of cattle & provisions), excellent, whence ~ly³ adv..~NESS n.; primary, fundamental; (Arith., of a number) having no integral factors except itself and unity (e.g. 2, 3, 5, 7, 11), (of numbers) having no common measure but unity; ~ COST¹, MOVER; ~ *vertical (circle)*, great circle of the heavens passing through E. & W. points of horizon & through zenith, where it cuts meridian at right angles; ~ *minister*, principal minister of any sovereign or State (now official title of first minister of State in Great Britain). [f. L *primus* first]

prime³, v.t. & i. (Hist.) supply (fire-arm, or abs.) with gunpowder for firing charge; wet (pump) to make it start working; equip (person with information etc.); fill (person with liquor); cover (wood etc.) with first coat of paint or with oil etc. to prevent paint from being absorbed; (of engine boiler) let water pass with steam into cylinder in form of spray. [?]

prim'er¹, n. 1. (usu. pri-). Elementary school-book for teaching children to read; small introductory book, as *P~ of Evolution, Latin P~*; (Hist.) prayer-book for use of laity esp. before Reformation. 2. (pri-). *Great, long,* ~, sizes of TYPE. [f. med. L *primarius* adj. (as PRIME², see -ER²(2)]

prim'er², n. In vbl senses of PRIME³, esp. cap, cylinder, etc., used to ignite powder of cartridge etc. [-ER¹]

prim'ero, n. (hist.). Gambling card-game fashionable in 16th & 17th cc. [f. Sp. *primera* fem. of *primero*, as PRIMARY]

primeur (prēmér'), n. First-fruits; fruit etc. before its season; early news. [F; affected by E journalists]

primev'al, -aeval, a. Of the first age of the world; ancient, primitive. Hence ~ly² adv. [f. L *primaevus* (*primus* first + *aevum* age) +-AL]

prim'ing¹, n. In vbl senses of PRIME³; also or esp.: gunpowder placed in pan of fire-arm; train of powder connecting fuse with charge in blasting etc.; mixture used by painters for preparatory coat; preparation of sugar added to beer; hasty imparting of knowledge, cramming. [-ING¹]

prim'ing², n. Acceleration of the tides taking place from neap to spring tides (cf. LAG¹). [f. rare vb *prime* f. PRIME²]

primip'arous, a. Bearing child for the first time. [f. L *primipara* ~ woman (also used in E) f. *primus* first + *parĕre* bring forth]

prim'itive, a. & n. 1. Early, ancient, as *the P~ Church* (Christian Church in its earliest times); old-fashioned, simple, rude; original, primary; (Gram., of words) radical, not derivative; (Math., of line, figure, etc.) from which another is derived, from which some construction begins, etc.; (of colours) primary; (Geol.) of the earliest period; (Biol.) appearing in earliest or very early stage of growth etc.; P~ *Methodist Connexion*, society of Methodists founded 1810 by Hugh Bourne by secession from main body, P~ *Methodist, Methodism*, member, principles, of this. 2. n. Painter of period before Renascence, picture by such painter; ~ word, line, etc.; P~ Methodist. Hence ~ly² adv., ~NESS n. [ME & F *primitif* f. L *primitivus* (as PRIME²)]

prī'mō (prē-), n. (mus.). Upper part in duet etc. [It.]

prī'mō¹ (prē-), adv. ~, sĕxŭn'dō, tĕr'tĭō (-shĭ-), In the first, second, third, place (written 1°, 2°, 3°). [L]

primogen'itor, n. Earliest ancestor. [med. L, f. L *primo* (at) first +*genitor* begetter (*gignere genit-* bring forth, see -OR²), after L *primogenitus* first-born]

primogen'iture, n. Fact of being the

first-born of the children of the same parents; (*right of*) ~*ure*, right of succession belonging to the first-born, esp. feudal rule by which whole real estate of intestate passes to eldest son. So ~AL, primus aa. [f. med. L *primogenitura* (as prec., see -URE)]

primórd'ial, a. Existing at or from the beginning; primeval; original, fundamental. Hence ~ITY (-ăl'), n., ~IУ adv. [f. LL *primordialis* (L *primordium* f. *primus* first + *ordiri* begin, see -AL)]

prim'rose (-z), n. Plant bearing pale yellow flowers in early spring; flower of this; (attrib.) of the colour of this flower; the ~ *path*, the pursuit of pleasure (w. ref. to *Haml.* I. iii. 50); ||*P~ Day, League*, anniversary of the death (Apr. 19th, 1881) of, Conservative association formed in memory of, Benjamin Disraeli Earl of Beaconsfield; *P~ League*; ~ *peerless*, two-flowered narcissus, (formerly) any species of narcissus. Hence **prim'rósy²** (-z-) a. [late ME *primerose* f. med. L *prima rosa* lit. first rose, sense unexpl.]

prim'ŭla, n. Kind of herbaceous perennial with yellow, white, pink, or purple flowers. [med. L, fem. adj. as n., dim. as PRIME²]

prīm'um mŏb'ĭle, n. Outermost sphere added in Middle Ages to Ptolemaic system, supposed to revolve round earth in 24 hours carrying with it the contained spheres; (fig.) prime source of motion or action. [med. L, lit. first moving thing]

prīm'us¹, a. & n. 1. ||(In boys' school) eldest (or of longest standing) of the name, as *Jones ~* (usu. written *Jones* i.: similarly *secundus* ii., *tertius* iii.; *quartus* iv., *quintus* v., *sextus* vi., *septimus* vii., *octāvus* viii., *nonus* ix., *děcimus* x.); (L) ~ *inter pārēs* (-z), first among equals, senior or spokesman of a board of colleagues. 2. n. ‖ Presiding bishop in Scottish Episcopal Church. [L, = first]

prim'us², n. Brand of stove burning vaporized oil for cooking etc. [P]

prince, n. 1. (Now rhet.) sovereign ruler; *P~ of Peace*, Christ; ~ *of darkness, the air, the world*, etc., Satan. 2. Ruler of small State, actually or nominally feudatory to king or emperor. 3. Male member of royal family, esp. (in Great Britain) son or grandson of king or queen (also ~ *of the blood*). 4. *P~ of Wales*, heir apparent to British throne (*P~ of Wales's feathers*, triple ostrich plume); *P~ Consort*, husband of reigning female sovereign being himself a ~; *P~ of Denmark*, Hamlet (*Hamlet without the P~ of Denmark*, thing robbed of its essence). 5. (As English rendering of foreign titles) noble usu. ranking next below duke; (as courtesy title in some connexions) duke, marquis, earl; (title of cardinal) ~ *of the (Holy) Roman) Church*. 6. (fig.) Chief, greatest,

(of novelists, liars, etc.), 7. *P~ *Albert* (collog.), frock-coat; ~ *bishop*, bishop who is also a ~; *P~ Regent*, ~ who acts as regent, e.g. George (afterwards IV); ~ *royal*, eldest son of reigning monarch; *P~ Rupert's drops*, pear-shaped lumps of glass bursting to pieces when thin ends are broken off; ~'*s feather*, kinds of plant esp. tall plant with feathery spikes of small red flowers; ~'*s metal*, alloy of copper & zinc. Hence ~'DOM (-sd-), ~'KIN (-sk-), ~'LET, ~'LING (2), (-sl-), nn., ~'LIKE (-sl-), a. [F, f. L *princeps* (*princes* first -*cip*-*is* taken]

prince'lĭ (-sl-), a. (Worthy) of a prince; sumptuous, splendid. Hence ~INESS n. [-LY¹]

prin'cess (or -ĕs' *ecc. when followed by name*), n. (Arch.) queen; wife of prince; (also ~ *of the blood*) daughter, granddaughter of sovereign; ~ *royal*, (title conferrable on) sovereign's eldest daughter; *P~ Regent*, ~ acting as regent, (also) wife of prince regent; ~ *dress, petticoat*, of which the lengths of bodice & skirt are cut in one piece. [ME & F *princesse* (as PRINCE, see -ESS²)]

prin'cipal, a. & n. 1. First in rank or importance, chief, as *their ~ food is potatoes, the ~ town of the district, the ~ persons concerned*; ~ *boy, girl*, actress who takes leading male, female, part in pantomime; main, leading, as *a ~ cause of his failure*. 2. (Of money) constituting the original sum invested or lent. 3. (gram.) ~ *sentence, clause*, one to which another is subordinate; ~ *parts of verb*, those from which the others can be derived. 4. n. Head, ruler, superior; head of some colleges (*lady ~*, female head), whence ~SHIP n. 5. Person for whom another acts as agent etc., as *I must consult my ~*; person directly responsible for crime, either (~ *in the first degree*) as actual perpetrator or (~ *in the second degree*) as aiding; person for whom surety; combatant in duel. 6. Any of the main rafters on which rest the purlins that support the common rafters. 7. Capital sum as distinguished from interest or from income. 8. Organ diapason stop sounding octave above normal. [f. L *principalis* adj. (as PRINCE, see -AL)]

principal'itý, n. Government of a prince; State ruled by a prince; || *the P~*, Wales; (pl.) an ORDER¹ of angels. [f. OF *princet-palité* f. LL *principālitātem* (as PRINCE, see -TY)]

prin'cipally, adv. For the most part, chiefly. [-LY²]

prin'cipāte, n. (Rom. Hist.) rule of early emperors while some republican forms were retained; State ruled by a prince. [f. L *principātus* (as PRINCE, see -ATE¹)]

prin'ciple, n. 1. Fundamental source

primary element, as *held water to be the first ~ of all things.* **2.** Fundamental truth as basis of reasoning etc., as *(first) ~s of political economy;* (Physics) general law (often with discoverer's name, as *Pascal's ~*); general law as guide to action, as *moral, conservative, ~s, a dangerous ~,* whence -**prin'ciplod²** (-ld) a.; (pl. & collect. sing.) personal code of right conduct, as *a man of high ~, has ability but no ~s, is everything; on ~,* from settled moral motive, as *I refuse on ~* (not from selfish motive etc.). **3.** Law of nature seen in working of machine etc., as *in all these instruments the ~ is the same.* **4.** (Chem.) constituent of a substance, esp. one giving rise to some quality etc., as *bitter, colouring, ~.* [f. L *principium* beginning, as PRINCE]

Prink, v.t. & i. Make (oneself etc.) spruce; dress oneself up. [cogn. w. PRANK²]

Print¹, n. **1.** Indentation in surface preserving the form left by pressure of some body, as *finger~, foot ~,* whence ~LESS a. **2.** Printed cotton fabric, as (attrib.) *~ dress.* **3.** Language embodied in printed form, printed lettering, as *large, small, clear, ~;* state of being printed; *book is in ~,* (1) in printed form, (2) on sale, not *out of ~* (sold out); (of writer) *rush into ~,* publish book, write to newspaper etc., on insufficient grounds; (chiefly U.S.) printed publication, esp. newspaper; picture, design, printed from block or plate; (Photog.) picture produced from negative. **4.** ~ *hand, letters* (imitating ~); *~-seller,* dealer in engravings etc., *~-shop,* his shop; *~-works,* factory where cotton fabrics are printed. [ME *prent* f. OF *priente, -nt,* p.p. of *preindre* press f. L *premere*]

Print², v.t. **1.** Impress, stamp, (surface, e.g. pat of butter, *with* seal, die, etc.; a mark or figure *on, in,* yielding or other surface); (fig.) impress (idea, scene, etc., *on* mind, memory). **2.** Produce (book, picture, etc., or abs.) by applying inked types, blocks, or plates, to paper, vellum, etc.; (of author or editor) cause (book, MS.) to be so ~ed; express, publish, in print, as *not bound to ~ every opinion you hold;* write (words, or abs.) in imitation of typography. **3.** Mark (textile fabric) with decorative design in colours; transfer (coloured design) from paper. **4.** (Photog., also *~ out, off*) produce (picture) by transmission of light through negative. Hence ~ABLE a. [ME *prenten,* prob. f. prec.]

prin'ter, n. In vbl senses, esp.: one who prints books; owner of printing business; printing instrument; *P~s' Bible* (with *P~s* for *Princes,* Ps. cxlv. 161); ~'s DEVIL¹; ~'s *mark* (device, trade-mark); ~'s *pie,* ~ = PIE³ n. [-ER¹]

prin'ting, n. In vbl senses; *~-ink,* ~ *press,* (for ~ on paper etc. from types etc.), [-ING¹]

pri'or¹, n. Superior officer of religious house or order; (in abbey) officer next under abbot, so ~ESS¹ n.; (Hist.) chief magistrate in some Italian republics. Hence or cogn. ~ATE⁴(1), ~SHIP, nn. [OE as foll.]

pri'or², a. & adv. **1.** Earlier; antecedent in time, order, or importance, *(to).* **2.** adv. *~ to,* before, as *existing ~ to his appointment.* So **prio'rity** n. (also, an interest having a ~ claim to consideration; in recent use freq. with qualification, as *a first, top, ~ing*). [L, f. OL *pri* before]

pri'ory, n. Monastery, nunnery, governed by prior(ess); *alien ~,* alien, (dependent on abbey in foreign country). [f. AF *priorie* f. med. L *prioria* (as prec., see -Y¹)]

|| **prise.** See PRIZE³.

pri'sm, n. Solid figure whose two ends are similar, equal, & parallel rectilineal figures, & whose sides are parallelograms; transparent body of this form, usu. triangular, with refracting surfaces at acute angle with each other; (loosely) spectrum produced by refraction through ~, (pl.) prismatic colours; *~-glasses,* binoculars (in which triangular ~s are used to shorten the instrument); PRUNE¹s &~. Hence **pris'mal** (-z-) a. [f. LL f. Gk *prisma -matos* thing sawn (*prizō* saw, see -M)]

prismat'ic (-z-), a. Of, like, a prism; *~ compass,* hand-compass used in survey work, with attached prism enabling the dial to be read while the sight is taken; *~ powder,* gunpowder whose grains are hexagonal prisms; (of colours) formed, distributed, etc., by transparent prism, (also) brilliant, so **pris'my²** (-z-), a.; *the ~ colours,* seven into which ray of light is separated by prism. Hence **prismat'-ICALLY** (-z-) adv. [as prec., see -IC]

pris'moid (-z-), n. Body like prism, with similar but unequal parallel polygonal ends. Hence **prismoid'al** (-z-a-) [-OID]

pris'on (-zn), n., & v.t. **1.** Place in which person is kept in captivity, esp. building to which person is legally committed while awaiting trial or for punishment; custody, confinement, as *lie, put* (person), *in ~;* *~-bird.* =GAOL-bird; *~-breaking,* breaking out of lawfully confined person from ~, so *~-breaker;* *~ editor,* editor of newspaper who takes legal responsibility for its contents & serves terms of imprisonment entailed by conviction; *~-house* (usu. rhet.), ~. **2.** v.t. (poet.). Imprison. [(vb f. n.) ME & OF *prisun, -on,* f. L *prensionem* (*pre(he)ndere prens-* seize, see -ION, -SON)]

pris'oner (-zn-), n. Person kept in prison; *~ at the bar,* person in custody on criminal charge & on trial; *~ of State, State~,* (confined for political reasons); (also *~ of war*)

one who has been captured in war; *take ~* (person) ~, *seize & hold as ~*; (fig.) *am a ~* (confined by illness etc.) *to my room or chair, made her hand a ~* (secured it); *~'s bars, base*, game played by two parties of boys etc., each occupying distinct base or home. [f. F *prisonnier*, as prec., see -ER(2)]

pris'tine, a. Ancient, primitive, good old. [f. L *pristinus*, cf. *priscus* ancient, *primus* first]

prith'ee (-dh-), int.(arch.), Pray, please, as *tell me, ~*. [=(I) *pray thee*)]

pri'vacy (also prī-), n. Being withdrawn from society or public interest, as *lived in absolute ~*; *must disturb your~*; avoidance of publicity, as *in such matters ~ is impossible*. [PRIVATE, -ACY]

priv'at-docent, -cent, (prévaht'dōtsênt'), n. (In German univ.) private teacher or lecturer recognized by university but not on salaried staff. [G]

pri'vate, a. & n. **1.** (Of person) not holding public office or official position; *~, (soldier)*, ordinary soldier without rank, one below non-commissioned officers (freq. prefixed, as *P~ Smith*); *~ member* of House of Commons (not member of Government). **2.** Kept, removed, from public knowledge, as *the matter was kept ~; had ~ reasons*. **3.** Not open to the public, as *~ door, news, came through ~ channels, ~ boarding-house, carriage, hotel, theatricals; ~ view* (of exhibition of pictures esp. before it is opened to the public). **4.** *~ house*, dwelling-house of a person (opp. to his shop or office, to public house, or to public building); *~ parts*, genitals (*~protector*, guard worn at cricket etc.); *~ school* (‖ carried on for owner's profit, cf. PUBLIC; *=schoolmaster* of or in this). **5.** One's own, as *my ~ goods, property*; individual, personal, not affecting the community, as *motives of ~ motive*; (Parl.) *~ bill, act* (affecting individual or corporation only). **6.** Confidential, as *asked for some ~ conversation, this is for your ~ ear* (confidential). **7.**(Of person) retired, secluded; (arch., of person) given up to retirement. **8.** *In ~, ~ly*, in ~ company or life. **9.** n. pl. *~ parts*. Hence ~LY² adv. [f. L *privatus*, orig. p.p. of *privare* deprive]

privateer', n. Armed vessel owned & officered by private persons holding commission from government (*letters of* MARQUE) & authorized to use it against hostile nation esp. in capture of merchant shipping, whence ~ING(1) n.; commander, (pl.) crew, of this. [f. prec. +-EER, prob. after *volunteer*]

priva'tion, n. Loss, absence, (of quality), as *cold is the ~ of heat*; want of the comforts or necessaries of life, as *died of ~, suffered many ~s*. [F, f. L *privationem* (PRIVATE, -ATION)]

priv'ative, a. Consisting in, marked by, the loss or removal or absence of some quality or attribute, as *cold is merely ~* (cf. prec.); (of terms) denoting privation or absence of quality etc.; (Gram. of particles etc.) expressing privation, as (Gk Gram.) *alpha ~* (*a-* =not-). Hence ~LY² adv. [f. L *privativus* (as PRIVATE, see -IVE)]

priv'et, n. Bushy evergreen shrub with small white flowers & small shining black berries, much used for hedges; *~-hawk*, large species of moth depositing eggs on

priv'ilege, n. & v.t. **1.** Right, advantage, immunity, belonging to person, class, or office (*~ of Parliament*, those of either House or its members; *breach of ~*, esp., infringement of any of these); special advantage or benefit, as *to commune with him was a ~*; *~* (BENEFIT) *of clergy; bill of ~*, (formerly) of peer demanding to be tried by his peers; *writ of ~*, writ to deliver ~d person from custody when arrested in civil suit; monopoly, patent, granted to individual, corporation, etc.; *~ cab* (admitted to stand for hire in private places esp. railway station). **2.** v.t. Invest with ~, allow (person to do) as ~; exempt (person from burden etc.). Hence priv'ileger² (-jd) a. (~b f. F *privilégier* f. med. L *privilegiare*) f. L *privilegium* bill, law, affecting an individual (*privus* private +*lex legis* law).

priv'ity, n. (Law) any relation between two parties that is recognized by law, e.g. that of blood, lease, service; being privy (to designs etc.). [f. OF *priveté* f. L *privus* private, see -TY]

priv'y, a. & n. **1.** (Of things, places, etc.) hidden, secluded; *~ parts*, external organs of sex; (of action) secret, *~ to*, in the secret of (person's designs etc.). **2.** ‖*P~ Council*, sovereign's private counsellors, (in Great Britain) body of advisers chosen by sovereign (now chiefly as personal dignity, most functions being performed by Cabinet, committees, etc.) together with princes of blood, archbishops, etc.; *~ counsellor, -cillor*, private adviser, esp. (abbr. P.C.) member of *P~ Council*; *~ purse*, allowance from public revenue for monarch's private expenses, keeper of this; *~ seal*, seal affixed to documents that are afterwards to pass, or that do not require, the Great Seal (keeper of the) *P~ Seal*. **3.** n. Private place of ease, latrine, (arch.); (Law) person having a part or interest in any action, matter, or thing. [f. F *privé* PRIVATE]

prize, n., & v.t. **1.** Reward given as symbol of victory or superiority to student in school or college who excels in attainments, to competitor in athletic contest, to exhibitor of best specimen of manufactured products, works of art,

etc., in exhibition; (fig.) anything striven for or worth striving for, as *many ~s in the Church, missed all the great ~s of life*; money or money's worth offered for competition by chance, in lottery, etc. **2.** (attrib.), ~ *ox, poem*, etc. (to which ~ is adjudged in show, competition, etc.). **3.** || ~ *fellowship* (given as reward for eminence in examination), ~ *fellow*, holder of this; ~*fight*, boxing-match for money, so ~*-fighter*, ~*-fighting*, nn.; ~*-man*, winner of (often specified) ~, as *Smith's ~man*, winner of Smith's P~; ~*-ring*, enclosed area (now usu. square) for, (fig.) practice of, ~-fighting. **4.** v.t. Value highly, as *we ~ liberty more than life*. Hence ~LESS a. [(n.) differentiation of PRIZE; (vb) f. OF *prisier, preisier*, PRAISE]

prize², n. & v.t. Ship, property, captured at sea in virtue of rights of war; || ~*-court*, department of admiralty court concerned with ~s; || ~*-money* (realized by sale of ~); *make ~ of* (cargo, ship, etc.), seize thus; *become* (*lawful* etc.) ~, be thus seized; (fig.) find or windfall (*see what a ~ I have found!*); (v.t.) make ~ of. [(vb f. n.) f. F *prise* taking, capture, f. Rom. *prensa* f. L *pre(he)ndere -hens-* seize]

|| **prize¹, -se**, v.t., & n. Force (lid etc. *up, out*, box etc. *open*) by leverage; (n.) leverage, purchase. [(vb f. n.) as prec.]

prō¹, prep. ~ *form'a* adv. & a., (done) for form's sake; ~ *hāc vī'cē*, for this occasion only; ~ *rāt'a* adv. & a., proportional(ly); ~ *rē rāt'a* adv. & a., for an occasion as it arises, as *a meeting held ~ re nata, a ~ re nata meeting*; ~ *tān'tō*, so far, to that extent; ~ *tēm'porē* adv. & a. (abbr. *pro tēm.*), for the time, as *made secretary pro tem.*, the *pro tem. secretary*. [L]

prō², n. (colloq.; pl. ~**s**), A PROFESSIONAL. [abbr.]

prō-¹, pref. (before vowel occas. in earlier form *prod-*)=L *pro* in front of, for, on behalf of, instead of, on account of. As living E pref. **1.** In sense ' substitute(d) for ', as ~*cathed'ral* a. & n., (church) used as substitute for cathedral, || ~*proc'tor*, assistant or deputy proctor in univ., ~*rec'tor*, vice-rector in univ., etc.; ~*leg*, fleshy abdominal limb of larvae of some insects, e.g. caterpillars. **2.** In sense 'favouring or siding with ' (cf. ANTI-), as ~*Bo'er* a. & n., ~*Brit'ish*, ~*educa'tional*, ~*neg'ro* a. & n., ~*pap'ist* a. & n., ~*slav'ery*, ~*ta'riff-reform*.

prō-², pref.=Gk *pro* before (in time, place, order, etc.) in wds f. Gk & in mod. scientific wds.

prō'a, n. Malay boat, esp. a type of sailing-boat. [f. Malay *prahu*, also used in F]

prō and cŏn', adv. & n. 1. (Of arguments or reasons) for & against, on both sides. **2.** n. pl. *Pros & cons*, reasons for & against. [f. L *pro et contra*]

probabil'iorism, n. (R.-C. casuistry). Doctrine that the side on which evidence

preponderates ought to be followed (cf. foll.). So ~IST n. [f. L *probabilior* more PROBABLE.+-ISM]

prŏb'abilism, n. Doctrine that where authorities differ any course may be followed for which recognized doctor of the Church can be cited (cf. prec.); theory that there is no certain knowledge, but may be grounds of belief sufficient for practical life. So ~IST n. [as PROBABLE +-ISM]

probabil'ity̆, n. Quality of being probable: *in all ~y*, most likely; *there is no ~y* (likelihood) *of his coming*; (most) probable event, as *what are the ~ies, the ~y is that he will come*; (Math.) likelihood of an event, measured by the ratio of the favourable cases to the whole number of cases possible, as *from a bag containing 3 red balls & 7 white the ~y of a red ball's being drawn first is 3/10*. [f. F *probabilité* f. L *probabilitatem* (as foll., see -TY)]

prŏb'able, a. & n. **1.** That may be expected to happen or prove true, likely, as *reckon the ~ cost, it is ~ that he forgot, gives a ~ account of the matter*. **2.** n. A ~ candidate, member, selection, etc. Hence **prŏb'ably²** adv. [f. L *probabilis* (*probare* PROVE, see -BLE)]

prŏb'ang, n. Surgeon's strip of whalebone with sponge, button, etc, at end for introducing into throat. [altered f. inventor's wd *provang* (etym. dub.), perh. on *probe*]

prŏb'ate, n. Official proving of will; verified copy of will with certificate as handed to executors; ~ *duty*, tax on personal property of deceased testator, now merged in estate duty. [f. L *probatum* neut. p.p. of *probare* PROVE]

proba'tion, n. Testing of conduct or character of person esp. of candidate for membership in religious body etc. (*on ~*), undergoing it before full admission etc.); moral trial or discipline; system of releasing young criminals esp. first offenders on suspended sentence during good behaviour under supervision of person (~ *officer*) acting as friend & adviser. [f. OF *probacion* f. L *probationem* (as PROVE, see -ATION)]

proba'tion̆ary (-sho-), a. Of, serving for, done in the way of, probation, so ~AL a.; undergoing probation. [-ARY¹]

proba'tioner (-sho-), n. Person on probation, e.g. hospital nurse at early stage of training; offender under PROBATION. Hence ~SHIP n. [-ER¹]

prŏb'ative, a. Affording proof, evidential. [f. L *probativus* (as PROVE, see -IVE)]

probe, n., & v.t. **1.** Blunt-ended surgical instrument usu. of silver for exploring wound etc.; *(fig.; f. vb) investigation. **2.** v.t. Explore (wound, part of body) with ~, penetrate (thing) with sharp instrument; (fig.) examine closely, sound, (person, motive, report, etc.). [(vb f. n.) f. LL *proba* PROOF]

pröb′ity, n. Uprightness, honesty. [f. L *probitas* (*probus* good, see -TY)]

pröb′lem, n. **1.** Doubtful or difficult question, as *how to prevent it is a ~, the question, as how to prevent it is a ~; the ~ of ventilation*: (attrib.) *~ play, novel* (in which social or other ~ is treated). **2.** Thing hard to understand, as *his whole conduct is a ~ to me*. **3.** (Geom.) proposition in which something has to be done (cf. THEOREM); (Log.) the question (usu. only implied) involved in a syllogism (Physics, Math.) inquiry starting from given conditions to investigate a fact, result, or law, as *Kepler's ~*; (Chess) arrangement of pieces on the board in which player is challenged to accomplish specified result, often under prescribed conditions. [f. F *problème* & L f. Gk *problēma -matos* f. PRO²(*ballō* throw), see -M]

problemăt′ic(al), aa. Doubtful, questionable, as *its success is ~, the whole question is ~*; (Log.) enunciating or supporting what is possible but not necessarily true. Hence **problemăt′ically²** adv. [f. F *problématique* f. LL f. Gk *problēmatikos* (as prec., see -IC)]

pröb′lemăt(ist, nn. One who studies or composes (esp. chess) problems. [-IST]

Prŏbŏscid′ean, -ian, aa. & nn. Having a proboscis; of, like, a proboscis; (mammal) of the order *Proboscidea*, containing elephant & extinct allies. [f. mod. L *Proboscidea*+-AN]

probŏs′cis, n. Elephant's trunk; long flexible snout of tapir etc.; elongated part of mouth of some insects; sucking organ in some worms; (joc.) human nose; *~ monkey* (with nose projecting far beyond mouth). So **probŏs′cidĭ′ferous, probŏs′cid′iform**, aa. [L, gen. *-cidis*, f. Gk *pro-boskis* f. PRO²(*boskō* feed)]

procē′dure (-dyer), n. Proceeding; mode of conducting business (esp. in parliament) or legal action. [f. F *procédure* (as foll., see -URE)]

proceed′, v.i. Go on, make one's way, (*to* place); go on (*with, in*, action, investigation, remarks, etc., *to* another subject, *to do*); adopt course of action, as *how shall we ~?*; take legal proceedings *against* person; (abs.) go on to say, as '*in either case*,' *he ~ed*; *our course is clear*'; ‖ ~ *to* (take) the degree of *M.A.*, ‖ (take degree of) *M.A.*.: (of action) be carried on, take place, as *the case, the play, will now ~*; come forth, issue, originate, as *sobs heard to ~ from next room, volumes ~ from the Pitt Press, exertions ~ from a false hope*. [f. F *procéder* f. L PRO²(*cedere cess-* go)]

proceed′ing, n. In vbl senses, esp.: action, piece of conduct, as *a high-handed ~, a shall institute legal ~s* (or bring ~s) (against) *~, legal ~s*, (steps taken in) legal action; (take) the ~s of *M.A.,* our course is clear'; ‖ (as title) *P~s of Royal Society* etc. [-ING¹]

prŏ′ceeds, n. pl. Produce, outcome, pro-

For other words in *pro-* see PRO-¹.

pröceleusmăt′ic, a. & n. (prosody). *~ foot*, metrical foot of four short syllables. [f. LL f. Gk *prokeleusmatikos* f. *prokeleus-ma* incitement f. PRO²(*keleuō* command)]

pröcellā′rian, a. & n. (Bird) of the genus *procella* storm, or family to which petrels belong. [f. L *procella* storm, see -ARIAN]

prŏ′cess¹, n., & v.t. **1.** Progress, course, *in ~ of construction* etc., being constructed, *in ~ of time*, as time goes on; course of action, proceeding, esp. method of operation in manufacture, printing, photography, etc.; natural or involuntary operation, series of changes. **2.** (Print from block produced by) method other than simple engraving by hand. **3.** Action at law, formal commencement of this, summons or writ (*~ -server*, sheriff's officer). **4.** (Anat., Zool., Bot.) outgrowth, protuberance. **5.** v.t. Institute legal (person); treat (material), preserve (food), reproduce (drawing), by a *~*. Hence *~ER¹, ~OR²,* nn. [vb partly thr. OF *processer*] f. F *procès* f. L *processus -ūs*, as PROCEED]

prŏ′cess², v.i. (colloq.) Walk in procession. [back formation f. foll.]

procĕs′sion (-shn), n., & v.i. & t. Proceeding of body of persons (or of boats etc.) in orderly succession, esp. as religious ceremony or on festive occasion, as *go, walk, in ~*; body of persons doing this; (fig.) ill-contested race; (Theol.) emanation of the Holy Ghost; *~ caterpillars,* kinds that go in ~, so ~ *moth, whence ~ARY¹ (-sho-) a.*: (v.i.) go in ~; (v.t.) walk along (street) in ~. [vb f. n.] f. F, f. L *processionem* (as PROCEED, see -ION]

2. n. ~ *hymn*: (Eccl.) office-book of ~ *hymns* etc. [f. med. L *processionale* a. -*le* n. (as prec., see -AL)]

procĕs′sional (-sho-), a. & n. **1.** Of processions; used, carried, sung, in processions.

prŏ′cess-verbal (prósā-̆verbahl′), n. (pl. **process-verbaux** (prósā-̆verbō). Written report of proceedings, minutes; (Fr. Law) written statement of facts in support of charge. [F]

prŏ′chronism (-k-), n. Referring of event etc. to an earlier than the true date, as *races held in June & called by a ~ the Mays*. [f. PRO-² on ANACHRONISM]

proclaim′, v.t. Announce publicly & officially (thing, *that*); declare (war, peace); announce officially the accession of (sovereign); declare (person, thing) publicly or openly (*traitor* etc.); declare (district etc.) under legal restrictions, prohibit (meeting etc.), by declaration. So **prŏclaim²**

fit, as *the ~ will be devoted to charity*. [f. PROCEED v.; sing. now obs.]

TION n., **proclaim'atory** a. [f. L PRO-¹ (*clamare* cry out)]

procli'tic, a. & n. (Gk gram.). (Monosyllable) closely attached in pronunciation to following word & having itself no accent. [f. PRO-² on ENCLITIC]

procli'vity, n. Tendency (*to*, *towards*, action or habit, esp. bad one, *to* do). [f. L *proclivitas* f. PRO-¹(*clivis* f. *clivus* slope); see -ITY]

procon'sul n. (Rom. Hist.) governor of Roman province, in later republic usu. an ex-consul; (under empire) governor of senatorial province; ∥ (rhet.) governor of modern colony etc.; (*pro-consul*) deputy consul. Hence or cogn.~AR¹ a.,~ATE²(I), ~SHIP, nn. [L, earlier *pro consule* (one acting) for consul]

procras'tin|ate, v.i. & t. Defer action, be dilatory; (rare) postpone (action). Hence or cogn. ~**ātingly²** adv., ~**A'TION**, ~**ātor¹** nn., ~**ātive**, ~**ātory**, aa. [f. L PRO-¹(*crastinare* f. *crastinus* of tomorrow f. *cras*), see -ATE³]

procre'|ate, v.t. Beget, generate, (offspring, or abs.). Hence or cogn. ~**ANT**, ~**ātive**, aa., ~**A'TION** n. [f. L PRO-¹(*creare* CREATE)]

Procrus'tean, a. Tending to produce uniformity by violent methods. [f. Gk *Prokroustēs*, lit. stretcher, name of fabulous robber who fitted victims to his bed by stretching or mutilation, see -AN]

∥ **proc'tor**, n. (Univ.) each of two officers (*senior*, *junior*, ~) appointed annually & charged with various functions esp. discipline of persons *in statu pupillari*; (Law) person managing causes in court (now chiefly eccl.) that administers civil or canon law; *King's*, *Queen's*, *P~*, official who has right to intervene in probate, divorce, & nullity cases when collusion or suppression of facts is alleged. Hence **proctor'IAL** a., ~**SHIP** n. [syncop. of PROCURATOR]

∥ **proc'toriz|e**, v.t. Exercise proctor's authority on (undergraduate etc.). Hence ~**A'TION** n. [-IZE]

procum'bent, a. Lying on the face, prostrate; (Bot.) growing along the ground. [f. L PRO-¹(*cumbere* lay oneself) fall forwards,-ENT]

procura'tion, n. Procuring, obtaining, bringing about, so **procur'AL**(2), **procur'ANCE**, nn.: function, authorized action, of attorney; ∥ (Eccl.) provision of entertainment for bishop or other visitor by incumbent etc., now commuted to money payment; (fee for) negotiation of loan; procurer's trade or offence. [F. f. L *procurationem* (as PROCURE, see -ATION)]

proc'urātor, n. (Rom. Hist.) treasury officer in imperial province; agent, proxy, esp. one who has power of attorney; ∥ magistrate in some Italian cities; ∥

fiscal, public prosecutor of district in Scotland. Hence or cogn. **procurātor'IAL** a.,~**SHIP** n. [L, as PROCURE, see -OR³]

proc'urātory, n. Authorization to act for another, esp. *letters of* ~. [f. LL *procuratorium* neut. adj. (as PROCURE, see -ORY)]

procū'ratrix, n. Inmate of nunnery managing its temporal concerns. [L, as foll.,-TRIX]

procū're, v.t. & i. Obtain by care or effort, acquire, as *must* ~ *a copy*, *cannot* ~ *employment*; (arch.) bring about, as ~*d his death by poison*; act as procurer or procuress. Hence **procū'ABLE** a., ~MENT (~ū'rm-) n. [f. F *procurer* f. L PRO-¹(*curare* see to)]

procū'r|er, n. In vbl senses, esp. man or woman who procures women for gratification of another's lust. So ~**ESS¹** n. [ME & AF *procuroür* f. L as PROCURATOR]

prŏd, v.t. & i. (-dd-), & n. **1**. Poke with pointed instrument, end of stick, etc.; (fig.) goad, irritate; make ~ding motion *at*. **2**. n. Poke, thrust, pointed instrument. [?]

prōdēli'sion (-zhn), n. (prosody). Elision of initial vowel (as in *I'm* for *I am*). [f. L *prod-*=PRO-¹+ELISION]

prŏd'igal, a. & n. Recklessly wasteful (person); lavish of; ~ *son*, repentant sinner, returned wanderer, etc. (*Luke* xv. 11-32). Hence or cogn. ~**TY** (-ă1ĭ-) **n.**, ~**LY²** adv. [obs. F, f. L *prodigus* f. *prodigere* squander (*prod-* PRO-¹+*agere* drive), -AL]

prŏd'igalize, v.t. Spend lavishly. [-IZE]

prodi'gious (-jus), a. Marvellous, amazing; enormous; abnormal. Hence ~**LY²** adv., ~**NESS** n., (-jus-). [f. L *prodigiosus* (as foll., see -OUS)]

prŏd'igy, n. Marvellous thing, esp. one out of the course of nature; wonderful example of (some quality): person endowed with surprising qualities, esp. precocious child, as (attrib.) *a* ~ *violinist*. [f. L *prodigium* portent (*prod-* PRO-¹, cf. ADAGE)]

prŏd'rom|e, n. Preliminary book or treatise (*to* another); (Med.) premonitory symptom (*of*), whence ~**AL**, **prodrōm'ic**, aa. [f. mod. L *prodromus*, pl. -*mi*, also in E, f. Gk PRO-²(*dromos* running, runner) **a.** & n.; E has also in mod. sense *prodroma* n. pl. & (improp.) n. sing. with pl. -*mata*]

prod'uce¹, n. Amount produced, yield, esp. in assay of ore; (also *raw* ~) agricultural & natural products collectively; result (*of* labour, efforts, etc.); (of ordinance or military or naval stores) *brought to* ~, broken up & assorted into classes to be disposed of. [f. foll.]

produce'², v.t. Bring forward for inspection or consideration, as *will* ~ *evidence*, *witnesses*, *reasons*, ~ *your tickets*; bring (play, performer, book, etc.) before the

For other words in *pro-* see PRO-¹.

prodū́ce, v.t. (Geom.) extend, continue, (line to a point); manufacture (goods) from raw materials etc.; bring about, cause, (a sensation etc.); (of land etc.) yield (produce); (of animal or plant) bear, yield, (offspring, fruit). So **prodū́cing**[2] n., **prodū́cible** a. [f. L PRO-¹(*ducere duct-* lead)]

prodū́cer, n. In vbl senses, esp.; (Pol. Econ.) one who produces article of consumption (cf. CONSUMER); (Cinemat.) person generally responsible for production of a film (apart from direction of the acting); ~ *gas*, combustible gas, properly that formed by passing air through red-hot carbon, but often used for the 'semi-water gas' formed by passing steam and air through red-hot carbon. [f. prec. + -ER¹]

prŏ́duct, n. Thing produced by natural process or manufacture; result, as *the ~ of his labours*; (Math.) quantity obtained by multiplying quantities together; (Chem.) compound not previously existing in a body but formed during its decomposition. [as PRODUCE²]

prŏdū́ction, n. Producing; thing produced, esp. literary or artistic work. [F, f. L *productionem* (as prec.; see -ION)]

prŏdū́ctive, a. Producing, tending to produce, as ~ *of fuss*, ~ *of great annoyance*; (Pol. Econ.) producing commodities of exchangeable value, as ~ *labour(er)*; producing abundantly, as *a ~ soil, mine*, *writer*. Hence ~LY² adv., ~NESS, productī́vITY, nn. [f. med. L *productivus* (as PRODUCE², see -IVE)]

prŏ́ēm, n. Preface, preamble, to book or speech; beginning, prelude. So profān-ĒM'IAL a. [f. OF *proeme* f. L f. Gk PRO-²(*oimon* f. *oimos* way or *oimē* song)]

profāne¹, v.t. Treat (sacred thing) with irreverence or disregard; violate, pollute, (what is entitled to respect). So **profān-**ATION n. [f. L *profanare*, as foll.]

profāne², a. Not belonging to what is sacred or biblical, as ~ *history, literature, writer*; not initiated into religious rites or any esoteric knowledge; (of rites etc.) heathen; irreverent, blasphemous, so **profań'ITY** n. Hence ~LY² adv., ~NESS n. [f. obs. F *prophane* f. L PRO-¹(*fanus* f. *fanum* temple) before i.e. outside the temple]

profèss, v.t. & i. Lay claim to (quality, feeling), pretend (to be or do), as *they ~ extreme regret, does not ~ to be a scholar; openly declare, as they ~ themselves quite content, I ~ (that) this is news to me;* affirm one's faith in or allegiance to (religion, God, Christ); make (law, medicine, flute-playing, the flute, etc.) one's profession or business; teach (subject) as professor; perform duties of a professor. [f. L PRO-¹(*fitēri fess- =fatēri* confess)]

profèss'ed (-st), a. Self-acknowledged, as *a ~ Christian*; alleged, ostensible, whence **profèss'edly**² adv.; claiming to be duly qualified, as *a ~ anatomist; ~ monk, nun* (that has taken vows of religious order), **profèss'ion** (-shn), n. Declaration, avowal, *as in practice if not in ~, accept my declaration of belief in a religion; vow* made on entering, fact of being in, a religious order; vocation, calling, esp. one that involves some branch of learning or science, *as the learned ~s* (divinity, law, medicine), whence ~LESS a.: the body of persons engaged in this, esp. (Theatr. sl.) actors, as *lets apartments to the ~*. [F, f. L *professionem* (as PROFESS, see -ION)]

profèss'ional (-sho-), a. & n. 1. Of, belonging to, connected with, a profession, as ~ *men, etiquette, jealousy; ~ politician, agitator,* etc. (making a trade of politics etc.); ~ *cricketer, golfer,* etc. (playing for money, cf. AMATEUR). 2. n. ~ *man*, esp. (abbr. *pro*) ~ cricketer, golfer, etc. Hence ~LY² adv. [-AL]

profèss'ionalism (-sho-), n. Employing professionals. So ~IZE(3) v.t. [-ISM]

profèss'or, n. ‖ One who makes profession (of a religion); public teacher of high rank, esp. holder of a chair in university (prefixed as title, abbr. *Prof.*), whence ~ATE¹(1), ~SHIP, nn. profèssṓr-IAL a., profèssṓr-IALLY² adv.; (as grandiose title) P~ *Smith's Boxing Dormice* etc.; (sl.) professional. [L (as PROFESS, see -OR²)]

profèr, v.t., & n. (literary) 1. Offer (gift, services, etc., arch. to do; esp. in p.p.). 2. n. Offer. [(n. f. AF *profre*) f. AF *profrer* (PRO-¹+OFFER)]

profic'ient (-shnt), a. & n. Adept, expert, (*in, at*, an art etc., *in doing*). Hence **profic'iency** n., ~LY² adv., (-shn-). [f. L PROFICIENS, see -ENT]

prṓfile (-fēl, -fīl), n., & v.t. 1. Drawing, silhouette, or other representation, of side view esp. of human face, whence ~IST n.; *drawn etc. in ~* (as seen from one side); side outline esp. of the human face; (Forti.) transverse vertical section of fort, comparative thickness of earthwork etc.; flat outline piece of scenery on stage. 2. v.t. Represent in ~, give a ~ to. [It. *profilo* (now *proff-*) f. It. *profilare* spin f. L *filare* f. *filum* thread]

prŏ́fit, n. Advantage, benefit, as *have studied it to may ~, no ~ in such pursuits;* pecuniary gain, excess of returns over outlay, (usu. pl.); (Book-keep.) ~ *& loss account,* account in which gains are credited & losses debited so as to show net ~ or loss at any time; ~-*sharing* (of system, between employer & employed). Hence ~LESS a., ~LESSLY² adv., ~LESSNESS n. [OF, f. L *profectus -ûs* f. PRO-¹(*ficere* advance)]

prŏ́fit², v.t. & i. (Of thing) be of ad-

vantage to (person etc. orig. indirect object), as *it will not ~ him, what will it ~ him?*; be of advantage; (of person etc.) be benefitted or assisted, as *hope to ~ by your advice, ~ed by his confusion to make my escape.* [f. F *profiter* as prec.]

prŏf′itable, a. Beneficial, useful, as *~ conservation*; yielding profit, lucrative, as *a ~ speculation*. Hence ~NESS n., **prŏf′it-ablY**[2] adv. [F (PROFIT[1]+-ABLE)]

profiteer′, v.i. & n. 1. Make inordinate profits out of the State's or the consumer's straits (esp. of contractors & traders in times of scarcity). 2. n. ~ing person. [PROFIT, -EER]

prŏf′ligate, a. & n. 1. Licentious, dissolute; recklessly extravagant. 2. n. ~ate person. Hence ~ACY n., ~atelY[2] adv. [f. L PRO[1](*figare=fligere* strike down) overthrow, ruin, see -ATE[3]]

profound′, a. & n. 1. Having, showing, great knowledge or insight, as *~ statesman, inquiry, treatise*; demanding deep study or thought, as *~ doctrines*; (of state or quality) deep, intense, unqualified, as *fell into a ~ sleep, take a ~ interest, simulated a ~ indifference*; having, coming from, extending to, a great depth, as *~ crevasses, a ~ (deep-drawn) sigh, ~ (deep-seated) gangrene*. 2. n. (poet.) *The vast depth (of ocean, futurity, the soul, etc.).* Hence or cogn. ~LY[2] adv., ~NESS, **profun′dity**, nn. [f. OF *profund* f. L PRO[1]-(*fundus* bottom) deep]

profuse′, a. Lavish, extravagant, (*in, of, gifts, promises, expenditure, etc.*); (of things) exuberantly plentiful. Hence or cogn. ~LY[2] (-sl-) adv., ~NESS (-sn-), **profu′sion** (-zhn), nn. [f. L PRO[1](*fundere fus-* pour)]

prŏg[1], n. (sl.) Food, esp. for journey or excursion. [?]

‖ **prŏg**[2], ‖ **prŏgg′ins** (-ginz), nn. & vv.t. (sl.), Proctor at Oxford or Cambridge; (v.t.) proctorize. [abbr.]

progén′itive, a. Capable of, connected with, the production of offspring. [as foll., -IVE]

progén′itor, n. Ancestor of person, animal, or plant; (fig.) political or intellectual predecessor, original of a copy. Hence ~ōr′ial a., ~ORSHIP, ~NESS[1], nn. [f. obs. F *progeniteur* f. L *progenitorem* f. PRO[1](*gignere genit-* beget), see -OR[2]]

progén′iture, n. (Begetting of) offspring. [as prec., -URE]

prŏ′gený, n. Offspring of person, animal, or plant; descendants; (fig.) issue, outcome. [f. obs. F *progenie* f. L *progenies* f. PRO[1](*gignere* beget)]

‖ **prŏg′gins**. See PROG[2].

proglŏtt′is, n. (pl. *~tdēs*). Sexually mature segment of tapeworm. [f. Gk PRO[2](*glōssis* f. *glōssa, -tta,* tongue), from its shape]

prŏg′nathous, a. With projecting jaws; (of jaws) projecting. So **prŏgnáth′ic** a., ~ISM(2) n. [f. PRO[2] + Gk *gnathos* jaw+ -OUS]

prŏgnŏs′is, n. (pl. *-ōsēs*). Prognostication, esp. (Med.) forecast of course of disease. [L, f. Gk PRO[2](*gnōsis* f. *gnō-* know)]

prŏgnŏs′tic, n. & a. 1. Pre-indication, omen, (*of*); prediction, forecast. 2. adj. Foretelling, predictive, (*of*). [(n. f. OF *pronostique*) f. med. L f. Gk *prognōstikos* f. PRO[2](*gignōskō* learn), -IC]

prŏgnŏs′ticāte, v.t. Foretell (event, that); (of things) betoken. Hence or cogn. ~ABLE, ~ātıve, ~ātorY, ~ātor[2], nn., ~A′TION, nn. [f. med. L *prognosticare* (as prec.), see -ATE[3]]

prŏg′ram(me), n., & v.t. 1. Descriptive notice of series of events, e.g. of course of study, concert, etc.; definite plan of intended proceedings; (colloq.) *what is the ~ for* (what are we going to do) *today?*; *~music* (intended to suggest series of scenes or events) *~ picture* (Cinemat.), film of some length forming part, but not the main feature, of the ~. 2. v.t. Make a ~ or definite plan of. [f. L f. Gk *programma* f. PRO[2](*graphō* write) write publicly, see -M; -me now usu., but cf. *diagram, telegram*, etc.]

prŏg′ress[1], n. Forward or onward movement in space, as *made slow ~, continued his ~; an inquiry is now in ~* (going on); advance, development, as *made no ~ in his studies, the ~ of civilization, disease made rapid ~*; ‖(arch.) state journey, official tour, esp. *royal ~*. [ult. f. L PRO[1]-(*gredi gress-=gradi* walk)]

progrèss′[2], v.i. Move forward or onward; be carried on, as *the controversy still ~es*; advance, develop, as *we ~ in knowledge, science ~es*. [f. prec.; Amer. revival of obs. E]

progrè′ssion (-shn), n. Progress, as mode of ~; (Math.) ARITHMETICAL, GEOMETRICAL, HARMONIC, ~; (Mus.) passing from one note or chord to another. Hence ~AL (-sho-) a., [F, f. L *progressionem* (as PROGRESS, see -ION)]

progrè′ssionist (-sho-), n. Advocate of progress e.g. in political or social matters (also **prŏg′rèssist** n.); one who holds that life on the earth has been marked by gradual progression to higher forms. [-IST]

progrèss′ive, a. & n. 1. Moving forward, successive; proceeding step by step, successive; *~ whist* etc. (played by several sets of players at different tables, certain players passing after each round to next table); advancing in social conditions, character, efficiency, etc., as *a ~ nation*; (of disease) continuously increasing; favouring progress or reform, as *~ principles, party*, whence **progrèss′ivism** n. 2. n. Advocate of ~ policy. Hence ~LY[2] adv., ~NESS n. [-IVE]

For other words in *pro-* see PRO[1].

prohibit

adv., ~NESS n. [F (-if, -ive), as PROGRESS¹, see -IVE]

prohib'it, v.t. Forbid, debar, (action, thing, person from doing). Hence or cogn. ~ER¹, ~OR² n. [f. L PRO¹(hibēre habit- = habēre hold)]

prohibi'tion (-bib-), n. Forbidding (as prec., see -ION); edict, order, that forbids; forbidding by law of sale of intoxicants for common consumption, whence ~IST (-ibisho-) n.; (Law) writ from High Court of Justice forbidding inferior court to proceed in suit as being beyond its cognizance. [f., f. L prohibitionem (as prec., see -ION)]

prohib'itive, a. Prohibiting; serving to prevent the use or abuse or purchase of a thing, as ~ tax, published at a ~ price. Hence or cogn. ~LY² adv., ~NESS n.

prohib'itory a. [F (-if, -ive), as PRO-HIBIT, see -IVE]

project'¹, v.t. & i. Plan, contrive, (scheme, course of action, etc.); cast, throw, impel, (body into space etc.); ~ oneself, go out of oneself into another's feelings, the future, etc. (Spirit.) make a phantom of oneself visible to a distant person; (Chem.) cast (substance into, on, etc.); cause (light, shadow) to fall on surface etc.; (fig.) cause (idea etc. to take shape); (Geom.) draw straight lines from a centre through every point of (given figure) to produce corresponding figure on a surface by intersecting it, draw (such lines), produce (such, corresponding figure); make projection (of earth, sky, etc.); (intr.) pro-trude. [f. L PRO¹(jicĕre ject- =jacĕre throw)]

project'² n. Plan, scheme. [as prec.]

projec'tile, a.&n. 1. Impelling, as~force; capable of being projected by force, esp. from gun. 2. n. ~ missile. [as prec. +-ILE]

projec'tion, n. 1. Throwing, casting. 2. Transmission of metals, as powder of ~, alchemists' powder of philosophers' stone. 3. Planning. 4. Protruding; pro-truding thing; thrusting forward. 5. (Geom.) Projecting of a figure (see PRO-JECT¹); ~ of a point, point in derived figure corresponding to point in original figure. 6. Representation on plane sur-face of (any part) of surface of earth or of celestial sphere, as Mercator's ~ (in which points of compass preserve same direction all over the map). 7. Mental image viewed as objective reality. 8. (Cinemat.) display of films by throwing image on screen, whence ~IST (-sho-) n. [f. L projectio (as prec. see -ION)]

projec'tive, a. (Geom.) of, derived by, projection, ~ property of a figure (un-changed after projection); mentally pro-jecting or projected, as ~ imagination. Hence ~LY² adv. [as prec., see -IVE]

projec'tor, n. One who forms a project; promoter of bubble companies; apparatus for projecting rays of light or throwing image on cinematograph screen. [as prec., see -OR²]

prolapse, v.i. & n. (path.), Slip forward or down out of place; (n.)=foll. [f. L PRO¹(labi laps- slip)]

prolap'sus n. (path.). Slipping forward or down of part of organ esp. of uterus or rectum. [L, gen. -ūs, as prec.]

prolate, a. (Geom., of spheroid) length-ened in direction of polar diameter (cf. OBLATE); growing, extending, in width; (fig.) widely spread; (Gram.)=foll. Hence ~LY² adv. [f. L PRO¹(ferre lat- carry)]

prolative, a. (gram.). Serving to extend or complete predication, as in ' you can go', go is a ~ infinitive. [f. LL prolativus (prec., -IVE)]

prolegom'enon, n. (usu. in pl.~a). Pre-liminary discourse or matter prefixed to book etc. Hence ~ARY¹, ~OUS, aa. [Gk prolegomenon neut. pass. part. of PRO³(legō say)]

prolep'sis, n. (pl. -psēs). Anticipation; (Gram.) anticipatory use of adjectives, as in So those two brothers & their mur-dered man Rode past fair Florence. Hence or cogn. **prolep'tic** a., **prolep'tically** adv. [Gk prolēpsis f. PRO²(lambanō take)]

proletaire', n. =foll. n. Hence **prole-tair'ISM**(2) n. [f. F prolétaire, as foll.]

proletar'ian, a. & n. (Member) of the proletariate. Hence or cogn. ~ISM(2) n. [f. L proletarius one who served the State not with property but with offspring (proles, see -ARY¹ & -AN)]

proletar'iate, n. (Rom. Hist.; & mod., often derog.) lowest class of community; (Pol. Econ.) Indigent wage-earners, labouring classes; dictatorship of the ~, Communist ideal of domination by the ~ after the suppression of capitalism & the bourgeoisie. [f. F prolétariat (as prec., see -ATE¹)]

prolicide, n. Killing of offspring, esp. before or soon after birth. Hence pro-**licid'AL** a. [f. L proles offspring+-CIDE]

prolif'erate, v.i. & t. Reproduce itself, grow, by multiplication of elementary parts; produce (cells etc.), thus. So ~A-TION n., ~ATIVE a. [back formation f. proliferous (proles offspring); see -FEROUS]

prolif'ic, a. Producing (much) offspring; abundantly productive of; abounding in. Hence ~ACY [irreg.], **prolif'ICITY**, ~NESS nn. [f. med. L prolificus (as prec., see -FIC)]

prolif'erous, a. (Bot.) producing leaf or flower buds from leaf or flower, (also) producing new individuals from buds; (Zool.) multiplying by budding; (Path.) spreading by proliferation. [f. med. L prolifer (proles offspring); see -FEROUS]

prolig'erous, a. Bearing offspring; gener-ative, [as prec. +L -ger- bearing +-OUS]

prol'ix (or prōliks'), a. Lengthy, tediously wordy, as ~ speech, writer. Hence or cogn. ~ITY¹ n., ~LY² adv. [f. L PRO¹(líxus be liquid)]

prol'ocutor (or prolō⁶-), n. Chairman || esp. of lower house of convocation of either province of Church of England. Hence ~SHIP n. [LL, f. PRO¹(loqui locut-speak).-OR²]

prol'ogize (-j-), **~guize** (-gīz), vv.i. Write, speak, a prologue. [(~gize) f. Gk prologizō as foll. (-pu-) f. foll.+-IZE]

prol'ogue (-ōg), n., & v.t. Preliminary discourse, poem, etc., esp. introducing play (cf. EPILOGUE); (fig.) act, event, serving as introduction (to); (v.t.) introduce, furnish, with a ~. [(vb f. n.) F, f. L f. Gk PRO¹(logos speech)]

prolong', v.t. Extend (action, condition, etc.) in duration; extend in spatial length; lengthen pronunciation of (syllable etc.). So **~ABLE** (-ngə-) a., **PROlongA'TION** (-nggə-) n. [f. OF prolonguer f. LL PRO¹(longare, as LONG¹)]

prolu'sion (-ōōzhn), n. Preliminary essay, article, or attempt. So **prolu'sory** (-ōō-) a. [f. L prolusio f. PRO¹(ludere lus- play) practise beforehand]

prom, n. (colloq.). =PROMENADE concert. [abbr.]

promenade' (-ahd, -ād), n., & v.i. & t. 1. Walk, ride, drive, taken for exercise, amusement, or display, or as social ceremony; place, esp. paved public walk, for this; ~ concert, one at which (part of) audience is not seated and can move about;~ deck, an upper deck on a liner, where passengers may~. 2. v.i. Make a ~, whence **promenad'ER¹**(-ahd-, -ād-) n. 3. v.t. Make a ~ through (place); lead (person) about a place esp. for display. [(vb f. n.) F, f. promener take for walk f. LL PRO¹(minare threaten) drive (beasts), -ADE]

prom'erops, n. S.-Afr. genus of birds, esp. Cape ~, small bird with long curved bill & very long tail. [PRO-² + Gk merops bee-eater]

Prometh'ean, a. Of, like, Prometheus in his skill or punishment. [f. Gk Prometheus (demigod who made man from clay, stole fire from Olympus & taught men the use of it & various arts, & was chained by Zeus to rock in Caucasus), see -AN]

prom'inent, a. Jutting out, projecting; conspicuous; distinguished. Hence or cogn. **~ENCE**, **~ENCY**, nn., **~ently²** adv. [f. L PRO¹(minēre, see EMINENT)]

promis'cuous, a. Of mixed & disorderly composition, as a ~ mass; (w. pl. n.) of various kinds mixed together; indiscriminate, as ~ massacre, hospitality; ~ bathing (of both sexes together); ~ sexual relations (unrestricted by marriage or cohabitation); (colloq) casual, as took a ~ stroll; (vulg., joc.) ~like, casually, for no particular reason. Hence or cogn. **promiscu'ITY** n., **~LY²** adv. [f. L PRO¹(miscēre mix)+-OUS]

prom'ise¹, n. Assurance given to a person that one will do or not do something or will give or procure him something; thing promised, as I claim your ~; BREACH¹ of ~; land of ~ (see foll.); (fig.) ground of expectation of future achievements or good results, as book, writer, of great ~. [f. L promissum p.p. of PRO¹ (mittere send) put forth, promise]

prom'ise², v.t. & i. Make (person) a promise to give or procure him (thing), as I ~ you a fair hearing; make (person) a promise (to do, that thing shall be done etc.); (abs.) cannot positively; ~ oneself, look forward to (a pleasant time etc.); (colloq.) I ~ (assure) you, it will not be so easy; (fig.) afford expectation of, as these discussions ~ future storms, seem likely (to do); (abs.) ~ well etc., hold out good etc. prospect; ~d land (also land of promise), Canaan (Gen. xii. 7 etc.), heaven, any place of expected felicity. Hence **prom'isER¹** n. [f. prec.]

prom'isee', n. (law). Person to whom promise is made. So **prom'isOR²** n. [-EE]

prom'ising, a. Likely to turn out well, hopeful, full of promise, as ~ boy, sky, beginning. Hence **~LY²** adv. [-ING²]

prom'issory, a. Conveying or implying a promise; (rare) full of promise (of); ~ note, signed document containing written promise to pay stated sum to specified person or to bearer at specified date or on demand. [f. med. L promissorius (as PROMISE¹, see -ORY)]

prom'ontory¹, n. Point of high land jutting out into sea etc., headland; (Anat.) kinds of protuberance in the body. Hence **~IED²**(-rid) a. [f. med. L promontorium altered (on mons -ntis mount) f. L pro-munturium (perh. as PROMINENT)]

promote', v.t. Advance, prefer, (person to position, higher office; was~d major, to be major, to the rank of major, to majority, not to major); help forward, encourage, (process, result); support actively the passing of (law), take necessary steps for passing of (local or private act of parliament); (Chess) raise (pawn) to rank of queen etc. Hence or cogn. **promo'TION** n., **promo'TIVE** a. [f. L PRO¹(movēre mot-move)]

promo'ter, n. In vbl senses, esp. (also company~) one who promotes formation of joint-stock company (freq. derog., whence ~ISM n.).

prompt¹, a., & n. 1. Ready in action, acting with alacrity, as a ~ assistant, made, done, etc., readily or at once, as ~ reply, decision, payment, whence or cogn. ~itude, ~ness, nn., ~ly² adv.; (Comm.) ~ for cash (on the spot); (Commerce, of goods) for immediate delivery & payment, as ~ iron. 2. n. Time limit for payment of account, stated on ~note, as what is the ~? [(n. f. adj.) f. L promere prompt-produce (PRO¹+emere take)]

prompt², v.t., & n. 1. Incite, move, (person etc. to action, to do); supply (actor,

reciter, or abs.) with the words that come next, assist (hesitating speaker) with suggestion; inspire, give rise to, (feeling, thought, action). 2. n. Thing said to help the memory esp. of actor; ~-*book*, copy of play for prompter's use; ~(*prompter's*) of). 3. Utter, articulate, (words, or abs.), *box on stage*; ~ *side* of stage (usu. to actor's left; abbr. *p.s.*). [f. L vb f. prec.]

prŏmp'ter, n. One who prompts, esp. (Theatr.) person stationed out of sight of audience to assist actor's memory. [-ER¹]

prŏmp'ting, n. In vbl senses, esp. the ~s *of conscience* etc. [-ING¹]

prom'ulgāte, v.t. Make known to the public, disseminate (creed etc.), proclaim (decree, news). Hence or cogn. ~A'TION, ~A'TOR² nn. [f. L *promulgare* perh. corrupt. of *pro¹*(*vulgare* publish f. *vulgus* the people), see -ATE³]

promülge' (-j), v.t. (arch.) = prec. [as prec.]

proná'ŏs, n. (Gk Ant.). Space in front of body of temple, enclosed by portico & projecting side walls. [L, f. Gk *pro²*(*naos* temple)]

prŏn'āte, v.t. (physiol.). Put (hand, fore limb) into prone position (cf. SUPINATE). So ~A'TION n. [f. LL *pronare* (as PRONE), see -ATE³]

prŏnā'tor, n. (anat.). Muscle that effects or helps pronation. [med. L (as prec., see -OR²)]

prŏne, a. Having the front or ventral part downwards, lying face downwards, (loosely) lying flat, prostrate, as *fell* ~, whence ~ly² (-nl-) adv.; (of ground) having downward aspect or direction, (loosely) steep, headlong; disposed, liable, (to quality, action, or condition, *to do*). Hence ~'NESS (-n-n-) n. [f. L *pronus*]

prŏng, n. & v.t. Forked instrument, [F] hay-fork; each pointed member of fork, whence (~)~ED² (-ngd) a.; (v.t.) pierce, stab, turn up (soil etc.), with ~; ~*buck*, -*horn*, -*horned* antelope, N.-Amer. deer-like ruminant. [?]

pronŏm'inal, a. Of (the nature of) a pronoun. Hence ~ly² adv. [f. LL *pronominalis* f. L *PRO¹*(*nomen -minis* noun), see -AL]

prŏn'oun, n. Word used instead of (proper or other) noun to designate person or thing already mentioned or known from context or forming the subject of inquiry (used also to include pronominal & other adjectives, see below); *personal* ~s (I, we, thou, you, he, she, it, they); *interrogative* ~s (who, what, which); *relative* ~s (who, that, which); *possessive* ~s, adjectives representing possessive case (*my, her, our*, etc., with absolute forms *mine, hers, ours*); *demonstrative* ~s (this, that); *distributive* ~s (each, every, either, etc.); *indefinite* ~s (any, some, etc.). [PRO-¹]

pronounce', v.t. & i. 1. Utter, deliver, (judgement, sentence, curse, etc., formally or solemnly), state, declare, as *one's opinion*, as *I ~ the pears unripe, cannot ~ him* (or *that he is*) *out of danger*, whence ~MENT (-sm-) n. 2. Pass judgement, give one's opinion, (*on, for, against, in favour of*). 3. Utter, articulate, (words, or abs.), *some* ~, *cannot ~ French*, whence ~'ment-ABLE (-sohl) a. [f. OF *pronuncier* f. LL *pro¹*-(*nuntiare* announce f. *nuntius* messenger)]

pronounced' (-st), a. In vbl senses, also, strongly marked, decided, as ~ *tendency, magenta, flavour*. Hence pronoun'cedly² adv. [-ED²]

pronoun'cing, n. In vbl senses: (attrib., ~ *dictionary* (in which pronunciation is indicated), [-ING¹]

***prŏn'tō**, adv. (sl.). Promptly, quickly. [Sp.]

prŏn'tosil, n. One of the sulphonamide group of drugs. [P]

pronunciamén'tō, n. (pl. ~s). Proclamation, manifesto, esp. (in Spanish-speaking countries) one issued by insurrectionists. [f. Sp. *pronunciamiento*, also used in It, f. L as PRONOUNCE, see -MENT]

pronuncia'tion, n. Mode in which a word is pronounced; a person's way of pronouncing words, as *his* ~ *is often faulty*. [f. L *pronuntiatio* (as PRONOUNCE, see -ATION]

prŏŏf, n. 1. Evidence sufficing or helping to establish a fact, as *this requires no* ~, *as a ~ of his esteem, ~ positive of his intention or that he intended*, whence ~LESS a.; spoken or written legal evidence. 2. Proving, demonstration, as *not capable of ~, in ~ of my assertion*. 3. || (Sc. law) trial before judge instead of by jury. 4. Test, trial, as *must be brought to the ~, will stand a severe ~, the ~ of the pudding is in the eating*. 5. (Place for) testing of fire-arms or explosives. 6. (arch.). Proved impenetrability, as *armour of* ~. 7. Standard of strength of distilled alcoholic liquors. 8. (Print.) ~, trial impression taken from type, in which corrections etc. may be made (cf. REVISE); ~-*reader*, ~-*reading*, (person employed in) reading & correcting ~s; ~-*sheet*, sheet of ~. 9. Each of a limited number of careful impressions made from engraved plate before printing of ordinary issue & usu. (also ~ *before letters*) before inscription is added; *artist's, engraver's*, ~ (taken for examination or alteration by him); *signed* ~, *early* ~ signed by artist. 10. Test-tube. 11. Rough edges left to some leaves of book to show it has not been cut down. 12. ~-*plane*, conductor fixed on insulating handle & used in measuring electrification of a body. [f. OF *prueve* f. LL *proba* (as PROVE]

prŏŏf², a., & v.t. 1. (Of armour) of tried strength; impenetrable, as ~ *against the severest weather, the pricks of conscience,*

esp. in comb., as *bomb, bullet, burglar, fire, rain, sound, thief, weather,* ~, WATER-I-~. **2.** v.t. Make (thing) ~, esp. make (fabric etc.) waterproof. [(vb f. adj.) f. prec.]

prop¹, n., & v.t. & i. (-pp-). **1.** Rigid support, esp. one not forming structural part of thing supported, e.g. pole; ||CLOTHES-~; (fig.) person etc. who upholds institution etc. **2.** v.t. Support (as) by ~ (lit. & fig.), hold up thus. **3.** v.i. (Of horse etc.) come to a dead stop with forelegs rigid. [(vb prob.f.n.) cf. Du. *proppe,* etym. dub.]

prop². See PROPOSITION.

propaedeut'ic, a. & n. (Subject, study) serving as introduction to higher study; (n. pl.) preliminary learning. Hence ~AL a. [f. Gk PRO²(*paideuō* teach f. *pais paidos* child), see -IC]

propagan'da, n. **1.** (*Congregation, College,* of) the P~, committee of cardinals in charge of foreign missions. **2.** Association, organized scheme, for propagation of a doctrine or practice; doctrines, information, etc. thus propagated; efforts, schemes, principles, of propagation. [It., f. mod. L *congregatio de propaganda fide* congregation for propagation of the faith]

propagan'dist, n. Member, agent, of a propaganda, whence ~ISM n., ~is'tic a. [f. prec.], ~IZE(2, 4) v.i. & t.; proselytizer: missionary, convert, of the Propaganda. [-IST]

prop'agate, v.t. **1.** Multiply specimens of (plant, animal, disease, etc.) by natural process from parent stock; (of plant etc.) reproduce (*itself,* or abs.). **2.** Hand down (quality etc.) from one generation to another. **3.** Disseminate, diffuse, (statement, belief, practice). **4.** Extend the operation of, transmit, (vibration, earthquake, etc.). Hence or cogn. ~A'TION, ~ATOR² nn., ~ATIVE a. [f. L *propagare* multiply plants from layers, f. PRO¹(*pago* perh. f. root of *pangere* fix, set), see -ATE³]

parox'ytone, a. & n. (Gk gram.). (Word) with acute accent on antepenult. [f. Gk PRO²(*paroxutonos* PAROXYTONE]

propel', v.t. (-ll-). Drive forward, give onward motion to, (lit. & fig.) JET²-~led. [f. L PRO¹(*pellere puls-* drive)]

propell'ant, -ent, a. & n. Propelling (agent); explosive that propels bullet or shell from fire-arm. [-ANT, -ENT]

propell'er, n. In vbl senses, esp. revolving shaft with blades usu. (*screw-*~) set at an angle & twisted like thread of screw, for propelling ship or aircraft. [-ER¹]

propen'sity, n. Inclination, tendency, (*to* condition, quality, thing, *to do, for doing*). [f. now rare *propense* t. L *propensus* inclined, p.p. of PRO¹(*pendēre* hang)+-ITY]

prop'er, a. **1.** (arch.). (Usu. w. possessive pron. & occas. w. *own*) own, as *with my own.*~ *eyes.* **2.** (astron.). ~ *motion,* that part of the apparent motion of fixed star etc. supposed to be due to its actual move-

ment in space. **3.** Belonging, relating, exclusively or distinctively (*to,* or abs. as ~ *psalms, lessons,* ~ *to particular day*). **4.** (gram.). ~ *noun* or *name,* name used to designate an individual person, animal, town, ship, etc. (e.g. *Jane, Smith, France, London*). **5.** Accurate, correct, as *in the* ~ *sense of the word.* **6.** (Usu. foll. its noun) strictly so called, real, genuine, as *within the sphere of architecture* ~; ~ *fraction* (less than unity). **7.** (colloq.). ~. Thorough, complete, as *will be a* ~ *row about this.* **8.** (arch.). Handsome, as *a* ~ *man.* **9.** Fit, suitable, right, as *choose the* ~ *time, do it the* ~ *way.* **10.** In conformity with demands of society, decent, respectable, as *she is so distressingly* ~, *would it be quite* ~? **11.** (her.). In the natural, not conventional, colours, as *a peacock* ~. [ME. & F *propre* f. L *proprius*]

propérispōm'enon, a. & n. (Gk gram.). (Word) with circumflex accent on penult. [Gk PRO²(PERISPOMENON]

prop'erly, adv. Fittingly, suitably, as *do it* ~ *or not at all;* rightly, duly, as *he very* ~ *refused;* with good manners, as *behave* ~; (colloq.) thoroughly, as *puzzled him* ~. [-LY²]

prop'erty, n. **1.** Owning, being owned, as ~ *has its duties;* thing owned, possession(s), as *the book is his* ~, *regards him as her exclusive* ~, *a man of (great)* ~, *has a small* ~ (estate) *in Norfolk,* PERSONAL, REAL, ~ ; ~ *qualification* (based on possession of ~), ~ *tax* (levied directly on ~). **2.** (theatr.). Article of costume, furniture, etc., used on stage; ~*man,* ~*master,* man in charge of stage properties. **3.** Attribute, quality, as *the properties of soda, has the* ~ *of dissolving grease;* (Logic) quality common to a whole class but not necessary to distinguish it from others. [f. OF *propriete* f. L *proprietatem* (as PROPER, see -TY)]

proph'ecy, n. Faculty of a prophet, as *the gift of* ~; prophetic utterance; foretelling of future events. [f. OF *profecie* f. LL f. Gk *prophēteia* (as PROPHET)]

proph'esy, v.i. & t. Speak as a prophet; foretell future events; (arch.) expound the Scriptures; foretell (event, that, who, etc.). [f. OF *profecier,* as prec.]

proph'ēt, n. Inspired teacher, revealer or interpreter of God's will; *the* ~, prophetical writers of O.T., *major* ~s, Isaiah, Jeremiah, Ezekiel, Daniel, *the 12 minor* ~s, Hosea to Malachi; *the P~,* Mohammed, (also) Joseph Smith, founder of Mormons; *Saul among the* ~s, person revealing unexpected gifts or sympathies (see I Sam. x. 11); spokesman, advocate, (of principle etc.); one who foretells events, as *am no weather-*~; (sl.) tipster. Hence ~ESS¹, ~HOOD, ~SHIP, nn. [f. F *prophète* f. LL(-*ta*) f. Gk PRO²(*phētēs* speaker f. *phēmi* speak) spokesman]

prophet'ic, a. Of a prophet; predicting,

containing a prediction of (event etc.). Hence ~AL a., ~ally² adv. [f. LL f. Gk *prophalaktikos* (prec., -IC)]

prophylac'tic, a. & n. (Medicine, measure) tending to prevent disease. [f. Gk *prophalaktikos* f. pro²(*phalassō* guard)]

prophylax'is, n. Preventive treatment of disease. [f. PRO-² + Gk *phalaxis* a guarding, after prec.]

propine', v.t. ...

propin'quity, n. Nearness in place; close kinship; similarity. [f. obs. F *propin-quité* f. L *propinquitatem* (*propinquus* near, *prope* near, see -TY)]

propi̅'tiate (-shi-), v.t. Appease (offended person etc.); make propitious. [f. L *pro-pitiare* (as PROPITIOUS, see -ATE²)]

propitia'tion (-shi-), n. Appeasement; atonement; (arch.) gift etc. meant to propitiate, as *he is the ~ for our sins*. [f. LL *propitiatio* (as prec., see -ATION)]

propi̅'tiatory (-sho-), a. & n. Serving, meant, to propitiate, as *a ~y smile*; (n.) the mercy-seat (esp. fig. of Christ). Hence ~ily² adv. [f. LL *propitiatorius* (as propitious, -ORY)]

propi̅'tious (-shŭs), a. Well-disposed, favourable, as *the fates were ~*; (of omens etc.) favourable; (of weather, occasion, etc.) suitable *for*, favourable *to*, (purpose). Hence ~LY² adv. [f. OF *propicius* f. L *propitius*, -OUS]

prop'olis, n. Red resinous substance got by bees from buds to stop up crevices with. [Gk PRO²(*polis*(city)suburb, bee-glue)]

propo̅'nent, a. & n. (Person) that puts forward a motion, theory, or proposal. [f. L as PROPOUND, see -ENT]

propor'tion, n. & v.t. **1.** Comparative part, share, as *a large ~ of the earth's sur-face, of the profits*; comparative relation, ratio, as *the ~ of births to the population*, (*to the labour etc.*, or abs.); due relation of one thing to another in various parts of a thing, as *windows are in admirable ~, his success bore no ~ to his abilities*, whence ~LESS (-sho-) a.; *was out of (all) ~ to*, too great for; (pl.) dimensions, as *athlete, building, of magnificent ~s*; (Math.) equality of ratios between two pairs of quantities, as *3, 5, 9, & 15 are in ~*, set of such quantities, (Arith.) RULE of three. **2.** v.t. Make (thing etc.) proportionate to, as *must ~ the punishment to the crime*, whence (-)~ED¹(-shond) a., ~MENT (-sho-) n. [f. F, f. L PRO(*portionem* PORTION); cf. OF *proportioner*]

propor'tional (-sho-), a. & n. **1.** In due proportion, corresponding in degree or amount, as *a ~al increase in the wages, resentment ~al to his injuries, ~al REPRE-SENTATION*, so ~ALLY, so ~ATELY, adv.; (of a proportion, as *5, 3, 10, 6, are ~als, 6 is a mean ~al between 3 & 12*. Hence or cogn. ~ÁLITY n., ~ally² (-sho-) adv. [f. LL *proportionalis* (as prec., see -AL)]

propo̅se' (-z), v.t. & i. Put forward for consideration, propound; set up as an aim, as *the object I ~ to myself*; nominate (person) as member of society etc.; offer (person's health, person) as toast; make offer of marriage (to); put forward as plan, as *we ~ (to make) a change, that a change should be made*; intend, purpose, (to do, doing); (abs.) *man ~s, God disposes*. [f. F PRO²(*poser*, see COMPOSE)]

proposi'tion (-z-), n. Statement, assertion, as *a ~ too plain to need argument*, esp. (Logic) form of words consisting of predicate & subject connected by copula; (Math., abbr. *prop*) formal statement of theorem or problem, other including the demonstration, as *Euclid, Book I, ~ 5*; proposal, scheme proposed; (sl.) task, job, problem, objective, occupation, trade, opponent, prospect, etc. Hence ~AL, (-zisho-) a. [f. F, f. L *propositionem* (as foll., see -ION)]

propound', v.t. Offer for consideration, propose, (question, problem, scheme, matter, etc., *to* person); produce (will) before proper authority in order to establish its legality. Hence ~ER¹ n. [earlier *propone* f. L PRO²(*ponere posit-* place), cf. *compound* etc.]

propræ'tor, n. (Rom. hist.), Ex-praetor with authority of praetor in province not under military control. [L, earlier *pro praetore* (one acting) for praetor]

proprie'tary, a. & n. **1.** Of a proprietor, as *~ rights*; holding property, as *the ~ classes*; held in private ownership, as *~ medicines* (sale of which is restricted by patent etc.). **2.** n. Proprietorship, as *an exclusive ~*; body of proprietors, as *the landed ~*. [f. LL *proprietarius* (as PRO-PERTY, see -ARY)]

proprie'tor, n. Owner. Hence ~O'rIAL a., ~O'riALY² adv., ~OTSHIP, ~TESS¹, nn. [altered in 17th c. f. prec.]

proprie'ty, n. Fitness, rightness, as *doubt the ~y of the term, of refusing him*; correctness of behaviour or morals, as *a breach of ~y*; (pl.) details of correct con-duct, as *must observe the ~ties*. [(in earlier senses) from earlier *propriety*. [f. F pro-priété PROPERTY]

prop'riётà mēträ (or *mäträ pröp'riö*), n. Form of papal bull without seal & used in the administration of the papal court. [L. = of our own motion, wds included in the formula]

props, n. pl. (sl.). Stage properties. [abbr.]

proptō'sis, n. (path.). Prolapse, protru-sion, esp. of eye. Hence ~ED¹(-st) a. [LL, f. Gk *proptōsis* f. pro²(*ptōsis* fall)]

propul'sion (-shn), n. Driving or pushing forward; JET² ~*ion*; (fig.) impelling influence. So ~IVE a. [F (as PROPEL, see -ION)]

propy'laee'um, n. (pl. ~a). Entrance to temple; *the* P~*a*, entrance to Acropolis at Athens. [L, f. Gk PRO²*pulaion* f. *pulē* gate)]

prop'ylite, n. Volcanic rock found in some silver-mining regions. Hence ~it'ɪc a. [f. foll. +-ITE¹, as opening a volcanic epoch]

prop'ylon, n. (pl. -*ons*, -*a*). = PROPYLAEUM. [L, f. Gk PRO²(*pulon* f. *pulē* gate)]

pros- in comb. = Gk *pros* to, towards, in addition.

prosa'ic (-z-; *also* pro-), a. Like prose, lacking poetic beauty; unromantic, commonplace, dull, as *a* ~ *life, person, view of things*. Hence **prosā'ically** adv., ~NESS n. [f. med. L *prosaicus* (as PROSE, see -IC)]

pros'ā'ist (-z-), n. Prose author; prosaic person. So ~ISM(4) n. [as PROSE, see -IST]

proscen'ium (*or* pro-), n. (pl. -*ia*). (In ancient theatre) the stage; (mod.) space between curtain or drop-scene & orchestra, esp. with the enclosing arch. [L, f. Gk PRO²(*skēnion* f. *skēnē* background of stage)]

proscribe', v.t. Put (person) out of protection of law; banish, exile, (esp. fig.); reject, denounce, (practice etc.) as dangerous etc. So **proscrip'tion** n., **proscrip'tive** a. [f. L PRO¹(*scribere scrip*-write)]

prose (-z), n., & v.i. & t. **1.** Ordinary nonmetrical form of written or spoken language (*Milton's* ~ *works*); (Eccl.)= SEQUENCE; ~ *poem*, ~ work of poetical style; plain matter-of-fact quality, as *the* ~ *of existence*; tedious discourse. **2.** v.i. Talk prosily (*about* etc.), whence **pros'ER¹** (-z-) n. **3.** v.t. Turn (poem etc.) into ~. [F, f. L *prosa* (*oratio*) straightforward (discourse), fem. of *prosus*, earlier *prorsus*, contraction of PRO¹(*versus* p.p. of *vertere* turn)]

prosec'tor, n. One who dissects dead bodies in preparation for anatomical lecture etc. [LL, = anatomist, f. PRO¹(*secare sect*- cut)]

pros'ecute, v.t. Follow up, pursue, (inquiry, studies); carry on (trade, pursuit); institute legal proceedings against (person), as *trespassers will be* ~*d*, (abs.) *shall not* ~. [f. L PRO¹(*sequi secut*- follow)]

prosecū'tion, n. Prosecuting (of pursuit etc.); (Law) institution and carrying on of criminal charge before court; carrying on of legal proceedings against person; prosecuting party, as *the* ~ *denied this*;

|| *director of public* ~*s*, English public prosecutor. [f. LL *prosecutio* (prec., -ION)]

pros'ecūtor n. One who prosecutes esp. in criminal court; *public* ~, law officer conducting criminal proceedings in public interest. Hence **prosecū'rɪx** n. (pl. -*ices* pr. -ɪsēz). [med.L (as PROSECUTE, see -OR²)]

pros'elyte, n., & v.t. **1.** Convert from one opinion, creed, or party, to another, as *made many* ~*es*; Gentile convert to Jewish faith, ~*e of the gate* (not submitting to circumcision etc.). **2.** v.t. (now rare). Make a ~*e* of (person, or abs.). Hence ~ISM(1, 2), ~IZER¹ nn., ~IZE(2) v.t. (often abs.). [(vb f. n.) f. LL f. Gk PROS(*ēlutos* f. *st. eluth*- come) one who has come, convert]

prosen'chyma (-ngk-), n. (bot.). Tissue of elongated cells placed with their ends interpenetrating (cf. PARENCHYMA), esp. fibro-vascular tissue. Hence ~tous (-ēngkɪm-) a. [f. Gk *pros* toward, as PARENCHYMA]

pros'ify (-z-), v.t. & i. Turn into prose, make (prosaic; write prose. [-FY]

pros'odɪy (*also* -z-), n. Science of versification. Hence ~ɪ'ᴬᴄᴬʟ, **prosōd'ɪᴀʟ, prosōd'ɪᴄ, aa.,** ~ɪsᴛ n. [f. L f. Gk PROS(*ōidia* as ODE)]

prosōpopoe'ia (-pēʲa), n. (rhet.). Introduction of pretended speaker; personification of abstract thing. [L, f. Gk PROS(*ōpopoïïa* (*prosōpon* person +*poieō* make)]

prospect, n., & v.i. **1.** (prŏs'pĕkt). Extensive view of landscape etc., as *a fine, striking,* ~; mental scene, as *opened a new* ~ *to his mind*; expectation, what one expects, as *offers a gloomy* ~, *his* ~*s were brilliant, no* ~ *of success, have nothing in* ~ *at present*, whence ~LESS a.; (Mining) spot giving ~*s* of mineral deposit, sample of ore for testing, resulting yield; possible or probable customer, subscriber, etc. **2.** (prospĕkt'). v.i. Explore region (*for* gold etc.), so **prospĕc'tor²** (*or* prŏs') n.; (fig.) look out *for,* (of mine) promise (*well, ill*); (v.t.) explore (region) for gold etc., work (mine) experimentally, (of mine) promise (specified yield). [(vb f. n.) as PROSPECTUS]

prospec'tive, a. Concerned with, applying to, the future (cf. RETROSPECTIVE), as *the law was held to be exclusively* ~, *implies a* ~ *obligation*; expected, future, some day to be, as ~ *peer, bridegroom, profit.* Hence ~ʟʏ² adv., ~NESS n. [f. med. L *prospectivus* (as foll., see -IVE)]

prospec'tus, n. (pl. ~*es*). Circular describing chief features of school, commercial enterprise, forthcoming book, etc. [L, gen. -*ūs*, = prospect, f. PRO¹(*spicere*= *spicere* look)]

pros'per, v.i. & t. Succeed, thrive, as

cheeds never ~, *nothing will ever ~ in his hands*; make successful, as *Heaven ~ our attempt*. [f. F *prospérer* f. L *prosperare*, as foll.]

prós'perous, a. Flourishing, successful, thriving, as a ~ *merchant, enterprise, voyage*; auspicious, as a ~ *gale, in a ~ hour*. adv. [f. obs. F *prospereux* f. L *prosperus*, see -OUS.]

prós'tate, n. Large gland, each of several small glands, accessory to male generative organs in mammals. Hence **prostat'ic** a. [f. med. L (-tâ) f. Gk PRO²(*statēs* f. *sta-* stand) one who stands before]

prós'thesis, n. (Gram.) addition of letter or syllable at beginning of word; (Surg.) making up of deficiencies (e.g. by false teeth or wooden leg) as a branch of surgery. So **prosthet'ic** a. [L, f. Gk *pros-thesis* f. *pros*(*tithēmi* put, vbl adj. *thetos*)]

prós'titute, n., & v.t. 1. Woman who offers her body to indiscriminate sexual intercourse esp. for hire. 2. v.t. Make a ~ of (oneself); (fig.) sell for base gain (one's honour etc.), put (abilities etc.) to infamous use. So **prostitū'tion** n. [f. L PRO¹(*stituere* -*ūt-*=*statuere* set up, place) offer for sale]

prós'trate (or -āt), a. Lying with face to ground, esp. as token of submission or humility; lying in horizontal position; overcome, overthrown, as *had laid the Whig party* ~; physically exhausted. (Bot.) lying flat on ground. [f. L p.p. as foll.]

prostrāte'² (or *prós'*), v.t. Lay (person etc.) flat on ground; cast oneself down prostrate (*at shrine, before person* etc.); (fig.) overcome, make submissive; (of fatigue etc.) reduce to extreme physical weakness. So **prostrā'tion** n. [f. L PRO¹(*sternere strāt-* lay flat)]

prós'tyle, n. & a. Portico of not more than four columns in front of Greek temple; (adj.) having a ~. [f. L (-os) f. Gk PRO²(*stūlos* STYLE²)]

prōs'ily² (-z-), a. Commonplace, tedious, dull, as ~*y talker*). Hence ~**ily²** adv. ~**INESS** n. [f. PROSE + -Y¹]

protag'onist, n. Chief person in drama or plot or story; leading person in contest, principal performer; (erron.) advocate, champion, *of course, method,* etc. [f. Gk *prōtagōnistēs* (*prōtos* first-+*agōnistēs* actor, as AGONIZE)]

prot'asis, n. (pl. -*ásēs*). Introductory clause, esp. clause expressing condition (cf. APODOSIS). So **protat'ic** a. [LL, f. Gk PRO¹(*tasis* f. *teinō* stretch) stretching forward, proposition.]

protéct', v.t. Keep safe, defend, guard, (person, thing, *from, against,* danger, injury, etc.); (Pol. Econ.) guard (home industry) against competition by imposts

on foreign goods; (Commerc.) provide funds to meet (bill, draft); provide (machinery etc.) with appliances to prevent injury from it, as ~*ed rifles*. [f. L PRO¹(*tegere tect-* cover)]

protec'tion, n. Protecting, defence, as *to your kind* ~; protecting person or thing, as *man, dog is a great ~ against burglars*; *live under X's ~*, (of a woman) be kept by; safe-conduct; U.S. certificate of American citizenship issued to seamen; (Pol. Econ.) system of protecting home industries, whence ~ISM(3), ~IST(2). [F, f. LL *protectionem* (as prec., see -ION)]

protec'tive, a. Serving or intended to protect; (of foods) protecting against deficiency diseases; ~ *custody*, (usu.) detention of persons in order to protect the State from their (real or supposed) subversive activities. Hence ~**ly²** adv. ~NESS n. [-IVE]

protec'tor, n. Person who protects; regent in charge of kingdom during minority, absence, etc., of sovereign, *Lord P~ of the Commonwealth*, title of Oliver Cromwell (1653-8) & Richard Cromwell (1658-9), whence ~AL, & ~SHIP n.; thing, device, that protects, as CHEST~, *point-* [as PROTECT, see -OR¹]

protec'torate, n. Office of protector or kingdom or State; period of this, esp. of the ~ of O. & R. Cromwell; protectorship of weak state by stronger one, esp. of territory inhabited by backward tribe; such territory. [-ATE¹]

protec'tory, n. (Rom. Cath.). Institution for care of destitute or vicious children. [as PROTECT, see -ORY]

protégé (prŏt'ezhā), n. (fem. ~*e*). Person to whom another is (usu. permanent) protector or patron. [F, p.p. of *protéger* PROTECT]

prōt'eid, n. = PROTEIN (1st sense). [-ID⁴]

prōt'eiform, a. Very changeable in form. [f. PROTEUS + -FORM]

prōt'ein, n. (chem.). (Now preferred in scient. use to *proteid*) albuminoid, kinds of organic compound (containing carbon, hydrogen, oxygen, & nitrogen, freq. also sulphur, occas. phosphorus) forming an important part of all living organisms, and the essential nitrogenous constituent of the food of animals; (orig.) supposed basis of albuminoids. Hence ~ACEOUS (-āshus), **protein'ic, prōt'einous,** aa. [G, f. Gk *prōteios* primary (*prōtos* first, see -IN]

prōt'er(o)- in comb. = Gk *proteros* former, anterior, as ~*an'drous*, ~*o'gynous*, having stamens (pistil) mature before pistil (stamens).

prōt'est¹, n. Formal statement of dissent

or disapproval, remonstrance, as *made a ~*, *paid it under ~*; || written statement of dissent from motion carried in H. of Lords signed by any peer of minority; written declaration usu. by notary public that bill that has been duly presented & payment or acceptance refused; solemn declaration. [obs. F, as foll.]

protest² ², v.t. & i. Affirm solemnly (one's innocence etc., *that*, or abs.); write a protest in regard to (bill, see prec.); make (often written) protest *against* (action, proposal), whence ~ER¹, ~OR², nn., ~ingly² adv. [f. F *protester* f. L PRO¹(*testari* aver f. *testis* witness)]

prot'estant, P~, n. & a. (Member, adherent) of any of the Christian bodies that separated from the Roman communion in the Reformation (16th c.) or their offshoots, whence P~ISM(3) n., P~IZE(3) v.t. & i.; (Hist., pl.) those who dissented from decision of Diet of Spires (1529), adherents of reformed doctrines in Germany; (*also* protȇs⁻) making, maker of, a protest. [F or G prec., -ANT]

protèsta'tion, n. Solemn affirmation (*of, that*); protest (*against*), [f. f. LL *protestatio* (as prec., see -ATION)]

Prot'eus (-tūs), n. Changing or inconstant person or thing; (earlier name for) amoeba; kinds of bacteria; kinds of tailed amphibian with eel-like body & four short legs. [L, f. Gk *Prōteus* sea-god taking various shapes]

prōthalăm'ium, **-iŏn**, n. (pl. *-ia*). Preliminary nuptial song. [(*-on*) made by Spenser on EPITHALAMIUM (PRO-²)]

prōth'ésis, n. (Placing of eucharistic elements on) credence-table, part of church where this stands; (Gram.)=PROSTHESIS, so **prothět'ic** a. [Gk *prothesis* f. PRO²(*thémi* place)]

protis'ta, n. pl. Kingdom of organized beings not distinguished as animals or plants, [Gk *prōtista*, neut. pl. double superl. f. *prōtos* first]

prōto- in comb.=Gk *prōtos* first. **1.** = chief, original, primitive, as: ~A'rabic, ~Cel'tic, etc., of the original Arabs etc.; ~genět'ic, ~gěn'ic, of first period of formation of growth; *prōt'ogine*, kind of granite found in Alps, assumed to be the most ancient; ~*hipp'us*, extinct quadruped related to ~horse; *prōt'omartyr* (-ter), first martyr (esp., of Christians, St Stephen); *prōtoph'yta* n. pl., the most simply organized plants, each consisting of a single cell, *prōt'ophyte*, such plant; ~*theria* n. pl., mammals of the lowest subclass, their hypothetical ancestors; ~zō'a n.pl., great division of animal kingdom comprising animals of simplest type consisting of single cell & usu. microscopic, ~zō'on, such animal; ~zō'al a., ~zō'an a. & n. (animal) of the ~zoa, (of disease) caused by parasitic ~zoon; ~zō'ic, (Geol., of strata) containing earliest traces of living beings, (also) = ~zoal; ~zōöl'ogy, study of ~zoa. **2.** In chem. names of compounds in which the element or radical combines in smallest proportion with another element, as ~chlor'ide, ~sulph'ide, prōt'oxide, compound containing minimum of chlorine, sulphur, oxygen.

prōt'ocŏl, n., & v.i. & t. (-ll-). **1.** Original draft of diplomatic document, esp. of terms of treaty agreed to in conference & signed by the parties; formal statement of transaction; (in France) etiquette department of Ministry of Foreign Affairs; official formulas at beginning & end of charter, papal bull, etc. **2.** vb. Draw up ~s; record in ~. [f. OF *prothocole* f. med. L f. Gk PROTO(*kolton* f. *kolla* glue) fly-leaf glued to book]

prōt'on, n. (physics). Unit of positive electricity, forming part (or, in hydrogen, whole) of the nucleus of the atom (cf. ELECTRON), [neut. of Gk *prōtos* first]

prōtonot'arȳ, **prōtho-**, (or **proton'o-**), n. Chief clerk in some law courts, esp. (Hist.) Chancery, Common Pleas, & King's Bench, (orig. in Byzantine court); P~ies *Apostolic(al)*, twelve prelates who register papal acts, direct canonization of saints, etc. [f. LL f. late Gk PROTO(*notarios* NOTARY)]

prōt'oplăsm, n. Semifluid semitransparent colourless substance consisting of oxygen, hydrogen, carbon, & nitrogen, basis of life in plants & animals. Hence **prōtoplăsmăt'ic**, **prōtoplăs'mic**, aa., (-z-). [f. G PROTO(PLASMA)]

prōt'oplăst, n. The first created man; original, model; unit or mass of protoplasm. Hence **prōtoplăs'tic** a. [f. LL f. Gk PROTO(*plastos* moulded, as PLASMA)]

prōt'otype, n. The original thing or person in relation to any copy, imitation, representation, later specimen, improved form, etc. Hence ~typal, ~typ'ic(al), aa. [f. Gk PROTO(*tupon* f. *tupos* TYPE)]

protract', v.t. Prolong, lengthen out, as ~*ed their stay for some weeks*, whence ~edry² adv.; draw (plan of ground etc.) to scale. [f. L PRO(*trahere tract-* draw)]

protrac'tile a. (zool.). (Of organ etc.) that can be extended. [-ILE]

protrac'tion, n. Protracting; action of protractor muscle; drawing to scale. [f. LL *protractio* (as PROTRACT, see -ION)]

protrac'tor, n. Instrument for measuring angles, usu. in form of graduated semicircle; muscle serving to extend limb etc. [med. L (as prec., see -OR²)]

protrude' (-ŏŏd), v.t. & i. Thrust forth, cause to project; (fig.) obtrude; stick out, project. Hence or cogn. **protru'dent**, **protru'sible**, **protru'sive**, aa., (-ŏō-), **protru'sion** (-ŏŏzhn) n. [f. L PRO¹(*trudere trus-* thrust)]

protru'sile (-ōō-), a. (Of limb etc.) that may be thrust forth. [as prec., see -ILE]

protub'er|ant, a. Bulging out, prominent (lit. & fig.). Hence **~ANCE** n. [f. L PRO¹, (*tuberare* f. *tuber* hump), see -ANT]

prot'yle, n. (chem.). Supposed original undifferentiated matter of which chemical elements may be composed. [f. PROTO-+-YL]

proud, a. & adv. 1. Valuing oneself highly or too highly, esp. on the ground of (qualities, rank, possessions, etc.; also **~-hearted**) haughty, arrogant; feeling oneself greatly honoured, as *am ~ of his acquaintance; of knowing him, to know him*; having a proper PRIDE, as *too ~ to complain*; HOUSE~; (of actions etc.) showing pride; of which one is or may be justly ~, as *a ~ day for us, a ~ sight*; (of things) imposing, splendid; (of waters) swollen, in flood; *~ flesh*, overgrown flesh round healing wound. 2. adv. (colloq.) *You do me ~* (honour me greatly). Hence **~ly²** adv. [OE *prūt*, -d, prob. f. OF *prud* (f *prēuz*) f. LL **prōdis* useful, cf. L *prōdesse* be of use]

prove (proov), v.t. & i. (arch. p.p.~en). (Arch.) test qualities of, try; subject (gun etc.) to testing process; (Arith.) test accuracy of (calculation); *~es the rule*; take proof impression of (stereotype plate etc.); make certain, demonstrate, (*that, the truth of, thing etc. to be, that*), whence **~'ABLE** a., **~'ableness** n., **~'abiy²** adv., (-oov-); (Sc. Law, as *abiy*) *not proven*; verdict in criminal trial) *not proven*, establish genuineness & validity of (will); (intr.) turn out (*to be, to do*), turn out to be, as *will ~e (to be) the heir, to know nothing about it*. [f. OF *prover* f. L *probare* test]

provēd'itor, provēdōre', nn. (-tor) officer of Venetian republic; caterer, purveyor. [f. obs. It. *proveditore*, Port. *provedor*, ult. f. L as PROVIDE, see -OR²]

prov'enance, n. (Place of) origin, as *vases of doubtful ~*. [F, f. *provenir* f. L PRO¹-, (*venire* come), see -ANCE]

Provençal (see Ap.), a. & n. (Inhabitant, language) of Provence. [F. as PROVINCIAL]

prov'ender, n. Fodder; (joc.) food for human beings. [f. OF *provend(r)e* corrupt. f. L as PREBEND]

proven'ience, n. =PROVENANCE. [f. L as PROVENANCE, see -ENCE]

prov'erb, n. Short pithy saying in general use, adage, saw; *ignorant etc. to a ~* (notoriously); *their fickleness is a ~* (notoriously); *he is a ~* (byword) *for inaccuracy*; play (usu. French) based on in (pl.) kinds of round game; *Book of P~s* (in O.T.). [f. F *proverbe* f. L *proverbium* f. *verbum* word]

prover'bial, a. Of, expressed in, proverbs, as *~ wisdom*; that has become a proverb, notorious. Hence **~ITY** (-ǎl-) n., **~ly²** adv. [f. LL *proverbialis* (as prec., see -AL)]

prov'iant, n. Food supply esp. of army. [G. ult. f. L as PROVENDER]

provide', v.i. & t. 1. Make due preparation (*for* person's safety, entertainment, etc., *against* attack etc., rarely *for* undesirable thing); (of person, law, etc.) stipulate (*that*); supply, furnish, (person *with* thing, thing *for* or *to* person); equip with necessaries, as *you must ~ your selves*; make provision, as (for) necessaries, family, etc. 2. (hist.) Appoint (incumbent *to* benefice); (of pope) appoint (successor *to* benefice). =foll. [f. L PRO¹ *ēvidēre* (*vīs-* see)]

provid'ed, a. & conj. 1. In vbl senses, as *~ school*, public elementary school or by local authority. 2. conj. On the condition or understanding, as *~ (that) all is safe, ~ (that) he does no harm*. [-ED¹]

prov'idence, n. Foresight, timely care; thrift; benefit care of God or nature special; particular instance of this; (P~), God. [F, f. L *providentia* (as foll., see -ENCE)]

provid'ent, a. Having or showing foresight; thrifty. Hence **~LY²** adv. [as PROVIDE, see -ENT]

prov'idēn'tial, a. Of, by, divine foresight or interposition; opportune, lucky. Hence **~LY²** (-sha-) adv. [f. L as PROVIDENCE+-AL]

provid'er, n. In vbl senses; *lion's ~*, jackal (lit. & fig.); || *universal ~*, tradesman dealing in all or many kinds of goods etc. [-ER¹]

prov'ince, n. (Rom. Hist.) territory outside Italy under Roman governor; principal division of country etc.; (Eccl.) district under archbishop or metropolitan; *the ~s*, whole of a country outside the capital; sphere of action, business, as (*is not within*) *my ~*; branch of learning etc., as *in the ~ of polite letters*. [F, f. L *provincia* official duty, province. etym. dub.]

provin'cial (-shl), a. & n. 1. Of a province; of the provinces; having the manners, speech, narrow views, etc., prevalent in these, whence **~ITY** (-shiǎl-) n. 2. n. Inhabitant of a province or the provinces (also **~IST** n.); countrified person; (Eccl.) head of, chief of religious order in, a province. Hence **~IZE** v.t., **~ly²** adv., (-sha-). [f. L *provincialis* (as prec., see -AL)]

provin'cialism (-sha-), n. Provincial manner, fashion, mode of thought, etc.; word, phrase, peculiar to county etc.; attachment to one's province rather than country. [-ISM]

provi'sion (-zhn), n., & v.t. 1. Providing (*for, against*), esp. *make ~*; provided amount of something. 2. pl. Supply of food, eatables & drinkables; whence **~LESS** (-zho-) a. 3. Legal or formal statement providing for something, clause of this. 4. (hist.) Appointment to benefice not yet vacant; *P~s of Oxford*,

ordinances for checking king's misrule drawn up by barons under Simon de Montfort in 1258. **5.** v.t. Supply with ~s, whence ~MENT (-zho-) n. [F, f. L *provisionem* (as PROVIDE, see -ION)]

provi'sional (-zho-), a. For the time being, temporary. Hence **provisionāl'ITY**, ~NESS, nn., ~LY² adv., (-zho-). [-AL] provis'o (-zō), n. (pl. ~s). Stipulation; clause of stipulation or limitation in document. [L, neut. abl. of P.P., = PROVIDED *that*]

provis'or (-z-), n. **1.** (hist.). Holder of a PROVISION; *Statute of P~s* (preventing pope from granting provisions). **2.** (R.-C. Ch.) vicar general. [f. AF *provisour* f. L *provisorem* (as PROVIDE, see -OR²)]

provi'sŏrỹ (-z-), a. Conditional; making provision, as ~y *care*. Hence ~LY² adv. [f. prec., see -ORY]

prŏvocā'tion, n. Incitement, instigation, irritation, as *did it under severe* ~. [F, f. L *provocationem* (as PROVOKE, see -ATION)]

prŏvŏc'ative, a. & n. (Thing) tending to provocation (*of* curiosity etc.); intentionally irritating. [f. LL *provocativus* (foll. -IVE)]

provōke', v.t. Rouse, incite, (person *to* anger, *to* do); irritate; instigate, tempt; call forth (indignation, inquiry, a storm, etc.); cause, as *will~e fermentation*. Hence ~ING² a., ~ingLY² adv. [f. L PRO-²(*vocare* call)]

prŏv'ost (*in mil. senses* prŏvō'), n. **1.** ‖ Head of some colleges at Oxford, Cambridge, etc.; (Hist.) head of chapter or religious community. **2.** ‖ Head of Scottish municipal corporation or burgh (in some cities, *Lord P~*). **3.** Protestant clergyman in charge of principal church of town etc. in Germany etc. **4.** ~ *marshal,* head of military police in camp or on active service, master-at-arms of ship on which court martial is to be held, chief police official in some colonies. (Hist.) French semi-military officer: ~ *sergeant,* sergeant of military police. Hence ~SHIP n. [OE has *profost, pra-* OF *provost, pre-*, G *probst,* ult. f. L *pro- positus=praepositus,* see PRAEPOSTOR]

prow¹, n. Fore-part immediately about stem of boat or ship; (Zool., also *prora*) ~-*like* projection in front. [f. F *proue* prob. ult. f. L *prora* f. Gk *prō(i)ra*]

‖ prow² a. (arch.). Worthy, gallant. [f. OF *prou, prod,* (F *preux*) f. LL as PROUD]

prow'ĕss, n. Valour, gallantry. [f. OF *proece* (as prec., see -ESS³)]

prowl, v.i. & t., & n. **1.** Go about in search of plunder or prey (also fig.); traverse (streets, place) thus. **2.** n. ~ing, esp. *on the* ~. Hence ~ER¹ n. [ME *prollen,* etym. dub.]

prŏx'imal, a. (anat.). Situated towards centre of body or of point of attachment (cf. DISTAL). Hence ~LY² adv. [f. L *proximus* nearest + -AL]

---

after (in place, order, time, connexion of thought, etc.); approximate. Hence ~LY² adv. [f. LL *proximare* draw near (as prec.), see -ATE²]

‖ prŏx'imĕ accĕs'sĭt (aks-), sent., & n. (pl. *-ĕssē'rŭnt*). (Placed in list after name of candidate for prize etc.) he came very near (the winner; m.) *I was, he got a,* ~ (was very near). [L]

prŏxim'itỹ, n. Nearness in space, time, etc. (*to*; ~ *of blood,* kinship. [f. F *proximité* f. L *proximitatem* (as PROXIMAL, see -ITY)]

prŏx'imō, a. (abbr. *prox.*). Of next month, as *the 3rd prox.* [L, = in next (*mense* month)]

prŏx'ỹ, n. Agency of substitute or deputy, as *married, voted, by~*; person authorized to act for another, *as made me his* ~; writing authorizing person to vote on behalf of another, vote so given; (attrib.) done, given, made, by ~. [f. obs. *procuracy* f. med. L *procuratia* (as PROCURATION, see -ACY)]

prūde (prōōd), n. Woman of extreme (esp. affected) propriety in conduct or speech. Hence or cogn. ~ERY(4), ~ish-NESS, nn., ~ish a., ~ishLY² adv., (-ōō-). [mod. F, f. OF *prude, prode,* good, modest, fem. adj. as *prud*hom(m)e, as n. perh. back formation f. *prudefemme*]

prū'dent (-ōō-), a. (Of person or conduct) sagacious, discreet, worldly-wise. Hence or cogn. ~ENCE n., ~entLY² adv. [f. L *prudens=providens* PROVIDENT]

prūdĕn'tial (-ōō-, -shl), a. & n. Of, involving, marked by, prudence, as ~ *motives, policy;* (n. pl.) ~ considerations or matters. Hence ~ISM(2), ~IST(2), nn., ~LY² adv., (-ōō-, -shə-). [f. PRUDENCE + -AL]

prud'homme (prüdôm'), n. Member of French tribunal appointed to decide labour disputes. [F]

prū'inōse (-ōō-), a. (nat. hist.). Covered with white powdery substance, frosted. [f. L *pruinosus* (*pruina* hoar-frost, see -OSE¹)]

prune¹ (prōōn), n. Dried plum; colour of its juice, dark reddish purple (esp. attrib.); ~*s & prism* (of mincing way of speaking etc., *Little Dorrit* II. v). [F, f. med. L *pruna* (L -*num*) f. Gk prou(m)*non* plum]

prune² (prōōn), v.t. Trim (tree etc., often *down*) by cutting away superfluous branches etc.; lop *off, away* (branches etc.); (fig.) remove (superfluities); *pruning-hook* (used for this purpose); clear (book etc. *of* what is superfluous). [f. OF *prooing(n)ier,* etym. dub.]

prune³ (prōōn), v.t. (now rare). = PREEN. [?]

prunĕll'a¹ (prŏō-), n. Strong silk or worsted stuff used formerly for barristers' gowns etc. & later for uppers of women's

shoes; LEATHER & ~. [etym. dub.; F has *prunelle*]

prunell'a² (prōō-), n. Kinds of fever &c. of throat disorder; ~ *salt*, preparation of fused nitre used for ~; genus of plants including the weed Self-heal used to cure etc., tool for applying this. [perh. dial. form of *prinel*]

prunell'o (prōō-), n. (pl. ~s). Finest kind of prune, made esp. from greengages. [f. obs. It. *prunella* dim. of *pruna* PRUNE¹]

prunt, n. Piece of (esp. blackberry-shaped) ornamental glass laid on to vase etc. [?]

pru'rient (-oor-), a. Given to indulgence of lewd ideas; (rare) having morbid desire or curiosity. Hence ~ENCE, ~ENCY, nn., ~ently adv. [f. L *prurire* itch, be wanton, see -ENT]

prurig'o, -ir'us, (-oor-), nn. (Diseased state of skin marked by) violent itching (-ū). So **pruri'ginous** (-oor-) a. [L (gen. *-ginis, -tis*), =itching, as prec.]

Pru'ssian (-shn), a. & n. (Native, inhabitant) of Prussia; ~ *blue*, a deep blue pigment; ~ *brown, green* (derived from or allied to this); ~ (small kind of) *corn*. Hence ~IZE(3) (-shə-) v.t., (esp.) assimilate to the ~ system of sacrificing the individual to the State. [f. med. L *Prussi* (also *Borussi*) + -AN]

pruss'ic, a. Of, got from, Prussian blue; ~ *acid* (HYDROCYANIC). [f. F *prussique* (*Prusse* Prussia, see -IC)]

pry¹, v.i. Look, peer, inquisitively (often *into, about* adv.); inquire impertinently (*into* (person's) affairs, conduct, etc.). Hence ~ING² a., ~ingly² adv. [ME *prien*, etym. dub.]

pry², v.t. Var. of PRIZE³.

prytane'um, n. (Gk Ant.). Public hall, esp. one in Athens for entertainment of ambassadors, presidents of senate, & specially honoured citizens. [L, f. Gk *prutaneion* (*prutanis* president, member of presiding division of BOULE)]

psalm (sahm), n. Sacred song, hymn; *the* (*Book of*) *P~s*, (pop.) *the P~s of David*, book in O.T.; ~*book*, book containing the P~s, metrical version of these for public worship. [f. L f. Gk *psalmos* song sung to harp (*psallō* twang, sing to harp)]

psalm'ist (sahm-), n. Author of a psalm (also as title of book of psalmody); *the P~*, David or author of any of the Psalms. [f. LL *psalmista* (as prec., see -IST)]

psal'mody (sahm-, sahm-), n. Practice, art, of singing psalms, hymns, anthems, etc., esp. in public worship, whence **psalmod'ic** (-ŏd-) a., **psal'modist** (sai-) n.; arrangement of psalms for singing, psalms so arranged. [f. LL *psalmodia* f. Gk *psalmōidia* singing to harp (as PSALM + *ō(i)dē* song)]

psal'ter (sawl-), n. The Book of Psalms; version of this, as *Latin, English, Prayer*-

book, Scotch, Metrical, P~; copy of the Psalms esp. for liturgical use. [AF *sauter*, f. L f. Gk *psaltērion* instrument played by twanging (*psallō* twang)]

psal'tery (sawl-), n. Ancient & medieval instrument like dulcimer but played by plucking strings with fingers or plectrum. [f. OF *saltere* f. L as prec.]

psephi'sm (sē-, sĕ-), n. (Gk Ant.). Decree enacted by vote of (esp. Athenian) public assembly. [f. Gk *psēphisma* (*psēphizō* vote f. *psēphos* pebble, -M)]

pseud'echis (or s-, -k-), n. (zool.). Gems of venomous snakes, as ~ *poisoning*. [f. PSEUDO- + Gk *ekhis* viper]

pseudepi'graph|a (or s-), n. pl. Spurious writings, esp. Jewish writings ascribed to various O.T. prophets etc. Hence ~AL, ~IC aa. [neut. pl. of Gk PSEUDEPI*graphos*, see EPIGRAPH]

pseud'o(o- (or s-) in comb.= Gk *pseudo-* false(ly), seeming(ly) or professed(ly) but not real(ly), in compp.f. Gk, & as living pref. (occas. written separately without hyphen as adj., as *the ~o penitent*), as: ~*o-arch'ic*, artificially archaic in style etc., so ~*o-awch'aism*, ~*o-arch'aist*; ~*o-carp* (Bot.), fruit formed from other parts besides the ovary; ~*o-cath'olic*; ~*o-Christ*; ~*o-Christian*; ~*o-class'ic*, pretending or wrongly held to be classic; ~*o-Goth'ic*, sham Gothic in style; ~*o-mart'yr*; ~*o-proph'et*.

pseud'ograph (or s-, -ahf), n. A spurious literary work. [f. LL f. Gk PSEUDO-(*graphos* -GRAPH)]

pseudol'oger (or s-), n. (joc.). Systematic liar. So **pseudol'ogi|al** a., ~IST n. [f. Gk PSEUDO(*logos*, see -LOGER)]

pseud'o|morph (or s-), n. False form, esp. (Mineral) crystal etc. consisting of one mineral with form proper to another. Hence ~*morph'ic*, ~*morph'ous*, aa. [PSEUDO- + Gk *morphē* form]

pseud'onym (or s-), n. Fictitious name, esp. one assumed by author. [f. Gk neut. adj. as foll.]

pseudon'ymous (or s-), a. Writings, written, under a false name. Hence ~*onym'ity* n. [f. Gk PSEUDO(*onuma* name)+-OUS]

pseud'o|scope (or s-), n. Optical instrument making convex object seem concave & vice versa. Hence ~*scop'ic* a. [-SCOPE]

pshaw (psh-, sh-), int., n. & v.i. & t. Int. expr. contempt or impatience; (n.) this exclamation; (v.i.) say ~ (often *at*) (v.t.) show contempt for (thing etc.). [natural]

psi, n. Greek letter (Ψ, ψ)= ps. [Gk]

psilan'throp|ism (or s-), n. Doctrine that Christ was a mere man. So **psilan'throp|ist** a., ~IST n. [f. eccl. Gk *psilan-thrōpos* merely human (*psilos* bare, mere, +*anthrōpos* man)+-ISM]

psilo'sis (or s-), n. (path.). Stripping bare.

e.g. of hair or flesh; = SPRUE². [Gk (prec., -OSIS)]

psitt'acine (or s-), a. Of parrots, parrot-like. [f. L *psittacinus* (*psittacus* parrot, see -INE¹)]

psittacō'sis (or s-), n. Epidemic disease somewhat resembling typhoid fever and pneumonia said to be caught by human beings from parrots. [f. L *psittacus* parrot +-OSIS]

psō'ās (or s-), n. ~ *magnus, parvus*, two hip muscles. [Gk, acc. pl. of *psoa*, taken as sing.]

psōr'a (or s-), n. A contagious skin disease, itch. [L, f. Gk *psōra*]

psōrī'asis (or s-), n. Skin disease marked by red patches covered with scales. [prec., -ASIS]

psyche (psīk[i, s-), n. 1. Soul, spirit, mind, (in Gk Myth. personified as beloved of Eros, & represented with butterfly wings). 2. Genus of dayflying moths. [f. Gk *psukhē* breath, life, soul]

psychī'atrist (psīk-, sīk-), n. One who treats mental disease. So **psychīat'rr-ō**(AL) aa., ~Y¹ n., (psīk-, sīk-). [f. Gk as prec. +*íatros* physician +-IST]

psych'ic (psīk-, sīk-), a. & n. 1. = foll.; ~ *force*, non-physical force assumed to explain spiritualistic phenomena. 2. n. Person susceptible to ~ influence, medium; (pl.) psychology; psychical research. [f. Gk *psukhikos* (as PSYCHE, see -IC)]

psych'ical (psīk-, sīk-), a. Of the soul or mind, whence ~-ly² adv.; of the animal life of man; of phenomena & conditions apparently outside domain of physical law, esp. ~ *research*, so **psych'icism**, **psych'icist**, nn., (psīk-, sīk-). [-AL]

psycho- (psīk-, sīk-), in comb.=Gk *psukhē* soul, mind, as: ~ō-anāl'ysis, the psychology of Freud, Jung, & Adler, dividing the mind into conscious & unconscious elements, & investigating the interactions of these (so ~ō-an'alȳse v.t., ~ō-dynām'ic(s) n., ~ō-(analyt'ic a.); ~ō-dynām'ic(s) n., (science) of the mental powers; ~ōgen'esis, ~ōg'ony, genesis of soul or mind, so ~ōgenēt'ic(al), ~ōgon'ical, aa.; ~'ogram, ~'ograph, instrument for writing this; ~'og'raphy, descriptive branch of psychology, (also) spirit-writing; ~'ōmancy, occult communication between souls or with spirits; ~ōm'etry, faculty of divining from physical contact or proximity the qualities of an object or of persons etc. that have been in contact with it, so ~ōmet'ric(al) aa.; ~ōmōt'or a., inducing movement by psychic action; ~ōneurōs'is, mental disease consisting in loss of balance between instincts & controlling power; ~ōpath, mentally deranged person, ~ōpath'ic, ~ōp'athist, ~ōpathol'ogy, ~ōp'athy, of, one who treats, science of, mental disease; ~ōphys'ics, science of general relations between mind & body, so ~ōphys'ical a., ~ōphys'icist n.; ~ōphysiōl'ogy, branch of physiology dealing with mental phenomena, so ~ōphysiōlo'gical a., ~ōphysiōl'ogist n.; ~ōtherapeut'ic, ~ōthē'rapy, (of) treatment of disease by hypnotic influence.

psycholō'gical (psīk-, sīk-), a. Of psychology; ~ *moment* [f. F mistransl. of G *moment* neut. potent element as *moment* masc. moment of time], the ~ly appropriate moment, (improp., esp. joc.) nick of time. Hence ~ly² adv. [-ICAL]

psychōl'ogy (psīk-, sīk-), n. Science of nature, functions, & phenomena, of human soul or mind; treatise on, system of, this. So ~IST n., ~IZE(2, 3) v.t. & i. [-LOGY]

psychōs'is (psīk-, sīk-), n. (pl. -osēs). Severe mental derangement involving the whole personality, mental disease. [f. late Gk *psukhōsis* (*psukhoō* give life to, as PSYCHE, see -OSIS)]

psychrōm'ēter (psīk-, sīk-), n. Wet-&-dry-bulb thermometer. [f. Gk *psukhros* cold +-METER]

ptarm'igan (t-), n. Bird of grouse family, with black or grey plumage in summer & white in winter. [~ is pseudo-etym. after Gk etym. dub.; p- is pseudo-etym. after Gk wds in pt-]

ptēridōl'ogy (pt-, t-), n. Study of ferns. So ~olō'gical a..., ~ōl'ogist n. [f. Gk *pteris -idos*, a feathery fern (*pteron* wing) +-o- +-LOGY]

ptēr'o- (pt-, t-) in comb.= Gk *pteron* wing, as: ~odac'tyl, extinct winged reptile; ~ōg'raphy, description of feathers, so ~ōgraph'ic(al) aa.; ~'opod, mollusc with middle part of foot expanded into pair of wing-like lobes; ~'osaur, extinct flying saurian reptile.

ptē'ropus (pt-, t-), n. (pl. -pī). FLYING fox. [f. Gk PTERO(*pous* foot) wing-footed]

ptē'rygoid (pt-, t-), a. ~ *process*, each of two processes descending from junction of body & great wing of sphenoid bone; connected with these. So **ptē'rygo-** comb. form. [f. Gk *pterygoeidēs* wing-like (*pterux -agos* wing, -OID)]

ptisan (tī'zn, tīzăn'), n. Nourishing decoction, esp. barley-water. [f. F *tisane* f. L f. Gk *ptisanē* peeled barley (*ptissō* peel)]

Ptolemā'ic (t-), a. Of Ptolemy, Alexandrine astronomer of 2nd c., esp. ~ *system* (of astronomy, in which earth was held to be the stationary centre round which sun and stars revolved, cf. COPERNICAN); of the Ptolemies, rulers of Egypt from death of Alexander the Great to Cleopatra. [f. Gk *Ptolemaios* +-IC]

ptomaine (tōm'ān, tōmān'), n. Kinds of (often poisonous) alkaloid body in putrefying animal & vegetable matter, esp. ~ *poisoning*. [f. It. *ptomaina* f. Gk *ptōma* corpse (*piptō* fall), -INE⁵]

ptōs'is (pt-, t-), n. Drooping of upper eye-

lid from paralysis of a muscle. [Gk *ptōsis* falling.]

¶**pūb**, n. (colloq.). Public house. [abbr.]

pūb'erty, n. The state of being functionally capable of procreation; *age of* ~, at which ~ begins; in England, legally, 14 in boys, 12 in girls). [f. L *pūbertas* (*puber* of the age of ~, see TY]

pūbes'cence, n. Arrival at puberty; soft down on leaves & stems of plants, downiness; soft down on parts of animals, esp. insects. So ~ENT a. [F, f. L *pubescere* become hairy, reach puberty (*pubes* groin, private parts, hair on these), see -ENCE]

pūb'lic, a. & n. 1. Of, concerning, the people as a whole, as ~ *offence, holiday* (Parl.), ~ *act, bill*; ~ *utility*, a supply or undertaking usu. available in large towns, e.g. water, gas, electricity, etc. 2. Done by or for, representing, the people, as ~ *prosecution, prosecutor, assembly*. 3. ~ *school*, one under ~ manage-ment. ‖ esp. endowed grammar (usu. boarding-)school preparing pupils chiefly for universities or ~ services, often maintaining discipline with help of pupils. 6. Open to general observation, done or existing in ~, as *made a* ~ *protest, gave it* ~ *utterance, whence* ~LY² adv. 7. Of, engaged in, the affairs or service of the people, as ~ *life, a* ~ *man, notary* ~; ~ *spirit*, patriotism, so ~-*spirited* a., ~-*spiritedly* adv. -*spi'ritedness* n. 8. Of the nations, international, as *pro-scribed Napoleon as a* ~ *enemy*. 9. n. The (members of the) community in general, as *the* ~ *is the best judge, are the best judges, the British, American,* ~; *section of the community, as the reading* ~, *the most gullible of* ~s; ‖ *in* ~ *house* (colloq.); *in* ~, *openly,* ~LY. [F, f. L *publicus*, earlier *poplicus* (*populus* people), earlier *poplus*, see -IC]

pū'blican, n. (Rom. Hist., & in N.T.) tax-farmer, tax-gatherer; ‖ Keeper of public house. [f. F *publicain* f. L *publi-canus* (as prec., see -AN)]

pūblicā'tion, n. Making publicly known; issuing of book, engraving, music, etc., to the public; book etc. so issued. [f. L *publicatio* (as PUBLISH, see -ATION)]

pūb'licist, n. Writer on, person skilled in, international law; writer on current public topics, esp. journalist. So ~ISM n. ~'is'tic a., ~-IZE v.t. [f. F *publiciste* (PUBLIC, -IST)]

pūblic'ity, n. Openness to general ob-servation, notoriety, (*avoid, court,* ~; *give* ~ *to*); the business of advertising

(both goods and persons); ~ *agent*, person employed to keep the name of an actor etc. constantly before the public. [f. F *publicité*, see PUBLIC, -ITY]

pūb'lish, v.t. Make generally known, noise abroad; announce formally, pro-mulgate (edict etc.); ask, read, (banns of marriage); (of author, editor, or pub-lisher) issue copies of (book, engraving, etc.) for sale to the public. Hence ~ABLE a. [f. OF *puplier* f. L *publicare* (as PUBLIC), altered on -ISH²]

pūb'lisher, n. In vbl senses, esp. one who produces copies of book etc. & distributes them to booksellers or to the public. [-ER¹]

pŭc'e, a. Flea-colour, purple-brown. [F, = flea (-colour), f. L *pulicem* (nom. *-ex*) flea.]

puc'coon, n. N.-Amer. plant yielding red or yellow dye. [native]

pŭck¹, n. (P~) the goblin *Robin Goodfellow* or *Hobgoblin*; any mischievous sprite or (fig.) child. Hence ~ISH¹, ~LIKE, aa. [OE *pūca*, cf. ON *pūki*, W *pwca*, Ir. *púca*]

pŭck², n. (Disease in cattle attributed to) nightjar, goatsucker. [?]

pŭck³, n. Rubber disk used for hockey on ice. [?]

pŭck'a, pŭkk'a, a. (Anglo-Ind.). Of full weight; genuine; permanent, solidly built. [Hind. (*pakkā*), = cooked, ripe]

pŭck'er, v.i. & t., & n. 1. Contract, gather, (t. & i. of brow, seam, material, often *up*) into wrinkles, folds, or bulges; intention-ally or as fault e.g. in sewing. 2. n. Such bulge etc. Hence ~Y² a. [prob. cogn. w. POKE¹, -ER²]

pŭd, n. (nursery). Child's hand; fore-foot of some animals. [?]

pu'ding, (pŏŏ-), n. Soft or stiffish mix-ture of animal or vegetable ingredients, esp. mixed or enclosed in flour or other farinaceous food, cooked by boiling, steaming, or baking (*batter, beefsteak, bread-&-butter, currant, HASTY, lemon, MILK, PLUM, suet, YORKSHIRE,* ~); intestine of pig etc. stuffed with oatmeal, blood, etc. (BLACK, *hog's, white,* ~); *more praise than* ~ (material reward); *the PROOF¹ of the* ~ etc.; thing of ~-like appearance etc.; (sl.) drugged liver etc. given by burglars to dogs; (Naut., also *pu'dening*) pad, tow binding, to prevent chafing etc.; ~*cloth*, cloth in which some ~s are tied up for boiling; ~*face*, large fat face; ~*-head, dolt*; ~*-heart, coward*; ‖ ~ *pie*, forms of pastry; ~*-stone*, composite rock of rounded pebbles in siliceous matrix. Hence ~Y² a. [ME *poding*, prob. conn. w. F *boudin*, etym. dub.]

pŭd'dle, n. Small dirty pool esp. of rain on road etc.; (colloq.) muddle, mess; clay (& sand) mixed with water as watertight covering for embankments etc. Hence dim. of OE *pudd* ditch, cf. G dial. *pf(*u*)udel*]

pŭd'dle³, v.i. & t. Dabble, wallow, (often *about*) in mud or shallow water; busy oneself in untidy way; make (water, also fig.) muddy; knead (clay & sand) into, make, line (canal etc.) with, PUDDLE¹; stir about (molten iron) to produce wrought iron by expelling carbon. Hence pŭd'dlER¹ (1, 2) n. [f. prec. & cf. Du. *poedelen*, G *pudd(d)eln, butteln*, dabble]

pŭd'encý, n. Modesty. [f. LL *pudentia* (as foll., see -ENCY)]

pūdĕn'dum, n. (usu. in pl. -*da*). Privy parts. Hence or cogn. pūdĕn'dAl, pŭd'IC, aa. [L (*pudēre* be ashamed, -ND¹)]

pŭdge, n. (colloq.). Short thick or fat person, animal, or thing. Hence pŭdg'ý² a. [etym. dub., cf. PODGE]

pŭd'sý (-z-), a. Plump. [cf. prec. & PUD] *pue'blō* (pwĕ-), n. (pl. -*s*). Spanish -Amer. town or village, esp. settlement of Indians. [Sp.]

pū'erile, a. Boyish, childish; trivial, whence or cogn.~LY² adv., pŭeril'ITY n.; ~ *breathing* (with loud pulmonary murmur as in children, usu. sign of disease in adult). [f. L *puerilis* (*puer* boy see -ILE)] pŭerp'eral, a. Of, due to, childbirth. [f. L *puerperus* (*puer* child + -*parus* bearing +-AL]

pŭff¹, n. 1. Short quick blast of breath or wind; sound (as) of this; small quantity of vapour, smoke, etc., emitted at one ~. 2. Round soft protuberant mass of material in dress, of hair of head, etc. 3. (Also *powder*~) small pad of down or the like for applying powder to skin. 4. Piece, cake, etc., of light pastry esp. of ~ paste. 5. Unduly or extravagantly laudatory review of book, advertisement of tradesman's goods etc., esp. in newspaper. 6.~*adder*, large venomous African viper inflating upper part of body when excited; ~*ball*, fungus with ball-shaped spore-case; ~*box* (containing powder & ~); ~ *paste*, light flaky paste; ~*bird* (nursery), steam-engine, train. [ME *puf*, imit.]

pŭff², v.i. & t. 1. Emit puff of air or breath; (of air etc.) come *out*, *up*, in puffs; breathe hard, pant, esp. ~ & *blow*; put out of breath, as *was rather* ~*ed*; ~ *out*, utter pantingly; (of steam-engine, person smoking, etc.) emit puffs, move with puffs, as ~*ed away at his cigar*, ~*ed out of the terminus*. 2. Blow (dust, smoke, light object, *out*, *up*, *away*, etc.) with puff; smoke (pipe) in puffs. 3. Blow *out*, *up*, inflate; become inflated, swell *up*, *out*; ~ *up*, elate, make proud, (esp. in p.p., *with pride* etc.). 4. Advertise (goods) with exaggerated or false praise; ‖ bid at auction to raise price. Hence ~'ER¹ n. [ME *puffen*, imit.]

pŭff'ery, n. Advertisement, puffing; puff frilling, puffs. [-ERY]

pŭff'in, n. N.-Atlantic sea-bird with large furrowed particoloured bill. [?]

---

pŭff'ý, a. Gusty; short-winded; puffed out; corpulent. Hence ~INESS n. [-Y²]

pŭg¹, n. 1. (Also ~*dog*) dwarf squat-faced breed of dog like bulldog, whence ~g'ISH¹,~g'Y² aa., (-g-); ~*nose(d)*, (with short squat or snub nose. 2. ‖ (Among servants) upper servant in large establishment. 3. (Quasi-proper name for) fox. 4. ‖ Small locomotive for shunting etc. [?]

pŭg², n., & v.t. (-gg-). Loam or clay mixed & prepared for brickmaking etc.; (v.t.) prepare (clay) thus, pack (space esp. under floor, to deaden sound) with ~, sawdust, etc.; ~*mill* (for preparing ~). Hence ~g'ING¹(8) (-g-) n. [?]

pŭg³, n., & v.t. (Anglo-Ind.). Footprint of beast; (v.t.; -gg-) track by ~8. [vb f. n.] f. Hind. *pag*]

pŭg⁴, n. (sl.). Pugilist. [abbr.]

pŭgg'(a)ree (-rĭ), n. Indian's light turban; thin scarf of muslin etc. worn round hat & sometimes falling down behind to keep off sun. Hence pŭgg'(a)reED²(-rĭd) a. [f. Hind. *pagri* turban]

pū'gilist, n. Boxer, fighter; (fig.) vigorous controversialist. So ~ISM n., ~is'TIC a., ~is'TICALLY adv. [f. L *pugil* boxer (*pugnus* fist) + (-IST)]

pugnā'cious (-shus), a. Disposed to fight, quarrelsome. Hence or cogn.~LY² adv., pugnăc'ITY n. [f. L *pugnax* (*pugnare* fight, see -ACIOUS]

puisne (pūn'ĭ), a. & n. ~ (*judge*), judge of superior court inferior in rank to chief justice; (Law) later, subsequent (*to*), as ~ *mortgagees, subsequent ~ to the plaintiff*. [OF (*puis* after f. L *postea* +*né* born f. L *natus*)]

pū'issant (or pūis⁴ or pwis⁴), a. (arch.). Having great power or influence, mighty. Hence or cogn.~ANCE n., ~antLY² adv. [F, f. Rom. *possentem* part. of L *posse* be able)]

pu'ja (pŏŏ-), pŏŏ'ja, n. Hindu religious rites (generally); (v.t.) do ~. [Hind. f. Skr. *pūjā*]

pūke, v.i. & t., & n. Vomit. [?]

pukka(h), a. =PUKKA.

pūle, v.i. Cry querulously or weakly, whine. Hence pūl'ing²LY² adv. [imit., cf. F *piauler*]

pull¹ (pŏŏl), v.t. & i. 1. Exert upon (thing) force tending to draw it to oneself, as *don't* ~ *my hair*, ~ *his ears or him by the ear* (as chastisement), ~ *his nose or him by the nose* (as insult), ~ *his sleeve or him by the sleeve* (to gain attention), ~ *the bell-rope or handle to ring the bell*, ~ *person's* LEG, ~ (=*draw*) *the* LONG -*bow*, ~ *the* STRINGS, WIRES. 2. Draw (thing etc.) towards oneself or in direction so regarded, as ~ *it nearer*, ~ *him into the room*, ~ *your cap over your ears*, ~ *off one's hat* (as salutation), ~ *on one's stockings*. 3. Attract or secure (support, custom). 4. ~ (thing) *to pieces*, separate its parts

forcibly, (fig.) criticize (person, thing) un-favourably. **5.** Exert ~ing force, as *horse ~s well*, *~ed (away) at the handle*; exert influence in favour of person. **6.** Proceed with effort (*up hill* etc.); (of horse) strain, esp. habitually, against bit; *~ devil*, ~ BAKER. **7.** Draw, suck, at (pipe, tankard). **8.** Pluck (plant, often *up*) by root. **9.** *~ed*, reduced in health or spirits; *~ed bread*, pieces from inside of new loaf, rebaked till crisp. **10.** ~ *caps*, (copy, proof), orig. in old hand-press by *scuffle, quarrel*. **11.** Tear, pluck, at (thing). **12.** Print upon (sheet), print move (boat), by *~ing oar*; (of boat) be rowed, be rowed by (so many) oars; as *she ~ed inshore, ~s 6 oars*; ~ (row with effect in proportion to) one's *weight*. **14.** (sl.) Arrest; make raid on (gambling-house etc.). **15.** Check (horse) esp. so as to make him lose race; *~ one's punches* (Boxing), fail to give full force to one's blows, also *fig.* **16.** (Crick.) strike (ball, or abs.) strike ball bowled by (bowler), from off to leg; (Golf) drive (ball, or abs.) widely to left (of right-handed player). **17.** ~ *a* FACE¹; *~ a sanctimonious* etc. *face*, assume such expression. **18.** *~ about*, ~ from side to side, treat roughly; *~ down*, demolish (building etc.), lower in health, spirits, price, etc.; *~ in*, (of train) enter station; *~ off*, win (prize, contest); *~ out*, row out, (of train) move out of station; *~ out of the fire*, save (game etc.) when the case seems hopeless; *~-over* n., sweater put on over head; *~ through*, adv. & prep. (danger, illness, etc., or abs.); *~-through* n., cord with which cleaning-rag is drawn through rifle; *~ oneself together*, rally, recover oneself; *~ together*, work in harmony; *~ up*, cause (person, horse, vehicle) to stop, reprimand, check oneself, advance one's relative position in race etc.; *~up* n., house of call for travellers. **19.** *~back*, retarding influence, check, contrivance for ~ing fullness of woman's skirt to back. [OE *pullian*, etym. dub.]

pull² (pool), n. **1.** Act of pulling, wrench, tug; force thus exerted; (fig.) means of exerting influence, interest with the powerful. **2.** (Print.) rough proof. **3.** Pulling at bridle to check horse esp. in racing. **4.** Spell of rowing. **5.** (Crick., Golf) pulling stroke. **6.** ||(In public house) supply of beer etc. exceeding that asked for. **7.** *Have the ~* (advantage) *of* (person). **8.** Deep draught of liquor. **9.** Handle etc. by which ~ is applied. **9.** BEER¹, BELL¹. ~. [f. prec.]

pu'ller (pool-), n. In vbl senses, esp.: kinds of instrument or machine for pulling; horse that pulls esp. against bit. [-ER¹]

pu'llet (pool-), n. Young fowl, esp. hen from time she begins to lay till first moult. [f. F *poulet* dim. of *poule* f. LL *pulla* fem. of L *pullus* young animal. L *pullus*.]

pu'lley (pool-), n. (pl. ~s), & v.t. **1.** Grooved wheel(s) for cord etc. to pass over, mounted in block & used for changing direction of power, one of the simple mechanical powers; wheel, drum, fixed on shaft & turned by belt, used esp. to increase speed or power. **2.** v.t. Hoist, furnish, work, with ~. [ME & OF *polie* ult. f. Gk +*polidion* pivot dim. of *polos* POLE²]

Pu'llicate, n. (Material for) coloured handkerchief, orig. one made at Pulicat on Madras coast.

Pu'llman (pool-), a. & n. *~ (car)*, railway saloon carriage usu. arranged for use as sleeping-car. [G. M. ~, designer]

pu'llulate, v.i. (Of shoot, bud) sprout out, bud; (of seed) sprout; (fig., of doctrines etc.) develop, spring up. Hence ~ANT a., ~ATION n. [f. L *pullulare* sprout (*pullulus* dim. of *pullus* chick), see -ATE³]

||**pu'lly-hau'ly** (pool-), a. & n. (colloq.), (Of pulling & hauling) ~. So **pu'lly-haul** (pool-) v.t. & i. [-Y²]

pu'lmo- in comb. = L *pulmo-monis* lung, as: *~obranch'iate*, with gills modified for air-breathing; *~om'eter*, instrument measuring capacity of lungs, so *~om'etry*.

pu'lmonary, a. Of, in, connected with, the lungs, as *~ artery*, main artery conveying blood from heart to lungs, *~ disease*; having lungs or lung-like organs, so **pu'lmonate²** a.; affected with, subject to, lung-disease. So **pulmon'ic** a. [f. L *pulmonarius* (*pulmo-monis* lung, see -ARY¹]

pulp, n. & v.t. & i. **1.** Fleshy part of fruit, any fleshy or soft part of animal body, e.g. nervous substance in interior cavity of tooth; soft formless mass, esp. that of rags, wood, etc., from which paper is made; ore pulverized & mixed with water. **2.** vb. Reduce to ~, remove ~ from (coffee-beans), whence ~'ER¹(2) n.; become ~y. Hence or cogn. ~'ER¹ v.t., ~'INESS n., ~'LESS, ~'OUS, ~'Y², aa. [f. L *pulpa*]

pu'lpit (pool-), n. Raised enclosed platform usu. with desk & seat from which preacher in church or chapel delivers sermon; *the* profession of preaching; preachers; (in title of book) collected sermons; (attrib.). *~ eloquence, orator, style*. [f. L *pulpitum* scaffold, platform]

pulpiteer' (pool-), n., & v.i. Professional preacher (usu. derog.), so ~AR¹AN a. & n.; (v.i.) preach, whence ~eer'ING¹ n. [-EER¹]

pulque (pool'kā), n. Mexican fermented drink from sap of agave etc.; *~ brandy*, intoxicant made from ~. [Sp.-Amer.]

pulsate (or pŭl-), v.t. & i. Expand & contract rhythmically, beat, throb (lit.

& fig.); vibrate, quiver, thrill; agitate (diamonds) with machine (pŭlsăt'ŏr² n.) to separate them from earth in which they are found. Hence or cogn. pŭlsă²-TION n., pŭl'satory a. [f. L *pulsare* push, beat, frequent. of *pellere puls-* drive, see -ATE³]

pŭl'satile, a. Of, having the property of, pulsation; (of musical instrument) played by percussion. [as prec. +-ILE]

pŭlsatil'la, n. The pasque-flower, its extract used in pharmacy. [med. L, dim. of *pulsata* fem. p.p. of *pulso* beat (as quivering in wind)]

pŭlse¹, n., & v.i. & t. 1. Rhythmical throbbing of arteries as blood is propelled along them esp. as felt in wrists, temples, etc.; *feel* person's ~ (as indicating by its rate & character his state of health, fig., sound his intentions etc.); each successive beat of arteries or heart; (fig.) throb, thrill, of life or emotion; rhythmical recurrence of strokes e.g. of oars; (Mus.) beat; single beat or vibration of sound, light, etc. 2. v.i. Pulsate (lit. & fig.); (v.t.) send *out, in,* etc., by rhythmic beats. Hence ~'LESS a., ~'lESSNESS n. (n.) ME & OF *pous* f. L *pulsus -ūs* f. *pellere puls-* drive; vb as PULSATE]

pŭlse², n. (Collective sing., sometimes with pl. vb) edible seeds of leguminous plants e.g. peas, beans, lentils; (with pl.) any kind of these. [f. OF *pols* f. L *puls -tis* pottage of meal etc.]

pŭlsim'eter, n. Instrument for measuring race or force of pulse. [f. PULSE¹+-I-+-METER]

pŭlsŏm'eter, n. Steam-condensing vacuum pump, so called from pulsatory action of the steam. [P; prec., -o-]

pŭltă'ceous (-shŭs), a. Of (the nature of) pap or a poultice, soft, pulpy. [as PULSE², see -ACEOUS]

pŭl'verize, v.t. & i. Reduce to powder or dust, divide (liquid) into spray, whence ~ātor²(2), ~ER²(2), nn.; (fig.) demolish, crush, smash; (intr.) crumble to dust. Hence ~ABLE a., ~A'TION n. [f. LL *pulverizare* (*pulvis eris* dust, see -IZE)]

pŭl've'rulent (-rōō-), a. Powdery, of dust; covered with powder; (of rock etc.) of slight cohesion, apt to crumble. [f. L *pulverulentus* (*pulvis -eris* dust, see -LENT]

pŭl'vinate, -āted, aa. (Archit., *-ed*) swelling, esp. (of frieze) with convex face; (Bot., Entom.) cushion-like, having cushion-like swelling; [f. L *pulvinatus* (*pulvinus* cushion), see -ATE²(2)]

pŭm'¹a, n. = COUGAR. [Sp. f. Peruv.]

pŭm'ice(-stōne), n., & v.t. (Piece of) light spongy kind of lava used for removing stains from hands etc., polishing, etc.; (v.t.) rub, clean, with ~; ~ *hoof* of horse, made spongy by disease. So **pŭmi'cĕous** a. [ME & OF *pomis* f. LL *pūmicem,* L *pū-* (nom. *-mex*)]

pŭmm'el, v.t. (-ll-). Strike repeatedly esp. with fist. [altered f. POMMEL]

pŭm'(m')elō. Var. of POMELO.

pŭmp¹, n. 1. Machine, usu. cylinder in which piston etc. is moved up & down by rod, for raising water; kinds of machine for raising or moving liquids, compressing or rarefying gases, etc. (fig. of heart, insect's suckers, etc.); AIR¹, FORCE¹, STOMACH, ~, *bicycle-*~ (for inflating tires); pumping, stroke of ~; attempt, person skilful, at pumping others. 2. ~-*brake,* handle of ship's ~ esp. with transverse bar for several persons to work at; ~-*handle* v.t. (colloq.), shake (person's hand) effusively; ~-*room,* building where ~ is worked esp. at spa where medicinal water is dispensed. [ME *pumpe,* cf. Du. *pomp*; etym. dub.]

pŭmp², v.t. & i. Work a pump; remove, raise, (water etc., usu. *out, up*) thus; make (ship, well, etc.) *dry by* ~*ing*; ~ *up,* inflate (pneumatic tire), inflate tires of (bicycle etc.); bring out, pour forth, (abuse etc. *upon*) as by ~ing; elicit information from (person), elicit (information, usu. *out of* person), by artful or persistent questions; (of exertion) put completely out of breath (esp. pass.); (of mercury in barometer) rise & fall instantaneously; ~*ship* (not in polite use), (v.i.) make water, (n.) urination. Hence ~ER¹ n. (esp., rail TROLLEY). [f. prec.]

pŭmp³, n. Kind of light shoe now usu. of patent leather & without fastening, worn with evening dress & for dancing. [?]

pŭ'mpernickel (pōō-), n. German wholemeal rye bread. [G, etym. dub.]

pŭmp'kin, n. (Cucurbitaceous plant bearing) large egg-shaped or globular fruit with edible layer next to rind, used in cookery & for cattle. [f. earlier *pumpion, po-,* f. obs. F *pom(p)on* f. L *pepo* f. Gk *pepōn* large melon+-KIN]

pŭn¹, n. & v.i. (-nn-). 1. Humorous use of word to suggest different meanings, or of words of same sound with different meanings, play on words. 2. v.i. Make ~s (*upon* word, subject). Hence ~'ing-LY² adv. [?]

‖ **pŭn²,** v.t. (-nn-). Consolidate (earth, rubble) by pounding or ramming; work up to proper consistency with PUNNER. [dial.=POUND³]

pū'na (pōō-), n. High bleak plateau in Peruvian Andes; difficulty in breathing caused by rarefied atmosphere. [Peruv., in first sense]

pŭnch¹, n. Instrument or machine for cutting holes in leather, metal, paper, etc., driving bolt etc. out of hole (*starting-*~), enlarging hole, forcing nail beneath surface (*driving-*~), etc.; tool or machine for impressing design or stamping die on material; *bell-*~, conductor's ticket-~ with bell to announce punching of ticket. [prob. var. of POUNCE², but cf. PUNCHEON¹]

pǔnch², v.t. & n. 1. Strike esp. with closed fist, as ~ *his head*; ~*ing-ball*, inflated ball held by elastic bands etc. & ~ed as form of exercise; prod with stick etc. esp. *drive* (cattle) thus; pierce (metal, leather, bus-ticket, etc.) as or with punch; pierce (hole) thus; drive (nail etc. *in*, *out*) with punch. 2. n. Blow with fist (*a*~*on the head*; PULL¹ one's ~es; ~ed, also transit.); (sl.) vigour, momentum, effective force. Hence ~ER¹(1, 2) n. [(n. f. v.b) as prec.]

pǔnch³, n. 1. ||(*Suffolk*) ~, thick-set draught horse; ||(dial.) short fat man or thing. 2. (P~) grotesque hump-backed figure in puppet-show called P~ & Judy, esp. as title of a London weekly comic paper; *as pleased, as proud, as P~* (much, very). [perh. different wds; in last sense abbr. of PUNCHINELLO]

pǔn'cheon¹ (-shn), n. Short post esp. one supporting roof in coal-mine; (now rare) =PUNCH¹. [f. OF *poinçon* f. LL *punctio-nem* (*puncta* point f. *pungere* punct- prick, see -ION²)]

pǔn'cheon² (-shn), n. (hist.), Large cask for liquids etc. holding from 72 to 120 gals. [identical in form w. prec. in E & OF]

Punchiněll'ō, n. (pl. ~s). Chief character in Italian puppet-show; short stout person. [f. It. *Pulcinella*]

pǔn'ctāte, a. (nat. hist., path.). Marked or studded with points, dots, or spots. So ~A'TION n. [f. L as POINT¹, see -ATE²(2)]

pǔnctil'iō (-lyō), n. (pl. ~s). Nice point of ceremony or honour; petty formality, cf. [It. *puntiglio* dim. of *punto* POINT¹, cf. F *pointille*]

pǔnctil'ious (-lyus), a. Attentive to punctilios. Hence ~LY² adv., ~NESS n. [f. F *pointilleux* (as prec., -OUS)]

pǔnc'tūal, a. Observant of appointed time; in good time, not late; (arch.) punctilious; (Geom.) of a point. Hence ~ITY (-ǎl²) n., ~LY² adv. [f. med. L *punctualis* (*punctus* as POINT¹ see -AL)]

pǔnc'tūāte, v.t. Insert stops in (writing), mark or divide with stops; (fig.) interrupt (speech) *with* exclamations etc.; (improp.) emphasize, accentuate, *as fixing it on the ground to* ~*e his refusal*. Hence or cogn. ~IVE a., ~OR¹ n. [f. med. L *punctuare* (as prec.), see -ATE³)]

pǔnctūā'tion, n. Insertion of vowel & other points in Hebrew etc.; practice, art, of punctuating. [f. med. L *punctuatio* (prec., -ATION)]

pǔnc'tūm, n. (pl. ~a). Speck, dot, spot of colour or elevation or depression on surface. So ~ULE n., whence ~a-, ~ŪLA'TION n. [L, =POINT¹]

pǔnc'ture, n., & v.t. & i. 1. Pricking, prick, esp. accidental pricking of pneumatic tire; hole thus made. 2. v.t. Prick, pierce(v.i. of tire, bicycle etc.), experience a ~; (v.b f. n.) f. L *punctura* (as POINT¹, -URE)]

pǔn'dit, n. Hindu learned in Sanskrit & in philosophy, religion, & jurisprudence, of India; (joc.) learned teacher. [f. Hind. *pandit*]

pǔn'gent (-j-), a. (Nat. Hist.) sharp-pointed; (of reproof, satire, etc.) biting, caustic; mentally stimulating, piquant; affecting organs of smell or taste, or skin etc., with pricking sensation, as ~ *gas, smoke, sauce*. Hence **pǔn'gency** n., ~LY² adv. (-j-). [f. L *pungere* prick, -ENT]

Pū'nic, a. & n. Carthaginian; ~ *Wars* (between Rome & Carthage); ~ *faith* (n.) = language. [f. L *Punicus, Poen-.(Poe-nus* f. Gk *Phoinix* Phoenician, see -IC)]

pǔn'ish, v.t. 1. Cause (offender) to suffer for offence; chastise; inflict penalty on (offender); inflict penalty for (offence). 2. (colloq.). Inflict severe blows on (opponent in boxing); (of race, competitor) tax severely the powers of (competitor); take full advantage of (weak bowling, bowler, stroke at tennis); make heavy inroad on (food etc.); whence ~ING² a. Hence ~ABIL'ITY, ~ER¹, ~MENT, nn., ~ABLE a., ~ABLY² adv. [f. F *punir* (-ISH²), f. L *punire (poena* = Gk *poinē* fine)]

pǔn'itive, a. Inflicting punishment, retributive, as ~ *justice, expedition*; ~ *police* (India), detachment of police sent to a particular district and paid for by the inhabitants. So **pǔn'itory** a. [f. med. L *puni-tivus* (as prec., see -IVE)]

pǔnk¹, n. (arch.). Prostitute. [?]

pǔnk², n. & a. 1. Rotten wood, fungus growing on wood, used as tinder; worth-less stuff, rubbish, tosh. 2. adj. (sl.). Worthless, rotten. [?]

pǔnk'a(h) (-kə), n. (E.-Ind.). Portable fan usu. of leaf of palmyra; large swinging cloth fan on frame worked by cord. [f. Hind. *pankhā*]

pǔnn'er, n. Tool for ramming earth about post etc. [f. PUN²+-ER¹]

pǔnn'et, n. Small round chip basket for fruit or vegetables. [?]

pǔn'ster, n. Inveterate maker of puns. [-STER]

pǔnt¹, n., & v.t. & i. 1. Flat-bottomed shallow boat, broad & square at both ends, propelled by long pole thrust against bottom of river etc. 2. v.b. Propel with or use ~pole; convey in a ~. Hence **pǔn'ter¹** [-ER¹], (vb f. n.) OE, f. L *ponto*, kind of Gallic transport]

pǔnt², v.t. & n. 1. Kick (football) after it

has dropped from the hands & before it reaches ground. **2.** n. Such kick; ~ *about*, kicking about of football for practice, ball so used. [?]

pŭnt³, v.i. & n. **1.** (At faro & other card-games) lay stake against bank; (colloq.) bet on horse etc. **2.** n. Player who ~s; point in faro. Hence **pŭn'ter²** [-ER¹] n. [f. F *ponte(r)*, etym. dub.]

pŭn'tў, pō~, n. Iron rod used in glass-blowing. [prob. f. F *pontil* prob. f. It. *pontello* dim. of *punto* POINT¹]

pūn'lў, a. Undersized; weak, feeble; petty. Hence ~INESS n. [-PUISNE]

pŭp, n., & v.t. & i. (-pp-). **1.** Young dog; *in* ~, pregnant; *conceited* etc. ~, swindle him esp. by selling this on prospective value. **2.** vb. Bring forth ~s; give birth to. [shortened f. PUPPY]

pūp'la, n. (pl. ~*ae*). Chrysalis. Hence ~AL a. [L, = girl, doll]

pūp'late, v.i. Become a pupa. Hence ~A'TION n. [-ATE²]

pū'pil, n. **1.** One who is taught by another, scholar; & under care of guardian; ~ *teacher*, boy, girl, teaching in elementary school under head teacher & concurrently receiving general education from him or elsewhere. **2.** Circular opening in centre of iris of eye regulating passage of light to the retina. So ~(l)AR¹, ~(l)ARY², aa. [f. F *pupille* f. L *pupillus*, -*illa*, ward, minor, (-*la*-) of eye]

pū'pil(l)age, n. Nonage, minority (fig.; of country, language, etc.); so ~A'RITY n. (law); being a pupil. So PŪP'IL-SHIP n. [-AGE]

pū'pil(l)ize, v.t. & i. [-IZE]

pŭpip'arous, a. (entom.). Bringing forth young already advanced to pupal state. [f. PUPA+L -*parus* -bearing]

pŭp'pet, n. Figure, usu. small, represent-ing human being, esp. one with jointed limbs moved by wires etc. in ~-show; ~ person whose acts are controlled by another; ~-play, -show (with ~s as characters); ~-clock, -valve, disk valve opened by lifting bodily from its seat, not hinged. Hence ~RY(4, 5) n. [ME *popet(te)* =F *poupette* doll dim. f. PUPA]

pŭp'pў, n. Young dog (also, childish, ~ *dog*); vain empty-headed young man, coxcomb, whence ~ISM n. Hence ~DOM, ~HOOD, nn. ~ISH¹ a. [prob. =F *poupée* doll, irreg. f. PUPA]

pur-, pref. AF form of OF *por-*, f. L *por-*, PRO-¹ (*purchase, purport, pursue*).

pura'na (poorah-), n. Any of a class of Sanskrit sacred poems. Hence **pura'nic** (poorah-) a. [f. Skr. *purana* of former times (*pura* formerly)]

Pŭr'beck, a. ~ *stone*, hard limestone from ~ in Dorset; ~ *marble*, finer quali-ties of this.

pŭr'blind, a., & v.t. Partly blind, dim-sighted; (fig.) obtuse, dull; (v.t.) make ~. Hence ~NESS n. [earlier *pur(e) blind*; *pur-* perh. = PURE in sense 'quite' or =PUR- intensive, with changed sense]

pŭr'chase¹, n. **1.** Buying; ~-money, price (to be) paid; (Hist.) practice of buying commissions in army; thing bought; annual return from land, *as sold at 20 years'* ~; (fig.) *life is not worth an hour's* ~, cannot be trusted to last an hour; (Law) acquisition of property by one's personal action, not by inheritance. **2.** Mechanical advantage, leverage, (often fig.); appliance for gaining this, esp. (Naut.) rope, windlass, pulley (*single, double, treble, ~ pulley*, with 1, 2, 3, sheaves). [ME, f. OF *porchas, pur-*, as foll.]

pŭr'chase², v.t. **1.** Buy; acquire (vic-tory, freedom, etc., *with one's blood, toil*, etc.). **2.** (Naut.) haul up (anchor etc.) by means of pulley, lever, etc. So ~ABLE a., ~ER¹ n. [ME, f. AF PUR(*chacer* CHASE¹), procure, bring about]

pŭr'dah (-dā), n. (E.-Ind.). Curtain, esp. one serving to screen women from sight of strangers; (fig.) Indian system of seclud-ing women of rank; striped material for curtains. [f. Hind. & Pers. *pardah*]

pūre, a. **1.** Unmixed, unadulterated, as ~ *white, air, alcohol, water*; (of sounds) not discordant, esp. (Mus.) perfectly in tune. **2.** Of unmixed descent; ~-blooded; ~ *mathematics* (not including practical applications, opp. to *applied, mixed*); (Gram., of vowel) preceded by another vowel, (of stem) ending in vowel, (of consonant) not accompanied by another. **3.** Mere, simple, nothing but, sheer, as *knowledge* ~ *& simple*; ~ *nonsense, pre-judice*. **4.** Not corrupt, as *his taste was severe &* ~; morally undefiled, guiltless, sincere; sexually undefiled. Hence ~lў² (-lī¹) adv. (rare exc. in senses *exclusively, solely, entirely*), ~NESS (-ūr-) n. [f. OF *pur*, fem. *pure*, f. L *purus*]

purée (pūrē'ā, & see Ap.), n. Soup of vegetables, meat, etc., boiled to pulp & passed through sieve. [F]

pŭr'fle, n., & v.t. (arch.). **1.** Border, esp. embroidered edge of garment. **2.** v.t. Adorn (robe) with ~; ornament (edge of building *with crockets* etc.); beautify. Hence **pŭr'fling¹** n., (esp.) inlaid border-ing on back & belly of fiddles. [f. OF *porfil(er)*, as PROFILE]

pŭrgā'tion, n. Purification; purging of bowels; spiritual cleansing, esp. (R.-C. Ch.) of soul in purgatory; (Hist.) clearing of oneself from accusation or suspicion by oath or ordeal. [f. OF or *purgation* f. L *purgationem* (as PURGE, see -ATION)]

pŭr'gative, a. & n. Aperient (medicine); serving to purify. [F (-*if*, -*ive*), f. LL *purgativus* (as PURGE, see -ATIVE)]

pŭr'gatorў, n. & a. **1.** Condition, place,

of spiritual purging, esp. (R.-C. Ch.) of souls departing this life in grace of God but requiring to be cleansed from venial sins etc.; place of temporary suffering or expiation. 2. adj. Purifying. So **pur̄**-**gātor'iAl** a. [f. LL *purgatōrius* a. (med. L. *-um* n.), as foll. See -ORY]

pŭrge, v.i., & n. 1. Make physically or spiritually clean (*of, from*, impurities, sin, etc.); remove by cleansing process (lit. & fig., often *away, off, out*); (of medicine) relieve (bowels, or abs.) by evacuation; clear (person, oneself, *of* charge, suspicion); (Law) atone for, wipe out, (offence, sentence) by expiation & submission; rid (political party, army, etc.) of persons regarded as undesirable. 2. n. Such clearance, purgation, (*Pride's P~*, hist., exclusion by Col. Pride of Presbyterian & Royalist members from Long Parliament); aperient. [(n. f. vb) f. OF *purger* f. L *purgāre*]

pŭrĭfĭcā′tion, n. Purifying; ritual cleansing, esp. that of woman after child-birth, enjoined by Jewish law, as *the P~* (*of the Virgin Mary*, Feb. 2nd (Virg. ii. 22). So PURIFY, see *-ATION*]

pŭr′ĭfĭcātŏr, n. (eccl.). Cloth used at communion for wiping chalice & paten & fingers & lips of celebrant. [as foll., see *-OR²*]

pŭr′ĭfy, v.t. Make pure, cleanse, (*of, from*, impurities, sin, etc.); make ceremonially clean; clear of foreign elements, whence **~IER²**(2) n. [f. F *purifier* f. LL *purificāre* (as PURE, see -FY)]

Pŭr′ĭm, n. Jewish festival commemorating defeat of Haman's plot (*Esth.* ix). [Heb., pl. of *pur*, perh. = lot]

pŭr′ĭst, n. Stickler for, affecter of, scrupulous purity esp. in language. So **~ISM** n., **~is′tĭc(Al)** aa. [f. F *puriste* (PURE, -IST)]

Pū′rĭtan, n. & a. 1. (Hist.; *P~*) member of the party of English Protestants who regarded reformation of Church under Elizabeth as incomplete & sought to abolish unscriptural & corrupt ceremonies etc.; member of any non-religious purist party; person of or affecting extreme strictness in religion or morals. 2. adj. Of the P~s; scrupulous in religion or morals. Hence **Pū′rĭtanĭ′ic**(Al) aa., **Pū′rĭtăn′ity**[²] n., **Pū′rĭtanīsm** n., **~īsm** n., **~ĬZE**(2, 3) v.i. & t. [f. foll. +-AN]

pū′rĭty, n. Pureness, cleanness, freedom from physical or moral pollution. [ME & OF *purté* f. LL *pūritātem* (as PURE, see -TY)]

pŭrl[¹], n. & v.t. & i. 1. Cord of twisted gold or silver wire for bordering; chain of minute loops, each loop of this, ornamenting edges of lace, ribbon, etc.; (Knitt., also *pearl*) inversion of stitches, producing ribbed appearance. 2. vb. Border (material or abs.) with ~; invert (stitches or abs.); invert stitches in purl(*in cord sense prob. = arch. & Sc. pirl*

twist, etym. dub.; other senses perh. different wds]

pŭrl[²], v.i., & n. 1. (Of brook etc.) flow with whirling motion & babbling sound. 2. n. Such motion or sound. [cf. Norw. *purla* bubble up, & perh. *pirl* (see prec.)]

pŭrl[³], n. (hist.). Ale or beer mixed with worm-wood infused; hot beer mixed with gin as morning draught, dog's-nose. [?]

pŭrl[⁴], v.t. & i., & n. (colloq.). 1. Turn (t. & i.) upside down, upset. 2. n. Cropper, heavy fall. [prob. var. of *pirl* (see PURL[¹])]

pŭrl′er, n. (colloq.). Throw, blow, that hurls one head foremost (*come, take, a ~*, fall headlong). [prec. + -ER¹]

pŭr′lieu (-lū), n. Tract on border of forest, esp. one earlier included in it & still partly subject to forest laws; one's bounds, limits; (pl.) outskirts, outlying region (lit. & fig.); squalid street or quarter of town. [prob. altered after LIEU f. *pur(a)ley* f. obs. & AF *pur(ali)ALLEY* f. *puralley* perambulation to settle bounda-ries]

pŭr′lin, n. Horizontal beam running along length of roof, resting on principals & supporting common rafters or boards. [?]

pŭr′ple, n., a., & v.t., & v.t. & i. 1. (Of) a colour mixed of red & blue in various proportions with some black or white or both; got from the molluscs *purpura & murex*, also *Tyrian* (ancient), *-red* etc., red etc. inclining to crimson. ~ 2. ~ robe, esp. as dress of emperor, king, consul, etc., as *born in the ~*, or of cardinal, as *raised to the ~* (cardinalate). 3. pl. Swine fever; disease in wheat. 4. ~ *emperor*, a butterfly. 5. vb. Make, become, ~. Hence **pŭrp′lĭsH**[¹], **pŭrp′ly**[²], aa. [ME *purpel* f. OE *purpur*(e) f. L PUR-PURA]

purpoint. See POURPOINT.

pŭrp′ort, n. Meaning, sense, tenor, of document or speech; (rare) object, purpose. [AF² as foll.]

pŭrpo̅rt′(2) (per-), v.t. (Of document or speech) have as its meaning, convey, state, (fact, *that*); profess, be intended to seem (*to do*), as *a letter~ing to be written by you, to contain your decision*. [f. AF & OF PUR(*porter* f. L *portāre* carry) extend, embody]

pŭrp′ose,[¹], n. Object, thing intended, as *could not effect my ~, this will answer (or serve) our (or the) ~, what was the ~ of this law?*; fact, faculty, of resolving on something, as *honesty of ~, is wanting in ~*; *novel with a ~, ~-novel*, (written to defend some doctrine etc.); *on ~* (to do, *that*), (abs. also *of set ~*) designedly, not by accident, whence *~LY²* (-li-) adv.; *to the ~*, relevant, useful for one's ~; *to little, some, no, ~*, with such result

or effect. Hence ~FUL¹ (-sf-), ~LESS (-sl-), aa., ~fully², ~lessly² adv., ~fulness, ~lessness, nn. [f. AF & OF *purpos*, as foll.]

purp'ose², v.t. Design, intend, as *I ~ (arranging or to arrange) an interview; ~ that an interview shall be arranged;* (arch.) *am ~d,* intend *(to do, doing, that).* [f. OF *purposer* PROPOSE]

purp'osive, a. Having, serving, done with, a purpose; (of person or conduct) having purpose & resolution. [-IVE]

pûrp'ura, n. Disease marked by purple or livid spots on skin; genus of molluscs including some from which purple dye was derived. [L, f. Gk *porphura* (shell-fish yielding) purple]

pûrpur'ic (per-), a. Of purpura, as *~ fever; ~ acid,* an acid the salts of which are purple. [-IC]

pûrp'urin, n. Red colouring-matter orig. got from madder. [f. PURPURA + -IN]

pûrr, v.i. & t., & n. **1.** (Of cat or other feline animal, fig. of person) make low continuous vibratory sound expressing pleasure; utter, express, (words, contentment) thus. **2.** n. Such sound. [imit.]

pû'rree, n. Yellow colouring-matter from India & China. [f. Hind. *peorī*]

pur sang (see Ap.), adv. (appended to classifying n. or adj.). Of the full blood, without admixture, through & through, genuine, (*is Welsh or a Welshman, militarist, a cynic, ~; the artist ~ is a rarity*). [F]

pûrse¹, n. **1.** Small pouch of leather etc. for carrying money on the person, orig. closed by drawing strings together; (fig.) money, funds, as *a common ~* (fund), *heavy* or *long ~,* wealth, *light ~,* poverty, *the public ~,* national treasury; || PRIVY ~; sum collected, subscribed, or given, as present or as prize for contest, as *will any gentleman give* or *put up a ~?*; (in Turk. empire) ~ *of silver, gold,* 500 piastres, 10,000 piastres; bag-like natural or other receptacle, pouch, cyst, etc. **2.** ~*-bearer,* one who has charge of another's or a company's money; || official carrying Great Seal before Lord Chancellor in ~; ~*-net,* bag-shaped net for catching rabbits etc., mouth of which can be closed with cords; ~*-proud,* puffed up by wealth; ~*-seine,* ~*-net* for fishing; ~*-strings,* strings for closing mouth of ~, (*hold the ~-strings,* have control of expenditure; *tighten, loosen, the ~-strings,* be sparing, generous, of money). Hence prob. f. LL *bursa* purse f. Gk *bursa* hide]

pûrse², v.t. & i. Contract (lips, brow, often *up*) in wrinkles; become wrinkled; (rare) put (often *up*) into one's purse. [f. prec.]

pûrs'er, n. Officer on ship who keeps accounts esp. in passenger vessel. Hence ~SHIP n. [f. PURSE¹ + -ER¹]

pûrs'lane (-in), n. Low succulent herb used in salads & pickled. [f. OF *porcelaine* altered f. L *porcillaca, portulaca,* on PORCELAIN]

pursū'ance (per-), n. Carrying out, pursuing, (of plan, object, idea, etc.), esp. *in ~ of,* [as foll., see -ANCE]

pursū'ant (per-), a. & adv. Pursuing; (adv.) conformably to (*the Act* etc.), whence ~LY² adv. [f. OF *porsuivant* part. as foll.]

pursūe' (per-), v.t. & i. Follow with intent to capture or kill; (fig., of consequences, penalty, disease, etc.) persistently attend, stick to; seek after, aim at, (pleasure etc., one's object); proceed in compliance with (plan etc.); proceed along, continue, (road, inquiry, conduct); follow (studies, profession); go in pursuit (*after,* or abs.). Hence **pursū'ABLE** (per-) a. [f. AF PUR-*suer* e. L PRO(*sequere, -ire* pop. varr. of *sequi* follow)]

pursū'er (per-), n. In vbl senses, also || (Civil & Sc. Law) prosecutor. [-ER¹]

pursuit' (persūt), n. Pursuing, esp. *in ~ of* (animal, person, one's object); profession, employment, recreation, that one follows. [f. AF PURSEUTE, fem. p.p. & n. as PURSUE]

|| **purs'uivant** (-sw-), n. Officer of College of Arms below herald; (poet.) follower, attendant. [f. OF *porsivant* (as PURSUE, see -ANT)]

pûr'sy¹ [y¹], a. Short-winded, puffy; corpulent. Hence ~INESS n. [earlier *-ive* f. OF *polsif* (*polser* breathe with labour as PULSATE)]

pûr'sy², a. Puckered. [f. PURSE¹ + -Y²]

pûrt'enance, n. (arch.) Inwards, pluck, of animal. [earlier form of PERTINENCE]

pū'rulent (-rōo-), a. Of, full of, discharging, pus. Hence or cogn. ~ENCE, ~ENCY, nn., ~ently² adv. [f. L *purulentus* (PUS, see -LENT)]

purvey' (pervā), v.t. & i. Provide, supply, (articles of food) as one's business; make provision, act as purveyor, (for person, army, etc.). [f. AF PURVEIER PROVIDE]

purvey'ance (pervā'ans), n. Purveying; || right of crown to provisions etc. at fixed price & to use of horses etc. [f. OF *porveance,* as PROVIDENCE]

purvey'or (pervā'er), n. One whose business it is to supply articles of food, esp. dinners etc. on large scale, as *P~ to the Royal Household;* (Hist.) officer making purveyance for sovereign. [f. AF *purveour* (as PURVEY, see -OR²]

pûr'view (-vū), n. Enacting clauses of statute; scope, intention, range, (of act, document, scheme, book, occupation, etc.); range of physical or mental vision. [f. AF *purveu* provided, p.p. as PURVEY]

pus, n. Yellowish viscid matter produced by suppuration. [L, gen. *puris*]

Pus'eyism (-zīī-), n. (Hostile term for) TRACTARIANISM. So ~ITE¹ (-zīīt) n. [E. B. Pusey d. 1882 + -ISM]

push¹ (poosh), v.t. & i. **1.** Exert upon

(body) force tending to move it away;
move (body *up*, *down*, *away*, *back*, etc.);
exert such pressure, as *do not* ~
against the fence; (Billiards) make push-
stroke; (of person in boat) ~ *off*, ~ *against
bank with an oar to get boat out into stream
etc. **2.** (Bibl.) butt (t. & i.) with the
horns. **3.** (Cause to) project, thrust *out*,
forth, etc., as *plants* ~ *out new roots*, *cape
~es out into sea*. **4.** Make one's way
forcibly or persistently, force (one's way
thus. **5.** Exert oneself esp. to surpass
others or succeed in one's business etc.,
whence ~'ing² a., ~'ingly² adv., (póō-).
6. Urge, impel, (often *on*, *to do*, *to effort*
etc.). **7.** Follow up, prosecute, (claim etc.,
often *on*); engage actively in making
(one's *fortune*); extend (one's *conquests*
etc.); ∥ ~ (matter) *through*, bring it to a
conclusion. **8.** Press the adoption, use,
sale, etc. of (goods etc.) by advertisement. **9.** (Press (person) hard, as *do
not wish to* ~ *him for payment*, esp. in pass.,
as *am* ~*ed for* (can scarcely find) *time*,
money). **10.** ~*-pin*, a child's game.
Hence ~'ING¹ (1, 2) (póō-), n. [~*er aeroplane*, with
air-screw behind, opp. *tractor*). [f. F
pousser as PULSATE]

push¹ (póŏsh), *n*. **1.** Act of pushing, shove,
thrust; (Billiards) stroke in which ball is
pushed, not struck; exertion of influence
to promote person's advancement. **2.**
Thrust of weapon or of beast's horn. **3.**
Vigorous effort, as *must make a* ~ *to get it
done*, *for home*, (Mil.) attack in force.
4. Continuous pressure of arch etc.;
pressure of affairs, crisis, pinch. **5.** Enterprise, determination to get on, self-
assertion, whence ~'FUL (póŏ-) a. **6.** (sl.)
Gang of thieves, convicts, etc. **7.** (sl.)
Give, get, the ~, dismiss, be dismissed.
8. ~*-ball*, game played with enormous
ball, pushed, not kicked, towards opponents' goal; ∥ ~*-bike* (sl.) bicycle worked
by pedaling (opp. *motor-bike*). [f. prec.]

Pūsh'tōō, -tu (-tōō), *n.* Afghan language.
[f. Pers. *pashto*]

pūsillăn'imous (-z-), *a.* Faint-hearted,
mean-spirited. Hence or cogn. **pūsillan-
im'ITY** n., ~*ly²* adv. [f. eccl. L *pusilla-
nimis* (*pusillus* petty + *animus* soul) +
-OUS]

puss (póōs), *n.* Cat (esp. as call-name);
(quasi-proper name for) hare, tiger; (colloq.) girl, as *sly* ~; ~ *moth*, large European moth. [cf. Du. *poes*, Norw. *puse*,
perh. orig. a call]

pu'ssy (póŏ-), *n.* (nursery). ~(*-cat*), *cat*;
(nursery) soft furry thing, e.g. hazel catkin; ~(*-foot*, P-*foot*, liquor-prohibi-
tion, advocate of this, (from nickname of
a U.S. prohibitionist). [-Y³]

pū'stūlate, *v.t. & i.* Form into pustules.
So ~ATE²(-ət) a., ~A'TION n. [f. LL *pustu-
lare*, as foll.]

pū'stūle, *n.* Pimple; *malignant* ~, disease caused by anthrax bacillus; (Bot.,

put¹ (póŏt), Zool., wart, wart-like excrescence. Hence
or cogn. ~AR¹, ~OUS, aa. [f. L *pustula*
(PUS)]

put¹ (póŏt), *v.t. & i.* (*put*). **I.** General
senses. **1.** Propel, hurl, (*the weight*, *shot*)
from hand placed close to shoulder as
athletic exercise. **2.** Thrust (weapon),
send (missile), as ~ *a knife into*, *stab*, *put
a bullet through*, *shoot*. **3.** (Coal-mining)
propel (tram or barrow of coal). **4.** (Naut.)
proceed, take one's course, *back*, *forth*, *in*
(to harbour etc.), *off* (*from shore etc.*), *out*,
in ship. **5.** Move (thing etc., lit. & fig.) so
as to place it in some situation, as ~ *it in
down the well*; ~ (mark, write) *a tick
against his name*, *your signature to it*; ~
the horse to (the cart), harness him; ~ *bull
to cow or cow to bull* (for breeding); ~ (convey) *him across the river*; ~ *the children to
bed*, ~ *him in prison*; *has* ~ (infused) *new
life into him*; ~ (present) *him in his wheel*,
clearly before her; ~ *a* SPOKE *in his wheel*;
~ *the words into his* MOUTH¹; ~ *one's* FOOT
in it, one's SHOULDER *to the wheel*, *hand to
the* PLOUGH¹, *the* LID *on*. **6.** (With less or no
idea of physical motion in space) bring
into some relation or state, as ~ *yourself
into my hands*; ~ *to go habitually to school*; ~ *it to
(offer it for) sale*, *on the market*; ~ '*Othello
on* (the stage), produce it; ~ (add) *milk to
your tea*; *should* ~ (price) *it at 2/6*; ~*s
(estimates) the circulation at 60,000*; ~
(translate) *it into Dutch*; *cannot* ~ *it into
words* (express it in) *words*; *what a way you have
of* ~*ting things*!; ~*s* (sets) *no value on my
advice*; *I* ~ (base) *my decision on the
grounds stated*; ~ (apply) *it to a good use*;
~ (imagine) *yourself in his place*; ~ (substitute) *the will for the deed*; ~ *a good
FACE¹ on it*; ~ *an end*, *period*, *stop*, *to it,
stop it*; ~ *a check or stopper on it*, *a veto
on it*, *check it*, *forbid it*; ~ *an end to
(destroyed) *himself or his life*; ~ *the wind
up one* (sl.), *frighten him*; ~ (stake) *money
on a horse*; ~ *his money into* (invested in
in) *land*; ~ & *take* (name of a gambling
game with teetotum); *I* ~ (submit) *the case
to him*, *to the vote*; *I* ~ *it* (appeal) *to you*,
I ~ *it to you* (invite you to acknowledge)
that you were after no good; *dues were* ~
(imposed) *on cattle*; *every insult was* ~
(inflicted) *on him*; *don't* ~ *it* ~ *upon
(victimized) *by him*; ~ (lay) *the blame on
me*; ~ *him* (caused him to be) *at his ease*,
in fear of his life, *out of temper*, *on his
guard*, *on his mettle*; ~ *him* (make him
speak) *on* (*his*) *oath*; ~ *the servants on
(allow them) *board wages*; ~ *the proposal
into shape*; ~ *his* NOSE¹ *out of joint*; ~
thing out of court (make it not worth discussing etc.); ~ *thing out of one's* head¹
(forget, make him forget it); *a few words
will* ~ (make) *the matter right*; *always
manages to* ~ *me* (make me appear) *in the
wrong*; ~ *out of* COUNTENANCE¹; *must*

have ~ (made) the clock fast (by advancing hands); *~ wise (sl.), disabuse or en-lighten; ~ (subject) them to death, torture, ransom, expense, inconvenience, the test or trial, the rack, the sword, confusion, shame; land was ~ into or under (sown with) turnips; ~ (set) him to mind the fur-nace; ~ my horse to or at (invited him to jump) the fence; (of horse &c, of per-son) must be ~ through (made to perform) his paces; ~ him (make him read) through a book of Livy; was ~ (forced, driven) to flight, to his shifts, to the BLUSH², was ~ to (forced to play) his trumps; surprising what he can do when he's ~ to it (pressed); was hard ~ to it (could scarcely) keep them off. **II.** Special senses with adv. **1.** ~ *about*: lay (sailing vessel) on opposite tack, cause (horse, body of men) to turn round, (of vessel) go about; (chiefly Sc.) trouble, distress. **2.** ~ *across*, execute or establish successfully (~ *it across*, succeed in doing). **3.** ~ *away*: (arch.) divorce; lay by (money &c.) for future use; (sl.) con-sume (food, drink); (sl.) imprison; (sl.) pawn. **4.** ~ *back*: check the advance of, retard; move back the hands of (clock); restore to former place. **5.** ~ *by*: evade (question, argument); ~ off (person) with evasion; lay aside esp. for future use. **6.** ~ *down*: suppress by force or autho-rity; take down, snub, put to silence; cease to maintain (expensive thing); account, reckon, as *I ~ him down for nine years old, at nine, as a fool, for a fool*; attribute, as ~ *it down to his nervousness*; ~ *one's* FOOT¹ *down*. **7.** ~ *forth*: exert (strength, effort, eloquence); ~ in circulation; (of plant) send out (buds, leaves, or abs.). **8.** ~ *forward*: thrust (oneself &c.) into prominence; advance, set forth, (theory &c.). **9.** ~ *in*: install in office &c., as ~ *in a caretaker, bailiff*, (hence) distress, execution; present formally (document, evidence, plea, claim, bail) as in law-court; ~ *in* (make) *an appearance*; make a claim (for election &c.); interpose (blow, shot, remark, quoted words), ~ *in one's* OAR; throw in (additional thing); perform (piece of work) as part of a whole; (colloq.) pass, spend, (time). **10.** ~ *off*: postpone engagement with (person); postpone (person, demand, often *with* excuse, compromise); hinder, dissuade, *from*; foist (thing *upon* person); remove, take off, (clothes); (of boat, crew, &c.) leave shore; ~ *off* n., evasion, postponement. **11.** ~ *on*: clothe oneself or another with; (colloq.) ~ *it on*, overcharge, simulate exaggerated emotion, suffering, &c.; assume, take on, (character, appearance); develop additional (flesh, weight); add (so much to price, runs &c. to score); stake (money *upon* horse &c.); advance the hands of (clock); bring into action, exert, (force, pressure, speed, STEAM¹, the SCREW¹); appoint, arrange for, (person) to

bowl &c., (train) to run &c. **12.** ~ *out*: dislocate (shoulder &c.); (Crick.) cause (batsman) to be out; extinguish (candle, gas, fire, &c.); disconcert, confuse; annoy, irritate; ~ *to inconvenience*; exert (strength &c.); lend (money) at interest, invest; give (work) to be done off the premises. **13.** ~ *over*, secure appreciation for (film, play, &c.); ~ (oneself) *over*, impress one's personality on (an audience). **14.** ~ *through*: carry out (task); place (person) in telephonic connexion with (*to*) another through exchange(s). **15.** ~ *together*: form (whole) by combination of parts; ~ *Two & two together*; ~ (*our* &c.) *heads together*, consult; (Crick.) compile (score). **16.** ~ *up*: person's *back up*, enrage him; ~ *one's* HAIR *up*; employ (person) as jockey; produce (play) on stage; cause (game) to rise from cover; raise (price); offer (prayer), present (peti-tion); propose for election; publish (banns); offer for sale by auction or for competition; pack up in parcel, place in receptacle for safe keeping; sheathe (sword); lodge & entertain (man, horse); take up one's lodging (*at inn* &c.); ~ *up* (*a good* &c.) *fight*, make a good &c. fight of it; ~ *up with* (arch. ~ *up*), submit to, tolerate, (insult, annoying person or thing); ~ (person) *up to*, inform him of, instruct him in, (also) instigate him (*to do, to doing*, or action); construct, build; con-coct (underhand piece of work); ~ *up a¹*, fraudulently concocted. Hence **pu'ttER¹** (poŏ-) n. [OE *putian* (late), *potian* (late), *pytan*, cf. Da. *putte*]

put² (poŏt), n. **1.** Throw, cast, of the weight or stone. **2.** Option of delivering fixed amount of a stock at fixed price within fixed time. [f. prec.]

put³, pūtt, v.i. & t. (**putted**), & n. **1.** Strike golf-ball; strike (golf-ball) gently with club to get it into hole on smooth piece of ground called *putting-green*. **2.** n. Such stroke. Hence **pūtt'ER¹**(1, 2) n. [differ-entiated f. PUT¹,²]

put⁴, n. (old sl.). Duffer, queer person, countryman, &c. [?]

pu'tative, a. Reputed, supposed, as *his ~ father*. Hence ~**LY²** adv. [f. LL *putativus* (*putare* think, see -ATIVE)]

pute, a. (arch.). Pure (&) ~, mere. [f. L *putus* in phr. *purus ac putus*]

put'eal, n. (Rom. Ant.). Stone curb round mouth of well. [L (*puteus* well, see -AL)]

put'log, -lŏck, n. Short horizontal tim-ber on which scaffold-boards rest. [?]

pu'trefy, v.i. & t. Become putrid, rot, go bad; fester, suppurate; become morally corrupt; (rare) cause to ~fy. So ~**FAC'TION** n., ~**FAC'TIVE** a. [f. F *putréfier* f. L *putre-facere* (*putrēre* be rotten, see -FY)]

pūtres'c|ent, a. In process of rotting; of, accompanying, this process. Hence ~**ENCE** n., ~**IBLE** a. [f. L *putrescere* incept. of *putrēre* rot, see -ENT]

putˈrid, a. Decomposed, rotten; foul, noxious; (fig.) corrupt; (sl.) of poor quality, highly distasteful; ~ *fever*, typhus; ~ *sore throat*, gangrenous pharyngitis, diphtheria. Hence ~ITY (-idˈ-), ~NESS, nn., ~LY² adv. [f. L *putridus* (*putre* rot, -ID¹)]

putsch (-ŏŏ-), n. Revolutionary attempt, *coup de main*. [G (Swiss)]

putt. See PUT³.

puttˈee (-i), n. Long strip of cloth wound spirally round leg from ankle to knee for protection & support. [f. Hind. *patti* bandage]

puttˈoo, n. (Anglo-Ind.) Fabric, plain or patterned, produced in Cashmere from coarse goat-wool. [native name]

puttˈy, n. & v.t. **1.** (Also *jewellers'* ~) powder of calcined tin (& lead) for polishing glass or metal; (also *plasterers'* ~) fine mortar of lime & water without sand; (also *glaziers'* ~) cement of whiting, raw linseed oil, etc., for fixing panes of glass, filling up holes in woodwork, etc.; *medal*, fit reward for small service (*you deserve a ~ medal*). **2.** v.t. Cover, fix, join, fill up, with ~. [f. F *potée* lit. Potful, see -Y¹]

puy (pwē), n. Small volcanic cone esp. in Auvergne. [F]

puzˈzle¹, v.t. & i. Perplex; be perplexed (*about, over,* problem etc.); make *out* (solution of problem etc.); MONKEY-~. Hence ~DOM (-id-), ~MENT (-lm-), **puzzˈ-i-ng²** adj. ~*pate(d)*, (person) with confused ideas; *patience*, as *Chinese* ~; ~*head(ed)*, ||~*peg*, piece of wood so fixed to dog's lower jaw as to prevent him from putting nose close to ground. [?]

puzˈzle², n. Bewilderment, perplexity; perplexing question, enigma; problem, toy, contrived to exercise ingenuity & patience. See POZZOLANA.

puzzuolaˈna. See POZZOLANA.

pyaemˈia, n. Blood-poisoning marked by formation of pus-foci. Hence ~IC a. [f. Gk *puon* pus + *haima* blood + -IA¹]

pycˈno- in comb. = Gk *puknos* thick, dense, as ~*style* a. & n., (building) with close arrangement of columns, i.e. at interval of one diameter & a half.

pyeˈdŏg, p͞ieˈ-, n. Ownerless mongrel of the East. [Anglo-Ind.; cf. Hind. *pāhi* outsider]

pygˈm͞y, p͞iˈ-, n. & a. **1.** One of a diminutive race of men said to have inhabited parts of Ethiopia or India; *the P~ies*, a dwarf race in equatorial Africa; dwarf (fig. of intellectual inferiority etc.); elf, pixy. **2.** adj. Of the ~ies, dwarf. So **pygma(e)ˈAN** (-ēˈȧn) a. [f. L f. Gk *pugmaios* (*pugmē* length from elbow to knuckles)]

||pyjaˈmas, *paj-.-(-ahmȧz), n. pl. Loose silk or cotton trousers tied round waist, worn by both sexes among Mohammedans & adopted esp. for night wear by Euro-

peans; sleeping-suit of loose trousers & jacket. [f. Pers. *pae jamah* (*pae, pay,* foot, leg, + *jamah* clothing)]

pylˈon, n. Gateway esp. of Egyptian temple; tall compound structure erected as support or boundary or decoration. [f. Gk *pulōn* (*pulē* gate)]

pyloˈrus, n. (anat.), Opening from stomach into duodenum; part of stomach where this is. Hence **pylorˈic** a. [LL, f. Gk *pulōros* gatekeeper (*pulē* gate + *ouros* warder)]

pyo- in comb. = Gk *puon* pus, as ~*genĕsis*, formation of pus; ~*rrhoĕa* (-rēȧ), purulent discharge (esp. as a dental disease). So **pyˈOID** a.

pyrˈacanth, n. Evergreen thorny shrub with white flowers & scarlet berries. [f. L f. Gk *puracantha*, etym. dub.]

pyrˈamid, n. **1.** Monumental (esp. ancient Egyptian) structure of stone etc., with polygonal or (usu.) square base, & sloping sides meeting at apex. **2.** Solid of this shape with base of three or more sides, **3.** ~-shaped thing or pile of things; fruit-tree trained in ~ shape. **4.** Poem whose successive lines increase or decrease in length. **5.** || pl. (Billiards) game played with (usu. 15) coloured balls & one cue-ball. Hence or cogn. **pyramˈidal** a., **pyramidiˈcal(ly)** a., ~WISE adv. [f. L f. Gk *puramis -idos*, perh. of Egypt. orig.]

pyrˈamidist, n. Student of structure & history of Egyptian pyramids. [-IST]

pyre, n. Heap of combustible material, esp. funeral pile for burning corpse. [f. L f. Gk *pura* (*pur* fire)]

pyrethˈrum, n. Name of kinds of chrysanthemum. [L, f. Gk *purethron.*]

pyretˈic (or pī-), a. Of, for, or producing, fever. [f. Gk *puretos* fever + -IC]

pyrˈex¹|ia (or pī-), n.(path.). Fever. Hence ~IAL, ~ICAL), aa. [f. Gk *purexis* (*puressō* be feverish, as prec.)]

pyrheliomˈeter (per-), n. Instrument for measuring heat given off by sun. [f. Gk *pur* fire + *hēlios* sun + -METER]

pyrˈidine (or pī-), n. (chem.). A volatile liquid alkaloid from dry distillation of bone-oil, used for asthma. [f. Gk *pur* fire +-ID⁴+-INE⁵]

pyrite (-z), n. (Also *iron* ~) either of two sulphides of iron; *copper* ~, double sulphide of copper & iron. Hence **pyritˈic, pyritifˈerous, pyrˈitous,** aa., **pyrˈitize** v.t., (pir-, or pī-). [L, f. Gk *puritēs* stone of fire

pyro- in comb. = Gk *pur* fire, as: ~*o-electric*, ~*o-electriˈcity*, (property of) becoming electrically polar when heated; ~*ogaliˈic acid* (abbr. *pyro*), acid used as reducing agent in photography etc.; ~*ogenetic*, productive of heat, esp. in the body, or (also ~*ogenˈic*) of fever; ~*genous*, (of rock) igneous, (of substance) produced by combustion of another:

~ŏg'raphy, = POKER[1] ~work; ~ogravure', piece of poker-work; ~ŏl'atry, fire-worship; ~otig'neous, produced by action of fire or heat on wood, as ~oligneous acid; ~omăn'ĭa, incendiary mania, so ~omăn'ĭac n., ~omani'acal a.; ~om'eter, instrument for measuring high temperatures, so ~o-met'rĭc(al) aa., ~omet'rically adv., ~ŏm'etry n.: ~ŏph'orous, substance that takes fire spontaneously on exposure to air, so ~ophŏ'rĭc, ~ŏph'orous, aa.; ~ophŏt'ograph, one burnt in on glass or porcelain, so ~ophotograph'ĭc a., ~ophotŏg'raphy n. Also in scientific wds denoting (Chem.) new substance formed from another (Min.) minerals etc. showing some property or change under action of heat, or having fiery red or yellow colour.

pȳr'ōpe, n. A deep-red garnet. [f. OF pirope f. L f. Gk purōpos gold-bronze, lit. fiery-eyed (pur fire + ōps eye)]

pȳrotech'nic (-těk-), a. & n. 1. Of (the nature of) fireworks, as ~ic display; (fig. of wit etc.), brilliant, sensational. 2. n. pl. Art of making, display of, fireworks (lit. & fig.). Hence or cogn. ~ICAL a., ~icalty[2] adv., ~IST, **pȳr'otechny**[1], nn., (-těk-). [f. PYRO- + Gk tekhnikos (tekhnē art, see -IC)]

pȳr'ŏxēne, n. (Kinds of) mineral composed mainly of the silicates of calcium and magnesium, a common component of igneous rocks. [f. PYRO- + Gk xenos stranger (because erron. supposed alien to igneous rocks)]

pȳrŏx'ylin, n. Nitrates of cellulose, esp. the explosive, gun-cotton, or the lower nitrate which when dissolved in ether & alcohol forms collodion & serves as the basis of varnishes, artificial leather, etc. [f. PYRO- + Gk xulon wood + -IN]

Py'rrhic[1] (-rĭk), p., n. & a. 1. ~ (dance), war dance of ancient Greeks. 2. The metrical foot ~ ; (adj.) consisting of such feet. [(in pros. sense f. L f. Gk pyrrhīkhios) f. purrhīkhē, said to be named f. Purrhīkhos, the inventor]

Py'rrhic[2] (-rĭk), a. ~ victory (gained at too great cost, like that of Pyrrhus king of Epirus over the Romans at Asculum). [f. Gk purrhīkos (Purrhos Pyrrhus, see -IC)]

Py'rrhonism (-ro-), n. Sceptic philosophy of Pyrrho of Elis (c. 300 B.C.), doctrine that certainty of knowledge is unattainable; scepticism, philosophic doubt. Hence or cogn. **Pyrrhon'IAN** (-rō-), **Pyrrhon'IC** (-rō-), aa. & nn., ~IST (-ro-) n. [f. Gk Purrhōn Pyrrho + -ISM]

pȳr'us, n. Genus of rosaceous trees & shrubs including pear & apple, esp. P~ japonica, scarlet ~. [med. L, = L pirus pear-tree]

Pythăg'orě'an, a. & n. (Follower of) Pythagoras, philosopher of Samos (6th c. B.C.) said to have believed in transmigra-

---

tion of souls; ~ proposition, Euclid I. 47. [f. L f. Gk Puthagoreios + -AN]

Pyth'ian (-dh-), a. & n. Of (Apollo's oracle & priestess at) Delphi; the ~, Apollo, his priestess at Delphi. [f. L f. Gk Puthios (Puthō, older name of Delphi) + -AN]

pȳth'on[1], n. (Gk Myth.) huge serpent or monster slain near Delphi by Apollo; large snake that crushes its prey. So **pȳthŏn'ic**[1] [-IC] a. [f. L f. Gk Puthōn]

pȳthŏn[2], n. Familiar spirit; person possessed by this. Hence or cogn. ~ESS[1] n., **pȳthŏn'ic**[2] [-IC] a. [f. LL (-ō-) f. N.T. Gk puthōn; connexion w. prec. unexpl.]

pyx, n., & v.t. I. (Eccl.) vessel in which consecrated bread is kept. 2. || Box at Royal Mint in which specimen gold & silver coins are deposited to be tested at the annual trial of the ~ by jury of Goldsmiths' Company; || (v.t.) deposit (coin) in ~, test (coin) by weight & assay. [vb f. n.[1], PYXIS]

pȳxid'ium, n. (bot.; pl. -ia). Capsule of which the top comes off like lid of box. [f. Gk puxidion, dim. as foll.]

pȳx'is, n. Small box, casket; = prec. [L, f. Gk puxis f. puxos box-tree]

Q (kū), letter (pl. Qs, Q's). (Skating) change of edge followed by turn (reverse Q, turn followed by change of edge); wind one's Ps & Qs, see P; Q-boat, Q-ship, = MYSTERY[1]-ship; Q department, that of Q.M.G.

quā, conj. As, in the capacity of, (objects to the Church not ~ Church, but ~ Establishment). [L, abl. fem. sing. of qui rel. pron.]

quack[1], v.i., & n. (Utter) harsh sound made by ducks; talk loudly & foolishly; ~ (nursery), duck. [imit.; cf. Du. kwaken, G quacken]

quack[2], n., & v.i. & t. 1. Ignorant pretender to skill esp. in medicine or surgery, one who offers wonderful remedies or devices, charlatan, (often attrib., as ~ doctor, remedies); hence ~ERY(4) n., ~ISH[1] a. 2. vb. Play the ~; talk pretentiously; puff or advertise(cure etc.). [abbr. of foll.]

quack'sălver, n. (Orig. form, now rare, of) QUACK[2] n. [Du. (QUACK[1], SALVE, -ER[1])]

quad (kwŏd), n. See QUADRANGLE, QUADRAT, QUADRUPLET.

qua'drable (-ŏd-), a. (math.). Capable of being represented by an equivalent square or expressed in finite number of algebraic terms. [as QUADRATE[2], -ABLE]

quadragēnăr'ian (-ŏd-), a. & n. (Person) forty years old. [f. L quadragenarius (quadrageni distrib. of quadraginta forty, -ARY[1])]

Quadrăgĕs'ima (-ŏd-), n. (Also ~ Sunday) first Sunday in Lent. [med. L (earlier sense, the forty days of Lent), fem. of

L *quadragesimus* fortieth (*quadraginta* forty)]

quadragēs'imal (-ŏd-), a. Lasting forty days (of fast, esp. Lent); Lenten. [f. LL *quadragesimālis* (prec., -AL)]

quadrangle (kwŏd'răngg'l), n. Four-sided figure, esp. square or rectangle; so **quadrang'ular¹** a., **quadrăng'ūlarly²** adv. (-ngg-); ‖ (also *quad*, pr. kwŏd) four-sided court (partly) enclosed by parts of large buildings, such court with buildings round it. [F. f. LL *quadrangulum* (QUADRI-, ANGLE)]

qua'drant (-ŏd-), n. Quarter of circle's circumference; plane figure enclosed by two radii of circle & arc cut off by them; quarter of sphere; thing, esp. graduated strip of metal, shaped like quarter-circle, instrument properly so shaped & graduated for taking angular measurements. Hence **quadran'tal** a. [f. L *quadrans -ntis* (QUADRI-)]

qua'drat (-ŏd-), n. (Also *quad*, pr. kwŏd) small metal block used by printers in spacing (*em ~, en ~*, broader, narrower, size). [var. of foll.]

qua'drate¹ (-ŏd-), a. & n. **1.** Square, rectangular, (chiefly in anat. names, as ~ *bone* in birds & reptiles' heads, ~ *muscle* in loins, thigh, forearm, etc.). **2.** n. Rect-angular block or plate (rare); ~ *bone* or *muscle*. [f. L *quadrātus* (foll., -ATE²)]

quadrāte'² (or kwŏd-), v.t. & i. (rare). Make square; (Math.) square (circle etc.); correspond or conform (*with*, or to or abs. *subj.*); make conform (*with*, or to or abs. *obj.*). [f. L *quadrare* (QUADRI-), -ATE³]

quadrăt'ic, a. & n. **1.** Square (rare) (Math.), involving second & no higher power of unknown quantity or variable (esp.~ *equation*). **2.** n. ~ equation; (pl.) branch of algebra dealing with these. [QUADRATE¹, -IC]

qua'drature (-ŏd-), n. (Math.) finding of square with area precisely equal to that of figure bounded by curve (esp. ~ *of the circle*); (Astron.) one of two points in space or time at which moon is 90° from sun, position of heavenly body in relation to another 90° away. [f. L *quadratura* (QUADRATE¹, -URE)]

quadrenn'ial, a. Occurring every, lasting, four years. [irreg. f. L *quadriennium* four-year period (foll., *annus* year), -AL]

qua'dri- (-ŏd-), L comb. form = four, in a few L words (*quadriduum* period of four days, *quadripartitus* ~partite), & in many of later L & mod. formation, esp. in scientific use: ~**fid,** a., cleft into four divisions or lobes: ~**lat'eral,** a. & n., four-sided (figure or land); *the Quadri-lateral*, four fortresses in N. Italy & district pro-tected by them); ~**ling'ual** (-nggw-), a., using, in, four languages; **quadrill'ion** (kwŏdril'yon), n., ‖ fourth power of a million (1 followed by 24 ciphers), *fifth power of a thousand (cf. BILLION); ~

quadrifo'lious a. (also *set of* ~s); piece of music for such dance. [F. f. Sp. *cuadrilla* (*cuadra* square)]

quadron', n. Offspring of white & mu-latto, person of quarter-negro blood; hybrid of similarly proportioned descent between other human, animal, or vege-table stocks. [f. Sp. *cuarteron* (*cuarto* fourth) w. assim. to QUADRI-]

quadru'manous (-rōō-), a. Four-handed, belonging to the order *Quadrumana* of mammals with opposable digit on all four limbs. [after foll. f. L *manus* hand]

qua'druped (-ŏdrŏŏ-), a. & n. **1.** Four-footed animal, esp. four-footed mammal; so **quadru'pedal** (-rŏŏ-), a. **2.** adj. Four-footed. [f. L *quadrupes -pedis* as n. & n. *quadru-* form of QUADRI- occas. used be-fore *p-, pes* foot]

qua'druple (-ŏdrŏŏ-), a., n., & v.t. & i. **1.** Fourfold, consisting of four parts or involving four parties, (~ *algebra*, using four independent units; ~ *rhythm* or *time*, with four beats to a measure; ~ *al-liance* etc.); amounting to four times the amount or number of, equivalent to four times in amount or number to, (*has a ~ight & heed ~*, or ~ *of* or *to*, *that of the earth*); hence **qua'druply²** (-ŏdrŏŏ-), adv. **2.** n. Number or amount four times greater than another(esp. *the* ~ *of*). **3.** vb. Multiply (t. & i.) by four. [F. f. L *quadru-plus* (prec., *-plus* as in *duplus* DOUBLE)]

qua'druplet (-ŏdrŏŏ-), n. (Pl.) four chil-dren at a birth (colloq. *quads*, pr. kwŏdz); four things working together; bicycle for four. [f. prec. after TRIPLET]

quadru'plicate¹ (-ŏŏ-), a. & n. **1.** Four-fold, four times repeated or copied. **2.** n. copies; four such copies. [f. L *quadruplicare* (*quadruplex*, DUPLEX), -ATE²]

quadru'plicate² (-ōō-), v.t. Multiply by

L comb. form = four. -AL]

quadri'ga, n. (pl. *-ae*). Ancient chariot with four horses abreast (as in sculpture or coins). [L (QUADRI-, *jugum* yoke)]

quadrille'¹ (kă-, kwŏ-), n. Fashionable 18th-c. game for four persons with forty cards. [F, perh. f. Sp. *cuartillo* w. assim. to foll.]

quadrille'² (kă-, kwă-), n. Square dance for four couples & containing five figures

noˈn'ial, a., consisting of four algebraic terms; ~**pär'tite,** a., consisting of four parts, shared by or involving four parties; ~**rēme,** n., ancient galley with four banks of oars; ~**syll'able,** n., word of four syllables; ~**syllăb'ic,** a., four-syllabled; **quadriv'alent** (kwŏ-), a. (chem.), capable of combining with four univalent atoms; **quadriv'ium** (kwŏ-), n. (hist.), medieval university course of arithmetic, geometry, astronomy, & music (cf. TRIVIUM).

qua'dric (-ŏd-), a. & n. (solid geom.) (Surface) of second degree. [as prec., -IC]

four; make four specimens of. Hence ~ATION n. [as prec., -ATE³]

quadruplicity (-dǐroŏ-), n. Fourfold nature, being fourfold. [f. L (-tas), as prec., -TY]

quaere (kwēr'), v.t. imperat., & n. (abbr. *qu.*). 1. Inquire (imperat.), it is a question, I should like to know. (*most interesting, no doubt; but—, is it true?*). 2. n. A question, query. [L, imperat. of *quaerere* ask]

quaes'tor, n. Ancient-Roman official, state-treasurer, paymaster, etc. Hence or cogn. **quaestor'IAL** a., **~SHIP** n. [L *quaere quaesit-* seek, -OR²]

quaff (-ah-), v.i. & t. Drink (t. & i.) drafn (cup etc.), in copious or long draughts. [?]

quag, n. Marshy or boggy spot, quaking bog. Hence **~g'Y¹** (-g-) a. [imit.; cf. WAG, SWAG]

quǎgg'a, n. S.-Afr. quadruped related to ass & zebra, less striped than latter; Burchell's zebra. [S.-Afr.]

quǎg'mīre, n. Quaking bog, fen, marsh, slough (lit. & fig.). [prob. f. QUAG, MIRE]

*****quahog, -haug**, (kwahog), n. Edible clam of Atlantic coast of N. America. [abbr. of Amer.-Ind. *poquauhock*]

‖ **quaich, quaigh**, (kwāч), n. (Sc.). Kind of drinking-cup, usu. of wood & having two handles. [f. Gael. *cuach* cup]

Quai d'Orsay (kādòr-), n. (Used for) the French Foreign Office.

quail¹, n. Kinds of migratory bird allied to partridge esteemed as food; **~-call**, **~-pipe**, whistle with note like ~'s for luring. Hence **~'ERY**(3) n. [f. OF *quaille* prob. f. Tent., cf. OHG *quatala* prob. imit.]

quail², v.i. & t. (Of person, or his heart, courage, spirit, or eyes) flinch, be cowed, give way *before* or *to*; (rare) cow, daunt. [etym. dub.; from 1440; common 1520–60; then disappears till revived prob. by Scott]

quaint, a. Attractive or piquant in virtue of unfamiliar, esp. old-fashioned, appearance, ornamentation, manners, etc., daintily odd. Hence **~LY²** adv., **~NESS** n. [earlier senses *wise, cunning, ingenious*; f. OF *cointe* f. L *cognitus* p.p. of *cognoscere* learn]

quāke, v.i., & n. 1. Shake, tremble, rock to & fro, (of earth with earthquake, person usu. *for* or *with* fear or cold, bog when trodden on, etc.); **~ing-grass**, kinds with slender foot-stalks trembling in wind. 2. n. Act of ~ing, (colloq.) earthquake. Hence **~'ingLY²** adv., **~'Y²** a. [OE *cwacian* cf. QUAG]

quāk'er, n. 1. (Q~). (Outsiders' name for) member of Society of Friends founded by George Fox 1648–50, & devoted to peace principles, plainness of dress (esp. the use of drab or grey), simplicity of speech (esp. the use of *thee* & avoidance of titles & words, such as the names of the days, suggestive of paganism), & peculiar priestless religious meetings. 2. *Dummy gun in ship or fort. 3. (Also **~bird**, **~moth**) kinds of plain-coloured bird & moth. 4. ~, or ~'s, **~meeting**, religious meeting of Friends, silent till some member is moved by the spirit, (transf.) silent meeting, company in which conversation flags. Hence **~DOM**, **~ESS¹**, **~ISM**(3,4), nn. **~ISH¹**, **~LY¹**, aa. [name given 1650 w. ref. to 'quaking at the Word of the Lord'; -ER¹]

qualifica'tion (-ŏl-), n. 1. Modification, recognition of contingency, restricting or limiting circumstance, detraction from completeness or absoluteness, (*statement with many ~s; hedged with ~s; requires ~; his delight had one ~*). 2. Quality fitting person or thing (*for* post etc., or abs.); condition that must be fulfilled before right can be acquired or office held (*the ~ for citizenship may be a certain income*); document attesting such fulfilment. 3. Attribution of quality (*the ~ of his policy as opportunist is unfair*). So **qualificator** (-ŏl-) a. [f. med. L *qualificatio* (foll., -FICATION)]

qua'lifỹ (-ŏl-), v.t. & i. 1. Attribute some quality to, describe as, (*~ documents as heretical, person as a scoundrel, proposal as iniquitous*; *adjectives ~ nouns*). 2. Invest or provide with the necessary qualities, make competent, fit, or legally entitled, (*for* being or doing, to be or do, *for* post or sphere, or abs.; *~ing examination*, to ascertain that candidates are not below a fixed standard, often followed by *competitive*); (intr.) fulfil some condition, esp. pass examination or take oath, to make oneself eligible (*for* office, or abs.). 3. Modify (statement, opinion), make less absolute or sweeping, subject to reservations or limitation. 4. Moderate, mitigate, make less complete or pleasing or unpleasing; diminish strength or flavour of (spirit etc. *with* water, also joc. water *with* spirit). [f. med. L *qualificare* (L *qualis* such as, -FY)]

qua'litative (-ŏl-), a. Concerned with, depending on, quality (opp. QUANTITATIVE, esp. ~ *analysis*). [f. LL *qualitativus* (foll., -ATIVE)]

qua'litỹ (-ŏl-), n. 1. Degree of excellence, relative nature or kind or character, (opp. QUANTITY; *of good, high, poor*, etc., ~y; *is made in three ~ies; ~y matters more than quantity*); general excellence (*has ~y*, is excellent). 2. Faculty, skill, accomplishment, characteristic trait, mental or moral attribute, (*give a taste of one's ~y*, show what one can do; *has many good ~ies, the* DEFECTS *of his ~ies, the ~ies of a courage*), 3. (arch. or vulg.) High rank or social standing (*people of, the, ~y*, the upper classes). 4. (Log.: of proposition) being affirmative or negative. 5. (Of sound, voice, etc.) distinctive character

apart from pitch & loudness, timbre.
[f. F *qualité* f. L *quālitātem* (prec.)]
kind, -TY]

qualm (-ahm, -awm), n. Momentary
faint or sick feeling, queasiness; misgiving, sinking of heart; scruple of conscience, doubt of one's own rectitude in
some matter. Hence ~ISH[1] a. [cf. G
qualm vapour (dial. swoon)]

quanda'ry (-on-; *also* kwŏn'dəri), n. A
state of perplexity, difficult situation,
practical dilemma, (*am in a* ~). [c.
1580; etym. dub.]

quand même (see Ap.), adv. Despite
consequences, even so, all the same. [F]

‖quant (kwŏnt), n., & v.t. & i. Punting-
pole with disk to prevent its sinking in
mud used by E.-coast bargemen etc.;(vb)
propel (boat), propel boat, with ~. [perh.
f. L f. Gk *kontos*]

qua'ntic (-on-), n. (math.). Rational integral homogeneous function of two or
more variables. [f. L *quantus* how much,
-IC]

qua'ntify (-ŏn-), v.t. 1. (Log.) define application of (term, proposition) by use of *all*,
some, etc.; determine quantity of.
Hence ~FIABLE a., ~FICA'TION n. [f. med. L
quantificāre (prec., -FY)]

qua'ntitative (-ŏn-; *or* -tā-), a. Measured
or measurable by, concerned with, quantity (opp. QUALITATIVE; esp. ~ *analysis*,
of, based on, the quantity of vowels (~ *accent*, *scansion*, *verse*, etc.). Hence ~LY[2]
adv. [f. med. L *quantitātīvus* (QUANTITY,
-IVE)]

qua'ntitive (-ŏn-), a. = prec. (rare). [foll.,
-IVE]

qua'ntity (-ŏn-), n. 1. The property of
things that is estimable by some sort of
measure, the having of size, extension,
weight, amount, or number, (*mathematics
is the science of pure* ~*y*; *stated in terms of
* ~*y*; *the* ~*y of a surface is its area*). 2.
Amount, sum, (*the* ~*y of the current
depends on the size of the plates*). 3. Specified or considerable portion or number
or amount of something, *the amount of
something present*, (*a small* ~*y of blood*;
a ~*y of baskets*; *buys in large* ~*ies*; *the
* ~*y of heat in an animal body*); (pl.) large
amounts or numbers, abundance, (*is
found in* ~*ies on the shore*). 4. (Pros.)
length or shortness of vowel sounds (see
LONG[1]; ~*y-mark*, put over vowel to
indicate ~*y*; FALSE ~*y*). 5. (Log.) extension given to subject of proposition. 6.
(Math.) thing having ~*y*, figure or symbol
representing it, (*incommensurable* ~*ies
have no adequat partis*; *unknown* ~, transf.,
person or thing whose action cannot be
foreseen; *negligible* ~, transf., person
etc. that need not be reckoned with).
7. **‖BILL[4]** *of* ~*ies*; **‖**~*y surveyor*, one
whose business it is to prepare bills of
~*ies*, measure and price work done, etc.

[f. OF *quantité* f. L *quantitātem* (*quantus*
how much, -TY)]

quantivalence (-ŏn-, -ăn-), n. (chem.)
Extent to which one of element's atoms
can hold other atoms in combination. [f.
L *quantus* how much, after *equivalence*]

qua'ntum (-ŏn-; *in* L *phr.* -ăn-, -ŏn-), n.
(pl. -*a*, rare). Amount; share, portion;
required, desired, or allowed amount; ~
lib'et or plu'ret, abbr. *q.l.*, *q.p.*, as much as
is desired (in prescriptions), as much as
abbr. *quant. suff.*, or *q.s.*, as much as
suffices (in prescriptions), (gen.) sufficient
quantity, to sufficient extent; ~ *theory*
(Physics), the hypothesis, according for
the stability of the atom & other phenomena, that in radiation & the energy of
electrons is discharged not continuously
but in discrete amounts or quanta. [L,
neut. of *quantus* how much, as much
as]

quaquaver'sal, a. (geol.). Pointing in
every direction. [f. LL *quāquāversus
(quaqua* wheresoever, *versus* towards)]

quarantine (kwŏ'rantēn), n., & v.t. 1.
(Period of) isolation imposed on voyagers,
travellers, sick persons, or infected ship,
that might spread contagious disease.
2. v.t. Impose such isolation on, put in
~. [prob. f. It. *quarantina* forty days
(*quaranta* f. L *quadrāgintā* forty)]

‖quæ'renda, -der, (kwě-), n. Kind of
Devonshire & Somerset apple. [?]

qua'rrel[1] (kwŏ-), n. (hist.). Short heavy
arrow or bolt used in crossbow or arbalest.
[OF, cf. It. *quadrello* dim. of *quadro* a
square (LL *quadrus* a.)]

qua'rrel[2] (kwŏ-), n. 1. Occasion of complaint against person or his actions (*have
no* ~ *against or with him*; *find* ~ *in a
strong, be captious; pick a* ~, invent or
eagerly avail oneself of such occasion to
commence hostilities; *espouse one's* ~,
fight one's ~*s for him*, assist him in getting
redress; *in a good* ~, justly taken up).
2. Violent contention or altercation
between persons, rupture of friendly relations. Hence ~SOME a., ~SOME'LY adv.,
~SOMENESS n. [f. OF *querele* f. L *querela*
complaint (*queri* complain)]

qua'rrel[3] (kwŏ-), v.i.(-ll-). Take exception,
find fault *with* (*I never* ~ *with Providence*;
~ *with one's bread & butter*, abandon employment by which one lives); contend
violently (*with person*; *about or for thing*),
fall out, have dispute, break of friendly
relations. [f. prec.]

qua'rry[1] (kwŏ-), n. Object of pursuit by
bird of prey, hounds, hunters, etc.; intended victim or prey. [f. OF *cuiree* (*cuir*
skin f. L *corium*, -Y[5]), orig. sense, parts of
deer placed on hide & given to hounds]

qua'rry² (kwŏ-), n., & v.t. & i. **1.** Excavation made by taking stone for building etc. from its bed; place whence stone, or fig. information etc., may be extracted; floor-tile; ~man, worker in ~. **2.** vb. Extract (stone) from ~; extract (facts etc.) laboriously from books etc.; expend toil in searching documents etc. (~ing in the Harleian MSS.). [f. med. L quareia, quadraria, (L quadrare to square)]

qua'rry³ (kwŏ-), n. Diamond-shaped pane of glass as used in lattice-windows. [later form of QUARREL¹]

quart¹ (kwôrt), n. Measure of capacity, quarter of gallon or two pints (put ~ into pint pot, make less contain greater); pot or bottle containing this amount (~ bottle of wine or spirit, ½ gal.); (abs. for) ~ of beer (still takes his ~); ~pot. [F, f. neut. of L quartus fourth]

quart² (kärt), n., & v.i. & t. **1.** A position in fencing, CARTE, (~ & tierce, fencing-practice); sequence of four cards in piquet etc. (~ major, ace, king, queen, knave). **2.** vb. Use the position ~; draw back (head etc.) in this. [f. F quarte f. fem. L as prec.]

quar'tan (kwôr-), a. & n. (Ague or fever) with paroxysm every third (by inclusive reckoning fourth) day. [f. F (fièvre) quartaine f. L (febris) quartana (quartus fourth, -AN)]

quartā'tion (kwôr-), n. Combining of three parts of silver with one of gold as preliminary in purifying gold. [L quartus fourth, -ATION]

quarte (kärt). Var. of QUART² (see etym.)

quar'ter¹ (kwôr-), n. **1.** Fourth part, one of four equal or corresponding parts, fourth part of, (divide the apples into ~s; ~ of a century, any period of 25 years; second etc. ~ of the century, 26th to 50th etc. years of it; ~ of an hour, any consecutive 15 minutes; bad ~ of an hour, short unpleasant experience; can get it at the stores for a ~ the or of the, or for ~ the price; is not a ~ as good as it should be; ~ mile, yard, etc., ~ of a mile etc.). **2.** (U.S., Can.) 25 cents or ~ dollar, as amount or coin. **3.** One of four parts, each including leg or arm, into which beast's or bird's carcass is divided (of beast, often fore, hind, ~); (pl.) similar parts of traitor quartered after execution; (usu. in pl., often hind-~s) haunch(es) of living animal or man. **4.** Either side of ship aft of main-chains (on the ~, between astern & on beam). **5.** (her.) One of four divisions of quartered shield (dexter & sinister chief, dexter & sinister base) & charge occupying ~ placed in chief. **6.** ‖ Grain-measure of eight bushels, used in stating large quantities, prices, etc.; (abbr. qr) fourth of cwt., 28 lb., 7. Fourth of fathom (& a ~ five, 5¼ fathoms; a ~ less five, 4¾). **8.** Fourth of year for which payments become due on ~-day; instalment of allowance etc. for the ~; (now (chiefly Sc.) school term. **9.** Fourth of lunar period; moon's position between first & second or third & fourth of these. **10.** Point of time 15' before or after any hour o'clock (at a ~ to, past, six; it is not the ~ yet; strikes the hours, half-hours, & ~s; it has gone the ~, clock has sounded for it). **11.** ‖ (Channel I.) unit of property or income, reckoned as £25, for assessment of taxes etc. **12.** (Region lying about) point of compass, direction, district, locality, source of supply or help or information, (wind blows from all four ~s at once; what ~ is the wind in? lit., & fig. how are things going? etc.; flocked in from all ~s; no help to be looked for in that ~; had the news from a good ~). **13.** Division of town, esp. one appropriated to or occupied by special class (the Jewish, manufacturing, residential, etc., ~). **14.** pl. Lodgings, abode, esp. place where troops are lodged or stationed (HEAD~s; winter ~s, occupied, esp. by troops, for winter; take up one's ~s, lodge in, with, etc.; BEAT¹ up ~s of; beat to ~s, Naut., summon crew to appointed stations as for action; at CLOSE¹ ~s). **15.** Exemption from death offered or granted to enemy in battle who will surrender (give, receive, ~; ask for or cry ~; no ~ to be given). **16.** ~mile race or running-distance (won the ~; has done the ~ in 50'). **17.** ~-bell, sounding the ~-hours; ~-binding of book, with narrow leather at back & none at corners, so ~bound a.; ~butt in billiards, cue shorter than half-butt; ‖~day, on which quarterly payments are due, tenancies begin & end, etc. (Lady Day 25 Mar., Midsummer Day 24 June, Michaelmas 29 Sep., & Christmas 25 Dec.; in Scotland, Candlemas 2 Feb., Whitsunday 15 May, Lammas 1 Aug., Martinmas 11 Nov.); ~-deck, part of upper deck between stern & after-mast, the officers (cf. LOW'er deck) of ship or navy; ~-ill, cattle & sheep disease causing putrefaction in one or more of the ~s; ~ left, right, (Mil.), ~ of a right angle to left, right; ~-light, window in body of closed carriage apart from door-window; ~-line (Naut.), disposition in which bow of each ship is abaft beam of one in front; ~-master, (Naut.) petty officer or rating in charge of steering, binnacle, signals, holdstowing, etc., (Mil., Q.M.) regimental officer with duties of assigning ~s, laying out camp, & looking after rations, clothing, etc. (Q~master-General, abbr. Q.M.G., staff officer at head of department controlling quartering, equipment, etc.); ~miller, runner whose distance is the ~; ~-plate, photographic plate 3¼ in. × 4¼, photograph produced from it; ‖~sessions, court of limited criminal & civil jurisdiction & of appeal held quarterly by justices of peace in counties & by re-

corder in boroughs; ~staff, stout pole 6–8 ft long formerly used by peasantry as weapon; ~tone; ~wind, blowing on ship's (most favourable sailing wind). [OF. f. L *quartus* fourth, see -ER²(2)]

quar·ter² (kwȯr-), v.t. **1.** Divide into four equal parts, divide (traitor's body) into quarters. **2.** (her.), Place or bear (charges or coats of arms) quarterly on shield; add (another's coat) to one's hereditary arms; place in alternate quarters *with*: divide (shield) into quarters or into divisions formed by vertical & horizontal lines. **3.** Put (esp. soldiers) into quarters, station or lodge in specified place. **4.** (Of dogs) range or traverse (ground) in every direction. [f. prec.]

quar·terage (-ȯr-) n. Quarterly payment, a quarter's wages, allowance, pension, etc. [-AGE]

quar·tering (-ȯr-), n. In vbl senses: esp. (Her., pl.) coats marshalled on shield to denote alliances of family with heiresses of others. [-ING¹]

quar·terly (-ȯr-), a., n., & adv. **1.** Occur-ring every quarter of a year. **2.** n. ~ review or magazine. **3.** adv. Once every quarter of a year; (Her.) in the four, or in two diagonally opposite, quarters of shield (~*quartered*, with one or more quarters divided in four). [-LY¹,²]

‖ **quar·tern** (-ȯr-), n. (Also ~-*loaf*) four-pound loaf. [f. OF *quartron* quarter; orig. sense, quarter of anything]

quartette(-ȯr-) n. Musical composition for four voices or instruments, players or singers rendering this (*piano*~, 3 stringed instruments with piano); set of four. [F (-te), f. It. *quartetto* (*quarto* fourth f. L *quartus*)-ETTE]

quar·to (-ȯr-), n. (also written 4to, 4°; pl. ~s). Size given by folding sheet of paper twice; book consisting of sheets so folded; ~ *paper*, so folded. [L (*in*) *quarto* (in) fourth (of sheet); abl. of *quartus* fourth]

‖ **quar·tus** (-ȯr-). See PRIMUS¹.

quartz (-ȯr-). n. Kinds of mineral, mas-sive or crystallizing in hexagonal prisms, consisting in pure form of silica or silicon dioxide, & occas. containing gold. [f. G *quarz* etym. dub.]

quash (kwŏsh), v.t. Annul, make void, reject as not valid, put an end to, (esp. by legal procedure or authority). [f. OF *quasser* (now *casser*) f. L *quassare* frequent. of *quatere* shake]

Quashee (kwŏ-), n. Negro (as national nickname). [f. Ashantee or Fantee *Kwasi*, common personal name]

quasi, conj. & pref. **1.** (Introducing etymological explanation, abbr. *qu.*) that is to say, as if it were, (*Earls of Wilbraham*, ~ *Wild boar ham*). **2.** (Hyphened esp. to noun or adj.) seemingly, not real(ly), practical(ly), half-, almost, (*engaged in a*

quat·er-centen·ary, n. Four-hundredth anniversary. [L *quater* four times]

quatern·ary, a. & n. **1.** Having four parts, esp. compounded of four chemical ele-ments or radicals; concerned with the number four; (Geol.) belonging to most recent period, subsequent to Tertiary. **2.** n. Set of four things; the number four; *the Pythagorean* ~, $1+2+3+4=10$, with mystic significance in Pythagoreanism. [f. L *quaternarius* (*quaterni* distrib. of *quattuor* four, -ARY¹)]

quatern·ion, n. Set of four sheets folded in two; Pythagorean quater-nary, mystic number 4 or 10 (see prec.); (Math.) quotient of two vectors or opera-tor that changes one vector into another (named as depending on four geometrical elements),(pl.) form of calculus of vectors in which this operator is used. [f. LL *quaternio* (prec.)]

quatern·ity, n. Being four; set of four persons (esp. of the Godhead in contrast to Trinity). [f. LL *quaternitas*]

quatorzain (kăt·erzān), n. Fourteen-line poem, irregular sonnet. [f. F *quatorzaine* (*quatorze* fourteen f. L *quattuordecim*)]

quatrain (kwŏt·rin), n. Stanza of four lines occas. with alternate rhymes. [F (*quatre* four f. L *quatuor*)]

quatre (kăt·er), n. =CATER¹.

quat·refoil (kăt·re-, kătr-), n. Four-cusped figure, esp. as opening in archi-tectural tracery, resembling symmetrical four-lobed leaf or flower. [f. OF *quatre* (QUATRAIN), FOIL¹]

quattrocen·tist (-ahtrŏch-), n. & a. (Artist etc.) of the quattrocento. [-IST]

quattrocen·to (-ahtrŏch-), n. Fifteenth century as period in Italian art. [It., lit. 400, but used=1400]

quav·er, v.i. & t. Vibrate, shake, tremble, (esp. of voice or musical sound); use trills in singing; sing (note, song) with trills, say (usu. *out*) in trembling tones. Hence ~**ingly**² adv. [f. obs. *quave* cogn. w. QUAKE, QUIVER²+-ER⁵]

quav·er², n. Trill in singing; tremulous-ness in speech, whence ~**y**¹ a.; ‖ (Mus.) note equal in length to half crotchet. [f. prec.]

quay (kē), n. Solid stationary artificial landing-place usu. of stone or iron lying alongside or projecting into water for (un)loading ships. Hence ~AGE(1, 4) (kē·ij) n. [earlier & OF *kay*, cf. Sp. *cayo* shoal, W *cae* hedge, w. assim. to F *quai*]

quean, n. (arch.). Impudent or ill-behaved girl, jade, hussy. [OE *cwene* woman, cf.

Du. *kwēsen* barren cow; cogn. w. Gk *guné* woman & w. QUEEN]

queas'|y [ÿ (-z-), a. (Of food) unsettling the stomach, causing or tending to sickness, fulsome; (of person, his stomach, or his conscience) easily upset, weak of digestion, overscrupulous or tender or delicate, in fastidious condition. Hence ~**INESS** n. [earlier *coisy*; etym. dub.; cf. OF *coisler* hurt]

quebra'chō (kābrah-), n. (Kinds of) American tree yielding very hard timber and medicinal bark; bark of this tree. [Sp., = axe-breaker]

queen¹, n. 1. King's wife (also ~ *consort* for distinction from next sense; ~ *dowager*, wife of late king; ~ *mother*, dowager who is mother of sovereign, & see next sense; also prefixed as title, as *Q~ Elizabeth*). 2. Female sovereign of kingdom (~*mother*, ~having child or children; also prefixed as title, as *Q~ Victoria*; *Q~ Anne is dead*, retort to stale news; *Q~ Anne's* BOUNTY; *Q~ Anne*, in the architectural or decorative style of *Q~ Anne's* time; *Q~ of Scots*, Mary Stuart). 3. Adored female, e.g. the Virgin Mary (*Q~ of grace* etc.); ancient goddess (*Q~ of heaven*, Juno, *of love*, Venus, *of night*, Diana, etc.); person's sweetheart or wife or mistress; majestic woman; belle, mock sovereign, on some occasion (*Q~ of the* MAY² etc.). 4. Personified best example of anything that can be regarded as fem. (*the ~ of watering-places, roses, nurses*). 5. Person, country, etc., regarded as ruling over some sphere (~ *of hearts*, any beautiful woman; ~ *of the Adriatic*, Venice; ~ *of the seas*, Gt Britain; ~ *of the meadows*, meadowsweet). 6. (Also ~ *bee, wasp*, and) perfect female of bee etc. 7. Piece in chess (~'s *bishop, knight, pawn*, etc., those placed nearest ~ at start; ~'s GAMBIT). 8. One of court-cards in each suit. 9.~*cake*, small soft currant cake often heart-shaped; ~*posts*, two upright timbers between tie-beam & principal rafters of roof-truss; || Q~'s BENCH, BOUNTY; || Q~'s COLOUR¹, COUNSEL¹, ENGLISH¹, EVIDENCE, HEAD¹; ~'s *pincushion*, flower of guelder rose; ||~'s SHILLING; ~-*stitch*, fancy stitch in embroidery; ||~'s-*ware*, cream-coloured Wedgwood; ||~'s *weather*, sunshine. Hence ~**DOM**, ~**HOOD**, ~**SHIP**, nn., ~**LESS**, ~**LIKE**, aa. [OE *cwēn*, cf. ON *kven*; cogn. w. QUEAN]

queen², v.t. & i. Make (woman) queen; ~ *it*, play the queen; (Chess) advance (pawn) to opponent's end of board & have it converted to queen or other piece, (intr., of pawn) be converted thus. [f. prec.]

|| **queen'ing**, n. Kind of apple. [-ING³]

queen'|ly, a. Fit for, appropriate to, queen; majestic, queenlike. Hence ~**INESS** n. [-LY¹]

Queens'berry (-z-), n. ~ *Rules*, standard rules of boxing drawn up by 8th Marquis of ~ in 1867.

queer, a., & v.t. 1. Strange, odd, eccentric; of questionable character, shady, suspect; out of sorts, giddy, faint, (esp. *feel* ~); || (sl.) drunk; *in Q~ street* (sl.), in a difficulty, in debt or trouble or disrepute; hence ~**ISH**¹ a., ~**LY**¹ adv., ~**'NESS** n. 2. v.t. (sl.). Spoil, put out of order, (|| esp. ~ *the pitch for one*, spoil his chance beforehand by secret dealings); make feel ~. [perh. f. G *quer* crosswise]

quell, v.t. (poet. & rhet.). Suppress, forcibly put an end to, crush, overcome, reduce to submission, (fear, opposition, rebellion, rebels, etc.). Hence (-)~¹**ER**¹ n. [OE *cwellan*, cf. G *quälen*]

quench, v.t. Extinguish (fire, light, eyesight; chiefly poet. or rhet.); ~ *smoking flax*, cut short promising development (see *Is.* xlii. 3); cool, esp. with water (heat, heated thing; poet. or rhet.); stifle, suppress, (desire, speed, motion; poet. or rhet.); slake (thirst); (sl.) reduce to silence, shut up, (opponent); cool (hot metal) in water. Hence ~**ABLE**, ~**'LESS**, aa. [cf. Fris. *kwinka*]

quen'cher, n. In vbl senses; esp. (sl.) something to drink (usu. a modest ~). [-ER¹]

quenelle' (ke-), n. Seasoned ball of fish or meat reduced to paste. [F, etym. dub.]

quer'ist, n. Person who asks question. [f. L *quaerere* ask, -IST]

quern, n. Hand-mill for grinding corn; small hand-mill for pepper etc.; ~-*stone*, millstone. [OE *cweorn*, cf. Du. *kwern*, Da. *kvern*.]

que'rulous (-rōō-), a. Complaining, peevish. Hence ~**LY**² adv., ~**NESS** n. [f. LL *querulosus* (L *querulus*, f. *queri* complain, -OSE¹)]

que'ry, n., & v.t. & i. 1. (Used abs. to introduce question; abbr. *qu.*) pray, one would like to know; *Q~, or qu., was the money ever paid?*). 2. A question, esp. of the nature of objection (*was prepared to suppress all queries*); mark of interrogation or the word ~ or *qu.* written against statement, or the word ~ interjected in speech, to question accuracy. 3. vb. Ask, inquire, (*whether, if*, etc.); put a question; call (thing) in question in speech or writing, question accuracy of. [anglicized form of QUAERE]

quest¹, n. 1. || Official inquiry or jury etc. making it (now only in vulg. *croaner's ~, coroner's inquest*). 2. Seeking or thing sought by inquiry or search, esp. object of medieval knight's pursuit (*in ~ of*, seeking). [f. OF *queste* f. pop. L p.p. of *quaerere* seek]

quest², v.i. & t. (Of dogs etc.) search for game (often *about*); go (*about*) in search of something; (poet.) search for, seek out. [f. OF *quester* (prec.)]

ques'tion¹ (-chon), n. **1.** Sentence adapted by order of words, use of interrogative pronoun or stop, or other means, to elicit answer, interrogative sentence, (*put a ~ to one*, ask him something; *~ & answer*, alternation of *~s & answers*, catechetic procedure; LEADING² RHETORI-CAL, ~; *indirect, oblique, ~*, made into dependent clause; *~-mark or -stop*, mark of interrogation). **2.** (Raising of) doubt about or objection to thing's truth, credibility, advisability, etc. (*allowed it without ~; beyond all or beyond, out of, past, without, ~*; certainly, undoubtedly; *there is no ~ but that it is so* etc., admit it; (-cho-) adv. & a. **3.** Problem requiring solution, matter or concern depending on conditions of, (EASTERN ~; *a difficult ~*; BEG *the ~; success is merely a ~ of time*, will certainly come, but may come sooner or later; *it is only a ~ of putting enough coffee in*). **4.** Subject being discussed or for discussion, thing to be voted on, (*the person in ~*, that we are referring to; *come into ~*, be discussed, become of practical importance; *that is not the ~*, is irrelevant; *the ~ is*, introducing or recall-ing exact matter of debate; *Q~!* in public assemblies, used to recall speaker from digression; *the PREVIOUS ~; out of the ~*, too impracticable to be worth discussing; *put the ~*, require supporters & opponents of proposal to record their votes, divide meeting etc.; OPEN ~). **5.** (arch.) Torture to elicit confession (*was put to the ~*). [OF f. L *quaestionem* (*quaerere* seek, -TION)]

ques'tion² (-chon), v.t. Ask questions of, interrogate, subject to examination, (person); seek information from study of (phenomenon, facts); call in question, throw doubt upon, raise objections to, (*~ the honesty, accuracy, fitness, etc., of; it cannot be ~ed but that or but*, it is certain that), whence ~ABLE a. (esp., doubtfully true, not clearly consistent with honesty or honour or wisdom), ~ABLY adv., (-cho-). Hence ~ingly² (-cho-) adv. [f. OF *questionner* (prec.)]

ques'tionnaire' (kĕ-, kwĕ-), **ques'tionary** (rare; -cho-), n. Formulated series of questions, an interrogatory. [(-aire F) f. med. L *questionarium*, see QUESTION, -ARY]

quĕt'zăl, n. Beautiful Central-Amer. bird. [Sp. f. Aztec *quetzalli* the bird's tail-feather]

queue (kū), n., & v.t. & i. **1.** Hanging plaited tail of hair or wig, pigtail; line of persons, vehicles, etc., awaiting their turn to be attended to or proceed. **2.** vb. Dress (hair) in ~; (of persons etc.) form up in, join on to, a ~. [F, f. L *cauda* tail]

quib'ble, n., & v.i. **1.** Play on words, pun; equivocation, evasion, unsub-stantial or purely verbal argument etc. esp. one depending on ambiguity of word. **2.** v.i. Use ~s; hence quib'bler¹ n.

quib'ling³ a. [perh. dim. of obs. *quib* f., L *quibus* abl. pl. of *qui* who (familiar f. use in legal documents)]

quick, a., n., & adv. **1.** Living, alive, (arch.; esp. *the ~ & the dead, go down ~ into hell; ~ with child*, orig. *with ~ child*, at stage of pregnancy when motion has been felt). **2.** Vigorous, lively, ready, sensitive, prompt to act, perceive, be affected, learn, think, or invent, (*a ~ eye, ear*, etc., whence ~EYED², ~-EARED³, aa.; *is ~ to take offence; has ~ child*, intelligent; *~ temper*, easily irri-tated, whence ~tempered² a.; *~ sight*, acute or alert, whence ~sighted² a.; ~ N.B. these compounds have stressed when attrib., unstressed when pred.). **3.** Moving rapidly, rapid, swift, done in short time or with little interval, (*~ succession; at a ~ trot; a ~ way of doing it; his ~ growth; a ~ one, a ~ drink; be ~!*, make haste; *did a ~ mile; was followed by a ~ vengeance*), whence ~ly² adv. **4.** *~-change*, (of actor etc.) ~ly changing costume or appearance to play another part; ~'TIME¹; *~ march* (Mil.), march in ~ time (see below; esp. as word of command for starting at usual pace); *~'sand*, (bed of) loose wet sand readily swallowing up ships, animals, etc.; *~'set*, (adj., of hedge) formed of living plants esp. hawthorn set in ground to grow, hedge formed of these; *~'silver*, (n.) mercury (fig.) mobility of temperament or mood; (v.t.) coat (mirror-glass) with amalgam of tin; *~ step*, step used in ~ time (Mil.), rate of marching reckoned at 128 paces of 33 in. to the minute or four miles an hour, the usual British-army rate; *~'step* (Danc-ing), a fast foxtrot. **5.** n. Tender or sensitive flesh below skin or esp. nails, tender part of wound or sore where healthy tissue begins, seat of feeling or emotion, (*bites his nails to the ~; probed it to the ~; the insult stung him to the ~; is a Tory to the ~*, through & through). **6.** adv. (*~er, ~est*, always after vb). At rapid rate, in comparatively short time, (*run as ~ as I could; who will be there ~est?*); (ellipt. for imperat. of *go, come, be, ~*) make haste; *~ly*, soon, (~ part. esp. in -*ing*) ~ly, soon, (*~-fading, -forgotten*, etc.; *~-firing gun*, or *~-fir'ER¹* n. gun with special mechanism for firing shots in ~ succession). [Aryan; OE *cwicu*, cf. Du. *kwik*, G *keck* pert, Skr. *jivá*, L *vivus*, Gk *bios* life]

quick'en, v.t. & i. **1.** Give or restore natural or spiritual life or vigour to, animate, stimulate, rouse, inspire, kindle, whence ~ING² a.; receive, come to, life; (of

woman or embryo) reach QUICK stage in pregnancy; accelerate, make or (of pace, motion, etc.) become quicker. [-EN³]

quick'ie, n. (colloq.). Cheap film made to satisfy the Films Quota Act. [QUICK, -Y³]

quick'ness, n. Readiness or acuteness of perception or apprehension; speed, rapidity, suddenness, (rare; esp. of single gesture or motion); hastiness of temper. [-NESS]

quīcūn̄ (gwē'vătt, n. The~, the Athanasian creed. [initial L wds, = whosoever will]

‖ **quid¹**, n. (sl.; pl. ~). A sovereign, £1, (at two ~ a week). [?]

quid², n. Lump of tobacco held in mouth & chewed. [var. of CUD]

quidd'ity, n. Essence of a thing, what makes a thing what it is; quibble, captious subtlety. [f. med. L quidditas (L quid what, -ITY]

quid'nunc, n. Newsmonger, person given to gossip. [f, L quid what, nunc now]

quid prō quō, n. Blunder made by using or putting one thing for another(nowrare); compensation, return made, consideration, (must ged, must fund him, a ~), [f. L quid something pro for quo something]

quies'cent, a. Motionless, inert, silent, dormant. Hence or cogn. ~ENCE, ~ENCY, nn., ~ently² adv. [f. L quiescere (quies QUIET¹, -ESCENT]

qui'et¹, n. Undisturbed political condition, public tranquillity; silence, stillness; being free from disturbance or agitation or urgent tasks, rest, repose, peace of mind; unruffled deportment, calm. [f. L quies-etis]

qui'et², a. (~er, ~est). With no or slight or gentle sound or motion; of gentle or inactive disposition; (of colour, dress, etc.) unobtrusive, not showy; not overt, private, disguised, (~ resentment; had a ~ dig at him; esp. on the ~, or sl. abbr. on the q.t., secretly); undisturbed, not interfered with or interrupted, free or far from strife or uproar; informal (a ~ dinner-party); enjoyed in quiet, tranquil, not anxious or remorseful. Hence ~nɪ² adv., ~NESS, qui'ETUDE, nn. [f. L quiētus p.p. (QUIESCENT]

qui'et³, v.t. & i. Reduce to quietness, soothe, calm; become quiet (rare; usu. ~ down). [f. med. L quietare (prec.)]

qui'eten, v.t. & i. = prec. (vulg.). [-EN⁶]

qui'etism, n. Passive attitude towards life with devotional contemplation & abandonment of the will as form of religious mysticism, non-resistance principles. So ~ISM(2) n. & a., ~is'tic a. [f. It. quietismo (QUIET² -ISM]

quiet'us, n. Acquittance, receipt, given on payment of account etc. (now rare); release from life, death, extinction, final riddance, (got, gave him, his ~), [f. med. L quietus (est he is) quit (QUIET⁵) used as receipt form]

‖ **quiff**, n. Curl plastered down on the

forehead, formerly affected particularly by soldiers. [etym. dub., cf. COIF]

quill¹, n. Hollow stem of feather, (also ~feather) whole large feather of wing or tail; pen (also ~ pen), plectrum, fishing-float, or toothpick, made of this; one of porcupine's spines; bobbin of hollow reed, any bobbin; musical pipe made of hollow stem; curled-up piece of cinnamon or cinchona bark; ~coverts, feathers covering base of ~feathers; ~driver, clerk or journalist or author. [etym. dub.; cf. LG quiele, G kiel]

quill², v.t. & i. Form into quill-like folds, goffer, whence ~ING¹(2) n.; wind thread or yarn on bobbin. [f. prec.]

‖ **quill'et**, n. (arch.). Quibble, nice distinction. [perh. abbr. of obs. quillity perh. corrupt. of QUIDDITY]

quilt, n., & v.t. 1. Bed-coverlet made of padding enclosed between two layers of linen etc. & kept in place by cross lines of stitching; any coverlet or counterpane (PATCH-work~). 2. v.t. Cover with padded material; make or join together after the manner of a ~; sew up (coin, letters, etc.) between two layers of garment etc.; ‖ compile (literary work) out of extracts or borrowed ideas; (sl.) thrash. Hence ~ING¹(1, 3) n. [f. OF cuilte f. L culcita cushion]

quin'ary, a. Of the number five; consisting of five things. [f. L quinarius (quini distrib. of quinque five, -ARY¹)]

quin'ate, a. (bot.). (Of leaf) composed of five leaflets. [f. L quini (prec., -ATE²]

quince, n. Hard acid yellowish pear-shaped fruit used as preserve or as flavouring, tree bearing it. [orig. pl. of obs. quine, coyn, f. OF cooin f. L cydoneum var. of cydonium neut. of Cydonius of Cydonia in Crete]

quincun̄'cial⁴ (-shl) a., **quincin̄'cially²** (-sha-) adv. [L, = 5/12 (quin-que five, uncia OUNCE), also ~ pattern]

quingenten'ary (-j-; or -jĕn'te-), a. & n. Of, in, 500th year; (n.) 500th anniversary. [f. L quingenti 500 after CENTENARY]

quin'ia, n. (med.). =QUININE. [f. Sp. quina f, Peruv. kina bark]

quinine' (-ēn, -īn), n. Alkaloid found esp. in cinchona bark & used as febrifuge, tonic, & antiperiodic; (pop.) sulphate of ~, the usu. form in which ~ is taken. So **quin'IZE(4)** v.t., **quin'ISM(5)** n. [as prec., -INE⁵]

quinquagena'rian, a. & n. (Person) fifty years old. [f. L quinquagenarius (quin-quageni distrib. of quinquaginta fifty, -ARY¹), -AN]

quinquagèn'arỹ (or -kwǎ'e-), a. & n. = prec. a. & n.; fiftieth anniversary. [prec.]

Quinquagès'ima, n. (Also ~ *Sunday*) Sunday before Lent. [f. med. L ~ (*dies*), lit. 50th (day), so called either as 50th day before Easter by incl. reckoning, or loosely (cf. *sexagesima*, *septuagesima*) as before QUADRAGESIMA]

quinqu(e)-, comb. form of L *quinque* five, in some wds taken f. L, & in many mod., esp. bot. & zool., formations. So ~**ǎng'ūlar** (-ngg-) five-angled; ~**ēcos'tāte** five-ribbed; ~**ēnn'iad**, ~**ēnn'ium** (pl. -*a*), five-year period; ~**ēnn'ial** five-year-long, five-yearly, whence ~**ēnn'ially** adv.; ~**ēlăt'eral** a.; ~**ēlŏb'āte** five-lobed (figure or object); ~**ēpart'īte** divided into, consisting of, five parts; **quinq'ūrēme** ancient galley with five banks of oars; ~**ēvăl'vūlar**, ~**ivalent**; **quinq'ūfid** cleft in five; ~**ivalent** capable of combining with five univalent atoms.

quinquī'na (kinkē², kwinkwī²), n. (Kinds of tree producing) Peruvian bark yielding quinine & other febrifuge alkaloids. [f. Peruv. *kinkina* redupl. form as QUINIA]

quins (-z), n. pl. (colloq.). Five children at a birth. [short for QUINTUPLETS]

quin'sỹ (-z-), n. Inflammation of throat, suppuration of tonsils. Hence ~**IED²** (-id) a. [f. med. L *quinancia* f. Gk *kunagkhē* (*kuōn* -dog, *agkhō* throttle)]

quint (*in sense 2 usu.* kint), n. **1.** Musical interval of fifth; organ-stop of tone one-fifth above normal. **2.** (Piquet) sequence of five of same suit (~ *major*, or ~ *minor*, of knave to seven). [f. F ten: ~ *minor*, of knave to seven). [f. F *quinte* f. L fem. of *quintus* fifth]

quin'tain (-tin), n. (Hist.) (Medieval military exercise of tilting at) post set up as mark & often provided with sandbag to swing round & strike unskilful tilter. [f. OF *quintaine* perh. f. L *quintana* (*quintus* fifth) camp market]

quin'tal, kin—, n. 100 lb.; 112 lb. or hundredweight; 100 kilograms. [OF, f. Arab. *qintār*]

quin'tan, a. & n. (Ague or fever) with paroxysm every fourth (by incl. reckoning fifth) day. [f. L (*febris*) *quintana* (*quintus* fifth), -AN) fifth-day (fever)]

quinte (kǎnht), n. Fifth fencing thrust or parry. [as QUINT]

quintèss'ence, n. **1.** (Ancient Philos.) fifth substance, apart from four elements, composing the heavenly bodies entirely & latent in all things. **2.** Most essential part of any substance, refined extract; purest & most perfect form, manifestation, or embodiment, of some quality or class. Hence **quintessèn'tial** (-shl) a. [f. med. L *quinta essentia*]

quintètte(')', n. (Performers of) piece for five voices or instruments (*piano*, *clarinet*, etc. ~, four stringed instruments plus

instrument named); set of five. [F (-*te*), f. It. *quintetto* (*quinto* fifth f. L *quintus*)]

quintill'ion (-lyon), n. ‖ Fifth power of million (1 with 30 ciphers) (U.S. & France) cube of million (1 with 18 ciphers). [L *quintus* fifth, MILLION]

quin'tūp'le, a., n., & v.t. ~**lỹ**, adv., ~**lět**, n.; **quintūp'licāte** (-āt), a. & n., (-at), v.t., **quintūplicā'tion**, n. Fivefold etc. (for detailed senses see QUADRUPLE & wds in *quadrupl*-, substituting *five* for *four*). [~*uple* F, f, L *quintus* fifth, after QUADRUPLE]

‖ **quin'tus**. See PRIMUS¹.

quip, n., & v.i. (-pp-). Sarcastic remark, clever hit, smart saying, verbal conceit; equivocation, quibble; (v.i.) make ~s. [var. of obs. *quippy* perh. f. L *quippe* forsooth]

quipu (kē²prŏŏ, kwē-), n. Ancient-Peruvian substitute for writing by variously knotting threads of various colours. [Peruv., = knot]

quire², n. Four sheets of paper etc. folded to form eight leaves as in medieval MSS.; any collection of leaves one within another in MS. or book (*in* ~*s*, unbound, in sheets); 24 sheets of writing-paper. [f. OF *quaer*, now *cahier* see QUATERNARY]

Quir'inal, n. (Used for) the Italian Government or Court (esp. as opp. VATI-CAN). [name of palace]

quirk, n. Quibble, quip; trick of action or behaviour; twist or flourish in drawing or writing; (Archit.) acute hollow between convex part of moulding & soffit or fillet. [etym. dub.; from 16th c.]

*****quirt**, n., & v.t. Short-handled riding-whip with braided leather lash; (v.t.) lash with this. [prob. f. Sp. *cuerda* cord]

quis'ling (-z-), n. Person co-operating with an enemy who has occupied his country, (pop.) traitor. Hence ~**ITE¹** a. & n. [f. Q~, renegade Norwegian Army officer]

quit¹, pred. a. Free, clear, absolved, (arch.; *the others can go* ~; *was* ~ *for a ducking*, got off with that); rid of (*glad to be* ~ *of the trouble*); ~*claim*, (n.) renunciation of right, (v.t.) renounce claim to, give up (thing) *to* ; ~*rent*, (usu. small) rent paid by freeholder or copyholder in lieu of service. [f. OF *quit(t)e* f. L *quietus* QUIET¹]

quit², v.t. (~*ted*, rarely ~ exc. U.S.). **1.** Rid oneself of (arch.). **2.** (refl.) (Usu. w. archaic ref. pron. without *self*) behave, acquit, conduct, oneself well etc. (esp. *you like men*; arch.). **3.** Give up, let go, abandon, (~ *hold of*, loose; ~ *office* etc.); ~*cease*, stop, as ~ *grumbling*. **4.** Depart from, leave, (place, person, etc.; ~*ted Paris at midnight*; ~*ted him in anger*); (abs., of tenant) leave occupied premises (esp. *give*, *have*, etc., *notice to* ~). **5.**

(poet.). Requite, repay, clear off, (~ *love with hate*; *death ~s all scores*). Hence **~'**t'ER¹, n, one who deserts his job or his post, shirker, poltroon. [f. OF *quit(t)er* QUIER³]

qui tám, n. (legal). (Action brought by) informer. [L, = *who as well* (for the King as for himself sues)]

quitch, n. (Also ~-*grass*) COUCH³-*grass*. [OE *cwice*, cf. Du. *kweek*, G *queeke*]

quite, adv. Completely, wholly, entirely, altogether, to the utmost extent, nothing short of, in the fullest sense, positively, absolutely, (~ *covers it*; *was ~ by myself*; ~ *other*, very different; ~ *another*, a very different; *is ~ a hero, disappointment, good thing*; *I ~ like him*; *is ~ too delightful*, colloq., i.e. to be done justice to in words; *is ~ the thing*, fashionable; *not ~ proper* rather improper; ||(ellipt., colloq.) *he, she, isn't ~*, *he, she, isn't ~ a gentleman, lady*; ~ *so* (& improp. ~), I grant the truth of that. [f. obs. *quite* a. = QUIT¹]

quits, pred. a. On even terms by retaliation or repayment (*will be ~ with him yet*, will have revenge; *now we are ~*; *cry ~*, acknowledge that things are now even, agree not to proceed further in quarrel etc.; DOUBLE² *or* ~). [perh. abbr. of med. L *quittus*=*quietus* QUIT¹; or = QUIT¹-=ES]

quitt'ance, n. (arch., poet.). Release from something; acknowledgement, receipt, (*omittance is no* ~, debt is not annulled by not being pressed); requital. [f. OF *quitance* (*quiter* QUIT²]

quiv'er¹, n. Case for holding arrows (*have an arrow, shaft, left in one's* ~, not be resourceless; ~ *full of children*, large family, see Ps. cxxvii. 5). Hence ~FUL(2) n. [f. OF *quivre* f. Teut. (OE *cocer*, cf. G *köcher*)]

quiv'er², v.i. & t., & n. **1.** Tremble or vibrate with slight rapid motion (of person, leaf, wing, voice, light, etc.; *with emotion*, *in the wind* etc.); (of birds, esp. skylark) make (wings) ~; hence ~ing₁y adv. **2.** n. ~ing motion or sound. [prob. imit., cf. QUAVER]

qui vive (kēvēv'). *On the* ~, on the alert, watching for something to happen. [F, =lit. (*long*) *live who?*, i.e. *on whose side are you?*, as sentry's challenge]

Quix'ote, n. Enthusiastic visionary, pursuer of lofty but impracticable ideals, person utterly regardless of his material interests in comparison with honour or devotion. Hence quixŏt'ıc a. (*quixotics* n. pl., quixotic sentiments), quixŏt'ı-CALLY adv., quix'otısm(2), quix'otRY(4), nn., quix'otıze(2, 3) v.t. & i. [hero of Cervantes's *Don* ~]

quiz, n., & v.t. (-zz-). **1.** || Odd or eccentric person, person of ridiculous appearance, (now rare); person given to ~zing; (orig. U.S.) interrogation, questionnaire, examination; hoax, ridicule, thing done to expose or burlesque another's oddities

(now rare); hence ~z'ICAL a., ~z'ıcally² adv. **2.** v.t. Make sport of (person or his ways), whence ~z'ABLE a.; regard with mocking air; look curiously at, observe the ways or oddities of, survey through an eye-glass or (now rare) ~*zing-glass*; *examine by questioning; hence ~z'ing-ly² adv. [?]

quŏ'dd, prep. As regards; ~ *hoc*, in this respect, so far as this goes. [L (*quo* whither, *ad* to)]

quŏd¹, n., & v.t. (sl.; -dd-). Prison (*in, out of*, ~); (v.t.) imprison. [?]

quŏd², neut. of L *qui* which (~ *érát démŏnstrán'dum* abbr. Q.E.D., ~ *érát facién'dum* (-shi-) abbr. Q.E.F., ~ *érát inveniēn'dum* abbr. Q.E.I., which was the thing to be proved, made or done, found; formulae in geometrical demonstrations, &c. esp. Q.E.D., in gen. use; ~ *vid'é*, abbr. q.v., which see, in cross & other references).

quoin (koin), n., & v.t. **1.** External angle of building; stone or brick forming angle, corner-stone, whence~'ıng-¹(3)n.; internal corner of room; wedge for locking type in forme, raising level of gun, keeping barrel from rolling, etc. **2.** v.t. Secure or raise with ~s. [var. of COIN]

quoit (koit, kwoit), n., & v.t. & i. Heavy flattish sharp-edged iron ring thrown to encircle iron peg or to stick in ground near it in game of ~s; (vb; rare) fling like ~, *play* ~s. [?]

quŏn'dam, a. That once had but no longer has the specified character, sometime, former, (*a ~ friend of mine*). [L, =formerly]

quŏr'um, n. Fixed number of members that must be present to make proceedings of assembly or society or board valid. [L, =*of whom* (we will that you etc. be)]

quŏt'a, n. Share that individual person or company is bound to contribute to or entitled to receive from a total; ~ QUICKIE. [f. L *quota* (*pars*) how great (a part); fem. of *quotus* how-manyeth (*quot* how many)]

quoťa'tion, n. (Print.). quadrat used for filling up blanks; quoting, passage quoted; amount stated as current price of stocks or commodities; ~-*marks*, inverted commas & apostrophes, single (' ') or double (" "), used to mark beginning & end of quoted passage. [f. med. L *quotatio* (QUOTE, -ATION)]

quŏt'ative, a. Of quoting; given to quotation. [foll., -ATIVE]

quŏte, v.t., & n. **1.** Cite or appeal to (author, book) in confirmation of some view, repeat or copy out passage(s) from; repeat or copy out (borrowed passage) usu. with indication that it is borrowed, (abs.) make quotations, (*from* author; book, speech, etc.); adduce or cite *as*; state price of (usu. *at* figure); hence quŏt'ABLE, ~'WORTHY, aa. **2.** n. (colloq.) Passage quoted; (usu. pl.) quotation-

mark(s). [earlier sense *mark-with numbers*, f. med. L *quotāre* (QUOTA)]

quoth, v.t. 1st & 3rd pers. past indic. (arch.). Said *I, he, she,* & rarely *we* or *they* (placed amidst, after, or before the words quoted; *quoth'a*, arch. for ~ *he*, used in quoting contemptuously=for-sooth). [past of obs. *quethe*, OE *cwethan*; cf. OHG *quedan*]

quotid'ian, a. & n. 1. Daily, of every day, (~ *fever, ague*, recurring every day); 2. commonplace, trivial. 2. n. ~ ague or fever. [f. L *quotidianus* (*quotidie* daily, -AN)]

quŏ̄ wearrī'tŏ (wŏ-), n. (hist.). Writ, formerly issued by the King's Bench Division calling on a person to show by what warrant he held or exercised an office or franchise. [med. L, = by what warrant]

quŏ'tient (-shnt), n. Result given by dividing one quantity by another. [erron. f. L *quotiens* how many times, by confusion w. -ENT]

R

R (är), letter (pl. Rs, R's). *The* r *months*, those with r in their names (Sep-Ap.) as season for oysters; *the three* Rs, reading, (writing, &) (a)rithmetic, as basis of elementary education.

rabb'et, n., & v.t. 1. Step-shaped reduction cut along edge or face or projecting angle of wood etc. usu. to receive edge or tongue of another piece. 2. Elastic beam arranged to give rebound to hammer striking it in ascent. 3. v.t. Join or fix with ~, make ~ in. [f. OF *rabat* abatement, recess, (*rabattre* REBATE[1])]

rabb'i, n. Jewish doctor of the law (as form of address by itself or prefixed to name, or as ordinary noun), esp. one authorized by ordination to deal with law & ritual & perform certain functions; *Chief* R~, || ecclesiastical head of British Jewish communities. [L, f. Gk f. Heb. =my master(*rabh* master+pronom.suf.)]

rabb'in, n. Rabbi (usu. *the* ~s, chief Jewish authorities on law & doctrine, most of them between 2nd & 13th cc.). Hence ~ATE[1], ~ISM(3), ~IST(2, 3), nn., **rabbin'ICAL** a., **rabbin'ically** adv. [F (prec.); n perh. originated as supposed Heb. pl. term]

rabb'it[1], n., & v.i. 1. Burrowing rodent of hare family, brownish-grey in natural state, also black or white or pied in domestication; || (colloq.) a poor performer at any game (esp. cricket, golf, or lawn tennis); ~*hutch, -warren*; WELSH[1] ~; hence ~y[2] a. 2. v.i. Hunt ~s. [cf. Walloon *robett*, Flem. *robbe*]

rabb'it[2], v.t. (vulg.). *Odd=it* etc., form of imprecation. [perh. alteration of -*rat* in DRAT]

rabb'le[1], n. Disorderly crowd, mob; con-

temptible or inferior set of people; the lower part of the populace. [etym. dub.; earlier sense *pack* or *string of animals* etc.]

rabb'le[2], n. Iron bar with bent end for stirring molten metal. [f. F *râble* f. L *rutābulum* (*ruere rut-* rake up) fire-shovel]

rabb'lement (-lm-), n. (now rare). (Tumult as of) a rabble. [-MENT]

Rabelais'ian -aes'ian, (-zyǎn), a. & n. 1. Of, like, Rabelais or his writings, marked by exuberant imagination & language & coarse humour & satire. 2. n. Admirer or student of Rabelais. [*Rabelais*, French humorist, -IAN]

rab'id, a. Furious, violent, (~ *hate*); unreasoning, insensate, headstrong, (~ *democrat*); (esp. of dog) affected with rabies, mad; of rabies. Hence rabid'ITY, ~NESS, nn., ~LY[2] adv. [f. L *rabidus* (*rabere* rave)]

rab'ies (-z), n. Canine madness, hydrophobia. [L (prec.)]

race[1], v.t. & n. 1. Onward sweep or movement, esp. strong current in sea or river (*tide set with a strong* ~; *the* Ra~ *of Alderney* etc.). 2. Course of sun or moon, course of life, (*ere he had run half his*~). 3. Channel of stream (esp. in comb., as *mill-*~). 4. Contest of speed between runners, ships, horses, etc., or persons doing anything; (pl.) series of these for horses at fixed time on regular course (SELLING ~); ~*ball*, dance held in connexion with ~s; ~-*card*, programme of ~s; ~*course*, ground for horse-racing; ~*horse*, bred or kept for racing; ~-*meeting*, horse-racing fixture. [f. ON *rás*, cf. OE *ræs* swift motion]

race[2], v.i. & t. Compete in speed with; indulge in horse-racing (*a racing man; the racing world, the turf*); go at full speed, (of propeller, paddle-wheel, etc.) work violently from diminished resistance=move out of the water; have race with, try to surpass in speed; cause (horse etc.) to ~ (~*d his bicycle against a motor-car*); make (person, thing) move at full speed (~*d me along at five miles an hour;* ~*d the Bill through the House*); fling (fortune etc.) away on horse-racing. [f. prec.]

race[3], n. 1. Group of persons or animals or plants connected by common descent; posterity of (person); house, family, tribe or nation regarded as of common stock; distinct ethnical stock (*the Caucasian, Mongolian,* etc., ~); genus or species or breed or variety of animals or plants, any great division of living creatures (*the human, feathered, four-footed, finny,* etc., ~). 2. Descent, kindred, (*of noble, Oriental,* etc., ~; *separate in language &* ~). 3. Class of persons etc., with some common feature (*the* ~ *of poets, dandies,* etc.). [f. F. It. *razza* etym. dub.]

race[4], n. Root (of ginger). [f. OF *rais* f. L *radicem* nom.-*īx* root]

racème, n. (bot.). Flower-cluster with the separate flowers attached by short equal stalks at equal distances along central stem. Hence **racémose**[1] a. (bot.), also anat. of compound glands). [f. L *racemus* grape-bunch]

rā'cer, n. In vbl senses: esp.: racehorse, yacht, bicycle, etc., used for racing; circular horizontal rail along which the traversing-platform of a heavy gun moves. [-ER[1]]

rā'chis, rhā-, (-k-), n. (pl. *-ides* pr. *-ēz*). Stem of grasses etc. bearing flower-stalks at short intervals; axis of pinnately compound leaf or frond; vertebral column or cord from which it develops, whence **rā'chi(o)-** (-k-) comb. form; feather-shaft, the part that bears the barbs. [f. Gk *rhakhis* spine; the E pl. *-ides* is irreg.]

rachit'is (-k-), n. (Learned form for) RICKETS. [f. Gk *rhakhitis* (prec., -ITIS)]

rā'cial (-shl), a. Of, in regard to, due to, race. Hence **~ISM** (-sha-) n., tendency to ~ feeling, antagonism between different races of men, **~LY**[2] adv. [RACE[3], -IAL]

rack[1], n., & v.i. 1. Driving clouds; (vb: of clouds) drive before wind. 2. Destruction (usu. *go to ~ & ruin*). [with sense 1 cf. Norw. & Sw. dial. *rak* wreckage; sense 2 perh. var. of WRACK, WRECK]

rack[2], n., & v.t. & i. 1. Fixed or movable frame of wooden or metal bars for holding fodder; framework with rails, bars, pegs, or shelves, for keeping articles on or in (*plate, hat, tool, pipe*, etc., ~); cogged or indented bar or rail gearing with wheel or pinion or worm, or serving with pegs etc. to adjust position of something; **~railway**, with cogged rail between bearing rails; **~-wheel**, cog-wheel. 2. vb. Fill up stable with hay or straw for the night (also trans.; ~ *up horse*, provide it thus); fasten (horse) up to ~; place in or on ~. [prob. f. MDu. *rec* (Du. *rek*, cf. G *reck*) rail etc. (*recken* stretch)]

rack[3], v.t., & n. 1. Stretch joints of (person) by pulling esp. with instruments of torture made for the purpose; (of disease or bodily or mental agony) inflict torture on (*a ~ing headache*; ~*ed with pain*); shake violently, injure by straining, task severely, (*cough that seemed to ~ his whole body*; ~ *one's brains for something to say, a plan*, etc.). 2. Exact utmost possible amount of (rent), exhaust (tenants) with excessive rent, exhaust (land) with excessive use; **~-rent**, (n.) extortionate rent equal or nearly equal to full value of land, (v.t.) exact this from (tenant) or for (land); **~-renter**, tenant paying or landlord exacting ~-rent. 3. n. Instrument of torture, a frame with roller at each end to which victim's wrists & ankles were tied so that his joints were stretched when rollers were turned (*on the ~, being ~ed*, lift, or fig. of person in distress or under strain). [prob. f. MDu. *recken* stretch]

rack[4], n. Arrack (esp. ~ *punch*). [for ARRACK]

rack[5], n., & v.i. 1. Horse's gait between trot & canter, both legs of one side being lifted almost at once, & all four feet being off ground together at moments. 2. v.i Progress thus. [?]

rack[6], v.t. Draw off (wine etc.) from the lees (often *off*). [f. Pr. *arracar* (*raca* stems & husks of grapes, dregs]

rack'et[1], **răc'quet** (-kĭt), n. Cat-gutted bat used in tennis, rackets, etc.; (pl.) ball-game for two or four persons played in plain four-walled court with ~s; snow-shoe resembling ~; **~-ball**, small hard kid-covered ball of cork & string; **~-press**, for keeping ~s taut & in shape; **~-tail**, kinds of small bird with ~-shaped tail. [f. F *raquette* etym. dub.]

rack'et[2], n., & v.i. 1. Disturbance, uproar, din; social excitement, gaiety, dissipation. 2. (sl.) Dodge, game, line of business, lay; (orig. U.S.) scheme for obtaining money, or effecting some other object, by illegal (and often violent) means, so **~eer**[1]**ING**[1] n., organized black-mall of traders etc. by intimidation & violence, **~EER'** n., one who practises this. 3. Ordeal, trying experience; (*stand the ~*, come successfully through test, face consequences of action); hence **~y**[2] a. 4. v.i. Live gay life (often *about*), move about noisily. [prob. imit.]

raconteur (see Ap.), n. (fem. *-euse*). Teller of anecdotes (usu. *good, skilful*, etc., ~). [F]

rac(o)oon', n. Greyish-brown furry bushy-tailed sharp-snouted American nocturnal carnivore. [Algonquin]

rā'cy, a. Having the qualities that characterize the kind in high degree (esp. ~*y flavour*); of distinctive quality or vigour, not smoothed into sameness or commonness, retaining traces of origin (esp. ~*y of the soil*, of homely directness, spirited, lively, piquant). Hence **~ILY**[2] adv., **~INESS** n. [RACE[3], -Y[2]]

rād. See RADICAL n.

rā'dar, n. System for ascertaining direction & range of aircraft, ships, coasts, and other objects, by means of the electro-magnetic waves which they reflect; apparatus used for this. [f. initial letters of *radio detection and ranging*]

răd'dle, n., & v.t. 1. Red ochre. 2. v.t. Paint with ~; plaster with rouge. [var. of RUDDLE]

rād'ial, a. & n. 1. Of, in, rays; arranged like rays or radii, having position or direction of a radius (~ *axle*, maintaining such direction to curve of track as car etc. travels round it); having spokes or radiating lines, whence **~ized** (-zd) a., **~izā'tion** n.; acting or moving along lines that diverge from a centre; relating

to the radius of the forearm (~ *artery*, ~ *vein*, *nerve*); hence ~IY² adv. **2.** n. ~ nerve or artery. [RADIUS, RADIUM, -AL]

rād'ian, n. Angle at centre of circle subtended by an arc whose length is equal to the radius. [RADIUS, -AN]

rād'iant, a. & n. **1.** Emitting rays of light, (of eyes or looks) beaming with joy or hope or love, (of light) issuing in rays, (of beauty) splendid or dazzling; whence or cogn. **rād'IANCE**, **rād'IANCY** (rare), nn., ~LY² adv.; operating radially (esp. ~ *heat*); (Bot. etc.) extending radially; radiating; ~ *point*, (Astron.) apparent focal point of meteoric shower. **2.** n. Point or object from which light or heat radiates; (Astron.) ~ point. [f. L *radiare* (RADIUS), -ANT]

rād'iate¹, a. Having divergent rays or parts radially arranged. Hence ~LY² adv. [as foll., -ATE²]

rād'iate², v.i. & t. Emit rays of light or heat, (of light or heat) issue in rays; transmit electro-magnetic waves; diverge or spread from central point; emit (light or heat) from centre; disseminate (life, love, joy, etc.). Hence or cogn. ~A'TION n., ~ATIVE a. [f. L *radiare* (RADIUS), -ATE³]

rād'iātor, n. In vbl senses; esp.: small chamber heated with hot air or otherwise & radiating warmth into room etc.; engine-cooling apparatus in motor-car. [-OR²]

rād'ical, a. & n. **1.** Of the root(s). **2.** Naturally inherent, essential, fundamental, (~ *humour*, *heat*, etc., in medieval philos. & still joc., moisture, heat, etc., essential to life; *a ~ error*; *the ~ rottenness of human nature*); (the ~ *idea* or *principles of a system*). **4.** Affecting the foundation, going to the root, root-&-branch, (~ *change*, *cure*, *reform*); (of politicians) desiring such reforms, || belonging to extreme section of Liberal party, (of measures etc.) advanced by or according to principles of ~ politicians, whence ~ISM(2) n., ~IZE(3) v.t. & i., ~IZA'TION n. **5.** (Math.) of the root of a number or quantity (~ *sign*, √, ∛, ∜, etc., indicating that square, cube, fourth, etc. root of number following is to be extracted). **6.** (Philol.) of the roots of words (~ *word*, not analysable into root & other known element). **7.** (Mus.) belonging to the root of a chord. **8.** (Bot.) of, springing direct from the root or the main stem close to it; hence ~LY² adv. **9.** n. (Philol.) root; fundamental principle; (Math.) quantity forming or expressed as root of another; also the ~ sign; (Chem.) element or atom, or group of these, forming base of compound & remaining unaltered during compound's ordinary chemical changes; (Pol.) also colloq. *rǎd*) person holding ~ views or belonging to ~ party. [f. Ll. *radicalis* (*radīx -īcis* root, -AL)]

-ANT]

rād'io-, comb. form of L RADIUS & E RADIUM, w. sense of *the radius*, *of rays or of radiation*, *of radium*, as: ~o-*carp'al*, of radius & wrist; ~o-*ac'tive*, undergoing spontaneous atomic disintegration, usu. with emission of rays & corpuscles capable of penetrating opaque bodies, affecting photographic plates, etc., (of rays) emitted by such bodies & having these properties, so ~o-*activ'ity*; ~o-*bol'ance*, instrument for measuring intensity of heat radiation; ~ogoniom'eter, apparatus for finding the direction of ships & aircraft from their wireless signals; ~ogram, picture obtained by X-rays, (also) = ~o-*telegram*, (also, in full ~o-*gram'ophone*) combined wireless receiving-set & gramophone reproducing records through loud speaker; ~ograph, instrument recording intensity & duration of sunshine, (also) ~og'raphy, ~og'rapher, ~og'raphy, ~ol'ogy, scientific study of X-rays, ~o-*loca'tion*, = RADAR; ~o-*therapy*, etc., so ~ol'ogist, ~olo'gical; ~om'eter, instrument illustrating conversion of radiant energy into mechanical force, (also) instrument for measuring intensity of radiation; ~o-*phone*, production of sound by radiant light or heat; ~os'copy, examination by X-rays or other forms of radiation, so ~o-*tel'egram*, message by wireless telegraphy; ~o-*the'rapy*, treatment of disease with X-rays or other forms of radiation, so ~o-*the'rapeut'ic(s)*.

rād'ish, n. (Cruciferous plant with) fleshy pungent root often eaten raw as relish in salads. [f. F *radis* f. L *radicem* root]

rād'ium, n. Radio-active metallic element obtained from pitchblende, widely used in radio-therapy; ~ *emanation*, RADON; ~-*therapy*, treatment of disease by the use of ~ or its products, [-UM]

rād'ius, n. (pl. -ĭī). **1.** Thicker & shorter bone of forearm in man, corresponding bone in beast's foreleg or bird's wing. **2.** (math.). Straight line from centre to circumference of circle or sphere; radial line from focus to any point of curve (~ *vector*, variable line drawn to curve from fixed point, esp. in Astron. from sun or planet to path of satellite). **3.** Any of a set of lines diverging from a point like

rād'icle, n. Part of plant embryo that develops into primary root; rootlet; (Anat.) rootlike subdivision of nerve or vein; (Chem.)—prec. n. Hence **radic'ūLAR¹** a. [f. L *radicula* (prec., -ULE)]

rād'io, n. (pl. ~s), & v.t. & i. (orig. U.S.). **1.** Wireless telegraphy or telephony; message so sent; broadcasting; a wireless receiving-set; (attrib.) designed for wireless telephony etc., sent by wireless. **2.** vb. Send (message), communicate, broadcast, by ~. [Short for *radiotelegraphy*]

radii of circle; object of this kind, e.g. spoke. **4.** Circular area as measured by its ~ (*knows everyone within a ~ of 20 miles*; ∥ *the four-mile ~*, that of which Charing Cross is centre). **5.** (Bot.) outer rim of composite flowerhead, e.g. daisy, also radiating branch of umbel. [L., = staff, spoke, ray]

rād'ix, n. (pl. *-ices* pr. *-ĭsēz*). Number or symbol used as basis of numeration scale (*ten is the ~ of decimal numeration, & of common logarithms*); source or origin of. [L., = root]

rād'ŏn, n. Gaseous radio-active element arising from the disintegration of radium (formerly known as *nīton*). [f. RADIUM after *argon* etc.]

Raffaelesque. = RAPHAELESQUE.

Raff'ia, n. Kind of palm; fibre from its leaves used for tying up plants and making hats, baskets, mats, etc. [Malagasy]

raff'ish, a. Disreputable, dissipated, fast-looking. Hence ~LY² adv., ~NESS n. [-ISH¹]

raff'le¹ n. & v.i. & t. **1.** Sale of article by taking entrance-fee from any number of persons & assigning it by lot to one of them. **2.** vb. Enter one's name in ~ *for* article; sell by ~. [earlier sense *kind of dice-game* f. F *rafle* etym. dub.]

raff'le², n. Rubbish, refuse, lumber, debris. [cf. OF *rifle ou rafle* anything whatever]

raft¹ (-ah-), n., & v.i. & t. **1.** Collection of logs, casks, etc., fastened together in the water for transportation; flat floating structure of timber or other materials for conveying persons or things, esp. as substitute for boat in emergencies; floating accumulation of trees, ice, etc.; ~-*s'man*, worker on ~. **2.** vb. Transport as or on ~; form into a ~; cross (water) on ~(s); work~. [f. ON *raptr* RAFTER²]

raf'ter¹ (-ah-), n. Man who rafts timber. [-ER²]

raf'ter² (-ah-), n., & v.t. **1.** One of the sloping beams forming framework on which slates etc. of roof are upheld. **2.** v.t. (Usu. in p.p.) provide with ~s; ∥ plough (land) so that contents of furrow are turned over on same breadth of unploughed ground next it, half-plough. [OE *ræfter*, cf. MLG *rafter*, ON *raptr*]

rag¹, n. **1.** Torn or frayed piece of woven material, one of the irregular scraps to which cloth etc. is reduced by wear & tear (*in ~s*, torn); (pl.) tattered clothes (*in ~s*, in old clothes); GLAD ~s; (usu. with neg.) smallest scrap of cloth or sail (*not a ~ to cover him*; *spread every ~ of sail*); (collect.) ~s used as material for paper, stuffing, etc. **2.** Remnant, odd scrap, irregular piece, (*flying ~s of cloud*; *cooked to ~s*, till it falls to pieces; *not a ~ of evidence*). **3.** (derog.) Flag, handkerchief, curtain, newspaper, etc. **4.** Jagged projection (rare). **5.** ~-*baby*, doll made of ~s; ~-*bag*, in which scraps of linen etc. are kept for use; ~-*bolt*, (n.) with barbs to keep it tight when driven in, (v.t.) join together with these; ~ *fair*, old-clothes sale held in Houndsditch; ~*paper*, made of ~s; ~*tag*, ~*tag & bob-tail*, the riff-raff, ragged or low or disreputable people; ~*time*, popular music of U.S. negro origin with much syncopation, (attrib.) farcical (*a ~time army*); ~-*wheel*, with projections catching in links of chain that passes over it, sprocket-wheel; ~*wort*, yellow-flowered ragged-leaved plant. [f. ON *rogg* tuft of fur]

rag², n. Large coarse roofing-slate; ∥ kinds of hard coarse stone breaking up in thick slabs (see CORAL.~, *Kentish*, *Rowley*, ~). [?]

∥ **rag³**, v.t. & i. (-gg-), & n. (sl.). **1.** Scold, reprove severely; tease, torment, play rough jokes upon, disarrange (person's room etc.) by way of practical joke; engage in bally-ragging, be noisy & riotous. **2.** n. Noisy disorderly scene. [cf. BALLYRAG]

rag'amuffin, n. Ragged dirty fellow. Hence ~LY¹ a. [prob. f. RAG¹ w. fancy termination]

rage¹, n. **1.** (Fit of) violent anger; violent operation of some natural force or some sentiment (*the ~ of the wind, of faction*). **2.** Vehement desire or passion for (*has a ~ for*, or *for collecting, first editions*); object of widespread temporary enthusiasm or fashion (*Mrs Siddons, the open-air cure, was the or all the ~*). **3.** Poetic or prophetic or martial ardour. [F, f. LL *rabia* f. L RABIES]

rage², v.i. & refl. Rave, storm, speak madly or furiously, (*at, against*, or abs.), be full of anger; (of wind, sea, passion, feeling, battle, pain, disease, etc.) be violent, be at the height, operate unchecked, prevail, whence **rā'ging**~² adv.; (refl., esp. of storm etc.) ~ *itself out*, cease raging. [f. F *rager* (prec.)]

ragg'ed (-g-), a. Rough, shaggy, hanging in tufts; of broken jagged outline or surface, full of rough or sharp projections; faulty, imperfect, wanting finish or smoothness or uniformity, (*~ rhymes, time* in rowing, etc.); rent, torn, frayed, (of persons) *in ~ clothes*; ~*robin*, crimson-flowered wild plant; ∥ ~ *school* (obs.), free school for poor children. Hence ~LY² adv., ~NESS n. [RAG¹, -ED²; cf. Norw. *ragget* shaggy]

rag(g)ee (rah'gē), n. A coarse kind of millet, the staple food in parts of India. [Hind. *rāgī*]

Rāg'lan, n. Overcoat without shoulder seams, the sleeve running up to the neck; also attrib., as ~ *sleeve*. [f. Lord ~, commander in Crimean war]

ragout' (-ōō), n. & v.t. Meat in small pieces stewed with vegetables & highly

seasoned; (vb) cook thus. [f. F *ragoût* (*ragoûter* revive taste of, see RE², ROAST¹)]

ra'hat lakoum' (rah-h-, -ōōm), n. Kinds of Turkish sweetmeat, esp. TURKISH *delight*. [Turk.]

raid, n., & v.i. & t. **1.** Sudden attack made by military party (orig. of mounted men), ship(s), or aircraft; predatory incursion in which surprise & rapidity are usu. relied upon, foray, inroad; sudden descent of police upon suspected premises or illicit goods. **2.** vb. Make ~ *into* etc.; make ~ *on* (person, place, cattle); hence ~'ER¹ n. [Sc. form of OE *ráid* GUST²)]

rail¹, n., & v.t. & i. **1.** Horizontal or inclined bar or continuous series of bars of wood or metal used to hang things on, as top of banisters, as part of fence, as protection against contact or falling over, or for similar purpose. **2.** Any horizontal piece (cf. STILE²) in frame of panelled door. **3.** Iron bar or continuous line of bars laid on ground as one side or half of ~way track (*off the ~s*, disorganized, out of order, not working right; *by ~*, *by* ~way); (pl.; St. Exch.) ~way shares. **4.** ~*chair*, iron holder, attached to sleeper, in which railway~ rests; ~*head*, farthest point reached by a ~way under construction. (Mil.) point on ~way at which road transport of supplies begins; ~*motor*, self-propelled ~way coach (also attrib.); *~*road*, (n.) ~way, (v.t.) rush (person, thing) *to*, *into*, *through*, etc.; ~*way*, || road laid with ~s for heavy horse-carts, track or set of tracks of iron or steel ~s for passage of trains of cars drawn by locomotive engine & conveying passengers & goods, (also ~way line) the tracks of this kind worked by single company or the whole of the organization & persons required for their working, (attrib. in many phrr., as ~*way accident*; ~*way act*, regulating duties & rights of ~way companies; ~*way bill*, proposal in Parliament esp. for constructing new ~way; ~*way bridge, carriage, company*; ~*way speed*, very quickly; ~*way rug*, ~*way stock, system, train, travelling, tunnel*), whence ~'WAYLESS a., ~way v.i., travel by ~; hence ~'LESS a. **5.** vb. Furnish or enclose (place) with ~ (often *in*, *off*); provide (bench etc.) with ~, whence ~'ING¹ [-ING¹³, 4)] n.; lay (~way route) with ~s; convey (goods), travel, by ~. [f. OF *reille* (L *regula* RULE)]

rail², n. Kinds of bird, esp. LAND~, *water*~. [f. F *râle*, etym. dub.]

rail³, v.i. Use abusive language (usu. *at against*, or arch. *upon*). Hence ~'ER¹ n., ~'ing² [-ING¹(1)] n., ~'ing³ adv. [f. F *railler*, etym. dub.]

rail'lery, n. (Piece of) good-humoured ridicule, rallying. [f. F *raillerie* (prec., -ERY)]

rail'ment, n. (poet. & rhet.). Clothing,

dress, apparel. [f. obs. *arrayment* (ARRAY¹ -MENT)]

rain¹, n. **1.** Condensed moisture of atmosphere falling visibly in separate drops, fall of such drops (~ *or shine*, whether it rains or not); (pl.) showers of ~, esp. *the R~s*, rainy season in tropical countries, (Naut.; *the R~s*, rainy region of Atlantic 4-10° N. lat.; (~like descent of) falling liquid or solid particles or bodies (*a ~ of ashes, frogs, pearls, rice, fire*; also fig., *a ~ of melody, kisses, congratulations*); ~*bird*, kinds of bird, esp. Green Wood-pecker; ~*boa*, theatre contrivance imitating sound of ~; ~*coat*, water-proof; ~*doctor*, producer of ~ by magic; ~*drop*, single drop of ~; ~*fall*, shower, quantity of ~ falling within given area in given time (usu. in inches of depth per annum); ~*gauge*, instrument measuring ~fall; ~*glass*, barometer; ~*water*, collected from ~, not got from wells etc.; ~*worm*, common earthworm. Hence ~'LESS, ~'PROOF², ~'TIGHT, aa. [com-. Teut.; OE *regn*, *rēn*, cf. Du. & G *regen*]

rain², v.i. & t. *It ~s*, rain comes down (*it ~ed hooks, frogs, invitations, tracts*, etc., there was a shower of them; *it ~s cats & dogs*, violently; *it never ~s but it pours*, events usu. happen several together; *it ~s in*, rain penetrates house etc.; *it has ~ed itself out*, rain has ceased); *God, the sky, the clouds, ~*, send down rain; fall or send down in showers or like rain (*flowers ~ed from their hands*; *tears ~ed down her cheeks*; *blows ~ upon him*; *his eyes ~ tears*; *he ~ed benefits upon us*). [OE *regnian* (prec.)]

rain'bow (-ō), n. Arch showing prismatic colours in their order formed in sky (or across cataract etc.) opposite sun by reflection, double refraction, & dispersion of sun's rays in falling drops of rain (*lunar ~*, similar effect from moon's rays, rarely seen; *sea~*, formed on sea spray; *second~*, additional arch with colours in reverse order formed inside or outside of ~ by double reflection & double refraction; *all the colours of the ~*, many colours); (attrib.) many-coloured. Hence ~'troot, Californian kind. [OE *rēnboga* (RAIN¹, BOW¹)]

rain'y, n. In or on which rain is falling or much rain usually falls (*~y weather, climate, day, month, county*, etc.; *~y day*, fig., time of esp. pecuniary need, as *provide against a ~y day*); (of clouds, wind, etc.) laden with, bringing, rain. Hence ~iLY² adv., ~iNESS n. [-Y²]

raise (-z), v.t. (often followed by *up* in most senses), & n. **1.** Set upright, make stand up, restore to or towards vertical position, rouse, (*~d him from his knees*; *~ the standard of revolt*; *~a pastry, pie*, etc., standing without support of dish at sides; *~ one from the dead*, restore him to life; *~ the country, city*, etc., rouse inhabitants in some emergency, often *against* or *upon*

enemy etc.; *the danger ~d his spirits*; *~ the wind*, fig., procure money for some purpose; *~ a dust*, lit., & fig. cause turmoil, also obscure the truth). **2.** Build up, construct, create, produce, breed, utter, make audible, start, give occasion for, elicit, set up, advance, (*~ palace, large family*, blister, *~ one's own vegetables*, storm, shout, hymn, controversy, prejudice, claim, demand, objection, question; *a deliverer was ~d up*, caused by Providence to appear; *~ a laugh*, cause others to laugh; *no one ~d his voice*, spoke). **3.** Elevate, put or take into higher position, extract from earth, direct upwards, promote to higher rank, make higher or nobler, cause to ascend, make (voice) louder or shriller, (Naut.) come in sight of (land, ship); increase amount of, heighten level of, (*~ one's hat*, bow; *~ one's glass to*, *drink health of*; *thousands of tons of coal were ~d*; *~ one's eyes*, look upwards; *~ one's eyebrows*, look supercilious or shocked; *~d him to the see of York*; *trying to ~ to a degraded class*; *undertook to ~ the spirit of King Solomon*, cf. LAY³; *~ Cain, hell, the devil, the mischief*, etc., make disturbance; *their voices were ~d as in anger*; *~ income-tax from 8s. 6d. to 10s.*; *~ cloth*, make nap on it; *~ bread*, cause it to rise with yeast; *~ one's reputation, ~ colour* in dyeing, brighten it). **4.** Levy, collect, bring together, procure, manage to get, (*~ tax, loan, subscription, money, army, fleet*). **5.** Relinquish, cause enemy to relinquish, (siege, blockade) remove (embargo). **6.** p.p. *(vulg.)*. Brought up, educated. **7.** n. Increase in salary, stakes at poker, bid at bridge, etc. [f. ON *reisa*; causative of RISE¹, cf. BAIT¹, BITE¹]

rais'in (-zn), n. Partially dried grape. [f. OF *raizin* f. L as RACEME]

raison d'être (see Ap.), n. Purpose etc. that accounts for or justifies or originally caused thing's existence. [F]

rait. See RET.

raj (rahj), n. (Anglo-Ind.). Sovereignty (*the British ~ in India*). [Hind.]

raja(h) (rah'jö), n. Indian king or prince (also as title of petty dignitary or noble in India, or Malay or Javanese chief), Hence **ra'jahship** (rahj'ŏsh-) n. [Hind. *rājā* f. Skr. *rājan* king (*rāj* to reign)]

Rajpoot, -put (rahj'pŏŏt), n. Member of Hindu soldier caste claiming descent from Kshatriyas. [Hind. (-*ut*), f. prec., *putra* son]

rake¹, n. Implement consisting of pole with cross-bar toothed like comb at end for drawing together hay etc. or smoothing loose soil or gravel, wheeled implement drawn by horse for same purpose; kinds of implement resembling ~ used for other purposes, e.g. by croupier drawing in money at gaming-table. [OE *raca,*

cf. Du. *raak*, G *rechen*, (also Goth. *rikan* heap up)]

rake², v.t. & i. Collect, draw together, gather up, pull out, clear off, (as) with rake (*~ out the fire*; *~ up* or *together all possible charges*; *~ off the leaves*); clean or smooth with rake; search (as) with rake, ransack, (*has ~d all history for proofs*); make level, clean, etc., with rake; scratch, scrape; sweep with shot, enfilade, send shot along (ship) from stem to stern, sweep with the eyes, (of window etc.) have commanding view of; use rake, search as with rake (*have been raking among* or *in* or *into old records*); *~-off* (colloq.) commission, rebate, share of profits (usu. in bad sense). [f. ON *raka* cogn. w. prec.]

rake³, n. Dissipated or immoral man of fashion. [for RAKEHELL]

rāke⁴, v.i. & t., & n. **1.** (Of ship or its bow or stern) project at upper part of bow or stern beyond keel; (of masts or funnels) incline from perpendicular towards stern; give backward inclination to (*bicycle's front forks are ~d*). **2.** n. Amount to which thing ~s, raking position or build. [?]

‖ **rāke'hěll** (-kh-), n. (arch.). = RAKE³. Hence ~*y*² a. (arch.). [RAKE², HELL]

rāk'ish¹, a. (As) of, like, a RAKE³. Hence ~LY² adv., ~NESS n. [-ISH¹]

rāk'ish², a. (Of ship) smart & fast-looking, seeming built for speed & therefore open to suspicion of piracy. [perh.=prec. with extra association of raking masts (RAKE⁴)]

rāle (rahl), n. (path.). Sound additional to that of respiration heard in auscultation of unhealthy lungs. [F, f. *râler* to rattle, etym. dub.]

‖ rallentän'dō, mus. direction. Gradually slower. [It.]

‖ **rāll'icâr't**(-t), n. Light two-wheeled driving-trap for four. [*Ralli*, first purchaser, 1885]

rāll'y¹, v.t. & i., & n. **1.** Reassemble, get together again, (t. & i.; esp. of army or company) after rout or dispersion, (cause to) renew conflict; bring or come together (as support or for concentrated action (*rallied his party, his party rallied, round* or *to him*); revive (faculty etc.) by effort of will, pull oneself together, assume or rouse to fresh energy; throw off prostration or illness or fear, regain health or consciousness, revive. **2.** n. Act of ~ing (intr.), reunion for fresh effort; recovery of energy after or in the middle of exhaustion or illness; (in tennis, rackets, etc.) strokes quickly exchanged. [n. f. vb, f. F *rallier* (RE-, ALLY¹)]

rāll'y², v.t. Banter, chaff. Hence ~**ing**LY¹ adv. [as RAIL³]

răm¹, n. **1.** Uncastrated male sheep, tup. **2.**(*Ram*) zodiacal sign Aries. **3.** = BATTER-, ...*ing~*; (battleship with) projecting beak at bow for charging side of other ships;

falling weight of pile-driving machine; rammer; hydraulic water-raising or lifting machine; battering machine. 2. v.t. press; plunger of force-pump. 4. ~'s horn, lit., also scroll ornament imitated from ~'s head & horns. [OE, also Du. & OHG; perh. cogn. w. ON *rammr* strong]

rām², v.t. (-mm-). Beat down (soil etc.) into solidity with wooden block etc.; (abs.) use ~mer; make (post, plant, etc.) firm by ~ming soil round it; drive (pile etc.) down, in, by heavy blows; force, dash or violently impel (thing) *against, at, on,* or *into* (~*med his head against the wall, his horse at a fence*); ~*rod,* for ~ming home charge of muzzle-loader. Hence ~m'ER¹(2) n. [f. L *ramus* branch.]

║ rām³, n. (naut.). Boat's length over all. [?]

Ramadān', n. Ninth month of Moham-medan year, during all daylight hours of which rigid fasting is observed. [Arab. (*ramaḍa* be hot); perh. orig. one of hot months, now passing through all seasons owing to lunar reckoning]

rām'al, a. (bot.). Of, proceeding from, a branch. [f. L *ramus* branch, -AL]

rām'ble, v.i. & n. 1. Walk (v. & n.) for pleasure & without definite route. 2. Wander in discourse, talk or write dis-connectedly. [?]

rām'bler, n. In vbl senses; also, kinds of climbing rose, esp. the Crimson R~. [-ER¹]

rām'bling, a. Peripatetic, wandering; disconnected, desultory, incoherent; (of plants) straggling, climbing; (of house, street, etc.) irregularly planned. Hence ~LY² adv. [-ING²]

rām'bunc'tious (-ngkshus), a. (colloq.). = RUMBUSTIOUS (of which it appears to be an alteration).

ramburr'an (-oot-), n. Red fruit of an E.-Indian tree, covered with soft spines and pleasant sub-acid pulp. [Malay, f. *rambut* hair, in allusion to spines]

rām'ekin, -quin (-kin), n. Small quantity of cheese with bread-crumbs, eggs, etc., baked in small mould. [F (-*quin*), etym. dub.]

rām'ie (-mē), n. Fine strong fibre ob-tained from a Chinese and E.-Indian nettle-like plant, woven into a durable material. [Malay *rāmi*]

rāmifica'tion, n. Ramifying, (arrange-ment of) tree's branches; subdivision of complex structure comparable to tree's branches (*the ~s of a river, society, trade, plot, inquiry,* etc.). [foll., -ATION]

rām'if[y], v.i. & t. Form branches or sub-divisions or offshoots, branch out; (usu. pass.) cause to branch out, arrange in branching manner (*railways were ~ied over the country*). [f. F *ramifier* f. med. L *ramificare* (L *ramus* branch, -i-, -FY)]

rāmm'ish, a. Rank-smelling. [RAM¹, -ISH¹]

ramose', a. Branched, branching. [f. L *ramosus* (*ramus* branch, -OSE¹)]

rāmp¹, n. Slope, inclined plane joining two levels of ground esp. in fortification, etc.; difference in level be-tween opposite abutments of rampant arch; upward bend in stair-rail. [f. F *rampe* (foll.)]

║ rāmp², v.i. & t. (-gl.). 1. (Chiefly of lion) stand on hind-legs with fore-paws in air, assume or be in threatening posture; (now usu. joc.) storm, rage, rush about. 2. (Archit.) (of wall) ascend or descend to different level; (Archit., Mil) furnish or build with ramp. [f. OF *ramper* etym. dub.]

rāmp³, n. & v.i. & t. (sl.). Attempt to extort payment of fictitious debt from bookmaker; (transf.) levying of exorbi-tant prices, as the *black-market ~ in...;* (vb) engage in, subject (person to). [?]

rām'page, v.i., & n. 1. Behave violently, storm, rage, rush about. 2. n. Violent be-haviour (esp. *be on the ~*). Hence ~ous (-jus) a., ~ously² adv., ~ousness n. [prob. imit.? cf. RAMP²]

rām'pant, a. (Chiefly of lion, esp. in Her.) ramping (in Her., & in allusive imitations, placed after nouns, as *lion ~, the snob ~*); violent or extravagant in action or opinion, arrant, aggressive, unchecked, prevailing, (*is a ~ theorist; poppery is ~ among us*); rank, luxuriant, (*a rich soil makes nasturtiums too ~*); (of arch etc.) having one abutment higher than the other, climbing. Hence rām'p-ANCY n., ~LY² adv. [F (RAMP², -ANT)]

rām'part, n., & v.t. Broad-topped & (usu. stone-parapeted defensive mound of earth; (fig.) defence, protection; (vb) fortify or protect (as) with ~. [f. F *rempart* (*remparer* fortify, f. RE-, *emparer* take possession of, f. L *ante* before,...

rāmp'ire, n., & v.t. (arch.). = RAMPART.

rāmp'ion, n. Kind of bell-flower with white tuberous roots used as salad. [cf. F *raiponce,* It. *ramponzolo,* etym. dub.]

║ rām'shackle, a. Tumbledown, crazy, rickety, (usu. of house or vehicle). [earlier ~*ed,* perh. p.p. of obs. *ransackle* RAN-SACK]

rām'son (-sn), n. (Root, eaten as relish, of) broad-leaved garlic. [prop. pl. in -*en* of OE *hramsa,* cf. G *rams,* Gk *kromuon* onion]

rān¹, n. A certain length of twine. [?]

rān². See RUN¹.

rance, n. Kind of red marble with blue & white veins & spots. [?]

ranch, n., & v.i. 1. Cattle-breeding establishment in U.S. 2. v.i. Conduct ~. [f. Sp. *rancho* mess, persons feeding together]

ranch'id, a. Smelling or tasting like rank stale fat. Hence **rancid'ity**, ~**NESS**, nn. [f. L *rancidus* stinking]

ranc'our (-ker), n. Inveterate bitterness, malignant hate, spitefulness. Hence **ranc'orous** a., **ranc'orously²** adv. [OF, f. L *rancorem* nom. -*or* (prec., -OR¹)]

rand, n. 1. Strip of leather between heel & shoe or boot. 2. (S.-Afr.) highlands on either side of river valley (the R~, Johannesburg). [OE & Du., = bank, rim]

randan'¹, n. Style of rowing for three men, the middle using sculls & the others oars; boat for such use. [?]

randan'², n. Spree (esp. *on the* ~). [var. of RANDOM]

ran'dem, adv. & n. With three horses harnessed tandem; (n.) carriage or team so driven. [prob. formed on *random* & *tandem*]

ran'dom, n. & a. 1. *At* ~, at haphazard, without aim or purpose or principle, heedlessly. 2. adj. Made, done, etc., at~; (of masonry) with stones of irregular size & shape; hence ~LY² adv. (rare). [orig. sense *great speed*; f. OF *random* (*randir* gallop); for -*m* cf. *ransom*]

ran'dy, a. ‖ Loud-tongued, boisterous, lusty, (Sc.); (of cattle etc.; dial.) wild, restive; lustful, in lustful mood. Hence ~**INESS** n. [prob. f. obs. *rand* var. of RANT, -Y²]

ranee (rahn'ī), n. Hindu queen. [f. Hind. *rānī* f. Skr. *rajñi* fem. of RAJAH]

rang. See RING².

range¹ (-j), v.t. & i. 1. Place or arrange in a row or ranks or in specified situation or order or company (usu. pass. or refl.; ~*d their troops*; ~*d themselves on each side*; *was* ~*d against, among, on the side of, with*, etc.; *trees* ~*d in an ascending scale of height*; ~ *oneself*, init. F, take up definite position in society, settle down, e.g. by marrying). 2. Run in a line, reach, lie spread out, extend, be found or occur over specified district (often *from . . . to*), vary between limits, (~*s north & south, along the sea*; *nightingale* ~*s from the Channel to Warwickshire*). 3. Be level (*with*; *a 12mo does not* ~ *well with a folio*); rank or find right place *with* or *among* (~*s with the great writers*). 4. Rove, wander, (often *over, along, through,* etc., *district* or *coast*; *his thoughts* ~ *over past, present, & future*; *ranging fancy*, inconstant affections). 5. (Of gun) throw projectile over, (of projectile) traverse, (distance) ~*s over a mile*). 6. Go all about (place), sail along or about (coast, sea). [f. OF *ranger* (*rang* RANK¹)]

range² (-j), n. 1. Row, line, tier, or series, of things, row (~ *of buildings* or mountains. 2. Lie, direction, (*the* ~ *of the strata is east & west*; *keep the two buoys in* ~ *with the lighthouse*). 3. Stretch of grazing or hunting ground. 4. Piece of ground with targets for shooting. 5. Area over which plant etc. is distributed, area included in or concerned with something, sphere, scope, compass, register, limits of variation, limited scale or series, distance attainable by gun or projectile, distance between gun etc. & objective, (*gives the* ~*s of the species; the thorniest question in the whole* ~ *of politics; the* ~ *of her voice is astonishing; his reading is of very wide* ~; *the* ~ *of the barometer readings is about 2 in.; Hebrew is out of my* ~; *there is a lower* ~ *of prices today; the enemy are out of* ~, *have found the* ~ *of our camp*). 6. Cooking fireplace usu. with oven(s), boiler(s), & iron top plate with openings for saucepans etc. 7. ~*-finder*, instrument for estimating distance of object to be shot at. [OF, =row, rank, (prec.)]

ran'ger (-j-), n. 1. In vbl senses; also; keeper of a royal park, whence ~**SHIP** n.; *(R~)* member of U.S. COMMANDO; (pl.) body of mounted troops or other armed men; senior girl guide. [-ER¹]

rank¹, n. 1. Row, line, queue, (now chiefly of cabs standing; in chess, row of squares across board, opp. FILE³). 2. Number of soldiers drawn up in single line abreast (usu. one ~ behind another, called *front, rear,* ~; *the* ~*s were broken,* could not keep the formation; *the* ~*s* or *the* ~ *& file,* common soldiers, i.e. privates & corporals, & transf. lower classes or ordinary undistinguished people; *rise from the* ~*s,* said of common soldier or sergeant who is given commission, or of selfmade man). 3. Order, array, (*keep* ~, *break* ~, remain, fail to remain, in line). 4. Distinct social class, grade of dignity, station, high station, (*people of all* ~*s; persons of* ~, *members of nobility;* ~ *& fashion,* high society; *the pride of* ~). 5. Place in a scale. [f. obs. F *ranc* (now *rang*), perh. f. OHG *hrinc* RING¹]

rank², v.t. & i. 1. Arrange (esp. soldiers) in rank; classify, give certain grade to; *take precedence of* (person) in respect to rank; have rank or place (~*s among the Great Powers, next to the king,* etc.); have a rightful place on the list of claims on, or claimants against, a bankrupt estate; (Mil.) march past of. [f. prec.]

rank³, a. Too luxuriant, gross, coarse, over-productive, choked with or apt to produce weeds, (*roses are growing* ~, *running too much to leaf; land too* ~ *to grow corn*); foul-smelling, offensive, rancid; loathsome, indecent, corrupt; strongly marked, unmistakable, flagrant, virulent, gross, (~ *treason, pedantry, poison, nonsense*). Hence ~'LY² adv., ~'NESS n. [OE *ranc* long & thin, ON *rakkr* slender, bold]

rank'er, n. (Commissioned officer who has been) a soldier in the ranks. [-ER¹]

rankle (răngʹk'l), v.i. (Of wound, sore, etc.) fester, continue painful, (arch.); (of envy, disappointment, etc., or their cause) be bitter, give intermittent or constant pain. [f. OF *rancler*, *rancle*, *drancle*, *dranchè*, festering sore = med. L *dracunculus* dim. of *draco* serpent)]

rân'sôck, n., & v.t. Thoroughly search (place, receptacle, person's pockets, one's conscience, etc.); pillage, plunder, (house, country, etc.). [f. ON *ramsaka* (rann house, *sǽkja* seek)]

rân'som, n., & v.t. 1. (Liberation of prisoner of war in consideration of) sum of money or value paid for release (hold one to ~, be willing to release him for such consideration; *worth a king's* ~, of immense value); blackmail, sum etc. exacted in return for privilege or immunity, (*graduated income-tax & death-duties are no more than a fair ~ paid by the rich*); ~-bill, -bond, undertaking, esp. on part of captured ship, to pay ~; hence ~LESS a. 2. v.t. Redeem, buy freedom or restoration of; atone for, explate; hold to ~, release for a ~; exact ~ from. [f. OF *ransoun(er)* f., *redemptionem* REDEMPTION]

rant, v.i. & t., & n. 1. Use bombastic language; declaim, recite theatrically; preach noisily, whence (esp. of Primitive Methodist) ~ER n. 2. n. Piece of ~ing, tirade; empty turgid talk. [f. obs. Du. *randten* rave, cf. G *ranzen* frolic]

ranünc'ulus, n. (pl. ~uses, ~i). Genus of plants including the buttercups, crow-foot. Hence ~A'CEOUS (-āshŭs) a. [L, orig. dim. of *rana* frog]

ranz-des-vaches (see Ap.), n. Swiss herdsmen's melody made of harmonic notes of Alpine horn. [Swiss dial.]

rǎp[1], n., & v.t. & i. (-pp-). 1. Smart slight blow (a ~ *on the knuckles*, punishment inflicted on child, also fig. reproof); sound made by knocker on door etc., or by some agency on table or floor in spiritualistic seances. 2. v.b. Strike (esp. person's knuckles) smartly; make the sound called a ~ (~*ped at the door, on the table*, etc.); ~ *out* (oath, pun, etc.), utter abruptly or on the spur of the moment, (v.i.) use strong language; (of spirits) ~ *out* (message, word), express by ~s. [prob. imit.]

rǎp[2], n. Skein of 120 yds of yarn. [?]

rǎp[3], n. An atom, the least bit, (*don't care a ~*). [earlier sense 18th-c. Irish counter-feit halfpenny; etym. dub.]

rapa'cious (-shŭs), a. Grasping, extortionate, predatory. Hence or cogn. **rapa'city** n. [f. L *rapax* (*rapere* snatch)]

rāpe[1], v.t., & n. 1. Take by force (poet.); ravish, violate, (woman). 2. n. Carrying off by force (poet.); ravishing or violation of a woman (also fig. of a country, as *the ~ of Austria*). [prob. f. L *rapere* seize]

‖ rāpe[2], n. Any of six administrative divisions of Sussex. [from 1086; etym. dub.]

rāpe[3], n. Plant grown as food for sheep; plant cultivated for its seed from which oil is made, coleseed (*wild* ~, charlock; ~-*cake*, ~-*seed* pressed into flat shape after extraction of oil & used as manure; ~-*oil*, made from ~-seed & used as lubricant & in making soap & Indiarubber. [f. L *rapum* turnip]

rāpe[4], n. Refuse of grapes after wine-making used in making vinegar; vessel used in vinegar-making. [f. F *râpe*, cf. Pr. *raspa*, It. *raspo*]

Rāphaēlĕsque' (-sk), **Rǎff-**, a. In style of Raphael. [*Raphael* (It. *Raffaello*), -ESQUE]

rǎph'ia, n. (Bot. name of) RAFFIA.

rǎp'id, a. & n. 1. Speedy, quick, swift; acting or completed in short time; (of slope) descending steeply; hence or cogn. ~ITY² n., ~LY² adv. 2. n. (usu. pl.) Steep descent in river-bed, with swift current. [f. L *rapidus* (*rapere* seize)]

rǎp'ier, n. Light slender sword for thrusting only, small-sword, (~-*thrust*, often fig. of delicate or witty repartee). [f. F *rapière* etym. dub.]

rǎp'ine, n. (rhet.). Plundering, robbery. [f. L *rapina* (*rapere* seize, -INE²)]

rǎpparee', n. (hist.). 17th-c. Irish irregular soldier or freebooter. [f. Ir. *rapaire*]

rǎppee', n. Coarse kind of snuff. [f. F (*tabac*) *râpé* RASPED (tobacco)]

rapport' (or rapōr'), n. Communication, relationship, connection, (*be in*, or F *en* pr. ahn, *come into*, or F *en*, ~ *with*), [*rapporter* f. RE-, AP-, *porter* f. L *portare* carry)]

rapprochement (see Ap.), n. Re-establishment or recommencement of harmonious relations, esp. between States. [F]

rǎpscǎll'ion (-lyon), n. (arch.). Rascal, scamp, rogue. [earlier *rascallion*, prob. f. RASCAL]

rapt, p.p. & a. Snatched away bodily or carried away in spirit from earth, from life, from consciousness, or from ordinary thoughts & perceptions (often *away, up*, etc.); absorbed, enraptured, intent, (esp. *listen with* ~ *attention*). [f. L *raptus* p.p. of *rapere* seize]

raptōr'ial, a. & n. (zool.). (Member) of the *Raptores*, an order of birds of prey; predatory, (as) of predatory birds or animals. [f. L *raptor* (prec.,-OR²) plunderer+-IAL]

rap'ture, n. Mental transport, ecstatic delight, (*be in, go into,* ~s, be enthusiastic; talk enthusiastically; ~s, be enthusiastic, pleasure or the expression of it); (esp. Theol.) act of transporting a person from one place to another (esp. heaven). Hence ~ v.t. (usu. in p.p.), **rap'turousLY²** adv., **rap'tured** (-tyerd), a. Enraptured, in ecstasy. [f. obs. *rapture* vb (prec.), -ED¹]

rā'/a ă'vĭs, n. Rarity, kind of person or thing rarely encountered. [L, = rare bird]

rāre¹, a. 1. Of loosely packed substance, not dense, (the ~ *atmosphere of the mountain tops*). 2. Few & far between, uncommon, unusual, exceptional, seldom found or occurring, (*it is ~ for person etc. to do*, or *it is ~ly that he* etc. *does*). 3. Of uncommon excellence, remarkably good, very amusing, (*a miracle of ~ device*; *had ~ fun with him*). 4. ~ *earths*, oxides of certain metals (e.g. cerium, lanthanum, yttrium) found in a few ~ minerals. Hence ~lȲ² (âr-) adv., (esp.) seldom, not often, finely, in an unusual degree, ~'NESS (âr̄n-) n. [f. L *rarus*]

*rāre², a. (Of meat) underdone. [var. of obs. *rear* half-cooked (of eggs), f. OE *hērer*]

rāre'bĭt (râr̄b-), n. See WELSH¹ *rabbit*.

rā'ee-shōw (-ō), n. Show carried about in a box; any show or spectacle. [perh. = *rare show* as pronounced by Savoyard showmen]

rār'ĕfȳ, v.t.&i. Lessen density or solidity of (esp. air); purify, refine, (person's nature etc.); make (idea etc.) subtle; become less dense. So ~FAC'TION, ~FICA'TION, nn., ~fāctīve a. [f. L *rarefacere* (for *rarifacere*) f. *rarus* rare, *facere* make]

rār'ĭtȳ, n. Rareness (see RARE¹); uncommon thing, thing valued as being rare. [f. L *raritas* (RARE¹, -TY)]

ra'scal (rah-), n. & a. 1. Rogue, knave, scamp, (often playfully to child etc.; *you lucky~!*). 2. adj. Belonging to the rabble (arch.; *the ~ rout*, the common people). Hence~DOM,~ISM(2),rascal'Ity nn.,~lȳ¹ a. [f. OF *rascaille* rabble, etym. dub.]

rase. See RAZE.

rash¹, n. Eruption of the skin in spots or patches. [cf. OF *rache* scurf, It. *raschia* itch; from 18th c. only]

rash², a. Hasty, impetuous, overbold, reckless, acting or done without due consideration. Hence ~lȳ² adv., ~'NESS n. [cf. Du. & G *rasch* quick]

rash'er, n. Thin slice of bacon or ham. [perh. f. obs. *rash* to slice, prob. var. of RAZE]

rasp (rah-), v.t.&i., & n. (Scrape with) coarse kind of file having separate teeth raised with pointed punch; scrape roughly; grate upon (person or his feelings), irritate; scrape *off* or *away*; make grating sound. Hence ra'sper (rah-) n., (esp., Hunting) high difficult fence. [f. OF *raspe(r)*, now *rôpe(r)*, perh. f. Teut.]

ra'spatory (rah-), n. Rasp used in surgery. [f. med. L *raspatorium* (*raspare* RASP, -TORY)]

ra'spberry (rahzb-), n. 1. (Plant bearing) white, yellow, or usu. red subacid fruit of many small juicy grains arranged on conical receptacle. 2.(sl.) Sound, gesture, or sign expressing dislike, derision, or disapproval; dismissal. 3. ~-*canes*, the plants; ~ *vinegar*, kind of syrup. [f. *rasp* (now Sc.& north.) *raspis*, etym. dub.]

rasse (răs'ĭ, răs'h), n. Kind of civet-cat. [f. Javanese *rase*]

răt¹, n. & v.i. (-tt-). 1. Rodent of some larger species of the mouse kind (MUSK, WATER, ~; *black* or *old-English ~*, variety now largely ousted by common *grey, brown,* or *Norway ~*; *smell a ~*, have suspicions; *like a drowned ~*, said of person wet through; *Rats!*, sl. nonsense!, incredible!, etc.). 2. (Pol.) person who deserts his party in difficulties as ~s are said to desert doomed house or ship, turncoat. 3. Workman who refuses to join strike, takes striker's place, or accepts less than trade-union wages. 4.~*catcher* (who rids houses of ~s), (sl.) unorthodox hunting dress; ~'*bane*, ~ poison (now only in literary fig. use); ~'*s-tail*, thing shaped like ~'s tail, e.g. kind of file; ~*tail*, (horse with) hairless horse's tail, whence ~*tailed²* a. (~*tail spoon*, with tail-like prolongation of handle along back of bowl); ~*-trap*, lit., also (cycle pedal) made of two parallel iron plates with teeth; hence ~t'ȳ² a. (in n. senses, &c, sl., snappish, irritable, touchy). 5.v.i. Hunt or kill ~s (of person or dog); play the ~ in politics; hence ~'tER¹ n. [OE *ræt*, cf. Du. *rat*, G *ratz*, also F *rat²*, etym. dub.]

răt², v.t. 3rd sing. pres. subj. (vulg.). = DRAT.

ra'ta (rah-), n. Large handsome New Zealand tree with crimson flowers & hard red wood. [Maori]

rāt'able, a. Proportional (arch.); liable to payment of municipal rates, whence ~abIl'ItY n. Hence~ably² adv. [RATE², -ABLE]

rataf'ia (-ēà), -fee', n. Liqueur flavoured with almonds or kernels of peach, apricot, or cherry; kind of biscuit similarly flavoured; kind of cherry. [F (-ía), etym. dub.]

rāt'al, n. Amount on which rates are assessed (also attrib., as *the ~ qualification for vestries*). [f. RATE¹, prob. after RENTAL]

rătaplăn', n., & v.t.&i.(-nn-). 1. Drumming sound. 2. vb. Play (as) on drum; make ~. [F, imit.]

rătch'ĕt, răĭch, nn., & v.t. 1. Set of teeth on edge of bar or wheel by which in combination with a catch motion in one direction may be prevented while possible in the other; (also ~*wheel*) wheel with rim so toothed. 2. v.t. Provide with ~, give ~ form to. [f. F *rochet* kind of lance-head, cf. ROCKET²]

rāte¹, n. 1. Statement of numerical proportion prevailing or to prevail between two sets of things either or both of which may be unspecified, amount etc. mentioned in one case for application to all similar ones, standard or way of reckon-

ing. (measure of) value, tariff charge, cost, relative speed, (*going at the ~ of six miles an hour; can have them at the ~ of 11-a thousand; the death-~ was 19 per mile; the ~ of interest, wages, etc., is to be regulated; the high ~s charged by the railways; at that ~, colloq., if this is a fair specimen, if this assumption is true, etc.; at any ~, in either or any possible case, even if a stronger statement is doubtfully true, etc.: the low ~ at which you value it; sell at a high ~; win success at an easy ~; went off at a great ~, speed; pauperism increases at a fearful ~*). 2. ‖ Assessment levied by local authorities for local purposes (*~s & taxes; a 6d. ~ is raised for the public library service*). 3. Class (in FIRST, THIRD, etc., ~). 4. ‖ ~payer, person liable to have municipal ~s exacted from him. [OF, f. med. L *rata* (L *pro rata parte* according to the *proportional share*, f. *ratus* p.p. of *reri* reckon)]

rate², v.t. & i. 1. Estimate worth or value of (*I do not ~ his merits high; each offence is ~d at a fixed sum by way of penalty;* esp. *in over~, under~*), assign fixed value to (coin, metals) in relation to monetary standard (*the copper coinage is ~d much above its real value*); consider, regard as, (*I ~ him among my benefactors*). 2. ‖ (Usu. in pass.), subject to payment of a local rate, value for purpose of assessing rates on, (*we are highly ~d for education, have to pay a high rate; houses are ~d at a sum smaller than the rent, the sum on which rates are charged is less*). 3. ~ *up*, impose higher insurance rate on (persons etc., liable to exceptional risks); consider, regard as, (class under a certain RATING¹, (intr.) rank or be ~d as. [f. prec.]

rate³, v.t. & i. Scold (trans.) angrily; (rare) storm at. [?]

rate⁴. See REE.

‖ rat'el, n. S.-Afr. carnivorous quadruped, honey-badger. [Cape-Du.]

-rat'er, n. Racing yacht of specified tonnage (*10-~, 2½-~*, etc.). [RATE¹, -ER¹]

‖ rath (raath), n. (Ir. Ant.). Prehistoric hill-fort. [Ir.]

‖ rathe (-dh), a. (poet.). Coming, blooming, early, in the year or day; ~-ripe, *with ripe*, ripening early, precocious, (fig. early kinds of pea, apple, etc. [f. obs. *rathe* adv.]. OE *hræthe* (*hræd* quick)]

ra'ther (rahdh-), adv. 1. More truly, to a greater extent, as a more accurate description or preferable account of the matter, or to be more precise, (*is ~ good than bad; derived ~ from imagination than reason; orderliness is not the result of reason, ~ it is the cause of it; late last night, or ~ early this morning*); the ~ that, so much the more because. 2. In a modified way, to some extent, slightly somewhat, (*I ~ think you know him; the performance was ~ a failure, was ~ good, fell ~ flat*). 3. By preference, for choice, sooner, as an

alternative chosen sooner than another of same grammatical form or than to (*would much ~ not go; he would ~ have died than refused; use soft water ~ than hard; the desire to seem clever ~ than honest; he re-signed ~ than stifle his conscience;* also with *had*, as *I had ~ err with Plato than be right with —*). 4. ‖ (colloq.). In answers most emphatically, yes without doubt, assuredly. (*Have you been here before?— R~?*). [compar. of obs. *rathe* adv., see prec.]

*ra'thskeller (rahts-), n. Beer-saloon or restaurant in basement. [G. = town-hall cellar]

rat'ify, v.t. Confirm or make valid (compact made in one's name) by formal consent, signature, etc. So ~FICA'TION n. [f. OF, f. med. L *ratificare* (RATE¹, -FY)]

ratine' (-ēn), n. Dress fabric resembling sponge cloth. [F]

rat'ing¹, n. In vbl senses of RATE²; also or esp.: ‖ amount fixed as municipal rate; (Naut.) person's position or class on ship's books, ‖ non-commissioned sailor, ‖ (collect.) all persons of a particular ~; ‖ portion of the classes into which racing yachts are distributed by tonnage. [RATE², -ING¹]

rat'ing², n. Angry reprimand. [RATE³, -ING¹]

ra'tio (-shiō), n. (pl. ~s). Quantitative relation between two similar magnitudes determined by the number of times one contains the other integrally or fractionally (*are in the ~ of three to two or 3:2; the ~s 1:5 & 20:100 are the same*). [L (RATE¹, -ION)]

ratio'cinate (or -shi-), v.i. Go through logical processes, reason formally, use syllogisms. So ~A'TION n., ~ATIVE a. [f. L *ratiocinari* (prec.), -ATE³]

ra'tion (*rǎ-), n. & v.t. 1. (Usu. pl.) fixed daily allowance of food served out esp. for members of Services (& formerly of food etc. for civilians in time of shortage of animals); fixed allowance of forage for animals; fixed allowance of food etc. for civilians in time of shortage (*~ book*, entitling holder to ~); single portion of provisions, fuel, clothing, etc., (pl.) provisions. 2. v.t. Limit (persons, food, clothing) to fixed ~. [f. L RATIO]

ra'tional (-sho-), a. & n. 1. Endowed with reason, reasoning; sensible, sane, moderate, not foolish or absurd or extreme; of, based on, reasoning or reason, reject-ing what is unreasonable or cannot be tested by reason in religion or custom, (*~ dress,* esp. formerly of knickerbockers worn by women instead of skirts; *has ~ leanings in religion*, has doubts about the truth of revelation, the possibility of miracles, etc.). 2. (Math.) of quantity or ratio) expressible without radical signs (opp. SURD); hence or express, ~ITY² (-ǎl-) n., ~LY² adv. 3. n. pl. or dress. [f. L *ratio-nalis* (prec., -AL¹)]

ra'tionale' (-shō-), n. Reasoned exposi-tion, statement of reasons, (now rare)

fundamental reason, logical basis, of. [L, neut. as prec.]

rā'tionalism (-sho-), n. Practice of explaining the supernatural in religion in a way consonant with reason, and of treating reason as the ultimate authority in religion as elsewhere; theory that reason is the foundation of certainty in knowledge (opp. empiricism, sensationalism). So ~IST(2) n. & a., ~IS'TIC a., ~IS'TICALLY adv. [-ISM]

rā'tionalize (-sho-), v.t. & i. Explain, explain away, by rationalism, bring into conformity with reason; be or act as a rationalist; (Math.) clear from surds; (Econ.) reform (an industry) by eliminating waste in labour, time, & materials, whence ~A'TION n. [-IZE]

rāt'ite, a. (ornith.). Belonging to the Ratitae, a genus including ostrich, emu, cassowary, etc., with keelless breastbone (opp. CARINATE). [f. L ratis raft, -ITE²]

rāt'lin(e), -ling, n. (usu. pl.). (One of) small lines fastened across ship's shrouds like ladder-rungs. [cf. OF radlingue small cordage strengthening sail-edge]

ratoon', n., & v.i. New shoot springing from sugar-cane root after cropping; (vb) send up ~s. [f. Sp. retoño sprout]

rat(t)an', n. Kinds of E.-Indian climbing palm with long thin many-jointed pliable stems; piece of ~ stem used as cane or for other purposes; ~s used as a material in building etc. [f. Malay rotan (raut pare)]

rat-tat', rat-a-tat', rat'-tat-tat', n. Rapping sound, esp. of knocker. [imit.]

‖ratt'en, v.t. Molest (workman or employer) by abstracting or injuring tools or machinery etc. in disputes. [?]

rat'tle¹, v.i. & t. Give out rapid succession of short sharp hard sounds, cause such sounds by shaking something (use ~d at the door); talk in lively thoughtless way (often on, away, along); move or fall with rattling noise, drive vehicle or ride or run briskly, (usu. down, along, past, etc.); (part.) brisk, vigorous, (a rattling wind, pace); (preceding good etc.) remarkably (had a rattling good run, dinner, etc.); make (chain, window, crockery, etc.) ~ (~ the sabre, threaten war); say or recite (verses, stories, lists, oaths) rapidly (usu. off, out, over, away, etc.); stir up from dullness; (sl.) excite, agitate, fluster, make nervous, frighten; make move quickly (~ fox, hunt it close; ~ up the anchor; ~ bill through the House). [ME & Du. ratelen, cf. G rasseln, prob. imit.]

rat'tle², n. 1. Instrument or plaything made to rattle esp. in order to give alarm or to amuse babies; set of horny rings in ~snake's tail; kinds of plant with seeds that rattle in their cases when ripe (esp. Yellow, Red, ~); rattling sound, uproar, bustle, noisy gaiety, racket, (death~, such sound in throat immediately before death; the ~s, croup); noisy flow of words, empty chatter, trivial talk; lively incessant talker. 2. ~bag, bladder, -box, ~s constructed of bag etc. with objects inside to rattle;~brain,-head,-pate,(person with) empty brain etc., whence ~brain-ED², ~headED², ~patED³ aa.; ~snake, venomous American snake with rattling apparatus in tail; ~trap n. & a., rickety (vehicle etc.), (pl.) curiosities, odds & ends. [f. prec.]

ratt'ler, n. In vbl senses; esp.: remarkably good specimen of anything; *rattle-snake. [-ER¹]

ratty, See RAT¹.

rauc'ous, a. Hoarse, harsh-sounding. Hence ~LY² adv. [f. L raucus, -OUS]

‖rauque (rawk), a. (rare). Raucous. [F (RAUCOUS)]

rav'age, v.t. & i., & n. 1. Devastate, plunder, (t. & i.), make havoc. 2. n. Devastation, damage; (esp. pl.) destructive effects of. [f. F ravage(r), vb f. n., (ravir RAVISH, -AGE)]

rave¹, v.i. & t., & n. 1. Talk wildly or furiously (as) in delirium (often about, against, at, of, for; raving mad, uncontrollably, so as to ~); (of sea, wind, etc.) howl, roar; speak with rapturous admiration about or of, go into raptures; utter with ravings (~ one's grief etc.); ~ oneself hoarse, to sleep, etc.; storm ~s itself out, to an end; hence (often pl.) rAV'ING¹(1) n. 2. n. Raving sound of wind etc. [perh. f. OF raver var. of rêver dream (REVERIE)]

rav'el¹, v.t. & i. (-ll-), & i. 1. Entangle or become entangled, confuse, complicate, (thread etc., or fig. question, problem; esp. in p.p., as the ~led skein of life); fray (t. & t.) out, whence ~LING¹(2) n.; disentangle, unravel, distinguish the separate threads or subdivisions of, (often out). 2. n. Entanglement, knot, complication; frayed or loose end. [prob. f. Du. ravelen]

rav'elin (-vl-), n. (fortif.). Outwork of two faces forming salient angle outside main ditch before curtain. [F, f. It. ravellino etym. dub.]

rav'en¹, n. & a. 1. Large black-plumaged hoarse-voiced bird of crow kind feeding chiefly on flesh, often kept tame, & popularly held of evil omen. 2. adj. Of glossy black (esp. ~ locks, black hair). [com.-Teut.: OE hræfn, cf. Du. raaf, G rabe]

rav'en², v.i. & t. Plunder (intr.), go plundering about, seek after prey or booty, prowl for prey; eat(t. & abs.) voraciously; have ravenous appetite (for). [f. OF raviner ravage (L rapina RAPINE)]

rav'enous, a. Rapacious (now rare); voracious (esp. ~ hunger, eagerness, etc.);

famished, very hungry. Hence ~LY² adv., ~NESS n. (rare). [f. OF -OUS)]

ravin, n. (poet., rhet.). Robbery, rapine; seizing & devouring of prey (*beast of ~*, of prey); spoil. [f. F *ravine* (now obs. in this sense) f. L *rapina* RAPINE]

ravine¹ (-ēn), n. Deep narrow mountain cleft. Hence ~ED² (-ēnd²) a. [F. = violent rush, ravine, (prec.)]

ravish, v.t. 1. Carry off (person, thing) by force (now rare); (of death, circumstances, etc.) take from life or from sight. 2. Commit rape upon, violate, (woman), whence ~ER¹ n. 3. Enrapture, charm, entrance, fill with delight, whence ~ING² a., ~ingly adv., so ~MENT n. [f. F *ravir* (L *rapere* seize), -ISH²]

raw, a., n., & v.t. 1. Uncooked (~ *cream*, got without scalding of milk; ~ *brick*, not hardened by fire); in unwrought state, not or not completely manufactured, (~ *silk*, as reeled from cocoons; ~ *cloth*, unfulled; ~ *hide*, untanned leather, also rope or whip of this; ~ *spirit*, undiluted; ~ *grain*, unmalted; ~ *material*, that out of which any process of manufacture makes the articles it produces, as *the finished product of one industry is the material of another*; ~ *army is men*); artistically crude; inexperienced, untrained, unskilled, fresh to anything, (*is a ~ lad*; ~ *recruits*); stripped of skin, having the flesh exposed, excoriated, sensitive to a touch from being so exposed; ~ *edge* of cloth, without hem or selvage; (of atmosphere, wind, day, etc.) damp & chilly; ~*-boned*, with bones almost exposed, gaunt; ~ *head*, with bones *& bloody bones*, nursery bugbear, death's-head & cross-bones, (attrib., of narrative style etc.), cruelly horrible; hence ~ISH¹ a., ~NESS n. 2. n. ~ place on person's or esp. horse's skin; *touch one on the ~*, wound his feelings on the points on which he is sensitive. 3. v.t. Rub (esp. horse's back) into ~ness. [com.-Teut.; cf. OE *hréaw*, cf. Du. *rauw*, G *roh*; cogn. w. L *cruor* blood, Gk *kreas* flesh]

ray¹, n. 1. Single line or narrow beam of light; (in scientific use) straight line in which radiant energy capable of producing sensation of light is propagated to given point (*Röntgen*, pr. rün'tyen, or X, ~s, form of radiation penetrating many substances impervious to ordinary light; *Becquerel* ~s, ~s emitted by RADIO-active bodies). 2. Analogous propagation-line of heat or other non-luminous physical energy; (fig.) remnant or beginning of enlightening or cheering influence (*a ~ of hope, truth, genius*, etc.). 3. Radius of circle (rare); any of the lines forming a pencil or set of straight lines passing through one point, any of a set of lines

radiating lines or parts or things. 4. (Bot.) marginal part of composite flower, as daisy; radial division of starfish. Hence ~ED² (rād.), ~LESS, aa., ~LET n. [f. OF *rai* (now *rais* f. L RADIUS)]

ray², v.i. & t. (Of light etc., or fig. of thought, hope, etc.) issue, come forth, or off or out, in rays; radiate (t. & i.; poet.). [f. prec.]

ray³, n. Kinds of large sea-fish allied to shark, with broad flat body, used as food, esp. the skate. [f. F *raie* f. L *raia*]

Ray'ah (rī'a), n. Non-Moslem Turkish subject. [f. Arab. *ra'īyah* flock (*ra'ā* feed)]

ray'on, n. Artificial silk made from cellulose. [F]

rāze, rāse (-z), v.t. Wound slightly, graze, scratch out, (rare exc. fig. as ~ *person's name from remembrance*); completely destroy, level with the ground, (town, house, walls, etc.; usu. *to the ground*). [f. F *raser* f. pop. L frequent. of L *radere ras-* scrape]

razee', n., & v.t. (hist.) Ship reduced in height by removal of upper deck(s); (vb) turn into a ~. [f. F *rasée* fem. p.p. as prec.]

ra'zor, n., & v.t. 1. Instrument used in shaving hair from skin (*safety ~*, kinds with guard to obviate risk of gashing skin). 2. ~*back*, back sharp as ~'s edge (often attrib., as ~*back whale* or RORQUAL; ~*back hill*, etc.), whence ~*backed²* a.; ~*bill*, kinds of bird with ~ *bill* (bill shaped like ~), whence ~*-billed²* a.; ~*-edge*, keen edge, sharp mountain ridge, critical situation, sharp line of division (*keep on the ~-edge of orthodoxy*; *be on a ~-edge* or ~*'s edge*, init. Gk, be in great danger); ~*-fish, -shell*, kinds of bivalve with shell like handle of ordinary ~; ~*-grinder*, lit., (also kinds of bird; ~*-strop*, 3. v.t. (rare). Use ~ upon, shave, cut down close. [f. OF *rasor* (prec., -OR²)]

rāz'zi-a (rǎ-), n. (sl.). Excitement, bustle, stir, spree; undulating merry-go-round. [f. OF *rasor* (prec., -OR²)]

R-boat, n. Fast German motor mine-sweeper. [R f. G *Räumen* to clear]

re¹ (rā), n. Second note of octave; (rare) note D, the second in natural scale of C major. [See GAMUT]

rē² (rē), abl. of RES. (As prep.) in the matter of (chiefly in legal & business use as first word of headline stating matter to be dealt with; also vulg. as substitute for *about, concerning*, in ordinary use); *re infectā*, without having accomplished one's object (esp. *return re infecta*).

re- (see †Pronunciation. **Hyphen, below, pref. f. L *re-, red-*, again, back, un-

Re- both forms part of large numbers of already compounded words borrowed f. L or Rom., & is treated as a living pref. In the latter capacity it may be prefixed for the occasion to any vb or vbl derivative; this is esp. common in such phr. as *traverse* & *re-traverse* = traverse again & again, *reckoning* & *re-reckoning*, *translation* & *re-translation*; but many vbs etc. that originated as nonce-wds have become established, often with restriction to one or some only of the simple word's senses; the more common or important words of this class, & others whose simplicity of meaning allows them to be grouped with it, are given with any necessary information under senses 8, 9, below. Those senses are the simple ones, found also in many of the wds compounded before being adopted by E; but in others of the pre-E compds the sense of the pref. has been so developed as to be obscure or unrecognizable, & senses 1-7 are given as a rough classification.

†Pronunciation:—rē in all wds (esp. all given under senses 8, 9) that are historically, or are capable of being taken for, simple modifications of existing E wds by one of those senses (even when a similarly spelt compd exists in senses not capable of being so regarded; so *récover* = cover again, cf. RECOVER[1], *récreation* second or new creation, cf. recreation in RECREATE[1]); rĕ before vowels, and before h (exc. in *rehearse*); rē also in *reflex*, *regress* n., *rescript*, *retail* n.; rē also in *recalesce*, *recrudesce*, *replicate*, & their derivv., & *retractility*: elsewhere, ri when the next syllable bears the word-accent (*reflect'*, *repos'itory*), & otherwise rĕ (*recollect'*, *rev'ocable*).

Hyphen:—The hyphen is often used when a writer wishes to mark the fact that he is using not a well-known compd vb, but re- as a living prefix (senses 8, 9) attached to a simple vb (*re-pair* = pair again, cf. *repair* mend); also usu. before e (*re-emerge*), & occas. before other vowels (*re-assure*, usu. *reassure*); also when the idea of repetition is to be emphasized, esp. in such phr. as *make* & *re-make*.

1-7: Special senses chiefly in pre-E compds.

1. In return, mutual(ly); *react, reciprocal, recompense, recrimination, rejoinder, remunerate, repartee, repay, requite, result, revenge*, etc.

2. Opposition: *rebel, recalcitrant, recusant, reluctance, remonstrate, repugnant, resist, revolt*, etc.

3. Behind, after: *relic, relinquish, relish, remain, remorse,* REST[n 3, 4], etc.

4. Retirement, secrecy: *recluse, recon-* dite, recourse, refuge, remote, repository, reticend, etc.

5. Off, away, down: *rebate, relax, release, relegate, remiss, renounce, repress, repudiate, rescind, reside, resolve, retail,* etc.

6. Frequentative or intensive: *redolent, redouble, redoubtable, redound, reduplicate, refine, refulgent, regard, rejoice, remark, renown, repine, repute, research, respect, resplendent, revere, revile, revolve*, etc.

7. Negative, un-: *reproach, reproof, reprobate, resign, reveal.*

8, 9: Ordinary senses as living prefix.

8. Once more, again, anew, afresh, repeated, (often with implication that previous doing etc. was deficient or erroneous or now requires alteration or improvement or renewal; many wds may be classed indifferently under 8 or 9); *readdress'* v.t., change address of (letter); *readjust'* v.t.; so *readjust'ment* n.; *reaffirm'* v.t.; so *reaffirma'tion* n.; *reappa'rel* v.t.; *rearm'* v.l. & t., esp. provide (troops) with arms of new pattern; so *rearm'ament* n.; *rearrange'* v.t.; so *rearrange'ment* n.; *reassert'* v.t.; so *reasser-tion* n.; *reassess'* v.t.; so *reassess'ment* n.; *reassign'* v.t.; *rebaptize'* v.t., lit., & fig. give new name to; so *rebaptism* n.; *re-birth'* n., esp. fresh incarnation; so *reborn'* p.p.; *redite'* v.t., (defective parts of etched etc. plate with acid); *rebuild'* v.t.; *re-capit'ulate* v.t., go over headings of, summarize, go quickly through again; so *recapitula'tion* n. (spec. in Biol., reproduction in embryos of successive forms in line of development), *recapit'ulative, recapit'ulatory,* aa.; *recast'* v.t., & n., (put into) new shape, improved); so *recommence'ment* arrangement etc. (of); *rechris'ten* v.t., = rebaptize above; *reclothe* v.t.; *recoal'* v.t.; *recoat'* v.t., put new coat of paint on; *recoin'* v.t.; so *recoin'age* n.; *recol'onize* v.t.; so *recoloniza'tion* n.; *recol'our* v.t.; *recombine'* v.t.; so *recombina'tion* n.; *recommence'* v.t. & i.; so *recommence'ment* n.; *recommit'* v.t., esp. refer back (bill etc.), for further consideration to committee; so *recommit'ment, recommit'al,* nn.; *recompose'* v.t.; *recompound'* v.t.; *reconsid'er* v.t.; so *reconsidera'tion* n.; *reconstit'uent* a. & n., (remedy) that builds up strength or tissue anew; *recon'stitute* v.t., esp. piece together (past events) into an intelligible whole; so *reconstitu'tion* n.; *reconstruct'* v.t.; so *reconstruc'tion* n., *reconstruc'tive* a.; *re-count'* v.t., (esp. votes at election as security against error), & see RECOUNT[1]; so *re-count'* n.; *re-cov'er* v.t., (esp. umbrellas etc.), & see RECOVER[1] v.t., create over again, & see in RECREATE[1]; so *recrea'tion,* & see in RECREATE[1]; *redirect'* v.t., esp.=readdress above; so *redirec'tion* n.; *redistrib'ute* v.t.;

For pronunciation & hyphening of re- see RE-; for words in re- not given see RE- 8, 9.

so *redistribu'tion* n., esp. of seats in Parliament or voting-power in elections, &c.; *redistrib'utive* a.; *redivide' v.t.; divi'sion* n.; *redo' v.t.; redye' v.t.; so re-ed'it v.t.; so re-edi'tion n.; re-en'gine v.t.,* with new engine(s); *re-exam'ine v.t.,* esp. of opening side's second examination of witness after opponents' cross-examination; so *re-examina'tion* n.; *reface' v.t.,* put new facing on (building); *refash'ion v.t.; so refashion- ment* n.; *refill' v.t. & i.,* restore (ship) by, (of ship) undergo, renewal & repairs; so *refit', refit'ment,* nn.; *refloat' v.t.,* supply new foot to (stocking); *refur'nish v.t.; regen'esis* n.; *reground' v.t.; rehash'* esp. = *recast* above; *rehang' v.t.,* (put) materials esp. of literary kind in new shape; *rehear'ing v.t., rehouse' v.t.,* provide with new house(s); *reincarn'ate v.t.; so re- incarna'tion* n., entrance of the soul, after death, into another human (or animal) body, *reincarn'ate* (-at) a.; *reink' v.t.; reinsure' v.t. & t.* (esp. of underwriter etc. devolving risk upon another); so *re- insur'ance* n.; *reinter' v.t.; reinves't* 1 (see also sense 9) v.t., shift (money) to other investment; so *reinvest'ment* n.; *reiss'ue reiss'ue* n., esp. part of already published edition to be sold with change of form or price; *reiter'ate v.t.,* say or do over again or several times, repeat; so *reitera'tion* n., *reit'erative* a.; *relabel' v.t.; reline' v.t.; reline' v.t. & t.; reload' v.t.; remake' v.t.; reman'* 1 (see also sense 9) v.t., equip with fresh men; *remar'gin v.t.,* (esp. of secondhand book- seller repairing worn book); *remar'ry v.i. & t.; so remed'rridge* n.; *remast' v.t.; re- mind' v.t.; remod'el v.t., remould' v.t.,* re- mint' v.t.; so *remed'rridge* n.; *re- mount' v.t.* (see also REMOUNT1) v.t., esp provide with fresh horse etc.; *rem'ount* n., supply of fresh horses for regiment etc., fresh horse; *rename' v.t.; renum'ber v.t.,* esp. change numbers of series etc.; *reorg'anize v.t.;* so *reorganiza'tion, org'anizer,* nn.; *repaper v.t.; reparti'tion,* n.; *repop'er v.t.; so repers'al* n.; *replant'* v.t.; so *replanta'tion* n.; *repot' v.t.* (esp. plant into larger pot); *repo'int v.t.; repr'int* n., book, article, etc., re- printed, reproduce v.t. & i., esp. (trans.) produce copy or representation of, (intr.) multiply by generation; so *reproduc'tion* n., *reproduc'ible, reproduc'tively* adv., *repro- duc'tive, aa., reproduc'tively* adv., *repro- duc'tiveness* n.; *reproval'tion, re- pub'lish v.t.* (esp. book etc.); so *republica'- tion* n.; *reread' v.t.; reseat' v.t.* (esp. provide church, theatre, etc., with fresh seats); *reseek' v.t.; reset' v.t.* (esp. gems); *reset'tle v.t.;* so *reset'tlement* n. (esp. cards); *resole' v.t.; reshape' v.t.; reship' v.t. (esp. spell phonetically); re- v.t.; so reset'tlement n.; reshape' v.t.; respell' v.t.,* esp. spell phonetically; *re-*

9. Back, with return to previous state after lapse or cessation or occurrence of opposite state or action, (often corre- sponding to compounds in DIS- or UN-; many words may be assigned indifferently to 9 or 8): *reaff'orest v.t.; so reafforesta'- tion n.; ream'inate v.t.; so reanima'tion n.; reappear' v.i.; so reappear'ance n.; reappoint' v.t.; so reappoint'ment n.; re- arise' v.i.; rearouse' v.t.; reascend' v.i. & t.; reassem'ble v.i. & t.; reassume' v.t.* (now rare, ousted by RESUME); so *re- assump'tion n.; reassure' v.t.,* restore to confidence, dispel apprehensions of; so *reassur'ing a.* (of words, manner, etc.), *reassur'ingly adv.; rebard'anize v.t.; re- bind' v.t.* (esp. book); *recap'ture v.t. & n.; re-cede' v.t.; so re-ce'ssion n.; recharge' v.t.; recharge' n.,* amount of substance used in recharging; *recog'nize v.t.; so recogni'tion n.; recom'fort v.t.; recon'- duct' v.t.; recon'quer v.t.; so recon'quest n.; reconnect' v.t.; so reconvere'sion n.; reconvert' v.t.; recross' v.t.; so recrossf* d.; *redd'ress'* 1 *v.t.; redecend' v.i.; redis- cover' v.t.; so redisco'very n.; redissolve'* v.t. & i.; so *redisso'verly n.; re-eleet' v.t.,* so *re-elec'tion n.; re-el'igible a.; re-embark'* v.i. & t.; so *re-embarka'tion n.; re-emerge' v.i.;* so *re-emer'gence n., re-emer'gent a.; re-ena'ble v.t.; re-enact' v.t.;* so *re-enact'- ment n.; re-en'ter v.i. & t.* (part. occas.= RE-ENTRANT); *re-en'trance n.; re-exist' v.t.; re-export' v.t.; re-ex'port n.,* commodity imported & then exported esp. without further manufacture; so *re-exporta'tion* n.; *refill' v.t., ref'ill* n., = *recharge* above; *refloat' v.t.* (stranded ship); *ref'luz n., backward flow; refo'rest v.t.,* turn into forest again; so *reforesta'tion n.; refurb'- ish v.t.; regild' v.t.; rehabil'itate v.t.,* restore to privileges, reputation, or proper condition; so *rehabilita'tion n.; reign'ite v.t.; reimport' v.t. & i.; reim- port'* 1 v.t., import (same goods) after exporting; so *reim'port n.; reimpose' v.t.,* reingra'tiate v.t.; *reinsert' v.t.;* so *reinser'- tion n.; reinvest' v.t.;* (see also sense 8) *reingra'tiate v.t.; reinvest'2* (see also sense 8) *reinves'titure n.; reinvig'orate v.t.;* so *reinvigora'tion n.; rekin'dle v.t. & i.; reline'*

stamp' v.t.; restart' v.t. & n.; restate' v.t., esp. put into more intelligible or convincing words; so *restate'ment n.; re- stock' v.t. & i.,* provide with or take in fresh stock; *resum'm'ons n.,* renewed legal summons; *resur'vey v.t.;* so *resur'vey n.; retaste' v.t.; retell' v.t.; retouch' v.t.* (esp. *retry' v.t.,* =release above; so *retri'al* n.; *returf' v.t.; reurge' v.t.; reuse' v.t.; revacc'inate v.t.;* so *revaccina'tion n.; revicr'tual v.t.; reves't it* (often ri-) v.t., *record v.t.,* change wording of; *rewrite' v.t.*

re-

v.t., renew lining of (esp. garment); reman'² (see also sense 8) v.t., restore to manhood or courage; remigrate' v.i., esp. return after migrating; so remigra'tion n.; reoc'cupy v.t.; so reoccupa'tion n.; reop'en v.t. & i.; repag'anize v.t.; repaint' v.t., restore paint or colouring of; repass' v.t. & i., pass again on way back; so repass'age n.; repeo'ple v.t.; repercu'ssion n., echo, recoil after impact, indirect effect or reaction of event or act; so repercuss'ive a.; repiece' v.t., put pieces of together again, reconstruct; repoint' v.t. (joints of masonry); repol'ish v.t.; repop'ulate v.t.; repossess' v.t.; so re-posse'ssion n.; repurch'ase v.t., & n.; repur'ify v.t.; repurch'ase n., v.t.; resad'dle v.t. & abs.; resale' n., esp. sale of thing bought; so resal'able a.; reseize' v.t.; so reseiz'ure n.; resell' v.t., esp. sell after buying; reshi̇p' v.t. & i., put, go, on board ship again; so reship'ment n.; restuff' v.t.; retake' n. (Cinemat.), a second photograph(ing) of a scene; retransfer' v.t.; so retrans'fer n.; retrans-form' v.t.; retranslate' v.t. (esp. back into the original language); so retransla'tion n.; retread' v.t.; reunite' v.t. & i.; revit'al-ize v.t.; revive' v.t.

're, colloq. abbr. of are appended to we, you, & they (we're, you're, they're).

reach¹, v.t. & i. 1. Stretch out etc., extend, (t. & i.; often out etc.; ~ed out his hand, its branches; a dominion ~ing from the Ebro to the Carpathians). 2. Stretch out the hand etc., make ~ing motion or effort lit. or fig., (you must ~ out further; mind ~es forward to an ideal; ship ~es ahead in race). 3. Get as far as, attain to, arrive at, (specified point or object of destination; also abs.), succeed in affecting, either simply or with the hand or instrument or missile or influence, (~ BOTTOM¹; ~ed land; could not ~ his enemy, esp. in fencing, boxing; how is her conscience to be ~ed?; labels that the ordinary law ~es; the steps by which you ~ the entrance; your letter ~ed me today; every syllable ~ed the audience; has ~ed middle age, its eighth edition; cannot ~ so high, far enough, down, up to it, etc.; as far as eye could ~; my income will not ~ to it). 4. Hand, pass or take with outstretched hand, (~ed him the book; ~ed down his hat). 5. ‖ ~me-down a. & n. (sl.), ready-made (garment). Hence ~'ABLE a. [OE rǣcan, cf. Du reiken, G reichen]

reach², n. 1. Act of reaching out. 2. Ex-tent to which hand etc. can be reached out, influence be exerted, motion be carried out, or mental powers be used, range, scope, compass, (within, above, out of, beyond, one's ~, possible, impossible, of attainment or performance; has a wide ~; within easy ~ of the railway; no help was within ~). 3. Continuous extent, esp. part of river that can be looked along at once between two bends. 4. (Naut.) length of tack. [f. prec.]

react', v.i. 1. Produce reciprocal or responsive effect, act upon the agent, (they ~ upon each other; tyranny ~s upon the tyrant, has effects upon him as well as upon his victims); (Chem., of substance applied to another) call out activity, cause manifestation, (nitrous oxide ~s upon the metal). 2. Respond to stimulus, undergo change due to some influence. 3. (Mil.) make counter-attack(s). 4. Be actuated by repulsion against, tend in reverse or backward direction. Hence reac'tive a., reactiv'ITY n. [RE-1]

reac'tion, n. 1. Responsive or reciprocal action (esp. action & ~); (Chem.) action set up by one substance in another; CHAIN ~. 2. Response of organ etc. to external stimulus; responsive feeling (what was his ~ to this news?). 3. Return of previous condition after interval of opposite (e.g. glow felt after cold bath, depression after excitement). 4. (Mil.) counter-stroke. 5. Retrograde tendency esp. in politics, whence ~ARY¹ (-sho-) a. & (= ~ary person) n., ~IST(2) (-sho-) n. & a. 6. (Wireless) method by which weak signals are strengthened. [RE-1]

read (rēd), v.t. & i. (read, pr. rĕd), & n. 1. Interpret mentally, declare interpreta-tion of or coming development of, divine, (~ dream, riddle, omen, futurity, men's hearts or thoughts or faces; ~ person's hand, as palmist; ~ the sky, as astrologist or meteorologist). 2. (Be able to) convert into the intended words or meaning (written or printed or other symbols or things expressed by their means, or abs.; ~s or can ~ hieroglyphs, shorthand, the clock, the Morse system, music, several languages; does not ~ or write). 3. Repro-duce mentally or (often aloud, out, off, etc., or with ind. obj.) vocally, while following their symbols with eyes or fingers, the words of (author, book, tale, letter, etc., or abs.; often over, through, advv.; ~s well, with good intonation etc., expressively; was ~ing Plato; it through six times; does he preach extempore or ~?; have no time to ~; the Bible is the most ~ of all books; ~ one a lesson, admonish him; the Bill was ~ for the first etc. time, was allowed its first etc. READING; invalid is ~ to for several hours daily; seldom ~s French, anything written in it). 4. Study (t. & i.) by ~ing (often up; is ~ing law; shall not ~ for honours; ‖ ~ing man, who devotes most of his time to study; has ~ much); (p.p. in active sense as adj. with well, deeply, slightly, little, etc.) versed in subject by ~ing, acquainted with litera-ture. 5. Find (thing) stated, find state-

ment, in print etc. (*revenge, we ~ 's wild justice; I have ~ somewhere that . . .*; have ~ *of it*). **6.** Interpret (statement, action) in certain sense (*may be ~ several ways*; *my silence is not to be ~ as consent*). **7.** Assume as intended in or deducible from writer's words, find, implications, (*you ~ too much into the text*; *in their pleas for reform I ~ Protection*; ~ *between the lines*, search for or discover hidden meanings). **8.** (Of editor) give as the word(s) probably used by author (*Bentley ~s peraeque*; *also joc. in correcting statements, as for white ~ black*, & *the account may be accepted*). **9.** Bring into specified state by ~*ing* (~ *me to sleep*; *himself stupid, hoarse*, etc.; || ~ *oneself in*, of incumbent, enter upon office by public recording of xxxix articles etc.). **10.** (Of recording instrument) present (figure etc.). to one ~*ing it* (*thermometer ~s 33°*). **11.** Sound or affect hearer or reader well, ill, etc., when ~ (*play ~s better than it acts*; ~*s like a threat, translation*, etc.). **12.** n. Time spent in ~*ing* (*have a short, long, day, good, quick, ~*). [com.-Teut., cogn. w. Skr. *rādh*- accomplish]

read'a̱ble, a. Interestingly written; (rare) legible. Hence rea̱dabil'ity, ~le-NESS, nn., ~LY² adv. [-ABLE]

readdress. See RE-8.

read'er, n. In vbl senses; also or esp. person employed by publisher to read & report on offered MSS.; printer's proof-corrector; person appointed to read aloud, esp. (often *lay* ~) parts of service in church; || lecturer in some universities etc. (~ *in Roman law* etc.); book of selections for use by students of a language etc. Hence ~SHIP n. [-ER²]

rea̱d'ily (-red-), adv. Without showing reluctance, willingly; without difficulty (*the facts may ~ be ascertained*). [READILY, -LY²]

rea̱d'iness (-red-.), n. Prompt compliance, willingness; facility, prompt resourcefulness, quickness in argument or action; ready or prepared state (*all is in ~*). [READY, -NESS]

read'ing, n. In vbl senses; also or esp.: literary knowledge (*a man of vast ~*); first, second, third, ~, successive occasions on which Bill must have been presented for acceptance to each House before it is ready for royal assent (*first ~*, permitting introduction; *second*, approving general principle; *third*, accepting details as amended in committee); entertainment at which something is read to audience (|| *penny ~*, formerly for poor of parish or found in MS. in text of a passage (*the right, true, best, MS.*, etc.; ~; *various ~s*); (specified quality of) matter to be read (*is good, dull, ~*; *there is plenty of ~ in it*); figure etc. shown by graduated instrument or indicated. (~ *money, coin, cash; the ~*)

Interpretation, view taken, rendering, (*what is your ~ of the facts?*; *his ~ of Iago was generally condemned*); ~*-desk, for supporting book etc., lectern*; ~*-room, in club etc. for persons wishing to read.* [-ING¹]

readjust etc. See RE-8.

rea̱d'ly̱ (-red-), a., adv., n., & v.t. **1.** With preparations complete, in fit state, with resolution nerved, willing, apt, inclined, about to, prompt, quick, facile, provided, beforehand, within reach, easily secured, unreluctant, easy, fit for immediate use, (*are you ~? Go!, formula for starting race*; ~, *present, fire*, successive orders, the first = make ready ~; *dinner is ~*; *are ~ to march*; *am ~ to risk my life*; *is too ~ to suspect*; *was ~ to swear with rage*; *a bud just ~ to burst*; *is ~ for death*; *the ministers of vengeance; is very ~ of excuses*; *has a ~ pen, wit*, whence ~WITTEN² a., etc.; *gave a ~ consent*; *found ~ acceptance*; *its ~ solubility in water*; *found an instrument ~ to hand*, *a ~ source of revenue*; *the readiest way to do it; make ~, prepare* **1.** & t., *as they made ~ for the attempt or to fight, or made everything ~*; ~ *money, actual coin*, also payment on the spot); ~ *reckoner, book of ~-reckoned computations of kind commonly wanted in business. **2.** adv. (chiefly with p.p., usu. hyphened, prop. & pred. use of adj.). Beforehand, so as not to require doing when the time comes, (*please pack everything ~; boxes are ~ packed or packed ~*; ~ *-built houses*; ~ *made clothes, made in standard shapes & sizes, not to customer's individual measure*; ~ *-made shop, selling these*); (rare exc. in comp. & superl.) quickly (the child that answers readiest). **3.** n. Position in which rifle is held before the present (*come down to the ~ etc.*) (sl.) ~ *money* (*plumbed* (horse) for good ~ *handicap in race by preventing its winning in another.* [ME *rædy*, perh. f. OE *geræde* = MHG *gereit*, cf. f. G *bereit*, +-Y² on false anal.]

reaffirm etc., see RE-8; reafforest etc., RE-9.

rea̱'gency̱ (-jen-), n. Reactive power or operation (see REACT).

rea̱'gent, n. (Chem.) substance used to detect presence of another by REACTION; reactive substance or force (see REACT).

re'al¹ (rē-, rǎ-), n. Former silver coin & money of account used in Spain and Spanish-speaking countries (the ~ *de plata* being worth 6½d., and the ~ *de vellon*, of base metal, 2½d.). [Sp., n. use of adj. f. L *regalis* REGAL]

rē'al² a. **1.** Actually existing as a thing or occurring in fact, objective, genuine, rightly so called, natural, sincere, not merely apparent or nominal or supposed or pretended or artificial or hypocritical or affected, (~ *money, coin, cash; the ~*)

presence, of Christ's body & blood in the Eucharist as disputed by theologians; *a ~ object & its image*; *~ & paper roses*; *effected a ~ cure*; *should like a ~ fine day*; *~ life*, that lived by actual people, opp. fictitious & dramatic imitations; *there is no ~ doubt about it*; *who is the ~ manager?*; *is a ~ man*, unaffected, also worthy of the name; *the ~ thing*, not a makeshift or inferior article). **2.** (Law; cf. PERSONAL) consisting of immovable property such as lands or houses (esp. *~ estate*). **3.** (Philos.) having an absolute & necessary & not merely contingent existence. **4.** abs. *The ~*, what is *~*, esp. the ideal (also rarely as n. with pl. = *~ thing*, as *I dead only with~9*). [f. LL *realis* (res thing, -AL)]

real′gar, n. Disulphide of arsenic, red arsenic, red orpiment, used as pigment & in fireworks. [med. L, f. Arab. *rehj al-ghār* powder of the cave]

re′alism, n. **1.** Scholastic doctrine that universals or general ideas have objective existence (cf. *nominalism, conceptualism*). **2.** Belief that matter as object of perception has real existence (cf. *idealism*). **3.** Practice of regarding things in their true nature & dealing with them as they are, freedom from prejudice & convention, practical views & policy, (cf. *idealism*). **4.** Fidelity of representation, truth to nature, insistence upon details. So *~IST*(2) n. & a., *~is′tic* a., *~is′tically* adv. [-ISM]

re′ality, n. Property of being real; resemblance to original (*reproduced with startling ~*); real existence, what is real, what underlies appearances, (*in~*, in fact, opp. *in words, in appearance*, etc.); existent thing; real nature of. [f. med. L *realitas* (REAL², -TY)]

re′aliz|e, v.t. **1.** Convert (hope, plan, etc.) into fact (usu. pass.). **2.** Give apparent reality to, make realistic, present as real, (*these details help to ~ the scene*); conceive as real, apprehend clearly or in detail (noun, that, how, etc.). **3.** Convert (securities, property) into money (often *abs.* = sell one's property); amass (fortune, specified profit); fetch as price. Hence *~ABLE* a., *~A′TION* n. [-IZE]

really (ri′ali), adv. In fact, in reality, (often *~ & truly*); positively, indeed, I assure you, I mean what I say, I protest; *~?*, do you mean it?, is that so? [-LY²]

realm (relm), n. Kingdom (chiefly rhet., & in some legal phrr., *as the laws of the ~, persons who are out of the ~*); sphere, province, domain, (*the ~s of fancy, poetry*, etc.). [f. OF *reaume* f. pop. L *+regālimen* (REGAL, -MEN)]

Realpolitik (rāahl′ pŏlĭtēk′), n. Policy of placing the material greatness and success of one's own nation before all other considerations. [G, = real politics]

•**re′altŏr**, n. Real-estate agent (prop. one who is a member or affiliated member of the National Association of Real Estate Boards). [U.S., f. foll. +-OR²]

re′alty, n. Real estate (cf. *personalty*). [-TY]

ream¹, n. Twenty quires or 480 sheets of paper (often 500, to allow for waste; *printers' ~*, 516); (often pl.) large quantity of paper (*wrote ~s & ~s of verse*). [ult. f. Arab. *rizmah* bundle, cf. Du. *riem*, OF *renme*, It. *risma*]

∥**ream²**, v.t. Widen (hole in metal) with borer or *~*ER²(2) n.; turn over edge of (cartridge-case etc.); (Naut.) open (seam) for caulking. [OE *rȳman* (ROOM), cf. G *räumen*]

∥**ream³**, n. (dial., esp. SW. Eng.). Raw cream. [OE]

reanimate etc. See RE- 9.

reap, v.i. & t. Cut (grain or similar crop), cut grain etc., with sickle in harvest; gather in thus or with machine or fig, as harvest (*~ as one has sown, sow wind & ~ whirlwind, ~ the fruits of*, take consequences of one's actions; *~ where one has not sown*, profit by others' toil); harvest crop of (field etc.); *~ing-hook*, sickle; *~ing-machine*, for cutting grain & often binding sheaves without manual labour. Hence *~*ER¹(1, 2) n. [OE *rīpan*, excl. E]

reappear etc., see RE- 8; **reappear** etc., re-**appoint** etc., RE- 9.

rear¹, n. Hindermost part of army or fleet (*hang on the ~ of*, follow with view to attacking; *back of*, space behind, position at back of, army or camp or person (*bring, close, up the ~*, come last; *take enemy in ~*, attack from behind; *saw them far in the ~, behind; was sent to the ~ for safety*); back part of anything (*at the ~ of*, behind); ∥ (colloq.) water-closet or latrine; *~*, attrib., hinder, back-; so *~MOST* a.; *~-admiral*, flag-officer below vice-admiral; *~guard*, body of troops detached to protect *~* esp. in retreats (*~guard action*, engagement between *~ guard & enemy*); *′ward* n. [f. AF *rereward = ~-ward*(1), or (esp. in prep. phrr.; *to ~ward of, in the ~ward*); *′ward* a. & adv., *′wards* adv., towards the *~*. [-WARD(S). [shortened f. ARREAR]

rear² *~*ER¹ & i. **1.** Raise, set upright, build, uplift, hold upwards, (rhet.; *~ a pillar, cathedral*, etc.; *~ed his mighty stature*; *~ed his head*, one's voice, a hand, etc.). **2.** Raise, bring up, breed, foster, nourish, educate, cultivate, grow, (cattle, game, children, crops, etc.). **3.** (Of horse etc., intr. & rarely refl.) rise, raise itself, on hind feet. Hence *~*ER¹ n. [OE *rǣran*, native form corresp. to & largely ousted by RAISE]

rear-arch, **rēr e′**, n. Inner arch of window or door opening when of different

For pronunciation & hyphening of *re-* see RE-; for words in *re-* not given see RE- 8, 9.

rearise, **rearose** etc., from the outer. [f. F *arrière* see ARREAR]

rear-vault, n. Vaulted space connecting arched window or door head with arch in inner face of wall. [as REAR-ARCH]

reascend. See RE- 9.

reas'on[1] (-z-), n. **1.** (Fact adduced or serving as) argument, motive, cause, or justification (*give ~s for; prove with ~s; the woman's ~, repetition of fact as its own explanation, as in I love him because I love him; for no other ~ than that I forgot, but this; there is no ~ to suppose; ~ of State, political justification esp. for im-moral proceeding; the ~ of your isolation, of eclipses, is that—; I failed by ~ of its bad organization; there was ~ to believe; I saw ~ to suspect him; he complains with ~; not unjustifiably*). **2.** (Log.) one of premisses of syllogism, esp. minor premiss when given after conclusion. **3.** The intellectual faculty characteristic esp. of human beings by which conclusions are drawn from premisses (*whether dogs have ~ is readily a question of definition; there can be no opposition between ~ & common sense*). **4.** Intellect personified (*God &c ~ are identical*); (as transl. of G *Vernunft* in Kant) faculty transcending the under-standing (*Verstand*) & providing *a priori* principles, intuition. **5.** Sanity (*has lost his, is restored to, ~s*). **6.** Sense, sensible conduct, what is right or practical or practicable, moderation (*without RHYME or ~; bring to ~, induce to cease from vain resistance; will do anything in ~, within the bounds of moderation; it stands to ~, cannot be denied without paradox, would be generally admitted; hear or listen to ~, suffer oneself to be per-suaded; as ~ was, as good sense bade; have ~, arch. or transl. of F, be right; there is ~ in what you say*). Hence ~LESS[a]. [f. OF *raisun* f. L *rationem* (see RATION); *consider*, -ION]

reas'on[2] (-z-), v.i. & t. **1.** Use argument with person by way of persuasion. **2.** Form or try to reach conclusions by con-nected thought silent or expressed (*from premisses: about, of, upon, subject, whence ~ED[1] n.; discuss what, whether, why, etc.; conclude, assume as step in argument, say by way of argument, that (or parenth.).* **3.** Express in logical or argumentative form (*a ~ed exposition, manifesto, article; ~ed amendment, in which reasons are embodied with a view to directing course of debate*). **4.** Per-suade by argument out of, into (*tried to ~ him out of his fears; led himself into perplexity*). **5.** Think out (*consequences etc.).* Hence ~ING[1]( ) n. [f. OF *raisoner* (prec.)]

reas'onable (-z-), a. **1.** Endowed with reason, reasoning. (rare). **2.** Sound of judgement, sensible, moderate, not expecting too much, ready to listen to reason. **3.** Agreeable to reason, not absurd, within the limits of reason, not greatly less or more than might be expected, inexpensive, not extortionate, tolerable, fair. Hence ~LENESS n., ~LY[2] adv. [f. OF *raisonable* (REASON[1], -ABLE)]

reassemble, see RE- 9; **reassert, re-assess** etc., **reassign, reassume, reassure** etc., see RE- 9.

Réaumur (see AP-), n. Name of French physicist appended (abbr. R.) to readings of the thermometer introduced by him with freezing-point 0° & boiling-point 80° (*a temperature of more than 55° R. or ~*). [F]

reave, reive, (rēv), v.i. & t. (arch., poet.; *v&f*). Commit ravages (usn. *reive*); whence **reiv'ER**[1] (rēv'-) n.; forcibly deprive of (esp. in p.p.); take by force, carry off, (*away, from*). [com.-Teut.; OE *réafian*, cf. Du. *rooven*, G *rauben*]

rebaptize etc., see RE- 8; **rebarbarize, rebaptize**, RE- 9.

‖ **rebate'**[1], v.t. (arch.). Diminish, reduce force or effect of; blunt, dull. [f. OF *rabattre* (RE- 5, ABATE)]

reb'ate[2] (*also ribāt'*), n. Deduction from sum to be paid, discount, drawback. [f. F *rabat* (prec.)]

rebate[3] (rǎb'it, ribǎt'), n., & v.t. = RABBET.

reb'eck(k), n. Medieval three-stringed in-strument, early form of fiddle. [f. F *rebec* var. of OF *rebebe* f. Arab. *rebâb*]

reb'el[1], n. Person who rises in arms against, resists, or refuses allegiance to the established government; person or thing that resists authority or control; (attrib.) rebellious, of ~s, in rebellion. [orig. a. & n.; the pred. a. use now obs.; f. F *rebelle* f. L *rebellis* (RE- 2, *bellum* war)]

rebel'[2], v.i. (-ll-). Act as rebel (*against*); feel or manifest repugnance to some custom etc. (*against*). [f. F *rebeller* f. L *rebellare* make war] revolt, RE- 2]

rebell'ion (-lyon), n. Organized armed resistance to established government (*the Great R~, period of English history 1642–60*); open resistance to any authority. [f. F *rebellion* f. L *rebellionem* (REBEL[1], -ION)]

rebell'ious (-lyus), a. In rebellion, dis-posed to rebel, insubordinate, defying lawful authority; (of diseases, things) dif-ficult to treat, unmanageable, refractory. Hence ~LY[2] adv., ~NESS n. [as REBEL[1] or prec. +-OUS]

rebell'ow (-ō), v.i. & t. (poet.). Re-echo loudly. [RE- 6; after L *reboare* bellow, BELLOW, -ANT]

rebind, see RE- 9; **rebirth** etc., **rebite**, RE- 8.

rebound'[1], v.i. Spring back after impact; have reactive effect, recoil upon agent,

rebound (*our evil example will ~ upon ourselves*). [f. OF *rebonder* (RE-1, BOUND³)]

rebound²*, n. Act of rebounding, recoil; reaction after emotion (*take one on* or *at the ~*, utilize such reaction to persuade him to contrary action etc.). [f. prec.]

rebuff', n., & v.t. **1.** Check given to one who makes advances, proffers help or sympathy, shows interest or curiosity, makes request, etc., repulse, snub. **2.** v.t. Give ~ to. [f. obs.F *rebuffe(r)* f.It. *ribuffo, ribuffare*, (RE-2, *buffo* puff)]

rebuild. See RE-5.

rebuke', v.t., & n. **1.** Reprove, reprimand, censure authoritatively; hence ~'ingₓ² adv. **2.** n. ~ing or being ~ed; a reproof. [f. ONF *re(buker*= OF *bucher* beat), RE-5]

reb'us, n. Enigmatic representation of name, word, etc., by pictures etc. suggesting its syllables. [prob.=abl. pl. of L *res* thing; origin of sense (in F & E) doubtful]

rebut', v.t. (-tt-). Force or turn back, give check to; refute, disprove, (evidence, charge), whence ~t'AL(2), ~MENT, ~t'ER⁴ (see SURREBUT), nn. [f. OF *re(buter* BUTT⁴), RE-9]

recal'citr|āte, v.i. Kick *against* or *at* rules etc., refuse compliance, be refractory. So~ANT(1) a. & n., ~ANCE, ~A'TION, nn. [f. L *re(calcitrare* strike with heel f. *calx -cis* heel), RE-2, -ATE³]

recal'ĕsce', v.i. Grow hot again (esp. in techn. use of iron allowed to cool from white heat, which recovers heat at certain point for short time). Hence ~ĕs'CENCE n. [f. L *re(calescere* grow hot), RE-9]

recall'¹ (-awl), v.t. Summon back from a place or from different occupation, inattention, digression, etc.; cancel appointment of (official sent to distance, esp. overseas); bring back to memory, serve as reminder of, recollect, remember; revive, resuscitate; revoke, annul, (action, decision), take back (gift). Hence ~ABLE a. [RE-9]

recall'²(-awl), n. Summons to come back; cancelling of appointment abroad; signal to ship etc. to return; possibility of recalling esp. in sense of annulling (esp. *beyond, past, ~*). [RE-9]

recant', v.t. & i. Withdraw & renounce (opinion, statement, etc.) as erroneous or heretical; disavow former opinion, esp. with public confession of error. Hence **recant**aᵗTION n. [f. L *re(cantare* sing) revoke, RE-7]

recapitulate etc., see RE-8; **recapture,** RE-9; **recast,** RE-8.

recēde', v.i. Go or shrink back or farther off; be left by observer's motion at increasing distance; slope backwards; withdraw (*from engagement, opinion, etc.*); decline in character or value. [f. L *re(cē-dere* go), RE-5]

receipt' (-sēt), n., & v.t. **1.** = RECEIPE. **2.** Amount of money received. **3.** Fact or action of receiving or being received into person's hands or possession (*on ~ of a postal order for 10/- the goods will be sent; beg to acknowledge ~ of your book; entrusted with the ~ of subscriptions*); written acknowledgement of such ~ esp. of payment of sum due. **4.** (arch.). Place where money is officially received, esp. ~ *of custom,* custom-house. **5.** v.t. Write or print ~ on (bill). [ME *receit* f. ONF *receite* f. L *recepta* fem. p.p. of *recipere* RECEIVE w. -p- inserted on L]

receive' (-sēv), v.t. **1.** Accept delivery of, take (proffered thing) into one's hands or possession, (*Lord, ~ my soul,* dying man's prayer; ~ *stolen goods,* as thief's accomplice; ~ *person's confession, oath,* consent to hear; ~ *a petition,* take it to consider; ~ *the sacraments,* eat & drink the bread & wine, also abs., as *attend without receiving*). **2.** Bear up against, stand force or weight of, encounter with opposition, (~d *his body in their hands; arch ~s weight of roof; ~d the sword-point with his shield; prepare to ~ cavalry,* order to infantry). **3.** Admit, consent or prove able to hold, provide accommodation for, submit to, serve as receptacle of, (*had to ~ the visits, attentions, of;* ~ *an impression, stamp, mark, etc.,* be marked lit. or fig. more or less permanently with it; *sensitive paper ~s the record of signals; the basin that ~d his blood; the house ~d a new guest; hole large enough to ~ two men; fitted to ~ the knowledge of God; has ~d our yoke; town ~s a French garrison; was ~d into the Church,* admitted to membership). **4.** Entertain as guest, greet, welcome, give specified reception to, (*shall not be ~d at my house; he that ~th me ~th him that sent me; you slay here & ~ him; how did she ~ his offer?; was ~d with cries of Judas; news was ~d with horror; I ~ it as certain, as a prophecy,* regard it in that light); (abs.) ~ *company,* hold reception. **5.** Give credit to, accept as true, (*an axiom universally ~d; they ~ not our report*), whence **received¹** (-sēvd') a. **6.** Acquire, get, come by, be given or provided with, have sent to or conferred or inflicted on one, (*have not yet ~d my dividend; ~ a letter, news; a window that has not ~d a frame; ~ the name of John;* ~ *Christ in baptism,* have Christian character conferred; *pleasant to ~ sympathy; deserves more attention than it ~s;* ~ *orders to march; ~d many insults, a thrust, a broken jaw, the contents of his pistol*); partake of. Hence **receiv'ABLE** (-sēv-) a. [f. ONF *receivre* f. L *re(cipere= capere* take) recover, RE-9]

receiv'er (-sēv-), n. In vbl senses, esp.: person appointed by court's *receiving-*

For pronunciation & hyphening of *re-* see RE-; for words in *re-* not given see RE-8, 9.

recen'sion (-shn), n. Revision of text, or light, wireless receiving-set. [-ER¹] text. [f. L *recensio* f. *recensēre* review], RE- 8]

rē'cent, a. Not long past, that happened or existed lately, late; not long established, lately begun, modern. Hence **rē'cENCY** n., **~LY²** adv., **~NESS** n. [f. L *recens -entis*]

recep'tacle, n. Containing vessel, place, or space; (Bot.) common base of floral organs, axis of cluster. [f. L *receptaculum* (*recipi-* p.p. st. of *recipere* RECEIVE)]

recep'tion, n. **1.** Receiving or being received (rare in gen. sense); receiving esp. of those being received, into a place or company (*the rooms were prepared for his* ~; *was honoured by* ~ *into the Academy*; || ~ *order*, authorizing or certifying lunatic in asylum). **2.** Formal or ceremonious welcome (*the* ~ *of the delegates is arranged for Monday next*); occasion of receiving guests, assembly held for this purpose, (*after the review there will be a* ~; ~*-room*, available for receiving company). **3.** Receiving of ideas or impressions into the mind (*has a great faculty of* ~, *but little originative power*); (rare) mental acceptance, recognition of something as true or advisable, (*the general* ~ *of the Newtonian hypothesis*). **4.** Welcome or greeting of specified kind, denomination of feeling towards person or project, (*warm* ~, *vigorous resistance or enthusiastic welcome*; *his* ~ *was frigid, all that he could desire*). **5.** Receiving of wireless signals, or the efficiency with which they are received. Hence **~IST** (3) (-sho-) n., person employed by photographer, dentist, etc., to receive clients. [f. L *receptio* (as prec.)]

recep'tive, a. Able or quick to receive impressions or ideas (*a mind more* ~ *than retentive or creative*); (rare) concerned with receiving. Hence **~LY²** adv., **~NESS,** **receptiv'ITY,** nn. [f. med. L *receptivus* (as prec.)]

recess', n. & v.t. **1.** Temporary cessation from work, vacation, esp. of Parliament; receding of water, land, glacier, etc., from previous limit, amount by which it recedes, recession, (rare); retired or secret place (*in the inmost* ~*es of the Alps, of the heart*); receding part of mountain chain etc., niche or alcove of wall; fold or indentation in organ. **2.** v.t. Place in a ~, set back; provide with ~(es). [f. L *recessus* (*recess-* p.p. st. of RECEDEre)]

reces'sion (-shn), n. Receding, with-

drawal, from a place or point; receding part of object, recess; *slump in trade. So **recess'IVE** a. & n., (also, Mendelism, of a) characteristic appearing in the second or later generation of hybrids, inherited from one of the original parents but suppressed in the first generation (cf. DOMINANT). [f. L *recessio* (as prec., -ION)]

reces'sional (-sho-), a. & n. (hymn or ~), hymn sung while clergy & choir withdraw after service (*the R~*, poem of Kipling in *The Five Nations* sung on imperial occasions) of the parliamentary recess. [-AL]

Rěch'abite (reshărb'it), n. Total abstainer. [*Rechab*, see Jer. xxxv. 6, -ITE¹(1)]

recharge. See RE- 8.

recherché (rĕsharsha'ă, & see Ap.), a. Warmed-up dish; rehash (RE- 8). [F] Devised or got with care or difficulty, choice, far-fetched, thought out, (esp. of meals or words). [F]

rechristen. See RE- 8.

récid'ivist, n. One who relapses into crime. So **~ISM** n. [f. F *récidiviste* f. L *recidivus* I. *re(cidere=cadere* fall), RE- 9, -IVE. -IST]

rěc'ipe, n. Medical prescription or remedy prepared from it; statement of ingredients & procedure for preparing dish etc.; something, nostrum, device for effecting something, [2nd sing. imperat. as used (abbr. Ṛ) in prescriptions of L *recipere* RECEIVE]

recip'ient, a. & n. **1.** Receptive, whence **~ENCY** n. **2.** n. Person who receives something. [f. L *recipere* RECEIVE, -ENT]

recip'rocal, a. & n. **1.** In return (*if I helped him, I had* ~ *help from him*); mutual (~ *love, protection, injuries*); inversely correspondent, complementary, (*I took the chamois for a man, & it made the* ~ *mistake*); (Gram.) expressing mutual action or relation ('*each other' is a* ~ *pronoun*), (formerly also) reflexive; hence **~LY²** adv. **2.** n. (math.). Function or expression so related to another that their product is unity (*1/5 is the* ~ *of 5*). [f. L *reciprocus* (prob. f. *re-* back & *pro* forward), -AL]

recip'rocate, v.t. & i. **1.** (Mech.) go with alternate backward & forward motion (~*ating engine* etc., with work done by part that moves thus, opp. *rotatory* see ROTATE²); give such motion to; give & receive mutually, interchange, (influence etc.); return, requite, (affection etc.), make a return (often *with* thing given in return). So **~A'TION** n. [f. L *reciprocare*]

reciproc'ity, n. Reciprocal condition, mutual action; principle or practice of give-&-take, esp. interchange of privileges between States as basis of commercial relations. [f. F *réciprocité* (RECIPROCAL, -ITY)]

recit'al, n. **1.** Detailed account of a

number of connected things or facts, relation of the facts of an incident etc., a narrative. **2.** Part of document stating facts. **3.** Act of reciting; performance of programme by one musician (*vocal, pianoforte*, etc., ~).

recitative' (-ēv), n. Musical declamation of kind usual in narrative & dialogue parts of opera & oratorio; words, part, given in ~. [f. It. *recitativo* (foll., -IVE²]

recite', v.t. & i. Repeat aloud or declaim (poem, passage) from memory esp. before audience, give recitation (*reciting-note*, that held on for indefinite number of syllables in chanting); (Law) rehearse (facts) in document; mention in order, enumerate. So **recita'TION** n. [f. L *re(citare* CITE], RE-8]

recif'er, n. Person who recites; book of passages for recitation. [-ER¹]

recivilize etc. See RE-9.

reck, v.i. & t. (rhet., poet., in neg. & interrog. sentences only). ~ *of*, pay heed to, take account of, care about; care, be troubled, concern oneself, (*if, though, that, how, whether*, etc., or abs.; also impers. ~*s it him that . . ?*). [com.-Teut.; OE *reccan*, cf. OHG *ruohen*, ON *rækja*]

reck'less, a. Devoid of caution, regardless of consequences, rash; heedless of danger etc. Hence ~LY² adv., ~NESS n. [OE *reccēlas* (prec., -LESS)]

reck'on, v.t. & i. **1.** Ascertain number or amount of, ascertain number or amount of, by counting or usu. by calculation, compute; *start from, go on to*, in counting (t. & i.); *count up, sum up* character of; arrive at as total (*I ~ 53 of them*). **2.** Include in computation, *count in*, place in class *among* or *with* or *in*, take *for*, regard *as*, consider *to be* (or with obj. & compl. as ~ *him wise, beyond redemption*). **3.** Conclude after calculation, be of the confident opinion, (*that*; also, chiefly U.S., parenth., cf. *calculate, guess*). **4.** Make calculations, cast up account or sum, (~ *without* one's HOST²), settle accounts *with* person. **5.** Rely or count or base plans *upon*. [OE *(ge)recenian*, cf. MDu. *rekenen*, G *rechnen*; cogn. w. RECK]

reck'oner (-kn-), n. In vbl senses; esp.: READY ~. [-ER¹]

reck'oning (-kn-), n. In vbl senses; esp.: *day of* ~, time when something must be atoned for or avenged; DEAD ~; *out in* one's ~, mistaken in a calculation or expectation. [-ING¹]

reclaim', v.t. & i., & n. **1.** Win back or away from vice or error or savagery or waste condition, reform, tame, civilize, bring under cultivation, whence ~ABLE a.; make protest, say in protest, (rare); so **reclama'TION** n. **2.** n. ~*ing*, reclamation, (rare, chiefly in *past* or *beyond* ~),

[f. OF *reclamer* f. L *re(clamare* shout) cry out against, RE-2]

reclame (rāk'lahm, & see Ap.), n. Art or practice by which notoriety is secured. [F]

rec'linate, a. (bot.). Bending downwards. [f. L *reclinatus* (foll., -ATE²]

recline', v.t. & i. Lay (esp. one's head, body, limbs) in more or less horizontal or recumbent position (p.p., of person, lying thus); assume or be in recumbent position, lie or lean, sit with back or side supported at considerable inclination; (fig.) rely confidently *upon*. [f. L *reclinare* (RE-9), see DECLINE¹]

reclothe. See RE-8.

recluse' (-ōōs), a., & n. (Person) given to or living in seclusion or retirement or isolation, esp. as religious discipline, hermit, anchorite or anchoress. [F'(-*us*, -*use*) p.p. of *reclure* f. L *re(cludere=claudere* shut), RE-4]

recoal, recoat. See RE-8.

recogni'tion, n. In vbl senses (RECOGNIZE). So **recog'nitory** a. (rare). [f. L *recognitio* (RECOGNIZE, -ION)]

recog'nizance (or -kon-², n. Bond by which person engages before court or magistrate to observe some condition, e.g. to keep the peace, pay a debt, or appear when summoned; sum pledged as surety for such observance. [f. OF *reconissance* (*reconoistre* RECOGNIZE, -ANCE)]

recog'nizant (or -kon-², a. Showing recognition (of favour etc.), conscious or showing consciousness of something. [as foll., see -ANT]

rec'ognize, v.t. **1.** Acknowledge validity or genuineness or character or claims or existence of, accord notice or consideration to, discover or realize nature of, treat *as*, acknowledge *for*, realize or admit *that*. **2.** Know again, identify as known before. Hence ~ABLE a., ~ABIL'ITY n., ~ABLY² adv. [f. OF *reconniss-* part. st. of *reconoistre* f. L *re(cognoscere -gnitum* learn), RE-8, w. assim. to -IZE]

recoil', v.i., & n. **1.** Retreat before enemy (now rare); start or spring back, shrink mentally, in fear or horror or disgust; rebound after impact, (of fire-arms) be driven backwards by discharge, kick. **2.** n. Act or fact or sensation of ~*ing*. [n. f. vb, f. OF *reculer* (RE-9, *cul* the posterior f. L *culus*)]

recoin etc. See RE-8.

recollect', v.t. Succeed in remembering, recall to mind, remember. [f. p.p. st. of L *re(colligere* COLLECT², RE-8]

recollec'tion, n. Act, power, of recollecting; thing recollected, reminiscence; person's memory, time over which it extends, (*it is in my ~ion that*, I remember that; *happened within my ~ion*). So ~IVE a. [f. med. L *recollectio* (prec., -ION)]

For pronunciation & hyphening of *re-* see RE-; for words in *re-* not given see RE-8, 9.

recolonize etc., recolour, recombine etc., see RE- 8; reconnoitre, RE- 9; recommence etc., see RE- 8; reconfort, RE- 9; recom-

recommend', v.t. 1. Give (oneself, one's spirit, a child, etc.) in charge to God or a person or his care etc. 2. Speak or write of or suggest as fit for employment or favour or trial (to person, or with ind. obj. as *can you ~ me a cook, a book?*; as servant etc.; *for post*). 3. (Of qualities, conduct, etc.) make acceptable, serve as recommendation of. 4. Advise (course of action or treatment, person to do, that thing should be done). Hence or cogn. ~ATION n., ~ABLE a., ~ATORY aa. [f. med. L *recommendare* COMMEND), RE- 5]

recommit etc. See RE- 8.

recompense, v.t., & n. 1. Requite, reward or punish, (person, action, person for action, person to person or with ind. obj.); make amends to (person) or for (another's loss, injury, etc., or rarely one's own misconduct). 2. n. Reward, requital, atonement or satisfaction given for injury, retribution. [f. OF *recompenser* f. LL *recompensare* COMPENSARE), RE- 1]

recompose, recompound. See RE- 8.

reconcile, v.t. 1. Make friendly after estrangement (persons to one another, person *to* or *with* another, person to oneself). 2. Make (consecrated place etc.) by special service after desecration. 3. Make resigned or contentedly submissive (*to* disagreeables, *to* doing, or abs.; usu. in pass.). 4. Heal, compose, (quarrel etc.). 5. Harmonize, make compatible, show compatibility of by argument or in practice, (apparently conflicting facts, statements, qualities, actions, or one such *with* or *&* or rarely *to* another). Hence or cogn. ~ABLE a., ~ABILITY, ~EMENT (-lm-), RECONCILIA'TION, nn. [f. L *reconciliare* CONCILIATE), RE- 9]

rec'ondite (or rikon'), a. (Of subjects of knowledge) abstruse, out of the way, little known; (of author or style) dealing in ~ knowledge or allusion, obscure. Hence ~LY² adv., ~NESS n. [f. L *reconditus* p.p. of *condere* hide), RE- 4]

recondi'tion, v.t. Overhaul & refit, rehabilitate, renovate. [RE- 8]

rec'onduct. See RE- 9.

reconnaissance (-nis-), n. Military or naval examination of tract by detachment to locate enemy or ascertain strategic features (~ *in force*, made by strong party); reconnoitring party; preliminary survey made by anyone for any purpose. [F (earlier *-oissance*) as foll. -ANCE]

reconnoi'tre(re(-ter), v.t. & i., & n. 1. Make reconnaissance of (enemy, district), approach & try to learn position & condition etc. of; make reconnaissance. 2. n. (rare). Reconnaissance. Hence ~ER¹ n. [f. F *reconnoître* f. L *recognoscere* RECOGNIZE]

reconquer etc., see RE- 8; **reconsider**

etc., reconstitute etc., reconstruct etc., RE- 8; reconvert etc., RE- 9.

record'¹, v.t. 1. (Of birds) practise (tune, or abs.), by singing in an undertone. 2. Register, set down for remembrance or reference, put in writing or other legible form, (*this thoughts have been ~ed for us by himself, his features by Watts, & his voice by the phonograph; ~ing angel*, who registers men's good & bad actions; *ménimum thermometer ~ed 10° below zero*). Hence ~ABLE a. [f. OF *recorder* f. L *recordare* (classical *-ari*) remember (RE-, *cor* heart)]

record'², n. 1. State of being recorded or preserved in writing esp. as authentic legal evidence (*is on ~*, legally or otherwise recorded; *matter of ~*, something established as fact by being recorded; *court of ~*, whose proceedings are recorded & valid as evidence of fact). 2. Official report of proceedings & judgement in cause before court of ~, copy of pleadings etc. constituting case to be decided by court (*travel out of, keep to, the ~*, introduce, abstain from introducing, irrelevant matter). 3. ||(Public) R~ Office, building in London in which State papers and other public documents are stored, calendared, etc. 4. Piece of recorded evidence or information, account of fact preserved in permanent form, document or monument preserving it; *off the ~*, unofficial(ly); object serving to ~ as memorial of something, portrait etc.; series of marks giving record of operation etc. on plate etc. containing these (*second-hand gramophone ~s for sale*). 5. Facts known about person's past (*has a ~*; attrib.) best hitherto recorded (*at ~ pace; the ~ height*). [OF (prec.)]

record'er, n. In vbl senses; also: city or borough magistrate with criminal & civil jurisdiction || & holding court of Quarter sessions, whence ~SHIP n.; recording-apparatus in instruments; vertical (English) flute [RECORD¹, 1st sense].

record'ing, n. In vbl senses, esp. (Wireless) process of registering sound for subsequent reproduction, material (disk, film, magnetic steel tape) on which sound has been registered, sound-programme registered & reproduced. [-ING¹]

recount'¹, v.t. Narrate, tell in detail. [f. ONF *reconter* COUNT²), RE- 8]

re-count'², v.t. & i. (Law) deduct, keep back, (part of sum due), make such deduction; compensate (person loss, person *for* loss, loss; ~ *oneself*, recover what one has expended or lost). Hence

~MENT n. [f. F re(*couper* cut, see COUP), RE-5]

recourse' (-ôrs), n. Resorting or betaking of oneself to possible source of help (*~ to brandy is deprecated*; usu. in phr. *have ~ to*, adopt as adviser, helper, or expedient); thing resorted to (rare; *their usual ~ is perjury*); *without ~* (Commerce, Law), formula used by indorser of a bill etc. to indicate that he disclaims responsibility for non-payment. [f. F *recours* f. L *re(cursus* COURSE¹), RE-9]

reco'ver¹ (-kŭ-), v.t. & i., & n. 1. Regain possession or use or control of, acquire to find (out) again, reclaim, (*has ~ed his kingdom, his friends' affection, the meaning of the hieroglyphs, the track, health, his appetite, his voice, much land from the sea*; *~ oneself*, regain consciousness or calmness or control of limbs or senses; *horse ~s itself after stumble*; *~ one's legs*, stand up after fall). 2. Secure restitution or compensation, secure (damages), by legal process (*plaintiff shall ~ according to verdict*; *his remedy is to ~ in a court of law*; *an action to ~ damages for false imprisonment*). 3. Bring or come back to life, consciousness, health, or normal state or position (*the ~ed slowly*; *the mention of a bucket of water ~ed her*; *I ~ed the head of my body with fomentations*; *corpse cannot be ~ed to life*; *~ed me from a lingering illness*; *am quite ~ed from my cold*; *sad down to ~ from his agitation*; *~ sword*, bring it back after thrust etc., or, Mil., hold it upright with hilt opposite mouth). 4. Retrieve, make up for, get over, cease to feel effects of (*must try to ~ lost time*; *never ~ed the blow, this faux pas*). 5. Make one's way back to (rare; *~ed the shore with difficulty*); hence ~ABLE a. 6. n. Position to which sword etc. is brought back in fencing or drill, act of coming to this. [f. OF *recover* f. L *recuperare* RECUPERATE]

re-cover². See RE-8.

reco'very¹ (-kŭ-), n. Act or process of RECOVER¹ing or being recovered. [f. OF *recovree* (RECOVER¹,-Y⁴)]

recré'ant, a. & n. (rhet., poet.). Craven, coward(ly), apostate. Hence ~ANCY n., ~antLY² adv. [OF, part. of *re(croire* f. L *credere* entrust), RE-6, yield in trial by combat]

re'créàte¹, v.t. & i. (Of pastime, relaxation, holiday, employment, etc., or refl. of person indulging in them) refresh, entertain, agreeably occupy, (*it ~ates him to invent histories for his neighbours*; *~ates himself with cricket, climbing, lying in a hammock, political argument*; amuse oneself, indulge in ~ation. Hence ~A⁴TION n., ~ATIVE a. [f. L *re(creare* CREATE), RE-8,-ATE³]

re-create² etc. See RE-8.

recré'ment, n. Waste product, refuse, (now rare); (Physiol.) fluid separated from blood & again absorbed in it, e.g. saliva, bile. Hence ~R'TIOUS¹ (-shus) a. [f. L *re(crementum* f. *cernere cret-* sift, RE-5,-MENT)]

recrim'inàte, v.i. Retort accusation, indulge in mutual or counter charges. So ~ATION n., ~ATIVE, ~ATORY a. [f. med. L *re(criminari* f. *crimen*, CRIME), RE-1]

recross'. See RE-9.

recrudèsce' (-ōō-), v.i. (Of sore, disease, etc., or fig. of discontent etc.) break out again. So ~ES'CENT a., ~ES'CENCE n. [f. L *re(crudescere* f. *crudus* raw, see -ESCENT), RE-8]

recruit'¹ (-rōōt), n. Newly enlisted & not yet trained soldier; person who joins a society etc.; tiro (often *raw ~*). [earlier sense *reinforcement*, f. obs. F *recruit* = *recrue* fem. p.p. of *re(croître*, OF *creistre*, f. L *crescere* increase), RE-8]

recruit'² (-rōōt), v.t. & i. 1. Enlist recruits for (army, regiment, crew, society, party), enlist (person) as recruit, get or seek recruits (esp. *~ing-sergeant*). 2. Replenish, fill up deficiencies or compensate wear & tear in, reinvigorate. 3. (Seek to) recover health etc. (*has gone to the country to ~*), whence ~AU(2) n. Hence ~MENT (-rōō-) n. [f. F *recruter* (obs. *recrue*, see prec.)]

rec'tal, a. Of or by the rectum. [-AL]

rec'tangle (-nggl), n. Plane rectilinear four-sided figure with four right angles, esp. one with adjacent sides unequal. [f. LL *rectangulus* (*rectus* straight, ANGLE¹) right-angled]

rectang'ular (-ngg-), a. Shaped, having base or sides or section shaped, like rectangle; placed, having parts or lines placed, at right angles. Hence ~ITY (-ă'r-) n., ~LY² adv. [as prec., -AR¹]

rec'tify, v.t. 1. Put right, correct, amend, reform, adjust, (method, calculation, statement, position, instrument). 2. Abolish, get rid of, exchange for what is right, (abuse, anomaly, error, omission, grievance). 3. (Chem.) purify or refine by renewed distillation or other process. 4. (Geom.) find straight line equal to (curve). Hence or cogn. ~fiABLE a., ~FICA'TION n., ~fiER¹(1, 2) n., (also, Wireless) thermionic valve or other device transforming an alternating to a direct current. [f. F *rectifier* f. LL *rectificare* (L *rectus* right, FY)]

rectilin'ëar, -ëal, aa. In or forming a straight line; bounded or characterized by straight lines. Hence ~ëa'rITY n., ~ëarLY adv. [f. LL *rectilineus* (L *rectus* straight, *linea* LINE²), -AR¹, -AL]

rec'titude, n. Moral uprightness, righteousness; (rare) correctness, rightness. [F, f. LL *rectitudo* (L *rectus* right, -TUDE)]

For pronunciation & hyphening of re- see RE-; for words in re- not given see RE-8, 9.

rec̄to, n. Right-hand page of open book; front of leaf (opp. VERSO). [L recto]

rec̄to- (fōto) in comb. = rectus

rec̄tor, n. 1. ∥ Parson of parish whose tithes are not impropriate (cf. VICAR). 2. Head of university, college, school, or religious institution (esp. abroad); in England only of heads of Exeter & Lincoln Colleges, Oxford; in Scotland of headmasters of some secondary schools etc., & see LORD ~), whence rec̄'tress¹ n. Hence ~ATE¹, ~SHIP, nn., rectō'RIAL a. [f. L (as recto-)]

rec̄tory, n. ∥ Rector's benefice; rector's house. [f. med. L rectoria (prec.—Y¹)]

rec̄tum, n. Final section of large intestine, terminating at anus. [f. L rectum (intestinum) straight (intestine)]

recum'b|ent, a. Lying down, reclining. Hence ~ENCY n., ~ently adv. [f. L recumbere lie), ~ently adv. [f. L recumbere lie]

recū'p|erate, v.t. & i. Restore, be restored or recover, from exhaustion, illness, loss, etc. So ~A'TION n., ~ATIVE a. [f. L recuperare, recip-, extended form of recipere RECEIVE, -ATE³]

recū'r, v.i. (-rr-: part. pr. -ū'ring or -ū'ring). Go back in thought or speech to; (of idea etc.) come back to one's mind etc., return to mind; (of problem etc.) come up again; occur again, be repeated, (~ring decimals, figures in decimal fraction that ~ in same order again & again); ~ring curve, that returns upon itself, e.g. circle. Hence recū'rrence n. [f. L recurrere run), RE-9]

recū'rrent, a. & n. 1. (Of nerve, vein, branch, etc.) turning back so as to reverse direction; occurring again or often or periodically; hence ~LY² adv. 2. n. ~ artery or nerve, esp. one of the two laryngeal nerves. [as prec., -ENT]

recu'rve, v.t. & i. Bend backwards. So ~ATE² a., ~ATURE n. [f. L recurvare bend), RE-9]

rec̄'usant (-z-), n. & a. (Hist.) (person) who refused to attend Church-of-England services; (person) refusing submission to authority or compliance with regulation (against). Hence ~ANCE, ~ANCY, nn. [f. L recusare REFUSE]

recuse' (-z), v.t. (now rare). Reject (person, his authority); object to (judge) as prejudiced. [f. L recusare (RE-², cause cause) refuse]

rěd, a. & n. I. Of or approaching the colour seen at least refracted end of spectrum, of shades varying from crimson to bright brown & orange, esp. those seen in blood, sunset clouds, rubies, glowing coals, human lips, & fox's hair, (~ as a rose etc.; blood, fiery, yellowish, deep, etc., ~; ~ with anger etc., flushed in face; ~ hands, bloodstained; ∥ all-~ route, line, cable, etc., traversing British terri-tory or under British control, w. ref. to ~

in maps as British colour; ~ gold, arch. & poet., real gold, money; *~ cent, smallest coin orig. of copper, esp. don't care a ~ cent; ~ eyes, bloodshot, or with ~ lids sore from weeping, also of bird etc. with ~ iris; as distinctive epithet with many varieties of animal & plant & mineral, as ~ deer, partridge, mullet, ant, CURRANT, campion, ARSENIC). 2. Having to do with bloodshed, burning, violence, or revolution (~ battle, ruin; SEE ~; a ~ republican; radical, anarchical). 3. Russian, Soviet, (the Red Army, Air Force). 4. ~ ADMIRAL; ~ bark, superior kind of cinchona; ~ blind, colour-blind to ~; ∥ ~book (contain-ing list of nobility & gentry); ~ box, used by Ministers for official documents; ~ breast, the robin; ~carp, ∥ military police-man; ~coat, British soldier; ~ cross, St George's cross or national emblem of England, also Christian side in crusades, also (emblem of) ambulance service organized according to Geneva Conven-tion; ∥ ~ ENSIGN, used by British merchant ships; ~eye, the fish rudd; ~fish, male salmon in spawning season, also (market name for) salmon (opp. white fish of all other kinds); ~ flag, symbol of revolution (the Red Flag, a modern revolutionary song), signal for battle, danger-signal on shooting-ranges, railways, etc.; ~ gum, teething-rash in children, also (kinds of eucalyptus yielding) ~dish resin; ~handed, in the act of crime (take ~handed); ~ hat, cardinal's, ∥ (also nick-name for) British staff-officer; ~ heat, temperature of, being ~hot thing; ~ herring, herring(s) dened by being cured in smoke (neither fish, flesh, nor good ~ herring, of ambigu-ous indefinite nature; draw a ~ herring across the track, divert attention from subject in hand by starting irrelevant but exciting question, with ref. to use of ~ herring in exercising hounds); ~hot, heated to ~ness, highly excited, enthusi-astic, furious; ~hot poker, garden plant with flame-coloured spikes of flower; ∥ ~lamp, (nursery name for) throat; ~ lead, lane, (nursery name for) throat; ~ lead, pigment made from ~ oxide of lead (v.t., coat with this); ~legged, with ~ legs (of birds etc., esp. the ~legged or French partridge); ~legs, kinds of bird, also the plant bistort; ~-letter, (of day) marked with ~ letter(s) in calendar as saint's day or festival, (fig.) memorable as date of joyful occurrence, (v.t., record as memo-rable for joy); ~ light, danger-signal on railways (see the ~ light, fig., realize approach of disaster); ~ man, N.-Amer. Indian; ~ meat, beef, mutton, etc. (opp. veal & pork & chicken); ~ mass, at which priest wears ~; ~poll, kinds of ~-crested bird, esp. male linnet, also (pl.) ~-haired polled cattle; ~ rag, thing that excites person's rage as ~ object enrages bull (is

a ~rag to him), ‖ also kind of rust in grain; ~ *rattle*, lousewort; ‖ ~ *ribbon*, ribbon, membership, of Order of Bath; ~ *sanders*, wood of E.-Ind. tree used in dyeing; ~*shank*, kind of snipe; ~-*short*, (of iron) brittle while ~ -hot; ~*skin*, = ~ *man* above; ~ *snow*, ~dened by kind of alga & common in Arctic & Alpine regions; ~ *soldier*, (pig affected with) kind of swine fever with ~ness of skin; ~ *spider*, insect infesting hot-house plants esp. vines; ~*start*, ~-tailed European songbird [OE *steort* tail]; ~-*streak*, kind of cider apple; ~ *tape*, excessive use of or adherence to formalities esp. in public business, whence ~tāp'ism, ~tāp'ist, nn.; ~*triangle*, (emblem of the) Y.M.C.A.; ~-*water*, malarial cattle & sheep disease with ~ urine; ~ *weed*, corn poppy; ~ *wing*, kinds of thrush & other birds; ~*wood*, kinds of tree; ~ *worm*, kind used as fishing-bait; hence ~d'EN⁶ v.t. & i., ~d'ISH¹(2), ~d'Y² aa., ~'LY² adv. (rare), ~'NESS n. **5.** n. ~ colour; a shade of ~; the ~ colour in roulette & rouge-et-noir; the ~ ball at billiards; *the debtor side of an account (*in the ~*, in debt); ~ one of former three squadrons or divisions (*the ~*, *white*, *blue*) of British fleet; radical or republican or anarchist. [com.-Teut.; OE *read*, cf. Du. *rood*, G *rot*; cogn. w. L *rufus*, *ruber*, Gk *eruthros*, Skr. *rudhird-*]

red-, pref. = RE-; only in wds of L origin.

rēdāct', v.t. Put into literary form, arrange for publication, edit. So **rēdāc'tor²** n. [in mod. use a back formation f. foll.]

rēdāc'tion, n. Preparing or being prepared for publication, revision, editing, rearrangement; new edition. [f. F *rédaction* f. L *red(igere -act- = agere* bring), RE-8, -ION]

rēdan', n. Field work with two faces forming salient angle. [F (RE-, *dent* tooth)]

‖ **rēdd**, v.t. (Sc.). Clear up, arrange, tidy, put right, settle, compose. [cf. Du. *redden* of same meaning; prob. related to READY]

rēd'dle, n., & v.t. Red ochre, ruddle; (vb) colour with ~. [var. of RUDDLE]

‖ **rēde¹**, n. (arch.). Counsel, advice; resolve, design; narrative. [OE *rǣd*]

‖ **rēde²**, v.t. (arch.). Advise (person, with inf. with or without *to*, or with imperat.); read (riddle, dream). [var. of READ]

rēdeem', v.t. **1.** Buy back, recover by expenditure of effort or by stipulated payment, (~ *one's rights, position, honour, mortgaged land, pledged goods*); compound for, buy off, (charge or obligation) by payment. **2.** Perform (promise). **3.** Purchase the freedom of (another, oneself), save (one's life) by ransom. **4.** Save, rescue, reclaim; (of God or Christ) deliver

from sin & damnation. **5.** Make amends for, compensate, counterbalance, (fault, defect; *has one ~ing feature*); save from a defect (*the eyes ~ the face from ugliness*). Hence ~ABLE a., (esp. of Christ, see above) ~ER¹ n. [f. L *red(imere -empt- = emere* buy), RE-8]

rēdēmp'tion, n. **1.** REDEEMING or being redeemed, esp. the deliverance from sin & damnation wrought by Christ's atonement (*past, beyond, without, ~*, so that is hopeless; *in the year of our ~ 1948 etc.*, A.D. 1948 etc.). **2.** Thing that redeems (*that blow was or proved his ~*). **3.** ‖ Purchase (*became a member of a livery company by ~*). Hence **rēdēmp'tive** a. [f. L *redemptio* (prec., -ION)]

rēdescend'. See RE- 9.

rēdīf', n. (Soldier of) Turkish military reserve. [Turk.]

rēd'ingōte (-ngg-), n. Woman's long double-breasted outer coat with skirts sometimes cut away in front. [F, = kind of (orig. man's) coat, corrupt. of E *riding-coat*]

rēdin'tegrāte, v.t. Restore to wholeness or unity; renew or re-establish in united or perfect state. So ~ATION n. [f. L *red(integrare* INTEGRATE²), RE- 9, -ATE³]

rēdirect' etc., see RE- 8; **rediscover** etc., RE- 9; **redistribute** etc., **redivide** etc., **redo**, RE- 8.

rēd'olent, a. Fragrant (now rare); having a strong smell, (fig.) strongly suggestive or reminiscent, *of*. Hence ~ENCE n. [f. L *red(olēre* smell), RE- 6, -ENT]

rēdou'ble (-dŭbl), v.t. & i., & n. **1.** Intensify, increase, make or grow greater or more intense or numerous, (~*e one's efforts; the clamour ~ed*). **2.** (Bridge) double again a bid already doubled by adversary; (n.) act or instance of ~ing. [f. F *re(doubler* DOUBLE³), RE- 6]

rēdoubt' (-owt-), n. Outwork or fieldwork usu. square or polygonal & without flanking defences. [f. F *redoute* f. med. L *reductus* refuge f. p.p. of L RE-DUCE⁶; -*b*- on false anal. of DOUBT]

rēdoubt'able (-owt-), a. (Of opponent, warrior, controversialist, etc.) formidable. [f. F *redoutable* f. *re(douter* DOUBT³) fear, RE- 6]

rēdoubt'ed (-owt-), a. (arch.). Dreaded, redoubtable. [f. obs. *redoubt* f. F as prec.]

rēdound', v.i. Contribute, *to* one's advantage, credit, etc. (*this procedure will ~ to our advantage; the tale, fact, ~s to their credit*); come as final result to, come back or recoil *upon*, person (*the benefits that ~ to us from his self-sacrifice; his praises ~ upon himself*). [earlier sense overflow, f. F *rédonder* f. L *red(undare* f. *unda* wave), RE- 6]

rēdrēss', v.t., & n. **1.** Readjust, set

For pronunciation & hyphening of re- see RE-.; for words in re- not given see RE- 8, 9.

straight again, (usu. ~ *the balance*, restore equality); set right, rectify, remedy, make up for, get rid of, rectify, (distress, wrong, damage, grievance, abuse). **2.** n. Reparation for wrong, ~*ing of grievances* etc. [n.f. v.b, f. F re(dresser DRESS), RE- 8]

réduce, v.t. & i. **1.** Restore to original or proper position, remedy by such restoration, (now only surg.; *had the shoulder, dislocation, ~d*); bring back to (~ *person to discipline, ~d*); **2.** Convert subject to such conversion, make suitable for classification or analysis to, (~ *rule to practice*, act on it; *observations taken at surface must be ~d to centre*; ~ *anomalies to rule*, discover formula covering them; *the facts may all be ~d to three heads*; ~*it the unwritten customs were ~d to writing*; *to English orthography & speed employee*; ~ *dissimilar quantities to one denomina-tion, integer to form of broken* ; *can we ~ these ripples to their mechanical ele-ments* ?; ~ *clods to powder, ore to metal, compound to components, surface by har-rowing*, or simply ~ *clods, compound*, etc.; ~ *syllogism of one form to another*), **3.** Compel to do (rare); bring by force or necessity to some state or action, subdue, bring back to obedience, (~ *the Crown to submission, the revolted towns, all the other Powers of the continent*; ~*d him to assert or usu. asserting an absurdity*; *was ~d to despair, to weakness, to borrow or usu. borrowing clothes, to borrowing*). **4.** Bring down, lower, weaken, impoverish, dimin-ish, contract, (~ *Pope to place of chief bishop*; *N.C.O. was ~d to the ranks, made a private*; *is in a very ~d state, feeble* ; *liquid to two-thirds of its bulk; this ~s the temperature; the 16 may be ~d to 5, by omission of 11, or by reclassification* etc.; *have ~d our outfit to almost nothing; he ~d himself into the least possible compass*; ~*d to be sold at ~d prices*; ~*d circumstances*, poverty after prosperity; ~ *the establish-ment*, dismiss officials or cut down ex-penses; ~*d officers* etc., dismissed in such reduction). **5.** intr. Lessen one's weight. Hence **redū̆′CER¹** n. (esp. Photog.) an agent for reducing (the density of nega-tives), **redū̆′CIBLE** a. [f. L *reducere duc*-bring, RE- 9]

redū̆c′tĭō ăd absŭrd′um (-shi-), n. Re-duction to absurdity (see foll.). [L]

redū̆c′tion, n. Reducing or being RE-DUCED; also: reduced copy of picture, map, etc.; ~ *to absurdity*, proof of the falsity of a principle etc. given by pro-ducing a logical consequence of it that is absurd, (loosely) pushing of a principle to unpractical lengths. [f. L *reductio* (REDUCE, -ION)]

réduit (redwē′), n. (fortif.), Keep for gar-rison to retire to & hold when outworks are taken. [f. F *réduit* REDOUBT]

redŭn′dant, a. Superfluous, excessive, pleonastic; copious, luxuriant, full. Hence or cogn. ~ANCE, ~ANCY, nn., ~antly² adv. [f. L as REDOUND, -ANT]

redū̆p′lĭcāte, v.t. Make double, repeat; (Gram.) repeat (letter, syllable), form (tense) by reduplication. So ~ATIVE a. [f. med. L *redŭplicare* DUPLICATE², RE- 8, -ATE³]

redū̆plĭcā′tion, n. Doubling, repetition; counterpart; (Gram.) repetition of syl-lable or letter in word-formation, part so repeated. [f. LL *redŭplicatio* (prec. -ATION)]

redye. See RE- 8.

ree. = REEVE².

reeb′ŏk, n. Small S.-African antelope with sharp horns. [Du. = roebuck]

rē-ĕch′ō (-k-), v.i. & t. Echo (t. & i.), echo again & again, resound. [RE- 6]

reed, n., & v.t. **1.** (Tall straight stalk of) kinds of firm-stemmed water or marsh plant (*broken ~*, unreliable person or thing; *lean on a ~*, put trust in weak thing or person), whence ~ED² a.; (collect.) ~*s* growing in a mass or used as material esp. for thatching; || wheat-straw prepared for thatching. **2.** (poet.) Arrow ; musical pipe of ~ or straw; pastoral poetry. **3.** Vibrating part, of various shape & material, inserted in some musical wind-instruments (esp. oboe, bassoon, clarinet, bagpipe, & some organ-pipes) to produce the sound; (usu. pl., cf. *strings*, *brass*) ~ instrument(s). **4.** Weaver's implement for separating warp-threads & beating up weft; (usu. pl.) set of semicylindrical adjacent mould-ings like ~*s* laid together. **5.** ~*babbler* or ~*warbler* or ~*wren*, ~*-bunting* or ~*sparrow*, two kinds of bird; ||~*mace*, cat's-tail ; ~*pheasant*, Bearded Titmouse; ~*pipe*, musical pipe of ~, also ~*ed* organ-pipe; ~*stop*, organ-stop consisting of ~-pipes. **6.** v.t. Thatch with ~; make (straw) into ~s; decorate with ~-moulding; fit (musical instrument or organ-pipe) with ~. [com.-WG; OE *hréod*, cf. Du. & G *riet*]

rē-ĕd′ĭfy, v.t. Rebuild (house etc.); build up again (hopes, wasted tissue, etc.). [RE- 8]

rē-ĕd′it etc. See RE- 8.

reed′ling, n. Bearded Titmouse. [-LING¹]

reed′y, n. Abounding with reeds ; made of reed (chiefly poet., as ~*y pipe, couch*); like a reed in weakness, slenderness, or (of grass etc.) thickness; (of voice) like reed-instrument in tone, scratchy, not round & clear. Hence ~INESS n. [-Y³]

reef¹, n., & v.t. **1.** One of three or four strips across top of square & bottom of fore-&-aft sail that can be taken in or rolled up to reduce sail's surface (*take in a ~*, lit., & fig. proceed cautiously; ~*knot*, consisting of two bights each enclosing the other's parallel-laid shanks, ordinary double-knot made symmetrically

for easy casting off (opp. GRANNY); ~ *point*, one of the short pieces of rope attached to a sail to secure it when ~ed. **2. v.t.** Take in ~(s) of (sail; *single, double, treble, ~ed*, with 1, 2, 3, ~s taken in); shorten (topmast, bowsprit, also paddles of paddle-wheel by shifting them nearer centre). [ult. f. ON *rif* in same sense, perh. a spec. use of *rif* rib]

reef², n. Ridge of rock or shingle or sand at or just above or below surface of water; (Gold-mining) lode of auriferous quartz, also the bedrock. [as prec., prob. through Du. *rif*]

reef'er, n. One who reefs; (sl.) midshipman; REEF¹-knot; (also *reefing-jacket*) close double-breasted stout jacket. [REEF¹, -ER¹]

reek, n. Smoke (Sc. & literary); vapour, visible exhalation, (chiefly Sc. & lit.); fetid foul or stale odour (*the ~ of tobacco*); (*~-coal* etc.) [REEF¹, -ER¹]
reek, n. Smoke (Sc. & literary); vapour, visible exhalation, (chiefly Sc. & lit.); fetid foul or stale odour (*the ~ of tobacco*), fetid atmosphere (*amid ~ & squalor*). Hence ~Y² a. (chiefly Sc. & literary; *Auld Reek'ie*, Edinburgh). [com.-Teut.; OE *réc*, cf. Du. *rook*, G *rauch*]

reek², v.i. Emit smoke (chiefly of houses after conflagration or object that has been burning in open air); emit vapour, steam, (of hot drink or food, sweating person etc., or shed blood or thing smeared with it); smell unpleasantly (usu. of; *~s of patchouli, tobacco, blood, or* fig., *of murder, affectation, etc.*). [OE *riocan*, cf. Du. *rieken*, G *riechen*, smell, & Du. *rooken*, G *rauchen*, smoke, & see prec.]

reel¹, n., & v.t. & i. **1.** Kinds of rotatory apparatus on which thread, silk, yarn, paper, wire, etc., are wound at some stage of manufacture; contrivance for winding up & unwinding line as required, esp. in fishing (*off the ~*, fig., straight off, without hitch or pause, in rapid succession); ‖small cylinder on which sewing-cotton etc. are wound for convenience; revolving part in various machines; (Cinemat.) quantity of positive film rolled on one ~ (often as rough unit of length, about 1,000 ft, complete films being termed *two-, three-, four-, etc., ~ers*). **2. vb.** Wind (thread, fishing-line, etc.) on ~; take (cocoon silk etc.) off, draw (fish, logline, etc.) *in* or *up*, by use of ~; rattle (story, list, verses) *off* without pause or apparent effort; (of grasshopper etc.) make clicking noise like~ in motion. [vb f. n., OE *hréol*, excl. E]

reel², v.i., & n. **1.** (Of eyes, mind, head) be in a whirl, be dizzy, swim; sway, stagger, stand or walk or run unsteadily, be shaken physically or mentally, (*his mind, the front rank, the ship, the tower, ~ed under the shock*; ~ *to & fro like a drunken man*; *went ~ing down the street*; *the State*

was ~ing to its foundations); seem to shake (*the mountains ~ before his eyes*); hence ~'inglY² adv. **2.** n. ~ing motion lit. or fig. (*without a ~ or a stagger*; *the ~ of vice & folly around us*). [perh. cogn. w. prec.]

reel³, n., & v.i. **1.** Lively esp. Scotch dance, usu. of two couples in line & describing circular figures. **2. v.i.** Dance ~. [perh. f. REEL² n.]

re-elect'ic, re-embark'etc., re-emerge etc. See RE- 9.

reen, n. = RHINE¹.

re-enable, **re-enact** etc., see RE- 9; **re-engine**, RE- 8; **re-enter** etc., RE- 9. **re-en'trant**, a. & n. (Angle) that points inward (opp. SALIENT; esp. in fortification). [RE- 9, ENTRANT]

ré-en'trY, n. Act of entering again; (Law) a retaking possession; *card of ~* (Whist & Bridge), high card that can be relied on to give holder the lead by winning a trick. [RE- 9, ENTRY]

re-establish etc. See RE- 9.

reeve¹, n. (Hist.) chief magistrate of town or district; (Canada) president of village or town council. [OE *geréfa*, etym. dub.; prob. unconnected w. obs. *grave* steward, *landgrave* etc. G *graf* count]

reeve², *ree*, n. Female of RUFF². [?]

reeve³, v.t. (naut.; past & p.p. *rôve* or *~d*). Thread (rope, rod, etc.) *through* ring or other aperture; pass rope through (a block etc.); fasten (rope, block, or other object) *in, on, round*, to, something by reeving; (of ship) thread (shoals, icepack). [perh. f. Du. *reven* REEF¹ vb]

re-examine etc., see RE- 8; **re-exist**, **re-export** etc., RE- 9; **reface**, **refashion** etc., RE- 8,

refec'tion, n. Refreshment by food or drink (*milk & eggs were offered for our ~*); slight meal, repast. [f. F *réfection* f. L *re(fectionem=factionem* FACTION), RE- 8]

refec'torY (or *in monastic use* refĕ'-), n. Room used for meals in monasteries etc. [f. med. L *refectorium* f. L *re(ficere -fect- =facere* make) refresh, RE- 8, -ORY]

refer', v.t. & i. (-rr-). **1.** Trace or ascribe to person or thing as cause or source, assign to certain date or place or class, (~ *decision) to person* etc. (*I ~ myself to your generosity; let us ~ the dispute to Socrates*; ~ *to drawer*, abbr. R.D., banker's note suspending payment etc. of cheque). **2.** Send on or direct (person), make appeal or have recourse, *to* some authority or source of information, (abs.) cite authority or passage, (*ostler ~red me to landlord*;

For pronunciation & hyphening of *re-* see RE-; for words in *re-* not given see RE- 8, 9.

for my proof I ~ to the facts of human nature, to 1 Kings vii. 7; ~red to his watch for the exact time). **4.** (Of statement etc.) have relation, be directed, (of hearer etc.) interpret (statement etc.) as directed, to (these remarks ~ only to involuntary offences, are not to be ~red to deliberate, are not thought of or meant); (of person speaking etc.) make allusion, direct attention, to (he several times ~red to the modern increase in expenditure; found myself on the peak ~red to). [f. L referre (re-, latum bring), RE- 9]

referee', n., & v.i. & t. **1.** Referring, Arbitrator, person to whom dispute is to be or is referred for decision; umpire esp. in football. **2.** vb. Act as ~ (for) esp. in football. [-EE]

re'ference, n., & v.t. **1.** Referring or matter for decision or settlement or consideration to some authority, scope given to such authority; (the peerage was) allowed without ~ to the House of Lords; the ~ is very wide, strictly limited; the Commission must confine itself to, that is a question outside, the ~. **2.** Relation, respect, correspondence, to (the parts of a machine all have ~ to each other; success seems to have little ~ to merit; in, with, ~ to, regarding, as regards, about; without ~ to, irrespective of). **3.** Allusion to (~, a or no ~, several ~s, to a previous conversation was or were made). **4.** Direction more or less precise to (page etc. of book etc. where information may be found (loads his pages with, does not give, ~s; cross ~, to another passage in same book; ~ bible, with marginal cross ~s ‖ legislation by ~, use in bill-drafting of ~s to previous statutes instead of restatement); mark used to refer reader of text to note or to part of diagram (usual ~ marks: asterisk *, obelisk †, double obelisk ‡, section §, parallel ‖, paragraph ¶). **5.** Act of looking up passage etc., or of referring another or applying to person, for information (~ or ~ed him; please give me a ~, I should like to make ~, to your last employer; book of ~, to be used not for continuous reading but to consult on occasion; ~ library, where books may be consulted without being taken away); person named by one applying for post or offering goods etc. as willing to vouch for him or them (who are your ~s?); (loosely) testimonial; hence **referen'tial** (-shl) a. **6.** v.t. Provide (book) with ~s to authorities. [-ENCE]

refe'ren'diary, n. (rare). Referee; assessor to commission; reporting or revising official. [f. med. L referendarius (foll., -ARY¹)]

referen'dum, n. Referring of certain political questions or of such questions under certain circumstances to the electorate for direct decision by a general vote on the single question. [L (REFERRE), -ND¹]

refill'. See RE- 9.

refine', v.t. & i. Free from dross or impurities or defects, purify, clarify; make elegant or cultured, imbue with delicacy of taste, polish manners or appearance of; become pure or clear or improved in thought or delicacy; employ subtlety of thought or language, make fine distinctions, discourse subtly (upon; improve (upon) by refinements. Hence ~EDIy² adv. [RE- 6, FINE¹ v.]

refine'ment (-nm-), n. Refining or being refined; fineness of feeling or taste, polished manners etc.; subtle or ingenious manifestation of, piece of elaborate arrangement, (all the ~s of luxury; a countermine was a ~ beyond their skill); piece of subtle reasoning, fine distinction. [-MENT]

refi'ner, n. In vbl senses; esp., person whose business is to refine metal, sugar, etc., whence ~ERY(3) n. [-ER¹]

refit'. See RE- 8.

refla'tion, n. Inflation of currency after a deflation, undertaken to restore the system to its previous condition. [f. RE- 9, after INFLATION, DEFLATION]

reflect', v.t. & i. **1.** Fold back (rare; ~ the corner of the paper). **2.** (Of surface or body) throw (heat, light, sound, rarely ball etc.) back, cause to rebound, (shine with ~ed light, not one's own, borrowed). **3.** (Of mirror etc., or transit,) show image of, reproduce to eye or mind, exactly correspond in appearance or effect to, (laws ~ the average moral attitude of a half century earlier). **4.** (Of action, result, etc.) bring back or cause to redound (credit, discredit, etc.), (abs.) bring discredit, (upon person or method responsible. **5.** Go back in thought, meditate, or consult with oneself (on, upon, or abs.), remind oneself of (that, how, etc.), whence ~ingly² adv. **6.** Make disparaging remarks upon. [f. L re(flectere flec- bend), RE- 9]

reflec'tion, -e'xion (-kshn), n. (-x- etym. correct but now rare exx. in scientific use). **1.** REFLECTING or being reflected; (angle of ~, made by reflected ray with perpendicular to surface); reflected light, heat, colour, or image. **2.** Reflex action. **3.** (Piece of) censure (usu. on or upon); thing bringing discredit(upon. **4.** Reconsideration (on, ~ I doubt whether I was right). **5.** Mental faculty dealing with products of sensation & perception. **6.** Idea arising in the mind, mental or verbal comment, apophthegm, (often on or upon). Hence ~AL, ~LESS aa., (-sho-), [f. LL reflexio (prec., -ION) w. assim. to reflect]

reflec'tive, a. **1.** (Of surface etc.) giving back reflection or image; (of light etc.) reflected (rare). **2.** (Gram.) reflexive (now rare). **3.** (Of action) reflex, reciprocal, (now rare). **4.** (Of mental faculties) concerned in reflection or thought;(of person,

mood, etc.) thoughtful, given to meditation. Hence ~LY² adv., ~NESS n. [REFLECT, -IVE]

reflec′tor, n. **1.** Body or surface reflecting rays, esp. piece of glass or metal usu. concave for reflecting in required direction; (telescope etc. provided with) apparatus for reflecting images. **2.** Person, book, etc., that gives or affords conscious or unconscious representation of prejudices, habits, etc. [-OR²]

reflet′ (-lā), n. Lustre, iridescence, esp. on pottery. [F]

ref′lex¹, n. **1.** Reflected light or colour or glory (*the fame of Greece was a ~ from the glory of Athens*); (Paint.) part of the picture represented as affected by the light or colour of another part. **2.** Image or reflection in mirror etc. **3.** Reproduction, secondary manifestation, correspondent result, (*legislation should be a ~ of public opinion; lamb & mint sauce is a popular ~ of the passover with bitter herbs*). **4.** A reflex action (*doctor tested patient's ~es*); CONDITIONED ~. [f. L L *reflexus -ūs* as REFLECT]

ref′lex², a. **1.** (rare). Recurved; (of light etc.) reflected. **2.** (Of thought etc.) introspective, directed back upon itself or its own operations; (of effect or influence) reactive, coming back upon its author or source. **3.** (Physiol.) ~ *action*, independent of the will, excited as involuntary response to nerve-stimulation. **4.** (Gram.) reflexive (now rare). **5.** ~ (*camera*), a hand camera in which, by means of a pivoted surface-silvered mirror, the reflected image can be seen and focused up to the moment of exposure. Hence ~LY² adv. [f. L L *reflexus* p.p. (REFLECT)]

reflexed′ (-kst), a. (bot.). Recurved. [f. obs. *reflex* vb=REFLECT]

reflex′ible, a. Capable of being reflected. Hence ~IBIL′ITY n. [as prec., -IBLE]

reflexion. See REFLECTION.

reflex′ive, a. & n. (gram.). (Word, form) implying agent's action upon himself; (verb) indicating identity of subject & object; (pers. pronoun or poss. adjective) referring to subject. Hence ~LY² adv. [as prec., -IVE]

refloat. See RE- 9.

ref′luent (-ōo-), a. Flowing back (~ *tide, blood*). Hence **ref′luence** (-ōo-) n. [f. L L *re(fluere* flow), RE- 9]

reflux, see RE- 9; **refoot,** RE- 8; **reforest** etc., RE- 9.

reform′¹, v.t. & i. Make (person, institution, procedure, conduct, oneself) or (of person or body of persons) become better by removal or abandonment of imperfections, faults, or errors (*~ed churches,* see REFORMATION²); abolish, cure, (abuse, malpractice). Hence ~ABLE a. [f. L L *re(formare* FORM²), RE- 8]

reform′², n. Removal of abuse(s) esp. in

politics (*R~ Bill, Act,* esp. those of 1831–2 amending parliamentary representation); improvement made or suggested; *R~ Club,* former headquarters of the Liberal party (cf. CARLTON, NATIONAL *Liberal*). [f. prec.]

re-form′³, v.t. & i. Form again. So **re-formā′tion¹** n. [RE- 8]

reformā′tion², n. Reforming or being reformed, esp. radical change for the better in political, religious, or social affairs; *the R~,* 16th-c. movement for reform of abuses in Roman Church ending in establishment of Reformed or Protestant Churches, whence ~AL (-sho-) a. [f. L L *reformatio* (REFORM¹, -ATION)]

reform′ative a., **reform′atory** a. & n. **1.** Tending or intended to produce reform. **2.** n. Institution to which juvenile offenders are sent for ~ purposes, approved school. [REFORM¹, -ATIVE, -ORY]

reform′er, n. In vbl senses; esp.: leader in the 16th-c. REFORMATION²; advocate of the REFORM² bill. [-ER¹]

refract′, v.t. (Of water, air, glass, etc.) deflect (light) at certain angle when it enters obliquely from another medium of different density (*~ing telescope,* with object-glass converging rays to focus; (Chem.) analyse (nitre) to discover percentage of impurities. Hence or cogn. **refrac′tion** n., **refrac′tional** (-sho-), **refrac′tive,** aa. [f. L L *re(fringere -fract- = frangere* break), RE- 5]

refract′or, n. Refracting medium or lens or telescope. [-OR²]

refrac′tory, a. & n. **1.** Stubborn, unmanageable, rebellious; (of wound, disease, etc.) not yielding to treatment; (of substances) hard to fuse or work. **2.** n. Substance specially resistant to heat, corrosion, etc. Hence ~LY² adv., ~INESS n. [f. L *refractarius* (REFRACT, -ARY¹) w. assim. to -ORY]

refrain′¹, n. Recurring phrase or line esp. at end of stanzas. [OF, ult. f. pop. L †*refrangere=refringere* REFRACT]

refrain′², v.t. & i. Put restraint upon, curb, (oneself, one's tears, soul, etc.; arch.); abstain from doing something, abstain *from act* or *doing.* [f. OF *refrener* f. L L *refrenare* f. *frenum* bridle), RE- 9]

refran′gible (-j-), a. That can be refracted. Hence ~IBIL′ITY n. [incorrect for *refringible* (REFRACT, -IBLE]

refresh′, v.t. & i. Make cool again (rare); reanimate, reinvigorate, (of food, drink, rest, amusement, etc., or person providing these esp. in ~ *oneself*; *~ing innocence* etc., interesting to blasé observer); freshen up (memory); restore (fire, electric battery, etc.) with fresh supply; take esp. liquid refreshment. Hence ~ing-LY² adv. [f. OF *refreschir,* see FRESH, RE- 9]

For pronunciation & hyphening of *re-* see RE-; for words in *re-* not given see RE- 8, 9.

refresh'er, n. In vbl senses; esp.: extra fee to counsel in prolonged case; (colloq.) a drink; attrib., as ~ *course* (of instruction in modern methods etc.). [-ER¹]

refresh'ment, n. Refreshing or being refreshed in mind or body; thing, esp. (usu. in pl.) drink or food, that refreshes (*the sight was a ~ to him; take some ~ or ~s; ~ room at railway station or car on train); R~ Sunday,* 4th in Lent with gospel St John vi. [f. OF *refreschement* (prec., -MENT)]

refri'gerate, v.t. & i. 1. Make, rarely become, cool or cold. 2. Expose (provisions) to extreme cold in order to freeze or preserve, whence ~ANT(2) a. & n., ~ATION n. [f. L *refrigerare* (prec.)]

refri'geratory, n. & a. 1. Cold-water vessel attached to still for condensing vapour; refrigerator. 2. adj. Refrigerant. [f. L *refrigeratorius* (prec., -ORY)]

reft. See REAVE.

ref'uge, n., & v.t. 1. (Place of) shelter from pursuit or danger or trouble (*seek ~; has found a ~; take ~ in a cave, in lying; city of ~,* see Josh. XX; *house of ~,* institution for the homeless etc.); person, thing, course, that gives shelter or is resorted to in difficulties (*he is the ~ of the distressed; books are the ~ of ...*); raised piece in middle of busy road for crossers to halt on. 2. vb (rare). Give ~ to; take ~. [F. f. L *refugium* f. *fugere* flee]

ref'ugee', n. Person escaped to foreign country from religious or political persecution. [f. F *réfugié* p.p. of *réfugier* (prec.)]

reful'gent, a. Shining, gloriously bright. Hence or cogn. ~ENCE n., ~ently² adv. [f. L *refulgere* shine), RE-6, *fulgere*]

refu'nd, v.t. & i. & n. 1. Pay back (money received or taken, expenses incurred by another); reimburse; make repayment; hence ~MENT n. 2. n. ~ment. [earlier sense *pour back, on.* 2. vb (rare). [f. L *refundere fus-* pour.]

refurb'ish, see RE-9; **refurnish,** RE-8, ~, is importunate); also, right or privilege of deciding to take or leave a thing before it is offered to others (*leave, stipulate for, give person, the ~ of*). [foll., -AL(2)]

refu'se¹ (-z), v.t. & i. 1. Say or convey by action that one will not accept or submit to or give or grant or gratify or consent (*~ offer, gift, chance, office, candidate, person* as husband, etc.; *horse ~s fence* ...; (-z-) n.; *~e orders, control,* etc.; *~e obedience, compliance; ~ed me satisfaction, may request; have never been ~ed, had request rejected; ~e to do*). 2. Make refusal; (Cards) not follow suit. Hence ~ABLE (-z-) a. [f. F *refuser* (L *refundere* see REFUND)]

refu'se², a. & n. (What is) rejected as worthless or left over after use. [perh. f. OF *refuse* p.p. as prec.]

re-fu'se³ (-z), v.t. Fuse again. [RE-9]

refu'te, v.t. Prove falsity or error of (statement, opinion, argument, person advancing it), rebut or repel by argument. Hence or cogn. **refu'table** a., ~AL(2), **refuta'tion,** n. [f. L *refutare* see CONFUTE, RE-9]

regai'n, v.t. Recover possession of (esp. ~ *consciousness*); reach (place) again; recover (*one's feet or footing or legs*). [RE-9]

re'gal¹, a. Of or by kings (~ *government, title, office*); fit for a king, magnificent, (*lives in ~ splendour*). Hence ~ly² adv. [f. L *regalis* (*rex regis* king, -AL)]

re'gal², a. & n. 1. Choice dainty; a dainty (rare); choice flavour (rare; *viands of higher~*). [f. obs. F *régale* f. It. *regalo* gift, etym. dub.]

regale'², v.t. & i. Entertain choicely (often iron.) with food or *with* talk etc.; feed oneself choicely (usu. *on ~*). Hence ~MENT(-lm-) n. [f. F *régaler* (prec.)]

regāli'a¹ (-lya), n. pl. Royal privileges (now rare); insignia of royalty used at coronations; insignia of an order, e.g. of Freemasons. [L, neut. pl. of REGALIS]

regāli'a² (-lya), n. Large cigar of good quality. [f. Sp. *regalia* royal privilege (REGAL², -A¹)]

rē'galism, n. Doctrine of sovereign's ecclesiastical supremacy. [-ISM]

regā'lity, n. Attribute of kingly power, being king; (*things that touch his ~*); monarchical State, kingdom, (rare); royal privilege. [f. OF *regalité* (REGAL², -ITY)]

regā'rd¹, v.t. & i. 1. Gaze upon (usu. with adv. phr. or adv.; *found him ~ing me with curiosity, intently*). 2. Give heed to, take into account, let one's course be affected by, (esp. in neg. context; *fears not God nor ~s men; does not ~ my advice*); give heed, pay attention, take notice. 3. Look upon or contemplate mentally with reverence, horror, etc., or with adv. specified sentiment (*I still ~ him kindly*). 4. Consider (usu. as with compl., also in the light of, under an aspect, etc., also vulg. with compl. & without *as* = consider; *is to be ~ed as a wild beast; ~ it as madness or indispensable, him as among my friends*). 5. (Of things) concern, have relation to, (*does not ~ me* etc., has nothing to do with; esp. *as ~s,* or *~ing* as part, or prep. = about, touching; *as ~s wheat, prices are rising; considerations ~ing peace; am innocent ~ing the former*). [f. F *regarder* (GUARD²), RE-6, cf. REWARD]

regā'rd², n. 1. Gaze, steady or significant look. 2. Respect, point attended to, (in *this* etc. ~; esp. *in ~ to or of,* (in) regarding, as touching, about; *in one's ~,* concerning or about or towards him),

3. Attention, heed, care, (to, for; ~ must be had or paid to general principles; the next object of ~ is his conduct; set without ~ to or for decency; pays no ~ to expostulations or adviser), whence ~FUL a. (of), ~LESS a. & adv. (of; also sl. as ellipt. adv. = ~less of expense, as got up ~less, expensively dressed), ~FULLY² (rare), ~LESS-LY², adv., ~FULNESS (rare), ~LESSNESS, nn. 4. Esteem, kindly feeling or respectful opinion, (for; have little, a great, ~ for him, no, a high, ~ for his judgement or advice); (pl.) expression of friendliness in letter etc., compliments, (kind ~s to you all; give him my ~s or best etc. ~s). [F (prec.)]

regard'ant, a. (Her.) looking backward; observant, with steady or intent gaze. [F (REGARD¹, -ANT)]

regel'āte', v.i. (Of fragments of ice, heaped snow, etc.) be fused by temporary thawing of surfaces into frozen mass. Hence ~ATION n. [RE-9, L gelare freeze, -ATE³]

re'gency, n. Rule, control, (rare); office of regent; commission acting as regent; regent's or regency-commission's period of office (the R~ in Eng. Hist., 1810-20). [REGENT,-ENCY]

regen'eráte, v.t. & i. Invest with new & higher spiritual nature; improve moral condition of, breathe new & more vigorous & higher life into, (person, institution, etc.); generate again, bring or come into renewed existence, (must ~ate his self-respect; polypus ~ates after extraction); reform oneself. Hence or cogn. ~ATE² (-ăt), ~ATIVE, aa., ~A'TION n. [f. L re(generare GENERATE), RE-8]

regen'erator, n. In vbl senses; also, fuel-saving fire-brick device in furnaces. [-OR²]

regenesis. See RE-8.

re'gent, n. & a. 1. Ruler, ruling principle, (rare); person appointed to administer kingdom during minority, absence, or incapacity of monarch; || (Oxford and Cambridge Univv.) Master of Arts who presided over disputations in the Schools (hist.); *member of the governing body of a State University. 2. adj. (following n.). Acting as ~ (Queen, Prince, etc., R~). [n. f. a., f. L regere rule, -ENT]

regerminate etc. See RE-9.

re'gicide, n. Killer or participator in killing of a king (the ~s, those concerned in trying & executing Charles I); king-killing. Hence regicid'AL a. [L rex regis king, -CIDE]

régie (rāzhē'), n. State monopoly or control of tobacco, salt, etc. [F]

régime, regime, (rāzhēm'), n. Method of government, prevailing system of things, (ancien régime, see AP, system of govern-

ment in France before the revolution, also transf. any now abolished or past method); under the ~ of purchase, privilege, protection, competition, Whig ascendancy, etc. [F (ré-) f. L REGIMEN]

rĕ'gimen, n. Rule, system of government, régime, (now rare); (Med.) prescribed course of exercise, way of life, & esp. diet; (Gram.) relation of syntactic dependence between words, government. [L (regere rule, -MEN)]

rĕ'giment (or -jm-), n., & v.t. 1. Rule, government, (now rare). 2. Permanent recruiting & training unit of army usu. commanded by (Lieut.-)Colonel & divided into several companies or troops or batteries & often into two, or in war-time into many, battalions; operational unit of artillery, tanks, armoured cars, etc.; Royal R~ (of Artillery), Royal Artillery; (often pl.) large array or number, legion, (usu. of). 3. v.t. Form (men) into ~ or ~s; organize (workers, labour) in groups or according to a system, whence regimentA'TION n. [f. LL regimentum (prec., -MENT)]

regimen'tal, a. & n. 1. Of a regiment; hence ~LY¹ adv. 2. n. pl. Dress worn by regiment, military uniform. [-AL]

Regin'a, n. (abbr. R.). Reigning queen (in signatures to proclamations, as V.R., Victoria ~, titles of crown law-suits, as ~ v. Jones, versus Jones, etc.). [L (rex regis king, -INA¹)]

regin'al, a. (rare). Queenly, of or befitting a queen. [f. med. L reginalis (prec., -AL)]

re'gion (-jn), n. Tract of country, space, place, of more or less definitely marked boundaries or characteristics (a desert, fertile, ~; the ~ between the Elbe & the Rhine; earth is divided into ~s characterized by different fauna & flora); separate part of world or universe (often pl.; lower ~s, hell, realm of the dead; upper ~s, sky, heaven; the ~ beyond the grave); sphere or realm of (you are getting into the ~ of metaphysics); upper, middle, lower, layer of atmosphere or sea; part of the body round or near some organ etc. (the lumbar, abdominal, etc., ~; the ~ of the eyes). Hence ~AL (-jo-) a. [f. AF regiun f. L regionem nom. -o direction (regere direct, -TON¹)]

rĕ'gister¹, n. 1. Book in which entries are made of details to be recorded for reference; official or authoritative list kept e.g. of births, marriages, & burials or deaths, of shipping, of qualified voters in a constituency (~ office, or in mod. use ~, a registry). 2. Slider in organ controlling set of pipes; compass of voice or instrument, part of voice-compass (head, chest, throat, upper, middle, lower, ~). 3. Adjustable plate for widening or narrowing

For pronunciation & hyphening of re- see RE-; for words in re- not given see RE-8, 9.

an opening & regulating draught esp. in fire-grate; recording indicator of speed, force, etc. **4.** (Print.) exact correspondence of printed matter on two sides of leaf (*in* ~ so corresponding); (Photog.) correspondence of focusing screen with plate or film. [f. med. L *regestrum* for *regestum* (LL *regesta* things recorded f. *regerere*, f. RE-8, L *gerere* carry)]

rĕ'gister², v.t. & i. **1.** Set down (name, fact, etc.) formally, record in writing; (fig.) make mental note of. **2.** Enter or cause to be entered in particular register (~ *letter*, entrust to post-office with special precautions for safety; ~ *oneself* or abs., put one's name on electoral register). **3.** (Of instrument) record automatically, indicate; (Cinemat.) express facially (emotion). **4.** (Print. etc.) correspond, make correspond, exactly. Hence or cogn. **rĕ'gistrā'TION** n. [f. med. L *registrare* (prec.)]

rĕ'gistrar, n. Official recorder, person charged with keeping register. Hence ~**SHIP** n. [prec., -AR²]

rĕ'gistrary, n. Registrar of Cambridge University. [REGISTER¹, -ARY¹]

rĕ'gistry, n. Registration; place, office, where registers are kept; *married at a* ~ or ~ *office* or *register office*, i.e. without religious ceremony; *servants'* ~ (*office*), shop etc. where lists of vacant situations & servants seeking them are kept; register (rare). [REGISTER¹, -RY]

‖**Rē'gius**, a. ~ *professor* of Greek etc., holder of chair at Oxf. or Camb. instituted by Henry VIII, or of later one placed on same footing. [L, = royal (*rex regis* king)]

rē'gnal, a. Of a reign (~ *year*, beginning with king's accession or an anniversary of it; ~ *day*, anniversary of accession). [f. med. L *regnalis* (REGN, -AL)]

rē'gnant, a. Reigning (*Queen R*~), ruling in her own right & not as consort; *Prince R*~ etc.); (of things, qualities, opinions, etc.) predominant, prevalent. [f. L *regnare* REIGN², -ANT]

regōrge', v.t. & i. Bring or cast up again, vomit, disgorge; gush or flow back from pit, channel, etc.; swallow again. [RE-9]

rēgrāte', v.t. (hist.). Buy up (goods, esp. victuals) with view to retailing at a profit (a practice formerly prohibited). Hence RE', ~'ER¹, ~'OR² nn. [f. OF *regrater* perh. f. astron.).

rē'gress¹, n. Going back; declension, backward tendency. [f. L *regressus* (foll.)]

regrēss², v.i. Move backwards (chiefly astron.). [f. L *regredi—gressi gress-* step], RE-9]

regrĕ'ssion (-shn), n. Backward movement, retreat; return of curve; relapse, reversion. So **regrĕss'IVE** a., **regrĕs'sively²** adv., **regrĕs'siveness** n. [f. L *regrĕdi=gredi gress-step*,

regrēt', v.t. (-tt-), & n. **1.** Be sorry for loss of, wish one could have again; be distressed about or sorry for (event, fact), grieve at, repent (action etc.); be sorry *to say* etc. or *that* (esp. in polite refusal of invitation etc.); hence ~**t'ABLE** a., ~**t'ablY²** adv. **2.** n. Sorrow for loss of person or thing (often *for*); repentance or annoyance concerning thing (left undone) (*has no* ~*s*; *express* ~ *for*, esp. make apology or ask pardon for); vexation or disappointment caused by occurrence or situation (*hear with* ~ *of* or *that*; *refuse with much* ~ or *many* ~*s*); hence (of person or feeling) ~**FUL** a., ~**fully²** adv. [f. F *regretter*), OF also *regreter*, *regrater*, etym. dub.]

regroup. See RE-8.

rē'gūlable, a. Admitting of regulation. [REGULATE, -ABLE]

rē'gūlar, a. & n. **1.** (Eccl.) bound by religious rule, belonging to religious or monastic order, (cf. SECULAR; *the* ~ *clergy* in R.-C. countries, monks as opp. parish priests etc.). **2.** (Of shape, structure, arrangement, or objects in these respects) following or exhibiting a principle, harmonious, consistent, systematic, symmetrical, (~ *nomenclature, formation, features, curve, figure, flower; the five solids*, tetrahedron or triangular pyramid bounded by 4 triangles, hexahedron or cube by 6 squares, octahedron by 8 triangles, dodecahedron by 12 pentagons, & icosahedron by 20 triangles). **3.** Acting, done, recurring, uniformly or calculably in time or manner, habitual, constant, not capricious or casual, orderly, (~ *working, steps, procedure, sequence, pulse, bowels, salary, orbit, bedtime, employ; keep* ~ *hours*; do same thing at same time daily; *a* ~ *life*; lived in orderly manner, esp. without excesses; ~ *people*, living ~ *lives*; also vulg. as adv., *as comes, happens,* ~). **4.** Conforming to a standard of etiquette etc., not transgressing conventions, in order, (*had no* ~ *introduction; the attitude of the Foreign Office has been quite* ~). **5.** (Gram.) of verbs, nouns, etc. following a normal type of inflexion. **6.** Properly constituted or qualified, not defective or amateur, devoted exclusively or primarily to its nominal function, (*cooks as well as a* ~ *cook; has no* ~ *profession*; ~ *soldiers*, opp. volunteers or militia or temporary levies; ~ *army*, of soldiers); (colloq.) complete, thorough, indubitable, (*as a* ~ *rascal, brick, hero; a* ~ *royal queen; had a* ~ *smash, overhauling,* etc.; also vulg. as adv., *as 'is* ~ *angry*); hence **regŭlā'rITY** n., ~**IZE**(3) v.t., ~**IZA-TION** n., ~**ary²** adv. **7.** n. One of the ~ clergy; ~ soldier; (colloq.) customer, visitor, etc.; (colloq.)person permanently employed. [f. L *regularis* (*regula* rule f. *regere* direct, -AR¹)]

rē'gŭlāte, v.t. Control by rule, subject to

restrictions, moderate, adapt to requirements; adjust (machine, clock) so that it
may work accurately. Hence ~ATOR¹(L,
2) n., ~ATIVE a. [f. LL regulare (L regula
rule), -ATE³]

regula'tion, n. Regulating or being regulated; prescribed rule, authoritative direction; (attrib.) fulfilling what is laid
down by ~s, of correct pattern etc.,
ordinary, usual, formal, (of the ~ size;
exceed the ~ speed; a ~ sword, cap; the ~
mourning). [prec., -ATION]

re'gulus, n. (pl. ~i). **1.** (R-us) bright star
in Leo. **2.** (Chem.) purer or metallic part
of mineral separated by sinking to bottom
in crucible, impure metallic product of
smelting various ores, whence ~INE¹ a.
3. Golden-crested wren. [L, dim. of rex
regis king; sense 2 orig. of metallic form
of antimony, perh. as title of honour due
to its readiness to combine with gold]

regur'gitate, v.i. & t. Gush back; (of
stomach or receptacle) pour or cast up
again. Hence ~A'TION n. [f. med. L
re(gurgitare f. L gurges -itis whirlpool),
RE- 9, -ATE³]

rehabilitate etc., see RE- 9; **rehandle, rehang, rehash, rehear**, etc., RE- 8.

rehears'al (-hěr-), n. Rehearsing; preparatory performance of play or other entertainment (dress ~, such ~ in costume, i.e.
when practice is far advanced). [-AL (2)]

rehearse' (-hěrs), v.t. Recite, say over, repeat from beginning to end, give list of,
recount, enumerate; have rehearsal of
(play etc. or part in it), practise for later
public performance. [f. OF rehercer prob.
f. RE- 8, hercer harrow (herse harrow f. L
hirpex rake)]

rehouse, see RE- 8; **rehumanize**, RE- 9.

Reich (rīx), n. The German common-
wealth as a whole (First ~, Holy Roman
Empire, 962-1806; Second ~, 1871-1918;
Third ~, Nazi régime, 1933-45); ~s'wehr
(-vār), (formerly) German armed forces.
[G, = kingdom]

Reichsrat(h) (rīxs'raht), n. Parliament of
the late Cisleithan Austria-Hungary. [G]

Reichstag (rīxs'tahg), n. The German
parliament; parliament of the late Trans-
leithan Austria-Hungary. [G]

reify, v.t. Convert (person, abstract concept) into thing, materialize. So **reifi-
CA'TION** n. [f. L res thing, -I-, -FY]

reign¹ (rān), n. Sovereignty, rule, sway,
(under the ~ of Queen Victoria; his ~ was
a gentle one; the ~ of law in nature; night
resumes her ~; R- of Terror, period of
sanguinary excesses by revolutionaries
or reactionaries, & see TERROR); realm,
sphere, (rare); period during which sovereign reigns (in the ~ of John; during five
successive ~s). [f. OF regne f. L regnum
(regere rule)]

reign² (rān), v.i. Hold royal office, be
king or queen lit. or fig.; (~ed over Great
Britain for 60 years; a king who desired to
rule as well as ~; better to ~ in hell than
serve in heaven; ~ing beauty, acknowledged as supreme for the time); hold
sway, prevail, (dissension & improvidence
~ed; silence ~s, all is quiet). [f. OF regner
f. L regnare (prec.)]

reignite. See RE- 9.

reimburse', v.t. Repay (person who has
expended money, out-of-pocket expenses,
person expenses). Hence ~MENT (-sm-) n.
[RE- 9, obs. imburse put in purse f. LL
imbursare (IM-¹, BOURSE)]

reimport, reimpose etc. See RE- 9.

rein (rān), n., & v.t. **1.** Long narrow strap
with each end attached to bit used to
guide or check horse etc. in riding or
driving, (fig.) means of control, (often pl.
in same senses; draw ~, stop one's horse,
pull up, abandon effort, retrench expenditure, etc.; give horse the ~s or ~; let it
go its own way; so throw the ~s to; give ~
or the ~s to one's imagination etc., let it
have free scope; assume, drop, the ~s of
government, enter upon, resign, office);
hence ~LESS a. **2.** v.t. Check or manage
with ~s; (fig.) govern, restrain, control;
pull up or back with ~s, hold in, with ~s
or fig. [vb f. n., f. OF resne, AF reidne,
cf. L retina, perh. ult. f. L as RETAIN]

reincarnate etc., see RE- 8; **reincorpo-
rate**, RE- 9.

rein'deer (rān-), n. (collect. sing. usu. for
pl.). Subarctic deer used for drawing
sledges & kept in herds for its milk, flesh,
& hide. [f. ON hreindýri (hreinn reindeer, DEER)]

reinforce', v.t., & n. **1.** Strengthen or
support by additional men or material or
by increase of numbers, quantity, size,
thickness, etc. (~ fortress, army, provisions, party, the basses etc. in band or
chorus, person's health etc. with food etc.,
one's argument with fresh points); ~d
concrete (with metal bars, gratings, or
wire, embedded in it); (rare) enforce
again, re-enforce. **2.** n. Thicker part of
gun next breech; strengthening part,
band, etc., added to object. [RE- 8, in-
force=ENFORCE]

reinforce'ment (-sm-), n. Reinforcing or
being reinforced; (often pl.) additional
men, ships, etc., for military or naval
force; anything that reinforces. [-MENT]

reingratiate, see RE- 9; **reink**, RE- 8.

reins (rānz), n. pl. (arch.). The kidneys;
the loins. [OF, f. L renes, sing. ren]

reinsert etc. See RE- 9.

reinstate', v.t. Restore to, replace in, lost
position, privileges, etc.; restore to health
or proper order. Hence ~MENT (-tm-) n.
[RE- 9, obs. instate (IN-¹, STATE n.)]

reinsure etc., **reinter**, see RE- 8; **reinvest**
etc., RE- 8, 9; **reinvigorate** etc., RE- 9.

For pronunciation & hyphening of *re-* see RE-: for words in *re-* not given see RE- 8, 9.

reis (rās), n. pl. Former Portuguese and Brazilian money of account of very small value. [Port., pl. of REAL¹.]

reissue etc., **reiterate** etc. See RE- 8.

reiver. See REAVE.

reject, v.t. & n. 1. (rijĕkt'). Put aside as not to be accepted, believed, chosen, used, compiled with, etc., doctrine, custom, evidence, candidate, vote; sorting-machine ~s all defective specimens; cast up again, vomit, evacuate. 2. n. (rē'jĕkt). Somebody or something that has been ~ed (e.g. person unfit for military service, article sold cheaply as not up to standard). Hence or cogn. rejec'TION, rejec'TOR¹, rejec'TER¹, nn. rejec'tamĕn'ta. [f. L rejicere (re-, jacĕre throw), as prec.]

rejectamĕn'ta (rē-), n. pl. Refuse, waste matters; things cast up by the sea; excrements. [mod. L (prec., -MENT)]

rejoice, v.t. & i. Cause joy to, make glad, (the news ~d him; I am ~d to hear it, that it should be so, at it, by it, etc.); feel great joy, whence **rejoi'cing¹** adv.; be glad that or to do, take delight in or at, (~ in, for have); make merry, celebrate some event, whence **rejoi'cings** (-z) [-ING] n. pl. [f. OF re(join-iss- JOY², -ING 6]

rejoin'¹, v.i. & t. (Law) reply to charge or pleading, esp. to plaintiff's replication; say in answer, retort; join (one's companion, regiment, etc.) again. [f. F re(joindre JOIN), RE- 9, or perh. partly as foll.]

re-join'², v.t. & i. Join (t. & i.) together again, reunite. [RE- 9 + JOIN, or as prec.]

rejoin'der, n. What is rejoin'ed or said in reply, retort. [as REJOIN¹, -ER⁴]

reju'venāte, **reju'venize**, (-ōō-), vv.t. & i. Make or become young again. Hence ~A'TION, ~ātor², nn. (-ōō-). [RE- 9, L juvenis young, -ATE³, -IZE]

rejuvenĕsce (-ōō-), v.i. & t. Become young again; (Biol., i. & t. of cells) get, fill with, fresh vitality. Hence ~ĕs'CENT a., ~ĕs'CENCE n., (-ōō-). [f. LL re(juven-escere f. L juvenis, -ESCENT), RE- 9]

-rel, also **-crel**, suf. of dim. & depreciating tendency, occas. repn. OF -erel, mod. F -ereau, but usu. in native wds of obscure origin.

relabel. See RE- 9.

relapse', v.i., & n. 1. Fall back, sink again, into wrong-doing, error, heresy, weakness or illness, quiescence or indolence, (often into). 2. n. Act or fact of ~ing, esp. deterioration in patient's condition after partial recovery. [f. L re(labi lapse- slip)]

relāte', v.t. & i. 1. Narrate, recount, establish relation between, (to, with, or abs.; cannot ~e the phenomena with or to

anything we know or to each other? (p.p.), connected, allied, akin by blood or marriage, (the law extends to several ~ed groups; is ~ed to the royal family), whence ~'EDNESS n. 3. Have reference to, stand in some relation to, (notices nothing but what ~es to himself; how parts ~e to parts). [f. L relāt- (REFER)]

relā'tion, n. 1. Narration, a narrative; (Law) laying of information before Attorney-General for him to take action upon (proceeding at the ~ of the Board of Trade). 2. What one person or thing has to do with another, way in which one stands or is related to another, kind of connexion or correspondence or contrast or feeling that prevails between persons or things, (the ~ is primarily expressed by prepositions are those of place & time; the outlay seems to bear no ~, is out of all ~, to the object aimed at; the ~ between them is that of guardian & ward; ~s are rather strained, cordiality is impaired; the report has ~ to a state of things now past; in or rarely with ~ to, as regards), whence ~AL a., ~ally² adv., (-sho-). 3. Kinship lit. or fig. (rare, now usu. ~SHIP n.). 4. Kinsman, kinswoman, relative (occas. with mixture of prec. sense, as is he any ~, what ~ is he, to you?; he is no ~), Hence ~LESS (-sho-) a. [f. L relātio (prec., -ION)]

relā'tive, a. & n. 1. Referring, & attaching a subordinate clause, to an expressed or implied antecedent (~ pronoun, as in The man whom you saw; ~ adjective, as in Which things are an ~ category; ~ adverb, as in The place where he died); (of clause) attached to antecedent by ~ word. 2. (rare). Having mutual relations, corresponding in some way, related to each other, (different get ~ designs). 3. (rare). Pertinent, relevant, related to the subject, (without some more ~ proof). 4. Comparative (what are the ~ merits of the two?; made the next attempt with ~ coolness); in relation to something else (their ~ positions are the same though they are miles apart); proportioned to something else (supply is ~ to demand); implying comparison (heat, speed, strength, are ~ words); correlative or essentially involving a different but corresponding idea (the conceptions of husband & wife are ~ to each other); not having absolute existence but conditioned (she is beautiful to me, but beauty is ~ to the beholder's eye). 5. Having reference, relating, to (detailed the facts ~ to the matter; also loosely as adv., as I wrote to him ~ to renewal of the lease); hence ~LY² (-vl-) adv. 6. n. (Gram.) ~ word, esp. pronoun (the principal ~s are who, which, that, what), whence relā'tivAL a.; (Philos.) ~ thing or term. 7. Kinsman, kinswoman, relation by blood or marriage. [f. L relātīvus (RELATE, -IVE)]

rel′ativ·ism, n. Doctrine that knowledge ls of relations only. So ~IST(2) n. [prec., -ISM]

Relativ′ity, n. Relativeness; (Philos.) Einstein's theory of the universe, based on the principle that all motion is relative, regarding space-time as a fourth dimension, & invalidating previous conceptions of gravitation, the ether, geometry, & other matters. [-ITY]

relat′or, n. Relater (now rare); (Law) maker of RELATION (legal sense). [L (RE-LATE, -OR²)]

relax′, v.t. & i. Cause or allow to become loose or slack or limp, enfeeble, enervate, mitigate, abate, (~ *the bowels, the muscles, one's grasp, discipline, a rule, one's attention, one's efforts; ~ed throat,* form of sore throat; *place has a ~ing climate,* opp. *bracing*); grow less tense or rigid or stern or ceremonious or energetic or zealous (*his hold, hands, severity, features, manner, endeavours, ~ed; must not ~ in one's efforts*). [f. L re(luxare see LAX), RE-9]

relaxa′tion, n. Partial remission of penalty, duty, etc.; cessation from work, recreation, amusements; diminution of tension, severity, precision, etc. [f. L relaxatio (prec., -ATION)]

relay′¹, n., & v.t. & i. 1. Set of fresh horses substituted for tired ones; gang of men, supply of material, etc, similarly used (~-*race*, between teams of which each person does part of the distance, the 2nd etc. members of teams starting when the 1st etc. end); (Teleg.) instrument reinforcing long-distance current with local battery. 2. vb. Arrange in, provide with, replace by, get, ~(s); (Wireless) broadcast (a message, programme, originating at, and received from, another station). [f. OF relais n., relayer vb, etym. dub.]

re-lay′², v.t. Lay again. [RE- 8]

release′¹, n., & v.t. 1. (Law) remit, surrender, make over to another, (debt, right, property), whence ~EE′, ~OR², nn. 2. Set free, liberate, deliver, unfasten, (from); (Cinemat.) issue (film etc.) for general exhibition. Hence ~′ABLE a. [f. OF relesser f. L RELAXare]

release′², n. 1. Deliverance, liberation, from trouble, sorrow, life, duty, confinement, or fixed position. 2. Written discharge, receipt; legal conveyance of right or estate to another, document effecting this. 3. Handle, catch, etc., that releases part of machine etc. [f. OF reles (prec.)]

rel′egate, v.t. Banish to some place of exile; consign or dismiss to some usu. inferior position, sphere, etc.; transfer (matter) for decision or execution, refer (person) for information etc., *to*. Hence ~ABLE a., ~A′TION n. [f. L re(legare send), RE- 5, -ATE²]

relent′, v.i. Relax severity, become less stern, abandon harsh intention, yield to compassion. Hence ~ingly² adv., ~LESS a., ~lessly² adv., ~lessness n. [ult. f. RE- 9, L lentus soft; cf. F ralentir]

rel′evant, a. Bearing upon, pertinent to, the matter in hand. Hence~ANCE,~ANCY, nn., ~antry² adv. [f. L relevare RELIEVE, -ANT: from 16th c.]

reli′able, a. That may be relied upon, of sound & consistent character or quality. Hence ~ABIL′ITY n. (~*ability trials,* long-distance trials of motor vehicles designed to test dependableness, endurance, etc. rather than speed),~ableness n.,~ably² adv. [RELY, -ABLE; from 16th c.; an established wd avoided by purists as irreg. formation]

reli′ance, n. Trust, confidence, (usu. *upon, on, in; have, place, feel, ~ upon* etc.; *my ~ is upon God*); thing depended upon (*the well is our chief ~*). So reli′ANT a. [RELY, -ANCE]

rel′ic, n. 1. Part of holy person's body or belongings kept after his death as object of reverence; memento, souvenir. 2. pl. Dead body, remains, of person; what has survived destruction or wasting, remnant, residue, scraps. 3. Surviving trace or memorial of a custom, belief, period, people, etc.; object interesting for age or associations. [f. F relique f. RELIQUIAE]

rel′ict, n. Widow (usu. *his* etc. ~, or ~ *of*); (rare) = prec. [f. p.p. of L re(linquere -lict- leave), RE- 3]

relief′¹, n. 1. Alleviation of or deliverance from pain, distress, anxiety, etc. (*the medicine brought ~; it is a ~ to come across an optimist*). 2. Feature etc. that diversifies monotony or relaxes tension (*a blank wall without ~; a comic scene follows by way of ~*). 3. Assistance given to the poor esp. || formerly under the Poor Law (*recipients of public ~ shall not be eligible*) or to persons in special danger or difficulty (*a ~ fund for the earthquake victims;* ~-*works,* building etc. operations started to give work to the unemployed). 4. Reinforcement & esp. raising of siege of besieged town. 5. (Replacing of person or persons on duty by) person(s) appointed to take turn of duty. 6. Redress of hardship or grievance. [OF (relever RELIEVE)]

relief′², n. Method of moulding or carving or stamping in which design stands out from plane or curved surface with projections proportioned & more or less those of objects imitated (*the profile of Julius in ~*); piece of sculpture etc. in ~; appearance of being done in ~ given by arrangement of line or colour or shading, distinctness of outline lit. or fig., vividness, (*stands out in ~; bring out the facts

For pronunciation & hyphening of re- see RE-; for words in re- not given see RE-8, 9.

in full ~); ~ map, map-model showing 'the elevations and depressions of the area dealt with, usu. on an exaggerated relative scale, (also) ordinary map indicating hills and valleys by shading, colouring, or hachures, rather than by contour lines alone. [f. It. rilievo (rilevare raise f. L as RELIEVE)]

relieve', v.t. 1. Bring, give, be a, RELIEF[1] to (town was ~ed; am much ~ed to hear it; devotes himself to ~ing distress or the distressed; ||~ing officer, parish or union official charged with care of the poor; ~ing arch, built in substance of wall to ~e part below from weight; ~e one's feelings, by strong language or some ebullition; ~e nature, evacuate bladder or bowels; ~e guard, come & take one's turn on guard; you shall be ~ed at 10.30; ~e one of load, take it off him, also joc., as a RELIEF[2], exhibit with appearance of solidity or detachment, (esp. in p.p., often against background). Hence ~ABLE a. [f. OF relever f. L relevare f. L levis light), RE-9]

relièvo, n. = RELIEF[2] esp. in lit. senses (ALTO, BASSO, MEZZO, ~). [f. It. rilievo RELIEF[2] w. anglicized spelling & pronunc.]

relig'ion (-jn), n. 1. Monastic condition, being monk or nun, (enter into, be in, ~); (rare) a monastic order. 2. (rare). Practice of sacred rites. 3. One of the prevalent systems of faith & worship (the Christian, Mohammedan, ~; established ~; all ~s are the same to him). 4. Human recognition of superhuman controlling power & esp. of a personal God entitled to obedience, effect of such recognition on conduct & mental attitude, (get ~, vulg. or joc., be converted to such belief). 5. Action that one is bound to do (make a ~ of doing). Hence ~LESS (-jon-) a. [f. L religio perh. connected w. religare bind), RE-9]

relig'ioner (-jon-), n. Member of monastic order: person zealous for religion. [-ER[1]]

relig'ionism (-jon-), n. Excessive religious zeal. So ~IST(2) n. [-ISM]

relig'ionize(-jon-),v.t. & i. Convert to or imbue with religion; exhibit religious zeal. [-IZE]

relig'iōse, a. Morbidly religious. [as RELIGIOUS, -OSE[1]]

religios'ity, n. Being religious or religiose. [f. L religiositas (foll. -ITY)]

relig'ious (-jus), a. & n. 1. Imbued with religion, pious, god-fearing, devout; of, belonging to, a monastic order; of, concerned with, religion; scrupulous, conscientious, (with ~ care, exactitude, etc.); hence ~LY[2] adv., ~NESS n. 2. n. (As sing. with a etc., & as pl. in same form with the, some, several, etc.) person bound

by monastic vows. [f. L religiosus (RELIGION, -OSE[2])]

relíne, v.t. See RE-9.

relin'quish, v.t. Give up, abandon, cease from, resign, surrender, (habit, plan, hope, belief, right, possession); loose hold of (object held). Hence ~MENT n. [f. OF reliquir f. L re(linquere leave), RE-3, -ISH[2]]

rel'iquary, n. Receptacle for relic(s). [f. F reliquaire (RELIC, -ARY[1])]

rel'iquæ, n. pl. Remains; (Geol.) fossil remains of animals or plants; (Bot.) withered remains of leaves decaying on stem. [L (reliquus remaining, f. relinquere RELINQUISH, -ISH[1])]

rel'ish, n. 1. Flavour, distinctive taste of; slight dash or tinge of some quality. 2. Appetizing flavour, attractive quality, (meat has no ~ when one is ill; horseplay loses its ~ after childhood); thing eaten with plainer food to add flavour. 3. Enjoyment of food or other things, zest, liking for, (eat, read, appreciate jest, etc., with great ~; has no ~ for poetry). [earlier reless, & OF reles aftertaste (relesser RELEASE)]

rel'ish[2], v.t. & i. Serve as relish to, make piquant etc.; get pleasure out of, like, be pleased with, (though he could ~ a lobster; does not ~ the prospect), whence ~ABLE a.; taste, savour, smack, suggest presence of; affect the lit. or fig. taste well, badly, etc. [f. prec.]

relive, reload. See RE-8.

rel'ucent (-ōō-), a. (rare). Shining, bright. [f. L re(lucēre shine), RE-6, -ENT]

reluct', v.i. (now rare). Feel or show reluctance, make opposition. (at, against). So ~ATE[3](in same sense) v.i., ~ATION[2] n. [f. L re(luctari struggle), RE-2]

reluc'tant, a. Struggling, offering resistance, hard to work or get or manage, (esp. poet.); unwilling, disinclined, to do or abs. (am very ~ to admit; gave me ~ assistance). Hence reluc'tANCE n., ~LY[3] adv. [as prec., -ANT]

relume' (-ōōm), v.t. (poet.). Rekindle (light or flame lit, or fig.); make (eyes etc.) bright again; light (sky etc.) up again. [RE-9, & as ILLUME]

rely', v.i. Put one's trust, depend with confidence, (up)on person or thing (is do it, its being done, today; you may ~ upon it that he will be here); [earlier senses rally, adhere to, be vassal of; f. OF relier bind together, f. L re(ligare bind), RE-9]

remain[1], v.i. 1. Be left over after abstraction or use of or dealing with the rest (the few pleasures that ~ to an old man; worse things ~ to be told; nothing ~s but to draw the moral). 2. Abide, stay in same place or condition, continue to exist, be left behind, (~ three weeks in Paris; let it ~ as it is; as things have been they ~; the Parthenon ~s to attest or

as a proof of it; this visit will always ~ in my memory; the luggage unfortunately ~ed on the platform; victory ~ed with the Thebans). **3.** (With compl.) continue to be (*one thing ~s certain; ~ faithful etc.; I ~ yours truly etc.,* formula concluding letter). [f. OF *remaindre* f. L *re(manēre* stay), RE-3]

remain'², n. 1. (Usu. pl.) what remains over, surviving members or parts or amount, (the ~*s of a nation, family, meal, stock, building,* of one's *conscience* or *strength,* etc.; also in pl. as sing., & in sing., as here *there is the ~s, a ~, of a temple*); (usu. pl.) relics or relic of obsolete custom or of antiquity. **2.** pl. Works, esp. those not before or yet published, left by author (rarely in sing. of single work). **3.** pl. Dead body, corpse. [OF (prec.)]

remain'der, n., a., & v.t. **1.** (Law) residual interest in estate devised to another (cf. REVERSION) simultaneously with creation of estate (~ *man,* devisee of ~), right of succession to title or position on holder's decease, whence ~SHIP n. **2.** Residue, remaining persons or things; (Arith.) number left after subtraction; (Bookselling) copies left unsold when demand has ceased & often offered at reduced price, (vb) treat or dispose of (edition) as~; (attrib.) left over. [AF (REMAIN²ᵘᵉ, -ER⁴)]

remake, see RE-8; **reman,** RE-8, 9.

remand', (-ah-), v.t., & n. **1.** Send back to, reconsign, (now rare in gen. sense); send back (prisoner) into custody to allow of further inquiry. **2.** n. Recommittal to custody. [f. LL *re(mandāre* commit), RE-9]

rem'anent, a. Remaining, residual, (now rare exc. in ~ *magnetism,* that left in iron after electric excitation). [f. L part. as foll., see -ENT]

rem'anět, n. Remaining part, residue; postponed lawsuit or parliamentary bill. [L, =it remains (REMAIN¹)]

remar'gin, v.t. See RE-8.

remark'¹, v.t. & i. **1.** Take notice of, perceive, regard with attention, observe, (person, thing, fact, *that* etc.); say by way of comment; make comment (*up*)on. [f. F re(*marquer* MARK²), RE-6]

remark'², n. Noticing, observing, (*worthy of ~,* remarkable), commenting (*is the theme of general ~; let it pass without ~*); a written or spoken comment, anything said, (*his ~s are often interesting; make a ~,* speak). [f. F *remarque* (prec.)]

remark'able, a. Worth notice, exceptional, striking, conspicuous. Hence ~LENESS n., ~LY² adv. [f. F *remarquable* (REMARK¹, -ABLE)]

remarque (rimàrk'), n. Mark, usu. marginal sketch, indicating certain state of engraving plate. [F]

remarry etc., **remast.** See RE-8.

remblai (rahnblā'), n. (Fortif.) earth used to form ramparts, parapets, etc.; earth brought to form railway embankments etc. [F, f. *remblayer* embank]

Rembrandtesque (-sk), a. & n. (After) the style of Rembrandt, with marked effects of light & shade. [-ESQUE]

rem'edy, n., & v.t. **1.** Cure for disease, healing medicine or treatment, means of removing or counteracting or relieving any evil (*for*), redress, legal or other reparation, whence or cogn. **remēd'IAL** a., **remēd'ially¹** adv., (now poet. or rhet.) **remēd'iless** (*or* rěm'ĭ·) a., **remēd'iless**LY² adv. **2.** Margin within which coins as minted may differ from the standard fineness and weight. **3.** v.t. Cure medically (now rare); rectify, make good; so **remēd'IABLE** a., [vb f. L *remediāre,* n. f. AF *remedie,* f. L *re(medium* f. *medēri* heal), RE-1]

remēm'ber, v.t. **1.** Retain in the memory, not forget, recall to mind, recollect, know by heart, (person, thing, fact, *that, to do, how to do, when, why,* etc., or abs.; ~ *oneself,* bethink oneself of one's manners or intentions after a lapse; also refl. with *me, him,* etc., arch., as *I ~ me that, they ~ed them of),* whence ~ABLE a. **2.** Make present to, tip, (~*ed me in his will; ~ the waiter*). **3.** Mention in one's prayers. **4.** Convey greetings from (person) to another (~ *me kindly to them; begs to be ~ed to you).* [f. OF *remembrer* f. LL *re(memorāri* f. L *memor* mindful), RE-9]

remēm'brance, n. **1.** Remembering or being remembered, memory, recollection, (*has escaped my ~; have in, call to, ~; put in ~,* remind; *have no ~ of it; more than once within my ~; a pillar in ~ of the exploit).* **2.** Keepsake, souvenir, memorial. **3.** pl. Greetings conveyed through third person. [F (prec., -ANCE)]

remēm'brancer, n. **1.** || *King's, Queen's, R~,* officer collecting debts due to sovereign; || *City R~,* representing Corporation of City of London before parliamentary committees etc. **2.** Reminder, memento, of. [AF (prec., -ER¹)]

remigrate etc. See RE-9.

remind', v.t. Put (person) in mind of, to do, *that, how,* etc., or abs. [RE-8, MIND vb]

remin'der, n. Thing that reminds or is meant to remind. [-ER¹]

remind'ful, a. Acting as a reminder, reviving the memory, of. [-FUL]

remin'iscence, n. **1.** Remembering, recovery of knowledge by mental effort, (*Platonic doctrine of ~,* that all knowledge is such recovery of things known to the soul in previous existences). **2.** Remembered (& related) fact or incident; (pl.)

For pronunciation & hyphening of *re-* see RE-; for words in *re-* not given see RE- 8, 9.

collection in literary form of incidents that person remembers. **3.** Point in thing reminding of or suggestive of other thing (*there is a ~ of the Greek type in her face*). Hence **rēmīnīscēn'tīAL** (-shl) a. [f. LL *rēmīnīscentīa* f. L *rēmīnīscī* cogn. w. MIND] remember, RE- 9, -ENCE]

rĕmĭnt′cent, a. Recalling past things, given to or concerned with retrospection, mindful or having memories of; remind-ing or suggestive of. Hence **-LY² adv.** [as prec., -ENT]

rĕmĭnt. See RE- 8.

rĕmīse′¹ (-ēz), a. & v.i. **1.** (arch.). Coach-house, carriage hired from livery-stable. **2.** (fenc.). Second thrust made for recovery from first; (v.i.) make ~. [F, vbl n. f. *remettre* REMIT]

rĕmīse′² (-īz), v.t. (legal). Surrender, make over, (right, property). [f. F *re-mise* p.p. as prec.]

rĕmĭss′, a. Careless of duty, lax, negli-gent; lacking force or energy. Hence **-LY² adv.**, **~NESS n.** [f. L *remissus*]

rĕmĭss′ĭble, a. That may be remitted. [f. L *remissibilis*]

rĕmĭss′ion (-shn), n. **1.** Forgiveness of sins etc., forgiveness of sins; remitting of debt, penalty, etc. **2.** Diminution of force, effect, degree, violence, etc. **3.** Act of remitting in other senses (rare). So **rĕmĭss′ĭve a.** [OF,f. L *remissionem* (toll, -ION)]

rĕmĭt′, v.t. & i. (-tt-). **1.** (arch.). Forgive, pardon (sins etc.); refrain from exacting or inflicting or executing (debt, punish-ment, sentence). **2.** Abate(t, & i.), slacken, mitigate, partly or entirely cease from or cease, (~ one's anger or efforts, the siege; pain, enthusiasm, begins to ~). **3.** Refer (matter for decision etc.) to some autho-rity, send back (case) to lower court. **4.** Send or put back (*in*)to previous state; postpone, defer, to or till. **5.** Transmit (money etc.), get conveyed by post etc., whence **~t′er¹** [-ER¹], **~tee′** nn. Hence **~t′AL(2) n.** [f. L *remittere miss-* send), -TON)]

rĕmĭtt′ance, n. Money sent to person; consignment of goods sent (rare); sending of money; ~*-man*, emigrant subsisting on ~s from home, person paid to stay abroad. [prec.,-ANCE]

rĕmĭtt′ent, a. & n. (Fever) that abates at intervals (cf. INTERMITTENT). [REMIT, -ENT]

rĕmĭtt′er², n. (legal; for *remitter*¹ see REMIT). Substitution, in favour of holder of two titles to estate, of the more valid for the other by which he entered on possession; remitting of case to other court; restoration to rights, rehabilita-tion, (rare). [-ER¹]

rĕm′nant, n. The little or few that re-main(s), small remaining quantity or piece or number of persons or things; surviving trace *of*; fragment, scrap, esp. piece of cloth etc. offered at reduced price

when greater part has been used up. [short for obs. & OF *remenant*, -*manant*, (*remanoir* REMAIN¹, -ANT)]

rĕmŏd′elze (or -mĭn-), v.t. Restore (metal etc.) to former position as legal tender. Hence **~mĭn′ATION** [RE- 9]

rĕmŏn′strance, n. (Hist.) formal state-ment of public grievances (the *Grand R~*, remonstrance, expostulation, a protest.

rĕmŏn′strate, v.i. & t. Make protest, ex-postulate, (*against*, *about a course, with person, on or upon matter, or abs.*); urge in remon-strance (*that* or *parenth.*). Hence or cogn. **~ANT a. & n.,~antIVE a.,~atingLY² adv.,~ATOR² n.** [f. med. L *re*(*mon-strare* show), RE- 2, -ATE²]

rĕmŏn′tant, a. & n. (Rose) blooming more than once in year. [F (*remonter* REMOUNT², -ANT)]

rĕmōr′a, n. The sucking-fish, formerly supposed to stay course of ship to which it adhered; obstruction, impediment, (now rare). [L (RE- 2, *mora* delay), = im-pediment, sucking-fish]

rĕmōrse′, n. Bitter repentance for wrong committed, whence **~FUL**(-sf-) a., **~fullY²** adv.; compunction, compassionate reluc-tance to inflict pain or be cruel, (chiefly in *without* ~), whence **~LESS** (-sl-) a., **~lessLY²** adv., **~lessNESS n.** [OF *remors*, f. LL *remorsus* -ûs f. *mordēre mors-* bite),

rĕmōte′, a. (~r, ~st). **1.** Far apart, far away or off in place or time, not closely related, distant or widely different or by nature separate *from*, (*lies ~ from the road; came from the ~st parts of the earth; memorials of ~ ages; a ~ ancestor, descendant, kinsman; ~ causes, effects; introduces considerations ~ from the sub-ject*). **3.** Out-of-the-way, secluded, (*a ~ village; lives ~*). **4.** (Chiefly superl., of idea etc.) slight(est), faint(est), least, (*have not the ~est*, *have only a very ~, conception of the ~ means*). Hence **~LY² (-tl-) adv.,** **~NESS (-tn-) n.** [f. L *remotus* (REMOVE¹)]

rĕmōunt′², rĕmount¹, v.t. & i. See RE- 8. (hill, ladder, horse, etc.), again; go up again, get on horseback again, make fresh ascent; go back to specified date, period, source. [f. OF *re*(*monter* MOUNT²), RE- 9]

rĕmō′vable (-mŏo-), a. & n. In vbl senses; esp. (of magistrate or official) subject to removal from office, holding office during pleasure of Crown or other authority; ||(n.) ~able magistrate in Ireland. Hence **~ablLITY n.** [foll.,-ABLE]

rĕmōve′¹ (-ŏov), v.t. & i. **1.** Take off or away from place occupied, convey to another place, change situation of, get rid of, dismiss, (~ *one's hat, the tea-things, all traces; ~ mountains, do miracle; cardi-nal was ~d by poison; ~ magistrate from*

office; boy is ~d from school, taken away by parents etc.; this will ~ all apprehension, the last doubts; ~ furniture, for persons changing house, as special trade, whence rěmō'ver¹ (-mŏŏ-) n.); ‖ (pass., of course at dinner etc.) be succeeded by (boiled haddock ~d by hashed mutton). 2. Change one's residence, go away from, (am removing from London to Oxford; truth has ~d from earth). 3. p.p. Distant or remote from (is not many degrees ~d from the brute); (of cousins) once, twice, etc., ~d, with difference of one, two, etc., generations (my first cousin once, twice, ~d, cousin's child or parent's cousin, cousin's grandchild or grandparent's cousin). Hence rěmō'VAL (-mŏŏ-) n. (not of cousinship). [f. OF removoir f. L re(movēre MOVE), RE-4]

rěmove'² (-ŏŏv), n. 1. ‖ Dish that succeeds another at table. 2. ‖ Promotion to higher form at school (has not got his ~); ‖ (in some schools) a certain form or division. 3. (rare). Change of residence, departure, removal; distance (at a certain ~ its shape seems to change). 4. Stage in gradation, degree, (is but one ~, few ~s, from), esp. in consanguinity (cf. prec.). [f. prec.]

rěmū'ner|āte, v.t. Reward, pay for service rendered; serve as or provide recompense for (toil etc.) or to (person). Hence ~A'TION n., ~ATIVE a., ~ATIVELY² adv., ~ATIVENESS n. [f. LL re(mūnerarī f. munus -eris reward), RE-1]

rěnais'sance (& see Ap.), n. Revival of art & letters under influence of classical models in 14th–16th cc., period of its progress, style of art & architecture developed by it, (often attrib., as ~ painters, architecture, church); any similar revival. [F (renaître be born again) after naissance birth, cf. RENASCENCE]

rěn'al, a. Of the kidneys. [f. LL renalis (ren kidney, -AL)]

rename. See RE-8.

rěnas'cence, n. Rebirth, renewal; = RE-NAISSANCE. [foll., -ENCE]

rěnas'cent, a. Springing up anew, being reborn. [f. L re(nasci be born), RE-8, -ENT]

rěncoun'ter, rěncôn'tre (-ter, & see Ap.), 1. (now rare). Encounter, battle, skirmish, duel; casual meeting. [f. F rencontre (rencontrer, see RE-, ENCOUNTER]

rěnd, v.t. & i. (rěnd). 1. Tear or wrench (off, away, out of, from, asunder, apart, etc., or abs.; arch. or rhet.; a province rent from the empire; ~ one's garments, hair, in sign of grief etc.; turn & ~ one, fig., abuse him unexpectedly). 2. Split or divide (t. & i.) in two or in pieces or usu. into factions (~ laths, make them by splitting wood; Europe was rent in two by the question; ~ the air, sound explosively;

heart is rent by contending emotions; the veil ~s). [OE rendan, cf. OFris. renda]

rěn'der, v.t., & v. n. 1. Give in return (~ thanks, good for evil). 2. Give back (arch.); (chiefly arch.; ~ to Caesar the things that are Caesar's; grave ~s up its dead: fortress was ~d on terms). 3. Pay (tribute etc.), show (obedience etc.), do (service etc.), (usn. to or with ind. obj.). 4. Produce for inspection, submit, present, send in, (account, reason, etc.; account ~d, bill previously sent in & not yet paid, phr. used as substitute for repetition of items). 5. Reproduce, portray, give representation or performance or effect of, execute, translate, (painter has hardly ~ed the expression; the quartet, Iago, the dramatist's conception, were well ~ed; how would you ~ solvitur ambulando?: poetry can never be adequately ~ed in another language; whence ~ING¹ (1, 2) n. 6. (With obj. & compl.) make, cause to be, convert into, (age had ~ed him peevish; the tone ~ed it an insult). 7. Melt (fat) down, extract by melting, clarify. 8. Cover (stone, brick) with first coat of plaster; ~set v.t., plaster (wall etc.) with two coats, n. & v., (plastering) of two coats. 9. n. (legal). Return in money or kind or service made by tenant to superior. [f. OF rendre ult. f. L reddere reddit- (RE-, dare give)]

rendez'vous (rŏn'divŏŏ), n. (pl. same, pr. -ŏŏz), & v.i. (~es, ~ed, ~ing, pr. -ŏŏz, -ŏŏd, -ŏŏing). 1. Place appointed for assembling of troops or ships; place of common resort; meeting-place agreed on, meeting by agreement (place of ~). 2. v.i. Meet at ~. [F, f. rendez vous (rendre, see prec.) betake yourselves]

rěndi'tion, n. 1. Surrender of place or person (now rare). 2. A translation; interpretation, rendering, of dramatic role, musical piece, etc. [F (obs.), f. rendre RENDER, -ION]

rěn'egade n. & v.i., rěněgād'ō (arch.) n. 1. Apostate, esp. from Christianity to Mohammedanism; deserter of party or principles, turncoat. 2. v.i. Turn ~; so rěněgā'TION n. [Sp. (-o), f. med. L re(negatus f. negare deny), RE-9]

rěneg(u)e' (-ēg), v.i. & t. (Cards) revoke; (arch.) deny, renounce, abandon. [f. med. L renegare f. RE-+negare deny]

rěnew', v.t. & i. 1. Restore to original state, make (as good as) new, resuscitate, revivify, regenerate, (nature dies & is ~ed; person's life, sorrow, energy; ~ the golden age; rose from her knees ~ed by the Holy Spirit; ~ed by baptism). 2. Patch, fill up, reinforce, replace, (coat ~ed in places; ~ the water in the bowl; ~ garrison, tires, etc.). 3. Get, begin, make, say, or give, anew, continue after

internission, (~ *one's youth*, *strength*, etc.; ~ *one's youth*, again; ~ *attack*, *corre-*
grow young etc. again; ~ *attack*, *corre-* *reditta* fem. p.-p. as RENDER]
spondence, *speech*, *game*, *efforts* ; ~ *one's* **rên´tal**, n. Income from rents; amount
vows, *statements*, etc.; ~ *lease*, *bill*, grant paid or received as rent. [AF (prec., -AL)]
or be granted continuation of it); (abs.) **rente** (*rahñt*), n. Income, esp. that con-
~ *lease* or *bill*. **4.** (rare). Become new sisting of life-annuity or dividends. [F]
again (*the clamour* ~*ed*; *feel my youth* ~*-* **sentier** (*rahñtiaã*), n. Person living on
ing). Hence ~ABLE a., ~AL(2) n. [RE-, NEW] rente, person not needing to earn his
rên´iförm, a. Kidney-shaped. [REINS, living. [F]
-FORM]   **renûm´ber.** See RE- 8.
rênûnci´ation, n. Renouncing, document
rênounce´, v.t. & i. & n. **1.** Consent expressing it; self-denial, giving up of
formally to abandon, surrender, give up, things. So **renûn´ciANT**(1) n. & a., (-*shi*-),
(claim, right, possession). **2.** Repudiate, **renûn´ciATORY** (-*sha*-), **renûn´ciATORY**
refuse to recognize longer, decline associa- (-*shŏri*), aa. [f. L *renuntiatio* (RENOUNCE,
tion or disclaim relationship with, with- -ATION)]
draw from, discontinue, forsake, (~ *treaty*, **reo-.** See RHEO-.
principles, *person's authority*, *all thought* **reoc´cupy** etc., **reopen**, see RE- 9; **reor-**
of, *design*, *attempt*, *son* etc., *friend*, *friend-* **reorganize** etc.. **repaint.** See RE- 9.
ship ; ~ *the world*, abandon society or **rep**[1], **repp**, **rêps**, n. Textile fabric with
temporal affairs). **3.** (Law) refuse or corded surface used in upholstery. [f. F
resign right or position esp. as heir *reps* etym. dub.]
or trustee. **4.** (Cards) follow with card of **rep**[2], n. (school sl.). Verse etc. learnt by
another suit for want of right one (cf. heart. [abbr. of *repetition*]
REVOKE). — (n.) playing of such card, **rep**[3], n. (sl.). Person of loose character.
opportunity of doing so (*has a* ~ *in heart*). [perh. for REPROBATE[2]]
Hence ~´MENT (-SM-) n. [F *renoncer* f. L **repaganize** etc., **repaint.** See RE- 9.
renuntiare ANNOUNCE), RE- 5] **repair´**[1], v.i. & n. **1.** Resort, have
rên´ovate, v.t. Make new again, repair, recourse, go often or in numbers, have
restore to good condition or vigour. **2.** n. (arch.). Resort (*have* ~ *to*); haunt;
Hence ~A´TION, ~ätor₂ nn. [f. L *renovare* being visited by numbers (*a place of great*,
f. novus new), RE- 9, -ATE[3]] *little*, ~). [f. OF *repaire(t)* f. LL *repadriare*
renown´, n. Celebrity, fame, high distinc- f. L *patria* native land), RE- 9]
tion, (*men*, *town*, etc., *of* ~ *or great* etc.~, **repair´**[2], v.t. Restore (building, machine,
famous). [AF *renoun* = OF *renon* f. re- garment, tissue, strength, etc.) to good
nommer make famous f. L *nominare* condition, renovate, mend, by replacing
NOMINATE), RE- 8] or refixing parts or compensating loss or
renowned´ (-nd), a. Famous, celebrated. exhaustion, whence ~ABLE a.; remedy,
[obs. *renown* celebrate f. OF *renommer* set right again, make amends for, (loss,
prec.] wrong, error). [f. OF *reparer* f. L *re-*
rent[1]. See REND. *parare* make ready), RE- 9]
rent[2], n. Tear in garment etc., opening in **repair´**[3], n. Restoring to sound condition
clouds etc. resembling tear; cleft, fissure, (*health*, *bicycle*, *house*, *boots*, *need* ~; *shop*
gorge. [f. obs. *rent* vb, var. of REND] *wait*); good condition, relative condition,
rent[3], n. & v.t. & i. **1.** Tenant's periodical for working or using (*is in*, *out of*, ~;
payment to owner or landlord for use of *must be kept in good*, *is in bad*, ~). [f.
land or house or room; payment for hire prec.]
of machinery etc.; ~*-charge*, periodical **repand´**, a. (bot., zool.). With undulating
charge on land etc. reserved by deed to margin, wavy. Hence ~o- comb. form.
one who is not the owner; ~*-free* a. & [f. L *re(pandus* bent), RE- 9]
adv., with exemption from ~; ~*-roll*, **repaper.** See RE- 8.
register of person's lands etc. with ~s due **rep´arable**, a. (Of loss etc.) that can be
from them, sum of one's income from ~; made good. [F, f. L *reparabilis* (REPAIR[2],
||~*-service*, (tenure by) personal service in -ABLE)]
lieu of or addition to ~; hence (of land **repara´tion**, n. **1.** Repairing or being
etc., with *low*, *high*, etc.) **-rên´tED**[2] a. repaired, repair, (pl.) repairs, (now usu.
2. vb. Take, occupy, use, at a ~; let or *repair*, *repairs*). **2.** Making of amends,
hire for ~; be let *at specified* ~; impose compensation (esp., pl., for war damages).
~ on (tenant); ~*s his tenants low*); hence So **rep´arATIVE** (or *ripä'r*-), a. [f. OF *re-*
~ABLE a., **rên´tER**[1] n. (esp.) wholesaler *paration* f. L *reparationem* (REPAIR[2],
                                                                                       -ATION)]
                                                                                       repartee´, n. & v.i. Witty retort; (mak-
                                                                                       ing of) witty retorts (*a great power*, *a*
                                                                                       storehouse, *of* ~); (vb, now rare) make ~s.
                                                                                       [f. F *repartie* fem. p.-p. of *re(partir* PART[2])
                                                                                       start fresh, RE- 8]

repartition, see RE- 8; **repass** etc., RE- 9.

repast¹ (-ah-), n. (Food supplied for or eaten at) meal (usu. *rich, plentiful, slight, delicate, luxurious*, etc., ~). [OF, f. *re-paistre* f. LL *re(pascere past- feed*), RE- 8]

repatriate, v.t. & i. 1. Restore or return to native land. Hence ~ATE¹ (-ǎt) n., one who has been ~ated, ~ATION n. [f. LL *re(patriare* t. L *patria* fatherland), RE- 9]

repay, v.t. & i.(-*paid*). Pay back(money); return, retaliate, (blow, visit, service, etc.); give in recompense *for*; make repayment to (person); make return for, requite, (action); make repayment. Hence ~ABLE a., ~MENT n. [f. OF *re(paier* PAY²), RE- 9]

repeal, v.t., & n. 1. Revoke, rescind, annul, (law etc.); hence ~ABLE a. 2. n. Abrogation, ~ing; (Irish Pol.) cancelling of the Union demanded by O'Connell etc., whence ~ER¹ n. (hist.). [f. OF *repel(er)* (RE- 9, APPEAL¹)]

repeat, v.t. & i., & n. 1. Say or do over again, recite, rehearse, report, reproduce, give imitation of, (~ *action, statement, poem, conversation, attempt, pattern, signal,* etc.; *action was ~ed several times*, whence ~*édly*² adv.; *language will not bear ~ing*, is too foul etc. to ~); (of watch etc., abs.) strike last quarter etc. over again when required (so ~*ing watch* etc. or ~ER¹ n.); (of firearms) fire several shots without reloading (~*ing rifle* etc.). 2. Recur, appear again or ~edly, (*the last three figures ~; food ~s*, is tasted intermittently for some time). 3.(refl.) Recur in same form, say or do same thing over again, (*history ~s itself; does nothing but ~ himself*); hence ~ABLE a. 4. n. ~ing, esp. of item in programme in response to encore; (Mus.) passage intended to be ~ed, mark indicating this; pattern ~ed in wall-paper etc.; (Commerc.) fresh consignment similar to previous one, order given for this. [f. F *répéter* f. L *re(petere* seek), RE- 8]

repel, v.t. (-ll-). 1. Drive back, repulse, ward off, refuse admission or acceptance or approach to, (~ *assailant, attack, temptation, weapon, blow, suggestion, plea, offer*, person's *advances; first attracts & then ~s the magnet*). 2. Be repulsive or distasteful to, exert mental repulsion upon, whence ~lENT 8., ~lENTLY² adv. [f. L *re(pellere puls-* drive), RE- 2]

repent¹, a. (chiefly bot.). Creeping, esp. growing along or just under surface of ground. [f. L *repere* creep, -ENT]

repent², v.t. & i. 1. (arch.). (Refl., with arch. refl. pron.) Feel regret or penitence about something or *of* (*I now ~ me; he ~eth him of the evil*); (impers.) affect with penitence or regret (*it ~s me that I did it*). 2. Think with contrition *of*, think with contrition *of*, be regretful about or *of*, be contrite, wish one had not done,

(*you shall ~ this, ~ of this*, or abs.; *have nothing to ~ of; ~ my kindness, setting off when I did*). So **repen'tance** n., **repen'tant** a., **repen'tantly²** adv. [f. F *re(pentir* f. L *paenitēre* make sorry), RE- 3]

repeople. See RE- 9.

repercussion etc. See RE- 9.

repertoire (-twar'), n. Stock of pieces etc. that company or performer knows or is prepared to give. [F (*ré*), f. L as foll.]

repertory, n. 1. Place for finding something, store or collection, esp. of information, instances, facts, etc. 2. = prec. (~ *theatre, company, system*, relying on ~ & not on long runs). [f. L *repertorium* (*reperire -pert-* find f. RE-, OL *parire* = L *parĕre* produce, -ORY)]

reperuse etc. See RE- 8.

repetend', n. Recurring figures of decimal; recurring word or phrase, refrain. [f. L as REPEAT, -ND¹]

repeti'tion, n. REPEATING or being repeated; piece set to be learnt by heart; copy, replica; ability of musical instrument to repeat note quickly. Hence ~IONAL, ~IONARY¹ (-sho-), ~IOUS (-shus), **repet'itive**, aa. (rare). [f. L *repetitio* (RE- 8, PETITION)]

repiece. See RE- 9.

repine, v.i. Fret, be discontented, (*at, against*, or abs.). Hence ~*ing*LY² adv. [RE- 6, PINE²]

repique' (-ēk), n., & v.t. & i. 1. Winning of 30 points on cards alone before beginning to play in piquet. 2. vb. Score ~ against (opponent); make ~. [f. F *repic* (RE-, PIQUE²)]

replace', v.t. Put back in place; take place of, succeed, be substituted for, (*pass.*) be succeeded or have one's or its place filled *by*, be superseded; fill up place of (*with, by*), find or provide substitute for. Hence ~ABLE (-sa-) a., ~MENT (-sm-) n., (also) person or thing that ~s another. [RE- 9, PLACE²]

replant etc. See RE- 8.

replay, v.t. Play (a match) over again; hence **rēplay** n., a ~ed match. [RE- 8]

replen'ish, v.t. Fill up again (*with* or abs.); (p.p.) filled, fully stored, full, (*with* or abs.). Hence ~MENT n. [f. OF *re(plenir* ult. f. L *plenus* full), RE- 9, -ISH²]

replete', a. Filled, stuffed, fully imbued, well stocked, *with*; gorged, sated, (*with*). So ~´tion n. (esp. *full to ~etion*). [f. L *re(plēre plet-* fill), RE- 6]

replev'in, n. Restoration or recovery of distrained goods on security given for submission to trial & judgement; writ granting ~; action arising out of ~. [AF, f. OF as foll.]

replev'y, v.t. Recover by replevin. [f. OF *re(plevir* etym. dub.; see PLEDGE¹), RE- 9]

rep'lica, n. Duplicate made by original

For pronunciation & hyphening of *re-* see RE-: for words in *re-* not given see RE- 8, 9.

artist of his picture etc.; facsimile, exact copy. [It. (*replicare* REPLY)]

rĕp′licate¹, n. Tone one or more octaves above or below given tone. [as foll.]

rĕp′licate², a. (bot.). Folded back on itself. [as foll., -ATE²]

rĕp′licate³, v.t. (rare). Repeat; make replica of; fold back. [L *replicare* fold back]

rĕplică′tion, n. 1. Folding back, fold, (rare). 2. Replying, rejoinder, answer, esp. reply to answer; (law) plaintiff's reply to defendant's plea. 3. Echo. 4. Copy, copying. [OF, f. L *replicationem* (prec., -ATION]

rĕply′, v.i. & t., & n. 1. Make answer, respond, in word or action (*to*; abs., *that* etc., or parenth.; *rose to ~ for the ladies*, represent them in returning thanks for toast; *the batteries replied to our fire; he replied that I must please myself; 'Please yourself' he replied*). 2. n. Act of ~ing (*what he says in ~*); what is replied, response; ~ *paid*, (of telegram) with cost of prepaid by sender. [f. OF *replier* f. L as REPLICATE³]

répondez s'il vous plaît (see A.P.) formula appended (usu. in abbr. R.S.V.P.) to invitation or other letter, = please answer. [F]

rĕpoint, **rĕpolish**. See RE- 9.

rĕpŏr′t¹, v.t. & i. 1. Bring back account of, state as ascertained fact, tell as news, narrate or describe or repeat esp. as eye-witness etc. (*to*), relate as spoken by another, make official or formal statement about, inform against (offence, offender) *to* authorities or abs., announce oneself as returned or arrived, (*~s open water at pole, pole to the accessible, that he reached pole; it is ~ed, commonly said; ~ed all details of the scene to me; my actual words & those ~ed to you were quite different; ~ed speech, oblique oration; chairman of committee ~s bill to House*, announces conclusion of committee's dealings with it between 2nd & 3rd reading; ||~ *progress*, state what has been done so far, *move to ~ progress in House of Commons*, propose that debate be discontinued, often for obstructive purposes; *all variations are to be ~ed daily; shall ~ you, your unpunctuality, to senior partner*). 2. Take down word for word or epitomize or write description of for publication (~ *law case, proceedings, meeting*; also abs., as *reports for The Times*). 3. Make, draw up, or send in report. 4. Give report of conveying that one is well or badly impressed (*~s well of the prospects; is badly impressed ~ed of*). Hence ~ABLE a., ~AGE n. [f. OF *reporter* f. L *reportare* bring; RE¹]

rĕpŏr′t², n. 1. Common talk, rumour, (*mere ~ is not enough to go upon; the ~* goes, it is said); way person or thing is spoken of, repute, (*things of good ~; faithful through good & evil ~*). 2. Account given or opinion formally expressed after investigation or consideration, description or epitome or reproduction of scene or speech or law case esp. for newspaper publication, ||(~ *stage in House of Commons*, treatment of bill when committee has reported, see prec.). 3. Sound of explosion (*went off with a loud ~*). [OF (*reporter* see prec.)]

rĕpŏs′e¹ (-z), v.t. Place (trust etc.) *in*. Hence ~AL (-zl) n. [f. L *re(ponere posit-* place), RE- 4, w. assim. to *depose*, foll.]

rĕpŏs′e² (-z), v.t. & i. & n. 1. Rest (oneself or abs.); lay (one's head etc.) to rest (often *on* pillow etc.); give rest to, refresh with rest; lie, be lying or laid, esp. in sleep or death (lie, *on*, or abs.), be supported or based *on* (*the whole system ~s on fear*); (of memory etc.) dwell *on*. 2. n. Rest, respite from toil, sleep, peaceful or quiescent state, stillness, tranquillity; (of) restful effect, harmonious combination in art, composure or ease of manner, (esp. *in lacks ~*); hence ~FUL (-zf-) a., ~fully² adv. [f. F *reposer* f. LL *repausare* PAUSE; RE- 5); meaning influenced by prec.]

rĕpŏs′itŏrў (-z-), n. 1. Receptacle; place where things are stored or may be found, museum, warehouse, store, shop, (*book, person, etc., is a ~ of curious information*); burial-place. 2. Recipient of confidences or secrets. [f. L *repositorium*, -ORY]

rĕpossĕss etc. See RE- 9.

rĕpost. See RIPOSTE.

rĕpŏst. See RE- 8.

rĕpŏussé (repoōs′ā), a. & n. (Ornamental metal work) hammered into relief from reverse side. [F p.p. of *re(pousser* PUSH¹), RE- 3]

rĕpp. See REP¹.

rĕpped (-pt), a. Having surface like rep. [-ED²]

rĕprĕhĕnd′, v.t. Rebuke, blame, find fault with. So ~ĕn′SIBLE a., ~ĕn′sibly² adv., ~ĕn′SION (-shn) n. [f. L *reprehendĕre* seize), RE- 2]

rĕprĕsĕnt′ (-z-), v.t. 1. Call up by description or portrayal or imagination, figure, place likeness of before mind or senses, serve or be meant as likeness of, (*can you ~ infinity to yourself?; can only ~ it to you by metaphors; picture ~s murder of Abel; is ~ed in hunting costume*). 2. Try to bring (facts influencing conduct) home (to), state by way of expostulation or incentive, (*~ed the rashness of it, that it could not succeed*). 3. Make out to be etc., allege that, describe or depict as, (*am not what you ~ me to be or as; in the corner is the Pope ~ed as a beggar; ~s that he*

has or himself to have seen service). **4.** Act (play etc.), play part of on stage. **5.** Symbolize, act as embodiment of, stand for, correspond to, be specimen of, (*sovereign ~s majesty of State; inch of rain ~s 100 tons to acre; globe ~s totality; camels are ~ed in the New World by llamas; Welsh football is ~ed in the team by Morgan*). **6.** Fill place of, be substitute or deputy for, be entitled to speak for, be sent as member to House of Commons by (*King was ~ed by the Duke of Norfolk; members ~ing urban constituencies*). Hence or cogn. ~ABLE a., ~A'TION (-z-) n. (*proportional ~ation*, electoral system so arranged that minorities are ~ed in proportion to their strength), ~ā'tionAL (-shon-) a. [f. L re(*praesentare* PRESENT⁵), RE-8]

repré'sen'tative (-z-), a. & n. **1.** Serving as portrayal or symbol of (*a group ~ of the theological virtues*); that presents or can present ideas to the mind (*imagination is a ~ faculty*); typical specimens of all or many classes, (*the truth of an allegory is ~, not literal; call a meeting of ~ men; a very ~ selection, collection*); consisting of (*~ chamber, house*, etc.), based on representation by such deputies (*~ government, institutions*); hence ~LY² adv., ~NESS n. **2.** n. Sample, specimen, typical embodiment, analogue, of; person's agent, delegate, substitute, successor, or heir; deputy in ~ chamber (*House of R~s*, lower house of U.S. Congress). [f. med. L *repraesentativus* (REPRESENT, -ATIVE)]

représs', v.t. Check, restrain, put down, keep under, quell, suppress, prevent from sounding or bursting out or rioting. So **repré'ssion** (-shn) n. (esp., in Psych., of natural promptings), ~IVE a., [f. L re(*primere*=*premere* PRESS⁵), RE-5]

reprieve|**e'**, v.t., & n. **1.** Suspend or delay execution of (condemned person); (fig.) give respite to. **2.** n. ~ing or being ~ed; (warrant for) remission or commutation of capital sentence; respite. [n. f. vb, earlier *reprieve, -pry*, in sense re-mand, first in p.p., prob. f. F re(*pris* p.p. of *prendre* f. L *prehendere* take), RE-8; -v- unexplained]

rep'rimand (-ah-), n., & v.t. Official(ly) rebuke (for fault). [f. F *réprimande(r)* f. *réprimer* REPRESS]

reprint. See RE-8.

repri'sal (-zl), n. **1.** (hist.). Forcible seizure of foreign subjects' persons or property in retaliation (*letters of ~*, official warrant authorizing this). **2.** Act of retaliation (usu. *make ~s* or ~). [f. OF *reprisaille* as foll. +-AL(2)]

reprise (-z), n. **1.** (Law) rent-charge or other payment to be made yearly out of estate (*beyond, besides, above, ~8*, remaining after all ~s have been paid). **2.** (rare). Resumption of action, one of the times devoted to something not done all at once. [F, fem. of *repris* see REPRIEVE]

reproach', v.t., & n. **1.** Upbraid, scold, (person, often *with* offence); rebuke (offence); (of look etc.) convey protest or censure to (*his eyes ~ me*); hence ~ingLY² adv. (rare for ~*fully*). **2.** n. Thing that brings disgrace or discredit (*to: the state of the roads is a ~ to civilization*), whence ~LESS a. (rare for *irreproachable*); opprobrium, disgraced or discredited state, (*live in ~ & ignominy; the things that had brought ~ upon him; has taken away my ~*); upbraiding, rebuke, censure, (*abstain from ~; heap ~es on; the made ~ in his eyes; term of ~*, word implying censure), whence ~FUL a., ~fullY² adv., ~fulNESS n.; (pl.) Good-Friday chiefly R.-C. set of antiphons & responses representing ~es of Christ to people. [f. F *reproche(r)* perh. ult. f. L re(*prope* REPROVE]

rep'robāte¹, v.t. Express or feel disapproval of, censure; (of God) cast off, exclude from salvation. Hence ~A'TION n. [f. L re(*probare* approve), RE-7, -ATE³]

rep'robate², a. & n. (Person) cast off by God, hardened in sin, of abandoned character, immoral. See RE-8.

reproduce etc. See RE-8.

reproof¹, n. Blame (*a word, glance, of ~; spoke in ~ of idleness*); a rebuke or expression of blame. [f. OF *reprove* (*reprover* REPROVE]

reproof², v.t. Render (coat etc.) waterproof again. [RE-9]

reprove'(-ōov), v.t. Rebuke, chide, (person, rarely sin etc.). Hence ~ingLY² (-ōōv-) adv. [f. OF *reprover* f. L L as REPROBATE¹]

reprovision. See RE-8.

reps. See REP¹.

rep'tant, a. (nat. hist.). Creeping. [f. L *reptare* frequent. of *repere* crawl, -ANT]

rep'tile, n. & a. **1.** Crawling animal; member of the *Reptilia* or class of animals including snakes, lizards, crocodiles, turtles, & tortoises, whence répti'lIAN (-lyan) a. & n., répti'liFORM, aa.; mean grovelling person. **2.** adj. (Of animals) creeping; mean & grovelling (*the ~ press*, subservient semi-official newspapers). [(n. f. *reptile* neut.) f. LL *reptilis* (*repere rept-* crawl, -IL]

repúb'lic, n. A State in which the government is carried on nominally & usu. in fact also by the people or its elected representatives, commonwealth; (fig.) society of persons or animals with equality between members (*the ~ of letters*, literary men, literature). [f. L *respublica* (abl. *republica*) f. *res* concern, PUBLICUS]

repúb'lican, a. & n. **1.** Of, constituted as,

For pronunciation & hyphening of *re-* see RE-; for words in *re-* not given see RE-8, 9.

characterizing, republic(s). **2.** (Person) advocating or supporting ~ government, or opposition, etc. **3.** (*hi~*). *(Member) of U.-S. political party favouring liberal interpretation of constitution, extension of central power, & protective tariff, opp. DEMOCRATIC(1). **4.** (Of birds) social, living in large communities. Hence ~ISM(3) n., ~IZE(3) v.t. [-AN]

republish etc. See RE- 8.

repu'diate, v.t. & i. **1.** Divorce (one's wife; esp. of the ancients or non-Christians). **2.** Disown, disavow, reject, refuse dealings with, deny. **3.** Refuse to recognize or obey (authority) or discharge (obligation, debt); (of State) ~ate public debt. Hence ~A'TION, ~ATOR², nn. [f. L *repudiare* (*repudium* divorce, cf. REPUDERE) be ashamed of)]

repugn' (-ūn), v.i. & t. (rare), opposition; strive against, strive against; affect disagreeably, be repugnant to. [f. L *re(pugnare* fight) oppose, RE- 2]

repug'nance, n. Inconsistency, incompatibility, of ideas, statements, tempers, etc. (*of, between, to, with*); antipathy, dislike, aversion, (*to, against*). [f. L *repugnantia* (prec., -ANCE)]

repug'nant, a. Contradictory (*to*), incompatible (*with*); (poet.) refractory, resisting; distasteful (*to*). [f. L as REPUGN + -ANT]

repū'llulāte, v.i. (rare). Sprout afresh, shoot out again; (of diseases) start again, recur. Hence ~A'TION n. [f. L *re(pullulare* PULLULATE), RE- 9, -ATE³]

repŭlse', v.t., & n. **1.** Drive back, (attack, attacking enemy) by force of arms, (fig.) foil in controversy; rebuff (friendly advances or maker of them), refuse (request, offer, or maker of it). **2.** n. ~ing or being ~ed, rebuff, (*inflict, meet with, suffer*, etc., ~ or usu. ~s). [n. f. L *repulsa* or *repulsus* -ūs) f. REPELLere]

repŭl'sion (-shn), n. **1.** Repulsing (rare). **2.** (Physics) tendency of bodies to repel each other or increase their mutual distance (opp. ATTRACTION; also fig.); *capillary* ~, tendency in some liquids (e.g. quicksilver in glass) to shrink from wall of capillary tubes so that inner surface is convex. **3.** Dislike, aversion, repugnance. [f. LL *repulsio* (REPEL, -ION)]

repŭl'sive, a. **1.** Offering resistance (poet.). **2.** (Physics) exercising repulsion. **3.** (Of behaviour etc.) repellent, cold, unsympathetic, (arch.). **4.** Exciting aversion or loathing, loathsome, disgusting, whence ~LY² adv., ~NESS n. [REPULSE v., -IVE]

repurchase, repurify. See RE- 9.

repū'table, a. Of good repute, respectable. Hence ~LY² adv. [REPUTE n., -ABLE]

repūtā'tion, n. What is generally said or believed about a person's or thing's character (*has not justified his* ~); state of being well reported of, credit, distinction, respectability, good fame, (*persons of* ~; *has a* ~ *for integrity*); the credit, or discredit of doing or of being (*has the* ~ *of wrecking his tenants, of being or of the best shot in England*). [f. L *reputatio* (REPUTE, -ATION)]

repūte', v.t., & n. **1.** (Rare in active) consider or reckon, (pass.) be generally considered or reported of, (with compl., *to be*, or *as*; *is* ~d *the best doctor or to be* or rarely *as the best*); (pass.) be generally well, ill, etc., thought or spoken of (p.p.), passing as but probably not being (*his* ~d *father, clemency*, etc.; ||~d *pint* etc., bottle of beer etc. sold as imperial pint etc. but not guaranteed as Imperial pint etc.); hence repū'tedly² adv. [f. F *re(puter*, or *repute* think), RE- 6]

request', n., & v.t. **1.** Act of asking for something, petition made, thing asked for, (*came at his* ~; *shall make two* ~s; *you shall have your* ~; *make* ~ *for*; *by* ~, in response to expressed wish); state of being sought after, demand, (*is now in great, come into,* ~). **2.** v.t. Seek permission to do; ask to be given or allowed or favoured with (~ *candid consideration* or *a person's presence*, etc.); ask *that*; ask (person) *to do*. [f. OF *requeste*(p), see RE- 6, QUEST]

requick'en. See RE- 9.

req'uiem, n. Special mass for repose of souls of the dead; musical setting for ~; dirge. [initial L wd.(=rest) of the mass]

requiēs'ce|t, n. Wish for dead person's repose (~*at*, ~*ant, in páce*, abbr. R.I.P., inscription=may he or she, they, rest in peace, used esp. on R.-C. tombs. [L, =may he rest]

require', v.t. & i. **1.** Order (person), demand (of person) to do (*they* ~ *me to appear*); demand or ask in words (person's action, act of person, thing at person's hands, *that*, etc.) esp. as of right (*they* ~ *my appearance, an oath of me, a gift at my hands, that I should appear*). **2.** Lay down as imperative (*had done all that was* ~d *by the Act*). **3.** Need, call for, depend on for success etc. on, (*the emergency* ~s *it, that it should be done; trying* ~s *care in its use; land* ~s *a 10 lb. of seed to the acre; place would* ~ *an army to take it; machine* ~s *no attention; it* ~d *all his authority to keep them in hand*). **4.** (rare). || Be necessary (*do not tie it more tightly than* ~s). Hence ~MENT (4Tfm-) n. [f. L *requirere* (-*quisit*-=*quaerere* seek), RE- 6]

requisite (-z-), a. & n. **1.** Required by circumstances, necessary to success etc., called for; hence ~NESS (-zitm-) n. **2.** n. Requirement, thing needed for accomplishment of some purpose (*for*). [f. L p.p. as prec.]

requisition (-z-), n. **1.** Requiring, demand made, esp. formal & usu. written demand that some duty should be

performed; order given to town etc. to furnish certain military etc. supplies; being called or put into service (*is under* or *in* ~, being used or applied; *put in, call into,* ~, *have recourse to*). **2.** v.t. Demand use or supply of esp. for military purposes; demand such supplies etc. from (town etc.); press into service, call in for some purpose. [f. L *requisitio* (REQUIRE, -ION)]

requite' (-z-), v.t. Make return for, reward or avenge, (service, wrong, injury, treatment; often *with*); make return to, repay with good or evil, (person; often *for* treatment received, *with* treatment given). Hence give in return (~*e like for like*). Hence ~AL(2) n. [RE- 1, *quite* var. of QUIT²]

re-read. See RE- 8.

rere'dos (rērd-), n. Ornamental screen covering wall at back of altar. [earlier *areredos* (REAR¹, F *dos* back f. L *dorsum*) **rēs** (-z-), n. (L). Thing (~ *judicata* (jōō-), =CHOSE JUGÉE); property (~ *angus'ta* (-ngg-) *domi'*, poverty).

resaddle, resale etc. See RE- 9.

rescind' (-z-), v.t. Abrogate, annul, revoke, cancel. So **resci'ssion** (-zhn) n. [f. L *re(scindere sciss-* cut), RE- 5]

res'cript, n. **1.** Roman emperor's written reply for guidance esp. from magistrate on legal point; Pope's decretal epistle in reply to question, any papal decision. **2.** Ruler's or government's or official edict or announcement. **3.** Thing rewritten, rewriting; palimpsest. [f. L p.p. neut. of *re(scribere script-* write)]

res'cue, v.t., & n. **1.** Deliver *from* or *from* attack, custody, danger, or harm; (Law) unlawfully liberate (person), forcibly recover (property); hence ~ER¹ n. **2.** n. ~ing or being ~ed, succour, deliverance, illegal liberation, forcible recovery; ~*e* (*bid*), a bid at bridge made to get one's partner out of a difficult situation. [f. OF *rescoure* (L RE-, EXcutere=*quatere* shake)]

research' (-sér-), n., & v.i. **1.** Careful search or inquiry *after* or *for*; (usu. pl.) endeavour to discover facts by scientific study of a subject, course of critical investigation, (*his* ~*es have been fruitful; is engaged in* ~). **2.** v.i. Make ~es; hence ~ER¹ n. [f. obs. F *recherche(r)*, now *recherché*, see RE- 6, SEARCH]

reseat. See RE- 8.

resect' (-z-), v.t. (surg.). Pare down (bone, cartilage, etc.). So **resec'tion** n. [f. L *re(secare sect-* cut), RE- 5]

resé'da, n. **1.** Genus of plants including mignonette & Dyer's weed. **2.** (usu. *réséda* F, pr. rāzādǎ'). Pale green colour as of mignonette. [L, perh. imperat. of *re(sedare* quiet) allay, RE- 5, used as first wd of charm in applying plant to tumours]

reseek, see RE- 8; **reseize** etc., **resell,** RE- 9.

resem'ble (-z-), v.t. Be like, have similarity to or feature(s) in common with or same appearance as, & so ~ANCE (*to, between, of*) n. ~ANT (*to*) a. (rare); (arch.) liken *to.* [f. OF *re(sembler* f. L *similare, simulare,* f. *similis* SIMILAR), RE- 1]

resent' (-z-), v.t. Show or feel indignation at or retain feelings about (insult or injury sustained). Hence ~FUL [perh. through obs. *resent* ~*ment*] a., ~fully² adv., ~MENT n. [f. F *ressentir* (RE- 1, L *sentire* feel]

reserva'tion (-z-), n. In vbl senses; also or esp.: (Eccl.) right reserved to Pope of nomination to vacant benefice, power of absolution reserved to superior, practice of retaining for some purpose a portion of the Eucharistic elements (esp. the bread) after celebration; (Law) right or interest retained in estate being conveyed, clause reserving it; *tract of land reserved esp. for exclusive occupation by native tribe; express or tacit limitation or exception made about something (*mental* ~, qualification tacitly added in making statement, oath, etc.); *booking (of berth on steamer, room in hotel, seat in train, etc.). [f. LL *reservatio* (foll., -ATION]

reserve'¹ (-z-), v.t. **1.** Postpone use or enjoyment or treatment of, hold over, keep back for later occasion, (~*e oneself for,* not put forth one's energies till). **2.** Secure or retain possession or control of esp. by legal or formal stipulation (*for* or *to* oneself or another; ~*ed seats at* entertainment etc., that may be booked; ||~*ed list,* of naval officers removed from active service but liable to be called out); (pass.) be left by fate *for,* fall first or only to. **3.** Set apart, destine, *for* some use or fate. **4.** (p.p. as adj.). Reticent, slow to reveal emotions or opinions, uncommunicative, whence ~'ediy² (-z-) adv. [f. OF *reserver* f. L *re(servare* keep), RE- 3]

reserve'² (-z-), n. **1.** Something reserved for future use, extra stock or amount, (*banker's* ~, amount kept on hand to meet probable demands; *has a great* ~ *of energy;* often attrib., as *his* ~ *strength*). **2.** (Mil., sing. or pl.) troops withheld from action to reinforce or cover retreat, forces outside regular army & navy & air force liable to be called out in emergencies, member of such forces (also RESERVIST (-z-) n.); (in games) extra player chosen in case substitute should be needed. **3.** Being kept unused but available (*has it in* ~). **4.** Place reserved for some special use. **5.** (At exhibitions) distinction conveying that exhibit will have prize if another is disqualified. **6.** Limitation, exception, restriction, or qualification, attached to something (*I accept your statement without* ~, fully; *sale or auction*

without ~, not subject to a fixed price's being reached; ~ *price*, than which less will not be accepted; *we publish this with all ~, all proper—s*, without endorsing it). 7. Self-restraint, abstinence from exaggeration or ill-proportioned effects, in artistic or literary expression; reticence, avoidance of plain speaking; coolness of manner, lack of cordiality; intentional suppression of truth. [f. F *réserve* (*réserver*, OF *reserver* RESERVE)]

rés'ervoir (-zervwǎr), n. & v.t. 1. Receptacle constructed usu. of earthwork or masonry in which large quantity of water is stored. 2. Any natural or artificial receptacle esp. for or of fluid, place where fluid etc. collects; part of machine or organ of body holding fluid (~ *pen*, containing its own supply of ink); reserve supply or collection of something e.g. knowledge or facts, etc. 3. v.t. Store in reservoir. [f. F *réservoir* (LL *reservatorium*, cf. COUNTER¹, PARLOUR) f. *réserver* see prec., -ORY(2)]

rését¹, v.t. & i. (-tt-; arch.). Receive (stolen goods); receive stolen goods. So ~'t'ER¹ n. [f. OF *receter* f. L *receptare* frequent. of *recipere* RECEIVE]

reset², resettle etc., reshape, see RE-8; reship etc., RE-9; reshuffle, RE-8.

reside (-z-), v.i. (Of persons) have one's home, dwell permanently, *at, in, abroad*, etc.; (of officials) be in residence; (of power, rights, etc.) rest or be vested *in* person etc.; (of qualities) be present or inherent *in*. [f. L *residēre* (*sedēre* sit), RE-3]

rés'idence (-z-), n. 1. Residing (*have, take up, one's ~, dwell, begin to dwell; honoured the place with her ~; ~ is required*, official etc. must live on the spot for certain periods or altogether; so *in ~*). 2. Place where one resides, abode of; house esp. of considerable pretension, mansion. (*desirable family ~ for sale*). [f. F *résidence* f. L *residentia* (prec., -ENCE)]

rés'idency (-z-), n. Official residence of Governor-general's representative at Indian native court. [as prec., -ENCY]

rés'ident (-z-), a. & n. 1. Residing (whether ~ *at home or abroad; the ~ population*);(of birds etc.) non-migratory; bound to residence, having quarters on the spot, (~ *surgeon, tutor, political agent*); inherent, located, in (*a right ~ in the nation; powers of sensation ~ in the nerves*). 2. n. Permanent inhabitant of town or neighbourhood (opp. *visitor*); Indian Governor-general's political agent residing at native court, British government agent in other semi-dependent State, whence ~SHIP n. [f. L (RESIDE, -ENT)]

résidén'tial (-z-, -shl), a. Suitable for or occupied by private houses (~ *estate, street, quarter*); connected with residence (*the ~ qualification for voters*).—[RESIDENCE, -AL]

résidén'tiary (-z-, -sho-), n. & a. 1. Ecclesiastic bound to residence. 2. adj. Bound to, requiring, of or for, official residence (usu. after n.; *Canon, Canonry, ~; at his ~ house*). [f. med. L *residentiarius* (RESIDENCE, -ARY¹)]

résid'ual (-z-), a. & n. 1. (Math.) resulting from subtraction (n., ~ *quantity*). 2. Remaining, left over, left as residuum (n., remainder, substance of the nature of a residuum). 3. (Of error in calculations) still unaccounted for or not eliminated. [RESIDUUM, -AL]

résid'uary (-z-), a. 1. Of the residue of an estate (~ *bequest, clause, legatee*, etc.); of, being, a residuum, residual, still remaining, (*mere ~ substances; the ~ aberration; some ~ odds & ends*). [RESIDUUM, -ARY¹]

résid'ue (-z-), n. Remainder, rest, what is left or remains over; what remains of estate after payment of charges, debts, & bequests. (Chem. etc.) residuum. [f. F *résidu* RESIDUUM]

résid'uum (-z-), n. (pl. -dua). What remains, esp. (Chem. etc.) substance left after combustion or evaporation, (in calculations) amount not accounted for or residual error; lowest stratum or dregs of population. [L, neut. of *residuus* remaining (RESIDE)]

résign¹ (-zīn), v.t. & i. 1. Relinquish, surrender, give up, hand over, (office, right, claim, property, charge, task, life, hope; often *to* person, *into* person's hands etc., ~ *oneself to another's guidance, to sleep, rest, meditation*, etc.). 2. Reconcile oneself, one's mind, etc. (*to one's fate* etc., *to doing*, or abs. = accept the inevitable without repining), whence ~ED¹ (-zīnd²) a., ~EDLY² (-zīn-) adv. 3. Give up office, retire. [f. OF *resigner* f. L *resignare* (seal) unseal, cancel, RE-7]

rē'sign² (-sīn), v.t. & i. Sign again. [RE-8, SIGN¹]

résigna'tion (-z-), n. In vbl senses (RESIGN¹); esp. resigning of an office, document conveying it (*give, send in*, one's ~); being resigned, uncomplaining endurance of sorrow or other evil. [f. F *résignation* (RESIGN¹, -ATION)]

résile' (-z-), v.i. (Of elastic bodies) recoil, rebound, resume shape & size after stretching or compression; have or show elasticity or buoyancy or recuperative power. Hence resil'ience, resil'iency, (n., resil'ient a., (-zilyen-). [f. L *re-* (*silire=salire* jump), RE-9]

rés'in (-z-), n., & v.t. 1. Adhesive substance insoluble in water (cf. GUM²) secreted by most plants & exuding naturally or upon incision esp. from fir & pine; kinds of similar substance got by chemical process. 2. v.t. Rub or treat with ~. Hence ~IF'EROUS, ~OUS, aa., [~OID a. & n., ~ATE¹(3) n., ~IFY v.t. & i., ~IFICA'TION n., ~-0- comb. form. [f. F *résine* f. L *resina* cogn. w. Gk *rhētinē*]

résipis'cence, n. Recognition of error, return to good sense. So ~ENT a. [f. L

(-ntia) f. re(sipiscere f. sapere see SAPIENT), RE-9]

resist[1] (-z-), v.t. & i., & n. **1.** Stop course of, successfully oppose, keep off or out, prevent from penetrating, repel, be proof against or unaffected or uninjured by, abstain from, (projectile, weapon, edge, frost, heat, moisture, attack, temptation, power, infection, influence, suggestion, etc.; who can ~ God's will ?; cannot ~ a joke, must make it if it suggests itself, or must be amused by it), whence ~IBLE a., ~LESS a. (poet.), ~lessLY² adv. **2.** Strive against, oppose, try to impede, refuse to comply with. **3.** Offer resistance, make opposition, whence or cogn. ~ANT, ~ENT, ~IVE, aa., ~ER¹ n. (|| passive ~er, person refusing on grounds of justice to pay education rate imposed by Act in 1902). **4.** n. Composition applied to surfaces for protection from some agent employed on them, esp. to parts of calico that are not to take dye. [f. L re(sistere redupl. of stare stand), RE-2]

resis'tance (-z-), n. **1.** (Power of) resisting (passive ~, refusal to comply; something with greater ~ for its weight than steel); ~ movement (esp. of unconquered people in a conquered country). **2.** Hindrance, impeding or stopping effect, exercised by material thing upon another (overcome the ~ of the air; ~ of fluids varies with their specific gravity; line of ~, direction in which it acts; take line of least ~, fig., adopt easiest method or course). **3.** (Electr., Magnet., Heat) non-conductivity; (Electr.) part of apparatus used to offer definite ~ to current. [f. F résistance (prec. -ANCE)]

resistibil'ity (-z-), n. Being resistible; power of offering resistance. [RESISTIBLE, -BILITY]

resole. See RE-8.

res'oluble (-z-; -lōō-, -lū-), a. That can be resolved, (usu.) analysable into, resolvable. [f. LL resolubilis (RESOLVE, & see SOLUBLE)]

res'olute (-z-; -lōō-, -lū-), a. (Of person or his temper or action) determined, decided, bold, not vacillating, unshrinking, firm of purpose. Hence ~LY² adv. [f. L p.p., see RESOLVE]

resolu'tion (-z-; -lōō-, -lū-), n. **1.** Separation into components, decomposition, analysis, conversion into other form; (Med.) disappearance of inflammation without suppuration; (Pros.) substitution of two short syllables for one long; (Mus.) making of discord to pass into concord; (Mech.) replacing of single force by two or more jointly equivalent. **2.** Solving of doubt, problem, question, etc. **3.** Formal expression of opinion by legislative body (cf. MOTION) or public meeting, form proposed for this. **4.** Resolve, thing resolved on, (good ~s, intentions that one formu-

lates mentally for virtuous conduct). **5.** Determined temper or character, boldness & firmness of purpose. [f. L resolutio (RESOLVE, -ION)]

res'olutive (-z; -lōō-, -lū-), a. & n. **1.** Having dissolving power, disintegrating, (chiefly med.); (n.) ~ application or drug. **2.** (Law) ~ condition, whose fulfilment terminates contract etc. [prec., -IVE]

resolve' (-z-), v.t. & i., & n. **1.** Dissolve (t. & i.; into), disintegrate, analyse, break up into parts, dissipate, convert or be converted into, reduce by mental analysis into, (used vinegar to ~ the rocks; blood first coagulates & then ~s; ~ thing, thing is ~d or ~s itself or ~s, into its elements; telescope ~s nebula into stars; inflammation, tumour, is ~d or ~s, passes away without suppuration; House ~s itself into a committee; might ~ Christianity into a system of morality); (Mus.) convert (discord) or be converted into concord. **2.** Solve, explain, clear up, settle, (all doubts were ~d; ~ me this, arch., answer this question; the problem of its origin has not yet been ~d). **3.** Decide upon, make up one's mind upon action or doing or to do, form mentally or (of legislative body or public meeting) pass by vote the resolution that, (of circumstances etc.) bring (person) to resolution to do or upon action or doing, (he ~d upon or rarely ~ amendment; ~d that nothing should induce him, that he would do, upon doing; the House began by resolving that . . .; this discovery ~d us on going or to go; p.p. used in minutes of meeting, = the following resolution was passed, namely that; p.p. as adj., resolute, whence **resólved**-LY² (-z-) adv.); hence **resól'vable** (-z-) a. **4.** n. Resolution come to in the mind (he she kept her ~); (poet.) resolution, steadfastness, (a mind, deeds, of high ~). [f. L re(solvere solut- SOLVE, RE- 5]

resól'vent (-z-), a. & n. (chiefly med. & chem.). (Drug, application, substance) effecting resolution of tumour etc. or division into component parts. [prec., -ENT]

res'onant (-z-), a. (Of sound) echoing, resounding, continuing to sound, reinforced or prolonged by vibration or reflexion; (of bodies, rooms, etc.) tending to reinforce or prolong sounds esp. by vibration; (of places) resounding with. Hence or cogn. ~ANCE n., ~antLY² adv. RE- 6, -ANT]

res'onàtor (-z-), n. Instrument responding to single note & used for detecting it in combinations; appliance for giving resonance to sounds. [as prec., -OR²]

resórb', v.t. Absorb again. Hence ~ENCE n., ~ENT a. [f. L re(sorbēre sorpt- ABSORB), RE- 9]

For pronunciation & hyphening of re- see RE-; for words in re- not given see RE- 8, 9.

resor'cin (-z-), n. Compound got by action of potash on resin used chiefly as dye-stuff. [RESIN, ORIGIN]

resorp'tion, n. Resorbing or being resorbed. [RESORB, -ION]

resort'¹ (-z-), v.i. **1.** Turn for aid to (~ *to force, experiment,* etc., or rarely concrete object or person). **2.** Go in numbers or often to (*visitors ~ed to him, to the shrine; by the hundred; watched the inn to which he was known to* ~). [f. OF *resortir* come out, etym. dub.), RE- 8]

resort'² (-z-), n. **1.** Thing to which recourse is had, what is turned to for aid, expedient. (*a carriage, repetition of the experiment, was the only* ~), **2.** Recourse (*cannot be done without* ~, *to compulsion; in the last* ~, *when all else has failed,* as final attempt). **3.** Frequenting or being frequented (*encouraged the* ~ *of scholars; a place of great* ~). **4.** Place frequented usu. for specified purpose or quality (*health, holiday,* ~; *mountain, seaside,* ~). [(prec.)]

ré-sôrt'³, v.t. Sort again. [RE- 8]

resound' (-z-), v.i. & t. **1.** (Of place) ring or echo (*with*); (of voice, instrument, sound, etc.) produce echoes, go on sounding, fill place with sound. **2.** (Of fame, event, etc.) be much talked of, produce sensation, (often *through Europe* etc.). **3.** Repeat loudly (usu. *the praises* etc. *of*); (of place) give back (sound). Hence ~**ingly²** adv. [RE- 9, SOUND, after L as RESONANT]

resource' (-sŏrs), n. **1.** (Usu. in pl.) means of supplying a want, stock that can be drawn on: (pl.) country's collective means for support & defence. **2.** (after French; now rare). Possibility of aid (*lost without* ~). **3.** Expedient, device, shift, (*flight was his only* ~; *am at the end of my* ~s). **4.** Leisure occupation (*reading is a great* ~; *a man of no* ~s). **5.** Skill in devising expedients, practical ingenuity, quick wit, (*is full of* ~). Hence ~**FUL** (-ŏrsf-), ~**LESS** (-ŏrsl-), aa., ~**fulNESS,** ~**lessNESS,** nn., ~**fully²** adv., ~**lessly²** adv. [f. F *ressource* f. OF *re(s)sourdre* f. *re-* 9, L *surgere* rise]

respect'¹, n. **1.** Reference, relation, (*to; the terms have* ~ *to position alone; is true with* ~ *to the French; with* ~ *to possible routes, there are three; ablative, accusative, of* ~ *in Lat. Gram.,* those translatable by *with* ~ or *as to*). **2.** Heed or regard to or of, attention to, (*have not had or paid* ~ *to anything but colour; did it quite without* ~ *to the results;* ~ *of persons,* partiality or favour shown esp. to the powerful). **3.** Particular, detail, point, aspect, (*of; is admirable in* ~ *of style; in all, many, some,* ~s: *in one, this,* ~), **4.** (arch.). Consideration that (*is out of the question, in* ~ *that it stultifies the whole plan*), **5.** Deferential esteem felt or shown towards person or quality (*has won the* ~ *of all; have the greatest* ~ *for him; is held in* ~; SELF-~).

respect'², v.t. **1.** Pay heed to (arch.; ~ *persons,* discriminate unfairly between them under influence of wealth etc., whence ~ER¹ n. *of persons*). **2.** Relate to, be concerned with, (now rare exc. in part., as *legislation* ~ing *property,* also used as prep., as *am at a loss* ~ing *his whereabouts*). **3.** Regard with deference; avoid degrading or insulting or injuring or interfering with or interrupting, treat with consideration, spare, (~ *oneself,* refrain from unworthy conduct or thoughts, have self-respect; ~ *innocence* or *the innocent,* refrain from offending or corrupting or tempting; ~*ed my silence,* let me remain silent; ~ *privileges, properly, neutral territory,* etc.). [f. L *respicere spect-* = *specere* look at), RE- 6]

respectabil'ity, n. Being, those who are, a person who is, socially respectable. [foll., -BILITY]

respec'table, a. & n. **1.** Deserving respect (*did it from* ~ *motives*). **2.** Not inconsiderable in amount etc., of some merit or importance, fairly good or many or much, tolerable, passable, (*a* ~ *hill, antiquity, painter, minority;* ~ *talents*). **3.** Of fair social standing, having the qualities necessary for such standing, not disreputable, honest & decent in conduct; (of pursuits, clothes, etc.) befitting ~ persons; hence **respec'tably²** adv. [f. LL *respectabilis* (RESPECT²)]

respect'ful, a. Showing deference (~ *behaviour; stood at a* ~ *distance*). Hence ~**LY²**adv., ~**NESS** n. [-FUL]

respec'tive, a. Each's own, proper to each, individual, several, comparative, (*go to your, put them in their,* ~ *places; were given places according to their* ~ *rank* or *ranks; A & B contributed the* ~ *sums of 4£. & 3£.; the election depends on the popularity of the candidates*). Hence ~**LY²** adv. [f. LL *respectivus* (RESPECT²)]

6. pl. (With *my, his,* etc.) polite messages or attentions (*give him my, sends his,* ~s: (*respicere* see foll.)]

respell. See RE- 8.

rés'pirable (or rĕspīr'-), a. (Of air, gas, etc.) that can be, fit to, be breathed. [f. LL *respirābilis* (RESPIRE, -ABLE)]

respira'tion, n. Breathing; single inspiration & expiration; plant's absorption of oxygen & emission of carbon dioxide. [f. L *respiratio* (RESPIRE, -ATION)]

rés'pirator, n. Apparatus of gauze etc. worn over mouth (& nose) to warm or filter inhaled air; (Mil.) kinds of chemical filtering-apparatus worn for defence against poison-gas. [f. L as foll. +-OR²]

respire', v.i. & t. Breathe, inhale & exhale, air; whence **rés'piratory** (or rispīr'at-) a.: breathe (air etc.); (rare) exhale (perfume, amiability, etc.); breathe again, take breath, recover hope or spirit,

get rest or respite. [f. L re(spirare breathe), RE- 9]

rés'pite, n., & v.t. **1.** Delay permitted in the discharge of an obligation or suffering of a penalty; interval of rest or relief. **2.** v.t. Grant ~ to, reprieve, (condemned person); postpone execution or exaction of (sentence, obligation); give temporary relief from (pain, care) or to (sufferer); (Mil., formerly) withhold (pay), withhold pay from. [f. OF respit f. L RESPECT¹us]

résplén'dent, a. Brilliant, dazzlingly or gloriously bright. Hence ~ENCE, ~ENCY, nn., ~ently² adv. [f. L re(splendére glitter), RE- 6, -ENT]

respónd'¹, v.i. **1.** Make answer (esp. of congregation making set answers to priest etc.); perform answering or correspond-ing action (~ed with a drop-kick, left-hander, etc.). **2.** Show sensitiveness to by behaviour or change (does not ~ to kind-ness; nerve ~s to stimulus, string to note, etc.). **3.** (rare) Correspond, be analogous, whence or cogn. ~ENCE, ~ENCY, nn. [f. L re(spondére spons- pledge) answer, RE- 1]

respónd'², n. **1.** (Eccl.)=RESPONSORY, also response to versicle. **2.** (Archit.) half-pillar or half-pier attached to wall to support arch. [OF (respondre answer, as prec.)]

respón'dent, a. & n. **1.** Making answer; responsive to; in position of defendant. **2.** n. One who makes answer, defends thesis, etc.; defendant esp. in divorce case, [as RESPOND¹, -ENT]

respónse', n. Answer given in word or act, reply, retort, (in ~ to; made no ~; the ~s of the oracles; his ~ was the proclama-tion of martial law); feeling, movement, etc., elicited by stimulus or influence (called forth no ~ in his breast); (Eccl.) = RESPONSORY, also any part of liturgy said or sung in answer to priest. [f. L responsum neut. p.p. (RESPOND¹)]

responsibil'it̄y̆, n. Being responsible (de-clines all ~y for it; will take the ~y of doing it; did it on his own ~y, without authori-zation; is not afraid of ~y, of having to act without detailed guidance); charge for which one is responsible (a family is a great ~y; asked to be relieved of his ~y or ~ies). [foll., -BILITY]

respón sib̆le, a. Liable to be called to ac-count, answerable (to person, for thing, or abs.; ~le ruler, government, not auto-cratic), morally accountable for actions, capable of rational conduct; of good credit or position or repute, respectable, apparently trustworthy; involving re-sponsibility (a~le office). Hence ~ly² adv. [obs. F (L RESPOND¹ére, -IBLE)]

|| **respón'sions** (-shnz), n. pl. First of three examinations for Oxford B.A. degree (also smalls colloq.; cf. moderations, greats, final schools). [RESPOND¹, -ION]

respón'sive, a. Answering, by way of answer, (of liturgy etc.) using responses; responding readily to or to some influence, impressionable, sympathetic. Hence ~LY² adv., ~NESS n. [f. LL responsivus (RESPOND¹, -IVE)]

respón'sory, n. Anthem said or sung by soloist & choir after lesson. [f. LL re-sponsoria neut. pl. (RESPOND¹, -ORY)]

ressaldár', n. Native captain in Indian cavalry regiment. [f. Hind. risaladar (risalah squadron f. Arab. arsala he sent, dar having)]

rest¹, v.i.& t. **1.** Be still, cease or abstain or be relieved from exertion or action or movement or employment, lie in sleep or death, be tranquil, be let alone, (waves that never ~; ~ (up)on one's oars, tem-porarily cease rowing or any exertion; never let your enemy ~; let us ~ here, cease walking etc.; ~ from one's labours; ~s in the churchyard, lies buried; let her ~ in peace; is too feverish to ~; could not ~ under an imputation, till he got his wish; land was allowed to ~, left fallow; the matter cannot ~ here, must be further examined etc.); give relief or repose to (stayed a day to ~ myself; ~ your men for an hour; says the goggles ~ his eyes; must ~ the ground; ~ or God ~ his soul, may God give it repose); (p.p.) refreshed or reinvigorated by ~ing (are you quite ~ed?). **2.** Lie, be spread out, be sup-ported or based, depend, rely, (of eyes etc.) alight or be steadily directed, (up)on (shadow, light, ~s on his face; roof ~s on four arches; their left ~ed on the river; hand ~ing on the table; science ~s on pheno-mena; I ~ upon your promise; his gaze ~ed on a strange object); be propped against; repose trust in (be content to ~ in God); place for support or foundation (up)on (~ one's elbow, load, on the table; ~ one's case on equity, unimpeachable evi-dence). **3.** ~ing-place, provided or used for ~ing (last ~ing-place, the grave). [OE restan, cf. G rasten, Du. rusten]

rest², n. **1.** Repose or sleep esp. in bed at night (go, retire, to ~; take ~ or one's ~). **2.** Abstinence or freedom from or absence of exertion or activity or movement or care or molestation, a period of such abstinence etc., (day of ~, Sunday; a ~ from work etc.; give person, horse, machine, etc., a ~; take a short ~; at ~, still, not agitated or troubled, often of the dead; set question, person's mind, at ~, settle, relieve; lay to ~, bury). **3.** Lodging-place or shelter provided for sailors, cabmen, or other class. **4.** Prop or support or steadying-piece, e.g. for gun in aiming, billiard-cue, cutting-tool in lathe, or foot on bicycle. **5.** (Mus.) appointed interval

For pronunciation & hyphening of re- see RE-; for words in re- not given see RE- 8, 9.

rest, of silence or sign denoting it; pause in elocution, caesura in verse. **6.** ~-*balk*, ridge left unploughed between furrows; (Mus.) ~-*cure*, ~ ust. of some weeks in bed as medical treatment; ~-*day*, day spent in ~, (rare) Sunday; ~-*house*, dawk-bunga-low. [OE *rœst*, cf. G *rast*, Du. *rust*]

rest², v.i. Remain over (arch.; *whatever ~s of hope*); ~ *with*, (*it ~s with you to propose terms*; *the management of affairs ~s with Wolsey*); remain in specified state (*the affair ~s a mystery*; ~ *assured, satisfied, etc.*; also arch. in epistolary forms, as *I ~ your devoted friend*). [f. F *rester* f. L *re(stare* stand), RE-8]

rest³, n. 1. *The remaining part(s)* or indi-viduals of, the remainder of some quantity or number, the others, (& *the* or *all the ~ of it*, & all else that might be mentioned; *for the ~*, as regards anything beyond what has been specially mentioned). **2.** ||(Banking) reserve fund; (Commerce), stocking & balancing; (Tennis etc.) spell of continuous returns. [f. F *reste* (prec.)]

rest⁴, n. (hist.). Check holding butt of medieval tilter's spear when couched for charging (*with, lay* or *set one's, lance in ~*). [for ARREST¹ & see REST³]

restamp, restart, restate etc. See RE-8.

rés'taurant (-tor-, & see AP.), n. Place where meals or refreshments may be had. [F (*restaurer* RESTORE, -ANT)]

restaurateur (restorätör'), n. Restaur-ant-keeper. [F]

rest'ful, a. Favourable to repose, free from disturbing influences, soothing. Hence ~LY² adv., ~NESS n. [-FUL]

rest'-härrow (-ö), n. A tough-rooted shrub, cammock. [obs. *rest* v. as REST⁵, HARROW¹]

|| **restif.** See RESTIVE.

rĕs'titūte, v.t. & i. (rare). Make restitu-tion (of). [f. L *restituere* -tut- = *stature* set up), RE-8]

rĕstitū'tion, n. Restoring of or of thing to proper owner, reparation for injury, (esp. *make ~*; ~ *of conjugal rights*, name of a matrimonial lawsuit); restoring of thing to its original state (esp. Theol. *the ~ of all things*); resumption of original shape or position by elasticity. [f. L *restitutio* (prec., -ION)]

rĕs'tive, || rĕs'tiff (arch.), a. (Of horse) refusing to advance, stubbornly standing still or moving backwards or sideways, jibbing, refractory; (of person) un-manageable, rejecting control; (erron.) restless. Hence **rĕs'tively²** (-vl-) adv., **rĕs'tiveness** (-vn-) n. [earlier sense *inert*; orig. form -iff, f. OF *restif* (REST¹, -IVE)]

rĕst'less, a. Finding or affording no rest, uneasy, agitated, never still, ever in mo-tion, unpausing, fidgeting. Hence ~LY² adv., ~NESS n. [REST², -LESS]

restock. See RE-8.

restora'tion, n. In senses of RESTORE; also or esp.: (period of) re-establishment of monarchy in 1660 (*the R~*); model or drawing representing supposed original form of extinct animal, ruined building, etc. [earlier *restauration* f. L *restauratio* (RESTORE, -ION) w. assim. to *restore*]

restora'tionism (-shon-), n. Doctrine that all men will ultimately be restored to happiness in the future life. So ~IST(2) n. [-ISM]

restor'ative, a. & n. 1. Tending to restore health or strength. **2.** n. ~ food, medicine, or agency. Hence ~LY² adv. [f. OF *restauratif -ive* (foll., -IVE)]

restore', v.t. 1. Give back, make restitu-tion of. **2.** (Attempt to) bring back to original state by rebuilding, repairing, repainting, emending, etc. (*church, pic-ture, text, has been ~ed, spoilt in ~ing, ~ed out of all recognition*, etc.); make repre-sentation of supposed original state of (extinct animal, ruin, etc.). **3.** Reinstate, bring back to dignity or right; bring back to or to health etc., cure (person). **4.** Re-establish, renew, bring back into use. **5.** Reinsert by conjecture (missing words in text, parts of extinct animal, etc.). **6.** Replace, put back, bring to former place or condition. Hence ~ABLE a., ~ER¹ n. [f. OF *restorer* f. L *restaurare*]

restrain'¹, v.t. Check or hold in *from*, keep in check or under control or within bounds, repress, keep down; confine, imprison. Hence ~ABLE a., ~ẽdly² adv., (esp. with self-restraint). [f. OF *re-strain(d)re* f. L *re(stringere* strict-tie), RE-2]

rē-strain'², v.t. Strain again. [RE-8]

restraint', n. Restraining or being re-strained, stoppage, check, controlling agency or influence, confinement esp. in asylum, (*without ~*, freely, copiously; *is under ~*, as lunatic); constraint or reserve of manner; self-control, avoid-ance of excess or exaggeration, austerity of literary expression; ~ *of princes*, em-bargo. [f. OF *restreinte* (RESTRAIN¹)]

restric', v.t. Confine, bound, limit, (*to, within*; *has a very ~ed application*; *am ~ed to advising*; *is ~ed within narrow limits*). Hence or cogn. **restric'tion** n., **restric'tive** a., ~ẽdly² adv., **restric'tively²** adv. [f. L, see RESTRAIN¹]

restruc'. See RE-9.

result' (-z-), v.i., & n. **1.** Arise as actual or follow as logical consequence (*from* con-ditions, causes, premisses, etc., or abs.); have issue or end in specified manner esp. in failure etc. (~*ed badly, in a large profit*). **2.** n. Consequence, issue, or outcome of something (*without ~*, in vain, fruitless), whence ~FUL, ~LESS, aa.; quantity, formula, etc., given by calculation. [n. f. vb. f. L *re(sultare=saltare* jump), RE-8]

resŭl'tant (-z-), a. & n. **1.** Resulting, esp. as total outcome of more or less opposed forces. **2.** In Composite effect of two or more forces acting in different directions at same point (esp. in Mech., also transf.). [prec., -ANT]

resŭme' (-z-), v.t. & i. **1.** Get or take again or back, recover, reoccupy, (~ one's spirits, sway, liberty, seat; ~ gift, grand, territory). **2.** Begin again (upon), go on (with) after interruption, begin to speak or work again, recommence t. & i., (the House ~d work or its labours, or ~d; ~ thread of one's discourse; ~ pipe, go on smoking again; No, it is hopeless,' he ~d). **3.** Make résumé of, recapitulate, summarize. [f. L re(sumere sumpt- take), RE-8]

résumé (räz'ŏŏmā, & see Ap.), n. Summary, epitome, abstract. [F, p.p. of résumer RESUME]

resŭm'mons. See RE-8.

resŭmp'tion (-z-), n. Resuming. So ~IVE a., ~ively² adv. [f. L resumptio (RESUME, -ION)]

resŭp'ināte, a. (bot.). (Of leaf etc.) inverted, bottom up. Hence ~A'TION n. [f. L re(supinare make SUPINE²), RE-9]

resŭrge', v.i. (rare exc. joc.). Experience resurrection, revive, rise or arise again. So (in ordinary use) **resŭr'gence¹** n. & a., **resŭr'gent** n. [f. L re(surgere surrect- rise f. SUR-¹, regere direct), RE-9]

resŭrrĕct' (-z-), v.t. (colloq.). Raise from the dead (rare); revive practice or memory of; take from grave, exhume. [back form. f. foll.]

resŭrrĕc'tion (-z-), n. **1.** (R~). (Festival in memory of) rising of Christ from the grave; rising again of men at the last day. **2.** Exhumation lit. or fig., resurrecting (~ man, BODY-snatcher), whence ~IST(1) (-sho-). n. **3.** Revival from disuse or inactivity or decay, restoration to vogue or memory, (|| ~ pie, made from remains of previous meals). Hence ~AL (-sho-) a. [f. LL resurrectio (RESURGE, -ION)]

resŭrvey'. See RE-8.

resŭs'citate, v.t. & i. Revive, return or usu. restore to life, consciousness, vogue, vigour, or vividness. Hence or cogn. ~A'TION, ~ātor²(1,2), nn., ~ATIVE a. [f. L re(suscitare CITE), RE-9, -ATE²]

rēt, rāte, raĭt, v.t. & i. Soften (flax, hemp) by soaking or exposing to moisture; (of hay etc., in pass. or intr.) be spoilt by wet, rot. [cf. Du. reten, roten, Sw. röta; cogn. w. ROT²]

retā'ble, n. Shelf, or frame enclosing decorated panels, above back of altar. [f. F rétable (RE-, TABLE), f. med. L retrotabulum]

rētaĭl¹, n. Sale of goods in small quantities (esp. by ~, or attrib., as ~ trading, dealer; also adv., esp. in conjunction w. wholesale, as do you buy wholesale or ~?).

[OF, = piece cut out f. re(taillier cut, see TAILOR], RE-5]

rētaĭl², v.t. & i. **1.** Sell (goods) by retail; (of goods) be ~ed (esp. at or for specified price). **2.** Recount, relate details of. Hence ~ER¹ n. [prob. f. prec.]

rētaĭn', v.t. **1.** Keep in place, hold fixed, (~ing wall, supporting & confining mass of earth or water; ~ing force, Mil., posted to keep part of enemy inactive etc.). **2.** Secure services of (esp. barrister) by engagement & preliminary payment (~ing fee, retainer). **3.** Keep possession of, not lose, continue to have; continue to practise or recognize, allow to remain or prevail, not abolish or discard or alter. **4.** Succeed in remembering, not forget. Hence ~ABLE a. [f. OF retenir f. L re(tinēre tend-=tenēre hold), RE-3]

rētaĭn'er, n. **1.** (Law) formal retention of something as one's own, authorization to retain thus; being retained to serve in some capacity; fee paid to barrister etc. for right to his services, if required. **2.** In vbl senses; esp. (hist.) dependant or follower of person of rank. [RETAIN + (sense 1) -ER¹, (sense 2) -ER²]

retake. See RE-8.

rētăl'iāte, v.t. & i. **1.** Repay (injury, insult, etc., rarely kindness etc.) in kind; retort (accusation) upon person. **2.** Do as one is done by, esp. return evil, make reprisals, (Pol. Econ.) impose duties on imports from foreign State in return for its import duties. Hence ~A'TION n., ~ATIVE, ~ATORY, (-lya-), aa. [f. L re(taliare f. talis such), RE-1]

rētärd', v.t. & i., & n. **1.** Make slow or late, delay progress or arrival or accomplishment or happening of. **2.** (Esp. of physical phenomena, e.g. motion of tides, waves, or celestial bodies) happen, arrive, behind normal or calculated time; hence or cogn. **retärda'TION**, ~MENT, nn., ~ATIVE, ~ATORY, aa., & n. **3.** n.=ation (~ of tide or high water, interval between full moon & following high water). [f. F retard(er) f. L re(tardare f. tardus slow), RE-3]

retaste. See RE-8.

rētch, v.i. (d.) & n. **1.** Make motion of vomiting esp. ineffectually & involuntarily. **2.** n. Such motion or sound of it. [OE hrǣcan spit (hrǣca spittle, cf. ON hrækja)]

retell. See RE-8.

rētĕn'tion, n. RETAINING: esp. (Med.) failure to evacuate urine or other secretion. [OF, f. L retentionem (RETAIN, -ION)]

rētĕn'tive, a. (Of memory, or rarely of person in that respect) tenacious, not forgetful; (of substances) ~ of moisture etc., apt to retain it (also ~ abs., ~ of moisture); (Surg., of ligature etc.) serving to keep something in place. Hence ~LY² adv., ~NESS n. [OF (-if, -ive), see RETAIN, -IVE]

For pronunciation & hyphening of re- see RE-; for words in re- not given see RE-8, 9.

retenue' (-nōō), n. Reserve, self-control. [F]

rē'tiary (-shǐ-), n. A net-making or geo-metrical spider. [f. L *retiarius* (gladiator) with net (*rēte* net, -ARY¹)]

retī'cence, n. Reserve in speech, avoid-ance of saying all one knows or feels; abstinence from over-emphasis in art; holding back of some fact; disposition to silence, taciturnity. So **~ENT** a. (*on, upon, about*), **~ENTLY** adv. [f. L *reticentia* f. *tacēre* be silent), RE- 4]

retī'cle, n. Network of fine threads or lines in object-glass of telescope to help accurate observation. [f. L RETICULUM]

retī'culate, v.t. & i. Divide or be di-vided in fact or appearance into a net-work, arrange or be arranged in small squares or with intersecting lines. So (see etym.) **~ATE²** (-āt) a., **~ATION** n. [f. L ~**ATION** n., ~**āte**- comb. form [vb by back form. f. *reticulated* f. *reticulate* a. (RETICULUM, -ATE²)]

retī'cule, n. 1. = RETICLE. 2. Lady's netted or other bag carried or worn to serve purpose of pocket. 3. (Astron.) a Southern constellation. [f. F *réticule* f. L (foll.)]

retī'culum, n. (pl. ~a). 1. Ruminant's second stomach or honeycomb. 2. Net-like structure, reticulated membrane etc., whence **~AR¹**, **~OSE¹**, aa., **~o**- comb. form. [L (*rēte* net, -CULE)]

retī'form, a. Netlike, reticulated. [f. L *rēte* net, +-, -FORM]

rĕt'ina, n. (pl. ~as, ~æ). Layer at back of eyeball sensitive to light. Hence **~AL** a., **~'ITIS** n. [med. L, perh. f. L *rēte* net]

rĕt'inūe, n. Suite or train of persons in attendance upon someone. [f. OF *retenue* fem. p.p. of *retenir* RETAIN]

retīre', v.i. & t., & n. 1. Withdraw (intr.), go away, retreat, seek seclusion or shelter, recede, go (as) to bed, (~ *from the world*, become recluse; ~ *into oneself*, be un-communicative or unsociable, whence **rĕtī'r-ING²** a., **rĕtī'rINGLY²** adv. **rĕtī'rING-NESS** n.; *the ladies* ~, leave dining-room after dessert; *always* ~*s before midnight*, often goes to rest, to bed, for the night, etc.; *general, army, was forced to* ~, ~*d in good order*, often from position, to place, before enemy, etc.; *background does not* ~ *as it should*; *retiring-room*, for retiring to, esp. lavatory); (p.p., f. obs. trans. use; pr. rĭtīr'd) withdrawn from society or observation, secluded, (*lives* ~*d*; *in a* ~*d life*; *in a* ~*d valley*), whence **~d'NESS** n. 2. Cease from or give up office or profession or employment or candida-ture, often from position, to place, before innings, (Cricket) voluntarily terminate one's (~ *from the army, from business, on a pension*; *batsman* ~*d hurt*; *was com-pulsorily* ~*d as incompetent*; *retiring pension*, allowed to one who ~*s at normal time*); (p.p., see -ED¹(2) for sense) that has ...

retort'¹, v.t. & i., & n. 1. Requite (humi-liation, insult, attack) in kind; turn (mis-chief etc.), fling (charge, sarcasm, jest), back (*on* or *upon* another or aggressor); make (argument) tell against or *against* its user; make, say by way of, repartee or counter-charge or counter-argument; (p.p.) recurved, twisted or bent back-wards. 2. n. Incisive reply, repartee; turning of charge or argument against its author; piece of retaliation. [f. L re(*torquere tort*- twist), RE- 9]

retort'², n., & v.t. 1. Vessel usu. of glass with long downward-bent neck used in distilling liquids; kinds of receptacle of various shapes & materials used in puri-fying mercury & making gas & steel. 2. v.t. Purify (mercury) by heating in ~. [f. med. L *retorta* fem. p.p. as prec.]

retor'tion, n. Bending back (lit. & fig.); subjects of another. [f. med. L *retortio* (RETORT¹, -ION)]

retouch'. See RE- 8.

retrāce', v.t. Trace back to source or beginning; look over again; recall the course of in memory; go back over (one's *steps* or *way*; often fig. of undoing actions). [f. F *retracer* (RE- 8, TRACE v.)]

retrăct', v.t. & i. 1. Draw (esp. part of one's body) back or in, (of such part etc.) shrink back or in or be capable of being ~ed, (*small* ~*s its horns*; *cat's claws* ~ *or can be* ~*ed*; *surgeon* ~*s skin with instru-ment*, *organ is* ~*ed by muscle*, called **retrac'tor²** n.; *if the piston is suddenly* ~*ed*); hence or cogn. **retrac'tABLE¹** [-ABLE] & (in same sense) **retrac'tIBLE** aa., **retrac'TILITY** n., **retrac'tive** a., **retrac'-tion¹** [-ION] n. 2. Withdraw, revoke, cancel, refuse to abide by f. acknowledge falsity or error of, expressly abandon, (statement, promise, opinion), (abs.) ~ opinion or statement); hence or cogn. **retrac'TABLE²** [-ABLE] a., **retrac'TION**, **retrac'tion²** [-ION] nn. [sense 1 f. L re(*trahere tract*- draw), RE- 4; sense 2 L *retractare* pull about or handle), RE- 8, as in arch. *retractation* rehandling, now only in title of Augustine's *Retractations*]

rē'tral, a. (nat. hist. etc.). Hinder, pos-terior, at the back. [RETRO-, -AL]

retransfer, retransform, retranslate etc., **retread¹**. See RE- 9.

rē-tread'[2] (-ĕd), v.t., & n. Furnish with a new tread; (n.) tire so renewed. [RE- 9]

rētreat', v.i. & t., & n. 1. Go back, retire, relinquish a position, (esp. of army etc.): (trans., chiefly in chess) move (piece) back from forward or threatened position; recede (a ~ing chin, forehead). 2. n. Act of, (Mil.) signal for, ~ing (sound the ~; ~ing, Mil.: beat a ~, ~, abandon undertaking; make good one's ~, get safely away; intercept ~ of, cut off; are in full ~); 3. Withdrawing into privacy or security, (place of seclusion; (Eccl.) temporary retirement for religious exercises; asylum for inebriates or lunatics or pensioners; lurking-place, place of shelter. [f. OF retraiter f. L as RETRACT(1)]

rētrench', v.t. & i. 1. Cut down, reduce amount of, (expenses, things causing outlay); cut off, remove, (~ed a year from the established period); make excisions in or of, shorten or remove, (literary work or passages in it); cut down expenses, introduce economies. 2. (fortif.) Furnish with inner line of defence usu. consisting of trench & parapet. Hence ~MENT n. [f. obs. F retrencher var. of retrancher (RE-, TRENCH)]

retrial. See RE- 8.

rētribu'tion, n. Recompense for evil or rarely for good done, vengeance, requital; (~). So **rētrib'ūtive** a., **rētrib'ūtiver**[2] adv. [f. L RE(tribuere -ut- assign, -ION), RE-1]

rētrieve', v.t. & i., & n. 1. (Of dogs, esp. of special breed) find & bring in (killed or wounded bird etc., or abs.), whence ~'ER[1] n. 2. Recover by investigation or effort of memory, restore to knowledge or recall to mind. 3. Regain possession of. 4. Rescue from bad state etc.; restore to flourishing state, revive, (esp. one's fortunes etc.). 5. Make good, repair, set right, (loss, disaster, error); hence ~'ABLE a., ~'AL(2) n. 6. n. Possibility of recovery (beyond, past, ~e). [f. OF retrover, trouver find, compose in verse, ult. f. L f. Gk tropos TROPE), RE- 9]

retrim. See RE- 8.

retro- (usu. rē- exc. in the commoner wds, esp. retrograde, retrospect), pref. f. L retro adv. & pref.: (1) chiefly in L derivatives (~act, ~grade) or wds formed on L anal. of L elements (~flex, ~ject) with senses backwards, back again, in return; (2) chiefly in scientific esp. anat. wds with sense behind (~sternal a., behind the breastbone), hinder (~choir, part behind high altar).

rētroact', v.i. React; operate in backward direction; have retrospective effect. Hence ~AC'TIVE a., ~ac'tivel[2] adv., ~activ'ITY, ~AC'TION, nn. [f. L RETRO-(agere act- act)]

rētrocēde'[1], v.i. Move back, recede; (of gout) strike inward. So ~cēd'ENCE n., ~cēd'ENT a. [f. L RETRO(cedere cess- go)]

rētrocēde'[2], v.t. Cede (territory) back again. [f. F rétrocéder (RETRO-, CEDE)]

rētrocē'ssion (-shn), n., **rētrocē'ssive**, a. In vbl senses (RETROCEDE[1, 2]). [-ION, -IVE]

rēt'rochoir (-kwīr), n. Part of cathedral or large church behind high altar. [f. med. L RETRO(chorus CHOIR)]

rētroflĕc'ted, **rēt'roflĕx, -flĕxed** (-kst), aa. (anat., path., bot., etc.). Turned backwards. So **rētroflĕ'xion** (-kshn) n. [f. L RETRO(flectere flex- bend)]

rētrogradā'tion, n. (Astron.) apparent backward motion of planet in zodiac, motion of heavenly body from E. to W., backward movement of lunar nodes on ecliptic; = (the now usu.) RETROGRESSION. [f. L RETRO(gradatio f. -gradare f. -gradus -walking, -ATION)]

rēt'rogrāde, a., n., & v.i. 1. (Astron.) in or showing RETROGRADATION; directed backwards (~ motion), retreating; reverting esp. to inferior state, declining; inverse, reversed, (in ~ order; ~ imitation in music, with notes of passage repeated backwards); hence ~LY[2] adv. 2. n. (rare), Degenerate person; backward tendency. 3. v.i. (Astron.) show RETROGRADATION; move backwards, recede, retire, decline, revert. [f. L RETRO(gradus, -gradare (prec.)]

rētrogrĕss', v.i. Go back, move backwards, deteriorate. Hence ~IVE a., ~ively[2] adv. [f. L RETRO(gradi gress- walk)]

rētrogrĕ'ssion (-shn), n. (Astron.) retrogradation; backward or reversed movement; return to less advanced state, reversal of development, decline, deterioration. [f. L (prec.)+-ION]

rēt'roject, v.t. Cast back (chiefly as opp. project in lit. senses). [RETRO-, & as PROJECT[1]]

rētropul'sion (-shn), n. (path.). Shifting of external disease to internal part. [RETRO-, L pellere puls- drive, -ION]

rētrŏrse', a. (nat. hist.). Turned back, reverted. Hence ~LY[2] (-sl-) adv. [f. L retrorsus=RETRO(versus n.p.p. of vertere turn)]

rēt'rospĕct, n. Regard (to be) had to precedent or authority or previous conditions; (rare) retrospective force, retroaction; backward view (is pleasant in the ~, when looked back on; a short ~ is now necessary). [f. L RETRO(spicere spect- = specere look) after PROSPECT n.]

rētrospĕc'tion, n. Action of looking back esp. into the past, indulgence or engagement in retrospect. [as prec., -ION]

rētrospĕc'tive, a. Of, in, proceeding by, retrospection; (of statutes etc.) not re-

For pronunciation & hyphening of re- see RE-; for words in re- not given see RE- 8, 9.

stricted to the future, licensing or punishing etc. past actions, having application to the past, retroactive (of view) lying to the rear. Hence ~IY² adv. [as prec., -IVE]

retroussé (rĕtrōōs'ā), a. Turned up (of nose). [F]

rĕt'rovĕrt, v.t. Turn backwards (esp. path. in p.p. of womb). So **rĕtrover'sion** (-shn) n. [f. LL RETRO(vertere vers- turn)]

rĕt'tĕry, n. See RE-8.

rĕt'fĕry, n. Flax-retting place. [REF, -ERY]

returf. See RE-8.

rĕtûrn'¹, v.i. & t. **1.** Come or go back (*gone never to ~; ~ home, the way one came;* the occas. as in -ED¹(2), as *a ~ed emigrant, they are* or usu. *have ~ed*). **2.** Revert (*~; ~ to one's old habits; properly ~s to original owner*). **3.** Bring, convey, give, yield, put, send, or pay, back or in return or requital (*fish must be ~ed to the water; ~ borrowed book* or *sum; investments ~ a profit; ~ sword to scabbard,* or *~ swords* (MIL.); *~ ball,* strike etc. it back in tennis etc.; *~ like for like,* the compliment, a blow, an answer; *~ thanks* express them esp. in grace at meals or in response to toast; *~ person's love, greeting,* etc., reciprocate it; *~ed empties,* packing-cases etc., sent back; *~ clubs* etc. or *partner's lead* at cards, lead from same suit). **4.** Say in reply, retort. **5.** State, mention, or describe, officially esp. in answer to writ or formal demand (*liabilities were ~ed at £5000; were all ~ed guilty, unfit for work;* || *~ing officer,* official conducting election & announcing name of person elected); (of constituency) elect as M.P. Hence ~ABLE a. [f. OF re(turner TURN), RE-9]

rĕtûrn'² **1.** Coming back (*this ~ was the signal for riots; ~ of* POST¹; || *~ ticket* or *~,* ticket for there-&-back journey, as *took a first-class ~ to Leeds; ~ passenger, voyage, cargo,* etc.; *many happy ~s of the day* or *~s,* birthday or festival greeting; *have had a, no, ~ of the symptoms*). **2.** (Archit.) part receding from line of front, e.g. side of house or of window-opening (*~ angle, side, wall,* etc.). **3.** (Coming in of) proceeds or profit of undertaking (often pl.; *the ~s were large; brings an adequate ~; small profits & quick ~s,* motto of cheap shop etc. relying on large trade). **4.** Giving, sending, putting, or paying, back, or thing so given etc.; || esp. sheriff's report on writ, (returning officer's announcement of) candidate's election as M.P., or formal report with statistics etc. compiled by order (*sheriff made a ~ of nulla bona; secured his ~ for Colchester; table littered with ~s & pamphlets; must ask for the ~ of the book* or *loan; received a ticket in ~ for his fare, neglect in ~ for attention; fencer's ~,* i.e. riposte, *is slow; fielder has a good ~,* in cricket, sends ball in fast &

straight; *~ match* or *game,* or *~,* between same sides as before; **5.** pl. || Kind of mild pipe-tobacco (orig. sense refuse of tobacco). Hence ~LESS a. [AF (prec.)]

rĕtûse', a. (bot., entom.). With broad end & central depression (of leaf or similar part). [L re(tundere tus- beat), RE-9]

rĕūn'ion (-nyon), n. **1.** Reuniting or being reunited, reunited state. **2.** Social gathering, esp. of intimates or persons with common interests (formerly often in F form ré-). [f. F réunion (RE-, UNION)]

rĕūn'ionist, -ism, (-nyon-), nn. Seeker, & advocate, of reunion between R.-C. & Anglican Churches. [-IST, -ISM]

reunite etc. See RE-8.

rĕv, n., & v.i. & t. (colloq.; -vv-). **1.** = REVOLUTION (of engine). **2.** vb. Revolve (with *up,* to increase in speed of revolution); (often with *up*) cause (engine) to run quickly (esp. when first starting). [abbr.]

rĕvalĕn'ta, n. Food prepared from lentil & barley flour. [orig. ervi- (L ervum lens LENTIL)]

rĕvaloriza'tion, n. Restoration of the value of a country's currency. [RE- 9 + VALORIZATION]

revalue etc. See RE-8.

revanche (revahnsh'), n. Return match (esp. as name of the revenge for the Franco-German war desired by France from 1870). [F]

rĕveal'¹, v.t. **1.** (Esp. of God) make known by inspiration or supernatural means (*~ed religion,* opp. *natural*). **2.** Disclose, divulge, betray, (*~ itself,* come to sight or knowledge). Hence ~ABLE a. [f. L re(velare t velum VEIL)]

rĕveal'², n. Internal side surface of opening or recess, esp. of doorway or window aperture. [f. obs. vb revale t. OF re(valer lower f. à val downwards f. L ad vallem to the valley), RE-4]

rĕveill'e (-vĕli, -vāli), n. Military waking-signal sounded in morning on bugle or drums. [f. F réveillez imperat. pl. of réveiller (RE-, veiller f. L vigilare watch, see VIGIL)]

rĕv'el, v.i. & t. (-ll-), & n. **1.** Make merry, be riotously festive, feast, carouse, whence ~LER¹ n.; take keen delight in; throw away (money, time) in ~ry. **2.** n. ~ling, (occasion of indulgence in) merry-making, (often pl., as *the ~s began; ~ rout,* party of ~lers f. obs. *~-rout~ry*); hence ~RY4, 5) n. [f. OF revel(er) riot f. L REBEL²lare]

rĕvela'tion, n. Disclosing of knowledge, knowledge disclosed, to man by divine or supernatural agency (*the R~s,* also pop. *R~s* or *the R~s,* abbr. Rev., last book of N.T., Apocalypse), whence ~AL (-shon-) a.; striking disclosure (*it was a ~ to me; what a ~*); revealing of some fact. [f. L

revelā'tionist (-shon-), n. The R~, author of Apocalypse; believer in divine revelation. [-IST]

revenant (rev'enahn), n. One returned from the dead or from exile etc. [F]

revendica'tion, n. (diplom.). Formal claiming back, or recovery by such claim, of lost territory etc. [F RE~, VINDICATION]

revenge'¹ (-j), v.t. & i. Satisfy oneself, (pass.) be revenged, with retaliation (for offence, on, upon, of, offender); retaliate, requite, exact retribution for, (offence) to oneself or another; on, upon, (offender) avenge (person); take vengeance. [f. obs. F re(venger f. L vindicare VINDICATE, RE-¹]

revenge'² (-j), n. 1. Revenging, act done in revenging; desire to revenge, vindictive feeling, whence ~FUL (-jf-) a., ~fulLY² adv., ~fulNESS n. 2. (Games) opportunity given for reversing former result by return game (give one his ~). [f. prec.]

rev'enue, n. 1. Income, esp. of large amount, from any source (pl. collective items of it, annual w. possess. as his ~s). 2. State's annual income from which public expenses are met (INLAND ~; ~ tax, imposed solely to raise ~, not to affect trade, opp. protective; ~ cutter, officer, etc., employed to prevent smuggling); department of civil service collecting it. [OF, p.p. of revenir f. L re(venire come) return. RE-9]

rèverb'eriàte, v.t. & i. 1. Return, beat back, echo, reflect, (t. & i. of sound, light, heat; ~ating furnace or kiln, constructed to ~ate heat on substance dealt with, whence ~atory a. & n.). 2. (rare). (Of emotion etc.) react upon; (of ball etc.) rebound. So ~A'TION n., ~ATIVE, ~ANT (poet.), aa. [f. L RE- 9(verberare beat), -ATE³]

rèverb'erātor, n. Reflector, reflecting lamp. [-OR²]

rèvêre', v.t. Regard as sacred or exalted, hold in deep & usu. affectionate or religious respect, venerate. [f. L RE(vereri fear)]

rev'erence, n., & v.t. 1. Revering (see prec.; hold in, regard with, ~; feel ~ for, pay ~ to); capacity for the rising generation lacks ~); (arch.) gesture showing it, bow, curtsy, obeisance; so rèverèn'tIAL (-shl) a., rèverèn'tialLY² adv. 2. Being revered (saving your ~, arch., apology for coarse term; your, his, ~, arch. or vulg. or joc., titles used to, of, clergyman). 3. v.t. Regard with ~, venerate. [f. L reverentia (prec., -ENCE)]

rev'erend, a. & n. 1. Deserving reverence by age, character, or associations (of person, place, custom, etc.; esp. as title, abbr. Rev., or otherwise, of clergyman;

Very R~, of dean; Right R~, of bishop; Most R~, of archbishop; the Right R~ John Smith or the Right R~ the bishop of ---; Rev. or the Rev. John or J. Smith, or vulg. Rev. or the Rev. Smith; the ~ gentleman, the clergyman in question; as n., usu. pl., = clergymen etc., as ~s & right ~s, clergy & bishops). 2. Of the clergy (~ utterances etc.). 3. (arch.). = foll. [f. L reverendus (REVERE, -ND⁷)]

rev'erent, a. Feeling or showing reverence. Hence ~LY² adv. [f. L reverens (REVERE, -ENT)]

rèv'erie, n. (Fit of) musing, day-dream(ing), (was lost in ~ or a ~); (arch.) fantastic notion or theory, delusion; [Mus.) dreamy instrumental piece. [OF (rever, resver, now rêver dream etym. dub., -ERY); cf. RAVE²]

revers (revār'), n. (pl. the same). Turned-back edge of coat, bodice, etc., displaying lining. [F]

rèverse'¹, a. Opposite or contrary (to, or abs.) in character or order, inverted, back or backward, upside down, (in the ~ direction to the time before; the ~ side etc. of a coin, picture, etc.; ~ Q; ~ fire, battery, etc., playing on enemy's rear or into works from rear; ~ flank, opposite to pivot end in wheeling). Hence ~LY² (-sll) adv. [f. L re(vertere vers- turn), RE-9]

rèverse'², v.t. & i. 1. Turn (trans.) the other way round or up or inside-out, invert, transpose, convert to opposite character or effect, (~e arms, hold rifles butt upwards; ~e motion, policy, order, etc.; ~e engine, make it work backwards). 2. Revoke, annul, (decree, attainder, etc.). 3. (Danc., esp. in waltz) begin to revolve in opposite direction. Hence ~AL(2) n., ~IBLE a., ~IBIL'ITY n. [f. F reverser (RE-, L versare frequent. of vertere turn)]

rèverse'³, n. 1. The contrary (of, or abs.; with others the ~ of this or the ~ happens; on the ~ in motoring, with car moving backwards; ~s opposite, as periphr. for its opposite, as made remarks the ~ of complimentary). 2. (Device on) subordinate piece of coin etc. (opp. OBVERSE) = VERSO. 3. = REVERSE¹ side (take in ~, subject to REVERSE¹ fire). 4. Piece of misfortune, disaster, esp. defeat in battle (the ~s of fortune; suffered a ~). [OF (-rs, -rse) as REVERSE¹]

rèver'si, n. Game on draught-board with counters coloured differently above & below. [F]

rèver'sion (-shn), n. 1. (Return to grantor or his heirs or passing to ultimate grantee or ~ER¹ (-sho-) n. of, also right of ultimate succession to) estate granted till specified date or event, esp. death of original grantee (in ~, on such conditions). 2. Sum payable on person's death esp. by

For pronunciation & hyphening of re- see RE-; for words in re- not given see RE- 8, 9.

way of life-insurance. **3.** Thing to which one has a right or expects to succeed, when relinquished by another. **4.** Return to a previous state, habit, etc., (Biol.) to ancestral type. Hence ~**AL**, ~**ARY**[1] aa., ~**aliy**[2] adv. (-sho-). [OF, f. L *reversionem* f. *vertere* vers- turn, -ION), RE- 9].

revert, v.i. & t. **1.** Go back (bare). **2.** (Of property, office, etc.,) fall in by REVERSION, whence ~**ER**[4] n. (legal). **3.** Return to former state etc., (cf. prec.). n. after *convert, pervert*, person who readopts his original faith): (abs.) fall back into wild state. **4.** Recur to subject in talk or thought. **5.** Turn (eyes, rarely steps) back. [f. OF *revertir* f. L as prec.]

rever′tible, a. (Of property) subject to reversion. [prec., -IBLE]

revêt′, v.t. (-tt-). Face (rampart, wall, etc.,) with masonry etc. Hence ~**MENT** n. (as prec.). [f. F *revêtir* f. L *revestire* clothe f. VESTIS), RE- 8]

revêt′ment, n. Retaining-wall or facing (as prec.). See RE- 8.

revic′tual, v. [f. F *revêtement* (prec., -MENT)]

review[1] (-vū), n. **1.** Revision (esp. legal; *is not subject to ~; court of ~*, before which sentences etc. come for revision), fleet, etc. (~ *order*, dress & arrangement usu. at ~s, & transf., full fig : *pass in ~*, fig. t. & i., examine or be examined). **2.** Display & formal inspection of troops, fleet, etc. (~ *order*, dress & arrangement usu. at ~s, & transf., full fig : *pass in ~*, fig. t. & i., examine or be examined). **3.** Retrospect, survey of the past. **4.** Critique of book etc.; periodical publication with articles on current events, new books, art, etc. **5.** Second view. [f. OF *reveue* (now -*vue*) orig. fem. p.p. of *revoir* f. L *re(vidēre* see), RE- 9]

review[2] (-vū), v.t. & i. **1.** View again, survey, glance over, look back on. **4.** Hold review of (troops etc.). **5.** Write review of (book etc.), write reviews, whence ~**ER**[1] (-vūer) n. Hence ~**ABLE** a., ~**AL**(2) n. [REVIEW]

revile, v.t. & i. **1.** Call by ill names, abuse, rail at; talk abusively, rail. Hence ~**ER**[1], ~**ING**[1](1), nn., ~**ingLY**[2] adv. [f. OF *reviler* (RE- 6, VILE)]

revise[e] (-z), v.t. & n. **1.** Read or look over or re-examine or reconsider & amend faults in (literary matter, printers' proofs, law, constitution, etc.; *R~ed Version*, Authorized or 1611 Version of Bible); hence or cogn. ~**ABLE**, ~**ORY**, (-z-), aa., ~**AL**(2) (-z-), **revi′sion** (-zhon) n., (esp. in pl. of authors of R.V.). **2.** n. Revision, ~ing, (rare): ~ed form (rare): (Print.) proof-sheet embodying corrections made in earlier proof. [n. f. vb, f. F *reviser* look at f. L *vidēre vis*- see), RE- 8]

revisit, see RE- 8.

revi′val, n. **1.** Bringing or coming back into vogue (~ *of learning, letters, etc.,* at Renaissance; ~ *of architecture, 19th-o.,* reversion to Gothic; ~ *of book, play, word, custom,* etc.). **2.** (Special effort with meetings etc. to promote) reawakening of religious fervour, whence ~**ISM**(3), ~**IST**(2), n. **3.** Restoration to bodily or mental vigour or to life or consciousness. [foll., -AL(2)]

revi′ve, v.i. & t. **1.** Come or bring back to consciousness, life, existence, vigour, notice, activity, validity, or vogue : (Chem.) restore (metal, esp. mercury) to natural form. Hence ~**ABLE** a. [f. L revivere live), RE- 8 : trans. use prob. f. *is* etc. revived as -ED[2](2)]

revi′ver, n. In vbl senses ; esp. : (sl.) stimulating drink ; preparation for restoring faded colour etc. [-ER[1]]

revi′vify, v.t. Restore to animation, activity, vigour, or life ; (Chem.)=REVIVE. Hence ~**FICA′TION** n. [f. LL *revivificare*]

revivis′cence, n. **revivis′cent**, a. Re-turning to life or vigour. [f. L RE- 8 (*viviscere* incept. of *vivere* live), -ENCE, -ENT]

‖ **revi′vor**, n. (law). Proceeding for revival of suit after death of party etc. [REVIVE, -OR[2]]

revoke, v.t. & i. & n. **1.** Repeal, annul, withdraw, rescind, cancel, (decree, consent, promise, permission ; also rarely abs., withdraw promise etc.), so **rev′oc-ABLE**, **rev′ocatory**, aa., **revoca′tion** n.; (Cards) make ~. **2.** n. Card-player's failure to follow suit though he could ; (rare) revocation (*beyond ~*). [f. L revo-care call), RE- 9]

revolt′, v.i. & t. & n. **1.** Cast of allegiance, make rising or rebellion, fall away *from* or rise *against* ruler, go over to rival power, (n., act of ~ing or state of having ~ed, rising, insurrection ; so *in ~*; p.p. as -ED[2], as *his ~ed subjects*). **2.** Feel revulsion or disgust *at*, rise in repugnance *against*, turn in loathing *from*, (common *sense, nature*, one's *heart*, ~s *at* or *against* or *from it* ; n., sense of loathing, rebellious or protesting mood). **3.** Affect with strong disgust, nauseate, whence ~**ING**[2] a., ~**ingLY**[2] adv. [f. F *révolter* f. L *volvere volut-* roll]

rev′olute[1] (-oot, -ūt), a. (bot. etc.). With back-rolled edges. [f. L REVOLVERE]

revolute[2] (-oot), v.i. (sl.). Engage in political revolution. [back formation f. foll.]

revolu′tion (-ōo-, -lū-), n. **1.** Revolving, motion in orbit or circular course or round axis or centre, rotation, single completion of orbit or rotation, time it takes, cyclic recurrence. **2.** Complete change, conditions, fundamental reconstruction, esp. forcible substitution by subjects of new ruler or policy for the old (*the R~*, expulsion of James II 1688 ; *French R~*,

overthrow of monarchy 1789 etc.; *American R~*, overthrow of British rule 1775 etc.), whence ~IZE(1, 3) v.t., ~ISM(3), ~IST(2), nn., (-óshǒ-, -ǔ-). [f. LL (-tio) as REVOLVE, -ION]

revolu′tionarў (-óshǒ-, -ū-), a. & n. (Instigator) of revolution; involving great & usu. violent changes; (rare) of rotation or revolving. [-ARY¹]

revolve′, v.t. & i. Turn (t. & i.) round or round & round, rotate, go in circular orbit, roll (intr.) along, (~ *problem, fact, in the mind* etc. or abs., ponder over it; *mechanism for revolving the turntable. Earth ~s both round or about sun & on its axis; seasons, years,* ~). [f. L *re(volvere volut-* roll), RE- 6]

revol′ver, n. Pistol with revolving mechanism enabling user to fire several shots without reloading (*policy of the big* ~, of threatening foreign States with retaliatory tariff). [-ER¹]

revue′, n. Loosely constructed play or series of scenes or spectacles presenting or satirizing current events. [F]

revul′sion (-shn), n. 1. Counter-irritation, treatment of one disordered organ etc. by acting upon another. 2. (rare). Drawing or being drawn away (*the ~ of capital from other trades*). 3. Sudden violent change of feeling, sudden reaction in taste, fortune, trade, etc. [f. L re(*vulsio* f. *vellere vuls-* pull), RE- 9]

revul′sive, a. & n. (chiefly med.). 1. Of, producing, revulsion. 2. n. Counter-irritant application. [prec., -IVE]

reward′ (-wǒrd), n., & v.t. 1. Return or recompense for service or merit, requital for good or evil, retribution; sum offered for detection of criminal, restoration of lost property, etc.; hence ~LESS a. 2. v.t. Repay, requite, recompense, (service or doer of it, offender, offence). [f. ONF *reward(er)* = OF REGARD¹(er)]

rewin, see RE- 9; **reword**, **rewrite**, RE- 8.

Rex, n. (abbr. *R.*). Reigning king (in use as REGINA). [L]

Rey′nard (rēn-, rān-), n. (Proper name for) the fox; a fox. [f. OF *Renart* name of fox in the *Roman de Renart*]

rhab′domancў, n. Use of divining-rod, esp. for discovering subterranean water or ore. [f. LL f. Gk *rhabdomanteia (rhabdos* rod, -MANCY)]

Rhadaman′thǔs, n. Stern & incorruptible judge. Hence ~INE² a. [name of judge in Gk Hades]

Rhae′tian (rēshn), a. & n. ~ *Alps*, part of Alps about the Engadine; ~ = RHAETO-ROMANIC a. & n. [L *Rhaetia*, -IAN]

Rhaet′ic, a. & n. (Of) *the* set of strata intermediate between lias & trias prevailing in Rhaetian Alps. [f. L *Rhaeticus* (prec., -IC)]

Rhaeto-Roman′ic, -ánce′, aa. & nn. (Of, in) any of the Romance dialects of SE. Switzerland & Tyrol, esp. Romansh & Ladin. [L *Rhaetus* Rhaetian, -O-]

rhap′sǒde, n. Ancient-Greek minstrel or reciter of epic poems. [f. Gk *rhapsōidos (rhaptō* stitch, ODE)]

rhap′sǒdize, v.t. & i. Recite (t. & i.) as rhapsode; talk or write rhapsodies (usu. *about, on,* etc.). So ~IST(1) n. [foll., -IZE]

rhap′sǒdў, n. 1. (Gk Ant.) epic poem, or part of it, of length for one recitation. 2. Enthusiastic extravagant high-flown utterance or composition, emotional irregular piece of music, whence **rhap-sōd′ICAL a., rhapsōd′icalLY² adv.** Hence **rhapsōd′IC a.** [f. L *rhapsodia* f. Gk *rhapsōidia* (RHAPSODE, -IA¹)]

rhat′anў, n. (Extract, used medicinally & in adulterating port, of root of) S.-Amer. shrub. [f. Port. *ratanhia* f. native *ratahá*]

rhe′a (rēa), n. S.-Amer. three-toed ostrich. [name of Gk goddess]

Rhēm′ish, a. Of Rheims (~ *Bible, Testament, version, translation,* N.T. translated by Roman Catholics of English College at Rheims 1582). [obs. E *Rhemes*, -ISH]

Rhēn′ish, a. & n. (arch.). 1. Of the Rhine & districts on its banks (now usu. *Rhine* attrib.). 2. n. ~ wine (now usu. *Rhine wine* or *hock*). [f. OF *rinois* or MHG *rīnisch* or MDu. *rijnsch* w. assim. to L *Rhenus* Rhine]

rhēn′ium, n. Rare metallic element of manganese group, discovered in 1925. [f. L *Rhenus* Rhine, -IUM]

rhēo-, rēo-, comb. form in chiefly electr. terms of Gk *rheos* stream, = current; as *rheol′ogy*, study of flow & deformation of matter; *rhe′ostat*, apparatus for controlling supply of current, esp. to electric motors when starting up, by introducing variable resistance.

rhē′sus, n. Small catarrhine monkey common in N. India. [arbitr. use of Gk *Rhēsus*, mythical king of Thrace]

rhē′tor, n. Ancient Greek or Roman teacher or professor of rhetoric; (mere) orator (rare). [L, f. Gk *rhētōr (eirō,* perf. *eirēka,* speak)]

rhet′oric, n. (Treatise on) the art of persuasive or impressive speaking or writing; language designed to persuade or impress (often w. implication of insincerity, exaggeration, etc.); persuasiveness of or of looks or acts. [f. L f. Gk *rhētorikē (tekhnē* art) of RHETOR, -IC]

rhetō′rical, a. Expressed with a view to persuasive or impressive effect, artificial or extravagant in language, of the nature of rhetoric, (~ *question,* asked not for information but to produce effect, as *who cares? for nobody cares*); of the art of

For pronunciation & hyphening of *re-* see RE-: for words in *re-* not given see RE- 8, 9. In words beginning with *rh-* h is mute.

rhetoric; given to rhetoric, oratorical. Hence ~LY² adv. [f. LL f. Gk *rhētorikos* (RHETOR, -IC) +-AN]

rhĕtŏrĭ'cian (-shn), n. = RHETOR; rhetorical speaker or writer. [f. OF *rethoricien* (RHETORIC, -IAN)]

‖ rheum (rōom), n. (arch.). Watery secretion or discharge of mucous membrane etc. such as tears, saliva, or mucus; catarrh; (pl.) rheumatic pains. [f. OF *reume* f. L f. Gk *rheuma* -*atos* stream (*rheō* flow, -M)]

rheumăt'ic (-ōō-), a. & n. 1. Of, suffering from, subject to, producing, or produced by, rheumatism (~*ic fever*, non-infectious fever with inflammation & pain in joints; ~*ic walk* etc., impeded by rheumatism); hence ~ICALLY adv., ~ICKY² a. (colloq.). 2. n. ~*ic patient*; (pl., colloq.) rheumatism. [f. L f. Gk *rheumatikos* (prec., -IC)]

rheu'matism (-ōō-), n. Disease marked by inflammation & pain in joints (*acute* ~, rheumatic fever). [f. L f. Gk *rheumatismos* (RHEUMA, -IZE, -ISM)]

‖ rheu'my̆ (-ōō-), a. (arch.). Consisting of, flowing with, rheum; (of air) damp, raw. [-Y²]

rhīn'al, a. (anat. etc.). Of nostril or nose. [RHINO-, -AL]

‖ rhīne¹ (rēn), n. (SW. dial.). Large open ditch. [prob. f. OE *ryne* = obs. *rune* stream]

Rhine², n. German river (~ *wine*, kinds esp. of white wine from ~ vineyards, cf. RHENISH; ~'*stone*, kind of rock-crystal, also paste gem imitating diamond).

rhīnŏ¹, n. (sl.). Money (often *ready*~). [?]

rhīnŏ²¹, n. (sl.; pl. ~s). (Short for) rhinoceros.

rhīnŏ⁻, comb. form of Gk *rhis rhinos* nostril, nose, as ~*opharynx'geal*, of nose & pharynx; ~*oplas'tic*, *rhin'oplasty*, (of) plastic surgery of the nose; *rhin'oscope*, ~*oscŏp'ic*, ~*ŏs'copy¹.

rhīnŏ'ceros, n. Large unwieldy African & S.-Asiatic quadruped with horn or two horns on nose & thick folded & plated skin. So rhinŏceroť'ic a. [f. LL f. Gk RHINO⁻ceros f. *keras* horn]

rhīzŏ⁻, comb. form of Gk *rhiza* root chiefly in bot. terms as ~*carp*, plant with perennial root but perishing stems.

rhīz'ōme, n. Prostrate rootlike stem emitting roots, rootstock. [f. Gk *rhizōma* (*rhizoomai* take root, as prec., -M)]

rhō, n. Greek letter (P, ρ) = r. [Gk]

Rhōde İs'land (ĭl-) Rĕd, n. American breed of reddish-black domestic fowl. [f. *Rhode Island*, State of U.S.]

Rhōdes schŏl'ar (rōdz sk-), n. Holder of any of 190 scholarships tenable at Oxford by members of British Dominions & Colonies or United States (formerly also by Germans). [Cecil *Rhodes*, founder]

Rhŏd'ian, a. & n. (Native) of Rhodes. [L *Rhodius* f. L f. Gk *Rhodos* Rhodes (f. -AN]

rhŏd'ium¹, n. (Also ~*wood*) scented wood of Canary convolvulus, rosewood. [f. mod. L, neut. adj. (sc. *lignum* wood) = roselike f. Gk *rhodon* rose]

rhŏd'ium², n. Hard white metal of platinum group (~*ium pen*, steel pen tipped with it). Hence ~IC, ~OUS, aa. (chem.). [Gk *rhodon* rose, -IUM, from colour of solution of its salts]

rhŏd'ō⁻, comb. form of Gk *rhodon* rose, as ~*sperm'ous* with red spores.

rhŏdŏdĕn'dron, n. Kinds of large-flowered evergreen shrubs akin to azalea. [L f. L f. Gk (prec., *dendron* tree)]

rhŏmb (-b usu. mute exc. before vowel), n. Oblique equilateral parallelogram, diamond or lozenge, object or part with such outline; (Cryst.) rhombohedron. Hence rhŏm'bĭc a., rhŏm'bo- comb. form. [f. L f. Gk *rhombos*]

rhŏmbŏhē'dron, n. (chiefly cryst.; pl. ~*a*, ~*ons*). (Crystal in shape of) solid bounded by six equal rhombs. Hence ~AL a. [RHOMBO- (prec.), Gk *hedra* base]

rhŏm'boid, a. & n. 1. Of or near the shape of a rhomb (~ *muscle*, connecting scapula with vertebrae). 2. n. Quadrilateral of which only opposite sides & angles are equal; ~ *muscle*. [f. LL f. Gk *rhomboeidēs* (RHOMB, -OID)]

rhŏmboid'al, a. Having shape of a rhomboid (prec., n.); = prec. (adj.). Hence ~LY² adv. [prec., -AL]

rhŏm'bus, n. (pl. -*buses*, -*bī*). 1. = RHOMB. 2. Kind of flat-fish including turbot & brill. [L (RHOMB)]

rhŏť'acism, n. rhŏť'acize v.i. (Speak with) excessive or peculiar pronunciation of r; conversion of, convert, other sounds into r. [n. f. L vb f. Gk *rhōtakizō* (RHO, -IZE)]

rhū'barb (rōō-), n. 1. (Purgative made from) root of Chinese & Tibetan plant (usu. *Chinese*, *East Indian*, *Russia*, or *Turkey* ~, from channels of importation). 2. (Fleshy leaf-stalks of) kinds of garden plant, cooked in spring as substitute for fruit (*occas. English*, *French*, *common*, or *garden* ~). 3. attrib. (Of colour) yellowish-brown like Chinese ~. Hence ~Y² a. [f. OF *rubarbe* f. med. L *rheubarbarum* foreign rha or rhubarb (*rha* Gk, perh. f. *Rha* the Volga, BARBAROUS), w. assim. to L Gk *rheon* rhubarb]

rhyme¹, rime, n. 1. Identity of sound between words or verse-lines extending from the end to the last fully accented vowel & not further (greet & deceit,

shepherd & leopard, quality & frivolity, stationary & probationary, is it & visit, give ~s, but seat & deceit, station & crustacean, visible & invisible, *do not*; *single* or *male* or *masculine*, *double* or *female* or FEMININE, *treble* or *triple*, *quadruple*, or *quintuple*, to number of syllables included; *imperfect* ~, as in *love & move*, *phase & race*; *without* ~ *or reason*, quite unaccountable, -bly). **2.** Verse marked by ~s (pl. or sing.), a poem with ~s, the employment of ~, (*should be written in* ~; *prefer blank verse to* ~; *am sending you some* ~s; NURSERY ~; *was reading an old* ~; *royal*, stanzas of seven ten-syllable lines with ~s as *ababbcc*, as in Chaucer's *Clerkes Tale* etc.). **3.** Word providing a ~ to another; *can't find a* ~ *to teacups*; *English is badly off for double* ~s). Hence [*rhyme* assim. to RHYTHM of earlier & OF *rime* f. L f. Gk *rhuthmos* RHYTHM] ~'LESS (-ml-) a., ~'lessNESS n.

rhỹme², rime f. *rime*, v.i. & t. Write rhymes, versify (intr.), whence **rhỹm'ER, rhỹme'-STER** (-ms-), nn.; put or make (story etc.) into rhyme (~d *verse*, opp. *blank verse*) while (time) *away* in rhyming; (of words or lines) exhibit rhyme, (of word) supply or act as rhyme *to* or *with*, (of person) treat (word) as rhyming *with*, select rhymes, (~s *carelessly*; ~s *law with four*; rhymING¹-*dictionary*, of words arranged by terminations for versifiers' use), whence **rhỹm'IST**(1) n. [f. OF *rimer* as prec.]

rhỹ'thm (-dhm, -thm), n. **1.** Metrical movement determined by various relations of long & short or accented & unaccented syllables, measured flow of words & phrases in verse or prose. **2.** That feature of musical composition concerned with periodical accent & the duration of notes. **3.** (Art) harmonious correlation of parts. **4.** (Physics, Physiol., & gen.) movement with regular succession of strong & weak elements. Hence or cogn. **rhỹth'-mic(AL)** aa., **rhỹth'micALLY²** adv., **rhỹthm'LESS** a., **rhỹth'misT**(3) n., (-dh-, -th-). [f. L f. Gk *rhuthmos* cf. *rheo* flow]

ri'ant, a. Smiling, cheerful, (of face, eyes, etc., & esp. of landscape). [F (*rire* f. L L *ridêre* laugh, -ANT)]

rib, n., & v.t. (-bb-). **1.** One of curved bones reaching from spine round upper part of body (*true, sternal, ~*, joined also to breastbone, opp. *false, floating, short, ~*; *poke one in the* ~s, to draw his attention facetiously; *smite under fifth* ~, Bibl., stab; ~ or ~s *of beef etc.*, as joint of meat; SPARE~; (joc. w. ref. to Gen. ii. 21) wife, woman. **2.** Ridge or long raised piece often of thicker material across thinner surface serving to support as part of framework or strengthen or adorn, e.g. vein of leaf, shaft of feather, spur of mountain, vein of ore, ridge between furrows, wave-mark on sand, raised line in knitting, one of ship's curved timbers to which planks are nailed or corresponding ironwork, arch supporting vault, groin, raised moulding on groin or across ceiling etc., wooden or iron beam helping to carry bridge, hinged rod of umbrella-frame. **3.** ~-*grass*, ~'*wort*, Narrow-leaved Plantain. Hence (-)~DED² (-bd), ~'LESS, aa. **4.** v.t. Provide with ~s, act as ~s of, whence ~b'ING¹(3, 6) n.; mark with ridges; plough with ~s between furrows, half-plough, rafter. [com-Teut., cf. ON *rif*, G *rippe*, Du. *rib*]

rib'ald, n. & a. **1.** Irreverent jester, user of scurrilous, blasphemous, or indecent language; so ~RY(4, 5) n. **2.** adj. (Of language or its user) scurrilous, obscene, irreverent. [earlier sense *low-born retainer, menial*, f. OF *ribaud, -auld*, etym. dub.]

rib'and n., **rib'anded** a. = RIBBON(ed). [f. F *riban* (now *ru-*), etym. dub.]

ribb'and, n. Wale, strip, scantling, or light spar, of wood, used esp. in ship-building to hold ribs in position, launching, & making of gun-platform or pontoon-bridge, [f. RIB, BAND, or var. of prec.]

ribb'on, n. **1.** (Piece or length of) silk or satin or other fine material woven into narrow band esp. for adorning costume; ~ of special colour etc. worn to indicate membership of knightly order, club, college, athletic team, etc. (BLUE¹; R~ *Society*, Irish R.-C. secret society formed in early 19th c. & associated with agrarian crime, whence R~ISM n.) **2.** Long narrow strip of anything, ~-like object or mark, (pl.) driving-reins, (*hang in, torn to,* ~-s, ragged strips; *handle, take, the* ~s, drive). **3.** ~-*building*, ~-*development*, the building of houses along a main road, extending outwards from a town; ~-*fish*, long slender flat kinds; ~-*grass*, slender-leaved kind; ~-*man*, member of R~ Society. Hence (-)~ED² (-nd) a. [var. of RIBAND]

rib'ĕs (-z), n. (bot.). Currant or gooseberry plant. [med. L, = sorrel, f. Arab. *ribas*]

Rib'ston pipp'in, n. Kind of dessert apple. [*Ribston* Park in Yorks.]

Ricăr'dian, a. & n. (Adherent) of the political economist Ricardo (d. 1823), according to his views. [-IAN]

rice, n. (Pearl-white seeds, used as staple food in many Eastern countries, & in Britain in puddings, cakes, etc., or as table-vegetable, of) chiefly oriental plant, grown in marshes; ~-*bird*, Java sparrow, also bobolink; ~-*milk*, boiled & thickened with ~; ~-*paper*, kind made from pith of a Formosan plant & used by Chinese artists for painting on (named after ~ in error). [f. OF *ris* f. It. *riso* (L f. Gk *oryza* prob. f. Oriental source)]

In words beginning with *rh-* h is mute.

rich, a. **1.** (Of persons, societies, States, etc.) wealthy, having riches, (also as n. in *the ~, ~ & poor*). **2.** (Of countries, periods, soil, etc.) abounding in or *in* natural resources or some valuable possession or production, fertile. **3.** Valuable (*~ offerings, a ~ harvest*). **4.** (Of dress, furniture, buildings, banquets, etc., & *fig.*) elaborate, (with lace, sculpture, etc.). **5.** (Of food or diet) containing or involving large proportion of fat, oil, butter, eggs, sugar, spice, etc. **6.** (Of colours, sounds, smells) mellow, deep, full, not thin. **7.** Abundant, ample. **8.** (Of incidents) highly amusing, full of entertainment or material for humour. **9.** *~, richly (~clad, ~bound, ~glittering,* etc.). Hence *~′EN⁶ v.t. & t.* (rare), *~′NESS* n. [com.-Teut.: OE *rīce,* cf. Du. *rijk,* G *reich,* ON *ríkr:* perh. early Teut. adoption of L *rex*]

Rich′ard, pers. name. *~ Rōe,* typical name for defendant in ejectment suit (cf. JOHN *Doe*); *Poor ~′s sayings,* maxims from almanacs issued by Benjamin Franklin *again* (†: Interpolation in Cibber's version of Shaks. *~ III*), said by or of person recovered from despondency, fear, illness, etc.

rich′es (-iz), n. (usu. as pl.). Abundant means, wealth, valuable possessions, being rich. [f. obs. & OF *richesse (riche* serves a thrashing, *to succeed*). [-IY²]

rich′ly, adv. In adj. senses; also (chiefly with *deserve*) fully, thoroughly. (*~ de-serves a thrashing, to succeed*). [-LY²]

rick[1], n., & v.t. **1.** Stack of hay, corn, peas, etc., esp. one regularly built & thatched; ||*~barton,* = *~yard; ~cloth,* canvas cover for unfinished *~; ~stand,* short wooden or stone pillars bearing joists to raise *~* from ground; *~yard,* enclosure for *~s.* **2.** v.t. Form into *~*(s). [OE *hrēac,* cf. Du. *rook,* Norw. *rauk*]

rick[2]. See WRICK.

rick′ets, n. (as sing. or pl.) *-et* in comb. etc., as *ricket-producing, rickety*). Children's disease with softening of bones, esp. of spine, & bow-legs etc., rachitis. [etym. dub.; taken by writer (1645) of treatise on it for corrupt. of RACHITIS, which he introduced as its scientific name]

rick′ety, a. **1.** Suffering from, of (the nature of), rickets. **2.** Feeble, shaky, tottering, weak-jointed, fragile, insecure, (of persons or things, esp. furniture). Hence *~INESS* n. [-Y²]

rick[3]. See WRICK.

ric′ochet (-shā, -shět), n., & v.i. & t. (-t-or -tt-, pr. -shād or -shětid, -shāing or -shěting etc.). **1.** Skipping on water or ground of projectile esp. shell or bullet, hit made after it (often attrib. as *~ fire, shot*). **2.** vb. (Of projectile) skip once or more; (of gun, gunner, etc.) hit or aim at with *~* shot(s). [vb f. n, F, etym. dub.]

rid, v.t. (past *ridded, rid*; p.p. *rid,* rarely *ridded*). Make (person, place) free, disencumber, of (usu. in p.p. with *be* or *get; glad to be, must get, ~ of him;* (arch.) *abolish, clear away, get ~* of, (arch.). Hence *~DANCE* n. (esp. *a good ~dance* as excl. of joy: person etc. *is a good ~dance, better away*). [earlier sense *clear* (land etc.): f. ON *rythja*]

rid′(d)el, n. (eccl.). Altar-curtain. [f. OF *ridel* (F *rideau*) curtain]

ridden. See RIDE.

rid′dle[1], n., & v.i. & t. **1.** Question, statement, or description, designed or serving to test the ingenuity of hearers in divining its answer or meaning or reference, conundrum, enigma; puzzling or mysterious fact, thing, or person. **2.** vb. Speak in, propound, (part.) expressed in, *~s,* often *~ me* as challenge). [OE *rǣdels* (READ), suf. *-els* as in BURIAL), cf. Du. *raadsel,* G *rätsel*]

rid′dle[2], n., & v.t. **1.** Coarse sieve for corn, gravel, cinders, etc.; plate with pins used in straightening wire. **2.** v.t. Pass (corn etc.) through *~,* sift, (*fig.*) test (evidence, truth); fill (ship, person) with holes esp. of gunshot, (*fig.*) pelt with questions, refute (person, theory) with facts. [OE *hriddel,* earlier *hridder (hrid-* shake), cf. RID.

ride, v.i. & t. (*rōde,* arch. *rid; ridden* pr. rī′dn, arch. *rid*) & n. **1.** Sit on & be carried by horse etc., go on horseback etc. or on bicycle etc. or in train or other public conveyance (cf. DRIVE¹), sit or go or be on something as on horse esp. astride, sit on & manage horse, lie at anchor, float buoyantly, (of sun etc.) seem to float, (of things normally level or even) project or overlap, (*~ a-*COCK-HORSE, BODKIN, ROUGH-*shod, 50 miles, full speed, a race; ~ to hounds, hunt; ~ for a fall, ~* or the act recklessly; *~ 12 st.* etc., weigh that in riding-trim; *~ over, ~* in horse-racing as WALK *over; ~ one down,* overtake him by riding, also put one's horse at him; *~ one off* at polo, edge him away; *~ off on a side issue,* use it to evade the main point; *~ & tie,* of two or more travellers sharing horse, one riding ahead & then leaving it tied to await the other; *riding on his father's shoulders, back, knee, foot; ~s well, cannot ~; learn to ~, riding-lessons or -school; bird, ship, ~s on the waves;~ out or the storm lit. &* *fig.,* come safely through it; *moon was riding high; bone ~s* in fracture, one part overlaps other; *rope ~s,* has one turn crossing over another); traverse on horseback etc., *~ over, ~ through, (~ the country, desert, etc.; ~ a ford, pass*

through it on horseback). **2.** ~ on, sit heavily on, oppress, haunt, dominate, tyrannize over, (~ *horse*; ~ *one's horse at* fence or enemy, urge it forward; ~ *one's horse*, & fig. hobby or method or jest, *to death*, kill or overdo it; *nightmare* ~*s sleeper*; ~ *the waves; ridden by fears, prejudices*, etc.; *priest* etc. *-ridden*). **3.** Give ~ to, cause to ~, (~ *child on one's back*; ~ *one on rail*, carry him astride on it as torture). **4.** (Of ground) be of specified character for riding on (~*s well, soft, hard*, etc.); hence **rid'**ABLE a. **5.** n. Journey in public conveyance, spell of riding on horse, bicycle, person's back, etc.; *take for a* ~ (sl.), drive (person) away in **6.** motor-car prior to murdering him. Road esp. through wood for riding on. **7.** (Mil.) batch of mounted recruits. [com. Teut.; OE *rīdan*, cf. Du. *rijden*, G *reiten*]

rid'el. See RIDDEL.

rid'er, n. In vbl senses; also or esp.: **1.** (Naut., pl.) additional set of timbers or iron plates strengthening ship's frame; (sing.) overlying rope or rope-turn. **2.** (Curl.) stone that ousts another. **3.** Additional clause amending or supplementing document, esp. parliamentary bill at third reading; corollary, naturally arising supplement; expression of opinion, recommendation etc., added to verdict. **4.** (Math.) problem testing student's mastery of principles on which its solution depends. **5.** Piece in machine etc. that surmounts or bridges or works over others. Hence ~LESS a. [OE *rīdere* (RIDE)]

ridge, n., & v.t. & i. **1.** Line of junction in which two sloping surfaces meet (*the* ~ *of a roof, the nose*, etc.); long narrow hill-top, mountain range, watershed; (Agric.) one of a set of raised strips separated by furrows; (Gard.) raised hot-bed for melons etc.; any narrow elevation across surface; ~*piece*, beam along ~ of roof; ~*-pole*, horizontal pole of long tent, also =~-*piece*; ~*-tile*, used for roof~; ~*-tree*, =~-*piece*; ~*way*, road along ~; hence **ridg'**Y² a. **2.** vb. Break up (land) into ~s; mark with ~s; plant (cucumbers etc.) in ~s; gather (t. & i. esp. of sea) into ~s. [com. Teut.; OE *hrycg*, cf. LG *rüg*, G *rücken*]

rid'icule, n., & v.t. **1.** Ridiculous thing, ridiculousness, (arch.); holding or being held up as laughing-stock, derision, mockery. **2.** v.t. Make fun of, subject to ~, laugh at. [f. L *ridiculum* neut. of *ridiculus* laughable (*ridēre* laugh)]

ridic'ulous, a. Deserving to be laughed at, absurd, unreasonable. Hence ~LY² adv., ~NESS n. [as prec. +-OUS, or f. L *ridiculosus*]

rid'ing¹, n. In vbl senses; also, road for riders, esp. green track through or beside wood; ~*breeches*; ~-HABIT¹; ~-*lamp*, *-light* (borne by ship at anchor). [-ING¹]

|| **rid'ing²,** n. Administrative division (East, W., or N., R~) of Yorkshire; similar division of other U.-K. or colonial county. [for *thriding* (THIRD, -ING³) third part, with loss of *th-* owing to preceding *-t(h)* of *east* etc.]

rĭaciment'ō (-ahch-), n. (pl. *-ti* pr. *-tē*). Remodelled form of a literary work or the like. [It.]

rife, pred. a. Of common occurrence, met with in numbers or quantities, prevailing, current, numerous, (usu. *be*, also *grow*, *wax*, etc.; ~ *with maxims*). Hence ~NESS n. [OE *rīfe*, cf. MIDu. *rijf*, ON *rīfr* (-fn-)]

Riff, a. & n. (Of) a Berber of the *Rif* district of Morocco. So~¹AN a. & n.

riff-raff, n. The rabble, disreputable persons. [earlier *riff & raff* f. F *rif et raf*]

rī'fle¹, v.t. & i. **1.** Search & rob, esp. of all that can be found in various pockets or storing-places; carry off as booty. **2.** Make spiral grooves in (gun or its barrel or bore) to produce rotatory motion in projectile (p.p. of projectile, with projections fitting such grooves). **3.** Shoot (t. & i.) with rifle. Hence **rif'**LING¹ n. [1 f. OF *rifler* graze, scratch; 2 (from 1635) ult. f. same source, cf. LG *rifeln*, G *riefeln*, Da. *rifle*, Sw. *reffla*; 3 f. foll.]

rī'fle², n. **1.** One of the grooves made in rifling a gun (obs.). **2.** (Formerly ~-*gun*) fire-arm with rifled barrel esp. one fired from shoulder; (pl.) troops armed with ~s. **3.** ~-*bird*, dark-green Australian bird; || R~ *Brigade*, regiment of British army; ~-*corps*, of volunteer ~men; ~(-)*green* n. & a., (of) dark green as in ~*man's uniform*; ~-GRENADE¹, ~*man*, soldier armed with ~, esp. member (R~*man* when prefixed = Private) of some ~ regiments in British army, also = ~-*bird*; ~-*pit*, excavation as cover for ~ men firing at enemy; ~*range*, distance ~ carries, place for ~-*practice*; ~-*shot*, distance~ carries, *good* etc.~-*marksman*, shot fired with~. [f. prec. 2]

rift, n., & v.t. **1.** Cleft, fissure, chasm, in earth or rock; rent, crack, split in an object, opening in cloud etc. (*little* ~ *within the lute*, often fig. of incipient madness or dissension); ~-*valley*, steep-sided formed by subsidence of earth's crust; hence ~LESS, ~Y² aa. **2.** v.t. (Usu. in p.p.) rend apart, cleave. [f. Scand.; cf. Da. *rift* a cleft, ON *ripta* to break (a bargain etc.)]

rig¹, v.t. & i. (-gg-), & n. **1.** Provide (ship), (of ship) be provided, with necessary spars, ropes, etc., or ~g¹ING¹(3) (g-) n., prepare (t. & i.) for sea in this respect; assemble & adjust parts of (aircraft); fit (*out, up,* or rarely abs.) with or *with* clothes or other equipment; set *up* (structure) hastily or as makeshift or by

utilizing odd materials; ~**ging-loft**, gallery in dockyard for fitting ~ging, (Theatr.) space over stage from which scenery is worked. **2.** n. Way ship's masts, sails, etc., are arranged, whence ~GED² (-gd) a.; (transf.) person's or thing's look as determined by clothes etc. (~*up*, *out*, such accessories). [etym. dub.; cf. Norw. *rigga* bind up]

rig⁴ n., & v.t. (-gg-). **1.** Trick, dodge, way of swindling; (Commerc.) = CORNER. **2.** v.t. Manage or conduct fraudulently (the market, cause artificial rise or fall in prices). [?]

Rig'a (or rē-), n. A port of the Baltic (~ *deal*, *hemp*, etc.; ~ *balsam*, essential oil distilled from kind of pine & used medicinally.

rigadoon', n. Lively dance for two persons; music for this dance. [F *rigaudon*]

rigs'cent, a. Growing rigid, rather stiff. So ~ENCE n. [f. L *rigescere* (*rigēre* be stiff, -ESCENT)]

rigg'er¹(-g-), n. In vbl senses (RIG⁴,²); also or esp. one who attends to the rigging of aircraft; (Mech.) hand-wheel; = OUT-RIGGER; = THIMBLE-~; ~, ship rigged in specified way. [-ER¹]

right (rīt), a., v.t. & i., n., & adv. **1.**(arch.), Straight (now only in ~ *line*, ~-*lined*). **2.** (Of angle) neither acute nor obtuse, of 90°, made by lines meeting not obliquely but perpendicularly, (*at* ~ *angles*, turning or placed with such angle, whence ~-ANGLED² (-ngzld) a.; involving ~ angle(s), not oblique, due ~ *sailing*, due N., S., E., or W.; ~ ASCENSION; ~ *cone*, *cylinder*, *prism*, etc., with ends or base perpendicular to axis). **3.** (Of conduct etc.) just, morally good, required by equity or duty, proper, (acted a ~ *part*; it is only ~ to tell you, that you should know), whence ~-**minded²** a., ~-**mind'edness** n. **4.** Correct, true, (~ *use of words*; did not give a ~ *account of the matter*; your opinions are ~ *enough*); the preferable or most suitable, the less wrong or not wrong, (which is the ~ *way* to —?; the ~ *man* in the ~ *place*; does no do it the ~ *way*; the ~ *heir*; cf. Mr, Miss, R~, destined husband, wife; took the ~ *way* to offend us; a fault on the ~ *side*; the ~ *side* of a fabric etc., that meant for show or use; so ~ *side up*; on the ~ *side of forty* etc., not yet 40 years old). **5.** In good or normal condition, sound, sane, satisfactory, well-advised, not mistaken, (in one's ~ *mind*, not mad etc.; is not ~ *in his head*; are you ~ *now*?, comfortable, recovered, etc.; all's ~ *with the world*; is as ~ *as a trivet*, *as rain*, etc., quite; set or put ~, *as a trivet*, restore to order, health, etc., also correct mistaken ideas of, also justify oneself usu. with person; get ~, bring or come into ~ state; ~, *you are*, forms of approval, or, & so also *all* ~, || ~ *oh!* sl., of assent to order or proposal), whence

|| ~'**EN⁶** (rīt-) v.t. (rare). **6.** (arch.), Right-ful, real, veritable, properly so called, (~ WHALE; ~ *cognac* etc.). **7.** (Of position) having the relation to front & back that equinoctial sunrise has to north & south, on or towards that side of human body of which the hand is normally more used, on or towards that part of an object which is analogous to person's ~ side or (with opposite sense) which is nearer to spectator's ~ hand, (cf. LEFT¹; ~ *side*, *eye*, etc.; ~ *wing* or *flank* of army etc.; ~ *bank*, on ~ side of one looking down stream; ~ CENTRE¹), **8.** ~ & *left²* adv., to or on both sides, on all hands, as the ground *divided*, *he was abused*, ~ & *left* adj., with or of contrary threads at two ends; n., ~ & *left shot*, also pugilist's two blows in quick succession with different hands. **9.** ~ *arm*, (fig.) one's most reliable helper. **10.** ~ *hand*; hand of ~ side; this as the better hand, as *put one's* ~ *hand to the work*; this w. ref. to hand-shaking, as *give the* ~ *hand of fellowship*; region or direction on this side of person, as *at*, *on*, *to*, one's ~ *hand*; one's indispensable or chief assistant; ~-*hand*, placed on the right hand, as ~-*hand man*, soldier on one's ~ hand in line, also assistant as above; ~-*hand screw*, with thread turning to ~; ~-*handed*, using ~ hand more than left; ~-*handed blow* etc., struck with ~ hand; ~-*handed tool* etc., made to suit ~ hand; ~-*handed rotation* etc.; ~-*hander*, ~-handed blow or person. **11.** ~ *turn*, into position at ~ angles with original one; ~-*about turn* or *face*, ~ turn prolonged to rear (see ABOUT¹ for mil. use); ~-*about*, ~-*about turn*, reversal of front, hurried retreat as in *send to the* ~-*about*, send packing, also as v.t. & i.=reverse or make reverse front; hence ~NESS (rīt-) n. **12.** vb. Restore to proper or straight or vertical position (~ *helm*, put it amid-ships; *boat* ~s *herself*; could not ~ the *boat*, *car*); ~ *oneself*, recover balance, (of ship) recover vertical position. **13.** Make reparation for to, avenge, (wrong, wronged person); vindicate, justify, re-habilitate. **14.** Correct (mistakes etc.), correct mistakes in, set in order, (often refl., as *that is a fault that will* ~ *itself*); hence ~ABLE (rīt-) a. **15.** n. What is just, fair treatment, (~ & *might*, ~ & *wrong*; *do one* ~, treat or think of him fairly; *by* ~ or *now now*; ~s, *if* ~ *were done*; *the* ~, the juster cause, as *God defend the* ~; *be in the* ~, have justice on one's side), the ~, have justice or truth on one's side. **16.** Justification, fair claim, being en-titled to privilege or immunity, (~ *to do*, *of doing*, *of search* etc.; ~ *divine* or DIVINE ~; *claims in* ~ *of his wife*; *reigns by* ~ *of worth*; *belongs to heir* or *by* ~); ~s & *duties*; *woman's* ~s, of equality with

men; ~ *of way*, ~ established by usage to pass over another's ground, also path subject to such ~; *Declaration* or *Bill of R~s*, ∥ constitutional settlement of 1689; *assert* or *stand on* one's ~s, refuse to relinquish them; *peeress in her own* ~, not by marriage; *admiration is her* ~), whence ~LESS (rit-) a. **17.** pl. ~ condition, true state, (*set* or *put to* ~s, arrange properly; *have not heard, do not know, the* ~s *of the case*). **18.** ~-hand part or region or direction (*is on your* or *the, to the,* ~; *to, from,* ~ *& left; work round the enemy's* ~); (Pol., usu. *R*~) conservative members of (orig. continental) parliament etc., whence ~WARD a. & adv., ~WARDS adv., (rit-). **19.** adv. Straight (*wind was* ~ *behind us*; *go* ~ *on; went* ~ *at him*; ~ *off, away*, chiefly U.S., immediately, without pause). **20.** All the way to, round, etc., completely (~ *round house; took gate* ~ *off hinges* ~ *round, turned* ~ *round*). **21.** Exactly, quite, (~ *in the middle*). **22.** Very, to the full, (*know* ~ *well; banqueted* ~ *royally; was* ~ *glad to hear*; ~ HONOURABLE, REVEREND). **23.** Justly, properly, correctly, aright, truly, satisfactorily, (*whether they act* ~ *or wrong*; *does not hold his pen, do the sum,* ~; *serves him* ~, is no worse than he deserves; *nothing goes* ~ *with me; if I remember* ~, *guessed* ~). **24.** To ~ hand (*eyes* ~!, order to soldiers dressing; *looks neither* ~ *nor left*). [com.-Teut., cf. Du. & G *recht* etc., also L *rectus* DIRECT²]

right·eous (rich´us), a. Just, upright, virtuous, law-abiding, (~ *person, life, action*). Hence ~LY² adv., ~NESS n. [OE *rihtwīs* (prec. n. + WISE a., or prec. a. + WISE n.) w. assim. to *bounteous* etc.]

right·ful (rīt-), a. (Of actions etc.) equitable, fair; (of persons) legitimately entitled to position etc. (*the* ~ *king, heir, owner*), (of office, property, etc.) that one is entitled to. Hence ~LY² adv., ~NESS n. [-FUL]

right·ly (rīt-), adv. Justly, fairly, properly, correctly, accurately, justifiably. [-LY²]

ri´gid, a. Not flexible, stiff, unyielding, (*a* ~ *bar, stem, frame, airship*); inflexible, harsh, strict, precise, punctilious, (~ *justice, principles, Catholics, adherence to rules, economy*). Hence or cogn. **rigid´ity** n., ~LY² adv. [f. L *rigidus* (as RIGOR)]

rig´marole, n. Rambling or meaningless talk or tale; (attrib.) incoherent. [prob. f. obs. *ragman roll*=catalogue, etym. dub.]

rig´or, n. (path.). Sudden chill with shivering before fever etc.; ~ *mort´is*, stiffening of body after death. [L (*rigēre* be stiff, -OR¹)]

rig´our (-ger), n. Severity, strictness, harshness, (pl.) harsh measures; strict enforcement of rules etc. (*with the utmost*

~ *of the law*); extremity or excess of weather, hardship, famine, etc., great distress; austerity of life, Puritanic strictness of observance or doctrine, so **rig´orism**(3), **rig´orist**(2), nn.; logical accuracy, exactitude. So **rig´orous** a., **rig´orously²** adv. [OF, f. L (prec.)]

rigs´dag (-z-), n. Danish Parliament. [Da.]

Rig-ve´da (-vā-), n. The chief VEDA. [f. Skr. *rigveda* (*ric* praise)]

·riks´dag, n. Swedish parliament. [Sw.]

rile, v.t. (sl.). Raise anger in, irritate. [var. of obs. & U.S. *roil* make muddy, cf. obs. F *ruiler* mix mortar]

rilie´vo (rēlyā-), n. = RELIEF², RELIEVO. [It.]

rill, n., & v.i. **1.** Small stream, runnel, rivulet; hence ~ET¹ n. **2.** v.i. Issue or flow as ~. [cf. Du. *ril*, G *rille*]

rille, n. (astron.). Trench or narrow valley of moon's surface. [G (prec.)]

rillètts´, -èttes´ (-ĕts), n. pl. Preparation of minced ham, chicken, fat, etc. [F (-*es*)]

rim¹, n., & v.t. (-mm-). **1.** Outer ring of wheel's framework, not including tire; frame of sieve; (poet.) circular object (*golden* ~, *crown*); (Naut.) surface of the water; raised edge or border, margin, verge, esp. of something more or less circular; ~*brake*, acting on ~ of wheel; hence ~LESS, (-)~MED² (-md), aa. **2.** v.t. Furnish with ~, serve as ~ to, edge, border. [OE *rima*, cf. ON *rime* ridge]

∥ **rim²**, n. (arch.). ~ (*of the belly*), peritoneum. [OE *rēoma*, cf. Du. *riem*, G *riemen*, strap]

rime¹ (RHYME), n., & v.t. & i. = RHYME¹˒². [earlier *rime* (RHYME) was corrected c. 1560 to RHYVHM, which served for senses *rhythm & rhyme* till *rhyme* was established c. 1700 as different.; obs. *rime* was revived c. 1870 & is often used by writers on prosody & literature]

rime², n., & v.t. (chiefly poet.). **1.** Hoarfrost; hence **rim´y²** a. **2.** v.t. Cover with ~. [OE & ON *hrīm*, cf. Du. *rijm*]

rim´er, n. = REAM²er. [dial. *rime* var. of REAM², -ER¹]

Rimm´on, n. Ancient deity worshipped at Damascus (*bow down in the house of* ~, compromise one's convictions). [2 *Kings* v. 18]

rim´ose, rim´ous, aa. (bot. etc.). Full of chinks or fissures. [f. L *rimosus* (*rima* chink, -OSE¹), -OUS]

rind, n., & v.t. Bark of tree or plant (vb, strip ~ from); peel of fruit or vegetable; harder enclosing surface of cheese or other substance; skin of bacon etc.; external aspect, surface. Hence ~´ED² a. [OE, cf. Du. *run*, G *rinde*]

rin´derpĕst, n. Disease of ruminants esp. oxen, cattle-plague. [G (*rinder* pl. of *rind* ox)]

ring¹, n., & v.t. & t. **1.** Circlet usu. of precious metal & often set with gem(s) worn round finger as ornament or token

(esp. of betrothal or marriage) or signet, or (usu. *nose*, *arm*, etc., ~) hung to or encircling other part of body. **2.** Circular appliance of any material & any (but esp., cf. *hoop*, no great) size. **3.** Raised or sunk or otherwise distinguishable line or band round, rim of, cylindrical or circular object. **4.** Circular fold, coil, bend, structure, part, or mark (~s of tree, concentric bands of wood corresponding in number to tree's years; *has lurid ~s round his eyes*; *puffing out ~s of smoke*; ~*s in water, circular ripples expanding from centre of agitation*). **5.** Persons, trees, etc., disposed in a circle, such disposition; (Commerce, etc.), combination of traders or politicians acting together for control of market or policy. **6.** Circular enclosure or space for circus-riding, prizefighting (PRIZE~), betting at races (*the ~*, bookmakers), showing of cattle, etc. **7.** Circular or spiral course (*make ~s round*, go or do things incomparably quicker than). **8.** ~*bark* v.t., cut ~ in bark of (tree) to kill it or to check its growth & bring it into bearing; ~*bolt*, bolt with ~ attached for fastening rope to etc.; ~*bone*, (horse-disease with) deposit of bony matter on pastern-bones; ~*cartilage*, ~*dove*, wood-pigeon; ORICOID; ~*fence*, completely enclosing estate etc.; ~*finger*, third esp. of left hand; ~*goal*, game in which light hoop is thrown towards goal with sticks; ~*haunt*, in which beasts are driven inwards by ~ of fire; ~*leader*, (one of) chief instigator(s) in mutiny, riot, etc.; ~*lock*, opened by right adjustment of several grooved ~s; ||~*man*, bookmaster; ~*master*, manager of circus performance; ~*neck*, ~*necked* plover or duck; ~*necked*, with band(s) of colour round neck; ~*net*, kind of salmon net, also of lace; ~*ouzel*, kind of bird allied to blackbird; ~*snake*, common European grasssnake (from coiling); ~*stand*, for keeping finger-~s on; ~*straked* (Bibl.), marked with ~s of colour round body; ~*tail*, female of hen-harrier, also golden eagle till its third year, also ~*tailed* opossum or phalanger; ~*tailed*, (of phalanger) with tail curled at end; ~*taw*, game with marbles in ~; ~*wall*, as ~*fence*; ~*worm*, skin-disease esp. of children in circular patches; hence (~)-ED² (-ngd). ~LESS, aa. **9.** vb. (Of hawk etc.) rise in spirals; (of hunted fox) take circular course. **10.** Encompass (usu. *round*, *about*, *in*; often in p.p.), hem in (game, cattle) by riding or beating in circle round them. **11.** Put ~ upon, put ~ in nose of (pig, bull), (~*the-bull*, game with ~ to be thrown or swung on to hook). **12.** ~-thrown or swung on to hook). **12.** ~-s, [com.-Teut.; OE *hring*, cf. ON *hringr*, Du. & G *ring*]

---

ring², v.i. & t. (*rang*, now rarely *rung*; *rung*), & n. **1.** Give forth clear resonant sound (as) of vibrating metal (*bell*, *trumpet*, *coin*, *sound*, ~*s*, often *out* etc.; *with a ~ing laugh*; *a shot rang out*; *a ~ing frost*, in which ground ~s under foot; ~ *true*, *false*, of coin tested by throwing on counter, & fig. of sentiments etc.); (of bell) ~ *to* or *for prayers*, *dinner*, etc., convey summons by ~ing, resound, re-echo, (*with sound*, *to sound* or its cause, *with fame* etc. or its theme, *with talk of*; often *again*). **3.** (Of utterance or other sound) ~ *in* one's *ears*, *heart*, etc., linger in one's hearing, haunt the memory. **4.** (Of ears) be filled with sensation as of bell-~ing (so *has a ~ing in the ears*) or *with sound*. **5.** Make (bell ~ (~ *the bell* (colloq.), be successful [from use of bell in machines for testing strength or skill], (also) strike a sympathetic note or ~*up bell*, raise church bell over beam & ~ it there; ~*ing engine*, pile-driver worked by ropes like peal of bells); throw (coin) on counter to test it. **6.** ~ bell as summons (~ *at door*, to get admittance etc.; *view*: ~ *off*, terminate telephone interview; ~ *curtain up* or *down* in theatre, direct it by bell to be raised or lowered). **7.** Sound (peal, knell, BOB² *major*, the CHANGE¹s) on bells (or with *bell* or *bells* as subj.; ~ *the knell of*, announce or herald abolition etc.). **8.** Announce (hour etc.) by sound of bell(s). **9.** Summon *up* etc. by ~*ing bell* (~ *up* on telephone, get or seek communication with; ~ *off*, terminate telephone interview; ~ *curtain up* or *down* in theatre, direct it by bell to be raised or lowered). **10.** Usher *in*, *out*, with bell-~ing. **11.** n. Set of (church) bells. **12.** ~ing sound, ~ing tone in voice etc., resonance of coin or vessel. **13.** Act of ~ing bell, ~ing bell (~ *up* on telephone, get or seek communication) ~ing sound so produced, (*three ~s for the hall porter*; *give bell a ~*; *heard a loud ~ at the door*); call on the telephone (*give me a ~*). [OE *hringan*, cf. ON *hringja*, G *ringen*, perh. imit.]

rin'gent (-j-), a. Gaping, grinning, (esp. bot. of wide labiate corolla). [as RICTUS, -ENT]

ring'er, n. 1. Quoit that falls round pin; fox that runs in ring when hunted. **2.** Bell~; device for ringing bell. [RING¹,², -ER¹]

ring'let, n. 1. (rare). Small ring, fairy ring on grass, ring-shaped mark etc. **2.** Curly lock of hair, curl, whence ~ED² -Y², aa. [-LET]

rink, n., & v.i. 1. Stretch of ice used for game of curling; sheet of natural or artificial ice, floor, for (roller-)skating. **2.** v.i. Skate on ~ esp. with roller-skates, whence ~ER¹ ¹n. [earlier sense *Jousting-ground*; from 14th c.; perh. f. OF *renc* RANK¹]

rinse, v.t. & n. **1.** Wash out or *out* (vessel, mouth) by filling with water etc., shaking, & emptying; pour liquid over or wash

lightly); put (clothes) through clean water to remove soap; clear (impurities) *out* or *away* by rinsing; wash (food) *down* with liquor. **2.** n. Rinsing (*give it a* ~). [f. F *rincer*, OF *raincer* perh.=med. L *re(sincerare* f. *sincerus* pure), RE- 8]

ri'ot, n., & v.i. & t. **1.** Loose living, debauchery. **2.** Loud revelry, a revel; unrestrained indulgence in or display or enjoyment of something (*a* ~ *of emotion, colour, sound*). **3.** (Hunt.) following of any scent indiscriminately (*run* ~, orig. of hounds doing this, now usu. fig. of person or his tongue or fancy throwing off all restraint). **4.** Disorder, tumult, disturbance of the peace, outbreak of lawlessness on part of a crowd || (*R*~ *Act*, by which persons not dispersing after official reading of part of it incur guilt of felony; *read the R*~ *Act*, lit., & joc. of parent etc. announcing that noise etc. is to cease); hence or cogn. ~**ous** a., ~**ously²** adv., ~**ousness**, (rare) ~**ry²**(2), nn. **5.** vb. Live wantonly, revel. **6.** Throw *away* (time, money), wear *out* (life), in dissipation. **7.** Make or engage in a political ~ or offence against the R~ Act, whence ~**ER²**(4) n. [f. OF *riote(r)*, cf. Pr. *riota*, It. *riotta*, etym. dub.]

rip¹, n. Worthless horse, screw; dissolute person, rake. [perh. var. of REP³]

rip², v.t. & i. (-pp-), & n. **1.** Cut or tear (thing) quickly or forcibly away from something (~ *out the lining*; ~ *the boards off*); make long cut or tear in, cut or tear vigorously apart (often *up*; *had his belly* ~*ped up*). **2.** Split (wood, rock), saw (wood) with the grain (~*saw*, used thus). **3.** Strip (roof) of tiles or slates or laths. **4.** Make (fissure, passage) by ~ping. **5.** Open *up* (wound, quarrel, sorrow, the past) again. **6.** Come violently asunder, split (intr.). **7.** Rush along (of ship, & transf.; so *let her* ~, do not check speed or interfere). **8.** || (part.; sl.; of, *rattling*). Fine, splendid, enjoyable, first-rate, (also as adv. with *good* etc., as *a* ~*ping good time*), whence ~**p'ing-ly²** adv. **9.** ~-**cord** (Aeron.), cord for releasing parachute from its pack. **10.** n. Act of ~ping; long tear or cut. [cf. Fris. *rippe*]

rip³, n. Stretch of broken water in sea or river, overfall. [perh. f. prec.]

ripa'rian, a. & n. **1.** Of, on, river-bank (esp. ~ *proprietor, rights*). **2.** n. ~ proprietor. [L *riparius* (*ripa* bank, -ARY²) + -AN]

ripe, a., & v.t. & i. **1.** Ready to be reaped, gathered, eaten, drunk, used, or dealt with, fully developed, mellow, mature, prepared or able *to* undergo something, in fit state *for*, (~ *corn, fruit, cheese, wine, seed;* ~ *lips, red & full like* ~ *fruit;* ~ *beauty,* of grown woman; ~ *scholar, scholarship, judgement, experience, understanding; die at a* ~ *age,* old; *persons of* ~ *years,* not immature; *opportunity* ~

to be seized; *is* ~ *to hear the truth; mood or person, plan, disease,* ~ *for mischief, execution, treatment; soon* ~ *soon rotten,* prov. depreciating precocity; hence **rip'en⁶** v.t. & i., ~**LY²**(-pl-) adv., ~'**NESS** (-pn-) n. **2.** vb. (chiefly poet.). = ~n. [OE *rīpe*, cf. Du. *rijp*, G *reif*]

ripo'ste, n., & v.i. **1.** Quick return thrust in fencing; (transf.) counterstroke, retort. **2.** v.i. Deliver ~. [F, f. It. *risposta* RESPONSE]

ripp'er, n. In vbl senses; esp.: tool for ripping roof; rip-saw; (sl.) ripping person or thing. [-ER¹]

rip'ple¹, n., & v.i. & v.t. **1.** Toothed implement used to clear away seeds from flax. **2.** v.t. Treat with ~. [cf. Du. *repel(en)*, G *riffel(en)*]

rip'ple² n., & v.i. & t. **1.** Ruffling of water's surface, small wave(s); wavy or crinkled appearance in hair, ribbons, etc.; gentle lively sound that rises & falls (esp. *a* ~ *of conversation*); ~*cloth*, soft woollen washing fabric with ~d surface used for dressing-gowns etc.; ~*mark*, ridge, ridged surface, left on sand or mud or rock by water or wind; hence **ripp'let¹** n., **ripp'ly³** a. **2.** vb. Form, flow *in*, show, agitate or mark with, sound like, ~s. [vb found earlier than n.; etym. dub.; cf. RIP³ (found later), -LE(3)]

Ripua'rian, a. Of the ancient Franks living on Rhine between Meuse & Moselle (esp. ~ *law*, code observed by them). [f. med. L *Rīpuarius* (perh. irreg. f. L *ripa* bank)+-AN]

Rip van Winkle (wing'kl), n. Person of utterly antiquated ideas or information. [hero of tale by W. Irving who slept 20 years]

rise¹ (-z), v.i. & t. (*rose* pr. rōz; ~n. pr. ri'zn; p.p., see ED¹(2), often with *is* etc.). **1.** Get up from lying or sitting or kneeling position, get out of bed, (of meeting etc.) cease to sit for business, recover standing or upright position, become erect, leave ground, come to life again or usu. *again or from the dead*, (~ *from table,* leave meal; *all rose to receive him; house,* i.e. theatre audience, ~*s at actress* etc., in universal applause; *found he could not, was too weak to,* ~; ~, *Sir Thomas* etc., formula in knighting; ~ *up early; Parliament will* ~ *next week; fell never to* ~ *again; the hair rose on his head; horse* ~*s on its hind-legs; horse* ~*s to a fence,* takes off for leap; *birds* ~ *well today*). **2.** Cease to be quiet, abandon submission, make revolt, (*if a wind should* ~; ~ *in arms, rebellion,* etc., *against oppression, oppressor; town rose on its garrison; gorge, stomach,* ~*s,* indignation or disgust is felt; *my whole soul* ~*s against it,* finds it intolerable). **3.** Come or go up, grow upwards, ascend, mount, soar, project or swell upwards, become higher, reach higher position or level or

amount, increase, incline upwards, come to surface, become or be visible above or above surroundings, develop greater energy or intensity; be progressive, (*sun, star, morning, dawn, ~s; the ~n sun; at owner's ~*, he to bear any contingent loss); *rising cupboard, kitchen lift; the rising generation, the young; smoke ~s; tree ~s 20 ft*, attains that height; *fabric rose like a dream; blisters ~*, form; *bread will not ~*, swell with yeast; *~s; should ~ above petty jealousies*, be superior to; *picture, idea, ~s before mind; river, tide, flood, level, rose 6 ft, is rising; the mercury, barometer or glass, is rising; spirits ~*, become more cheerful; *prices, demands, ~; a rising lawyer; a man likely to ~; ~ in the world*, attain higher social position; *~ to greatness; rising ground*, sloping up; *~ in a rising series; ~s in a gentle curve; the interest ~s with each ad; bubbles ~; fish ~s*, comes to surface to feed; *drowning man ~s three times; in the foreground ~s a castle; does not ~ above mediocrity; the wind is rising; her colour rose*, became brighter or deeper; ‖*rising 5, 14*, getting on for that age). 4. Develop powers equal to (*does not ~ to an occasion; rose to the emergency*, require). 5. Have origin, begin to be, flow, from, in, at, etc. (*river ~s from a spring, in the Grampians, etc.; earth & heaven rose at His word; the difficulty ~s from misapprehension*). 6. (rare, usu. poet.) Arise (*a feud, rumour, rose*). 7. ((Causative in spec. senses) make or see (*did not ~ a fish, a bird, all day; ~ ship*, see it appear from top downwards in approaching it). [com.-Teut.; OE *rīsan* (usu. *arīsan* ARISE), cf. Du. *rijzen*, G (of sun) *reisen*]

rise² (-z), n. 1. Coming up of sun etc. (rare; *at ~ of sun, day*; cf. *sun~* etc.). 2. Ascent, upward slope, knoll, hill, (*came to a ~ in the road; chapel stands on a ~*). 3. Social advancement, upward progress, increase in power, rank, value, price, amount, height, pitch, (*wages, price, had a ~ in life; the ~ & fall of statesmen; the ~ of the tide is 30 ft*; ‖*rates rise for a ~*, higher wages; *prices are on the ~*, increasing). 4. Movement of fish to surface (*not a sign of a ~*; fig., *get or take a ~ out of one*, draw him into display of temper or other foible). 5. Vertical height of step, arch, incline, etc., (also **ris'er¹** (-z) n. f. prec.), vertical piece connecting two treads of staircase. 6. Origin, start, (*has, takes, its ~ in, from; give ~ to*, occasion, suggest). [f. prec.]

ris'ible (-z-), a. Inclined to laugh, so **ris'IB'ILITY** (-z-) n.; of laughter (*~ nerves, faculties*, etc.); (rare) laughable, ludicrous. [f. LL *rīsibilis* (*rīdēre rīs-* laugh, -IBLE)]

ris'ing (-z-), n. In vbl senses: esp.: *~ (-again)*, resurrection; insurrection, re-volt; boil, pimple. [-ING¹]

risk, n. & v.t. 1. Hazard, chance of or of bad consequences, loss, etc., exposure to mischance, (*there is the ~ of his catching cold; run ~s, a ~, the ~*, often *~*, expose oneself or be exposed to loss etc.; *take ~s* etc., expose oneself so; *at the ~ of his life; at owner's ~*, he to bear any contingent loss); *~-money*, allowance to cashier to cover accidental deficits; hence *~ful*, injury or loss; venture on, take the chances of, (*~ the jump, a battle, a sprained ankle*). [f. F *risque(r)* f. It. *risco* n., *riscare* dub.]

risott'ō (-z-), n. Stew made with rice, chicken, onions, etc. [It.]

ris'kẏ, a. 1. Hazardous, full of risk. 2. (Also, & after, F *risqué* pr. rēs'kā) involving dangerous suggestion of indecency, offending against propriety, (of story), dramatic situation, etc.). Hence ~ILY adv., ~INESS n. [f. 2]

riss'ōle, n. Fried ball or cake of meat or fish mixed with bread-crumbs etc. [F, perh. ult. f. L *russeolus* reddish]

ritardan'dō (rē-), a. mus. direction. Slower. [It.]

rite, n. (Form of) procedure, action required or usual, in) a religious or solemn ceremony or observance (*the ~s of hospitality; the ~ of confirmation; burial or funeral ~s; conjugal or nuptial ~s*, sexual intercourse between husband & wife; *the ~*, body of usages characteristic of a Church). Hence ~LESS (-t-) a. [f. L *rītus -ūs*]

rit'ual, a. & n. 1. Of, with, consisting in, involving, religious rites; hence ~LY¹ adv. 2. n. Prescribed order of performing religious service; book containing this; performance of *~* acts, whence (w. implication of excess) ~ISM(3), ~IST(2), nn.; ~istically adv., ~ISTIC(2, 3) v.i. & t. [f. L *ritūalis* (prec., -AL)]

‖**riv'age**, n. (poet.). Coast, shore, bank. [F (OF *rive* f. L *rīpa* bank, -AGE)]

riv'al, n., attrib. a., & v.t. & i. (-ll-). 1. Person's competitor for some prize (esp. a woman's or man's love) or in some pursuit or quality (also of things; *without a ~*, unapproached for excellence etc.); hence ~RY(2, 4), ~SHIP, nn. 2. adj. That is a *~* or are *~s*. 3. vb. Vie with, be comparable to, seem or claim to be as good etc. as; (rare) be in ~RY. [f. L *rivālis* (*rīvus* stream) orig.=on same stream]

rive, v.t. & i. (~d; *~n* pr. rī'vn, rarely ~d). Rend, cleave, wrench *away* or *off* or *from*, strike asunder, (arch., poet.); (of artisan) split (wood, stone), make (laths) by splitting, whence **rīv'er¹** ['ER¹(1)] n.; be split, gape under blow etc., (of wood etc.), admit of splitting. [f. ON *rīfa* perh. cogn. w. G *reiben* rub]

‖**riv'el**, v.i. & t. (arch.; -ll-). Wrinkle, crumple, shrivel. [prob. back formation

f. **rivelled**, OE *rifelede* perh.f. +*rifel* a fold +.-ED²]

riven. See RIVE.

riv'er², n. (for *river*¹ see RIVE). Copious stream of water flowing in channel to sea or lake or marsh or another ~ (||*the* ~ often prefixed to name, as *the* ~ *Thames*; *the boundary between life & death*; copious flow or stream of (*a* ~ *of lava*; ~*s of blood*, much bloodshed); (attrib., prefixed to many names of animals, plants, & things) living in, situated or used on, ~(s); ~-BED¹(2); ~-*god*, mythological being dwelling in & personifying a ~; ~-*horse*, hippopotamus; ~-*side*, ground along ~'s bank (often attrib., as *a* ~*side villa*). Hence (-)~ED²(-erd), ~LESS, aa. [f. OF *rivere* f. pop. L +*riparia* (L *ripa* bank, -ARY¹)].

riv'erain, a. & n. **1.** Of river or its neighbourhood; situated, dwelling, by river. **2.** n. Person dwelling by river. [F (*rivière* as prec., -AN)]

riv'erine, a. Of, on, river or its banks, riparian. [-INE¹]

riv'et, n., & v.t. **1.** Nail or bolt for holding together metal plates etc., its headless end being beaten out or pressed down after passing through two holes. **2.** v.t. Clinch (bolt); join or fasten with ~s (*together, down, to, into, on* adv. or prep., etc.); fix, make immovable, (eyes, attention, etc., *upon*); engross (attention) of; hence ~ER¹(1, 2) n. [vb f. n., OF (*river* clinch, etym. dub.)]

rivière (-ēā, or rēvyā'r), n. Gem necklace, esp. of more than one string. [F, as RIVER²]

roach¹, n. Small freshwater fish allied to carp (*sound as a* ~, in firstrate health etc.); ~-*backed, -bellied* (convex in profile). [f. OF *roche* etym. dub.]

roach², n. (naut.). Upward curve in foot of square sail. [?]

roach³, n. = COCKROACH. [abbr.]

road¹, n. **1.** (Usu. pl.; also ~*stead*) piece of water near shore in which ships can ride at anchor. **2.** Line of communication between places for use of foot-passengers, riders, & vehicles (*on the* ~, travelling; *take the* ~, set out; *the* ~, the highway; ||*take the* ~ *to the* ~, arch., become highwayman; *rule of the* ~, custom regulating side to be taken by vehicles, riders, or ships, meeting or passing each other). **3.** Way of getting to the (~ *to York, ruin, success*; *royal* ~ *to*, way of attaining without

trouble). **4.** One's way or route (*in the, my,* etc. ~; colloq., obstructing someone or something; *so get out of the, my,* etc., ~). **5.** ~-*book*, describing ~s of country etc., itinerary; ~ *fund* (for construction & maintenance of ~s & bridges); ~ *hog*, reckless or inconsiderate motorist or cyclist; ~ *house*, inn on main ~ in country district; ~'*man* (repairing ~s); ~-*sense*, capacity for safe handling of vehicles on the ~; ~'*side*, border of ~ (esp. attrib., as ~*side plants, inn*); ~'*way*, ~, central part of ~ (opp. *side-path*), part of bridge or railway used for traffic; ~'*worthy*, fit to be used on the ~. Hence (-)~ED², ~LESS, aa. [OE *rdd* (*vidan* RIDE)]

road², v.t. (Of dog) follow up (game-bird, or abs.) by foot-scent. [?]

road'ster, n. Ship at anchor in roadstead; horse, bicycle, etc., for use on the road; experienced traveller. [-STER]

roam, v.i. & t., & n. Ramble (v., & rarely n. as *a half-hour's* ~), wander; walk or travel unsystematically over or through or about (country, seas, etc.). [?]

roan¹, a. & n. **1.** (Of animal) with coat of which the prevailing colour is thickly interspersed with another, esp. bay or sorrel or chestnut mixed with white or grey (often with chief colour prefixed, as *black, blue, red,* ~). **2.** n. ~ horse, cow. [OF, cf. Pr. *rouan*, It. & Sp. *roano*]

roan², n. Soft sheepskin leather used in bookbinding as substitute for morocco. [perh. f. *Rouen* in France]

roar (rōr), v.i. & t., & n. **1.** (Utter, send forth) loud deep hoarse sound (as) of lion, person or company in pain or rage or loud laughter, the sea, thunder, cannon, furnace, etc., (*the* ~ *of the waves*; ~*s of laughter*; *lions* ~*ing after their prey*; ~*ed with pain or laughter or for mercy*; *you need not* ~, talk so loud; *set table in a* ~, make company laugh loud). **2.** (Of horse) make loud noise in breathing due to disease, whence ~ER¹, ~ING¹, (rōr-), nn. **3.** (Of place) be full of din, re-echo, (often *again*). **4.** Say, sing, utter, (words, chorus, oath, etc., often *out*) in loud tone. **5.** Make *deaf, hoarse,* etc., put *down*, by ~ing. **6.** (part.). Riotous, noisy, boisterous, brisk, (*a* ~*ing night*, stormy, also spent in revelry; *a* ~*ing blade*, arch., fast liver; *the* ~*ing game*, curling; ~*ing forties*, see FORTY; *in* ~*ing health*; *drive a* ~*ing trade*). [n. f. vb, OE *rárian*, cf. LG *raren*, G *rehren*, prob. imit.]

roast, v.t. & i. (p.p. in vb forms ~ed, as adj. ~), & n. **1.** Cook (esp. meat) by exposure to open fire or now usually in oven (*prefers* ~ *beef, his mead* ~*ed*); heat or calcine (ore) in furnace; heat (coffee-beans) as preparation for grinding; expose (victim for torture, oneself or some part for warmth) to fire; ridicule,

banter, chaff; undergo ~ing; (part.) very hot; ~*ing-jack*, appliance keeping meat in motion while ~ing. **2.** n. ~ meat or a dish of it (*rule the* ~, be master); opera-tion of ~ing. [n. partly f. OF *rost*, partly f. vb, f. OF *rostir* f. Teut. (OHG *rôsten* f., *rôst* gridiron)]

roast′er, n. In vbl senses: esp.: kind of oven for roasting; ore-roasting furnace; coffee-roasting apparatus; pig, potato, etc., fit for roasting. [-ER¹]

rob, v.t. (-bb-). Despoil (person etc.) of or of property by violence, feloniously plunder (person, place, often *of*), deprive of what is due, (~ PETER); (abs.) commit robbery. So ~b′er [-ER¹], ~b′ERY(2, 4), n. [f. OF *rob(b)er* f. Teut. (REAVE)]

robe, n. & v.t. & i. **1.** Any long loose outer garment (rare, poet., metaph.); (trade name of) kind of lady's dress in one piece; outer garment of baby in long-clothes; (often pl.) longer outer garment worn as indication of wearer's rank, office, profession, etc., gown, vestment, (*the long* ~, *legal or clerical dress*; *gentle-men of the long* ~, lawyers); ~*de-chambre* (F.), dressing-gown, wrapper. **2.** vb. Invest (person) in ~, dress; assume one's ~s or vestments. [OF, conn. w. prec., orig. sense *booty*]

▌Rôb′ert, n. (colloq.). A policeman. [see BOBBY]

rob′in, R~, n. (Also ~ *redbreast*) small red-breasted bird; (with or without dis-tinctive epithet) kinds of Amer. Colonial, & Indian bird; ~, ~ *s*, in plant names, eye, herb-Robert; ground-ivy, ‖~*'s-eye*, ‖*R~-run-the-hedge*, ‖~*'s-eye*, sportive goblin; *R~ Goodfellow*, a medieval forest outlaw; ROUND¹~, (type of fam. for *Robert*]

rôb′orant, a. & n. (med.). Strengthening (drug). [L *roborare* (*robur -oris* strength)]

-ANT]

rob′ôt, n. **1.** An apparently human auto-maton, an intelligent & obedient but im-personal machine; (transf.) machine-like person. **2.** Automatic traffic signal. **3.** Flying bomb. [term in Capek's play R.U.R.; cf. Pol. *robotnik* workman]

rôb′urite (-ber-), n. A strong flameless ex-plosive. [L *robur* strength, -ITE¹(2)]

robust′, a. (~er, ~est). Of strong health & physique, not slender or delicate or weakly,(of persons, animals, plants, body, health, etc.); (of exercise, discipline, etc.) tending to or requiring strength, in-vigorating, vigorous; (of intellect, etc.) sensible, straightforward, not given to nor confused by subtleties. Hence ~LY² adv., ~NESS n. [f. L *robustus* (*robur* strength)]

robus′tious, a. Boisterous, self-assertive, noisy. [earlier in common use = prec.; now chiefly w. ref. to *Hamlet* III. ii. 10] Arab. *rokh*]

---

rôc′ambôle, n. Kind of leek, Spanish garlic. [F, etym. dub.]

rôch′et, n. Surplice-like vestment used chiefly by bishops & abbots. [OF f. Teut. (G *rock* coat)]

rock¹, n. **1.** Solid part of earth's crust underlying soil (*dug down to the living* ~; often *bed-*~; *built, founded, on the* ~, lit., & fig. secure; *R~ of ages*, Christ); mass of this projecting & forming a hill, cliff, etc., or standing up into or out of sea etc., from bottom (*the R~*, Gibraltar; *run upon the* ~, *see* ~*s ahead*, etc., of lit. or fig. shipwreck or danger of it; *on the* ~*s*, sl., hard up; ~*of water etc.*, ref. to *Numb.* xx. 11). **2.** Stone as a substance (*a mass, needle, etc.*), large detached stone, boulder; (Geol.) any particular igneous or stratified mineral constituent of earth's crust including sands, clays, etc. **3.** Kinds of hard sweetmeat (usu. *almond etc.* ~). **4.** (Also *blue* ~) = ~*pigeon*. **5.** ~*bed*, base of ~, rocky bottom; ~*bird*, esp. puffin; ~*bottom*, (colloq., of prices etc.) very lowest; ~*cake*, bun with hard rough surface; ~*cork*, variety of asbestos; ~*crystal*, transparent colourless silica or quartz usu. in hexagonal prisms; ~*dove*, ~*pigeon*; ~*drill*, ~*boring tool or machine*; ~*English*, mixed language of Gibraltar; ~*fever*, kind of enteric pre-valent at Gibraltar; ~*fish*, kinds of goby, bass, wrasse, etc.; ~*garden*, artificial mound or bank of stones with ~*plants* etc. planted in the interstices, garden in which ~*eries are the chief feature*; ~*goat*, ibex; ~*hewn*, cut out of the ~; ~*leather*, as ~*cork*; ~*ling* [-LING¹], kinds of fish esp. sea-loach; ~*oil*, native naphtha or petroleum; ~*whistler*, Alpine marmot; ~*wood*, as ~*cork*; ~*work or* ~*ERY(3) n., pile of rough stones with soil in interstices for growing ferns etc. on, also natural group or display of* ~*s. Hence* ~*LESS, ~LIKE, aa., ~′LET n.* [f. OF *roke, rocque, roche*, etym. dub.]

rock², n. (hist.). Distaff. [cf. Du. *rokken*, G *rocken*, It. *rocca*]

rock³, v.t. & i.; & n. **1.** Move (t. & i.) gently to & fro (as) in cradle, set or keep (cradle etc.) or (of cradle etc.) be in such motion, (~ *him to sleep*; *ship* ~*ing on*, ~*ed by the waves*; *sat* ~*ing himself or* ~*ing in his chair*; ~*ed in security, hopes, etc.*); (Gold-min.) work (CRADLE), work cradle; shake in cradle; sway (t. & i.) from side to side, shake, oscillate, reel, (*earthquake*

~s house, house ~s, a ~ing gait). 2. ~ing-chair, mounted on rockers, or with seat arranged to ~; ~ing-horse, wooden horse on rockers for child; ~ing-stone, poised boulder easily ~ed; ~ing-turn in skating, from any edge to same in opposite direction with body revolving away from convex of first curve (counter-~ing-turn or -rocker or counter, same turn with body revolving away from concave); ~-shaft, that oscillates about axis without making complete revolutions; ~-staff, part of apparatus working smith's bellows. 3. n. ~ing motion, spell of ~ing. [OE roccian; cf. Du. rukken, G rücken, tug]

rock′er, n. In vbl senses; esp.: one of the curved bars on which cradle etc. rocks (off one's ~, sl., crazy); gold-miner's cradle; skate with highly curved blade (Skat.). ~, counter-~=(counter-)ROCK³ing-turn. [ROCK³,-ER¹]

rock′et¹, n. Kinds of plant of which some are used as salad & some grown for flowers (Garden, Roman, etc., ~; R-gentle; Base ~, wild mignonette; Blue ~, kinds of wolfsbane & larkspur, also blue-bell). [f. F roquette f. It. ruchetta (ruca f. L eruca,-ETTE)]

rock′et², n., & v.t. & i. 1. Cylindrical paper or metal case that can be projected to height or distance by ignition of contents, used in firework displays, for signalling, to carry line to ship in distress, etc.; projectile containing its own propellant & depending for its flight on the reaction set up by a continuous jet of rapidly expanding gases released in the propellant by ignition (e.g. of cordite) or by the mixture of two liquids (e.g. alcohol & liquid air). 2. vb. Bombard with ~s; (of horse or its rider) bound upwards or dart like ~; (of prices etc.) rise steeply; (of pheasant etc.) fly straight upwards, fly fast & high, whence ~ER¹ n. [f. F roquet or It. rocchetta (rocca ROCK², w. ref. to cylindrical shape),-ETTE]

rock′(ȳ, &c.) (pl.). 1. Of rock, full of or abounding in rocks, (the R-y Mountains, or as n. the R-ies, western N.-Amer. range); like rock in ruggedness, firmness, solidity, etc. 2. (rare). Unsteady, tottering. Hence ~ilY² adv., ~iNESS n. [ROCK¹³,-Y²]

rococo, a. & n. 1. Of a style of art prevalent in Europe c. 1730–80. 2. (Of furniture, architecture, etc., also of literary style) highly ornamented, florid. 3. (obs.). Antiquated, out of date. 4. n. The ~ style of art. [F, perh. f. rocaille pebble-work]

rod, n. 1. Slender straight round stick growing as shoot on tree or cut from it or made from wood, switch, wand, (occas. as symbol of office etc., see esp. BLACK¹ ~; AARON'S- ROD; divining, dowsing, ~, see DOWSING). 2. Such stick, or bundle of twigs, for use in caning or flogging (the ~,

use of this; spare the ~ & spoil the child; make etc. a ~ for one's own back, prepare trouble for oneself; kiss the ~, take punishment meekly or gladly; have a ~ in pickle for, be ready to punish when time comes). 3. =FISH²ing-~. 4. (Also ~′man & ~′STER n.) angler. 5. (As measure)=PERCH². 6. Slender metal bar, connecting bar, shaft, (curtain, piston, etc., ~). 7. (Physiol.) ~-shaped structure. Hence ~′LESS, ~′LIKE, aa., ~′LET n. [OE rodd, cf. ON rudda club]

rode. See RIDE.

rōd′ent, a. & n. 1. (Animal) of the order Rodentia with strong incisor & no canine teeth, whence **rōden′tial** (-shl) a. 2. Gnawing (esp. in Path. of ulcers). [f. L rodere ros-gnaw]

rōde′o (-dāō), n. A round-up of cattle on a western American range for branding etc., enclosure for this; exhibition of motor-cycle feats etc. [Sp., f. rodear go round]

rōdomontā̄de′, n., a., & v.i. 1. Boastful, bragging, (saying or talk). 2. v.i. Brag, talk big; hence ~ER¹ n. [vb & adj. f. n., F (Rodomont f. It. Rodomonte character in Orlando Furioso,-ADE]

rōe¹, n.(collect. sing. occas. for pl.). Small kind of European & Asiatic deer; ~′buck, ~′deer, ~ ~; ~′deer, ~ ~. [com.-Teut.; OE rāha, cf. Du. ree, G reh]

rōe², n. Mass of eggs (also hard ~) in fish's ovarian membrane (~-corn, one egg); soft ~, male fish's milt; ~-stone, oolite. Hence (-)rōeD²(rōd)a. [cf. MDu., MLG, MHG, roge]

rogā′tion, n. 1. (Eccl., usu. pl.) litany of the saints chanted on the three days before Ascension Day (R-~ days, these; R-~ week, Sunday, including, preceding, them; ~ flower, milk-wort), whence ~AL (-shon-) a. 2. (Rom. Ant.) law proposed before the people by consul or tribune (Licinian etc. ~s, proposed by Licinius etc.). [f. L rogatio (rogare ask,-ATION)]

Rō′ger, n. Male name (the jolly ~, pirates' black flag; ~ or Sir ~ de Coverley (de kŭv′erli), a country-dance & tune).

rōgue (-g), n., & v.t. 1. Idle vagrant (arch.); knave, rascal, swindler, (often playfully of mischievous child or waggish or arch-mannered person). 2. Inferior plant among seedlings (vb, weed out ~s from). 3. (Also ~ elephant, buffalo, etc.) wild beast, esp. elephant, driven or living apart from the herd & of savage temper. 4. Shirking racehorse or hunter. Hence **rōg′uERY(4) (-ger-) n., rōg′uISH¹(-gi-) a., rōg′uISHNESS** n. [16th-c. cant wd, etym. dub.]

roi (rwah), n. (F for) king; ~ fainéant (see Ap.; lit. = King Do-nothing), ruler, chairman, etc., who is a mere figure-head like the Merovingian kings whose power was usurped by mayors of the palace; le ~ le veult, le ~ s'avisera, (see Ap.), forms

of giving, refusing, the royal assent to parliamentary bill, = the king wills it, will consider.

roi`nek`, roo`i-, n. New-comer, esp. British or European immigrant, in S. Africa; (in Boer war) British soldier. [S.-Afr.-Du. (*rooi-*), = red-neck]

rois`ter, v.i. Revel noisily, be uproarious; (esp. in part. as adj.). Hence ~ER¹, ~ING¹, n. [f. obs. *roister* roisterer f. F *rustre* var. of *ruste* cf. L RUSTICUS]

Rol`and, n. Name of nephew of Charlemagne celebrated in legend often with his comrade Oliver (*a ~ for an Oliver*, effective retort).

role, rôle (rōl), n. Actor's part; one's function, what one is appointed or expected or has undertaken to do. [F *rô-*, as foll.]

roll¹, n. **1.** Cylinder formed by turning flexible fabric such as paper or cloth over & over upon itself without folding (*~s of carpet, printing-paper*, etc.; SWISS ~); (in Ionic capital) *volute.* **2.** Document, esp. official record, in this form (∥ *Master of the R~s*, judge of Court of Appeal with charge of certain public records; ∥ *the R~s*, buildings in which these were formerly kept now superseded by Public Record Office, also court of Master of the R~s); register or catalogue (*in the ~ of saints; a long ~ of heroes; on the ~ of fame*; RENT-~; ~ *of honour*, esp. list of those who have died for their country in war); ∥ the official list of qualified solicitors (*strike off the ~s*, debar from practising for dishonesty etc.; a list of persons esp. soldiers or schoolboys used to detect absentees (*~-call*, calling over of this). **3.** More or less (semi)cylindrical straight or curved mass of anything however formed (*a ~ of butter, soap, straw, tobacco, hair; has ~s of fat on him; ~ of bread or* usu. *~, small loaf esp. for breakfast use*); (Archit., also *~-moulding*) moulding of convex section. **4.** Turned-back edge of something, e.g. coat-collar. **5.** (Bookbind.) revolving patterned tool for marking cover. **6.** Cylinder or roller. [f. OF *rolle* (now *rôle*) f. L *rotulus* collat. form of *rotula* (foll.)]

roll², v.t. & i., & n. **1.** Move (t. & i.) or send or go in some direction by turning over & over on axis often with aid of gravitation (*~ barrel; barrel started ~ing; ball, coin, ~ed under the table, into a hole; river ~s down stones; ~ing stone GATHERS no moss; planets ~ on their courses; years ~ on or by; go smoothly; ~ one over, send him ~ing or sprawling; ~ make revolve between two surfaces* (*~ing a marble between his palms*); wrap usu. up in by *~ing motion* (*~ed himself up in the blankets*). **2.** Change direction (of) with rotatory motion (*his eyes ~ strangely; ~ed his eyes on us*). **3.** Wallow, turn about in fluid or loose medium, (of horse etc.)

lie on back & kick about, (*porpoise, swimmer, ~s in the water; ~ing in money, luxury, ease; mule tried to ~*, as way of getting rid of rider or load). **4.** Sway or rock (t. & i.), walk with swaying gait as of sailor, reel, (*~ed himself from side to side; ship ~s & pitches; he ~ed up to her*). **5.** Undulate, show undulating surface or motion, go or propel or carry with such motion, (sea, river, ~s; river ~s its waters to sea; waves ~ in; smoke ~s up; chimney ~s up smoke; the mist ~ed away; a ~ing expanse or plain). **6.** Utter or be uttered, sound, with vibratory or undulating or trilling effect (*~ out verses, song*, etc.; *thunder, drum, organ, voice, echo, ~s; ~ one's r's*). **7.** (Of wheeled vehicle) advance or convey usu. *along, by*, etc., (of person) be so conveyed, (*carriage ~ed along, ~ed them by; he ~ed past in his carriage; ~ing-stock*, railway company's wagons & trucks). **8.** Flatten by passing roller over or by passing between rollers (*~ lawn, metal, paste for pies*, etc.; *~ed gold*, thin coating so applied; *~ing-pin*, roller for paste; *~ing-press*, copperplate-printer's press with revolving cylinder, also press with rollers for various purposes). **9.** Turn (t. & i.) over & over upon itself into more or less cylindrical shape (*~s itself into a ball or ~s up*). **10.** Form (t. & i.) (into) cylindrical or spherical shape, or accumulate into mass, by rolling (*~ the way to a greatcoat; hedgehog ~s itself into a ball or ~s up*). **11.** ~*-top desk*, with flexible cover sliding in curved grooves. **12.** ~ *up*, (Mil.) drive flank of (enemy line) back & round so that line is shortened or surrounded, (intr., colloq.) appear on the scene, turn up; hence ~ABLE a. **13.** n. ~*ing motion* (*the ~ of the sea, ship*); (Aeron.) complete revolution about the longitudinal axis; spell of ~ing (*a ~ on the grass*); ~*ing gait*. **14.** Quick continuous beating of drum; long peal of thunder or shout; rhythmic flow of words. [f. OF *roller* f. ROLL¹]

(L *rotula* dim. of ROTA)

roll`er, n. **1.** In vbl senses; esp.: cylinder of wood, stone, metal, etc., & of various proportions used alone or as rotating part of machine for lessening friction, smoothing ground, pressing, stamping, crushing, spreading printer's ink, rolling up cloth on etc.; (usu. ~ *bandage*) long surgical bandage rolled up for convenience of applying; kind of tumbler-pigeon; long swelling wave; brilliant-plumaged bird allied to crows, also German breed of canary, [G. f. *rollen* to roll]; ~ *skating* (~ *towel*, endless, working on ~.

roll`ey. See RULLEY.

roll`ick, v.i., & n. **1.** Be jovial, indulge in

high spirits, enjoy life boisterously, revel, (esp. in part. as adj.). **2.** n. Exuberant gaiety; frolic, spree, escapade. [?]

rol'y-pol'y, n. & a. **1.** (Also ~ *pudding*) pudding made of sheet of paste covered with jam etc., formed into roll & boiled. **2.** adj. (Usu. of child) podgy, plump. [prob. formed on ROLL²]

Rom, n. (pl. ~*a*). Male gipsy, (pl.) gipsies. [Romany wd]

Romā'ic, a. & n. (Of, in, etc.) the vernacular language of modern Greece. [f. Gk *Rōmaïkos* Roman (used esp. of Eastern empire)]

Romā'ïka, n. National dance of modern Greece. [mod. Gk (-*kē*), orig. fem. adj. (prec.)]

Rōm'an¹, n. **1.** Citizen, soldier, native, or inhabitant, of (ancient Rome, member of ancient~State, (*King, Emperor, of the~s*, sovereign head of Holy Roman Empire); inhabitant of medieval or modern Rome. **2.** pl. Christians of ancient Rome (~s, or in full *Epistle to the ~s*, N.-T. book, abbr. *Rom.*). **3.** (Print.) roman¹ type (abbr. in press-correcting, *rom.*). **4.** = ROMAN CATHOLIC. [f. L *Romanus* (ROME, -AN)]

Rōm'an², a. **1.** Of ancient Rome or its territory, people, or (rarely; usu. *Latin*) language (~ *Empire*, that established by Augustus 27 B.C. & divided by Theodosius A.D. 395 into WESTERN or LATIN & eastern or Greek empires, of which the eastern lasted till 1453, & the western, after lapsing in 476, was revived 800 by Charlemagne & continued to exist as the *Holy ~ Empire* till 1806; ~ *law*, code developed by ancient Romans & forming basis of many modern codes; ~ *pottery, bricks, road*, etc., surviving from period of ~ rule; ~ *cement*, trade name for a hydraulic cement named after ancient~ kind; ~ *balance, beam*, or *steelyard*, ordinary steelyard; ~ *simplicity, honesty, virtue, patriotism*, etc., as of Romans of early Republic; ~ *nose*, with high bridge, aquiline, whence~, of person or horse, ~-**nōsed²**(-zd) a.; ~ *letters* or *type*, of the plain upright type used in ordinary print, opp. *Gothic* or *black letter* & *italic*; ~ *alphabet*, that used by Romans & still with slight modifications in W. Europe; ~ *numerals*, the letters I, V, etc. used in composing number-symbols, see below* for mod. use, & cf. ARABIC; ~ *architecture*, COMPOSITE, & see ORDER¹; ~ *history, historian*, etc., of ancient Rome). **2.** Of papal Rome, esp.= ROMAN CATHOLIC, whence~ISH²(2) a., ~IZER¹ n. **3.** Of medieval or modern Rome (~ *school*, painting school of Raphael; ~ *fever*, malaria prevalent at Rome; ~ SNAIL; ~ *vitriol*, sulphate of copper; ~ CANDLE). Hence ~ISM²(3, 4), ~IST²(2,3), nn., ~is'tic a., ~IZE²(2, 3, 4) v.t. & i., ~IZĀ'TION n. **Roman²o-** comb. form. *Mod. use of ~ numerals, differing in

some respects from the ancient: The only symbols now used are I=1, V=5, X=10, L=50, C=100, D=500, M=1000; the letters composing a number are ranged in order of value, & the number meant is found by addition, e.g. MDCLXVI = 1666; if a letter or set of letters is placed before a letter of higher value, it is to be subtracted from it before the addition is done, e.g. IIC=98, MCM=1900; IIII is usu. preferred to IV on clock-faces. [as prec.]

Rōm'an Cath'olic, a. & n. (Member) of the Church of Rome. Hence **Rōman-Cath'olicly**, **Rōman-Cath'olicism²** adv., **Rōman-Cath'olicism³**(3) n. [f. c. 1600, perb. orig. as non-controversial compromise between *Roman(ist)*, *Romish*, etc., & *Catholic*]

romance', n. & a., & v.i. **1.** (R~), Vernacular language of old France mainly developed but distinguished from Latin, corresponding language of Spain, Provence, etc.; (collect.) the languages descended from Latin. **2.** adj. (R~; of languages) thus descended. **3.** Medieval tale usu. in verse of some hero of chivalry (named as written in R~). **4.** Prose or rarely verse tale with scene & incidents remote from everyday life, class of literature consisting of such tales; set of facts, episode, love affair, etc., suggesting such tales by its strangeness or moving nature; atmosphere characterizing such tales, mental tendency to be influenced by it, sympathetic imaginativeness, whence ~LESS (-sl-) a. **5.** (An) exaggeration, (a) picturesque falsehood. **6.** (Mus.) short piece of simple character. **7.** v.i. Exaggerate or distort the truth, draw the long-bow. [f. OF *romanz* f. pop. L +*romanice* (opp. *Latīne* in Latin) adv. f. ROMANICUS]

român'cer, n. Medieval or other writer of romances; fantastic liar. [f. *romance* vb (prec.) partly in obs. sense]

Rōm'anĕs, n. Gipsy language. [Gipsy (adv.)]

Rōmanēsque' (-k), a. & n. = ROMANCE 1 & 2. **2.** (archit.). (In) style of building prevalent in Romanized Europe between the classical & Gothic periods. [-ESQUE]

Rōmān'ic, a. & n. **1.** Descended from Latin, Romance (a. & n.). **2.** Descended from, inheriting civilization etc. of, the Romans, Romance-speaking. [f. L *Rōmānicus* (ROMAN¹, -IO)]

Rōmān'ity, n. (rare). Civilization & influence of Roman empire. [ROMAN², -ITY]

Rōmansh', **Rou-**, **Ru-**, (ro-, rōō-), n. & a. = ROMANCE 1 & 2. (In) the RHAETO-ROMANIC tongue of NW. part of E. Switzerland; = *Rhaeto-Romanic*. [as ROMANCE]

român'tic, a. & n. **1.** Characterized by or suggestive of or given to romance, imaginative, remote from experience, vision-

-ary (a ~ story, scene, adventure, girl).
2. (Of music) subordinating form to
theme, imaginative, passionate. 3. (Of
projects etc.) fantastic, unpractical,
quixotic, dreamy. 4. (Of literary or
artistic method etc.) preferring grandeur
or picturesqueness or passion or irregular
beauty to finish & proportion, subordinating whole to parts or form to
matter, (opp. CLASSIC, CLASSICAL), whence
~ISM(2, 3) n.; hence románt'ICALLY adv.,
~IST(2) n.; (pl.) ~ ideas or talk. [f. F roman-
tique (romant tale, now roman, var. of
romance ROMANCE.-IO)]

Róm'any, n. & a. 1. Gipsy (n. & a.); (pl.,
also collect. sing.) the gipsies, (pl.) gipsies.
2. The gipsy language. [f. Gipsy Romani
fem. & pl. of Romano adj. (ROM)]

roma'unt, n. (arch.). A romance or tale
of chivalry etc. [f. OF romant see Ro-
MANTIC]

Róme, n. 1. City or ancient State of ~ (~
was not built in a day, encouragement to
fainthearted; do in ~ as ~ does, as the
Romans do, adapt oneself to surroundings); Roman empire. 2. Church of ~,
whence ~'WARD a. & adv., ~'WARDS adv.
(-nw-), Rōm'ish[1] a. (chiefly derog.). [OF,
f. L Romā]

rōmp, v.i., & n. 1. (Of children etc.) play
about together, chase each other, wrestle,
etc.; (Racing sl.) get along, past, etc.,
without effort, come in or home as easy
winner. 2. n. Child or woman fond of ~-
ing, tomboy; spell of ~ing, boisterous
play, (come game of ~s); hence ~'Y[2] a.
[perh. n. f. vb, var. of RAMP[2]]

rōmp'er, n. (sing. or pl.) child's overall.
[prec.-ER[2]]

rōn'deau (-dō), n. Ten-line or thirteen-
line poem with only two rhymes throughout & opening words used twice as
refrain. [F, earlier RONDEL]

rōn'del, n. (Special form of) RONDEAU.
[F, rond ROUND[1]-LE(2)]

rōn'dō, n. (pl. ~s). Piece of music with
leading theme which returns from time to
time. [It., f. F RONDEAU]

rōn'dure, n. (poet.). Round outline or
object. [f. F rondeur (ROUND[1], -URE[1])]

rōne, n. (Sc.). Gutter to carry off rain
from roof. [?]

|| Rön'tgĕn, n., & v.t. Machine for duplicat-
ing letters, circulars, etc., in numbers;
(v.t.) reproduce with a ~. [P]

Rön'tgenogram (röntgén-), n. Photograph taken by Röntgen rays. [foll., -o-,
GRAM]

Röntgen rays. See RAY[1].

rōōd, n. 1. The cross of Christ (arch.; often
in oaths, as by the R~); crucifix, esp. one
raised on middle of ~-screen, wooden or
stone carved screen separating nave &
choir; ~-arch, between nave & choir; ~-
beam, cross-beam, usu. as head of ~-
screen, supporting ~; ~-cloth, veiling ~
in Lent; ~-loft, gallery on top of ~-
screen. 2. Quarter of an acre (esp. as
loose term for small piece of land: not a
~ remained to him). [OE rōd cross, cf.
OFris. rōde, cogn. w. ROD]

roof, n., & v.t. 1. Upper covering of house
or building usu. supported by its walls
(under one's ~, in one's house, esp. w.
ref. to hospitality; also fig., as the ~ of
heaven; ~ of the world, high mountain
range; ~ of the mouth, palate; under a ~,
of foliage); top of covered vehicle esp.
when used for outside passengers; ~ of
garden, on flat ~ of building; ~-tree,
ridge-pole of ~; hence ~AGE(1) n.,(~)ED[2]
(-ft), ~LESS aa. 2. v.t. Cover with ~, be
~ of, (often in, over); hence ~ING(1)(3) n.
[OE hrōf, cf. OFris. rhōof, MDu. roof]

roof'er, n. (colloq.). Letter of thanks
for entertainment sent by departed
visitor. [prec.-ER[1]]

rook[1], n., & v.t. 1. Black hoarse-voiced
bird of crow tribe nesting in colonies;
sharper, esp. at dice or cards, person who
lives on inexperienced gamblers etc., (cf.
PIGEON); ~ pie, of young ~s; ~-rifle, of
small bore for ~-shooting; hence ~'ERY,
~'ING[1], nn., ~-Y[2] a. 2. v.t. Win money
from at cards etc. esp. by swindling;
charge (customer) extortionately. [OE
hrōc, cf. Du. roek, G ruch; prob. imit.]

rook[2], n. (chess). = CASTLE[1]. [f. OF roc
ult. f. Pers. rukh]

rook'ery, n. 1. (Clump of trees with)
colony of rooks. 2. Colony of penguins
etc. or seals. 3. Crowded cluster of mean
houses or tenements. [-ERY]

rook'ie, n. (army sl.). Recruit. [corrupt.
of recruit]

room, n., & v.i. 1. Space that is or might
be occupied by something, capaciousness
or ability to accommodate contents,
(takes up too much ~; there is plenty of ~;
no ~ to turn in, to swing a CAT[1]; would
rather have his ~ than his company, wish
him away; we have no ~ here for idlers';
make ~, vacate standing-ground etc. or
post etc. for or for another, withdraw,
retire, also clear a space for person or
thing by removal of others; ~ for, arch.,
elliptically command to make way for some
one; in one's ~, in the ~ of, instead of, in
succession to, as substitute for, whence
~'Y[2] a., ~'INESS n., ~'ILY[2] adv. 2. Opportunity, scope, to do or for (~ to deny
ourselves; no ~ for dispute; leave ~ for
evasion; there is ~ for improvement, things
are not as good as they should be). 3.
Part of house enclosed by walls or partitions, floor, & ceiling; (pl.) set of these
occupied by person or family, apartments
or lodgings; (transf.) the company in a
~ (set the ~ in a roar); whence ~FUL(2) n.,
~ED[2](-md) a. 4. *v.i. Have ~(s), lodge,
whence ~'ER[1] n.; ~ing-house,
lodging-house. [com.-Teut.; cf.
G raum, Sw. & Da. rum]

roost¹, n., & v.i. & t. **1.** Bird's perching or resting place, esp. hen-house or part of it in which fowls sleep, (transf.) sleeping-accommodation, bed(room), (*go to ~*, retire for the night; *at ~*, perched, in bed; *curses come home to ~*, recoil upon curser). **2.** vb. (Of birds or persons) settle for sleep, be perched or lodged for the night; provide with sleeping-place. [vb f. n., OE *hrōst*, cf. MDu. *roest*]

‖ roost², n. Tidal race about Orkneys & Shetlands. [f. ON *rost*]

roos'ter, n. Domestic cock. [-ER¹]

root¹, n. **1.** Part of plant normally below earth's surface & serving to attach it to earth & convey nourishment from soil to it, (pl.) such part divided into branches or fibres, corresponding organ of epiphyte, part attaching ivy to its support (also ✓'LET n.), permanent underground stock of plant, small plant with ~ for transplanting, (plant, such as turnip or carrot, with) edible ~, (*pull up by the ~s*, uproot lit. & fig.; *take, strike, ~*, begin to draw nourishment from soil, fig. get established; *lay axe to ~ of tree* or institution, set about destroying it; ~ *& BRANCH¹*). **2.** (Bibl.) scion, offshoot, (*there shall be a ~ of Jesse*). **3.** Imbedded part of some bodily organ or structure, part of thing attaching it to greater or more fundamental whole, (~ *of tongue, tooth, nail*, etc.; ~ *of a gem*, esp. of emerald, cloudy part by which it adhered to stone; ~*s of mountain*, its base). **4.** Source or origin (of; *love of money is the ~ of all evil*; *a ~ of bitterness*: ~*fallacy, idea*, etc., the one ~ of things; *has the ~ of the matter in him*, is essentially sound, w. ref. to *Job* XIX. 28). **7.** (Math.) ~ *of*, number or quantity that when multiplied by itself a usu. specified number of times gives (specified number etc.; *square* or *second* ✓ 4, or ellipt. ✓ *of* 4 *or* ~ 4, symbol √4, *is* 2; ³√ *is irrational*; *cube* or *third* ~ *of* 27, symbol ³√27, *is* 3). **8.** (Philol.) ultimate analysable element of language, basis (whether itself existing as a word or not) on which words are made by addition of prefixes or suffixes or by other modification, (symbol ✓, as *sopor is from* ✓SWEP). **9.** (Mus.) fundamental note of chord. **10.** ~*-stock*, = RHIZOME, also primary form whence off-shoots have arisen. Hence ✓AGE¹(, 3) n., ~'LESS, ~'ŷ¹ [-Y¹], aa. [OE f. ON *rót*; cogn. w. L *radix*, & w. WORT]

root², v.t. & i. **1.** (Cause to) take root, fix firmly to the spot, establish, (*some kinds ~ freely; take care to ~ them firmly; fear ~ed him to the ground*; esp. in p.p., as *her affection was deeply ~ed*, ~*ed objections to*, obedience ~*ed in fear*, whence ~*'edly²* adv., ~*'edNESS n.*). **2.** Drag or dig *up* by the roots; ~ *out*, exterminate; uproot, tear away, *from* (poet.). [f. prec.]

root³, rout, v.i. & t. **1.** (Of swine etc.) turn up ground with snout, beak, etc., in search of food; turn *up* (ground) thus. **2.** (transf.) Search *out*, hunt *up*, rummage (*among, in*). **3.** *(sl.).* Be active *for* another by giving encouraging applause or support. [earlier *wroot*, f. OE *wrótan (rót* ROOT¹)]

root'ery, n. Pile of roots & stumps for growing garden plants on (cf. ROCK'ery). [-ERY]

rope, n., & v.t. & i. **1.** (Piece of) stout cordage (prop. over 1 in. in circumf., cf. CABLE¹, CORD) made by twisting strands of hemp, flax, hide, or wire, into one (*the ~*, halter for hanging person, also = TIGHT~; *on the HIGH ~s; the ~s*, those enclosing prize-ring or other arena: *know, learn, put one up to, the ~s*, the conditions in some sphere of action; *give one ~*, etc., *enough to hang himself, plenty of ~*, etc., not check him, trust to his bringing about his own discomfiture; ~ *of sand*, delusive security; ~ *of onions, ova, pearls*, these strung together; *on the ~*, of mountaineers, ~'d together). **2.** Viscid or gelatinous stringy formation in beer or other liquid. **3.** ~*dancer, -dancing, -performer*, performing, on tight~: ~*-drill*, in which a ~ stretched by two men represents company etc.: ~*-ladder*, two long ~s connected by short cross-~s as ladder; ~*-manship*, skill in ~-walking or -climbing; ~*-moulding*, cut spirally in imitation of ~-strands; ~*-quoit*, ring of ~ used in quoits played on board ship; ~*'s-end*, short piece of ~ used to flog (esp. sailor) with; ~*-walk*, long piece of ground used for twisting ~; ~*-walker, -walking*, =~-dancer, -dancing; ~*-yard, -making establishment; ~*-yarn*, (piece of the) material (esp. when unpicked) of which ~-strands consist, mere trifle; hence ROP'ING⁴(6) n., ROP'Y² a., ROP'iNESS n. **4.** vb. Fasten or secure (party) with ~, attach (person) to ~, put on ~; use ~s in towing etc.; enclose, close *in*, (space) with ~; ~ *in*, secure adherence of, decoy. **5.** ‖ (Racing) check (horse), check horse, (of athlete) not put forth full powers, in order to lose race. **6.** Become ropy or viscid. [com.-Teut.; OE *rāp*, cf. Du. *reep*, G *reif*, Icel. & Norw. *reip*]

‖ roque (rōk), n. Kind of French croquet. [~ in France]

roque'laure (-kelōr'), n. (hist.). Man's cloak reaching to knees (18th c.). [F (Duke of *R~*)]

Roq'uefort (-kfōr), n. Kind of French cheese of goats' & ewes' milk resembling Stilton. [~ in France]

roq'uet (-kī), v.t. & i.(~*ing, ~ed*, pr. -ing,

-id], & n. **1.** Cause one's ball to strike; (of ball) strike, another ball at croquet; strike another ball thus. **2.** n. Act or fact of ~ing. [arbitrary f. CROQUET² & orig. in same sense]

rŏr'qual, n. Whale with dorsal fin, fin-back. [F. f. Norw. *röyrkval* (*raud* red, *kval* whale)]

rō'ry-tŏr'y, raught'y (-awt-), a. (sl.). Enjoyable (*had a ~ time*); fond of amusement & excitement. [?]

rō̆sā'rian, n. **1.** Rose-fancier. **2.** (R.-C. Ch.) member of a Confraternity of the Rosary. [f. L *rosarium* ROSARY, -AN¹]

rō̆sā'ceous (-āshus), a. Of the family Rosaceae, of which the rose is the type. So **rŏsā'CEAN** (-zshǎn) n. [f. L *rosaceus* (ROSE, -ACEOUS)]

rō̆sā'rian, n. **1.** Rose-garden, rose-bed. **2.** (R.-C. Ch.) form of prayer in which fifteen decades of Aves are repeated, each decade preceded by Paternoster & followed by Gloria; book containing this; string of 165 beads for keeping count in this (*lesser ~, of* 55). [f. L *rosarium* (ROSE, -ARIUM)]

Rō̆s'cian (-shǐ-), a. Like or worthy of Roscius, famous Roman actor of 1st c. B.C. [-AN¹]

rōse (-z), n., a., & v.t. **1.** (Prickly bush or shrub bearing) a beautiful & usu. fragrant flower usu. of red or yellow or white colour (BLUSH², BRIER¹, CABBAGE, DAMASK, MOSS¹, MUSK, TEA, etc.; *~*; also in names of other flowering plants, as ROCK¹~, CHRISTMAS ~, R~ of *Jericho*, the Resurrection plant with dried fronds unfolding under moisture, R~ of *Sharon*, unidentified eastern flower, R~ of *May*, white narcissus; ATTAR, OTTO, of *~*; *red as a ~; gather ~s or life's ~s, seek pleasure; path, stream with ~s, life of delights; bed of ~s, pleasant easy post or condition, esp. in is no bed of ~s; so is not all ~s; ~ without a thorn, impossible happiness, unalloyed delight; the ~ of with place-name, most beautiful girl or woman in; Wars of the R~s, 15th-c. civil wars between Yorkists with white & Lancastrians with red ~ as emblem; under the ~, = SUB² rosa), whence **rōs'ERY(3)** (-z-) n. **2.** Representation of the flower in heraldry or decoration (esp. as national emblem of England, cf. THISTLE, SHAMROCK, LEEK or DAFFODIL, Golden ~, ornament blessed by Pope on 4th Sunday in Lent & sent as compliment to some R.-C. sovereign, city, etc.); etc.; the ~ of with access-name, ...; ~-shaped design. **3.** Rosette worn on shoe or clerical hat. **4.** Protuberance round base of animal's horn or some

birds' eye. **5.** Sprinkling-nozzle of water-ing-pot or hose, whence (·)RŌSEE)² (·zd) a. **6.** = ~ diamond; = ~ window. **7.** Light crimson colour, pink, (usu. pl.) rosy complexion (*has quite lost her, spoiled her natural, ~s*). **8.** The ~, erysipelas. **9.** ~-apple, tropical tree cultivated for foliage & fruit, its fruit; ~-bay, oleander, rhododendron, azalea, willow-herb; ~-bud, bud of ~ (often attrib., as ~-bud mouth), pretty girl, *débutante*; ~-bush, ~ plant; ~-chafer, green or copper-coloured beetle frequenting ~s; ~-colour, rosy red, pink, (fig.) pleasant state of things or outlook (*life is not all ~-colour*); ~-coloured, rosy, (fig.) optimistic, sanguine, cheerful, (*takes ~-coloured views; see things through ~-coloured spectacles*); ~-cut, cut as a ~ diamond, hemispherical with curved part with red blotches; ~-drop, skin-disease in triangular facets; ~-drop, appendage to lathe for engraving curved patterns; ~-gall, excrescence on dog-~ etc. made by insect; ~-leaf, leaf, usu. petal, of ~ (*crumpled ~-leaf, slight vexation alloying general felicity*); ~-tipped, with rosy lips; ~ (or ~-head) nail, with head shaped like ~ diamond; ~ noble, 15th-16th c. gold coin of varying value stamped with ~; ~-pink, pigment of chalk or whiting coloured with Brazil-wood decoction, also coloured with Brazil-wood decoction, also ~-coloured(ed) lit. & fig.; ~-rush, = ROSEO-LA; ~-red a. & n., red as (of) a ~; ~-root, kinds of plant with root smelling like ~, when dried or bruised; ~-tree; ~ vinegar, infusion of ~s in vinegar for application in headache etc.; ~-water, perfume made from ~s, (fig.) compliments, gentle handling, etc. (~water surgery; revolutions are not made with ~water); ~ window, circular, usu. with spokelike tracery; ~wood, kinds of cabinet wood named from their fragrance; hence ~LESS, ~LIKE, (-z-), aa. **10.** adj. Coloured like a ~ pale red ~, of warm pink. **11.** v.t. Make (face, snow-slope, etc.) rosy (esp. in p.p.). [OE ròse, ròse, f. L rosa prob. f. Gk *rhodea* rose-tree (*rhodon* rose)]

rōse², see RISE¹.

rō̆s'ēate (-z-), a. = ROSE-coloured (lit. & fig.). Hence ~LY² adv. [f. L *roseus* (ROSE¹) rosy + -ATE²]

rōse'mary (-zm-), n. Evergreen fragrant shrub with leaves used in perfumery etc. & taken as emblem of remembrance. [earlier *rosmarine* f. L *ros marinus* (*ros* dew, MARINE) w. assim. to *rose, Mary* (prob. the Virgin)]

rō̆s'ēo- (-z-), comb. form in names of salts etc.; German measles. Hence ~AR¹, ~OUS, aa. [mod. L (*proc*, -*ola* dim. termination)]

rō̆s'ēola (-z-), n. Rosy rash in measles etc.; German measles. Hence ~AR¹, ~OUS, aa. [mod. L (*proc*, -*ola* dim. termination)]

rōsětte (-z-), n. Rose-shaped ornament for dress or harness made of ribbons,

leather strips, etc.; (Archit.) carved or moulded conventional rose on wall etc., also rose-window; (Biol.) roselike cluster or organs, markings resembling rose; = ROSE *diamond*; roselike object or arrangement of parts. Hence ~ED² a. [F (ROSE¹, -ETTE)]

Rŏsĭcrū'cian (-zĭkrōōshn), n. & a. (Member) of a society devoted to occult lore & magic said to have been founded 1484 by Christian Rosenkreuz. Hence ~ISM(3) n. [f. L *rosa* rose, *crux crucis* cross, + -AN, as latinization of *Rosenkreuzian*]

rŏs'ĭn (-z-), n., & v.t. **1.** =RESIN : solid residue after distillation (of oil of turpentine from crude turpentine); hence ~Y² a. **2.** v.t. Smear, seal up, rub (esp. bow or string of fiddle etc.), with ~. [changed f. RESIN]

Rŏsĭnăn'tē (-z-), **Rŏz-**, n. Worn-out horse, jade. [f. Sp. *Rocinante* (*rocín* jade, cf. obs. E *rouncy* riding-horse), Don Quixote's horse]

rŏsŏl'ĭō (-z-), n. A S.-Europ. sweet cordial. [It., f. L *ros* dew, *solis* of the sun, cordial being orig. made from plant sundew]

rŏs'ter, n. List or plan showing turns of duty for individuals or companies esp. of a military force. [f. Du. *rooster* list, orig. gridiron (*roosten* ROAST), w. ref. to parallel lines]

rŏs'tral, a. (Of column etc.) adorned with beaks actual or sculptured etc. of ancient war-galleys; (Zool. etc.) of, on, the rostrum. [f. LL *rostralis* (ROSTRUM, -AL)]

rŏs'trāt'ĕd, a. (Of column etc.) = prec.; (Zool. etc.) having, ending in, a rostrum. [f. L *rostratus* (ROSTRUM, -ATE²)]

rŏs'trum, n. (pl. ~*a*, ~*ums*). **1.** (Sing., or pl. ~*a* or ~*ums*) platform for public speaking (orig. that in Roman forum adorned with beaks of captured galleys); pulpit, office, etc. that enables one to gain the public ear. **2.** (Rom. Ant.) beak of war-galley (pl. usu. ~*a*). **3.** (Zool., Entom., Bot.) beak, stiff snout, beaklike part, whence ~ATE² a., ~IFORM, aa., ~O- comb. form. [L; = beak (*rodere* gnaw)]

rŏs'ŭlate (-z-), a. (bot.). **(Of leaves)** packed over each other like rose-petals. [LL *rosula* (ROSE¹, -ULE), -ATE² see -UL-]

rŏs'ỹ (-z-), a. Coloured like a red rose (esp. of complexion as indicating health, of blush, wine, sky, light, etc.), (fig.) = ROSE-*coloured*; (now rare) smelling like a rose, made of or covered or strewn with roses; ~ *cross*, emblem of ROSICRUCIANS; ~*-fingered*, epithet of *dawn* etc. Hence **rŏs'ĭLỸ²** adv., **rŏs'ĭNESS** n., (-z-). [-Y²]

rŏt¹, n. & int. **1.** Decay, putrefaction, rottenness, (esp. in timber, cf. DRY1-~). **2.** Virulent liver-disease of sheep (usu. *the* ~). **3.** (sl.). (Also *tommy-*~) nonsense, absurd statement or argument or proposal

(often as int. of incredulity or ridicule), foolish course, undesirable state of things, (*don't talk* ~; *it is perfect* ~ *to trust him*; *what tommy* ~ *that it is not open on Sundays!*). **4.** (Cricket, War, etc.) sudden series of unaccountable failures on one side (*a* ~ *set in*). [prob. f. Scand. (Icel. Norw., *rot*), cogn. w. foll.]

rŏt², v.i. & t.(-tt-). **1.** Undergo natural decomposition, decay, putrefy, (~ *off*, drop from stem etc. through rottenness); (fig., of society, institutions, etc.) gradually perish from want of vigour or use, (of prisoner) pine away (*left to* ~ *in gaol*). **2.** Cause to ~, make rotten; (sl.) spoil or disconcert (*has* ~*ted the whole plan*). **3.** ||(sl.). Chaff, banter, tease: (abs.) talk ironically (*he is only* ~*ting*). **4.** ~*gut* a. & n., (liquor) injurious to stomach. [com.-Teut.; OE *rotian*, cf. Fris. *rotsje*, Du. *rotten*, Icel. *rota*]

rō'ta, n. **1.** List of persons acting, or duties to be done, in rotation, roster. **2.** (R.-C. Ch.: *R*~) supreme ecclesiastical & secular court. [L, = wheel]

rō'tar̄y, a. & n. **1.** Acting by rotation. **2.** n. ~machine. **3.** (*The*) *R*~, *R*~ *Club*(s), a world-wide society with many branches for international service to humanity, orig. named from clubs entertaining in rotation, whence **Rotar̄'ĬAN** a. & n., (member) of R~. [f. LL *rotarius* (prec., -ARY²)]

rō'tāte¹, a. (bot.). Wheel-shaped. [ROTA, -ATE²]

rōtāte'², v.i. & t. Move (t. & i.) round axis or centre, revolve; arrange (esp. crops) or take in rotation. Hence **rō'tAtive**, **rō'tAtory**, ~ABLE, aa. [f. L ROTAre, -ATE³]

rōtā'tion, n. Rotating; recurrence, recurrent series or period, regular succession in office etc., (often *in*, *by*, ~; ~ *of crops*, growing of different crops in regular order to avoid exhausting soil). Hence ~AL (-sho-) a. [f. L *rotatio* (prec., -ATION)]

rōtā'tor, n. (Anat.) muscle that rotates a limb etc.; revolving apparatus or part. [L ROTATE², -OR²]

rŏtch(e), n. The little auk. [earlier *rotge*, cf. Fris. *rotgĭes* brent-geese]

rōte, n. Mere habituation, knowledge got by repetition, unintelligent memory, (only *by* ~; *say*, *know*, *do*, *by* ~). [perh. OF, = ROUTE]

rō'tĭfer, n. Wheel-animalcule, member of class *Rotifera* with rotatory organs used in swimming. [L ROTA, -FEROUS]

rō'tŏgraph (-ahf), n. Print of MS. page etc. got by sensitized roll. [prec., -GRAPH]

rō'tor, n. Rotary part of machine; horizontally-rotating vane of helicopter. [irreg. f. ROTATOR]

rŏt'ten, a. **1.** Decomposed or decomposing, putrid, perishing of decay, falling to pieces or friable or easily breakable or tearable from age or use. **2.** (Of sheep) affected with the rot. **3.** Morally, socially,

or politically corrupt, effete, (‖~ BOROUGH; *something is ~ in the state of Denmark*; *Haml.* I. iv. 90, things are unsatisfactory). **4.** Inefficient, worthless; (sl.: of state of things, plan, etc.) disagreeable, regrettable, beastly, ill-advised. **5.** ~-stone, decomposed siliceous limestone used as polishing-powder. Hence ~LY² *adv.*, ~NESS n. [f. ON *rotinn* cogn.w. ROT² RET]

Rött′en Row (rŏ). n. (Now usu. *the Row*) track in Hyde Park, fashionable resort for riding. [perh. f. prec.]

‖ **rött′er.** n. (sl.). One who is objectionable on moral or other grounds, useless or inefficient or disliked person. [ROT², -ER¹]

rotund′. a. Circular, round, (rare), whence **rotún′dᴬᵀᴱ² a.**, **rotún′da., rotún′do-**, comb. forms, (bot.): (of mouth) rounded in speaking etc., (of speech, literary style, etc.) as from ~ mouth, sonorous, sounding, grandiloquent; (of persons) plump, podgy. Hence or cogn. **rotún′dír̄y n.**, ~LY² *adv.* [f. L *rotundus* cogn. w. ROTA]

rotún′da. n. Building of circular ground-plan. esp. one with dome; circular hall or room. [earlier *rotonda*, It., fem. of *ro-tondo* = prec.]

roturier (see Ap.). n. Plebeian. [F (*voture* plebeian tenure, prob. f. L *ruptura* break-ing. -ER¹]

rouble (rōo-). n. The Russian monetary unit (formerly a silver coin = 2/1½). [F. f. Russ. *ruble*]

roucou (rōōkōō′). n. (W.-Ind. tree yielding) orange dye. [F. f. Braz. *urucú*]

roué (rōō′ā). n. Debauchee, rake. [F. p.p. of *rouer* break on wheel, = one deserving this]

rouge¹ (rōōzh). a., n., & v.t. **1.** Red (only in R~ *Croix* pr. krwah. R~ *Dragon*, two pursuivants of English College of Arms, & in ~*royal marble*, reddish Belgian kind). **2.** n. Fine red powder made from safflower & used for colouring cheeks & lips; plate-powder of oxide of iron; revolutionary politician; ~*-et-noir* (-ā-nwah′r′), card-game played on table with red & black marks on which money staked is laid (~, the red in this). **3.** vb. Colour, adorn oneself, with ~. [F, f. L *rubeus* cogn. w. RED]

‖ **rouge²** (rōōj), n. Scrummage, also touchdown counting as point to opponents, in Eton football (field game). [?]

rough (rŭf). a., adv., n., & v.t. **1.** Of uneven or irregular surface, not smooth or level or polished, diversified or broken by prominences, hairy, shaggy, coarse in texture, rugged, (~ *skin*, *hands*, *paper*, *bark*, *road*, *cloth*, *country*; *book with ~ edges*, in which edges of original sheets are left untrimmed; ~ *leaf*, ‖ first true leaf of springing plant after the smooth leaves or cotyledons, *in the ~ leaf*, at this stage; ~ *rice*, unhusked rice, paddy). **2.** Not mild or quiet or gentle, unrestrained, violent, stormy,

disorderly, riotous, inconsiderate, harsh, unfeeling, drastic, severe, grating, astringent, (~ *manners*, *soldier*, *play*; ~ *water*, *sea*, *weather*, *wind*; ~ *words*; ~ *element of the population*, *quarter of the town*; ~ *usage*, *handling*; ~ *remedies*; ~ *baritone voice*; ~ *clarel*; ~ *tongue*, *habit of rude-ness*; *gave him a tick with the ~ side of my tongue*, spoke severely to him; ~ *passage*, *crossing over ~ sea*; ~ *work*, *violence*, *also task requiring it*, & *see below*; *have a ~ time*, *suffer* ~ *handling or hardship*; *a horse has ~ paces*, *jolts rider*; *fact etc. is* ~ *luck*, *or* ~, *on person*, *worse luck than he deserves*; ~ MUSIC). **3.** Deficient in finish or elaboration or delicacy, incomplete, rudimentary, entirely or partly unwrought, merely passable, inexact, approximate, preliminary, (~ *nursing*, *style*, *welcome*, *kindness*, *plenty*, *accommodation*, *sketch*, *drawing*; ~ *work*, & *see above*; ~ *state*, *attempt*, *makeshift*, *circle*; ~ *stone*, not dressed; ~ DIAMOND; ~ *justice*, ~ *translation*, *estimate*; ~ *copy of picture etc.*, reproducing only essentials; ~ *draft*; ~ COPY¹; ~ *coat*, first coat of plaster laid on; ~ *coating*, ~*cast*; ~ *& ready*, not elaborate, just good enough, not over-particular. **4.** ~*-é-tum′ble*, (adj.) irregular, effective; ~*-é-tum′ble*, (adj.) irregular, scrambling, disorderly, regardless of procedure-rules, (n.) haphazard fight, scuffle; ~*cast*, (adj., of wall etc.) coated with mixture of lime & gravel, (of plan etc.) imperfectly elaborated, (n.) plaster of lime & gravel for walls, (v.t.) coat(wall) with ~cast, prepare (plan, essay, etc.) in outline; ~*-dry*, dry (clothes) without ironing etc.; ~*-footed*, with feathered feet (in names of birds); ~*-grind*, give preliminary grinding to (edged tool etc.); ~*-hew*, shape out ~ly, give crude form to, (p.p., uncouth, unrefined); ~*-hound*, kind of dogfish; ~*house* (sl.), disturbance, row, horseplay; ~*-house*, (v.t.) handle (person) ~ly, (v.i.) make a disturbance, act violently; ~*-legged*, with hairy or feathered legs (of breeds of horse & bird); ~*neck* (sl.), a rowdy; ~*rider*, horsebreaker, man who can ride unbroken horses, (Mil.) irregular cavalryman; ~*shod*, (of horse) having shoes with the nail-heads projecting (*ride ~shod*, domineer *over*); ~*spoken*: ~*-wrought*, with the earlier processes done; hence ~EN⁶ (rŭf′n) v.t. & i., ~ISH⁴(2) a., ~LY² *adv.*, (~*ly SPEAKING*), ~NESS n., (rŭf′). **5.** *adv.* In ~ manner (*land should be ploughed* ~; ~*play* = chiefly in compds, of which some are given above). **6.** n. ~ ground (esp. *over ~ & smooth*), (Golf) the ~ ground outside the fairway between tees & greens; one of the spikes inserted in ~*ing* horse; hard part of life, piece of hardship, (usu. *the* ~ *& the smooth*, *the* ~ *s & the smooths*); ~ *& the smooth*, *the* ~ *s & the smooths*); ‖ rowdy, hooligan, man or boy of lower classes ready for lawless violence; the

unfinished or the natural state, *the general way, (shape it from the ~; is true in the ~).* **7.** v.t. Turn up (feathers, hair, etc.) by rubbing against the grain (~ *one up the wrong way*, irritate him); secure (horse or its shoes) against slipping by insertion of spikes or project-ing nails in shoes; ~ *it*, do without ordi-nary conveniences of life; break in (horse); shape or plan *out* ~ly; sketch in ~ly; tune *up* (piano) ~ly; give first shaping to (gem, lens, etc.). [OE *rūh*, cf. Du. *ruig*, G *rauh*]

roughage (rŭf'ij), n. (Dietetics) bran of cereals and other forms of cellulose con-sidered valuable as a mechanical stimu-lant to the bowels. [-AGE (1)]

roulade (rōōlahd'), n. Florid passage of runs etc. in solo vocal music, usu. sung to one syllable. [F (*rouler* ROLL², -ADE)]

rouleau (rōōlō'), n. (pl. ~x or ~s, pr. -z). Cylindrical packet of gold coins; coil or roll. [F (*rôle* ROLL¹)]

roulette (rōō-), n. **1.** Gambling game on table with revolving centre. **2.** (Math.) curve generated by point on rolling curve. **3.** Device for keeping hair in curl. **4.** Revolving toothed wheel used in engraving, similar wheel for perforating postage stamps. [F, dim. of *rouelle* dim. of *roue* f. L *rota* wheel]

R(o)um'an, R(o)umān'ian, (rōō-), nn. & aa. (Native or language) of R(o)umania. [f. F *Roumain* f. native *Român* f. L ROMAN *-us*; -IAN]

Roumansh. See ROMANSH.

R(o)umē'līōte (rōō-), n. Native of R(o)u-melia. [-OT²]

roun'cival, n. (Also ~ *pea*) large variety of pea. [from 16th c.; perh. f. *Ronces-valles* place-name]

round¹, a. **1.** Spherical or circular or cylindrical or approaching these forms, presenting convex outline or surface, (*the ~ world; ~ shot*, spherical ball for smooth-bore cannon; ~ *buckler, hole, mat,* of cir-cular outline; ~ *table*, with disk top; *the R~ Table*, at which Arthur & his knights sat that none might have precedence; ~*table conference*, held at ~ table for same purpose; ~ *game*, proper for ~ table, players being of any number & without sides or partners; ~ *face*, as broad as long; ~ *jacket*, cut level below, without skirts; ~ *hand* or *text*, writing with bold curves; ~ *tower, post, limbs;* ~ *arch*, semicircular as in Romanesque, opp. *pointed;* ~ *cheeks*, plump, not hollow; ~ *shoulders*, so bent forward that back is convex, whence **~shoul'dered²** (-shŏl'derd) a.; ~ *towel* in Phonet., pro-nounced with rounded lips). **2.** Done with or involving circular motion (~ *dance*, waltz; ~ *trip, voyage,* with return **to** starting-point; ~ or ~*arm* or ~*hand* bowling, with arm swung horizontally, cf. *underhand, overhand;* ~ *towel,* endless or

roller; ~ *robin*, written petition with signatures in circle to conceal order in which they were written). **3.** Entire, continuous, all together, not broken or defective or scanty, sound, smooth, plain, genuine, candid, outspoken, (~ *dozen, score,* that & no less, so many together; ~ *numbers,* tens, hundreds, etc., with neglect of minor denomina-tions, whence=roughly correct; *a ~ sum,* considerable; *a ~ style,* flowing; *at a ~ trot,* vigorous; *a ~ voice,* not harsh; ~ *unvarnished tale,* the plain truth; *be ~ with one,* arch., speak home-truths to him; *a ~ oath,* unmistakable). **4.** ~ *head,* member of Parliament party in 17th-c. civil war (from custom of wearing hair close cut); ~*house,* (Hist.) lock-up or place of detention, (Naut.) cabin or set of cabins on after part of quarterdeck chiefly in old sailing-ships); ~*top,* plat-form about masthead, formerly circular; ~ *turn* (Naut.), single turn of rope round post etc. (hence, transf., *bring up with a ~ turn,* check with a sudden jerk, check abruptly). Hence ~'ISH²(2) a., ~'NESS n. [f. OF *rund, rond-* (F *rond*), f. L RO-TUNDUS]

round², n. **1.** Round object (*this earthly ~,* earth; ~*s of ladder,* rungs; ~ *of beef,* thick disk from haunch as joint; ~ *of toast,* disk etc. cut across loaf). **2.**(Sculpt.) solid form as opp. *relief; in the ~* (fig.), with all the features etc. fully shown. **3.** Circumference, bounds, extent, of (*in all the ~ of Nature*). **4.** Revolving motion, circular or circuitous or recurring course, circuit, cycle, series, (*the earth in its daily or yearly ~; the daily ~,* ordinary occupa-tions of the day; *go for a good ~,* long walk out & home; *a ~ of days, pleasures, visits; make, go,* one's ~s, take customary walk esp. of inspection; *make the ~,* of, go round; *news, story, goes the ~,* is passed on); (Mil., pl.) watch that goes round inspecting sentries or circuit it makes (*visiting, grand ~s,* orderly, field, officer's inspection of guard & sentries); (Golf) playing of all holes in course once; (Mus.) kind of perpetual canon at the unison for equal voices. **5.** Allowance of something distributed or measured out, one of set or series, one bout or spell, one stage in competition, (*serve out a ~ of spirit, 20 ~s of ball cartridge; never fired a single ~; after ~ of cheers; a fight of ten ~s; threw up the sponge after the third ~; the winners in the first ~ are paired for the second*). **6.** ||~s'*man,* tradesman's employee going round for orders & with goods. [f. F *rond* (prec.) & prec.]

round³, adv. & prep. **1.** With more or less circular motion, with return to starting-point after such motion, with rotation, with change to opposite position lit. or fig., (*sun goes, summer comes, ~; brings us ~ to winter; sleep the clock ~,* for twelve or

twenty-four hours; *all the year* ~; *6 in.* ~, *soon won him* ~). **2.** To or as of affecting area or members of a company etc., in every direction from a centre or within a radius, (*glasses* ~, for all present to drink; *Rule all* ~, for each nationality; *Home man*, one of varied talents; *show one* ~, take him to all points of interest; *room hung* ~ *with portraits*; *spread destruction* ~; *all the neighbours for a mile* ~). **3.** By circuitous way (*will you jump or go* ~?; *go a long way* ~; *ask one* ~, out of his house into one's own). **4.** *All* ~ *right* ~ & ~, emphatic forms of ~; ~ *about*, in a ring (about), all ~ (adv. & prep.), on all sides (of), with change to opposite position, circuitously; ~'*about*, (n.) circuitous way, place where all traffic has to follow a circular course (also attrib.), piece of circumlocution; ~ *the world*; *has a wrapper* ~ *her*). **6.** With successive visits to, at or to end where you began after ups & downs, points on the circumference of, (*hawks them* ~ *the cafés*; *station them* ~ *the table*). **7.** In various directions from or with regard to (*diffuses cheerfulness* ~ *her*; *shells bursting* ~ *me*), *seated* ~ *the fire.* **8.** Having as axis of revolution or central point (*turns* ~ *its centre of gravity; argue* ~ *a subject*; not come to close quarters with it; *write book* ~ *a subject*). **9.** So as to double or pass in curved course, having result from thus passing, (*go, be, find person,* ~ *the corner; GET* ~). **10.** *All* ~, *right* ~, & ~, emphatic forms of ~. [f. ROUND¹,²]

round⁴, v.t. & i. **1.** Invest with, assume, round shape (~*ed eyes, mouth; her form is* ~*ing;* ~ *vowel*, pronounce it with ~ed lips; ~ *off* or ~ *the angles*, make them less sharp; ~ *dog's ears*, crop them). **2.** Bring to complete (often symmetrical or well-ordered state (often *off-*)~ *off* or ~ *a sentence, estate, career*). **3.** Gather up (cattle, & transit.) by riding round, whence ~'*-up* n. **4.** Pass round, double, (cape etc.). **5.** Turn (t. & i.) round (rare, chiefly Naut.; ~*ed on his heel to look at me;* ~ *bout* off etc., turn her to meet wave etc.; *ship* ~*s to*, comes to wind & heaves to). **6.** ~ *on*, make unexpected retort to (friend etc.), (of informer) peach upon. [f. ROUND¹,³]

round⁵, v.i. & t. (arch.). Whisper (t. & i.; chiefly w. double obj., as ~*ed him in the ear that*, told him secretly that). [OE *rūnian* (rūn RUNE)]

roun'del, n. Small disk, esp. decorative medallion etc.; rondeau or rondel. [f. OF *rondel*, see ROUND¹, -EL²]

round'elay, n. Short simple song with refrain; bird's song. [f. F *rondelet* (RONDEL, -ET²) w. assim. to LAY¹]

round'er, n. In vbl senses of ROUND⁴; || also, (pl.) game with bat & ball between two sides with ~ (or complete run of player through all the bases arranged in a round) as unit of scoring. [ROUND⁴,²]

round'ly, adv. In thorough-going manner (*go* ~ *to work*); bluntly, with plain speech, without qualification, severely, (*told him* ~ *that he would not*; ~ *asserts it is true*; *vas* ~ *abused*); in circular way (~ *oval*; *swells on* ~). [-LY²]

roup¹ (roop), n. (Sc. & north.). **1.** v.t. Sell by auction. **2.** n. An auction. [n. ~ [orig. sense *shout*], cf. Icel. *raupa* boast]

roup² (roop), n. Kinds of poultry-disease (a) with swelling on rump, (b) with purulent catarrh. Hence **roup'y¹** (roo-) a. [(a) etym. dub., (b) perb. imit. of hoarse breathing]

|| **rouse¹** (-z), n. (arch.). Draught of liquor, bumper, toast, revel, drinking-bout, (*take one's* ~, carouse; *give a* ~, propose or drink toast). [prob. for CAROUSE, perb. f. wrong division of *drink carouse*]

rouse² (-z), v.t. & i., & n. **1.** Startle (game) from lair or cover. **2.** Wake or stir up or from sleep or inactivity (often *up*, or confidence or carelessness (often *up*, etc.; ~ *oneself*, overcome one's indolence; ~ *from, out of, to action, to energy, to do,* etc.; *wants rousing*, is indolent; *a rousing cheer, song, sermon, lie*). **3.** Provoke temper of, inflame with passion, (*is terrible when* ~*d*). **4.** Evoke (feelings). **5.** Stir (liquid, esp. beer while brewing). **6.** (Naut.) haul vigorously *in, out, up*). **7.** Cease to sleep, become active, (usu. *up*). **8.** n. (mil.). || The reveille. [orig. as hunting term; etym. dub.]

rouse³ (-z), **rō̆se** (-z), v.t. Sprinkle (herring etc.) with salt in curing. [earlier *arrouse* f. OF *arrouser* f. L AD(*rorare* f. L *ros roris* dew)]

rous'er (-z-), n. In vbl senses of ROUSE²; esp.: implement for rousing beer; outrageous or rousing lie. [-ER¹]

Rousseau'ism (roosō-), n. (Adherence to) views on religion, politics, education, etc., of Jean Jacques Rousseau, French author 1712-78. So ~IAN, ~ISH¹, ~AN, aa., ~IST(2), ~ITE(1), nn. & aa. [-ISM]

Roussillon (rōōseyawn), n. A red wine. [~, old French province]

roust'about, n. *Wharf labourer, deck hand; (Austral., also *rousedabout*) handy man. [f. dial. & U.S. *roust* rout out]

rout¹, n. & v.t. **1.** Assemblage or company of revellers or rioters. (Law) assemblage of three or more persons engaged in unlawful act; riot, tumult,

disturbance, clamour, fuss. **2.** (arch.) || Large evening party or reception (~ *seat*, light bench hired out for ~s). **3.** Disorderly retreat of defeated army or troops (*put to* ~, utterly defeat). **4.** v.t. Put to ~. [f. OF ROUTE in senses obs. in F]

rout³, v.i. & t. =ROOT³; also, force or fetch out (of bed or from bed or house or hiding-place). [var. of ROOT³]

route (root, *mil. freq.* rowt), n., & v.t. **1.** Way taken in getting from starting-point to destination; (Mil.) marching orders (*get, give, the* ~, *column of* ~, *march*, training march of battalion etc.; *en* ~ (F; pr. ahn), on the way (*is, did it, en* ~). **2.** v.t. Send, forward, direct to be sent, by a certain ~. [F (now=road), f. L *rupta* (*via* way) fem. p.p. of *rumpere* break, with other senses in OF; see ROUT¹]

routin|e (rooten), n. Regular course of procedure, unvarying performance of certain acts; (attrib.) performed by rule (~*e duties* etc.). Hence ~ISM(3), ~IST(2), nn., (-én²). [F (prec., -INE⁴)]

rōve¹, v.i. & t., & n. **1.** Wander without settled destination, roam, ramble (*roving sailor*, kinds of creeper), (of eyes) look in changing directions; wander over or through; *roving commission*, authority given to person(s) conducting an inquiry to travel as may be necessary; (Angling) troll with live bait. **2.** n. Act of roving (esp. *on the* ~). [orig. term in archery = shoot at casual mark with range not determined; etym. dub.]

rōve², n., & v.t. **1.** Sliver of cotton, wool, etc., drawn out & slightly twisted. **2.** v.t. Form into ~s; hence **rōv'er¹** [-ER¹] n. [?]

rōve³, n. Small metal plate or ring for rivet to pass through & be clinched over. [f. ON *ró*]

rōve⁴. See REEVE³.

rōv'er² (for *rover¹* see ROVE²), n. **1.** (Archery) mark chosen at undetermined range, also mark for long-distance shooting, (usu. *shoot at* ~s); wanderer; (Croquet) ball that has passed all hoops but not pegged out, its owner. **2.** Sea robber, pirate; senior boy scout. [1 f. ROVE¹, -ER¹; 2 MDu. (*roven* rob cogn. w. REAVE, -ER¹)]

row¹ (rō), n. Number of persons or things in a more or less straight line (*in a* ~, ~*s*, so arranged); ~ *of houses*, street with this on one or each side (|| often in street names); || *the Row*, ROTTEN ROW; line of seats in theatre etc. (*in the front, third*, etc., ~); ~ *of plants* in garden (**a hard ~ to hoe*, difficult task). [OE *rāw*, cf. G *reihe*]

row² (rō), v.i. & t., & n. **1.** Propel boat, propel (boat), convey (passenger) in boat, with oars or sweeps (~ *over*, WALK over in boat-race; also with cogn. obj., as ~ *a* race, a few strokes, a fast stroke, 30 to the minute); ~ race with; ~ *down*, overtake in ~ing, esp. bumping, race; ~ *out*, exhaust by ~ing (*the crew were completely ~ed out at the finish*); be oarsman of specified number in boat (~ *s 5 in the Oxford crew*); (of boat) be fitted with (so many oars); ~*boat*, ~*ing-boat*. **2.** n. Spell of ~ing, boat-excursion. Hence ~ER¹ (rō'er) n. [OE *rōwan*, cf. Du. *roeijen*, ON *róa*; cogn. w. L *remus*, Gk *eretmon*, oar]

row³, n., & v.t. (colloq.). **1.** Disturbance, commotion, noise, dispute, (*what's the* ~?, what is the matter?; *make, kick up, a* ~, raise noise, also make protest); shindy, free fight, (*town-&-*GOWN ~); being reprimanded (*shall get into a* ~). **2.** v.t. Reprimand; rate; hence ~ING-¹(1) n. [from 1787; etym. dub.]

row'an (rō-, row-), n. (Sc. & north.) (Scarlet berry of) mountain ash (also ~*tree*). [f. Scand. (Sw. *rön*, Icel. *reynir*) imit.]

row-de-dow', n. Din, uproar. [imit.]

rowd'|y, n. & a. Rough & disorderly & noisy (person); so ~*y-dowdy* a. Hence ~INESS, ~YISM(2), nn., ~YISH(2) a. [U.S., etym. dub.; orig. sense *backwoodsman*]

row'el, n., & v.t. (-ll-). **1.** Spiked revolving disk at end of spur (vb, urge with ~). **2.** Circular piece of leather etc. with hole in centre inserted between horse's skin & flesh to discharge humours (vb, insert ~ in). [f. OF *rouel* f. L *rota* wheel, -EL²(2)]

row'lock (rŭl-), n. Pair of thole-pins or other contrivance on boat's gunwale serving as fulcrum for oar. [prob. assim. of earlier *oarlock*, OE *árloc* (OAR, LOCK²), to ROW²]

Rŏx'burghe (-tra), n. Style of bookbinding with plain leather gilt-lettered backs, cloth or paper sides, & leaves with untrimmed edges & bottoms. [Duke of ~ 1740-1804]

roy'al, a. & n. **1.** Of, from, suited to, worthy of, belonging to family of, in service or under patronage of, a king or queen (after its noun in some phrr., *as the blood*~, *family*, RHYME¹~, PRINCESS R~, cf. *R~ Princess* used of any of ~ family; ~ *charter, warrant*, etc.; *the* ~ *anger, hands*, etc., the sovereign's; R~ ACADEMY; R~ AIR¹ *Force*; *R~ Armoured Corps*, armoured fighting vehicles and tanks; *R~ Army* ORDNANCE *Corps*; *R~ Army Service Corps*, commissariat and transport branch of army; *R~ Artillery*; ~ *blue*, a deep pure vivid shade; ~ *burgh*, holding charter from Crown; *R~ Corps of Signals*, army organization dealing with communication in the field; *R~ Courts of Justice*, building in Strand, London, in which superior courts of law & appeal are held; *R~ Electrical & Mechanical Engineers*, instituted in 1942 to do some of the work previously done by the *R~ Army Ordnance Corps*

& the R~ Army Service Corps; R~ Engineers, engineer branch of army; ~ *evil*, =
KING¹'s evil; R~ *Exchange*, building in
Cornhill, London, for dealings between
merchants; R~ *Flying Corps*, now absorbed by R~ Air Force; R~ HIGHNESS;
R~ HORSE¹ *Artillery*; R~ HUMANE *Society*;
R~ *Institution*, founded 1799 for diffusion
of scientific knowledge; R~ *Irish Constabulary*, Imperial semi-military police in
Ireland, disbanded 1921; R~ *Marine Artillery*, R~ *Marine Light Infantry*, now
united in R~ *Marines*, soldiers serving on
warships; R~ *Military Academy*, formerly
at Woolwich for Engineer & Artillery
cadets, R~ *Military College*, formerly at
Sandhurst for infantry & cavalry cadets,
now amalgamated into R~ *Military Academy* at Sandhurst; R~ *Naval Air Service*,
former naval branch of R~ Air Force;
R~ *Naval Division*, military force raised
in the 1914–18 war from surplus sailors &
marines; R~ *Naval Reserve*, drawn from
mercantile marine; R~ *Naval Volunteer
Reserve*, drawn from landsmen used to
the sea; R~ *Navy*, Navy, ~ *oak*, in which
Charles II hid after Worcester; R~ *Observer Corps*, civilian organization for
observing aircraft; ~ ROAD *to*; R~
SOCIETY; ~ *standard*, square banner with
~ arms). **2.** Kingly, majestic, stately,
splendid, firstrate, on great scale, of
exceptional size etc., (~ *magnanimity*;
gave us ~ *entertainment*; *tn* ~ *spirits*; *had
a* ~ *time*; BATTLE¹; ~ *paper*, 24 × 19 in.
for writing & 25 × 20 for printing; ~
octavo etc., folded from this; ~ *fern*,
osmund; ~ *stag*, with head of 12 or more
points; ~ *sail, mast*, above topgallant sail
& mast; ~ *arch*, degree in free-masonry);
hence~·LY² adv. **3.** n. Member of ~ family
(colloq.); ~ *stag*; ~ *sail* or *mast*; (the R~-s,
the R~ Scots, (also) the R~ Marines. [f.
OF *roial* f. L *regalis* (rex king, -AL)]
roy'alist, n. **1.** Monarchist, supporter of
monarchy as an institution or of the
royal side in civil war etc. (also attrib.).
2. *Die-hard (esp. in phr. *economic ~ist*).
So ~·ISM(3) n., ~is'tic a. [-IST]
roy'alty, n. **1.** Office or dignity or power
of king or queen, sovereignty; royal person; member of royal family (usu. in
pl.); (usu. in pl.) prerogative(s) or privilege(s) of the sovereign. **2.** Royal right
(now esp. over minerals) granted by
sovereign to individual or corporation.
(hist.) lessee's payment to land-owner for
privilege of working mine; sum paid to
patentee for use of patent or to author
etc. for each copy of his book etc. sold.
[f. OF *rotalté* (ROYAL, -TY)]
∥**Roy'ston crow** (-ō), n. Hooded or grey
crow. [place-name]
rub¹, v.t. & i.¹ (-bb-), & n. **1.** Subject to
friction, slide one's hand or an object
along over or up & down the surface of
one, (~ *one's hands*, each with the other usu.

in sign of keen satisfaction; ~ *shoulders*,
come into contact with other people; ~
noses, of some savages, greet each other;
~ *the wrong way*, stroke against the grain,
irritate or repel as by stroking cat up
wards). **2.** Polish, clean, abrade, chafe,
make *dry, sore, bare,* etc., by ~bing.
3. Reproduce design of (sepulchral brass
or stone) by ~bing paper laid on it with
coloured chalk etc., whence ~b'ING(2) n.
4. Slide (hand, object) *against* or *on* or *over*
something, (objects) *together* or *together*,
with friction. **5.** Bring (stain etc.) *out*,
(nap etc., or fig. novelty, shyness, etc.)
off or *away*, force (liniment etc., or fig.
lesson, humiliating fact, etc.) *in* or *into*,
bring size or level of *down*, spread (ointment etc.) *over*, groom (horse, oneself)
down, freshen or brush (tarnished object,
or fig. one's memory, Greek, etc.) *up*, mix
(chocolate, pigment, etc.) *up* into paste,
~ *by ~bing* lit. or fig. **6.** Come into or be in
sliding contact, exercise friction, *against*
or *on*. **7.** (Of bowl) be retarded or diverted
by unevenness of ground, (fig. of person,
process, etc.) go *on, along, through*, with
more or less restraint or difficulty. **8.** (Of
cloth, skin, etc.) get frayed or worn or
sore or bare with friction. **9.** ~ *stone*,
(piece of) stone used for sharpening,
smoothing, etc. **10.** n. Spell of ~bing
(*give it a* ~, ~ *up*, ~ *down*, etc.). **11.**
(Bowls) inequality of ground impeding or
diverting bowl, the being diverted etc.,
by this (prov., *those who play at bowls
must look for* ~*s*); (transf.) impediment or
difficulty (*there's the* ~, that is the point at
which doubt or difficulty arises; *the* ~*s
& worries of life*); (Golf) ~ *of* or *on the
green*, accidental interference with course
or position of ball. [etym. dub.; cf. LG
rub². See RUBBER².]
rub-a-dub, n. & v.i. (Make) rolling
sound of drum. [imit.]
rubato (roōbah-), a. & n. (mus.). (Tempo)
~, time varied for expression. [It., =
robbed]
rubb'er¹, n., & v.t. In vbl senses: also or
esp.: masseur or masseuse; Turkish-bath
attendant; implement used for, part of
machine operating by, rubbing; caoutchouc or india-~ (often attrib.; vb, coat
with ~); superior soft brick that can be
rubbed down to any desired shape; *(pl.)
galoshes; ~*neck* (sl.), gaping sightseer,
inquisitive person. [~ER¹, India-~ sense
from use in rubbing out pencil-marks]
rubb'er², n. Three successive games between same sides or persons at whist,
bridge, cribbage, backgammon, etc.
(*have a* ~ *of whist* etc., or *a* ~); *the* ~ (also
abbr. *the rub*), winning of two games in
~, third game when each side has won
one. [etym. dub.; as term in bowls from
c. 1600; in early use often *a rubbers*]

rubb'ish, n. & int. Waste material, debris, refuse, litter; worthless material or articles, trash, (*a good riddance of bad* ~, esp. at departure of person one dislikes) absurd ideas or suggestions, nonsense (often as excl. of contempt), whence ~y² & colloq. in same sense ~**ing**, aa. [ME *roboUS, robeUS*, perh. AF pl. of foll.]

rubb'ble, n. Waste fragments of stone, brick, etc., from old houses; pieces of undressed stone used, esp. as filling-in, for walls; (Geol.) loose angular stones etc. as covering of some rocks, also water-worn stones. Hence **rubb'ly²** a. [cf. Icel. *rubb(i)* refuse]

*****rube** (rōō-), n. (colloq.). Country bumpkin, hick. [abbr. of *Reuben*]

ru'befy, -ify, (rōō-), v.t. Make red; (Med., of counter-irritant) stimulate (skin etc.) to redness, so **rubefa'cient** (-āshent) a. &c., see -ENT(2), n., **rubefac'tion** n. (rōō-). [ult. f. L *rubefacere* (*rubēre* be red, -FY)]

ru'bicelle (rōō-), n. Orange-red precious stone, kind of spinel ruby. [F, prob. dim. of *rubis* or *rubace* RUBY]

Ru'bicon (rōō-), n., & v.t. **1.** *The boundary by passing which one becomes committed to an enterprise* (usu. *pass* or *cross the* ~). **2.** (r~; Piquet) winning of game before opponent has scored 100; (v.t.) defeat (opponent) thus. [name of stream limiting Caesar's province & crossed by him before war with Pompey]

ru'bicund (rōō-), a. (Of face, complexion, or person in these respects) ruddy, high-coloured. Hence ~ITY (-tĭn-) n. [f. L *rubicundus* (*rubēre* be red, -ND¹)]

rubid'ium (rōō-), n. Soft silvery metallic element grouped with caesium, lithium, potassium, & sodium. [L *rubidus* red (w. ref. to spectrum lines), -IUM]

rubi'ginous (rōō-), a. Rust-coloured. [L *rubigo -inis* rust, -OUS]

ru'bious (rōō-), a. (poet.). Ruby-coloured. [-OUS]

ru'bric (rōō-), n. **1.** Heading of chapter, section, etc., also special passage or sentence, written or printed in red or in special lettering. **2.** Direction for conduct of divine service (prop. in red) inserted in liturgical book, whence ~AL a., ~ALLY² adv., **rubri'CIAN** (-ĭshn), ~ISM(2), nn., (rōō-). **3.** (Red-letter entry in) calendar of saints (now rare). [f. L *rubrica* (*ruber rubr-* red)]

ru'bricate (rōō-), v.t. Mark with, print or write in, red; furnish with rubrics. Hence ~A'TION, ~ātor², nn. [L *rubricare*, -ATE³]

ru'by (rōō-), n. & a., & v.t. **1.** Rare precious stone (also *true* or *Oriental* ~) of colour varying from deep crimson to purple to pale rose (*balas, spinel,* ~, stones of less value resembling ~; *above rubies*, of inestimable value). **2.** (Of glowing purple-tinged red colour. **3.** Red pimple

on nose or face. **4.** Red wine; (Pugil.) blood. **5.** A size of TYPE. **6.** ~ *glass,* coloured with oxides of copper, iron, lead, tin, etc.; ~*-tail,* insect of deep metallic bluish-green with upper side of abdomen bright red (also *Gold wasp*). **7.** v.t. Dye or tinge ~-colour. [f. OF *rubi(s)*, prob. ult. f. L *rubeus* red]

ruche (rōōsh, & see AP.), n. Frill or quilling of gauze, lace, etc. Hence **ruched²** (rōōsht) a. [F]

ruck¹, n. Main body of competitors left out of the running. [earlier senses *stack of fuel, heap, large quantity*; perh. cogn. w. RICK¹]

ruck², ‖ **ruc'kle¹**, nn., & vv.i. & t. Crease, wrinkle, (as vb usu. ~ *up*). [ruck(le³) f. n., f. ON *hrukka*; ruck(le³) f. *ruck*, -LE(3)]

ruc'kle², v.i., & n. (Make) gurgling sound esp. in throat of dying person. [f. Scand. (Norw. dial. *rukla* vb)]

ruc'ksack (rōō-), n. Bag slung by straps from both shoulders & resting on back for carrying walker's or climber's necessaries. [G]

ruc'tion, n. (sl.). Disturbance, tumult, row, (*there will be* ~s, things will not be allowed to proceed quietly). [from 1825; etym. dub.]

rudbeck'ia, n. (Kinds of) composite garden plant of the aster family native to N. America. [f. *Rudbeck*, surname of two Swedish botanists (c. 1700), -IA¹]

rudd, n. Freshwater fish resembling roach, red-eye. [prob. f. obs. *rud* red colour; cogn. w. RED]

rudd'le, n., & v.t. **1.** Red ochre, esp. of kind used for marking sheep. **2.** v.t. Mark or colour (as) with ~. [as RUDD]

rudd'ock, n. Robin redbreast. [OE *rud-duc* (RUDD, -OCK)]

ridd'y, a., & v.t. & i. **1.** (Of face or its owner) freshly or healthily red, rosy, (~*y health, youth,* etc., marked by ~iness); (of light, fire, sky, object lighted up, etc., also in animal names as ~*y plover, squirrel*) reddish; ‖(sl.) bloody, damnable; hence ~ily² adv., ~iness n. **2.** v.b. Make or grow ~y. [OE *rudig* (*rud* see RUDD, -Y²)]

rude (rōōd), a. **1.** Primitive, simple, unsophisticated, in natural state, rugged, unimproved, uncivilized, uneducated, roughly made or contrived or executed, coarse, artless, wanting subtlety or accuracy, (~ *times, men, simplicity, ignorance, chaos;* ~ *produce, ore;* ~ *scenery;* ~ *plough, beginnings, methods;* ~ *path, verses, drawing;* ~ *fare, plenty;* ~ *writer, style;* ~ *observer, version, classification*),

2. Violent, not gentle, unrestrained, startling, sudden, abrupt, (~ *passions, blast, shock, awakening, reminder*). **3.** Vigorous, hearty (~ *health*). **4.** Insolent, impertinent, offensive (~ *remarks; say ~ things; be ~ to*, insult). Hence ~ly² adv., ~NESS, (colloq.) ru'derY(4), nn., ru'd-ISH¹(2) a., (colloq.) ~(2).

Rü'deshei·mer (rŏŏdés-hī-), n. A white Rhine wine. [G (*Rü-*)]

ru'diment (rŏŏ-), n. (Pl.) elements or first principles of or of knowledge or some subject; (pl.) imperfect beginning of something that will develop or might under other conditions have developed, (sing.) part or organ imperfectly developed as having no function (e.g. the breast in males). Hence **rudimén'tal, aa., ~rudimén'tary, aa.**, (rŏŏ-). [f. L *rudimentum* (RUDE, -MENT)]

rue¹ (rŏŏ), v.t. & n. **1.** Repent of, bitterly feel the consequences of, wish undone or unbefallen, (*got shall ~ it; ~ the day, hour, etc., when ~*). **2.** n. (arch.). Repentance, dejection at some occurrence, whence (in ordinary & esp. joc. use) ~'FUL a. (*Knight of the ~ful countenance*, Don Quixote), ~'fully² adv., ~'FULNESS n.; compassion, ruth. [OE *hréow(an)*, cf. Du. *rouw(en)*, G *reu(en)*]

rue² (rŏŏ), n. Perennial evergreen shrub with bitter-strong-scented leaves formerly used in medicine. [F, f. L *ruta* f. Gk *rhutē*]

|| **rue·rá'ddy** (rŏŏ-), n. Belt or rope passed over shoulder to drag something with. [?]

ruffes'cent (rŏŏ-), a. (zool. etc.). Reddish. [L *rufescere* (*rufus* red, -ESCENT)]

ruff¹, n. **1.** Deep projecting frill of several folds of linen or muslin starched & separately goffered worn round neck esp. in 16th c.; projecting or conspicuously coloured ring of feathers or hair round bird's or beast's neck; whence (-)~ED² a. **2.** Kind of domestic pigeon. [perh. shortened f. RUFFLE]

ruff², n. (fem. *reeve*). Bird of sandpiper kind of which male has RUFF¹ & ear-tufts in breeding season. [perh. f. prec.; but vowel change (cf. *fox vixen*) suggests that it is an older wd & separate]

ruff³ n. Small freshwater fish of perch family with prickly scales. [perh. f. ROUGH]

ru'ffian, n. Brutal violent lawless turbulent person, desperado, bully, rough. Hence ~ISM(2) n., ~ly¹ a. [OF, cf. Pr. & Sp. *rufian*, It. *ruffiano*, etym. dub.]

ru'ffle, v.t. & i., & n. **1.** Disturb smoothness or tranquillity of (feathers, hair, water, temper or person in regard to it, brow; *~es up its feathers*, in anger or to keep off cold; *nothing ever ~ed him*). **2.** (of sea, hair, temper, etc.: rare) suffer ~ing, lose smoothness or calmness; swagger about, behave arrogantly or quarrelsomely, whence ~ER¹ n. **2.** n. Perturbation, bustle, (rare; *without ~e or excitement*); rippling effect on water; ornamental gathered or goffered frill of lace etc. worn at opening of garment esp. about wrist or breast or neck, RUFF¹ of bird etc., whence ~ED² (-feld) a.; (now rare) a contention, dispute; (Mil.) vibrating drum-beat. [etym. dub.; cf. LG *ruffelen* crumple, goffer; senses *swagger* etc. perh. independent]

ru'fous (rŏŏ-), a. (chiefly nat.-hist.) Reddish-brown. So ~I-, ~O-, comb. forms. [L *rufus*, -OUS]

rug (rŏŏ), n. **1.** Large wrap or coverlet of thick woollen stuff. **2.** Floor-mat or ornamental piece of thick material or thick pile, (often *hearth-~*) laid down before fireplace. [perh. f. Scand. (Norw. dial. *rugga* coverlet, Sw. *rugg* ruffled hair)]

Rüg'by·an (-bĕan), n. & a. (Member) of Rugby School.

rug'by², n. ~ *football* or ~, also **rügg'Er¹** (-g-) n. (sl.), one of the two chief forms of football, distinguished from *Association*, or *soccer* esp. by players' being permitted to carry the ball & to hold opponent doing this; ~ *Union*, of clubs using ~ football rules. [~ *school*]

rügg'ed (-g-), a. Of rough uneven surface (*~ bark; ~ ground, country*, full of abrupt ups & downs, craggy, wooded, etc.; *~ features*, strongly marked, of irregular outline); unsoftened, unpolished, lacking gentleness or refinement, harsh in sound, austere, unbending, involving hardship, (*~ manners, grandeur, kindness, honesty, character, verse, times, life*). Hence ~ly² adv., ~NESS n. [prob. f. Scand. cogn. w. RUG, RAG¹, ROUGH]

rugger². See RUGBY.

rugóse' (rŏŏ-), a. (chiefly nat.-hist.). Wrinkled, corrugated. Hence or cogn. ~ly² adv., **ru'gate²**, **ru'gŌus**, aa., **rugos'iTY** n., (rŏŏ-). [f. L *rugosus* (*ruga* wrinkle, -OSE¹)]

ru'in (rŏŏ-), n., & v.t. & i. **1.** Downfall or fallen or wrecked or impaired estate, lit. (of building or structure: *the crash of ~; tumble, lie, lay, in ~*) or fig. (*the ~ of my hopes; bring to ~*, complete loss of property or position; *dates her ~ from his arrival*; RACK¹ & ~); (often pl.) what remains of building, town, structure, etc., or fig. of person, that has suffered ~ (*the ~s of Rome*, remains of ancient Rome or of the Roman imperial system; *'is but the ~ of what he was; lies in ~s; is a ~; lives in an old ~*); what causes ~, destroying agency or havoc, (*will be the ~ of us*; BLUE¹ ~;

rapine & red ~), so [f. obs. *ruinate* vb]
ruin^'tion (rŏŏ-) n. **2.** vb. Reduce (place)
to ~s (esp. in p.p.); bring to ~ (*her extravagance ~ed him*; so ~ oneself; ~ *girl*,
seduce her ; ~ *one's new hat, prospects*);
(poet.) fall headlong or with a crash. [f. F
ruine(r) f. (vb thr. med. L *ruinare*) L
ruina (*ruere* fall, -INE⁴)]
ru'inous (rŏŏ-), a. In ruins, dilapidated ;
bringing ruin, disastrous, (~ *folly, expense*), whence ~**LY²** adv. Hence ~**NESS**
n. [f. L *ruinosus* (prec. -OSE¹)]
rule (rŏŏl), n., & v.t. & i. **1.** Principle to
which action or procedure conforms or is
bound or intended to conform, dominant
custom, canon, test, standard, normal
state of things, (*deduce ~s of action*; *the
~s of decorum, cricket*, etc.; ~ *of the
ROAD¹*; *there was a ~ that ~* : *standing ~*,
made by corporation to govern its procedure ; ~ *of thumb*, based on experience
or practice, not theory, often ~*-of-thumb*
attrib.; ~ *of three*, method of finding
number that bears same ratio to one
given as exists between two others given ;
also attrib., as ~*-of-three sum*; GOLDEN ~ ;
by ~, in regulation manner, mechanically ;
WORK² *to* ~ ; *hard & fast* ~, rigid formula ;
EXCEPTION *proves* ~; *large families law the
exception & not the* ~ ; *as a* ~, usually,
more often than not). **2.** Sway, government, dominion, (*bear* ~, *hold sway*;
under British ~ ; *the ~ of force*; *entrusted
with the ~ of half the tribe*). **3.** (Eccl.) code
of discipline observed by religious order.
4. (Law) order made by judge or court w.
ref. to particular case only (~ NISI ; ~
absolute, making ~ *nisi* no longer contingent). **5.** (Hist.) *the* ~s, limited area
outside Fleet & King's-Bench prisons in
which prisoners were allowed to live on
certain terms. **6.** Graduated often jointed
straight measure used by carpenters etc.
(*often foot~, 2 ft* ~, etc.). **7.** (Print.) thin
slip of metal for separating headings,
columns, etc.; also short (*en* ~) or long
(*em* ~) dash in punctuation etc. **8.** ~
joint, of kind usual in jointed carpenter's
~ ; hence ~**'LESS** (rŏŏl-l-) a. **9.** vb. Exercise
sway or decisive influence over, keep
under control, curb, (person, conduct,
one's passions; *ruling passion*, motive
that habitually directs one's actions);
(pass.) consent to follow *advice*, be
guided *by*. **10.** Be the ruler(s) or have the
sovereign control of or over, bear ~, (~
the ROAST; ~*s over many millions*; *kings
should ~ by love*). **11.** (Of prices, or goods
etc. in regard to them or to quality etc.)
have a specified general level, be for the
most part, (*corn, prices, the market, ~d
high* etc.; *crops ~ good*; *ruling prices*,
those current). **12.** Give judicial or
authoritative decision (usu. *that*; also ~
person or thing out of order; ~ *out,
exclude*, pronounce irrelevant or ineli-
gible), whence **ru'lING¹(2)** (rŏŏ-) n. **13.**

Make parallel lines across (paper), make
(straight line), with ruler or mechanical
help. [f. OF *riule(r)* f. L *regula, regulare*,
see REGULAR]
ru'ler (rŏŏ-), n. **1.** Person or thing bearing
(esp. sovereign) rule (often *of*), whence
~**SHIP** n. **2.** Straight strip or cylinder
usu. of wood used in ruling paper or lines.
[-ER¹]
‖ **rŭll'ey, rŏl', röl',** n. (pl. ~s). Flat four-
wheeled dray, lorry. [?]
rŭm¹, n. **1.** Spirit distilled from sugar-
cane; ~**SHRUB². 2.** *Any intoxicating
liquor (usu. with hostile sense); *~
runner* (colloq.), smuggler of intoxicants,
or ship engaged in the traffic; *~ row*
(colloq.), position outside the prohibited
area taken up by ~*-running* vessels.
[formerly *rumbullion, rumbustion, rumbo*,
etym. dub.]
rŭm², rŭmm'y¹, aa. (sl.). Odd, strange,
queer; ~ *customer*, (esp.) person or animal
that is dangerous to meddle with ; ~ *start*
(sl.), surprising occurrence. Hence **rŭm!**
LY² adv., **rŭm'NESS,
rŭmm'iNESS,** nn. [16th-c. cant, orig.
=*fine, spirited*, perh. var. of ROM¹; -Y²]
Ruman(ian). See ROMANSH.
Rumansh. See ROMANSH.
rŭm'ba (or rŏŏ-), n. Cuban negro dance;
ballroom dance imitative of this. [Sp.]
rŭm'ble¹, v.i. & t., & n. **1.** Make sound
(as) of thunder, earthquake, heavy cart,
air in the bowels, etc.; *go along, by*, etc.,
making or in vehicles making such
sound; utter, *say out, give forth*, with
such sound. **2.** n. Rumbling sound ; hind
part of carriage arranged as extra seat or
for luggage; ~*tumble*, lumbering vehicle,
rough motion. [ME *romblen*, cf. Du.
rommelen, G *rummeln*, prob. imit.]
‖ **rŭm'ble²,** v.t. (sl.). Get to the bottom
of, see through, detect. [?]
rŭmbŭs'tious, a. (colloq.). Boisterous,
uproarious. [perh. var. of ROBUSTIOUS]
Rumeliote. See ROUMELIOTE.
ru'měn (rŏŏ-), n. Ruminant's first STOM-
ACH. [L, =throat]
ru'minant (rŏŏ-), n. & a. **1.** Animal that
chews cud. **2.** adj. Belonging to the ~s ;
contemplative, given to or engaged **in**
meditation. [foll. -ANT]
ru'miňāte (rŏŏ-), v.i. & t. Chew the cud ;
meditate, ponder, (i., rarely t.; often *over,
about, of, on*), whence or cogn. ~**ATIVE** a.,
~**ATIVELY²** adv., ~**ĀTOR²** n. So ~**A'TION**
(rŏŏ-) n. [f. L *ruminari* (RUMEN), -ATE³]
rŭmm'age, v.t. & i., & n. **1.** Ransack
(ship, house, pockets, records, book),
make search in or *in*, make search; fish
out or *up* from among other things; disarrange, throw *about*, in searching. **2.**
Things got by ~*ing*, miscellaneous accumulation ; ~*ing*, search (esp. of ship by
Customs officer); ~*e sale*, clearance sale
of unclaimed articles at docks etc., sale of
odds & ends contributed to raise money

for charity bazaar. [n. in mod. senses f. vb : vb orig. f. n. in obs. sense *arranging of casks etc. in hold.* f. OF *arrumage* (now *arri-*) f. *arrumer* etym. dub.]

rŭm'er, n. Large drinking-glass. [f. WFlem. *rummer* or Du. *römer* etym. dub.] perh. = Roman glass]

rummy. See RUM³.

rŭm'my², n. Simple card game resembling COON-CAN, played with two packs. [?]

rumour (rōōm'er), n., & v.t. **1.** General talk, report, or hearsay of doubtful accuracy; *a* or *the current but unverified statement or assertion* (often *that, of*). **2.** v.t. (usu. in pass.). Report by way of ~ (*it is ~ed that—; he is ~ed to be etc.; the ~ed disaster*). [OF, f. L *rumorem* nom. *-or*]

rump, n. **1.** Tail-end, posterior, buttocks, of beast or bird or rarely of person, whence (of tailless fowl) ~LESS a. **2.** Small or contemptible remnant of a parliament or similar body, esp. the R~ (hist.), that of Long Parliament either after its restoration 1659 or from Pride's Purge 1648 to its first dissolution 1653. **3.** ~ *steak*, cut from ox's ~. [prob. f. Scand. (Da. *rumpe*, Sw. & Norw. *rumpa*)]

rŭm'ple, v.t. Wrinkle, crease, tousle, disorder. (fabric, leaves, garment, hair, etc.). [cf. MDu. *rompelen*, MLG *rumpen*]

rŭm'pus, n. (sl.). Disturbance, brawl, row, uproar. [?]

||**rŭm'py**, n. Manx tailless cat. [RUMP, -Y²]

rŭm-tŭm', n. Light sculling-boat on lower Thames. [?]

run, v.i. & t. (-nn-, *ran*; p.p. rarely as -ED²(2), as a *fresh~ salmon*). **I.** General senses. **1.** (Of men) progress by advancing each foot alternately never having both on ground at once (cf. WALK¹; ~*ning jump*, in which jumper ~*s* to the take-off); (of animals) go at quicker than walking pace, amble, trot, canter, gallop, etc. **2.** (Start to) cross cricket pitch to score run. **3.** Flee, abscond, (chiefly now in ~ *for it, cut & ~* sl.; ~*ning fight*, Naut., kept up by retreating ship or fleet with pursuer). **4.** Go or travel hurriedly, precipitately, etc., (~ *to meet one's troubles*, anticipate them; ~ RIOT; ~ *to help another*; ~ *over* or *down* or *up*, to place for flying visit; *he who ~s may read*, said of easily intelligible exposition etc.). **5.** Be allowed to grow or stray *wild*. **6.** Compete in or race (~ *second* etc., come pete in); seek election etc. (for parliament, president, etc.). **7.** (Of fish, ship, etc.) go straight & fast (in ~*ning whale; salmon* ~, go up river from sea; *ship* ~*s before the wind, into port, ashore, on the rocks*, FOUL *of* or *aboard* another). **8.** Advance (~*ing on wheels*, spin round or along, revolve (as) on axle, go with sliding or smooth or continuous or easy motion, be in action, work freely, be current or be street

operative, (*ball, carriage, wheel, spindle, sledge, time,* ~*s; rope* ~*s in pulley; his life* ~*s smoothly;* ~*ning knot, that slips along rope & enlarges or diminishes* ~*ning noose;* ~*ning hand*, writing in which pen etc. is not lifted after each letter; *how your tongue* ~*s!*, how incessantly you talk!; *verse* ~*s,* is smooth; *tune* ~*s in head,* seems to be heard over & over again; *lease, contract,* ~*s for seven* etc. *years; play ran 100 nights,* was kept on stage; *courage* ~*s in the family,* is found in all members of it; *the works have ceased* ~*ning; place where writs do not* ~, are not valid or respected). **9.** (Of public conveyance by land or water) ply (*from, to, between*). **10.** (Of colour in fabric) spread from the dyed to the undyed parts, (of thought, eye, memory, etc.) pass through one's head; *eyes* ~ *over object;* ~*ning commentary*, touching on a point here & there, broadcast report by eye-witness of ceremonial, sporting event, etc.; ~ *back over the post*, survey it summarily. **11.** (Of thought, eye, memory, etc.) pass in transitory or cursory way (*thoughts* ~*ning through one's head; eyes* ~ *over object; ~ning commentary*). **12.** (Of liquid, grain, sand, etc.) flow, be wet, drip, flow with, (*till the blood ran; ran blood; foundations* ~ *wine; is* ~*ning with oil; tide* ~*s strong; river* ~*s clear, thick; feeling ran high; one's blood* ~*s cold,* he is horrified; *the sands are* ~*ning out,* time of grace etc. is nearly up; ~*ning sore,* suppurating; *nose, eyes,* ~, drop mucus or tears; ~ *at the nose;* ~ *with sweat;* ~ *dry,* cease to flow, be exhausted; ~ *low, short,* become scanty; *candle* ~*s, gutters*). **13.** Extend, be continuous, have a certain course or order, progress, proceed, have a tendency or common characteristic or average price or level, (*fence* ~*s round the house;* phr. applied to immemorial tradition or custom; ~*ning account,* = *current* ACCOUNT; *road* ~*s at right angles to, those; the ridge's story, title, document,* ~*s in those words; must not* ~ *to extremes;* ~*s to sentiment; our pears* ~ *big this year,* are so for the most part; *prices* ~ *high; oats* ~ *44 lb. to the bushel*); (in part, placed after pl. n.) following each other without interval, in succession. (*happened three days, hit the bull's-eye seven times,* ~*ning*). **14.** (With cogn. obj.) pursue, follow, traverse, cover, make way swiftly through, or over, wander about in, perform, essay or be exposed or submit to, (*course, way, race, a mile,* run at cricket; *things must* ~ *their course,* be left to themselves; ~ *a scent,* follow it up; ~ *the streets,* be street

arab; ~ *errands, messages,* be a messenger; *the Derby was* ~ *in a snow-storm;* ~ *the* GAUNTLET†; ~ RISKS; ~ s a chance of being, may be; ~ *rapids,* shoot them; ~ *croquethoop,* send ball clear through it; ~ BLOCKADE†). 15. Sew (fabric) slightly. 16. Chase, hunt, have ~ning race with, (~ *fox five miles;* ~ *to earth,* chase to its lair, & often fig. = discover after long search; *will* ~ *you for £50 a side;* ~ *one hard* or *close,* press him severely in race, competition, or comparative merit etc.). 17. (In causative senses) make ~ or go (~ *cattle* etc., turn out to graze; ~ *brandy* etc., smuggle it in by evading coastguard etc.; ~ *ship aground, to New York;* ~ *boat down to the water;* ~ *cart into wall;* ~ *one's head against;* ~ *cart into wall;* ~ *sword, pin, into;* ~ *one's hand, eye, along, down, over,* something; ~ *rope through eyelet;* ~ *coach, steamer, business, person,* keep them going, manage them, conduct their operations; ~ *the show,* sl., dominate in an undertaking etc.; ~ *horse,* send him in for race, so ~ *candidate;* ~ *metal into mould;* ~ *the water off;* ~ *parallel, simile,* etc., *too far; ran his fingers, comb, through his hair;* ~ *thing fine,* leave very little margin of time or amount concerning it). 18. ~'*about,* (a.) roving, (n.) light motor-car; ~'*away* n. & a., fugitive, bolting (horse), ~*away match* or *marriage,* after elopement, ~*away ring* or *knock,* given at door by practical joker who immediately makes off. II. With prepp. 1. ~ *across,* fall in with. 2. ~ *after,* pursue with attentions, seek society of, give much time to (pursuit etc.). 3. ~ *against,* fall in with. 4. ~ *at,* assail by charging or rushing. 5. ~ *in* (incur) *debt.* 6. ~ *into,* fall into (practice, absurdity, etc.), be continuous or coalesce with, have collision with, reach or attain (*some length, five editions,* etc.). 7. ~ *on,* be concerned with (*talk, mind,* ~ *s on a subject*). 8. ~ *over,* review, glance over, peruse, recapitulate; touch (notes of piano etc.) in quick succession. 9. ~ *through,* examine cursorily, peruse, deal successively with; consume (estate etc.) by reckless or quick spending, pervade. 10. ~ *to,* reach (amount, number, etc.); have money or ability or (of money etc.) be enough for (some expense or undertaking); fall into (ruin); (of plants) tend to develop chiefly (seed); (of persons) indulge inclination towards (coarseness etc.). 11. ~ *upon,* (of thoughts etc.) be engrossed by, dwell on; (of person) encounter suddenly. III. With advv. 1. ~ *about,* bustle, hurry from one person to another, (esp. of children) play or wander without restraint. 2. ~ *away,* flee, abscond, elope; (of horse) bolt, (of horse or person) get clear away from competitors in race. 3. ~ *away with,* carry off (per-

son, stolen property, etc.); accept (notion) hastily; (of expense etc.) consume (money etc.); (of horse etc.) bolt with (rider, carriage or its occupants). 4. ~ *down,* (of clock etc.) stop for want of winding; (of person or his health etc.) become enfeebled from overwork, poor feeding, etc. (also in p.p. as *is, feels, much* ~ *down*); knock down or collide with (person, ship, etc.); overtake (game, person) in pursuit, discover after search; disparage. 5. ~ *in,* (of combatant) rush to close quarters; (Rugby footb.) carry ball over opponents' goal-line & touch it down; pay short visit (to person or house); (colloq.) arrest & take to prison; (colloq.) secure election of (candidate); bring (new machinery) into good working order by ~ning it. 6. ~ *off,* flee, flow away, digress suddenly; write or recite (poem, list, etc.) fluently; drain (liquid) off; decide (race) after tie or trial heats. 7. ~ *on,* be joined together (of written characters); continue in operation; elapse; speak volubly, talk incessantly; (Print.) begin (t. & i. of sentence etc.), in same line as what precedes. 8. ~ *out,* come to an end (of period, also of stock of something or its owner; ~ *out of,* exhaust one's stock of); escape from containing vessel; advance from block to hit ball in cricket; pass or be paid out (of rope); jut out; come out of contest in specified position etc. or complete required score etc.; complete (race); advance (gun etc.) so as to project; put down wicket of (batsman while ~ning); exhaust oneself by ~ning. 9. ~ *over,* overflow (of vessel or contents); recapitulate, review, glance over. 10. ~ *through,* pierce with sword etc.; draw line through (written words). 11. ~ *up,* grow quickly, rise in price, amount to; be RUNNER-UP; accumulate (number, sum, debt) quickly; force (rival bidder) to bid higher, force up (price or commodity in that respect); erect (wall, house) to great height or in unsubstantial or hurried way; add up (column of figures). [ME *rinnen, rennen,* prob. f. ON *rinna,* cf. MDu. & G *rinnen;* OE has *rinnan* very rarely, & usu. the metathetic forms *irnan* intr. & *æornan* trans.]

run², n. 1. Act or spell of RUN²ing (*have a* ~ *for one's money,* get some enjoyment etc. out of expenditure or effort, orig. w. ref. to scratching of horse after bets; *had a good* ~, esp. in hunting or on ship, train, etc.; *on the* ~, fleeing, also bustling about; *at a* ~, running; *a* ~ *on the Continent, to Paris,* etc., short excursion or visit); distance travelled by ship in specific time (usu. 24 hours). 2. (Cricket) traversing of pitch by both batsmen without either's being put out, point scored thus or otherwise, notch. 3. Rhythmical motion, way things tend to move, direction, (*cannot get the* ~

of the metre, or of some process or opera-tion, see how it goes: *the ~ of the market was against us*; *the ~ of the hills is NW.*). **4.** Rapid fall (*come down with a ~*, of building etc. prices, mercury in barometer etc., prices, etc.). **5.** (Mus.) rapid scale passage. **6.** Continuous stretch or spell or course, long series or succession, general demand, (*a 500 ft ~ of pipe*; *a long ~ of power, office*; *a ~ of luck*; *in the* LONG *~*; *a ~ on the bank*, sudden demand from many customers for immediate payment; *~ on rubber, book*, etc., great demand for it; so *book etc. has a considerable ~ on it*; *the red in rouge-et-noir, its coming many times running*; *play has a ~ of 50 nights*, *a long ~*, etc.). **7.** Common, general, average, or ordinary type or class (*the common ~ of men*, average men); class or line of goods: batch or drove of animals born or reared together, shoal of fish in motion. **8.** Regular track of some animals, enclosure for fowls etc., range of pasture (usu. *sheep* etc. *~*). **9.** Trough for water to run in. **10.** Part of ship's bottom narrowing towards stern. **11.** Licence to make free use of (*allowed him the ~ of their books, house*; *the ~ of one's teeth*, free board). **12.** (Of aircraft) flight on a straight and even course at a constant speed before or while dropping bombs (also *~-in* or *~-up*). **13.** *~-in*, act of run-ning in (see prec.), at football, see also sense 12; *~-off*, deciding race after dead heat; *~-up*, race between greyhounds up to hare's first turn, see also sense 12. [f. prec.]

run·agate, n. (arch.). Vagabond. [as-sim. of RENEGADE to *run* & obs. *agate* away]

run'cinate, a. (bot.). Saw-toothed, with lobes curved towards base. [L *runcina* plane (wrongly supposed to be saw), -ATE²]

‖**run·dale**, n. Joint occupation of (esp. Irish) land, each holder having several strips not contiguous. [RUN¹, obs. *dale* north. var. of DOLE¹]

rune (rōōn), n. **1.** Any letter of earliest Teutonic alphabet used esp. by Scandi-navians & Anglo-Saxons, dating from as early as 2nd c. & formed by modifying Roman or Greek characters to suit carv-ing; similar mark of mysterious or magic significance. **2.** (Division of) Finnish poem. **3.** *~-staff*, magic wand inscribed with *~s*, also runic calendar. [f. ON *rún*, cogn. w. OE *rún* whisper, secret counsel, whence ROUND⁵]

rung¹, n. Short stick attached at each end as rail, spoke, or cross-bar in chair etc. or esp. in ladder (often fig., as *the lowest, topmost, ~ of Fortune's ladder*). Hence ~ED²(g'd), ~'LESS, aa. [OE *hrung*, cf. Du. *rong* & G *runge*]

rung², **rung³**. See RING¹.

ru'nic (rōō-), a. & n. **1.** Of, in, marked with, runes; (of poetry etc.) of the ancient Scandinavian type; (of ornament) inter-lacing as on *~ monuments & metal-work*. **2.** n. *~ inscription*; kinds of (Print.) ornamental type of thick face & con-densed form. [-IC]

run·let¹, n. (arch.). Cask of varying size for wine etc. [f. OF *rondelet* dim. of *rondelle* dim. of *ronde* (ROUND¹)]

run·let², n. Small stream. [RUN¹, -LET]

runn·el, n. Brook, rill; gutter. [OE *rynel* f. RUN¹, -LE(1)]

rünn·er, n. In vbl senses: also or esp.: **1.** Messenger, scout, collector, or agent for bank etc., tout; (Hist., esp. Bow-STREET *~*) police-officer. **2.** The bird water-rail. **3.** =BLOCKADE¹. **4.** Revolv-ing millstone. **5.** =BLOCKAGE¹. **6.** Creeping stem that issues from main stem of strawberry & other having book & takes root; kinds of twining bean, esp. SCARLET *~*. **7.** Ring etc. that slides on rod, strap, etc.; one of the long pieces of wood etc. on which sledge etc. slides, (blade of) FEN *~*; groove or rod for thing to slide along; roller for moving heavy article. **8.** *~-up*, dog beaten only in final heat at coursing; competitor similarly beaten at golf etc. [-ER¹]

‖**run·rig**, n. (Sc.). =RUNDALE. [RUN¹, Sc. & north. *rig* RIDGE]

rün·ning, n. In vbl senses: esp.: (w. ref. to racing) *make, take up, the ~*, take the lead, set the pace, (lit., & fig. of talk etc.), *in, out of, the ~*, (of competition) with good, no, chance of winning; *~-board*, footboard on either side of a locomotive, motor-car, etc.; *~ powers*, right granted by railway to another to run trains over its line. [-ING¹]

rün·way, n. **1.** Trail to animals' watering-place. **2.** Incline down which logs are slid. **3.** Gangway (usu. of special kind). **4.** Specially prepared surface in airfield, for taking off and landing. [RUN¹]

rü·pee (rōō-), n. Indian monetary unit & silver coin, par 1s. 6d. (*pl. abbr.* Rs; *Rx*, tens of *~s*, in statistics etc.). [f. Hind. *rupiyah* f. Skr. *rupya* wrought silver]

rüp·ture, n. & v.t. & i. **1.** Breach of harmonious relations, disagreement & parting; (Path.) tumour formed by pro-trusion of part of an organ through breach in wall of containing cavity esp. in abdomen, hernia; breaking, breach. **2.** vb. Burst, break, (cell, vessel, mem-brane); sever (connexion, marriage, etc.); affect with hernia; suffer *~*. [f. L *ruptura* (*rumpere rupt-* break, -URE)]

rur·al (rōōr-), a. In, of, suggesting, the country (opp. URBAN), pastoral or agri-cultural, (*~* DEAN; *in ~ seclusion*; *~ policeman, ~ constituency, ~ sports*, etc.).

Hence **rurál** THY n., ~IZE(2, 3) v.i. & t., ~IZA'TION n., ~LY[2] adv. [f. L *ruralis* (*rus ruris* country, -AL)]

ruridécan'al (roor-; *also* -dēk'a-) a. Of rural DEAN[1] or deanery. [L *rus* (prec.), -I-]

Rúritā'nia (roor-), n. Imaginary Central-European kingdom, the novelist's and dramatist's locale for court romances in a modern setting; hence ~IAN a. & n. [scene of Anthony Hope's novel *The Prisoner of Zenda*]

rū'sa (rōō-), n. Large E.-Ind. deer. [Malay]

ruse (rōōz, & see AP.), n. Stratagem, feint, trick. [OF (*ruser* drive back, retreat, cogn. w. RUSH[2])]

rusé (see AP.), a. (fem. -ée). Given to ruses, sly, cunning, (of person, procedure, look, etc.). [F]

rush[1], n., & v.t. 1. Marsh or water-side plant with naked slender tapering pith-filled stems (prop. leaves) formerly used for strewing floors & still for making chair-bottoms & plaiting baskets etc., *a* stem of this, (collect.)~es as a material; thing of no value (*don't care, not worth, a ~*). 2. ‖ (~-*bearing*, annual northern festival on occasion of carrying ~es & garlands to strew floor & decorate walls of church; ~ *candle*, made by dipping pith of a ~ in tallow; ~*light*, ~ candle (usu. fig. of feeble glimmer of intelligence, scanty information, etc.); ~ *ring*, made of (~es) formerly used in (esp. mock) weddings; hence ~LIKE, ~Y[2] aa. 3. v.t. Supply (chair-bottom), strew (floor), with ~es. [OE *risc* & rare *rysc*, cf. MDu. *risch*, also Du. & G *rusch*]

rush[2], v.t. & i., & n. 1. Impel, drag, force, carry along, violently & rapidly (~*ed them into danger, round the sights; ball is ~ed down the field; ~ bill through*, get it hurriedly passed; *refuse to be ~ed*, insist on doing things at one's own pace). 2. (Mil.) take by sudden vehement assault. 3. Pass (obstacle, stream, fence, etc.) with a rapid dash. 4. Swarm upon & take possession of (goldfield, platform at meeting, etc.). 5. (sl.). Charge (customer) exorbitant price (*they ~ you shockingly, ~ed us £1 a head*). 6. Run precipitately, violently, or with great speed, go or resort without proper consideration (*in*)*to*, (*into, out of, the room; ~ at*, charge; *dark horse ~ed past the favourite; ~ into extremes; ~ into print*, write to newspaper, publish book, etc.). 7. Flow, fall, spread (intr.), roll (intr.), impetuously or fast (*river ~es past; a ~ing mighty wind; avalanches ~ down; blood ~ed to his face; his past life ~ed into his memory*). 8. n. Act of ~ing, violent or tumultuous advance, spurt, charge, onslaught, (*the ~ of the tide; carry the citadel with a ~; a ~ of blood to the head; carry the head; great ~ of business*); (Footb.) combined dash of several players

with the ball; sudden migration of large numbers esp. to new goldfield; strong run on *or* for some commodity; ~*hours* (at which traffic is busiest). [n. f. vb, AF *russher* f. OF *re*(*h*)*usser, ruser*, perh. f. L *re*(*fundere fus-* pour), RE- 9, cause to flow back]

rusk, n. Piece of bread pulled or cut from loaf & rebaked. [f. Sp. or Port. *rosca* twist, coil, roll of bread]

Rúskin'ian, a. & n. After the manner or principles, follower, of John Ruskin writer on art & social subjects d. 1900. So ~INESE' (-ēz), ~INESQUE' (-ēsk), aa. & nn., ~INISM(3) n., ~INIZE(2, 3, 4) v.i. & t. [-IAN]

Russ, n. & a. 1. A Russian; the Russian language. 2. adj. Russian. Hence ~IFY v.t., ~IFICA'TION n., ~O- comb. form, ~'OPHIL n. & a., ~ŎPH'ILISM(3) n., ~'O-PHOBE n. & a., ~OPHO'IA n. [f. Russ. *Rusi* Russian people or country]

Rúss'ell cōrd), n. Ribbed fabric of cotton & wool used for scholastic gowns etc. [?]

russ'et, n. & a. 1. (Hist.) coarse homespun reddish-brown or grey cloth worn by peasants; reddish brown; kind of rough-skinned ~-coloured apple. 2. adj. Reddish-brown (also ~Y[2] a.); (arch.) rustic, homely, simple. [f. OF *rousset* (*rous* red f. L *russus,* -ET[1])]

Rū'ssia (lea'ther) (-sha; lēdh-), n. Durable bookbinding leather from skins impregnated with birch-bark oil. [*Russia*]

Rū'ssian (-shn), n. & a. 1. Native, language, of Russia. 2. adj. Of or from Russia (~ *boots*, loosely enclosing calf); (of or in ~; hence ~IZE(3) (-sha-) v.t. [f. med. L *Russianus* (prec.-AN)]

Rúss'niák, n. & a. (Member, language) of the Little Russian or Ruthenian race in Galicia. [f. native *Rusnyaḱ*]

rŭst, n., & v.i. & t. 1. Yellowish-brown coating formed on iron or steel by oxidation esp. as effect of moisture & gradually corroding the metal, similar coating on other metals; (fig.) impaired state due to disuse or inactivity, inaction as deteriorating influence. 2. (Plant-disease with ~coloured spots caused by) kinds of fungus, blight, brand; hence ~LESS a. (~*less steel*, esp. ferro-chromium alloys used for stainless cutlery etc.). 3. vb. Contract ~, undergo oxidation or blight; (of bracken etc.) become ~coloured; lose quality or efficiency by disuse or inactivity (*better wear out than ~ out*, exhortation to maintain activity in old age etc.); affect with ~, corrode. [OE *rūst*, cf. Du. *roest*, G *rost*; cogn. w. RED]

rús'tic, a. & n. 1. (Now less usual for) rural. 2. Having the appearance or manners of country-people, characteristic of peasants, unsophisticated, unpolished, unrefined, uncouth, clownish (~

seed, bridge, work, of untrimmed branches or rough timber); (of lettering) irregularly formed; (Archit.) with rough-hewn or roughened surface or with chamfered joints (~work, such masonry); hence or cogn. **rus'ticALLY** n. 4. n. Countryman, peasant. **rusti'cITY** n. [f. L *rusticus* (*rus* the country)]

rus'ticate, v.i. & t. 1. Retire to, sojourn in, the country, lead a rural life; send down temporarily from university as punishment; country. 2. Mark (masonry) with sunk joints or roughened surface. Hence ~A'TION n. [f. L *rusticari* live in the country (prec.), ~LY²]

rus'tle (-sl), v.i. & t. 1. (Give forth) sound (as) of dry leaves blown, rain pattering, or silk garments in motion; go with ~e (*along* etc.; ~*e in silks*, be clad in silk); cause to ~e by shaking etc.; hence ~inglY (-sl-) adv. 2. *(colloq.).* Hustle, move energetically; hence ~e by (cattle or horses); hence ~ER¹ (-sl-) n. [n. f. vb, imit.; cf. Du. *ridselen*]

rus'ty¹, a. Rusted, affected with rust; of antiquated appearance; (of voice) croaking, creaking; stiff with age or disuse, antiquated, behind the times, impaired by neglect, in need of furbishing, (*this Greek is a little ~*); (of black clothes) discoloured by age; rust-coloured. Hence ~lilY² adv., ~iNESS n. [-Y¹]

rus'ty², a. Rancid (esp. of bacon). [=obs. *resty* a. OF *resté* left over, stale]

rut¹, n., & v.i.(-tt-). 1. Periodic sexual excitement of male deer (also of goat, ram, etc.). heat. 2. v.i. Be affected with ~. Hence ~T'ISH¹(1) a. [OF, also *ruit*, f. L *rugitus -ūs* (*rugire* roar)]

rut², n., & v.t.(-tt-). 1. Track sunk by passage of wheels; established mode of procedure, beaten track, groove; hence p.p. [?] 2. v.t. Mark with ~s (usu. in p.p.). [?]

ruth (rōōth), n. (arch.). Pity, compassion. Hence (mod.) ~LESS a., ~lessLY² adv., ~lessNESS n., [~LESS a., ~less¹² adv.,]

ruthē'nium (rōō-), n. Rare metallic element of the platinum group. [f. med. L *Ruthenia* Russia (from its discovery in the Urals)]

‖ **rüx** n. (school sl.). Temper, passion. [?]

-ry, suf., shortened form of -ERY (which see for numbered meanings), as in *chandry poultry, jewel(l)ery*; occas. also in direct formations, as *rivalry*. [ME *chaunnerie, jewry, bottomry, foundry,*]

rye, n. (Grain of) a N.-Europ. cereal used for bread in northern Continental countries & for fodder in U.K. [OE *ryge*, cf. ON *rugr*, Da. *rug* etym. dub. w. assim.]

rye'-grass (rīgrahs), n. Kinds of fodder grass. [f. obs. *ray* etym. dub. w. assim. to prec.]

‖ **rye'peck** (rīp-), n. Ironshod pole for securing punt etc. [?]

S (ĕs), letter (pl. *Ss, S's*). (Also) S-shaped object (*collar¹ of S, Ss, SS*, or *esses*) or curve (*river makes a great S*); **'s**, used for (1, arch.) *God's* in '*sblood* & other oaths; (2, colloq.) *is* in '*he's, she's, it's, Smith's*, etc.; (3, colloq.) *has* as in (2), esp. before p.p. as *he's done it*; (4, colloq.) *does*, as *what's he say about it?*

Sa'baïsm n. Star-worship. [f. Heb. *çabā* host, -ISM]

Sabæ'an (-bē-), a. & n. (Native) of ancient Yemen; (erron.)=SABIAN. [f. L.f. Gk *Sabæus* (*Saba* f. Arab. *Saba'* people of Yemen) +-AN]

‖ **rȳm'er**, n. One of the posts in weir or lock holding paddles. [?]

ry'ot, n. Indian peasant. [f. Hind. *raiyat* f. Arab. as RAYAH]

S

Sab'aŏth, n. pl. *Lord of* ~ in N.T. & *Te Deum*, Lord of Hosts. [f. Heb. pl. (prec.)]

sābbatā'rian, n. & a. 1. Sabbath-keeping Jew; Christian who accepts (& inculcates) the obligation to observe Sunday strictly as sabbath; member of sect observing Saturday as sabbath, seventh-day baptist etc.; hence ~ISM(3) n. 2. adj. Of ~ tenets. [f. L *sabbatarius* (toll., -ARY¹) + -AN, see -ARIAN]

săb'bath, n. 1. (Also ~ *day*) seventh day of week as day of religious rest appointed for Israel (~-*day's journey*, distance Israelite might travel on ~, about ⅞ m.; also transf. easy journey). 2. (Also ~ *day*) Christian Sunday esp. as day of obligatory abstinence from work & play (chiefly in Presbyterian, nonconformist, & distinctively protestant use, or joc.; *keep, break, the ~*; ~-*breaker*, whence ~LESS a. 3. Period of rest. 4. (Usu. *witches'* ~) annual midnight orgy of the devil, demons, sorcerers, & witches. [f. L *sabbatum*, Gk -*ton*, f. Heb. *shabbāth* (*shābath* to rest)]

sabbăt'ic(al), aa. Of, appropriate to, the sabbath (~*al river*, one in Jewish legend flowing except on sabbath; ~*al year*, seventh year in which Israelites were to cease tilling & release debtors & Israelite slaves). Hence ~alLY² adv. [f. Gk *sabbatikos* (prec., -IC), -AL]

Sabĕl'lian¹, a. & n. (Rom. Hist.), (Member) of the group of tribes in ancient Italy including Sabines, Samnites, Campanians, etc. [f. L *Sabelli* SABINES + -IAN]

Sabĕl'lian², a. & n. (Holder) of the doctrine of Sabellius (3rd c.), that the three Divine persons are merely aspects of one. [-AN]

Sāb'ian, a. & n. **1.** (Member) of a sect classed in Koran with Moslems, Jews, & Christians, as believers in the true God. **2.** (erron.). (Adherent) of SABAISM. [f. Arab. *çabi'* (perh. f. Aram. **vb**=baptize) +-AN]

sāb'icu (-kōō), n. Cuban timber-tree; its valuable hard durable wood. [Cuban Sp.]

Sāb'ine, a. & n. (One) of the ~s, ancient Italians of central Apennines. [f. L *Sabinus*]

sā'ble¹, n. Small brown-furred arctic & subarctic carnivorous quadruped allied to martens; its skin or fur; fine paint-brush made of ~ hair. [OF, = ~-fur, prob. f. Slav. (Pol. & Czech *sobol*, Hung. *czoboly*, the ~)]

sā'ble², n. & a. **1.** Black as a heraldic colour (poet., rhet.) the colour black; (poet. & rhet.; pl.) mourning garments, whence **sā'blED**² (-beld) a. **2.** (Also ~ *antelope*) large stout-horned antelope of which male is black. **3.** adj. (poet. & rhet.). Black, dusky, gloomy, dread, (of Negro, sky, sea, night, Fate, etc.; *his* ~ *Majesty*, the devil); hence **sāb'lY**² adv. [f² (her.), peth. f. prec.]

sāb'ot (-ō), n. **1.** Shoe hollowed out from one piece of wood worn by French lower classes; wooden-soled shoe. **2.** (Mil.) wooden disk riveted to spherical, metal cup strapped to conical, projectile (Mech.) shoe or armature of pile, boring-rod, etc. Hence ~ED² (-bōd) a. [F, cf. *savate* shoe, etym. dub.]

sāb'otage (-ahzh, -ij), n., & v.t. & i. **1.** Malicious or wanton destruction, esp. doing of damage to plant etc. by work-men on bad terms with their employers (*the derailing of the train is attributed to* ~; *acts of* ~). **2.** vb. Commit ~ (on); (fig.) destroy, render useless, as ~ *a scheme*. [F]

sā'bre (-er), n., & v.t. **1.** Cavalry sword with curved blade (*the* ~, military force or rule); (in pl.) cavalry unit (cf. *rifle*); cavalry soldier & horse, (*had 3000* ~s); copper tool for skimming molten glass; ~*-bill*, -*wing*, kinds of bird; ~*-cut*, blow with ~, wound made or scar left by it; ~*-toothed lion or tiger*, extinct mammal with long ~-shaped upper canines. **2.** v.t. Cut down or wound with ~. [F, earlier *sable* f. G *sabel* prob. of Oriental orig.]

sā'bretache (-ertăsh), n. Cavalry officer's satchel on long straps from left of waist-belt. [F, f. G *säbeltasche* (prec., *tasche* pocket)]

sabreur (sahbrĕr'), n. Cavalryman with sabre, esp. (often *beau* ~) cavalry officer of dashing appearance. [F]

sāb'ūlous, a. Sandy, of sand, (pedant.); (Med., of secretions esp. in urinary or-gans) granular. [f. L *sabulosus* (*sabulum* sand, -OSE¹)]

sabū'rra, n. (med.). Foul granular matter deposited in stomach. [L, =sand, cf. prec.]

sāc, n. Baglike membrane-enclosed cav-ity in animal or vegetable organism; membranous envelope of hernia, cyst, tumour, etc.; (of dress)=SACK¹. [f. L *saccus* SACK¹]

sacc'āte, a. (Bot.) dilated into bag; con-tained in sac. [f. med. L *saccatus* (prec., -ATE²)]

sacc'har- (-kar-), stem, f. Gk *sakkharon* SUGAR, of many words chiefly in scientific use; ~ATE¹(3), salt of *sacchā'rIC acid*, a dibasic acid formed by the action of nitric acid on dextrose; ~IDE, (now more com-monly used in chem.) ~OSE; ~¹F'EROUS, sugar-bearing; ~IFY, convert (starch) into sugar; ~¹FICA'TION; ~¹M'ETER, instrument for testing sugars by polarized light; ~¹M'ETRY; ~IN(e) n., intensely sweet sub-stance got from coal-tar & used to sweeten food for the gouty, diabetic, etc.; ~INE¹ a., sugary, of or containing or like sugar; ~O-, sugar-&-; ~OID a. (Geol.) granular like sugar, (n.) sugarlike substance; ~ó-M'ETER, hydrometer used, esp. in brewing, to estimate amount of sugar in solution by specific gravity; ~OSE², ordinary sugar, cane-sugar.

sāc'cifŏrm (-ks-), a. Sac-shaped. [SAO, -FORM]

sāc'cule, n. Small sac or cyst. Hence (see -UL-) ~AR¹, ~ATE², ~āted, aa., ~AC-TION n. [f. L *sacculus* (SAC, -ULE)]

sā'cerdŏçy, n. (rare). Sacerdotalism (*sa-cerdos -otis* priest lit. sacrifice-giver f. *sacer* holy, *dare* give)]

sā'cerdŏtage, n. (joc.). Sacerdotalism; priest-ridden state. [as prec. w. ref. to *dotage*, cf. *anecdotage*]

sacerdŏt'al, a. Of priest(s) or priesthood, priestly; (of doctrines etc.) ascribing sacrificial functions & supernatural powers to ordained priests, claiming excessive authority for the priesthood. Hence ~LY² adv., ~ISM(3), ~IST(2), nn., ~IZE(3) v.t. [F, f. L *sacerdotalis* (as SACERDOCY, -AL)]

sāch'ĕm, n. Supreme chief of some Amer.-Ind. tribes; big-wig, eminent per-son. [Amer.-Ind.]

sā'chet (-shä), n. Small perfumed bag; (packet of) dry perfume for laying among clothes etc. [F, dim. of *sac* f. L SACCUS]

sāck¹, n., & v.t. **1.** Large usu. oblong bag for storing & conveying goods usu. open at one end & made of coarse flax or hemp (*give one, get, the* ~, dismiss him, be dis-missed, from service, cf. '*On tuy a donné son sac*, hee hath his passport given him', in Cotgrave), whence ~ING(3) n.; ~ with contents (usu. *of*; also ~¹FUL n.); amount of corn, coal, flour, wool, potatoes, etc.) usu. put in ~ as unit of measure or weight (*at 12/- the* ~). **2.** (Of dress; also as pseudo-F *sacque, sac*) kind of lady's loose gown (arch.); pleated silk appendage attached to shoulders of dress & falling to

ground & forming train; man's or woman's loose-hanging coat not shaped to back. **3.** ~*cloth*, coarse fabric of flax or hemp, ~*ing*, (fig.) mourning or penitential garb (esp. in ~*cloth & ashes* Bibl.). ~*race*, between competitors tied in ~s up to the neck. **4.** *v.t.* Put into ~(*s*); (colloq.) give the ~ *to*, dismiss from service; (colloq.) defeat in match or fight. [OE *sacc* f. L f. Gk *sakkos* f. Heb. *saq*]

sack[2], *v.t. & n.* **1.** (Of victorious army or its commander) plunder, give over to plunder, (captured city etc.); (of burglars etc.) carry off contents of. **2.** *n.* ~*ing* of captured place, w. ref. [f. F phr. *f. n. f.* It. *sacco* phr. *mettre à sac* put to sack, f. It. *sacco* etym. dub. (perh. f. *saccare* put in SACK[1])]

sack[3], *n.* (hist.). Kinds of white wine formerly imported from Spain & the Canaries (*sherry, Canary, etc.*; ~; ~ *posset*, whey, etc., beverages containing it; *half-pennyworth of bread to intolerable deal of*, absurd excess of the unessential, w. ref. *seck*, f. F *vin sec* dry wine]

sack'but, *n.* (Old name for) trombone. [f. F *saquebute* sackbut from 15th c., prob.=ONF *saqueboute* hook for pulling man off horse (*saquier* pull, *boute* of doubtful sense); in *Dan.* iii ~ is mistransl. of Aram. *sabbeka* (a stringed instrument) due to accidental likeness of the wds]

‖ **sack'less**, *a.* (arch., Sc. & north.). Innocent (*of*), harmless, feeble-minded. [OE *sacléas* (*sacu* litigation, -LESS]

sac'ra (săk). See SACK[1].
sac'ral, *a.* (Anat.) of the sacrum; (Anthropol.) of or for sacred rites. [SACRUM, -AL]

sac'rament, *n. & v.t.* **1.** Religious ceremony or act regarded as outward & visible sign of inward & spiritual grace (applied by the Eastern, pre-Reformation Western, & R.-C. Churches to the seven rites of baptism, confirmation, the eucharist, penance, extreme unction, orders, & matrimony; restricted by most Protestants to baptism & the eucharist; *the* ~, *the* ~ *of the altar, the Blessed* or *Holy S*~, the eucharist, also the consecrated elements esp. the bread or Host; *take, receive, the* ~ *to do* or *upon*, as confirmation of some promise or oath). **2.** Thing of mysterious & sacred significance, solemn engagement taken. **4.** *v.t.* (esp. in p.p.). Bind by oath. [f. F *sacrement* f. L *sacramentum* military oath, legal caution-money, f. *sacrare* (*sacer sacr-* SACRED). -MENT, used in Christian L as transl. of Gk *mustērion* MYSTERY[1]]

sac'ramen'tal, *a. & n.* **1.** Of (the nature of) a or the sacrament, whence ~ITY (-ăl'-) *n.*; (of doctrine etc.) attaching great importance to the sacraments, whence ~ISM(3), ~IST(2), *nn.*; hence ~LY[2] *adv.* **2.** *n.* Observance analogous to but not reckoned among the sacraments, e.g. use of holy water or sign of the cross. [f. LL *sacramentalis* (prec., -AL)]

sacramentar'ian, *a. & n.* **1.** (hist.), (of, the sacramentary) denying, denier of, Real Presence (as holding that 'body & blood of Christ' was used only in a sacramental, i.e. symbolic, sense). **2.** Holding or involving, holder of, high sacramental doctrine, whence ~ISM(3) *n.* [f. SACRAMENT(*arius* -ARY), see -ARIAN]

sacra'rium, *n.* (pl. *-ia*), (Rom. Ant.) shrine, adytum, room of Penates in house; (also *sanctuary*) part of church within altar-rails; (R.-C.) piscina. [L (*sacer sacr-* holy, -ARIUM)]

sacré (-ā), *v.i.* (*-créd, -créing*). (Of Frenchman) say *sacré*, swear. [f. F *sacré* interj. =foll.]

sac'red, *a.* (rarely ~*est*). **1.** Consecrated or held dear to a deity, dedicated or reserved or appropriated to some person or purpose; made holy by religious association, hallowed, (~ *book, writings, beasts* etc. now or once ~ *to* some god, as ~ *ibis, monkey, beetle*). **2.** Safeguarded or required by religion or reverence or tradition, indefeasible, inviolable, sacrosanct, (*His most S*~ *Majesty the King; the* ~ *right of insurrection; regards it as a* ~ *duty; their property, persons, will be held* ~; *no place was* ~ *from him, from outrage*). Hence ~LY[2] *adv.*, ~NESS *n.* [p.p. of obs. *sacre* consecrate f. F *sacrer* f. L *sacrare* (*sacer sacr-* holy)]

sac'rifice, *n. & v.t. & i.* **1.** Slaughter of animal or person, surrender of a possession, as offering to a deity, (fig.) act of prayer or thanksgiving or penitence as propitiation; what is thus slaughtered or surrendered or done, victim, offering; (Theol.) the Crucifixion, the Eucharist as either a propitiatory offering of the body & blood of Christ or an act of thanksgiving. **2.** Giving up of thing for the sake of another that is higher or more urgent, thing thus given up, loss thus entailed, (*will gain nothing by the* ~ *of your principles; at some* ~ *of regularity; surplus stock for sale at a large* ~; *his health was the* ~ *demanded of him; the great* or *last* ~, esp. death for one's country in war; SELF-~); so **sacrifi'cial** (-shl) *a.*, **sacrifi'cially** (-she-) *adv.* **3.** *v.t.* Offer (as) ~ (*to*); give up, treat as secondary or of inferior importance, devote, *to* (*has* ~*d herself, her whole life, her pleasures, to his interest; ~ accuracy to vividness*); resign oneself to parting with, (*has* ~*d sacrificium* (*sacrificus* as prec., -FICE[1])]

sac'rilege, *n.* Robbery or profanation of sacred building, outrage on consecrated

person or thing, violation of what is sacred. Hence **sacrilé'gious** (-jus; *or* -ij'us) a., **sacrilé'giously** (-jus-) adv.; **sacrilé'gist**(1) n. (rare). [OF, f. L *sacrilegium* f. *sacrilegus* (SACRED, *legere* collect)]

sác'ring, n. (arch.). Consecration of elements in the mass; ordination & consecration of bishop, sovereign, etc.; ~ **bell**, rung at elevation of Host. [obs. *sacre* (SACRED), -ING[1]]

sác'rist, n. Official keeping sacred vessels etc. of religious house or church. [OF (-é), f. L *sacrista* (SACRED, -IST)]

sác'ristan, n. Sexton of parish church (arch.); = prec. [f. med. L SACRISTANUS (-AN)]

sác'risty, n. Repository for vestments, vessels, etc., of a church. [F (-ie), f. med. L *sacristia* (SACRIST, -IA[1])]

sác'rosanct, a. (Of person, place, law, etc.) secured by religious sanction against outrage, inviolable. Hence **sácrosānc'tity** n. [f. L *sacrosanctus* (*sacro* abl. of *sacrum* SACRED rite, SAINT a.)]

sác'rum, n. Composite triangular bone of anchylosed vertebrae forming back of pelvis. Hence ~**AL** a., ~**o-** comb. form. [f. L os *sacrum* sacred bone (from sacrificial use)]

sàd, a. (-dd-). Sorrowful, mournful, showing or causing sorrow, (a ~*der* & *a wiser man*, of one who has had bitterest experience; *in* ~ *earnest*, seriously); (derog., usu. joc.) shocking, deplorably bad, incorrigible, (*is a* ~ *slut, coward*, etc.; ~ *dog*, rake, scapegrace; *writes* ~ *stuff*); (of pastry, bread, etc.) heavy, doughy; (of colour) dull, neutral-tinted; ~**-iron**, solid flat-iron. Hence ~**d'ish**[1](2) a. & i., ~**LY**[2] adv., ~**NESS** n., ~**d'ish**[1](2) a. [earlier senses *sated, weary, solid, serious*, com.-Teut.; OE *sæd* cf. Du. *zat*, G *satt*, cogn. w. L *sat*(is), Gk *hadēn*, enough]

sàd'dle, n. & v.t. 1. Rider's seat placed on back of horse etc. (usu. concave-shaped of leather with side-flaps & girths & stirrups) or forming part of bicycle etc. or of some agricultural machines (PACK[1], SIDE, ~; *in the* ~, mounted, fig. in office or control; *put* ~ *on right, wrong, horse*, blame right, wrong, person). 2. Part of shaft-horse's harness that bears shafts. 3. ~-shaped thing, e.g. ridge between two summits, support for cable or wire on top of suspension-bridge pier or telegraph pole, joint of mutton or venison consisting of the two loins. 4. ~*back*, (Archit.) tower roof with two opposite gables, ~-backed hill, kinds of bird (esp. the Grey Crow) & fish, (adj.) ~-backed; ~-backed, with upper outline concave, (Archit.) having ~*back*, one of pair of bags laid across horse behind ~, kind of carpeting (in imitation of Eastern ~-bags of camels) used in upholstering chairs etc.; ~-*boiler*, of concave form used in heating-apparatus; ~-*bow* (-bō), arched

front of ~ [BOW[1]]; ~-*cloth*, laid on horse's back under ~; ~-*fast*, firmly seated in ~; ~-*horse*, for riding; ~-*pin*, by which bicycle etc. ~ fits into socket; ~-*tree*, frame of ~, also N.-Amer. tulip-tree(with ~-shaped leaves); hence ~**LESS** a. 5. v.t. Put ~ on (horse etc.); burden (person) *with* task, responsibility, etc.; put (burden) *on or* upon (person). [com.-Teut.; OE *sadol*(*ian*), cf. Du. *zadel*(*en*), G *sattel*(*n*); perh. cogn. w. SIT]

sàdd'|er, n. Maker of or dealer in saddles & other equipment for horses; (Mil.) man in charge of cavalry regiment's ~ery. Hence ~**ERY**(1, 2, 3) n. [-ER[1]]

Sàdd'ūcee, n. Member of a Jewish sect or party (cf. PHARISEE, ESSENE) of time of Christ that denied resurrection of the dead, existence of spirits, & obligation of the traditional law. Hence or cogn. **Sàddūcē'AN** a., ~**ISM**(2) n. [f. LL f. Gk *Saddoukaios* f. Heb. *Çaddūqī* prob. = descendant of *Zadok*]

sādhu (sah'dŌŌ), n. (India) holy man. [Skr., =pious]

sa'd|ism (sah-), n. Form of sexual perversion marked by love of cruelty. So ~**ISM**(2) n., ~**is'tic** a. [f. F *sadisme* (Count de *Sade* 1740–1814, -ISM)]

safa'ri (-ahr-), n. Hunting expedition (esp. in phr. *on* ~); sportsman's or traveller's caravan. [Swahili, f. Arab. *safar* journey]

safe[1], n. (Also *meat*~) ventilated cupboard for provisions; fireproof & burglar-proof receptacle for valuables. [orig. *save*, f. SAVE[1]]

safe[2], a. 1. (Pred., after *come, arrive, bring, keep*, etc.) uninjured (*parcel came* ~; *saw them* ~ *home*; often ~ *& sound*); secure, out of or not exposed to danger (*from*, (*now we are, can feel*, ~; *is* ~ *from his enemies*). 2. Affording security or not involving danger(*put it in a* ~ *place*; *is it* ~ *to leave him*?; ~ *custody, convoy*, etc.; *err, error, on the* ~ *side*, with margin of security against risks; *dog is not* ~ *to touch*; *it is* ~ *to say*, may be said without risk of exaggeration or falsehood); debarred from escaping or doing harm (*have got him* ~). 3. Cautious & unenterprising, consistently moderate, that can be reckoned on, unfailing, certain to do or be, sure to become, (*a* ~ *critic, statesman*; ~ *methods*; *a* ~ CATCH[2]*, winner*; *is a* ~ *first*, sure to take a first class; *is* ~ *to win, be there*); hence ~**NESS** (-fn-) n. 4. ~ *conduct*, (document conveying) privilege granted by sovereign, commander, etc., of being protected from arrest or harm on particular occasion or in district; ~ *deposit*, building containing strong-rooms and safes let separately; ~-*guard*, = *conduct*, (also & usu.) proviso or stipulation or quality or circumstance that tends to prevent some evil or protect, (v.t.) guard, protect, (esp. rights etc.) by precaution

or stipulation (||~-guarding duties, on imports, against competition held to be unfair); ~ keeping, custody. Hence ~**ly²** (-li) adv. [ME & F *sauf* f. L *salvus* uninjured cogn. w. Gk *holos* WHOLE]

safe'ty (-ti), n. 1. Being safe, freedom from danger or risks, (*there is ~ in numbers* prov.; *is in ~*; *cannot do it with ~*; *play for ~*, avoid risks in game or fig.; *~ first*, motto inculcating caution). 2. Safeness, being sure or likely to bring no danger, (*is the ~ of the experiment certain?*; *~ factor* or *coefficient of ~* in engineering, ratio of materials' strength to strain to be allowed for). 3. (Also ~-bolt) contrivance for looking gun-trigger, gun with this. 4. (Also ~-bicycle) bicycle of usual low-saddled modern form (opp. *ordinary*). 5. ~-curtain, fireproof curtain cutting off the auditorium in a theatre from the stage; ~-film, cinematographic film on slow-burning or non-inflammable base (esp. in sub-standard sizes); ~-FUSE² containing a slow-burning composition for firing detonators from a distance, (Electr.) protective FUSE¹; ~-glass, TRIPLEX glass; ~-lamp, miner's so protected as not to ignite fire-damp; ~-match, only igniting on prepared surface; ~-pin, with point that returns to head & is caught in a guard so that wearer may not be pricked nor pin come out; ~-razor, kinds with guard to prevent cutting skin; ~-valve in steam-boiler, opening automatically to relieve excessive pressure, (fig.) means of giving harmless vent to excitement etc. (*sit on the ~-valve*, follow policy of repression). [f. F *sauveté* f. med. L *salvitatem* (prec.; -1-, -TY)]

saffian, n. Leather of goatskin or sheepskin tanned with sumach & dyed in bright colours. [f. Russ. *safyanu*]

saf'flower (-owr), n. A thistle-like plant yielding red dye used esp. in rouge; its dried petals; the dye made from them. [f. Du. *saffloer* f. OF *saffleur* f. early It. *saffiore*, etym. dub.]

saff'ron, n., a., & v.t. 1. Orange-coloured stigmas of the Autumnal Crocus used for colouring & flavouring confectionery & liquors (*Bastard S~*, the plant safflower). 2. adj. & n. ~-colour(ed), whence ~y² a.; ~ cake, cake flavoured with ~, also tablet of pressed ~. 3. v.t. Colour with or like~. [f. F *safran* ult. f. Arab. *za'farān*]

saf'ranin, n. Colouring-matter of saffron; yellowish-red coal-tar colour. [prec., -IN]

sag, v.i. & t. (-gg-), & n. 1. Sink or subside under weight or pressure; hang sideways, be lopsided, (*gate, bridge, ~s*); have downward bulge or curve in middle (*ceiling, beam, stretched rope, ladder, ~s*); (trans.) cause to curve thus; (Commerce) decline in price; (of ship) drift from course (esp. *~ to leeward*); hence ~g¹,² (-g'-) a. 2. n. Amount that rope etc. ~s, distance from middle of its curve to straight line be-

tween supports; sinking, subsidence; decline in price; (Naut.) tendency to leeward. [cf. Du. *zakken* subside, Da. *sakke* lag; perh. cogn. w. SINK]

saga (sah-), n. A medieval Icelandic or Norwegian prose narrative, esp. one embodying history of Icelandic family or Norwegian king; (transf.) story of heroic achievement or adventure; series of connected books giving the history of a family etc. [ON, = narrative, cogn. w. SAY²]

sagā'cious (-shus), a. Mentally penetrating, gifted with discernment, practically wise, acute-minded, shrewd; (of sayings, plans, etc.) showing sagacity; (of animals) exceptionally intelligent, seeming to reason or deliberate. Hence or cogn. ~LY² adv., **sagā'cīty** n. [f. L *sagax* (*sagire* discern acutely), -ACIOUS]

sage¹, n. Aromatic herb with dull greyish-green leaves; its leaves used in cookery (*~ & onions*, stuffing used for goose, duck, pork, etc.); ~-brush, growth of alkaline plants characterizing some sterile districts of U.S.(~-cock, ~-grouse, ~-hare, etc., found in these); ~ cheese, flavoured & mottled by addition of ~-infusion to the curd; ~-green, colour of ~-leaves; ~ tea, medicinal infusion of ~-leaves. Hence **sā'gy²** a. [ME & F *sauge* f. L *salvia*]

sage², a. & n. 1. Wise, discreet, judicious, having the wisdom of experience, (of or indicating profound wisdom, (often iron.) wise-looking, solemn-faced; hence ~LY² (-ji-) adv., ~NESS (-ji-) n. 2. n. Profoundly wise man (often iron.), esp. any of the ancients traditionally reputed wisest of their time (*the seven ~s*, 7 Greeks each credited with a notable saying); hence ~SHIP (-ji-) n. [f. F com.-Rom. *sabio* f. pop. L *sapius* (L *sapere* be SAPIENT)]

sagg'ar, n. Case of baked fireproof clay enclosing pottery while it is baked. [perh. contr. of *safeguard*]

Sagitta, n. A northern constellation, the Arrow. [L, = arrow]

sa'gittate, a. (bot., zool.) Shaped like arrow-head. [SAGITTA, -ATE²]

Sagitta'rius, n. Constellation & ninth sign of zodiac, the Archer. [L (prec., -ARY¹)]

sago, n. (pl. ~s). (Kinds of palm & cycad with pith yielding) kind of starch used as food in puddings etc. [Malay *sagu*]

||sahaa (sz-hah'), int. Goodbye. [Maltese]

Sahā'ra (sz-hah-), n. Great Libyan desert; arid tract (lit. & fig.). Hence ~IC, aa. [f. Arab. *çahrā*]

Sahib, n. (fem. *mēm'sahib*). 1. (India) European as spoken of or to by Indians; an honorific affix (*Colonel ~, Jones ~, Raja~, Khum~*). 2.(colloq.; s~), gentleman (*pukka s~*). [Hind., f. Arab. *çahib* friend]

said¹. See SAY².

Said² (sĕd). Var. of SEID.

saig'a (or sī-), n. Antelope of steppes. [Russ.]

sail¹, n. 1. Piece of canvas or other textile material extended on rigging to catch wind & propel vessel, (collect.) some or all of ship's ~s (CARRY, CROWD², *hoist*, *lower*, MAKE¹, SET¹, SHORTEN, STRIKE, ~; *take in* ~, fig., moderate one's ambitions; *take* WIND¹ *out of* ~s; *full* ~ adv., with all ~ spread lit. & fig.; *under* ~, with ~s set). 2. (collect.) Ships (in giving number of ships in squadron or company; *a fleet of twenty* ~). 3. Ship (esp. in ~ *ho!*, cry announcing that ship is in sight). 4. pl. (naut. sl.; hist.). ‖ Chief petty officer in charge of rigging; one who makes or repairs ~s. 5. Wind-catching apparatus, now usu. set of boards, attached to arm of windmill. 6. ~fish's dorsal fin, tentacle of nautilus. 7. (Also *wind-*~) funnel-shaped bag on ship's deck or above mine giving ventilation. 8. ~*arm*, arm of windmill; ~*axle*, on which ~arms revolve; ~*cloth*, canvas for ~s, also dress-material; ~*fish*, kinds with large dorsal fin, esp. Basking shark. Hence (-)~ED² (-ld), ~LESS, aa. [com.-Teut.; OE *seg(e)l*, cf. Du. *zeil*, G *segel*]

sail², v.i. & t. & n. 1. (Of vessel or person on board) travel on water by use of sails (~*ing-ship, -vessel*, opp. *steamer*; ~ *close to or near the wind*, nearly against it, also fig. come near transgressing a law or moral principle); (of vessel or person on board) travel on water by use of sails or engine-power, start on voyage, (*we* ~ *next week*; list of ~ING¹s *from London*; ~*ing orders*, instructions to captain for departure, destination, etc.). 2. (Of bird, cloud, moon, etc.) glide in air; (esp. of women) walk in stately manner. 3. Travel over or along, navigate, glide through, (*the sea, Spanish main, sky*, etc.). 4. Control navigation of (ship; *plain* ~ING¹, used pred. to describe task etc. that is not perplexing; ~*ing-master*, officer navigating yacht); set (toy-boat) afloat. 5. ~*into* (sl.), inveigh against, scold, rate, attack. 6. n. Voyage or excursion in ~ing-vessel (*go for a* ~); voyage of specified duration (*is ten days'* ~ *from Plymouth*). [OE *siglan, segl(i)an*, (prec.)]

sail'er, n. Ship of specified sailing-power (*fast, good, bad,* ~). [-ER¹]

sail'or, n. Seaman, mariner, esp. one below rank of officer (*good, bad,* ~, person not, very, liable to sea-sickness); ~*hat*, of straw with straight narrow brim & flat top worn by women, also with turned-up brim in imitation of ~'s worn by children; ~*man*, (vulg. & joc. for) ~; ~*s' home*, institution for lodging ~s cheaply ashore; ~*'s knot*, way of tying neck-tie. Hence ~ING¹(l) n., ~LESS, ~LY¹, aa. [var. of prec., see -ER¹, -OR²]

‖ saint, v.t. (arch.). Make sign of the cross on, bless, protect by divine power or enchantment. [OE *segnian*, cf. G *segnen* bless, f. L *signare* mark (SIGN¹sm)]

sain'foin, n. Low-growing herb used as fodder. [F (*sain* SANE, *foin* hay f. L *faenum*)]

saint, a. (unstressed sent, snt; abbr. St, S, *in pl.* Sts, SS.), n., & v.t. 1. Holy, canonized or officially recognized by the Church as having won by exceptional holiness a high place in heaven & veneration on earth, (usu. as prefix to name of person or archangel as *St Paul, St Michael*, whence ellipt. names of churches as *St Peter's*, & of towns called after their churches often with loss of possessive sign as *St Andrews* & *St Albans*, & many Christian & family names taken either from patron ~ or from local names as above; also in some names of churches not called after ~s, as *St Saviour's, Sepulchre's, Faith, Cross*); *St* ~*'s day*, Church festival in memory of particular ~. 2. *St Andrew*, patron ~ of Scotland (*St A.'s day*, 30th Nov.); *St Anthony's*, *St B.'s*, *St Bartholomew*; *St B.'s, Elmo's,* FIRE¹. *St Bernard, St B.'s*, (used for) St B.'s Hospital in London, abbr. *Bart's*; *massacre of St B.*, of Huguenots in France on St B.'s day, 24 Aug., 1572. *St Bernard (the Great, Little, St B., Alpine passes)*; *St Bernard dog or St Bernard*, breed kept by monks of Hospice on Great St Bernard pass for rescue of travellers. *St Cecilia*, patron ~ of music; *St Charles*, King Charles I as canonized martyr; *St David, St D.'s*, patron ~ of Wales (*St D.'s day*, 1st Mar.); *St Denis*, patron ~ of France. *St George*, patron ~ of England (*St G.'s day*, 23rd Ap.); *St G.'s*, (used for) St G.'s Hospital in London; *St G.'s, Hanover Square*, London church at which many West-end weddings take place; *St G.'s cross*, the Greek CROSS¹. *St Germain* (or *Faubourg St G.*), aristocratic quarter of Paris; *St Gotthard* (the *St G.*, the Alpine pass of St G. or the tunnelled railway used instead of it). *St Helén'a*, (used for) place of exile (w. ref. to Napoleon, 1815–21). *St James's* (or *the Court of St James's or St James*), the British court (esp. in distinction from foreign courts; w. ref. to St James's Palace in London); (also) fashionable district in London about St James's Palace. *St-John's-wort*, kinds of yellow-flowered wild & garden plant. *St Leger*, horse-race at Doncaster for three-year-olds, f. founder's name; *St Lubbock's day*, any of the BANK²-holidays instituted 1871 by Sir J. Lubbock's Act; *St Luke's summer*. *St Mark's*, (used for) St M.'s church in Venice; *St Martin's-le-Grand*, (used for) the General Post Office; *St Martin's summer*; *St Michael & St George*, order of knighthood; *St Michael*, kind of orange, f. one of the Azores so called; *St Monday*.

St Patrick, patron ~ of Ireland (St P.'s Day, 17th Mar; order of St P., Irish order of knighthood); St Peter's, cathedral of see of London; St Peter in the Vatican in Rome; St Peter's chair, (used for) the office of Pope. St Sophia, (used for) the mosque of St S. in Constantinople; St Stephen's, (used for) Parliament (w. ref. to former use of St S.'s chapel, Westminster, for meetings of House of Commons); St Swithin's, the day (15th July) whose rain or absence of rain presages the same for 40 days. St Thomas's, (used for) St Thomas's Hospital in London. St VALENTINE's day; St Vitus's DANCE². **3.** n. One of the blessed dead or other member of the company of heaven (departed ~, phr. used by or attributed to mourners, = deceased person); canonized person (see adj. sense; patron ~, selected as heavenly protector of person or place, esp. church, often named after him); (Bibl., arch., & with some mod. sects) one of God's chosen people, member of the Christian Church or speaker's branch of it; person of great real or affected holiness (would provoke, try the patience of, a ~; young ~s old devils or sinners, early piety is no good sign; LATTER-day ~s); ~'s-day, Church festival in memory of a ~, often observed as holiday at schools etc.; hence ~'DOM, ~'HOOD (-t-h-), ~'SHIP, ~'LING⁴ nn., ~LIKE, ~'LY¹ aa., ~'LINESS n. **4.** v.t. Canonize, admit to the calendar of ~s; call or regard as a ~; (p.p.) worthy to be so regarded; ~'ly life, (of place etc.) sacred. [vb f. n. f. adj., OF f. L sanctus p.p. of sancire consecrate]

Saint-Simón'ian, a. & n. (Advocate) of the socialism of the Comte de Saint-Simon (1760–1825) with State control of property & distribution of produce. So **Saint-Sim'onism**(2), **Saint-Sim'onre**¹(1), **Saint-Sim'onism**(3), ~ISM²(3), ~-IAN]

saith. See SAY².

Saïtic, a. Of Saïs, ancient capital of Lower Egypt (~ dynasties, 26th–30th of Egyptian kings). [f. L f. Gk Saïtikos (Saïtēs f. Saïs, -TE')]

sake, n. For the ~ of —, for —'s or my etc. ~, out of consideration for, in the interest of, because of, owing to, in order to please or do honour or get or keep, (common n. with sibilant ending does not take the extra syllable of the possessive before ~, but has usu. the apostrophe, as for peace, conscience', goodness', ~, cf. for God's sake, children's, Phyllis's, ~; for my own ~ as well as yours; for both, all, our ~s rarely ~; for his name's ~, because he bears the name he does or in the interest of his reputation; persecuted for opinion's ~; for any ~ in entreaties, for one reason or another; for old ~'s ~, in memory of old days). [OE sacu contention, charge,

---

fault, sake, cf. Du. zaak lawsuit, cause, thing, G sache affair, also OE sacu to quarrel; cogn. w. SEEK]

sä'ké (-ā), n. Japanese fermented liquor made from rice. [f. Jap. sake]

säk'er, n. **1.** Large lanner falcon used in hawking, esp. the female larger than the male or ~ET¹ n. **2.** (hist.) Old form of cannon. [f. F sacre (in both senses) f. Sp., Port., sacro prob. f. Arab. çaqr]

sa'ki (sah-), n. S.-American monkey with long non-prehensile tail, and neck-ruff. [native name, through F]

sä'kia (sah-), n. Eastern water-wheel for irrigation. [Arab. sāqiya (saqā irrigate)]

sal (sahl), **saul,** n. Valuable Indian timber (tree). [Hind.]

salaam' (-lahm), n. & v.i. & t. **1.** Oriental salutation 'Peace'; Indian obeisance with this, low bow of head & body with right palm on forehead. **2.** vb. Make ~ (to). [f. Arab. salām]

sä'lable, a. Fit for sale, finding purchasers; ~ price, that article will fetch. Hence sä'laBILITY n. [-ABLE]

salā'cious (-shus), a. Lustful, lecherous. Hence or cogn. ~LY² adv., ~NESS, salā'CITY, nn. [f. L salax (salire leap) -ACIOUS]

sal'ad, n. Cold dish of various mixtures of raw or cooked vegetables or herbs usu. seasoned with oil, vinegar, etc., & eaten with or including cold fish, meat, hard-boiled eggs, etc.; vegetable or herb suitable for eating raw; ~days, inexperienced youth; ~dressing, mixture of oil, vinegar, cream, etc., taken with ~; ~-oil, kinds of oil for ~-dressing. [f. OF salade ult. f. L sal salt, -ADE(1)]

sal'amander, n. **1.** Lizard-like animal supposed to live in fire; person who can endure great heat, fire-eating soldier etc.; spirit living in fire (cf. sylph, gnome, nymph). (Zool.) kinds of tailed amphibian, whence **salamän'drod** a. & n. **2.** Red-hot iron for firing gunpowder, hot iron plate for browning omelettes etc. Hence **salamän'drian, salamän'drine,** aa. [F (-dre), f. L f. Gk salamandra]

sala'mé (-lah-), n. Italian sausage highly salted and flavoured often with garlic. [It.]

sal-ammon'iac, n. Ammonium chloride. [L sal salt, AMMONIAC]

sal'angane (-ngg-), n. Swallow making edible nest. [F, f. salanga name in Luzon]

salā'riat, n. The salaried class. [F]

sal'ary, n., & v.t. **1.** Fixed periodical payment made to person doing other than manual or mechanical work (cf. wages). **2.** v.t. Pay ~y to (chiefly in p.p. ~ied pt. -rid). [AF (-ie), = OF salaire f. L salarium orig. soldier's salt-money (sal salt, -ARY¹)]

sale, n. Exchange of a commodity for money or other valuable consideration, selling (on, for, ~, offered for purchase;

~ &, or, return, arrangement by which retailer takes quantity of goods with right of returning all that he fails to sell; amount sold (the ~s were enormous); public auction (put up for ~, offer at auction); rapid disposal at reduced prices of shop's stock at end of season; BILL³ of ~; ~ring, ring of buyers at auction; ~'s*man*, ~s'*woman*, person engaged in selling goods in shop or as middleman between producer & retailer, whence ~s'manship (-lz̥) n., skill in this art; ~s resistance, the opposition or apathy of the prospective customer etc., to be overcome by ~smanship. [OE *sala* prob. f. ON *sala* cogn. w. SELL]

‖ Sāl'em, n. Nonconformist chapel. [*Heb.* vii. 2]

sāl'ep, n. Nutritive meal from dried tubers of some orchidaceous plants. [F f. Turk., f. Arab. *tha°leb*]

*sāl'erātus, n. Impure bicarbonate of potash or sodium bicarbonate as ingredient in baking-powders. [f. mod. L *sal aerātus* AERATED salt]

Sāl'ian¹, a. Of the Salii or priests of Mars. [L *Salii* pl. (*satire* leap), -AN]

Sāl'ian², a. & n. (Member) of Frankish tribe near Zuyder Zee from which the Merovingians were descended. [LL *Salii* the tribe, -AN]

Sāl'ic, Salique' (-ēk), aa. (Form *-ic*) =prec., adj. (~ *law*, Frankish law-book extant in Merovingian & Carolingian times); (*-ic*, *-ique*) ~ *law*, law excluding females from dynastic succession, esp. as alleged fundamental law of French monarchy (based on a quotation, not referring to such succession, from the law-book above). [F *-ique*) f. *Salii* (prec.), -IC]

sāl'icin, n. Bitter crystalline principle got from willow-bark & used medicinally. So sāl'ICIN, sāl'ICYL¹CᵒA. (*salicylic acid*, used as antiseptic & for rheumatism), salī'CYLATE³(3) n., sali'CYLISE(5) n. same sense salī'CYLATE³ vv.t., sali'CYLISM(5) n., sali'CYLOUS (chem.) a. [F (-*ine*), f. L *salix* -*icis* willow, -IN]

sāl'icional (-shon-), sāl'icĕt, nn. Organ stop of soft reedy tone as of willow pipe. [G, f. L *salix* (prec.) w. suff.]

sāl'ient, a. & n. 1. Leaping or dancing (pedant., joc.), (of water etc., poet.) jetting forth, (~ *point*, arch., initial stage or origin or first beginning, from old med. use=heart as it first shows in an embryo); (of angle, esp. in Fortif., opp. RE-ENTRANT) pointing outwards; jutting out, prominent, conspicuous, most noticeable, (~ *points, features, characteristics*). 2. n. A ~ angle or part in fortification (*the S~*, that at Ypres in the 1914–18 war). Hence sāl'IENCE, sāl'IENCY, nn., ~LY² adv. [f. L *satire* leap, -ENT]

sāli'ferous, a. (geol.). (Of strata) containing much salt. [L *sal* salt, *-i-*, -FEROUS]

sāl'ine (or *salin*'), a. & n. 1. (Of natural waters, springs, etc.) impregnated with salt or salts, whence sālinōm ETER n.; (of taste) salt; (of chemical salts, of the nature of a salt; (of medicines) containing salt(s) of alkaline metals or magnesium; hence salin'ITY n., salin'ō- comb. form. 2. n. Salt lake, spring, marsh, etc.; salt-pan; salt-works; ~ *substance*; ~ *purge*; solution of salt & water. [prec., -INE¹]

Salique. See SALIC.

sāliv'a, n. Colourless liquid given by mixed secretions of salivary & mucous glands discharged into mouth & assisting mastication, spittle. So sāl'ivary¹ a. [L]

sāl'ivāte, v.t. & i. Produce unusual secretion of saliva in (person) usu. with mercury; secrete or discharge saliva esp. in excess. So ~A'TION n. [f. L SALIVARE, -ATE³]

salle (sahl), n. Hall, room, (of foreign countries); ~*à-manger* (see Ap.), dining-room, coffee-room; ~*d'attente* (see Ap.), waiting-room at station. [F]

sāll'enders, n. pl. Dry eruption inside hock of horse's hind-leg (cf. MALANDERS). [cf. F *solandre*; etym. dub.]

sāll'ow¹ (-ō), n. Willow-tree, esp. of low-growing or shrubby kinds, whence ~y² (-ōi) a.; a shoot, the wood, of this. [OE *sealh*, cf. OHG *salaha*, ON *selja*, also L *salix*, Gk *helikē*]

sāll'ow²(-ō), a. (-*er*, -*est*), n., & v.t. & i. 1. (Of human skin or complexion or person in these respects, rarely of foliage) of sickly yellow or pale brown; hence ~ISH⁴(2) (-ōi·) a., ~NESS (-ōn·) n. 2. n. ~ hue. 3. vb. Make or grow ~. [OE *salo*, cf. MDu. *salu* discoloured, OHG *salo* dark]

sāll'y¹, n., & v.i. 1. Rush of besieged upon besiegers, sortie: a going forth, excursion; sudden start into activity, outburst; escapade (rare); witticism, piece of banter, lively remark esp. by way of attack upon person or thing or of diversion in argument; ~*port*, opening in fortification for making ~ from. 2. v.i. Make military ~ (often *out*); go *forth* or *out* on a journey, for a walk, etc.; issue, come out, suddenly (rare). [vb f. n., f. F *saillie* (*saillir* issue, in OF also dance, f. L *satire* leap)]

sāll'y², n. First movement of bell when set for ringing (also *hand-stroke*, opp. *back-stroke*), bell's position when set; part of bell-rope prepared with inwoven wool for holding; ~*hole*, through which bell-rope passes. [perh. f. prec. in obs. sense *swinging motion*]

Sāll'y³, fam. for *Sarah* (AUNT ~; ‖ ~ *Lunn*, sweet light tea-cake served hot, perh. f. name of girl hawking them at Bath c. 1800).

sālmagŭn'di, n. Dish of chopped meat, anchovies, eggs, onions, etc., & seasoning;

general mixture, miscellaneous collection, of articles, subjects, qualities, etc. [f. F *salmigondis* etym. dub.]

salmi (-ē), n. Ragoût esp. of game-birds. [F. prob. short for prec.]

salmon (săm'on), n. (collect. sing. usual for pl.), & a. 1. Large silver-scaled pink-fleshed anadromous fish much prized for food & sport; ~-colour(ed), (of) the orange-pink colour of ~-flesh; ~*ladder*, *-leap*, *-pass*, *-stair*, series of steps or other arrangement for allowing ~ to pass dam & ascend stream; ~ *peel* (or *peal*), small grilse; ~ *steak*, fried slice of ~; ~ *trout*, N.-Europ. fish resembling ~. 2. adj. ~-*coloured*, orange-pink. [AF *saumoun* f. L *salmonem* nom. -o prob. cogn. w. *salire* leap]

Salomonic, Salomōn'ian, aa. Of, as of, Solomon. [L *Salomon* Solomon, -ic, -IAN]

salon, n. 1. Reception-room, esp. in continental Ap.], n. Reception-room in great house; ~ (reception-room in) reception-room of (esp. Parisian) lady of fashion; *the S~*, annual exhibition of living artists' pictures in Paris; ~ *music*, light music for drawing-room. [F]

saloon, n. 1. Hall or large room, esp. in hotel or place of public resort, fit for assemblies, exhibitions, etc. 2. Large cabin for first-class or for all passengers on ship; cabin for passengers in large aircraft. 3. || (Also ~-*car*, -*carriage*) luxurious railway carriage without compartments furnished as drawing-room etc. (also *sleeping, dining,* ~). 4. || Public room(s) or gallery for specified purpose (*billiard, shaving, shooting, etc.,* ~). 5. *Drinking-bar. 6. || ~ *bar*, first-class bar in English public-house; ||~ *deck*, and no partition behind driver; ~ *deck*, reserved for ~ passengers; *~-*keeper*, of range practice in shooting~. [f. prec. f. It. *salone* (*sala* hall f. Teut. cf. G *saal*)

Salop'ian, a. & n. (Native) of Shropshire; (member) of Shrewsbury school. [*Salop* Shropshire f. AF *Sloppesberie* corrupt. of OE *Scrobbesbyrig* Shrewsbury, -IAN]

salpiglos'sis, n. Herbaceous showy-flowered garden-plant allied to petunia. [irreg. f. Gk *salpigx* trumpet, *glossa* tongue]

sal'sify, n. British & Continental plant with long cylindrical fleshy roots eaten as vegetable, Purple Goat's-beard. [f. F *salsifis,* cf. It. *sassefrica* etym. dub.]

salt (sawlt, sŏlt), n., a., & v.t. 1. (Often *common* ~) substance that gives sea-water its characteristic taste got in crystalline forms from strata consisting

of it or by evaporation of brine pumped from these or of sea-water & used for seasoning or preserving food & other purposes, sodium chloride, (BAY-SALT, SEA-, ROCK~; *white* ~; refined for household use from the brownish rock~; *table* ~, powdered or easy to powder for the ~cellar; *in* ~, sprinkled with ~ or immersed in brine as preservative; *eat* ~ *with, be guest of; eat one's* ~, be his guest, efficient, worth keeping; *drop pinch of* ~ *on tail of,* capture, w. ref. to directions given children for catching bird; *take with a grain of* ~, regard as exaggerated, be incredulous about, believe only part of; *am not made of* ~, can go out in rain without fear of dissolving; *the* ~ *of the earth,* people or classes for whose existence the world is better, moral élite, see *Matt.* v. 13). 2. Sting, piquancy, pungency, wit, (*no* ~ *in such tears; talk full of* ~; ATTIC~). 3. (Old Chem.) solid soluble non-inflammable sapid substance (obs. exc. in some compd names, as ~ *of LEMON*[1], GLAUBER'S SALT, SMELLING ~s, EPSOM ~); (Chem.) compound of basic & acid radicals, acid with whole or part of its hydrogen replaced by a metal. 4. = *cellar* (chiefly now in trade use; & hist. ~*cellar* [assim. of obs. *saler* (f. OF *salier* ~*box* f. L as SALARY) to *cellar*), vessel holding ~ for table use, (also, colloq. specially deep hollow above collar-bone in woman's neck (regarded as disfigurement; usu. pl.); ~*glaze,* glaze on stoneware made by throwing ~ into furnace; ~*-lick,* place where animals collect to lick earth impregnated with ~; ~-*mine,* yielding rock~; ~-*pan, depression near sea, vessel, used for getting* ~ by evaporation; ~-*pit,* pit yielding ~; ~-*pond,* natural or artificial for evaporating sea-water; ~-*spoon,* usu. with short handle & roundish deep bowl for helping ~; ~-*well, bored well yielding brine; ~-*works,* ~*manufactory;* ~*work,* kinds of maritime & ~*marsh plants;* hence ~ LESS, ~Y[2]. aa., ~*INESS* n. 9. adj. Impregnated with, containing, tasting of, cured or preserved with ~; (of marshes, (of tears, grief, etc.) bitter, afflicting; (of wit etc.) pungent; (of stories, jests, etc.) indecent, spicy; (of bill, charge, etc.: sl.) exorbitant; ~ *horse* (Naut. sl.), ~ *beef;* ~ JUNK[1]; ~-*water, sea-water, tears;* ~-*water,* of, living

in, the sea; hence ~'ISH¹(2) a., ~'LY² adv., ~'NESS n. **10.** v.t. Cure or preserve with ~ or brine (~ *down money or stock*, sl., put it by); sprinkle (esp. snow to melt it in street) with ~; make ~, season, (lit. & fig.); (p.p.; of horses or persons) proof against diseases incident to climate or special conditions by habituation hardened; treat (esp. paper in Photog.) with solution of ~ or mixture of ~s; (Commerce, sl.) ~ *an account* etc., put down extreme price for articles, ~ *the books*, represent receipts as larger than they have been; (Mining, sl.) ~ *a mine*, introduce extraneous ore etc. to make it seem rich. [com.-Teut.; OE *sealt(an)*, cf. Du. *zout(en)*, G *salz(en)*, cogn. w. Gk *hals*, L *sal*]

saltarel'lo, n. Italian & Spanish dance with sudden skips for one couple. [It. & (-*elo*) Sp.]

salta'tion, n. Leaping, dancing, a jump; sudden transition or movement. So **sal'tatory**, **saltato'rial**, aa., [f. L *saltatio* frequent. of *salire* salt- leap, -ATION]

salt'er (sawlt-, sŏl-), n. Manufacturer of, dealer in, salt; =DRY-L~; workman at salt-works; person who salts fish etc. [OE *sealtere* (SALT n. & v., -ER¹)]

salt'ern (sawlt-, sŏl-), n. A salt-works; set of pools for natural evaporation of sea-water. [OE *sealtern* (SALT, *ern* hut)]

sal'tigrade, a. & n. (Spider) with legs adapted for jumping. [L *saltus -ūs* leap (*salire* salt-), -gradus -walking]

saltimban'co, n. Mountebank, quack. [It.]

salt'ire, n. (her.). Ordinary formed by bend & bend sinister crossing like a St Andrew's cross (*in ~*, *per ~*, so arranged); ~ Hence ~WISE (-ĕrwiz) adv. [f. OF *sautoir* stile, saltire, f. L *saltatorium* (SALTATION, -ORY)]

saltpetre (sawltpět'er, sŏl'-), n. Potassium nitrate, nitre, white crystalline salty substance used as constituent of gunpowder, in preserving meat, & medicinally (*Chili* or *cubic* ~, sodium nitrate); ~ *paper*, TOUGH-paper; ~ *rod*, white efflorescence on new or damp walls. [earlier & OF *salpetre* f. med. L *salpetra* prob. for *sal petrae* salt of stone (i.e. found as incrustation) w. assim. to *salt*; *petrae* f. LL f. Gk *petra* rock]

sal'tus, n. (pl. -ūs). Sudden transition, breach of continuity. [L, = leap]

salu'brious (-lōō-, -lū-), a. Healthy (chiefly of climate, air, etc.; rarely of food, exercise, etc.). Hence or cogn.~LY² adv., **salu'brity** n., (-lōō-, -lū-). [L *salubris* (as SALUTARY), -OUS]

Salu'ki (-lōō-), n. Breed of dog, Arabian gazelle-hound. [Arab.]

sal'utary, a. Salubrious (now rare); producing good effects, beneficial. [f. L *salutaris* (*salus -utis* health, -AR¹), -ARY²]

saluta'tion, n. (Use of) words spoken or written to convey interest in another's health etc., pleasure at sight of or communication with him, or courteous recognition of his arrival or departure, (rarely, now usu. *salute*) gesture of similar import, (*the Angelic S~*, the Ave Maria). Hence or cogn. ~AL (-shо-), **salu'tatory** (-lōo-, -lū-), aa. [OF (-*cion*), f. L *salutationem* (foll., -ATION)]

salute' (-ōōt, -ūt), v.t. & i., & n. **1.** Make salutation to; greet; (rare) hail as (king etc.); perform ~ to or *to*, perform ~; (arch.) kiss (person, cheek, hand) esp. at meeting or parting; accost or receive *with* a smile, oath, volley, etc.; become perceptible to (eye, ear, person arriving). **2** n. Gesture expressing respect, homage, or courteous recognition, to person esp. when arriving or departing; (Mil., Naut.) prescribed movement or position of body or weapons, or use of flag(s) or discharge of gun(s) in sign of respect; (*a ~ of 7 guns was fired; the ~*, attitude taken by individual soldier, sailor, policeman, etc., in saluting; *take the ~*, esp. of highest officer present, acknowledge it as meant for him by gesture); (Fenc.) formal performance of certain guards etc. by fencers before engaging; kiss given, prop. as greeting (arch. or joc.; often *a chaste ~*). [vb f. L *salutare* (*salus -utis* health); n. f. F *salut* partly f. L *salutem* nom. *-us* & partly f. com.-Rom. & L *salutare*]

salutif'erous (-lōō-, -lū-), a. (now rare). Promoting health. [f. L *salutifer* (prec., -FEROUS)]

sal'vage, n., & v.t. **1.** (Payment made or due for) saving of a ship or its cargo from loss by wreck or capture (also *attrib.*, as ~ *money*); rescue of property from fire etc.; property ~d; saving & utilization of waste paper, scrap-metal, etc.; materials ~d. **2.** v.t. Make ~ of, save from wreck, fire, etc. [OF (L *salvare* SAVE¹, -AGE]

sal'varsan, n. Drug used esp. in syphilis. [P]

salva'tion, n. **1.** Saving of the soul; deliverance from sin & its consequences & admission to heaven brought about by Christ (*find ~*, be converted, also joc. discover formula that will enable one to abandon one's principles etc.). **2.** Preservation from loss, calamity, etc., thing that preserves from these (esp. *be the ~ of*). **3.** *S~ Army*, organization on military model for revival of religion among the masses, whence (& w. ref. to religious revivals in general)~ISM(3), nn., (-shо-). [OF (-*cion*), f. L *salvationem* (SAVE¹, -ATION)]

salve¹ (sahv, sălv), n., & v.t. **1.** Healing ointment for sores or wounds (now chiefly poet. & in *lip-~*). **2.** Mixture of tar & grease for smearing sheep. **3.** Something that soothes wounded feelings or uneasy

conscience or (arch.) glozes over discrepancy or (arch.) palliates fault (usu. *for*). **4.** v.t. Anoint (wound etc.; arch.; exc. in fig. use=*soothe* as below). **5.** Smear (sheep). **6.** Smooth over or make good (defect, disgrace, etc.; arch.); soothe (pride, self-love, conscience, etc.). **7.** Account for, dispose of, harmonize, vindicate, (difficulty, doubt, discrepancy, person's honour). **8.** Save (ship, cargo) from loss at sea or (property) from fire, whence ~VABLE a. [n. in 1st sense OE *sealf*, cf. Du. *zalf*, G *salbe*, cogn. w. Skr. *sarpis* clarified butter & perh. Gk *olpē* oil-flask, f. L *salvāre* SAVE esp. as connected w. SALVO¹, & in last sense back formation f. SALVAGE]

sǎl've², n. (Also S~ *regina*) R.-C. antiphon beginning with ~ recited after Divine Office from Trinity Sunday to Advent, music for it. [L (vb imperat. = hail)]

sǎl'ver, n. Tray usu. of gold, silver, brass, or electroplate, on which servants hand refreshments, letters, cards, etc. [f. F *salve* tray for presenting certain things to king f. Sp. *salva* assaying of food (*salvo* in sǎl'vē²)+-ER¹]

sǎl'via, n. (Kinds of) gamopetalous plant of the sage family (including several garden flowering plants). [L, =SAGE¹, f. *salvus* safe (from the medicinal properties of the herb)]

sǎl'vō¹, n. (pl. ~s). Saving clause, reservation, (often *of*; *with an express ~ of their rights*); tacit reservation, quibbling evasion, bad excuse; expedient for saving reputation or soothing pride or conscience. [f. L abl. of *salvus* SAFE² as used in *salvo jure* etc. without prejudice to the right etc.]

sǎl'vō², n. (pl. ~es, ~s). Simultaneous discharge of pieces of artillery or other fire-arms esp. as salute, or in seafight; number (*of bombs*) released from aircraft at the same moment, cf. STICK; round or volley of applause. [earlier f. It. *salva* salutation, perh. com.-Rom. f. L SALVE²]

sǎl volāt'ile, n. (Aromatic solution, taken for faintness etc., of) ammonium carbonate. [mod. L, =volatile salt]

sǎl'vor, n. Person, ship, making or assisting in salvage. [SALVE¹ vb, -OR²]

Sǎm, n. (sl.). *Stand ~*, bear the expense esp. of drink; || *upon my ~*, asseveration. [?]

Samā'ritan, n. & a. **1.** Native, language, of Samaria (*good ~*, genuinely charitable person, w. ref. to *Luke* x. 33 etc.); adherent of the ~ religious system. **2.** adj. Of Samaria or the ~s (*the ~ pentateuch*, recension used by ~s of which MSS. are in use), ~ or archaic-Hebrew characters). Hence ~ISM(2, 3, 4) n. [f. LL *Samaritanus* f. Gk *Samareites* (*Samareia* Samaria)+-AN]

sǎm'bō, n. (pl. ~s, ~es). Half-breed esp. of Negro & Indian or European blood; (S~; nickname for) Negro. [1st sense f. Sp. *zambo* perh. = *zambo* bandy-legged]

Sǎm Browne, n. Army officer's belt & straps. [f. Gen. Sir S. J. *Browne*]

sǎm'bŭr, n. Indian elk. [f. Hind. *sā(m)-bar*]

same, a. **1.** Monotonous, uniform, unvarying, (*the life is perhaps a little ~*), whence ~NESS (-mn-) n.; (with *this, these, that, those*; often w. depreciatory intention) aforesaid, previously alluded to or thought of, (*what is the use of this patience?*); (vulg. or commerc.) = the ~, a., pron. & adv.: (adj.) identical, not different, indifferent, unchanged, (also *the very*), *just the ~*, & in sing. *one & the ~*; *the ~ causes produce the ~ effects*; *the difference between a body in motion & the body at rest*; *the ~ observations are true of the others also*; *all planets travel in the ~ direction*; *belong to one & the ~ class*; *say the ~ thing twice over*; *several of the very ~ birds*; *bigotry is the ~ in every age*; *she was always the ~ to me*; *it is all, just, the ~ to me*, makes no difference; *much the ~*, not appreciably different; *at the ~ time*, often introducing fact etc. in apparent conflict with what precedes but also true or to be remembered; *by the ~ TOKEN*; identical with (*words of the ~ nature with those he had first heard*; *expectation of pleasure is the ~ thing with desire*); (emphatic substitute—before full or elliptical relative clause with *that, where*, etc., or esp. as *Pisa; gave the ~ answer as before*) *the ~ person* (now rare exc. in *To, From, the ~* as heading of letter or poem addressed to or coming from person as the preceding one), *the ~ thing* (*we must all say, do, the ~*; *would do the ~*), the aforesaid thing or person (arch., legal, commerc., & vulg.; occas. in commerce, & vulg. use with omission of *the*; *grace & power faithfully to fulfil the ~*; *the ~ shall endure unto the end, the ~ shall be saved*; *& never met, found, the ~ again*; *to repairing sleeve of ~ 1/3*); (adv.) in the ~ manner (*think the ~ of, feel the ~ to, remain in the ~ mind regarding*; *we take what pleasure we can get the ~*, or vulg. ~, *as you do*; *all the ~*, nevertheless, notwithstanding, even under different circumstances; *just the ~*, in spite of changed conditions). [ON, cf. OHG & Goth. *sama*; cogn. w. Skr. *sama*, Gk *homos*]

săm'el, a. (Of brick, tile) imperfectly baked, soft, from being outmost in the baking. [perh. f. OE sam- half, cogn. w. SEMI-, *ǣlan* burn]

Sam'ian, a. & n. (Native) of Samos (~ ware, fine pottery found on Roman sites). [L, f. Gk *Samios* (*Samos*), -AN]

săm'isēn, n. Long three-stringed Japanese guitar, played with plectrum. [Jap., f. Chin. *san-hsien* (*san* three, *hsien* string)]

săm'ite, n. (arch.). Rich medieval dress-fabric of silk occas. interwoven with gold. [f. (OF *samit* or) med. L *samitum* f. late Gk *hexamiton* (*hex* six, *mitos* thread) perh. = fabric in which weft-threads are caught only at every sixth warp-thread, cf. DIMITY]

săm'let, n. Young salmon. [SALMON, -LET]

Săm'nite, n. & a. **1.** Member of an ancient-Italian people at war with republican Rome. **2.** adj. Of the ~s. [f. L *Samnites* pl.]

Samo'an, a. & n. (Native, language) of Samoa. [-AN]

sămovar', n. Russian tea-urn with interior heat-tube. [f. Russ. *samovaru* = self-boiler]

Sam'oyed (-mo-), n. Member of a race of Siberian Mongols (also attrib.); their language; white Arctic breed of dog. [f. Russ. *Samoyedu*]

Samoyed'ic (-mo-), a. & n. Of the Samoyeds; (n.) their language. [-IC]

săm'pān, n. Any small boat of Chinese pattern. [f. Chin. *san-pan* (*san* three, *pan* board)]

săm'phire, n. Cliff plant with aromatic saline fleshy leaves used in pickles. [earlier *sampere* f. F (*herbe de*) *St Pierre* St Peter('s herb)]

sa'mple (sah-), n., & v.t. **1.** Small separated part of something illustrating the qualities of the mass etc. it is taken from, specimen, pattern, (esp. as offered by dealer in commodities sold by weight or measure; also of immaterial things, as *if that is a fair ~ of his proceedings*); ~ *card*, card with ~(s) of goods attached. **2.** v.t. Take or give ~s, try the qualities, get a representative experience, of; hence **sa'mpler¹** [-ER¹] n. [f. obs. *essample* var. of EXAMPLE]

sa'mpler² (sah-), n. **1.** Piece of embroidery worked by girl as specimen of proficiency & often preserved & displayed on wall etc. **2.** Young tree left standing when others are cut down. [f. OF *essemplaire* f. L *exemplaris* (EXAMPLE, -AR¹, -ER²)]

Săm'son, -pson, n. Person of great strength or resembling ~ (*Judg.* xiii–xvi) in some respect; (Naut.) ~'s-post, strong pillar passing through hold or between decks, post in whale-boat to which harpoon rope is attached. [L, f. Gk (-*psōn*) f. Heb. *Shimshon*]

săm'urai (-oori), n. (Jap.; pl. same). Military retainer of daimios, member of military caste (hist.); army officer. [Jap.]

săn'ad, n. (India). Deed of grant; charter, warrant. [Hind. & Arab., = signature, deed]

săn'ative, -torȳ, aa. Healing, of or tending to physical or moral health, curative. [-ive f. med. L *sanativus*, -ory mod., f. L *sanare* cure, -IVE, -ORY]

sănatōr'ium, n. (pl. -ia). Establishment for treatment of invalids esp. convalescents & consumptives; place with good climate etc. frequented by invalids. [as prec., -ORY(2)]

sănbéni'tō (-né-), n. (pl. ~s). Penitential scapular-shaped yellow garment with red St Andrew's cross before & behind worn by confessed & penitent heretic under Spanish Inquisition; similar black garment painted with flames & devils worn by impenitent heretic at auto-da-fé. [Sp. (*samb-*), f. *San Benito* St Benedict (shaped like scapular introduced by him)]

sănc'tifȳ, v.t. Consecrate, set apart or observe as holy; purify or free from sin (p.p. often iron. = sanctimonious; *such ~fied airs*); impart sanctity to, make legitimate or binding by religious sanction, give colour of innocence to, justify, sanction (*the end ~fies the means*); make productive of or conducive to holiness. So ~FICATION n. [f. OF *saintifier* f. eccl. L *sanctificare* (L *sanctus* holy, -FY)]

sănctimōn'ious, a. Making a show of sanctity or piety. Hence ~LY² adv., ~NESS n. [foll., -OUS]

sănc'timonȳ, n. Sanctimoniousness. [OF (-ie), f. L *sanctimonia* sanctity (*sanctus* SAINT, -MONY)]

sănc'tion, n., & v.t. **1.** Law, decree, (hist.; PRAGMATIC ~). **2.** Penalty (also *vindicatory* or *punitive* ~) or reward (also *remuneratory* ~) for (dis)obedience attached to a law, clause containing this; (Eth.) consideration operating to enforce obedience to any rule of conduct. **3.** Confirmation or ratification of law etc. by supreme authority, express authoritative permission, countenance or encouragement given to action etc. by custom etc.; hence ~LESS a. **4.** v.t. Ratify, invest with authority, make binding; authorize, countenance (action etc.); attach penalty or reward to (law). [vb f. n., f. L *sanctio* (*sancire sanct-* make sacred, -ION)]

sănc'titūde, n. (now rare). Saintliness. [f. L *sanctitudo* (SAINT, -TUDE)]

sănc'titȳ, n. Holiness of life, saintliness, (ODOUR of ~y); sacredness, being hallowed, right to reverence, inviolability; (pl.) sacred obligations, feelings, etc. (*the ~ies of the home*). [f. OF *sainctelé* f. L *sanctitatem* (SAINT, -TY)]

sănc'tuarȳ, n. **1.** Place recognized as holy, church, temple, tabernacle, HOLY place, HOLY of holies, SACRARIUM, pene-

tralia, inmost recess, (lit. & fig.). **2.** Sacred place by retiring to which fugitive from law or debtor was secured by medieval Church law against arrest or violence, place in which similar immunity was established by custom or law, asylum or place of refuge (*London, the ~ of political refugees*); (right of affording) such immunity (*violate* or *break ~*, *seek*, etc., ~; *resort to a* ~; *rights* etc. *of* ~). **3.** Place for protection of birds & wild animals. [f. OF *sanctuarie* f. L *sanctuarium* (*sanct-*, see SAINT), -ARY²]

sanc'tum (sǎngk'tŭm), n. **1.** Holy place (~), HOLY of holies (~ *sanctorum*), in Jewish temple (usu. transf. of inner retreat, esoteric doctrine, etc.). **2.** Person's private room, study, den. [L, transl. of Heb.]

sanc'tus, n. The hymn 'Holy, holy, holy' closing the Eucharistic preface, music for this; ~ *bell*, bell in turret at junction of nave & chancel, or handbell, rung at the ~. [L, = holy]

sand, n., & v.t. **1.** Minute fragments resulting from wearing down of esp. siliceous rocks & found covering parts of the seashore, riverbeds, deserts, etc. (also pl.) shoal or submarine bank of ~, (usu. in pl.) grain of ~, (pl.) expanse or tracts of ~ (*numberless as the ~* or ~*s*; ROPE *of* ~; *built* etc. *on* ~, unstable; PLOUGH *the* ~ or ~*s*; *the* ~*s are running out* etc., time of grace etc. is nearly at end, w. ref. to hour-glass etc.; *children playing on the* ~*s*; *scour saucepan, adulterate sugar, dry ink* or *writing, with* ~). **2.** *(colloq.)* Firmness of purpose, grit. **3.** ~*bag* n. filled with ~ for use (a) in fortification for making temporary defences, (b) as ballast for boat or balloon, (c) as ruffian's weapon inflicting heavy blow without leaving mark, (d) as support for engraving-plate, (e) to stop draught from window or door; ~*bag* v.t., barricade or defend, provide (window, chink), with ~*-bag(s)*, fell with blow from ~*bag*; ~*bank*, shoal in sea or river; ~*bar*, ~*bank* at mouth of harbour or river; ~*-blast*, jet of ~ impelled by compressed air or steam for giving rough surface to glass etc.; ~*-box*, castor for sprinkling ~ over wet ink (hist.), mould of ~ used in founding, box of ~ on locomotive for ~ used in teeing; ~*boy*, receptacle for ~ used in teeing; ~*boy*, (prob.) boy hawking ~ for sale (now only in *folly as a ~boy*); ~*cloud*, driving ~ in simoom; ~*crack*, disease of horses' hoofs, crack in human foot from walking on hot ~; ~*eel*, an eel-like fish; ~*-fly*, kind of midge, kind of fishing-fly; ~*glass*, wasp-waisted reversible glass with two bulbs

containing enough ~ to take a definite time (*hour, minute*, etc., *glass*) in passing from upper to lower bulb; ~*hill*, dune; ~*-hopper*, small marine crustacean, common on seashore; ~*man*, (also *dust-man*) power causing children's eyes to smart towards bedtime; ~*martin*, kind nesting in side of ~*-pit* or sandy bank; ~*paper*, with ~ stuck to it for polishing, (v.t.) polish with ~*paper*; ~*piper*, kinds of bird haunting open wet sandy places; ~*-pump*, for clearing drill-hole, caisson, etc., of wet ~; ~*-shoes*, usu. of canvas with rubber or hemp soles for use on ~*s*; ~*-spout*, pillar of ~ raised by desert whirlwind; ~*stone*, rock of compressed ~, (*old, new, red, ~stone*, series of British rocks below, above, carboniferous); ~*-storm*, desert storm of wind with clouds of ~. **4.** v.t. Sprinkle with ~; overlay with, bury under, ~; adulterate (sugar, wool, etc.) with ~; polish with ~. [com. Teut.: OE; cf. G *sand*, Du. *zand*]

sǎn'dal¹, n., & v.t. (-ll-). **1.** Sole without uppers attached to foot by thongs passing over instep & round ankle (worn chiefly by ancient Greeks & Romans, by some Orientals, & as modern revival esp. by children); strap for fastening low shoe passing over instep or round ankle. **2.** v.t. Put ~*s* on (feet, person; esp. in p.p.). fasten or provide (shoe) with ~. [f. L f. Gk *sandalon* cf. *sandalon*, etym. dub.]

sǎn'dal²wood, n. Kinds of scented wood (*white, yellow, red,* ~); *sandal-tree*, the Malabar white ~-tree. [f. med. L *sandalum*, cf. Arab. *çandal*]

sǎn'darǎc, n. = REALGAR; (also *gum* ~) varnish & pounce. [f. L f. Gk *sandaraké*]

sǎnd²blind, a. (arch.). Dim-sighted, purblind. [prob. for *sǎmblind* cf. SAMEL]

sǎn'derling, n. A small wading bird. [?]

sǎn'ders, Saun., n. [| =SANDALWOOD; RED ~, [f. OF *sandre* var. of *sandle* SANDAL²]

Sǎnd'hūrst (-d-h-), n. (Used for) Royal Military College or Academy ~, for army cadets. [~ in Berkshire]

sǎn'diver, n. Glass-gall, liquid saline matter given off in glass-making. [prob. f. F *suin de verre* exhalation (*suer* sweat) of glass]

sǎnd'wich, n., & v.t. **1.** Two slices of bread with meat or other relish between (*ham, egg, caviare, cucumber*, etc., ~; fig., as *a ~ of good & bad*); (usu. ~*-man*, *-boy*, etc.) man etc. walking street with two advertisement-boards hung one before & one behind; ~*-board*, one of such boards; ||~*-boat* in bumping race, boat rowing last in higher & first in lower division on same day. **2.** v.t. Insert (thing, statement, etc.) between two of another character. [perh. f. Earl of S~ while gaming for 24 hrs]

sǎn'dy, a. In n. senses; also, (of hair)

yellowish-red, (of person) with such hair. Hence ~INESS n., ~ỹISH²(2) a. [-Y²]

Sän'dỹ², n. (Nickname for) Scotsman. [usual Sc. shortening of *Alexander*]

sāne, a. Of sound mind, not mad; (of views etc.) moderate, sensible. Hence ~lY² (-nl-) adv. [f. L *sanus* healthy]

sang¹. See SING.

sǎng'ar(r) (-ngg-), n. Stone breastwork used by Indian hill-tribes. [f. Hind. *sunga*]

sängaree' (-nggˑ), n. Cold drink of wine diluted & spiced. [f. Sp. *sangría* (lit. bleeding) drink of lemon-water & red wine]

sang-de-bœuf (sahñdebŭf'), n. & a. (Of) a deep red colour found on old Chinese porcelain. [F, = ox's blood]

sang-froid (see Ap.), n. Composure, coolness, in danger or under agitating circumstances. [F, = cold blood]

sangrail, -real. See GRAIL².

sänguifica'tion (-nggwi-), n. Formation of, conversion of food into, blood. [L *sanguis* blood, -FICATION]

sǎng'uinarỹ (-nggwi-), a. Attended by, delighting in, bloodshed or slaughter, bloody, bloodthirsty, (of laws) inflicting death lightly; ‖ (euphem., substituted in reporting foul language, or used orig. as milder form, for) bloody. Hence ~iLỸ² adv., ~INESS n. [f. L *sanguinarius* (*sanguis -inis* blood, -ARY¹)]

sǎng'uine (-ngwin), a., n., & v.t. 1. Blood-red (literary, & in Nat. Hist.: ~ L *sanguineus*, as ~ *ant, sponge, turtle*); of blood (rare; ~ *rain*), sanguinary (rare; ~ *slaughter*); (Hist.) of the temperament in which the blood predominates over the other HUMOUR's, with ruddy complexion & courageous hopeful amorous disposition; (of complexion) bright, ruddy, florid; habitually hopeful, confident, expecting things to go well, whence (& rarely in other senses) ~ilỸ² adv., ~NESS n. 2. n. Crayon coloured red with iron oxide; a drawing in red chalk. 3. v.t. (poet.). Stain with blood, stain red. [f. F *sanguin(e)* f. L *sanguineus* (prec.)]

sänguin'eous (-nggwi-), a. Of blood (Med.); blood-coloured (esp. Bot.); full-blooded, plethoric. [f. L as prec., -OUS]

sǎn'hedrim (nĭ-), n. Highest court of justice & supreme council in ancient Jerusalem, of 71 members. [f. late Heb. *sanhedrin* f. Gk *sunedrion* (SYN-, *hedra* seat)]

sǎn'icle, n. An umbelliferous plant. [OF, f. med. L *sanicula* prob. f. L *sanus* SANE]

sǎn'ifỹ, v.t. Make healthy, improve sanitary state of, (place). [f. L *sanus* healthy, -I-, -FY]

sǎn'itarỹ, a. Of the conditions that affect health esp. with regard to dirt & infection; free from or designed to obviate influences deleterious to health; ~ *towel* (of kind used in menstruation). Hence

sǎnitā'riAN (-ār-) n. & a., ~ilỸ² adv., ~INESS n., ~ỹISM²(2) n. [f. F *sanitaire* (L as SANITY, -ARY¹)]

sänitā'tion, n. Improving of sanitary conditions. Hence ~ist(2) (sho-) n., (by back formation) **sǎn'itāte** v.t. & i. [irreg. f. SANITARY, -ATION]

sǎn'itỹ, n. Being sane, mental health; tendency to avoid extreme views. [f. F *sanité* f. L *sanitatem* (SANE, -TY)]

sǎn'jǎk, n. One of the administrative districts of a Turkish vilayet. [Turk.]

sank. See SINK¹.

san(n)yasi (sŭnyah'sĭ), n. (Also *sunnyasee*) Indian religious mendicant. [Hind., f. Skr. *sannyāsin* laying aside]

sans, prep. Without (as E wd, pr. sǎnz, now chiefly w. ref. to Shaks. *A. Y. L.* II. vii. 166, ~ *teeth*, ~ *eyes*, ~ *taste*, ~ *everything*. As F wd, pr. as F, in phrr. & compounds, for pronunc. of which see Ap.: ~ *cérémonie* adv., with rude or hurried or kindly neglect of usual formalities; ~*culotte'*, pr. as F or E, lit. = breechless, republican of Parisian lower classes in French Revolution, any extreme republican or revolutionary, whence ~*culott'erie* [-ERY(4, 5)] n., ~*culott'ic* a., ~*culott'ism* n.: ~ *façon* adv., outspokenly, unceremoniously; ~*gêne* n., absence of constraint, familiarity, making oneself at home; ~ *peur et* ~ *reproche* a., of chivalrous character, cf. BAYARD; ~ *phrase* adv., in a word, without qualification; ~*souci* n., gay carelessness, unconcern). [OF, ult. f. L *sine*]

sǎns'rif, n. & a. (Form of type) without serifs. [prob. f. prec. + SERIF, but found earlier than *serif*]

Sǎn'skrit, -scrit, n. & a. (Of, in) the ancient & sacred language of India, oldest known member of INDO-European family. Hence **Sǎnskrit'ic** a., **Sǎn'skritist**(3) n. [f. Skr. *saṃskṛta* composed (*saṃ* together, cogn. w. SAME, *kṛ* make)]

Sǎn'ta Claus' (-z), n. Personage who fills children's stockings with Christmas presents by night. [U.S., f. Du. *Sint Klaas* St Nicholas]

sǎn'tŏn, n. Mohammedan monk or hermit. [Sp. (*santo* SAINT)]

sǎntŏn'ica, n. Kind of wormwood. [L (*Santones* Aquitanian tribe, -IC)]

sǎn'tonin, n. Extract of santonica used as anthelmintic. [-IN]

Saorstat Eireann (sayŏr'stath är'an), n. Republic of Ireland. [Ir.]

săp¹, n.., & v.t. (-pp-). 1. Vital juice circulating in plants (also fig., as *the ~ of youth*, *there is no ~ in a written constitution*); (also ~*wood*) soft outer layers of wood, alburnum; ~*green* n. & a., pigment made from buckthorn berries, (of) colour of this; ~*lath*, made of ~-wood; hence ~'FUL, ~'LESS, ~'rỸ², aa., ~p 'iNESS n. 2. v.t. Drain or dry (wood) of (~); (fig.) exhaust, vigour of (*his energy, constitution, belief,*

had been ~ped by; cf. foll.); remove ~ wood from (log). [OE *sæp*, cf. Du. *sap*, G *saft*; perh. cogn. w. L *sapere* taste]

sap², n., & v.i. & t. (-pp-). **I.** Making of trenches to cover assailants' approach to besieged place, (fig.) insidious or slow undermining of belief, resolution, etc.; covered siege-trench; ~-head, front end of ~; ~-roller, large gabion covering ~-head. **2.** vb. Dig ~, approach (i. & t.) by ~; undermine, make insecure by removing foundations, (fig.) destroy insidiously (cf. prec.), (walls, cliffs, ~ped by the stream, tide; heath ~ping old beliefs). [cf. F *sappe* or It. *zappa* spade, sap, etym. dub.]

sap³, v.i. (-pp-), & n. (school sl.). **I.** ∥ Be studious, work hard at books or lessons. **2.** n. ∥ Studious or hardworking person; ∥ tiresome task, trouble, grind, (it is such a, too much, ~.); *(sl.) simpleton. [prob. fig. use of prec.]

sap'ajou (-jōō), n. Small S.-Amer. monkey often kept as pet. [F, earlier -ŏu, said to be Cayenne wd]

sap'an-wŏŏd, -pp-, n. A red dye-wood obtained from an E.-Ind. tree. [Malay *sapan*, cf. Tamil *shappangam*]

sāp'id, a. Having (esp. agreeable) flavour, savoury, palatable, not vapid or uninteresting, (fig.) not vapid (of talk, writing, etc.). So **sapid'ITY** n. [f. L *sapidus* (*sapere* taste, -ID³)]

sā'pient, a. Wise (now rare); would-be wise, of fancied sagacity, airing wisdom. Hence or cogn. **sā'pIENCE** n., **~LY²** adv. [f. L *sapient-* part. st. of *sapere* be wise]

sapien'tial (-shl), a. Of wisdom (esp. the ~ books, Prov., Eccl., Ecclus., Cant., Wisd., etc.). [f. eccl. L *sapientialis* (L *sapientia* wisdom as prec., -AL)]

sāp'ling, n. Young tree; (fig.) a youth, greyhound in first year (~ stakes in coursing). [SAP¹, -LING²]

sāpodil'la, n. Large evergreen tropical-Amer. tree with durable wood & edible fruit (~-plum or NASEBERRY). [f. Sp. *zapotilla* dim. of *zapote* f. Mex. *zapotl*]

sāponā'ceous (-shus), a. Of, like, containing, soap, soapy (lit. &, in joc. use, fig.). [f. L *sapo -onis* soap, -ACEOUS]

sāpon'ifY, v.t. & i. Turn (f. & i. of fat or oil) into soap by decomposition with alkali. Hence or cogn. **~FICA'TION** n. [f. F *saponifier* (prec., -FY)]

sap'or, n. Quality perceptible by taste, e.g. sweetness; sensation of taste, distinctive taste of substance. [L *sapor*, -OR³]

sapp'er, n. In vbl senses of SAP¹,²,³; also, ∥ officer or man of Royal Engineers, as official term, private (Royal S~s & Miners, former title of R.E.). [-ER¹]

Sapph'ic (săf'ik), a. & n. **I.** Of Sappho (Lesbian lyric poetess 600 B.C.; ~ vice, also **Sapphism** (săf'izm) n., unnatural sexual relations between women; ~ verse, stanza, in Gk metres invented by Sappho & imitated in L by Horace, esp. the four-line stanza with short fourth line roughly copied in E light verse as *Needy knife-grinder, whither do you wander?*). **2.** n. pl. Verse in ~ stanzas. [f. F *sapphique* f. L f. Gk *Sapphikos* (Sapphō, -IC)]

sapphire (săf'īr), n. & a. **I.** A transparent blue precious stone, (Mineral.) any precious native crystalline alumina, including ~ & ruby; bright blue of ~, azure; (attrib.) of humming-bird; so **sapphire²** (săf'īr-) a. **2.** adj. Of ~ blue. [f. OE *safir* f. L f. Gk *sappheiros* lapis lazuli]

sappy. See SAP¹.

sapr-(o)-, comb. form of Gk *sapros* rotten in scient. terms: ~dem'ia, septic poisoning, so ~æm'ic a., [Gk *haïma* blood]; ~ogen'ic, causing or produced by putrefaction; ~ophile a. & n., (bacterium) inhabiting putrid matter; ~ophyte, vegetable organism living on decayed organic matter.

∥ **sâr²**, n. A fish, the sea bream. [F, f. L *sargus*]

sắr'ābānd', n. Stately old Spanish dance; music for this or in its rhythm, in triple time freq. with long note on second beat of bar. [F (-de), f. Sp. *zarabanda* prob. of oriental orig.]

Sā'racen, n. & a. **I.** (General name among later Greeks & Romans for) nomad of Syro-Arabian desert; Arab or Moslem of time of crusades; ∥ ~ corn, buckwheat; ~'s head, as heraldic charge or inn-sign; hence (esp. of Moslem archit.) **Saracēn'IC** a. **2.** adj. = ~ic. [f. LL f. late L f. Gk *Sarakēnos* etym. dub.]

Sāra'tōg'a (trŭnk), n. Lady's large travelling-trunk. [prob. f. Saratoga Springs, New York watering-place]

sarc-, sarco-, comb. form of Gk *sarx sarkos* flesh; ~ology, anatomy of fleshy parts of body; ~oplasm, interfibrillar substance of muscle.

sarc'āsm, n. Bitter or wounding remark, taunt, esp. one ironically worded; language consisting of, faculty of uttering, use of, such remarks; so **sarcās'tIC** a., **sarcās'tICALLY** adv. [f. LL f. late Gk *sarkasmos* (*sarkazō* gnash the teeth, tear flesh, see SARCO-, -asm corresp. to -ISM)]

sarc'ast, n. (rare). Sarcastic person. [as prec., -ast f. -ist]

sarce'lle, n. Kinds of small duck or teal. [f. OF *cercelle* f. L *querquedula*]

sar'cenet, sar'senet, n. Fine soft silk material used esp. for linings. [AF *sarzinett*, perh. dim. of *sarzin* SARACEN as = Saracen cloth]

sar'cōde, n. Animal protoplasm. [prec. + -ODE]

sarcōm'a, n. (pl. ~ta). Tumour of embryonic connective tissue. [f. Gk *sarkōma* (*sarkoō* see SARCO- become fleshy, -M)]

sarcoph'agus, n. (pl. -gi, pr. -gī, -jī). Stone coffin usu. adorned with sculpture or inscription. [L, f. Gk *sarkophagos* orig. = flesh-consuming (stone) as SARCO- + -phagos -eating]

sarc'ous, a. Consisting of flesh or muscle. [SARCO-, -OUS]

sard, n. Yellow or orange cornelian. [F (-e), f. L sarda, L f. Gk sardios (Sardis in Lydia)]

Sardanapā'lian, a. As of, like, Sardanapalus king of Nineveh notorious for effeminate luxury. [-IAN]

sardelle', n. Fish like & treated like sardine. [f. It. sardella dim. of L sarda SARDINE²]

sard'ine¹, n. Precious stone in *Rev.* iv. 3. [prob. erron.; R.V. gives sardius (SARD)]

sardine² (-ēn), n. Small fish of herring kind found off Sardinia & Brittany, or young pilchard of Cornish coast, cured & tinned in oil (packed like ~s, of crowded company). [f. F, f. It. f. L sardina (sarda f. Gk sardō cf. Sardō Sardinia)]

Sardin'ian, a. & n. (Inhabitant) of the island or of the kingdom (1720–1859, including also Piedmont etc.) of Sardinia. [-AN]

sardón'ic, a. Bitter, scornful, mocking, sneering, cynical, (of laugh, laughter, affected merriment, etc.). Hence ~**ically** adv. [f. F sardonique f. L f. Gk sardonios assim. of Homeric sardanios etym. dub. to Sardonios Sardinian, owing to belief that convulsive laughter ending in death resulted from eating a Sardinian plant, +-IC]

sard'onyx, n. Onyx with white layers alternating with sard. [L, f. Gk sardonux (SARDIOS, ONYX)]

sargass'ō, n. (pl. ~s, ~es). (Also *gulf-weed*) kinds of seaweed with berry-like air-vessels found floating in island-like masses in the Gulf-stream & esp. in N. Atlantic region called S~ *Sea*. [f. Port. sargaço]

sa'ri (sah-), n. Length of cotton or silk wrapped round body, worn as main garment by Hindu women. [Hind.]

sarissa, n. (Gk Ant.; pl. ~s, ~es). Long lance of ancient Macedonians. [Gk]

‖ **sark**, n. (Sc.). Shirt or chemise. Hence ~'**ING¹** n., boarding between rafters & roof. [OE serc, cf. ON serkr]

Sarma'tian (-shn), a. & n. (Inhabitant) of ancient Sarmatia (Russia & Poland): (poet.) Pole, Polish. [-AN]

sarm'entōse, -en'tous, aa. (bot.). With long thin trailing shoots. [f. L sarmentosus (sarmenta pl. twigs, brushwood, f. sarpere prune, -MENT, -OSE¹, -OUS]

sarong', n. Malay national garment, a long strip of (often striped) cotton or silk worn by both sexes tucked round waist. [Malay sārung]

sarsaparil'la, n. Kinds of tropical American smilax esp. the Jamaica (so called as chief source of the medicinal ~ for which Jamaica was emporium); dried roots, or extract of these used as tonic etc., of (esp. Jamaica) ~. [f. Sp. zarzaparilla (zarza bramble, perh. + dim. of zarza vine)]

sars'en, n. Sandstone boulder on chalk downs esp. in Wilts. [prob. f. SARACEN]

sars'enet, sär'c-, (-sn-), n. Fine soft silk material now used chiefly for linings. [AF sarzinett (prob. f. sarzin SARACEN + -ET¹ after OF drap sarrasinois Saracen cloth)]

sar'torial, a. Of tailor, tailoring, or men's clothes. [f. L sartorius (sartor tailor f. sarcire patch), -AL]

Sar'um, n. eccl. name of Salisbury (~ *use*, order of divine service used in diocese of Salisbury from 11th c. to Reformation). [med. L, prob. f. misread abbr. of L Sarisburia Salisbury, cf. viz for videlicet]

sash¹, n. Ornamental scarf worn by man usu. as part of uniform or insignia over one shoulder or round waist or by woman or child round waist. Hence ~**ed¹** [-ED²] (-sht) a. [earlier sense turban-band, f Arab. shash muslin]

sash², n. Frame usu. of wood holding pane(s) of glass & usu. made to slide up & down in grooves of window aperture, glazed sliding light of glass-house or garden-frame, (opp. CASEMENT); (rare)= casement; ~*cord*, *-line*, strong cord attaching ~weights to ~; ~*pocket*, space on each side of window-frame in which ~weights run; ~*pulley*, for ~cord to work over; ~*tool*, kinds of glazier's & painter's brush; ~*weight*, attached to each end of ~ to balance it at any height; ~*window*, with ~ or usu. two ~es, of which one or each can be slid over the other to make opening. Hence ~**ed²** [-ED²] (-sht), ~**LESS**, aa. [corrupt. of CHASSIS prob. taken for pl.]

sās'in, n. Indian antelope. [Nepalese]

sassā'by, n. Large S.-Afr. antelope. [native]

sāss'afrās, n. (Small N.-Amer. tree-yielding) a bark used medicinally; infusion of this. [Sp. (sasa-), etym. dub.]

Sāssān'ian, Sāss'anid, nn. & aa. (Member, esp. a king) of family of Sa(s)san, rulers of Persian empire A.D. 211–651. [-IAN, -ID³]

Sāss'enach (see Ap.), n. & a. (Sc. & Ir. for) English(man). [thr. Gael. & Ir. f. Saxon]

sat. See SIT.

Sāt'an, (arch.) **Săt'anăs**, n. The Devil, Lucifer. [L f. Gk, f. Heb. sāṭān enemy]

Satān'ic, a. Of, like, or befitting Satan, diabolical, hellish, (his ~ majesty, Satan; ~ school, orig. Byron, Shelley, etc., also any set of writers accused of defiant impiety etc.). Hence ~**ally²** adv. [-IC, -ICAL]

Sāt'anism, n. Deliberate wickedness, pursuit of evil for its own sake, diabolical disposition, so ~IZE(3) v.t.; characteristics of SATANIC school; (esp. French 19th-c.) professed worship of Satan. So ~IST(2) n. [-ISM]

Sătănŏl'ŏgy, n. (History or collection of) beliefs concerning the Devil. [-o-, -logy]

satăr'a, n. Heavy broadcloth with hori-zontal rib. [S~ in India]

sătch'el, n. Small bag usu. of leather & hung from shoulder with strap for carry-ing books etc. esp. to & from school. Hence ~lnĐ² (-ld) a. [f. OF sachel f. L saccŭlus (SACK¹, -EL)]

sāte, v.t. Gratify, surfeit, person feeling it) to the full; cloy, surfeit, weary with over-abundance (~d with). Hence ~LESS (-ti-) a. (poet.). [earlier sade, OE sadian (SAD), assim. to L sat(is) enough]

sateen', n. Cotton or woollen fabric with glossy surface. [f. SATIN after VELVETEEN]

sāt'ellīte, n. Person's follower or hench-man or hanger-on, member of great man's retinue, underling; heavenly body revolving round another (often fig.), whence ~IC'to a.; (attrib.) secondary, minor. [F., f. L satellitem nom. -les guard]

săti. See SUTTEE.

sā'tiāte¹ (-shyāt), a. Satiated. [L satiare]

sā'tiāte² (-shi-), v.t. = SATE. So **sā'tIARIE** (-shō-) a. (rare), **satIA'TION** (săsī-, săshī-) n. [as prec., -ATE³]

satī'ety, n. Glutted or satiated state, feel-ing of having had too much of something, also kind of moth; ~ or white ~, sl., gin, cloyed dislike of, (to ~, to extent beyond what is desired); (rare) over-abundance. [f. F satiété f. L satietatem (satis enough, -TY)]

sătīn, n. & a., & v.t. **1.** Silk fabric with glossy surface on one side got by catching warp-threads only at intervals (Denmark ~, smooth worsted material used for ladies' slippers); white ~, the plant Honesty, also kind of moth; ~ or white ~, sl., gin. **2.** adj. Smooth as ~. **3.** ~ beauty, carpet, kinds of moth; ~ cloth, a woollen cloth woven like ~; ~ finish, polish given to silver with metallic brush; ~ flower, Hon-esty; also Greater Stitchwort; ~ gypsum, fibrous kind with pearly lustre; ~ paper, fine glossy writing-paper; ~ pug, pygmy, kinds of moth; ~ sheeting, fabric of waste silk & cotton; ~ spar, fibrous carbonate of lime; ~-stitch, giving appearance of ~ in embroidery & wool-work; ~-stone, ~ gypsum; ~-strew, soft & flexible for hats; ~ white, artificial sulphate of lime; ~ wood, choice timber of a tropical tree; hence ~Y² a., ~ETTE'(2) & in same sense ~ET¹ nn. **4.** v.t. Give glossy surface to (paper). [F, prob. ult. f. L sēta silk, -INE¹]

săt'īre, n. (Rom. Ant.) poetic medley, esp. poem aimed at prevalent vices or follies; a composition in verse or prose holding up vice or folly to ridicule or lampooning individual(s), this branch of literature, (often upon); thing that brings ridicule upon something (our lives are a ~ upon our religion); use of ridicule, irony, sarcasm, etc., in speech or writing for the ostensible purpose of exposing & discouraging vice or folly. [f. L satira in 1st sense above, var. of satura (lanx satura full dish)]

satĭr'ic, a. Of satires or satire, containing satire, writing satire, (~ verse, poem, poet, writer, intent, stroke). [F (-que), f. LL satĭricus (prec., -IC)]

satĭr'ical, a. = prec.; given to the use of satire in speech or writing or to cynical observation of others, sarcastic, humor-ously critical. Hence ~LY² adv. [prec., -AL]

săt'irist, n. Writer of satires; satirical person. [-IST]

săt'irize, v.t. Assail with satire, write satire(s) upon, describe satirically. [f. F satiriser (SATIRE, -IZE)]

săt'is, Latin adv. & n. = enough, used in phr. făm.~ already enough, ~ superque (pr. sūpĕr'kwi), enough & too much.

satisfăc'tion, n. **1.** Payment of debt, fulfilment of obligation, atonement (for), thing accepted by way of, (Eccl.) perfor-mance of penance, (Theol.), atonement made by Christ for sins of men, (make ~; in.~ of; enter ~; legal, place on record of court that payment ordered has been made; Christ is the ~ for our sins). **2.** Op-portunity of fighting duel with person not be done; would be a ~ to me; thirsts only of present ~). [F, f. L satisfactionem (SATISFY)]

satisfăc'torўy, a. **1.** (Theol.) serving as atonement for sin. **2.** Satisfying expecta-tions or needs, leaving no room for com-plaint, causing satisfaction, adequate, (~y proof, method, result, pupil, pair of boots, expedition, marriage, compromise). Hence ~ILY² adv., ~INESS n. [f. F satis-factoire f. med. L satisfactorius (SATISFY, -ORY)]

satisfy, v.t. & i. **1.** Pay (debt, rarely creditor), fulfil (obligation), comply with (with), demand no more than or consider it enough to do, (rest ~ied, make or take no further demands or steps). **4.** intr. Give satisfaction, leave nothing to be de-sired. **5.** Dispose of (an appetite or want), rid (person) of an appetite or want, by sufficient supply. **6.** Furnish with ade-quate proof, convince, (of fact, that it is

so; ~*y oneself*, attain to practical certainty). 7. Adequately meet (objection, doubt, request, conditions). Hence ~iABLE, ~YING,² aa., ~YINGLY² adv. [f. OF *satisfier* f. L SATIS *facere fact* -FY]

satrangi (sat'rŭnji, satrŭn'ji), n. Cheap Indian cotton carpet. [Bengali]

sat'rap, n. Holder of provincial governorship or ~y¹ in ancient-Persian empire, viceroy; modern subordinate ruler, colonial governor, etc. (esp. rhet. with implication of luxury or tyranny). [f. L f. Gk *satrapēs* f. OPers. *khsatra-pava* province-guardian]

Sat'sŭma, n. (Also ~ *ware*) creamcoloured Japanese pottery. [name of province]

sat'urate (or -cher·), v.t. Impregnate, soak thoroughly, imbue *with*; overwhelm (defences, target area) by concentrated bombing; (Chem. etc.) charge (substance, air, vapour, metal) with or cause to combine with or absorb or hold the greatest amount possible of another substance, moisture, magnetism, electricity, etc.; (p.p., of colour) free from admixture of white, full, rich. Hence or cogn. ~ATE² (-at) a. (poet. exc. of colour), ~ABLE a., ~A'TION n. [f. L *saturare* (*satur* full cogn. w. SATIS), -ATE³]

Sat'urday (-erdi), n. Seventh day of week (HOLY, HOSPITAL,); ~*-to-Monday*, =the now usu. WEEK-*end*). [OE *Sætern(es)dæg* transl. of L *Saturni dies* day of SATURN]

Sat'ŭrn, n. 1. (Rom. Ant.) Italic god of agriculture later identified with Greek Cronos father of Zeus, ruler of the world in a golden age of innocence and plenty. 2. A planet, the furthest off of the 7 anciently known, with 10 moons & broad flat ring, credited in astrology with producing cold sluggish gloomy temperament in those born under its influence. [f. L *Saturnus* (severe *sat-* sow)]

Saturnā'lia (-ter·), n. pl. &(see below) sing. Ancient-Roman festival of Saturn in December observed as time of unrestrained merrymaking with temporary release of slaves, predecessor of modern Christmastide (S~); scene or time of wild revelry or tumult (also S~; often as sing. as *a ~ of crime*). Hence saturnā'lian(-ter·) a. [L, neut. pl. of *Saturnalis* (prec., -AN)]

Satŭrn'ian, a. & n. 1. Of the god or the planet Saturn; ~ *age*, GOLDEN age; ~ *metre*, *verse*, metre used in early Latin poetry before introduction of Greek metres & generally taken to have been an iambic dimeter catalectic followed by three trochees (e.g. *dabunt·malum Metelli·Naevio poetae*). 2. n. Inhabitant of Saturn; (pl.) ~ verse. [f. L SATURNius, -AN]

satŭrn'ic, a. (path.). Affected with leadpoisoning. So Sat'urnism(5) (-ter·) n. [SATURN in aloh. sense *lead*, -IC]

sat'urnine (-ter·), a. Of sluggish gloomy temperament, (of looks etc.) suggestive of or produced by such temperament, whence ~LY² adv.; of lead (a ~ *poultice*, *red*, etc.); of, affected by, lead-poisoning (~ *patients*, *symptoms*). [SATURN (cf. prec.), -INE¹]

satyagraha (sahtyah'grahah), n. (Indian pol.). Passive resistance. [Skr., f. *satya* faithful + *āgraha* obstinacy]

sat'yr (-er), n. 1. One of a class of Greek woodland deities in human form with horse's ears & tail (or, as represented by Romans, with a goat's ears, tail, legs, & budding horns); lustful or beastlyminded man; (rare) orang-utan. [f. L f. Gk *saturos*]

sătyri'asis (-ter·), n. Excessive sexual desire in males. [f. Gk *saturiasis* (prec., -ASIS]

săty'ric, a. Of satyrs (esp. ~ *drama*, kind of Greek play with chorus of satyrs). [f. L f. Gk *saturikos* (SATYR, -IC)]

sauce, n., & v.t. 1. Liquid preparation taken as relish with some article of food (*bread*, *egg*, *mint*, *parsley*, *tomato*, etc.~, with these as prominent ingredient; *while ~, of melted butter, flour*, etc.; *hunger is the best ~; for the* GANDER; *serve with the same ~*, subject to same usage); (fig.) something that adds piquancy (*is tame without the ~ of danger*). 2. Solution of salt & other ingredients used in some manufacturing processes. 3. Sauciness, impertinent speech, cheek, (*none of your ~*). 4. ~*alone*, hedge-weed formerly used to flavour salads &~s; ~*boat*, vessel in which ~ is served; ~*box*, impudent person; ~*pan* (-an), metal vessel usu. cylindrical with long handle projecting from side for boiling things in cookery; hence ~LESS a. 5. v.t. Season with ~s or condiments (rare); (fig.) make piquant, add relish to; (vulg.) be impudent to, cheek, (person). [vb f. n., f. f. pop. L *salsa* fem. of *salsus* (*sal(e)re sals-* to salt f. *sal* salt)]

sau'cer, n. Shallow vessel for standing cup on to intercept spillings of tea. etc. (~ *eye*, large & round as a ~, whence ~EYED² a.); vessel placed under flowerpot to prevent water from running away at once; any small shallow round vessel resembling tea~. Hence ~FUL(2) n., ~LESS a. [earlier sense *condiment-dish*, f. OF *saussier* (SAUCE, -ARY¹)]

sau'cy, a. Impudent to superiors, cheeky, (sl.) sprightly, smart, stylish. Hence ~ILY² adv., ~INESS n. [earlier sense *savoury*; SAUCE, -Y²]

sauerkraut(sowr'krowt), n. German dish of pickled cabbage. [G]

saul. See SAL.

Saumur (sōm'ūr), n. White wine produced near ~ in France.

saunders. See SANDERS.

saun'ter, v.i. & n. 1. Walk in leisurely way or without destination, stroll, (also fig., as ~ *through life*); hence ~ER¹ n.,

~ingu² adv. **2.** n. Leisurely ramble or gait. [²]

Saur′|ian, a. & n. (One) of the *Sauria* or order of lizards including crocodiles, alligators, & extinct kinds such as ichthyo- (part.) redeeming (by the saving grace of souls); form, **~OID** a. & n. [Gk *sauros* lizard, -IAN]

saur′y, n. A long-billed sea-fish. [prob. f. mod. L f. Gk *sauros* lizard]

saur′sage (sos-), n. Pork or other meat minced, seasoned, & stuffed into long cylindrical cases prepared from entrails & divided when full into lengths of a few inches by twisting or tying, a length of this, (*Bologna ~*, large kind made of bacon, veal, pork-suet, etc., & sold ready for eating cold); (army sl.) KITE balloon; **~-filler, -grinder, -machine,** appliances; **~-meat,** meat & bread etc. minced & seasoned for use in **~s** or as a stuffing etc.; **~ roll,** **~-meat** enclosed in a pastry & cooked. [f. ONF *saussiche* f. LL *salsicia* (L *salsus* see SAUCE)]

sauté (sōt′ā), a. (in fem. **-ée**; pl. **-és, -ées;** pronunc. the same in all forms). Quickly fried in hot pan with little grease. [F]

Sauterne (sōtårn′), n. Kinds of sweet white French wine. [place-name]

sauve-qui-peut (sōvkēpœ′), n. Precipitate flight in various directions. [F, f. phr. *sauve qui peut* let him find safety who can]

sav′age, a., n., & v.t. **1.** Uncultivated, wild, (arch.); *a ~ scene*); uncivilized, in primitive state, (~ *tribes, life*); fierce, cruel, furious, (~ *persecution, persecution, revenge, criticism, blow*); (colloq.) angry, out of temper; (Her.: of human figure) naked; hence or cogn. **~LY²** (-ijli) adv., **~NESS** (-ijn-), **~GERY**(2, 4) (-ijri), nn. **2.** n. Member of a ~ tribe esp. of one living by hunting & fishing, whence **~DOM** (-ijd-) n.; brutally cruel or barbarous person. **3.** v.t. (Of horse) attack & bite or trample (person; *was ~d by his horse*). [earlier & OF *salvege* f. L *silvaticus* (*silva* a wood, -ATIC, cf. -AGE)]

sav′àn|a(h) (-nə), n. Grassy plain with scattered trees in tropical & subtropical regions. [f. Sp. *zavana* perh. of Carib. orig.]

Savant (see Ap.), n. Man of learning, esp. distinguished scientist. [part. of F *savoir* know, as SAPIENT]

savate′ (-aht), n. French boxing in which feet & head are used as fists. [F]

save¹, v.t. & i., & n. **1.** Rescue, preserve, deliver, from (or from danger or misfortune or harm or discredit (~*d my life, me from drowning, the State; ~ me or God me from my friends etc.,* comment upon well-meant inopportune officiousness; ~ *us!,* excl. of surprise; ~ one's BACON, FACE¹; ~ the situation, find or provide way out of difficulty, avert disaster; ~*

appearances, put a good face on something*); (Footb. etc.) prevent opponents from scoring. **2.** Bring about spiritual salvation of, preserve from damnation, (*who then can be ~d?; the saving of souls*); God; has the saving grace of humour); **3.** Keep for future use, husband, reserve, abstain from expending, lay by money, live economically, (~ one's breath, be silent; *a saving housekeeper; is saving his strength; has never ~d,* put by money; economy; *you may ~ your pains or economy; need, need not take, will take in vain, whence* **SAV′ER¹(1)** n., **SAV′ING¹(2)** n. (usu. in pl.), **SAV′ING¹²** adv. **4.** Relieve (person) from need of expending (money, trouble, etc.) or from exposure to (annoyance etc.), obviate need of, reduce requisite amount of, (*that will ~ me £50; his secretary ~d him much time or labour; get enough runs to prevent it; whence in cricket, time ~s nine; soap ~s rubbing*), whence losing, be in time for, succeed in catching, (*write hurriedly to ~ the post; shall we ~ the tide?, get in or out while it serves*). **5.** Avoid (**~SAVER¹(2)** n., **~SAVING²** a.) **6.** Make reservation concerning, make reservation, (esp. *saving clause,* containing stipulation of exemption etc.; *saving your reverence,* apology for unseemly expression etc., cf. ~ *the MARK¹);* (part. as prep.) except, with the exception of, **SAVE².** **7.** n. (Footb. etc.) act of preventing opponents from scoring; (Bridge) action taken to prevent heavy losses. **8.** ~*cul*, pan with spike for burning up candle-ends; *savings-bank,* receiving small deposits & conducted solely in depositors' interests (*Post-office savings-bank,* with branches at local post offices). Hence **SAV′ABLE** a. [f. OF *salver* f. L *salvare* (*salvus* safe)]

save², prep. & conj. **1.** Except, but, (with n. in obj. case, or with *that* clause; poet., or with formal or pretentious effect, in ordinary writing, also pleonast. in ~ *except; forty stripes ~ one; all ~ him, & see conj.; I am well ~ that I have a cold).* **2.** conj. (arch.). Unless, but, (thou seest no ~ *only he; happy ~ for one vent).* **[f.** SAVE¹ after F *sauf* & SALVO¹]

sav′eloy, n. Highly seasoned dried sausage. [earlier & OF *cervelat* f. It. *cervellata* (*cervello* brain f. L CEREBELLUM, named as orig. made of pig's brain)]

sav′in, n. (Tree or shrub with) tops yielding a volatile oil used medicinally. [f. OF *savine* f. L *sabina* (*herba*) SABINE (herb)]

sav′iour (-vyer), n. Deliverer, redeemer (*the, our, S~,* Christ), person who saves a State etc. from destruction etc. [f. OF *sauveour* (SAVE¹ -IOUR)]

savoir faire (săv′wär fâr′), n. Quickness

to see & do the right thing, address, tact. [F]

savoir vivre (sǎv'wǎr vē'vr), n. Good breeding, being at home in society. [F]

sav'ory, n. Herb of mint family used in cookery. [ult. f. L *satureia* prob. w. assim. in F to foll.]

sav'our (-ver), n., & v.i. & t. **1.** Characteristic taste, flavour, relish, or (now rare) smell, power to affect the taste (lit. or fig.); quality suggestive, perceptible admixture, suspicion, smack, of (a *not unpleasing ~ of preciosity*); hence ~LESS (-ver-)a. **2.** vb. Appreciate or perceive the lit. or fig. taste of (arch.); give flavour to (rare); smack, suggest the presence, of (*the offer ~s of impertinence*). [f. OF *savour(er)* f. L *saporem* (*sapere* taste, -OR¹)]

sav'oury (-veri), a. & n. **1.** With appetizing taste or smell; (of places etc.; only w. neg.) free from bad smells; (of dishes etc.) of salt or piquant & not sweet flavour (*sweet or ~y omelette*); hence ~ILY² adv., ~INESS n. **2.** n. ∥~y dish, esp. one served at beginning or end of dinner as stimulant or digestive. [f. OF *savouré* p.p. (SAVOUR)]

savoy', n. Kind of cabbage with wrinkled leaves. [*S~* in France]

Savoy'ard (-oi-), n. & a. **1.** (Native) of Savoy. **2.** Member of the Savoy Theatre company who acted in the original productions of the Gilbert and Sullivan operas. [F (*Savoie* Savoy, -ARD)]

sav'vy̆, corrupt. of Sp. *sabe* knows, in sl. use = do you understand? (*no*~, I do, he etc. does, not know or understand), also as n. = understanding, wits, savoir faire.

saw¹, n., & v.t. & i. (p.p. ~n, rarely ~ed). **1.** Implement usu. of steel worked by hand or mechanically & with variously shaped blade or edge having teeth of various forms cut in or attached to it for dividing wood, metal, stone, etc., by reciprocating or rotatory motion (*annular*, *crown*, *cylinder*, ~, cylinder with toothed edge for making circular hole; BAND¹, BOW¹, FRAME², FRET¹, ~; CIRCULAR ~; *cross-cut*, *rip*~, ~, for cutting wood across, along, the grain; *hand*~, held with one hand; HACK²~; *jig*~, *frame*~ worked mechanically in connexion with table holding the wood etc. *jig*~*puzzle*, of pieces sawn with jig~ to be put together; *musical or singing* ~, ordinary ~ played on by performer by means of violin bow; *pit*~, worked by two men one above & one in pit; *reciprocating* ~, worked mechanically with backward & forward strokes; *stone*~, toothless frame~ cutting stone by friction with sand & water). **2.** (Zool. etc.) serrated organ or part. **3.** ~*doctor*, machine for making teeth of ~; ~*dust*, wood fragments produced in ~ing used in packing, pugging, stuffing, drying moisture, etc. (*let the*

~*dust out of*, fig., expose pretentiousness or unsubstantial character of, w. ref. to doll's stuffing); ~*fish*, large kind with toothed snout used as weapon; ~*fly*, kinds injurious to plants with serrated ovipositor; ~*frame*, in which ~-blade is held taut; ~*gate*, ~*frame*; ~*gin*, cotton-GIN¹ with ~-teeth; ~*horse*, rack supporting wood for ~ing; ~*mill*, driven by water or steam for mechanical ~ing; ~*pit*, in which lower of two men working pit~ stands; ~*set*, tool for wrenching ~-teeth in alternate directions to give kerf wider than blade & let ~ work freely; ~*wort*, plant yielding yellow dye named from serrated leaves; ~*wrack*, a serrated sea-weed; ~*wrest*, ~-set. **4.** vb. Cut (wood etc.) with, make (boards etc.) with, use, ~; move (t. & i.) backward & forward, divide (the air etc.) with motion as of ~ or person ~ing; (quasi-pass.) admit of being ~n *easily*, *badly*, etc.; (Bookbind.) make incisions to receive binding-bands in (gathered sheets); ~*bones* (sl.), surgeon. [vb f. n., OE *sagu*, cf. Du. *zaag*, G *säge*, cogn. w. L *secare* cut]

saw², n. Proverbial saying, old maxim, (usu. *old or wise* ~). [OE *sagu*, cogn. w. SAY²]

saw³. See SEE¹.

sawd'er, n. *Soft* ~, compliments, flattering speeches, blarney. [=SOLDER]

Sawn'ey, n. (Nickname for) Scotsman; simpleton. [prob. as SANDY²]

saw'yer, n. Man employed in sawing timber (TOP~); * uprooted tree floating or stranded in river (named as sawing up & down); kinds of wood-boring larva. [f. *saw* + -YER]

săx, zăx, n. Slater's chopper, with point for making nail-holes. [OE *seax* knife]

săx'atile, a. (nat. hist.) Living, growing, on or among rocks. [f. L *saxatilis* (*saxum* rock, -ATILE)]

săxe, n. ∥ Kind of photographic paper; a colour, = SAXON *blue*. [F, = Saxony (place of origin)]

săx'horn, n. Brass instrument made in seven sizes, the lowest three being considered tubas. [A. *Sax*, inventor]

săxic'oline, -lous, a. (nat. hist.), = SAXATILE. [L -*cola* inhabitant of (*colere* inhabit)]

săx'ifrage (or -āj), n. Kinds of Alpine or rock plant with tufted foliage & panicles of white or yellow or red flowers. [OF, f. L *saxifraga* spleenwort (*saxum* stone, *frangere* break) prob. named as growing in rock-clefts]

Săx'on, n. & a. **1.** Member, language (often *Old* ~), of the Teutonic N.-German people by which Britain was conquered in 5th & 6th cc.; = ANGLO-SAXON, whence ~DOM n.; native of modern Saxony; Teutonic (opp. Latin or Romance) elements of English. **2.** adj. Of the ~s (

architecture, rude Romanesque preceding Norman in England); in ~ (~ *words* in English, of Teutonic origin), whence ~ISM(2, 4), ~IST(2) nn.; ~ *blue*, solution of indigo in sulphuric acid as dye; hence ~IZE(2, 3) v.t.& t. [F, f. L *Saxonem* f. WG (OE *Seaxan* pl., perh. f. *seax* knife)]

saxony, n. Fine kind of wool, cloth made from it. [f. S~ in Germany]

saxophone, n. Keyed brass instrument in several sizes, having a reed like that of a clarinet. [as SAXHORN, Gk *phōnē* sound]

saxtuba, n. Large SAXHORN. [PUBA]

say¹, n. (now rare). Fine serge-like cloth. [f. F *saie* f. L *saga* pl. of *sagum* military cloak]

say², v.t.& i. (*said* pr. sĕd; 3rd sing. pres. *says* pr. sĕz, arch. *saith* pr. sĕth; arch. 2nd sing. pres. ~st or ~est, past *saidst* rarely *saidest*), & n. 1. Utter, make(specified remark), recite, rehearse, in ordinary speaking voice (~ *the word*, give the order etc.; ~ WHEN; ~ *no more*, cease speaking; ~ *a good word for*, commend; named ~ *to be said or sung*; ~ *no*, *yes*, refuse, grant, request, also deny, confirm or accept, statement; ~ *out*, express fully or candidly; ~ *one nay*, refuse him something; *has said his* ~, finished what he had to ~; ~ *lesson*, repeat it to teacher; ~ *grace*, *prayer*; ~ *something*, ~ *grace*, also make a speech; *that is to* ~, in other words, as *the whole family, that is to* ~ *four persons*, also ~ or at least, *as he never went, that is to* ~ *it is not recorded that he did*, also elliptic. ~ in giving sum in words after figures, as £500, ~ *five hundred pounds*; *he said 'You lie'*, ~ *or said he* etc., *said I*, ~s *I* colloq., forms inserted in repeating conversation; ~ing & doing, speech & action; || *I* ~, excl. used to draw attention, open a conversation, or express surprise, as *I* ~, *who was that?*, *I* ~, *what a beauty!*, or in same sense *I* ~! alone). 2. State, promise, prophesy, (*he* ~s *all men or that all men are liars*; *you said you would*; DARE ~; *they* ~; *it is said*, forms introducing rumour; *it* ~s *in the Bible*, *the Bible* ~s; *goes without* ~ing, is too obvious to need mention; *hear* ~, hear it reported; *so he* ~s, *he* ~s *so*; *you may well* ~ *so*, your statement is fully justified). 3. Speak, talk, (rare; ~ *away*, ~ *what you have to* ~; *he said, & turned his back*, in narrative poetry etc.). 4. Put into words, express (*that was well said*). 5. Adduce or allege in argument or excuse (*there is much to be said on both sides*; *have you nothing to* ~ *for yourself?*). 6. Form & give opinion or decision as to or abs. (*there is no* ~ing, *it is hard to* ~; *who would I cannot* ~, do not know whether etc., or abs.; *do* ~ *which you will have*; *what* ~ *you to a theatre?*, are you inclined for it?; *& so* ~ *all of us*, *& that is our opinion too*). 7. Select as example, assume, take (specified number etc.) as near enough. (*let us* ~, or usu. elliptic. ~; *any country, let us* ~ *Sweden, might do the same*; *well, ~ it were true, what then?*; *a few of them, ~ a dozen* (or so). 8. n. (Opportunity of, ~ing) what one has to ~, share in decision, (~ *your* ~; *let him have his* ~; *had no* ~ *in the matter*). [OE *secgan*, cf. ON *segja*, G *sagen*]

say'ing, n. In vbl senses; esp., sententious remark, maxim, adage, (*as the* ~ *is*, form used in quoting proverb or phrase). [-ING¹]

Say'(y)id (sä'yïd), **Said** (säd), nn. Varr. of SEID.

scab, n., & v.i. (-bb-). 1. Dry rough incrustation formed over sore in healing, cicatrice; mange, itch, or similar skin-disease; kinds of fungous plant-disease; mean dirty fellow (arch.); (Trade unionism) workman who refuses to join strike or union or takes striker's place, blackleg; ~wort, cleanpanea; hence ~BED² (-bd), ~b'y¹ aa., ~b'ily² adv., ~b'iNESS n. 2. v.i. (Of sore) form ~, heal over. [f. ON (Da. *skab*, Sw. *skabb*, cf. OE *sceab*, *sceeb*), (SHABBY)]

scab'bard (zb·), n. Sheath of sword, bayonet, etc. (*fling, throw, away the* ~, commit oneself to fighting a matter out to *commit* end); ~fish, silvery-white sea-fish shaped like sword~. [earlier *scauberk*, cf. AF *escaudre* (prob. ult. f. Teut., (SHELL, HAUBERK)]

scab'ies (-z), n. The itch. [L (*scabere* scratch)]

scab'ious, a. & n. 1. Scabby, affected with mange, itch, etc. 2. n. Kinds of wild & cultivated annual or perennial herb with blue, pink, or white, pincushion-shaped flowers. [(n. f. *scabiosa herba* named as specific against itch) f. L *scabiosus* (prec., -OSE¹]

scad, n. Kind of fish called also horse-mackerel. [?]

scaf'fold, n., & v.t. **scaf'folding** n. 1. Elevated platform of timber usu. for execution of criminals (~*the* ~, death by executioner's hands) or rarely (~, ~ing) for display of something or accommodation of spectators; (usu. ~ing) temporary structure of poles & planks providing workmen with platform(s) to stand on while building or repairing house etc., (~ing) materials for this; (Anat., Embryol.; ~, ~ing) framework outlining parts to be formed on it later (*the* ~ *of the skull*); ~ing-pole, mastlike pole helping to support building-platform. 2. v.t. Attach ~ing to (house), [f. OF *escadfaut*

(now *échafaud*) perh. f. EX-+It. *catafalco* CATAFALQUE]

scag′lia (or skahl′ya), n. Reddish Italian limestone. [It.]

scagliola (skălyōl′ă), n. Imitation stone of plaster mixed with glue & variously coloured or diversified. [It. (*-uola*)]

scal′able, a. In vbl senses of SCALE¹, ², ³. [-ABLE]

scala′riform, a. (bot., zool.). Ladder-shaped (of veins in insect's wings, or of alternating thick & thin strips in structure). [L *scalaria* staircase (neut. pl. of *scalaris* f. *scala* SCALE¹, -AR³), -FORM]

scal′awag, scal′la~, scall′y~, n. Undersized or ill-fed animal; good-for-nothing person, scamp, scapegrace. [U.S., etym. dub.]

scald¹ (-aw-), v.t. & n. 1. Injure or pain (skin, or person or animal or part in regard to it) with hot liquid or vapour (*was ~ed to death by the steam*; *~ing tears, of bitter grief*); raise (milk) to near boiling-point (*~ed cream*, from milk ~ed & allowed to stand), whence ~ER²(2) n.; cleanse (vessel; often *out*) by rinsing with boiling water. 2. n. Injury to skin by ~ing (*for ~s & burns*). [f. ONF *escader* f. LL EX(*caldare* f. L *calidus* hot)]

scald² (-aw-), sk-, n. Ancient-Scandinavian composer & reciter of poems in honour of great men. Hence **sca′ldic** (-awl-) a. [ON *skáld* etym. dub.]

scald′head (-awld-hěd), n. Scalp-disease of children. [SCALL, -ED³]

scald′inō (-ahldē-), n. (pl. *-nī* pr. -ē). Small earthenware brazier used in Italy for warming the hands etc. [It.]

scale¹, n., & v.t. & i. 1. One of the thin horny overlapping plates protecting the skin of many fishes & reptiles. 2. Plate or thin outer piece with some resemblance to fish~ in organic or other object, e.g. pod, husk, rudimentary leaf or feather, bract, metamorphosed hair of lepidoptera, bulb-layer, flake of skin, scab, lamina on surface of rusty iron. 3. (Without *a*) incrustation inside boiler etc., tartar on teeth. 4. *~-armour*, of metal ~s attached to leather etc.; *~-board*, very thin for back of mirror, picture, etc.; *~-borer*, machine for removing ~ from boiler-tubes; *~-fern*, ceterach; *~-insect*, kinds that cling fast to plants & secrete a shieldlike ~ as covering; *~-moss*, kinds of plant with ~like leaves resembling moss; *~-winged*, lepidopterous; *~-work*, overlapping arrangement, imbrication; hence(-)**scaled(**-ĭd), **scal′y²** aa., **scal′iness** n. 5. vb. Take away *~(s)* from (~ *fish, almonds, peas, teeth, iron*); (of skin, metal, etc.) form, come off in, drop, *~s*; (of *~s*) come off. [f. OF *escale* f. OTeut. *skalā*; cogn. w. foll.]

scale², n., & v.t. 1. Dish of simple balance (*throw sword into ~*, back claim with arms; *turn the ~*, of motive or circum-

stance, be decisive); (Astron.), the *S~s*, = LIBRA; (pl.) a simple balance (also *pair of ~s*) or weighing-instrument (*hold the ~ even*, be impartial judge). 2. v.t. Weigh in *~s* (rare); (of thing weighed) show (specified weight) in the *~s* (*~s 10 st., 100 lb.*). [f. ON *skál* bowl f. OTeut. *skǣlā*; cogn. w. OE *scealu* shell & w. prec.]

scale³, n., & v.t. & i. 1. Series of degrees, ladderlike arrangement or classification, graded system, (*is high in the ~ of creation or social, intellectual, etc.; ~; sink in the ~*, fall to lower rank or level; *at the top, bottom, of the ~*; *sliding ~*, see SLIDE¹), 2. (Mus.) steplike ordered arrangement of all notes used in any system of music (DIATONIC, CHROMATIC, MAJOR², MINOR², ~; *play, sing, run over one's*, *~s*, as exercise for fingers or voice). 3. (Often ~ *of notation*) basis of numerical system as shown in ratio between units in different places of number (the *ordinary* or *denary* or *decimal ~*, with successive places denoting units, tens, hundreds, etc.; *binary ~*, denoting units, twos, fours, etc.; *ternary ~*, denoting units, threes, nines, etc.; thus fourteen is written in binary ~ 1110 i.e. nought+two+four+eight, in ternary ~ 112 i.e. two+three+nine, in septenary ~ 20 i.e. nought+two sevens, & in denary ~ 14 i.e. four+ten). 4. Relative dimensions, ratio of reduction & enlargement in map etc., (*philanthropy, armies, on a vast ~*; *a building of small ~ to ~*, with uniform reduction or enlargement; *the ~ to be one to fifty thousand, an inch to the mile*, 1/1000, etc.). 5. Set of marks at measured distances on a line for use in measuring or making proportional reductions & enlargements, rule determining intervals between these, piece of metal etc. or apparatus on which they are marked (GUNTER'S ~). 6. vb. Climb (wall, steep place, or abs.) with ladder (*scaling-ladder*) or by clambering. 7. Represent in dimensions proportional to the actual ones, reduce to common ~, (*~ up, down*, make larger, smaller, in due proportion). 8. (Of quantities etc.) have common ~, be commensurable. [f. L *scala* ladder (*scandere* climb)]

scalene′, a. & n. 1. Unequal-sided (~ *triangle*, with no two sides equal; ~ *cone, cylinder*, with axis inclined to base; ~ *muscle*, any of several connecting spine & ribs). 2. n. ~ triangle or muscle. [f. LL f. Gk *skalēnos*]

scall (-awl-), n. (arch.). Scaly eruption on skin (*dry ~*, the itch; *moist ~*, eczema). [f. ON *skalle* bare head]

scallawag. See SCALAWAG.

scall′ion (-yon), n. Kind of onion or shallot. [f. AF *scaloun* = OF *eschalogne* SHALLOT]

scall′op, scŏ-, scŏ′-, n., & v.t. 1. Bivalve mollusc with shell divided into grooves &

ridges radiating from middle of hinge & edged all round with small semicircular lobes; (also ~*shell*) one valve of this (hist.) as pilgrim's badge, (mod.) as utensil in which oysters, shredded fish, mince, etc., are cooked & served, small shallow pan similarly used; (pl.) orna-mental edging cut in material in imitation of ~*-edge*. 2. v.t. Cook in ~; ornament (edge, material) with ~s or ~ING[6] n. [f. OF *escalope* f. Teut. (Du. *schelp* cogn. w. SCALE[1,2] SHELL)]

scallywag. See SCALAWAG.

scalp, n. & v.t. 1. Top of head; skin with hair etc. of head excluding face, this as part of it cut as trophy from enemy's head by Red Indians (*take* ~; *out for* ~s, on the war-path, often fig. = in aggres-sive or pugnacious or savagely critical mood); bare rounded hill-top; whale's head without lower jaw; ~*-lock*, single lock on Red Indian's shaven head left as challenge to enemies; hence ~LESS a. 2. v.t. Take ~ of; criticize savagely. [cf. MSw. *skolp*, ON *skálpr*, sheath, MDu. *schëlpe* shell; cogn. w. SCALLOP, SCALE[1], SHELL]

scal'pel, n. Surgeon's small light knife shaped for holding like pen. [f. L *scalpel-lum* (*scalprum* chisel, f. *scalpere* scrape, -EL)]

scal'per, scaup'er, n. Gouge used by en-gravers. [f. L *scalprum* (prec.)]

scal'priform, a. Chisel-shaped (of in-cisor teeth). [L *scalprum* see SCALPEL, -I-FORM]

scămm'ony, n. (Kind of Asiatic con-volvulus yielding) a gum resin used as drastic purgative. [f. L Gk *skammōnia*]

scămp[1], n. Rascal, knave, (also in play-ful use as term of endearment). Hence ~ISH[1] a., [prob. of same orig. as SCAMPER]

scămp[2], v.t. Do(work etc.)in perfunctory or inadequate way. [prob. var. of SCAMP[1]]

scămp'er, v.i., & n. 1. Run impulsively like (or of) frightened animal or playing child; take ~ *through*. 2. n. Hasty run; gallop on horseback for pleasure; rapid tour or course of reading (*through Nor-mandy, Dickens,* etc.). [earlier sense flee (of army etc.), f. ONF (s')*escamper* (EX-, L *campus* field)+-ER[5]]

scăn, v.t. & i. (-nn-). 1. Test metre of (line etc.) by examining number & quantity of feet & syllables, read over with emphasis on rhythm; be metrically correct(*line does not~*), admit of rhythmic reading(*line will not ~ smoothly, badly*). 2. Look intently at all parts successively of (face, horizon, etc.). 3. (Television) resolve (a picture) into its elements of light and shade for purposes of transmis-sion. [f. L *scandere* climb, perh. with loss of *-d* by confus. w. -ED[1]]

scăn'dal, n. (Thing that occasions) general feeling of outrage or indignation esp. as expressed in common talk, opprobrium, (*it is a ~ that such things should be possible*; *a grave ~ occurred*; *gave rise to ~*); malicious gossip, backbiting, whence ~-MONGER n.; (Law) public affront, irre-levant abusive statement in court, (med.) LIBEL, SLANDER). So ~OUS a., ~OUSLY[2] adv., ~OUSNESS n. [ME *-dle*, f. ONF *escandle* f. eccl. L f. Gk *skandalon* snare, stumbling-block]

scăn'dalize[1], v.t. Offend moral feelings, sense of propriety, or ideas of etiquette, of; shock. [f. F *scandaliser* f. eccl. L f. Gk (-ize) as prec., see -IZE]

scăn'dalize[2], v.t. (naut.). Reduce area of (a sail). [corrupt. of obs. SCANTelize]

scăn'dălum măgnā'tum, n. (hist.) Defamation of magnates. [med. L]

Scăndinā'vian, a. & n. (Native, family of languages, of) Scandinavia (Denmark, Norway, Sweden, & Iceland). [-AN]

scăn'sion (-shn), n. Metrical scanning, way verse scans. [f. L *scansionem* (*scandere* scans- climb, -ION)]

scansō'rial, a. Habitually climbing, adapted for climbing, (of birds, their feet, etc.). [L *scansorius* (prec. -ORY), -AL]

scănt, a., & v.t. 1. Barely sufficient, de-ficient, with scanty supply of, (arch., poet., & in isolated phrr. as *with ~ courtesy*, *~ of breath*); hence ~IY[2] adv. 2. v.t. (arch.). Skimp, stint, provide grudgingly, (supply, material, person). [f. ON *skamt* short, whence also SCAMP[2]]

scănt'ling, n. Specimen, sample, (arch.); modicum, small amount, one's necessary supply of; small beam under 5 in. in breadth & depth; size to which stone or timber is to be cut; set of standard dimensions for parts of structure esp. in shipbuilding; trestle for cask. [f. OF *escantillon* etym. dub.]

scănt'ly a. Of small extent or amount, barely sufficient. (opp. *ample*). Hence **scănt'ily[2]** adv., ~INESS n. [-Y[2]]

scănt'y a., & n. & v.t. (arch.). Escape (still in **scāpe[2],** n. (Bot.). radical stem bearing fructification; & no leaves as in primrose; (Entom.) base of antenna; shaft of fea-ther: spring: usu. with curve, of column from base. [f. L *scapus* cf. SCEPTRE]

scāpe'goat (-pg-), n. (O.T.) goat allowed to escape when Jewish chief priest had laid sins of people upon it (*Lev.* xvi); person bearing blame due to others. [SCAPE[1]]

scāpe'grāce (-pg-), n. Harebrained person, esp. child, who constantly gets into trouble. [= one who gets no grace (SCAPE[1])]

scāph'oid, a. & n. (anat.). 1. Boat-shaped (~ *bone*, one in tarsus & one in carpus). 2. n. ~ bone. [f. Gk *skaphoeidēs* (*skaphos*, bowl, boat, -OID)]

scăp'ula, n. (pl. -ulae), SHOULDER-blade. [LL, sing. of L *scapulae*]

scăp'ular, a. & n. **1.** Of shoulder or shoulder-blade (~ *arch.,* = *shoulder-* GIRDLE'; ~ *feathers,* growing near insertion of wing). **2.** n. Monastic short cloak covering shoulders; badge of admission to an ecclesiastical order, consisting of two strips of cloth hanging down breast & back & joined across shoulders (also ~*y*); bandage for shoulder-blade; ~ feather. [(n. in first sense f. F *scapulaire*) f. LL *scapularis* (prec., -AR¹)]

scăp'ŭlo-, comb. form of SCAPULA, as ~*hŭm'eral,* ~*răd'ial,* ~*ŭl'nar,* of scapula & humerus, & radius, & ulna. [-O·]

scăr¹, n., & v.t. & i.(-rr-). **1.** Mark left after healing of wound or burn or sore, cicatrice, (also fig. of abiding effects of grief etc.); mark on plant left by fall of a leaf etc., hilum; hence ~*less* a. **2.** vb. Mark with ~ or ~s (esp. in p.p.); heal (i. & t.) over, form ~. [f. OF *escare* f. LL *eschara* f. Gk *eskhara* hearth, burn]

scăr², scaur (-ôr), n. Precipitous craggy part of mountain side. [f. ON *sker* isolated rock in sea, cogn. w. SHEAR¹]

scăr'ab, n. Sacred beetle of ancient Egypt; =foll.; ancient-Egyptian gem cut in form of beetle & engraved with symbols on flat side. [f. F *scarabée* f. L *scarabaeus*]

scărabae'id, n. Member of *Scarabaeidae,* family of beetles including prec., cockchafer, etc. [prec., -ID³]

scărabae'oid, a. & n. Like a scarab or a scarabaeid; (n.) counterfeit scarab. [-OID]

scă'ramouch, n. (arch.). Boastful poltroon, braggart. [F(-e), f. It. *Scaramuccia* stock character in Italian farce]

scarce, a. & adv. **1.** Insufficient for the demand or need, not plentiful, scanty, (usu. pred., & of food, money, or other necessaries of life); whence **scar'city** n. (of, or abs. =dearth of food); seldom met with, rare, hard to find, (*a ~ book, moth; make oneself ~,* colloq., retire, make off, keep out of the way); whence ~*ness* (-sn-) n. **2.** adv. (arch., poet., rhet.). Scarcely. [f. ONF *escars,* cf. It. *scarso* perh. f. LL *scarpsus* for L EX(*cerptus*= *carptus* f. *carpere* pluck) *select*]

scarce'ly (-slĭ), adv. Hardly, barely, only just, (*is ~ seventeen years old; had ~ arrived when he was told that —; I know him*); surely not, not unless the unlikely happens or is true, (*you will ~ maintain that; he can ~ have said so*); (mild or apologetic substitute for) not (*I ~ think so, know what to say*). [-LY²]

scarce'ment (-sm-), n. Set-back in a wall, ledge resulting from this. [SCARCE + -MENT]

scare, v.t., & n. **1.** Strike (esp. child, foolish person, or animal) with sudden terror, frighten (as) with a bugbear, (~*d face, expression,* etc., betraying terror; ~ *away,* drive off by fright); keep (birds) off,

field to keep birds away, bugbear, badly dressed or grotesque-looking or skinny person. **2.** n. Unreasoning terror, esp. baseless general apprehension of war, invasion, etc., whence ~'MONGER n.; commercial panic; ~*head(ing),* extravagantly sensational newspaper headline. [ME *skerre,* f. ON *skirra* (*skiarr* timid)]

scarf¹, n. (pl. -*fs*, -*ves*). Long narrow strip of material worn for ornament or warmth round neck, over shoulders, or baldricwise; man's necktie (|| ~*pin, ~ring,* usu. of gold or jewelled for holding ends of this together); ~*loom,* for weaving narrow fabrics; ~*skin,* outermost layer of skin constantly scaling off (esp. of that adhering to base of nails); ~*wise,* baldricwise. Hence ~ED² (-ft) a. [prob. f. ONF *escarpe* f. Teut., cogn. w. SCRIP¹]

scarf², v.t., & n. **1.** Join ends of (pieces of timber, metal, or leather) by bevelling or notching so that they overlap without increase of thickness & then bolting, brazing, or sewing them together; flench (whale). **2.** n. Joint made by ~ing timber or leather (also ~*joint*) or metal (also ~*weld*); notch, groove. [n. f. vb, perh. f. Sw. *skarfva* join (*skarf* seam)]

scar'ifier, n. In vbl senses: esp.:=prec.; agricultural machine with prongs for stirring without turning soil; spiked roadbreaking machine. [foll., -ER¹]

scar'ify, v.t. (Surg.) make superficial incisions in, cut of skin from, (fig.) pain by severe criticism etc.; stir (soil) with scarifier. So ~FICA'TION n. [f. F *scarifier* f. L *scarificare* by assim. to -*ficare* -FY of *scarifare* f. Gk *skariphaomai* (*skariphos* style, cogn. w. L *scribere* write)]

scar'ious, a. (bot.). Thin, dry, & membranaceous (of bracts etc.). [f. F *scarieux* f. mod. L *scariosus* etym. dub.]

scarlati'na (-tē-), n. Scarlet fever. [It. (-t-), f. *scarlatto* SCARLET]

scar'let, n. & a. (Of) brilliant red colour inclining to orange; ~ cloth or clothes (*dressed in* ~); ~ *admiral,* kind of butterfly; ~ *fever,* infectious fever with ~ rash, (joc.) tendency to fall in love with soldiers; ~*grain,* scale-insect from which red dye is made in Russia & Turkey; ~ *hat,* cardinal's, (allus.) cardinalate; ~ *rash,* roseola; ~ *runner,* ~-flowered trailing bean-plant; ~ *woman, whore,* pagan Rome, papal Rome, or the worldly spirit (acc. to interpretation put on *Rev.* xvii), ~ *cloth* (also *saqlatun,* whence ME *ciclatoun*)]

scar'roid (or skär-), a. & n. (Fish) of scarus genus, resembling scarus. [-OID]

scarp, n., & v.t. **1.** Inner wall or slope (cf. COUNTERSCARP) of ditch in fortification;

any steep slope. **2.** v.t. Make (slope) per-pendicular or steep, provide (ditch) with steep~ & counter~; (fig. etc.) still steep, precipitous. [f. It. *scarpa*]

scar'us, n. Kinds of bright-hued fish with parrotlike beak (also *parrotfish*) of wrasse family. [L, f. Gk *skaros*]

scathe (-dh), v.t., & n. **1.** Injure esp. by blasting or withering up (now rare exc. in part. used by exag. of severe speech, as ~*ing sarcasm, ridicule, remarks,* whence ~**ing**²·(-dh-)adv.); (in neg. context) do the least harm to (*shall not be* ~*ed;* esp. *unscathed*). **2.** n. (rare, & usu. in neg. context). Harm, injury, (*without, guard from,* ~*e*), whence ~e'**LESS** (-dhl-) a. [f. pred.). f. ON *skathe* n., *skatha* vb, cf. Gk *askēthēs* unharmed, in which *a-*=*a-* (7)]

scatol'ogy, n. Study of coprolites. [Gk *skōr skatos* dung, -LOGY]

scatoph'agous, a. Feeding on dung. [prec. Gk *-phagos* -eating]

scätt'er, v.t. & i. **1.** Throw here & there (~ *gravel*), strew (~ *gravel on road, road with gravel*), sprinkle; disperse (t. & i.), turn routed); dissipate (cloud, hopes); diffuse (light); (of gun) send charge, send (charge), in spreading manner; (p.p.) not situated together, wide apart, sporadic, (~*ed hamlets, garrisons, instances*); ~-*brain,* heedless person; ~-*brained,* heedless, desultory. Hence ~**ingly**² adv. [ME, etym. dub.]

scaup(-dück), n. Kinds of duck named from frequenting mussel-scaups or beds of mussels exposed at low tide. [var. of SCALP]

scaup'er. See SCAR².

scaup'er. Var. of SCALPER.

scäv'engler(-j-), n., & v.i. **1.** Person employed to keep streets clean by carrying away refuse; animal feeding on carrion (esp. ~*er-beetle, -crab*), writer etc. delighting in filthy subjects; hence ~**e** (-j-; by back formation) v.t. & i., (also) expel exhaust gases etc. from cylinder of internal-combustion engine, ~**ER** (2, 5) (-j-) n. **2.** v.i. Be, act as, ~*er.* [earlier *scavager* (cf. *messenger, passenger*) inspector of imports (AF *scawage* inspection f. ONF *escauwer* inspect f. Tent. cf. SHOW+-AGE, -ER¹)]

scäz'on, n. Greek & Latin iambic, ending with ~--˘ instead of ˘-˘-˘, used in short poems, choliamb; other metres of usu. limping recitative. [It.]

scena'rio (shä-), n. (pl. ~s), (Table of) scene-distribution, appearances of characters, etc., in dramatic work, skeleton libretto; (usu. pr. *sēnār'iō*) written version

of play, details of scenes, etc., in film production. [It.]

scend. See SEND².

scène, n. **1.** Stage of theatre (arch.; still in fig. use *quit the* ~, esp. = die); place on stage (*this world is a* ~ *of strife*). **2.** Place in which events set forth in drama or tale are supposed to occur; locality of event, (*the* ~ *is laid in India; the* ~ *of the disaster was the North Sea*). **3.** Portion of a play during which action is continuous or (esp. of French plays) in which no intermediate entries or exits occur; subdivision (or rarely the whole) of an act, (*in the third* ~ *of Act II; Act II, ii, 220; the famous duel* ~; CARPENTER~); (transf.) description with more or less abrupt beginning & end of an incident or part of a person's life etc. (~*s of clerical life, from a goldfield,* etc.), actual incident that might occasion such description (*distressing* ~*s occurred*), agitated colloquy esp. with display of temper (*now don't make a* ~). **4.** Any of the pieces of painted canvas, woodwork, etc., used to help in representing ~ of action on stage, or whole of these together (*behind the* ~*s,* among the stage machinery or the actors off the stage, usn. fig.=having information not accessible to the public; CARPENTER~; ~ *is painted by* —; *set* ~, made up of many parts fitted together; DROP-SCENE); (transf.) landscape or view spread before spectator like ~ in theatre (*a sivran, desolate,* ~; *a* ~ *of destruction, change of* ~, variety of surroundings esp. secured by travel). **5.** ~-*dock,* space near stage where ~s are stored; ~-*painter,* ~*painting* of theatre ~s; ~-*shifter,* person helping to change ~s in theatre. [f. F *scène* f. L f. Gk *skēnē* tent, stage]

scèn'ery, n. Accessories used in theatre to make stage resemble supposed scene of action; spectacles presented by natural features of a district (*the* ~ *is imposing, tame*). [earlier *scenary* f. It. *scenario* f. L *scenarius* (prec., -ARY²) of the stage, assim. to -ERY]

scèn'ic, a. Of, on, the stage (~ *performances*); of the nature of a show, picturesque in grouping; (of picture etc.) telling a tale, crystallizing an incident; (of emotion etc.) dramatic, affected, put on; ~ *railway,* miniature railway running through artificial picturesque scenery, as attraction at large fairs etc. Hence **scèn'ically** adv. [f. F *scénique* f. L f. Gk *skēnikos* (SCENE, -IC)]

scěnog'raphy, n. Drawing or painting in perspective (esp. of representing building not in ground-plan or elevation, but as spectator sees it). So ~OGRAPH(I), ~ōG'RAPHER, nn., ~ōGRAPH'IC, a., ~ōGRAPH'ICALLY adv. [f. L f. Gk *skēnographia* (SCENE, -GRAPHY)]

scent, v.t. & i., & n. **1.** Discern by smell

(~ *game* etc.), (fig.) begin to suspect presence or existence of (~ *treachery, a job*); ~ *out*, discover by smelling about ~ or search; make fragrant or rank (*rose, carrion*), ~ *s the air*), apply perfume to (handkerchief etc.; ~*ed dames, cigarettes*) exercise sense of smell, apply this to, (*goes ~ing about; lifts its head & ~ s the air*). 2. n. Odour, esp. of agreeable kind, proceeding from or belonging to something (*the ~ of hay*), whence ~'LESS a.; (Hunt.) trail perceptible to hounds' sense of smell left by animal (often fig.; *follow up, lose, recover,* etc., *the ~, lit., &* of investigation; *on the ~*, having clue; *put off the ~*, deceive by false indications; COLD[1], HOT[1], ~); power of detecting or distinguishing smells or of discovering presence of something, flair, (*some dogs have practically no ~; keen~ed; has a wonderful ~ for snobbery; young talent,* etc.). liquid perfume distilled from flowers etc. 3. ~*-bag*, pouch containing special odoriferous substance in some animals, also bag of aniseed etc. as substitute for fox in hunting; ~*-bottle*, for perfume; ~*-gland*, secreting musk, civet, etc.; ~*-organ*, ~*-bag* or ~*-gland*; hence (-)~'ED[2] a., (~*ed caper*, kind of tea; ~*ed fern*, kind smelling like citron). [n. f. vb, earlier *sent*, f. F *sentir* perceive, smell, f. L *sentire* perceive]

scép′sis (sk-), *sk-, n. Philosophic doubt, sceptical philosophy. [f. Gk *skepsis* inquiry (*skeptomai* examine)]

scep′tic (sk-), *sk-, n. Ancient or modern holder of PYRRHONISM; person who doubts truth of the Christian or of all religious doctrines, agnostic, (pop.) atheist; person of sceptical habit of mind, or unconvinced of truth of particular fact or theory, or who takes cynical views. So ~ISM(3) (sk-) n. [ult. f. Gk *skeptikos* (prec., -IC)]

scep′tical (sk-), *sk-, a. Inclined to suspense of judgement, given to questioning truth of facts & soundness of inferences, critical, incredulous; accepting PYRRHONISM, denying possibility of knowledge; holding, designed to support, inspired by, the ideas of SCEPTICS. Hence ~LY[2] adv. [-AL]

scep′tr|e (-ter), n. Staff borne as symbol of personal sovereignty; royal or imperial authority. Hence ~ED[2] (-terd). ~eLESS (-terl-), aa. [OF,f.L f. Gk *skēptron* (*skēptō* prop)]

schadenfreude (shah′denfroide), n. Malicious enjoyment of others' misfortunes. [G, f. *schade* damage + *freude* joy]

schappe (shāp′, shah′pe), n. Fabric or yarn made from waste silk. [G, = silk waste]

sched′ule (||sh-, *sk-), n., & v.t. 1. Tabulated statement of details, inventory,

list, etc., esp. as appendix or annexe to principal document; *time-table*; ~ *time*, that stated in time-table (*on ~, to ~ time*). 2. v.t. Make ~ of, include in ~, [ME & OF *cedule* f. LL *scedula* (L *sceda* papyrus-strip, -ULE)]

scheik. = SHEIK.

schēm′|a (sk-), n. (pl. ~*ata*), Synopsis, outline, diagram; (Log.) syllogistic figure; (Gram., Rhet.) figure of speech; (Kantian Philos.) general type, essential form, conception of what is common to all members of a class. So ~**ăt′Ic**[ICALLY] adv., (sk-). [med. L, f. Gk *skhēma -atos* shape (*ekhō, skh-*, hold, be)]

schēme (sk-), n., & v.i. & t. 1. Systematic arrangement proposed or in operation (~ *of colour*, principle on which colours have been chosen & grouped in picture etc.), table of classification or of appointed times, outline, syllabus; plan for doing something; artful or underhand design. 2. vb. Make plans, plan esp. in secret or underhand way (*to do, for, or abs.*), intrigue, whence ~'ER[1] n., ~'ING[1] a., (sk-); plan to bring about. [f. L SCHEMA]

scher·zăn′dō (skāts-), mus. direction. In playful manner. [It.]

scher·zo (skāɐ̆t′sō), n. (pl. ~s). Vigorous (prop. light & playful) composition, independent or as movement in works of sonata type. [It., f. Teut. (G *scherz* jest)]

Schiedăm′ (skid-), n. Holland gin. [place]

schill′ing (sh-), n. Modern (1925–88) Austrian coin (par about 7*d.*), 100 groschen. [G]

schipp′erke (sk-, sh-), n. Kind of lapdog. [Du.]

schism (si′zm), n. Division of a community into factions (rare in gen. sense), esp. separation of a Church into two Churches or secession of part of a Church owing to difference of opinion on doctrine or discipline; offence of causing or promoting such separation. [f. OF *sisme* f. eccl. L f. Gk *skhisma -atos* (*skhizō* split, -M)]

schismăt′ic (siz-), a., & n., -IClal, a. 1. Tending or inclined to, guilty of, schism; hence ~ALLY[2] adv. 2. n. Holder of opinions, member of ~ faction or seceded branch of a Church. [f. OF *scismatique* f. eccl. L f. Gk *skhismatikos* (prec., -IC), -AL]

schist (sh-), n. Kinds of foliated rock presenting layers of different minerals & splitting in thin irregular plates. Hence ~'OSE[1] (sh-) a. [f. F *schiste* f. L f. Gk *skhistos* split (SCHISM)]

schizăn′thus (sk-), n. Kinds of flowering annual with handsome white, violet, or crimson flowers & much-divided leaves. [Gk *skhizō* split, *anthos* flower]

schizomȳcēte′ (sk-), n. Any of the *Schizomycetae*, a class of minute often single-cell vegetable organisms between algae &

schizophre′nia (skĭ-), n. Mental disease marked by disconnexion between thoughts, feelings, & actions. Hence **~′ēn′ĭc** a. & n. [as prec., Gk *phrēn* mind]

schnäp(p)s (shn-), n. A spirit resembling Holland gin. [G]

schnauzer (shnow′tser), n. German breed of house-dog with close wiry coat. [G]

Schneid′er Troph′y (shni′-), n. International trophy open to seaplanes of all nations presented in 1913 by Jacques Schneider, in 1931 won outright by Great Britain.

schnŏr′rer (shn-), n. Jewish beggar. [Yiddish, f. G dial. *schnurrer* beggar]

schŏl′ar (skŏ-), n. **1.** Schoolboy, schoolgirl, (arch. or vulg.). **2.** Person's disciple (rhet.). **3.** Person who learns (*proved an apt, dull,* ~; *at 90 he was still a* ~). **4.** Learned person, person versed in literature esp. that of ancient Greece & Rome, (*a* ~ *& a gentleman*, person of good education & breeding; *whence* ~LY a., whence ~SHIP (3) n. **5.** (Univ., Pub. Schh.) under-graduate or boy admitted to foundation usu. after competitive examination & receiving education gratis or for reduced fees (RHODES ~), whence ~SHIP(1) n. [AF *escoler* (SCHOOL¹, -ER¹) refash. on Ll *scholaris* (-AR¹)]

scholăs′tic (skŏ-), a. & n. **1.** Of universities, schools, schooling, dons, or school-masters, education, academic, pedantic, formal, (*a* ~ *education, life*; ~ *agent, dātire, manners, precision, life*; ~ *agent, finding posts for teachers*). **2.** (As) of the SCHOOL-men, dealing in logical subtleties, (~ *theology,* much concerned with precise definition of & deduction from dogma); hence or cogn. **scholăs′tically** adv., **~ISM** (2, 3) n. **3.** In SCHOOL¹man; modern theologian of ~ tendencies; Jesuit be-tween novitiate & priesthood. [f. Ll f. Gk *skholastikos* (*skholazō* be at leisure, see SCHOOL¹, -IC)]

scholī′ast (skō-), n. Commentator, esp. ancient grammarian who wrote scholia, on the classics. Hence **~ăs′tic** a. [f. Gk *skholiastēs* (*skholiazō* write scholia, foll.)]

scholī′um (skō-), n. (pl. *-ia*). Marginal note, explanatory comment, esp. one by ancient grammarian on passage in classical author. [f. med. L f. Gk *skholion* (*skholē* see foll.)]

schŏŏl¹ (skō-), n., & v.t. **1.** Institution for educating children or giving instruction usu. of more elementary or more technical kind than that given at universities (BOARD¹, BOARDING, DAY, GRAMMAR, MIXED, NIGHT, NORMAL, PRIMARY, PRIVATE, PUBLIC, RAGGED, SECONDARY, SUNDAY, ~; ll *national* ~, one founded by the National Society started 1811 to promote education of the

poor; *continuation* ~, at which those who have left esp. primary ~ for an occupation can have further teaching in leisure time; *evening* ~ = *night* ~; *free* ~, open without fees; *high* ~, secondary ~, or chief ~ of a town etc.; *technical* ~, giving TECHNICAL education; *keep a* ~, manage private ~); buildings of such institution, any of its rooms used for teaching in (the *fifth-form, chemistry,* ~), its pupils (the *whole* ~ *knows*); time during which teaching is done (*there will be no* ~ *today*; *go to* ~, *attend lesson*). **2.** Being educated in a ~ (*go to, leave,* ~, *begin, cease, this*; *go to, leave, be at, etc.,* ~, *begin, cease, this*; (fig.) *circumstances or occupation serving to discipline or instruct (in the* ~ *of adversity;* ~ *learnt his generalship in a severe* ~; *the duel is a good* ~ *of manners*). **3.** Medieval lecture-room (the ~s, medieval universities & their professors & teaching & disputations, ~men); ll any of the branches of study with separate examinations at university (the ~ *of ll history, mathematical, Greats,* ~); hall in which university examinations are held; (pl.) such examination (*in the* ~s, undergoing or conducting this at Oxford; ll *in for his* ~s, of candidate). **4.** Disciples or imitators or followers of philosopher, artist, etc., band or succession of persons devoted to some cause or principle or agreeing in typical characteristics, (*left no* ~ *behind him;* ~ *of Epicurus, Raphael, etc.*; *Bolognese, Venetian, Roman, British, etc.,* ~, of painters; *lake, romantic, etc.,* ~, of literature; *peripatetic, Hegelian, etc.,* ~, of philosophy; *laissez-faire, blue-water, etc.,* ~, of politics, strategy; *Tübingen* ~, of rationalistic theological criticism; *a gentleman of the old* ~, according to the older acceptation of the word). **5.** (Mus.) manual of (~'s *violin* ~, ~ *of counterpoint*). **6.** ll *Old* ~ *tie,* necktie worn by former members of a ~, (fig.) sentimental or excessive local or class loyalty; ~*board,* local education authority ll respon-sible (1870-1902) for providing BOARD¹~s; ~*book,* for use in ~s; ~*boy, boy at* ~ (often attrib., as ~*boy slang, mischief, spirits*); ll ~*dame,* keeper of old-fashioned DAME~; ~*days,* time of being at ~ esp. as looked back upon; ~ *divine, scholastic theologian, so ~divinity*; ~ *feés*, amount periodically paid by pupil's parent etc.; ~*fellow, member past or present of same* ~; ~*girl* (as ~*boy*); ~*house, building of* esp. *village* ~; ll ~ *house, headmaster's or* central boarding-house at public ~; ~*inspector,* reporting on efficiency of ~s provided at public expense; ~*marm* collog. ~*mistress;* *~-ma'am,* ~*man, mistress*; ~*master,* head or assistant male teacher in

~, pedagogue; ~'made, contemporary at same~; ~ miss, inexperienced or bashful girl; ~'mistress (as ~master'); || ~ pence, money formerly brought weekly by elementary~ child as fee; ~'room, used for lessons in ~ or private house; ~-ship, training-ship; ~-teacher, master or mistress esp. in primary ~; ~-teaching; ~-time, lesson-time at ~ or home, also = ~-days. **7.** v.t. Send to ~, provide for education of (rare), whence (in common use) ~'ING¹ n.; discipline, bring under control, deliberately train or accustom to, induce to follow advice, (must ~ his temper; ~ oneself to patience, to take an interest in; will not be ~ed). [OE scōl f. L schola school f. Gk skholē leisure, philosophy, lecture-place]

school² (sk-), n., & v.i. **1.** Shoal of fish; ~fish, kinds that ~, esp. the menhaden. **2.** v.i. Form ~s. [Du., cf. SHOAL²]

school'able (sk-), a. Liable by age etc. to compulsory education. [-ABLE]

schoon'er (sk-), n. **1.** Fore-&-aft-rigged vessel with two or more masts; PRAIRIE-~. **2.** *Tall beer-glass; || measure for beer. [perh. f. an alleged Sc. & New-England scun, scoon, skim or skip; orig. (c. 1713) scooner, name given by first designer, now sch- by assim. to its derivative Du. schooner]

schörl (sh-), n. Black tourmaline. [f. G schörl]

schottische (shótésh'), n. (Music for) kind of slower polka. [G -sch), = Scottish]

sciag'raphy (sī-), skī-, n. Art of shading in drawing etc.; photography by X-rays (usu. sk-); (Archit.; also & usu. -graph) vertical section showing interior of house etc.; (Astron.) finding of time by shadows as in sundial. So **sci'agram** n., X-ray picture, **sciagrammāt'ic** a., ~**ically** adv., **sci'agraph**(1, 2, 3) n. & v.t., **sciäg'GRAPHER** n., SCIAGRAPH'IC a., **sciägraph'ICALLY** adv., sci-) [f. Gk skiagraphia (skia shade, -GRAPHY]

sciam'achy (sī-, -ki), skī-, n. Fighting with shadows, imaginary or futile combat. [f. Gk skiamakhia (prec., -makhos -fighting f. makhomai fight, -IA¹)]

sciat'ic (sī-), a. Of the hip (~ nerve, artery, etc.); of, affecting, the ~ nerve; suffering from or liable to sciatica. Hence **sciät'roALLY** adv. [f. F sciatique f. LL sciaticus f. L f. Gk iskhiadikos subject to sciatica (iskhias -ados loin-pain f. iskhion socket of thigh-bone)]

sciat'ica (sī-), n. Neuralgia of hip & thigh, pain in sciatic nerve. [med. L, fem. of LL as prec.]

sci'ence (sī-), n. **1.** Knowledge (arch.), whence (in mod. use) **sciēn'tial** (-shl) a., **scién'tially²** adv. **2.** Systematic & formulated knowledge (moral, political, natural, etc., ~, such knowledge in reference to these subjects); pursuit of this or principles regulating such pursuit (man of ~). **3.** (Also natural ~) the physical or natural ~s collectively (~ now shares the curriculum with literature, history, & mathematics). **4.** (With a & pl.) branch of knowledge, organized body of the knowledge that has been accumulated on a subject, (the ~ of optics, ethics, philology; exact~, admitting of quantitative treatment; pure ~, one depending on deductions from self-evident truths, as mathematics, logic; natural, physical, ~, one dealing with material phenomena & based mainly on observation, experiment, & induction, as chemistry, biology, whence esp. **sci'entist, sci'entism,** nn.; the dismal~, political economy). **5.** Expert's skill as opp. strength or natural ability, esp. in pugilism or other fighting. [F, f. L scientia (scire know, -ENCE)]

sciēn'ter (sī-), adv. (legal). Wittingly. [L (prec., -ENT, -er adv. term.]

scientif'ic (sī-), a. (Of investigations etc.) according to rules laid down in science for testing soundness of conclusions, systematic, accurate; of, used or engaged in, esp. natural science (~ic instruments, books, terminology, men); (of act or agent) assisted by expert knowledge (a ~ic boxer, game; ~ic cruelty). Hence ~**ICALLY** adv. [f. LL scientificus, see SCIENCE, -FIC]

sci'icět (sī-), adv. (abbr. sc., scil.). To wit, that is to say, namely, (introducing word to be supplied or explanation of ambiguous one). [L, = scire licet it is allowed to know]

Scillōn'ian (sī-), a. & n. (Native, inhabitant) of the Scilly Isles. [f. Scill(y) + -onian (perh. after Devonian)]

scim'itar (sī-), n. Oriental curved sword usu. broadening towards point. [f. Rom (It. scimitarra, F cimeterre) perh. f. Pers shamshir]

scintill'a (sī-), n. Spark, atom, (esp. no ~ of evidence etc.). [L]

scin'tillate (sī-), v.i. Sparkle, twinkle emit sparks. So ~**ANT** a., ~**A'TION** n. [f L scintillare (prec., -ATE²]

sci'olist (sī-), n. Superficial pretender to knowledge, smatterer. Hence or cogn. ~**ISM(2)** n., ~**IS'TIC** a. [f. LL sciolus smatterer (scire know), -ISF]

sciol'tŏ (shō-), adv. mus. direction. In free manner, according to taste; staccato. [It.]

sciomachy. See SCIAMACHY.

sci'on (sī-), n. Shoot of plant, esp. one cut for grafting or planting; descendant, young member of (esp. noble) family. [F (earlier also cion), etym. dub.]

Sci'ŏt(ē) (sī-), a. & n. (Inhabitant) of Scio, the ancient Chios. [-OT²]

scir'e fā'ciăs (sīrī -shī-), n. Writ to enforce or annul judgement, patent, etc. [L, =let (party) know]

scirocco. See SIROCCO.

scirrhus (sī'rus, skī-), n. Hard tumour as early stage of cancer. Hence or cogn.

scissel (sĭs'l), n. ~'OID, aa., ~ŏs'ITY n. [LL, f. Gk *skir(r)os* [SKIRROS hard)]

sciss'el, (sĭs'-), n. Waste clippings of metal or remainder of metal plate from which disks have been punched in coining. [f. F *cisaille* f., *ciseler* CHISEL, -AL(2)]

sciss'ile (sĭs'-), a. Able to be cut. [f. L *scissilis* (*scindere sciss-* cut, -IL)]

scission (sĭ'shn), n. Cutting, being cut, division, split. [F. f. LL *scissionem* (prec., -ION)]

sciss'or (sĭz'or), v.t. Cut (*off, up, into,* etc.) with scissors; clip out or *out* (cutting from book etc.), whence ~ING⁴(2) n. [f. foll.]

sciss'ors (sĭz'orz), n. pl. Instrument for cutting fabrics, paring nails, etc., made of two blades with handles for thumb & one finger or the fingers & so pivoted that their cutting edges work by leverage against each other (often *pair of* ~; *I want a pair of some,* ~; *where are my* ~?; *buttonhole* ~, *with gaps in blades near pivot so that cutting begins inside edge of cloth; lump, nail,* ~, *of special shapes for trimming wicks, nails;* ~ *& paste, compiling of books out of cuttings from others);* ~ *scissor-bill,* the bird SKIMMER; *scissor-bird* or *-tail,* kinds of bird with long forked tail esp. fork-tailed fly-catcher; *scissor-tooth,* tooth in carnivora acting like* ~ *against one in other jaw. Hence* **sciss'orwise** (sĭz'or-) adv. [ME *cisoures* f. OF *cisoires* f. L *cisorium* (as CHISEL, -ORY)]

scī'urine (sī-), a. Of the squirrel tribe; squirrel-like. So ~OID a. [f. L Gk *skiouros* squirrel (*skia* shade, *oura* tail), -INE¹]

Sclav, Sclavonic, etc. See **Slav** etc.

sclĕr'a, n. = SCLEROTIC n. (anat.). Hence ~IT'IS, ~ŎT'OMY, nn. [f. fem. of Gk *sklēros* hard]

sclerī'asis, n. (path.). Hardening of tissue. [f. Gk *sk-*), = induration of eyelid (foll., -ASIS)]

scler'(o), comb. form of Gk *sklēros* hard; *~ench'yma* (*-ngk-*), hard tissue of coral, tissue forming hard parts of plants such as nut-shell or seed-coat; *~oderm'(a)ous,* with hard outer skin (of reptiles, fish, etc.); *~ogen,* hard matter deposited on inner surface of plant-cells, e.g. that lining walnut shell; *~omēn'inx,* DURA MATER; *~oskel'eton,* hard parts resulting from ossification of tendons as in turkey's leg etc.; *~os'teous,* of the nature of *~o-*skeleton.

sclĕr'oid, a. (bot., zool.). Of hard texture. [f. Gk *sklēroeidēs* (prec., -OID)]

sclĕrō'ma, **sclĕrō'sis**, nn. (pl. *-mata, -sēs)* Morbid hardening of tissue; (Bot.; -sēs) hardening of cell-wall by SCLEROGEN. Hence **sclĕrō'sed²**(-st) a. [Gk *sk-*), see SCLERO-, -M, -OSIS]

sclĕrŏt'ic, a. & n. **1.** Of, with, sclerosis; of the *~.* **2.** n. Membrane coating eye

---

round iris, white of eye; hence **sclĕrŏt'i'tis** n. [SCLERO-, -OTIC]

sclĕr'ous, a. (path., anat., bot.,). Indurated, bony. [Gk *sklēros* hard, -OUS]

scŏbs, n. Sawdust, shavings, filings, dross. [L]

scŏff¹, n. & v.i. **1.** Mocking words, taunt, gibe; object of ridicule, laughing-stock. **2.** v.i. Speak derisively esp. of religion or object of respect; aim ~s or mockery *at;* hence ~ER¹ n., ~INGLY² adv. [vb f. n., ME *scof,* cf. ON *skop*]

scŏff², n., & v.t. & i. (sl.), **1.** Food, meal, grub. **2.** vb. Eat greedily. [Cape Du., corrupted f. Du. *schoff* quarter of a day (hence, meal); vb orig. a. var. of dial. *scaff*]

scŏld, v.i. & t., & n. **1.** Find fault noisily, rail; rate, rebuke, (chiefly of parent, employer, speaking to child, servant), whence **scŏl'ding²**(-l) n. **2.** n. Railing or nagging woman. [vb f. n., f. ON *skáld* SCALD²]

scŏl'ex, n. (pl. *-ēcēs*). Head of larval or adult tapeworm. [f. Gk *skōlēx* worm]

scŏlĭō'sis, n. Lateral curvature of spine. Hence ~ŏt'ic a. [Gk *sk-*), f. *skolioō* make crooked (*skolios*), -OSIS]

scŏllop. See SCALLOP.

scŏlopā'ceous (-shus), a. Of, like, the snipes. [Gk *skolopax -akos* snipe]

scŏlopĕn'drium, n. Kinds of fern, hart's-tongue etc. [L, f. Gk *skolopendrion* (prec.)]

scŏm'b'er, n. Mackerel or kinds of fish allied to it. Hence ~RID⁴(1) n., ~ROID a. & n. [L, f. Gk *skombros*]

scŏnce¹, n. Flat candlestick with handle; bracket candlestick to hang on wall; [earlier sense, lantern; f. OF *esconse* dark lantern f. med. L *sconsa* f. L *absconsa* var. of ABSCONDITA fem. p.p.]

scŏnce², n. (Old joc. term for) head, crown of head (*a crack on the* ~), a use of prec. or foll.]

scŏnce³, n. Small fort or earthwork, usu. covering a ford, pass, etc.; (arch.) shelter, screen; (dial.) fixed slab seat by fireplace. [f. Du. *schans,* etym. dub.]

sconce⁴, v.t., & n. **1.** (At Oxford) inflict forfeit of beer etc. for offence against quotations are, ~d); (hist., of university officials etc.) fine for breach of discipline (*Vice-Chancellor ~d all that were without their hoods).* **2.** n. The forfeit. [?]

scŏne, n. Soft cake of barley-meal or wheat-flour of size for single portion & usu. triangular cooked on griddle. [perh. f. MDu. *schoon(bro)* fine (bread)]

scoop, n., & v.t. **1.** Short-handled deep

shovel for taking up & transferring such things as grain, sugar, coal, specie; large long-handled ladle-shaped dipping-vessel for liquids; gouge-like instrument e.g. for surgical use or for helping cheese; coal-scuttle; motion as of, act of, ~ing (*with a, at one,* ~); (sl.) large profit made quickly or by anticipating competitors; (sl.) exclusive piece of news for newspaper; ~*net*, formed for sweeping river-bottom, also hand-net for catching bait; ~*wheel*, with buckets on circumference raising water for irrigation etc. **2. v.t.** Lift (usn. *up*), hollow (usn. *out*), (as) with ~; (sl.) secure (large profit etc.) by sudden action or stroke of luck; (sl.) forestall (rival newspaper, reporter, etc.) with ~. [cf. Du. *schoep* bucket & *schop* shovel, G *schüpfen* draw (water); cogn. w. SHOVE]

scoop'er, n. In vbl senses; esp.: engraver's tool; kind of avocet. [-ER¹]

scoot, v.i. (sl.). Run, dart, make off. Hence ~ER¹(2) n., child's toy, a footboard with two tandem wheels on which one foot is set while the other propels & a long handle (*motor* ~*er*, similar machine propelled by motor). [earlier *scout* in naut. use; reimported as *scoot* f. U.S.]

scop'a, scop'ūla, nn. (entom.; pl. *-ae*). Small brushlike tuft of hairs esp. on bees' legs. Hence **scop'ATE²**, **scop'ULATE²**, **scop'iFORM, scop'ULIFORM, scop'iFEROUS,** aa. [*scopa* sing. of L *scopae* broom, *-la* mod. sing. of L *scopulae* pl.]

scope, n. **1.** End aimed at, purpose, intention, (now rare). **2.** Outlook, purview, sweep or reach or sphere of observation or action, tether, extent to which it is permissible or possible to range, opportunity, outlet, vent, (*mind, undertaking, of wide* ~; *is beyond my* ~; *gives no, ample,* ~ *for expatiating, to ability; seeks* ~ *for his energies*). **3.** (Naut.) length of cable out when ship rides at anchor. [earlier sense *target* (perh. thr. It. *scopo*) f. Gk *skopos* mark to shoot at, watcher, (*skeptomai* look at, cf. L *specere*)]

-scope, suf. repr. Gk *skopos* watcher (prec.). *Horoscope* is f. Gk *hōroskopos* (watcher of a nativity). *Telescope* is f. Gk *teleskopos* far-seeing. In wds of mod. formation the suf. usn. has the sense *instrument for observing or showing,* as *stetho~, gyro~, laryngo~,* and the hybrid *muto~.* Hence **-scop'ic,** adj. suf., pertaining to the *-scope,* occas. w. extended meaning also, as in TELESCOPIC, MICROSCOPIC; **-scopy,** n. suf., use of or examination by the *-scope,* as *laryngoscopy.*

scorbū'lic, a, & n. Of, like, (person) affected with, scurvy. Hence ~ICALLY adv. [f. F *scorbut* scurvy prob. f. MLG *schorbūk* (*schoren* break, *būk* belly) +-IC]

scorch, v.t. & i. & n. **1.** Burn surface of with flame or heat-rays so as to discolour or injure or pain, affect with sensation of burning (*a vit that* ~*es*), whence ~ING¹ a., ~ingLY² adv.; ~*ed earth policy,* burning crops etc. and removing or destroying anything that might be of use to an enemy occupying the country; become discoloured etc. with heat. **2.** (sl.) (Of motorist or cyclist) go at utmost speed; (n.) spell of such driving or riding. [earlier *scorken* perh. f. ON *skorpna* be shrivelled]

scorch'er, n. In vbl senses; also, (sl.) fine specimen of its kind. [-ER¹]

score, n., & v.t. & i. **1.** Notch cut or line cut or scratched or drawn (*rock covered with* ~*s or striations; the* ~*s of the whip showed on his back; made a* ~ *in the tally; lightning had made* ~*s in the mountain side*); mark showing starting-point in race or standing-place in shooting-match (now rare; hence perh. *go off at* ~, start off vigorously esp. to discourse on pet subject); (Naut.) groove in block or deadeye to hold strap. **2.** Running account kept by ~s against customer's name esp. for drink in old inns, reckoning esp. for entertainment, (*pay one's* ~, settle reckoning; *death pays all* ~*s; pay off old* ~*s,* fig., pay person out for past offence; so *quit* ~*s with*). **3.** Number of points made by player or side in some games, register of items of this, (*make a good* ~; *what is the* ~ *now?;* ~*book, -card, -sheet,* prepared for entering esp. cricket~ in; *keep* ~, register it as it is made). **4.** (Mus.) copy of a composition on set of staves braced & barred together (named from bar drawn through all staves: *full* ~, with separate staff for each part; *compressed, close, short,* ~ in vocal music, with treble & alto on one staff, tenor & bass on another; *in* ~, with parts arranged below each other & corresponding). **5.** Twenty, set of twenty, (for use of ~, s, see DOZEN; *three* ~ *& ten,* phr. for normal length of human life; ~*s of people,* great numbers). **6.** Category, head, (*rejected on the* ~ *of making cheap* ~*s*); piece of good fortune (*what a* ~/). **7.** ||(sl.). Remark or act by which person ~s off another (*given to absurdity,* as being absurd; *you may be easy on that* ~, so far as that matter is concerned). **8.** vb. Mark with notches or incisions or lines, slash, furrow, make (line etc.) with something that marks, (~ *out words,* draw line through them; ~ *under,* underline). **9.** Mark *up* in inn~, enter (item of debt *against* or *to* customer; often *up*); (fig.) mentally record (offence *against* or *to* offender); record (point in cricket etc. ~; abs., keep the ~, whence **scor'ER¹** n.). **10.** Win & be credited with (*has* ~*d a success, a century at cricket*), make points in game (*failed to* ~), secure an advantage or have scored good luck (*that is where he* ~*s; we shall* ~ *by it*); || ~ *off* (sl.), worst in argument or repartee, inflict some humiliation on. **11.** (Mus.) orchestrate, whence **scor'ING¹** (6) n., arrange

for another instrument, write out in ~. [OE *scora* twenty f. ON *skor* twenty, notch; cogn. w. SHEAR; sense *twenty* perh. from twentieth notch's larger size]

scor′ia, n. (pl. ~*iae*). Cellular lava or fragments of it. Hence ~IA′CEOUS (-āshus) a. [L. f. Gk *skōria* refuse (*skōr* dung)]

scor′ify, v.t. Gk Reduce to dross, assay (precious metal) by ~fying a portion of its ore fused with lead & borax. Hence ~FICA⁴ TION, ~FIER¹ (2), nn. [prec., -FY]

scorn, n., & v.t. **1.** Disdain, contempt, derision, (*think* ~ *of*, despise; LAUGH to ~); whence ~FUL a., ~fully² adv., ~fulNESS n.; object of contempt, (usu. ~ *to, the* ~ *of*, persons etc.). **2.** v.t. Hold in contempt, consider beneath notice, abstain from or refuse *to do* as unworthy (~s *lying, a lie, to lie*); hence ~ER¹ n. (arch. exc. w. *of*). [ME *skarn* n., *scarne* vb, f. OF *escarn(ir)* f. Teut. cf. Du. *scherm(en)* ridicule n. & v.]

scorp′io, n. Zodiacal constellation & eighth sign of zodiac, the Scorpion. [L, also *scorpius* f. Gk *skorpios* scorpion, *skorpíōn* ballista]

scorp′ioid, n. & a. (bot.). (Inflorescence) curled up at end like scorpion's tail & uncurling as flowers develop. [f. Gk *skorpioeidēs* (prec., -OID)]

scorp′ion, n. **1.** Arachnid with lobsterlike claws & jointed tail that can be bent over to inflict poisoned sting on prey held in claws, falsely reputed to sting itself to death if encircled with fire & to contain a substance serving as antidote for its poison. **2.** (Bibl.) whip armed with metal knobs (1 *Kings* xii. 11). **3.** (*S~*) = SCORPIO. **4.** Kind of ballista. **5.** ~*broom*, kind of genista: ~*-fish*, kind with spines on head & fins: ~*-plant*, Javan orchid with creamy white flower, also ~*-broom*: ~*shell*, kind of shellfish with long spines fringing outer lip of aperture: ~*-thorn*, ~*-broom*. [F, f. L *scorpiōnem* SCORPIO]

scor′zoner′a, n. Black salsify or Viper's-grass, a plant with parsnip-like root used as vegetable. [It., prob. f. *scorzone* adder 'because it doeth heele the bytinges of this beast']

scot¹, n. (hist.). Payment corresponding to modern tax, rate, or other assessed contribution (*pay* ~ *& lot*, share pecuniary burdens of borough etc.); ~*-free* (in mod. use), not having to pay (rare), (usu.) unharmed, unpunished, safe, (esp. *go* ~*free*). [f. OF *escot* f. ON *skot* shot, contribution, cf. OE *sceot* whence SHOT³]

Scot², n. (pl.). Gaelic tribe that migrated from Ireland to Scotland about 6th c. (often PICTs & ~s); native of Scotland, (often *Scots* pl., f. LL *Scotus*)

[OE *Scottas* pl., f. LL *Scotus*]

Scotch¹, a. & n. **1.** Of Scotland or its inhabitants, in the dialect(s) of English spoken in Lowlands of Scotland, (the ~ themselves usu. prefer the form *Scottish*, also used by the English esp. in dignified

style or context, or *Scots* rare in Engl. use exc. in compliment to ~ bearers; *the* ~, ~ **people** *or* **nation**; ~ FIR, KALE, MIST; POUND¹ *Scots*; ~ *broth*, soup or liquid stew with pearl barley and vegetables; ~ *cap*, of shapes worn with Highland costume, Glengarry, Tam-o'-Shanter, etc.; ~ *catch or snap* in music, short note on the beat followed by long one occupying remainder of beat; ~ *terrier*, small rough-haired short-legged kind; ~ *whisky*, kind distilled in Scotland esp. from malted barley; ~ *pebble*, kinds of agate & jasper, cairngorm, etc.; ~ *collops*, steak & onions; ~ *woodcock*, eggs on anchovy toast; ~*-d-English*, prisoners' base); *~'man, Scots′man, ~woman, Scots′-woman*, natives of Scotland (*Flying Scots′man*, a London–Edinburgh express). **2.** n. The ~ dialect of English (Sc. *Scots*; also *Lowland* ~; BROAD ~); ~ whisky (~ *& soda*, glass of this with soda-water). [contr. of SCOTTISH]

scotch², v.t., & n. (arch.). **1.** Make incisions in, score, wound without killing, slightly disable, (lit.); 'We have ~'d the snake, not killed it', see *Macbeth* III ii. 13). **2.** n. Slash, mark on ground for HOP²-, [?]

scotch³, n. & v.t. **1.** Wedge or block placed before wheel etc. to prevent motion downhill. **2.** v.t. Hold up (wheel, barrel) with ~. [perh. var. of *scotch* stilt, see SKATE²]

sco′tia, n. Large sea-duck. [?]

sco′tia, n. (-sho), n. Concave moulding esp. in base of column. [L, f. Gk *skotia* darkness (SCOTO-) w. ref. to shadow produced]

Scot′ism, n. (hist.). Metaphysical doctrines of Duns Scotus (d. 1308). So ~IST(2) n. [L *Scotus* the Scot, -ISM]

Scot′land Yard. (Used for) the London police, the headquarters of the detection of crime. [*Great, New*, ~, successive headquarters of metropolitan police]

scot′o-, comb. form of Gk *skotos* darkness; ~*graph*, machine for writing in darkness.

scotom′a, n. (path.; pl. ~*ta*). Obscuration of part of the field of vision. [LL, f. Gk *skotōma* f. *skotoō* darken (prec., -M)]

Scots. See SCOTCH¹; (in regimental titles) *Royal* ~, *Royal* ~ *Fusiliers, Greys*, ~ *Guards*. [ME *Scottis* SCOTTISH]

Scot(t)ice (skŏt′isē), adv. In Scotch. [med. L (LL *Scot(t)icus* Scotch)]

Scot′ticism, -ôti-, n. Scotch phrase, word or idiom. [as prec., -ISM(4)]

Scot′ticize, -ôti-, v.i. & t. Imitate the Scotch in idiom or habits; imbue with, model on, Scotch ways. [prec., -IZE]

Scot′tish, a. See SCOTCH¹; (in regimental titles) *King's Own* ~ *Borderers*, ~ *Rifles*, *London* ~. [OE *Scottisc*]

scoun′drel, n. Unscrupulous person, villain, rogue, rascal. Hence ~DOM, ~ISM(3), nn., ~LY¹ a. [?]

scour¹ (-owr), v.t., & n. **1.** Cleanse or brighten by friction (~ *metal*, with sand etc.; ~ *clothes* etc., with soap or chemicals); (of water, or person with water) clear out (channel, harbour, pipe, etc.) by flushing or flowing through or over; (of drug, physician, etc.) purge (bowels) drastically (~ *worms*, purge them by placing in damp moss etc. to fit them for bait); clear (rust, stain, etc.) *away, off*, by rubbing etc. (also fig.); ~*ing-rush*, kind of HORSE¹-tail with silicious coating used for polishing wood etc.; hence (-)~ER¹(1, 2) n. **2.** n. Clearing action of swift current on channel etc. (*the ~ of the tide*); diarrhoea in cattle; substance used for ~ing fabrics. [prob. f. MLG *schüren* (G *scheuern*) f. OF *escurer* f. med. L *scurare* (L EXcuratus taken good care of, see CURE⁵)]

scour² (-owr), v.i. & t. 1. Rove, range, go along hastily, esp. in search or pursuit; hasten over or along, search rapidly, (~ *the plain, coast, woods*). 2. v.t. Use whip on (arch.). [f. earlier *skūr* a storm, & cogn. w. SHOWER]

scourge (skerj), n., & v.t. **1.** Whip for chastising persons (arch.); person or thing regarded as instrument or manifestation of divine or other vengeance or punishment (e.g. barbarian conqueror, pestilence, war; *the white~*, consumption as an endemic disease). **2.** v.t. Use whip on (arch.); chastise, afflict, oppress, harass. [m.f. AF *escorge* f. p.p. (=thong) of LL EX(*corrigere* f. *corium* hide); vb f. OF *escorgier* perh. f. the LL vb=flay]

scout¹, n., & v.i. **1.** (Mil. etc.) man sent out to get information about enemy or surroundings (*boy ~*, member of organization intended to develop character, resourcefulness, & public spirit); || A.A. or R.A.C. patrol-man; ship designed for reconnoitring; small fast aircraft; || (Oxf.) college servant (cf. GYP¹, SKIP²); || (Crick., arch.) fielder; act of seeking (esp. mil.) information (*on the ~*); kinds of bird, auk, guillemot, puffin; ~'*master*, officer directing ~s or boy~s. **2.** v.i. Act as ~(esp. *out ~ing*). [vb f.n., f. OF *escoute* spy, eavesdropper, (*escouter* listen f. L as AUSCULTATION)]

scout², v.t. Reject (proposal, notion) with scorn or ridicule. [cf. ON *skúta* a taunt, Sw. *skjuta* to shoot; prob. cogn. w. SHOOT]

scow, n. Kind of flat-bottomed boat. [f. Du. *schouw* ferry-boat]

scowl, v.i. & t., & n. **1.** Wear sullen look, look sour, frown ill-temperedly; ~ *down*, master or overbear (person, opposition, etc.) with ~; hence ~ingLY² adv. **2.** n. ~ing aspect, angry frown. [cf. Da. *skule* look down]

scrab'ble, v.i. Scrawl, scribble, (Bibl.); scratch or grope about to find or collect something (usu. *about*). [f. Du. *schrabbelen*, dim. of *schrabben* SCRAPE]

scrăg, n., & v.t. (-gg-). **1.** Lean skinny person, animal, plant, etc.; bony part of animal's carcass as food, || esp. neck of mutton or inferior part of it; (sl.) person's neck; hence ~g'rY²(-gĭ) a., ~g'ĭlY² adv., ~g'ĭNESS n., (-gĭ-). **2.** v.t. Put to death by hanging, garotte, wring neck of, (sl.); (Footb.) tackle by the neck; (school sl.) squeeze neck of with arm by way of torture. [prob. f. obs. (& Sc.) *crag* neck (cf. Du. *kraag*, G *kragen*) with acquired s-]

***scrăm**, int. (sl.). Be off! [f. foll.]

scrăm'ble, v.i. & t., & n. **1.** Make way as best one can over steep or rough ground by clambering, crawling, etc.; take part in physical or other struggle to secure as much as possible of something from competitors (usu. *for*; ~ *for pennies*, of children etc. among whom coin is thrown; ~ *for place, wealth, a living*); throw (coins etc.) to be ~d for; cook (eggs) by breaking into pan with butter, milk, etc., stirring slightly, & heating; hence scrăm'blingLY² adv. **2.** n. Climb or walk over rough ground etc.; eager struggle or competition for or for something. [f. 16th c., etym. dub.]

scrăn, n. (sl.). Food, eatables, broken victuals; *bad ~ to —!* (Anglo-Ir.), bad luck to —. [?]

|| **scrănn'el**, a. (arch.). (Of sound) weak, reedy, feeble, (chiefly w. allus. to Milton, *Lycidas* 124). [cf. Norw. *skran* thin, lean, dry]

scrănn'y, ***scrawn'y**, a. (chiefly dial.). Lean, scraggy. [cf. prec.]

scrap¹, n., & v.t. (-pp-). **1.** Small detached piece of something, fragment, remnant, (pl.) odds & ends, useless remains, whence ~pY² a., ~p'ĭlY² adv., ~p'ĭNESS n.; picture, paragraph, etc., cut from book or newspaper for keeping in a collection (~-*book*, for pasting these into); ~ *of paper*, negligible promise etc. (w. ref. to violation of Belgian neutrality 1914); (collect.) rubbish, waste material, clippings etc., of metal collected for reworking (also ~-*iron*, ~-*metal*), (~-*heap*, collection of waste stuff, also fig.; ~-*heap policy*, practice of discarding promptly what is past its prime); (sing. or pl.) residuum of melted fat or of fish with the oil expressed (~-*cake*, compressed fish ~). **2.** v.t. Consign to ~-heap, condemn (ships, supplies, etc.) as past use, discard. [f. ON *skrap* (SCRAPE)]

scrap², n., & v.i. (sl.: -pp-). **1.** Fight, scrimmage, esp. of unpremeditated kind (*had a bit of a ~ with*). **2.** v.i. Have a ~. [?]

scrāpe, v.t. & i., & n. **1.** Level surface of, clear of projections, abrade, smooth, polish, shave, or graze, by drawing sharp or angular edge breadthwise over or by causing to pass over such edge (~ *one's bottom*, clear of barnacles etc.; ~ *one's chin*, shave; ~ *one's boots*, remove dirt from soles by drawing over scraper; ~

one's plate, leave no food on; *ship ~d her side, putné, against the pier*; ~ **away**, reduce by scraping; ~ **down**, ~ **away**, also ~ **all over**, & see below). 2. Take (projection, stain, etc.) **off**, **out**, or **away**. 3. Excavate (hollow) by scraping (often *out*). 4. Draw along with scraping sound, produce such sound from, emit such sound, (*~er's feet*, in restlessness or to drown speaker's voice, also ~ *abs.*, esp. = draw back foot in making clumsy formal bow; ~ **down**, silence by scraping feet; ~ *bow across fiddle-strings*, also ~ *abs.* = play fiddle etc.; *branches scraping against the window*). 5. Pass along something so as to graze or be grazed by it or just avoid doing so (*~d against, along, the wall*; ~ **through** adv. or prep., get through with a squeeze or narrow shave, often fig. of passing examination etc.). 6. Amass by scraping or with difficulty or by parsi- mony, contrive to gain, (usu. *up*; *together*; *must ~ up enough for*; *~penny*, miser; *~ acquaintance with*, thrust one's acquain- tance on); hence **scrap(e) economy** (*work & ~ as one may*); hence **scrap²ING¹** (esp. 2), **scrap²ER¹**(1, 2), nn. 7. n. Act or sound of scraping (*a ~ of the pen*, writing of a, esp. important, word or two e.g. signa- ture); scraping of foot in bowing; awk- ward predicament or fix resulting from escapade. [f. ON *skrapa*; cogn. w. OE *screpan* scratch]

scratch¹, v.t. & i., n., & a. 1. Score surface of, make long narrow superficial wounds in, with nail, claw, or something more or less pointed, (*threatened to ~ my face*; *~ the surface of*, not penetrate far into; *~ a Russian, & you find a Tartar*; *stones ~ed with rude letters or pictures*; *much ~ed with thorns*), get (some part of one) ~ed (*Have ~ed my hands badly*); form (letters, representation), excavate (hole), by ~ing, scribble (a few lines etc.); scrape without marking esp. with nails to relieve itching (*~ one's head*, esp. as sign of per- plexity; *~ my back & I will ~ yours*, = CLAW me, (abs.) = oneself, ~ **ground** etc. in search (*~ about for stray seeds, evidence, etc.*); scrape together or up; score (written words etc.) **out** or **through**, strike off with pencil etc., ||erase (horse's name in list of entries for race, com- petitor's name), withdraw (horse, candi- date, or intr. for refl.) from competition; ~ **along**, sl., manage to live etc. 2. n. Mark or sound made by ~ing (*a ~ of the pen*, signature or written order easily given); spell of ~ing oneself, etc. 3. (Racing) line from which competitors in race start (*toe, come to or up to, the ~*, put in appearance at; right time, not shirk, often transf.; *~ race*, with all on equal terms, opp. handi- cap; *~ man or ~*, competitor in handi- cap receiving no start); (pl.) horse-disease

with dry chaps above heel; (also *~urg*) wig, covering part only of head; *~cat*, spiteful child or woman; *~work*, graffito decoration. 3. adj. Collected by hap- hazard, *~ed together*; heterogeneous, (*a ~ crew, collection, team*). [perh. mixture AF of ME *scrattle* (cf. MSw. *kratta* scrape w. AF pref. es- EX¹) with ME *cracche* (cf. M.Du. *kratsen*)]

Scratch², n. Old ~, the devil. [f. obs. *scrat* hermaphrodite=ON *skratta* goblin]

scratch'y, a. (Of drawing etc.) done in hurried more or less illegible way; mark (paper etc.) *over, all over*, with bad writing or lines like writing. 2. n. Piece of bad writing, hurried note or letter. [earlier senses, sprawl, crawl; perh. = crawl w. acquired s-]

||**scray**, n. Common tern, sea swallow. [cf. W *yscraen*]

Scream, v.i. & t., & n. 1. Utter piercing cry expressing terror, pain, or pretence of these, (of steam-engine etc.) whistle or hoot shrilly; laugh uncontrollably (usu. *~ with laughter*; *~ING¹ farce, fun, etc.* causing spectators to *~*, intensely funny); utter, say, in ~ing tone (usu. *out*; *~ed that she did not dare jump*; *~ out a curse, order, etc.*); hence **~ingʰ¹** adv. 2. n. (sl.) irresistibly comical affair; (without article) violent over-emphasis in style or sentiment, whence **~ʸ¹** a., **~ʰ¹ʸ²** adv., **~ɪɴᴇss** n. [ME *scramen* etym. dub.]

||**Scree**, n. (Mountain slope covered with) small stones that slide down when trod- den on (often pl. in same sense). [f. ON *skritha* (*skritha* glide)]

screech, v.i. & t., & n. Scream (vb & n.) with, of, fright or pain or anger, or in harsh or uncanny tones (usu. derog. or joc., & esp. w. ref. to disagreeable nature of sound); *~out*, kinds that ~ instead of hooting, ||esp. the BARN-owl. [limit.; earlier *scritch, scrike*, etc.]

screed, n. Long tiresome harangue (esp. list of grievances) or letter; ||one of the fillets of mortar or strips of wood by which a surface to be plastered is divided into compartments. [var. of SHRED]

screen, n. & v.t. 1. Partition of wood or stone separating without completely cut- ting off one part of church or room from another, esp. that between nave & choir of cathedral etc. (ROOD~), decorated wall

enclosing court etc., façade of church. **2.** Movable piece of furniture designed to shelter from excess of heat, light, draught, etc., or from observation (*fire, window, folding,* etc., ~). **3.** Any object utilized as shelter esp. from observation, expression of face or measure adopted for concealment, protection afforded by these, (*prepared the attack behind a ~ of trees; put on a ~ of indifference; a cavalry ~,* cavalry thrown out to keep enemy's scouts from getting in touch with main body; *under ~ of night*). **4.** Board, often with wire-netting cover, on which notices are posted. **5.** White surface on which moving or televised pictures or lantern slides are projected; *the ~,* moving pictures collectively. **6.** Body proof against electric or magnetic induction or having property of interrupting other such physical processes. **7.** Large sieve or riddle esp. for sorting coal etc. into sizes. **8.** (Photog.) transparent finely-ruled plate used in process of half-tone reproduction. **9.** (Cricket) one of two large movable white wood or canvas erections placed near boundary in line with wicket to assist batsman's sight of the ball. **10.** v.t. Afford shelter to, hide partly or completely, (*from*; often fig. of protecting another from deserved censure etc. by taking blame upon oneself or diverting it). **11.** Show (object, scene) on lantern or cinema~. **12.** Riddle (coal etc.; *~ed coal,* from which dust etc. has been removed; *~ings,* refuse separated by sifting); (fig.) sift & investigate (persons). [cf. OF *escren* prob. f. OHG *skirm* (G *schirm*) shelter]

screeve v.i., **screev′er** n. (sl.) (Be) pavement artist. [nlt. f. L *scribere* write]

screw¹ (-ōō), n., & v.t. & i. **1.** Cylinder with spiral ridge called the thread running round it outside (MALE or *exterior ~*) or inside (FEMALE or *interior ~*), metal male ~ with slotted head & sharp point for fastening pieces of wood together with more security than nail (also *wood-, common, ~*) or with blunt end to receive nut & bolt things together (also *~bolt*), wooden or metal male or female ~ as part of appliance or machine acting as one of the MECHANICAL powers to exert pressure in various ways, (ARCHIMEDEAN *~*; *endless* or *perpetual ~,* threaded revolving shaft engaging with & working cogwheel; *differential* or *Hunter's ~,* arrangement of *~*s with threads of different pitch working inside each other giving great lifting-power; *left-handed ~,* advanced by turning leftwards contrary to usu. arrangement; *right-&-left ~,* cylinder with threads in opposite directions at the two ends; *interrupted ~,* with parts of thread cut away; *have, there is, a ~ loose,* phrr. suggesting that something, esp. person's brain, is out of working

order; *put the ~ on,* exert pressure esp. in way of extortion or intimidation). **2.** (Also *~propeller*) revolving shaft with spiral blades projecting from ship or airship at stern & propelling it by acting on ~ principle upon water or air. **3.** (Also *~ steamer,* abbr. *s.s.*) steamer propelled by ~ or ~s. **4.** One turn of a ~ (*give it another ~*). **5.** ‖ Oblique curling motion or tendency as of billiard-ball struck sideways. **6.** ‖ Small twisted-up paper of tobacco etc. **7.** Miser, stingy or extortionate person. **8.** ‖(sl.). Amount of salary or wages. **9.** *~ coupling, right-&-left female ~* for joining ends of pipes or rods; *~cutter,* hand-tool for cutting ~s; *~driver,* tool like blunt chisel for turning ~s by the slot; *~eye, ~* with loop for passing cord etc. through instead of slotted head; *~ gear, endless ~* with cogwheel or pinion; *~hook,* hook to hang things on with ~ at end of shank to fasten it in with; *~jack,* dentist's implement for regulating distance between crowded teeth, (also) carriage JACK¹ worked by ~; *~pile,* with ~ at lower end, & sunk by rotation; *~pine,* plant with leaves arranged spirally & resembling those of pineapple; *~plate,* metal plate for holding *~*cutting dies, also steel plate with threaded holes for making male~s; *~pod,* kind of mesquit with spirally twisted pods; *~ press,* press worked by simple ~ used esp. by printers & binders; *~tap,* tool for making female ~s; *~valve,* stopcock opened & shut by ~; *~wheel,* valve moved by ~; *~wheel,* worked by endless ~; *~wrench,* for turning ~s with angular head or nuts, also wrench with jaws worked by ~. **10.** vb. Fasten, tighten, etc., by use of ~ or ~s (*~ up door,* make fast, esp. as practical joke at university; *~ up person, ~ up his door; boards are ~ed down; his head is ~ed on the right way,* he has sense). **11.** Turn (~), twist round like ~, (w. ref. to twisting pegs of fiddle; usu. *up*) make tenser or more efficient (*~ one's courage to the sticking-place, ~ up one's courage, gather resolution; he, the management, wants ~ing up*). **12.** Put the ~ upon, press hard on, oppress. **13.** Be miserly. **14.** Squeeze, extort, (consent, money, etc.) *out of.* **15.** Contort, distort, contract, (*~ one's face into wrinkles; ~ up one's eyes*). **16.** (Of ~) revolve (*~ stiffly, to the right,* etc.). **17.** (Of rolling ball, also of person etc.) take curling course, swerve; hence *~′ABLE* (-ōōa-) a. [f. OF *escro(u)e* etym. dub.; cf. SCROLL]

screw² (-ōō), n. Vicious, unsound, or worn-out horse. Hence *~′Y²* (-ōōĭ) a. (also, sl., slightly crazy, having a screw loose). [perh. f. prec.]

screwed (-ōōd), a. (sl.). Drunk, drunken. [prob. f. SCREW¹, -ED¹]

scribā′cious (-shus), a. (rare). Given to writing. [f. L *scrībere* write, -ACIOUS]

scrib'ble¹, v.t. & i. & n. **1.** Write (t. & i.) hurriedly or carelessly in regard either to handwriting or composition; be a journalist or author (w. implication, often mock-modest, of inferiority), write poetry etc., whence **scrib'bler¹** [-ER¹] n.; ∥ *scrib-bling-paper, -diary*, etc. for casual jottings; hence **~MENT** n. (rare). **2.** n. Careless handwriting or thing written in it, scrawl, hasty note, etc. [f. med. L *scribillare* dim. of L *scribere* write]

scrib'ble², v.t. Card (wool, cotton) coarsely, pass through scribbling-machine or **scrib'bler²** [-ER²] n. [prob. f. LG, cf. Sw. *skrubbla*; cogn. w. SCRUB²]

scribe, n. & v.t. **1.** Person who writes or can write (rare; *am no great ~*, do not write well). **2.** (Bibl.) ancient-Jewish maker & keeper of records etc., also Jewish theologian & jurist of type prevalent in time of Christ; hence **scrib'AL** a. **3.** (Also *~-awl*) pointed instrument for marking lines on wood, bricks, etc., to guide saw etc., or writing words on barrel etc. **4.** v.t. Mark with ~; *scribing-com-pass*, for scratching circles etc.; *scribing-iron*, **scrib'ER¹** n., = (sense 3). [vb.f. n., f. L *scriba* (*scribere* write)]

scrim, n. Lining-cloth in upholstery etc. [?]

scrim'mage, scrum, n., & v.i. & t. **1.** Tussle, confused struggle, row, brawl, skirmish, (usu. scri-). **2.** (Rugby footb.; usu. scru-; also abbr. *scrum*) tight mass of all the forwards with ball on ground in middle; *scrum half*, the half-back who puts the ball into the scrum. **3.** vb. Engage in a ~. [var. of SKIRMISH]

scrimp, v.t. & i. Skimp. Hence **scrim'py¹** a. [f. 18th c. only; cf. SHRIMP]

∥ **scrim'shank**, v.i. (mil. sl.). Shirk duty. Hence **~ER¹** n. [f. 1890; etym. dub.]

scrim'shaw, v.t. & i., & n. **1.** Adorn (shells, ivory, etc.), adorn shells etc., with carved or coloured designs (as sailors' amusement at sea). **2.** n. Piece of such work. [perh. f. person's name]

scrin'ium, n. (Rom. Ant.; pl. *-ia*). Cylindrical or other box for rolled MSS. [L, see SHRINE]

∥ **scrip¹**, n. (arch.). Beggar's or traveller's or pilgrim's wallet, satchel. [prob. f. OF *escrepe*; cf. SCARF¹]

scrip², n. Provisional certificate of money subscribed to bank or company entitling holder to formal certificate in due time & to dividends etc.; (collect.) such certificates. [abbr.; =(sub)scription receipt]

scrip³, n. **1.** (Law) original document (*copy, copy*). **2.** Handwriting, written characters (opp. *print*); printed cursive characters, imitation of handwriting in type. **3.** Text of broadcaster's announcement or talk; typescript of film-play. **4.** ∥ Examinee's written answer. [f. L *scrip-tum* thing written (*scribere* script- write)]

scriptor'ium, n. (pl. *-s, -ia*). Room set apart for writing esp. in monastery. [med. L (prec., -ORY)]

scrip'tural, a. Founded on, reconcilable with, laying stress on, appealing to, doctrines contained in the Bible, whence **~ISM(3), ~IST(2)**, nn. of, taken from, the Bible (rare; usu. now *scripture* attrib.); Hence **~LY²** adv., **~NESS** n. [foll., -AL]

scrip'ture, n. **1.** The Bible with or without the Apocrypha (usu. without article; also *Holy S~* or the *S~s*; *a doctrine not found in S~ or the S~s*; *a doctrine* taken from the quotation from the Bible; (attrib.) taken from or relating to the Bible (*a ~ text, lesson*; *~reader*, person employed to read the Bible to the poor in their homes. [f. L *scriptura* (SCRIPT-, -URE)]

scriv'ener, n. (hist.). Writer, drafter of documents, notary, broker, money-lender; (in mod. use) *~'s palsy*, WRITER'S cramp. [f. OF *escrivein* f. L L *scribanus* (SCRIBE, -AN) + -ER¹]

scrobic'ulate, -ated, aa. (bot., zool.). Pitted, furrowed. [L L *scrobiculus* (*scro-bis* ditch, -CULE), -ATE²]

scrof'ula, n. Morbid constitutional condition with glandular swellings & tendency to consumption. Hence **~OUS** a., **~OUSLY²** adv., **~OUSNESS** n. [med. L sing. f. L L *scrofulae* scrofulous swelling, orig. dim. of *scrofa* a sow]

scroll, n. & v.t. & i. **1.** Roll of parchment or paper, book or volume of the ancient roll form; (arch.) schedule or list. **2.** Ornamental design esp. in architecture carved or drawn or otherwise made to imitate ~ or parchment more or less exactly, volute of Ionic capital or of chair etc., head of fiddle, flourish in writing, ribbon bearing heraldic motto, etc. **3.** Any tracery of spiral or flowing lines. **4.** *~-bone*, turbinated; *~ gear*, with *~wheel*; *~-head*, volute at ship's bow; *~-lathe*, for spiral work; *~-saw*, fretsaw; *~-wheel*, cogwheel in shape of disk with cogs in spiral lines on one side causing variation of pace according as outer or inner parts are in action; *~-work*, ornament of spiral lines esp. as cut by *~-saw*. **5.** vb. Curl up (t. & i.; rare) like paper; adorn with *~s* (chiefly in p.p.). [earlier *scrow* dim. of ME *scrowe* f. OF *escro(u)e* (cf. SCREW¹) f. Teut.; cogn. w. SHRED]

scroop, n., & v.i. (Make) grating noise. [imit.]

scro'tum, n. (pl. *~a*). Bag containing testicles. Hence **~AL** a., **~ITIS, ~OCELE**, nn. [L]

scrounge (-j), v.i. & t. (sl.). Appropriate things; cadge; acquire thus. Hence **scroun'gER²** (-j-) n. [?]

scrub¹, n. (Ground covered with) brush-wood or stunted forest growth; worn

or short-bristled brush or moustache; stunted or insignificant person, animal, or plant; ~*oak*, American dwarf kinds. Hence ~**b'y**[2] a., ~**b'iness** n. [var. of SHRUB[1]]

scrub[2], v.t. & i. (-bb-), & n. **1.** Rub hard to clean or brighten esp. with soap & water applied with ~**bing-brush**; use such brush (*would rather ~ for my living*); eliminate, or extract for use, certain components from (coal-gas); hence ~**b'er**[1] (esp., apparatus for ~bing gas), ~**b'ing**[1], nn. **2.** n. ~bing or being ~bed (*give it, he wants, a good ~*). **3.** *(colloq.)*. [f. LL f. L 1, 2]

scruff, n. Back *of the neck* as used to grasp & lift or drag animal or person by (*take by the ~ of the neck*). [corrupt. of SCUFF[2]]

scrum(mage). See SCRIMMAGE.

scrump'tious (-shus), a. *(sl.)*. Delightful, delicious, firstrate. [arbitrary; cf. SCRUMPTIOUS]

scrunch. = CRUNCH. [*s-* as in SCRAG etc.]

scru'ple (-ōō-), n., & v.i. & t. **1.** Weightunit (in apothecaries' wt) of 20 grains; very small quantity (arch.); feeling of doubt or hesitation on grounds of morality or propriety about acting or approving of action, conscientious objection, (*make no ~ to do*, do without such hesitation or with easy conscience; *have ~s about doing*; *man of no ~s*, unscrupulous; *did it without ~*). **2.** v.b. Feel or be influenced by ~s (rare); be deterred from or hindered in (*doing or a ~* of action; arch.; *would ~ lying or a lie*) by ~s; hesitate owing to ~s *to do* (esp. w. neg.; *does not ~ to say*). [vb f. n., f. F *scrupule* f. L *scrupulus* (*scrupus* sharp stone, -ULE]

scru'pulous (-ōōp-), a. Careful to offend in nothing, conscientious even in small matters, not neglectful of details, punctilious, marked by extreme thoroughness, unfailing, (*~ persons*; *~ honesty, cleanliness, care, methods, respect, attention,* etc.); over-attentive to details, esp. to small points of conscience, whence **scrupulos'ity** (-ōōp-) n. Hence ~**LY**[2] adv., ~**NESS** n. [f. F *scrupuleux* f. L *scrupulosus* (prec., -OSE[1])]

scru'tin'or (-ōō-), n. Person given to scrutiny (chiefly as signature to newspaper letters etc.). [L (SCRUTINY, -OR[2]]

scrutin (skrōōtǎṅ), n. *~ d'arrondissement, de liste,* (dǎrawṅdǎsmahṅ', də lēst'), contrasted methods by which voter votes for one or more representatives of small district only, or for large number representing wide area. [F]

scrutineer' (-ōō-), n. Person examining ballot papers for irregularities. [SCRUTINY, -EER]

scrutin'ize (-ōō-), v.t. Look closely at, examine in detail. Hence ~**ingLY**[2] adv. [foll., -IZE]

scru'tiny (-ōō-), n. Critical gaze, close investigation, examination into details; official examination of votes cast in election to test their validity when closeness of contest or suspicion of irregularity makes it desirable (*demand a ~*). [f. LL *scrutinium* (*scrutari* search f. *scruta* broken pieces)]

scry, v.i. Use the crystal in CRYSTAL-*gazing*. Hence ~**ER**[1] n. [= (DE)SCRY]

scud, v.i. (-dd-), & n. **1.** Run or fly straight & fast esp. with smooth or easy motion, skim along; (Naut.) run before the wind. **2.** n. Spell of ~ding; vapoury driving clouds. [f. 16th c., etym. dub.]

scu'dō (or -ōō-), n. (pl. -**dī** pr. -dē). Old Italian silver coin of about 4/-. [It., f. L *scudum* shield]

scuff[1], v.i. Walk with dragging feet, shuffle with the feet. [f. 18th c., etym. dub.]

scuff[2], n. Nape (now usu. *scruff*). [also *scuft, scruft*, etym. dub.]

scuf'fle, v.i., & n. (Engage in) confused struggle in which disputants chiefly push each other about, disorderly fight. [prob. f. Scand. orig. & cogn. w. *shove, shuffle*]

scug, n. *(schoolsl.)*. Person lacking spirit, sociability, manners, sportsmanship, etc. [?]

scull, n., & v.t. & i. **1.** One of pair of small oars used by single rower each with one hand; oar resting in nick on boat's stern & worked with twisting strokes to propel like ship's screw. **2.** vb. Propel (boat), propel boat, with ~(s). [f. 14th c., etym. dub.]

scull'er, n. User of scull(s); boat intended for sculling. [-ER[1]]

scull'ery, n. Back kitchen, room for washing up dishes etc. [f. OF *escuelerie* f. L *scutella* (SCUTTLE)+-ERY]

scull'ion (-yon), n. (arch., poet., rhet.). Cook's boy, washer of dishes & pots. [perh. assim. to prec. of F *souillon* scullion, orig. dirty fellow (as SOIL[2])]

sculp, v.t. *(colloq. for)* SCULPTURE. [f. L *sculpere*; now regarded as abbr.]

scul'pin, n. Kinds of small American seafish with large spiny head. [perh. corrupt. of obs. *scorpene* f. L f. Gk *skorpaina* a fish]

sculp'sit, sculpser'unt, (abbr. *Sc.* or *sculps.*), v. sing. & pl. 3rd pers. (So-&-so) carved or sculptured or engraved (this work; used with artist's signature). [L, see SCULPTURE]

sculp'tjor, n. One who sculptures. Hence ~**RESS**[1] n. [L (foll., -OR[2])]

sculp'ture, n., & v.t. & i. **1.** Art of forming representations of objects in the

round or in relief by chiselling stone, carving wood, modelling clay, casting metal, or similar processes; (*Zool., Bot.*) raised or sunk markings on shell etc.; hence ~AL, ~ESQUE (-ĕsk²) aa., ~ally² adv., (-cher-). 2. v.b. Represent in ~e; adorn with ~e; be a sculptor, do ~e; (p., P., *Zool.* & *Bot.*) having ~e. [vb.f. L f. *sculptura* (*sculpere sculpt-*, perf. *sculpsi*, -URE)]

scum, n., & v.t. & i. (-mm-). 1. Impurities that rise to surface of liquid esp. in boiling or fermentation, floating film; (fig.) worst part, refuse, offscouring, (*of*); hence ~m'y² a. 2. vb. Take ~ from, skim; be or form a ~ on; (of liquid) develop ~. [Teut. (cf. G *schaum*, Da. *skum*) perh. Thr. OF *escume*; see also SKIM]

scún'cheon (-chon), n. Stones or arches across angles of square tower supporting alternate sides of octagonal spire. [f. OF *escoinson* (EX-, COIN²)]

scúm'ble, v.t., & i. (-bl-). 1. Soften (oil-painting) by covering with very thin coat of opaque colour. 2. n. Softening of tints produced. [prec., -LE(3)]

‖ **scümm'er²**, n., & v.t. & i. (Sc.). 1. Strong dislike (esp. *take ~ at, against*), object of loathing. 2. vb. Sicken, disgust; feel sick, be nauseated. [?]

scúpp'er¹, n. Hole in ship's side to carry off water from deck. [perh. f. SCOOP vb + -ER¹]

‖ **scúpp'er²**, v.t. (sl.). Surprise & massacre, sink (ship, crew), do for. [perh. f. prec.]

scúrf, n. Flakes on surface of skin cast off as fresh skin develops below, esp. those of head (also *dandruff*); any scaly matter on a surface. Hence ~y², & i., ~INESS n. [OE, cogn. w. *sceorfan* scarify, cf. Sw. *scorp*]

scúrr'ilous, (arch.), **scúrr'ile(e)**, aa. Grossly or obscenely abusive (of person or language), given to or expressed with low buffoonery. Hence or cogn. ~ously adv., ~ITY (-il'-) n. [f. obs. *scurril* f. L *scurrilis* (*scurra* buffoon), -OUS]

scúrr'y, v.i., & n. 1. Run hurriedly esp. with short quick steps, scamper, (*the ~ing mice*). 2. n. Act or sound of ~ing; short fast horse-race (*polo~*, race for polo-ponies). [perh. shortened f. *hurry*]

scúr'v|y, a. & n. 1. Paltry, low, mean, dishonourable, contemptible, (*a ~y trick, fellow*); hence ~ily² adv. 2. n. Deficiency disease with swollen gums, livid spots, & prostration, attacking sailors & any who feed on salt meat & lack vegetables; ~y-grass [corrupt. of -*cress*], plant of mustard family used against ~y; hence ~IED² (-vid) a. [In (expressing pitiful state) f. adj. orig.=scurfy (SCURF, -Y²)]

scut, n. Short tail esp. of hare, rabbit, or deer. [etym. dub.; cf. Icel. *short fox's tail*]

scūt'age, n. (hist.), Money paid by feudal landowner in lieu of personal service. [f. med. L *scutagium* (*scutum* shield, -AGE)]

scūtch, v.t., & n. 1. Dress (fibrous material, esp. retted flax) by beating; ~-blade, ~-ing-sword, ~ER²(2) n, implements for ~ing flax. 2. n. ~er; coarse tow separated f. ... [perh. f. OF *escousser* f. L EX(*cutere cuss-* = *quatere* shake)]

scútch'eon (-chon), n. = ESCUTCHEON; plate for name or inscription. [short for ESCUTCHEON]

scute. See SCUTUM.

scūt'ell|um n. (nat. hist.; pl. ~a). Small shield, plate, or scale, in plants, insects, birds, etc., esp. one of the horny scales on birds' feet. Hence scūt'ellate² ~AR¹, aa., ~ATION n. [mod. L, dim. of SCUTUM]

‖ **scŭtt'er**, v.i., & n. Scurry. [var. of SCUTTLE³]

scútt'le¹, n. (Usu. *coal~*) metal or other vessel in which small supply of coal esp. for single fireplace is brought & kept. [OE *scutel* dish f. L *scutella* salver, dim.

scútt'le², n., & v.t. 1. Hole with lid in wall or roof of house or ship's deck, side, or hatchway-covering; section of motor-car connecting bonnet and body; ~butt, ~cask, water-butt usu. on deck with hole in top for dipping from. 2. v.t. Make hole(s) in (ship), open sea-cocks of (ship), esp. for purpose of sinking. [cf. F *escoutille*, Sp. *escotilla*, hatchway; perh. all f. Du. *schutten* to shut]

scútt'le³, v.i., & n. 1. Hurry along, scurry, run away, make off, fly from danger or difficulty. 2. n. Hurried gait, precipitate flight or departure. [earlier also *scuddle*, f. SCUD, -LE(3)]

scūt'um, n. (pl.-a), (Rom. Ant.) legionary's shield of oblong, oval, or semi-cylindrical shape; (Anat.) knee-pan; (*Zool.* etc.; also *scute*) shieldlike plate or scale, piece of bony armour in crocodile, sturgeon, turtle, armadillo, etc., whence ~AL, ~ATE³ aa. Hence ~IFORM a. [L, cogn. w. Gk *skutos* hide, SKY, SCUM, etc.]

Scyll'a, n. ~ & *Charybdis*, six-headed monster living on a rock, & whirlpool, so placed on opposite sides of Straits of Messina that it was hard to steer clear of one without being caught by the other (see Homer, *Od.* xii).

scýph'us, n. (pl. ~ī). (Gk Ant.) footless drinking-cup with two handles not higher than rim; (Bot.) cup-shaped part as in narcissus flower or in lichens, whence ~OSE¹ a. Hence ~IFORM a. [L, f. Gk *skuphos*]

scythe (sīdh), n., & v.t. 1. Mowing & reaping implement of long slightly curved blade swung over ground by usu. crooked pole about 5 ft long with two short handles projecting at right angles from

it; blade continuing axle of ancient war-chariot at each end, whence **SCYTHED²** (-dhd) a.. **2.** v.t. Cut with ~. [OE *sīðhe*, cf. Du. *zeis*, ON *sigðr*; cogn. w. L *secare* cut, SICKLE]

Scyth'ian (sidh-, -th-), a. & n. (Inhabitant) of ancient Scythia, the region north of the Black Sea; = TURANIAN. [L f. Gk *Skuthia* (*Skuthēs* a ~), -AN]

‖ **'sdeath** (zdēth), int. (arch.) expressing anger, surprise, etc. [short for *God's death*]

se-, L pref. = apart, without.

sea, n. **1.** Expanse of salt water that covers most of earth's surface & encloses its continents & islands, the ocean, any part of this as opposed to dry land or fresh water, (*by ~ & land*; *at the bottom of the ~*; *jumped into the ~*; *on the ~*; *in ship* etc., also situated on ~*shore*; *go to ~*; become sailor; *follow the ~*, be sailor; *put to ~*, leave port or land; *arm of the ~*, deep gulf; *at~*, away from & esp. out of sight of land, also fig. = perplexed, not knowing conditions etc. or what to do; *between* DEVIL *& deep ~*; *as good* FISH¹ *in the ~*; *when the ~ gives up its dead*, at the resurrection; also pl. in same sense, as *beyond, over, ~ or ~s*, to or in countries separated by ~; *the high ~s*, the open ~ outside the three-mile limit to which nearest country's jurisdiction extends; *mistress of the ~ or ~s*, chief naval power at any time). **2.** Particular tract of ~ partly or sometimes wholly enclosed by land & usu. distinguished by special name *the North, Mediterranean, Caspian, Dead, Sea*; *inland ~*, entirely landlocked as the Caspian, also rarely of great fresh-water lakes; *closed ~*, = MARE¹ *clausum*; *the seven ~s*, Arctic, Antarctic, N. & S. Pacific, N., & S. Atlantic, & Indian, Oceans; ‖ *the four ~s*, those enclosing Great Britain). **3.** Local motion or state of the ~, swell, great billow, (*a heavy ~ with great waves*; *~s mountains high*; (of boat etc.) *ship a ~*, be flooded by a wave; *long ~*, with long regular waves; *short ~*, choppy & irregularly agitated; *~ like looking-glass* or *sheet of glass*, quite smooth; *half ~s over*, having drunk too much). **4.** Vast quantity or expanse of (*a ~ of troubles, care, flame, upturned faces*; also pl., as *~s of blood*, ruthless bloodshed). **5.** (Bibl.) *brazen*, or *molten ~*, = LAVER². **6.** (attrib., & in comb.). Living or used in or on, near, like, the ~ (often prefixed to name of animal, fruit, etc., to form name of marine thing with merely superficial resemblance to what it is named after, as ~ *canary, cucumber, -fox, raven*, below); ~ *acorn*, barnacle; ~ *air*, air at ~side esp. as recommended for invalids etc.; ~*anchor*, DRAG²-anchor; ~ANEMONE; ~*angel*, ANGEL-fish; ~*arrow*, flying squid; ~*barrow*, skate's egg-case;

~ *bathing*, in ~; ~ *bear*, polar bear, also of fur-seal; ~-*bells*, ~ shore bind-weed; ~-*bell*, sweet fucus, a ~weed with beltlike fronds; ~*board*, ~shore, coast region, line of coast; ~-*boat*, ship etc. of specified ~going qualities (*is a good, bad, etc., ~boat*), boat which can be lowered quickly in an emergency at ~; ~*born*, born of the ~ (poet., esp. of Aphrodite); ~*borne*, conveyed by ~ (~*borne commerce, goods*); ~*bow*, rainbow effect in ~-spray; ~-*breeze*, blowing landward from ~ esp. during day in alternation with land-breeze at night; ~ *breeze*, any breeze at ~; ~-*calf*, common seal; ~ *canary*, white whale (from its whistling); ~ *captain*, (poet., rhet.) great sailor or commander at ~, (in ord. use, chiefly where army-captain is to be excluded) past or present captain of ship in navy or merchant service; ~ *change*, trans-formation (w. ref. to *Tempest* I. ii. 400); ~ *chestnut*, ~-urchin; ~-*cloth*, used in theatre to represent ~ shore; ‖ ~ *coal*, arch, coal (orig. of coal brought from Newcastle by ~, opp. charcoal etc.); ~ *coast*, ~*cock*, kinds of bird & fish, also valve by which ~water can be let into ship's interior; ~ *colander*, brown ~weed with fronds perforated like colander; ~ *cook*, naut. term of abuse; ~*cow*, sirenian, also walrus; ~ *crow*, kind of gull; ~ *cucumber*, any holothurian, esp. *bêche-de-mer*; ~*devil*, kinds of fish; ~-*dog*, kinds of seal, also dogfish, also old sailor (esp. of the Elizabethan ~captains); & see ~-DOG; ~ *eagle*, kinds of fishing eagle, also osprey; ~-*ear*, ormer; ~ *elephant*, large kind of seal with proboscis; ~-*fan*, kind of coral; ~*faring* a. & n., traversing the ~ esp. habitually (~*faring man*, sailor), so ~**farer¹** n. (rare); ~ *fennel*, samphire; ~-*fight*, between warships; ~-*flower*, ~ anemone; ~ *fog*, caused by difference of land & ~ temperature & extending only short way inland; ~-*fowl*; ~-*fox*, long-tailed shark; ~ *front*, part of town facing ~; ~ *furbelow*, kinds of brown ~weed; ~-*gauge*, ship's draught, also kind of sounding-instrument; ~ *gherkin*, ~ cucumber; ~ *gilliflower*, pink; ~-*girt*, surrounded by ~ (poet., rhet., of island etc.); ~*god(dess)*; ~*go-ing*, (of ship) for crossing ~, not coasting, (of person) ~faring; ~ *grape*, shrub allied to firs, also gulf-weed, also (pl.) cuttle-fish eggs; ~-*green* a. & n., (of) bluish green as of ~; ~-*gull*; ~ *hedgehog*, ~-urchin; ~-*hog*, porpoise; ~-*horse*, creature harnessed to ~god's chariot having horse's head & fish's tail, also walrus, also hippocampus; ~-*island cotton*, fine quality of long-stapled cotton originally grown on islands off Georgia and S. Carolina; ~ *kale*, kind of perennial with young shoots used as table vegetable; ~ *kidney*, kidney-shaped polypidom; ~-*king*, medi-

eval Scandinavian pirate chief; ~ kind of ~weed with long cordlike fronds; ~ lawyer, (naut. term of contempt for captious person); ~-legs, ability to walk on deck of rolling ship (has not yet got his ~legs); ~ lemon, a yellow oval mollusc; ~ leopard, kinds of spotted seal; ~ letter, official protective letter carried by neutral ship in war-time, describing her cargo, crew, etc.; ~ level, level continuous with that of ~ (halfway between high & low water (also mean ~ level) as used in reckoning height of hills etc. & for barometric standard (corrected to ~ level); ~ lily, crinoid; ~ line, horizon at ~; ~ lion, kinds of large eared seal, esp. one with mane; || Sea Lord, naval member of the Board of Admiralty; ~-men, sailor, (Nav.) rating of executive or upper-deck branch (ABLE-bodied ~man, ordinary ~man, below rating of A.B.), matters, whence ~'manïkE,~'manïy¹, aa. ~'mansHIp(3) n.; ~ mark, beacon, lighthouse, etc., or elevated conspicuous object, used to direct course at ~; ~-mad, polyzoon forming flat matted coralline; ~ melon, kind of holothurian; ~ mew, gull; ~ mile, geographical MILE; ~ mon-ster, any huge, terrible, or strange animal; ~ moss, mosslike polyzoan or ~weed; ~-mouse, an iridescent ~-worm; ~weed; ~mud, saline deposit of salt marshes etc, used as manure; ~ necklace, string of ~ egg-cases; ~ needle, garfish; ~ nettle, jellyfish; ~nymph; ~ook, kind of ~weed; ~ooze, ~ mud; ~orange, globose orange-coloured holothurian; ~orb, globe-fish; ~ otter, kind with very valu-able fur; ~owl, = LUMP², ~-oz, walrus; ~-pay, for active service at ~; ~ peach, pear, kinds of ascidium; ~pen, feather-shaped polyp; ~ pie (bird); ~-pig, porpoise, also neutral ship's passport in time of war; meat etc., || also a shore-bird, the oyster-catcher; ~piece, picture of scene at ~; ~pi'et, ~ pie (bird); ~-pig, porpoise, also ~-poacher, a small fish; ~port, town with harbour; ~ power, ability to control and make successful use of the ~; ~ pumpkin, ~ melon; ~purse, skate's egg-case; ~ raven, sculpin; ~ robin, red gurnard; ~-room, clear space at ~; allow-ing ship to turn etc.; ~ rover, pirate or piratical ship; ~salt, got by evaporating ~ water; ~-scape, ~piece; ~ scouts; serpent, kinds of snake living in ~, also (the ~ serpent) enormous serpentine maritime auxiliary to boy scouts; ~ ~ monster occasionally reported as seen but disbelieved in by naturalists; ~

shore, land close to ~, (Law) space between high & low water marks; ~sick, vomiting or inclined to vomit from motion of ship etc., whence ~SICKNESS n.; ~side; places or some unspecified place close to ~ as permanent or esp. as holiday residence (do you like the ~side?; must go to the ~side); ~sleeve, cuttlefish; ~ snail, small slimy fish, the unctuous sucker, also periwinkle or similar shell-fish; ~ snipe, the dunlin, also the snipe-fish; ~ squirt, any ascidium; ~ straw-berry, kind of polyp; ~ sunflower, anemone; ~ swallow, tern; ~-tangle; kinds of ~weed; ~-toad, the angler; ~-urchin, echinus; ~-vall, wall or embank-ment made to check encroachment of ~; ~ ware, ~weed collected for manure or other uses; ~water; ~-way, ship's pro-gress, also place where ship lies in open water (in a ~way); ~weed, any alga or other plant growing in ~; ~-whip, whip-shaped coral; ~ whipcord, kind of ~ weed; ~-wife, fish allied to wrasse; ~-wind, =~breeze; ~-wing, a bivalve mol-lusc; ~withwind, ~-bells; ~-wolf, elephant, also kinds of fish, also viking or pirate; ~worthy, (of ship) in fit state to put to ~, strong & well rigged etc., whence ~WORTHINESS n. Hence ~WARD aa., adv., & n., ~WARDS (-z) adv. [OE sæ]

seal¹, n. & v.i. 1. Kinds of carnivorous amphibious marine mammal with short limbs modified to serve chiefly for swim-ming but having fur or hair & beastlike face, feeding on fish & hunted for their oil & skin & the valuable fur of some species (eared ~ or otary, kinds distin-guished from common ~ by having visible external ears, & including the larger kinds, as sea bear, sea lion, sea elephant, & the fur-~s); ~skin; ~-fishery or ~ERY n.; ~-rookery, ~s' breeding-place; ~ skin, skin of ~, or usu. prepared for ~s as material for women's jackets etc., jacket of this. 2. v.i. Hunt ~s. [OE seolh, cf. ON selr, Da. sæl]

seal², n. & v.t. 1. Piece of wax, lead, or other such material, impressed with de-vice & attached in some way to document usu. in addition to signature as guarantee of authenticity (given under my hand &~, signed & ~ed by me; set one's to, authorize or confirm) or to envelope or to any receptacle such as box or room or house to prevent its being opened with-out knowledge of owner etc, (leaden ~ stamped piece of lead holding ends of a wire used as fastening; under ~ of con-fession, confidence, silence, etc., fig. of communications for which secrecy is stipulated or obligatory); impression stamped on or paper disk stuck to docu-ment as symbol equivalent to wax ~. 2. (fig.). Significant or prophetic mark (has the ~ of death in his face). 3. Gem,

piece of metal, etc., serving as stamp to produce ~ on wax etc. or paper (~*ring*, finger-ring with ~; ‖ *the* ~**s**, those held during tenure of office by Lord Chancellor or Secretary of State; ‖*Great S*~, = in charge of Lord Chancellor or Lord Keeper used in ~ing Parliament-writs, treaties, & Important State papers; ‖*PRIVY S*~; *Fisher's S*~, papal ~ with St Peter fishing as device), **4.** Act done, thing given, event regarded, as confirmation or guarantee of (~ *of love*, kiss, birth of child, etc.; *baptism & the Lord's Supper are* ~*s of God's covenant with us*). **5.** Substance used to close aperture etc., esp. water standing in drain-trap to prevent ascent of foul air (~*pipe*, DIP²-pipe). **6.** ~*wort*, SOLOMON'S ~. **7.** v.t. Affix to ~, stamp or fasten with ~, certify as correct with ~ or stamp (*S~ed Book*, one of perfect copies of Book of Common Prayer certified by Great S~ under Charles II); show genuineness of (devotion etc.) *with* one's life etc. **8.** Close securely or hermetically, stop up or up, (*my lips are* ~*ed*, *a* ~*ed book to me*, is something of which I have & can get no knowledge; *windows must be* ~*ed up*, e.g. by pasting paper along all crevices; ~ *up tin*, solder it so that air has no access; ~ *pipe* etc., provide it with water~ by means of trap etc.), **9.** Set significant mark on, set apart, destine, decide irrevocably, (*death has* ~*ed her for his own*; *is* ~*ed to or for salvation, damnation*, etc.; *his fate is* ~*ed*); (of Admiralty etc.) officially adopt (design); ‖~*ed pattern*, standard pattern of equipment, clothing, etc., approved for issue by the Admiralty etc. (also fig.). **10.** Confine securely (often *up*); fix (staple etc.) into wall etc. with cement etc. **11.** ~*ing-wax*, mixture of shellac & rosin with turpentine & pigment used for ~s. [vb f. n., f. OF *seel* f. L *sigillum* see SIGILLATE]

seal'er, n. In vbl senses of SEAL¹, ²; esp., ship or man engaged in seal-hunting. [-ER¹]

Seal'yham (-liəm), n. ~ (*terrier*), a breed of terrier. [place]

seam, n., & v.t. **1.** Line of junction between two edges esp. those of two pieces of cloth etc. turned back & sewn together or of boards fitted edge to edge, fissure left by gaping of parallel edges (*ship's* ~*s want caulking*); scar, cicatrice; line of separation between two strata; thin stratum of coal etc. between thicker strata; (Anat.) suture; ~*-lace*, ~*ing-lace*; ~*-presser*, agricultural implement for flattening down furrow-ridges after the plough, also tailors' goose; hence ~LESS a. **2.** v.t. Unite with ~ (rare); mark or score with ~, fissure, or scar (*chiefly* in p.p.; ~*ed with wounds, cracks*, etc.); (Knitting) make ridges in (stocking

etc.; ~*ing-lace*, galloon or other trimming sewn over ~s in upholstery etc. [OE *seam*, cf. Du. *zoom*, G *saum*; cogn. w. SEW]

seam'stress, semp⁴** (sĕms-), n. Sewing-woman. [OE *sēamestre* (prec., -STER) + -ESS¹]

seam⁴**y, a. Showing seams (~ *side*, inside of garment etc. where turning-back of seams is visible, chiefly fig. of the less presentable or attractive aspect of life etc.). [-Y²]

Seanad Eireann (shăn'ădh âi'ən), n. Upper Chamber of the legislature of Eire. [Ir., = senate of Ireland]

se'ance (sā-), *séance* (see AP.), n. Sitting of a society or deliberative body; meeting for exhibition or investigation of spiritualistic phenomena. [F, f. L *sedēre* sit]

sear¹ a. & v.t., **sēre** a. **1.** (Of leaves, flowers, etc., & fig. of age etc.) withered, dried up (*the* ~, *the yellow leaf*, old age). **2.** v.t. Wither up, blast; (rare): scorch surface of esp. with hot iron, cauterize, brand; make callous (*a seared conscience*); *searing-iron*, for cauterizing. [vb f. adj., OE *sēar*, cf. ODu. *sore* dry; cogn. w. Gk *auos* dry, & AUSTERE]

sear²**, See SERE¹.**

search (sĕr-), v.t. & i., & n. **1.** Look or feel or go over (person or his face or pockets, receptacle, place, book) for what may be found or to find something of which presence is suspected, probe (lit. & fig.; ~ *a wound, men's hearts*); * ~ *me!*, int. implying that the speaker does not know (the answer to some inquiry, what to do, etc.); (of shrapnel, gunners) penetrate all recesses of (trench etc.); (arch.) look for, seek out or (still current) *out*; make ~ or investigation (*for* or abs.); (part., of examination etc.) thorough, leaving no loopholes, whence ~'ing**LY¹** adv.; hence ~ER¹(1, 2) n., ~LESS a. (poet.). **2.** n. Act of ~ing, investigation, quest; (*am in* ~ *of*, trying to find; *the* ~ *for* or *of*; *right of* ~ in internat. law, belligerent's right to stop neutral vessel & ~ it for contraband); ~*light*, electric arc-light with concentrated beam that can be turned in any direction for use esp. for discovering hostile aircraft, enemy movements, etc.; ~*party*, persons going out to look for lost or concealed person or thing; ~*warrant*, granted by justice of peace to enter premises of person suspected of concealing stolen property etc. [ME *serchen, cerchen*, f. OF *cerchier* (F *chercher*) f. LL *circare* go round (CIRCUS)]

searching (sĕr-), n. In vbl senses; esp., ~*s of heart*, misgivings caused by guilt or otherwise. [-ING¹]

seas'on (-zn), n., & v.t. & i. **1.** Proper time, favourable opportunity, time at which something is plentiful or in vogue or active, (*a word in* ~, advice given

when it is likely to be taken or is needed; in ~ & out of ~, at all times without selection; oysters, venison, strawberries, are in ~, to be had in good condition & without special difficulty; the holiday ~, any of the times when most people keep holiday. || esp. Christmas, Easter, Whit-suntide, or August; the London, Brighton, Parisian, ~, when society is busy or visitors many there; when society is busy or visitors many there; the theatrical, publishing, cricket, ~; close, open, ~, when hunting etc. of some animal is prohibited, permitted). 2. Period of indefinite or various length (may endure for a ~; a ~ of inaction). || ~ticket, issued at reduced rates for any number of journeys taken, performances attended, etc., within a year, six months, or other period). 3. One of the divisions of the year with distinguishable characteristics of temperature, rainfall, vegetation, etc. (the four ~s, spring, summer, autumn, winter, beginning astronomically each at an equinox or solstice but popularly having different dates in different countries; the dry, rainy, ~, two ~s recognized in the tropics instead of the four of temperate countries); hence ~AL, ~LESS, aa., ~ally² adv., (z-). 4. vb. Bring into efficient or sound condition by habituation, acclimatization, exposure, special preparation, use, or lapse of time, inure, mature, (~ed soldiers, timber, wine). 5. Make palatable or piquant by introduction of salt, condiments, wit, jests, etc., give zest to, flavour, (highly ~ed dishes; conversation ~ed with humour); whence ~ER¹(2), ~ING¹(4), nn., (-z-); temper, moderate, (let mercy ~ justice). 6. Become fit for use by being ~ed. [vb f. n. f OF seson, f. L sationem (serere sat-]

sow, ~ING in LL sense season]

seas'onable (-z-), a. Suitable to, of the kind usual at, the season (esp.~le weather, frost etc. in winter); opportune, meeting the needs of the occasion, (~le aid, counsel, conversation ~ed with humour; dishes); etc.; the ~le arrival of). Hence ~leNESS n., ~ly² adv. [prec., n., -ABLE]

seat, n. & v.t. 1. Thing used, esp. one made, for sitting on, chair, throne, stool, bench, or other sitting-accommodation, (the ~s are uncomfortable), occupation (take a ~, sit down), whence ~ING¹(6) n., ~ER¹ n. (motor-car, aeroplane, etc. with ~ for specified number). 2. Part of chair etc. on which sitter's weight directly rests, part of machine that supports another part (~ of valve, surface etc. on which it slides or works). 3. The buttocks, part of trousers etc. covering them. 4. Site or location, temporary or permanent scene, abiding-place, (of the liver is the ~ of disease; the disease has its~in the liver; the ~ of war is mountainous; seat a ~ in with park or large grounds (has a ~ in

Norfolk; the country ~s of England). 6. Right to sitting-accommodation or to sit as member of board or esp. House of Commons (have taken two ~s for Macbeth; has a ~ on the Board; lost his or the ~, failed to secure re-election to Parliament). 7. Manner of sitting horse, bicycle, etc. (has a good, firm, graceful, ~; hence ~LESS a. 8. v.t. Make sit, place oneself in sitting posture, (p.p) sitting, (took up the child & ~ed him on the bookcase; ~ himself or oneself in state; found him ~ed on a reversed bucket; pray be ~ed, sit down). 9. Fit or provide (church, room, etc. with ~s (is ~ed for 5000); (of room etc.) have ~s for (number). 10. Mend ~ of (chair, trousers). 11. Establish in position, fix in particular place (~ machinery, put it on its supports; a deep~ed disease; the Turks ~ed themselves on the Bosphorus). [yh f. n., f. ON sǣti, cogn. w. SIT]

sebā'ceous (-shus), a. Of tallow or fat, fatty, (~ gland, follicle, duct, secreting or conveying oily matter or ~ humour to lubricate hair & skin). [L sebaceus (sebum tallow), -OUS]

sēbes'ten, -en, n. Plumlike fruit of the tree Cordia Myxa, used medicinally in the East & formerly in Europe. [Arab. sebastān]

sěc., a. (Of wine) dry. [F]

sē'cant, a. & n. (math.). 1. Cutting. 2. n. ~ line, esp. radius of circle produced through end of are to meet tangent to other end, ratio of are to radius, ~ of angle, ratio of greater to less of its containing lines as bounded by a perpendicular to either (abbr. sec; see 60° =2). [L secare cut, -ANT]

sĕcateur (sěkátēr), n. Pair of pruning clippers. [F, irreg. f. L secare cut]

sec'co, n. Tempera-painting. [It.]

secc'otine (-ēn), n., & v.t. A liquid substitute for glue; (v.t.) stick with ~ (on, together, etc.). [P]

sēcēde', v.i. Withdraw formally from membership of some body, esp. a Church or federal or other State. Hence ~ER¹ n. [f. L sēcēdere cess- go)]

secern'ent, a. & n. (physiol.). 1. That secretes or can secrete. 2. n. Secreting organ; drug that promotes secretion. [as SECRETE, -ENT]

sēcě'ssion (-shn), n. Act of seceding (War of S~), American civil war of 1861-5 caused by ~ of eleven Southern States). Hence ~ISM(3), ~IST(2), nn. (-shon-). [f. L secessionem (SECEDE, -ION)]

seclude (-ōōd), v.t. Keep (person, place, esp. oneself) retired or away from company or resort (~e oneself from society; a ~ed spot, life, etc.). Hence ~ed ly² (-ōō-) adv. [f. L sēclūdere -clūs- = claudere shut)]

seclu'sion (-ōozhn), n. Secluding or being secluded, retirement, privacy, avoidance

of intercourse, whence ~IST(2) n.; se-cluded place. [f. med.L seclusionem (prec., -ION)]

sec'ond, a., n., & v.t. **1.** Next after first (*the, a,* ~, often as n. with ellipse of n., esp. = day of month; often further defined, as *the* ~ *man you meet, was the* ~ *to come; in the* ~ *place,* secondly; ~ *to none,* sur-passed by no other; ~ CLASS; ~ *cabin,* class accommodation in passenger-ship; *come in, finish,* ~, *be* ~ *in race;* ~ *floor,* that two floors above ground-floor; ~ *distance,* space in landscape between fore-ground & background). **2.** Other besides one or the first, additional, supplemen-tary, (~ *advent,* return of Christ esp. as preliminary to His expected personal reign on earth, whence ~**ad'ventist** n.; ~ *ballot,* electoral method by which, if the winner on the first ballot has not polled more than half the votes cast, a ~ is taken in which only he & the next candi-date are eligible; ~ *chamber,* upper House in bicameral parliament; ~ *coming,* ~ ad-vent; ~ DIVISION; ~ *nature,* acquired tendency that has become instinctive, as *habit is* ~ *nature, self-sacrifice is now* ~ *nature with him;* ~ SELF; ~ *teeth,* those of adults, cf. MILK[1] *teeth;* ~ *thoughts,* opinion or resolution formed on reconsideration; ~ WIND[1]). **3.** Of secondary kind, sub-ordinate, derived, unoriginal, imitative, metaphorical, (~ *cause,* that is itself caused; ~ CHILDHOOD, COUSIN; ~ *Daniel, Solomon,* etc., person comparable to these; ~ *fiddle, violin,* etc., lower of two employed in score, esp. fig. in *play* ~ *fiddle,* be of only secondary importance, often *to* other person; *at* ~ *hand,* by hearsay, not actual observation etc.; ~ INTENTION, SIGHT[1]). **4.** ~-*best,* of ~ quality (*come off* ~-*best,* get the worst of it); ~ *class,* of ~ of inferior position or quality (|| ~-*class passenger, ticket,* using, entitling to use of ~-class railway-carriage etc.); || ~-*hand,* (of clothes, books, furniture, etc.) bought after use by a previous owner; (of information etc.) taken on another's authority & not got by original observation or research; ~ *lieutenant,* army OFFICER; || ~-*pair back, front,* room on ~ floor in back, front, of house (see PAIR[2]); ~ PERSON (gram.); ~ *rate,* not of superior quality, (of ship, also as n.) rated in ~ class. **5.** n. ~ person etc. in race etc. (*a good* ~, close up); || ~ class in examination for honours, person who takes this. **6.** Another person or thing besides the previously mentioned or principal, whether regarded as next, inferior, or equal. **7.** (Mus.) interval of which the span involves only two alpha-betical names of notes, harmonic com-bination of the two notes thus separated. **8.** pl. Goods of ~ quality, esp. coarse flour or bread made from it. **9.** Supporter chosen by principal in duel or pugilism

to see fair play etc. **10.** Sixtieth part of a MINUTE of time or angular measurement (see etym.), (loosely) short time (*wait a* ~). **11.** ~ *in command,* officer next in rank to commanding officer; ~ *of* EX-CHANGE[1]; ~-*mark,* extra hand in some watches & clocks recording ~s; ~-*mark,* mark (") used with ~figures in state-ments of angular measurement or time (*1° 6' 40"; 1 h. 35' 15"*), or denoting linear inches. **12.** v.t. Supplement, support, back up, (~ *words with deeds; will you* ~ *me if I ask him?*). **13.** (Of member of debating body) give the necessary formal support to (motion etc. or its proposer) by rising with or without speech to show that mover is not isolated, whence ~ER[1] n. **14.** (*pr.* sĭkŏnd'). || (Mil.) put (officer) into temporary retirement with a view to staff or other extra-regimental appoint-ment; || transfer (official) temporarily to another department. [F, f. L *secundus* (*sequi* follow); ~ of time etc. f. F *seconde* f. med.L (*minuta*) *secunda* secondary minute, i.e. minute of a minute]

sec'ondarly, a. & n. **1.** Next below, coming in place or time after, depending on or derived from, of less importance or originality than, what is primary, of the second rank etc., supplementary, of in-ferior rank or importance to, (~y COLOUR[1]; ~y *education, school,* for those who have received elementary or primary instruc-tion but not yet proceeded to university or occupation, esp. boys & girls over 11; ~y *planet,* planet's satellite; (Geol.) = MESOzoic; hence ~LY[2] adv. **2.** n. Deputy or delegate; || minor cathedral dignitary; ~y *planet;* feather growing on second joint of wing; insect's hind wing; ~y *strata.* [f. L *secundarius* (prec., -ARY[1])]

sec'onde, n. Fencing-position. [F (SECOND)]

sec'ondly, adv. In the second place (in enumerations). [-LY[2]]

secon'do, n. Second performer or lower part in duet (cf. PRIMO[1]). [It. (as SECOND)]

sec'recy, n. Keeping of, ability to keep or habit of keeping, secrets (*be promised* ~; *can rely on his* ~; *the gift of* ~; *done with great* ~); tendency to concealment, se-cretiveness; unrevealed state, being kept secret, (*there can be no* ~ *about it; in* ~, in secret). [earlier *secretee, -tie* (toll., -TY)]

sec'ret, a. & n. **1.** (To be) kept private, not (to be) made known or exposed to view, privy, (~ *treaty, understanding, errand, door, passage, sin, process, arrival, influence; the* ~ *parts,* parts of body of which exposure is avoided esp. the geni-tals; || ~-*service money,* applied to Government to securing information etc. without obligation to state details of expenditure), whence ~LY[2] adv.; given to or having faculty of secrecy, secretive, close, reticent, not leaky; (of place etc.) secluded, retired. **2.** n. Thing (to be) kept

~ (*keep a ot the* ~, abstain from revealing it); thing known only to a limited number (*in the* ~, among the number of those allowed to know it; *open* ~, thing ~ only to those who do not trouble to learn it); mystery, thing of which explanation is sought in vain, (*the* ~*s of nature*); true but not generally recognized method for attainment of (*the* ~ *of health, success, happiness, salvation, is temperance, to try again,* etc.); secrecy (only in *in* ~, ~*ly*). (R.-C. Ch.) celebrant's private prayer in Mass. (pl.) ~ parts of body. [F. f. L *secretus* f. *se(cernere cret-* sift) put apart]

secrétaire', n. Escritoire. [F (-crè-), as foll.]

secrétar'iate), n. Office of secretary; members of a government administrative office collectively; administrative office collectively; administrative office building. [f. foll. -ATE¹]

sĕc'rétarў, n. **1.** Person employed by another to assist him in correspondence, literary work, getting information, & other confidential matters (often *private* ~; *unpaid* ~, esp. of person acting as ~ to prominent politician for sake of experience). **2.** Official appointed by society or company or corporation to conduct its correspondence, keep its records, & deal in the first instance with its business (*honorary* ~, amateur hon. sec., unpaid ~ usu. of society not conducted for profit). **3.** Minister in charge of a Government Office (*the S~ of State for Foreign Affairs, War, Air, the Colonies, the Dominions,* (formerly) *now Commonwealth Relations), India* (formerly), *Burma* (formerly), *Scotland,* or the *Home, Foreign, Colonial, Indian,* etc., *S~; under~,* one of two permanent manager of the connected office, the other usu. as representative in other House of the *S~* of State; *ll permanent ~, under~* as above; ~ *of legation* or *embassy,* ambassador's chief subordinate & deputy; *S~ of State,* (in U.S. & Vatican) chief ~ & foreign minister. **4.** Secretaire, escritoire. **5.** (Print.) script type imitating engrossing-hand. **6.** ~ bird, African bird preying on snakes, with crest likened to pen stuck over writer's ear. Hence **secrétār'IAL** a., ~shIP(1) n. [earlier sense *confidant;* f. med.L *secretarius* (SECRET, -ARY¹)]

secréte', v.t. Put (object, person, one-self) into place of concealment; (Physiol.; of gland or organ or the person etc. of which it is part) produce by secretion, whence ~OR¹(2) n., ~ORY a. [f. L SECRETUS]

secré'tion, n. Act of concealing (*the* ~ *of stolen goods*); (Physiol.) process by which special substances are separated from blood or sap for service in the organism or for rejection as excretions, any substance produced by such process, as

saliva, urine, resin. [F (*sécré-*), f. L *secretionem* (SECRET, -ION)]

secré'tive (or sĭkrē-), a. Given to making secrets, intentionally uncommunicative, needlessly reserved. Hence ~NESS n. (or sĭkrē-). [f. SECRET + -IVE]

sĕct, n. Body of persons agreed upon religious doctrines usu. different from those of an established or orthodox Church from which they have separated & usu. having distinctive common worship, nonconformist or other Church as described by opponents, party or faction in a religious body, religious denomination, so ~AR'IAN a. & n., ~AR'IANISM(2, 3) n., ~AR'IANIZE(3) v.t.; followers of a particular philosopher or philosophy or school of thought. [f. L *secta secut-* follow, cf. *sectari* pursue]

sĕcta'rў, n. (arch.). Member of a sect, esp. of the Independents, Presbyterians, etc., at time of the Civil War. [f. F *sectaire* f. med.L *sectarius* (prec. -ARY¹)]

sĕc'tile, a. Able to be cut (esp. of soft minerals such as talc). [F, f. L *sectilis* (*secare sect-* cut, -IL)]

sĕc'tion, n. & v.t. **1.** Separation by cutting. **2.** Part cut off from something, one of the parts into which something is divided arbitrarily or may naturally be considered as divided (e.g. length of cane-stem between two rings), one part of a structure such as boat or wooden house that is made in parts for transportation, one of the minor subdivisions of a book, usu. indicated by the ~*mark* (§; §20), (Mil.) subdivision of the platoon, part of community having separate interests or characteristics (whence ~alISM n., ~alize v.t.), (*microscopic* ~, thin slice cut from something for examination with microscope; *subject falls into five* ~*s; last* ~ *of the journey; conveyed to Tanganyika in* ~*s;* ~*s have been preferred to chapters;* ~ *with all* ~*s & classes*). **3.** Cutting of solid by plane (*conic* ~*s,* study of curves of intersection produced by allowing plane to cut cone at various angles); representation of internal structure of something supposed to be cut thus (*vertical, horizontal, longitudinal, oblique,* etc., ~) according to position chosen for plane). **4.** (Nat. Hist.) group, esp. sub-genus. **5.** The ~ *mark* (see above) used as mark of marginal reference or with or without number to indicate beginning of ~; hence ~AL (-shon-) a., ~alrў² adv. **6.** v.t. Arrange(n, divide into, ~s. [f. L *sectionem* (prec. -ION)]

sĕc'tor, n. **1.** Plane figure enclosed between two radii of circle, ellipse, etc., & the arc cut off by them (~ *of sphere* etc., solid generated by revolution of plane ~ round one radius). **2.** (Mil.) any of the parts into which the space occupied by

opposing armies is distributed according as each lies within the tactical purview of a headquarters at the focus or centre in rear. **3.** Mathematical rule of two flat pieces working on rule-joint with lines representing sines, tangents, etc., radiating from centre of joint for use in making diagrams etc. Hence ~**AL** a. [LL. =sector f. L=cutter (prec., -OR²)]

sectō'rial, a. & n. (Carnivore's tooth) acting with tooth in opposite jaw like scissors (of specialized molar or premolar). [prec., -IAL]

sec'ular, a. & n. **1.** Occurring once in or lasting for an age or a century (~ *games*, ancient Roman festival held at long intervals; ~ *hymn*, composed for this; *the* ~ *bird*, phoenix). **2.** Lasting or going on for ages or an indefinitely long time (opp. *periodical*, *cyclic*; ~ *change*, going on slowly but persistently; ~ *cooling* or *refrigeration*, that of the earth from fluid state; ~ *acceleration*, slow increase in motion of heavenly body; ~ *fame*, enduring; *the* ~ *rivalry between France & England, Church & State*, etc.). **3.** Concerned with the affairs of this world, worldly, not sacred, not monastic, not ecclesiastical, temporal, profane, lay, (~ *affairs, education, music; the* ~ *clergy*, parish priests etc., opp. *regular*; *the* ~ *arm*, hist., civil jurisdiction to which criminal was transferred by ecclesiastical courts for severer punishment); sceptical of religious truth or opposed to religious education etc., whence ~**ISM**(3)n., ~**IST**(2)n. & a., ~**IZE**(3) v.t., ~**IZATION** n.; hence **secula'r**ITY n., ~**LY²** adv. **4.** n. ~ *priest*. (in senses lay, worldly, f. OF *seculer* f. L *saecularis* (*saeculum* generation, age, perh. f. st. of *serere* seed- sow)]

secund', a. (bot. zool.). Arranged on one side only (as flowers in lily-of-the-valley). Hence ~**LY²** adv. [f. L as SECOND]

secun'do. See PRIMO².

secun'dum, L prep. = according to: ~ *art'em*, artificially, also skilfully or scientifically; ~ *natūr'am*, naturally, not artificially; ~ *quid*, in some respect only, not absolutely or generally, with limitations.

secure', a., & v.t. **1.** Untroubled by danger or apprehension (*a quiet* ~ *existence*; *dwell* ~); (arch.) confident or unsuspecting (*a* ~ *fool, dupe* etc.; *the* ~ *hope of salvation*); safe against attack, impregnable; reliable, certain not to fail or give way, (*a* ~ *foundation, fastening, foothold, grasp*); (usu. pred.) in safe keeping, firmly fastened, (*have got him* ~; *are you sure it is* ~?); having sure prospect of, safe against or from, (~ *of victory*; ~ *against assault*; ~ *from interruption*); hence ~**LY²** (-rli) adv. **2.** v.t. Fortify (town, harbour, etc., usu. with wall etc.); confine, enclose, fasten, or close, ~ly (~ *prisoner, valuables, buckle, window*; ~ *vein* etc. in surgery, compress to prevent bleeding; ~ *arms*, Mil., hold rifles with lock in armpit to guard from rain); guarantee, make safe against loss, (*loon~d on landed property* etc.; *how can I* ~ *myself against the consequences?*; *to* ~ *the labourer the or in the fruits of his labour*); succeed in getting, obtain, (esp. something coveted or competed for, as *have* ~*d front places, a first-class cook, the prize, my ends*); hence **secur'**ABLE a. [vb f. a., f. L SE(*curus* f. *cura* care)]

secur'iform, a. (esp. nat. hist.). Axe-shaped. [L *securis* axe (*secare* cut). -i-, -FORM]

secur'ity, n. In adj. senses; also or esp. over-confidence; thing that guards or guarantees (*pride should at least be a* ~ *against meanness*; *in* ~ *for*, as guarantee for); thing deposited or hypothecated as pledge for fulfilment of undertaking or payment of loan to be forfeited in case of failure, document as evidence of loan, certificate of stock, bond, exchequer bill, etc. [f. L *securidadem* (SECURE, -TY)]

sedan', n. (Also ~-*chair*) 17th & 18th c. vehicle seated for one & carried by two chairmen with poles; enclosed motor-car for four or more persons including driver. [?]

sedate', a. (Of person or his manner, look, speech, or writing) tranquil, equable, composed, settled, not impulsive or lively. Hence ~**LY²** adv., ~**NESS** n. [L *sedare* settle (*sedēre* sit), -ATE²]

sed'ative, a. & n. (Drug, influence, etc.) tending to soothe. [f. F *sédatif* as prec. +-IVE]

sē dēfendēn'dō, adv. In self-defence (as plea in cases of homicide). [L]

sed'entary, a. & n. **1.** Sitting (~*y posture, statue*); (of person) inclined by nature or driven by occupation to, (of occupation) involving, (of life etc.) characterized by, much sitting, whence ~i**LY²** adv., ~i**NESS** n.; (Zool. etc.) not migratory, free-swimming, etc., (of spider) lying in wait till prey is in web. **2.** n. ~*y person*; ~*y spider*. [f. F *sédentaire* f. L *sedentarius* (*sedēre* sit, -ENT, -ARY²)]

sed'erunt, n. Sitting of ecclesiastical assembly or other body, or of a company over the wine or in talk (*had a long* ~). [L, = (the following persons) sat]

sedge, n. Kinds of grasslike plant with jointless stems growing in marshes or by waterside, bed of such plants; ~*warbler*, -*wren*, kind of warbler frequenting ~. Hence **sēdg'y²** a. [OE *secg*, cf. LG *segge*; cogn. w. SAW¹, SECTION, prob. w. ref. to swordlike blades]

sedil'ia, n. pl. (sing. *sedil'ē*, rare). Set of usu. three stone seats for priests in S. wall of chancel often canopied & otherwise decorated. [f. L *sedile* seat (*sedēre* sit)]

sed'iment, n. Matter that settles to bottom of liquid, lees, dregs. Hence

~ARY¹ (-ĕrĭ) a. [F (sé-), f. L seditionem (prec., -MENT)]

sedi'tion, n. Agitation directed against the authority of a State's executive, conduct or speech tending to rebellion or breach of public order. So **~ious** (-shus) a., **~iously** adv., **~iousness** n. [OF, f. L seditionem (sed- = SE-, ire it- go, -ION)]

sedu'ce', v.t. Lead astray, tempt into sin or crime, corrupt; persuade (woman) into surrender of chastity, debauch. Hence **~ER¹** n., **~ingLY²** adv., **~e'MENT** (-sm- rare), **~ER¹**, nn. [f. L SEducere duct- lead]

sedu'ction, n. Seducing or being seduced; thing that tends to seduce, tempting or attractive quality of (often with merely playful or no imputation of blame), (the ~ions of a great capital, of beauty, the country, etc.). So **~IVE** a., **~ively²** adv., **~iveness** n. [F (sé-), f. L seductionem (prec., -ION)]

sed'ulous, a. Diligent, persevering, assiduous, (of action etc.) deliberately & consciously continued, painstaking, (with ~ care; ~ flattery, attentions; play the ~ ape, acquire literary style by imitation). Hence or cogn. **~ITY²** adv., **sedū'lITY**, **~NESS**, nn. [L sedulus, -ous]

See¹, v.i. & t. (saw, seen). **1.** Have or exercise the power of discerning objects with the eyes (~s best at night; cannot ~ till the ninth day; ~ into millstone, through brick wall, fig. of preternatural acuteness of intelligence; ~ing is believing, one's own observation is the best evidence; ~ DOUBLE¹ adv.; ~ red, sl., ~ things as blood-coloured, be filled with homicidal fury; ~ing ye shall ~ & shall not perceive; ~ through, fig., not be deceived by, penetrate, detect nature of). **2.** Descry, discern by sight, observe, look at or over, (come where we cannot be ~n; children should be ~n & not heard; please ~ whether it is there, where it is; ~ the light, be born or alive; things ~n, not imaginary etc.; ~ visions, be a seer etc.; ~ things, have hallucinations etc.; ~ stars, have dancing lights before eyes from blow on head; was ~n to fall or falling; saw him fall or falling; ~ the back, be quit of visitor, invader, etc.; cannot ~ my way; ~ one's way to do or to doing, manage, contrive; over house etc., go round examining; ~ the sights, town, etc., as SIGHT-seer; ~ worth ~ing, notable; ~ p. 15 etc., look at, vide; ~ thing done, supervise doing of it). **3.** Learn from the newspaper (I ~ that another speed record was broken yesterday). **4.** Discern mentally, attain to comprehension of, apprehend, exogitate, ascertain by search or inquiry or reflection, consider, (cannot ~ a or the joke, point; do you ~ what I mean?, also ~? ellipt. In same sense colloq.; you ~?, parenth. as you no doubt understand,

also = I must explain; I ~, now that you have explained I understand; I can ~, to the best of my understanding or belief; must ~ what can be done; do not ~ the good, fun, advantage, etc., of doing; do not ~ how to do it; you ~ what it is to have faith); (part. as prep. or conj.) considering or inasmuch as (~ing that course is open to us). **5.** Experience, go through more or less observantly, have presented to one's observation, contemplate & abstain from interference with, (shall never ~ death; have ~n five reigns; will never ~ 50 etc. again, is over that age; ~ life, gain experience of men & manners esp. by dissipation etc.; so perh. well ~n, archi, accomplished in, as intr. p.p.; have ~n the day when, in drawing attention to past state of affairs; never saw such doings; has ~n service, is expert or worn; has ~n better, or its etc. best, days, has declined; you will not ~ me shot like a dog?; ~ person or thing blored or damned, before one will do what he asks or trouble about it; ~ thing through or out, not abandon undertaking before it is completed). **6.** Grant interview or be at home to, pay visit to, secure interview with, (refused to ~ me; can I ~ you on business?; when will you come & ~ us?; must ~ the lawyer, doctor, etc.; can ~ you for five minutes). **7.** Call up picture of, imagine, (cannot ~ myself submitting to it). **8.** Recognize as tolerable, consent willingly to, (do not ~ being made use of. **9.** Escort, conduct, stand by & countenance, (may I ~ you home?; mind you ~ him off the premises; saw him off by the M.carretania; will you ~ me through the difficulty?). **10.** Take view of, have opinion, (~ life,

things, it, differently now; ~ good, consider it right or expedient to do; ~ EYE¹ to eye). **11.** Make provision, take care, give attention, (~ that it is done; ~ you don't catch your foot; ~ to one's business; ~ to it that, take care that). **12.** Make examination, hold inquiry, (must ~ into it). **13.** Reflect, take time to consider, (esp. let me ~), appeal for time to think before making answer or giving particulars, or confession that coming statement may need reconsideration; will ~ about it, form for declining to act at once, & see above). **14.** (Gambling etc.) accept or take on (challenge to bet or competition, person offering it). **15.** ~ bright, the plant clary (w. ref. to use as eye-salve founded on pop. etym. of clary as = clear-eye). Hence sé'ER¹ n. [OE sēon, cf. Du. zien, G sehen]

see², n. What is committed to (archi-bishop, (archi-)episcopal unit, (usu. the ~ of Norwich, Canterbury, Rome, etc.; Holy See, See of Rome, the Papacy or Papal court; cf. BISHOPRIC, DIOCESE; several new

~s were created). [f. OF se(d) f. L sedes seat (sedēre sit)]

seed, n., & v.i. & t. **1.** Flowering plant's unit of reproduction or germ capable of developing into another such plant, (collect.)~s in any quantity esp. as collected for sowing, (its ~s are, ~ is, black; is full of ~; drops its ~s or ~ everywhere; to be kept for or as ~; go, run, to ~, cease flowering as ~ comes, fig. grow shabby etc.). **2.** Male fecundating fluid, semen, milt. **3.** (Bibl.) offspring, progeny, (raise up ~, beget children; the ~ of Abraham, Hebrews). **4.** Germ, prime cause, beginning, (~s of strife, vice; sow the ~s of). Initiate]. **5.** ~-cake, containing whole ~s esp. caraway as flavouring; ~-coral, in small ~like pieces; ~-corn, reserved for ~; ~-drill, DRILL²; ~-eater, kind of bird; ~-fish, ready to spawn; ~-leaf, primary leaf or developed cotyledon; ~-lobe, cotyledon; ~-oysters, young ones for planting; ~-pearl, small; ~-plot, piece of nursery-ground, (fig.) hotbed of sedition etc.; ~s-man, dealer in ~s; ~-time, sowing season; ~-vessel, pericarp; ~-wool, raw cotton before ~s have been removed from fibre; hence ~LESS a. **6.** vb. Go to ~, produce or let fall ~; sprinkle (as) with ~. **7.** Remove ~s from (fruit etc.). **8.** Separate ~ from straw of (flax). (Sport) sort stronger from weaker (competitors) to secure good later matches in tournament. **9.** ~ing-machine, mechanical ~sower; ~ing-plough, with hopper depositing ~ in furrow as made. [OE sǣd, cf. Du. zaad, G saat; cogn. w. SOW¹]

seed'er, n. Seed-drill; apparatus for seeding raisins etc.; || spawning fish. [-ER¹]

seed'ling, n. Plant raised from seed & not from cutting etc.; young tender plant. [-LING¹]

seed'|y, a. Full of seed, going to seed; (of brandy) having flavour attributed to weeds among the vines; (colloq.) shabby-looking, in worn clothes, || out of sorts, feeling ill, whence ~iLY² adv.; ~y-toe, disease of horse's foot. Hence ~iNESS n. [-Y²]

seek, v.t. & i. (sought pr. sawt). **1.** Make search or inquiry for, try or be anxious to find or get, ask (thing of person), aim at, pursue as object, endeavour to do, make for or resort to (place, person, for advice, health, etc.), (what are you ~ing?; ~s a situation as cook, wealth, scope for his energies, etc.; sought of him a sign; ~s my aid; ~s my life or to kill me; came ~ing advice; sought his bed, a fortune-teller, the shore; ~ dead!, order to retriever to find killed game; ~ out, single out for pursuit etc., esp. make special efforts to secure society of). **2.** Search (place, receptacle) through. **3.** Make search or inquiry after or for (sought-after, much in demand, generally desired or courted). **4.** (arch.), Resort in numbers to (person, place),

5. Is etc. to ~ or much to ~, is deficient, wanting, or not yet found (politeness is much to ~ among them; is to ~ in intelligence, grammar; an efficient leader is yet to ~). Hence(-)~ER¹n. [OE sēcan, cf. Du. zoeken, G suchen; cogn. w. L sāgīre perceive, Gk hēgeomai consider]

seel, v.t. (arch.). Close eyes (eye), close eyes of (hawk), by sewing up lids; (fig.) hoodwink. [f. OF siller, c-, (cil eyelid f. L as CILIA)]

seem, v.i. **1.** Have the air or appearance or sensation of being, appear or be apparently perceived or ascertained to do or have done, (be what you ~ to be or ~; the man who ~ed the ringleader; ~s to be tired, a hopeless absurdity; ~s to be a good fellow, saind, etc.; I ~ to be or ~ deaf today, ~ to see him still; do not ~ to, sl., somehow do not, as I do not ~ to like him, fancy it; ~ good to, be adopted as best course by; what ~eth him good, arch., what he chooses; ~s to have died at 35). **2.** Appear to be true or the fact (with antlcipatory it & following that-clause, or parenth. with it only, often with implication of anger or remonstrance; it ~s to me that it will rain, such talk is absurd, we had better make up our minds to it; so we are to get nothing, it ~s; it ~s you were lying; also it should or would ~ in same senses; me~s, ~eth, ~ed, arch., it ~s, ~ed, to me). **3.** (part.). Ostensible, apparent only, apparent but perhaps not real, apparent & perhaps real, (the ~ing & the real; a ~ing friend; with ~ing sincerity; ~ing-virtuous etc., usu. with suggestion of falsity), whence ~'ingLY² adv. [ME seme f. ON (Icel. sēma conform to), cogn. w. SAME]

seem'l|y, a. & adv. **1.** Decent, decorous, becoming; hence ~iNESS n. **2.** adv. (rare). Decorously. [f. ON sœmiligr (sœmr becoming f. sœmr SAME, -LY²)]

seen. See SEE¹.

seep, v.i. Ooze out, trickle, leak; also fig. Hence ~'AGE(3) n. [orig. dial.; cf. OE sipian to soak]

seer¹, n. Prophet, person who sees visions, person of preternatural insight esp. as regards the future. [different. in sense & pronunc. of se'er (SEE¹, -ER¹)]

seer², n. Indian (varying) measure of weight (in most parts = 2 lb.); Indian liquid measure (about one litre). [Hind., ser]

seer³, n. Indian blue-&-white-striped linen. [f. Pers. shīr o shahkar lit., milk & sugar]

seer'-fish, seir- (sēr-), n. Common Indian scombroid fish. [corruption of Port. serra saw]

seer'sucker, n. Indian blue-&-white-striped linen. [f. Pers. shīr o shahkar lit., milk & sugar]

see'saw, n., a., adv., n., & v.i. **1.** With backward & forward motion as of a saw (~ motion; to ~, vacillate or alternate). **2.** n. Game in which two persons sit one at each end of long board balanced on

seethe (-dh), v.t. & i. (~ed; arch. past sod; arch. p.p. SODDEN) Cook (t. & i.) by boiling (arch.; prov. *thou shalt not ~e a kid in his mother's milk*); (fig.) boil, bubble over, be agitated, (the ~*ing waters; India was* ~*ing with discontent;* ~*ing in his brain*). [OE *sēothan*, cf. Du. *zieden*, G *sieden*]

seg'ment, n. & v.t. & i. **1.** Part cut off or separable or marked off as though sepa-rable from the other parts of something (e.g. one ring of a worm, one division of a limb or the skull, one wedge of orange-pulp); (Geom.) part cut off by line or plane from any figure (~ *of circle*, part enclosed between arc & chord; ~ *of sphere*, part cut off by any plane not passing through centre), ~ *of line*, part included between two points; ~-*gear*, ~-*rack*, *-wheel*, with cogs occupying arc of circle only; ~-*saw*, with teeth extending over ~ of circle, also circular saw made up of ~al saw-plates, also saw for cutting into ~al shapes; ~-*valve*, closed by slide turning radially across seat; hence ~AL (-ĕn²), ~ARY¹, aa., ~ARIY² (-ĕn²) adv. **2.** vb. Divide (i. & t.) into ~s, (of embryo) undergo cleavage or divide into parts; (Physiol.) reproduce by gemmation; hence ~A'TION n., (esp.) formation of many cells from a single cell. [f. L *segmentum* (*secare* cut, -MENT)]

seg're·gate¹, v.t. & i. Put apart from the rest, isolate; (Intr.; Crystallog.) separate from a mass & collect about centres or lines of fracture. Hence or cogn. ~A'TION n., ~ATIVE a. [f. L SEgregare f. *grex gregis* flock), -ATE¹]

seg're·gate², a. Set apart, separate, (arch.); (Zool.) simple or solitary, not compound; (Bot.) ~ *polygamy*, inflores-cence in which each floret within common calyx has its own perianth also. [prec., -ATE²]

seiche (sāsh), n. Oscillation of lake waters due to changes in barometric pressure. [Swiss F, etym. dub.]

Seid'litz powd'er (sed-), n. Aperient medicine of two powders mixed separate-ly with water & then poured together giving effervescence. [named as sub-stitute for mineral water of *Seidlitz* in Bohemia]

Sei'di (sā-, or sed), n. Descendant of Mo-hammed through Fatima & Ali. [f. Arab. *seyyid* prince]

seigneur (sānyer'), **seignior** (sān'yor), n. Feudal lord, lord of manor, whence **seigneur'IAL** (sānyōr') a.; *grand seigneur* (see Ap.), person of high rank or whose demeanour etc. correspond to popular ideal of great nobleman; *the Grand Seignior*, = GRAND *Signior*, [F (*-eur*), as SENIOR].

seignior'age (sān'yorïj), n. Something claimed by sovereign or feudal superior as prerogative, esp. Crown's right to percentage on bullion brought to mint for coining. [OF (-*norage*, see prec., -AGE]

seigniory (sān'yori), n. Lordship, sover-eign authority; seignior's domain; muni-cipal council of medieval Italian republic. [f. OF *seignorie* (SEIGNEUR, -Y¹)]

seine (sān, sēn), n., & v.t. & i. **1.** Fishing-net for encircling, with floats at top & weights at bottom edge, & usu. hauled ashore; ~-*gang*, set of men working ~; ~-*needle*, for netting ~s; ~-*roller*, cylinder over which ~ is hauled. **2.** vb. Fish, catch, with ~, whence **sein'er¹** n. [OE *segne*, f. L L (f. Gk *sagēnē*]

seise, seisin. See seiz-.

seis'mic, seis'mal (rare), (sīz-), aa. Of earthquake(s). [Gk *seismos* earthquake (*seiō* shake), -IC]

seis'mo- (-sīz-), comb. form = earth-quake:- ~*ogram*, record given by ~OGRAPH (2) or ~METER or ~OSCOPE, instruments showing force, place, etc., of earthquake; so ~*óg'raphy*, ~*óg'rapher*, ~*ográph'ic(al)*, ~*óm'ĕtry*, ~*omĕt'ric(al)*, ~*oscóp'Ic*; ~*ól'ogy*, ~*ól'ogist*, ~*oló'gical(ly)*. [prec., -o-]

seize (sēz), v.t. & i. **1.** (Law; also *seise*) put in possession of (chiefly in p.p. ~*d* or *seised of*, having in legal possession, &, fig., aware or informed of; often *seised of*...). **2.** Take possession of (contraband goods, documents, etc.) by warrant or legal right, confiscate, impound, attach, whence **seiz'OR²** n. (legal), **seiz'ABLE** a., **3.** Lay hold of forcibly or suddenly, snatch, grasp with hand or mind, com-prehend quickly or clearly, (~ *fortress, sceptre, person by the neck etc., person's hand, opportunity or occasion, an idea, a distinction, the point, the essence of the matter; was* ~*d by apoplexy, with remorse or panic*). **4.** Lay hold eagerly upon (~ *upon a chance or pretext*). **5.** (Naut.) lash, fasten with several turns of cord, (~ *one up*, lash him to rigging for flogging; ~ *ropes together*), whence **seiz'ING**(4) (sēz-) n. (usu. pl.). **6.** (Of machinery) become stuck, jam, from undue heat or friction. [f. OF *seisir, sai-*, give seizin, f. LL *sacire* take possession of (perh. f. Teut. & cogn. w. SET¹)]

seiz'in, seis'in, (sēz-), n. (legal). Posses-sion of land by freehold; act of taking such possession; what is so held. [f. OF *seisine, sai-* (prec., -INE¹)]

seizure (sēzher), n. In vbl senses; esp. sudden attack of apoplexy etc., stroke. [-URE]

se'jant, a. (her.). Sitting with forelegs upright. [AF *seiant* (*seter* var. of OF *seoir* f. L *sedēre* sit, -ANT)]

se'kŏs, n. (archaeol.). Sacred enclosure esp. of ancient temple, adytum. [Gk (sēkos)]

selāch'ian (-k-), n. & a. 1. Any fish of shark or dogfish kind. 2. adj. Of like such fishes. [Gk selakhos shark, -IAN]

sela'dăng (-ahd-), n. Large wild ox of Malay countries; Malayan tapir. [native name]

sel'ah, Hebrew word of unknown meaning retained in Bible version of Psalms & supposed to be a musical direction. [Heb]

sela'mlĭk (-ah-), n. Men's part of Mohammedan house. [Turk.]

sel'dom, adv. (rarely ~er, ~est). Rarely, not often, (~ or never; very ~; not ~). [OE seldan, cf. Du. zelden, G selten; -om by assim. to adv. dat. ending as in whilom]

selĕct', a., & v.t. 1. Chosen for excellence, choice, picked, got by rejection or exclusion of what is inferior; (of society etc.) exclusive, cautious in admitting members; hence ~NESS n.; ~ committee, small parliamentary committee appointed to conduct some special investigation; *~man, one of the annually elected councillors in a New England town(ship). 2. v.t. Pick out as best or most suitable; hence selĕc'tive a. (*~ive service, conscription), selĕc'tively² adv. & L SE(ligere lect-=legere pick)]

selĕc'tion, n. Selecting, choice; what is selected (a fine ~ of summer goods; what is your ~ for the Derby?; the new headmaster is a good ~); (Biol.) sorting out in various ways (natural, sexual, physical, artificial, methodical, unconscious, ~) of the types of animal or plant better fitted to survive or multiply regarded as a factor in evolution. [f. L selectio (prec., -TON)]

selĕctiv'ity, n. (Of wireless receiving-sets etc.) power to respond to any particular wave-length without interference from others. [SELECTIVE + -ITY]

selenite, n. 1. (sĕl'īn-). Sulphate of lime or gypsum occurring as transparent crystals or thin plates; (Chem.) salt of selenium. 2. (S~; sĭlē'). Inhabitant of moon. Hence **selēnit'ic** a. [f. Gk selēnitēs (lithos) moon(-stone) f. Selēnē moon; -ITE¹]

selē'nium, n. Non-metallic element of sulphur-tellurium group, characterized by the fact that its electrical resistance varies with the intensity of the illumination falling on it. Hence **selēn'io** a., **sĕl'enāte²**(3) n., **selēn'ious** (chem.) a. [Gk Selēnē moon, -IUM; named w. ref. to TELLURIUM]

selēn[i]'(o)-, comb. form of Gk selēnē moon; ~ocen'tric, a. (as seen etc. from centre of moon; ~odont, (mammal) with crescent-ridges on crowns of teeth; selēnŏg'RAPHY, study or mapping of the moon, so ~o-

GRAPH(1), selēnŏg'rapher, ~ographic; selēnŏl'ogy, selēnŏl'ogist; ~oʻtrŏp'ic, curving towards the moon (of plant-organs influenced in growth thus), so selēnŏ'tropism, selēnŏ'tropy¹.

Seleu'cid, n. (pl. ~s, ~ae). One of the dynasty founded by Seleucus that governed Syria c. 312–64 B.C. [-ID³]

sĕlf, n. (pl. -ves) & a. 1. Person's or thing's own individuality or essence, person or thing as object of introspection or reflexive action, (the study of the ~; the consciousness of ~; one's former, better, etc., ~, oneself as one formerly was, one's nobler impulses etc.; one's second ~, intimate friend, right-hand man; chiefly his, its, etc., own or very ~ as form of himself etc. when difficult: Caesar's pity'd, etc., ~, rhet. for Caesar himself, pity id-self); one's own interests or pleasure, concentration on these, (cares for nothing but, refers everything to, ~; ~ is a bad guide to happiness); flower of uniform, or of the natural wild, colour; (commerce., vulg., joc.) = myself, yourself, himself, etc. (cheque drawn to ~; a ticket admitting ~ & friend); our noble selves (joc., as toast). 2. adj. (Of colour) uniform, the same throughout,(of flower)~coloured. 3. HER-SELF, HIMSELF, ITSELF, MYSELF, ONE~, OUR-SELF, THEMSELVES, YOURSELF. [OE, cf. Du. zelf, G selbe; etym. dub.; orig. appended, as adj. or in apposition, to pronoun & declined with it, he self, his selfes, dat. him selfum, acc. hine selfne; in ME also adj.=same, very]

sĕlf-, pref. (prec.) expr. direct or indirect reflexive action, automatic or independent action, or sameness; freely used as living pref.; the more established wds are given alphabetically with references to the numbered classes following:

1. Expressing direct reflexive action with part. of any vb that can have self for object, & hence with the p.p. in sense by oneself or itself, & with vbl nn. & adji. & advv. in sense of -self; so from 'I accuse myself' come ~accusing, ~accused, aa., ~accuser, ~accusation, nn., ~accusatory aa., ~accusingly, ~accusatorily, advv.

2. By extension it is prefixed also to any word, whether participle or other vbl deriv. or not, to which self might be attached by a preposition; in a large class (2a) the sense is without external agency or assistance; so from 'acts by or of itself' come ~acting, ~action, ~activity; from 'evident of itself' comes ~evident; in other wds (2b) the relation expressed is various; so from 'conceited about one self' ~conceited & ~conceit, from 'be absorbed, confide, in oneself' ~absorbed, ~absorption, ~confidence, from 'inflict on oneself' ~inflicted, from 'be conscious, despair, of oneself' ~consciousness, ~despair, from 'depend on oneself' ~dependence, from 'righteous as seen by

oneself', ~righteous, from 'seek things for oneself'; ~seeker, 'seeking a. & n. from 'suffice, use violence, to oneself'; etc., l:~ing, suffi'cient, ~violence.

3. To a few nn. & their deriv's. in -ED² self- is prefixed with sense uniform, or natural & not artificially produced.

~aban'donment, ~abase'ment, ~abho'r-rence, ~abnega'tion, 1:~absorbed, ~absorp'tion, 2b:~accusa'tion, ~accus'atory, etc., l:~act'ing, ~action, ~activ'ity, 2a, automatic (action): ~adjust'ing, ~adjust'ment, l, of machinery etc.; automatic (action): ~adjust'ing, admin'istra'tion 1(Psych), re-cognition and assertion of the existence of the conscious self: ~aggran'disement, ~ap-point'ed, ~apprecia'tion, ~appro'val, appro-ba'tion, 1:~ASSER'ting, ~asser'tive, asser'tion, etc., 1:~assumed' 2b, of title etc. not conferred but taken esp. without right:~begot'ten 1, by exag. for not begotten by another; ~betray'al 1:~col-bin'der 2a, reaping-machine with auto-matic arrangement for binding sheaves; ~blind'ed 1:~born 1, as ~begotten:~cen'tredness) 2b, preoccupied with one's own personality or affairs; ~clos'ing 1: ~cock'ing 1, of gun in which hammer is raised by trigger, not by hand; ~col-lect'ed 2b, having or showing presence of mind or composure; ~col'our(ed) 3, of flower or material in which colour is uni-form throughout, or flower whose colour has not been changed by cultivation etc.; ~command' 1, power of controlling one's emotions; ~commun'ion 2b, meditation esp. upon one's own character or conduct; ~compla'cent, ~compla'cency, 2b, of person too easily pleased with himself; ~con-ceit'(ed) 2b:~condemned', ~condemna'tion, 1:~con'fidence, ~con'fident(ly), 2b; ~con'gratula'tion, ~congt'uest, 1; ~con'scious(ness) 2b, esp. of person embar-rassed or made theatrical by inability to forget himself in society, also philos. etc. of man as having faculty of ~con-templation; ~conss'tent, ~consis'tency, 2b; ~con'stituted 1, esp. of person who assumes function without right to it; ~con-suming 1:~contained' 1, not com-municative, also compact or complete in itself; ~contempt', ~contemp'tuous(ly), 1:~content' n., ~conten'ted, 2b:~contradic'tion, ~contradic'tory, ~control', ~convict'ed, 1:~cover'ed, ~crea'tion, 1, as ~begotten, 1:~crit'ical, ~crit'icism, ~cul-ture, ~decei'ving, ~decei'ver, ~deceit', ~decep'tion, 1:~defence' 1 (in ~defence, not by way of aggression; art of ~defence, boxing): ~delu'sion 1; ~DENY'ing (~denying ordinance, resolution of Long Parliament 1645 depriving mem-bers of Parliament of civil & military office; also often used allusively), deni'al, 1:~depen'dent, -ence, 2b; ~deprecia'tion, 1:~despair' 2b; ~destroy-

ing, ~destruc'tion, etc., 1: ~determ'ining, ~determina'tion, etc., 1, esp. w. ref. to free will as opp. fatalism etc., &, in recent Pol., of a nation's right to determine its own policy; ~devel'opment 1: ~devo'tion 1, devoting of oneself to person or cause; ~dis'cipline, ~disparage'ment, ~display', ~dispraise', ~distrust'(ful), ~edu'cated, educa'tion, efface'ment, 1:~elec'tive 1, esp.~proceeding etc. by co-optation; ~esteem' 1: ~ev'ident(ly) 2a, without need of demonstration: ~examina'tion 1:~ex'ecuting 1, not needing legislation etc. to enforce it; ~exis'tent 2a; ~explain' ing, ~explan'atory, 1; ~feed 3, (of stone) unhewn, undressed; ~feed'ing, ~feed'er, 1, (furnace, machine, etc.) that renews its own fuel or material automatically; ~fert'ilizing, ~fert'ilized, 1, ~fert'ile, ~fertil'ity, 2a, of plants fertilized by their own pollen, not from others: ~flat'tering, ~flat'tery, 1:~forget'ful(ness) 1, unselfish-(ness): ~gen'erating 1:~glazed 3, (of porcelain) covered with glaze of one tint; ~glorifica'tion 1; ~go'verning (esp. tha ~go'vernment, 1:~gradua'tion 1, ~heal'ing, ~governed colonies opp. CROWN ~colony), of extra current in that circuit; ~in-duce'tion 2a, (Electr.) (capable of) pro-duction of plant named as enabling patient to do without doctor: ~help' 1, working for oneself without waiting for external aid; ~humilia'tion, ~immola'tion, 1:~import'ant, ~import'ance, 2b, in one's own eyes, & hence pompous etc.; ~imposed' 2b, of task etc.; ~im'potent 2a, opp. ~fertile; ~improve'ment 1:~induc'tive, ~fructify etc.:~mas'tery, mortifica'tion, vulgarity etc.; ~mas'tery, mortifica'tion, 1:~mov'ing, ~motion, ~murd'er(er), 1; ~opin'ion, ~opin'ioned, ~opin'ionated, 2b, of stubborn adherence to one's own opi-nions; ~par'tial, ~partial'ity, 2b, of ~pit'y, ~pleas'ing a. & n., 1:~poised' 2a, portrait (literary or pictorial) made by a person of himself; ~pos'sessed, ~posse'ss-ion, 1, coolness), composed, composure, in agitating circumstances etc.; ~praise' 1 (~praise is no recommendation); ~preserva'tion 1, esp. the primary in-stinct impelling conscious beings to go on living & avoid injury; ~prof'it 2b;

~prop'agating 1; ~propelled' 1; ~rak'er 2a, reaping-machine with set of rakes automatically preparing corn for binding; ~realiza'tion 1, development of one's faculties esp. as ethical first principle; ~record'ing 2a, of scientific instrument etc.; ~regard'ing, ~regard', 1, opp. altruism etc. without the censure implied in selfish etc.; ~re'gistering 2a, as ~recording; ~reg'ulating 1, of machinery; ~reli'ant, -ance, 2b; ~renuncia'tion 1, unselfishness; ~repre'ssion, ~reproach' (ful), 1; ~repug'nant 2b, inconsistent; ~respect'ing, ~respect', ~respect'ful, 1, of person who has & acts up to a standard of worthy conduct; ~restrained', ~restraint', ~reveal'ing a., ~revela'tion, 1; ~rev'erence, rev'erence, 1, rhet., poet., theol., etc., for ~respect etc.; ~right'eous(ness) 2b; ~right'ing a, 1, of boat; ~sac'rificing a., ~sac'rifice, 1, postponing private interest & desires to those of others; ~same 3, emphatic form of same; ~sat'isfied, -satisfac'tion, 2b, conceit(ed); ~scorn 1; ~seek'ing a. & n., ~seek'er, 2b; ~slaught'er 1; ~sown' 1, sprung from seed that has dropped without human agency; ~start'er 2a, electric appliance for starting motor-car without use of crank-handle; ~ste'rile, -steril'ity, 2a, as ~impotent; ~styled' 1, having taken the name without right etc., pretended, would-be; ~suffi'cing 2b, requiring nothing from outside, independent for ~suffi'cient, -ency, 2b, = ~suffi'cing, also & usu. sufficient in one's own opinion, presumptuous; ~sugges'tion 2b, reflexive suggestion of the mesmeric or hypnotic kind; ~support'(ing), ~surren'der, ~sustain'ing, -sustained', -taught', -torment'ing etc., -tor'ture etc., 1; ~vi'dence 2b, esp. suicide; ~will(ed) 2b, as ~opinion etc.; ~wind'ing 1, of clock with automatic winding apparatus; ~wor'ship 1.

self'hood, n. (rare). Personality, separate & conscious existence. [-HOOD]

self'ish, a. Deficient in consideration for others, alive chiefly to personal profit or pleasure, actuated by self-interest, (of ~motives etc.) appealing to self-interest (~ theory of morals, that pursuit of pleasure of one kind or another is the ultimate spring of every action). Hence ~LY² adv., ~NESS n. [-ISH¹]

self'less, a. Oblivious of self, incapable of selfishness. Hence ~NESS n. [-LESS]

self'ness, n. (rare). = SELFHOOD. [-NESS]

Seljuk' (-ōok), n. Member of 11th–13th-c. Mohammedan dynasties in central & Western Asia descended from the chieftain Seljuk. Hence ~IAN a. & n.

sell, v.t. & i. (sōld), & n. 1. Make over or dispose of in exchange for money (of, BUY, BARTER; ~ one's life dearly, fig., kill or wound assailants before being killed; ~ing-race, -handicap, etc., in which winning horse must be sold to highest bidder; ~ one a pup, sl., swindle him), 2. Keep stock of for sale or be a dealer in (do you ~ candles?; bookselling etc.). 3. Betray for money or other reward (~ one's country etc.). 4. Prostitute for money or other consideration, make a matter of corrupt bargaining, (~ justice, oneself, one's honour or chastity). 5. (sl.). Disappoint by not keeping engagement etc., by failing in some way, or by trickery (sold again!, excl. used by or to disappointed person). 6. (Of goods) find purchasers (will never ~; ~ing like wildfire, hot cakes). 7. ~ off, ~ remainder of (goods), clear out stock, at reduced prices; ~ out, leave army by ~ing commission (hist.), ~ (all or some of one's shares in company, whole stock-in-trade, etc., or abs.); ~ up, ~ goods of (debtor) by distress or legal process. 8. n. (colloq.). Disappointment (what a ~!). Hence (-)~ER¹ n. [OE sellan, cf. ON selja, OHG sellen deliver up; cogn. w. SALE]

sellanders. See SALLENDERS.

selt'zer, n. (Also ~ water) medicinal mineral water from Selters in Germany; artificial substitutes for this, soda-water. selt'zogène, n. = GAZOGENE. [f. F selzogène (prec., -GEN)]

sel'vage, -edge, n. Edge of cloth so woven that it cannot unravel, border of different material or finish along edge of cloth intended to be torn off or hidden, list; edge-plate of lock with opening for the bolt. Hence sel'vaGED² (-ijd) a. [f. MDu. selfegge (SELF, EDGE)]

sel'vagee' (-j-), n. Hank of rope-yarn bound together, used as a sling etc. [f. prec.]

selves. See SELF.

seman'tic, a. & n. 1. Relating to meaning in language. 2. n. pl. Branch of philology concerned with meanings. [f. Gk sēmantikos significant (sēmainō mean)]

sem'aphore, n., & v.i. & t. 1. Signalling apparatus of post with oscillating arms, arrangement of lanterns, etc., for use (esp. now on railways) by day or night; military signalling by operator's two arms or two flags. 2. vb. Signal, send, by ~. Hence semaphō'rIC a., semaphō'rI-CALLY adv. [irreg. f. Gk sēma -atos sign, pherō bear]

sēmasiōl'ogy, n. Semantics. So ~o-lō'gical a. [f. Gk sēmasia meaning + -LOGY]

sēmat'ic, a. (nat. hist.). (Of colour or markings in animals) significant, serving to warn off enemies or attract attention. [prec., -IC]

|| sem'blable, a. (arch.). Having semblance of something, seeming. [OF (foll., -ABLE)]

sem'blance, n. What looks like, the outward appearance of, something (put on a ~ of anger; bears the ~ of an angel & the heart of a devil). [F (sembler f. L as SIMULATE, -ANCE)]

semée, semé, (sem'i), a. (her.). Covered with small bearings of indefinite number (e.g. stars, fleurs-de-lis) arranged over field. [F. p.p. of *semer* sow (SEMEN)]

semeiology. Semeiotics. See semio-.

sémé'on, n. Generative fluid of male animals. [L, genit. -*ōnis*, = seed (*serere* sow, -MEN)]

sémès'ter, n. Half-year course or term in German & other universities. [G., f. L *semestris* six-monthly (*sex* six, *mensis* month)]

sém'i-, pref. = L *semi-* half- [cf. Gk *hēmi-*, OE *sām-*, Skr. *sāmi*, perh. cogn. w. SAME], attached to any E wd as living pref. (cf. Br-. Di-.² DEMI-, HEMI-): the more estab-lished or illustrative wds are given alpha-betically w. ref. to the following num-bered senses: **1.** the half of (~*circle*); **2.** on one of two sides (~*detached*), in one of two directions (~*infinite*), in some particular directions (~*vowel*): **3.** little more or better than (~*barbarism*): **4.** rather less than (~*official*), in low degree (~*civilized*), not quite deserving the description (~*smile*); **5.** imperfectly (~*bull*, ~*double*); **6.** occurring, published, etc., each half — or twice in a —(~*annual*; cf. Br- 1e): ~*ann'ual(ly)* 6; ~*barbār'ism*, *-bar'arism*, 3; || ~*brēve* 1, longest note in common use, equalling two minims (see BREVE); ~*circle*, instrument for measuring angles; ~*bull* 5, issued by Pope after election & before coronation with one side of seal left blank; ~*centen'ial* 6, occurring etc. every fifty years; ~*chor'us* 1, half or part of choir, passage given by it; ~*circle*, ~*cir'cular* a., 1, (amounting to, arranged as or in, shaped like) half of a circle or of its circumference, set of ob-jects ranged in or object forming a ~circle, ~*col'on* 4, punctuation-mark (;) now used as the chief stop (the colon being mostly reserved for special uses) of intermediate value between comma & full stop; ~*cyl'inder*, ~*cylin'drical*, 1, (of, forming, etc.) half of a cylinder cut longitudinally; || ~*demi-semiquaver* 1: ~*detached* (-cht) 2, (of house) joined to another by party-wall on one side only; ~*dome* 1, 4, half-dome formed by vertical section, part of structure more or less resembling dome; ~*dou'ble* 5 (Bot.), having outer stamens only converted to petals; ~*fin'al* 4, match or round preceding the final (~*fin'alist*, competitor in this); ~*fluid* a. & n. 4, viscous (fluid); ~*fūsed* 5; ~*in'fidel* 3; ~*in'finite* 2, limited in one direction & stretching to infinity in the other; ~*lun'ar* 1, 4, halfmoon-shaped, crescent shaped, (esp. in anat. names, as ~*lunar* bone, cartilage, fold, fossa, lobe, valve); ~*month'ly* 6; ~*mute* a. & n. 3, (person) practically dumb owing to (esp. congeni-tal) deafness; ~*offi'cial(ly)* 4, esp. of com-munications made to newspapers by official with stipulation that they shall not be formally attributed to him; ~*plume* 2, feather with firm stem but downy web; ~*pré'cious* 4, of stones; || ~*quaver* 1 (Mus.), note half length of quaver ~*ri'gid* 4, (of airship) having a stiffened keel attached to a flexible gas container; ~*smile* 4; ~*tone* 1 (Mus.), smallest interval in normal European music, half length of tone (*diatonic* ~*tone*, occurring in major or minor scale; *chroma-tic* ~*tone*, not so occurring); ~*transpā'rent* 4; ~*trop'ical* 4, (as) of regions bordering on the tropics; ~*tū'bular* 1, shaped like half a tube cut longitudinally; ~*un'cial* a., 2, sound, or letter representing it, intermediate between vowel & con-sonant that is not a vowel (e.g. *l, m, z*); ~*week'ly* 6.

sém'inal, a. Of seed or semen or repro-duction, germinal, reproductive, propa-gative, (~ *fluid*, semen); *in the* ~ *state*, rudimentary still undeveloped; ~ *prin-ciples*, pregnant with consequences. Hence ~*LY²* adv. [F (*sé-*), f. L *seminalis*]

sém'inar'y, n. Place of education (for-merly in pretentious use for *school*, cf. ACADEMY; now rare exc. either fig. as a ~ *of vice* etc., or of R.-C. & esp. Jesuit schools, whence ~*IST* n.). [f. L *seminarium* seed-plot (SEMEN, -ARY¹)]

sémina'tion, n. (bot.). Process, plant's manner, of seeding. [f. L *seminatio* (*semi-nare*, f. SEMEN, -ATION)]

séminif'erous, a. Bearing seed; convey-ing semen. [SEMEN, -i-, -FEROUS]

sémiol'ogy, sémiot'ics, -meio- (-miō-), nn. Branch of pathology concerned with symptoms. [Gk *sēmeion* sign (*sēma* mark), *sēmeiōtikós* of signs, -LOGY, -ICS]

Sem'ite, n. & a. (Member) of any of the races supposed to be descended from Shem (*Gen.* x. 21 foll.) including esp. the Hebrews, Arameans, Phoenicians, Arabs, & Assyrians. So **Sémit'ic** a., (also n. = title languages), ~*ISM*(2, 4), ~*ITIST*(3), nn., ~*ITIZE*(3) v.t. [LL f. Gk *Sēm* Shem, -ITE]

|| **sémm'it**, n. (Sc.). Undershirt. [?]

sémoli'na (-lē-), **sém'ola**, n. Hard grains left after bolting of flour, used in puddings etc. [*-ina* f. It. *semolino* dim. of *semola* bran f. L *simila* fine flour]

sémpiter'nal, a. (Rhet. for) eternal; everlasting, never to end, (rare). [OF (*-nel*), f. L *sempiternus* (*sempi-* for *semper* always, w. suf. as in *aeternus* eternal) +]

sém'pre (-chā), adv. (Mus.). direction. [It.]

sempstress. See SEAMSTRESS.

sén, n. Japanese copper coin, 1/100 of yen.

sénar'ius, n. (pl. -*iī*). Latin verse of six

feet, esp. iambic trimeter. [f. L (versus) senarius (seni six each, -ARY)]

sēn'arỹ, a. On basis of six, by sixes, (~ SCALE, cf. BINARY). [f. L as prec.]

sen'ate, n. 1. State-council of the ancient-Roman republic & empire dividing legislation with the popular assemblies, administration with the magistrates, & judicial power with the equites. 2. Upper & less numerous branch of the legislative assembly in various countries; (rhet.) any legislature or its proceedings or members (the ~, the pulpit, & the press). 3. Governing body of Cambridge Univ. & other institutions; S~-house (esp. at Cambridge). [f. OF senat f. L senatus (sen-old, -ATE[1])]

sen'ator, n. Member of senate. Hence or cogn., sēnatōr'IAL a., sēnatōr'ially[4] adv., ~SHIP n. [OF (-our), f. L senatorem nom., -or (prec., -OR[2])]

sēnā'tus, n. 1. The ancient-Roman senate & people of ancient Rome, abbr. S.P.Q.R., official name of ancient Rome as a State; ~ consult'(um), (hist.) decree of the ~). 2. || (In full academ'icus) governing body in some universities. [L, = SENATE]

send[1], v.t. & i. (sent). 1. Bid go, secure conveyance of, to some destination (destination given by to or other prep. or by ind. obj. of person, or merely implied; ~ message or messenger to; sent me a book; ~ an army; ~ goods all over or round the world; ~ COALS to Newcastle; ~ word, have message taken that, to do, etc.; ~ up or in one's name, an exhibit, etc., enter oneself or it for competition). 2. (Of God, providence, etc.) grant, bestow, inflict, bring about, cause to be so-&-so, (~ rain, a judgement, pestilence; God ~ it may not be so!; ~ him victorious!). 3. Propel, cause to move, (~ bullet; sent his temperature up, down; ~ out or forth leaves, steam, odour). 4. Dismiss, with or without force (with off, away, or compl. or adv. phr.; sent him away, packing, flying, about his business, to the right-about; ~ to COVENTRY; || ~ down, rusticate or expel from university; ~ off letter, parcel, etc., get it off one's own hands & started on its way; ~ off person, witness his departure as sign of respect etc., so ~-off n., also laudatory review of book etc.). 5. Drive mad or crazy. 6. ~ message or letter (send to warn me, depose him, to me to take care; ~ for him, telling him to come; ~ for the book, ordering it as purchase). Hence ~'ER[1] n. [OE sendan, cf. Du. zenden, G senden]

send[2], sc, n., & v.i. (naut.; ~ed). 1. Impulse given by the down slope of a wave (usu. ~ of the sea). 2. v.i.(Of vessel) plunge or pitch owing to this. 3. n. Such plunge. [prob.= prec., with sc- by confusion with descend]

sēn'dal, n. Medieval silken fabric used for rich dresses, pennons, etc. [Rom. (OF, Sp., Port., cendal) prob. ult. f. Gk sindōn fine linen]

sēn'ega, -ka, n. (Drug, used in cough-mixtures, made from root of) American plant called also S~-snake-root. [f. name of Seneca Indians]

senēs'cent, a. Growing old. Hence ~ENCE n. [f. L senescere (SENIOR, -ESCENT)]

sēn'eschal (-shl), n. Steward or major-domo of medieval great house, [OF, f. Teut. (Goth. +sins old, found in sinista oldest, cogn. w. L senex, skalks servant, cf. MARSHAL)]

sēn'green (-n-g-), n. = HOUSE[1]-leek. [OE singrēne evergreen]

sēñor, señora, señorita, (sānyō̃r', -ō̃r'a̤, -orēt'a̤), used of or to Portuguese as SIGNOR etc.

sēn'ile, a. Showing the feebleness etc. of, incident to, old age (~ atrophy, apathy, garrulity, dementia, etc.). Hence senil'ITY n. [f. L senilis (foll., -IL[1])]

sēn'ior, a. & n. 1. More advanced in age or older in standing, superior in age or standing to, of higher or highest degree, (opp. JUNIOR; || the ~ service, Navy as opp. Army; the ~ members of the family, university, etc.; the ~ partner, head of firm; || ~ optime, see WRANGLER; || ~ classic, competitor placed highest in classical tripos when names were arranged according to merit; || ~ WRANGLER; is two years ~ to me), so sēnio'rITY n. 2. (Appended to name for distinction; abbr. sen., sr; opp. JUNIOR) ~ to another of same name (esp. with father's Christian name & surname when son has same, as John Smith sen., or at school with surname when two or more boys have same, as Smith sen.). 3. n. Person of advanced age or comparatively long service etc.; one's elder or superior in length of service, membership, etc. (is my ~); || ~ wrangler,|| classic, or man. [L, = older, old(ish) man, compar. f. st. of senex senis old (man)]

sēniō̃r'ēs priō̃r'ēs (-z, -z), L sentence (= elders first) used in reminding the young of precedence due to seniority.

sēnn'a, n. (Dried leaflets, used as laxative, of) kinds of cassia. [f. Arab, sanā]

sēnn'et, n. (hist.). Signal call on trumpet (in stage-directions of Shaksperian & other plays). [var. of SIGNET]

sēnn'ight (-īt), n. (arch.). Week (esp. Tuesday etc.~). [for seven-night]

sēnn'it, sinn'ĕt, n. (naut.). Braided cordage-made in flat or round or square form from 3-9 cords (common i.e. flat, round, square, ~). [?]

señor, señora, señorita, (sānyō̃r', -ō̃r'a̤, -orēt'a̤), used of or to Spaniards as SIGNOR etc.

Sēnoûs'si(s)'i̤ (-ōō-), n. Religious & political Mohammedan fraternity in N. Africa

named after founder (usu. *the* ~ *as sing.* *or pl.*).

sensā'tion, n. **1.** Consciousness of per- ceiving or seeming to perceive some state or affection of one's body or its parts or senses or of one's mind or its emotions, contents of such consciousness, (*had a* ~ *of giddiness, heat, pain, comfort, thirst, falling, soreness, deafness, bridle, stupid- ity; pressing the eyeball in the dark will produce the* ~ *of light or of seeing light; in search of a new* ~). **2.** Stirring of emotions common to many people or of eager interest among them, display of intense common emotion or interest, literary or other use of material calculated to excite it, (*made a great* ~, *was eagerly discussed or viewed; among the audience, shown by deep silence, applause, or other general manifestation; a three- days'* ~; *what is the latest* ~?; *the essence of melodrama is* ~; *deals largely in* ~). Hence ~AL (-shon-) a., ~ALLY² adv. [f. med. L *sensātio* (L *sens-* SENSE, -ATE², -ION)]

sensā'tionalism (-shon-), n. (Philos.) theory that ideas are derived solely from sensation; pursuit of the sensational in literature, political agitation, etc. So ~IST(2) n. [-ISM]

sense, n. & v.t. [-ISM] **1.** Any of the special bodily faculties by which sensation is roused (*the five* ~s, *sight, hearing, smell, taste, & touch; sixth or muscular* ~, pro- ducing sensation of muscular effort; *has quick, keen,* ~s, *a dull* ~ *of smell*; (pl.) person's sanity or ordinary state of mind regarded as secured by possession of these (*have you taken leave of, are you out of your* ~s?, *are you mad?; he will soon come, we must bring him, to his* ~s, *out of mad folly; frightened out of his* ~s, *into loss of faculties; in one's* ~s, *sane*). **2.** Ability to perceive or feel or to be conscious of the presence or properties of things, sensitiveness of all or any of the ~s, (~-*perception; errors of* ~, *mistakes in perception; the pleasures of* ~, *those depending on sensation; has a great* ~). **3.** Consciousness of (*a* or *the* ~ *of pleasure, pain, gratification, having done well, one's own importance, shame, responsibility; labouring under a* ~ *of wrong, feeling wronged*). **4.** Quick or accurate apprecia- tion of, instinct regarding or insight into specified matter or habit of squaring conduct to such instinct, (~ *of locality, distance, the ridiculous, humour, duty, beauty, gratitude; a keen* ~ *of honour; the religious, moral, aesthetic,* ~). **5.** Prac- tical wisdom, judgement, common ~, conformity to these, (*sound, good,* COM- MON¹, ~; *a man of* ~, *sagacious; had not the* ~ *to do; has plenty of* ~; *what is more* ~ *than to do; now you are talking* ~). **6.** Meaning, way in which word etc. is to be under-

stood, intelligibility or coherence or possession of a meaning, (*in what exact* ~ *we shall rise again is doubtful; the* ~ *of the word is clear; does not make* ~, *is unintel- ligible; in the strict, limited, literal, figura- tive, moral, metaphorical, legal,* PICK- WICKIAN, *proper, full,* ~; *in a vague, in every,* ~; *in a* ~, *provided the statement is taken in a particular way, under limitations, as what you say is true in a* ~; *make* ~ *out of nonsense*). **7.** Prevailing sentiment among a number of people (*take the* ~ *of the meeting,* ascertain this by putting question etc.). **8.** ~-*body,* -*cap- sule,* -*cavity,* -*cell,* -*centre,* -*organ,* parts of animals concerned in producing sensa- tion; hence ~'LESS (-sl-) a. (esp.=foolish; *knock* ~-*less,* stun), ~'lessLY² adv., ~- LESSNESS n. **9.** v.t. Perceive by ~, (esp.) be vaguely aware of. [f. F *sens* f. L *sensus -ūs* (*sentīre sens-* feel)]

sensibi'lity, n. Capacity to feel (*skin lost its* ~); exceptional openness to emotional impressions (*sense &* ~), delicacy of feel- ing, susceptibility (~ *to kindness* etc.), over-sensitiveness; (pl.) susceptibility in various directions. [f. L *sensibilitātem* (foll., -TY)]

sēn'sible, a. Perceptible by the senses (~ *phenomena, things*); great enough to be perceived, appreciable, (*a* ~ *difference, increase*); (arch.) sensitive (*to*); aware, not unmindful, of, (*was* ~ *of his peril, your kindness*); of good sense, reasonable, judicious, moderate, practical, (*a* ~ *man, course, compromise; that is very* ~ *of him*). Hence **sēn'sibLY²** adv. ~NESS n. [F, f. L *sensibilis* (SENSE, -BLE)]

sēn'sitive, a. & n. **1.** Of the senses, sensory (rare); having sensibility (*to,* very open to or acutely affected by external impressions esp. those made by the moods or opinions of others in relation to one- self; (of instrument etc.) readily respond- ing to or recording slight changes of condition (~*ive market,* liable to quick changes of price); (Chem.) readily affected by or responsive to appropriate agent, (Photog.)~*ive paper,* prepared to receive impressions from light, whence ~IZE(3) v.t., ~IZA'TION, ~IZER¹(2), ~OM'ETER, nn.; ~*ive plant,* kind of mimosa whose leaves curve downwards & leaflets fold together at nightfall or when touched; hence ~*ively²* adv., ~*iveness,* ~*iv'ity* (chem., photog., physiol., psychol.) n. **2.** n. (Hypnotism etc.) person~*ive* to hypnotic etc. influences. [f (-*ĕ,* -*ive*), f. med. L *sensitīvus,* irreg. f. L *sentīre sens-* feel, -IVE]

sēnsō'rium, n. (pl. -*ia,* -*s*). The seat of sensation, the brain, brain & spinal cord, or grey matter of these; (Biol.) whole sensory apparatus including nerve-system etc. [LL (foll.)]

sēn'sory, sēnsō'rial, aa. Of the senso- rium or of sensation or the senses. [SENSE, -ORY, -AL]

sen'sual (*or* -shōō), a. Of sense or sensation, sensory, (rare); of or depending on the senses only & not the intellect or spirit, carnal, fleshly, (~ *pleasures*); given to the pursuit of ~ pleasures or gratification of the appetites, self-indulgent in regard to food & sexual enjoyment, voluptuous, licentious; (Philos.) holding the doctrine of, according to, of, sensationalism. Hence or cogn. ~IZE(3) v.t., ~ĪZA'TION, ~ISM(2, 3), ~IST(1, 2), nn., ~LY² adv. [f, LL *sensualis* (SENSE, -AL)]

sen'suous, a. Of, derived from, affecting, the senses (chiefly as substitute, free of implied censure, for prec.; cf. *non-moral* & *immoral*). Hence ~LY² adv., ~NESS n. [SENSE, -OUS]

sent. See SEND¹.

sen'tence, n., & v.t. 1. (arch.) One's opinion for or against some course or conclusion (*my ~ is for war*); pithy saying, briefly expressed thought, maxim, proverb. 2. Verdict (rare); (declaration of) punishment allotted to person condemned in criminal trial (also transf.). 3. (Gram.) set of words complete in itself, containing subject & predicate (either, or part of either or both, occas. omitted by ellipsis), & conveying a statement, question, or command (e.g. *I go, will you go?*, *go* = *go thou or you, what?* = *what did you say?*, *hearts trumps* = *hearts are trumps*; *simple ~*, with single subject & predicate; *compound ~*, with more than one of either or both; *complex ~*, with subordinate clause or clauses), so SENTEN'TIAL (-shl) a. (rare); (loosely in Gram.) usu. *subordinate ~*) subordinate clause. 4. Small amount of speech, usu. that between two full stops often including several grammatical ~s (e.g. *I went & he came*). 5. v.t. State ~ of (condemned criminal, or transf.), declare condemned *to*. [OF, f. L *sententia* (for *sentie-*) f. *sentire* be of opinion, -ENCE]

senten'tious (-shus), a. Aphoristic, pithy, given to the use of maxims, affecting a concise impressive style; (of style) affectedly formal; (of persons) fond of pompous moralizing. Hence ~LY² adv., ~NESS n. [prec., -OUS]

sen'tient (-shi-), a. Having the power of sense-perception. Hence SEN'TIENCE (-shi-) n., ~LY² adv. [L *sentire* feel, -ENT]

sen'timent, n. 1. A mental feeling, the sum of what one feels on some subject, a tendency or view based on or coloured with emotion, such feelings collectively as an influence, (*the ~ of pity, patriotism*; *animated by noble ~s*; *my ~ towards him is a one of respect*; *~ unchecked by reason is a bad guide*; *these are, often joc. them 's, my ~s, that is what I think about it*). 2. (Art) moving quality resulting from artist's sympathetic insight into what is described or depicted. 3. Tendency to be swayed by feeling rather than by reason,

emotional weakness, mawkish tenderness or the display of it, nursing of the emotions, whence **sentimen'tăl** a., **sentimĕn'tălly** adv., **sentimĕntăl'ITY**, **sĕntimĕn'talism**, **sĕntimĕn'talist**, nn., **sĕntimĕn'talize**(2, 3) v.i. & t. 4. (Sense intended to be conveyed by) the expression of some desire or view esp. as formulated for a toast etc. (*the ~ is good though the words are injudicious etc.*; *I call upon Mr Jones for a song or a ~*). [OF (-tement) f. med.L *sentimentum* (L *sentire* feel, -MENT)]

sen'tinel, n., & v.t.(-ll-). 1. Soldier posted to keep guard (cf. foll.); (also ~ *crab*) Indian-Ocean crab with long eye-stalks. 2. v.t. Keep guard over or in (poet.); station ~s at or in (rare). [f. OF *sentinelle* f. It. *sentinella*, both fem. & perh. orig. = watchtower]

sen'try, n. (Term in ordinary mil. use for) sentinel; ~-*board*, platform for ~ outside ship's gangway; ~-*box*, wooden cabin large enough to hold ~ standing; ~-*go*, duty of pacing up & down as ~. [perh. f. *centrinel* 16th-c. var. of prec.]

sĕn'za (-tsa), It. prep.=without, in mus. directions as ~ *tĕm'pō*, not in strict time.

sĕp'al, n. One of the divisions of the calyx, calyx-leaf, (cf. PETAL). [assim. of L *separ* separate to term. of *petal*]

sĕp'arate, a. & n. 1. Physically disconnected, forming a unit that is or may be regarded as apart or by itself, distinct, individual, of individuals, (*from*, or abs.; *the ~ members of the body*; *the ~ volumes may be had singly*; *live in ~ rooms*; *live ~*; *the two questions are essentially ~*; *one is quite ~ from the other*; *~ & corporate or common ownership*; *~ estate*, married woman's property when not subject to husband's control; *~ maintenance*, husband's allowance to wife from whom he lives ~ by consent, cf. *alimony*; hence ~LY² adv., ~NESS n., & (esp. w. ref. to political or ecclesiastical independence, opp. *unionism*, *-ist*) **sĕp'aratism**(3) n., **sĕp'aratist**(2) n. & a. 2. n. Copy of single article etc. reprinted from proceedings of society, magazine, etc., for ~ distribution. [f. L SE(*parare* arrange), -ATE²]

sĕp'ar|āte², v.t. & i. Make separate, sever, disunite, keep (trans) from union or contact, part (t. & i.), secede *from*, go different ways, disperse (intr.); sort or divide (milk, grain, ore, fruit, light, etc.) into constituent parts or sizes, get (cream etc.) by such process for use or rejection, whence ~ĀTOR²(2) n. Hence ~ABLE, ~ATIVE, ~ATORY (rare), aa., ~ABLY² adv., ~ABIL'ITY, ~ableNESS, nn. [as prec., -ATE³]

separā'tion, n. In vbl senses; esp. partial divorce, divorce from bed & board without dissolution of marriage tie (*judicial ~*, ordered by court); ~ *allowance*, that made by soldier etc., with larger Govern-

ment augmentation, to his wife etc. [OF, f. L *separationem* (prec., -ION)]

Sephardi, n. (pl. **-im**), Spanish or Portuguese Jew. [f. Heb. *Sephārdī* (see *Obad.* 20) Spain.]

sẹp'ia, n. Black fluid of CUTTLE-fish; brown pigment prepared from this used in monochrome drawing & in water-colours (*warm* ~, mixture of this with some red), dark reddish-brown colour; (also ~-*drawing*) a drawing done in ~. [L f. Gk (*sē-*), = cuttle (or its ink)]

sẹp'oy, n. Native Indian soldier disciplined by European methods, esp. one of those serving in British-Indian army (~ *mutiny*, = Indian MUTINY). [f. Hind. *si-pāhī* native soldier f. Pers. *sipāhī* soldier (*sipāh* army)]

seps, n. Kinds of skink, serpent lizard. [Gk (*sē-*), f. *sēpō* rot, w. ref. to effect of bite]

sẹp'sis, n. (med.). Putrefaction, contamination from festering wound etc., blood-poisoning. [Gk (*sē-*), as prec.]

sept, n. Clan, esp. in Ireland. [f. OF *septe* var. of SECTE]

sept-, septĕm-, septi-, comb. forms of L *septem* seven (in **sept'an**, (of fever) recurring every 6th (inclus. 7th) day; **septangular**, -*angulār*; heptagon(al); ~**ĕmpar'tite**, divided into 7 parts; ~**enār'ius**, verse (esp. Latin) of 7 feet esp. trochaic tetrameter catalectic; ~**ēn'ary** a. & n., of or involving the number 7, on basis of 7, by sevens; ~**ennial**, set of 7; **septĕnnāte** (Bot.), having 7 parts; ~**ĕnn'āte**, (arrangement made for) period of 7 years; ~**ĕnn'ial(l)y**, of, for, (recurring) every, 7 years; ~**ĕnn'ium** (pl. -*ia*), period of 7 years; ~**ĕtt(e)'**, (composition for) group of 7 singers or players, (transf.) any set of 7; ~**foil**, the plant tormentil, seven-lobed figure esp. as R.-C. symbol of the 7 sacraments; ~**ilāt'eral**, seven-sided; ~**ill'ion** (-lyon), ‖ seventh power of a million, 1 with 42 ciphers; ~**isẏll'able**, word of 7 syllables; **sept'tuple** a. & n. & v.t. & i., sevenfold (amount), multiply by 7, increase sevenfold.

Septĕm'ber, n. Ninth month of year. [OF (-*bre*), f. L *September* (SEPT-, cf. DE-CEMBER)]

Septĕm'brist, n. Participator in the massacres in Paris Sept. 2, 3, 1792. [F (-*e*), see -IST]

sĕp'tĭc, a. & n. (med.). **1.** Of or involving sepsis, putrefying; ~ *tank* (in which sewage is disintegrated through bacterial activity); hence **sĕp'TICALLY** adv., **sĕp**-ti'city n. **2.** n. substance. [f. L f. Gk *sēptikos* (*sēptos* f. *sēpō* rot, -TIC)]

sĕptĭcæm'ia (-sēm-), n. (path.). Blood-poisoning. Hence ~**ic** a. [mod. L, f. Gk *sēptikos* see prec., *haima* blood, & -IA¹]

sĕp'tĭmal, a. Of the number 7. [f. L *septem* seven, after *decimal*]

sĕp'timus. See PRIMUS.]

sĕptuāgēnar'ian, a. & n. (Person) between 69 & 80. [foll., -AN]

sĕptuāgēnar'y, a. Of seventy. [f. L *septuagenarius* (*septuageni* seventy each f. *septuaginta* seventy, -ARY¹)]

Septū'āgēs'ima, n. (Also ~ *Sunday*) Sunday before Sexagesima. [L, = seventieth (day), prob. named loosely as before SEXAGESIMA]

Septū'āgint, n. Greek version of O.T. including the Apocrypha said to have been made about 270 B.C. by seventy-two translators. [f. L *septuaginta* seventy]

sĕp'tum, n. (anat., bot., zool.; pl. -*ta*). Partition such as that between the nostrils or the chambers of a poppy-fruit, dissepiment. [L (also *sae-*), = fence (*sae-pire saept-* f. *saepes* hedge)]

sĕp'tūple. See SEPT-.

sĕpŭlch'ral (-kral), a. Of sepulchre(s) or sepulture (~ *mound*, *pillar*, etc.; *customs*); suggestive of the tomb, funereal, gloomy, dismal, (*a* ~ *look*, *voice*). Hence ~**LY²** adv. [f. L *sepulcralis* (foll., -AL)]

sĕp'ulchre (-ker), n., & v.t. **1.** Tomb esp. cut in rock or built of stone or brick, burial vault or cave, (*the Holy S*~ in which Christ was laid; *whited* ~, hypocrite, w. ref. to *Matt.* xxiii, 27). **2.** v.t. Lay in ~, serve as ~ for. [OF (-cre), f. L *sepulcrum* (*sepelire sepult-*, suf. -crum cf. *simulacrum*)]

sĕp'ulture, n. Burying, putting in the grave. [OF, f. L *sepultura* (prec., -URE)]

sĕquā'cious (-shus), a. (pedant.). Inclined to follow, lacking independence or originality; servile; (of reasoning or argument, logical inference, conclusion. [OF (-lle), as foll.]

sĕquel'a, n. (path.; usu. in pl. -*ae*). Morbid condition or symptom following upon some disease. [L (*sequī* follow)]

sē'quence, n. **1.** Succession, coming after or next, set of things that belong next each other on some principle of order, series without gaps, (*shall follow the* ~ *of events*, *give the facts in historical* ~; *cala-mities fell in rapid* ~; *a* ~ *of clubs* etc. in

cards, three or more next each other in value; *the ~ spring, summer, autumn, winter*). **2.** Mere succession without implication of causality (*~ is related to consequence as post hoc to propter hoc*; *is causality, is a law of nature, anything beyond invariable ~?*), so (& rarely in other senses) **sĕq'uĕnt**, **sĕquĕn'tial** (-shl), aa., **sĕquĕn'tiallʏ²** adv., **sĕquĕn'tiăl'ɪtʏ** (-shĭ-) n. **3.** (Cinemat.) incident in a film story recorded consecutively (corresponding to a scene in a play). **4.** (Mus.) succession of similar melodic phrases at different pitches. **5.** (Gram.) *~ of tenses*, accommodation of subordinate vb in tense or mood according to certain rules to tense or mood of principal vb (e.g. *I should think you were satisfied now*). **6.** (Eccl.) hymn said or sung after the Alleluia that precedes the Gospel (also *prose*). [f. LL *sequentia* (prec., -ENCE)]

sĕquĕn'tĕs, **sĕquĕn'tia** (-shia), (abbr. *seq.* or *seqq.*), L wds = (&) the following lines, (&) what follows, appended (with or without *et* and) to line or page numbers in references. [pl. part. of L *sequi* follow]

sĕquĕs'ter, v.t. & i. **1.** Seclude, isolate, set apart, (*~ oneself from the world*; esp. in p.p.; as *a ~ed life, retreat, cottage*). **2.** (Law; also **sĕquĕs'trᴀᴛᴇ³**, *or* **sĕk'wĭs-**, v.t.) seize temporary possession of (debtor's estate etc.), remove (debatable property) from control of party to lawsuit, (intr.; of widow) renounce concern in husband's estate. **3.** (Also *sequestrate*) confiscate, appropriate; hence *or* cogn. **sĕquĕstrᴀ'ᴛɪᴏɴ**, **sĕq'uĕstrᴀᴛᴏʀ²**, nn., **sĕquĕs'ᴛʀᴀʙʟᴇ** (*or* sĕk'wĭs-) a. [f. LL *sequestrare* commit for safe keeping (L *sequester* trustee, agent, cf. *secus* apart)]

sĕquĕs'trum, n. (pl. *~a*). Piece of dead bone detached from living bone but remaining in place. Hence ~L̄a., **sĕquĕstrŏᴛᴏ'ᴍʏ** n. [neut. of L *sequester* adj. standing apart]

sĕq'uin, n. (Hist.) Venetian gold coin of about 9/4; coinlike ornament of silver, lit. etc., sewn on to dresses etc. [F, f. It. *zecchino* (*zecca* mint f. Arab. *sikka* die)]

sĕquoi'a, n. Kinds of Californian coniferous tree of great height. [f. *Sequoiah*, a Cherokee pers. name]

sĕrac (sĕrăk', n. One of the castellated masses into which a glacier is divided at steep points by the crossing of crevasses (usu. in pl.). [Swiss F, orig. name of a cheese]

sera'glio (-ahlyŏ), n. (pl. *~s*). Walled palace, esp. (hist.) that of Sultan with government offices etc. at Constantinople, harem. [f. It. *serraglio* enclosure (*serrare* lock, f. LL *serare* f. L *sera* bolt f. *serere* join, -aglio=L-*aculum*)]

serai' (-rī, -rahī'), n. =CARAVANSERAI.

serăng', n. (Anglo-Ind.). Native head of a Lascar crew. [f. Pers. *sarhang* commander]

sĕ'raph, n. (pl. *~im*, *~s*). Celestial being; one of the highest ORDER¹ of ninefold celestial hierarchy gifted esp. with love & associated with light, ardour, & purity; (*Order of the S~im*, Swedish order of knighthood). Hence **sĕrăph'ɪᴄ** a. (*the S~ic Doctor*, St Bonaventura), **sĕrăph'icALLY** adv. [earlier *-in* etc. as with CHERUB; f. Heb. *seraphim* pl., seraphs, perh. f. *sāraph* to burn]

sĕ'raphine (-ēn), n. Early form of harmonium. [prec., -INE¹]

sĕ'ruskier', n. Turkish general commanding, commander-in-chief, or minister of war; *~ảt*, war office. [Turk. f. Pers. = head of army]

Sĕrb a. & n., **Sĕrb'ian** a. & n. (Native, language) of Serbia. Hence **Sĕrbo-** comb. form. [f. Serb. *Srb*, *Serb*]

Serbŏn'ian bŏg, n. Treacherous bog formerly existing between delta of Nile & isthmus of Suez, (fig.) situation from which escape is difficult. [Gk *Serbōnis*, -IAN]

sĕre¹, **sear²**, n. Catch of gun-lock holding hammer at half or full cock. [f. OF *serre* lock (*serrer* f. LL *serare* see SERAGLIO)]

sere². See SEAR¹.

serein (serăⁿ'), n. Fine rain falling in tropical climates from cloudless sky. [F]

serĕnă'dᴇ, n. & v.t. **1.** Evening song or instrumental piece sung or played by lover at his lady's window; = foll. **2.** v.t. Sing or play *~e* to; hence *~*ᴇʀ¹ n. [OF, f. It. *serenata* (*sereno* open air f. L as SERENE)] see -ADE]

serĕna'ta (-nah-), n. (mus.). Cantata with pastoral subject; simple form of orchestral or wind-band suite. [It. (prec.)]

serĕndip'ity, n. The faculty of making happy and unexpected discoveries by accident. [coined by Horace Walpole after *The Three Princes of Serendip* (Ceylon), a fairy-tale]

serēne', a. & n., & v.t. **1.** (Of sky, air, etc.) clear & calm, (of sea etc.) unruffled; placid, tranquil, unperturbed, (*a ~ temper, look, life*); !! (sl.) *all ~*, all right; *His, Her, Their, Your, S~ Highness(es)*, abbr. H.S.H., T.S.H., titles used of or to certain continental princes; hence *or* cogn. *~*ʟʏ² adv., **serēn'ity** n. (*your* etc. *Serenity, S~ Highness*). **2.** n. *~* expanse of sky, sea, etc. **3.** v.t. (poet.). Make (sky, brow, etc.)*~*. [f. L *serenus*]

sĕrf, n. Villein, person whose service is attached to the soil & transferred with it (cf. SLAVE); oppressed person, drudge. Hence *~*ᴀɢᴇ, *~*ᴅᴏᴍ, *~*ʜᴏᴏᴅ, nn. [OF, f. L *servus* slave]

serge, n. Kind of durable twilled worsted fabric used esp. for rough wear (*silk ~*, used for tailor's linings). [orig. a silk stuff; OF, f. L *serica* fem. of *sericus* silken (*Sericus* Chinese f. Gk *Sēres* pl. the Chinese, -IC)]

sergeant, **-j-**, (sȧrj'ănt), n. **1.** (Hist.)

lawyer of high rank (~); **2.** (Mil.: ~; abbr. *Sergt*) non-commissioned officer above corporal, employed to teach drill, command small detachments, etc. (~*major* or *regimental* ~; ~*major*, warrant officer assisting adjutant of regiment or battalion; *company* ~*major*, *C.S.M.*, highest non-comd officer of company; *lance*~, corporal acting as ~). **3.** Police officer ranking between inspector & constable (~g-). **4.** *Serjeant-at-arms*, title of certain officials with ceremonial duties; city officials with parliamentary, & *Common Serjeant*, officer of City of London; ~-*fish* (g-), sea-fish with lateral stripes suggesting chevron. Hence ~SHP n. [f. OF *serjant* f. L *servientem* nom. *-ens* servant (L *servire* SERVE, -ENT)]

sergette (-j-), n. Thin serge. [F (SERGE, -ETTE)]

sēr'ial, a. & n. **1.** Of, in, forming, a series, whence ~ITY (-ăl'-) n.; (of story etc.) issued in instalments (~ *rights*, copyright in regard to story etc. so issued), whence ~IST (1) n.; (of publication) periodical; hence ~LY² adv. **2.** n. ~ *story*; a ~ *publication*; periodical. (rare). Hence [SERIES, -AL]

sēr'iate, a. **-ated**, aa., **sēr'iate** v.t. (Arrange) in the form of a series, in orderly sequence. Hence **sēr'iaᵀᴵᴼᴺ** n. [L SERIES, -ATE², ³]

sēr'iatim (*or* sēr-), adv. Point by point, taking one subject etc. after another in regular order, (*consider, examine, discuss, take*, etc., ~). [med. L (prec., *-im* adv term).]

Sēr'ic, a. (rhet. etc.). Chinese. [f. L as SERGE]

sēri'ceous (-shəs), a. (bot., zool.). Of silky or satiny surface, soft & shiny, covered with glossy down. [f. L *sericeus* silken (*sericum* silk, see SERGE), -OUS]

sē'ri(ci)culture, n. Silkworm-breeding, production of raw silk. Hence ~**cûl'tur**Aʟ a., ~**cûl'tur**ɪsᴛ(3) n., (-cher-). [F (-ci-), see prec., -t-, CULTURE]

sēriēm'a, n. Sonorous-voiced Brazilian bird of heron size preying on serpents. [native]

sēr'iēs (-z), n. (pl. same). **1.** Number of things of which each is similar to the preceding or related to it as to its predecessor, sequence, succession, order, row, set, (*a* ~ *of kings, misfortunes*; *in* ~, in ordered succession; ~ *of stamps, coins*, etc., of different denominations but issued at one time, in one reign, etc.; *the whole* ~ *of reform acts*). **2.** (Bibliog.) set of successive issues of a periodical, of articles on one subject or by one writer, etc., esp. (*first, second*, etc., ~) when numbered differently from a preceding or following set, also set of independent books in common *format* or under common title or supervised by common general editor, (*Guesses at Truth, 2nd S*~; *the Men-of-*

Letters ~). **3.** (Geol.) set of strata with common characteristic. **4.** (Chem.) set of elements with common properties or of compounds with common radical. **5.** (Math.) set of terms constituting a progression or having the several values determined by a common relation (*arithmetical, geometrical*, ~, one in ARITHMETICAL, GEOMETRICAL, progression). **6.** (Electr.) set of batteries etc. having positive electrode of each connected with negative of next. **7.** (Zool.) number of connected genera, families, etc. (used vaguely like GROUP). [L (*serere* join, cf. Gk *eirō* bind)]

sē'rif, (now rare) **cē'riph**, n. Cross-line finishing off a stroke of a letter (esp. in SANSERIF; *This has* ~s: *This is sanserif*, [?]

sē'rin, n. Central-Europ. finch related to canary. [F, etym. dub.]

sērinette', n. Instrument for teaching cage-birds to sing; kind of small barrel-organ, musical box, etc. [F (*seriner* teach to sing f. prec., -ETTE)]

sēring'a (-ngg-), n. Brazilian rubber-tree. [F = SYRINGA; kinds of f. LL SYRINGA]

sēriō-cöm'ic, a. Combining the serious & the comic, jocular in intention but counterfeiting seriousness or vice versa. Hence ~ICALLY adv. [-o-]

sēr'ious, a. **1.** Thoughtful, earnest, sober, sedate, responsible, not frivolous or reckless or given to trifling, (*has a* ~ *look, air*; *a* ~ *young person's* ~ *politician*, who gives his best energies to politics; ~ *thought*, real deliberation). **2.** Important, demanding consideration, not to be trifled with, not slight, (*this is a* ~ *matter, question, step*; *made a* ~ *alteration*; *have a* ~ *rival in her affections*; ~ *illness, danger, wound, damage, accident, defeat*). **3.** Sincere, not ironical or jesting in earnest, (*are you* ~?, *do you mean what you say?*; *made a* ~ *attempt*, not merely perfunctory; *& now to be* ~). **4.** Concerned with religion or ethics, not worldly or secular, (~ *subjects* etc.); (now chiefly joc.) religious-minded, with thoughts concentrated on salvation. Hence ~LY² adv. (esp. as preface to sentence implying that irony etc. is now to cease), ~NESS n. [f. LL *seriosus* (L *serius* etym. dub., -OSE-]

sē'riph, n. = SERIF.

serjeant, n. See SERGEANT.

sěr'mon, n., & v.t. **1.** Extempore or written discourse delivered from the pulpit by way of religious instruction or exhortation, similar discourse (often *lay* ~) on religious or moral subject delivered elsewhere or published, (*S*~ *on the Mount*, Matt. v-vii); discourse of Christ reported Matt. v-vii); moral reflection suggested by natural objects etc. (esp. ~*s in stones*); piece of

admonition or reproof, lecture. **2.** v.t. Administer such ~ to. Hence ~ETTE', ~ET¹, nn., ~IZE(1, 2) v.t. & i., ~IZER¹ n. [OF., f. L *sermonem* nom. -o speech]

sēro-, comb. form of SERUM: ~**púr'ulent,** of serum & pus; ~**sanguin'olent,** & blood- **sē'rotine,** n. Chestnut-coloured European bat. [F (*sé-*), f. L *serotinus* late (*serus* late)]

sēröt'inous, a. (bot.). Appearing late in season. [prec., -OUS]

sē'rous, a. Of or like serum, watery, whey-like. Hence **sēros'ITY** n. [f. F *séreux* f. L *serosus* (SERUM, -OUS)]

sẽrp'ent, n. Scaly limbless reptile, snake esp. of the larger kinds. (preferred to SNAKE chiefly in rhet. use; *the, the old, S~,* the devil, w. ref. to *Gen.* iii, *Rev.* xx); (fig.) treacherous person esp. one who worms himself into favour for base ends; *the S~,* a northern constellation; obsolete wind-instrument, a wooden tube with several bends giving powerful note; *Pharaoh's* ~, chemical toy of small cone that when ignited issues in long coiling ~like ash; ~*charmer,* person who charms ~s esp. by music; ~*eater,* SECRETARY-bird; ~*grass,* Alpine bistort; ~*lizard,* seps; ~*s-tongue,* ADDER's-tongue. Hence **sẽrpēn'tiFORM, ~LIKE,** aa. [OF., f. L *serpentem* nom. -ens, orig. part. of *serpere* creep, cogn. w. Gk *herpō* creep, Skr. *sarpa* snake]

sẽrp'entine, a. & n., & v.i. **1.** Of or like a serpent lit. or fig., writhing, coiling, tortuous, sinuous, meandering, cunning, subtle, treacherous, (~ *windings,* of stream, road, etc., or of insinuation; ~ *motion,* ~ *wisdom,* profound, w. ref. to *Matt.* x. 16; ~ *dance,* with sinuous movements enhanced by special drapery; ~ *verse,* line beginning & ending with same word; || *the S~,* ornamental water in Hyde Park). **2.** n. Kinds of hydrous silicate of magnesium, soft rocks of dark green & other colours sometimes mottled or spotted like serpent's skin, taking high polish & used as decorative material; (Skating) wavy line produced by meander of edge. **3.** v.i. Move sinuously, meander. [f. OF *serpentin* a., *serpentine* n., f. L *serpentinus -a* (prec., -INE¹)]

serpi'ginous, a. (path.). Affected with herpes; (of skin-disease etc.) creeping from one part to another. [obs. & med. L *serpigo -ginis* ringworm (L *serpere* creep), -OUS]

sẽrp'ūla, n. (pl. *-ae*). Kinds of marine worm inhabiting beautifully coloured tortuous calcareous tubes often massed together. [LL, = small serpent (L *serpere* creep)]

sẽr'ra, n. (anat., bot., zool.; pl. *-ae*). Serrated organ, structure, or edge. [L, = saw, perh. f. *secare* cut]

sẽrradill'a, n. Kind of clover grown as fodder. [Port., dim. of *serrado* SERRATE a.]

sẽr'rate a., **sẽrrāte'** v.t. (chiefly anat., bot., zool). **1.** Notched like saw. **2.** v.t. (Usu. in p.p. as adj.) provide with saw-like edge. Hence **sẽrrā'TION** n. [f. L SERRA(tus -ATE²), -ATE³]

sẽr'refile, n. (mil.; usu. in pl.). Person in, (pl.) the line of supernumerary & non-commissioned officers in, rear of squadron or troop. [F, f. *serrer* (see SERRIED) + file (see FILE³)]

sẽr'ri, comb. form (-i-) of SERRA: ~*corn,* (beetle) with serrate antennae; ~FEROUS; ~FORM; ~*rost'rate,* (of bird) with serrated bill.

sẽr'ried (-rid), a. (Of ranks of soldiers, rows of trees, etc.) shoulder to shoulder, without gaps, close. [angliciz. of F *serré* p.p. of *serrer* close f. LL *serare* see SERA-GLIO]

sẽr'rulāte (-roo-), **-āted,** aa. Finely serrate, with series of small notches. Hence ~A'TION n. [L *serrula* (SERRA, -ULE), -ATE²]

sẽr'um n. **1.** Whey; thin transparent part of the blood; chyle, lymph, watery animal fluid; (Path.) blood ~ of an animal used as therapeutic agent; ~ *sickness,* skin eruption, fever, etc., sometimes following injections of ~. [L, cf. Gk *oros* whey, Skr. *sara(s)* flowing]

sẽrv'al, n. Tawny black-spotted African tiger-cat. [F, f. Port.]

sẽrv'ant, n. **1.** Person who has undertaken usu. in return for stipulated pay to carry out the orders of an individual or corporate employer, esp. one who lives in house of master or mistress receiving board & lodging & wages & performing domestic duties (*public* ~s, State officials; || *railway company's* ~s, its employees; *civil* ~, member of the civil service; *outdoor* ~, groom, gardener, etc.; *indoor* ~, cook, butler, footman, housemaid, etc.; *domestic,* GENERAL, LIVERY¹, ~; ~*girl,* ~*maid; the* ~ *question,* problem of getting & controlling ~s; *keeps three* ~s; ~*s' hall,* room in which ~s of large household have meals etc.; ~ *of* ~s, lowest of dependants, esp. as title assumed by Popes, transl. of *servus servorum Dei; a good* ~ *but a bad master,* of things that should be treated as means & not ends). **2.** Devoted follower, person willing to serve another, (*a* ~ *of Jesus Christ;* || *your humble* ~, arch. form of ironical courtesy; || *your obedient* ~, epistolary form preceding signature now used only in letters of official type). [OF (SERVE, -ANT)]

sẽrve, v.t. & i., & n. **1.** Be servant (to), do service (to), be useful (to), (~ *two masters,* be divided between two conflicting principles etc.; ~ *the Lord or God,* be religious or virtuous; ~ *the devil,* be wicked; ~ *tables,* postpone spiritual to bodily needs, see *Acts* vi. 2; ~ *at table,* act as waiter; *has* ~*d his generation; would do much* ~ *to you; indiscretion sometimes* ~*s us well;* ~ *in army, navy,* etc., be employed in it; *has* ~*d in India,* been employed

esp. as soldier). **2.** Meet needs (of), avail (t. & i.), suffice (t. & i.), satisfy, perform function, be suitable, do what is required for, (~ *a purpose*; ~*s the purpose of*, take place of, be used as; *to* ~ *some private ends*; ~*s the or one's turn or need*, does well enough; *it will* ~, do what is absolutely necessary; *that excuse will not* ~ *you*; *it* ~*s to show the folly of*; 1 *th.* ~*s him for a week*; *nothing would* ~ *him* or ~ *but absolute submission*; *a sofa serving him*, or *serving*, *as or for a bed*; *as memory* ~*s*, whenever one remembers; *as occasion* ~*s*, when it is favourable; *the tide* ~*s*, is suitable for getting out of harbour etc.; *curate* ~*s two parishes*, does the work; ~ *an office*, go through a tenure of it; ~ *one's apprenticeship*, go through training; ~ *one's time*, hold office for normal period, also ~ *a sentence*; ~ *time*, undergo imprisonment etc.; ~ *gun, battery*, keep it firing; ~ *mare etc.*, cover, esp. of stallion etc. hired for purpose; ~ *rope etc.*, Naut., bind with small cord to save fraying). **3.** Dish up, set (food) on table, set out ready, distribute rations, etc., *out or round*; *was serving a customer with stockings*, *serving in the shop*; *have them* ~*d with soup*; ~ *with the gun, battery, etc.*; = ~ *writ etc. on*; ~ *warrant, writ, notice, process, attachment, etc.*, usu. *on person*, deliver document to person concerned in legally formal manner; ~*s well, badly, etc.*, sends ball to opponent in first stroke of round). **4.** Treat, treat to, pay (person) out, (*has* ~*d me shamefully*; *you may* ~ *me as you will*; ~*d them a trick*, played it on them; ~ or ~*s him right*, excl. of satisfaction at sight of offender getting his deserts; *shall manage to* ~ *him out*, retaliate). **5.** || *Serving-man*, male servant. Hence (-)SERV'ER¹(1, 2) n. (also, Eccl.) celebrant's assistant. **6.** n. (Tennis etc.) first stroke of round, turn for delivering this (*whose* ~ *is it?*). [f. OF *servir* f. L *servire* (*servus* slave)]

Servian¹. Var. of, & till 1914 more usual than, SERBIAN.

Servian², a. (Rom. Ant.). Of Servius Tullius sixth king of Rome (~ *wall*, built by him & still existing in parts). [-AN]

ser'vice¹, n., & v.t. **1.** Being servant, servant's status, master's or mistress's employ, (*girl etc. goes out to*, *goes into*, ~; *a trick, played it on them*; ~ or ~*s him right*, excl. of satisfaction at sight of offender getting his deserts; *shall manage to* ~ *him out*, retaliate). **2.** Meet

work done to meet some general need, persons engaged in it, employment in it, (*the fighting*, or *the*, ~*s*, navy, army, & air force ; *the public* ~*s*; *the* CIVIL, COVENANTED, consular, SECRET, *bus, railway, etc.*, ~; *the preventive* ~, coastguards, custom-house, etc.; *is on* ~, *in active* ~, actually engaged in such employ; *see* ~, have experience esp. as soldier or sailor); (attrib.) of the kind issued to the ~ (*the* ~ *rifle*). **3.** Person's duty or behalf (*at your etc.* ~, ready to obey orders or to be used; || *on his, her, Majesty's* ~, abbr. O.H.M.S., frank stamped on official letters etc.). **4.** What employee or subordinate is bound to, work done or doing of work on behalf of employer, benefit conferred on or exertion made on behalf of someone, expression of willingness to confer or make these, (*personal* ~*s*, feudal obligation or homage etc.; *feudal, menial, willing, YEO-MAN'S,* ~ ; *has a right to my* ~; *asks for my own* ~*s*; *will you do me a* ~ ; *exaggerates his own* ~*s*; *has seen* ~, been much used, shows signs of wear; *my* ~ *to him*, form of respectful message). **5.** Use, assistance, (*can I, will it, be of* ~ *to you?*). **6.** Liturgical form or office appointed for use on some occasion, (whole proceedings, usu. including one such ~ or more, of) single meeting of congregation for worship, musical setting of all or several of the invariable parts of a liturgy adapted for such treatment, (*the communion, burial, etc.*, ~; *special* ~*s*; *divine* ~ usu. without *a*, meeting for worship; *holds four* ~*s every Sunday*; *are you going to* ~ or *the* ~?; ~'*s* ~, setting by particular composer; *full* ~, performed by choir without solos, also ~ *with music* wherever possible; *plain* ~, read or monotoned; ~ *book*, book of offices of a Church, e.g. the Book of Common Prayer; CHURCH¹ ~). **7.** Legal serving of or writ etc. (*personal* ~, delivery with announcement of contents to person affected; ~ *by publication, substitution*, publishing of writ etc. by posting up or insertion in newspaper or by handing to neighbour etc. recognized as sufficient under some conditions; ACCEPT ~). **8.** Set of dishes, plates, etc., required for serving meal (*dinner, dessert, tea, etc.*, ~). **9.** (Traffic) set of trains, steamers, buses, etc., plying at stated times. **10.** (Single act of) serving in tennis etc. Serve, manner of serving, person's turn to serve, (*his* ~ *is weak, terrific*; *whose* ~ *is it?*; ~-*line*, marking limit short of which serve must fall). **11.** Expert assistance or advice given to customers after sale by manufacturers or vendors of an article, e.g. a motor-car or wireless set (so ~ *department, depot, station*). **12.** ~ *area* (Wireless), area round broadcasting station within which satisfactory reception may be expected; ~ *dress*, ordinary uniform (opp. *full dress*); ~ *flat*

(in which domestic ~ and meals are provided by the management); ||~ *hatch* (through which dishes are passed to dining-room); ~ *pipe* (conveying water or gas from the main to a building). **13.** v.t. Maintain or repair (car etc.) after sale. [OF, f. L *servitium* (*servus* slave)]

sĕr'vice², n. (Usu. ~-*tree*) European tree rare in England with leaves like those of mountain-ash & small pear-shaped fruit (~-*berry* or ~) eaten when over-ripe. [f. *serves* pl. of obs. *serve* f. L *sorbum* berry of the *sorbus* taken as sing. & assimilated to prec.]

sĕr'viceable (-sabl), a. Of use, useful, willing & able to render or capable of rendering service, (*a~le person, reminder, instrument*); durable, suited for rough use or ordinary wear rather than for ornament. Hence ~LY² adv., ~leNESS n. [f. OF *serviçable* (SERVICE¹, -ABLE)]

servĭĕtte', n. Table-napkin (chiefly used by & to waiters or servants). [F]

sĕr'vile (or -īl), a. Of, being, a slave or slaves, slave-, (~ *war*, between revolted slaves & their owners; ~ *class, labour*; ~ *letter*, fig, having no other function than to indicate pronunciation of another, as *e* in manageable, saleable); as of a slave, slavish, cringing, mean-spirited, menial, completely dependent, (~ *spirit, creature, submission, flattery, fear, imitation*), so ~LY² adv. ~ *works* (Eccl.), menial or mechanical work forbidden on Sundays and major Church festivals. Hence ~LY² adv. [f. L *servilis* (*servus* slave, -IL)]

sĕr'vitor, n. Attendant, henchman, servant, (arch., poet.); ||(Oxf. Univ.; hist.) undergraduate assisted from college funds & performing menial duties in return, whence ~SHIP n. [OF f. LL (SERVE, -OR²)]

sĕr'vitude, n. Slavery lit. or fig., subjection esp. involuntary to a master, bondage (PENAL ~); (Law) subjection of tenement to an easement. [F, f. LL *servitudo* (*servus* slave, -TUDE)]

Serv-o- Serbo- (see SERBIAN).

sĕr'vo-mō'tor, n. Auxiliary motor, esp. one for operating the reversing gear of a large marine engine. [f. F *servo-moteur* (L *servus* slave)]

sĕs'amé, n. Annual herbaceous tropical & subtropical plant with seeds used in various ways as food & yielding an oil used in salads & as laxative; its seeds; *open ~*, (w. ref. to Arabian-Nights tale) magical or mysterious means of commanding access to what is usu. inaccessible. [f. L f. Gk *sēsamē*]

sĕs'amoid, a. & n. **1.** Shaped like a sesame-seed, nodular, (esp. of small independent bones developed in tendons passing over angular structure, as the knee-pan & the navicular bone). **2.** n. Such bone. [f. L f. Gk *sēsamoeidēs* (prec., -OID)]

sĕs'eli, n. Genus of white-flowered umbelliferous perennial plants. [OF, f. L f. Gk]

sĕs'qui-, L pref. (perh. f. *semis-que* & a half), = one & a half (~*pedalis* a foot & a half long), proportioned as $n+1: 1$ or $3:2$ (~*alter*), proportioned as $n+1: n$ (~*tertius*, ~*quartus*, etc., in ratios $4:3, 5:4$, etc.). Hence in E: **1.** *Chem.* wds (of compounds in which there are three equivalents of the named element to two of others, as ~*ox'ide*, ~*sulph'ide*; ~*bas'ic*, (of salt) with three of base to two of acid. **2.** *Math.* wds expressing ratios as above, ~*al'teral* $3:2$, ~*ter'tial* $4:3$, ~*quar'tal*, ~*quin'tal*, ~*sex'tal*, ~*sep'timal*, ~*octav'al*, ~*non'al* $10:9$. **3.** *Mus.* wds in ~*a* corresponding to the above & expressing intervals ~*al'tera* interval having ratio $2:3$, ~*ter'tia* $3:4$, etc.). **4.** Miscellaneous wds, as ~*centenn'ial*, (of) a one-hundred- & -fiftieth anniversary; ~*ocell'us* (Entom.), large spot with smaller one within it (also ~*alter*); ~*pedal'ian*, (of word) 1½ ft long, cumbrous & pedantic; *sesquip'li-cate*, in ratio of cube to square; ~*tone*, musical interval of 1½ tone.

sess. See CESS.

sĕss'ile, a. (bot., zool.). (Of flower, leaf, eye, etc.) attached directly by the base without stalk or peduncle. [f. L *sessilis* (*sedēre* sess- sit, -IL)]

sĕ'ssion (-shn), n. **1.** Being seated, sitting posture, (rare). **2.** Being assembled esp. for transaction of deliberative or judicial business, single uninterrupted meeting for such purpose, period during which such meetings are held daily or at short or regular intervals, period (usu. one in a year) between meeting & prorogation of Parliament, (*in ~*, sitting or assembled for business, not keeping vacation; *had a long ~*, sat assembled a long time; *autumn ~*, incorrectly for *autumn sitting*, resumption of ... of Parliament occas. required by pressure of business after long adjournment in summer without prorogation); (esp. Sc. & U.S.) university term. **3.** || QUARTER-~s; || BREWSTER-SESSIONS; || *petty ~s*, meeting of two or more justices of the peace for summary trying of certain offences; ||*Court of S~*, supreme civil court of Scotland; KIRK-~. Hence ~AL (-shon-) a. (~*al order*, Parl., valid only for, renewable each, ~). [F, f. L *sessionem* (prec., -ION)]

sĕs'tĕrce, sĕstĕr'tius (-shus; pl. *-iī*), nn. Ancient-Roman silver (& later bronze) coin & money of account = ¼ denarius or 2½ (later 4) asses. [f. L (-*ius*) orig. adj. with *nummus* coin = 2½ (*semistertius* half-third)]

sĕstĕr'tium (-shm), n. (pl. *-ia*). Ancient-Roman money of account = 1000 sesterces. [orig. gen. pl. of prec. after *mīlla* thousands]

sĕstĕt', n. =SEXTET; last six lines of

sonnet. [f. It. *sestetto* (*sesto* f. L *sextus* sixth, -ET²)]

sestína (-tē-), n. Form of rhymed or unrhymed poem with six stanzas of six lines & final triplet, each stanza having same words as the others ending its lines but in different order. [It., (prec., -INE²)]

set, v.t. & i. (set). I. (*set*) I. General senses. 1. Put, lay, stand (trans.), (usu. with adv. or adv] phr.; ~ *load or passenger down, statue up, meat before person, flowers in water, one brick on another, his bow in heaven*; ~ *foot, tread on*; ~ *thing against another, balance, reckon as counterpoise or compensation*; *separate*; ~ *aside, reserve, reject, disregard, annul*; ~ *by, reserve, save for future use*; ~ *stone out, lay it with edge projecting beyond one below*; ~ *person over others or thing, put in authority*). 2. Apply (thing) to (~ *pen to paper, bugle to one's lips, spurs to horse*; ~ *one's hand, seal to document, sign, seal*; ~ *one's hand to task, begin*; ~ *fire to, kindle*; ~ *the axe to, wits to question, try to solve*; ~ *one's wits to another's, argue with him*; ~ SHOULDER *to wheel*). 3. Station, place ready, place or turn in right or specified position or direction, dispose suitably for use or action or display, (~ *a* or naut. *the watch, put sentinels etc. in place*; ~ *chairs, for visitors etc.*; ~ *clock or watch, put hands to right time*; ~ *alarum, provide for its sounding at desired time*; ~ *hen, cause to sit on eggs*; ~ *eggs, place for hen to sit on*; ~ *seed, plant, put in ground*; QUICK-~; ~ *butterfly etc., place as specimen*; ~ *sail, hoist, also = start on voyage*; ~ *trap*; ~ *razor, give even edge to after grinding*; ~ *saw, give teeth alternate outward inclination*; ~ *table, lay for meal*; ~ *up type, arrange it in words etc.*; ~ *up MS., put it in type*; *spaces between words or letters*; ~ *out*, ~ *wide*; ~ *one's cap¹ (at*). 4. Join, attach, fasten, fix, determine, decide, appoint, settle, establish, (~ *leg, bone, joint, put parts into right relative position after fracture or dislocation, also by extension* ~ *fracture or dislocation*; ~ *eyes on, catch sight of*; ~ *diamond etc., insert in gold etc. as frame or foil*; ~ *stake in ground*; *close*-~, *inserted with little interval*; *close*-~, *one's heart, mind, hopes, etc., on, aspire confidently to, expect, be resolved to get*; ~ *one's life on a chance etc. metaph. from gambling, risk it*; ~ *price on, announce salable value of*; ~ *person against another or a thing, fill with settled dislike for*; ~ *price on one's life or head, offer specified reward for his killing*; ~ *store or much by,* & ellipt. ~ *by, estimate or value highly*; ~ *one's face or oneself against, steadfastly oppose or disfavour; countenance*; ~ *one's teeth, clench them,*

esp. fig. = make up one's mind inflexibly; often in p.p.; ~ *smile, eyes, look, purpose*; *of* ~ *purpose, intentionally, deliberately*; ~ *time, pre-arranged*; ~ *scene, built up of more or less solid material*; ~ *piece in fireworks, built up to scaffolding*; ~ *forms of prayers etc., not extempore*; ~ *speech, composed beforehand*; ~ *fair, of weather, fine without sign of breaking*; ~ *on or upon, determined to get, absorbed in*; *baissan is damp so that it dries in waves.* 6. Bring by placing, arranging, impelling, or other means, into specified state (~ *things right, to rights, in order, in motion*; ~ *one's house in order, often fig., introduce reforms*; ~ *question, person's heart, at rest*; ~ *machine going, cask abroach*; ~ *person on his feet* lit. & fig., *box on its end*; ~ *one in the way, direct him*; ~ *one on his way, arch., go part way with him*; ~ *one right, disabuse him of error, correct, often with implication of officiousness etc.*; ~ *one at ease, relieve his anxieties or bashfulness*; ~ *at liberty*, ~ *free, release*; ~ *persons by the ears, at variance or loggerheads, produce quarrel*; ~ *on fire, kindle*; ~ *Thames on* FIRE¹; ~ *movement etc. on foot, start it*; ~ *table, company, laughter*; ~ *teeth on* EDGE¹; ~ *at defiance, defy*; ~ *at naught, mock, disregard.* 7. Make sit down to task, order to apply energies to doing, cause to work, apply oneself to work, (~ *him to dictation, wood-chopping, work at his Greek*; *shall* ~ *to work now, begin*; ~ *oneself to do, make up one's mind, resolve or undertake*). 8. Exhibit or arrange as pattern or as material to be dealt with (often w. ind. obj.; ~, ~ *person, an example, task, problem, etc., to be followed, done, solved, by him*; ~ *the fashion, the pace, determine it by leading*; ~ *paper, draw up questions to be answered by examinees*; ~ *the* TEMPERAMENT *in piano-tuning, arrange intervals of one octave as standard for the rest*). 9. ~ (*to music*), provide (song, words) with music usu. composed for the purpose. 10. Make insertions in (surface) with (gold, field, sky, ~ *with gems, daisies, stars*; *shall* ~ *top of wall with broken glass, this bed with geraniums*). 11. Turn (l. rarely t.) to solid or hard or rigid from liquid or soft or mobile state, curdle, solidify, harden, take shape, develop (usu. intr.) into definiteness or maturity, (*egg* ~*s, by cooking or incubation*; HARD-~; ~ *blossom* ~*s, forms into fruit*; *fruit* ~*s, develops out of blossom*; *tree* ~*s, develops fruit*; *plaster of Paris* ~*s quickly*; *the jelly, a boy's muscles prematurely*; *eyes* ~, *become motionless in death, swoon, etc.*). 12.

Sink below horizon (*sun, moon,* ~*s; the star of Rome, his star, has or is* ~, greatness is departed). **13.** (Of tide, current, etc., & transf. of feelings, customs, etc.) have motion, gather force, sweep along, show or feel tendency, (*tide* ~*s in, out; current* ~*s strongly, eastwards; opinion is* ~*ting against it; his soul* ~ *to grief*). **14.** (Of sporting dog) take rigid attitude indicating presence of game; (of dancers) take position facing partners (often = *to partners*). **15.** (Of garment) adapt itself to figure, sit, *well, badly,* etc. **16.** (In some games) fix the number of points to decide the game. **17.** SHARP[1]. **II.** Special senses with adv. & prepp. **1.** ~ *about,* begin, take steps towards, (task, doing). **2.** ~ *back,* impede or reverse progress of, *(sl.)* cost (person) so much. **3.** ~ *down,* put in writing, attribute to, explain or describe to oneself as. **4.** ~ *forth,* make known, declare, expound, adorn, begin journey or expedition. **5.** ~ *forward,* assist progress of, begin going forward *(arch.)*. **6.** ~ *in,* arise, get vogue, become established, *(reaction, rain,* ~ *in; it* ~ *in to rain*). **7.** ~ *off,* act as adornment or foil to, enhance, make more striking, start (person) laughing or talking on pet subject, begin journey. **8.** ~ *on* adv., ~ *on* prep., urge (dog etc.) to attack (person etc.), attack. **9.** ~ *out,* embellish, demonstrate, exhibit, declare, begin journey. **10.** ~ *to* adv., begin doing something vigorously, esp. (usu. w. pl. subj.) fighting or arguing. **11.** ~ *up,* develop figure of by physical training (esp. in p.p., as *a well* ~ *up man*), start (institution, business, one's carriage, etc.), occasion (soreness etc.), establish (person) or provide with means of establishment or establish oneself in some capacity (*his father, £500,* ~ *him up as a tobacconist or in the tobacco trade; shall* ~ *up as a dentist*), provide adequately *in* or *with* some article (*am* ~ *up with novels for the winter*), place (standard, notice, etc.) in view, begin uttering (protest, shriek, etc.) loudly, propound (theory), restore from ill-health or depression; ~ *up for,* make pretensions to the character of (~*s up for a scholar, moralist,* etc.). **12.** ~ *upon,* = ~ *on* prep. [OE *settan* (*sittan* SIT), cf. Du. *zetten,* G *setzen*]

set³, *n.* **1.** Number of things or persons that belong together as essentially similar or as complementary to each other, group, clique, collection, (~ *of studs, chairs, golf-clubs, fire-irons, lectures;* ~ *of teeth,* natural or artificial; *a fine* ~ *of men, players; toilet* ~*; dinner* ~*; dinner* SERVICE[1]*; toilet* ~, vessels of washhand-stand; *the fast, best, racing, smart, literary, political,* etc., ~, sections of society consorting together; ~ *of quadrilles* or ~, figures that make up a

quadrille; ~ *of dancers* or ~, number needed to make up square dance; *a, the first,* etc., ~ in tennis etc., group of games counting as unit to side that wins more than half the games in ft; ~ *point,* state of a ~ in lawn tennis when one side needs only one more point to win it; ~ *of exchange,* first etc. of EXCHANGE[1] collectively). **2.** Slip or shoot for planting; young fruit just set. **3.** Setting *of* sun or day (poet.). **4.** Way current or wind or opinion etc. sets, drift or tendency of, (*the* ~ *of the current, public feeling,* etc.; *the* ~ *of his mind is towards intolerance*). **5.** Configuration, conformation, habitual posture, way head etc. is set on or carried, way dress etc. sits or flows, (usu. *of; the* ~ *of the hills, his head, the drapery*); warp or bend or displacement caused by continued pressure or position (*has got a* ~ *to the right*). **6.** (Amount of) alternate deflection of saw-teeth. **7.** Last coat of plaster on wall. **8.** Timber frame supporting gallery etc. in coal-mine. **9.** Amount of margin in type causing letters to be close or wide set. **10.** Number of eggs in nest, or number laid before bird sits, clutch. **11.** Setter's pointing in presence of game (often *dead* ~*; make dead* ~ *at,* transf., combine to attack esp. by argument or ridicule). **12.** ∥ Badger's burrow. **13.** Granite paving-block. **14.** Kinds of wrench & punch. **15.** (Theatr.) set scene; (Cinemat.) built-up scene. **16.** (Wireless) receiving apparatus. **17.** ~*back,* reversal or arrest of progress, relapse; ~*down,* rebuff, snub; ~*off,* thing set off against another, thing of which the amount or effect may be deducted from that of another of opposite tendency, counterpoise, counter-claim, thing that embellishes, adornment *to* something, (Archit.) sloping or horizontal member connecting lower and thicker part of wall etc. with upper receding part; ~*out,* commencement or start (esp. *at the first* ~*out*), things set out, equipment, display of food or utensils or goods; ~*to,* combat esp. with fists; ~*up,* erectness or carriage of body, (colloq., orig. U.S.) structure or arrangement of an organization etc. [in 1st sense prob. corrupt. of SECT; in others f. prec.]

sētā′ceous (-shus), *a.* Bristly, having bristles, shaped like a bristle. Hence ~**LY**[2] *adv.* [f. L *sēta* bristle, -ACEOUS]

sētī′ferous, sētī′gerous, sētōse′, aa. Having bristles. [L *sēta* bristle, *setiger, setosus,* bristly, -FEROUS, -GEROUS, -OSE[1]]

sĕt′on, *n.* (surg.). Skein of cotton or the like passed below skin and left with ends protruding to maintain an artificial issue as counter-irritant etc. esp. in veterinary practice; ~*needle,* for inserting ~. [f. med. L *sētonem* silk (L *sēta* bristle)]

set square, *n.* Draughtsman's appliance consisting of a triangular plate of wood or

metal with angles of 90°, 60°, 30°, or of 90°, 45°, 45° for drawing lines at such angles. [p.p. of SET¹]

sett. Arbitrary var. of SET² in some of its more technical senses.

settee¹, n. Long seat, variously constructed to seat more than one person, esp. kind of double arm-chair or short sofa that ends alike for tête-à-tête. [perh. irreg. dim. f. SETTLE¹; see EE]

settee², n. Mediterranean sharp-prowed lateen-sailed vessel with two or three masts. [f. It. *saetta* (*saetta* f. L SAGITTA)]

setter, n. In vbl senses; esp. dog trained to stand rigid on scenting game; ~*on*, instigator. [SET¹, -ER¹; dog named from native habit of crouching on same occasion]

setterwort (-ĕrt), n. A plant, Bear's-foot or Fetid Hellebore. [prob. f. MLG or MHG (*sitro, sutten,* etc., WORT)]

setting, n. In vbl senses; esp.: the music of a song etc.; the metal or other frame in which a gem is set, (transf.) surround of any object regarded as its framework or as accessories setting it off, environment, (Theatr.) way a play is put on the stage, scenery, properties, costumes, etc.; ~*board*, on which entomological specimens are set; ~*box*, in which ~ boards are kept like shelves or drawers; ~*-lotion*, used to damp the hair before it is set; ~*-needle*, needle in wooden handle used in setting specimens; ~*-rule*, brass rule or steel plate with which type is kept temporarily in place as it is set up; ~*stick*, used in setting type. [-ING¹]

settle¹, n. Bench with high back & arms & often with chest from seat to floor. [OE *setl,* cf. Du. *zetel,* G *sessel*; cogn. w. SIT, SET¹]

settle², v.t. & i. **1.** Establish or become established in more or less permanent abode or place or way of life (often *down*), (cause to) sit down or down to stay for some time, cease from wandering or mobility (often *down*), bring to or attain fixity or composure or certainty or clarity or decision, determine, agree upon, decide, appoint, (*he ~d detachments of Jews in Assyria; shall ~ in London, Australia; feet in stirrups, plant's root well down in ground, invalid among pillows, oneself in chair; ~ down to dinner, whist, reading, married life; ~d down to defensive play, a series of skirmishes; marry & ~ down; cannot ~ to work, to anything, of restless or excited or desultory person; bird ~s on tree, alights; stand beer to ~, get clear; let the excitement ~ down; things will soon ~ into shape; must get it ~d up, finally arranged; ~ coffee, soup, with white of egg, clarify; ~ man, expression, etc., melancholy; ~d order, state, habitation, government, weather; a liqueur to ~ one's* dinner, facilitate digestion; *~ the day, fix date; ~ quarrel, question, doubts, etc., pattern of, waverers; what have you, ~d on or ~d; ~ the succession, determine who shall succeed; that ~s the matter or question, there is no more to be said; ~ one's affairs, esp. before death by making will etc.*). **2.** Colonize, establish colonists in, ~ as colonists in, (country). **3.** Subside, sink to bottom of liquid or into lower position, (*the solid matter soon ~s; soil, house, foundation, etc., comes gradually to lower level by gravitation & giving way of what is below; ship ~s, shows loss of buoyancy, tends to sink*). **4.** Deal effectively with, dispose or get rid of, for, pay (bill), pay bill, (*~ person, get rid of his importunity or obstruction by argument or conflict or killing; let us ~ up our accounts or ~ up, draw up & liquidate balance; ~ person's HASH or business; ~d, written on paid bill in acknowledging payment; will you ~ for me?, pay the bill; ~ with creditors, pay their bills or such proportion as they will agree to accept; ~ settling-day, esp. fortnightly account day at Stock Exchange*). **5.** Bestow legally for life on (*I am annuity on him; all his property on his wife; ~d estate, held by tenant for life under specified conditions*). [OE *setlan* (prec.), perh. with admixture of OE *sahtlian* reconcile (*saht* reconciliation)]

settlement (-tlm-), n. In vbl senses; estate(s) in, property to make provision for one or more beneficiaries differing from what would result from simple conveyance or statutory inheritance (*marriage ~*, usu. made in favour of wife, her children, etc.); company of persons aiming at social reform who establish themselves in a poor district to live in intimate relations with the working class; newly settled tract of country, colony; subsidence of building, house, etc.; *Act of S~*, statute of 1701 vesting crown in Sophia of Hanover & her heirs. [-MENT]

settler, n. In vbl senses; esp.: one who settles in new colony, early colonist; (sl.) decisive blow, argument, or event. [-ER¹]

settlor (-awl), n. (Law) conveyance of, or creation of estate(s) in, property to make provision for one or more beneficiaries differing from what would result from simple conveyance or statutory inheritance. [-ER¹]

setwall (-awl), n. Kind of valerian formerly in medicinal use. [AF *zedeuale,* as ZEDOARY]

seven, adj. & n. **1.** One more than six, 7, VII, (often agreeing with understood n., as ~ *of the men, ~ of them, ~ o'clock or ~; one & ~, 1/7 ; & sir, 7/6; twenty ~ or ~-&-twenty, & so on to ~ & ~, ninety; was ~ last birthday, years old; one-&-~-penny etc., costing 1/7 etc.; the ~ SAGES or wise men; the ~ sleepers, Christians who fell asleep in a cave while hiding from Decian persecution & woke 200 years later when Roman Empire was Christian; the ~ VIRTUES, deadly SINS, WONDER's*

of the world; **~-league boots**, giving wearer power of going 7 leagues at each stride; **seventy times ~**, large indefinite number, w. ref. to *Matt.* xviii. 22; **~-gills**, kind of shark; hence **~FOLD** a. & adv., **~TEEN** a. & n. (*sweet ~-teen*, age of girlish beauty), **~TEENTH²** a. & n. **2.** n. The number 7, the symbol 7, set of 7 persons or things esp. 7-pipped card, (*twice ~ is 14; make a large ~; by ~s*, in sets of 7; *at sixes & ~s*). [Aryan: OE *seofon*, cf. Du. *zeven*, G *sieben*, L *septem*, Gk *hepta*, Skr. *saptá*]

sev'enth, a. & n. **1.** Next after sixth (*the, a, ~* often as n. with ellipse of n., esp. *the ~* = 7th day of month; *~ day*, Saturday in Quaker speech & with sects keeping Saturday instead of Sunday on sabbath (*~-day*, sabbatarian; *S~-day Adventists*, a millenarian sect); *in the ~ HEAVEN*, in the greatest happiness or satisfaction; *~ part*, one of 7 equal parts into which thing may be divided). **2.** n. ~ part; (Mus.) interval of which the span involves 7 alphabetical names of notes, harmonic combination of notes thus separated. [-TH²]

sev'enthly, adv. In the 7th place (in enumerations). [-LY²]

sev'enty, a. & n. **1.** Seven times ten, 70, LXX, (*~y-one* etc., or *one-&-~y* etc.; *~y-first* etc.; *the ~y*, the disciples of *Luke* x, also the sanhedrim, also the Septuagint translators; *~y-four* (French 75 mm. gun, 74 guns; *~y-five*, French 75 mm. gun, = *soixante-quinze*; hence **~IETH** a. & n. **2.** n. The number or symbol 70; *the ~ies*, years between 69 & 80 in life or century. [-TY²]

sev'er, v.t. & i. Separate, divide, part, disjoin, disunite, (t. & rarely i.; *~husband & wife, friends or friendship, rope, neck, connexion; sea ~s England & or from France; the rope ~ed under the strain*); cut or break off, take away, (part) from or from whole (*~ed his head, his head from his body; ~ oneself from the Church*); (Law; of person in joint action) conduct case independently of the rest. Hence **~ABLE** a., **~ANCE** n. [f. OF *sever* f. L as SEPARATE]

sev'eral, a. & pron. **1.** Separate, diverse, distinct, individual, respective, (*all of us went their ~ ways*; *each has his ~ ideal*; *went their ~ ways*; *indictment of three counts; the ~ members of the Board; each ~ skip sank her opponent*; *collective & ~ responsibility*, of persons as a body & as individuals; *joint & ~ bond* etc., signed by more than one person, of whom each is liable for whole sum; *~ estate*, not shared with others), whence **~LY²** adv.; a few, more than two but not many, (*have called ~ times; myself & ~ others*). **2,** pron. A moderate number, more than two but not many, of the previously mentioned or implied persons or things

(*~ of you have seen him; went mushroom-hunting & found ~*). [AF, f. med. L *separale* separate thing (L *separ* SEPARATE, -AL)]

sev'erally, n. Individual or unshared tenure of estate etc. (usu. *in ~*). [-TY]

severe', a. (*~er, ~est*). **1.** Austere, strict, harsh, rigorous, unsparing, (*~ look, discipline, critic, master, sentence, inspection, self-control; ~ upon*, hard on). **2.** Violent, vehement, extreme, (*~ weather*, very cold or stormy; *a ~ winter; a ~ attack of gout*). **3.** Trying, making great demands on endurance, energy, skill, or other quality, (*~ test, pain, competition, requirements*). **4.** Unadorned, stripped of all that is unessential, without redundance, restrained, terse, (*~ architecture, beauty, simplicity, style*). **5.** Sarcastic or satirical (*~ remarks; you are pleased to be ~*). Hence or cogn. **~LY²** (-rli) adv. (*leave* or *let ~ly alone*, abstain from dealing with as mark of disapproval, also joc. avoid meddling with as too formidable or difficult), **sevÈr'ITY** n. (w. pl. = treatment). [f. L *severus* etym. dub.]

sev'ery, n. (archit.). Compartment of vaulted ceiling. [f. OF *civoire* f. L CIBORIUM]

Séville o'range (-rinj), n. The bitter orange, used for marmalade. [*Seville*, in Spain]

Sèvres (see Ap.), n. Porcelain made at ~. [*Sèvres*, in France]

sew (sō), v.t. & i. (p.p. *sewn, sewed*, pr. sŏn, sōd). Fasten (material, pieces) by passing thread again & again through holes made with threaded needle or with awl etc. (*~ cloth, calico, leather, pieces together, sheets of book*), whence **~ING¹** (5) (sōi-) n.; make by ~ing (*~ seam, plead, shirt, book, boot, buttonhole*); fasten on or in, attach, by ~ing (*~ on a button; can you~ buttons?; ~ in a patch, band, gusset, rib,* etc.); close up (hole, rent, wound, bag) by ~ing; enclose, fasten up, by ~ing receptacle (*~ up money in a bag; ~ money into one's belt*); *~ one up*, sl., utterly exhaust, (esp. in p.p.) intoxicate; use needle & thread or ~ing-machine; *~ing-machine*, apparatus in which needle is worked mechanically by crank or treadle; *~ing-press*, apparatus for ~ing books. Hence **~er¹** [-ER¹] (sō'er) n. [Aryan: OE *siwian*, OHG *siuwen*, L *suere*, Gk *sassuō* (CATA-), Skr. *sīv*]

sew'age, n., & v.t. **1.** Matter conveyed in sewers; *~farm*, on which ~ is used as manure, esp. one that utilizes & disposes of a town's ~; *~-grass*, grown on ~d land. **2,** v.t. Manure with ~. [prob. formed f. SEWER³ by change of (supposed) -ER¹ f. -AGE]

sewel'lel, n. Small burrowing rodent of the W. coast of U.S. [Amer.-Ind.]

sewer¹. See SEW.

sew'er², n. (hist.). Person who set out table, placed guests, carried & tasted

dishes, etc. [f. AF *assewer* f. OF *assewer* f. L AS(*sidère*=*sedère* sit) sit beside]

sewer³, n. & v.t. 1. Conduit or channel for carrying off the drainage & excrementitious matter of a town, public drain; ~*gas*, foul air of ~s; ~*rat*, common brown or Norway rat; hence ~AGE(¹) n. 2. v.t. Drain, provide, with ~s. [f. OF *seuwiere* sluice f. L EXsequaria (*aqua* water, -ARY¹) cf. EWER]

sewin, -en, n. Kind of salmon trout. [?]

sewn. See SEW.

sex, n. Being male or female or hermaphrodite (*what is its* ~?; *does not matter*; ~ *without distinction of age or* ~), whence ~*less* a., ~'*lessNESS* n.; males or females collectively (*all ranks & both* ~*es*; *the fair, gentle, softer, weaker,* ~, & joc. *the* ~, *women; the sterner* ~, *men; is the fairest of her* ~); (attrib.) arising from difference, or consciousness, of ~ (~ *antagonism,* ~ *instinct,* ~ *urge*); ~ *appeal*, (usu. of women) attractiveness arising from difference of ~. [f. L *sexus* -ūs]

Sex-, sexi-, comb. forms of L *sex* six, in derivatives of L compds & in mod. formations: ~'*angle*, hexagon; ~*ang'ular(ly)*, hexagonal(ly); ~*cent'enary* (or -sē') n., of 600, 600-year, 600th anniversary; ~*di'gitate*, six-fingered; ~*enn'ial(ly)*, lasting, (occurring) once in, six years; ~'*fid* (Bot.), cleft in 6; ~'*foil*, 6-lobed figure in architectural or other decoration, also 6-leaved plant; ~*till'ion* (-lyon), [6th power of a million, 1 with 36 ciphers; ~'*syllab'ic*, ~*tsyll'able*, (word) of 6 syllables; ~'*valent* (Chem.), combining with 6 atoms of hydrogen, having 6 combining equivalents; ~*part'ite*, divided in 6; ~'*tuple* a. & n. & v.t. & i., sixfold (amount), multiply by 6.

sexagenār'ian, a. & n. (Person) between 60 & 70. [L *sexagenarius* (foll.), -AN]

sexāgĕn'ary, a. & n. Of 60, going by sixties. [f. OF *sexagenaire* f. L *sexagenarius* (*sexagenī* 60 each f. *sexaginta* 60, -ARY¹)]

Sexāgĕs'ima, n. (Also ~ *Sunday*) Sunday before Quinquagesima. [L, fem. = 60th (day), prob. named loosely as preceding QUINQUAGESIMA]

sexāgĕs'imal, a. & n. Sixtieth, of 60, proceeding by sixties, (~ *fractions*, or ~s n., with denominations proceeding in ratio of 60 as in the divisions proceeding of the circle & hour). Hence ~ITY² adv. [f. LL *sexagesimalis* f. L *sexagesimus* 60th (*sexaginta* 60), -AL]

sext, sĕxte, n. (eccl.). The office of the 6th hour, recited at noon. [f. fem. *sexta* (*hora* hour) of L *sextus* sixth]

sex'tain, n. Stanza of 6 lines. [L *sextus* sixth, after QUATRAIN]

sex'tan, a. (Of fever etc.) recurring every fifth (by inclusive reckoning sixth) day. [as prec.]

sex'tant, n. Sixth part of circle (obs.); instrument including a graduated ~ used in navigation & surveying for measuring angular distances. [f. L *sextans* -ntis sixth part (*sextus* divide by 6)]

sextet(te)', n. (Musical work for) 6 voices, singers, instruments, or players, in combination; (transit.) any set of 6. [f. L *sextus* sixth, as QUARTE(T)TE)]

sextill'ion (-lyon), n. = SEXILLION. [f. prec. BILLION)]

sĕxtō, n. (pl. ~s). Book formed by folding sheets in six. [f. L *sextus* sixth, as QUARTO]

sextodē'cimō, n. (abbr. 16mo, usu. read sixteenmo). Sheet of paper folded in 16 leaves; this way of folding (in ~); book made by folding thus, [orig. *in* ~ L (IN ⁶, *sextus decimus* 16th)]

sex'ton, n. Officer charged with care of church, its vessels, vestments, & churchyard, & often with duties of parish clerk & grave-digger; ~ *beetle*, kinds that bury carrion to serve as nidus for eggs. [ME *sekesteyn* etc., corrupt. of SACRISTAN]

‖ **sex'tus.** See PRIMUS¹.

sex'ual (or -kshŏo-), a. Of sex, a sex, or the sexes (~ *organs, genitals*; ~ *intercourse* or *commerce*, copulation; ~ *affinity*, mutual attraction of two individuals of opposite sexes; ~ SELECTION; ~ *appetite, indulgence, for, in,* ~ *intercourse*); (Bot.; of classification) based on the distinction of sexes in plants, whence ~ITY² n. Hence ~LY² adv. [f. LL *sexualis* (SEX, -AL)]

sexuālize (or -kshŏo-), v.t. Attribute sex to. Hence ~A'TION n. [-IZE]

Seym (sām), n. The Polish parliament. [Pol.]

sforzando' (-ts-), mus. direction. With sudden emphasis. [It.]

sfu'mato (-ǒomah-), a. (paint.). With indistinct outlines. [It., lit. smoked]

shabb'y, a. Scurvy, contemptible, paltry, dishonourable, (*played me a* ~*y trick*); close-fisted, mean; worn, threadbare, dilapidated, seedy, in bad repair or condition; ~*y-genteel*, retaining traces of better days, attempting to keep up appearances. Hence ~ILY² adv., ~INESS n., ~'ISH²(2) a. [OE *sceab, sceabb*, SCAB, +-Y²]

shăb'rack, n. Cavalry saddlecloth. [f. G *schabracke* of E. Europ. orig.]

shăc'kle, n., & v.t. 1. Metal loop or staple bow of padlock, link closed by bolt for connecting chains etc., coupling link; long link joining pair of wrist or ankle rings, (pl.) fetters, impediments, or restraints (*the* ~s *of convention*); link of insulator for telegraph wires; ~*bolt*, for closing ~, also bolt with ~ at its end; ~*joint*, in some fishes, formed by bony ring passing through hole in other bone. 2. v.t. Fetter, impede, trammel. dub.]

shad, n. Kinds of anadromous deep-bodied fish, of which the American or White S~, is much esteemed as food. [OE *sceadd*, cf. Ir. & Gael. *sgadan*, W *ysgadan*, herrings]

shadd'ock, n. (Fruit, sometimes weighing 15 lb., of) orig. Malayan & Polynesian tree of orange kind. [S~, introducer to W. Indies]

shade[1], n. 1. Comparative darkness (& usu. coolness) caused by interception of light (& usu. heat) rays; (fig.) comparative obscurity (*throw into the* ~, outshine). 2. (Often pl.) place sheltered from sun, cool or sequestered retreat; (pl.) wine vaults; (pl.) darkness of night or evening. 3. Darker part of picture (*without light &* ~, *of paintings, also fig. of descriptions or characters, monotonous, uniformly glaring or sombre*). 4. A colour esp. with regard to its depth or as distinguished from one nearly like it, gradation of colour, material so coloured, (*in all* ~s *of purple*; *I want the same colour in a lighter* ~; *all the* ~s *of opinion, delicate* ~s *of meaning*). 5. Slight difference, small amount, (*am a* ~ *better today*). 6. Unsubstantial or unreal thing (*is the shadow of a* ~, delusive). 7. Soul after death (*spoke with the* ~ *of Homer*; *went down to the* ~s, died, visited Hades; S~ *of Priscian etc.!*, exclamation at blunder, crime, etc., that would have outraged person invoked). 8. Screen excluding or moderating light, heat, etc. (usu. in comb., as SUN, candle, lamp, ~), eye-shield, glass cover for object. Hence ~LESS (-dl-) a. [Aryan: SHADOW; OE *scead, sceadu*, cf. Du. *scha-duw*, G *schatten*, Gk *skotos*]

shade[2], v.t. & i. 1. Screen from excessive light (*~d his eyes with his hand*; *trees* ~ *the street*). 2. Cover, keep off, or moderate power of (luminous object, light) with or as intervening object. 3. Make dark or gloomy (*a sullen look* ~*d his face*). 4. (Drawing) darken (parts of object represented) esp. with parallel pencil lines to give effects of light & shade or gradations of colour, whence **shad'ING**[1](6) n. 5. (Of colour or light, & fig. of opinion, practice, etc.) pass off by degrees into (*or into*) other colour or variety, make (colour etc.) pass thus *into* another. 6. Modify pitch of (organ-pipe). [f. prec.]

shadoof, n. Pole with bucket & counterpoise used esp. in Egypt for raising water. [f. Arab, *shādūf*]

shad'ow[1](-dō), n. 1. Shade (*sitting in the* ~; *the* ~ *of death is on his face*; VALLEY *of the* ~ *of death*; *the* ~s *of night*; *under the* ~ *of misfortune*; dark part of picture, room, etc. 2. Patch of shade, dark figure projected by body that intercepts light rays, this regarded as person's or thing's appendage (*may your* ~ *never grow less!*, nor consequently you thin); (fig.) one's inseparable attendant or companion. 3. Reflected image. 4. Type, faint representation, adumbration, premonition (*coming events cast their* ~ *before*). 5. Slightest trace (*without a* ~ *of doubt*). 6. Unsubstantial or unreal thing & counterfeit (*what* ~s *we are!*; *catch at* ~s *having only the* ~ *of freedom*); phantom ghost, (is but the ~ *of his former self*; *worn to a* ~; *a terrible* ~ *with uplifted hand*). 7. Privacy, obscurity, (*content to live in the* ~). 8. Shelter, protection, (*under the* ~ *of the Almighty*). 9. (Yacht.) kind of light sail used in fair winds. 10. ~*boxing*, (against imaginary opponent as form of training); || ~ CABINET: ~ *factory*, one planned or built for possible reserve production against the emergency of war. ~*stitch*, kind of ladder-work in lace making. Hence ~LESS (-ōl-), ~Y[2] (-ōi) aa., ~NESS (-ōi-) n. [OE *sceadu*, see SHADE[1]]

shad'ow[2] (-dō), v.t. Overspread with shadow (chiefly poet.); set *forth* dimly, in outline, allegorically, or prophetically dog, secretly watch all movements of [f. prec.]

shad'y, a. Giving, situated in, shade, (of actions, conduct, etc.) shunning the light, disreputable, of dubious honesty; *on the ~y side of forty* etc., more than. Hence ~ILY[2] adv., ~INESS n. [-Y[2]]

shaft (-aft-), n. 1. (Slender pole of) lance or spear. 2. Long-bow arrow (often CLOTH-*yard*; ~s fig., as ~s *of satire, ridicule, envy*). 3. Ray of light, bolt or stroke of lightning. 4. Stem, stalk, column between base & capital, one of group of clustered columns, spire, part of chimney above roof, rib of feather, part more or less long & narrow & straight supporting or connecting part(s) of greater thickness etc. 5. (Mech.) large axle, revolving bar transferring force by belts or cogs, whence ~'ING[1](3, 6) n. 6. Handle of tool etc. 7. One of pair of bars between which horse of vehicle is harnessed (~*horse*, so placed, opp. LEADER in tandem). 8. Vertical or inclined excavation giving access to mine; tunnel of blast-furnace; (also *ventilating* ~) upward vent for smoke or bad air from tunnel, drain, etc. [OE *sceaft* spear-shaft, perh. orig. shaven rod (SHAVE, suf. -t), cf. Du. *schacht*, G *schaft*]

shag[1], n. 1. Rough growth or mass of hair etc., whence ~g[2]ED[2](gid) a. (rare); (arch.) long-napped rough cloth. 2. Coarse kind of cut tobacco. [OE *sceacga*, cf. ON *skegg* beard (prob. f. *skaga* jut out)]

shag[2], n. Crested cormorant. [prob. f. prec.]

•**shag'bark**, n. The white hickory. [SHAG[1]]

shagg'y (-g-), a. Hairy, rough-haired; (of hair) coarse, wildly abundant, un-kempt; (of land etc.) overgrown with

forest or rough vegetation; (of trees etc.) with rough branches or twigs; (Bot., Biol.) villous. Hence **~ly²** adv., **~iness** n. (-g-). [-y²]

shagreen, n. Kind of untanned leather made from skin of horse, ass, camel, etc., & usu. dyed green; shark-skin rough with natural papillae used for rasping & polishing. [as CHAGRIN, which is differentiated in sense]

shah, n. King of Persia, padishah. [Pers., =ruler; cf. CHECK¹]

shake¹, v.t. & i. (*shook, shaken*). **1.** Move (thing, person) violently or quickly up & down or to & fro with the hand(s) etc. (*like a terrier shaking a rat*; deserves a *good* shaking¹(1) n.; ~ *hands*, ~ *one by the hand*, clasp right hands with or without shaking at meeting or parting, in reconciliation or congratulation, or over concluded bargain; ~ *one's head*, move it from side to side in refusal, denial, disapproval, or concern over or at or abs.; ~ *with fear, cold, etc.*, tremble violently; ~ *in one's shoes*, tremble with apprehension). **2.** (Make) tremble or rock or vibrate or quiver or oscillate; ~ *one's fist, stick, etc., in person's face or at*, threaten with fist etc.; ~ *a LEG*; ~ *feet, look, ~y*). **3.** Agitate, shock, disturb, (*was much ~n by, with, at, the news*; ~ *him out of his lethargy; shook the earth shook; hand ~s, is unsteady, (~ the house; wave, jolt, jar, brandish, (~ the house; tremble with apprehension*). **4.** Weaken, impair, make less convincing or firm or stable or courageous, (*the firm's credit was ~n; shook the witness's evidence; his faith in Providence was greatly ~n; the ranks were shaken (~ not broken*). **5.** (Of voice, musical note, singer, etc.) make tremulous sounds, change pitch or power with rapid alternations, trill, (*his voice shook with emotion; must learn to ~*). **6.** (imperat.: colloq., chiefly U.S.), ~ *hands*. **7.** ~ *down*, fetch or send down by shaking (fruit from tree; straw or blankets etc. on floor for bed, whence **~'down** n.; grain etc. in vessel into least compass), (intr.) become compact, get comfortably settled or into harmony with associates or circumstances; ~ *off*, get rid of (dust etc. & fig. undesirable companion or worry) by shaking (~ *out of the DUST¹ from one's feet*; ~ *out*, empty (vessel, garment, etc.) of contents or dust, (contents) from vessel etc., spread or open (sail, flag, reel); ~ *up*, mix (ingredients), restore (pillow etc.) to shape, by shaking, rouse from stagnant or lethargic or convention-ridden state. Hence **shakᴀʙʟᴇ** a. [OE *scacan*, cf. ON & Sw. *skaka*]

shake², n. **1.** Shaking or being shaken (see prec.); *all of a ~*, trembling; *the ~s*, ague); *a ~; with a ~ of the head*; give it, had, jolt, jerk, shock. **2.** *A glass of milk, or milk and eggs, flavoured and shaken up (short for milk-~)*. **3.** Trill, quick alternation of two notes with voice or on instrument. **4.** Moment (*in two etc. ~s of a lamb's tail* etc., or *~s*, very quickly, in no time). **5.** Crack in growing timber. **6.** (sl.) *Is no great ~*, not very good or efficient. **7.** ~*-out* (St. Exch.), crisis in which weaker speculators are driven out of market; ~*-up*, shaking or being shaken up. [f. prec.]

shak·er, n. In vbl senses; also (S~) member of religious sect founded in Manchester, & still existing in U.S., holding that Christ's second coming has taken place (named from religious dances), whence **Shak'eress¹**, **Shak'erism(3)**, nn. [-ER¹]

Shak(e)spea'rian (-kspẽr-), a. (In the style of Shakespeare. So **~ᴀɴ²ᴀ** n. pl. [-IAN]

shak'o, n. (pl. ~s). Form of military hat, more or less cylindrical with peak & upright plume or tuft. [f. Magyar *csákó*]

shak'y, a. Unsteady, apt to shake, trembling; unsound, infirm, unreliable, tottering, wavering; (*a ~y hand, table, old man, house; ~y credit, voters, courage; feel, look, ~y*). Hence **~iʟʏ²**, **~iɴᴇss**, nn. [-Y²]

shale, n. Kinds of clayey stone splitting readily into thin plates & resembling slate but softer & less solid; ~*-oil*, kind of naphtha got from bituminous ~. Hence **shal'ʏ²** a. [prob. f. obs. *shale* shell f. OE *scealu*, cf. SCALE²]

shall (unstressed shal, shl), v. aux. (pres. I, he, we, you, they, ~, *thou shalt*; past & condit., I, he, we, you, their, *should* pr. shŏŏd, *thou shouldst* pr. shŏŏdst, neg. forms *shall not* or *shan't* pr. -ah-, *should not* or *shouldn't*; no other parts used.) **1** In first person, to form a plain future or conditional statement or question (*we ~ hear about it tomorrow; I should have been killed if I had let go; ~ I hear from you soon?*); **2** in 2nd & 3rd persons (1st having *will, would*) to form a future or conditional statement expressing speaker's will or intention (*you ~ not catch me again; he should not have gone if I could have prevented it*); **3** alternatively with *will, would*, in sentences of type 1 changed in reporting from 1st to other person (*he says or said, you say or said, that he, you, ~ or should never manage it*; now more (*or now will, would*) or from other person to 1st (*he says I ~ or will never manage it*, reporting *you will never; will* now rare); **4** in reporting sentences of type 2 that contained ~ or *should* (*you promised to type 1, should not catch you at it again*); **5** in 2nd-person questions corresponding to type 1, by attraction to expected answer (*~ you be going to church?*); **6** in any person to form statements or

questions involving the notions of command & future or conditional duty, obligation, etc. (*thou shalt not steal*; *I, you, he, should really have been more careful*; ~ *I, he, open the door?*; *why should I, you, he, obey?*); **7** in all persons to form conditional protasis or indefinite clause (*if, when, we ~ be defeated or defeat ~ overtake us*; *any one who should say*; *if you should happen to be there*; & with inversion *should I, you, he, be there, it would be talked about*); **8** alternatively with *may, might,* in all persons in final clauses (*to the end that I, you, he ~ or should not be able*); **9** in some miscellaneous idioms (*it should seem, it seems*; *you ~ find,* arch. ~ *be sure you will find*; *it is surprising* etc. *that I, you, he, should be or have been so foolish*). [OE *sceal*, cf. Du. *zal*, G *soll*, cogn. w. G *schuld* debt, guilt]

shalloon', n. Light cloth for coat-linings & women's dresses. [f. *Chalons* in France]

shall'op, n. Light open boat. [f. F *chaloupe* SLOOP]

shal(l)ot', n. Plant of onion kind with cloves like, but of milder flavour than, those of garlic. [earlier *eschalot* f. F *eschalotte* dim. of *escaloigne* f. L *ascalonia* orig. fem. adj. f. *Ascalon* in Palestine]

shall'ow (-ō), a. (~er, ~est), n., & v.i. & t. **1.** Of little depth (lit. & fig.; ~ *water,* a ~ *stream, dish*; a ~ *mind, argument, love, man,* superficial, trivial; so ~-*brained, -hearted, -pated*); hence ~LY² adv., ~NESS n. **2.** n. ~ place, shoal. **3.** vb. Become ~er, make ~. [15th-c. *schalowe* etym. dub.; cf. SHOAL¹]

shalt. See SHALL.

sham, v.t. & i. (-mm-), n., & a. **1.** Feign, simulate. (~ *illness, sleep, a faint, fear*; *is only ~ming*); pretend to be (~*med ill, dead, asleep*); hence ~m'ER¹ n. **2.** n. Imposture, pretence, humbug, (*this age of ~s*); person or thing pretending or pretended to be something that he or it is not; (also *sheet, pillow,* ~) embroidered linen laid on bed in day for show. **3.** adj. Pretended, counterfeit, (~ *fight,* imitation battle for training troops; ~ *plea* etc. in law, advanced only to gain time). [17th-c. sl., etym. dub.]

Sham'anism, n. Religion of Siberian tribes involving belief in secondary gods & in power of shamans or priests to influence these. [f. G *schamane* of Mongol origin,-ISM]

sham'ble, v.i., & n. **1.** Walk or run in shuffling or awkward or decrepit way (~*ing gait,* of person who ~es). **2.** n. ~ing gait. [prob.f.obs. *shamble* adj. straddling, wry, perh. f. *shamble* bench (see foll.) w. ref. to straddling trestles]

sham'bles (-lz), n. pl. (often w. sing. constr.). Butchers' slaughter-house; scene of carnage (*the place became a ~*); (loosely, esp. in journalistic use) mess, muddle (with no implication of blood or

death). [pl. of obs. *shamble* stool, OE *scamel* f. L *scamellum* dim. of *scamnum* bench]

shame¹, n. **1.** Feeling of humiliation excited by consciousness of guilt or shortcoming, of having made oneself or been made ridiculous, or of having offended against propriety, modesty, or decency, (*flushed with ~*; *begin with ~ to take the lowest room*). **2.** Restraint imposed by, desire to avoid, such humiliation (*for ~!,* appeal to person not to disregard or reproof for disregarding this; *cannot do it for very ~*; *is quite without or lost to ~*), whence ~'LESS (-ml-) a., ~'LESS-LY² adv., ~'LESSNESS n. **3.** State of disgrace or ignominy or discredit (~ *on you!*; *put one to ~,* disgrace him esp. by exhibiting superior qualities etc.), person or thing that brings disgrace (*is a ~ to his parents*; *would think ~ to do it*; *is a sin & a ~*), whence ~'FUL (mf-) a., ~'fulLY² adv., ~'fulNESS n. [OE *sc(e)amu*, cf. Da. *skam*, G *scham*]

shame², v.i. & t. Be ashamed, refuse from shame, (~ *to*; arch.; usu. with negative, as *he ~d not to say*); bring shame on, be a shame to, make ashamed; put (superior) to his blush by outdoing (*a dog's fidelity ~s us*) frighten by shame *into* or *out of doing,* conduct, etc. [OE *sc(e)amian* (prec.)]

shame'faced (-āmfāst), a. Bashful, shy, (poet., etc.) modest, retiring, inconspicuous. Hence ~LY² adv., ~NESS n., (-āmfāsd-, -āst-). [f. obs. *shamefast,* OE *scamfæst* (SHAME, FAST⁴) by confusion w. ~faCED²]

shammy, sham'oy, n. =CHAMOIS(2).

shampoo', v.t., & n. **1.** Subject (body etc.) to kneading or massage after hot bath (orig. sense, now rare); lather, wash, & rub (head, hair). **2.** n. A ~ing of the head; *dry ~,* alcoholic saponaceous preparation for cleaning the hair, powder for similar purpose, ~ing with these. [f. Hind. *chāmpnā* press, shampoo]

sham'rock, n. Kinds of trefoil or clover serving as national emblem of Ireland (cf. *rose, thistle, leek*). [f. Ir. *seamróg* trefoil, dim. of *seamar* clover]

shan'drydan, n. Light two-wheeled cart; old rickety vehicle. [?]

shan'dygaff, n. Mixed drink of beer & ginger-beer or lemonade. [?]

shanghai' (-hī), v.t. (naut. sl.). Drug & ship as sailor while unconscious. [S~ in China]

shank, n., & v.i. & t. **1.** Leg (*S~'s mare,* one's own legs as opp. riding etc.); leg from knee to ankle; shin-bone; upright part of bird's foot; footstalk of flower; leg of stocking; shaft of pillar etc., shank of tool between head etc. & handle, stem of key, spoon, anchor, etc., straight part of fish-hook, narrow middle of boot-sole; hence (~)ED² (-kt) a. **2.** vb. ~ *off,* (of flowers) fall off by decay of ~; (Golf)

shanny, n. Oblong olive-green European sea-fish, the smooth blenny. [?]

shan't. See SHALL.

shan'tung, n. A soft undressed Chinese silk (usu. undyed). [S~, Chin. province]

shan'ty¹, n. Hut, cabin, mean dwelling. [f. Canad.-F *chantier* log hut f. F=work-shop]

shan'ty², n. Var. of CHANTY.

shape¹, n. 1. Configuration, form, total effect produced by thing's outlines, (spherical in ~; has the ~ of a boat). 2. Appearance, guise, (monster in human form, in the ~ of a boot). 3. Concrete presentment, embodiment, (intention took ~ in action; showed me politeness in the ~ of an invitation). 4. Kind, description, sort, (made no overtures in any ~ or form). 5. Symmetrical or definite form, orderly arrangement, proper condition, (get one's ideas into ~; LICK into ~; give ~ to), whence ~'LESS (-pl-) a., ~'LESSLY² adv., ~'LESSNESS n. 6. Person considered as impressing the sight, & esp. as indistinctly seen or imagined, apparition, ghost, (a ~ loomed through the mist; a grim mysterious ~ stalked towards me). 7. Pattern for work-man etc., mould for shaping hats etc.; jelly, blancmange, etc. shaped in mould; padding worn by actor. Hence (-)**shap-ed²** a. [OE *gesceap* (Y-, prec.)]

shape'ly² (-pl-), a. Well formed or proportioned, of the right or a pleasing shape. Hence ~**iNESS** n. [-LY¹]

shap'er, n. In vbl senses; esp., kinds of machine for turning, planing, stamping, moulding, etc. [-ER¹]

shard, sherd, n. [arch.] Potsherd (still used by gardeners of fragment put over hole of flowerpot); beetle's wing-cover. [OE *sceard* (SHEAR, SHARE-⁴)]

share¹, n. 1. Portion detached for individual from common amount (must get a ~ of the plunder). 2. Part one is entitled to have or bound to contribute, equitable portion, (that is your fair ~; took, bore, my or more or less than my ~ of the burden); as ~s, make equitable division with others; ~ and ~ alike, with equal division; LION's ~). 3. Part one gets or contributes in bringing it about, but no ~ of the credit). 4. Part-proprietorship of property held by joint owners (has a ~ in the bank, estate, etc.), esp. one of the equal parts into which company's capital is divided entitling holder to proportion of profits (holds 50 ~s in; an issue of 10,000 ~s); deferred ~s, on which lower dividend or none is to be paid till fixed date of contingent event; preference or preferred ~s, on which fixed dividend is guaranteed before payment begins on ordinary ~s; ~holder, owner of ~s; ||~-list, of current prices of ~s in various companies; ~-pusher, colloq., pedlar of (usu. worthless) ~s. 5. *~-cropper, tenant farmer who pays his rent with a part of his crop. [OE *scearu* (scean SHEAR-⁴)]

share², v.t. & i. Apportion (food, property, task, etc.) among others, give each a share of; give away part of (would ~ his last crust); get or have share of, possess or use or endure jointly with others; have share(s), be sharer(s), (will ~ with you in the undertaking; we must ~ alike); ~ out, distribute, whence ~ out n., provident club's distribution. Hence **shar'er¹** n.

share³, n. Ploughshare; blade of seeding-machine or cultivator; ~-beam, part of plough in which ~ is fixed. [OE *scear* (scean SHEAR-⁴)]

shark, n., & v.t. & i. 1. Kinds of long-shaped lateral-gilled inferior-mouthed sea-fish many species of which are large & voracious (Basking, Man-eating, White, Blue, Dusky, Bonnet-headed, etc., S~); rapacious person, swindler, (LAND-~); *(college sl.) brilliant student; ~moth, kinds of moth named from shape; ~-oil, got from ~'s liver & used like cod-liver oil; ~'s-mouth, opening in awning for mast etc. 2. v.b. Play the swindler, adventurer, etc. (~s for a living); whence ~'ING² a.; gather up by dishonest or dishonourable means; swallow vora-ciously. [f. 16th c., etym. dub.]

sharp, a., n., & adv. 1. With fine edge or point, not blunt; peaked, pointed, edged, (~ gable, summit, ridge). 2. Well-defined, clean-cut, (~ outline, distinction, impression, features; so ~ed). 3. Abrupt, angular, (~ turn, incline). 4. Keen, vigilant, clever, (~ eyes, ears, intelligence, attention; ~-sighted, -witted, etc.; keep a ~ look-out; a ~ remark, child; as a ~ needle, very intelligent). 6. Quick to take advantage, bent on winning, artful, unscrupulous, dishonest, (was too ~ for me, overreached me; ~ practice, barely honest dealings). 7. Vigorous, speedy, (take a ~ walk;

~'s the word, exhortation to be quick; ~ work, said of matter quickly dispatched or fight etc. that takes all one's energy). **8.** (Phonet., of mutes) unvoiced, hard. **9.** (Mus., opp. FLAT[2]) above true pitch (*piano is* ~; *B, D*, etc., ~, a semitone higher than *B, D*, etc.), (of key) having ~(s) in signature. **10.** ~-*shooter*, skilled shot posted where marksmanship is required; hence ~EN[6] v.t. & i., (-)~/en-ER[1](1, 2) n., ~'LY[2] adv., ~'NESS n. **11.** n. Sewing-needle of slender make; (Mus.) note raised a semitone above pitch, symbol indicating this raising, ~s & FLAT[2]s; ~ *consonant*; (colloq.) swindler, cheat (*billiard*-~); *(joc.) expert (*mining*-~); || (pl.) middlings (between flour & bran). **12.** adv. Punctually (*at six o'clock* ~); (Mus.) above true pitch (*is singing* ~); LOOK[1] ~-*set*, hungry; ~-*shod*, calked. [OE *scearp*, cf. Du. *scherp*, G *scharf*]

sharp[2], v.t. & i. Sharpen, whet, (arch. or vulg.); raise pitch of (note) or mark as sharp; play sharply, swindle, at cards etc., whence ~ER[1] n. [f. prec.]

Sha'stra (-ah-), n. One of the sacred Hindu writings. [Skr. *çāstra*]

shatt'er, v.t. & i. Break (t. & i.) suddenly & violently in pieces; utterly derange, destroy, dissipate, (~*ed nerves, constitution, hopes*). [f. 14th c., etym. dub.]

shave[1], v.t. & i. **1.** Remove (hair), free (chin etc.) of hair, relieve (person) of hair on chin etc., with razor (*has* ~*d off* or ~*d his beard, now wears none; a* ~*n chin*); (intr.) oneself (*he does not* ~ *every day*). **2.** Pare surface of (wood etc.) with spokeshave, plane, etc., whence SHAV'ING[1](2) n. **3.** Pass close to without touching, skirt, miss narrowly, nearly graze. ~-*hook*, tool for scraping surface of metal before soldering; *shaving-brush*, for lathering chin etc. before shaving; *shaving-horse*, bench with clamp for holding wood to be ~*d*. [OE *sc(e)afan*, cf. Du. *schaven*, G *schaben*, perh. cogn. w. L *scabere* scratch, Gk *skaptō* dig]

shave[2], n. **1.** Having one's beard etc. shaved (*must have a* ~; *a sixpenny* ~). **2.** Close approach without contact, narrow miss or escape or failure, (*had a close* ~ *of it*). **3.** Knife-blade with handle at each end for shaving wood etc. **4.** || Trick, deception, hoax. [(the tool f. OE *sceafa*) f. prec.]

shave'ling (-vl-), n. (arch.). Shaven person, monk, friar, priest. [-LING[1]]

shav'er, n. In vbl senses; also (colloq.), lad, youngster, (usu. *young* ~). [-ER[1]]

Shā'vian, a. (In the manner) of G. B. Shaw, dramatist. [-IAN]

|| **shaw**, n. (arch. & poet.). Thicket, wood. [OE *sceaga*, cogn. w. SHAG[1]]

shawl, n. & v.t. **1.** Rectangular garment, often square to be folded into triangle,

chiefly worn by women as outer covering for shoulders; ~-*dance*, in which dancer waves a ~; ~-*pattern*, variegated design like that of Oriental ~. **2.** v.t. Put ~ on (person). [f. Pers. *šāl*]

shawm, n. Obsolete musical instrument with reed. [f. OF *chalemie* f. L f. Gk *kalamos* reed]

shay, n. (Arch. joc., or vulg., for) CHAISE. [back form. f. *chaise* taken for pl.]

shē, pron. (obj. HER[1], possess. HER[2]; pl. THEY etc.), n., & a. **1.** The female (or thing personified as female, e.g. ship or train) previously mentioned or implied or easily identified. **2.** n. Female, woman, (*the not impossible* ~, woman one might love; *is the child a he or a* ~; *had a litter of two* ~*s & a he*, two bitches & a dog). **3.** adj. (usu. hyphened). Female (~-*goat, -ass, -bear*, etc.; ~-*devil, -cat*, malignant or spiteful woman; ~-*oak*, kinds of Australian shrub, esp. BEEFwood; ~-*pine*, Australian conifer). [OE *sēo* fem. of def. art., orig. demonstr. pron., *se*; cf. Du. *zij*, G *sie*, Gk *hē*]

shea (shē), n. N.-Afr. tree yielding a vegetable butter (~-*butter*). [native]

shead'ing, n. Any of the six administrative divisions of the I. of Man. [SHED[1], -ING[1]]

sheaf, n. (pl. -*ves*), & v.t. **1.** Bundle of things laid lengthwise together & usu. tied (~ *of papers, arrows*, etc.), esp. armful of corn-stalks tied after reaping (~*binder*, tool for tying these). **2.** v.t. Make into sheaves, sheave. [OE *scéaf*, cf. Du. *schoof*, G *schaub*; cogn. w. SHOVE]

sheal'ing. Var. of SHEILING.

shear[1], v.t. & i. (past ~*ed* & arch. *shore*; p.p. *shorn*, rarely ~*ed*). **1.** Cut with sword etc. (poet.; t. & i.; *shore off his plume; shore through the bone*); clip, cut with scissors or shears, (trans.; ~ *sheep*, clip its wool; also abs., *shall be* ~*ing*, i.e. my sheep, tomorrow; ~ *cloth*, remove or reduce nap by clipping); (fig.) fleece, strip bare, (*come home shorn; shorn of wool, glory*, etc.). **2.** (Of structure, material, etc.) be distorted or broken by the strain called a shear, (of pressure) distort or break thus. **3.** ~-*water*, kinds of low-flying sea-bird. Hence ~ER[1] n. [OE *sceeran*, cf. Du. & G *scheren*, Gk *keirō* shave; cogn. w. SHARD, SHARE[2], etc.]

shear[2], n. **1.** (pl.) clipping-instrument with two meeting blades pivoted as in scissors or connected by spring & passing close over each other edge to edge (*hand me the* ~; *want a pair of* ~; ~ in comb. or attrib., as ~*bill*, the bird scissorbill or skinner; ~-*grass*, kind with sharp-edged leaves; ~-*legs*, SHEER's; ~ *steel*, cut of special quality fit for ~s & other cutting tools; ~-*tail*, humming-bird with tail like ~s). **2.** (Mech.) kind of strain produced by pressure in structure of a substance, its successive layers being

shifted laterally over each other. [OE *scēar* sing (prec.)]

shear'ling, n. Sheep once shorn. [-ING[1]]

shear'fish. n. Largest European fresh-water fish. [f. G *scheidfisch* (*scheid* of doubtful etym. & meaning)]

sheath, n. (pl. pr. -dhz). Close-fitting cover, esp. for blade or weapon or tool; (Bot., Zool., Anat.) investing membrane, tissue, skin, horny case, etc.; structure of loose stones for confining river within banks. Hence ~LESS a. [OE *scǣth*, cf. Du. *scheede*, G *scheide*; cogn. w. SHED[1]]

sheathe (-dh), v.t. Put into sheath (~ *the sword*, cease from war, & fig.); encase, protect with casing or **sheath**ING[3] n. [f. prec.]

sheave[1], n. Grooved wheel in pulley etc., for rope to run on. [cf. G *scheibe* slice, disk, Icel. *skīfa* slice n. & v.]

sheave[2], v.t. Gather (corn etc.) into sheaves, sheaf. [f. SHEAF]

sheaves. See SHEAF.

*****shebáng**[1], n. (sl.). House (esp. gambling-house), store, saloon; any matter of present concern; business (*the whole* ~). [perh. var. of foll.]

‖**shebeen**[1], n. Pot-house, unlicensed house selling drink. [Ir.]

shed[1], v.t. (shed). Part with, let fall off, (*tree, stag, snake, crab, Prime Minister,* ~s *leaves, horns, skin, shell, colleagues*); drop (~ *tears*, weep); ~ *one's blood for one's country*, be wounded or killed); cause (others blood) to flow; disperse, diffuse, spread abroad, (~ *light on*, illuminate, esp. fig.: ~ *love, radiance, perfume, etc., around one*); (Electr.) reduce (the LOAD[1]). Hence ~d'ER[1] n. [OE *scēadan* part, cf. Du. & G *scheiden*, prob. cogn. w. Gk *skhizō*, L *scindere*]

shed[2], n. One-storeyed shelter for storing goods or vehicles or keeping cattle etc. or for use as workshop etc. & consisting of roof with some or all or no sides open. [var. of SHADE]

sheen, n. Splendour, radiance, brightness. Hence ~y[1] [-Y[2]] a. (poet.). [f. obs. adj. *sheen* beautiful, OE *scīene*, cf. G *schön*; sense affected by confusion with unrelated *shine*]

sheen'y[3], n. (sl.). Jew (derog.). [?]

sheep, n. (pl. the same). **1.** Kinds of wild or domesticated timid gregarious woolly occas. horned ruminant mammal of which male is named *ram*, female *ewe*, & young *lamb* (~ & *goats*, the good & the bad, see *Matt.* xxv. 33; BLACK[1] ~; *cast* ~'*s eyes*, glance amorously at; *follow like* ~, said of persons with no initiative or independence: *as well be hanged for a* ~ *as a* LAMB[1]; ~ *that have no shepherd*, helpless crowd etc.; WOLF *in* ~'*s clothing*). **2.** Bashful embarrassed person (so ~'ISH a., ~'ishly[2] adv., ~'ishNESS n.). **3.** (Usu. pl., now chiefly joc.) member(s) of minister's flock, parishioners etc. **4.** = ~-

skin leather. **5.** ~bot, fly & larva injurious to ~; ~cote (arch.), -fold, -pen (rare), enclosure for penning ~; ~dip, preparation for cleansing ~ or vermin or preserving their wool; ~dog, collie, also breed of rough-coated short-tailed dog used by shepherds; ‖~farmer, -master, breeder of ~; ~-hook, shepherd's crook; ~louse, -tick, kinds of parasite on ~; ~pox, ~-run, extensive ~-walk, esp. in Australia; ~'s-bit, plant resembling small-scabious; ~'s fescue, a pasture grass; ~'s-wash, lotion for killing vermin or preserving wool on ~; ~shank, bight & hitches used to shorten rope's length temporarily; ~'s-head lit., also kind of sea-fish used for food; ~-shearing, (festival at) shearing of ~; ~'skin, garment or rug of ~'s skin with wool on, also leather of it or ~'s skin used in bookbinding etc., also parchment of it or deed or diploma engrossed on this; ~-walk, tract of land on which ~ are pastured; ~wash, lotion for killing vermin or preserving wool on ~. [OE *scēap*, cf. Du. *schaap*, G *schaf*, etym. dub.]

sheer[1], a. & adv. **1.** Mere, simple, unassisted, unmitigated, uncompounded, (*did it by* ~ *force; is* ~ *waste, nonsense, folly: a* ~ *impossibility*); (of rock, fall, ascent, etc.) perpendicular, unrelieved by slope; (Commerc., of textiles) diaphanous. **2.** adv. Plumb, perpendicularly, outright, (*fell 3000 ft* ~; *torn* ~ *out by the roots; rises* ~ *from the water*). [ME *schere*=ON *skærr* bright (*skína* SHINE v.), cogn. w. OE *scír* bright]

sheer[2], v.i. (Naut.) deviate from course; (also in gen. use) ~ *off*, part company, depart, esp. from person one dislikes or fears or is offended by. [perh. f. Du. *scheren* SHEAR[1]]

sheer[3], n. Upward slope of ship's lines towards bow & stern; deviation of ship from course. [perh. f. SHEAR[1]]

sheer[4], n. (pl.; also ~-*legs* or *shear-legs*) hoisting-apparatus of two (or more) poles attached at or near top and separated at bottom for masting ships or putting in engines etc., used in dockyards or on ~-*hulk*, dismasted ship used for the purpose. [var. of SHEAR[2]; named from resemblance to pair of shears]

sheet[1], n. **1.** Rectangular piece of linen used in pairs as inner bed-clothes (*between the* ~s, in bed); whence ~ING[3] n. **2.** Broad more or less flat piece of some thin material (*a* ~ *of iron, glass*, etc., **3.** Wide expanse of water, snow, ice, flame, colour, etc. **4.** Complete piece of paper of the size in which it was made (*book is in* ~s, printed but not bound; ~ *of notepaper*, usu. folded once for writing on: ~ *of quarto* etc., the four etc. leaves given by folding a ~ twice etc.); newspaper (*a penny, scurrilous,* etc., ~). **5.** Rope or chain at lower corner of sail

for regulating its tension etc. *(flowing ~, not close-hauled, eased for free wind; a three ~s, in the wind. sl., rather, very, drunk).* **6. ~anchor** [see etym.], second anchor orig. carried outside waist of ship for use in emergencies, (fig.) last dependence or security; ~ *copper, iron, metal, etc.,* spread by rolling, hammering, etc., into thin ~s; ~ *glass,* kind made first as hollow cylinder, which is cut open & flattened in furnace; ~ LIGHTNING; ~ *music* (published in ~s, not in book form) [OE *scíete, scýte,* linen cloth, with mixture of sense of OE *scéat* corner, fold, all cogn. w. SHOOT; orig. sense *projection;* ~*anchor,* earlier *shut(t)e-, shot(e)-, shott-,* may be f. obs. *shot* spliced cables]

sheet², v.t. Furnish with sheets; cover with sheet *(the ~ed dead);* form into sheets *(~ed rain);* secure (sail) with sheet (esp. ~ *home).* [f. prec.]

sheik(h) (-ēk, -āk), n. Chief, head of Arabian or Mohammedan tribe, family, or village; (transf.) masterful husband or lover; *S~ ul Islam,* grand mufti at Constantinople, chief authority on sacred law in Turkish empire. [Arab. *shaikh,* =elder, chief]

shekarry. See SHIKAREE.

shek'el, n. Jewish weight & silver coin; (pl.) money, riches, pelf. [f. Heb. *sheqel* (*shāqal* weigh)]

Shekin'ah, -ch-, n. Visible glory of Jehovah resting over mercy-seat. [Heb. (-k-), f. *shākhan* dwell]

shel'drake, n. (fem. occas. *shelduck*). Kinds of bright-plumaged wild duck. [prob. f. dial. *sheld* piebald = MDu. *schillede,* DRAKE²]

shelf, n. (pl. *-ves*). Projecting slab of stone or board let into or hung on wall to support things, one of the boards in cabinet, bookcase, etc., on which books etc. stand, *(on the ~,* put aside, done with, esp. of person past work); ledge, horizontal steplike projection in cliff face etc.; reef or sandbank under water. Hence SHELVED² (-vd) a., ~'FUL(2) n. [prob. f. LG *schelf,* cogn. w. OE *scylfe* of doubtful meaning & *scylf* crag]

shell¹, n. **1.** Hard outer case enclosing nuts, kinds of seed or fruit, eggs, some animals or parts of them, etc., husk, crust, pod, carapace, scale, conch, wing-case, pupa-case, *(come out of one's ~,* throw off reserve, become communicative). **2.** Walls of unfinished or gutted house, ship, etc. **3.** Outline of plan etc. **4.** Inner coffin. **5.** Light racing-boat. **6.** Hollow metal or paper case to contain explosives for fireworks, cartridges, etc.; explosive projectile or bomb for use in big gun or mortar, whence ~'PROOF² a.; ~'cartridge. **7.** Handguard of sword. **8.** Lyre (poet.). **9.** ∥ (At schools) intermediate form. **10.** Outward show, mere semblance. **11.** (Short for) ~*-jacket.*

12. ~*back* (Naut. sl.), old sailor; ~*-bark,* kinds of hickory; ~*-bit,* gouge-shaped boring-bit; ~ *button,* made of two metal disks enclosed in cloth etc.; ~*fish,* aquatic ~ed mollusc (oyster etc.) or crustacean (crab, shrimp, etc.); ~*-heap* or *-mound,* kitchen MIDDEN; ~*-jacket,* army officer's undress jacket reaching only to waist behind; ~*-lime,* fine quality produced by burning sea~s; ~*-marble,* kinds containing fossil ~s; ~*shock,* disorganization of mental faculties, power of speech, etc., resulting from exposure to bombardment & other war strains; ~*-work,* ornamentation of ~s cemented on wood etc. Hence (-)~ED² (-ld), ~'LESS, ~'Y² aa. [OE *scell,* cf. Du. *schel;* cogn. w. SCALE¹]

shell², v.t. & i. **1.** Take out of shell, remove shell or pod from, *(~ peas).* **2.** Provide, cover, or pave, with shell(s). **3.** Bombard (town etc.), fire at (troops) with shells, whence ~'ING⁴(1) n. **4.** (Of metal etc.) come *off* in scales. **5.** ~ *out* (sl.), pay up (t. & i.), hand over required sum; ~*-out* n., the game of pyramids played by three or more persons. [f. prec.]

shellac', n., & v.t. (*-king-, -ked*). **1.** LAC¹ melted into thin plates, used for making varnish. **2.** v.t. Varnish with ~. [SHELL¹, LAC¹]

Shel'ta, n. Ancient hybrid cant language of Irish gipsies and pipers, Irish and Welsh travelling tinkers, etc. (largely BACK¹-*slang*). [?]

shel'ter¹, n. Thing serving as shield or barrier against attack, danger, heat, wind, etc. (ANDERSON, MORRISON, ~); screen or cabin built to keep off wind & rain *(cabman's ~);* place of safety or immunity; shielded condition *(find, take, ~).* Hence ~'LESS a. [f. 16th c. only, etym. dub.; perh. f. *shield* vb + -URE¹]

shel'ter², v.t. & i. Act or serve as shelter to, protect, conceal, harbour, defend *from* blame, screen, shield; ~ *oneself under, beneath, behind,* etc., use the protection afforded by; take shelter *under, in, from;* ~*ed trades,* those not exposed to foreign competition, e.g. building & inland transport. [f. prec.]

∥ **shel'ty, -tie,** n. (Sc.). Shetland pony. [prob. f. ON *Hjalti* Shetland]

shelve¹, v.t. Put on shelf (books etc.), (fig.) abandon or defer consideration of (plan etc.), cease to employ (person); fit (cupboard etc.) with shelves, whence **shel'ving²(3)** n. [f. SHELF]

shelve², v.i. Slope gently. [cf. WFris. *skelf* oblique; unconnected w. *shelf*]

shelves. See SHELF.

Shema' (-ah), n. The *Hear, O Israel, Jews'* confession of faith. [the initial wd, Heb. = hear]

She'ōl, n. Hebrew Hades, place of the dead, the grave. [Heb.]

shep'herd (-perd), n. & v.t. 1. Man who tends sheep at pasture, pastor (lit., & fig., esp. of minister in relation to his flock; *the good S~, Christ); ~'s-club, -joy, -knot, 'purse, -rod, etc., plants; ~'s crook, staff with hook at one end and used by ~s; ~'s pie, minced meat baked under mashed potatoes; ~'s plaid, small black & white check pattern in cloth; hence ~ESS¹ (-per) n. 2. v.t. Tend (sheep, also fig.) as ~; marshal or conduct or drive (crowd etc.) like sheep. [SHEEP, HERD²]

|| shepp'y, n. Sheep-cote. [f. SHEEP; a pseudo-archaism]

She'raton, n. Severe 18th-c. style of furniture (often attrib., as ~ chairs). [~ maker & designer]

she'rbet, n. Eastern cooling drink of diluted fruit-juices (in pop. Engl. use, made effervescent). [Turk. & Pers., f. Arab. shariba to drink]

sherd. See SHARD.

sherif (-ef), -eef, n. Descendant of Mohammed through Fatima, entitled to wear green turban or veil; chief magistrate of Mecca. [f. Arab. sharif lofty]

she'riff, n. ||Chief officer of crown in county or shire, charged with the keeping of the peace, administering justice under direction of the courts, executing writs by deputy, presiding over elections, etc.; *elective officer responsible for keeping the peace in his county. [OE scir-gerefa (SHIRE, REEVE²)]

she'riffalty, she'riffdom, she'riffhood, she'riffship, nn. Shrievalty, office of sheriff. [-alty after shrievalty; -DOM, -HOOD, -SHIP]

she'rry, n. White wine of Xeres or of South Spain (brown ~, dark varieties); ~-glass, wineglass containing about four table-spoons; ~ COBBLER. [earlier sherris, f. Xeres]

She'tland, n. Group of islands NNE of Scotland (~ lace, openwork woollen trimming; ~ pony, small hardy breed; ~ wool, fine kind).

shew. See SHOW¹; ~'bread, see SHOW¹.

Shi'ah, Shi'ite, (shē-), nn. Member of the Mohammedan sect (cf. Sunni, see SUN-NAH) that regards Ali as first Imam or successor of Mohammed & rejects first three Sunni Caliphs. [Arab. = sect]

shibb'oleth, n. Test word or principle or behaviour or opinion, the use of or inability to use which betrays one's party, nationality, etc. (see Judg. xii. 6); old-fashioned & generally abandoned doctrine once held essential. [Heb.]

shield, n., & v.t. 1. Variously shaped & sized detached piece of armour made of leather, wood, or metal, for wearing on left arm to receive thrust or stroke, esp. (cf. buckler, target) one of elongated form (cf. other side of the ~, the aspect of a question etc. that is less obvious, or that is not the one lately presented); protective plate or screen in machinery etc.; person or thing that protects one; ~like part in animal or plant; (Her.) drawing etc. of ~ used for displaying person's coat of arms; ~-fern, common handsome fern with ~-shaped covers to fruit-dots; ~-hand (arch.), left hand; hence ~LESS a. 2. v.t. Protect, screen, esp. from censure or punishment (often with implication of illegitimate concealment of facts). [OE scéld, cf. Du. & G schild]

||shie'ling, n. (Sc.), Grazing-ground for cattle; roughly constructed hut for shepherds or sportsmen; sheep-shelter. [f. Sc. shiel hut (etym. dub.)+-ING¹]

shi'er, -est. See SHY¹.

shift¹, v.t. & i. 1. Change or move (t. & i.) from one position to another, substitute one specimen of for another, undergo such substitution, change form or character, (~one's ground, take up new position in argument etc.; ~one's lodging; ~load into other hand;) ~the scene, the scene shaken out of place; often ~about, ~off, etc., arch., change it; cargo ~ed, got shaken out of place; often ~about, ~off, transfer to another; wind~s round to the E.). 2. Use expedients, take whatever course is available, contrive to do something, manage or get along or make a livelihood, (must ~ as I can, for himself). 3. Equivocate, practise evasion, (rare; ~& prevaricate); ~ as I can, for himself). [OE sciftan divide, cf. Du. schiften divide, ON skipta divide, shift]

shift², n. 1. Change of place or character, substitution of one thing for another, vicissitude, rotation, (rare; the ~s & changes of life; ~ of crops, rotation). 2. Relay of workmen, time for which it works. 3. New device, expedient, resource, whence ~LESS a., ~LESSLY adv., ~LESSNESS n. 4. Dodge, trick, artifice, piece of evasion or equivocation, whence ~Y² a. (~y eyes, deceitful), ~ILY² adv., ~INESS n. 5. Make ~, or a long somehow (must make ~ without it). 6. (arch.). Chemise. 7. Arrangement by which joints of successive tiers in brickwork etc. do not coincide. [ME schift cogn. w. prec.; cf. ON skipti division, exchange, Sw. skift spell, relay]

Shii'te. See SHIAH.

shika'r', n. (Anglo-Ind.). Hunting. [Hind.]

shika'ri (-ri), shekā'rry, n. (Anglo-Ind.). Hunter; native attendant of sportsman. [Hind.(-i), f. prec.]

shille'lagh (-âlo), -alah, n. Irish cudgel of blackthorn or oak. [Shillelagh in Ireland]

||shill'ing, n. (abbr. s., as 3s.). British silver coin & money of account=1/20 of pound or twelve pence (1/1/6, a ~ & six-pence; £1, 1s. 1d.; take King's or Queen's ~, enlist as soldier, w. ref. to now obs.

method of recruiting; *cut off* one's heir etc. *with a* ~, leave one's property to others; ~'s-WORTH[1]. [OE *scilling*, G *schilling*; cf. Du. *schelling*, G *schilling*; perh. = thin slice (SKILL, -LING)]

shil'ly-shal'ly, n., a., & v.i. **1.** Inability to make up one's mind, indecision, vacillation. **2.** adj. Vacillating. **3.** v.i. Vacillate, be undecided, hesitate to act or choose one's course. [f. *shall I? w.* redupl.]

shily. See SHY[1].

shim, n. & v.t. (-mm-). Thin slip or wedge used in machinery etc. to make parts fit; (vb) fit or fill up thus. [?]

shim'mer, v.i., a., & n. (Shine with) tremulous or faint diffused light. [OE *scymrian*, cf. G *schimmern*]

shim'my[1], n. (Colloq., nursery, etc., for) CHEMISE.

***shimm'y[2],** n., & v.i. **1.** Kind of fox-trot accompanied by tremulous motions of body. **2.** v.i. Dance a ~. [?]

shin, n., & v.i. & t. (-nn-). **1.** Front of leg below knee (~*bone,* tibia; ~ *of beef,* ox's shank); (~*guard,* worn at football. **2.** vb. Climb *up* (tree, wall, ladder, etc.; or with *up* adv.); kick ~s of, hack. [OE *scinu,* cf. Du. *scheen,* G *schiene;* perh. orig. = thin slice]

shin'dy, n. Brawl, disturbance, row, noise, (often KICK[2] *up a* ~). [perh. f. Sc. *skinny* or *shinty* kind of hockey]

shine, v.i. & t. (*shone*). Emit or reflect light, be bright, glow, (lit. & fig.; *face shone with soap or with gratitude* etc.); impair brilliance or newness of, also throw into the shade by surpassing; (sl.) disturbance, shindy, sensation; *take a* ~ *to* (sl.), take a fancy for. [f. prec.]

shin'er, n. (sl.). A coin, esp. sovereign, (pl.) money. [SHINE[1], -ER[1]]

shingle[1] (shing'gl), n., & v.t. **1.** Rectangular slip of wood used like roof-tile on roofs, spires, etc.; *small signboard;* ~d hair, this style of hairdressing. **2.** v.t. Roof with ~s; cut (hair of head) so that ends are exposed like roof—s, cut hair of (head, person) thus. [n. f. L *scindula,* earlier *scandula*]

shingle[2] (shing'gl), n. Small rounded pebbles lying on sea-shore. Hence **shing'ly[2]** (-ngg-) a. [earlier *ch-*, perh. imit., cf. *chink*]

shingles (shing'glz), n. pl. Skin-disease forming inflamed band often round right half of body at waist. [f. med. L *cingulus* f. L *cingulum* girdle (*cingere* gird)]

Shin'tō, n. Japanese religion partly ousted by Buddhism. Hence ~ISM, ~IST, nn. [f. Chin. *shin tao* way of the gods]

shin'ty, shinn'y, n. Variation of hockey played in Scotland and N. England; stick or ball used in it. [perh. f. Gael. *sinteag* a bound; cf. SHINDY]

shin'y, a. Glistening, polished, rubbed bright, (~*y hat, boots,* etc.; ~*y coat, seams,* with nap worn off). Hence ~INESS n. [-Y[2]]

ship, n. (regarded as femn. w. pron. *she, her*). **1.** Vessel with bowsprit & three, four, or five square-rigged masts; (cf. sea-going vessel of considerable size (BATTLE[1]-, ~ *of the* LINE[2], MERCHANT~, SAIL[?]*ing*~, WAR[1]~; *sister* ~, built on same plan as another; ~ *of the desert,* camel; ABOARD[2] ~; PUMP[2] ~; *take* ~, embark; *on* BOARD[1] ~; *when my* etc. ~ *comes home,* when I etc. make my etc. fortune); (sl.) boat, esp. racing-boat; ~*aircraft; on* ~ *board, on* board ~. **2.** ~('s) *biscuit,* hard coarse kind made for keeping used on board ~; ~*breaker,* contractor who breaks up old ~s; ~*broker,* agent transacting ~'s business in port, dealer in ~s, marine-insurance agent; ~*builder,* ~*building;* ~*canal,* for conveying ~s inland; ~-CHANDLER(y); ~*fever,* typhus; ~*letter,* conveyed by other than mail~; ~*load,* whole quantity of something forming cargo; ~*mate,* person belonging to or sailing on same ~ as another, esp. fellow sailor; ~*money* (hist.), impost for providing ~s for navy, revival of which by Charles I was a cause of Great Rebellion; ~*owner,* person owning (shares in) ~(s); ~*railway,* for transportation of ~s over-land from water to water; ~*rigged,* as ~ in first sense; ~'s *articles,* terms on which seamen take service on her; ~'s COM-PANY[1]; ||~'s CORPORAL[3]; ~*shape* adv. or pred. a., in good order (& see BRISTOL); ~'s *husband,* ~*broker* in first sense; ~'s *papers,* documents establishing owner-ship, nationality, nature of cargo, etc., of ~; ~*way,* inclined structure on which ~ is built & down which it slides to be launched; ~*worm,* mollusc boring into ~ timbers; ~*wreck* n, destruction of ~ by storm, foundering, stranding, striking rock, etc., (fig.) ruin (*make* ~*wreck,* be ruined; *make or suffer* ~*wreck of* one's *hopes* etc.); ~*wreck* v.t. & i., inflict ~wreck lit. or fig. on (person, hopes, etc., rarely ~), suffer ~wreck; ~*wright,* ~builder; ~*yard,* ~building establishment. Hence ~*LESS* a. [OE *scip,* cf. Du. *schip,* G *schiff*]

ship[2], v.t. & i.(-pp-). Put, take, or send away (goods, passengers, sailors) on board ship; (Commerc.) deliver (goods) to forwarding agent for conveyance by land or water; step (mast), fix (rudder etc.), in its place on ship (~ *oars,* take from

rowlocks & lay inside boat); (of ship or boat) ~ *a sea*, be flooded by wave; take ship, embark, (of sailor) take service on ~. [f. prec.]

-ship, suf. f. OE *-scipe* (cf. Du. *-schap, -schoft*) f. Teut. root *skap* form, make, forming abstract nn. on adj.; as *hard~*, *vor~* (*worth* adj.) & on nn. as *lord~*, *friend~*, *scholar~*, *apprentice~*; in the latter use it has a living suf.; meaning, (1) being so-&-so, status, office, honour, capacity. *Landscape* also contains the suf.

ship'ment, n. Putting of goods etc. on ship; amount shipped, consignment. [SHIP²-MENT]

||shipp'en, -on, n. (chiefly dial.), Cowhouse, cattleshed. [OE *scyppen*; cogn. w. SHOP]

shipp'er, n. Merchant etc. who sends or gets goods by ship. [-ER¹]

shipp'ing, n. In vbl senses; also; ships, esp. the ships of a country, port etc.; *~agent*, person acting for ship or line of ~, also loose term for ships at a port etc.; *~articles*, agreement between captain & seamen as to wages etc.; *~bill*, manifest of goods shipped; *~master*, official in whose presence *~articles* are signed, paying off is done, etc.; *~office*, *~agent's* or *~master's*. [-ING¹]

||shire (as suf. pr. -sher) n. County (chiefly now as suf. in names of certain counties & districts, as *Hamp~*, *Hallam~*, *Devon~* or *Devon*, & in pl. the *~s*, band of counties stretching NE from *Hamp~* & *Devon~* ending in ~, also loose term for midland counties, &; for the hunting district including Leics. & Rutland & Northants.); *~bred horse*, *~horse*, largest breed of draught horse raised esp. in ~. Lincoln~ & Cambridge~; KNIGHT of the ~. [OE *scir* business, administration, province, etym. dub.; not connected w. *shear, share*]

shirk, v.t. & n. 1. Avoid meanly, get out of, shrink selfishly from, (duty, responsibility, fighting, etc.; also abs.); hence ~ER¹ n. 2. n. ~er. [f. obs. *shirk* n. sponger, sharper, perh. f. G *schurke*]

*shirr, n. & v.t. 1. Elastic webbing; elastic thread woven into fabric; gathered thread trimming, gathering in costumery. 2. v.t. Gather (material) with parallel threads run through; hence **shirr'ing¹** n. [?]

shirt, n. Man's sleeved under-garment worn under cloth clothes, extending from neck to thighs, usu. visible at collar & wrist-bands, & made of linen, cotton, flannel, or silk (NIGHT~); *~ sleeves*, *in one's ~ sleeves*, without coat & waistcoat, coat; *near is my ~*, *but nearer is my skin*, self is the first consideration; *keep one's ~ on*, sl., keep one's temper; *get one's ~ off*, sl., make him angry; *put one's ~ on*, sl., bet all one has upon; *give one a wet ~*, work him till he sweats); woman's blouse with stiff collar & cuffs; *~front*, breast of ~, usu. stiffened & starched (*~front cricket pitch*, also dicky; *true & smooth ~*, also lordly~). Hence ~ED² ², ~LESS aa., ~ING¹ (3) n.

shirt'y¹ a. (sl.), In a rage, annoyed. [OE]

shit, v.i., v.t., & n. (vulg.). 1. Evacuate bowels. 2. n. Ordure (& as term of abuse). [earlier *sc(h)~*), cf. ON *skita*, Du. *schijten*, G *scheissen*]

shiv'er¹, v.i. & n. 1. Experience or show quick slight vibrating movement (such as is) caused by sensation of cold, tremble with cold; *~ing-fit*, as in ague; hence ~ingry² adv. 2. n. Momentary ~ing movement (often pr., as *gives me the ~s*), whence ~Y² a. [ME *chiveren*, etym. dub.]

shiv'er², n. (usu. pl.), & v.t. & i. 1. (One of) the many small pieces into which thing is shattered by blow or fall. 2. vb. Break (t. & i.) into ~s (*~ my timbers*, reputed naut. imprecation). [ME *scifre* cf. obs. *shive* slice, & G *schiefer* slate]

shoal¹, n., a., & v.i. 1. Shallow, not deep, (only lit., of water). 2. n. Shallow place, submerged sandbank esp. one that shows at low water, (fig., usu. pl.) hidden danger(s) or impediment(s), whence ~Y² a., ~INESS n. 3. v.i. Get shallower. [OE *sceald*]

shoal², n. & v.i. 1. Multitude, crowd, great number, esp. of fish swimming in company (also SCHOOL²), (*~s of people*; *gets letters in ~s*). 2. v.i. (Of fish) form ~. [perh. f. OE *scolu* troop of soldiers, cf. OSax. *scola* multitude; but prob. a re-adoption f. Du. of SCHOOL²]

shock¹, n. 1. Violent collision, concussion, felt; or impact (*three ~s of earthquake were felt*; *clashed with a mighty ~*; *~ tactics*, use of cavalry to charge in masses; *~troops*, troops specially trained for the offensive). 2. Sudden & disturbing physical or mental impression (*news came upon me with a ~*; *was a great ~*; *electric ~*, stimulation of nerves by passage of current through body); (Path.) state of prostration following overstimulation of nerves by sudden pain as at wound etc. or violent emotion (*died of ~*; *is the more dangerous than the loss of blood*). 3. Injury inflicted on credit, stability, etc., great disturbance of organization or system. 4. *~brigade*, *~workers*, (in U.S.S.R.) body of workers selected or volunteering for some specially arduous task. [f. F *choc* (*choquer*, see foll.)]

shock², v.t. & i. Affect with indignation, disgust, or horror, appear improper or outrageous or scandalous to (*was ~ed at, by, to hear*, etc.), whence ~ING² a. & adv. (*~ing bad* etc., colloq.); ~ingry²

adv., ~ingness n.; collide violently (poet.). [f. F *choquer* clash. etym. dub.]

shock³, n., & v.t. **1.** Group of usu. twelve corn-sheaves stood up close together in field. **2.** v.t. Arrange (corn) in ~s. [cf. MDu. *schok* ~, sixty, MHG *schok* heap, sixty, MSw. *skokk* crowd]

shock⁴, n. Unkempt or shaggy mass of hair; *~head*, rough head of hair, whence *~-headed²* a. [perh. f. obs. *shock-dog* or *shough* poodle, etym. dub.]

‖**shŏck'er**, n. (colloq.). Very bad specimen of anything; sensational cheap novel. [-ER¹]

shŏd. See SHOE³.

shŏd'dy, n. & a. **1.** Fibre made from old cloth etc. shredded; inferior cloth made partly of such fibre; anything of worse quality than it claims or seems to have. **2.** adj. Counterfeit, pretentious, trashy. [prob. f. OE *sceddan* SHED¹]

shoe¹ (-ōo), n. **1.** Outer foot-covering, esp. not reaching above ankle (*that's another pair of ~s*, another matter; *dead men's ~s*, property or position as looked forward to by expectant successor; *be in person's ~s*, in his plight; *die in one's ~s*, by violence, esp. hanging; *where the ~ pinches*, hardships of one's own lot; *put the ~ on the right foot*, apportion blame etc. truly). **2.** Metal rim nailed to hoof of horse etc. **3.** Thing like ~ in shape or use, e.g. wheel-drag, socket, ferrule, mast-step. **4.** *~s & stockings*, bird's-foot trefoil; ‖*~black*, boy or man who blacks ~s of passers-by; *~buckle*, buckle for fastening over instep (now used only as ornament); *~horn*, instrument of horn, metal, etc., for helping ~ on to foot; *~leather*, *-string*, for lacing up ~; *~latchet* (Bibl.), fastening of ~; *~maker*, maker of boots & ~s. Hence ~LESS (-ōol-) a. [OE *scōh*, cf. Du. *schoen*, G *schuh*; perh. cogn. w. SHADE, SKY]

shoe² (-ōo), v.t. (*shŏd*; part. *~ing*). Fit with shoe(s) (esp. with horse etc. as obj., or in p.p. as *nearly shod feet*, *pole shod with iron*). [f. prec.]

shŏg'un (-ōon), n. (hist.). Japanese hereditary commander-in-chief & virtual ruler for some centuries until the office was abolished 1868. Hence ~ATE¹ n. [Jap. ~ = general]

shone. See SHINE¹.

shoo, int., & v.i. & t. (Utter) sound used to frighten birds away; drive *away* thus. [imit.]

shook¹. See SHAKE¹.

shook², n., & v.t. **1.** Set of staves & headings for cask ready for putting together. **2.** v.t. Pack in ~s. [prob. p.p. of *shake*; *shaken cask* is used in same sense]

shoot, v.i. & t. (*shŏt*). **1.** Come vigorously or swiftly out, forth, along, up, etc., or abs., sprout, dart, (*boat shot out from the* creek; *~ing* STAR¹; *flash ~s across sky*; *~ ahead*, come quickly to front of competitors etc.; *buds are ~ing*; *tree ~s*, puts forth buds; *fountain, flame, ~s up*; *prices shot up*, rose suddenly; *cricket-ball ~s*, darts along ground when it touches, instead of bouncing; *child is ~ing up*, growing tall; *pain ~s through nerves etc.*; *corn, tooth, ~s*, inflicts intermittent pain). **2.** Project abruptly out (*mountain-spur, cape, ~s out*). **3.** Send out, discharge, propel, emit, violently or swiftly (*~rubbish* etc., let it slide from cart or receptacle; *bow, gun, ~s arrow, shell*; *passengers were shot out of coach*; *sun ~s its rays*; *~ out one's lips*, Bibl., protrude in scorn; *~ one's linen*, display wristbands by shaking them down; *~ the cat*, sl., vomit; *~ fishing-net*, extend it across river etc.; *~ bolt of door*, send it home; *tree ~s out branches*). *~/ (sl.), say what you have to say. **4.** Discharge (bullet etc.) from gun etc., cause (bow, gun, etc.) to discharge missile, discharge gun etc., make use *well* etc. of gun etc., kill or wound (person, animal) with missile from gun etc., hunt game etc. habitually or on one occasion with gun, *~ the game over estate* etc., *~ game on* (estate etc.), (of gun etc.) go off, send missile *straight* etc., (*fool's* BOLT¹ *is soon shot*; *I'll be shot if* —, form of negative asseveration; *can army or sportsman, does gun, ~ straight?*; *was shot for a spy*; *~ a match*, engage in *~ing-match*; *will ~ the coverts tomorrow*; *neither rides nor ~s*; *was out ~ing*; *have shot away all our ammunition*). **5.** (Cinemat.) photograph. **6.** (Assoc. Footb., Hockey, etc.) take a shot at goal. **7.** *~ up*, terrorize (village, district) with punitive rifle-shooting, firing of houses, etc.; *~ the sun* (Naut.), take its altitude with the sextant at noon; ‖*~ the moon* (sl.), remove one's goods by night to avoid paying rent. **8.** Be, have one's boat, swept swiftly under or down (bridge, rapid fall; *~ Niagara*, attempt desperate enterprise). **9.** (Joinery) plane (edge of board) accurately (hence *shot edges*). **10.** p.p. (Of coloured material) so woven etc. as to show different colours at different angles (*shot silk*; *crimson shot with maize-colour*). **11.** ‖*~ing-box*, sportsman's lodge for use in *~ing-season*; *~ing-coat, -jacket, -boots*, of patterns useful in *~ing* game; *~ing-iron*, (sl.), fire-arm; *~ing-range*, ground one in which there is *~ing* (opp. *cold war* or WAR¹ *of nerves*). Hence ~ABLE a. [OE *scēotan*, cf. Du. *schieten*, G *schiessen*]

shoot, n. Young branch or sucker; rapid in stream; inclined plane down which water etc. may flow or things slide, chute; shooting party or expedition or practice or ~(= SHOOTING) land. [f. prec.]

shoot'er, n. In vbl senses; esp.: ball that

shoots at cricket; (in comb.) shooting-
implement at cricket; (in comb.) ~; *six* etc., ~, revolver
firing six etc. shots), [-ɪŋ¹]

shoot′ing, n. In vbl senses (for compounds see SHOOT¹); ~ *right of* ~ over
particular land; estate etc. rented to
shoot over. [-ɪŋ¹]

shop, n., & v.i. & t. (-pp-). **1.** Building,
room, etc., for retail sale of some commodity (*chemist's, butcher's, fruit*, ~;
come to the wrong ~, transl., apply to
wrong person etc.), or in which manufacture or repairing is done (*engineering*
~; *fitting, pattern*, etc., ~), departments
of manufactory. **2.** ‖(sl.). Institution,
establishment, etc., (e.g. one's school,
university, etc.; esp. formerly of R.M.A.,
Woolwich; *the other* ~, rival institution;
SMELL *of the* ~), whence ~p′y⁴ a. **3.** One's profession, trade, or business,
things connected with it, or talk about it,
(*CLOSE* a/d ~; *shut up* ~, cease doing something; *talk* ~; *sink the* ~, refrain from
talking ~, also conceal one's occupation:
SMELL *of the* ~), whence ~p′y⁴ a. **4.** *All
over the* ~ (sl.), in disorder, in every
direction, wildly, (*have looked for it all
over the* ~; *my books are all over the* ~;
hitting, steering, etc., *all over the* ~).
5. ~*-bell*, on door to give notice of customer's entrance; ~*-boy, -girl*, assistants
in ~; ~*-keeper*, owner of ~ (*nation of* ~
keepers, the English); ~*-lifter*, pretended
customer who steals goods in ~; ~*-man*
~keeper or his assistant; ~*-soiled*, = ~
worn; ‖~*-steward*, person elected by his
fellow workmen in a factory or branch of
work etc.; ‖~*-walker*, attendant in large
~ who directs customers; ~ *window*,
window of ~ used for display of wares
(*has everything in the* ~ *window*, transf.,
is superficial); ~*-worn*, soiled or faded by
being shown in ~. **6.** vb. Go to (-ɛɪ) to
make purchases, visit ~; ~ *a person*, (sl.)
imprison, (of informer) cause (accomplice)
to be imprisoned. [OE *sceoppa* booth, cf.
G. *schopf* porch, shed]

shore¹, n. Land that skirts sea or large
body of water (*in* ~, on the water near or
nearer to ~); (law) land between ordinary high & low water marks. Hence
~*LESS* (-ʊ̄l-) a., ~*WARD* (-ɔ̄w-) a. & adv.
[ME *schore*, cf. Du. *schoor* prob. cogn. w.
SHEAR¹]

shore², n., & v.t. **1.** Prop, beam set
obliquely against ship, wall, tree, etc., as
support. **2.** v.t. (Support, hold *up*, with
~(s). Hence SHŌ′RING¹(3) n. [ME *schore*,
cf. Du. *schoor*, ON *skortha*]

shore³, abs. p.t. of SHEAR¹.

shorn, p.p. of SHEAR¹.

short, a., adv., n., & v.t. **1.** Measuring
little from end to end in space or time,
soon traversed or finished, (*a* ~ *way off*;
a ~ *time ago*; ~ *story*, of the character of
a novel but less lengthy; ~ *CUT¹*; ~ *circuit*,
electric circuit made through a small
resistance, esp. one acting as a shunt to

one of greater resistance, form of this due
to a fault that allows current's escape to
earth; ~*-circuit* v.t., establish ~ circuit
in, cut off current from thus; ~ DIVISION;
~ *drink*, cocktail etc. esp. before a meal;
~*er CATECHISM*; ~ *rib*, ~ *sea*, ~ *broken
SHRIFT*; ~ *WHIST³*; *a* ~ *sea*, ~ broken
waves); *make a* ~ *work of*, dispose of or
destroy or consume quickly; *he, his joy
etc., had but a* ~ *life*, whence ~*-LIVED² a.*;
~ *temper*, self-control that is soon or
easily lost, whence ~*-tempered² a.*; ~
waist in dress, made high up, whence
~*-WAISTED² a.*; ~ *wind*, easily exhausted
breathing-power, inability to run long or
fig. to talk or write at any length, whence
~*-WINDED² a.*, ~*-wind′EDNESS n.*; ~
clothes or *coats*, dress of child too old for
long-clothes, whence ~*-coat v.t.* **2.** Of
small stature, not tall, (usu. *of* human
beings, or of upright things, as chimney,
tower, tree). **3.** Not far-reaching, acting
near at hand, deficient, scanty, in want
of, below the degree of abruptly finished,
(~ *sight*, not seeing clearly at distance or
fig. into the future, whence ~*-SIGHTED²
a.*, ~*-sight′EDLY² adv.*, ~*-sight′EDNESS
n.*; *at* ~ *range*; *take* ~ *views*, consider the
present only; ~ *date*, early date for maturing of bill etc., whence ~*-dated² a.*; ~
bill, paper, etc., dated for early payment; ~ *LEG, SLIP*, in cricket; *has a* ~
memory; *are* ~ *of hands*, have not enough
workmen, whence ~*-handED² a.*; ~ *of
breath*, panting, ~*-winded*; ~ COMMONS;
in ~ *supply*, scarce; ~ *weight*, less than it
is represented to be; *a* ~ *ten miles, mile,
hour*, etc., less or seeming less than that;
cut ~, bring to end before natural time;
come ~, disappoint expectations etc., fall
of one's duty or proper development,
whence ~*-COMING¹ n.*; *fall* ~, be insufficient or inadequate; *run* ~, have or
be too little, as *our tea run* ~, *we ran* ~ *of
tea*; *an escape nothing* ~ *of marvellous*).
4. Concise, brief, curt, sullenly or snappishly reticent, (*the* LONG¹ *& the* ~ *of it*,
in ~, to use few words, without circumlocution, to give the conclusion briefly;
is called Bob for ~, by way of ~ name;
was very ~ *with me*, uncivil). **5.** (Phonet.,
Pros.; of vowel or syllable) (prop.) having
the less of the two recognized durations
(pop.) unstressed, (also, of vowel) having
the *or* an other sound than that called
LONG¹ (e.g. those in *met, pull, but*). **6.** (Of
pastry, clay, etc.) friable, crumbling, not
tenacious, (cf. COLD-SHORT). **7.** (St. Exch.
etc.; of stocks, stockbroker, crops, etc.)
sold, selling, etc., when the amount is not
in hand in reliance on getting the deficit
in time for delivery. **8.** *Something* ~, a
drink of spirits etc.; ~*bread*, ~*cake*,
brittle dry cake made with flour & much
butter & sugar; ~*fall*, deficit; ~*hand*,
methods of compendious writing used
for taking verbatim reports of speeches

etc., stenography; ~ *head* (Racing), distance of less than length of horse's head (also ~*-head* v.t., beat by this distance); ~*horn*, name of ~*-horned* breed of cattle; ~ *metre*, hymn stanza of 4 lines (6, 6, 8, 6 syllables); ~ *suit* (of less than four cards); ~ *time*, condition of working less than the regular number of hours per day or days per week; ~ TON¹; ~ *wave* (Wireless), having a wave-length of from 10 to 100 metres; hence ~ˈISH¹ (2) a., ~ˈNESS n. **9. adv.** Abruptly, before the natural or expected time, in ~ manner, (*took him up* ~, interrupted him; *stop* ~, suddenly cease, not go on to the end; *bring, or pull, up* ~, check or pause abruptly; *be taken* ~, have sudden motion of bowels; ~*-spoken*, given to brevity of speech; *sell* ~, when one has not the articles in hand, see the adj.); ~ *of*, except, putting out of the question, (~ *of committing suicide he does his best to keep out of the way*). **10. n.** ~ syllable (LONG¹'s & ~s) or vowel; mark indicating that vowel is ~, as ă; ~ *film*; (colloq.) a ~ circuit; (pl.) garment like trousers cut ~ worn by athletes, boy scouts, boys, etc. **11.** v.t. (colloq.). To ~-circuit. [OE *sceort*, cf. OHG *scurz*, cogn. w. SKIRT, SHIRT]

shortˈage, n. (Amount of) deficiency (*there is* no ~, a ~ *of 100 tons*). [-AGE]

shortˈen, v.i. & t. Become or make actually or apparently shorter or short, curtail; reduce the amount of *sail* spread; put (child) into short clothes. Hence ~ˈING¹ (3) n., fat used for making pastry crisp. [-EN⁶]

shortˈly, adv. Before long, a short time *before* or *after*; in few words, briefly; curtly. [-LY²]

shot¹, n. (pl. ~s, also ~ see below), & v.t. (-tt-). **1.** Single missile for fire-arm or big gun, non-explosive projectile, (usu. with qualification or in comb., as *round, solid,* CHAIN-, GRAPE-, CASE², BUCK¹-, ~, *chilled* ~, *case-hardened for armour-piercing*; *a ~ in the* LOCKER); (pl. usu. ~) small lead pellets of which a quantity is used for single charge or cartridge esp. in sporting guns, such pellets collectively; (~ *does or do well for cleaning decanters*; *put three or ~s of different sizes on the gut*; ~ *is made in various ways*; *about a dozen no 10* ~ *were extracted from his leg*). **2.** Discharge of fire-arm or big gun (*several ~s were fired, heard,* etc.); attempt to hit with projectile or missile or fig. to make stroke in game or guess or do something (*at each* ~ *he was nearer the bull's-eye*; *a beautiful* ~ *from cover-point took off the bails*; *a lucky* ~ *at goal*; *made a bad* ~, *guessed wrong*; *am going to have a good* ~ *at winning*; *snap* ~, discharging of rifle etc. with momentary aim, cf. SNAPSHOT; *flying* ~, at bird on wing or moving object; PARTHIAN, *random,* ~; (-)~, range, reach, distance to or at which thing

will carry or act, as *bow, rifle, ear,* ~). **3.** Possessor of specified skill with rifle, gun, pistol, etc. (*is a good, bad, crack* or *first-class,* or *no,* ~). **4.** Dose of cocaine, injection of morphine, etc.; (colloq.) dram of spirits. **5.** Photograph taken with cinematograph camera. **6.** ~*-tower*, in which ~ is made from molten lead poured through sieves at top & falling into water at bottom; hence ~ˈPROOF² a. **7.** v.t. Load, weight, etc., with ~. [OE *gesceot* (Y-, *scēotan* SHOOT¹), cf. G *schoss*]

shot². See SHOOT¹.

shot³, n. Reckoning, (one's share of) bill at inn etc., (usu. *pay* one's ~). [var. of SCOT¹]

shoulᵈ. See SHALL.

shoulˈder (shŏl-), n., & v.t. & i. **1.** Part of body at which arm or foreleg or wing is attached, either lateral projection below or behind neck, (also ~*-joint*) combination of end of upper arm with those of collarbone & blade-bone, (pl.) upper part of back, (pl.) body regarded as bearing burdens, (of slaughtered animal) foreleg with parts usu. kept with it in dismembering, (HEAD¹ & ~s; *dislocate* one's ~; ~ *to* ~, with closed ranks or united effort; *has broad* ~s, is strong, can bear much weight or responsibility; *old head on young* ~s, youthful wisdom, wise young person; *put, set,* ~ *to wheel*, make effort; *straight from the* ~, said of well-directed blow or telling invective; ~*-of-mutton sail*, triangular fore-&-aft sail hoisted abaft mast; COLD¹ ~; COLD¹~ v.t.; *lay the blame, burden,* etc., *on the right* ~s). **2.** Part of mountain, bottle, tool, etc., projecting like human ~. **3.** (Mil.) position of soldier who has ~ed arms (see vb). **4.** ~*-belt*, baldric, bandolier, or other band passing over one~ & under opposite arm; ~*-blade*, either large flat bone of upper back, scapula; ~*-brace*, contrivance for flattening round back of child etc.; ~*-knot*, of ribbon or metal lace worn on ~ by livery servant; ~*-pegged*, (of horse) stiff in ~s; ~*-strap*, band from ~ tip in soldier's uniform, keeping ~-belts in place & bearing name or number of regiment etc.; hence (-)~ED² (-erd) a. **5. vb.** Push (t. & i.) with ~, jostle, make way thus; take (burden lit. or fig.) on one's ~s; (Mil.) ~ *arms*, hold rifle vertical supported by right hand at lock (cf. SLOPE v.). [OE *sculdor*, cf. Du. *schouder*, G *schulter*, etym. dub.]

shout, v.i. & t., & n. **1.** Make loud articulate or inarticulate cry or vocal sound, speak loudly, (~*ed with laughter*; ~ *for joy*; ~ *at*, speak loudly to etc.; *all is over but the* ~*ing*, contest is virtually decided); say loudly, call out, express in loud tones, (~ *approbation*; ~*ed that the coast was clear*; ~*ed to for me to come*; '*Go back*' *he* ~*ed*). **2.** n. Loud utterance or vocal sound from individual or com-

pany expressing joy, (dis)approval, defiance, etc., or calling attention (my ~, sl., turn to order drink etc. for the company). [f. 14th c., etym. dub.]

shove (-ŭv), v.t. & i., & n. **1.** Push (t. & i.) vigorously, move (t.) along by hard or rough pushing; make one's way along, past, through, etc., by pushing, jostle (person); ~-halfpenny, modern gambling form of shovelboard; (colloq.) put some-where (~ it in the drawer); ~ off, start from shore in boat. **2.** n. Push (give one a ~ off, help him to start); woody centre of flax-stem. [OE scūfan, G schieben]

sho'vel (-ŭv-), n. & v.t. (-ll-). **1.** Scooping implement for shifting coal, earth, etc., often in form of spade with sides of blade turned up; ~ hat, broad-brimmed as worn by Anglican dignitaries; ~ head, kinds of sturgeon & shark, also ~ nose; hence ~FUL(2) (shŭv'elfool) n. (pl. ~fuls), **2.** v.t. Shift (coal etc.) with or as with ~ (~ food into one's mouth, eat greedily). [OE scofl, cf. Du. schoffel hoe, G schaufel; cogn. w. prec.]

shovelboard (shŭv'elbŏrd), n. Game played (now esp. on ship's deck) by impelling disks (formerly coins) with hand or mace over marked surface. [earlier shoveboard, ~groat (SHOVE)]

sho'veller (-ŭv-), n. In vbl senses; also, the spoonbill duck. [-ER[1]]

show[1] (-ō), v.t. & i. (p.p. ~n, rarely ~ed; also spelt, now rarely, shew, shewn, disclose, w. pron. shō etc.). **1.** Let be seen, disclose, manifest, offer (thing, person thing, thing to person) for inspection, exhibit, produce, give (treatment, person treatment, treatment to person), reveal, (clothes ~ signs of wear; an aperture ~s the inside; ~ed neither joy nor anger, that he was annoyed, how much he felt it, etc.; ~ oneself, be seen in public; ~ me, I was ~n, a specimen; has nothing to ~ for it, no token of achievement etc.; ~ your tickets, please; got prizes for all the dogs he ~ed; (colloq.) ~ a leg, get out of bed; ~ a CLEAN[1] pair of heels; ~ the white FEATHER[1]; ~ the fire, slightly heat it). **2.** Be visible or noticeable, come into sight, appear in public, have some appearance, (the blood ~s through her skin; stain will never ~; buds are just ~ing; her husband never ~s at her at-homes, colloq.; ~s white, like a disk, from here). **3.** Demonstrate, prove, expound, point out, cause (person) to understand (thing), (has ~n the falsity of the tale, that it is false, how false it is, to be false; ~ one the way, by words, point-ing, or going with or before him, also encourage by doing thing first; ~ person how to write, what to do, etc.; ~ person the DOOR; it only ~s how little you know; on your own ~ing, even according to your own admission or contention). **4.** Conduct (~ed us round the house; one out or in, esp. open door for his exit or entrance). **5.** ~ down, (Poker) laying down of cards with faces up, (fig.) final test, disclosure of achievements or possibilities; ~ forth (arch.), exhibit, ex-pound; ~ off (trans.) display to advan-tage, (intr.) try to make impression by exhibiting one's wealth or skill; ~ up, make or be conspicuous or clearly visible, expose (fraud, impostor); shew'bread, shew'-bread, twelve loaves displayed in Jewish temple & renewed each sabbath; ~ case, glazed case for exhibiting goods, curiosities, etc.; ~ room, ~ window, in which wares are kept, hung up, for inspection; ~ place, that tourists etc. go to see. [OE scēawian see, make see, cf. Du. schouwen, G schauen; cogn. w. L cavēre be cautious, Gk koeō observe.]

show[2] (-ō), n. **1.** Showing (voted by ~ of hands; DUMB[1] ~). **2.** Spectacle, exhibi-tion, pageant, display, collection of things shown esp. for money to entertain (flower, horse, etc.; ~ ll Lord Mayor's ~; procession of symbolic cars etc.; a fine ~ of blossom); (colloq.) any kind of public entertainment. **3.** Outward appearance, semblance, impression produced, parade, ostentation, pomp, display, (piece be-neath the ~s of things; there is a ~ of reason in it; good enough in outward ~; did it for ~; is fond of ~; ll S~ Sunday, that before Commemoration at Oxford; give him a fair ~). **6.** (Obstetr.) discharge indicating approach of labour. **7.** ~ boat (orig. U.S.), (river) steamboat in which theatrical performances are given; ~ girl, actress whose role is decorative rather than histrionic; ~ man, proprietor or manager of menagerie or other such ~; ~ manship, the art of the ~ man, (fig.) capacity for exhibiting one's wares or one-self to the best advantage. [f. prec.]

show'er, n., & v.t. & i. **1.** Brief fall of rain, or of hail, arrows, bullets, dust, stones, etc. (also fig., as a ~ of gifts, honours; letters come in ~s); ~ bath, in which water descends from above through perforated plate; hence ~Y[2] a., ~INESS n. **2.** vb. Discharge (water, missiles, etc. in a ~, bestow (gifts etc. usu. upon); descend or come in a ~. [OE scūr, cf. Du. schoer, G schauer]

ll **shram**, v.t. (dial.; -mm-: usu. in p.p.). Benumb with or with cold. [perh. cogn. w. OE scrimman shrivel]

shrank. See SHRINK.

shrăp′nel, n. Bullets or pieces of metal contained in shell timed to burst slightly short of objective & let them fly on in shower; part of bomb etc. so scored as to break & scatter. [inventor's name]

shrĕd, n., & v.t. (-ded, arch.~). 1. Scrap, fragment, rag, strip, torn or broken piece, small remains, least amount, (*tore it to* ~*s; without a* ~ *of clothing on him; not a* ~ *of evidence, reputation,* etc.; *tear* an argument etc. *to* ~s, completely refute it). 2. v.t. Tear or cut into ~s. [OE *scrēade* n., *scrēadian* vb, cf. G *schrot;* cogn. w. SHROUD, doublet of SCREED]

shrew (-ōō), n. 1. Scolding woman, whence ~´ISH¹ (-ōō´-) a., ~´ISHLY² adv., ~´ISHNESS n. 2. (Also ~-*mouse*) small long-snouted mammal, like mouse, feeding on insects. [OE *scrēawa* ~mouse]

shrewd (-ōōd), a. (Of pain, cold, etc.) sharp, biting, (literary, esp.~ *blow, knock, thrust, turn*); sagacious, sensible, discriminating, astute, judicious, (*can make a* ~ *guess; a* ~ *observer;* ~ *face* etc., sagacious-looking). Hence ~´LY² adv., ~´NESS n. [ME *shrewed* (prec., -ED², cf. *dogged, crabbed*)]

shriek, n. & v.t. & i., & n. (Utter) shrill & usu. inarticulate cry of terror, pain, etc., screech, scream; laugh uncontrollably (usu. ~ *with laughter*); ~ *out,* say in shrill agonized tones. [var. of SCREECH]

shriev′alty, n. Sheriff's office or jurisdiction, tenure of this. [as SHERIFF n. F suf. as COMMONALTY]

shrift, n. (Arch.) Confession to priest, confession & absolution, (now only in *short* ~, little time between condemnation & execution or punishment). [OE *scrift* (SHRIVE)]

shrike, n. Kinds of bird called also *butcher-bird* with strong hooked & toothed bill & habit of impaling its prey of small birds & insects on thorns. [prob. f. OE *scríc* missel-thrush or perh. any shrill-voiced bird; cogn. w. SHRIEK]

shrill, a., & v.i. & t. 1. Piercing & high-pitched in sound; (fig.) importunate, insisting on being heard esp. in complaint or accusation; hence shrill′LY² (-l-ll) adv., ~´NESS n. 2. vb. (poet. or rhet.) (Of cry etc.) sound ~y; (of person etc.) utter, send *out,* (song, complaint, etc.) ~y. [f. 14th c.; cf. Sc. *skirl,* LG *schrell*]

shrimp, n., & v.i. 1. Kinds of long-tailed ten-footed saltwater crustacean of which the common British species is about two inches long of translucent greenish-grey while alive & brown when cooked; diminutive person. 2. v.i. Go catching ~s; hence ~´ER¹ n. [f. 14th c.; cf. MHG *schrimpen* shrink up]

shrine, n., & v.t. 1. Casket, esp. one holding sacred relics; tomb usu. sculptured or highly ornamented of saint etc.; altar or chapel of special associations; place

hallowed by some memory. 2. v.t. (poet.), Enshrine. [OE *scrín* f. L *scrinium* chest for writing-materials (*scribere* write]

shrink, v.i. & t. (*shrank; shrunk* & rarely in vbl, commonly in adj., use *shrunken*), & n. 1. Become of ~AGE(3) n.; grow smaller, whence ~´AGE(3) n.; recoil, retire from observation, (~ *into oneself,* become reserved), flinch *from,* whence ~´ING¹ adv.; be averse *from doing;* make smaller (esp. in pass.; *his face has a shrunken look*), make ~ (flannel etc., in order that it may not do so later; ~ *wheel-tire* etc. *on,* slip it on while expanded with heat & let it tighten as it cools), whence ~´ABLE a. 2. n. (rare). ~ing (*how much must we allow for the* ~?). [OE *scrincan,* cf. MDu. *schrinken*]

shrive, v.t. (arch.; *shrōve, shrĭven*). Hear confession of, assign penance to, & absolve; (of penitent) submit oneself to priest for this purpose. [OE *scrīfan* prob. f. L *scribere* write]

shrĭv′el, v.i. & t. (-ll-). Contract or wither (i. & t.) into wrinkled, folded, rolled-up, contorted, or dried-up state. [cf. Sw. dial. *skryvla*]

shrŏff, n., & v.t. 1. Banker or money-changer in the East; (Far East) native expert employed to detect base coin. 2. v.t. Examine (coin). [corrupted f. Arab. & Pers. *ṣarrāf*]

shroud, n., & v.t. 1. Winding-sheet, garment for the dead, whence ~´LESS a.; concealing agency (*wrapped in a* ~ *of mystery*); (pl.) set of ropes forming part of standing rigging & supporting mast or topmast. 2. v.t. Clothe (corpse) for burial; cover & conceal or disguise. [OE *scrúd* garment, cogn. w. SHRED]

Shrove Tues′day (tūz′dĭ), n. Day before Ash Wednesday, on which & the preceding days or *Shrovetide* it was customary to be shriven. [*shrove* formed f. SHRIVE (cf. ABODE), = SHRIFT]

shrŭb¹, n. Woody plant of less size than tree & usu. divided into separate stems from near the ground. Hence ~b′Y² a., ~b′ERY(3) n. [OE *scrybb,* cf. Norw. *skrubba* dwarf cornel]

shrŭb², n. Cordial made of fruit-juice & spirit (usu. *rum-*~). [f. Arab. *sharāb;* cogn. w. SHERBET, SYRUP]

shrŭg, v.t. & i. (-gg-), & n. 1. Slightly & momentarily raise (shoulders), raise shoulders, to express indifference, helplessness, contempt, vexation, etc. 2. n. This motion (*of the shoulders,* or abs.). [f. 1400, etym. dub.]

shrunk(en). See SHRINK.

shŭck, n., & v.t. 1. Husk, pod. 2. v.t. Remove ~s of, shell. [?]

shŭdd′er, v.i., & n. (Experience) sudden shivering due to fear, horror, repugnance, or cold; feel strong repugnance etc. (*I* ~ *to think what might happen*). Hence ~´ing-LY² adv., & *schaudern,* cf. G *schaudern*]

shŭffle, v.i. & t. & n. **1.** Move (t. & i.) with scraping or sliding or dragging or difficult motion (~s along rheumatically; ~s his feet; ~ cards, slide them over one another so as to change their relative positions; so ~ things of any sort, intermingle, confuse; ~ the cards, fig., change the parts, try new policy, etc.); slip (clothes, burden) off or on (~ off responsibility upon others; ~d on his clothes); keep shifting one's position lit. or fig.; fidget, vacillate, prevaricate, whence shŭff'lĭng¹ adv. = SHOVELBOARD; hence shŭff'lĭngly² adv. **2.** n. Shuffling movement; shuffling of cards, general change of relative positions; piece of equivocation or sharp practice; quick scraping movement of feet in dancing (double ~, executed twice with one & then the other foot). [perh. f. LG schüffeln, cogn. w. SCUFFLE]

shŭn, v.t. (-nn-). Avoid, keep clear of, eschew. Hence ~LESS a. (poet.). [OE scunian, etym. dub.]

'shŭn¹, abbr. of attention ! as word of command.

shunt, v.t. & i., & n. **1.** Divert (train, electric current, etc.), ||(of train etc.) diverge, on to a side track, esp. to clear line for more important traffic, whence ~'ER¹ n.; postpone or stifle discussion of (subject), lay aside (project), leave (person) inactive. **2.** n. Turning or being turned on to side track; (Electr.) conductor joining two points of circuit, over which more or less of current may be diverted. [perh. f. SHUN]

shut, v.t. & i. (shut). **1.** Move (door, sash, lid, lips, etc.) into position to stop an aperture (~ the door upon, refuse to consider, make impossible). **2.** ~ door etc. of, window, box, eye, mouth, etc.; ~ your eyes; ~ one's eyes or by extension ears to, pretend not or refuse to see or hear. **3.** Become or admit of being closed, swing or fall or contract into closed position, (the door ~s with a bang; lid ~s automatically; pimpernels ~ in rainy weather). **4.** Keep (person, sound, etc., out or in by ~ting door etc., send (person) into or out of room etc. & fasten door etc. against him, bar (person) out from hope etc. **5.** Be ~ of (person (sl.), be rid of. **6.** Catch or pinch (finger, dress, etc.) by ~ting something on it (~ his finger into the door-hinge). **7.** Bring parts of together (~ his teeth, a knife, etc.). **8.** ~ down, push or pull (window-sash etc.), down into closed position, (of factory etc.) cease working; ~ in, (of hills, houses, sea, etc.), enclose, prevent free prospect or egress from or access to; ~ off, check flow of (water, gas, etc.), by ~ting valve, separate from society etc.; ~ out, exclude (landscape etc., from view, prevent (possibility etc.).; ~ to adv., close (door etc., or intr. of bid; ~ up, close (door etc., or door etc.) tight; ~ up, close all doors & windows of or bolt & bar (house; ~ up shop, cease business for the day or permanently, close (box etc., securely or decisively or permanently), imprison (person); put (thing) away in box etc., desist (colloq.; esp. ~ up imperat.), reduce to silence by rebuke or refutation. [OE scyttan cogn. w. SHOOT (f. shooting of bolt)]

shŭt'ter, n., & v.t. In vbl senses of prec.; esp.: one of a set of wooden panels or iron plates, hinged, sliding, folding, or detachable, placed inside or outside glass of window to keep out light or burglars or permanently; structure of jointed laths or metal slats on rollers serving same purposes; blind of swell-box in organ for regulating loudness; piece that opens & closes lens of photographic camera; hence ~LESS a.; (v.t.) provide with ~s, put up ~s of. [-ER¹]

shut'tle, n. Weaving-implement shaped like cigar with two pointed ends by which weft-thread is carried or shot across between threads of warp; carrier of lower thread in lock-stitch sewing-machine; ~ armature (Electr.), armature with a single coil wound on an elongated iron bobbin; ~cock, cork stuck with feathers & struck to & fro in BATTLEDORE & ~ [-cock prob. f. flying motion]; ~ train (running a short distance to and fro, usu. on branch-line), so ~ service. [OE scytel bolt, cogn. w. SHOOT, SHUT, see -LE(1)]

shy¹, a. (~er, ~est, rarely shi-). (Of beasts, birds, fish, etc.) easily startled, timid, avoiding observation; bashful, coy, uneasy in company; avoiding company of person, chary of doing, (might ~ of); elusive, hard to find, catch, interpret, etc.; (sl.) short (of), in the position of having lost (I'm ~ three quid); -shy, (in comb.) indicating fear of or distaste for (first element of comb.), as in GUN-~, WORK¹-~. Hence ~LY² adv., ~NESS n.

shy², v.i., & n. Start suddenly aside (at object or noise, or fig. at proposal etc.) in alarm (usu. of horse, or fig. of person). Hence ~ER¹ n. [f. prec.]

shy³, v.t. & i., & n. (colloq.). **1.** Fling, throw. (stone etc., or abs.). **2.** n. Act of ~ing (have a ~ at, try to hit with missile, jeer at, make an attempt to get). [?]

Shy'lock, n. Hard-hearted money-lender. [character in Merchant of Venice]

shy'ster, n. (sl.). Person without professional honour, esp. tricky lawyer. [?]

si (sē), n. (mus.). Seventh note of octave. [added perh. c. 1600 to names of hexachord; see GAMUT; perh. f. initials of Sancte Johannes in sapphics given under gamut]

sī'amăng (or sē-), n. Kind of gibbon from Sumatra & Malay peninsula. [Malay]

Siamese (-z), a. & n. (pl. same). (Native, language) of Siam; ~ *twins*, two ~ (d. 1874) joined by cartilaginous band from one's right to other's left side, (fig.) inseparable friends etc.; ~ *cat*, cream-coloured short-haired breed with brown or blue points. [-ESE]

sib, a. (arch. & Sc.). Related, akin, (*to*). [OE *sib(b)*, cf. MDu. *sib(be)*, OHG *sippi*]

Siberian (sibē-), a. & n. (Inhabitant) of Siberia (~ *dog*, of breed much used for sledging). [-AN]

sib'ilant, a. & n. 1. Hissing, sounded with a hiss (esp. of letter or set of letters, as s, sh); hence ~ANCE, ~ANCY, nn. 2. n. ~ant letter(s). [f. L *sibilare* hiss (*sibilus* a hissing), -ANT]

sib'ilate, v.t. & i. Pronounce with hissing sound. Hence ~ATION n. [as prec., -ATE³]

sib'yl, n. One of the women who in ancient times acted at various places (*Cumaean, Erythraean*, etc., ~) as mouthpiece of some god, & to whom many collections of oracles & prophecies were attributed, pagan prophetess; old fortune-teller, sorceress, or hag. [f. L f. Gk *Sibulla*]

sib'ylline, a. Issuing from an ancient sibyl, oracular, mysteriously prophetic; the ~ *books*, collection of oracles belonging to ancient-Roman State & often consulted by magistrates for guidance, (fig., with ref. to story of their acquisition) thing that one refuses & is afterwards glad to get on worse terms. [f. L *Sibyllinus* (prec., -INE¹)]

sic, Latin adv. = so, appended in brackets after a word or expression in a quoted passage as guarantee that it is quoted exactly, though its incorrectness or absurdity would suggest that it was not. Also in the phr. ~ *vōl'ō* ~ *jub'eō* (jŏō-; such is my will & command) used as n. = arbitrary order; ~ *vōs nōn vōb'īs* (so ye not for yourselves) used w. ref. to work of which the credit etc. falls to another than the doer.

Sican'ian, a. 1. Aboriginal inhabitant of Sicily (cf. *Sicel, Siceliot, Sicilian*). 2. adj. Of the ~s. [f. L *Sicanus* (L f. Gk *Sikanoi* pl.), -AN]

sic'cative, a. & n. (Substance etc.) of drying properties, esp. one mixed with oil-paint to dry it. [f. LL *siccativus* (DESICCATE, -ATIVE]

sice¹, n. The six on dice. [f. OF *sis* six]

sice², **syce**, n. (Anglo-Ind.). Groom. [f. Hind. f. Arab. *sā'īs*]

Si'cel, Sik'el, Siceil'ian, nn. & aa. 1. Member of race that immigrated into Sicily perh. c. 11th c. B.C., native as opposed to Greek ancient Sicilian (cf. foll.). 2. adj. Of the ~s. [f. Gk *Sikeloi* pl., & L *Siculi* pl., -AN]

Siceil'iot, Sik-, n. & a. 1. Ancient-Greek settler in Sicily. 2. adj. Of the ~s. [f. Gk *Sikeliōtēs* (*Sikeleia* Sicily, -OT²)]

Sicil'ian, a. & n. 1. Of Sicily or its inhabitants (~ *Vespers*, massacre of French residents by natives in 1282, with vesper bell as signal). 2. n. Native of Sicily. [f. L *Sicilia* Sicily +-AN]

sick¹, a. 1. Ill, incapacitated by illness, feeling effects of some disease, (*a ~ man; the S~ Man*, Turkish Empire (hist.); ~ *of a fever; the ~*, those who are ill; || *be, feel, make*, ~ in mod. use, vomit, be disposed or cause to vomit; *turn ~*, feel as if about to vomit). 2. Disordered, perturbed, suffering effects of, disgusted, pining for, (*am ~ at heart; ~ of love, love~; makes me ~ to think of it; is awfully ~ at being beaten; for a sight of home*). 3. Surfeited & tired of (~ *of flattery, rain, waiting*). 4. (Of ship) needing repair (esp. ~BAY³; ~*bed*, invalid's bed, as *nail~, pain~*). 5. ~BAY³; ~*bed*, invalid's bed, invalid state; ~*benefit*, allowance made to worker absent from work through illness; ~*call*, military summons on bugle etc. for men to attend; ~*flag*, yellow, indicating presence of disease at quarantine station or on ship; ~*headache*, due to biliousness; ~*leave*, leave of absence granted for reason of health; ~*list*, of the ~ esp. in regiment, ship, etc. (*on the ~list*, laid up); ~*room*, occupied by ~ person, or kept ready for the ~. Hence ~ISH¹(2) a. [OE *sēoc*, cf. Du. *ziek*, G *siech*]

sick², v.t. Set upon (usu. in imperat. *him!* etc. urging dog to worry rat etc.). [var. of SEEK]

sick'en, v.i. & t. Begin to be ill, show symptoms of illness (*child is ~ing for something*); feel nausea or disgust at, to see, etc.; affect with inclination to vomit, loathing, or disgust (*a ~ing sight*) or with weariness or despair of (*was ~ed of trying to make peace*), whence ~ER(²) n., ~ingLY² adv. [-EN⁶]

sic'kle, n. Reaping-hook, short-handled semicircular - bladed implement now chiefly used for lopping & trimming, formerly for cutting corn; *the* constellation Leo; ~*bill*, kinds of bird with ~-shaped bill; ~*feather*, one of long middle feathers of cock's tail; ~*wort*, the plant Heal-all. [OE *sicol*, cf. Du. *sikkel*, G *sichel*, perh. f. L *secula* (*secare* cut)]

sick'ly, a., & v.t. 1. Apt to be ill, chronically ailing, of weak health; suggesting sickness, as of sick person, languid, faint, pale, (~*y look, smile, complexion*); causing ill health, inducing or connected with nausea, (~*y climate, smell, taste*); mawkish, weakly sentimental. 2. v.t. Cover over or o'er with a ~*y* hue (w. ref. to *Haml.* III. i. 85). Hence ~INESS n. [-LY¹]

sick'ness, n. 1. Being ill, disease. 2. A disease (FALL¹*ing ~; sleeping ~*, fatal African disease, *morbus dormitivus*, marked by somnolence & nerve-paralysis, caused by certain trypanosomes intro-

duced by kinds of tsetse; **sleepy ~**, epi-demic encephalitis or *encephalitis lethar-gica*, acute inflammation of the brain, not yet traced to a parasitic cause, but distinct from sleeping ~, though lethargy is a mark of both). **3.** Vomiting or inclination to vomit. [-NESS]

Siculian. See SICEL.

Sic′ŭlo-, comb. form of L *Sĭcŭlī* Sicilians, as ~*-Arabian*, Arabian as modified in Sicily. [-o-]

side, n. **1.** One of the flat(tish) surfaces bounding an object (*cube has six ~s*), esp. a more or less vertical outer or inner sur-face (~ *of house, cave, mountain, etc.*; so perh. COUNTRY-~); such surface as distin-guished from top & bottom, or front & back, or ends (*four, or two, ~s of box; two ~s of house*). **2.** Either surface of thing re-garded as having only two (*two ~s of sheet of paper, board, etc.; sent him six ~s of argument*, pages of notepaper so filled; the INSIDE & OUTSIDE of a bowl; *right, wrong, ~ of cloth*, etc., surface meant, not meant, to be visible; BACK′*side*; SHADY, SEAMY, SILVER, ~). **3.** (Math.) bounding line of superficial figure (*opposite ~s of a parallelogram*). **4.** Part of person or animal that is on his or its right or left, esp. that of it which extends from armpit to hip or from foreleg to hindleg (~ *of mutton, bacon*, etc., this part of carcass; BLIND) ~; ~ *by* ~, standing close together; *laugh heartily*; ~*-splitting*, causing violent laughter, amusing). **5.** Part of object turned in same direction as ob-server's right or left & not directly to-wards or away from him, or turned in specified direction (*right, left, ~; debit, credit, ~*, in account book; *epistle, gospel, ~, south, north, end of altar*; DECANI, CANTORIS, ~; *the north, landward, ~*). **6.** Part or region near margin and remote from centre or axis of thing, subordinate or less essential or more or less detached part, (~ *of room, road, table*, etc.; (attrib) ~ *issue, point that distracts attention*; ~ *line*, work etc. carried on apart from one's main work, see also sense 14); *on the* ~, as a ~ *line*, in addition to one's regular work. **7.** Region external but contiguous to, specified direction with relation to, person or thing (*on one* ~, aside; *look on all* ~*s; came from all* ~*s or every* ~; *standing at my* ~; *on the north* ~ *of*). **8.** Partial aspect of thing, aspect differing from or opposed to other aspects (*study all* ~*s of the question; has many* ~*s to his character; the* ~ *of the moon visible to us*); *on the* ~ (so-and-so), rather (so-and-so), as *prices were on the high* ~. **9.** (Cause represented by, position in company with) one of two sets of oppo-nents in war, politics, games, etc. (*the Lord is on my* ~; *there is much to be said, there are faults, on both* ~*s; take* ~*s*, decide to

espouse one or other cause; *join the win-ning* ~; ON[1], OFF, ~; *Cambridge has a strong* ~, team for cricket, football, etc.). **10.** Position nearer or farther than, right or left of, dividing line (*on this* ~ *of*, or *on this* ~, *the Alps; on this* ~ *the grave*, in life; *on the right, wrong,* ~ *of forty, below, above,* 40 years of age; *on the wrong* ~ *of the door*, shut out; *on the wrong* ~ *of the* BLANKET[1]). **11.** Line of descent through father or mother (*well descended on the mother's or maternal* ~; DISTAFF or spindle, SPEAR, ~). **12.** ∥(Billiards) spin-ning motion given to ball by striking it on ~. **13.** ∥(sl.). Assumption of superio-rity, swagger, (*puts on, has too much,* ~, whence sid′Y². **14.** ~*-arms*, swords or bayonets; ~*-bet*, bet between opponents, freq. in card-games; ~*-board*, table or flat-topped chest at ~ of dining-room for supporting and containing dishes, decan-ters, etc.; ~*-bone*, (in carving fowls) either small forked bone under wing, ~*-car*, = JAUNTing-car, (also) car for passenger(s) at-tachable to ~ of (motor-)cycle; ~*-chapel*, in aisle or at ~ of church; ~*-dish*, extra dish often of elaborate kind at dinner etc.; ~*-drum*, small double-headed drum in military band hung at drummer's ~; ~*-light*, light from ~, (fig.) incidental illustration etc., (Naut.) red port or green starboard light on ship under way; ~*-lines*, (space immediately outside) lines bounding football-pitch, tennis-court, etc., *at the* ~*s*, see also sense 6; ~*-note*, ... (vb) or motion broadside on instead of forward, also shoot of tree & (fig.) illegi-timate child, also (Theatr.) division at ~ of stage for working scenery; ~*s′man*, deputy churchwarden; ~*-step*, (n.) step taken sideways, step for getting in & out of carriage etc., (v.t.) avoid by stepping sideways; ~*-stroke*, stroke towards or from a ~, incidental action, kinds of swimming action opp. breast-stroke; ~*-track*, siding, (v.t.) turn into siding, shunt, postpone treatment or consideration of, (chiefly U.S.); ~*-view*, view obtained sideways, profile; ~*-walk*, path at ~ of road for foot-passengers (chiefly U.S.); ~ *wind*, wind from a ~, indirect agency or influ-ence. Hence (-)sid′ED[2] a., (-)sid′ED[1]² a. adv. (-)sid′EDNESS n. ~′LESS (-dl-) a. [OE *side*, cf. Du. *zijde*, G *seite*, & prob. OE *sid* spacious]

side², v.i. Take part, be on same side, *with* disputant etc. [f. prec.]

side′long (-dl-), adv. & a. Inclining to one side, oblique(ly), (*move* ~; *a* ~ *glance*).
[-LONG]

sider'eal, a. Of the constellations or the fixed stars (~ *day*, time between successive meridional transits of star, esp. of first point in Aries, about 4' shorter than solar day; ~ *year*, time in which earth makes one complete revolution round sun, longer than tropical year by difference due to precession; ~ *time*, measured by apparent diurnal motion of stars). [f. L *sidereus* (*sidus -eris* star), -AL]

si'di (sē-), n. An African; negro (chiefly in comb. ~-*boy*). [Urdu *sīdī*, f. Arab. (see SEID); orig. title of honour given in India to African Moslems]

sid'ing, n. Short track by side of railway line & opening into it at one end or both for shunting purposes. [-ING¹]

si'dle, v.i. Walk obliquely, esp. in timid or cringing manner (often *along*, *up*). [back formation f. obs. *sideling* (now SIDELONG)]

Sidon'ian, a. & n. (Inhabitant) of Sidon. [f. L f. Gk *Sidōnios* (*Sidōn*), -AN]

siege, n., & v.t. 1. Operations of encamped attacking force to take or compel surrender of fortified place, period during which these last, besieging or being besieged, (often fig.; *push the* ~, continue it vigorously; *raise the* ~ f, abandon attempt to take; *lay the* ~ *to*, begin besieging; ~ *lasted 100 days*; *stood a long* ~, before or without surrendering); persistent attempt to force or persuade reluctant person to do something; ~-*basket*, gabion; ~-*gun*, used in ~s, too heavy for field use; ~-*train*, artillery & other appliances for besieging; ~-*works*, trenches, shelters, etc., of besiegers. 2. v.t. (arch.). Besiege. [OF, orig. = seat, ult. f. L *sedes*]

Sieg'fried line, n. German fortified line along Franco-German border. [person]

Sien(n)ese' (-z), a. & n. (pl. same). (Inhabitant) of Siena (~ *school*, of 13th-14th-c. painters). [-ESE]

sienn'a, n. Ochrous earth used raw or burnt as pigment of brownish-yellow (*raw*~) or reddish-brown (*burnt*~) colour. [f. It. (*terra di*) *Siena* (earth of) Sienna]

sie'rra, n. Long jagged mountain-chain; Spanish mackerel. [Sp., f. L *serra* saw]

sies'ta, n. Midday nap or rest in hot countries. [Sp., f. L *sexta* (*hora*) sixth hour]

sieve (siv), n., & v.t. 1. Utensil for separating finer from coarser particles by letting finer pass when shaken through holes too small for coarser, usu. a shallow wooden cylinder with cross wires or hairs stretched across bottom; coarsely plaited basket often used as measure; person who cannot keep secrets. 2. v.t. Put through, sift with, ~. [OE *sife*, cf. Du. *zeef*, G *sieb*]

siffleur' (sēflér'), n. (fem. *-euse*, pr. *-ēz*). Whistling artiste. [F]

sift, v.t. & i. Separate into finer & coarser parts with sieve, separate (finer parts *from* material or its coarser parts or *out*, sprinkle (sugar etc.) from perforated spoon etc.; closely examine details of (evidence, facts, etc.) with regard to credibility or authenticity or relevance, analyse character of; (of snow, light, etc.) fall as from sieve. Hence (-)~ER¹(1, 2) n. [OE *siftan* (*sife* SIEVE)]

sigh (sī), v.i. & t., & n. 1. Draw deep audible breath expressive of sadness, weariness, aspiration, relief from tension, cessation of effort, etc.; *yearn for* (person or thing desired or lost); utter or express with ~s (usu. *out*); (of wind etc.) make sound like ~ing; hence ~'ingLY²(sī'i-) adv. 2. n. Act of, sound made in, ~ing (*a* ~ *of relief*). [ME *sīhen* prob. f. OE *sīcan*]

sight¹ (sīt), n. 1. Faculty of vision (*long*, *short* or *near* ~, requiring objects to be unusually far, near, for clear definition; *short* ~, fig., lack of discernment or foresight; *has good*, *bad*, ~; *know by* ~, be familiar with appearance only of; *loss of* ~, becoming blind; *second* ~, power of internal vision by which future or distant occurrences are presented), whence (-)~'ED³ (sīt-) a., (-)~'EDLY² adv., (-)~'EDNESS n. 2. Seeing or being seen, way of looking at or considering thing, (*catch*, *lose*, ~ *of*, begin, cease, to see; *have lost* ~ *of Jones*, no longer know his movements etc.; *get a* ~ *of*, manage to see; *take a* ~ (*of*, *at*), sl., cock a snook; *at*, *on*, ~, as soon as person or thing has been seen; *plays music at* ~, without preliminary study or practice of piece; ~-*singing*, reading vocal music at ~; *payable at* ~, of draft etc.; *at first* ~, *prima facie*; *the* ~ *of her distress unmanned him*; *she found favour in his* ~; *do what is right in one's own* ~). 3. Range or unobstructed space within which person etc. can see or object be seen (*is in*, *out of*, ~, visible, not visible; HEAVE¹ *in* ~; *the millennium is in* ~, clearly near at hand; *put out of* ~, hide, ignore; *came in* ~ *of the fort*, so as to see it or be seen from it; *out of* ~ *out of mind*, we forget the absent; *out of my* ~!, rhetorical order to depart). 4. Thing seen, visible, or worth seeing, display, show, spectacle, (*a sad* ~ *awaited us*; *a* ~ *for sore eyes*, person or thing one is glad to see, esp. welcome visitor; *went to see the* ~s, noteworthy features of town etc., whence ~'SEER¹, ~'seeing¹, nn.; *the daffodils were a* ~ *to see* or *a* ~; *his face is a perfect* ~, disfigured with wounds etc.; *make a* ~ *of oneself*, dress in bizarre fashion etc.). 5. (colloq.). Great quantity (*will cost a*

~ *Of money; is a long* ~ *better*). **6.** (Kinds of device for assisting) precise aim with gun or observation with optical instrument (*forgot to put up the leaf of his back* ~, *in rifle-shooting; took a careful* ~ *before firing; the* ~s *of, a* ~ *with, quadrant or compass*). **7.** ~**worthy**, worth seeing. [OE *gesiht* (χ-, SEE-, TH²), cf. G *sicht*]

sight² (sīt), v.t. Get sight of, esp. by coming near (~ *land, game*); take observation of (star etc.) with instrument; provide (gun, quadrant, etc.) with sights; adjust sights of (~*ing shot*, experimental one to guide rifleman etc. in this); aim (gun etc.) by means of sights. [f. prec.]

sight'less (sīt-), a. Blind; (poet.) invisible.

sight'ly (sīt-), a. Not unsightly. Hence ~**INESS** n. [-LY¹]

si'gillate, a. (Of pottery) with impressed patterns; (Bot.) having seal-like marks. [f. LL *sigillatus* (*sigillum* seal dim. of SIGNUM, -ATE²)]

si'gma, n. Greek letter (Σ or ς or s) corresponding to s. [Gk, perh. f. *stzō* hiss, -M.]

si'gmate¹, a. Sigma-shaped; S-shaped. [-ATE²]

si'gmate², v.t. Add sigma or s to. Hence ~A'TION n. [-ATE²]

sigma'tic, a. Formed with sigma (esp. ~ *aorist*). [SIGMA-*atos*, -IC]

si'gmoid, a. & n. **1.** (Chiefly anat.) curved like the uncial sigma (C), or (now usu.) like S. **2.** n. Reversed or inverted curve. [-OID]

sign¹ (sīn), n. **1.** Mark traced on surface etc. (esp. *the* ~ *of the cross*, made by Christian priests in blessing or laymen in reverence with finger on forehead or breast; ~ *manual*, signature written with person's own hand). **2.** Written mark conventionally used for word or phrase, symbol, thing used as representation of something, (*positive* or *plus* ~, +; *negative* or *minus* ~, - : *words are the* ~s *of ideas; a sacrament is an outward & visible* ~ *of an inward & spiritual grace*). **3.** (Thing serving as) presumptive evidence or indication or suggestion or symptom of or that, distinctive mark, token, guarantee, password, miracle evidencing supernatural power, portent, (*violence is a* ~ *of weakness or that one is weak; shows all the* ~s *of decay; gave earth & water in* ~ *of submission; by this* ~ *ye shall know them; did* ~s & *wonders;* ~ & *counter*~, secret sentences etc. by which confederates recognize each other; ~s *of the times*, things showing the tendency of affairs); (Path.) objective evidence or indication of disease (often with defining word, as *Babinski's, Oppenheim's,* ~). **4.** (Often ~ *board*) fanciful device usu. painted on a board displayed formerly by traders of any sort & still by many inns & some barbers etc. as advertisement of their business (*at the* ~ *of the White Hart* etc., formerly used as address). **5.** Natural or conventional motion or gesture used instead of words to convey information & esp. order or request (*gave him a* ~ *to withdraw; deaf-&-dumb* ~s, those used in finger-talk; *make no* ~, seen unconscious, not protest, etc.). **6.** Any of twelve divisions of ZODIAC named from constellations formerly situated in them. **7.** ~**painter, -writer**, of ~*boards*, shop-front inscriptions, etc.; ~**post**, at cross-roads etc. with names of places on each road. [f. F *signe* f. L *signum*]

sign² (sīn), v.t. & i. **1.** Mark with sign (esp. ~ *infant* etc. *with the sign of the cross in baptism*). **2.** Acknowledge or guarantee (letter, deed, picture, book, article, petition, etc., or abs.) by writing one's own name or initials or recognized mark (*the will had never been* ~ed; *a* ~ed *masterpiece of Turner's;* ~ed *as usual with a dickybird; does not* ~ *his contributions to the press; nothing shall induce me to* ~), whence ~**ABLE** (sīn-) a. **3.** Write (one's name) as signature; convey (right, property, etc.) away by ~ing deed etc.; take, acknowledge being taken, on for some employment to which employee binds himself by signature. **4.** Communicate by gesture (~ *assent*), give order or make request by gesture to person to do (~ed *to come*). [f. L *signare* (*signum*, see prec.)]

sig'nal¹, a. Remarkably good or bad, conspicuous, noteworthy, exemplary, condign, (~ *victory, defeat, reward, punishment, virtue, example*). Hence ~**IZE**... [f. L *signum*]

sig'nal², n. & v.t. & i. (-ll-). **1.** Preconcerted or intelligible sign conveying information or direction esp. to person(s) at a distance, message made up of such signs, (*the* ~ *was to be the dropping of a handkerchief;* ~s *are made by day with flags & by night with lights; gave the* ~ *for advance;* esp. from ship made by firing guns; help, esp. from ship made at meteorological station; *code of* ~s, ~*book, body of* ~s *arranged for sending complicated messages* esp. in naval & mil. use); immediate occasion for some general movement (*the earthquake was the* ~ *for an outbreak of the primitive instincts*); ~**man** (.. ROYAL CORPS of S~s; ~*box*, hut on railway with ~*ling-apparatus;* ~*er*). ~ *strength*, strength of reception of wireless ~s (varying with the time of day etc.). **2.** vb. Make ~(s), make ~(s) to, transmit (order, information) by ~, announce (event, that) by ~; direct (person to do) by ~; hence ~**LER¹** n. [F, f. med. L *signale* (orig. neut. adj. as prec.]

sig'nalize, v.t. Make noteworthy or

remarkable, lend distinction or lustre to, (*his accession was* ~*d by an amnesty*). [SIGNAL¹, -IZE]

sig'nator|y, a. & n. (Party, esp. State) that has signed an agreement esp. a treaty (*the* ~*ies or* ~*y powers to the treaty of Berlin*). [f. L *signatorius* of sealing (*signare* mark, -TORY)]

sig'nature, n. **1.** (arch.). Significant appearance or mark (*has the* ~ *of passion, of early death, in his face*; *herb's yellow flowers are a* ~ *indicating that it will cure jaundice*). **2.** Person's name or initials or mark used in SIGN'ing. **3.** Letter or figure placed by printer at foot of first page of each sheet of book as guide in making up for binding, such sheet after folding. **4.** (mus.). Key ~, clef with sharps or flats at beginning of each staff; *time* ~, fraction placed at beginning of composition, numerator giving number of beats in each bar and denominator duration of each. **5.** ~ *tune*, special tune used in broadcasting to announce a particular turn etc. [F, f. med. L *signatura* (prec., -URE)]

sig'net, n. Private seal for use instead of or with signature as authentication (*the* ~, royal seal formerly used for special purposes; || WRITER *to the* ~; ~*-ring*, finger-ring with seal set in it. [OF (SIGN¹, -ET¹)]

signif'icance, n. Being significant, expressiveness, (*there is no* ~ *in his eyes*; *with a look of deep* ~); covert or real import, what is meant to be or may be inferred, (*those were the words, but what is their* ~?); importance, noteworthiness, (*what he thinks about it is of no* ~). [OF, f. L *significantia* (SIGNIFY, -ANCE)]

signif'icant, a. Having a meaning (-kin *is a* ~ *termination*); expressive, suggestive, with pregnant or secret sense, inviting attention esp. from part only of company; noteworthy, of considerable amount or effect or importance, not insignificant or negligible, (usu. in negative contexts, as *the only* ~ *event was* —). Hence ~LY² adv. [as SIGNIFY, -ANT]

significa'tion, n. Act of signifying (rare); exact meaning or sense (usu. ~ *of something*, esp. of a word or phrase). [OF, f. L *significationem* (SIGNIFY, -ATION)]

signif'icative, a. Offering signs or presumptive evidence of. [OF (-*if*, -*ive*), see foll., -ATIVE]

sig'nif|y̆, v.t. & i. Be a sign or indication or presage of (*a long upper lip* ~*ies obstinacy*; *a halo* ~*ies rain*); mean, have as meaning, (*D.D.* ~*ies doctor of divinity*); communicate, make known, (*he* ~*ied his reluctance, that he could not consent*); be of importance, matter, (esp. in negative contexts, as *it does not* ~*y*). [f. F *signifier* f. L *significare* (SIGN¹, -FY)]

Signior, Signora, Signorina. See GRAND.

Signor, Signora, Signorina, (sēn'yŏr,

sēnyŏr'a, sēnyorēn'a), nn. (pl. -*ri* pr. -rē, -*re* pr. -rā, -*ne* pr. -nā). Titles used of or to Italians corresponding to Sir & Mr, Madam & Mrs, young lady & Miss. [It.]

Sikh (sēk, sĭk), n. Member of Hindu community founded as monotheistic sect c. 1500 in Punjab & after achieving independence annexed 1849 to British India. Hence ~'ISM n., the (religious) tenets of the ~s. [Hind., = disciple]

sil'age, n., & v.t. **1.** = ENSILAGE. **2.** v.t. Put into silo. [SILO, -AGE]

sil'ence, n., & v.t. **1.** Abstinence from speech or noise, being silent, taciturnity, non-betrayal of secret etc., fact of not mentioning a thing, (*the* ~ *of Scripture on the subject*; ~ *gives consent*; ~ *is golden*; *keep, break,* ~, abstain from speaking, speak; *put to* ~, esp. refute in argument); absence of sound, stillness, (*in* ~, without speech or other sound); oblivion, state of not being mentioned, (*have passed into* ~); S~! (order to cease from speech or noise). **2.** v.t. Make silent by force, superior argument, etc. (~*d the enemy's batteries, the best debaters in the House, the voice of conscience*). Hence **sil'encer¹** n., kinds of device for rendering (comparatively) noiseless the escape of gas from gun, oil-engine, etc. [vb f. n., OF, f. L *silentium* (*silēre* be silent)]

sil'ent, a. Not speaking, not uttering or making or accompanied by any sound, (~ *letter*, one written but not pronounced, e.g. *b* in *doubt*; ~ *film*, without sound accompaniment; ~ *partner*, with no voice in management of business; *the* ~ *system* in prisons, by which prisoners are never allowed to speak); taciturn, speaking little; saying nothing on some subject (*history is* ~ *upon it*). Hence ~LY² adv. [f. L *silēre* be silent, -ENT]

Silē'nus, n. Rollicking drunken bloated old man. [L, f. Gk *Seilēnos* name of one of Bacchus's attendants]

silē'sia (-sha), n. Kinds of thin cloth used for blinds & dress-linings. [orig. made in Silesia]

silhouětte' (-lŏŏ-), n., & v.t. **1.** Portrait of person in profile showing outline only, all inside the outline being usu. black on white ground or cut out in paper; appearance of person or object as seen against light so that outline only is distinguishable (*in* ~, so seen or placed). **2.** v.t. Represent or (usu. pass.) exhibit in ~. [named after French minister of finance 1759 w. ref. to his parsimony]

sil'ic|a, n. Silicon dioxide, occurring as quartz & as principal constituent of sandstone & other rocks (~*os'TS* n., disease caused by inhalation of quartz dust, so ~OT'IC a. & n.). Hence **silĭ'cɪᴄ,** ~ɪʀ'ᴇʀᴏᴜꜱ, **silĭ'cɪᴏᴜꜱ** or **silĭ'cɪᴏᴜꜱ** (-shus), aa., ~ᴀᴛᴇ¹(ȧ) n., ~ɪ⁻, ~ᴏ⁻, comb. forms. [f. L *silex -icis* flint]

sil'icātĕd, a. Coated, mixed, combined,

or impregnated, with silica. [prec., -ATE³, -ED¹]

sili̇ci̇fy̆, v.t. & i. Impregnate with silica, turn (t. & i.) into silica, petrify. Hence **~FICA̍TION** n. [SILICA, -FY]

sili̇con, n. Non-metallic element of very common occurrence in the compound SILICA. [as SILICA]

sili̇ʹqua (pl. -ae), **sili̇que**' (-ēk), n. Pod of plants of mustard family. Hence **sili̇ʹqu-**ose¹, **sili̇ʹquous**, (-kw-), aa. [L]

silk, n. **1.** Fine soft thread produced in making cocoon by ~'worm or larva of kinds of moth feeding esp. on mulberry leaves (spun ~, see SPIN; thrown ~, ORGAN-ZINE); similar thread spun by some spiders etc. or (artificial) made from cellulose, rayon) thread or yarn made from cellulose, K.C. or Q.C. & exchange stuff for ~ gown); (pl.) robes, or garments made, of such cloth. **3.** || (colloq.) K.C. or Q.C. **4.** Peculiar lustre seen in some sapphires & rubies. **5.** (attrib., now usu. preferred to silken). Made of ~; stockings etc.; make a ~ purse out of a sow's ear, get better results from a person than his qualities admit of). **6.** || ~-foot, breed with silky plumage; ~-gland, secreting the substance produced as ~; ~-reel, -winder, for unwinding ~ from cocoon &, winding it as thread. [OE seolc f. L sericum neut. adj. (L f. Gk Sēres prob. the Chinese, -IC)]

sil̍ken, a. Made of silk (arch., poet.); clad in silk; soft, lustrous, as silk; (of manner etc.), suave, insinuating. [-EN⁵]

sil̍ky, a. Like silk in smoothness, softness, fineness, or lustre (~y manner etc., suave). Hence **~INESS** n. [-Y¹]

sill, n. Shelf or slab of stone or wood at foot of door or window; horizontal timber at bottom of dock or lock entrance, against which the gates close. [OE syll(e), cf. ON syll, svill, Da. syld, G schwelle]

sil̍labub, n. Dish made of cream or milk mixed with wine etc. into soft curd &, sometimes whipped or solidified with gelatine. (also sillibouk (& merribouk), perh. f. SILLY (& merry)+dial. bouk belly)

||**sil̍ler**, n. (Sc.) Silver; money. [= SILVER]

sil̍lery, n. Kinds of sparkling & still champagne. [place-name]

sil̍ly, a. & n. **1.** || Innocent, simple, helpless, (arch.); foolish, weak-minded, imprudent, unwise, imbecile; || the ~y season, August & September as the season when newspapers start trivial discussions for lack of news; ~y point, short leg (placed close up to batsman). **2.** n. (colloq.) A ~y person. Hence **~ILY²** adv., **~INESS** n. [earlier sense fortunate; OE sǣlig-ga, cf. Du. zalig, G seelig, blessed]

sil̍o, n. (pl. ~s), & v.t. **1.** Pit or airtight structure in which green crops are pressed & kept for fodder, undergoing fermenta-

tion. **2.** v.t. Make ensilage of. [Sp., f. L f. Gk siros]

silt, n., & v.t. & i. **1.** Sediment deposited by water in channel, harbour, etc. **2.** vb. Choke or be choked with ~ (usu. up; the passage has or is ~ed up). [cf. Du. zult, W. salt]

Silu̇ʹri̇an, a. & n. **1.** Of the Silures, a people of ancient Britain. **2.** (Of) a series of rocks forming a subdivision of Palaeozoic immediately underlying the Devonian, named as first investigated in district of the Silures. [f. L Silures, -IAN]

Sil̍van, Sȳ-, a. Of the, having, woods; rural. [f. L silvānus (silva wood, -AN)]

sil̍ver¹, n. **I.** A white lustrous precious metal used chiefly with alloy of harder metals for coin, plate, & ornaments, & in chem. combinations for photography etc.(German ~, nickel ~, etc., white alloys used as substitutes for ~ in table articles etc., or for coating with ~; fulminating ~, an explosive powder; OXIDIZED ~). **2.** ~ coins (have you any ~ on you?). **3.** ~ vessels or implements or articles of furniture (melted down all his ~ in the king's service). **4.** Any of the salts of ~ used in sensitizing photographic paper. **5.** attrib. or adj. (usu. now preferred to ~n a. arch. see -EN⁵). Made of ~, second-best, (~ age, see BRAZEN¹; also spec. the period of Latin literature that followed the Augustan; so ~ Latin; a ~ cup; speech is ~ or ~n, but silence is golden, better be silent than speak); (as substitute for ~y² a., whence ~INESS n.) resembling ~ in whiteness, lustre, ringing sound, etc., (~ hair, white & lustrous; has a ~ or ~y tone; has a ~ tongue, is eloquent, whence **~-tongued** a.; every cloud has a ~ lining, misfortune has its consolations). **6.** ~-bath, (tray for holding) solution of ~ nitrate used for sensitizing; ~ fir, kind with two ~ lines on under side of leaves; ~-fish, kinds of fish, esp. a colourless variety of gold-fish, (also) ~y insect found in books & mouldy places; ~ FOIL; ~ fox, variety of common fox with black grey-tipped fur; ~ gilt, gilded over, also imitation gilding of yellow lacquer over ~ leaf; ~-grey, lustrous grey; ~ LEAF; ~ paper, fine white tissue-paper, (loosely) tin foil; ~ plate, vessels, spoons, etc., of ~; ~ point, (process of sketching on prepared paper with) ~-pointed style (a head in ~ point); ~ print, photographic positive on paper sensitized by a salt of ~; ~ sand, fine kind used in gardening; ~ screen, superior type of cinematograph(ic) screen, (also) film-pictures collectively; ~ side, best side of round of beef; ||~smith, worker in ~, manufacturer of ~ articles; ~ solder, solder for joining ~; ~ standard, use of ~ money alone as full legal tender; ~ streak, the English channel; ~ thaw, field-officer of Life Guards on palace duty;

glassy coating on the ground, exposed woodwork, etc., caused when rain freezes as it falls, or when a sudden thaw (after hard frost) is succeeded by a light frost; ~-top, a disease in grasses; ~-weed, yellow-flowered roadside plant with ~y lower leaf-surfaces. [OE seolfor, cf. Du. zilver, etym. dub.]

sil'ver², v.t. & i. Coat or plate with silver; provide (mirror-glass) with backing of tin foil, mercury, etc.; (of moon or white light) give silvery appearance to; (with hair as obj. or subj.) turn (t. & i.) grey or white. [f. prec.]

sil'viculture, sy̆-, n. The growing and tending of trees as a branch of forestry. [f. L silva a wood + CULTURE]

sim'ian, a. & n. 1. (Zool.). (Of) one of the Simiidae or anthropoid apes. 2. Ape-(like), monkey(-like). So ~OID a. [f. L simia ape, -AN]

sim'ilar, a. & n. 1. Like, alike. having mutual resemblance or resemblance to, of the same kind; (Geom.) shaped alike; hence or cogn. ~ITY (-ă'r~) n., ~LY² adv. 2. n. Thing resembling another; (pl.) ~ things. [f. F similaire (L similis like, -AR)]

simi̇le, n. The introduction, esp. in poetry or poetical style, ostensibly for explanatory or illustrative purposes but often in fact for ornament only, of an object or scene or action with which the one in hand is professedly compared or usu. connected by a comparative conjunction such as as (a style rich in ~ & metaphor); a comparison of this kind (by ~ of the dome of many-coloured glass; cf. METAPHOR, ALLEGORY, PARABLE). [f. L neut. of similis like]

simili'tude, n. Likeness, guise, outward appearance, (in, assume, the ~ of); simile, comparison, (talks in ~s); counterpart, facsimile, (rare; is the very ~ of). [OF f. L similitudo (prec., -TUDE)]

sim'ilize, v.i. & t. Use simile; illustrate by simile(s). [SIMILE, -IZE]

simm'er, v.i. & t., & n. 1. Be, keep (trans.), on the point of boiling, boil (t. & i.) very gently; (fig.) be in a state of suppressed anger, indignation, or laughter. 2. n. ~ing state (esp. at a or on the ~). [earlier simper, prob. imit.]

‖ sim'nel-cāke, n. Rich ornamental boiled cake made esp. at Easter, Christmas, and Mid Lent. [f. OF simenel f. L simila finest flour, cf. Gk semidalis]

simōn'iăc, n. Person guilty of simony. [f. OF simoniaque (SIMONY, -AC)]

simoni'acal, a. Guilty, of the nature, of simony. Hence ~LY² adv. [-AL]

Sim'on Pūre, a. The real or genuine person or article (usu. the real ~). [character in Centlivre's Bold Stroke for a Wife]

sim'ony, n. Buying or selling of ecclesiastical preferment. [OF simonie f. med. L simonia f. Simon (Magus, see Acts viii. 18, -Y¹]

simoom', n. Hot dry suffocating dust-laden wind moving in straight narrow track and passing in a few minutes, chiefly in Arabian desert. [f. Arab. semūm (samm to poison)]

*simp, n. (colloq.). Simpleton. [abbr.]

sim'per, v.i. & t., & n. 1. Smile affectedly, smirk; express by or with ~ing (~ed consent); hence ~inglY² adv., ~ER¹ n. 2. n. Affected smile. [cf. Da. & Norw. semper, G zimpfer, delicate, affected]

sim'ple, a. & n. 1. Not compound, consisting of one element, all of one kind, involving only one operation or power, not divided into parts, not analysable, (~ sentence, without subordinate clauses; ~ INTEREST¹; a ~ quantity, expressible by single number; induction by ~ enumeration, based merely on random examples without selection or tests; ~ addition, of numbers of one denomination; ~ equation, not involving the second or any higher power of unknown quantity, cf. QUADRATIC; ~ machine, any of the MECHANICAL powers; ~ leaf, of one blade; ~ pistil, of one carpel; ~ eye, of insect, OCELLUS; ~ fracture, breaking of bone only, cf. COMPOUND²; ~ idea, that cannot be analysed into elements). 2. Not complicated or elaborate or adorned or involved or highly developed (the style is ~ and devoid of ornament; ~ diet; the ~ life, practice of doing without servants & luxuries, attempt to return to more primitive conditions; the greatest works of art are the ~st; in ~ beauty, unadorned; a ~ form of pump; ~ forms of life, creatures low in scale of evolution). 3. Absolute, unqualified, mere, neither more nor less than, just, (to give an infant alcohol is ~ murder or madness; his ~ word is as good as an oath; pretends to be no more than a ~ gentleman; FREE ~). 4. Plain in appearance or manner, unaffected, unsophisticated, ingenuous, natural, artless, (a ~ person; a ~ attire; a ~ heart or mind, whence ~-hearted², ~-minded², aa., ~-mind-edness n.). 5. Foolish, ignorant, inexperienced, (am not so ~ as to suppose). 6. Easily understood or done, presenting no difficulty, (gave a ~ explanation; the problem is very ~; can be cured by a ~ device). 7. Of low rank, humble, insignificant, trifling, (GENTLE & ~; her ~ efforts to please); hence or cogn. ~NESS (rare), simpli'city, nn., sim'plY² adv. 8. n. A herb used medicinally, the medicine made from it; be cut for the ~s, undergo operation for cure of folly. [OF, f. L simplic- st. of simplex onefold (sim- one-, cf. semel once, simul at once, singuli one by one, + plic-, + plic-, cf. plicare to fold)]

sim'pleton (-plt-), n. Foolish, gullible, or half-witted person. [fancy noun f. prec.]

simplī'citer, adv. Absolutely, univer-

sally, without limitation, not relatively or in certain respects only (cf. SECUNDUM quid). [L.]

sim'plify, v.t. Make simple, make easy to do or understand. So ~FICA'TION n. [f. L *simplus* simple, -FY]

sim'plism, n. Affected simplicity. [-ISM]

simulae'rum, n. (pl. -ra). Image of something; shadowy likeness, deceptive substitute; mere pretence. [L (SIMULATE)]

sim'ulant, a. Having the appearance of (spec. biol., as *stamens ~ of petals*). [foll., -ANT]

sim'ulate, v.t. Feign, pretend to have or feel, put on, (~ *virtue, indignation*, etc.); pretend to be, act like, resemble, wear the guise of, mimic, (of word) take or have an altered form suggested by (word wrongly taken for its source), (*actor ~s king* etc.; *chameleon ~s its surroundings*; *amuck*, for *amok*, ~s the English *muck*). So SIMULA'TION n. [f. L *simulare* (*similis* like), -ATE[3]]

simulta'neous, a. Occurring or operating at the same time (*with*). Hence simultanē'ITY, ~NESS, nn., ~LY[2] adv. [f. L *simul* together, -ANEOUS, perh. after L *momentaneus* f. *momentum*]

sin[1], n. & v.i. & t. (-nn-). 1. Transgression, against divine law or principles of morality (ORIGINAL ~; *living in open ~; deadly or mortal ~*, such as kills the soul or is fatal to salvation; *the seven deadly ~s*, pride, covetousness, lust, anger, gluttony, envy, sloth; *one's besetting ~*, to which one is especially tempted; *for my ~s*, joc., as a judgement for something or other; *the unpardonable ~*, that described Matt. xii. 31-2; *man of ~*, arch. or joc., reprobate, also Antichrist; *like ~*, sl., vehemently); offence against good taste, propriety, etc.; ~*-eater*, one hired to take on himself a dead person's ~s by eating bread and drinking ale placed on the bier; ~*-offering*, sacrifice etc. in expiation of ~; hence ~'FUL, ~LESS, aa., ~'fully, ~'lessly, advv., ~'fulness, ~'lessness nn. 2. vb. Commit ~; offend against (*more ~ned against than ~ning*, see *King Lear* III. ii. 60, often of victim of seduction); (~) *one's mercies*, be ungrateful for good luck; hence ~'NER n. (often joc., as *you young ~ner; as I am a ~ner*, form of asseveration). [vb f. n., OE *syn*, cf. Du *zonde*, G *sünde*; perh. cogn. w. L *sons sontis* guilty]

Sinai'tic, a. Of Mount Sinai or the peninsula of Sinai. [f. mod. L *Sinaiticus*]

Sinánthrŏp'us, n. Apelike man of the type represented by remains found near Peking. [mod. L f. SINO-+Gk *anthrōpos* man]

sin'apism, n. Mustard plaster. [f. F *sinapisme* f. L f. Gk *sinapismos* (*sinapizō* cover with *sinapi* mustard)]

since, adv., prep., & conj. 1. After specified or implied past time, throughout (usu. *ever ~*) or at some or any point in the period, between such time & that which is present or being dealt with, (*has or had been healthy ever ~; has ever been cut down; than ever before or ~; ~ then more flourishing; have or had not seen him ~*); ago (*happened many years ~; how long ~ is it?; saw him not long ~*). 2. prep. After (specified past time or event), through or in period between time present or being dealt with & (such time). (*has or had been going on, has happened, ~ yesterday; ~ seeing you I have or had heard ~*). 3. conj. From the past time when, through or in the period between time present or being dealt with & that when (*what have you done ~ we met?; nothing has happened, there had been a disturbance, ~ we parted*); seeing that, inasmuch as, (~ *that is so, there is no more to be said*; (ellipt.) as being (*a more dangerous, ~ unknown, foe*). [earlier *sith-ence* f. OE *siththan* after that (*sith* after, cf. G *seit*, then instr. case of demonst. pron.)+-ES]

sincere', a. Free from pretence or deceit, the same in reality as in seeming or profession, honest, frank. Hence or cogn. sincere'TY n., ~LY[2] (-rli) adv. (esp. in *yours ~ly* before signature of letter). [f. L *sincerus*, etym. dub.]

sin'ciput, n. Head from forehead to top (cf. OCCIPUT). [L (*semi-* half, *caput* head)]

sine[1], n. (trigon.). (~ *of arc*) line drawn from one extremity of arc perpendicularly to radius which meets other extremity; (~ *of angle*) ratio of the perpendicular subtending the angle A to radius (abbr. *sin*, as *sin A*, ratio of the hypotenuse; *versed ~*, abbr. *vers*, unity minus the cosine). [f. L *sinus* curve]

sin'e[2], L prep. Without (~ *di'e*, without date, of business indefinitely adjourned; ~ *quā non*, indispensable condition or qualification).

sin'ecure, n. Office of profit or honour without duties attached, esp. benefice without cure of souls. Hence ~ISM (3), ~IST(2), nn. [f. L *sine cura* without care]

sin'ew, n. & v.t. 1. (Piece of) tough fibrous tissue uniting muscle to bone, tendon; (pl. loosely) muscles, bodily strength, (fig.) what forms the framework, resources, (esp. *the ~s of war*, money, armaments, etc.); hence ~LESS a. 2. v.t. (poet.). Serve as ~s of, sustain, hold together. [OE *sinu*, cf. Du *senuw*, G *sehne*]

sinfoni'a (-fe'a), n. (In early Italian operas) overture. [It. = symphony]

sing, v.i. & t. (*sang* or, now rare, *sung*; *sung*). 1. Utter words, utter (words, in

tuneful succession, esp. in accordance with a set tune (~ one's *praises*), be always praising him), whence (*birds were* ~*ing*; ~ *another song or tune*, ~ *small*, become more humble, be crestfallen). **3.** Make inarticulate melodious or humming or buzzing or whistling sounds (*wind, kettle, bee,* ~*s*); (of ears) be affected as with buzzing sound (also *have a* ~*ing in one's ears*). **4.** Compose poetry, celebrate (hero, beauty, great event, etc.) in verse. **5.** Usher (esp. old or new year) *out* or *in* with ~*ing*; ~ *to sleep, into good humour,* etc., with ~*ing*; ~ *out* t. & i. call out loudly, shout. **6.** ‖ ~*ing-man* [-ING²], paid ~er; ~*ing-master* [-ING-¹], teacher of ~ing; ~*ing-voice* [-ING-¹], voice as modulated in ~ing. Hence ~ER¹ n. [OE *singan*, cf. Du. *zingen*, G *singen*]

singe (-j), v.t. & i. (~*ing*), & n. **1.** Burn (t. & i.) superficially (~ *person's hair*, burn off tips as hairdressing operation; ~ *pig, fowl*, burn off bristles, down, after killing or plucking; *King of Spain's beard*, harry his coasts; *your dress is* ~*ing*; *his reputation is a little* ~*d*; ~ *one's feathers* or *wings*, take some harm esp. in venturesome attempt). **2.** n. Superficial burn (rare). [OE *sengan*, G *sengan* perh. related to prec. w. ref. to hissing sound made in burning; cf. Du. *zengen*, G *sengen*] (Now usu. form of) CINGALESE.

Singhalese (-nggaléz'). **Singhalese** (-nggaléz'). (Now usu. form of) CINGALESE.

single¹ (sing'gl), a. & n. **1.** One only, not double or multiple, united, undivided, designed for or used or done by one person etc. or one set or pair, (~ COMBAT, ENTRY, FILE³; ~ *flower*, that grows one on a stem, also that has not double corolla; ~ *game*, with one player on each side; ~ *wicket*, rudimentary form of cricket; ~ *court* in lawn tennis, fives, etc., of size etc. for ~ *game*; ~ *bed, room*, for one person; ~ *eye-glass*, for one eye, monocle; *a multitude inspired with a* ~ *purpose*; (of ticket) valid for outward journey only. **2.** Solitary, lonely, unaided, (*a* ~ *tree stands on the ridge; paid either by instalments or in a* ~ *sum*; ~ *life, state, man, woman*, unmarried; ~ *blessedness*, joc., unmarried state). **3.** (In negative contexts) not to speak of more (*did not see a* ~ *one, a* ~ *person; can a* ~ *argument be advanced for it?*). **4.** Free from duplicity, sincere, consistent, guileless, ingenuous, (*a* ~ *eye*, devotion to one purpose, whence ~-eyeD³ a.; ~ *heart* or *mind*, simplicity of character, whence ~-heartED², ~-mindED², aa., ~-mind'edNESS n.). **5.** ~-*acting*, (of engine etc.) with steam admitted only to one side of piston; ~-*breasted*, (of coat etc.) with only one set of buttons & buttonholes, not overlapping & buttoning either way; ~-*cut*, (of file) with grooves cut in one direction only, not crossing; ~-*fire*, (of cartridge)

not meant to be recharged after use; ~-*handed* a. & adv., (done etc.) without help from other persons (*by his* ~-*handed efforts; cannot be done* ~-*handed*), also with or for one hand (*the men played* ~-*handed against the women with both hands*; *two-handed &* ~-*handed swords*); ~-*loader*, breechloading rifle without magazine; ~-*stick*, (fencing with) basket-hilted stick of about sword's length; hence ~NESS n., sing'LY² adv., (-ngg-). **6.** n. ~ *game*; ~ *ticket*; hit for one in cricket; (short whist) game won by 5−4; (pl.) twisted threads of silk. [OF, f. LL *singulus* (L *singuli* one by one, cf. SIMPLE)]

single² (sing'gl), v.t. Choose *out* as an example or as distinguishable or to serve some purpose. [f. prec.]

‖ **sing'let** (-ngg-), n. Garment worn below shirt, vest. [SINGLE¹, -ET¹; prob. orig. = unlined garment on anal. of DOUBLET]

sing'leton (-nggit-), n. The only card of a suit at bridge etc.; single thing, only child, etc. [f. SINGLE on anal. of *simpleton*]

sing'song, a. & n., & v.i. & t. **1.** In, recited with, monotonous rhythm. **2.** n. Monotonous rhythm; ‖ impromptu vocal concert, meeting for amateur singing. **3.** vb. Recite (verse etc.), speak, in manner. [SING, SONG]

sing'ular (-ngg-), a. & n. **1.** (Gram.) of the form used in speaking of a single person or thing, not dual or plural; single, individual, (esp. *all & ~*, all whether taken together or separately); unexampled, unique, (now rare); unusual, remarkable from rarity, much beyond the average in degree, extraordinary, surprising; eccentric, unconventional, strangely behaved. **2.** n. (gram.). The ~ NUMBER¹; a word in the ~ number. Hence ~LY² adv. [f. F *singulier* f. L *singularis* (*singuli* one by one, -AR¹)]

singula'rity (-ngg-), n. In adj. senses; esp. uncommonness, being remarkable, odd trait or peculiarity. [f. F *singularité* f. L *singularitatem* (prec., -TY)]

sing'ularize (-ngg-), v.t. Strip (word) of termination mistaken for that of plural (*pease & Chinese are* ~*d into pea, Chinee*). Hence ~A'TION n. [-IZE]

Sinhalese (-nalez'), = CINGALESE.

sin'ister, a. (Her.) on left side of shield etc. (in on right as seen by observer; BEND¹, BAR¹, ~; cf. DEXTER); (joc.) left; of evil omen; (usu. of person in regard to his appearance, or of his face or look) ill-looking, of malignant or villainous aspect; wicked, flagitious, (a ~ *design*). Hence ~LY² adv. [f. OF *sinistre* f. L *sinistrum* nom. -*ter* left]

sinis'tral, a. Of, on, the left (rare); (of spiral shells) with whorls going to left & right. Hence ~ITY² adv.

sinistro-, comb. form of L *sinister* left,

as ~*ce'rebral*, of the left hemisphere of the brain; ~*rse*, with leftward motion or aspect (esp. in Bot. of climbing plants etc.).

sink, v.i. & t. (*sank* or in adj. use usu. *sunken* or now rarely *sunk*; *sunk* or in adj. use usu. *sunken*). **1.** Fall slowly downwards, decline, disappear below surface of liquid or below horizon, come gradually to lower level or pitch, droop, despond, subside, settle down, gradually expire or perish or cease, (*sun is ~ing*, *sank*; *my heart*, *spirits*, *sank*; *ship ~s*, *goes to the bottom*; *her eyes sank*, *were turned downwards*; *his head*, *chin*, *sank on his shoulder*, *chest*; *voice ~s*, *becomes lower-pitched*, *or quieter*; *sick man*, *life*, *is ~ing*, *becoming weaker*, *dying*; *prices ~*, *become lower*; *storm*, *river*, *~s*, *subsides*; *ground ~s*, *slopes down*, *also comes to lower level by subsidence*; *darkness sank upon the scene*, *descended*; *~ into feebleness*, *degradation*, *the grave*, *a quicksand*, *a chair*; *~ in one's estimation*, *lose credit with him*; *his eyes*, *cheeks*, *have sunk in or sunk*, *fallen inwards*, *become hollow*; *so sunken cheeks*, *eyes*; *here goes*, *~ or swim*, *said in running risks & taking chances*). **2.** Penetrate (intr.), make way *in* or *into* (*bayonet sank in to the hilt*; *impression*, *lesson*, *~s into the mind or memory*, *becomes fixed*; *dye the grave*, ...). **3.** Cause or allow to ~*s in*, is absorbed). **3.** Cause or allow to droop; *drought had sunk the streams*; ~ *one's title*, *name*, *office*, etc., keep it temporarily secret, not obtrude it; ~ *the* **SHOT**; ~ *a fact*, keep it quiet; ~ *oneself or one's own interests*, be altruistic; SINKING-*fund*; ~ *a die*, engrave it; ~ *money*, invest it in undertaking from which it cannot be readily withdrawn, also lose it by such investment; *sunk* **FENCE**). Hence *~*ABLE **a.** [OE *sincan*, cf. Du. *zinken*, G *sinken*]

sink², n. In vbl senses; esp.: weight used to sink fishing or sounding line (HOOK¹, *line*, & ~); DIE¹, ~. [-ER¹]

sink'ing, n. In vbl senses; also: internal bodily sensation caused by hunger or apprehension; ~*fund*, moneys set aside for the purpose of sinking or wiping out a State's or corporation's debt by degrees (*the ~*fund, *surplus of revenue over expenditure*, devoted to payment of

national debt; *raid the ~*fund, use such surplus in any year for other purposes).

sinn'er. See SIN.

Sinn Fein (shin fān), n. A 20th-c. patriotic movement & party in Ireland aiming at national revival in language etc. as well as political independence. [Ir., = we ourselves]

Sin'o-, comb. form of Gk *Sīnai*, the Chinese; ~*PHOBE* n., a hater of, hating, the Chinese; ~*PHOI'LA*; also with another adj. of nationality, with the meaning 'Chinese and' (~*Japanese*).

sin'ologue (-*ŏg*, -*ōg*), n. Person versed in sinology. [F (foll. -LOGUE)]

sinŏl'ogy, n. Knowledge of the Chinese language, history, customs, etc. Hence **sinŏl'ogIST** n. [SINO-, -LOGY]

sin'ter, n. Siliceous or calcareous rock formed by deposit of springs. [G, cf. CINDER]

sin'uate, a. (esp. bot.). Wavy-edged, with distinct inward & outward bends along edge. Hence ~*LY*² adv., SINUA'TION n. [f. L *sinuare* (SINUS) bend, -ATE²]

sinuŏs'ity, n. Being sinuous; a bend, esp. in a stream or road. [foll., -ITY]

sin'uous, a. With many curves, serpentine, tortuous, undulating. Hence ~*LY*² adv. [f. L *sinuosus* (SINUS, -OUS)]

sin'us, n. (pl. *~uses*, *-ūs*). (Anat., Zool.) cavity of bone or tissue, pouch-shaped hollow; (Path.) fistula; (Bot.) curve between lobes of leaf. [L, = bosom, recess]

-sion (-shn, -zhn), suf. forming nn. of action or condition (= -s- of L p.p. st. + -ION, & see -ATION; as *tension* (*tendere tens-*).

Sioux (sōō, sū), n. (pl. the same, pr. sōō, sū, sōōz, sūz), & a. **1.** Member of a N.- Amer. Indian tribe. **2.** adj. Of the ~. [F, f. native name]

sip, v.t. & i. (-pp-), & n. **1.** Drink (t. & i.) in repeated tiny mouthfuls or by spoonfuls. **2.** n. Small mouthful of liquid imbibed (*a ~ of brandy*). [f. 14th c.; perh. dim. in form & sense of SUP]

si'phon, n., & v.t. & i. **1.** Pipe or tube shaped like inverted V with unequal legs for conveying liquid over edge of vessel & delivering it at lower level by utilizing atmospheric pressure; (also *~bottle*) aerated-water bottle from which liquid is forced out by pressure of gas through ~ tube; (Zool.; also *siphuncle*) canal or conduit etc. in molluscs or shells, suck- ing-tube of some insects etc.; ~ *barometer*, with tube bent at bottom like inverted ~; ~*cup*, lubricating apparatus with oil led over edge of reservoir by capillary action through wick; ~ *gauge*, glass ~ attached to reservoir & containing mercury for indicating pressure etc. in- side reservoir; hence ~*AL*, **siphŏn'**ic, aa.

2. vb. Conduct or flow (as) through ~ (*water is ~ing from the vase on to the tablecloth*); hence ~AGE(3) n. [f. L f. Gk *siphōn* tube]

siph'onet, n. One of two tubes through which aphides exude honeydew. [prec., -ET¹]

siph'uncle (sīfŭngkl), n. See SIPHON. [f. L *siphunculus* (SIPHON, -UNCLE)]

sipp'et, n. Small piece of bread etc. soaked in liquid; one of the pieces of toast or fried bread served round mince etc. [perh. dim. of SOP, see -ET¹]

si quis, n. Notice posted in ordination candidate's parish church serving similar purpose to banns. [L,=if anyone (know an impediment)]

sir, n., & v.t. (-rr-). 1. Used as vocative in addressing a master or superior, the Speaker of the House of Commons either in his own person on points of order or in debate, any male whose name is or is to be understood to be unknown to speaker, or boy etc. who is to be rebuked (pl. ~s, for which *gentlemen* is usu. substituted), 2. Used as titular prefix to name of knight or baronet, always followed by Christian name, or its initial & surname, or the whole name (*Sir John Moore, Sir J. Moore*, or, in familiar use esp. as vocative, *Sir John*), 3. v.t. Address as ~ (*don't ~ me*). [shortened f. SIRE]

sirc'ar, n. (Anglo-Ind.). The Government of India; head of government or household; house-steward; native accountant. [f. Hind. f. Pers. *sarkār* (*sar* head, *kār* work)]

sir'dar, n. (In India etc.) person in command, leader; (in Egypt) commander-in-chief (formerly a British officer) of army. [f. Hind. f. Pers. *sardār* (prec., *-dār* holding)]

sire, n., & v.t. 1. Father or male ancestor (poet.); male parent of beast, esp. stallion kept for breeding; (voc.) Your Majesty (in addressing king or sovereign prince). 2. v.t. Beget (esp. of stallions). [OF, f. L SENIOR]

sir'en, n. 1. (Gk Myth.; pl.) women, or half women & half birds, living on a rocky isle to which they lured unwary seafarers with enchanting music. 2. Sweet singer. 3. Dangerously fascinating woman, temptress, tempting pursuit etc.; (attrib.) irresistibly tempting, as of a ~. 4. = SIRENIAN. 5. Instrument used in acoustic experiments & for making loud sound as warning etc. by revolution of perforated disk over jet of compressed air or steam; instrument for giving warning of air raids. [f. OF *sereine* f. LL *Sirena* f. Gk *Seirēn* etym. dub.]

siren'ian, a. & n. (Member) of the *Sirenia*, an order of fishlike mammals resembling cetaceans, including manatee & dugong. [mod. L *Sirenia* (prec.), -AN]

sirg'ang, n. Bright-green Asiatic bird, the green jackdaw. [E.-Ind.]

sir'iasis, n. Sunstroke; sun-bath as medical treatment. [L, f. Gk *seiriasis* (*seiriaō* be hot, -ASIS)]

Sir'ius. See DOG¹. [L, f. Gk *Seirios*, cf. prec.]

sirk'ar. =SIRCAR.

sirl'oin, n. ? Upper part of loin of beef, with meat both above & (*undercut* or *fillet*) below the bone. [corrupt. of *surloin* (1554) f. F *surlonge* (SUR-² LOIN)]

siroc'ō, sci-, n. (pl. ~s). (Italian name for) Sahara wind or simoom when it reaches Italy, (also for) warm sultry rainy wind prevailing in winter. [It., f. Arab. *sharq* the East]

sir'rah (arch.), *sir'ree'**, nn. voc. replacing *sir* in imperious or contemptuous use. [f. SIR]

sirup. See SYRUP.

sirvente (sērvahnt'), n. Medieval usu. Medieval form. satirical lay of special metrical form. [orig. sense *service-song* (i.e. not love-song), F, f. Pr. *sirventes* (L *servīre* serve, -ENT, -ESE]

sis'al, n. Fibre prepared from leaves of agave, used for cordage, ropes, etc.; the plant. [S~, port of Yucatan]

sis'kin, n. Olive-green songbird, kind of finch, often kept in cage. [f. G dial. *sisschen* prob. of Slav. orig., cf. Pol. *czyżik*]

siss'ōō, n. Valuable Indian timber(-tree). [Hind. *sīsū*]

siss'y. See CISSY.

sis'ter, n. 1. Daughter of same parents (also ~ *german*) or (strictly *half-*~) parent as another person (the latter usu. specified by *my* etc. or possessive case; *the Fatal S~s* or *S~s three* or *three S~s*, the Fates; *S~ Anne*, person watching on behalf of another for an arrival, w. ref. to *Bluebeard*); (prop. ~-*in-law*) one's husband's or wife's ~ or brother's wife. 2. Close female friend, female fellow member of class or sect or human race. 3. Member of religious community of women (~ *of* CHARITY; ~ *of mercy*, member of nursing sisterhood, esp. of R.-C. one founded in Dublin 1827; *little S~s of the poor*, French R.-C. charitable sisterhood; IAY²). 4. Hospital nurse in authority over others. 5. Personified quality or thing regarded as female that closely resembles another (*prose, younger ~ of verse; ~ ships*, built on same design). 6. ~-*hook*, double hook that opens to admit rope etc. & closes into a figure 8. Hence ~LESS, ~LY¹, aa., ~LINESS n. [Aryan; OE *swuster*, cf. Du. *zuster*, G *schwester*, L *soror*, Skr. *svasā*]

sis'terhood, n. Being a sister or sisters; relation between sisters; society of women bound by monastic vows or devoting themselves to religious or charitable work. [-HOOD]

Sis'tine, a. Of one of the popes called Sixtus (~ *chapel*, in Vatican, with frescoes by Michelangelo; ~ *Madonna*, picture by Raphael removed from church of San Sisto in Piacenza). [f. It. *Sistino* (*Sisto* Sixtus, -INE¹)]

sis'trum, n. (pl. **-tra**), Jingling instrument or rattle used by ancient Egyptians, esp. in rites of Isis. [L, f. Gk *seistron* (*seiō* shake)]

sisyphe'an, a. As of Sisyphus, Greek condemned in Tartarus to push a stone up hill & begin again when it rolled down, everlastingly laborious. [f. L, f. Gk *Sisupheios* (*Sisyphus*), -AN]

sit, v.i. & t. (**sit**). **1.** Take or be in position in which body is supported more or less upright by buttocks resting on ground or raised seat (*~s well*, has good seat in riding; *~ tight*, colloq., remain firmly in one's place, not be shaken off or moved away or yield to distractions); be engaged in some occupation in which this position is usual (*~ in judgement*, assume right of judging others, be censorious; *~ for one's portrait*, give painter interviews or sit for it; *~ for fellowship* etc., undergo examination for it; *~ for borough* etc., represent it in Parliament; *Courts, &c., are ~ting*, in session; *~ under*, ... his principles *~ loosely on him*). **2.** (Of birds & some animals) be inactive, rest with legs bent & body close to ground or perch (*shoot bird, hare, ~ting*, when not on wing or running); remain on nest to hatch eggs (*~ting hen*, engaged in hatching; *wants to ~*, is broody). **3.** (Chiefly of inanimate things) be in more or less permanent position (*~s the wind there?*, is that the quarter?, is that the state of affairs?; *food ~s heavy on the stomach*, is not soon digested; *her dress, temperateousness, etc., ~s well on her*, suits, fits; *~ting tenant*, one in present occupation; *his principles ~ loosely on him*). **4.** Keep one's seat on (horse etc.; *he could not ~ his mule*). **5.** *~ down*, take seat after standing (also refl. arch., as *sat him, pray ~ you, down*), (Mil.) encamp before place to besiege it; *~-down strike*, one in which strikers refuse to leave the place where they are working; *~ down under*, submit tamely to (insult etc.). **6.** *~ on* or *upon*, (of jury etc.) hold session concerning; *~ on his head* (as way of keeping fallen horse quiet); (sl.) repress or rebuke or snub (*he wants ~ting upon*). **7.** *~ out*, take no part in something, esp. in particular dance (also trans., as *sat out the next dance*), also *~ outdoors*, (trans.) outstay (other visitors) or stay till end of (performance). **8.** *~ over* (player), (Bridge) be on his left hand (and so in advantageous position). **9.** *~ under* (minister), be one of congregation preached to by (minister). **10.** *~ up*, rise from lying to ~ting posture, remain (late, etc.), out of bed, ~ erect without lolling (*make one ~ up*, colloq., subject him to hard work, pain, surprise, etc.); *~ up & take notice* (colloq.), have one's interest (suddenly) aroused. **11.** *~fast* n., horny sore on horse's back. [Aryan; OE *sittan*, cf. Du. *zitten*, G *sitzen*, L *sedēre*]

site, n. & v.t. **1.** Ground on which town or building stood, stands, or is to stand. **2.** v.t. Locate, place. [f. L *situs*]

||**sith**, conj. (arch., bibl.), Since. [see SINCE]

sit(i)o-, comb. form of Gk *sitos, sition*, food, as *~ol'ogy* dietetics, *~ophō'bia* morbid aversion to food.

sit'ter, n. In vbl senses; esp. person sitting for portrait; *good, bad, ~*, hen that sits well etc.; (sl., from *to shoot bird sitting*) easy shot, thing easily done.

sit'ting, n. In vbl senses; esp.: time during which one sits continuously (*wrote the whole poem at a ~; all-night ~ of House of Commons; can you give me one ~s?*, for portrait); clutch of eggs; seat in church appropriated to a person; *~ room*, space enough to accommodate seated persons, also a room used for sitting in (opp. *bedroom*). [-ING¹]

sit'uated, sit'uate (arch.), aa. In specified situation (*situated on the top of the hill; awkwardly situated*, in a difficult ...). [f. LL *situatus* (L *situs* position,...) -ATE²,³]

situa'tion, n. Place, with its surroundings, occupied by something (*house stands in a fine ~; unrivalled for ~*); set of circumstances, position in which one finds oneself, (*came out of a difficult ~ with credit*); critical point or complication in drama (*curtain falls on a strong ~*); employee's, esp. domestic's, place or paid office (*cannot find a ~*). [F precr., -ATION]

sitz-bath. See BATH¹.

Si'va (sē'-), n. Hindu god held supreme by his special votaries, & by others associated as principle of destruction with Brahma & Vishnu in a triad. Hence *~is'fic* [-ism, -ic] a., *~ISM¹(†)* n. & a. [Hind., f. Skr. *çiva* propitious]

six, a. & n. **1.** One more than five, 6, vi, (often agreeing with understood noun, as *~ of the men, ~ of them, ~ o'clock* or *~ to one*, long odds; *two & ~*, half-a-crown; ||*~ & eightpence*, lawyer's common item in solicitors' bills; ||*~ & ~*, 6/6; *it is ~ of one & half-a-dozen of the other*, difference is merely nominal; *twenty~* or *~-& twenty*, & so on to *~-&-ninety; am not ~ yet*, years old); *~-footer*, person 6 ft in height, thing 6 ft long; ||*~pence*, (silver coin worth) 6d. (*have not got a ~pence*); ||*~penny* a., costing or worth 6d. (*~penny bit*, or *~penny* as n., the coin; *~pence* etc.); ||*~seven-&~-penny* bits, costing 7/6 etc.); *~-shooter*, ~penny revolver; hence *~'FOLD* a. & adv. **2.** n. The

number ~ (*twice* ~ *is twelve*; *at* ~*es & sevens*, in confusion); card or die-face of ~ pips (*the* ~ *of spades*; *double* ~*es*, die-throw of two ~es); || (pl.) candles made ~ to the lb. [Aryan; cf. Du. *zes*, G *sechs*, L *sex*, Gk *hex*, Skr. *shash*]

six'ain, n. Six-line stanza. [F (*six* f. L *sex*)]

six'er, n. Hit for six in cricket. [-ER¹]

sixte, n. One of the positions in fencing. [F, f. L *sexte* sixth]

sixteen', a. & n. 1. One more than fifteen, 16, xvi; ~*mo* or *16mo*, = SEXTODECIMO; hence ~TH³ a. & n. 2. n. The number ~ (*twice* ~ *is thirty-two*). [-TEEN]

sixth, a. & n. 1. Next after fifth (*the, a,*~, often as n. with ellipse of noun, esp. *the* ~ = 6th day of month; || ~ FORM¹); ~ *part*, one of six equal parts into which thing may be divided. 2. n. = ~ part; || *the* ~ *form*; (Mus.) interval of which the span involves six alphabetical names of notes, harmonic combination of notes thus separated. [OE *sixta*, w. assim. to FOURTH, see TH³]

sixth'ly, adv. In the sixth place (in enumerations). [-LY¹]

six'ty, a. & n. 1. Six times ten, 60, lx, (~*one, -eight*, etc.; ~*first, fourth*, etc.); *four-mo*, (size of) book or page given by folding sheet six times into 64 leaves (for L *in quarto et sexagesimo*); hence **six'ti-ETH** a. & n. 2. n. The number ~; *the sixties*, years between 59 & 70 in life or century. [OE *sixtig* -TY³]

siz'able, a. Of large size. [SIZE¹,-ABLE]

|| **siz'ar**, n. Student at Cambridge or Trinity College, Dublin, paying reduced fees & formerly charged with certain menial offices. Hence ~SHIP n. [foll. = ration, -ER¹ (cf. *scholar*)]

size¹, n., & v.t. & i. 1. (hist.). Standard of weight or measure for some article esp. of food or drink; || (Camb. Univ.; also **siz'ING²** n.) ration of food or drink from buttery. 2. Dimensions, magnitude, (*is of vast, diminutive,* ~, very large or small; ~ *matters less than quality; are both of a*, i.e. the same, ~; *is the* ~ *of*, i.e. as big as; *an egg; what* ~, i.e. how big, *is it?; that's about the* ~ *of it*, colloq., a true account of the matter); one of the usu. numbered classes into which things, esp. garments, otherwise similar are divided in respect of ~ (*is made in several* ~*s; takes* ~ 7 *in gloves; is quite a* ~, *three* ~*s, too big*; OUT ~). 3. Implement for sizing pearls. 4. ~ *stick*, shoemaker's measure for taking length of foot; hence (-)SIZED² (-zd) a. 5. v.t. Group or sort in ~s or according to ~, whence **siz'ER(2)** n.; ~ *up*, estimate ~ of, (colloq.) form judgement of (person etc.), 6. v.i. || (Camb. Univ.) order ~. [f. OF *sise* shortened f. *assise* ASSIZE]

size², n., & v.t. 1. Gelatinous solution used in glazing paper & stiffening textiles & in many manufacturing processes;

hence **siz'Y²** a. 2. v.t. Glaze or stiffen or treat with ~. [perb. = prec.]

siz'zle, v.i., & n. (colloq.). 1. Make sputtering sound as in frying. 2. n. Such noise. [imit.]

sjam'bok (sh-), n., & v.t. 1. Rhinoceros-hide whip. 2. v.t. Flog with ~. [S.-Afr. Du. f. Malay *chamboq* f. Pers. *chābuk* whip]

skald. See SCALD².

skat (-aht), n. A three-handed card-game popular in Germany. [G, f. It. *scarto* a discard]

skate¹, n. Kinds of ray-fish, esp. rhomboidal long-tailed kind. [f. ON *skata*]

skate², n., & v.i. & t. 1. One of pair of implements, each with steel blade or set of rollers, attached beneath boots & enabling wearer to glide in curves over ice or (*roller*~e) hard floor. 2. vb. Move, perform (specified figure), on ~es (~e *about thin ice*, talk on subject needing tactful treatment); ~*ing-rink*, piece of ice artificially made, or floor reserved, for ~ing; hence ~ER¹ n. [earlier *schates* pl. f. Du. *schaatsen* pl. f. ONF *escache* stilt]

skean, skène, skain, n. Gaelic dagger used in Ireland & Scotland; ~*dhu* (-dōo), dagger stuck in stocking as part of Highland costume. [f. Gael. *sgian* knife, *dubh* black]

skedad'dle, v.i., & n. (colloq.). 1. Run away, disperse in flight. 2. n. Hurried flight or dispersal. [U.S., etym. dub.]

skee. See SKI.

skein (-ān), n. Bundle of yarn or thread or silk made by coiling it many times, drawing it out to the coil's length, & folding it; flock of wild geese etc. in flight; (fig.) tangle, confusion. [f. OF *escaigne*, etym. dub.]

skel'eton, n. 1. Hard internal or external framework of bones, cartilage, shell, woody fibre, etc., supporting or containing an animal or vegetable body, whence **skel'etAL** a., **skel'éto-** comb. form, **skeléto'RAPHY** n., etc. 2. Dried bones of human being or other animal fastened together in some relative positions as in life (~ *at the feast*, something that alloys pleasure, intrusive care; ~ *in the cupboard, family*~, discreditable or humiliating fact concealed from strangers); part of anything that remains after its life or usefulness is gone. 3. Framework or essential part of anything (~ *crew, regiment*, etc., permanent nucleus ready for filling up, cadre; ~ *drill*, with companies etc. represented by two men separated by long rope; ~ *key*, fitting many locks by having interior of bit hollowed; ~ or ~-*face type*, with thin strokes). 4. Outline sketch, epitome, abstract. 5. (By exag.) thin person. [Gk, orig. neut. of *skeletos* dried-up (*skello* parch)]

skel'etonize, v.t. Reduce to skeleton or abstract by destroying flesh, the tissue

between veins of leaves, etc., or by omitting details. [-IZE]

‖ **skep**, n. Kinds, varying locally, of wooden or wicker basket; straw or wicker bee-hive. [f. ON *skeppa*, cf. Du. *schepel*]

skene. See SKEAN.

skepsis, skeptic, etc. See SCE-.

sketch, n. & v.t. & i. **1.** Preliminary, rough, slight, merely outlined, or unfinished drawing or painting often as experiment for, or memorandum for use in, regular picture; brief account without many details conveying general idea of something; rough draft, general outline; slight play often of musical kind or short descriptive article; musical composition of single movement; ~-book, ~book, arrangements of drawing-paper leaves for doing series of ~es on; ~-map, outlines but little detail; hence ~y² a., ~INESS n. **2.** vb. Make or give ~ of; make ~es esp. ~ [-IZE²]; ~ly² adv., ~s of; hence ~ER¹ n. [f. Du. *schets* f. It. *schizzo*, perh. f. L f. Gk *skhedios* off-hand, extempore]

skew, a. & n. **1.** Oblique, slanting; sideways, distorted, (now chiefly in Archit., Mech., & Math.; ~ bridge, with line of arch not at right angles to abutment; ~ chisel, with oblique edge; ~ wheel, bevel wheel, with oblique teeth; ~ curve, in three dimensions); askew. **2.** n. Sloping top of buttress; coping of gable; stone element on opposite sides; ~back, sloping face of an abutment on which the extremity of an arch rests; ~bald, (esp. of horse) with irregular patches of white & some colour (prop. not black, cf. *piebald*); ~-eyed, squinting; ‖~whiff (colloq. & dial.), askew. **2.** n. Sloping top of buttress; coping of gable; stone built into bottom of gable to support coping. [f. obs. *skew* vb side, shy, f. ONF *eskiuwer* = OF *eschever* ESCHEW]

skew'er, n. & v.t. **1.** Pin of wood or iron for holding meat compactly together while cooking; (joc.) sword etc. **2.** v.t. Fasten together, pierce, (as) with ~. [f. 17th c.; also *skiver*; etym. dub.]

ski (skē, shē), n. (pl. ~s), & v.i.(~d pr. skēd; ~ing pr. skē'ing). **1.** One of pair of wooden runners about 8 ft long & 4 in. broad fastened under feet for travelling over snow esp. in Scandinavia; ~toring (-yör'ing), winter sport in which the skier is towed by a horse. **2.** v.i. Go on ~. [Norw., f. ON *skíth* billet, snow-shoe, cf. SKID]

skiagraphy etc. See scia-.

skid, n., & v.t. & i. (-dd-). **1.** Piece of frame or timber serving as buffer, support, or drag; wooden or metal shoe preventing wheel from revolving used as drag (also ~-pan), other kinds of wheel-

locking contrivance; slip or slide of wheel on muddy ground. **2.** vb. Support or move or protect or check with ~; (of wheel or vehicle) slide forwards or backwards or sideways on slippery ground. [perh. cogn. w. ON *skíth* billet, cf. ME *shide* slip of wood, & SHEATH]

skier (skē'er), n. Person using SKI (cf. SKYER).

skiff, n. Light rowing or sculling boat. [f. F *esquif* prob. f. OHG self SHIP]

skil'ful, a. Having or showing skill (*at*, *in*), practised, expert, adroit, ingenious. Hence ~ly² adv. [foll.-FUL]

skill, n. Expertness, practised ability, facility in doing something, dexterity, tact. [f. ON *skil* discernment (*skilja* to separate), cf. Sw. *skäl* reason]

skilled (-ld), a. Having or showing skill, skilful, (rare exc. in phr. ~ *labour*, *workmen*, etc. = trained, or followed by *in*). [-ED²]

skil'let, n. Small metal pot with long handle & usu. legs used in cooking. [f. 15th c., etym. dub.]

skill²less, a. (rare). Without skill, knowing nothing of. [-LESS]

skills, v.i. 3rd sing. impers. (arch.). It ~ *not*, makes no difference, is of no use, (usu. *to do*). [f. ON *skilja*, see SKILL]

skil'ly, n. Thin broth or soup or gruel usu. of oatmeal & water flavoured with meat often served out in prisons, workhouses, etc. [earlier *skilligalee*, *-galee*, etym. dub.]

skim, v.t. & i. (-mm-), & a. **1.** Take scum or cream or floating layer from surface of (liquid), take (cream etc.) from surface of liquid, (~ *the cream off*, often fig. take best part of; ~ming-dish, sl., flat-bottomed racing yacht, fast light motor-boat); keep touching lightly or nearly touching (surface) in passing over, (intr.) go thus over or *along* surface, glide along in air; read (t. & i.) superficially, look over cursorily, gather salient facts contained in. **2.** adj. = milk, from which cream has been ~med. [prob. f. OF *escumer* (*escume* SCUM]

skimmer, n. In vbl senses: esp. ladle etc. for skimming liquids; fast light motor-boat; kinds of water-bird, esp. Black S~, with flat mandibles. [-ER¹]

skimp, v.t. & i. Supply (person *with* or *in* food, money, etc.; material, expenses, etc.) meagrely, stint; be parsimonious. Hence ~INGLY² adv. [f. 19th c. only; cf. SCRIMP]

skin, n. **1.** Flexible continuous covering of human or other animal body (*with a whole* ~, unwounded; *save one's* ~, get off safe; *change one's* ~, undergo impossible change of character etc.; *would not be in his* ~, should not like to be he; *is only* ~ & *bone*, very thin, & so ~n'y² a., ~n INESS n.; *escape with the* ~ *of one's teeth*, narrowly; *thick*, *thin*, ~, imperviousness,

sensitiveness, to affront or criticism; *fair*, *dark*, etc., ~, complexion; *near is my* SHIRT, *nearer my* ~; (Anat.) one layer of this (*true* or *inner* ~, derma; *outer* ~, epidermis). **2.** Hide of flayed animal with or without the hair etc.; material prepared from ~s esp. of smaller animals (cf. *hide*). **3.** Vessel for wine or water made of animal's whole ~. **4.** Outer coating of plant, fruit, etc., rind. **5.** Planking or plating of ship or boat inside or outside ribs. **6.** GOLD-*beaters'* ~. **7.** ~-*bound*, with ~ tightly stretched over flesh; ~-*deep*, (of wound, also of emotion, impression, beauty, etc.) superficial, not deep or lasting; ~-*effect* (Electr.), tendency of high-frequency alternating current to flow through the outer layer only of a conductor; ~-*friction*, lateral resistance to way of ship etc. passing through water; ~-*ful* (*of wine* etc., or abs.), as much liquor as one can hold; ~-*game* (sl.), swindle; ~-*grafting*, surgical substitution of ~ cut from another part or person for damaged part. Hence (-)SKINNED²(-nd), ~'LESS, aa. [f. ON *skinn*, cogn. w. G *schinden* flay]

skin², v.t. & i. (-nn-). Cover (sore etc., usu. *over*) as with skin, (of wound etc.) form or become covered with new skin, cicatrize, (usu. *over*); strip of skin, withdraw skin from, flay, (*keep your eyes* ~*ned*, sl., be watchful or cautious); (colloq.) strip oneself, strip (another), of tight garment such as jersey; (sl.) fleece, swindle; ~*flint*, niggard, miser. [f. prec.]

skink, n. Kinds of small-limbed lizard. [f. L f. Gk *skinkos*]

skin'ner, n. In vbl senses; esp., (now chiefly in name of a city company) dealer in skins, furrier. [-ER¹]

skip¹, v.i. & t. (-pp-), & n. **1.** (Of lambs, kids, children, etc.) jump about, gambol, caper, frisk, move lightly from one foot on to the other; (of children, esp. girls) use ~*ping-rope*; shift quickly from one subject or occupation to another, be desultory, (usu. *off*, *from*, etc.); (sl.) make off, disappear; omit, make omissions, in dealing with a series or in reading (*do them all without* ~*ping any* or ~*ping*; *always* ~ *the descriptions*; ~*s as he reads*; ~ *every tenth row*); ~-*jack*, jumping toy made of bird's merrythought, also kinds of fish & butterfly & beetle named from their movements; ||~*ping-rope*, length of rope with two wooden handles used in girls' game of ~*ping*: hence ~p'ingly² adv. **2.** n. ~ping movement, esp. quick shift from one foot to other (HOP², ~, & jump). [f. Scand., cf. MSw. & Norw. *skoppa* vb]

skip², n. College servant, scout, esp. at Dublin. [perh. f. obs. *skip-kennel* lackey]

skip³, n. Captain or director of side at bowls & curling. [perh. for SKIPPER²]

skip⁴, n. Cage, bucket, etc., in which men or materials are lowered & raised in mines & quarries. [var. of SKEP]

skipp'er¹, n. In vbl senses; esp., (Zool.) =SKIP-*jack*. [-ER¹]

skipp'er², n. Sea captain, esp. master of small trading vessel; ~*s daughters*, (with pun on prec.) tall white-crested waves; captain of an aircraft; (transf.) captain of side in games. [f. MDu. *schipper* (*schip* SHIP¹, -ER¹)]

skipp'et, n. (hist.). Small cylindrical wooden box used to enclose and protect large seal attached by ribbon to deed. [?]

skirl, v.i., & n. (Make) sound characteristic of bagpipes. [Sc., prob. f. Scand.]

skirm'ish, n., & v.i. **1.** Piece of irregular or unpremeditated fighting esp. between small or outlying parties, slight engagement; encounter of wit, argument, etc. **2.** v.i. Fight in small parties, loose order, or unpremeditated way; hence ~ER¹ n. [n. f. vb, f. OF *eskermir* (-ISH²) fence, f. OHG *scirman* (*scirm*, whence G *schirm* shelter); cf. *scrimmage*]

ski'rret, n. Kind of water parsnip formerly much used as table vegetable. [prob. f. OF *eschervis* var. of *carvi* CARAWAY]

skirt, n., & v.t. & i. **1.** Part of coat or shirt that hangs below waist; woman's outer garment shaped like petticoat from waist downwards (*divided* ~, loose trousers resembling ~), whence ~'ING²(③) n.; (vulg. sl.) woman (esp. in *bit of* ~); edge, border, extreme part, (often pl.; *the* ~*s of London*, just inside or outside of it); ~ *of beef* etc., the diaphragm & other membranes as cheap food-material; ~-*dance(r)*, -*dancing*, with full ~ waved about giving graceful effects; hence ~ED², ~'LESS, aa. **2.** vb. Go along or round or past the edge of, be situated along; go along coast, wall, etc.; ~-*ing-board*, along bottom of room-wall. [f. ON *skyrta*; cogn. w. SHORT, & doublet of SHIRT]

skit¹, n. Light piece of satire, burlesque, literary squib, (often *upon*). [f. obs. *skit* shoot, dart, jump, perh. f. Scand., cf. ON *skjóta* SHOOT]

skit², n. (colloq.). A number, crowd (esp. in pl., heaps, lots). [etym. dub.; cf. U.S. *scads* in same sense]

skitt'er, v.i. (Of wild-fowl) go splashing along water in rising or settling; fish by drawing bait along surface. [as SKIT¹, -ER¹]

skitt'ish, a. (Of horses etc.) nervous, inclined to shy, excitable, playful, fidgety; (chiefly of women) capricious, coquettish, flirting, lively, given to amusement, gadding about, affecting youthfulness, wanton. Hence ~LY² adv., ~NESS n. [as SKIT¹, -ISH¹]

skit'tle, n., & v.t. **1.** ||~s, game played

with nine pins (~s or ~pins) set up at end of ~valley or ~ground to be bowled down with ~ball (beer &~s, amusement, as life is not all beer &~s); (sl., as int.) ~s!, rubbish, nonsense. 2. v.t. & i. (Cricket) get (batsmen) out rapidly in succession. [formerly also kittlepins; etym. dub.]

skive, v.t. Split or pare (hide, leather); grind away surface of (gem). [f. ON skífa]

skiver, n. Knife for skiving leather; thin leather got by skiving. [-ER¹]

‖**skivvy**, n. (colloq.). Female domestic servant (usu. derog.). [?]

skua, n. Kinds of gull kind, esp. the *Great S~*, largest of gull kind, chiefly dark-coloured. [f. ON skūfr]

skulk, v.i. Lurk, keep oneself concealed, esp. in cowardice or with evil intent, stay or sneak away in time of danger, shirk duty, avoid observation. Hence ~ER¹ & ~ingly² adv. (in same sense) **skulk**, nn., ~ingly² adv. [f. Scand., cf. Da. skulke, Norw. skulka]

skull, n. Bony case of the brain, frame of the head, cranium, (~ & cross-bones, representation of bare ~ with two thigh-bones crossed below it as emblem of death); ~cap, close-fitting cap usu. of velvet worn indoors chiefly by old men, also kinds of plant with helmet-shaped flower. Hence (-)~ED²(-ld) a. [f. 13th c., etym. dub.]

skunk, n. Black white-striped bushy-tailed American carnivorous animal about size of cat able to emit powerful stench from liquid secreted by anal glands as defence; its fur; stinking or contemptible fellow. [f. Amer.-Ind. segongw]

Skupshtina (-ōŏp-), n. Jugoslav parliament. [Serb., = assembly]

sky, n. & v.t. 1. (The vault of) heaven (blue, clear, cloudy, overcast, etc., ~; if the ~ fall we shall catch larks, unlikely cataclysms are not worth providing against; under the open ~, out of doors; often pl., as land to the skies, highly; was raised to the skies, taken up to heaven). 2. Climate, atmosphere, (try what a warmer ~; warmer skies, will do for you). 3. ~blue a. & n. (blue etc.); ~born, poet., of divine birth; ~clad, joc., naked; ~high adv. & a., so as to reach, reaching the ~; ~lark n., lark that flies spirally upwards (singing, v.i. (with pun on LARK¹,² & perh. of naut. orig., w. ref. to clambering about rigging), frolic, play tricks or practical jokes, ballyrag, etc.; ~light, window set in plane of roof or ceiling; ~line, outline of hill etc. defined against ~ (is on the ~line, seen outlined on ~); ~ pilot, sl., parson; ~rocket, discharged upwards; ~sail, light sail above royal in square-rigged ship; ~scape, picture chiefly representing ~; ~scraper, joc. = ~sail, also building of many storeys, tall chimney, etc.; ~

writing, legible smoke-trails made as advertising method by aeroplane; hence ~er², ~LESS, aa., ~WARD(S) adv. & a. 4. v.t. Hit (cricket-ball) high up; hang (picture) high on wall, treat picture of (artist) so. [earlier sense cloud; f. ON ský]

Skye (tē'rrier), n. Small long-bodied short-legged long-haired slate or fawn coloured variety of Scotch terrier, named from Skye.

skyer, n. High hit at cricket (cf. SKIER).

slab¹, n., & v.t. (-bb-). 1. Thin flat usu. square or rectangular piece of stone or other rigid material; (of timber) outer cut sawn from log; ~sided, long & lank; ~stone, kinds of stone that split readily into ~s. 2. v.t. Remove ~s from (log, tree) to prepare it for sawing into planks; ~bing-gang, set of saws for doing this. [f. 13th c., etym. dub.]

‖**slab²**, a. (arch.). Viscous, (of liquid) thick & sticky, (chiefly w. ref. to *Macbeth* IV. i. 32). [f. prov. E slab puddle, cf. Icel., Sw., & Norw. slabb mud]

slabber. = SLOBBER.

slack, a., adv., n., & v.t. & i. 1. Sluggish, remiss, relaxed, languid, loose, inactive, negligent, (~ water, about turn of tide, esp. low tide; ~ in stays, Naut., slow in going about; a ~ rope, not taut; keep a ~ hand or rein, ride, or fig. govern, carelessly; ~ trade, business, market, with little doing; ~ weather, inclining to indolence; ~ time, slaked lime; hence ~EN⁶ v.t. & i., ~LY² adv., ~NESS n. 2. adv. (In comb. w. slow, baked, etc.) slowly, insufficiently, (~-dried hops; to ~-bake bread). 3. n. part of rope (haul in the ~); ~ time in trade etc.; (colloq.) spell of inactivity or laziness (I'm going to have a good ~ this afternoon); (dial.) cheek, impertinence; (pl.) trousers; [perh. f. G schlacke slag] coal-dust used chiefly for making brick. 4. v.t. & i. ~en; make loose (rope; often off, away); (colloq.) take a rest, be indolent, whence ~ER n.; = SLAKE (lime); ~ off, abate vigour; ~ up, reduce speed of train etc. before stopping. [OE sleac, cogn. w. LAX; & cf. ON slakr]

slag, n., & v.i. (-gg-). 1. Dross separated in fused state in reduction of ores, vitreous smelting-refuse, clinkers; volcanic scoria; ~-wool, = mineral WOOL; hence ~like mass. [f. MLG slagge, cogn. w. Sw.

slake, v.t. Assuage, satisfy, (thirst, & rhet. revenge etc.), whence ~LESS(-li) a. (poet.); (also slack) combine (lime) chemically with water. [var. of SLACK]

sla'lom (-ah-), n. Ski-race down course defined by artificial obstacles. [Norw.]

slam, v.t. & i.(-mm-).& n. 1. Shut (t. & i.) of door etc.; often to adv) with loud

slan'der (-ah-), n., & v.t. **1.** False report maliciously uttered to person's injury; uttering of such reports, calumny; (Law) false oral defamation (cf. LIBEL, SCANDAL); hence or cogn. ~OUS a., ~OUSLY² adv., ~OUSNESS n. **2.** v.t. Utter ~ about, defame falsely; hence ~ER¹ n. [f. OF esclandre f. L SCANDALum]

slang, n., a., & v.t. **1.** Words & phrases in common colloquial use, but generally considered in some or all of their senses to be outside of standard English; words & phrases either entirely peculiar to or used in special senses by some class or profession, cant, (*racing, thieves', artistic, schoolboy*, etc., ~). **2.** v.t. Use abusive language to. [cant word, etym. dub.]

slang'¹ly, a. Of the character of, given to the use of, slang. Hence ~ILY² adv., ~INESS n. [-Y²]

slant (-ah-), v.i. & t., a., & n. **1.** Slope (i. & t.), diverge from a line, lie or go obliquely to a vertical or horizontal line; hence ~ing¹y² adv. (Joc. on *perpendicular*) ~in(g)dic'ular or ~endic'ular a. **2.** adj. (chiefly poet.). Sloping, inclined, oblique. **3.** n. Slope, oblique position, (*on the* or *a ~*, aslant), whence ~WISE (-ahntwiz) adv.; ||(arch.) indirect censure, disparaging remark; (Naut.) *a ~ of wind*, favourable breeze; *way of regarding a thing, point of view. [f. ON (Norw. *slent* n. side-slip, *slenta* vb)]

slap, v.t. (-pp-), n., & adv. **1.** Strike with palm of hand, smack; (part. as adj. & adv.) very fast, big, good, etc. (*a ~ping pace, great girl, dinner*). **2.** n. Such stroke (~ *in the face* lit., also fig. rebuff, insult). **3.** adv. With the suddenness or effectiveness or true aim of a blow, suddenly, just quite, full, (*ran ~ into him; hit me ~ in the eye*). **4.** ~-*bang*¹ violently, noisily, headlong; ~-*dash*¹ adv., vehemently, recklessly; ~*dash*¹ (adj.) impetuous, random, happy-go-lucky, (n.) such action or work, also =ROUGHcast, (v.t.)=ROUGHcast; ~*up* a. (sl.), quite up to date, in the latest fashion, with all modern appliances. [imit., cf. LG *slapp* sounding blow]

*slap'jack, n. Kind of pancake cooked on a griddle; =FLAPJACK, [SLAP v. +JACK]

slap'stick, n. Flexible divided lath used by harlequin; (fig.) boisterous low comedy of the roughest kind (also attrib.). [SLAP v. +STICK]

slash, v.i. & t., & n. **1.** Make sweeping or random cut(s) with sword, knife, whip, etc. (~*ing criticism*, with outspoken condemnation); make long narrow gashes in (~*ed sleeve* etc., with slits cut to show lining or puffing of other material); lash (person etc.) with whip, crack (whip); (Mil.) fell (trees) to form abatis. **2.** n. (Wound or slit made by) ~*ing* cut; debris resulting from the felling or destruction of trees. [perh. f. OF esclachier break in pieces.]

slat¹, n. Thin narrow piece of wood, esp. used in sets in Venetian blinds, lath. [f. OF esclat = esclate, see SLATE¹]

slat², v.i. & t. (-tt-). (Of sails, cordage, etc.) flap against mast etc. with reports; strike noisily with or on a surface. [f. SLAT¹, or imit.]

slāte¹, n., a., & v.t. **1.** Kinds of grey, green, or bluish-purple rock easily split into flat smooth plates; piece of such plate used as roofing-material; piece of it usu. framed in wood used, by schoolchildren, small shopkeepers, etc., for writing on with ~*pencil* or small rod of soft ~ (*clean the ~*, rid oneself of or renounce obligations); ~*black, -blue, -grey*, modifications of these tints such as occur in ~; ||~*club*, mutual benefit society with small weekly contributions; ~*colour(ed)*, (of) dark bluish or greenish grey; hence slāt'Y² a. **2.** adj. (Made) of ~. **3.** v.t. Cover with ~s esp. as roofing; hence slāt'ER¹ n. [f. OF esclat(e)(now éclat) f. esclater shiver in pieces, etym. dub.]

slāte², v.t. (colloq.). Criticize severely (esp. author in reviews), scold, rate. Hence slāt'ING¹(1) n. [?]

slātt'ern, n. Sluttish woman. Hence ~LY¹ a., ~LINESS n. [perh. for *slattering* (dial. *slatter* be wasteful)]

slaughter (-awt-), n., & v.t. **1.** Slaying, esp. of many persons or animals at once, carnage, massacre, (~ *or massacre of the* INNOCENTS); ~*house*, shambles, place for killing cattle or sheep, place of carnage; hence ~OUS a. (rhet.), ~OUSLY² adv. **2.** v.t. Kill (people) in ruthless manner or on great scale; butcher, kill for food; hence ~ER¹ n. [f. ON *slátr* meat, cogn. w. SLAY]

Slav (-ahv), n. & a. **1.** One of a race spread over most of Eastern Europe and including Russians, Bulgarians, Illyrians, Poles, Silesians, Pomeranians, Bohemians, etc.; hence ~OPHIL, ~OPHOBE, nn. & aa., ~ISM(2, 3) n., (-ahv-). **2.** adj. Of the ~s, Slavonic, Slavonian. [earlier *Sclave* f. med. L *Sclavus*, late Gk *Sklabos*, f. Slavonic]

slāve, n., & v.i. **1.** Person who is the legal property of another or others and is bound to absolute obedience, human chattel (WHITE¹ ~); helpless victim *to* or *of* some dominating influence (*is a ~ to drink, the ~ of his wife's caprices*, etc.; *the ~s of fashion*); drudge, person of no leisure; mean contemptible person. **2.** ~*bangle* (of gold, glass, etc., worn by ladies above elbow); ~*born* (in slavery, of ~*parents*); ~*driver*, overseer of ~s at

work, (transit.) hard taskmaster; ~, (of commodities) produced by ~ labour; ~holder, owner of ~s; ~hunter, person who hunts ~s. Negroes to sell them as ~; ~ship, employed in ~-trade; ~ *Stades*, southern States of N. America, in which slavery prevailed before civil war; ~-trade, procuring, transporting, & selling as ~s, of human beings, esp. African Negroes; so ~-trader. 3. v.i. Work like ~, drudge. [f. OF *esclave* f. med. L *sclavus* Slav captive, see prec.]

slaver¹, n. Ship or person engaged in slave-trade. [-ER¹]

slaver², v.i. & t., & n. 1. Let spittle flow from mouth; let one's spittle fall upon (garment etc., or another's cheek in kissing). 2. n. Spittle running from mouth. (fig.) fulsome or servile flattery; hence (fig.) ~y¹ [-y²] a. [f. Scand. (Icel. *slafra* n., *slafur* n., LG *slabbern*]

slaver³, n. Condition of a slave; slave-holding; exhausting labour, drudgery. [-ERY]

‖ **slāv´ey**, n. (sl.; pl. ~s), Maid-servant, esp. in lodgings or boarding-house. [-Y³]

Slā´vic (-ah-), a. & n. (Language) of the Slavs, Slavonic. [-IC]

slāv´ish, a. As of, having the character-istics of, slaves, abject, servile, base, (~ imitation, without any attempt at de-velopment or originality). Hence ~LY² adv., ~NESS n. [-ISH¹]

Slavōn´ian, a. & n. (Language, member) of the Slav race; (inhabitant) of the former Austrian district Slavonia. [f. med. L *Sc(l)avonia* country of Slavs, -AN¹]

Slavōn´ic, a. & n. (Language) of the Slavs. Hence ~IZE(3) v.t. [as prec., -IC]

***slaw**, n. Salad of sliced cabbage. [Du. *sla*, shortened f. *salade* salad]

slay, v.t. (slew pr. -ōo, slain). Kill (chiefly poet., rhet., or joc.; often also, as *used forth ~ing & spoiling*). Hence (-)~ER¹ n. [OE *slēan*, cf. Du. *slaan*, G *schlagen*, strike]

sleaz´y, a. (Of textiles, & rarely transl.) flimsy. [f. 17th c., etym. dub.]

sled, slédge¹, sleigh (slā), nn., & vv.i.& t. 1. Vehicle on runners instead of wheels for conveying loads or passengers esp. over snow drawn by horses or dogs or reindeer or pushed or pulled by hand, toboggan, (sled now little used in Eng-land except of structure on runners for dragging loads in agriculture; *sleigh* chiefly of runner-carriage for driving over snow; *sledge* in all senses); *sleigh-bell*, one of the tinkling bells often attached to harness of ~-horse etc. 2. vv.i.& t. Travel, go, convey, in ~. [*sled* f. MDu. *sledde* cogn. w. SLIDE; *sledge* f. MDu. *sleedse*; *sleigh* (vh arbitrary) shortened f. *sled*, cf. Du. *slee* for *sled*]

slédge², n. (Also ~-hammer) blacksmith's large heavy hammer (~-hammer blows, argu-attrib. & fig., as ~-hammer blows, argu-

ments, styles). [OE *slecg* (*slēan* smite, SLAY), cf. Du. *sleggel*]

sleek, a., & v.t. 1. Smooth & soft & glossy (of hair, fur, skin, or animal or person with such hair etc.); hence ~LY² adv., ~NESS n. 2. v.t. Make ~ esp. by stroking or pressing down. [var. of SLICK, ME *slike*, cf. OE *slician* & Icel. *slíkja* make ~]

sleep¹, n. Bodily condition, normally re-curring every night & lasting several hours, in which nervous system is in-active, eyes are closed, muscles relaxed, & consciousness nearly suspended, pro-longed similar condition of hibernating animals, (BEAUTY ~); in one's ~, while asleep; the ~ of the just, sound, ~ that knows not breaking, death; broken ~, with disturbed intervals; go to ~, fall asleep; fall on ~, arch., go to ~, fig. die); a period of or single indulgence in ~ (shall try to get a ~); (fig.) rest, quiet, negligence, death, etc.; ~walker, -walking, somnam-bulist, -ism. Hence ~LESS¹ a., ~lessly² adv., ~lessness n. [OE *slēp*, cf. Du. *slaap*, G *schlaf*, cogn. w. LG *slap*, G *schlaf*, loose]

sleep², v.i. & t. (slept). 1. Be immersed in sleep, fall or be asleep, (let ~ing dogs lie, avoid stirring up trouble; ~ like a log or top, soundly; ~ on, upon, over, a ques-tion, leave it till tomorrow; ~ the clock ROUND~). 2. Spend in or affect by ~ing (~ the hours away; slept off his vacation, headache, debauch). 3. Be inactive or dor-mant (sword ~s in the scabbard; top ~s, spins so steadily as to seem motionless). 4. Lie in the grave. 5. Sojourn for the night at, in, etc.; have sexual intercourse with. 6. Provide ~ing accommodation for (lodging-house ~s 300 men). 7. ~ing-bag, for ~ing out of doors in; ~ing-car(riage), railway wagon provided with beds; ~ing-draught, opiate; ~ing-sick-NESS; ~ing-suit, pyjamas. [OE *slēpan*, cf. Du. *slapen*, G *schlafen*, & see prec.]

sleep´er, n. In vbl senses; also, ‖ wooden beam or piece of other material used as support for rails etc.; = SLEEP²ing-car. [-ER¹]

sleep´y, a. Drowsy, ready for sleep; habitually indolent, unobservant, etc.; without stir or bustle (a ~y little town); (of fruit, esp. pears) insipid & dry with incipient decay; ~ghead, ~y or inatten-tive person (esp. in voc.); ~y SICKNESS. Hence ~ILY² adv., ~INESS n. [-Y²]

sleet, n., & v.i. impers. 1. Hail or snow falling mixed with rain. 2. vb. It ~s etc., ~ falls. Hence ~Y² a., ~INESS n. [f. 14th c.; cf. G *schlosse* hailstone]

sleeve, n. 1. Part of garment that covers arm (LAWN¹~s; LEG-of-mutton ~; manda-rin~, loose & open below elbow; laugh in one's ~, secretly; have card, plan, etc., up one's ~, in reserve, concealed but ready for use; turn, roll, up one's~s,

prepare to fight or work; *wear* one's HEART *upon* one's ~). **2.** Tube enclosing rod or smaller tube. **3.** = WIND[1].*sock*. **4.** ~-*coupling*, tube for connecting shafts or pipes; ~-*fish*, kind of cuttlefish, squid; ~-*link*, two buttons joined for fastening wristband; ~-*nut*, long nut with right-hand & left-hand screw-threads for drawing together pipes or shafts conversely threaded; ~-*valve* (in the form of a cylinder with sliding movement). Hence (-)sleeved[2] (-'vd), ~LESS (-vl-), aa. [OE *slíefe*, *slíf*, cf. MDu. *slove*, *sloof*, covering]

sleigh. See SLED.

sleight (slīt), n. Dexterity, cunning, deceptive trick or device or movement, (arch.); ~*-of-hand*, juggling, legerdemain, prestidigitation, quickness of hand in fencing etc. [f. ON *slœgth* (*slœgr* SLY, -TH[1])]

slen'der, a. Of small girth or breadth, slim, not stout, (~ *stem*, *waist*, *pillar*, *girl*, *hand*); scanty, slight, meagre, inadequate, relatively small, (~ *hopes*, *means*, *store*, *income*, *acquaintance with subject*, *foundations for belief*). Hence ~LY[2] adv., ~NESS n. [f. 14th c., etym. dub.]

slept. See SLEEP[2].

sleuth-hound (-lōō-, -lñ-), n. Bloodhound (lit. & fig.); (also *sleuth*, esp. U.S.) detective. [*sleuth* var. of SLOT[2]]

slew[1], **slue**, (slōō), v.t. & i., & n. **1.** Turn or swing forcibly or with effort out of the forward or ordinary position (often *round*, *to the left*, etc.). **2.** n. Such change of position. [naut. wd, etym. dub.]

slew[2]. See SLAY.

slice, n., & v.t. & i. **1.** Thin broad piece or wedge cut off or out esp. from meat, bread, or cake; share, part taken or allotted, (*a* ~ *of territory*, *of the profits*, etc.); kinds of implement with thin broad blade e.g. (also *fish*-~) for helping fish, (also ~-*bar*) for clearing furnace-bars of clinker, or for lifting things out of frying-pan etc. **2.** vb. Cut (often *up*) into ~s, cut (piece) *off* adv. or prep., go through (air etc.) with cutting motion; make incorrect slicing motion with oar (also trans. ~ *the water*) or golf-club (also trans. ~ *the ball*, hit it a glancing blow so that it curves off to the right of a right-handed player). [vb f. n., f. OF *escice* splinter (*esciCier* f. OHG *skízan*, G *schleissen*, cogn w. SLIT)]

slick, a. & adv. (colloq.), & v.t. **1.** Dexterous, not marred by bungling, carried smoothly through. **2.** adv. Directly, exactly, completely, (*came* ~ *into the middle of them*; *hit him* ~ *in the eye*; *bowled his middle stump* ~ *out of the ground*). **3.** v.t. Make sleek. Hence ~'ER n. [var. of SLEEK]

slide[1], v.i. & t. (*slid*). **1.** Progress along smooth surface with continuous friction on same part of object progressing (cf. ROLL; *slid sitting down a grass slope*; *piston* ~*es*

noiselessly *up & down*), make move thus (~*e the drawer into its place*). **2.** Glide over ice on both feet without skates with momentum got by running (~ *over delicate subject*, barely touch upon it); glide, go smoothly along. **3.** Go without interference (*let things* ~*e*, be negligent). **4.** Go unconsciously or by imperceptible degrees (~*es into sin*; ~*e from one note to another* in music). **5.** ~*ing door*, drawn across aperture on slide instead of turning on hinges; ||~*ing keel*, CENTRE-board; ~*ing*, ~*e-*, *rule*, graduated, with ~*ing* part for doing certain mathematical processes automatically; ~*ing scale*, schedule for automatically varying one thing (esp. tax, wages, prices) in direct or inverse proportion to fluctuations of another; ~*ing seat*, mounted on runners esp. in racing boats to lengthen rower's or sculler's stroke. Hence ~'ER[1] (1, 2) n., ~'ABLE a. [OE *slídan*, cf. SLED]

slide[2], n. **1.** Track on ice made by persons sliding; slope prepared with snow or ice for tobogganing. **2.** Act of sliding. **3.** Inclined plane down which goods etc. slide to lower level, chute. **4.** (Also ~*way*) part(s) of machine on or between which sliding takes place. **5.** Part of machine or instrument that slides, (also ~-*valve*) sliding piece that opens and closes aperture by sliding across it. **6.** Thing slid into place, esp. glass holding object for microscope or magic-lantern picture. [f. prec.]

slight[1](-īt), a. Slender, slim, frail-looking, (*saw a* ~ *figure approaching*); supported by *a* ~ *framework*); a or some inconsiderable (*has a* ~ *cold*; *took a* ~ *repast*; *have made a* ~ *inquiry*, *some* ~ *inquiries*, *into it*); not much or great or thorough, inadequate, scanty, not even the smallest, (*after* ~ *inquiry*; *did it with* ~ *inconvenience to himself*; *there is not the* ~*est excuse for it*; *a conclusion based on very* ~ *observation*; *a structure raised on* ~ *foundations*; *paid him* ~ *attention*). Hence~'ISH[1,2) a., ~'LY[2] adv., ~'NESS n., -(it-). [cf. ON *sléttr*, Du. *slecht*, G *schlecht* bad, *schlicht* smooth]

slight[2](-īt), v.t., etc., & n. **1.** Treat or speak of (person, branch of study, etc.) as not worth attention, fail in courtesy or respect towards, markedly neglect; hence ~'ingLY[2](-it-) adv. **2.** n. Marked piece of neglect, omission of due respect etc., (*put a* ~ *upon*, slight). [f. prec.]

sli'ly. Var. of SLYLY.

slim, a., & v.i. (-mm-). **1.** Of small girth or thickness, slenderly built, of slight shape; (f. S.-Afr. Du.)clever,instratagem, crafty, unscrupulous. **2.** v.i. Reduce one's figure by dieting and exercises. Hence~'LY[2]adv.,~'MISH[1,2)a.,~'NESS n. [Du., = sly, bad, cf. G *schlimm* bad, cunning]

slime, n., & v.t. & i. **1.** Fine oozy mud or other substance of similar consistence,

e.g. liquid bitumen or mucous exudation of fish etc.; ~-gland in molluscs etc.; secreting ~; ~-pit, of liquid bitumen. 2. vb. Cover with ~ (esp. of snake preparing prey for gorging); ||(sl.) get through, away, past, out of it, etc., by physical or moral slipperiness. [OE *slim*, cf. Du. *slijm*, G *schleim*, also L *līmus* mud.]

slim'ly, a. Of the consistence of slime; covered or smeared with or full of slime; slippery, hard to hold; cringingly dishonest; repulsively meek or flattering. Hence ~IRY² adv., ~INESS n. [-Y²]

sling, v.t. & i. (*slang*), & n. [1]. Throw (rare; ~-*ink*, sl., be an author or journalist, write); hurl (stone etc.) from ~, use ~, whence ~ER¹ n.; suspend with ~, allow to swing suspended, arrange so as to be supported from above, hoist or transfer from axletree; *shung shot*, metal ball attached by thong to wrist & used esp. by criminals as weapon. 2. n. Strap or string used with the hand to give impetus to small missile; kinds of apparatus used to support hanging weight, e.g. injured arm, rifle, ship's boat, goods being transferred; ~-*dog*, one of pair of hooks used to grapple goods for hoisting. [vb f. ON *slyngva*, cf. G *schlingen* entwine, twist; n. cogn., but prob. f. various Teut. mn.]

sling², n. (chiefly U.S.). Kind of toddy (esp. *gin*~). [?]

slink¹, v.i. (*slunk* or rarely *slank*, *slunk*). Go in secretive manner or with guilty or ashamed or sneaking air (usu. *off, away, by*, etc.). [OE *slincan* creep, cf. G *schlinken*]

slink², v.t. & i., & n. 1. (Of animal) miscarry, produce (young, or abs.) prematurely. 2. n. Animal, esp. calf, so born; its flesh; ~-*butcher*, who deals in ~. [perh. = prec., perh. var. of SLING¹]

slip¹, v.i. & t. (-pp-). 1. Slide unintentionally for short distance, lose footing or balance or place by unintended sliding, (~*ped in the mud or over the edge and fell; blanket* ~*ped off bed; foot* ~*s out of stirrup; ring off finger*). 2. Go with sliding motion (*as the door closes the catch* ~*s into place*; ~ *along*, sl., go at great speed; ~ *into*, sl., pummel, belabour, eat heartily of). 3. Escape restraint or capture by being slippery or hard to hold or by not being grasped (*eel, opportunity,* ~*ped through his fingers; let reins* ~ *out of his hands; let* ~ *the dogs of war*, poet., begin war). 4. Make way unobserved or quietly or quickly (*how time* ~*s away!*; ~ *by, past*; ~ *out of the room*; ~ *off or away*, depart without leave-taking etc.; *just* ~ *across to the baker's; errors will* ~ *in*). 5. Make careless mistake (~ *some & then in his grammar*). 6. Let go from restraint of some kind (~ *greyhounds*, from leash; ~ *anchor*, detach ship from it; *cow* ~*s its*

calf, produces it prematurely). 7. Pull (garment etc.; hastily *on, off*). 8. Insert stealthily or casually or with gliding motion (~*ped half a crown into the porter's hand, a white powder into her glass, the papers into his pocket, a marker between the pages*). 9. Escape from, give the slip to, (*dog* ~*s his collar, prisoner his guard; the point had* ~*ped my attention*). [ME; = escape, glide, prob. f. MLG *slippen*; & cf. OE *slipor* SLIPPERY]

slip², n. 1. Act of slipping, blunder, accidental piece of misconduct, (*a* ~ *on a piece of orange-peel may be fatal; there's many a* ~ *'twixt the cup & the lip*, nothing is certain till it has happened; *give one the* ~, escape from him; ~ *of the tongue, pen*, thing said or written accidentally for something else; *a few* ~*s in youth are inevitable*). 2. Kinds of loose covering or garment, e.g. pillow-case, under bodice, petticoat, pinafore. 3. Leash for slipping dogs, device for suddenly loosing clip or attachment. 4. Artificial slope of stone as landing-stage; inclined plane on which ships are built or repaired. 5. Long narrow strip of thin wood, paper, etc, printer's proof on such paper. 6. Cutting taken from plant for grafting or planting. 7. One of the fielders (*short, long,* ~) stationed for balls glancing off bat to off side behind batsman; (sing. or pl.) this part of ground (*was caught in the* ~*s or at* ~). 8. (Without pl. or article) semifluid clay for coating or making pattern on earthenware. 9. (Theatr.; pl.) part from which scenes are slipped on, part where actors stand before entering. 10. pl. Bathing-drawers. 11. Small sole (flat-fish). 12. Loss of distance travelled by aircraft arising from nature of medium in which its propeller revolves. [chiefly f. prec.; senses *scion, strip*, prob. f. MDu. *slippe* strip]

slip-, comb. form of SLIP¹, ². ||~*carriage*, railway carriage on express for casting loose at station where rest of train does not stop; ~*cover*, of calico etc. for furniture out of use; ~-*galley*, long narrow tray for holding composed type; ~-*hook*, with contrivance for loosing it readily at need; ~-*knot*, that can be undone by a pull, also knot that slips up & down string & tightens or loosens loop; ~-*rope*, with both ends on board so that casting loose either end frees ship from moorings; ~*shod*, having shoes down at heel, slovenly, (fig., of speech, writing, speaker, writer, method of work, etc.) negligent, careless, unsystematic, casual, loose in arrangement; ~'*slop*, n. (as redupl. of *slop*) washy stuff lit. or fig., weak drink, slops, sentimental talk or writing; ~*stream*, stream of air driven astern by aircraft's propeller(s); ~-*up* n. (colloq.),

blunder; ~way, shipbuilding or landing slip.

slipp'er, n., & v.t. **1.** Loose comfortable indoor shoe (HUNT¹-the~; bed- ~ ~-shaped BED¹-pan), whence ~ED²(-erd) a.; skid or shoe placed under wagon-wheel as drag; person who slips greyhounds in coursing-match; ~-bath, shaped like ~, with covered end; ~wort, calceolaria. **2.** v.t. Chastise (child etc.) with ~; hence ~ING¹(¹) n. [-ER¹]

slipp'erЎ, a. (Of ground) hard to stand on, causing slips by its smoothness or muddiness, (fig., of subject) requiring tactful handling; (of object or person) hard to hold firmly owing to polish or sliminess or elusive motion, (fig.) unreliable, incalculable, shifty, unscrupulous. Hence ~ILY² adv., ~INESS n. [f. OE slipor slippery (cf. SLIP¹), -Y²]

slipp'Y̆, a. Slippery (vulg.); look or be ~ (sl.), look sharp, make haste. [-Y²]

slit, v.t. & i. (slit), & n. **1.** Cut or (t. & i.) tear lengthwise, make long incision or rent in, cut into strips, (threatened to ~ his nose, tongue, etc.; ~ one's weasand, cut his throat; ~ hide into thongs, sheet of metal into strips or rods; if you strain it too hard it will ~; has ~ my coat-sleeve from shoulder to wrist); ~-ling-rollers, ribbed pair fitting into each other & ~ing metal sheet by pressure. **2.** n. Long incision; long narrow opening comparable to cut (a ~ is provided for the coin to drop through; the windows are mere ~s; the ~s on the neck are gill-openings); trench, narrow trench for soldier or weapon. [ME slitten (w. change of vowel) schleissen & schlitzen slit; cogn. w. SLICE]

slith'er (-dh-), v.i. (colloq.). Slide unsteadily, go with irregular slipping motion. [var. of obs. slidder, OE slidrian, cf. SLIDE & OE slidor slippery]

sliv'er, n., & v.t. & i. **1. 1.** Piece of wood torn from tree or timber, splinter, (vb, break t. & i. off as ~, break t. & i. up into ~s). **2.** (In fishing) side of small fish cut off as bait (vb, cut ~s from). [f. obs. slive vb f. OE slīfan split +-ER¹]

slobb'er, v.i. & t., & n. **1.** Run at the mouth in infantile helplessness or maudlin emotion; wet (clothes, other person in kissing) with saliva; do (task) badly, botch, bungle. **2.** n. Running saliva; maudlin talk, emotion, or kisses; hence ~Y² a., ~INESS n. [cf. Du. slobberen be messy]

slob'ice, n. (Newfoundland). Floating ice mixed with snow. [f. slob=SLAB²]

sloe, n. (Small bluish-black wild plum, fruit of) BLACK-thorn (~gin, liqueur of ~s steeped in gin). [OE slā, cf. Du. slee]

sloe-worm. Var. of SLOW-WORM.

slŏg, v.i. & t. (-gg-), & n. **1.** Hit (i. & t.) hard & wildly esp. in boxing & at cricket; walk or work doggedly (usu. on, away);

hence ~g'ER¹(-g-) n. **2.** n. Hard random hit. [?]

slŏg'an, n. Highland war-cry; party cry, watchword, motto; short catchy phrase used in advertising. [f. Gael. sluaghghairm (sluagh host, gairm outcry)]

sloid, sloyd, n. A system (orig. Swedish) of manual training, esp. by means of wood-carving, used in schools. [f. Sw. slöjd skill, cogn. w. SLEIGHT]

slŏŏp, n. Small one-masted fore-&-aft-rigged vessel with mainsail & jib, & usu. gaff topsail & forestaysail; ‖ small warship used for general purposes & esp. for police work on foreign stations; ‖ ~ of war (hist.), cutter-rigged ship mounting guns; ~rigged, rigged like ~. [f. Du. sloep perh. f., perh. the source of, F chaloupe SHALLOP]

sloot. Var. of SLUIT.

slŏp, n. (in pl. only), & v.i. & t.(-pp-). **1.** (Pl.) dirty water or liquid, waste contents of kitchen or bedroom vessels; (pl.) liquid food, as broth, gruel, etc., non-alcoholic drinks; ~basin, for receiving dregs of cups at table; ~pail, for removing bedroom ~s. **2.** vb. Spill (i. & t.), (allow to) flow over edge of vessel, (often over, out); make mess with ~s (or with ~s as subj.) upon (clothes, floor); ~ over (fig.), gush, be maudlin, (earlier sense in sing. puddle; OE -sloppe liquid droppings, cf. sluppe in COWSLIP]

slŏp², n. (in pl. only). (Arch.) wide knickerbockers; ready-made clothing, clothes & bedding supplied to sailors in navy; ~room, from which ~s are issued aboard ship; ~seller, -shop, of ready-made clothes. [f. ON sloppr gown (cf. OE oferslop upper garment)]

‖**slŏp³**, n. (sl.). Policeman. [=ectlop (police spelt backwards)]

slōpe, n., & v.i. & t. **1.** Inclined position or direction, the having of one end or side at higher level than the other, difference in level between two ends or sides of thing, the lying in a line neither parallel nor perpendicular to level ground or a line serving as standard, (there is always a certain ~ in a ship's deck; cut this side straight & the other with a ~ to the right; the whole ~ may amount to 2 ft); piece of rising or falling ground, incline; position of soldier with rifle ~d (come to the ~); hence ~WISE(-pwiz) adv. **2.** v.b. Have or show ~, lie or tend obliquely esp. to ground level, slant esp. up or down, whence slōp'inglЎ adv.; place or arrange or make in or at a ~(~arms, place rifle at a ~ over shoulder; must ~ the sides of the pit); (sl.) make off, go away, also saunter, walk about. [n. & v. 17th & 16th c. formations f. obs. or arch. adj. slope, which was perh. for slopen p.p. of slip, or perh. for ASLOPE]

slŏp'pЎ, a. (Of road) wet with rain, full of puddles; (of floor, table, etc.) wet with

slops, having water etc. spilt on it; (of work) unsystematic, not thorough; (of sentiment or talk) weakly emotional, mawkish. Hence ~ILY² adv., ~INESS n. [stop¹, -Y²]

slosh, n., & v.t. 1. =SLUSH. 2. v.t. (sl.). Beat, thrash. [see SLUSH]

slot¹, n., & v.t. (-tt-). 1. Groove, channel, slit, or long aperture, made in machine etc. to admit some other part, esp. slit for penny or other coin that sets working a ~-machine or automatic retailer of small wares; stage trapdoor. 2. v.t. Provide with ~(s). [f. OF *esclot* hollow of the breast, etym. dub.]

slot², n. Track of deer etc. esp. as shown by footprints. If. AF & OF *esclot* hoof-print prob.f. ON *slóth* trail, cf. SLEUTH-HOUND]

sloth, n. 1. Laziness, indolence, whence ~FUL a., ~FULLY² adv., ~FULNESS n. 2. Kinds of S.-Amer. mammal with curved long-clawed feet living entirely in trees & capable only of very slow motion on ground. 3. ~-bear, large-lipped black shaggy honey-eating bear of India & Ceylon; ~-monkey, kind of loris. [ME *slouthe* (SLOW, -TH¹)]

slouch, v.i. & t., & n. 1. Droop, hang down negligently; go or stand or sit with loose ungainly attitude; bend one side of brim of (hat) downwards (opp. *cock*); hence ~ingly² adv. 2. n. ~ing attitude or walk, stoop, downward bend of hat-brim (opp. *cock*); (sl.) incompetent or slovenly worker or operator or performance (esp. *is no ~ at, this show etc. is no ~*); ~ hat, with ~ed brim. [cf. Icel. *slókr* ~ing fellow, etym. dub.]

slough¹ (slow), n. Quagmire, swamp, miry place, (*the S~ of Despond*, state of hopeless floundering in sin). Hence ~y¹ [-Y²] (-owy) a. [OE *slóh*, etym. dub.]

slough² (sluf), n., & v.i. & t. 1. Snake's cast skin, any part that an animal casts or moults; dead tissue that drops off from living flesh etc.; (fig.) habit etc. abandoned; hence ~y² [-Y²] (slufi) a. 2. v.b. Drop off (t. & i.; often *off, away*, esp. in intr. sense) as ~; cast off ~. [cf. LG *sluwe* husk]

Slovak, n. & a. (Member) of a Hungarian Slavic people. [Boh.]

slov'en (-uv-), n. Personally untidy or dirty, careless & lazy, or unmethodical person. Hence ~LY¹ a., ~INESS n., ~LY² adv. (arch.), ~RY n., [-iuv-]. [perh. f. Du. *slof* careless +-*ain* -AN]

Slovene (or slōv-), n. **Slovén'ian**, a. & n. (Member) of a southern Slavic people in Jugoslavia; (-*ian*) language of the Slovenes. [G, f. OSlav. (*slovo* word), whence also SLAV]

slow (-ō), a., adv., & v.t. & t. 1. Not quick, deficient in speed, taking a long time to traverse a distance or do a thing, (~ & steady wins the race; ~ & sure, haste is risky; ~ march, of troops in funeral procession etc.; ~ music), gradual (~ growth, reluctant, lingering, (*was not ~ to defend himself*), not hasty or easily moved (*is ~ to anger*); (of clock etc., usu. pred.) behind correct time (*is 20' ~*); dull-witted, stupid (*is ~ of speech, of wit*); deficient in interest or liveliness, dull, tedious, (*entertainment was voted ~*); (of a photographic lens) of small aperture (and so necessitating long exposure); (of surfaces) tending to cause ~ness (*a ~ pitch, tennis-court, billiard-table*); ~coach, person ~ in action, dull of wit, or behind the times in opinions etc.; ~match, ~-burning for igniting explosives; ~-motion, (attrib., of a film) greatly increased (~*ing down the motion* when projected at the normal rate); ~-worm, see foll.; hence ~NESS (-ōn-) n. 2. adv. (~er, ~est). At ~ pace, ~ly, (being ousted by ~ly, but still common when the adv. & not the vb gives the essential point, as *how ~ he climbs!, please read or go ~ or ~er, watch goes ~*, cf. *I saw a man climb ~ly up*; placed always after vb exc. in excl. with *how* or ~ in comb. with part. as ~-*going, -moving*). 3. vb. Reduce one's speed, reduce speed of (train, ship, etc.), (usu. *down, up, off*). [OE *sláw*, cf. Du. *slee(uw)*, Sw. *slö*, & perh. L *laevus* & Gk *laios* left]

slow-worm (slō-wêrm), n. Small harmless reptile between snakes & lizards, blindworm. [OE *slá-wyrm*, cf. MSw. *slá*, Norw. *slo*, slow-worm]

sloyd. See SLOJD.

slub, n., & v.t. (-bb-). 1. Wool slightly twisted as preparation for spinning. 2. v.t. Twist thus. [?]

slubb'er, v.t. & i. Do carelessly or bunglingly; slaver, slobber. [cf. Da. *slubbre*, G *schlubbern*, & SLOBBER]

sludge, n. Thick greasy mud; sewage. Hence **sludg'y²** a. [see SLUSH]

slue. See SLEW¹.

slug¹, n. & t. (-gg-). 1. Kinds of shell-less snail destructive to small plants; (vb) collect & destroy ~s in garden etc. 2. Bullet of irregular shape; roundish lump of metal; line of type in linotype printing. [sense 1 f. obs. n. = SLUGGARD; sense 2 either f. 1 w. ref. to shape, or as 1 w. ref. to weight]

*slug², v.t. & i. (-gg-), & n. = SLOG. [cf. SLOG]

slug-a'bed, n. (arch.). Person who lies late in bed. [as foll., ABED]

slugg'ard, n. Lazy sluggish person. [f. obs. *slug* be slothful f. Scand. +-ARD]

slugg'ish (-gi-), a. Inert, inactive, torpid, indolent, slow-moving (*a ~ stream, circulation, temper, person*). Hence ~LY² adv., ~NESS n. [obs. *slug* SLUGGARD, -ISH¹]

sluice (-ōōs), n., & v.t. & i. **1.** (Also ~gate, -valve) sliding gate or other contrivance for changing level of a body of water by controlling flow into or out of it, floodgate; water above or below or issuing through floodgate; (also ~-way) artificial water-channel; a rinsing. **2.** vb. Provide with ~(s); flood with water from ~; rinse; pour or throw water freely upon; (of water) rush out etc. (as) from ~. [f. OF escluse f. LL exclusa floodgate (orig. fem. p.p. see EXCLUDE]

sluit (-ōōt), **slōōt**, n. (S. Africa). Narrow water-channel. [Du. sloot ditch]

slum[1], n., & v.i. (-mm-). **1.** Dirty back street or court or alley in city. **2.** v.i. Go about the ~s to visit or examine condition of inhabitants; hence ~m'ER[1] n. [cant wd, etym. dub.]

slum[2], n. Non-lubricating part of crude oil; gummy residue formed in lubricating oil during use. [?]

slum'ber, v.i. & t., & n. Sleep (distinguished in sense only by an implication of comfort or ease, which is not invariable, e.g. fell into a troubled ~; & in use by a rhet. or poet. tinge; the n. is often in pl., ~ as his ~s were interrupted by a knock); ~ away, waste (time) in ~; ~-suit (shop), pyjamas. Hence **slum'b(e)rous** a., **slum'b(e)rousLY**[2] adv., ~ER[1] n. [earlier sense doze; in n. f. vb, f. ME slumen (slume n. f. OE slúma) +-ER[5]; -b- as in NUMBER; cf. G schlummern]

slum'mock, v.t. & i. (colloq.). Swallow greedily, wolf down; move or speak in awkward disorderly way. [cf. dial. slammakin sloven]

slump, n., & v.i. **1.** Sudden or rapid or great fall in prices or diminution of demand for commodity or interest taken in subject or undertaking. **2.** v.i. Undergo ~, fall in price, fall through, fail utterly. [earlier (17th-c.) sense be bogged; prob. imit., cf. PLUMP[2]]

slung. See SLING[1].

slunk. See SLINK[1].

slur, v.t. & i. (-rr-), & n. **1.** Write (t. & i.) or pronounce (t. & i.) indistinctly with letters or sounds running into one another; (Mus.) perform legato, mark (notes) as to be so performed; pass (fault, fact, etc.) lightly over, conceal or minimize; (arch.) put ~ upon (person, character), make insinuations against. **2.** n. Imputation, blame, stigma, (he put a ~ upon me; it is no ~ upon his reputation that he should have or to say that); piece of ~ring in handwriting, pronunciation, or singing; curved mark used in musicwriting to show that two or more notes are to be sung to one syllable or played or sung legato. [f. obs. slur thin mud, etym. dub.]

slu'rry, n. Liquid mixture of materials for Portland cement manufacture; semifluid mixture of ganister and fire-clay

used in repairing converter-linings etc. [as prec.]

slush, n. Watery mud or thawing snow (cf. SLUDGE); (fig.) silly sentiment. Hence ~'Y[2] a. [f. 17th c., w. varr. sludge & slutch, also 19th c. slosh; etym. dub.]

slut, n. Slovenly woman, slattern; (joc.) girl. Hence ~t'ERY(4) n., ~'ISH[1] a., ~t'ishLY[2] adv., ~t'ishNESS n. [perh. f. Scand., cf. Sw. dial. slåta, Norw. slott idler]

sly, a. (~er, ~est). Cunning, wily, hypocritical; practising concealment (~ dog, person who keeps his peccadilloes or pleasures quiet), done etc. in secret (on the ~, privately, without publicity); knowing, arch, bantering, insinuating, ironical; ~'boots, ~ person (in playful use, esp. to or of child or animal). Hence ~LY[2] adv., ~'NESS n. [ME sleigh f. ON slœgr, perh. cogn. w. SLAY; cf. SLEIGHT]

slype, n. Passage from cathedral transept to chapter-house or deanery. [var. of SLIP[2]]

smack[1], n. & v.i. **1.** Flavour, taste that suggests presence of something; barely discernible amount of some food-material etc. or of a quality etc. present in dish or person's character, tinge, tincture, spice, dash, of, (has a ~ of ginger, of the cask, in it, of recklessness, of the old Adam, in him). **2.** v.i. Have a slight curious or unexpected or secondary taste (rare); taste slightly of, suggest by taste or otherwise the presence or effects of, (wine ~ing of the cork; his manner ~ed of supercilious-ness). [vb f. n., OE smaec, cf. G geschmack n., schmecken vb]

smack[2], n., v.t. & i., & adv. **1.** Slight explosive report as of surface struck with palm, of lips parted suddenly, or of whip cracked; blow with palm, slap; hard hit at cricket; loud kiss (gave her a hearty ~); have a ~ at (colloq.), make trial of (something), have a go at. **2.** vb. Slap (person's face etc.) with palm; part (t. & i. of lips) noisily in eager anticipation or enjoyment of food or other delight; crack (t. & i. of whip). **3.** adv. (colloq.). With a ~, in sudden direct violent way, outright, exactly, (went ~ through windows, into ditch; hit him ~ on the nose). [prob. imit., & unconnected w. prec.; cf. MDu. smack n., smacken vb]

smack[3], n. Sloop esp. for fishing; ~s-man, sailor on ~. [f. MDu. smacke, etym. dub.]

smack'er, n. (sl.). Loud kiss; sounding blow; ‖large or remarkable specimen of anything; *dollar. [SMACK[2], -ER[1]]

small (-awl), a., n., & adv. **1.** Not large, of deficient or comparatively little size or strength or power or number, consisting of minute units (~ rain), (of agent) not doing thing on large scale, (usu. without emotional implications of LITTLE, e.g. not a dear ~ pony or a dirty ~ scoundrel;

~ farmer, shopkeeper, on ~ scale; has a ~ voice (~ FRY¹, ~ HOURS; ~ & early, party with few guests & not kept up late; the still ~ voice, conscience; coal is ~ or too ~ for me; ~ craft, boats; came in ~ numbers; this beer is very ~, weak, watery). ~er kind (~-sword, rapier or sword for thrusting only; ~ beer, arch., of light beer; ~ talk of trifles as important; look, feel, ~ be humiliated; think no ~ beer of oneself, be conceited; chronicle ~ beer, talk of trifles as important; look, feel, ~ be humiliated; trivial remarks; ~ gross, ten dozen; ~ letters, not capitals; ~ change, copper & silver coins, (transf.) ARM²s, portable fire-arms; ~ capitals, of less height than the fount's regular capitals; ~ pica, size of TYPE; ~ hand, ordinary writing, opp. text-hand; || ~ debt, not above largest amount recoverable in county court; ~ piece of land between one and fifty acres in extent let or sold by a county council to a ~ holder for cultivation. ~ 3. Not much of (& ~ blame to him, & ~ wonder), comments on account etc, just described; *there was no ~ excitement about it; has ~ Latin, knows little of it). 4. Unimportant, trifling, (~ talk, ordinary society conversation; the ~ worries of life; is great in ~ matters). 5. Socially undistinguished, poor, obscure, humble, (great & ~, all classes; lives in a ~ way, unpretentiously; have experimented with radium in a ~ way). ~ people love to talk of great). clothes, arch., knee-breeches; (~ holding, 6. Morally mean, ungenerous, petty, paltry, (this ~ spiteful nature; only a ~ man would think of that at such a time; I call it ~ of him to remind me of it), whence ~'mind'ED² a. 7. ~'poor, highly pustules; hence ~'ISH'(2) a., ~'NESS n. (-awl). 8. n. The slenderest part of something, esp. ~ of the back, hinder part of waist; ~ (pl., at Oxford) responsions; || (pl., colloq.) ~ articles of laundry. 9. adv. SING~. [OE smæl, cf. Du, Da, & Sw. smal, G schmal, thin]

small'age (-awl-), n. Wild celery. [prec., F ache f. L apium parsley]

smalt (-awlt), n. Glass coloured blue with cobalt; pigment made by pulverizing this. [F. f. It. smalto f. Teut., cogn. w. SMELT¹]

|| **smarm'y̆**, a. (colloq.). Unctuously ingratiating, fulsome. [f. smarm var. of dial. smalm smooth down (as with grease),-Y²]

smart¹, v.i., & n. 1. (Of person or part of him, or of wound lit. or fig. or the missile or insult etc. that has inflicted it) feel or give acute pain, rankle, (my finger ~s; rushed off ~ing with nettle-stings, under disappointment, etc.; with the gibe yet ~ing in his brain; ~ for, be paid out for, suffer consequences of, esp. as threat you shall ~ for this). 2. n. Bodily or mental sharp pain, stinging sensation.

3. ~money, paid or exacted as penalty or compensation; ~ weed, the Water Pepper. [OE smeortan, cf. Du. smarten, G schmerzen; cogn. w. L mordēre bite, Gk smerduleos terrible]

smart², a. 1. Severe, sharp, vigorous, lively, brisk, (gave him a ~ rap over the knuckles; had a ~ skirmish, walk, bout of toothache; went off at a ~ pace). 2. Clever, ingenious, showing quick wit or ingenuity, keen in bargaining, quick to take advantage, (a ~ talker, retort, saying, device, invention; a ~ officer, servant, lad, ready & intelligent; ~ dealing, selfishly clever to verge of dishonesty); unscrupulously clever; *a ~ aleck, a would-be clever person. 3. Bright & fresh in appearance, spruce, in perfect order or repair, in gay or fashionable clothes, well groomed, showing bright colours or new paint, (~ clothes, a ~ garden; ~ person, house, ship, looks quite ~). 4. Conspicuous in society, leading the fashion, stylish, (~ people; the ~ set). Hence ~'LY², ~'NESS n., adv. [prec.]

smash, v.t. & i., n., & adv. 1. Break (t. & i.) utterly to pieces (often up), shatter, bash in with crushing blow, (a ~ing blow, ~es shop-window and grabs valuables behind it). 2. n. Breaking to pieces; violent fall or collision or disaster (go to ~, be spoilt or disorganized or ruined); ~ing stroke in lawn tennis (see vb); violent blow with fist etc.; bankruptcy, series of commercial failures; drink of spirit & water iced & flavoured (usu. brandy-~); ~-up, complete ~. 3. adv. (With vbs of motion) with a ~ (went ~ into a goods train). [prob. imit.]

smash'er, n. In vbl senses: esp. (sl.), convincing argument or smashing blow or heavy fall. [-ER¹]

|| **smatch**, n. (now rare). =SMACK¹ n.

smatt'er|ing, n. Slight superficial knowledge of a language or subject. So ~ER¹ n. [f. obs. smatter talk ignorantly, prate, earlier (14th c.) dette, etym. dub.]

smear, v.t. & i., & n. 1. Daub with greasy or sticky substance or with something that stains, (of grease etc.) make marks on, make a ~; blot, obscure outline of, (writing, drawing); defame, sully. 2. n. Blotch made by ~ing; hence ~'Y² a., ~'INESS n. [OE smerian (smeru n., fat, cf. G schmeer); cogn. w. Gk maron ointment]

smec'tite, n. Kind of whitish clay used for taking out grease from cloth etc. [f. Gk smēktis fuller's earth (smaō wipe), -ITE¹(2)]

|| **smeech**, **smitch**, n. (dial.). Smell of burning or smouldering. [OE *smēc*, *smic*, cogn. w. *smoke*]

smĕg′|ma, n. Sebaceous soaplike secretion in folds of the skin, esp. of the prepuce. Hence ~**mằt′ic** a. [f. Gk *smēgma* *-atos* soap(*smēkhō=smạ̄ō* see SMECTITE, -M)]

smĕll, n., & v.t. & i. (*smelt* or rarely ~*ed*). **1.** Nasal sense by which odours are perceived (~ *is less acute in man than in most animals; has a fine sense of* ~; *is perceptible to* ~ *as well as sight*); quality in substances that affects this sense, odour, (*has no, a sweet, pungent, disgusting, peculiar, close,* ~; *the* ~ *of thyme, carrion*); bad odour, whence ~′**y²** a. (colloq.); act of inhaling in order to ascertain ~ (*take a* ~ *at it*); hence ~′LESS a. **2.** vb. Perceive ~ of, detect presence of by ~, (*am sure I* ~ *gas; horses smelt the water a mile off; a rat*, fig., suspect foul dealing etc.), whence ~′ABLE a.; inhale ~ of, set one's sense of ~ to work at (*smelt it or at it to see if it was high; came up & smelt at my calves*); (of dog) hunt out by ~, (fig. of person) find out (secret, plotter, etc.) by investigation, (of dog or fig. of person) sniff or search *about*; perceive ~s, have sense of ~ (*can, do, fishes* ~?); emit ~ usu. of kind specified by adj. or adv., suggest or recall the ~, (*flowers that do not* ~; ~*s sweet, nice, disgustingly, of garlic, of brandy*; ~ *of the lamp, seem to have been composed laboriously at night*; ~ *of the shop*, be over-technical; ~ *of jobbery, nepotism*, etc., suggest these); stink, be rank; seem from the ~ to be (*dish, milk,* ~*s good, sour*); ~*ing-bottle*, pocket phial of ~*ing-salts*, ammonium carbonate mixed with scent to be sniffed as cure for faintness etc. [ME *smel(len)*, excl. E]

smĕll′er, n. In vbl senses; also (sl.) the nose; severe blow esp. on the nose. [-ER¹]

smĕlt¹, v.t. Extract (metal) from (ore) by melting; extract (metal) from ore by melting. [cf. Da. *smelte*, G *schmelzen*, & the prob. connected MELT²]

smĕlt², n. Small fish allied to salmon & prized as food. [OE, cf. Du. *smelt*, G *schmelte*, *sand-eel*]

smĕlt³. See SMELL.

smew, n. Kind of fishing duck. [also *smee*, *smeath*, etym. dub.]

smī′lăx, n. Genus of climbing shrubs some of which yield sarsaparilla; a Cape vine much used in decoration. [L f. Gk]

smīle, v.i. & t., & n. **1.** Relax features often by parting lips into pleased or kind or gently amused orindulgently contemptuous or sceptical expression or forced imitation of these, look (*up*)*on* or *at* with such expression, (~*e sweetly, indulgently, cynically, bitterly*; ~*e at the claims of,* ridicule or show indifference to ~*ing*, whence ~′**ingly²** adv.; express by ~*ing* (~*e welcome, consent, appreciation*, etc.); give *a* ~*e* of specified kind (~*ed an ironical, a curious,* ~*e*); drive (person's vexation etc.) *away*, bring (person) *into* or *out of* a mood, by ~*ing*; *come up* ~*ing*, face fresh difficulty (w. ref. to boxer beginning new round); be or appear propitious, have bright aspect, seem to look propitiously (*up*)*on*, (*fortune, occasion,* ~*es on us*; *all nature looks* ~*ing & gay*). **2.** n. Act of ~*ing*, ~*ing* expression or aspect; hence ~′LESS (-l-) a. [cf. MHG *smielen*]

smĭrch, v.t., v.i. & n. Stain, soil, smear, spot, (lit., & fig. as *a* ~*ed reputation*). [perh. f. OF *esmorcher* torture, brand]

smĭrk, v.i., & n. (Put on or wear) affected or silly smile, simper. [OE *smercian*, excl. E]

smīte, v.t. & i. (*smōte* & arch. *smit*, *smitten* & arch. *smit*), & n. **1.** Strike, hit, (chiefly arch. or joc.; *whosoever shall* ~ *thee on thy right cheek*; *smote his hands together*; *smote the harpstrings*; ~ *off his head*; *smote the first ball for four*; *an idea smote him*, suddenly came); inflict severe defeat on (~ *them hip & thigh*, utterly defeat them; *we hope to* ~ *them*); chastise (*God shall* ~ *thee*; *his conscience smote him*); (chiefly in p.n.) strike or seize or infect or possess *with* disease or desire or fascination (*city, person, smitten with plague, palsy*; *am smitten with her charms or her or abs.*; *smitten with a desire to*); come forcibly or abruptly (*up*)*on* (*wave smote upon the cliff*; *sun's rays smiting upon him*; *sound* ~*s upon the ear*); hence **smĭt′ER¹** n. **2.** n. Blow, stroke, attempt. [OE *smītan*, cf. Du. *smijten*, G *schmeissen* (OHG *smīzan* to stroke, smear)]

smĭth, n. Worker in metal esp. one who forges iron, blacksmith, (the gen. sense chiefly in comb., as *gold, silver, tin, white,* ~). [OE cf. Du. *smid*, G *schmied*]

smĭth|ereens′ (-dh-), **smĭth′ers** (-dh-), nn. pl. Small fragments (*smash* etc. *to* or *into* ~). [19th c. only, etym. dub.; *-een* Ir. dim. ending]

smĭth′ery, n. Smith's work; (esp. in Admiralty dockyards) smithy. [-ERY]

Smĭth′field, n. (Used for) the London meat market. [~ in London]

smĭ′thy (-dhĭ), n. Blacksmith's workshop, forge. [f. ON *smidhja*, cf. obs. E *smithe* f. OE *smiththe*]

smĭtten. See SMITE.

smŏck, n., & v.t. **1.** Chemise (arch.); child's overall; ~*frock*, field-labourer's outer linen garment of shirtlike shape & with upper part closely gathered; ~*mill*, windmill of which the cap only & not the body revolves. **2.** v.t. Adorn with SMOCK-ING. [OE *smoc* (*smūgan* creep into), cf. OHG *smocco*]

smŏck′ing, n. Honeycomb ornamentation on garment of which the basis is close gathers as on smock-frock. [-ING¹]

smōke¹, n. **1.** Volatile products of com-

bustion, esp. visible vapour with carbon etc. in suspension emitted by burning substance (*a column, cloud, of* ~; *end, go up in* ~, come to nothing; *no* ~ *without* FIRE[1]; *from* ~ *into smother*, from one evil to another or a worse; *like* ~, sl., without check or difficulty, rapidly, easily). **2.** Spell of tobacco-smoking (*must have a* ~). **3.** (sl.) Cigar(ette). **4.** ~*-ball*, projectile filled with material emitting dense ~ used to conceal military operations etc., also for inhaling vapour from in asthma etc.; ~ *-bell*, suspended over lamp etc. to protect ceiling; ~*-consumer*, apparatus for utilizing instead of releasing ~ of furnace or fireplace, &c.; ~*-dried*, cured in ~; ~*-jack*, machine for turning roasting-spit by use of current of hot air in chimney; ~*-plant, -tree*, ornamental shrub with feathery ~like fruit-stalks; ~*-rocket*, contrivance for injecting ~ into drain to discover leak; ~*-screen* (Mil., Nav.), ~ diffused to hide operations; ~*-stack*, funnel & steam-escape pipes of steamer; ~*-stone*, cairngorm. Hence ~'LESS (-kl-) a., ~'lessLY adv., ~'less- n. [OE *smoca*, cf. *sméocan* to smoke; cogn. w. Du *smook*, G *schmauch*]

smōke', *v.i. & t.* **1.** Emit smoke or visible vapour, reek, steam, (*altars* ~*e*; *his* ~*ing blade, steeds; meat* ~*ing on the board*; *lamp is* ~*ing*, not burning clear), (of chimney or fire) discharge smoke into room. **2.** Colour or darken or obscure, spoil taste of in cooking, preserve or cure, suffocate, rid of insects etc., with smoke (*lamp* ~*es ceiling*; ~*ed wood*, fumed; ~*ed glass*, darkened with smoke for looking at sun etc.; *the porridge is* ~*ed*; ~*ed ham, haddock*, etc.; ~ *insects, plants*, kill, cleanse, them by fumigation; ~*e out wasps, wasps'-nest*, etc., destroy by injecting smoke). **3.** Inhale & exhale smoke of (tobacco-pipe, cigar, cigarette, tobacco, opium, stramonium, cane; brown paper; *put that in your pipe &* ~ *it*, reflect upon what has been said, esp. some admonition or rebuke), whence ~'ABLE a.; ~*e tobacco* (~*es too much or like a chimney; will you* ~*e?*), bring oneself into specified state by ~ing (*has* ~*ed himself ill, sick, stupid, into tranquillity*). **4.** Get inkling, become suspicious or aware, of; || (arch.) quiz, make fun of, (person etc.). **5.** || ~*e-room*, = ~*ing-room*; ~*ing-cup*, *-jacket*, of ornamental kind worn while one ~*es*; ~*ing-car(riage)* or compartment, reserved for smokers on railway-train; || ~*ing-concert*, concert at which ~ing is allowed; ~*ing-mixture*, blend of tobaccos for ~ing in pipe; ~*ing-room*, in hotel or house kept for ~ing; ~*ing-room talk* etc., such as is suited for men only; ~*ing-tobacco* (esp. for use in pipes). [OE *smocian* (prec.)]

smōk'er, n. In vbl senses; also or esp.: person who habitually smokes tobacco (~*'s heart, throat*, ailments due to excessive smoking); smoking-carriage on train; || smoking-concert. [-ER[1]]

smōk'y, a. Emitting, veiled or filled with, obscure (as) with, stained with or coloured like, smoke (*a* ~*y fire, city, room, hue, ceiling*). Hence ~*Ily*[2] adv., ~*INESS* n. [-Y[2]]

smōlt, n. Second-year salmon at stage between parr & grilse after development of silvery scales. [cf. OE *smolt* serene?]

smōoth[1] (-dh), a. **1.** Of relatively even & polished surface, free from perceptible projections or lumps or indentations or roughness or (of liquid) undulations, not wrinkled or pitted or scored or hairy, that can be traversed without check, (~*skin, surface, morocco, brow, chin; am now in* ~ *water*, have passed obstacles or difficulties; *bring the paste to a* ~ *consistence; had a* ~ *passage, across sea; course of true love never did run* ~; ~ *hair*, esp. flattened down on head). **2.** Free from harshness of sound or taste (~ *verse, spirit, etc.*; ~ *breathing* in Gk Gram., unaspirated sound of initial vowel, also symbol of this). **3.** Equable, unruffled, polite, conciliatory, complimentary, that tering, (~ *temper, manners*; ~ *face*, esp. hypocritically friendly, whence ~*faced* a.; ~ *things*, esp. flattery or insincere encouragement, whence ~*SPOKEN*, ~*tongued*[2], aa.). **4.** ~*-bore*, gun with unrifled barrel. Hence ~*LY*[2]adv., ~*NESS* n. (-dh-). [OE *smōth* (rare, usu. *smēthe*) excl. E]

smōoth[2] (-dh), *v.t. & i. & n.* **1.** Make smooth (often *out, over, down, away*; ~ *over* or *away differences, perplexities, difficulties*, etc., reduce or get rid of in fact or appearance); free from impediments or discomfort (~ *the way; will* ~ *his declining years*); cloak over faults etc.; become smooth (usu. *down; sea presently* ~*ed down*). **2.** n. ~ing touch or stroke (*gave his hair a* ~); ~*ing-iron*, implement usu. heated to ~ linen etc.; ~*ing-plane*, small plane for finishing the planing of wood. [f. prec.]

smōte. See SMITE.

smŏth'er (-udh-), *n. & v.t. & i.* **1.** Smouldering ashes etc. (arch.; *from the* SMOKE *into the* ~); cloud of dust, spray, smoke, etc., or obscurity caused by it (rare). **2.** *vb.* Suffocate, stifle, kill by stopping breath of or excluding air from, (~*ed mate* in chess, when king having no vacant space to move to is checked by knight); overwhelm *with* kisses, gifts, kindness, etc.; put out or keep down (fire) by heaping with ashes etc.; suppress, conceal or secure concealment of, keep from notice or publicity, burke, (often *up*; ~ *a yawn*;

with ~ed curses; the facts, the recommendations of the committee, were ~ed up); cover entirely *in (strawberries ~ed in cream);* (rare) perish of suffocation, have difficulty in breathing. [vb f, n, ME *smorther* (OE *smorian* stifle, cf. Du. *smoren* stew, G *schmoren* stew, +agent-suf. *-ther*)]

smo'thery (-dh-), a. Stifling. [-Y²]

smoul'der (smō-), v.i., & n. 1. Burn without flame, burn inwardly or in suppressed way or unseen; (of feelings etc.) exist, operate, be nursed, undetected or without conspicuous effects (*~ing discontent, hatred, rebellion*), 2. n. ~ing combustion (*the ~ will soon be a flame*). [n. f, vb, ME *smolderen* (obs. *smolder* n. smoke), etym. dub.]

smidge¹, smútch (arch.), v.t. & i., & n. 1. Smear or blot or blur lines of (writing, drawing); make dirt-mark or confused blot or smear on (face, paper, surface); (usu. *-tch*) defile, sully, stain with disgrace, impair purity of, (person's record, fame, etc.); (of ink, drawing, etc.) become blurred (*smudges easily*). 2. n. Dirt-mark lit. or (esp. *-tch*) fig., blotted line, blurred mark; hence **smidg'y²** a., **smúdg'iɴʏss** n. [*-ge* older as vb (1430), *-tch* as n. (1580); etym. dub.]

smidge², n. Outdoor fire with dense smoke made to keep off insects etc. [?]

smug, a. & n. 1. Of commonplace respectable narrow-minded self-satisfied comfortable unambitious unimaginative character or appearance; hence ~ɴɛss n. 2. n. (chiefly univ. sl.) ‖ Person ill fitted for society or without athletic pursuits or interests. [?]

smug'gle, v.t. Import or export (goods, or abs.) illegally, esp. without payment of customs duties (often *in, out, over*), whence ~ɛʀ¹, ~ɪɴɢ¹, nn.; convey secretly *in, out,* etc., or put *away* etc. into concealment. [f. LG *smuggelen*]

smút, n. & v.t. & i. (*-tt-*). 1. (Spot or smudge made by) small flake of soot; *ditto, brother* ~ (nursery etc.); tu quoque retort to criticism; obscene talk or words or stories; disease of corn by which parts of the ear change to black powder; ~*ball,* kinds of fungus; ~*mill,* machine for cleansing grain from ~; hence ~*t'ʏ²* a., ~*t'ɪɴʏss* n. 2. vb. Mark with ~(s); infect (corn) with, (of dog), cf. *schmutz* dirt, G *schmutz* dirt, the corn-disease]

smútch. See SMUDGE.

Smyrn'iot(e) (-őt-), a. & n. (Native or inhabitant) of Smyrna. [-oт²]

snáck, n. Slight or casual or hurried meal; *go ~s,* go shares (*~sl,* claim to share). [orig. sense *snap* n. & v. (of dog), cf. MDu. *snac* n., *snacken* vb, snap]

snaf'fle¹, n. Bridle consisting of ~*e-bit,* or plain slender jointed bit without curb, & single rein; *ride one on the ~e* (fig.,

---

manage him gently. Hence ~ᴇᴅ²(-ld) a. [cf. Du. *snavel,* G *schnabel,* mouth, beak]

‖ **snäf'fle²,** v.t. (sl.). Appropriate, purloin, pinch. [?]

snäg, n., & v.t. (*-gg-*). 1. Jagged projecting point, e.g. irregular or broken tooth, stump of branch remaining on tree, pointed root or stump poking out of ground, piece of rough timber or rock embedded in river or sea bottom & impeding navigation; (fig.) unexpected obstacle or drawback; hence ~ᴳᴱᴅ²(-gd). ~ᴳ'ʏ²(-gl), aa. 2. v.t. Run (ship) on ~; clear (land, waterway, tree-trunk) of ~s. [prob. f. Scand. (Norw. *snag* spike)]

snail, n., & v.t. & i. 1. Kinds of slimy slow-creeping gasteropod mollusc, most of them with spiral shell & horns or retractile eye-stalks, some used as food esp. in France, whence ~ᴇʀʏ(3) n., & many destructive in gardens (*Roman ~,* the chief edible kind; ~*s gallop, pace,* very slow locomotion); (also ~*wheel*) notched wheel in clock resembling ~ in outline determining number of strokes in striking the hours; (also ~*clover, -trefoil*) kinds of leguminous plant including lucerne with spiral pods; ~*fish, slow snail* as a ~; hence ~*ʟɪᴋᴇ* a. 2. vb. Rid (garden) of, hunt for, ~s. [OE *snægl,* cf. OHG *snegil,* ON *snigill*]

snäke, n., & v.i. 1. Serpent (commoner in ordinary speech, more loosely applied so as to include ~like lizards etc., & specially used of the common British harmless kind; ~ *in the grass,* hidden danger or secret enemy; *warm, cherish,* etc., *a ~ in one's bosom,* meet with ingratitude or receive evil for good; SCOTCH² *the ~; see ~s,* have delirium tremens; *raise or wake ~s,* make disturbance, start violent quarrel; *S~sl,* int. of anger). 2. Treacherous cold-hearted person. 3. ~*bird,* fish-eating bird with long slender neck; ~*charmer, -charming,* see SERPENT; ~*fence* (of horizontal tree-trunks only), laid zigzag with overlapping ends to support each other); ~ *lizard,* kinds of lizard with rudimentary or no legs; ~*locked,* with ~s instead of hair; ~*root,* one of several American plants having roots reputed to be ~-poison antidotes; ~*s'head,* the fritillary plant; ~*stone, ammonite; ~*weed, bistort; ~*wood,* (wood of) a S.-American timber-tree (from its ~like markings). 4. v.i. Move, twist, etc. like a ~. [OE *snaca,* cf. MLG *snake,* ON *snákr,* Sw. *snok*]

snäk'|ʏ, a. Infested with snakes; snake-like in appearance or in such attributes as venom, guile, coldness, ingratitude; ~*y hair* (of the Furies with snakes for hair). Hence ~ɪɴᴇss n. [-Y¹]

snäp, v.t. & i.(*-pp-*), & n. 1. Make sudden audible bite (*dog ~ped viciously; ~ at,* try to bite, also speak irritably to; ~ *at*

bark, offer, chance, etc., accept eagerly, (fig.), say Ill-tempered or spiteful things (~ *out*, say irritably), whence ~p¹ish¹ a., ~p¹ishᴸy adv., ~p¹ishness n.; bite off (~ *off one's nose*, esp. fig. interrupt him angrily or rudely). 2. Pick *up* (scraps, or fig. bargain etc.) hastily, whence ~p¹ᴱR-up n.; take up (interjection etc.) without letting him finish. 3. (Cricket) catch (batsman) smartly at the wicket. 4. Break (t. & i.) with sharp crack (~ *the string, a stick; can, wire*, ~*s*). 5. Produce report from, emit report or crack, (~ *pistol, whip*); ~ *one's fingers*, make audible fillip esp. at person etc. in contempt; *pistol* ~*s*, either in going off or in missing fire); close (t. & i.) etc. with ~ping sound (~ *the clasp, one's teeth together; the door* ~*ped to*). 6. Take instantaneous photograph of (esp. unconscious or unwilling subject). 7. ~ *into it* (sl.), start moving quickly; ~ *out of it* (sl.), get rid of a moody habit, etc. 8. ~*ping turtle*, ferocious American freshwater kind. 9. n. Act or sound of ~ping (also quasi-adv., as ~ *went an oar*). 10. Spring-catch fastening bracelet etc. 11. ‖ Kinds of small crisp cake. 12. A card-game. 13. (Usu. *cold* ~) sudden spell of frost. 14. Crispness of style, fresh vigour or liveliness in action, go, dash, spring, whence ~p¹y² a. (*make it* ~*py*), colloq., be quick about it. 15. = ~*shot* n. (see below) 16. *(sl.) Easy task (esp. *soft* ~). 17. (Theatr.) short engagement as actor. 18. attrib. (Esp. of parliamentary or other deliberative proceedings) taken by surprise, brought on without notice, etc. 19. ~*bolt, -lock*, ...; ~*shot*, (n.) Instantaneous photograph taken with hand camera, (v.t., also -*shoot*) take such photograph of. [f. MLG *snap-pen* (snared beak), cf. G *schnappen*]

snare, n., & v.t. 1. Trap for catching birds or animals, esp. one made with cord; (Surg.) wire loop for catching & extracting polypi etc.; device for tempting the enemy or dupe to expose himself to capture, defeat, failure, disgrace, loss, etc.; thing that acts as a temptation (*popularity is often a* ~); (pl.) twisted strings of gut or hide stretched across lower head of side-drum to produce rattling sound. 2. v.t. Catch (bird etc.) in ~, whence (-)snar̄er n.; get (person) into ~ (less common, than *ensnare*). [f. ON *snara*, cf. Du. *snaar* string]

snatch (middle-column continuation) ... (also quasi-adv., as ~ *went an oar*) ... decide, crisis, vote, etc.). 19. (~ *division*, whence snatchen, etym. dub.; perh. cogn. w. SNACK, SNECK]

snatch, v.t. & i., & n. 1. Seize quickly, eagerly, or unexpectedly, esp. with suddenly outstretched hand(s), resene narrowly *from*, secure with difficulty, carry suddenly *away* or *from*, (~*ed his gun up, down; wind* ~*ed my cap off; child* ~*es its foot*; ~ *less, opportunity*, etc.; *was* ~*ed from the jaws of death*; ~ *a half-hour's repose*; ~ *by premature death*); ~ *at*, try to seize (also fig.; as ~ *at offer*, *at help, to seize; hence* ~*block* (Naut.), block with hinged flap admitting rope to sheave. 2. n. Act of ~ing (*made a* ~ *at it*); (usu. pl.) fragment(s) or short burst(s) of song or recitation or talk, short spell(s) of action (*only works by* ~*es, fits & starts*), whence ~y² a., ~ily² adv. [ME *snacchen*, etym. dub.; perh. cogn. w. SNACK, SNECK]

snaᴿk, n. Chimerical animal of ill-defined characteristics and potentialities. [from *The Hunting of the S*~ by 'Lewis Carroll' (1876)]

snarl¹, v.i. & t., & n. 1. (Of dog) make high-pitched quarrelsome growl; (of person) speak cynically, make ill-tempered complaints or criticisms; ~ *out*, utter in ~ing tone; express (discontent etc.) by ~ing; hence ~ᴱR¹ n., ~ingᴸy² a. 2. n. Act or sound of ~ing; hence ~ᴱR¹ n., ~ingᴸy² adv. [frequent. of earlier *snar*, cf. MHG & MLG *snarren* (G *schnarren*)]

snarl², v.t. & i., & n. 1. Twist, entangle, become entangled, (a ~*ed skein*, intricate business); adorn exterior of (narrow metal vase) with raised work made by indirect internal hammering with ~*ing-tron*. 2. n. Knot, tangle. [frequent. of SNARE]

sneak, v.i. & t., & n. 1. Slink, go furtively, (often *in, out, past, round, about, off, away*, etc.), whence ~*ers* n. pl. (sl.), silent shoes; (part.) furtive, not avowed, (*have a* ~*ing kindness for him*, an affection that one cannot justify by reason); 2. n. Mean cowardly underhand person; ‖(school sl.) informer, telltale; (Cricket) ball bowled along the ground; ~*thief* (stealing from open doors or windows). [f. 16th c. etym. dub.]

‖ **sneck**, n., & v.t. (chiefly Sc.). Latch. [ME (n.), perh. cogn. w. SNACK, SNATCH]

sneer, v.i. & t., & n. 1. Smile derisively (often *at*); utter derisive words esp. of a covert or ironical kind (usu. *at*); put (person) *down*, out of countenance, etc., take *away* (person's reputation, happiness, etc.), by ~ing; hence ~ᴱR¹ n., ~ingᴸy² adv. 2. n. ~ing look or remark. [earlier sense *snort*; cf. NFris. *smeer* a taunt, *sneere* to scorn]

sneeze, v.i. & n. 1. Make explosive sound in involuntarily expelling anything that irritates interior of nostrils (*not to be* ~*d ...*

ad, passable, not contemptible); ~ *into a basket* (euphem.), be guillotined. **2.** n. Act. or sound of sneezing. [ME *snesen*, var. of *fnese* (due to misreading of *f* as *ʃ* when *fnese* had been made unfamiliar by substitution of *neeze*) f. OE *ge-fnǣsan* cf. Du. *fniezen*, Gk *pneō* breathe]

snick, v.t. & n. **1.** Cut small notch or make small incision in; (Cricket) slightly deflect course of (ball) with bat. **2.** n. Slight notch or cut; (Cricket) ~ing touch with bat. [?]

snick'er, v.i., & n. Whinny, neigh; = SNIGGER. [imit.]

snickersnee', n. (joc.). Knife, esp. one usable as weapon. [perh. f. obs. *snick-or-snee*, earlier *stick or snee*, f. Du. *steken* thrust, *snijen* cut]

snide, a. & n. (sl.). **1.** Counterfeit, bogus. **2.** n.= jewellery or coin(s); ~s'man, utterer of false coin. [cant word, etym. dub.]

Snid'er, n. (Also ~ *rifle*) early pattern of breechloading rifle. [inventor]

sniff, v.i. & t., & n. **1.** Draw up air audibly through nose to stop it from running or as expression of contempt (~ *at*, try the smell of, also show contempt for or discontent with, also, of dog, show disposition to bite person's *calves*); draw up or *up* (air, liquid, scent), draw up scent of (flower, brandy, meat, etc.), into nose. **2.** n. Act or sound of ~ing, amount of air etc. ~ed up. [imit.: f. 14th c.]

sniff'y, a. (colloq.). Disdainful, contemptuous; (of thing that should be odourless) slightly malodorous. [-Y[2]]

sniff'ing-valve, n. Air-escape valve in steam-engine cylinder. [f. obs. *sniff* = SNIFF]

snigg'er (-g-), v.i., & n. (Give) half-suppressed secretive laugh esp. of cynical kind or of amusement at obscenity or indecency. [imit., cf. SNICKER]

snig'gle, v.i. Fish *for eels* by pushing bait into hole. [f. dial. *snig* eel, etym. dub.]

snip, v.t. & i. (-pp-), & n. **1.** Cut with scissors or shears esp. in small quick strokes (~ *cloth, a hole*; ~ *off the ends*; ~ *at*, make ~ping strokes at), whence ~p'ING[1](2) n. **2.** n. Act of ~ping; piece ~ped off; (colloq.) tailor; (Racing sl.) certainty (also *dead* ~). [cf. Du. *snippen*]

snipe, n. (collect. sing. usu. for pl.), & v.i. & t. **1.** Kinds of gamebird with long straight bill & angular flight frequenting marshes (*common* or *whole, great* or *double* or *solitary, small* or *half* or *jack*, ~, British kinds); ~*eel, -fish,* etc., kinds with long slender snout; hence snip'y[2] a. **2.** Vb. Go ~-shooting; (Mil.) fire shots from hiding usu. at long range into enemy's camp or at individuals, kill or hit thus, whence **snip'ER[1]** n. [cf. Icel. *-snīpa*, Da. *sneppe*, G *schnepfe*]

snipp'et, n. Small piece cut off, snipping; (pl.) detached fragments of knowledge or information, odds & ends, whence ~Y[2] a., ~INESS n. [-ET[1]]

snip'-snap-snor'um, n. A round card-game. [f. LG *snipp-snapp-snorum*]

sniv'el, v.i. (-ll-), & n. **1.** Run at the nose; be lachrymose, affect contrition, show maudlin emotion; hence ~ER[1] n., ~ING & a. **2.** n. Running mucus; whining & weeping; hypocritical talk, cant. [ME *sneevlen* (OE *snofl* mucus)]

snob, n. || Man of low birth or breeding or social position (arch.); || (at universities & public schools; arch.) townsman; person with exaggerated respect for social position or wealth & a disposition to be ashamed of socially inferior connexions, behave with servility to social superiors, & judge of merit by externals, whence ~b'ISH[1] a., ~b'ISHLY[2] adv., ~b'ISHNESS n., ~b'ERY(4, 5), ~'LING[1](2), ~oc'RACY, nn. [earlier sense in dial. *cobbler's man*, etym. dub.]

snoek (-ook), n. (S. Afr.). Large edible sea-fish (cf. SNOOK). [Du.]

snood, n. **1.** (Sc. & literary) fillet worn by maidens in Scotland to confine hair, whence ~ED[2] a. **2.** Any of the short lines attaching hooks to a main line in sea fishing. [OE *snōd*, etym. dub.]

snook[1], n. Kinds of fish esp. the sea pike (cf. SNOEK). [f. Du. *snoek*]

snook[2], n. (sl.). Contemptuous gesture with thumb to nose & fingers spread out (*cock, cut, make, a* ~ or ~*s; S~s!*, int. of contempt). [?]

snook'er, n. Game on billiard-table combining pool & pyramids (~*ed*, having one's object-ball covered by another). [?]

snoop, v.i. & t. (orig. U.S., colloq.). Pry into matters one is not concerned with; sneak *around* looking for infractions of the law; steal. Hence ~ER[1] n. [f. Du. *snoepen* enjoy stealthily]

snooze, v.i. & t., & n. (Take) short sleep esp. in day-time; pass time in lazy indifference; ~ *time* etc. *away*, spend it indolently. [?]

snore, v.i. & t., & n. (Make) hoarse rattling or grunting noise in breathing esp. during sleep; pass time *away* in ~ing; bring *oneself awake, into a nightmare,* etc., by ~ing. Hence ~ER[1] n. [prob. imit.; cf. foll.]

snort[1], v.i. & t., & n. (Make) explosive noise due to sudden forcing of breath through nose & usu. expressing anger or indignation or incredulity, or (of steam-engine etc.) noise resembling this; express (defiance etc.) by ~ing (often *out*), throw *out* (words) with ~ing. [prob. imit.; cf. prec.]

snort[2], n. Device for enabling submarines to take in air for engines & crew when submerged to periscope depth. [?]

snort'er, n. In vbl senses; also (sl.): boisterous gale; performance etc. conspicuous for vigour or violence. [-ER[1]]

snot, n. (vulg.). Mucus of the nose (also of person as low term of abuse); ~handkerchief, [OE *gesnot*, cf. Du. & Da. snot; cogn. w. SNOUT]

snot't'[y], a. & n. 1. Running or foul with snot (vulg.; also as low abusive epithet); (colloq.) annoyed, short-tempered; hence ~iy² adv.; ~iness n. 2. n. (nav. sl.). Midshipman. [-y²]

snout, n. Nose (& mouth) of animal or (derog.) human being; (~ of something, nozzle, (~ of glacier, of battleship's ram, etc.); ~beetle, kinds with beaked head; ~ring, inserted in pig's ~ to prevent rooting. Hence (-)~ED² a. [cf. *snitten* blow the nose] Du. *snuit*, G *schnauze*; cogn. w. OE

snow¹ (-ō), n. & v.i. & t. 1. Atmospheric vapour frozen into ice crystals & falling to earth in white flakes or spread on it as a white layer (*red ~*, see below); (pl.) falls or accumulations of ~ (*where are the ~s of last year?*). 2. Substance etc. resembling ~ esp. in whiteness (*her breast of ~*; *the ~s of seventy years*; white hair; *apple, chestnut*, etc., ~, kinds of pudding); (sl.) cocaine. 3. ~ball, (n.) mass of ~ pressed into hard ball esp. for use as missile, || fund each subscriber to which finds n others, || kinds of pudding e.g. apple enclosed in rice, (v.t. & i.) pelt or have pelting-match with ~balls; ~-ball-tree, guelder-rose; ~-berry, garden shrub with white berries; ~-bird, kinds of white or partly white finch, esp. the ~ bunting (~-blindness), unable, inability, to see owing to exhaustion of retina, by reflection of light endured in traversing ~-fields etc.; ~-blink, reflection in sky of ~ or ice fields; ~-boots, over-boots of rubber & cloth; ~-bound, kept from going out or travelling by ~; ~-cap, white-crowned humming-bird; ~-capped, (of mountain) covered at top with ~; ~-drift, bank of ~ heaped by wind; ~-drop, early spring white-flowered plant; ~-fall, esp. amount of ~ that falls on one occasion or in a year at any place as measured by ~gauge; ~-field, esp. permanent wide expanse of ~ in mountainous or polar regions; ~-flake, one of the small collections of crystals in which ~ falls; ~-goggles, spectacles worn by mountaineers etc. to prevent ~-blindness; ~-goose, arctic white goose with black-tipped wings, the wavy ~; ~-grouse, ptarmigan; ~-ice, opaque white ice formed from ~-slush; ~-leopard, ounce; ~-line, level above which ~ lies permanently at any place; ~-man, figure made of ~ by children etc. & set up; ~-on-the-mountain, kinds of white-flowered garden plant; ~, or usu. red ~, microscopic alga growing in ~ & colouring it red; ~-plough, contrivance for clearing road or track by pushing ~ aside; ~ plume, fringe of blown ~ driven from mountain-top or ridge; ~ shoes, racket-heads or (also ski) long narrow boards attached to feet & enabling wearer to traverse ~ without sinking in; ~shovel, large wooden shovel for ~; ~slip, avalanche; ~storm, heavy fall of ~ esp. with wind; ~white, white as ~; hence ~LESS (-ō-), ~y² (-ō), aa., ~iy² adv., ~iness n., (-ō-). 4. vb (impers.) *it ~s, will ~,* etc., ~ falls etc.; under, cover (as) with ~, overwhelm with numbers etc. (esp. in pass. of election candidate defeated by huge majority); ~ed up, in, ~bound, blocked up with ~. [AryaN.: OE *snāw*, cf. Du. *sneeuw*, G *schnee*, L *nix nivis*, Gk *nipha* accus.]

snow² (-ō), n. Small brig-like sailing vessel with supplementary trysail mast. [L Du. *snauw*]

snub¹, v.t. (-bb-) & n. 1. Rebuff, reprove, put down, humiliate, with sharp words or marked want of cordiality, whence ~b¹ING¹(1) n., ~b¹ingɪʏ² adv.; check way of (ship) esp. by rope wound round ~. 2. (naut.) ~(bing)-post or bollard. 2. n. ~bing), rebuff. [n. f. vb, f. ON *snubba* chide]

snub², a. & n. 1. (Of nose) short & stumpy or turned up, whence ~-nosed² a. 2. n. (rare). ~ nose. [f. prec. vb in old sense check growth of]

snuff¹, v.i. & t. & n. 1. = (the now more usu.) SNIFF vb; also, take ~, whence ~ER¹ n. 2. n. = (the now more usu.) SNIFF n.: also; powdered tobacco taken by sniffing as stimulant or sedative (*give person ~*, deal sharply with him; *take thing in ~*; arch., take offence at it; *up to ~*, sl., not childishly ignorant or innocent), whence ~y² a.; ~iness n.; medicinal powder taken by sniffing; ~-(&-)butter, brownish-yellow; ~-colour(ed), (of) dark yellowish-brown; ~-mill, for grinding ~; || also ~box; ~-taking. [n. f. vb, f. MDu. *snuffen* clear the nose, cf. G *schnauben* snort; sense tobacco prob. f. Du. *snuf* abbr. of *snuftabak* snuffing-tobacco]

snuff², v.t. & i. & n. 1. Trim ~ from (candle or its wick) with fingers or scissors or esp. ~ers n. pl., kind of scissors with box to catch ~ (~ out v.t., extinguish by trimming, also fig. as *I was nearly, his hopes were, ~ed out*; ~ out v.i., sl., die; *can ~ a candle with a pistol*, shoot off top of wick without putting flame out); ~er-tray, holding ~ers. 2. n. Charred part of candle-wick, esp. in bad wick, black excrescence obscuring light; ~-dish, ~-tray. [n. f. vb, etym. dubl.]

snuff³le, v.i. & t. & n. 1. Sniff (intr.), make sniffing sounds; speak nasally, whiningly, or like one with a cold, esp. as form of religious affectation ascribed to puritans & dissenters, whence ~ER¹ n.; ~e out, utter with ~ing; hence ~ingɪʏ²

adv. **2. n.** Sniff; ~ing sound, tone, or talk. [SNUFF¹, -LE(³)]

snug, a. Sheltered from weather & cold, well enclosed or packed in or fixed in place, comfortably situated, cosy, (as ~ *as a bug in a rug*); (of income, dinner, etc.) good enough for modest requirements. Hence ~LY² *adv.*, ~NESS *n.* [cf. ON *snøggr* smooth (of hair), Sw. *snygg* neat]

snugg'ery (-g-), *n.* Snug place, esp. person's private room or den; bar-parlour of inn. [-ERY]

snug'gle, *v.i. & t.* Shift one's position or lie close up *to* for warmth; draw (child etc.) close to one, cuddle. [f. obs. *snug* vb (SNUG) +-LE(³)]

so, *adv., conj., int., & pron.* **1.** To the extent or in the manner set forth by preceding or following *as*-clause or implied in context, thus, equally, similarly, analogously, (now used to express degree before *as*-clause only with negative, as *I am not so eager, but I am as eager, as you; as the tree falls, so must it lie; as bees love sweetness, so flies love rottenness*; rarely used twice correlatively, as *so many men so many minds; when he saw her so frightened; why are you panting so?; so & so only can it be done; stand just so; did not expect to live so long; did not get it by force & ought not to be so deprived of it;* often in sentence appended as explanation, as *I paid him double, I was so pleased; ever* or *never so bad* etc. in condit. clause, as bad etc. as possible, *so far,* up to this time or point or extent, as *so far it has not happened, so far you are right; so* or *in so far as* or arch. *so far forth as,* to whatever extent; *& so forth, & so on,* et cetera, & the like; *so long as,* with the proviso, on the condition, that; *so be it,* form of acceptance, resignation, etc.; *so long,* good-bye till we next meet; *so much for,* that is all that need be done or said about; *is only so much rubbish,* all rubbish; *at so much a week, a head,* etc., a definite but unspecified sum etc.; similarly *so much of one ingredient & so much of another; not so much as,* less than, not even; *is not so much discontented as unsatisfied*). **2.** To the degree or in the manner or with the intent or result set forth by following *that*-clause or *but*-clause or *as to* (*so high that you cannot reach it; so run that ye may obtain; warned him so that he might avoid the danger; all precautions have been taken, so that we expect to succeed; not so deaf but he can hear a gun; was so fortunate as to escape; put it so as not to offend him; it so happens that he was not there*). **3.** To a degree that demands exclamatory emphasis (*so many worlds, so much to do!; I am so glad, tired; she is so beautiful; so kind of you!;* also colloq. or vulg. with *ever,* as *that is ever so much* better, *he is ever so angry!*). **4.** On condition that or that, on condition set forth in *as*-clause or implied, (*so that* or *so it is done, it matters not how; so may you find forgiveness as now you forgive me!; so help me God!,* form of asseveration). **5.** Accordingly, consequently, therefore, as appears or results from preceding or implied statements or fact, (*he says he was not there, so he doubtless was not; so* or *and so I cannot come; so you are back again; so that's that,* colloq. winding up of statement or discussion; *so WHAT?; so look to yourself*). **6.** (Accompanying emphasis on some later word) moreover, also, as well, in actual fact, (*well, so I did; you said it was good, & so it is; yes, I denied it, but* or *& so did you; 'your birthday? yes, so it is'*). **7.** (As substitute, often preceding vb, for obj. of *say, call, speak, tell, think, hope, suppose, do,* etc.) it, this, that, the same, this is what, (*so he said; so spake Achilles,* i.e. what precedes, *& Patroclus so,* i.e. what follows; also ellipt., as *So Satan, whom the archangel thus rebukes; do you think so?; & so say all of us; I suppose so,* form of agreement; *I told you so,* warned you in vain; *she is ill & he thinks himself so; so-called,* epithet questioning accuracy of description; *so to say* or *speak,* apology for exaggeration, metaphor, neologism, etc.; *you don't say so?,* formula of surprise). **8.** In that state or condition, actually the case, (*he, it, is better so; God said Let there be light, & it was so; must it be so?; but perhaps it is not, even if it were, so; though it was,* or *things were, ever* or *never so,* vulg., however bad the state of things; also with omission of *it is* etc., as *how so?, why so?; if so, not so;* also ellipt. for *is that so?* chiefly in init. of German, as '*He went off yesterday.*' '*So?*'; *quite so, just so,* forms of agreement). **9.** (arch.). *And so,* after which I, they, etc., proceeded (*& so to dinner, to bed,* etc.); *so please you,* by your favour, if you please. **10.** (Ellipt. after conditional clause; arch.) let it be so, very well, (*if you are content, so*). **11.** (As int., also *soh*) that will do, stay as you are, stand still, be quiet. **12.** (In comb. with relative words) *-ever* (also with *-ever* appended, as *whoso, whosoever*). **13.** *So-&-so,* particular person or thing not needing to be specified (*never mind what so-&-so says; tells me to do so-&-so*); *so so,* pred. adj. or adv., not more than passable, *-bly;* or so, or thereabouts (after expressions of quantity or numbers; *send me ten or so; 1lb. or so will do*). [OE *swā,* cf. Du. *zoo,* G *so*]

soak, *v.t. & i., & n.* **1.** (Of absorbent substance) take *up* or suck *in* (liquid); place or leave or lie in or in liquid for saturation, steep t. & i., make or be wet through, (of rain etc.) drench, whence ~ING⁴(1) *n.*; (of moisture) make way *in(to)* or *through,*

~ make its *way*, by saturation, whence
~ AGE(3) n.; (sl.) extract money from by
extortionate charge, taxation, etc. (~ *the
rich*); drink persistently; hard drinking. 2. n. ~-
ing; drinking-bout; hard drinker. [OE
socian (*sūcan* SUCK)]
soak'er, n. in vbl senses; esp.; hard
drinker; drenching shower. [-ER²]
soap, n., & v.t. & i. 1. Compound of fatty
acid with soda or potash or (insoluble
~-s) with an earth or metallic oxide, of
which the soluble kinds yield when
rubbed in water a lather used in washing
(*soft* ~ made with potash & remaining
liquid, also fig. flattery); ~-*berry, nut,
-plant, -pod, -root, -wort*, kinds of plant
yielding substances serving purpose of
~; ~-*boiler, -boiling*, manufacture(r) of
~; ~-*box*, box for holding ~, makeshift
stand for street orator; ~-*bubble*, iridescent globe of air enclosed in film of
soapy water made by blowing through
pipe dipped in ~-*suds*; ~-*earth*, ~-*stone*,
steatite; ~ *opera* (sl.) radio serial; ~
suds; ~-*works*, ~ manufactory; hence
~LESS a. 2. vb. Apply ~ to, scrub or
rub with ~; use ~ upon oneself. [OE
sāpe, cf. Du. *zeep*, G *seife*]
soap'|y², a. Like, smeared or impregnated
with, suggestive of, soap; (of person or
his manners or talk) unctuous, flattering.
Hence ~ILY² adv., ~INESS n. [-Y¹]
soar (sör), v.i. Fly high (lit. & fig.), mount
to or be at a great height above earth,
hover or sail in the air without flapping
of wings, (~*ing eagle, spire, thoughts,
ambition, ideals*). Hence ~ingLY² adv.
[f. *essorer* f. L1 EX(*aurea* f. *aura* breeze)]
sŏb, v.i. & t. (-bb-), & n. 1. Draw breath
in convulsive gasps usu. with weeping
under mental distress or physical exhaustion (~ *out*, utter with ~-s); hence
~bingLY² adv. 2. n. Convulsive drawing
of breath esp. in weeping; ~-*stuff*, pathos, sentimental writing; [prob. imit.]
sŏb'er, a., & v.t. & i. 1. Not drunk (as ~
as a judge; *appeal from Philip drunk
to Philip* ~, suggest that opinion etc.
represents passing mood only); temperate in regard to drink (*is a* ~ *man*);
moderate, well-balanced, sane, tranquil,
self-controlled, sedate, not vehement or
passionate or excited (or wayward or
fanciful or exaggerated, (of colour) quiet
& inconspicuous, (*in* ~ *fact*, in fact as
opp. fancy; *a* ~ *estimate*; ~-*minded*;
~-*sides*, sedate person; ~-*suited*, poet,
clad in ~ colours), whence ~LY² adv.
2. vb. Make or become ~ or less wild,
reckless, enthusiastic, visionary, etc.
(often *down*). [f. OF *sobre* f. L *sobrius*
perh. f. *so-, se-*, apart from L *ēbrius* drunk,
etym. dub.]
Sŏbra·njě(-ahnyě), n. Bulgarian national
assembly. [Bulg.]

sŏbri'ety, n. Being SOBER. [f. F *sobriété*
f. L *sobrietatem* (SOBER, -TY)]
sŏb'riquet (-kā), **sou-** (sōō-), n. Nickname, assumed name. [F, etym. dub.]
sŏc(c)'age, n. Feudal tenure of land
involving payment of rent or other
service to superior. [AF, f. OE *sōc* jurisdiction (*sēcam* SEEK) +-AGE]
sŏcc'er (-k-), n. (colloq.) Association
football, form of football in which (cf.
RUGBY) ball may not be touched with hand
except by goalkeeper. [ASSOCIATION, -ER¹]
sŏ'ciable (-sha-), a. & n. 1. Fitted for
companionship, ready & willing to converse, not averse to society, communicative, liking company; (of meeting etc.)
marked by friendliness, not stiff or
formal; hence sŏciABI'lITY n., ~LY² adv.,
(-sha-). 2. n. Open carriage with facing
side seats; tricycle for two riders side by
side; S-shaped couch allowing two
occupants to face each other. [F, f. L
sociabilis (*sociare* f. *socius* fellow cogn. w.
sequi follow, see ABLE)]
sŏ'cial (-shl), a. & n. 1. Living in companies, gregarious, not fitted for or not
practising solitary life, interdependent,
co-operative, practising division of labour,
existing only as member of compound
organism, (*man is a* ~ *animal*; ~ *bees,
wasps*, kinds having common nests etc.;
~ *birds*, building near each other in communities; ~ *plants*, kinds that grow
thickly together & monopolize ground
they grow on; ~ *polypeta*). 2. Concerned
with the mutual relations of men or
classes of men (~ *problems, science, morality, students, philosophers; the* ~ *contract*
or rarely *compact*, agreement among men
to exchange the individual freedom of
the state of nature for legal restriction,
assumed by 18th-c. thinkers as basis of
political society; ~ *democrat*, politician
aiming at improving condition of lower
classes by gradual advance towards
socialism; ~ *security*, freedom from unemployment & want; *the* ~ *evil*, prostitution). 3. Of or in or towards society (~
*intercourse, life, code, etiquette, pleasures,
duties; one's* ~ *superiors & inferiors;
rank, position, distinctions; has* ~ *tastes;
a* ~ *evening, gathering*). 4. Of or with
allies (*the S~ war* in Rom. Hist.). 5. n.
~-gathering, esp. one organized by club,
congregation, etc. Hence or cogn.
sŏ'cialLY² adv. [f. L
socialis (*socius* see prec. -AL)]
sŏ'cialism (-shz-), n. Principle that
individual freedom should be completely
subordinated to interests of community,
with any deductions that may be correctly
or incorrectly drawn from it, e.g. substitution of co-operative for competitive
production, national ownership of land
& capital, State distribution of produce,
free education & feeding of children, &
abolition of inheritance (*Christian* ~*ism,*

attempt to apply Christian precepts in ordinary life resulting in some approximation to the aims of ~ism). Hence ~ISM(2) n. & a., ~IS'TIC a., ~IS'TICALLY adv., (-sha-). [-ISM]

so'cialize (-sha-), v.t. Make social; arrange socialistically. Hence ~A'TION n. [-IZE]

soci'ety, n. **1.** Social mode of life, the customs & organization of a civilized nation, (the progress of ~ is an evolution; the pests of ~, persons who prey on the community). **2.** Any social community (no ~ can retain members who flout its principles). **3.** The upper classes of a community whose movements & other doings are more or less conspicuous, the socially distinguished, fashionable & well-to-do & well-connected people, (was welcomed by ~; the customs of polite ~; ~ does not approve; leaders of ~; often attrib., as ~ lady, people, gossip, news, journal; ~ verse, of light topical witty kind). **4.** Participation in hospitality, other people's houses or company, (goes a great deal into, avoids, is at his best or embarrassed in, ~). **5.** Companionship, company, (~ & solitude; always enjoy his ~; seek, avoid, the ~ of). **6.** Association of persons united by a common aim or interest or principle (S~ of Friends, Quakers; S~ of Jesus, abbr. S.J., see JESUIT; FRIENDLY ~; Royal S~, founded 1662 for improving natural knowledge; S~ for the Propagation of the Gospel, abbr. S.P.G.; DORCAS ~; building, co-operative, ~). [f. OF societé f. L societatem (socius see SOCIABLE, -TY)]

Soci'nian, a. & n. (Follower, following of) the doctrine) of the 16th-c. Italian theologians Laelius & Faustus Socinus, whose opinions resemble those of modern unitarians. Hence ~ISM(3) n. [-IAN]

sociol'ogy, n. Science of the development & nature & laws of human society. Hence **sóciolo'gical** a., **sóciolo'gically²** adv., (-sho-), **sóciol'ogist** n. [F (-gie), f. L socius see SOCIABLE, -LOGY]

sock¹, n. (shop pl. soz). Short stocking not reaching knee (|| pull up your ~s!, brace yourself for an effort); removable inner sole put into shoe for warmth etc.; ancient comic actor's light shoe (also used allusively for comedy etc., cf. BUSKIN). [OE socc f. L soccus comic actor's shoe]

sock², v.t., n., & adv. (sl.). **1.** Fling (ball, stone) at; hit (person) with hand-flung missile. **2.** n. Blow inflicted by missile or fist (esp. give him ~s!). **3.** adv. With such blow, plump, right, (hit him ~ in the eye). [?]

|| **sock³**, n., & v.t. & i. (school sl.). **1.** Sweets, pastry, etc., eaten at odd times, tuck, grub. **2.** vb. Treat to ~, indulge in ~; give (person thing). [?]

*sockdol'oger, -lag-, n. (sl.). Decisive blow or argument. [perh. corrupt. of doxology]

sock'er. Var. of SOCCER.

sock'et, n. & v.t. **1.** Natural or artificial hollow for something to fit into or stand firm or to revolve in (eye-~; or ~ of the hip; candle too large for ~; BALL¹ & ~); ~ joint, = BALL¹-&-~ joint; ~pipe, with enlarged end to receive another. **2.** v.t. Place in, fit with, ~; (Golf) hit (ball) with heel of club. Hence ~ED² a. [f. OF soket dim, of soc ploughshare]

sock'eye (-kī), n. The blue-back salmon. [Amer.-Ind. sukai]

so'cle, n. (archit.). Plain low rectangular block serving as support for pedestal, vase, statue, etc. [F, f. It. zoccolo f. L soccŭlus (soccus SOCK¹, -ULE)]

Socrat'ic, a. & n. **1.** Of, like, following, etc., Socrates (~ic method, dialectic, procedure by question & answer; ~ic irony, pose of ignorance assumed in order to entice others into display of supposed knowledge). **2.** n. Follower of Socrates. Hence ~ICALLY adv. [f.L f. Gk Sōkratikos (Sōkratēs, -IO)]

sod¹, n., & v.t. (-dd-). **1.** Turf, upper layer of grass land including blades & roots & earth, (under the ~, in the grave); piece of turf pared off; hence ~d'y² a. **2.** v.t. Cover (ground) with ~s (~ding mallet, spade, implements used); pelt with ~s. [cf. Du. zode, LG sode]

sod². See SEETHE.

sod³, n. (vulg.). Sodomite (esp. as vague term of abuse). [abbr.]

sod'a, n. **1.** One of the compounds of sodium in common use, esp. sodium carbonate or bicarbonate. **2.** (Also ~water) water made effervescent by impregnation with carbonic acid under pressure & used alone or with spirit or wine or milk as a drink (orig. made with sodium bicarbonate; some ~-water; some or a brandy & ~; ~fountain, vessel in which ~-water is stored under pressure to be drawn out, shop, *store, or counter equipped with this apparatus). [med.L, etym. dub.]

sodal'ity, n. A confraternity or association esp. of religious character (chiefly in titles of R.-C. societies). [f. L sodalitas (sodalis comrade, -TY)]

sodd'en, a., & v.t. & i. **1.** Saturated with liquid, soaked through; (of bread) doughy, heavy & moist; stupid or dull in fact or appearance with habitual drunkenness; hence ~NESS n. **2.** vb. Become or make ~. [orig. p.p. of SEETHE]

sod'ium, n. A soft silver-white metallic element found in soda, salt, & other compounds, which in its pure form decomposes water. Hence **sŏd'ɪo** a. [SODA, -IUM]

sod'omite, n. Person practising sodomy.

[f. L f. Gk *Sodomitēs* inhabitant of Sodom, see -ITE¹(1)]

sŏd'omỹ, n. Copulation between male persons. [f. L *Sodomie* f. *Sodoma* Sodom, see *Gen.* xix. 4 foll. -Y²]

sōēv'er, suf. occas. separable usu. appended to relative pronouns, adverbs, or adjectives, but sometimes following them at an interval, to give indefinite meaning (*whosoever, howsoever*, etc.; *how great ~ it may be; with what end ~ he did it*). [SO, EVER]

sō'fa, n. Couch with raised ends & back on which several persons can sit or one lie; *~ bed(stead)*, piece of furniture serving as *~* by day & bed by night. [f. Arab. *soffah* bench]

sŏff'it, n. Lower surface of architrave, arch, balcony, etc. [f. F *soffite* f. It. *soffitta* ceiling, fem. p.p. = fixed under (L SUB², *figere* fix)]

soff(sm). See SUFI(sm).

soft(sāw-, sŏ-), a., n., adv., & int. **1.** Comparatively wanting in hardness, yielding to pressure, malleable, plastic, easily cut, (*~ as butter; ~ stone, iron; ~ coal*, bituminous, opp. *anthracite; ~ corn*, moist thickening of skin between toes confused with CORN³; *~* (opp. HARD) *currency; ~ tissues* of body, not bony or cartilaginous; *~ palate*, hinder part of palate; *~wicket* &c cricket, moist or sodden turf; || *~ goods*, textiles; *~ solder*, kinds used for easily fusible metal, cf. SAWDER; *~* SOAP; *~ tack*, Naut., bread, opp. *hard tack* or biscuit; *~ roe*, of male fish). **2.** Of smooth surface or fine texture, not rough or coarse, (*~ skin, hair, raiment*). **3.** Mellow, mild, balmy, not noticeably cold or hot, (*~ air; a ~ winter*). **4.** || Rainy or moist or thawing (*~ weather; a ~ day*). **5.** (Of water) free from mineral salts & so good for washing or cooking. **6.** Not astringent or sour or bitter (*~ claret* etc.). **7.** Not crude or brilliant or dazzling (*~ colours, light, eyes*); not strident or loud, low-toned, (*a ~ voice; ~ music; ~* PEDAL¹; *~pedal* v.i. & t.); not sharply defined (*a ~ outline*). **8.** Gentle, quiet, conciliatory, complimentary or amorous, (*~ rein; ~ drink*, colloq., non-alcoholic; *~ manners; a ~ answer*, esp. a good-tempered one to abuse or accusation; *~ nothings*, amorous talk). **9.** Sympathetic, compassionate, (*has a ~ heart, ~hearted²* a., *~heart'edNESS* n.). **10.** Tranquil (*~ slumbers*). **11.** (sl.), Easy (*has a ~ job; a ~ option; ~ thing*, light well-paid office etc.). **12.** Flabby, weak, feeble, unstrung, effeminate, silly, (*the national character has gone ~; a ~ luxurious people; ~ muscles; ~headed,*

~witted, half idiotic); hence *~ISH¹* a., *~'LY²* adv., *~'NESS* n. **13.** n. Silly weak person, also *~Y³* n. **14.** adv. (commoner in compar. than in posit.), -ly (*play ~; ~er; ~whispering* etc.). **15.** int. (arch.), Wait a moment; hush! [OE *sŏfte* (usu. adv.), *sēfte* a., cf. G *sanft*, Du. *zacht*]

sŏf'ta, n. Moslem student of sacred law & theology. [Turk.]

sŏft'en(saw'fn, sŏ-), v.i. & t. Become or make soFT or softer; (also *~ up*) reduce strength of (defences) by bombing etc.; *~ing* (morbid degeneration) *of the brain*. Hence *~ER¹*(1, 2) n. [-EN⁶]

sŏgg'ỹ(-g-), a. Sodden, saturated, dank. Hence *~INESS* n. [f. dial. *sog* a swamp, etym. dub.]

sŏh. See so.

sohō'(-), int. used in quieting horse etc. [AF hunting-cry]

Soho², n. District in London associated with foreign restaurants etc.

soi-disant (see Ap.) a. Self-styled, pretended. [F]

soigné (swahn'yā), (fem. *~e*), a. (Chiefly of a woman's toilet) exquisite in detail, carefully finished or arranged. [p.p. of F *soigner* take care of (*soin* care)]

soil¹, n. The ground, upper layer of earth in which plants grow consisting of disintegrated rock usu. with admixture of organic remains, mould, (*good, poor, clayey, alluvial, light, rich*, etc., *~*; NIGRU-*~*; *one's native ~*, ground of one's native land or place). Hence(*~*)*~ED²*(2d) a. [AF, f. L *solium* seat confused w. *solum* ground]

soil², v.t. & i., & n. **1.** Make dirty, smear or stain with dirt, tarnish, defile, (*~ed linen; would not ~ my hands with it* fig.), so *~URE* n. (arch.); admit of being *~ed* (*~s easily*). **2.** n. Dirty mark, stain, smear, defilement. **3.** *~pipe*, discharge-pipe of water-closet; hence *~'LESS* (-l-) a. [n.f.vb, OF *souiller* defile, perh. f. L *suculus* dim. of *sus* pig: doublet of SULLY]

soil³, v.t. Feed (cattle) on fresh-cut green fodder (orig. for purging). [perh. f. SOIL²]

soirée (swah'rā), n. Social evening, evening gathering esp. for music, conversation, the advancement of some society's objects or the like. [F, = evening (*~party*) f. L *serus* late, *-ata* see -ADE(1)]

soixante-quinze (see Ap.), n. French 75 mm gun, famous in the 1914-18 war. [F, = 75]

sojourn (sŭj'ern, sŏ-), v.i., & n. (Make) temporary stay *in*, or *in* (loosely *at* or *with* or *among*) person(s). Hence *~ER¹* n. [f. OF *sojourner* (L SUB-, *diurnus* f. *diurnal*)]

Sŏl¹, n. (joc.), The sun. [L]

sŏl², n. (mus.), Fifth note of octave. [ist syl. of L *solve*, see GAMUT]

sō'la, n. Pithy-stemmed tropical swamp

plant (~ tŏp'4, Indian sun-helmet of the pith). [f. Hind. sholā]

sŏl'ace, n., & v.t. Comfort (v. & n.) in distress or disappointment or tedium (~ oneself with, find compensation or relief in; tobacco, once the poor man's ~; found ~ in religion). [f. OF solas f. L solacium (solari CONSOLE[1])]

sŏl'an(-gōose, n. The gannet. [f. ON sula, perh. + ond duck]

solān'um, n. Large genus of plants including potato, nightshade, & many kinds (often spoken of as ~) cultivated as ornamental creepers or for flowers or foliage. [L, = nightshade]

sŏl'ar, a. Of, concerned with, determined by, the sun (~ DAY, eclipse, spectrum, time, YEAR; ~ flowers, that remain open only for some hours in the day; ~ month, an exact twelfth of the year; ~ myth, tale explained as symbolizing ~ phenomena; ~ plexus, the complex of nerves at pit of stomach; ~ system, the sun & the heavenly bodies whose motion is directly or indirectly determined by it). [f. L solaris (sol sun, -AR[1])]

sŏl'arism, n. Belief in solar myths as chief source of mythology. So ~IST(2) n. [-ISM]

solār'ium, n. (pl. -ia). Place often enclosed in glass for enjoyment or esp. medical use of sun's rays. [L, = sun-dial, sunning-place (SOLAR, -ARY[1])]

sŏlā'tium, n. (pl. -tia). Thing given as compensation or consolation. [L, = SOLACE]

sold. See SELL.

sŏldanĕll'a, n. Kinds of Alpine plant some of which (esp. the Blue moonwort) are grown in gardens. [It., etym. dub.]

sŏl'der (or sŏd'er), n., & v.t. 1. Kinds of fusible alloys used to join edges of less fusible metals (hard, SOFT, ~; fusible at higher, lower, temperature &c so serving for different metals), (fig.) cementing agency. 2. v.t. Join with ~ (~ing-iron, tool used hot for applying). [vb f. n., f. OF soudure (souder f. L solidare f. SOLIDUS, -URE)]

sŏl'dier (-jer), n., & v.i. 1. Member of army (lit. & fig.; ~s & sailors; po, enlist, for a ~; play at ~s, of children, also of volunteers etc.; tin, toy, ~s; ~ of Christ, active or proselytizing Christian; the unknown S~, see WARRIOR; every INCH[1] a ~; old ~, lit., also person of experience, also empty bottle, also cigar-end; come the old ~ over, claim to dictate to in virtue of greater experience; ~ of fortune, ready to take service under any State or person that will hire him; red ~, pig-disease; ~'s wind, Naut., fair wind for going & returning; private or N.C.O. in army (both officers & ~s; often

common ~; military commander of specified ability (a great, fine, poor, ~; no~), whence ~SHIP(3) n.; hence ~LIKE a., ~LY[1,2] a. & adv., ~LY[2]. 2. (sl.) (Naut.) man, esp. sailor, who shirks work; red herring. 3. (Also ~ ant) one of fighting section of ant or termite colony; (also ~ beetle) kinds of ant or reddish-coloured insect with carnivorous larvae; (also ~ crab) kind of hermit crab; ~ orchis, kind with helmet-shaped sepals. 4. v.i. Serve as ~ (chiefly in gerund, as go, tired of, ~ing). (Naut., sl.) shirk work. [OF (soude pay f. SOLIDUS, -ARY[2])]

sŏl'diery (-jeri), n. The soldiers (of a State, in a district, etc.); a set of troops of specified character (a wild, licentious, etc., ~). [-ERY]

sŏl'do, n. (pl. -dī, pr. -dē). Italian halfpenny. [It., f. SOLIDUS]

sōle[1], n., & v.t. 1. Lower surface of human or other plantigrade foot; part of shoe, sock, etc. below foot; bottom or foundation of various things, e.g. plough, carpenter's plane, wagon, golf-club head; ~-channel, groove in ~ of boot etc. in which sewing is sunk; ~-leather, compressed for use in ~s; ~-plate, bed-plate of engine etc.; hence -SŌLED[2] (-ld) a. 2. v.t. Provide (shoe etc.) with ~. [OF, f. med. L sola f. L solea]

sōle[2], n. Kind of flat-fish much esteemed as food (LEMON[2] ~). [OF, f. L solea (prec.)]

sōle[3], a. One & only, exclusive, (his ~ reason is this; on my own ~ responsibility); (Law) unmarried (only in FEME SOLE); ||(arch.) alone, unaccompanied, (went forth ~; CORPORATION ~). Hence ~LY[2] (-l-l-) adv. [OF sol f. L solus]

sŏl'ecism, n. Offence against grammar or idiom, blunder in the manner of speaking or writing; piece of ill breeding or incorrect behaviour. So ~IST(1) n., ~is'tic a. [f. L f. Gk soloikismos (soloikizō f. soloikos barbarous, said to be f. Soloi town in Cilicia noted for bad Attic, -oikos -dwelling, -IZE), -ISM]

sŏl'emn (-m), a. Accompanied with ceremony, done etc. in due form, formally regular, (~ feast-day, sacrifice, oath; the S~ League & COVENANT; probate the ~ form); mysteriously impressive (~ silence, a ~ cathedral); full of importance, weighty, (a ~ occasion, truth, warning); grave, sober, deliberate, slow in movement or action, (~ music, a ~ promise, ~ looks; a ~ pace); pompous, affecting gravity or importance, dull, (put on a ~ face; a ~ fool). Hence ~LY[2] (-ml) adv., ~NESS n. (rare). [ME & OF solempne f. L sollemnis, etym. dub.]

solĕm'nity, n. Rite, celebration, festival, piece of ceremony; being solemn, solemn character or feeling or behaviour. [f. OF solempnete f. LL sollemnitatem (prec., -TY)]

sŏl'emnize, v.t. Celebrate (festival etc.); duly perform (marriage ceremony); make

solemn. Hence ~ATION n. [f. OF
solempniser (SOLEMN, -IZE)]

sōl′en, n. A bivalve, the Razor-shell.
[L, f. Gk *sōlēn* tube, shellfish]

solen′oid, n. Cylindrical coil of wire
which, when an electric current is passed
through it, behaves as a bar magnet, &
can magnetize a piece of iron or steel
placed inside it. [f. F *solénoïde* (prec.,
-OID)]

sōl′fa (-ah), v.i. & t., & n. = SOLMIZATE,
SOLMIZATION; TONIC ~. [SOL² FA]

sōlfĕg′gio (-jō), n. (pl. -gi), n. (pl. -ji),
Solmization, sol-fa; sol-fa exercise for
voice. [It., (prec. + suf. *eggio*)]

sōlfer′nō (-ē-), n. A purplish-red colour
made from rosaniline. [discovered in
year of battle of S~, cf. MAGENTA]

sōl′icit, v.t. & i. Invite, make appeals or
requests to, importune, (*marvels ~ his
attention or senses*; *we ~ you for your
custom*; *was known to have ~ed the judges*;
(of prostitute) entice (man, or abs.) in
public place; ask importunately or
earnestly for (~ *favours, office, custom*).
So ~ATION n. [f. OF *solliciter* f. L *sollicitare* (*sollicitus* anxious perh. f. *solus* whole,
ciēre cit- rouse)]

sōli′citor, n. One who solicits (rare);
|| member of the legal profession com-
petent to advise clients & instruct &
prepare causes for barristers but not to
appear as advocate except in certain
lower courts (cf. BARRISTER, LAWYER,
ATTORNEY); *canvasser*; || S~-General,
Crown law officer below Attorney-General,
& like him appointed by the Government
of the day & advising & representing it in
legal matters. [f. OF *solliciteur* (prec.,
-OR²)]

sōli′citous, a. Eager *to do*; desirous *of*;
anxious, troubled, (*about, concerning, for,
etc., or* abs.). Hence ~LY² adv. [f. L
sollicitus see SOLICIT, -OUS]

sōli′citude, n. Being solicitous, anxiety,
concern. [OF, f. L *sollicitudo* (prec.,
-TUDE)]

sŏl′id, a. & n. 1. Of stable shape, not
liquid or fluid, having some rigidity, (~
food; *water becomes ~ at 32° F.*). 2. Of
substance throughout, not hollow, without internal cavities or interstices, uninterrupted, whole, (~ *sphere or ball*; ~
tire, without central tube; ~ *square*, Mil.,
formation of equal depth & length; ~-
hoofed, -horned, etc.; *~-drawn, of tubes
etc., pressed or drawn out from a ~ bar
of metal*; *~ printing*, without leads
between lines; *a ~ hour, day, etc.*). 3.
Strongly constructed, not flimsy, (~
house, pier, furniture; man of ~ build).
4. Homogeneous, alike all through, (*of ~
silver etc.*; ~ *colour*, covering the whole
of an object, without pattern etc.; *a ~
vote etc.*, unanimous, undivided; *go or be
~ for*, be united in favour of; *the ~ South*,
southern States of U.S. consistently

voting for Democratic party). 5. Well
grounded, sound, reliable, real, genuine,
not fancied or pretended or showy, (~
arguments, sense, comfort; *a ~ man,
sensible but not brilliant, also of sound
financial position*; *have ~ grounds for
supposing*; ~ *consideration*, thing that
can fairly be regarded as an inducement
in contracts etc.). 6. Of three dimensions
(~ *foot etc., cubic*; ~ *angle*, formed by
three or more plane angles in different
planes meeting at point; ~ *number*,
integer with three prime factors), 7. Concerned with ~s (~ *geometry*; ~ *measure*).
~ *problem*, Math., involving curves that
are sections of ~s & requiring cubic
equation); hence or cogn. **solid′ify** v.t.
& i., **solidifiable** a.; **solid′ity** n.,
sol′idly adv. 8. n. Body consisting of particles that maintain their
relative positions against some degree
of pressure; (Geom.) body or magnitude
having three dimensions (cf. *point, line,
surface*; *regular ~, bounded by equal
& regular planes equally inclined, see
REGULAR*). [f. OF *solide* f. L *solidus* cogn.
w. Gk *holos*, Skr. *sarvá(s)*, whole]

sŏlidar′ity, n. Holding together, mutual
dependence, community of interests,
feelings, & action. So **sŏl′idary** a. [f.
F *solidarité* (*solidaire* f. *solide* = prec.,
-ARY¹, -TY)]

sŏlid′ungular (-ngg-), -ate, aa. Solid-
hoofed, of horse family; equine. [f. L
solidus, ungula hoof, -AR¹, -ATE²]

sŏl′idus, n. (pl. -dī). (Hist.) gold coin
introduced by Roman Emperor Constantine; (only in abbr. s.) shilling(s),
as 7s. 6d., £1 1s.; the shilling line (for /
or long s) as in 7/6. [L, a noun use of
SOLIDUS]

sŏlif′idian, a. & n. (Holder) of doctrine
that faith by itself suffices for salvation.
[L *solus* alone, *fides* faith, + -IAN]

sŏlil′oquy, n. Talking without or regardless of the presence of hearers (*a ~y,
piece of this esp. on part of character in
play*). Hence ~IZE(2) v.i., ~IST(1) n. [f. L
soliloquium (*solus* alone, *-I-, loqui* speak)]

sŏl′ipĕd, a. & n. Solidungulate (animal).
[L *solus* alone, *pes pedis* foot]

sŏl′ipsism, n. (metaphys.). View that
the self is the only knowable, or the only
existent, thing. So ~IST n. [f. L *solus*
alone, *ipse* self, -ISM]

sŏlitaire′, n. Ear-ring, shirt-stud, etc.,
having a single gem; shirt-cuff fastening
in one piece; game played by one person
with marbles on special board; (now
usu. *patience*) kinds of card-game for
one player; kinds of W.-Ind. & Amer.
thrush; (now rare) a recluse. [F, see
foll.]

sŏl′itarȳ, a. & n. 1. Living alone, not
gregarious, without companions, unfrequented, secluded, single, lonely, sole,
(*~y ants, bees, etc., kinds not living in

communities; *a~y life, walk, valley, instance; ~y confinement*, isolation in separate cell; hence **~li**Y² adv. **~lNESS** n.
2. n. Recluse, anchoret. [f. L *solitarius*
(*solus* alone)]

sŏl'itude, n. Being solitary; lonely place.
[OF, f. L *solitudo* (SOLE³ -TUDE)]

sŏl'mizate, v.i., **sŏlmizā'tion**, n. (Use)
system of associating each note of scale
with particular syllable (see GAMUT), in
fixed-do system C always being do &
other syllables accordingly, in *movable-do*
system key-note always being do & other
syllables accordingly. [-ate f. F *solmiser*
(SOl², MI, -ISH)]

sŏl'ŏ, n. (pl. -os, in sense 1 also -*i* pr. -ē),
a, & adv. **1.** Vocal or instrumental piece
or passage performed by one person with
or without subordinate accompaniment
(also attrib., as ~ *passage*; ~ *stops* on
organ, stops specially suitable for playing
~ passages accompanied by other stops;
~ *organ*, fourth manual on large organ,
with stops of this kind); whence **~IST**(1) n.
2. (cards). Kind of whist in which one
player opposes three or undertakes other
tasks; similar varieties of other games;
declaration or playing to win five tricks
at ~ *whist*. **3.** (aviation). An unaccompanied flight; (adj. & adv.) unaccompanied, alone, (a ~ *flight; flying* ~). [It.,
as SOLE³]

Sŏl'omon, n. King of Israel reputed
wisest of men (*is no* ~; SONG *of* ~),
whence **Sŏlomŏn'ic** a.; *~'s seal*, kinds
of flowering plant with some likeness to
lily of the valley.

Sŏl'on, n. Sage, wise legislator. [name of
Athenian lawgiver]

sŏl'stice, n. Either time (*summer, winter*,
~, about 21st June, 22nd Dec.) at which
sun is farthest from equator & appears
to pause before returning; (also *solstitial
point*) point in ecliptic reached by sun at
~. So **sŏlsti'tial** (-ĭsh) a. [OF, f. L
solstitium (SOL¹, *sistere* -stit- make stand
f. *stare* stand)]

sŏl'us, pred. a. (fem. *sola*), Alone, unaccompanied, (esp. in stage directions,
as *enter king* ~; also joc., as *found myself*
~). [L]

solu'tion (-lōō-, -lū-), n., & v.t. **1.** Separation, dissolution, abolition of union,
(chiefly in ~ *of continuity*, Surg., separation of tissues by fracture etc., & transf.).
2. Dissolving or being dissolved, esp. conversion of solid or gas into liquid form by
mixture with liquid called the solvent or
menstruum (*chemical*~, involving change
in chem. properties of components;
mechanical ~, without such change);
state resulting from this (*held in* ~ etc.;
his ideas are in ~, in a state of flux,
unsettled); liquid & solid or gas so mixed
(*a* ~ *of alum; strong, weak,* ~, with small,
large, proportion of solvent). **3.** Resolution, solving, answer, method for the
solving, of a problem, puzzle, question,
doubt, difficulty, etc. (*of, for, to*). **4.** (In
full *rubber* ~) dissolved caoutchouc. **5.**
v.t. Coat with rubber ~. [OF, f. L
solutionem (as SOLVE, -ION)]

solu'tionist (-lōōshon-, -lū-), n. Professional solver of newspaper puzzles. [prec.
+-IST (3)]

Solu'trian, a. (archaeol.). Of the palaeolithic period represented by remains
found at the Solutré cave, Saône-et-
Loire, France.

sŏlve, v.t. Untie, loosen, unravel,
dissolve, (knot, tangle, cohesion, etc.;
arch.); find answer to (problem) or way
out of (difficulty). Hence **sŏl'**VABLE a.,
sŏlVABIL'ITY n. [f. L *solvere solut-*
(*se-* apart, *luere*, cf. Gk *luō*, loosen)]

sŏl'vent, a. & n. **1.** Having the power of
dissolving or forming SOLUTION with
something or fig. of weakening the hold
of traditions or beliefs; having money
enough to meet all pecuniary liabilities,
whence **sŏl'VENCY** n. **2.** n. liquid or
substance, menstruum, (see SOLUTION;
water is the commonest ~; *alcohol is the*
~ *of resinous substances*); dissolving or
weakening agent (*science as a of
religious belief*). [f. L SOLVERE, -ENT]

-som. See -SOME.

sŏmăt'ic, a. Of the body, corporeal,
physical, (opp. *mental, spiritual, psychic;
~ death*, comb. form (prec. -o-) =of
body or the human body, as *~ogĕn'ic*,
originating in the body, *~ŏl'OGY*, science
of living bodies physically considered,
also physiog, also human anatomy &
physiology.

sŏm'bre (-ber), a. Dark, gloomy, dismal,
as a ~ *sky*, ~ *prospect, man of* ~ *character*.
Hence **~**liY² adv., **~NESS** n., **sŏm'brous**
(poet.) a. [F, etym. dub.; cf. Sp. *sombrio*
sombre, *sombra* shade]

sŏmbrer'o (-āro), n. (pl. -s). Broad-
brimmed felt hat common in America.
[Sp. (*sombra*, see prec.)]

some (sŭm, sum), a., pron., & adv.
1. Particular but unknown or unspecified
(person or thing), as ~ *fool has locked the
door, saw it in* ~ *book (or other)*, *ask*
~ *experienced person*, ~ *(people) say yes &*
~ *(or others or other people) say no*. **2.** A
~ certain quantity or number of (~
thing), as *drink* ~ *water, eat* ~ *bread,
bring* ~ *pens, I have* ~ *already, have* ~
more, ~ *of it is spoilt*, ~ *of them were late,
can we can't we have* ~ *milk? (but we
cannot have any milk; if I find* ~ *(or any)
I will send them;* *& *then* ~ *(sl., & plenty

more than that. **3.** An appreciable or considerable quantity of, as ~ went ~ miles out of our way, had ~ trouble in arranging it, ~ years ago, that is ~ guide, test, proof; (emphat., in meiosis, U.S. & sl.) such in the fullest sense, ~thing like (a), as this is ~ war!, I call that ~ poem. **5.** (Usu. stressed) not quite no, as do have ~ mercy on our nerves, has after all ~ sense of decency. **6.** Approximately so many or much (~stone), as wanted ~ 20 minutes, scales ~ 15 stone, we were ~ 60 in all; ABBR.&-. **7.** adv. (sl.) as he seemed annoyed ~. **8.** ~body, ~ person, (w. pl. -dies) person of consequence. **9.** ~'how, in ~ reason or other, as he ~how dropped behind, ~how or other I never liked him, (stressed) no matter how, as must get it finished ~how. **10.** ~'one, = ~body (not in pl.); ~ one, any particular (one), as choose ~ one place as a centre, take ~ one as a type. **11.** ~thing, ~ thing (esp. or ~thing as vague substitute for noun, adj., vb. or adv.), as have ~thing to tell you; we hope to see ~thing of (occasionally meet) them, has lost ~thing or other, take a drop of ~thing (liquor), he is or has ~thing (~ official, employment) in the record office, can spare ~thing out of so much, there is ~thing (truth, point) in what you say, thinks himself ~thing (of ~ consequence), felt there was a little ~thing wanting, ~thing of precocity in his style, am ~thing (of (am in ~ sense or degree) a carpenter, it is ~thing (~ comfort) to be safe home again, his temper is, his fads are, ~thing awful, was made a bishop or ~thing, has sprained his ankle or ~thing (~ other part), is neurotic or ~thing, lost his train or (did) ~thing, turned the tap too soon or too hard or (too) ~thing; (adv., arch. exc. ~thing like) in ~ degree, as was ~thing impatient, ~thing troubled, sharped ~thing like a cigar; (colloq. w. stress on like) this is ~thing like a (is a large or good) pudding, that's ~thing like (is capital)! **12.** ~ time adv., for ~ time, as have been waiting ~ time, at ~ time, as must see him about it ~ time; ~'time adv. & a. (arch.), former(ly), as was ~time mayor of Barnstaple, (the) ~time sheriff; ~'times adv., at times hot & ~times cold. **13.** ~'way, in ~ way. **14.** ~'what, (adv.) in ~ degree, as it is ~what difficult, was ~what puzzled, answered ~what hastily, (pron., arch. exc. when in disting.: f. adv.) found ~what to detain him, loses ~what (perh. adv.) in what telling, loses ~what of its force. **15.** ~-when (rare, affected), at ~ time or other. **16.** ~'where, in, at, to, ~ place, as lives ~where near us, sent him ~where, Burton says ~where in the Anatomy, will see him ~where (in hell etc.) first. **17.** ~whither

(arch.), to ~ place, [OE *sum*, cf. ON *sumr*, Da. *somme* pl.]

-some, -som, suf. forming adji., OE -sum. repr. Du. -zaam, G -sam; joined to nn. w. sense 'adapted to, productive of', as *handsome, quarrelsome, gladsome* (f. *lissom, glad* n.), to adji., as *tithesome* (also *lissome*), *blithesome, fulsome,* & to trans. vbs w. sense 'apt to', as *tiresome, win-some, wearisome, gruesome* (f. *grue* in *two, three,* -om in *lissom, buxom,* etc.; in *two, three, four, -some* that was orig. the pronoun OE *sum some*; -som in RANSOM not orig.

so'mersault, -set¹, (sŭ-), n. & v.i. **1.** Spring, bound, in which person turns heels over head (*double, treble,* ~, twice, thrice) in the air; turn a ~, make such spring. **2.** v.i. Turn ~. [f. OF *sombre saut* f. Pr. *sobresaut* f. L *supra* above + *saltus* -ûs leap (*salire*)]

‖ **so'merset²** (sŭ-), n. Paddled saddle esp. for one-legged rider. [f. Lord F. S~, who used one]

So'merset House (sŭ-), n. Building in London containing chief place of deposit of proved wills, & inland revenue offices, & often mentioned allusively in these connexions.

sŏ'mite, n. Segment of (esp. articulate or vertebrate) animal body; metamere. Hence **sŏmit'ic** a. [f. Gk *sōma* body + -ITE¹(²)]

sŏmnam'būlĭsm, n. Walking or performing other action during sleep; condition of brain inducing this; *artificial ~ism,* hypnotism. Hence or cogn. ~ANT (rare), ~is'tĭc, aa., ~ATE³ v.i. (rare), ~IST n. [f. L *somnus* sleep + *ambulare* walk]

sŏmni- in comb. = L *somnus* sleep, as: ~ferous, inducing sleep, narcotic; ~'o-quence, ~'loquism, ~'loquy, habit of talking in sleep; ~'loquous, ~'loquist, (person) given to this; ~p'athist, hypnotic subject; ~p'athy, hypnotic sleep.

sŏm'nolent, a. Sleepy, drowsy; inducing drowsiness; (Path.) in state between sleeping & waking. Hence or cogn. ~ENCE, ~ENCY, nn., ~ently² adv. [f. L *somnolentus, -lent-* (*somnus* sleep, see -LENT)]

sŏm'nŏlĭsm, n. Hypnotic sleep. [f. prec. +-ISM]

son (sŭn), n. **1.** Male child of a parent (~ & heir, esp. eldest ~); ~-in-law, one's daughter's husband; *he is his father's ~* (like, worthy of, his father). **2.** The Son of Man, (N.T.) Christ, the Messiah, (O.T.) descendant of Adam, esp. as form of address in *Ezekiel; the ~S of men,* mankind; the Son (of God), = GOD¹ the Son. **3.** ~ of a GUN; every MOTHER¹'s ~. **4.** Descendant, as ~s of Abraham. **5.** (As form of address esp. of old man to young man, confessor to penitent, etc.) my ~.

6. ~ *of the soil*, recognizable native of a district, worker on the land, dweller in the country. **7.** Native of a country, as *Britain's* ~s. **8.** Person viewed as inheriting an occupation, quality, etc., as ~ *of toil*, ~ *of Mars* (soldier), ~ (= *man*) *of* BELIAL, ~s *of light, darkness*, etc.; *Sons of Liberty, of the* (*American*) *Revolution*, etc., American patriotic etc. organizations. Hence ~LESS a., ~'SHIP n. [f. SON, ON *sonr*]

-son, suf., = -TION in some wds t. F, as *reason, season* (F *raison, saison*, L *rationem, sationem*), *treason* (OF *traison*, L *traditionem*), *benison* (OF *beneison*, L *benedictionem*), POISON, VENISON, ORISON, COMPARISON.

sŏn|ant, a. & n. (Sound, letter) capable of being sounded continuously, accompanied by vocal vibration, voiced, not surd, (e.g. *b, d, g, j, v, z*). Hence ~ANCY n. [f. L *sonare* sound (*sonus*), see -ANT]

sŏnā'ta (-nah-), n. Composition for one instrument (e.g. piano) or two (e.g. piano & violin), normally with three or four movements (one or more being usu. in ~ *form*) contrasted in rhythm & speed but related in key; ~ *form*, type of composition in which two themes ('subjects') are successively set forth, developed, & restated. [It. (as prec., see -ADE)]

sŏnati'na (-tē-), n. Simple or short form of sonata. [It., dim. of prec.]

sŏng, n. **1.** Singing, vocal music, as *burst forth into* ~; musical cry of some birds (~-*birds*). **2.** Short poem set to music or meant to be sung; short poem in rhymed stanzas; poetry, verse, as *renowned in* ~. **3.** (Mus.) ~ *form*, mode of composition usu. in three sections, the first & third being nearly the same & the second contrasted with the first. **4.** *Bought, sold, it for a* ~ *or an old* (~ mere trifle); *nothing to make a* ~ *about* (colloq.); ~ of very trifling importance; *S~ of* DEGREES *or of* ~s, *S~ of Solomon*, Canticles; ~-PLUG²*ging*; ~-THRUSH¹; ~-*sparrow*, hedge-sparrow & other birds. Hence ~LESS a. [OE, Da., G, *sang*, cf. Du. *zang*; as SING]

sŏng'ster, n. Singer; song-bird; poet. Hence ~TRESS¹ n. [-STER]

sonif'erous, a. Conveying or producing sound. [f. L *sonus* sound +-FEROUS]

sŏnn'ĕt, n. Poem of 14 lines (usu. rhyming thus; *pig bat cat wig jig hat rat fig; lie red sob die bed rob or tie red die bed pie wed*; or otherwise e.g. as in Shakspere's ~s); ~ *sequence*, a set of ~s connected in theme; (now rare) any short lyric. So ~EER' (usu. derog.), (n.) composer of ~s, (v.i. & t.) compose ~s, celebrate in ~s address ~s to. [F, f. It. *sonetto* (*suono* SOUND² n. -ET¹)]

sŏ'nny (sŭ-), n. Familiar form of address to a boy. [f. SON +-Y³]

sŏnŏm'ĕter, n. Kinds of instrument for testing deaf person's hearing, measuring sounds, etc. [f. L *sonus* sound +-METER]

sŏnōrĕs'çīent, a. (Of hard rubber etc.) emitting sounds corresponding to pulsations of radiant heat or light. So ~ENCE n. [as SONOROUS +-ESCENT]

sŏnōrif'ic, a. Producing (esp. other than vocal) sound. [as foll. +-FIC]

sonō'rous, a. Resonant, loud-sounding; (of speech, style, etc.) high-sounding, imposing; ~ *figures* (formed in layer of sand etc. by sound-vibration); ~ *râle* (heard in some diseases). Hence or cogn. **sonō'rity**, ~NESS, nn., ~LY² adv. [f. L *sonorus* (*sonor* sound f. *sonare* vb) +-OUS]

∥ **sŏn'sý**, a. (Sc.). Plump, buxom; of cheerful disposition (esp. in phr. ~ *lass*). [ult. f. Gael. *sonas* good fortune]

sŏoj'ee (-jǐ), n. Flour ground from Indian wheat; food resembling semolina prepared from this. [Hind. *sūjī*]

sōon, adv. **1.** Not long after the present time or time in question or after specified time, in a short time, as *shall* ~ *know the result, was* ~ *convinced of his error, arrived* ~ *after four*, ~ *after the gate was closed, least said* ~*est mended*. **2.** As (or *so*, esp. after negative, or when causality ~ or other close connexion is suggested) ~ *as*, the moment that, not later than, as early as, *as came as* (or *so*) ~ *as I heard of it, will get there as* ~ *as they* (*do*), *did not arrive so* (or *as*) ~ *as I expected, drops his fine theories so* (or *as*) ~ *as they clash with his interests, so* ~ *as* (*ever*) *there is any talk of paying he cools down*. **3.** (With expressed or implied comparison) willingly, as *I would just as* ~ *stay at home* (as *go*), *would* ~*er die than let him* (or *than that he should*) *find it out, which would you* ~*est do?* **4.** Early, as *what makes you come so* ~?; *you spoke too* ~; *we had no* ~*er sat down than* (the moment we sat down) *she burst into tears; no* ~*er said than done*, it was done the moment it was proposed etc.; *the* ~*er the better; you will repent it* ~*er or later* (some day, in the long run). [OE *sōna*, cf. OHG *sān*]

sōot, n., & v.t. **1.** Black substance rising in fine flakes in the smoke of wood, coal, oil, etc., during combustion & sticking to sides of chimney etc., used as fertilizer; ~-*cancer*, ~*wart*, disease of scrotum in sweeps. Hence ~ILY² adv., ~'INESS n., ~'LESS, ~'Y² aa. **2.** v.t. Cover with ~. [OE & ON *sōt*, cf. Da. *sod*]

∥ **sōot'erkin**, n. (arch.). Dutch woman's false birth produced by sitting over stove; (fig.) abortive scheme. [?]

∥ **sōoth**, n. (arch.). Truth, fact, esp. *in* (*good*), ~, really, truly. [OE *sōth* (for *santh*), cf. ON *sannr*, Sw. *sann*, Da. *sand*, true]

sōōth'e (-dh) v.t. Calm (person, nerves, passions); soften, mitigate, (pain); flatter, humour, (person, his vanity); flatter. ~ER¹ (-dh-) n. (in vbl senses, & esp. rubber teat for child to suck), ~ingly² (-dh-) adv. [OE *(ge)sōthian* confirm, assent to (*ge-* Y- + *sōth* SOOTH)]

sōōth'fast (-ah-), a. (arch.). Truthful; true; loyal, steadfast. [OE *sōthfæst*]

sōōth'sayer, n. One who foretells the future, diviner. Hence **sōōth'say** v.i. [SOOTH+SAY+-ER¹]

sŏp, n., & v.t. & i. (-pp-). 1. Piece of bread etc. dipped in broth etc. (~ *in the pan*, fried bread); MILK ~; something given (to formidable or troublesome animal, person, etc., esp. to Cerberus) to pacify, bribe. 2. v.t. Soak (bread etc. in broth etc.), take *up* (water etc.) by absorption. 3. v.i. Be drenched, as *am* ~*ping with rain*, *clothes* ~*ping* (vbl n. as adv.) wet, whence ~**pY**² a., || also (colloq.) full of mawkish sentiment. [OE *sopp* n., *soppian* vb, cf. -M)]

sŏph'ism, n. False argument intended to deceive (cf. PARALOGISM). [ME & OF *sophisme* f. L f. Gk *sophisma* (as foll, see -M)]

sŏph'ist, n. Ancient-Greek paid teacher of philosophy & rhetoric; captious or fallacious reasoner, quibbler. Hence or cogn. **sophis'tic(al)** aa., **sophis'tically²** adv. ~RY(4, 5) n. [f. L f. Gk *sophistēs* (*sophizō* instruct f. *sophos* wise, -IST)]

sŏph'ister, n. (hist.). Student of varying seniority at some English & American universities. [f. OF *sophistre* var. as prec.]

sophis'ticate, v.t. & i. Involve (subject) in sophistry; mislead (person); thus; deprive (person, thing) of simplicity; make artificial; (p.p., of person) worldly-wise; tamper with (text etc.) for purposes of argument etc.; use sophistry; adulterate (wine etc.). So ~'TION n. [f. med. L *sophisticare* (*sophisticus* sophistic), see -ATE³]

*sŏph'omore, n. Second-year university student. [prob. f. *sophom* obs. var. of SOPHISM+-OR²]

Sŏph'ỹ, n. (hist.). Ruler of Persia in 16th & 17th cc. [f. Pers. *Cafi* surname of dynasty]

sŏp'orif'ic, a. & n. (Drug) tending to produce sleep. So ~if'EROUS a. [f. L *sopor* sleep + -i- + -FIC]

soprā'nō (-rah-), n. (pl. ~*nos*, ~*ni* pr. -nē). (Music for) highest female or boy's voice, treble (often attrib.); (also ~IST n.) singer with this. [It. (*sopra* above f. L *supra*)]

-sor, suf. forming agent-nn. on L f.p.p. st. in -s-, as *professor*: see -OR².

sō'ra, n. Bird frequenting marshes of Carolina etc. in autumn & used as food. [native]

sŏrb, n. Service-tree; (also ~*apple*) its fruit. Hence ~ATE¹(3) n., ~'IC a. (chem.). [f. L *sorbus*]

sŏrbe'tient (-shnt), a. & n. (med.). (Drug etc.) causing absorption. [f. L *sorbēre* suck in f.+FACIENT]

sŏrb'et, n. Flavoured water-ice; = SHER-BET. [F, as SHERBET]

Sorbonne', n. (Hist.) theological faculty in University of Paris having great influence in 16th & 17th cc.; the faculties of *Académie* of Paris & of the cities of science & literature. [F, f. R. de Sorbon, founder about 1250]

sŏr'cerer, n. User of magic arts, wizard, enchanter (often fig.). So ~ESS¹, SŎRCERY (4, 5), nn. [earlier *sorcer* t. OF *sorcier* t. LL *sortiarius* caster of lots (*sors* -*rtis* lot, see -ARY¹)+-ER¹]

sŏrd'ament, adv. (mus.). In a muffled manner. [It.]

sŏrd'id, a. Mean, niggardly; ignoble, base; (Bot., Zool., of colours) impure, muddy, as ~ *blue*; (arch.) dirty, squalid. Hence ~ly² adv., ~NESS n. [f. F *sordide* f. L *sordidus* (*sordēre* be dirty, *sordes* filth, see -ID)]

sŏrd'ine (-ēn), n. (mus.). Mute for bowed or wind instruments; damper of piano string. [f. It. *sordina* f. L as SURD]

sōre, a., n., & adv. 1. (Of parts of body, person) morbidly tender, as *has a* ~ *arm*, *is* FOOT¹~, (*clergyman's*) ~ THROAT, *touched him on a* ~ *place* (often fig.), *a sight for* ~ *eyes* (welcome, pleasant); *like a bear with a* ~ *head* (grumpy); irritated, aggrieved, touchy, as *is very* ~ *about his defeat*; arousing painful feelings, irritating, esp. *a subject*; (arch., poet.) distressing; grievous, severe, as *in distress*, *a* ~ *struggle*, *affliction*; *he bore*, whence ~ly² (-tl-) adv. 2. n. painful memory, *old* ~*s*; ~ place on body e.g. where skin or flesh is bruised or inflamed; (fig.) ~ subject, BED¹~; EYE¹~. 3. adv. Grievously, severely, as ~ *oppressed*, *bested*, *afflicted*. Hence ~NESS (-rn-) n. [(n. & adj.) OE *sār* painful, cf. Du. *zeer* sore, ON *sárr* painful, rel. to sore, Q *sehr* sorely, very]

sorel, See SORREL².

sŏr'ghum (-gum), n. Kinds of grass including millet & Chinese sugar-cane. [mod. L f. It. *sorgo* etym. dub.]

sŏr'icine, a. Of, related to, the shrew-mouse. [f. L *soricinus* (*sorex* -*icis* shrew-mouse, -INE¹)]

sŏrī'tēs (-z), n. Chain-syllogism (e.g. a cat is a quadruped, quadruped is an animal, animal is a substance; therefore a cat is a substance); form of sophism leading by gradual steps from truth to absurdity & based on the absence of precise, esp. numerical, limits to terms (e.g. a man with only 1 hair is bald, therefore a man with 2, 3, 4, ... 10,000, hairs is bald). So **sorit'ICAL** a. [f. L f. Gk *sōritēs* lit. heaper (*sōros* heap, see -ITE¹) its

‖ **sŏrn**, v.i. (Sc.). Obtrude oneself *on* (person) for bed & board. Hence ~ER¹ n. [f. obs. Ir. *sorthan* free quarters]

sŏrŏp'timist, n. Member of an international association of women's clubs. [app. f. L *soror* sister + OPTIMIST]

sorŏ'rity, n. Devotional sisterhood; *women's society in college or university. [f. med. L *sororitas* (L *soror* sister), after *fraternity*]

sorŏ'sis, n. (bot.). Fleshy compound fruit, e.g. pineapple, mulberry. [as SORUS +-OSIS]

‖ **sŏ'rra**, adv. (Ir., sl.). Not, never, (~ *a one, a bit,* etc., = the devil a). [= *sorrow*]

sŏ'rrel¹, n. Kinds of acid-leaved herb allied with dock. [f. OF *sorele* f. L *sūr* SOUR]

sŏ'rrel², a. & n. (Of) reddish-brown colour; ~ animal esp. horse; (also *sorel*) buck of third year. [f. OF *sorel* ~ horse, dim. of *sor* ~ (horse), etym. dub.]

sŏ'rrow (-ō), n. & v.i. 1. Grief, sadness, caused by loss of good or occurrence of evil, whence ~FUL (-rōf-) a., ~fully² adv., ~fulNESS n.; occasion of this, misfortune, trouble, as *has had many ~s, much ~; the Man of S~s,* Christ; ~*-stricken* (with ~); lamentation, as *his ~ was loud & long.* 2. v.i. Grieve, feel ~, (*at, over, for,* misfortune etc., *for,* i.e. on behalf of, person etc.), mourn (*after, for,* lost person or thing), whence ~ER¹ (-ōer¹) n., ~ING² (-rōi-) a. [ME *sorwe*, OE & ON *sorg,* cf. Du. *zorg,* G *sorge*]

sŏ'rry, a. Feeling regret, regretful, as *will be ~ for this some day, felt ~ for him* (on his account), ~ *for* (regret) *that, am so ~ (that) you must go, am ~ to hear it,* (as informal apology for trifling offence) ~*!*; (literary) wretched, paltry, shabby, of poor quality, as *a ~ fellow, in a ~ plight, in ~ clothes, a ~ excuse,* whence **sŏ'rrilY**² adv., **sŏ'rriNESS** n. [OE *sārig* (SORE, -Y²); not connected w. prec.]

sŏrt, n. 1. Group of things etc. with common attributes, class, kind, species, as *biscuits of several ~s, a new ~ of bicycle, people of every ~ & kind; of ~s,* (in inventories etc.) unassorted, mixed. 2. (In foll. uses = KIND¹) *nothing of the ~, coffee of a ~, what ~ of tree?,* (colloq.) *these ~ of men, a ~ of stockbroker* etc., *I ~ of expected it; a ~ of war* etc., *a war* etc. *of a ~* or colloq. *of ~s,* not fully deserving the name; (colloq.) *an awfully good ~* (of person), *that's your ~* (the way to do it). 3. (arch.). Manner, way, as *in seemly, courteous,* etc., ~; *after or in a ~* (= FASHION); *in some* (literary), *to a certain* extent. 4. (Print.) any letter or piece in fount of type, as *copy is hard* (or *runs*) *on ~s* (requires many of some ~s). 5. *Out of ~s,* out of health, spirits, or temper, (Print.) short of ~s. [f. OF *sorte* f. L *sortem* (nom. *sors*) lot, chance, state

sŏrt², v.t. & i. 1. Separate into sorts (often *over, out*); select (things of one sort) from miscellaneous group, as ~*ed out those of the largest size.* 2. (arch.). Correspond or agree with (*his actions* ~ *ill, well, with his profession*). Hence ~'ABLE a., ~'ER¹ n. [f. prec.]

sŏrt'ēs (-z), n. pl. ~ *Virgiliān'ae, Biblicae* or *Sac'rae, Homē'ricae,* divination by chance selection of passages from Virgil, the Bible, or Homer. [L, pl. as SORT¹]

sŏrt'ie (-tē) n. 1. Sally esp. of beleaguered garrison. 2. Operational flight by one aircraft. [F, f. *sortir* go out, etym. dub.]

sŏrt'ilège, n. Divination by lots. [f. OF *sortilege* f. med. L *sortilegium* f. L *sortilegus* a. (as SORT¹ + *legere* choose, read)]

sŏrti'tion, n. Casting of lots, [f. L *sortitio* (*sortiri* cast lots)]

sŏr'us, n. (bot.; pl. *sŏr'ī*). Heap, cluster, esp. of spore-cases on back of fern-frond. [f. Gk *sōros* heap]

-sory, suf., a spec. form of -ORY in aa. or nn. f. L vbs that form p.p. in -s-, as *accessory (cedere cess-), promissory (mittere miss-).*

S O S (ĕs'ōĕs'), n. Wireless code-signal of extreme distress; broadcast appeal to (otherwise untraceable) person (to visit dying relative etc.); (transf.) any despairing cry or action. [arbitrary]

sŏ-sō, pred. a. & adv. Not very good. [so]

sŏstenu'tō (-nōō-), adv. (mus.). In sustained or prolonged manner. [It.]

sŏt, n., & v.i. (-tt-). 1. Confirmed drunkard, person stupefied by habitual drunkenness. 2. v.i. Tipple. Hence ~**t'isH**¹ a., ~**t'isHLY**² adv., ~**t'isHNESS** n. [OF, = fool, etym. dub.; cf. Du. *zot,* med. L *sottus*]

Sŏth'eby's (sŭthe-), n. A sale-room in London for books, MSS., etc.

Sŏth'ic, a. Of the dog-star, esp. ~ *year* (Egyptian), ~ *cycle* (of 1460 ~ or 1461 solar years). [f. Gk *Sōthis* f. Egypt. name of dog-star]

sŏtt'ō vŏ'ce (-chĕ), adv. In an undertone, aside. [It., = beneath the voice]

sou (sōō), n. (pl. -s pr. -z). (Hist.) French coin of various values; (loosely) five-centime piece; (colloq.) *hasn't a ~* (a farthing, any money). [F]

soubrette (sōōbrĕt'), n. Maid-servant or similar character (esp. w. implication of pertness, coquetry, intrigue, etc.) in comedy. [F]

sou'cār (sow-), **sow'kār**, n. Hindu banker or money-lender. [Hind. *sāhūkār* great merchant]

sou'chong (sōōsh-), n. Kind of black tea made from youngest leaves. [F, f. Chin. *siao* small+*chung* sort]

S(o)udanese (sōōdanēz'), a. & n. (pl. same),

(inhabitant) of the Soudan, district of Africa, south of Sahara. [-ESE]

souffle (sōō'fl) n. (med.). Low murmur heard in auscultation of various organs etc. [F.f. *souffler* blow f.L *suf*(*flare* blow)]

soufflé (sōō'flā) a. & n. Made light & frothy, as *omelet* ~. 2. n. Such dish, usu. made with beaten whites of eggs. [F, p.p. as prec.]

sough (sŭf, sow), n., & v.i. (Make) moaning, whistling, or rushing sound as of wind in trees etc. [OE *swōgan* resound, prob. imit.]

sought. See SEEK.

soul (sōl), n. 1. The immaterial part of man, as *immortality of the* ~, *commend one's* ~ *to God* (person at point of death), emotional part of man, as *his whole* ~ *revolted from it*, CURE¹ *of* ~s, *has a* ~ *above sherry & bitters*. 3. Intellectual part of man, vital principle & mental powers of meaner ~s of antiquity, *left that to animals* including man, as *keep* BODY¹ *& ~ together, cannot call his* ~ *his own* (is dominated by another). 4. Animating or essential part, person viewed as this, as *he was the* (*life* &) ~ *of the party*. 5. Person viewed as embodying moral or intellectual qualities, *as the greatest* ~*s of antiquity*. 6. (Often without a) emotional or intellectual energy e.g. as revealed in work of art, as *the fellow has no* ~, *his pictures lack* ~. 7. (Of persons) personification or pattern of (*is the* ~ *of honour*, *is incapable of dishonourable conduct*), embodied spirit, as ALL S~s' Day; disembodied spirit. 9. Person, as *not a* ~ *to speak to for miles round*, *ship went down with 200* ~s; (expr. familiarity, patronage, pity, contempt, etc.) *my good* ~, *there's a good* ~, *the poor little* ~ *had lost her way*. 10. (In comb.) ~-*destroying*, -*stirring*, -*subduing*, etc. Hence (-)~ED² (bodily, &c.), ~'LESS (sŏl-), a., ~'lESSLY² adv., ~'lESSNESS n. [OE *sāwel*, -ul, -ol, cf. Du. *ziel*, G *seele*]

soulful (sōl-), a. Having, expressing, appealing to, the (esp. higher) emotional or intellectual qualities. Hence ~LY² adv., ~NESS n. [-FUL]

sound¹, a. & adv. 1. Healthy, not diseased nor injured nor rotten, as *a* ~ *body*, ~ *mind*, ~ *in life & limb*, ~ *fruit*, ~ *timbers*, ~ *ship*; correct, logical, well-founded, judicious, as ~ *doctrine*, *theologian*, *argument*, *views*, *policy*, *is he* ~ *on free trade?*; (Commerc., of company etc.) solvent; thorough, unqualified, as *a* ~ *sleeper*), *flogging*. 2. adv. ~*ly*, as *a* ~ (fast) *asleep*, *will sleep the* ~*er for it*. Hence ~'LY² adv., ~'NESS n. [ME, Da., Sw., *sund*, cf. OE & G *gesund*, Du. *gezond*]

sound², n. & v.i. & t. 1. The sensation produced through the ear, what is or may be heard; vibrations causing this sensation; *musical* ~ (produced by con-

tinuous & regular vibrations, opp. to *noise*); any of a series of articulate utterances, as *vowel*, *consonant*, ~s; *mere words* (~ *& fury*); (fig.) mental impression produced by oral or other statement etc., as *will have a queer* ~, *don't like the* ~ *of it*. 2. ~-*board*, ~-*bow*, thick edge of bell against which tongue strikes; ~-*film*, cinema film with audible dialogue, songs, etc. recorded on ~-*track*; ~-*hole*, *post*, hole in belly, small prop between belly & back, of some stringed instruments; ~-*PROOF²*; ~-*track*, on side of cinema film record-ing ~; ~-*wave* (of condensation & rare-faction, by which ~ is propagated in elastic medium e.g. air). 3. v.b. Give forth ~, as *the trumpets* ~; (w. ref. to impression created, often fig.) ~ *to me like something cracking*, ~ *as if a tap were running*, ~*s as if he wanted to back out of it, will* ~ *very strange to say you hadn't time, that* (excuse etc.) ~ *is very hollow, that* (report, explanation) ~*s all right* (promising, plausible, etc.); (part.) *having more* ~ *than sense or truth, as ~ing rhetoric, promises, imposing, as ~ing titles*; make (trumpet etc.) ~; utter, as ~ *a note of alarm*; pronounce (*the h in hour is not* ~*ed*); give notice of (*an alarm, the retreat*, etc.) with bell etc.; cause to resound, make known, as ~ *his praises far & wide*; test (railway-carriage wheel etc., lungs etc.) by noting ~ produced direct ~ towards audience, thin plate of wood in musical instrument increasing ~. Hence ~'LESS a. [(n.) AF *soun* f. OF *son*, f. L *sonus*; for -d cf. LEND, ROUND¹, HIND²; (vb) f. OF *soner* f. L *sonare*]

sound³, v.t. & i. & n. 1. Test the depth of (sea, channel, pond, etc. or abc.) & the quality of its bottom with ~*ing-line* or -*apparatus* or -*machine* (often furnished with cup etc. for bringing up sample); find depth of water in (ship's hold) with ~*ing-rod*; get records of temperature, humidity, pressure, etc. from (upper atmosphere) with ~*ing-balloon*; (Med.) examine (bladder etc.) with probe; (of fish, esp. whale) dive to the bottom; inquire esp. in cautious or reserved manner into the sentiments or inclination of (person *about*, *on*, *as to*). 2. n. Surgeon's probe. [(n. f. vb) f. F *sonder* (*sonde* SOUND⁴)]

sound⁴, n. 1. Narrow passage of water connecting two seas or sea with sea or strait. 2. Fish's air-bladder; cuttle-fish. [OE, ON, Da., Sw., G, *sund*, cogn. w. SWIM. = variously swimming, water, sea, strait, air-bladder, ferry]

sound'er², n. ‖(Arch.) herd of wild swine; (pseudo-arch.) young wild boar. [f. OF *sundre* f. Teut., cf. OE *sunor*, OHG *sunar*]

sound'er², n. In vbl senses of SOUND², esp. telegraphic receiving instrument for reading message by sound. [-ER¹]

sound'er³, n. In vbl senses of SOUND³; *echo~*, apparatus for sounding by measuring time-interval between transmission of a note & receipt of its echo from the sea-bed; *flying ~*, sounding apparatus that can be used without reducing ship's speed. [-ER¹]

sound'ing, n. In vbl senses of SOUND³, also (pl.) place near enough to shore to admit of ~, as *be in, come into, ~s*. [-ING¹]

soup (soop), n. Liquid food made of stock & other ingredients (*in the ~*, sl., in difficulties); || (legal sl.) prosecution brief given to junior barrister at Quarter Sessions etc.; *~-kitchen*, public establishment for supplying ~ gratis to the poor; *~-ticket* (entitling holder to ~ at *~-kitchen*); *~ maigre* (-ger), thin chiefly of vegetables; *~-plate*, deep kind for ~; *pea~*. Hence ~Y² a. [f. F *soupe* (*souper* SUP)]

soupçon (see AP.), n. Very small quantity, dash, (of flavouring, quality, etc.). [F]

sour (sowr), a., & v.i. & t. **1.** Of acid taste, esp. as result of unripeness, as *~ apples*, ~ GRAPES, or of fermentation, as *~ milk, bread*; (of soil) dank; (of person or temper) harsh, peevish, morose; *~ dock*, common sorrel. **2.** vb. Make, become, ~, (esp. fig.), as *~ed by misfortune*. Hence ~ISH¹ a., ~'LY² adv., ~'NESS n. [OE *sūr*]

source (sawrs), n. Spring, fountain-head, from which stream issues, as *the ~s of the Nile*; origin, place from which thing comes or is got, as *the ~ of all our woes, reliable ~ of information, drawn from all ~s*; *~-book* [transl. of G *quellenbuch*], book or collection of original documents serving as material for the historical study of a subject. [f. OF *sorse*, fem. p.p. as n. of *sourdre* rise f. L *surgere*]

sourdine (soorden'), n. Harmonium stop producing soft effect; = SORDINE. [F, cf. SORDINE]

*sourdough (sowr'dō), n. One who has spent one or more winters in Alaska; old-timer. [dial, ~ = leaven; SOUR + DOUGH]

sour-sop (soor'sop), n. A W.-Ind. fruit & tree. [SOUR + SOP]

souse, n., v.t. & i., & adv. **1.** Pickle made with salt; food in pickle, esp. head, feet, & ears, of swine; dip, plunge, drenching, in water. **2.** vb. Put in pickle, as *~d mackerel*; plunge (t. & i., *into* liquid), soak (thing *in* liquid), throw (liquid *over* thing); (p.p.) drunk (sl.). **3.** adv. With swift descent, headlong, as *came ~ into our midst*. [vb f. n., OF *sous* pickle f. OHG *sulza* (*salzan* to SALT); adv. partly f. obs. *souse* swoop cogn. w. *source*]

soutache (soo'tahsh), n. Ornamental braid for sewing on fabric in designs. [F, f. Hung. *sújtás* ringlet]

soutane (sootahn'), n. (R.-C. Ch.) Priest's cassock. [F]

souteneur (sŏotĕner'), n. Man cohabiting with & living on the earnings of a prostitute. [F, = protector]

south, adv., n., a., (abbr. S.), & v.i. **1.** (Towards, at, near) point of horizon directly opposite to north; point of compass opposite north; DUE¹ ~, BY¹ *east* or *west*¹; *~ of*, farther than; *~-east, ~-west*, etc., adv., aa., & nn., POINT¹s of the compass, corresponding regions, (with uses & derivatives corresp. to those of ~, e.g. *~-easterly*); ||southern part of, England, Scotland, Ireland, or Europe; the Southern STATE¹s; ~ (*wind*), wind from the ~; *~-east, ~-west*, (abbr. S.E., S.W.) London postal districts. **2.** adj. Situated or dwelling in, looking towards, the ~; *S~ Downs* (of Hampshire & Sussex); *~down* a. & n., (sheep) of a breed originating on S~ Downs esteemed for their flesh; *S~ Kensington*, (used for) the museums of S~ Kensington or the atmosphere of culture & art & instruction associated w. them; *S~ Sea* (hist.), the Pacific; *S~ Sea Bubble*, scheme for trading in Spanish America, which collapsed in 1720. **3.** v.i. Move towards ~, (of moon etc.) cross the meridian of a place. Hence ~'WARD a. & n., ~'WARD(S) adv. [OE *sūth*, cf. ON *suthr*]

southeas'ter, south'er, nn. Wind from SE. from S. [-ER¹]

sou'therly (sŭdh-), a. & adv. Towards the south; (of wind) blowing from the south. [f. SOUTH, as EASTERLY]

sou'thern (sŭdh-), a. & n. **1.** Of, in, the south; *S~ HEMISPHERE, CROSS¹, CONFEDERACY, STATES*; looking south, as *~ aspect*; (of wind, rare)= prec. **2.** n. Inhabitant of the south, esp. of the S~ States, whence ~ER¹ n.; *~wood*, kind of wormwood with scented leaves. Hence ~'MOST a. [-ERN¹]

south'ing, n. In vbl senses, also (Naut.) difference of latitude made in sailing south. [-ING¹]

sou'thron (sŭdh-), a. & n. (arch. Sc.). English, Englishman, (usu. derog.). [var. of SOUTHERN]

southwes'ter, n. Wind from SW.; (usu. **sou'wes'ter**) waterproof hat with broad brim behind to protect neck. [-ER¹]

souvenir (sŏov'ĕner), n. Thing given, kept, etc., to recall the past, memento (of occasion, place, etc.; also in the 1914–18 war, as French children's request for keepsake to foreign soldiers). [F (n. f. vb), = remember, souvenir, f. L SUB-(*venire* come) occur to the mind]

sov'ereign (-vrin), a. & n. **1.** Supreme, as *~ power, the ~ good* (= SUMMUM BONUM); lofty, as *with ~ contempt*; possessing power, as *~ States*, royal, as *our ~ LORD*, whence ~TY (-vrin-) n.; very good, esp.

a ~ *remedy*; hence ~LY² adv. (arch.). 2. n. Supreme ruler, esp. monarch; ∥(colloq. abbr. **sov**) English gold coin worth £1; ∥half ~, gold coin worth 10s. [n. f. adj.), f. OF *soverain* f. LL SUPER- (*anus* -ANᵈ); -*v*- by assoc. w. *reign*]

sŏv'iĕt, S-, n. Any of the councils elected by the workers & soldiers of a district in revolutionary Russia, or of a smaller number elected by these, or the all-Russian congress of delegates from these; hence (S~) the *revolutionary government of Russia*; *the S~ Socialist Republics*; *Union of S~ Socialist Republics* (abbr. **U.S.S.R.**), the revolutionary government of Russia. So ~ISM, ~IST, nn. [OE *sǣwan*, cf. Du. *zaaien*, G *säen*, ON *sā*]

sow¹ (sō), v.t. (~ed, ~n or ~ed). Scatter (seed, or abs.) on or in the earth for purpose of growth; (fig.) ~ (*the seeds of*) *dissension* etc.; *as a* ~ (*completely*). 2. (Also ~*bug*) wood-louse. 3. Main through through which molten iron runs into side-channels to form pigs, large block of iron that solidifies in this. 4. ~*back*, low ridge of sand thickly with seed) by ~*ing*; (fig.) cover etc.; ~*bread*, kind of cyclamen; ~ *thistle*, plant with small yellow flowers & milky juice. [OE *sugu*, cf. Du. *zog*, G *sau*, ON *sȳr*]

sow², n. 1. Adult female hog; *get the wrong* ~ *by the ear*, fix on wrong person or thing; *reach wrong conclusion; as drunk as a* ~ (*in the wind* (see WHIRL); plant molten iron runs into side-channels to form pigs. [OE *sugu*, cf. Du. *zog*, G *sau*]

sowar' (sǝwär'), n. Indian cavalry trooper. [Hind. & Pers. *sawār* horseman]

soy, n. Kind of sauce made in Japan & China (from the SOYA BEAN. [f. Jap. *shoyu*]

soy'a, (now rarely) **soy, bean,** n. (Seed of) a leguminous plant of south-eastern Asia, yielding an edible oil (~ *oil*) & *soya flour* used for cattle & human food. [prec.]

sŏz'zled (-ld), a. (sl.). Very drunk. [p.p. of *sozzle* dial. to mix sloppily (prob. imit.)]

spa (-ah, -aw), n. (Place where there is a) mineral spring. [*Spa*, place in Belgium]

space, n. 1. Continuous extension viewed with or without reference to the existence of objects within it. 2. Interval between points or objects viewed as having one, two, or three dimensions, *as separated by* a ~ *of 10 ft, clear a* ~ (*area*), *box occupies too much* ~, *would take up too much* ~ (on paper) *to go into detail.* 3. (Print.) blank between words etc., type securing this. 4. Interval of time, *as in the* ~ *of an hour, after a short* ~, *let us rest a* ~, ~*bar,* bar in typewriter for making ~ between words; ~*time* (Philos.), a fusion of the concepts of ~ & time, regarded as a continuum in which the existent exists, & as the fourth dimension non-recognition of which confines the Euclidean or three-dimensional geometry to the range

of practical experience & leaves it philosophically assailable beyond that range; ~*writer,* ~*writing* (in newspaper, paid according to area occupied). Hence ~*LESS* (-sl-) a. [f. F *espace* f. L *spatium*]

space², v.t. & t. Set at intervals, put spaces between, (esp. words, letters, lines, in printing); make a space between words on typewriter etc., *as don't forget to* ~, *more* or *wider spaces between.* Hence **spā'cING**¹(1), n. [f. prec.]

spā'cious (-shŭs), a. Enclosing a large space, roomy. Hence ~LY² adv., ~NESS n. [f. F *spacieux* f. L *spatiosus* (as SPACE¹, see -OUS)]

spāde, n., & v.t. 1. Tool for digging & cutting ground, turf, etc., with sharp-edged iron blade & wooden handle used with both hands; *call a* ~ *a* ~, call things by their names, speak plainly or bluntly; tool of similar shape for various purposes, e.g. for removing blubber from whale; ~ *bayonet* (with broad blade, used as both ~ & weapon); ~ *husbandry* (with deep ~ digging instead of subsoil-ploughing). 2. (Playing-card with) black figure(s) shaped like heart with small handle; (pl.) suit of these cards; ~ *guinea* (of George III with shield shaped like ~ on cards). 3. ~*work,* (fig.) hard work with attention to details. 4. v.t. Dig over (ground), cut blubber from (whale), with ~. Hence ~*FUL* (-dfōōl) n. [OE *spadu* perh. f. LG *spade,* Sw., Norw., *spade*), cogn. w. L f. Gk *spathē* broad blade; in card sense f. It. *spade* Sp. *espada* sword]

spade'ful, n. (sl.). Corrupt. of SPARROW. [II.]

spādille' n. Ace of spades in ombre & quadrille. [F f. Sp. *espadilla* dim. as SPADE]

spād'īx, n. (bot.; pl. ~*ices* pr. -īs'ēz), Spike of flowers closely arranged round fleshy axis & usu. enclosed in a spathe. Hence or cogn. ~*ICEOUS* (-ish·ŭs), ~*ICOSE*¹, aa. [f. Gk, = palm-branch]

spād'ō, n. (law). Person incapable of procreation. [L, f. Gk *spadōn* eunuch]

spaghett'i (-gě'), n. Kind of macaroni. [It.]

spahi, -ee (spah'hē) n. Member of 14th-c. Turkish irregular cavalry; member of native Algerian cavalry in French service. [f. Turk. f. Hind. *sipahi* SEPOY]

spall (-awl), v.t. & t. & n. Splinter, chip; (Mining) prepare (ore) for sorting by breaking it up. Hence *spall'ᴅEᴿ¹ (-awl-) n. [f. obs. vb. *spald,* etym. dub.; cf. G *spellen*]

spam, n. (tr.). Mean fellow, rascal. U.S. [P; f. *spiced ham*]

span¹, v.t. & t. (-nn-). (Of bridge, arch, etc., fig., of memory etc.) stretch from side to side of, extend across, (river etc., fig. period etc.), (of builder etc.) bridge

(river etc.); measure, cover, the extent of (thing) with one's grasp etc.; (Naut.) confine (booms etc.) with ropes; move in distinct stretches like span-worm. [f. OE *span* n... see foll.]

span², n. **1.** Full extent from end to end, as ~ *of a bridge, of an arch, our brief* ~ (*of life*), *the whole* ~ *of Roman history*. **2.** Each part of a bridge etc. between piers or supports. **3.** Greenhouse or similar structure with ~ roof. **4.** Maximum distance between tips of thumb & little finger, esp. as a measure = 9 in. **5.** Short distance, as *our life is but a* ~. **6.** (Naut.) rope fastened by both ends to take a purchase in the loop, double rope connected with thimbles. **7.** (Colon., U.S.) pair of horses or mules, yoke of oxen. **8.** ~-*dogs*, pair of iron bars with claws for grappling timber; ~ *roof* (with two inclined sides, opp. to pent-roof or lean-to); ~-*worm*, larva of GEOMETER. [senses *measure, extent*, f. OE *span* (of the hand); senses 6 & 7. f. Du. *span* (*spannen* fasten)]

spangle (spăng'gl), n., & v.t. **1.** Small piece of glittering material esp. one of many as ornament of dress etc.; any small sparkling object; (also *oak-*~) spongy excrescence on oak-leaves, oak-apple. **2.** v.t. Cover with ~es (esp. in p.p.). Hence ~**y²** a. [f. earlier *spang* f. M Du. *spange* metal clasp +-LE]

spaniard (-yard), n. Native of Spain. [f. OF *Espaignard* (*Espaigne* Spain, -ARD)]

spaniel (-yel), n. Kinds of dog with long silky coat, drooping ears, & docile & affectionate disposition, some used by sportsmen & some kept as pets (*King Charles's* ~, small black-&-tan kind); (fig.) fawning or cringing person. [ME, f. OF *espaigneul* f. Sp. *español* Spanish f. *España* Spain f. L *Hispania*]

Spanish, a. & n. **1.** Of Spain or the Spaniards or their language; ~ (=*Invincible*) ARMADA; ~ *black, brown, red, white*, pigments; ~ CHESTNUT; ~ *fly*, bright green insect dried & used for raising blisters, as aphrodisiac, etc.; ~ *fowl*, breed of domestic fowl with glossy greenish-black plumage; ~ *grass*, esparto; ~*main* (hist.), NE coast of S. America between Orinoco river & Panama, & adjoining part of Caribbean sea; ~ *windlass*, use of stick as lever for tightening cord or bandage; *War of the* ~ *succession* (between France & Bavaria on one side & England, Prussia, & United Provinces on the other, on death of Charles II of Spain without issue, 1701–14). **2.** n. ~ language. [ME *Spanisc* (*Spain*, see -ISH¹)]

spank, v.t. & i., & n. **1.** Slap on buttocks with open hand or slipper etc., whence ~*ing¹* [-ING¹] n.; urge forward esp. by slapping or whipping; (of horse etc.) move briskly esp. at a step between trot & gallop. **2.** n. Slap, blow with open hand etc., on buttocks. [imit.]

spank'er, n. In vbl senses; also or esp.: fast-going horse; (colloq.) person or thing of notable size or quality, stunner, whopper; (Naut.) fore-&-aft sail set on after side of mizzenmast. [-ER¹]

spanking¹, See SPANK.

spank'ing², a. & adv. In vbl senses; also: (colloq.) striking, notable, excellent, as *had a* ~ *time, a* ~ (*strong*) *breeze*, (adv.) *a* ~ *fine woman*. [-ING², cf. *whacking, thumping, whopping*]

span'less, a. (poet.). Beyond measure. [-LESS]

spann'er, n. In vbl senses; also: instrument for turning nut on screw etc.; cross-brace of bridge etc.; connecting-rod in parallel motion of engine; = SPAN²-*worm*. [-ER¹; mech. sense f. G *spanner*]

spar¹, n., & v.t. (-rr-). **1.** Stout pole esp. such as is used for mast, yard, etc., of ship; ~-*buoy* (made of a ~ with one end moored so that other stands up); ~-*deck*, upper deck extending from bow to stern, including quarterdeck and forecastle. **2.** v.t. Furnish with ~, help (ship) over shallow bar with ~s. [ME *sparre*, cf. Du. *spar*, G *sparren*, ON *sparri*]

spar², n. Kinds of crystalline mineral, easily cleavable & non-lustrous, as *calcareous* ~, calcite, *Derbyshire* (= FLUOR) ~, *Iceland* ~, transparent calcite much used for optical purposes. [f. MLG *spar*, cogn. w. OE *spæren* gypsum]

spar³, v.i. (-rr-), & n. **1.** Make motions of attack & defence with closed fists, use the hands (as) in boxing, (often *at* opponent; ~*ring partner*, boxer employed to practise with another in training for a fight); (fig.) bandy words, as *they are always* ~*ring* (*at each other*); (of cocks) fight esp. with protected spurs. **2.** n. ~*ring motion*, boxing-match, cock-fight. [orig. = (of cock) strike out with spurs; etym. dub.]

spa'rable, n. Headless nail for soles & heels of boots. [corrupt. of *sparrow-bill*]

spare¹, a. & n. **1.** Scanty, frugal, as *diet*, lean, thin, as *man of a* ~ *frame*, whence ~*ly²* (-rl-) adv., ~*ness* (-rn-) n.; ~*rib*, upper part of ribs of pork with small amount of meat adhering; that can be spared, not required for ordinary use, as *how to use your* ~ *time, have no* ~ *cash*; reserved for emergency or extraordinary use, as *always take a* ~ *cap*, ~*room* (bedroom for visitor). **2.** n. ~ part for substitution in machine. [OE *spær*, cf. ON *sparr*, Da. *spar*(*som*), Sw. *spar*(*sam*)]

spare², v.t. & i. Be frugal or grudging of, as ~ *the rod & spoil the child, must not*

~ *expense*, whence **spär'ingly²** adv., **spär'ingness** n.; dispense with, do without, as *cannot ~ him just now*, ~ *me a penny, could have ~d the explanation*; ‖ (arch.) forbear (*to do*); abstain from inflicting (with double object), as ~ *me these protestations*; abstain from killing, hurting, wounding, etc., as ~ (do not kill) *me*, ~ *my life*, ~ *his feelings*, (loosely) ~ (do not provoke) *his blushes*; be frugal. [OE *sparian*, cf. prec., & Du. & G sparen]

spär'ger, n. Sprinkling-apparatus, esp. in brewing. [f. rare vb *sparge* f. L *spargere*, -ER¹]

spärk¹, n. **1.** Fiery particle thrown off from burning substance, or still visibly alight in ashes, or struck out by impact from flint etc. (*as the ~s fly upward*, with the certainty of a law of nature), as *bright object or point* e.g. in gem. **3.** (fig.) Brilliant emanation of wit etc., esp. *strike ~s out of* person, provoke him to lively or original conversation. **4.** (Usu. neg. or quasi-neg.) particle of fire or (fig.) of quality etc., as *not a ~ of generosity in you, if you had a ~ of life remained*, **5.** (Electr.) luminous effect of sudden disruptive discharge, electric ~ serving to fire explosive mixture in oil-engine or motor etc., as *advance, retard, the ~* (in the cycle of operation in the engine), **6.** *S~s*, (nickname for) wireless operator; *fairy ~s*, phosphorescent light from decayed vegetable matter etc.; ~*-arrester*, device for preventing (injury from) SPARK³ing in electrical apparatus, netting etc. to catch ~s on steam-engine; ~*LESS* a., ~*LET* n., small ~, carbonic-acid charge for use in some gazogenes. [OE *spearca*, cf. MDu. *sparke*, & ON *sprakka*, Da. *sprage*, crackle; perh. f. crackle of burning wood etc.]

spärk², v.i. Emit sparks of fire or electricity; ‖ ~*ing-plug*, device for firing explosive mixture in motor-engine; (Electr.) produce sparks at point where continuity of circuit is interrupted. [prob. f. prec.]

2. v.i. Play the gallant. Hence ~*ISH³* a. [prob. fig. use of SPARK¹]

spärk³, n. & v.i. **1.** Gay fellow; gallant. **2.** v.i. Play the gallant. [ME *sparke* n.; ? f. SPARK¹²⁺-ER¹(3)]

spär'kle, v.i. & n. **1.** Emit sparks, (of gems etc. & fig. of wit etc.) glitter, glisten, scintillate, whence ~*ER¹* n., ~*ingly²* adv.; ~*ing wines* (giving out carbonic-acid gas in small bubbles, cf. STILL). **2.** n. ~*ing*, gleam, spark. [ME *sparkle* n.; ~*klen* vb, f. SPARK¹²⁺-LE¹(3)]

spär'row (-ō), n. Kinds of small plain-coloured bird, esp. *house ~*, European kind noted for attachment to human dwellings, prolificness, and pugnacity; ~*-bill*, = SPARABLE; ~*-grass* (vulg.), asparagus; ~*-hawk*, kinds of small hawk preying on ~s etc. [OE *spearwa*, cf. ON *sporr*, Da. *spurv*]

spär'ry, a. Of, like, rich in, SPAR². [-Y²] **spärse**, a. (Of population etc.) thinly scattered, not dense; (Bot., Zool.) placed, occurring, at distant or irregular intervals. Hence ~*ly²* (-sl-), ~*NESS* (-sn-) n. [f. L *spargere spars-* scatter]

Spärt'acist, a. & n. (Member) of the Spartacus group of extremists in the German revolution in 1918. [*Spartacus*, leader in anc.-Roman servile war, -IST]

Spärt'an, a. & n. (Native) of Sparta (esp. w. allusion to supposed characteristics of ~s, as ~ *endurance, simplicity*). [f. L *Spartanus* (*Sparta* f. Gk *Spartē*, see -AN)]

spä'sm, n. Excessive muscular contraction (CHRONIC, TONIC, ~); sudden convulsive movement, wrench, or strain; as *a ~ of coughing*, (fig.) ~*s of grief* etc.; *functional ~*, nervous disorders caused by contraction, as *writer's cramp*. Hence ~*ōī'OGY* (-āz-) n. [f. L f. Gk *spasmos* (*spaō* draw)]

spasmō'd|ic (-āz-), a. Of, caused by, subject to, spasm(s), as *a ~ic jerk*, ~*ic asthma*; occurring, done, by fits & starts, as ~*ic efforts*. Hence ~*ICALLY* adv. [f. Gk *spasmōdēs* (as SPASM, see -OID)+-IC]

spā'stic, a. (med.), = prec. [f. L f. Gk *spastikos* drawing (*spaō* draw, see -IC)]

spät¹, n. & v.i. & t. (-tt-). **i.** Spawn of shellfish esp. oyster. **2.** vb. (Of oyster etc.) spawn(s); shed (spawn). [prob. cogn. w. SPIT²]

spät², n. (usu. pl.). Short gaiter covering instep & reaching little above ankle. [for SPATTER*dash*]

spät³. See SPIT².

spätch'còck, n., & v.t. **1.** Fowl killed & cooked in a hurry. **2.** v.t. (colloq.). Insert (words) hastily in telegram etc. [usu. expl. as *dispatch-cock*, but perh. f. contus. w. SPITCHCOCK]

späte, n. River-flood, esp. *river is in ~*. [orig. Sc., etym. dub.]

spä'tial (-shl), a. Of space, as ~ *relations, extent*. Hence **spätiăl'ITY** (-shl-) n., ~*LY²* adv. [f. L *spatium* SPACE+-AL]

spä'ttee, n. Woollen legging worn by women and children over shoes and stockings. [f. SPAT² after *puttee*]

spätt'er, v.t. & i., & n. **1.** Scatter (liquid, mud, etc.) here & there in small drops; splash (person *with* mud, slander, etc.) drops. **2.** n. ~*ing*, splash (of mud etc.), quick succession of light sounds, pattering. **3.** ~*dashes* (or now usu. *spats*), cloth or other leggings to protect stockings etc. from mud etc. [of. Du. *spatten* burst, spout, -ER¹]

spät'üla, n. Broad-bladed instrument for working pigments etc.; surgeon's

instrument for pressing tongue down or to one side. [L, dim. as SPATHE]

spatʹule, n. (zool.). Broad racket-shaped formation or part, esp. end of bird's tail-feather. Hence ~AR¹, ~ATE², ~IFORM, aa. [OF. f. L as prec.]

spavʹin, n. Disease of horse's hock-joint; *blood, bog,* ~, distension of the joint by effusion of lymph within it; *bone* ~, deposit of bony substance uniting the bones. Hence ~ED² (-nd) a. [f. OF *espavain, esparvain,* etym. dub.]

spawn, v.t. & i., & n. 1. (Of fish, frog, mollusc, crustacean, derog. of human being or other animal) produce (eggs, or abs.), generate; (of eggs or young of fish etc.) be produced, issue. 2. n. Eggs of fish etc.; (derog.) human or other offspring (~ *of the devil, of Cobden,* scoundrels, free-traders); white fibrous matter from which fungi are produced, mycelium, as *mushroom* ~. [(n. f. vb) f. OF *espandre* EXPAND]

spay, v.t. Castrate, remove ovaries of, (female animal). [f. AF *espeier* (OF *espee* sword)]

speak, v.i. & t. (*spoke,* arch. *spake*; *spoken*). 1. Use articulate utterance in ordinary (not singing) voice, as *child is learning to ~, wish you would ~ distinctly;* (D.D., as stage direction) to be said, not sung (also as n., such part). 2. Hold conversation (*with, to, person, of, about, thing*), as *have heard him ~ of it, will ~ to him about it; portrait ~s* (is lifelike), so ~*ing likeness.* 3. Make oral address, deliver speech, before assembly, magistrate, tribunal, etc. 4. Utter (words), make known (one's opinion, *the truth,* etc.), thus, esp. ~ *one's mind* (bluntly etc.). 5. Use (specified language) in ~*ing,* as *cannot ~ French,* whence **French'** etc. ~ER¹ n., ~ING² a. 6. *Strictly, roughly, generally,* ~*ing* (quasi-adv.), in the strict, rough, etc., sense of the word(s), as *am not strictly* ~*ing a member of the staff; legally* etc. ~*ing,* from the legal etc. point of view. 7. (As an apology for loose or strong or figurative expression) *so to* ~ if I may use such an expression. 8. Hall & hold communication (with ship). 9. (arch.). (Of conduct, circumstance, etc.) show (person) to be (so-&-so), as *his conduct* ~*s him generous;* be evidence of, as *this* ~*s a little mind.* 10. (Of fact etc.) ~ *volumes,* be very significant; ~ *volumes* etc. *for,* well *for,* be abundant evidence of, place in favourable light, as ~*s volumes for his forbearance.* 11. (Of mus. instrument etc.) sound. 12. fig. (Of dog) bark esp. when ordered. 13. Make mention in writing of. 14. ~ *by the* or *like a* BOOK¹; ~ (person) *fair,* use polite language to ~; *for,* act as spokesman of, state the sentiments of; ~ *of,* mention; *nothing to* ~ *of,* nothing worth mentioning, practically nothing; ~ *out* (also *up*), ~ freely,

~ one's whole opinion; ~ *to,* address (person etc.), ~ in confirmation of or in reference to, as *I can* ~ *to his having been there, will* ~ *to that point later;* ~ *up* (also *out*), ~ louder; ~ *without book,* give facts etc. from memory; *fair, smooth, ill, well,* etc., -*spoken* [as if -*speech*ED²], (given to) using such language: *~easy* (sl.), illicit liquor shop. [OE *sp(r)ecan,* cf. Du. *spreken,* G *sprechen*]

speakʹer, n. One who speaks esp. in public; (S~) presiding officer in House of Commons charged with preservation of order etc. & having casting vote in case of equal division, similar officer in U.S. House of Representatives etc., whence S~SHIP n. [-ER¹]

speakʹing, n. In vbl senses: ~ *acquaintance,* person one knows well enough to exchange conversation with him, this degree of familiarity: *not on* ~ *terms,* not, esp. no longer, having ~ acquaintance *with* (usu. implying estrangement): ~ *trumpet,* instrument for conveying voice to a distance; ~ *tube,* tube for conveying voice from one room or building to another. [-ING²]

spear, n., & v.t. & i. 1. Hunter's or foot-soldier's thrusting or hurling weapon consisting of stout staff with point usu. of steel (cf. LANCE, PIKE): (poet.) = *man*; sharp-pointed & barbed instrument for stabbing fish etc.; ~*head,* (esp. fig.) individual or group chosen to lead a thrust or attack; ~*man,* person esp. soldier who uses ~; ~*mint,* common garden mint; ~ *side,* male branch of family (cf. DISTAFF). 2. v.t. Pierce, strike, with ~. 3. v.i. Shoot into a long stem. [(vb f. n.) OE *spere,* cf. Du. & G *speer*]

spec, n. (colloq.). Speculation, speculative enterprise, as *it turned out a good* ~, *did it on* ~. [abbr. of SPECULATION]

speʹcial (-shl), a. & n. 1. Of a particular kind, peculiar, not general, (cf. ESPECIAL), as *lacks the* ~ *qualities required, word used in a* ~ *sense, what is your* ~ *work?, its* ~ *charm did not appeal to him, anatomy* (of particular organs of human body), ~ JURY, ~ *hospital* (for particular class of diseases). 2. For a particular purpose, as ~ *appointed* ~ *agents, received* ~ *instructions.* 3. (Also *especial*) exceptional in amount, degree, intensity, etc., as *took* ~ *trouble, find no* ~ *excellence in his work.* 4. ~ *case,* written statement of facts submitted by litigants to court; (also) exceptional or peculiar case; ~ *constable* (sworn in to assist in maintaining public peace in time of emergency); ~ *correspondent* (appointed by newspaper to report on ~ facts); ~ *edition* (including later news than ordinary edition of newspaper); ‖ ~ *licence* (enabling priests to marry ~ parties without publication of banns or at time or place other than those usually necessary); ~ *logic,* rules for

thinking concerning ~ class of objects; ~ *pleader*, member of Inns of Court whose business it is to give verbal or written opinions on matters submitted to him & to deal with various proceedings out of usual course; ~ *pleading*, (Law) allegation of ~ or new matter as opp. to denial of allegations of other side. (pop.) specious but unfair argument, statement of case designed to favour speaker's point of view rather than to discover the truth; ~ *train*, extra train for ~ purpose; ~ VERDICT. **5.** n. ~ constable, train, examination, edition of newspaper (esp. EXTRA-~), etc. Hence ~LY² (shɛ-) adv. [f. OF (e)*special* f. L *specialis* (species, see -AL)]

spē'cialist (-shɛ-), n. One who devotes himself to particular branch of a profession, science, etc. Hence or cogn. ~ISM n. ~is'tic a. [-IST]

spēciā'lity (-shi-), n. Special feature or characteristic; (also *specialty*) special pursuit, product, operation, etc., thing to which a person gives special attention, as *jam-making is our* ~. [f. OF (e)*speciaité* f. LL *specialitatem* (as SPECIAL, see -TY)]

spē'cialize (-shɛ-), v.t. & i. Make specific or individual.; modify, limit, (idea, statement); (Biol.) adapt, set apart, (organ etc.) for particular purpose, differentiate; be differentiated, become individual in character; be(come) a specialist. Hence ~ATION n. [f. F *spécialiser* (SPECIAL, -IZE)]

spē'cialty (-shl-), n. (Law) Instrument under seal, sealed contract; = SPECIALITY (2nd sense). [f. OF *specialté* (as SPECIALITY)]

spē'cie (-shē, -shē), n. (no pl.). Coin as opp. to paper money, as ~ *payments, paid in* ~, *shortness of* ~. [f. L abl. of foll. in phr. *in specie*]

spē'cies (-shēz, -shēz), n. (pl. same). **1.** (Nat. Hist.) group subordinate in classification to *genus* (cf. CLASS) & having members that differ only in minor details; *the* ~ *or* ~, mankind. **2.** (Logic) group subordinate to GENUS & containing individuals agreeing in some common attribute(s) & called by a common name. **3.** Kind, sort, as *has a* ~ *of cunning, a* ~ *of dogcart.* **4.** (Law) form, shape, given to materials. **5.** (Eccl.) the sensible form of each of the elements of consecrated bread and wine used in the Eucharist. [L, = appearance, kind, beauty, f. *specere* look]

spĕcí'fic, a. & n. **1.** Definite, distinctly formulated, as *a* ~ *statement, has no* ~ *aim*; of a species, as *the* ~ *name of plant* or ~; *the* ~ *difference* (what differentiates a species); possessing, concerned with, the properties that characterize a species, as *the* ~ *forms of animals, draws a* ~ *distinction between them*; relating to particular subject; peculiar, as *has a* ~ *style, a style* ~ *to that school of painters*; (of a duty or tax) assessed by quantity or amount, not

ad valorem.; ~ *cause* (producing a particular form of disease); ~ *centre*, place or period at which differentiation from a common stock takes place; ~ GRAVITY, HEAT¹; ~ *medicine*, having distinct effect in curing a certain disease. **2.** n. medicine or remedy. Hence spĕcí'f'c-ALLY adv. spĕcí'f'cITY, ~NESS, nn. [f. med. L *specificus* (as SPECIES, see -FIC)]

spĕcificā'tion, n. Specifying; specified detail, esp. (pl.) detailed description of construction, workmanship, materials, etc., of work undertaken by architect, engineer, etc.; description by applicant for patent of the construction & use of his invention; (Law) working up of materials into a new product not held to be the property of the owner of the materials. [f. med. L *specificationem* (foll., FICATION)]

spĕ'cify, v.t. Name expressly, mention definitely, (items, details, ingredients, etc.; often *abs.*); include in (e.g. architect's) specifications, as *a slate-course was* ~ *ied*. Hence ~IABLE a. [f. OF *specifier* f. med. L *specificare* (as SPECIFIC, see -FY)]

spĕ'cimen, n. Individual or part taken as example of a class or whole, esp. individual animal or plant or piece of a mineral etc. used for scientific examination, as ~*s of copper ore, zoological* ~*s*, *fine* ~ *of the Swallow-tail, of mosaic work, a* ~ *of his skill, generosity,* ~ *page* (of book, printed in prospectus to show size, type, etc.); (colloq. *derog.*) *what a* ~ (person) ! [L, = characteristic mark (*specere* look, -MEN)]

spĕciŏ'logy (-shi-), n. Science of (origin etc. of) species. Hence ~olŏ'gICAL a. [-LOGY]

spē'cious (-shus), a. Of good appearance, plausible, fair or right on the surface, as ~ *argument, tale, speech, appearance*. Hence or cogn. spē'cios'ITY (-shi-), ~NESS, nn. ~LY² adv. [f. L *speciosus* beautiful (SPECIES, see -OUS)]

speck¹, n., & v.t. **1.** Small spot, dot, stain; particle (*of* dirt etc.): spot of rottenness in fruit. **2.** v.t. Mark with ~s (esp. in p.p.). Hence ~ LESS a. [OE *specca*, cf. SPECKLE]

speck², n. (U.S. & S. Afr.). Fat meat, bacon, pork; fat of seals, whales, etc., blubber. [f. Du. *spek* or G *speck*, cf. OE *spic* bacon]

spĕ'ckle, n., & v.t. **1.** Small spot or stain. **2.** v.t. Mark with ~s or patches (esp. in p.p.). [SPECK¹+-LE: cf. Du. *spikkel*]

spĕcktioneer', -si-, (-shon-), n. (whaling) Chief harpooner. [f. Du. *speksnijder*]

spĕcs, n. pl. (colloq.). Pair of spectacles. [abbr.]

spĕc'tacle, n. **1.** Public show, whence spĕctăc'ūlar¹ a., spĕctăc'ūlar'ly² adv. **2.** Object of sight, esp. of public attention, as *a charming* ~, *drunken woman is a*

deplorable ~, *sure to make a* ~ (= EXHIBITION) *of himself.* **3.** (Pair of) ~s or colloq. **specs**, pair of lenses to correct or assist defective sight, set in frame without spring (cf. EYE¹-*glass*) constructed to rest on nose & ears; (fig.) *sees everything through rose-coloured etc.* ~s, *takes cheerful etc. views*; (Cricket) *pair of* ~s, two DUCK⁴s. [OF, f. L *spectaculum* show (*spectare* see, frequent. of *specere* look)]

spec'tacled (-ld), a. Wearing spectacles; (of animals) marked in a way that suggests spectacles, esp. ~ **bear**, the S.-Amer. bear. [-ED²]

spectāt'or, n. One who looks on esp. at a show, game, etc., as *the* ~s *were moved to tears, was a mere* ~, *an unconcerned* ~, (as title of paper) *The S~*. Hence **spectāt'ress¹** n. [L (*spectare*, see SPECTACLE & -OR²)]

spec'tral, a. Ghostlike; of ghosts; of spectra or the spectrum, as ~ *colours, analysis*. Hence ~LY² adv. [SPECTRUM, -AL]

spec'tre (-ter), n. Ghost; haunting presentiment (*of ruin, war, madness, etc.*); ~ *of the Brocken*, huge shadowy image of the observer projected on mists about mountain-top, first observed on the Brocken; (in names of animals compared to ~ from thinness of body etc.) ~*bat*, ~*crab*, ~*insect*, ~*lemur*, ~*shrimp*. [F, f. SPECTRUM]

spec'trio- in comb. = SPECTRUM, as: ~*o-graph*, apparatus for photographing or otherwise reproducing the spectrum, ~*ogram*, representation obtained by this, so ~*ograph'ic* a., ~*og'raphy* n.; ~*ohel'io-graph*, instrument for taking photographs of the sun from light of one wave-length only; ~*ohel'ioscope*, instrument for viewing sun in light of one wave-length only; ~*om'eter*, instrument for measuring refraction of light-rays in passing through prism.

spec'troscope, n. Instrument for forming & analysing the spectra of rays, consisting usu. of collimating tube, prism or diffraction grating, small telescope, & measuring apparatus. Hence ~*oscop'ical₁*, ~*ŏs'copist* (*or* spĕ⁴), ~*ŏs'copy¹* (*or* spĕ⁴), nn. [F ɪꜱᴛ (*or* spĕ⁴), ~ŏs'copy¹ (*or* spĕ⁴)...] [SPECTRO- + -SCOPE]

spec'trum, n. (pl. -ra). (Also *ocular* ~) image of something seen continuing when the eyes are closed or turned away; image formed by rays of light or other radiation in which the parts are arranged in a progressive series according to their refrangibility, i.e. according to wave-length; *diffraction, prismatic*, ~ (produced by means of diffraction grating, by means of prism); *solar* ~ (formed from rays of sun); ~ (*or spectral*) *analysis*, chemical analysis by means of spectroscope. [L, = appearance, image, f. *specere* look]

spec'ular, a. Of (the nature of) a speculum, esp. reflecting, as ~ *surface*. [f. L *specularis* (SPECULUM, see -AR¹)]

spec'ulāte, v.i. 1. Pursue an inquiry, meditate, form theory or conjectural opinion, (*on, upon, about, question, the nature, cause, etc., of a thing, or abs.*). 2. Make investment, engage in commercial operation, that involves risk of loss, as *has been* ~*ing in stocks, in rubber*, (esp. w. implication of rashness) *is believed to* ~ *e a good deal*. Hence or cogn. ~IVE a... ~ively¹ adv., ~IVENESS, ~OR², nn. [f. L *speculari* spy out, observe, (*specula* watch-tower as SPECULUM), see -ATE³]

specula'tion, n. 1. Meditation, inquiry into, theory about, a subject, as *much given to* ~, *sorry to disturb your* ~s. 2. Speculative investment or enterprise, practice of speculating, in business, as *ruined by (a single unlucky)* ~, *bought it as a* ~ (or *on* SPEC, rarely *on* ~). 3. Game in which cards are bought & sold. [f. L *speculationem* as prec., see -ATION]

spec'ulum, n. (pl. -la). (Surg.) instrument for dilating cavities of human body for inspection; mirror, usu. of polished metal e.g. ~-*metal* (alloy of copper & tin), esp. in reflecting telescope; (Ornith.) specially coloured area on wing of some birds, also = OCELLUS. [L, = mirror (*specere* look)]

sped. See SPEED.

speech, n. 1. Faculty of speaking. 2. Thing said, remark, as *after this unlucky* ~ *he remained silent*. 3. Public address, as *after-dinner*, MAIDEN, ~, ~ *for the defence, a set* ~; ||*King's or Queen's* ~, *make* (*deliver*) *a* ~; ~ *from the throne*, brief statement of the chief foreign & domestic affairs & of the chief measures to be considered by Parliament, prepared by Government & read by sovereign in person or by commission at opening of Parliament. 4. Language of a nation. 5. Act of sounding in organ-pipe etc. 6. FIGURE¹ *of* ~; PART¹s *of* ~; ~-*read-ing*, deaf person's interpretation of ~ by watching speaker's lips; ||~-*day*, annual day for delivering prizes in schools usu. marked by recitations etc. [OE *spǣc*, earlier *sprǣc*, as SPEAK]

speech'ify, v.i. (derog.) Make speeches, hold forth in public. Hence ~FICA'TION, ~FIER¹, nn. [-FY]

speech'less, a. Dumb; temporarily deprived of speech by emotion etc., as ~ *with rage*; (sl.) dead drunk. Hence ~LY² adv., ~NESS n. [OE *spǣclēas*, see -LESS]

speed, n., & v.t. & i. (spĕd, exc. as below). 1. Rapidity of movement, as *with all* ~, *more haste less* ~, *at full* ~; rate of progress or motion, as *attains a high* ~, *depends on the* ~ *required, three-*~ *engine, bicycle, etc.* (with adaptable gear for going at different ~s); AIR¹, GROUND¹, ~

2. (arch.). Success, prosperity, as *send*
me good ~ (cf. GOD[1]*~*), **3.** *~boot*, motor-
boat designed for high *~*; *~cone*, contrivance for adjusting ratio of *~* between
parallel shafts by means of belt; *~cop*
(orig. U.S., sl.), police motor-cyclist
detailed to check motorists' *~*; *~way*,
arena for motor-cycle racing; *~road* or
track reserved for fast motor traffic;
~well, kinds of herb with creeping or
ascending stems & bright-blue flowers.
4. vb. Go fast, as *sped down the street* (now
chiefly literary); (arch.) send fast, send on
the way, as *~ an arrow from the bow*, *~ the
parting guest*. **5.** (arch.). Be or make
prosperous, succeed, give success to, as
how have you sped?, *God ~ you!* **6.** (past
& p.p. *~ed*). Regulate *~* of (engine etc.),
cause to go at fixed *~*; *~ up*, cause to
work at greater *~* (*the train service usually
~ing up*); (of motorists) travel at illegal
or dangerous *~*. [vb f. OE *spēdan* OE]
spēd (*spōwan prosper*), cf. Du. *spoed*,
OHG *spuot*, *spōt*, success]

speed'er, n. Kinds of device for regulating or increasing speed of machinery.
[-ER[1]]

speedöm'eter, n. Appliance indicating
the speed at which motor-car etc. is
moving. [SPEED, -o-, -METER]

speed'ly, a. Rapid; expeditious, prompt,
coming without delay, as *~y answer*,
vengeance. Hence *~ILY*[2] adv., *~INESS* n.
[-Y[2]]

speiss (-īs), n. Compound of arsenic, iron,
etc., found in smelting some lead ores.
[f. G *speise* food, amalgam, f. pop. L
spesa EXPENSE]

spelae'an, a. Of, dwelling in, caves. So
speleol'ogy, (~Ōl'OGY, nn. [f. L f. Gk *spē-
laion* cave (*speos* cave) + -AN]

spelicans. See SPILLIKIN.

spell[1], n. Words used as charm, incantation or its effect (*under a ~*, mastered by
or as by a *~*); attraction, fascination,
exercised by person, pursuit, quality,
etc.; *~binder*, political speaker who can
hold audiences *~bound*; *~bound*, bound
(as) by a *~*. [OE *spell(l)* saying, story, cf.
ON *spjal*; cogn. w. foll.]

spell[2], v.t. (*spelt* or *~ed* pr. -lt). Write
or name the letters that form (a word,
as *how do you ~ 'analyse' ?*, *must not be
spelt with a z*, *can't ~ his own name*, (abs.)
wish you would learn to ~ (correctly);
make out or over, make out (words, writing)
laboriously letter by letter; *~ backward*,
repeat or write the letters of (word) in
reverse order, (fig.) misinterpret, pervert
meaning of; (of letters) make up, form
(word), as *what does* c a t *~* ?; (fig., of circumstances, scheme, etc.) have as necessary result, involve, as *these changes ~
ruin to the farmer*. [f. OF *espeler* f. Teut.
(OE *spellian* tell f. prec.)]

spell[3], n. & v.t. **1.** Turn of work, as *did
a ~ of carpentering*; short period, as *wait*

(*for*) *a ~*. **2.** v.t. (rare). Relieve, take
the place of, (person) in work etc. [OE
spelian vb, *gespelia* & *spala* nn. = sub-
stitute]

spell'er, n. In vbl senses of SPELL[2]; also
= SPELLING-*book*. [-ER[1]]

spell'ing, n. In vbl senses, as *his ~ is
weak*, *not sure of the ~ of 'aneurysm'*;
another *~ of the same word*; *~bee*, competition in *~*; *~book*, (for teaching *~*).
[-ING[1]]

spelt[1], n. Kind of wheat giving very fine
flour, German wheat. [OE, f. LL *spelta*]

spelt[2]. See SPELL[2].

spel'ter, n. (now commerc.). Zinc. [cf.
OF *espeautre*, Du. & G *spiauter*, & PEW-
TER]

|| **spence**, *-se*, n. (arch.). Buttery, larder.
[OF short for *despense* (see DISPENSE)]

spen'cer[1], n. Short woollen jacket. [f.
Earl S~ (d. 1834)]

spen'cer[2], n. (naut.). = TRYSAIL. [?]

Spen'cerism, n. Doctrine of Herbert
Spencer(d. 1903)referring the ordered universe to the necessary laws of mechanics,
synthetic philosophy. So **Spen'cerian**
a., **Spen'cerianism** n. [-ISM]

spend, v.t. & i. (*spent*). **1.** Pay out (money)
for a purchase etc. (also abs., as *~ profusely*). **2.** Use, use up, consume, as *our
ammunition was all spent, shall ~ no more
breath, trouble, etc., on him, how do you ~
your time ?, spent a pleasant day*; exhaust,
wear out, as *his anger will soon ~ itself,
storm is spent, spent common-ball* (with
little impulse left). **3.** (Naut.) lose (mast).
4. Be consumed, as *candles ~ fast in
draught*. **5.** Emit spawn; *spent herring
etc.* (that has deposited its spawn).
6. *~thrift*, extravagant person, prodigal,
(often attrib.). Hence *~ABLE a., ~ER[1]*
n. [OE *spendan* f. L EX(*pendere weigh)
spend]

Spen'low and Jor'kins(-lō, -z), n. Plan
of attributing one's (S.'s) hard dealings
to a supposed hard partner (J.) kept in
background. [persons in Dickens's *David
Copperfield*]

|| **spense**. See SPENCE.

Spen'serian, a. & n. **1.** Of the poet
Edmund Spenser (d. 1599), esp. *~ stanza*,
that used in the *Faerie Queene*. **2.** n. pl.
~ stanzas. [-IAN]

spent. See SPEND.

sperm[1], n. (Also *~whale*) cachalot,
whale yielding spermaceti; = foll. [abbr.]

spermacet'i, n. White brittle fatty substance contained in solution in heads of
sperm-whale etc., used for candles &
ointments. [med. L, = SPERM[1] + *ceti* of
whale f. Gk *kētos* (*~* being regarded as
whale-spawn)]

sperm'ary, n. Male germ-gland, testicle
or equivalent organ. [SPERM[1] + -ARY[1]]

spermat'ic, a. Of SPERM¹ or the spermary. [f. OF *spermatique* f. L f. Gk *spermatikos* (as SPERM¹, see -IC)]

spĕrm'at|o- in comb. = SPERM¹, as: ~*oblast*, germ of a ~*ozoon*; ~*ogen'esis*, development of ~*ozoa*, so ~*ŏ'genous* a., ~*ŏ'geny* n.; ~*ŏt'ogĭst*, ~*ŏt'ogy*, student, study of sperm, so ~*ŏt'gĭcal* a.; ~*ophore*, capsule containing ~*ozoa*; ~*orrhœ'a* (-rēa), involuntary seminal discharge; ~*ozō'ŏn* (pl. -zōa), male fertilizing element contained in semen of animals, similar element in lower plants, so ~*ozō'al*, ~*ozō'an*, aa.

spĕrm'|o- in comb. = Gk *sperma* seed, semen, as: ~*oblast* = SPERMATOBLAST; ~*ŏl'ogy*, = SPERMATOLOGY, (Bot.) study of seeds, so ~*ŏt'gĭcal* a., ~*ŏt'ogĭst* n.

spew, **spūe**, v.t. & i. Vomit (t. & i.); (of gun) droop at muzzle from too quick firing. [OE *spēowan*, *spīwan*, cf. ON *spȳja*, G *speien*, L *spuere*, Gk *ptuō*]

sphā cēliate, v.t. & i. Affect, be affected, with gangrene or necrosis. Hence ~A'TION n. [f. Gk *sphakelos* gangrene + -ATE²]

sphaer(o)- in comb.= Gk *sphaira* ball, in many scientific esp. nat. hist. terms.

sphăg'num, n. (bot.; pl. -na). Kinds of moss growing in bogs and peat, and used as packing etc. [mod. L f. Gk *sphagnos* a moss]

sphĕn'|(o)- in comb. = Gk *sphēn* wedge, chiefly in sense 'of the sphenoid bone'; also: ~*ogram*, cuneiform character, so ~*ographĭc* a.

sphĕn'oid, a. & n. (anat.). Wedge-shaped, esp.~ (*bone*), compound bone at base of skull. ~ Hence **sphĕnoid'**AL a., **sphēnoid'o-** comb. form. [f. Gk *sphenoeidēs* (*sphēn* wedge, -OID)]

sphēre, n., & v.t. 1. Solid figure generated by revolution of semicircle about its diameter, or every part of whose surface is equidistant from a point within called the centre. 2. Ball, globe; (poet.) the heavens, the sky; any heavenly body; globe representing the earth or the apparent heavens. 3. Each of the revolving globe-shaped shells in which the heavenly bodies were formerly supposed to be set, esp. *music*, *harmony*, *of the* ~s (produced by movements of the ~s). 4. One's field of action, influence, or existence, one's natural surroundings, one's place in society, as *has done much within his peculiar* ~, *earnest young lady in search of a* ~, *great mistake to take him out of his* ~, *moves in quite another* ~, *State's* ~ (claimed or recognized area) *of influence in Africa.* 5. *Celestial* ~, surface on which heavenly bodies appear to lie; *doctrine of the* ~, spherical geometry & trigonometry; *great, small, circle of* ~, section made by plane passing, not passing, through its centre; *oblique, right, parallel,* ~ of apparent heavens at a place where there is oblique angle, right angle, no angle, between equator & horizon. 6. v.t. Enclose (as) in ~, make ~-shaped; (poet.) exalt to the (celestial) ~. Hence **sphēr'**Y² a. (poet.). [(vb f. n.) f. OF *espere* f. L f. Gk *sphaira* ball, globe]

sphēr'ic, a. & n. 1. (Poet.) of the heavens, celestial, exalted; (rare) =foll. 2. n. pl. Geometry & trigonometry of the sphere. [f. L f. Gk *sphairikos* (as prec., see -IC)]

sphēr'ical, a. Shaped like a sphere, globular, whence or cogn. ~LY² adv., **sphēri'**CITY n.; of spheres, as ~ *geometry*; ~ *lune*, *triangle*, *polygon* (bounded by arcs of great circles of sphere). [-AL]

sphēr'ograph (-ahf), n. Stereographic projection of the earth on disk, with meridians & parallels of latitude marked in single degrees. [SPHERE +-o- + -GRAPH]

sphēr'oid, n. Sphere-like but not perfectly spherical body; solid generated by revolution of ellipse about its major (*prolate* or *oblong* ~) or minor (*oblate* ~) axis, as *the earth is an oblate* ~. Hence **sphēroid'**ALY² adv., **sphēroid'**IC(O)AL aa., **sphēroid'io-** comb. form. [f. L f. Gk *sphairoeidēs* (as SPHERE, see -OID)]

sphērŏm'eter, n. Instrument for finding radius of sphere & for exact measurement of thickness of small bodies. [f. F *sphéromètre*, see SPHERE, -METER]

sphē'rule (-ōōl), n. Small sphere. Hence ~AR¹, ~ATE²(2) (entom.), aa. [f. L *sphaerula* (as SPHERE, see -ULE)]

sphē'rulite (-rōō-), n. Vitreous globule as constituent of some rocks. Hence ~it'ic a.; ~itIZE(3) v.t. [f. prec.+-ITE¹]

sphinc'ter, n. Muscle surrounding & serving to close an opening or tube. Hence ~AL, **sphinctē'rIAL**, **sphinctē'rio**, aa. [L f. Gk *sphinktēr* (*sphiggō* shut tight)]

sphinx, n. 1. (Gk Myth., S~) winged monster of Thebes with woman's head & lion's body who proposed a riddle to the Thebans, killed all who could not guess it, & on Oedipus's solving it threw herself from the rock on which she sat & died. 2. (Egypt. Ant.) figure with lion's body & man's or animal's head (*the S*~, colossal ~ near the pyramids at Gizeh). 3. Enigmatic person. 4. Hawk-moth; kind of baboon. [L.f. Gk *sphigx*, perh.f. *sphiggō* strangle]

sphrăgis'tics, n. pl. (often treated as sing.). Study of engraved seals. [f. Gk *sphragistikos* (*sphragizō* seal vb f. *sphragĭs*]

sphyg'm|o- in comb. = foll. as: ~*ograph*, instrument for showing character of pulse in series of curves; ~*ogram*, record so produced, so ~*ograph'ic* a., ~*ography* n.; ~*ŏt'ogy*, study of the pulse; ~*omanóm'eter*, ~*ophone*, ~*oscope*, instrument for making audible, visible, the action of the pulse.

sphyg'mus, n. (physiol.). Pulse, pulsation. [mod. L f. Gk *sphugmos* f. *sphuzō* throb]

spic'|a, n. (Bot.) spike, whence ~āted, aa.; (Surg.) spiral bandage with reversed turns. [L. = spike, ear of grain]

Spice, n., & v.t. 1. Aromatic or pungent vegetable substance used to flavour food, e.g. cloves, pepper, mace; ~s collectively; as dealer in ~, sugar & ~ & all that's nice; so spi'cery) n.; (fig.) smack, dash, flavour, (of malice etc. in person's character, writings, etc.); ~'bush, aromatic American shrub of laurel family. 2. v.t. Flavour with ~. [vb f. n.] f. OF espice spice f. L SPECIES]

Spick, a. ~ & span, smart & new, brand-new. [earlier ~-&-span-new, redupl. of ME span new f. ON spán-nýr = chip-new]

spic'ūle, n. Small hard sharp-pointed body; (Zool.) small hard body esp. in framework of sponge; (Bot.) small or fragmentary spike. Hence ~AR¹, ~ATE²(2), aa. [f. L spiculum dim. of spica]

spic'|y, (fig.) Of, flavoured or fragrant with, spice; (fig.) piquant, pungent, improper. adv. ~(y story), showy, smart. Hence ~iIY² adv. ~INESS n. [-Y²]

spi'der, n. 1. Eight-legged animal of the order Aranéida, many species of which spin webs esp. for capture of insects as food (~ & fly, fig., ensnarer & ensnared); kinds of arachnid like ~. 2. Thing compared to ~ esp. as having prominent legs, e.g. kind of three-legged gridiron. 3. Sulky with very large light wheels. 4. ~-catcher, kinds of bird; ~-crab, crab with long thin legs; ~-line, thread of ~'s web substituted for wire in scales etc. for minute work; ~-monkey, kind with long limbs & long prehensile tail; ~-wasp, wasp that stores its nest with ~s for its young. Hence ~LIKE a., ~Y² a. (esp. of writing; legs, spokes, etc.) very thin. [ME spíþre (spin²+-ther agent suf.)]

spieg'eleisen (-lîzn), n. Kind of cast iron containing manganese, much used in Bessemer process. [G spiegel mirror f. L speculum+eisen iron]

*spiel, n., & v.i. & t. (sl.). 1. Speech, story. 2. vb. Hold forth, orate; reel of (patter, yarn, tale of misfortune). [G. = play, game]

spif(f)'lic|āte, v.t. (sl.). Trounce, do for. Hence ~A'TION n. [?]

spig'ot, n. Small peg or plug esp. one for insertion into gimlet-hole in cask; plain end of pipe fitting into socket of next one. [f. OFr. espiga ear of corn f. L spica]

Spike, n. & v.t. 1. Sharp point; pointed piece of metal e.g. one of a set forming top of iron fence etc. or worn in bottom of shoe to prevent slipping; large stout nail esp. as used for railways; (Bot.) flower-cluster of many sessile flowers arranged closely on long common axis; separate sprig of any plant in which flowers form ~like cluster; ‖ (colloq.) a 'spiky' Anglican [back

formation f. L spika)]; ~ oil (got from lavender); ~ plank, bridge before mizzen-mast of vessel meant for arctic service. 2. v.t. Fasten with ~s, furnish with ~s; plug up vent of (cannon) with ~, (fig.) make useless. Hence ~'LET(-kī-) n., (bot.,) ~'WISE(-kw-) adv., spik'y²a. (also, colloq.) of hard un-yielding 'high-church' views. [ME, cf. Sw. & Norw. spik, Du. spijker, nail; partly also f. L spíca ear of corn]

spike'nard (-kn-), n. (Ancient costly aromatic ointment made chiefly from) peren-nial herb allied to valerian; kinds of fragrant oil. [f. LL spíca nardi (of NARD)]

spile, n., & v.t. 1. Wooden peg, spigot; large timber for driving into ground, pile. 2. v.t. Make ~-hole in (cask). [(vb f. n., cf. Du. spijl spile, bar, G spell skewer; in sense spile perh. corrupt. of PILE¹]

spil'ing, n. Set of piles; (Naut.) edge-curve of plank in vessel's hull. [f. prec. +-ING¹; partly dub.]

spill¹, v.t. & i. (spilt or ~ed) & n. 1. Allow (liquid, substance in small particles) to fall or run out from vessel, as spill the salt, no use crying over spilt milk, (of liquid etc.) fall or run out; ~ blood, be guilty of bloodshed, ~ the blood of, kill; ~ money (sl.), lose it in betting etc.; (Naut.) empty (belly of sail) of wind. ~ the beans (sl.), give the show away. divulge information indiscreetly; throw from saddle or vehicle, as horse spilt him, was spilt from a dog-cart. 2. n. Such throwing, as had a nasty ~; ~'way, passage for surplus water from dam. [OE spillan destroy, cf. ON spilla, Du. spillen, G (ver)spillen, also OE spildan (the orig. form)]

spill², n. Thin strip of wood, spiral tube etc. of paper for lighting candles etc. [ME, perh. cogn. w. SPILE]

spill'er n. Seine put into a larger one to take out fish when the larger cannot be hauled ashore. [?]

spill'ikin, n. Splinter of wood, bone, etc. used in some games; (pl. also spellicans) game played with ~s. [f. SPILL², see -KIN]

spilt. See SPILL¹.

spilth, n. (arch.). What is spilt; excess, surplus. [-TH¹]

spin, v.t. & i. (span or spun, spun) 1. Draw out & twist (wool, cotton, or abs.) into threads; make (yarn) thus. 2. (Of spider, silkworm, etc.) make (web, gossamer, cocoon, or abs.) by extrusion of fine viscous thread. 3. Form (cup etc.) in lathe or similar machine. 4. (fig.) Produce, compose, (narrative, literary article, etc.; often out i.e. at great length, esp. ~ a yarn (orig. Naut.), tell a story. 5. ~ out, spend, consume, (time, one's life, etc., by discussion etc., in occupation etc.); prolong (discussion etc.). 6. Cause (top etc.) to whirl round, (of top

whirl round, turn (person, thing) quickly round, (of person etc.) turn thus, e.g. as result of blow, as *sent him ~ing*. **7.** Fish in (stream, pool) with swivel or spoon-bait. **8.** || (sl.). Reject (candidate) after examination. **9.** p.p. (sl.). Tired out, done. **10.** *Spun glass* (spun when heated into filaments that remain pliant when cold); *spun gold, silver, gold, silver, thread prepared for weaving*; *spun silk*, cheap material of short-fibred & waste silk often mixed with cotton; *spun yarn* (Naut.), line formed of rope-yarns twisted together. [OE *spinnan*, cf. Du. & G *spinnen*, ON *spinna*, cogn. w. SPAN]

spin², n. Spinning motion, whirl; (Aviation) diving descent combined with rotation; secondary revolving motion esp. as developed in rifle bullet, or in billiard or tennis ball struck aslant; (Cricket) twisting motion given to ball when bowled (*~ bowler*, expert at this); brisk or short run or spell of driving, rowing, bicycling, etc., as *went for a ~*. [f. prec.]

spin´ach, ~age, (-nij), n. Garden vegetable with thick succulent leaves used when boiled as food; other plants similarly used. Hence **spina´ceous** (-āshəs) a. [f. OF *espinache, -age*, perh. f. Arab. *isfīnāj* f. Pers. *isfānāj*, but usn. assoc. w. L *spina* thorn]

spin´al, a. Of the spine, as *~ curvature, complaint; ~ column, spine; ~ cord*, cylindrical structure within *~ canal*, a part of the central nervous system. [f. LL *spinalis* (SPINE, -AL)]

spin´dle, n., & v.i. **1.** Pin in spinning-wheel used for twisting & winding the thread; small bar serving same purposes in hand-spinning; pin bearing bobbin of spinning-machine; pin, axis, that revolves or on which a thing revolves; *live* (revolving) *~, dead* (non-revolving) *~*; slender thing or part; varying measure of length for yarn. **2.** *~-shanked*, with long thin legs, *~-shanks*, person with such legs; *~-shaped*, of circular cross-section & tapering towards each end; *~-tree*, shrub or small tree with hard wood used for *~*; hence **spind´ly** a., slender, attenuated. **3.** v.i. Have, grow into, long slender form. [(vb f. n.) OE *spinl*, as SPIN¹+phonetic *-d-* +-LE(1)]

spin´drift, n. Spray blown along surface of sea; *~ clouds*, light feathery clouds. [var. of *spoon-drift* or *spoon-drift*, etym. dub.]

spine, n. The series of the vertebrae, backbone; *railway ~e*, concussion of *~e* due to railway accident; (Bot.) stiff sharp woody process due to degeneracy or modification of some organ; sharp ridge or projection; the part of a book's cover or jacket visible when it is in place on a shelf; *~e-back*, kinds of fish with *~es* in or in front of dorsal fins. Hence

[f. OF *espine* thorn f. L *spina* thorn, backbone]

spin´el, n. Kinds of mineral of various colours occurring in regular crystals; *~ ruby*, valuable red variety. [f. OF (e)*spinelle*, etym. dub.]

spine´less (-nl-), a. Having no spine, invertebrate; (fig.) limp, weak, having no backbone; (of fish) having no fin-spines. [-LESS]

spin´et (or *-ět´*), n. (hist.). Small wing-shaped harpsichord with one string to each note. [f. F *espinette* (now *épinette*) prob. f. G. *Spinetti*, inventor]

spin´i- in comb. = L *spina* thorn, back-bone, as: *~aci´rebrate*, having brain & spinal cord; *~if´erous*, having or producing spines; *~iform*.

spinn´aker, n. Large jib-shaped sail carried on mainmast of racing-yacht running before wind. [f. *Sphinx*, name of yacht using it]

spinn´er, n. In vbl senses, esp.: thread-spinning machine; person who shapes vessels etc. in lathe; (also *~et¹* n.) spinning-organ in spider, silkworm, etc.

|| **spinn´ey,** n. (pl. *~s*). Small wood, thicket. [f. OF *espinaye* (espine, see SPINE)]

spinn´ing, n. In vbl senses; *~-house* (chiefly hist.), house of correction for prostitutes; *~-jenny,* mechanism for spinning more than one strand at a time; *~-machine*, (esp.) machine that spins fibres continuously; *~-wheel* (hist.), household implement for spinning yarn or thread, with fly-wheel driven by crank or treadle. [-ING¹]

So *~ist* n., *~is´tic* a. [-ISM]

spin´ster, n. Unmarried (esp. elderly in pop. use) woman. Hence *~HOOD* n. [ME, orig. = woman who spins (SPIN¹, see -STER)]

spintha´riscope, n. Screen of zinc blende showing incidence of alpha particles (of ALPHA *rays*) by fluorescent flash. [f. Gk *spintharis* spark+-SCOPE]

spin´ule n. (bot., zool.). Small spine. Hence *~IF´EROUS, ~OSE¹, ~OUS,* aa. [f. L *spinula* (as SPINE, see -ULE)]

spin´|y, a. Full of spines, prickly, esp. in names of animals, as *~y crab, lobster, rat*; (fig.) perplexing, troublesome, thorny. Hence *~INESS* n. [-Y²]

spir´acle, n. (zool.). Kinds of breathing-hole in animals, e.g. blow-hole of cetaceans. Hence **spirac´ular,** **spirac´ulate²,** aa. [f. L *spiraculum* (also used in E) f. *spirare* breathe]

spiraea, n. Kinds of rosaceous plant with small white or pink flowers. [L, f. Gk *speiraia* meadowsweet (*speira* coil)]

Spinoz´|ism, n. Doctrine of B. **de** Spinoza, a Spanish Jew (d. 1677), that there is one sole & infinite substance of which extension & mind are attributes & individual beings are changing forms.

spīr′al, a., n., & v.t. (-ll-). **1.** Coiled; winding continually about & constantly receding from a centre, whether remaining in same plane like watch-spring or rising in a cone; winding continually & advancing as if along cylinder, like thread or screw; ~ *spring*; ~ *wheel* (with teeth cut at angle to axis). **2.** n. Plane or other ~ *curve*, ~ *spring*, ~ *formation in shell* etc.; (fig.) gradual but progressive rise or fall (*the vicious* ~ *of rising prices and wages*). **3.** v.t. Make ~. Hence ~ITY (-ăl-) n., ~LY² adv. [f. med. L *spiralis* (as SPIRE², see -AL)]

spīr′ant, a. & n. (phonet.) (Consonant) uttered with perceptible expulsion of breath & in producing which the organs are near together but not wholly closed, continuable (consonant) (cf. EXPLOSIVE), e.g. *f, v, th, dh,* & occas. *w, y,* & others. [f. L *spirāre* breathe, see -ANT]

spīre¹, n., & v.i. & t. 1. Tapering structure in form of tall cone or pyramid rising above tower; continuation of tree trunk above point where branching begins; any tapering body, e.g. stalk of grass. **2.** v.i. Shoot up. **3.** v.t. Furnish with ~. Hence **spīr′y²** a. [OE *spīr,* cf. Du. & G *spier*]

spīre², n. Spiral, coil; single twist of this. Hence **spīr′y²** a. [F, f. L f. Gk *speira* coil]

spīrill′um, n. (pl. *-la*). Group of bacteria characterized by a spiral structure; any member of this. [dim. of L *spīra* SPIRE²]

spĭr′it¹, n. 1. Intelligent or immaterial part of man, soul; in (the) ~, inwardly, as *groaned in* ~, *was vexed in* ~, *shall be with you in* (the) ~. **2.** Person viewed as possessing this, esp. w. reference to particular mental or moral qualities, as *one of the most ardent* ~*s of his time, a meeting of choice* ~*s; a master*~, person of commanding intellect etc. **3.** Rational or intelligent being not connected with material body, disembodied soul, incorporeal being, elf, fairy, as *God is a* ~, *the Holy S*~ (third person of the Trinity) *has seen a* ~, *~s must have been at work, peace to his departed spirit*; **4.** Person's mental or moral nature or qualities, as *a man of an unbending* ~; *the poor in* ~, *the meek*. **5.** Courage, self-assertion, vivacity, energy, dash, as *if you had the* ~ *of a mouse, do shoot a little* ~, *went at it with* ~, *infused* ~ *into his men, people of* ~. **6.** Person viewed as supplying this (= *soul,* but usu. w. adj.), as *was the animating* ~ *of the rebellion.* **7.** Mental or moral condition or attitude, mood, as *took it in a wrong* ~, *depends on the* ~ *in which it is done, did it in a* ~ *of mischief, objections made in a captious* ~. **8.** Real meaning opp. to verbal expression, as *must consider the* ~ *of the law, not the letter, have followed out the* ~ *of his instructions.* **9.** Animating principle or influence, mental or moral tendency, as *cannot resist the* ~ *of the age or times, governing vital phenomena,* whence (mod.) ANIMAL ~*s; high or great* ~*s, cheerfulness & buoyancy; poor or low* ~*s, depression.* **11.** (Usu. pl.) strong distilled liquor esp. alcohol, e.g. brandy, whisky, gin, rum, as *glass of* ~ *& water,* ARDENT~*s, touches no* ~ *but gin.* **12.** Solution (of volatile principle) in alcohol, tincture; ~*s of salt,* hydrochloric acid; ~ *or* ~*s of wine,* alcohol; METHYLATED ~; **13.** ~ *duck,* kinds of duck diving rapidly at flash of gun etc.; || ~*lamp* (burning alcohol instead of oil); ~*level,* glass tube partly filled with ~ for testing horizontality; ~*rapper, person professing to hold intercourse with departed* ~*s by means of their raps on table etc., so* ~*rapping;* ~*room (Naut.), paymaster's store-room, formerly used for* ~*s.* [f. L *spīritus* breath, spirit, f. *spirāre* breathe]

spĭr′it², v.t. Convey (usu. *away, off,* etc.) rapidly and secretly (as) by agency of spirits; cheer (person, usu. *up*). [f. prec.]

spĭr′ited, a. Full of spirit, animated, lively, brisk, courageous, as *a* ~ *translation, attack, reply;* having specified spirit, as *high, mean, proud, jealous,* ~; having specified spirits, as *low*~. Hence (-)~LY² adv., ~NESS n. [-ED²]

spĭr′itless, a. Wanting in courage, vigour, or vivacity. Hence ~LY² adv., ~NESS n. [-LESS]

spĭr′itual, a. & n. 1. Of spirit as opp. to matter; of the soul esp. as acted on by God, as ~ *life;* of, proceeding from, God, holy, divine, inspired, as ~ *songs, the* ~ *law; the* ~*man,* inner nature of man, (also esp. in N.T.) regenerate man (opp. to *natural, carnal*); concerned with sacred or religious things, as *our* ~ *interests, lords* ~, bishops & archbishops in House of Lords; having the higher qualities of the mind. **2.** n. Religious song peculiar to American negroes(also *negro*~). Hence ~LY² adv., ~NESS n. [f. OF *spirituel* f. L *spiritualis* (as SPIRIT, see -AL)]

spĭr′itualism, n. Belief that departed spirits communicate with & show themselves to men. (also *modern* ~*ism*) at seances by means of spirit-rapping, -handwriting, etc., so **spĭr′itism, spĭr′itist,** nn.; (Philos.) doctrine that spirit exists as distinct from matter or that spirit is the only reality (cf. MATERIALISM). Hence or cogn. ~ISM n., ~IST²¹ a. & n. [-ISM]

spirituǎl′ity, n. Spiritual quality; (usu. pl.) what belongs or is due to the Church or to an ecclesiastic as such, as *the* ~*ies of his office,* ~ *of benefices, tithes of land etc.* [f. OF *spiritualité* f. LL *spiritualitātem*]

spiri'tualiz|e, v.t. Make spiritual, elevate, (character, person, thoughts); (rare) infuse life into, animate; attach spiritual as opp. to literal meaning to. Hence ~A'TION n. [f. F spiritualiser (as SPIRITUAL, see -IZE)]

spiritüe'(le)', a. (Chiefly of women) marked by refinement, grace, or delicacy of mind. [F. as SPIRITUAL]

spi'rituous, a. Containing much alcohol, distilled (not fermented, as ~ liquors (also used loosely of beer etc.). Hence ~NESS n. [f. OF spiritueux f. L as SPIRIT, -OUS]

spir'itus, n. (Gk gram.). = ăs'per, lēn'īs, = rough, smooth, BREATHING[1]. [L]

spir'ivalve, a. Having spiral shell; (of shell) spiral. [f. L spīra SPIRE[2] + valva door]

spīrk'eting, n. Inside planking between top of waterways & lower sills of ports. [f.obs. spirket, spur-, etym. dub.]

spīro-[1] in comb. = Gk speīra coil, as ~chaete (-kēt'ē), spiral-shaped bacterium. **spīr'o-[2]** in comb. (irreg.) = L spīro breathe in sense ' breath', as: ~ograph, instrument for marking breathing movement; ~om'eter, ~oscope, instrument for measuring lung capacity, &c. ~ometric a., ~ometry n.; ~ophore, instrument for inducing respiration in cases of suspended animation.

spurt, spŏrt, v.i. & t., & n. 1. Gush out in a jet or stream; cause (liquid etc.) to do this. 2. n. Sudden gushing out, jet. [?]

spit[1], n., & v.t. (-tt-). 1. Slender bar on which meat that is to be roasted is made to rotate before fire; small point of land running into sea; long narrow underwater bank. 2. v.t. Thrust a ~ through (meat etc.); (fig.) pierce, transfix, with sword etc. [(vb f.n.) OE spitu, cf. Du. spit, G spiess]

spit[2], v.i. & t. (spat or arch. spit), & n. 1. Eject saliva (~ & ~ polish, furbishing work of soldier etc.): eject (saliva, blood, food etc. out) from mouth; (fig.) utter (oaths, threats, etc.) vehemently (~ it out, sl., exhortation to speak or sing louder); (of cat etc., fig. of person) make noise as of ~ting as sign of anger or hostility; (of rain) fall lightly, (of fire, candle, pen) send out sparks, stray ink, etc.; ~ at or upon, (fig.) treat with ignominy; ~'fire, person of fiery temper, (also ~'devil) toy cone of wet gunpowder ~ting when ignited. Hence ~t'ER[1] n. 2. n. ~ting (spittle; the (very) ~ of (exact counterpart of, likeness of, as he is the very ~ of his father). [(n. f. vb) OE spittan, also spǣtan (whence past & p.p. spat): prob. cogn. w. ON spýta, Da. spytte, Sw. spotta, and w. SPOUT]

spit[3], n. Spade-depth (dig it two ~s or ~ deep). [Du., cf. OE spittan dig]

spitch'cŏck, n. & v.t. 1. Eel split & broiled. 2. v.t. Prepare thus (eel, fish, bird). [f. 16th c., etym. dub.]

spite, n., & v.t. 1. Ill will, malice, as did it from pure ~ or in or out of ~; grudge, as has a ~ against me; (in) ~ of, notwithstanding. 2. v.t. Thwart, mortify, annoy, as does it to ~ me, cut off one's nose to ~ one's face, injure oneself by vindictive or resentful conduct. Hence ~'FUL (-tf-) a., ~'fully[2] adv., ~'fulness n. [(vb f. n.) short for DESPITE]

spit'tle, n. Saliva esp. as ejected from mouth. [OE spǣtl (spǣtan SPIT[2])]

spittoon', n. Vessel to spit into, usu. round metal or earthenware vessel with funnel-shaped top. [irreg. f. SPIT[2] + -OON]

spitz, n. (Also ~dog) small kind of dog with pointed muzzle, Pomeranian. [G spitz(hund) f. spitz pointed, hund dog]

‖ **spiv,** n. (sl.). Shady character who avoids honest work & lives by his wits esp. in black-market traffic. [?]

splanch'nic (-ngk-), a. Of the entrails, intestinal. So ~o- comb. form, ~oï'ŏGY, ~OT'OMY, nn. [f. Gk splagkhnikos (splagkhna entrails, see -IC)]

splatter (person etc. with water, mud, etc.); dash, spatter, (liquid about, on or over person etc.); (of liquid) fly about in drops or scattered portions; (of person) cause liquid to do this, make one's way, move across, along, etc., thus; step, fall, plunge, etc., into (water etc.) so as to ~ it; decorate with scattered ornamentation. 2. n. ~ing; quantity of liquid ~ed; resulting noise, as we heard a ~; ‖(colloq.) small quantity of soda-water etc. (diluting whisky etc.); spot of dirt etc. ~ed on to things; patch of colour esp. on animal's skin; make a ~, (fig.) attract much attention, create sensation; complexion powder usu. of rice-flour; ~-board, guard in front of wheeled vehicle to keep mud off occupants. Hence ~'Y[2] a. [=FLASH with emphat. s- (= OF es- f. L EX-)]

splash'er, n. In vbl senses; also: kinds of guard placed over wheels of locomotive etc. to keep off mud etc.; screen behind wash-stand to protect wall. [-ER[1]]

splătt'er, v.i. & t. Make continuous splashing sound; speak (a language, or abs.) unintelligibly; ‖~dash, noise, clamour; ‖~dashes, = SPATTERdashes. [prob. var. of SPATTER]

splay, v.t. & i., & n., & a. 1. Construct (aperture) with divergent sides (~ed loop-hole, window, doorway, with opening wider at one side of wall), (of aperture or its sides) be so shaped or set; dislocate (esp. horse's shoulder). 2. n. Surface making oblique angle with another, e.g. ~ed side of window, embrasure. 3. adj. Wide & flat, turned outward; ~ foot n. & a., (having) broad flat foot turned outward; ~ mouth, wide mouth, mouth stretched wide in grimace. [(n. & adj. f. vb) ME splayen, short for DISPLAY]

spleen, n. 1. Organ producing certain

modifications in the blood of most vertebrates, situated in mammals at left of
stomach. 2. Lowness of spirits, ill temper,
spite, as *a fit of* ~, *vented his* ~,
~'FUL, ~'ISH¹, ~'Y², aa., ~'fully,
~'ishly¹ adv. 3. ~'*wort*, kinds of fern
formerly used for ~ disorders. Hence
~'LESS a. [f. L f. Gk *splēn*]

splēn'dent, a. (mineral., entom.). Having
bright metallic lustre. [f. L *splendēre*
shine, see -ENT]

splēn'did, a. Magnificent, gorgeous,
sumptuous, glorious, brilliant, as *a* ~
palace, gift, achievement, victory; (of person) affecting splendour (*in surroundings*
etc.); (colloq.) excellent, capital, as *here's
a* ~ *chance of escape.* Hence ~'LY² adv.
[f. L *splendidus* (as prec., see -ID¹)]

splen'dour (-der), n. Great or dazzling
brightness; magnificence, grandeur;
(Her.) *sun in* ~ (with rays & human face).
[OF., f. L *splendorem* (as SPLENDENT, see
-OR¹)]

splenif'ic, a. & n. 1. Ill-tempered,
peevish, whence ~'ICALLY adv.; a. of the
spleen. 2. n. Medicine for, sufferer from,
disease of the spleen. [f. L f. L *splenicus*
(as SPLEEN, see -ETIC)]

splēn'ial, a. (anat.). Acting like a splint;
of the splenius. [-AL]

splēn'ic. a. Of, in, the spleen, as ~ *fever,*
anthrax. So **splēn'OID** a. [f. L f. Gk
splēnikos (as SPLEEN, see -IC)]

splēn'ius, n. (pl. -ii). (Either section of)
muscle on back & sides of neck serving to
draw back the head. [f. Gk *splēnion*
bandage]

spleniza'tion, n. Conversion of lung into
substance resembling spleen. [-IZE,
-ATION]

splice, v.t., & n. 1. Join ends of (ropes) by
interweaving strands; join (pieces of timber etc.) in overlapping position; (colloq.)
join in marriage, as *when did he or they
get* ~*d* ?; ~ *the* MAIN³ *brace.* 2. n. Junction of two ropes or pieces of wood etc.
by splicing; EYE¹-~; *sit on the* ~ (Cricket,
sl.), play a cautious defensive game,
stonewall. [(n. f. vb) MDu. *splissen*
perh. cogn. w. SPLIT]

spline, n., & v.t. 1. Rectangular key
fitting into grooves in hub & shaft of
wheel & allowing longitudinal play; slat;
flexible wood or rubber strip used in
drawing large curves esp. in railway work.
2. v.t. fit with ~. [?]

splint, n. & v.t. 1. Strip of rigid or flexible material for holding broken bone

when set or for basketwork etc.; (Anat.,
also ~*-bone*) either of two small bones in
horse's foreleg lying behind & in close
contact with cannon-bone, (in man)
fibula; tumour on, callus due to disease
of, ~*-bone* of horse; ~*-coal*, cannel coal
of slaty structure. 2. v.t. Confine (broken
limb etc.) with ~s. [(vb f. n.) f. MDu. or
MLG *splinte* metal plate or pin]

splin'ter, n. & v.t. & i. 1. Split (t. & i.)
into long thin pieces, shiver. 2. n. Sharp-
edged or thin piece broken off from wood,
stone, etc.; ||~*-bar*, cross-bar in vehicle
supporting springs or to which traces are
attached; ~*-bone,* fibula; ~*-proof* (against
~s of bursting shells or bombs). [(n. f.
vb) MDu., cf. prec.]

splin'tery, a. Of splinters; splinter-like;
apt to splinter. [-Y²]

split, v.t. & i. (*split*). 1. Break forcibly,
be broken, into parts esp. with the grain
or plane of cleavage. 2. Divide into parts,
thicknesses, etc., as ~ *it into three layers,*
the job, sum, etc., was ~ (usu. *among*
6 *of us,* ~ *one's* vote, vote for each of opposed candidates, ~ *the difference,* take
mean quantity etc. between two proposed; ~ *hairs,* draw over-subtle distinctions, so HAIR-~ting. 3. Divide (t. & i.)
into disagreeing or hostile parties (*on*
question etc.). 4. ~ (one's *sides or intr.)
be convulsed with laughter, so *side-~ting*
a. & n., *side-~ter* (person or joke); *head
is* ~*ting* (feels acute pain), a ~*ting* (acute)
headache. 5. ~ *on* (sl.), betray the secrets
of (accomplice etc.). 6. ~ *cloth* (Surg.),
bandage with several tails esp. for head
& face; ~ *gear, wheel* (made in halves for
removal from shaft); ~ *infinitive* (with
adverb etc. inserted between *to* and verb,
e.g. *seems to partly correspond*); ~ *mess,*
kinds of which capsules ~ at maturity;
~ *pease*(-) (dried & ~ in half for cooking);
~ PIN¹; ~ *ring* (usu. of steel on the pattern of those used for bunches of keys);
~ *second,* a very short period of time;
~ *shot, stroke, stroke* at croquet driving
two touching balls in different directions.
Hence (-)~TER¹(1, 2) n. [f. MDu. *splitten,*
cf. Du. *splitten* & *splijten,* G *spleissen*]

split², n. 1. Splitting; fissure, rent, crack.
2. Separation into parties, schism, rupture. 3. Split osier etc. for parts of basket-
work; each of the strips of steel, cane,
etc., of reed in loom; single thickness of
split hide. 4. (In faro) turning up of two
cards of equal value so that stakes are
divided. 5. Half bottle of aerated water,
half glass of liquor. 6. pl. Acrobat's trick
of sitting on ground with legs spread out
laterally, as *do* ~s. [f. prec.]

splosh, n. (colloq.). A quantity of water
suddenly dropped or thrown down; ||(sl.)
money. [imit.]

splotch, splōdge, nn. Daub, smear.
Hence **splōtch'y²,** a. [*ch* t. 17th, *dge*
19th, c.; etym. dub.]

splurge, n., & v.i. (Make) noisy display or effort. [U.S. wd., prob. imit.]

splütt'er, v.i. & t. & n. =SPUTTER. Hence **~ER¹** n. [for -t- cf. SP(L)ATTER]

Spode, n. A fine pottery. [J. ~, maker, d. 1827]

spoff'ish, a. (sl.), Bustling, fussy. [?]

spoil, n. **1.** (Usu. pl. or collect. sing.) plunder taken from enemy in war, (fig.) profit, advantage, accruing from success in contest etc., emoluments of public office etc. **2.** *~s system*, practice of giving public offices to adherents of successful party, whence *~s'man*, advocate of, one who seeks to profit by, this. **3.** A draw in the game of *~five*, in which each player has five cards. **4.** Earth etc. thrown or brought up in excavating, dredging, etc. [f. OF *espoille* f. L *spolium* skin stripped off animal, (usu. pl.) spoil]

spoil², v.t. & i. (~*t* or ~*ed*). **1.** (arch., literary; never ~*t*). Plunder, deprive (person of thing), by force or stealth, as ~ *the Egyptians* (persons regarded as one's natural enemies etc.; *Exod.* xii. 36). **2.** Impair the qualities of, or person's enjoyment of, as *was quite ~t by the rain*, *will ~ all the fun, always ~t by the news ~t his dinner, ~ one's beauty for him* (with black eye etc.). **3.** Injure character of (person etc.) by indulgence, as *spare the rod & ~ the child, are determined to ~ me, is the ~t child of fortune*. **4.** (sl.). Maim or kill or do for (person). **5.** (Of fruit, fish, etc., fig. of joke etc.) decay, go bad, as *will not ~ with keeping, dog is ~ing* (ripe, eager) *for a fight*. **6.** *~sport*, one who ~s sport. Hence ~**ER¹** n. [f. OF *espoillier* f. L *spoliare* strip, plunder (as prec.)]

spoil'age, n. Paper spoilt in printing. [-AGE]

spoke¹, n., & v.t. **1.** Each of the bars running from hub to rim of wheel, whence ~*WISE* (-kw-) adv.; rung of ladder; each radial handle of steering-wheel of vessel; bar used to prevent wheel from turning esp. in going down hill, as (fig.) *put a ~ in person's wheel*, thwart his purposes; ~*bone*, radius of forearm; ~*shave*, plane-bit between two handles, used for ~s & other esp. curved work where ordinary plane is not available. **2.** v.t. Furnish with ~s, check (wheel) with ~; *spoking-machine* (for giving uniform inclination to ~s of wheel). [(vrb f. n.) OE *spāca*, cf. Du. *speek*, G *speiche*]

spoke², **spoken**, **-spoken**. See SPEAK. **spokes'man** (-ks-), n. (pl. *-men*). One who speaks for others, representative. [irreg. f. SPOKE² +-ES +MAN]

spōl'ia opīm'a, n. (Rom. Ant.) arms stripped from hostile general by Roman commander in single combat; (fig.) supreme achievement or distinction. [L, =rich spoils]

spolia'tion, n. Plunder, pillage, esp. of

neutral vessels by belligerent, (fig.) extortion; (Eccl.) taking of fruits of benefice under pretended title, *writ of ~* (for recovery of these); (Law) destruction, mutilation, alteration, of document to prevent its being used as evidence. Hence or cogn. **spōl'iātor²** n., **spōl'ia-tory** a. [f. L *spoliationem* (as SPOIL², see -ATION)]

spondā'ic, a. Of spondees; (of hexameter) having spondee as fifth foot. [f. F *spondaïque* ult. f. Gk *spondeiakos* (as foll., see -AO)]

spon'dee (-dī), n. Metrical foot – –. [f. L f. Gk *spondeios* (*pous* foot) used in making treaty (*spondai* n. pl. f. *spendō* make libation)]

****spondü'ricks**, n. pl. (sl.). Money. [?] **spon'dyl(e)**, n. Joint of backbone, vertebra. Hence ~(O)- comb. form. [F (-le), f. L f. Gk *spondulos* (prop- *spho-*)]

sponge¹ (-ŭnj), n. **1.** Aquatic animal of low order with pores in the body-wall, whence **spōngōl'OGIST**, **spōngōl'OGY**, (-nġĕ-), nn. **2.** Skeleton of a ~ or colony of ~s (whence **spo'ngi**FORM (-ĭnj-) a.), esp. elastic kind chiefly from the Levant used as absorbent in bathing, cleansing surfaces, etc.; *throw up the ~*, (of boxer or his attendant) throw into the air as token of defeat (the ~ used between rounds, fig.) abandon contest, own oneself beaten; *pass the ~ over*, agree to forget (offence etc.). **3.** Thing of ~like absorbency or consistence, e.g. piece of leavened dough, ~*gourd*, *vegetable ~*, kind of gourd used in Turkish baths as rubber or towel, loofah; ~ *tent*, compressed ~ for keeping wound etc. open; ~*free*, spiny tropical shrub of bean family with globose heads of fragrant yellow flowers. [OE, f. L f. Gk *spoggia* var. of *spŏbggos*, cf. FUNGUS]

sponge² (-ŭnj), v.t. & i., & n. **1.** Wipe, cleanse, with sponge; sluice water over (parts of body etc., or abs., often *down*, *over*) with sponge; wipe out, efface, (writing, fig. memory of thing etc., usu. *out*) with sponge; absorb, take *up*, (water etc.) with sponge; gather sponges; procure by sycophantic arts; ~ *on*, live as the parasite of, be meanly dependent on (person *for* thing). **2.** n. Sponging, bath with sponge, as *had a ~ down*. Hence **spo'ng**ER¹(1, 2)(-ĭnj-) n. [(n.f.vb) f. LL *spongiare* (as prec.)]

spo'nging (-ĭnj-), n. In vbl senses; ~*house* (hist., in arch. sense *sneezing*), bailiff's house for temporary lodging of arrested debtor. [-ING¹]

spongiopiline (spŭnji-), n. Substitute for poultice made of sponge & fibre backed with rubber. [as SPONGE¹ + Gk *pīlos* felt + -INE⁴]

spongy (-ĭnjĭ), a. Like sponge; porous, compressible, elastic, absorbent, as sponge; (of metal) finely divided & loosely coherent. Hence ~INESS n. [-Y²]

spónsion (-shn), n. Being surety for another; (Internat. Law) engagement made on behalf of State by agent not specially authorized. [f. L *sponsio* (*spon-dēre spons-* promise, see -ION)]

spónson, n. Projection from side of warship to enable gun to be trained forward & aft; triangular platform before & abaft paddle-box. [?]

spónsor, n. & v.t. 1. Godfather or god-mother; person who makes himself responsible for another; advertiser who pays for a broadcast programme into which advertisements of his wares are introduced. 2. v.t. Be ~ for. Hence ~SHIP n. [L (*spondēre spons-* promise, see -OR²)]

spontáné̈ous, a. 1. Acting, done, occur-ring, without external cause; voluntary, without external incitement, as *made a ~ offer of his services*; (of sudden move-ments etc.) involuntary, not due to conscious volition; growing naturally without cultivation; (Biol., of structural changes in plants, muscular activity in esp. young animals) instinctive, auto-matic, prompted by no motive; (of bodily movements, literary style, etc.) gracefully natural & unconstrained. 2. ~ *combustion*, ignition of mineral or veget-able substance (e.g. heap of rags soaked with oil, mass of wet coal) from heat en-gendered by rapid oxidation; ~ *genera-tion*, production of living from non-living matter as inferred from appearance of life (due in fact to bacteria etc.) in some in-fusions; ~ *suggestion* (from association of ideas without conscious volition). Hence or cogn. spóntané̈ITY, ~NESS nn., ~LY² adv. [f. L *spontaneus* (*sponte* of one's own accord, see -ANEOUS)]

spontóon, n. (hist.). Kind of halberd used by some British infantry officers. [f. F *sponton* f. It. *spontone* f. *puntone*, *punto*, point]

spoof, v.t. & n. (sl.). Swindle, humbug, hoax; (attrib.) faked or fabricated. Hence ~'ER¹ n. [arbitrary]

spook, n. (joc.). Ghost. Hence ~'ISH, ~'Y² aa. [Du., cf. G *spuk*]

spool, n. & v.t. 1. Reel for winding yarn, photographic film, etc., on; revolving shaft of angler's reel. 2. v.t. Wind on ~. [f. MDu. *spoele*, cf. Sw *spole*, G *spule*]

spoon, n., & v.t. 1. Utensil consist-ing of round or usu. oval bowl & a handle for conveying esp. liquid food to mouth, usu. of silver or plated metal for table use (*tea, dessert, table, ~, of small,* medium, large, size, esp. as recognized measure for medicine; APOSTLE ~, EGG¹, *salt, mustard, ~*; *narrow-~*, for getting marrow from bones) & of wood or iron for cooking etc.; BORN *with silver ~ in mouth*; *long ~ & the devil* (see SUP); *wooden ~* (hist.), (wooden ~ given to) last man in Cambridge mathematical tripos; EGG¹-*&-~ race*; *~-shaped thing*, esp. (oar with) broad curved blade, wooden golf-club with more loft than driver & brassie. 2. ~ (*-bait*), bright revolving ~-shaped piece of metal used as lure in fishing; *~-beak, -bill*, kinds of bird; *~-drift*, see SPINDRIFT; *~-fed*, (fig., of industries etc.) artificially encouraged by bounties or import duties; *~-meat*, liquid food, food for infants (also fig.); *~-net*, angler's landing-net. 3. vb. Take (liquid etc., usu. *up, out*) with a ~; fish with ~-bait; (Cro-quet) make pushing stroke; (Cricket) strike (ball) feebly, send *up* (ball, a catch). Hence (-)~FUL n. [vb f. n.) OE *spōn*, cf. Du. *spaan*, G *span*]

spoon², n., & v.i. & t. (sl.). 1. Simpleton; silly or demonstratively fond lover; *be ~s on*, be sillily in love with. 2. vb. Behave amorously, behave thus towards (girl etc.). [f. prec.]

spooner'ism, n. Accidental transposi-tion of initial letters etc. of two or more words (e.g. *has just received a blushing crow*, for *real enjoyment give me a well-boiled icycle*). [f. Rev. W. A. *Spooner* (d. 1930), esteemed for ~s, + -ISM]

spoon[ý s a. & n. (sl.). 1. Soft, silly; senti-mental, amorous, sweet (*upon*. 2. n. Mild simpleton. Hence ~ILY² adv., ~i-NESS n. [prob. f. SPOON², -Y²]

spoor, n., & v.t. & i. 1. Track, scent, of animal. 2. vb. Follow by ~. Hence ~'ER¹ n. [Du., perh. cogn. w. SPUR, cf. OE & ON *spor*, G *spur*]

sporádic, a. Occurring only here & there, separate, scattered. Hence ~AL a. (rare), ~ALLY² adv., ~ALNESS n. [f. med. L f. Gk *sporadikos* (*sporas -ados* scattered, cf. *speirō* sow, see -IC)]

sporán'gium, n. (bot.). Case in which spores are produced. [f. Gk *spora* SPORE + *aggeion* vessel]

spore, n. (Bot., in cryptogamous plants) single cell that becomes free & capable of individual development; (Biol.) min-ute organic body that develops into new individual; (fig.) seed, germ, of any-thing. [f. Gk *spora* sowing, seed, f. *speirō* sow]

sporo- in comb. = prec., as: *~ogen'esis*, spore-formation; *~o'genous*, producing spores.

spo'rran, n. Pouch, usu. covered with fur etc., worn by Highlander in front of kilt. [f. Gael. *sporan*]

sport, n., & v.i. & t. 1. Amusement, diversion, fun; *in ~*, jestingly; *make ~ of*, turn into ridicule, make fun of; *be the ~*

(plaything, butt) of *Fortune* etc.; pastime, game; outdoor pastime, e.g. hunting, fishing, racing; *have good ~s*, esp. make good bag or basket when shooting etc.; *athletic ~s*, running, jumping, putting weight, etc., meeting of athletes to compete in these, as *school ~s, inter-university ~s* (*~s coat, jacket*, giving freedom of movement; *~s field; ~s car*, for racing); animal, plant, deviating suddenly or strikingly from normal type; (sl.) good fellow, *~sman; ~s'man, ~s'woman*, person fond of *~s* esp. hunting, shooting, or fishing, (fig.) person who regards life as a game in which opponents must be allowed fair play, person ready to play a bold game, whence *~s'manship* n.; *~s'man-like*, befitting, worthy of, a *~sman*. 2. vb. Divert oneself, take part in pastime; (part.) interested in *~*, as *a ~ing man, ~smanlike*, as *~ing conduct, ~ing offer*, whence *~ing*LY² adv.: (Bot., Zool.) become or produce a *~*; wear, exhibit, produce, esp. ostentatiously, as *~ed a gold tie-pin; || ~ one's* OAK. [short for DISPORT]

spor'tive, a. Playful. Hence ~LY² adv., ~NESS n. [-IVE]

spo'rule, n. Spore; small spore. Hence ~AR¹ a. [-ULE]

spot¹, n. 1. Particular place, definite locality, as *dropped it on this precise ~, the ~ where William III landed; a tender ~*, (fig.) subject on which one is touchy. 2. Small part of the surface of a thing distinguished by colour, texture, etc., usu. round or less elongated than a streak or stripe, small mark or stain, pimple, as *a blue tie with pink ~s*, SUN~, *can the* LEOPARD *change his ~s?*; (fig.) moral blemish, stain, as *without a ~ on his reputation*. 3. Kinds of fish & domestic pigeon. 4. (sl.) Act of spotting winner etc.; horse etc. so spotted. 5. (colloq.). Small quantity of anything (*a ~ of leave, lunch*); a drink. 6. (billiards), Small round black patch near each end of table equidistant from sides; || *~-stroke*, pocketing red ball when placed on *~* remote from balk; || *~-barred game* (in which successive *~-strokes* are not allowed); *~ (-ball)*, white ball distinguished from the other by black *~*. 7. *On the ~*, without delay or change of place, then & there, (of person) wide awake, equal to the situation, in good form at game etc.; •*put on the ~* (sl.), decide on the assassination of, murder. 8. (commerc.). *~ cash, cotton, wheat, prices* (to be paid or delivered immediately on sale); *~s*, commodities sold for *~ cash*. 9. *~light* (Theatr.), beam of light thrown on a particular actor, or the projector used for this purpose (also fig., as LIMELIGHT). Hence ~LESS, ~LY², aa., ~'lessLY² adv., ~'lessNESS, ~'iNESS, nn. [ME, cf. MDu. *spotte, spot*]

spot², v.t. & i. (-tt-). 1. Mark, stain, soil, with spots (lit., & fig. of character etc.); (of material etc.) be (liable to be) marked with spots. 2. (colloq.). Single out beforehand (winner of race etc., horse etc. as winner for event); detect, recognize nationality etc. of, as *~ted him at once as an American, can always ~ a dun*. 3. (Mil.) locate enemy's position (esp. from the air; whence ~t'ER¹ n, aviator detailed for such work, also person trained in aircraft recognition). 4. (p.p.). Marked with spots, esp. in names of animals; || *~ted dog* (sL.) =PLUM-duff; *~ted fever*, cerebro-spinal meningitis. Hence ~t'edNESS n. [f. prec.]

spouse (-z), n. Husband or wife. [f. OF *sp(o)us* masc., *spuse* fem., f. L p.p. of *spondere* promise]

spout, v.t. & i., & n. 1. Discharge, issue, forcibly in a jet, as *blood ~s from wound, wounds ~ blood, whale ~s water*; utter (verses etc., or abs.) in declamatory manner, speechify; (sl.) pawn. 2. n. Projecting tube through which liquid etc. is poured from teapot, kettle, gutter of roof, etc.; sloping trough down which thing may be shot into receptacle, esp. *is up the ~* (in pawn); jet, column, of liquid or grain etc.; WATER¹~; (also *~hole*) spiracle of whale. Hence ~ER¹ n, ~LESS a. [ME *spouten* vb, *spoute* n., cf. Du. *spuiten*; oogn. w. SPIT²]

sprag, n. Billet of wood or similar device for checking wheel of car etc. [?]

sprain, v.t., & n. 1. Wrench (ankle, wrist, etc.) violently so as to cause pain & swelling but not dislocation. 2. n. Such wrench, resulting inflammation & swelling. [f. 17th c., etym. dub.]

|| **spraints**, n. pl. Otter's dung. [f. OF *espraintes* lit. out-pressings f. OF *espreindre* f. L EX(*primere*=*premere* press)]

sprang. See SPRING¹.

sprat, n., & v.i. (-tt-). 1. Small European herring-like fish much used as food; other kinds of fish, e.g. sand-eel, young herring; *throw a ~ to catch a herring or mackerel or whale*, risk a little to gain much; (joc.) thin child; ||*~-day*, Nov. 9, on which *~* season begins in England. 2. v.i. Fish for *~s*, whence~t'ER¹, ~t'ING, nn. [(vb f. n.) OF *sprot*, cf. G *sprott*, Du. *sprot*]

sprawl, v.i. & t., & n. 1. Spread oneself, spread (one's limbs), out in careless or ungainly way; (of writing, plant, etc.) be of irregular or straggling form; open out (troops) irregularly. 2. n. *~ing* movement or attitude. [OE *spreawlian*, cf. NFris. *sprauweli*]

spray¹, n. Branch of tree with branchlets or flowers, esp. slender or graceful one, sprig of flowers or leaves; ornament in similar form, as *a ~ of diamonds* etc.; ~drain, drain in field etc. made by filling

trench with branches. Hence ~**ey**¹ a.
[cf. CLAYEY]. [ME, etym. dub.]

spray² n., & v.t. 1. Water or other liquid
flying in small drops from force of wind,
dashing in small drops, or action of waves, or
etc.; medical or other liquid preparation
to be applied in this form with atomizer
etc. 2. v.t. Throw (liquid, or abs.) in form
of ~, sprinkle (object) thus. 3. ~'**board**
(on boat's gunwale to keep off ~). Hence
~'EN¹(1, 2) n., ~'**ey²** a. [cf. MDu.
sprueyen, MHG *spræjen*, to sprinkle]

spread (~ĕd), v.t. & i.(**spread**). 1. Extend
the surface of, cause to cover larger
surface, by unrolling, unfolding, smearing, flattening out, etc., (fig.) display
thus to eye or mind, as *peacock ~s its tail*,
~ *oneself* (sl., = talk bumptiously), ~ *a
banner*, ~ *out a rug on the grass*, ~ *butter
on bread*, *map lay ~ out on the table*, *the
~ view ~ out before us*, whence ~'ER¹(2) n.
2. Show extended or extensive surface,
as *river here ~s out to a width of half a
mile*, *on every side ~ a vast desert*, *~ing
years*. 3. Diffuse, be diffused, as *his name
~ fear in every quarter*, *rumour ~ from
mouth to mouth*, *has ~ a malicious report*.
4. Cover surface of, as *slices of bread ~
with jam*, *a table ~ with every luxury*,
meadow ~ with daisies. 5. ~ **eagle**, figure
of eagle with legs & wings extended as
seen on coins etc., skating movement on
both inside edges at once one forward
& the other back, (colloq.) fowl split open
down the back & broiled, (Naut.) person
lashed in rigging with arms and legs ~
out as punishment, (fig., ~-**eagle**) bombastic, esp. noisily patriotic, whence ~-
ea'gleism n. 6. ~-**over** (*system*), elasticity
in accommodating restricted work-hours
to special needs. [OE *sprædan*, cf. Du.
spreiden, G *spreiten*]

spread² (~ĕd), n. Spreading; capability of
expanding, as *inferior to the eagle in ~ of
wings*; increased bodily girth, as *middle-
age ~*; breadth, compass, as *arches of
equal ~*; diffusion (*of education* etc.);
(colloq.) feast, meal, as *had no end of a ~*;
*(Commerce.) difference between cost of
manufacture & selling price. [f. prec.]

spree, n., & v.i. Lively frolic, bout of
drinking etc., as *is on the* (having a) ~;
(v.i.) *have a ~*. [19th-c. sl., etym. dub.]

||**sprent**, a. (arch.). Sprinkled, over-
spread, (with drops, particles, etc.). [p.p.of
obs. *spreng* f. OE *sprengan* make SPRING¹]

sprig, n., & v.t.(-gg-). 1. Small branch,
shoot; ornament of ~ form; small headless nail: (usu. derog.) youth, young man,
as *who is this ~ ?*, *a ~ of the nobility*. 2.
v.t. Ornament with ~s, as *~ged muslin*.
3. ~'**tail**, kinds of duck & grouse with
pointed tail. Hence ~g'Y²(-g-) a. [sense
nail f. 14th, shoot f. 15th, c.; prob. two
wds; etym. dub.]

spright¹]ȳ(-īt-), a. Vivacious, lively, gay.
Hence ~IYNESS n. [f. SPRITE + -LY¹]

spring¹, v.i. & t. (**sprang**, **sprung**). 1.
Leap, jump, move rapidly or suddenly,
(often *up*, *down*, *out*, *over*, *through*, *away*,
back, etc.), as *sprang* (*up*) *from his seat*,
sprang through the gap, *at his throat*, *to
their assistance*, *blood sprang to her cheeks*.
2. Move rapidly as from constrained position or by action of a spring, as *branch
sprang back*, *door sprang to*. 3. Come into
being (usu. ~ *up*), arise (often *from
source*), appear, as *a breeze sprang up*,
the piers from which the arches ~, *is spring
from or of a royal stock*, *the buds are
~ing*, *the belief has sprung up*, *his actions
~ from a false conviction*; (to person
arriving suddenly or unexpectedly or
whose presence is only now realized)
where do or did you ~ from ? 4. (Of wood)
warp; (t. & i. of wood) split, crack, as
bat is or has sprung, *have sprung my
racket*. 5. p.p.(colloq.). Tipsy. 6. Rouse
(game) from earth or covert. 7. Cause to
act suddenly by means of a spring,
produce or develop suddenly or unexpectedly, as *~ a trap*, *has sprung a new
theory*, *loves to ~ surprises on us*. 8. Provide (motor vehicle etc.) with springs
(usu. as p.p.). 9. Cause (mine) to burst.
10. (Naut., of ship) *~ a butt*, loosen part
of plank by labouring in heavy sea,
~ a leak, develop leak from starting of
timbers, || *~ the* or *her luff*, yield to helm
& sail nearer to wind. [OE *springan*, cf.
Du. & G *springen*, ON *springa* burst]

spring², n. 1. Leap, as *took a ~*, *rose with
a ~*. 2. Season in which vegetation
begins, season preceding summer (esp.
from about March 21 to June 22). 3.
Place where water or oil wells up from
earth, basin so formed, as *hot*, *mineral*,
~s. 4. Backward movement from constrained position, recoil, e.g. of bow.
5. Elasticity, as *his muscles have no ~ in
them*. 6. Elastic contrivance usu. of
bent or coiled metal used esp. as motive
power in clockwork etc. or for preventing
jar as in vehicle, as *bow ~* (bow-shaped),
CEE ~, *air* or *pneumatic ~* (working by
compression of air), HAIR~, MAIN².
7. (fig.). Motive actuating person etc.,
source, origin, as *the ~s of human action*,
the custom had its ~ in another country.
8. Upward curve of beam etc. from
horizontal line. 9. Starting of plank.
10. Springing of leak. 11. Mooring-rope.
12. pl. Period of ~ tide. 13. ~ **balance**
(measuring weight by tension of ~); ~
beam, beam stretching across wide space
without intermediate support, elastic bar
used as ~ in tilt-hammer etc.; ~-**bed**,
mattress, mattress formed of spiral ~s in
wooden frame; ~-**board**, elastic board
giving impetus in leaping, diving, etc.;
~-**carriage**, ~-**cart** (mounted on ~s); ~
(contrived to go off when trespasser or
animal stumbles on it); ~-**halt**, convulsive
movement of horse's hind leg in walking;

~ *tide*, high tide occurring shortly after new & full moon in each month; ~*tide*, ~*time*, season of ~; ~*water* (from ~), opp. to river or rain water). Hence ~LESS, ~LIKE, aa., ~LET n. [OE, f. prec.]

|| **spring'al(d)**, n. (arch.). Youngster. [f. 15th c., etym. dub.]

spring'bŏk, n. S.-Afr. gazelle with habit of springing in play or when alarmed; S~s, (nickname for) S. Africans, S.-African football team etc. [S.-Afr. Du.]

springe (-j), n. Noose, snare, for small game. [ME (SPRING¹)]

spring'er, n. In vbl senses; also or esp. (Archit.) part of arch where curve begins, lowest stone of this part, bottom stone of coping of gable, rib of groined roof or vault; kind of spaniel used to spring game; grampus; springbok. [-ER¹]

spring'ly, a. (Of movement or substance) elastic. Hence ~INESS n. [-Y²]

sprinkle (spring'kl), v.t. & i., & n. 1. Scatter (liquid, ashes, crumbs, etc.) in small drops or particles, whence **sprink'-LER¹**(2) n.; subject (ground, object) to sprinkling (with liquid etc.); (of liquid etc.) fall thus on. 2. n. Light shower (of rain etc.), so **sprink'LING¹**(2) n. (esp., fig., *a few here & there of*). [(n. f. vb) earlier *sprenkle*, cf. Du. *sprenkelen*, G *sprenkeln*]

sprint, v.i. & t., & n. 1. Run short distance, run (specified distance), at full speed. 2. n. Such run. Hence ~ER¹ n. [cf. ON *spretta*]

sprit, n. Small spar reaching diagonally from mast to upper outer corner of sail; ~*sail* (-sāl, -sl), sail extended by ~, (formerly) sail extended by yard set under bowsprit. [OE *sprēot* pole, cogn. w. SPROUT]

sprite, n. Elf, fairy, goblin. [ME, as SPIRIT]

sprŏck'ĕt, n. Each of several teeth on wheel engaging with links of chain; ~*wheel*, such wheel, e.g. for engaging bicycle chain. [?]

sprout, v.i. & t., & n. 1. Begin to grow, shoot forth, put forth shoots; spring up, grow to a height; produce by ~ing, as *has ~ed horns, a moustache*. 2. n. Shoot of plant; BRUSSELS ~s. [(n. f. vb) OE *sprūtan*, cf. Du. *spruiten*, G *spriessen*]

spruce¹(-ōōs), a., & v.t. 1. Neat in dress & appearance, trim, smart. 2. v.t Smarten (oneself etc., usu. *up*). Hence ~LY² adv., ~NESS n. [prob. as foll., w. ref. to Prussian leather]

spruce²(-ōōs), n. (Also ~ *fir*) kinds of fir; ~*-beer* (made from leaves and small branches of ~, useful as antiscorbutic). [f. AF *Pruce* (F *Prusse*) Prussia, cf. med. L *Sprucia*, used attrib. = Prussian]

sprue¹ (-ōō), n. Passage through which metal is poured into mould; metal filling ~. [?]

sprue² (-ōō), n. Tropical disease (also *psilosis*) with ulcerated mucous membrane of mouth & chronic enteritis. [f. Du. *spruw* THRUSH²]

spruit (-rāt), n. (S. Africa). A small watercourse, usu. almost dry except in the wet season. [Du., see SPROUT]

sprung. See SPRING¹.

sprỹ, a. (~er, ~est). Active, lively. [dial. & U.S., etym. dub.]

spŭd, n., & v.t. (-dd-). 1. Kinds of small spade for cutting roots of weeds etc.; short thick thing, whence ~d'y² a.; (sl.) potato. 2. v.t. Remove (weeds, often *up*, *out*) with ~. [f. 15th c., etym. dub.]

|| **spŭd'dle**, v.i. (dial.). Dig lightly, dig about, (of amateur gardeners etc.). [orig. alteration of *puddle*; now assoc. w. prec.]

spue. See SPEW.

spŭm|e, n., & v.i. Froth, foam. Hence ~ĕs'CENCE, ~INESS, nn., ~ES'CENT, ~'OUS, ~Y², aa. [f. L *spūma*]

spun. See SPIN¹.

spunge. (Arch. for) SPONGE.

spunk, n. Courage, mettle, spirit; anger. Hence ~Y² a. [orig. = spark, tinder; obs. *funk* (cf. G *funke*), & *punk*, spark are perh. the same word]

spŭr, n., & v.t. & i. (-rr-). 1. Pricking instrument with point or (also *rowel~*) rowel worn on horseman's heel [*put* or *set ~s to*, = ~ vb; *need the ~*, be sluggish, also of persons); *win one's ~s*, (hist.) gain knighthood, (fig.) gain distinction, make a name; (fig.) stimulus, incentive; *on a (or the) ~ of the moment*, impromptu, on a momentary impulse; ~shaped thing, e.g. hard projection on cock's leg, steel point fastened to this in cockfight, projecting mountain (range), climbing-iron, wall crossing part of rampart and joining it to interior work, slender hollow projection from some part of flower. 2. [~*royal*, coin of James I bearing ~like sun with rays; ~*wheel*, cog-wheel with radial teeth; ~*wort*, plant with whorls of leaves like rowel of ~. 3. vb. Prick (horse) with ~s (~ *a willing horse*, fig., be needlessly importunate), incite (person *on to* effort, *to do*, etc.), furnish (person, boots, gamecock, esp. in p.p.) with ~s; (intr.) ride hard (*on, forward*, etc.). Hence ~LESS a. [(vb f. n.) OE *spura, spora*, cf. Du. *spoor*, G *sporn*; perh. cogn. w. SPOOR]

spurge, n. Kinds of plant with acrid milky juice. [f. OF *espurge* (*espurger* purge, as EXPURGATE)]

spū'rious, a. Not genuine, not being what it pretends to be, not proceeding from the pretended source, as ~ *coin*, (*reading in*) *MS, affection*; (Zool.) resembling an organ etc. but not having its function, having the function of organ etc. but morphologically different, as ~ *eyes, legs*. Hence ~LY¹ adv., ~NESS n. [f. L *spurius* +-OUS]

‖ **spür'ing-line**, n. (naut.). Line from steering-wheel to telltale in cabin for showing position of helm. [?]

spür'rier (or spür'i), n. Spur-maker. [-ER¹]

spür'ry, -rey, n. Kinds of herb of pink family, esp. corn-~, a weed in cornfield etc. [f. Du. *spurrie*, cf. med. L *spergula*]

spürt¹, v.i., & n. (Make) short sudden violent effort esp. in racing. [var. of SPIRT, etym. dub.]

spurt². See spirt.

spŭt'ter, v.t., & i., & n. **1.** Emit with spitting sound; speak, utter, (words, threats, a language, etc.) rapidly or incoherently; speak in hurried or vehement fashion (often *at* person etc.). **2.** Such speech. Hence ~ER¹ n., ~ingⱽ² adv. [imit., cf. Du. *spütteren*]

spŭt'um, n. (pl. *-ta*). Saliva, spittle; expectorated matter esp. as characteristic of disease. [L, neut. p.p. of *spuere* spit]

spy, n., & v.t. & i. **1.** Person who goes, esp. in disguise, into enemy's camp or territory to inspect works, watch movements, etc., & report the result; person who keeps (esp. secret) watch on movements of others, as *refuse to be a ~ on his conduct*. **2.** v.t. Discern, make out, esp. by careful observation, as *spied a horseman approaching, is quick at ~ing his neighbours' faults, I ~ STRANGERS*; ~ *out*, explore secretly, discover by this means; (v.i.) *play the ~*, keep close & secret watch (*upon* person, movements, etc., *into* secret etc.); ~*glass*, small telescope; ~*hole*, peep-hole. [ME *spie* n., *spien* v.b. f. OF *espíe* n., *espíer* v.b ESPY]

squab (-ŏb), a., adv., & n. **1.** Short & fat, squat, whence ~by² (-ŏ-) a. **2.** adv. With heavy fall, as *come down ~ on the floor*. **3.** n. Short fat person; young esp. unfledged pigeon; stuffed cushion; ottoman; ~*-chick*, unfledged bird; ~ *pie*, pigeon-pie, pie of mutton, onions, & apples. [cf. Sw. dial. *squab* loose flesh, *swabb²* fat woman, etc.]

squa'bble (-ŏ-), v.i. & t., & n. **1.** Engage in petty or noisy quarrel (*with* person *about* thing); (Print.) disarrange (composed type). **2.** n. Petty or noisy quarrel. Hence ~ER¹ n. [prob. imit., cf. Sw. dial. *skvabbel* n. dispute]

squăc'cŏ, n. (pl. ~s). Small crested heron of S. Europe, Africa, & Asia. [f. It. *squacco*]

squad (-ŏd), n. (Mil.). small number of men assembled for drill etc. (~ *drill*, elementary); *awkward ~* (of recruits not yet competent to take place in regimental line, also fig.); small party of persons; FLYING ~. [f. F *escouade* var. of *escadre*

squa'dron (-ŏd-), n., & v.t. **1.** Principal division of cavalry regiment or mechanized formation, consisting of two troops. **2.** Any orderly body of persons. **3.** Detachment of warships employed, on particular service, as *flying ~* (equipped for rapid cruising). **4.** Unit of Royal Air Force (10 to 18 machines); ~*-leader* (see also AIR¹ *Force*), **5,** v.t. Form (men) into ~s. [f. It. *squadrone* (prec. -ONE)]

‖ **squail**, n. (Pl.) game with small wooden disks (~s) on round table or board (~ *board*), [?]

‖ **squail'er**, n. Stick with leaded knob for striking or throwing at squirrels etc. [f. dial. *squail* strike with ~+-ER¹]

squa'lid (-ŏl-), a. Dirty, mean, poor, in appearance. Hence or cogn. ~ITY (-ĭd-), ~NESS, **squa'lor**, nn., ~LYⱽ² adv., (-ŏl-). [f. L *squalidus* (*squalere* be stiff or dirty, -ID¹)]

squall (-awl), v.i. & t., & n. **1.** Cry out, scream, violently as in fear or pain; utter in screaming or discordant voice. Hence ~ER¹ n. **2.** n. Sudden & violent gust or successive gusts of wind, esp. with rain or snow or sleet (*arched ~*, ~ occurring near equator with sudden collection of black clouds in form of arch & usu. violent thunderstorm; *black ~*, with dark cloud; *white ~*, arising in fair weather without formation of clouds), whence ~Y² (-aw-) a.; *look out for ~s*, (fig.) be on one's guard against danger or trouble. [f. the v.b] discordant cry, scream. [imit., kind of sea-fish. [mod. L) genus of sharks.

squal'oid, a. Like a shark. [f. L *squalus*,

squa'nder (-ŏn-), v.t. Spend (money, time, etc.) wastefully; dissipate (fortune etc.) thus. Hence ~ER¹ n., ~ingⱽ² adv., ~OUS, aa., ~ULE n. [L]

squa're, n., a., & adv., & v.t. & i. **1.** Equilateral rectangle; object (approximately) of this shape; quadrilateral area planted with trees etc. or ornamentally laid out in streets, as *Trafalgar S~, Russell S~*, bounded by four streets; L-shaped or (*T~~*) T-shaped instrument for obtaining or testing right angles; *out of ~*, not at right angles; standard, pattern, (usu. fig., & arch. exc. *on the ~*, fairly, honestly, as *can be trusted to act on the ~, by the ~*, exactly; product of a number multiplied by itself, as *the ~ of 9 is 81, of 2² is z⁴, 9 is a perfect ~* (has rational root); body of infantry drawn up in rectangular form, *hollow ~*, so drawn up with space in

middle for baggage etc., or with files facing inwards to receive orders from officers in central space; (also word~) set of words (to be guessed from description &) arranged in a ~ so as to read alike across & downwards (e.g. *cab ace bed*); MAGIC ~; 100 ~ ft as measure of flooring etc. **2. adj.** Of ~ shape; ~ *foot, inch*, etc., (area equal to that of) ~ whose side is a foot, inch, etc.; ~ *measure* (expressed in ~ feet etc.): *a table 4 ft* ~ *has an area of 16* ~ *ft*; rectangular, as *table with* ~ *corners*; at right angles to; ~ *number*, ~ of an integer, e.g. 1, 4, 9, 16, etc.: ~ *root* of a given number, number of which it is the ~, *as the* ~ *root of 9 is 3, of x² is x*; √2 *is irrational*; ~ *dance*, game (in which four couples, players, face inwards from nearly equal to the length or height than is usual, as *a man of* ~ *frame*; angular, not round, as ~ *peg in round* HOLE¹ *has a* ~ *jaw*; properly arranged, in good order, uncompromising, as *was met with a* ~ *refusal, made a* ~ *meal*; fair, honest, as *his play is not always quite* ~, *a* ~ *deal*, fair bargain, fair treatment; *be on the* ~, be a freemason; on a proper footing, even, quits, as *am now* ~ *with all the world, get* ~ *with* (pay, compound with) *our creditors*; (Golf) *they were* ~ *or all* ~ (had won the same number of holes) *at the turn*. **3.** ~*-built*, of comparatively broad shape; ||~'*face* (sl.), gin; ~'*head*, Scandinavian in U.S. or Canada (cf. DAGO); ~ *leg* (Cricket), fielder at some distance on batsman's leg-side & nearly opposite wicket, his place, as *was put at* ~ *leg*; ~-*rigged*, with principal sails extended by horizontal yards slung to mast by the middle, opp. to fore-&-aft rigged; ~ *sail*, four-cornered sail extended on yard slung to mast by middle esp. on fore-&-aft rigged vessel; ~-*shouldered*, with broad & not sloping shoulders, esp. opp. to round-shouldered; ~-*toed*, (having boots) with ~ toes, (fig.) formal, prim; ~-*toes*, ~-toed person. Hence ~'LY² (-rl-) adv., ~'NESS (-rm-) n., squar'ISH¹ a. **4. adv.** ~'ly, as *sat* ~ *on his seat, hit him* ~ *on the jaw, do you think he plays* ~ (fair)?, FAIR² & ~. **5. vb.** Make ~; make rectangular, give rectangular edges to; (timber); multiply (number) by itself, as *3* ~*d is 9, x* ~*d is written x²*; adjust, make or be suitable to or consistent with, reconcile, as *decline to* ~ *my conduct to or with his interests, his practice does not* ~ *or he does not* ~ *his practice with his principles*; settle, pay, (bill etc.), esp. ~ *accounts with* (fig. have revenge on), (abs. in some senses) ~ *up*; (colloq.) pay, esp. bribe, as *can you* ~ *the porter?, has been* ~*d to hold his tongue*; secure acquiescence etc. of (person) thus; assume attitude of boxer, move up to (person) thus; ~ *the circle*, construct ~ equal in area to given circle, express area of circle exactly in ~ measure, (fig.) perform demonstrable impossibility; (Golf) make the score of (a match) equal, make the scores equal; (Naut.) lay (yards) at right angles with keel making them at same time horizontal, get (dead-eyes) horizontal, get (ratlines) horizontal & parallel to one another. [f. OF *esquarre* n. (cf. It. *squadra*), *esquarré* a., *esquarre* vb, f. pop. L +EX(*quadra* n., -*are* vb, square, cf. QUADRI-)]

squa'rrose, -ous, (-ōr-), aa. (bot., zool.), Rough with scalelike processes. [f. alleged LL *squarrosus* prob. mistake for *squamosus* (as SQUAMA, see -OSE¹, -OUS)]

|| **squaˈsh'on**, n. (joc.). Squire & parson in one. [portmanteau wd]

squash¹ (-ŏ-), v.t. & i., & n. **1.** Crush, squeeze flat or into pulp; pack tight, crowd; (fig.) silence (person) with crushing retort; squeeze one's way (*into* etc.). **2. n.** ~ed thing or mass, whence ~'INESS n., ~'Y² a.; crowd; (sound of) fall of soft body; (also ~ *rackets*) game played with rackets & soft ball in fives-court; LEMON¹ ~; ~ *hat* (of soft felt etc.). [f. OF *esquasser* f. pop. L +EX(*quassare* see QUASH)]

squash² (-ŏ-), n. Kinds of gourd. [f. Amer.-Ind. *askutasquash*]

squat (-ŏt), v.i. & t. (-tt-), a., & n. **1.** Sit on ground etc. with knees drawn up & heels close to or touching hams, crouch with hams resting on backs of heels; put (oneself, person) into this position; (of animals) crouch close to ground; (colloq.) sit (*down, on*, etc.). **2. adj.** in ~ting posture; (of person etc.) short & thick, dumpy. **3. n.** ~ting posture; ~ person. [(adj. & n. f. vb) f. OF *esquatir* flatten (es- EX+*quatir* f. L L *coactus*, see COGENT)]

squa'tter (-ŏt-), n. In vbl senses; also: (Austral.) person who gets right of pasturage from government on easy terms, also, any stock-owner; person who settles on new esp. public land without title; person who takes unauthorized possession of unoccupied premises. [f. prec. +-ER¹]

squaw, n. Amer.-Indian woman or wife; ~-*man*, white married to ~. [f. native *squa*]

squawk, v.i. & n. **1.** (Chiefly of birds) utter harsh cry of pain or fear. **2. n.** Such cry. [imit.]

squeak, v.i. & t., & n. **1.** Utter short shrill cry as of mouse or unoiled hinge; utter (words) shrilly; (sl.) turn informer, peach. **2. n.** Short shrill sound, whence ~'ILY² adv., ~'Y² a.; (*narrow*) ~, narrow escape, success barely attained; BUBBLE¹ *and* ~. [limit., cf. Sw. *sqväka* croak]

squeak'er, n. In vbl senses; also, young bird esp. pigeon. [-ER¹]

squeal, v.i.&t.,& n. **1.** Utter shrill cry as of child from pain, fear, anger, joy, etc.; utter (words) thus; (sl.) protest excitedly

e.g. against taxation; (sl.) turn informer; *make* one ~ (sl.), blackmail him. **2.** n. Shrill cry of child, pig etc. [imit.]

squeal'er, n. In vbl senses; also, young bird esp. pigeon. [-ER¹]

squeam'ish, a. Easily nauseated; fastidious, overnice, overscrupulous in questions of propriety, honesty, etc. Hence ~LY² adv., ~NESS n. [earlier *squeamous* f. ~LY² adv., ~NESS n.]

squee'gee (or -ē'), **squil'gee,** nn. & v.t. **1.** Rubber-edged implement for sweeping wet deck or road; small similar instrument or roller used in photography. **2.** v.t. Treat with ~. [*squee-* f. *squid-*?]. etym. dub. (also *squillagee*, altered on SQUEEZE]

squeeze, v.t. & i., & n. **1.** Exert pressure upon (sponge, lemon, etc.) in order to extract moisture, compress with hand or between two bodies, as ~ person's hand (as sign of sympathy, affection, etc.), ~*d orange* (fig.) person, thing, from whom or which no more is to be had, *was ~d to death in the crowd*; thrust (oneself, person, thing, *into* vehicle, room, etc., *out of*, etc.) forcibly; make one's way by squeezing (*into* etc.); harass by exactions, extort money etc. from; constrain, bring pressure to bear on, as *could ~ the government to any extent*; get (money etc. *out of* person etc.) by extortion, entreaty, etc.; produce with effort (*a tear* etc.); take impression of (coin etc.) esp. with sheets of damp paper or prepared wax. **2.** n. Application of pressure, as *gave him a ~ (of the hand)*; crowd, crush, as *we all got in, but it was a (tight) ~*; impression of coin etc., esp. as above; forced exaction by Asiatic official, illicit commission, percentage on goods purchased extorted by native servant. **3.** ~ *play*, (Bridge) leading winning cards until opponent is forced to discard important card, (Baseball) hitting ball short to infield to enable runner on third base to get home as soon as ball is pitched. Hence **squeeze'ABLE** a. [cf. obs. *queose, queise, squize, equiss*, & OE *cwésan*]

squeez'er, n. In vbl senses; also or esp.: machine for expressing air-bubbles etc. from puddled iron; (pl.) playing-cards with value shown at top right-hand corner so that they need not be opened out. [-ER¹]

squelch, v.t., & i., & n. (colloq.). **1.** Stamp on, crush flat, put an end to; disconcert, silence; make sucking sound as of hoof drawn out of thick mud. **2.** n. Act or sound of ~ing. [imit.]

squib, n. & v.t. & i. (-bb-). **1.** Firework thrown by hand & exploding like rocket or burning with hissing sound; tube of gunpowder used to fire a charge; short satirical composition, lampoon. **2.** vb. Write, attack with, lampoons. [f. 16th c., etym. dub.]

squid, n., & v.i. (-dd-). **1.** Kind of cuttle-fish used as bait; kinds of artificial bait. **2.** v.i. Fish with ~. [?]

‖**squiff'er,** n. (sl.). Concertina. [?]

squiff'y, a. (sl.). Slightly drunk. [?]

squil'gee. See SQUEEGEE.

squill, n. Plant of lily family; its bulb, used as diuretic, purgative, etc.; (also ~*fish*) a crustacean. [f. L *squilla* f. Gk *skilla*]

squinch, n. Straight or arched structure across interior angle of square tower as support for side of octagon. [var. of obs. *scunch* abbr. of SCUNCHON]

squint, v.i. & t., n., & a. **1.** Have the eyes turned in different directions, have strabismus; look obliquely (*at* etc.); close (eyes) quickly, hold (eyes) half-shut. Hence ~'ER¹ n. **2.** n. Affection of eyes in which their axes are differently directed, as *has a fearful ~*; stealthy or sidelong glance; (colloq.) glance, look, as *let's have a ~ at it*; leaning, inclination, (*to, towards*, etc.); oblique opening through wall of church esp. affording view of altar from transept. **3.** adj. ~*ing*, looking different ways; ~*-eyed*, (fig.) malignant. [f. obs. adv. *squint* obliquely, ...]

squire, n. & v.t. **1.** Country gentleman, esp. the chief landed proprietor in a district; woman's escort or gallant; ~*d dames*, man who is attentive to or frequents company of women; attendant on knight (hist.). **2.** v.t. (Of man) attend upon, escort, (woman). Hence ~HOOD, ~LER, ~LING¹, ~SHIP, nn., ~LY¹ a. [as ESQUIRE]

squire'archy (-ki), n. Government by, landed proprietors esp. before Reform Bill of 1832; the class of landed proprietors, so ~'**arch** (-k) n. Hence ~'**archAL**, ~'**archICAL**, adj. (-k-). [f. prec. + Gk *-arkhia* rule f. *arkhō*]

‖**squireen',** n. Small landed proprietor esp. in Ireland. [f. SQUIRE + *-een* dim. suf.]

squirm, v.i. & n. **1.** Wriggle, writhe; (fig.) show, feel, embarrassment or discomfiture. **2.** n. Wriggling movement; (Naut.) twist in rope. [imit.]

squirr'el, n. Kinds of rodent quadruped of active arboreal habits with bushy tail & pointed ears; *burking ~*, prairie-dog; ~*fish*, kinds of fish covered with sharp spines; ~*hawk*, large hawk preying on ~s; ~*monkey*, marmoset & other small monkeys; ~*tail*, kinds of grass allied to barley. [f. OF *escureul* f. med. L *scurellus* irreg. dim. of L f. Gk *skiouros* (pop. explained as f. *skia* shadow + *oura* tail)]

squirt, v.t. & i., & n. **1.** Eject (liquid, powder) in a jet as from syringe; (of liquid etc.) be discharged thus. **2.** n. Syringe; jet of water etc.; (also ~*-gun*) kind of toy syringe; (colloq.) insignificant self-assertive fellow. [im. f. vb) cf. LG *swirtjen*]

squish, n. (colloq.). Marmalade. [imit.]

squit, n. (sl.). Small insignificant person. [?]

St. For St Andrew etc. see SAINT.

stab, v.t. & i. (-bb-), & n. **1.** Pierce, wound, with (usu. short) pointed weapon e.g. knife or dagger; aim blow with such weapon (*at*); (fig.) inflict sharp pain on (person, his feelings, conscience, etc.), aim blow *at* (reputation, person, etc.); ~ (vb & n.) *in the back*, slander; roughen (brick wall) with pick before plastering. **2.** n. Blow, thrust, with knife etc., wound thus made, blow or pain inflicted on person's feelings. Hence ~**b'er**[1] n. [m.f. 15th, vb f. 16th, c.; etym. dub.]

Stab'at Mater (or stah-. mah-), n. (Musical setting for) Latin hymn on agony of the Virgin Mary at the crucifixion. [L, = the mother was standing, first wds of the hymn]

stā'ble[1], a. Firmly fixed or established, not easily to be moved or changed or destroyed, as *doubt whether the structure is* ~, firm, resolute, not wavering nor fickle, as *the only* ~ *politician of his day*; ~ EQUILIBRIUM. Hence or cogn. **stabil'ity**, **stābiliza'tion** (also, esp.) maintenance of the purchasing power of a country's currency by fixing its value in terms of gold, ~**NESS**, nn., **stāb'ilize**[3] v.t., **stāb'ilizer**[1] n. (esp. = aircraft's fixed horizontal tailplane), **stā'biLY**[2] adv. [f. OF *estable* f. L *stabilis* (*stare* stand, see -BLE)]

stā'ble[2], n., & v.t. & i. **1.** Building set apart & adapted for lodging & feeding horses or (less usu.) cattle; racehorses of particular ~; (pl. Mil.) duty or work in the ~s, (also) = (~*call*; AUGEAN ~s; ~*boy*, ~*man* (-mn), (employed in ~); ~*call*, cavalry signal for grooming & watering horses; ~*companion*, horse of same ~, (colloq.) member of same school, club, etc. **2.** v.t. Put, keep, horse in ~, as *where can we* ~ *our horses?*; (v.i., of horse etc., fig. of person) be ~d, as *must* ~ *where they can*. [f. OF *estable* f. L *stabulum* (*stare* stand)]

stā'bling, n. In vbl senses of prec., esp. accommodation for horses etc. [-ING[1]]

||**stāb'lish**, v.t. (arch.). Fix firmly. [as ESTABLISH]

stacca'tō (-aht-), a. & adv. (To be played) in abrupt sharply detached manner, cf. LEGATO; ~ *mark*, dot above or below ~ note. [It.]

stack, n. & v.t. **1.** Circular or rectangular pile of grain in sheaf of hay, straw, etc., usu. with sloping thatched top; ~*funnel*, pyramidal frame ventilating centre of ~; ~*stand* (on which ~ is built for dryness & exclusion of vermin); as measure of wood) pile of 108 cub. ft; pile, heap of anything; (colloq.) large quantity, as *have* ~s, *a whole* ~, *of work to get through first*; pyramidal group of rifles, pile; number of chimneys standing together; (also *smoke*~) chimney, funnel, of locomotive or steamer; || high detached rock esp. off coast of Scotland & Orkneys. **2.** v.t. Pile in ~; ~ (= PILE[9]) *arms*. [vb f. n.) f. ON *stakkr* haystack, cf. Sw. *stack*]

stacte, n. A sweet spice used by ancient Jews in making incense. [f. L f. Gk *staktē* oil trickling from myrrh etc. (*stazō* drip)]

stactom'eter, n. Tube for measuring a liquid in drops. [f. Gk *staktos* vbl adj. f. *stazō* drip +-METER]

stad'ium, n.(pl.-*ia*). **1.**(Gk Ant.) measure of length, about 202 yds; course for footrace. **2.** Modern athletic or sports ground. **3.** (med.). Stage, period, of disease. [L, f. Gk *stadion* (*sta*-stand)]

stad'tholder (stahd-. staht-. stä-), n. (hist.). Viceroy or governor of province or town in Netherlands; chief ~magistrate of United Provinces. Hence ~SHIP n. [altered f. Du. *stadhouder* deputy (*stad* STEAD+*houder* HOLDER)]

staff[1] (-ahf), n. (pl. now ~s exc. Mus. *staves*) & v.t. **1.** Stick, pole, for use in walking or climbing or as weapon (now chiefly fig.), as *bread is the* ~ (support) *of life*, *you are the* ~ *of his old age*, QUARTER[1]. ~, **2.** This as sign of office or authority, as *pastoral* ~ (borne by or before bishop etc.). **3.** Shaft, pole, as support or handle, as FLAG[1]~. **4.** Stick used in surveying etc., esp. JACOB's ~. **5.** Kinds of instrument for taking altitude at sea, as *back*, *cross*, *fore*, ~s. **6.** Surgeon's steel instrument for guiding knife into bladder. **7.** Token delivered to engine-driver on single-line railways as authority to proceed over a given section of line (~ *system*, this method of working). **8.**(mil.). Body of officers assisting officer in high command & concerned with army or regiment as a whole, as *regimental* ~; *general* ~ (at main headquarters of army, acting as personal ~ of commander-in-chief); ~ *officer*. -*serpeant*, (serving on ~); ~ *college* (in which officers are prepared for ~ as opp. to regimental duties). **9.** Body of persons carrying on work under manager etc., as *editorial* ~ *of newspaper*, *diplomatic* ~; whence (-)~ED[2] (-ahft) a. **10.** (mus.). Set of five parallel lines on any one or between any two of which a note is placed to indicate its pitch; ~ *notation* (by means of ~, esp. opp. to TONIC *sol-fa*). **11.** v.t. Provide (institution etc.) with ~. [OE *stæf*, cf. Du. *staf*, G *stab*, ON *stafr*]

staff[2] (-ahf), n. Mixture of plaster-of-Paris, cement, etc., as building-material. [?]

stag, n. **1.** Male of red deer or of other large kinds of deer; bull castrated when (nearly) full-grown. **2.** || (St. Exch.) person who applies for allotments in new con-

cerns with a view to selling at once at a profit; ||(sl.) irregular dealer in stocks. 3. ~-beetle (with branched mandibles like ~'s antlers); ~-evil, lockjaw in horses; ~-horn, kinds of club-moss & coral; ~-hound, large kinds of hound hunting deer by sight or scent; ~-party (of men only). [cf. ON *stǽgr*, *ǿ*, he-bird]

stage¹, n. **1.** Raised floor or platform, e.g. scaffold for workmen's use in building, *painters' use), *landing~* (at quay etc. for landing from vessel) surface on which object is placed for inspection through microscope. **2.** Platform on which plays etc. are exhibited. **3.** (fig.) The drama, dramatic art or literature, actor's profession, as *went on the ~, became actor, the French ~.* **4.** (fig.) Scene of action, as *quitted the ~ of politics, the ~ of his operations, a larger ~ opened to him.* **5.** Point or period in development etc., as *reached a critical ~, at this ~ an interruption occurred, passed through a long ~ of inactivity, is in the hoyden ~, larval ~.* **6.** Regular stopping-place in route, distance between two of these, as *travelled by easy ~s, got down at the next ~.* **7.** ~-coach, coach running regularly by ~s between two places, ~-coachman, driver of this; ~-craft, skill or experience in writing or staging plays; ~ direction, written or printed instruction in play as to movement, position, tone, etc., of actor; ~ door, actors' & workmen's entrance at back of ~; ~ effect, effect produced in acting or on the ~, artificial or theatrical effect produced in real life; ~ fever, inordinate desire to go on the ~; ~ fright, nervousness on facing audience esp. for first time; ~ manager, person superintending production of play, managing rehearsals, etc.; ~ right, exclusive right to perform particular play; ~-struck, struck with ~ fever; ~ whisper, whisper meant to be heard by others than the person addressed. [f. OF *estage* f. L +*staticum* (*stare* stand)]

stage², v.t. & i. **1.** Put (play) on stage; arrange to take place dramatically (~ *a* COME¹-*back, recovery*); (of play) lend itself to representation, as *does not ~ well.* [f. prec.]

stä'ger, n. *Old~*, experienced person, old hand, [STAGE¹+-ER¹]

stäg'gard, n. -t, n. Stag four years old. [-ARD]

stäg'ger (-g-), v.i. & t., & n. **1.** Walk or stand unsteadily, totter; hesitate, waver in purpose; cause to totter, as *received a ~ing blow*; cause to hesitate or waver, as *the question ~ed him, his resolution*; arrange in zigzag order, esp. set (spokes of wheel) leaning alternately to right & left; arrange (holidays, hours of work, etc.) so that they differ from those of others. Hence ~ing₂ adv. **2.** n. Tottering movement; (Mech.) overhanging or slantwise or zigzag arrangement of like parts in a structure etc.; (pl., also *blind ~s*) kinds of disease of brain & spinal cord esp. in horses & cattle; (pl.) giddiness, frequent. of *staka* push) [(n. f. vb) earlier *stacker* f. ON *stakra*

stägg'erer (-g-), n. In vbl senses, esp. disconcerting argument, objection, event, etc. [-ER¹]

stä'ging, n. Putting play on stage; driving or running stage-coaches; scaffolding. [-ING¹]

Stä'girīte, n. *The ~*, Aristotle. [f. L f. Gk *Stageirītēs* native of *Stageira* (-ITE¹)]

stäg'nāte, v.i. (Of liquid) become motionless, have no current, cease to flow; (of life, action, mind, business, person) be(come) dull or sluggish. Hence or cogn. ~ANCY, ~A'TION, nn., ~ANT a., ~ANTLY² adv. [f. L *stagnare* (*stagnum* pool), -ATE³]

stäg'nolous, a. Living in swamps or stagnant water. [f. L *stagnum* pool + *colere* inhabit +-OUS³]

stä'g'ỹ, a. Theatrical in manner, style, appearance, etc. Hence ~INESS n. [f. STAGE¹+-Y²]

staid, a. Of steady & sober character; sedate. Hence ~'LY² adv., ~'NESS n. [= *stayed* p.p. of STAY]

stain, v.t. & i., & n. **1.** Discolour, make foul, soil, as *cigarettes ~ the fingers, wine will ~ the cloth, warranted not to ~ clothes*; (fig.) sully, blemish, (reputation, name, person); p.p. often in comb., as *guilt, sin, ~-ed*); colour (wood, glass, etc.) by process other than painting or covering the surface; impregnate (substance) for microscopic examination with colouring matter that acts more powerfully on some parts than on others; print colours on (wall-paper). Hence ~ABLE a., ~ER¹ n. **2.** n. Discoloration, spot or mark caused esp. by contact with foreign matter, as *cloth is covered with tea-~s*; ~*ing-material*; (fig.) blot, blemish, as *without a ~ on his character*. Hence ~'LĔSS a., (usu. of reputation, also of kind of chromium-steel alloy immune to rusting & corrosion), ~'lĔSSLY² adv. [(n. f. vb) also obs. *distain* f. OF *desteindre* f. L *tingere* dye]

stair, n. Each of a set of (now usu. indoor) steps, as *the top~ but one*; (now usu. pl.) set of these, as *passed him on the ~ down a winding ~*; flight, pain, of ~s, set of ~s in continuous straight line or from one landing to another; *below ~s*, belonging to servants, as *was cooly discussed below ~s* (by the servants); *down, up, ~s*, on, to, the lower, upper, floor(s) of house; BACK¹~; ~*case*, (upper, of building containing) flight of ~s, *cork-screw ~case* (winding round central pillar); ~-*rod* (for securing ~-carpet in

angle between two steps); ~'way, way up a flight of ~s, ~case. [OE *stǣger*, cf. Du. *steiger*, cogn. w. OE *stīgan*, OHG *stīgan*, ON *stiga*, & Gk *stekhō*, go up, go]

|| **staith, staithe** (-dh), n. Waterside coal depot equipped for loading vessels. [ON *stöth* berth, OE *stæth* bank]

stake, n. & v.t. **1.** Stick sharpened at one end & driven into ground as support, boundary mark, etc.; post to which person is bound to be burnt alive, (fig.) death by burning, as *was condemned to, suffered at, the* ~. **2.** Tinsmith's small anvil fixed on bench by pointed end. **3.** Money etc. wagered on an event, esp. deposited with third party (~'*holder*) by each of those who make a wager, (pl.) money to be contended for esp. in horse-race, (pl.) such race, as *maiden, triad,* ~s; *have a* ~ *in the country*, be materially concerned in its welfare, e.g. as landowner; (fig.) principle etc. contended for, as *consider the immensity of the* ~; *at* ~, at issue, in question, risked, as *life itself is at* ~. **4.** ~-*boat* (anchored to mark course for boat-race etc.); ~-*net*, fishing-net hung on ~s. **5.** v.t. Fasten, secure, support, with ~ or ~s; mark off, out (area) with ~s, as ~ *out a claim*. **6.** Wager, risk, (money etc. on event etc.). [(vb f. n.) OE *staca*, cf. MDu. *stake*; cogn. w. STICK]

stal'actite (or stalác²), n. Deposit of carbonate of lime, usu. in form like large icicle, hanging from roof of cave etc. & formed by trickling of water. Hence **stalac'tic, stalactif'erorm, stălactif'ic**, aa. [f. mod. L *stalactītēs* (Gk *stalaktos* vbl adj. f. *stalassō* drip, see -ITE²)]

Stal'ag, n. German prison camp, esp. for non-commissioned officers and men. [G]

stăl'agmite (or stalǎk²), n. Deposit as STALACTITE on floor of cave etc. often uniting with stalactite. Hence **stălagmit'ic** a., **stălagmit'ically** adv. [f. mod. L *stalagmītēs* (Gk *stalagmos* dripping, as STALACTITE)]

stale¹, a., n., & v.t. & i. **1.** Not fresh, insipid, musty, or otherwise the worse for age; ~ *bread* (musty; also, not of the day's baking, as ~ *bread is best for toast*); (fig.) lacking novelty, trite, as ~ *joke, news, devices*; (of athlete) overtrained; ~'*mate* (Chess), draw resulting from player's having no move available, his king not being in check, (v.t.) reduce (player) to this position, (fig.) bring to a standstill. Hence ~'LY² (-l-li) adv., ~NESS (-l-n-) n. **2.** v.t. Make ~ or common: (of horse etc.) make water. [n. f. vb, prob. f. OF *estaler* make water, cf. It. *stallare*, Du. & MHG *stallen*, Sw. *stalla*, Da. *stalle*; adj. perh. also f.vb (cf. Flem. *stel* adj., used of beer & urine), or f. Teut. *sta-* stand; *stale(mate)* perh. f. OF *estaler* f. OE as STALL¹ vb]

|| **stăle²**, n. (arch.). Decoy bird; dupe,

laughing-stock. [prob. f. AF *estale* of Teut. orig, cf. OE *stæl(hrán* reindeer) decoy reindeer f. *stellan* to place]

stalk¹(-awk), v.i. & t.,&n. **1.** Stride, walk in stately or imposing manner (often *along* etc.); steal up to game under cover; pursue (game) stealthily; ~*ing-horse*, horse behind which hunter conceals himself, (fig.) pretext. **2.** n. ~*ing* of game, imposing gait. Hence (-)~ER¹ n. [OE *stealcian* walk warily, cogn. w. STEAL]

stalk²(-awk), n. (Bot.) stem, main axis, of plant, (loosely) any support of an organ; ~*like* support of organ etc. in animals; stem of wine-glass etc.; (Archit.) ornament like ~ of plant; tall chimney of factory etc.; ~-*eyed*, (of crab etc.) having the eyes mounted on ~s. Hence (-)~ED² (-awkt), ~'LESS, aa., ~'LET n. [ME *stalke* perh. dim. f. OE *stalu* side or rung of ladder]

stall¹(-awl), n. & v.t. & i. **1.** (Single compartment for one animal in) stable, cow-house; FINGER-~; booth in market etc., compartment in a building, for sale of goods, table in this on which goods are exposed, as *picked it up in or on a book-*~; fixed seat in choir or chancel of church more or less enclosed at back & sides & often canopied, esp. one appropriated to clergyman, as *canon's, dean's,* ~, (fig.) office, dignity, of canon etc., as *how long has he had his* ~?; || each of a set of seats in theatre usu. between pit & stage; working-compartment in coal-mine; ~-*feed*, fatten (cattle) in ~, so ~-*fed* a. **2.** vb. Place, keep, (cattle etc.) in ~ esp. for fattening, as a ~*ed ox*; furnish (stable etc.) with ~s; (of horse or cart) stick fast as in mud or snow, (of motor-engine) stop working, (of aeroplane or airman) become unstable by loss of pace. [(vb f. n.) OE *steal(l)*, cf. Du. *stal*, G *stall*, ON *stallr*; cogn. w. STABLE²]

stall²(-awl), n., & v.i.& t. **1.** Pickpocket's confederate who diverts attention during theft & assists thief's escape etc. **2.** vb. *Fence conversationally; *block, delay, obstruct, (~ *off*, get rid of by evasive tactics or trick). [var. of STALL²]

|| **sta'llage** (-awl-), n. Space for, rent for, right to erect, stall(s) in market etc. [AF *estalage* (*estal* STALL¹, -AGE)]

stall'ion (-yon), n. Uncastrated male horse, esp. one kept for breeding. [f. OF *estalon* (OHG *stal* STALL¹, see -OON), so called because kept in stall]

sta'lwart (-awl-), a. & n. **1.** Strongly built, sturdy; courageous, resolute, determined, as ~ *supporters*. **2.** n. (polit.) Strong party man. Hence ~LY² adv., ~NESS n. [earlier *stalworth*, OE *stǣl-wyrthe*, prob. for *statholwyrthe* (*stathol* foundation + *wyrthe* WORTH)]

stăm'en, n. Male organ of flowering plants, organ containing pollen. Hence

stamina (-) ~ED² (-nd), **stamin'eal, stamin'eous,** aa. [L. gen. *-inis,*

stamin'iferous, aa. [L. gen. *-inis,* = warp in upright loom, thread]

stam'ina, n. Staying-power, power of endurance. [L.pl. of prec. now usu. as sing.]

stam'inal, a. Of stamens or stamina. [-AL]

stam'inate, a. Having stamens but no pistils; having staminens. [-ATE²(2)]

stamm'er, v.i. & t. & n. 1. Speak (habitually, or on occasion from embarrassment etc.) with halting articulation esp. with rapid repetitions of same syllable; whence ~ER¹ n., ~INGLY¹ adv.; utter (words) thus, as ~*ed out an excuse.* **2.** n. ~*ing speech, tendency to* ~. [OE *stamerian,* cf. Du. *stameren,* G *stammeln*]

stamp, v.t. & i. & n. 1. Impress pattern, name, mark, upon (metal, butter, paper, etc.) with die or similar instrument of metal, wood, rubber, etc.; affix postage or other ~ to (envelope, document); crush, pulverize, (ores etc.); bring down one's foot, bring down (foot), heavily on ground; ~ *out* (foot), put an end to, crush, destroy, (rebellion etc.); assign a character to, characterize, (*as this alone* ~*s the story as*) *a slander*; impress on the memory. Hence (-) ~ER¹(1, 2) n. **2.** n. Instrument this; impression of official mark required to be made for revenue purposes on deeds, bills of exchange, etc., as evidence of payment of tax; piece of paper impressed with official mark as evidence of payment of tax or fee & meant to be affixed to letter, postcard, receipted account, etc.; mark impressed on, label etc. affixed to, commodity as evidence of quality etc., (fig.) characteristic mark, impress, as *bears the* ~ *of genius*; character, kind, as *avoid men of that or his* ~; block that crushes ore in ~-mill; heavy downward blow with foot. **3.** ~ *act,* act concerned with ~-duty, esp. that imposing duty on American colonies in 1765 & repealed in 1766; ~-*collector* (of postage~s as curiosities); ~-*duty* (imposed on certain kinds of legal instrument); ~-*machine* (for beating rags etc. into pulp for paper); ~-*mill* (for crushing ore etc.); ~-*office* (for issue of government ~s & receipt of ~-duty etc.). [ME *stampen,* cf. Du. *stampen,* G *stampfen;* or f. OF *estamper* f. Teut.]

stampede´, n. & v.i. & t. **1.** Sudden fright & scattering of a number of horses or cattle; sudden flight or hurried movement of people due to panic; *(Polit.)* unconcerted movement of many persons by common impulse. **2.** vb. (Cause to) take part in ~. [f. Sp. *estampida* crash]

stance, n. Position taken for stroke. [OF. f. It. *stanza*]

stanch, staunch, (-ahr-, -aw-), v.t. Check the flow (esp. of blood); check the flow from (esp. wound). [f. OF *estanchier,* cf. It. *stancare* to weary, perh. f. L. as STAGNATE]

stanch² etc. See STAUNCH¹ etc.

sta´nchion (-ahnshn), n. & v.t. **1.** Post, pillar, upright support, vertical strut; upright bar, pair of bars, for confining cattle in stall. **2.** v.t. Supply with ~, fasten (cattle) to ~. [vb f. n.] f. OF *estanchon* dim. of OF *estance* prop f. pop.

I as stanza

stand, v.i. & t. (*stŏŏd*). **1.** Have or take or maintain upright position, be set upright, as *tell him to* ~ *up,* ~ *at EASE*, ~ *EASY,* ~ *in person's* LIGHT¹, *in the* BREACH¹, *stood there till I was tired, was too weak to* ~, *chair will not* ~ *on two legs, hair* ~*s on end* (with terror). **2.** Be of specified height, as ~*s six foot three, the cups* ~ *on the top shelf, here once stood a huge oak.* **4.** Assume stationary position, as ~ *still, was commanded to* ~; *(deliver)*, highwayman's order. **5.** Maintain position, avoid falling or moving or being moved, as *don't* ~ *there arguing, house will* ~ *another century, whether we* ~ *or fall, has stood through worse storms, pillars, a stronger stood in the doorway,* ~*ing* (Naut. & transit.), *fast,* ~ *firm; all lower sails or prepare, taken by surprise.* **6.** *It* ~*s to reason, it is logically demonstrable* (*that),* (pop.) I shall lose my temper if you deny *(that).* **7.** Hold good, remain valid or unaltered, as *the former conditions may* ~, *the passage must* ~, *the same remark* ~*s good.* **8.** Be, find oneself, in specified situation, rank, etc., as ~*s convicted of treachery, in need of help, in an awkward position, under heavy obligations;* I ~ *corrected* (accept correction); *thermometer stood at 90°; corn* ~*s higher* (is dearer) *than ever; the matter* ~*s thus; he* ~*s first on the list, alone among his contemporaries, in the same relation to both parties,* ~*s well* (is on good terms or in good odour) *with the authorities; how do we* ~ *in the matter of* (have we enough or suitable) *horses*?; I ~ *prepared to dispute it,* ~ *in awe of,* have often stood his friend,* ~ *at* BAY¹. **9.** Move to & remain in specified position, as ~ *back, clear, aside, aloof, away;* (Naut.) hold specified course, as ~ *in for the shore;* (of dog) point, set. **10.** Place, set, in upright or specified position, as ~ *the jug on the table, it against the wall, shall* ~ *you in the corner* (as punishment). **11.** Endure without succumbing or complaining; as *nerves could not* ~ *the strain, how does he* ~ *pain?, could never* ~ *the fellow, shall* ~ *no nonsense, can't* ~ *these French matches;* ~ *fire* (receive fire of enemy without giving way); *failed to* ~ *the test;* ~ *one's ground,* maintain one's position (lit., & fig. of argument etc.). **12.** Undergo (trial), be faced with (CHANCE¹). **13.** Provide at one's expense, as *stood him a drink, stood a bottle to the company, who is going to* ~

tread? **14.** ~ **by** (prep.), uphold, support, side with, (person), adhere to, abide by, (terms, promise), (Naut.) take or ~ ready to take hold of (anchor etc.); ~ **by** (adv.), ~ near, be a bystander, & look on, as *will not* ~ *by* & *see him ill-treated*, (orig. Naut.) ~ ready, be on the alert; ~**by**, thing, person, that one can depend upon. **15.** ~ **down**, retire from witness-box or similar position, (Mil.) go off duty after ~ ing to. **16.** ~ **for**, represent, signify, imply, as *P.O.*~s *for postal order, tariff reform* ~s *for a great deal more than that*, ‖ be candidate for (office), be candidate for representation of (constituency) in Parliament, espouse the cause of (free trade etc.), (colloq.) endure, tolerate, acquiesce in. **17.** ~ (person) **in** (sum), cost, as *coat stood me in* £20, *wife* ~s *him in* £50 *yearly for motor tires*; ~ (person) *in good* STEAD; ~ *in with*, be in league with. **18.** ~ **off**, move away, keep one's distance, (colloq.) dispense with the services of (employee) temporarily; ~**off** (*half*), (Rugby football) half-back who forms a link between the scrum-half and the three-quarters; ~ *off* & *on* (Naut.), sail alternately away from & towards shore so as to keep a point in sight. **19.** ~ **on** (prep.), insist on, observe scrupulously, esp. ~ *on ceremony*; ~ **on** (adv., Naut.), continue on same course. **20.** ~ **out**, hold out, persist in opposition (*against*) or endurance, be prominent or conspicuous. **21.** ~ **over**, be postponed. **22.** ~ **to** (prep.), abide by (promise etc.), stick to, not desert, (one's post, guns, esp. fig., duty, etc.), ~ *to it*, maintain stoutly (*that*), ~ *to sea* (Naut.), sail out to sea; ~ **to** (adv.), (arch.) fall to, set to work, (Mil.) take post in preparation for an attack (esp. before dawn & after dark); ~ *to win, lose*, have one's bets or other dispositions so made that one is sure to win or lose something or a specified amount (*whoever loses, I* ~ *to win; how much do you* ~ *to lose?; if Ladas is scratched I* ~ *to win* £5000). **23.** ~ **up**, rise to one's feet from sitting or other position, maintain erect position; ~ *up for*, side with, maintain, support, (person, cause); ~ *upon*, = *on*; ~ *up to*, meet, face, (opponent) courageously, (of things) remain unimpaired despite the effects of (hard wear etc.); ~ *up with*, take one's place with (partner) for dance, dance with. **24.** ~**off'ish** a., distantly reserved, not affable, whence ~**offishly** adv., ~**offishness** n.; ~**up** a., (of collar) upright, high, opp. to *turn-down*, (of fight) thorough, fair & square. [OE *standan*, ON *standa*; cogn. w. L *stare*, Gk *histēmi* (st. *sta-*)]

stand², n. **1.** Cessation from motion or progress, stoppage, as *came, was brought, to a* ~; *be at a* ~ (arch.), be unable to proceed, be in perplexity. **2.** Stationary condition assumed for purpose of resis-tance, esp. *make a* ~ (against enemy, for, against, principle etc.). **3.** Position taken up, as *took his* ~ *near the door, I take my* ~ (base argument etc., rely) *on the precise wording of the act*. **4.** Table, set of shelves, rack, etc., on or in which things may be placed, as *music, hat, umbrella,* ~; INK~, (WASH-hand-)~. **5.** Stall in market etc., as *fruit*~. **6.** Standing-place for vehicles etc., as CAB~. **7.** Raised structure for persons to sit or stand on, as BAND¹~, GRAND ~; *witness-box, take the* ~. **8.** Standing growth (of clover etc.). **9.** (Theatr.) each halt made on a tour to give performances (*a one-night* ~). **10.** (Austral.) a forest, or its timber, regarded commercially. **11.** ~ *of arms*, complete set for one man; ~ *of colours*, regiment's flags. **12.** ~ *camera* (for use on a tripod); ~*pipe*, vertical pipe for various purposes; ~*point*, point of view; ~*rest*, high stool with sloping top for supporting person standing at easel etc.; ~*still*, stoppage, inability to proceed, as *am brought to a* ~*still*. [f. prec.]

stan'dard, n. **1.** Distinctive flag, esp. flag of cavalry regiment (opp. to *colours* of infantry), as *the* (*English*) *royal* ~ (square banner with national arms); (fig.) rallying principle (*raise the* ~ *of revolt, free trade*). **2.** Weight or measure to which others conform or by which the accuracy of others is judged (often attrib., as ~ *pound, yard,* etc.); thing serving as basis of comparison. **3.** Degree of excellence etc. required for particular purpose (*does not come up to the* ~: *must set a low* ~; *of living*, minimum of material comfort with which a person or class or community may reasonably be content); ~ *novels* (those of admitted merit); grade of classification in primary schools. **4.** Average quality, as *work was of a low* ~. **5.** *Monetary* ~, proportion of weight of fine metal & alloy in gold or silver coin (*gold, silver,* ~) or in both (*double* ~); *multiple, tabular,* ~, of value obtained by averaging prices of a number of products. **6.** Measure of timber. **7.** Upright support (often attrib., as ~ *lamp*, set on rail usu. telescopic pillar; upright water or gas pipe; tree, shrub, that stands alone without support; shrub grafted on upright stem & trained in tree form. **8.** ~*bearer*, soldier who bears ~ (fig.) prominent leader in a cause; ‖~ *bread* (wheaten, of mixed flours). [MiF, f. OF *estandard* & *estendard* (f. L as EXTEND + -ARD); partly also f. STAND¹]

stan'dardiz|e, v.t. Make to conform to standard; (Chem.) obtain by analysis specific value of (solution etc.) for purposes of comparison. Hence ~A'TION n. [-IZE]

stan'ding¹, n. In vbl senses; esp.:

estimation in which one is held, repute, position, as *men of high* ~, *is of no* ~; duration, as *a dispute of long* ~; **~-room**, space to stand in. [-ING²]

stan'ding², n. In vbl senses, esp.: established, as *a* ~ *rule*, *has become a* ~ (stock) *jest*; permanent, not made, raised, etc., for the occasion, as ~ *army*, ~ *orders* (esp. those respecting manner in which business shall be conducted in Parliament); ~ *rigging* (fixed stays); ~ *corn* (not cut); ~ *jump* (performed without preliminary run); ~ (stagnant) *water*, [STAND²]

stän'dish, n. (arch.). Inkstand. [STAND² + DISH]

*stand'patter, n. Politician who is for strict adherence to party platform, esp. on tariffs. [f. *stand pat*¹]

stan'hope (-nop), n. Light open carriage of 2 or 4 wheels: (also S~) printing press invented by Lord S~; S~ *lens* (with convex surfaces of different curves). [name of inventors]

stän'iel (-yel), n. Kestrel. [OE *stângella* (*stân* stone + *gellan* YELL)]

stank. See STINK v.

‖**stänn'ary**, n. & a. Tin-mine; tin-mining district; ~ *court* (for regulation of tin-mines in Cornwall & Devon). [f. med. L *stannaria* n. (LL *stannum*, *stag-*, tin, see -ARY)]

stänn'ic, a. (chem.). Of tin esp. in its higher valence, as ~*ic acid*. So ~ATE(3) n., ~IʹFEROUS, ~OUS, aa. [f. LL *stannum* n.+-IC]

stan'za, n. Group of (usu. four or more) rhymed lines, as *Spenserian* ~; group of four lines in some Greek & Latin metres, esp. *Alcaic*, *Sapphic*, ~. Hence (-)~'d, ~ED³ (-ad), **stänz'a'ic**, aa. [It., = chamber, stanza, f. pop. L *stantia* f. *stand*. abode (*stāre* stand, see -ANCE)]

stä'ple¹, n., & v.t. 1. Hoop-shaped bar or piece of wire with pointed ends for driving into post etc. to take point of hook, hasp, etc.; box-shaped part into which lock of door etc. shuts; metal tube holding the reeds of oboe & similar instruments; bent wire used in wire-stitching. 2. v.t. Furnish, fasten, with ~; ~ *stapling-machine*. [vb f. n.] OE *stapol*, cf. Du. *stapel* chair-leg, Da. *stabel* stake, G *staffel* rung, step, *stapel* stake; prob. cogn. w. STEP]

stä'ple², n., a., & v.t. 1. Important or principal article of commerce, as *the* ~*s of that country*, (fig.) chief element or material; (fig.) chief element or material; *as formed the* ~ *of conversation*; fibre of cotton, wool, etc., viewed as determining its quality, as *cotton of fine, short*, ~. 2. adj. Principal, as ~ *commodities*. 3. v.t. Sort, classify (wool etc.) according to fibre, whence **stä'pler¹** n. [vb & adj. f. n.) = market, f. OF *estaple* f. MLG *stapel*, = prec.]

stär¹, n. 1. Celestial body appearing as luminous point; (also *fixed* ~) such body so far from earth as to appear motionless except for diurnal revolution of the heavens; *double, multiple*, ~, group of two, of three to six, fixed ~s appearing to naked eye as one; *binary* ~, two ~s revolving round one another; EVENING ~, MORNING ~; *day* ~ (poet.), morning ~; LODE~; *north, polar*, ~ (= POLE²); *shooting* ~, small meteor appearing like moving rapidly and disappearing. 2. Thing suggesting ~ by its shape, esp. figure or object with radiating points e.g. as decoration of an order; ~*s & stripes*, U.S. national flag; asterisk; white spot on forehead of horse etc. 3. ‖(Pool) additional life bought by player whose lives are lost. 4. Principal actor or actress in a company (*film* ~; *the* ~ *system*, of relying on a ~ or two to make up for weak company); ~ *turn*, principal item in an entertainment or performance; brilliant or prominent person, as *literary* ~, *bright particular*~ (object of one's devotion). 5. Heavenly body considered as influencing person's fortunes etc., as *born under an unlucky*~, *his* ~ *was in the ascendant*, *you may thank your* ~*s you were not there*, *the* ~*s were against it* (cf. ILL~-red). 6. ~-*apple*, edible applelike fruit of W.-Indian tree, with a stellate section; S~ *Chamber* [perh. diff. wd.], court of civil & criminal jurisdiction primarily concerned with offences affecting crown interests, noted for summary & arbitrary procedure, & abolished 1640;~-*drift*, common proper motion of a number of fixed ~s in same region; ~'*finch*, redstart; ~'*fish*, echinoderm with five or more radiating arms; ~-*gazer* (joc.), astronomer; ~'*light*, star of ~s, as *walked home by* ~*light*, (adj., also of ~*lit*) lighted by the ~s as *a*~*light night*; ~ *of Bethlehem*, plant of lily family with like white flowers striped with green on outside; S~ *of India*, order of knighthood instituted 1861 to commemorate assumption of direct government of India,~ *shell*, kind designed to burst in air & light up enemy's position; ~-*spangled*, spangled with ~s (esp. of U.S. flag); ~-*stone*, kind of sapphire; ~-*stream*, present as a theatrical, film, etc., star. 3. ‖(Pool) buy additional life. [f. prec.]

stä'board (-berd), n. & v.t. 1. Right side of vessel looking forward (cf. PORT⁵; LAR-BOARD; often attrib.). 2. v.t. Turn, put, (helm) to ~. [vb f. n.) OE *stēorbord*

(stǣor rudder, see STEER¹, + bord BOARD], early Teut. ships being steered with a paddle over the right side]

starch, a., n., & v.t. **1.** (now rare). Pre-cise, prim, whence ~LY² adv., ~NESS n. **2.** n. White odourless tasteless powder procured chiefly from corn & potatoes but found in all plants except fungi & valuable in digestion; preparation of this with usu. boiling water for stiffening linen etc. before ironing; (fig.) stiffness of manner, formality. Hence ~INESS n., ~Y² a., (lit. & fig.). **3.** v.t. Stiffen with ~ (often fig, esp. in p.p., whence ~´EDIY² adv., ~´EDNESS n.); CLEAR¹.~ Hence (~)~ER¹ ² n. [adj. f. n. f. vb, ME *sterche* stiffen f. STARK]

star│e, v.i. & t., & n. **1.** Look fixedly with eyes wide open (*at, upon,* etc., or abs.) from surprise, admiration, bewilderment, stupidity, horror, impertinent curiosity, etc.; (chiefly in part.) be unpleasantly prominent or striking, as a *~ing waist-coat, tie was of a ~ing red,* (adv.) *stark ~ing mad;* reduce (person) to specified condition by *~ing,* as *~ed him out of countenance, into silence, dumb; ~e down,* outstare; *~e(person) in the face,* be evident or imminent, as *the facts ~e us in the face, ruin ~ed him in the face.* Hence ~´ingⁿ² adv. **2.** n. ~ing gaze. [(n. f. vb) OE *starian,* cf. Du. *staren,* ON *stara*]

stark, a. & adv. **1.** Stiff, rigid, as *~ & stiff, lies ~ in death;* (poet.) strong; (poet.) stubborn, resolute; downright, sheer, as *~ madness.* **2.** adv. Quite, wholly, (chiefly in *~ mad, naked*). [OE *stearc* strong, stiff, cf. Du. *sterk,* G *stark,* ON *sterkr; ~ naked* was orig. *start* (= tail) *~naked* (OE *steort* tail, cf. REDSTART & Du. *staart,* G *stjert,* ON *stertr*)]

star│ling¹, n. Bird of blackish-brown plumage with light speckles & metallic purple & green reflections, of great imitative powers & easily tamed. [OE *stærlinc* (*stær* starling, cf. G *staar,* Da. *stær,* L *sturnus*)+-LING¹]

starling², n. Protective piling round pier of bridge. [f. 17th c., perh. corrupt. of obs. *staddling,* OE *staðolung* (*staðo-lian* establish f. *staðol* foundation, -ING¹)]

starry. See STAR¹.

start¹, v.i. & t. **1.** Make sudden movement from pain, surprise, etc., as *~ed in his seat, ~ed at the sound of my voice;* change position abruptly as from shock or sudden impulse, as *~ aside, from one's chair.* **2.** (Of timbers etc.) spring from proper position, give way. **3.** Set out, begin journey, as *we ~ed at six;* make a beginning (on journey, enterprise, book, cigar, etc.); begin, commence, (work etc., *doing, to do*). **4.** *~ in* (colloq.), begin (*to do*); *~ out* (colloq.), take steps as intending (*to do*); *~ up,* rise suddenly e.g. from seat, arise, come into existence or action, occur to the mind, as *many difficulties, rivals, have*

~ed up, (trans.) cause (engine) to begin running. **5.** Rouse (game) from lair etc. **6.** Originate, set going, (enterprise, news-paper, business, clock after winding, objections, quarrel, etc.); cause to begin doing (*this ~ed me coughing*); cause or enable (person) to commence business etc.; give signal to (persons) to ~ in race. **7.** Cause or experience the starting of (timbers, tooth, etc.). **8.** (Naut.) pour out (liquor) from cask. **9.** *To ~ with,* in the first place, as *you have no right to be here, to ~ with;* at the beginning, as *had 6 members to ~ with.* [ME *sterte,* perh. f. OE *styrtan,* cogn. w. Du. *storten,* Da. *styrte,* G *stürzen,* hurl etc.]

start², n. **1.** Sudden movement of sur-prise, pain, etc.; (pl.) intermittent or spasmodic efforts or movements, esp. (*works*) *by fits & ~s.* **2.** Beginning of journey or action or race, as *shall make an early ~ for town, is difficult work at the ~, the ~ is fixed for 3 p.m.;* starting-place of race. **3.** Advantage conceded in race, as *will give you 60 yards~, 15 seconds~;* advantageous position gained in business etc., as *got a good ~ in life, got the ~ of rivals* (gained advantage over) *his rivals.* **4.** *A rum ~* (colloq.), surprising occurrence. [ME *steort,* as prec.]

start´er, n. In vbl senses, esp.: one who gives signal to start in race; horse, com-petitor, starting in race, as *list of probable ~s;* SELF-~. [-ER¹]

start´ing, n. In vbl senses: *~-gate,* re-movable barrier for securing fair start in horse-races; *~-post* (from which com-petitors start in race); *~ prices* in horse-races, final odds at start. [-ING¹]

start´le, v.t. Cause (person etc.) to start with surprise or sudden alarm, give shock to, take by surprise, whence (of person, news, etc.), start´lER¹ ¹ n.; (part.) surprising, alarming, as *startling news, discovery, development,* whence start´lingLY² adv. [ME *startlen, ster-,* f. START¹, see -LE(3)]

starv│e, v.i. & t. **1.** Die of hunger; suffer from lack of food; suffer extreme poverty; (colloq.) feel hungry, as *am simply starving;* ‖(now rare) perish with, suffer from, cold; (fig.) suffer mental or spiritual want, feel strong craving for (sympathy, amusement, knowledge, etc.). **2.** Cause to perish with hunger; deprive of, keep scantily supplied with, food (lit. & fig.); compel (garrison etc. *into sur-render* etc.) thus; ‖cause to perish, affect severely, with cold. Hence starva´TION n. [OE *steorfan* die, cf. Du. *sterven,* G *sterben,* die]

starve´ling (-l-), n. & a. **1.** Starving or ill-fed person or animal. **2.** adj. Starving. [-LING¹]

stas´is, n. (path.). Stoppage of circulation of any of the fluids of the body. [Gk, = standing]

-stat, terminal element in names of certain instruments. f. Gk *statos* stationary; as AERO~, PHOTO~, THERMO~.

state¹, n. & a. **1.** Condition in which a thing is, mode of existence as determined by circumstances, as ~ *of life* (one's rank & occupation), *in a* ~ *of health*, stated, as *the* ~ *is unfounded*; formal *found him in the same* ~, *in a* ~ *of deep depression, things were in an untidy* ~, *in a bad* ~ *of repair, what a (dirty, untidy)* ~ *you are in!*, (colloq.) *he was in quite a* ~ (quite excited or anxious) *about it*. **2.** (Often *S~*) organized political community forming part of federal republic, esp. *the United S~s (of America)*. **3.** pl. Legislative body in Jersey & Guernsey. **4.** Civil government, as *Church & S~*. **5.** Rank, dignity, as *in a style befitting his* ~, **6.** Pomp, as *arrived in great* ~; *keep* ~, maintain one's dignity, be difficult of access; *in* ~ (with all due ceremony). **7.** (arch.) Throne (also *chair of* ~), dais, canopy over throne. **8.** (Of dead person) *lie in* ~, be placed on view in public place. **9.** (Bibliog.) one of two or more differing portions of a single edition of a book. **10.** (Impression taken from) an etched or engraved plate at a particular stage of its progress. **11.** *Free, Slave, S~, S~* in which slavery did not, did, exist; *Southern S~s* (in southern part of U.S.); *S~s of the Church, Papal S~s*, former temporal dominions of Pope chiefly in central Italy; *S~s General*, legislative bodies of (1) the Netherlands before 1648, (2) France before 1789; *~-craft*, art of conducting affairs of S~. **12.** adj. Of, for, concerned with, the S~, as *~ criminal, political offender*; *~ documents, service; ~ prisoner*, person under arrest for felony, also political prisoner; *~ trial*, prosecution by S~ esp. for political offence; **S~ Department* (of foreign affairs); **S~ rights*, rights & powers not delegated to United S~s but reserved to individual S~s; **S~ socialism, socialist*, policy, advocate, of S~ control of manufactures, railways, etc. for the benefit of the masses. **13.** Reserved for, done on, occasions of ceremony, as *~ apartments, carriage; ~ call* (colloq.) formal visit; *~ room*, room so reserved, also, private sleeping-apartment on steamer. [f. n. f. OF *estat* f. STATUS]

state², v.t. Express, esp. fully or clearly, in speech or writing, as *have ~d my opinion, must ~ full particulars, this condition was expressly ~d, no precise time ~d, did not ~ why, ~s that arrangements are complete*; fix, specify, (date etc.), as *at ~d intervals*, whence **stat'edLY²** adv.; (Alg.) express the conditions of (problem, relation, etc.) in symbols. Hence **stat'ABLE** a. [f. prec.]

state'lĭy̆ (-tli-), a. (Of manner, language, person, literary style, rhythm, building, proportions, etc.) dignified, imposing, grand. Hence **~iNESS** n. [as STATE¹, see -LY¹]

state·ment (-tm-), n. Stating, expression in words, as *requires clearer* ~; thing stated, as *the* ~ *is unfounded*; formal account of facts, e.g. of liabilities & assets, as *the Bank issues monthly* ~s. [-MENT]

stat'er, n. Ancient Greek coin of various values, esp. gold coin worth 20 drachmae. [L, f. Gk *stater* (*sta-* stand, *histēmi* weigh)]

states'man (-ts-), n. Person taking prominent part, person skilled, in management of State affairs; sagacious far-sighted practical politician; ‖ (North.) small working landowner; ‖ *Elder Statesmen*, the Japanese statesmen who mainly directed the evolution of Japan between the re-establishment of the Mikado (1868), & the end of the 19th c., also transf. Hence ~LIKE, ~LY¹ aa., ~SHIP(3) n. [= *state's man*]

stat'ic(al), a. Concerned with bodies at rest or forces in equilibrium, whence **stat'ics** n. pl. (or as sing.), also = atmospheries: acting as weight but not moving, as *~ pressure; ~ electricity* (at rest); *static ataxia*, inability to stand without falling or swaying; *static water*, local supply not under pressure. Hence **stat'ically²** adv. [f. Gk *statikos* (*sta-* stand, see -IC & -AL)]

sta'tion, n. & v.t. **1.** Standing, being still, (opp. *motion*; now rare; *a ~ like the herald Mercury*). **2.** Place, building, etc., in which person or thing stands or is placed esp. habitually or for definite purpose, as *was assigned a ~ in the valley, returned to their several ~s, took up a convenient ~, coastguard ~* (occupied by coastguards-men), POLICE ~, ‖ *lifeboat ~* (where lifeboat is kept); *naval ~*, place affording shelter or harbour for ships with dock-yard etc.; (pl. Nav.) posts assigned to members of ship's complement in readiness for battle. **3.** Subordinate depot or office serving local needs. **4.** Stopping-place on railway with buildings for accommodation of passengers & goods or ‖ (*goods~*) of goods only. **5.** Position in life, (high) rank, status, employment, as *occupied a humble ~, men of (exalted) ~, the duties of his ~*. **6.** (Surv.) point from which measurements are made, standard distance usu. 100 or 66 ft. **7.** Military post esp. in India, officers or society residing there. **8.** (Austral.) sheep-run or its building. **9.** (eccl.). Fast on Wed. & Frid. (hist.); (also *~ of the cross*) each of series of 14 images or pictures representing Christ's passion before which devotions are performed in some churches; church esp. in Rome to which pilgrims etc. go for devotions. **10.** (Bot., Zool.) nature of the habitat of plant or animal

in respect of climate, soil, etc. **11.** ~-**bill** (Naut.), list of appointed posts of ship's company; ‖ ~-**calendar,** board showing successively the starting-time of trains at each platform; ~-**house,** police-station; ‖ ~-**master,** official in charge of railway ~; ~-**pointer,** three-armed protractor for locating place on chart from certain data. **12.** v.t. Assign to, place (person, one-*self*) in ~. [vb f. n.) F, f. *stationem (stare stand,* -ATION)]

sta'tionary (-sho-), a. & n. **1.** Remaining in one place, not moving, as *balloon was now* ~; not meant to be moved, not portable, as ~ *engine, troops;* (of planet) having no apparent motion in longitude; not changing in magnitude, number, quality, efficiency, etc., as ~ *temperature, population, intelligence;* ~ *air* (remaining in lungs during ordinary respiration); ~ *diseases,* local diseases due to atmospheric conditions & disappearing after a period. **2.** n. ~ person, esp. (pl.) ~ troops. Hence **sta'tionariNESS** (-sho-) n. [f. L *stationarius* (as prec., see -ARY[1])]

sta'tioner (-sho-), n. One who sells writing-materials etc.; ‖ *S~s' Hall* (of *S~s'* Company in London, at which book was formerly *entered,* i.e. registered, for purposes of copyright). Hence **sta'tion-ERY** (1) (-sho-) n. [earlier = bookseller (as prec. in med. L sense *shopkeeper* as opp. *pedlar*)]

sta'tist, n. Dealer in statistics. [earlier = politician, f. STATE[1] +-IST]

statis'tics, n. pl. Numerical facts systematically collected, as ~*ics of population, crime;* (treated as sing.) science of collecting, classifying, & using ~ics. So ~IC(AL) aa., ~ICALLY[2] adv., **statisti'CIAN** (-ishn) n. [prec. +-ICS]

statisto'r, n. (electr.). Stationary portion of a generator or motor; ~ *armature* (non-rotating). [L, f. *stare* stand]

sta'toscope, n. Aneroid barometer for showing minute variations of pressure. [f. Gk *statos* fixed *(sta-* stand) +-SCOPE]

sta'tuary, a. & n. **1.** Of or for statues, as ~ *art,* ~ *marble* (fine-grained white). **2.** n. Sculptor; (art of making) statues. [f. L *statuarius* (as foll., see -ARY[1])]

sta'tue, n. Sculptured or cast or moulded figure of person or animal (esp. one not much below life size, opp. to ~ETTE' n.); EQUESTRIAN ~*e.* Hence ~ED[2] (-ūd) a. [OF, f. L *statua (stare* stand)]

statuesque' (-k), a. Like, having the dignity or beauty of a statue. Hence ~LY[2] (-k-) adv., ~NESS (-kn-) n. [-ESQUE]

stat'ur|e (-yer), n. Height of (esp. human) body, as *undersized* in ~*e,* of *mean* ~*e.* Hence (-)~ED[2] (-yerd) a. [OF, f. L *statūra* standing posture *(stare stat-* stand, see -URE)]

sta'tus, n. (pl. prob. not used). Social position, rank, relation to others, relative importance, *(his* ~ *is a matter of doubt,*

their ~ *is wholly different, his ~ among novelists*); (Law) person's relation to others as fixed by law; position of affairs, esp. ~ (*in*) *quo,* unchanged position (cf. IN[5] *statu quo)* or (also ~ *quo ante*) the previous position. [L, gen. -*ūs,* = standing *(stare* stand)]

sta'tut|able, a. = STATUTORY. Hence ~LY[2] adv. [-ABLE]

stat'ute, n. A written law of a legislative body, e.g. Act of Parliament; *S~ of Westminster* (in 1931, conferring equality of status on the self-governing British Dominions); ~ *law,* a ~, (collect.) the ~s (opp. to COMMON[1] *law*); ordinance of corporation, founder, etc., intended to be permanent, as *University* ~s; (Bibl.) divine law, as *kept thy* ~s; *declaratory* (fixing interpretation of existing law); *private* (affecting individuals, opp. to *general, public,* ~); ~-*book,* book(s) containing the ~ law; ~-*roll,* engrossed ~, ~-*book;* ~s *at large* (in full as originally enacted). [f. F *statut* f. LL *statutum* neut. p.p. as n. of L *statuere* establish *(stare* stand)]

stat'utory, a. Enacted, required, imposed, by statute, as ~ *provisions, mini-mum.* [-ORY]

staunch[1], stanch, (-awr-, -ah-), a. Trust-worthy, loyal, as ~ *friend, supporter;* (of ship, joint, etc.) watertight, airtight. Hence ~LY[2] adv., ~'NESS n. [earlier also = watertight, f. OF *estanche* fem. adj. as STANCH[1]]

staunch[2]. See STANCH[1].

staur'oscope, n. Instrument for examining effects of polarized light on crystals. [f. Gk *stauros* cross +-SCOPE]

stave[1], n. Each of the curved pieces of wood forming sides of cask etc.; each of the boards forming curb of well or hollow cylinder; rung of ladder; stanza, verse; (Mus.) = STAFF; ~-*rhyme,* alliteration esp. in old Teut. poetry. [var. of STAFF, due to pl. *staves*]

stave[2], v.t. *(slōve* or ~*d*). Break a hole in (cask, boat; often *in* adv.); (usn. ~ *in*) crush or bash (hat, box) out of shape; furnish, fit, (cask etc.) with staves; ~ *off,* avert, ward off, defer, (ruin, exposure, etc.); make (metal etc.) firm by compression. [f. prec.]

staves'acre (-vzāker), n. Kind of lark-spur whose seeds are used as poison for vermin. [f. L *staphisagria* (Gk *staphis* dried grapes +*agria* wild)]

stay[1], v.t. & i., & n. **1.** (Now chiefly literary) check, stop, (progress, inroads of disease etc.). **2.** ~ one's *stomach,* appease hunger esp. temporarily. **3.** Postpone (judgement, decision). **4.** Support, prop (often *up*) as or with buttress etc. **5.** Remain, as ~ *here till I return, will not* ~ *where it is put* (also, *will not* ~ *put*), *has come to* (colloq.), must be regarded as permanent; (w. adv.) *away, on, out-*

etc.; ~-in strike, (of miners); ~-down strike, = SIT-down strike; (colloq.) wait long enough to partake of (can you ~ supper?); dwell temporarily (at hotel etc., in town etc., with person). 6. Pause in movement, action, speech (esp. in imperat.), etc., as get him to ~ a minute, ~!—you forget one thing. 7. Show endurance esp. in race, as does not seem able to ~, whence ~'ER¹ n. 8. ~-at-home a. & n., (person) remaining habitually at home, 9. n. Remaining, esp. dwelling, in a place, duration of this, as made a long ~ in London, your ~ has been very short. 10. Suspension of judicial proceedings (esp. of execution, i.e. of carrying out judgement given). 11. (Chiefly literary) check, restraint, (will endure no ~, a ~ upon his activity). 12. Endurance ~ing-power, 13. Prop, support, (you have been the ~ of my old age). 14. pl. Corset, whence ~-LESS a. 15. ~-bar, -rod, support in building or machinery; ~-lace, -maker (of corsets). [f. vb, prob. f. OF ester f. L stare stand; sense support v. & n. perh. f. OF estaye(r), f. Teut. as foll., in transferred uses]

stay¹, n., & v.t. (naut.). 1. Rope supporting mast or spar; ship is (hove) in ~s (going about from one tack to another); miss ~s, fail in endeavour to tack; ~sail (-sāl, Naut. -sl), any sail extended on a ~. 2. v.t. Support (mast etc.) by ~s; put (ship) on other tack. [vb f. n. OE stæg, cf. G, Du., & ON stag, cogn. w. STEER]

stead (stěd), n. (now chiefly literary) Stand (person) in good ~, be advantageous or serviceable to; in person's ~, instead of him, as his substitute. [OE stede, town, & w. SPAN?; seen in bedstead, homestead.]

steadfast (stěd-), a. Constant, firm, unwavering. Hence ~LY² adv., ~NESS n. [OE stedefæst (prec., FAST²)]

steading (stěd-), n. Farmstead. [-ING¹]

stead'y (stěd-), a., n., & v.t. & i. 1. Firmly fixed or supported or standing or balanced, not tottering, as not ~ on his legs, must level table's legs to make it ~, as a rock, has not acquired a ~ seat on bicycle; done, moving, acting, happening, in uniform & regular manner, as went off at a ~ pace, had a ~ wind behind us, requires a ~ light, observe a ~ increase in the numbers; (as command or warning) ~!, be ~, abstain from erratic or boisterous behaviour, premature action, hasty inference, etc., (Naut., also keep her ~, keep direction of ship's head unchanged; not changeable, as ~ in his principles, ~one, stop!; constant in mind or conduct, allegiance; of industrious & temperate habits. 2. n. Kinds of support for hand or tool; *(colloq.) regular sweetheart. Hence stea'dily² adv., stea'diness n., (stěd-). 3. vb. Make, become, ~, as ~ the

boat, boat steadied, adversity will ~ him, he will soon ~ (down). [STEAD +-Y¹]

steak (stāk), n. Slice of beef, pork, venison, or fish, cut for broiling etc., as beef ~, RUMP-, PORTER²-house, ~, fillet ~ (from undercut of sirloin); Hamburg ~, cake of chopped & seasoned beef cooked in covered frying-pan. [f. ON steik (steikja roast on spit)]

steal, v.t. & i. (stōle, stōlen). 1. Take away (thing, or abs.) secretly for one's own use without right or leave, take feloniously, as who ~s my purse ~s trash, stolen fruit; obtain surreptitiously or by surprise, as stole a kiss, a stolen interview; ~ one's THUNDER; get, ~ (away) win, get possession of, (esp. person's heart) by insidious arts, attractions, etc.; ~ a march on, get the start of, anticipate. 2. intr. Move (in, out, away, up, by, etc.) secretly or silently, as stole out of the room, mist stole over the valley. Hence (~)ER¹ n. [OE stelan, cf. Du. stelen, G stehlen]

stealth (stělt), n. Secrecy, secret procedure, esp. by ~, surreptitiously. Hence ~'ILY² adv., ~'INESS n. ~'Y² a., [-TH¹]

steam¹, n. 1. Vapour of water, esp. the gas into which water is changed by boiling, largely used as motive power owing to its elasticity; saturated ~ (in contact with, & at same temperature as, boiling water); superheated ~ (having higher temperature at given pressure, & greater volume for a given weight, than saturated ~); wet, dry,~ (containing, not containing, mechanically suspended particles of water); visible particles of water resulting from condensation of water vapour, as get up ~, summon energy for special effort, so put on, let off, work off, vaporous exhalation. 2. (colloq.). Energy, as get up ~, summon energy for special effort, so put on, let off, work off, ~. 3. ~-boat, vessel propelled by ~; ~-boiler, vessel in which water is boiled to generate ~ esp. for working engine; ~-box, -chest (through which ~ passes from boiler to cylinder); ~ brake, crane, gun, hammer, plough, whistle, winch, etc., (worked by ~); ~-cock (used in heating ~-boilers); ~-colour (fixed on printed cloth by action of ~); ~-cylinder (in which piston of ~-engine moves); ~-engine, locomotive or stationary engine in which the motive power depends on elasticity & expansion or rapid condensation of ~; ~-gas, superheated ~; ~-gauge (attached to boiler to show pressure of ~); ~-heat, heat required to produce given out by ~ from radiators etc.; ~-jacket, casing round cylinder etc. with space between to be filled by ~ for heating the cylinder etc.; ~-navvy, excavating machine; ~-port, each of two oblong passages from ~-chest into cylinder, any passage for ~; ~-power, force of ~ applied to machinery etc.; ~-roller, heavy slow-moving locomotive with wide wheels

used in road-making, (fig.) a crushing power or force (v.t., crush as with a ~ roller); ~ ship (propelled by ~); ~ tight, capable of resisting passage of steam; ~ tug, steamer for towing ships etc. Hence ~'INESS n., ~'Y² a. [OE steam, cf. Du. stoom, etym. dub.]

steam², v.t. & i. Cook (food) by steam; treat with steam, soften (timber) for bending by steam; give out steam or vapour, as a sirloin ~ed on the table, water ~ing hot; rise in vapour; move by agency of steam, as we, the vessel, ~ed down the river; (colloq.) work vigorously, make great progress, esp. ~ ahead, away. [OE stéman (prec.)]

steam'er, n. In vbl senses; also or esp.: vessel propelled by steam; fire-engine worked by steam; vessel in which things are steamed, esp. cooked by steam: boiler is a bad ~ (generator of steam). [-ER¹]

ste'arin, n. Chief ingredient of suet & tallow; (pop.) stearic acid separated from ~ by steam & used for candles. Hence **ste'arate**(3) n., **steá'ric** a. [f. Gk stear fat+-IN]

ste'arinery, n. Manufacture of stearin (products). [-ERY]

ste'atite, n. Kind of talc, soapstone. Hence **steati'ro** a. [f. L steatites (f. Gk as foll., -ITE¹)]

steat(o)- in comb. = Gk stear-atos fat.

steed, n. (poet., rhet., or joc.). Horse, esp. war-horse. Hence ~'LESS a. [OE stéda (stod STUD²)]

steel, n., & v.t. 1. Kinds of malleable alloy of iron & carbon largely used as material for tools, weapons, etc., & capable of being tempered to many different degrees of hardness (often attrib., as ~ pen), whence ~'IFY v.t.; BESSEMER ~; cold ~, sword etc. as opp. to firearm; a grip, muscles, a heart, of ~ (very tight, strong, hard); rod of ~, usu. tapering & roughened, for sharpening knives; strip of ~ for stiffening corset or expanding skirt; (poet., rhet., not in pl.) sword (a foe worthy of one's ~). 2. ~ cap, simple form of helmet; ~-clad, clad in armour; ~ engraving, engraving on, ~ plate; ~work, ~ articles, ~ for these. 3. v.t. Harden (oneself, one's heart, etc., to do, to action, against compassion etc.). [OE stýle & stéli, cf. Du. staal, G stahl, ON stál, cogn. w. STAY²]

steel'y, a. Of, hard as, steel; inflexibly severe, as ~y glance, composure. Hence ~'INESS n. [-Y²]

steel'yard, n. Kind of balance with short arm to take the thing weighed & long graduated arm along which a weight is moved till it balances this. [prob. f. STEEL & YARD; but usu. taken as f. beam, i.e. balance of Hanseatic 'Steelyard' (MI.G státhof = sample-house mistranslated) in London]

steen'bōk (stán-, stén-), n. Kinds of small African antelope. [Du., lit. stone buck]

steen'ing, n. Stone lining of well. [f. dial. steen pave (OE sténan to STONE) +-ING¹]

steen'kirk, n. (hist.). Cravat, other articles of dress etc., named in allusion to Battle of Steenkerke in Belgium 1692.

steep¹, a. & n. 1. Having decided slope, sheer, as ~ hills; (colloq.) of demand, price, etc.) exorbitant, unreasonable, as seems a bit ~ that we should take both the trouble & the expense, (of story etc.) exaggerated, incredible. 2. n. ~ slope, precipice. Hence ~'EN¹ v.i. & t., ~'LY³ adv., ~'NESS n., ~'Y² (poet.) a. [OE stéap, cf. OFris. stáp, cogn. w. STOOP]

steep², v.t., & n. 1. Soak in liquid; bathe with liquid; ~ in (fig.), impregnate with, pervade with, as ~ed in Greek & Latin, misery, slumber. 2. n. Process of ~ing (esp. in ~), liquid in which thing is ~ed. [ME stepen, cf. Sw. stöpa; perh. cogn. w. STOUP]

steep'er, n. Vessel in which things are steeped. [-ER¹]

stee'ple, n. Lofty structure, esp. tower surmounted with spire, rising above roof of church; ~chase, horse-race (perh. orig. with ~ as goal) across tract of country with ditches, hedges, etc., to jump, (also) cross-country foot-race; ~chaser, rider in ~chase, horse trained for ~chase; ~chasing, the sport of riding in ~chases; ~-crowned hat (with tall pointed crown); ~jack, man who climbs ~s etc. to do repairs etc.; ~-top, polar whale with spout-holes ending in cone. Hence **stee'plerd²** (-ld) a., ~'WISE adv. [OE stépel & stýpel (as STEEP¹)]

steer¹, v.t. & i. Guide (vessel) by rudder or helm, guide vessel in specified direction, (~ing-wheel, vertical wheel with handles along rim for controlling rudder); guide (motor, aircraft, etc.) by wheel etc.; (chiefly colloq. or poet.) direct (one's course), direct one's course, in specified direction, as ~ed his flight heavenwards, we ~ed (our course) for the railway station, ~ clear of (avoid) the local meteorologist; ~s'man, one who ~s vessel, ~s'manship, skill in ~ing. Hence ~'ABLE a., ~'ER¹(1, 2) n. [OE stéran, stéoran (stéor rudder, cf. Du. stuur, G steuer, ON stýri, cogn. w. ON staurr, Gk stauros, stake)]

steer², n. Young male of ox kind, esp. castrated bullock raised for beef. [OE stéor, cf. Du. & G stier bull, ON þjórr]

steer'age, n. (Now rare) steering; (Naut.) effect of helm on ship, as ship went with easy ~; part of ship allotted to ~ passengers (travelling at cheapest rate), variously placed; (hist.: in warship) part of berth-deck just forward of wardroom, quarters of junior officers, clerks, etc.; ~-way, amount of headway required by vessel to enable her to be controlled by helm. [-AGE]

steeve¹, v.i. & t. & n. (naut.). 1. (Of bowsprit) make angle with horizon; cause (bowsprit) to do this. 2. n. Such angle. [perh. f. OF *estive* ploughstaff f. L *stiva*]

steeve², n. & v.t. (naut.). 1. Long spar used in stowing cargo. 2. v.t. Stow with this. [(n. f. vb) f. OF *estiver* cram f. L *stipare*]

Stein'berger (stīn-, -ger), n. White wine grown on Rhine near Wiesbaden.

stein'böck (stīn-), n. A wild goat, the Alpine ibex. [G. = stone buck]

stel'e, n. (Gk archaeol.; pl. -ae). Upright slab or pillar usu. with inscription & sculpture, esp. as gravestone. [Gk]

stel'lar, a., Of stars. So ~if'erous, ~i-FORM, aa. [f. LL *stellaris* (*stella* star, see -AR¹)]

stel'late, -ated, aa. Arranged like a star, radiating, esp. (Bot.) ~ *leaves* (surround stem in a whorl). Hence stell'ately² adv. [f. L *stellare* set with stars (*stella* star), see -ATE²]

I stell'enbösch(-sh), v.t.(mil. sl.). Supersede without formal disgrace by appointing to unimportant command. [f. S~ in S. Africa, military base so utilized]

stell'ular, a. Shaped like, set with, small *stella* star +-AR¹]

stem¹, n., & v.t. & i. (-mm-). 1. Main body or stalk (usu. rising into light & air but occas. subterranean) of tree, shrub, or plant; slender stalk supporting fruit, flower, or leaf, & attaching it to main stalk or branch or twig. 2. ~-shaped part, e.g. slender part of wine-glass between body & foot, vertical line rising or falling from head of note in music, various winding-parts of watch (~-*winder*, ~ not by key), tubular part of tobacco-pipe. 3. Part of noun, verb, etc. (derived from & occas. identified with a root) to which case-endings etc. are added, part that appears or would originally appear unchanged throughout the case of a noun, persons of a tense, etc. 4. Line of ancestry, branch of family, etc. [OE *stefn, stemn* f. Gmc, cf. Du. *stam* trunk, *stem* of ship, Da. *stamme*, G *stamm*, trunk]

stem², v.t. (-mm-). Check, dam up, (stream etc., lit. & fig.); make headway against (tide, current, etc., lit. & fig.). [sense check f. ON *stemma*, cf. Da. *stemme*,

G *stemmen*, cogn. w. STAMMER; 2nd sense f. prec.]

stemm'a, n. (pl. ~ta). Family tree, pedigree; lineal descent; (Zool.) simple eye, facet of compound eye. [L, f. Gk *stemma* wreath (*stephō* wreathe, see -M)]

stem'ple, n. Each of several cross-bars in shaft of mine serving as supports or steps. [cf. G *stempel*]

Stën (gün), n. A light-weight machine-gun. [f. S and T (initials of inventors' surnames, Shepherd and Turpin) + -en for England)]

stench, n. Offensive smell; ~-*trap* (in sewer etc., to prevent upward passage of G *stench* (any) smell, cf. Du. & G *stank*, cogn. w. STINK]

stén'cil, n. & v.t. (-ll-). 1. (Also ~-*plate*) thin plate of metal etc. in which pattern (interrupted when necessary by a thin bar of the material left to prevent piece from falling out) is cut out; decoration, lettering, etc., produced by ~. 2. v.t. Produce (pattern) on surface, ornament (surface) with pattern, by brushing paint etc. over a ~-*plate* laid on the surface. Hence ~ler¹ n. [perh. f. OF *estenceler* sparkle, cover with stars, f. *estencele*, see TINSEL]

sténo- in comb. = Gk *stenos* narrow, chiefly in scientific wds.

sténóch'romy(-k-), n. Art of printing in several colours at one impression. [f. STENO-+Gk *khrōma* colour +-Y¹]

stén'ograph (-ahf), n. Character used, piece of writing, in shorthand; kinds of machine for writing in shorthand. Hence stěnóg'rapher¹, stěnóg'raph-ist, stěnóg'raphy¹, nn., stěnóg'raph¹ic a., stěnógraph¹ICALLY adv. [STENO-+ -GRAPH]

Stěn'tor, n. Person with powerful voice, herald in Trojan war. Hence stěntór¹IAN a. [L f. Gk *Stentōr*, herald in Trojan war]

stén'torphone, n. Specially powerful loud speaker. [prec.+Gk *phōnē* sound]

step¹, v.i. & t. & (-pp-). 1. Shift & set down foot or alternate feet (~ *out, short, long, short, steps*; ~ *through a dance*, perform its steps; ~ *high*, lift feet high esp. of trotting horse, so HIGH-*stepper*); go short distance or progress in some direction by ~ping (~ *back, forward, across the road, into the boat*; ~ *this way*, polite formula for come here; ~ *in, out*, enter, leave, room or house; ~ *in*, fig, intervene to help or hinder; ~ *up, down*; ~ *aside*, lit. & fig. = make digression); ~ *on the gas*; hence ~ *on it* (sl.), hurry. 2. Perform (dance; also ~ *it*, dance), measure (distance) by ~ping. 3. (Naut.; prob. f. n.) set up (mast) in step. 4. ~-*in* n. & a., (garment, esp. woman's undergarment) put on by being ~ped into; in stream or muddy place to enable passengers to cross dryshod, (fig.) means

to an end; ~ up (trans.), increase the rate, volume, etc. of, (Electr.) increase voltage of (current) by transformer. [OE *steppan* plant foot, go, cf. Du. *stappen*, G *stapfen*]

step², n. **1.** Complete movement of one leg in walking or running or dancing, distance gained by it, mark left by foot down, manner of stepping as seen or heard, simultaneous stepping with corresponding legs by two or more persons or animals, (fig.) measure taken esp. as one of a series in some course of action, (*took a ~ back or forward; ~ by ~, gradually, cautiously, by degrees; that is a long ~ towards success; it is but a ~ to my house, from life to death, exagg. for short distance or quick transition; do not move a ~; turn one's ~s, go in a specified direction; found his ~s or usu. foot~s in the soil; in his etc. ~s, following his etc. example; do you hear a, know her, ~?; walks with a rapid ~; one~, two~, dance names; in, out of, ~, stepping, not stepping, in time with others or with drum-beat etc.; keep, break, ~, keep in, get out of, ~; keep ~ with person, to band etc.*; FALSE ~; *must take ~s in the matter, to prevent it, etc.; a rash, ill-advised, prudent, etc., ~; mind, watch, your ~, be careful*). **2.** Surface provided or utilized for placing foot on in ascending or descending, e.g. tread or riser & tread of staircase, block of stone or other platform before door or altar etc., rung of ladder, notch cut for foot in ice-climbing, attached piece of vehicle for stepping up or down by, (pl., also ~ladder or pair or set of ~s) kind of short ladder with flat ~s & prop used without being leant against wall etc, (fig.) one of the degrees in some scale of precedence or advancement, advance from one of these to another, (*staircase of 50 ~s; one ~ of the ladder; run down the ~s; cutting ~s with his ice-axe; when did you get your ~?*; promotion esp. in army; *give him a ~ in the peerage*). **3.** (Naut.) socket or platform supporting mast; (Carpentry) piece of timber with another fixed upright in it; (Mech.) lower socket or bearing for shaft. **4.** ~-dance, in which the ~s are peculiar or difficult or of more importance than the figure, usu. danced as display by one performer. Hence ~PED² (-pt) a., ~'WISE adv. [OE *stæpe* (prec.)]

step-, pref. = holding nominal relationship, analogous to that specified owing to death of one and remarriage of the other of a married pair; ~child, ~son, ~daughter, one's wife's or husband's child by previous marriage; ~father, ~mother, ~parent, one's parent's later husband or wife; ~mother or arch. ~dame, harsh or neglectful mother lit. or fig., whence ~'motherly a., ~brother, ~sister, child of previous marriage of one's ~parent. [OE *steop* orphaned, cf. Du. & G *stief*, OHG *stiufan* deprive of parents or children; applied first to child & later extended to parent etc.]

stephanot'is, n. Climbing hotbouse plant with fragrant waxy flowers. [Gk fem adj. = fit for a wreath (*stephanos*)]

step'ney, n. (pl. ~s). Spare spokeless wheel formerly carried by motorists [said to be from S~ street, Llanelly, where made]

steppe, n. Level plain devoid of forest esp. in Russia & Siberia. [f. Russ. *stepi*]

-ster, suf. forming agent nn.; OE *-estre*, cf. Du. & Fris. *-ster*. In OE the suf. was orig. confined to the fem., but this restriction appears in mod. E only in *spinster*. Exx.: *brew~, huck~* (which however seems to have existed before the obs. vb *huck*), *game~, malt~, pun~,* & perh. *hol~, bol~*. In *seamstress* -ESS¹ is added to *-ster*; *-ster* in *lobster* is of different orig., but perh. assimilated.

stercora'ceous (-shus), **sterc'oral,** aa. Of ordure or faeces. [L *stercus -oris* dung, -ACEOUS, -AL]

stere (stēr), n. A cubic metre (about 35·3 cu. ft). [F (-ère), f. Gk *stereos* solid]

ste'reō, n. & a. (colloq.: pl. ~s). Stereotype (often attrib., as ~ *plate*); stereoscope; (adj.) stereoscopic. [shortening]

ste'reo-, comb. form of Gk *stereos* solid, stiff: ~bate, solid platform on which a building is erected; ~chem'istry, branch dealing with composition of matter as affected by relations of atoms in space; ~gram, ~graph, (one of) a pair of photographs for use in a ~scope; ~scope, instrument for viewing pair of photographs of scene, object, etc. taken at slightly different angles, each with one eye, thus producing by the combination of these images an impression of depth & solidity, so ~scōp'IC(ALLY), ~scopY¹ (-ŏs²).

ste'reotype, n., & v.t. **1.** Printing-plate cast from a papier-mâché or other mould of a piece of printing composed in movable type; making, use, of such plates; (fig.) fixed mental impression; ~e-block, on which ~e is mounted for use; hence ~IST(1), ~Y¹, ~ŏG'RAPHY, nn. **2.** v.t. Make ~es of; print by use of ~es; (fig.) make unchangeable, impart monotonous regularity to, fix in all details, formalize; hence ~ER¹ n. [f. F *stéréotype* a. & n. (prec., TYPE)]

ste'rrile, a. Unfruitful, unproductive, barren, not producing crop or fruit or young, or complete seed or result (~e land, cow, plant, year, effort, discussion); ~e free from living germs esp. bacilli or bacteria or microbes (usu. ~ized); (of style)jejune, bald. Hence or cogn. ~IZE(3) (-il~) v.t., (esp.) render free from microorganisms, render incapable of producing offspring, ~izA'TION, ~iZER¹(2), steril'ITY,

m. [f. L *sterilis*, cogn. w. Skr. *starĭ*, Gk *steira* barren cow]

stérˈlet, n. Kind of small sturgeon. [f. Russ. *sterlyadĭ*]

stérˈling, a. & n. **1.** (Of coins & precious metals) genuine, of standard value or purity, (abbr. *stg*; with coins, chiefly appended to sum expressed in pounds without odd money, as *£20 stg*; *is of ~ gold, silver*); (transf.) of solid worth, not showy, that is what it seems to be, (*is a ~ fellow*; *~ sense, qualities, character*; *the ~ nature of*). **2.** n. Genuine British money; British money as dist. from foreign money, (orig. as n., = the English silver penny; etym. dub.; the derivation f. *Easterling* is unlikely, requiring loss of the stressed syllable; perh. = little star, w. ref. to star found on some early Norman pennies; see -LING (2))

stérn¹, a. Severe, grim, rigid, strict, enforcing discipline or submission, not compassionate or indulgent or yielding, (*~ countenance, ruler, treatment, rebuke, virtue, father, tutor*; *~er SEX*). Hence ~LY², ~NESS nn. [OE *styrne*; perh. cogn. w. STEREO-, STARE]

stérn², n. **1.** Hind part of ship or boat (opp. *bow, stem*; *from stem to ~*, throughout ship); *~ chase*, pursuit of ship by another straight behind it; *~ foremost*, moving backwards, (fig.) with *~ presented*; by *~-way*, backward motion or impetus of ship; *~-wheeler*, steamer propelled by one large paddle-wheel at ~. **2.** Buttocks, rump; tail esp. of foxhound. **3.** ~-CHASE¹(v); *~fast*, rope or chain securing ~ to quay etc.; *~-post*, central upright timber or iron of ~ usu. bearing rudder; *~ sheets*, space in boat aft of rowers' thwarts often with seats for passengers. Hence (-)~ED²(-nd), ~MOST aa., ~WARD (-z) adv., ~WARDS (-z) adv. [f. ON *stjórn* steering cogn. w. STEER¹]

stérn(o)-, comb. form of foll. esp. in names of muscles etc. connecting sternum with other part; *~al/gia*, chest-pain, esp. angĭna pectŏris; *~oclavĭcŭlar*, of sternum & clavicle; *~ofăcĭal*; *~ohy̆oĭd*, *~othy̆roĭd*, etc. [f. Gk *sternon* breast]

stérnˈum, n. (pl. ~a). Bone running from neck to stomach & having ribs articulated with it, the breastbone. Hence ~AL¹ a. [mod. L, f. Gk *sternon*]

stérnūtāˈtion, n. Sneezing, sneeze. [f. L *sternutātio* (*sternuĕre* frequent. of *sternuĕre* sneeze cf. Gk *ptarmumai*), -ATION]

stérnuˈtative a., **stérnuˈtatory** a. & n. (Substance, e.g. snuff) causing to sneeze. [L *sternuāre* (prec.), -IVE, -ORY]

stértˈorous, a. (Of breathing or breather, esp. in apoplexy etc.) making snorelike sounds. Hence ~LY² adv., ~NESS n. [LL *stertere* snore, cogn. w. stertive snore, -OR², -OUS]

stĕt, proof-correcting direction, & v.t. **1.** Let it (i.e. the original form) stand (in margin to cancel a correction). **2.** v.t. Write ~ against, cancel correction of. [L, 3 sing subj. of *stare* stand]

stĕth´oscōpe, n. **1.** Instrument used in auscultation esp. of the heart. **2.** v.t. Examine with ~oscope. Hence ~ōsˈcopist, ~ōsˈcopy¹ nn., ~ōscoˈpic a., ~ōscoˈpˈĭcally adv. [F (*sté-*), f. Gk *stēthos* breast, -SCOPE]

stĕt´son, n. Slouch hat of type worn by Anzac soldiers. [maker's name]

stévˈedore, n. Man employed in loading & unloading ships. [f. Sp. *estivador* (*estivar* f. L *stipare* pack tight, -TOR)]

stew¹, n. Brothel (usu. the *~s*). [earlier sense (cf. BAGNIO) bath room or house, f. OF *estuve* f. med. L *stupha*(va) etym. dub.; prob. cogn. w. E STOVE, G *stube* room]

stew², v.t. & i. & n. **1.** Cook (t. & i.) by long simmering in closed vessel with little liquid (*let person, thing, ~ in his etc. own juice or grease*, abstain from helping etc.; *~ING¹ pears* etc., fit for eating *~ed*, not raw; *the tea is ~ed*, is bitter or strong by too long soaking); (fig.) be oppressed by close or moist warm atmosphere, (sl.) = SWOT; *~-pan, -pot*, shallow saucepan, covered crock, used for *~ing*. **2.** n. Dish made by *~ing* (*Irish ~*, of mutton, potato, & onion); (fig., colloq.) *in a ~*, agitated with perplexity, anxiety, or anger. [n. f. vb, f. prec. in sense *hot bath*]

stew³, n. ‖ Fishpond, tank for keeping fish alive in; artificial oyster-bed. [f. OF *estui* (*estuier* shut up)]

stewˈard, n. **1.** Person entrusted with management of another's property, esp. paid manager of great house or estate. **2.** Purveyor of provisions etc. for a college, club, guild, ship, etc. **3.** Passengers' attendant & waiter on ship. **4.** Any of the officials managing a race-meeting, ball, show, etc. **5.** ‖ *Lord High S~ of England*, official managing coronation or presiding at trial of a peer; ‖ *Lord S~ of the Household*, high court officer. Hence ~ESS¹, ~SHIP, nn. [OE *stíweard* (*stig* house etc.)]

sthén´ic, a. (path.) (Of disease etc.) with morbid increase of vital action esp. of heart & arteries. [Gk *sthenos* strength, -IC]

stich´omyth, **stichomyth´ia**, (-k-), n. Dialogue in alternate lines of verse as employed in Greek plays. [f. Gk *stikhomuthiā* (*stikhos* line, MYTH)]

stick, v.t. & i. (stuck), & n. **1.** Thrust point of into or through (*~ the spurs in*; *~ bayonet, pin, into or through*). **2.** Insert pointed thing(s) into, stab, (*~ pigs*, of butcher, also of mounted sportsman spearing wild pig; *will pull out a knife & ~ you*; *tipsy-cake stuck over or stuck with almonds*; *cushion stuck full of pins*). **3.** Fix (upon pointed thing, be fixed (as) by point into) or on (to), (colloq.) put in specified position, (*heads were stuck on*

spikes of gateway; *arrows ~ in target; work with needle ~ing in it; ~ feather, rose, in cap, buttonhole; ~ pen behind one's ear; ~ up a target, erect it; ~ your cap on ~ them in your pocket; ~ a few commas in; ~ just ~ it on the table, down anywhere). **4.** (With *out, up*) protrude, (cause to) project, be or make erect, (~ one's head out of window; his hair ~s straight up; ~-up collar, not turned down; ~ out one's chest; how his stomach ~s out!; this ~s out a mile, sl., is very obvious; stuck-up, conceited, insolently exclusive, prob. f. carriage of head; ~ up to, not humble oneself before, offer resistance to; ~ up for, maintain cause or character of esp. absent person). **5.** Fix or become or remain fixed (as) by adhesion of surfaces, (cause to) adhere or cleave, (~ postage-stamp on; this envelope will not ~; if you throw MUD enough, some of it will ~; innocence is not proof against scandal; limpet ~s to rock; ~ to the point, not digress; ~ to business, avoid distractions; the name stuck to him or stuck, was not forgotten; friend that ~eth closer than a brother; can you ~ on a horse?, escape being thrown; some of the money stuck in or to his fingers, was appropriated or embezzled by him; friends should ~ together; ~ to friend, resolve, promise, word, etc., abide by, remain faithful to; || ~ bills, post placards on wall etc., esp. ~ no bills, notice forbidding placarding of wall; ~ photographs, paste them in book etc.; ~s like a bur, is not to be got rid of; are you going to ~ in or indoors all day?, remain at home; so perh. ~ out for higher price, better terms, etc., refuse to take lower). **6.** ~ it out or ~ it (sl.), endure the conditions (could not ~ it any longer). **7.** ~ it on (sl.), make high charges, exaggerate in narration. **8.** Lose or deprive of power of motion through friction, jamming, suction, difficulty, or other impediment (~ in the mud lit., & fig. be unprogressive; ~-in-the-mud, (adj.) slow, unprogressive, (n.) person of such kind; also sl. Mrs etc. S~-in-the-mud, Mrs. etc. So-&-so; ~s in my throat, I cannot swallow it, lit. or fig.; ~ in one's gizzard, cannot be digested fig.; ~ fast, be hopelessly bogged etc.; is stuck on a sandbank; got up to the fourth form, through some ten lines, & there stuck; ~ at nothing, allow nothing, esp. no scruples, to deter one; || stuck up, sl., completely at a loss; that will ~ him up, puzzle him; ~ up bank, mail-coach, etc., sl., terrorize officials, passengers, etc., in order to rob). **9.** Provide (plant) with ~ as support or to climb up. **10.** Set (type) in COMPOSING~, whence ~FUL(2) n. **11.** ~ing-place, -point, at which screw becomes jammed (usu. fig. w. ref. to Macbeth I. vii. 60); ~ing-plaster, adhesive plaster for wounds etc.;

|| ~jaw (sl.), toffy etc. hard to masticate. **12.** n. Shoot of tree cut to convenient length for use as walking-cane or bludgeon, staff, wand, rod, piece of wood whether as part of something or separate more or less resembling these in shape & size, (cut a ~ from the hedge; cannot walk without a ~; gathering ~s to make a fire, twigs; any ~ to beat a dog, hatred makes unscrupulous; BROOM¹, DRUM¹, FIDDLE, GOLD, rocket, SINGLE¹, SWORD, umbrella, ~; riding on broom~, witch's way of transporting herself through air; house was pulled down & not a ~ left standing; a few ~s of furniture, chairs etc. of simple kind; wants the ~, should be caned; as CROSS³ as, DEVIL¹ on, two ~s; in a cleft ~, see CLEAVE¹; CUT² one's ~; (Naut., joc.) mast or spar; (Mus.) conductor's baton; (fig.) person of no vigour or intelligence or social qualities. **13.** Slender more or less cylindrical piece of sugar-candy, sealing-wax, shaving-soap, etc. **14.** (Short, with aid of context, for) fiddle~, drum~, composing-~, etc. **15.** Number (of bombs) released in rapid succession from aircraft, cf. SALVO². **16.** ~-insect, = WALKING~-insect. [vb a mixture of ME *sticien* (OE *stician*) & ME *steken*; cogn. w. Gk *stizō* prick, L *instigare* INSTIGATE, Skr. *tigmá* sharp; n., OE *sticca* (*stician*), orig. = peg]

stick'er, n. In vbl senses; also or esp. *pig~*, long-bladed sharp-pointed knife; BILL~; batsman who scores slowly & is hard to get out; person who stays too long on visit; *adhesive label; (Organ-build.) wooden rod transmitting motion between ends of two reciprocating levers. [-ER¹]

stic'kleback (-klb-), n. Small fish with sharp spines on back. [OE *sticela* prickle, sting, f. *stician* STICK, -LE(1), BACK¹]

stick'ler, n. ~ *for*, person who insists on or pertinaciously supports or advocates (*is a great, am no, ~ for authority, precision, etc.*). [f. obs. *stickle* be umpire, prob. f. ME *stightlen* arrange f. OE *stihtan* make, found, cf. MDu. *stichten*, G *stiften*; -ER¹]

stick'|y, a. Tending to stick to what is touched, glutinous, viscous; unbending, critical, making or likely to make objections (*he was very ~y about giving me leave*); (sl.) highly unpleasant & painful (*he'll come to a ~y end*); ~y-back, small photograph with gummed back. Hence ~iny² adv., ~iness n. [-Y²]

stiff, a. & n. **1.** Rigid, not flexible, unbending, unyielding, uncompromising, obstinate, (~ shirt-front; lies ~ in death; has a ~ leg, incapable of bending at knee; ~-necked, stubborn; keep a ~ upper lip, show firmness of character; ~ ship, heeling little under sail, not crank; ~ market, with prices remaining firm; met the charge with a ~ denial). **2.** Lacking ease or grace or graciousness or spontaneity,

constrained, reserved, haughty, formal, ~ manners; a ~ reception, bow, etc.; ~ movement, attitude, etc.; writes in a ~ style). 3. Not working freely, sticking, offering resistance.(a~hinge, piston, etc.; ~ un, veteran athlete etc., (sl.) corpse; ~ neck, rheumatic affection in which patient cannot turn head without pain; (of muscle, limb, etc., or person in regard to them) aching when used as result of previous exertion. 4. Hard to cope with, calling for strength or capacity of some kind, trying, (~ examination, climb, slope, breeze; a ~ price, high; a ~ glass of rum, strong; a ~ subject, requiring application to master it). 5. (Of moist clay, batter, etc.) thick & viscous, not fluid, in or approaching plastic state. 6. (colloq.) (In pred. use) to the point of exhaustion, almost to death, as bore, scare, ~. 7. ~ bit, horse's bit made of unjointed bar with rings at ends; hence ~LY[1] adv., ~NESS n., ~'ISH[2] a., ~'ENING[1](1, 4), n. 8. n. (sl.). Negotiable paper; corpse; hopeless or incorrigible person. [OE stif, cf. Du. stijf, G stejf; cogn. w. L stipes stem, stipare pack]

stiffle, v.t. & i. = SMOTHER vb. Hence (preferred to corresp. wds f. a. smother) **stiff'ling[1]** a., **stiff'lingLY[2]** adv. [earlier stuf(f)le, perh. f. OF estouffer, -LER[3])]

stiffle[2], n. (Also ~joint) joint of horse's hind leg between hip & hock; disease of ~joint or ~bone, whence **stif'led[2]** (-ld) a.; ~bone, bone of ~joint, horse's knee-pan; ~shoe, kind with which ~d horse is shod on sound leg to make it use & so strengthen the weak one. [?]

stig'ma, n. (pl. ~s, & ~ta as specified below). 1. (arch.). Mark branded on slave, criminal, etc. 2. Imputation attaching to person's reputation; stain on one's good name. 3. (Path.) definite characteristic of some disease; (Anat., Zool.) spot, pore, small natural mark on skin etc.; small red spot on person's skin (pl. ~ta) that bleeds periodically or under mental stimulus; (Bot.) part of style or ovary-surface that receives pollen in impregnation, so **stig-mat'ic**, ~tose[1], aa. 4. (Eccl.; pl. ~ta; usn. in pl.) mark(s) corresponding to those left by the nails & spear at the Crucifixion, developed by St Francis of Assisi & others (whence ~TIST n.) & attributed to divine favour. [L f. Gk, genit. -atos (st'izō prick, brand, -MA)]

stig'matize, v.t. Use opprobrious terms of, describe opprobriously as, (shall not ~e him as he deserves; ~e him, it, as a coward, cowardice); produce stigmata on (person) by hypnotic suggestion etc. Hence ~A'-TION n. [f. med. L f. Gk stigmatizō (prec., -IZE)]

stikké (stīk'i), n. Game resembling both squash rackets & lawn tennis played in court surrounded by 9 ft walls, with central net. [prob. f. term. of Sphæris-

tiké, original (1873) name of lawn tennis]

stile[1], n. Steps or some provision other than gate enabling passengers to get over or through fence or wall but excluding cattle etc. (help lame DOG[1] over ~). [OE stigel f. stīgan climb, cf. G steigern. -LE(1)]

stile[2], n. Vertical piece (cf. RAIL[1]) in frame of panelled door, wainscot, etc. [?]

stilett'o, n. (pl. ~s, ~es), & v.t. 1. Small dagger (vb. stab with ~). 2. Pointed implement for making eyelets etc. [It., dim. of stilo f. L stilus STYLE[1], -ET[1]]

still[1], a., n., v.t. & i., & adv. 1. Without or almost without motion or sound or both (stand, sit, lie, keep, ~, motionless; a ~ lake, unruffled; ~ WATER's run deep; thing is!; the ~ evening; now ~ every-thing is!; the ~ meditation; ~ small voice, 12; all sounds are ~, hushed; ~ life in painting, representation of inanimate things such as fruit & furniture; ~ hock etc., not sparkling; ~ birth, delivery of dead child, so ~born); ~bugle, naval call next call; hence ~'y[1] (-lī) [-LY[1]] adv. (rare), ~NESS n. 2. n. Deep silence (in the ~ of night); an ordinary photograph, as distinct from a motion picture. 3. vb. Quiet, calm, appease, assuage, silence; (rare) grow calm (when the tempest ~s). 4. adv. || Constantly, habitually, (arch.); then or now or for the future as before, even to this or that past or present or future time; nevertheless, for all that, on the other hand, all the same; (with com-par.) even, yet. [OE stille adj. & adv., stillan vb., cf. Du. stil(len), G stillen)]

still[2], n., & v.t. 1. Distilling-apparatus, esp. for making spirituous liquors, consisting essentially of a boiler & a condensing chamber, the vapour from the former passing into a spiral tube or worm surrounded by cold water or other refrigerating matter that fills the latter & issuing in drops as it condenses; || ~room, room in large house. 2. v.t. Distil (poet.); make (spirit) in ~. [vb in 2nd sense f. n.; n. f. vb in 1st sense, partly short for DISTIL, partly f. L stillare drip]

still'age, n. Bench, frame, etc., for keeping articles off floor while draining, waiting to be packed, etc. [prob. f. Du. stellage (stellen to place, -AGE)]

still'ing, still'ion (-yon), n. Support for cask. [perh. f. Du. stelling scaffold (as prec., -ING')]

stilly[1]. See STILL[1].

stilly[2], a. (poet.). Still, quiet, [STILL[1], -LY[1]]

stilt, n. Pole with rest for foot used generally in pairs with upper part of pole bound to leg or held with hand & raising user from ground (on ~s lit, & fig.—

bombastic, stilted); (also ~-bird or -plover or -walker) long-legged bird resembling plover in having three-toed feet; ~petrel, -sandpiper, long-legged kinds. [cf. Sw. stylta, Du. stelt, G stelze]

stil'ted, a. (As) on stilts; (of literary style etc.) pompous, bombastic, whence ~ly² adv., ~NESS n.; (of arch) with pieces of upright masonry between imposts & feet of the true arch. [-ED²]

Stil'ton, n. Superior kind of cheese named from ~ in Huntingdonshire.

stilus. See STYLUS.

stim'ulant, a. & n. 1. Stimulating (rare in gen. sense); (Med.) producing rapid transient increase of vital energy in organism or some part of it. 2. n. = agent or substance, as warmth, electricity, joy, etc., or exciting drug or article of food esp. alcoholic drink; *never takes~s*, usu. = drinks no alcohol. [f. L as foll., -ANT]

stim'ulate, v.t. Apply stimulus to, act as stimulus upon, animate, spur on, excite to (more vigorous) action. Hence or cogn. ~ATING², ~ATIVE, aa., ~A'TION, ~ATOR², nn. [f. L *stimulare* (foll.), -ATE³]

stim'ulus, n. (pl. ~ī). 1. Thing that rouses to activity or energy (*so lethargic that no ~us affects him*); rousing effect (*under the ~us of hunger*). 2. (Physiol.) thing that evokes functional reaction in tissues; (Bot.) sting, whence ~OSE¹ a. 3. (Eccl.) point at end of crosier, pastoral staff, etc. [L, = goad]

stim'y, n., & v.t. (Var. of) STYMIE.

sting, v.t., & i. (*stung*), & n. 1. Wound with ~ (*a bee, nettle, stung him, his finger*); affect with acute physical or mental pain (*pepper ~s one's tongue; the cane, his bad-handle, the blow, his conscience, the imputa-tion, stung him; stung by reproaches, with envy or desire; a ~ing 'insult*), whence ~ingly² adv.; (of part of one's body) feel acute pain or communicate it to sensorium (*my hand, tooth, ~s*); be able to ~, have a ~ (*some bees do not ~*; ~ing-nettle, opp. DEAD-nettle); (sl.) involve in expense, (usu. pass.) be caught, swindled, involved in expense (*he was stung for a fiver*). 2. n. Sharp-pointed weapon often tubular & connected with poison-gland in some insects & other animals (in tail as with bee, in head as with gnat, in claws as with centipede; also of snake's poison-fang) & plants (projecting as hair from surface as in nettle); infliction of wound with ~, wounded so made, pain caused by it, wounding quality or effect, rankling or acute pain of body or mind, keenness or vigour, (*was hurt by a ~; face covered with ~s; the ~ of hunger, ~s of pleasure; a jest with a ~ in it; this air, boxing, has no ~ in it*, is relaxing, feeble). 3. ~-bull or -fish, kind of weever; ~-nettle, ~ing-nettle; ~-ray, kinds of fish with flexible tail having sharp serrated projecting spine used as weapon; ~-winkle, beaked shell-fish that bores holes in other shellfish; hence ~LESS a. [OE *stingan*, cf. Da. *stinge*, Sw. & ON *stinga*]

sting'aree (-ngg-), n. = STING-ray. [corrupt.]

sting'er, n. In vbl senses; esp. smart painful blow. [-ER¹]

sting'o (-nggō), n. (arch.). Strong beer. [SING, w. ref. to pungency, with fancy ending]

stin'gy (-jī), a. Meanly parsimonious, niggardly. Hence~ily² adv.,~iNESS n. [spec. sense & pronunc. of obs. *stingy* (-ngī) nipping (of wind etc.) f. STING, -Y¹]

stink, v.i. & t. (*stank* or *stunk, stunk*), & n. 1. (Have or emit) strong offensive smell (~ in NOSTRILS of; ~ one out, drive him from room etc. by ~), whence ~'inglY² adv.; (sl.) ~ of money, be notoriously rich; (sl.) perceive ~ of (*can ~ it a mile off*); || (n. pl., sl.) chemistry, natural science, as subject of study; (part., sl.) objectionable in any way, that one dislikes; (part., as distinctive epithet of animals or plants) having recognizable & usu. disagreeable smell (~ing camomile; ~ing cedar or yew, savin & allied trees; ~ing crane's-bill, hellebore, horehound, nightshade, etc.; ~ing weed or -wood, kind of cassia; ~ing badger, teledu). 2. ~-alive, the fish bib (from rapid putrefaction after death); ~-ball, vessel containing explosives etc. generating noxious vapours used formerly in naval warfare & still by Eastern pirates; ~-bomb (emitting nauseating smell on exploding); ~-horn, kinds of ill-smelling fungus; ~-pot, any receptacle containing something that ~s, also = ~-ball, also as abusive term for person or thing; ~-stone, kind of lime-stone giving off fetid smell when quarried; ~-trap, appliance to prevent escape of effluvia from drains when opened. [OE *stincan*, cf. Du. & G *stinken*; cogn. w. STENCH]

stink'ard, n. Stinking person or animal, esp. the teledu. [-ARD]

stink'er, n. Stinkard, stinkpot; kinds of large petrel; (sl.) anything peculiarly offensive, irritating, or rousing (esp. of a letter, as *I wrote him a ~*). [-ER¹]

stint, v.t., & n. 1. Cease *doing* or *to do* (arch.); keep on short allowance (~ one-self or person or animal *in* food etc.); supply or give in niggardly amount or grudgingly (~ *food, money, service*, etc.); hence ~inglY² adv. 2. n. Limitation of supply or effort (usu. *without, no, ~; laboured without ~*, without sparing effort), whence ~'LESS a. 3. Fixed or allotted amount of or of work (*do one's daily ~*); area of coal-face to be worked in a shift. 4. Kinds of small sandpiper, esp. dunlin. [OE *styntan* (*stunt* short of wit, dull, cf. OE *stuntr* short)]

stip'ate, a. (bot.). Crowded, close-set. [L *stipare* pack, -ATE²]

stipe, stip'es (-z), n. (bot., zool.). Stalk or stem (in Bot. esp. support of carpel, stalk of frond, stem of fungus). [*stipe* F. f. L *stipes* stem]

stip'el, n. (bot.). Secondary stipule at base of leaflets of compound leaf. Hence ~LATE² a. [f. F *stipelle* (prec.,-EL)]

stip'end, n. Fixed periodical money allowance for work done, salary, esp. clergyman's official income. [f. OF *stipende* f. L *stipendium* (for *stipip-*) f. *stipem* alms etc. in small coin, *pendēre* pay]

stipen'diary, a. & n. (Person) receiving stipend, paid, not serving gratuitously; ~ (*magistrate*), paid police magistrate in large towns appointed by Home Secretary. [f. L *stipendiarius* (prec.,-ARY²)]

stipes. See STIPE.

stip'ple, v.t. & i. & n. 1. Engrave (plate, thing portrayed), paint or draw, in dots, not lines; use this method; hence ~ER¹(1, 2), ~ING¹, nn. 2. n. Dotted work; ~e-graver, engraver's ~ing-tool. [f. Du. *stippelen* (*stippen* to prick, f. *stip* point)]

stip'ulate¹, v.t. & i. ~ate for, mention or insist upon as essential part of agreement; demand as part of bargain or agreement *that*; (p.p.) laid down as part of the terms of an agreement (*is not of the ~ated quality*). So ~ā'tion¹ [-ATION¹], ~ātor², nn. [f. L *stipulari* (OL *stipulus* firm, cogn. w. *stipes*) bargain, -ATE³]

stip'ule, n. Small leaflike appendage to leaf usu. at base of leaf-stem. Hence ~A'CEOUS (-āshus), ~AR¹, ~ARY¹, ~ate² [-ATE²],-ULE] n.

stir, v.t. & i. (-rr-), & n. 1. Set, keep, or (begin to) be, in motion (*not a breath ~s the lake, leaves*; *sit without ~ring a foot* etc. or ~ring; *if you ~, I shoot*; *never ~red abroad or out of the house, went out*; *it's not ~ring yet, is still in bed*; ~ *the fire*, use poker; ~ *your stumps*, colloq., make haste, walk etc. faster; ~ *tea, porridge, soup, etc.*, move spoon etc. round & round in to mix ingredients, keep from burning in pot, etc.; *there is no news ~ring*, going about; *lead ~ring life*, be busy; ~ *up*, mix well by ~ring; ~ *up the mud, sediment, etc.*, make it rise from bottom of liquid by ~ring; rouse (up), excite, animate, inspirit, (~ *up strife, mutiny, discontent, curiosity*; *person wants ~ring up*, is indolent or torpid; ~ *one's blood*, excite him to enthusiasm, desire, etc.; ~ *one's wrath, bile, etc.*, enrage, disgust, etc.; ~*ring events, times, music, etc.*, exciting, stimulating; *a ~ring speech, picture, tale*), whence ~ringly² adv.; ~*about*, (n.) porridge. (adj.) bustling; hence ~rer¹(1, 2) n. 2. n. Commotion, bustle, disturbance, excitement, sensation, (*full of ~ & movement*; *person, event, etc. makes a great ~, is much discussed* etc.); slightest movement (*not a ~*), whence

~LESS a.; act of ~ring (*give the fire a ~*). [OE *styrian*, cf. Norw. *styrja*; perh. cogn. w. Du. *storen*, G *stören*, disturb, & w. STORM]

stir², n. (sl.). Prison. [?]

stirk, n. (Sc. & dial.). Yearling bullock or heifer. [OE *stirc*]

stirp'iculture, n. Breeding of special stocks or strains. [foll., -i-, CULTURE]

stirps, n. (law) progenitor of family; (zool.) classificatory group. [L, = stock]

stirr'up, n. Rider's foot-rest usu. consisting of iron loop with flattened base hung by a strap or ~-leather from ~-bar, iron attachment let into saddle; (Naut.) rope with eye giving hold in reefing; ~-bone, small bone, ~-shaped in man, in mammal's ear; ~-cup, of wine etc. presented to person mounted for departure; ~-iron, ~ with-out ~-leather; ~-piece in carpentry etc., hanging support; ~-pump (with foot-rest & nozzle for producing either jet or spray of water, used for extinguishing small fires). [OE *stigráp* (*stígan* climb, cf. STILE, ROPE)]

stitch, n. & v.t. & i. 1. Acute internal pain in the side such as often results from running etc. soon after eating. 2. Single pass of needle in sewing (*a ~ in time SAVE's nine*); result of it or of single complete movement in knitting, crochet, embroidery, etc. (*if one ~ gives the rest will*; *what long ~es!*; *has not a dry ~ on him, is wet through*); *drop a ~* in knitting, let loop fall off needle-end spoiling the continuity; *put a ~ or ~es in* in surgery, sew up wound with gut, silk, wire, etc.; method followed in making ~es or kind of work produced (*am learning a new ~*; LOCK³, *buttonhole*, HERRING-bone, etc., CROSS-STITCH). 3. ~-wheel, harness-maker's notched wheel for pricking leather in places where ~es are to go; ~wort, kinds of chickweed, esp. one with erect stem & white star flowers (named as cure for ~ in side). 4. v.b. Sew (t. & i.; = *up*, usu. mend by sewing; ~*ing-horse*, harness-maker's clamp for holding work). [vb f. n., OE *stice* pricking (*stician* pierce), cf. STICH, *stichen* vb]

stith'y (-dhi), n. (arch. & poet.). Smith's shop, forge. [f. ON *stethi* (Teut. *sta-* stand)]

stiv'er, n. Even the smallest coin (usu. *don't care, has not a ~*). [f. Du. *stuiver* small obsolete coin]

stō'a, n. (pl. -æ). Portico in ancient-Greek architecture (*the ~*, the PORCH, see STOIC). [Gk]

stoat¹, n. The ermine, esp. in its summer coat (also as general name for ermine & allied kinds, weasel, ferret, etc.). [f. 15th c., etym. dub.]

stock, n. & v.t. & i. & l. Stump, butt, main

trunk, plant into which graft is inserted, body-piece serving as base or holder or handle for working parts of implement or machine, (source of) family or breed, raw material of manufacture, store ready for drawing on, equipment for trade or pursuit, *(they nest in the ~s of trees*, arch. use; *~s & stones*, inanimate things, lethargic persons; *laughing, gazing, etc., ~*, butt for ridicule etc.; *must be grafted on a sound ~; ~ of rifle, plane, plough*, main part, usu. of wood, into which barrel, blade, share, etc., are fastened; *~ of anchor, cross-bar; lock, ~, & barrel*, fig., completely; *root & branch; comes of a good*, Puritan, treacherous, etc., *~*, family of distinct character; *polyp* etc. ~ in Zool. aggregate organism; *paper* etc., rags etc. from which paper etc. is made; *soup~* or usu. ~, liquor made by stewing bones etc. as basis for any sort of soup; *has a great ~ of information, hardware;* ROLL²ing ~; *take over a farm with the ~*, its animals, also *live ~*, & implements, also *dead ~; fat ~*, fit for slaughter as food; *~-in-trade*, all requisites for a trade, also fig., *as the politician's ~-in-trade of a dozen catchwords; renew one's ~; lay in a ~ of; have in ~*, have ready without need of procuring specially; *take ~*, review one's ~ for accurate knowledge of what one has in ~; so *~taking* n.; *take ~ of*, fig., observe with a view to estimating character etc. of; *~*, one that requires no fresh thought but is always at hand & perpetually repeated whether by individual or by people in general). **2.** Kinds *(common* or *ten-weeks*, *Virginia*, etc., ~) of fragrant-flowered usu. hoary-leaved garden plant (orig. ~-*gilliflower*, named as having stronger stem than clove-gilliflower or pink). **3.** pl. Timber frame with holes for feet & occas. hands in which petty offenders were confined in sitting position. **4.** pl. Timbers on which ship rests while building *(on the ~s*, in construction or preparation, often transt.). **5.** Stiff wide band of leather or other material formerly worn round neck, now displaced in general use by collar & tie, but surviving in some military uniforms & occas. revived in modified forms by fashion. **6.** (Finance) money lent to a government & involving payment of fixed interest to lenders or whomsoever their rights have passed to by purchase etc. *(buy, hold, ~*, the right to receive such interest on some amount of ~; || *the ~s*, State's funded debts as a whole; *has money, £50,000, in the ~s; take ~ in*, fig., concern oneself with); capital of corporation or company contributed by individuals for prosecution of undertaking & divided into (esp. £100) **shares** entitling holders to proportion of profits (also JOINT²-~; *bank, railway*, etc., ~; PREFERENCE or *preferred* ~; ~ *certificate*; WATER² ~). **7.** Best quality clamp-burnt brick (also of certain kiln-burnt bricks, as *malm ~*). **8.** || ~*-account*, *-book*, showing amount of goods laid in & amount disposed of; || *~-breeder*, raiser of live ~; *~broker*, *~broking*, (person engaged in) buying & selling for clients on commission of ~s held by ~jobbers; *~car*, cattle-truck; *~ company*, one semi-permanently engaged at a particular theatre; *~dove*, European wild pigeon smaller & darker than rockdove [perh. from breeding in ~s of trees]; *~ exchange*, place where ~s & shares are publicly bought & sold, || esp. *the S~ Exchange*, (building in London occupied by) association of dealers in ~s conducting business according to fixed rules *(is on the S~ Exchange*, a member of this association); *~farm(er)*, that breeds live ~; *~fish*, cod & similar fish split & dried in sun without salt; *~gang*, gang of saws in frame cutting log into boards at one passage; *~jobber*, *~jobbing*, *~jobbery*, || (person engaged in) speculating in ~s with view of profiting by fluctuations in price, cf. *~broker*; *~list*, daily or periodical *~-exchange* publication giving current prices of ~s etc.; *~ lock* (enclosed in wooden case, usu. on outer door); *~man* (Austral.), man in charge of live ~; *~-market*, exchange or transactions on it; ||*~-owl*, the great eagle owl; *~-pot*, for making or keeping soup~; *~rider* (Austral.), herdsman on unfenced station; *~-still*, motionless; *~-whip*, with short handle & long lash for herding cattle; *~yard*, enclosure with pens etc. for sorting or temporary keeping of cattle; hence *~LESS a*. (esp. of gun, anchor, etc.). **9.** vb. Fit (gun etc.) with ~. **10.** (US). Confine in the ~s. **11.** Provide (shop, farm, etc.) with goods or live ~ or requisites *(a well-~ed larder*, *library*, etc.); keep (goods) in ~ *(we do not ~ the out sizes*). **12.** Fill or cover (land) with permanent growth esp. of pasture-grass; (of plant) = TILLER³. [OE *stocc*, cf. Du. *stok*, G *stock*]

stockāde, n., & v.t. (Fortify with) breastwork or enclosure of upright stakes. [f. F *estacade* f. Sp. *estacada* f. *estaca* f. Teut., see STAKE², -ADE(1), w. assim. to prec.]

Stock'holm tar' (-hōm), n. Kind of tar prepared from resinous pinewood, used esp. in shipbuilding. *[Stockholm* in Sweden]

stock'inet, n. Elastic knitted material used esp. for underclothing. [foll., -ET¹; or corrupt. of older *stocking-net*]

stock'ing, n. Tight covering usu. knitted or woven of wool or cotton or silk or nylon for foot & leg up to or slightly above knee (usu. in pl., esp. *pair of ~s; is or stands six feet in his ~s or ~feet*, when measured without his shoes; *elastic ~*,

stockist (cont.)
surgical appliance of elastic webbing like ~ or part of it worn for varicose veins, strained muscles, etc.; white etc. ~ in horse etc., lower part of leg differently coloured from rest); ~-frame, -loom, -machine, knitting-machine. Hence ~-LESS a. [STOCK, -ING³] formerly also stock(s) short for nether-stock(s) opp. upper-stock(s)= knee-breeches, stock having sense docked part of the original hose or single garment for abdomen & legs])

stock'ist, n. One who stocks (certain) goods for sale. [-IST (3)]

stöck'y, a., || stügg'iy (-g-; colloq.), a. Thickset, short & strongly built, (of person; also in Bot. & Zool.). Hence ~ily² adv., ~iNESS n. [-Y²]

stödge, n., & v.i. & t. (school sl.). 1. Food esp. of heavy kind; full meal, feast; greedy eater. 2. vb. Eat greedily. [perh. init.]

stödg'iy, a. (Of food) heavy, filling, indigestible; (of receptacle) packed, bulging; (of book, style, etc.) over-full of facts or details, wanting in lightness or interest. Hence ~iNESS n. [-Y²]

stoep (-ōōp), n. (S.-Afr.). Terraced veranda in front of house. [Du., cogn. w. STEP]

*****stōg'y, -gie,** (-gi), n. Kind of heavy boot or shoe; long roughly-made cigar. [orig. stoga, short for Conestoga (Penn.)]

stō'ic, n. Philosopher of the school founded at Athens c. 308 B.C. by Zeno making virtue the highest good, concentrating attention on ethics, & inculcating control of the passions & indifference to pleasure & pain (S~); often attrib., as S~ philosopher, doctrines, indifference; person of great self-control or fortitude or austerity; whence ~AL a., ~ality² adv. Hence S~ISM(2, 3), ~ISM, n. [f. L f. Gk stōikos (stoa porch, w. ref. to Zeno's teaching in Stoa Poecile Painted Porch at Athens. -IC)]

stōke, v.t. & i. Feed & tend (furnace), feed furnace of (engine etc.), act as stoker; (fig.; colloq.) take food esp. in hurried way; ~hole, ~hold, compartment in which steamer's fires are worked. [back form, f. foll.]

stōk'er, n. Man who tends furnace esp. that of steamer or steam-engine (mechanical ~ automatic feeder for furnace). [Du. (stoken stoke)]

stōle¹, n. (Rom. Ant.; also L stola pl. -ae) outer dress of ancient-Roman matron; ecclesiastical vestment, a strip of silk or other material hanging from back of neck over shoulders & down to knees (worn by deacon over left shoulder only); woman's wrap similarly worn; ||groom of the ~ [orig. stoole, i.e. king's close-stool, first LORD of the Bed-chamber. Hence (-)stōlen² (-ld) a. [f. L f. Gk stolē stolē robe (stellō array)]

stōle² = STOLEN.

stōle³, stolen. See STEAL.

stōl'id, a. Phlegmatic, unemotional, lacking animation, not easily agitated, hard to stir, obstinate, apparently stupid. Hence or cogn. stōlid'ITY n., ~iy³ adv. [f. L stolidus]

stōl'on, stōle, n. Reclined or prostrate branch that strikes root & develops new plant; underground shoot of mosses developing leaves; (Zool.) rootlike creeping growth. Hence stōl'onATE², stōlonif-EROUS, aa. [f. L stolo -onis]

stō'mach (-tmak), n., & v.t. 1. Internal cavity in which chief part of digestion is carried on, being in man a pear-shaped enlargement of the alimentary canal extending from end of gullet to beginning of gut (coat of the ~, its mucous innost lining; coats of the ~, the peritoneum or serous coat, the muscular, submucous, & mucous layers); (in some animals, esp. ruminants), one of several digestive cavities either of similar character or differing in action or function (ruminant's ~s, first ~ or paunch or rumen, second ~ or honeycomb or reticulum, third ~ or psalterium or omasum, fourth or true ~ or reed or abomasum; muscular ~, acting by grinding or squeezing, as the gizzard; glandular ~, acting esp. by gastric juices); (loosely) belly, abdomen, lower front of body, (pit of the ~, depression below bottom of breastbone, the wind or mark; what a ~ he has got!, corporation). 2. Appetite for or for food (STAY¹ one's~). 3. Taste or readiness for sufficient spirit for (or arch. to) controversy, conflict, danger, or an undertaking (had no ~ for the fight), proud or high ~, haughtiness. 4. ~-ache, pain in belly, esp. in bowels; ~-cough, caused by irritation of ~ or small intestine; ~-pump, kind of syringe for emptying ~ or forcing liquid into it; ~-staggers, apoplexy in horses due to paralysis of ~; ~-tooth, lower canine milk-tooth in infants, cutting of which often disorders ~; ~-tube, for introducing through gullet into ~ to wash it out or empty it by siphon action; hence ~AL, ~LESS, aa., ~FUL (2) n. 5. v.t. Eat with relish or toleration, find sufficiently palatable to swallow or keep down, (fig.) pocket or put up with (affront etc.), (usu. w. neg., as cannot ~ it). [ME stomak f. F estomac f. L f. Gk stomachos gullet, dim. of stoma mouth]

stomach'ic (-k-), a. & n. 1. Of the stomach; aiding ~ action, promoting digestion or appetite. 2. n. ~ drug, bitters etc. [f. L f. Gk stomachikos (STOMACH, -IC)]

stō'macher (-tmach-), n. (hist.). Front-piece of 16th-17th-c. female dress covering breast & pit of stomach, ending downwards in point often lapping over skirt, & often set with gems or richly embroidered. [f. AF or OF estomacher (prec.), whence the pronunc.]

stomatit'is, n. Inflammation of the mucous membrane of the mouth. [as foll.+-ITIS]

sto̅matic-, comb. form of Gk *stoma -atos* mouth, as ~*gastric*, of mouth & stomach.

sto̅ne, n., a., & v.t. **1.** Piece of rock of any shape usu. detached from earth's crust & of no great size, esp. a pebble, a cobble, or a single piece used or usable in building or roadmaking or as missile (STOCKS & ~*s*; *built of great ~s*; *as hard as a ~*; ROLL³*ing* ~; ROCK³*ing* ~; SERMONS *in* ~*s*; ~*s will cry out*, wrong is great enough to move inanimate things; *give a ~ for bread*, offer a mockery of help; *mark with a white* ~, record as a joyful day, w. ref. to ancient-Roman use of chalk; *meteoric* ~, *meteorite*; *leave no* ~ *unturned*, try every possible means, often to do; *break* ~*s*, get living by preparing road metal, as phr. for being reduced to extremities; *cast, throw, ~s or a ~ at*, lit., & = make aspersions on character etc. of; *those who live in glass houses should not throw ~s*, aspersion provokes retort; *shower of ~s*, thrown, or rolling down hill etc.; *kill two BIRDS with one ~*; ~'*s cast or throw*, distance ~ can be thrown). **2.** (Usu. *precious* ~) a gem (*no* ~ *in it worth less than £100*; *Bristol* ~, Bristol DIAMOND; CAIRNGORM ~). **3.** ~*s* or rock as a substance or material (often with defining pref., as SAND, LIME¹, ~; *Bath, Caen, Portland*, ~, kinds of building-~; *built of* ~*ware*; ~ *buildings* etc.; ~ *jar* etc., of ~*ware*; ~JUG¹; HOLYSTONE; ~ *kaolin; has a heart of* ~, is hard-hearted; *harden into* ~, petrify lit. or fig.; *the* ~ *age*, stage of civilization at which implements & weapons were of ~, not metal; PHILOSOPHERS' ~). **4.** Piece of ~ of definite & designed shape (often with ~ purpose specified by word in comb., or easily supplied from context; GRIND, GRAVE¹, HEARTH, MILL¹, WHET, ~; ~; *Moabite, Rosetta*, ~, stelae with historically important inscriptions). **5.** Thing resembling ~ in hardness or pebble in shape, e.g. calculus (as single concretion or as *the malady*), hard case of kernel in drupe or ~*fruit*, seed of grape, testicle, pellet of hail, GALL¹.~; *underwent an operation for* ~ *or the* ~, *remove the* ~*s from plums, grapes*, etc.; *hail-storm with* ~*s as big as marbles*). **6.** ‖ Weight of 14 lb. or of other amounts varying with the commodity (*rides 12* ~, weighs that in the saddle; *give a* ~ *& a beating to*, orig. Racing sl., surpass easily; ~ *of mead or fish 8 lb.*, ~ *of cheese 16 lb.*, etc.). **7.** ~*axe*, with two obtuse edges for hewing ~; ~*blind* (quite); ~*blue*, compound of indigo with starch or whiting; ~*boiling*, primitive method of boiling by putting heated ~*s into water*; ~*borer*, kinds of mollusc; ~*break, saxifrage*; ~*buck, steenbok*; ~*butter*, kind of alum; ~*cast*, = ~'*s cast*

above; ~*CHAT²*; ~*coal, anthracite*; ~ *cold* (quite); ~*crop*, kinds of low creeping plant growing esp. on walls & rocks; ~ *curlew*, thick-knee or thick-kneed plover; ~*dead, -deaf* (quite); ~*eater*, = ~*borer*; •~*fence* (sl.), whisky & cider, or similar mixed drink; ~*fern, ceterach*; ~*fly*, insect with aquatic larvae found under ~*s*, used as bait for trout; ~*fruit*, with seeds enclosed in hard shell surrounded by pulp, drupe, e.g. plum, peach, cherry; ~*gall*, round mass of clay in variegated sand~; ~*horse* (arch.), stallion; ~ *man, cairn*; ~*marten*, = BEECH *marten*; ~ *mason*, dresser of or builder in ~; ~ *parsley*, a hedge plant; ~*pine*, S.-Ital. kind with branches at top spreading like umbrella; ~*pit, quarry*; ~*pitch*, inspissated pitch; ~*plover*, large kind called also *thick-knee &* ~*curlew*; ~*race* (of runners who must pick up ~*s* laid at intervals); ‖ ~*rag*, kind of lichen; ~*rue*, kind of fern; ~*saw*, untoothed iron blade stretched in saw-frame for cutting ~ with aid of sand; ~*weed, gromwell*; ~*snipe*, large N.-Amer. kind; ~*wall* v.i. & t., obstruct by ~*walling*; ~*ware*, pottery made from very silicious clay or from composition of clay & flint; excessively cautious batting, (Politics, esp. Austral.) parliamentary obstruction; ~*work, masonry*; ~*wort*, kinds of plant, esp. ~*parsley*; hence (-)STONED² (-nd). ~'*LESS* (-nl-), aa. **8.** adj. Made of ~. **9.** v.t. Pelt with ~*s* (~ *to death*). **10.** Free (fruit) from ~*s*. **11.** Face, pave, etc., with ~. [OE *stān*, cf. Du. *steen*, G *stein*]

sto̅n'|ȳ, a. & adv. **1.** Full of, covered with, having many, stones; hard, rigid, fixed, as stone (*a* ~*y stare*, refusing response or recognition; ~*y heart*, obdurate or unfeeling heart, also *hard core* or *interior*, whence ~*y-hearted²* a.); hence ~iry² adv., ~*iness* n. **2.** adv. Utterly (only in ~*y BROKE²*). [-Y²]

stood. See STAND.

stooge, n., & v.i. (sl.). **1.** *Butt, foil, esp. for a comedian; a deputy; person learning to fly.* **2.** v.i. Move, esp. fly, *about, around*, etc. [?]

stook, n., & v.t. (chiefly Sc. & north.). =SHOCK³. [ME *stouk*, cf. MLG *stūke*]

sto̅ol, n., & v.i. **1.** Backless seat for one, often consisting of wooden slab on three legs (*office* ~, high ~ used by clerks etc.; MUSIC, CAMP¹, ~; *three-legged* ~; *folding* ~, made to fold up; ~ *of repentance*, orig. that on which fornicators etc. were set to receive rebuke in churches in Scotland, & now transf.; *fall between two* ~*s*, fail from vacillation between two courses etc.); low bench for kneeling on; = FOOT~; **2.** (Archit.) window-sill. **3.** (Place for) evacuation of bowels, faeces evacuated (*go to* ~; CLOSE¹, NIGHT¹, ~). **4.** Root or stump of plant from which shoots spring. **5.** Piece of wood to which decoy-bird is

attached. **6.** ~*ball*, old game resembling cricket still played in Sussex esp. by girls; ~*pigeon*, pigeon used, person acting, as decoy. **7.** v.i. Throw up shoots from root; (arch.) go to ~, evacuate bowels. [OE *stól*, cf. Du. *stoel*, G *stuhl*; cogn. w. STAND]

stoop[1], v.i. & t., & n. **1.** Bring one's head nearer the ground by bending down from standing position, (fig.) deign or condescend to do, descend or lower oneself to some conduct (~ *to conquer*, gain power or one's end by preliminary self-abasement); carry one's end by ...; carry one's head & shoulders bowed forward, whence ~'*ing*[1] *adv.*; (of hawk etc., & transf.; arch., poet.) swoop, pounce; incline (head, neck, shoulders, back) forward & down; tilt (cask) forward. **2.** n. ~ing carriage of body; (arch.) swoop of hawk etc. [OE *stúpian*, cf. MDu. *stūpen*, ON *stúpa*; cogn. w. STEEP[1, 2]]

stoop[2] n. =STOUP.

stoop[3] n. (U.S., Can.). Uncovered platform in front of house (cf. STOEP). [f. Du. STOEP]

stop[1], v.t. & i. (-pp-). **1.** Stuff up or up, prevent or forbid passage through, make impervious or impassable, close, bar, stifle, stanch, (~ *a leak, hole, etc.*; ~*ped pipe* in organ, with upper end plugged, giving note an octave lower; ~ one's *ears*, put fingers in to avoid hearing, also fig, refuse to listen; || ~ *a tooth*, fill cavity in it with ~'p[1]ng[1] n. of gold, amalgam, cement, etc.; ~ *a wound*, stanch its bleeding; ~ one's *mouth*, fig., induce him by bribery or other means to keep silence about something; ~ *the way*, serve to meet a temporary need; ~ *a gap*, be or act as obstruction, prevent progress). **2.** Put an end to (motion etc.), completely check progress or motion or operation of, effectively hinder or prevent, (~ *progress* etc.; ~ *horse* etc., esp. when running away; ~ *ball*, esp. of batsman or field in cricket; ~ *thief!*, cry of pursuer; ~ *blow*, parry it in boxing; ~ *blow with one's head* one, be shot; *thick walls* ~ *sound*, render it inaudible; ~ one's *breath*, kill him by smothering or otherwise; ~ *clock, factory*, etc., make it cease working; ~ *person's doing*, person *from doing*; *shall* ~ *that nonsense*, not allow it to go on). **3.** Cut off, suspend, decline customary giving of or permission for, (*shall* ~ *your wages* or *holidays, meetings; the cost must be* ~*ped out of his salary*; ~ *payment of a cheque, direct one's banker not to cash*; ~ *payment*, declare oneself unable to meet obligations, break financially; *why has our gas, water, been* ~*ped?*). **4.** Obtain desired note from (string of violin etc.) by pressing finger, so shortening vibrating length. **5.** Cease, come to an end, cease from *doing*, discontinue (one's action), cease from motion or speaking or action,

make a halt or pause, (*noise, annuity, etc.*; ~*s; do not* ~, go on, continue; ~ *dead* or *short*, cease abruptly; *shall* ~ *playing, subscribing, my visits, my endeavours; to* ~ *grumbling, your complaints, that noise; he* ~*ped in the middle of a sentence; my watch has* ~*ped; train does not* ~ *at, before, Exeter; he never* ~*s to think*). **6.** (colloq.) Remain, stay, sojourn, (*shall* ~ *in bed, at home*; ~ *up*, not go to bed; *shall you* ~ *for the sermon?*; *have been* ~*ping in Cornwall with friends*). **7.** Provide with (*cable etc.*) (Etching) ~ *out*, cover (parts that are to be protected from action of acid) with defensive coating (~*ping-brush*, for doing this); (Photog.) ~ *down*, obscure part of (lens) with diaphragm; (Founding) ~ *off*, fill in (part of mould not to be used) with sand. Hence ~'P AGE(3) n. [OE (*for*)-*stoppian* f. pop. L *stuppare* (*stup(p)a* of Gk *stuppē* tow)]

stop[2], n. **1.** Stopping or being stopped, pause, check, (*put a* ~ *to; make, come to, bring to, a* ~; *is at a* ~, not proceeding or unable to proceed; *train runs from London to Crewe without a* ~). **2.** Punctuation-mark, esp. comma, semicolon, colon, or period (*full* ~, period; *come to a full* ~, transf., cease completely). **3.** (Mus.) change of pitch effected by stopping (see prec.), (in organ) row of pipes of one character brought into action by a ~-*knob* or small ~-*key*; (fig.) manner of speech adopted to produce particular effect (*can put on* or *pull out the pathetic, blustering, virtuous, etc.,* ~ *at will*). **4.** Batten, peg, or the like, meant to stop motion of something at fixed point. **5.** (Opt., Photog.) diaphragm; (Phonet.) mute consonant sound made by closure of organs concerned (as k, t, p); (Naut.) small line used as lashing, also projection of lower mast-head supporting trestle-trees. Hence ~'LESS a. [f. prec.]

stop[3], comb. form of STOP[1, 2]: ~*cock*, externally-operated valve inserted in pipe to regulate passage of contents; ~*collar, -gap*, temporary substitute; ~*key, -knob*, see prec. (sense 3); ~*order*, order to stockbroker to buy or sell on stock's reaching specified price; ~*plate*, limiting play of axle on bearings; || ~*press*, (news) inserted in paper after printing has begun; ~*valve*, closing pipe against passage of liquid; ~*volley* (Lawn Tennis), checked volley close to net, dropping ball dead on other side; ~*watch*, with mechanism for starting & stopping it at will, used in timing races etc.

stopp'er, n., & v.t. In vbl senses: esp.: plug for closing bottle etc. usu. of same material as the vessel (*put a* ~ *on*

something, bring about cessation of it); *tobacco*~, implement for pressing down tobacco in pipe-bowl; (Naut.) rope, clamp, double claw, etc., for checking & holding rope cable or chain cable; ~ *bolt*, ring-bolt in deck to which ~s are secured; ~*knot*, finishing of end of ~rope made by interlacing its strands; (vb) close or secure with ~. [-ER¹]

stŏp'ple, n., & v.t. 1. Stopper of bottle or other vessel. 2. v.t. Close with ~. [STOP¹, -LE(1)]

stŏr'age, n. Storing of goods, method of doing this (*cold* ~, in refrigerators etc.); space available for it; cost of warehousing; ~*battery*(Electr.), apparatus for storing electrical energy in a chemical form. [STORE+-AGE]

stŏr'ăx, n. (Tree yielding) a resinous vanilla-scented balsam formerly much used in medicine & perfumery; *liquid* ~, a balsam got from the Oriental sweetgum tree. [L, f. Gk *sturax*]

stŏre, n., & v.t. 1. Abundance, provision, stock of something ready to be drawn upon, (sing. with or, arch. exc. of intangible things, without a, & pl.; *has* ~, *good* ~, *a* ~, *or* ~*s*, *of wine, wit, anecdote, wisdom*; *in* ~, laid up in readiness, about to come, destined, as *I have, tomorrow has, a surprise in* ~ *for you*). 2. Place where things are kept for sale, = *ordinary shop (~ clothes etc., esp. = ready-made; book etc. ~), ||large commercial establishment selling goods of many different kinds usu. for cash & at low prices (the ~s, these opp. ordinary shops, as I get most things at the ~s; co-operative ~ or ~s; Army & Navy, etc., ~s, orig. selling only to members, who must have specified qualification). 3. pl. Articles of particular kind or for special purpose accumulated for use, supply of things needed, (military, naval, etc., ~s; marine ~s, old ship materials). 4. attrib. Kept for future use (~ cattle etc., not yet being fattened). 5. Set ~ by, reckon precious or important, esp. set no great ~ by. 6. ~'house, place where things are ~d up, granary etc., esp. fig. (person, book, is a ~house of information etc., cf. MINE¹); *~keeper, *shopkeeper; ~room, in which household requisites are kept; ~ship, carrying ~s for fleet, garrison, etc. 7. v.t. Stock or furnish with or with something (usu. with knowledge or the like; ~ your mind with facts; a well-~d memory). 8. Lay up or up for future use (harvest has been ~d, got in; ~ up a saying in one's heart); deposit (furniture etc.) in a warehouse for temporary keeping. 9. (Of receptacle) hold, keep, contain, have storage-accommodation for (a single cell can ~ 2,000,000 foot-pounds of energy); hence stŏr'ABLE a. [vb f. n., f. OF estor f. estorer build f. L IN(staurare cf. RESTORE renew)]

stōr'ey (pl. ~eys), **stōr'ĕy** (pl. ~ies), n. Any of the parts into which a house is divided horizontally, the whole of the rooms etc. having a continuous floor, (*fell from a third~ey window; a house of five ~eys; upper~ey or ~eys*, fig., the brain, as *is a title wrong in the upper ~ey*); ~*ey-post*, upright supporting a beam on which rests a floor or wall. Hence (-)~EYED² ~ied, (-rid), a. [f. 13th-c. Anglo-L *hystoria, istoria*, perh. orig. meaning tier of storied windows or sculpture, & = STORY¹; spelling ~ey is for different. f. STORY¹]

stŏr'iāted, a. (Of title-pages etc.) with elaborate decorative designs. [for HISTORIATED]

stŏr'ied (-rid), a. Celebrated in legend, associated with legends or stories or history; adorned with legendary or historical representations. [STORY¹, ED²]

stŏrk, n. Tall stately wading bird allied to heron, the best-known species pure white except for black wing-tips & reddish bill & feet, occas. half domesticated & nesting on buildings, & credited with peculiar affection both to its young & its parents (*King S~*, oppressively active ruler, cf. *King* log¹); ~*s-bill*, kinds of plant. [OE *store*, cf. Du. *stork*, G *storch*]

storm, n., & v.i. & t. 1. Violent disturbance of the atmosphere with thunder, strong wind, or heavy rain or snow or hail, a tempest, (*cyclonic* ~; *thunder, rain, snow, wind,* ~; ~ *in a teacup*, great excitement over small matter); (Meteorol.) atmospheric disturbance intermediate between whole gale & hurricane. 2. Violent disturbance of the established order in human affairs, tumult, agitation, war, invasion, dispute, etc. (~ *& stress*, period of fermenting ideas & unrest in person's or nation's life, f. G *Sturm und Drang*, name of a play characteristic of the literary movement in Germany 1770-82). 3. Vehement shower of missiles or outbreak of hisses, applause, indignation, etc. 4. Direct assault by troops on fortified place, capture of place by such assault, (*take by* ~, of such capture, & transf. of captivating audience or person rapidly). 5. ~*-beaten*, battered by lit. or fig. ~s; ~*-belt*, tract in which ~s are frequent; ~*-bird*, stormy petrel; ~*'bound*, prevented from leaving port or continuing voyage by ~s; ~*-card*, chart assisting navigator of ship in ~ to conjecture position of ~-centre & so to direct course: ~*-centre*, point to which wind blows spirally inward in cyclonic ~, (fig.) subject etc. upon which agitation or disturbance is concentrated; ~*-cloud*, heavy rain-cloud, state of affairs that threatens disturbances; ||~*-cock*, kinds of bird, esp. missel-thrush, fieldfare, or green woodpecker; ||~*-cone*, tarred-canvas cone

hoisted as warning of high wind, upright for north & inverted for south; ~door, additional outer door for protection in bad weather or winter; ~drum, cylinder added to ~-cone for expected ~ of great violence; ||~finch, stormy petrel; ~glass, sealed tube containing a solution of which the clarity is affected by tempera-ture formerly regarded as efficient weather-glass; ~petrel, stormy petrel; ~-sail, of smaller size & stouter canvas than the corresponding one used in ordi-nary weather; ~signal, ~-cone, ~-drum, or other device for warning of an ap-proaching ~; ~-tossed, lit. & fig.; ~troops, shock-troops, (also) a Nazi semi-military organization (~-trooper, member of this); ~-belt; hence ~'LESS, ~'PROOF² aa. 6. vb. (Of wind, rain, etc.) rage, be violent. 7. Talk violently, rage, bluster, fume, scold (intr.), (often *at* object of dis-pleasure). 8. Take by ~ (~*ing-party*, detachment told off to begin assault; so ~ER¹ n.). [yb f. n., OE, also Du. Sw., & Da., cf. G *sturm*; cogn. w. STIR]

storm'|y, a. Of marked violence, raging, vehement, boisterous, (~*y wind, sea, waves, passions, temper, abuse*); infested or troubled with lit. or fig. storms (*a ~y coast, sea, night, debate, life*); associated with or threatening storms (~*y petrel; a ~y sunset*). Hence ~ily² adv., ~INESS n. [-Y²]

stôr'|t(h)ing (-ti-), n. Norwegian Parlia-ment. [Norw. (-ti-), f. *stor* great, *t(h)ing* assembly]

stôr'|y¹, n. 1. History (arch.; *versed in classic ~*). 2. Past course of person's or institution's life (*his ~ is an eventful one; in our rough island~*). 3. Account given of an incident (*they all tell the same ~; according to his own ~*, suggestion of doubt as to his veracity; *to make a long ~ short*, formula excusing omission of details; *it is quite another ~ now*, we now hear a different account, esp. = things have changed; *the ~ goes*, it is said). 4. Piece of narrative, tale of any length told or printed in prose or verse of actual or fictitious events, legend, myth, anec-dote, novel, romance, (*tell me a ~; but is the ~ true?*; *short ~*, relating usu. a single incident & published as article in magazine or as one of a collection; *good, funny, ~*, amusing anecdote often em-bodying witticism or ludicrous situation; *but that's another ~*, formula for breaking off & tantalizing reader with allusion; 5. Main facts or plot of novel or epic or play (*reads only for the ~; the ~ is the least part of the book*). 6. Facts or experi-ences that deserve narration (*that face must have a ~; ~belonging to ~*). 7. (Nursery) fib, liar (*oh you ~!*). 8. ~book, con-taining ~ or stories; Eastern ~-teller, making a living by telling stories to

audience, writer of stories, retailer of anecdotes in society. (Nursery) liar. [AF *estorie* f. OF *estoire* f. L as HISTORY]

stoup (-ōōp), n. (arch.), Flagon, beaker, drinking-vessel; holy-water basin. [f. ON *staup*, cf. Du. *stoop*, OE *stēap*]

story². See STOREY.

|| **stôt**, n. (north. dial.). Young ox, steer. [OE]

stout, a. & n. 1. Brave, doughty, resolute, vigorous, sturdy, stubborn, staunch, strongly built, (~ *fellow*, arch., good at fighting etc.; *a ~ heart*, courage, whence ~**heart'ED²** (-häd-) a., ~**heart'EDLY** adv., ~**heart'EDNESS** n.; *a ~ resistance*; *a ~ opponent*; *a ~ stick, ship*, etc.); corpulent, bulky, tending to fat-ness; hence ~'ISH¹(2) a., ~'LY² adv., ~'NESS n. 2. n. Strongest kind of porter. [f. OF *estout* f. L Teut. (Du. *stout*, G *stolz*, proud), perh. f. L *stultus* stupid]

stōve¹, n., & v.t. 1. Kinds of closed ap-paratus in which heat is produced by con-sumption of wood, coal, charcoal, oil, gas, or other fuel, for use in warming rooms, cooking, etc.; (Gardening) hot-house with artificial heat; (~*pipe*, con-ducting smoke & gases from ~ to chimney (~*pipe hat*, tall silk hat). 2. v.t. Force, raise, (plants) in ~; [earlier sense *heated room, bath*; prob. f. MDu. *stove*, cf. OE *stofa* hot-air bath, G *stube* room, & STEW¹]

stove². See STAVE².

stow (-ō), v.t. Pack (goods etc.) in right or convenient places without waste of room (~ *thing away*, place it where it will not cause obstruction); fill (receptacle) with articles compactly arranged; (sl., usu. in imperat.) abstain from, cease to indulge in, (~ *larks, that nonsense*, etc.); (~*away*, person getting free passage by going aboard ship & hiding till she is at sea (~ *away* as v.i., do this); ~*wood*, billets used for chocking casks in ship's hold. Hence ~AGE(1, 3, 4)(-ĭj) n. [ME, f. OE *stōw* a place, cogn. w. STAND]

strabot'omy, n. Operation of cutting eyeball muscle to cure squint. [prec., -TOMY]

strabis'mus (-z-), n. Squinting, squint, (*cross-eyed ~us*, with eye or eyes turning inward; *wall-eyed ~us*, outward). Hence ~IC, ~AL, aa. [mod. L, f. Gk *strabismos* (*strabos* squinting, -ISM)]

strad'dl|e, v.i. & t., & n. 1. Take or be in attitude with legs wide apart; stand or sit across (thing) thus (*cannot ~ his horse*; widely, *~ing the ditch*); part (one's legs) widely. (Nav.) drop shots short of & beyond (target, enemy) esp. to find range; drop bombs from side to side across (target); (fig.) vacillate between two poli-cies etc., sit on the fence. 2. n. Act of ~ing lit. or fig.; (St. Exch.) contract giv-ing holder the right of either calling for or delivering stock at fixed price. [STRIDE, -LE(3)]

Strădivā'rius (or -âr-), (colloq.) **Străd,** n. Violin or other stringed instrument made by ~ of Cremona (d. 1737). [Bombard, worry with shells, bombs, sniping, etc.; reprimand or abuse or thrash. **2.** n. Piece of strafing (*the morning* ~ ; gunfire at dawn). [joc. adaptation of G 1914 catchword *Gott* ~ (God chastise) *England*]

străf (-âhf; * -âf), v.t., & n. (sl.) **1.** Bombard, worry with shells, bombs, sniping, etc.; reprimand or abuse or thrash. **2.** n. Piece of strafing (*the morning* ~ ; gunfire at dawn). [joc. adaptation of G 1914 catchword *Gott* ~ (God chastise) *England*]

străg'gle, v.i. Stray from the main body, fail to remain compact, get dispersed, proceed in scattered irregular order, be sporadic, occur here & there, (*crowd* ~*ed along; plant* ~*es,* grows long & weedy; ~*ing village, houses,* etc.). Hence ~ᴱᴿ¹ n., **~inglʸ**² adv., ~ʏ² a. [perh. f. ME *straken* cogn. w. STRETCH, -LE(3)]

straight (-āt), a., n., & adv. **1.** Without curve or bend, extending uniformly in same direction, (~ *line* in Geom., lying evenly between any two of its points; ~ *arch,* shaped like inverted V without curves; *a* ~ *back,* not bowed; *a* ~ *knee,* not bent; ~ *legs,* not bandy or knock-kneed; ~ *hair,* not curly); (of aim, look, blow, course) going direct to the mark; (*are the pictures* ~? ; *put things* ~, get rid of disorder; *accounts are* ~ , made up in due form; *a* ~ *race, fight,* etc., in which competitors do their best to win); direct from source (~ *tip,* hint esp. as to likely winner of race or prospects of investment got from good authority); *neat* (*a whisky* ~), undiluted, unmixed; *the* ~ *ticket,* the party programme without modification; ~*for'ward,* honest, open, frank, (of task etc.) presenting no complications; so ~*for'wardly* adv. ~*for'wardness* n.; ~*way* (arch.), at once, immediately; hence ~ᴱᴺ⁶ v.t. & i., ~*NESS n., (-āt-).* **2.** n. condition (*is out of the* ~ , crooked); ~ part of something, esp. concluding stretch of racecourse (*they were even as they reached the* ~); sequence of cards in poker. **3.** adv. In a ~ line, direct, without deviation or circumlocution, (*go* ~ ; *hit* ~ *from the shoulder,* in boxing, also fig.; *ride* ~ , taking fences etc. instead of going round; *come* ~ *from Paris; 'tis making* ~ *for a precipice; told it him* ~ *out*); in right direction, with good aim, (*shoot* ~); correctly (*does not see* ~); (arch.) at once (also in ~ *away,* sl., immediately; ~ *off,* without hesitation, deliberation, etc., as *cannot tell you* ~ *off*). **4.** ~*-cut,* (tobacco) cut lengthwise ~*edge,* bar with one edge accurately ~ , used for testing; ~*-eight,* motor vehicle with eight cylinders in line; ~ *eye,* ability to detect deviation from the ~ ; ~ *face* (intentionally inexpressive); ~ *fight* (Pol.), direct contest between two candidates. [ME *stregt,* p.p. of *streccan* STRETCH]

strain¹, v.t. & i. **1.** Stretch tightly, make taut, exercise to greatest possible or beyond legitimate extent, press to extremes, wrest or distort from true intention or meaning, (~ *parchment across the aperture;* ~ *rope to breaking-point;* ~ *every nerve,* do one's utmost; ~ *one's ears, eyes, voice,* etc., listen etc. to best of one's power, & see below; ~ *one's authority, powers, rights,* etc., or *the law* etc., apply them beyond their province or in violation of their true intention ; ~ *a point,* go further than one is entitled or can be expected to, esp. in the way of concession, or sense, got by pressing some rule of grammar etc. too far; ~*ing-beam, -piece,* horizontal beam used as strut between tops of queen-posts). **2.** Hug (person) to oneself or one's breast etc. **3.** p.p. Produced under compulsion or by effort, artificial, forced, constrained, not spontaneous, (*the quality of mercy is not* ~*ed,* mercy should be spontaneous ; ~*ed manner, laugh, cordiality,* etc.). **4.** Overtask, injure or try or imperil by over-use or making of excessive demands, (*take care not to* ~ *your eyes, voice,* etc.; *for fear of* ~*ing his followers' loyalty; has* ~*ed a muscle, his leg, his heart,* etc.; *ship is* ~*ed,* has had parts wrenched out of rigid state; ~*ed relations,* over-sensitiveness between parties who have tried each other's forbearance too far). **5.** Make intense effort, strive intensely *after, tng at,* hold out with difficulty under or under pressure, (*the* ~*ing horses, masks; plants* ~*ing upwards to the light; dogs, horses, rovers,* ~ *at the leash, collar, oar; porter* ~*ing under his load;* ~*s too much after epigram, effect,* etc.). **6.** Clear (liquid) of solid matter by passing through sieve or other ~ᴱᴿ²(2) n.; filter (solids) *out* from liquid; (of liquid) percolate. **7.** ~ *at,* be over-scrupulous about (ref. to *Matt.* xxiii. 24, prop. ~ *out,* see R.V., in prec. sense). Hence ~'ABLE a. [ME *streinen* f. OF *estreindre estreim-* f. L *stringere strict-*]

strain², n. **1.** Pull, stretching force, tension, demand upon or force that tries cohesion or strength or stability or resources, exertion required to meet such demand or to do something difficult, injury or change of structure resulting from such exertion or force, (*the* ~ *on the rope was tremendous; was a great* ~ *on my resources, attention, credulity; the* ~ *of modern life; is suffering from* ~ *or over-* ~ ; *all his senses were on the* ~ , exerted to the utmost; *is epigrammatic without* ~ , appearance of undue effort; *has a* ~ *in his leg*). **2.** (Physics, Mech.) condition of a body subjected to stress, molecular displacement. **3.** (poet. & rhet., usu. in pl.). Burst or snatch of music or poetry

(*martial, inspiriting, pathetic*, etc., ~s, music or poetry of such character; *the ~s of the harp, of the Elizabethan poets*, etc.). **4.** Tone or style adopted in talking or writing, tendency of discourse, (*the went on in another ~; & much more in the same ~*). **5.** Moral tendency forming part of a character (*there is a ~ of weakness, ferocity, mysticism, in him*). **6.** Breed of animals, human stock or family, (*comes of a good ~*). [first sense from prec.; last f. OE *strēon* gain, product, progeny; others of mixed orig.]

strait, a. & n. **1.** Narrow, limited, confined or confining, (arch. exc. in ~ *jacket*, ~ *waistcoat*, = *jacket* or usu. *waistcoat*, to *Matt.* vii. 14, ~ *jacket* or usu. *waistcoat*, strong garment put on maniacs to confine arms, which are either in sleeves so long that the ends can be tied or strapped within body of jacket, & in ~-*laced* now fig. only, severely virtuous, morally scrupulous, puritanic). **2.** Strict (arch. exc. in ~*est sect of our religion, Acts* xxvi. 5; hence ~ly² adv. (arch.), ~NESS n. (arch.), ~ EN⁶ v.t. (~*ened circumstances*, poverty; *is ~ened for*, ill supplied with). **2.** n. Narrow passage of water connecting two seas or large bodies of water (usu. in pl. when used of particular ~ with name, as *the S~s of Messina, Dover; S~s Settlements*, Crown colony on S~s of Malacca & Singapore; *the S~s*, formerly of Gibraltar, now usu. of Malacca); (usu. pl.) difficult position, need, distress, (esp. *in ~s*), *streit* f. OF *estreit* f. LL p.p. as STRAIN¹]

strake, n. Continuous line of planking or plates from stem to stern of ship (GAR-BOARD ~). [var. of STREAK]

stramineous, a. (arch.). Of, light or worthless as, coloured like, straw. [L *stramineus* (*stramen -inis* straw f. *sternere* strew- -MEN), -OUS]

stramonium, n. (Drug, much used in asthma, from seeds or leaves of) kind of datura. [mod.L, etym. dub.]

strand¹, n. & v.t. & i. **1.** Margin of sea, lake, or river (rhet., poet.). **2.** vb. Run (t. & i. of ship) aground; (p.p.) in difficulties, unable to get along esp. for want of funds or other resources, left behind while others advance. [com.-Teut.; OE, Du., G, Sw., & Da., *strand*; etym. dub.]

strand², n. & v.t. **1.** One of the strings or wires by twisting which a rope is made; (fig.) element or strain in any composite whole. **2.** v.t. Break a ~ in (rope). [cf. OF *estran* rope]

strange (-j), a. **1.** Foreign, alien, not one's own, not familiar or well known (to), novel, queer, peculiar, eccentric, singular, surprising, unaccountable, unexpected, (*in a ~ land; worship; gods; cannot play on a ~ ground, with a ~ racket; it is a ~ thing, story; how ~ that you should not have heard!; wears the ~st clothes; is very ~ in his manner, seems mad* etc.; *truth is*

~*r than fiction; repeating the question with* ~; *persistency; feel* ~, not in one's usual condition, esp. dizzy etc.; *it feels* ~, is a novel sensation), whence ~ly² (-jli) adv. **2.** Fresh or unaccustomed to, unacquainted, bewildered, (*am* ~ *to the work;* ~). [first sense from prec.; last f. OE EXTRANEUS]

stranger (-j-), n. Foreigner, person in a country or town or company that he does not belong to, person unknown to or to one (in U.S. as rustic voc. = *sir* etc.), person entirely unaccustomed to some feeling or experience or experience, (*am a ~ here, do not know my way about etc.; here, do not know my way about etc.;* ∥ *spy or see ~s in House of Commons,* demand withdrawal of all but members or officials; *make a, no, ~ of,* treat distantly, cordially; *you are quite a ~, seldom show yourself here; is a, no, ~ to me, I know, do not know, him; is a, no, ~ to,* unacquainted with; *the little ~,* newborn child). [f. OF *estrangier*, see prec.. -ER²(2)]

strangle (stràng-gl), v.t. Throttle, kill by squeezing windpipe; (of collar etc.) squeeze (neck); (fig.) suppress (movement, impulse, etc.); ~*hold*, deadly grip (usu. fig. in Pol. or commerce); [f. OF *estrangler* f. L *strangulare* f. Gk *straggaloō estrangle* halter f. *straggos* twisted]

strangles (stràng-glz), n. pl. (usu. treated as sing.). Infectious catarrh in horse, ass, etc. [f. prec.]

strangulate (-nggu-), v.t. Strangle (rare); (Path., Surg.) prevent circulation through (vein, intestine, etc.) by compression. Hence ~A°TION n. [f. L as STRANGLE, -ATE³]

strangury (-nggu-), n. Disease in which urine is passed painfully & in drops; disease produced in plants by bandaging. So **strangū°rious** (-nggu-) a. [f. LL Gk *straggouria* (*stragx -ggos* drop, *ouron* urine)]

strap, n., & v.t. (-pp-). **1.** Strip of leather; strip of leather or other flexible material with buckle or other fastening for holding things together or other purpose (SHOULDER-~; ~ *rug, umbrella*, etc., ~ *pair of ~s* with holder joining them for making bundle); strip of metal used for securing or connect, leaf of hinge, etc.; (Bot.) tongue-shaped part in ligulate floret; *the ~*, chastisement with a ~. **2.** ~*hanger*, bus or train passenger who has to stand & hold on by ~ for want of sitting space; ~-*laid*, (of rope) made by laying ropes side by side & joining them into a flat band; ~-*oil*, beating given with a ~; ~-*work*, ornamentation imitating plaited ~s; ~-*wort*, kind of white-flowered knotgrass. **3.** v.t. Secure with ~ (often *up, down*, etc.; ~*ped trousers*, held down by ~ passing below instep for riding

etc.); strop, whet, (razor, knife); (Surg.) close (wound), bind (part), up or *up* with adhesive plaster or ~p'ɪɴɢ⁴(4) n.; flog with ~; (part. as adj., of *thumping, whacking, whopping*) big, lusty, tall, (*a ~ping girl, fellow*), whence ~p'ᴇʀ¹ n. [OE *strop* prob. f. L *struppus*, cf. Gk *strophos* band (*strophō* twist)]

strappad'ō, n. (pl. ~s), & v.t. 1. Torture inflicted by securing person's hands or other part in ropes, raising him, & letting him fall till brought up by taut rope. 2. v.t. Subject to ~. [f. F *strapade* f. It. *strappata* (*strappare* pull); for -o see -ADO(2))]

sträss, n. Paste used in making artificial gems. [G, f. name of inventor, Josef *Strasser*]

strata. See STRATUM.

strat'agem, n. (An) artifice, trick(ery), device(s) for deceiving enemy, (*devised a* ~; *must be effected by* ~). [f. F *stratagème* f. l. f. Gk *stratēgēma* (*stratēgeō* be STRATE-GUS, -Mᴛ)]

strate'gic, a. Of, dictated by, serving the ends of, strategy (~ *skill, considerations, movement, position*); (of bombing) designed to disorganize the enemy's internal economy & to destroy morale. Hence ~ᴀʟ a. (now rare), ~ᴀʟʟʏ² adv., **strate'gics** n. [f. Gk *stratēgikos* (foll., -ɪᴄ)]

strate'gus, n. (Gk Ant.; pl. -gi n. -gī or -jī). Military commander, esp. one of annually appointed board of ten at Athens. [L, f. Gk *stratēgos* (*stratos* army, *agō* lead)]

strat'egy, n. Generalship, the art of war, (lit. & fig.); management of an army or armies in a campaign, art of so moving or disposing troops or ships as to impose upon the enemy the place & time & conditions for fighting preferred by oneself, (cf. TACTICS). Hence ~ɪsᴛ(3) n. [f. F *stratégie* f. Gk *stratēgia* (prec., -ɪA¹)]

sträth, n. (Sc.) Broad mountain valley; ~spey' (-ā), (music for) a lively Scottish dance (named f. *Strathspey* valley of the Spey). [f. Gael. *srath*, cf. W *ystrad*]

strat'icŭlate, a. (geol.). Arranged in thin layers. [STRATUM, -I-, -CULE, -ATE²]

strat'ifӯ, v.t. Arrange in strata (esp. p.p.). Hence ~FICA'TION n. [f. F *stratifier* (STRATUM, -I-, -FY)]

strāto-, comb. form of STRATUS, as ~ci'rrus, ~cŭm'ŭlus.

stratoc'racӯ, n. Military government, domination of soldiers. [Gk *stratos* army, -CRACY]

strat'osphēre, n. The layer of atmosphere air lying above the TROPOSPHERE, in which the temperature ceases to fall with height, remaining constant. [STRATO- +SPHERE]

strāt'um, n. (pl. -~a). (Geol.) layer, or set of successive layers, of any geological substance; (transf.) social grade (*the various ~a of society*). Hence ~ᴀʟ, **strāt'i**-FORM, aa., **stratig'RAPHY(2)** n., **strāti-GRAPH'IC** a., **strātigräph'ICALLY** adv. [L, =spread thing, coverlet, neut. p.p. of *sterněre* strew]

strāt'us, n. (pl. -tī). Continuous horizontal sheet of cloud. [assim. of prec. to termination of *cumulus* & other CLOUDS]

straw, n., & v.t. 1. Dry cut stalks of kinds of grain as material for bedding, thatching, packing, hats, etc. (*made of, thatched* etc. *with*, ~; *a load of* ~; ~ *mattress, hat, rope*, etc.; *in the* ~, arch., in childbed; *man of* ~, stuffed effigy, imaginary person set up as opponent etc., person without substantial means); ~ *hat*; single stalk or piece of ~, insignificant trifle, (*with a* ~ *in his mouth; lemonade sucked through* ~; *draw* ~s, draw lots with ~s of different lengths; *make bricks without* ~, of persons set to work without adequate means, see *Exod.* v. 7; *catch at a* ~, resort to utterly inadequate expedient like drowning man; *the last* ~, slight addition that makes something no longer tolerable as with camel's load; *a* ~ *shows which way the wind blows*, slight hint may suggest much; *is not worth, don't care, a* ~). 2. ~-*board*, coarse cardboard made of ~; ~-*colour(ed)*, (of) pale yellow; ~-*stem*, wineglass with stem not made separately & attached but drawn out of bowl; *~ *vote* (Pol.), unofficial balloting as test of strength; ~-*worm*, caddis; hence ~ʏ² a. 3. v.t. (arch.). Strew. [OE *strēaw*, cf. Du. *stroo*, G *stroh*; cogn. w. STREW (of which the vb is perh. a var.; & L *sterněre* strew]

straw'berry, n. (Kind of perennial plant throwing out runners & producing) pulpy red fruit having surface studded with yellow seeds (*crushed* ~, kind of dull crimson; || *the* ~ *leaves*, ducal rank, w. ref. to ornamentation of (duke's coronet); ~-*mark*, soft reddish birthmark; ~ *pear*, (fruit of) W.-Ind. cactaceous plant; ~*roan*, red ROAN¹; ~-*tree*, evergreen arbutus bearing ~-like fruit. [OE *strēawberige* (prec., w. ref. to runners, BERRY]

stray, v.i. (p.p. as -ED¹, 2), n., & a. 1. Wander, go aimlessly, deviate from the right way or from virtue, lose one's way, get separated from flock or companions or proper place. 2. n. ~ed domestic animal; WAIFS & ~s; || property of deceased person escheating to crown in default of heirs; (Wireless, usu. in pl.) ATMO-SPHERICS. 3. adj. (no comp. & sup.). ~ed; scattered, sporadic, occurring or met with now & then or casually or unexpectedly, (*a few* ~ *instances; a* ~ *customer or two came in; hit by a* ~ *bullet*). [(n. & a. f. AF *estrai*, stray) f. OF *estraier* prob. ult. f. L as EXTRAVAGANT]

streak, n., & v.t. & i. 1. Long narrow irregular line or band or layer-edge, esp. one distinguished by colour, visible on a surface (*black with red* ~s; *a* ~ *of light above the horizon; bacon with* ~s *of fat &*

lean; ~ of *lightning*, flash; *like a* ~ *of lightning*, or *a* ~, swiftly; || *the silver* ~, English Channel; *superstition*, etc., *in him*, strain of element; hence ~'Y²a., ~'LIY²adv., ~'INESS ment; 2. vb. (Usu. in p.p.) mark with ~(s); (intr.) move very rapidly (like a ~ of *lightning*). [OE *strica* stroke, line, cf. G *strich*; cogn. w. STRIKE]

stream, n. & v.i. & t. **1.** Body of water running in bed, river, or brook; (*on the banks of a* ~; *a* ~; *up, down*, ~, moving or situated upwards, downwards, on river; *whence* ~'LESS a., ~'LET n.; flow of any liquid, onward moving fluid mass or crowd, (sing. or pl.) large quantity of or of something that flows or moves along; (*saw a* ~ *of lava*; *came out, went by, in a* ~ *or* ~*s*; *a* ~, ~*s*, *of blood, tears, people*); current, direction of flow, (GULF-~); with ~*line*, (n.) natural course of water or air currents (~*line shape* in aircraft, motor-car, etc., that calculated to cause least resistance), (v.t.) give a ~*line* form to; hence ~*lined* (a.(rare). **3.** vb. Flow or move as a ~; run with liquid (~*ing eyes, windows, umbrella*); (of banner, loose hair, etc.) float or wave in the wind; emit ~ of (blood etc.). [OE *strēam*, cf. Du. *stroom*; cogn. w. Skr. *sru*, Gk *rheō*, flow]

stream'er, n. Pennon, ribbon attached at one end & floating or waving at the other; column of light shooting up in aurora. [-ER¹]

street, n. Town or village road that has houses on one side or both, this with the houses, (*go down, across, the* ~; *main, side, broad*, etc., ~; *live in the* ~, be constantly outside one's house; *lives in a fashionable* ~); MAN¹ *in the* ~; *not in the same* ~ *with*, colloq. utterly inferior to in ability etc.; *window looks on the* ~; *in the* ~, said of St.-Exch. business done after closing hours; *on the* ~*s*, living by prostitution; ~ *Arab*; || ~ *cries*, of hawkers; ~ *orderly, scavenger*; (arch.) paved road, highway (as *Watling S*~); WALL STREET; *the* ~, = Fleet S~; *Wall S*~; ~*door*, opening on ~; ~*-sweeper*, esp. machine with revolving brush for cleaning ~*s*; ~ *walker*, common prostitute. Hence (-)~ED²a., ~'WARD adv. & a. [OE *strēt* f. LL *strāta* (*via*) paved (way) f. *sternere strāt-*lay]

strength, n. **1.** Being STRONG, degree in which person or thing is strong; (*the* ~ *of a man, rope, beam, fortress, current, argument, wind, fleet; the* ~ *of wine, acid, tea, evidence; the* ~ *of body, mind, will, memory, judgement; his* ~ *is in endurance; has the* ~ *of a horse, is as strong; has not the* ~ *to lift a cup, walk upstairs; that is beyond*

human, too much for my ~; MEASURE² *one's* ~ *with; on the* ~ *of, encouraged by or relying on or arguing from, as I did it on the* ~ *of your promise; as I did makes strong (God is our* ~; *his* ~ *patience*). **3.** Proportion of whole number present (*were then in great, full*, ~; *taken is, on the* ~). Hence ~'LESS a. **4.** || (Mil.) *on the* ~, on the muster-roll (*was strength is*). [OE *strengthu* (*strang* STRONG, -TH¹)]

streng'then, v.t. & i. Make or become stronger; ~ *one's hands* (fig.), encourage him to vigorous action. [-EN¹]

stren'uous, a. Energetic, unrelaxing, ardently persistent. Hence ~LY² adv., ~NESS n. [L. *strenuus*, cf. Gk *strēnēs strong*, +-OUS]

Strěph'on, n. Fond lover (~ & *Chloe*, pair of lovers). [character in Sidney's *Arcadia*]

strěp'tó-, comb. form twisted. [Gk *streptos torque* (*strephō turn*)]

strěptocòc'cus, n. (pl. -ci). Any of a group of bacteria which, as they remain attached after fission, are usu. found in chains. [Gk *streptos* torque (*strephō turn*) *kokkos* a grain]

strě'ptÓ,mus. direction. Noisily. [It.]

strèss, n. & v.t. **1.** Constraining or impelling force of (*under, driven by*, ~ *of weather, poverty*, etc.). **2.** Effort, demand upon energy, (STORM & ~; *subjected to great* ~; *times of slackness & times of* ~). **3.** Emphasis (*lay* ~ *on*, convey that one attaches importance to); accentuation, emphasis laid on syllable or word, or the accent, (~ *& quantity are different metrical principles; the* ~ *is on the first syllable, on the word 'permissive'*). **4.** (Mech.) force exerted between contiguous bodies or parts of a body; hence ~'LESS a. **5.** v.t. Lay the ~ on, accent, emphasize; subject to mechanical ~. [vb in present sense f. n., which is partly aphetic for DISTRESS¹ & partly f. the vb f. OF *estrecier* f. pop. L *†strictiare* see DISTRESS²]

strětch, v.t. & i. & n. **1.** Make taut, tighten, straighten, place somewhere in tight-drawn or outspread state, (*the rope must be* ~*ed tight*; ~ *a wire across the road*; ~ *a canopy over them*; ~ *trousers, frame*; ~ *creases etc. by pulling out in frame*); ~ *oneself or* ~ *abs.*, tighten muscles after sleeping etc. by extending limbs etc. in various directions; ~ *one's legs*, straighten them by walking as relief from sitting etc.; ~ *one on the ground*, knock him prostrate (p.p.) *lying at full length, on the lawn, etc.; ~ *oud hand, foot, leg*; ~ *out, abs.*, reach out hand, also begin to lengthen stride); **2.** Strain, exert to utmost or beyond legitimate extent, make the most of, do violence to, exaggerate, (~ *a point, a principle, one's powers, one's credit*, = *strain*; ~ *the truth* or ~ *abs.*,

exaggerate, lie). **3.** Have specified length or extension, be continuous between points or to or from a point, (~*es from end to end, across the sky, to infinity; road* ~*es away, memory* ~*es down, from* or *to place* or *period*). **4.** Draw, be drawn or admit of being drawn, out into greater length or extension or size (*gloves, boots, want* ~*ing; ti~es like elastic*); (sl.) hang (person). **5.** n. ~ing or being ~ed (*with a* ~ *& a yawn*, whence ~Y² a., ~INESS n.; *by a* ~ *of authority, language,* etc.; *with every faculty on the* ~). **6.** Continuous expanse or tract or spell (*a* ~ *of road, open country,* etc.; *works ten hours at a* ~): (Naut.) distance covered on one tack; (sl.) imprisonment for a year, any term of imprisonment or penal servitude. [OE *streccan*, cf. Du. *strekken*, G *strecken*; perh. cogn. w. STARK]

stretch'er, n. In vbl senses; esp.: brick or stone laid with side in face of wall (cf. HEADER); board in boat against which rower presses feet; appliance, often of canvas stretched on oblong frame, for carrying disabled person on; (sl.) exaggeration, lie; ~bond, method of building in which all bricks are ~s but joints of contiguous courses do not coincide. [-ER¹]

strew (-ōō), v.t. (p.p. ~n, ~ed). Scatter (sand, flowers, small objects) over a surface; (partly) cover (surface, object) with small objects scattered. [OE *streawian* (STRAW) cf. G *streuen*; prob. cogn. w. L *sternere strat-*]

stri'a, n. (anat., zool., bot., geol.: pl. ~ae). Linear mark on surface, slight ridge or furrow or score. Hence ~ATE² a., ~ATE³ v.t., ~ATE°'ly adv., ~ATION, ~ATURE, nn. [L]

stricken. See STRIKE.

stric'kle, n. Rod used in STRIKE-*measure*; whetstone. [OE *strícel* (STRIKE)]

strict, a. Precisely limited or defined, accurate, tense, without irregularity or exception or deviation, requiring implicit obedience or exact performance, not lax, (*in the* ~ *sense; keep* ~ *watch;* ~ *time in music; lives in* ~ *seclusion; was told me in* ~ *confidence; gave* ~ *orders; a* ~ *code of laws or customs;* ~ *morals,* admitting no laxity; ~ *parents, schoolmaster, discipline*). Hence ~LY² adv., (~*ly speaking,* if one is to use words in their ~ sense), ~NESS n. [f. L *stringere strict-* tighten]

stric'ture, n. (Usu. in pl.) piece of censure, critical remark, (usu. on or upon); (Path.) morbid contraction of some canal or duct in the body, whence ~RD² (-kcherd) a. [f. L *strictura* contraction (*stringere*, see prec. & STRIGIL, -URE]

stride, v.i. & t. (past strode, rare p.p. stridden or strid), & n. **1.** Walk with long steps; pass over (ditch etc.) with one step; bestride, straddle (trans.). **2.** n. Single step esp. in respect of length, gait as determined by length of ~, (*walks with vigorous* ~*s* or *a vigorous* ~; *take obstacle in one's* ~, clear it without changing step to jump, (fig.) find no serious impediment in it; *get into one's* ~, (fig.) settle down steadily to the job in hand); distance between feet parted either laterally or as in walking. [OE *stridan*, cf. Du. *strijden*, G *streiten*, contend]

strid'ent, a. Loud & harsh in sound. Hence ~LY² adv. [L *stridere* creak, -ENT]

strid'ulate, v.i. (entom.). Make shrill jarring sound by rubbing together hard parts of body (of cicadas, grasshoppers, etc.). So ~ANT a., ~A'TION, ~ātOR²(I, 2), nn. [L *stridulus* creaking (prec.), -ATE³]

strife, n. Contention, state of conflict, struggle between opposed persons or things. [f. OF *estrif*, cf. *estriver* STRIVE]

stri'gil, n. Skin-scraper used by ancients at bath. [f. L *strigilis* (*stringere* graze), cf. Gk *stleggis, strangle*]

strig'ose, strig'ous, aa. (bot.). With short stiff hairs or scales. [L *striga* swath, -OSE¹, -OUS]

strike, v.t. & i. (*struck, struck* & as specified below *stricken*), & n. **1.** Hit, hit upon or (upon, deliver blow(s) or stroke(s), (*struck me in the mouth, with his fist;* ~ *ball out of court* etc., send it with blow; ~ *weapon up* or *down* or *aside*, divert it by blow; ~ *one's foot against a stone, one's hand on the table;* ~ *while* IRON¹ *is hot; striking-force*, esp. military body ready to deliver blow at short notice; *within striking-distance*, near enough to ~; ~ *a blow,* or ~, *for freedom; hammer* ~*s on* or ~*s bell; ship* ~*s rock* or *on rock* or ~*s*, runs on it; ~ *hands*, arch., touch or clasp them in sign of agreement; *was struck by a stone, lightning; a stricken heart*, afflicted by strokes of grief; *stricken with fever, pestilence, paralysis,* etc.; *a stricken field*, pitched battle or scene of it; *stricken in years*, enfeebled by age; ~ *out*, hit from the shoulder, also use arms & legs in swimming or feet in skating; ~ *upon an idea, plan,* etc., have it luckily occur to one; ~ OIL¹; *light* ~*s upon object*, illuminates it; ~ *at*, aim blow at; ~ *at the root of*, threaten destruction to; ~ *back*, return blow; ~ *home*, get blow well in; ~ *all of a heap*, colloq., dumbfound; ~ *fish* or ~ abs., jerk tackle in order to secure hook in mouth; ~ *the track*, come upon it). **2.** Produce or record or bring into specified state by stroke(s) or striking (~ *coin*, make it by stamping; ~ *bargain*, make it as by striking hands; ~ *sparks, fire, light, out of flint;* ~ *a match*, ignite by striking against something; ~ *a light*, produce by striking match; *clock* ~*s not* ~, give light when struck; *clock* ~*s the hour, five,* etc.; *the hour has struck, clock has struck it,* & fig. *the critical moment has come* or *gone;* ~ *one blind, deaf,* etc., blind, deafen, etc., him at one

strike. ~ *me dead!*, vulg., form of asseveration.; ~ *down*, fell with blow lit. or fig.; ~ *his head off*, behead; ~ *out plan* etc., forge or devise; ~ *out a line for oneself*, be original.; ~ *item or name out or off*; ~ *word through*, expunge with pen-stroke; ~ *up an acquaintance*, start it rapidly or casually.; *band or person* ~s *up a tune* or makes as by stamping). **3.** Arrest attention of, occur to mind of, produce mental impression on, impress as, (*what struck me was the generosity of the offer; it* ~s *me he* or *that he may have misunderstood; an idea suddenly struck me; how does it* ~ *you?*, what do you think about it?; ~s *me as ridiculous, absolutely perfect*); (part.) sure to be noticed, arresting, impressive, whence **strik'ingly**[2] adv. **strik'ing**NESS n. **4.** Lower or take down (flag, sail, tent), signify surrender by striking flag, surrender, (~ *one's flag*, surrender ship or fortress to enemy, also resign a naval command; ~ *tents*, break up camp; *town, ship,* ~s, surrenders). **5.** Cease (work), cease work, (of workmen) refuse to go on working unless employer accedes to some demand (cf. LOCK[3] *out*; ~ *for higher pay, against long hours*, etc.). **6.** (Cause to) penetrate (*struck a knife, terror, into his marrow; cold* ~s *through his clothes, into his* roots *into the soil*; ~s *root*, or ~s abs.; ~ *through fog; struck with terror, panic, dizziness*, etc., suddenly filled with). **7.** Direct one's course somewhere, take specified direction, diverge to, start into, (*then* ~ *to the right*; ~ *into* or *out of a track*, with suggestion etc.; ~ *in*, intervene in talk, often interior instead of extremities; ~ *into a gallop*, begin galloping). **8.** Level (grain etc. or the measure) in ~ *measure* (see n.); ascertain (balance) by deducting credit or debit from the other; arrive at (average) by equaling all items; compose (jury) by allowing both sides to reject same number. **9.** Suddenly & dramatically assume (attitude). **10.** ~*-a-light*, apparatus for getting light from flint. Hence **strik'ER**[1] (1, 2) n. **11.** n. Concerted refusal to work by employees till some grievance is remedied (*on* ~, acting on such refusal; ~*-breakers*, workmen brought in to replace strikers; ~ *pay*, allowance for subsistence made by trade union to workmen who have struck; *general* ~, by workmen of all or most trades with a view to securing some common object by paralysing business; *sit-down, stay*[1]*-in,* ~; *sympathetic* ~, by unaggrieved trade to give moral support to one on ~). **12.** =STRICKLE (~ *measure*, when grain etc. is measured by passing a rod across top of heaped vessel to secure that it shall be full & no more). **13.** *Sudden success at finding gold, etc., or in financial operations. **14.** (Baseball) batsman's actual or constructive attempt to hit pitched ball. [OE *strícan* go, cf. Du. *strijken*, G *streichen*, smooth, stroke, cogn. W. L *stringere* graze]

string, n. & v.t. & i. (*strung*). **1.** Twine or fine cord, piece of this or of leather, ribbon, webbing, or other material, used for tying up, lacing, drawing or holding together, actuating puppet, etc., (*want some* ~ *& brown paper*; APRON, bonnet, BOW[1], kite, etc., ~; *two* ~s *to one's* BOW[1]; *first, second,* ~, person or thing that one's chief, alternative, reliance is set on, W. ref. to prec. phr.; *pull the* ~s, be the real actuator of what another does; *have person on a* ~, have under one's thumb; cf. the WIND?), whence (-)~ED[2] (-ngd) a. **2.** Tough piece connecting two halves of pod in beans etc. **3.** Stretched piece of catgut, cord, or wire, yielding musical tone(s) in piano, harp, violin, & other instruments (*harp-, fiddle-*, etc.; ~ *touch the* ~s, play; *harp on one* ~, dwell on single subject; *touch a* ~, fig. excite particular feeling in person's heart; *the* ~s, the ~ed instruments in a band or part contributed by them to the effect, cf. *the* WIND?), whence HEART[1]~s). **4.** Set or usu. of objects strung together or persons or things of one kind coming one after another (*a* ~ *of beads, onions, pearls; filed past in a long* ~; *a* ~ *of porters, horses, oaths, lies*). **5.** (Billiards) scoring-board with buttons sliding on wires, the score, stroke made in ~*ing for lead*. **6.** The racehorses, collectively, under training at a particular stable, etc. **7.** pl. *Conditions attached to a gift, offer, etc. **8.** ~ *alphabet*, code for the blind in which special knots on ~ represent letters; ~ *band*, (prop.) of ~ed instruments only; ~*-bark*, STRINGY-bark; ~*-board*, supporting timber in which ends of staircase steps are set; ~*-course*, raised horizontal band or course running round or along building; ~*-halt*, = SPRING[2]*-halt*; ~*-piece*, long timber supporting & connecting the parts of a framework. Hence ~'less a. **9.** vb. Supply with ~(s), tie with ~. **10.** Secure (bow) in state ready for use by bending it & slipping loop of ~ into notch; (fig., chiefly in p.p.) tighten up or make ready or sensitive or excited (senses, nerves, resolution, or person in regard to them; *was strung up to do the deed; high-strung* or *highly strung* nerves or person, neurotic, susceptible, over-sensitive). **11.** Thread (beads etc.) on a ~; strip ~s from (beans). **12.** *(colloq.). Hoax. **13.** ~ *up* (colloq.), kill by hanging. **14.** (Of glue etc.) become stringy. **15.** (Billiards) make the preliminary strokes that decide which player shall begin. [OE *streng*, G *strang*, cf. STRANGLE, STRICT]

stringĕn'dō (-ji-), mus. direction. With increasing speed. [It.]

strin'ģient (-ji-), a. (Of rules, stipulations, etc.) strict, precise, requiring exact performance, leaving no loophole or discretion; (of money-market etc.) tight, hampered by scarcity, unaccommodating, hard to operate in. Hence ~ENCY n., ~ently² adv. [L stringere draw tight, -ENT]

string'er (-ng-), n. In vbl senses; also, STRING-BOARD. [-ER¹]

string'ly (-ngi), a. Fibrous, like string, (~y-bark, kinds of gum-tree); (of liquid) viscous, ropy. Hence ~INESS n. [-Y¹]

strip¹, v.t. & i. (-pp-). 1. Denude, lay bare, deprive of covering or appurtenance or property, (~ one to the skin, leave him no clothes; ~ped, naked; ~ped of fine names, it is a swindle; ~ house, ship, tree, remove furniture, rigging, bark & branches; ~ cow, milk to last drop; ~ tobacco, remove stems from; ~ screw, tear thread from it); pull or tear (covering lit. or fig., appurtenance, property) off or off from or from something; put off one's clothes, undress (~tease, an entertainment in which a woman gradually ~s before an audience). 2. (Of screw) lose thread; (of projectile) issue from rifled gun without spin. 3. ~leaf, tobacco with stems removed. Hence ~p'ER¹(1, 2) n. [OE strīpan, cf. Du. stroopen, G streifen]

strip², n. Long narrow piece (a ~ of card, paper, cloth, garden, territory, board); AIR¹-~. [prob. f. MLG strippe strap]

stripe, n. 1. Long narrow band usu. of uniform breadth on a surface from which it differs in colour or texture (black with a red ~; STAR¹s & ~s; ~s on soldier's trousers; sergeant's, corporal's, ~s, symbols of rank; get, lose, one's ~s, be promoted, degraded; zebra's ~s), whence (-)strīped²(-pt), strip'Y², aa., strip'iness n. 2. (arch.) Blow with scourge (usu. in pl.) (pl.) flogging. 3. pl. (colloq.) Tiger. [prob. f. MDu. stripe, cf. G streifen, ON strip striped fabric, also STRIP¹; sense blow perh. as STRIP²]

strip'ling, n. Lad, young man whose figure has not yet filled out. [prob. f. STRIP² -LING¹]

strive, v.i. (strōve, strĭven). Struggle, endeavour, try hard, make efforts, contend, vie, (to do, for or after desired end, with or against opponent or temptation or difficulty; ~ together, or with each other, quarrel, dispute pre-eminence etc.). [f. OF estriver (from, or whence, estrif strife), prob. f. Teut. (Du. strǎven, G strêben)]

strōb'ĭle, n. Cone of pine etc. [f. L f. Gk strobilos (strephō twist)]

strode. See STRIDE.

strōke¹, n., & v.t. 1. Blow, shock given by blow, (to receive 20 ~s of the birch; with one ~ of his sword; killed by a ~ of lightning or lightning-~; finishing ~, coup de grâce, final & fatal blow; ~ of paralysis or apoplexy, or ~, sudden disabling attack; SUN-~). 2. Single effort put forth, one complete performance of a recurrent action or movement, time or way in which such movements are done, (has not done a ~ of work; ~ of wing, oar, etc., whole of motion till starting-position is regained; ~ of piston, whole motion in either direction; golfer does hole in five ~s, successive single dealings with ball; row a fast, slow, long, etc., ~; vary the ~; second boat is gaining at every ~ or ~ by ~). 3. Method of striking in games etc., specially successful or skilful effort, (invented a new ~ in cricket; ~ of genius, original idea; ~ of wit, diplomacy, etc.; ~ of business, profitable transaction; a clever ~; MASTER-~); ~ of luck, unforeseen opportune occurrence. 4. Mark made by movement in one direction of pen or pencil or paint-brush, detail contributing to general effect in description, (up, down, ~, part of letter so written; HAIR-~; thick, thin, horizontal, etc., ~; dash off picture with a few ~s; could do it with a ~ of the pen by exag., by writing signature; finishing ~s, finishing touches; description is full of ~s when the life). 5. Sound made by striking clock (it is on the ~ of nine, nine is about to strike; was there on the ~, punctually). 6. (Also, now rarely, ~ oar) oarsman rowing nearest stern & setting time of ~(row, pull, ~, act as ~). 7. v.t. Act as ~ to (boat, crew). [ME strōk, strŏk, (STRIKE)]

strōke², v.t., & n. 1. Pass the hand gently, & usu. repeatedly in same direction, along surface of (~e one or one's hair the wrong way, irritate him; ~e one down, mollify his anger etc.); hence ~'ingLY adv. 2. n. Act or spell of ~ing. [OE strācian, cf. Du. streeken, G streichen; cogn. w. STRIKE]

strŏll, v.i. & t., & n. 1. Saunter, go for short leisurely walk; go from place to place giving performances etc., traverse the country thus, (~ing players; a ~ing company). 2. n. Short leisurely walk (go for, take, a~). Hence ~ER¹ n. [f. 17th-c., etym. dub.]

strŏm'a, n. (biol.; pl. -ta). Framework of an organ or cell. usu. of connective tissue. Hence strōmăt'ic a. [L f. Gk (-ŏ-), = coverlet (strōnnumi spread, -M]

strŏng, a. (comp. & sup. pr. -nng-). 1. Having power of resistance, not easily broken or torn or worn or injured or captured, tough, healthy, firm, solid, (~ china, stick, cloth; a ~ constitution, not liable to, able to overcome, disease; ~ nerves, proof against fright, irritation, etc.; ~ fortress, town, etc.; ~ box, -room, proof against burglars etc. for keeping valuables in; ~ those who have good health; are you quite ~ again?, restored to health;

a ~ *foundation*; a ~ *market*, steadily high or rising *prices*; ~ *meat*, doctrine or measures acceptable only to vigorous or instructed minds. **2.** Capable of exerting great force or doing much, muscular, powerful by size or numbers or resources, or quality or ability, convincing, striking, powerfully affecting the senses, (~ *to do*, *suffer*, *labour*, *save*, etc.; *is* ~ *enough to*; *in judgement*, *Greek*, *numbers*, *health*, well equipped in these respects; ~ *eyes*, *memory*, etc.; a ~ *man*, muscular; *by the* ~ *arm* or *hand*, by force; *is as* ~ *as a horse*, can do or stand much work; *the* ~ *army*, *fleet*, etc., numerous & well equipped; a ~ *detachment*, numerous; *a company* 200 ~, numbering 200; *how many* ~ *are you?*, what are your numbers?; *a* ~ *combination*, set capable of doing much when united; *a* ~ *candidate*, likely to win; ~ *tea*, *toddy*, *waters*, alcoholic liquors; ~ *drink*, made with large proportion of the flavouring element; ~ *situation*, conjuncture in play or story calculated to move audience deeply; ~ *voice*, loud or penetrating; ~ *mind*, capable of sound reasoning; ~ *-minded*, having such mind, also & usu. in spec. sense of woman, claiming mental & legal equality with men; ~ *evidence*, *argument*, *case*; ~ *light*, *shadow*, *colour*, *flavour*; ~ *cheese*, *onion*, pungent; ~ *butter*, *bacon*, rancid; ~ *breath*, ill-smelling). **3.** Energetic, effective, vigorous, decided, (a ~ *wind*, *tide*, *attraction*; *have a* ~ *hold upon* or *over*, be able to influence; *a* ~ *literary style*, vivid & terse; *has a* ~ *inclination to*; ~ *language*, forcible expressions esp. of abusive or blasphemous kind; *give* ~ *support to*, support with all one's power; *a* ~ *partisan*, *Tory*, *advocate*; ~ *man*, administrator who acts without hesitation, masterful person; ~ *measures*, drastic action; *is* ~ *against compromise*, will have nothing to do with it; *going vigorously*, also in good health or trim; *come* or *go it* ~, sl. go to great lengths in something). **4.** (Gram., of vbs) forming inflexions by vowel-change within stem rather than by addition of suffix (e.g. *swim swam*, *give gave*, *break broke*, cf. *float floated*). **5.** ~ *hold*, fort, fastness, citadel, place where some cause or sentiment still prevails (*Liverpool was a* ~*hold of protestantism*). Hence ~ *~ly²* adv. [OE *strang*, cf. ON *strengr*, Du. *streng*, G *streng* strict; cogn. w. L *stringere* STRAIN]

stron′tia (-sha) n. **stron′tian** (-shn) n. & a. An oxide of strontium of which the nitrate is used in fireworks to colour flame red; (adj.) of strontia or strontium. [-*a* f. foll.; -*an* (n.) f. *Strontian* in Argyll, (adj.) f. foll. +-AN]

strontium (-shm), n. A soft silver-white metallic element. [*Strontian* (prec.), -IUM]

strop, n., & v.t. (-pp-). 1. Strip of leather on which razor is sharpened, implement or machine serving same purpose; collar of leather or spliced rope or iron used in slinging pulley etc. **2. v.t.** Sharpen on or with ~. [as STRAP]

strophan′thin, n. Poisonous drug extracted from varieties of the tropical plant *Strophanthus*, used as a heart-tonic. [f.Gk *strophos* twisted cord + *anthos* flower + -IN]

stroph′e, n. (Lines recited during) turn made in dancing by ancient Greek chorus (~, *antistrophe*, *epode*, three sections of a choral ode or of one division of it, ~ & antistrophe exactly corresponding in metre). So **stroph′ic** a. [Gk (-ē), orig. = turning (*strephō* turn)]

strove. See STRIVE.

strow (-ō), v.t. (p.p. ~*n* or ~*ed*). (Arch. for) STREW.

struck. See STRIKE.

struc′ture, n. Manner in which a building or organism or other complete whole is constructed, supporting framework or whole of the essential parts of something, make, construction, (*the* ~ *of a house*, *machine*, *animal*, *organ*, *poem*, *sentence*; a *sentence of loose, a rock of columnar,* ~*e*; *its* ~*e is ingenious*; *ornament should embellish & not disguise the lines of* ~*e*; *whence* ~AL, (-*cher*-), ~LESS, (-~ED² (-*cherd*), aa., ~AL²RY² adv.; thing constructed, complex whole, a building, (a *fine marble* ~*e*; *a lumbering* ~*e drawn by six horses*). [f. L *structura* (*struere struct-* build, -URE)]

strug′gle, v.i. & n. 1. Throw one's limbs about in violent effort to get free or escape grasp (*child* ~*ed & kicked*); make violent or determined efforts under difficulties, strive hard to do, contend with or against opponent or obstacle or difficulty, (~*ed to express himself, control his feelings*; ~*ing with his infirmity, against superior numbers or the forces of nature*); make one's way with difficulty through, (*a* ~*ing artist* etc.); hence ~*ingly²* adv., *~ling²* n. **2. n.** Spell of ~*ing*, confused dirty *games*; (part,) experiencing difficulty in making a living or getting recognition as an element in natural selection. [ME *strogelen*, cf. Norw. *stru* retractory]

strid′bu̇g, n. One of those cursed with immortality in *Gulliver's Travels*. [arbitrary]

strum, v.i. & t. (-mm-), & n. 1. Touch notes or twang strings of piano or other stringed instrument (esp. unskilfully); ~ *on* (piano, guitar, etc.). **2. n.** Sound made by ~*ming* (*the* ~ *of a guitar*). [imit., cf. THRUM]

strum'a (-ōō), n. (pl. ~ae). Scrofula; (Bot.) cushion-like dilatation of an organ. So ~ōSE¹, ~OUS, aa. [L, = scrofulous tumour]

strüm'pĕt, n. Prostitute. [f. 14th c., etym. dub.]

strung. See STRING.

strŭt' v.i. (-tt-), & n. (Walk with) pompous or affected gait. Hence ~t'ing LY² adv. [OE *strūtian* project, cf. foll.]

strŭt², n., & v.t. (-tt-). 1. Piece of wood or iron inserted in a framework & intended to bear weight or pressure in the direction of its length, brace, esp. one set obliquely from rafter to king-post or queen-post. 2. v.t. Brace with ~(s). [cf. ON *strútr* conical cap, Norw. *strut* spout, Sw. *strut* paper cornet]

struth'ious (-ōō-), a. Of or like an ostrich, of the ostrich tribe. [L *struthio* f. Gk *strouthiōn* ostrich (*strouthos* sparrow)\n~OUS]

strych'n|ine, (arch.) **strych'n|ĭa,** (-k-), nn. Vegetable alkaloid got from plants of genus *Strychnos*, very bitter to the taste & highly poisonous & used in minute doses as nerve-stimulant. Hence ~IC a., ~(in)ISM(5) nn. [L *strychnos* f. Gk (*strukhnos* kind of nightshade, -INE⁵]

Stŭ'art, n. *The* ~s, sovereigns James I, Charles I & II, James II, Mary & Anne. [f. L *studēre*]

stŭb, n., & v.t. (-bb-). 1. Stump of tree, tooth, etc., left projecting; remnant of pencil, cigar, dog's tail, or similar object; ~*iron*, used for gun-barrels & made of old horseshoe or other nails; ~*mortise, -tenon*, going only part of the way through; hence ~b'Y² a. 2. v.t. Grub up (~) by the roots; clear (land) of ~s; ~ one's *toe*, hurt it by striking against something; (also ~ *out*) extinguish (cigar, cigarette) by pressing lighted end of ~ against some object. [OE *stybb*, cf. Du. *stobbe*, ON *stubbr*, Gk *stupos*]

stŭb'ble, n. Stumps of grain left sticking up after harvest, cropped hair or beard. Hence **stŭbb'lY²** a. [f. OF *estuble* f. LL *stupula* f. L *stipula* (*stipes* stock, -ULE]

stŭbb'orn, a. Obstinate, unyielding, obdurate, inflexible, refractory, intractable, (*facts are ~ things*, will not adapt themselves to theory). Hence~LY² adv., ~NESS n. [ME *stoborn, stiborn*, perh. f. OE *stybb* STUB w. unexplained snf.]

stŭcc'ō, n. (pl. ~es), & v.t. 1. Kinds of plaster or cement used for coating wall surfaces or moulding into architectural decorations. 2. v.t. Coat with ~. [It., f. OHG *stukki* a crust (whence G *stuck* piece)]

stuck(-up). See STICK.

stŭd¹, n., & v.t. (-dd-). 1. Large-headed nail, boss, or knob, projecting from a surface esp. for ornament; rivet, crosspiece in each link of chain-cable; two-headed button for use with two button-holes ‖ esp. in shirt-front (*collar-~, long*

kind going through four holes); post to which laths are nailed, whence~d'ING¹ n., woodwork of lath-&-plaster wall. 2. v.t. Set with ~s by way of strengthening or usu. of decorating, (p.p.) thickly set or strewed *with (door, lawn, sea, sky, ~ded with nails, trees, islands, stars*); be scattered over or about (surface). [OE *studu* post, cf. ON *stoth*, Sw. *stöd*, G *stütze* prop]

stŭd², n. Number of horses kept for some purpose as breeding, racing, hunting, coaching; ~*book*, containing pedigrees of horses; ~ *farm*, place where horses are bred; ~*-horse*, stallion. [OE *stōd*, cf. ON *stóth*, G *gestüt*; cogn. w. STAND]

studding-sail (stŭn'sl), n. Sail set on small extra yard & boom beyond leech of square sail in light winds. [etym. dub.]

stŭd'ent, n. 1. Person studying in order to qualify himself for some occupation or devoting himself to some branch of learning or under instruction at university or other place of higher education or technical training (*medical, theological, historical*, ~; ~ *interpreter*, civil servant qualified or qualifying for consular service in China, Persia, etc., by study of the language required; *a ~ of archaeology, law, botany, manners; numbers its ~s by the thousand*). 2. Person of studious habits. 3. ‖ (At some colleges) recipient of stipend from foundation, fellow or scholar, whence ~SHIP n. [L *studēre* (*studium* STUDY¹), -ENT]

stŭd'io, n. (pl. ~s). Working-room of painter, sculptor, photographer, etc., often with skylights or windows specially designed to secure suitable light; room in which cinema-play is staged; (pl.) cinema-~s of a film company with auxiliary buildings; one of the rooms in a broadcasting station used for transmissions. [It., f. L STUDY¹]

stŭd'ious, a. Given to study, occupied with reading; taking care to do, anxiously desirous of doing; studied, deliberate, intended, zealous, anxious, painstaking, (*with ~ care, attention, politeness*). Hence ~LY² adv., ~NESS n. [f. L *studiosus* (foll., -OSE²]

stŭd'y¹, n. 1. Thing to be secured by pains or attention (*it shall be my ~ to please, to write correctly; your comfort was my ~; make a ~ of, try to secure*). 2. (Now usu. *brown ~*) fit of musing, reverie, (*there he stood for an hour in a ~; is in a brown.~, too intent on his thoughts to observe what is passing*). 3. Devotion of time & thought to acquiring information esp. from books (often pl.), pursuit of some branch of knowledge, (*gives his hours to ~; make a ~ of, investigate carefully; my studies have convinced me that; the ~ of mathematics, morals; continue your studies, go on with your lessons*). 4. Thing that is or deserves to be investigated (*the proper ~ of mankind is man; his face was a ~,*

5. (Paint. etc.) sketch made for practice in technique or as preliminary experiment for picture or part of it (*this studies are exquisite, but his finished work disappoint-ing*); a ~ of a head; (Mus.) composition designed to develop skill in some particular branch; (Theatr.) *good, slow,* etc., learner of parts (UNDERSTUDY). **6.** Room used for literary occupation, transaction of business etc. (*you will find him in his, the, ~*). [AF & OF *estudie* f. L *studium*]

stud′y², v.t. & i. **1.** Make a study of, take pains to investigate or acquire knowledge of (subject) or to assure (result sought); scrutinize or earnestly contemplate (visible object), (~ *law, French, philo-sophy; ~ book,* read it attentively; ~ one's *part,* try to learn it by heart; ~ *up,* get up for examination etc.; ~ *out,* succeed in finding out by hard thinking; *studies others' convenience, his own inter-ests; ~* person's *face or character, a map, the stars*). **2.** Apply oneself to study esp. reading (~ *for the bar,* read law). **3.** (arch.) Meditate, muse. **4.** Be on the watch, try constantly to manage, to do (*studies to avoid disagreeable topics*). **5.** p.p. De-liberate, intentional, affected, (*a studied insult; with studied politeness, rudeness, unconcern, abandon,* whence **stud′iedly²** (-di-) adv. [f. OF *estudier* f. med. L *studiare* t. L as prec.]

stuff, n. & v.t. & i. **1.** Material that thing is made of or that is or may be used for some purpose (*the~ that dreams, heroes, are made of; has good~ in him,* sterling quali-ties; *some~ they call beer; this punch, book, is good, sorry, ~; household~,* arch. furniture etc.; *bread, food, ~s,* things made into bread, used as food; *green, garden~,* vegetables; *doctors', physic; ~inch~,* boards 1 in. thick; *the~,* colloq., available supply of something, e.g. timber, money, shells). **2.** Any woollen fabric (opp. silk, cotton, linen; || ~ *gown,* worn by barrister who has not taken SILK). **3.** Valueless matter, refuse, trash, nonsense (n. & int.), (*take that~ away; Smith a liar? ~ & non-sense!; what~ he writes!*). **4.** (sl.) **Do your~,* perform your tricks, get on with your job; HOT ~; *the ~ to give 'em* or the *troops,* the way to proceed etc. **5.** vb. Pack, cram, stop up, fill, distend, (~ one's *ears with wool, cushion with down; ~ed birds, beasts,* skin with interior removed & replaced by enough material to restore original shape; ~*ed food, turkey, haddock,* with minced seasoning inserted be-fore cooking; **~ed shirt,* colloq., a pom-pous nonentity; *a head ~ed with romance, facts, folly*), whence ~ING(4) n. (~*ing-box,* chamber in machinery through which rod can work without allowing passage of air etc., all *vacant space being filled*

with ~*ing*). **6.** Ram or press into recep-tacle (~*ed his necessaries into a small bag, his fingers into his ears, the food into his mouth*). **7.** Gull with lies, hoax. **8.** Gorge oneself, eat greedily; hence (-)~ER¹ n. [vb f. n.; OF *estoffe,* cf. Pr., Sp., & Port. *estofa* cloth, It. *stoffa* woven piece, etym. dub.; G & Sw. *stoff,* Da. *stof,* are f. the OF]

stuff′y, a. (Of valley, room, etc., or atmosphere in it) lacking fresh air or ventilation, close, hard to breathe in, fusty; **disapproving,* pompous, boring. Hence ~**INESS** n. [-Y²]

stug′gy etc. See **stock-.**

stul′tify, v.t. (Of act, statement, agent, speaker) reduce (previous act etc., to absurdity, exhibit (act etc. or oneself) in ridiculous light, make (act etc.) of no effect, neutralize (oneself) as agent, by later inconsistent act etc. Hence ~**FICA′TION** n. [f. LL *stultificare* (L *stultus* foolish, *-fy*)]

stum, n. & v.t. (-mm-). **1.** Unfermented grape-juice, must. **2.** v.t. Prevent from fermenting, secure (wine) against further fermentation in cask, by introduction of antiseptic. [f. Du. *stom* n., *stommen* vb antiseptic]

stum′ble, v.i. & t. & n. **1.** Lurch for-ward, have partial fall, from catching or striking foot or making false step (~*e along, ~e* go with frequent ~es); make blunder(s) in doing something (~*es in his speech; ~e through a recitation*); be of-fended, feel scruples, *at*; come accident-ally (*up)on or across*; (arch.) give pause to, excite scruples in; ~*ing-block,* obstacle, circumstance that causes difficulty or hesitation or scruples; hence ~**ing**r² adv. **2.** n. Act of ~ing. [f. 14th c.; cf. Norw. *stumla,* & STAMMER]

|| **stüm′er,** n. (sl.). Worthless cheque, counterfeit coin or note. [?]

stump, n. & v.i. & t. **1.** Projecting rem-nant of cut or fallen tree, corresponding remnant of broken branch or tooth or amputated limb, useless end of cigar or pencil, worn-down brush or other imple-ment, stub; (pl. joc.) legs (usu. STIR one's ~*s*). **2.** ~ of tree used by orator to address meeting from (*on the ~,* colloq., engaged in political speech-making or agitation; ~ *ordory,* of kind suitable for such speeches). **3.** (Cricket) one of the three uprights of a wicket (OFF, *middle,* LEG, ~). **4.** Cylinder of rolled paper or other material with conical ends for softening pencil-marks & other uses in drawing. **5.** vb. Walk stiffly & noisily as on wooden legs. **6.** (Of question etc.; colloq.) pose, be too hard for, (*am ~ed,* at a loss, at my wits' end), whence ~ER¹(2) n. **7.** (Cricket) put (batsman who is not in his ground) out by disturbing wicket while holding ball, whence ~ER¹(1) n. (sl., = wicket-keeper). **8.** Make ~ speeches, traverse (district) doing this. **9.** Use ~on (drawing,

line, etc.). **10.** || ~ *up* (sl.), pay over the money required, produce (sum). [cf. Du. *slomp*, G *stumpf*; perh. cogn. w. STAMP, STUB]

stump'|ў, a. Thickset, stocky, of small height or length in proportion to girth, (*a ~y man, book, tail, pencil*). Hence **~ILY²** adv., **~INESS** n. [-Y²]

stŭn, v.t. (-nn-). (Of sound) deafen temporarily, bewilder; (of blow lit. or fig.) knock senseless, reduce to insensibility or stupor, benumb, overwhelm; (part. as adj., sl.) ravishingly good in some respect, splendid, delightful, ripping, whence **~n'ing**LY² adv., & so **~n'ER¹** n. [prob. f. OF *estoner* ASTONISH]

Stun'dism, Stun'dist, (-ŏŏ-), nn. Doctrines, adherent, of a religious body in Russia, orig. of peasants, rejecting ceremonies of Orthodox Church & basing itself on the Bible as translated 1861 into modern Russian. [G *stunde* hour, lesson (the movement originating with German colonists). -ISM, -IST]

stung. See STING.

stunk. See STINK.

stun'sail, stŭns'l, n. =STUDDING-SAIL.

stŭnt, v.t. Check growth or development of, dwarf, cramp, (esp. in p.p.). [f. OE *stunt* a. dull, cf. ON *stuttr* short]

stŭnt, n., & v.i. (colloq.). 1. Special effort, feat, show performance, display of concentrated energy; advertising device. 2. v.i. Perform ~s esp. aerobatics. [etym. dub.; first in U.S. college athletics]

stupe¹, n., & v.t. 1. Flannel etc., wrung out of hot water & applied as fomentation; pledget of soft material used as surgical dressing. 2. v.t. Apply ~ to, foment. [f. L *stup(p)a* tow]

stupe², n. (sl.). Fool. [for STUPID]

stup'efy, v.t. Make stupor or torpid, deprive of sensibility, (~*fied with drink*, *narcotics, grief,* etc.). Hence or cogn. **~FA'CIENT** (-āshnt) a. & n. (med.), **~FAC'TION, ~FIER¹**(1, 2), nn., **~fäctive** a. [f. F *stupefier* f. L *stupefacere* (*stupēre* be torpid, -FY)]

stupen'dous, a. Amazing, prodigious, astounding, esp. by size or degree (*a ~ structure, error, achievement; ~ folly*). Hence **~LY²** adv., **~NESS** n. [L *stupendus* (*stupēre* be amazed at, -ND¹), -OUS]

stu'pid, a. & n. 1. In a state of stupor or lethargy; dull by nature, slow-witted, lacking in sensibility, obtuse, crass, characteristic of persons of this nature, (*a ~ person, joke, idea, book, fright; what a ~ place to put it in!*), whence **stupid'ITY** n.; uninteresting, dull, (*a ~ place, visit, time*). 2. n. (colloq.). ~ person. Hence **~LY²** adv. [f. L *stupidus* (as STUPENDOUS, -ID¹)]

stu'por, n. Dazed state, torpidity, whence

~OUS a. (med.); helpless amazement. [L (as STUPENDOUS, -OR¹)]

stup'ose, a. (bot., zool.). With tow-like tufts of long hair. [as STUPEOUS, -OSE¹]

stŭr'd|ў¹, a. Robust, hardy, vigorous, lusty, strongly built, (*~y child, opponent, legs, frame, resistance, courage; ~y beggar*, arch., able-bodied but not working). Hence **~ILY²** adv., **~INESS** n. [earlier sense *reckless*; f. OF *estourdi* amazed, etym. dub.]

stŭr'd|ў², n. Vertigo in sheep caused by tapeworm in brain. Hence **~IED²**(-id) a. [f. OF *estourdie* giddiness (prec.)]

stŭr'geon (-jn), n. Kinds of large anadronous fish resembling shark in general shape, having mailed body & head, yielding caviare & isinglass, & esteemed as food. [f. OF *esturgeon* f. med. L *sturionem* nom. ~o f. OHG *sturio*, cf. OE *styrga*; perh. cogn. w. STIR]

Sturm und Drang (shtoorm ŏŏnt drahng'). See STORM & stress.

stŭtt'er, v.i. & t., & n. 1. Keep repeating parts, esp. initial consonants, of words in effort to articulate; utter in this way (often *out*); hence **~ER¹** n., **~ing**LY² adv. 2. n. Act or habit of ~ing. [obs. *stut* in same sense (cf. G *stossen* strike) + -ER⁵; cf. Du. *stotteren*, G *stottern*]

stȳ¹, n. (pl. -*ies*), & v.t. & i. 1. (*Pig'~*), enclosure for keeping pig(s) in, (fig.) mean or dirty hovel or room, place of debauchery. 2. vb. Lodge (t. & i.) in ~. [OE (& ON) stī]

stȳ² (pl. -*ies*), **stȳe,** n. Inflamed swelling on edge of eyelid (usu. *a ~ in one's eye*). [prob. f. obs. *styany* (= *styan eye* f. OE *stigend* sty, lit. riser, f. *stigan* rise + *eye*) shortened as though = sty on eye]

Sty'gian, a. (As) of the Styx or of Hades, murky, gloomy. [L f. Gk *Stugios* (STYX), -AN]

style¹, n., & v.t. 1. Ancient writing-implement, a small rod with pointed end for scratching letters on wax-covered tablets & blunt end for obliterating (whence **STY'LIFORM** a.); pen or pencil; (transf.) thing of ~-like shape as etching-needle or styloid process in Anat. 2. Manner of writing, speaking, or doing, esp. as opposed to the matter to be expressed or thing done (*the ~ is better than the matter; written in a florid, cumbrous, lucid, delightful, ~; different ~s of rowing; slashed about him in fine ~; good, bad, ~, =good, bad,* FORM³). 3. Collective characteristics of the writing or diction or artistic expression or way of presenting things or decorative methods proper to a person or school or period or subject, manner exhibiting these characteristics, (*in the ~ of Shakspere, Raphael, Wagner; the epic, lyric, dramatic, ~; lapidary or monumental ~*, fit or resembling that fit for inscriptions on stone; *pre-Raphaelite, impressionist, ~*, in painting; *baroque,*

Louis XIV, rococo, renaissance, ~, in architecture or furniture or dress; GOTHIC, classical, ROMANESQUE, ~, in architecture; Norman, early English, decorated, perpendicular, ~s, kinds of esp. ecclesiastical architecture prevailing successively in England 1066-1189, 1189-1272, 1272-1377, 1350-1400, & marked respectively by round arches & heavy pillars, pointed arches & lancet windows & simple tracery, slender pillars & vast windows divided by vertical & horizontal lines; Tudor, Jacobean, Queen Anne, ~s, kinds of esp. domestic architecture). **4.** Descriptive formula, designation of person or thing; full title, (is entitled to the ~ of Right honourable, King, Esquire; did not recognize him under that ~; my ~ is plain John Smith; regret that I am not acquainted with your proper ~; old, new, ~, abbr. O.S., N.S., appended to dates; = so called when reckoned by the Julian, GREGORIAN, CALENDAR'). **5.** Noticeably superior quality or manner esp. in regard to breeding or fashion, distinction, (there is no ~ about her, she looks commonplace; let us do the thing in ~ if we do it at all), whence STYL'ISH 1 a. styl'ishY 2 adv. STYL'ISHNESS n. **6.** Kind, sort, esp. with regard to appearance (what ~ of house, servant, do you require ?; a gentleman of the old ~). **7.** Make, shape, pattern, (this ~ 3/6; in all sizes & ~s). **8.** v.t. Use specified designation of (is ~d king, duke, folly). [ME stile t. OF stile, style, t. L stilus incorrectly spelt stylus by late writers w. assin. to Gk (foll.)]

style² n. Gnomon of sun-dial; (Bot.) narrowed extension of ovary supporting stigma. [f. Gk stulos pillar]

style³ n. (Incorrect spelling for) STYLE.

styl'et, n. Slender pointed instrument, stiletto; (Surg.) stiffening wire of catheter, probe. [f. F. f. It. STILETTO]

styl'ist, n. Person with or aiming at good literary style. [-IST]

stylis'tic, a. Of literary style. Hence ~ICALLY adv. [-IC]

styl'ite, n. Medieval ascetic living on top of a pillar. [f. late Gk stulitēs (STYLE², -ITE¹)]

styl'ize, v.t. (Usn. in p.p.) conform (artistic representation) to the rules of a conventional style. [-IZE]

styl'o, n. (colloq.; pl. ~s). Stylograph. [abbr.]

stylo-, comb. form of styloid in names of muscles = of the styloid process & ~, as ~hyoid, ~maxillary. [f. L as STYLE¹, -O-]

styl'obate, n. Continuous basement supporting a row or rows of columns. [f. L f. Gk stulobatēs (STYLE², batnō stand)]

styl'o|graph (-ahf), n. Kind of pen containing reservoir of ink & marking with point instead of split nib. Hence ~graph'ic a., ~graph'ically adv. [STYLE¹, -o-; -GRAPH]

stylo'id, a. & n. ~ (process), spine projecting from base of temporal bone. [STYLE¹, -OID]

styl'us, stil'us, n. **1.** = STYLE¹ (writing implement). **2.** = STYLE¹ 2. [see STYLE¹]

stym'ie, n., & v.t. (golf). **1.** Condition on putting-green when a player's ball lies between opponent's ball & the hole, if the balls are at least six inches apart, as I laid him a ~. **2.** v.t. Put (opponent, opponent's ball, oneself) into the position of having to negotiate a ~; also fig. [?]

styp'tic, a. & n. (Substance) that checks bleeding. [f. LL f. Gk stuptikos (stuphō contract)]

styr'ax, n. Kinds of tree & shrub, some of which yield valuable gums. [L, f. Gk sturax]

Sunbian. See SWABIAN.

Styr'ian, a. & n. (Native) of Styria. [-AN¹] **Styx**, n. (Gk Myth.) River encompassing Hades (cross the ~; die; black etc. as ~).

su'able, a. That can be sued. Hence **suabil'ITY** n. [-ABLE]

sua'sion (swā'zhn), n. Persuasion as opposed to force (esp. moral ~). So **suas'IVE** (swā-) a. [f. L suasionem nom. -o (suadēre suas- urge, cogn. w. foll., -ION)]

suave, (swāv), a. Bland, soothing, mollifying, polite, (~ person, speech, manners, wine, medicine). Hence or cogn. ~LY² adv., ~NESS n. [F, f. L suavis cogn. w. SWEET]

sua'viter (swā-), ~ in mŏd'ŏ, fŏr'titer in rē, gently but firmly, with iron hand in velvet glove. [L, = suavely in manner, strongly in matter]

sub¹, n., & v.i. (-bb-; colloq.). **1.** Subaltern; submarine; subscription; substitute. **2.** v.i. Act as substitute for someone. [abbr.]

sub² 1 L prep., = under, in some L phrr.: ~ fīnem (albr. s.f.), towards the end (of the chapter etc. referred to); ~ jūdĭcĕ (jōō-), under judicial consideration (news-paper comment on cases ~ judice etc. is prohibited), not yet decided, still debatable (the matter is still ~judice; cf. RES judicata); ~ rōsā (-z-), (of communications, consultations, etc.) in confidence, under express or implied pledge of secrecy [lit. under the rose, as emblem of secrecy]; ~ silen'tio (-tiō, -shiō), in hushed-up manner, privately; ~ vō'cĕ, abbr. s.v., (in references to dictionaries etc.) under the word in question, under the word —. **sub-** (sub, sub), pref. f. L sub prep. & sub-pret. = under.

1. Many words are from L compounds, in which ~ (or often by assim. suc-, suf-, sug-, sum-, sup-, sus-, sur-) expresses clearly or obscurely the ideas of lower position (~jacent, ~ordinate, ~scribe, ~sist, ~stance), motion to this (~ject,

~jugate, ~junctive, ~merge, ~mit, ~side, succumb, suppose, suppress) or from this (~tract, succinct, suspect, suspend, suspire), covertness or secrecy or tacitness (~audition, ~orn, summon, surreptitious), inclusion (~sume), closeness (~join, ~junctive, ~time, ~sequent, ~urb, succeed), inferiority (~altern, ~serve, succour, succentor, support (~sidy, ~vention, succour, suffer, suffice, sustain), addition (suffix, supplement), or substitution (~stitute, supplant, ~surrogate).

2. ~, without the above changes into suc- etc., is also used as a living pref. with more definite senses:

a. On anal. of L subterraneus underground (sub terra below the earth), adjj. are formed from sub, the abl. of any L noun, & an adj. ending, esp. as anat. terms with sense situated under the — (~sternal f. L sub sterno below the breastbone); in others ~ has the secondary sense below in degree (~normal below normal), & in some having this sense, as in b below, ~ is prefixed directly to a derived E adj. (~human less than human, as from sub homine).

b. On anal. of L subacidus slightly acid, adjj. & rarely nn. are formed by prefixing ~ to E adjj. & nn. whether of L orig. or not, the pref. having an effect equivalent to rather (~acid), more or less (~aquatic), roughly (~cylindrical), incipient (~delirium), not quite (~conscious), approaching the specified character (~erect), on the borders of (~alpine).

c. On anal. of med. L subprior underprior, ~ is prefixed to nn. & vv. with sense under-, subordinate(ly), secondary -ily, further, (~prefect, ~heading, ~species, ~divide, ~let).

d. On anal. of subst[ruction f. L substructio, ~ is rarely prefixed to E nn. with sense underlying (~soil, ~way).

e. With multiplicative adjj. (double, triple, quadruple, octuple, sextuple, septuple, octuple, decuple) ~ inverts the sense; so, double, triple, expressing the ratios 2:1, 3:1, ~double, ~triple, = 1:2, 1:3.

The following list contains, with letters of reference & further explanation when necessary, the words in ~ whether compounded in L or in E that fall under 2; the L wd needed to give the meaning of wds marked a will be found by reference to the simple adj. that is left when ~ is removed, or to wd added in brackets:—~abdom'inal, a; ~a'cid, ~acid'ity, b, (lit., & fig. of pine etc.); ~a'gent, ~a'gency, c; ~al'pine, b; ~ān'al, a; ~ande'an, b (of Andes mountains); ~ap'ennine, b; ~apostol'ic, b, of period after that of apostles; ~aquat'ic, b, of more or less aquatic habits or kind, also a, underwater; ~aqueous, a; ~are'ic, b; ~as'tral, a, terrestrial; ~aur'al, a; ~ax'il-

lary, a; ~branch, ~breed, nn., c; ~caud'-al, a; ~cen'tral, a, b; ~ce'rebral, a (esp. of reflex action in which the spinal cord is concerned, but not the brain); ~class, c; ~clav'ate, b; ~clā'vian, ~clavic'ular, a (CLAVICLE); ~commis'sion(er), ~committ'ee, c; ~conc'ave, ~con'ical, ~con'scious(ly, -ness), b; ~con'tinent n., b, region whose size & importance would justify the name continent if it were not part of one, e.g. India, S. Africa; ~con'tract n., ~contract' v.i., ~contrac'tor n., c; ~con'trary a. & n. pl., ~contrar'ety n., b, contrary in some degree only (esp. in logic, as ' some men are mortal' & ' no man is mortal' are contraries, whereas ' all men are mortal' & ' no man is mortal' are not contraries); ~con'vex, b; ~cord'ate, b; ~corn'eous, b, rather horny, also a, placed under horn, nail, etc.; ~cort'ical, ~cos'tal, ~crin'ial, a; ~crys'talline, b; ~cutân'eous(ly), ~cutic'ular, a; ~cylin'drical, b; ~deac'on, ~deac'onship, ~dean', ~dean'-ery, ~decân'al, c; ~dec'uple, e; ~deli'r-ium, b, incipient or mild or intermittent; ~derm'al, a (DERM); ~diac'onate, c; ~divide', v.t. & i. [f. L subdividere], ~divi'sion, c; ~dom'inant n. (Mus.), a, note below dominant, fourth of diatonic scale; ~dors'al, a; ~dou'ble, ~dup'licate, e; || ~ed'it, ~ed'itor, c; ~epiderm'al, a (EPIDERMIS); ~eq'ual, b (esp. of quantities in a group such that no one is as large as the sum of the rest); ~equi-lat'eral, b; ~erect', b; ~fam'ily, c (in zool. classif.); ~feb'rile, b; ~flavour, b; ~form, c; ~fuse, b, dusky, dull-coloured [f. L suffuscus see FUSCOUS]; ~gelat'inous, b; ~gēnus, ~gene'ric, c; ~gla'cial, a; ~glob'ular, ~gradiator'ial, b; ~group, ~head (in classif.), ~head'ing, c; ~hep-at'ic, a, b; ~himalay'an, b; ~hūm'an, ~hūm'eral, a (HUMERUS); ~infeuda'tion, ~inspec'tor, c; ~intes'tinal, a (INTESTINE'); ~joint, c, one of ~divisions of regular joint in leg etc. of insect etc.; ~kingdom, c, main division of animal or vegetable kingdom; ~lan'ceolate, b; ~lease n., ~lease' v.t., ~lessee', ~less'or, ~let' v.t., ~librar'ian, ||~lieuten'ant, c; ~līm'inal, a (LIMEN; of sensations so faint that subject is not conscious of them; ~liminal self, the ~conscious mind as a distinct part of the individual's personality); ~ling'ual, a; ~lit'toral, b; ~lun'ar (poet.), ~lun'ary, a, of this world, earthly; ~machine-gun, a, large automatic pistol; ~mamm'ary, a (MAMMA²); ||~master, c, second master in some schools; ~maxil-l'ary, a (MAXILLA); ~med'iant n. (Mus.), a, sixth note of diatonic scale; ~mem'bra-nous, b; ~men'tal, a (MENTAL²); ~metal-l'ic, b; ~mon'tane, a; ~muc'ous, b; ~mul'tiple a. & n., e; ~narcot'ic, b; ~nās'al, ~na'tural (opp. supernatural), ~norm'al, e; ~occip'ital (OCCIPUT), ~ocean'ic, a; ~ocell'-ate, b (OCELLUS); ~oc'tuple, e; ~oc'ular, ~

oesopha'geal(OESOPHAGUS), ~ory'ical(ORBIT),
a.; ~'order, ~ordi'nal, a (in bot. & zool.
classif.); ~ov'al, b; ~pari'etal, ~pharyn'-
geal (PHARYNX), ~plever'ic, a; ~pri'ose, b;
~pleur'al, a; ~pol'ar, b, of nearly polar
character or situation, also a, directly
below pole of heavens (astron.); ~préfec'-
(ture), ~pri'or, c; ~pyram'idal, ~quadran-
g'ular, ~quad'ruple, b; ~quad'ruple, ~
quin'tuple, e; ~ram'ose, b; ~reader, c (in
Inns of Court); ~rectang'ular, b; ~rector,
c, rector's deputy; ~rectang'ular region, a
faunal region; ~rent v.t., c; ~ret'inal, a
(RETINA); ~rhomboid'al, b; ~sac'ral, a
(SACRAL); ~sat'urated, ~saturation, b;
~scap'ular; a; ~section, c; ~sen'sible, b,
below the reach of the senses; ~sep'tuple, e;
e; ~ser'ous, ~ses'ile, b; ~sev'entuple, e;
~'soil, d; ~species, ~specif'ic a., c; ~
sphe'rical, ~spin'ous (SPINE), b; ~station,
c; ~stern'al, a (STERNUM); ~strat'um (pl.
-ta rare), d, what underlies something,
lower layer, foundation, basis, (often fig.,
as it has a ~stratum of truth); ~struc'tion
or ~struc'ture, ~struc'tural, d; ~term'inal,
b (of climate etc.); ~tenant, ~tenancy, c;
~trop'ical, b (of climate, fauna, flora, etc.);
~ung'ulate, b, hoofed, but with several
digits; ~urs'ine, b; ~variety, c(in classif.);
~vert'ebral, a; ~vertical, ~vit'reous, b;
~way, d, ∥covered usu. underground
way, "underground railway."
[L]

subahdar'(sŏŏbaa')n.(Anglo-Ind.). Chief
native officer of company of sepoys.
[Hind. (subah province, dār master)]

sub'altern, a. & n. 1. Of inferior rank.
(Log., of propositions) particular, not
universal. 2. n. (mil.). Junior officer below rank of captain. [f. LL SUB(alternus
ALTERNATE')]

subaud'i, v. imperat. Supply (specified
word or words) by way of subaudition.
[L]

subaudi'tion, n. Mental supplying of
omitted word(s), understanding of what
is not expressed, reading between the
lines. [f. L subauditio f. SUB(audire hear)]

subdúce, subdúct', vv.t. (rare). Withdraw, deduct, subtract. So **subdúc'tion**
n. [f. L SUB(ducere -duct- draw)]

subdúe', v.t. Conquer, subjugate, overcome, vanquish, master, tame, bring into
subjection, discipline, (~ enemies, nature,
rough land, one's passions; (~ by kindness); soften, make gentle, tone down,
mitigate, (esp. in p.p., as ~d colour, light,
tone, effect, mood, manners, satisfaction,
whence ~d'NESS (-dū'd-) n.). Hence **sub-**

dū'ABLE a., **subdū'al**(2) n. [ME sodeue
f. OF soduire repr. in form L SUBDUCERE,
but in sense of L SUBDUCERE, while the E vb
has the sense of L SUB(dere duct; conquer]

**súber'eous, súbe'ric, súb'erōse, aa.
Corky, of or like cork. [(-ous f. LL
suberus + -OUS) f. L suber cork, -IC, -OSE¹]

subjä'cent, a. & adv. 1. (arch., poet.). Sub-
jacent (survey the ~ plains). **2.** Under
government, not independent, owing
obedience to, (a ~ province, tribe; is held
~, in subjection; has long been ~ t
France; States ~ to foreign rule; we are di
~ to the laws of nature, the law of the land).
3. Liable or exposed or prone to (thing);
persons ~ to gout; is very ~ to damage,
envy, etc.). **4.** ~ (a. & adv.) to, condi-
tional(ly) upon, on the assumption of,
without precluding; (treaty is ~ to ratification, not valid unless ratified; the
arrangement is made, or is, ~ to your
approval; ~ to correction, these are the
facts). [ME & OF suget, f. L p.p. of SUB-
(jicère -ject- = jacère throw)]

sub'ject², n. 1. Person subject to political
rule, any member of a State except the
Sovereign, any member of a subject State,
(rulers & ~s; the ~s of the Sultan; the
loyalty of my ~s; the liberty of the ~, such
immunities as are secured to ~s under
constitutional rule; fig., as the ~s of King
Shakespeare). **2.** (Log., Gram.) that member
of a proposition about which something
is predicated, the noun or noun-equivalent with which the verb of a sentence is
made to agree in number etc., (~ &
predicate are the essential parts of a
sentence; every verb has a ~ expressed or
understood, not every verb has an object).
3. (Metaphys.) thinking & feeling entity,
the mind, the ego, the conscious self, as
opp. all that is external to the mind (~ &
object, the ego & the non-ego, self & not-
self, the consciousness & what it is
or may be conscious of); what it is
or substratum of anything as opp. its
attributes. **4.** Theme of or of discussion
or description or representation, matter
(to be) treated of or dealt with, (never
talks on serious ~s; proposed a ~ for the
debate; on the ~ of, concerning, about; a
tabooed, ticklish, interesting, dull, ~; what
is the ~ of the poem, story, picture?; constantly wanders from the ~; pastoral, genre,
marine, historical, etc., ~ in painting; ~
of piece of music, theme of fugue or sonata,
leading phrase, motif; ~ for dissection, or
~, dead body; was made the ~ of an
experiment; could write if I could think of
a ~; change the ~, talk of something else,
esp. as way out of embarrassment;
5. Circumstance that gives occasion for

specified feeling or action (*is a ~ for ridicule, pity, rejoicing, congratulation*). **6.** Person of specified usu. undesirable bodily or mental tendencies (*a sensitive, bilious, plethoric, hysterical, ill-conditioned, etc., ~*). **7.** ~-*heading*, in index collecting references to a ~; ~-*matter*, matter treated of in book etc.; ~-*object*, object of sense or thought as it is conceived of (opp. *object-object*, as it is in fact). Hence ~LESS a. [f. L masc. & neut. p.p. (prec.)]

subjec't², v.t. Subdue (nation etc. usu. *to* one's sway etc.); expose, make liable, treat, *to* (*rudeness ~s one to retorts in kind; must be ~ed to great heat; shall ~ it to criticism*). So **subjec'tion** n. [f. OF *subjecter* f. L as SUBJECT¹]

subjec'tive¹, a. & n. **1.** (Philos.) belonging to, of, due to, the consciousness or thinking or perceiving subject or ego as opp. real or external things; (pop.) imaginary. **2.** (Of art & artists) giving prominence to or depending on personal idiosyncrasy or individual point of view, not producing the effect of literal & impartial transcription of external realities, whence ~NESS. **subjectiv'ity**, nn. **3.** (Gram.) of the subject (~ *case*, or ~ as n., the nominative; cf. ~ *genitive*, as in 'by the act of *God*', cf. OBJECTIVE). Hence ~LY² adv. [f. LL *subjectivus* (SUBJECT², -IVE)]

subjec'tivism, n. Doctrine that knowledge is merely subjective & that there is no external or objective test of truth. So ~IST(2) n. & a. [prec., -ISM, -IST]

subjoin', v.t. Add at the end, append, (illustration, anecdote, etc.). [f. OF *subjoindre* f. L SUB(*jungere junct-* join)]

sub'jugate (-jŏŏ-), v.t. Subdue, vanquish, bring under bondage or into subjection. Hence or cogn. ~ABLE a., ~A'TION, ~ātor², nn. [f. L *subjugare* bring under the yoke (SUB² *jugum* yoke)]

subjunc'tive, a. & n. ~ *mood* or ~, a verbal MOOD², obsolescent in English, named as being used in the classical languages chiefly in subordinate or subjoined clauses (cf. CONJUNCTIVE; the two names denote the same forms & are occas. used indifferently; occas. ~ is restricted to the subordinate uses while *conjunctive* either includes all uses or is restricted to principal-clause verbs, as in apodosis of conditional sentence). Hence ~LY² adv. [f. L *subjunctivus* (SUBJOIN, -IVE)]

sublapsar'ian, a. & n. =INFRALAPSARIAN. [SUB-2a]

sub'limate¹, v.t. Convert from solid state to vapour by heat & allow to solidify again; (fig.) refine, purify, idealize. Hence ~A'TION n. [as foll., -ATE³]

sub'limate², a. & n. Sublimated (substance); *corrosive* ~, mercuric chloride. [f. L *sublimare* SUBLIME², -ATE²]

sublime'¹, a. Of the most exalted kind, so distinguished by elevation or size or nobility or grandeur or other impressive quality as to inspire awe or wonder, aloof from & raised far above the ordinary, (~ *mountain, scenery, tempest, ambition, virtue, heroism, self-sacrifice, love, thought, beauty, genius, poet, etc.*; ~ *indifference, impudence, etc.*, as of one too exalted to fear consequences; *the S~* PORTE; *the* ~, *all that is* ~, sublimity), whence or cogn. ~LY² adv., **sublim'ITY** n.; (Anat.) lying near the surface, not deep-sunk. [F. f. L *sublimis*, perh. f. SUB², *limen* lintel, =reaching up to the lintel]

sublim'le², v.t. & i. Sublimate (lit.), whence~ ER(2) n.; undergo sublimation; purify or elevate, become pure, as by sublimation; make sublime. [f. OF *sublimer* f. L *sublimare* in med. L sense sublimate (prec.)]

sub'man, n. Man of markedly inferior development or capacity (opp. SUPERMAN). [SUB-2 c]

sub'marine (-ēn; *adj. also* -ēn'), a. & n. **1.** Existing, acting, used, constructed, etc., under the surface of the sea, as ~e *plant, volcano, cable*. **2.** n. A ~e vessel, esp. a warship capable of operating either on or under the surface, equipped with torpedo-tubes, guns, & periscope, & propelled by diesel engines or electric motors. Hence ~ER¹ (-ēn-) n. [SUB-2 a]

submerge', v.t. & i. Place below water, flood with water, inundate, (also fig.; *the* ~d *tenth*, the part of the population that is plunged in debt or permanently in distress); (of submarine or its crew or commander) dive, go below surface. Hence or cogn. **submer'gence**, **submer'sion** (-shn), nn. [f. L *submergere mers-* dip)]

submers'le', v.t. & a. (rare). **1.** Submerge (rare exc. in p.p. used in Bot. of parts of plants growing under water). **2.** adj. (rare; bot.).~ed. Hence (in common use) ~IBLE a., [f. L p.p. (prec.)]

submi'ssion (-shn), n. Submitting or being submitted (*shall be satisfied with nothing short of complete* ~; *demands the* ~ *of the signature to an expert*); (in legal use) theory etc. submitted by counsel to judge or jury (*my* ~ *is that*, I submit that); humility, meekness, resignation, acceptance of authority, obedient conduct or spirit, so **submiss'IVE** a., **submiss'ive-LY²** adv., **submiss'iveNESS** n. [f. L *submissionem* (foll., -ION)]

submit', v.t. & i. (-tt-). Surrender oneself for control etc. to (*wives* ~ *yourselves unto your own husbands*); present for consideration or decision (*should like to* ~ *it to your inspection*; ~ *a case to the court*); urge or represent deferentially that (*I* ~ *that a material fact has been passed over*:

For words in *sub-* not given see SUB-.

also parenth., as *that*, I ~, *is a false in-ference*); give way, make submission, yield, cease or abstain from resistance, (*will never* ~, ~ *to indignity*, ~ *to being parted from you*; *had to* ~ *to defeat, God's will*). [f. L SUB(*mittere miss-* send)]

subŏr'dĭnate¹, a. & n. 1. Of inferior importance or rank, secondary, sub-servient, (*to*; ~ *clause*, sentence made by addition of a conjunction or by position to serve as a noun or adj. or adv. in another sentence); hence ~LY² adv. 2. n. Person working under another (*leaves everything to, never trusts,* ~*s or his* ~*s*). [f. med. L SUB(*ordinatus* f. L *ordinare* ORDAIN)]

subŏr'dĭnāte², v.t. Make subordinate, treat or regard as of minor importance, bring or put into subservient relation, (*to*). Hence ~A'TION n., ~ATIVE a. [as prec., -ATE³]

subŏrdĭnā'tionism (-shŏ-), n. (theol.) Doctrine that second & third persons of Trinity are inferior to the Father as regards (orthodox view) order only or (Arian view) essence. [-ISM]

subŏr'n, v.t. Induce by bribery or other-wise to commit perjury or other unlawful act. Hence or cogn. subŏrnA'TION, ~ER¹, nn. [f. L SUB(*ornare* equip) or incite secretly]

subpœn'a (-pēn-), n., & v.t. (~*ed pr. -ad,* ~*d*). 1. Writ commanding person's atten-dance in court of justice. 2. v.t. Serve ~ on. [orig. two words, L. = under penalty, the first in the writ]

subrĕp'tion, n. Obtaining of something by surprise or misrepresentation. [f. L *subreptio* purloining f. SUB(*ripere -rept-* =*rapere* snatch)]

subrŏgā'tion, n. (law). Substitution of one party for another as creditor. [f. L *subrogatio -onis* election as substitute; cf. SURROGATE]

subscrī'be', v.t. & i. 1. Write (one's name or rarely other inscription) at foot of document etc. (*the* ~*ed names carry weight*; *someone has* ~*ed a motto*); write one's name at foot of, sign, (document, picture, etc.). 2. Express one's adhesion to an opinion or resolution (*cannot* ~ *e to that*). 3. Enter one's name in a list of contributors, make or promise a contri-bution, contribute (specified sum), to or to a common fund or for a common ob-ject, raise or guarantee raising of by ~ing thus, (~*e to a charity, for a testi-monial, £10*; ~*e for a book*, engage before it is published to take copy or copies; ~*e to a newspaper*, engage to take it for specified time; *the sum needed was* ~*ed several times over*). Hence or cogn. ~ER¹ (*the* ~*er*, the under-signed), subscrip'-TION, nn. [f. L SUB(*scribere script-* write)]

sŭb'scrĭpt, a. ((Gk gram.). Written below (only in *iota* ~, small iota written below ā, ē, & ō). [f. L p.p. (prec.)]

subsĕll'ĭum, n. (*pl. -ia*). =MISERICORD (last sense). [L (SUB², *sella* seat)]

sŭb'sĕquent, a. That follow(s) or fol-lowed the event etc. indicated in the context, of later time or date than some-thing. Hence or cogn. subsĕquENCE n., ~LY² adv. [f. L SUB²(*sequi* follow), -ENT]

subsĕrve', v.t. Serve as means in promoting (purpose, end, etc.). [f. L SUB²(*servire* SERVE)]

subsĕr'vĭent, a. Useful as means, having merely instrumental relation, (*to*); cring-ing, obsequious. Hence ~ENCE, ~ENCY, nn., ~ENT·LY² adv. [f. L as prec., -ENT]

subsīde', v.i. (Of water, esp. flood) sink in level, run off, disappear; (of ground) cave in, sink; (of building, ship, etc.) settle down lower in ground or water; (of suspended matter) fall to bottom, be precipitated; (of person, usu. *joc.*) sink into sitting or kneeling or lying posture (~*d into an armchair*); cease from activity or agitation, become tranquil, abate, (*storm, tumult, apprehension, excitement,* ~*s*). Hence sŭb'sĭdENCE (or *subsī'*) n. [f. L *subsīdere* settle cogn. w. *sedēre* sit)]

subsĭd'iarÿ, a. & n. 1. Serving to assist or supplement, auxiliary, supplementary, (*to*); (of money etc.) supplementary con-tributed by another holding more than 50 per cent. of its issued share capital; (of troops) subsidized, hired by another nation. 2. n. (Usu. *pl.*). ~y thing or per-son, accessory; ~y company. [f. L *sub-sidiarius* (SUBSIDY, -ARY¹)]

sŭb'sĭdīze, v.t. Pay subsidy to. [foll., -IZE]

sŭb'sĭdÿ, n. (Hist.) parliamentary grant of money to the sovereign for State needs, tax levied on particular occasion; money grant from one State to another in re-turn for military or naval aid or other equivalent; money contributed by State to expenses of commercial undertaking, charitable institution, etc., held to be of public utility. [f. L *subsidium* reserve troops f. SUB²(*sidēre=sedēre* sit)]

subsĭst', v.i. & t. Exist, continue to exist, remain in being; keep oneself alive, sup-port life, be kept in life, find sustenance, (*on vegetables, charity*, etc., *by begging* etc.); provide sustenance for (*undertook to clothe, arm, & ~ 1000 men*). [f. F *sub-sister* f. L SUB²(*sistere* stand, causal f. *stare* stand)]

subsĭs'tence, n. Subsisting; means of supporting life, livelihood, what one lives on or by; ~ *money*, allowance or advance of pay granted for maintenance. [f. LL *subsistentia* substance (prec., -ENCE)]

sŭb'stance, n. 1.(Metaphys.) the substra-tum that the cognizable properties or qualities or attributes or accidents of things are conceived as inhering in or affecting, the essential nature underlying phenomena, (~ *& accidents in metaphysics*

correspond to subject & predicate in logic; *a ~ is a being subsisting in itself & subjected to accidents; being of one ~ with the Father*); essence or most important part of anything, pith, purport, real meaning, (*I agree with you in ~, generally, apart from details; the ~ of his remarks; the ~ of religion*). **2.** Material as opposed to form (the ~ *is good, but the style repellent*). **3.** Reality, solidity, solid worth, actual possessions, (*sacrifice the ~ for the shadow; there is no ~ in him; an argument of little ~; a man of ~*, with property, cf. *man of* STRAW; *waste one's ~*, be spendthrift). **4.** Particular kind of matter (*a heavy, porous, yellow, transparent, ~; the small number of ~s that make up the world*). [OF, f. L substantia (SUB² *stare* stand, -ANCE)]

substan'tial (-shl), a. Having substance, actually existing, not illusory, (*the ghost proved ~ after all*); of real importance or value, of considerable amount, (opp. *nominal, verbal; a ~ argument, point; made a ~ contribution, ~ progress, ~ concessions*); of solid material or structure, not flimsy, stout, (*a ~ house; a man of ~ build*); possessed of property, well-to-do, commercially sound, (*a ~ yeoman; deal only with ~ firms*); deserving the name in essentials, virtual, practical, (~ *truth, agreement, success, performance of contract*). Hence or cogn. ~**ITY** (-shiǎl'-) n., ~**IY²** adv. [f. LL substantialis (prec., -AL)]

substan'tialism (-sha-), n. (philos.). Doctrine that behind phenomena there are substantial realities. So ~**IST**(2) n. [-ISM]

substan'tialize (-sha-), v.t. & i. Invest with or acquire substance or actual existence. [-IZE]

substan'tiate (-shi-), v.t. Prove the truth of, give good grounds for, (charge, statement, claim). Hence ~**A'TION** (-si-, -shi-) n. [SUBSTANCE, -ATE³]

sub'stantive, a. & n. **1.** Expressing existence (*the ~ verb*, the vb *be*); having a separate & independent existence, not merely inferential or implicit or subservient or parasitic, (~ *enactment, motion, etc.*, made in due form for the noun in the now usual sense distinguishing it from the *noun adjective* now called *adjective* simply); ~ *rank* (Mil.), permanent rank in the holder's branch of the army (as opp. *brevet, honorary,* or *temporary rank*); hence ~**LY²** adv. (esp. in gram., = *substantivally*). **2.** n. Noun in the now usual sense excluding adjectives; so **substan'tival** a., **substan'tivally²** adv. [OF (*-if, -ive*), f. LL substantivus adv. [OF (-*if, -ive*), f. LL substantivus self-existent (SUBSTANCE, -IVE)]

sub'stitute, n., & v.t. **1.** Person or thing performing some function instead of

another. **2.** v.t. Make (person or thing) fill a place or discharge a function for or for another; (vulg.) replace (person or thing) *by or with* another; put in exchange (*for*); so ~**U'TION** n., ~**u'tional**(-sho-), ~**u'tion-ARY**¹ (-sho-), ~**U'TIVE**, aa., ~**u'tionally**² adv. [f. L SUB(*stituere -ut- = statuere* see STATUTE)]

subsume', v.t. Include (instance etc.) under a rule or class. Hence **subsump'-TION** n. [SUB-, L *sumere sumpt-* take]

subtend', v.t. (geom.). (Of chord, side of triangle) be opposite to (arc, angle). [f. L SUB(*tendere tens-* stretch)]

subtense', n. Line subtending arc or angle. [f. L p.p. (prec.)]

subter-, pref. = under, less than, esp. in wds formed as opposites to compounds of SUPER-, as ~*position*, ~*human*, ~*natural*. [L (SUB² *-ter* as in INTER²)]

sub'terfuge, n. Attempt to escape censure or defeat in argument by evading the issue, statement etc. resorted to for such purpose, use of such statements etc. [f. L *subterfugium* f. SUBTER(*fugere* flee)]

subtile (sŭt'l, sŭb'tīl), a. (Arch. for) SUBTLE. Hence or cogn. **subt'ilize**(2, 3) v.t. & i., **subtiliza'tion** n., (sŭt-), **subtilry** (sŭt'ĭtī) n. Same f. L *subtilis* perh. orig. = fine-woven (SUB², *tela* web)]

subtle (sŭt'l), a. Tenuous or rarefied (arch.), pervasive owing to tenuity, (*the ~ air, a ~ vapour*; of *~ texture, a ~ perfume*); evasive, mysterious, hard to grasp or trace, (~ *magic, charm, power, art; a ~ distinction*); making fine distinctions, having delicate perception, acute, (~ *senses, perception, insight; a ~ observer, philosopher, intellect, mind*); ingenious, elaborate, clever, (*a ~ device, fancy, workman, explanation, policy; ~ fingers*); crafty, cunning, (*now the serpent was more ~ than any beast; a ~ enemy*). Hence **subt'LY²** (sŭt-) adv. [ME & OF sotil f. L as prec.]

subtlety (sŭt'lti), n. In adj. senses; also, a fine distinction, a piece of hair-splitting. [f. OF *soutilté* f. L *subtilitatem* (SUBTIL, -TY)]

subtract', v.t. Deduct (part, quantity, number) from or from whole or greater quantity or number, esp. in arithmetic or algebra. Hence or cogn. **subtrac'TION** n., **subtrac'tive** a. [f. L SUB(*trahere tract-* draw)]

sub'trahend, n. What is to be subtracted in a subtraction sum. [L as prec., ND¹]

sub'ulate, sub'uliform, aa. (bot., zool.). Awl-shaped. [L *subula* awi (*suere* sew), -ATE², -T-, -FORM]

sub'urb, n. Outlying district of city (*the ~s*, all or one of such districts, as *a house in the ~s*, also the environs). So **subŭrb'-AN** a. [f. OF *suburbe* f. L SUB(*urbem* f. *urbis* city)]

For words in *sub-* not given see SUB-.

Suburb'ia, n. (usu. derog.), (Quasi-proper name for) the suburbs (esp. of London) & their inhabitants. [-IA¹]

subven'tion, n. Grant of money in aid, subsidy. [OF. f. LL *subventionem* f. SUB-(*venire, vent-* come) assist, -ION]

subvert', v.t. Overturn, upset, effect destruction or overthrow of, (religion, morality), the constitution, principles, monarchy). Hence or cogn. **subver'sion** (-shn) n., **subver'sive** a. [f. L SUB(*vertere* -s- turn)]

suc-, = SUB- in L compounds of sub with words in c- & their derivatives.

succade' (-dz), n. pl.(commerc.), Candied fruits in syrup. [f. OF *succade, chucade*, etym. dub.]

succedan'e|um (-ks-), n. (pl.~a), Substitute, thing or rarely person that one falls back on in default of another. So ~ous a. [neut. of L *succedaneus* (foll. -ANEOUS)]

succeed' (-ks-), v.t. & i. 1. Take the place previously filled by, follow (t. & i.) in order, come next (to), ensue, be subsequent (to), come by inheritance or in due order to or to office or title or property, (*day's day or to day; agitation ~ed calm or ~ed; ~ing ages will reverence his memory; Elizabeth ~ed Mary, ~ed to the throne, ~ed*). 2. Have success (in doing etc.), be successful, prosper, accomplish one's purpose; (of plan etc.) be brought to successful issue. [f. F *succéder* f. L SUC(*cedere cess-* go)]

success' (-ks-), n. Issue of undertaking (rare); *with good or bad* ~; favourable issue, accomplishment of end aimed at, attainment of wealth or fame or position, (*have inquired for it without* ~; *military* ~*es; spoilt by* ~; *nothing succeeds like* ~, *one* ~ *leads to others*), whence ~FUL a., ~fully² adv.; thing or person that turns out well (*the experiment is a* ~; *was a great* ~ *as a bishop*); crammer's pupil who passes his examination. [f. L *successus -ūs* (SUCCEED)]

succe'ssion (-kseshn), n. 1. A following in order (esp. *in* ~; *in* ~; *three great victories in* ~; running; without intervening defeat). 2. Series of things *in* ~ (*a* ~ *of disasters*, several running). 3. (Right of) succeeding to the throne or any office or inheritance, set or order of persons having such right, (*laws regulating the* ~; *claimed, was excluded from, the* ~; *in* ~ *to*, as successor of; *the* ~ *must not be broken; is second in the* ~; *was left to him & his* ~, heirs; passes his examination.

succent'or (-ks-), n. Precentor's deputy in some cathedrals. [LL, f. L SUC(*cinere -cent-* = *canere* sing), -OR²]

succès d'estime (see Ap.), n. Passably cordial reception given to performance or work from respect rather than appreciation. [F]

success'ion, (See Ap.) n. Success marked by wild enthusiasm. [F]

of spiritual authority through bishops from the apostles downwards; *law of* ~, regulating inheritance esp. in cases of intestate decease; ~ *duties*, taxes on property passing by ~; *the S~ States*, those resulting from the partition of Austria-Hungary. 4. (Biol.) order of descent in development of species. Hence ~AL, ~IST n., ~IVE¹² a. [f. L *successionem* (SUCCEED, -ION)]

succe'ssive (-ks-), a. Following one after another, in uninterrupted succession, consecutive. Hence ~ly² adv., ~NESS n. [f. med. L *successivus* (SUCCEED, -IVE)]

success'or (-ks-), n. Person or thing that succeeds to another (*to, of*; cf. PREDECESSOR). [OF f. L(SUCCEED, -OR²)]

succinct' (-ks-), a. Terse, concise, briefly expressed. Hence ~LY² adv., ~NESS n. [f. L *succinctus* f. SUC(*cingere cinct-* gird, tuck up)]

succ'ory, n. = CHICORY.

*suc'cotash, n. Dish of green maize & beans (& salt pork) boiled together. [f. Amer.-Ind. *msiquatash*]

succ'our (-ker), v.t. & n. 1. Come to the assistance of, give aid to, (person in danger or difficulty). 2. n. Aid given at time of need; (pl. arch.) reinforcements, troops coming to the rescue; hence ~LESS a. [vb f. OF *sucurre* f. L SUC(*currere curs-* run); n. f. OF *socors* f. med. L *succursus -ūs* (*succurrere*)]

succ'u|ba, -bus, n. (pl. -bae, -bi). Female demon having sexual intercourse with sleeping men. [LL (-ba) & med. L (-bus) f. SUC(*cumbere* lie)]

succ'ulent, a. Juicy (of lit. or fig. food); (Bot.) thick & fleshy, having such leaves or stems. Hence ~ENCE n., ~ently² adv. [f. L *succulentus* (*succus* juice, -LENT)]

succumb' (-m), v.i. Be overcome, have to cease from resistance or competition or other effort, be forced to give way to, die owing to, die, (*to one's enemies; superior numbers, grief, temptation*). [f. OF *succomber* f. L SUC(*cumbere* lie)]

such, a. (no comp. or sup.; placed not between a & n. but before or after them), & pron. 1. Of the same kind or degree as (~ *people, people* ~, *as these;* ~ *beauty as yours; experiences* ~ *as this are rare;* ~ *grapes as you never saw;* ~ *also* = *of the one a kind that, was a scarlet as makes the eyes ache*). 2. So great, so natural in some respect, as to do or that (*is* ~ *as to make one despair; had* ~ *a fright that she hardly survived it*). 3. Of the kind or degree already described or implied or intelligible from the context or circumstances (*never had* ~ *sport; there are no* ~ *doings now;* ~ *things make one despair; don't be* ~ *are the privileges of fatherhood;*

in ~ a hurry; how could you leave him at ~ a time?; saw just ~ another yesterday; long may he continue ~!; often colloq. preceding the adj. & n. with the effect of so modifying the adj., as ~ horrid language, language so horrid, was it ~ a long time ago?, don't want ~ a big one or ~ big ones; also rarely used twice as relative & correl., as ~ master ~ servant, the servant is ~ as the master is). **4.** (In legal or formal style) (whoever shall make ~ return falsely). **5.** So great!, of a kind that demands exclamatory description, (we have had ~ sport!, ~ an enjoyable evening!). **6.** Of a kind or degree sufficient to account for the preceding or following statement (he cannot come too often, he gives ~ pleasure; there was ~ a draught, it is no wonder he caught cold). **7.** (Also ~-&-~) particular, of particular kind, but not needing to be specified (~ an one, ~ a one, arch., ~-&-~ a person, someone, so-&-so; ~-&-~ results will follow from ~-&-~ causes). **8.** ~-like, of ~-kind (now chiefly vulg.; & see below). **9.** pron. ~ as, those who (chiefly arch. or poet. or rhet.: ~ as sit in darkness). **10.** That, the action etc. referred to, (I may have offended, but ~ was not my intention). **11.** As ~, as being what has been named (in country places a stranger is welcome as ~); all ~, persons of ~ character (so perish all ~!). **12.** (Also ~like; chiefly vulg.) things of ~ kind (do not hold with theatres & balls & ~ or ~like). **13.** (vulg. or commerc.). The aforesaid thing(s), it, they or them, (those who leave parcels in the train cannot expect to recover ~). [OE swylc, swelc, G solch f. OHG solih]

suck, v.t. & i., & n. **1.** Draw (milk, liquid) into mouth by making vacuum with muscles of lips etc., (fig.) imbibe or gain (knowledge, advantage, etc.; also ~ in knowledge, ~ advantage out of); draw milk or liquid or sustenance or advantage from (~ dry, exhaust of contents thus; ~ the breast of; the mother whom he ~ed; ~ed orange, thing in which there is no goodness left; ~ one's brains, extract his ideas for one's own use); roll the tongue about, squeeze in the mouth, (~ sweets, one's teeth, etc.); (of absorbent substance) ~ in or up, absorb; (of whirlpool etc.) ~ in, engulf; ~ the breast or udder (part., not yet weaned, as ~ing child, ~ing-pig; also fig., unpractised, budding, as ~ing barrister, saint); ~ something, use ~ing action, make ~ing sound, (sat ~ing at his pipe; pump etc. ~s, makes gurgling or drawing sound; ~ing-disk, sucker); ||~-up (schoolboy sl.), play toady (to; ~-up n., a toady). **2.** n. Opportunity of ~ing the breast (give ~, of mother or nurse or animal suckling child etc.); drawing action of ~ing (at breast etc.: spell of ~ing with lips or in mouth (take a ~ at it); small

draught of or of liquor; ||(schoolboy sl., pl.) sweets; (schoolboy sl.) disappointment, fiasco, (what a ~!, ~s!, intl. expr. amusement at another's failure after confidence). [OE sūcan, cf. L sugere sucʰ-, G saugen, Du. zuigen]

suck'er, n., & v.t. & i. **1.** Person or thing that sucks, esp. sucking-pig or new-born whale; (sl.) person of immature mind, greenhorn; kinds of fish that suck in food or have mouth suggesting suction or adhere by sucking-disk. **2.** Piston of suction-pump; pipe through which liquid is drawn by suction. **3.** (Also *sucking-disk*) flat or concave surface (as organ in some animals, also *acetabulum*, or artificial of rubber etc. in machinery or appliances) that adheres by suction & atmospheric pressure to what it is placed against. **4.** (bot.). Shoot springing from subterranean part of stem, from part of root remote from main stem, from axil, or abnormally from bole or branch. **5.** vb. (bot.). Remove ~s from; produce ~s. [-ER²]

suc'kle, v.t. Give suck to. [perh. back form.-f. foll.]

suck'ling, n. Unweaned child or animal (*babes & ~s*, the utterly inexperienced). [SUCK VB, -LING¹]

suc'rose, n. Cane-sugar or any of the sugars of the same composition & properties. [F sucre SUGAR, -OSE²]

suc'tion, n. Sucking; production of partial vacuum by removal of air etc. for purpose of enabling external atmospheric pressure to force in liquid or produce adhesion of surfaces; ~-chamber, -pipe, in ~-pump; ~-fan, for withdrawing chaff etc. from grain by ~; ~-plate, holding set of artificial upper teeth & adhering to palate by ~; ~-pump, drawing water through pipe into chamber exhausted by piston. [L sugere suct- SUCK, -ION]

suctor'ial, a. (zool.). Adapted for or capable of sucking, having sucker for feeding or adhering. [mod. L suctorius (prec., -ORY), -AL]

Sudanese (sōōdanēz'). =SOUDANESE.

sudar'ium, n. (pl. *-ia*). Kerchief of St Veronica miraculously stamped with face of Christ; any miraculous portrait of Christ; napkin about Christ's head (*John* xx. 7). [L, = handkerchief (*sudor* sweat, -ARY¹)]

sudator'ium, n. (pl. *-ia*). Hot-air bath. [L neut. as foll.]

sud'atory, a. & n. **1.** Promoting perspiration. **2.** n. ~ drug; =prec. [f. L *suda-torius* (*sudare* SWEAT, -ORY)

sudd, n. Floating plants, trees, etc., impeding navigation of White Nile. [Arab., = barrier]

sudd'en, a. & n. **1.** Occurring or coming without warning, abrupt, abnormally rapid, hurried, (~ death, need, fear; a ~

resolve, departure, change, turn of the wrist, bend in the road; is very ~ in his movements); ~ death, (also, colloq.) decision by a single toss of a coin (as against the best of three); decision of a tennis set at lawn tennis by the issue of the next game; a, rarely on the, ~, -ly. [f. OF or on ~ hence ~-LY² adv., ~-NESS n. 2, n. Of or on a, rarely on the, ~, -ly. [f. OF or on ~ f. L subitaneus (subitus sudden f. SUB-ire -it- come up, -ANEOUS)]

sudorif'erous, a. Sweat-producing (of glands). [f. LL sudorifer (sudor sweat, -FEROUS)]

sudorif'ic, a. & n. (Drug) causing sweat. [L sudor sweat, -i-, -FIC]

Sud'ra (soō-), n. Lowest of four great Hindu castes. [Skr.]

suds (-z), n. pl. Froth of soap & water (usu. soap-~). [perh. f. MDu. sudse marsh]

sue, v.t. & i. Prosecute (person) in law-court; entreat (person to, for); make entreaty or application to person or law-court, (for redress or a favour, esp. woman's hand in marriage); ~ out, make petition in law-court for & obtain (writ, pardon, etc.). [f. AF siwir f. L OF sivre (now suivre) follow f. pop. L +sequere for L sequi]

suede (swād), n. Undressed kid as used for gloves, shoes, etc. (usu. attrib.). [f. F (gants de) Suède (gloves of) Sweden]

su'et, n. Hard fat of kidneys & loins of oxen, sheep, etc. Hence ~Y² a. [OF seu f. L sebum tallow, -ET¹]

suf-, =SUB- in L compds with wds in f- & their derivatives.

suff'er, v.t. & i. 1. Undergo, experience, be subjected to, (pain, loss, grief, defeat, change, punishment, wrong, etc.); undergo pain or grief or damage or disablement (~s acutely; ~ing mortals; was ~ing from neuralgia; your reputation will ~; the engine ~ed severely; trade is ~ing from the war), whence ~ER¹, ~ING¹(l), nn. (often pl.). 2. (Of condemned man) be executed (was to ~ the next morning). 3. Permit to do, allow to go on, put up with, tolerate, (~ them to come; should not ~ it for a moment; how can you ~ him or his insolence?, whence, chiefly w. neg., ~ABLE a.). [f. OF soffrir f. L SUF(ferre bear)]

suff'erance, n. ‖ (Arch.) submissiveness; tacit consent, permission or toleration implied by abstinence from objection, (esp. on ~, in virtue of such toleration). [f. OF suffrance f. LL sufferentia (SUFFER, -ENCE)]

suffete, n. One of two chief magistrates of ancient Carthage. [f. L sufes -etis f. Punic]

suffice', v.i. & t. Be enough (to do, for person or purpose, or abs.), be adequate, (your word will ~; that ~s to prove it; ~ it to say that, I will content myself with saying that); satisfy, meet the needs of, (half-a-dozen ~d him). Hence suffic'-ingly² adv. [ME suffisen f. OF suffire (part. -fisant) f. L SUF(ficere=facere make)]

suffic'iency (-shn-), n. ‖ (Arch.) being sufficient, ability, efficiency; adequate resources, a competence, a sufficient amount of or of something. [f. L suffic-entia (foll., -ENCY)]

suffic'ient (-shnt), a. & n. 1. Sufficing, adequate esp. in amount or number to the need, enough, (is ~ to feed a hundred men; had not ~ courage for it; has impudence ~ for anything; have you ~ provisions?), whence ~-LY² adv.; ‖ (arch.) competent, of adequate ability or resources; SELF-~. 2, n. Enough, a sufficient quantity, (chiefly vulg. for enough; have you had ~?). [f. L part. (SUFFICE, -ENT)]

suff'ix, n., & v.t. 1. Append (letter, syllable) in word-formation. [f. L SUF(figere fix)]

suff'ix, n. Suffixed letter or syllable (cf. prefix, affix). [f. L F.p. (prec.)]

suff'ocate, v.t. & i. Choke or kill by stopping respiration (of person, superincumbent mass, fumes, etc.); produce choking sensation in, impede breath or utterance of, (~ated by or with grief, excitement, etc.); feel ~ated, gasp for breath. Hence or cogn. ~atingly² adv., ~A'TION n. [f. L suffocare (SUB-², fauces throat)]

suff'ragan, a. & n. ~ bishop or ~, bishop consecrated to assist bishop of see by managing part of his diocese, also any bishop in relation to his archbishop or metropolitan (~ see etc., of ~ bishop). Hence ~SHIP n. [OF, f. med. L suffraga-neus assistant (bishop) f. L suffragari support with vote (foll.)]

suff'rage, n. Vote, approval or consent expressed by voting, (the electors gave their ~s for free trade; also transf., as the horse has my ~; I think it preferable); the right of voting in political elections (the ~, or manhood, woman, universal, etc., ~; extended to women as well as men; universal, ~, extended to all adults); (Eccl.) short petition of congregation, esp. one said in response to priest, (arch.) an intercessory prayer. [F, f. L suffragium]

suffragette', n. Woman who agitated for woman suffrage. [incorrect use of -ETTE]

suff'ragist, n. One who attaches importance to (esp. some extension of) suffrage (woman-~ etc.). [-IST]

suffuse' (-z), v.t. (Of colour or moisture) well up from within & colour or moisten (a blush, tears, ~d her cheeks, eyes; often in p.p., as skies ~d with amethyst). So **suffu'sion** (-zhn) n. [f. L SUF(fundere fus-pour)]

Sufi (soō-), **sōf'i,** n. Mohammedan pantheistic mystic. Hence ~ic a., ~ISM (3) n. [f. Arab. çūfī man of wool (çūf wool)]

sug-, = SUB- in L compds w. wds in g- & their derivatives.

su'gar (shoō-), n., & v.t. & i. 1. Kinds of sweet crystalline substance prepared

from various plants esp. the ~cane &
beet for use in cookery, confectionery,
brewing, etc. (*cane*, *beet*, *maple*, etc., ~,
named from plant of origin; *brown*, *white*,
powdered, LUMP¹, CASTOR³, LOAF¹, ~).
2. Sweet words, flattery, anything serving
purpose of ~ put round pill in reconciling
person to what is unpalatable. **3.** (chem.).
Kinds of soluble sweet-tasting ferment-
able carbohydrate divided according to
their composition into glucoses & saccha-
roses. **4.** ‖ ~*basin*, holding ~ for table
use; ~*beet*, kinds of pulse & kidney-
bean; ~*bird*, kinds that suck flowers; ~
candy, candy; ~*cane*, a grass with
jointed stems 18–20 ft high from which ~
is made; ~*daddy* (sl.), elderly protector
and source of revenue of a (female) GOLD-
digger; ~*gum*, Australian gum-tree with
sweet foliage; ~*house*, establishment in
which raw ~ is made; ~-LOAF¹; ~*maple*,
tree from sap of which ~ is made; ~*mill*,
for crushing ~cane & expressing ~; ~
mite, kind intesting unrefined ~; ~
orchard, of ~maples; ~*plum*, sweetmeat,
esp. small ball of boiled ~; ~*refiner(y)*,
refines raw ~; ~*tongs*, small tongs for
taking up lump~ at table; hence ~Y²,
~LESS, aa., ~INESS n. **5.** vb. Sweeten with
~ lit. or fig. **6.** (sl.). Used in pass. as
euphem. imprecation. **7.** ‖ (sl.). Work
lazily, not do one's full share of work, not
put forth all one's strength, whence ~
ER¹ n. [f. OF *zucre* f. Arab, *sukkar*;
cf. Pers. *shakar*, Skr. *çarkara* gravel,
candy, & Gk *sakkharon*]

suggest¹ (sujˊ), v.t. Cause (idea) to present itself, call up the idea of by mention
or association, (*thing* ~*s itself*, comes into
the mind); propose (theory, plan, often
expressed in *that*-clause) for acceptance
or rejection, set up the hypothesis *that*,
(~*ed a retreat*, *that they should retreat*;
I ~ *that*, formula of examining counsel in
imputing motives etc. = *I put it to you*, as
I ~ *that you had a secret understanding
with them*). [f. L SUG(*gerere gest-* bring)]

suggesˊtˊible (sujˊ-), a. That may be suggested; open to hypnotic suggestion.
Hence ~IBILˊITY n. [-IBLE]

suggesˊtˊiōˊfalˊsō (sujˊ-), n. Positive misrepresentation not involving direct lie
but going beyond concealment of the
truth (cf. SUPPRESSIO VERI). [L]

suggesˊtion (sujēsˊchon), n. Suggesting
(*full of* ~, suggesting many ideas, stimulating reflection); theory or plan suggested; suggesting of prurient ideas; in-
sinuation of a belief or impulse into the
mind of a hypnotic subject, such belief
or impulse. So **suggesˊtive** a. (*of*), **sug-
gesˊtiveˊly**² adv., **suggesˊtiveˊness** n.
(-ION)]

suˊi¹, genit. of L *suus* his, her, its, or their;

own: ~ *génˊeris* pred. a., not classifiable
with others, unique; ~ *jurˊis* (-oor-) pred.
a., of full age & capacity, independent.

suˊiˊcide, n. **1.** Person who intentionally
kills himself; (Law) ~ of years of discretion & sane mind. **2.** Intentional self-
slaughter (in law, as in **1**; esp. *commit* ~,
kill oneself); action destructive to one's
own interests or continuance in some
capacity (*commit political* ~, ruin one's
prospects as a politician; *race*~, failure
of a people to maintain its numbers);
hence **suicidˊal** a., **suˊicidˊallˊy**² adv.
[formed on false anal. of *fratricide* etc. f. L
sui genit. of *se* self, -CIDE(1, 2]

suˊiˊllˊine, a. Of the hog family. [L *suillus*
of pigs (*sus* pig). -INE¹]

suit (sūt), n., & v.t. & i. **1.** Suing, petition,
seeking of woman's hand in marriage,
(*make* ~, urge a humble request; *with
lowly* ~; *has a* ~ *to the king*; *press, push,
etc., one's* ~; *prosper in one's* ~). **2.** Legal
prosecution of a claim, action in law-
court, (also *law*~; ~ *at law*; *criminal,
civil, etc.,* ~). **3.** Any of the four sets
(hearts, diamonds, spades, clubs) into
which pack of cards is divided (*follow* ~,
play from ~ that was led, fig. conform to
another's movements; *player's holding*
in it (*long, short,* ~ in whist, of more than
three, less than four, cards). **4.** Set of
man's clothes esp. when of same cloth,
consisting usu. of coat, waistcoat, &
trousers or knickerbockers or breeches
(often ~ *of clothes*; *dress* ~, for evening
dress; ~ *of dittos*; ~*case*, kind of small
portmanteau), whence ~ING¹(3) n.; (in
recent use, usu. **2, 3, 4,** -*piece* ~) woman's
costume. **5.** Set of sails, set of armour,
for simultaneous use. **6.** vb. Accommodate, adapt, make fitting or appropriate, to (~ *the action to the word*; ~ *one's
style to one's audience*; (p.p.) appropriate *to*, well adapted or having the right
qualities *for*, (*democracy is not* ~*ed to* or
for Negroes; *is not* ~*ed to be* or *for an
engineer*). **7.** Satisfy, meet the demands or
requirements or interests of, (*does not* ~
all tastes; *it* ~*s me* or, prob. w. ref. to
betting, *my book to put up with him*; ~
yourself, do as you choose, also find something that satisfies you, esp. as servant's
formula in giving warning); (of food, climate, etc.) improve or be consistent with
the health of, agree with, (*cold, asparagus,
does not* ~ *me*). **8.** Comport with or with,
go well with appearance or character of,
become, (*red does not* ~ *with* or ~*s her complexion*; *the part* ~*s him admirably*; *mercy
* ~*s a king*). **9.** Be convenient (*that date
will* ~). [vb t. n., f. OF *suatte* following f. med. L *secuta* (L *sequi secut-* follow)]

suitˊˊable (sūtˊ-), a. Suited to or for, well
fitted for the purpose, appropriate to the
occasion. Hence ~ABILˊITY, ~ableNESS,
nn., ~ablˊy² adv. [prec., -ABLE]

suite (swēt), n. Retinue, set of persons in attendance; set of things belonging together, esp. ~ *of rooms* or *furniture*; (Mus.) instrumental composition, orig. succession of movements in dance style. [F, as SUIT]

suit′or (sūt-), n. Party to lawsuit; petitioner; wooer, man who asks for woman's hand in marriage. [AF *seutor* f. LL *secutor* (L *sequi* follow, -OR²)]

suivez (swēv′ā), mus. direction instructing accompanist to suit his time etc. to soloist's performance. [F]

Suk′ey (sōō-), n. (colloq.). ~ or *black* ~, kettle. [*Susan*]

sŭl′cāte, a. (bot., anat.). Grooved, fluted, channelled. [L *sulcus* furrow, -ATE²]

sŭlk, n., & v.i. **1.** Sulky fit (usu. pl., esp. *in the* ~*s*). **2.** v.i. Be sulky. [f. 18th c. only; etym. dub.]

sŭl′k|y̆, a. & n. **1.** Sullen, morose, silent or inactive or unsociable from resentment or ill temper; hence ~ĭLY² adv., ~ĭNESS n. **2.** n. Light two-wheeled one-horse vehicle for single person. [-Y²]

sŭll′age, n. Filth, refuse, sewage. [prob. f. F as SOIL² + -AGE]

Sŭll′an, a. (Rom. hist.). Of, enacted by, L. Cornelius Sulla. [-AN]

sŭll′en, a. & n. **1.** Passively resentful, unforgiving, gloomy-tempered, unsociable, not responding to friendliness or encouragement or urging, stubbornly ill-humoured, morose, of dismal aspect; hence ~LY² adv., ~NESS n. **2.** n. pl. *The* ~*s*, ~ frame of mind, ill temper, depression. [ME *soleyn* lonely (L *solus* SOLE³, -AN)]

sŭll′y̆, v.t. Soil, tarnish, (chiefly poet.); diminish the purity or splendour of (reputation, character, victory, etc.), disgrace. [prob. f. F *souiller* SOIL²]

sŭl′ph|(o)-, comb. forms of SULPHUR: ~*ăm′ic*, derived from an amic acid of sulphuric acid, so ~*am*ATE¹(3); ~*āte*, salt of sulphuric acid (~*ate of copper*, blue vitriol; ~*ate of iron*, green vitriol; ~*ate of magnesium*, Epsom salts; ~*ate of sodium*, Glauber's salts; ~*ate of zinc*, white vitriol); ~*īde*, compound of sulphur with element or radical; ~*īte*, salt of sulphurous acid; ~*ocyăn′ic*, containing sulphur & cyanogen; ~*onal*, a hypnotic & anaesthetic drug; ~*ōnăm′īdes*, group of synthetic chemical compounds acting as anti-bacterial agents when circulating in the blood-stream or applied locally; ~*ŏn′ic acid*, any of a group of acids produced by the action of sulphuric acid (~*ona′tion*) on various aromatic compounds; ~*ovĭn′ic*, of sulphuric acid & alcohol.

sŭl′phur (*-er*), n., a., & v.t. **1.** Pale-yellow non-metallic element occurring in crystalline & amorphous modifications, burning with blue flame & stifling smell, & used in making gunpowder, matches, vulcanite, & sulphuric acid, & in medical treatment of skin-diseases (*flowers, milk, of* ~, yellow, white, powders got by treating ~ in certain ways; *roll, stick,* -~, ~ refined & cast in moulds, brimstone). **2.** Kinds of yellow butterfly. **3.** Material of which hell-fire & lightning were held to consist. **4.** ~*-bottom* (*whale*), Pacific rorqual with yellow belly; ~ *ore*, iron pyrites; ~*-spring*, of water impregnated with ~ or its compounds; ~*-wort*, yellow-flowered herb formerly used in medicine; hence ~Y² a. **5.** adj. Of pale slightly greenish yellow. **6.** v.t. Apply ~ to, fumigate with ~. [f. OF *soufre* f. L *sulfur, -phur*]

sŭl′phūr|āte, v.t. Impregnate or fumigate or treat with sulphur, esp. in bleaching. Hence ~A′TION, ~**ā**TOR²(2), nn. [f. LL SULPHUR(*atus* -ATE²), -ATE³]

sŭlphūr′ėous, a. Of, like, suggesting, sulphur; (Bot.) sulphur-coloured. [L *sulphureus* (SULPHUR), -OUS]

sŭlphūrĕtt′ėd, a. Having sulphur in combination (chiefly in ~ *hydrogen*, a transparent colourless fetid gas). [obs. *sulphuret* (SULPHUR, -ET¹) sulphide, -ED²]

sŭlphūr′ic, a. (chem.). Containing sulphur in its higher combining proportion (cf. SULPHUROUS; ~ *acid*, oil of vitriol, a dense oily colourless highly acid & corrosive fluid much used in the arts; ~ *ether*, = ETHER in chem. sense). [f. F *sulfurique* see SULPHUR, -IC (chem.)]

sŭl′phūrīz|e, v.t. = SULPHURATE. Hence ~A′TION n. [-IZE]

sŭl′phūrous, a. = SULPHUREOUS; (Chem.; *pr.* -ūr′*us*) containing sulphur in its lower combining proportion (cf. SULPHURIC; ~ *acid*). [f. L SULPHUR(*osus* -OSE¹)]

sŭl′tan, n. **1.** Moslem sovereign (*the S*~, hist., ~ of Turkey), whence ~ATE¹ n. **2.** Kinds of gorgeously coloured bird of rail family; variety of white domestic fowl from Turkey; *sweet, yellow,* ~, kinds of garden flower. [F, f. Arab.]

sŭlta′na (-tah-), n. **1.** Sultan's mother, wife, or daughter. **2.** Mistress of king etc. **3.** Sultan-bird. **4.** Kind of seedless raisin grown at Smyrna & used in puddings & cakes. [It., f. *sultano* (prec.)]

sŭl′tanėss, n. = prec. (first sense). [-ESS¹]

sŭl′tr|y̆, a. (Of atmosphere or weather) hot & close or oppressive; (of temper etc.) passionate. Hence ~ĭLY² adv., ~ĭNESS n. [f. obs. *sulter* vb prob. = SWELTER, -Y⁴]

sŭm, n., & v.t. & i. (-mm-). **1.** Total amount resulting from addition of items, brief expression that includes but does not specify details, substance, summary, (also ~ *total*; *the* ~ *of all my wishes is happiness*; *the* ~ *of two & three is five*; ~, *remainder, product, quotient*, results of addition, subtraction, multiplication, division; *the* ~ or ~ *& substance of his objections is this*; *in* ~, briefly & comprehensively put); particular amount of money (*what* ~ *would you give for it?*; ***for the* ~ *of 15/-; a good, round, considerable,***

~; LUMP¹ ~); (working out of) an arith-metical problem (*good at ~s; did a rapid ~ in his head*). **2.** vb. Collect into or express or include as one total or whole (often *up*), gather up (evidence, points of argument etc., already treated in detail) into brief review; ~ *up* (intr.), make recapitulation of evidence or argument (esp. of judge after both sides have been heard; so ~*ming-up* n.). [f. OF *somme(r)* f. L *summa* n. orig. fem. of *summus* highest (SUPER-), *summare* vb]

sŭm'ăc(h) (-k; *also* shŏŏm'ăk), n. (Dried & ground leaves, used in tanning & dye-ing, of) kinds of shrub. [F (-*ac*) f. Arab. *summāq*]

Sŭmē̆r'ian, a. & n. (archaeol.). **1.** Of the non-Semitic element in the civilization of Babylonia. **2.** n. The ~ language, a ~ per-son. [f. *Sumer*, a district of Babylonia]

sŭmm'ar̄ize, v.t. Make or be a summary of, sum up. So ~ĭSN(1) n. [foll., -IZE]

sŭmm'ar̄y̆, a. & n. **1.** Compendious, brief, dispensing with needless details or formalities, done with dispatch, (*a ~y ac-count; ~y methods, jurisdiction*, etc.); hence ~ĭLY² adv. **2.** n. Brief account, abridgement, epitome. [n. f. L *summarium*, adj. f. med. L *summarius*, (L *summa*; see SUM, -ARY¹)]

sŭmmā'tion, n. Addition, finding of total or sum. [f. L *summare*, -ATION]

sŭmm'er¹, n., & v.i. & t. **1.** Second or hot season of the year, May–July (Astron., 21 June–21 Sep.); INDIAN, ‖ St MARTIN'S, ~; ‖ *St Luke's* ~, period of fine weather ex-pected about 18th October. **2.** (Usu. in pl. with number etc.) year of life or age (*a child of ten ~s*). **3.** attrib. Characteristic of or fit for ~ (~-*house*, light building in garden etc. for sitting in; ~ *school* long-vacation meeting for lectures etc., esp. at university; ~-*time* or ~*time*, the weather or season of ~; ‖ ~-*time*, that indicated by clocks advanced in ~ to facilitate use of daylight; ‖ (British) *double ~ time*, two hours in advance of Greenwich mean time); hence ~LY¹, ~Y², ~LESS, aa. **4.** vb. Pass the ~ usu. at or in place; pasture (cattle) *at* or *in*. [OE *sumor*, cf. Du. *zomer*, G *sommer*, Skr. *samā* half year]

sŭmm'er², n. (Also ~-*tree*) horizontal bearing beam, esp. one supporting joists or rafters. [see BREASTSUMMER]

summersault, -set. = SOMERSAULT.

sŭmm'it, n. Highest point, top, apex, highest degree, (*the icy ~s of the Alps; at the ~ of power; the ~ of my ambition is*). Hence ~LESS a. [f. OF *somet, sommette*, (*som* top f. L *summum* neut. of *summus*, -ET¹)]

sŭmm'on, v.t. Demand the presence of, call upon to appear, esp. as defendant or witness in lawcourt, cite, convoke, in-vite; call upon (town etc.) to surrender; ~ *up*, gather courage, spirit, etc., usu. *to*

do or *for* undertaking. [f. OF *somondre* f. L SUB(*monēre* warn]

sŭmm'ons (-z), n. (pl. ~es), & v.t. **1.** Authoritative call or urgent invitation to attend on some occasion or to something. **2.** Citation to appear before judge or magistrate. **3.** v.t. Serve with ~. [f. OF *somonse* f. a pop. L fem. p.p. (*summonsea*) f. L as prec.]

sŭmm'um bŏn'um, n. The chief good, esp. as the end or ultimate determining principle in an ethical system. [L]

sŭmp, n. Pit or well for the reception of (esp. superfluous) water, oil, or other liquid in mines, machines, etc.; cesspool. [earlier sense, now dial., marsh; f. MLG *sump* marsh; cf. SWAMP]

sŭmp'ter, n. (Arch.) pack-horse or its driver; ~-*horse, -mule, -pony*, pack-animals. [f. OF *sommetier* pack-horse driver f. LL †*sagmatarius* (=*sagmarius* f. Gk *sagma -atos* pack-saddle (*sattō* pack, -M)]

sŭmp'tion, n. Major premiss of syllogism. [f. L *sumptiō* f. *sumere sumpt-* take = SUB-, *emere* take, buy, -ION]

sŭmp'tuary, a. Regulating expenditure (~ *law, edict*, etc., limiting private ex-penditure in the interest of the State). [f. L *sumptuarius* (*sumptus -ūs* cost as prec.)]

sŭmp'tuous, a. Rich & costly, suggesting lavish expenditure. Hence ~LY² adv., ~NESS n. [f. OF *somptueux* f. L *sumptuosus* (prec., -OSE¹)]

sŭn, n., & v.t. & i. (-nn-). **1.** The heavenly body that the earth travels round & receives warmth & light from, such light or warmth or both, (~ *rises, sets, is brought by earth's revolution above, below, the horizon; his, its*, etc., ~ *is set*, time of prosperity or existence is over; *rise with the* ~, get up early; *Order of the Rising Sun*, Japanese order; *hail* or *adore the rising* ~, curry favour with new or coming power; *empire* etc. *on which the* ~ *never sets*, world-wide; *let not the* ~ *go down upon your wrath*, limit it to one day; *the midnight* ~, seen in arctic & antarctic regions; *nothing new under the* ~, in the world; *mock* ~, parhelion; *Sun of right-eousness*, Christ; *see the* ~, be alive; *make* HAY *while the* ~ *shines; hold a candle to the* ~, prov. of superfluous action; *take*, or sl. *shoot, the* ~ (Naut.), ascertain its altitude in order to fix latitude; *with, against, the* ~, CLOCK-wise, counterclockwise, whence ~'WISE (-z) adv.; ~'s *eyelashes*, ~'s *back-stays* (Naut.), ~ *drawing water*, pheno-menon given by rays piercing aperture in cloud & illuminating suspended particles in parallel lines; ~ & *planet*, system of gearing in which cogged wheel on recipro-cating rod both rotates on its axis & travels round the wheel that it engages & communicates motion to; *exclude, let in, the* ~; *in the* ~, exposed to ~'s rays; *a*

place in the ~, fig. favourable situation or conditions; take the ~, expose oneself to ~light). **2.** Any fixed star with satellite(s). **3.** (poet.) Day or year. **4.** (Also ~ burner) set of gas-jets, electric lights, etc., massed as one great light in ceiling. **5.** ~-bath, exposure of naked body to ~; bright-plumaged Old-World birds with resemblance to humming-birds; || ~-blind, window-shade; ~-bonnet, of linen etc. with projection & pendent back to shade face & neck; ~-bow, prismatic bow given by ~light on spray etc.; ~burn, tanning of face etc. by exposure to ~, so ~burnt or -burned a.; ~burst, firework or piece of jewellery imitating ~ and rays; ~-dance, of N.-Amer. Indians in honour of ~; ~'dew, kinds of small bog-plant with hairs secreting drops of moisture; ~-DIAL; ~-DOG; ~'down, ~set; ~'downer, Australian tramp who times his arrival at a station for the evening, (colloq.) a drink at ~set; ~-dried, dried by ~ & not by artificial heat; ~fish, large fish of almost spherical shape; ~flower, kinds of tall garden-plant with showy golden-rayed flowers; ~-glow, whitish or faintly coloured corona of light oceas. seen round ~; ~-god, the ~ worshipped as a deity; ~-hat, -helmed, adapted by material or shape to keep ~ off; ~light; ~lit; ~myth, SOLAR myth; ~-rays, ultra-violet rays used therapeutically as substitute for ~light; ~'rise, (moment of) ~'s rising; ~set, (moment of) ~'s setting, western sky with colours characterizing ~set (attrib., resembling these), (fig.) declining period of life; ~-shade, parasol, also awning of shop-window; ~'shine, light of ~ (~shine recorder, instrument recording duration of ~shine; ~shine roof, sliding roof of saloon motor-car), surface illuminated by it, fair weather, (fig.) cheerfulness or bright influence, so (~shiny a.; ~-snake, ornament found in early N.-Europ. art shaped like S with small circle at centre; ~-spot, one of the dark patches, changing in shape & size & lasting for varying periods, oceas. observed on ~'s surface; ~-star, red starfish with many rays; ~-stone, kinds of quartz (esp. cat's-eye) & feldspar; ~stroke, acute prostration from excessive heat of weather; ~-up (dial.), ~rise; ~-worship(per); hence ~'LESS a., ~'lESSNESS n., ~'LIKE, ~'PROOF², aa., ~'WARD a. & adv., ~'WARDS (z) adv. **6.** v.b. Expose to the ~ (~ oneself; bask in ~light); ~ oneself. [OE sunne, cf. Du. zon, G sonne, ON sunna; cogn. w. L sol, Goth. sauil, ON sôl]

*sun'dae (-di), n. Portion of ice-cream mixed with crushed fruit, nuts, etc. [?]

Sun'day (-di), n. First day of week, Lord's day, observed as day of rest & worship (HOSPITAL, LOW¹, PALM¹, ROGATION, SHOW²; ~; month of ~s, long period; ~ letter, dominical letter; ~ best, usu. joc., best clothes kept for ~ use; ~-school, for religious instruction on ~s). [OE sunnan dæg day of the sun]

sun'der, v.t. & i. (arch., rhet., poet.). Separate (t. & rarely i.), sever, keep (trans.) apart. Hence ~ANCE n. (rare). [OE sundrian (sundor asunder), cf. ON sundra, G sondern]

sun'dry, a. & n. **1.** Divers, several, (chiefly arch. & joc.; all & ~, each & all, everyone collectively & individually). **2.** n. (Austral.) an extra in cricket; (pl.) oddments, accessories or items not needing special mention. [OE syndrig (sundor see prec., -Y²)]

sung. See SING.

sunk(en). See SINK¹.

sünn, n. (Also ~ hemp) E.-Ind. hemplike fibre, [f. Hind. san f. Skr. sana]

Sünn'[a(h] (-na), n. Traditional portion of Mohammedan law based on Mohammed's words or acts, but not written by him, accepted as authoritative by the orthodox (~ITE¹ or ~i pr. -ē, nn.) & rejected by the Shiites. [Arab. (-a), = tradition]

sunn'ud. Var. of SANAD.

sünn'[ly, a. Bright with or as sunlight; of the sun (rare); exposed to, warm with, the sun (the ~y side, side of house etc. that gets sun, also fig. the more cheerful aspect of circumstances etc.); cheery, bright in disposition, diffusing cheerfulness. Hence ~iLY² adv., ~iNESS n. [-Y¹]

sunnyasee. Var. of SAN(N)YASI.

sup¹, v.t. & i. (-pp-), & n. **1.** Take (soup, tea, etc.) by sips or spoonfuls (the must have a long spoon that ~s with the devil, parleying with doubtful characters is risky); take supper (on, off, specified food); (north. of liquid (esp. mother or bite nor~). [OE sūpan, OHG sūfan; partly also f. OF souper see SUPPER]

sup², = SUB- in L compds w. wds in p- &c.

sup'er, n. & a. (colloq., shop). **1.** Supernumerary actor, (fig.) extra or unwanted or unimportant person etc.; superintendent; expensively produced film designed for exhibition as the principal item in cinema programmes (in full ~-film); (Commerc.) superfine cloth or manufacture. **2.** adj. Superfine; (of measure) superficial, in square (not linear or solid) measure (120 ~ ft. or 120 ft ~). [abbr. supernumerary, superfine, superficial]

sup'er-, pref. f. L super prep., super-pref., over, beyond [compar. form f. SUB² pref., cf. Gk hyper, Skr. upari]. **1.** In adji. (& their derivv.) formed on anal. of L supernumerarius f. L phr. consisting of super numerarius f. L phr. consisting of super numerum = being governed by it; super numerum = beyond the number, ~numerary = being

beyond the number. The distinguishable varieties of meaning are:

a. situated directly over, as ~*columnar* above columns, ~*humeral* over the shoulder;

b. not in or under but above, as ~*aqueous*, ~*terrene*, ~*celestial*, above water, earth, sky;

c. exceeding, going beyond, more than, transcending, too exalted for contact or connexion with, as ~*normal* beyond the norm, ~*natural* beyond what nature will account for, ~*sensible* out of reach of sense, ~*ethical* above the sphere of ethics.

2. In vbs & adjj. & their derivv. adapted from or made on anal. of L wds to which ~ was prefixed with advl sense. Varieties of meaning are:

a. on the top of something, as ~*impose*, ~*scribe*, ~*stratum*;

b. observation from above, as ~*intend*, ~*stition*, ~*vise*;

c. besides, in addition, as ~*add*, ~*erogation*, ~*fetation*;

d. to a degree beyond the usual or the right, as ~*eminent*, ~*saturate*, ~*subtle*.

3. In nn. & their derivv. on anal. of L *superficies* (*facies* face) in which ~ is prefixed w. adj. force;

a. upper or outer, as ~*canopy*, ~*cilious*, ~*hive*;

b. of higher kind, in higher than the ordinary sense, esp. in names of classificatory divisions, as ~*class* group including more than one class;

c. in the second degree, as ~*parasite* the parasite of a parasite, ~*tuberation* the forming of tubers on tubers.

4. In math. wds expressing ratio on anal. of L *superpertius* exceeding by ⅓, ~*bipartient* or ~*bitertial* = exceeding by ⅔ or in the ratio 5:3, ~*biquintal* in ratio 7:5, ~*tripartient* or ~*triquartal* = in ratio 7:4, ~*quadripartient* or ~*quadriquintal* = in ratio 9:5, ~*sesquialteral* in ratio 5:2, ~*sesquitertial* in ratio 7:3.

~abound' v.i., ~abún'dance n., ~abún'dant a., ~abún'dantly adv., 2d; ~add' v.t., ~addi'tion n., 2c; ~altar (-awl-) n., 3a, slab of stone consecrated & placed on unconsecrated altar; ~ān'al a., la (ANUS); ~ăngĕl'ic a., 1c; ~ănn'ūate v.t., 1c (L *annus* year), declare too old for work or use or continuance, dismiss or discard as too old, require the removal from school of (a pupil who has failed to reach a certain educational standard), send into retirement with pension, (p.p.) past work or use, so ~ănnūā'tion n.; ~ā'quéous a., 1b; ~bĭpȧr'tient, ~bĭquĭn'tal, ~bĭtĕr'tial (-shl), aa., 4; ~căr̄gō n. (pl. -oes), 1, person in merchant-ship managing sales etc. of cargo [f. Sp. *sobrecargo*]; ~cĕlĕs'tial a., 1b, also 1c= ~ăngĕl'ic; ~chȧr̄ger n., 2d, pump used in motor-cars & aeroplanes to force an extra quantity of explosive mixture into cylinders of engine & so increase the power output; ~cĭl'iȧr̄ȳ a., 3a (L *supercilium* eyebrow f. *cilium* eyelid cf. Gk *kutla* parts below eye), of the brows, over the eye; ~cĭl'ious a., ~cĭl'iouslȳ adv., ~cĭl'iousnĕss n., 3a [f. LL *superciliosus* w. ref. to raised eyebrows, see prec.], contemptuous, showing haughty indifference, assuming superiority; ~cĭv'ĭlized (-zd) a., 2d; ~class (-ah-) n., 3b; ~cŏlūm'nar a., 1a; ~cŏlūmniā'tion n., 1a, placing of one architectural order over another; ~cool v.t., 2d, cool (a liquid) below its freezing point, without solidification; ~dread-nought (-drĕd'nawt) n., 1c, battleship more powerful than the Dreadnought type; ~ĕlĕvā'tion n., 3b, amount by which outer rail at a curve is higher than inner; ~ĕm'inent a., 2d; ~ĕrogā'tion n., 2c [f. L *supererogare* pay out beyond what is expected], doing of more than duty requires (esp. *works of ~erogation* in Theol., such as form a reserve fund of merit that can be drawn on in favour of sinners), so ~ĕrŏg'atŏr̄ȳ a.; ~ĕth'ical a., 1c; ~ĕx'cellent a., ~ĕx'cellence, ~ĕxcĭtā'tion, nn., 2d; ~fămily n. (biol.), 3b; ~fătt'ed a., 2d (of soap); ~fĕcundā'tion, ~fĕtā'tion, nn., 2c, second conception occurring during gestation; ~fĭ'cial (-ishl) a., ~fĭcial'itȳ (-sht-) n., ~fĭ'ciallȳ adv., 3a (foll.), of or on the surface only, not going deep, without depth, (*~ficial colour, resemblance, knowledge, wound, accomplishments; a ~ficial person,* with no reserve of knowledge or feeling behind what he shows), (of measure) square (see SUPER a.); ~fĭ'cies (-shĭēz) n. (pl. the same), 3a [L, f. *facies* face], a surface; ~fine a., 2d, (commerce.) of extra quality (gen.) affecting great refinement; ~flu'itȳ (-lōō-) n., 2d (foll.), ~fluous amount (*give of one's ~fluity*) thing not needed; ~fluous (sŏōpĕr'flŏō-) a., ~fluouslȳ adv., ~fluousnĕss n., 2d (L *superfluus* f. *fluere* flow), more than enough, redundant, needless; ~heat' v.t., 2d, (esp.) heat (steam) to temperature higher than that of boiling water, so ~heat'ER-²(2) n.; ~hive n., 3a, removable upper compartment of hive; ~hūm'an a., ~hūm'anlȳ adv., 1c; ~hūm'eral n., 1a (L HUMERUS), Jewish ephod, also amice¹, also archiepiscopal pallium; ~impōse', (-z) v.t., 2a, lay on or on something else; ~imprĕgnā'tion n., 2c, ~fecundation; ~incŭm'bent a., 2a, lying on something; ~indūce' v.t., 2c, develop or bring in as an addition; ~institū'tion n., 2c, institution of person into benefice already occupied; ~intĕnd' v.t. & 1, 2b (L INTEND ere attend to), have the management (of), arrange & inspect working (of), so ~intĕn'dence n., ~intĕn'dent n., person who ~intends, ∥ police officer above rank of inspector; ~jā'cent a., 2a (L *jacĕre* lie), ~incum-

super-

bent; **~lative,** a. & n., 2d [f. LL *superlativus* f. *ferre lat-* carry)]. of the highest degree (**~lative** *wisdom, beauty,* etc.; ~*lative degree* in Gram, the forms of the adjective & adverb by which the highest or a very high degree of a quality is expressed, as *bravest, most absurdly),* so **~latively** adv., **~lativeness** n. (n.) the ~*lative degree* or form (*not used in the ~lative: what is the ~lative of shy?),* a word in the ~*lative (this talk is all ~latives,* be exaggerates); (of a ~*lative* n. Gram.) MAN; **~médial,** la.; **~médien,** 3b, compound molecule, combination of molecules acting as physical unit; **~min'dāne** a., 1c, above earthly things; **~nāc'ūlum** adv. & n., 1 [mod. L nā'culum finger-nail f. G *nagel),* ‖ *drink- ing* to the bottom (w. ref. to pour- ing of the last drop on thumbnail), (n.) choice wine worthy of being so drunk; **~nat'ant** a., 2a (NATATION), floating on sur- face; **~nat'ural,** (-cher-) a., **~nā'turally** adv., **~nā'turalness** n., 1c, due to or manifesting some agency above the forces of nature, outside the ordinary operation of cause & effect, so **~nā'turalism,** **~nā'turalist** n., belief, believer, in the ~natural, **~nā'turalize,** elevate into the ~natural region; **~nôrm'al** a., 1c; **~nūm'erary** a. & n., 1c, (person or thing) in excess of the normal number, esp. extra person engaged for odd jobs; **~organ-stop** two octaves above principal; **~ōrd'inary** a., 1c; **~ōrgān'ic** a., 1c (of psychical things considered apart from the organisms in which they are mani- fested), also, 3b, social, organic in a higher metaphorical sense; **~ōxyġĕnā'tion** n., 2d; **~pā'rasite** n., **~pārasīt'ic** a., 3c; **~phŏs'phate** n., 2d, phosphate with greatest possible proportion of phos- phoric acid; **~phys'ical** (-z-) a., 1c; **~pose'** (-z) v.t., **~posi'tion** (-z-) n., 2a, lay (thing) on or (up) on another; **~sā'cral** a., la (SACRUM); **~scribe** v.t., 2a [f. LL **rā'tion** n., 2d; **~scribe** v.t., 2a [f. LL *superscribere script-* write)]. write (in- scription) at top of or outside something, write inscription over or on (thing), so **~scrip'tion,** written above the line, super- ior, **~scrip'tion** n., **~scribed** word(s); **~sēde** v.t. 2d; **~scribe** v.t., **~sā'ti- rā'tion** n., 2d; **~scribe** v.t., 2a [f. LL *superseder* desist f. l. *super sedēre sess-* sit) desist from], set aside, cease to employ, adopt or appoint another person or thing in place of, (of person or thing appointed or adopted) take the place of, oust, supplant; **~sen'sible** a., 1c; **~sen'sitive** a., 2d; **~sen'sual,** a., 1c, **~sen'suous,** aa., 1c, **~sensible;** **~sĕs- quiăl'teral, ~sĕsquiēr'tial** (-shl), aa., 4; **~sĕs'sion** (-shn) n., ~*seding* or being

~seded; ~sŏl'ar a., 1b; **~sŏl'id** n., 3b, a solid of more than three dimensions; **~sŏn'ic** a. & n., 1c (L *sonus* sound), relat- ing to sound-waves of such a high fre- quency as to be inaudible, (of speed) greater than that of sound, (of aircraft etc.) travelling at **~sonic** speed, (n. pl.) high-frequency sound-waves, study of these; **~spi'ritual** a., **~spiritual'ity** n., 2d; **~sti'tion** n., 2b [OF, f. L *super- (stitionem* f. *stare std-* stand) perb. orig. = standing over in awe), credulity regard- ing the ~natural, irrational fear of the unknown or mysterious, misdirected reverence, a religion or practice or parti- cular opinion based on such tendencies, so **~sti'tious** (-shus) a., **~sti'tiously** adv., **~sti'tiousness** n.; **~strāt'- um,** **~strŭc'tion** or **~strŭcture** nn., **~strŭc'tural** (-cher-) a., 2a; **~sub- stăn'tial** (-shl) a., 1c; **~suble** (-sŭt'l) a., **~subtlety** (-sŭt'lti) n., 2d; ‖ **~tăx** n., 3b, (1909-29) tax on incomes above £5,000 p.a. levied in addition to ordinary income tax; **~tĕllū'ric** a., 1b (L *tellus -uris* the earth); **~tĕm'poral** a., 1a, above the temples of the head, also 1c, transcending time; **~tĕrrēne',** **~terrĕs'trial,** aa., 1b; **~tŏnic** n., 1c, tone in musical scale next above tonic; **~tōnic** n. (L *vise* (-z) v.t., 2b (L *vidēre vīs-* see), direct or watch with authority the work or proceedings or progress of, oversee, so **~vī'sion** (-zhn) n., **~visor** (-z) n., **~vis'ory** (-z-) a.

sū'perable, a. Not insuperable. [f. L *superabilis* f. *superare* overcome (super over, see prec.).] **-ABLE**

supĕrb', a. 2d [f. L *superbus* (super over)]. Of the most im- pressive or splendid or exalted kind, grand,(~ *beauty, courage, impudence; a ~ view, display, collection, specimen, voice, binding).* Hence **~LY** adv. [f. L *superbus* proud.]

superhĕt'erodyne, n. & a. (Using) a system of wireless reception in which a local variable oscillator is tuned to beat at a constant ultrasonic rate with carrier- wave frequencies, thus making it un- necessary to tune the amplifier & securing great selectivity; abbr. *superhět'.* [f. SUPER(SONIC) + HETERODYNE]

supĕr'ior (sŏŏ-, sū-), a. & n. 1. Upper, in higher position, (of higher rank, (~ *officer, rank, court);* ~ LIMB[1]; ~ *genus,* higher in the classificatory series & so more com- prehensive; ~ *wings,* folding over others; ~ *figures* or *letters,* written or printed above the line; ~ *limb* of sun etc., upper

For words in *super-* not given, see SUPER-.

edge; (Bot., of calyx or ovary) placed above the ovary or calyx). **2.** Better or greater in some respect, related as the better or greater to, (by ~ *wisdom, cunning,* etc.; *is* ~ *in speed to any other machine;* ~ *numbers,* esp. more men or their presence, *as was overcome by* ~ *numbers*). **3.** Of quality or qualities above the average, having or showing consciousness of such qualities, (*made of* ~ *leather; may cook is a very* ~ *woman;* ~ *persons,* the better educated etc., also & usu. iron., prigs; *he remarked with a* ~ *air*). **4.** Above giving attention or yielding or making concessions to (~ *to bribery, temptation, revenge, fortune; rise* ~ *to,* be unaffected by); hence or cogn. **superio'rity** (or -pē-) n., **~LY**[2] adv. (chiefly in position in Bot., Anat., etc.). **5.** n. One's better, person ~ to one, in rank or in some respect (*is deferential to his* ~*s; you are my* ~ *in ability & I yours in application; has no* ~ *in courage*). **6.** Head of monastery etc. (often *Father, Mother, Lady, S~*), whence **~ESS**[1] n. (rare). [OF, f. L *superiorem* nom. *-or,* comp. of *superus* high (*super* above, see SUPER-)]

supern'al, a. (poet., rhet.). Heavenly, divine, of the sky, lofty. [OF, f. L SUPER*nus,* -AL[1]]

supersed'eds, n. Writ staying proceedings. [L 2 sing. pres. subj. as SUPER*sede*]

sup'ināte, v.t. Turn (hand) palm upward (cf. PRONATE). Hence or cogn. **~A'TION** n., **~ātor'**[2] n. (as name of two muscles). [L *supinare* (foll.), -ATE[3]]

sup'ine[1] (or -īn'), a. Lying face upward (cf. PRONE); disinclined for exertion, indolent, lethargic. Hence **supine'LY**[2] adv.. **supine'NESS** n. [f. L *supinus* (st. of SUPER-, -INE[1])]

sup'ine[2], n. (L gram.). Verbal noun with accusative in *-um* & ablative in *-u* formed from p.p. st. of L vbs & used in special constructions. [f. L (*verbum*) *supinum* (prec., sense doubtful)]

supp'er, n. A meal taken at the end of a day, the last meal of the day when dinner is not the last. Hence ~NESS a. [f. OF *soper* (now *souper*) f. *soper* take supper, etym. dub.]

supplant' (-ah-), v.t. Oust & take the place of esp. by underhand means. Hence **~ER**[1] n. [f. OF *supplanter* f. L SUP(*plantare* f. *planta* sole) trip up]

sup'ple, a., & v.t. & i. **1.** Easily bent, pliant, flexible; given to compliance, avoiding overt resistance, wanting in sturdiness of character, artfully submissive, fawning; (~*jack,* (walking-cane of) kinds of strong twining shrub; hence ~NESS n.. **sup'plY**[2] adv.. **2.** vb. Make or grow ~ (~ *horse,* train him to obey slightest touch of rein). [f. OF *souple* f. L SUP(*plex-plicis* f. *plicare* fold) submissive]

sup'plement[1], n. Thing added to supply deficiencies, esp. fuller treatment of special subject issued with newspaper etc.; (Math.) the angle that added to another will make the sum two right angles. Hence ~AL, ~ARY[1] aa., -(mēn[4]-). [f. L SUP(*plementum* f. *plēre* fill, -MENT)]

supplement[2], v.t. Make addition(s) to. Hence **~A'TION** n. [f. prec.]

supp'liant, a. & n. **1.** Supplicating, expressive of supplication; hence ~LY[2] adv. **2.** n. Humble petitioner. [F (*supplier* f. L as foll., -ANT)]

supp'licāte, v.t. & i. Make humble petition to or to person or for or for thing. Hence or cogn. **~ātingLY**[2] adv., **~A'TION** n., **~atory** a. [f. L *supplicare* (*supplex* SUPPLE), -ATE[3]]

supply', v.t., & n. **1.** Furnish, provide, (thing needed, or person, receptacle, etc., with or *with* thing needed), whence **suppli'ER**[1] n.; make up for, meet, serve to obviate, (deficiency, need, loss); fill (place vacancy, pulpit) as substitute. **2.** n. Providing of what is needed (*Committee of S~,* House of Commons discussing details of estimates for public service; ~ *department,* charged with ~*ing* some need, esp. stores & provisions for army etc.); stock, store, amount of something provided or at hand or get-at-able, (~ *& demand* in Pol. Econ., chief factors regulating price of commodities; *an inexhaustible* ~ *of fish, coal,* etc.; *goods are in short* ~, scarce; *water &c.~*), (pl.) collected necessaries for army etc.; (pl.) grant of money by Parliament for cost of government, money allowance to person (*his father cut off the supplies*). [n. f. vb, f. OF supploier f. L SUP(*plēre* fill)]

support', v.t., & n. **1.** Carry (part of) weight of, hold up, keep from falling or sinking, (*foundation, buttress,* ~*s house, wall;* ~*ed by a lifebelt; had to be* ~*ed home*). **2.** Enable to last out, keep from failing, give strength to, encourage, (*what* ~*ed him or his strength was a glass of brandy, a good conscience, hope, your approval; too little food to* ~ *life*). **3.** Endure, tolerate, (~*s fatigue well; I can* ~ *life, such insolence, no longer*), whence ~ABLE a., ~abLY[2] adv. **4.** Supply with necessaries, provide for, (~ *a family*). **5.** Lend assistance or countenance to, back up, second, further, (~ *a cause, policy, team, leader, candidate;* ~ *actor or other performer,* take secondary part to him; ~*ing film, picture,* less important one in programme; ~ *resolution* etc., speak in favour of it; ~ *lecturer* etc., appear on his platform; ~ *institution,* subscribe to its funds). **6.** Bear out, tend to substantiate, bring facts to confirm, (statement, charge, theory, etc.). **7.** Keep up or represent (part, character) adequately.

For words in *super-* not given, see SUPER-.

8. ~ing or being ~ed (*give~ to; requires ~; gets no ~; trench, the second of three lines, between fire-trench & reserve or thing that ~s (*shelf must have another ~; he is the chief ~ of the cause); hence ~LESS a. [f. F supporter f. L supportare carry]

support'er, n. In vbl senses; esp., (Her.) representation of living creature holding up or standing (with SUPPER- 1a, as an escutcheon. [-ER¹]

suppōse' (-z), v.t. 1. Assume as a hypothesis (*let us ~ a second flood; well, ~ it was so; in part, or imperat. with conjunctional force = if, as supposing white were black you would be right; ~ your father saw you what would he say ?; also in imperat. as formula of proposal, as ~ we went for a walk, ~ we try another). 2. (Of theory, result, etc.) require as a condition (*that ~s mechanism without flaws; design in creation ~s a creator). 3. Take for granted, presume, assume in default of knowledge, be inclined to think, accept as probable, (*I ~ we shall be back in an hour; you cannot ~ I don't ~ he will come; what do you ~ he meant?; I ~ so, form of hesitating assent; also abs. in parenth. as you will not be there, I ~). 4. Be ~d, have as a duty (*he is not ~d to clean the boots). 5. P.p. Believed to exist, believed to have specified character, (*the ~d music of the spheres; his ~d brother, generosity); whence supposedly (-z-) adv. Hence or cogn. suppōs'ĕdlỹ² (-z-) adv. Hence or cogn. suppōs'ABLE (-z-) a., supposi'TION [see below], suppōsi'TIONAL (-zishǒ-) a., suppōsi'TIONALLY² adv., suppōsi'tious(2) (-zishǔs) a., hypothetical, assumed. [f. F supposer POSE¹); suppposition etc. f. L suppositiōnem f. L ponere posit- place, -TION), cf. DEPOSITION] suppōsiti'tious (-zitishǔs), a. Substituted for the real, spurious, (~ child, writings). Hence ~LY² adv., ~NESS n. [f. L suppositicius f. SUP(ponere posit- place) substitute, -ITIOUS¹]

suppōs'itory (-z-), n. (med.)., Cone or cylinder of medicinal substance introduced into rectum or vagina or uterus & left to dissolve. [f. L SUP(positorium (prec., -ORY)]

suppress', v.t. Put down, quell, put an end to activity or existence of, (rebellion, sedition, agitators, conscience, piracy, monasteries, etc.); restrain, keep in, not give vent to, withhold or withdraw from publication, keep secret, not reveal, (groan, yawn, feelings, name, book, evidence, facts); (p., of a disease) checked in its normal course (~ed measles etc.). So ~IBLE a., suppress'ION (-shn), ~OR², nn. [f. L SUP(primere press- = premere press)]

suppress'stō eŭr'ĕ, n. Suppression of

truth, misrepresentation by concealment of facts that ought to be made known. [L]

supp'ūr̆iāte, v.i. Form pus, fester. So ~ATION n., ~ATIVE a. [L SUP(purare f. PUS), -ATE²]

sǔp'ra, adv. Above; previously, before (in a book or writing). [L, =above]

sūpra-, pref. f. L supra adv. & prep. above, freely used in forming anat. terms indifferently with SUPER- 1a, as ~clavic'ular above the clavicle, ~orb'ital above the eye-sockets, ~rēn'al above the kidney, or with SUPER- 3a, as ~maxill'ary a. & n., (of) the upper jaw; also in other wds w. sense over, beyond, before, after, often in contrast with compds of INFRA-, SUB-, as ~mun'dane above or superior to the world, ~lapsār'ian(ism) a. & nn., (holding, holder of) doctrine that God's decrees of election & reprobation were not due to the Fall but preceded it & his prescience of it (cf. INFRALAPSARIAN); ~prof'est, acceptance or payment of bill by third person after protest for non-acceptance or non-payment.

suprēm'acy (sū-, sū-), n. Being supreme, highest authority, (*Act, oath, of ~, securing ecclesiastical ~ to the Crown & excluding the authority of the Pope), [foll., -ACY(2)]

suprēme' (sōō-, sū-), a. & n. Highest in authority or rank (*the S~ Being or the S~ as n., God; S~ Council of the Allies, small body, also the Big Four, Five, settling by conference the Allied common policy 1919-21, each Great Power having a representative; S~ Court of JUDICATURE; ~ end or good, SUMMUM BONUM; ~ Pontiff, the Pope); greatest possible, uttermost, extreme, last & greatest or most important, (~ wisdom, courage, etc.; the ~ test of fidelity; a or the ~ hour, moment, etc.). Hence ~LY² adv. [f. L supremus superl. of superus see SUPRA-]

sur-¹, =SUB- in some L compds w. wds in r- & their derivatives, as surge, surreptitious.

sur-², =SUPER- in many wds taken into E f. OF, as surcharge, surface, surloin, surprise, surrender, also sometimes for SUPRA-renal.

sura(h)² (soor'a), n. Chapter of Koran. [Arab.]

sūr'ah¹ (-ǎ), n. Kind of soft twilled usu. one-coloured silk. [perh. f. Surat in India]

sū̆r'al, a. Of the calf of the leg (~ artery etc.), [L sura calf, -AL]

surat' (sōō-), n. Kind of cotton grown, kind of cotton cloth made, in the Bombay Presidency. [place-name]

|| surcease' (ser-), n., & v.i. (arch.). 1. Cessation. 2. v.i. Cease. [AF sursise delay, orig. fem. P.p. of OF surseoir f. L as SUPERsede, w. assim. to cease]

surcharge, n., & v.t. 1. (ser'chärj).

Excessive or additional load or burden or amount of money charged; supply of force, electricity, etc., in excess of what is required; additional charge made by assessors as penalty for false returns of taxable property; mark printed on postage-stamp changing its value; amount in official account not passed by auditor & having to be refunded by person responsible; showing of omission in account for which credit should have been given. **2.** v.t. (serchárý). Overload, fill or saturate to excess; (of assessor, auditor) exact ~ from, exact (sum) as ~, fine (person sum) as ~; show omission of credit in (account). [f. OF *surcharge(r)*, see SUR-²]

sur'cingle, n., & v.t. Band round horse's body rarely as saddlegirth, usu. to keep blanket etc. in place; girdle of cassock; (vb) gird (horse), fasten (blanket etc.) with ~. [f. OF SUR²*cengle* girth f. L *cingula* f. *cingere* gird)]

surc'oat, n. (hist.). Loose robe worn over armour, 15th–16th-c. woman's jacket. [OF SUR²*cote* COAT]

surc'ulóse, -lous, aa. (bot.). Producing suckers. [f. L *surculosus* (*surculus* sucker, -OSE¹), -OUS]

surd, a. & n. **1.** (math.). Irrational (a. & n.). **2.** (phonet.). (Consonant, consonantal sound) uttered with the breath & not the voice (as p, f, s, cf. *sonant* or *vocal* of b, v, z). [f. L *surdus* deaf, noiseless; math. sense by mistransl. into L of Gk *alogos* (1) irrational, (2) speechless]

sure (shoor), a. & adv. **1.** Having or seeming to have adequate reason for belief, convinced of or (*that*), having certain prospect or confident anticipation of or satisfactory knowledge of, free from doubts of, (*are you* ~?; *you may be* ~ *of his honesty, he is or that he is honest; he feels or is* ~ *of success; I did not feel* ~ *of my company, could not feel* ~ *about it; if one could be* ~ *of living to* 70; *I'm* ~ *I didn't mean to hurt you,* form of asseveration; *well, I'm* ~!, excl. of surprise). **2.** Safe, reliable, trusty, unfailing, (*sent it by a* ~ *hand; put it in a* ~ *place; a* ~ *draw,* marksman who never misses; *a* ~ *shot,* covert certain to yield fox, remark etc. certain to draw person; ~ *card,* scheme etc. certain to succeed; SLOW & ~; *there is only one* ~ *way;* ~-*footed,* never stumbling or making false step lit. or fig.). **3.** To be relied on, certain, to do (*is* ~ *to turn out well; would be* ~ *to dislike him*). **4.** Undoubtedly true or truthful (*one thing is* ~; *to be* ~, formula of concession = to avoid over-statement, *as to be* ~ *she is not perfect, is pretty, is ugly,* as excl. of surprise, *as so it is, to be* ~!, *well, to be* ~!; *make* ~, ascertain absolutely that something is as supposed, take measures to secure that something is as desired; *make* ~ *of,* establish the truth or ensure the happen-

ing of; also *make* ~ *of or that,* have confident but often false anticipation of or that); hence ~'NESS n. **5.** adv. (Arch.) I admit, you will admit, (*'tis pleasant,* ~, *to see one's name in print*); *(colloq.) certainly (it* ~ *was cold*); as certainly as (*as* ~ *as eggs is eggs, as* ~ *as a gun,* colloq. forms of asseveration; ~ *enough,* in fact as well as in prospect (*I said it would be, &* ~ *enough it is*), with practical certainty (*he will come* ~ *enough*); *~ *thing* (colloq.), a certainty, (as int.) certainly! [f. OF *sur* f. L *securus* SECURE]

sure'ly (shoor'li), adv. With certainty or safety (*he knows full* ~ *that; will diminish slowly but* ~; *mule plants its feet* ~); it strong belief or experience or probability or right is to count for anything (*it* ~ *cannot have been he;* ~ *I have met you before; there is no truth in it,* ~; ~ *you will not desert me;* (in answers, arch.) certainly, undoubtedly, (' *Should you be willing to try?' S*~'). [-LY²]

sure'ty (shoor'ti), n. (Arch.) certainty (esp. of a ~, certainly); thing pledged as security for payment or performance (now rare); person who makes himself responsible for another's appearance in court or payment of sum or performance of engagement (*stand* ~, become so responsible, go bail, for another; *find* ~ or *sureties,* said of person primarily liable); whence ~SHIP n. [f. OF *seurté* f. L *securitatem* (SURE, -TY]

surf, n., & v.i. **1.** Foam & commotion of sea breaking on shore or reefs; ~-*bird,* coast-bird related to sandpiper; ~-*boat,* of buoyant build for use in ~; ~-*man,* skilled in managing ~-boats; ~-*riding* (on boards, as a sport). **2.** v.i. Go ~-riding. Hence ~Y² a. [earlier *suffe,* etym. dub.]

surf'ace (-is), n., & v.t. & i. **1.** The outside of a body, (any of) the limits that terminate a solid, outward aspect of material or immaterial thing, what is apprehended of something upon a casual view or consideration, (*has a smooth, uneven,* ~; *presents a large* ~ *to view; its upper* ~ *is as cold as ice; looks only at the* ~ *of men & things; his politeness is only of or on the* ~; *one never gets below the* ~ *with him*), (attrib.) of the ~ only (~ *plausibility, impressions,* etc.); the ~ of the sea (~ *mail,* opp. air mail; ~ *craft, raider, ship,* opp. submarine). **2.** (geom.). That which has length & breadth but no thickness (*plane* ~, that contains the whole of the straight line connecting any two points in it; *curved* ~, that may be so cut by a plane through any point in it that the line of section shall be a curve; *developable* ~, that may be unfolded into a plane without doubling or separation of parts, e.g. ~ of cone or cylinder). **3.** ~-*colour,* used in ~-printing, printing from raised ~ as with ordinary type or woodcuts & not from incised lines; ~-*man,* keeping per-

manent way of railway in order; ~
tension, tension of a liquid causing it to
act as an elastic enveloping membrane
seen in drop or bubble; ~*water*, that
collects on & runs off from ~ of ground
etc.; hence (-)*surf̃aced²* a. **4.** vb. Put
special ~ on (paper etc.); bring (submarine) to the ~; (of submarine) rise to
the ~. [f. SUR-² FACE]

sūr̃feit (-fĭt), n. & v.t. & i. **1.** Excess esp.
in eating or drinking, oppression or
satiety resulting; ~ of. Overfeed (t. & i.),
(cause to) take too much of something,
cloy, satiate *with*. [vb f. n., f. OF *sorfeit*
(so *do*)]

sūr̃ge, v.i. & n. **1.** Move up & down or to
& fro (as) in waves (of sea, crowd, standing
corn, emotion, etc.); (Naut., of rope or
chain on windlass) slip back with a jerk;
(of wheel) revolve without advancing
on rail or road. **2.** n. Waves, a wave,
surging motion. [n. f. vb, f. OF *sourdre*
sourge- f. L *surgere* rise, contraction of
surrigere (*regere* direct)]

sūr̃geon (-jn), n. Medical man treating
injuries & deformities & diseases by
manual operation (*house-~*, on staff of
hospital), person skilled in surgery;
medical practitioner having a diploma
qualifying him to practise surgery (~
dentist, dentist thus qualified); (formerly,
opp. *physician*) general practitioner dispensing drugs & attending out-patients
& not confining himself to consultation;
medical officer in navy or army or military hospital; ~*-fish*, kind named from
lancet-shaped spines on each side of tail.
[AF *surgien* f. OF *cirurgien* (*cirurgie* f. L
f. Gk *kheirourgia* handiwork, surgery, f.
kheir hand, -o-; *ergō* work)]

sūr̃gery, n. **1.** Manual treatment of
injuries or disorders of the body, operative therapeutics, surgical work, (*antiseptic, clinical, plastic*, etc., ~; *conserva-
tive~*, avoiding amputations etc.). **2.** Doctor's consulting-room & dispensary. [f.
OF *cirurgerie* (*cirurgie* see prec., -ERY)]

sūr̃gical, a. Of surgeons or surgery (~
skill, operations, instruments; ~ *fever*,
caused by ~ operation through sepsis).
Hence ~ly² adv. [as SURGEON, -ICAL]

sūr̃icate, n. S.-Afr. animal resembling
polecat & ferret. [native]

sūr̃loin, obs. form of SIRLOIN.

sūr̃l̄y¹, a. Uncivil, given to making rude
answers, showing unfriendly temper,
churlish. Hence ~ily² adv., ~iness n.
[earlier *sirly* (SIR, -LY) = masterful]

‖ sûr̃master (-ah-), n. Second master or
vice-master in St Paul's School. [SUR-²]

surmise (sermīz'), n., & v.t. & i. **1.** Conjecture, suspicion of the existence or
guess at the nature of something. **2.** vb.
Infer doubtfully, suspect the existence of;
make a guess, try to divine something.
[vb f. n., OF, orig. fem. p.p. of SUR²(*mettre*

put f. L *mittere miss-* send) lay to person's
charge]

surmount' (ser-), v.t. Cap, be on the top
of, (usu. in pass.; *peaks ~ed with snow*);
overcome, get over, (difficulty, obstacle,
etc.; now esp. in p.p.). Hence ~**ABLE** a. [f. OF SUR²(*monter*
MOUNT²)]

surmū̃llet (ser-), n. The red mullet. [f.
OF *surmulet* perh. f. *sor* SORREL² MULLET]

sûr̃name, n. & v.t. **1.** Additional name
of descriptive or allusive kind attached to
a person & occas. becoming hereditary;
the name common to all members of a
family (cf. CHRISTIAN *name*). **2.** v.t. Give
~ to; give (person ~); (p.p.) called by
way of additional name, having as
family name. [SUR-², NAME, after F
SUR²(*nom* f. L *nomen* see NOMINAL)]

surpass' (serpahs'), v.t. Outdo, excel,
be greater than, exceed. Hence ~**ING²** a.,
~**ingly²** adv. [f. F
SUR²(*passer* PASS¹)]

sūr̃pl̄ice (-s), n. Loose full-sleeved white-
linen vestment descending to hips or
knees or ankles & worn usu. over cassock
by clergy & choristers at divine service;
~*ed* (-st) a. If. OF SUR²*plis* f. med. L
SUPER(*pelliceum* f. L *pellicius* see PELISSE)]

sūr̃plus, n. What remains over, what is
not required for the purpose in hand, esp.
excess of public revenue over expenditure
for the financial year, (opp. *deficit*; often
attrib., as ~ *population*). So ~**AGE**(1) n.
[OF, f. med. L SUPER(PLUS)]

surprise (serprīz'), n., & v.t. & i. **1.** Catching
of person(s) unprepared (*the lord was taken,
the truth must be discovered by ~; was taken,
to attempt a ~; a ~ visit*, without notice);
emotion excited by the unexpected;
astonishment, (*full of ~; his ~ was visible;
to my great ~*, much against my expectations; ~ *packet*, with unexpected contents, e.g. packet of sweets with coin,
also often fig.); event etc. that excites ~
(*was a great ~ to me; I have a ~ for you*,
piece of unexpected news, unexpected
gift, etc.; *what a ~!*). **2.** v.t. Capture
(place, person) by ~, attack at unawares,
come upon (person) off his guard (~*d him
in the act*); affect with ~, astonish, turn
out contrary to expectations of (~*d you
to find ~ to learn—?; I am
~d at you*, shocked, scandalized; *more
~d than frightened*), whence **surpris'ING²**
a., **surpris'ingly²**, **surpris'edly²**
adv. (serprīz'-): hurry (person) by ~ *into
conduct or act or doing* (~*d me into rudeness, consent, dropping the reins*); hence
surpris'AL(2) (serprīz'-), n. [OF, orig. fem.
p.p. of SUR²(*prendre* f. L *prehendere* take)]

surra (sŭr'ra, soor'a), n. Form of pernicious anaemia affecting horses & cattle
in the tropics. [Marathi *sūra*]

sûr̃r̄eal'ism, n. Twentieth-century
movement in art & literature purporting to express the subconscious mind by

Images etc. in sequences or associations such as may occur in dreams. So ~ist a. & n. [SUR-², REAL², -ISM]

surrebut' (-tt-), **surrejoin'**, vv.i. (Of plaintiff) reply, make **surrebutt'er**⁴, **surrejoin'der**⁴, nn., to defendant's rebutter, rejoinder (order of pleadings at common law: Plaintiff's *declaration*, Defendant's *plea*, P.'s *replication*, D.'s *rejoinder*, P.'s *surrejoinder*, D.'s *rebutter*, P.'s *surrebutter*). [SUR-²]

surren'der, v.t. & i., & n. **1.** Hand over, give into another's power or control, relinquish possession of, esp. upon compulsion or demand (~ *fortress, army, ship, freedom, hopes, chastity, privilege, office,* etc.; ~ *insurance policy,* abandon claim in return for repayment of part of premiums); give *oneself* over to habit, emotion, influence, etc.; (of fortress, ship, or force, or its commander) accept enemy's demand for submission; give oneself up, cease from resistance, submit, (~ *to one's bail,* appear in court after being admitted to bail). **2.** n. ~ing or being ~ed (~ *value,* amount payable to one who ~s insurance policy). [f. OF SUR²(*vendre* RENDER)]

surrepti'tious (-*ĭshus*), a. Underhand, kept secret, done by stealth, clandestine. Hence ~LY² adv. [L *surrepticius* f. SUR-¹ (*ripere -rept- = rapere* snatch), -ITIOUS¹]

*su'rrey, n. (pl. ~s). Light two-seater four-wheeled carriage. [Engl. county]

su'rrogate, n. ‖ Deputy, esp. of bishop or his chancellor. Hence ~SHIP n. [L SUR-¹ (*rogare* ask) elect as substitute, -ATE²]

surround', v.t., & n. **1.** Come or be all round, invest, enclose, encompass, encircle, environ, (*the ~ing country,* the neighbouring district; ~*ed with* or *by*). **2.** n. Floor-covering between walls & carpet. [earlier sense overflow; f. OF SUR²(*onder* f. L *undare* see AROUND); present sense by confus. w. *round*]

surroun'dings (-z), n. pl. Sum total or general effect of all that is in the neighbourhood of a person or thing (*picturesque, healthy, degraded, cultured,* ~). [-ING¹]

sūrs'um côrd'a, L phr. Priest's exhortation to the people before the Preface in the Latin Mass. [lit. 'up hearts'; in Book of Common Prayer ' Lift up your hearts ']

surt'ax, n., & v.t. (Impose) additional tax (on); ‖ graduated tax on incomes above £2,000 in addition to ordinary income tax, imposed in 1929–30 in place of supertax. [f. F SUR²(*taxe, -taxer,* TAX)]

surt'out (-tōō), n. (now rare). Overcoat, esp. of frock-coat shape. [F, f. *sur tout* over all]

surveill'ance (*servāl'ans, -'l'yans*), n. Supervision, close observation, invigilation, (esp. *under~,* not trusted to work or go about unwatched). [F, f. SUR²(*veiller* f. L as VIGILANT)]

survey'¹ (*servā'*), v.t. Let the eyes pass over, take general view of, form general idea of the arrangement & chief features of; examine condition of (building etc.); collect by measurement etc. all facts needed for determining the boundaries, size, position, shape, contour, ownership, value, etc., of (country, coast, district, estate, etc.), whence ~ING¹(1) n. [AF SUR²(*veier* f. OF *veoir* f. L *vidēre* see)]

sūrv'ey²(-vā), n. General view, casting of eyes or mind over something; inspection of the condition, amount, etc., of something, account given of result of this; department carrying on, operations constituting, piece of, surveying of land etc. (see prec.), map or plan setting forth results of such ~(ORDNANCE ~). [f. prec.]

survey'or (*servā'er*), n. Official inspector of (~ *of weights & measures* etc.), whence ~SHIP n.; person professionally engaged in SURVEYing. [AF *surveour* (SURVEY¹ -OR⁸)]

surviv'al (*ser-*), n. Surviving (~ *of the fittest,* process or result of natural SELECTION); person or thing that has remained as a relic of an earlier time. [foll., -AL(2)]

survive' (*ser-*), v.t. & i. Outlive, be still alive or in existence after the passing away of, come alive through or continue to exist in spite of, (~ one's *children, contemporaries,* etc.; ~ one's *usefulness;* ~ *all perils*); continue to live or exist, be still alive or existent. Hence **surviv'or⁸** (*ser-*) n., **surviv'orship** n. (esp. right of joint tenant to whole estate on other's death). [f. F *survivre* f. LL SUPER(*vivere* live)]

sus-, =SUB- in L compds w. wds in ǒ- (also SUC-, *cf.* succeed, susceptible), in p- (also SUP-, *cf.* suppose, suspend), & in t-, & their derivatives. [for subs var. of *sub*; *cf.* ABS-]

suscep'tible, a. (Pred.) admitting of (*passage is ~le of another interpretation; facts not ~le of proof*), open or liable or accessible or sensitive to (*very ~le to pain, injury, kindness, female charms*); impressionable, sensitive, readily touched with emotion, touchy. Hence or cogn. susceptIBIL'ITY n. (often in pl. = sensitive points of person's nature), ~LY² adv. [f. med. L *susceptibilis* f. L SUS(*cipere -cept-=capere* take), -BLE]

suscep'tive, a. Concerned with the receiving of emotional impressions (*cf.* prec. & receptive; *the ~ faculties, nature*). [f. med. L *susceptivus* as prec., -IVE]

sus'i (sŏō-), n. E.-Ind. cotton fabric with stripes of different-coloured silk. [Hind.]

suspect'¹, v.t. **1.** Have an impression of the existence or presence of (*danger, a plot, foul play, collusion, a causal relation*); half believe to be (I ~ *him to be my brother, a liar, dying*); be inclined to think that, or that (I ~ *you once thought otherwise;* also parenth., *as you, I ~, don't care*). **2.** Incline to mentally accuse of or incul-

pate, doubt the innocence of, distrust, (I ~ him, of lying, of deep designs; a ~ed criminal, person ~ed of being one; ~ed person; the ignorant ~ everybody). 3. Hold to be uncertain, mistrust, doubt the genuineness or truth of, (~ the authenticity of the evidence). Hence ~ABLE a. (rare). [f. L suspect-(toll.)]

sus'pect², pred. a. & n. 1. Of suspected character, subject to suspicion, not un-impeachable, (the statement of an interested party is naturally ~). 2. n. Suspected person (political ~s are kept under sur-veillance). [F., f. L suspicere suspect-(SUB- specere look)]

suspénd´, v.t. 1. Hang up, (p.p., of solid particles, or body in fluid medium) sustained somewhere between top & bottom (a balloon ~ed in mid-air; ~ed particles of dust), so suspénd'ed a., suspénsibil'ity n. 2. Keep in undecided or inoperative state for a time, defer, or inoperative state for a time, defer, temporarily annul, adjourn, debar tem-porarily from office or function or privi-lege or membership, (~ judgement, one's indignation, the rules, the Habeas-Corpus Act, proceedings, a clergyman; ~ payment, fail to meet financial engagements, admit insolvency; ~ed animation, state of insensibility without death). [f. L sus-(pendère pens- hang)]

suspénd'er, n. In vbl senses; esp., (pl.) *pair of braces, || pair of (sets of) attach-ments to which tops of socks or stockings are hung. [-ER¹]

suspénse´, n.   State of usu. anxious uncertainty or expectation or waiting for information (deep one in ~, delay acquainting him with what he is eager to know); (Law) suspension, temporary cessation of right etc.; ~ account in book-keeping (in which items are temporarily entered till proper place is determined). [OF, f. p.p. of L suspendere]

suspén'sion (-shn), n.   In vbl senses (SUSPEND); esp. ~sion bridge, in which roadway is hung across stream etc., usu. on wire or chain cables passing over towers & anchored, without support from below. So ~SIVE a. (~sive veto, operat-ing only for a time, not definitive), ~SORY a., ~sivery² adv. [f. LL suspensionem (SUSPEND, -ION)]

sus'pĭrcôll', n. The entry recording that a person is to be hanged (often joc. = hanged, hanging). [abbr. of L suspendatur per collum, let him be hanged by the neck]

suspĭ'cion (-shn), n., & v.t. 1. Feeling of one who suspects, suspecting or being suspected (above ~, too obviously good etc. to be suspected; partial or uncon-firmed belief esp. that something is wrong or someone guilty; hence ~LESS a. 2. v.t. (dial.). Have ~ that or ~LESS a. 2. v.t. (dial.). Have ~ that or that. [AF suspecioun (OF souspecon) f. med. L suspectionem f. L suspicere sus-PECT. -ION]

sustain´, v.t. 1. Bear weight of, hold up, keep from falling or sinking (cf. support), 2. Enable to last out, keep from failing, give strength to, encourage, (exx. as in SUPPORT; ~ing food, that keeps up the strength). 3. Endure without giving way, stand, bear up against, (~ed the shock of the enemy's cavalry; will not ~ comparison with). 4. Undergo, experi-ence, suffer, (~ a defeat, severe contusion, loss, etc.). 5. (Of court or other authority) allow validity of, give decision in favour of, uphold, (~ the objection, the applicant in his claim, etc.). 6. Bear out, tend to sub-stantiate or corroborate, confirm, (state-ment, charge, theory, etc.). 7. Keep up or represent (part, character) adequately. 8. Keep (sound, effort, etc.) going con-tinuously (a ~ed note, effort). Hence ~ABLE a., ~MENT n. (rare). [f. OF sustenir f. L sustinēre tent-=tenère hold]

sus'tenance, n.   Nourishing (now rare; given for the ~ of our bodies); nourishing quality, subsistence, food lit. or fig., (there is no ~ in it; how shall we get ~?; lived a week without ~ of any kind). [OF (sos-), f. sostenir SUSTAIN, -ANCE]

sustentā'tion, n.   Support of life (rare); ~ fund, collected to support indigent clergy). [OF, f. L sustentationem (susten-tare frequent. of sustinère SUSTAIN, -ION)]

susurrā'tion n., susŭ'rrous a., (rare). Whispering, rustling.   [L susurrare, susurrus a. (susurrus a whisper), -ATION, -OUS]

sut'ler, n.   Camp-follower selling pro-visions etc.   [f. Du. soeteler (soeten befool, cf. G sudeln to sully)]

Sut'ra (soo-), n.   Set of aphorisms in Sanskrit literature. [Skr., orig. = string, cogn. w. SEW]

suttee´, satī´ (-ē), n.   Hindu widow who immolates herself on her husband's funeral pyre; custom requiring such im-molation, also suttee'ISM(2) n.   [Skr. (sa-), = virtuous wife]

sū'turje, n., & v.t. 1. Seamlike articula-tion of two bones at their edges, esp. one of those in the skull, similar junction of parts in Bot., Entom., etc.; (Surg.) uniting of edges of wound by stitching, thread or wire used for this. 2. v.t. Stitch (wound). Hence ~AL(~chief) a., ~ally² (-ted) a. [F, f. L sutura (suere sut- sew, -URE)]

sü´zerain, n.   Feudal lord, lord para-mount, sovereign or State having nominal sovereignty or right of general control

suspi'cious (-shus), a.   Prone to, feeling, indicating, suggesting or justifying, suspicion (with a ~glance; under ~ circumstances; the ignorant are ~; he became suspicious). Hence ~LY² adv., ~NESS n. [OF, f. L suspiciosus (prec., -OSE¹)]

suspice´, v.i. (poet.). Sigh. So süspirā'-TION n.   [f. L suspirare (SUB-, spirare breathe]

over semi-independent or internally autonomous State. So ~TY n. [F., f. *sus* above f. L *su(r)sum* upward (SURSUM) on anal. of *souverain* SOVEREIGN]

svelte, a. Lightly built, lissom, supple, (chiefly of human, esp. female, figure). [F., f. It. *svelto* pop. L p.p. of L *vellere* pull)]

swab (-ŏb), v.t. (-bb-), & n. **1.** Mop or other arrangement of absorbent material on handle for cleaning; absorbent pad used in surgery; specimen of morbid secretion etc. taken with a ~ for bacteriological examination. **2.** (naut. sl.). Officer's epaulet; clumsy fellow, also ~**b′ER**[1] n. **3.** v.t. Clean with ~, as ~ (*down*) *the deck*; take *up* (moisture) with ~. [back form. f. *swabber* f. Du. *zwabber* ship-drudge, cf. MLG *swabben* to splash in mud]

Swā′bian, Sua-, a. & n. (Inhabitant) of Swabia (~ *emperors*, Hohenstaufens, 1138–1254). [*Suabia* (mod. L f. G *Schwaben*), -AN]

Swade′shī (-ahdā-), n. Movement in India, originating in Bengal, advocating the boycott of foreign, esp. British, goods. [Bengali, = own country]

swag, n. (sl.). Booty carried off by burglars etc., (transf.) gains made by political or other jobbery; (Austral.) tramp's, miner's, or bush-traveller's bundle. [f. obs. *swag* vb hang swaying (of bundle, fat belly, etc.), prob. f. Scand., & cogn. w. SWAY]

swage, n., & v.t. **1.** Kinds of die or form for shaping wrought iron etc. by hammering or pressure; ~*block*, with variety of perforations, grooves, etc., for this purpose. **2.** v.t. Shape with ~. [vb f. n., f. OF *souage* etym. dub.]

swägg′er (-g-), v.i. & t., & n. & a. **1.** Walk like a superior among inferiors, show self-confidence or self-satisfaction by gait, go *about, in, out,* etc., with such walk; behave in domineering or defiant way; talk boastfully (*about* prep.) or in hectoring manner; bluff (person) *into, out of,* etc.; hence ~**ER**[1] n., ~**ing**ly[2] adv. **2.** n. ~*ing* gait or manner or talk; dashing or confident air or way of doing something, freedom from tameness or hesitancy, smartness; ||~*cane*, carried by soldiers when walking out. **3.** adj. (colloq.). Smart, fashionable, (~ *clothes, society,* etc.). [obs. SWAG vb, -ER[5]]

swain, n. Young rustic; bucolic lover; (joc.) lover, suitor. [f. ON *sveinn* lad, cf. OE *swán* swineherd]

|| **swa′llet** (-ŏ′-), n. (dial.). Underground stream; hole into which a stream flows, SWALLOW[1]-hole. [prob. f. foll.]

swa′llow[1] (-ŏlō), v.t. & i., & n. **1.** Cause or allow (food etc.) to pass down one's throat (~ *a* CAMEL, make no difficulty about something incredible or impossible or outrageous); engulf, absorb, exhaust, draw in, make away with, (usu. *up*; *the earth* ~*ed them up*; *the expenses more than* ~ *up the earnings*; *death is* ~*ed up in victory*); accept (statement) with ready credulity (*will* ~ *anything you tell him*); put *up* with, pocket, stomach, (affront); recant (one's words); perform muscular operation of ~*ing* something. Hence ~ABLE a. **2.** n. Gullet; act of ~*ing*; amount ~*ed at once*; || (also ~*hole*) funnel-shaped cavity in limestone. [ME *swolouen* f. OE *swelgan*, cf. Du. *zwelgen*, G *schwelgen* gorge]

swa′llow[2] (-ŏlō), n. **1.** Kinds of usu. migratory, long-winged, swift-flying, wide-gaped, weak-legged, fork-tailed, insectivorous bird associated with summer (*one* ~ *does not make a summer*, warning against hasty inference). **2.** || ~ *dive* (with arms outspread till close to water); ~*fish*, kind of gurnard; ~*hawk*, -*plover*, -*strike*, etc., fork-tailed kinds of hawk etc.; ~*tail*, deeply forked tail, kinds of butterfly & humming-bird having this, points of burgee, (sing. or pl.) ~*-tailed* coat; ~*tailed*, with deeply forked tail (of butterflies, birds, etc.; ~*tailed coat*, kind with tapering tails formerly worn in ordinary costume & still in evening dress); ~*wort*, milk-weed, also celandine. [OE *swealwe*, cf. Du. *zwaluw*, G *schwalbe*]

swam. See SWIM.

swa′mi (-ah-), n. Hindu idol; Hindu religious teacher (esp. as form of address to Brahmin); ~ *work*, silver articles ornamented with figures of Hindu deities. [Hind., = master, prince, f. Skr. *svāmin*]

swamp (-ŏ-), n., & v.t. **1.** Piece of wet spongy ground, bog, marsh, (attrib., in many names of plants & animals found in ~s); hence ~**Y**[2] a. **2.** v.t. Entangle in ~ (usu. in p.p.); (of water) overwhelm, flood, soak, (boat or its crew or contents, house, provisions, etc.); make helpless with excessive supply of something (*am* ~*ed with letters, applications, work*); (of greater quantity or numbers) swallow up, make invisible etc., prevent from being noticed or taking effect. [f. 17th c. in Virginia; prob. cogn. w. SUMP; cf. OHG & MLG *swamp*, OE & Goth. *swamm*, sponge or fungus, & Gk *somphos* spongy]

swan (-ŏn), n. **1.** Kinds of large water-bird with long flexible neck, webbed feet, and in most species snow-white plumage, formerly supposed to sing melodiously at point of death (*white, black-necked, black,* *mute* or *tame* or *common, hooper* or *hooping, trumpeter,* etc., ~; *black* ~,

name given before discovery of black species to extreme rarity; *all his geese are ~s*, see GOOSE); (fig., w. ref. to dying-ness of ~ing water; of dying song) poet (esp. *S~ of Avon*, Shakspere). **2.** The constellation *Cygnus*. **3.** *~dive*, = SWALLOW[2] *dive*; ~*flower*, kind of orchid; ~*goose*, long-necked China goose; ~*herd*, royal officer having charge of ~-marks; ~*mark*, cut in skin of beak to show ownership; ~*s-neck*, curved end of discharge-pipe; ~*s-down*, down of ~ used in trimmings & esp. in powder-puffs, also kind of fine thick cloth with soft nap on one side; ~*shot*, of large size; ~*skin*, kind of fine twilled flannel; ~*song*, of dying ~, also person's last production etc.; ||~*upping*, annual taking up & marking of Thames ~s. Hence ~*LIKE* a., ~*n*[1]ERY(3) n. [OE, cf. *Du. zwaan*, *G schwan*; perh. cogn. w. Skr. *svan*, L *sonare*, sound.]

swank, n., & v.i. (sl.). Show(ing) off, swagger, bounce, bluff. [dial. wd (=strut), etym. dub.]

swap. See SWOP.

Swaraj' (-ah'), n. Home-rule or self-government as the watchword of Indian Nationalists. Hence **swaraj'IST** (-ahj-) n. & a. [f. Skr. *svarāj* self-ruling; cf. L *suas* one's own, & see RAJ]

sward (-ôrd), n. Expanse covered with short grass, lawnlike ground; turf, whence ~*ED*[1] a. [OE *sweard* skin, cf. Du. *zwoord* bacon-rind, G *schwarte* bark, bacon-rind.]

sware. See SWEAR.

swarm[1] (-ôrm), n., & v.i **1.** Large number of insects, birds, small animals, sharp-shooters, horsemen, etc., moving about in a cluster or irregular body esp. round prey or enemy (~s, great numbers of children, stars, people, bills, etc.); cluster of honey-bees emigrating from hive with queen bee to establish new home; ~*cell*, ~*spore*, zoospore. **2.** v.i. Move in a ~ (~ *round*, *about*, *over*, etc.); (of bees) cluster for emigration (prepp.)., (of places) be very numer-ous; (of places) be overrun, be crowded, abound, *with* (*road*, *hills*, *house*, ~*ing with beggars*, *rebels*, *fleas*). [OE *swearm*, cf. Du. *zwerm*, G *schwarm*, perh. cogn. w. Skr. *svara* to sound, L *susurrus* whisper]

swarm[2] (-ôrm), v.i. & t. Climb (rope etc., tree or pole (always *up*), climb (rope etc., or *up* rope etc.), by clipping with knees & hands. [?]

swart (-ôrt), a. (arch.). Dark-hued, swarthy, cf. Du. *zwart*, G *schwarz*]

swar'thly(-ôrdhi), a. Dark-complexioned. Hence ~*iLY*[2] adv., ~*iNESS* n. [obs. *swarth* var. of prec., -Y[1]]

swash (-ô-), v.t. & i., & n. **1.** (Arch.) strike violently (~*buckler*, bully, bravo; ~*ing* *blow*, hard); (of water etc.), wash about, make sound of washing or rising & falling; ~*plate*, inclined disk revolving on axle

& communicating up-&-down motion to bar whose end rests on it. **2.** n. Motion or sound of ~ing water. [imit.]

swas'tika (*or swos̆*), n. Fylfot. [Skr., lit. =fortunate (*sŭ* well, *astí* being)]

swat (-ot), v.t. (-tt-). Slap, crush (fly etc.). [U.S.]

swath (-aw-); *pl. pron.*-dhz), n. Ridge of grass, corn, etc., lying after being cut, or space left clear after one passage of mower etc. [OE *swæth*, *swathu*, track, cf. Du. *zwad*, G *schwad*; cogn. w. LG *snode* scythe]

swathe (-dh), v.t., & n. **1.** Bind with bandages, enclose in wraps or cloths of one side or in different directions by turns, have unsteady swinging motion, oscillate irregularly, waver, vacillate; give ~*ing* motion to, govern the motion of, wield, control direction of, have influence over, govern, rule over, (*wind* ~*s trees*; ~ *sceptre*, *cricket-bat*, *sword*; *his speech* ~*ed votes*; *is too much* ~*ed by the needs of the moment*; ~*s a fifth of mankind*; (p.p. of horse, also ~*backed*) with back abnormally hollowed. **2.** n. ~*ing* motion or position; rule, government. [f. LG *sudjen* be blown to & fro, cf. Sw. *svaja*, G *schweien*, Du. *zwaaien*]

swear (swâr), v.t. & i. (*swore* or arch. *sware*; *sworn*), & n. **1.** State something on oath, take oath (*to*, that *of that*), promise (*conduct*, *to* do) on oath, take (oath), (colloq.) say emphatically that, (*will you* ~ *it*, ~ *to it*, ~ *you or that you were not there*, *on the Testament*; ~ *fidelity*; *had sworn*, *or sworn a solemn oath*, *to return*; *I* ~ *it is too bad of him*; ~ *to or by*, appeal to as witness & guarantee of oath; ~ *by*, colloq., profess or have great belief in, regularly resort to or recom-mend; ~ *off drink* etc., take oath to abstain). **2.** Use profane oaths to express anger or as expletives (often *at*). **3.** Cause to take oath, administer oath to, (~ *witness* etc.; ~ *person to secrecy*; *sworn brothers or friends*, close intimates; *sworn enemies*, open & irreconcilable; *sworn broker*, admitted to profession with oath against fraud etc.; ~ *in*, induct into office by administering oath); (p.p.) of evidence etc.) given on oath. **4.** Make sworn affir-mation of (offence) *against* (~ *treason against*; ~ *the peace against*, make oath that one is in danger of bodily harm from); hence ~*ER*[1] n. **5.** n. Spell of profane ~*ing* (*relieved his feelings by a hearty* ~); (colloq., also ~*word*) a profane oath. [OE *swerian*, cf. Du. *zweren*, G *schwören*]

sweat (-ĕt), n., & v.i. & t. **1.** Moisture exuded from the skin, perspiration (*running*, *dripping*, *wet*, *with* ~; *in or*

by the ~ of one's brow or face, by dint of toil; *bloody* ~, exudation of blood mixed with ~); ~*ing state*, spell of ~ing, piece of exercise that induces ~, (*in a*, colloq. *all of a*, ~; *nightly* ~*s*; *a cold* ~, as in death, swoon, terror, etc.; *a* ~ *will do him good*); (colloq.) state of anxiety (*in a* ~); (chiefly colloq.) drudgery, toil, effort, a laborious task or undertaking, (*cannot stand the* ~ *of it*; *says it is a horrid* ~; *will not take the* ~); *old* ~ (sl.), old soldier; drops exuding from or condensing on any surface. **2.** ~-*band*, leather or flannel lining of hat or cap; ~*cloth*, esp. thin blanket under horse's saddle or collar; ~-*duct*, by which ~ exudes from ~-*gland*, secreting ~ below skin; ~-*shop*, in which ~ed workers are employed; hence ~¹ɴᴇss, ~ʏ² aa., ~ɪʟʏ² adv., ~ɪɴᴇss n. **3.** vb. Exude ~, perspire; (fig.) be in state of terror or suffering or repentance (*he shall* ~ *for it*, repent it); emit (blood, gum, etc.) like ~; (of wall etc.) exhibit surface moisture; toil, drudge; make (horse, athlete, etc.) by exercise; employ (labour, workers) at starvation wages for long hours, exploit to the utmost by utilizing competition, (~*ed clothes etc.*, made by ~*ed workers*), (of workers) work on such terms: subject (hides, tobacco) to fermentation in manufacturing; deprive (coins) of part of metal by shaking in bag; remove ~ from (horse) by scraping; fasten (metal part) *on* or *in* by partial fusion. **4.** ~-*ing-bath*, for producing ~; ~-*ing-iron*, for scraping ~ from horse; ~-*ing-room*, in Turkish bath; ~-*ing-sickness*, epidemic fever prevalent in 15th & 16th cc. [vb f. n., OE *swāt*, cf. Du. *zweet*, G *schweiss*; cogn. w. Skr. *svēdas*, Gk *hidrōs*, L *sudor*]

swea'ter (-ĕt-), n. In vbl senses; esp. sweating employer; thick woollen jersey worn during or after exercise to reduce weight or prevent chills. [~ᴇʀ¹]

swede, n. Native of Sweden (*S*~); ‖ Swedish turnip. [MLG, MDu.]

Swedenbor'gian, a. & n. (Adherent) of the Swedish philosophical & religious mystic Emanuel Swedenborg (1688-1772) or his doctrines or New Church. Hence ~ɪsᴍ(3) n. [-ɪᴀɴ]

Swed'ish, a. & n. (Language) of Sweden or its inhabitants. [sᴡᴇᴅᴇ, -ɪsʜ¹]

*sween'y, n. Atrophy of muscle, esp. of shoulder, in horse. [prob. f. dial. G *schweine* atrophy]

sweep, v.i. & t. (*swept*), & n. **1.** Glide swiftly, speed along with impetuous unchecked motion, go majestically, extend (intr.) in continuous curve or line or slope, (*eagle* ~*s past*; *wind* ~*s along*; *cavalry* ~*s down on the enemy*; *she swept out of the room*; *his glance* ~*s from right to left*; *with a* ~*ing stroke*; *coast* ~*s northward*; *plain sweeps away to the sea*). **2.** (part.). Of wide range, regardless of limitations or exceptions, (~*ing remark, generalization*, etc.), whence ~'ɪɴɢʟʏ¹ adv., ~'ɪɴɢɴᴇss n. **3.** Impart ~ing motion to, carry *along* or *down* or *away* or *off* in impetuous course, clear off or away or out of existence etc. or *from*, (*swept his hand across*; *river* ~*s away bridge*, ~*s logs down with it*; *was swept away by an avalanche*; *the plague swept off thousands*; ~ *away slavery, feudalism*, abolish swiftly; *he swept his audience along with him*, won enthusiastic support; ~ *all obstacles from one's path*). **4.** Traverse or range swiftly, pass lightly across or along, pass eyes or hand quickly along or over, scan, scour, graze, (~ *the seas*, traverse in all directions, & see below; *wind* ~*s the hillside*; ~ *the strings, lute*, etc., of hand or its owner; ~ *the horizon*, of eyes or their owner; *river-bottom* etc., drag it to find something; *dress* ~*s the ground*). **5.** (Of artillery etc.) include in line of fire, cover, enfilade, rake, (*battery* ~*s the approaches, glacis, street*). **6.** Clear everything from, clear of dust or soot or litter with broom (often *up*), gather *up* or collect (as) with broom, push *away* etc. (as) with broom, (~ *the seas*, drive all enemies from them, & see above; ~ *floor, carpet, chimney*; ~ *up the room*; ~ *away the snow*; *swept & garnished*, generally renovated, w. ref. to *Luke* xi. 25; ~ *the board*, win all the money on gaming-table, & transf. win all possible prizes etc.; ~ *a constituency* etc., receive nearly all votes, have large majority; ~*s everything into his net*, seizes all that comes; ~ *up litter* etc., whence ~'ɪɴɢ¹(2) n. usu. in pl.). **7.** Propel (barge etc.) with ~s. **8.** ~-*net*, long fishing-net, also entomologist's net; ~-*seine*, large seine; ~*stake*(s), form of gambling on horse-races etc. in which the sum composed of participators' stakes goes to the drawer(s) of winning or placed horse(s) etc.; hence ~ᴇʀ¹(1, 2) n., (also, India) domestic servant employed on sanitary & scavenging duties. **9.** n. ~ing motion or extension, curve in road etc., piece of curving road etc., (*with a* ~ *of his arm, eyes, scythe*; *a* ~ *of mountain country*; *river makes a great* ~ *to the left*; *house is approached by a fine* ~ *or carriage* ~). **10.** Range or compass of something that has ~ing motion (*within, beyond, the* ~ *of the scythe, net, telescope, eye, human intelligence*). **11.** Act of ~ing (as) with broom (*give it a thorough* ~ *or* ~-*up or* ~-*out; make a clean* ~, have complete riddance of old furniture, officials, etc.). **12.** Long oar worked by standing rower(s) on barge, becalmed sailing-ship, etc. (*had to get out the* ~*s*). **13.** Long pole mounted as lever for raising bucket from well. **14.** Man who ~s chimneys (often *chimney-*~). **15.** (colloq.) = ~*stake*. [ME *swepen*, derivative vb f. OE *swāpan* sᴡᴏᴏᴘ: cf. ON *sveipa*, G *schweifen*, E sᴡɪᴘᴇ]

sweet, a. & n. **1.** Tasting like sugar or honey (~ *apples* etc.; ~*stuff*, ~*meats*; *likes her tea* ~, with much sugar; *a* ~ *tooth*, a liking for things; ~ *wine*, opp. DRY¹; ~ *tastes* ~, *has* ~ *taste*). **2.** Smelling like roses or perfumes, fragrant, (*smells* ~; so ~-SCENTED² a.; *air is* ~ *with thyme*; ~ *violet*, of scented kind, opp. *dog-violet*; ~ *breath*). **3.** Melodious or harmonious in sound (*has a* ~ *voice*; *sounds* ~; ~ *song*, *singer*, etc.). **4.** Fresh & sound, not salt or salted or sour or bitter or rancid or high or stinking, (~ *water*, fit for drinking, neither salt nor bitter nor putrid; *is the meat, milk, butter, still* ~?; *keep the room clean &* ~). **5.** Highly agreeable or attractive or gratifying, inspiring affection, charming or delightful; (colloq.) pretty or charming or delightful, (*'tis* ~ *to hear one's own praises*; ~ *toil*, that one loves; ~ *love, dalliance, idleness, sleep*; *what a* ~ *nature, face*, etc.; *a* ~ *girl*, lovable, affectionate; ~ *one*, voc., darling; *a* ~ *one*, sl., painful blow with fist etc.; in smooth-going carriage). **6.** *At one's own* ~ *will*, just as or when one pleases, arbitrarily, at random; ~ (*up*)*on* (colloq.), (inclined to be) in love with, very fond of. **7.** ~*bread*, pancreas (*belly* ~*bread*) or thymus-gland (*throat* or *neck* ~*bread*), esp. of calf as food; ~BRIER¹; ~ GALE¹; ~*heart*, either of pair of lovers, (vb) be engaged in love-making (esp. *go* ~*heart-ing*); ~*john*, kinds of pink or of narrow-leaved ~*william*; ~*meat*, shaped morsel of confectionery usu. consisting chiefly of sugar or chocolate, a fruit preserved in sugar, bonbon, sugarplum, goody; ~ *oil*, (esp.) olive oil; ~ *pea*, garden annual with showy ~*scented* flowers; ~ POTATO; ~*root*, liquorice; ~*rush*, kind of sedge with thick creeping aromatic rootstock used in medicine & confectionery; ~*sop*, (~pulped fruit of) an evergreen shrub of tropical America; ~ SULTAN; ~*water*, kind of white hothouse grape; ~*will¹iam*, a garden-plant, kind of pink with close-clustered flowers often particoloured in zones; ~*willow*, ~ *gale*; hence ~EN⁶ v.t. & I., ~ening¹(4) n., ~ISH¹(2) a., ~LY¹ adv., ~NESS n. **8.** n. ~ part (*the* ~ *& the bitter* or ~*s & bitters of life*); ~ a ~meat, bonbon, (also ~s¹ n.); ~ (usu. pl.) dishes) such as puddings, tarts, creams, jellies, forming a course at table; (usu. pl.) fragrance (*flowers diffusing their* ~*s on the air*); (pl.) delights, gratifications, pleasures, (*the* ~*s of office, domestication, flattery, success*); (chiefly in voc.) darling. [Aryan; OE *swēte*, cf. Du. *zoet*, G *süss*; Skr. *svādús*, Gk *hēdus*, L *suāvis* pleasant, *suādēre* persuade]

sweet'ing, n. Kind of sweet apple; (arch.) darling. [-ING³]

swell, v.i. & t. (p.p. swollen, arch. swoln, rarely ~ed) & n. & a. **1.** (Cause to) grow bigger or louder, dilate, expand, rise or raise up from surrounding surface, bulge out, increase in volume or force or intensity, (*wrist began to* ~ *up or* ~, *the injured wrist began to* ~; ~*ing scuts*; whence ~ING¹(2) n.; *the* ~*ing oratory*, of inflated kind; *sound* ~*s on the breeze*; *murmur* ~*ed into a roar*; *ground* ~*s into an eminence*; ~ *heart* ~*s*, feels like bursting with emotion; ~ *with pride, indignation*, etc., be or seem hardly able to contain it; *wind* ~*s the sails*; *the* ~*ing tide*; *expendi-ture swollen by extravagance*; *swollen voices* ~ *the sound*; *items* ~ *the total*; ~ *note crescendo & diminuendo*; *emotion* ~*s & subsides*; ~*ed head*, sl., conceit). **2.** n. Act or condition of ~ing (*the* ~ *of the hymn floated past*; *the* ~ *of the ground*). **3.** Heav-ing of sea with waves that do not break after storm. **4.** Part of any more or less cylindrical object that ~s out (*the* ~ *of the fore-arm*). **5.** (mus.). Mechanism in organ (operated by ~*pedal*) for obtaining crescendo or diminuendo by opening or closing slats in front of ~*box* containing pipes of the ~*manual*. **6.** (colloq.). Person of distinction or ability, member of good society, person of dashing or fashionable appearance, (*is a* ~ *in politics, at cricket*, etc.; *what a* ~ *you are!*, how finely dressed; *has been asked to dinner by some* ~*s*), whence ~DOM n. **7.** ~*fish*, kinds that can inflate themselves into nearly globular form; ~ *mob(smen)*, (class of) pickpockets dressed like gentlemen; ~*organ*, set of pipes enclosed in ~*box*; ~*rule* in printing, dash ~ing into diamond in middle & tapering towards ends. **8.** adj. (colloq.). Of distinction (*a* ~ *pianist*; ~ *parties, society*, etc.); smart, finely dressed, (~ *clothes*; *looks very* ~); hence ~ISH¹(2) a. [OE *swellan*, cf. Du. *zwellen*, G *schwellen*]

swept. See SWEEP.

swell'ter, v.i., & n. **1.** Be faint or moist or languid or oppressive with heat (of atmosphere etc., or of things or persons suffering from it; *under a* ~*ing sky*; *city* ~*ed in the plain*; ~*ing horses*). **2.** n. ~ing atmosphere or conditions (*in the* ~ *of the Indian night*). [OE *sweltan* die, cf. ON *swelta*, Goth. *swiltan*, OHG *swelzan* be consumed by fire or love, ~MR¹]

swerve, v.i. & t. & n. **1.** Diverge from regular line of motion, go off in changed direction, dodge, (*never* ~*s an inch from his duty*; *bird, ball,* ~*s in the air*; *horse, three-quarters at football,* ~*d suddenly*; *cause* (ball) *to* ~ in the air. **2.** n. Diver-gence from course, swerving motion; hence ~LESS (-vl-) a. [OE *sweorfan* rub,

swift, file, cf. Du. *zwerven*, swerve, OFris. *swera* creep, ON *sverfa* file]

swift, a., adv. (~er, ~est), & n. **1.** Fleet, rapid, quick, soon coming or passing, not long delayed, (now chiefly poet. & rhet.; ~ *runner, movement, feet, retribution, anger, laughter, response, riddance*; so ~**FOOTED**², ~**WINGED**¹, aa.); prompt, quick to do, (*has a ~ wit*; *to anger*; *be ~ to hear, slow to speak*; so ~**HANDED**² a.); hence ~'**LY**² adv., ~'**NESS** n. **2.** adv. ~ly (*he answered* ~; *they that run ~est*; esp. in comb., as ~*coming, ~passing*). **3.** n. Kinds of very long-winged & ~-flying insectivorous bird with resemblances to swallows, whence ~'**LET** n. (small kind); kinds of small lizard; the common newt; ‖ breed of pigeons; kinds of moth; revolving frame for winding yarn etc. from. [OE *swift* (move quickly, cf. ON *svifa*, cogn. w. **SWEEP**)]

swig, v.t. & i. (-gg-), & n. (sl.) **1.** Take draughts (of). **2.** n. (Act of taking) a draught of liquor. [vb f.n. (16th c.) in obs. sense *liquor*, etym. dub.]

swill, v.t. & i., & n. **1.** Rinse, pour water over or through, flush, (often *out*); drink (t. & i.) greedily. **2.** n. Rinsing (*give it a ~ or ~ out*); bout of drinking (rare); inferior liquor; hog-wash, slops. [OE *swilian* wash, etym. dub.]

swim, v.i. & t. (*swăm, swum*), & n. **1.** Float on or at surface of liquid (**SINK**¹ or ~; *vegetables ~ming in butter; with bubbles ~ming on it*). **2.** Progress at or below surface of water by working legs, arms, tail, webbed feet, fins, flippers, wings, body, etc., traverse or accomplish (stream, distance, etc.) thus, compete in (race) thus, compete with thus, cause (horse, dog, etc.) to progress thus, (fig.) go with gliding motion, (~ *on* one's *chest, back, side*, methods of human ~*ming; ~ across, out, back, the channel, a mile, a race, person a hundred yards*, one's *horse across; cannot ~ a stroke; ~ with the tide or stream*, act with the majority; ~ *to the bottom or like a stone or tailor's goose*, joc., sink; *she swam into the room; moon ~s in sky*), whence ~'**m**ER¹ n. **3.** Appear to undulate or reel or whirl, have dizzy effect or sensation, (*everything swam before his eyes; my head ~s; has a ~ming in the head*). **4.** Be flooded or covered with or in moisture (*eyes, deck, ~ming with tears, water*; ~*ming eyes; floor ~ming in blood*). **5.** ~*ming-bath*, large enough to ~ in; ~*ming-bell, bell-shaped ~ming organ of jellyfish etc.; ~ming-bell*, to keep learner afloat; ~*ming-bladder, fish's sound; ~ming-stone*, kind of spongy quartz. **6.** n. Spell of ~ming; ~*ming-bladder* (rare); deep pool frequented by fish in river; (fig.) main current of affairs (esp. *in the ~*, engaged in or acquainted with what is going on). [OE *swimman*, cf. Du. *zwemmen*, G *schwimmen*]

swimm'eret, n. Swimming-foot in crustaceans. [*swimmer*, -**ET**¹]

swimm'ingly, adv. With easy & unobstructed progress (esp. *go on ~*). [-**LY**²]

swin'dle, v.t. & i., & n. **1.** Cheat (person, money out of person, person out of money etc., or abs.); so ~**ER**¹ n., ~**ingIY**² adv. **2.** n. Fraudulent scheme, imposition, piece of ~ing, person or thing represented as what it is not. [back formation f. *swindler* f. G *schwindler* visionary projector, swindler, (*schwindeln* be dizzy, f. OHG *suindan* waste away)]

swine, n. (pl. the same). Kinds of ungulate non-ruminant omnivorous mammal, pig (which name has displaced it exc. in poet., rhet., zool., agricult., & U.-S. use), whence **swin'ERY**³ n.; person of greedy or bestial habits; ~*bread*, the truffle, also ~**SOW**²*bread*; ~*fever*, ~*plague*; ~*herd*, tender of ~; ~*plague*, infectious lung-disease of ~; ~*pox*, form of chicken-pox; ~'s-*snout*, dandelion. Hence **swin'ISH**¹ a., **swin'ishIY**² adv., **swin'ishNESS** n., (chiefly of persons & their habits). [OE *swīn* (sing. & pl.), cf. Du. *zwijn*, G *schwein*; perh. orig. an adj. form, cf. L *suīnus* of pigs (*sus* **SOW**, -**INE**¹)]

swing, v.i. & t. (*swung* or rarely *swang, swung*), & n. **1.** Move (t. & i.) with to-&-fro or curving motion of object having fixed point(s) or side but otherwise free, sway (t. & i.) or so hang (t. & i.) as to be free to sway like a pendulum or door or branch or tree or hammock or anchored ship, oscillate, revolve, rock, wheel, (*he shall ~ for it*, be hanged; *door swung to*, closed; *boat, boom, ~s round, across; ship ~s at anchor*; ~ *child etc.*, work the ~ in which he sits; *sat on table* ~*ing his legs*; ~ one's *arms, a bell, Indian clubs, bat, basket*; ~ *a hammock*, suspend it by ends; *no room to* ~ *a* **CAT**¹; *officer* ~*s his company, company ~s, into line*, brings, comes, by wheeling). **2.** part. (Of gait, melody, etc.) vigorously rhythmical (*at a long ~ing trot*; *a ~ing chorus*). **3.** Go with ~ing gait (*he swung out of the room*; ~*along, past, by, etc.*), whence ~'**ing**IY² adv. **4.** ‖~ *the lead* (Service sl.), malinger or scrimshank. **5.** n. Act of ~ing, oscillation, ~ing movement, (*work is in full ~*, active; *the ~ of the pendulum*, fig., tendency to alternation, esp. tendency of electorate to put parties in power alternately). **6.** ~*ing gait* or rhythm (*goes with a ~*); (also ~ *music*) kind of jazz in which time of melody is freely varied, with simple harmonic accompaniment in rigid rhythm. **7.** Normal duration of activity (*let it have its ~*, have free course till it rests of itself like pendulum). **8.** Seat slung by ropes or chains for ~ing in (~ *& round³abouts*), spell of ~ing in this. **9.** Compass to which thing ~s (*has a ~ of 3 ft*). **10.** ~*boat*, boat-shaped carriage hung from frame for ~ing in; ~ *bridge*,

that can be swung aside as a whole or in sections to let ships etc. pass; ~ without wheels. [OE *swingan*, cf. Sw. *svinga*, G *schwingen*]

swinge (-j), v.t. (~ing). Strike hard, beat, (arch. exc. in a ~ing *blow* etc.); (part.) huge (~ing *majority, lie, damages*; cf. *thumping, whopping*, etc.), [OE *swengan*, causal of prec.]

swingle (swing'gl), n., & v.t. **1.** Wooden instrument for beating flax & removing woody parts from it; swinging part of flail; ∥~*tree*, crossbar pivoted in middle to ends of which traces are fastened in cart, plough, etc. **2.** v.t. Clean (flax) with ~; *swingling-tow*, coarse part of flax. [f. MDu. *swinghel*, as SWING, (*-ncan*) cogn. w. SWING]

∥ **swink**, v.i., & n. (arch.). Toil. [OE *swincan*]

swipe, v.i. & t., & n. **1.** Hit at or hit hard & recklessly, slog; (sl.) steal by snatching; hence **swip'ER**¹ n. **2.** n. Reckless hard hit or attempt to hit at cricket etc., slog. [var. of SWEEP]

∥ **swipes** (-ps), n. pl. Washy or turbid or otherwise inferior beer. [f. prec. in obs. sense *drink off*]

swirl, v.i. & t., & n. **1.** Eddy, carry (object) or be carried with eddying motion. **2.** n. Eddying motion of water, air, etc., commotion made by fish etc. rushing through water. [cf. Norw. *svirla* frequent. of *sverra* hum, whirl, & G *schwirren*.]

swish¹, v.t. & i., & n. ∥ Flog with birch; audibly cut the air with (cane etc.), cut (flower etc.) *off* thus; make such audible cut with cane etc.; (make, move with) sound as of cane or lash or swift bird cutting the air or of scythe cutting grass; ∥ a stroke of a birch or cane or lash. [imit.]

∥ **swish**² a.(colloq.). Smart, swagger. [?]

Swiss, a., & n.(pl. the same). (Native) of Switzerland (~ *French, German*, dialects of French & German spoken in Switzerland; ~ *guards*, ~ mercenaries formerly employed in France etc. & still at the Vatican; ~ *roll*, kind of jam sandwich baked & rolled up). [f. F *Suisse* f. MHG *Swīz*]

switch, n., & v.t. & i. **1.** Flexible shoot cut from tree, tapering rod resembling this. **2.** Tress of dead hair tied at one end used in hairdressing. **3.** Kinds of mechanism for making & breaking connexion between corresponding parts of a system by which railway trains are diverted from one line to another, electric circuits completed or interrupted, etc. **4.** ∥*~back*, zigzag railway for ascending or descending steep slopes, also railway (chiefly used for amusement at fairs etc.) in which train's ascents are effected solely by momentum acquired in previous descents; ~*bar*, part of railway or electric ~; ~*board*,

arrangement for varying the connexion between a number of electric circuits; ~*lever*, handle & lever operating a ~; ~*man*, in charge of railway ~es; ~*signal*, flag or lantern or semaphore board indicating position of railway ~. **5.** vb. Whip with ~. **6.** Swing (thing) round quickly, snatch suddenly, whisk, (con ~*es her tail*; *I ~ed my head round*; *he ~ed it out of my hand*). **7.** Transfer (train, current) with ~; (fig.) direct (thoughts, talk) to another subject; (Bridge) change to another suit in bidding. **8.** Turn (electric light, current) *off* or *on*; put (user of telephone) *on to* or cut (him) *off* from another (~ *off* intr., cut off connexion). [f. LG *zwukse* n., *zwuksen* vb to bend or swish]

∥ **swith'er** (-dh-), v.i., & n. (So.). **1.** Hesitate. **2.** n. Flurry, doubt, uncertainty. [?]

Switzer, n. (arch.). A Swiss. [MHG (G *Schweizer*) Du. *Zwitser*] f. *Switz* Switzerland.]

swiv'el, n., & v.t. & i. (-ll-). **1.** Ring & pivot serving as connexion between two parts of something & enabling one of them to revolve without the other (~*chain, bookrest, gun, -hook, -joint, rowlock*, etc., provided with ~); ~*eye(d)*, (with) squinting eye. **2.** vb. Turn (f. & i.) on ~. [OE *swīfan* see SWIFT, -LE¹]

swob(ber), var. of SWAB(ber).

swoll, **swoln** (arch.), p.p. of SWELL.

swoon, v.i., & n. (Have) fainting-fit (~*ed for joy, with pain*, etc.); (of music etc.) die languidly away, whence ~*ing*-LY¹ adv. [n. f. vb, ME *swowne* perh. back form. f. *iswowene* (*swogan* to choke) = OE *geswogen* fainted(*swogan* to choke)+-ING¹]

swoop, v.i. & t., & n. **1.** Come down or down with the rush of a bird of prey, make sudden attack from a distance, (often *upon* prey, place, etc.); (colloq.) snatch *up*, snatch, the whole of, at one swoop. **2.** n. Sudden attack or downward plunge as of bird of prey; snatching action carrying off many things at once; *at one fell ~* (in describing completeness & extent & suddenness of catastrophe & see *Macb*. IV. iii. 219). [n. f. vb, OE *swāpan* rush, cf. ON *sveipa*, G *schweifen*]

swop, **swap** (-op), n. & v.t. & i.(-pp-), & n. (sl.). Exchange (v.t. & i., & n.) by way of barter (*never ~ horses while crossing the stream*, leave changes till crisis is past; ~*ped my knife for bread*; *will you ~ places* etc.?, or abs.; *shall we try a ~?*). [f. 14th c. in obs. sense *hit*, prob. imit.]

sword (sōrd), n. **1.** Offensive weapon consisting of long variously shaped blade for cutting or thrusting or both & hilt with hand-guard (BROAD~; *cavalry ~*, sabre; *court dress, ~*, worn with court dress; *double-edged, two-handed*, etc., ~; *duelling, small, ~*, kind with straight edgeless

blade of triangular section used for thrusting only; SCUTCHING~~; || ~ of State, borne before sovereign on State occasions; *the ~ of the spirit*, the word of God; *cross* or *measure ~s*, have fight or controversy or open rivalry, often *with*; *draw, sheathe, the ~*, begin, cease from, war; *throw one's ~ into the scale*, back claim etc. with arms; *put to the ~*, kill, esp. of victors or captors; *fire & ~*, rapine, destruction spread by invading army; *the ~*, war, the arbitrament of war, military power, sovereign power; (army sl.) bayonet. 2. ~*-arm*, right; ~*-bayonet*, kind with short ~-blade & hilt; ||~*-bearer*, person carrying sovereign's or other great person's ~ on some occasions; ~*-belt*, to which scabbard is attached; ~*-bill*, long-billed humming-bird; ~*-cane*, hollow walking-stick enclosing ~-blade; ~*-cut*, wound given with ~-edge, scar left by it; ~*-dance*, in which ~s are brandished, or women pass under men's crossed ~s, or performer treads about ~s laid on ground; ~*-fish*, large Atlantic & Mediterranean kind with upper jaw elongated into sharp weapon capable of piercing other fish or ship's timbers; ~*-flag*, esp. yellow iris; ~*-flighted*, (of birds) having flight-feathers of separate colour & looking when closed like ~ worn at side; ~*-grass*, gladiolus, kinds of sedge with ~-like leaves; ~*-guard*, part of ~-hilt that protects hand; ~*-hand*, right; ~*-knot*, ribbon or tassel attached to ~-hilt orig. for securing it to wrist; ~*-law*, military domination; ~*-lily*, gladiolus; ~*-play*, fencing, (fig.) repartee, cut-&-thrust argument; ~*s'man*, person of (usu. specified) skill with ~, whence ~*s'manship*(3) n.; ~*-stick*, ~-cane. Hence (-)~ED², ~'LESS, ~'LIKE, ~'PROOF², aa. [OE *sweord*, cf. Du. *zwaard*, G *schwert*, etym. dub.]

swore, sworn. See SWEAR.

swot, swat, v.i. & t. (-tt-), & n. (school sl.). 1. Work hard esp. at books, sap; ~ (subject) *up*, study it hurriedly. 2. n. Hard study; (thing that demands) effort, a swot, (*it is too much a ~*; *what a ~!*); person who works hard esp. at learning, a sap. [var. of SWEAT]

swum, swung. See SWIM, SWING.

sy-, = SYN- in Gk compds with wds in s- followed by consonant or in z- & their derivatives.

syb'ar'ite, n. & a. 1. (S~ite). Inhabitant of ancient-Greek colony of Sybaris in Italy noted for luxury. 2. Luxurious & effeminate (person). Hence ~it'ic a., ~it'ICALLY adv. [f. L (-ta) f. Gk *Subarītēs* (*Subarīs*, -ITE')]

syb'il, n. (Erron. for) SIBYL.

syc'amine, n. (bibl.). The black mulberry-tree. [f. L f. Gk *sukamīnos* mulberry-tree f. Heb. *shiqmah* sycamore]

syc'amore, n. (Also ~ *fig* or *Egyptian* or *oriental ~*), kind of fig-tree growing in Syria & Egypt; (also ~ *maple*) large timber-tree allied to maple. [f. OF *sicamore* f. L f. Gk *sukomoros* (*sukon* fig, *moron* mulberry)]

syce. See SICE⁵.

syce', n. (Also ~ *silver*) ingots of pure silver bearing banker's or assayer's seal & used in China for payments by weight. [f. Chin. *si sa²* fine silk (as capable of being drawn out fine)]

sychnocárp'ous (-k-), a. (bot.). Bearing fruit several times before dying, perennial. [Gk *sukhnos* numerous, *karpos* fruit, -OUS]

sy̆con'ium, n. (bot.; pl. -ta). Fleshy hollow receptacle developing into multiple fruit as in fig. [mod. L (Gk *sukon* fig)]

syc'ophant, n. Flatterer, toady, parasitic person. So ~ANCY n., ~ăn'tIC a. [f. L (-ta) f. Gk *sukophanēs* informer, perh. f. *sukon* fig, *phainō* show (informing against export of figs or plunder of sacred fig-trees)]

sy̆cōs'is, n. Skin-disease of bearded part of face or scalp also called *barber's itch*. [f. Gk *sukōsis* figlike ulcer (*sukon* fig, -OSIS)]

sy̆en'ite, n. Grey crystalline rock of feldspar & hornblende with or without quartz. Hence ~it'IC a. [F (*syé-*), f. L *Syenites* (*lapis* stone) of Syene in Egypt, see -ITE¹]

syl-. = SYN- in Gk compds w. words in l- & their derivatives.

syll'abary, n. List of characters representing syllables & serving the purpose, in some languages or stages, of an alphabet. [L *syllaba* SYLLABLE, -ARY¹]

syllăb'ic, a. Of syllable(s) (often in comb., as *mono, di, tri, quadri,* -*ic*, having 1, 2, 3, 4, syllables); (of symbols) representing a whole syllable; articulated in syllables. Hence ~ICALLY adv. [f. Gk *sullabikos* (SYLLABLE, -IC)]

sylláb'icāte, sylláb'ify, syll'abīze, vv.t. Divide into or articulate by syllables. Hence **sylláb'icā'TION, syllăbIFICA'TION,** nn. [Gk *sullabē* see foll., -IC, -ATE³, -FY, -IZE]

syll'able, n., & v.t. 1. Unit of pronunciation forming a word or part of a word & containing one vowel sound & often consonant(s) preceding or following or preceding & following this; (transf.) so much as a word, the least amount of speech, (*not a ~e!*, do not speak); hence (-)~ED² (-ld) a. 2. v.t. Pronounce by ~es, articulate distinctly; (poet.) utter (name, word). [f. OF *sillabe* f. L f. Gk *sullabē* (syl-, *lambanō* take); for -le cf. PRINCIPLE, PARTICIPLE]

syllabub. See SILLABUB.

syll'abus, n. (pl. -bī, -buses). 1. Abstract giving heads or main subjects of a lecture, course of teaching, etc., conspectus or programme of hours of work etc. 2. (R.-C.

Ch.) summary of points decided by an ecclesiastical decree, esp. catalogue of specially heretical doctrines or practices or institutions condemned by Pius IX in 1864. [mod. L based on a prob. non-existent Gk *sullabos*]

syllep′sis, n. (gram.; pl. ∼*ses*). Application of a word to two others in different senses (e.g. *in a flood of tears & a sedan chair*) or to two of which it grammatically suits one only (e.g. *neither you nor he knows*). So ∼tic a., ∼**tically** adv. [LL, t. Gk *sullēpsis* (*sullambanō* see SYLLABLE) comprehension]

syll′ogism, n. Form of reasoning in which from two given or assumed propositions called the premis(s)es & having a common or middle term a third is deduced called the conclusion from which the middle term is absent (FIGURE, 1 WOOD²), *of* ∼*ism*: *false* ∼*ism*, one whose conclusion does not necessarily follow from its premisses because it fails to fulfil the rules of logic regarding the nature & mutual relations of the major & minor & middle terms necessary if the inference is to be sound); (transf.) deductive reasoning as opp. induction. So ∼**is′tic** a., ∼**is′tically** adv. [f. OF *silogime* f. L.f. Gk *sullogismos* f. *sullogizomai* (SYL-, *logizomai* to reason f. *logos* reason), -ISM]

syll′ogize, v.i. & t. Use syllogisms; throw (facts, argument) into syllogistic form. [f. med. L *syllogizāre* f. Gk *sullogizomai* (prec.)]

sylla sylvan. See SILVAN.

sylph, n. Elemental spirit of the air (cf. nymph, gnome, salamander, of water, earth, fire) in Paracelsus's system, whence ∼**LIKE** a.; (transf.) slender girl; kinds of long-tailed humming-bird. [f. mod. L *sylphes* or G *sylphen* (pl.), prob. invented by Paracelsus]

sylvan. See SILVAN.

sylviculture. See SILVICULTURE.

syn-, =SYN- in Gk compds with words in b-, m-, p-, as: ∼*biont(t)*, organism living in ∼**biosis** [Gk *bíōn -ontos* part. of *bios* f. *bios* life]; ∼*bíō′sis*, permanent union between organisms each of which depends for its existence on the other as the fungus & alga composing lichen [f. Gk as *symbiōn*, -OSIS], whence ∼*biō′tic* a., ∼*biō′tically* adv.; ∼*pod′mograph*, apparatus exhibiting sound-curves usu. by double pendulum with style attached [Gk *patmos* vibration f. *pallō* brandish]; ∼*pet′mous*, (of bird) having tendons of toe-flexors united at a point [Gk *pélma* sole]; ∼*pet′alous*, having petals united; ∼*phyll′ous*, with leaves united [Gk *phnllon* leaf]; ∼*phys′is*, growing together, (place or line of) union between two correspond-ing bones or other parts, coalescence, [Gk *phnō* grow], whence ∼*phys′eAL* a.; ∼*pössóm′ētĕr*, instrument for measuring force of current of water, also barometer in which atmospheric pressure is balanced

partly by column of liquid & partly by elastic pressure of confined gas [Gk *piestō* f. *piezō* press]; ∼*pod′eAL* a., stem whose successive sections are strictly branches each springing from the preceding, as in the vine [Gk *pous podos* foot], so ∼*pod′eAL* a., ∼*pod′eALy²* adv.

sym′bol, n. & v.t. (-ll-). 1. Thing regarded by general consent as naturally typifying or representing or recalling something by possession of analogous qualities or by association in fact or thought (*white, the purity, courage, Zeus, Christianity; values the handle to his name only as a* ∼). 2. Mark or character taken as the conventional sign of some object or idea or process, e.g. the astronomical signs for the planets, the letters standing for chemical elements, letters of the alphabet, the mathematical signs for addition & infinity, the asterisk; hence or cogn. ∼**iza′tion, symbol(I)er′ory, symbol(I)-ōr′ArRY,** nn. 3. vb (rare, also & usu. ∼*ize*). Be the ∼ of; represent by means of (a symbol); as ∼*ic* & not literal. Import ∼*ism* (f. *L symbole* f. LL.f. Gk *sumbolos* etc.) as ∼*ic* & not literal. Import ∼*ism* (f. *L symbole* f. LL.f. Gk *sumbolos*, -on, token, watchword, f. *sumballō* (SYM-, *ballō* throw) agree]

sym′metry, n. 1. (Beauty resulting from) right proportion between the parts of the body or any whole, balance, congruity, harmony, keeping. 2. Such structure as allows of an object's being divided by a point or line or plane or radiating lines or planes into two or more parts exactly similar in size & shape & in position relatively to the dividing point etc., repetition of exactly similar parts facing each other or a centre, whence (in art) ∼-OPHOR′IA n. 3. Approximation to such structure, possession by a whole of corresponding parts correspondingly placed; (Bot.) possession by flower of sepals & petals & stamens & pistils in (multiples of) the same number. Hence or cogn. **sym′met′ric(AL)** aa., **symmet′ricALY²** adv., ∼**IZE**(3) v.t., ∼**iza′TION** n. [f. LL.f. Gk *summetria* f. SYM(*metros* measure) commensurate, symmetrical ∼-OPHOR′IA, n.

sympathĕt′ic, a. & n. 1. Of, full of, exhibiting, expressing, due to, effecting, sympathy (∼ *heart, person, conduct, words;* ∼ *landscape* etc., that touches the feelings by association etc.; ∼ *pain* etc., caused by pain or injury to someone else or in another part of the body; ∼ *sound, resonance, string,* sounding by vibration communicated through the air or other medium from vibrating object; ∼ *STRIKE; ∼ *nerve,* any, esp. either of two extending the length of the vertebral column, of a

system of nerves uniting viscera & blood-vessels in common nervous action; ~ink, writing done with which is invisible till brought out by warmth or other agency); (as Gallicism, & in critics' slang) capable of evoking sympathy, appealing *to reader* etc.; hence **sympathet'ically** adv. **2.** n. ~ nerve or system; person peculiarly sensitive to hypnotic or similar influence. [f. late Gk *sumpathetikos* (SYMPATHY, PATHETIC)]

sym'pathiz|e, v.i. Feel or express sympathy, share feeling or opinion *with* person etc., agree *with* sentiment. Hence ~ER¹ n. [f. F *sympathiser* (foll., -IZE)]

sym'pathy, n. Being simultaneously affected with the same feeling, tendency to share or state of sharing another person's or thing's emotion or sensation or condition (*with*), mental participation in another's trouble (*with*), compassion (*for*), agreement in opinion or desire. [f. LL f. Gk *sumpatheia* f. *sumpathēs* f. *pathos* feeling) sympathetic]

sym'phony, n. (Arch.) harmony, consonance of sounds, whence **symphōn'ious** a. (rare); (Mus.) SONATA for full orchestra, (also) opening or closing instrumental passage in song. Hence **symphōn'ic** a. [f. OF *simphonie* f. L f. Gk *sumphōnia* f. SYM(*phōnos* f. *phōne* sound) harmonious]

sympōs'iärch (-k), n. President of symposium, toast-master, feast-master. [f. Gk *sumposiarkhos* (foll., -*arkhos* -ruler f. *arkhō* rule)]

sympōs'ium (-z-), n. (pl. ~a). **1.** Ancient-Greek after-dinner drinking-party with music, dancers, or conversation; any drinking-party. **2.** Philosophical or other friendly discussion; set of contributions on one subject from various authors & points of view in magazine etc. Hence ~AL a. [f. L f. Gk *sumposion* f. SYM(*pinō* drink, cf. *posis* drinking) drink together]

symp'tom, n. Perceptible change in the body or its functions indicating disease (*subjective, objective*, ~s, directly perceptible only to patient, to others); sign or token of the existence of something. Hence or cogn. ~āt'ic a., ~atŏl'ogy n. [f. F *symptome* f. L f. Gk *sumptōma -atos* f. SYM(*piptō* fall, -M)]

syn-, pref. (appearing also as SYL-, SYM-, *syr-* before F-, *sus-*, before s- not followed by consonant, & *sy-*; the Gk change of *sun-* to *sug-* before gutturals is disregarded in mod. derivatives) repr. Gk *sun* prep. & pref. *with, together* or *alike*, in wds derived directly f. Gk wds (*syncope*) or made f. Gk (*syngnathous*) or very rarely f. non-Gk (*synovial*) elements:—~(a)er'esis (contraction of two vowels or syllables into one [Gk *haireō* take]; ~allagmät'ic, (of treaty or contract) imposing reciprocal obligations [Gk *allassō* exchange]; ~al(o)eph'a (-lē-), elision or obscuration of final before initial vowel [Gk *aleiphō* smear]; ~an'therous, with stamens coalescent by the anthers; ~an'thous, with flowers & leaves appearing simultaneously [Gk *anthos* flower]; ~aphe(i)'a (-ĕa), continuity between lines or scansion of lines in verse, allowing the ordinary rules of elision & quantity to operate with the final syllable [Gk *haptō* join]; ~arthrŏs'is (pl. -ōsēs), immovable articulation, as in sutures of skull & socketing of teeth; ~carp, aggregate or multiple fruit, e.g. blackberry, fig, so ~carp'ous a. [Gk *karpos* fruit]; ~chondrŏs'is (-k-), (nearly) immovable articulation of bones by layer of cartilage, as in spinal vertebrae; ~clas'tic, concave, or convex, all over (opp. *anticlastic*, partly concave & partly convex) [Gk *klaō* break]; ~clīn'äl, (~clīn'al of strata) dipping towards a common line or point (opp. *anticlinal*, dipping away); ~cotylēd'onous, with cotyledons united; ~'crĕt-ĭsm, attempt to sink differences & effect union between sects or philosophic schools, so ~crĕt'ic, ~crĕtīst', ~crĕtis'tic, ~crĕtīze v.t. & i. [Gk *sugkrētizō* etym. dub., combine against common enemy]; ~eğĕt'ium (pl. -ia), mass of protoplasm with several nuclei but not forming one cell [-CYTE]; ~dac'tyl(ous) aa., with digits united as in webbed feet etc., so ~dac'tylism; ~desmŏs'is, articulation by ligaments, so ~desmŏt'ic, ~desmŏl'ogy, ~desmog'raphy [Gk *desmos* bond f. *deō* bind]; ~dět'ic, of, using, conjunctions [ASYNDE-TON]; ~'drome (-mī), concurrence of, set of concurrent, symptoms in disease; ~ec'doche (-kǐ), extended acceptation by which when a part is named the whole it belongs to is understood, as in *50 sail* (for ships) [Gk *ek* out, *dekhomai* accept]; ~'esis, violation of grammatical rule due to influence exerted by the sense (as *neither of them are right*) [Gk *sunesis* understanding (*hiēmi* send)]; ~gen'esis, formation of embryo partly from the male & partly from the female element; ~'gnathous, (of fish) with jaws united into tubular snout; ~izēs'is (pl. -ĕsēs), pronunciation of two vowels not making a diphthong as one syllable [Gk *hizō* to seat]; ~oe'cious (-nēshus), having male & female organs in one inflorescence or receptacle, as in composite flowers & mosses [Gk *oikos* house]; ~osteŏl'ogy, science of the joints of the body; ~ost(e)ōs'is, anchylosis, so ~ostŏt'ic a.; ~ŏv'ia, albuminous fluid secreted by membranes in interior of joints & in other places needing lubrication, so ~ŏv'ial a. [invented by Paracelsus from unknown elements].

syn'agogue (-ŏg), n. Jewish congregation with organized religious observances & instruction, its place of meeting. Hence **synagŏg'ĭcAL** (-gǐ-, -jǐ-) a. [f. LL f. Gk *sunagōgē* (prec., *agōgē* bringing f. *agō* bring]

synch'ronize (-ngk-), v.i. & t. Occur at the same time, be simultaneous or ~ous a. (whence ~ously² adv.), (with); ascertain or set forth the correspondence in date of (events); cause (clocks) to show, (of clocks) show, a standard or uniform time. Hence or cogn. ~ISM(1) n, (also) coordination of the audible and visible components in cinematography, television, etc., ~IzA'TION, n. [f. Gk (SYN-, *khronos* time, -IZE)]

'yn'copist, v.t. Shorten (word) by dropping interior letter(s) or syllable(s), as in *symbology for symbolology*, *Gloster for Gloucester*; (Mus.) displace beats or accents in (passage) so that what was 'strong' becomes 'weak', & vice versa. Hence ~A'TION n. [f. *syncopate* swoon (foll.), -ATE³]

syn'copē, n. (Gram.) syncopated spelling or pronunciation; (Med.) fainting, loss of consciousness from fall of blood-pressure, whence **syncop'(t)ic** a.; (Mus.) syncopation, also such combination of voice-parts that two or more notes in one coincide with one in another. [f. (Mus.) syncopa- (SYN-, *koptō* strike)]

sýnc'ro-mĕsh, a. & n. (System of gear-changing, esp. in motor-cars) in which the sliding gear-wheels are provided with small friction clutches which make contact with the non-sliding wheels before engagement, thus facilitating gear-changing by making both wheels revolve at the same speed. [for *synchronized mesh*]

syn'dic, n. Official of kinds differing in different countries & times; ‖(Camb. Univ.) member of special committee of senate. [F, f. LL f. Gk *sundikos* f. *dikē* justice) advocate]

syn'dicalism, n. A movement among industrial workers having as its object the transfer of the means of production & distribution from their present owners to unions of workers, the method generally favoured for the accomplishment of this being the general strike. [f. F *syndica-lisme* (*syndicated* trade union, SYNDICATE, -ISM)]

syn'dicate, n. (-*ǎt*), & v.t. (-*āt*). **1.** Body of syndics (esp. at Camb.); combination of commercial firms etc. associated to forward some common interest; combination of persons for the acquisition of literary articles etc., and their simultaneous publication in a number of periodicals. **2.** v.t. Form (parties) into ~; deal with (news etc.) by ~. Hence **syndica'TION** n. [vb f. n., f. F *syndicat*, -ISM¹)]

sýne, Sc. for *since* (*auld lang* ~ the days of long ago, esp. as title & refrain of song sung at parting etc.).

syn'od, n. **1.** Ecclesiastical council (*oecumenical or general, national, provincial, diocesan,* ~, attended by bishop(s) &

delegated clergy of all nations, a nation, a province, a diocese); (Presb.) ecclesiastical court above presbyteries & subject to General Assembly; any meeting for debate. **2.** (astron.). Conjunction of planets or stars. So ~AL, synōd'IC(AL), aa., synōd'ICALLY adv. [f. LL f. Gk *sunodos* (SYN-, *hodos* way) meeting]

sýn'onym, n. Word identical & coextensive in sense & usage with another of the same language (as *caecitis*, cf. *typhlitis*); word denoting the same thing(s) as another but suitable to different context (as *deep*, *slay*, cf. *jump*, *kill*) or containing different suggestion (as *blind-worm*, cf. *slow-worm*); word equivalent to another in some only of either's senses (as *ship*, cf. *vessel*). Hence or cogn. **synonym'ITY** n., **synon'ymous** a. (*with*), **synon'ym-ously²** adv. [f. LL f. Gk *sunōnumos* of like sense (SYN-, *onoma* -*dos* name)]

synonym'ic, a. Of or using synonyms. [prec., -IC]

sýnon'ymy, n. Synonymity; collocation of synonyms for emphasis (as *in any shape or form*); system or collection of, treatise on, synonyms. [f. LL f. Gk *sunōnumia* (SYNONYM, -Y)]

synop'sis, n. (pl. -*psēs*). Summary, conspectus. [f. LL f. Gk SYN(*opsis* seeing f. *op*- see)]

synop'tic, a. & n. **1.** Affording a conspectus or general survey (~ *gospels*, those of Matthew, Mark, & Luke); of the ~ gospels (~ *chart* (Meteor.), weather map; hence ~AL a., ~ally² adv. **2.** n. (Also **synop'tist**) writer of a ~ gospel. [f. Gk *sunoptikos* (prec., -IC)]

synovi'tis, n. Inflammation of the membrane that secretes the lubricating fluid in a joint. [f. SYNovia +-ITIS]

syntac'tic, a. & n. **1.** Of, according to, syntax; hence ~ICALLY adv. **2.** n. pl. Branch of mathematics relating to the number of ways of putting things together under conditions. [f. Gk *suntak-tikos* (foll.)]

syn'tax, n. Sentence-construction, the grammatical arrangement of words in speech or writing, set of rules governing this. [F (-*xe*), f. LL f. Gk *suntaxis* f. *tassō* order) marshalling, syntax]

syn'thĕsis, n. (pl. ~*sēs*). Combination, composition, putting together, (opp. *ana-lysis*); building up of separate elements esp. of conceptions or propositions or facts, into a connected whole, esp. a theory or system; (Chem.) artificial production of compounds (called 'synthetic rubber, indigo', etc.) from their constituents as opp. extraction from plants etc.; (Gram.) making of compound & derivative words, preference of composition to inflexion to use of prepositions etc.; (Surg.) joining of divided parts. Hence or cogn. **synthet'IC(AL)** aa., **synthet'ICALLY** adv., **synthet'IZE**, vv.t., ~**tism**(1), ~**tize**, vv.t., ~**tist**(1),

~sist, nn. [L, f. Gk *susthesis* (SYN-, *tithēmi* put); the irreg. ~size more used than the correct ~tize]

sypher'er, v.t. Join (planks) with overlapping edges into flush surface; ~joint, thus made. [var. of CIPHER in obs. sense]

syph'ilis, n. Pox, a contagious venereal disease affecting first some local part (*primary ~is*), secondly the skin & mucous membrane (*secondary ~is*), & thirdly the bones & muscles & brain (*tertiary ~is*). Hence ~it'IC,~OUS,~OID, aa.,~IZE(5) v.t., ~OL'OGY n. [F, f. *Syphilus*, (character in) 16th-c. Latin poem on the subject]

syphon, syren, erron. for si-.

Sy'riac, n. & a. (In) the language of ancient Syria, western Aramaic. Hence ~ISM(4) n. [f. L f. Gk *Suriakos* (*Suria* Syria f, *Suros* a Syrian, -AC)]

Sy'rian, a. & n. (Native) of Syria. [*Suria* -AN]

syring'a (-ngga), n. The mock orange, a shrub with strong-scented white usu. clustered flowers. [SYRINX (w. ref. to use of stems cleared of pith as pipe-sticks). -A]

sy'ringe (-j), n., & v.t. 1. Cylindrical tube with nozzle & piston into which liquid is first drawn by suction & then ejected in fine stream used in surgery, gardening, etc., squirt, (*hypodermic ~*, needle-pointed for hypodermic injections). 2. v.t. Sluice or spray (ears, plants, etc.) with ~. [f. med. L *siringa* f. Gk as foll.]

sy'rinx, n. (pl. -es, -ngēs). Pan-pipe; (Archaeol.) narrow rock-cut gallery in Egyptian tombs; (Anat.) Eustachian tube from throat to drum of ear supplying latter with air, whence **syringī'tis** (-j-) n., lower larynx or song-organ of birds, whence **syrin'gēal** (-j-) a.; (Surg.) fistula, whence **syringot'omy** n. [L, f. Gk *suriṅx* pipe]

Sy'ro-, comb. form f. Gk *Suros* Syrian, as ~arab'ian, ~phoeni'cian. [-O-]

syr'tis (sĕr-), n. (pl. -tēs). Quicksand. [L, f. Gk *surtis* (*surō* draw)]

sy'rup, *si-, n. Water (nearly) saturated with sugar, this combined with flavouring as beverage or with drug(s) as medicine; condensed sugarcane-juice, part of this remaining uncrystallized at various stages of refining, molasses, treacle, (|| *golden ~*, trade name for pale kind). Hence ~y² a. [f. OF *sirop* f. Arab. *sharāb* beverage, cf. SHERBET]

sȳssarcō'sis, n. Connexion between bones by intervening muscle. [f. Gk *sussarkōsis* (SYN-, *sarkoō* f. *sarx sarkos* flesh, -OSIS)]

sȳssit'ia, n. pl. (Gk Ant.). Public messes of Spartans & some other Dorians at which citizens were required to feed with a view to the promotion of patriotism, military efficiency, discipline, & simplicity. [Gk (*su-*) pl. of *sussition* (SYN-, *sitos* food]

systal'tic, a. Contracting & dilating by turns, having systole & diastole, pulsatory. [f. LL f. Gk *sustaltikos* (SY-, *stellō* place, -IO]

sys'tem, n. 1. Complex whole, set of connected things or parts, organized body of material or immaterial things, (*~ of pulleys*, several arranged to work together; *~ of philosophy*, set of co-ordinated doctrines; *mountain ~*, range or connected ranges; *river, railway, ~*, river, railway, with its tributaries or branches, also rivers, railways, of a country, continent, etc.; *solar ~*, sun & planets; *nervous, muscular, etc., ~*, the nerves, muscles, of a person's or animal's body; *digestive* etc. *~*, all bodily parts subserving digestion etc.; *the ~*, the body as a functional whole, as *the poison has passed into the or his ~*; *Ptolemaic* etc. *~*, set of hypotheses or principles composing Ptolemy's etc. theory; *Devonian* etc. *~*, set of strata etc. so named). 2. Method, organization, considered principles of procedure, (principle of) classification, (*~ of government*; *what ~ do you go on ?*; *lacks, works with, ~*; *Linnaean, natural, etc., ~*; classifications with different criteria, whence ~LESS a. 3. (mus.). Braced staffs of score. [f. LL f. Gk *sustēma -atos* (SY-, *histēmi* set, -M]

systemat'ic, a. Methodical, according to a plan, not casual or sporadic or unintentional, (*~ie worker, liar, insolence, nomenclature*). Hence or cogn. ~ICALLY adv., sys'tematIZE(3) v.t., sys'tematISM(1), sys'tematizER(1), sys'tematiz'ATION, nn. [f. LL f. late Gk *sustēmatikos* (prec., -IO]

systēm'ic, a. (physiol.). Of the bodily system as a whole, not confined to a particular part. Hence ~ICALLY adv. [-IC]

sys'tolē, n. (physiol.). Contraction of heart etc. alternate with DIASTOLE. Hence systōl'IC a. [f. Gk *sustolē* (*sustellō*, see SYSTALTIC)]

sys'tyle, a. With columns set comparatively close together. [f. L f. Gk SY(*stulos* STYLE²]

sys'tylous, a. (bot.). With styles united. [as prec., -OUS]

syz'ygy, n. (astron.). Conjunction or opposition. [f. LL f.G k *suzugia* f. *suzeugnumi* (SY-, *zeugnumi* f. *zugon* yoke]

T

T, t, (tē), letter (pl. Ts, T's, T's). T-shaped thing, esp. attrib., as *T-bandage, -bar, -bolt, -joint, -pipe, -SQUARE*; *suits me, hit it off*, etc., *to a T*, exactly, to a nicety; *cross the T's*, (fig.) be minutely accurate, also, emphasize a point.

|| ta (tah), int. (nursery, vulg.). Thank you, as *ta muchly, must say ta*. [?]

taal (tahl), n. The ~, earlier Afrikaans. [Du. = language, cogn. w. TALE]

tāb, n. Small flap, strip, tag, or tongue, as part of or appendage to garment etc., e.g. metallic binding at end of boot-lace, (also *ear-*~) flap at side of cap to protect ear; (Mil.) mark on collar distinguishing staff-officer; (colloq.) account, tally, check (esp. in phr. *keep* ~ (or ~*s*) *on*, keep account of, have under observation or in check). [?]

tăb'ard, n. (Hist.) coarse outer garment worn by the poor, knight's garment worn over armour; herald's coat blazoned with arms of sovereign. [OF, etym. dub.]

tăb'aret, n. Upholstery fabric of alternate watered-silk stripes. [mod. trade wd, perh. f. TABBY]

tăbasheer', -shir (-ēr), n. Kind of opal found in joints of bamboo & used in E. Ind. medicine. [Hind. & Arab. (-ir)]

tăb'by, n., & v.t. 1. Watered fabric esp. silk (often attrib.). 2. (Also ~ *cat*) brindled or mottled or streaked cat, esp. of grey or brownish colour with dark stripes; cat, esp. female. 3. Gossiping woman esp. old maid. 4. (Also ~ *moth*) kind of moth. 5. Kind of concrete. 6. v.t. Give wavy appearance to (fabric). [(vb f. n.) f. F, *tabis* f. Arab. *'attābiy* a quarter of Bagdad, some senses perh. f.*Tabitha*]

tăbefăc'tion, n. Emaciation due to disease. [f. LL *tabefacere* (*tabēre* f. TABES, *facere* f., see -FACTION)]

¶ **tăb'erdăr**, n. Scholar of Queen's College, Oxford. [= *tabarder* (TABARD + -ER), from former dress]

tăb'ernacle, n., & v.t. & i. 1. (Bibl.) fixed or movable habitation usu. of slight construction, (fig.) human body; *Feast of T~es*, Jewish autumn festival commemorating the dwelling of the Jews in wilderness; (Jewish Hist.) tent used as sanctuary before final settlement of Jews in Palestine. 2. (often contempt.), Place of public worship. 3. Receptacle for pyx or eucharistic elements. 4. (archit.), Canopied stall, niche, or pinnacle, ~*e-work*, series, tracery characteristic, of such ~*es*, whence ~ED²(-ld) a. 5. Socket or double post for hinged mast that requires lowering to pass under bridges. 6. vb. (fig.), Provide with shelter; dwell temporarily. So **tăberna'cŭlar²** a. [(vb f. n.) F, f. L *tabernaculum* tent (*taberna* hut, see -CULE)]

tăb'ēs (-z), n. (med.). Emaciation; *dorsal* ~, wasting disease of spinal cord, locomotor ataxia. [L]

tabĕt'ic, a. & n. Of, affected with, ~ tabes. 2. n. ~ patient. So **tabes-CENCE**, **tăb'ĭFORM**, nn., **tabes'CENT**, **tăb'ĭD**, aa., **tăb'ĭDly²** adv. [irreg. f. prec. + -t + -io)]

tăb'ĭnĕt, n. Watered fabric of silk & wool. [as TABARET]

tăb'lature, n. (arch.). Mental picture; graphic description. [F (as see foll. -URE)]

tā'ble, n., & v.t. 1. Article of furniture consisting of flat top of wood or marble etc. & one or more usu. vertical supports esp. one on which meals are laid out, articles of use or ornament kept, work done, or games played; *breakfast, luncheon, dinner, tea, supper,* ~, used for such meals or on which such meal is laid out (*at* ~, while taking meal at ~, as *refused to talk politics at* ~; *under the* ~, esp. drunk after dinner); each half of folding backgammon-~; *billiard-*~ (or billiards, with slate top covered with green cloth); LORD'S, ROUND¹, KNEE¹,-*hole*, DRESSING-, TOILET-, ~. 2. Part of machine-tool on which work is put to be operated on. 3. Slab of wood, stone, etc. 4. Matter written on this, esp. *the two* ~*s* or *the* ~*s of the law or covenant or testimony*, ten commandments, *the twelve* ~*s*, laws promulgated in Rome 451-450 B.C., principal source of Roman jurisprudence. 5. Level area, plateau. 6. (archit.) Flat usu. rectangular surface, horizontal moulding esp. cornice. 7. Flat surface of gem, cut gem with two flat faces. 8. Palm of hand, esp. part indicating character or fortune. 9. Each of two bony layers of skull. 10. Company seated at (dinner- etc.), as *kept the* ~ *amused*. 11. (Quantity & quality of) food provided at ~, as *keeps a good* ~, *expenses of his* ~. 12. List of facts, numbers, etc., systematically arranged esp. in columns, matter contained in this, as *mathematical-*~*s* (of logarithms, trigonometrical ratios, etc.), ~*s of weights & measures, knows his multiplication* ~ *up to 12 times 12,* ~ *of* CONTENT¹s. 13. *Lay, lie, on the* ~, postpone (measure, report, etc., in Parliament etc.), be postponed, indefinitely; *turn the* ~*s* (on person, or abs.), reverse relations (between), esp. pass from inferior to superior position [f. backgammon sense of ~s]. 14. ~-*beer*, ordinary beer used at ~; ~-*book*, ornamental usu. illustrated book kept on ~; ~-*clamp* (for fastening thing to ~); ~-*cloth* (of white linen etc. for use at meals, of coloured material for use at other times); ~-*cut*, (of gem) cut with flat top; ~-*flap*, hinged end of ~-top, lowered when not in use; ~-*knife*, steel knife for use at ~; ~-*land*, extensive elevated region with level surface, plateau; ~-*leaf*, piece that may be inserted in top of ~ to increase its length, also, ~-*flap*; ~-*lifting, -moving, -rapping, -tipping, -turning*, lifting etc. of ~ apparently without physical force, as spiritualistic phenomenon; ~-*linen*, ~-cloths, napkins, etc.; ~-*money*, allowance to higher officers in army etc. for official hospitality, charge to members of club for use of dining-room; ~-*spoon*; ~-*talk*, miscellaneous talk at ~ (often as

title of book); ~ *tennis*, ping-pong; ~ *tomb*, flat-topped chest-like tomb in Roman catacombs; ~*ware* (for use at~); ~*-water*, mineral water bottled for use at ~. Hence ~FUL n. **16.** v.t. Lay (measure etc., as above) on the ~. **16.** v.t. Lay (timbers etc.) together with alternate grooves & projections in each to prevent shifting. **17.** Strengthen (sail) with wide hems. Hence **táb'ling**¹(1, 2) n. [[vb partly f. OF *tabler*) F, f. L *tabula* board, tablet, etc.]

táb'leau (-lō) n. (pl. ~*eaux* pr. -ōz). Picturesque presentation, esp. (also ~ *vivant*, see Ap.; pl. ~*x vivants*; lit. living picture) silent & motionless group of persons etc. arranged to represent a scene; dramatic or effective situation suddenly brought about; (as int., after description of incident) picture the scene!; ~ *curtains* (Theatr.), pair of curtains to draw across & meet in the middle of the stage in place of the usual drop-curtain. [F, = picture, dim. of prec.]

table d'hôte (tahbl-dōt'), n. Common table for guests at hotel; ~ *dinner* etc. (served in hotel etc. at fixed hour & price). [F, = host's table]

táb'let, n. **1.** Thin sheet of ivory, wood, etc., for writing on, esp. each of a set fastened together; (usu. pl.) such set. **2.** Small slab esp. with or for inscription, as *votive* ~. **3.** Small flat piece of prepared substance, esp. fixed weight or measure of a drug brought by pressure or addition of gum into convenient shape. **4.** (Also *tablette*) projecting horizontal coping of wall. [f. OF *tablete* (TABLE, -ETTE)]

táb'lier' (-lyā), n. Woman's small apron or apron-like part of dress. [F]

táb'loid, n. **1.** = TABLET (sense 3; P). **2.** Newspaper that gives its news in concentrated & easily assimilable form; also attrib., as ~ *journalism*. [-OID]

taboō', n., a., & v.t. **1.** (Among Polynesians etc.) system, act, of setting apart person or thing as accursed or sacred; ban, prohibition. **2.** adj. Under a ban, prohibited, consecrated. **3.** v.t. Put (thing, practice, etc.) under ~, exclude or prohibit by authority or social influence, as *the subject was* ~*ed*. [[vb f. n.) f. Polynes. *tapu* a. & n.]

táb'or, n. (hist.). Small drum, esp. one used to accompany pipe. [f. OF *tabour* perh. f. Arab., cf. TAMBOUR]

táb'ouret (-borit), n. Small seat usu. without arms or back. stool; embroidery-frame. [OF, = stool, dim. as prec.]

tabu. Var. of TABOO.

táb'ula, n. (pl. -ae). (Anat.) hard flat surface of bone etc.; ~ *rās'a*, erased tablet, (fig.) human mind at birth viewed as having no innate ideas. [L, = board, table, pl. tablets]

táb'ular, a. Of, arranged in, computed etc. by means of, tables, as *a* ~ *statement*, ~ *values, results, computations, arranged in* ~ *form*, ~ *difference* (between successive logarithms etc. in mathematical tables); ~ broad & flat like a table, as ~ *surface*; (formed) in thin plates, as ~ *structure*. Hence ~LY² adv. [f. L *tabularis* (prec., see -AR¹)]

táb'ulāte, v.t., & a. **1.** Arrange (figures, facts) in tabular form, whence ~A'TION, ~ātor² nn.; give flat surface to. **2.** adj. (-āt). Having flat surface, composed of thin plate. [f. TABULA + -ATE²,³]

tac'amahāc (-unā-), n. Gum resin from some S. Amer. & other trees; the balsam poplar. [Sp. (-ca), f. Aztec *tecomahiyac*]

tăc-au-tăc' (-ō-), n. (fencing). Parry combined with riposte; rapid succession of attacks & parries. [F, imit.]

tǎ'cět, v.i. imperat. Be silent (~ *is Latin for a candle*, veiled injunction = MUM¹). [L]

tǎ'cět, mus. direction indicating silence of voice or instrument. [L, =is silent]

tāch(e), n. (bibl.). A clasp, link. [see TACK]

tachōm'ẽter (-k-), n. Instrument for measuring velocity. So **tachōM'ETRY** n. [f. Gk *takhos* speed + -METER]

tǎchỹcǎrd'ia (-ki-), n. (path.). Abnormally rapid heart-action as a disease. [f. Gk as foll., & see CARDIAC]

tǎchỹg'raphỹ (-k-), n. Stenography, esp. that of ancient Greeks & Romans. Hence ~ER¹ n., **tǎchỹgrǎph'ic**(AL) aa. [f. Gk *takhus* swift + -GRAPHY]

tǎch'ỹlỹte (-k-), n. A vitreous form of basalt. Hence ~**lỹt'ic** a. [as prec. + -*lutos* f. *luō* loose, from ready fusion under blowpipe]

tǎchỹm'ẽter (-k-), n. Surveyor's instrument for rapid location of points. [as prec. + -METER]

tǎ'cit, a. Understood, implied, existing, without being stated, as ~ *consent, agreement, understanding*; ~ *abstaining from speech or action* (~ *spectator*). Hence ~LY¹ adv. [f. L *tacitus* silent (*tacēre* be silent)]

tǎ'citūrn, a. Reserved in speech, not given to much speaking. So **tacitūrn²-ITY** n. [f. L *taciturnus* as prec.]

tǎck, n., & v.t. & i. **1.** Small sharp flatheaded nail of iron, copper, etc., for securing carpet etc. (*tin-*~, *iron* ~ coated with tin; BRASS ~s). **2.** pl. Long stitches as temporary fastening in needlework. **3.**(naut.). Rope for securing corner of some sails, corner to which this is fastened; direction in which vessel moves as determined by position of sails (*port, starboard*, ~, with wind on port, starboard, side); temporary change of direction in sailing to take advantage of side wind etc., esp. each of several alternate movements to port & starboard (~ *&* ~, *by successive* ~s). **4.** (fig.). Course of action or policy, as *must change our* ~, *am on the right or wrong* ~, *try another* ~. **5.** =foll.

(parl. sense). **6.** Sticky condition of varnish etc., whence ∼INESS n. ∼′Y² a. **7.** [prob. diff. wd.]. Food, fare, esp. HARD ∼; *soft* ∼; bread, good fare. **8.** ∼*driver*, machine that automatically places & drives ∼s; ∼*hammer*, light hammer for shifting ∼s, usu. with claw for extracting ∼s. **9.** vb. Fasten (carpet etc., often *down*) with ∼s, stitch (pieces or parts of cloth etc.) lightly together; (fig.) annex, append, (thing *to* or *on to* another, *on*, as in foll.). **10.** Change ship's course (often *about*) by shifting ∼s & sails (cf. WEAR³); (fig.) change one's conduct, policy, etc. Hence ∼ER¹(1, 2) n. [vb f. n.; n. f. AN.-F. TACHE, & G *zacken* prong; Du. *tak* twig]

tacking, n. In vbl senses, esp.: (Law) priority of a third or subsequent mortgage etc. to a second of which notice was not given; ‖(Parl.) appending of an extraneous clause to a money bill to secure its passing House of Lords, which cannot amend money bills. [-ING¹]

tac′kle, n., & v.t. & i. **1.** Mechanism esp. of ropes, pulley-blocks, hooks, etc., for lifting weights, managing sails or spars, etc. (*naut. pr.* tā′kl); windlass with its ropes & hooks; requisites for a task or sport, as *fishing-*∼; grasping or holding or obstructing esp. of opponent in football; ∼*-block*, pulley over which rope runs; ∼*-fall*, rope connecting blocks of a ∼. **2.** vb. Grapple with, grasp with endeavour to hold or manage or overcome, (opponent, awkward thing or business, problem); running with ball); secure by means of ∼. (Footb.) obstruct or seize & stop (player ∼*s* (colloq.), fall to work vigorously, set to. Hence **tack′ling**¹(1, 3, 6) n. [vb f. n.] ME & LG *takel* f. MLG *taken* lay hold of, cogn. n. TAKE]

tact, n. Intuitive perception of what is fitting esp. of the right thing to do or say, adroitness in dealing with persons or circumstances, whence ∼′FUL, ∼′LESS, aa. ∼*fully*² adv., ∼′lessness n. [f. L *tactus* -*ūs* (sense of) touch (*tangere tact-* touch)]

tac′tical, a. Of tactics; (of bombing) carried out in immediate support of military or naval operations; adroitly planning or planned. Hence ∼*ly*² adv. [f. Gk *taktikos* (foll.)+-AL]

tac′tics, n. (As sing. or pl.) art of disposing military or naval forces esp. (cf. STRATEGY, LOGISTICS) in actual contact with enemy; (pl.) procedure calculated to gain some end, skilful device(s), as *cannot approve these* ∼; so occas. in sing. form **tac′tic** n. Hence **tactic′ian** (-ĭshn) n. [f. Gk *taktika* neut. pl. (*tassō* arrange, see -IC)]

tac′tile, a. Of, perceived by, connected with, the sense of touch, as ∼ *impression*, ∼ *organ*, so **tac′tual** a., **tac′tually**¹ adv.; tangible; (Paint.) producing or having to do with the effect of solidity (∼ *values*

etc.). Hence **tactil′ity** n. [f. L *tactĭlis* (*tangere tact-* touch, see -ILE)]

tad′pole, n. Larva of batrachian, e.g. frog, from time it leaves egg till loss of gills & tail; ∼*-fish*, European fish with large flat head. [ME *tadpolle* (TOAD +POLL¹, f. size of head)]

tae′dium vit′ae, n.(path.). Weariness of life with tendency to suicide. [L]

tael (tāl), n. Chinese ounce (=1⅓ oz avoirdupois) esp. of silver as former monetary unit. [Port., f. Malay *tahil* weight]

taen′ia, n. (pl.-*ae*). (Arch.), fillet on top part esp. of brain; roller bandage; tapeworm; (Gk & Rom. Ant.) fillet, headband. Hence ∼OID a. [L, f. Gk *tainia*]

taff′eta, n. Kinds of silk or linen fabric esp. thin glossy silk of plain texture. [f. F *taffetas* f. Pers. *tāftah* (*tāftan* twist)]

taff′rail, **taff′erel** (-ĭrl), n. Rail round stern of vessel; (*-erel*) upper part of stern. [f. Du. *tafereel* dim. of *tafel* f. L as TABLE, assim. to RAIL¹]

Taff′y¹, n. (colloq.). Welshman. [W pron. of *Davy* = *David*]

taff′y,² See TOFFEE.

tafi′a, n. (W. Ind.). Kind of rum distilled from molasses etc. [native]

tag, n., & v.t. & i. (-GG-). **1.** Metal point at end of lace. **2.** Loop at back of boot used in pulling it on. **3.** Address label, esp. one for tying on. **4.** Loose or ragged end of anything; ragged lock of wool on sheep. **5.** Appendage; (Theatr.) closing speech addressed to audience; trite quotation, stock phrase, refrain of song. **6.** (Tip of) animal's tail. **7.** [perh. diff. wd]. Children's game in which one chases the rest (*cross-*, *long-*, etc.), ∼, forms of this). **8.** ∼*-rag*, = RAG¹. ∼*-sore*, pustular disease of sheep; ∼*tail*, kind of worm, sycophant. **9.** vb. Furnish (lace etc., literary composition) with a ∼. **10.** Join (thing, esp. piece of writing, *to* or *on to* another, things *together*), find rhymes for (verses), string (rhymes) together. **11.** Shear away ∼s from (sheep). **12.** (colloq.). Follow closely or persistently. **13.** Touch (person pursued) in game of ∼. [vb f. n.: f. 14th c., etym. dub.]

tag′etes (-jētēz), n. Kinds of plant of aster family with showy yellow or orange flowers. [f. L *Tages*, Etruscan divinity]

tag′ger (-g-), n. In vbl senses; also or esp.: pursuer (also called *it*) in game of tag; (pl.) thin sheet iron, whether coated with tin or (*black-*∼s) not. [-ER¹]

tahsil′ (-ĕl), n. Territorial subdivision in India for revenue purposes. Hence ∼*dar′* n., native collector of revenue in ∼. [Hind. & Arab., = collection; Pers. *dār* holder]

taiga (tī′gah), n. Coniferous forest between tundra & steppe. [Russ.]

tail¹, n., & v.t. & i. **1.** Hindmost part of animal esp. when prolonged beyond rest

of body, as dog WAG¹s his ~, tail WAG¹s dog, dog has his ~ between his legs (as sign of alarm or dejection; often fig. of person); ~s up (in good spirits; turn ~, turn one's back, run away; twist the LION's ~, drop pinch of SALT on ~ of, PASHA of three etc. ~s. **2.** Thing like or suggesting ~ in shape or position, hind or lower or subordinate or inferior part, slender part or prolongation, as ~ (luminous train) of comet, ~ (outer corner) of the eye, ~ (end) of procession etc., ~ (weaker members) of the XI (or other sports team), ~ margin (at foot of page), followed by a ~ (long train of attendants, at the ~ (back) of a cart, ~ (string & paper appendage at lower end) of a kite, cow's~, frayed end of rope etc., ~ (= STEM¹) of musical note, ~ (part below line) of a g etc., ~ (exposed end) of slate or tile in roof, ~ (unexposed end) of brick or stone in wall, ~ (slender backward prolongation) of butterfly's wing, ~ (comparative calm at end) of a gale, ~ (calm stretch following rough water) of a stream, ~ of the trenches (Fortif.), part first made by advancing party, make HEAD¹ or ~ of, PIGTAIL. **3.** pl. = ~coat, as boys go into ~s at sixteen. **4.** (In tossing) ~ or usu. ~s, reverse of coin turned upwards (see HEAD). **5.** ~bay, part of canal lock between ~gate & lower pond; ~board, hinged or removable back of cart; ~braid (for protecting hem of skirt); ~coat, man's morning or evening coat with long skirt divided at back into ~s & cut away in front; ~gate, lower gate of canal lock; ~light (carried at back of train, car. cycle, etc.); ~piece, decoration in blank space at end of chapter etc., triangular piece of wood to which lower ends of strings are fastened in some musical instruments; ~pipe, suction-pipe of pump, (v.t.) fasten something to ~ of (dog, fig. person); ~race, part of mill-race below water-wheel; ~spin (Aviation), kind of spinning dive. Hence (-)~ED²(-ld), ~²LESS, aa. **6.** v.b. Furnish with ~, **7.** (colloq.). Remove the ends of (fruit). **8.** Join (thing on to another). **9.** ~ after, follow closely; ~ away or off, (of persons, dogs, etc.) fall behind or away in scattered line; ~ in, fasten (timber) by one end into wall etc..; ~ to the tide, ~ up and down stream, (of anchored vessel) swing up & down with tide. [(vb f.n.) OE tæg(e)l, cf. ON tagl, Sw. tagel, dial. G zagel]

tail², n. & a. (law). **1.** Limited ownership (in~, on those terms); estate limited to a person & heirs of his body. **2.** adj. So limited, esp. estate ~, FEE~~. [f. OF taille notch, cut, tax, f. taillier cut f. LL taliare (L talea slip of wood)]

tail'ing, n. In vb¹ senses of TAIL¹: also or esp.: unexposed end of brick or stone or beam in wall; (pl.) refuse or inferior part of grain, ore, etc.; blur or other fault in calico-printing. [-ING¹]

tail'or, n., & v.i. & t. **1.** Maker of (esp men's garments esp. to order (the~makes the man; nine~s go to a man; ride like a~ badly); ~bird, kinds of small bird sewing leaves together to form nest; ~made. (esp. of woman's dress) made by ~ usu. w. little ornament & w. special attention to exact fit; ~'s chair (without legs), for sitting cross-legged as ~ at work; ~'s cramp (in fingers & thumbs); ~'s twist, kind of strong silk thread. Hence ~ESS¹ n. **2.** vb. Be, work as, a~, whence ~ING¹ n.; make clothes for (chiefly in p.p., as well~ed); (sl.) kill (bird) badly. [f. OF tailⁱour f. LL talidorem (talidre TAIL², -OR²)]

tain, n. Thin tin plate; tin foil for backing mirror. [F, = étain tin]

taint, n., & v.t. & i. **1.** Spot, trace, of decay or corruption or disease (lit. & fig.), corrupt condition, infection, as there was a ~ of insanity in the family, the moral ~ had spread among all classes, without ~ of commercialism. **2.** vb. Introduce corruption or disease into, infect, be infected, as ~ed meat, ~s all it touches, meat will ~ readily in hot weather, his mind was ~ed; ~ed goods (in trade-unionism), goods that members of a union must not handle because non-union labour has been employed on them or for similar reasons. Hence ~LESS a., ~²lĕssly² adv. [f. F teint n. & p.p. of teindre TINGE; partly also aphetic f. ATTAINT]

Tai'ping', **Tae~**, (ti-), n. One of those who took part in a rebellion in China (1850–64). [f. Chin. t'ai p'ing great peace]

taj (tahj), n. Tall cap of Mohammedan dervish. [Pers. f. Arab.]

take', v.t. & i. (took, ~n), **I. General senses. 1.** Lay hold of with the hand(s) or other part of the body or with any instrument (lit. & fig.), grasp, seize, capture, catch by pursuit or surprise, captivate, win, gain, as ~ it between your finger & thumb, took him by the throat, ~ it up with the tongs, ~ the BULL¹ by the horns, deuce ~ it!, ~ BIT¹ between teeth, ~ a fortress, ~ by STORM, took 113 prisoners, was ~n prisoner or captive, took his bishop (at chess), ~ the odd trick (at cards); ~s (gains, receives in payment) £40 a week, took (gained) little by this move, took first prize, ~ the CAKE or biscuit (sl.), rabbit ~n in trap, took (surprised, caught) him in the act or at a disadvantage, was ~n ill or colloq. bad. ~n aback, what ~s (captivates) my fancy, was much ~n (charmed) with or by her manners, novel did not ~ (become popular), vaccine did not ~ (operate). **2.** Assume possession of, procure e.g. by purchase, acquire, avail oneself of, use, use up, consume, require as instrument, material, agent, etc., as ~s whatever he can lay his hand on, wish you would not ~ my bicycle.

~ (assume or enjoy as one's right); *prece-dence*, took his degree, ~ ORDER-s, ||~ SILK, *shall* ~ *a holiday*, (cooking direction) *I ox of curry-powder*, *do you* ~ (buy regu-larly, subscribe to) *Punch ?*, *am not taking any* (sl.), *decline offer*, ~ (engaged) *seats in advance*, *must* ~ *lessons*, *lodgings*, *a cab*, *will* ~ (buy) *2 lb.*, ~ *legal*, *medical*, *etc.*, *advice*, *consult lawyer etc.* (& see *below*), ~ (as *instance*) *the French Revolu-tion*, *has* ~ *a partner*, *a wife*, (arch.) *took to* (as) *wife*, *Jane Smith*, ~ *a* BACK! *seat*, *took his seat on the bench*, must ~ the *liberty of differing from you*, *must* ~ *leave to differ*, *took a mean advantage*, *do not* ~ *advantage* (avail yourself unfairly) *of his youth*, ~ *the opportunity*, *will* ~ (drink) *a cup of tea*, ~*s too much alcohol*, *these things* ~ *time*, ~ *your time*, *do not hurry*, *it* ~*s a lot of doing* (is hard to do), ~*s a poet to translate Virgil*, *transitive verbs* ~ *an object*. **3**. Cause to come with one, carry with one, conduct, convey, remove, conduct, convey, remove, dispossess person etc. of, as ~ *the letters to the post*, *the dog for a walk*, *the children to the pantomime*, *the corkscrew from the shelf*, ~ *for a* RIDE, ~*s his readers with him* (engrosses their attention), ~ *him through* (make him read) *a book of Livy*, *took him into partnership*, ~*s all the fun out of it*, ~ *to* TASK, ~ *in hand*, undertake, start doing or dealing with, undertake the control or reform of (*the boy wants taking in hand*). (see also special uses w. adv. & prep.). **4**. Catch, be infected with, (cold, fever, etc.). **5**. Conceive, experience, indulge, give play to, exert, as ~ *offence*, *umbrage*, *a fancy to*, ~ *a pride in his work*, *a pleasure in contradicting*, ~ *pity on him*, ~ *no notice*, ~ *heed*, *pains*, *trouble*. **6**. As-certain (person's measure, height, tem-perature, address, etc.) by inquiry, measurement, etc. **7**. Apprehend, grasp mentally, infer, conclude, understand, interpret, as *I* ~ *your meaning* or (arch.) *you*, *I* ~ *this to be ironical*, *I* ~*it that we are to wait here*, ~ *person at his* WORD!, *how would you* ~ (translate, interpret) *this passage ?*, ~ *it for granted*, assume it, *do you* ~ *me for* (think me) *a fool ?* **8**. Treat or regard in specified manner, adopt specified attitude towards, as ~ *things coolly*, ~ *it easily*, *should* ~ *it kindly if you* (be obliged) *if you would answer my letter*, *must not* ~ *it ill of him* (resent his conduct), ~ *to* HEART, ~ *as read*, dispense with the actual reading of (minutes etc.). **9**. Accept, put up with, submit to, adopt, choose, receive, derive, as ~ *the offer*, ~ *what you can get*, *the bet was* ~*n*, ~*a & offered betting odds*), *I took him* (his bet), *must* ~ *us as you find us*, *will* ~ *no nonsense*, ~ *a hint*, ~ *advice*, *act on it like a lamb*, *will not* ~ *this treatment*, *took it like a lamb*, (& see *above*), *you may* ~ *it from me or* ~ *my word for it*, I, I, a well-informed person,

assure you, ~ *sides*, join one of two parties, ~ (hold, adopt) *a different view*, ~*s its name from the inventor*. **10**. Perform, execute, make, undertake, negotiate, deal with, as *took work for a friend*, ~ *notes*, *a photograph*, *took a sudden leap*, *horse will not* ~ *fence*, ||~ (be ex-amined in) *the mathematical tripos*, ~ (conduct) *the evening service*, ~ *a glance round*, *took a deep breath*, ~ *an oath*, ~ *account of*, include, *does not* ~ *well*. **12**. ~ *account of*, include, direct weapon or missile (*at* object); ~ *earth*, (of fox etc., fig. of person) escape into hole; ~ EFFECT!, EXCEPTION, HEART (of *grace*), HOLD[2], ~ *it* (colloq.), endure punishment etc.; ~ LEAVE[1] (of); ~ *one's life in one's hand*, risk it; ~ *person's* esp. *God's name in vain*, use it lightly or pro-fanely; ~ PART!; ~ *place*, happen; ~ STOCK (of, in); ~ *the* WALL, ~ WIND!. **11**. Spec. uses w. prep., adv., & adv. phr. **1**. ~ *after*, resemble (person, esp. parent or relation) in character, feature, etc. **2**. ~ *back* (colloq.), retract (words). **3**. ~ *down*, write down; ~ *down* (lower) *one's* esp. ~ *person down a peg* or *two*; swallow (food etc.) esp. with difficulty or relu-tance; remove (building, structure) by tak-ing it to pieces. **4**. ~ *from*, diminish, lessen, weaken, as *such faults do not* ~ *from his credit as a historian*. **5**. ~ *in*: admit, receive, (lodgers, guest, etc.); ~ (lady) *in* (often to dinner), conduct from drawing-room to dining-room & sit beside; receive (washing, sewing, typewriting, etc.) to be done at home; include, comprise; re-duce (garment etc.) to smaller compass, furl (sail); understand, digest mentally; believe (false statement); deceive; cheat; || ~ (newspaper etc.) by subscription; ~ *in*, a fraud, deception, piece of humbug. **6**. ~ *into*: ~ *into one's con-fidence*, confide in; ~ *into one's head*, conceive, get hold of, (idea), imagine, adopt the belief, (*that*, *it...that*), resolve (*to do*). **7**. ~ *off*: remove (clothes, hat, etc.) from the body (~ *off one's hat to*, fig., applaud as admirable); remove, conduct away, as *took him off to the station*, *took himself off*, went off; deduct (part of price); drink off; ridicule by imitation, mimic; jump, spring, (*from*, *at*, place); (Aviation) start from rest & become air-borne; ~*off* n., caricature, spot from which one jumps, (Aviation) becoming airborne, (Croquet) stroke causing one's

own ball to go forward while touching but scarcely moving another. **8.** ~ *on* : undertake (work, responsibility); ~ *person on at golf* etc., play with him; (colloq.) show violent emotion, make a fuss. **9.** ~ *out* : cause to come out, bring or convey out, as ~ *him out for a walk, books must not be ~n out of the library*; remove (stain etc.); (Bridge) remove (one's partner from the suit he has called by bidding a fresh suit or no trumps; ~ *the nonsense* etc. *out of* person, cure him of it; accept payment of (debt etc.) or compensation for (injury etc.) *in*, as *took it out in cigars & drinks*; ~ *it out of*, have revenge on, get satisfaction from, exhaust the strength of; procure, get issued, (patent, summons, etc.). **10.** ~ *over*, succeed to management or ownership of (business etc.). **11.** ~ *to*: begin, fall into the habit of, begin to busy oneself with, as *took to humming a tune*, ~ *to bad habits, literature*; conceive a liking for (person etc.). **12.** ~ *up*: lift up; absorb, occupy, engage, as *sponges* ~ *up water*, ~*s up all my time, my attention*; *train stops to* ~ *up* (admit) *passengers*: ~ into custody; adopt as protégé; interrupt or correct (speaker); enter upon (profession, subject); pursue (matter, inquiry) further; secure, fasten, (dropped stitch, artery, etc.); furnish the amount of (loan etc.); ~ *up with*, consort with; ~ *up the* CUDGELS, GAUNTLET, GLOVE; ~*up* n. (Mech.), kinds of device for tightening band etc. in machine, drawing up slack of thread, removing material that has been operated on, etc. **13.** ~ (*it*) *upon* or *on one to*, venture, presume, to. [late OE *tacan* f. ON *taka*, cf. Sw. *taga*, Da. *tage*, cogn. w. TACKLE]

tāke², n. Amount (of fish, game, etc.) taken or caught; (Print.) amount of copy set up at one time; takings, esp. money received at theatre for seats; (Cinemat.) a scene that has been or is to be photographed; GIVE² & ~. [f. prec.]

tāk'er, n. In vbl senses, esp. one who takes a bet, as *no* ~*s, a few* ~*s at 5 to 4.* [-ER¹]

ta'kin (tah-), n. Tibetan horned ruminant. [native]

tāk'ing¹, n. In vbl senses, esp.; (pl.) money taken in business, receipts; (arch.) state of agitation, as *was in a great* ~. [-ING¹]

tāk'ing², a. Attractive, captivating; catching, infectious. Hence ~LY² adv., ~NESS n. [-ING²]

tāl'apoin, n. **1.** Buddhist monk in Ceylon, Siam, etc. **2.** Kind of monkey. [f. Port. *talapão*, of E.-Ind. orig.]

tal'botype (tawl-), n. Photographic process invented by W. H. Fox Talbot in 1840, the basis of that now used. [TYPE]

tālc, n., & v.t. 1. A magnesium silicate usu. found in flat smooth often transparent plates & used as lubricator etc.; (pop. commerc.) mica esp. as glazing-material. Hence tāl(c)k'Y², ~OID, ~OSE¹, ~OUS, aa. [F, f. Arab. *talq*]

tāl'cite, n. A massive variety of talc. [-ITE¹]

tāl'cum, n. = TALC; ~ *powder*, powdered talc for toilet use, usu. perfumed. [med. L]

tāle, n. **1.** True or usu. fictitious narrative esp. one imaginatively treated, story, as *tell him a* ~, *a true* ~ *of the Crusades, old wives'* ~*s, marvellous legendary* ~*s*; ~ *of a tub*, idle fiction; *prefer to tell my own* ~ (give my own account of the matter); *thing tells its own* ~ (is significant, requires no comment, explains itself). **2.** Malicious report whether true or false, as *all sorts of* ~*s will get about, if all* ~*s be true* (esp. as preface to scandal); *tell* ~*s (out of school)*, report esp. with malicious intention what is meant to be secret; ~*bearer*, person who does this, so ~*bearing* a. & n.; ~*teller*, one who tells ~*s* (in either sense). **3.** ‖ (arch., rhet., poet.), Number, total, as *the* ~ *is complete, shepherd tells his* ~ (of sheep). [OE *talu* narrative, cf. Du. TAAL, ON *tala* talk, tale, number, G. *zahl* number, cogn. w. TELL]

tāl'ent, n. **1.** Special aptitude, faculty, gift, (for music etc., *for doing*; see *Matt.* xxv. 14–30), high mental ability, whence ~ED², ~LESS, aa. **2.** Persons of ~, as *all the* ~ *of the country, looking out for local* ~; (Sport. sl.) *the* ~, those who take odds etc. relying on their own judgement. **3.** Ancient weight & money of account among Greeks, Romans, Assyrians, etc., of varying value, as *Attic* ~ (about £243. 15s.). **4.** ~*money*, bonus to professional cricketer etc. for especially good performance. [f. L *talentum* f. Gk *talanton* balance, ~(weight, money), cogn. w. *talas* adj. enduring, *tla-* endure, sustain]

tāl'es (-z), n. (law), Writ for summoning jurors, list of persons who may be so summoned, to supply deficiency; *pray a* ~*man* (or -lz-), person so summoned. [L ~ (*de circumstantibus*) such (of the bystanders), first wds of writ]

Tāliacō'tian (-shn), a. ~ *operation*, formation of new nose by means of flap taken from arm or forehead but severed only after union has taken place. [f. *Tagliacozzi*, Italian surgeon d. 1599 + AN]

tāl'ion, n. (Also L *lex tāltōn'is*) the law of retaliation inflicting punishment of same kind & degree as injury (see *Lev.* xxiv. 20). Hence **tāliōn'ic** a. [F, f. L *talio -onis* (*talis* such)]

tāl'iped, a. & n. **1.** Club-footed; (Zool., of sloth etc.) having feet twisted into unusual position. **2.** n. ~ person or animal. [as foll.]

tāl'ipēs (-z), n. Club-foot(edness); taliped formation. [mod. L(TALUS, pes pedis foot)]

tāl'ipŏt, -ūt, n. A fan-leafed palm. [f. Hind. tālpāt f. Skr. tālapatra (tāla palm + patra leaf)]

tăl'isman (-z-), n. Charm, amulet, thing capable of working wonders; (Astrol.) magical figure cut or engraved & capable of benefiting its possessor. Hence **tālis-mān'ic** (-z-) a. [f. Arab. tilsam f. late Gk telesma rite (Gk teléō pay f. telos end, initiation. -M]

talk (tawk), v.i. & t., & n. 1. Converse, communicate ideas, by spoken words, as ~ing with or to a friend, what are you ~ing about?, now you're ~ing (sl. =I welcome that offer etc.), you can't ~ (colloq. =you are just as bad yourself); communi-cate by wireless signals. 2. Have the power of speech, as child is learning to ~, parrots can ~; use this to excess, as is always ~ing. 3. Express, utter, discuss in words, as you are ~ing nonsense, ~ treason, philo-sophy, SHOP; ~(cold) turkey (colloq.), tell the plain truth. 4. Use (language), as ~ French, ~'s nothing but English. 5. Bring into specified condition etc. by ~ing, as ~ himself hoarse, ~ person round, persuade him, ~ed him out of his resolu-tion, into his grave, would ~ a horse's hind leg off, is talkative. 6. ~about, discuss, as do not want to be ~ed about (made sub-ject of gossip); ~at, address to one of a company remarks covertly hostile to & meant to be heard by (another); ~away, consume (time) in ~ing; ~back, reply defiantly; ~down, silence (person) by superior loudness or persistency; ~of, discuss, mention, as ~ing of muffins, what time do you have tea?, express some intention of (doing); ||~out (bill, motion, in Parl.), get rid of it by prolonging discussion till time of adjournment; ~over, discuss at some length, win over by ~ing; ~round, discuss (subject) at length without reaching conclusion; ~through one's hat (sl.), exaggerate or bluff or make wild statements; ~to, speak to, (colloq.) re-prove, give a piece of one's mind to, so gave him a ~ing-to; ~up, discuss (sub-ject) in order to rouse interest in it. 7. n. Conversa-tion, as let us have a ~, SMALL ~, it will end in ~ (nothing will be done); short address or lecture in conversational style (esp. when broadcast by wireless); theme of gossip, as they, their quarrels, are the ~ of the town. [(n. f. vb) ME talken (OE tal-as in TALE + frequent. -k)]

Hence **ta'lkative** (tawk-), a. Fond of ~, ~NESS n. [-ATIVE]

ta'lkee-ta'lkee (tawki), n. Incessant chat-ter; broken English of Negroes etc. [TALK]

ta'lkies (tawkiz), n. pl. (sl.) = SOUND². films. [f. TALK, after MOVIES]

ta'lking (tawk-), a. In vbl senses, having the power of speech, as ~eyes.; expressive, as ~eyes.

tall (tawl), a. & adv. 1. (Of person) of more than average height; (of tree, steeple, mast, etc.) higher than the average or than surrounding objects; of specified height, as he is six feet ~ (new chest of drawers 5 ft or more high some-times in lower & upper sections or mounted on legs or on dressing-table, kind of chimney-pot; (sl.) extravagant, boastful, excessive, as a ~story, ~talk, a ~order (exorbitant or unreasonable demand). 2. adv. (sl.) In a ~way, as talk ~, boast. Hence ~NESS n. [prob. f. OE getæl quick, prompt, cf. OHG gizal quick]

tall'(i)age, n. (hist.) Form of taxation abolished in 14th c. [ME & OF taillage (tailler cut, see TAIL² & -AGE)]

tall'ith, n. Scarf worn by Jews esp. at prayer. [Heb.]

tall'ow (-ō), n. & v.t. 1. Substance got by melting the harder & less fusible kinds of (esp. animal) fat, used for making candles & soap, greasing machinery, etc.; ~vegetable ~, kinds of vegetable fat similarly used; ~-chandler, maker, vendor, of ~candles, so ~ER¹(-ōer) n.; ~-drop, style of cutting precious stones with dome on one or both sides; ~-face, pale person; ~-tree, kinds of tree yielding vegetable ~. Hence ~ISH¹, ~Y²(-ōi), aa. 2. v.t. Grease with ~; fatten (sheep). [(vb f. n.) ME talgh, cf. G, Da., Sw. talg]

tall'y, n. & v.t. & i. 1. Piece of wood scored across with notches for the items of an account & then split into halves of which each party kept one; account so kept, score, reckoning; mark made to register a fixed number of objects deli-vered or received, such number used as unit, as buy goods by the ~ (dozen, hun-dred, etc.); (in counting goods aloud as delivered) 16, 18, ~ (20), 96, 98, ~ (100); ticket, label of wood or metal or paper with name etc. attached to thing for identification, as horticultural tallies, pliant labels; corresponding thing, coun-terpart, duplicate, (of). 2. ||~man, one who keeps a ~ or ~-shop, one who sells goods by sample; ~-sheet, paper on which ~ is kept; ||~system, trade (of sales on short credit with account kept by ~). 3. vb. Record, reckon, by ~; (Naut.) haul(sheet) taut; agree, correspond, (with), as goods do not ~ with invoice. Hence **tall'IER¹** n. [(vb f. n.) AF taille f. L talea, see TAIL²]

tall'y-hō', int., n., & v.t. & i. 1. Hunts-man's cry to hounds on viewing fox. 2. vb. Utter, urge (hounds) with, this.

tal'ma, n. Woman's or man's long cape or cloak in first half of 19th c. [F. J. T~, French tragedian]

tăl'mi-gŏld, n. Brass thinly coated with gold. [G, etym. dub.]

Tăl'mud, n. Body of Jewish law & legend comprising the Mishnah (precepts of the elders codified c. 200 A.D.) & the Gemara (commentary on the Mishnah in recensions at Jerusalem c. 400 & at Babylon c. 500), (also, in limited sense) the Babylonian Gemara. Hence **Talmŭd′Ic(ăl)**, aa. [late Heb., = instruction (*lāmad* teach)]

Tăl′mudist, n. Compiler, adherent, or (now usu.) student, of the Talmud. Hence ~**ĭs′tic** a. [-IST]

tăl′on, n. 1. Claw esp. of bird of prey. 2. Cards left after deal. 3. Shoulder of bolt against which key presses in shooting it; ogee moulding; heel of sword-blade. Hence (-)~**ED³**(-nd) a. [OF, = heel, f. LL *talo* -*ōnis* ankle f. L *talus* heel]

taluk′ (-ōōk), -**ook**, n. District in India subject to revenue collection by native officer; tract of proprietary land in India; ~*dar*, such officer, proprietor of ~. [Hind. (-*uk*)]

tăl′us, n. (pl. -*lī*). 1. (Anat.) ankle(-bone) form of club-foot. 2. Slope of wall that tapers to the top or rests against bank; (Geol.) sloping mass of fragments at foot of cliff. [L, = ankle, heel (in sense *slope*, thr. OF *talu*)]

tamăn′dŭa, tăm′anoir(-wär), nn. Kinds of ant-eater. [(-*ua*) Braz., (-*oir*) F corrupt.]

tăm′arăck, n. Kinds of Amer. tree, esp. = HACKMATACK. [Amer.-Ind.]

tăm′arin, n. Kinds of S.-Amer. marmoset. [native]

tăm′arind, n. (Tropical tree with) fruit whose pulp is used in making cooling drinks etc.; ~*fish*, preparation of fish with ~ pulp. [ult. f. Arab. *tamr* ripe date + *Hind* India]

tăm′arisk, n. Kind of plant, esp. *common* or *French* ~, evergreen shrub with feathery branches & white or pink flowers suitable for planting near sea. [f. LL *tamariscus*, etym. dub.]

tama′sha (-mah-), n. (Anglo-Ind.). A show or entertainment or function. [Arab.]

tăm′bour(-oor), n., & v.t. 1. Drum, esp. bass drum; circular frame on which silk etc. is stretched to be embroidered, stuff so embroidered; (Archit.) cylindrical stone in shaft of column, circular part of various structures, ceiled lobby with folding doors in church porch etc. to obviate draught; kinds of fish making drumming noise or like drum in shape; (Fortif.) palisaded defence for road, gate, etc. 2. v.t. Decorate, embroider, (stuff or abs.) on ~. [(vb f. n.) F, f. Arab. *tambūr* lute, drum]

tăm′bourin(-bor-), n. Long narrow drum used in Provence; (music for) dance accompanied by this. [F, dim. of prec.]

tămbourine′ (-borēn), n. 1. Small drum made of wooden or metal hoop with parchment stretched over one end & loose jingling metal disks. 2. Kind of African pigeon. [prob. f. prec.]

tāme, v.t., & a. 1. Make gentle & tractable, domesticate, break in, (wild beast, bird, etc.); subdue, curb, reduce to submission, humble, (person, spirit, courage, ardour, etc.). Hence **tāma-BIL′ITY**, **tăm′ablENESS**, (-)**tāmer**¹, nn., **tăm′ABLE**, ~**LESS** (-ml-: poet.), aa. 2. adj. Made tractable, domesticated, not wild, (~ *cat*, fig., person tolerated as useful hanger-on); (colloq., of land or plant) produced by cultivation; submissive, spiritless, inert, feeble, flat, insipid, as the ~*st of slaves*, ~*acquiescence*, *scenery*, *description*. Hence ~**LY** (-ml-) adv., ~**NESS** (-mn-) n. [OE *temian* vb, *tam* a., cf. Du. *tam*, G *zahm*, cogn. w. L *domare*, Gk *damaō*]

Tăm′Il, n. Language, member, of a race inhabiting S. India & Ceylon. Hence **Tamil′IAN** a. [native]

Tămm′any, n. Central organization of democratic party in ~ *Hall*, New York (often implying political corruption). Hence ~**ISM** n.

tăm-o′-shăn′ter, tăm′m′y, n. Round woollen or cloth cap fitting closely round brows but large & full above. [f. Burns's *Tam o' Shanter*]

tămp, v.t. Pack (blast-hole) full of clay etc. to get full force of explosion, whence ~**′ING**¹(3) n.; ram down (road material etc.). Hence ~**ER**¹ n. [var. of TEMPER]

tăm′pion, n. Wooden stopper for muzzle of gun; plug e.g. for top of organ-pipe. [f. F as foll.]

tăm′pon, n., & v.t. 1. Plug used to stop haemorrhage; pad for the hair. 2. v.t. Plug (wound etc.) with ~. [(vb f. n.) F, var. of *tapon* (*tape* bung, -OON)]

tămponāde′, n. Use of tampon for wound etc. So **tăm′ponAGE, tăm′ponMENT**, nn. [-ADE]

tamtam. See TOMTOM.

tăn¹, v.t. & i. (-nn-), n., & a. 1. Convert (raw hide) into leather by soaking in liquid containing tannic acid or by use of mineral salts etc., whence ~**n′ABLE** a., ~**n′AGE**(3), ~**n′er**¹[-ER¹(1)], ~**n′ERY**(2, 3), nn.; treat (imitation marble, fish-nets, etc.) with hardening process; (sl.) beat, thrash. Hence ~**n′ING**⁴(1) n. 2. Bark of oak or other tree bruised & used for ~ning hides; colour of this, yellowish-

brown; the bronze of sunburnt skin; the ~ (sl.), the circus; (also spent ~) from which tannic acid has been extracted, used for covering roads etc.; ~-balls (of spent ~, used for fuel); ~-liquor, -ooze, -pickle, liquid used in ~ning; ~-yard, ~nery. 3. adj. Of ~ colour; black¹ & ~. [(vb f. n.) F, prob. f. Celt.; cf. Bret. tann oak]

tan². See TANGENT.

Tăn'agra, n. City of ancient Greece; (in full, ~ statuette, figurine) terracotta statuette found, or of the type found, in tombs near ~. [f. Hind. thānā]

tăn'ager, n. Kinds of Amer. birds of finch family & mostly of brilliant plumage. Hence ~RINE, ~ROID, aa. [f. Braz. tangara]

tan². See TANGENT.

tăn'dem, adv., n., & a. 1. (Of horses in harness) one behind another; drive ~ (with horses so harnessed). 2. n. (Carriage with) horses ~; bicycle or tricycle with seats for two or more one behind another. 3. adj. (Of bicycle) so arranged. [L, = at length (of time), orig. joc. use in E]

tănd'stícker, n. Swedish wooden lucifer match. [f. Sw. tandsticka match, pl. -or (tända kindle + sticka splinter)]

tăng¹, n., & v.t. 1. Point, projection, esp. part of chisel etc., that goes into handle. 2. Strong taste or flavour, characteristic property, whence ~(y²-(ngi) a. 3. v.t. Furnish or affect with a ~. [ME, f. ON tange point]

tăng², n. Kinds of seaweed. [cf. Norw. & Da. tang, Icel. thäng]

tăng³, v.t. & v.i. 1. Ring, twang, sound loudly, (t. & i.); induce (bees) to settle by striking pieces of metal together. 2. n. Twang. [imit.]

tăn'gent (-j-), a. & n. 1. Meeting a line or surface at a point but not (when produced if necessary) intersecting it. 2. n. Straight line ~ to a curve at any point; fly, go, off at a ~, diverge impetuously from matter in hand or from normal line of thought or conduct.; (Trig., abbr. tan) ~ of an angle, ratio of the perpendicular subtending it in any right-angled triangle to the base. 3. ~balance (showing weight by position of beam as shown on graduated arc), Hence tăn'genCY n., tăn'gen'tIAL(-shen) a., tăn'gen'tIALly² adv. [f. L tangere touch, see -ENT]

Tăn'gerine' (-jerēn), a. & n. (Native) of Tangier; ~ (orange), small flattened kind. [f. Tanger Tangier, see -INE¹]

tăn'ghin (-nggin), n. Madagascar tree the fruit of which has poisonous kernel formerly used in ordeals. [f. f. native tanghena]

tăn'gible (-j-), a. Perceptible by touch; definite, clearly intelligible, not elusive or visionary, as ~ible advantages, scheme,

distinction; (Law) corporeal. Hence or cogn. ~IBIL'ITY, ~ibleNESS, nn., ~ibly² adv. [f. L tangibilis (tangere touch, see -BLE)]

tangle¹ (tăng'gl), v.t. & i. & n. 1. Intertwine (threads, hair, etc.), become entangle; complicate, as a ~d affair; ~foot (sl.), whisky or intoxicants. 2. n. Confused mass of intertwined threads etc.; confused state, as skein, business, is in a ~; device used in dredging for delicate forms of marine life. Hence ~SOME, tăng'ly² (-ngg²-), aa. [n. f. vb, ME, var. of tagle entangle, prob. of Scand. orig.]

tangle² (tăng'gl), n. = TANG².

tăng'ó (-nggʒ), n. (pl. ~s), & v.i. A S.-Amer. dance; (v.i.) dance the ~. [?]

tăn'gram (-ngg²-), n. Chinese puzzle square cut into seven pieces to be combined into various figures. [?]

tăn'ist, n. (hist.) Celtic chief, usu. most vigorous adult of his kin. [f. Ir. tánaiste heir]

tăn'istry, n. Celtic mode of tenure according to which a lord's successor was chosen from his family by election (abolished in Ireland under James I). [-RY]

tănk, n. 1. Large metal or wooden vessel for liquid, gas, etc.; part of locomotive tender containing water for boiler; (E.-Ind.) storage-pond, reservoir for water. 2. (mil.) Armoured motor vehicle moving on caterpillar tracks & mounted with guns (~-buster, sl, aircraft with anti-~ cannon). 3. ~ drama (Theatr. sl.), sensational drama in which water is used for representing rescue from drowning etc.; ~ engine, railway engine carrying fuel & water receptacles on its own frame, not in tender. [f. Port. tanque f. LL as STANCH; or perh. f. Ind. org.]

tănk'age, n. (Charge for) storage in tanks; cubic content of tank(s); kind of fertilizer got from refuse fats etc. [-AGE]

tănk'ard, n. Large drinking-vessel usu. of silver or pewter & often with cover; contents of, amount held by, this, as a ~ of ale; COOL¹ ~; ~ turnip, kinds with oblong rootmu, rising high above ground. [cf. Du. tanckaert, F tanquart, etym. dub.]

tănk'er, n. Ship with tank(s) for carrying liquids, esp. mineral oils, in bulk. [-ER¹]

tăn'ner¹. See TAN¹.

tăn'ner², n. (sl.). A sixpence. [?]

tănn'ic, a. Of tan; ~ic acid (also ~IN n.), astringent substance got chiefly from bark etc. of oak & other trees & used in preparing leather & yielding-ink & in medicine. So ~IN¹(3) n. (chem.), ~irrous a. [-IC]

tan'rec. See TENREC.

tăn'sy (-zi), n. Herb with yellow flowers & finely-toothed bitter aromatic leaves

used in medicine & cookery. [f. OF *tantesie* f. med. L f. Gk *athanasia* immortality (*a-* not +*thanatos* death)]

tan'talize, v.t. Torment, tease, (person etc.) with hopes that seem continually on point of fulfilment or with object almost within his grasp or with imperfect information etc. Hence ~A'TION n., ~ingLY² adv. [f. TANTALUS +IZE]

tan'talum, n. A rare white metallic element highly resistant to heat & to action of acids. [f. foll. w. ref. to its non-absorbent quality +-UM]

Tan'talus, n. 1. (Gk Myth.) son of Zeus condemned in Tartarus to stand up to chin in water that receded whenever he stooped to drink. 2. (~). Kinds of ibis; spirit-stand in which decanters are locked up but visible. 3. ~cup, toy cup containing figure of man illustrating principle of siphon. [L, f. Gk *Tantalos*]

tan'tamount, a. Equivalent, as *his message was ~ to a flat refusal.* [orig. as vb, f. AF *tant amunter* AMOUNT to so much (*tant* f. L *tantus* so great)]

tanta'ra, n. Succession of notes on trumpet or horn. [imit.]

tantiv'y, n., a., adv., & v.i. (arch.). 1. Hunting cry; swift movement, gallop, rush. 2. adj. Swift. 3. adv. Swiftly. 4. v.i. Hurry, rush. [perh. imit. of hoof-strokes]

tan'tra, n. Each of a class of recent Sanskrit religious works dealing chiefly with magic. Hence **tān'trism**(3), **tān'trism**(2), nn. [Skr., =loom, groundwork, doctrine]

Taoism (tah'ō-, tow'-), n. Religious doctrine of Lao-tsze, Chinese philosopher (c. 500 B.C.). [f. Chin. *tao* way +-ISM]

tap¹, n., & v.t. & -(pp-). 1. ‖Cock through which liquid is drawn from cask or flows from pipe; plug used to close opening in cask; liquor of a particular brewing etc. w. ref. to quality, as *an excellent ~, you know the ~;* =~room, as *found him in the* ~; instrument for cutting threads of internal screws; *on* ~, (of cask) furnished with ~, (of liquor) in such cask, ready to be drawn, ‖(of Treasury bills etc.) obtainable when & as required at a fixed rate; ~borer, auger for boring tapering hole in cask; ‖~'room (in which liquor is sold & drunk); ~root, chief descending root of plant. 2. v.t. Furnish (cask) with cock; pierce (cask etc.) to let out liquid, let out fluid from; (Surg.) give vent to (fluid accumulated in body); operate thus on (person); draw sap from (tree) by cutting into it; penetrate to, get into communication with, establish trade etc. in, (district etc.); apply to, solicit, (person for); broach (subject); divert part of current from (telegraph wires etc.) to intercept message; make internal screw-thread in.

[vb OE *tæppan* f. n.) OE *tæppa*, cf. Du. *tap*, ON *tappi*, G *zapfen*]

tap², v.t. & i.(-pp-), & n. 1. Strike lightly, as ~ *the door with your knuckles, pavement with your stick, ~ped his forehead knowingly;* cause (thing) to strike lightly against etc., as ~*ped his stick against the window;* strike gentle blow, rap, (at door etc.); apply leather to (heel of shoe). 2. n. Light blow, rap; sound of this, as *heard a ~ at the door;* (pl.) men's dinner-call in barracks, *signal on drum or trumpet for lights to be put out in soldiers' quarters; ~dancing, stage-dancing characterized by rhythmical ~ping of the feet. [(n. & f. vb) imit., perh. thr. F *tap(p)er*]

ta'pa (tah-), n. Bark of a tree used in Pacific Islands for clothes, mats, etc. [native]

tape, n., & v.t. 1. Narrow cotton or linen strip used for tying up parcels & in dressmaking etc. (RED ~); such strip stretched across racing-track between winning-posts, as *breast the* ~, win race; narrow band of strong fabric rotating on pulleys etc. in machinery; continuous strip of paper in receiving instrument of recording telegraph; =~measure, ~worm; (sl.) spirituous liquor. 2. ~line, ~measure, strip of ~ or thin flexible metal marked for use as measure, & often coiled up in cylindrical case; ~worm, kinds of ~-like many-jointed worm infesting alimentary canal of man & most vertebrates. Hence ~'LESS a. 3. v.t. Furnish, tie up, with ~; join sections of (book) with bands of ~; *have person ~d* (sl.), have summed him up. [(vb f. n.) OE *tæppe*]

tap'er, n., a., & v.i. & t. 1. Slender candle, wick coated with wax etc. 2. adj. (now chiefly poet. or rhet.). Growing gradually smaller towards one end like cone or pyramid, as ~ *fingers,* whence ~NESS n., ~WISE adv. 3. vb. (Often = *off*) make or become ~, (cause to) grow gradually less, as *the upper part~s* or *is ~ed off to a point,* whence ~ingLY² adv. [vb f. adj. f. n., w. ref. to shape) OE]

tap'estry, n. Textile fabric in which woof is supplied with spindle instead of shuttle, with design formed by stitches across warp, used for covering walls, furniture, etc.; *Bayeux* ~, ancient roll of linen representing scenes in life of William I preserved at Bayeux; *Russian* ~y, stout linen ~ used for blinds etc. Hence (-)~ied²(-rĭd) a. [f. F *tapisserie* (*tapisser* furnish with ~y, f. TAPIS, see -ERY]

tapio'c'a, n. Starchy substance in hard white grains got by heating cassava & used for puddings etc. [Port., f. Braz. *tipioca* juice of cassava (*tipi* dregs +*oka* pinch, squeeze)]

tap'ir (-er), n. Hoofed swinelike mammal with short proboscis, allied to rhinoceros. Hence ~OID (-er-) a. & n. [f. Braz. *tapira*]

tā´pis (-ē, -ĭs), n. (Of subject) *be, come, on the ~* (under consideration or discussion), on machinery to impart intermittent motion; ~ *loom* (in which hammers are worked by ~s). [perh. f. TAP¹+-STER¹]

tā´p ster, n. Person employed at a bar to draw & serve liquor. [OE *tæppestre*, orig. fem. TAP¹.]

tapu. See TABOO.

tā¹, n., & v.t. (-rr-). **1.** Dark viscid liquid got by dry distillation of wood, coal, etc., & used as preservative of timber & iron, antiseptic, etc.; *a touch of the~brush,* admixture of Negro blood as shown by colour of ~red rope etc.; ~*macadam,* roadmaterials of stone or slag with ~; ~*water,* cold infusion of ~ used as medicine, also, tarry ammoniacal water obtained in gas-manufacture. **2.** v.t. Cover with ~; ~ *& feather,* smear with ~ & then cover with feathers as punishment; ~*red with the same brush* or *stick,* having the same faults. [vb f. n.) ON *tjara,* Da. *tjære,* cogn. w. TREE]

tā², n. (Also *Jack ~*) sailor. [abbr. of TARPAULIN]

tā´radiddle, tarra-, n. (colloq.). Fib, lie. [?]

tā´a-fêrn, n. Edible fern of New Zealand etc. [Tasmanian]

tarantāss´, n. Springless four-wheeled Russian vehicle. [f. Russ. *tarantass*]

tarantĕll´a, -ĕlle´, n. (Music for) rapid whirling Ital. dance once held a cure for tarantism. [F (-*le* f. It. -*la*), as foll.]

tă´rantism, n. Dancing mania, esp. that originating in S. Italy among those who (thought they) had been bitten by the tarantula. [f. It. *Tarentum,* S. -Ital. town. -ISM]

tarăn´tūl a, n. Large spider of S. Europe whose bite was formerly held to cause tarantism; other kinds of spider. Hence ~*AR¹ a.* [f. It. *tarantola,* as prec.]

tă´ratantara (*or* -ăntă´ra), n. Sound of trumpet or bugle. [imit., cf. TANTARA.]

tarăx´acum, n. Kinds of plant of aster family including dandelion; drug prepared from this. [prob. of Arab. or Pers. orig.]

tā´boosh´, n.   Cap like fez. [f. Arab. *farbūsh*]

Tā´denoĭs´ĭan (-z-), adv. Slowly. [It.] **Tā´denoĭs´ian** (*or* -ăntă´o), n. Of the mesolithic period represented by remains at Tardenois, Aisne, France. [-IAN] **tā´dĭgrāde,** a. & n. (zool.). Slow-moving

(animal). [f. L *tardigradus (tardus* slow +*gradi* walk)]

tā´d l³y, a. & adv. (mus.). Slow(ly). [It.]

tā´d l¹y, a. & adv. (mus.). Slow-moving, slow, coming or done late, amends, reform; (of person etc.) reluctant, hanging back. Hence ~y retribution, slow, see -IVE]

adv., ~INESS n. [f. F *tardif* f. L *tardus* slow, see -IVE]

tāre¹, n. Kinds of vetch, esp. common vetch (in *Matt.* xiii. 25, 36, perh.=darnel). [ME, etym. dub.]

tāre², n., & v.t. **1.** Allowance made for weight of box etc. in which goods are packed, as *real, customary, average,* ~; weight of motor vehicle without fuel etc.; ~ *& tret,* arithmetical rule for computing ~ etc.; (Chem.) weight of vessel in which substance is weighed. **2.** v.t. Ascertain weight of (box etc.). [F f. Arab. *tarḥah* what is rejected (*taraḥa* reject)]

tārge. See foll.

tā´gĕt (-g-), n. **1.** Circular stuffed pad with concentric circles painted on surface as mark in archery; similar usu. rectangular mark for fire-arms; anything that is fired at (also attrib., as ~ *area*); (fig.) objective, result aimed at, as *export, fuel, savings,* ~ (also attrib.); (fig.) person, thing, serving as mark *for* (scorn etc.). **2.** Circular railway signal e.g. at a switch. **3.** Neck & breast of lamb as joint. **4.** (Also *targe* arch.) shield, buckler, esp. small round one, whence ~ED² a. **5.** ~*card* (coloured like ~, for keeping archer's score); ~ *skep,* old ship used as ~. [f. OF *targuete* dim. of *targue* (also *targe*) f. ON *targa,* cf. OHG *zarga* frame, border]

tā´riff, n., & v.t. **1.** List of duties or customs to be paid on imports or exports; such duties collectively; law imposing these; duty on particular class of goods; *preferential* ~, reduced duties on imports from favoured country; *retaliatory* ~, import duties levied by a nation to balance foreign duties imposed on its exports; ~ *reform,* removal of inequalities etc. in ~ ((esp. as name given by opponents of free trade in U.K. to their policy); ~ *wall,* ~-created national trade barrier; list of charges, as *railway, telegraph,* ~; duties on (goods); put a valuation on. **2.** v.t. Make ~ of duties on (goods); put a valuation on. [vb f. n.) f. It. *tariffa* arithmetic, ratebook, f. Arab. *ta´rif* notification (*´arafa* notify)]

tā´latan, n. Thin kind of muslin. [f. F *tarlatane* earlier *tarn-,* etym. dub.]

tā´rm´ac, n.=TAR¹ *macadam;* part of airfield surface made of ~. [abbr.; P]

tarn, n. Small mountain lake. [f. ON *tjörn,* cf. Sw. dial. *t(j)ärn*]

tărn², See TERN¹.

tărn'al, *tărnā'tion, aa. & advv. (sl.) Confounded(ly). [(-ation on damnation) corrupt. of ETERNAL]

tărn'ish, v.t. & i., & n. 1. Lessen or destroy the lustre of, lose lustre, as has been ~ed by damp, will ~ if exposed, does not easily ~, (fig.) a ~ed reputation. 2. n. Loss of lustre, blemish, stain; (Mineral.) film of colour formed on exposed surface of mineral. Hence ~ABLE a. [(n. f. vb) f. F ternir (terne dark), see -ISH²]

ta'rŏ (tah-), n. (pl. ~s). Kinds of tropical plant of arum family with root used as food esp. in Pacific islands. [native]

ta'rŏc, -ot (-ō), n. Game played with, each card of, a pack of 78 cards. [f. F tarot f. It. tarocchi, etym. dub.]

tărp'ăn, n. Wild horse of Tartary. [native]

tărpaul'in, n. Waterproof cloth esp. of tarred canvas; sheet of this as covering; sailor's tarred or oiled hat; (arch.) sailor. [f. TAR-+palling covering f. pall vb cover f. PALL¹]

Tărpei'an (-pēan), a. ~ rock, cliff from which ancient-Roman criminals were hurled. [f. L Tarpeius of Tarpeia (who was buried at foot of ~ rock)+-AN]

tărp'on, n. Large game-fish common on south coast of U.S. [?]

tă'rradiddle. See tara-.

tă'rragon, n. Plant allied to wormwood & used in salads & in making ~ vinegar. [f. Arab. ṭarkhōn perh. f. Gk as DRAGON]

Tărrăgo'n'a, n. Spanish wine like port. [~ in Spain]

tă'rras, n. See TRASS.

tă'rrock, n. Young kittiwake; common tern; guillemot. [?]

tăr'ry¹, a. Of, like, smeared with, tar. [-Y²]

tă'rry², v.i. & t. (now literary). Remain, stay lodge, (at, in, etc.); wait (often for); delay to come or appear, be late; wait for. [f. 14th c., etym. dub.]

tărs'ia, n. Kind of mosaic woodwork. [It.]

tărs'ier, n. Small large-eyed nocturnal lemur. [F (foll., from structure of foot)]

tărs'/us, n. (pl. ~ī). 1. Collection of bones between lower leg & metatarsus, ankle; shank of bird's leg; (Entom.) terminal segment of limb. 2. Plate of connective tissue in eyelid. Hence ~AL a., ~r-, ~o-, comb. forms. [mod. L, f. Gk tarsos flat of the foot]

tărt¹, a. Sharp-tasting, acid; cutting, biting, as a ~ rejoinder. Hence ~LY² adv., ~'NESS n. [OE teart, perh. cogn. w. TEAR¹]

tărt², n. 1. || Pie containing fruit, as apple, cherry, ~; jam ~, piece of pastry with jam on top. 2. (sl.) Girl, woman, esp. of immoral character. So ~'LET n. [f. OF tarte perh. var. of to(u)rte f. L torquēre tort- twist]

tărt'an, n. & a. 1. Woollen fabric with stripes of various colours crossing at right angles esp. as worn by Scottish Highlanders; (other fabric) so striped, as silk ~ velvet; Scottish plaid with distinctive pattern of a clan. 2. (rare) Highlander; Highland troops. [f. 16th c., etym. dub.]

tărt'an², n. Kind of single-masted vessel used in Mediterranean. [f. F tartane f. It. tartana]

tărt'ar¹, n. Pink or red deposit from completely fermented wine, forming hard crust on side of cask, whence tărtă'RIC, ~OUS, aa. (chem.), ~IZA'TION n., ~IZE(5) v.t.; CREAM² of ~; incrustation of saliva, calcium phosphate, etc., forming on the teeth; ~ emetic, double tartrate of potassium & antimony used as emetic, purgative, etc. [f. F tartre perh. f. Arab.]

Tărt'ar², Ta'tar (tah-), a. & n. 1. (Native) of Tartary, (member) of a group of peoples including Turks, Cossacks, etc., so Tărtă'rIAN a. 2. (Tar-) intractable or savage person (catch a ~, meet with person who is more than a match for one). [cf. Pers. Tātār, perh. the native form, whence Tar-, the usu. spelling, by assoc. w. foll.]

Tărt'arus, n. (Gk Myth.). Abyss below Hades where Titans were confined; place of punishment in Hades. So Tărtă'reăn a. [L, f. Gk Tartaros]

tărt'rate, n. Salt of tartaric acid. [f. TARTAR¹+-ATE¹]

Tărtuf(f)e' (-oof), n. Religious hypocrite. Hence~'ISM n. [character in Molière's ~e]

task (tah-), n., & v.t. 1. Piece of work imposed; lesson to be learnt at school, as has done his ~; a work voluntarily undertaken, as an arduous ~, undertook the ~ of classification; take person to ~, accuse him of fault, rebuke him for (doing); ~ force, specially organized unit for a special ~; ~'master, ~mistress, one who imposes ~. 2. v.t. Assign ~ to; exact labour from, put strain upon, tax, (powers, intellect, etc.). [(vb f. n.) f. ONF tasque (OF tasche) TAX]

Tasmā'n'ian (-z-), a. & n. (Inhabitant) of Tasmania; ~ devil, DASYURE peculiar to the island; ~ wolf, nocturnal carnivorous wolflike marsupial. [after Abel Tasman, discoverer]

|| tăss¹, n. (Sc.) Small draught (of brandy etc.). [f. OF tasse cup prob. f. Arab. tass basin]

Tăss², n. Telegraph agency of the Soviet Union. [f. initials of Russian title]

tăss'el, n., & v.t. (-ll-). 1. Tuft of loosely hanging threads or cords as ornament for cushion, cap, etc.; ~-like head of some plants, esp. staminate inflorescence at top of stalk of Indian corn; ribbon sewn into book to be used as bookmark; =TORSEL. 2. v.t. Furnish with ~; remove ~s of (Indian corn) to strengthen plant. [(vb f. n.) OF, perh. f. L taxillus small die]

taste¹, v.t. & i. 1. Learn flavour of (food

etc., or abs.) by taking it into the mouth, as ~ *this cheese, he ~s teas* (professionally, *for Smith & Co.* **2.** Eat small portion of or arch. of (esp. after negative, as *must just ~ a snack, has not ~d food for 3 days.* **3.** Perceive the flavour of, as *can ~ nothing when you have a cold, fancy I ~ garlic.* **4.** (arch.). Relish, enjoy, as *can ~ a joke against himself.* **5.** Experience, have experience of, as *shall not ~ (of) death, has never ~d (of) success.* **6.** (Of food etc., fig.) have a flavour ~ of, *smack of, as ~s of mint, his writings ~ of the schools.* Hence **tast'ABLE** a. [f. OF *taster* handle, ult. f. L *taxare* TAX]

taste², n. **1.** Sensation excited in certain organs of mouth by contact of some soluble things, flavour, as *cannot endure the ~ of onions, white of egg has no ~.* **2.** Sense by which this is perceived. **3.** (rare). Act of tasting. **4.** Small portion (of food etc.) taken as sample (*give him a ~ of the whip,* enough to show how it feels). **5.** Liking, predilection, for, as *has no ~ for sweet things, a ~ for drawing, ~s differ, there is no accounting for~s, add pepper etc. to ~* (to the amount desired). **6.** Faculty of discerning & enjoying beauty or other excellence esp. in art & literature, as *is a man of ~, true, false, ~, remark was in bad ~.* **7.** Disposition or execution of work of art, choice of language, conduct, etc., dictated by or seen in the light of this faculty, *as is composed in admirable ~, the remark was in bad ~.* [ME, f. OF *tast* as prec.]

taste'ful (-tf-), a. (Of person, work of art, etc.) having, showing, done in, good taste. Hence **~LY²** adv., **~NESS** n. [-FUL]

taste'less (-tl-), a. Having no flavour; insipid; lacking the physical sense of taste; lacking artistic taste; (of language, conduct, etc.) not in good taste. Hence **~LY²** adv., **~NESS** n. [-LESS]

tās'ter, n. In vbl senses, esp.: person employed to judge of teas, wines, etc., by taste; (fig.) publisher's reader; (hist.) person employed to taste food before it was touched by his employer; small cup used by wine~; instrument for extracting small cylindrical sample from a cheese. [-ER¹]

tās'ti'y, a. (colloq.). Savoury, of pleasant flavour; (now vulg.: of dress, decoration, etc.) in good taste. Hence **~ily²** adv. [-Y²]

tät', v.i. & t. (-tt-). Do tatting; make by tatting. [prob. back formation f. TATTING]

tāt', tärt'ōō', n. (Anglo-Ind.). Pony. [f. Hind. *ṭaṭṭū*]

Tatar. See TARTAR².

ta-ta (tätä'), int. Good-bye.

Tate Gall'ery, n. London public gallery with permanent exhibition of pictures & sculpture by British & modern foreign artists. [Sir H. *Tate,* donor]

etc. **2.** Rag; torn piece, of cloth, paper, dub.), ragged fellow. Hence **~ED²** (-vrl) **~Y²** aa. [cf. ON *tǫturr* rags]

Tät'tersall's (-z), n. (Used for) head-quarters of horse-dealing & betting rendezvous (*knows his ~ better than his Greek Testament*). [R. *Tattersall,* founder of firm]

tät'ting, n. Kind of knotted work used for trimmings etc. [?]

tät'tle, v.i. & t., & n. **1.** Prattle, chatter, gossip, whence **tät'tling²** adv.; utter (words) idly. **2.** n. Trivial talk. [(n. f. vb) perh. f. MFlem. *tatelen,* cf. MLG *tateren*]

tät'tler, n. **1.** Prattler, gossip, (arch. *Tatler,* periodical of Steele & Addison). **2.** Sandpiper. [f. prec. +-ER¹]

tattōō¹ (tättōō'), n., & v.t. **1.** Beat of drum, or bugle-call, at 10 p.m. recalling soldiers to quarters, elaboration of this with music & marching as entertainment; *beat the devil's ~,* drum idly with fingers etc. **2.** v.i. Rap quickly & repeatedly, beat the devil's~. [(vb f.n.) f. Du. *taptoe*]

tät'tōō², n. (Anglo-Ind.). Matting of cuscus-grass hung & kept wet to cool & perfume the air. [f. Hind. *ṭaṭṭī* wicker frame]

tattōō³ (tättōō'), v.t., & n. **1.** Mark (skin etc.) with indelible patterns by inserting pigments in punctures. **2.** n. Such mark. [(n. f. vb) f. Tahitian *tatau* n.]

tau (taw, tow), n. Greek letter (T, τ)=t; kinds of fish etc. marked with *or* suggesting this; (attrib.) T-shaped, as *~ cross.* [Gk]

Tauch'nitz (towk-), n. (Used for) any volume in the Library of British & American authors published by Tauchnitz of Leipzig, much used by travellers on the Continent.

taught. See TEACH.

taunt¹, v.t., & n. **1.** Reproach, upbraid, (person etc. *with* conduct etc.) contemptuously, whence **~'ingly²** adv. **2.** n. Contemptuous reproach, object of this, as *endured the ~s of, became a ~ to, his neighbours.* [f. OF *tanter, tenter,* provoke, TEMPT; or f. F phr. *tant pour tant* so much for so much, tit for tat, f. L *tantum* so much]

‖**taunt²,** a. (naut.). (Of mast) tall. [f. *ataunt* adv. naut. fully rigged f. F *autant* as much]

taur'ine, a. Bull-like, bovine, so~iform, a.; of the zodiacal sign Taurus. [f. L *taurinus* (*taurus* bull; see -INE²)]

taurōm'achy (-ki), n. Bull-fight(ing). [f. Gk *tauromakhia* (*tauros* bull + *makhē* fight)]

Taur'us, n. A constellation; second sign of zodiac. [L, = bull]

taut, a. (naut.). (Of rope) tight, not slack;

(of vessel etc.) in good order or condition. Hence ~ENᵉ v.t. & i., ~LY² adv., ~NESS n. [ME *togt*, perh. = TIGHT w. assim. to p,p, of ROW]

tauto- in comb.= Gk *tauto, to auto*, the same, as; ~*ochrōne* (-k-) [f. Gk *khronos* time], curve on which body starting from lowest point in same time from whatever point it starts, so ~*och'ronism* (-k-) n., ~*och'ronous* (-k-) a.; ~*oph'ony*, repetition of same sound.

tautol'og|y, n. Saying of the same thing twice over in different words (e.g. *arrived one after the other in succession*). Hence **tautolo'gical²** aa., **tautolo'gically²** adv., ~IST(1) n., ~IZE(2) v.i. [f. LL f. Gk TAUTO(*logia* -LOGY)]

tāv'ern, n. Public house for supply of food & drink. [f. OF *taverne* f. L *taberna* hut, tavern]

taw¹, v.t. Make (hide) into leather without use of tannin, esp. by soaking in solution of alum & salt. Hence ~ERᴵ, ~ERY(3), nn. [OE *tawian* prepare, cf. Du. *touwen* curry, MHG *zouwan* make, prepare]

taw², n. Game at marbles; limit line in playing marbles; a marble. [f. 18th c., etym. dub.]

tawd'r|y, a. & n. **1.** Showy but worthless, gaudy, having too much or ill-judged ornament, whence ~ILY² adv., ~INESS n. **2.** n. Cheap or excessive or tasteless finery. [f. *St Audry's* fair held in Isle of Ely (*Audry* corrupt. of *Etheldrida*, who founded Ely Cathedral)]

tawn'|y, a. Brownish-yellow, tan-coloured. Hence ~INESS n. [f. OF *tané* TANᴵ-ned]

taws(e) (-z), n. sing. or pl. (Sc.). Slit thong for chastising children. [prob. related to TAW¹; a sing. *taw* is much later]

tax¹, v.t. Impose tax on (subjects, citizens, etc., commodity, land, etc.), so ~A'TION n.; (N.T.) register (person) for purpose of imposing tribute; make demands upon, demand exertion from, (person's resources, powers, ingenuity, etc.); *cannot ~ my memory*, cannot undertake to recollect the facts wanted; (Law) examine & (dis)allow items of (costs etc.); ~ed (also ~) *cart*, two-wheeled cart usu. for agricultural or trade purposes on which only reduced duty (& later none) was charged; charge (person *with* fault, *with doing*); ||~*ing-master*, law court official who ~es costs. Hence ~ABH/ITY, ~ableNESS, nn., ~ABLE a., ~'abiᴵ² adv. [f. OF *taxer* f. L *taxare* censure, charge, compute, cf. TASK, TASTE¹]

tax², n. Contribution levied on persons, property, or business, for support of government, as DIRECT², INDIRECT, *capitation*, INCOME, *poll-*; *single~*, proposed sole ~, on value of land irrespective of improvements; strain, heavy demand,

(*upon* (person, his energies etc.); ||~*cart*, see prec.; ~*collector*, official who collects~es; ~*farmer*, one who buys from government the right to collect certain ~es; ~*free*, exempt from ~es; ~*gatherer*, =~*collector*; ~*payer*. Hence ~LESS a. [f. prec.]

tax'i¹, n. & t. **1.** Motor-cab plying for hire & fitted with taximeter (also ~*cab*), other motor-car of similar pattern; ~*man*, driver of ~; ~*plane*, light aeroplane for public hire (also ~). **2.** vb. Ge or convey in ~; (Aeron., of aircraft or pilot) go along ground or water under machine's own power before or after flying. [abbr. TAXIMETER]

tax'idērm|y, n. Art of preparing & mounting skins of animals in lifelike manner. Hence **taxidēr**ᴹAL, **taxidēr**ᴹ'IC, aa., ~IST(3) n. [f. TAXIS+DERM]

taxim'eter, n. Automatic device fitted to cab & indicating fare due at any moment. [f. F *taximètre* (*taxe* tariff, TAX²-METER)]

tax'in, n. Resinous substance from yew leaves. [f. L *taxus* yew+-IN]

tax'is, n. (Surg.) manual pressure applied to restore parts to their place; (Gk Ant.) various divisions of troops; (Zool.) classification; (Gram., Rhet.) arrangement. [Gk, f. *tassō* arrange]

tax|on'omy, n. (nat. hist.). (Principles of) classification. Hence or cogn. ~ol'OGY, ~on'omIST(3), nn., ~onŏm'IC(AL) aa., ~onŏm'ically² adv. [f. F *taxonomie* (TAXIS-f. Gk -*nomos* f. *nemō* manage)]

taz'za (talit'sa), n. Saucer-shaped cup esp. one mounted on a foot. [It.]

tchick, n., & v.i. (Make) sound produced by pressing tongue against roof of mouth & quickly withdrawing it, esp. as used in urging horse. [imit.]

tea, n., & v.i. & t. **1.** (Also ~*plant*) shrub or small tree of camellia family grown in China, India, etc.; leaves of this dried & prepared for use (*black, green, ~, congou, souchong, pekoe*, etc., kinds of black, *hyson, gunpowder*, etc., ~, kinds of green; *tile ~*, in BRICK form). **2.** Infusion or decoction of ~-leaves as beverage; infusion etc. of leaves of other plants or of other substance, as BEEF, CAMOMILE, ~. **3.** Light afternoon meal with ~, esp. *five-o'-clock ~*; (also *high ~, meat ~*) solid evening meal with ~. **4.** ~-CADDY; ~*cake*, kinds of cake eaten toasted or otherwise at ~; ~*chest*, light lead-lined wooden box in which ~ is exported; ~*cloth* (for ~-table or -tray, also drying-cloth for cups etc.); ~*cup*, cup in which ~ is drunk (*storm in a ~-cup*, commotion in circumscribed circle or about trivial matter), (as measure, also ~*cupful*) gill; ~*fight* (colloq.), ~*party*; ~*garden* (in which ~ is served to the public); ~*gown*, woman's loose gown worn at ~ etc.; ~*house* (in which ~ etc. is served in China

& Japan): ~-kettle (used in making ~); ~-leaf, leaf of ~ esp. (pl.) after infusion or soaking, used in sweeping floors; ~-partly (at which ~ is served); ~-pot, vessel in which ~ is made; ~-rose, kinds with scent compared to that of ~; ~-service, -set, ~-pot, cups etc., used in serving ~; ~-SPOON; ~-table (often attrib., as ~-table conversation); ~-things, ~-set; ~-tray (on which ~-set is used or carried); ~-urn, for boiling or holding water for ~. 5. vb. Take ~, as we ~ at 4; give ~ to (person). [vb f. n.) earlier as tay, tee, f. Chin. dial. t'e, f. Chin. ch'a]

teach, v.t. & i. (*taught* pr. tawt). 1. Enable or cause (person etc. to do) by instruction & training, as ~ *him to swim, dog was taught to beg, misfortune has taught him to be thankful for small mercies, this taught him to speak the truth,* etc., (intr.) be a ~er. **4.** Give instruction to, educate; (intr.) be a ~er. **4.** Explain, show, state by way of instruction, (fact etc., how, that, etc., to person or w. double obj.), as *taught that we must forgive our enemies. I was taught that two sides of a triangle were greater than the third, was taught otherwise, was never taught this, who taught you that?* Hence ~ER, ~ership, nn. [OE *tǣcan,* cogn. w. TOKEN]

teach'able, a. Apt to learn, docile; (of subject etc.) that can be taught. Hence ~ABILITY, ~ableness, nn. [-ABLE]

teach'ing, n. In vbl senses, esp. what is taught, doctrines, as *the ~s of the Church.* [-ING¹]

Teague (-g), n. (derog.). Irishman. [f. *Tadhg,* common Irish name]

teak, n. (E.-Ind. tree with) heavy durable timber that does not warp or shrink or corrode iron, much used in shipbuilding. [f. Port. *teca* f. Malayalam *tēkka*]

teal, n. (pl. same). Kinds of small fresh-water duck. [ME *tēle,* cf. Du. *taling, te-,* etym. dub.]

team, n. & v.t. 1. Two or more beasts of burden harnessed together, whence ~WISE adv.; set of players on one side in some games e.g. football; set of persons working together; ~-work, combined effort, organized co-operation. **2.** v.t. Harness (horses etc.) in ~; give out (work) to contractor who employs ~ of workmen, whence ~ING¹ n. [OE *tēam* family, set, cf. Du. *toom,* ON *taumr,* rein, G *zaum* bridle, cogn. w. L *ducere* lead]

team'ster, n. Driver of a team. [-STER]

teap'oy, n. Small three- or four-legged table esp. for tea. [f. Hind. *tīn* three +

Pers. *pāē* foot; sense & spelling influenced by TEA]

tear¹ (tār), v.t. & i. (*tore, torn*) & n. 1. Pull apart, rend, lacerate, as *tore up the letter, has torn his coat,* ~ *it in half, in two, in pieces, torn to pieces by a tiger,* (fig.) *country was torn by factions, heart torn by conflicting emotions;* make (hole, rent) thus; ~ *it* (sl.), spoil one's chances, foil one's plans, put the lid on (*that's torn it*); pull violently (lit. & fig.), as *tore down the notice,* ~ *out a page,* ~ *off the cover, tree torn up by the roots, was torn* (forcibly parted) *from her parents, babe torn from the breast, could not* ~ *myself* (make up my mind to go) *away;* pull violently at, as *tear at the cover of the parcel;* ~ *one's hair,* pull it in anger or perplexity or despair; ~ lend itself to ~ing, as *~s easily, will not* ~. **2.** Run or walk hurriedly or impetu-ously, as *tore down the hill, was simply ~ing.* **3.** ~*away* a., impetuous. **4.** n. Rent in cloth etc. [fn. f. vb) OE *teran,* cf. Goth. *gatairan* break, G *zehren* con-sume, Gk *derō* flay]

tear² (tēr), n. (Also ~*drop*) drop of saline liquid ordinarily serving to moisten & wash the eye but falling from it as result of grief or other emotion or of coughing or laughter, as *the ~s fell down her cheeks, wept bitter ~s of remorse, laughed till the ~s came, ~s were her only argument, a ~-stained face, found her in ~s* (weeping); ~-like thing, e.g. drop of fluid, solid drop of resin etc.; *~s of strong wine,* drops forming on inside of partly-filled glass of port etc.; CROCODILE ~s; ~-gas, lach-rymatory poison gas used in warfare; ~ ~. (= LACHRYMATORY) shell. [OE *tēar,* cf. ON *tār,* Da. *taar,* cogn. w. L *lacrima,* Gk *dakru(on)*]

tear'ful (tēr-), a. Shedding tears, so **tear'-LESS** a.; (of event, news, etc.) mournful, sad. Hence ~LY² adv., ~NESS n. [-FUL]

tear'ing (tār-), a. In vbl senses (TEAR¹), also, violent, overwhelming (~ *pace, rage*). [-ING²]

teas|e (-z), v.t. & n. 1. Assail playfully or maliciously, vex, with jests, questions, or petty annoyances, whence ~ingly² (-z-) adv.; importune (person *for thing, to do*); pick into separate fibres, comb, card, (wool, flax, etc.); dress (cloth etc.) with teasels. **2.** n. Person given to ~ing. [OE *tǣsan* pluck, pull, cf. Du. *teezen*]

teas'el (-z-), **-zel,** n., & v.t. 1. Kinds of plant with large prickly heads used in dressing cloth; such head; machine substituted for ~s. **2.** v.t. Dress (cloth) with ~s, whence ~ER¹ (-zel-), **teaz'ler,** nn. [OE *tǣsel* (as prec. +-LE¹)]

teas'er (-z-), n. In vbl senses, esp.: teasing person; (colloq.) difficult question or problem or task, thing hard to deal with. [-ER¹]

teat, n. Mammary nipple through which milk passes, pap of woman, dug of beast.

Hence (-)~ED² ~¹IKE, aa. [f. OF *tete* prob. f. Teut. (OE *tā*, MDu. *title*)]

tec, n. (sl.). Detective. [abbr.]

tech′nic (-k-), a. & n. **1.** adj. (rare). = foll. **2.** n. = TECHNIQUE; (usu. pl.) doctrine of arts in general; (pl.) technical terms, details, methods, etc. Hence **techni′cian** (těknĭ′shn) n., person skilled in the technique of a particular art, or in ~s generally, ~IST n. [f. L f. Gk *teknikos* (*teknē* art, see -IC)]

tech′nical (-k-), a. Of or in a particular art, science, handicraft, etc., as ~ *terms*, *skill*, *difficulty*; of, for, in, the mechanical arts, as ~ *education*, *school*; legally such, in the eyes of the law, as ~ *assault*. Hence ~LY² adv., ~NESS n. [-AL]

technical′ity (-k-), n. Technicalness, technical expression, distinction, etc., as *legal ~ies*. [-ITY]

Technicolor (těk′nĭkŭler), n. (cinemat.). Process of colour photography in which the colours are separately but simultaneously recorded & then transferred to a single positive print. [**P**; f. TECHNI(CAL) + COLOUR]

technique (těknēk′), n. Mode of artistic execution in music, painting, etc.; mechanical skill in art. [F, as TECHNIC]

tech′nocracy (-k-), n. Organization and management of a country's industrial resources by technical experts for the good of the whole community. Hence **tech′nocrat** (-k-) n., advocate of this. [f. Gk *teknē* art + -CRACY]

technol′ogy (-k-), n. Science of the industrial arts; ethnological study of development of arts. Hence **technolo′gical** a., ~IST n. [f. Gk *teknologia* (*teknē* art, -LOGY)]

techy. See TETCHY.

tecto′logy, n. Structural morphology, i.e. that which treats an organism as composed of organic individuals. Hence **tectolo′gical** a. [irreg. f. Gk *tektōn* carpenter + -LOGY]

tecton′ic, a. & n. **1.** Of building or construction; (Geol.) due to a change in structural conditions caused by deformation. **2.** n. pl. Whole art of producing useful & beautiful buildings, furniture, vessels, etc. [f. LL f. Gk *tektonikos* (*tektōn -onos* carpenter, see -IC)]

tecto′rial, a. Forming a covering, esp. ~ *membrane*. [f. L *tectorius* (as foll., see -ORY) + -AL]

tectri′ces (-z), n. pl. (ornith.). Covering feathers of wings & tail. [f. L *tegere tect-* cover, -TRIX]

ted, v.t. (-dd-). Turn over & spread out (grass, hay) to dry. Hence ~D ER ¹(1, 2) n. [f. Icel. *teðja* spread manure (*taðh*)]

Ted′dy bear (bâr), n. Child's toy bear (named after *Theodore* Roosevelt).

Te De′um, n. (Music for) hymn beginning, ~ *laudamus*, 'We praise thee, O God', sung at morning service, or on special

occasions as thanksgiving; *sing ~*, (fig.) exult, triumph. [L]

te′dious, a. Wearisome, irksome, tiresome. Hence ~LY² adv., ~NESS n. [f. LL *taediosus* (as foll., see -OUS)]

te′dium, n. Tediousness. [f. L *taedium* (*taedet* it wearies)]

tee¹, n. Letter T; T-shaped thing esp. pipe.

tee², n., & v.t. & i. **1.** Mark aimed at in quoits, bowls, curling. **2.** (golf). Cleared space from which the ball is struck at beginning of play for each hole (also ~*ing-ground*); small pile of sand or small appliance of wood, rubber, etc. on which ball is placed before being struck. **3.** v.t. Place (ball) on ~; (v.i.) ~ *off*, start from ~, (fig.) start, begin. [?]

tee³, n. Umbrella-shaped usu. gilded ornament crowning tope or pagoda. [f. Burm. *h'tī* umbrella]

teem, v.t. & i. || (Arch.) bear (offspring); be prolific, be stocked to overflowing *with*, as *forests ~ with snakes*, *book ~s with blunders*; be abundant, as *fish ~ in these waters*. [OE *tӯman* (TEAM)]

teem², v.t. (dial., tech.). Empty, discharge, pour out, (vessel, cart, coal, molten metal, etc.). Hence ~ER ¹ n. [f. ON *tœma* (*tōmr* adj. empty)]

|| teen, n. (arch.). Grief; trouble; harm. [OE *tēona* injury; cf. ON *tjón*]

-teen, suf. of numbers from 13 to 19 implying addition of ten (stress is variable like that of -ED³ compounds). [OE *tēne*, *tӯne*, pl. of TEN]

teens (-z), n. pl. (Also *teen age*, *years*) years of one's age from 13 to 19, esp. *in* one's ~; *teen-age* a., in the ~. [f. prec.]

tee′ny. See TINY.

teeth. See TOOTH.

teethe (-dh), v.i. Grow or cut teeth. Hence **teeth′ing¹** (-dh-) n. [f. prec.]

teeto′tal, a. Of, advocating, total abstinence from intoxicants, as ~ *meeting*, *pledge*, whence ~ISM n.; (colloq.) total, entire, whence ~LY² adv. [redupl. of *total*; from about 1833]

teeto′taller, n. Total abstainer. [-ER¹]

teeto′tum, n. Children's four-sided top with sides lettered to determine gain or loss of the spinner; any top spun with the fingers (*like a ~*, spinning). [f. T (the letter on one side) + L *totum* the whole (stakes), for which it stood]

teg, n. Sheep in its second year. [f. 16th c., etym. dub.]

teg′ular, a. Of or like tiles. Hence or cogn. ~**arly²** adv., ~**ated** [-ATE²] a. [f. L *tegula* tile (*tegere* cover) + -AR¹]

teg′ument, n. Natural covering of (part of) animal body. Hence ~AL, ~ARY¹, aa., (-ěn-). [f. L *tegumentum* (*tegere* cover, see -MENT)]

tehee′, n., & v.i. **1.** Restrained or contemptuous laugh. **2.** v.i. Laugh thus, titter. [imit.]

Tē′ian, Tē′an, a. Of (the poet Anacreon born at) Teos. [f. L *Tēius* (f. Gk *Tēōs*) + -IAN]

tē- in comb. See TELE-.

tēd, see TEND.

tēknŏn′ymŷ, n. (anthrop.). Practice of naming parent from child. So ~ous a. [f. Gk *teknon* child + -ōnumos -named + -Y[1]]

tēlaesthē′sia, n. (psych.). Direct perception of distant occurrences or objects not effected by the recognized senses. Hence ~ĕt′ic a. [mod. L f. TELE- + Gk *aisthēsis* perception, & -IA[1]]

tēlamŏn, n. (archit.; pl. ~es pr. -ēz), Male figure as bearing pillar(cf. CARYATID). [L, f. Gk *Telamōn* mythal. person]

tēlaut′o̱graph (-ahf), n. Telegraph that reproduces writing etc. So ~GRAM (5) n. [f. TELE- + AUTO- + -GRAPH]

tēle-ărch′ics (-k-), n. pl. Art of wireless control (of aircraft) from a distance. [TELE-, Gk *arkhikos* governing (*arkhō* rule)]

tēlecommūnicā′tion, n. Communication at a distance, as by cable, telegraph, telephone, or radio. [TELE-]

tēl′edu (-ōō), n. Stinking badger of Java and Sumatra. [native]

tēlĕg′onŷ n. (biol.). Influence of previous sire seen in subsequent sire's progeny by same mother. Hence tēlĕgŏn′ic a. [f. TELE- + Gk *-gonia* begetting]

tēl′egrăm, n. [-GRAM]

tĕl′egraph[1] (-ahf), n. **1.** Apparatus for transmitting messages or signals to a distance esp. by electrical impulses. **2.** Semaphore. **3.** (In titles of newspapers) *Daily T~* etc. **4.** ~ (-board), board on which numbers of horses running in race, cricket scores, etc., are put up so as to be visible at distance; ~-*key*, device for making and breaking electric circuit of ~; ~-*line*, -*pole* or -*post*, -*wire* (used in forming telegraphic connection); ~-*plant*, E.-Ind. plant whose leaves have spontaneous jerking motion. [f. F *télégraphe* (TELE-, -GRAPH)]

tĕl′egraph[2] (-ahf), v.t. & i. Send (message) to person, (or abs.) by telegraph, as ~ *the news to your father*, ~ *me the result*, ~ *to him to come, that we cannot come*; make signals (to person to do, that, etc.), [as prec.]

tēlĕg′rapher (or tĕl′i-), n. Person skilled or employed in telegraphy. So ~IST n. [-ER[1]]

tēlegraphēse′ (-z), n. & a. (In) the elliptical style usual in telegrams. [-ESE]

tēlĕgrăph′ic, a. Of telegraphs or telegrams; of ~ie brevity, economically worded, with unessential words omitted; ~*ie address*, abbreviated or other registered address for use in telegrams. Hence ~ICALLY adv. [-IC]

tēlĕg′raphŷ, n. Art of constructing, practice of communicating by, telegraph; *wireless* ~, transmission of signals through space by means of electromagnetic waves. [-Y[1]]

tēlekinē′sis, n. (psych.). Movement at a distance from the motive cause or agent without material connexion. [mod. L, f. TELE- + Gk *kinēsis* motion (*kineō* move)]

tēlemărk, n. Expert swing turn in skiing used to change direction or to stop short. [f. *T~*, district in Norway]

tēlemēchăn′ics (-k-), n. pl. Art of transmitting power by radio, & so controlling machinery from a distance. [TELE-]

tēleŏl′ogŷ, n. Doctrine of final causes, view that developments are due to the purpose or design that is served by them. So tēleolŏ′gic(AL) aa., tēleolŏ′gically[2] adv., ~ISM, ~IST, nn. [f. Gk *telos* -eos end-+ -LOGY]

tēleosaur′us (-sŏ-), n. Genus of fossil crocodiles. [f. Gk *telos* complete + *sauros* lizard]

tēlep′athŷ, n. Action of one mind on another at a distance through emotional influence without communication through senses. Hence tēlepăth′ic a., tēlepăth′ically adv., ~IST(2) n., ~IZE(1, 2) v.t. & i. [TELE- + -PATHY]

tēlĕphone, n. & v.t. & i. **1.** Apparatus for transmitting sound esp. speech to a distance by wire or cord, esp. by means of electricity; *the* ~, system of communication by a network of ~s (*on the* ~, having an instrument connected with this; *also*, by use of or while using the ~). **2.** vb. Send (message etc.), speak (*to person*) by ~. Hence tēlephŏn′ic a., tēlephŏn′ically adv., tēleph ŏns(3), tēlĕph′onŷ(3), tēl′ephon[1] n. [(vb f. n.), f. TELE- + Gk *phōnē* sound]

tēlephŏtŏg′raphŷ, n. Photographing of distant objects by means of a combination of telescope & ordinary photographic lens. So ~photŏg′raph′ic a. [TELE-]

tēl′eprinter, n. Telegraph instrument for transmitting messages by typing over the telephone exchange system. [TELE-]

tēl′ergy, n. (psych.). Force conceived as operating on the brain in telepathy. [TELE- + (*en*)*ergy*]

tēl′escope, n., & v.t. & i. **1.** Instrument for making distant objects appear nearer & larger, whence *tēlĕs′copist*(3), tēlĕs′copȳ[1], nn. **2.** vb. Press, drive, (sections that one slides into another like sections of small telescope); together so as to close into one another, be capable of closing, thus. [(vb f. n.) f. It. *telescopio*

tĕlĕscŏp′ic, a. Of, made with, a telescope, as ~*ic observations*; visible only through telescope, as ~*ic stars*; consisting of sections that telescope, as ~*ic funnel* (of steamer), so ~IFORM a. Hence ~ICALLY adv. [-IC]

tĕl′ĕsème, n. System of electrical signalling including annunciator, used in hotels etc. [f. TELE- + Gk *sēma* sign]

tĕl′ėvision (-zhn), n. A system employing mechanical, photo-electrical, & wireless processes for reproducing scenes, objects, performers, etc., visually at a distance; vision of distant objects obtained thus. Hence **tĕl′ėviewer** (-vūer) n., one who uses a ~ receiver, **tĕl′ėvise** (-z) v.t. & t., transmit by ~, **tĕl′ėvisor²** (-z-) n., ~ apparatus. [TELE-]

tĕll, v.t. & i. (*tŏld*). **1.** Relate in spoken or written words, as ~ *me a tale*, ~ *a story*. **2.** Make known, divulge, state, express in words, as ~ *me what you want*, ~ *me all about it, will* ~ *you a secret*, ~ *it not in Gath* (let this news not reach & gladden the enemy, usu. joc. w. ref. to 2 *Sam.* i 20), ~ *that to the* (HORSE²)-*marines*, *told him my candid opinion*, ~ *me your name*, *glad I was*, ~ FORTUNES. **3.** Utter, as *you told me a lie*, *a* STORY¹, *are you* ~*ing the truth?* **4.** Give information or description, as *told me of or about his difficulties, he told of foreign lands, that* ~*s a tale* (is significant, reveals something); (childish) *don't* ~ *on* (inform against) *me*. **5.** Decide, determine, as *how do you* ~ *which button to press?, you never can* ~ (appearances & probabilities are deceptive). **6.** Distinguish, as *cannot* ~ *them apart, him from his brother*. **7.** Assure, as *I can* ~ *you, it is not so easy*. **8.** Produce marked effect, as *every blow* ~*s, strain begins to* ~ *on him*, whence ~′ING² a., ~′ING²ᴸʸ adv. **9.** Count (votes esp. in House of Commons, *one's* BEAD²s; *we were 18 men all told*; *a hundred*; ~*s over his money every night*). **10.** Direct (person) *to do something* (~ *him to wait for me*). **11.** *~ person good-bye*, say good-bye to; ~ *off*, count off, detach, for duty, as *6 of us were*, *I was, told off to get fuel*, ‖ (sl.) ~ (person) home truths, recite misdoings of; ~ *the tale* (sl.), pitch a pitiful yarn to evoke sympathy; *~ the world*, announce openly, assert emphatically, *you're* ~*ing me!* (sl.), I am fully aware of that. Hence ~ABLE a. [OE *tellan* (TALE), cf. Du. *tellen*, G *zählen*]

tĕll′er, n. In vbl senses, esp.: any of four persons appointed (two for each side) to count votes in House of Commons; person appointed to receive or pay out money in bank etc. Hence ~SHIP n. [-ER¹]

tĕll′tāle, n. One who tells about another's private affairs, tattler; (fig.) thing, circumstance, that reveals person's

thoughts, conduct, etc., esp. attrib., as ~ *blushes, face, the* ~ *clay on his shoes*; kinds of mechanical device for recording person's attendance at specified time etc., giving warning that cistern is full, etc.; (Naut.) index near wheel to show position of tiller, (also~*compass*) compass hung usu. in captain's cabin for checking ship's course.

tĕllū′rian, a. (Inhabitant) of the earth. So ~AL a. [as foll. + -IAN]

tĕllū′rion, n. Instrument for illustrating succession of day & night & changes of seasons. [f. L *tellus -ūris* earth]

tĕllū′rium, n. (chem.). A rare brittle silver-white metallic element. Hence ~′ŪRATE¹³(3), ~′ŪRIDE, nn., ~′ŪRĒTED¹, ~′ŪROUS, aa. [as prec. + -IUM]

tĕl′ŏtype, n. Printing electric telegraph; telegram so printed. [TELE-, -O-, TYPE]

tĕl′pher, a. Serving to transport (esp. goods) by electric locomotion, as ~ *line*. Hence ~AGE(1, 2) n. [for TELE-(PHORE)]

tĕl′son, n. Last joint in abdomen of Crustacea. [Gk, = limit]

tĕm′ĕnŏs, n. (Gk Ant.; pl. -*nē*). Sacred enclosure, temple precinct. [Gk (*temnō* cut)]

tĕmerā′rious, a. (literary). Reckless, rash. [f. L *temerarius* (*temere* rashly) + -OUS]

tĕmĕ′rĭtỹ, n. Rashness. [f. L *temeritas* (*temere* at random, rashly, see -TY)]

tĕmp., abbr. (now usu. as playful pedantry) of L *tempore* in the time of, as ~ *Henry I.*

Tĕmpē′an (or tĕ′), a. Of or like Tempe, beautiful vale in Thessaly celebrated by Gk & L poets. [-AN¹]

tĕm′per¹, v.t. & i. **1.** Prepare (clay etc.) by moistening, mixing, & kneading. **2.** Bring (metal, esp. steel), (of metal) come, to proper hardness & elasticity by successive heating & cooling. **3.** Modify, mitigate, (*justice* etc.) by blending *with* (*mercy* etc.); moderate, restrain, tone down. **4.** (mus.). Tune, modulate, (piano, organ) in particular TEMPERAMENT. Hence ~ABLE, ~ATIVE, aa., ~ER¹ n. [OE *temprian* f. L *temperare* (perh. f. *tempus -oris* time, due season)]

tĕm′per², n. **1.** Mixture, esp. suitable combination of ingredients (*of* mortar etc.); resulting condition or consistence. **2.** Condition of metal as to hardness & elasticity. **3.** Habitual or temporary disposition of mind, as *vas of a saturnine, frigid, fiery, placid*, ~, *persons of congenial* ~, *found him in a good* ~ (not irritable or angry), *in a bad* ~ (peevish, angry); irritation, anger, as *fit of* ~, *what a* ~ *he is in!, naughty* ~!; *show* ~, be petulant; *lose one's* ~, become angry; *keep, control, one's* ~, not lose it; *out of* ~, angry. Hence (-)~ED² (-erd) a., (-)~edɪʀ² adv. [f. prec.]

tĕm′pera, n. = DISTEMPER³. [It.]

těm'perament, n. 1. Individual charac- ter of one's physical organization perma- nently affecting the manner of acting, feeling, & thinking, as a *nervous ~, the artistic ~; sanguine, lymphatic or phleg- matic, choleric or bilious, ~* (formerly attributed to predominance of blood, lymph, yellow bile, black bile). 2. (mus.) Adjustment of tuning of piano etc. so as to fit the scale for all keys, esp. *equal ~,* in which the 12 semitones are at equal intervals. Hence ~AL (-ĕnt) a. (in n. senses, & esp., of persons, liable to peculiar moods). [f. L *temperamentum* (as TEMPER¹, see -MENT)]

těm'perance, n. Moderation, self- restraint, in speech, conduct, etc., esp. in eating & drinking; moderation in use of, ~ total abstinence from, alcoholic liquors as beverages; *~ hotel* (not supply- ing alcoholic drinks); *~ movement, society, league* (for restriction or abolition of use of alcoholic drinks). [AF (-*ounce*), f. L *temperantia* (as TEMPER¹, see -ANCE)]

těm'perate, a. Moderate, self-restrained; abstemious; of mild temperature, as *north, south, ~ zone* (between tropic of Cancer & arctic circle, Capricorn & ant- arctic). Hence ~LY² adv., ~NESS n. [f. L TEMPER¹*atus*]

těm'perature, n. Degree or intensity of sensible heat of a body or of the atmo- sphere esp. as shown by thermometer, as *high, low, ~;* (Med.) internal heat of the body (*normal ~* in man, 98·4°; *take one's ~,* ascertain his variation from this in illness etc.); *absolute zero of ~; ~ curve* (showing variations of ~). [f. L *tempera- tura* (as TEMPER¹, see -URE)]

těm'pest, n. Violent storm of wind often with rain, snow, etc.; (fig.) violent tumult or agitation. [f. OF *tempeste* f. L *tem- pestas* time, weather, storm (*tempus* time, see -TY)]

těmpěs'tuous, a. (Of weather, time, etc., and fig. of person or mood) stormy, violent. Hence ~LY² adv., ~NESS n. [f. LL *tempestuosus* (prec., -OUS; for -*u*- cf. VOLUPTUOUS)]

těm'plar, n. 1. (T~) member of religious military order (*Knights T~s*) for protec- tion of pilgrims to Holy Land, suppressed in 1312. 2. Lawyer, law student, with chambers in the Temple. 3. *Good T~s,* temperance society. [f. OF *templier* = med. L *templarius* (TEMPLE¹, -ARY¹)]

těm'ple¹, n. See TEMPLET.

těm'ple², n. 1. Edifice dedicated to service of (esp. ancient Greek, Roman, Egyptian) god. 2. Any of three successive religious edifices of the Jews in Jerusalem. 3. Place of Christian public worship, esp. Protestant church in France; (fig.) place in which God resides (1 *Cor.* vi. 19). 4. *Inner, Middle, T~,* two INNS of Court on site of the *T~* (establishment of Knights Templars) in London; *T~ Bar,* gateway (removed 1879) that marked the westward limit of the City Corporation's jurisdiction, at junction of Fleet Street & Strand in London. [f. L *templum* cogn. w. Gk TEMENOS]

těm'ple³, n. Flat part of either side of head between forehead & ear. [OF, f. L *tempora* the ~s (sing. *tempus*)]

těm'ple⁴, n. Device in loom for keeping cloth stretched. [F. = foll.]

těm'plet, -āte, n. Pattern, gauge, usu. thin board or metal plate, used as guide etc.; timber or plate used to distribute weight in wall or under beam etc.; wedge for building-block under ship's keel. [perh. f. L *templum* rafter + -ET¹]

těm'pō, n. (mus., pl. -pī pr. -pē). Time, rapidity of movement; (fig.) rate of motion or activity (*the ~ of the war is quickening*); characteristic style of move- ment, as *~ di menuetto.* [It.]

těm'poral, a. & n. 1. Of this life, secular, esp. opp. to *spiritual,* as *~ affairs, interests,* whence ~LY² adv., ~NESS n. 1; *~ lords,* peers of realm, ~NESS n.; *~ power,* of ecclesiastic etc. Pope in *~ matters.* 2. Of or in or denoting time (*~ & spatial,* of time & space); *~ conjunctions,* when etc.); (Gk Gram.) *~ augment* (made by leng- thening initial vowel). 3. Of the temple(s) of the head, as *~ artery, bone.* 4. n. (Law) temporalities. [F, f. L *temporalis* (*tempus -oris,* time, see -AL)]

tempŏrăl'ity, n. A secular possession, esp. properties & revenues of religious corporation or ecclesiastic (usu. pl.); (Law) temporariness. [f. LL *temporali- tātem* (as prec., see -TY)]

těm'porally, adv. In time; = prec. (1st sense). [f. OF *temporalité* as prec.]

těm'porarÿ, a. Lasting, meant, only for a time, as *~y buildings, relief, possession, office.* Hence ~ILY² adv., ~NESS n. [f. L *temporarius* (prec. -ARY¹)]

těm'poriz/e, v.i. Pursue indecisive or time-serving policy; avoid committing oneself, act so as to gain time; comply temporarily with requirements of occa- sion. Hence ~ATION, ~ER¹, nn., ~INGLY² adv. [f. F *temporiser* f. L *tempus -ŏris* time + -IZE]

těm'poro- in comb. = L *tempora* temples of head, as *~făcial,* of temporal & facial regions.

tĕmpt, v.t. (Arch., Bibl.) test, try the resolution of, as *God did ~ Abraham;* entice, incite, (to do, to action esp. evil one); *I am ~ed* (strongly disposed) *to question this;* allure, attract, whence ~'ingly² adv.; (arch., Bibl.) provoke, defy, as *shalt not ~'the Lord.* Hence or cogn. ~ABIL'ITY n., ~'ABLE a. [f. OF *tempt-,* f. L *tentāre, temptt, tempt,* handle, test, try]

tempta'tion, n. Tempting or being tempted (*the T~,* see *Matt.* iv); thing that

attracts, attractive course. [f. OF *temptacioun* f. L *temptationem* (prec., -ATION)]

tempt'er, n. One who tempts; the *T~er*, the devil. So **~RESS¹** n. [ME *temptour* f. L *temptatorem* (as prec., see -OR³)]

ten, a. & n. One more than nine, 10, X; (as round number) *~ times as easy*, *~ to one he forgets it*; HART of *~*; UPPER *~*; *~PENNY nail*; *~-pounder* (hist.), person having vote in parliamentary election by occupation of property of rental value of £10. Hence **~FOLD** a. & adv., **~TH²** a. & n., **~THly²** adv. [OE *tien* cf. Du. *tien*, G *zehn*, & L *decem*, Gk *deka*]

ten'able, a. That can be maintained or defended against attack, as *a ~ position*, *fortress*, *theory*; (of office etc.) that can be held *for* specified time, *by* person, etc. Hence **tenabil'ITY**, **~NESS** nn. [F (*tenir* hold f. L *tenēre*, see -ABLE)]

ten'ace (-is), n. (cards). (Holding of) two cards, one next above, the other next below, the opponents' highest of the suit (*major*, *minor*, *~*, variations of this variously defined). [f. Sp. *tenaza* lit. pincers]

tena'cious (-shus), a. Holding fast; keeping firm hold (of property, rights, principles, etc.); (of memory) retentive; adhesive, sticky; strongly cohesive. Hence or cogn. **~NY²** adv., **~NESS**, **tena'CITY**, nn. [f. L *tenax* (*tenēre* hold, see -ACIOUS)]

tenac'ulum, n. (pl. *-la*). Surgeon's sharp hook for picking up arteries etc. [L, = holding instrument (*tenēre* hold)]

tenail', **-aille'** (-āl), n. (fortif.). Outwork in main ditch in front of curtain between two bastions. [F (*-le*), f. prec.]

ten'ant, n., & v.t. **1.** One who occupies land or tenement under a landlord; (Law) person holding real property by private ownership, also defendant in real action; occupant (*of* any place); *~ farmer* (cultivating farm he does not own); || *~ right*, right of *~* to continue tenancy, as long as he pays rent & acts according, without injurious increase of rent, & to receive compensation from landlord if turned off. **2.** v.t. Occupy as *~* (esp. in p.p.). Hence or cogn. **ten'ANCY** n., **~LESS** a. [F, f. L *tenēre* hold, see -ANT]

ten'antable, a. Fit to be occupied by a tenant. [-ABLE]

ten'antry, n. Tenants. [-RY]

tench, n. A European freshwater fish of carp family. [f. OF *tenche* f. LL *tinca*]

tend¹, v.i. Be moving, be directed, hold a course, lit. & fig.; as *~s in our direction*, *downwards*, *this way*, *towards the coast*, *to the same conclusion*; be apt or inclined, serve, conduce, (*to* action, quality, etc., *to do*). [f. OF *tendre* stretch f. L *tendere tens-* or *tent-*]

tend², v.t. & i. Take care of, look after, (flocks, invalid, machine); wait *upon*; (Naut.) watch (ship at anchor) so as to keep turns out of her cable. So **ten'd-ANCE** n. (arch.). [shortened f. ATTEND]

ten'dency, n. Bent, leaning, inclination, (*towards*, *to*, thing, *to do*). [f. med. L *tendentia* (as TEND¹, see -ANCE)]

tenden'tious (-shus), a. (Of writing etc.) having an underlying purpose, calculated to advance a cause. [f. G *tendenziös* (TENDENCY, -OUS)]

ten'der¹, n. In vbl senses of TEND²; also: vessel attending larger one to supply her with stores, convey orders, etc.; carriage attached to locomotive & carrying fuel, water, etc.; small water reservoir fixed to mop etc. [-ER¹]

ten'der², v.t. & i., & n. **1.** Offer, present, give in, (one's *services*, *resignation*, etc.); offer (money etc.) as payment; make a *~* (*for* supply of thing or execution of work). **2.** n. Offer, esp. offer in writing to execute work or supply goods at fixed price, as *are open to receive ~ for*; *plea of ~* (that defendant has always been ready to satisfy plaintiff's claim & now brings the sum into court); *legal ~*, currency that cannot be refused in payment of debt, as *silver is not legal ~ above 40s.* [(n. f. vb) as TEND¹]

ten'der³, a. (*~est*). **1.** Soft, not tough or hard, as *~ steak*; easily touched or wounded, susceptible to pain or grief, as *a ~ heart*, *conscience*, *place* (in body); delicate, fragile, (lit., & fig. of reputation etc.; *of ~ age*, immature, young); loving, affectionate, fond, as *~ parents*, *wrote ~ verses*; solicitous, considerate, (of one's honour, good name, etc.); afraid of (doing wrong thing); requiring careful handling, ticklish, as a *~ subject*. **2.** *~-eyed*, having gentle eyes, weak-eyed; *~-foot* (colon. & U.S. sl.), new-comer in bush etc., novice; *~-hearted*, having *~* heart, so *~-heartedly* adv., *~-heartedness* n.; ***~-loin**, undercut of sirloin, (*T~loin*) amusements district of New York & other cities. Hence **~LY²** adv., **~NESS** n. [f. OF *tendre* f. L *tener*]

ten'don, n. Strong band or cord of tissue forming termination or connexion of fleshy part of muscle; *~foot of Achilles* (akil'ēz; L *tendo Achillis*), connecting heel (where alone Achilles was vulnerable) with calf. So **ten'dinous** a. [f. med. L *tendo -inis* f. Gk *tenōn* w. assim. to *tendere* stretch]

ten'dril, n. Slender leafless plant-organ attaching itself to another body for support. Hence **~LED²-id)** a. [cf. F *tendrillon* dim. of *tendron* bud (as TENDER³)]

ten'ebrae, n. pl. (R.-C. Ch.). Matins & lauds for last three days of Holy Week, at which candles are successively extinguished. [L, = darkness]

tenebrif'ic, a. Making darkness, as *~ stars* (believed to cause night). [f. prec., see -FIC]

ten'ebrous, a. (arch.). Dark, gloomy. [f. OF *tenebrus* f. L *tenebrosus* (TENEBRAE, -OUS)]

ten'ement, n. Piece of land held by an owner; (Law) any kind of permanent

property, e.g. lands, rents, peerage, held of a superior, so ~ARY¹ (-mén²) a.; dwelling-house; set of apartments used by one family (~house, containing ~s). Hence ~AL (-mén²) a. [OF. f. med. L *tenementum* (*tenére* hold, see -MENT)]

tenes'mus (-z-), n. (path.). Continual inclination to void the bowels or bladder accompanied by painful straining. [med. L f. Gk *tēnesmos* straining (*teinō* stretch)]

tén'et, n. Principle, dogma, doctrine, of a person or school. [L, = he holds; formerly also *tenent*, = they hold]

tén'ner, n. (colloq.). ‖ Ten-pound, dollar, note. [-ER¹]

tén'nis, n. Game for 2, 3, or 4 persons played by striking ball with rackets over net stretched across walled court; ~ LAWN ~; ~ *arm, elbow,* affection of arm caused by ~; ~*-ball, -court* (for ~). [15th c. *tenetz,* prob. f. F orig., perh. = *tenez* hold, take this, play (as foll.)]

tén'on, n., & v.t. 1. End of piece of wood fitted for insertion into corresponding cavity (esp. MORTISE) in another piece; ~*-saw* (small, with strong brass or steel back, for fine work). 2. v.t. Cut into a ~, join by means of ~, whence ~ER¹(1, 2) n. [F. f. *tenir* hold f. L *tenére*]

tén'or¹, n. 1. Settled or prevailing course or direction, esp. fig. of one's life, way, etc.; general purport, drift, (of speech, writing, etc.). 2. (Law) true intent, (also) exact copy. 2. (Music for, singer with) highest ordinary adult male voice, between baritone & alto (often attrib. as ~ *voice*); instrument, esp. viola, of which range is roughly that of ~ *voice*; ~ *bell* (largest of peal or set). So ~IST(3) n. (mus.). [f. OF *tenour* f. L *tenorem* holding on, (med. L) chief melody (formerly assigned to adult male voice), f. *tenére* hold, see -OR¹]

tenot'omý, n. Tendon-cutting, esp. as remedy for club-foot. [irreg. f. Gk *tenōn, -ontos* tendon (*teinō* stretch)+-TOMY]

tén'réc, tän', n. Hedgehog-like tailless insectivorous mammal of Madagascar. [F (*tanr-*), f. Malagasy *tràndraka*]

tense², n. (gram.). Form taken by verb to indicate the time (also continuance or completeness) of the action etc., as *present, future, past,* (*imperfect, pluperfect, aorist,* ~, *primary, historic,* ~s; set of such forms for the various persons; SEQUENCE of ~s. Hence ~LESS a. [f. OF *tens* f. L *tempus* time]

tense², a. & v.t. & i. 1. (Of cord, membrane, nerve, fig. of mind, emotion) stretched tight, strained to stiffness. 2. v.b. Make or become ~. Hence ~LY² adv., ~NESS, tén'sITY, nn. [f. L as TEND¹]

tén'sible a. [as prec., see -LE]

tén'sion (-shn), n., & v.t. 1. Stretching, being stretched; tenseness; mental strain or excitement; strained (political, social, etc.) state; (Mech.) stress by which bar, cord, etc. is pulled when it is part of a system in equilibrium or motion; expansive force of gas or vapour; electromotive force. 2. v.t. Subject to ~. Hence ~AL a. [f. L f. LL *tensio* (as TEND¹, see -ION)]

tén'son, -zon, n. Contest in verse between troubadours; subdivision of poem composed for this. [F (-son), = It. *tenzone,* as prec.]

tent¹, n. (anat.). Muscle that tightens or stretches a part. [as TEND¹, see -OR²]

tent¹, n., & v.i. & t. 1. Portable shelter of canvas, cloth, etc., supported by pole(s) & stretched by cords secured to ~*-pegs* driven into ground; with one pole in middle; (Photog., also *dark* ~) portable dark room for outdoor use. 2. ~*-bed* (with a ~*-like* canopy); ~*-fly,* piece of canvas stretched over ridge pole of ~ leaving open space but keeping off sun & rain; ~*-pegging,* cavalry exercise in which rider tries at full gallop to carry off on point of lance ~*-peg* fixed in ground; ~*-stitch,* series of parallel diagonal stitches suggesting ~. 3. vb. Cover (as) with ~; encamp in ~. [ME & OF *tente* neut. pl. p.p. as TEND¹]

tent², n. Deep red wine chiefly from Spain, used esp. as sacramental wine. [f. Sp. *tinto* deep-coloured f. L as TINGE]

tén'tacle, n. Feeler, long slender flexible process or appendage of animal, used for exploration, prehension, or locomotion; (Bot.) sensitive hair or filament. Hence ~D² (-ld), téntăc'ŭlar, téntăc'ŭlate², ~ated, téntăc'ŭliform, téntăc'ŭli-errous, aa. [f. L as TEMPT + -*culum* seen in *spectaculum* etc.]

tén'tative, a. & n. 1. Done by way of trial, experimental. 2. n. Experimental proposal or theory. Hence ~LY² adv. [f. med. L *tentativus* (as TEMPT, see -IVE)]

tén'ter¹, n. Person in charge of something; ‖ Sc. *tend* var. of TEND²+-ER¹]

tén'ter², n. Machine for stretching cloth to set or dry; ~(*hook*), each of the hooks that hold the cloth; *be on* ~*hooks* (arch.) *on the* ~s (in state of suspense or mental torment). [earlier also *tenture,* prob. f. L *tentura* (TEND¹, -URE) cf. BORDER]

tén'uis, n. (pl. -es pr. -ēz). Hard or surd mute (k, p, t), cf. MEDIA. [L, = thin]

tenu'ity, n. Slenderness; (of style) rarity, thinness; (of air, fluid) absence of grandeur. [f. L *tenuitas* (as

tĕn′ūous, a. (rare). Thin, slender, small; (of distinctions etc.) subtle, over-refined. [f. L TENUIS +-OUS]

tĕn′ure (-yer), n. Kind of right or title by which (esp. real) property is held, as ALLODIAL, FEUDAL, ~, military~ (involving military service); (period of) holding, possession, enjoyment, as during his ~ of office, holds life on a precarious ~; (Hist.) ~horn, -sword (produced on certain occasions as evidence of ~ of estates). [OF (tenir hold f. L tenēre, see -URE)]

tĕnu′tō (-ōō-), a. (mus.). Sustained, given its full time value (cf. STACCATO). [It. = held]

Tĕōdit′i, n. Temple of Mex. & other Amer. aborigines, usu. on truncated pyramid. [Mex. (teotl god +calli house); also teopan]

tēp′ee, teep′ee, n. Conical tent or lodge of the American Indians, formerly made of skins, now of cloth or canvas. [native name]

tĕp′ěfy, v.t. & i. Make, become, tepid. Hence ~FAC′TION n. [f. L tepefacere (as TEPID, see -FY)]

tĕph′igram, n. (meteorol.). Diagram showing state of atmosphere at different levels in terms of temperature & entropy. [t. symbol t for temperature + symbol phi for entropy +-GRAM]

tĕph′rite, n. Kinds of modern volcanic rock. [f. Gk tephra ashes, -ITE¹]

tĕp′id, a. Slightly warm, lukewarm (lit. & fig.). Hence or cogn. tĕp′idITY, ~NESS, nn., ~LY² adv. [f. L tepidus (tepēre be lukewarm, see -ID³)]

tĕpĭdā′rium, n. (Rom. Ant.; pl. -aria). Intermediate room of moderate temperature in Roman baths; boiler for heating hot bath. [L(as prec., see -ARIUM)]

tĕ′raph, n. (bibl.; only in pl. ~īm, used as sing. or collective sing.). Small image(s) as domestic oracle of ancient Hebrews. [Heb.]

terce. See TIERCE.

tĕr′cel, tier′cel, n. Male falcon. [OF. f. pop. L tertiolus dim. of tertius third (hawk's third egg being held to produce small male)]

tẽrcĕn′tenarÿ (or -entēn-), -tĕnn′ial, aa. & nn. Of 300 years; (n.) 300th anniversary. [TER]

tẽr′cĕt, n. (Mus.; Pros.; also tiercet)=

TRIPLET. [f. It. terzetto (terzo third f. L tertius)]

tĕ′rēbēne, n. A hydrocarbon prepared by treating oil of turpentine with sulphuric acid, used as disinfectant etc. [f. foll. +-ENE]

tĕ′rēbinth, n. Turpentine-tree, yielding Chian turpentine; oil of ~, oil of turpentine. [f. OF therebinthe f. L f. Gk terebinthos]

tĕrēbin′thine, a. Of the terebinth; of turpentine, so tĕrĕb′ic a. [f. L f. Gk terebinthinos (as prec., see -INE²)]

tĕ′rĕbrla, n. (pl. ~ae). Boring ovipositor of some insects. Hence ~ATE²(2) a. [L, = borer]

tĕrĕd′ō, n. (pl. ~s). Ship-worm, mollusc that bores ships etc. [L, f. Gk terēdōn (teirō rub)]

tẽrg′al, a. Of the back, dorsal. [f. L tergum back +-AL]

tẽrgĕm′inate, a. (bot.). (Of leaf) having at base a pair of leaflets & forking with a pair on each branch. [f. L TER(geminus born together) +-ATE²]

tẽr′givĕrsāte, v.i. Turn one's back on oneself, turn one's coat, apostatize, change one's party or principles; make conflicting statements. So ~A′TION, ~ātor², nn. [f. L tergiversari turn one's back (tergum back +vers- f. vertere turn), see -ATE³]

term¹, n. 1.(arch.). Boundary, limit, esp. of time, as set a ~ to his encroachments, awaited the ~ of his existence, whence ~LESS a. (poet., rhet.). 2. Limited period, as for a ~ of 5 years, his ~ of office expired. 3.(Univ~, School, Law) period during which instruction is given || or court holds sessions, as Michaelmas, Hilary, Easter, Trinity, ~ (w. ref. to administration of justice, now sittings), will end it next ~, during ~ (-time), || EAT one's ~s. 4. Appointed day, || esp. QUARTER¹-day. 5.(law). (Also ~ of or for years) estate or interest in land to be enjoyed for fixed period. 6.(math.). Antecedent or consequent of ratio, part of expression joined to the rest by + or − (e.g. $3x^2 - b + cz$ has three~s). 7.(logic). Word(s) that may be subject or predicate of a proposition, as MAJOR³ MINOR, MIDDLE¹, ~. 8. Word used to express a definite conception esp. in particular branch of study etc., as technical, scientific, law~, ~ in ~s of (in the language peculiar to), CONTRADICTION in ~s, set (definite) ~s. 9. pl. Language employed, mode of expression, as in the most flattering ~s. 10. pl. Conditions, as cannot accept his ~s, do it on your own ~s; esp. charge, price, as his ~s are 2 guineas a lesson, INCLUSIVE ~s; come to ~s, yield, give way, (also make ~s) conclude agreement (with); bring person to ~s, cause him to accept conditions; ~s of reference, points referred to an individual or body of persons for decision or report, scope of

an inquiry. **11.** pl. Relation, footing, as ~~am on good, bad, familiar~~ ~s with him, are not on speaking ~s. [f. F terme f. L TERMINUS]

term², v.t. Denominate, call, as the music ~ed plain-song, I forget how or what he ~s it, this he ~ed sheer robbery. [f. prec.]

term'agant, n. & a. **1.** (hist.; T~). Imaginary Mohammedan deity of turbulent character, often appearing in morality plays. **2.** Brawling woman, shrew, scold. **3.** adj. Boisterous, turbulent, shrewish, whence **term'agancy** n., ~ly² adv. [f. OF tervagant f. It. trivigante, -vag-, perh. = wandering under three names (Selene, Artemis, Persephone), f. L tri- thrice + vagari wander, -ANT]

term'inable, a. That may be terminated; coming to an end after certain time, as ~ annuity. Hence ~NESS n. [f. obs. termine, or TERMINATE, see -ABLE]

term'inal, a. & n. **1.** Of, forming, a limit or terminus, as ~ station; (Math.) value, most concise form of an expression; (Bot.) borne at end of stem etc.; (Zool. etc.) ending a series, as ~ joints; of, done each term, as ~ accounts, subscription; ~ (TERMINUS) figure. **2.** n. Terminating thing, extremity, esp. point of connexion in electric circuit; *railway terminus. Hence ~LY² adv. [f. L terminalis (TERMINUS, see -AL)]

term'inate¹, v.t. & i. Bound, limit; bring, come, to an end; (of word) end in (such letters or syllable). Hence or cogn. ~atively² adv. [f. L terminare (TERMINUS, see -ATE³]

term'inate², a. Coming to an end, bounded, as a ~ decimal. [as prec., see -ATE²]

termina'tion, n. (In vbl senses, see TERMINATE¹ & esp.) word's final syllable or letter or group of letters esp. as an element in inflexion or derivation; put a ~ to, bring to a ~, make an end of. Hence ~AL a. (gram.). [f. L terminationem (TERMINATE¹, -ATION)]

term'inator, n. Person, thing, that terminates; dividing line between light & dark part of heavenly body. [LL (as prec., -OR²)]

term'iner. See OYER.

term'inism, n. Doctrine that everyone has limited term for repentance; = NOMINALISM. So ~IST n. [f. TERMINUS +-ISM]

termin|öl'ogÿ, n. Science of proper use of terms; terms used in an art etc. Hence ~olö´gical a. (~ological inexactitude, joc. lie), ~olö´gically² adv. [f. TERMINUS +-LOGY]

term'inus, n. (pl. ~uses, -ī). **1.** (Now rare) final point, goal. **2.** || Station at end of main or branch railway. **3.** (Rom. Ant., T~) god of boundaries. **4.** Figure of human bust ending in square pillar. **5.** ~ ad quem, ā quō, terminating, starting,

-point (of argument, policy, period, etc.). [L, cf. Gk terma limit]

termitar'ium, term'itarÿ, nn. Nest of, cage for, termites. [f. foll. +-ARIUM, -ARY¹]

term'ite, n. Social insect, chiefly tropical & very destructive to timber, pop. but erron. called white ant. [f. LL termes -itis wood-worm f. terere rub]

term'lÿ, a. & adv. (rare). (Occurring, paid, etc.) by the term, terminal(ly). [-LY¹]

term'or, n. (law). One who holds lands etc. for a term of years, or for life. [AF termer (TERM, see -OR² s.f.)]

tern¹, tärn, n. Kinds of sea-bird like gull but usu. smaller & with longer bill. [cf. Da. terne, Swed. tärna, ON therna]

tern'arÿ, a. Composed of three, so ~AT a.; (Math.) having three variables. [f. LL ternarius (L terni three each, see -ARY¹)]

tern'ate (or -āt), a. Arranged in threes, esp. (Bot., of leaves) having three leaflets, whorled in threes. Hence ~LY² adv. [-ATE²]

tern'e, n. (Usu. ~-plate) inferior tin-plate alloyed with much lead. [prob. f. F terne dull, see TARNISH]

Terpsichore'an (-ko-), t., a. Of Terpsichore, the Muse of dancing, as the ~ art. [f. Gk Terpsikhorē +-AN]

te'rra, n. Earth (in various L & It. phrr.); ~ cotta, tripolli, rotten-stone; terrae fī'lius, son of the soil, humbly-born person; ~ fī'rma, dry land; ~ incōg'nita (in-k-), unknown region; ~ Japon'ica, gambier [orig. thought to be earth from Japan]; ~ nera (nā'rā), pigment used by ancient artists [It., = black earth]; ~ verde (vār'dā), green earth used as pigment. [It. L]

te'rrace, n. & v.t. **1.** Raised level space, natural or artificial; (Geol.) raised beach. **2.** || Row of houses along top or face of slope (also as fancy name of street etc.). **3.** v.t. Form into, furnish with, ~; ~d roof, flat roof of an Indian or Eastern house. [F (prec., -ACEOUS)]

terracott'a, n. Hard pottery used as ornamental building-material & in statuary (often attrib.); statue, figurine, of this; (a. & n.) its brownish-red colour. [It., = baked earth]

terrain', n. A tract of land as regarded by the physical geographer or the tactician. [F, as TERRENE]

terramare' (-ahr, -ār), n. Kinds of earthy deposit containing bones, phosphates, etc., & useful as fertilizer; S.-Europ. prehistoric deposit like kitchen MIDDEN. [F, f. dial. It. TERRA mara (marra marl)]

terra'ceous, a. (bot.). Growing on land. [f. TERRA, see -ACEOUS]

te'rrapin, n. Kinds of freshwater tortoise,

esp. salt-marsh ~ (also *diamond-back*), kind valued as food. [prob. of Amer.-Ind. orig.]

terraq'ueous, a. (Of the earth) comprising both land & water. [TERRA, AQUA, -EOUS]

terrène', a. Of earth, earthy; terrestrial. [f. L *terrenus* (TERRA)]

terreplein (târ'plān), n. (fortif.) Surface of rampart behind parapet, where guns are mounted; base above, on, or below, the ground level, on which a battery is placed in field-works. [F (*terre* earth f. TERRA+*plein* f. L *plenus* full); orig. sense *earth-pack, talus*]

terres'trial, a. & n. 1. Of the earth, esp. opp. to *celestial*, as *the ~ seasons, the ~ globe* (representing earth), *~ MAGNETISM*; of this world, worldly, as *~ aims, interests*; of land opp. to water; (Zool.) living on the ground, opp. to *aquatic, arboreal, aerial*. 2. n. Inhabitant of earth. Hence ~LY² adv. [f. L *terrestris* (TERRA)+ -AL]

te'rret, -it, n. Each of loops or rings on harness-pad for driving-reins to pass through. [f. OF *toret* dim. of TOUR]

te'rrible, a. Exciting or fit to excite terror, awful, dreadful, formidable; (colloq.) excessive, as *a ~ bore*; ENFANT TERRIBLE. Hence ~NESS n, **te'rribLY²** adv. (esp., sl., very). [F, f. L *terribilis* (*terrère* frighten, see -BLE)]

terric'olous, a. Living on or in the earth, esp. of the *Terricolae*, group of annelids including earthworm. [f. L *terricola* (TERRA+*colere* inhabit)+-OUS]

te'rrier¹, n. 1. Kinds of active & hardy dog with digging propensity; *black-&-tan*, BULL¹, FOX¹, ~, short-haired kinds; *Cairn, Irish, Scotch, Skye, Yorkshire,* ~, rough-haired kinds; *Maltese, toy,* ~, small toy kinds. 2. (colloq.). || Member of Territorial Army. [F, f. L sa foll.]

te'rrier², n. Book recording site, boundaries, etc., of land of private persons or corporations; (Hist.) collection of acknowledgements of vassals or tenants of a lordship. [OF = rent-roll, = med. L *terrarius* (*liber* book) of lands]

terrif'ic, a. Causing terror, terrible. Hence~ICALLY adv. [f. L *terrificus* (*terrère* frighten, see -FIC)]

te'rrify, v.t. Fill with terror, frighten. [f. L *terrificare* (as prec, see -FY)]

terri'genous, a. Produced by the earth, as *~ deposits, ~ metals*, metallic bases of earths, e.g. aluminium. [f. L *terrigenus* born of earth (TERRA + *genus* =-born f. *gigno*)+-OUS]

territ. See TERRET.

terrine' (-ēn), n. Earthenware vessel containing and sold with some table delicacy, as *terrin earthen*. [F, fem. of OF *terrin* earthen (L TERRA, -INE²)]

te'rritor'ial, a. & n. 1. Of territory, as *~ possessions, acquisitions*; limited to a district, as *the right was strictly ~*; (T~) of (any of) the U.S. Territories; (Eccl.) *~ system* (in which civil rule claims supremacy as a natural right, whence ~ISM n.); || *T~ Army* or *Force*, force organized for home defence to replace the older bodies of militia, yeomanry, and volunteers. 2. n. || Member of T~ Army. Hence ~LY³ adv. [f. LL *territorialis* (as TERRITORY, see -AL)]

territor'ialize, v.t. Extend by addition of, reduce to state of, territory. [-IZE]

te'rritory, n. Extent of land under jurisdiction of sovereign, State, city, etc.; (Commerce) area over which a commercial traveller operates; large tract of land; *(T~)* organized division of the country not yet admitted to full rights of a State. [f. L *territorium*, etym. dub.]

te'rror, n. Extreme fear; *~-stricken, -struck* (with ~); person, thing, that causes this, as *a ~ to evildoers*; (colloq.) *here comes this ~* (troublesome child) again; *king of ~s*, death (*Job* xviii. 14); *Reign of T~, the T~*, period of French Revolution, 1793-4 (& of similar periods marked by sanguinary excesses of revolutionaries, also *Red T~*, or reactionaries, also *White T~*). [f. F *terreur* f. L *terrorem* (*terrère* frighten, see -OR¹)]

te'rrorist, n. One who favours or uses terror-inspiring methods of governing or of coercing government or community, esp. (1) Jacobin under Reign of Terror, (2) Russian revolutionary. Hence or cogn.~ISM(2, 3),~IZA'TION, nn.,~IS'TIC a., ~IZE(1) v.t. [F'(-e), prec, -IST]

te'rry, n. A pile fabric with the loops uncut (also attrib.). [perh. f. F *tiré* draw f. LL *tirare* etym. dub.]

terse, a. (Of speech, style, writer) free from cumbrousness and superfluity, smooth and concise. Hence ~LY² (-sl-) adv., ~NESS (-sn-) n. [f. L *tergere* ters-wipe, polish]

ter'tian (-shn), a. & n. (Fever, disease) whose paroxysms occur every other day, as *~ ague*. [f. fem. of L *tertianus* (*tertius* third, see -AN)]

ter'tiary (-sha-), a. & n. 1. Of the third order, rank, formation, etc. 2. n. (Ornith.) flight-feather of third row, so **ter'TIAL** (-sl) a. & n.; (T~) member of third order of monastic body; *the T~*, third geological period. [f. L *tertiarius* (prec, -ARY¹)]

ter'tio (-shiō). See PRIMO.

ter'tium quid (-shi-), n. A third something, esp. between mind and matter or between opposite things. [L]

ter'tius (-shus), a. || (In schools) *Jones* etc. ~ (third of the name); *~ gaud'ens* (L, = glad third), third party expecting to profit by two others' quarrel. [L]

terza rima (tàrt'sa rēm'a), n. (pl. -ze -me, pr. -ā). Arrangement of (hen)decasyllabic triplets rhyming thus (bat pig cat fig box wig ox etc), as in Dante's *Commedia*; such triplets. [It.]

terzet'tŏ (tĕärts-), n. (mus.). Vocal trio. [It.]

Tĕs'la, n. ~ **coil**, form of induction coil for high-frequency alternating currents such as are used in diathermy. [Nikola ~, Amer. scientist]

tĕss ellāt'ed, a. Formed of tesserae, as ~*ated pavement*; (Bot., Zool.) regularly checkered. So ~**AR¹** a., ~**ATION** n. [f. L *tessellatus* (*tessella* dim. of foll., see -**ATE³**)]

tĕss'erͺa, n. (pl. ~*ae*). Small square unit, cubic block used in mosaic, whence ~**AL** a.; (Rom. Ant.) small square of bone etc. used as token, ticket, etc. [L, f. Gk *tessares* four]

tĕss'itŭr'a (-oorͺa), n. (mus.). Range within which most tones of a voice-part fall. [It., = TEXTURE]

tĕst¹, n. **1.** Critical examination or trial of person's or thing's qualities, as *has stood the ~* (undergone) *the successive ~s of poverty and riches*, *must put it to the ~*; *a ~ case* (serving to show the principle involved). **2.** Means of so examining, standard for comparison or trial, circumstances suitable for this, as *success is not a fair ~*. **3.** Ground of admission or rejection, as is *excluded by our ~*. **4.** (chem.). Reagent, substance employed to reveal presence of an ingredient in a compound, *as galls are a ~ of or for iron*. **5.** Movable hearth in reverberation furnace used in separating silver from lead. **6.** (collog.). ~**match**. **7.** *T~ Act* (of 1672, requiring all persons before holding office to *take the ~*, i.e. the oaths of supremacy and allegiance or equivalent ~; repealed in 1828); ~**match**, one of the matches in a cricket tour etc. that are to count towards the total result; ~**glass**, *-mixer*, *-paper*, *-tube*, (for ~s or other chem. purposes). [OF, f. L *testum* earthen pot, esp. (med. L) one for trying metals in]

tĕst², v.t. Put to the test, make trial of, (person, thing, quality); try severely, tax, (one's powers of endurance etc.); refine (metal); (Chem.) examine by means of reagent. Hence ~**ABLE** a., tĕs'ter² [-ER¹(.2)] n. [f. prec.]

tĕst³, n. Shell, hard covering, of some animals. [f. L *testa* tile, jug, shell, etc., cogn. w. *testum* TEST¹]

tĕst⁴, n. *= testa*; so tĕstā'CEAN (-āshn) a. & n., tĕstācĕol'ogͺy n.; with a hard continuous shell. (Bot., Zool.) of red brick colour. [f. L *testaceus* (TEST³)]

tĕs'taͺcy, n. Being testate. [-ACY]

tĕs'tament, n. **1.** = WILL³ (last sense) as MILITARY ~, so ~**ary¹** (-ĕnͺ) adv., ~**ARY¹** (-ĕr) a. **2.** (Bibl.) covenant, dispensation; *Old, New, T~*, the portion of the Bible dealing with the Mosaic, Christian, dispensation; (T~) copy of the N.T. [f. L *testamentum* will (TESTATE, -MENT); bibl. sense f. LL mistransl. of Gk *diathēkē* covenant, will]

|| **tĕstām'ur**, n. (univ.). Certificate that one has passed examination. [L, = we testify]

tĕs'tāte (or -ͺt), a. & n. (Person) who has made a will (and died leaving it in force). So **tĕstā'tor**², **tĕstā'trix**, nn. [f. L *tes-tari* testify, make will, (*testis* witness), see -ATE²]

tĕs'ter¹. See TEST².

tĕs'ter², n. Canopy, esp. over FOUR-poster. [f. OF *testere* (*teste* head, as TEST³)]

tĕs'ter³, n. Shilling of Henry VIII; (arch., joc.) sixpence. [var. of earlier and OF *teston* (as TEST³, see -OON)]

tĕs'ticle, n. Each of two glands in male that secrete spermatozoa etc. Hence **tĕstic'ŭlͺar¹** a. [f. L *testiculus* dim. of *testis* a.~]

tĕstic'ŭlate, a. Having, shaped like, testicles; (Bot.) having a pair of organs so shaped. [f. L *testiculus* (prec., -ATE²)]

tĕs'tifͺy, v.t. & t. (Of person or thing) bear witness (*to* fact, state, assertion, *against* person etc., *arch. of* or *concerning* matter); (Law) give evidence; affirm, declare, (one's regret etc., *that*, *how*, etc.); (of things) be evidence of, evince. [f. L *testificari* (*testis* witness, see -FY)]

tĕstimō'nial, n. Certificate of character, conduct, or qualifications; gift, money, presented to person, esp. in public, as mark of esteem, in acknowledgement of services, etc. [OF (adj.), f. LL *testi-monialis* (TESTIMONY, -AL)]

tĕstimō'nialͺize, v.t. Present (person) with testimonial. [-IZE]

tĕs'timonͺy, n. Evidence, demonstration, as *called him to ~*, *produce ~* (*to*, *of*), *we have his ~ for that*; (Law) oral or written statement under oath or affirmation; declarations, statements, as *must rely on the ~ of history, of historians*; (arch.) solemn protest, as *for a ~ against them*; (Bibl.) the decalogue, esp. *the tables of the ~*; (sing. or pl.) the Scriptures. [f. L *testimonium* (*testis* witness, see -MONY)]

tĕstudinͺā'rious, a. Mottled with red, yellow, and black, like tortoise-shell. [f. TESTUDO, see -ARIOUS]

tĕstū'dinate, a. Arched like carapace of tortoise. [f. LL *testudinatus* (TESTUDO, see -ATE²)]

tĕstūdin'eous, a. Like carapace of tortoise. [f. L *testudineus* (foll., -EOUS)]

tĕstū'dŏ, n. (pl. ~*os*, ~*ines*). **1.** (Rom. Ant.) screen formed by body of troops in close array with overlapping shields; similar screen used by miners where ground is likely to cave in. **2.** Genus of tortoises, whence ~**inͺal** a. [L, gen. *-dinis*, = tortoise-shell (TEST³)]

tĕs'tͺy, a. Irritable, touchy. Hence ~**iͺly¹** adv., ~**iͺness** n. [f. AF *testif*; OF has *testu* heady (TEST³)]

tĕtan'ic, a. & n. **1.** Of, such as occurs in, tetanus, as ~ *spasm*. **2.** n. Remedy acting

on the muscles through the nerves, e.g. strychnine. [f. L f. Gk *tetanikós* (as foll., see -IC)]

tet´anus, n. Disease marked by spasm of many or all muscles of voluntary motion, e.g. lockjaw; *artificial* ~*us* (induced by strychnine etc.). Hence or cogn. ~IZA´TION n., ~IZE(3) v.t., ~OID a. [L. f. Gk *tetanos,* redupl. f. st. of *teinō* stretch]

tet´ch|y [¹]´ÿ, a. Peevish, irritable. Hence ~ILY´ adv., ~INESS n. [f. 16th c., etym. dub.]

tête-à-tête (tât´ahtât´), adv., a., & n. 1. Together in private. 2. adj. Private, confidential. 3. n. Private interview or conversation usu. between two; sofa for two. [F, lit. head-to-head]

tĕth´er (-dh-), n., & v.t. 1. Rope, chain, halter, by which grazing animal is confined; (fig.) scope, extent of one's knowledge, authority, etc. (*was beyond, at the end of, his* ~). 2. v.t. Tie (esp. grazing animal) with ~. [vb f. n., prob. f. ON *tjóðr* (Sw. *tjuder*)]

tĕtra- in comb. = Gk *tetra-* comb. form of *tettares* four, as: ~*chord* (-k-), scale series of half-octave (esp. in ancient mus.), so ~*chord´al* a.; ~*cyc´lic* (Bot.), of four circles or whorls; ~*dac´tyl* a. & n., ~*dac´tylous* a., four-toed (animal); ~*gon,* plane rectilineal figure of four angles & four sides, so *tĕtrăg´onal* a.; ~*grăm,* word of four letters; ~*grăm´maton,* word written in four letters; *tĕtră´gynous* (-ji-), of four pistils; ~*hēd´ron* (-a-h-), four-sided solid, esp. triangular pyramid, so ~*hēd´ral* (-a-h-) a.; *tĕtrăl´ogy,* group of four dramatic or operatic works, esp. (Gk Ant.) three tragedies & satyric drama; *tĕtrăm´eral, tĕtrăm´erous,* having four parts; *tĕtrăm´eter,* verse of four measures (cf. DIMETER);~*morph* (Christian art), union of attributes of four evangelists in one winged figure; ~*pet´alous,~phyll´ous,* of four petals, leaves; ~*pŏd* a. & n., *tĕtrăp´odous* a., (butterfly) with only four perfect legs; ~*stich* (-k), group of four lines of verse; ~*style* a. & n., (building) with four pillars esp. forming portico in front or supporting roof; ~*syllăb´ic* a. *tĕtr´ăd,* n. The number four; set of four; atom, element, with combining-power of four atoms of hydrogen. [f. Gk *tetras -ados* (as prec., see -AD)]

tĕtrăn´drous, a. (bot.). Having four stamens. [f. TETRA-+Gk *anēr andros* male +-OUS]

tĕtr´arch (-k), n. (In Rom. empire) governor of fourth part of a country or province, subordinate ruler, whence or cogn. ~ATE(1), ~Y¹ nn. *tĕtr´ărch´|cal* a., (-k-); commander or subdivision of ancient Greek phalanx. [f. LL *tetrarcha*

f. Gk *tetrarkhēs* (TETRA-+-*arkhēs* f. *arkhō* rule)]

tĕtt´er, n. Kinds of skin-disease; ~*work,* larger celandine (supposed to cure these). [OE *teter,* cf. OHG *zittaroh,* G dial. *zitteroch*]

Teuc´rian, a. & n. Ancient Trojan. [f. L *Teucri*+-AN]

Teut´o-, comb. form (irreg.) of foll., as ~MAN´IA(0), ~PHIL(E), ~PHOB´IA, ~PHOB´IC. **Teut´on,** n. Member of any of the Teutonic nations or (Hist.) of the tribe of ~s first mentioned in 4th c. B.C. & dwelling perh. near mouth of Elbe. [f. L *Teutoni,-nes;* of Teut. orig., cf. DUTCH]

Teutŏn´ic, a. & n. 1. Of the Teutons; of the Germanic peoples (including, in widest sense, Scandinavians & Anglo-Saxons as well as German races); ~*languages,* High & Low GERMAN² & Scandinavian. 2. n. Languages of the Teutons collectively. Hence ~ISM(4), -IZE. **Teut´onISM**(2, 4), **TeutonIZ**A´TION, nn., **Teut´onIZE**(3) v.t. [f. L *Teutonicus* (prec., -IC)]

tĕxt, n. Original words of author esp. opp. to paraphrase of or commentary on them, as *there is nothing about this in the* ~, *the* ~ *is hopelessly corrupt* (altered by copyists); passage of Scripture quoted as authority or esp. chosen as subject of sermon etc. ~ *subject, theme; stick to one's* ~, *not digress; main body of the* ~; *book;* opp. to notes, pictures, etc.; ~*book;* (also ~*hand*) large kind of handwriting; CHURCH¹, GERMAN², ~; ~*book,* manual of instruction, standard book in a branch of study. [f. F *texte* f. L *textus -ūs* (in med. L = Gospel) f. L *texere text-* weave]

tĕx´tile, a. & n. 1. Of weaving, as *the* ~ *art;* woven, suitable for weaving, as ~ *fabrics, materials.* 2. n.~ material. [f. L *textilis* (as prec., see -ILE)]

tĕx´tual, a. Of, in, the text, as ~ *criticism, errors.* Hence ~LY² adv. [ME & AF *textuel* (as TEXT, see -AL)]

tĕx´tual|ist, n. One who adheres strictly to the letter of the text, so ~ISM n.; ready quoter of scriptural texts. [-IST]

tĕx´ture, n. Arrangement of threads etc., in textile fabric, as *loose* ~*e;* arrangement of constituent parts, structure, (of skin, rock, literary work, etc.); representation of surface of objects in works of art; (Biol.) tissue, structure of this. Hence ~AL (-cher-, -tūr-) a. [f. L *textura* (as TEXT, see -URE)]

tĕx´tureless (-cherl-, -tūrl-), a. Without discernible texture, amorphous. [-LESS]

-th¹, suf. forming nn. = -NESS; usu. f. adj. (*truth, wealth, breadth, broad*); corrupted to -*t* in *drought, height;* also f. vv. (*tilth, ruth, growth*), meaning result or process, & (by assim. to *ruth* etc.) f. nn., as *faith* (OF *feid*). [of var. orig.]

-th², -eth after -*ty,* suf. forming ordinal

numbers (adj., & nn. expr. fractions), as *fourth*, *tenth*, *thirtieth*, *hundredth*, *millionth*; in *fifth*, *sixth*, etc., assim. f. earlier -t; in *eighth*, united w. end of stem. [OE -*tha* (-db-) (later -*th*), -*thon*, cf. numbers by assim.] f. OTeut. -*thon*, cf. Gk -*tos*, L -*tus*]

thăl'amus, n. (pl. -*mi*). (Gk Ant.) inner room, women's apartment; (Anat.) place where nerve emerges from brain, esp. optic ~; (Bot.) receptacle of flower. [L, f. Gk *thalamos*]

thā'ler (tah-), n. German silver coin. [G, see DOLLAR]

Thalī'a, n. Muse of comedy & pastoral poetry. Hence ~AN a. [L, f. Gk *Thaleia* (*thalō* bloom)]

thall'ium, n. Rare soft white metallic element used in making a highly refractive optical glass. Hence ~IC, ~OUS, aa. [f. foll. (from green line given in spectrum) +-IUM]

thall'us, n. Plant-body without root, stem, or leaves. Hence ~OID a. [L, f. Gk *thallos* young shoot (*thalō* bloom)]

than (dhan, -ăn), conj. (& quasi-prep.) introducing second member of comparison, as *you are taller ~ he* (is), (colloq.) *taller ~ him*, *I know you better ~ he* (does), *better ~ I* (know) *him, it is better to use hot water ~ cold, do anything rather ~ let him get off, would do anything rather ~ that he should get off, a man ~ whom no one has better able to judge*. [OE, = THEN, than; *A is better than B* orig.=*A is better, then B*]

thane, thane'. Rank of, land granted to, thane. [-AGE]

thăn'atoid, a. Deathlike, apparently dead; deadly. [as prec.+-OID]

thāne, n. (In early Eng. Hist.) member of a rank between ordinary freemen and hereditary nobles. Hence ~'DOM, ~'HOOD, ~'SHIP, nn. [OE *thegn* soldier, servant, thane, cf. OSax. *thegan*, ON *thegn*, cogn. w. Gk *teknon* child]

thank[1], v.t. Express gratitude to (person for thing); ~ *you, I~ you* (polite formula acknowledging gift, service, offer accepted or refused); (as contempt. refusal) ~ *you for nothing*; (anticipatory) ~ *you (for that bell)!, please throw it here*; (as polite formula, now usu. iron. implying reproach) *I will ~ you to shut the door, wipe your boots, leave my affairs alone; he may ~ himself, has only himself to ~, for that, it is his own fault*. [OE *thancian*, tho-, (foll.) cf. Du. & G *danken*]

thănk[2], n. (now only in pl.) (Expression of) gratitude, as *give ~s to Heaven, pressed his heartfelt ~s, she bowed her ~s, small* (iron. *much*)~*s I got for it*;~ *offering* (Bibl.) Jewish offering made as act of thanksgiving; (as formula) ~*s*, thank you;~*s to* (as the result of) *my foresight, your obstinacy*.

thank'ful, a. Grateful; (of words or act) expressive of thanks. Hence ~LY adv., ~NESS n. [-FUL]

thank'less, a. Not feeling or expressing gratitude; (of a task (not likely to win thanks), unprofitable. Hence ~LY adv., ~NESS n. [-LESS]

thanks'giving, n. Expression of gratitude esp. to God; form of words for this, as *General T~* (in Book of Common Prayer); *T~ day* (set apart in U.S. for ~ to God, usu. last Thursday of November): (Bibl.) offering made as ~.

thar (tar), n. Goat antelope of Nepal. [native]

that, a., pron., & adv. 1. demonstr. adj. & pron. (pr. dhăt; pl. *those* pr. dhoz). The (person, thing), the person or thing, pointed to or drawn attention to or observed by the speaker at the time, or already named or understood or in question or familiar, as *observe ~ dog in the next field, who is ~* (woman) *in the garden?, what was ~ noise?, what noise is ~?, don't roll your eyes like ~* (as you are doing) *or in ~ imbecile fashion, I knew all ~ before, talked about responsibilities & all ~* (similar commonplaces), ~ (your action, the action you tell me of) *is not fair, ~'s right!* (formula of approval, also vulg. = yes), (colloq.; also *there's*) ~'*s* (you, in view of present or future compliance etc., are) *a dear!, I use ~* (or *the*) *term in a special sense, much to the disgust of ~* (or *the*) *monarch, was cured from ~ hour, things were easier in those days, so ~'s ~* (formula closing narrative or discussion), *come out of ~* (sl. form ordering person etc. to clear out), *wouldn't give ~* (a finger-snap) *for it*, AT ~; (with *other* (various doctors), *this, ~, & the other* (various things), *put this & ~* (various facts etc.) *together*; (as pron. replacing the w. noun, w. sense completed by rel. pron. expressed or, in obj. case & arch. in subj., omitted) *those who drink water think water, those may try it who choose, had ~ in his eye which forbade further trifling, all those* (~) *I saw, all those* (usu. *the*) *specimens ~ I saw, those* (usu. *the*) *few* (books) ~ *I had, a different pattern to ~* (which) *I was used to*; (or by adj. or equivalent) *those used for use, those below the standard, a tunic like ~ described above, those* (usu. *the*) *persons most injured by the tax, like most of those issuing from German workshops, cost of*

[OE *thone, thonc*, cf. Du. & G *dank*, cogn. w. THINK]

oil is less than ~ of gas; (foll. by that conj.) such, such *a*, *as has ~ confidence in his theory that he would put it into practice tomorrow, was wounded to ~ degree that he resigned.* **2.** adv. (pr. dhăt). To such a degree, so, as (colloq.) *will go ~ far, have done ~ much,* (vulg.) *I was angry I could have struck him.* **3.** rel. pron. (pl. same; pr. dhăt; used, exc. arch., rhet., poet., only to introduce defining-clause essential or rhet. viewed as essential to identification; now largely replaced by WHO & to some extent by WHICH, esp. after antecedent ~; in obl. case, & in arch. use in subj., ~ is often omitted; prep. governing ~ is always placed after it & usu. at end of clause). Exx.: *the book* (~ *or which*) *I sent you, the box* (~ *or which*) *you put them in, the man* (~ *or usu. whom*) *you stopped, the people* (~) *you got it from or from whom you got it, the meanest flower* (~ *rarely which*) *blows, the best ~* (not *which*) *you can do, no one* (~; not *whom*) *I ever heard of could see any difference*; (colloq.) *Mrs Smith, Mary Jones* (not *who*) *was* (=whose maiden name was Mary Jones). [OE *thæt* that, THE, cf. Du. *dat*, G *das*; for those see THIS]

that² (*dhat, occas. -ăt*), conj. introducing subordinate clauses: (of statement or hypothesis) *they say* (~) *he is better, there is no doubt* (~) *he meant it, it is suggested ~ the mistake was intentional, it is hoped ~ all will go well, it is monstrous* (~) *he should expect further help, to think* (~) *he may eat, he withdrew* (in order) ~ *the dispute might cease*; (of result) *am so sleepy* (~) *I cannot keep my eyes open, his language was such ~ ve declined further dealings with him, what have I done ~ he should cut me?, where is he, ~ you come without him?*; (of reason or cause) *it is rather ~ he has not the time, not ~* (I do not say this because) *I have any objection*; (of wish) (O) ~ *that were all!*, (O) ~ *I knew the truth!*; (arch. or literary) *in ~, since, in so far as*; *now* ~, *since now, as you ought to write now* ~ *you know the address.* [OE, neut. as prec.]

thătch, n., & v.t. **1.** Roof-covering of straw, reeds, or (in tropical countries) coconut & other leaves; (colloq.) thick hair of the head. **2.** v.t. Cover (roof, house, or abs.) with ~. [vb f. OE *theccan* f.) OE *thæc*, cf. Du. *dak*, G *dach*, cogn. w. Gk *tegos*, *stegē*, roof, L *toga* robe, *tegere* cover, etc.]

thaum'atrŏpe, n. Disk etc. on which are depicted images that appear to go through various movements when disk revolves. [irreg. f. Gk *thauma* wonder + *-tropos* -turning]

thaumatur'ge, n. Worker of miracles, wonder-worker. Hence or cogn. **thau-matūr'gic**(AL)aa., ~*ist*, ~*y¹*, nn. [f. med.

L f. Gk *thaumatourgos* a. (*thauma -matos* wonder +*o-*+*ergos* -working)]

thaw, v.i. & t., & n. **1.** (Of ice, snow, frozen thing) pass to liquid state, melt, dissolve; (of weather, *it*) become so warm as to melt ice etc., rise above 32° Fahr.; (fig.) be freed from coldness or stiffness, unbend, become genial; cause to ~ (lit. & fig.). **2.** n. ~*ing*, warmth of weather that ~s, as *a ~ has set in.* Hence ~'LESS, ~'Y', aa. [(n. f. vb) OE *thawian*, cf. Du. *dooien*, OHG *douwen*]

the (before vowel dhī, before consonant dhe, emphat. dhē), a. & adv. **1.** adj. Applied esp. to person(s) or thing(s) already mentioned or under discussion, or from the nature of the case actually or potentially existent, or unique (as class or individual), or familiar, or otherwise sufficiently identified, as *tried to soothe child, gave ~ fellow a shilling, shall let ~ matter drop, how is ~ game or score?, what is ~ time?, depends on ~ weather, Devil, sun, moon, stars, Thames, inflammation of ~ lungs, pulled ~ trigger, what was ~ result?, you will be ~ loser, revised by ~ author, find their way to ~ sea, went to ~ baths, theatre, rink, ~ King, ~ Home Secretary, ~ McGregor etc.* (chief of clan), *story does not lose in ~ telling*; to sing, n. as repr. species, class, etc., as ~ *lion, ~ domestic cat, philosopher, cucumber, gavotte, general reader, man in the street, new woman,* (rhet., esp. Bibl.) ~ *oppressor, ~ locust*; to some nn. used in restricted sense, esp. fig. repr. a pursuit etc., as ~ *gloves, ribbons, bottle, pulpit, fancy, platform, hustings, table, stage, theatre, plat-* to names of diseases etc. (now partly arch.), as ~ *smallpox, measles, toothache, pout, fidgets, blues* (depression), ~ *hump,* (vulg.) ~ (habit of) *drink*; to nn. expr. a unit, as *10d.* ~ (or *a* or per) *pound, yard, etc., £15* ~ *coat & skirt, allow 8 minutes* (to) ~ *mile, 16 oz to* ~ *pound*; with sense completed by rel. clause or adj. or equivalent, as ~ *book* (that) *you borrowed, ~ best* (that) *I can do for you, has no* ~ *nerve for motoring, wonder you have ~ impudence* (to ask it expr. or understood), (exclam.) ~ *impudence of fellow!, ~ cup on* ~ *top shelf, ~ one with a broken handle, ~ bottom of a well, ~ best way, ~ only way, ~ way out, ~ upper classes, ~ better man of* the *two*; w. adji. used abs., as *none but* ~ *brave* (brave men) *deserve* ~ *fair, ~ beautiful* (beauty), ~ *sublime*; w. adji. rhet. viewed as part of definition, as ~ *virtuous & talented Duchess of X., details of ~ shocking disaster, ~ enraged animal*; (dhe; italics) applied to the person or thing best known or best entitled to the name, as *no relation to the Browning, ~ the tobacco is* (advertiser's). **2.** adv. (a) rel., only in comb. w. (b). In whatever degree. (b) In that degree, by that amount, on that account. Exx.: ~ *more*

he gets, ~ *more he wants; I play ~ worse,
~ more I practise; am not* (or *none*) *~ more
inclined to help him because he is poor, on
that account, for what you tell me; none ~
better for seeing you; that makes it all ~
worse* (in the full degree to be expected
from what you say etc.); *that* (tautologically)
so much ~ worse for him. [f. OE *hwón*
worse, for him. [f. OE *hwón*
se), fem. *théo* (earlier *séo*), neut. *that*; cf.
Du. *de*, G *der*, *die*, *das*, L *iste*, *-a*, *-ud*,
Gk *ho*, *hé*, *to*, Skr. *tá*. 2. OE *thý*, *thé*,
instrumental case]

theǎn'dric, a. Of the union, by joint
agency, of divine & human nature in
Christ. [f. eccl. Gk *theandrikos* (*theos*
god, *anér andros* man, -IC)]

theǎnthrŏp'ic(al), aa. Both divine &
human; tending to embody deity in
human form. [f. eccl. Gk *theanthrópos*
god-man f. *theos* god + *anthrópos* man +
-IC]

theǎr'chy (-ki), n. Government by god(s);
class, order, of gods, as *the Olympian ~*.
[f. eccl. Gk *thearkhia* rule of god (Gk
theos god + *-arkhia* f. *arkhó* rule)]

the'atre (-ter), n. Building for dramatic
spectacles, playhouse: || *patent ~* (estab-
lished by letters patent, not licensed by
Lord Chamberlain): room, hall, for
lectures etc. with seats in tiers (*operating
~*, for surgical demonstrations); dramatic
literature or art: scene, field, of operation,
as *the ~ of war: good ~* (pred.), effective
on the stage; *~-goer*, *-going*, frequenter,
frequenting, of *~s*. [(perh. thr. OF) f. L
f. Gk *theatron* (*theaomai* behold f. *thea*
spectacle)]

theǎt'rical, a. & n. 1. (Of manner, speech,
gesture, person) calculated for effect,
showy, affected; of or suited to the
theatre, of acting or actors, so **theǎt'ri**-
a. (rare). 2. n. pl. ~ performances, esp.
private (amateur) *~s*. Hence ~ISM(2, 4),
~ITY (-ǎl-), nn., ~IZE(3) v.t., ~LY² adv.
[f. L f. Gk *theatrikos* (as prec., see -IC)
+ -AL]

Thēbā'id (or thē'), n. Territory around
Thebes (in Egypt); (also L *~is*) poem on
(siege of) Thebes (in Greece), esp. that
of Statius. [f. L f. Gk *Thēbaïs -ïdos*
(*Thēbai* Thebes)]

Thēb'an, a. & n. (Inhabitant) of Thebes.
[-AN]

thee. See THOU.

theft, n. Stealing; larceny. [OE *théoft*
(*théóf* THIEF + -TH²)]

the'ic, a. & n. One who drinks tea to excess.
So ~ism¹ [-ISM(6)] n. [mod. L *thea* tea,
-IC]

the'ine, n. = CAFFEINE. [as prec. +-INE¹]

their (dhār), possessive case of, & adj.
corresponding to, THEY, with absolute
form **theirs** (for uses cf. HER²). [f. ON
theira gen. pl. of *tá*]

theism¹. See THEIC.

the'ism², n. Belief in existence of a god

supernaturally revealed to man (cf.
DEISM) & sustaining a personal relation
to his creatures. So ~IST n., ~is'TIC(AL)
aa. [f. Gk *theos* god + -ISM]

then. See THEY.

themǎt'ic, a. (Mus.) of themes, as *~
treatment*, *~ catalogue* (giving opening
themes as well as names etc.); (Gram.) of,
belonging to, a theme, as *~ vowel, form*.
Hence **themǎt'ICALLY** adv. [f. Gk *thema-
tikos* (as foll.-IC)]

theme, n. Subject on which one speaks,
writes, or thinks; school composition,
essay, on given subject; (Gram.) stem of
noun or verb, part to which inflexions
are added; (Mus.) melodic subject usu.
developed with variations; (Hist.) any
of 29 provinces in Byzantine empire;
~ song, recurrent melody in musical play
or film. [f. L f. Gk *thema -matos* (*tithēmi*
set, place, see -M)]

Them'is, n. (Gk Myth.) goddess of law
& justice; these personified. [L f. Gk
Themis law]

themselves (dhemsělvz'), pron. Emphat.
& reflex. form corresp. to THEY (for use, cf.
HIMSELF). [THEM +pl. of SELF]

then (dhěn), adv., conj., a. & n. 1. adv.
At that time, as *was ~ too much occupied,
~ comes the trouble, the ~ existing ordinances*; next, afterwards, after that, as
*it must ~ soak for two hours, & ~ the
operation is complete; non & ~*, at one
time & another, from time to time.
2. conj. In that case, therefore, it follows
that, (often *well, ~*), as *~ you should have
said so, ~ it is no use your going*, (but) *~
(if what you say is true) why did you take
it?* ; (of grudging or impatient concession)
if you must have it so, as *take it ~,
between you & I . . . 'me', ~*; (resump-
tively, not as first word) accordingly, as
the new Governor, ~, came prepared; NOW
~. 3. adj. Existing *~* at that time, as
the ~ Duke, secretary. 4. n. That time, as
before, till, by, from, ~; every now & ~,
from time to time. [OF *thenne, tho-*,
tho-, cogn. w. THAT¹, THE, cf. Du. *dan*, G
dann]

thence (dh-), adv. (Arch.) from that
place, from there; (somewhat arch.) from
that source, for that reason, as *a discrepancy ~ results, it ~ appears*; *~forth*,
~forward, advv. & nn., from (or from)
that time forward. [ME *thenne* (OE
thanon, tho-, f. root of *this, that, then*)
+-ES]

then'ar, n. (anat.) Palm of hand, sole of
foot; (also attrib.*~ prominence, eminence*)
ball of thumb. [Gk *thenar*]

the'o- in comb. = Gk *theos* god, as:
~oc'racy, government or State governed
by God directly or through a sacerdotal
class etc., *the Theoc'racy*, Jewish commonwealth from Moses to the monarchy;
theoc'rat, ruler in, subject under, *~ocracy*,
so **theocrat'ic** a.; *~oc'ratist*, believer in

direct intervention & authority of God through revelation in government of society; **~og'rasy** (or thē'okrăsĭ) [f. Gk *kratos* mixture], union of soul with God through contemplation (among Neoplatonists, Buddhists, etc.); **~ŏd'ĭcy**, vindication of divine providence in view of existence of evil; **~ŏg'ony**, (poem dealing with) genealogy of the gods, so *theogón'ĭc* a.., *~ŏg'onĭst* n.; **~ŏm'achy** (-kĭ), strife against or among the gods; *theŏmăn'ĭa*, insane belief that one is God, also, religious insanity, so *theŏmăn'ĭac* n.; **~ŏph'any**, appearance of God to man, so *theŏphăn'ĭc* a.; *theŏphĭlăn'thrŏpĭst*, member of a society formed in Paris in 1796 with object of replacing Christianity by a form of deism, also, one who professes to unite love to God with love to man, so *theŏphĭlăn'thrŏpĭsm*, *theŏphĭlăn'thrŏpy*, nn.; *theŏpneus'ty*, divine inspiration, so *theŏpneus'tŏs* a.; *thē'osŏphy* (-k-), supernatural machinery; *theŏtech'nĭc* (-k-) a.

theŏd'olĭte, a. Surveying-instrument for measuring horizontal and vertical angles by means of telescope. Hence **~ĭt'ĭc** a. [orig. *-delite*; observe, *dēlos* plain]

Théŏdōs'ĭan, a. Of the emperor Theodosius (I, II, or III), esp. **~ code** (published under Theodosius II, d. 450). [-AN]

theŏlo'gĭan, n. Person skilled in, professor of, theology. [F (-ien), as foll. + -AN]

theŏl'ogў, n. Science of (esp. Christian) religion; *natural ~* (dealing with knowledge of God as gained from his works by light of nature & reason); *positive, revealed, ~* (based on revelation); *dogmatic ~* (dealing with authoritative teaching of the Scriptures & the Church); *speculative ~* (giving scope to human speculation, not confined to revelation); *systematic ~*, methodical arrangement of the truths of religion in their natural connexion. Hence or cogn. **theŏl'ogĭcAL** a., **theŏl'ogĭcallў** adv., **theŏl'ogŭe**(1, 2) v.t. & i. [ME & OF *theologie* f. L f. Gk THEO(*logia* -LOGY)]

theŏrb'ō, n. (pl. ~s). Two-necked musical instrument of lute class much used in 17th c. [f. F *téorbe* f. It. *tiorba* etym. dub.]

thē'orĕm, n. (Math.) proposition to be proved by chain of reasoning, a truth to be established by means of accepted truths, (cf. PROBLEM); algebraical or other rule, esp. one expressed by symbols or formulae, as *binomial ~em*, formula for raising binomial to any power without multiplication; a speculative truth. Hence **~ĕmăt'ĭc(AL)** aa., **~ĕm'atĭsT**(3) n. [f. LL f. Gk *theōrēma* (*theōreō* see THEORY & -M)]

theŏrĕt'ĭc, a. & n. **1.** = foll. **2.** n. pl. Speculative parts of a science etc, so **~ĕt'ĭcAL** (-ĭshn) n. [f. LL f. Gk *theōrētikos* (as THEORY, see -ETIC)]

theŏrĕt'ĭcal, a. Concerned with knowledge but not with its practical application, speculative; based on mere theory, not dealing with facts as presented by experience. Hence **~LY²** adv. [-AL]

thē'orў, a. (Gk Ant.). Of, for, public spectacles, esp. **~ fund** (for providing free seats at theatre for poor citizens etc.). [f. Gk *theōrikos* (as THEORY, see -IC)]

thē'orў, n. Supposition explaining something, esp. one based on principles independent of the phenomena etc. to be explained, opp. to HYPOTHESIS; a speculative view, as *one of my ~ies* (often implying fancifulness); the sphere of speculative thought, as *this is all very well in ~y, but how will it work in practice?*; exposition of the principles of a science etc., as *the ~y of music*; (Math.) collection of results designed to illustrate principles of a subject, as *~y of chances, equations*. Hence **~IST**(3), **~IZA'TION**, nn.. **~IZE**(2) v.i. [f. LL f. Gk *theōria* f. *theōreō* behold, contemplate (*theōros* spectator f. *thea* spectacle)]

theŏs'ophў, n. Any of various ancient & modern philosophies professing to attain to a knowledge of God by spiritual ecstasy, direct intuition, or special individual relations. Hence or cogn. **thē'osŏph**, **~ER¹**, **~IST**(2), nn., **theōsŏph'ĭc(AL)**, **theŏsophĭs'tĭcAL**, aa., **~IZE**(2) v.i. [f. med.L f. late Gk *theosophia* f. THEO(*sophos* wise)]

-ther, -ter, suf. in pronominal & other wds w. idea of distinction or comparison (*other, either, whether*; NETHER, FURTHER; *hither* etc.; AFTER); *neuter, alter* vb, have the cogn. L suf. [cf. Gk *-teros*, L *-ter*, G *-der*]

thèrapeut'ĭc, a. & n. **1.** Curative; of the healing art. **2.** n. pl. Branch of medicine concerned with treatment of disease & action of remedial agents in disease or health. Hence **~ĭcAL** a., **~ĭcallў** adv., **~IST**(3) n. [f. Gk *therapeutikos* (*therapeuō* wait on, cure, f. *theraps* servant, see -IC)]

-thē'rapў, suf. f. Gk *therapeia* service, medical treatment, denoting medical treatment as indicated by first element of wd; also as n. (*occupational therapy*).

there (dhâr, dher *as below*), adv., n., & int. **1.** In or at that place, as *put it down ~*, *what is that dog doing ~?*, *lived ~ some years*, *have been ~ before* (sl.), *know all about it*, *all ~* (sl.), in one's senses, sane, *~ it is—on the sofa*, (calling attention) *you ~!*; at that point in argument, progress of affairs, situation, etc., as *~ I agree with you*, *~ is* (or *comes in*) *the difficulty*, *you had* (the advantage of) *him ~*, *~ it* (the trouble) *is, you see*; HERE &~, *neither* HERE *nor* ~; to that place, as *go~ every day*, *got ~ in two minutes*, *get ~* (sl.),

succeed; **~ or ~abouts**, (transf.) about that amount, time, etc. ('was it two years ago?' 'T~ or ~abouts'; will come to £100, ~ or ~abouts); (merely expletive or introductory, usu. dher; preceding, or in interrog. or neg. or quasi-neg. sentence following, verb that normally precedes its subject, esp. *be*; in poet. or exclam. use subject may stand first) ~ *was plenty to eat*, ~ *was nothing ~*, ~ *was a cart close by*, ~ *was nothing ~*, *what is ~ for supper?*, *not a sound was ~ to indicate their presence*, *seldom has ~ been more fuss*, ~ *fell a deep silence, a knight ~ was, a nice mess ~ is or seems to be!*; ~ 's (=THAT's) *a dear* etc. **2.** n. That place, as *was brought from ~, lives somewhere near ~, tide comes up to ~, passed by ~*. **3.** int. Expr. confirmation, triumph, dismay, etc., as ~! *what did I tell you?*, or used to soothe child etc., as ~, ~, *never mind*. **4.** ~abouts(') near that place, or ~abouts; ~after (arch.), after that, according to that matter; ~at' (arch.), at that place, on that account, after that; ~by (or dha'rbi), by that means, as result of that (& ~by hangs a tale, in which connexion there is something to be told, see *As You Like It*, II. vii. 28); ~for' (arch.), for that object or purpose; ~fore, for that reason, accordingly, consequently; ~from' (arch.), from that or it; ~in' (arch.), in that place, in that respect; ~ind'ter, ~before', later, earlier, in same document etc.; ~in'to (arch.), into that or it; ~of' (arch.), of that or it; ~on' (arch.), on that or it (of notion & position); ~out' (arch.), out of that, from that source; ~through' (arch.), through that; ~to' (arch.), to that or it, in addition, to boot; ~un'to (arch.), to that or it; ~upon', in consequence of that, soon or immediately after that, (arch.) upon that (of motion or position); ~with', (arch.) with that, ~upon; ~withal', in addition, besides. [OE *thæt, thær*, cf. Du. *daar*, G *da*; f. stem ef THAT¹]

theri'ac, n. (Also **theri'aca Andróm'achí** pr. -áki, *Venice treacle*) antidote to bites of poisonous animals compounded of many drugs. [f. Ll. f. Gk *thériaké* antidote, fem. adj. as n. (*thérion* dim. of *thér* wild beast, see -AC)]

theri'ànthrop'ic, a. Of, worshipping, beings represented under form of man & beast. So ~àn'thropism(3) n. [f. Gk *thérion* beast+*anthrópos* man+-IC]

therm, n. Statutory unit of calorific value in gas-supply (100,000 B.Th. units; see THERMAL). [f. Gk *thermé* heat]

therm'ae, n. pl. (Gk & Rom. Ant.). Hot springs or (esp. public) baths. [Ll. f. Gk *thermai*, pl. as prec.]

therm'al, a. & n. **1.** Of heat, as ~ *unit* (for measuring heat); *British ~ unit* (abbr. B.Th.U.), amount of heat required to raise 1 lb. of water at maximum density through 1° Fahr.; ~ *equator*, line along which greatest heat occurs on earth's surface; ~ *springs*, hot springs of thermae. **2.** n. (Usu. pl.) rising current of heated air (used by gliders). Hence ~LY² adv. [as THERM+-AL]

therman'tidŏte, n. Apparatus for cooling the air, used in India. [as THERM + ANTIDOTE]

therm'ic, a. Of heat, as ~ *rays, conditions*. [as THERM+-IC]

Thermidōr'ian, n. Any of those who effected or favoured Robespierre's overthrow on Thermidor 9th, 1794. [f. F *thermidorien* (*thermidor*, republican month July-August, as THERM+Gk *dōron* gift), see -IAN]

therm'ion, n. An ION emitted by an incandescent substance. Hence **thermi-ŏn'ic** a. (~*ic valve or vacuum tube*, appliance giving copious flow of electrons used esp. in wireless transmission & reception. [THERMO-+ION]

therm'ite, -mit, n. Mixture of finely powdered aluminium and oxide of iron that produces a very high temperature on combustion (used in welding and as a composition for incendiary bombs). [G (-mit), f. foll.+-ITE¹]

therm'o- in comb. = Gk *thermos* warm, *thermé* heat, esp.: ~chem'istry (-kem-), branch of chemistry dealing with the quantities of heat evolved or absorbed during chemical reactions; ~(electric) couple, =~pile; ~dynam'ics, science of the relations between heat & mechanical work; ~electri'city, electricity produced by difference of temperature, so ~electric a.; ~gen'esis, production of heat aa.; ~gram, record made by ~graph (self-registering thermometer); ~pile, electric battery esp. arranged for measuring small quantities of radiant heat; ~scope, instrument for detecting differences of temperature without measuring, so ~scop'ic(al) aa.; ~stat, automatic instrument for regulating temperature, so ~stăt'ic a.; ~stăt'ics, theory of the equilibrium of heat; ~thăr'ia, regulation of heat or temperature esp. in warm-blooded animals; ~tăc'tic, ~tăx'ic, aa.; thermot'ropism, involuntary movement of animal or plant towards or away from source of heat.

thermom'eter, n. Instrument for measuring temperature, usu. glass tube with small bore containing mercury or alcohol, & variously graduated (Fahrenheit, Réaumur, Celsius or Centigrade, ~, with freezing-point at 32°, 0°, 0°; boiling-point of water at 212°, 80°, 100°); clinical ~ (small, with range of 25° or less, for taking temperature of the body); MAXIMUM, MINIMUM, ~. Hence thĕrmomĕt'ric(al)

aa., **thermomět'rically²** adv., **ther-mǒm'etry** n. [THERMO- + -METER]

therm'os, n. T~ *flask* or ~, kind of VACUUM flask. [P]

ther'oid, a. (Esp. of idiot) having beast-like propensities. [f. Gk *thēr* wild beast + -OID]

therŏl'ogy, n. Science of mammals, mammalogy. So ~IST n. [as prec. + -LOGY]

thesaur'us, n. (pl. *-ri*). Lexicon, cyclo-paedia. [L, f. Gk *thēsauros* treasure (*thithēmi* place)]

thes'is (or *thē- as below*), n. (pl. *thēses* pr. *-ēz*). **1.** Proposition to be maintained by dissertation, esp. one by candidate for degree; school or college exercise. **2.** (*Also* thē-) unaccented syllable in English scansion (cf. ARSIS). [Gk (*-k-*), = thing laid down, (Pros.) thesis or ARSIS, f. *tithēmi* place]

Thes'pian, a. & n. **1.** Of Thespis, semi-legendary Greek dramatic poet of 6th c. B.C.; *the ~ art,* the drama. **2.** n. Actor or actress. [f. Gk *Thespis + -AN*]

thē'ta, n. Greek letter (θ, θ)=th. [Gk]

the'urgy, n. Supernatural agency esp. in human affairs; art of securing this; magical science of Neoplatonists; pro-duction of effects by supernatural agency opp. natural magic. Hence or cogn. **theür'gic(AL)** aa., **~IST(3)** n. [f. L f. Gk *theourgia* miracle f. *theourgos* (*theos* god + -ergos* -working)]

thews (-z), n. pl. Sinews, muscles; (fig.) mental or moral vigour. Hence **thew**ED² (-ŭd), **thew'**LESS, **thew'Y¹,** aa. [OE *thēaw* habit, (pl.) manners]

they (dhā), pron. (obj. *them* pr. *dhem*, -ŏm, poss. THEIR), Pl. of HE, SHE, IT; ~ (the persons) *who;* ~ (people in general) *say;* (joc.) *them's* (those are) *my sentiments.* [ME *thei* f. ON *thei-r* pl. of *sd* = OE SE THE

thick, a., n., & adv. **1.** Of great or specified depth between opposite surfaces, as *bread is* (*cut*) *too ~, spread the butter ~, a board two inches ~, how ~ was it?;* (of line etc.) broad, not fine, (of script, type, etc.) consisting of ~ lines. **2.** Arranged closely, crowded together, as ~ *hair, forest, crowd grew ~er;* numerous, as *fell ~ as peas;* abounding, packed, *with,* as *trees ~ with leaves, air ~ with snow;* (of firm consistence, as ~ *paste, soup;* turbid, muddy, cloudy, not clear, as ~ *puddles, weather is still ~;* **3.** Stupid, dull; (of voice) muffled, indistinct. **4.** (colloq.). Intimate, esp. ~ *as thieves.* **5.** *Lay it on ~,* (sl.) be profuse esp. in compliments; || *a bit ~, rather ~, a little too ~,* etc. (sl.), going beyond what is reasonable, too much of a good thing; || *~ ear* (sl.), external ear swollen as result of blow (esp. in *give person a ~ ear*). **6.** ~ *head,* **blockhead;** ~*headed, stupid; ~'set, set or growing close together, heavily or

solidly built, (n., ~*set*) kind of stout fustian, (also ~*set hedge*) close-grown hedge; ~*skinned,* (fig.) not sensitive to reproach, insult, etc., stolid; ~*skulled, ~witted,* stupid; || ~ *'un* (obs. sl.), sovereign (coin). **7.** n. The ~ part of anything, esp. fig, *in the ~ of it* (of fight etc.); (colloq.) stupid person; || (sl.) cocoa; *through ~ & thin,* under all conditions, resolutely, so ~*&-thin* a., as ~*&-thin supporters.* **8.** adv. ~*ly,* as *snow was falling ~, blows came fast & ~, heart beats ~.* Hence ~ISH¹ a., ~LY² adv. [OE *thicce,* cf. Du. *dik,* G *dick*]

thick'en, v.t. & i. Make or become thick; make (gravy etc.) of stiffer consistence, whence ~ING¹(3) n.; *plot ~s* (becomes more intricate). [-EN²]

thick'et, n. Number of shrubs, trees, etc., growing close together. [OE *thiccet* (as THICK)]

thick'ness, n. Being thick; dimension other than length & breadth; piece of material of known ~, as *three ~es of card-board will suffice.* [-NESS]

thief, n. (pl. *-ves*). **1.** One who steals esp. secretly & without violence, whence **thiev'**ERY(4), **thiev'ishNESS,** nn., **thiev'**ISH¹ a., **thiev'ishLY²** adv.; *thieves'* LATIN. **2.** Projection in wick of candle causing it to gutter. [OE *thēof,* cf. Du. *dief,* G *dieb*]

thieve, v.i. & t. Be a thief, practise steal-ing; steal (thing). [OE *thēofian* (as prec.)]

thigh (thī), n. Part of human leg between hip & knee, corresponding part in other animals; *smite* HIP¹ *and ~; ~-bone,* single bone of ~, femur. Hence (-)~ED²(-ĭd) a. [OE *thēoh,* cf. Du. *dij,* OHG *dioh*]

thill, n. Shaft of cart or carriage; (also ~ER¹ n.) *~horse* (but between ~s). [f. 14th c., etym. dub.]

thim'ble, n. **1.** Metal cap (occas. open at end) worn to protect finger & push needle in sewing; (Mech.) short metal tube, as ~ *joint, coupling;* metal ring concave on outside & fitting in rope to prevent chafing. **2.** ~*ful* (-bl-fŏŏl), small quantity (of brandy etc.) to drink; ~*pie, rapping on head with ~,* as punishment; ~*rig* n., & v.i., (play) sleight-of-hand trick with three ~-shaped cups & pea, by-standers betting which cup covers pea, ~*rigger,* one who plays this, sharper. [OE *thymel,* as THUMB + -LE(1)]

thin¹, a. Having opposite surfaces close together, of small diameter, slender, as ~ *wire, string, board, sheet;* not dense, as ~ *air;* not full or closely packed, as ~ *house* (theatre); of slight consistency, as ~ *gruel;* lacking in important ingredient, as ~ *beer, blood, voice, humour, eloquence;* (fig.) shallow, transparent, flimsy, as ~ *disguise, excuse,* (colloq.) *that's too ~;* lean, not plump; (of lines) narrow, fine, (of script, type, etc.) consisting of ~ lines; (sl.) uncomfortable, distasteful, (esp. *have a ~ time*); *through* THICK *and ~;

~-skinned, (fig.) sensitive; || ~ *captain*, *doing* (avoid hasty action), ~ *twice before doing* (avoid hasty action), ~ *in German* etc., I ~ I'll try. **8.** ~ *about*, consider, esp. consider the practicability of (scheme, doing); ~ *aloud*, utter one's thoughts in the order of their occurrence; ~ *fit or good*, choose (to do esp. arbitrary or foolish thing); ~ *of*, consider, imagine, propose to oneself, entertain the idea of, hit upon, as *have many things to ~ of*, *to ~ of* (one can hardly imagine) *his not guessing it!*, *must be ~ing of going*, *couldn't ~ of such a thing*, ~ *of a word beginning with* B, *would have telephoned if I had thought of it*; ~ *better of*, decide on second thoughts to abandon (intention), (also) have higher opinion of (person, esp. than to believe etc.); ~ *little or nothing of*, consider insignificant or contemptible, as ~ *nothing of 30 miles a day*, I ~ *nothing of your friend Jones*; ~ *much*, *well*, *highly*, *meanly*, etc., *of*, esteem thus, ~ *no small BEER of*; ~ *out*, consider carefully, devise (plan etc.); ~ *over* (adv. or prep.), reflect upon, as ~ *over what I have said*, *will ~ it over*. Hence ~'ABLE, ~'ING² (*all ~ing men*, all who accept my view), aa., ~'ER¹ n. [OE *thencan*, past *thohte*, cf. ON *thekkja*, G *denken*; cogn. w. THANK²]

thi(o)-, comb. form of Gk *theion* sulphur, as ~*o-acid*, acid in which oxygen is replaced by sulphur.

third, a. & n. **1.** Next after second, whence ~'LY² adv. **2.** *, ~ DEGREE, ~ ESTATE, ~ *of EXCHANGE*¹; ~ *-class*, *-rate*, (loosely) inferior, poor; (Crick.) ~ *man*, (place of) fielder diagonally behind point away from wicket; ~ *party or person* (see PERSON for gram. sense), another besides the two principals, bystander etc., (~ *party risks* in insurance, damage to another than the insured, which the underwriter contracts to meet). **3.** n. One of three equal divisions of a whole. **4.** Sixtieth of a second of time or angular measurement. **5.** (mus.) Interval of which the span involves three alphabetical notes, harmonic combination of the notes thus separated. **6.** ~ part of husband's personal property, going to widow in certain cases. [OE *thridda*]

thine, n. *(fig.)* & i. (-mr-). Make or become thin, reduce in bulk or numbers, as *his hair is ~ning*, *nation had ~ned under* (or been ~*ned by*) *proscription*; remove some young fruit from (vine, tree) to improve growth of rest (also ~ *out seedlings* etc.). [OE *thynnian*, as prec.]

thine. See THY.

thing, n. **1.** Whatever is or may be an object of thought (including or opp. to person), as: (of animate objects, esp. persons, expr. contempt, pity, affection, etc.) *poor* ~, *spiteful* ~, *a dear old* ~, *dumb* ~*s*, (sl.) OLD ~, *-&-the like*, etc.); (of inanimate material object) *take those* ~*s off the table*, *platinum is a costly* ~, *got my* ~*s* (clothes) *wet*, *pack up your* ~*s* (personal belongings); (of act, fact, idea, course, task, affair, circumstance) *a foolish* ~ *to do*, SOFT ~, PUT-*up* ~, *strange* ~ *that you cannot hold your tongue*, *that is not the same* ~, *the only* ~ *now is to take a cab*, *the* ~ (to aim at) *is to improve the pace*, ~*s begin to look brighter*, *has made a mess of* ~*s*, *takes* ~*s too seriously*; (of specimen or type of work etc.) *the latest* ~ *in hats*, *a sweet* ~ *in coalscuttles*, *a little* ~ *of mine I should like to read to you*; *not the* (conventionally proper) ~; *am not feeling at all the* ~ (well); (Law.) ~*s personal*, *real*, *personal*, *real*, *property*; (pl. with adj. following, often joc.) all that is not so describable (~*s Japanese*, *political*, *feminine*, *scholastic*, etc.). **2.** *Do the handsome* ~ *by*, treat handsomely; *have a* ~ *about* (colloq.), be obsessed by; *know a* ~ *or two*, be experienced or shrewd; *make a good* ~ *of*, make good profit by; [OE. = thing, cause, sake, office, council, cf. Du. & G *ding*.]

ON *thing*]

thing'amy, **thing'umajig**, **thing'um-bob**, **thing'ummy**, nn. Person, thing, whose name one forgets or treats as known, what's-his-name, what-d'you-call-it. [prec.]

think, v.t. & i. [*thought* pr. thawt). **1.** Consider, be of opinion, as *we ~ (that) he will come*, *we do not ~ it probable*, *I ~ it a shame*, *it is not thought fair*, *is thought to be a fraud*, *I don't* ~ (sl. addition to ironical statement, as *you are a pattern of tact*, *I don't* ~). **2.** Intend, expect, as ~*s to deceive us*. **3.** Form conception of, as ~*-s off my* ~*s* *as cannot ~ the infinite*, (colloq.) *I can't* ~ *how you do it*. **4.** Recognize presence or existence of, as *the child thought no harm*. **5.** Reduce to specified condition etc. by ~*ing*, as *cannot ~ away a toothache*, *will otherwise than by passive reception of another's ideas*, as *let me ~* (appeal for

time before answering etc.), ~ *twice before thirst*, n. & v.i. **1.** Suffering caused by want of drink, desire for drink (*have a* ~, colloq., want a drink); (fig.) ardent desire, craving, (*of*, *for*, *after*, glory, person's blood, etc.). **2.** v.i. Feel ~ (no chiefly fig. *for*, *after*). Hence ~LESS a. [OE *thyrstan* vb, *thurst* n., cf. Du. *dorst*, G *durst*, ON *thorsti*, cogn. w. L *torrēre* parch]

thirst'y, a. Feeling thirst (*be* ~*y*, *current* E for *thirst* vb); fond of drink; (of country or season) dry, parched; (colloq.) causing thirst, as *this is* ~*y work*. Hence ~*iLY*¹ adv. [OE *thurstig* (prec., -Y¹)]

thirteen', a. & n. One more than twelve, 13, xiii; *the ~ superstition* (that ~ as the number of persons at table, or of one's room etc., brings ill luck). Hence ~TH² a. & n. [OE *thrēotēne, -tÿne* (as THREE, see -TEEN)]

thirty, a. & n. Three times ten, 30, xxx; *~one* etc., *~first* etc.; *T~-nine Articles* (subscribed to by person taking orders in Ch. of Eng.); *~two-mo*, 32mo, book with 32 leaves to the sheet. Hence **thir'tieth, ~fold** (see -FOLD), aa. & nn. [OE *thrītig, thrittig* (*thrī* THREE, see -TY²)]

this (dh-), a. & pron. (pl. *these* pr. dhēz). The (person, thing), the person or thing, close at hand or touched or pointed to or drawn attention to or observed by the speaker at the time, or already named or understood or in question or familiar (seldom idiomatically interchangeable with THAT¹, but often only equally applicable to the facts, the implication of greater nearness, familiarity, etc., being purely idiomatical), as *observe ~ dog on the hearthrug, who are these people in the next room ?, what is all ~ noise ?, fold it like ~, I knew all ~ before, ~* (your action, the action I am speaking of) *is not fair, ~ term is liable to much abuse, things are easier in these days; ~* and THAT¹: *~ much, ~ amount* (esp. *~* what I am about to state, as I *know ~ much, that the thing is absurd*); *~,* THAT¹, *& the other;* (of time) *~ day, today, shall be or have been busy all ~ week, ought to be ready by ~* (time), *before ~* (time), *have been asking for it these* (or *~*) *three weeks* (just past). [OE masc. *thes*, fem. *thēos*, neut. *this*, prob. f. root of *that* (see THE); OE pl. *thēs* gave *these, thós* gave *those* (now used as pl. of THAT¹)]

this'ness (dh-), n. Quality of being this. [=HAECCEITY. -NESS]

tho', See THOUGH.

thi'stle (-sl), n. Kinds of prickly composite plant with globular or cylindrical heads with purple, yellow, or white flowers, Scottish national emblem (cf. ROSE); *Order of the T~*, a Scottish order of knighthood. Hence **thi'stlY²**(-sl) a. [OE *thistel*, cf. Du. & G *distel*, ON *thistill*]

thith'er (dhidh-), adv. (arch.). To that place, there (of motion). Hence ~WARD(S) adv. [OE *thider, thyr-,* f. root of THE, cf. hither]

thôle¹, v.t. (arch.). Undergo, endure, suffer, (pain, grief, etc., or abs.); permit, admit of. [OE *tholian*, cf. ON *thola*, Da. *taale*, G *gedulad* patience, cogn. w. Gk †*tlaō* suffer, L *tolerare*]

thôle², n. (Also *~-pin*) pin in gunwale of boat as fulcrum for oar; each of two such pins between which oar plays. [OE *thol*, cf. Du. *dol*, ON *thollr* tree, peg]

Thom'ism (tō- 1874), a scholastic philosopher and theologian, or of his followers. So ~IST n., ~ is'TIC(AL) aa. [-ISM]

thong, n., & v.t. **1.** Narrow strip of leather used as halter, reins, lash of whip, etc. [OE] **2.** v.t. Provide with~, strike with~. [OE *thwang*, cf. ON *thwengr*, cogn. w. TWINGE]

Thôr, n. Scandinavian god of thunder, war, & agriculture; *~'s hammer*, flint axe (-hammer). [f. ON *Thórr*]

thôr'ax, n. (Anat., Zool.) part of trunk between neck & abdomen or tail; whence **thora'cic** a., **thorá'ci-, thorá'cico-, thorác'o-**, comb. forms; (Gk Ant.) breastplate, cuirass. [L, f. Gk *thōrax-akos*]

thôr'ite, n. A black compact mineral found in Norway. [THOR+-ITE¹]

thôr'ium, n. Radio-active metallic element, the oxide of which is used in gasmantles. [THOR+-IUM]

thôrn, n. **1.** Prickle, spiny process on plant, esp. abortive branch; kinds of *~y* shrub or tree, as *haw~, white~, black~; a ~ in one's flesh or side*, constant source of annoyance; *be, sit, on ~s*, be continuously uneasy esp. in expectation of being detected etc. at any moment. **2.** Name of the obs. E letter þ (th). **3.** *~back*, ray with spines on back and tail, British spider crab; *~bill, ~tail*, kinds of humming-bird; *~tree* (S. Afr.), kinds of acacia. Hence ~LESS, ~Y² (often fig. of affair, = hard to handle), aa. [OE & ON, cf. Du. *doorn*, G *dorn*]

thorough (thŭ'ro), a., n., prep., & adv. **1.** Complete, unqualified, not superficial, out-&-out, as *his work is seldom ~, has caught a ~ chill, wants a ~ change, a ~ scoundrel*. **2.** n. (hist.). Uncompromising policy of Strafford & Laud under Charles I. **3.** prep. & adv. (arch.). Through. **4.** *~bass*, bass part accompanied by signs esp. numerals to indicate the general harmony, such system of signs, (loosely) harmonic composition; *~brace*, strap between C-springs of vehicle; *~bred* a. & n. (animal, esp. horse) of pure breed, high-spirited, mettlesome, (also fig. of persons); *~fare*, road, street, esp. one through which much traffic passes; *no ~fare*, (as notice at end of obstructed or private road) no passage; *~going*, uncompromising, out-&-out; *~paced*, (lit., of horse) trained to all paces, (fig.) complete, unqualified, as a *~paced rascal*; *~pin*, swelling in hollow of horse's hock. Hence ~LY² (-rŏlĭ) adv., ~NESS (-rŏnĕs) n. [=THROUGH]

thôrp(e), n. Village, hamlet, (esp. in place-names). [OE & ON (-þ), cf. Du. *dorp*, G *dorf*]

those. See THAT¹.

thou (dhow), pron. (object. *thee*, pl. YE, YOU), & v.t. & i. Sing. pron. of 2nd pers., now arch. or poet. exc. in addressing God & (usu. *thee* as used by Quakers: v.t.) address (person) as ~; (v.i.) use ~ instead of *you*.

though² See THINK.

[OE & ON *thēah*, cf. Da. & G *thō*, *thō*], **conj.** (Also **although**), notwithstanding the fact that, as *he finished first ~ he began last*, *~ it was late we decided to go*; (also *although*) on the supposition that, as *it is better to ask him* (*even*) *~ he* (*should*) *refuse or refuses*; what does it matter if) *the ~ way is what* (arch. *be*) *long?*; *as ~*, *as it*, *as it is as ~ man should ask alms of a beggar*, *he acts as ~ he were mad*, *it looks as ~ he meant* (vulg. *means*) *business*; (introducing what is virtually an independent sentence) & yet, as *I have no doubt he will understand however*, as *I wish you had told me*, *~ ~ you never know*; (abs. or as adv.) [ME *thogh*, cf. ON *thō*, Du. & G *doch*]

thought¹ (thawt), n. **1.** Process, power, of thinking; faculty of reason; sober reflec- tion (*in ~*, meditating); consideration, as *take ~* (consider matters), *after serious ~*, *acts without ~*; idea, conception, chain of reasoning, etc., produced by thinking, as *an essay full of striking ~s*, *a happy ~*; well-timed or apposite idea or suggestion; half-formed intention, as *had* (*some*) *~s of resigning*, *had no ~ of offending him*; (usu. pl.) what one thinks, one's opinion, as *will tell you my ~s of the matter*; subject of one's ~s, as *his one ~ is to get away*, *~s, I often think of you*. **2.** A ~, a little, somewhat, as *cut it a ~ shorter*, *seems to me a ~ arrogant*; FREE¹ ~; quick ~; *second ~s are best*, *on second ~s I will take a cab*; second ~, ~reader, ~reading, of person's ~s by telepathy; ~wave, undula- tion of the supposed medium of ~-trans- ference. Hence (-)~ED² (-awt-) a. [OE *gethoht* (THINK)]

thought². See THINK.

thought'ful (-awt-), a. Engaged in or given to meditation; (of book, writer, remark, etc.) giving signs of original thought; (of persons or conduct) consider- ate, not haphazard or unfeeling. Hence ~LY² adv., ~NESS n. [-FUL]

thought'less (-awt-), a. Careless of con- sequences or of others' feelings; due to want of thought. Hence ~LY² adv., ~NESS n. [-LESS]

thous'and (-z-), a. & n. Ten hundred, 1000, M (for uses cf. HUNDRED); (loosely) many, as *a ~ times easier*, *one in a ~* (esp. rare or excellent one); (*a*) ~ & one, myriad, numberless (*the ~ & one small worries of life*; *made a ~ one excuses*); a ~ thanks, pardons, apologies, etc. (forms of polite exaggeration); UPPER ten ~. Hence ~FOLD a. & adv., (-)~TH² a. & n. [OE *thūsend*, cf. Du. *duizend*, G *tausend*]

thrall (-awl), n., & v.t. **1.** Slave (*of, to*, person or thing, lit. & fig.); bondage, esp.

su, tu]

in ~, **2.** adj. (arch.), Enslaved (to). **3.** v.t. Enslave. Hence **thra'l|DOM** (-awl-) n. [OE *thrǽl*, f. ON *thrǽll*, f. Da. *trǽl*]

thrash, thresh, v.t. & i. **1.** (usu. -esh). Beat out or separate grain from (corn etc.) on threshing-floor or in threshing-machine; (fig.) *~ out*, arrive at, obtain, (the truth, rhyme, etc.) by repeated trial. **2.** (Of paddle-wheel, branch, etc.) act like flail, deliver repeated blows, (of ship) keep striking the waves, make way against wind or tide (usu. -ash, *~ to windward*). **3.** (-ash). Beat esp. with stick or whip, conquer, surpass, whence **thrāsh'ing¹** n. [OE *therscan*, G *dreschen*]

thrāsh'er, thrē~, n. Kind of shark; (usu. thre-) person, machine, that threshes; (thra-) one who thrashes. [-ER¹]

thrāson'ical, a. Bragging. Hence ~LY² adv. [f. L *Thraso -onis*, character in Terence, f. Gk *thrasus* bold, +-ICAL]

thread¹ (-red), n. **1.** Spun-out filament of cotton, flax, silk, wool, etc., yarn, (*has not a dry ~ on him*, is wet through); thin cord of twisted yarns; gold ~ (of silk etc. with gold wire wound round it); LISLE THREAD; ~ & THRUM¹; ~-shaped thing, long slender body, e.g. spiral part of screw; thin seam or vein of ore; (fig.) *the ~* (course) *of life*; *hang by a ~*, (of person's life etc.) be in a precarious state, (of momentous issue etc.) be determin- able either way by something still in doubt; *lost the ~* (chain, connexion) *of his argument*; *resume or take up the ~ of*, proceed with after interruption; *gather up the ~s*, bring the divisions of subject etc. into relation after separate treat- ment. **2.** ~bare, (of cloth) worn so that nap is lost & ~ visible, wearing such clothes, (fig.) well-worn, hackneyed, whence ~bareness n.; ~ lace (made of ~); ~mark, mark made in bank-note paper with highly coloured silk fibres to prevent counterfeiting; ~needle, child- ren's game (OLD *Lady of T~needle St*); ~paper (strip of) soft thin paper used for rolling up ~; ~worm, kinds of ~like worm, esp. one infesting rectum of children. Hence ~INESS n., ~Y² a., [OE *thrǽd* (as THROW), cf. Du. *draad*, G *draht*]

thread² (-red), v.t. Pass thread through eye of (needle); string (beads etc.) on thread, make (chain etc.) thus; pick one's way through (maze, streets, crowded place, etc.), make one's way thus; streak (hair etc.) as with threads. [ME *threden*, as prec.]

threat (-ret), n. Declaration of intention to punish or hurt; (Law) such menace of bodily hurt or injury to reputation or property as may restrain person's free- dom of action; indication of coming evil (*there is a ~ of rain*). [OE *threat* crowd, calamity, threat, cf. *thréotan*, past *thréat*,

afflict, urge, & Du. *verdrieten* vex, cogn. w. L *trudere* push]

threa'ten (-ĕtn), v.t. & i. Use threats towards (person etc., or abs.; *with the evil* ~*ed*, *as* ~*ed me with death*, *am* ~*ed with a visit*; *give warning of the* infliction of (injury etc., or abs.), announce one's intention (*to do*), as punishment or in revenge etc., as ~*s every kind of torment*, ~ *to resign*, (fig.) *clouds* ~ (*an interruption* or ~ *to interrupt us*), *the practice* ~*s to become general*. Hence ~ing**LY²** adv. [OE *thréatnian* (THREAT)]

three, a. & n. 1. One more than two, 3, iii; (Skat.) any of four turns in which direction & edge are both changed; (Rugby footb.) ~*quarter*; ~*times* ~, cheers thrice repeated; *the* ~ *R's*, reading, writing, arithmetic; RULE of ~. 2. ~*bottle man*, old-fashioned hard drinker; ~*card trick* (in which bets are made on which is the queen among ~ cards lying face downwards; also *find the lady*); ~ *colour process* (of reproducing natural colours by combining photographs in red, blue, & yellow); ~*cornered*, triangular, (of contest etc.) between ~ parties each for himself; ~*deck'er*, war-vessel with ~ gun-decks, ~*storeyed* pulpit; ~*handed*, with ~ hands, played by ~ persons, as ~*handed euchre*; ~ *halfpence*, 1½d.; *T*~ *in One*, the Trinity; ~*legged race*, of couples each having a right & left leg tied together; ~*mast'er*, vessel esp. schooner with ~ masts; ||~*pair*, (of room) up ~ pair of stairs (usu. ~*pair back or front*); ||~*pence* (thrĕp-, ip-), sum of ~ pence; ||~*penny* (*bit*) (same pron.), the ~ *pence*; (*the*) ~*per-cents*, coin worth ~ pence; ~*per-cents*, (government) bonds bearing that interest; ~*PHASE*; ~*ply*, of ~ strands, webs, or thicknesses, (as n.) ~*ply wood made by gluing together 3 layers with grain in different directions*; ~*point landing* (Aeron.), landing of an aircraft on the two wheels & the tail skid simultaneously; ~*quar'ter(s)*, (adj.) of ~ fourths of normal size or numbers, (of portrait) going down to hips, showing ~ fourths of face, (n.) ~*score* (age) of sixty (~*score & ten*, age of 70 as normal limit of life). Hence ~*FOLD* a. & adv. [OE *thréo, thri*, cf. Du. *drie*, G *drei*, L *tres*, Gk *treis*]

three'some, n. & a. (chiefly Sc.). 1. Set of three persons: game etc. for three. 2. adj. Of three. [-SOME]

thrĕnmatŏl'ogȳ, n. Science of breeding animals & plants. [f. Gk *thremma -matos* nursling (*trephō* nourish, -M), -O-, -LOGY]

thrēn'ŏde, -odȳ, nn. (Song of) lamentation esp. on person's death. Hence or cogn. ~ETIC, ~ĕt'ICAL, ~ŏd'IST, ~ŏd'IO, aa., ~ŏdIST(3) n. [f. L f. Gk *thrēnōidia* (*thrēnos* wailing+ōidē ODE)]

thresh etc. See THRASH etc.

thresh'ŏld, n. Plank or stone at bottom of door in dwelling-house, church, etc.; (loosely, esp. fig.) entrance, *as at the* ~ *of a discussion, on the* ~ *of a revolution, of a new century*; ~ *of consciousness* (Psych.). =LIMEN. [OE *therscold* (*therscan* THRASH +-LE)]

threw. See THROW.

thrice, adv. (arch. or literary). Three times (now chiefly in comb. = highly, as ~*blessed*, -*favoured*), [ME *thries* (THREE, -ES)]

thrid, v.t. (arch.; -dd-). =THREAD².

thrid'ace, n. Inspissated juice of lettuce, used as sedative. [f. Gk *thridax -akos* lettuce]

thrift, n. 1. Frugality, economical management, whence ~LESS.a., ~'lessLY² adv., ~'lessNESS n. 2. n. Kinds of plant, esp. sea-pink. [ME & ON (as THRIVE, see -TH¹)]

thrif'tȳ, a. Frugal, economical; thriving, prosperous. Hence ~ilY² adv. [-Y²]

thrill, v.t. & i. & n. 1. Penetrate (person etc.) with wave of emotion or sensation, *as his voice* ~*ed the listeners*; be thus penetrated or agitated (*with horror* etc.); (of emotion etc.) pass *through, over, along, as fear* ~*ed through my veins*: quiver, throb, (as) with emotion. 2. n. Wave of emotion or sensation, *as a* ~ *of joy*: throb, pulsation; (Med.) kinds of tremor or resonance observed in auscultation; (sl.) sensational story. Hence ~ER¹(2) n. (esp. sensational play or tale), ~'ingLY² adv., ~'ingNESS n. [ME *thrillen*, f. OE *thyrlian* (*thyrel* a. & n. bored, hole, f. *thurh* THROUGH]

thrips, n. Kinds of insect, esp. (improp.) some injurious to vines etc. [L f. Gk, = woodworm]

thrive, v.i. (*thróve* rarely ~*ed*, *thriven* rarely ~*ed*). Prosper, flourish; grow rich; (of animal or plant) grow vigorously. Hence ~ingLY² adv., ~'ingNESS n. [ME *thriven*, past *throf*, -*of*-, f. ON *thrfa* grasp, cf. Da. *trives*, Sw. *trivas*, thrive]

thro', thro. See THROUGH.

throat, n., & v.t. 1. Front of neck between chin & collar-bone, jugular region, (*cut one's* ~, esp. with intent to kill him; *take by the* ~, try to throttle); gullet; windpipe, as *words stuck in my* ~; ~*shaped* thing, e.g. narrow part of river between rocks, (also in many naut. wds); *sore* ~, inflammation of lining membrane of gullet etc., *clergyman's* (*sore*) ~, form of this affecting those who speak much in public, often of nervous origin; *cut one's own* ~, *one another's* ~*s*, adopt suicidal, mutually destructive, policy; *lie in one's* ~, lie grossly; *give person the lie in his* ~, accuse him of lying grossly; *thrust thing down one's* ~, force it on his attention. 2. v.t. Channel, groove. Hence (-)~ED² a., perh. cogn. w. Du. *strot* throat & ON *throti* swelling]

throat'ly, a. Guttural, uttered in the throat; having prominent or capacious throat. Hence ~**INESS** n. [-Y²]

throb, v.i. (-bb-), & n. (Of heart, bosom, temples, etc.) palpitate, pulsate, beat with more than usual force or rapidity; (fig.) quiver, vibrate, (as) with emotion. 2. n. Palpitation, pulsation, as *heart~s, ~s of pleasure*. Hence ~**bing-**ly² adv. [ME *throbben*; excl. & perh. imit.]

thrōe, n., & v.i. 1. (Usu. pl.) violent pang(s), esp. of childbirth lit. & fig.; anguish; (pop.) *in the ~s of* (struggling with) *spring-cleaning*. 2. v.i. (rare). Be in agony. [ME *throwe* n., etym. dub.]

‖**Thrōgmŏr'ton Street**. (Used for) the London Stock Exchange or its members or operations.

thrŏmbōs'is, n. Coagulation of blood in blood-vessel or organ. Hence ~**ŏr'ic** a. [Gk *thrombōsis* curdling (*thrombos* lump, see -OSIS)]

thrōne, n., & v.t. 1. Chair of state for sovereign, bishop, etc., usu. decorated & raised on dais; sovereign power, as *come to the ~, lost his ~*; (pl.) third ORDER¹ of angels. 2. v.t. (poet. exc. in p.p.). Enthrone (lit. & fig.). Hence ~**LESS** (-nl-) a. [f. OF *trone* f. L f. Gk *thronos* seat, chair]

throng, n., & v.i. & t. 1. Crowd of people; multitude esp. in small space (of people or things). 2. v.b. Come, go, press, (round etc.) in multitudes; fill (street etc.) with a crowd or as crowd does; (arch.) press hard upon (person). [vb f. n.) OE *(ge)throng* f. *thringan* vb crowd, cf. Du. & G *dräng*]

thrō'stle (-sl) n. 1. Song-thrush. 2. (Also ~-frame) machine for spinning wool, cotton, etc. [OE, cf. MHG *drostel*, cogn. w. L *turdus* thrush]

thrŏt'tle, n., & v.t. 1. Throat, gullet, windpipe; (also ~-valve) valve controlling flow of steam etc. in engine. 2. v.t. Choke, strangle; control (steam etc., engine) with ~-valve; ~ *down*, reduce speed of (engine, car) thus. [vb (f. 1400) perh. f. THROAT+-LE(3); n. (f. 1550) perh.f. north.]

through, thro', thro. (-rōō), prep., adv., & a. 1. From end to end or side to side of, between the sides or walls or parts of, as *marched ~ the town, arrow went ~ his arm, see ~ a telescope, look ~ the window, pass ~ the doorway, swam ~ the waves, pushes his fingers ~ his hair*; (fig.) *went ~ many trials, got ~ his examinations, saw ~ his hypocrisy, wait ~ ten long years, flashed ~ his mind*; by reason of, by agency, means, or fault of, as *it all came about ~ his not knowing the way, concealed it ~ shame, it was all ~ you that we were late*. 2. adv. From side to side, from end to end, from beginning to end, as *let us stroll ~, would not let us ~* (gate etc.), *ice gave & I went ~, read it carefully ~, read*

it ~ & ~ (again & again), *looked him ~ & ~* (observed searchingly), *lasted all ~* (all the time); (colloq.) *are you ~* (with *that job*)?, *have you finished* (it)? ; CARRY, *drop* or FALL¹, PULL¹, ~; GO¹ ~ *with*, 3. adj. Going, concerned with going, ~, as a ~ *bolt*, ~-*stone*, = BOND¹-*stone*; esp. (of railway or steamboat travelling) going all the way without change of line etc., going over different companies' lines with the same ticket, as~ *carriage, train, passenger, ticket* (for ~ *passenger*), *fares*. [OE *thurh* prep. & adv., cf. Du. *door*, G *durch*, cogn. w. Goth. *thairh* through & *thairkō* hole]

through'ly(-ōōl), adv. (arch.). Thoroughly. [f. THROUGH+-LY²]
[OUT]

throughout' (-rōō-owt), adv. & prep. 1. Right through, in every part, in all respects, as *timber was rotten ~, followed in sound policy ~*. 2. prep. Right through, from end to end of, as ~ *the length & breadth of the land*, ~ *the 18th century*.

thrŏve. See THRIVE.

throw¹ (-ō), v.t. & i. (*threw* pr. -ōō, ~n pr. -ōn). 1. Release (ball, object) with imparting motion, propel through space, send forth or dismiss esp. with some violence, fling or hurl or cast (lit. & fig.), as *must not ~ stones* (lit., & fig. = cast imputations), *threw the ball over his head, learnt to ~ a fly* (in fishing), *mortars ~n from his horse, was ~n into a dilemma or upon his own resources*, ~ COLD¹ *water on*, ~ a SOP *to*; ~ *light on the matter*, help to explain it; ~ *down the* GLOVE, ~ DUST¹ *in person's eyes*; ~ *oneself, one's daughter, at the head of* (openly seek as husband); ~ (as FLING) *in one's teeth*; ~ *good money after bad* (lose more in trying to recoup a loss); ~n. ind. obj.) ~ *me a rope*, ~ *one a kiss* (wave hand to him after kissing it); (Cricket, of bowler) deliver ball with sudden straightening of elbow (*was no-balled for ~ing*). 2. (Of wrestler, horse) bring (antagonist, rider) to the ground. 3. Put (clothes etc.) carelessly or hastily *on, off, over one's shoulders* etc.; (of snake) cast (skin). 4. (Of animals, e.g. rabbits, pigeons) bring forth (young). 5. Make (specified cast) with dice, as *threw deuce-ace*. 6. Twist (silk etc.) into threads. 7. Shape (round pottery) on potter's wheel. 8. Turn, direct, move esp. quickly (esp. part of body), as *threw his eyes to the ground, a glance backwards, his arms up, his head back*; ~ *a chest* (sl.), stand erect with chest expanded. 9. *Lose (contest, race, etc.) intentionally. 10. Have (a fit), give (a party). 11. ~ *away*, (fig.) part with needlessly or recklessly, lose by neglect, as *threw away all his advantages, an excellent offer*; (p.p.) wasted, as *the advice was ~n away upon him*. 12. ~ *back*, revert to ancestral character; ~*back* n.,

reversion to ancestral character, example of this. **13.** ~ *oneself down*, lie down. **14.** ~ *in*, (also ~ *into the bargain*) add (thing) to a bargain without extra charge; interpose (word, remark) by way of parenthesis or casually; ~ *in one's hand*, lit. in card games esp. Poker, (fig.) give up, withdraw from a contest; ~ *in one's lot with*, decide to share the fortunes of **15.** ~ *oneself into*, engage vigorously in. **16.** ~ *off*, discard (acquaintance etc.); contrive to get rid of (illness, troublesome companion); abandon (disguise); produce, deliver, (poem, epigram) in offhand manner; (of hounds or hunt, also transf.) begin hunting, make a start, begin speaking, playing, etc.; (& see above). **17.** ~ *oneself on, upon*, place one's reliance on (*the mercy of the court* etc.). **18.** ~ *open*, open suddenly or wide; make accessible (*to* all comers etc.); ~ *open the door to*, make possible. **19.** ~ *out*, cast out; build (wing of house, pier, projecting or prominent thing); suggest, insinuate; reject (bill in Parliament); distract (person speaking, thinking, or acting) from the matter in hand so that he blunders or stops; (Cricket, of fielder) put out (batsman) by ~*ing* at wicket. **20.** ~ *over*, desert, abandon. **21.** ~ *overboard*. see OVER-(2). **22.** ~ *up*, lift up (window-sash); resign (office); vomit (t. & i.); ~ *one's eyes up* (as sign of horror or outraged propriety); ~ *up the* SPONGE. Hence (-)~**ER**¹ (-ōer) n. [OE *thrāwan*, past *thrēow*, twist, hurl, cf. G *drehen*, Du. *draaien*, twist, whirl]

throw² (-ō), n. **1.** Throwing, cast; cast of dice; cast of fishing-line; distance a missile is or may be thrown, as *record ~ with the hammer*; *a stone's ~*, (loosely) slight distance; fall in wrestling; (Cricket) bowler's illegitimately delivered ball. **2.** (Geol, Mining) fault, leap, in strata. **3.** Machine, device, giving rapid rotary motion. **4.** ~-*off*, start in hunt or race; ~-*stick*, club, stick, meant to be whirled from the hand, e.g. boomerang. [f. prec.]

throw·ster (-rō-), n. One who throws silk. [-STER]

thrum¹, n., & v.t. (-mm-). **1.** Fringe of threads remaining on loom when web has been cut off; single thread of this; any loose thread or tuft; *thread & ~*, all alike, good & bad. **2.** v.t. Make of, cover with, ~s. Hence ~**m'Y²** a. [OE, cf. ON *thrǫmr* edge, Du. *dreum*, G *trumm*, end, thrum]

thrum², v.i. & t. (-mm-), & n. **1.** Play monotonously or unskilfully on or *on* (stringed instrument); drum, tap idly on or *on* (table etc.). **2.** n. Such playing, resulting sound. [imit.]

thrush¹, n. Family or genus of birds, esp. European *song-~*, throstle. [OE *thrysce*]

thrush², n. Disease, esp. of children, marked by pearl-coloured fungous vesi-cles in mouth & throat; disease affecting frog of horse's foot. [f. 17th c., etym. dub.; cf. Da. *troske*]

thrust, v.t. & i. (thrust), & n. **1.** Push with sudden impulse or with force (lit. & fig.), as ~ *his fist into my face*, ~ *the letter into his pocket*, ~ *a pin into the cushion*, *I ~ out my hand*, ~ *him forth* (out of room etc.), *was ~ from his rights*; ~ *oneself* or *one's nose in*, obtrude, interfere; pierce (person etc.) through; make sudden push *at* (person etc. *with* dagger etc.); force oneself *through, past*, etc.; make one's *way* thus; hence ~**ER¹** n. (|| esp., foxhunter who endangers others or the hounds in securing a forward place). **2.** n. Sudden or forcible push, (Mil.) strong attempt to penetrate enemy's line or territory; remark aimed at a person (*a shrewd*, HOME¹, ~; *he parried the ~*); stress between two bodies esp. parts of structure, e.g. arch, rafters; crushing of coal-mine pillars by weight of roof; ~-*block*, (esp.) casting or frame carrying or containing the bearings on which the collars of a propeller-shaft press; ~-*hoe* (worked by ~, not pull). [(n. f. vb) ME *thrusten* f. ON *thrysta*, perh. cogn. w. L *trudere*]

thud, v.i. (-dd-), & n. (Make, fall with) low dull sound as of blow on soft thing. [prob. imit.; but cf. OE *thyddan* strike, thrust]

thug, n. Member of a religious organization of assassins in India suppressed about 1825; cut-throat, ruffian. [f. Hind. *thag, -ag*]

thugg'ee (-gē), n. The practice of the thug. So ~**ERY**, ~**ISM**, nn., (-g-). [f. Hind. *thagi* as prec.]

Thū'lē, n. Name given by Pytheas of Massilia to some (island) north of Gt Britain; *ul'tīma* (=farthest) ~, any faraway unknown region.

thumb (-m), n., & v.t. **1.** Short thick finger set apart from & opposite to the others on human hand; digit of other animals corresponding to this in position; ~*s up!* (sl. excl. of satisfaction); RULE *of* ~; *his* FINGERS *are all* ~*s; under person's*~ (influence, domination). **2.** ~-*blue*, washing indigo in small lumps; ~-*index*, set of lettered grooves cut in front edges of a book's leaves to facilitate reference; ~-*latch* (raised by pressing end of lever with ~); ~-*mark* (made by ~ esp. on leaf of book); ~-*nail sketch*, portrait of ~*nail* size, hasty word-picture; ~-*nut* (shaped for ~ to turn); ~-*print*, impression of ~, as used for identification; ~-*screw*, instrument of torture for squeezing ~s; ~-*stall*, sheath, pad, etc., to protect~. **3.** v.t. Wear, soil, (pages etc.) with~; handle (piano keys etc.) or play (music) awkwardly. Hence ~**LESS** (-ml-) a. [OE *thūma*, cf. Du. *duim*, G *daumen*, L *tumēre* to swell]

thŭmm'im. See URIM.

thump, v.t. & i. & n. 1. Beat heavily esp. with fist; deliver heavy blows *at, on,* etc.; ~ *on a cushion* (of vehement preacher emphasizing his words with blows on pulpit cushion). 2. n. Heavy blow, bang. [imit.]

thŭm'pier, n. In vbl senses, also: (colloq.) large, striking, or impressive person or thing, esp. lie, so ~ING² a. [-ER¹.]

thŭn'der, n., & v.i. & t. 1. Loud noise following flash of lightning & due to discharge of electricity through the air; ~*bolt*, as *Jove's* ~s; (fig.) loud noise, as ~s *of applause, blood-&-*~, (of novel etc.) sensational; (pl.) authoritative censure or threats (*the* ~s *of The Times, the Church*). 2. v.i. Give forth ~, usu. *it* ~s; make loud noise, as *voice* ~*ed in my ears*; utter violent threats etc. *against* etc. 3. v.t. Emit (threats etc.) in loud or impressive manner. 4. *Stead person's* ~, (fig.) forestall him (by telling the story he meant to tell, making profitable use of his invention before he can, & the like; from remark of John Dennis when the stage ~ he had intended for his own play was used for another); ~-*&-lightning*, = OXFORD mixture; ~*bolt*, flash of lightning with crash of ~, imaginary bolt or shaft viewed as substance of lightning, kinds of stone or fossil supposed to be such bolt, formidable threat etc.; ~*clap*, crash of ~ (esp. fig. or in simile of sudden terrible event or news; *the* ~*clap of Napoleon's escape; the news came on me like a* ~*clap*); ~*cloud* (producing ~); ~*storm* (with ~); ~*struck*, struck by lightning, amazed. Hence ~LESS, ~OUS, ~Y² aa., ~ously² adv. [vb., OE *thunrian*) OE *thunor*, cf. Du. *donder*, G *donner*, ON *thōrr* (cf. THOR), cogn. w. L *tonare* thunder, Gk *sténō*

thŭn'derer, n. In vbl senses, esp. *the T*~, Jupiter, ||(joc.) *The Times* newspaper. [-ER¹.]

thŭn'dering, a. & adv. In vbl senses, also or esp.: (colloq.) unusual(ly), remarkably, decidedly; as *a* ~ *nuisance, was* ~ *glad to get back, a* ~ *great fish; the T*~ *Legion*, Roman legion containing Christian soldiers whose prayers were held to have procured a thunderstorm that terrified the enemy. Hence ~LY² adv. [-ING².]

thŭr'i-, in comb. = L *thus thuris* frank-incense, as: ~'*ifer*, acolyte who carries censer; ~'*iferous*, producing frankincense; ~'*ification*, burning of incense.

thū'rible, n. Censer. [f. L *thuribulum* containing ... *thūs*, see prec. f. Gk *theos* f. *thuō* sacrifice).]

Thŭrs'day (-zdi), n. Fifth day of week; HOLY, MAUNDY, ~. [OE *thures dæg* THOR's day f. ON *thors-dagr*, on L *dies Jovis* Jupiter's day]

thus (dh-), adv. In this way, in the way (to be) indicated, whence ~NESS n. (joc.); accordingly, as a result or inference; to this extent, so, as ~ *far*, ~ *much*. [OE, cf. Du. *dus*, prob. cogn. w. THAT!]

thwack, v.t. & n. = WHACK. [imit.]

|| **thwaite**, n. Piece of wild land made arable (now in place-names, as *Es*~, *Stone*~). [f. ON *thveit* paddock, cogn. w. OE *thwītan* cut, WHITTLE]

thwart (-ôrt), adv., prep., & a., (arch.), v.t. & n. 1. Across, athwart; (Naut.) ~*hause*, across the hawse, ~*ship* a., ~*ships* adv., (lying across ship; (adj.) lying across, transverse. 2. v.t. Frustrate, cross, (wish, purpose), whence ~'ingLY² adv. 3. n. Oarsman's bench placed across boat. [ME (adv.), f. ON *thvert*, cf. OHG *twer*, G *quer*; cogn. w. L *torquēre* twist]

thỹ, thine, (dh-), pron. & a. Possessive case of, & adj. corresp. to, THOU (now arch., etc., as THOU; before vowel usu. thy, also (*thine*) in abs. use, as *it was thy fault, lift thine eyes, the fault is thine, thin*, cf. ON *thinn*, G *dein*; thy by loss of *-n*]

thỹl'ăcine, n. Zebra wolf, a Tasmanian carnivorous marsupial. [F, f. Gk *thulakos* pouch, -INE¹]

thyme (tim), n. Kinds of plant, esp. *common garden* ~, shrub with pungent aromatic leaves used in cookery, *sheep herd's* or *wild* ~, kind with mildly aromatic leaves. Hence thym'oι n. (a powerful antiseptic), thym'Y² (i-) a. [f. F *thym* f. L f. Gk *thumos* (*thuō* sacrifice)]

thỹm'us, n. (anat.; pl. -mi). (Usu. ~ *gland*,) a ductless gland situated near the base of the neck (in man disappearing on the approach of puberty). [f. Gk *thumos*]

thỹr'oid, a. & n. (anat., zool.). Shield-shaped, as ~ *cartilage*, large cartilage of larynx projection of which in man forms Adam's apple; connected with the ~ cartilage, as ~ *artery*; ~ *body* or *gland*, large ductless organ of no known function situated on larynx & trachea, the seat of goitre (~ *gland* or ~, drug prepared in various forms from the ~ gland of animals & used in cretinism & other diseases); having shield-shaped markings, as ~ *woodpecker*. Hence thỹro- comb. form (anat.). [irreg. f. Gk *thureoeidēs* (Galen) f. *thureos* shield f. *thura* door, see -OID]

thyrs'us (-ér-), n. (Gk Ant.; pl. -si). Staff tipped with ornament like pine-cone, an attribute of Bacchus. [L, f. Gk *thursos*]

thỹsêlf' (dh-), pron. Reflexive & emphatic form corresp. to *thou, thee*. [THY+SELF]

ti (té), n. Kinds of tree with edible roots. [Polynesian name]

tiăr'a, n. Ancient Persian turban worn erect by king, depressed by others; Pope's diadem pointed at top & surrounded by three crowns, (fig.) the papa-

office; ornamental coronet. Hence ~'d [-ED²] a. [L.f. Gk, prob. of Pers. orig.]

tib'ia, n. (anat.; pl. ~æ pr. -ē). The shin-bone; fourth joint of leg in insects; drumstick of fowl. So ~AL a., ~o- comb. form. [L (ti-)=shin-bone, flute]

tic, n. Habitual spasmodic contraction of muscles esp. of face; (in full ~douloureux pr. dŏloróō', & see Ap., lit. painful ~) severe form of facial neuralgia with convulsive twitchings. [F, etym. dub.]

tical (in Siam tikahl'; in Burma ti'kl), n. Former Siamese silver coin (roughly = 1 rupee) or its weight; similar Burmese and Chinese weight. [Port. tical]

ticc'a, a., (Anglo-Ind.). Engaged on contract, hired (esp. in ~gharry, hackney-carriage). [Hind. ṭhikā, hire, fare]

tice, n. =YORKER. [f. obs. tice ENTICE]

tick¹, v.i. & t., & n. 1. (Make) slight recurring click, esp. that of watch or clock (to or on the ~, with exact punctuality); (colloq.) moment, instant; ~-tack, pulsating sound esp. of the heart (see also TICK-TRACK), kind of manual semaphore signalling practised by racecourse touts; ~~, (nursery for) watch. 2. Small mark set against items in list etc. in checking; (v.t.) mark (item, usu. off) with ~. 3. (Of clock etc.) ~away (the time etc.); ~off (sl.), reprimand; (of tape-machine) ~out (news etc.); ~over, (of int.-comb. engine) run slowly with gears etc. disconnected. [ME tek light touch, cf. Du. tik(ken) n. & vb, touch, pat; in sense 'click' perh. imit.]

tick², n. Arachnid or insect parasitic on various animals, as dog, sheep, cattle, ~. [OE ticia (once), perh. erron. for theca), ME teke, cf. MDu. teke, G zecke]

tick³, n. Cover, case, of bedding; (also ~ING¹ n.) stout usu. striped linen or cotton material used for this. [earlier teke f. L f. Gk thēkē case (tithēmi place)]

tick⁴, n. & v.i. & t. (colloq.). 1. Credit, as buy goods on ~. 2. vb. Give ~; buy or sell (thing) on ~; give (person) ~. [abbr. of TICKET]

tick'er, n. In vbl senses of TICK¹, esp.: (colloq.) watch, telegraphic tape; (joc.) the heart. [-ER¹]

tick'et, n., & v.t. 1. Written or printed piece of card or paper entitling holder to admission to place of entertainment etc., conveyance by train etc., or other right, as concert, theatre, bath, lottery, railway, excursion, SEASON, THROUGH, RETURN, ~; ‖(Mil. sl.) discharge (get one's ~); label attached to thing & giving price or other particulars; notice, usu. of card, set up in window etc. of house to let etc.; the ~ (colloq.), the proper thing, as not quite the ~; *(Polit.) list of candidates put forward by a party, (fig.) principles of a party, as the democratic ~. 2.‖(of leave (allowing liberty with certain restrictions to prisoner or convict who has served part of his time), ‖~-of-leave man, holder of such ~; ‖~-day (St. Exch.), day before settling-day, when names of actual purchasers are handed to stockbrokers; ~-night, performance at theatre proceeds of which are divided among several persons in proportion to number of ~s disposed of by each; ‖~-porter, licensed porter identified by badge; ‖~-punch (for punching ~s). 3. v.t. Put ~ on (article for sale etc.). [f. OF e(s)tiquet(te) ticket, bill, f. OLG sekan to STICK]

tick'ey, -ky, **tikk'ie**, -ky, n. (S.-Afr. colloq.). Threepenny-bit. [?]

tic'kle, v.t. & i., & n. 1. Apply light touches to (person, part of his body, or abs.) so as to excite the nerves & usu. produce laughter & in extreme case convulsion, as ~him with a feather, ~the soles of her feet, feel this sensation, as my foot ~s; excite agreeably, amuse, divert, (person, his sense of humour, vanity, etc.), as I was highly ~d at the idea, this will ~his palate; catch (trout etc.) with the hand. 2. n. Act, sensation, of tickling. [ME tikelle, perh. by metath. f. ON kitla, cf. KITTLE]

tick'ler, n. In vbl senses, also: puzzling or delicate question or matter; feather etc. used by revellers to tickle faces. [-ER¹]

tick'lish, a. Easily tickled, sensitive to tickling; (of question or thing to be dealt with) difficult, critical, delicate, requiring careful handling. Hence ~LY¹ adv., ~NESS n. [-ISH¹]

ticpolong'a (-ngg-), n. Venomous serpent of India & Ceylon. [f. Cingalese tit-polongā spot-viper]

tid'al, a. Of tide(s); ~air (passing in & out of lungs at each respiration); ~basin, dock, harbour (subject to rise & fall of tide); ~friction (of ~wave, retarding diurnal rotation of earth); ~river (affected by tide to some distance from mouth); ~wave, wave following sun & moon from east to west & causing tides, (improp.) any extraordinary ocean wave e.g. one attributed to earthquake, (fig.) widespread manifestation of feeling etc. Hence ~LY² adv. [-AL]

tid'bit. See TITBIT.

tidd'ly-winks, n. Game in which counters are flicked into tray etc. on centre of table. [?]

tide¹, n. 1. Time, season, (now chiefly in even-~, Whitsun-~, Christmas-~, yule-~, etc., otherwise arch.); period of time, as work double ~s (night & day). 2. Periodical rise (flood-~) & fall (ebb-~) of sea due to attraction of moon & sun, whence tidŏl'ogy n.; high, low, ~, completion of flood, ebb, ~; spring, neap, ~, maximum, minimum, ~ when solar & lunar ~s act together, act 90° apart; LAG¹ping, PRIMING² of the ~s; meteorological ~ (due to regular alternations of wind etc.); (fig.) trend of opinion or

fortune or events (*go with the ~, the ~
turns*). 3. ~**gate** (opened to admit water
or let vessels pass during rising ~; closed
to keep water in during ebb); ~**gauge**
(showing extremes or present level of ~);
~**lock** (between tidal harbour & basin
behind it); ~**rip(s)**, rough water caused
by opposing ~**s**; ~**water**, customs
officer who boards ship on arrival to
enforce customs regulations; ~**way**,
channel where ~ runs, ebb or flow in such
channel. Hence ~'**LESS** (-dl-) a. [OE *tīd*
time, cf. Du. *tijd*, G *zeit*, ON *títh*]

tid'ings (-z), n. pl. (now chiefly literary;
treated as sing. or pl.), (Piece of) news,
as *the* ~ *come(s) too late*. [OE *tīdung* (as
prec.), ME *tidinde* f. ON *títhindi* f.
prec.), ME *tidinde* f. ON *títhindi* f.
prec.]

tid'y, a., n., & v.t. 1. (Of dress, room,
person, habits) neatly arranged, neat,
orderly; (colloq.) pretty large, considerable, as *left a ~ sum behind him, a ~ day's
work*; (dial.) fairly well in health, as *am
feeling pretty* ~. 2. n. Detachable usu.
ornamental cover for chair-back etc.,
receptacle for odds & ends (*street* ~, bin
for paper etc.). 3. v.t. Make (room, table,
etc., oneself, or abs.; often *up*) neat, put
in good order. Hence **tid'ily** adv.,
tid'iNESS n. [ME, = seasonable, tidy,
(TIDE¹+-Y²)]

tie, v.t. & i. (*tying*). 1. Attach, fasten,
with cord or the like, as ~ *the dog to the
railings*, RIDE *&* ~, ~ *his legs together*, ~
up a parcel; secure (shoe, bonnet) by
tightening & knotting its strings; arrange
(string, ribbon, tie, etc.) to form knot,
bow, etc., as ~ *your tie*, ~ *it in a bow*;
form (knot, bow) thus; ~ (dress fish-hook
to look like) *a fly*; bind (rafters etc.) by
crosspiece etc.; restrict, bind, (person etc.,
to, down to, conditions, occupation, etc.),
2. ~*d to woman's* APRON*-strings*; ~ person's *tongue*, secure, compel, his silence;
~ *up*, restrict, esp. annex conditions to
(bequest etc.) to prevent its being sold or
diverted from its purpose; ||~*d house*,
public house bound to deal exclusively
with one firm. 3. (mus.). Unite (notes)
by tie. 4. Make equal score or run dead
heat or draw game (*with* competitor,
for place or prize). [OE *tīgan*, as foll.]

tie², n. 1. Cord, chain, etc., used for fastening; = NECK¹-~; *old* SCHOOL¹-~; (fig.)
thing that unites persons, bond, obligation, as ~*s of blood, friendship*; rod, beam,
holding parts of a structure together,
rail sleeper; ~*beam*, horizontal beam
connecting rafters; small fur necklet,
2. (mus.). Curved line above two notes
of same pitch that are to be joined as one.

---

3. Equality of score or draw or dead heat
among competitors in game or contest;
play, shoot, etc., off a ~, play further game
etc. to decide between such competitors; match between any pair of several
competing players or teams, as *cup-~s
(in competition for cup)*. 4. ~*up*, obstructed situation, standstill, esp. *strike
of railway men etc.; ~*wig* (tied behind
with ribbon). [OE *tēah* rope f. *tēohan*]

tier, n., & v.t. 1. Row, rank, esp. one of
several placed one above another as in
theatre; ~*s of cable*, circles it forms when
coiled. 2. v.t. Pile (often *up*) in ~**s**.
[vb f. n.) f. OF *tire* sequence (*tirer* to
draw)]

tierce, n. One third of a pipe as old
wine-measure, cask containing certain
quantity (varying with the goods) esp. of
provisions; (Mus.) = THIRD; sequence of
three cards; (Fencing) third position for
guard, parry, or thrust (~ *& quart*, fencing); (Eccl., also *terce*) office of third hour.
[ME, f.F *tiers, fem. ~rce, third, f. L TERTIUS]

tiercel. See TERCEL.

tiers état (tyārz ātah'), n. = *third* ESTATE.
[F]

tiff, n., & v.t. & i. 1. || Draught of liquor;
fit of peevishness, slight quarrel. 2. v.t.
|| Sip, drink. 3. v.i. Be in a pet; (Anglo-
Ind.) lunch. [different wds, etym. dub.,
last sense f. TIFFIN]

tiff'any, n. Kind of gauze muslin. [orig.
dress for Twelfth Night, f. OF *tiphanie*
f. LL *THEOphania* manifestation of God.
EPIPHANY]

tiff'in, n., & v.i. (Anglo-Ind.), (Take) light
meal esp. of curried dishes & fruit, lunch.
[TIFF vb+-ING¹; orig. in sense ' drinking ']

tige (tēzh), n. (Archit.) shaft of column;
(Bot.) stem, stalk. [F, f. L TIBIA]

tig'er (-g-), n. 1. Large Asiatic striped
feline quadruped, esp. *Bengal ~; American
~, jaguar; red ~, cougar; *work etc. like a
~ (with fierce energy); (colloq.) formidable
opponent in a game, opp. RABBIT; dissolute swaggerer or bully, whence ~ISM(2)
n.; groom accompanying master in light
vehicle; *(sl.) yell supplementary to
three cheers, final burst. 2. ~*beetle,
predacious kinds with spotted or striped
wing-covers; ~*cat, any moderate-sized
feline beast resembling the ~, e.g. ocelot,
serval, margay; ~*(s)eye, a gem of
brilliant lustre; ~*lily, garden kind with
flowers of dull orange spotted with black
or purple; ~*moth, kinds with richly
streaked hairy wings suggesting ~'s skin;
~*wood (imported from Brit. Guiana for
cabinet-making). So **tig'ress¹** n. [ME &
OF *tigre* f. L f. Gk *tigris* of oriental. orig.]

tight (tīt), a., n, & adv. 1. Closely &

firmly put together, as ~ ship; impermeable, impervious, esp. (in comb.) to
specified thing, as air, gas, water, wind,
~; closely held, drawn, fastened, fitting,
etc., as ~ knots, cork is too ~, corn caused
by a (too) ~ shoe; neat, trim, compact, as
a ~ lass (arch.), ~ little island; tense,
stretched so as to leave no slack, as ~
rope (~ rope, one on which rope-dancers
etc. perform); (colloq.) drunk; money is
~ (not easily obtainable), a ~ money-
market (in which money is ~); produced
by, requiring, great exertion or pressure,
as a ~ squeeze, am in a ~ place (usu.
fig., difficult situation); ~-fisted, stingy;
~*-wad (sl.), close-fisted or stingy person.
2. n. pl. Close-fitting garments as used by
acrobat etc. 3. adv. ~ly, as squeeze it,
hold it, ~. Hence ~EN⁵ (tit-) v.t. & i.
(~en one's belt, joc., go without food),
~NESS¹(1, 2), ~NESS, nn., ~LY² adv.
[earlier thight f. ON théttr, cf. G dicht]

tike. See TYKE.

tikkie,-ky. See TICKEY.

til (tēl), n. The TILDE in Port. use (over
vowel, repr. lost nasal n).

til'bury, n. (hist.). Kind of gig. [maker]

til'de (-ā), n. Mark (~) put over Spanish
n, when it is pronounced ny (so señor).
[Sp., var. of tildo TITLE¹]

tile, n., & v.t. 1. Thin slab of baked clay
for roof, pavement, drain, etc.; similar
slab glazed & often decorated for hearth,
fireplace, wall, etc.; have a ~ loose (sl.), be
rather mad; on the ~s (sl.), on a debauch;
Dutch ~ (painted usu. in blue & with
scriptural subjects); PANTILE; plain ~, flat
roofing-~ usu. about 10¼ × 6¼ in.; (colloq.)
silk hat; ~ TEA ; ~ stone, kinds of flagstone
serving when split for ~s. 2. v.t. Cover
(roof etc., or abs.) with ~s; (Freemasonry)
guard (lodge, meeting) against intrusion
by placing tiler at door, whence (gen.)
bind (person) to secrecy; ~ in, enclose in
~s. Hence til'ING⁴(1, 2, 6) n. [(vb f. n.;
in Freemasonry sense f. foll.) OE tigele
f. L tēgula f. tegere cover]

til'er, n. One who makes or lays tiles,
whence til'ERY(3) n.; (Freemasonry, also
arch. tyler) doorkeeper of lodge. [-ER¹]

till¹, v.t. Cultivate (soil). Hence ~ABLE
a., ~AGE(3) n. [OE tilian, teolian, strive
for, till, f. til useful, cogn. w. foll., cf. Du.
telen breed, till, G zielen aim at]

till², prep. & conj. 1. Up to, as late as,
(specified day, hour, season), as wait ~
evening, four o'clock, then, Monday, next
week; up to the time of (event expected
to happen sooner or later), as was true ~
death, waited ~ the end, ~ his return, arrival, departure (but not ~ his accident).
2. conj. Up to the time when, as ring ~
you get an answer, walk on ~ you come to
the gate. [f. ON til to, orig. a noun =OE
till fixed point, cf. G ziel]

till³, n. Money-drawer in shop counter.
[f. 15th c, etym. dub.]

till⁴, n. Stiff clay with boulders, sand,
etc., boulder-clay. Hence ~Y² a. [?]

till'er¹, n. One who tills. [-ER¹]

till'er², n. Lever fitted to head of rudder
for steering; ~-chain, -rope (connecting ~
with wheel). [f. OF telier crossbow-stock,
orig. weaver's beam, f. L tēla web, -ARY¹]

till'er³, n., & v.i. 1. Shoot of plant
springing from bottom of original stalk;
sapling; sucker. 2. v.i. Put forth ~s.
[OE telgor, cf. Du. telg, MHG zelch]

tilt¹, v.i. & t., & n. 1. (Cause to) assume
sloping position, heel over, as table is apt
to ~ over, don't ~ the table, cask wants
~ing (to facilitate emptying); (Geol., t.
& i. of strata) turn up at steep angle.
2. Make a charge with lance (often at opponent, esp. fig.); ~ at the ring (suspended
for horseman to carry off on point of
lance). 3. Hammer (steel etc.) with ~.
4. n. ~ing, sloping position. 5. Charging
with spear against antagonist or mark
(~-yard, place used for this). 6. Device
of crossed sticks etc. for showing when
fish has taken hook. 7. Full ~, at full
speed, with full force, esp. come, run, full
~ against. 8. ~ (-hammer), heavy pivoted
hammer used in forging. Hence~ER¹
(1, 2) n. [(n. f. vb) ME tilten f. OE tealt
unsteady, cf. Norw. tylten unsteady, Sw.
tulta waddle]

tilt², n., & v.t. 1. Covering of canvas etc.
esp. for cart. 2. v.t. Furnish with~. [OE
teld, cf. MDu. telde, G zelt, ON tiald]

tilth, n. Tillage, cultivation; depth of soil
affected by this. [OE (TILL¹+-TH¹)]

tim'bal, -ul, tý-, n. Kettledrum. [f. F
timbale, earlier attabale f. Arab. al ṭabl the
drum]

timbale (tánbahl'), n. Drum-shaped
raised pie in crust of paste or macaroni.
[F]

tim'ber, n. 1. Wood prepared for building, carpentry, etc.; trees suitable for
this; woods, forest; piece of wood, beam,
esp. (Naut.) any of the curved pieces
forming ribs of vessel, whence (invoking
destruction) shiver my ~s; || (Hunting)
fences & gates. 2. ||~-cart (large four-wheeled
with tackle for lifting ~); ~-head, top end
of ~ rising above deck & used for belaying
ropes etc.; ~-hitch, knot used in attaching
a rope to a spar; ~-toe(s), colloq.. person
with wooden leg; ~-wolf, large American
grey wolf; ||~-yard (lit., &, in cricket sl.,
batsman's wicket). Hence (-)~ED²(-erd)
a., ~ING¹(2, 3) n. [OE, cf. Du. dial.
timmer, G zimmer room, timber, ON timbr,
cogn. w. Gk demō build, L domus house]

timbre (tám'ber, & see Ap.), n. Characteristic quality of sounds produced by each
particular voice or instrument, depending
on the number & character of the over-
tones. [F, = timbre, clock-bell, drum, f.
TYMPANUM]

tim'brel, n. Tambourine. [dim. of ME
timbre f. prec.]

time[1], n. **1.** Duration, continued existence; progress of this viewed as affecting persons or things, as ~ *will show who is right*, *has stood the test of* ~, (personified) *assaults of* (*old, Father*) T~. **2.** More or less definite portion of this associated with particular events or circumstances, with particular events or circumstances, historical or other period, as *the* ~*s of the Stuarts*, *the* ~ *of the Black Death*, *for the* ~ BEING, *prehistoric* ~*s*, *those godless* ~*s*, ~ (colloq.=tax your powers); *give me* ~ & *I will pay*; (colloq.) *got there* ~ (soon enough to see him; *gain* ~, *procure it esp. by temporizing measures*. **4.** Moment or definite portion of this; ~ *destined or suitable for a purpose etc.*, *as there is a* ~ *for everything*, *will fix a* ~ *for seeing him*, *now is the* ~ *to press your point*, *now is your* ~ (opportunity), *I must bide my* ~, *it is* ~ (HIGH ~) *to go*, *for lunch, lunch*~, *it is* ~ *I was going* (for me to go), *in the* NICK[1] *of* ~, ~, ~ (for boxing-round etc.), *is up*, (umpire's call) ~*!*, *is serving his* ~ (as apprentice etc.), *is doing* ~ (in prison), *is far on in her* ~ (of gestation), *is near her* ~ (of childbirth), *my* ~ (death) *is drawing near*. **5.** (Often pl.) conditions of life, prevailing circumstances of a period, as *hard, bad, good*, ~*s* (esp. hard etc. to get a living in); *had a good* ~, *enjoyed myself*; *those were* (the) ~*s!*; *what a* ~ (trouble) *you will have getting him home!* **6.** Occasion, as *the first* ~ *I saw him, wait till next* ~, *did it seven* ~*s running*, *have told you a dozen* ~*s*, ~*s out of number*, ~ & *again*, *many a* ~, *after* ~, *for the last* ~ *of asking*; *three, four, etc.* ~*s* (but twice, not two ~*s*) *9 is 27 etc.*, *is three* ~*s the size of mine*, *ten* ~*s easier or as easy*. **7.** Past, present, future, ~, *the portions into which all* ~ *may at any moment be accurately or loosely divided* (esp. Gram., with reference to tenses). **8.** (Amount of) ~ as reckoned by conventional standards, as *the* ~ *allowed was four years, months, minutes, did a mile in record* ~, *astronomical* (mean solar) ~, *apparent* (SOLAR) ~, SIDEREAL ~, *esp. stated in hours & minutes of the day, as the* ~ *fixed was 4.30, what is the* ~*?*, *is that the correct* (GREENWICH) ~*?*, *at this* ~ *of day* (fig., at this late stage in history), *in the negotiations, etc.*). **9.** Duration of a note as indicated by semibreve, minim, etc.; style of movement depending on number & accentuation of beats in a bar, as *binary, ternary, ~* (with two, three, beats in bar), COMMON[1] ~; *rate of execution*, =*tempo*. **10.** *Against* ~, *with utmost speed, as working, riding, against* ~; *ahead of, (born) before, one's* ~ or ~*s, having notions too enlightened to*

be appreciated or put into practice; *all the* ~, *during the whole of the* ~ *referred to* (*they were laughing all the* ~), *at all* ~*s* (*is a business man all the* ~), *at the same* ~, *simultaneously, notwithstanding, all the same*; *at* ~*s, now & then*; *at one* ~, *during a known but unspecified past period* (*at one* ~ *we met frequently*); *beat* ~, *indicate, follow* ~ *of music with stick, hand, etc.*; *civil* ~ (expressed by CIVIL year etc.); CLOSE[1] ~; *from* ~ *to* ~, *occasionally*; *in* ~, *not late, early enough* (to do, *for thing), eventually, sooner or later, in accordance with, following, the* ~ *of music etc.*; *in no* ~, *rapidly, in the twinkling of an eye*; *keep* ~, *walk, dance, sing, etc., in* ~, (of clock etc.) *keep good, bad, etc., record* ~ (inaccurately; *mean* ~, (regulated by average); *one, two, etc., at a* ~, *each, each two etc., separately*; *out of* ~, *unseasonable, unseasonably, too late, day, hour by clock*, (colloq.) *pass the* ~ *of day*, *exchange greeting etc.* (with person), (sl.) *so that's the* ~ *of day* (the state of affairs, your little game, etc.); *the* ~ *of one's life, a period of exceptional enjoyment or pleasant or unpleasant excitement* (have the ~ *of one's, give one the* ~ *of his, life*); *what* ~ (poet.), *while, when; The* T~*s, the newspaper so named, esp.* (shall write to The T~*s) as used by correspondents for ventilating grievances etc. **11.** ~-*ball* (dropped from top of staff at observatory to indicate fixed moment of mean ~); ~-*bargain*, contract for sale of stock etc. at future ~ (often a form of gambling); ~-*bomb* (designed to explode some ~ after being dropped or put in position); ~-*book, -card, -sheet* (for recording workmen's hours of work); ~-*fuse* (calculated to burn for or explode at given ~); ~-*honoured*, venerable by antiquity; ~-*keeper*, one who records esp. ~ of workmen, *watch etc. is good, bad*, ~-*keeper* (keeps good, bad,); ~-*lag*, interval of ~ between cause etc. & result or consequence; ~-*piece*, measuring instrument esp. portable but stationary clock; ~-*server*, one who, esp. for selfish ends, adapts himself to opinions of the ~*s or of persons in power, so* ~-*serving* & n.; ~-*table, scheme of school work etc., table showing* ~*s of trains*; ~-*work* (paid for by ~, not PIECE-*work*). [OE *tīma*, cf. ON *tími*, Da. *time*, cogn. w. TIDE]

time[2], v.t. & i. Choose the time for, do at chosen time, as *must* ~ *your blows, remark was ill, well,* ~*d*; arrange time of arrival of, regulate rate of travelling of, (train etc.); ascertain the time taken by (race, runner, etc.), whence **tīm**′**ER**[1], nn. [f. prec.]

tim′**ING**[1], n.: keep time, harmonize,

time'less (-ml-), a. (rare). Unending; untimely. [-LESS]

time'ly¹ (-ml-), a. Seasonable, opportune. Hence ~liNESS n. [-LY¹]

tim'eō Dăn'aōs ĕt dōn'a ferĕn'tēs, phr. inculcating or expressing distrust of a conciliatory enemy. [L, = I fear the Greeks, even when bringing gifts]

‖ **time'ous** (-mus), **tim'ous**, a. (chiefly Sc.). Timely. Hence ~LY² adv. [f. TIME¹+-OUS]

tim'id, a. Easily alarmed; shy. Hence or cogn. timid'ITY, ~NESS, nn., ~LY² adv. [f. L *timidus* (*timēre* fear, ~ID¹)]

timoc'racy, n. Form of government in which there is a property qualification for office. So **timocrăt'IC** a. [f. OF *timocracie* f. med. L f. Gk *timokratia* (*timē* honour, worth, value, see -CRACY)]

tim'orous, a. Timid, easily alarmed. Hence ~LY² adv., ~NESS n. [f. L *timor* fear f. *timēre*, -OUS]

tim'othy, n. (Also ~ grass). A fodder grass. [? ~ Hanson, who introduced it in N. America]

‖ **tim'ous**. See TIMEOUS.

tim'pan|ō, n. (pl. ~i pr. -ē). A kettle-drum. So ~IST n., one who plays the percussion instruments in an orchestra. [It., see TYMPANUM]

tin, n., & v.t. (-nn-). **1.** White highly malleable metal taking high polish, little affected by atmosphere, & much used for cooking-utensils etc. esp. in form of ~ *plate* (sheet iron coated with ~); ‖ vessel etc. of ~, esp. for preserving meat, fruit, etc., as *sardine~*; (attrib.) made of ~ or of iron covered with ~; (sl.) money; *cry of ~*, crackling sound it makes if bent; *salt of ~*, ~*liquor*, solutions of ~ used as mordants by dyers etc. **2.** ~ *fish* (Naut. sl.), torpedo; ~ *foil*, foil of ~ or ~like alloy, used as wrapper for soap, tobacco, etc., (v.t.) cover or coat with this; ~ *god*, object of mistaken veneration; ~ *hat* (army sl.), modern soldier's steel helmet; ~ *Lizzie*, nickname for Ford motor-car; ‖ ~*opener*, tool for opening ~s; ~*plate* v.t. coat with ~; ~*man*, ~*smith*, worker in ~ plate, so ~n'ER¹ n.; ~*pot* a. (derog.), cheap, inferior; ~*stone*, principal ore of ~; ~*ware*, vessels etc. of ~ or ~ plate; ~ *whistle*, = penny WHISTLE. Hence ~n'Y² a. **3.** v.t. Cover, coat, with ~; ‖ pack (meat, fruit, etc.) in ~s for preservation. [OE, ON, Du., Da., cf. G *zinn*; not conn. w. L *stannum*, *stag-*, whence F *étain*.]

tin'amou (-ōō), n. S.-Amer. quail-like game-bird. [F, of S.-Amer. orig.]

tinc'al,-kal, (-ngkl), n. Unrefined borax. [f. Malay *tingkal* f. Skr. *tankana*]

tincto'rial, a. Of colour or dyeing, producing colour. [f. L *tinctorius* (TINGE, -ORY)+-AL]

tinc'ture, n., & v.t. **1.** Alcoholic solution of some (usu. vegetable) principle used in medicine, as ~ *of quinine*; slight flavour, spice, smack, (of thing, fig. of moral quality etc.); tinge (of colour); (Her.) inclusive term for the metals, colours, & furs in a coat of arms. **2.** v.t. Colour slightly, tinge, flavour; (fig.) affect slightly (*with* quality). [(vb f. n.) f. L *tinctura* dyeing (as TINGE, see -URE)]

tin'dal, n. (India). Native petty officer of Lascars. [Malayalam *taṇḍal*]

tin'der, n. Dry substance readily taking fire from spark, esp. charred linen etc. used in ~*box* (containing ~), flint, & steel, for kindling fire); *German* ~.=AMADOU. Hence ~Y² a. [OE *tynder* (-*tendan* kindle, cf. Da. *tænde*, Sw. *tända*)]

fine, n. Point, prong, e.g. of antler, harrow, or fork. Hence (-)**tineD²** (-nd) a. [OE *tind*, cf. ON *tindr*, Sw. *tinne*]

ting, n., & v.i. (Make) tinkling sound as of bell. [imit.]

tinge (-j), v.t., & n. **1.** Colour slightly (*with* red etc.); (fig.) modify by mixture (*with* envy etc.). **2.** n. Tint, slight colouring, flavour (lit. & fig.). [f. L *tingere tinct-* dye, stain]

tingle (ting'gl), v.i. & t., & n. (Feel) prickling or stinging sensation; cause this, as *the reply ~d in his ears*; (rare) make (ear etc.). ~. [var. of TINKLE]

tink'er, n., & v.t. **1.** ‖ Mender (esp. itinerant) of kettles, pans, etc. (*don't care a ~'s damn or cuss*, at all); rough-&-ready worker, botcher; patching, botching, as *had an hour's ~ at it*. **2.** Kinds of fish, bird, & seal. **3.** vb. Repair (metal-work), patch (anything, lit. & fig., often *up*) roughly; work in amateurish or clumsy fashion *at* (thing) in the way of repair or alteration. Hence ~LY¹ a. [(vb f. n.) f. 13th c., etym. dub.]

tinkle (ting'kl), v.i. & t., & n. (Make) succession of clinking sounds; make (bell etc.) ~; (obs.) tingle. [(n. f. vb) f. obs. *tink* to chink +-LE(3)]

tink'ler, n. In vbl senses, esp.: (sl.) small bell. [-ER¹]

tinn'i|us, n. (med.). Ringing in the ears. [L f. *tinnire -it-*, imit., cf. TING]

tinny. See TIN.

tin'sel, n., a., & v.t. (-ll-). **1.** Kinds of glittering metallic substance made in thin sheets & used in strips, threads, etc., to give sparkling effect; dress-fabric etc. adorned with ~; (fig.) superficial brilliancy or splendour. **2.** adj. Showy, gaudy, cheaply splendid. **3.** v.t. Adorn with ~ (lit. & fig.). [a. & vb f n.) f. MF *estincelle*, *ét-*, spark (for loss of é- cf. *ticket*) f. L *scintilla* perh. corrupted to *stincilla*]

tint, n., & v.t. **1.** A variety of a colour, esp. one made by diluting with white; (rare) tendency towards, admixture of, a different colour, as *red or* or *with a blue ~*; *autumn ~s* (of dying leaves); (Engrav.; set of parallel lines cut with ~*tool* to give uniform shading; ~*block*, block bearing design to be printed in faint colour as

background, *ruled, crossed,* ~; surface of this with parallel, crossing, lines. **2.** v.t. Apply ~ to, colour. Hence ~'LESS a. [f. It. *tinta* (as TINGE); earlier also *tinct* f. L]

tin'ter, n. Person who tints; instrument for tinting; magic-lantern slide of plain coloured glass. [-ER²]

tintinnăbŭlā'tion, n. Tinkling of bells. [f. foll.+-ATION]

tintinnă'bŭlum, n. (pl. ~*a*). Bell, esp. small tinkling one, whence ~ARY¹), ~OUS, aa.; rattle made of small bells or metal plates. [L., = bell, f. *tintinnare* redupl. form as TINNITUS]

tintŏm'eter, n. Instrument for determining tints. [-METER]

tin'tỹ, a. Discordantly tinted. [-Y²]

tin'ỹ, teen'ỹ (nursery), a. Very small, as *a ~ little boy, little ~ boy.* [earlier *tine, tyne,* used as n. & adj., a bit, little, etym. dub.]

-tion, suf. of nn. of action or condition (=-*t*- of L p.p. stem +-ION, cf. -ATION), as *attention.*

tip¹, n., & v.t. (-pp-). **1.** Extremity, end, esp. of small or tapering thing, as *the ~s of the fingers, walk on the ~s of your toes, ~ of a cigar, bird measures 15 in. from the ~ of my tongue, was just going to say it*; kinds of brush used in gilding; small piece or part attached to end of thing, e.g. ferrule. **2.** ~*staff* (hist., pl. ~*staves*), (metal-tipped staff as badge of) sheriff's officer; ~-*tilted,* (of nose) turned up at the toes, (v.i.) walk ~*toe*; ~*top',* (n.) highest point of excellence. (a. & adv.) first-rate. **3.** v.t. Furnish with ~. [ME. ~ ~*toe,* (adv., also on *the ~s* of ...) Du., Da.]

tip², v.t. & i. (-pp-), & n. **1.** (Cause to) lean or slant, tilt, topple, (*over, up,* etc. esp. with slight effort. **2.** Strike or touch lightly (~ *& run,* form of cricket in which batsman must run if bat touches ball; ~-*&-run raid,* one in which the raider appears suddenly and makes off immediately after attacking). **3.** Overturn, cause to overbalance, (person *into* pond etc.); discharge (contents of jug etc. *out, into,* etc.); thus. **4.** (sl.). Throw lightly, hand, give, communicate, in informal manner, as ~(throw) *us a copper,* ~ *us your fin,* shake hands, ~ *us a song, a yarn, might have ~ped me the wink* (given me warning wink); ~ *off,* give (person) warning, so ~-*off* n., a hint; (Sport.) give secret information about horse etc. to. **5.** Make usu. small present of money to, as *must ~ the porter, ~ped me* (now rarely *with*) *half-a-crown.* **6.** n. Small money present. **7.** Secret information about horse-racing, money-market, etc., as *will give you the straight ~; good ~,* useful dodge or recipe for doing something; *miss one's ~,* fail in one's object. **8.** Slight push; light stroke esp. in baseball. **9.** Place where refuse is ~ped. **10.** ~-*cart,* ~-*cart* (pivoted for ~ping), ~'*cat,* (game with) short piece of wood tapering at ends & struck with stick; ~-*up seat,* (to allow of free passing. Hence ~'PER'¹(1, 2) n. [of doubtful & prob. various orig.]

Tipperar'y, n. Refrain specially associated with the B.E.F. of 1914. [*It's a long way to ~* first wds of chorus]

tipp'ét, n. Cape, muffler, of fur etc. covering shoulders & coming down to some distance in front, worn by women & as part of official costume by judges, clergy, etc. [f. 1300; prob. f. TIP¹+-ET¹]

tipp'le, v.i. & t., & n. **1.** Drink (liquor) habitually; drink (liquor) slowly & repeatedly. **2.** n. Strong drink. Hence **tipp'ler¹** n. [cf. Norw. *tipla* frequent. of *tippa* drip from tip]

tipp'ỹ, a. (Of tea) containing a large proportion of 'golden tips' (leaf-buds). [TIP¹+-Y²]

tip'ster, n. One who gives tips about races etc. [-STER]

tip'sỹ, a. Intoxicated; proceeding from, showing, intoxication, as *a ~y lurch*; ~*y-cake,* sponge-cake soaked in wine & served with custard. Hence ~IFY v.t., ~ily² adv., ~iNESS n. [prob. f. TIP² ~inclined to lean, unsteady; for -*sy* cf. *tricksy*]

tirade', n. Long vehement speech esp. of censure; long passage of declamation etc. [F, = long speech, f. It. *tirata* drawing, pulling, f. It. & LL *tirare* draw, see -ADE]

tire¹, v.t. & i. Make or grow weary; *am ~d,* have had enough of, am sick of, (thing, doing), am exhausted *with.* Hence ~'d'NESS (tīrd-) n., ~less a. also (poet.), ~'less¹ (tīr-) a., ~'lessly² adv. [OE *tēorian, tē-;* excl. E]

tire², ||tyre, n., & v.t. **1.** Band of metal, rubber, etc., placed round rim of wheel to strengthen it or prevent jar; PNEUMATIC ~. **2.** v.t. Place ~ on (wheel). Hence (-tīred² (tīrd.), ~less² (tīr-) [-LESS², aa. [prob.=foll.]

||tire³, n., & v.t. (arch.). **1.** Head-dress; attire. **2.** v.t. Adorn, attire, as *she ~d her head*; ~'*less woman* (arch.), woman employed to dress another. [for ATTIRE]

tire'some (tīrs-), a. Tending to tire, fatiguing; tedious; annoying, as *how ~! —I have left my watch behind.* Hence ~LY¹ adv., ~NESS n.

'tis (-z), contraction of *it is.*

tisane' (-zän), n. =PTISAN. [F]

tiss'ue (-shoo or -shū, -sū), n. Any fine

woven fabric; (Biol.) substance of an organ, fabric formed of cells & cell-products, as *adipose, connective, muscular, nervous*, ~; (fig.) interwoven series, set, collection, (*of lies, crimes*, etc.); ~(*-paper*), thin soft unsized paper for wrapping or protecting delicate articles, engraving in book, etc. Hence (-)**tĭss′ŭed**[2] (-tĭd, -shŭd) a. [f. F *tissu* woven (thing) f. +*tistre* weave (mod. F *tisser*) f. L *texere*]

tĭt[1], n. **1.** Kinds of small bird, including ~*lark* &~*mouse* (both also called~*ling*); *bearded, blue, cole, crested, great, long-tailed, marsh*, ~. **2.** (arch.). Small or poor horse; child, girl. [prob. imit. of littleness; cf. Icel. *tittr* pin, titmouse]

tĭt[2], n. ~ *for tat*, blow for blow, retaliation. [perh., = earlier *tip for tap*]

tĭt[3], n. (colloq.) = TEAT.

Tī′tan, n. (Gk Myth.) each of a gigantic race, the children of Uranus & Ge, (also) the sun-god, brother of Helios; the *weary* ~, British or other large empire (w. ref. to ATLAS); person of superhuman size, strength, intellect, etc., whence ~**ĔSS**[1] n. So ~**ĔSQUE′** (-ĕsk), **tĭtăn′ĬC**, aa. [f. L f. Gk] **tī′tan′ium**, n. A dark-grey metallic element. Hence **tĭt′anĀTE**[3](3) n. [prec. + -IUM]

tĭt′bĭt′, n. Delicate bit, choice morsel. [earlier *tidbit* f. dial. *tid* delicate, wanton]

tithe (-dh), n., & v.t. **1.** Tax of one-tenth, esp. one payable in kind; || (often pl.) tenth part of annual proceeds of land (*predial* ~s) & personal industry (*personal* ~s) taken for support of clergy & church; || *mixed* ~s (from pigs, sheep, etc., fed on the land); || ~ *commissioners* (arranging commutation of ~s etc.); ||~*pig*, tenth pig set apart for ~; (rhet.) tenth part, esp. *not a* ~ *of*. **2.** v.t. Subject to ~s. Hence **tithe′ABLE** (-dh-) a. [vb OE *tēothian*) OE *tēotha* (as TEN, see -TH[2])

tīth′ing (-dh-), n. Taking tithe: (Hist.) ten householders living near together & bound over as sureties for each other's peaceable behaviour. [OE *tēothung* (*tēothian*, prec., -ING[1])]

Tī′tian (-shn), n. Venetian painter (d. 1576); one of his pictures; (attrib., esp. of hair) bright golden auburn. Hence ~**ĔSQUE′** (shanĕsk) a., in the style of ~.

tĭt′illāte, v.t. Tickle; excite pleasantly. So ~**ATION** n. [f. L *titillare*, see -ATE[2]]

tĭt′ivāte, **tĭtt′i-**, v.t. & i. (colloq.). Adorn, smarten, (oneself etc.); adorn oneself. [earlier *tid-*, perh. f. *tidy* after *cultivate*]

tĭt′lĀrk. See TIT[1].

tī′tle, n. **1.** Distinguishing appellation placed at head of chapter, poem, etc.; contents of ~-page of book, short essential part of these used in reference (e.g. *Adam Smith's Wealth of Nations*). **2.** Formula at head of legal document, statute, etc.; division of statute etc. **3.** Personal appellation, hereditary or not, denoting or implying office (e.g. *king, queen, judge,*

mayor, rector, captain) or nobility (e.g. *duke, marquis, earl, viscount, baron*, any of which exc. *duke* may be COURTESY ~ of son etc. of duke etc.) or distinction or merit (e.g. *baronet, knight*) or (usu. *degree*) qualification (e.g. *D.D., M.A.*) or used in addressing or referring to person (e.g. *Lord, Lady, Sir, Mrs, Miss, Doctor, Professor*, prefixed to name; *your* or *her* or *his Majesty, Grace*, etc.). **4.** (Law) right to ownership of property with or without possession, the facts constituting this, (also ~*deed*) legal instrument as evidence of right; just or recognized claim *(to)*; service, merit, etc., that constitutes this. **5.** Fineness of gold as expressed in carats. **6.** Fixed sphere of work & source of income as condition to ordination. **7.** (Distinct attached to) parish church in Rome. **8.** ~*-page*, page at beginning of book giving particulars of subject, authorship, publication, etc.; ~*-role*, part in a play that gives its name (e.g. *Othello*). Hence ~**LESS** a. [OF, f. L *titulus*]

tī′tled (-ld), a. Having title of nobility.

tĭt′ling[1], n. See TIT[1]. [f. ON *titlingr* (as TIT[1], see -LING[1])

tĭt′ling[2], n. Impressing of title in gold-leaf etc. on back of book. [-ING[1]]

tĭt′mouse, n. (pl. *-mice*). = TIT[1]. [ME *tit-mōse* (TIT[1]+OE *māse* ~, cf. Du. *mees*, G *meise*]

tĭt′ĕr′lāte, v.t. Determine quantity of given constituent in (compound) by observing quantity of a standard solution necessary to convert this constituent into another form. So ~**ATION** n. [f. F *titre* TITLE + -ATE[2]]

tĭtt′er, v.i., & n. **1.** Laugh, giggle, in restrained manner. **2.** n. Such laugh. Hence ~**ER**[1] n. [imit.]

tĭt′tle, n. Particle, whit, esp. *not one jot or* ~. [ME, = stroke over word or letter, f. L as TITLE, cf. TILDE]

tĭt′tlebăt (-lb-), n. Stickleback. [corrupt.]

tĭt′tle-tăttle, n., & v.i. Gossip. [redupl. f. *tattle*]

tĭtt′up, v.i., & n. **1.** Go *along* etc., move, conduct oneself, in lively or frisky fashion; || (Naut. etc. sl.) toss for drinks. **2.** n. Spring, prance. Hence ~(p)Y[2] a. [perh. imit. of hoof-beat]

tĭtū′ba′tion, n. (med.). Fidgetiness esp. as caused by nervous irritation. [f. L *titubatio* (*titubare* totter, see -ATION]

tĭt′ular, a. & n. **1.** Held by virtue of a title, as ~ *possessions*; existing, that is such, only in name, as ~ *sovereign*(*ty*); ~ *bishop*, (R.-C. Ch.) bishop bearing name of a former Christian see esp. in Mohammedan countries; ~ (*saint*), patron saint of church. **2.** n. Holder of office etc. esp. of benefice without corresponding functions or obligations. Hence ~LY[2] adv. [f. L as TITLE +-AR[1]]

titýre-tû (-rä), n. Member of gang of London street-ruffians in time of Charles II. [*Titýre, tu*, first wds of first eclogue of Virgil.]

tmésis, n. (gram.). Separation of the parts of a word by intervening word(s) (e.g. *to us-ward, what things soever*). [Gk *tmēsis* cutting f. *temnō* cut]

T.N.T., TNT, n. = TRINITROTOLUENE.

to¹ (before consonant tŏ, before vowel tŏŏ or at end of clause tŏŏ, emphat. tŏŏ), prep. **1.** In the direction of (place, person, thing, condition, quality, etc.; with or without the implication of intention or of arrival), *the station, fled to Rome, throw it to me, got us walking over to Bath, on his way to the house by four, to bed with you, fluttered to the pavement, was committed to the flames, house looks to the south, held it to the light, to arms!, hand to hand, told him to his face, was carried to destruction, letter has come to hand, fell to work, fell to musing, tends or has a tendency to indolence, slow to anger, appointed to a post, born to a great fortune, all to no purpose, to his shame be it said.* **2.** As far as; not short of, as *true to the core, fought to the last gasp, but it to the end, cut him to the heart, a Home-ruler to the boundary, correct to a hair's-breadth, suits him to a T, acted his part to perfection, might run to £5, drank himself to death, might argue to all eternity, & so on to the end of the chapter.* **3.** (Of comparison, ratio, adaptation, reference, etc.) *this is nothing to what it might be, 3 is to 4 as 6 is to 8, ten to one he will find it out, two to one is not fair play, not up to the mark, equal to the occasion, made to order, drawn to scale, not to the point, true to life, will speak to that question later, sang to his guitar, cannot do it to his liking*; *corresponding, compared, inferior, etc., to.* **4.** (arch.). For, by way of, as *took her to wife, has a duke to his father-in-law.* **5.** (Introducing indirect object of vb, recipient, possessor, etc., or person or thing affected by the action, quality, etc.; alternative constr. as shown) *tend it or them, or this etc., or your knife etc., to John or to him* (also *lend John or him this etc. or your knife or rarely it or them, lend it or rarely them him or rarely John, but not lend this etc., or your knife him, or John, nor lend etc. to him or John it or them*, nor in ordinary prose *lend to him or John this etc. or your knife*); *write to me, explain it to me, apply to the secretary, seems to me absurd, to my mind or thinking, revolting to sane minds, pleasant to the taste, impervious to weather, obedient to command, unkind to him, has been a good father to them, what's that to you?, drink to me only with thine eyes, here's to you (your health), broken in to the saddle, accustomed to it, next door to us, ready to his hand, has not a shilling to his name, takes no vine to his dinner* (arch.), *there is a moral to it, there is no end to it*; *would to God* (I wish it were or had been God's will) *that*-. **6.** (As sign of infinitive, expressing purpose, consequence, etc., limiting the meaning of adj., or rarely forming verbal n.; omitted after *can, do, may, must, shall, will*, &c as shown, cf. also DARE, NEED, GO) *he proposes to stay, declines to go, wants to know, began to sing* (or *began singing*), *fail to understand, does it to annoy, the matter is difficult to explain, it is useless to rebel* (rebellion is useless), *alas seen to fall* (but *I saw him fall*), *was heard to complain* (but *I heard him complain*), *floor was felt to tremble* (but *felt the floor tremble*), *was never known or found it* (to) *fail, have sometimes known or found it* (to) *fail, make him repeat it, he was made* (usu. to) *repeat it, help me* (to) *lift this, please* (to) usu. omitted) *shut the door, was pleased* (thought fit) *to be angry, I prefer to go* (but *had rather go, had as lief go*), *had my work to do, had to do my work* (but *will not have you talk such nonsense*), *was about to protest*, (arch.) *he is much to seek* (deficient) *in that respect*, (arch.) *what went ye out for to see?*, to WIT¹. **7.** (As substitute for infinitive) *meant to call but forgot to, had no time to, you promised to.* **8.** Included, contained, or involved in (*that's all there is to it, it's that and no more*), *the door is to* (just not shut); *to & FRO*. [f. prec.]

to² (tŏŏ), adv. To the normal or required position or condition, esp. to a standstill, as BRING, COME, FALL, GO, HEAVE, LIE³ *to; the door is to* (just not shut); *to & FRO*. [OE *tō* prep. & sign of gerund as distinct from infinitive, cf. Du. *toe*, G *zu*]

toad, n. **1.** Amphibian like frog but with clumsy & usu. warty body & not aquatic except when breeding; detestable or disgusting person. **2.** ~ *in* (or *the*) *hole*, beef baked in batter. **3.** ~-*eater*, sycophant, obsequious parasite, so ~-*eating* a. & n.; ~-*flax*, perennial plant with spurred yellow flowers marked with orange spot; ~-*spit*, = CUCKOO-spit; ~-*stone*, stone, occas. precious, supposed to resemble or to have been formed in body of ~, formerly used as amulet etc. [f. G *tottes gestein* dead rock] kind of volcanic rock; ~-*stool*, kinds of umbrella-shaped fungus. Hence ~ISH¹ a. [OE *tādige*, etym. dub.]

toad'y, n. & v.t. **1.** = TOAD-eater. **2.** v.t. Fawn servilely upon (person, or abs.). Hence ~ISM¹ a., ~ISM n. [19th c. wd, perh. shortened f. TOAD-eater]

toast, n. & v.t. & i. **1.** (Slice of) bread browned on each side esp. at the fire (*anchovies etc. on* ~, so served at table; *have one on* ~, sl., have him at one's mercy; *as warm as a* ~, glowing with warmth); (arch.) *a* ~, piece of ~ in cup of wine. **2.** Person esp. woman whose health is drunk, thing, sentiment, similarly named in drinking, as *was a great* ...

~ in her day. **3.** ~-list, ~-master, (person who announces) ~s at public dinner; ||~-rack (for holding slices of ~ at table); ~-water (in which ~ has stood, used as cooling drink; also ~ & water). **4.** vb. Brown, cook, (bread), muffin, cheese, bacon, or intr. of these) before fire; warm (one's feet etc.) thus. **5.** Drink to the health or in honour of. Hence ~ER¹ (1, 2) n. [(vb f. n.) ME *tost* f. OF *toster* vb f. L *tostus* p.p. of *torrēre* parch; drinking sense of anecd. orig.]

toast'ing, n. 1 in vbl senses; ~-fork, long fork for making toast, (joc., also ~-iron) sword. [-ING¹]

tobacc'ō, n. (pl. ~s). **1.** (Also ~-plant) plant of Amer. origin with narcotic leaves used for smoking, chewing, or snuff; its leaves esp. as prepared for smoking etc. **2.** ~-cutter, instrument for shredding ~; ~-heart, disorder of heart caused by excessive use of ~; ~-pipe¹; ~-pouch (for carrying about small quantity of ~); ~-stopper, instrument for pressing down ~ in pipe. [f. Sp. *tabaco*, of native orig.]

tobacc'onist, n. Dealer in tobacco. [irreg. f. prec. + -IST; ~a- perh. after *Platonist* etc.]

toboggʼan, n., & v.i. **1.** Long narrow sled used for going downhill esp. over snow or ice; ~-shoot, -slide, slide for ~s, usu. divided into different courses to prevent collision. **2.** v.i. Go in ~. Hence ~ER¹, ~ING¹, nn. [of Amer.-Ind. orig.]

tob'ȳ, n. Jug or mug usu. in form of old man with three-cornered hat (also *T~ Fillpot*); || ~ collar, broad turned-down goffered collar like the frill of Punch's dog T~. [pers. name]

tocca'ta (-kah-), n. (mus.). Kind of rapid brilliant composition for piano, organ, etc. [It. f. *toccare* TOUCH, see -ADE]

Tōc H, n. Society with many branches carrying on comradeship from the 1914-18 war. [signallers' letter T, +H, for *Talbot House* started at Ypres in memory of Gilbert Talbot]

Tochar'ian (-k-), a. & n. (Of, in) an extinct Indo-European language. [f. *Tochari* a Scythian tribe (in Strabo)]

||**tochʼer** (-χ-), n. (Sc.). Marriage portion, dowry. [f. Gael. *tochar*]

||**tōc'ō, -kō,** n. (sl.). A thrashing; chastisement. [f. Hind. *ṭōkō* imperat. of *ṭoknā* censure, blame]

tōc'sin, n. (Bell rung as) alarm-signal (now chiefly fig.). [f. OF *toquassen* f. Pr. *tocasenh* (*tocar* TOUCH + *senh* signal-bell f. L as SIGN)]

||**tōd¹,** n. (arch.). Bush; mass of foliage; weight for wool, usu. 28 lb. [f. 15th c.; cf. ON *toddi* piece, Du. *tod(de)* rag, G *zotte* tuft]

||**tōd²,** n. (dial.). Fox. [f. 12th c., etym. dub.]

today', to-day', adv. & n. (On) this present day, as *saw or shall see him ~*, *~ is his birthday*. [OE *tō dæge* on (this) day (*tō* TO¹ + dat. of DAY); so *tonight, tomorrow*]

tod'dle, v.i. & t., & n. **1.** Walk with short tottering steps, as child learning to walk; make (one's way), perform (distance), thus; take casual or leisurely walk (*round, to,* etc.). **2.** n. ~ing walk; (colloq.) ~ing child. Hence tōdd'lER¹ n. [c. 17th c., etym. dub.]

todd'ȳ, n. Sap of some kinds of palm, from which when fermented arrack is obtained; sweetened drink of spirits & hot water. [f. Hind. *tāṛī* (*tār* palm f. Skr. *tāla* palmyra)]

to-dō' (-dōō), n. = ADO. [TO¹+DO]

tōd'ȳ, n. W.-Ind. bird related to kingfisher. [f. F *todier* f. L *todus*, a small bird]

tōe, n., & v.t. & i. **1.** Digit of foot; part of stocking, shoe, boot, that covers the ~s. **2.** Fore part of hoof; piece of iron under front of horseshoe to prevent slipping. **3.** Projection from foot of buttress etc. to give stability; outer end of head of golf-club; (Mech.) lower end of vertical shaft resting in a step, arm on cam. **4.** *Ball* (callous fleshy pad on under side) of ~; *great, little,* ~, *largest, smallest,* of human foot; *tread on person's ~s,* offend his feelings or prejudices; *the light fantastic ~,* (joc.) dancing; (sl.) *turn up one's ~s,* die; *from top to ~,* from head to foot, completely; *heel-&-~* WALK'ing; ~ cap, outer covering of ~ in boot or shoe; ~-drop, inability to raise ~s, from paralysed muscles; ~-nail, nail of human ~, metal nail driven obliquely through end of board etc. **5.** vb. Furnish with ~, mend ~ of, (stocking, shoe); (school sl.) kick (person etc.); touch (*the line, mark, scratch*) with ~ before starting in race (~ *the line,* fig., conform esp. under pressure to the requirements of one's party); (Golf) strike (ball) with part of club *toe* near ~; ~ *in, out,* turn ~s in, out, in walking. Hence (-)TOED (tōd), ~LESS, aa. [OE & ON *tā,* cf. G *zehe*]

tō-fall (tōō'fawl), n. (arch., poet.), Close, decline, (of day etc.). [TO²+FALL]

||**tō'ff,** n. (sl.). Distinguished person, swell. [perh. corrupt. of TUFT]

||**tōff'ee** (-fi), **-fȳ,** n. Kinds of sweetmeat made of sugar, butter, etc., as *almond ~*; *can't shoot etc. for ~* (sl.), is no shot etc. (cf. NUT). [earlier, & still Sc. & U.S., *taffy,* etym. dub.]

||**tōft,** n. (law). Homestead; land once occupied by this; ~man (hist.), occupier of ~. [OE, f. ON *topt*]

||**tōg,** n., & v.t. (sl.; -gg-). **1.** (Usu. pl.) garment(s); (Naut.) *long ~s,* shore-clothes. **2.** v.t. Dress (person, oneself, often *out*). Hence ~gᵉRY(5)(-g-), n. [perh. f. foll.]

tōg'a, n. Ancient Roman's loose flowing outer garment, esp. w. allusion to Roman

citizenship, to civil career, or (also ~
vðrli̇̄es, manly ~) to its assumption as
sign of manhood (at age of 14). Hence
~'d, ~ED² (*ad*), a. [L, cogn. w. Hence
cover]

togéth′er (-dh-), adv. In company or conjunction, as *walking* ~, *lived* ~; simultaneously, as *both* ~ *exclaimed*; *compared*
~ (one with another); into conjunction,
so as to unite, as *sew them* ~, *tied* ~, GET,
HANG¹, ~, *put* TWO *&* two ~; uninter-
ruptedly, on end (he *would keep sober for*
weeks ~); ~ *with*, as well as, & also, as
sent a host of foot-soldiers ~ *with some*
cavalry. [OE *tŏgædere* (tŏ TO¹+*gædre*
together, cf. GATHER)]

∥tŏg′gle, n. (Naut.) pin put through eye
of rope etc. to keep it in place etc.; pair
of rods or plates hinged together by ~-
joint (knee-joint) so as to transmit pressure at right angles; ~-*iron*, harpoon
with movable blade instead of fixed
barbs; ~-*press* (acting by means of ~-
joints); ~-*rope* (with wooden handle at
one end & loop at the other). [perh. cogn.
w. TUG & TANGLE]

toil¹, v.i., & n. 1. Work long or laboriously
(*at, on, through,* task); move painfully or
laboriously (*up* hill etc., *along*). 2. n.
Labour, drudgery; ~-*worn* (by ~). Hence
~ʳER¹, ~ʳSOMENESS, nn., ~ʳFUL, ~ʳLESS
(-l-), ~ʳSOME, aa., ~ʳfully² & ~ʳsomely²
adv. [(n. f. vb) prob. f. OF *toilier* mix,
pester, prob. f. L *tudiculāre*, stir up f.
tudicula olive-bruising machine (*tudes*
mallet f. *tundere* beat, -CULE)]

toil², n. (now only in pl.). Net, snare, (lit.
& fig.), as *taken in the* ~*s.* [f. OF *toile*
cloth, (pl.) toils, f. L *tela* web f. *texere*
weave]

toile (twahl), n. ~*cirée* (sērā′), fine kinds
of oilcloth; ~ *coll′bert* (-bar), canvas for
embroidery; ~ *d'Alsace'* (-alss), *de Vichy*
(vēshē′), linen materials for woman's
summer dress. [F, see prec.]

toil′et, n. 1. Process of dressing, arranging
the hair, etc., as *make one's* ~; (style of)
dress, costume, as *an elaborate* ~, *a*
white satin ~ (also ~-*table*) dressing-table
usu. with looking-glass; lavatory or
water-closet; ~-*cover*, cover for ~-*table*;
~-*paper* (for water-closet); ~ *powder*,
dusting powder used in making one's ~;
~-*set* (of utensils for ~); ~ *soap* (for use
in ~); ~ *vinegar* (aromatic kind for mixing
with washing-water). 2. (med.). Cleansing of a part after operation. [F (-*ette*),
orig. = cloth, clothes-bag, dim. of prec.]

toison d'or (twahzawŭ′ dŏʳ), n. = *Golden*
FLEECE. [F]

Tokay, n. Rich aromatic wine made at
Tokaj in Hungary; kind of grape.
∥tŏke, n. (sl.). Food (esp. dry bread). [?]
tŏk′en, n. 1. Sign, symbol, evidence, (*of*
affection etc.; often *in* ~ *of*); memorial
of friendship, keepsake; ring, coin, etc.,

---

serving as proof of authenticity; BOOK¹
~. 2. (bibl.). Preconcerted signal (*Mark*
xiv. 44; 2 (hist.). Piece of metal like &
used instead of coin, but worth much les-
than nominal value & issued by trades-
men, bank, etc., without sanction of
government. 4. (arch. or joc.). *By* (*this,*
what I say, 5. ~ *money*, coins of higher
nominal than intrinsic value but exchangeable for full-standard money at
the higher rate; ~ *payment*, (Polit.)
payment of small proportion of sum due
(esp. from one country to another) as
indication that debt is not repudiated,
(loosely) nominal payment; ~ *vote*,
Parliamentary vote of money in which
the amount stated *pro formâ* is not meant
to be binding. Hence ~LESS a. [OE
tāc(e)n, cf. Du. *teeken*, G *zeichen*, ON
teikn, cogn. w. TEACH]
∥tŏk′ō. See TOCO.

tŏl′a, n. Unit of weight in India, = 180
grains troy. [Hind., f. Skr. *tulā*]
told. See TELL.
Toled′o (-lē-), n. (pl. ~s). Fine sword(-blade)
made at ~ in Spain.

tŏl′erable, a. Endurable; fairly good, not
bad, as *am in* ~*le health, had a* ~*le passage*.
Hence ~LENESS n., ~LY² adv. [F (-*lé-*), f.
L *tolerābilis* (as foll., see -BLE)]
tŏl′erate, v.t. Endure, permit, (practise,
action, person's *doing*); forbear to judge
harshly or rigorously (person, religious
sect, opinion); endure society of or intercourse with; sustain, endure, (suffering
etc.), esp. (Med.) sustain use of (drug etc.
without harm. Hence or cogn. ~ANCE,
~ANT² nn., ~ANT¹ a., ~antly² adv. [f. F
tolérer f. L *tolerāre, -āt-* (-ATE³)]
tŏleră′tion, n. Tolerating; forbearance;
recognition of right of private judgement
in religious matters, liberty to uphold
one's religious opinions & forms of worship or to enjoy all social privileges etc.
without regard to religious differences
whence ~IST(2) n.; *Act of T*~ (conditionally freeing Dissenters from some restrictions on the exercise of their forms of
worship, 1689). [F (-*lé-*), f. L *tolerationem*
(as prec., see -ATION)]

toll¹, n. & v.i. 1. Tax, duty, paid for use
of market, public road, etc., or for service
rendered; ~ *road* (~ (fig.), road casualties;
(Law) ~ *thorough*, (taken by town for
use of highway, bridge, etc.,); ~ *traverse*
(for passing over private land); ~ grain
retained by miller as compensation for
grinding (still, fig., in *take* ~=abstract a
portion of). 2. ~-*bar*, -*gate*, bar or usu.
gate across road to prevent passage of
person, vehicle, etc., without paying ~;
~-*booth* (arch., Sc.), town gaol [orig.
temporary structure for collection of
market ~s & detention of those who did
not pay & others]; ~*house* (occupied by
collector at ~-gate), ~

[OE (also *tolm*), cf. Du. *tol*, G *zoll*, ON *tollr*, perh. f. L f. Gk *telōnion* ~house (*telos* tax)]

toll² v.t. & i., & n. **1.** Cause (bell, or abs.) to ring with slow uniform strokes; (of bell or clock) give out (stroke, knell, hour of day), give out measured sounds, ring on account of (person, his death, etc.). **2.** n. ~ing, stroke, of bell. [ME *tollen* draw, entice, etym. dub.]

toll'able a. (Of person or goods) subject to toll. [TOLL¹+-ABLE]

|| **tol(l)'booth.** See TOLL¹.

tol-lol', a. (sl.). In fair state, so-so, middling. [f. *tol(erable)* w. redupl.]

|| **tŏll'y**, n. (school sl.). Candle. [perh. f. TALLOW]

Tŏl'tēc, n. One of a race traditionally held to have ruled in Mexico before the Aztecs. Hence ~AN a. [Mex.]

tolu' (or tō), n. Balsam got from a S. Amer. tree & used in perfumery & medicine. Hence ~IC a., **tŏl'ūīne** & **tŏl'ūŏl** nn., colourless inflammable liquid hydrocarbon of the benzene series, used in the preparation of dyes & T.N.T. [name of place]

tom, n. **1.** (*Tom*) abbr. of *Thomas*; *Tom, Dick, & Harry*, persons taken at random, ordinary commonplace people. **2.** Male animal, esp. ~(-*cat*). **3.** *Long* ~ (Naut.), long gun esp. one carried amidships on swivel-carriage; *Old Tom*, strong kind of gin; *Tom & Jerry*, rum & water beaten up with eggs etc.; ~'*boy*, romping girl, hoyden; ~'*fool*, fool, trifler, (v.l.) play the fool, act in trifling manner (~*fool'ery*, foolish trifling, foolish knick-knacks etc.); *Tom Fool* (type of witlessness, esp. in proverb *there's more knows Tom Fool than Tom Fool knows* = notoriety is not honour); ~*nodd'y*, blockhead, fool; *Tom Thumb*, a legendary dwarf, any diminutive person, dwarf variety of various plants; *Tom Tiddler's ground*, children's game, place where money can be had for the picking up; || ~'*tit*', kinds of small bird, esp. titmouse.

tom'ahawk (-a-h-), n., & v.t. **1.** War-axe of N.-Amer. Indian, with head of horn, stone, or steel; *bury the* ~ *or hatchet*. **2.** v.t. Strike, kill, with ~; criticize savagely in review. [f. native orig.]

tomáll'ey (-ĭ), n. Soft greenish substance (called the liver) in lobster, used as sauce. [Carib]

tonan' (-ahn), n. Persian gold coin. [Pers.]

toma'to (||-ah-, *-ā-), n. (pl. ~es). (Plant with) red or yellow pulpy edible fruit; *currant* ~ (with small fruit about size of currant); *tree*~, kind that grows erect & sustains fruit without support. [f. Sp. *tomate* f. Mex. *tomatl*; formerly called *love-apple*]

tomb (tōōm), n., & v.t. **1.** Hole (made) in earth or rock to receive dead (esp. human) body, grave; subterranean or other vault for the dead; sepulchral monument; (fig.) *the* ~, death; ~'*stone*, monumental stone placed over grave. **2.** v.t. Enclose as or in or as in ~. Hence ~'LESS a. [f. OF *tumbe* f. LL *tumba* f. Gk *tumbos* sepulchral mound]

tom'băc, -k, n. Kinds of copper-&-zinc alloy, used under various names as material for cheap jewellery. [F (-c), f. Malay *tambāga* copper]

tom'bola, n. (In France & southern U.S.) kind of lottery with fancy articles for prizes. [It., perh. f. *tombolare* TUMBLE]

tome, n. Volume, esp. large heavy one. [F, f. L f. Gk *tomos* section f. *temnō* cut]

-tome, suf. f. (1) Gk *tomē* a cutting, or (2) *-tomos* cutting, (1) denoting section, segment, & (2) used in designations of surgical instruments (for corresponding operations in -TOMY).

tomen't|um, n. (Bot.) kind of pubescence composed of matted woolly hairs; (Anat.) flocculent inner surface of pia mater. Hence **tŏm'entōsE¹**, ~OUS, aa. [L, =padding of wool etc.]

tomm'|y, n. **1.** (*T~*) familiar form of TOM; || *T~ Atkins*, the British soldier, whence *T~* or ~ (sl.), private in army. **2.** (mech.). Kinds of wrench or turn-screw, (also ~*bar*) short bar for working box-spanners. **3.** Bread, provisions, esp. as given to workman in lieu of wages; this system of payment, truck system (now illegal); ~*shop*, (formerly) in which ~ was enforced, (now) shop in works where provisions may be bought, any baker's shop; || food carried by workmen. **4.** *~*gun*, sub-machine gun [f. inventor J. T. Thompson]; ~ROT¹; *soft* ~ (Naut.), soft or fresh bread (cf. HARD *tack*). [-Y³]

tomorr'ow, to-mō'rrow, (-ō), adv. & n. (On) the day after today, as *will write* ~, (prov.) ~ *never comes*; (attrib.) ~ *morning, afternoon*, etc. (used as nn. & advv.; ~ *week*, eight days hence). [TO¹+MORROW, cf. TODAY]

tom'pion. Var. of TAMPION.

tŏm'tŏm, n., & v.i. (-mm-). **1.** Native Indian drum; gong. **2.** v.i. Beat ~. [f. Hind. *tamtam*, imit.]

-tomy, suf. = Gk *-tomia* -cutting (*temnō* cut), chiefly in names of surgical operations (*anat~, phlebo~, tracheo~*).

ton¹ (tŭn), n. **1.** Measure of weight, 2240 or *(also *short* ~) 2000 lb. avoirdupois; *metric* ~, 1000 kilograms (2204·6 lb.). **2.** Measure of capacity (often varying for timber (40 ft), stone (16 cub. ft), salt (42 bushels), lime (40 bushels), coke (28 bushels), wheat (20 bushels), wine (see TUN), etc. **3.** Unit of internal capacity (100 cub. ft) or carrying capacity (40 cub. ft) of ship. **4.** (colloq.). Large number or amount, as *bag weighs (half) a* ~ (several pounds, ounces, etc.), ~*s of people, have asked him* ~*s of times*. [var. of TUN]

ton² (tawn), n. Prevailing mode, fashion, as in *the* ~, BON TON. [F]

tôn'al, a. Of tone or tones; of tonality. Hence ~IY² adv. [f. med. L *tonālis*]

tonăl'ity (tō-), n. (Mus.) character of tone; colour scheme of picture. [-ITY]

‖ to-náme (tōō-), n. (chiefly Sc.). Name added esp. to person's Christian name & surname for distinction. [OE *tō-nama* (TO¹, NAME)]

tŏn'dō, n. (pl. *-di* pr. -dē). Easel painting, or relief, of circular form. [It. = round (place) f. L *rotundus* round]

tone¹, n. **1.** Sound, esp. w. ref. to pitch, quality, & strength; *heart* ~s, sounds of heart heard in auscultation. **2.** Modulation of voice to express emotion, sentiment, et.., as *impatient, lively, imploring, despondent, bantering, suspicious,* ~. **3.** (gram.). Stress on one syllable of word. **4.** (Mus.). Musical sound, esp. with ref. to pitch, quality, & strength (FUNDAMENTAL ~); interval of major second, e.g. C–D, E–F sharp; *whole~, ~s*, consisting entirely of ~s, with no *semitones*; *Gregorian* ~s, traditional plain-song chants for psalms. **5.** (med.). Proper condition of the bodily organs, state of health in which animal functions are duly performed, as *has lost, recovered,* ~. **6.** Prevailing character of morals, sentiments, etc., as *the* ~ *of the nation must be raised, gave a flippant* ~ *to the debate.* **7.** General effect of colour or of light & shade in picture; tint, shade of colour; degree of luminosity of colour; (Photog.) colour of finished positive picture. **8.** ~*-arm,* tubular arm connecting sound-box of gramophone to the horn; idea, painting in which the ~s are harmonized poetically. Hence ~'LESS (-nl-) a., ~'lESSNESS n. [f. F *ton* f. L f. Gk *tonos* thing strung stretched, tone, f. root of *teinō* stretch.]

tone², v.t. & i. **1.** Give tone or quality (of sound or colour) to (~*d paper, colour*); pale amber tint). **2.** (mus.). Adjust (part of instrument, e.g. padded surface of hammers of piano) so as to produce desired quality of sound. **3.** (photog.). Give (picture) (of picture) receive, altered colour in finishing by means of chemical solution. **4.** Harmonize (usu. intr.), as *does not* ~ *with the wallpaper.* **5.** ~ *down,* soften colouring of (picture); render (statement, expression, etc.) less pronounced or confident; (intr.) become softer, less pronounced, etc.; ~ *up,* give, receive, higher tone or character or greater vigour. [f. prec.]

tông'a (-ngg'-), n. A Chinese guild or secret society. [Chin. *t'ang* meeting-place]

tŏng'a (-ngg²-), n. Light two-wheeled vehicle used in India. [f. Hind. *tāngā*]

tŏngs (-z), n. pl. (Also *pair of* ~) kinds of instrument for grasping & holding usu. with two limbs pivoted together near either end or connected by spring piece, as *fire*~(for grasping coal etc.), *asparagus, sugar, blacksmith's, wire,* LAZY, ~; HAMMER¹ & ~; *would not touch* (repulsive person or thing) *with a pair of* ~ (still less without). [OE *tangé*) sing., cf. Du. & Da. *tang,* G *zange,* cogn. w. Gk *dáknō* bite]

tongue¹ (tŭng), n. **1.** Fleshy muscular organ in the mouth, serving purposes of taste, mastication, swallowing, & (in man) of speech (*put out one's* ~, as grimace, or for doctor's inspection; *on the* ~*s of men,* much talked of; *furred or dirty* ~, symptom of illness). **2.** This as article of food, as *ox-, sheep's, reindeer* &, ~; *smoked, rolled,* ~. **3.** Faculty of, tendency in, speech, as *have a ready or fluent* ~, *sharp, caustic, dangerous, long* (talkative), ~; *put, speak with, one's* ~ *in one's cheek, speak ironically, humour one's hearer; keep a civil* ~ *in one's head,* avoid rudeness. **4.** Language or a nation etc., as *the German* ~, *one's mother* ~; *gift of* ~*s,* power of speaking in unknown ~s esp. as miraculously conferred on early Christians; *confusion of* ~*s (Gen.* xi. 1–9). **5.** Thing like ~ in shape (esp. tapering) or function, e.g. long low promontory, strip of leather closing gap in front of shoe, clapper of bell, pin of buckle, projecting edge of MATCH¹-board, slip connecting two grooved boards etc., index of scale or balance, vibrating slip in reed of some musical instruments, jet of flame, pointed rail in railway-switch. **6.** *Have lost, find,* one's ~, be too bashful, recover power of speech; *give or throw* ~, (of hounds) bark esp. on finding scent; *hold one's* ~, be silent; *on the TIP of one's* ~; *say one's ~*, talk indiscreetly or volubly; ~*-bit* (with plate preventing horse from getting ~ over mouthpiece); ~*-bone,* = HYOID; ~*-tie, impediment in speech due to shortness of fraenum of* ~; ~*-tied,* having this. (fig.) debarred from speaking out. Hence (-)tŏngUED¹*) (tŭngd),* ~'LESS, aa., ~'LET n. [OE *tunge,* cf. ON & Sw. *tunga,* Du. *tong,* G *zunge,* cogn. w. L *lingua,* OL *dingua*]

tongue² (tŭng), v.t. & i. Produce staccato etc. effects with (flute etc.) by use of tongue, use tongue thus; ~ *& groove,* furnish (MATCH¹-board etc.) with tongue & groove. [f. prec.]

tŏn'ic, a. & n. **1.** (Of medicine, medical treatment, etc., fig. of success, misfortune, punishment) serving to invigorate, bracing; (Mus.) of tones, esp. of the keynote); ~ *accent,* stress on syllable; ~ *sol-fa* (-ah), system of sight-singing & notation in which keynote of all major keys is *doh* (& other notes correspondingly, as *ray, me, fah, sol, lah, te*) & keynote of all minor keys *lah* (& other

notes correspondingly, as *te, doh*, etc.), with time-values shown by vertical lines, colons, etc.; ~ *spasm*, continuous musoular contraction (cf. CLONIO). 2. n. ~ medicine etc. (lit. & fig.): (Mus.) keynote. Hence tōn'ICALLY adv. [f. Gk *tonikos* (as TONE[1], see -IC)]

tōni'city, n. Tone; being tonic; healthy elasticity of muscles etc. [-ITY]

tonight', to-night', (-nīt), adv. & n. (On) the present night, (on) the night of today. [TO[1] + NIGHT, cf. TODAY]

tōn'ish, tonn-, a. (now rare). In the TON[2], modish, stylish. Hence ~NESS n. [-ISH[1]]

tōn'ite, n. A powerful gun-cotton explosive. [f. L *tonare* thunder + -ITE[1]]

‖tŏnk, v.t. (sl.). Hit (bowling, person) hard, defeat easily in contest. [?]

Tŏnk'a bean, t-, n. Fragrant seed of a tree found in Guiana etc., used in perfumery etc. [native *tonka*, the bean]

tŏ'nnage (-tŭ-), n. Internal cubic capacity, or freight-carrying capacity, of ship in TON[1]s; total freightage esp. of a country's merchant marine; duty on vessels formerly reckoned on ~, now on registered size; charge per ton on cargo or freight; ~ *& poundage* (hist.), customs duties on the tun of wine & the pound's worth of merchandise imported or exported, granted as subsidies (orig. for the defence of the realm) at intervals in the 14th–18th cc, & levied unconstitutionally by Charles I without consent of Parliament; ~*-deck* (upper of two, second of three or more). [TON[1], -AGE]

tŏnn'eau (-nō), n. Part of some motorcars that contains the back seats. [F, lit. cask, tun]

-to'nner (tŭ-), n. Vessel of so many tons, as *two-thousand-*~. [-ER[1]]

tŏnŏm'eter, n. Tuning-fork or other instrument for measuring pitch of tones. [as TONE[1] + -METER]

tŏn'sil, n. Either of two oral organs on each side of the fauces. Hence tŏn'sillAR[1] a., tŏnsillī'TIS n. [f. L *tonsillae* pl.]

tŏnsō'rial, a. (joc.). Of a barber or his work. [f. L *tonsorius* (*tondēre tons-* shave, see -OR[2]) + -AL]

tŏn'sure (-sher), n., & v.t. 1. Rite of shaving the crown (R.-C. Ch.) or whole head (Gk Ch.) of person entering priesthood or monastic order; bare part of monk's or priest's head; (fig.) admission to holy orders. 2. v.t. Shave crown of, give ~ to. [f. L *tonsura* (as prec, see -URE)]

tŏntine' (-ēn), n. Annuity shared by subscribers to loan, the shares increasing as subscribers die till last survivor gets all; ~ *policy of insurance* (in which associated policy-holders agree to receive no dividend, return-premium, etc., till end of fixed period called ~ *period*). [f. It. *tontina* (Lorenzo *Tonti*, originator of ~ about 1653)]

tŏō, adv. & a. 1. In a higher degree than is

admissible for a specified or understood purpose, standard, etc. (not used to qualify vb, cf. VERY), as ~ *ripe for cooking*, ~ *good to be true*, allows ~ *long an interval*, ~ *long intervals*, ~ *large for me, my taste*, ~ *my purpose, is* ~ *fond of comfort*, ~ MANY *for*; ~ *much (of a good thing)*, intolerable (*this is really* ~ *much or* ~ *much of a good thing*). 2. (In affected or gushing use) *is quite* ~, *is* ~ ~, (*delightful* etc., often omitted). 3. Also, as well, as *take the others* ~, *mean to do it* ~ (as well as threaten). 4. Moreover, as *achieved,* ~, *at small cost*. 5. adj. ~~, gushing. [= TO[1]]

tŏŏk. See TAKE.

tŏŏl[1], n. 1. Mechanical implement, as *carpenter's, joiner's, gardener's, engraver's, mason's,* ~*s*; (pl.) implements & munitions of war; machine used in making machinery, e.g. lathe. 2. (fig.). Thing used in an occupation or pursuit, as *literary* ~*s*, *the* ~*s of one's trade*; person used as mere instrument by another, cat's-paw. 4. Separate figure in tooling of book. 4. *Broad* ~, = TOOLER[1], *edged*, ~; ~*-holder*, device for holding ~ in lathe, handle for use with different ~s; ~*-post, -rest*, holder or support for cutting-~ in lathe. [OE *tōl*, cf. ON *tôl* pl., OE *tawian* prepare, Goth. *taujan* make, cause]

tŏŏl[2], v.t. & i. 1. Dress (stone) with chisel; ornament (edges of book-cover) with tooling; work with ~; (sl.) drive (coach etc.), (intr.) drive, ride, (often *along* etc.) esp. in casual or leisurely manner. [f. prec.]

tŏŏl'er, n. In vbl senses, esp. stone-mason's broad chisel for tooling. [-ER[1]]

tŏŏl'ing, n. Stone-dressing in parallel lines; ornamentation of edges of book-cover with designs impressed by heated tools (*blind* ~, without gilding). [-ING[1]]

tŏŏn, n. E.-Ind. tree with close-grained red wood much used for furniture etc. [f. Hind. *tun*]

tŏŏt, v.t. & i. & n. 1. Sound, esp. produce harsh or dismal sound with, (horn, cornet, whistle, etc.); sound horn etc. thus; (of horn etc.) give out such sound; (of grouse) call. 2. n. Sound of horn, trumpet, etc. [imit., cf. G *tuten*, Du. *tuyten*]

tŏŏth, n. (pl. *teeth*), & v.t. & i. 1. Each of several hard dense structures growing in jaws of vertebrates & used for mastication; CANINE, EYE[1], INCISOR, MILK[1], MOLAR[1], WISDOM, ~; *false, artificial*, ~ (made by dentist). 2. ~-shaped projection or thing, e.g. cog, point, etc., of gear-wheel, saw, comb, rake. 3. SWEET ~; *cast thing in person's teeth*, reproach him with it; *in the teeth of*, in spite of (opposition etc.), in opposition to (directions etc.), in the face of (the wind etc.); *armed to the teeth* (completely, elaborately); *cut one's eye-teeth*, gain worldly wisdom; *escape by the skin of one's teeth* (narrowly); *fight, struggle,* ~ *& nail* (with utmost effort);

from the teeth outwards (arch.), insincerely; not from the heart; LIE² *in one's teeth*; *long in the* ~, old (orig. of horses; from recession of gums with age); *set one's teeth on* EDGE¹; *show one's teeth*, take threatening tone; *take the* BIT¹ *between one's teeth*. 4. ~*ache*, ache in ~; ~*-billed*, (of bird) having ~*-like* process(es) on cutting edges of bill; ~*-brush* (for cleaning teeth); ~*-comb* (with fine close-set teeth); ~ *ornament*, = DOG¹-~; ~*-paste*, *-powder*, (for cleaning or preserving teeth); ~*-pick*, small sharp instrument of quill, wood, gold, etc., for removing matter lodged between teeth. 5. v.b. Furnish with teeth: (of cog-wheels) interlock. Hence (-)~ED² (-tht), ~LESS, aa., ~LET n. [OE *tóth*, cf. Du. *tand*, G *zahn*, L *dens -ntis*, Gk *odous -ontos*, f. root *ed-* EAT]

tooth/**ful** (-ŏŏ), n. Small draught of spirit [-FUL]. ~**some**, a. Pleasant to eat. Hence ~LY² adv., ~NESS n. [-SOME]

tootle, v.i. Toot gently or repeatedly esp. on flute. [-LE³(3)]

toot'sy(-wootsy), n. (nursery). Foot. [?]

top¹ n. & a. 1. Summit, highest part, as *the* ~, *of a hill, hill*~, *at the* ~ *of the tree* (fig., of the ~, win distinction; *on* ~, above; *on the* ~ *of*, in addition to. 2. Leaves etc. of plants grown for the root, as *turnip-*~s. 3. Surface (of ground), upper surface (of table etc). 4. Upper part of shoe: cover of carriage; lid of saucepan etc.; head (of page in book); upper edges of book, as *gilt* ~. 5. (Person occupying) highest rank, foremost place, as *came out (at the)* ~ *of the school, the* ~ (upper end, head) *of the table*. 6. Utmost degree, height, as *realized the* ~ *of my ambition, called at the crown of the head, as from* ~ *to toe; the* ~ *of the morning* (to you), Irish morning greeting. 7. (naut.). Platform round head of lower mast serving to extend ~mast shrouds, as *main*~, *fore*~, *mizzen*~. 8. pl. Two highest cards of a suit in Bridge. 9. (In motoring) highest gear (usu. *on* ~). 10. pl. Metal buttons plated etc. only on face. 11. Bunch of hair, fibres, etc. as *measure* = 1⅓ lb. 12. adj. Highest in position or degree, as *the* ~ *rail, at* ~ *speed*, ~ *dog* (sl.) = victor, master, opp. *under dog*), whence ~MOST a. 13. ~*boot* (also ~), boot with high ~ usu. of different material or colour & made to look as if turned down; ~*coat*, overcoat; ~*dress*, apply manure on the ~ of (earth) instead of ploughing it in; ~*-dressing*, this process, manure so applied ; ~*gallant* (tŏng-), *tŏp'*), mast, sail, yard, rigging, immedi-

ately above ~mast & ~sail; ~ *hamper*, light upper sails & rigging; ~ *hat*, tall silk hat; ~*-heavy*, overweighted at ~ so as to be in danger of falling (often fig. of scheme etc.); ||~*-hole* (sl.), first-rate; ~*knot*, knot, bow of ribbon etc., tuft, crest, worn or growing on head; ~ *lantern*, *-light*, light displayed from mizzen~ of flagship; ~*man*, ~*sawyer* (lit.), (Naut., also ~*s'man*) man doing duty in a ~; ~*mast* (-àst) (next above lower mast); ~*sail* (sl), square sail next above lowest; ~*-saw'yer*, sawyer in upper position in saw-pit, (fig.) person in superior or high position; ~*sides*, sides of ship above water-line. [OE, Du., ON *toppr*, G *zopf* tuft, tree-top]

top², v.t. (-pp-). 1. Provide with top or cap: (Naut.) raise one end of (yard etc.) above the other. 2. Remove top of (plant) to improve growth etc. 3. Reach the top of (hill etc.). 4. Be higher than ; be superior to, surpass, as ~ *s all I ever saw*, whence ||~*p'ing*² a., ~*p'ingly*² adv.; ~ *one's part*, act or discharge it to perfection. 5. (golf). Hit (ball) at top instead of true. 6. ~ *off* *or up*, put an end or a finishing touch to (thing, or a ob.); ~ *up*, (also) fill up (partly empty container). 7. Be of (specified height), as *he* ~*s 6 ft*. 8. ~*ping-lift*, rope from lower mast-head to end of boom (for raising it). [f. prec.]

top³, n. Kinds of wooden or metal toy, usu. conical, spherical, or pear-shaped, rotating on sharp point at bottom when set in motion by hand, spring, or string; HUMMING, PEG, WHIP¹*ping or whip-*, SLEEP² *like a* ~ (sound); *old* ~ (sl.), old chap, old fellow ; ~*-shell*, kinds of shell-fish with ~-shaped shell. [cf. MHG *top*, MlG *doppe*]

top'áz, n. 1. A transparent or translucent mineral, a silicate of aluminium, yellow, white, green, blue, or colourless; *false* ~, kind of yellow quartz. 2. Kind of humming-bird. [f. OF *topaze* f. L f. Gk *topazos -zion*, etym. dub., cf. Skr. *tapas*]

topaz'olite, n. Yellow or green kind of garnet. [prec. + -o- + -LITE]

tope¹, v.i. Drink alcoholic liquors to excess (esp. habitually. Hence **top'ER**¹ n. [perh. f. F *tôper* cover stake in dicing, whence (je) *tôpe!* int. agreed!, done!, (in drinking) I pledge you]

tope², n. (Anglo-Ind.). Mango or other grove. [f. Tamil *tōppu*]

tope³, n. Buddhist monument, usu. dome or tower. [f. Hind. *tōp* f. Skr. *stūpa* mound]

tope⁴, n. Small species of shark, dogfish. [?]

toph, toph'us (pl. *-phî*), nn. Gouty deposit of calcareous matter round teeth & at surface of joints. Hence **topha'ceous** (-āshus) a. LL (*-us*),=sandstone, tufa]

Tŏph′ĕt, n. Place in Valley of Hinnom near Jerusalem used for idolatrous worship & later for depositing refuse, for consumption of which fires were kept burning; hell. [f. Heb. *topheth* etym. dub.]

tŏp′i, tŏp′ee (-ĭ), n. (Anglo-Ind.). Hat. [see SOLA]. [Hind. *topī*]

tŏp′ĭᵃ, n. Ancient-Roman style of mural decoration with heterogeneous landscape scenes. [L, = landscape gardening or painting, f. Gk *topos* place]

tŏp′iarÿ, a. The ~y art (of clipping shrubs etc. into ornamental shapes). Hence **tŏpiar′ıaN n.** [f. L *topiarius* landscape gardener (as prec., see -ARY¹)]

tŏp′ic, n. Theme for discussion, subject of conversation or discourse; (Logic, Rhet.) class of considerations from which arguments can be drawn. [f. L f. Gk (*ta*) *topika* topics, as title of a treatise of Aristotle (*topos* place, see -IC)]

tŏp′ical, a. Of topics; dealing with esp. current or local topics, as ~ *allusion, song*; local, esp. (Med.) affecting a part of the body. Hence ~LY² adv. [-AL]

topŏg′raphÿ, n. Detailed description, representation on map etc., of natural & artificial features of a town, district, etc.; such features; (Anat.) mapping of surface of body with reference to the parts beneath. Hence ~ER¹ n., **tŏpō-graph′ic(AL) aa., tŏpŏgraph′icaLLy²** adv. [f. LL f. Gk *topographia* (*topos* place, see -GRAPHY)]

topŏn′ymÿ, n. Study of the place-names of a region. [f. Gk *topos* place, *onuma* name, -Y¹]

tŏpp′er, n. 1 In vbl senses, also: (colloq.) =TOP¹ *hat*; (colloq.) a good fellow, good sort; (commerc.) fine fruit etc. put at top of stock for show. [f. TOP² + -ER¹]

tŏp′ple, v.i. & t. (Cause to) totter & fall (often *over, down*). [f. TOP¹ + -LE(3)]

tŏpsÿtûrv′ÿ, adv., a., n., & v.t. 1. Upside down; (in)utter confusion. 2. v.t. Turn ~y. Hence (joc.) ~ÿDOM, ~ÿFICA′TION, nn., ~ÿFY v.t. [f. 16th c., prob. containing TOP¹ + obs. *terve* overturn cogn, w. OE *tearflian* turn, roll over]

tŏque (-k), n. 1. Small kinds of man's & woman's cap or bonnet (hist.); woman's small hat with little or no or turned-up brim. 2. Kinds of monkey with caplike arrangement of hair. [F, cf. It. *tocca*, Sp. *toca*]

tŏr, n. Hill, rocky peak, esp. on Dartmoor. [OE, cf. W *tŵr* heap]

-tor, suf. forming agent nn. on L p.p. stems in -t- (*doctor, narrator*); see -OR².

tŏr′ah, n. Revealed will of God, esp. Mosaic law; Pentateuch. [Heb. *tōrāh* instruction]

tŏrch, n. Piece of resinous wood or twisted flax etc. soaked in tallow etc. for carrying lighted (~ *of Hymen*, passion of love); other appliance for this purpose, e.g.

oil-lamp on pole; *electric* ~, portable electric lamp; ~-*fishing*, (also ~ING¹ n.) mode of catching fish by ~light; ~-*race*, ancient-Greek festival performance of runners handing lighted ~es to others in relays; *~-singer*, woman who sings *~-songs* (sentimental ditties of unrequited love); *hand on the* ~, keep knowledge etc. alive (w. ref. to ~-race). [f. F *torche* perh. ult. f. L *torquēre tort*- twist]

torchon (see Ap.), n. attrib. ~ *paper*, paper with rough surface used esp. for water-colours; ~ *board* (covered with ~ paper); ~ *mat*, MAT² of ~ paper; ~ *lace*, peasants′ bobbin lace with geometrical designs. [F, = dish-cloth (*torcher* wipe)]

tore¹. See TEAR¹.

tore². = TORUS (first sense).

tŏr′eadŏr, n. Spanish (usu. mounted) bullfighter. [Sp. (*torear* engage in bullfight f. *toro* bull f. L *taurus*, see -OR²)]

toreu′tic (-rōō-), a. & n. 1. Of chasing, carving, & embossing, esp. metal. 2. n. pl. This art. [f. Gk *toreutikos* (*toreuō* bore, chase, see -IC)]

tŏr′g′ŏch (-x), n. Red-bellied char. [W (*tor* belly + *coch* red)]

torii (tō′riē, tōr′iē), n. Gateway of Shinto temple. [Jap.]

tŏrm′ent¹, n. Severe bodily or mental suffering, as *was in*~, *suffered* ~s; source of this, as (colloq.) *the child is a positive* ~. [OF, f. L *tormentum* engine for hurling stones, rack, torment, (*torquēre* twist, see -MENT)]

torment′², v.t. Subject to torment, as ~*ed with neuralgia, suspense, inquiries.* Hence ~ingLY² adv. [f. OF *tormenter* (prec.)]

tŏrm′entil, n. Low herb with bright yellow flowers & highly astringent root-stock used in medicine. [f. med. L *tormentilla* f. TORMENT¹; sense-connexion unknown]

tŏrm′ent′o̧r, n. Person, thing, that torments, whence ~RESS¹ n.; long fork used on ship for taking meat from coppers; kind of harrow on wheels. [-OR²]

tŏrm′ina, n. Griping pains in bowels, colic. [L *torquēre* twist)]

torn. See TEAR¹.

tŏrnād′ō, n. (pl. ~es). Violent storm of small extent, esp. in W. Africa at beginning & end of rainy season & in U.S. from April to July, having usually a rotary motion, & often accompanied by funnel-shaped cloud; (fig.) outburst or volley of cheers, hisses, missiles, etc. Hence **tŏr-nād′ıᴄ a.** [perh. assim. of Sp. *tronada* thunderstorm (*tronar* to thunder) to Sp. *tornar* to turn]

tŏr′ous, torōse′, aa. (Bot.) cylindrical with bulges at intervals; (Zool.) knobby. [f. L *torosus* (TORUS, see -OSE¹, -OUS]

tŏrpēd′ō, n. (pl. ~es), & v.t. 1. Electric ray, a fish with electric apparatus for numbing or killing its prey etc. 2. Kinds of explosive mine or petard; cigar-shaped

self-propelling submarine missile that can be aimed at a ship etc. & explodes on touching it (*aerial* ~, discharged from aircraft; ~*-boat*, small fast warship for carrying or discharging ~es; ~*(-boat)-catcher*, ~ *gunboat*, large vessel intended to catch ~-boat; ~*(-boat) destroyer*, small fast warship orig. designed to destroy ~-boats & carry ~es, later used for fleet & convoy anti-submarine escort as well as for general offensive purposes; ~*net* (hung round ship to intercept ~es or ~-boat); ~*-tube* (from which ~es are discharged). **3.** v.t. Destroy, attack, with ~; (fig.) paralyse, make (policy, institution, etc.) ineffective. [(vb f. n.) fish (*torpère* be numb)]

tôrp'lid, a. & n. **1.** (Of hibernating animal) dormant; numb; sluggish, dull, apathetic. **2.** n. pl. || Hilary term boat-races at Oxford between second crews of colleges; (sing.) boat rowing in these. Hence or cogn. ~**id'ITY**, ~**idNESS**, ~**OR**, n., ~**idLY²** adv., ~**IFY** v.t., ~**OrIFIC³** a. [f. L *torpidus* (prec., -ID³)]

Torps, n. (nav. sl.). Ship's torpedo officer. [abbr.]

torq'uate, -ated, aa. (zool.). With ring of peculiar colour or texture of hair or plumage about the neck. [f. L *torquatus* (foll., -ATE²)]

torque (-k), **tôrc**, n. Necklace of twisted metal, esp. of Gauls; (Mech., -que) twisting-MOMENT. [f. L *torques* necklace, as TORE]

tô'rrêfy, v.t. Parch with heat, roast, dry, (metallic ores, drugs). So ~**FACTION** n. [f. F *torréfier* f. L *torrefacere* (*torrère* parch, see -FY)]

tô'rrent, n. Rushing stream of water etc.; (pl.) great downpour of rain (also *rain falls in* ~*s*); (fig.) violent flow (of abuse, grief, questions). Hence **tôrrēn'tiAl**(-shl) a., **tôrrēn'tiaLY²** adv. [f. L *torrentem* lit. boiling stream (*torrère* parch, see TORE)]

Torricell'ian, a. ~ *experiment* (with mercury in tube, leading to principle on which barometer is made); ~ *tube* (used for this). [E. *Torricelli* d. 1647 + -AN]

tô'rrid, a. (Of land etc.) parched by sun, very hot; ~ *zone*, part of earth's surface between tropics. Hence ~**ITY**(-dǐ-), ~**NESS**, nn. [f. L *torridus* (*torrère* parch, see TORE)]

tôrs'el, n. Twisted ornament e.g. scroll; block of wood in brick wall for joist etc. to rest on. [prob. var. of TASSEL]

tôr'sion (-shn), n. Twisting; (Bot.) state of being spirally twisted, so **tôrs'IVE** a.; (Med.) twisting of cut end of artery after operation etc. to check haemorrhage; ~ *balance* (for measuring minute forces by means of fine twisted wire). Hence ~**AL**, ~**LESS**, aa., ~**ally²** adv. (-sho-), [F, f. LL *tortionem*, -si- (as TORT, see -ION)]

tôrsk, n. Fish of cod family. [Sw. & Da.]

tôrs'ŏ, n. (pl.~s). Trunk of statue apart from head & limbs; human trunk; (fig.) unfinished or mutilated work. [It., = stalk, stump, torso, f. L THYRSUS]

tôrt, n. (law). Private or civil wrong. [F, = wrong, harm, f. L *torquère tort-* twist]

tôrticoll'is, n. (path.). Rheumatic affection of muscles of neck, stiff neck. [f. L as prec. + *collum* neck]

tôrt'ile, a. Twisted, curved; (Bot.) coiled. Hence **tôrtil'ITY** n. [f. L *tortilis* (TORT, -ILE)]

tôrtill'a (-elya), n. Flat maize cake, Mexican equivalent of bread. [Sp.]

tôrt'ious (-shus), a. (law). Constituting a tort, wrongful. Hence ~**ly²** adv. [AF *tortious* (TORSION, -OUS), assoc. in sense w. tort]

tôrt'oise (-tus), n. Land (& freshwater) varieties of turtle, reptile encased in two scaly or leathery shields forming a box; ~*shell* (perh. as TORT, w. ref. to ~'s crooked feet]
2. *Hare &* ~, ability beaten by persistence; ~-*shell*, mottled & clouded outer shell or scale of some sea-turtles used for combs etc., ~*shell cat, butterfly* (with black & yellow markings suggesting ~*shell*. [ME *tortuce*, *tortu* (thr. OF *tortue*), f. LL *tortuca* (perh. as TORT, w. ref. to ~'s crooked feet]

tôrt'uous, a. Full of twists or turns, so **tôrt'uose¹** a. (bot.); (fig., of policy etc.) devious, circuitous, crooked, not straightforward. Hence or cogn. **tôrtŭŏs'ITY**, ~**NESS**, nn., ~**ly²** adv. [AF f. L *tortuosus* (*tortus -ās* twist, foll., -OUS)]

tôr'ture, n. & v.t. **1.** Infliction of severe bodily pain e.g. as punishment or means of persuasion etc *as was put to the* ~*e, instruments of* ~*e* (rack, thumbscrew, etc.); severe physical or mental pain. **2.** v.t. Subject to ~e, as ~*ed with neuralgia*; wrest from natural position or state, pervert meaning of (words, passage). Hence ~**ABLE** a., ~**OUS** aa., ~**Er¹** n., ~**ingLY²** adv. [(vb f. n.) F, f. L *tortura* twisting (*torquère tort-* twist, see -URE)]

tôr'ŭla, n. (pl.~ae). Kinds of yeastlike fungus; chain of spherical bacteria, whence ~**FORM** a.; (Bot.) small torus. [mod. L dim. of TORUS]

tôr'us, n. (pl.~ī). Large moulding of semicircular profile esp. as lowest member of base of column; (Bot.) receptacle of flower, modified end of stem; (Anat.) smooth ridge as of muscle. [L, = protuberance, bed]

Tôr'y, n. & a. (now chiefly in colloq. or hostile use). (Member) of the party that opposed the exclusion of the Duke of York (James II), inclined to the Stuarts after 1689, accepted George III and the established order in Church & State, opposed Reform Bill of 1832, & has been succeeded by Conservative party (cf. WHIG). Hence ~**ISM** n. [orig. = Irish

robber, f. Ir. *tóraidhe* pursuer (*tóir* pursue).

-tory, suf., most freq. form of -ORY, in wds f. L vbs w. p.p. stem in -t- (*amatory, factory*).

tŏsh, n. (sl.). Rubbish, twaddle; (Cricket, lawn tennis, etc.) easy bowling or service. [?]

‖ tŏsh'er, n. (sl.). Unattached student (see UNATTACHED). [corrupt.]

tŏss, v.t. & i. (~ed or poet. *tost*), & n. 1. Throw up (ball etc.) with the hand esp. with palm upward, (of bull etc.) throw (person etc.) up with the horns. 2. Throw (thing to person, *away, aside*, etc.) lightly or carelessly. 3. Throw (coin) into air to decide choice etc. by way it falls, settle question or dispute with (person *for* thing) thus, as *will* ~ *you for* (or *who has*) *the umrachair*. 4. Toss (person) *in blanket*, jerk him upwards out of it by pulling suddenly on all corners; ~ *one's head*, throw it back esp. in contempt or impatience: ~ *a pancake*, jerk it up so that it returns upside down to pan. 5. Throw (thing, *oneself*) about from side to side, throw oneself about thus in bed etc., roll about restlessly; (of sea, ship, branch, etc.) roll or swing with fitful to-&-fro motion. 6. Separate heavy from light parts of (tin ore) by agitation in vessel. 7. ~ *oars* (of boat's crew bringing oars to upright position blades upward as salute); ~ *off*, drink off at a draught, dispatch (work) rapidly or without apparent effort; ~ *up*, ~ coin as above, prepare (food) hastily; ~*pot* (arch.), toper. 8. n. ~ing of coin, head, etc., as *win the* ~, have its decision in one's favour; *a contemplatious* ~ *of the head*; *full* ~, a full pitch at cricket; ~-*up*, ~ing up of coin, doubtful question, as *is quite a* ~-*up whether he comes or not*; PITCH² -&-~. 9. ‖ Throw from horseback etc. (*take a* ~, be thrown). [n. f. vb) f. 16th c., etym. dub.]

tŏt¹, n. Small child, esp. *a tiny* ~; (colloq.) dram of liquor. [f. 18th c., etym. dub.]

tŏt², n. & v.t. & i. (colloq.; ~s, etym. dub.) 1. ‖ Set of figures to be added. 2. vb. Add usu. *up*; (of items) mount *up* (~ *up to*, amount *to*). [abbr. of foll. or of L *totum* the whole]

tŏt'al, a... n... & v.t. & i. (-ll-). 1. Complete, comprising the whole, as *the* ~ *number of persons*, ~ *population, sum* ~, ~ *tonnage*; absolute, unqualified, as *was in* ~ *ignorance of it; resulted in* ~ *loss of his fortune*, ~ ABSTINENCE, abstainer; ~ *eclipse* (in which whole surface is obscured); ~ *war* (in which all available weapons & resources are employed). 2. n. ~ number or amount. 3. vb. Find the ~ of (things, set of figures), amount in number to, as *the visitors* ~*led* 131; amount *to*, mount *up to*. Hence totaL'ITY n. (esp., time for which an eclipse is ~). [f. F f. LL *totalis* (*tōtus* entire, see -AL)]

totalitār'ian, a. Relating to a polity that permits no rival loyalties or parties; ~ *State* (with only one, the governing, party). [-ARIAN]

tŏt'alizator, n. Device showing number & amount of bets staked on race with a view to dividing the total among betters on winner. [foll. -ATE³ -OR²]

tŏt'alize, v.t. & i. Collect into a total, find the total of; use totalizator in betting. Hence ~A'TION n. [-IZE]

tŏt'alizer, n. (sl.). =TOTALIZATOR. [abbr.]

*tōte¹, n. (sl.). =TOTALIZATOR. [abbr.]

*tōte², v.t. Carry (a gun, supplies, timber, etc.). [f. 1676: etym. dub.]

tŏt'em, n. Natural object esp. animal assumed among N. Amer. Indians as emblem of clan or individual on ground of relationship; image of this; ~*post* (on which ~s are carved or hung); ~ *stage*, stage of mental development in which ~s are taken as clan-names & objects of worship. Hence totEM'IC, ~IS'TIC, aa., ~ISM(3), ~IST(2), nn. [of native orig.]

†to'ther, to'ther, (tudh-), a. & pron. The other; *tell* ~ *from which* (joc. variant of *tell one from the other*). [earlier *the tother* f. wrong division of ME *thet* (THAT) *other*; now understood as=*the other* & usu. used without *the*]

tot'tĕm vĕr'ō·v'ĭs, adv. In so many words, in these very words, as *he said*, ~, *that he would write in either case*. [L]

tŏt'ĭes quŏt'ĭēs (or tŏsh'ĭēs kwŏsh'ĭēs), adv. On each occasion, every time, as *offer was refused*. [L, = as often as]

tŏt'ō cuel'ō (sĕ-), adv. *Differ* ~ (by an immense distance). [L, = by the whole heaven]

tott'er, v.i. Stand or walk unsteadily (esp. of child learning to walk); (part. of steps) unsteady; (of tower etc., fig. of State, system, etc.) be shaken, be on the point of falling. Hence ~ER¹ n., ~ingLY¹ adv., ~Y² a. [f. 1200, etym. dub.; cf. Norw. dial. *totra* quiver, Du. *touteren* swing]

toucan (toōkahn', toō'kn), n. Kinds of tropical American bird with immense beak. [f. Braz. *tucama*]

touch¹ (tŭch), v.t. & i. 1. Be separated at one or more points by no intervening space or object from (thing etc.), be in or come into contact with, bring part of body esp. hand into contact with, establish this relation towards (thing *with one's head, stick*, etc.), cause (two things) to come into contact, (of two things) be in contact, as *two rocks* ~ (*each other*) *at the bases, you are* ~*ing wet paint*, ~ *pitch*, have to do with shady transaction or person, *he* ~*ed me on the shoulder*, ~ *him* (unpleasant person) *with a barge-pole, just* ~*ed them together & they cracked, I never* ~*ed him* (hostility); *can just* ~ *bottom* (of water with toes), ~ BOTTOM¹, ~*ed his hat* (as salutation), *was* ~*ed by the*

king (to cure KING1's evil), ~ wood (to propitiate Nemesis after boasting etc.), ~ the spot (find out, or do, exactly what is requisite). 2. (geom.) Be a tangent to (circle etc.). 3. Apply slight force to, as he ~ed (rang) the bell; strike (keys, strings, of musical instrument), strike keys or strings of. 4. Delineate, mark lightly, put in, (features etc.) with brush, pencil, etc. 5. Reach, as can just ~ the ceiling; (fig.) approach in excellence etc., as no one can ~ him in light comedy, in the spot-barred game, for purity of style. 6. Affect to the heart, was visibly ~ed by her appeal; rouse painful or angry feeling in, as ~ed him on a raw or tender place (also lit.). 7. Treat of (subject) lightly or in passing. 8. Con-cern, as the question ~es you nearly. 9. (Chiefly neg.) have to do with, as refuses to ~ (drink) beer. 10. Injure slightly, as flowers are a little ~ed with the east wind. 11. P.p. Slightly crazy. 12. Affect slightly, modify, as morality ~ed with emotion; (neg.) produce slightest effect on, cope with, as brass polish won't ~ these candlesticks, couldn't ~ the algebra paper. 13. (sl.) ~ one for £5, (sum) out of him (~ed me for £5; cf. TAP1). 14. ~ at (Naut.), call at (port etc.); ~ down, (Rugby footb.) ~ ball on ground either behind one's own or the opponents' goal, (of aircraft) alight; ~ off, make (sketch) hastily, make hasty sketch of, (also) discharge (cannon); ~ on or upon, treat (subject) briefly; refer to or mention casually; ~ up, correct, give finishing touches to (picture, writing, etc.), stimulate (horse) with whip, jog (memory). 15. ~wood1 (see also foll.), children's game in which ~ing wood gives immunity from pursuit. Hence ~ABLE a. [ME, f. OF tochier, cf. Pr., Sp., & Port. tocar, It. toccare]

touch2 (tŭch), n. 1. Act or fact of touch-ing, contact, as gave him a ~, felt a ~ on my arm, royal ~ (for KING1's evil), at a ~ (it touched, however lightly). 2. Sense by which contact is perceived, whence ~'LESS a. 3. Light stroke with pencil, brush, etc., in drawing etc., as added a few ~es, finishing ~es, (often fig. of writing, management of business, etc.). 4. Small amount, slight tinge or trace, as wants a ~ of salt, an occasional ~ of irony, felt a ~ of rheumatism. 5. Performer's manner of touching keys or strings of musical instrument, manner or degree in which keys etc. respond to this, manner or style of workmanship in carving etc. or in writing, as has a light or firm ~ on piano, piano is wanting in ~, writer has light ~ (produces required effect simply, without laboured emphasis, etc.); the Nelson ~, Nelson's unique handling of a situation. 6. Mental correspondence, sympathy,

communication, esp. keep in ~, remain in sympathy or not cease from correspon-dence or personal intercourse (with). 7. Magnetization of steel bar by repeated contact with magnet. 8. (arch.). ~stone, test, as put it to the ~. 9. Near ~, close shave, narrow escape. 10. (med.) Ex-ploration of organs etc. by sense of ~. 11. (footb.). Part of field outside the side limits (~-lines) & between goal-lines produced; ~-in-goal, each of the four outside corners enclosed by ~-lines & goal-lines; ~-down, touching down (as in prec.). 12. ~-&-go, (adj.) of uncertain event, risky, placed in risky circum-stances, as it was ~-&-go whether we got past, as ~-&-go business, we were ~-&-go all the time, (n.) such situation; ~-body, -corpuscle (concerned in sense of ~); ~hole, small hole in cannon by which it was fired; ~last, children's game; ~needle, needle of gold alloy of known composition used as standard in testing other alloys on ~stone; ~ of nature, natural trait, (pop.) exhibition of feeling with which others sympathize (f. mis-interpretation of Shaksp. T. & C. III. iii. 175); ~paper (steeped in nitre, for firing gunpowder etc.); ~stone, fine-grained dark schist or jasper used for testing alloys of gold etc., (fig.) standard, cri-terion; ~wood2 (see also prec.), soft substance into which wood is changed by some fungi, used as tinder. [f. prec.]

tou'cher (tŭ'-), n. In vbl senses, also : [(sl.) near ~, close shave, as near as a ~, very nearly, almost exactly. [-ER1]

tou'ching (tŭ'-), a. & prep. 1. Affecting, pathetic, as a ~ incident, shows the most ~ confidence in us, whence ~ING1 adv., ~NESS n. 2. prep. (arch. or literary) (Also as ~) concerning, about. [-ING2]

tou'chy (tŭ'-), a. Apt to take offence, over-sensitive. Hence ~ILY2 adv., ~INESS n. [perh. corrupt. of TETCHY]

tough (tŭf), a. & n. 1. Flexible but not brittle, hard to break or cut, as a beef-steak as ~ as leather, requires the ~est steel; (of clay etc.) stiff, tenacious; able to endure hardship, hardy; unyielding, stubborn; difficult, as found it a ~ job; (collog., of work etc.) hard, severe, un-pleasant; *ruffianly, turbulent & crimi-nal. 2. n. *Street ruffian. Hence ~'EN v.t. & i., ~'ISH1 a., ~'LY2 adv., ~'NESS n., (tŭf-). [OE tôh, cf. Du. taai, G zähe(l)]

toupee' (tōō'-), n. Wig or artificial patch of hair worn to cover bald spot. [f. F toupet dim. of toupe tuft (as TOP1)]

toupet' (tōō'pā), n. Front of false hair. [F, see prec.]

tour (toor), n., & v.i. & t. 1. Journey through a country from place to place; the grand ~ (hist.), journey through France, Italy, etc., as finishing touch to education; rambling excursion, short journey, walk, as a ~ of observation

through the town; ‖ (Mil.) spell of duty on service, time to be spent at a station; ~ *de force* (de), feat of strength or skill. **2.** vb. Make ~ (*through*, *about*, etc.); make a ~ of, travel through, (country etc.). Hence ~ER¹ n., ~ing-car. [F, = turn, round, tour, f. *tourner* TURN]

tour'acŏ (toor-), n. (Kinds of) large African bird with crimson & green plumage & prominent crest. [F, f. native name]

tourbillion (toorbil'yon), n. Kind of firework spinning in air so as to look like scroll or spiral column of fire. [f. F *tourbillon* whirlwind]

tour'ist (toor-), n. Person who makes a tour, as *place is overrun with* ~*s*; ~ *ticket*, railway etc. ticket issued to ~ on special terms, esp. return ticket available for extended period. So **tour'ism** (toor-) n., organized touring. [f. F *touriste* (TOUR, see -IST)]

tour'maline(e)(toor-),n. Mineral of various colours possessing powerful electric properties & used as gem; ~ *granite* (containing ~). [F, f. Cingalese *tōramalli*]

tour'nament (toor-, tẽr-), n. **1.** (hist.). Pageant in which two parties of mounted & armed men contended with blunted weapons. **2.** Any contest of skill between a number of competitors, as *chess, lawn-tennis,* ~. [f. OF *torneiement (torneier* TOURNEY, see -MENT)]

tour'nay (toor-), n. Printed worsted upholstering-material. [f. *Tournay*, in Belgium]

tour'ney (tẽr-, toor-), n. (pl. ~s), & v.i. (*now* dial. *or* obs., cf. *Touzer* as dog's name). ME *tusen*, cf. G *zausen*, +-LE(3)]

tous-les-mois (toolamwah'), n. Food starch got from tubers of species of canna. [F, lit. = every month, prob. corrupt. of S.-Amer. *toloman*]

tous'y (-zĭ), a. Rough, shaggy, dishevelled. [f. *touse* (TOUSLE) +-Y²]

tout (towt), v.i., & n. **1.** Solicit custom, pester possible customers with applications (*for* orders); ‖ spy out movements & condition of horses in training. **2.** n. Instance of, (*also* ~ER¹ n. *rare*) person employed in, ~ing. [ME *tolen* peep, pry, OE *tōtian* project, peep out, cf. ON *tūta* peak, Sw. *tut* point, Da. *tud* spout]

tout court (too koor), adv. (Of name etc.), without addition or explanation. [F, lit. = quite short]

tout ensemble (see Ap.), n. See EN-SEMBLE. [F]

tow¹ (tō), v.t., & n. **1.** (Of vessel, horse on bank, etc.) pull (boat, barge, etc.) along in water by rope or chain; pull (person, thing) along behind one; drag (net) over surface of water, drag net over (water), to collect specimens. **2.** n. ~ing, being ~ed, esp. *take, have, in* or *on* ~, (fig.) assume direction of, take possession of, (person); ~(*ing*)*-line, -rope* (used in ~ing); ~(*ing*)-*net* (for dragging water); ~(*in*)-*path* (along river or canal for use in ~ing). Hence ~AGE(3, 4) (tō'ĭ) n. [OE *togian*, cf. ON *toga* pull, OHG *zogōn* draw, cogn. w. G *ziehen* draw & w. L *ducere* lead, draw]

tow² (tō), n. Coarse & broken part of flax or hemp. Hence ~Y² (tō'ĭ) a. [f. 14th c., etym. dub.; cf. ON *tó* tuft of wool for spinning]

toward¹ (tō'ĕrd), a. (arch.). Docile, apt. Hence ~LY¹ a., ~NESS n., (arch.). [as foll.]

towards, toward², (tō'rdz, tō'ĕrdz, twôrdz, towôrdz), prep. (-s now more usu. in prose & colloq.). In the direction of, *as looks* ~ *the sea, set out* ~ *town, I look* ~ *you* (in drinking health); as regards, in relation to, *as felt some animosity* ~ *him, his attitude* ~ *Home Rule*; (arch. esp. bibl.) *to usward*, ~ us; for, for the purpose of, *as saved something* ~ *his education; near, as* ~ *noon, the end of our journey;* (arch., as adv.) *feast is toward* (coming); (arch.). [OE *tōweard* a. future (TO, -WARD), see -ES]

tow'el, n., & v.t. & i. (-ll-). **1.** Cloth for drying oneself after washing; *throw in the* ~ (Boxing, & fig.), admit defeat (cf. SPONGE¹); *roller* ~, endless ~ on revolving bar; ~*horse,* frame for hanging ~s on; (old sl.) *lead* ~, bullet, *oaken* ~; endgel. **2.** vb. Wipe (oneself etc.) with ~; ‖ (sl.) thrash; wipe oneself with ~. Hence ~ING·(1, 3) n. [f. OF *toaille* f. OHG *dwahila* (G dial. *zwehle*) f. *twahan* wash, cf. OE *thwéan*]

tow'er, n., & v.i. **1.** Tall usu. equilateral (esp. square) or circular structure, often forming part of church or other large building; (fig.) place of defence, protector (~ *of strength*, champion, comforter, etc.); *ivory* ~, shelter from the harsh realities of life; MARTELLO ~; *water-*~, pipe used to secure high head of water at fires, (also) ~ supporting tank for distribution of water at high pressure; ‖ *the T* ~ (*of London*), assemblage of buildings now used as repository of objects of public interest, orig. a fortress & palace & later used as State prison. **2.** v.i. Reach high (*above* surroundings, often fig. of eminent person, *as* ~*s above his contemporaries*),

(of eagle etc.) soar or be poised aloft, (of wounded bird) shoot straight up; (part.) high, lofty, (fig.) a ~ing (violent) rage, passion. Hence ~ED² (erd), ~Y², aa. [vrb f. n.] f. OF *tur* f. L *turris*]

town, n. **1.** (hist.). Collection of houses enclosed by wall or hedge. **2.** Considerable collection of dwellings etc. (larger than *village*; often opp. to *country*), esp. one not created a CITY. **3.** The people of a ~; as *the whole ~ knows of it*, *is the talk of the ~*). **4.** (talked about by everyone in the ~). **4.** (Without *the*) London or the chief city or ~ in speaker's neighbourhood, as *went up to ~* in London; *from York, is not in ~, is out of ~*. **5.** *Man about ~*, fashionable idler esp. in London; PAINT² *the ~ red*; COUNTY (~) & GOWN. **6.** ~ *clerk*, official who makes & keeps ~ records; ~ *councillor*(lor), (member of) governing body in municipality; ~ CRIER; ~ *hall*, building for transaction of official business of ~, often also used for public entertainment etc.; ~ *house*, one's (as opp. to *country*) residence; ~ *major* (hist.), chief executive officer in a garrison~ or fortress; ~*s folk*, inhabitants of a particular ~ or of ~s; ~*s'man*, inhabitant of a town, fellow citizen; ~*talk*, the talk of the ~. Hence ~LESS, ~'WARD, aa., ~'LET n., ~'WARD(S) adv. [OE *tūn*, cf. Du. *tuin*, G *zaun* hedge]

townee', n. (univ. sl.), Inhabitant of university town who is not a member of the University. [-EE]

town'ship, n. (Hist.) community inhabiting a manor, parish, etc., manor or parish as a territorial division, small town or village forming part of a large parish, or being one of the parishes into which a larger one had been divided; (U.S. & Can.) division of county with some corporate powers, district six miles square; (Austral.) site laid out for town. [OE *tūnscipe*, see TOWN, -SHIP]

towy. See TOW².

tóxaem'ia, n. Blood-poisoning. [as TOXIC + Gk *haima* blood + -IA¹]

tóx'ic, a. Of poison, as ~ *symptoms*; poisonous; ~ *anaemia, epilepsy*, etc. (caused by poison). Hence tóx'ICALLY, ~óló'gICALLY, advv., ~ANT a. & n., ~óló'gICAL a., tóxi'CITY, ~óló'GIST, ~ól'OGY, ~OMAN'IA, ~ōSIS, tóxiPHOB'IA, nn. [f. L f. Gk *toxikon* poison, orig. for dipping arrows in, neut. of *toxikos* (*toxa* bow & arrows, -IC)]

tóx'in, n. A poison, esp. one secreted by a microbe & causing some particular disease. [prec., -IN]

tóxiph'ilite, n. & a. (Student, lover) of archery. Hence ~ir'ic a. [f. Gk *tozon* bow + -PHIL + -ITE¹]

toy, n., & v.i. **1.** Plaything esp. for child; knick-knack, thing meant rather for amusement than for serious use, as *the spendthariscope is a pretty ~*; occupation followed in trifling or unpractical manner, hobby, as *she makes a ~ (amuses herself with needless elaboration) of housekeeping*. **2.** ~*box* (for keeping one's ~s in); ~ *dog, spaniel, terrier*, small kinds kept as pets or curiosities; ~ *shop*; ~ *soldier* (of lead etc., or of an army that has no fighting to do). **3.** v.i. Trifle, amuse oneself; ~ *with*, deal with, handle, in trifling or fondling or careless manner, as ~*ed with a plate of strawberries*, whence ~'ingLY² adv. [vrb f. n.] etym. dub.; once in 1303. = amorous play; common f. 1530, cf. Du. *tuig* tool, stuff, trash, (*speeltuig* toy), & G *zeug* (*spieltzeug* toy)]

Toyn'bee Hall (hawl), n. Institution in Whitechapel founded in 1884 by members of Oxf. & Camb. Univv. as a SETTLE MENT in memory of A. Toynbee, social reformer.

tra-, pref. alternating with TRANS- before consonants in some wds of L orig.

trabe̅a'tion, n. Use of beams (not arches or vaulting) in construction. So **trab'éate** [-ATE²(2)], **-āted**, aa. [f. L *trabs* beam +-ATION]

trabéc'üla, n. (pl. ~cae), (Anat.) supporting band or bar of connective tissue etc., (Bot.) beamlike projection or process. Hence ~AR¹, ~ate [-ATE²(2)], ~āted, aa. [L, dim. of *trabs* beam]

trăcass'eries (trahkahsre'), n. pl. Petty worries & entanglements & quarrels. [F]

trace¹, v.t., & n. **1.** Delineate, mark out, sketch, write esp. laboriously, as ~*d (out) a plan of the district*, ~*d the words with a shaking hand*, (fig.) *the policy ~d (out) by him was never followed*. **2.** (Also ~ *over*) copy (drawing etc.) by following & marking its lines on superimposed sheet (esp. of *tracing-paper* made transparent with oil of turpentine etc.) through which they are visible or on sheet placed below with carbon paper between. **3.** Follow the track or path of (person, animal, footsteps, etc., *along, through, to*, etc.). **4.** Ascertain position & dimensions etc. of (ancient road, wall, etc.) by its remains. **5.** Observe or find vestiges or signs of, as *his resentment can be clearly ~d in many passages*, *cannot (often = do not think I received) any letter of that date*. **6.** ~ *back*, go back over the course of, as *have ~d his genealogy back to (the time of) William I*, *the report has been ~d back to you*. **7.** Pursue one's way along (path etc.). Hence ~ABIL'ITY, ~ABLENESS, nn., ~ABLE a., ~ably¹ (-sa-), adv., trā'CER¹(1, 2) n. (esp. Mil., projectile whose course is made visible by flame etc. emitted, so ~*r bullet, shell*), trā'CING¹ n., *tracing-cloth* (transparent linen sized on one side). **8.** n. Track left by person or animal walking or running, footprints (usu. other visible signs of course pursued (usu.

pl.). **9.** Visible or other sign of what has existed or happened, as *of these buildings no ~ remains, sorrow has left its ~s on her face, ~s of Italian influence abound in his earlier works*; (loosely) small quantity, as *contains ~s of soda*. Hence ~'LESS (-sĭ-) a., ~'lessLY² adv. [f. F *trace(r)* vb & n. ult. f. L *trahere tract-* draw]

trace², n. Each of the two side-straps or chains by which horse draws vehicle; *in the ~s*, in harness (lit. & fig.); *kick over the ~s*, (fig., of person) become insubordinate; *~horse* (that draws in ~s or by single ~s, esp. one hitched on to help up hill etc). [ME *trays* f. OF *trais*, orig. pl. of TRAIT]

trā'ceriȳ, n. Stone ornamental open-work esp. in head of Gothic window; decorative pattern or natural outline (e.g. in insect's wing) suggesting this. Hence ~ıED² (-rĭd) a. [f. TRACE¹+-ERY]

trache'a (-kēa; or trăk'ĭa), n. (pl. -ae). Principal air-passage of body from larynx to bronchial tubes; each of the passages by which air is conveyed from the exterior in insects, arachnids, etc.; (Bot.) duct, vessel. Hence **trăch'EAL, trăch'EAN, trăch'EATE²**(2), aa., **trăch'ēo-** comb. form, **trăch'ēoCELE, trăchēO'TOMY, trāchēī'TIS,** nn., (-k-). [med. L f. Gk *trakheia* (*artēria*), lit. rough artery, f. *trakhus* rough]

trachēī'O- (-k-) in comb. = Gk *trakhēos* neck.

trachōm'a(-k-), n. Disease of eye marked by granular excrescences on inner surface of lids. Hence **~ōm'atous** a. [f. Gk *trakhōma* roughness (*trakhus* rough, see -M)]

trăchy- (-k-) in comb. = Gk *trakhus* rough, as **~ğhōn'ia** hoarseness.

trăch'yte (-kīt), n. Light-coloured volcanic rock rough to the touch. Hence **trachÿt'IC** (-k-) a. [F. f. Gk *trakhutēs* roughness (*trakhus* rough) on wds in -ITE, -M)]

trăck, n., & v.t. & i. **1.** Continuous line, series of marks, left by person, animal, or thing, in passing along, (pl.) such marks, esp. footprints, as *watched the ~ of departing ship, followed his brood ~ through the snow, am on his ~* (in pursuit of him, fig. in possession of clue to his conduct, designs, etc.), *presently came on some more of his ~s, keep ~ of* (follow the course or development of). **2.** Course taken, as *followed in his ~, indicated the ~ in which we were to go, ~ of a comet*. **3.** Path, esp. one beaten by use, (fig.) course of life or routine, as *a rough ~ runs round the hillside, covered with sheep-~s, afraid to leave the beaten ~* (of ordinary life; also lit.). **4.** Prepared racing-path, esp. *cinder-~* (for runners). **5.** Continuous line of railway, as *single, double, ~, one pair, two pairs, of rails*. **6.** Wheelband of tank, tractor, etc., whence (of vehicle) ~ED²

(-kt) a. **7.** Transverse distance between a vehicle's wheels. **8.** *In one's ~s* (sl.), where one stands, there & then; *make ~s* (sl.), go or run away, make off; *make ~s for* (sl.), go in pursuit of, go after; *off the ~*, off the scent, (fig.) away from the subject; *~clearer*, kinds of device attached to locomotive, mowing-machine, etc., for clearing ~ in front or behind. Hence ~'LESS a., ~'lessLY² adv. ~'lessNESS n. **9**, vb. Follow the ~ of (animal, person, to lair etc.); *~ down*, reach, capture, by ~ing; trace, make *out*, (course, development, etc.) by vestiges. **10.** Tow (boat) by rope etc. from bank. **11.** (Of wheels) so run that the ~ is exactly in the first's ~. Hence ~'ER¹ n. (in vbl senses. & esp. wooden connecting-rod in organ mechanism). [f. OF *trac* perh. f. MDu. *treck* (*trecken* draw); vb f. n., but in sense *tow* direct f. Du.]

trăck'age, n. Towage; railway-tracks collectively, amount of these. [-AGE]

trăct¹, n. Region, area, of indefinite (usu. large) extent, as *a ~ of sand, pathless ~s*; (Anat.) area of organ or system, as *olfactory, optic, respiratory, ~*; ||(arch.) period (of time etc.). [f. L *tractus -ūs*, vbl n. f. *trahere tract-* draw]

trăct², n. Short treatise or discourse esp. on religious subject; (R.-C. Ch. &c.) a form of anthem; *T~s for the Times, Oxford T~s*, see TRACTARIANISM. [abbr. of TRACTATE]

trăc'table, a. (Of persons, rarely of materials etc.) easily handled, manageable, pliant, docile. Hence ~ABIL'ITY, ~ableNESS, nn., ~abLY² adv. [f. L *tractabilis* (*tractare* handle, frequent. of *trahere tract-* draw, -BLE)]

Tractăr'ian, a. & n. (Adherent, promoter) of Tractarianism. [TRACT²+-ARIAN]

Tractăr'ianism, n. (Also *Oxford movement*) High-Church reaction towards primitive Catholicism & against rationalism & formalism, voiced by Newman, Pusey, Keble, Froude, etc., in 90 tracts (*Tracts for the Times*) published at Oxford 1833–41. [-ISM]

trăc'tāte, n. Treatise. [f. L *tractātus -ūs* (*tractare*, see TRACTABLE)]

trăc'tion, n. Drawing of a body along a surface, as *electric, steam, ~*; *line of ~*, that in which the force of ~ acts, *angle of ~* (between line of ~ & plane in which body is drawn); contraction e.g. of muscle, as *~ aneurysm* (produced by ~); *~-engine*, movable steam-engine for dragging heavy load on ordinary road, or gang of ploughs etc.; *~-wheel*, driving-wheel of locomotive etc. Hence or cogn. ~AL (-sho-), ~tıVE, aa. [f. med. L *tractionem* f. L *trahere tract-* draw, see -ION]

trăc'tor, n. **1.** Traction-engine; stationary or locomotive motor engine for hauling. **2.** Aeroplane with engine in

front (opp. *pusher*). [LL, = puller (*trahere* draw)].

trade, n., & v.i. & t. **1.** Business, esp. mechanical or mercantile employment, opp. to *profession*, carried on as means of livelihood or profit; *be in* ~, be a retailer, keep a shop; JACK¹ *of all* ~s; *two of a* ~ *never agree*; *trick of the* ~, device for attracting custom, gaining advantage of rival, etc.; ∥ *the* ~, (colloq.) the licensed victuallers, (naut. sl.) submarine branch of Navy. **2.** Exchange of commodities for money or other commodities, commerce, as *foreign* ~, exportation & importation of goods from & to home country or exchange of commodities of different countries, *domestic or home* ~ (carried on within a country); *is good, bad, for* ~, induces, discourages, buying; *carrying* ~, transportation of goods from one country to another by water. **3.** The persons engaged in a ~, as *the* ~ *will never submit to it, is unpopular with the book* ~. **4.** *Board of T* ~, ∥ committee of Privy Council supervising commerce & industry; BALANCE¹ *of* ~; FREE¹ ~; FAIR² ~. **5.** = *wind* (chiefly pl.). **6.** *T* ~ *Board*, statutory body for the settlement of disputes, wage claims, etc., in certain industries; ~ *cycle*, recurring succession of ~ conditions alternating between prosperity & depression; ~ *hall* (for meetings of traders etc.); ~ *mark*, device or word or words legally registered (or, formerly, established by use) as distinguishing a manufacturer's or trader's goods; ~ *name*, that by which a thing is called in the ~, (also) name given by manufacturer to proprietary article; ~ *price* (charged by manufacturer etc. to dealer for goods that are to be sold again); ~ *show*, private exhibition of new film to renters & critics; ~*sman*, person engaged in ~, esp. shopkeeper; ~*s'people*, ~*smen & their families*; ~ *union*, organized association of workmen of a ~ formed for protection & promotion of common interests, ~*un'ionism*, this system of association, ~*un'ionist*, advocate of this, member of ~ union; ~ *wind*, wind blowing continually towards thermal equator within parallels 30° N. & 30° S. in Atlantic & Pacific & deflected westwardly by rotation of earth, (pl.) the ~ *wind & the* (30°-60°) ANTI-TRADE. **7.** vb. Buy & sell, engage in ~ (*in commodity, with person*); have a transaction (*with person for thing*); carry merchandise (*to place*); exchange in commerce, barter, (goods); make a ~ *of* one's political influence, make corrupt bargains in politics, (esp. in part.). **8.** ~ *on*, take (esp. unscrupulous) advantage of (*person's good-nature, one's knowledge of a secret, etc.*). [(vb f. n.) ME f. MLG, orig. = path etc.]. (as TREAD].

trad'er, n. Person engaged, vessel regularly employed, in trade. [-ER¹]

tradi'tion, n. **1.** Opinion or belief or custom handed down, handing down of these, from ancestors to posterity. **2.** (theol.). Doctrine etc. supposed to have divine authority but not committed to writing, esp. (1) laws held by Pharisees to have been delivered by God to Moses, (2) oral teaching of Christ not recorded in writing by immediate disciples, (3) words & deeds of Mohammed not in Koran. **3.** Artistic or literary principle(s) based on accumulated experience or continuous usage, as *stage* ~, *the* ~*s of the Dutch School*. **4.** (law). Formal delivery. Hence (-sho-) ~AL, ~ARY¹, aa., ~ALLY² adv., ~ALIST⁴ n. [f. OF *tradicion* f. L *traditionem* (*dit-=dare* give), delivery, tradition, f. TRA(*dere* *-OR²*]

tradi'tionalism (-sho-), n. (Excessive) respect for tradition esp. in religion; philosophical system referring all religious knowledge to divine revelation & tradition. So ~(a)list nn., ~alis'tic a. [-ISM]

tradi'tor, n. (pl. ~s, ~es pr. -ōr'ēz). Early Christian who to save his life surrendered copies of Scripture or Church property to persecutors. [L (*tradere*, see TRADITION, -OR²)]

tradu'ce, v.t. Calumniate, misrepresent. Hence tradu'cer¹, ~ment (-sm-), nn., tradu'cible a. [f. L TRA(*ducere* duct- lead) bring over, display, disgrace, propagate]

tradu'cian(ist), nn. One who believes that soul as well as body is propagated (cf. CREATIONISM, 1st sense). So ~ISM n. [f. L *traducianus* f. L *traduc-ucis* layer of vine (as prec.), see -AN]

Trafal'gar Square, n. London square often made use of for popular demonstrations, with plinth of Nelson column as platform.

traf'fic, v.i. & t. (-ck-), & n. **1.** Trade (in commodity lit. & fig.), carry on commerce; barter (esp. fig.). Hence ~KER¹ n. **2.** n. Trade (in commodity lit. & fig.), as *the ~ in raw hides, unscrupulous in lucrative appointments*; transportation of goods, coming & going of persons or goods by road, rail, steamship route, etc., number or amount of persons or goods conveyed, *as there is little ~ on these roads, the ~-returns (periodical statements of ~) on all railways show marked decrease, apply to the superintendent of ~ (on railway)*. Hence ~LESS a. [(n. f. vb) f. F *trafiquer* f. It. *trafficare* perb. = TRANS- + -*ficare* -FY in sense transact]

trag'acanth, n. White or reddish gum from certain herbs, used in pharmacy, calico-printing, etc. [f. F *tragacanthe* f. L f. Gk *tragakantha*, name of shrub (*tragos* goat + *akantha* thorn)]

traged'ian, n. Writer of tragedies; (w. fem. ~enne) actor in tragedy. [f. OF *tragedïane* fem.-*enne*, or f. foll.+-AN]

trag'edy, n. **1.** Drama in prose or verse

of elevated theme & diction & with unhappy ending (~ *queen*, *tragic actress*). (T'~.) personified. **2.** Sad event, calamity, serious accident or crime. [ME & OF *tragedie* f. L (-*oed*-) f. Gk *tragōidia* f. *tragōidos* lit. goat-singer (*tragos* goat + *ōidos* singer f. *aeidō* sing), hist. doubtful]

tra'gic(al), aa. **1.** (-*ic*). Of, in the style of, tragedy, as ~ *drama*, *the* ~ *stage*, *in a* ~ *voice*, ~ *actor*; ~ *irony*, used in Gk tragedy of words having an inner esp. prophetic meaning for audience unsuspected by speaker. **2.** Sad, calamitous, distressing, as a ~(*al*) *tale*, *event*, *scene*. Hence ~**allY²** adv., ~**alNESS** n. [f. L f. Gk *tragikos* (*tragos* see prec., -IC, -AL)]

tragicom'edY, n. Drama of mixed tragic & comic elements. So ~**IC** a., ~**ICALLY** adv. [f. F *tragicomédie* f. L *tragicocomoedia* (as prec., see COMEDY)]

trag'opān, n. Horned pheasant. [L f. Gk, name of fabulous bird (*tragos* goat, *Pan*, Gk god)]

trail, n., & v.t. & i. **1.** Part drawn behind or in the wake of a thing, long (real or apparent) appendage, as *engine left a* ~ *of smoke behind it*, *the* ~ *of a meteor*; lower end of gun-carriage; track left by thing that has moved or been drawn over surface, as *slimy* ~ *of a slug*; track, scent, followed in hunting, as *got on*, *off*, *the* ~; beaten path esp. through wild region; *at the* ~ (Mil.), with arms ~ed (see vb). **2.** vb. Draw along behind one esp. on the ground, as *was* ~*ing a toy cart*, ~*ed her dress through the mud*, ~*ing clouds of glory*; follow the ~ of, pursue; (Mil.) ~ *arms*, let rifles hang balanced in one hand (*right*, *left*, ~) parallel to ground; tread down (grass etc.) so as to make path; be drawn along behind, as *skirt* ~*s on the ground*; drag (one's limbs) along, walk wearily, lag, straggle; hang loosely; (of plant) grow to some length over ground, wall, etc.; ~*ing edge*, rear edge of aircraft's wing; ~*ing wheel*, either hind wheel of carriage. [cf. ONF *traille* & Du. *treil* tow-line, f. L *tragula* drag-net, sledge, f. *trahere* draw]

trail'er, n. In vbl senses; also or esp.: trailing plant; set of short extracts from a film exhibited to advertise it in advance; wheeled vehicle drawn by another. [-ER¹]

train, v.t. & i., & n. **1.** Bring (person, child, animal) to desired state or standard of efficiency etc. by instruction & practice, as ~ *up a child in the way he should go*, *was* ~*ed for the ministry*, *a* ~*ed nurse*, *soldier*, ~*ed faculties*, *did not escape his* ~*ed eye*. **2.** Teach & accustom (person, animal, to, to action), as *dog is* ~*ed to jump through hoop*, ~*ed to all outdoor exercises*. *to obey or obedience*. **3.** Bring (horse, athlete, oneself), come, to physical

efficiency by exercise & diet, as *is* ~*ing for the boat-race*, ~*s horses*, *is only half-* ~*ed*, *is over*, *under*, ~*ed*, ~ *down* (to lower weight); ~ *fine* (into exact condition required; t. & i.), *always* ~*s on vegetarian diet*; cause (plant) to grow in required shape (often *up*, *over*, *wall* etc.). **4.** Point, aim, (gun etc. *upon* object etc.). **5.** (arch.). ‖ Entice, lure, (*away*, *from* post etc.). **6.** (now rare). ‖ Draw along (esp. heavy thing). **7.** (colloq.). Go by ~, perform (journey) thus, as *shall* ~ *from York to Leeds*, *the rest of the way*, *we* ~*ed it all the way*. **8.** ~ *off* (of shot) go off obliquely. Hence ~'**ABLE** a., ~'**EE** n. **9.** n. Thing drawn along behind or forming hinder part, esp. elongated part of woman's skirt trailing on ground or of official robe, long or conspicuous tail of woman's skirt or conspicuous tail of bird. **10.** Body of followers, retinue, as *formed part of his* ~, *a* ~ *of admirers*. **11.** Succession or series of persons or things, also *long* ~ *of sightseers*, *of camels*, *by an unlucky* ~ *of events*, *suggested a whole* ~ *of ideas*, *painful* ~ *of thought*, *in the* ~ *of* (as a sequel of; *war with pestilence in its* ~). **12.** Series of railway carriages drawn by same engine(s), as *missed my* ~, *put on a special* ~, EXPRESS¹, *fast*, *slow*, UP, DOWN⁵, THROUGH, CORRIDOR, PARLIAMENTARY, ~; *train de luxe* (see Ap.). **13.** Line of combustible material to lead fire to mine etc. **14.** (arch.). Ordered arrangement, condition, as *matters were in a fine* ~. **15.** Series of connected wheels or parts in machinery. **16.** ~'*band* (hist.), each division of London citizen soldiery in Stuart period; ~*bearer*, person employed to hold up ~ of robe; ~*ferry*, vessel that conveys a (usu. loaded) ~ across a piece of water; ~*mile*, mile run by a ~, as unit of work in railway accounts. Hence ~'**LESS** a. [(n. f. F *traine* & *train*), f. *trainer* vb trail, draw, f. L *trahere* draw]

train'er, n. In vbl senses, esp. one who trains horses, athletes, etc., for races etc. [-ER¹]

train'ing, n. In vbl senses; *be in* (process of) ~, *go into* ~, (for race etc.); ~*bit*, gagbit for vicious horse; ~*college*, *school*, (for training teachers); ~*ship* (on which boys are taught seamanship etc.). [-ING¹]

train-oil, n. Oil got from blubber of whale (esp. of the right whale). [earlier also *trane*, *train*, f. MDu. *traen* tear, ~, cf. G *träne* tear, exudation from vine]

traipse. Var. of TRAPES.

trait (‖ -â, *-ât*), n. Distinguishing feature in character, physiognomy, habit, or portrayal; stroke, touch, (of humour etc.). [f. F *trait* n. & p.p. of *traire* draw f. L *trahere tract*- draw]

trait'or, n. One who violates his allegiance or acts disloyally (*to country*, *king*, *cause*, *religion*, *principles*, *himself*, etc.). Hence or cogn. ~**OUS** a., ~**OUSLY²** adv.,

~OUSNESS, trait'ress¹, nn. [OF. f. L *tra-ditionem (tradere, see TRADITION & -OR²)]

traje'c'tory (or trā'jĕ'e·), n. Path described by projectile moving under given forces; (Geom.) curve or surface cutting system of curves or surfaces at constant angle. [f. L TRA(*jicere ject-=jacĕre throw), see -ORY]

trăm¹, n., & v.t. & t. (-mm-). 1. ‖ (Also ~car) passenger car running on rails laid in public road; such rail; ‖ (also ~way, ~line) line consisting of such rails; four-wheeled car used in coal-mines; ‖~-lines (collog.), either pair of long parallel lines bounding a lawn-tennis court, the inner of each pair being the single-court boundary; ~-road (hist.), road with wooden, stone, or metal wheel-tracks. 2. vb. Convey in, travel (journey) in ~; go in ~. [= LG *tram balk, beam, barrowshaft; in E prob. first = shaft of car]

trăm², n. Kind of double silk thread used for some velvets & silks. [f. F *trame wett]

trămm'el, n., & v.t. (-ll-). 1. Kinds of net for fish, esp. (also ~net) triple drag-net; shackle, esp. one used in teaching horse to amble; hook in fireplace for kettles etc.; instrument for drawing ellipses etc.; beam-compass; (usu. pl.) impediment(s) to free movement or action (chiefly fig.), as ~s of *etiquette, *official routine. 2. v.t. Confine, hamper, entangle with ~s (usu. fig.) (p.p., of horse) with white marks on fore & hind feet of same or (cross-~led) different sides. [vb f. n.] f. OF *tramail f. med. L *tramacula perh. f. tri- triple + *macula MAIL¹]

trāmonta'na (-ah-, -ahl-), n. (In Mediterranean) north wind; cold blighting wind in the Archipelago. [It., see foll.]

trāmon'tāne, a. & n. 1. (Situated, living) on other side of the Alps (fig., from It. point of view) foreign, barbarous. 2. n. ~ person, also =prec. [f. It. *tramontano f. L TRANS(*montanus f. *mons -ntis mountain) beyond the mountains]

trămp, v.i. & t., & n. 1. Walk heavily, as *heard him ~ing about overhead; walk, go on foot, perform (journey), traverse (country), on foot (usu. w. implication of reluctance, weariness, etc.), as *have ~ed up & down all day looking for you, decline to ~ ten miles in this heat, have ~ed the whole country in my time, missed the train & had to ~ it. 2. Be a ~. 3. n. Sound of person(s) walking or marching or of horse's steps. 4. Journey on foot, walk. 5. Iron plate protecting sole of boot from wear & tear of spade in digging. 6. Person who ~s the roads in search of work or as vagrant, this mode of life (esp. on the ~). 7. Freight-vessel running on no regular steps. 8.~*pick, lever for turning up hard soil. [ME & G *trampen, cf. Da. *trampe, Sw. *trampa]

trăm'ple, v.t. & i., & n. 1. Tread under

foot, crush thus, as ~ed to death by elephants; ~e on, tread heavily on, (fig.) treat roughly or with contempt, show no consideration for, (person, feelings, etc.). 2. n. Sound, act, of ~ing. Hence ~ER¹ n. [-LE(3)]

trance¹, n. = TRANS- before s.

trance²(-ah-), n., & v.t. 1. State suggesting that the soul has passed out of the body; ecstasy, rapture, extreme exaltation; (Path.) state of insensibility to external surroundings with partial suspension of vital functions, catalepsy; also, hypnotic state. 2. v.t. (poet.) = ENTRANCE². [vb f. n.] f. OF *transe f. *transir fall into trance f. L TRANS(*ire go) go over]

trăn'quil, a. Calm, serene, unruffled, not agitated, as *preserved a ~ *mind, ~ *scene, ~ *surface of pond. Hence or cogn. ~ITY, ~liza'TION, ~lizER¹ nn., ~lIZE(3) v.t., ~lizing̍ly², ~LY² adv. [f. L *tranquillus]

trans-, pref. (before s usu. *trans-, before other consonants occas. *tra- in wds of L orig.), = L *trans- across, beyond, on or to the other side, through, into a different state or place, (~*mit, ~*end, ~*fer, ~*fix, ~*form, ~*late); as living pref, chiefly in sense 'on other side of', as~*Appalachian, ~*Caucasian, ~*frontier (esp. of India), ~*Gangetic (of the Ganges).

trănsâct' (-z-), v.t. & i. Perform, carry through, (business); carry on business (with person). So ~âc'TOR (-z-) n. [f. L TRANS(*agere act-=agere ACT)]

trănsâc'tion (-z-), n. Management of business, as *left the ~ of the matter to him; piece of esp. commercial business done, the ~s of a firm, the ~ will not pay; looking into, mixed up in, shady ~s; (pl.) reports of discussions, papers read etc., at meetings of some learned societies, as *Philosophical T~s (esp. of Royal Society of London); (Law) adjustment of dispute by mutual concessions, any act affecting legal rights. [f. L *transactionem (as prec., see -ION)]

trănsâl'pine (-z-), a. & n. (Person living) beyond the Alps (usu. from Ital. point of view). [f. L TRANS(*alpinus ALPINE)]

trănsatlăn'tic (-z-), a. Beyond the Atlantic, American; crossing the Atlantic, as ~ *flight, *line, *steamer. [TRANS-]

trănscĕnd', v.t. & i. Be beyond the range or domain or grasp of (human experience, reason, description, belief, etc.); (t. & i.) excel, surpass. [f. L TRAN(*scendere=*scandere climb)]

trănscĕn'd'ent, a. & n. 1. Excelling, surpassing, as ~ent *merit, *genius. 2. (scholastic philos.), Higher than, not included under any of, the ten categories. 3.(Kantian philos.). Not realizable in experience. 4. (Usp. of God) existing apart from, not subject to limitations of, the material universe. 5. n. (philos.). ~ent thing. Hence or cogn. ~ENCE, ~ENCY, nn., ~ently² adv. [as prec., see -ANT, -ENT]

transcendĕn′tal, a. & n. **1.** = prec. (second sense). **2.** (Kantian philos.). Of a priori character, presupposed in & necessary to experience, as ~ *cognition*, a priori knowledge, ~ *object*, real (unknown & unknowable) object, ~ *unity* (brought about by cognition). **3.** Explaining matter & objective things as products of the subjective mind (esp. in Schelling's philosophy). **4.** (pop.). Abstruse, vague, obscure, visionary. **5.** (math.). (Of functions) not capable of being produced by the algebraical operations of addition, multiplication, & involution, or the inverse operations; ~ *curve* (represented by ~ function). **6.** n.~term, conception, etc. Hence ~ĪY² adv. [f. med. L *transcendentalis* (prec., -AL)]

transcendĕn′talism, n. Transcendental philosophy, esp. that of Schelling & his followers, e.g. Emerson. So~IST n., ~IZE(3) v.t. [-ISM]

transcontinĕn′tal (-z-), a. Extending across a continent, as~*railway*. [TRANS-]

transcrībe′, v.t. Copy out in writing. Hence or cogn. ~ĬB′ER¹, ~ĬP′TION, nn., ~ĬP′TIONAL, ~ĬP′TIVE, aa. [f. L TRAN-(*scribere script-* write)]

trăn′script, n. Written copy. [as prec.]

trănscū′rrent, a. (nat. hist.). Set or running crosswise. [f. L TRANS(*currere* run), -ENT]

trănsĕc′tion, n. Cross-section. [TRAN-]

trăn′sĕpt, n. Transverse part of cruciform church, either arm (*north*, *south*, ~). Hence **trănsĕp′tal** a. [f. TRAN-+SEPTUM]

trănsfĕr′¹, v.t. (-rr-). Convey, remove, hand over, (thing etc. *from* person or place *to* another); make over possession of (property), ticket etc. conferring rights, *to* person); convey (drawing etc.) from one surface to another esp. to lithographic stone by means of transfer-paper; remove (picture) from one surface to another esp. from wood or wall to canvas. Hence **trănsferabi′lity, trăns-ferĕr**², **trănsfĕror**², **ferōr′**, nn., **trănsfĕrable** a. (*the ~able vote*, electoral method for securing that elected candidate shall represent a majority, each voter signifying on his ballot-paper to which candidate his vote shall be ~red if no candidate has an absolute majority of first preferences), **trănsfĕrĕn′tial** (-shal) a. [f.L TRANS(*ferre lat-* bear)]

trăns′fer², n. 1. Transferring; conveyance of property or right, document effecting this; design etc. (to be) conveyed from one surface to another; small toy coloured picture or design transferable from paper on which it is sold to other surface; ∥ soldier exchanged from one regiment etc. to another. **2.** ~*book*, register of ~s of property, shares, etc.; ∥~*days* at Bank of England, days for ~ of consols

etc. free of charge (all but Sat. & Sun.); ~*ink* (for making designs on lithographic stone or ~*paper*); ~*paper* (specially coated to receive impression of ~ink & transfer it to stone). [f. prec.]

trănsfigūrā′tion, n. Change of form or appearance, esp. that of Christ (*Matt.* xvii. 1-9); (*T*~) festival of Christ's ~, Aug. 6. [f. L *transfigurationem* (as foll., see -ATION]

trănsfig′ure (-ger), v.t. Change in form or aspect esp. so as to elevate or idealize. [f. OF *transfigurer* f. L TRANS(*figurare* FIGURE]

trănsfix′, v.t. Pierce with lance etc.; (of horror etc.) root (person) to the spot, paralyse faculties of. [f. L TRANS(*figere fix-* fix)]

trănsfix′ion (-kshon), n. Piercing through; (Surg.) amputation by piercing transversely & cutting outwards. [-ION]

trănsfōrm′, v.t. Make (esp. considerable) change in the form, outward appearance, character, disposition, etc., of, as *caterpillar is* ~*ed into butterfly, 10 years is India have* ~*ed him* (in character or physique), *a beard may* ~ *a man beyond recognition.* Hence ~ABLE, ~ATIVE, aa. [f.L trans(*formare* FORM²), TRANS-]

trănsformā′tion, n. Transforming, being transformed, as *has undergone a great* ~; metamorphosis esp. of insects; change from solid to liquid or from liquid to gaseous state or vice versa; (Math.) change from one figure or expression to another equal in quantity; change in blood during passage through capillaries of vascular system; morbid change of tissue into form proper to some different part; (shop) woman's artificial head of hair; ~*scene*, elaborate spectacular scene in which chief pantomime characters are supposed to change into chief actors of the harlequinade that follows. [f. LL *transformationem* (as prec., see -ATION)]

trănsfōrm′er, n. In vbl senses, esp. apparatus for reducing or increasing the voltage of an alternating current. [-ER¹]

trănsfōr′mism, n. Fact, doctrine, of the development of one species from another; theory of development of complex animals from free organisms united into a colony & changed into organs of a complex whole. So~IST n. [F(-*me*), as TRANS-FORM, -ISM]

trănsfūse′ (-z), v.t. Cause (fluid, fig. quality etc.) to pass from one vessel etc. to another; (Med.) transfer (blood) from veins of person or animal to those of another person, inject (liquid) into blood-vessel to replace lost fluid. Hence or cogn. ~**fū′SION** (-zhn) n., ~**fūs′IVE** a. [f. L TRANS(*fundere fus-* pour)]

trănsgrĕss′ (-z-, -s-), v.t. Violate, infringe, (commandment, law; often abs.). So **trănsgrĕ′ssion** (-shn), ~OR², nn. [f.

tranship, = *trans-ship*.

tranship'ment, n. See TRANS-SHIP.

transhū'mance, n. Seasonal moving of live-stock to another region. [TRANS-, L *humus* ground., -ANCE]

trän'sient (-z-), a. Not permanent, as *the ~ affairs of this life*; of short duration, momentary, hasty, as *a ~ gleam of hope, snatched a ~ glance*; (Mus.) passing. Hence **trän'sienCE, trän'sienCY,** ns., **trän'sientLY²** adv., **~NESS** n. [f. L *transire* (see TRANSIT)]

trànsil'ient, a. [f. L TRANS(*silīre go*), see -ENT] Extending across from one point of support to another. [f. L TRANS(*silīre=salīre* leap), see -ENT]

trànsillūmin'ātion (-z-), n. (med.). Throwing of strong light through organ etc. for purpose of diagnosis. [TRANS-]

tränsī'rē (-z-), n. Custom-house permit for removal of goods. [L TRANS(*īre* go) go across]

trän'sit (-z-), n, & v.t. **1.** Going, conveying, being conveyed, across or over or through, as *allowed 2 days for the ~ by rail*, *the lake, improved methods of ~*; *goods delayed in ~, loses quality in (the) ~*; passage, route, as *the overland ~*; *~-circle, -compass, -instrument*; apparent passage of heavenly body across meridian of place; passage of heavenly body (esp. of Venus as determining solar parallax, or of Mercury) across sun's disk etc. **2.** observing ~ of heavenly body across meridian; *~-compass*, surveyor's instrument for measuring horizontal angle; *~-circle, -instrument*, instruments for observing ~ of heavenly body across meridian; *~-duty* (paid on goods passing through a country) **3.** v.t. Cross the disk of (sun etc.). [(vb f. n.) f. L *transitus -ūs* f. TRANS(*īre it-* go)]

trànsi'tion (-z-), n. Passage, change, from one place or state or act or set of circumstances to another; as *came by an abrupt ~ into hilly country, made a hurried ~ to indifferent topics, is subject to frequent ~s from high spirits to depression*; (Mus.) modulation of momentary character; (Art) change from one style to another, esp. (Archit.) from Norman to Early English, as (attrib.) *~ stage, period*; *~ tumour* (tending, on recurrence after removal, to become malignant). Hence **~AL, ~ARY¹,** aa., **~aliY²** adv., (-zisho-).

trän'sitive, a. & n. (gram.). (Verb) taking a direct object expressed or understood (e.g. *pick* in: *pick peas, pick till you are tired*; opp. to intransitive as in *picked at the hole to make it bigger*). Hence **~LY²** adv., **~NESS** n. [f. LL *transitivus* (as TRANSIT, see -IVE)]

trän'sitorY, a. Not permanent, lasting only a short time; *~y action* (Law), one that can be brought in any country irrespective of where the transaction etc. occurred. Hence **~ilY²** adv., **~INESS** n.

[f. *transgressor* f. L TRANS(*grědi gress-* walk)]

trànslāte' (-s-, -z-), v.t. **1.** Express the sense of (word, sentence, book) in or into another language, as *has ~ed Homer (into English, from the Greek), has this work been ~ed into French*; (fig.) render, *~ (say what you mean in plain words)*; (quasi-pass., of language, style, etc.) lend itself well etc. to translation. **2.** Convey, introduce, (idea, principle) *from* one art etc. *into* another. **3.** Infer or declare the significance of, interpret, (signs, movements, conduct, hint, etc.), as *this I ~ed as a protest, ~ed his gestures to the bystanders*. **4.** Remove (bishop) to another see; (Bibl.) convey to heaven without death; (arch.) transform; (Teleg.) retransmit (message); (Mech.) cause (body) to move so that all its parts follow same direction, impart motion without rotation to. Hence or cogn. **~ABLE, trànslātā'TIONAL** (mech.), aa., **translā'TION, ~OR²(1, 2),** nn. [f. OF *translater* f. L *translater* (as TRANSFER)]

trànslit'erāte(-z-), v.t. Represent (word, or abs.) in the more or less corresponding characters of a different language. Hence **~A'TION, trànsliter'ātor²** n. [f. TRANS-+ L *litera* letter+-ATE³]

trànslū'cent (-zlōō-), a. Transmitting light but not transparent; (loosely) transparent. Hence **~ENCE, ~ENCY,** nn. [f. L TRANS(*lucēre* shine), see -ENT]

trànsmarī'ne (-z-, -ēn), a. Situated beyond the sea. [f. L TRANS(*marīnus* MARINE)]

trän'smigrāte (or -ig'ā), v.i. (Of soul) pass into, become incarnate in, a different body; migrate. So **~ANT** & n. (esp. alien passing through one country on way to another), **~ātor²** n. **trànsmig'ratorY** a. [f. L TRANS(*migrāre* MIGRATE)]

trànsmigrā'tion, n.= METEMPSYCHOSIS, whence **~ISM(3)** n.; migration. [f. LL *transmigrationem* (as prec., see -ATION)]

trànsmit' (-z-), v.t. (-tt-). Pass on, hand on, transfer, communicate, as *will ~mit the parcel, shall ~mit daily despatches, will ~mit the title, the disease, the faculty, to his descendants, his writings have ~mitted the principle to posterity*; suffer to pass through, be a medium for, serve to communicate, (heat, light, sound, electricity, emotion, news). Hence or cogn. **~missi-BIL'ITY, ~mi'ssion** (-zmĭshn), **~missi-BL'ITY, ~mi'ssion** (-zmĭshn), **~mitt'ER¹(1, 2),** nn. **~miss'IBLE, ~mitt'AL, ~miss'IVE,** aa. [f. L TRANS-...]

trànsmŏg'rifY (-z-), v.t. (joc.). Transform esp. in magical or surprising manner. Hence **~FICA'TION** n. [etym. dub.; perh. thr. the n. as corrupt. of *transmigration* (of souls)]

trànsmutā'tion (-z-), n. Transmuting; change into another form, nature, or substance; (Alch.) change of baser metals into gold etc.; (Geom.) change of

figure or body into another of same area or content; (Biol.) change of one species into another, whence ~IST(2) n.; ~ *glaze*, iridescent porcelain glaze. [OF (as foll., see -ATION)]

transmute' (-z-), v.t. Change the form, nature, or substance, of. Hence or cogn. ~ABIL'ITY, ~ER¹, nn., ~ABLE, ~ATIVE, aa., ~ABLY² adv. [f. L TRANS(*mutare* change)]

transnorm'al (-z-), a. Beyond, exceeding, what is normal. [TRANS-]

transocean'ic (-zōsh-), a. Situated beyond the ocean; crossing, concerned with crossing, the ocean, as ~ *flight of birds*. [TRANS-]

trän'som, n. ‖ Horizontal (cf. MULLION) bar of wood or stone across window or top of door; ~ *window* (divided by ~ or placed above ~ of door); each of several beams fixed across stern-post of ship; beam across saw-pit; strengthening cross-bar. Hence ~ED² (-md) a. [f. L TRANS(*trum*, agent-suf.)]

trans'pădăne, a. Situated beyond (usu. =north of) the Po. [f. L TRANS(*padanus* f. *Padus* Po, see -AN)]

transpar'ency, n. Being transparent, so ~; ‖ TRANSPAR'ENCE n.: picture, inscription, etc., painted on canvas or muslin & shown up by light behind, wooden framework supporting such picture: (Photog.) positive picture on glass hung in window as ornament or used as lantern slide; porcelain relief whose parts vary in thickness & ~; *his* etc. T~ (burlesque title = G *Durchlaucht*, cf. SERENITY). [f. med. L *transparentia* (as foll., see -ENCY)]

transpar'ent, a. Transmitting rays of light without diffusion so that bodies behind can be distinctly seen; (fig., of disguise, pretext, etc.) easily seen through, (of motive, quality, etc.) easily seen through attempted disguise; bright, clear, (fig.) free from affectation or disguise, frank; ~ *colours*, (in painting) such as when laid lightly on do not hide underlying colours & forms, (in stained glass) appearing only by transmission of light. Hence ~LY² adv., ~NESS n. [f. med. L *transparēre* appear, TRANS-, see -ENT]

transpierce', v.t. Pierce through. [f. F TRANS(*percer* PIERCE)]

transpire', v.t. & i. **1.** Emit through excretory organs of skin or lungs, pass off in vapour; be emitted thus, pass off as in insensible perspiration. **2.** (Of gas or liquid) move through capillary tube under pressure; (Bot., of plant or leaf) exhale watery vapour. **3.** (fig.) (Of secret etc.) ooze out, come to be known; (vulg.) happen. Hence or cogn. ~ABLE, ~atory, aa., transpira'tion n. [f. TRAN- + L *spirare* breathe]

transplant' (-lah-), v.t. Plant in another place; remove & establish, esp. cause to live, in another place; (Surg.) transfer (living tissue) & implant in another part of

body or in another person's body. Hence or cogn. ~ABLE (-lah-) a., **transplant-A'TION** n. [f. L TRANS(*plantare* PLANT]

transpla'nter (-lah-), n. In vbl senses, esp.: hand-tool for lifting plants, machine for removing trees, with ball of earth about roots. [-ER¹]

‖ **transpon'tine**, a. Of the part of London on Surrey side of Thames; cheaply melodramatic, like the plays formerly popular in ~ theatres. [f. TRANS-+L *pons -ntis* bridge +-INE¹]

transport¹', v.t. **1.** Convey (person, goods, troops, baggage, etc.) from one place to another, whence ~ER¹ n. **2.** (hist.). Convey (criminal) to penal colony. **3.** Carry away by strong emotion (chiefly in pass., as ~*ed with joy, anger, fear*), whence ~ingLY² adv. [f. L TRANS(*portare* carry)]

trans'port², n. **1.** Conveyance, transportation, from place to place; means of ~, as *motor* ~. **2.** Vessel employed to carry soldiers, stores, etc., to destination. **3.** (hist.). Transported convict. **4.** Vehement emotion, as *in a* ~ *of rage, was in* ~*s* (usn. of joy). [f. prec.]

transport'able, a. That may be transported, whence ~ABIL'ITY n.; (of offender or offence) punishable by transportation. [-ABLE]

transporta'tion, n. Conveying, being conveyed, from place to place; removal to penal colony (hist.). [-ATION]

transpose' (-z), v.t. Cause (two or more things) to change places; (Alg.) transfer (term) with changed sign to other side of equation; change the natural or the existing order or position of (words, a word) in sentence; (Mus.) write, play, in different key, as ~*ed from G to B*; ~*ing instrument* (producing notes different in pitch from the written notes), ~*ing piano* (on which transposition may be effected mechanically). Hence ~AL, ~ER¹, nn, (-z-). [f. F TRANS(*poser*, see COMPOSE]

transposi'tion (-zi-), n. Transposing, being transposed. Hence or cogn. ~AL, ~zi'TIVE, aa., (-zi-). [F, f. med. L *transpositionem* f. TRANS(*ponere posit-* place), see -ION]

trans-ship' (-nsh-), v.t. (-pp-). Transfer from one ship or conveyance to another. Hence ~MENT n. [TRANS-]

transubstan'tiate (-shi-), v.t. Change from one substance into another (esp. as foll.). [f. med. L TRANS(*substantiare*, as SUBSTANCE), see -ATE³]

transubstantia'tion (-shi-, -si-), n. Change from one substance into another, esp. (Theol.) conversion of whole substance of eucharistic bread & wine into body & blood respectively of Christ (cf. CONSUBSTANTIATION). [f. med. L *transubstantiationem* (as prec., see -ATION)]

transude', v.i. (Of fluid) pass through pores or interstices of membrane etc.

Hence ~ʌ'TION n., ~'ATORY a. [TRAN-, L *sudāre* sweat]

transvers'al (-nz-), a. & n. 1. (Of line) cutting a system of lines. 2. n. ~ line. Hence ~-LY² (-āl-) n., ~-LY² adv. [f. med. L *transversālis* (foll. -AL)]

transverse' (-z-; also trā-), a. & n. 1. Situated, arranged, acting, in crosswise direction, as ~ *artery, ligament, magnet* (whose poles are at sides not ends), *section, axis.* 2. n. ~ *muscle.* Hence ~-LY² adv., **transverse'ly** (-z-) comb. form. [f. L TRANS(*vertere vers-* turn)]

tran'ter, n. (dial.) Carrier; hawker. [f. med. L *trāvetārius*, etym. dub.]

trap¹, n., & v.t. & i. (-pp-). 1. Pitfall or enclosure or mechanical structure for catching animals, affording entrance but not exit & often baited & having door or lid actuated by spring; FLY¹, RAT¹, ~; (fig.) trick for betraying person into speech or act, as *is always setting ~s for me, walked straight into the ~, is this* (question etc.) *a ~?* 2. Contrivance for suddenly releasing bird, or throwing ball etc. into air, to be shot at; shoe-shaped wooden device with pivoted bar that sends ball from its heel into air on being struck at other end with bat, ~*-ball,* game played with this. 3. U-shaped or other section of pipe so arranged as to prevent return flow of gas by means of liquid replaced whenever ~ is used. 4. ∥ Kinds of wheeled vehicle, e.g. dog-cart. 5. = ~*-door.* 6. □ ~*-cellar,* space under stage of theatre; ~*-door,* door in floor or roof (~*door spider,* kind that makes hinged ~*door* at top of nest), (fig.) L-shaped tear in cloth etc. 7. vb. Catch (animal, fig. person) in ~; furnish (stage) with ~s for a play; set ~s in (wood, hedge, etc.); arrest (gas) in ~; supply (drain etc.) with ~; (of steam) be impeded in pipe etc. [OE *treppe, træppe*, cf. MDu. *trappe*, med. L *trappa*, Olr *trapa*; relation between Teut. & Rom. wds. & w. G *treppe*, Sw. *trappa*, stair, doubtful]

trap², n. Dark-coloured eruptive rock of columnar structure; (pl.) portable step-ladder. [f. Sw. *trapp* (*trappa* stair, see prec.)]

trap³, v.t. (-pp-), & n. 1. Furnish with trappings. 2. in pl. Personal belongings, baggage, as *pack up your ~s.* [f. F *drap-*(*er*) cloth(e)]

trapan. See TREPAN².

trapes (-ps), **traipse**, n., & v.i. (collog. & dial.) 1. Slattern; a tiresome walk. 2. v.i. (Esp. of women) tramp or trudge wearily or in draggletailed way, go about on errands. [vb earlier also *traipe*; perh. cogn. w. Du. *trappen* tread]

trapé|ze', n. Cross-bar(s) suspended by cords used as swing for gymnastic exercises; = foll., whence ~ɪFORM a. [f. F *trapéze*, = foll.]

trapé'z|ium, n. Any irregular quadri-lateral esp. one with one pair of opposite sides parallel, cf. foll. [mod. L, f. Gk *trapezion* (*trapeza* table)]

trapé'zoid, n. & a. 1. Quadrilateral no two of whose sides are parallel, cf. prec. 2. adj. Of, in the form of, a ~. Hence ~AL (-oid'-) a. [f. late Gk *trapezoeides* (prec. -OID)]

trapp'|ean, a. Of the nature of the rock TRAP². So ~OID, ~OSE¹, aa. [-EAN]

trapp'er, n. One whose business is to trap animals esp. for furs; one who tends air-doors in mines. [f. TRAP¹ +-ER¹]

trapp'ings (-z), n. pl. Harness of horse esp. when ornamental; (fig.) ornamental accessories (of office etc.). [f. TRAP³ +-ING¹]

Trapp'ist, n. Member of a Cistercian order founded 1140 at Soligny-la-Trappe, & noted for silence & other austerities. [-IST]

trapp'istine, n. Trappist abbey of Grâce-Dieu in France. Hence ~INESS n.

trash, n. & v.t. 1. Worthless or waste stuff, rubbish, refuse; loppings of trees etc., (W. Ind.) stripped leaves of sugar-cane used as fuel; thing, e.g. literary production, of bad workmanship or material; nonsensical talk; *come~,* refuse of crushed sugarcanes & dried leaves & tops, used as fuel; ~*-house* (on sugar-plantation, for storing bagasse & cane-~); ~*-ice,* broken ice mixed with water; *white~,* the poor white population in the Southern States. 2. v.t. Strip (sugar-canes) of outer leaves. Hence ~ERY(1), ~INESS, nn., ~ɪʟʏ² adv., ~ʏ² a. [f. Icel. *tros* rubbish, leaves & twigs as fuel]

träss, tä'rras, n. A volcanic earth formerly imported as cement-material. [Du. *tarras, tras*, f. Rom. (L *terra* earth). -ACEOUS]

trättori'a (-ēa), n. Italian eating-house. [It.]

traum'a, n. (pl. ~*ta*, ~s). Morbid condition of body produced by wound or external violence; (Psych.) emotional shock. So ~TISM n. [f. Gk *trauma -matos* wound]

traumat'ic, a. & n. Of, (medicine) for, wounds. [f. LL f. Gk *traumatikos* (as prec., see -IC)]

travail', n., & v.i. (arch.). 1. (Suffer) pangs of childbirth; (make) painful or laborious effort. [(vb f. OF *travailler*) OF, = toil, prob. f. LL *trepalium* instrument of torture (L *tres* three, *palus* stake)]

trav'el, v.i. & t. (-ll-), & n. 1. Make a journey esp. of some length tc distant countries, as *ordered to ~ for his health, spend his life in ~ling;* act as

COMMERCIAL traveller (*for firm, in commodity*); (of machine or part) move (*along bar* etc., *in groove* etc.); pass esp. in deliberate or systematic manner from point to point, as *his eye ~led over the scene, mind ~s over the events of the day*; (of deer etc.) move onwards in feeding; move, proceed, in specified manner or at specified rate, perform (distance), as *horse ~s slowly, light ~s faster than sound, train ~s thousands of miles per second, train ~led 1,000 miles a day*; journey through, as *~led France from end to end*; cause (herds etc.) to ~; (p.p.) experienced in ~ling, as *is a ~led man*; ~ *out of the record*, wander from subject; *~ling-cap, -dress*, etc. (of form convenient for ~ling). **2.** n. ~ling esp. in foreign countries, as *is much improved by ~, has returned from his ~s, is going to publish (account of) his ~s, cannot read books of ~ or ~s*; range, rate, mode, of motion of a part in machinery, as *has extended, improved, the ~ of the valves*; (of person, clothes, etc.) *~soiled, -stained, -worn*, etc. (as result of ~). [differentiated f. preo.]

tra'veller, n. In vbl senses, esp.: kinds of moving mechanism (esp. overhead crane on rails); = COMMERCIAL; ‖ *bona fide ~*, one entitled to call for refreshment on Sunday at public house by having travelled 3 miles; FELLOW-~; *tip person the ~*, impose on him, tell him lies; *~'s tale*, presumable lie; *~'s-joy*, a climbing plant. [-ER¹]

tra'velogue (-ŏg), n. Illustrated lecture-narrative of expedition etc. [irreg. f. *travel*+-LOGUE]

tra'verse, a., n., & v.t. & i. **1.** (Arch. in gen. use) = TRANSVERSE; (Her.) crossing shield from side to side; ~ *sailing* (on zigzag track). **2.** n. Thing, esp. part of structure, that crosses another; (Fortif.) earthwork in form of parapet protecting covered way etc., double or quadruple right-angle in trench (⌐, ⌐⌐) to prevent enfilading; gallery from side to side of church etc.; (Geom.) transversal line; single line of survey (usu. plotted from prismatic-compass bearings & chained or paced distances between angular points); (Naut.) zigzag line taken by ship owing to contrary winds or currents (*work, solve, a ~*, compute direct distance so covered); sideways movement of part in machine; sideways movement across face of precipice from one practicable line of ascent or descent to another, place where this is necessary; (Law) denial esp. of allegation of matter of fact; ‖ (arch.) thwarting circumstance; turning (~ *of gun*) to required direction; ~*table*, nautical table used in solving ~s, platform for shifting engine etc. from one line of rails to another. **3.** vb. Travel or lie across, as *must ~ a vast extent of country, district ~d by canals, wall ~d by beam*; make a ~ in climbing; (fig.) consider, discuss, the whole extent of (subject); turn (gun); plane (wood) across grain; deny esp. (Law) in pleading; thwart, frustrate, oppose, (plan, opinion); (of needle of compass etc.) turn (as) on pivot; (of horse) walk crosswise; *travers-ing pulley* (running over rope etc. that supports it). [(vb f. F *traverser*, n. partly thr. adj.) f. F *travers -rse*, f. L as TRANSVERSE]

tra'verser, n. In vbl senses, esp. railway traverse-table. [-ER¹]

tra'vertin(e), n. Porous light-yellow rock, a calcareous deposit from springs, hardening on exposure and used in Italy for building. [f. It. *travertino* f. L *tiburtinus* (*lapis* stone) of Tibur (Tivoli), see -INE¹]

tra'vesty, v.t., & n. **1.** Make (subject etc.) ridiculous (intentionally or not) by treatment of it; (of person or thing, e.g. literary work) be a ridiculous imitation of (another). **2.** n. Such treatment, such imitation, (*of*). [(vb & n. f. obs. adj.) f. F *travesti* p.p. of *travestir* disguise, change the clothes of, f. It. *travestire* clothe f. L *vestire* f. *vestis* clothing]

trawl, v.t. & i., & n. **1.** Drag (~net), catch fish in ~net. Hence ~ING¹ n. **2.** n. (Also ~net) large bag-net with wide mouth held open by beam (*beam-~*) or otherwise, meant to be dragged along the bottom by boat; *(also ~line) long sea-fishing line buoyed & supporting short lines with baited hooks; ~anchor (for anchoring ~line); ~boat (for setting ~line or drawing ~net). [f. 16th c., etym. dub.]

trawl'er, n. Person who trawls; trawl-boat. [-ER¹]

tray, n. Flat shallow vessel usu. of wood or metal for placing or carrying esp. small articles on, as *tea-~, pen-~, developing-* (in photography); metal or other container on desk for correspondence, as *in, out, ~*; shallow lidless box forming a compartment in trunk. Hence ~FUL n. [OE *trīg*, cogn. w. TREE]

trea'cherous (-ĕch-), a. Violating allegiance, betraying trust, perfidious; not to be relied on, deceptive, as *~ memory, ~ ice* (apt to give). Hence or cogn. ~LY² adv., ~NESS, **trea'chery¹** (-ĕch-), n. [f. OF *trecherous* (*trecheur* a cheat f. *trechier* deceive perh. cogn. w. TRICK, -OUS]

trea'cle, n. Syrup got in refining sugar; (loosely)= MOLASSES; kinds of saccharine fluid, e.g. sap of birch. Hence **treac'ly²** a. [earlier=THERIAC; f. OF *triacle* f. L as THERIAC]

tread (-ĕd), v.i. & t. (trŏd, arch. *trode*; *trodden*), & n. **1.** Set down one's foot, walk, step, (of foot) be set down, as *do lightly*, (fig.) deal cautiously with delicate subject; *where no foot may ~, where angels fear to ~*; in person's (*footsteps, (fig,)

follow his example; ~ *on person's corns* or ~; ||*~felony*, attempt to depose sovereign ~ *on a person's corns* on ~, offend him; ~ *on the heels of*, or levy war in order to compel change of (lit., & fig. of event etc.) come closely or measures, intimidate parliament, or stir immediately after; ~ *or seem to* ~ *on air* up foreign invasion. Hence ~OUS a. [f. (of person transported with joy); ~ *on* OF *traison*, as TRADITION]

as on eggs (of person in situation requiring **treas'onable** (-z-), a. Involving the much tact); ~ (*set* one's foot lit. or fig. as crime, guilty, of treason. Hence ~leness ~ AWRY. 2. *Walk* upon, press or crush n., ~LY² adv. [-ABLE]

with the feet, as ~*s a perilous path*, trod **treas'ure** (-ēzher), n., & v.t. 1. Precious the room from end to end; ~ *grapes* (in metals or gems, hoard of these, accumumaking wine), *vine*. 3. *Perform*, execute, lated wealth, as *buried* ~, had amassed (of person etc., as *trod a dozen hurried* *great* ~ *or* ~*s*, *a voyage in quest of* ~, (not *paces*, ~ *a measure* (in dancing). 4. (Of now in colloq. use); thing valued for cock) copulate with (hen, or abs.). 5. ~ rarity, workmanship, associations, etc., *down*, press down with feet, trample on, as *art* ~*s, absorbed in his latest* ~ (book, destroy, as ~ *down Saten under our feet*; ~ picture, etc.); (colloq.) beloved person *in walking etc., as trod a dozen* ~. *In* esp. child, as (voc.) *my* ~; (colloq.) or into earth etc. with feet; ~ *in*, press *highly efficient or satisfactory person*, *stamp out* (fire, grain) with feet; ~ *the* e.g. servant, *as the girl is a perfect* ~. press out (wine, grain) with feet; ~ *out* 2. v.t. *Store* (usn. *up*) as valuable; re*stage* or *boards*, be an actor, appear on ceive, regard, as valuable, store (usn. *up*) on *stage*; ~ *under foot*, (fig.) destroy, treat in memory, (person's words, looks, etc.). contemptuously; ~ *under foot*, (fig.) 3. ~*-city* (Bibl.), city for stores & magaupright position in deep water. 6. n. zines; ~*-house*, place where ~s (esp. fig.) Manner, sound, of walking, as *recognized* are kept; ~ *trove* [see TROVER], gold etc., *his heavy* ~, *approached with cautious* ~. found hidden in earth & of unknown 7. (Of male bird) copulation. 8. (Also ~ ownership. [f. OF *tresor* f. L f. Gk *board*) top surface of step or stair, each *thesauros*] step of ~mill. 9. Piece of metal or rubber placed on step to lessen wear or sound. **treas'urer** (-ēzher-), n. 1. Person in charge of 10. Part of wheel that touches ground or funds of society, company, club, etc.; rails, part of rail that wheels touch. 11. officer authorized to receive & disburse Part of stilt on which foot rests. 12. public revenues; *Lord High* T~ (hist.), Part of boot-sole that rests on ground. crown officer with duties now discharged 13. Distance between pedals of bicycle. by Lords of the Treasury; ||T~ *of the* 14. Cleatriole of egg (formerly supposed *Household*, official ranking next to Lord to appear only in fecundated eggs). Steward. Hence ~SHIP n. [f. OF *tresor(i)er* 15. ~*mill*, appliance for producing f. LL *thesaurarius* (as prec., see -ARY¹, motion by the stepping of man or horse -IER)] etc. on movable steps on revolving cylinder, esp. kind used in prisons as **treas'ury** (-ēzher-), n. 1. Place, building, punishment, (fig.) monotonous routine; where treasure is stored; (fig.) book, ~*wheel*, ~mill or similar appliance. [f. person, etc., viewed as repository of t. vb] OE *tredan*, cf. Du. *treden*, G *treten*. information etc. 2. Place where public ON *trotha*] revenues are kept; department managing public revenue of a country, officers of

trea'dle (-ĕdl), n., & v.i. 1. Lever moved this; ||T~ *Board*, *Lords* (*Commissioners* by foot & imparting motion to machine, *of the* T~, board in charge of British pube.g.: lathe, sewing-machine, bicycle, reed- lic revenue, viz. *First Lord of the* T~, organ; ~*machine*, *-press*, printing-press usn. prime minister, *Chancellor of the* worked by ~. 2. v.i. Work ~. Hence *Exchequer*, & 3 junior lords; T~ *bench*, **tread'ler¹** (-rĕd-) n. [vrb f. n.] OE *tredel* front bench on right hand of Speaker in step (as prec.) House of Commons, occupied by First **treas'on** (-z-), n. 1. (Also *high* ~) violation Lord of T~ (if a commoner), Chancellor of by subject of allegiance to sovereign or to Exchequer, & other members of Governchief authority of State (e.g. compassing ment. 3. ||~ *bill*, bill of exchange or intending sovereign's death, levying issued by the T~ to raise money for war against him, adhering to his enemies, temporary needs & sold to highest bidder; killing his wife or her, violating his wife ~ *note*, = CURRENCY note, *note issued by or eldest unmarried daughter or heir's T~, & receivable for government dues; wife, killing chancellor or treasurer or T~ *warrant* (issued by T~ for sums disjustice, abetting marriage of sovereign bursed by Exchequer). [f. OF *tresorie* (as under 18 years of age without written TREASURE, see -Y¹)] consent of regent & parliament). 2. **treat**, v.t. & i., & n. 1. Act towards, Breach of faith, disloyalty, (*to cause*, behave to, *as how did they* ~ *you*, ~*ed* friend, etc.). 3. *Constructive* ~ (held in *me abominably, kindly, as if I were a child*, law as equivalent to ~ though not in *better* ~ *it as a joke*. 2. Deal with (person,

tended or realized as such); MISPRISION¹ *of* process

to, subject to chemical agent etc., as ~ed him for smallpox, how would you ~ a sprained ankle?, must next be ~ed with sulphuric acid. **3.** Manipulate, present, express, (subject) in literature or art. **4.** Give (person) food or entertainment at one's expense, as *I will ~ you all, think you might ~ me to an ice, a theatre,* (of candidate for election) give food etc. or cause these to be given to (electors) in order to influence election, whence ~'ING¹ n. **5.** Negotiate terms (*with* person); ~ *of*, handle, discuss, (subject). **6.** n. Thing that gives great pleasure, as *pantomime is a great ~ to him, what a ~ it is not to have to get up early;* entertainment designed to do this, as *school-~, picnic* etc. for (esp. Sunday-) school children; *stand ~*, bear expense of entertainment. Hence ~'ABLE a., ~'ER¹ n. [(n. f. vb) f. OF *traitier* f. L *tractare* handle frequent. of *trahere tract-* draw]

treat'ise (-z, -s), n. Literary composition dealing more or less systematically with definite subject. [AF *tretis* (*traitier* as prec.)]

treat'ment, n. (Mode of) dealing with or behaving towards a person or thing, as *received strange ~ from him, must vary the ~, is now ready for ~ with an acid.* [as TREAT, see -MENT]

treat'y, n. Formally concluded & ratified agreement between nations; agreement between persons (*to do* etc.); *be in ~* (negotiating) *with* (person *for* purchase etc.); ~ *port*, one that a country is bound by ~ to keep open to foreign trade. [f. F *traité* p.p. of *traiter* (OF *-ter*) TREAT]

tre'ble, a. & n., & v.t. & i. **1.** Threefold, triple, whence **tre'bly**¹ʏ² adv.; multiplied by three, three times (amount etc., as *the enemy had ~ our numbers*); (esp. of boy's voice or boy)=SOPRANO. **2.** n. (In short whist) game won by 5 to 0 counting three points; = SOPRANO. **3.** vb. Multiply, be multiplied, by three, as *has ~d its value, its value has ~d.* [(vb & n. f. adj.) OF, f. L *triplus* TRIPLE; mus. sense from early contrapuntal music in which ~ was third part]

treb'ŭchĕt (-sh-), **treb'ŭckĕt**, n. (Hist.) military engine for throwing stones etc.; tilting balance for weighing light articles; kind of trap for small birds etc. [OF, f. *trebucher* tumble, f. TRANS- + OF *buc* trunk of body f. WG *bûh* belly (G *bauch*)]

trecĕn'to|ō (-äch-), n. The 14th century in Italian art & literature. So ~ISN(2, 3) n. [It., = three (for thirteen) hundred]

tree, n., & v.t. **1.** Perennial plant with single woody self-supporting stem or trunk usu. unbranched (cf. SHRUB¹) piece or framework of wood for various purposes, e.g. AXLE, BOOT¹, ROOF, SADDLE, SWINGLE, ~, CROSS-TREES; (arch.) gibbet, cross used for (esp. Christ's) crucifixion; CHRISTMAS~;(Math.) diagram of branching lines; *family* or GENEALOGICAL ~; *up a ~*, (fig.) cornered, nonplussed; *at the top of the ~*, at the top of one's profession. **2.** ~ *agate* (with ~like markings); ~ *calf*, calf binding for book stained with ~like design; ~ *creeper*, kinds of small bird; ~ *fern*, kinds of fern attaining size of ~; ~*frog*, (pop. name for) ~*toad*; ~*goose*, = BARNACLE (1); ~*milk*, juice of a shrub used in Ceylon instead of milk; ~*nail*, pin of hard wood for securing planks etc.; ~ *of knowledge of good & evil* (Gen. iii); ~ *of liberty* (dedicated to liberty & set up in public place); ~ *of life* (Gen. ii. 9); ~*toad*, arboreal amphibian with adhesive disks on digits enabling it to climb. Hence ~'LESS a., ~'LESSNESS n. **3.** v.t. Force (animal, fig. person) to take refuge in ~; stretch (boot) on boot~. [(vb f. n.) OE *trēo* tree, timber, cf. ON *trē*, Da. *træ*, Sw. *trä*]

trēf'oil, n. & a. Kinds of leguminous plant with leaves of three leaflets & flowers of various colours, clover; kinds of plant with similar leaves; three-lobed ornamentation in tracery etc.; (thing) arranged in three lobes, whence ~ED² (-ld) a. [f. OF *trifoil, trefoil*, f. L TRI(*folium* leaf)]

trēha'ia (-ah-), n. Manna of starch, sugar, & gum, excreted in cocoon form by an insect in Turkey & Persia. [f. native *tigalah*]

trĕk, v.i. (-kk-), & n. (S.-Afr.). **1.** (Of ox) draw vehicle, pull load; travel by ox-wagon; migrate; proceed slowly. **2.** n. Such journey, each stage of journey; organized migration. Hence ~k'ER¹ n. [f. Du. *trekken* vb, *trek* n.]

trĕll'is, n., & v.t. **1.** (Also ~*work*) lattice, grating, of light wooden cross-bars nailed together where they cross, similar structure of wire or metal; summer-house, screen, etc., made of ~*work*. **2.** v.t. Furnish, support (vine etc.), with ~. [(vb f. n.) f. OF *treliz* f. L TRI(*licem*, nom. *-ix*, f. *licium* warp-thread) three-ply]

trĕm'ble, v.i., & n. **1.** Shake involuntarily from fear, agitation, physical weakness, etc., as *he ~ed with anger, voice ~ed with excitement, hands ~e from over-smoking* etc.; (fig.) be in state of extreme agitation, fear, suspense, etc., as *I ~e to think what has become of him, ~e at the thought, no cause to ~e before his judge, hear & ~e* (be duly impressed)! *I ~e* (am alarmed) *for his safety, in ~ing un-certainly;* move in quivering manner, as *leaves ~e in the breeze*, ~*ing* POPLAR; (fig.) *his fate, life,* etc., *~es in the balance* (has reached a critical point, is in extreme danger). Hence or cogn. ~EMENT n. (poet., rare), ~ingLY² adv., ~'ʏ¹² a. **2.** n. ~ing, quiver, as *there was a ~e in her voice*, (colloq.) *was all of a ~e* (=ing all over); (pl.) kinds of (esp. cattle-) disease, with

~ing. [(n. f. vb) f F *trembler* f. med. L *tremulare* as TREMULOUS]

trèm'bler, n. In vbl senses; also or esp.: automatic vibrator for making & break-ing electric circuit; electric bell. [-ER¹]

trèm'ellose, a. (bot.), Jellylike, shaking like jelly. [f. mod. L *Tremella*, genus of jellylike fungi, +-OSE¹]

trèm'endous, a. Awful, fearful, over-powering, (colloq.) considerable, as a ~ *explosion, revolution, makes a ~ difference; a — (huge) bluebottle.* Hence ~LY² adv., ~NESS n. [f. L *tremendus* (*tremere* tremble, see -ND) +-OUS¹]

trèmŏlăn'dō, adv. (mus.), Tremulously. [It.]

trèm'olant, -ūlant, n. Device in organ for producing tremolo effect. [(-ŏl- f. It. *tremolante* f. med. L as TREMBLE, see -ANT)]

trèm'olō, n. (mus.), Tremulous effect in singing or in playing bowed instruments etc.; = prec. [It., as TREMULOUS]

trèm'or, n. (Of leaf, part of body, voice, person) shaking, quivering; thrill (of fear, exultation, etc.); *intention* ~ (in part of body when it moves to do something); *metallic* ~, trembling palsy of metal-workers. Hence ~LESS a. [ME & OF, f. L *tremorem* (*tremere* tremble, *tremere*)]

trèm'ulous, a. Trembling, quivering, as ~ *leaves, voice, hand; ~ line* (drawn by ~ hand); timid, vacillating. Hence ~LY² adv., ~NESS n. [f. L *tremulus* (*tremere* tremble, shake) +-ous¹]

trenail. Var. of TREENAIL.

trench, v.t. & i. & n. 1. Dig ditch in (ground); turn over the earth of (field etc.) by digging succession of contiguous ditches; || cut groove in (wood etc.); pro-ceed, make one's way, (*down, along,* etc.) by ~ing; encroach (*up)on* (person's rights, privacy, etc.); verge or border closely (*up)on* (heresy, vulgarity, etc.). Hence ~'er¹ [-ER¹] n. 2. n. Deep furrow or ditch; (Mil.) ditch often 7 ft deep with earth thrown up to form parapet, as *open* (begin digging) *the* ~*es, mount* (guard in) *the* ~*es.* 3. ~*cart,* hand-cart on low wheels for use in ~es; ~ *coat,* soldier's mackin-tosh; ~ *foot,* affection of feet or legs with sloughing etc. caused by much standing in water; ~ *mortar,* light simple kind throw-ing heavy charge of high explosive short distance for use in ~es. [f. OF *trenchier* ditch; prob. ult. f. L *truncare* TRUNCATE]

trench'ant, a. Sharp, keen, as ~ *sword, blade,* (now rare in lit. sense); (fig., of style, language, policy, etc.) penetrat-ing, incisive, decisive, vigorous. Hence **trench'ancY** n., ~LY² adv. [OF, part. as prec.]

trencher¹. See TRENCH.

trench'er², n. Wooden platter now chiefly used for cutting bread on at table; (arch.) the pleasures of the table, eating, (chiefly attrib. or in comb., as ~ *com-panions,* ~-*valiant; good, poor,* etc., ~-*man,*

trend, v.i. & n. 1. Have specified general direction, bend or turn away in specified direction, as *coast* ~*s (towards the) south;* (fig.) be chiefly directed, have general tendency, (*towards* etc.). 2. n. General direction & tendency (esp. fig. of events, opinion, etc.). [(n. f. vb) OE *trendan* cf. Da. & Sw. *trind* a. round]

trèn'tal, n. Set of 30 successive daily masses for the dead. [f. med. L *trentāle* f. L *trigínta* thirty +-AL]

trente-et-quarante (see AP.), n. = ROUGE¹-ET-NOIR. [F, = 30 & 40]

trepan¹, n. & v.t. (-nn-). 1. Surgeon's cylindrical saw for removing part of bone of skull to relieve brain; borer for sinking shafts. 2. v.t. Perforate (skull) with ~. So **trèpana'TION** n., ~n'ING¹, n. [f. F *tré-panier* f. med. L *trepanum* f. Gk *trupanon* (*trupaō* bore f. *trupaō* hole)]

trepan², v.t. (-nn-). Trap, ensnare, be-guile, (*into, from,* place etc., *into doing*). [f. obs. *trepan* a decoy; perh. connected w. *trap*]

trepang', n. Edible sea-slug used in China for soup. [f. Malay *trīpang*]

trephine', (-ēn, -īn), n. & v.t. 1. Improved form of trepan with guiding centre-pin, ends w. ret. to its shape] 2. v.t. Operate on (skull, eyeball, person) with this. So **trèphina'TION** n. [(vb f. n.) f. L *tres fines* three assim. of TREPAN¹ to L *tres fines* three ends]

trepida'tion, n. Alarm, flurry; trembling of limbs e.g. in paralysis; (hist.) oscilla-tion of ecliptic formerly assumed to account for precession of equinoxes etc. [f. L *trepidātiōnem* (*trepidāre* be agitated, tremble, f. *trepidus* flurried, see -ATION)]

trĕs'pass, v.i. & n. 1. Make unlawful or unwarrantable intrusion (*on, upon,* land, rights, etc., or abs.; ~ *on one's pre-serves,* fig., meddle in a matter that he has made his own); make unwarrantable claim on (chiefly in polite formulas, as *shall ~ on your hospitality*); offend (*against* person, law, principle, rights; now lite-rary), as *forgive them that ~ against us.* Hence ~ER¹ n. 2. n. Transgression of law or right; (Law) any transgression that is not (misprision of) treason or felony; ~*ing* (see vb, 1st sense) on another's land with damage; (also *action of* ~) common-law action for recovery of damages for ~; ~-*offering,* sacrifice atoning for ~ against Mosaic law. [in f. OF *trespass*] f. OF *trespasser* pass over, trespass (*tres-* TRANS-+*passer* PASS)]

tress, n., & v.t. 1. Portion, lock, plait, of hair of human esp. woman's or girl's head; (pl.) hair of esp. woman's or girl's head. Hence (-)ED² (-st), ~Y², aa. 2. v.t. Arrange (hair) in ~es (chiefly in

p.p.). [(vb f. F *tresser*) f. F *tresse*, cf. med. L *trecia* perh. f. Gk *trikha* threefold (TRI-)]

tre'stle (-sl), n. Supporting structure for table or flat form or carpenter's work etc., consisting of bar supported by two divergent pairs of legs or of two frames fixed at an angle or hinged; (also ~*work*) open braced framework of wood or metal for supporting bridge etc.; (Naut. also ~*tree*) each of a pair of horizontal pieces on lower mast supporting topmast etc. [f. OF *trestel* ult. f. dim. of L *transtrum* TRANSOM]

‖ **tret**, n. (hist.). Allowance of extra weight formerly made to purchasers of some goods for waste in transportation. [perh. f. OF *traite* transportation etc. (as TRAIT)]

trevet. See TRIVET.

trews (-ōoz), n. pl. Tartan trousers, esp. as worn by some Scottish regiments. [Ir. *trius* f. *trouse* see TROUSERS]

trey (trā), n. Card, die, with three spots. [f. OF *treis* three f. L *tres*]

tri-, pref.—L & Gk *tri-* three-, having or composed of three, triple, as: ~*adelph'ous*, with stamens in 3 sets; ~*an'drous*, with 3 stamens; ~*ap'sidal*, with 3 apses; ~*bas'ic*, with 3 hydrogen atoms replaceable by base or base radical; ~*brach'ial* (-k-), three-armed implement; ~*carp'a* flint implement; ~*cap'sular* (Bot., Zool.), with 3 capsules (to each flower); ~*carp'ous*, bearing 3 fruits or carpels; ~*centen'ary*, =TERCENTENARY; ~*chord* (-k-) a. & n., three-stringed (instrument esp. lute); ~*chromat'ic* (-kr-), three-coloured (~*chromatic photography*, THREE-*colour process*), (of the eye) having the normal three colour sensations, i.e. red, green, & purple, so ~*chrom'atism* (-kr-) n.; ~*corn*, having 3 horns, (n., also ~*corne*) three-cornered cocked hat; ~*corp'oral*, ~*corp²orate* (Her.) having 3 bodies & one head; ~*cotyled'onous*, with 3 cotyledons; ~*crot'ic*, (of pulse) with 3 beats; ~*cus'pid*, with 3 cusps or points, as ~*cuspid valve* of heart, ~*cuspid murmur* (heard when this is deranged); ~*dac'tyl(ous)*, with 3 fingers or toes; ~*den'tate*, with 3 teeth or prongs; ~*di'gitate*, =~*dactyl*; ~*dimen²sional*, of 3 dimensions; ~*fa'cial* a. & n., (of) the trigeminus; ~*flor'al*, ~*flor'ous*, bearing 3 flowers; ~*fo'liate*, ~*fo'liolate*, (of compound leaf) with 3 leaflets, (of plants) having such leaves; ~*fo'liated*, (Bot.) =prec., (Archit.) trefoiled; ~*form(ed)*, formed of 3 parts, having 3 forms or bodies; ~*furc'ate* (-āt) a., divided into three forks, (v.t. & i., -āt) divide thus; ~*gem'inal* a. & n., triple, (of) the ~*geminus* or ~*gem'inus*, cranial nerve with the 3 functions of motion, common sensation, & taste; ~*goneut'ic* (Entom.), having 3

broods in a year; ~*gram*, ~*graph*, group of 3 letters representing one sound; ~*gynous* (trij-), having 3 pistils; ~*hed'ral*, with 3 surfaces; ~*jug'ate*, ~*jug'ous*, (-jōō-), (Bot.), having, arranged in, 3 pairs; ~*lat'iate*, three-lipped; ~*lam'inar*, of 3 layers; ~*lat'eral* a. & n. (adv. -*lly*), of 3 sides, (of dealings) to which there are 3 parties, (n.) triangle; ~*lemm'a*, choice between 3 things; ~*lin'ear*, of 3 lines; ~*ling'ual* (-nggw-), of, expressed in, 3 languages; ~*lit'eral*, of 3 letters, (of Semitic languages) having (most of) their roots in 3 consonants, so ~*lit'eralism*, ~*literal'ity*, nn.; ~*lith*, monument of 3 stones, esp. two upright & one across their tops, so ~*lith'ic* a.; ~*lob'ate*, three-lobed; ~*lobite*, member of palaeozoic group of animals with body in 3 main divisions, so ~*lobit'ic* a.; ~*loc'ular*, with 3 cells or compartments; ~*men'sual*, ~*mes²trous*, of 3 months; *trim²erous*, of 3 members or joints (also 3-*merous*); ~*morph'ism*, ~*morph'ous*, (Biol., Bot., Crystallog.), existence, existing, in 3 distinct forms; ~*nerved*, three-nerved; ~*nōd'al* (Anat., Bot.), having 3 joints; ~*nōm'ial* a. & n., (technical name, algebraical expression) consisting of 3 terms; ~*nom'ialism*, use of 3 terms in naming objects in natural history; ~*oe'cious* (-ēsh-), having male, female, & hermaphrodite flowers each on different plants; ~*ox'ide*, oxide containing 3 oxygen atoms; ~*penn'ate*, =~*pinnate*, ~*pet'alous*, having 3 petals; *triph'thong*, 3 vowels forming one sound; *triphthong'al* (-nggl), so formed; ~*phyll'ous*, three-leaved; ~*pinn'ate*, having 3 series of leaflets; ~*rad'ial*, ~*rad'iate(d)*, radiating in 3 directions; ~*sēr'ial*, ~*sēr'iate*, (Anat., Bot.) disposed in 3 rows; ~*sperm'ous*, containing 3 seeds; ~*spor'ous*, ~*spor'ic*, having 3 spores; *tris'tichous* (-k-), arranged in 3 vertical rows; ~*stigmat'ic*, ~*styl'ous*, (Bot.), having 3 stigmas, styles; ~*sulc'ate*, (Bot.) three-grooved, (Zool.) divided into 3 digits or hoofs; ~*tern'ate*, (Bot.) thrice ternate, having 27 leaflets; ~*tone*, (Mus.), interval of 3 tones; *triv'alent* (Chem.), having combining power of 3.

tri'able, a. That may be tried. [-ABLE]

triacontahéd'ral, a. Having 30 sides or surfaces. [f. Gk *triakonta* 30+*hedra* seat, -AL1]

tri'ad, n. Group of three; (Chem.) element, radical, with combining power of three; (Mus.) chord of three notes, common chord; Welsh form of literary composition depending on arrangement in groups of three. Hence **triād'ic** a. [f. L f. Gk *trias -ados* (*treis* three, see -AD)]

‖ **tri'age**, n. Refuse of coffee-beans. [F, =sifting (as TRY, see -AGE)]

tri'al, n. 1. Process or mode of testing the

For other words in *tri-* **see TRI-.**

qualities of a thing, experimental treat-ment, test, as *made ~ of his strength, was found on ~ to be incompetent, shall subject* or *put it to further ~, will make the ~* (try the experiment), *has been making ~s* or (attrib.) *~ ascends with an aeroplane; ~ of the PYX; bicycle is hired, clerk employed, on ~* (to be retained only if efficient), *will give you a ~* (employ you on ~); = ~ HEAT; = ~ match. **2.** Trying thing or experience or person, esp. hardship, *will find the boy, the piano next door, a great ~*. **3.** Judicial examination & determination of issues between parties by judge with or without jury or on reference etc., as *was on his ~* or *stood* or *underwent ~ for murder, granted a new ~* (on ground of error or injustice in former ~). **4.** *~ balance* (of ledger in double-entry book-keeping), comparison reveals certain errors in posting; *~ eights*, two experimental crews tried against each other with a view to selection of crew for boat-race; *~ match*, game of cricket, football, etc., in which players who may be selected for an important team take part; *~ trip*, new vessel's trip to test sailing qualities etc., (fig.) experi-ment. [AF [TRY, -AL]]

triangle (-nggl), n. **1.** Figure (esp. plane) bounded by three (esp. straight) lines, as *equilateral, isosceles, scalene, right-angled, ~*; *spherical ~* (formed on surface of sphere by intersection of three great circles); any three points not in one straight line together with the imaginary lines joining them. **2.** Implement etc. of this shape, e.g. right-angled ~ as drawing-implement, (Naut.) device of three spars for raising weights, (Mus.) rod of polished steel in form of ~ open at one angle sounded by striking with steel rod, (hist.) frame of three halberds joined at top to which soldier was bound for flogging; *the* ETERNAL ~; *~s of the neck* (regions into which it is divided for surgical purposes); **3.** *Solution of a ~*, finding of the remaining angles & sides when some are given; *~ of forces*, (T~) a northern constellation. **3.** *~ numbers*, sums of the series 1, 2, 3, etc., taken to any number of terms, e.g. 1, 6, 28, 55 (w. ref. to mode of disposing such number of points in form of equi-lateral triangle); *~ pyramid* (with ~ base). Hence ~ITY (-nggl...) n., ~LY² adv. [f. LL *triangulāris* (as prec., see -AR¹)]

triang'ulate¹ (-nggr-), v.t. Make tri-angular; divide (area etc.) into triangles for surveying purposes; determine (height, distance, etc.) thus. Hence ~A'TION n. [f. TRIANGLE + -ATE³]

triang'ulate² (-nggr-), a. (zool.). Marked with triangles. Hence ~LY² adv. [f. med. L *triangulātus* (prec., -ATE²)]

tri'as, n. (geol.). Division of rocks under-lying the Jurassic. Hence TRIASS'IC a. [as TRIAD, f. threefold subdivision in Ger-many]

triat'ic stay, n. (naut.). Stay connecting masts in fore-&-aft-rigged ships. [?]

trib'adism, n. Unnatural vice between women. [f. L f. Gk *tribas -ados* lewd woman (*tribō* rub) + -ISM]

trib'alism, n. Tribal organization. [-ISM]

tribe, n. **1.** Group of families or clans under recognized chiefs; (Rom. Hist.) each of the political divisions (orig. three, probably representing clans, ultimately 35) of the Romans; any similar division whether of natural or political origin, e.g. *the twelve ~s* of the Israelites (*the ten ~s*, those without Judah & Benjamin; *the lost ~s*, the ten ~s after deportation by Shalmaneser). **2.** (zool., bot.). Group of plants or animals usu. ranking between genus & order. **3.** (usu. derog.). Set, number, of persons esp. of one profession etc., as *the whole ~ of parasites, actors, the scribbling ~*. **4.** *~s'man*, member of a ~ or of one's own ~. Hence trib'AL a., trib'ALLY² adv. [f. L *tribus*, etym. dub.]

trib'let, trib'olet, n. Mandrel used in making tubes, rings, etc. [f. F *triboulet*, etym. dub.]

tribom'eter, n. Sledlike apparatus for measuring friction. [f. F *tribomètre* f. Gk *tribos* rubbing + -METER]

trib'rach (-k), n. Metrical foot ◡◡◡. Hence tribrach'ic a. [f. L f. Gk *tríbrakhus* short)]

tribula'tion, n. Severe suffering or trial. [OF (-cion), f. LL *tribulātiōnem* (*tribulāre* press, oppress, f. *tribulum* sledge for threshing, f. *terere trit-* rub, see -ATION)]

tribu'nal, n. Judgement-seat, seat or bench for judge(s) or magistrate(s); court of justice (chief, & often fig., as *before the war*) local board bearing claims for exemption from military service. [L (as TRIBUNE¹, see -AL)]

trib'une¹, n. **1.** (Rom. hist.). (Also *~ of the people*) each of (orig. two, ultimately ten) officers chosen by the people to protect their liberties against senate & consuls; kinds of military, fiscal, & other officers. **2.** (transf.). Popular leader or demagogue (the T~e, often as newspaper title). Hence or oogn. ~ATE¹(1), ~ESHIP, n., ~ARY¹, ~Í'CIAL, ~Í'CIAL(-shl), ~Í'CIAN (-shn), aa. [f. L *tribūnus* (as TRIBE)]

trib'une², n. Raised floor for magistrate's chair in apse of Roman basilica; bishop's

throne, apse containing this, in basilica; platform, pulpit, esp. that used by speakers in French Chamber of Deputies. [F, f. med. L *tribuna* (prec.)]

trib′ūtar̄y, a. & n. **1.** Paying, subject to, tribute, as ~*y States*; contributory, auxiliary; (of river) serving to swell a larger river. **2.** n. ~*y* State, person, stream. Hence ~ily² adv., ~iness n. [f. L *tributarius* (as foll., see -ARY¹)]

trib′ūte, n. Money or equivalent paid periodically by one prince or State to another in acknowledgement of submission or as price of peace or protection, or by virtue of treaty; state of being subject to ~, as *was laid under* ~; (fig.) contribution, esp. thing done, said, given, etc., as mark of respect etc., as *the ~ of a tear, will not withhold my ~ of praise, the* ~*s* (gifts, compliments, attentions) *of her admirers, floral* ~*s* (flowers to actress, at funeral, etc.); ‖ (Mining) proportion of ore, its equivalent, paid to miner for his work, ~-*work* (so paid). [f. L *tributum* (*tribuere -ut-* give)]

tric′ar̄, n. Three-wheeled motor-car. [TRI-]

trice¹, v.t. (naut.). Haul up (usu. *up*); haul up & secure in place (usu. *up*); tie up (usu. *up*). [f. MDu. *trisen* hoist, etym. dub.]

trice², n. *In a* ~, in a moment. [prob. f. prec., but cf. Sp. *en un tris* in a trice (*tris* clink of breaking glass)]

tri′cĕps, a. & n. **1.** (Of muscle) three-headed. **2.** n. ~ muscle, esp. large muscle of back of arm. [L (TRI-+*caput -itis* head)]

trich′ī. See TRICHINOPOLI.

trichī′asis (-k-), n. Urinary disease in which hairlike filaments appear in urine; disease affecting breasts in child-bearing women; inversion of eyelashes; disease marked by matted state of hair. [LL, f. Gk *trikhiasis* (as foll., see -ASIS)]

trich′in̄a (-k-), n. (pl. ~*ae*). Hairlike worm parasitic in body of man, swine, rat, etc., usu. introduced into human body by use of imperfectly cooked pork, & causing often fatal disease. Hence ~i′, ~i′ASIS, ~izA′TION, ~oS′IS, nn., ~IZE(3) v.t., ~ōSED²(-sd), ~oT′IC, ~OUS, aa. [f. Gk *trikhinos* of hair (TRICHO-, -INE²)]

trichinŏp′oli, trich′i, n. Kind of Indian cheroot. [*Trichinopoli* in India]

trich′o(o- -(-k-) in comb. = Gk *thrix trikhos* hair, as: ~*ŏ′genous* a., (preparation) promoting growth of hair; ~*ŏ′logy*, study of the hair; ~*opath′ic* a., ~*ŏp′athy* n., (treatment) of diseases of hair.

trichōs′is (-k-), n. Any disease of hair. [as TRICHO-+-OSIS]

trichŏt′om‖ȳ (-k-), n. Division into three, esp. of human nature into body, soul, & spirit. Hence ~OUS a. [f. Gk *trikha* threefold (*treis three*)+-TOMY]

trick, n., v. & v.t. & i. **1.** Fraudulent device or stratagem, as *I suspect some* ~, *of the* TRADE, *shall not serve me that* ~ *twice*. **2.** Feat of skill or dexterity, knack, precise mode of doing or dealing with a thing, as *conjurer's* ~*s*, *do the* ~ (sl., = accomplish one's purpose), *my dog knows no* ~*s*, *I know a* ~ *worth two of that* (better expedient), *shall soon get or learn the* ~ *of it* (best way of doing or handling it), (attrib.) ~ *cyclist* etc. **3.** Peculiar or characteristic practice, habit, mannerism, as *has a* ~ *of repeating himself, these are private-school* ~*s, style is disfigured by* ~*s, must cure himself of the* ~ *of archaism*. **4.** Mischievous or foolish or discreditable act, practical joke, prank, as *is always playing mad* ~*s, a dirty or shabby or dog's* ~ *to play on anyone*. **5.** (cards). The cards played in a round, as *take up the* ~; such round, point gained as result of this, as *won, lost, saved, the* ~; *the* ODD ~. **6.** (naut.). Man's turn at helm, usu. two hours. **7.** ~-*line*, cord used in making changes in pantomime; ~ *scene* (made without dropping curtain); ~ *wig* (of which hair can be made to stand on end). **8.** vb. Deceive by ~, cheat, (person, often *out of* thing, *into doing*, etc.); (of thing) foil, baffle, disappoint the calculations of, take by surprise; play ~*s*; (usu. ~ *out or up*) dress, decorate, deck. Hence ~ER¹, ~ERY (4, 5), ~′STER, nn., ~′ISH (now rare, ~TRICKY) a. [vb f. n., f. OF *trique=triche* (*trichier* see TREACHEROUS)]

trick′le, v.i. & t., & n. **1.** (Of liquid) flow in drops or in small stream, as *tears* ~*ed down her cheeks, water* ~*es through crevice*, (fig.) *the information* ~*ed* (came gradually) *out*; cause (liquid) to do this, pour out in drops; ~*e charger*, accumulator charger that works at a low rate. **2.** n. ~*ing* stream. Hence ~EF¹ n., ~Y² a. [ME *triklen*, etym. dub.]

trick′sў, a. Playful, frolicsome; quaint. [perh. f. *tricks* pl.+-Y², but cf. *tipsy, cocksy, Betsy*]

trick-tăck, tick-tăck, n. Complicated form of backgammon. [f. F *trictrac*, prob. imit. of sound]

trick′ȳ, a. Crafty, prone to deceit; skilful at evasion, resourceful, adroit; (of task etc.) requiring adroitness, full of pitfalls, ticklish. Hence ~ily² adv., ~iness n. [TRICK+-Y²]

triclin′ium, n. (Rom. Ant.; pl. -*ia*). Dining-table with conches along three sides, room containing this. [L, f. Gk TRI(*klinion* f. *klinē* couch)]

For other words in *tri-* see TRI-.

tric'oline, n. Fine cotton poplin resembling silk. [P]

tri'colour, -or, (-ŭler), a. & n. 1. (Also ~ed² a.) of three colours. 2. n. Flag of three colours in about equal proportions, esp. French national standard of blue, white, & red, adopted during Revolution. [f. F TRI(colore f. L as COLOUR)]

tricot (trēk'ō), n. Hand-knitted woollen fabric, imitation of this; kind of ribbed cloth; ~-stitch, kind of crochet stitch. [F, = knitting]

tri'cycle, n., & v.i. (Ride on) three-wheeled cycle. Hence ~IST(1) n. [vb f. n.] F(TRI-)]

trid'ent, n. Three-pronged implement e.g. fish-spear; such spear or sceptre as attribute of Poseidon or Neptune. [f. L TRI(dens -ntis tooth)]

Triden'tine, a. & n. 1. Of the Council of Trent (1545-63) esp. as basis of Roman Catholic doctrine & practice, as ~ theology. 2. n. Roman Catholic. [f. med. L Tridentum Trent +-INE¹]

triduo (trēd'ōō), **trid'uum,** n. (R.-C. Ch.). Three days' service of prayer in preparation for saint's day or for obtaining saint's intercession. [(-o It.) f. L TRI(duum f. dies day) space of three days]

trien'nial, a. & n. 1. Lasting, happening or done every, three years, as ~ plants, parliaments; repealed 1716). 2. n. ~ plant; mass performed daily for three years for soul of dead person; every third anniversary of event. Hence ~LY² adv. [f. L TRI(ennium f. annus year) space of three years +-AL]

tri'er, n. In senses of TRY, esp. (also trior) person appointed to decide whether challenge to juror is well founded. [-ER¹]

tri'erarch (-k), n. (Gk Ant.). Commander of trireme; wealthy person compelled to build & equip trireme at his own expense. Hence ~AL (-k-) a. [f. L f. Gk triērarchos f. triērēs trireme +archō rule]

tri'erarchy (-k-), n. Office, duty, of trierarch; (Athenian formation of fleet at expense of) the trierarchs. [f. Gk triērarchia (prec., -Y¹)]

trifid, a. (bot., zool.). Partly or wholly divided into three, three-cleft. [f. L TRI(fidus f. root of findere cleave)]

trifle, n., & v.i. & t. 1. Thing, fact, circumstance, of slight value or importance, as urges time on us, the merest ~ puts him out, (iron.) shall probably break our necks, but that is a ~; small amount esp. of money, as spare a ~ for the porter. (adv.) seems a~ (rather) angry; confection of whipped cream or white of eggs, with pastry etc. soaked in wine, fruit, almonds, etc.; common pewter; ~-ring. 2. vb. Talk or act frivolously; ~ with, treat (person, thing, matter) with flippancy or derision, refuse to take seriously, (also) occupy oneself carelessly with, toy with, (novel, cigarette, etc.); throw or fool away (time, energies, money, etc. on object); (part.) a trifling error, correction, circumstance, etc. (unimportant). Hence **tri'fler¹** n., **tri'fling¹** a. [vb f. n.] ME & OF truffle mockery, var. of trufle jest, etym. dub.]

trifo'rium, n. (pl. -ia). Gallery, usu. in form of arcade, above arches of nave & choir (& transepts) of church. [med. L, fores door, being applied f. 12th to 18th c. only to Canterbury, where the openings are not triple]

trig¹, a., & n. (-gg-), & n. 1. Trim, spruce, smart. 2. v.t. Smarten, deck, (often up, out); || check, stop, (wheel) with skid, stone, etc.; prop up. 3. n. Obstacle etc. used. [cf. ON tryggja vb (tryggr firm)]

trig², n. school abbr. of trigonometry.

trig'amous (-g-), a. Thrice married or having three wives or husbands at once, whence or cogn. ~ISM, ~Y¹, nn.; (Bot.) having male, female, & hermaphrodite flowers in same head. [f. Gk TRI(gamos -married) +-OUS]

trigg'er (-g-), n. Device for releasing spring or catch & so setting mechanism in action, esp. projecting tongue in firearm that liberates hammer of lock; HAIR ~. Hence (-)~ED²(-gerd) a. [earlier tricker f. Du. trekker (trekken pull, cf. TREK)]

trig'lyph, n. Each of the grooved tablets alternating with metopes in Doric frieze. Hence ~AL, **trigly'phic(AL)** aa. [f. L f. Gk TRI(glŭphos f. glŭphō carve)]

trig'on, n. (Astrol.) each of four groups (watery, earthy, airy, fiery, ~) of three signs of zodiac; triangular instrument used in dialling; =TRINE; (Gk Ant.) game at ball for three persons, (also trigon'on) triangular lyre or harp; (Math.) triangle, whence **trigo'nal** a. [f. L f. Gk TRI(gōnia angle)]

trigon'al, a. (Math.) triangular; (Bot., Zool.) triangular in cross-section, as ~al stem, antennae. Hence or cogn. ~ally adv., ~OUS a. [-AL]

trigonom'eter, n. Instrument for solution of plane right-angled triangles by inspection. [TRIGON +-o- +-METER]

trigonom'etry, n. Branch of mathematics dealing primarily with relations of sides & angles of a triangle, much used in astronomy, surveying, & navigation. Hence ~omet'ric(AL) aa., ~omet'rically² adv. [TRIGON +-o- +-METRY]

trike, n. & v.i. (colloq.). =TRICYCLE. [abbr.]

tril'by¹, n. || ~ (hat), soft felt kind (colloq.); (pl., sl.) feet. [f. G. du Maurier's novel T~ (1894)]

trill, v.i. & t. & n. 1.(Of person or thing) give forth sound with tremulous vibration, as ~ing laughter; sing (b. & i.) in quavering manner, esp. (Mus.) with shake.

2. n. Quavering sound, esp. (Mus.) quick alternation of two notes a (semi)tone apart, shake; consonant pronounced with ~ing sound, e.g. r. [(n. f. vb) f. It. trillare imit.]

trill'ing, n. Compound crystal of three individuals; each of three children born at a birth. [f. L tres three +-LING¹]

trill'ion (-lyon), n. & a. ‖ A million million million; *(after F) a million million. Hence ~TH² &a. & n. [f. TRI- on MILLION, cf. BILLION]

tril'ogў, n. (Gk Ant.) set of three tragedies to be performed in immediate succession; set of three literary compositions, speeches, etc., each complete in itself but with common theme. [f. Gk TRI(logia -LOGY]

trim, a., v.t. & i. (-mm-), & n. **1.** In good order, well arranged or equipped, neat, spruce, whence ~LY² adv., ~NESS n. **2.** vb. Set in good order, make neat or tidy, remove irregular or superfluous or unsightly parts from, (lamp or strictly its wick, hedge, beard, etc.); remove (such parts, often off, away) by clipping, pruning, planing, etc.; make (person, oneself, often up) neat in dress & appearance; ornament (dress etc. with ribbon, lace, etc.); (of school of fish) ~ (move along close to the shore; (Naut.) adjust balance of (ship, boat) by distribution of cargo or passengers etc., arrange (yards, sails) to suit wind, as ~ BY¹ the head, stern; hold middle course in politics or opinion, attach oneself to neither of contesting parties, be a time-server; (colloq.) rebuke sharply, thrash, cheat out of money, worst in bargain etc.; (colloq.) person's jacket, flog him. **3.** n. State, degree, of adjustment or readiness or fitness, as found everything in perfect ~, am in no ~ (state of dress, health, etc.) for rough work, in fighting ~, (of ship, & fig.) ready for battle; good order (esp. Naut.), as in, out of ~; (Naut.) (relative position) of the masts. ((n. f. vb, OE trymian make firm, set in order) f. OE trum strong, cf. LG trim]

trim'eter, n. & a. (Verse) consisting of three measures (see DIMETER), esp. iambic ~, six-foot iambic line usual in ancient Greek dramatic dialogue. Hence trimēt'ric(AL) aa. [f. L f. Gk tri(metros f. metron measure)]

trimm'er, n. In vbl senses, esp.: one who trims articles of dress, as coat, hat, ~; person who stands neutral, time-server, (orig. of party following Marquis of Halifax 1680-90); kinds of instrument for clipping etc.; piece of timber framed across opening (e.g. for hearth) to carry ends of the truncated joists. [-ER¹]

trimm'ing, n. In vbl senses, esp.: ornamentation of lace etc. on dress etc.; (pl,

colloq.) leg of mutton etc. & ~s (accessories). [-ING¹]

trine, a. & n. **1.** Threefold, triple, made up of three parts, whence trīn'AL, trīn'ARY¹, aa.; ~ immersion or immersion, thrice sprinkling in baptism; (Astrol.) of a ~, in ~. **2.** n. (astrol.) Aspect of two planets 120° apart; in ~, so related (to). [f. F trīn, brīne f. L trīnus three-fold (tres three)]

tringle (tring'gl), n. Curtain-rod; supporting rod for canopy of bedstead; (Archit.,) small square moulding or ornament; (Gunnery) bar on traversing-platform to check recoil. [F, of unkn. orig.]

trinitrotōl'üene, -ūōl, n. A high explosive (abbr. T.N.T. or TNT). [f. TRI-, NITRO-, TOLU-, -ENE, -OL]

trin'ity, n. **1.** Being three; group of three; the T~, union of three persons (Father, Son, Holy Spirit) in one Godhead, doctrine of this, whence Trinitar'ian(ISM nn.; symbolical representation of the T~ in art. **2.** ~ ring, kinds of ancient bronze ring with three bosses etc. found in Ireland; T~ Sunday, next after Whitsunday; ‖T~ Brethren, members of T~ House, association concerned with licensing of pilots, erection of lighthouses, etc.; ‖T~ term. [f. OF trinite f. LL trinitatem (as TRINE, see -TY)]

trink'et, n. Trifling ornament, jewel, etc., worn on the person; small fancy article. Hence ~RY(1, 5) n. [f. 16th c., etym. dub.; cf. obs. trenket (TRENCH) small knife, & trick]

tri'o (-ēō, -iō), n. (pl. ~s), **1.** (mus.). Composition for three vocal or instrumental parts; set of three performers; second division of minuet, march, etc., orig. performed by ~ of instruments; piano ~, for violin, violoncello, & piano. **2.** Set of three persons etc.; three aces, kings, queens, or knaves, in piquet. [F f. It., f. L tres three]

tri'ōde, a. (Of wireless valves) having three electrodes. [TRI- + Gk hodos way]

tri'ōle (trē-), n. (mus.). = TRIPLET. [dim. of TRIO]

tri'olet (or trē-), n. Poem of 8 (usu. 8-syllabled) lines with rhymes as shown, first line recurring as fourth & seventh & second as eighth (cat dog bat cat fat hog cat dog). [F (-LET)]

Triōn'ēs (-z), n. pl. = CHARLES'S WAIN. [L, = plough-oxen]

trior. See TRIER.

trip, v.i. & t. (-pp-), & n. **1.** Walk or dance with quick light tread, (fig., of rhythm etc.) run lightly, whence ~p'ingLY² adv. **2.** (arch.) Take journey or excursion, whence (in mod. use) ‖~p'ER¹ n., person who goes on a ~ esp. for a day to seaside or other resort. **3.** Make false step, stumble, (often over obstacle); make mistake, commit inconsistency or inac-

For other words in tri- see TRI-.

curacy or moral delinquency, as *caught him ~ping in his dates, all apt to ~*; (of person or obstacle) cause (person) to stumble by entangling his feet (often *up*); detect (person) in blunder (often *up*). 4. (Naut.) arresting his feet (often *up*); detect (person) in blunder (often *up*). 4. (Naut.) loose (anchor) from bottom by means of cable, turn (yard etc.) from horizontal to vertical position; release (part of machine) suddenly by withdrawing catch etc. 5. n. Journey, voyage, excursion, esp. for pleasure, as *round ~* (to a place & back), *cheap~s to the Riviera*. 6. Nimble step. 7. Stumble (lit. & fig.); ~ping or being ~ped up. 8. The fish caught during a voyage. 9. ~*hammer*, kind of TILT-hammer. [(n. f., + vb.) f. OF *treper*, *trip(p)er*, f. Teut., cf. M Du. *trippen*, G *treppe* step]

tripar′tie (or trip²), a. Divided into 3 parts; (Bot., of leaf) divided into 3 segments almost to the base; ~ *indenture* (with 3 corresponding parts or copies); made, existing, between 3 parties, as ~ *treaty*. Hence ~LY² adv., **tripartī′tion** n. [f. L *tripartītus* p.p. of *partīrī* divide f. *pars ~tis* part)]

tri′plane, n. Aeroplane with three planes. [TRI-, PLANE³]

tri′ple, a., & v.t. & i. 1. Threefold, of three parts (often in comb., as ~*-headed*, ~*-nerved*); T~ *Alliance*, (1) between England, Sweden, & Netherlands, in 1668 against Louis XIV, (2) between France, Great Britain, & Netherlands, in 1717 chiefly against Spain, (3) between Germany, Austria, & Italy, in 1882–3 against Russia & France; ~ *crown*, pope's tiara; T~ ENTENTE (Mus.) ~ *time* (of 3 or 9 beats in bar). 2. vb. Increase (t. & i.) threefold; be three times as great or many as; alter (engine) to ~ expansion. [vb f. adj.) F, f. L *triplus* f. Gk *triplous*]

trip′let, n. Set of three things; 3 verses rhyming together; (Mus.) 3 notes performed in the time of two; (colloq.) each of 3 children born at a birth; (Naut.) 3 links of chain between cable & anchorring. [f. prec. +-ET¹]

trip′lex, a. & n. 1. Triple, threefold; ~ *glass* (P; also ~) unsplinterable glass used in motor-cars etc., consisting of a transparent sheet of plastic material between two sheets of glass. 2. n. (mus.) Triple time; composition in three parts. [L TRI(*plex ~plicis* f. *plicare* fold) three-fold]

trip′licate¹, a. & n. 1. Threefold, esp. of which three copies are made, as ~ *certificate*; ~ *ratio* of two numbers, ratio of their cubes. 2. n. Each of a set of 3 copies or corresponding parts, state of being ~, as *document drawn up in ~*. [f. L *triplicāre* (TRIPLEX), -ATE²]

trip′licāte², v.t. Treble, make triplicate. So ~A′TION, ~ATURE, nn. [-ATE²]

trip′lice (-chā), n. =TRIPLE alliance (3). [It., =triple]

trip′licity, n. State of being triple. [f. L L *triplicitātem* (TRIPLEX, -ITY)]

trip′od, n. Stool, table, utensil, resting on three feet or legs, whence ~AL a.; three-legged stand for supporting camera etc.; (Gk Ant.) bronze altar at Delphi on which priestess sat to utter oracles, imitation of this esp. as prize in Pythian games etc. [f. L *tripus* f. Gk *tri(pous podos* foot)]

trip′oli, n. =ROTTEN-stone. [f. T~ in Africa]

∥ **trip′os**, n. (Camb. univ.). (List of successful candidates in) honours examination. [as TRIPOD, w. ref. to stool on which B.A. sat to deliver satirical speech at commencement]

trip′per, n. See TRIP.

trip′tych (-ik), n. Picture or carving on three panels side by side, set of three associated pictures so placed or set of writing-tablets hinged or tied together. [f. Gk TRI(*ptuchon* f. *ptussō* fold) three-layered, neut. adj. as n.]

∥ **tripu′diāte**, v.i. (pedant.). Dance for joy; dance in triumph or contempt *upon*. [f. L *tripudiāre* (*tripudium* a dance, perh. f. *pes pedis* foot), -ATE³]

triquē′tra, n. (pl. *-ae*). Symmetrical ornament of TRI(*quetrus* unexpl.) three-cornered. [L, fem.]

triquē′trous, a. Three-cornered, esp. having 3 acute angles. [f. L as prec. +-OUS]

trirē′me, n. Ancient esp. Greek warship with three banks of oars. [f. L TRI(*rēmis* oar)]

Trisa′gion (-g-), n. Hymn esp. in Oriental Churches with triple invocation of God as holy. [f. Gk *trisagios* (*tris* thrice + *hagios* holy)]

trisē′ct, v.t. Divide (line, angle, etc.) into three esp. equal parts. Hence **trisē′ction** n. [f. TRI-+L *secāre sect-* cut]

trist′ful, a. (arch.). Sad. [obs. *trist* f. OF *triste* f. L *tristis* sad +-FUL]

trisy′llable, n. Word of three syllables. **trisylla′bic** a., **trisylla′bically** adv. [f. n. f. TRI-+SYLLABLE; adj. f. L f. Gk TRI(*sullabos*, see SYLLABLE) adj.]

tri′tagōnist (or *-agō*-), n. Third actor in Greek play (cf. DEUTERAGONIST). [f. Gk *tritagōnistēs* (*tritos* third + *agōnistēs* actor, see AGONISTIC)]

trite, a. (Of expression, sentiment, quotation, etc.) commonplace, hackneyed, worn out. Hence ~LY² adv., ~NESS n. [f. L *terere trit-* rub]

tri·the|**ism**, n. Doctrine that there are (esp. that Father, Son, & Holy Spirit are) 3 Gods. So ~IST n., ~**is'tic**(AL) aa. [TRI-]

Tri'ton, n. (Gk Myth.) son of Poseidon & Amphitrite, each of a race of minor sea-gods usu. represented as men with fishes' tails & occas. with forefeet of horse & carrying shell-trumpet; ~ *among the* MINNOWS; (*t*~) kinds of gastropod & salamander. [L, f. Gk *Tritōn*]

tri'tu|**rate**, v.t. Grind to fine powder; grind with molar teeth, masticate thoroughly. Hence or cogn. ~RABLE a., ~A'TION, ~**ā'tor²**(1, 2), nn. [f. LL *triturare* f. L *tritura* rubbing, as TRITE, see -URE & -ATE³]

tri'umph, n., & v.i. **1.** (Rom. Ant.) procession & ceremony in honour of victory & victorious general; state of being victorious or successful; signal success, great achievement, thing that constitutes this, as *returned home in* ~, *has achieved great* ~*s*, *the* ~*s of science, that is a* ~ *of ugliness*; joy at success, manifestation of this, exultation, as *great was his* ~ *on hearing* etc., *could detect no* ~ *in his eye*. **2.** v.i. (Rom. Ant.) enjoy a ~; gain victory, be successful, prevail, (*over* enemy, opposition, etc.); exult (*over* fallen enemy etc., or abs.), whence ~**ing**LY² adv. [vrb f. OF *triumpher*) f. OF *triumphe* f. L *triumphus* cf. Gk *thriambos* hymn to Bacchus]

tri'umph'al, a. Of, used in, celebrating, a triumph, as ~*car*, *progress*, *hymn*; ~*crown* (Roman general's laurel wreath); ~*arch* (built to commemorate victory etc.). [f. F *triomphal* f. L *triumphalis* (as prec., see -AL)]

tri'umph'ant, a. Victorious, successful; (of person), speech, voice, etc.), exulting. Hence ~LY² adv. [f. F *triomphant* (as TRIUMPH Vb, see -ANT]

tri'umvir, n. (pl. ~s, ~ī). (Rom. Ant.) each of three men united in office; (Rom. Hist.) each member of first or second triumvirate. Hence ~AL a. [L (*trium*, gen. *of tres* three, +*vir* man)]

tri'umvirate, n. Office of a triumvir; set of triumviri; (Rom. Hist.) *first* ~, (coalition 60 B.C. between) Pompey, Julius Caesar, & Crassus, *second* ~, (that in 43 B.C. between) Mark Antony, Octavian, & Lepidus; party, set, of three. [f. L *triumviratus* (prec., see -ATE¹)]

tri'une, a. Three in one, as ~ *Godhead*. Hence **triun'**ITY n. [f. TRI- +L *unus* one]

triv'et, n. Iron tripod for holding cooking-vessels by the fire; iron bracket designed to hook on to bars of grate for similar purposes; *right* (orig. = steady) *as a* ~, (colloq.) all right (adj. & adv.), in good

health or position or circumstances; ~ *table* (with three feet). [earlier also *tre-*; f. L TRI(*pes pedis* foot) three-footed]

triv'ial, a. Of small value or importance, trifling, as ~ *matters*, *a* ~ *loss* (of something ~), *raised* ~ *objections* (of person) trifling, shallow, lacking ability or moral qualities; commonplace, humdrum, as *the* ~ *round* (of daily life etc.); (Bot., Zool., of name) popular, not scientific, also, specific opp. to *generic*. Hence or cogn. ~ISM(2, 4), **triviā'l**|ITY, ~NESS, nn., ~IZE(3) v.t., ~LY² adv. [f. L *trivialis* commonplace f. TRI(*vium* f. *via* road) cross-road, see -AL]

triv'ium, n. (hist.). (In medieval schools) the first three liberal arts, grammar, rhetoric, & logic. [see prec.]

-**trix**, suf. forming fem. agent nn. corresp. to masc. nn. in -TOR, f. L *-trix -tricis*, chiefly in legal terms (*executrix*, *administratrix*).

troat, v.i., & n. (Make) cry of rutting buck. [imit.]

troc'ar, n. (med.). Instrument used in dropsy etc. for withdrawing fluid from body. [F (*trois* three + *carre* side f. L *quadra* square)]

trocha'ic (-k-), a. & n. **1.** (Composed) of trochees, as ~ DIMETER, TETRAmeter. **2.** n. pl. ~ verse. [f. L f. Gk *trokhaikos* (as TROCHEE, see -IC)]

troch'al (-k-), a. (zool.). Wheel-shaped. [f. Gk *trokhos* wheel (*trekhō* run) +-AL]

trochan'ter (-k-), n. (anat., zool.). Each of several bony processes on upper part of thighbone; second joint of insect's leg. [F, f. Gk *trokhantēr* ball of hip-bone (*trekhō* run)]

troch'ee (-k-), n. Metrical foot ~◡. [f. L f. Gk *trokhaios* (*pous*) running foot (*trekhō* run)]

troch'il(us) (-k-), n. Kinds of small bird esp. (1) humming-bird, (2) bird mentioned by ancient writers as picking crocodile's teeth. [f. L f. Gk *trokhilos* (*trekhō* run)]

troch'i'le̱a (-k-), n. (anat.: pl.~*ae*). Pulley-like part or arrangement. Hence ~AR¹ (anat., bot.), ~ATE² (bot.), aa. [f. L *trochlea* pulley, cf. Gk *trokhilia*]

troch'oid (-k-), a. & n. **1.** (Anat.) rotating on its own axis; (of curve) generated by a point in the plane of one curve that rolls on another; (Conch.) top-shaped. **2.** n. ~ joint, ~ curve, kinds of gasteropod. Hence **trochoid'AL** (-k-) a. [f. L f. Gk *trokhoeidēs* wheel-like (TROCHAL, -OID)]

trochom'e̱ter (-k-), n. =HODOMETER, [as TROCHAL +-METER]

trod(den), See TREAD.

For other words in *tri-* see TRI-.

trŏg'lodȳte, n. Cave-dweller, esp. of pre-historic W. Europe (often attrib.); (fig.) hermit; kinds of wren & anthropoid ape. Hence or cogn. **trŏglodȳt'ĬC**(AL) aa., **~ĬSM**(2) n. [f. L (-ta) f. Gk *trōglē* cave+*duō* enter)]

trŏi'ka, n. (Vehicle with) team of three horses abreast. [Russ.]

trois-temps (see Ap.), a. & n. **~** (*waltz*), waltz in ordinary time (cf. DEUX-TEMPS). [F. = three-time]

Trōj'an, a. & n. (Inhabitant) of Troy; **~** *War* (between Greeks under Agamemnon & **~**s under Priam); (fig.) person who works or fights or endures courageously, esp. *like a ~*. [f. L *Trojānus* f. *Trōja* Troy; f. L f. Gk *Trōs* Trojan, see -AN]

trŏll', v.t. & i., & n. 1. Sing out in care-free spirit; fish for, fish in (water), fish with rod & line & dead bait or with spoon-bait (**~***ing-spoon*) drawn along behind boat; (arch.) cause (bottle) to circulate at table etc. 2. n. Song sung in successive parts, catch; reel of fishing-rod; **~***ing-spoon*. [(n. f.vb) earlier sense *roll*, f. OF *troller*, perh. f. G *trollen* roll, troll]

trŏll', n. Supernatural being, giant or (later) friendly but mischievous dwarf, in Scandinavian mythology. [ON & Sw., cf. Da. *trold*]

trŏll'ey (pl. ~s), **trŏll'ȳ** n. Kind of truck that can be tilted; || costermonger's cart pushed by hand or drawn by donkey; || low truck worked by hand-lever along the rails for conveying railwaymen to work; (also ~*-table*) small table usu. on castors for use in serving food; wheel used for collecting current in electric street-railway (~*-pole*, with ~ at upper end for this purpose); (also ~*-lace*) lace of which the pattern is outlined with thick thread; || ~*-bus*, trackless electric bus running on a highway; ~*-car*, electric street-car. [prob. f. TROLL[1]]

trŏll'op, n. Slatternly woman; prostitute. Hence ~ISH[1], ~Y[2], aa. [perh. f. TROLL[1]]

trŏm'ba, n. (mus.). Trumpet. [It.]

trŏm'bōn/e, n. Large musical instrument of trumpet family with sliding tube or with valves. Hence ~ĬST(3) n. [It. (as prec., see -ONE)]

trŏmm'el, n. (mining). Revolving cylin-drical sieve for cleaning ore. [G.=drum]

trŏmŏm'ēter, n. Instrument for measur-ing very slight earthquake shocks. [f. Gk *tromos* trembling (*tremō* tremble)+ -METER]

trŏmpe, n. Apparatus for producing blast in furnace. [F. = TRUMP[1]]

trŏop, n. & v.i. & t. 1. Assembled com-pany, assemblage of persons or animals, as a **~** of *school-children*, of *antelopes*, *surrounded by* **~**s *of friends*; (pl.) soldiers, as *lost a third of his* **~**s, HOUSEHOLD **~**s; cavalry unit usu. consisting of cavalry unit usu. consisting of with two lieutenants & captain (cf. COM-PANY), command of this (*get one's ~*, be promoted captain); unit of artillery & armoured formation; particular call of drum as signal for marching; company of performers, troupe; **~***-carrier*, large air-craft for transporting **~**s; **~***-horse*, cavalry horse; **~***-ship*, transport. 2. vb. Assem-ble, flock together, (often *up, together*, etc.); move along in a **~** (*along, in, out*, etc.); (w. pl. subject) walk hurriedly off; (of troops, ceremony) Into **~**s; **~***-ing the colour*, ceremony at public mounting of garrison guards. [(vb f. n.) f. F *troupe*, OF *trope*, f. LL *troppus* flock, etym. dub.]

trŏop'er, n. Horse-soldier, private soldier in cavalry; *swear like a ~* (much); cavalry horse; troopship. [-ER[1]]

trōpe, n. Figurative (e.g. metaphorical, ironical) use of a word; (Eccl.) phrase or verse introduced as embellishment into some part of the mass. [F. f. L f. Gk *tropos* turn, way, trope, (*trepō* turn)]

trŏph'ic, a. Concerned with nutrition, as **~** *nerves*. [f. Gk *trophikos* (*trophē* nourish-ment f. *trephō* nourish +-ic)]

tropho- in comb. = Gk *trophē* food, as **~***-neuros'is*, defective nutrition due to nervous derangement.

trŏph'ȳ, n. (Gk Ant.) arms etc. of van-quished enemy set up on field of battle or elsewhere to commemorate victory; Ro-man memorial of victory in imitation of this but usu. permanent; anything, e.g. captured standard, kept as memorial of victory (lit. & fig.); prize; memento; ornamental group of symbolic or typical objects arranged on wall etc. Hence (-)~IED[2] (-id) a. [f. F *trophée* f. L f. Gk *tropaion* (*tropē* rout f. *trepō* turn)]

trŏp'ic, n. & a. 1. Parallel of latitude 23° 27' north (**~** *of Cancer*) or south (**~** *of Capricorn*) of the equator; *the* **~**s, region between these; each of the two corre-sponding circles on celestial sphere where sun appears to turn after reaching greatest declination; **~***-bird*, kinds of bird like tern seen usu. in the **~**s. 2. adj. = foll. exc. last sense. [f. L f. Gk *tropikos* (*tropē* turn, circle) f. *tropē* turning; see -IC]

trŏp'ical, a. Of, peculiar to, suggestive of, the tropics, as **~** *plants, diseases, heat, abscess* (of liver, induced by residence in hot climate); **~** *year* (between two succes-sive passages of sun through same equi-nox); (fig.) fervid, passionate; [f. TROPE] figurative]. Hence ~LY[2] adv. [-AL]

tropicopŏl'Ĭtan, a. & n. (Animal, plant) confined & common to the tropics. [f. TROPIC on *cosmopolitan*]

tropŏl'ŏgy, n. Figurative use of words; figurative interpretation esp. of the Scriptures, so **trŏp'īsm(2)** n. Hence **trŏpŏlŏ'gi-cal** a., **trŏpŏlŏ'gically** adv. [f. LL *tropologia* (TROPE, -LOGY)]

trŏp'opause (-z), n. Narrow layer between troposphere & stratosphere. [f. Gk *tropos* turn +PAUSE]

trŏp'osphēre, n. Layer of atmospheric air extending about seven miles upwards from the earth's surface, in which temperature falls with height (cf. STRATO-SPHERE). [f. Gk *tropos* turn + SPHERE]

trŏp̄p'ō, adv. (mus.). Too, as *andante* etc. *ma non-* ~ (but not too much so). [It.]

trŏt, v.i. & t. (-tt-), & n. **1**. (Of horses etc.) proceed at steady pace faster than walk lifting each diagonal pair of legs alternately with brief intervals during which body is unsupported; cause (horse etc.) to do this; (of person) run at moderate pace esp. with short strides (often *along* etc.); perform (distance) by ~ting; bring (person, horse, etc.) to specified condition by ~ting, as ~*led him off his legs, to death*; ~ *out*, cause (horse) to ~ to show his paces, (fig.) produce, introduce, (person, thing, superior information, subject) to excite admiration. **2**. n. Action, exercise, of ~ting, as *proceeded at a* ~, *went for a* ~; (fig.) brisk steady movement or occupation, as *kept him on the* ~ (*busy*); || toddling child. [f. OF *trot*(*er*), *trotter*; f. OF *trotter*, it. *trottare*]

trŏth, n. (arch.). Truth, esp. (*in*) ~, truly, upon my word; *plight* one's ~, pledge one's word esp. in betrothal. [OE *trēowth* TRUTH]

trŏt'ter, n. In vbl senses; also or esp.: horse of special breed noted for trotting; (pl.) animal's feet used as food, as *pigs', sheep's*, ~*s*; (joc.) human foot. [TROT, -ER[1]]

trŏubadour' (-ōo-, -oor), n. Lyric poet of a class originating in Provence (cf. TROU-VÈRE) in 11th c. [F, f. Pr. *trobador* f. *trobar*=F *trouver* find f. LL *tropare* make poetry (as TROPE) or f. L *turbare* (cf. CON-TRIVE), see -OR[2]]

trŏu'ble (trŭb-), v.t. & i., & n. **1**. Agitate, disturb, be disturbed or worried, as ~*d waters, don't let it* ~ *you, don't* ~ *about it, has been* ~*d about or with money matters* a. ~*d countenance*; afflict, as *am* ~*d with neuralgia, how long has it been troubling you?*; subject, be subjected, to inconvenience or exertion (chiefly in polite formulas), as *may I* ~ *you to shut the door?, to mind your own business?, will* ~ *you for* (to pass) *the mustard, sorry to* ~ *you, don't* ~ (*to explain etc., or abs.*), *why should I* ~ (*myself*) *to explain?* **2**. n. Vexation, affliction, as *has been through much* ~, *till this great* ~ *came upon them, life is full*

of *small* ~*s*; disease, as *liver, digestive, ~s*; inconvenience, unpleasant exertion, source of this, as *did it to spare you* ~, *shall not put you to any* ~ *in the matter, fear the child is a great* ~ *to you, will never take the* ~ *to write, is incapable of taking* ~, *an omelette is no* ~ (*to make*), *French beans are a great* ~ *to prepare*, (as polite formula) *no* ~ (*at all*); *ask* or *look for* ~ (sl.), meddle, be rash, etc.; *be in, get into*, ~, incur censure, punishment, etc.; (Mining) small fault. [f. OF *trouble*(r), *toubler*, ult. f. L *turba* crowd]

trou'blesome (trŭbls-), a. (Of person or thing) causing trouble, vexatious. Hence ~**LY[2]** adv., ~**NESS** n. [-SOME]

trou'blous (trŭb-), a. (arch.). Full of troubles, agitated, disturbed, as ~ *times*. [f. OF *troubleus* (TROUBLE, -OUS)]

trough (-ŏf, -awf, -ŭf), n. Long narrow open wooden or other receptacle for kneading water or food for sheep etc., kneading dough, washing ore, etc.; wooden or other channel for conveying liquid; ~ *of the sea*, hollow between two waves; ~ *of barometric depression*, line of greatest depression in area of moving barometric pressure. [OE, Du., ON, G, *trog*, cogn. w. TREE]

trounce, v.t. Beat severely, castigate, (lit. & fig.). Hence **troun'cing[1]** n. [cf. OF *troncer* cut back (as TRUNK]

troupe (-ōo-), n. Company of actors, acrobats, etc. Hence ~**ER[1]** n., member of a theatrical ~ *s*. [F, see TROOP]

trous-de-loup (trōo de loo'), n. pl. Small conical pits with stake in centre of each as defence against cavalry. [F, lit. wolf-holes]

trous'er (-z-), n. (Pl., also *pair of* ~s) two-legged outer garment reaching from waist to ankles; (vulg.) pair of ~s, as *here, again, is a smart & dressy* ~; ~-*button* (of certain sizes & materials); ~ or ~*s pocket* (esp. as holding one's money, or hands when idle); ~-*stretcher*, apparatus for stretching ~s to preserve shape; early 19th-c. woman's long frilled drawers reaching to ankles. Hence~**ED[2]** (-zerd) a., ~**ING[1](3)** n. [pl. form (cf. *tweezers*) of obs. *trouse* sing. (cf. TREWS) f. Ir. *triubhas* a Celtic garment of close breeches, occas. w. stockings attached]

trousseau (trōosō', trōō'sō), n. (pl. ~s, or ~ *x* pr. -z). Bride's outfit of clothes etc. [F, lit. bundle, OF *troussel* dim. as TRUSS]

trout, n. (pl. usu. same), & v.i. **1**. Kinds of freshwater fish esteemed as food & game; ~-*coloured*, (of white horse) speckled with black, bay, or sorrel. **2**. v.i. Fish for ~. Hence ~**LET**, ~**LING[1]**, nn., ~**Y[2]** a. [OE *truht* f. L *tructa* f. Gk *trōktēs* lit. gnawer (*trōgō* gnaw), a sea-fish]

trouvaille (trōovah'), n. Lucky find, windfall. [F]

trouvère (trōovar'), n. Epic poet of a class

trove. See TREASURE-.

trov'er, n. (law). Acquisition of personal property; common-law action to recover value of personal property wrongfully taken or detained. [OF, F *trouver* (TROU-BADOUR, -ER⁴)] originating in N. France (cf. TROUBADOUR).

‖ **trow¹** (-ō, -ow), v.t. (arch.). Think, believe; (added to question) *what ails him,* (I) ~ (I wonder)? [OE *triwian* (*triwa* faith), *tréowian* (*tréowe* faith)]

trow'el, n., & v.t. (-ll-). **1.** Mason's or bricklayer's flat-bladed tool for spreading mortar etc.; *lay it on with a ~,* (fig.) flatter grossly; gardener's scoop for lifting plants etc. **2.** v.t. Apply (plaster etc.) with ~. [vb f. n.] f. F *truelle* f. LL *truella* dim. of L *trua* ladle, cf. *trulla* spoon]

troy, n. (Also ~ *weight*) system of weights used for gold & silver (cf. AVOIRDUPOIS), as *weighs 3 lb. 5 oz. ~; pound contains 12 oz., 5760 grains.* [prob. f. *Troyes,* town in France]

tru'ant (-ōō-), n., a., & v.i. **1.** One who absents himself from place of work, esp. child who stays away from school without leave; *play ~,* stay away thus; ~-*school* (hist.), industrial school for ~ children. **2.** adj. (Of person, conduct, character, thoughts, etc.) shirking, idle, loitering, wandering. **3.** v.i. Play ~. Hence **tru'ANCY** n. [ME *truant* a. f. OF, prob. f. Celt. (W *truan,* Gael. *truaghan,* wretched)]

truce (-ōō-), n. (Agreement for) temporary cessation of hostilities (FLAG⁴ *of~*); respite from pain etc., rest from work etc. (*a ~ to ~,* arch., demand that — shall cease); ~ *of God* (hist.), suspension of private feuds esp. during certain church festivals etc. Hence ~'LESS a., **tru'CIAL** (-ōōshl) a., of or bound by a ~ (only in ref. to ~ *States,* 1835 between Britain & certain Sheikhs of Oman Peninsula, as in *trucial chiefs*). [ME *treuwes,* pl. of OE *tréow* compact, faith, see TRUE]

truck¹, v.i. & t., & n. **1.** Make an exchange, trade, bargain, (*with* person *for* thing); exchange (thing *for* another); hawk, (wares) about. **2.** n. Exchange, barter, traffic, (*have no ~ with,* avoid dealing with); small wares; *market garden produce; (colloq.) rubbish, (fig.) nonsense, as *shall stand no ~;* (also ~ *system, tommy*) practice of paying workmen in goods instead of money or in money on the understanding that they will buy provisions etc. of their employers, *T~ Acts* (of 1831 & 1870, providing for suppression of or inquiry into ~ system); ~ *shop* (conducted on ~ system). [f. F *troque(r)* étym. dub.]

truck², n., & v.t. **1.** Strong usu. four- or six wheeled vehicle for heavy goods; ~ open railway wagon; motor vehicle for transporting troops etc.; porter's two-, three-, or four-, wheeled barrow for luggage at railway station etc.; set of wheels in framework for supporting whole or part of railway-carriage etc.; (Naut.) wooden disk at top of mast with holes for halyards; (now rare) small tireless wheel; ~*bolster,* crossbeam on car-~ supporting one end. **2.** v.t. Convey on ~. Hence ~'AGE(3, 4) n. [f. L f. Gk *trokhos* wheel (*trekhō* run)]

truc'kle, v.i., & n. **1.** Submit obsequiously, cringe, (*do*), whence **truck'lER⁴** n. **2.** n. (Usu. ~-*bed*) low bed on wheels that may be wheeled under another, esp. as formerly used by servants etc. [(vb. earlier ~*sleep in ~-bed,* f. n.) f. TROCHILE]

truc'ulent (or -ōō-)a. Of or showing bellicose aggressive merciless temper. Hence ~'ly adv. f. cogn. ~ENCE, nn., ~ENCY, [f. L *truculentus* (*trux trucis* fierce, see -LENT)]

trudge, v.i. & t., & n. **1.** Walk esp. laboriously, perform (distance) thus. **2.** n. Such walk. [f. 16th c., etym. dub.]

trudg'en, n. ~ (*stroke*), swimming with alternate right & left over-arm strokes & ordinary leg action. [J. T~, person]

true (-ōō-), a., adv., & v.t. **1.** In accordance with fact or reality, not false or erroneous, as *his story is~, that is only too ~, is it~ that he refused?; his words have come ~* (been realized in fact); (as formula of concession) ~, *it would cost more.* **2.** In accordance with reason or correct principles or received standard, rightly so called, genuine, not spurious or hybrid or counterfeit or merely apparent, having all the attributes implied in the name, as ~ *judgement, frog is not a ~ reptile, is a ~ benefactor, the ~ heir,* ~*ribs* (complete, articulating with breast-bone, not floating), ~ HORIZON. **3.** Accurately conforming *to* (type etc.), ~ (of voice) in perfect tune. **5.** Loyal, constant, adhering faithfully (*to* one's word, friend, one-self, etc.; often ~ *as steel*). **6.** (Of wheel, post, beam, etc.) in correct position, balanced or upright or level. **7.** (arch.) Not given to lying, veracious; honest, as ~ *men.* **8.** ~ *bill,* bill of indictment endorsed by grand jury as being sustained by evidence; ~*blue* a. & n. (person) of uncompromising principles or loyalty; ~*born,* of genuine birth, truly such by birth, as a ~-*born Englishman;* ~*bred,* of genuine or good breed; ~-*hearted*(ness); ~*love,* person truly loved or loving, sweetheart, plant with four leaves arranged like ~-*love('s) knot* (kind of double knot with interlacing bows on each side); ~-*penny* (arch.), honest fellow. **9.** adv. Truly (rare exc. w. certain vbs, as *tell me, aim, breed,* ~). **10.** v.t. Bring (tool, wheel, frame, etc.) into exact position or form required. Hence ~NESS n. [f. OE *tréowe* (*tréow,* see TRUCE), cf. Du. *getrouwa,* G *treu,* ON *tryggr*]

truf'fle (or trōō-), n. Subterranean fungus used for seasoning dishes. Hence ~ED² [-ïd] a. [f. OF *trufle* prob. f. L *tubera* pl. of *tuber*]

‖ **trug**, n. Wooden milk-pan; shallow garden basket made of wood strips. [perh. var. of TROUGH]

tru'ism (-ōō-), n. A self-evident or indisputable truth; proposition that states nothing not already implied in one of its terms (e.g. *I don't like my tea too hot=I don't like it hotter than I like it*); hackneyed truth, platitude. [f. TRUE +-ISM]

trull, n. (arch.). Prostitute. [cf. G *trulle*, Swiss *trolle*]

tru'ly (-ōō-), adv. Sincerely, genuinely, as *am ~ grateful*, *a ~ alarming state of affairs, a ~ courageous act*; (as purely neutral formula for closing letter) *yours (very) ~ W. Jones*, (hence, joc.) *won't do for yours* ~ (me); (usu. parenthet., & now chiefly literary or arch.) really, indeed, as ~, *I should be puzzled to say*; faithfully, loyally, *as has served him* ~; accurately, truthfully, as *it has been* ~ *stated, is not ~ represented*. [OE *trēowlīce* (as TRUE, see -LY²)]

trumeau (trōōmō'), n. (archit.; pl. ~x). Piece of wall, pillar, between two openings, e.g. pillar dividing large doorway. [F]

trump¹, n. (arch., poet.). Trumpet, its sound, as *last ~, ~ of doom*. [f. F *trompe*, etym. dub.]

trump², n., & v.t. & i. 1. Each card of a suit temporarily ranking above others, as *a call for ~s* (conventional signal to partner to lead ~s); ~ *card*, card turned up to determine which suit shall be ~s, any card of this suit, (fig.) valuable resource; (colloq.) person of admirable courage, resource, generosity, etc., excellent fellow; *gnd person to his ~s*, (fig.) reduce him to his last resources; *turn up ~s* (colloq.), turn out better than was expected, (also) have a stroke of luck. 2. vb. Defeat (card) with a ~, play a ~ (also fig.); ~ *up*, fabricate, forge, (story, excuses, etc.). [f. F *triomphe* TRIUMPH, a game of cards]

trump'ery, n. & a. 1. Worthless finery; rubbish; nonsense. 2. adj. Showy but worthless, delusive, shallow, as ~ *furniture, arguments*. [f. F *tromperie* (*tromper* deceive, etym. dub., -ERY)]

trump'et, n., & v.t. & i. 1. Wind instrument of brass, the developed orchestral form having valves (occas. slides) increasing the sounding length of the tube & thus giving extra harmonic series, so making all notes instantaneously available; reed-stop in organ imitating this; trumpeter, esp. (hist.) one sent as envoy; EAR, SPEAKING, ~; ~-shaped thing e.g. kind of funnel; sound (as) of ~; *feast of ~s*, Jewish festival celebrating beginning of year; FLOURISH² of ~s; BLOW¹ one's own ~. 2. ~-*call*, call by sound of ~, (fig.) urgent summons to action; ~-*conch, -shell, sea-~*, kinds of gasteropod with turreted shell; ~-*flower, -leaf*, kinds of plant with ~-shaped flowers, leaves; ~ *major*, head trumpeter of cavalry regiment. 3. vb. Proclaim (as) by sound of ~ (usu. fig., = celebrate), blow ~, (of elephant etc.) make loud sound as of ~. [(vb f. n.) F *trompette* dim. as TRUMP¹]

trump'eter, n. 1. One who sounds a trumpet, esp. cavalry soldier giving signals with trumpet (*be one's own* ~, = BLOW¹ one's own *trumpet*). 2. Kind of domestic pigeon with peculiar coo, esp. birds making trumpetlike sound, esp. (also ~ *swan*) a large N.-Amer. swan.

trunc'al, a. Of the trunk of a body or tree. [f. L as TRUNK +-AL]

trunc'ate, v.t., & a. 1. Cut the top or end from (tree, body, cone, pyramid, fig. quoted passage etc.); (Cryst.) replace (edge) by plane. 2. adj. ~ated, (Bot., Zool., of leaf, feather, etc.) ending abruptly as if cut off at tip, whence ~ately² adv. So ~A'TION, ~ATURE (zool.), nn. [f. L *truncare* (TRUNK), -ATE² ³]

trun'cheon (-shn), n. ‖ Short, club or cudgel e.g. that carried by policeman; baton, staff of authority, esp. (Her.) that of Earl Marshal. [f. OF *tronchon* dim. as TRUNK]

trun'dle, n., & v.t. & i. 1. Small broad wheel, e.g. castor; small wheel with cylindrical teeth; low-wheeled truck; (also ~-*bed*)=TRUCKLE-*bed*; head of lower drum of double capstan. 2. vb. Roll (t. & i., of hoop, truck, etc.. often *along, down*, etc.); (sl.) bowl at cricket; hence ~ER¹ n. (esp., sl., bowler). [(vb f. n.) var. of OE (& MHG & MLG) *trendel* circle, cogn. w. TREND]

trunk, n., & v.t. 1. Main body of tree opp. to branches & roots; human or animal's body without head & limbs & tail; main part of any structure. 2. (Also ~-*line*) main line of railway or canal, telephone main line (esp. of lines from town to town). 3. Box with hinged lid, often covered with leather, for carrying clothes etc. on journey. 4. Kinds of shaft, conduit, or trough, usu. rectangular & of wood, for ventilation, separation of ores, etc. 5. Open cylinder used instead of piston-rod in some marine & other engines (~-*engines*). 6. Proboscis esp. of elephant. 7. pl. (Also ~ *hose*)16th–17th-c. breeches from waist to middle of thigh. 8. ‖ ~-*call*, telephone call on ~-line with special charges according to distance; ~ *drawers* (shop), drawers reaching only to knees; ~-*nail*, nail with large ornamental head for ~; ~-*coffin*, etc.; ~-*road*, main road. Hence ~'FUL n., ~'LESS a. 9. v.t. Separate (ore) by use of ~. [(vb f. n.) f. OF *tronc* f. L *truncus* a. & n., maimed, trunk]

trunnion, trun′ion (-yon), n. Cylin-drical projection on each side of cannon or mortar; hollow gudgeon supporting cylinder in steam-engine & giving passage to steam. Hence ~ED² (-yond) a. [f. F *trognon* core, stump, etym. dub.]

truss, v.t. & n. 1. Support (roof, bridge, etc.) with ~ (see below). 2. Fasten (wings of fowl etc.), before cooking, tie arms of (person) to his sides; (arch.) fasten, tighten, (gar-ment, usu. *up*), hang (criminal, usu. *up*), (of hawk etc.) seize (bird). 3. n. Support-ing structure or framework of roof, bridge, etc., e.g. pair of rafters with tie-beam, king-post, & struts (~-*bridge* etc., so strengthened). 4. Bundle of old (56 lb.) or new (60 lb.) hay or (36 lb.) straw. 5. Com-pact terminal flower-cluster. 6. Large corbel supporting monument etc. 7. (naut.) Heavy iron fitting securing lower yards to mast. 8. (surg.) Padded belt or encircling spring used in rupture. [f. F *trousse(r)* perh. f. L *tors-* p.p. st. of *torquēre* twist]

trust, n., & v.t. & i. 1. Firm belief in the honesty, veracity, justice, strength, etc., of a person or thing; as *our ~ is in God, I repose considerable ~ in him, put no ~ in* (naut.); confident expectation (*that*). 2. Per-son, thing, confided in, as *he is our sole ~.* 3. Reliance on truth of statement etc. without examination, as *takes everything on ~.* 4. Commercial credit, as *supplied with goods on ~.* 5. Responsibility arising from confidence reposed in one, as *am in a position of ~.* 6. (law.) Confidence reposed in person by making him nominal owner of property to be used for another's benefit; right of the latter to benefit by such property; property so held, legal relation between holder & property so held, as *have accepted a ~, the property is held merely a ~, is held in,* (attrib.) ~-*money*, merc.). 7. Thing, person, committed to one's care, resulting obligation, as *would not desert his ~, have fulfilled my ~.* 8. (com-merc.). Organized association of several companies for purpose of defeating com-petition etc., the shareholders in each transferring all or most of the stock to central committee & losing their voting power while remaining entitled to profits. 9. BRAINS T~; ~-*deed*, deed by debtor conveying property to trustee for pay-ment of his debts, deed conveying pro-perty to creditor to sell & pay himself & restore the residue, any instrument of conveyance that creates a ~. 10. vb. Place—*In*, believe in, rely on the character or behaviour of, as *have never ~ed him, if we may ~ this account, do not ~ him with* (let him use) *your typewriter, cat cannot be ~ed with* (will steal) *milk*, whence ~ *him with untold gold*, whence ~ingly² adv., ~ingness n. 11. Consign (thing to person etc.), place or leave (thing *with* person etc., *in* place etc.), without misgiving. 12. Allow credit to (customer *for* goods). 13. Entertain an earnest or (rarely) confident hope, as *I ~ he is not hurt(?), I ~ to hear better news.* 14. Place reliance *in*; ~ *to*, place (esp. undue) reliance on, as *we must ~ to meeting someone who knows, does not do to ~ to memory for these things,* whence ~, trusten vb. [f. ON *treost* n. (*treustr* strong), *treysta* vb. (cf. G *trösten* to comfort)]

trustee′, n. Person who holds property in trust for another (|| *the Public T~*, State official charged, since 1908, with executing wills & trusts when invited); (pop.) each of a body of men, often elective, managing affairs of college etc. Hence ~SHIP n.

trust′ful, a. Full of trust, confiding. Hence ~LY² adv., ~NESS n. [-FUL]

trust′worthy (-erdhi), a. Worthy of trust, reliable. Hence ~iNESS n.

trust′y, a. & n. 1. (Chiefly arch.) trust-worthy, as ~*y steed, sword, servant*, whence ~LY² adv., ~iNESS n. 2. n. Well-behaved & privileged convict. [-Y²]

truth (-ōō-), n. (pl. pr. -dhz). Quality, state, of being true or accurate or honest or sincere or loyal or accurately shaped or adjusted, as *the ~ of the rumour is doubted, there is ~ in what he says, may depend on his ~, which is out of ~; what is true*, as *have told you the* (whole) *~, the ~ is that I forgot, am a lover of ~* (or T~ personified), *fundamental ~s, home ~s* (unpalatable facts about oneself), GOD's *~*, GOSPEL *~*; *in ~* (literary), *of a ~* (arch.), truly, really; *to tell the ~, ~ to tell*, formulas introduc-ing confession (as TRUE, see -TH²)]

truth′ful (-ōōth-), a. Habitually speaking truth, veracious (of tale etc.), true. Hence ~LY² adv., ~NESS n. [-FUL]

truth′less (-ōōth-), a. (Of statement) false; (of person) faithless, not adhering to promise etc. Hence ~NESS n. [-LESS]

try, v.t. & i., & n. 1. Test (quality), test the qualities of (person, thing) by experi-ment, subject (person etc.) to suffering or hard treatment (as if) for this purpose (whence ~ING² a., ~ingly² adv.), as *~ (the effect of) soap & water, ~ (buy) our ginger ale, did you ever ~ quinine* (as cure) *for it?, (strength of) rope must be tried before it is used, each machine is tried before it leaves the shops, ~ your hand (skill) at, this will ~ his courage, patience has been sorely tried, should not ~ your eyes with that small print.* 2. Make experi-ment in order to find out, as *~ how far you can throw, let us ~ which takes longest, whether it will break*; ~ CONCLUSIONS, a FALL². 3. Investigate (case, issue) judici-ally, subject (person) to trial (*for* murder etc., also *for his life*). 4. Settle (question, disputed point) by examination or experi-ment. 5. Attempt to achieve or perform, as *tried a jump & fell, better ~ something*

easier; attempt, endeavour, (to do or abs.; colloq. often & do, seldom after past tense), as *do ~ to* (or &) *attend, must ~ to* (or &) *get it finished tonight, if at first you don't succeed ~, ~, ~ again, no use ~ing to persuade him, don't ~ to* (rarely &) *palliate it, have often tried to mend it.* 6. (Also *~ up*) dress (roughly-planed board) with *~ing*-plane to give fine surface. 7. (Also *~ out*) purify (metal, fat, oil) by melting or boiling. 8. *~ back*, =HARK (intr.) *back*, lit. & fig. *~ for*, aim at (a calmer tone etc.), apply or compete for (appointment etc.); *~ on*, put (clothes etc.) on to test fit, begin (*it*, one's *games, tricks*, etc., often *with* person) experimentally to see how much will be tolerated, as *no use ~ing it on with me*; *~on* n. (colloq.), an attempt to deceive; *~out* n., experimental trial, test of popularity etc. (*he gave the play a ~-out at Brighton*). 9. *~'sail* (-sl), small fore-&-aft sail set with gaff in heavy weather on mainmast or foremast or supplementary mast instead of mainsail or foresail [f. obs. naut. sense of vb.; = lie to]; *~(ing)-square*, carpenter's square usu. with one wooden & one metal limb: *~-works*, apparatus for *~ing* blubber. 10. n. Attempt (colloq.), as *have* (*make*) *a ~ at it, for it, to catch it*; (Rugby footb.) right to carry ball in front of goal & *~ to kick* goal. [n. f. vb f. OF *trier* etym. dub.]

tryp'anosŏme, n. Kinds of blood-parasite some of which cause sleeping-sickness & other diseases. [f. Gk *trupanon* auger, *sōma* body]

tryp'sin, n. Chief digestive ferment of the pancreatic juice. [f. Gk *tripsis* friction (because first obtained by rubbing down the pancreas with glycerin)+-IN]

tryst, n., & v.t. & i. (arch.). 1. Appointed meeting, appointment, as *keep, break, ~*. 2. vb. Engage to meet (person), appoint (time, place) for meeting; make a *~*. [f. OF *trist(r)e* station to watch in hunting, prob. of Scand. orig. cogn. w. TRUST]

tsar etc. Usu. modern form of CZAR etc.

tset'sĕ, n. African fly whose bite is often fatal to horses, cattle, dogs, etc. [native]

tuan (tŏŏahn'), n. Lord, master (title of respect given by Malayans to Europeans). [Malay *tuan, tuwan*]

tub, n., & v.t. & i.(-bb-). 1. Open wooden usu. round vessel of staves held together by hoops used for washing (*wash-~*) or holding butter, liquids, etc. (*let every ~ stand on its own bottom*, everyone look to himself); varying measure of capacity for butter, corn, tea, etc. 2. Sponge-bath, bath taken in this, as *jumped into his ~, seldom has a ~, a cold ~ would do him good*. 3. (Mining) kinds of bucket or box for conveying ore, coal, etc. 4. Clumsy slow boat (derog.); boat used for practice rowing, as *~-pair, -eight*, etc. (for so many oarsmen). 5.*~-thumper*, ranting preacher or orator, so *~-thumping* a. & n.; *~-wheel*, bowl-shaped water-wheel, rotating drum for washing skins etc. in. Hence *~'*FUL n. 6. vb. Bathe (t. & i.) in *~*; plant in *~*; row in *~*, coach (oarsman, -men) in *~-pair*; (Mining) line (shaft) with wood or iron casing. Hence *~b'*Ing-V(1, 2) n. [(vbf. n.), cf. MDu. *tobbe, tubbe*]

tŭb'a, n. Bass brass instrument of various sizes & pitches; an organ reed-stop. [L, =trumpet]

tŭbb'|y, a. Tub-shaped, fat & round, corpulent, so *~*ISH¹ a.; (of musical instrument) sounding dull, lacking resonance. [-Y¹]

tūbe, n., & v.t. 1. Long hollow cylinder esp. for conveying or holding liquids etc.; cylinder of thin flexible metal with screw cap for holding paint etc. (*~ colours, beef in ~s*). 2. Main body of wind instrument. 3. (Anat.) hollow *~*-shaped organ, esp. one conveying air, as *bronchial ~*, whence **tŭb'**AL, **tŭb'**AR¹, aa. 4. *Thermionic valve. 5. || Each of several tubular electric railways in London. 6. *Crookes's ~*, vacuum *~* for showing certain phenomena connected with gases; *pneumatic ~* (for pneumatic dispatch); TEST¹-*~*; *~ flower*, ornamental E.-Ind. shrub of vervain family; *~-shell*, kinds of bivalve forming shelly *~*; *~-well*, iron pipe with sharp point & perforations at bottom for getting water from underground. 7. v.t. Furnish with, enclose in, or *~s*; *~d horse* (that has had a metallic *~* inserted in the air-passage). Hence **tŭb'**Ing-V(2) n. [(vb f. n.) F, f. L *tubus*]

tŭb'er, n. Short thick part of an underground stem covered with modified buds, e.g. potato, artichoke, whence *~*IFEROUS, *~*IFORM, aa.; kinds of underground fungus, truffle; (Anat.) swelling part, prominence. [L, =bump, tumour]

tŭb'ercle, n. Small rounded projection esp. of bone; small granular tumour or nodule formed within the substance of an organ tending to degeneration & (in lungs etc.) to production of pulmonary consumption etc.; (Bot.) wartlike excrescence, small tuber. Hence *~*ED² (-ld), **tŭbĕrc'ŭl**AR¹, **tŭbĕrc'ŭl**ATE², aa., **tŭbĕrc'ŭl**IN n., liquid prepared from cultures of *~e* bacillus, used esp. as a test for tuberculosis, **tŭbĕrc'ŭl**OID, **tŭbĕrc'ŭl**OSE¹, **tŭbĕrc'ŭl**OUS, aa. [F, f. L TUBER-*culum* (-CULE)]

tŭbĕrcŭlā'tion, n. Formation, set, system, of tubercles. [-ATION]

tŭbĕrc'ŭl(ar/iz)e, vt.t. Infect with tuberculosis. Hence *~*A'TION n. [-IZE]

tŭbĕrcŭlō's'is, n. Disease affecting most tissues of the body marked by tubercles & thus the presence of a characteristic bacillus; *pulmonary ~*, consumption. Hence **tŭbĕrc'ŭl**ŌSĕD²(-st) a. [-OSIS]

tūb'erōse, a. & (pop. pron. tūb'rōz) n. Covered with tubers, knobby; of the nature of a tuber; bearing tubers. Hence or cogn. ~OS'ITY, ~OUSNESS, nn. ~OUS a. 2. n. Garden & greenhouse bulb with creamy-white fragrant flowers. [(n. f. L fem. adj.) f. L *tuberosus* (TUBER, see -OSE)]

tūb'i- in comb. = L *tubus* tube, as: ~*corn,* s. & n. (ruminant) with tubular tongue. ~FORM; ~*ling'ual,* with tubular tongue.

tūb'ūlar, a. Tube-shaped; having, consisting of, contained in, tube(s), as ~*ar boiler* (in which heat or water to the heated passes through many tubes), ~*ar bridge,* rectangular tube through which railway etc. passes; (of sound in breathing) like sound of air passing through tube. So ~OSE, ~OUS, aa. [f. foll. +-AR¹]

tūb'ūle, n. Small tube. Hence **tūb'ūli-** comb. form. [f. L *tubulus* dim. as TUBE]

tuck¹, v.t. & i., & n. 1. Gather (material) into flat folds for stitching; draw or thrust or roll the parts of (cloth etc. *up, in*) close together, as ~ *in the loose ends,* ~*ed up his shirt-sleeves* (so as to leave arms bare); draw together into small compass, as ~*ed in his head under his wing;* ~ *up* (person, oneself) snugly & compactly in bed, as ~ *a child, himself up in bed,* ~ *away* (thing *in corner* etc., *away* etc.). (of spare material etc., be disposed of by ~*ing away*; empty (seine) by means of small one; (sl.) hang (criminal) up; ~ *in* (sl.), eat heartily (at food, or abs.). 2. n. Flat fold, often one of several parallel folds, in fabric fixed in place by stitches as ornament or to dispose of spare material, as *make a ~ in sleeves* (when too long); (Naut.) part of vessel's hull where after planks meet; || (sl.) eatables esp. pastry & sweets, ~*-in,* ~*-out,* full meal, ~*-shop* (where ~ is sold); ~*-net, -seine,* small net for taking fish from larger one; ~*-point-ing,* method of pointing brickwork with coloured mortar, a central groove in which is filled with fine white lime putty, projecting slightly. [(n. f. vb) ME *tukken,* cf. LG *tukken, to-,* G *zucken,* & TOUCH]

tuck², n. (arch.). Blast, flourish, of trumpet; (Sc.) ~ (beat) of drum. [f. Picard *toquer* var. of F *toucher* TOUCH]

tuck'er¹, n. In vbl senses; also or esp. piece of lace, linen, etc., covering neck & shoulders of woman in 17th & 18th c. (*best HB² &c ~*); part of sewing-machine used in making tucks. [TUCK¹ +-ER¹]

***tuck'er²,** v.t. (colloq.). Tire, weary (usu. ~*out*). [f. TUCK¹ (vb)]

tuck'et, n. (arch.). Flourish on trumpet. [cf. TUCK², & It. *toccata* prelude (*toccare* TOUCH, cf. -ADE)]

tuc'um (too-), n. Brazilian palm with fibre used for cordage etc. [Braz.]

-tude, suf. forming abstract nn. f. L adj. & p.p., usu. ending in -*ti-* (*desu~, con-* *sue~,* for -*suetitude*); in wds direct f. L (*alti-~*), thr. F (*apti-~, atti-~*), or in L anal. (*correctl~*). [F, f. L -*tudin-em*]

Tud'or, a. Of the (period of the) ~s, English sovereigns from Henry VII to Elizabeth, as ~ (late perpendicular) *style* in architecture, ~ *rose,* five-lobed flower, ~ *flower,* trefoil ornament, used in ~ style. [Owen ~ of Wales, grandfather of Henry VII]

Tuesday (tūz'di), n. Third day of week; SHROVE ~. [OE *Tiwes dæg* (*Tiwes* genit. of *Tiw* god of war, cogn. w. L *deus* god, Gk *Zeus* Jupiter+*dæg* DAY]

tūf'a, n. Rock of rough or cellular texture of volcanic or other origin. Hence **tūf'á-CEOUS** (-ashus) a. [It., as foll.]

tūff, n. Kinds of volcanic fragmentary rock; ~*-cone* (of ashes etc. round volcanic opening). [f. F *tuf* f. It. *tufo, tufa,* f. L *tophus* soft sandy stone]

tuft, n., & v.t. & i. 1. Bunch, collection, of threads, grass, feathers, etc., held or growing together at the base, whence **tufty²** a.; (Anat.) bunch of small blood-vessels; imperial (beard); || titled under-graduate [from ~ formerly worn on cap]; ~*-hunter, -hunting,* one who seeks, practice of seeking, society of titled persons. 2. vb. Furnish with ~ or ~s; make depressions at regular intervals in (mattress etc.) by passing thread through; grow in ~s. [(vb f. n.) f. F *touffe* prob. of Teut. orig., cf. G *zopf*]

tug, v.t. & i. (-gg-), & n. 1. Pull with great effort or violently; make vigorous pull at; tow (vessel) by means of steam ~, (of steam ~) tow (vessel); (fig.) drag (subject etc. *in* etc.) forcibly. 2. n. ~*ging,* violent pull, as *gave a ~ at the bell;* violent or painful effort, esp. fig., as *felt a great ~ at parting, parting was a ~, had a great ~ to persuade him.* 3. || (Eton sl.) colleger. 4. (Also ~*boat*) small powerful steam-vessel for towing others. 5. Loop from saddle supporting shaft or (in double harness) trace; ~*-spring,* spring-frame in which this is fastened to lessen jerk in starting etc. 6. (Mining) iron hoop to which a tackle is fixed. 7. ~ *of war,* contest in which each of two groups of persons holding same rope tries to pull the other across line marked between them, supreme contest. [(n. f. vb) ME *toggen,* cogn. w. OE *tēon* draw, & TAUT, TIGHT, TIE, TOW¹, TOUGH]

tū'ism, n. Doctrine that all thought is addressed to a second person, esp. to one's future self as this. [f. L *tu* thou +-ISM]

tū'ition, n. Teaching, esp. as a thing to be paid for; fee for this. Hence ~AL, ~ARY¹, aa., (-sho~). [OF, f. L *tuitionem* (*tuēri tuit-* watch, guard, see -ION)]

tul'a (too-), n. (Also ~*-work*) = NIELLO. [Tula, in Russia]

|| **tūl'chan, -in,** (-ҳ-), n. (Sc.). Calf-skin stuffed with straw or spread on mound

beside cow to make her give milk; ~ *bishops* (hist.), titular bishops in whose names revenues of Scottish sees were drawn by lay barons after Reformation. [Gael., = mound]

tūl′ip, n. Kinds of plant with brilliant bell-shaped flowers of various colours; bell-shaped outward swell of muzzle of gun; ~*root*, disease of oats causing base of stem to swell; ~*tree*, N.-Amer. tree with flowers like large greenish-yellow ~s, marked with orange inside. [thr. F *tulippe* or It. *tulipa(no)* f. Turk. *tulband* f. Pers. *dulband* TURBAN]

tūlipo|mān′ia, n. Craze for tulips, esp. that in Holland about 1634. Hence ~MAN′IAC n. [prec. + o- + -MANIA]

tulle (tōōl, & see Ap.), n. Fine silk net used for veils & dresses. [*T*~, city in France]

tūl′wär, n. Sabre used by some N.-Indian tribes. [Hind. *talwār*]

tum, tŭm′tŭm, n. Sound of banjo or similar instrument. [imit.]

tŭm′ble, v.i. & t., & n. **1.** Fall (*down, over, off, from,* etc.) suddenly or violently; (of waves, sick person, etc.) roll, toss, up & down, or from side to side; move, walk, run, in headlong or blundering fashion (*came tumbling along,* ~*d up the stairs,* ~*d into* or *out of bed*); perform acrobatic feats; pull about; disorder, rumple, (clothes, hair, etc.); overturn, fling head-long, throw or push (*down, out, in,* etc.) roughly or carelessly; bring down (bird, hare, etc.) by shooting; polish (castings etc.) in tumbling-box. **2.** ~ *in,* fit (piece of timber) into another, (Naut., also ~ *home,* of ship's sides) incline inwards above extreme breadth, (sl.) go to bed; ~ *to* (sl.), understand, grasp, (idea etc.). **3.** n. Fall, as *had a slight, nasty,* etc., ~; somersault or other acrobatic feat; untidy or confused state, as *things were all in a* ~. **4.** ~*bug,* kinds of dung-beetle; ~*down,* dilapidated. [(n. f. vb) f. OE *tumbian* + -LE(3), cf. Du. *tuimelen,* G *taumeln, tummeln,* stagger]

tŭm′bler, n. In vbl senses; also or esp.: one who turns somersaults etc., acrobat; kind of pigeon that turns somersaults during flight; toy figure of sitting man-darin etc. contrived to rock when touched; flat-bottomed stemless drink-ing-glass (formerly with rounded bottom so as not to stand upright), whence ~FUL n.; part of the mechanism of a lock or gunlock. [-ER¹]

tŭm′brel, -il, n. (hist.), Two-wheeled covered cart for carrying tools, ammuni-tion, etc.; dung-cart; open cart used in

French Revolution to convey victims to the guillotine; instrument of punishment perh. the same as CUCKING-STOOL. [f. OF *tumb(e)rel* (mod. F *tombereau*), f. *tumb(e),* cf. TUMBLE]

tŭm′e|fy, v.t. & i. (Cause to) swell, inflate; be inflated, (lit. & fig.). So ~FA′CIENT (-āshnt) a. (path.), ~FAC′TION n. (path.). [f. F *tuméfier* ult. f. L *tumefacere* (*tumēre* swell, see -FY)]

tūm′id, a. (Of parts of body etc.) swollen, inflated, so **tūmēs′CENCE** n., **tūmēs′CENT** a.; (fig., of style etc.) inflated, bombastic. Hence or cogn. **tūmid′ITY,** ~NESS, nn., ~LY² adv. [f. L *tumidus* (*tumēre* swell, -ID¹)]

tŭmm′y, n. (nursery). =STOMACH. [-Y³]

tūm′our (-mer), n. Local swelling ~ from morbid growth; *malignant* ~ (tend-ing to recur after removal & cause death, opp. to *benign* ~). [f. L *tumorem* (*tumēre* swell, -OR¹)]

tŭm′tŭm¹, n. W.-Ind. dish of boiled plantains beaten soft in a mortar; (Anglo-Ind.) light vehicle, dog-cart. [?]

tumtum², See TUM.

tūm′ult, n. Commotion of a multitude esp. with confused cries etc.; noisy up-rising of mob etc.; uproar; confused & excited state of mind, as *the* ~ *within him had subsided.* Hence or cogn. **tūmŭl′tūARY¹** (esp. undisciplined, rio-tous), **tūmŭl′tūOUS** (esp. vehement, uproarious), aa., **tūmŭl′tūOUSLY²** adv.. **tūmŭl′tūOUS**NESS n. [f. L *tumultus* (as foll.)]

tūm′ŭl|us, n. (pl. ~ī). Sepulchral mound often enclosing masonry. Hence or cogn. ~AR(Y)¹ aa. [L (*tumēre* swell)]

tŭn, n., & v.t. (-nn-). **1.** Large cask for wine, beer, etc., esp. formerly as measure of capacity (252 wine gallons); brewer's fermenting-vat; ||~*dish,* kind of funnel esp. in brewing. **2.** v.t. Store (liquor) in ~. [(vb f. n.) OE *tunne,* cf. Du. *ton,* G *tonne,* ON *tunna*]

tūn′a, n. The Californian TUNNY. [Sp.-Amer.]

||**tŭnd,** v.t. (Winch. Coll. sl.). Thrash with stick. [f. L *tundere* beat]

tun′dra, n. Barren arctic regions where subsoil is frozen. [Lappish]

tūne, n., & v.t. & i. **1.** Melody with or without harmony, air; as *psalm, hymn,* ~; correct intonation in singing or play-ing, due adjustment of instrument for this, as *piano is out of* ~, *sings out of* ~, *must learn to sing in* ~. **2.** Agreement, concord, harmonious relation, as *in, out of,* ~ *with one's surroundings or company;* suitable mood (*for purpose* etc.). **3.** *Change one's* ~, *sing another* ~, assume a different style of language or manner, e.g. change from insolent to respectful tone; *to the* ~ (serious or exorbitant amount) *of £5* etc. **4.** vb. Put (violin, piano, etc.) in ~, whence **tūn′ER¹(1, 2) n.;**

(fig.) adjust, adapt, (thing to standard, purpose, circumstances, etc.); be in harmony (*with*, lit. & fig.); (poet.) produce (music), as *tune a his song*; express, celebrate, in music. 5 ~ *in*, set wireless instrument to right wave-length; ~ *up*, (of orchestra) bring instruments to common pitch, begin to play or sing, (joc., of child) begin to cry. Hence tūn´ABLE² a., tūn´ABLENESS n., tūn´ABLY² adv. [XIVth c. var. of TONE n.]

tūne´ful (-nf-), a. Melodious, musical. Hence ~LY² adv., ~NESS n. [-FUL]

tūne´less (-nl-), a. Not in tune; unmelodious, silent. [-LESS]

tūng´-oil, n. An oil used chiefly for varnishing woodwork, obtained from the Chinese *tung-tree*. [Chin. *t'ung yu*]

tūng´sten, n. A steel-grey heavy metallic element with very high melting-point, used for the filaments of electric lamps. [Sw. (*tung* heavy + *sten* stone)]

tūn´ic, n. 1. Ancient Greek or Roman body-garment reaching about to knees; woman's loose blouse or coat gathered or belted at waist; close-fitting short coat of uniform of soldier, policeman, etc. 2. (Zool.) leathery envelope of ascidia etc.; (Anat.) membrane enclosing an organ; (Bot.) any of the layers of a bulb, integument of a part; whence ~ATE¹(3) a., (Zool., anat., bot.), & n. (Ecol.)=foll. [f. OF *tunique* f. L *tunica*]

tūn´icle, n. Fine or delicate tunic (esp. ?, zool.); (Eccl., esp. R.-C. Ch.) short vestment of deacon at eucharist etc., (pl.) this & dalmatic worn by bishop. [f. L *tunicula* dim. as prec.]

tūn´ing, n. In vbl senses; ~-*fork*, two-pronged steel fork designed to give particular note (esp. middle C) when struck; ~-*hammer*, hammer-shaped wrench for altering tension of strings in piano etc. by turning the pegs (~-*pegs*, -*pins*) to which they are attached. [-ING¹]

tunnage. See TONNAGE.

tūnn´el, n. & v.t. & i. (-ll-). 1. Artificial subterranean passage through hill etc. or under river etc.; subterranean passage dug by burrowing animal; (Mining) adit or level open at one end; main flue of chimney; ~-*borer*, kinds of machine for making ~s; ~-*net*, fishing-net wide at mouth & narrow at other end. 2. vb. Make a ~ through (hill etc.); furnish with ~; make one's way (*through, into*, etc.), make one's way (*through, into*, etc.). [f. OF *tonnel* dim. of *tonne* TUN]

tūnn´y, n. Large oceanic scombroid fish used as food. [f. F *thon* f. L f. Gk *thunnos*]

tūn´y, a. (Of music) having marked or catchy tunes. Hence ~INESS n. [-Y²]

tŭp, n. & v.t. (-pp-). 1. Male sheep, ram; striking-face of steam hammer etc.

2. v.t. Copulate with (ewe). [ME *tupe*, etym. dub.]

tuque (-k), n. Kind of Canadian cap. [Canad. F form of TOQUE]

tū´quo´que, n. The retort *So are* (or *did* etc.) *you too*. [L, =you too]

Tūrā´nian, a. & n. Of the Asiatic languages that are neither Semitic nor Indo-European, esp. of the Ural-Altaic group of languages. [f. Pers. *Tūrān* region beyond Oxus. + -IAN]

tŭr´ban, n. Oriental man's head-dress of scarf wound round cap; modification of this, esp. early-19th-c. European woman's head-dress; (later) woman's or child's hat with narrow or no brim; spire of univalve shell; ~-*shell*, kinds of gasteropod or shell; ~-*stone*, Mohammedan pillar tombstone with ~ carved on top; ~-*top*, kind of mushroom. Hence ~ED² (-nd) a. [f. Turk. *tulband* f. Pers. *dulband*]

tŭr´bary, n. Right of digging turf on another's ground; place where turf or peat is dug. [f. OF *torberie* (*tourbe* TURF f. Tent., -ERY)]

tŭr´bid, a. (Of liquid or colour) muddy, thick, not clear; (fig.) confused, disordered. Hence ~ITY (-id-), ~NESS, nn. ~LY² adv. [f. L *turbidus* (*turbare* disturb f. *turba* crowd, tumult, see -ID¹)]

tŭr´binate, a. Shaped like a top or inverted cone, so ~IFORM, ~OID, aa.; (Anat., esp. of some nasal bones) of scroll-like formation; whirling like a top. So ~AL a., ~A´TION n. [f. L *turbinatus* (as foll., see -ATE²)]

tŭr´bine, n. Kinds of water-wheel driven by impact or reaction or both of a flowing stream of water; *air* ~, wheel of similar form driven by wind or by air from tube, *gas* ~ (driven by gas), *steam* ~ (driven by steam jets); ~ *boat* etc. (driven by ~s). [F, f. L *turbo -inis* wheel, top, whirlwind.]

tŭr´bit, n. Kind of domestic pigeon with flat head & short beak. [perh. f. L as prec., w. ref. to shape]

tŭr´bot, n. Large kind of flat-fish esteemed as food. [f. OF *tourbout*, as TURBINE.]

tŭr´bulent, a. Disturbed, in commotion; tumultuous; insubordinate, riotous. Hence or cogn. ~ENCE n., ~ENTLY² adv. [f. L *turbulentus* (*turba* tumult, see -LENT)]

Tŭrc´ō, n. (hist.; pl. ~s). Algerian tirailleur in French service. [F]

Tŭrco-, Tŭrko-, in comb. Of the Turks. So Tŭrc´oPHIL, Tŭrc´oPHIL´ISM, Tŭrc´oPHOBE, nn. f. med. L as TURK. -o-]

tŭrd, n. (not in polite lang.). Ball or lump of excrement. [OE *tord*, cf. MDu. *torde*]

tŭr´dine, a. Thrushlike. So ~IFORM, etc. [f. L *turdus* thrush + -INE¹]

tūreen´, n. Deep covered dish for holding soup etc. at table. [earlier *terreen* f. F TERRINE]

turf, n., & v.t. **1.** Surface earth filled with matted roots of grass etc.; piece of this cut from the ground, sod; (in Ireland) peat; *the* ~, the race-course, occupation or profession of horse-racing, esp. *on the* ~, so occupied; ~*-bound*, (covered with ~); ~ *drain* (covered with ~); ~ *man*, person interested in horse-racing, so ~'ITE¹ n. **2.** v.t. Cover (ground) with ~; (sl.) throw (person or thing) *out*. Hence ~'INESS n., ~'Y² a. [OE & Du., cf. ON & Sw. *torf*, Da. *tørv*]

tur'gid, a. Morbidly swollen or inflated or enlarged, whence ~ĒS'CIBLE a.; (fig., of language) pompous, bombastic, inflated. Hence or cogn. ~ĒS'CENCE, ~id'ITY, nn., ~ĒS'CENT a., ~idly² adv. [f. L *turgidus* (*turgēre* swell, see -ID¹)]

tur'ion, n. (bot.). Young scaly shoot rising from ground as in asparagus, hops, etc. Hence ~iF'EROUS a. [f. L *turio -onis* shoot]

Turk, n. **1.** Ottoman, Osmanli; member of the race from whom the Ottomans are derived; (transf.) ferocious, wild, or unmanageable person (now chiefly joc. of children); Mohammedan; Turkish horse. **2.** ~'*s cap*, kinds of lily & other plants; ~'*s head*, head on post for sword displays; turbanlike ornamental knot, kinds of round brush or broom, kind of baking-pan for cakes. Hence ~'ISM n. [cf. F *Turc*, med. L *Turcus*, Pers. & Arab. *Turk*]

turk'ey, n. (pl. ~s). **1.** Large (esp. domestic) gallinaceous bird native of America related to pheasant, esteemed as food & associated with Christmas festivities. **2.** (T~). Country of the Turks. **3.** ~ *buzzard, vulture*, an American vulture; T~ *carpet* (made entirely of wool, & of velvety appearance); ~*cock*, male of (*red as a* ~*cock*, of person flushed with anger etc.), (fig.) pompous or self-important person; T~ *corn*, maize; ||T~ *leather*, kind treated with oil before the hair side is removed; ~*poult*, young of ~; T~ *red*, a pigment or colour, cotton cloth dyed with this; T~ *stone*, kind of oilstone for sharpening knives etc.; ~ *trot*, kind of dance. [cf. F *Turquie* Turkey (prec., -IA¹), whence the bird was held to come (as prec.)]

Turk'ish, a. & n. **1.** (Language) of Turkey or the Turks. **2.** ~ *bath*, hot-air bath followed by soaping, washing, rubbing, kneading, etc., (also pl.) building used for this; ~ (=TURKEY) *carpet*; ~ *delight*, a sweetmeat in gelatinous slabs coated with powdered sugar; ~ *music* (produced with instruments of percussion); ~ *pound* (usu. written £T, as £T 50), coin formerly worth about 18/2; ~ *towel* (rough with long nap usu. of uncut loops). [-ISH¹]

Turk'oman, Turk'man, Turc'o-, n. (pl. ~s). Member of any of various Turkish hordes in Turkestan, Afghanistan, Persia, & Russia; ~ *carpet*, rich-coloured kind with soft long nap. [f. Pers. *Turkumān* (*Turk*, *mān-dan* resemble)]

turm'alin(e). See TOURMALIN.

turm'eric, n. E.-Ind. plant of ginger family; powdered root of this as dye-stuff, stimulant, & condiment esp. in curry-powder; ~*paper* (saturated with ~ & used as test for alkalis). [f. F *terre-mérite* perh. corrupt. of Arab. as CURCUMA]

turm'oil, n., & v.t. **1.** Agitation, trouble. **2.** v.t. (arch., chiefly in p.p.), Agitate, trouble. [f. 16th c., etym. dub.]

|| **tûrn'ut**, var. of *turnip* used by writers as characteristic of rustic speech.

turn¹, v.t. & i. **I.** General senses. **1.** Move (t. & i.) on or as on axis, give rotary motion to, receive such motion, as *crank* ~*s wheel, wheel* ~*s*, or the ~ *key in the lock*, ~ *the tap, tap will not* ~, *he* ~*ed on his heel*(8), ~ *person round one's* FINGER, *everything* ~*s* (depends) *on his answer*. **2.** Execute (somersault etc.) with rotary motion. **3.** Change from one side to another, invert, reverse, (fig.) revolve mentally, as ~*s everything upside down or inside out* (into state of confusion), *whole world has* ~*ed topsy-turvy, umbrella* ~ *inside out*, ~*ed the body with its face upwards*, ~*ed* (inverted) *comma*, ~*ed period* (·), ~ TURTLE, ~ *the* TABLES *on*, ~ *over pages of book* (to read on other side), ~ *over new* LEAF, *not* ~ *a* HAIR, *dress must be* ~*ed* (the soiled outside becoming the inside), ~ *one's* COAT, ~ *an honest* PENNY, *have* ~*ed the matter over & over in my mind*. **4.** Give new direction to, take new direction, adapt, be adapted, as ~ *your face this way, river* ~*s to the right*, ~*ed his flight northwards, scarcely know where or which way to* ~ (fig. what course to follow, where to seek help), ~*ed to God in her trouble*, ~*one's* BACK² *on*, ~ *a* DEAF *ear to*; ~ *the edge of* (knife etc., fig. remark etc.), blunt; ~ *your attention to this; have often* ~*ed my thoughts, thoughts have often* ~*ed, to the subject; can* ~ *his hand to* (learn to do) *anything*; ~*s even his errors to account* (profits by them); *all* ~*s* (tends) *to his profit; tide* ~*s* (at ebb or flow). **5.** Move to other side of, go round, flank, as ~ *the* CORNER; ~ *the scale*, cause it to sink, (fig.) decide question in suspense; ~ (the flank or position of) *an army*, pass round so as to attack it from flank or rear; ~ *person's flank*, outwit him, defeat him in argument etc. **6.** Be ~*ed* (have passed the age)(*of*) *40 etc.* **7.** Cause to go, send, put, as *was* ~*ed adrift in the world, he* ~*ed it out into a basin, never* ~*ed* (away) *a beggar from his door, will* ~ (resist or divert) *a bullet.* **8.** Change (t. & i.) in nature, form, condition, etc., change for the worse, (cause to) become, as ~*ed water into wine, has been* ~*ed into a joint stock company, fear he will* ~ *crusty, has* ~*ed traitor, Mohammedan, botanist, joy is*

or has ~ed to bitterness, ~ (translate) it into French, how would you ~ this passage?, milk will ~ (sour), thunder will ~ milk (sour), ~ed gate at the thought, they thought ~s me pale, sight of raw meat ~s (nauseates) my stomach, stomach ~s at the sight, success has ~ed his head (intoxicated him), head has ~ed with success, head ~s (with giddiness), overwork has ~ed his brain. **9.** Shape (object) in lathe, (of material) lend itself (easily, well, etc.) to treatment in lathe. **10.** Give (esp. elegant) form to, as can ~ a compliment, could ~ a Latin verse in my day, well-~ed phrase, exquisitely-~ed wrist. **II.** Spec. uses with advv. & prepp. **1.** ~ about, ~ so as to face in new direction. **2.** ~ against, become hostile to. **3.** ~ down, fold down; place (playing-card) face downwards; reduce flame of (gas, lamp, etc.) by ~ing tap etc.; refuse (proposal), its maker, bed. **4.** ~ in, fold inwards; incline inwards, as his toes ~ in, (colloq.) go to bed. **5.** ~ off, check passage of (water, gas, etc.), by means of tap etc.; achieve, produce, (epigram, piece of work); dismiss (servant etc.) from employment; (sl.) hang (criminal), marry (couple). **6.** ~ on (adv.), give free passage to (water etc.) by ~ing tap; (colloq.) give free scope to, as ~ on the underworks, begin to cry. **7.** ~ on (prep.), depend upon; face hostilely, become hostile to. **8.** ~ out, expel; cause to point or incline outwards, as ~ out your toes; produce (manufactured goods etc.); ~ inside out, bring to view, as made him ~ out his pockets; assemble for duty etc., as 15 men ~ed out; get out of bed; (Mil.) ~ out the guard, call them from guard-room; be found, prove to be the case, as this ~s out to be true, he ~ed out a humbug, it ~s out that he was never there, we shall see how things ~ out. **9.** ~ over, cause to fall over, upset; transfer the conduct of (thing to person); do business to the amount of, as ~s over £500 a week. **10.** ~ round, face about; adopt new opinions or policy. **11.** ~ to (prep.), apply oneself to, set about, (work, doing). **12.** ~ to (adv.) begin work. **13.** ~ up (Cards) expose (trump card); disinter, as plough ~s up skulls; make one's appearance, as ~ed up an hour late, unexpectedly; (of event, opportunity, etc.) happen, present itself; (colloq.) cause to vomit, as the sight ~ed me up. **14.** ~ upon, = ~ on. **III.** Comb. ~bench, watch-maker's portable lathe; ~buckle, device for connecting parts of metal rod.; ~cap, revolving chimney-top; ~cock, one who ~s his coat; ~cock, person employed to ~ on water for mains etc.; ~down, (of collar) doubled down; ~key, person in charge of prison keys; ~out, ~ing-out eep. for duty, strike of employees, assembly of persons to see spectacle etc., equipage, quantity of goods manufac-

tured etc. in given time.; ~over, upsetting of carriage etc., semicircular pie or tart, amount of money ~ed over in business, || newspaper article running on to next page; ~pike, defensive frame of pikes (hist.), gate set across road to stop carts etc. till toll is paid, such road; ~round, (of ship) process of entering port, discharging cargo, reloading, & leaving port; ~screw, screwdriver; ~side, giddiness in dogs; ~sole, kinds of plant supposed to ~ with the sun; ~spit, long-bodied short-legged dog formerly used to ~ spit; ~stile, post at entrance of building etc. where admission fee is charged ing cap, ~stile, post at entrance of building round as person passes through; ~stone, bird allied to plover; ~table, circular revolving platform for reversing loco-motives etc.; ~up, thing ~ed up. (colloq.) commotion. [OE *tyrnan*, *turnian*, f. L *tornare* turn in lathe (*tornus*= Gk *tornos*)]

turn², n. **1.** Rotary motion, changed or change of direction or position or tendency, deflection, deflected part, bend, as a single ~ of the handle, a ~ of Fortune's wheel (change of luck), with a neat ~ of the wrist, took a sudden ~ to the left, complaint took a favourable ~, milk is on the ~ (just turning sour), tide is on the ~ (turning), gave a new ~ to the argument, path is full of ~s & twists, walked along a ~ of the river; (Mil. as wds of command) right, left, about, ~!; any of the THREE (~ A, B, C, D) in figure-skating. **2.** Character, tendency, disposition, formation, as was of a humorous ~, do not like the ~ of the sentence, the ~ of an ankle, have a fine, pretty, etc., ~ of speed etc., be able to go very fast etc. on occasion. **3.** Short walk, stroll, drive, ride, or performance, as take a ~ in the garden, on a bicycle, took a ~ of work; short ~s (songs, recitations, etc., in music-hall etc.) **4.** Opportunity, occasion, privilege, obligation, coming successively to each of several persons etc., as it is your ~ to watch, it was now my ~ to be angry, must not speak out of (before or after) your ~, will hear you all in ~ (succession); we dug by ~s (in rotation of individuals or groups); take ~s, work etc. alternately or by ~ ; ~ about (alternately), went hot & cold by ~s; did not serve my ~ (service, disservice); one good ~ deserves another; **5.** (mus.) Kind of grace consisting of principal note with those above & below it. **6.** pl. Menses. **7.** Each round in coil of rope etc. **8.** (print.). Inverted type as temporary substitute for missing letter, letter turned wrong side up. **9.** (colloq.) Nervous shock, as gave me quite a ~. **10.** To a ~, exactly, perfectly, as meat is done to a ~ (enough & not too much). [f. prec.]

turn'er, n. In vbl senses; also or esp.

one who works with lathe, so ~ERY (1, 2, 3) n.; ‖ kind of tumbler-pigeon. [-ER¹]

turn'ing, n. In vbl senses, esp.: use of lathe; place where road meets another, such road, as *stop at the next ~, take the second ~ to the left*; ~*-point*, point in place, time, development, etc., at which decisive change occurs, as *has reached the ~-point, this may be the ~-point of his life.* [-ING¹]

turn'ip, n. Biennial plant of mustard family; its fleshy globular root used as vegetable for feeding cattle etc.; ~*-top*, growing top of ~ used as vegetable. Hence ~Y² a. (esp. tasting of ~s). [OE *nǣp* f. L *napus*; tur- perh. = turn or F TOUR, w. ref. to shape]

turp'entine, n. & v.t. **1.** Oleo-resin secreted by several coniferous trees & (*Chian* ~) by terebinth, used in mixing paints & varnishes & in medicine; (also pop. *turps*) oil or spirit of ~; ~*-tree*, terebinth. **2.** v.t. Apply ~ to. [f. OF *ter(e)bentine* f. L f. Gk *terebinthinos* (as TEREBINTH, see -INE²)]

turp'eth, n. Cathartic root of an E.-Ind. plant. [f. OF *turbith* f. Arab. & Pers. *turbid*]

turp'itūde, n. Baseness, depravity. [F, f. L *turpitūdinem* (*turpis* base, see -TUDE)]

turps. See TURPENTINE.

turquoise (-koiz, -kwoiz), n. Opaque sky-blue or greenish-blue precious stone; ~ *green*, pale colour between green & blue. [F, fem. of *turquois* Turkish (*Turc* TURK)]

turr'et, n. Small tower connected with main building whether rising from ground or projecting from wall or corbels; (Mil.) low flat usu. revolving tower for gun & gunners in ship or fort; (Hist.) square many-storeyed building on wheels used in attacking fortified place; ~*-gun* (for ~s in revolving ~); ~*-ship* (with guns in ~s). Hence ~ED² a. [f. F *tourette* dim. of *tour* TOWER]

turr'icŭlate, -āted, aa. (conch.). (Of shell) having a long spire. [f. L *turricula* (*turris* tower, see -CULE, -ATE²)]

turt'le¹, n. (Now usu. ~*-dove*) kinds of dove, esp. a common wild kind noted for soft cooing & affection for mate & young. [OE f. L *turtur*, imit.]

turt'le², n., & v.i. **1.** Marine reptile encased as tortoise & with flippers used in swimming, esp. (also *green* ~) kind much used for soup; MOCK² ~; *turn* ~ (naut. sl.), capsize; ~*-shell*, tortoise-shell, esp. dark kind used for inlaying, (also ~*cowry*) large handsome kind of cowry. **2.** v.i. Hunt for ~s, whence **turt'LER¹, turt'LING⁴**, nn. [=*tortu(e)* TORTOISE, assim. to PREC.]

Tus'can, a. & n. (Language, inhabitant) of Tuscany; ~ ORDER¹; ~ *straw*, fine yellow wheat-straw used for hats etc. [f. LL *Tuscānus* (L *Tuscus*, see -AN¹)]

tush¹, int., n., & v.i. (arch.). Pshaw. [imit.]

tush², n. Long pointed tooth, esp. canine tooth of horse. [var. of TUSK]

tush'ery, n. (literary). Use of archaisms such as TUSH¹. [-ERY; word made by R. L. Stevenson]

tusk, n., & v.t. **1.** Long pointed tooth, esp. protruding from closed mouth as in elephant, walrus, etc.; ~like tooth or part in harrow, lock, etc. Hence (-)~ED³ (-kt), ~Y² aa. **2.** v.t. Gore, thrust, tear up, with ~ or ~s. [(vb f. n.) OE *tusc, tux*, cf. OFris. *tusk*]

tusk'er, n. Elephant with developed tusks. [-ER¹]

tuss'er, -ur, -ōre, n. Oak-feeding silkworm yielding strong but coarse silk; (also ~*-silk*) silk of this & some other silkworms. [f. Hind. *tasar* f. Skr. *tasara* shuttle]

tuss'ive, a. (med.). Of a cough. [f. L *tussis* cough, see -IVE]

tuss'le, n., & v.i. Struggle, scuffle, (*with* person, *for* thing). [as TOUSLE]

tuss'ock, n. Clump, hillock, of grass etc.; tuft, lock, of hair etc.; (also ~*-moth*) kinds of moth with tufted larvae; ~*-grass*, tall elegant grass on boggy ground in Patagonia etc. Hence ~Y² a. [f. 16th c., etym. dub.]

tuss'ōre. See TUSSER.

tut, tŭt-tŭt, int., n., & v.i. (-tt-). **1.** Int. expr. impatience, contempt, or rebuke. **2.** n. This exclamation. **3.** v.i. Exclaim ~. [instinctive]

‖ **tŭt'²**, n. (mining). Job; ~*-work*, piece-work (cf. TRIBUTE). [?]

tut'elage, n. Guardianship; (period of) being under this. [f. L *tutela* (*tuēri tuit-* or *tut-* watch) +-AGE]

tut'elar(y̆), aa. Serving as a guardian, protective; (of a guardian, as ~ *authority*. [f. LL *tutelārius* (as prec., see -ARY¹)]

tut'enăg, n. Zinc imported from China & E. Indies; white alloy like German silver. [f. Marathi *tuttināg* perh. f. Skr. *tuttha* blue vitriol+*nāga* tin]

tut'or, n., & v.t. & v.i. **1.** Private teacher, esp. one having general charge of person's education; ‖ (Eng. Univ.) college official, usu. a fellow, directing studies of undergraduates assigned him; (Law) guardian of a minor. Hence or cogn. ~AGE(2), ~ESS¹, ~SHIP, nn., **tŭtō̆r'IAL** a. (also n., period of instruction given by a college ~), **tŭtō̆r'IALLY²** adv. **2.** vb. Act as ~ to, instruct; exercise restraint over (oneself, one's passions, another); make one's living as ~. [f. OF *tutour* f. L *tutorem* (*tuēri tut-* watch, see -OR²)]

tut'san, n. St-John's-wort, plant once held to heal wounds etc. [earlier *tolsane* f. L *totus* whole, *sanus* sound, prob. thr. F]

tutti (tŏŏt'ē) mus. direction, & n. All (voices, instruments) together; (n.) passage for these. [It.]

tutti-frutti (tŏŏt'ĭ frŏŏtē), n. Confection, ice-cream, of mixed fruits. [It., = all fruits]

tut'tȳ, n. Impure zinc oxide used as polishing-powder. [f. OF *tutie* f. Arab.]

tü'um. See MEUM.

tu-whit', tu-whoo' (tōō-) n., & v.i. (Make) cry of owl. [imit.]

tixéd'ō, n. (pl. ~s, ~es). Dinner-jacket. [?~, place-name]

tuyère (twēyǎr', tóōyǎr', twēr), **twȳ'er**, n. Pipe through which air is forced into furnace etc. [F (*tu-*) = nozzle]

twa'ddle (-ŏ-), v.i., & n. (Indulge in) senseless, feeble, or prosy talk. Hence **twa'ddler** (-ŏ-), n.

twa'ddell (-ŏ-), n. Kind of hydrometer for liquids heavier than water. [?~, inventor's name]

twain, a. & n. (arch.). Two; two persons or things; *cut* etc. *in* ~ (in two). [see TWO]

twang, v.i. & t., & n. 1. (Cause to) make ringing metallic sound as of string of musical instrument or bow when plucked, (derog.) play on or on (fiddle etc.) thus, as *the fiddles* ~*ed,* ~*ed* (*on*) *his fiddle,* ~*ed his bow,* whence ~LE(3) (-ăng-ĕl) v.i. & t.; speak, utter, with nasal sound. 2. Sound of tense string when plucked, nasal tone. [imit.]

twänk'ay, n. Kind of green tea. [f. Chin. *Tun-ki,* name of a stream]

'twas (-ŏz), contraction of *it was.*

tway'blade, n. Kinds of orchid with green or purple flowers & single pair of leaves. [*way* var. of TWAIN + BLADE]

tweak, v.t., & n. 1. Pinch & twist sharply, pull with sharp jerk, twitch. 2. Such sharp pull, pinch. Hence ||~ER¹ n. (sl.), boy's catapult. [f. 17th c., cf. TWITCH]

tweed, n. Twilled woollen or wool-&-cotton fabric with unfinished surface & usu. two colours combined in the yarn, used esp. for men's clothes & largely made in S. Scotland; (pl.) suit of this. [anecdot. explained as corrupt. of *twill* (Sc. *tweel*) helped by assoc. with *Tweed*]

twee'dle, n. Sound as of fiddle; ~*dum & ~dee* (-ld-), things differing only or chiefly in name. [prob. imit.]

'tween, adv. & prep. Between, esp. ~-*decks* (space) between decks. [abbr.]

||**tween'ȳ**, n. (colloq.). Servant assisting two others e.g. cook & housemaid. [prec. + -Y³]

tweet, n. & v.i. Chirp (of bird). [imit.]

tweez'er, n. & v.t. 1. (Pl., also *pair of* ~s) minute pair of tongs for taking up small objects, plucking out hairs, etc. 2. v.t. Extract (hair, thorn, etc.) with ~s. [vb f. n.) f. obs. *tweese,* pair of tweeses, case, esp. folding case, for small instruments, f. F ÉTUI]

twelfth, a. & n. 1. Next in order after eleventh (*the* ~, of August, as beginning minute of grouse-shooting); T~-*day* (after Christmas, festival of Epiphany); T~-*night,* night of this, celebrated with various festivities etc.; T~-*cake,* eaten by T~-night. 2. n. Each of 12 equal parts. Hence ~1LY² adv. [OE *twelfta* (foll., -TH²)]

twelve, a. & n. One more than eleven, 12, xii; *the* T~ (apostles); T~ TABLES; *in* ~s (duodecimo); *long, square,* ~s, duodecimo pages of sheet variously folded; ~FOLD a. & adv.; ~*mo,* 12mo, = DUODECIMO; ||~*month, year,* as *has been there a ~month ago*; ||~*pence,* shilling (pl.). [OE *twelf,* lit. two over (as TWO + -*lif* cogn. w. LEAVE²)]

twén'tȳ, a. & n. Twice ten, 20, xx; *have told him* (several) *times*; ~-*one,* ~-*two,* etc., *or one, two,* etc., & ~; ~-*five,* 25 (Rugby football, Hockey), line drawn across ground 25 yds from each goal, ground between this & goal-line; ~*mo,* ~*fourmo,* (20mo, 24mo), leaf of sheet folded into 20, 24, equal parts, book made up of such leaves. Hence **twén'ti**ETH a. ~FOLD a. & adv. [OE *twentig* (*twegen*...

'twere (-er), contr. of *it were.*

||**twerp**, n. (sl.). Bounder, cad. [?]

twi- in comb. = two, double, in TWILIGHT & in some arch. or pseudo-arch. forms as: ~*bill,* double-bladed battle-axe, kind of mattock; ~*blade,* = TWAYBLADE; ~*fold* a. = twofold; ~*folded*; ~*forked*; TWO, see -ES)]

twice, adv. Two times (esp. of multiplication), on two occasions, as ~ *3 is 6, told him* ~; doubly, in double degree or quantity, as ~ *as strong, has* ~ *the strength, is* ~ *the man he was* (~ *as strong* etc.); (colloq.) *did it in* ~ (two attempts or instalments). [ME *twies,* written -ce to show pronunc. (-s *not* -z), OE *twiges* (as TWO, see -ES)]

twid'dle, v.t. & i., & n. 1. Twirl idly, esp. ~ *one's thumbs* (for lack of occupation); trifle *with* (object); *twiddling-line,* string attached to compass-gimbal & pulled to make compass-card play freely. 2. n. Slight twirl. [perh. dim. of *twist* or *twirl*]

||**twi'fer**, n. Compositor who is also pressman. [f. prec. + -ER¹]

twig¹, n. Small shoot or branch of tree or plant; (Anat.) small branch of artery etc.; (Electr.) small distributing conductor; *divining-rod,* esp. *work the* ~; ~*-LESS,* ~-ḡ'Y² (-g-), aa. [OE, cf. Du. *twijg,* G *zweig,* cogn. w. TWO]

twig², v.t. & i. (colloq.: -gg-). Understand, catch the meaning of, (person, words, plan, *that* etc., or abs.); perceive, observe. [f. 18th c., etym. dub.]

twi'light (-īt) n., & v.t. (~*ed*). 1. Light from sky when sun is below horizon in morning or (usu.) evening; faint light; (fig.) state of imperfect knowledge, understanding, etc.; ~ *arch*() or *curve* (bound...

atmosphere receives solar rays direct); ~ *of the gods* (Norse myth.), conflict in which gods & giants destroyed each other; ~ *sleep*, name of a method of making child-birth painless. [ME (TWI-+LIGHT¹)]

twill, n., & v.t. **1.** Textile fabric in which weft-threads pass alternately over one warp-thread & under (not one as in plain weaving but) two or more, thus producing diagonal lines. **2.** v.t. Weave (material) thus (esp. in p.p.). [OE TWIL, cogn. w. OHG *zwilih*, two-threaded, after L BI(*lix* f. *licium* thread)]

twill, contr. of *it will*.

twin, a., n., & v.t. & i. (-nn-). **1.** Forming, being one of, a closely related or associated pair esp. of children born at a birth, as ~ *children, brother(s), sister(s), the T~ Brothers or Brethren*, Castor & Pollux, ~ *bed(s)*; (Bot.) growing in pairs; consisting of two closely connected & similar parts; ~ *boat, steamer* (with two hulls supporting one deck & having paddle-wheel between them); ~ *flower*, slender creeping evergreen bearing a pair of fragrant flowers; ~ *screw*, pair of ships having two propellers on separate shafts having opposite twists. **2.** n. Each of a closely related pair esp. of children born at a birth; exact counterpart of person or thing; compound crystal one part of which is in a reversed position with reference to the other; *The T~s*, Gemini; SIAMESE ~s. Hence ~ING¹ ~SHIP, nn. **3.** vb. Join intimately together, couple, pair, (*with*; t. & i.); ~*ning-machine, -saw* (for cutting out teeth of combs, these being cut in pairs). Hence ~N'ING¹ n., formation of ~ crystals. [(vb & t. f. adj.) OE *twinn* double, cf. ON *tvinnr*, cogn. w. Two]

twine, n., & v.t. & i. **1.** String of two or more strands of hemp, manilla, etc., twisted together; coil, twist, as *snaky* ~*es*; interlacing, tangle. **2.** vb. Form (thread) by twisting strands together, whence ~'ER¹ (2) n.; form (garland etc.) of interwoven material, garland (brow etc.) *with*; interweave; coil, wind, (thing *about, round, another*); (of plant, snake) coil itself or itself (*round*). Hence ~'ING¹³ adv. [(vb ME *twinen* cogn. w.) n. OE *twin*, cf. Du. *twijn*, ON *tvinni*, G *zwirn*, cogn. w. TWO]

twinge (-j), v.t. (rare), & n. (Affect with) sharp darting pain, as *conscience* ~*d him, a ~ of toothache, rheumatism, conscience, remorse*. [(n. f. vb) OE *twengan*, etym. dub.]

twinkle (twing'kl), v.i. & t., & n. (Of light, star, etc.) shine with quick gleams, sparkle; (of eyelids, feet in dancing, etc.) move rapidly up & down or to & fro; blink, wink, (one's eyes, or intr. of person or eye); (of eyes) sparkle (*at* jest etc.); emit (light) in quick gleams. Hence ~ER¹ n.

2. n. Twitching of eyelid, blink, wink; sparkle, gleam, of the eyes, as *a humorous, mischievous,* ~*e*; short rapid movement e.g. of feet in dancing; quick tremulous light, glimmer. [(n. f. vb) OE *twinclian*; cf. obs. *twinken* & G *zwinken* to wink]

twink'ling, n. In vbl senses, esp. *in a* ~, *in the* ~ *of an eye, in the* ~ *of a* BED'*post*, in a moment, very quickly. [-ING¹]

twirl, v.t. & i., & n. **1.** Revolve (t. & i.) rapidly, spin, whirl, (often *round*); turn (one's *thumbs* etc.) round & round in purposeless way, twiddle. **2.** n. Rapid or idle circular motion, flourish or curl made with pen etc. [(n. f. vb), f. 16th c. etym. dub.]

twist, n., & v.t. & i. **1.** Thread, rope, etc., made by winding two or more strands etc. about one another; kinds of strong silk thread & of cotton yarn; roll of bread, tobacco, etc. in form of ~; paper packet with screwed-up ends. **2.** Act of ~ing, condition of being ~ed, as *give it a* ~, *has a curious* ~, *full of turns &* ~*s*. **3.** Manner or degree in which thing is ~ed, e.g. inclination of rifle-grooves, whirling motion given to ball in cricket etc. to make it take special curve. **4.** Peculiar tendency of mind, character, etc. **5.** ~ing strain, (angle showing) amount of torsion of rod etc., forward motion combined with rotation about an axis. **6.** ∥ Kinds of mixed drink, as *gin* ~. **7.** ∥ (colloq.). Appetite, as *had a tremendous* ~. **8.** *Damascus* ~, process of ~ing Damascus iron to form gun-barrel; ~ *of the wrist*, (fig.) dexterity, knack. **9.** vb. Wind (strands etc.) one about another; form (rope etc.) thus; interweave (thing *with* or *in with* another). **10.** Give spiral form to (rod, column, etc.) as by rotating the ends in opposite directions; receive, grow in, spiral form. **11.** Cause (ball, esp. in billiards) to rotate while following curved path. **12.** Twine (flowers etc. *into* garland etc.), make (garland etc.), thus. **13.** Make one's *way*, make one's *way*, (*through* crowd etc., *along*, etc.) in winding manner. **14.** Wrench out of natural shape, distort, as *limbs* ~*ed on the rack, features* ~*ed with pain*, (fig.) *wants to* ~ *my words into an admission of error*; ~ one's *arm*, force his hand or wrist round as torture. **15.** ~ *off*, break off (piece) by ~ing; ~ *up*, ~ (paper etc.) into spiral form. Hence ~'ABLE a., (vb ME *twisten* cogn. w.) n. OE *twist* (in *mæst-twist* mast-rope), f. root of TWO]

twis'ter, n. In vbl senses; also or esp.: twisting ball in cricket or billiards: girder, inner part of thigh as proper place to rest upon on horseback. [-ER¹]

twit, v.t. (-tt-). Reproach, upbraid, taunt, (person *with* fault etc.). Hence ~'ting-LY² adv. [OE *ætwitan* (æt at + *witan* blame)]

twitch, v.t. & i., & n. **1.** Pull (thing *off*

etc.) with light jerk; pull at, jerk at, (person's sleeve etc.); esp. to call attention; (of features, muscles, limbs) move or contract spasmodically. 2. n. Sudden involuntary contraction or movement, sudden pull or jerk; veterinary appliance for stilling horse during operation. (In f. vb) ME *twicchen*, cf. G *zwicken*.

twitch, n. = QUITCH. [dial. var.]

twite, n. Kind of linnet. [perh. imit. of cry]

twitt'er, v.i. & t., & n. 1. (Of bird) utter succession of light tremulous sounds, chirp; utter, express, thus. 2. n. Such series of sounds; (colloq. also ~A'TION n.) excited state. [(n. f. vb) ME *twiteren*, cf. G *zwitschern*]

'twixt, prep. = BETWIXT. [abbr.]

two (tōō), a. & n. 1. One more than one, 2, ii; *one or* ~, a few (also lit.); *cut, divide,* etc., *in* ~ (into ~ parts); ~ *can play at that game,* threat of retaliation; *put* ~ & *together,* make inference from data; *in* ~s, in a very short time. 2. ~**-cleft** (Bot.), divided nearly to the middle in ~ parts; ~**-edged**, (of sword etc.) having an edge on each side, (fig., of argument, compliment, etc.) cutting both ways, ambiguous; ~**-faced**, (fig.) insincere; ~**-fold** a. & adv., double, doubly; ~**-handed**, having ~ hands, (of sword) requiring to be used with both hands, (of saw, game, etc.) to be worked, played, etc., by ~ persons; ~**-legged**, specified, as ~**-line** a. (Print.), having a depth double that of the size specified, as ~*-line pica*; ||~**-pence** (tŭ'ns), sum of, silver coin (now only as maundy money) worth, ~ pence (~*pence coloured,* cheap &, as opp. *penny plain,* gaudy); ||~**-penny** (tŭp'eni), (adj.) worth or costing ~pence, cheap, worthless, (n.) kind of beer orig. sold at ~pence a quart (hist.); ~**-penny-halfpenny** (tŭp'eni hāp'eni); contemptible, insignificant; ~**-ply**, of ~ strands, layers, or thicknesses, as ~*-ply rope, carpet;* ~**-sided**, having ~ sides, aspects, etc.; ~**-speed**, adapted for ~ rates of speed, as ~*-speed gear, bicycle;* ~**-step**, kind of round dance in march or polka time; ~**-tongued**, double-tongued, deceitful; ||~**-way**, (Electr., of switch) permitting current to be switched on or off from either of ~ points, (Plumbing, of cock) permitting fluid to flow in either of ~ channels, (Math.) having double mode of variation. Hence ~'NESS n. [OE *twā* (fem. & neut.), *twēgen* masc., *twū* neut., cf. Du. *twee*, G *zwei*, ON *tveir*, L *duo*, Gk *dúo*]

two'some (tōō-), a. & n. (Game, dance, etc.) for two persons. [-SOME]

'twould, contr. of *it would*.

twy-, pref., var. of TWI-.

twyer. See TUYERE.

-ty¹, -ity, -ety, suff. in abstract nn., repr. F *-té* f. L *-tātem* (nom. *-tas*). L adj. or n. stems in *-t-* took *-tas* without change, as *felicitas, doctilitas, civitas*; adj. stems in *-o-* changed *-o-* to *-i-* or when preceded by *-i-* to *-e-*, as *aequitas, benignitas, pietas* (*pius*), *varietas* (*varius*), *satietas* (as if f. *satias*); consonantal stems (nn. or rarely adjj.) occas. added *-t-*, as *auctoritas* but *paupertas*; nn. f. comparatives, as *priority, seniority, majority, superiority,* date only f. med. L; in *plenitas, bonitas,* F dropped *-t-*, & this type was followed in E *plenty, bounty, fealty, loyalty, penalty*, etc.

-ty², suff.= *-tens,* as *twenty, thirty, ninety,* (two, three, etc. tens); OE *-tig,* cogn. w. *ten* & Goth. *tigjus,* Gk *dekas* (*deka* ten), decade.

Tyb'ûrn, n. (hist.), Place of execution in London; ~ *ticket* (hist.), exemption from parish offices etc. granted to one who prosecuted a felon to conviction; ||~ *tippet,* halter; ||~ *tree,* gallows. Hence **Tÿbû'ria** n., fashionable London district north of Hyde Park.

Tychǒn'ic (-k-), a. Of the Danish astronomer Tycho Brahe (d. 1601) or his system. [-IC]

tycoon', n. Title applied by foreigners to shogun of Japan 1854-68; *(colloq.) business magnate. [f. Jap. *taikun* great prince]

tying. See TIE¹.

tyke, ti-, n. Cur; ||low fellow; *Yorkshire* ~, Yorkshireman. [ME, f. ON *tik* bitch]

tyler. See TILER.

tȳ'loped, a. & n. (Animal) with padded not hoofed digits; e.g. camel. Hence **tȳlǒp'odous** a. [f. Gk *tulos* knob + *pous podos* foot]

tylō'sis, n. (Path.) Inflammation of eyelids with hardening of the margins; roof-timber in mine. [abbr. of foll.]

tymp, n. Crown of opening in front of hearth in blast-furnace; short horizontal roof-timber in mine. [abbr. of foll.]

tym'pan, n. Stretched sheet of membrane or thin material; frame for equalizing pressure in some printing-presses; (Anat., Archit.)=TYMPANUM. [OF. f. TYMPANUM]

tympan'ic, a. Like, acting like, a drumhead; (Anat.) of the tympanum; ~*mem-brane,* drum-membrane of ear; ~ (*bone*), bone of ear supporting this. [-IC]

tympanist, n. Var. of TIMPANIST.

tympani'it'ēs (-z), n. Swelling of abdomen caused by air in intestine etc. Hence **tympani'it'ic** a. [LL f. Gk *tumpanítēs* of *tumpanon* drum]

tympani'tis, n. Inflammation of lining membrane of tympanum. [-ITIS]

tym'panum, n. (pl. *-na*). (Anat.) middle ear, (also *tympanic membrane*) ear-drum; modified end of trachea in ducks etc.; (Archit.) triangular space forming field of pediment, similar space over door between lintel & arch, door-panel; drumwheel for raising water from stream; kind of treadmill. [L, f. Gk *tumpanon* drum]

Tyn'wald (-ōld), n. Isle of Man legislature. [f. ON *thing-vollr* place of assembly (*thing* field+*vollr* field)]

type[1], n. 1. Person, thing, event, serving as illustration, symbol, prophetic similitude, or characteristic specimen, of another thing or of a class, as *vader may serve as a ~ of instability, paschal lamb is a ~ of Christ, these things are a ~* (have a prophetic significance), *the treatment he received is but a ~ of what patriots must expect, person is an admirable ~ of modern athleticism or of the modern athlete*. 2. Class of things etc. having common characteristics, as *her beauty was of or belonged to another ~, dislike men of that ~*. 3. (biol. etc.). main division of animal or vegetable kingdom characterized by this, as *the vertebrate ~*; organism having the essential characteristics of its group (so *~ genus*, genus giving its name to & having the characteristics of a higher group, e.g. a family); whence **typ'AL** a. 4. (chem.). Compound whose structure illustrates that of many others, esp. hydrochloric acid, water, ammonia, & marsh-gas. 5. Object, conception, work of art, serving as model for subsequent artists. 6. Device on either side of medal or coin. 7. (print.). Piece of metal or wood having on its upper surface a letter or character for use in printing, (collect. sing.) set or supply or (with pl.) kind of these, as *wooden ~s are or ~ is now used only for posters, run short of ~, short of certain ~s, was printed in various ~s* (kinds or sizes of ~), *printed in large ~, a large ~ Bible; brilliant, diamond, pearl, ruby, nonpareil, emerald, minion, brevier, bourgeois, long primer, small pica, pica, English, great primer, canon, ~* (principal sizes in ascending order); BLACK[1]-*letter*, CHURCH[1]-*text*, CLARENDON, GERMAN[2]-*text*, GOTHIC, ITALIC, ROMAN[2], RUNIC, SCRIPT, (in) FOUNT[2] of ~*. 8. ~*-bar*, line of ~s in solid bar as cast in some ~-setting machines; ~-*high*, (of woodcut etc.) of proper height to print with ~; ~-*metal*, alloy used for printing~s; ~'*script*, ~written matter; ~*setter*, compositor, (also) composing machine; ~'*setting*, setting of ~s in proper order for printing, ~-*setting machine* (for simplifying this process, occas. including the making of ~s as they are needed); ~-*wheel*, wheel bearing letters in relief as used in some ~writers & telegraphs; ~*write*, print (copy etc., or abs.) with ~writer; ~*writer*, machine for producing printed characters on paper as substitute for handwriting, (now rare) typist. [F, f. L f. Gk *tupos* blow, impress, model, f. *tuptō* strike]

type[2], v.t. Be a type of; typewrite. [prec.]

typhlī't'is, n. Inflammation of caecum & vermiform appendix. Hence ~**it'ic** a. [f. Gk *tuphlos* blind, w. ref. to CAECUM, +-ITIS]

typh'oid, a. & n. Like typhus; ~ (*fever*), infectious fever with eruption of red points on chest & abdomen & severe intestinal irritation, enteric; ~ *bacillus*, germ causing~; ~ *condition* (of depressed vitality, occurring in many acute diseases); ~ *pneumonia* (combined with ~). Hence **typhoid'AL** a. [f. TYPHUS +-OID]

typhomān'ia, n. Muttering delirium characteristic of typhus. [Gk (*tuphō*-) f. *tuphos* TYPHUS, -MANIA]

typhoon', n. Violent hurricane in the China seas occurring esp. from July to October. Hence **typhōn'ic** a. [partly f. Arab. *tūfān* perh. f. Gk *tuphōn* whirlwind, partly f. Chin. *tai fung* big wind]

typh'us, n. Fever marked by eruption of purple spots, great prostration, & usu. delirium; *malignant, simple, ~, severe, mild*, form of ~. Hence **typh'ous** a. [mod. L f. Gk *tuphos* smoke, stupor]

typ'ic, a.=foll. (first sense). [f. F *typique*, f. L f. Gk *tupikos* (as TYPE[1], see -IC)]

typ'ical, a. Serving as a type or characteristic example, representative, symbolical, emblematic, (of), as *a ~ genus, plant, Scotsman, is ~ of the genus, was ~ of* (foreshadowed) *Christ's second coming*; characteristic of, serving to distinguish, a type, as ~ *markings, structure, phraseology*. Hence ~LY[2] adv., ~NESS n. [f. med. L *typicalis* (prec. -AL)]

typ'ify, v.t. Represent by a type, foreshadow; be a type of, embody the characteristics of. Hence ~FICA'TION, ~FIER[1], m. [as TYPE[1]+-FY]

typ'ist, n. User of typewriter. [f. TYPE[1] +-IST]

typ'ō, n. (sl.; pl. ~s). =TYPOGRAPHER, [abbr.]

typ'o- in comb.=TYPE[1], as: ~*ograph*, machine for making & setting type; ~*olite*, stone impressed with figure of animal etc., fossil; ~*ol'ogy*, doctrine, interpretation, of (esp. biblical) types, so ~*olo'gical* a.; ~*onym* (Biol.), name based on a type, so ~*ōn'ymal*, ~*ōnȳm'ic*, aa. **typŏg'raphy̆**, n. Art of printing, whence ~ER[1] n.; character, appearance, of printed matter, as *faults of ~y, the ~y was admirable*. Hence **typŏg'raphIc(AL)** aa., **typŏgraph'icalLY[2]** adv. [F (-*ie*), =TYPE +-o-+-GRAPHY]

tyrann'ĭc(al), a. (~*-ic* rare). Acting like, characteristic of, a tyrant; arbitrary, imperious, despotic. Hence or cogn.

~ically², tỹr̃annously², adv., ~ical-
NESS n., tỹr̃annous a. [~ic f. F tyran-
nique f. L f. Gk turannikos (TYRANT, -IC)
+-AL]

tỹr̃ann'icide, n. Killer, killing, of a
tyrant. Hence ~cid'AL a. [F, f. L tyran-
nicida, -cidium (as TYRANT, see -CIDE)]

tỹr̃annize, v.i. & t. Play the tyrant, rule
despotically or cruelly (over person etc.);
(now rare) rule (person etc.) despotically.
[f. F tyranniser (TYRANT, see -IZE)]

tỹr̃anny, n. Despotic or cruel exercise
of power; instance of this, tyrannical
act or behaviour; rule of (Greek) tyrant,
period of this. [f. OF tyrannie f. med. L
(-ia) f. Gk turannia, -ïs, as tyrant. L
-ANT]

tỹre, n. (Anglo-Ind.). Curdled milk &
cream. [Tamil tayir]

tỹre². See TIRE².
tyr̃'ō. See TIRO.
Tyrolese' (-z), a. & n. (pl. same). (Native)
of the Tyrol. [-ESE]

Tyr̃ölienne', n. Dance of Tyrolese peasants, song suitable for this. [F]

tỹr̃ot'ox'icon, n. A ptomaine produced in
milk or cheese. [f. Gk turos cheese +
toxikon poison]

Tyr̃'rhēne, Tyrrhēn'ian, (-rē-), aa.& nn.
Etruscan. [f. L f. Gk Turrhēnos +-IAN]

tzar etc. See CZAR etc.
tzetze. See TSETSE.
Tzigane (tsĭgàne'), a. & n. 1. Of the
Hungarian gipsies or their music. 2. n.
Hungarian gipsy. [F, f. Magyar czigány]

U

U, u, (ū), letter (pl. U's, Us'), U-boat,
German submarine [G untersee, under-
water]; U-bolt, -tube, etc. (shaped like
U); U.P. (sl. pronunc. of up adv., esp. it's
all U.P.).

ūbī'ety, n. Being in definite place, local
relation, whereness. [f. L ubi where,
see -TY]

ūbiquitār'ian, a. & n. (theol.). Of, believer in, the omnipresence of Christ's
body. Hence ~ISM n. [foll., -ARIAN]

ubiq'uit'y, n. Omnipresence; being
everywhere or in an indefinite number of
places at same time; ‖~y of the king
(Law), his official presence in courts in
the person of his judges. Hence ~OUS a.,
~OUSLY² adv., ~OUSNESS n. [L ubique
everywhere f. ubi where, -ITY]

ud'al (ū'dăl), n. Kind of freehold right based on

uninterrupted possession prevailing in
N. Europe before feudal system & still
in Orkney & Shetland (often attrib., as
~ tenure); ~man, holder of property by
~, so ~ER¹ n. [f. ON ōthal, cf. OHG
uodil inherited property]

ūdd'er, n. Mammary glands of cattle etc.
esp. when large & having more than one
teat. Hence (-)~ED² (-erd), ~LESS, aa.
[OE ūder, cf. Du. uijer, G euter, cogn. w.
L ūber, Gk outhar]

ūdom'eter, n. Rain-gauge. Hence ūdo-
mēt'ric a. [f. F udomètre f. L udus damp
+-O-+-METER]

ugh (ōōh), int. expr. disgust or horror.

ūg'ly, a. & n. 1. Unpleasing or repulsive
to sight, as an ~ beast of a bulldog must
not make ~ faces, the ugliest house I have
seen, has an ~ scar on the forehead;
morally repulsive, vile, discreditable, unpleasant, unpleasantly suggestive, threatening, unpromising, as ~ vices, his
conduct has an ~ look, ~ rumours are
about, an ~ (awkward) job, an ~ customer,
formidable person, cloud has an ~ look, ~
have had ~ weather, an ~ gash; ~
duckling, person who turns out the genius
etc. of the family after being thought
the dullard etc. (w. ref. to cygnet in brood
of ducks in an Andersen tale). Hence
ūg'lily v.t., ūg'lily² adv., ūg'liNESS n.
2. n. ‖ Shade worn as appendage to bonnet
about middle of 19th c. [f. ON uøglígr
fearful (uggr fear +-lígr -LY¹)]

Ug'rian, Ug'ric, (ōō'-), aa. Finnic.
name of a tribe +-IAN, -IC]

uh'lan (ōō-, ū-), n. (hist.),. Cavalryman
armed with lance in some European
armies. [G, f. Pol. ulan f. Turk. oghlān
son, child]

Uitlander (āt'länder), n. (S. Africa),.
Foreigner, alien. [Du., f. uit out+land
land; cf. OUTLANDISH]

ūkāse', n. Edict of Czarist Russian
government; any arbitrary order. [f.
Russ. ukaz' ordinance, edict]

ukulele (ūkŭlā'lē), n. Four-stringed
Hawaiian guitar. [native]

-ul- in comb. = -ULE, forming derivative
adji. etc. with or without dim. sense &
often preferred to direct formations from
parent noun (glanduler, globulin, nodu-
lose).

ul'cerate, v.i. & t. Form, convert or be
converted into, affect with, an ulcer (lit. &
fig.). Hence or cogn. ~ABLE, ~ATIVE, aa.,
~ATION n. [f. L ulcerare (prec.), -ATE³]

ul'cer, n. Open sore on external or internal
surface of body with secretion of pus
etc.; (fig.) moral blemish, corrupting influence, etc. Hence or cogn. ~ED² (-erd),
~OUS a., ~OUSLY² adv., ~OUSNESS n. [f.
L ulcus -eris sore, cf. Gk helkos wound,
sore]

-ule, suf. of dimin. f. L wds in ulus, -ula,
-ulum, as globule (L globulus f. globus),
granule, pustule, & in mod. wds on L

enal. *anguillule*; also *-le*, as *angle*. In *pendule*, *-ule* has diff. orig.

U'léma (ŏŏ-), n. Moslem doctors of sacred law & theology esp. in former Turk. empire. [f. Arab. *'ulamā* pl. of *'alim* learned f. *'alama* know]

-ulent, suf. of adj. f. L, repr. L *-ulentus*, the normal form of *-lentus* -LENT, as in *fraud~, turb~, truc~*. Hence n. suf. *-ulence*.

uli'ginōse, a. (bot.). Growing in muddy places. [f. L *uliginosus* (*uligo -ginis* moisture, see -OSE¹)]

ull'age, n. (commerc.). What a cask etc. wants of being full. [AF *ulliage*, OF *oullage* (*ouiller* fill up, -AGE)]

ul'min, n. (chem.). Black gummy substance found on elm & other trees & in vegetable mould etc. Hence ~IC, ~OUS, aa. (chem.). [f. L *ulmus* elm +-IN]

ul'na, n. (pl. ~ae). Inner of two bones of forearm (cf. RADIUS). Hence ~AR¹ a., ~o- comb. form. [L, =elbow, cf. Gk *ōlenē*, & ELL]

ulōt'rich|an a. & n., **~ous** a., (-k-). Woolly-haired; (member) of the woolly-haired division of mankind. [f. Gk *oulos* woolly +*thrix trikhos* hair +-AN, -OUS]

ul'ster, n. Long loose overcoat often with belt orig. of U~ frieze, whence ~ED² (-erd) a.; U~ custom, form of tenant-right in Ireland. [place]

ulte'rior, a. Situated beyond; more remote, not immediate, in the future, in the background, beyond what is seen or avowed, (~ *views, object, plans*). Hence ~LY² adv. [L, compar. of adj. seen in ULTRA-]

ul'tima, a. Last, most remote, (in phrr.: ~ *ra'tiō* (-shi-), final argument esp. force; ~ *ratio rēg'um*, last argument of kings, resort to arms; ~ THULE). [L, fem. of *ultimus*, superl. as prec.]

ul'timate, a. Last, final, beyond which no other exists or is possible, as ~ *result, analysis*; fundamental, primary, as ~ *basis*, ~ *principles, truths*, ~ *cause* (beyond which no other can be found), *the* ~ *facts of nature* (beyond reach of analysis). Hence ~LY² adv., ~NESS n. [f. LL *ultimare* come to an end (*ultimus*, as prec.), see -ATE²]

ul'timatum, n. (pl. -tums, -ta). Final proposal or statement of terms, rejection of which by opposite party may lead to rupture, declaration of war, etc.; ultimate conclusion; fundamental principle. [neut. p.p. as prec.]

ul'timō, adj. (usu. abbr. ult.). In the month preceding that now current (cf. PROXIMO, INSTANT¹), *as your letters of 28th ult. & 3rd inst.* [L, = in last (*mense* month), see ULTIMA]

ultimogē'niture, n. System in which youngest son (cf. PRIMOGENITURE) takes inheritance, = BOROUGH-ENGLISH. [f. L *ultimus* (see ULTIMA) on PRIMOGENITURE]

ul'tra, a. & n. Favouring, advocate of, extreme views or measures. [orig. as abbr. of F *ultra-royaliste*]

ultra-, pref. = L *ultra* beyond, on the other side of, esp. as living pref. to adj. & their derivatives w. sense 'excessively, beyond what is usual or natural or reasonable', as ~classical, ~conservatism, ~conservative, ~cosmopolitan, ~critical, ~fashionable, ~partisan, ~Protestant(ism), ~religious; applied to instruments for very minute measurements or observations, as ~micrometer, ~microscope; ~microscopic, beyond the range of any microscope; ~short wave (Wireless), having a wave-length below 10 metres.

ul'traïst, n. Holder of extreme opinions (in politics, religion, etc. So ~ISM n. -IST]

ultramarine' (-ēn), a. & n. 1. Situated beyond the sea. 2. n. Blue pigment got from lapis lazuli; *artificial* ~ (made by mixing clay, carbonate of soda, sulphur, & resin); ~ *ashes*, residuum of lapis lazuli after extraction of ~, used by old masters for neutral flesh-tints etc. [f. med. L ULTRA(*marinus* MARINE); n. sense from fact that lapis lazuli was brought from beyond sea]

ultramon'tane, a. & n. 1. Situated south of the Alps; Italian; favourable to the absolute authority of the Pope in matters of faith & discipline, whence ~anism, ~anist, nn. 2. n. One who resides south of the Alps, person holding ~ane views. [f. med. L ULTRA(*montanus* f. L *mons -ntis* mountain +-ANE); earlier in senses, 'north of Alps', 'unfavourable to Pope', etc., cf. TRAMONTANE, CIS-montane]

ultramun'dāne, a. Beyond the world or the solar system; of another life. [f. LL ULTRA(*mundanus* MUNDANE)]

ultra-vi'olet, a. (Of invisible rays of the spectrum) beyond the violet rays. [ULTRA-]

ul'tra vir'es (-z), adv. or pred. a. Beyond one's power or authority. [L]

ul'ulāte, v.i. Howl; hoot. So ~ANT a., ~A'TION n. [f. L *ululare*, see -ATE³]

-um. See -IUM.

um'bel, n. (bot.). Flower-cluster in which stalks nearly equal in length spring from common centre & form a flat or convex or concave surface as in parsley. Hence ~LAI, ~LAR¹, ~LATE²(2), ~LIF'EROUS, ~bell¹IFORM, aa., ~LET¹, ~umbell'ULE, nn. [f. L *umbella* sunshade dim. of UMBRA]

um'ber, n., a., & v.t. 1. Natural pigment like ochre but darker & browner (*raw* ~, this in natural state, of dark yellow colour, *burnt* ~, redder & deeper in colour), whence ~Y² a.; ~*bird* (also *umbrelle'*), whence ~Y² a.; ~ *grayling*; ~*bird* allied to stork & heron. 2. adj. Of ~colour, dark, dusky. 3. v.t. Colour with ~. [(vb & adj. f. n.) f. OF *ombre* (or *terre d'ombre*) f. L *Umber* Umbrian shade, or f. fem. of L *Umber* Umbrian]

ŭmbĭl'ical (or -īk'al), a. Of, situated near, the umbilicus, as ~ cord, ropelike structure passing from foetus to placenta; central; connected through the female line, as an ~ ancestor. [f. med. L umbili-calis (UMBILICUS, -AL)]

ŭmbĭl'iciate, a. Shaped like a navel, whence ~A'TION n.; having an umbilicus. [f. L umbilicatus (UMBILICUS, -ATE²)]

ŭmbĭl'icus, n. Navel, whence ŭmbĭl'-ĭf'ĕrous, ŭm'bĭlĭfŏrm, aa.; (Bot., Zool., Conch.) navel-like formation; (Geom.) point in a surface through which all lines of curvature pass; (Rom. Ant.) boss at each end of stick on which MS. was rolled. [L, cogn. w. Gk omphalos, & NAVEL]

ŭm'bō, n. (pl. ~s, ~nes pr. -ōn'ēz). Boss of shield, esp. in centre; (Bot., Zool., etc.) boss, knob, protuberance. Hence ŭm'-bonal, ŭm'bonate² ŭmbon'ic, aa. [L, gen. -ōnis]

ŭm'br|a, n. (pl. ~ae). (Astron.) total shadow (cf. PENUMBRA) cast by the earth or moon in an (eclipse); dark central part of sun-spot (cf. PENUMBRA); (Rom. Ant.) uninvited guest brought by a guest. Hence ~AL a. [L, = shade]

ŭm'brage, n. Sense of slight or injury, offence, as give, take, ~; (chiefly poet.), shade, what gives shade, so ŭmbrāge'-ous (-jus) a. [f. F ombrage f. L umbra-ticum (UMBRA, see -AGE)]

ŭmbrĕll'a, n. 1. Light circular canopy of silk or other material attached to radia-ting folding frame sliding on stick carried in the hand as protection against rain or (now usu. sunshade, parasol) sun; (fig.) a screen of fighter aircraft or (in full ~ barrage) a curtain of fire put up as pro-tection against enemy aircraft; gelatinous disk of jellyfish etc. by contraction & expansion of which it swims; (also ~ shell) gastropod with ~like shell. 2. ~ bird, kinds of S.-Amer. bird with radiating crest; ~-stand (for holding closed ~s, usu. with pan at bottom to catch drippings); ~-tree, small kind of magnolia with leaves in ~like whorl at end of branch, (colloq.) tree so grafted or trained that its branches droop in ~ form. Hence ~'d [-ED²] a. [f. It. ombrella, dim. of ombra shade f. UMBRA]

umbrette. See UMBER.

Um'brian (ŭ-), a. & n (1). Of (ancient or modern) Umbria; ~ school, school of painting to which Raphael & Perugino belonged. 2. n. Language, inhabitant, of ancient Umbria. [-AN]

ŭmbrĭf'erous, a. Affording shade. [f. L umbrifer (UMBRA, see -FEROUS)]

um'iak (ŏŏm'yăk), n. Eskimo boat worked by women. [Esk.]

um'laut (ŏŏm'lowt), n., & v.t. 1. (In Germanic languages) vowel change due to ε or u (now usu. lost or altered) in following syllable (e.g. German mann

männer, fuss füsse, English man men). 2. v.t. Modify (form, sound) by the ~. [G (um- around + laut sound)]

ŭm'pire, n., & v.t. & t. 1. (Law) third person called in to decide between arbi-trators who disagree; person chosen to decide (question); person chosen to enforce rules & settle disputes in cricket or other game. Hence ŭm'pīrage(3), ~SHIP, nn. 2. v.i. Act as ~ (for persons, in game etc.), act as ~ in (game). [(vbl n.) ME nompere third man, odd man, (non not + per PEER³); for loss of n- cf. ADDER]

ŭmp'teen, n. (sl.). Several, many, a lot of. [joc. form. on -TEEN]

'un, pron. (colloq.). One, as that's a good 'un, he's a tough 'un, stiff 'uns race.

ŭn-¹, pref. of vbs w. neg. sense & usu. denoting action contrary to or annulling that of the simple vb. The pref. being unlimited in use, only a selection of the existing vbs & derivative vbs is here given. Adj. in -able, -ed, & -ing, are identical in form with wds in UN-² with or without material difference in mean-ing; an un-²coiled rope must be coiled before it can be un-¹coiled; an unbridled¹ horse may (un-¹) or may not (UN-²) have been previously bridled, in either case he is now un²bridled². As a rule, the UN-² forms of such adj. are current, the others not. The stress in the foll. wds is not marked, being the same as in the un-¹ simple vb or n. or, where that is mono-syllabic, falling on the second syllable (undeceive', unsay'); but p.pp. or adj. in -ed, whether in un-¹ or UN-², tend in attrib. use to take stress on un- (cf. -ED²), as an un'masked villain, an un'muzzled hound, villain was unmasked, dog was unmuzzled.

1. Wds formed upon a simple verb & with contrary sense (rarely w. intensified negative sense, as unloose). The distinc-tion between some of these & the vbs in the following groups, which appear to be formed rather on a noun, is neces-sarily arbitrary, the assumed simple vb (identical in form with the noun, from which it is usu. derived) being often rare or non-existent in the required senses of ', furnish with', 'place in', etc. Exx.: unanchor v.t. & i.; unattire v.t. & i.: unbalance v.t.; unbank v.t., cause (fire) to burn briskly by removing ashes from top; unbar v.t., remove bar from (gate etc.), unlock, open, (often fig.); unbear v.t., take off or relax bearing-rein of (horse); unbend v.t. & i., change from bent position, straighten, relax (mind

etc.) from strain or exertion, rid oneself of constraint, be affable, whence unbending¹ a., (Naut.) unfasten (sails) from yards & stays, cast (cable) loose, untie (rope); unbeseem v.t., be unbecoming to; unbias v.t., free from bias; unbind v.t., release from bonds or binding; unblindfold v.t.; unblock v.i. & t. (Cards), play high card to avoid interrupting partner's long suit, give free scope to (partner's suit) by such play; unbolt v.t., release (door etc.) by drawing back bolt; unbonnet v.i. & t., take off cap etc. e.g. in salutation, remove the bonnet of; unbosom v.i. & t., disclose one's secret feelings, disclose (thoughts etc.); unbrace v.t., remove the braces of, free from tension, relax (nerves etc.); unbraid v.t., separate the strands of; unbreech v.t., free the breech of (cannon) from fastenings etc.; unbridle v.t., remove bridle from (horse, fig. person, tongue, etc.); unbuckle v.t., release the buckle of (strap, shoe, etc.); unburden v.t., relieve of burden, relieve (oneself, conscience, etc.) by confession etc. to person; unbutton v.t., open (coat etc.) by withdrawing buttons from buttonholes; unchain v.t.; unchristianize v.t.; unclasp v.t., loosen the clasp of; unclench, -inch, v.t. & i.; unclog v.t.; unclose v.t. & i., open; unclothe v.t.; uncock v.t., let down hammer of (gun) softly so as not to explode charge; uncoil v.t. & i.; uncord v.t.; uncork v.t., draw cork from (bottle), (colloq.) give vent or expression to (feelings etc.); uncouple v.t., release (dogs, railway-cars, etc.) from couples or couplings; uncover v.t. & i., remove covering from, lay bare, disclose, take off one's hat or cap, (Mil., of front line) expose (the line behind) by wheeling to right or left; uncreate¹ v.t., annihilate; uncross v.t., remove (legs, arms, knives, etc.) from crossed position; uncurb v.t.; uncurl v.t.; undeceive v.t., free from deception, whence undeceived¹ a.; undeify v.t.; undo v.t., annul (cannot ~ the past, our past actions), untie or unfasten or unloose (coat, button, parcel), unfasten the buttons or garments or stays of (person), ruin the prospects or reputation or morals of, whence undoer, undoing, nn., undone¹ a.; undomesticate v.t.; undrape v.t.; undress¹ v.t. & i., take off the clothes of, take off one's clothes, whence undressed¹ a.; unentangle v.t.; unequalize v.t.; unfasten v.t., whence unfastened¹ a.; unfetter¹ a.; unfeudalize v.t.; unfile v.t., remove (paper) from file; unfit¹ v.t., whence unfix v.t. & i., make unsuitable (for); unfix v.t., whence unfixed¹ a.; unfold v.t., open the folds of, spread out, (fig.) reveal (thoughts, designs), become opened out, develop; unform v.t.; unfurl v.t. & i., spread out (sail), become spread out; ungear v.t., strip of gear, throw out of

gear; ungild v.t.; ungird v.t.; unglaze v.t.; unhallow v.t., profane, desecrate; unhand v.t., take one's hands off, release from one's grasp; unhang v.t., remove from hanging position, strip (wall etc.) of hangings; unharness v.t.; unhasp v.t., loose from hasp; unhinge v.t., take (door) off its hinges, disorder (mind etc.), whence unhinged a.; unhitch v.t.; unhook v.t., remove from hook, open (dress etc.) by detaching its hooks; unhoop v.t.; unhouse v.t., deprive of shelter, drive from house; unhumanize v.t.; unjoin v.i.; unjoint v.t., separate joints of (fishing-rod etc.); unkink v.t. & i.; unknit v.t.; unlace v.t., loose or open by undoing lace(s) of (boot, stays, etc.); unlade v.t.; unlash v.t. (Naut.); unlatch v.t., release latch of (door); unlay v.t. (Naut.), untwist; unlearn v.t., expel from one's memory, forget the knowledge of, rid oneself of (esp. false or misleading information, habit, etc.); unline v.t., remove lining of; unlink v.t.; unload v.t., remove load from (ship, cart, etc., or abs.), remove (load) from ship etc., (Stock Exch.) get rid of (stocks or shares), sell out, withdraw charge from (gun etc.); unlock v.t., release lock of (door, box, etc., fig. mind etc.), (fig.) disclose (secret etc.); unlodge v.t., dislodge; unloose v.t., loose; unmake v.t., destroy, annul; unmask v.t. & i., remove the mask from, expose (villain, villainy), take off one's mask, reveal one's true character etc.; unmew v.t. (poet., rhet.), release; unmoor v.t., loose the moorings of (vessel etc. or fig., also abs.), weigh one of two or more anchors of (vessel); unmortise v.t.; unmould v.t., change the form of; unmuffle v.t. & i., remove muffler from (face, bell, etc.), remove muffler etc. from one's face; unmuzzle v.t., (esp., fig.) relieve of obligation to remain silent; unnaturalize v.t., make unnatural; unnerve v.t., deprive of nerve or strength or resolution, whence unnerved a.; unpack v.t., open & remove contents of (package, box, etc., or abs.), take out (contents) from package etc.; unpeg v.t., remove the peg(s) from or of, open thus; unpeople v.t., depopulate; unpick v.t., undo (stitches, garment, etc.) by picking, open with pick; unpin v.t., unfasten by removing pins; unplait v.t.; unplug v.t.; unpreach v.t., recant in preaching; unravel v.t., separate (threads etc.), separate (lit. & fig.) (material), disentangle (lit. & fig.); unreel v.t. & i., unwind, become unwound, from reel; unreeve v.t. (Naut.); unrein v.t., give the rein to (often fig.); unriddle v.t., solve or explain (riddle, mystery); unrig v.t. (Naut.); unrip v.t., rip open or apart; unrivet v.t.; unroll v.t. & i., open (roll of cloth etc.), (of roll) be opened, display, be displayed; unromanize v.t.; unroot v.t., pull up by root; unsaddle v.t. (often

abs.); **unsay** v.t., retract (statement), whence unsaid[1] a.; **unscrew** v.t., unfasten by removing screws, loosen (screw); **unseal** v.t., break the seal of, open (letter etc.); **unseam** v.t., rip open (garment etc.) at seam; **unseat** v.t., remove from seat, throw from seat on horseback, depose (M.P. etc.) from seat, whence unseated[1] a.; **unset** v.t., remove (gem) from its setting; **unsettle** v.t., disturb orderly arrangement of, discompose, disincline to routine etc. (*holidays ~ me*), derange (intellect), whence unsettled[1] a.; **unshackle** v.t.; **unsheathe** v.t.; **unship** v.t. (Naut.), remove (oar, tiller, etc.) from place where it is fixed or fitted, whence unshipped[1] a.; **unsling** v.t. (esp. Naut.); **unspeak** v.t., retract; **unsteel** v.t., soften, relax, (resolution, person); **unstick** v.t., separate (one thing) from another; *come unstuck*, sl., come to grief, fail); **unstitch** v.t., undo stitches of; **unstock** v.t., deprive of stock, remove (gun-barrel) from stock; **unstop** v.t., free from obstruction, remove stopper from; **unstrap** v.t., remove or undo the strap(s) of; **unstring** v.t., remove the strings of, loosen strings of (harp etc.), take (beads etc.) off string, weaken (nerves), weaken nerves of (person etc.), whence unstrung a.; **unswaddle** v.t.; **unswathe** v.t.; **unswear** v.t., recant by oath; **untack** v.t., disjoin, separate, (thing tacked to another); **untangle** v.t.; **unteach** v.t.; **untemper** v.t., take away the temper of (metal etc.); **unthink** v.t., retract in thought; **unthread** v.t., take thread out of (needle), find one's way out of (maze); **untie** v.t., undo (knot etc.), undo the cords etc. of (bundle, package, etc.), liberate from bonds, whence untied[1] a.; **untruss** v.t.; **untuck** v.t.; **untune** v.t., put out of tune (lit. & fig.); **untwist** v.t. & i.; **unveil** v.t. & i., remove veil from, remove one's veil, remove concealing drapery from (statue etc.) with ceremonies; **unvote** v.t., retract by vote (what has been voted); **unwarp** v.t., restore from warped state; **unweave** v.t., take to pieces (textile fabric), separate (woven threads); **unwill** v.t., will the reverse of (what one has willed); **unwind** v.t. & i., draw out at length (what is wound), become thus drawn out, whence unwound[1] a.; **unwish** v.t., retract in thought, undo, destroy; **unwrap** v.t. & i., **unwrinkle** v.t.; **unyoke** v.t. & i., release (as from) yoke, (fig.) cease work.

2. Vbs formed on n. or vb⁻—see (1)—& having sense 'deprive of', 'separate from'. A simple vb sometimes exists in same sense, e.g. (*un*)*bone*, (*un*)*husk*, (*un*)*shell*. Exxs.: **unappareled** v.t.; **unarm** v.t., deprive of arms or armour, whence unarmed[1] a.; **unballast** v.t.; **unbell** v.t.; **unbone** v.t.; **unboot** v.t. & i.; **unbowel** v.t.; **uncap** v.t.; **uncloak** v.t.; **uncowl** v.t., uncover (face) by removing cowl, un-monk; **uncrown** v.t., deprive (esp. fig. king etc.) of crown; **unedge** v.t., destroy edge of, blunt; **unface** v.t., expose; **un-feather** v.t.; **unfence** v.t.; **unflesh** v.t.; **unflower** v.t.; **unframe** v.t.; **unfrock** v.t., deprive of frock or (fig.) of ecclesiastical rank; **ungirdle** v.t.; **unglove** v.t. & i., deprive of, take off one's gloves; **ungown** v.t.; **ungum** v.t.; **unhair** v.t.; **unhat** v.t. & i.; **unhead** v.t. (Print.), remove leads from (types); **un-helm** v.t.; **unhusk** v.t.; **unkennel** v.t.; **unland** v.t.; **unleash** v.t.; **unman** v.t., deprive (esp. ship) of men, see also (4); **unmask** v.t., take nails out of, un-fasten (box etc.), thus; **unplume** v.t.; **unprop** v.t.; **unring** v.t.; **unrobe** v.t. & i., undress; **unroof** v.t.; **unrumple** v.t.; **un-scale** v.t., remove scales of; **unself** v.t., rid of self, unegoize; **unsex** v.t., deprive (usu. woman) of the qualities of the sex; **unshell** v.t.; **unshoe** v.t., remove shoe(s) of (horse etc.); **unshot** v.t., remove shot from (gun); **unshudder** v.t.; **unsister** v.t.; **unslumber** v.t.; **unsolder** v.t.; **unspar** v.t.; **unstarch** v.t., free from starch or (fig.) stiffness or reserve; **unstopper** v.t.; **unfile** v.t.; **untin** v.t.; **untooth** v.t.; **unturf** v.t.; **untomb**

3. Vbs similarly formed with sense 're-lease from', 'take out of', 'displace from'. Exxs.: **unbag** v.t.; **unbed** v.t.; **unbit** v.t. (Naut.); **unbox** v.t.; **uncage** v.t.; **uncart** v.t.; **uncase** v.t.; **unchurch** v.t., excommunicate; **uncloister** v.t.; **uncoop** v.t.; **undock** v.t.; **unearth** v.t., drive (fox etc.) from an earth, dig up, (fig.) bring to light; **unfold²** v.t., release (sheep) from fold; **unhive** v.t.; **unhorse** v.t., throw from horse, (of horse) throw (rider), cause to dismount; **unleash** v.t.; **unnest** v.t.; **unpen** v.t.; **unperch** v.t.; **unroost** v.t.; **unsnare** v.t.; **unspell** v.t.; **unstep** v.t. (Naut.); **untent** v.t.; **unthrone** v.t.; **untomb** v.t.

4. Occasional vbs formed chiefly f. nouns with sense 'cause to be no longer', 'degrade from the position of'. Exxs.: **unbishop** v.t.; **unduke** v.t.; **unking** v.t.; **unprince** v.t.; **unqueen** v.t.; **un-squire** v.t.; **unvicar** v.t.; **unpope** v.t.; **unprelate** v.t.; **unpriest** v.t.; **unlord** v.t.; **unman** v.t., deprive of manly qualities, break the courage of, dishearten, emasculate, see also (2).

ün-², pref. giving negative sense to adj., with their derivative nn. & advv., & to a miscellaneous group of in-dependent formation.

1. Of the many adj. formed with *un-*, esp. of those in *-able*, *-ed*, *-ing*, for which cf. UN-¹, only a selection is here given. The sense of *un-* is either simply 'not' (as in most adj. in *-able*, *-ed*, *-ing*, & in some others, as *unofficial*) or more com-monly 'the reverse of', with implication

of praise, blame, etc. Between *un-* & *in-²* a differentiation has been suggested according to which *inartistic* means ' contrary to rules of art,' such as an artist would condemn', & *unartistic* means ' not concerned with rules of art'; & pairs of words may be found that bear out the distinction, esp. where one of the pair has long been restricted to the proposed sense & the other has been manufactured or revived to supply its deficiencies (*immoral, unmoral*). But the purely neutral sense thus ascribed to *un-* is not that found in many of the most familiar adj. (*unbeautiful, unfair, ungraceful, ungracious, unkind, unjust, ungenerous, untrue, unscrupulous, unmanly, unscholarly, unladylike, unchristian*), including some of the exact type of *unartistic* (*unscientific, unphilosophical*): when we say that a thing is *undrue*, we do not mean that it does not matter for our purpose whether it is true or not, but that it is culpably inconsistent with truth. Apart from the adj. in *-able, -ed, -ing*, both *un-* & *in-* more commonly have this implication of blame etc., the purely neutral sense being often given by NON-(5). IN-² is preferred to *un-* with certain terminations of L orig., e.g. *-ate, -ite, -ant, -ent, -ble* (exc. *-able*, now a living E suf.), *-ed¹* (*indigested* etc., part arch. with *-ed¹,²*, but cf. *inexperienced*), and is not used with *-ing, -ful, -like, -ly*, etc. Derivatives in *-ly, -ness, -ity*, etc., are briefly recorded, but for adj. in *-ed* see UN-¹. Exx.: **unabashed**; unabated; unabbreviated; unabetted; unabiding; **unable**, not able (to do); unabridged; unabsorbable; unabsorbed; unabsorbent; unaccented; unaccentuated; unacceptable; unaccommodating; **unaccompanied**, not accompanied, (Mus) without accompaniment; **unaccomplished**, not accomplished or achieved, lacking accomplishments; unaccordant; **unaccountable** (*-bility, -bleness, -bly*), that cannot be explained, strange, not responsible; unaccredited; unaccented; unaccused; **unaccustomed**, not accustomed (to), not usual (*his ~ silence*); unachievable; unachieved; unacknowledged; unacquainted; unacquirable; unacquired; unacted; unadaptable; unadapted; unaddicted; unaddressed; unadjudged; unadjusted; unadministered; unadmired; unadmonished; **unadopted**, ||(esp., of new roads) not taken over for maintenance by the local authority; unadorned; unadulterated; unadventurous; unadvisable (*-bility*); **unadvised** (*-edly*), indiscreet, rash, without advice; un-ffable; **unaffected** (*-ly, -ness*), free from affectation, genuine, sincere, not affected (*by*); unaffiliated; unafflicted; unaggressive; unaided; unalarmed; unalleviated; unallotted; unallowable; unalloyed; **unalterable** (*-bility,*

-bleness, -bly); unaltered; unamazed; unambiguous (*-ly, -ness*); unambitious (*-ly, -ness*); unamenable; unamendable; **unAmerican**, not American, foreign to American customs or ideas; unamiable (*-bility, -bleness, -bly*); unamusing; unanalysable; unanalysed; unanimated; unannounced; **unanswerable** (*-bility, -bleness, -bly*), that cannot be answered or refuted; unanswered; unanticipated; unapocryphal; **unapostolic**, contrary to apostolic usage, not having apostolic authority; unappalled; unapparelled; unapparent; unappeasable; unappeased; unappetizing (*-ly*); unapplied; unappreciated; unappreciative; unapprehended; unapprehensive; unapprised; unapproachable (*-bility, -bleness, -bly*); **unappropriated** (*~ blessing*, joc., old maid); unapproved; unapproving (*-ly*); unapt (*-ly, -ness*); unarmed²; unarmoured; unarranged; unarrayed; unarrested; **unartificial** (*-ly*), not artificial, natural; unartistic; unascertainable; unascertained; unashamed; unasked; unaspirated; unaspiring (*-ly*); **unassailable**, not assailable, (of statement etc.) against which nothing can be said; unassayed; unassignable; unassimilated; unassisted; **unassuming**, making little of one's merits or status; **unattached**, not attached, (Law) not seized for debt, (Mil.) not assigned to regiment or company, (Univ., of student) belonging to no college; unattainable (*-ness*); unattempted; unattended; unattested; unattractive (*-ly, -ness*); unaugmented; unauthentic (*-ity*); unauthenticated; unauthorized; unavailable; **unavailing** (*-ly*), ineffectual; unavenged; unavoidable (*-bly*); unavowed; **unaware**, not aware (*of, that,* etc.); **unawares** (ŭnawâr'z) [-ᴇs] adv. & n., unexpectedly, by surprise, unintentionally, as *was taken ~ by his question, must have dropped it ~*, (n.) *at ~*, unexpectedly; **unbacked**, not supported, having no backers (esp. in betting); unbaptized; **unbroken**, not taught to bear rider; **unbalanced**, (esp., of the mind) disordered, violently impulsive; unbaptized; **unbearable** (*-bly*); **unbeaten**, not beaten, not surpassed (*~ record* etc.); **unbeautiful**, ugly; **unbecoming** (*-ly, -ness*), indecorous (*an ~ speech*), not befitting (person, *to* or *for* person), not suited to the wearer (*are ~ hat*); unbefitting; unbefriended; unbegotten; **unbeknown, -knownst** [-ᴇs], (colloq.), not known, esp. *~ to* quasi-adv., without the knowledge of, as *did it ~ to him*; unbelievable; **unbelieving** (*-ly*), not believing esp. in divine revelation; unbeloved (*-ed*); **unbending²** (*-ly, -ness*), not bending, inflexible, firm, austere; unbeneficed; unbeseeming (*-ly*); unbesought; unbespoken; unbias(s)ed; **unbiblical**, not in or authorized by the Bible; **unbidden**, not commanded, not invited; unbigoted; unbleached; unblemished; unblest; **unblooded**, (of horse etc.) not thoroughbred; unblush-

ing (-ly, -ness); unbookish; un-born; un-bounded (-ly, -ness), not bounded (by, or abs.), infinite; ~ by, unbred; unbridled (-ly, -ness), not bridled, esp. fig., as ~ inso-lence, tongue; unbroken, not broken, esp. fig., as ~ ness), not broken, not subdued, not interrupted (~ slumber, peace), not surpassed (~ re-cord), not broken in (~ horse); unbrother-ly; unburdened; unburied; unbusinesslike;

uncalled, not called, esp. ~ for, imperti-nently obtruded, as the remark was ~ for, his ~-for remark; uncanal; uncandid (-ly); unceremonious (-ly, -ness), informal, familiar, abrupt in manner, wanting in courtesy; uncertain (-ly, -ty), not cer-tainly knowing or known (am ~ which he means, ~ of his meaning, is of ~ age, the result is ~, not to be depended on (is ~ in his aim), changeable (~ temper, weather); uncertificated; un-challenged; unchancy (chiefly Sc.), un-lucky, unseasonable; unchangeable (-bly, -ness); uncharitable (-bly, -ness), cen-sorious, severe in judgement; unchar-chastened; unchary; unchaste (-ly, -tity); un-ness), not Christian; uncircumstantial, heathen, unregenerate; uncircumstantial, (fig.) not going into details; uncivil (-ly), ill-mannered, rude; uncivilized, unclad; un-claimed; unclean (-ness), not clean, foul, unchaste, ceremonially impure (in Jew-ish law); unclerical; unclothed; unclouded (esp. ~ of happiness etc., cf. cloudless); uncoloured, not coloured, (fig.) not exaggerated or heightened in descrip-tion (~ account etc.); uncombed; uncome-at-able(-kumāt-), colloq., not accessible or attainable; uncomely (-iness); uncomfor-table (-bly); uncommercial, not commercial, contrary to commercial principles; un-committed; uncommon (-ly, -ness) a. & colloq. adv., not common, unusual, re-markably (adv.) remarkably (un ~ fine girl); uncommunicative (-ly, -ness), re-served, taciturn; uncompanionable; un-completing (-ly, -ness); uncomplaisant (-ly); uncomplicated; uncomplimentary; uncompounded; uncompromising (-ly), not admitting of compromise, decided, in-flexible, unyielding; unconcerned (-edly), free from anxiety or agitation; uncon-demned; unconsidered; unconditional (-ly, -ness, -ity), not subject to conditions, ab-solute, (~ surrender, refusal); uncondi-tioned, not subject to conditions (the U~, Philos, that which is not subject to the conditions of finite existence or inborn response to Psych, instinctive

a stimulus); unconfirmed (esp. of rumour etc.); unconformable (-bly, -ness); uncon-genial; unconquerable (-bly, -ness); uncon-quered; unconnected; unconquerable (-ly, -bly)) unconquered; unconscientious (-ly, -ness); unconscionable (-bly, -ness), wholly unreasonable, not guided or restrained by conscience, (Law) ~ bargain, contract too grossly unfair to be enforced, (prob. f. conscience, formed as sing. of conscience taken as pl.); unconscious (-ly, -ness), not conscious, as was ~ of any change, lay for some hours, ~ CEREBRATION, the ~ (as n.; see PSYCHO-analyst); unconsecrated, unconsidered, disregarded; unconstitu-tional (-ly, -ty), (of measures, acts, etc.) opposed to a country's constitution; uncon-strained (-edly); unconstrained; uncon-taminate(d); uncontaminated; uncontemplated, not expected; uncontested; uncontra-dicted; uncontrollable (-bly, -ness); un-controlled; uncontroversial (-ly); uncon-ventional (-ly, -ty); unconverted; uncon-victed; unconvinced; unconvincing (-ly, -ness); uncooked; uncoordinated; uncor-roborated; uncorrected; uncorroborated; uncorrupt(ed); uncorrupted; uncountable, not uncoupled; uncourtly; uncouth; uncourteous, uncouth; uncoursed, uncovenanted, not promised by or based on a covenant (~ mercies of God), not enjoying a covenant (~ civil service in India); uncovered; un-covered; uncreated, not yet created, (also arch. uncreate²) existing without being created; uncritical (-ly), disinclined or incompetent to criticize, uncrossed, not to principles of criticism; uncrossed, not crossed ((~ cheque etc.), not thwarted, uncrowned (~ king, not yet crowned, also having power but not name of king); unculled; uncultivable; uncultivated; un-cultured; uncurbed; uncurled; uncush-ioned; uncustomed, not liable to duty, having paid no duty; uncut, not cut, esp. (of book) with full untrimmed margins (~ covert), uncreated, not yet created, un-

undamaged; undated, not dated; un-daunted (-ly, -ness), not daunted, fearless; undebauched; undebauched; undeceived (-ly), irresolute (he stood ~); undecipherable; undecided (-ly), not settled (point is still ~), undefended, (esp. of suit) in which no defence is put in; undefiled; undemonstra-tive, not given to showing strong feelings, reserved; undeniable (-bly), that cannot be denied or disputed, decidedly good; undenominational (~ education); unde-pendable; underived; undeplored; un-deposed; undepraved; undepreciated; un-depressed; underserved; undervalued; undeserving; undesignated; undesigned (-edly), not designed, esp. not intended; undesirable (-bility, -bleness, -bly) a. & n. not desirable, unpleasant, inconvenient, (n.) ~ person; undesired, not desired or soli-cited; undestroyed; undetachable; undetected; undetermined, not settled, irresolute; undeveloped; undeviating (-ly);

undevout (-ly); undifferentiated; undiffused; undigested (esp. fig., of ill-arranged facts etc.); undignified, lacking or inconsistent with dignity; undiluted; undiminished; undimmed; undiplomatic; undirected; undiscerned; undiscerning (-ly); undischarged; undisciplined; undisclosed; undiscomfited; undisconcerted; undiscoverable (-bly); undiscovered; undiscriminating (-ly); undiscussed; undisguised (-dly), not veiled, open, (~ reluctance etc.); undismayed; undispelled; undispersed; undisplayed; undisputed; undissected; undissembled; undissolved; undistinguishable (-bly, -ness); undistinguished; undistracted; undistressed; undistributed (~ middle, fallacy resulting from failure to DISTRIBUTE middle term); undisturbed (-dly); undiversified; undivided; undivorced; undivulged; undomesticated; undone², not done; undoubted; undoubtedly adv., without doubt (implying certainty on speaker's part, cf. DOUBTLESS); undoubting (-ly); undraped; undreamed-of, -nt-of; undressed²; undrilled; undrinkable; undue (-duly), excessive, disproportionate, (spoke with ~ warmth), improper (~ influence, by which person, e.g. testator, is induced to do what he would not of his own free will; (of bill etc.) not yet due; undurable (-bly); undutiful (-ly, -ness); undying (-ly), immortal (~ fame etc.);

unearned, not earned (~ increment, increased value of land due to external causes e.g. increased population, not to owner's labour or outlay); unearthly (-iness), not earthly, supernatural, ghostly, weird, (~ cry, pallor), (colloq.) absurdly early (why call me at this ~ hour?); uneasy (-ily, -iness), disturbed or uncomfortable in body or mind (you seem ~ passed an ~ night), disturbing (had an ~ suspicion); uneatable; uneaten; unecclesiastical; uneclipsed; uneconomic, (esp., of rent) too low to repay owner & builder; uneconomical; unedifying, (esp.) tending to suggest evil or offend moral delicacy; unedited; uneducated; uneffaced; uneffected; unelated; unelected; unelucidated; unemancipated; unembarrassed; unemphatic (-ally); unemotional (-ally); unemployable a. & n., (person) unfitted by character, by age, or otherwise, for paid employment; unemployed, not used, lacking employment, out of work & wages (~ capital, energies, the ~); unempowered; unenclosed; unencumbered (~ estate, having no liabilities on it); unendangered; unending (-ly, -ness), having no end; unendorsed; unendowed; unendurable (-bly); unenforced; unenfranchised; unengaged; un-English, not (characteristic of) the English; unenjoyable; unenlightened; unenrolled; unenslaved; unenterprising; unentertaining (-ly, -ness); unenthusiastic (-ly, -ness); unenumerated;

rated; unenviable (-bly); unenvied; unequable; unequal (-ly), not equal (to), of varying quality; unequalled; unequipped; unequivocal (-ly, -ness), not ambiguous, plain, unmistakable; unerased; unerring (-ly, -ness), not erring or failing or missing the mark (~ judgement, wisdom, aim); unescapable; unespied; unessayed; unessential a. & n., not essential, not of the first importance, (n.) ~ part or thing; unestablished; unestimated; unestranged; unevangelical; unevaporated; uneven (-ly, -ness), not level or smooth, not uniform or equable (makes ~ progress, has an ~ temper), (of number, rare) odd; uneventful (-ly); unexamined; unexampled, without precedent; unexcelled; unexceptionable (-bly, -ness), with which no fault can be found; unexcised, not subject to excise; unexclusive (-ly); unexecuted; unexemplified; unexercised; unexhausted; unexpected (-ly, -ness); unexpensive; unexpiated; unexpired, (of lease etc.) still running; unexplained; unexplored; unexpressed; unexpounded; unexpressed; unexpurgated; unextended, not extended, occupying no space, dimensionless;

unfadable, that cannot fade; unfading (-ly, -ness); unfailing (-ly, -ness), not failing, not running short (~ supply), not disappointing one's expectations etc. (~ resource, supporter, etc.); unfair (-ly, -ness), not equitable or honest or impartial (an ~ advantage, got by ~ means, ~ play); unfaithful (-ly, -ness), (esp.) not faithful in wedlock; unfaltering (-ly); unfamiliar (-ity, -ly); unfashionable (-bly, -ness); unfashioned, not brought into shape; unfashioned¹; unfathered, (poet.) fatherless, (fig.) not acknowledged by its author (~ theory etc.); unfatherly; unfathomable (-bly); unfathomed; unfavourable (-bly, of person etc.) developed; unfleshed, not FEED³; unfeeling (-ly, -ness), lacking sensibility, harsh, cruel; unfeigned (-edly); unfelt, not FELT²; unfeminine; unfermented; unfertilized; unfettered²; unfigured, not marked with figures (~ muslin, vase); unfilial (-ly); unfilled; unfiltered; unfinished; unfit (-ly, -ness), not fit (to do, for purpose, for a doctor etc., to be one); unfitted, not fit, not fitted, not furnished with fittings; unfitting (-ly); unfixed²; unflagging; unflattering (-ly); unflavoured; unfledged, not yet fledged or (fig., of person etc.) developed; unfleshed; unflinching (-ly); unfordable; unforeseen; unforgettable; unforgivable; unforgiven; unforgiving (-ly, -ness); unforgotten; unformed, not formed, shapeless; unformulated; unfortified; unfortunate (-ly) a. & n., the reverse of fortunate, unlucky, unhappy, (n.) ~ person; unfounded, without foundation (~ rumour, hopes); not yet founded; unfrequented; unfriended, lacking friends; unfriendly (-iness); unfruitful (-ly, -ness); unfulfilled; unfunded, (of debt

floating, not funded.; **unfurnished**, not supplied (*with*), without furniture; **un-fused** (FUSE¹, ²).

ungallant, not gallant to women; **ungarnished**; **ungathered**; **ungauged**; **un-generous** (-ly); **ungenteel**; **ungentle** (-ness, -ly); **ungentlemanly** (-iness); ungentlemanly of a gentleman, rude, ill-bred; unworthy of a gentleman, rude, ill-bred; **ungodly** (-ly, -iness); **ungovern-able** (-bly), unruly, licentious, wild, violent, (~ *passions*); **ungraceful** (-ly, -ness); **ungracious**, not kindly or courteous (~ *reply, reception*); **ungrudg-ing** (-ly); **unguarded** (-ly), not guarded, incautious, thoughtless (*an ~ expression, admission*);

unhackneyed; **unhallowed**; **unhampered**; **unhandsome** (-ly, -ness), (of appearance, conduct, etc.) not handsome; **unhandy** (-ily, -iness), awkward to handle, incon-venient, (of person) clumsy; **unhanged**, (esp.) who has escaped hanging (*the greatest scoundrel ~*); **unhappy** (-ily, -iness), not happy, unlucky, wretched; **unharmed**; **unhatched** (HATCH², ³); un-**healthy** (-ily, -iness); **unhealthy** (-ly, -iness),(esp.) Mil. sl., of places) dangerous, exposed to fire; **unheard**, not heard (~ *of*, unprecedented); **unheeded**; **unheedful** (-ly); **unheeding**; **unhelpful** (-ly); **un-hemmed**; **unheralded**; **unheroic**; **unhesitat-ing** (-ly); **unhewn** (lit., & fig., rough, incondite); **unhidden**; **unhistoric(al)**,(esp.) merely legendary; **unholy** (-ily, -iness), not holy, impious, wicked, (colloq., as intensive epithet) frightful, hideous (*what an ~ row to kick up!*); **unhonoured**; **un-human**, not human; **unhung**; **unhurt**;

unidea'd, having no ideas; **unideal**, not ideal, prosaic, ordinary, dull, interior; **unidentified**; **unilluminated**; **unillustrated**; **unimaginable**; **unimaginative** (-ly, -ness); **unimpaired**; **unimpassioned**; **unimpeach-able** (-bility, -bleness, -bly), giving no opening to censure, beyond reproach or question; **unimpeded**; **unimportant**(-ance); **unimposing**; **unimpressionable**; **unim-pressive** (-ly, -ness); **unimproved**, (esp. of land) not improved; **unimpregnated**; **un-indexed**; **unindicated**; **uninfected**; **uninfluenced**; **uninflected**; **uninformed**,(esp.)ignorant; **uninhabitable**; **uninhabited**; **uninitiated**; **uninjured**; **uninspired**, (esp. of oratory etc.) commonplace; **uninstigated**; **un-instructed**; **uninstructive**; **uninsulated**; **unintelligent** (-ly); **unintelligible** (-bility, -bleness, -bly); **unintentional** (-ly, -ness); **uninteresting** (-ly, -ness); **unintermittent** (-ly); **unintermitting**(-ly); **uninterpretable**(-bly); **uninterrupted**(-ly); **uninvestigated**(-ly); **uninvited**; **un-**

unviting (-ly), unattractive, repellent; **uninvolved**; **uninvoked**; **unirrigated**; **un-isolated**; **unissued**; **unjaundiced**; **unjust** (-ly), contrary to justice, not just; **unjusti-fiable**(-bly, -ness).

unkind (-ly, -ness), not kind, harsh, cruel; **unkindled**; **unknightly** (-iness); **unknowable** (-bility, -bleness, -bly) (*the U~*, the First Cause or ultimate reality, which is beyond finite apprehension); **unknowing** (-ly) not knowing, uncon-scious, (of, or abs.) unknowns, n.,&adv., not known (*he, his purpose, what he wanted, that district was ~ to me, a youth to fame ~, of ~ ingredients, x & y denote the ~, equation of two ~s,* (adv.) ~ *to, without the knowledge of; did it ~ to me*).

unlabelled; **unlaboured**, (of style etc.) easy, spontaneous; **unladylike**; **un-lamented**; **unlawful** (-ly, -ness); **un-learned**, not LEARNED; **unlearnt** (pr. -nd), not learnt; **unleavened** (lit. & fig.), **unlettered**, illiterate; **unlicensed**; **unlicked**, not licked into shape, unmannerly; **unlike** (-ness) a. & prep., not like (*is ~ both his parents, the two are ~, plays quite ~ anyone I have heard before*); **unlikely** (-lihood, -iness), improbable, unpromising, (~*tale, errand*); **unlimited** (-ly, -ness), boundless, unre-stricted, very great or numerous (*has ~ scope, possibilities, his powers are ~, expense of sea, drinks ~ coffee*); **unlined**, (esp.) with no lining, (of face etc.) not wrinkled; **unliquidated**; **unlit**; **unlocated**; **unlooked-for**, not expected; **unlopped**; **un-lovable**; **unloved**; **unlovely** (-iness), not amiable or attractive; **unloverlike**; **un-loving**; **unlucky** (-ly), not lucky or for-tunate or successful, hapless, wretched, unsuccessful, bringing bad luck, ill-timed, ill-contrived, (~ *toss of coin, always ~ at cards, ~ fellow, asked in an ~ hour, single magpie is ~, his ~ efforts to please, an ~ expedient*).

unmade; **unmaidenly**; **unmailable**, that must not or cannot be sent by post; **unmaintainable**; **unmalleable** (-bility); **unmanageable** (-bly, -ness), not (easily) to be managed or manipulated or controlled (~ *child, material, situation*); **unmanful**(-ly); **unmanlike**, not like a man, esp. womanish or childish; **unmanly** (-iness); **unmannerly** (-iness), rude, ill-bred; **unmarked**, not marked, not noticed; **unmarketable**; **unmarriageable** (-ness); **unmarried**; **unmasculine**, not masculine or manly; **unmatchable**; **unmatched**; **unmeaning** (-ly, -ness), without meaning, senseless; **un-measured**, (poet.) immeasurable; **unme-chanical**; **unmeet** (-ly, -ness), arch., **not**

fit (to do, for purpose); *unmelodious* (-ly, -ness); *unmelted*; *unmendable*; *unmentionable* (-ness) a. & n., that it is improper to mention, (n. pl., joc.) trousers; *unmerchantable*; *unmerciful* (-ly, -ness); *unmerited*; *unmethodical*; *unmetrical* (-ly), not metrical, violating requirements of metre; *unmilitary*; *unmindful* (-ly, -ness); *unmined*; *unmirthful* (-ly); *unmistakable* (-bly), that cannot be mistaken or doubted, clear; *unmitigated*, unqualified, absolute, (~ *blackguard, lie*); *unmixed*; *unmodernized*; *unmodified*; *unmodulated*; *unmolested*; *unmoral* (-ity), non-moral; *unmortgaged*; *unmotherly*; *unmounted*, not mounted (~ *police, picture, jewel*); *unmourned*, *unmoved*, not moved, not changed in purpose, not affected by emotion; *unmown*; *unmurmuring* (-ly), not complaining; *unmusical* (-ly, -ly), not pleasing to the ear, unskilled in or indifferent to music; *unmutilated*;

unnamable, (esp., of vices) too horrible to be named; *unnamed*; *unnational*; *unnatural* (-ly, -ness), contrary to nature, monstrous, (~ *crimes, vices*), lacking natural feelings (~ *parent, child*), artificial, forced, affected; *unnaturalized* (-ly) a. & n., not naturalized; *unnavigable*; *unnecessary* (-ily) a. & n., not necessary, more than is necessary (with ~ *care*), (n., usu. pl.) ~ thing(s); *unneedful* (-ly); *unnegotiable*; *unneighbourly* (-iness); *unnoticed*; *unnourished*; *unnumbered*, not marked with number, not counted, countless;

unobjectionable (-bly); *unobliging*; *unobliterated*; *unobscured*; *unobservant*; *unobserved*; *unobstructed*; *unobtainable*; *unobtrusive* (-ly, -ness); *unoccupied*; *unoffending*, harmless, innocent; *unoffered*; *unofficial*, (esp., of news) not officially confirmed; *unofficinal*; *unopened*; *unopposed*; *unordained*; *unorganized*; *unoriginal*, not possessing originality, derived; *unornamental*, not ornamental, unsightly; *unornamented*; *unorthodox*; *unostentatious* (-ly, -ness); *unowned*;

unpacified; *unpaged*, with pages not numbered; *unpaid*, (of sum, bill, debt, or person) not paid (|| *the great* ~, magistrates or justices); *unpaired*; *unpalatable* (-bly); *unparalleled*, having no parallel or equal; *unpardonable* (-bly, -ness); *unpared*; *unparental*, unworthy of a parent; *unparliamentary* usage (~ *language*, oaths, abuse); *unpatented*; *unpatriotic* (-ally); *unpatronized*; *unpaved*; *unpawned*; *unpeaceful*; *unpedantic*; *unpedigreed*; *unpeeled*; *unpensioned*; *unperceived*; *unperforated*; *unperformed*; *unperjured*; *unpersuadable*; *unpersuaded*; *unpersuasive*; *unperturbed*; *unperused*; *unperverted*; *unphilosophical* (-ly, -ness), not according to philosophical principles, wanting in philosophy; *unpicked*, not selected, (of flowers) not plucked; *unpicturesque*; *unpiloted*; *unpitied*; *unpitying* (-ly); *unplaced*, not placed esp. in race or list; *unplagued*; *unplanned*; *unplanted*; *unplastered*; *unplastic*; *unplaited*; *unplausible* (-bly); *unplayable* (esp. of ball or serve in games); *unpleasant* (-ly), not pleasant, disagreeable; *unpleasantness* n., in adj. senses, also, misunderstanding, quarrel, *the late ~* (joc.), the civil war; *unpleasing* (-ly); *unpliable* (-bly); *unpliant* (-ly); *unploughed*; *unplucked*; *unplumbed*; *unpoetical* (-ly, -ness); *unpointed*, having no point, not punctuated, without vowel points (in Hebrew etc.), (of masonry) not pointed; *unpolished*; *unpolitical*, not concerned with politics; *unpolled*, *unpolluted*, *unpopular* (~ *elector, vote*), not popular, esp. not liked by the public; *unportioned*, portionless; *unpossessed*, not possessed, not *unposted*, uninformed, ||(of letter) not posted; *unpractical*(-ity,-ly);(of person, plan, method, etc.) not practical; *unpractised*, not experienced or skilled, not put into practice; *unpraised*; *unprecedented*, for which there is no precedent, unparalleled; *unprefaced*; *unprejudiced*, (esp.) impartial; *unprelatical*; *unpremeditated* (-ly), not previously thought over, not deliberately planned, unintentional; *unpreoccupied*; *unprepared* (-ness), not prepared (*found everything* ~, *was* ~ *for this objection, delivered an* ~ *speech*); *unprepossessing*; *unprescribed*; *unpresentable*, not presentable, not fit to be seen; *unpresented* to company, not fit to be seen; *unpresuming*; *unpresumptuous*; *unpretending* (-ly), *unpretentious* (-ly, -ness), aa., not given to display, making little show; *unpreventable*; *unpriced*, with the price(s) not fixed or marked or stated (~ *goods, catalogue*); *unpriestly*; *unprimed*; *unprincely*; *unprincipled*, lacking or not dictated by good moral principles (~ *person, conduct*); *unprintable*, (esp.) too blasphemous, indecent, etc., to appear in print; *unprinted*; *unprivileged*; *unprized*, not valued; *unproclaimed*; *unprocurable*; *unproductive* (-ly, -ness); *unprofaned*; *unprofessional* (-ly), not pertaining to one's profession, not belonging to a profession, contrary to professional etiquette etc., (*knows nothing of* ~ *matters, ask any* ~ *man,* ~ *conduct*); *unprofitable* (-bly, ~ness; ~ *servants*, persons content to do no more than their duty); *unprogressive* (-ness), not progressive, conservative; *unprohibited*; *unprolific*; *unpromising*; *unprompted*, spontaneous; *unpromulgated*; *unpronounceable*; *unpropagated*;*unprophetic*;*unpropitious*(-ly, -ness); *unproportional*, not proportional; *unproposed*; *unprosperous*(-ly, -ness); *unprotected*; *unprotestant*; *unprovable*; *unproved, -en*; *unprovided*, not supplied (*with money* etc.), not prepared; *unprovoked*;

(of person or act) without provocation; unprovoked; unpublished, not made public; (of MS. etc.) not published; unpractical (-tice, -ly); unpunished; unpurified; unqualified;

unqualified (-ly); unqualified (-ly), not competent, not legally or officially qualified, not modified, (am ~ to serve, an ~ practitioner, gave his ~ assent); unquelled; unquenchable (-bly); unquenched; unquestionable (-bly), that cannot be questioned or doubted, not disputed or doubted, not interrogated; unquestioning (-ly), asking no questions (~ obedience etc.), yielded without questions asked); unquiet, restless, agitated, (~ spirit, times); unquotable (as unprintable); unquoted.

unransomed; unrazored, unshaven, (of book etc.) not read, (of person) not well-read; unreadable (-bly), not readily, not prompt in action; unreal (-ity, -ly), illusive, sham, visionary; unrealizable; unrealized; unreaped; unreasonable (-bly, -ness), not reasonable, exceeding the bounds of reason (~ demands, conduct, etc.), not guided by or listening to reason; unreasoned, not rationally thought out; unreasoning (-ly), not using or guided by reason; unrebated; unrecallable; unrebuked; unrecalled; unreceipted; unreceived; unreciprocated; unreckoned; unreclaimed; unrecognizable (-bly); unrecognized; unrecompensed; unreconciled; unrecorded; unredeemed, not redeemed, (of promise) not fulfilled, (of bills etc.) not recalled (by payment, not taken out of pawn, (of faults etc.) not mitigated or relieved (by merits etc., or abs.); unredressed; unrefined, not refined (~ sugar, manners); unreflecting; unreformed; unrefuted; unregal; unregarded; unregenerate; unregistered; unregretted; unregulated; unrehearsed (esp. of results that surprise their authors); unrelated; unrelaxed; unrelenting (-ly, -ness); unreliable (-bility, -bleness, -bly); unrelieved, (esp.) lacking the relief given by contrast or variation; unreligious, not concerned with religion; unremembered, unremitting (-ly), not abating, incessant, unremorseful; unremunerative, not profitable; unrenowned; unrenewed; unrepealed; unrepentant (-ance); unrepining (-ly); unreplenished; unrepresentative; unrepresented; unreproached; unreproved; unrequited, not requited (~ love); unreserved; unreserved (-edly, -ness), without reservation (~ compliance etc.), open, frank, (an ~ nature), not reserved; unresented; unresenting (~ affection); unresisted; or returned; unresisting (-ly); unresolved, not having formed a decision, not solved or cleared up (~ doubts, problem), not separated into

constituent parts; unrespected; unresponsive (-ness); unrestful (-ly, -ness); unresting (-ly); unrestrained; unrestricted; unrestrained (-edly, -ness); unrestricted (-ly); unretarded; unretentive; unrevenged; unrevealed; unrevoked; unrewarded; unrhymed; unrhythmical, without (satisfactory) rhythm; unridable; unrighteous (-ly, -ness), not upright or honest or just, evil, wicked; unripe (-ness), not ripe (lit. & fig.; unrisen; unrivalled, having no equal, peerless; unromantic (-ally); unroofed; unroyal (-ly), unlike or unworthy of a king; unruffled, unruled, not governed, not ruled with lines; unru'ly (-iness), lawless, refractory, [f. rare ruly RULE, -Y³]);

unsafe (-ly, -ness), dangerous; unsaid²; unsaleable; unsaluted (-bility, -bleness); unsalaried; unsalted; unsanctified; unsanctioned; unsanitary, unhealthy; unsated; unsatisfactory (-ily, -ness); unsatisfied; unsatisfying (-ly); unsavoured, not saved (esp. in religious sense); unsavoury (-ily, -ness), uninviting, disgusting, (an ~ dish, smell, theme); unsayable; unscalable, that cannot be climbed; unscannable, that cannot be scanned; unscathed, without injury suffered (~ verses); unscholarly; unschooled, unscientific (-dly), (esp.) transgressing scientific principles; unscorched; unscoured; unscreened (esp. of coal); unscriptural (-ly), not in accordance with Scripture; unscrupulous (-ly, -ness), having no scruples shameless, unprincipled; unsculptured, not covered with sculpture, (Zool.) smooth; unsealed; unsearchable, beyond the reach of search; unsearched; unseasonable (-bly, -ness); unseasoned; unseated² not provided or furnished with seat(s); unseaworthy (-iness); unseconded; unsectarian (-ism), free from sectarian limitations; unsecured; unseduced; unseductive; unseeing, blind, unobservant; unseemly (-iness) a. & (arch.) adv.; unseen a. & n., not seen (the ~, the world of spirits), (translation) translation of unprepared passages as school exercise; unseizable; unselect, promiscuous, mixed; unselected; unselfish (-ly, -ness), regardful of others' interests rather than of one's own; unsensational (-ly); unsent; unsentenced; unsentimental; unseparated; unserviceable (-bly, -ness); unset, not set (sun, gem, trap, broken leg, is ~); unsettled², not settled, liable to change, open to further discussion, not paid, having no fixed abode, (of lands) not occupied by permanent inhabitants, (his mind is still ~; ~ weather; the point, the bill, is ~); unsevered; unshackled; unshaded; unshadowed; unshaken, not shaken esp. in resolution; unshapely; unshared; unshaven; unshed; unsheltered; unshipped;

unshocked; unshod; unshorn, not shorn or shaven; unshown; unshrinkable, that will not shrink (~ flannel); unshrinking (-ly), unhesitating, fearless, firm; unshrunk; unshut; unshuttered; unsifted; unsighted, not sighted (ship is still ~), not furnished with sights (~ gun), precluded from seeing (the umpire was ~ when Jones was caught); unsightly (-iness), repulsive to the sight, ugly; unsigned; unsisterly (-iness); unsized, not stiffened with size; unskilful (-ly, -ness); unskilled, not possessing or requiring skill or special training (~ labour; simple forms of manual labour); unskimmed; unsleeping, unslumbering, (fig.) watchful; unsmoked; unsociable (-bility, -bleness, -bly); unsocial; unsoiled; unsolaced; unsold; unsoldierly; unsolicited (esp. ~ testimonial); unsolicitous; unsolid (-ity); unsolvable; unsolved; unsoothed; unsophistical, unsophisticated (-ness), artless, innocent, simple, not adulterated, not artificial; unsorted; unsought; unsound (-ness), not sound, diseased, morbid, rotten, ill-founded, erroneous, fallacious, unreliable, (~ lungs, fruit, doctrine, policy, argument; ~ mind, insane); unsounded, unfathomed; unsoured; unsown; unsparing (-ly, -ness), profuse, lavish, (~ praise, ~ of or in praise, ~ in his efforts), merciless; unspeakable (-bly, -ness), that words cannot express, good, bad, etc., beyond description (~ joys, an ~ bore); unspecified; unspeculative; unspent; unspilt; unspiritual (-ity, -ly); unspliced; unspoiled, -lt; unspoken; unspontaneous, forced, artificial; unsportsmanlike (colloq. also unsporting); unspotted, not spotted or (fig.) contaminated; unsprung, (of vehicles, furniture, etc.) not provided with springs; unsquared; unstable; unstaid; unstained, not stained (esp. fig.); unstamped, without stamp (~ deed, letter); unstarched; unstartled; unstated; unstatesmanlike; unstatutable (-bly), not warranted by statute; unsteadfast (-ly, -ness); unsteady (-ily, -iness); not steady or firm, shaking, reeling, changeable, fluctuating, of irregular habits, (an ~ hand, walked with ~ steps, ladder is ~, was ~ in his adherence, ~ winds, is notoriously ~, dissipated); unstigmatized; unstimulated, unstinted, unstirred; unstocked (with, or abs.); unstopped; unstored, unstrained, not forced, not subjected to strain, not put through a strainer; unstratified; unstressed, not pronounced with stress; unstudied, easy, natural, spontaneous, (~ ease, eloquence); unstuffed; unstung; unsubdued; unsubjugated; unsubmissive (-ly, -ness); unsubscribed; unsubstantial (-ity, -ly), having little or no solidity or reality (~ air, visions, forms, an ~ building); unsubstantiated, not confirmed or established (~ rumours); unsuccessful (-ly); unsugared; unsuggestive; unsuitable (-bility,

-bly); unsuited, unfit (for purpose), not adapted (to); unsullied; unsummoned (to); unsung, not sung or (poet.) sung of; unsunned, not lighted by sun; unsupplied; unsupportable (-bly, -ness); unsupported; unsuppressed; unsure; unsurgical; unsurmised; unsurmounted; unsurpassable (-bly); unsurpassed; unsurrendered; unsurveyed; unsusceptible; unsuspected(-ly); unsuspicious (-ly, -ness); unsustainable; unsustained (-ly, -ness); unswathed, not controlled or influenced; unsweetened; unswept; unswerving (-ly); unsworn, not sworn (~ oath, witness); unsymbolical; unsymmetrical (-ly), failing in or not characterized by symmetry; unsympathetic (-ally); unsympathizing (-ly); unsystematic (-ally);

untainted; untalented; untamable(-ness); untamed; untarnishable; untarnished; untasked, untasted; untaught, (of person etc. or subject etc.) not taught, ignorant; untaxed; unteachable (-ness); untechnical; untempered, not tempered (~ mortar, steel, severity); untempted; untenable (-bility,-bleness); untenantable, not fit to be occupied; untenanted; untended; untendered, not offered; unterrified; untested; untethered; unthanked; unthankful (-ly, -ness); unthatched; unthinkable, that cannot be conceived in thought, (colloq.) unlikely; unthinking (-ly), thoughtless; unthought, not thought, esp. ~-of; unthoughtful (-ness); unthrashed; unthreadable; unthreaded; unthreshed; unthrifty; unthwarted; untidy(-ily,-iness); untied¹; untidied; untidiable; untimbered; untimely (-iness) a. & adv.; || untim(e)ous (Sc.), untimely; untinctured; untinged; untired; untiring (-ly); untithed, not subject to tithes; untitled; untold, not counted, beyond count (~ gold); untormented, untorn; untortured; untouchable, that may not be touched, (n.) a non-caste Hindu (whom a caste man may not touch); untouched; untoward (arch.), perverse, refractory, awkward, unlucky, (an ~ generation, accident); untraceable; untraced; untracked, not followed by means of or marked with tracks; untragic, not tragic or suited to tragedy; untrained, not trained or practised or instructed, not prepared by exercise, diet, etc., for race etc.; untrammelled; untransferable, that cannot or must not be transferred; untranslatable (-bility, -bleness, -bly); untranslated; untransmutable; untransportable; untravelled, that has not travelled; untraversable; untried, (esp.) inexperienced; untrodden; untroubled, not troubled, calm; untrue (-uly), not true, contrary to the fact, false, not faithful or loyal (to person, principle, etc.), deviating from correct standard; untrussed; untrusty (-iness); untrustworthy (-iness); untruthful (-ly, -ness);

untuned; untuneful (-ly); unturned, not turned or altered (leave no STONE ~); untaught or schooled.

unused; unusual(-ly,rare, -ness, -ly),not usual, remarkable; unutilized; unutterable (~ torment, joy, etc., an ~ fool); unuttered; unvaccinated; unvalued, not esteemed or prized, not estimated or priced; unvanquished; unvaried; unvariegated; unvarnished or embellished (~ surface, the ~ truth); unvarying (-ly); unvenerable; unvenomous; unventilated; unveracious; unverified; unverifiable; unversed or skilled (in); unvexed; unvibrating; unvindicated; unviolated; unvisited; unvitiated; unvoiced, not spoken or uttered, (Phonet.) not voiced; unvouched, not touched (usu. -for).

unwak(en)ed; unwanted; unwarlike; unwarmed; unwarned; unwarped; unwarrantable (-bly, -ness), indefensible, unjustifiable, improper; unwarranted, unauthorized, not guaranteed; unwary (-ily, -iness); unwashed, not washed (the great ~, the rabble); unwatched; unwatchful (~-ness); unwatered, not watered or diluted (~ milk, horse, capital); unwavering (-ly); unwearied; unweary; unwearying (-ly), not growing weary, persistent, (~ efforts etc.); unwedded; unweary-weighed; unwelcome; unwelcomed; unwell, not in good health, indisposed, menstruating; unwept (rhet., poet.), not wept for; unwetted; unwhipped; unwhitewashed; unwholesome (-ly, -ness); unwifely; unwilling (-ly, -ness), not willing or inclined (to do, for thing to be done, that, or abs.); unwinged; unwinking, not winking, vigilant, unwise (-ly), foolish, imprudent; unwished, unwished (usu. -for); unwithdrawn; unwithered, not written (~ law, resting originally on custom or judicial decision, not on written statutes etc., also assumption that homicide in defence of personal honour etc. is justifiable); unwooded; unworkable; unworldly, (~-minded etc.), not worldly, spiritual, (~-minded etc.), not worn or impaired by wear; unworshipped; unworthy (-ily, -iness), not worthy or befitting the character (of), discreditable, unseemly; unwound²; unwounded; unwoven; unwrinkled; unwritten, not written (~ law, resting etc.; unyielding (-ly, -ness), firm, obstinate; unyoked; ungouthful; unzealous.

2. Nouns are occas. formed either directly on a simple noun (unbelief, unfriend,

unrepair) or by back formation or otherwise on corresp. adj. Exx.: unbelief, incredulity, disbelief esp. in divine revelation or in a particular religion, so unbelief er; unchast'ity; uncircumci'sion, not being circumcised, (N.T.) the ~, the Gentiles; unconcern', freedom from anxiety, indifference, apathy; unconstraint', freedom from constraint; undress²', ordinary dress opp. to full dress of uniform, loose negligent dress, (often fig. & attrib.) loose negligent dress opp. to full dress or uniform; unease' (arch.), uneasiness, distress, discomfort; unemploy'ment, lack of employment, state of things in which many workers cannot find work or wages (~ benefit, payment made to unemployed worker under an insurance act, or by a trade union); un'faith' (rare), want of faith; unfriend' (arch.), enemy; un'reas'on, lack of reason, nonsense, folly (ABBOT of U~); unre'serve', absence of reserve, frankness; unrest', lack of rest, disturbed or agitated condition of person or nation (the ~ in Turkey); unrestraint'; unright' (arch.), wrong, injustice; un'truth', untruth, being untrue, falsehood, lie, (the manifest ~ of this statement, told me an ~); unwis'dom, lack of wisdom, folly, imprudence. [OE & G, cf. Du. on-, cogn. w. L IN-² & NE, α(n)-, NE-.]

|| **ún**'a, n. Small catboat-rigged sailing yacht. [name of first boat of the kind seen in England]

unadopted, see UN-¹(1); **unanchor**, UN-¹(1).

unanim'ous, a. All of one mind, agreeing in opinion, as we were, the meeting was, ~ (for reform, as to the policy to be pursued, in protesting, etc.); (of opinion, vote, etc.) formed, held, given, with one accord. Hence or cogn. **unanim'ity, ~NESS, nn., unan'imously** adv. [f. L unanimus, -mis, (unus one+animus mind)+-OUS]

unapparel, unarm, unarmed¹, see UN-¹(2); **unattire**, UN-¹(1).

ún'au (-aw), n. Brazilian two-toed sloth. [Braz.]

unbag, see UN-¹(3); **unbalance**, UN-¹(1); **unballast**, UN-¹(2); **unbank**, unbar, **unbear**, UN-¹(1); **unbed**, UN-¹(3); **unbe-knownst**, UN-¹(1); **unbelief, unbe-liever**, UN-¹(2); **unbelt**, UN-¹(2); **unbend**, **unbending**¹, UN-¹(1).

unbewail'ed (õonbewõo-), a. Unsummoned (in E use as deprecating Nemesis after boastful remark etc.). [G]

unbeseem, unbias, unbind, see UN-¹(1); **unbishop, unbias, unbind**, see UN-¹(4); **unbitt**, UN-¹(3); **un-blindfold, unblock, unbolt**, UN-¹(1);

unbone, UN-¹(2); unbonnet, UN-¹(1); unboot, UN-¹(2); unbosom, UN-¹(1); unbowel, UN-¹(2); unbox, UN-¹(3); unbrace, unbraid, unbreech, unbridle,
unbuckle, unburden, unbutton, UN-¹
(1); uncage, UN-¹(3); uncanny, UN-²
(1); uncap, UN-¹(2); uncart, uncase,
UN-¹(3).

uncate. See UNCINATE.

unchain, see UN-¹(1); unchastity, UN-²
(2); unchristianize, UN-¹(1); unchurch,
UN-¹(3).

ŭn'cia (-shia), n. (Rom. ant.; pl. -ae).
Twelfth part, esp. (as coin or amount) of
the as; ounce; inch. [L]

ŭn'cial (-shl), a. & n. 1. Of, written in, a
kind of majuscule writing found in MSS.
of 4th to 8th c. with characters partly resembling modern capitals. 2. n. ~ letter
or MS. [f. L uncialis (prec., see -AL), in
sense inch-high, large]

ŭn'cinate, a. (Also ŭnc'āte) hooked,
crooked. So ŭncif'EROUS, unc'iFORM,
~AL, aa. [f. L uncinatus (uncinus hook f.
L uncus hook, see -ATE²]

uncircumcision, see UN-²(2); unclasp,
UN-¹(1).

uncle (ŭng'kl), n. Father's or mother's
brother; aunt's husband; *(as familiar
mode of address) U~ Tom's Cabin etc.,
U~ Sam, government or typical citizen
of U.S.; (sl.) pawnbroker; (colloq., often
w. name added, as voc. or not) elderly
friendly person, e.g. B.B.C. announcer;
talk to (person) like a Dutch ~ (with kindly
severity). Hence ~SHIP n. [AF, f. L
avunculus maternal uncle (avus grandfather, see foll.)]

-uncle, suf. in nn. of L orig. or in L anal.,
repr. L -unculus, -la, a special form of
-culus -CULE prob. due to use of -culus w.
stems in -on-, as sermunculus (sermo-),
carbunculus (carbon-), oratiuncula, etc.,
and its extension to other stems (avunculus, st. avo-, furunculus, st. fur-). E
has also -uncule (homuncule), & L -culus
is sometimes kept (ranunculus).

unclench, -inch, see UN-¹(1); uncloak,
UN-¹(2); unclog, UN-¹(1); uncloister,
UN-¹(3); unclose, unclothe, UN-¹(1).

‖ŭnc'ō, a., n. (pl. ~s), & adv. (Sc.). 1.
Strange, unusual; notable. 2. n. Stranger; (pl.) news. 3. adv. Remarkably,
very; the ~ guid, rigidly religious people
(usu. derog.). [dial. var. of UNCOUTH]

uncock, uncoil, see UN-¹(1); unconcern,
UN-²(2); unconditioned, unconscionable, UN-²(1); unconstraint, UN-²(2);
uncoop, UN-¹(3); uncord, uncork,
uncouple, UN-¹(1).

uncouth' (-ōō-), a. (Obs. or arch.) not
known of, unfamiliar, unusual; (of places)
now literary) unfrequented, desolate,
wild, (of life) uncivilized, comfortless; (of
persons, looks, conduct, etc.) strange,
awkward, clumsy, uncultured, (of language) harsh, rugged, pedantic. Hence
~LY² adv., ~NESS n. [OE uncūth unknown (UN-² +cūth p.p. of cunnan know,
CAN²)]

uncover, see UN-¹(1); uncowl, UN-¹(2);
uncreate, uncross, UN-¹(1); uncrown,
UN-¹(2).

ŭnc'tion, n. Anointing with oil or unguent for medical purposes or as religious
rite or ceremonial (EXTREME ~): thing
used in anointing, unguent, (fig.) soothing
or flattering words or thought or circumstance (see FLATTER); fervent or sympathetic quality in words or tone caused
by or causing deep religious or other
emotion; simulation of this, affected
enthusiasm, gush; excessive suavity;
keen or lingering enjoyment in narration,
gusto, (told the story with much ~). [f. L
unctionem (ungere unct- anoint, see -ION)]

ŭnc'tŭous, a. Full of (esp. simulated)
unction; greasy, esp. (of minerals) having
a soapy feel when touched. Hence ~LY²
adv., ~NESS n. [f. med. L unctuosus f. L
unctus -ūs anointing (as prec.), see -OUS]

uncurl, uncurl, see UN-¹(1).

ŭn'dé (-ā), ŭn'dée, a. (her.). Wavy. [f. F
ondé (L undā wave, -ATE²]

undeceive, undeceived¹, undeify, see
UN-¹(1).

ŭn'der, prep., adv., & a. 1. In or to a
position lower than, below, as it lay, fell,
~ the table, assembled ~ (at the foot of) the
castle wall, struck him ~ the left eye,
nothing new ~ the sun (anywhere), ~
FOOT¹, ~ HATCH¹es, ~ one's NOSE, ~ (in
& covered by) water, ~ one's WING,
2. Within, on the inside of, (surface etc.),
as inserted a knife-blade ~ the bark,
was seen to blush ~ his dusky skin, with a
good meal ~ his belt (in his stomach), ~ the
LEE of 3. Inferior to, less than, as no one
~ a bishop, incomes £400, cannot be done
~ (at less cost than) £5, total falls ~ what
was expected, speak ~ one's breath (in a
whisper). 4. In the position or act of supporting or sustaining, subjected to, undergoing, liable to, on condition of, subject
to, governed or controlled or bound by,
in accordance with, in the form of, in the
time of, as sank ~ the load (lit. & fig.),
a ~ a CLOUD, groaning ~ tyranny, is now ~
repair, ~ examination, a few acres ~
(planted with) corn, ~ FIRE¹, ~ (propelled
by) sail, ~ WAY, ~ ARM¹s, forbidden ~
pain of death, a criminal ~ sentence of
(condemned to) death, have sat ~ (attended sermons of) famous preachers,
country prospered ~ him or his rule, might
succeed ~ other conditions, is ~ a delusion, was ~ the impression, ~ the circumstances, ~ the rose, =SUB¹rosa, ~FAVOUR,
~ (attested by) one's hand & seal, was ~
a vow, known ~ an assumed name, ap-

For adjj. in un- not given see UN-²(1).

pears ~*various forms*, ~*pretence of ignor-ance*, *lived* ~ *the Stuarts*. **5.** adv. In or to a lower place or subordinate condition, as BRING, KEEP¹, KNOCK¹, KNUCKLE, GO¹, ~*, a cloth, should be spread* ~ (usu. *beneath*). **6.** adj. Lower (now largely merged in foll.), as the ~ *jaw*, ~ *layers*, ~ *servants*; ~ *dog* (sl.), dog, person, who has the worst of an encounter. Hence ~MOST a. [com.-Teut. cf. Du. *onder*, G. *unter*, ON *undir*, cogn. w. L *infra* below]

under-, pref. =prec. prep. or adv. in

1. As prep. governing the noun to which it is prefixed. w. sense ' below ', *under-* forms a few adv. & adji. as: **un'deram** a., (Cricket)=UNDERHAND, (Lawn Tennis, of service or stroke) made by swinging racket below shoulder-level; ~**co'ver** a., surreptitious (~*cover agent*, one trying to secure evidence of illegal activities by associating with the suspected wrong-doers); ~**foot'** adv., under one's feet; UNDERGROUND; UNDERHAND; **un'derproof** a., with less alcohol than proof spirit.

2. *Under-* is prefixed to vbs & their de-rivatives w. adv. or prep. force in sense ' beneath ', ' lower than ', ' below ', as: ~**drain'** v.t., make lower bid than (person), drain (ground) by forming channels be-neath it; ~**lay'** v.t. & t., lay something under (thing), esp. (Print.) lay paper under (types) to raise them, (Mining, intr.) incline from the vertical; **un'derlay** n., paper laid under types, waterproof paper, sheet, etc., for laying under carpet or mattress, (Mining) = inclined lode or shaft; ~**let'** v.t., let below true value, (word) to secure emphasis or to indicate italics; ~**line'** v.t., draw line under (ball) so that it rises high & does not roll far on alighting, (Commerc.) offer lower terms than (competitor); ~**pin'** v.t., place support of masonry etc. under (wall, overhanging bank, etc.); ~**play'** v.i. (Cards), play low card while retaining high one of same suit; **un'derplay** n., ~*playing*; ~**prop'** v.t., put prop under; ~**quote'** v.t., quote lower prices than (person), quote lower prices than others for (goods etc.); ~**run'** v.t. & t., run or pass under, (Naut.) overhaul or examine (a cable etc.) by lifting it on board and passing it along by hand; ~**score'** v.t., ~*line*; ~**sell'** v.t., sell cheaper than (person); **un'derseller**; ~**set'** v.t., sup-port (masonry etc.) by prop; **un'dershot** a., (of wheel) worked by water pass-ing under it. =UNDERHUNG; ~**signed** a., *I, we, the* ~*signed*, (whose signatures appear below); ~**trump'** v.t., play lower trump than (person, trump played).

3. *Under-* in sense ' insufficiently ', ' in-completely ', is prefixed to vbs (used in p.p.) & to some adji. w. their derivatives. Adji. & p.p. tend in attrib. use (cf. UN-¹, -ED²) to take stress on first syllable (*beef was* ~*done'*, *hate* **un'derdone** *beef*; *an* **un'der-exposed** *or* **un'der-exposed** *nega-tive*). Exx. ~**act'** v.t., act (a part, or abs.) inadequately; ~**bred** a., ill-bred, vulgar; ~**charge'** v.t., charge too little for (thing) or to (person), put insuffici-ent charge into (gun etc.); **un'dercharge** n., insufficient charge; ~**devel'op** v.t. (photog.); ~**do'** v.t., cook insufficiently, esp. in p.p. ~*done*; ~**dose'** v.t.; ~**draw'** v.t., depict inadequately; ~**dress** v.t. & t., dress too plainly or too lightly; ~**es'timate** v.t., form too low an estimate of; ~**es'timate** (-at), ~**ation**, nn.; ~**expose'** v.t., ~**exposure** n. (photog.); ~**feed'** v.t. & t.; ~**fired'** a., (of pottery) not baked enough; ~**grown** a.; ~**man'** v.t., furnish (ship etc.) with too few men; ~**manned'** a.; ~**pay** v.t., pay (workmen etc.) inadequately; ~**production** n., production less than is usual or required; ~**rate'** v.t., ~*esti-mate*; ~**reck'on** v.t.; ~**ripe'** a.; ~**sized'** a., of less than the usual size, dwarfish; ~**state'** v.t., ~**state'ment** n.; ~**stock'** v.t., supply (farm, shop, etc.) with insufficient stock; ~**timed'** a.; ~**val'ue** v.t.,

4. *Under-* in adj. relation with noun re-places or is interchangeable with *under* a., in senses situated beneath, sub-ordinate '. In the less-established com-pounds the hyphen is usu. retained & the stress variously placed on either com-ponent or both. Exx.:~**growth** n., **un'der-brush** n. = ~*growth*; **un'dercarriage**, aircraft's landing gear; **un'derclay** n., clay bed under coal; ~**clerk(ship)** nn.; **un'der-cliff** n., terrace or lower cliff formed by a landslip; **un'derclothes**, **un'derclothing**, nn., clothes worn under others esp. next to skin; ~**drain²** n., drain placed under-ground; **un'derflow** n., current flowing beneath surface; **un'dergarment** n., gar-ment worn under others; **un'dergrowth** n., shrubs or small trees growing under larger ones; ~**king** n., inferior or sub-ordinate king; ~**lease** n., lease granted by lessee for shorter term than his own; **un'derline²** n., advance announcement of production of subsequent play at foot of play-bill, descriptive line(s) under an il-lustration; **un'derlinen**, linen or (loosely) other ~*garments*; **un'derload** n., sub-ordinate plot in play or novel; **un'der-sec'retary(ship)** nn.; || (*Parliamentary Under-Secretary*), member of Govern-ment; *Permanent Under-Secretary*, mem-ber of Civil Service & head of a depart-ment); ~**servant** n., **un'dersel²** n. (Naut.), undercurrent in contrary direction to that of wind or surface water; ~**shirt** n.; ~**sheriff** n., sheriff's deputy; ~**sheriff**

shrub n., plant like shrub but smaller; detached one, worn under another; *un'dersoil* n.; *un'derstrapper* n., inferior agent, underling; ~*stratum* n.; ~*tenant* n., tenant's tenant; ~*tenancy* n.; *un'dertint* n., subdued tint; *un'dertone* n., subdued tone esp. in speaking, thin or subdued colour; *un'dertow* n., backward flow of wave breaking on beach, = ~*set*; underneath; *un'derwear* n. (clothes meant for) wearing underneath; *un'derwing* n., kinds of moth with conspicuous markings etc. on under wings; *un'derwood* n., = ~*growth*; *un'derworld* n., antipodes, infernal regions, lowest social stratum.

underact, see UNDER- 3; **under-agent**, UNDER- 4; **underarm**, UNDER- 1; **under-bid**, UNDER- 2; **underbred**, UNDER- 3; **underbrush, undercarriage**, UNDER- 4; **undercharge**, UNDER- 3; **underclay, undercliff, underclothes, underclothing**, UNDER- 4; **undercover**, UNDER- 1.

un'dercroft (-aw-), n. Crypt. [UNDER, ME *croft* f. L *crupta* CRYPT]

un'dercurrent, n. Current below the surface; (fig.) unperceived influence or feeling of different or contrary tendency; (Mining) large shallow box beside main hydraulic sluice serving to aid in saving gold. [UNDER- 4]

undercut[1]. See UNDER- 2.

un'dercut[2] n. || Under side of sirloin; upward blow in boxing. [UNDER- 4]

under-develop, underdo, underdose, see UNDER- 3; **underdrain**[1] v.t., UNDER- 2; **underdrain**[2] n., UNDER- 4; **under-draw, underdress, underestimate, underestimation, under-expose, under-exposure, underfeed, under-fired**, UNDER- 3; **underflow**, UNDER- 4; **underfoot**, UNDER- 1; **undergarment**, UNDER- 4.

undergō', v.t. Be subjected to, suffer, endure esp. with firmness, as *has undergone many trials, undergoing a rapid change, an operation*. [OE UNDER(*gān* GO)]

undergrād'ūate, n. Member of university who has not taken his first degree (often attrib.). Hence ~**ateship** n., ~ETTE[1] n. (joc.) female ~ate. [UNDER- 4]

underground', adv., a., & n. 1. Beneath surface of earth. 2. adj. (in attrib. use ūn[2]). Situated ~, as ~ *railway*; (fig.) hidden, secret, as ~ (secret resistance) *movement*. 3. n. (ūn[2]). || ~ railway; ~ movement. [UNDER- 1]

undergrown, see UNDER- 3; **under-growth**, UNDER- 4.

underhand', adv., & a. (in attrib. use ūn[2]). Clandestine(ly), secret(ly), not above-board; (Crick., of bowling) (performed) with hand underneath both elbow & ball, as *bowls* ~, ~ *bowling*. [UNDER- 1, 4]

underhüng' (in attrib. use ūn[2]), a. (Of lower jaw) projecting beyond upper jaw; having ~ *jaw*. [UNDER- 2]

under-king, see UNDER- 4; **underlay** v.t. & i. & n., UNDER- 2; **under-lease**, UNDER- 4; **underlet**, UNDER- 2.

underlie', v.t. Lie, be situated, under (stratum etc., or abs.); (fig., of principle etc.) be the basis of (doctrine, law, conduct, etc., or abs. esp. in part.). [UNDER- 2]

underline[1] v.t., see UNDER- 2; **under-line**[2] **underlinen**, UNDER- 4.

un'derling, n. Subordinate (usn. derog.). [ME (-LING[1])]

undermine, undermanned, see UNDER- 3; **undermentioned**, UNDER- 2.

undermine', v.t. Make mine or excavation under, wear away base or foundation of, as *rivers* ~ *their banks*, ~ *the walls*; injure (person, reputation, influence, etc.) by secret means; injure, wear out, (health etc.) insidiously or imperceptibly. Hence ~ER[1] n. [UNDER- 2]

underneath', adv., prep., a., & n. 1. At or to a lower place (than), below (not in fig. senses). 2. adj. & n. Lower (surface, part). [OE *underneoðan* (UNDER, cf. BENEATH]

underpay, see UNDER- 3; **underpin, underplay** v.i., & n., UNDER- 2; **underplot**, UNDER- 4; **under-production**, UNDER- 3; **underproof**, UNDER- 1; **underprop, underquote**, UNDER- 2; **underrate, under-reckon, under-ripe**, UNDER- 3; **underrun, underscore**, UNDER- 2; **under-secretary(ship)**, UNDER- 4; **underseller**, UNDER- 2; **under-servant**, UNDER- 4; **underset**[1] v.t., UNDER- 2; **underset**[2] n., **under-sheriff, under-shirt**, UNDER- 4; **undershot**, UNDER- 2; **undershrub**, UNDER- 4; **undersigned**, UNDER- 2; **undersized, undersoil, underskirt, undersleeve, undersoil**, UNDER- 4.

understand', v.t. & i. (-stood; arch. p.p. -standed). 1. Comprehend, perceive the meaning of, (words, person, or language etc.), as *does not* ~ *what you say, do you* ~ *me?, French; tongue not* ~*ed of the people, foreign language.* 2. Grasp mentally, perceive the significance or explanation or cause or nature of, know how to deal with, as *do not* ~ *why he came, what the noise is about, the point of his remark; quite* ~ *your difficulty; cannot* ~ *him, his conduct, his wanting to go; thoroughly* ~*s children, could never* ~ *mathematics;* (abs.) *you don't* ~ (the situation etc.). 3. Infer esp. from information received, take as implied, take for granted, as *I* ~ *that doors open at 7.30, that they are almost destitute, him to be or that he is a distant relation, I quite understood that expenses were to be paid, no one could* ~ *that from my words, what*

For adjj. in un- not given see UN-[2](1).
For other words in *under-* see UNDER-.

did you ~ him to say (~ from his words)?; (expr. uncertainty or surprise or indigna-tion) do I ~ (you to say) that or am I to ~?; (you to say) that or am I to ~ that you refuse?; (introducing warning or threat) now ~ me, he gave or I was given to ~ (I thought he said or meant) that it was done. 4. Supply (word) mentally, as the verb may be either expressed or under-stood. [OE UNDER(standan STAND)]

understand'ing¹, a. Having insight. [-ING²]

understand'ing², n. In vbl senses, esp.: intelligence, as has an excellent ~, men of abstract thought, (often opp. to reason); agreement, harmony, union of sentiments, convention, thing agreed upon, as must come to an ~ with him, disturbed the (good) ~ between them, had a secret ~ with other firms, consented only on this ~, on the distinct ~ that; (pl., sl.) feet, legs, shoes, etc. [-ING¹]

understate'(ment), understock, under-stratum, UNDER- 3; **understrapper, under-** UNDER- 3.

understud'y, n. & v.t. 1. One who studies theatrical part in order to play it at short notice in absence of the usual actor. 2. v.t. Study (part) thus, act as ~ to (actor). [UNDER- 4]

undertake', v.t. & i. Bind oneself to per-form, make oneself responsible for, en-gage in, enter upon, (work, enterprise, responsibility); accept an obligation, promise, (to do); accept, argument, etc., (person) in combat, argument, etc.; guarantee, affirm, as I will ~ that he has not heard a word, that you shall or will be no loser by it; (arch.) be guarantee for (person, fact); (colloq.) manage funerals. [ME UNDER(taken TAKE)]

undertak'er, n. In vbl senses, esp.: one who manages funerals; (Hist.) influential person who undertook to procure parti-cular legislation esp. to obtain supplies from Commons if king would grant some concession. [-ER¹]

undertak'ing, n. In vbl senses, esp.: work etc. undertaken, enterprise, as a serious ~; management of funerals (fun'.). [-ING¹]

under-tenant, under-tenancy, see UN-DER- 4; **under-timed**, UNDER- 3; **under-tint, undertone, undertow**, UNDER- 2; **undertrump**, UNDER- 2; **undervalua-tion, undervalue**, UNDER- 3; **under-wear, underwing, underwood, under-world**, UNDER- 4.

underwrite' (-rīt), v.t. & i. Execute & deliver (policy of insurance esp. on marine property), practise marine insurance, engage to buy all stock in (company etc.), not bought by the public, whence un'derwriter¹ n.; write below, as the underwritten names. [UNDER- 2]

un'dies (-dīz), n. pl. (colloq.) [Esp. women's) underclothing. [abbr. -y³]

undine' (-ēn), n. Female water-sprite who by marrying a mortal & bearing a child might receive a soul. [f. L unda wave + -INE¹]

undo, see UN-¹(3); **undock**, see UN-¹; **undoer, undoing, undomesticate, un-done¹**, UN-¹(1).

un'dose, a. (entom.). Wavy, undulating. [f. L undosus (unda wave, see -OSE¹)]

undrape, undress¹ v.t. & i., see UN-¹(1); **undress²** n., UN-²(2); **undressed¹**, UN-¹(1); **unduke**, UN-¹(4).

un'dulate¹, v.i. Have wavy motion or look. Hence ~ANT a. (esp. ~ant fever, Malta fever), ~atingLY² adv. [as foll., -ATE³]

un'dulate², a. Wavy, going alternately up & down or in & out, as leaves with ~ margins. Hence~LY² adv. [f. L undulatus (unda wave, see -UL-, -ATE²)]

undula'tion, n. Wavy motion or form, gentle rise & fall, each wave of this; set of wavy lines; (Path.) sensation of un-dulating movement in the heart. [as prec.+-ATION]

un'dulatory, a. Undulating, wavy; of, due to, undulation; ~ theory of light (that light is propagated through the ether by wave-motion imparted to the ether by molecular vibrations of the radiant body), so ~ undulā'tionIST²(-sho-) n. [-ORY¹]

unearth, see UN-¹(3); **unease**, UN-²(2); **unedge**, UN-¹(2); **unegoize**, UN-¹(1); **un-employment**, UN-²(2); **unentangle, un-equalize**, UN-¹(1); **uniace**, UN-¹(2); **un-faith**, UN-²(2); **unfasten, unfastened¹**, UN-¹(3); **unfeather, unfence, unfetter, unfettered¹, unfeudalize, un-file, unfit, unfix, unfixed¹**, UN-¹(1); **un-flesh, unflower**, UN-¹(2); **unfold¹**, UN-¹(1); **unfold²**, UN-¹(3); **unfold³**, UN-¹(1); **unframe**, UN-¹(2); **unfriend**, UN-²(2); **unfrock**, UN-¹(2); **unfurl**, UN-¹(1).

ungain'ly, a. & adv. (Of persons or animals or their movements) ill-made, awkward-looking, clumsy; (adv.) in ~Y manner. Hence ~NESS n. [prec.²+obs. gain a. f. ON gegn straight +-LY¹]

ungear, ungild, ungird, UN-¹(1); **un-girdle**, UN-¹(2); **unglaze**, UN-¹(1); **un-glove, ungown**, UN-¹(2).

ung'ual (-nggw-), a. Of, like, bearing, a nail or hoof or claw. So ung'uicular, ung'uic'ulate², [-CULE, usu. without dim. force], ung'ui'ferous, ung'uiform, aa. [f. L unguis claw, nail, +-AL]

ung'uent (-nggw-), n. Any soft substance used as ointment or for lubrication. So ~ARY¹ a. [f. L unguentum (unguere anoint)]

ung'uis (-nggw-), n. (pl. ~ue), Hoof, claw, talon, whence ~ATE²(2) a. & n. (zool.); hooked instrument for extracting dead foetus; cone, cylinder, with top cut off by plane oblique to base. Hence ~AR¹ a. [L, dim. as UNGUAL]

ung'um, unhair, see UN-¹(2); **unhallow,**

unhand, unhang, unharness, unhasp, UN-¹(1); **unhat, unhelm,** UN-¹(2); **unhinge(d), unhitch,** UN-¹(1); **unhive,** UN-¹(3); **unhook, unhoop,** UN-¹(1); **unhorse,** UN-¹(3); **unhouse, unhumanize,** UN-¹(1); **unhusk,** UN-¹(2).

ūni-, in comb. = L *unus* one, as: *~artic'ulate,* single-jointed; *~ax'(ī)al,* having a single axis, whence *~ax'ially* adv.; *~cam'eral,* of only one chamber (of Parliament etc.); *~cap'sular,* of one capsule; *~cell'ular,* one-celled; *~col'our(ed),* of one colour; *~corn'ous,* one-horned; *~cos'tate,* single-ribbed; *~cus'pid* & n., (tooth) of one cusp; *ūn'icycle,* single-wheeled vehicle; *~flor'ous,* bearing one flower; *~fo'liate,* having one leaf; *~lat'eral,* one-sided (*~lateral leaves,* leaning to one side of stem, *~lateral contract,* binding one party only), whence *~lat'erally* adv.; *~lit'eral,* consisting of one letter; *~loc'ular* n., *loc'ulate,* (Bot., Zool.), single-chambered; *ūnip'arous,* producing one at a birth, (Bot.) having one axis or branch; *~part'ite,* not divided; *ūn'iped,* single-footed; *~pers'on'ed,* (of Deity) existing only in one person, (of verb) used only in one person; *~plān'ar,* lying in one plane; *~pol'ar,* (Biol.) having only one pole, (Electr.) showing only one kind of polarity, whence *~polā'rity* n.; *~rād'iate(d),* having only one arm or process; *~se'rial,* set in one row; *~sex'ual,* of one sex, not hermaphrodite, having stamens or pistil but not both, whence *~sexual'ity* n., *~sex'ually* adv.; *~sul'cate* (Bot., Zool.), single-grooved; *ūniv'alent* (Chem.), having a combining power of one, whence *univ'alence, univ'alency,* nn.; *ūn'ivalve* a. & n. (mollusc) of one valve; *ūniv'ocal* & n., (word) of only one proper meaning, whence *ūniv'ocally* adv.

Un'iat, -āte, (ū-), n. Member of any community of Oriental Christians that acknowledges Pope's supremacy but retains own liturgy etc. [f. Russ. *uniyat* f. L *unus* one]

ūn'icŏrn, n. 1. Fabulous animal with horse's body & single straight horn (in *Deut.* xxxiii. 17 mistransl. of Heb. *re'ēm,* a two-horned animal); heraldic representation of this, with goat's beard & lion's tail. 2. (Also *~fish, ~whale, sea-~*) narwhal. 3. Kind of single-horned beetle; caterpillar with hornlike prominence on back (*~ moth,* of this). 4. Pair of horses with third horse in front, turn-out with these. 5. (Also *~shell*) kinds of gastropod with spine on lip of shell. [f. L UNI(*cornis* f. *cornu* horn)]

ūn'ifŏrm, a., n., & v.t. 1. Not changing in form or character, the same, unvarying, as *present a ~ appearance, ~ size & shape, keeps a ~ temperature, behaved with ~ moderation, ~ acceleration* (not varying

with time); (of tax, law, etc.) not varying with time or place; conforming to same standard or rule. 2. n. ~ dress worn by members of same body, e.g. by soldiers, sailors, policemen. 3. v.t. Make ~, clothe in ~. Hence *~LY³* adv. [(n. & vb f. adj.) f. F *uniforme* f. L UNI(*formis* -FORM)]

ūnifŏrm'ity, n. Being uniform, sameness, consistency; *Act of U~* (for securing ~ in public worship, esp. that of 1662); *doctrine of ~* (that ~ has prevailed in physical causes & effects in all ages, opp. to CATASTROPHISM), whence *unifŏrmitā'rian*(*ism*) nn. [f. L *uniformitas* (as prec., see -TY)]

ūn'ify, v.t. Reduce (things, or abs.) to unity, or uniformity. Hence or cogn. *~FICA'TION, ~FIER²,* nn. [f. med. L UNI-(*ficare* -FY)]

Unigen'itus (ū-), n. (hist.). Bull of Clement XI against Jansenism in 1713. [mod. L, = only-begotten, its first wd]

unintelligible. See UN-²(1).

ūn'ion (-yon), n. 1. Uniting, being united, coalition, junction, as *effected a ~, the ~ of the parts was imperfect, ~ by first or second INTENTION; the U~* (of England & Scotland in 1706, also, of Great Britain & Ireland in 1801). 2. Matrimony, marriage. 3. Concord, agreement, as *lived together in perfect ~.* 4. A whole resulting from combination of parts or members, esp. (1) the U.S., (2) the United Kingdom, (3) South Africa; TRADE ~; POSTAL ~. 5. ‖ (Formerly) two or more parishes consolidated for administration of poor-laws, (in full *~ workhouse*) workhouse erected by such ~. 6. ‖ Association of independent (esp. Congregational or Baptist) churches for purposes of co-operation. 7. (U~) general club & debating society at some universities, buildings of such society. 8. Part of flag with device emblematic of ~ normally occupying upper corner next staff (*ensign hoisted ~ down,* with ~ below as signal of distress); *U~ Jack* or *flag,* national ensign of United Kingdom formed by ~ of crosses of St George, St Andrew, & St Patrick. 9. Kinds of joint or coupling for pipes etc.; shallow vat in which beer is left to clear; fabric of mixed materials, e.g. cotton with linen or silk or jute. 10. *~ suit,* combinations (garment). [F, f. LL *unio* unity (*unus* one, see -ION)]

ūn'ionist (-nyo-), n. 1. Member of a trade union, advocate of trade unions. 2. Person opposed to rupture of legislative union between Great Britain & Ireland, opponent of home rule in Ireland, as LIBERAL *~ist,* (attrib.) *~ist party, principles; *(Hist.)* one who during the civil war opposed secession. So *~ISM* n., *~is'tic* a. [-IST]

ūnique' (-ēk), a. & n. 1. Unmatched, unequalled, having no like or equal or paral-

For adjj. in *un-* not given see UN-².

For other words in *uni-* see UNI-.

lel, as *his position was ~*, *this ease is so far as is known ~*, (vulg.) *the most ~ (remark-able) man I ever met*. **2.** *n.* **~'thing.** Hence **L~IY²** (-ēk'li) *adv.*, **~NESS** (-ēk'nis) *n.* [f. L *unicus* (*unus* one)]

ū'nison, *a. & n.* **1.** (Mus.) coinciding in pitch, whence or cogn. **ūnis'onant, ūnis'onal, ūnis'on-ance** n.; **~ string** & meant to be sounded with it). **2.** *n.* Unity of pitch (in unison of notes or tones, (Mus.) this regarded as an interval; state of sounding at same pitch, esp. *in ~*; = ~ *string*) concord, agreement, as *acted in perfect ~*. [f. LL. UN(*sonus* sound)]

ū'nit, *n.* Individual thing or person or group regarded for purposes of calcula-tion etc. as single & complete, each of the individuals or groups into which a com-plex whole may be analysed, as *take the family as the ~ of society*; quantity chosen as a standard in terms of which other quantities may be expressed, as *abstract ~*, *the number one* (1), *C.G.S. system of ~s* (in which centimetre, gramme, second, are the ~s of length, mass, & time). [shortened f. UNITY]

ūnitā'rian, *n. & a.* **1.** (U~) one who, member of a Christian body that, main-tains against the doctrine of the Trinity that God is one person, whence **U~ISM** n, **U~ISE** v.t.; advocate of unity or central-ization e.g. in politics. **2.** *adj.* Of the U~s, as (U~ *Church*; = foll. [-ARIAN]

ū'nitary, *a.* Of a unit or units, as ~ *method*, a rule in arithmetic used for same purpose as rule of three; marked by unity or uniformity. [-ARY¹]

ūnite', *v.t. & i.* **1.** Join (t., t.) together, make or become one, combine, consoli-date, amalgamate, as *~ the parts with cement*, *give the parts time to ~*, *the two nations gradually (became) ~d*, *oil will not ~ with water*; U~d *Brethren*, the MORAVIAN sect; U~d *Irishmen*, Irish society formed in 1791 for purposes of parliamentary reform etc.; U~d KINGDOM; U~d *Nations*, (orig.) those ~d against the AXIS powers (in 1942) those ~d against the AXIS powers in the 1939-45 war, (later) an organization of almost all 'peace-loving States'; U~d *Provinces*, Holland, Zealand, & 5 other provinces ~d in 1579 & forming basis of republic of Netherlands, (also, hist.) one of the major Indian administrative divisions, com-prising Agra and Oudh; U~d STATE's. **2.** Agree, combine, co-operate, (*in senti-ment, conduct, doing*). Hence **unīt'edly²** adv., **ūn'ITIVE** a. [f. L *ūnīre* -it- (*unus* one)]

ū'nitism, *n.* = MONISM. [-ISM]

ū'nitize, *v.t.* Reduce to, treat as, a unit. [-IZE]

ū'nity, *n.* Oneness, being one or single or individual, being formed of parts that constitute a whole, due interconnexion &

coherence of parts, as *disturbs the ~ of the idea*, *pictures lack ~*, *national ~*; thing showing such ~, thing that forms a complex whole, as *a person regarded as a ~*; (Math.) the number one, factor that leaves unchanged the quantity on which it operates; *the dramatic unities*, *unities of time, place, & action*, limitation of sup-posed time of drama to that occupied in acting & to a single day, use of same scene throughout, & abstention from all plot; harmony, concord, between persons etc., as *dwell together in ~*, *at ~ with*; (Law) joint tenancy of different tenants, joint possession by one person of different rights. [f. L *ūnitātem* (*unus* one, see -TY]

ūnivers'al, *a. & n.* **1.** Of or belonging to or done etc. by all persons or things in the world or in the class concerned, appli-cable to all cases, as *the terror was ~*, *met with ~ applause*, *has the ~ sanction of philosophers*, *the rule does not prevent to be ~*, ~ *agent* (empowered to do all that can be delegated), ~ PROVIDER, ~ *compass* (with legs that may be extended for large circles), ~ *coupling* or *joint* (trans-mitting power by a shaft at any selected angle), ~ *legatee* (to whom the whole of a property is bequeathed), ~ *proposition* (in which the predicate is affirmed or denied of the entire subject). Hence or cogn. **ūniversâl'ITY, ~īZA'TION,** nn., **~IZE(3)** v.t., **~ĪY²** adv. **2.** *n.* (Logic) ~ proposi-tion; (Philos.) general notion or idea, thing that by its nature may be pre-dicated of many. [f. OF *universel* f. L *universalis* (as UNIVERSE, see -AL.)]

ūnivers'alist, U~, *n.* One who holds, esp. member of an organized body of Christians who hold, that all mankind will eventually be saved. Hence or cogn. **~ISM** n., **~is'tic** a. [-IST]

ū'niverse, *n.* All existing things; the whole creation (& the Creator); all man-kind; (Logic) all the objects under con-sideration. [f. F *univers* f. L *universum* neut. of *universus* p.p. of *vertere* turn combined into one, whole]

ūnivers'ity, *n.* Educational institution designed for instruction or examination or both of students in all or many of the more important branches of learning, conferring degrees in various faculties, & often embodying colleges & similar institutions; members of this collec-tively; team, crew, etc., representing a ~, as *the ~ had four wickets to fall*; U~ EXTENSION; U~ *Test Act* (abolishing subscription to Thirty-nine Articles etc. as requisite to taking of degree, 1871). [f. OF *universite* f. L *universitas* whole, universe, corporation, (as prec., see -TY)]

ūniversŏl'ŏġy, *n.* Science of all created things; science of all that is of human

interest. Hence ~olō′gical a., ~ōl′ogıst n. [f. UNIVERSE + ō- + -LOGY]

unjoin, unjoint, see UN-¹(1).

unkémpt′ (ŭn-k-), a. Uncombed, dishevelled; untidy, of neglected appearance; (of language) careless, rough, incondite. [UN-² + ME kempt p.p. of kemben comb, OE cemban]

unking, see UN-¹(4); **unkink, unknit,** unknot, **unlace, unlade, unlash, un-** latch, **unlay,** UN-¹(1); **unlead,** UN-¹(2); **unlearn,** UN-¹(1); **unleash,** UN-¹(3).

unléss′, conj. If not, except when, as shall (not) go ~ I hear from him, ~ absolutely compelled, always walked ~ I had a bicycle; ~ & until (verbose for until in condit. use, cf. if & when). [earlier onless (ON +LESS) = on less provocation than my hearing, short of my hearing, cf. F à moins que or de]

unlimber, see UN-¹(2); **unline, unlink,** unload, **unlock, unlodge, unloose,** UN-¹(1); **unlord,** UN-¹(4); **unmake,** UN-¹(1); **unman,** UN-¹(2, 4); **unmantle,** UN-¹(2); **unmask, unmew,** UN-¹(1); **unmonk,** UN-¹(4); **unmoor, unmortise,** unmould, **unmuffle, unmuzzle,** UN-¹ (1); **unnail,** UN-¹(2); **unnaturalize, un-** nerve(d), UN-¹(1); **unnest,** UN-¹(3); **un-** pack, unpeg, UN-¹(1); **unpen,** UN-¹(3); **unpeople,** UN-¹(1); **unperch,** UN-¹(3); **unpick, unpin, unplait, unplug,** UN-¹ (1); **unplume,** UN-¹(2); **unpope,** UN-¹(4); **unpreach,** UN-¹(1); **unprejudice,** UN-² (2); **unprelate, unpriest, unprince,** UN-¹(4); **unprop,** UN-¹(2); **unqueen,** UN-¹(4); **unravel,** UN-¹(1); **unreason,** UN-²(2); **unreel, unreeve, unrein,** UN-¹ (1); **unrepair, unreserve, unrest, un-** restraint, UN-²(2); **unriddle, unrig,** UN-¹(1); **unright,** UN-²(2); **unring,** UN-¹ (2); **unrip, unrivet,** UN-¹(1); **unrobe,** UN-¹(2); **unroll, unromanize,** UN-¹ (2); **unroof,** UN-¹(2); **unroost,** UN-¹(3); **unroot,** UN-¹(1); **unrumple,** UN-¹(2); **unsaddle, unsaid¹, unsay,** UN-¹(1); **unscale,** UN-¹(2); **unscrew, unseal,** unseam, **unseat, unseated,** UN-¹(1); **unself,** UN-¹(2); **unset, unsettle, un-** settle(d)¹, UN-¹(1); **unsex,** UN-¹(4); **shackle, unsheathe,** UN-¹(1); **unshell,** UN-²(2); **unship, unshipped¹,** UN-¹(1); **unshoe, unshot, unshutter, unsinew,** unsister, UN-¹(2); **unsling,** UN-¹(1); **unsnare,** UN-¹(3); **unsolder, unspar,** UN-¹(2); **unspeak, unspell,** UN-¹(1); **unsphere,** UN-¹(3); **unsprung,** UN-²(1); **unsquire,** UN-¹(4); **unstarch,** UN-¹(2); **unsteel,** UN-¹(4); **unstep,** UN-¹(3); **un-** stick, **unstitch, unstock, unstop,** UN-¹(1); **unstopper,** UN-¹(2); **unstrap,** unstring, **unstrung,** UN-²(2); **unsuc-** cess, **unsuspicion,** UN-²(2); **unswaddle,** unswathe, **unswear,** UN-¹(1); **unsym-** metry, UN-²(2); **untack, untangle,**

unteach, untemper, UN-¹(1); **untent,** UN-¹(3); **untether, unthink, unthread,** UN-¹(1); **unthrift,** UN-²(2); **unthrone,** UN-¹(3); **untie, untied¹,** UN-¹(1).

until′, prep. & conj. =TILL² (preferred when its clause or phrase stands first, as ~ you told me I had no idea of it, & occas. in leisurely or dignified or pompous style, as unless & ~). [ME untill f. ON und as far as +TILL²]

untile, untin, see UN-¹(2).

ŭn′to (-ŏŏ), prep. (arch.). =TO¹ (in all uses except as sign of infinitive). [as UNTIL, w. TO¹ substituted for TILL²]

untomb, see UN-¹(3); **untooth,** UN-¹(2); **untouchable,** UN-²(1); **untruss,** UN-¹(1); **untruth,** UN-²(2); **untuck, untune,** UN-¹ (1); **unturf,** UN-¹(2); **untwine, untwist,** unveil, **unturf,** UN-¹(2); **unvicar,** UN-¹(4); **un-** vote, unwarp, **unweave,** UN-¹(1).

unwiel′d|y, a. Slow or clumsy of movement, difficult to use or manage, owing to size or weight or shape. Hence ~ILY² adv., ~INESS n. [UN-² + obs. wieldy (obs. wield n. control, cf. WIELD v., -+-Y²) vigorous]

unwill, unwind, see UN-¹(1); **unwisdom,** UN-²(2); **unwitting(ly),** UN-²(1); **un-** wound¹, **unwork, unwrap, unwrinkle,** unyoke, UN-¹(1).

up, adv., prep., a., n., & v.i. 1. To or in a higher place, position, degree, amount, value, etc., to or in a capital or university or place farther north or otherwise conventionally regarded as high(er), as bird flew up to the eaves, high up in the air, what is he doing up there ?, horse might have won with a better jockey up (in saddle), lives four floors up, a few feet further up, flames mount up, total mounts up, tide is coming up, water came up to his chin, a hundred up (on scoring-board, scored in game), it is up to (incumbent on) us to foot the bill, sums up to £5, lives up to (spends all) his income, up to the MARK¹, up against (confronted with) a hard job, am not up to (fit for) travelling, custom is traced up (back) to the Stuarts, up to DATE²; lift up your head, as far up (north) as Aberdeen, I stayed up (at Oxford etc.) for the vacation, ran up to town (London) for the day, was had up (before magistrate) on a charge of drunkenness, sailed up (towards source) as far as the river was navigable, corn is up (at high price), is high up in the school, went up three places in class, ran up a bill, have looked for it up & down (in every direction). 2. To the place in question or in which the speaker etc. is, as child came up & asked me the time, went straight up to the door, sure to TURN¹ up late. 3. To or in erect or vertical position (lit. & fig.) esp. as favourable to activity, out of bed or lying or sitting or kneeling posture, in(to)

For adj|n in un- not given see UN-²(1).

condition of efficiency or activity, as *sprung up from his seat, stand up* (with *get, stand, etc.* understood) *up!, up with you, up, get up, up with it, put it up, up* (opp. *down with*) *the Bolsheviks!, was* (already) *up early this morning, was* (still) *up late last night, must be up & doing, Home Secretary is up* (has risen to speak, is speaking). ‖*Parliament is up* (no longer sitting, prorogued), *stir up sedition, GET up, screw up your courage, wind up watch, put the helm up* (so place it as to force ship away from wind), *his blood is up* (anger or spirit roused), *is up* (going on)?, *what tricks have you been up to* (playing)?, *up to SNUFF! do not feel up* (equal) *to work, this cigar is not up to much* (is poor); ‖ (at Eton Coll.) *he is up to* (in the form of) *Mr A.* **4.** (Expr. complete or effectual result etc.) *eat, drink, burn, dry, tear, up; speak up* (loudly); *hunt up, find by hunting; follow up; praise up, accumulate by saving; pack, PUT[1], bind, store, up; lock, chain, tie, fasten, fix, nail, seal, up* (securely); *time is up* (exhausted); GIVE[1] *up, hurry up,* MAKE[1] *up, cheer up, clear up; it is all up* (& sl. U.P.) *with him, his case is hopeless;* HARD*-up.* **5.** prep. To a higher point of, on or along in ascending direction, as *climbed up the ladder, up the hill, smoke goes up chimney, sailed up river* (towards source of) *the river, walked up* (towards higher or more central part of, or simply along) *the street, up hill & down dale, up & down in every direction, taking the country as it comes; at or in a higher part of, as *lives further up the road, saw him sitting half-a-mile up the river, saw him sitting half-a-mile up the* SPOUT. **6.** adj. Moving, sloping, going, towards a higher point or to the capital, as *up stroke, up hill, up train.* **7.** n. *On the up-&-up* (colloq.), improving, on the level, honest; *ups & downs, rises & falls, undulating ground, alternately good & bad fortune.* **8.** v.i. (colloq. & dial.; -pp-). Start up, begin abruptly to say or do something (*he ups & says*); (with *with*) raise, pick up, as *he upped* (or *up*) *with his fist, with his stick.* [OE *up(p)* adv., cf. Du. op, G *auf*]

ŭp-, pret. = prec. **1.** Adv. pref. to vbs (esp. in p.p.) & vbl nn., chiefly arch. (UPBRAID etc.), poet., or rhet., exc. a few given separately (UPHEAVE etc.), as : *upbear'* v.t., hold up, sustain aloft, esp. in p.p. *upborne; upbind'* v.t. ; *upblaze'* v.i.; *up'bringing* n. (mod.), bringing up, education ; *upcast'* (-ah-) v.t. ; *up'cast* n., casting up, upward throw, (Mining) shaft through which air

passes out of mine ; *up'growth* (-ōth) n.; *growing(up, development, what grows up ; upheav'* (-p-h-) v.t.; *upheav'al* (-p-h-) n. (mod.), heaving up, esp. (Geol.) of part of earth's crust, (fig.) vast social or other change; *upheave'* (-p-h-) v.t. & i.; *up'keep* n. (mod.), (cost, means, of) maintenance ; *uplift'* v.t.; *up'lift* n. (esp. U.S.), (mod.), raising esp. in rebellion etc., influence, edifying effect, moral inspiration ; *uprise'* v.i.; *upris'ing* n., rising esp. from bed, rebellion, riot; *uproot'* v.t., tear up by roots (lit. & fig.); *upstan'ding,* well set up, erect, (of wages) fixed, not variable ; *up'take* n., lifting, (orig. Sc.) understanding, apprehension, as *quick in the uptake; up'throw* (-ō), n., throwing up (country adv.); *uphill'* (-p-h-) adv., up country districts (cf. f. nn., as : *up-country* (-kŭ-) a., toward the interior, inland, as *up-country advr. & adj.*) ; *uphill'* (-p-h-) adv., with upward slope along hill or slope in upward direction, as *road runs uphill, riding uphill; up'hill* (-p-h-) a., sloping upwards, (fig.) arduous, difficult, laborious, as *uphill work; up'stage* a. (colloq.), standoffish: *upstairs'* (-z) adv., *up'stair(s)* a., on, to, an upperstorey: *up'stream' adv., up'stream adv.*, (moving, done) against the current. **3.** With adj. force, as : *up'land* a. & n. (sing. or pl.), (of) the higher or inland parts of a country ; *up'stroke,* upward line made in writing.

upa'nĭshăd (ŏŏpah-, ōōpă-), n. Each of a series of Sanskrit philosophical treatises forming a division of the Vedas. [Skr.]

ŭp'as, n. (Also *~-tree, antiar*) Javanese tree yielding milky sap used as arrow-poison & held fatal to whatever came beneath its branches, (fig.) pernicious influence, practice, etc.; poisonous sap of this & other trees. [Malay. = poison]

ŭpbraid', v.t. Chide, reproach (person & *with, for,* fault etc.). [ME *upbraid,* ~ING[1] n., ~ingly[2] adv. [OE *UP(reg)den* BRAID[2]); orig. = bring up or adduce (a fault).]

ŭp-énd', v.t. & i. (dial). Set on end; stand, or rise, up. [UP adv.]

ŭphōld' (-p-h-), v.t. Hold up, keep erect, support; give support or countenance to (person, practice, etc.); maintain, confirm, (decision, verdict). Hence ~ER[1] n. [UP-]

ŭphōl'ster (-p-h-), v.t. Furnish (room etc.) with hangings, carpets, furniture, covering, padding, springs, etc., cover (chair etc.) with textile covering, (chair etc. *with, in,* tapestry etc.). [back formation f. foll.]

ŭphōl'sterer (-p-h-), n. One whose trade

For other words in *up-* see UP-.

it is to upholster; **~-bee**, kind that furnishes its cell with cut leaves etc. So **uphŏl′stery**(1, 2) n. [earlier *uphold(st)er* repairer (UPHOLD, -STER) or dealer; + -ER¹]

ûph′rŏe, n. (naut.). Long wooden block with holes through which cords are rove for adjusting an awning. [f. Du. *juffrouw* young lady, (Naut.) ornamental pulley, etc. (*jong* young + *vrouw* woman)]

upŏn′, prep. = ON (*on* & *~* are perhaps always idiomatically interchangeable; *on* is perhaps the commoner word esp. in colloq. use; *~* is perhaps preferred when the prep. follows its object, as *had no evidence to go ~, nothing to depend ~ not enough to live ~*, but cf. *which table did you leave it on?*; other idiomatic preferences are perhaps rightly shown in *~my word, on the whole, tier ~ tier of seats, fell ~ him unawares, had him on toast, came at once on receiving your message, take it on trust, will go on the chance, went on the spree, thrown ~ his own resources, stretched ~ the rack*). [formerly also as adv.; ME (UP + ON)]

ûpp′er, a. & n. **1.** Higher in place, situated above, as *~ lip, ~ storey* (of house, also fig.= brain, as *something wrong in his ~ storey*). *~* (right-hand side of) keyboard, *~* CASE²; *have* or *get the ~ hand* (mastery); *~ works* (Naut.), parts of ship above water when she is balanced for voyage; *~-cut* (Boxing), short-arm blow delivered upwards inside opponent's guard, (v.t.) hit with *~-cut*; *~* PARTIALS. **2.** Higher in rank, dignity, etc., as *the ~ servants, the U~ House*, House of Lords, *the ~ ten (thousand)*, the aristocracy, *the U~ Bench* (hist.), Court of King's Bench during exile of Charles II.; *~ crust* (colloq.), the aristocracy. **3.** n. *~* part of boot or shoe, as *be on one's ~s* (poor, in difficulties); (pl.) cloth gaiters. [ME (UP + -ER²)]

ûpp′ermost, a. & adv. **1.** Highest in place or rank, so **ûp′MOST** a. **2.** adv. On or to the top, as *said whatever came ~* (first suggested itself). [prec. + -MOST]

~LY² adv., ~NESS n. [f. UP + -ISH¹]

ûp′right (-rīt; *in pred. use also* ûprīt′), a., adv., & n. **1.** Erect, vertical, as *an ~ post, posture,* PIANO³ (pred. a. or adv.) *stood ~, set it ~*; righteous, strictly honourable or honest, whence ~LY² adv., ~NESS n., (-rīt-). **2.** n. Post or rod fixed ~ esp. as support to some structure. [OE UP(*riht* RIGHT)]

ûp′roar (-ôr), n. Tumult, violent disturbance, clamour. Hence **ûproar′ious** a. (often of laughter, high spirits, etc.), **ûproar′iously**² adv., **ûproar′iousNESS** n., (-ôr-). [f. Du. *oproer* (*op* up + *roer* a stir, cf. G *ruhr*)]

ûp′rush, n. An upward rush; (esp.,

Psych.) a sudden emergence into consciousness from the subliminal. [UP-1]

upsĕt′¹, v.t. & i., & n. **1.** Overturn, be overturned, as *carriage (was) ~*; disturb the composure or temper or digestion of, as *the news quite ~ him, ate something that ~ him*; shorten & thicken (metal, esp. tire) by hammering or pressure. **2.** n. (ûp′sĕt), *~ting, being ~*. [UP-]

ûp′sĕt², a. *~ price*, lowest selling price of property in auction etc, reserve price. [UP-]

ûp′shŏt, n. Final issue, conclusion; general effect, the long & short, (of a matter). [UP-]

ûp′side-down′, adv. & a. With the upper part under, inverted, in total disorder, as *everything was (turned) ~, an ~ arrangement*. [altered f. ME *up so down*, lit. up as if down; cf. TOPSY-TURVY]

∥**ûpsī′des** (-dēz), adv. (dial.). *Get ~ with*, turn the tables on, avenge oneself upon. [UP-]

ûpsil′on, n. Greek letter (T, v)=u. [Gk (*psīlos* bare)]

ûp′start, n. Person who has risen suddenly from humble position (often attrib.); person who assumes arrogant tone. [UP-]

ûp′ward a., **ûp′ward(s)** (-z) adv. **1.** Directed, moving, towards a higher place (lit. & fig.), as *an ~ glance, prices show an ~ tendency*, whence ~LY² adv. **2.** adv. In ~ direction, as *look, move, ~(s)*, followed *the stream ~(s)* (towards source); *children of 6 years old &~(s)* (more); *found ~(s) of* (more than) *40 specimens*. [-WARD(S)]

ûraem′ia, n. (path.). Morbid condition of blood due to retention of urinary matter normally eliminated by kidneys. Hence ~IC a. [f. Gk *ouron* urine + *haima* blood]

ûrae′us, n. Serpent as head-dress of Egyptian divinities & kings. [mod. L f. Gk *ouraios* repr. the anc.-Egypt. wd for cobra]

Ur′al-Altā′ic (ūral-ăl-), a. Of (the people of) the Ural & Altaic mountain ranges; (Philol.) of a family of Finnic, Mongolian, & other agglutinative languages of N. Europe & Asia.

uranian. See VENUS.

ûrā′nium, n. Radio-active white metallic element, the heaviest of the elements occurring in nature, used as a source of atomic energy & (in the isotope U 235) in atomic bombs. Hence **ûrā′nic**, **ûr′anous**, aa. [f. URANUS + -IUM]

ûran̳o- in comb.= Gk *ouranos* heaven, as: *~ŏg′raphy*, descriptive astronomy, so *~ŏgraph′ic(al)* aa., *~ŏg′raphist* n.: *~ŏl′ogy*, astronomy; *~ŏm′etry*, measurement of stellar distances, map showing positions and magnitudes of stars.

Ûr′anus (Ūr-; or ūr̄an-), n. (Gk Myth.) son of Ge (Earth) & father of Cronus (Saturn), the Titans, etc.; planet dis-

For other words in *up-* see UP-.

urban, a. Of, living or situated in, a city or town, as ~ *districts, population*, in a city or town. [f. L *urbanus* (as prec.)]

urbane', a. Courteous, suave, elegant or refined in manner. Hence ~ly² adv. [as prec.]

urban'ity, n. Courtesy, polished manners; || (arch.) polished wit or humour. [f. L *urbanitas* (as prec., see -TY)]

ur'ceolate, a. (bot.). Pitcher-shaped, with large body & small mouth. [f. L *urceolus* dim. of *urceus* pitcher + -ATE²]

urch'in, n. 1. Roguish or mischievous boy; boy, youngster. 2. (Usu. *sea~*) = ECHINUS; || (arch.) hedgehog, goblin. [f. ONF *heriçon* f. L *ericius* hedgehog]

Urdu (oor'dŏō), n. Hindustani. [Hind., lit. = camp (language), as originating between Mohammedan conquerors & their subjects]

-ure, suf. forming nn., repr. F -*ure*, L -*ura*, added to p.p. stems of vbs (*aperture, capture, censure, dictature*), rarely to others (*figura*). Wds in -*dtura* lost +- in F (*armâture* F *armure, tornatura* F *tour-nure, capellatura* F *chevelure*), &. -*ure*, thus appearing to be added to pres. st., became living suf. in F forming nn. on vbs in -*er* not always of L orig. (*procedure, leisure, tenure*), are F infinitives in -*ir* adopted in E. *Seizure, pleasure, failure, manure, brochure*), many of which are as legislature, (3) term of (official) agency, as (rarely) *judicature*.

ur'ea, n. (chem.). Soluble colourless crystalline compound contained esp. in urine of mammals. [f. Gk *ouron* urine]

-uret, suf. (chem.) of nn. & their derivatives indicating combination, now for the most part replaced by -IDE. [mod. L as prec.]

uret'er, n. Duct by which urine passes from kidney to bladder etc. Hence ~ic'(-et'-) a. [f. Gk *ourētēr* (*oureō* make water)]

ureth'ra, n. Duct by which urine is dis-charged from bladder. Hence ~AL a., ~R'IS, ~ōCELE, ~ŌT'OMY, nn. [LL, f. Gk *ourēthra* (as prec.)]

urge, v.t. & n. 1. Drive forcibly, impel, hasten, cause to proceed with effort, as ~ *his horse forward*, ~*d him on, we ~d our flight northwards*; (fig.) entreat or earnestly or persistently, as ~ *haste in action, to take steps*; advocate (measure etc.) pressingly; ply (person etc.) hard with argument or entreaty; dwell per-

sistently or emphatically upon, as *in vain you* ~ *his youth, ~d the difficulty of getting supplies, argument was ~d in vain*. 2. n. Impulsion, yearning. [f. L *urgēre* press, drive]

ur'gency, n. Being urgent; || (Parl.) formal declaration, by vote of three to one in house of not less than 300, that matter is urgent & shall take precedence of all others. [f. foll., see -ENCY]

ur'gent, a. Pressing, calling for imme-diate action or attention, as *am in ~ need, the matter is* ~, *an* ~ *demand*; im-portunate, earnest & persistent in demand, as *was* ~ *with me for* (or *to disclose*) *further particulars*. Hence ~ly² adv. [F (as URGE, see -ENT)]

ur'ic, a. Of urine; ~ *acid* (found in small quantities in healthy urine of man & quadrupeds, chief constituent in that of birds & reptiles). [f. F *urique* (URINE, -IC)]

ur'im, n. ~ *& thumm'im*, objects of un-known nature connected with breast-plate of high priest (*Exod.* XXVIII. 30). [Heb. *urim* pl. of *ur* light, *tummim* pl. of *tom* perfection]

ur'inal, n. Fixed vessel or receptacle for use of persons requiring to pass urine; public or private place containing such receptacles; vessel used by invalid for passing water in bed; glass vessel for containing urine for inspection. [OF, f. L (URINE, -AL)]

ur'inary, a. Of urine, as ~ *organs, diseases*. 2. n. Reservoir for urine as manure; (Mil.) barrack building contain-ing several urinals. [-ARY¹]

ur'inate, v.i. Pass urine. Hence ~A'TION n. [f. med. L *urinare* (as foll.). See -ATE³]

ur'ine, n. Pale-yellow fluid secreted from the blood by the kidneys, stored in bladder, & discharged through urethra. So ~OUS a. [OF, f. L *urina*, cogn. w. Gk *ouron*, see -INE⁴]

ur'ino- in comb. = prec., as ~*ōl'ogy, study of the urine*; ~*ōm'eter*, instrument show-ing specific gravity of urine, so ~*ōmét'ric* a., ~*ōm'ĕtry* n.; ~*ōs'copy*, inspection of urine, so ~*ōscŏp'ic* a.

urn, n., & v.t. 1. Vase with foot & usu. with rounded body, esp. as anciently used for storing the ashes of the dead or as vessel or measure; (fig.) anything in which dead body or its remains are pre-served, e.g. grave; vase-shaped vessel with tap in which tea, coffee, etc., is kept hot, e.g. by means of spirit-lamp; ~*flower*, kinds of bulbous plant with ~-shaped flower. Hence ~FUL n. 2. v.t. Enclose in ~. [(vb f. n.) f. L *urna* (*urere* burn]

uro- in comb. = URINO-, as *ūrŏl'ogy* etc.

uro-² in comb. = Gk *oura* tail, in anat. terms.

Ursa (er-'), n. ~ *Major, Minor,* Great, Little, BEAR¹. [L., = she-bear]

Urs'ine, a. Of, like, a bear. [f. L *ursinus* (*ursus* bear, see -INE¹)]

Urs'uline (er-), a. & n. (Nun) of an order founded in 1537 for nursing the sick & teaching girls. [f. St *Ursula* +-INE¹]

ūrti·cārĭa, n. (path.). Nettle-rash. [f. L *urtica* nettle]

ūr'tĭcāte, v.t. Sting like a nettle; whip (paralytic limb etc.) with nettles to restore feeling. So ~ATION n. [f. med. L *urticare* (L *urtica* nettle) see -ATE³]

ūru·bū (ōō'rōōbōō), n. American black vulture. [Brazilian]

ūr'us, n. Kind of wild bull described by Caesar, = AUROCHS. [L., = Gk *ouros*]

us (ŭs, ŭs), pl. obj. of I² (abbr. *'s,* as *let's go;* occas. poet. & arch., = ourselves, as *let's get us from the mole*), [OE *ūs,* cf. Du. *ons,* G *uns,* L *nos,* Gk *hēmas,* Skr. *asmān*]

us'age (-z-), n. Manner of using or treating, treatment, as *med with harsh ~, damaged by rough ~;* habitual or customary practice resp. as creating a right or obligation or standard, as *sanctified by ~, an ancient ~, contrary to the ~ of the best writers;* (Law) habitual but not necessarily immemorial practice. [ME & OF, f. med. L *usaticum* (as USE¹, see -AGE)]

ūs'ance (-z-), n. (commerc.). Time allowed for payment of foreign bills of exchange, as *the ~ on Indian bills is 4 months, bill drawn at half or double ~.* [OF (as USE² see -ANCE)]

use¹ (ūs), n. **1.** Using, employment, application to a purpose, as *should recommend the ~ of a file, taught him the ~ of the globes, put it to a good ~, is meant for not ornament, is in daily ~, becomes easier with ~, worn & polished with ~, made of* (employed) *a quibble, pray make ~ of my telephone.* **2.** Right or power of using, as *stipulated for the ~ of the piano, lost the ~ of his left arm.* **3.** Availability, utility, purpose for which thing can be used, as *a blunt knife 's of ~ for this work, a foot-rule will be found of* (great) *~, it is* (of) *no ~ talking or to talk, what is the ~ of talking?, talking is no ~, find a ~ for banana-skins, I have no ~ for it.* **4.** Custom, wont, familiarity, as *long ~ has reconciled me to it, in such matters ~ is everything, according to his ~ in emergencies, ~ & wont.* **5.** Ritual & liturgy of a church, diocese, etc., as *Sarum, Anglican, Roman, ~.* **6.** (Law) benefit or profit of lands & tenements in the possession of another who holds them solely for the beneficiary. [f. OF *us* f. L *usus* -ūs (as foll.); (in legal sense) AF *oes* f. L *opus* employment, need]

use² (ūz), v.t. & i. **1.** Employ for a purpose, handle as instrument, consume as material, exercise, put into operation, avail oneself of, as *seldom ~ a knife, should ~ oil for frying, we seem to ~ a great deal of butter, never ~ a dictionary, learn to ~ your hands, ~ your wits, must ~ the services of an agent, shall ~ every means, must ~ your opportunities, ~ your discretion, should at least ~ some moderation, may I ~ your name* (quote you as authority, reference, etc.)?, *do not fail to ~* (in argument, pleading, etc.) *this damaging fact, has ~d my absence to poison everyone against me.* **2.** Treat in specified manner, as *has ~d me like a dog, how did he ~ you?, ~d me ill, ill-~d me.* **3.** (Now only in past, usu. pron. ūst; esp. when followed immediately by *to*) be accustomed, have as one's constant or frequent practice, as *I ~d to take the bus, does not come as often as he ~d* (to), *bell ~d always to ring at one, what ~d he to say?, ~d not* (colloq. *didn't ~*) *to answer.* **4.** (Now only in p.p., pron. as last sense) accustomed, as *am not ~d to this sort of thing, to being called a liar, have become ~d to a vegetarian diet.* **5.** ~ *up,* consume the whole of (material etc.), find a use for (remaining material etc.), exhaust, wear out e.g. *with overwork.* Hence **ūs'ABLE** a., **ūs'er¹** [-ER¹] n., (-z-). [f. OF *user* f. LL *usare* frequent. of L *uti us-* use]

ūse'fŭl (-sf-), a. Of use, serviceable, producing or able to produce good result, as *~ arts, ratchet-brace will be found ~, gave me some ~ hints, must make himself generally ~* (perform miscellaneous services); (sl.) highly creditable or efficient, as *a pretty ~ performance, is pretty ~ at Greek iambics.* Hence ~LY² adv., ~NESS n. [-FUL]

ūse'lĕss (-sl-), a. Serving no useful purpose, unavailing, as *a mass of ~ erudition, contents were rendered ~ by damp, protest is ~;* (sl.) out of health or spirits, unfit for anything, as *am feeling ~.* Hence ~LY² adv., ~NESS n. [-LESS]

ūs'er¹. See USE².

ūs'er² (-z-), n. (law). Continued use or enjoyment of a right etc.; *right of ~,* (1) right to use, (2) presumptive right arising from ~. [OF (as USE² see -ER³)]

ūsh'er, n., & v.t. **1.** Officer or servant acting as doorkeeper of a court etc., showing persons to seats in public hall etc., || or walking before person of rank, as (gentleman ~ of the) BLACK¹ rod; || (now usu. derog.) under-teacher, assistant schoolmaster. Hence ~ETTE¹, ~SHIP, nn. **2.** v.t. Act as ~ to, precede (person) as ~, announce, show in etc., as *was at length ~ed* (into his presence, *star ~s in the dawn.* [(vb f. n.) AF *usser,* f. OF *(h)uissier* f. L *ostiarius* doorkeeper (*ostium* door, see -ARY¹)]

ūs'quebaugh (-aw), n. Whisky; Irish cordial made of brandy etc. [f. Ir. *uisge beatha* water of life (*uisge* water, WHISKY, + *beatha* life)]

ustulā'tion, n. Drying of moist substance by means of fire. [f. L *ustulare* (*ustus* burn, -ATION)]

ū'sual (-zhŏŏ-), a. Such as commonly occurs, customary, habitual, as *asked the ~ questions*, customary; *with his ~ disregard of convention*, the courtesy ~ *with him, it is ~ to tip the waiter, came earlier than (was) ~, have forgotten something as (is) ~* or (vulg. joc.) *as per ~*. Hence ~LY² adv., ~NESS n. [f. OF *usuel* f. L *usualis* (as USE¹, see -AL)]

ūsucap'tion (-z-), n. (civil law). Acquisition of the title or right to property by uninterrupted & undisputed possession for prescribed term. [also -*cāpion*, f. L *usucapio -onis* f. *usucapere* acquire by prescription (*usu* by USE¹ + *capere capt-* take)]

ū'sufruct (-z-), n. & v.t. Right of enjoying the use & advantages of another's property short of destruction or waste of its substance; (vb) hold in ~. [(vb f. n.) t. L *usus/fructus* use & enjoyment (*usus* USE¹ + *fructus* FRUIT)]

ūsufruc'tuary (-z-), a. & n. Of, one who has, usufruct. [f. LL *usufructuarius* (prec., -ARY¹)]

ū'surer (-zhər-), n. One who lends money at exorbitant interest. [AF, f. med. L *usurarius* (as USURY, see -ER²)]

ūsûrp' (-z-), v.t. & i. Seize, assume, (throne, office, power, property, etc.) wrongfully; (rare) encroach (up)on. Hence or cogn. **ūsurpā'TION** (zer-), ~ER¹, n., ~ingly² adv. [f. OF *usurper* f. L *usurpare* use, usurp, etym. dub.]

ū'sury (-zhŭr-), n. Practice of lending money at exorbitant interest esp. at higher interest than is allowed by law, whence **ūsūr'ious** (-z-, -zh-) a., **ūsūr'iously** adv., **ūsūr'iousness** n.; such interest; (now usu. fig.) interest, as *the service was repaid with ~*. [f. med. L *usuria*, L *usura* (USE¹, -URE²)]

ut¹ (ŏŏt), n. Key-note of a scale (now usu. DO¹). [see GAMUT]

ūt², adv. Ut¹ *sūp'ra, in'fra*, as shown or stated above, below. [L]

ūten'sil, n. Instrument, implement, esp. one in domestic use, as *kitchen, cooking-, ~s*. [f. OF *utensile* f. L *utensilis* usable]

ū'terine, a. Of the uterus; born of same mother but not same father (*his ~ brother*). [f. LL *uterinus* (foll., -INE¹)]

ū'terus, n. (pl. ~ī). The womb. Hence **ū'ter·us**, [f. L]

ūtil'itar'ian, a. & n. Of, consisting in, utility; (holder) of utilitarianism. [-ARIAN]

ūtilitar'ianism, n. Doctrine that actions are right because they are useful; doctrine that greatest happiness of greatest number should be sole end of public action. [-ISM]

ūtil'ity, n. Usefulness, profitableness, useful thing; = *public ~*; = prec.;

(Theatr., also ~-*man*) actor of the smallest parts in plays; (attrib.) made or serving for ~, severely practical, (~ *clothes, furniture*, etc.). [f. F *utilité* f. L *utilitatem* (*utilis* useful f. *uti* use, see -TY)]

ū'tilize (-līz), v.t. Make use of, turn to account, use. Hence ~ABLE a., ~A'TION n. [f. F *utiliser* (*utile* f. L *utilis*, see prec.)]

ut'ī possidē'tis, n. Principle that leaves belligerents in possession of what they have acquired. [LL. = as you possess]

ū'tmost, a. & n. 1. Furthest, extreme, as *the ~ limits*; that is such in the highest degree, as *showed the ~ reluctance*. 2. n. One's ~, all one can do. [OE *ūtemest*, double superl. of *ūt* OUT, cf. AFTERMOST]

Ūtō'pian (ū-), a. & n. (Inhabitant) of Utopia; (characteristic of an) ardent but unpractical reformer etc., whence **ūtō'pianism** n. [-AN]

Ūtō'pia (ū-), n. (Book published by Sir T. More in 1516 describing) imaginary island with perfect social & political system; ideally perfect place or state of things. [=nowhere, f. Gk *ou* not+*topos* place]

ū'tricle, n. Cell of animal or plant; small bag or cavity in the body, esp. one in the inner ear. Hence **ūtric'ūlar¹** a. [f. L *utriculus* dim. of *uter* leather bag]

ŭtt'er¹, a. Complete, total, unqualified, as ~ *misery, saw the ~ absurdity of it, an ~ denial*; ||~ *barrister* (junior, addressing court from outside bar within which K.C. pleads). Hence ~LY² adv., ~MOST a., ~NESS n. [OE *ūttera*, compar. adj. f. *ūt* OUT]

ŭtt'er², v.t. Emit audibly (cry, groan, sigh, etc.); express in spoken or written wds (one's sentiments, a lie, the truth, etc.); put (notes, base coin, etc.) into circulation. [f. OUT, cf. Du. *uiteren* (*uit* out), G *äussern* (*aus* out)]

ŭtt'erance¹, n. Uttering, expressing in words, as *gave ~ to his rage*; power of speech, as *defective ~*; spoken words, as *his pulpit~s*. [-ANCE]

||ŭtt'erance², n. (literary). Fight etc. *to the ~* (bitter end). [f. OF *outrance* (*outrer* surpass, as ULTRA-)]

ū'vula (ū-), n. (pl. ~ae). Pendent fleshy part of soft palate; similar processes in bladder & cerebellum. Hence ~AR¹ a. [med. L dim. of L *uva* bunch of grapes]

ūxŏr'ious, a. Excessively fond of one's wife. Hence ~LY² adv., ~NESS n. [f. L *uxorius* (*uxor* wife) + -OUS]

Uz'bĕg (ū-), n. Member of a Turkish race in central Asia. [native]

V

V, v, (vē), letter (pl. Vs, V's, Vees). V-shaped thing, e.g. joint; (Roman numeral) 5, as IV 4, VI 6, viii 8, viii (now usu. ix) 9, xv 15, lv 55; *V sign*, made by hand with fingers clenched except the

first and second outspread to form the letter V (for *Victory*).

vac'ancy, n. Being vacant or empty or unoccupied; emptiness of mind, idleness, listlessness; unoccupied post, as *has a ~ on his staff, in his warehouse, must fill the ~*. [f. LL *vacantia* (as foll., see -ANCY)]

vac'ant, a. Empty, not filled or occupied, as *house is still ~, a ~ smoking-compartment, have no ~ space, will amuse your ~ hours, applied for a ~ post in the Treasury*; not mentally active, not rationally occupied, empty-headed, thoughtless, listless, stupid, as *his mind seems completely ~, received the news with a ~ stare, given up to ~ frivolities*, whence ~LY² adv. [OF (as foll., see -ANT)]

vacate', v.t. Go away from so as to leave empty or unoccupied, give up occupation or possession of, (military position, place, house, throne, office); annul (law, contract, etc.). [f. L *vacare* be empty (cf. VACUOUS), see -ATE³]

vaca'tion, n. Vacating (of house, post, etc.); holiday, fixed period of cessation from work, esp. in law-courts & universities, as *Christmas, Easter, Whitsun, long or summer ~*. [OF, f. L *vacationem* (as prec., see -ATION)]

vac'cinate (-ks-), v.t. Inoculate with vaccine to procure immunity from small-pox or with modified virus of any disease in order to produce it in mild form & so prevent serious attack. Hence ~A'TION (1, 2)(-ks-), nn. [f. foll. + -ATE³]

vac'cine (-ks-), a. & n. 1. Of cows or cowpox or vaccination. 2. n. Virus of cowpox as used in vaccination (*bovine, humanized, ~*), got direct from cow, got from human subject), modified virus of any disease similarly used, whence **vac'cinal, vaccin'io,** (-ks-), aa.; ~*-farm* (where ~ is cultivated by inoculation of heifers); ~*-point*, pointed instrument used in inoculation. [f. L *vaccinus* a. (*vacca* cow, see -INE¹)]

vaccin'ia (-ks-), n. (med.), Cowpox, esp. inoculated. [mod. L, f. prec.]

vac'illate, v.i. Move from side to side, oscillate, waver; fluctuate in opinion or resolution. Hence or cogn. ~a'tingly² adv., ~A'TION n. [f. L *vacillare*, see -ATE³]

vac'u̇ole, n. (biol.). Minute cavity in organ etc. containing air, fluid, etc. Hence ~oLAR¹, ~oLATE²(2), aa. [F, dim. of VACUUM]

vac'uous, a. Empty, void; unintelligent, expressionless, vacant, as *a ~ stare, remark*. Hence or cogn. **vacū'ITY**, ~NESS, nn. [f. L *vacuus* +-OUS]

vac'uum, n. (pl. ~ums, -a). 1. Space entirely devoid of matter, as *nature abhors a ~*; space, vessel, from which air has been almost exhausted by air-pump etc. (*Guerickian, Torricellian, ~*, produced by air-pump, by mercury-pump as in mercurial barometer); (loosely) partial diminution of pressure below normal atmospheric pressure. 2. ~ *brake*, continuous train-brake in which pressure is caused by exhaustion of air from bellows pulling brake-rod; ~ *cleaner*, apparatus for removing dust etc. by suction; ~ *flask*, with two walls separated by jacket so that liquid in inner receptacle retains its temperature; ~*-gauge* (for testing pressure consequent on production of ~); ~*-tube*, sealed glass tube with almost perfect ~ for observing passage of electric charge (see also THERMION). [L, neut. as prec. used as n.]

vad'e-mec'um, n. Handbook or other thing carried constantly about the person (often in title of book). [L, = go with me]

vae vic'tis, int. Woe to the vanquished (expressing victor's intention of exacting full fruits of victory). [L]

vag'abond, a., n., & v.i. 1. Having no fixed habitation, wandering; driven, drifting to & fro; (of spider) not sedentary. 2. n. Wanderer, vagrant, esp. idle & worthless one; (colloq.) scamp, rascal. 3. v.i. (now colloq.). Wander about, play the ~. Hence ~AGE(2, 3), ~ISM(2), nn., ~ISH¹ a., ~IZE(2) v.i. [f. L *vagabundus* (*vagari* wander)]

vaga'ry, n. Whimsical or extravagant notion; caprice; freak. [ult. f. L *vagari* wander]

vagi'na, n. Sheath, sheathlike covering, esp. (Anat.) sexual passage in female from uterus to external orifice, whence **vaginr'is, vaginör'ory,** nn.; (Bot.) sheath formed round stem by, base of leaf. Hence **va'ginal, va'ginATE², va'ginated,** aa. [L]

vag'rant, a. & n. 1. Wandering, roving, strolling, itinerant, as *a ~ musician, indulging in ~ speculations*. 2. n. Wanderer, idle rover, vagabond; (Law) idle & disorderly person of any of three grades liable to various terms of imprisonment. Hence **vag'rancy** n., ~LY² adv. [earlier *vagarant*, perh. f. AF *wakerant, walcrand*, of Teut. orig.; altered on L *vagari* wander]

vague (-g), a. Indistinct, not clearly expressed or identified, of uncertain or ill-defined meaning or character, as *returned only a ~ answer, has some ~ idea of going to Canada, have not the ~st notion of his reasons, yield to ~ terrors, heard a ~ rumour to that effect*. Hence ~LY² (-gl-) adv., ~NESS (-gn-) n. [f. L *vagus* wandering]

vail¹, v.t. & i. (arch., poet.). ‖ Lower or doff (one's plumes, pride, crown, etc.) esp. in token of submission; yield, give place, uncover as sign of respect etc. [f. F *avaler* see AVALANCHE]

‖**vail²**, n. (arch.; usu. pl.). Gratuity, tip; present given for corrupt purpose. [=-AVAIL]

vain, a. 1. Unsubstantial, empty, trivial,

as ~ **boasts, ~ triumphs, distinctions**; useless, unavailing, followed by no good result, as *in the ~ hope of dissuading him, all resistance was ~, to resist is ~, it is ~ to resist*; conceited, having too high an opinion of one's beauty, ability, etc. **2.** *In* ~, to no purpose, as *we protested in ~, it was in ~ that we protested*; TAKE¹ *person's name in* ~. **3.** ~**ness**, excessive vanity, whence ~**glor'ious**ness, ~**glor'iously** adv., ~**glor'ious**ness n. Hence ~**LY²** adv., ~**NESS** n (rare). [OF., f. L *vanus* empty, vain]

vair, n. (her.), ... [F., f. L as VARIOUS]

Vaisya (vī'syə), n. (Member of) the third of the four great Hindu castes, comprising the merchants and agriculturists. [Skr. *vaiśya* peasant]

eakeet', **-ti** (-ēt), n. (E.-Ind.), Ambassador, commissioner, residing at a court; native attorney or deputy. [Hind. (-ti)]

val'ance, **val'ence¹**, n. Kind of damask frame or canopy of bedstead. Hence **val'anced²** (-st) a. [perh. f. AF *valer* descend f. OF *avaler* see AVALANCHE]

vale¹, n. Valley (now chiefly poet. or in names as *V~ of the White Horse*); ∥ small trough or channel carrying off water from pump etc. [f. OF *val*, f. L *vallis*]

vale², int. & n. Farewell. [L, imperat. of *valēre* be well, be strong]

vâledic'tion, n. (Words used in) bidding farewell. So ~**ORY** a., (also, as n. *farewell oration delivered by senior scholar on graduation etc.) [f. L *valēdicere dict-* say) bid farewell, see -ION]

val'ence¹, n. (chem.). See VALANCE.

val'ence², n. See VALENCY.

Valen'cia (-shə), n. Province of Spain; (usu. pl.) mixed fabric with wool weft and silk, cotton, or linen warp, usu. striped; (pl.) ~ almonds or raisins.

Valenciennes' (-sǐenz, & see Ap.), n. Rich kind of lace. [~, in France]

val'ency, n. (chem.). Unit of combining capacity, as *carbon has 4 ~ies*; =VALENCE². [-ENCY]

val'entine, n. *St V~'s day*, day on which St V~ was beheaded & on which birds were supposed to pair, Feb. 14; sweetheart chosen on this; amatory or satirical letter or picture sent to person of opposite sex on *St V~'s day*. [f. L *Valentinus*, proper name]

valer'ian, n. Kinds of plant, esp. *common* ~, herb with small pink or white flowers & strong odour esteemed by cats & rats; root of this used as mild stimulant etc., whence **val'erate¹**(3) n., **valer'ic** a., (chem.). [f. OF *valeriane*, etym. dub.]

val'et (or -lā) n., & v.t. **1.** (Also ~ *de chambre*, pr. vǎl'ā de shahn'br) manservant, who attends on man's person; ~ *de place* (vǎl'ā de plahs), courier esp. in France. **2.** v.t. Act as ~ to. [(vb f. n.) OF, var. of VARLET]

valetūdinǎr'ian, a. & n. **1.** Of infirm health; seeking to recover health; unduly solicitous about health. **2.** n. ~ person. Hence or cogn. ~**ISM** n., **valētūd'inǎry** a. & n. [f. L *valetudinarius* (*valetudo -dinis* health f. *valēre* be well, see -TUDE & -ARY¹)]

Valhǎl'la, n. (Norse Myth.), palace in which souls of slain heroes feasted; building used as final resting-place of the illustrious, or containing their statues etc. [f. ON *valhöll*, hall of the slain (*valr* slain + *höll* HALL)]

val'iant (-ya-), a. (Of person or conduct) brave, courageous. Hence ~**LY²** adv. [f. OF *vaillant* part. of *valoir* be worth f. L *valēre* be strong]

val'id, a. (Of reason, objection, argument, etc.) sound, defensible, well-grounded; (Law) sound & sufficient, executed with proper formalities, as ~ *contract, the marriage was held to be* ~. Hence or cogn. **valid'ITY** n., ~**LY²** adv. (see -ID¹)]

val'idāte, v.t. Make valid, ratify, confirm. So ~**A'TION** n. [f. med. L *validus* strong (as prec.), see -ATE³]

valise' (-ēs, -ēz), n. Kind of small portmanteau; (Mil.) soldier's kitbag. [F, cf. med. L *valisia*, etym. dub.]

valkyr (val'kyr), **vǎlkē'rǐa**, **-ǐe**, n. (Norse myth.; pl. **-kyrs**, **-kyries**). Each of Odin's handmaidens who selected those destined to be slain in battle. Hence **vǎlkyr'IAN** a. [f. ON *valkyrja* lit. chooser of slain (*valr* slain + *-kyrja* chooser cogn. w. CHOOSE)]

val(l)or'ia, n. Acorn-cups of the ~ *oak*, used in tanning, dyeing, & making ink. [f. It. *vallonia* ult. f. Gk *balanos* acorn]

val'lum, n. (Rom. ant.). Rampart. [L]

val'orize, v.t. Raise or stabilize the value of (a commodity etc.) by government action. Hence ~**A'TION** n. [f. L *valor* worth + -IZE (3)]

val'our (-ler), n. (now chiefly poet., rhet., or joc.). Personal courage esp. as shown in fighting; prowess. So **vǎl'orous** a., ~**ously²** adv. [OF, f. LL *valorem* worth, courage (*valēre* be strong, see -OR¹)]

valse (vahls), n. Waltz; ~ *à* DEUX-TEMPS, waltz with two beats (instead of three) in a bar, each divided into three smaller beats. [F, f. G as WALTZ]

val'uable, a. & n. **1.** Of great value or price or worth, as ~ *property, land, furniture, information, assistance*; capable of valuation, as *a service not* ~ *in money*. **2.** n. (usu. in pl.) ~ thing(s), esp. small article(s) of personal property, as *sent all her* ~*s to the bank*. [f. VALUE + -ABLE]

valua'tion, n. Estimation (esp. by professional valuer) of a thing's worth, worth so estimated, price set on a thing, as ~ *of land, disposed of at a low* ~, *sets too high a* ~ *on his abilities*. [OF, as foll vb + -ATION]

val'ue, n., & v.t. **1.** Worth, desirability, utility, qualities on which these depend, as *now learnt the* ~ *of fresh water, a friend, quinine, accuracy, regular exercise*; worth as estimated, valuation, as *sets a high* ~ *on his time*; *commercial, economic, exchange(able)* ~, *in exchange, purchasing power, power of a commodity to purchase others, amount of (pop.) money or (Pol. Econ.) other commodities for which thing can be exchanged in open market*; SURPLUS ~, *surplus production of labour after subsistence of labourer & family*; the equivalent of a thing, what represents or is represented by or may be substituted for a thing, as ~ *received* (see BILL[4] *of exchange*), *got good* ~ *for* (something well worth) *his money, paid him the* ~ *of his lost property, the precise* ~ (meaning) *of a word, acute accent has not always its full time* ~, (the full time indicated by it); (Paint.) relation of one part of picture to others in respect of light & shade, as *out of* ~, *too light or dark*; amount, quantity, denoted by algebraical term or expression; (Biol.) rank in classification. **2.** v.t. Estimate the ~ of, appraise (professionally), whence **val'uer[1]** n., or otherwise), as *should* ~ *the whole at £2000*; have high or specified opinion of, attach importance to, prize, esteem, appreciate, value oneself on, as ~ *sincerity (beyond all things), a* ~*d friend,* ~*s himself on his conversational powers, do not* ~ *that a brass farthing*. [(vb f. n.) OF fem. p.p. of *valoir* be worth f. L *valēre* be strong]

val'ueless (-li-), a. Worthless. Hence ~NESS n. [-LESS]

valve, n. Kinds of automatic or other device for controlling passage of liquid or gas or the like through pipe etc., as *clack, rotary, screw, sliding, throttle,* ~, *key* ~ (of organ, flute, etc.), SAFETY-~; THERMIONIC ~; (Anat., Zool.) membranous part of organ etc. allowing flow of blood etc. in one direction & not in another, as ~*s of the heart, veins, pulmonary* ~*s*, whence **val'vŭlar** [-UL-] n.; (Conch.) each of two or more separable pieces of which shell consists, whole shell in one piece; (Bot.) each of the segments into which a capsule dehisces, each half of an anther after its opening; (now rare) receiver with thermionic ~(s) (opp. *crystal set*). Hence or cogn. **val'val** (bot.), **val'vate** (anat., bot.), (-)val'ved[2] (-vd), ~LESS (-vl-), val'viform, val'vŭlate (anat., bot.), aa. [f. L *valva* leaf of folding door]

vam'brace, n. (hist.). Armour for forearm. [AF *vand-bras (avant* before, see ADVANCE[1] + *bras* arm f. L *brachium*)]

vamose, -oose, v.i. & t. (sl.). Begone, decamp; decamp from (place). [f. Sp. *vamos* let us go]

vamp[1], n., & v.i. & t. **1.** Upper front part of boot or shoe; patch designed to make old thing look new; improvised accompaniment. **2.** vb. Put new ~ to (boot, shoe); repair, furbish usu. *up*; make *up* (literary article etc.) out of odds & ends; improvise accompaniment to, improvise accompaniments. Hence ~'ER[1] n. [(vb f. n.) ME *vaumpe* f. MF *avant-pied (avant* before, see ADVANCE[1], + *pied* foot f. L *pedem* nom. *pes*]

vamp[2], n., & v.t. & i. (colloq.). **1.** Adventuress, woman who exploits men; unscrupulous flirt. **2.** vb. Allure, exploit; act as ~. [abbr. of foll.]

vam'pire, n. Ghost (usu. of wizard, heretic, criminal, etc.) that leaves grave at night & sucks blood of sleeping persons; person who preys on others; = prec. n.; (in full ~ *bat*) kinds of bat, some of which suck blood of horses, cattle, & sleeping persons; (Theatr.) small spring trap of two flaps used for sudden (disappearances of one person. Hence **vam'pir'ic** a. [F, f. Magyar *vampir* perh. of Turk. orig.]

vam'pirism, n. Belief in existence of vampires; blood-sucking (lit. & fig.). [-ISM]

vam'plate, n. (hist.). Iron plate protecting hand when lance was couched. [f. AF *vand-* (as VAMBRACE) + PLATE]

|| van[1], n., & v.t. (-nn-). **1.** (Arch.) winnowing-machine; (arch., poet.) wing. **2.** v.t. Test quality of (ore) by washing on shovel or by machine, whence ~n'ER[1] (1, 2) n.; (n.) such test. [var. of FAN[1]]

van[2], n. Foremost division of army on the march or of fleet when sailing; front of army in line of battle; (fig.) leaders of a movement etc., as *in the* ~ *of civilization*; ~*guard*, detachment of army marching in front to guard against surprise (also fig.). [abbr. of *vanguard*, f. OF *avant-warde, -garde (avant* before, see ADVANCE[1], WARD, GUARD)]

van[3], n., & v.t. (-nn-). Large usu. covered vehicle for conveying furniture or other goods; || railway carriage for luggage

(luggage ~) or for use of guard (guard's ~); (vb) convey in ~. [abbr. of CARAVAN, cf. bus, wig]

vanad'ium, n. Hard grey metallic element used in small quantities for strengthening some steels. Hence vanad'-ATE[3] n., vanad'ic, vanad'ous, aa. (chem.). [f. ON *Vanadis* goddess in Scand. myth. + -IUM]

Van'dal, a. & n. (Member) of a Germanic race that ravaged Gaul, Spain, N. Africa, & Rome, destroying many books & works of art; (fig., also v~) wilful or ignorant destroyer of works of art etc., whence ~ISM(2), v~, n. Hence Vandal'ic, v~, a. [f. L *Vandalus* pl. of Teut. orig.]

vandyke, n., a., & v.t. 1. (V~; prop. *Van Dyck*) Flemish painter d. 1641, picture by him; each of a series of large points forming a border to lace, cloth, etc., (also V~ *cape, collar*) cape, collar, with ~s. 2. adj. (usu. V~). In the style of dress, esp. with pointed borders, common in V~'s portraits; V~ (pointed) *beard*; V~ *brown*, deep rich brown. 3. v.t. Cut (cloth etc.) in ~s.

vane, n. Weathercock; similar device exposed to current of water etc. as in water-meter; (also *dog-~*) cone or other device used on shipboard as weathercock; blade of windmill, screw propeller, etc.; sight of surveying instruments, sight of quadrant etc. Hence väne²(-nd), ~LESS, aa. [OE *fana* small flag, cf. Da. *fane*, G *fahne*]

väng, n. (naut.). Each of two guy-ropes running from end of gaff to deck. [var. of FANG[4]]

van'gee (-jē), n. Contrivance for working ship's pumps by barrel & crank-brakes.

vanill'a, n. Kinds of tall orchid with fragrant flowers; (also ~*a-bean*) fruit of this; extract obtained from ~a-bean & used for flavouring ices, chocolate, etc. Hence ~ATE[3] n., ~(d a. (chem.). [f. Sp. *vainilla* pod dim. of *vaina* sheath, pod, f. VAGINA]

vanill'ism, n. Eruptive itching skin-disease common among workers in vanilla. [-ISM(5)]

van'ish, v.i. & n. 1. Disappear suddenly; disappear gradually, fade away; pass away; cease to exist; (Math.) become zero (~*ing fraction*, one that becomes zero for a particular value of the variable it contains); (Perspect.) ~*ing-point*, point in which all parallel lines in same plane tend to meet, ~*ing-line*, that which represents the line at infinity in which given plane cuts all parallel planes; ~*ing cream*, emollient that leaves no trace when rubbed into the skin. 2. n. (phonet.). Slight sound with which a principal sound ends (e.g. oo, i, at end of ō, ā). [aphetic f. OF as EVANISH]

van'ity, n. Futility, unsubstantiality, un-reality, emptiness, unsubstantial or unreal thing, as *the ~ of worldly wealth, of political distinction, of human achievements, these things are ~ or vanities, all is ~, pomps & ~ of this wicked world, V~ Fair*, the world (allegorized in *Pilgrim's Progress*) as a scene of ~; empty pride, conceit, based on personal attainments or attractions or qualities (~ *bag, case*, carried on the person & containing small mirror, powder-puff, etc.); ostentatious display; (O.T.) heathen deity, as *the vanities of the Gentiles*. [f. OF *vanite*, f. L *vanitatem* (as VAIN, see -TY)]

vanquish, v.t. Conquer, overcome, (lit. & fig.; now chiefly rhet.). Hence ~ABLE a., ~ER[1] n. [f. OF *veincre* (past *veinquis*, see -ISH[2], f. L *vincere*]

van'tage (vah-), n. = ADVANTAGE (now chiefly in tennis use & in ~-*ground*, coign of ~). [AF var.]

vap'id, a. Insipid, flat, as ~ *beer, conversation, moralizings*. Hence vapid'ITY, ~NESS, nn., ~ly² adv. [f. L *vapidus*]

vap'or|ize, v.t. &i. Convert, be converted, into vapour. Hence or cogn. ~ABIL'ITY, ~iza'TION, ~izER²(2), nn., ~(IZ)ABLE aa. [-IZE]

vap'our (-per), n. & v.i. 1. Moisture in the air e.g. mist, (loosely) light cloudy substance e.g. smoke, (Physics) gaseous form of a normally liquid or solid substance (cf. GAS), whence vap'ori²FEROUS, vap'ori²FIC, vap'ori²FORM, aa., vap'ori-M'ETER n.; (Med.) kinds of remedial agent to be inhaled, as ~ *of iodine*; unsubstantial thing, vain imagination; (arch.) empty boasting; || (pl., arch.) depression, spleen, hypochondria, whence ~ISH¹(-per-), ~ishNESS n.; ~ *bath* (also VAPORAR'IUM n.), apparatus for vaporizing a hydrocarbon for lighting or heating purposes; ~*engine* (driven by steam or other elastic fluid). Hence or cogn. vap'orOSE, vap'orOUS, ~Y²(-per-), aa., vap'orOS'ITY, vap'orOUSNESS, nn., vap'orOUSly² adv. 2. v.i. Emit ~; utter idle boasts or empty talk, whence ~ER¹(-per-) n. [(n.) AF, f. L *vaporem* nom. -or; (vb) f. L *vaporare*

vap'ula'tion, n. (rare). Flogging. So vap'ulATORY a. [f. L *vapulare* be flogged + -ATION]

vaquer'o (-kār-), n. (pl. ~s). Mex. or U.-S. herdsman. [Sp., f. med. L *vaccarius* (*vacca* cow, -ARY[3])]

Varan'gian (-j-), n. Norse rover, esp. of those who ravaged Baltic coasts about 9th c.; ~ *guard*, bodyguard of Byzantine emperors formed partly of ~s. [f. med. L *Varangus* f. ON *Væringi* lit. confederate (*vārar* pl. oaths)]

va'rec, n. Seaweed; kelp. [f. F *varech* prob. as WRECK]

va'riable, a. & n. 1. That can be varied

or adapted, as rod of ~ length, *the pressure is* ~, *a word of* ~ *construction*, ~ **gear** (designed to give varying speeds), e.g. slow advance & quick return); apt to vary, not constant, fickle, unsteady, as ~ *wind, mood, temper, fortune*; (Astron., of stars) periodically varying in brightness or magnitude; (Math., of quantity) indeterminate, able to assume different numerical values; (Bot., Zool., of species) including individuals or groups that depart from the type; (Biol., of organism) tending to change in structure or function. Hence vā'riabIL'ITY, ~NESS, nn., vā'riablY[2] adv. 2. n. ~ thing esp. quantity; (Naut.) shifting wind, (pl.) region between NE & SE trade-winds. [OF, f. L *variabilis* (VARY, -BLE)]

vā'ria lec'tiō, n. Variant reading. [L]

vā'riance, n. Disagreement, difference of opinion, dispute, lack of harmony, as *on that point we are at* ~ (*among ourselves*), *at* ~ *with the authorities, have had a slight* ~ *with him, this theory is at* ~ *with all that is known on the subject*; (Law) discrepancy between pleadings & proof or between writ & declaration. [OF, f. L *variantia* difference (as foll., see -ANCE)]

vā'riant, a. & n. 1. Differing in form or in details from the one named or considered, differing thus among themselves, as *a* ~ *reading in some MSS.*, *40* ~ *types of pigeon*; variable, changing. 2. n. ~ form, spelling, type, reading, etc., as *valet is a* ~ *of varlet, difficult to choose between these* ~s. [OF (as VARY, see -ANT)]

vāriā'tion, n. Varying, departure from a former or normal condition or action or amount or from a standard or type, extent of this, as *is as is not liable to* ~, *repeated* ~s *of temperature, is subject to a* ~ *of several degrees, estimates the* ~ *in value at 20 per cent*; (Gram.) inflexion; (Astron.) deviation of heavenly body from mean orbit or motion (*periodic, secular,* ~, compensated in short, in very long, period); (of magnetic needle) = DECLINATION (~**chart**, with lines drawn through places that have same ~); (Biol.) structural or functional deviation from type; (Alg.) (theory of) relation between quantities that VARY as each other; thing that varies from a type, as *the season is a* ~ *of* or *on the ordinary iambic trimeter*, esp. (Mus.) tune or theme repeated in a changed or elaborated form. Hence ~AL (-sho-) a. [OF, f. L *variationem* (VARY, -ATION)]

vā'ricāted, a. (conch.) Having varices. So vā'ricA'TION n. [f. VARIX, see -ATE²(2)]

vā'ricĕll'a, n. = CHICKEN-POX. Hence ~AR¹, ~OID, aa. [mod. L, irreg. dim. of VARIOLA]

vā'ricocēle, n. Tumour composed of varicose veins of spermatic cord. [as VARIX+-CELE]

vā'ricoloured (-kŭlerd), a. Variegated in colour; of various or different colours. [as VARIOUS]

vā'ricōse, a. Of, affected with, designed for cure of, varix, as ~*e ulcer, vein, bandage*, whence ~ED¹ (-st) a., vāricōs'ITY n.; = VARICATED. [f. L *varicosus* (VARIX, see -OSE¹)]

vā'riegāte, v.t. Diversify in colour, mark with irregular patches of different colours (chiefly in p.p., esp. Bot. of leaves partly pale from suppression of chlorophyll or of plants with such leaves, as ~*ated geranium*). Hence ~A'TION n. [f. L *variegare* (as VARIOUS+*agere* drive, make, cause), see -ATE¹]

vāri'ety, n. 1. Being various, diversity, absence of monotony or uniformity, many-sidedness, as *was struck by the* ~ *of his attainments, of his conversation, of the scene, London has for me the charm of* ~, *cannot live without* ~. 2. Collection of different things, as *turned over a* ~ *of silks, for a* ~ *of reasons*; entertainment or show (consisting of dances, songs, acrobatic feats, etc.), ~ *theatre* (for ~ shows etc.). 3. (Specimen, member, of a) class of things differing in some common qualities from the rest of a larger class to which they belong. 4. (biol.). Individual or group usually fertile with any other member of the species to which it belongs but differing from the type in some qualities capable of perpetuation, subspecies, as *climatic* ~ (produced by climatic influences), *geographical* ~ (confined to given area), whence varī'etāL a., varī'etalLY² adv. [f. L *varietatem* (as VARIOUS, see -TY)]

vā'rifōrm, a. Having various forms. [-FORM]

vā'riōla, n. Smallpox. Hence ~AR¹, variōl'IC, ~OUS, aa. [med. L, as VARIOUS]

variōlā'tion, n. Inoculation with smallpox virus. [f. prec.+-ATION]

vā'riōle, n. (zool., bot.). Shallow pit like smallpox mark. Hence ~OLATE², -oliāted, aa. [f. med. L VARIOLA]

vā'riolite, n. Rock with concretionary structure causing on surface an appearance like smallpox pustules. Hence ~it'IC a. [as prec.+-ITE¹]

vā'riolOID, a. & n. 1. Like smallpox. 2. n. Mild form of smallpox esp. as modified by previous inoculation. [as prec.+-OID]

variōm'eter, n. (electr.). Device for varying the inductance in an electric circuit. [as VARIOUS+-METER]

vāriōr'um, a. & n. 1. With notes of various commentators, as *a* ~ (*edition of*) *Horace*. 2. n. A ~ edition. [L, gen. pl. as VARIOUS]

vā'rious, a. Different, diverse, as *the modes of procedure were* ~, *types so* ~ *as to defy classification*; separate, several, more than one, as *came across* ~ *people, for* ~ *reasons*; (vulg., abs. or quasi-pron.) several, as *among the letters are* ~ *anent motor-*

driving, this is denied by ~; ~ have assured me. Hence ~ly¹ adv., ~NESS n. (rare). [f. L *varius* + -OUS]

Var'ix, n. (pl. *vä'rĭcēs*), (Path.) permanent abnormal dilatation of vein or other vessel, vein etc. thus dilated; (Conch.) each of the ridges across the whorls of a univalve shell. [L]

Var'let, n. (Hist.) medieval page preparing to be a squire; (arch., esp. joc.) menial, low fellow, rascal. [OF, earlier *vaslet*, prob. dim. as VASSAL]

Var'mint, n. (vulg., joc.). Mischievous or discreditable person or animal; (Hunt. sl.) the fox. [corrupt. of VERMIN]

Var'nish, n. & v.t. 1. Kinds of resinous solution applied to wood, metal, etc. to give hard shiny transparent surface; to glaze on pottery etc.; artificial or natural glossiness; superficial gloss of manner; favourable appearance given to misconduct etc.; palliation, whitewash; ~*tree*, kinds from which ~ is obtained. 2. v.t. Apply ~ to (wood, picture, etc., fig. character, person, action, account, or abs.); ~*ing-day*, day before exhibition at which pictures may retouch or ~ their pictures already hung. [(vb f. OF *vernir*, see -ISH²; earlier *vernisser*) f. OF *vernis* etym. dub.]

Warsaw (*Varsovie*?)

Var'us¹, n. Deformity involving inward bending of distal part of limb; bandy-legged person. [L. = bent]

Var'us², n. = ACNE. [L]

Var'y, v.t. & i. Change, make different, modify, diversity, as *can ~y the* (direction, amount, etc., of) *pressure at will, seldom ~ies the routine, ~ies the treatment according to circumstances, never ~ies his style, style is not sufficiently ~ied, a ~ied scene*; (Mus.) make VARIATIONS of (theme); suffer change, become(s) different in degree or quality, be of different kinds, as *he, his mood, ~ies from day to day, climate ~ies, tried with ~ying success, ~ies from the type, opinions ~y on this point; ~y* (directly) *as, ~y inversely as*, increase, decrease, in proportion or correspondingly to the increase of, as *attraction of bodies ~ies* (directly) *as their masses & inversely as the square of their distances. A ~ies as* (symbol ∝) *B, A ~ies as B & C jointly* (as their product). [f. L *variare* (as VARIOUS)]

Vas, n. (anat.; pl. *vas'a*), Vessel, duct, as ~ *déferens*, excretory duct of testicle. Hence **vas'cular**. a. Of, made up of, containing, vessels or ducts for conveying blood, sap, etc., as ~ *functions, tissue*, ~ (circulatory) *system*, ~ *plants*. Hence ~ITY (-ǎr'-), ~IZATION, nn., ~IZE(3) v.t., ~LY² adv. [f. L VASCULUM & -AR¹]

vas'culose, n. & a.¹. Chief substance of vessels of plants; (adj.) = prec. [foll., -OSE²+¹]

vas'culum, n. (pl. *-la*), Botanist's (usn. tin) collecting-case; (Anat.) small vessel, penis. [L, dim. of VAS]

vase (vahz; arch. vawz, arch. & U.S. vās, -z), n. Vessel of baked clay or other material used for various purposes but primarily ornamental, as *flower~*; large usn. sculptured vessel of marble etc. used to decorate gate-post etc.; ~*painting*, decoration of ~s with pigments esp. among ancient Greeks, instance of this. Hence ~FUL n. [F. f. L *vas*]

vas'eline, n. Unctuous substance got from petroleum & used in ointments etc. [P: irreg. f. G *wasser* water + Gk *elaion* oil + -INE⁵]

vāsi-, vāso-, in comb. = VAS, as: *vas'i-form* (*great, rear*); (*vaso-*) *vasoconstric'tor, -dilat'or, -mo'tor*, aa. & nn. (nerve, drug) causing constriction, dilatation, either, of blood-vessels; *vasoconstric'tion*, dilatation sensation to vessels.

vas'al, n. (Hist.) holder of land by feudal tenure (*great, rear*), ~, holding directly from king, holding from great ~); (rhet.) slave, humble dependant. [OF, f. med. L *vassallus, vassus*, cf. Breton *goaz*, servant, W & Corn. *guas*, ŎIr. *foss*]

vass'alage, n. (Hist.) condition, obligations, service, of a vassal; servitude, dependence; fief; (rare; also ~RY n.) vassals collectively. [f. OF *vasselage* (prec., see -AGE)]

vas'al, a. (colloq. now rare). = UNIVERSAL. [corrupt.]

Vasovienne' (-vyen), n. (Music for) dance resembling mazurka. [F, = (dance)]

vast (vah-), a. & n. 1. Immense, huge, very great, as *a ~ expanse of water, ~ plains, shook his ~ frame, a ~ multitude, scheme*; (colloq.) *gave him ~ satisfaction, makes a ~ difference*. Hence ~LY² adv. (esp. colloq.), ~NESS n. 2. n. (poet., rhet.), ~ *space*, as *the ~ of ocean, of heaven*. [f. L *vastus* empty, waste, huge]

vat, n. & v.t.(-tt-). 1. Large tub, cistern, or other vessel, esp. for holding liquids in manufacture, as *fermenting, tan~*, ~, whence ~FUL n. 2. v.t. Place, treat, in ~. [earlier *fat*: OE *fæt*, cf. Du. *vat*, G *fass*, ON *fat*, cogn. w. MDu. *vatten*, G *fassen*.]

Vat'ican, n. Palace & official residence of Pope on ~ hill in Rome; (fig.) papal government; ~ *Council*, oecumenical council held 1869-70 & proclaiming infallibility of Pope when speaking *ex cathedra*, whence ~ISM(3), ~IST(2), nn. [f. L *Vaticanus* ~ hill]

vati'cinate, v.t. Prophesy (often abs.). So ~A'TION, ~A'TOR, nn. [f. L *vaticinari* (*vates* prophet + *-canere* sing)-ATE³]

vaude'ville (vōdr-), n. || Slight dramatic sketch interspersed with songs & dances;

variety entertainment; French popular e.g. topical song with refrain; (Hist.) convivial song esp. any of those composed by O. Basselin, poet born at Vau de Vire in Normandy, d. 1418. Hence ~IST(3) n. [F. f. *Vau* or *Val de Vire* Valley of the Vire]

Vaudois¹ (vō̆dwah'), a. & n. (pl. same). (Inhabitants, dialect) of Vaud in Switzerland. [F (*Vaud* +-*ois* -ESE)]

Vaudois² (vō̆dwah'), a. & n. (pl. same). (Member) of the Waldenses. [F, as WALDENSES]

vaudoo. See voodoo.

vault¹, n., & v.t. **1.** (Archit.) arched roof, continuous arch, set or series of arches whose joints radiate from central point or line; ~like covering, as *the ~ of heaven*; arched apartment; arched or other cellar or subterranean chamber as place of storage (*wine-~* etc.), of interment beneath church or in cemetery (*family ~*), etc.; (Anat.) arched roof of a cavity. **2.** v.t. Make in form of, furnish with, ~ or ~s (esp. in p.p.). Hence ~ING¹(3) n. [(vb f. n.) ME *voute*, f. OF *voûte*, *volte*, vault, turn, fem. adj. as n. f. L *volutus* p.p. of *volvere* roll]

vault², v.i. & t., & n. **1.** Leap, spring, esp. while resting on the hand(s) or with help of pole, as *~ over the gate, from the saddle, upon a horse*; spring over (gate etc.); thus; *~ing-horse*, wooden horse for practice in ~ing. Hence ~ER¹ n. **2.** n. Leap so performed. [(n. f. vb) f. OF *volter* leap, w. assim. to prec.]

vaunt, v.i. & t., & n. **1.** Boast, brag; boast of. **2.** n. Boast. Hence ~ER¹ n., ~ingly² adv. [f. F *vanter* f. pop. L *vanitare* (as VANITY]

vaunt-courier (-kŏ̄-), n. = AVANT-COURIER.

vav'asory⁴, n. (hist.). Tenure, lands, of a vavasour. [-Y¹]

vav'asour (-ōr, -er, -oor), n. (hist.). Vassal holding of a great lord & having other vassals under him. [f. OF *vavassour* f. med. L *vassus vassorum* VASSAL of vassals]

've, colloq. abbr. of *have* appended to *I, we, you, they, & who* (*I've* etc.).

veal, n. Flesh of calf as food, as ~ *cutlet*. Hence ~Y² a., like~, *(colloq.)immature. [f. OF *veel* f. L *vitellus* dim. of *vitulus* calf]

vec'tor, n. (In quaternions etc.) line conceived 'to have fixed length & direction but no fixed position, quantity determining position of one point in space relative to another (~ *quantity*, one that may be represented by a ~); carrier of disease or infection; RADIUS ~. Hence vĕctŏr'IAL a. [L, =carrier (*vehere* veet-convey, see -OR³)]

Ve'da (vā-), n. (Also in pl.) ancient Hindu scriptures written in old form of Sanskrit (*Rig, Sama, Yajur, Atharva, ~*, four collections of hymns etc. composing the ~). Hence **Ve'dic**(vā-)a. [Skr. lit. knowledge]

Vedān'ta (vā-), n. Hindu philosophy founded on the Veda. Hence ~IO a, ~IST(3) n. [Skr. (*veda*+*anta* end)]

Vĕd'da (vĕd'a), n. Member of primitive race living in the Ceylon forests. [Sinhalese, = hunter]

vedětte', vĭ-, n. Mounted sentry placed in advance of an outpost. [F (*ve-*). f. It. *vedetta* prob. f. *vedere* see f. L *vidēre*]

veer, v.i. & t. Change direction esp. (of wind, cf. BACK²) sunwise; (fig.) change one's mind, turn round in opinion or conduct or language; (Naut.) slacken, let out, as ~ *away, out, the cable*; = WEAR³; & haul, tighten & slacken (rope etc.) alternately, (of wind) change alternately, (fig.) vacillate in opinion etc. Hence ~ingly² adv. [partly f. F *virer* to turn, etym. dub.; partly f. MDu. *vieren* let out]

ve'ga¹ (vā-), n. Low moist tract in Spain or Cuba; tobacco-field. [Sp., etym. dub.]

Veg'a², n. The brightest star in the constellation Lyra. [med. L f. Arab. *wāqia* falling]

ve'gĕtable, a. & n. **1.** Of (the nature of), derived from, concerned with, comprising, plants, as ~ *colic* (caused by use of unripe fruit), IVORY, *jelly* (=PECTIN), KINGDOM, MARROW, *naphtha, oyster* (= SALSIFY), *physiology*, SPONGE¹. Hence ve'gĕtal¹TRY n. **2.** n. Plant, esp. herbaceous plant used for culinary purposes or for feeding cattle, e.g. cabbage, potato, turnip, bean; (often attrib., as ~ *diet, soup*). [f. L *vegetabilis* animating (as VEGETATE, see -BLE)]

ve'gĕtal, a. & n. **1.** Of (the nature of) plants, so ~o- comb. form; common to animals & plants, as the ~al *functions* (of growth, circulation, generation, etc.). **2.** n. Plant, vegetable. Hence ~ăl'ITY n. [f. L *vegetare* VEGETATE +-AL]

vĕgĕtār'ian, n. One who uses or advocates a diet of vegetable food (usu. with addition of milk, eggs, etc.) to the exclusion of meat (often attrib., as ~ *food, diet, principles, craze*). Hence ~ISM n. [-ARIAN]

ve'gĕtāte, v.i. Grow as plants do, fulfil vegetable functions; (fig.) live an idle or monotonous life. So ~IVE a., ~ively¹ adv., ~iveness n. [f. L *vegetare* enliven (*vegetus* lively f. *vegēre* move, quicken), see -ATE³]

vĕgĕtā'tion, n. Vegetating (lit. & fig.); plants collectively; plant life, as *luxuriant ~, no sign of ~ for miles round*; (Path.) excrescence of surface of body. [f. med. L *vegetationem* (as prec., see -ATION]

ve'hĕment (vēim'-), a. Showing or caused by strong feeling, impetuous, ardent, passionate, as a ~ *desire, protest, man of ~ character*; acting with great force, violent, as a ~ *wind, onset*. Hence or cogn. **ve'hĕmence** (vēim'-) n., ~ly¹ adv. [OF, f. L *ve(he)mentem*, nom. -*ns*, perh. f. *ve-* apart from + *mens* -*ntis* mind]

ve'hicle (vēî), n. Carriage, conveyance, of any kind used on land; liquid etc. used as a medium for pigments, drugs, etc.; thing, person, used as a medium for thought or feeling or action, *as used the pulpit, the press, as a* ~ *for his political opinions, will not be used as the* ~ *of your resentment.* So **vehic'ūlar**[1] a. [f. L *vehiculum* (*vehere* carry, see -CULE[1])]

vehmgericht (fām'gerixt), n. German system of irregular tribunals prevailing esp. in Westphalia in 14th & 15th cc. & trying the more serious crimes in secret night sessions; such tribunal. Hence **veh'mic** (fām') a. [G, also f., f. *feme* punishment, tribunal, + *gericht* judgement, law]

veil (vāl), n., & v.t. 1. Piece of usu. more or less transparent material attached to woman's bonnet or hat or otherwise forming part of head-dress, esp. one serving to conceal the face or as protection against sun, dust, etc., *as raised, dropped, her* ~; *scarf on pastoral staff;* (Bot., Zool.) = VELUM; slight huskiness of voice, natural or due to a cold etc. Hence ~ING[3] (so as to uncover, cover, face), *took the* ~; *became nun; curtain (the* ~ *of the temple; beyond the* ~, in the unknown state of after death); (fig.) disguise, pretext, *as under the* ~ *of religion; draw a* ~ *over,* avoid discussing or calling attention to. **2.** v.t. Cover (one's face, etc. ~ *of the temple*...); (fig.) disguise, pretext, as ~*ed resentment.* [vb f. n., AF *veile* (OF *voile*) f. L *vela* pl. of VELUM]

vein (vān), n., & v.t. **1.** Each of the membranous tubes that convey blood to the heart (cf. ARTERY; *pulmonary* ~*s,* returning oxygenated blood from lungs to left side, *systemic* ~*s,* returning venous blood from all parts to right side); (pop.) any blood-vessel; (Entom., Bot.) rib of insect's wing or of leaf; (Geol., Mining) fissure in rock filled with deposited matter (~*stone,*.); = GANGUE); streak, stripe, of different colour in wood, marble, etc.; distinctive character or tendency, cast of mind or disposition, mood, *as was of an imaginative* ~; *said in a humorous* ~, *other remarks in the same* ~, *am in the* ~ *for high play, am not in the* ~ *for just now.* Hence ~LESS, ~LIKE, ~Y[2] aa., ~LET n. **2.** v.t. Fill or cover (as) with ~ or ~s (esp. in p.p.). Hence ~AGE(1), ~ING[1](6), nn. [vb f. n.), f. OF *veine* f. L *vena*]

vēlām'en (pl. -*mina*), **vēlamen'tum** (pl. -*ta*), nn. Enveloping membrane esp. of brain. [L, = covering (*velare* f. VELUM, -MEN, -MENT)]

vēl'ar. a. Of a veil or velum, as ~ *gutturals,* sounds produced by aid of soft palate (e.g. gw, kw). [f. L *velaris* (VELUM, see -AR[1])]

veld (fĕlt), n. S.-Afr. open country neither cultivated nor true forest. [Du.,=FIELD]

vēlĭtā'tion, n. (arch.). Slight skirmish, controversy. [f. L *velitatio* (*velitari* skirmish, as foll., see -ATION)]

vel'ĭte, n. (Rom. ant.). Light-armed soldier. [f. L *veles -itis*]

vellē'ĭty, n. Low degree of volition not prompting to action. [f. med. L *velleitas* (L *velle* vb wish, see -TY)]

vell'ĭcāte, v.t. & i. (rare). Twitch. Hence **vellicā'tion** n., ~ātive[3] a. [f. L *vellicare* (*vellere* pluck), see -ATE[3]]

vell'um, n. Fine parchment orig. from skin of calf; manuscript written on this; ~ *paper* (imitating ~). Hence ~Y[2] a. [f. OF *velin* (VEAL, -INE[1])]

vēlō'ce (-chā), adv. (mus.). With great rapidity. [It.]

vēlŏcĭpēd|e, n. Kinds of light vehicle impelled by rider (now chiefly hist. of obs. types e.g. hobby, also as general term = CYCLE). Hence ~IST(3) n. [f. F *vélocipède* f. L *veloc* swift + *pes pedis* foot]

vēlŏ'cĭty, n. Quickness, rate, of motion or, inanimate things, as *uniform* ~; (Mech.) speed in a given direction; *initial* ~, ~ of a body at starting; *muzzle* ~, ~ of projectile issuing from fire-arm. Hence **vēlocim'ETER** n. [f. F *vélo-cité* f. L *velocitatem* (*veloc -ocis* swift, see -TY)]

vēlours' (-oor), n. Kinds of plush used for hats etc. [F (OF -*our*, -*ous*), as VELVET]

vēloutine' (-ōōtēn), n. Kinds of corded fabric & of toilet-powder. [F]

vēl'um, n. (anat., bot., zool.; pl. -*la*). Kinds of membrane or membranous covering, esp. the soft palate. [L, = sail, veil, f. *velere* carry]

vēlu'rė, n. & v.t. Velvet or similar fabric; velvet or other pad for smoothing silk hat; (vb) smooth with ~. [vb f. n.) f. OF as VELOURS]

vēlū'rinous, a. (bot., entom.). Velvety. [f. L as VELVET + -INE[1] + -OUS]

vel'veret, n. Bad kind of velvet. [irreg. dim. of foll.]

vel'vet, n. & a. **1.** Closely woven fabric wholly (also *silk* ~) or partly (*cotton* ~) of silk with thick short pile on one side (*terry* ~, with pile uncut); furry skin covering a growing antler; (transf.) profit, gain; *on* ~, in an advantageous position (now chiefly in sporting sl. use, of a favourable betting position); ~ *pile,* fabric with pile like that of ~. **2.** adj. Of, soft as, ~ (often in names of animals & plants, as ~ *ant, osier*); ~ *glove,* outward gentleness cloaking inflexibility (*with an iron hand in a* ~ *glove*); ~ *paw,* of cat, fig. of cruelty etc. veiled under suave manner; ~ *tread,* soft. Hence ~ED[2], ~Y[2] aa. [f. med.L *velvetum* ult. f. L *villus* shaggy hair]

velveteen', n. Cotton fabric with pile like velvet; kind of velvet made of silk & cotton ; || (pl., transf.) gamekeeper. [prec. + -*een* (-INE[1])]

vel′veting, n. Velvet goods collectively; pile, nap, of velvet. [-ING[1]]

vel′nal, a. (Of person) that may be bought, ready to sell influence or services or to sacrifice principles from sordid motive (of conduct etc.) characteristic of ~ person. Hence or cogn. **venal′ITY** n., **~LY[2]** adv. [f. L *venalis* (*venus, -um,* sale, see -AL)]

vena′tion, n. Arrangement of veins on leaf, insect's wing, etc. Hence **~AL** a. [as VEIN + -ATION]

vend, v.t. Sell (now chiefly legal, whence or cogn. **~EE′, ~OR** & **DOR[2]**, nn.); offer (small wares) for sale, so (-)**věn′DER[1]** n. Hence or cogn. **~IBIL′ITY** n., **~′IBLE** a., **~′IBLY[2]** adv. [f. L *vendere = venumdare (venum* sale, *dare* give)]

ven′dace, n. Small & delicate fish found in some British & Continental lakes. [f. OF *vendese* dace, etym. dub.]

Vendé′an, a. & n. (Native) of Vendée, department of W. France; (member) of ~ royalist party in 1793-5. [f. F *Vendéen* (*Vendée,* see -AN)]

vendětt′a, n. Blood-feud in which family of injured or murdered man seeks vengeance on offender or his family; this practice as prevalent in Corsica etc. [It., f. L *vindicta,* see VINDICTIVE]

veneer′, v.t. & n. 1. Cover (wood, furniture, etc.) with thin coating of finer wood; cover (pottery etc.) with thin coat of finer substance; (fig.) disguise (character etc.) under superficial polish of manner etc. **2.** n. Thin outer coating, ~ing (lit. & fig.); ~-*moth,* kinds whose colouring suggests ~. [f. G *furniren* f. F as FURNISH]

ven′erable, a. Entitled to veneration on account of character, age, associations, etc., as ~*able priest, relics, beard, ruins, river* (also in Ch. of Eng. as title of archdeacons, abbr. *Ven.*; in R.-C. Ch. as title of one who has attained first of three degrees of sanctity but is not canonized). Hence ~**ABIL′ITY, ~ABLENESS,** nn., **~ABLY[2]** adv. [OF, f. L *venerabilis* (as foll., see -ABLE)]

ven′erate, v.t. Consider worthy of & regard with deep respect or warm approbation; revere. So **~OR[2]** n. [f. L *venerari,* -ATE[3]]

venera′tion, n. Profound respect, reverence; (Phren., often joc.) faculty of feeling reverence, as *organ, bump, of* ~. [f. L *venerationem* as prec., see -ATION]

vener′eal, a. Of sexual intercourse, as ~ *desire;* a. Of disease, communicated by sexual intercourse; ~ *remedies* (for disease). [f. L *venereus* of VENUS + -AL]

ven′ery[1], n. (arch.) Hunting. [f. OF *venerie* (*vener* hunt f. L *venari,* see -ERY)]

ven′ery[2], n. (arch.) Sexual indulgence. [VENUS, -Y[1]]

věn′esěct, v.t. & i., **věněsěc′tion,** n. = PHLEBOTOMIZE, PHLEBOTOMY. [vb f. n., f. L *venae sectio* cutting of vein]

Věně′tian (-shn), a. & n. **1.** Of Venice; ~ *blind,* window blind of slats of wood that may be turned so as to admit or exclude light; ~ *carpet* (of worsted, usu. with striped pattern); ~ (=FRENCH) *chalk;* ~ *glass,* glassware made at or near Venice, (also *Venice glass*) cup of this said to be destroyed by contact with poison; ~ *lace,* kind of point lace; ~ *mast,* spirally painted pole for use in street decorations; ~ (solid artificial) *pearl;* ~ *window* (with three separate openings). **2.** n. Native of Venice; (usu. ~s) blind, whence **věně′tianeD[2]** (-shа-) a., (pl.) kind of tape for holding slats of this. [f. med. L *Venetianus* f. L *Venetia* country of the *Veneti,* -AN]

věn′geance (-jəns), n. Punishment inflicted, retribution exacted, for wrong to oneself or to person etc. whose cause one espouses, as *will exact ample* ~, *took a bloody* ~ *on the murderer or for the murder of his children, you lay yourself open to his* ~; *with a* ~, in a higher degree than was expected or desired, in the fullest sense of the word(s), & no mistake, as *this is punctuality with a* ~. [F (*venger* avenge f. L as VINDICATE, see -ANCE)]

věnge′ful (-jf-), a. Disposed to revenge, vindictive. Hence **~LY[2]** adv., **~NESS** n. [f. obs. *venge* vb (as prec.) + -FUL]

věn′ial, a. (Of sin or fault) pardonable, excusable, not very wrong, (Theol.) not mortal. Hence **věnial′ITY, ~NESS,** nn., **~LY[2]** adv. [OF, f. L *venialis (venia* pardon, see -AL)]

Věn′ice, n. (attrib.). (=VENETIAN) *glass; ~ treacle,* = THERIAC.

věni′rĕ (*fū′cīas*) (-sh-), n. (law). Writ directing sheriff to summon jury. [L, = make come]

věn′ison (-nzon), n. Deer's flesh as food. [f. OF *veneisun* f. L *venationem* hunting (*venari* hunt, see -ATION, -SON)]

Věnī′tě, n. (Musical setting of) *Ps. xcv.* [L, = Come ye, first word of psalm]

věn′om, n. Poisonous fluid secreted by serpents, scorpions, etc., & introduced into system of victim by bite or sting; (fig.) malignity, virulence, of feeling or language or conduct. Hence or cogn. **~ED[2]** (-md), ~ous, aa., **~ously[2]** adv., **~OUSNESS** n. [ME & OF *venim* f. L *venenum* poison]

věnŏs′ity, n. Excess of venous blood in organ etc.; deficient aeration of venous blood in lungs with afflux of venous blood into arteries. [as foll., see -OSITY]

věn′ous, -ōse, aa. (anat., zool., bot.). Of, full of, contained in, veins, as ~ (opp. to arterial) *blood,* ~ *congestion,* accumulation, of ~ blood in organ etc. Hence **věn′ously[2]** adv. [f. L *venosus* (as VEIN, see -OSE[1], -OUS)]

věnt, n., & v.t. & i. **1.** Hole or opening allowing passage out of or into confined space, e.g. touch-hole of gun, hole in top

of barrel to admit air while liquid is being drawn out, finger-hole in musical instrument (also **věn'tĭdge** n.), flue of chimney, loophole in embattled wall; =~-faucet; **anus** esp. of animals below mammals; (fig.) outlet, free passage, free play, as *gave* ~ *to his indignation, impatience found* ~; ~|-ing of otter etc. (see vb); =~-faucet, hollow gimlet for making ~ in cask etc.; ~-hole, ~; ~-peg, peg for stopping ~ of barrel, also =~-faucet; ~-plug, plug for ~ of gun. Hence ~'LESS a. (1st sense). [f. OF *fente* f. L *findere*]

věn'tĭdŭct, n. (archit.). Air-passage, esp. subterranean one. [f. L *ventus* wind + DUCT]

věn'tĭl, n. Valve in musical instrument; shutter for regulating air in organ. [G, f. med. L *ventile* sluice f. L *ventus* wind]

věn'tĭlāte, v.t. Cause air to circulate freely in (room etc.); purify by air, **oxygenate**, (blood); submit (question, subject, grievance, etc.) to public consideration & discussion. Hence or cogn. ~'TION, ~'ātŏr²(2, 1 esp., appliance for ~-ating room), nn. **-ătĭvE a.** [f. L *ventilat-* blow, winnow (*ventus* wind), see -ATE³]

věn'tral, a. & n. (zool., bot.). Of the belly; on the belly (opp. DORSAL); ~ (fin), either of the abdominal fins. Hence **~LY² adv.** [F, f. L *ventralis* (VENTER, see -AL)]

ventre à terre (see Ap.), adv. At full speed (lit. with belly to ground). [F]

věn'tricle, n. (anat.). Any cavity of the body, hollow part or organ, as ~*s of the brain, right, left,* ~ (*of the heart*). Hence **ventric'ūlar, věntric'ūlous,** aa. [f. F *ventricule* f. L *ventriculus* dim. of VENTER]

věn'tricōse, -ous, aa. Having a protruding belly; (Bot.) distended, inflated. [f. VENTER + -IC + -OSE¹, -OUS]

věntrĭl'oquism, n. Act, art, of speaking, or uttering sounds in such a manner that the voice appears to come from some other source than the speaker. So **věntrĭloc'ūtion,** ~ISM(1), ~Y¹, nn., **věntriloquïal,** ~is'tic, ~ous, aa., **věntri-** [f. L *ventriloquus* ventriloquist (VENTER [f. L *ventriloquus* ventriloquist (VENTER) speak].

věn'tre- in comb. =VENTER, as ~*dors'al*, extending from belly to back.

věn'ture, n. & v.t. & i. 1. Undertaking of a risk, risky undertaking, as *declined the* ~, *ready for any* ~; commercial

speculation, as *one lucky* ~ *made his fortune, failed in all his* ~*s*; (arch.) thing at stake, property risked; *at a* ~, at random. **2.** v.b. Dare, not be afraid, make bold, as *did not* ~ *to stop him, I* ~ *to differ from you; dare to make or advance* or put forward, a guess, a step; expose to risk, cause, as *men who* ~ *their lives for the* opinion, a guess, a step; expose to risk, undertake risk; ~ *five shillings on it;* (abs.) undertake risk or make. as *shall* ~ *on a mild protest, will you* ~ *on a slice of* in or grapple with or make, as *shall* ~ *on* cucumber? Hence **věn'turer¹** n., (esp. Hist.) one who undertakes or shares in a trading ~, **~SOME** (-chers-) a., **~some¹y²** adv., **~SOMENESS** n. [aphetic f. ADVENTURE]

věn'ue, n. (law). Country within which jury must be gathered & cause tried (orig. neighbourhood of crime etc.), as *change the* ~ (to avoid riot, prejudiced jury, etc.); statement in indictment etc. indicating this; (pop) rendezvous, (OF, = coming, f. *venir* come f. L *venire*)

Vē'nus, n. (Rom. Myth.) goddess of love; a PLANET; (*uranian, pandemian* ~, spiritual, sensual, sex love): a beautiful woman; *Mount of* ~ (palmistry), base of thumb; ~'*s basin, bath,* common teasel; ~'*s comb,* plant of parsley family with combine fruit; ~'*s fly-trap,* herb with leaves that close on insects etc.; ~'*s slipper,* =LADY'*s-slipper.* [L, gen. -*eris*]

vērā'cious (-shus), a. Speaking, disposed to speak, the truth; (of statement etc.) true, not (meant to be) false. Hence or cogn. **~LY² adv., vērā'cĭty** n. [f. L *verax* (*verus* true, see -ACIOUS)]

vēran'dah (-da), n. Open portico or gallery along side of house with roof supported on pillars. [f. Port. *veranda*]

vē'rātrĭne, n. Poisonous compound from hellebore used esp. as local irritant in neuralgia & rheumatism. So ~ATE²(3) n., **vērā'trĭc a.** ~INE(5) v.t. [F (*vē-*), f. L *veratrum* hellebore + -INE¹]

verb, n. (gram.). Part of speech that predicates, word whose function is predication (e.g. italicized words in *Time flies, Salt is good. You surprise me*); copulative or *substantive* ~; be; AUXILIARY, DEPONENT, IMPERSONAL, (IN)TRANSITIVE, NEUTER, REFLEXIVE, ~. [f. L *verbum* WORD, verb]

věrb'al, a. & n. 1. Of, concerned with, words, as ~ *distinctions, subtleties, criticism, accuracy,* INSPIRATION: (loosely) oral, not written, as *a* ~ *communication, contract,* ~ *evidence;* (of translation) literal, word for word; ~ *note* (diplomacy), unsigned memorandum on matter that is not urgent but must not be overlooked; (Gram.) of (the nature of) a verb, as ~ inflexions, used in all the ~ senses (of verb), ~ *noun,* noun derived from verb & partly sharing its constructions (e.g. F

nouns in -ING¹. **2.** n. ~ noun. Hence ~LY²adv. [f. L *verbalis* (as prec., see -AL)]

verb'alism, n. Minute attention to words, verbal criticism. [-ISM]

verb'alist, n. Person concerned with words only, verbal critic. [-IST]

verb'alize, v.t. & i. Make (noun etc.)into a verb, so **verb'ify** v.t.; be verbose. Hence ~ATION n. [-IZE]

verbat'im, adv. & a. Word for word, as *copied it* ~, *a* ~ *reprint*. [med. L (adv.), as VERB, cf. LITERATIM]

verben'a, n. Kinds of plant of vervain family, as *lemon*(-scented) ~, [L, = sacred bough, of olive etc., VERVAIN]

verb'iage, n. Needless accumulation of words, verbosity. [F (as VERB, see -AGE)]

verb'icide, n. (joc.), Word-butcher(y). [as VERB+-CIDE]

verbose', a. Using, containing, more words than are wanted, prolix. Hence ~LY² adv., ~NESS, **verbos'ITY**, nn. [f. L *verbosus* (as VERB, see -OSE¹)]

Verb'um (săt) săpiĕn'ti, sent. (abbr. *verb. sap.*), A word is enough to the wise. [L]

verd'ant, a. (Of grass etc.) green, fresh-coloured; (of field etc.) covered with ~ grass etc.; (of person) unsophisticated, raw, green. Hence **verd'ANCY** n., ~LY² adv. [perh. f. *verdure*+-ANT]

verd-antique' (-ēk), n. Ornamental usu. green building-stone formed chiefly of serpentine; green incrustation on ancient bronze. [OF (*verd* green f. L *viridis* + ANTIQUE)]

verd'erer, -or, n. (hist.) Judicial officer of royal forests. [AF *verder* (*verd* f. L *viridis* green)+-ER¹, -OR²]

verd'ict, n. Decision of jury on issue of fact in civil or criminal cause, as *brought in a* ~ *of not guilty, a* ~ *for the plaintiff, open* ~ (reporting commission of crime but not specifying criminal), *partial* ~ (finding prisoner guilty of part of the charge), *privy* or *sealed* ~ (written = delivered to clerk of court when court has adjourned during deliberation of jury), *special* ~ (stating facts as proved but leaving court to draw conclusion from them); decision, judgement, as *the* ~ *of the public was in its favour, does not dispute your* ~. [ME & AF *verdit* f. L *vere dictum* thing truly said (*vere* truly+DIC-TUM]

verd'igris (or -ēs), n. Green crystallized substance formed on copper by action of acetic acid & used in medicine as pigment etc.; green rust on copper. [ME *verdegrese, verte grece*, f. AF *vert de Grece* green of Greece (as VERDURE+*Greece* f. L *Graecia*)]

verd'iter, n. Blue, green, ~, pigments got from copper nitrate. [f. OF *verd de terre* green of earth (as foll. + *terre* f. L *terra* earth)]

verd'ur|e, n. (-dyer), n. Greenness of vegeta-tion, green vegetation, whence ~ED² (-dyerd), ~ELESS, **verd'urous**, aa.; (fig.) freshness; French tapestry with prominent foliage. [F (OF *verd* green, f. L *viridis*, see -URE)]

verein (feriin'), n. Association of persons or parties, organized body. [G]

Verey¹, Var. of VERY².

verge¹, n. Extreme edge, brink, border, (usu. fig.), as *drew near to the very* ~ *of the stream, on the* ~ *of 70, destruction, betray-ing his secret*; grass edging of flower-bed etc.; wand, rod, carried before bishop, dean, etc., as emblem of office; kinds of shaft or spindle in various mechanisms; (Archit.) shaft of column, edge of tiles projecting over eaves, ~*board*, = BARGE-board; (Hist.) area of jurisdiction of Marshalsea. [OF, f. L *virga* twig, rod]

verge², v.i. Incline downwards or in specified direction (*the now verging sun*; ~ *towards old age, to a close*); ~ *on*, border on, approach closely, as *path* ~*s on the edge of a precipice, a solemnity verging on the tragic*. [f. L *vergere* bend, incline: sense influenced by prec.]

|| **vergée'** (-jē), n. Channel-Island measure of area, four-ninths of acre. [f. F *verge* measured (VERGE¹)]

ver'gency, n. (optics). Reciprocal of focal distance of lens as measure of divergence or convergence of rays. [VERGE²-ENCY]

ver'ger, n. Official in a church who shows persons to their seats etc.; || officer who bears staff before bishop, vice-chancellor of university, etc. Hence ~SHIP n. [prob. as VERGE¹ cf. med. L *virgarius* rod-bearer]

verid'ic|al, a. Truthful (usu. iron.); (Psych. Spirit.; of visions etc.) coinciding with realities. Hence or cogn. ~ally adv., ~OUS a. [f. L *veridicus* (*verus* true + *dicere* say)+-AL]

ver'ify, v.t. Establish the truth of, examine for this purpose, as *must* ~*fy the statement, his figures, am now* ~*fying the items*; (of event, action, etc.) bear out, make good, fulfil, (prediction, promise); (Law) append affidavit to (pleadings); support (statement) by proofs. Hence or cogn. ~fiABIL'ITY, ~FICA'TION, ~fIER¹, nn., ~fIABLE a. [f. OF *verifier* f. med. L *veri-ficare* (*verus* true, see -FY]

ver'ily, adv. (arch.). Really, truly, in very truth. [f. VERY¹+-LY²]

verisimil'itude, n. Air of being true, semblance of actuality, (*the* ~ *of the tale*; ~ *is not proof*); a thing that seems true. So **verisim'ILAR¹** a. [f. L *verisimilitudo* f. *verisimilis* probable (*veri* gen. of *verus* true+*similis* like), see -TUDE]

ve'ritable, a. Real, rightly so called, as *a* ~*le boon*. Hence ~LY² adv. [OF (as VERITY, see -ABLE)]

ve'ritas, n. (Also *bureau véritas*) French ship register like Lloyd's. [F (*vé-*), f. L as foll.]

ve'rit|y, n. Truth (of statement etc.); true statement; really existent thing, as *these*

things, alas! are ~ies; of a ~y (arch.), in truth, really. [f. OF verite f. L veritatem]

verjuice (vē'rjŏos), n. Acid liquor got from crab-apples, sour grapes, etc., & used in cooking. Hence ~ED² (-st) a. [f. OF verjus (verd, see VERDURE, +jus JUICE)]

ve'rmeil (-mil), n. Silver gilt; varnish used to give lustre to gilding; orange-red garnet; (poet.) vermilion. [OF, see VER-MILION]

ve'rmi- in comb. = L vermis worm, as: ~cide, drug that kills worms, so~icid'al a.; ~form, worm-shaped (~form APPENDIX), structurally allied to worms; ~ifuge, drug that expels intestinal worms, so ~if'ugal a.; ~igrade, moving like worm, wriggling along; ~ve'rous, feeding on worms.

ve'rmian, a. Of worms, wormlike. [f. L vermis worm +-AN¹]

vermice'lli, n. Paste of same materials as macaroni made in slender threads. [It., pl. of vermicello dim. f. L vermis worm]

vermi'cular, a. Like a worm in form or movements, as~(=VERMiform) appendix; marked with close wavy lines. [f. med. L vermi-cularis (L vermiculus dim. of vermis worm, see -AR¹)]

vermi'culate, a. = prec. (rare, usu. fig.), [f. L vermiculari be full of worms (prec.), -ATE².³]

vermicula'tion, n. Being eaten or infested by or converted into worms; vermicular marking; worm-eaten state. [f. L vermiculatio (prec., -ATION)]

vermi'lion (-lyon), n., a., & v.t. 1. Cinnabar; brilliant red pigment made by grinding this or artificially; (of) this colour. 2. v.t. Colour (as) with~. [(vb f. n.) f. OF vermillon vermilion, kermes insect (vermeil vermilion f. L vermiculus dim. of vermis worm, see -OON)]

verm'in, n. (usu. treated as pl.). Mammals & birds injurious to game, crops, etc., e.g. foxes, weasels, rats, mice, moles, owls, etc.; noxious insects, e.g. fleas, bugs, lice; parasitic worms (or insects); (fig.) vile persons, as the~ that infest recesses. So ~OUS a., ~ously² adv. [ME & OF vermine vb.l. f. L vermis worm]

verm'inate, v.i. Breed vermin, become infested with parasites. So ~A'TION n. [f. L verminare (vermis worm), see -ATE³]

verm'inous, a. Infested with, caused by, of nature of, vermin. [f. L verminosus (vermis), see -OUS]

verm'outh (-ōōth; or vĕrm'ōōt), n. White wine flavoured with wormwood. [f. F vermout f. G wermuth wormwood]

vernac'ular, a. & n. 1. (Of language, idiom, word) of one's native country, native, indigenous, not of foreign origin or of learned formation; (of disease)= ENDEMIC. 2. n. The language or dialect of the country, as Latin gave place to the~. Hence ~ISM(4), ~ITY(-ăt'r-)~IZA'TION, nn., ~IZE(3) v.t., ~LY² adv. [f. L vernaculus native (verna home-born slave, see -CULE)+-AR¹]

vern'al, a. Of, appearing or occurring in or done in, spring, as ~ breezes, flowers, EQUINOX, migration; ~ (malarial) fever; ~ grass, sweet-scented grass grown among hay. Hence ~LY² adv. [f. L vernalis (vernus f. ver spring, see -AL)]

verna'tion, n. (bot.). Arrangement of leaves (cf. AESTIVATION) within leaf-bud. [f. L vernare (ver spring, see -ATION)]

vern'ier, n. Small movable scale for obtaining fractional parts of the subdivisions on fixed scale of barometer, sextant, etc. [f. F. P. Vernier, inventor, d. 1637]

Vèronèse' (-z), a., & n. (pl. the same). (Inhabitant) of Verona. [-ESE]

veron'ica, n. 1. Kinds of herb or shrub with blue, purple, pink, or white flowers. 2. Cloth with representation of Christ's face, esp. one miraculously so impressed after being used by St.~ to wipe sweat from Christ's face. [V~, woman's name]

verru'ca (-rōō-), n. (path., zool., bot.; pl. -ae pr. -sē). Wart, wartlike elevation. Hence or cogn. ~IFORM (-rōō-), vĕrru-COSE¹ (-rōō-), vĕrru'cous (-rōō-)~ŭlose¹ aa. [L]

ve'rsant, n. Extent of land sloping in one direction, general slope of land. [F, f. L versare frequent. of vertere vers-turn]

vers'atile, a. Turning readily from one subject or occupation to another, capable of dealing with many subjects, as ~ author, genius, disposition, mind; capable of being moved or turned as on hinge, as ~ spindle; (Bot., Zool.) moving freely about or up & down on a support, as ~ anther, head, antennae; changeable, in-constant. Hence or cogn. ~LY² adv., vĕrsati'LITY n. [F, f. L versatilis (as prec., see -ATILE)]

vers de société (vār de sosiătā'), n. SOCIETY verse. [F]

vèrse, n., & v.t. & i. 1. Metrical line containing definite number of feet, as quoted some ~s of the Iliad, had a good ~ here & there, CAI² ~s; group of definite number of ~s, stanza; metrical composition in general, particular type of this, as wrote pages of ~, expressed in indifferent ~, what is not prose is ~, a price for Latin ~, BLANK¹, SOCIETY, elegiac, iambic, trochaic, etc., ~; each of the short divisions of chapter in Bible (CHAPTER & ~); short anthem etc.; ~-monger(ing), maker, making, of bad. Hence ~LED¹ (-sl-) n. 2. vb. Express in ~, make~s. [(vb f. n.) OE fers f. L versus -us turning, line, row, verse, f. vertere vers-turn]

versed (-st), a. Experienced, skilled, proficient, (in subject, occupation, etc.); reversed (now only in ~ SINE). [adapta-tion of L versatus p.p. of versari be engaged

-in, see VERSANT; trig. sense f. L *versus* p.p. as prec.]

vĕr'sĕt, n. (mus.). Short prelude or interlude for organ. [OF, dim. of *vers* VERSE]

vĕrs'icle, n. Short verse, esp. of each series of short verses in liturgy said or sung alternately by minister & people. [f. L *versiculus* (as VERSE, see -CULE)]

vĕrs'icolour(ed)(-ŭlerd), aa. Variegated; changing from one colour to another in different lights. [f. L *versicolor* (*vertere vers-* turn + *color* COLOUR)]

versic'ular, a. ~ *division* (into verses). [as VERSICLE (see -UL-) + -AR[1]]

vĕrs'ify, v.t. & i. Turn (prose) into verse; express in verse; make verses. Hence or cogn. ~ICA'TION, ~FIER[1], nn. [f. OF *versifier* f. L *versificare* (as VERSE, see -FY)]

vĕr'sion (-shn), n. **1.** Book etc. translated into another language, as *Authorized, Revised, V~* (of the Bible, made 1604–11, 1870–84; abbr. *A.V., R.V.*). **2.** Piece of translation, esp. into foreign language, as *now let me have your own ~ of the affair*. **3.** Account of a matter from particular person's point of view, as *Turning of child awkwardly placed for delivery so that head or feet may be first presented.* Hence ~AL (-sho-) a. [F, f. L *versionem* (L *vertere vers-* turn, see -ION)]

vers libre (vǎrē'br'e), n. Versification or verses in which different metres are mingled, or prosodical restrictions disregarded, or variable rhythm substituted for definite metre. Hence **versli'brist** (vǎrēē-) n., writer of ~. [F]

vĕrs'ō, n. (pl. ~s). Any left-hand page of book (cf. RECTO); reverse of coin. [L, abl. p.p. as VERSE]

vĕrs'us, prep. (abbr. *v.*). Against, as (Law) *Jones v. Smith*, (Cricket etc.) *Surrey v. Kent*. [L, = towards, against]

vĕrt[1], n. (Law, Hist.) all that bears green leaves in forest, right to cut this; (Her.) the tincture green. [OF, f. L *viridis* green]

‖ **vĕrt**[2], n., & v.i. (colloq.). Convert or pervert; (vb) leave one Church for another. [coined as neutral form]

vĕr'tĕbra, n. (pl. ~*ae*). Each segment of backbone (*false* ~4, fixed, as os sacrum & coccyx in man, *true* ~*a*, movable; neither expression now used in human anat.). Hence ~AL a., ~ally[2] adv., ~o- comb. form. [L (*vertere* turn)]

vĕr'tĕbr|ate, a. & n. (Animal) having a spinal column or a notochord, esp. (member) of the division *Vertebrata*, including mammals, birds, reptiles, amphibians, & fishes. Hence ~**āted** (-ATE[2]). a. [f. L *vertebratus* jointed (as prec., see -ATE[2]]

vĕrtĕbrā'tion, n. Formation of, division into, vertebrae or similar segments. [-ATION]

vĕr'tĕx, n. (pl. usu. *-ĭcēs*). Highest point, top, apex; (Anat.) crown of head; (Geom.) each angular point of triangle, polygon, etc., ~ *of an angle*, meeting-point of lines that form it. [L, gen. *-icis*, = whirlpool, head, vertex, (*vertere* turn)]

vĕr'tical, a. & n. **1.** Of, at, the vertex or highest point; at the zenith; perpendicular to plane of horizon; (Anat.) of the crown of the head; ~ *angles*, each pair of opposite angles made by two intersecting lines; ~ (= AZIMUTH-) *circle*; ~ *fins* (dorsal, anal, & caudal); ~ *plane*, plane perpendicular to the horizon. Plane or circle) ~-LY[2] adv. **2.** n. ~ line, plane, or circle; *out of the* ~, not ~. [F (prec., see -AL)]

vĕr'ticil, n. (bot., zool.). Whorl, set of parts radiating from axis. Hence **verti̇'cillate[2]** a., **verti̇'cillatery[2]** adv. [f. L *verticillus* whorl of spindle, dim. of VERTEX]

verti̇'gō (or *vertī*, *-tē̆*), n. (pl. ~s). Giddiness, dizziness, as *subjective, objective,* (in which patient feels as if he, as if surrounding objects, were turning round), *essential* ~ (without apparent cause). Hence **verti̇'ginous** a., **verti̇'ginously** adv., **verti̇'ginousness** n. [L, gen. *-ginis*, = whirling, dizziness, (*vertere* turn)]

vertu. See VIRTU.

vĕr'vain, n. Kinds of weedy plant with small blue, white, or purple flowers, formerly believed to have various virtues & used as amulet etc. [f. OF *verveine* f. L VERBENA]

verve (vǎrv), n. Enthusiasm, energy, vigour, in artistic or literary work. [F, etym. dub.]

vĕr'vet, n. A small S.-Afr. monkey often employed by organ-grinders. [F, etym. dub.]

vĕr'y̆, a. & adv. **1.** Real, true, genuine, that is such in the truest or fullest sense, as ~ *God of* ~ *God*, *has shown himself a* ~ *knave*, *the veriest simpleton knows that*, *must consent from* ~ *shame*, (somewhat arch. exc. in foll. uses); (with *the, this, that,* or *possessive* adj., emphasizing identity, coincidence, significance, or extreme degree) *this is the* ~ *spot I found it on, speaking in this* ~ *room, the* ~ *man I am looking for, a needle is the* ~ *thing (for our purpose), come here this* ~ *minute, grieves me to the* ~ *heart, the* ~ *stones cry out, his* ~ *servants bully him, drank it to the* ~ *dregs*; (with *a*) *a* ~ *little more will do, give me only a* ~ *little*. **2.** adv. (Perh. orig. adj., with superl. adj. often abs., or with *may* etc. *own*) in the fullest sense, as *drank it to the* ~ *last drop, the* ~ *last thing I expected, did the* ~ *best I could, did my* ~ *utmost, may keep it for your own*; (used with advv. & the positive of non-verbal adjj.; with partt. established as independent adjj., as *a* ~ *dazzling effect,*

effect *was ~ dazzling*, *a ~ trying time*; with
p.pp. in attrib. use applied to what is not
the real object of the vbl action, *as were a
~ pained, puzzled, troubled, vexed,
annoyed, surprised, etc.*, *expression*, but
not his expression was ~ pained etc.; *&*
colloq. with the same p.pp. in pred. use
applied to the true object & fulfilling
purely vbl function, *as I was ~ pleased,
surprised, annoyed, etc.*; not otherwise
used with vbs) in a high degree, *as that is
much easily done*, *~ often fails*, *~ easily done*, *~ much use, find ~ few instances, gives
~ little trouble, but not ~ better etc.* **3.**
~ *well*, formula of consent or approval.
[adv. f. adj.) ME & OF *verai* ult. f. L
verus true]

vẽr'rȳ², n. (attrib.). ~ *light* (projected
from ~ *pistol* for signalling or temporarily
illuminating part of battle-field etc.).
[S. W. ~, inventor]

vesic̃a, n. (anat. &c.) **1.** Bladder, cyst,
sac, esp. (whence vẽs'icoele, vẽsico̅t'-
omy, nn.) urinary bladder. **2.** (~ *piscis or
piscium* = fish's or fishes'), the pointed
oval (⬭) used as an aureole in medieval
sculpture & painting. Hence vẽs'ic̃al a.,
vẽs'ico- comb. form. [L]

vẽs'ic̃ate, v.t. Raise blisters on. Hence
~ANT(2), ~ĀTORY, aa. & nn., ~ĀTION n.
[f. prec. +-ATE³]

vẽs'ic̃le, n. (anat., bot., geol.), Small
bladder, cell, bubble, or hollow structure.
Hence vẽsic̃'ŪLAR¹, vẽsic̃'ŪLATE¹, vẽsi-
c̃ŪL'IFEROUS, vẽsic̃'ŪLIFORM, vẽsic̃'ULOSE¹
vẽsic̃'ULOUS, aa., vẽsic̃ULA'TION n., vẽsic̃'
ūlo- comb. form. [f. L *vesicula* dim. of
prec.]

VESICA

vẽs'per, n. (V~) Venus as evening-star.
(poet.) evening; (pl.) sixth of the seven
canonical hours of the breviary, EVEN-
song; ~(-*bell*), bell that calls to ~s;
Sicilian V~s, massacre of French residents in Sicily in 1282, begun at stroke of
~-bell. [L, cf. HESPERUS]

vẽs'pertine, a. Of, done in, the evening;
(Bot., of flowers) opening; (Zool.) flying,
in the evening; (Astron.) descending towards horizon at sunset. [f. L *vespertinus*
(VESPER)]

vẽs'piary, n. Nest of wasps. [irreg. f. L
vespa wasp, after *apiary*]

vẽs'pine, a. Of wasps. So vẽs'piFORM a.
[f. L *vespa* wasp +-INE¹]

vẽssel, n. **1.** Hollow receptacle esp. for
liquid, e.g. cask, cup, pot, bottle, dish.
2. Ship, boat, esp. large one. **3.** (Anat.)
duct, canal, holding or conveying blood or
other fluid, esp. *blood-~*; (Bot.) chain of
cells that have lost intervening partitions,
duct. **4.** (Bibl. or allus. use.), Person
viewed as recipient or exponent, as *chosen
~ (Acts ix. 15), weaker ~, woman* (1 Pet.
iii. 7), *~s of wrath (Rom.* ix. 22). Hence
dim. of VAS]
~-FUL n. [AF, f. OF *vaissel* f. L *vascellum*

vẽst¹, n. (Shop) waistcoat; (also *under~*)

4895

‖ knitted or woven undergarment; piece,
usu. V-shaped, on front of body of woman's gown; ‖(arch.) clothing, dress;
~-*pocket*, (attrib. of small articles, esp.
hand-cameras) of a size suitable for the
pocket (as a size of plate or film, 6×4·5
cm.). Hence ~ING²(3) n. [f. F f. It. *veste*
f. L *vestis* garment, cogn. w. Gk *esthēs*
dress]

vẽst², v.t. & i. Furnish (person *with*
authority, powers, property, etc.); ~
(property, power) *in* (person), confer formally on him an immediate fixed right of
present or future possession of it (~*ed
rights, interests, estate, etc.*, possession of
which is determinately fixed in a person
& is subject to no contingency); (of
property, right, etc.) ~ *in* (person), come
to him; (poet.) clothe. [f. OF *vestir* f. L
vestire -it- clothe (as prec.)]

vẽs'ta, n. (Rom. Myth., V~) goddess of
the hearth; (Astron., V~) an asteroid;
short wooden or (*wax ~*) wax match.
[L, cf. Gk *Hestia*]

vẽs'tal, a. & n. Of the goddess Vesta or
the ~ *virgins*; ~ (*virgin*), virgin consecrated to Vesta, vowed to chastity, &
charged with care of sacred fire perpetually burning on her altar, hence, woman
of spotless chastity, esp. one who devotes
her life to religion, nun. [f. L *Vestalis* a.
& n. (as prec.)]

vẽs'tibule, n. Ante-chamber, hall, lobby,
next to outer door of house & from which
doors open into various rooms; porch
of church etc.; *~e (*=CORRIDOR) *train*;
(Anat.) chamber or channel communicating with others, esp. ~*e of the cœr*, central
cavity of labyrinth of internal ear. Hence
vẽstib'ULAR¹, vẽstib'ULATE², (anat.),~ED²
ARY¹, aa. [f. f. L *vestibulum* (esp. biol.)]

vẽs'tibure, n. (zool.), Hair, scales, etc.,
covering a surface. [f. med. L *vestitura*
f. L as VEST²-URE]

vẽs'tige, n. Footprint (now only fig.),
track, trace, evidence, sign, as ~*s of an
earlier civilization, found no ~s of his
presence*; (loosely, w. neg.) atom, particle,
as *without a ~ of clothing (has not a ~ of
evidence for this assertion*); (Biol.) part,
organ, now degenerate & of little or no
utility but ancestrally well developed.
Hence vẽstig'IAL (esp. biol.), vẽstīg'-
ARY¹, aa. [F f. L *vestigium* footstep,
etym. dub.]

vẽs'tment, n. Garment, esp. official or
state robe; any of the official garments of
clergy, choristers, etc., worn during divine
service, esp. chasuble; altar-cloth. [f.
OF *vestement* f. L *vestimentum* (as VEST²,
see -MENT)]

vẽs'try, n. Room, building, attached to
church in which vestments are kept &
put on; chapel attached to non-liturgi-
cal church & used for prayer meetings
etc.; ‖(also *common, general, ordinary, ~*)
ratepayers of a parish, (also *select ~*)

Z Z

representatives of these, assembled for dispatch of parochial business; ‖ (room used for) meeting of either of these bodies; ‖ ~ clerk, officer chosen by ~ to keep parish accounts etc.; ~ man, member of a ~. Hence **vēs′trāL** a. [f. OF *vestiarie* f. L *vestiārium* wardrobe (as VEST¹, see -ARIUM)] ‖ **vēs′trydom**, n. (Corrupt, inefficient) government by vestry. [-DOM]

vēs′ture, n., & v.t. (poet., rhet.). 1. Garments, dress, clothes; covering. 2. v.t. Clothe. [OF, as VESTITURE]

vēs′turer (-cher-), n. Church official in charge of vestments; sub-treasurer of cathedral or church. [f. prec.+-ER¹]

Vĕsū′vian, a. & n. 1. (V~). Of Vesuvius; volcanic. 2. n. Kind of fusee match (obs.); (also ~ITE¹ n.) brown or green mineral first found on Vesuvius. [f. L *Vesuvius*+-AN¹]

vĕt, n., & v.t. (colloq.; -tt-). 1. =VETERINARY. 2. v.t. Examine or treat (beast), (fig.) check & correct. [abbr.]

vĕtch, n. Kinds of plant of pea family largely used, wild or cultivated, for forage, esp. *common* ~, tare. Hence ~Y² a. [f. ONF *veche* f. L *vicia*]

vĕtch′ling, n. Plant allied to vetch. [-LING¹]

vĕt′eran, a. & n. ‖ (Person) who has grown old in or had long experience of (esp. military) service or occupation, as *Wellington's* ~ s, a ~ *golfer*; *ex-service man*; of a ~, composed of ~ s, as ~ *service*, *troops*. Hence ~IZE(3) v.t. [f. L *veteranus* a. & n. (*vetus -eris* old, see -AN)]

vĕt′erinărẏ, a. & n. 1. Of, for, (the treatment of) diseases & injuries of domestic animals, as ~ *surgeon*, *science*, *college*. 2. n. (abbr. *vet*). A ~ surgeon; also **vĕterinā′rIAN** n. [f. L *veterinarius* f. *veterinae* cattle]

vĕt′ō, n. (pl.~es), & v.t. 1. Constitutional right of sovereign, president, governor, upper house of legislature, etc., to reject a legislative enactment (*suspensory* ~, suspending but not necessarily preventing completion of measure), whence ~ISM(2) n.; (official message conveying) such rejection; prohibition, as *interposed his* ~, *put a* or *his* ~ *on the proposal*. 2. v.t. Exercise ~ against (bill etc.), forbid authoritatively. [L, = I forbid, w. ref. to its use by tribune of the people in nullifying measures]

vĕttū′ra (-ōōra), n. (pl. *-re* pr. -rā). Italian four-wheeled carriage. [It.]

vĕx, v.t. Anger by slight or petty annoyance, irritate, as *this would ~ a saint, how ~ing!*, whence ~′edLY², ~′ingLY², advv. (arch.) grieve, afflict; (poet., rhet.) put (sea etc.) into state of commotion; *a ~ed* (much discussed) *question*. [f. OF *vexer* f. L *vexare*]

vĕxā′tion, n. Vexing, being vexed; harassing by means of malicious or trivial litigation; state of irritation or distress, as

conceive my ~, *in* ~ *of spirit*; annoying or distressing thing, as *subjected to many* ~ s. Hence **vĕxā′tious** (-shus) a., **vĕxā′tiousLY²** adv., **vĕxā′tiousNESS** n. [f. L *vexationem* (as VEX, see -ATION)]

vĕxill′um, n. (pl. *-illa*). (Rom. Ant.) military standard esp. of maniple, body of troops under this; (Bot., also **vĕx′il** n.) large upper petal of papilionaceous flower; web of a feather, whence **vĕx′illATE²** a.; (Eccl.) flag on or wound round bishop's staff, processional banner or cross. Hence or cogn. **vĕx′illaR(Y)¹** aa. [L (*vehere vect-* carry)]

vī′a, n. & prep. 1. *Via Lāc′tea*, Milky Way; ~ *mĕd′ia*, mean between extremes (esp. of Anglican church as placed between Romanism & extreme Protestantism). 2. prep. (Also *via*) by way of, through, as *from Exeter to York* ~ *London* (also joc. of connected subjects etc.). [L, = way, road]

vī′able, a. (Of foetus or new-born child) capable of maintaining life; (of plant, animal, etc.) able to live or exist in particular climate etc., (of seed) able to germinate. So **viabil′ITY** n. [F (*vie* life f. L *vita*, see -ABLE)]

vī′aduct, n. Long bridgelike structure, esp. series of arches, for carrying road or railway over valley or dip in ground; such road or railway. [f. L *via* way, after AQUEDUCT]

vī′al, n. Small (usu. cylindrical glass) vessel for holding liquid medicines etc.; LEYDEN ~ (=jar); *pour out* ~ s *of wrath*, take vengeance (*Rev.* xv. 7), (colloq.) give vent to anger. Hence ~FUL n. [as PHIAL]

vī′and, n. (usu. in pl.). Article(s) of food, victual(s). [AF *viande*, = meat, food, f. L *vivenda* things to live on (neut. pl. gerund. of *vivere* live, taken as fem. sing.)]

viăt′icum, n. (Rom. Ant.) supplies or sum of money allowed to officer for journey on State service; eucharist as given to dying person; portable altar. [L (*via* way, see -ATIC)]

vībrā′cūl̆um, n. (pl. *~a*). Filamentous appendage of some polyzoa serving to bring food within reach by lashing movements. Hence ~AR¹ a. [f. L as foll.]

vīb′rant, a. Vibrating; thrilling *with something*; (of sound) resonant. [f. L *vibrare* (foll.), -ANT]

vīb′rāte, v.i. & t. Move to & fro like pendulum, oscillate; (of sound) throb (on ear, in memory, etc.); (Physics) move unceasingly to & fro, esp. rapidly; thrill, quiver, (with passion etc.); cause to oscillate; (of pendulum) measure (seconds etc.) by vibrating. Hence **vīb′ratĬve**, **vīb′ratory**, aa. [f. L *vibrare* shake, swing, see -ATE³]

vīb′ratile, a. Capable of vibrating. Hence **vībratil′ITY** n. [-ILE]

vibrā'tion, n. Vibrating, oscillation; (Physics) rapid motion to & fro esp. of the parts of a fluid or an elastic solid whose equilibrium has been disturbed (*amplitude of ~*, maximum departure of vibrating body from position of rest; *forced, free, ~,* whose period is, is not, modified by an outside force). Hence ~AL a. **vibrā'tiUNCLE** n. dim. [f. L *vibrationem* (as VIBRATE, see -ATION)]

vĭb′ro̅scope, n. Instrument for observing vibrations. [-SCOPE]

vĭbū̆r′num, n. Kinds of shrub of honeysuckle family. [L]

vĭc, n. (sl.). V-shaped formation of aircraft. [L]

vĭc′ar, n. ‖ Priest of a parish the tithes of which belong to chapter or religious house or layman (cf. RECTOR); ~ *of Bray,* systematic turncoat, w. ref. to 17th-c. song; *clerk, lay, secular, ~,* cathedral officer singing some parts of service; ‖ *choral, clerical* or *lay assistant* in some (esp. musical) parts of cathedral service; ‖ ~ *general,* (Ch. of Eng.) official assisting (arch)bishop in ecclesiastical causes etc. (usn. his chancellor), (R.-C. Ch.) bishop's assistant in matters of jurisdiction etc.; (R.-C. Ch.) *cardinal ~,* Pope's delegate acting as bishop of diocese of Rome, ~ *apostolic,* missionary or titular bishop (whence **vĭcā̆r′IATE** [t] n.), ~ *fō̆r′ane,* dignitary appointed by bishop to exercise limited local jurisdiction. *V~ of (Jesus) Christ,* Pope. Hence ~SHIP n. [f. OF *vicaire* f. L *vicarius* deputed, deputy, (as VICE, see -ARY[t])]

vĭc′arage, n. Benefice, residence, of vicar. [-AGE]

vĭcā̆r′ial, a. Of, serving as, a vicar. [-AL]

vicā̆r′ious, a. Deputed, delegated, as ~ *authority;* acting, done, for another, as ~ *work, suffering,* ~ *sacrifice* (of Christ in place of sinner). Hence ~LY[t] adv., ~NESS n. [f. L as VICARIUS +-OUS]

vice[1], n. Evil esp. grossly immoral habit or conduct, (particular form of) depravity, serious fault, as *has the ~ of gluttony, drunkenness is not among his ~s,* ~ *is daily punished & virtue rewarded in fifth act, has no redeeming ~* (to relieve overpowering rectitude); defect, blemish, (of character, literary style, etc.) fault, bad trick, in horse etc., as *has no ~s, is free from ~, has*

one ~; (now rare) morbid state of physical system, as *inherited ~s of constitution;* (V~) buffoon in a MORALITY. [OF, f. L *vĭtium*]

vice[2], n. & v.t. **1.** Instrument with two jaws between which thing may be gripped usn. by operation of screw so as to leave the hands free for working upon it, as *bench* (attached to carpenter's or machinist's *bench), instantaneous-grip ~, grips like a ~.* **2.** v.t. Secure (material to be worked upon, or fig.) in ~. [vb f. n.] [ME, = screw, winding-stair, f. OF *vis* f. L *vītis* vine]

vice[3], n. (colloq.). = VICE-*president* etc. [abbr.]

vī′cĕ, prep. In the place of, as *gazetted as captain C. vice vice vicis* change]

vice-, pref. (= prec.) forming nn. w. sense ‘person acting or qualified to act in place of or next in rank to’, w. their deriv., as : ~*ad′miral,* ADMIRAL of third grade; ~*ad′miralty,* office of ~-admiral ‖ (~*admiralty courts,* tribunals with admiralty jurisdiction in British colonial possessions); ~*ch̄air′man(ship);* ‖ ~*chamberlain* (esp. deputy of lord chamberlain); ~*cham′cellor,* (Univ.) deputy chancellor discharging most administrative duties, (Law, formerly) judge in chancery division of High Court of Justice, (R.-C. Ch.) cardinal at head of the branch of chancery in charge of bulls etc.; ~*cham′cellorship;* ~*con′sul(ship);* ~*dean′,* subdean; ~*go̅′ernor;* ~*king′-dency;* ~VICEROY; ~*-pres′ident(ship);* ~*prin′cipal;* ~*queen* (rare), woman acting as viceroy, viceroy's wife; ~*re′gent;* ~*reine* (-srān), viceroy's wife; ~*she′riff;* ~*thre′asurer(ship);* ~*warder̄n.* [-ENT]

vicĕn′nial, a. Lasting, happening every, twenty years. [f. L *vicennium* period of 20 years (*vigĭnti* 20+*annus* year) +-AL]

vice′roy, n. Ruler exercising royal authority in colony, province, etc., as ~ *of India.* Hence **vicere̅g̅ AL,** **viceroy′ALTY,** **~SHIP,** nn. (-sī-). [OF (VICE- + *roy* king f. L *regem* nom. *rex*)]

vīce′ vē̆r′sâ, adv. or ellipt. sent. (The same is true), with the corresponding supposition, etc.) with the order of terms changed, the other way round, as *the man blames his wife & ~* (she him), *calls black the dog's dinner & ~* (he hers), *calls black white & ~* (white black). [L, (VICE, ablat. fem. p.p. of *vertere* turn)]

Vichy (vēshē), n. A mineral water. [*Vichy* in France]

vic′inage, n. Neighbourhood, surrounding district; relation of neighbours.

[refash. f. OF *voisinage* (*voisin* neighbouring f. L *vicinus* f. *vicus* village, quarter, +
-AGE)]

vicin′ity, n. Surrounding district; nearness in place (*to*); close relationship (*to*).
[f. L *vicinitatem* (as prec., see -TY)]

vi′cious (-shŭs), a. Of the nature of vice, morally evil or injurious, as ~ *tendencies, courses, life*; addicted to vice, as ~ *companions*; (of horse etc.) having vices; (of language, reasoning, etc.) incorrect; faulty, unsound, corrupt, as *a* ~ *style*; *a notoriously* ~ *manuscript*, ~ CIRCLE¹; ~ *union* (Surg.), faulty joining of fractured ends of bone, resulting deformity; bad-tempered, spiteful, as ~ *dog, mood, remarks*. Hence ~LY² adv., ~NESS n. [f. L *vitiosus* (as VICE¹, see -OUS)]

viciss′itude, n. Change of circumstances esp. of fortune, as *a life marked by* ~*s*; (arch., poet.) regular change, alternation. Hence **vicissitu′dinous** a. [f. L *vicissitudo -dinis* (*vicissim* by turns, as VICE¹, see -TUDE)]

vic′tim, n. Living being sacrificed to a deity or in performance of religious rite; person, thing, injured or destroyed in pursuit of an object, in gratification of a passion etc., or as result of event or circumstance, as *the* ~*s of his relentless ambition, fell a* ~ *to his own avarice, the* ~*s of disease, fell a* ~ *of a railway accident*; prey, dupe, as *held the* ~ *in his talons, the numerous* ~*s of the confidence trick*. [f. L *victima*]

vic′timize, v.t. Make (person etc.) the victim of a swindle etc. or of one's ambition, loquacity, etc.; (Trade-Un.) make (ringleader etc.) suffer by dismissal or other exceptional treatment. Hence ~A′TION n. [-IZE]

vic′tor, n. (rhet.). Conqueror in battle or contest (also attrib., as ~ *troops, sword*). Hence **vic′tress¹** n. [L (*vincere vict-conquer*, -OR²)]

victo′ria, n. 1. Low light four-wheeled carriage with seat for two & raised driver's seat & with falling top. 2. Kinds of gigantic water-lily. 3. Kinds of domestic pigeon. 4. *V~ Cross* (abbr. *V.C.*, pr. vē sō), decoration for conspicuous act of bravery founded by Queen V~ in 1856. [L, = victory (as prec.)]

Victo′rian, a. & n. Of, (person esp. author) living in, the reign of Queen Victoria (1837–1901); =EARLY-~; ~ *Order* (founded by Queen Victoria in 1896 & conferred usu. for great service rendered to sovereign). [-AN]

victorine′ (-ēn), n. (hist.). Woman's fur tippet with long narrow ends. [f. 1849; perh. named f. Queen Victoria]

victo′rious, a. Conquering, triumphant; marked by victory (~ *day* etc.). Hence ~LY² adv., ~NESS n. [f. OF *victorieux* f. L *victoriosus* (VICTORIA, -OUS)]

victory, n. Defeat of enemy in battle or opponent in contest, as *battle ended in a*

decisive ~, *fought hard for* ~, *hero of many victories*, (fig.) *gained a* ~ *over his passions, Cadmean* or PYRRHIC² ~, MORAL ~; (*V~*), (statue of) goddess of ~ (*winged* etc. *V~*). [f. OF *victorie* f. L VICTORIA]

victual (vī′tŭl), n., & v.t. & i. (-ll-). 1. (Usu. pl.) food, provisions. 2. vb. Supply with ~s, obtain stores, eat ~s. Hence ~LESS a. [(vb f. n.) ME & OF *vitaille* f. LL *victualia* neut. pl. (taken as fem. sing.) of *victualis* of nourishment (L *victus -ūs* food f. *vivere* live, see -AL)]

victualler (vī′tler), n. One who furnishes victuals, || esp. *licensed* ~, public-house-keeper licensed to sell spirits etc.; ship employed to carry stores for other ships. [f. OF *victuailleur* (prec., -OR²)]

victualling (vī′tling), n. In vbl senses; ||~*bill*, custom-house warrant for shipment of bonded stores; ||~*note* (Nav.), order authorizing ship's steward to victual a seaman; ||~*office* (for supplying provisions to navy); ||~*yard* (adjoining dockyard, for naval stores). [-ING¹]

vicu′gna, -u′ña, (-kōōnya), n. S.-Amer. mammal allied to llama & hunted for its flesh & wool; ~ *wool* (Commerce), mixture of wool & cotton, also wool of the ~. [Sp. f. Peruv.]

vid′e (or -ē), vb imperat. (abbr. *v.*). (In formal or joc. reference to passage in book etc.) see, as ~ *supra, infra*, see above, below, QUOD² , ~ *the press passim*. [L, imperat. of *vidēre*]

vide′licet, adv. (abbr. *viz*, usu. spoken as *namely*). That is to say, in other words, namely, (usu. following words that promise or more or less clearly require explanation etc. as: *under the following conditions, viz that etc.*; *a permanent board of three, viz etc.*; *opp. to i.e.*, which introduces rather optional explanation). [L (*vidēre licet* one may see)]

|| **vidette**. See VEDETTE.

vid′imus, n. (pl. ~*es*). Inspection of accounts etc.: abstract of document etc. [L, = we have seen (*vidēre*)]

vie, v.i. (*vying*). Strive for superiority, carry on rivalry, (*with* another *in* quality, *in doing*). [ME (*en*)*vien* f. OF *envier* IN-VITE]

Vienne′se′ (-z), a. & n. (pl. same). (Inhabitant) of Vienna. [-ESE]

vi et arm′is, adv. (law). With force & arms, with violence. [L]

view (vū), n., & v.t. 1. Inspection by eye, survey, (of surroundings etc.) (Law) inspection by jury of place, property, etc., concerned in a case, or of dead body. 2. Power of seeing, range of vision, as *stood in full* ~ *of* (visible to) *the crowd, came in* ~ *of* (where one could be seen from or see) *the castle, passed from our* (sight); what is seen, scene, prospect, as *a superb* ~; picture etc. representing this. 3. Mental survey, as *take a general* ~ *of the subject*; manner of considering a sub-

-ject, opinion, mental attitude, as *takes a different* ~, *his* ~ *is that we are the aggressors*, *takes a favourable* ~ *of her conduct*, *holds extreme* ~*s* (in politics etc.). **4.** Intention, design, as *will this meet your* ~*s?*, *cannot fall in with your* ~*s*, *cat has* ~*s upon the larder*. **5.** *In* ~ *of*, having regard to, considering, as *in* ~ *of recent developments we do not think this step advisable*, (vulg.) = *with a* ~ *to* (1), (see also above); *on* ~, open to inspection; *with a* ~ *to*, (1; also *with the* ~ *of*) for the purpose of, as a step towards ~; *dissolving* ~*s* (see DISSOLVE); *have in* ~, as *with a* ~ *to further hostilities*, (2) in the hope or on the chance of getting, with an eye to, as *said this with a* ~ *to the vacant secretaryship*, (3, vulg.) = *in* ~ *of*. *to* ~, openly, in public. **6.** MIND'S-eye ; POINT¹ *of* ~; *private* ~ (of picture, open only to exhibitors' friends, critics, etc.); ~*finder*, part of camera showing limits of picture; ~*halloo'*, huntsman's shout on seeing fox break cover. **7.** v.t. Survey with the eyes; form mental impression or judgement of, as *subject may be* ~*ed in different ways*, *does not* ~ *the matter in the right light*, *he or the proposal is* ~*ed unfavourably*. Hence ~ABLE (vū'abl) a., ~ER¹ (vū'er) n., (esp.) televiewer. [(vb) f. n.] AF. f. OF *veue* p.p. as n. f. *voir* see 1. L *vidēre*]

view'less, a. (poet., rhet.). Invisible. [-LESS]

view'ly (vū-), a. (colloq.). Given to odd or fanciful views, faddy. Hence ~INESS n. [-Y²]

vig'il, n. Keeping awake during the time usually given to sleep, watchfulness, as *eve* ~; (usu. pl.) nocturnal devotions; eve of a festival, esp. eve that is a fast. [f. OF *vigile* f. L *vigilia* (*vigil* awake)]

vig'ilance, n. Watchfulness, caution, circumspection, so~ANTE-. ~*ance committee*, organized body for maintenance of order etc. in imperfectly organized community. [F. f. L *vigilantia* (*vigilare*]

vigilan'te, n. Member of a vigilance committee. [Sp.]

vignette (vēnyĕt'), n., & v.t. **1.** (Archit.), ornament of leaves & tendrils; flourishes round capital letter in MS.; engraved illustration, esp. on title-page of book, not enclosed in definite border; photograph or portrait showing only head & shoulders with background gradually shaded off; (fig.) character sketch. **2.** v.t. Make portrait of (person) in ~e style, shade off (portrait) thus, whence ~'IST, n¹. [F, dim. as VINE]

vigoro'so, adv. (mus.). With vigour. [It.]

vig'our (-ger), n. Active physical strength or energy ; flourishing physical condition ; healthy growth, vitality, vital force; mental strength or activity as shown in thought or speech or literary style, forcibleness, trenchancy, animation, &c. Hence or cogn. **vig'orous**, ~LESS (-ger-), aa., **vig'orously²** adv., **vig'orous**NESS n. [AF. f. L *vigorem* (*vigēre* be lively, see -OR¹)]

vik'ing, n. Northern sea robber of 8th to 10th c. Hence ~ISM(2) n. [ON *víkingr*; perh. f. OE *wícing* (*wíc* camp, -ING³)]

vila'yet (-läh-), n. Province of Turkish empire. [Turk., f. Arab. *weláyet* district]

vile, a. Worthless; morally base, depraved, shameful, abject, as *the* ~ *trade of an informer*, *sycophant's* ~ *practices*, *the* ~*-st of mankind*; (colloq.) abominably bad, as *a* ~ *pen*, ~ *pastry*. Hence ~ly², ~²NESS n. [OF *vil* (*vile*), f. L *vilis*]

vil'ify, v.t. Defame, traduce, speak ill of; (rare) degrade, debase. Hence ~FI-CA'TION, ~FIER¹, nn. [f. L *vilificare*]

vil'ipend, v.t. (literary). Treat contemptuously, disparage. [f. L *vilipendere* (as VILE+*pendere* weigh)]

vill'a, n. Country residence; detached suburban house. Hence ~DOM n., suburban society. [L, = farmhouse, cf. *vicus* village]

vill'age, n. Assemblage of houses etc. larger than hamlet & smaller than town. [ME & OF f. L *villaticus* of a VILLA (see -AGE)]

vill'ager, n. Inhabitant of a village (usu. implying rusticity). [-ER¹]

vill'ain (-ǒn), n. & a. **1.** Person guilty or capable of great wickedness, scoundrel, as *has played the* ~, *plays the* ~*s in the melodramas*, (colloq. playful) *you little* etc. ~ (rascal) ; ||(arch.) rustic, boor; (Hist., also *villein* & n.) feudal serf, tenant holding by menial services, so **vill'ain**AGE (-ǒn-), ~e(h)nage(-lin-), n. **2.** adj. Of, done by, a ~, as ~ *services*. [ME & OF *vilein* f. pop. L +*villanus* farm-servant (as VILLA, see -AN)]

vill'ainous (-ǒn-), a. Worthy of a villain, vile, wicked, so **vill'ainy²** (-ǒn-) n.; (colloq.) abominably bad, as *a* ~ *scrawl*, ~ *style, hotel*. Hence ~LY² adv., ~NESS n. [-OUS]

villanelle', n. Form of (esp. French) poem of 19 lines on two rhymes. [F, f. It. *villanella*]

villegiatu'ra (-jetaoora), n. Stay, retirement, in the country. [It.]

vill'ein (-lin), n., & n. See VILLAIN.

vill'us, n. (pl. ~ī), (Anat.) each of the short hairlike processes on some membranes esp. on mucous membrane of intestine ; (Bot., pl.) long soft hair covering fruit, flower, etc. Hence or cogn. ~IFORM, ~OID, ~OSE¹, ~OUS, aa., ~ŎS'ITY n. [L, = shaggy hair]

vim, n. (colloq.). Vigour. [L, acc. of VIS]

vim'inal, a. (bot.). Of, producing, twigs or shoots. So **vimin'eous** a. [f. L *viminalis* (*vimen -minis* osier)]

vi'na (vē-), n. Indian seven-stringed musical instrument with fretted finger-board & a gourd at each end. [Hind.]

vina'ceous (-shŭs), a. Of wine or grapes; wine-red. [f. L *vinaceus* (*vinum* wine, -ACEOUS)]

vinaigrette' (-nĭg-), n. Bottle for holding aromatic vinegar etc., smelling-bottle. [F, dim. of *vinaigre* VINEGAR]

vin'cible, a. (rare). Not invincible. [f. L *vincibilis* (*vincere* conquer, see -BLE)]

vin'cilum, n. (pl. *-la*). (Alg.) line drawn over several terms to show that they have a common relation to what follows or precedes (e.g. $\overline{a+b} \times c = ac + bc$, but $a + b \times c = a + bc$; $\overline{a-b+c} = a-b-c$). [L, = bond (*vincire* bind)]

vin'dicate, v.t. Maintain the cause of (person, religion, etc.) successfully; establish the existence or merits or justice of (one's veracity, courage, conduct, character, assertion). Hence or cogn. ~ABIL'ITY, ~A'TION, ~ATOR² ~ATRESS¹, nn., ~ABLE, ~ATIVE, aa. [f. L *vindicare* (VIM +*dicare* assert, proclaim) lay claim to, see -ATE³]

vin'dicatory, a. Tending to vindicate. [-ORY]

vindic'tive, a. Revengeful, given to revenge; ~ (or *exemplary*) *damages* (awarded as punishment to defendant). Hence ~LY² adv., ~NESS n. [f. L *vindicta* vengeance (VINDICATE) +-IVE]

vine, n. Climbing woody-stemmed plant whose fruit is the grape (*under one's* ~ & FIG¹-*tree*); any plant with slender stem that trails or climbs, as *hop*, *melon*, ~; ~*borer*, kinds of insect destroying ~; ~*disease*, due to PHYLLOXERA etc. Hence **vin'Y²** a. [f. OF *vigne* f. L *vinea* vineyard (*vinum* wine)]

vin'egar, n., & v.t. 1. Acidliquid got from wine, cider, etc., by acetous fermentation & used as condiment or for pickling (fig., often attrib., as type of sourness, as *a* ~ *countenance*); *aromatic* ~ (holding camphor etc. in solution); *toilet* ~, aromatic ~ used for mixing with washing-water etc.; MOTHER³ *of* ; V~ *Bible*, 1717 ed. with *parable of the* ~ (for *vineyard*) above *Luke* XX; ~-*EEL*; ~-*plant*, microscopic fungus producing fermentation. Hence ~ISH¹, ~Y², aa. 2. v.t. Apply ~ to, make sour like ~ (lit. & fig.). [f. OF *vinaigre* (*vin* wine f. L *vinum* +*aigre*, see EAGER)]

vin'ery, n. Vine greenhouse. [-ERY]

vin'eyard (-nĭ-), n. Plantation of grape-vines. [VINE +YARD]

vingt-et-un (see Ap.), n. Card game in which the object is to reach the number of 21 pips without exceeding it. [F =21]

vini- in comb.=L *vinum* wine, as ; ~*cul-ture*, cultivation of vines, so ~*cul'turist*;

vinif'erous, (of district) wine-producing; ~*ficator*, apparatus for collecting alcoholic vapours in wine-making.

vinom'eter, n. Apparatus for measuring alcohol in wine. [f. L *vinum* wine +-METER]

vin ordinaire (see Ap.), n. Cheap (usu. red) wine as drunk in France mixed with water. [F]

vin'ous, a. Of, like, due to, wine, as ~ *flavour, fermentation, eloquence.* So **vinos'-ITY** n. [f. L *vinosus* (*vinum* wine, see -OUS)]

|| vint'¹, v.t. Make (wine). [f. VINTAGE]

vint'², n. A Russian card-game. [Russ., =screw]

vin'tage, n. Season of gathering grapes; (wine made from) season's produce of grapes; ~ *wines* (of well-known ~s); (poet., rhet.) wine. [f. OF *vendange* f. L *vindemia*; altered on *vintner*]

vin'tager, n. Grape-gatherer. [prec.,-RR¹]

vint'ner, n. Wine-merchant. [earlier *vinter* f. OF *vinetier* f. L *vinum* wine, *vinetum* vineyard, see -ARY¹]

vi'ol, n. Medieval (usu. 6-)stringed musical instrument, predecessor of violin etc. (*treble, tenor, bass*,~); *bass*~ (mod.), = VIOLONCELLO. [f. OF *viele*, *viole*, etym. dub., cf. LL *vitula*, & FIDDLE]

viol'a¹, n. 1. Kind of large violin, alto or tenor violin. 2. (hist.) = prec.; ~ *da braccio*,~, (alto) violin;~ *da gamba*, bass viol. [It., as prec.]

vi'ola², n. Kinds of plant including pansy, esp. of single colour, & violet. [L, = violet]

viola'ceous (-shŭs), a. Of violet colour; of violet family. [f. L *violaceus* (prec., -ACEOUS)]

vi'ollate, v.t. Transgress, infringe, act against the dictates or requirements of (oath, treaty, law, terms, conscience); treat profanely or with disrespect (sanctuary etc.); break in upon, disturb, (person's privacy etc.); commit rape upon, ravish. So ~ABLE a., ~A'TION, ~ATOR², nn. [f. L *violare* (VIS), see -ATE³]

vi'olence, n. Quality of being violent; violent conduct or treatment, outrage, injury, as *was compelled to use* ~, *did* ~ *to* (outraged, acted contrary to) *his feelings, our principles;* (Law) unlawful exercise of physical force, intimidation by exhibition of this. [OF, f. L *violentia* (as foll., see -ENCE]

vi'olent, a. Marked by great physical force, as *a* ~ *storm, came into* ~ *collision*, ~ *blows*; *death* (resulting from external force or from poison, cf. NATURAL); marked by unlawful exercise of force, as *laid* ~ *hands on him*; intense, vehement, passionate, furious, impetuous, as ~ *pain, sickness, abuse, controversy, discrepancy, revulsion, contrast, dislike, shock, apt to form* ~ *attachments, is of or was in a* ~ *temper;* ~ *presumption* (Law), one resting

violet on almost conclusive evidence. Hence ~-LY² adv. [OF, f. L *violentus* (VIS- -LENT)]

vi'olet, n. & a. 1. Kinds of plant chiefly of genus VIOLA, with blue, purple, white, or other flowers, as *common blue* ~, *sweet* ~, *dog-*~. 2. (Of) the colour seen at end of spectrum opposite red, produced by slight admixture of red with blue, so VIOLE⁴CENT a. 3. Kinds of ~ (colour). [f. It. *violetto* dim. of VIOLA¹ etc.] ~ (playing separate parts in orchestra, etc.). [f. OF *violete* (flower) & *violet* or other perfume; ~*-wood*, myall & other kinds. [f. OF *violette* dim. of *viole* f. L VIOLA²]

violin¹, n. Musical instrument with 4 strings of treble pitch played with bow; (also ~IST n.) player on ~, as *first*, *second*, ~ (playing separate parts in orchestra, etc.). [f. It. *violino* dim. of *viola*¹]

violin², **-ine**, n. Emetic substance contained in sweet violet. [f. F *violine* (VIOLA²+-IN²)]

vi'olist, n. Performer on viola¹. [-IST]

violoncell'o (vē-, -che-), n. (usu. abbr. *'cello*; pl. ~os). Bass violin, 4-stringed instrument held between player's knees. Hence ~IST(3) n. [It., dim. of *violone* large viol (VIOLA¹, see -ON)]

vi'per, n. Kinds of venomous snake esp. common ~, adder, the only poisonous snake in Gt Britain; (fig.) malignant or treacherous person. Hence or cogn. ~IFORM, ~INE¹, ~ISH¹ (fig.), ~OID, ~OUS (fig.), aa. [f. OF *vipere* f. L *vipera*, perh. as VIVIPAROUS]

virag'o, n. (pl. ~s). Turbulent woman, termagant; || (arch.) woman of masculine strength or spirit. [L, = female warrior (*vir* man)]

vi'relay, n. Kinds of (esp. old French) poem with two rhymes to a stanza variously arranged. [f. OF *virelai*, -lē]

vire'o, n. (Kinds of) small greenish-coloured American singing bird (also *greenlet*). [L, perh. = greenfinch]

vires'cence, n. Greenness; (Bot.) abnormal greenness in petals etc. normally of some bright colour. So ~ENT a. [f. L *virescere* become green (*virēre* be green), see -ESCENT, -ENCE]

virg'ate¹, a. (nat. hist.) Slim, straight, & erect. [f. L *virgatus* rodlike (*virga* rod, -ATE²)]

virg'ate², n. (hist.) A varying measure of land. [f. L *virga* rod + -ATE¹, cf. VERGE²]

Virg'ilian, a. Of, in the style of, the Roman poet Virgil (d. 19 B.C.). [f. L *Virgilianus* (*Virgilius* Virgil, -AN)]

vir'gin, n. & a. 1. Person esp. woman who has had no sexual intercourse, whence or cogn. ~HOOD, virg'in'ITY, nn.; member of any order of women under a vow to remain ~s; *the* (*Blessed*) *V~* (*Mary*) (abbr. B.V.M.), mother of Christ; picture, statue, of the B.V.M.; female insect producing eggs without impregnation; (Astron. V~) = VIRGO; ~*'s bower*, = TRAVELLER'S joy.

befitting, as a ~, as ~ *modesty*; spotless; not yet used or tried, as ~ *soil*, ~ *clay* (not fired); (of insect) producing eggs without impregnation; ~ *comb* (that has been used only once for honey & never for brood); ~ *honey* (taken from ~ comb, also, drained from comb without heat or pressure); ~ *queen*, unfertilized queen bee; *the V~ Queen*, Queen Elizabeth. [f. OF *virgine* f. L *virginem*, nom. -go, etym. dub.]

virg'inal, a. & n. 1. That is or befits or belongs to a virgin, whence ~LY² adv. 2. n. (Also ~s, *pair of* ~s) square legless spinet used in 16th-17th cc. [(adj.) OF, f. L *virginalis* (as prec., see -AL);

Virgin'ia, n. One of the U.S.; tobacco from ~a; ~ *creeper*, a woody vine cultivated for ornament. Hence ~AN a. & n. [f. VIRGIN (Queen)+-IA¹]

virg'o, n. 1. Sixth zodiacal sign; a constellation. 2. ~ *intac'ta* (L law), virgin with hymen intact. [L, = virgin]

virides'cent, a. Greenish, tending to become green. Hence ~ENCE n. [f. LL *viridescere* (*viridis* green, see -ESCENT)]

virid'ity, n. Greenness, esp. of oysters etc. after feeding on certain vegetable organisms. [f. L *viriditas* (*viridis* green, see -TY]

vi'rile (also vī°-), a. Of man as opp. to woman or child; of, having, procreative power; (of mind, character, literary style, etc.) having masculine vigour or strength. So Viril'ITY n. [OF (-il, -ile), f. L *virilis* (*vir* man, see -ILE)]

virile'scent, a. (Of female animal) assuming in advanced age some male characteristics. So ~ENCE n. [f. L as prec., -ESCENT]

viru'lose, a. (Bot.) Poisonous, full of virus, so ~OUS a.; (Bot.) having fetid smell. [f. L *virosus* (VIRUS, see -OSE²)]

virtu' (vēr-), n. Love of fine arts; *articles of* ~ (interesting from workmanship, antiquity, rarity, etc.). [f. It. *virtù* VIRTUE, virtu]

vir'tual, a. That is such for practical purposes though not in name or according to strict definition, as *is the ~ manager of the business*, *take this as a ~ promise*, *constitutes a ~ exculpation*; ~ *focus* (Optics), point at which the lines or a pencil of rays would meet if produced; ~ *velocity* or *displacement*, infinitesimal displacement of the point of application of a force measured in the direction of that force. Hence ~ITY(-il) n., ~-LY² adv. [f. med. L *virtualis* (irreg. as foll., see -AL)]

vir'tue, n. Moral excellence, uprightness, goodness, as ~ *is its own reward*, *make a ~ of necessity*, feign alacrity or sense of duty while acting under

compulsion; particular moral excellence, as patience is~, ~she has every~, the (seven) cardinal ~s (natural ~s, justice, prudence, temperance, fortitude; theological ~s, faith, hope, charity); chastity esp. of women, as a woman of ~; good quality, as has the ~ of being adjustable, of resisting temperature; inherent power, efficacy, as no ~ in such drugs; (pl.) seventh ORDER¹ of angels; by or in ~ of, on the strength of, on the ground of, as claims it in ~ of his long service, is entitled to it by ~ of his prerogative. Hence ~LESS (-til-) a. [f. F vertu f. L virtutem nom. -tus (vir, see VIRILE)]

virtuōs'ō, n. (pl. -si pr. -sē). Person with special knowledge of or taste for works of art or virtu; person skilled in the mechanical part of a fine art. Hence virtuōs'ITY, ~SHIP, nn. [It. (as VIRTU, see -OSE¹)]

vir'tuous, a. Possessing, showing, moral rectitude, chaste. Hence ~LY² adv., ~NESS n. [f. OF vertuous f. LL virtuosus for -tuosus (as VIRTUE, see -OUS)]

vir'ulent (or -rōō-), a. Poisonous, caused by or containing virus, as ~ent ulcer, so [irreg.] ~IFEROUS a. (med.); malignant, bitter, as ~ent animosity, tone, abuse. Hence or cogn. ~ENCE n., ~ently² adv. [f. L virulentus (foll., see -LENT)]

vir'us, n. Morbid poison, poison of contagious disease, as smallpox ~; (fig.) moral poison; (fig.) malignity, acrimony. [L, = poison]

vis, n. (mech.). ~ INERTIAE; ~ mort'ŭa, ~ vīv'a, living force (= mass × square of velocity) of moving body. [L, = force]

visa. Now usu. form of visé.

vis'age (-z-), n. (now chiefly literary). Face, countenance. Hence (-)~ED² (-zijd) a. [OF, f. L visus look (vidēre vis- see), see -AGE]

visard. See VISOR.

vis-à-vis (vēz'àhvē'), adv. & n. 1. In a position facing one another; opposite to. 2. n. Person facing another esp. in some dances; kinds of carriage & couch in or on which persons sit facing each other. [F, =face to face (vis face f. L as VISAGE)]

vis'cāch'a, viz-, n. S.-Amer. burrowing rodent with valuable fur. [of native orig.]

vis'cer'a, n. pl. The interior organs in the great cavities of the body (e.g. brain, heart, liver), esp. in the abdomen (e.g. the intestines). Hence ~AL a., ~I~, ~o-, comb. forms. [L, pl. of viscus -eris]

vis'cerāte, v.t. Disembowel. [prec., -ATE²]

vis'cid, a. Sticky; semifluid. So ~ITY (-id²) n. [f. LL viscidus (L viscum mistletoe, birdlime, & see -ID²)]

vis'cin, n. Sticky substance got from mistletoe & used in birdlime. [F, f. viscum, prec., -IN²]

vis'cōse, n. (In the manufacture of rayon) cellulose reduced to a viscous state (suitable for drawing into yarn) by treatment with sodium hydroxide solution & carbon disulphide. [f. obs. viscose a. f. L as VISCOUS]

viscos'ITY, n. Stickiness; (Physics, of fluids, semifluids, & gases) internal friction, power of resisting a change in the arrangement of the molecules, whence viscōm'ETER, viscōm'ETRY, viscosIM'ETER, nn. [f. OF viscosité (as VISCOUS, see -TY)]

visc'ount (vik-), n. Noble ranking between earl & baron. Hence or cogn. ~OY, ~ESS¹, ~SHIP or ~Y⁴, nn. (vik-). [f. OF visconte (VICE-+counté COUNT³)]

vis'cous, a. Sticky; (Physics) having viscosity. Hence ~NESS n. [f. L viscosus (as VISCID, see -OUS)]

visé (vēz'ā), visa (vēz'a), n., & v.t. (-ēd, -sē'd, -sa'd). 1. Indorsement on passport etc. showing that it has been found correct. 2. v.t. Mark with ~. [(-sē) p.p. f. F viser inspect f. L vidēre vis- see]

vis'ible (-z-), a. That can be perceived or ascertained, apparent, open, as has no ~ means of support, spoke with ~ impatience; prepared to receive callers (is she ~?); the ~ church, whole body of professed believers; ~ horizon, the line that bounds sight; ~ speech, system of alphabetical characters designed to represent all possible articulate utterances. Hence or cogn. visIBIL'ITY (in adj. senses, & esp., Meteorol. Naut. conditions of light & atmosphere as regards distinguishing of objects by sight), ~NESS, nn., vis'IBLY² adv., (-z-). [OF, f. LL visibilis (vidēre vis- see, see -BLE)]

vi'sion (-zhn), n., & v.t. 1. Act or faculty of seeing, sight, as beyond our ~, has impaired his ~, the field of ~, all that comes into view when the eyes are turned in some direction, reflected, refracted, ~ (as affected by reflected, refracted, rays of light); thing seen in dream or trance; supernatural or prophetic apparition, phantom; thing seen in the imagination, as romantic ~s of youth, had ~s of roast beef & plum pudding; (without article) imaginative insight, statesmanlike foresight, political sagacity. 2. v.t. See, present, (as) in a ~. [(vb f. n.) OF, f. L visionem (vidēre vis- see, see -ION)]

vi'sionary (-zho-), a. & n. 1. Given to seeing visions or to indulging in fanciful theories; existing only in a vision or in the imagination, imaginary, fanciful, unpractical. 2. n. (Also ~IST n.) ~ary person. Hence or cogn. ~AL a., ~alLY³ adv., ~arINESS n., (-zho-). [-ARY¹]

vis'it (-z-), v.t., & n. 1. Go, come, to see (person, place, etc., or abs.) as act of friendship or ceremony, on business, or from curiosity, as have never ~ed us, had no time to ~ the Tower, hope to ~ Rome;

go, come, to see for purpose of official inspection or supervision or correction; (of disease, calamity, etc.) come upon, attack; (Bibl.) punish (person, sin), avenge (*his sins* etc.) *upon* person, community, bless, (person *with* salvation etc.). **2.** n. Call on a person or at a place, temporary residence with person or at place, as *was on a ~ to some friends, paid him a long ~, during his second ~ to the East*; formal or official call for purpose of inspection etc., as DOMICILIARY *~*, *pay* VISITATION. Hence **~ABLE** a. [(n. f. F *visite*) f. OF *visiter* f. L *visitare* frequent. of *visere* f. *videre vis-* see]

visitant (-z-). a. & n. **1.** (poet.). Visiting; **2.** n. Migratory bird; (poet., rhet.) visitor; (*V~*) member of an order of nuns concerned with education of young girls. [f. L as prec., -ANT]

visita′tion (-z-), n. Official visit of inspection or the like esp. bishop's examination of the churches of his diocese; (colloq.) unduly protracted visit or social call; boarding of vessel belonging to another State to learn her character & purpose (*right of ~ or visit*, right to do this, not including right of search); divine dispensation of punishment or reward, notable experience compared to this; (Eccl.) festival in honour of visit of B.V.M. to Elizabeth (*Luke* i. 39); (Zool.) unusual & large migration of animals; *V~* = VISITANTS; *V~ of the Sick*, office of the Anglican Church. [OF. f. LL *visitationem* (as VISIT, see -ATION)]

visiting (-z-), n. Paying visits, making calls; *have a ~ acquaintance with, be on ~ terms with*, know well enough to visit; *~-book* (for names of persons to be called upon); ‖*~-card*, small card with one's name, address, etc., left in making call etc. [-ING]

vis′itor (-z-), n. One who visits a person or place; ‖(in colleges etc.) official with the right or duty of occasionally inspecting & reporting, whence or cogn. **visit′ing-house**, etc., in which *~s* write remarks. [f. OF *visiteur* (as VISIT, -OR)]

vis′or (-z-), **-zor**, **vis′ard** (-z-), **-zard**, n. (Hist.) movable part of helmet covering face; projecting front part of cap; (Hist.) mask. Hence **vis′ored**[2] (-zerd), **vis′or-LESS** (-z-), aa. [ME & AF *viser* (F *vis-*... as VIS-À-VIS)]

vis′ta, n. Long narrow view as between rows of trees; long succession of remembered or anticipated events etc., mental prospect or retrospect, as *opened up new ~s or a new ~ to his ambition, searched in the dim ~ of his childhood*. Hence **~'d** a. [f. It. *vista* sight, n. & fem. p.p. of *vedere* see f. L *videre*]

vis′ual (-zhyŏŏ- or -zū-), a. Of, concerned with, used in, seeing, as *~ nerve, organ*; *~ angle* (formed at the eye by rays from the extremities of an object viewed); *~ field* (of vision); *~ rays*, lines of light supposed to come from object to eye; *~ point*, point in the horizontal plane in which the *~ rays* unite. Hence **~ITY** (-ăl′-) n., **~IZE**[2], **~LY**[2] adv. [OF. f. LL *visualis* (*visus -ūs* sight f. *videre* see, see -AL)]

vis′ualize (-zhyŏŏ- or -zū-), v.t. Make visible to the eye, give outward & visible form to, (mental image, idea, etc.); call up distinct mental picture of (thing imagined or formerly seen, or abs.). Hence **~A′TION** n. [-IZE]

vit′a glass (-ah-), n. Kind of glass by which the ultra-violet vitalizing rays of sunlight are not excluded as by ordinary glass. [P]

vit′al, a. & n. **1.** Of, concerned with or essential to, organic life, as *~ energies, functions*, *~ power* (to sustain life), *wounded in a ~ part*; essential to existence or to the matter in hand, as *a ~ question, the success of ~ importance, secrecy is ~ to this*; fatal to life or to success etc., as *a ~ wound, error*; *~ centre* (Med.), part in which wound appears to be instantly fatal, esp. respiratory nerve-centre in medulla oblongata; *~ force or principle* (assumed to account for organic life); *~ statistics* (of birth, marriage, death, etc.). Hence **~LY**[2] adv. **2.** n. (pl.) *~s*, e.g., lungs, heart, brain. [OF. f. L *vitalis* (*vita* life, cogn. w. *vivere* live & Gk *bios* life, see -AL)]

vit′alism, n. (biol.). Doctrine that life originates in a vital principle distinct from chemical & other physical forces. So **~IST** n., **~IS′TIC** a. [-ISM]

vital′ity, n. Vital power, ability to sustain life; (fig.) (of institution, language, etc.) ability to endure & to perform its functions. [f. L *vitalitas* (as VITAL, see -TY)]

vit′alize, v.t. Endow with life. [-IZE]

vit′amin, n. Any of a number of accessory food factors chiefly of very complex chemical composition, present in many food-stuffs esp. in the raw state, & essential to the health of man & other animals; their absence from the diet is associated with malnutrition in various parts of the body or deficiency diseases. [f. L *vita* life + AMINE]

vitell′in, n. (chem.). Chief protein constituent of yolk of egg. [f. foll.+-IN]

vitell′us, n. (pl. *~*). Yolk of egg; *~plasmic* contents of ovum. Hence **vit′ellary**[2], **~INE**, aa., **~I-**, **~O-**, comb. forms. [L.,= yolk]

viti- in comb.=L *vitis* vine, as:*~cide*, insect etc. destructive to vines; *~culture*, grape-growing, so *~cul′tural* a., *~cul′turist*, nn.

viti′ate(-shi-), v.t. Impair the quality of, corrupt, debase, contaminate, as *constitu-tion ~ed by excess, ~ed air, blood, mind*,

judgement; make invalid or ineffectual, as *a word may ~e a contract.* So **vitia'TION**, **~OR²** nn., (-shi-). [f. L *vitiare* (as VICE¹), see -ATE³]

vit'reous, a. Of (the nature of) glass; like glass in hardness, brittleness, transparency, structure, etc.; *~ body* or *humour*, transparent jellylike tissue filling ball of eye; *~* ELECTRICITY. Hence or cogn. **vitrEOS'ITY**, **~NESS**, **vitrES'CENCE**, nn., **vitrES'CENT**, **vit'riFORM**(1), aa. [f. L *vitreus* (*vitrum* glass)+-OUS]

vit'riFy, v.t. & i. Convert, be converted, into glass or glasslike substance. Hence or cogn. **~FAC'TION**, **~fiABIL'ITY**, **~FICA¹ TION**, nn., **~fiABLE** a. [f. F *vitrifier* (as prec., see -FY)]

vit'riol, n. Sulphuric acid or any of its salts; (fig.) caustic speech, criticism, etc.; *blue* or *copper ~*, copper sulphate; *white ~*, zinc sulphate; *oil of ~*, concentrated sulphuric acid; *~throwing*, throwing *~* in person's face as act of vengeance etc. Hence **vitriOl'ic**, **~INE¹**, aa. [ME & OF, f. med. L *vitriolum*, dim. of L *vitrum* glass]

Vitru'vian (-ōō-), a. Of Vitruvius, Roman architect of the Augustan age; *~ scroll*, scroll pattern in frieze decorations etc. [-AN]

vitt'a, n. (pl. *-ae*). (Rom. Ant.) fillet, garland, as decoration of priest, victim, statue, etc.; lappet of mitre; (Bot.) oiltube in fruit of some plants; (Zool.) strips of colour. So **~ATE²** a. [L]

vitŭp'erāte, v.t. Revile, abuse, Hence or cogn. **~A'TION**, **~ātOR²**, nn., **~ATIVE** a., **~ativeLY²** adv. [f. L *vituperare* (*vitu-*, cogn. w. *vitium* VICE¹ + *parare* prepare), see -ATE³]

vī'va¹ (vē-), int. & n. (The cry) long live —. [It. 3rd pers. imperat. of *vivere* live, VIVA²]

viva². See VIVA VOCE.

vivace (vēvah'chā), adv. (mus.). In a lively manner. [It.]

vivā'cious (-shus), a. Lively, sprightly, animated, whence or cogn. **~LY²** adv., **vivā'CITY** n.; (Bot.) tenacious of life, surviving winter, perennial. [f. L *vivax* (*vivere* live, ~ACIOUS)]

vivandière (vēvahndyā'r'), n. (hist.). Woman attached to continental esp. French regiment & selling provisions & liquor. [F]

vivā'rium, n. (pl. *-ia*). Place artificially prepared for keeping animals in their natural state, zoological garden or the like. [L(*vivus*, see VIVIFY &-ARIUM]

vī'vā, int. & n. (The cry) long live, as *~ rex, regina*, long live the king, queen. [L, 3rd sing. subj. of *vivere* live]

vī'va vō'cē, adv., a., & n. **1.** Oral(ly).

2. n. (abbr. *viva*), Oral examination. Hence **vī'vā(-vō'cē)** v.t., examine *~*. [L, = with the living voice]

vive (vēv), int. Long live, as *~ le roi* (the king), QUI VIVE. [F, 3rd sing. imperat. of *vivre* live f. L *vivere*]

|| **vivErs** (-z), n. pl. (Sc.). Food, victuals. [f. OF *vivres* (*vivre* live f. L *vivere*]

vives (-vz), n. An ear disease esp. of young horses at grass. [f. F *avives* f. Sp. *avivas* f. Arab. *adhdhibah* (*al* the +*dhibah* she-wolf)]

viv'id, a. (Of light or colour) bright, intense, glaring, as *~ flash of lightning*, of *a ~ green*; (of mental faculty or impression) clear, vigorous, strongly marked, as *has a ~ imagination, gave a ~ description*. Hence **~LY²** adv., **~NESS** n. [f. L *vividus* (*vivere* live, see -ID)]

viv'iFY, v.t. Give life to, enliven, animate, (chiefly fig.). [f. F *vivifier* f. L *vivificare* (*vivus* living f. *vivere* live, see -FY)]

vivip'arous, a. (Zool.) bringing forth young alive, not hatching by means of eggs, (cf. OVIPAROUS); (Bot.) producing bulbs or seeds that germinate while still attached to parent plant. Hence **vivipa'rITY**, **~NESS**, nn., **~LY²** adv. [f. LL *viviparus* (*vivus*, see prec., +*parĕre* bring forth)+-OUS]

viv'isECT, v.t. Dissect (animal, or abs.) while living. [f. foll.]

vivisEc'tion, n. Dissection of or (loosely) inoculation etc. tried upon living animals. Hence **~AL** a., **~IST**(2, 3), **viv'isECTOR²**, nn. [f. L *vīvus*, see VIVIFY, +SECTION]

vix'en, n. She-fox; quarrelsome woman, termagant. Hence **~ISH¹**, **~LY¹**, aa. [OE +*fyxen*, fem. of FOX, cf. G *füchsin*]

viz. See VIDELICET.

vizard. See VISOR.

vizcacha. See VISCACHA.

vizi(e)r' (-zēr), n. High official, esp. State minister, in Mohammedan countries; *grand ~*, prime minister in Turkish empire & other countries. Hence **~ATE¹**(1), **~SHIP**, nn., **~IAL** a. [f. Turk. *vezīr* f. Arab. *wazīr* counsellor, orig. porter (*wazara* bear burden]

Vlach (-āk), a. & n. Member of a SE. European Latin-speaking people, Walachian or Roumanian. [Slav., ult. f. OHG *Walah* foreigner, Celt, Italian, Latin]

vlei (flā), n. (S. Afr.). Hollow in which water collects during rainy season. [Du. dial., f. Du. *vallei* valley]

vōc'able, n. Word, esp. w. ref. to form rather than meaning. [F, f. L *vocabulum* (*vocare* call, cogn. w. *vox vocis* voice)]

vocăb'ŭlARY, n. (List, arranged alphabetically with definitions, of) the (principal) words used in a language or usu. in a particular book or branch of science etc., or by a particular author, as *a Lévy with notes & ~, a word not found in the*

Chaucerian ~, the ever-increasing scientific ~, his ~ (range of language) is limited. [f. med. L vocabularius (as prec., -ARY¹)]

vŏc'al, a. & n. **1.** Of, concerned with, uttered by, the voice, as a ~ communication, ~ auscultation (of the sounds of the voice as heard through walls of chest), ~ cords, folds of lining membrane of larynx about the opening of the glottis, ~ music (written for or produced by the voice with or without accompaniment), ~ thrill or fremitus, vibration of wall of chest in audible speech; (poet., of trees, water, etc.) endowed (as) with a voice; (Phonet.) voiced, sonant, (also) of vowel character. Hence or cogn. vŏcAL'ITY n., ~LY² adv. **2.** n. Vowel, whence vŏcAL'IC a.; (R.-C. Ch.) person entitled to vote in certain elections. [f. L vocalis (as VOICE, see -AL)]

vŏc'alism, n. Use of voice in speaking or singing; vowel sound. [-ISM]

vŏc'alist, n. Singer (opp. to instrumentalist).

vŏc'alīz|e, v.t. & i. Form (sound), utter (word), with the voice, esp. make sonant, as f is ~ed into v; write (Hebrew etc.) with vowel points; (joc.) speak, sing, hum, shout, etc.; (Mus.) sing florid passage to a vowel. So ~A'TION n. [-IZE]

vocā'tion, n. Divine call to, sense of fitness for, a career or occupation, as felt no ~ (for the ministry), has never had the sense of ~, little or no ~ to literature; employment, trade, profession, as mechanical ~s, all ~s are overcrowded, mistook his (chose the wrong) ~. Hence ~AL (-sho-) a., ~ally² adv. [f. L vocationem (vocare, see -ATION)]

VOCABLE & -ATION]

vŏc'ative, a. & n. (gram.). (Case) employed in addressing person or thing. [f. L vocativus (vocare, see VOCABLE & -ATIVE)]

vŏcif'erāte, v.t. Utter (words etc., or oaths) noisily, shout, bawl. Hence or cogn. ~ANCE (rare), ~A'TION, nn., ~ANT(1) a. & n. [f. L vociferari (as VOICE + ferre bear)]

vŏcif'erous, a. (Of person, speech, etc.) noisy, clamorous. Hence ~LY² adv., ~NESS n. [f. prec. + -OUS]

vŏd'ka, n. Kind of fiery brandy distilled from rye etc. & drunk in Russia. [Russ.]

‖ **vŏe**, n. [Shetland]. Small bay, creek. [f. ON vágr]

vogue (vōg), n. & v.i. **1.** (Now chiefly literary) the prevailing fashion, as the ~ of large hats, large hats are the ~; popular use or reception, as has had a great ~; in ~, in fashion, generally current. **2.** v.i. ~ la galère (-âr), here goes (lit. let the galley set forth). [F, orig. = course, f. voguer f. It. vogare row in galley]

voice, n., & v.t. **1.** Sound uttered by the mouth, esp. human utterance in speaking, shouting, singing, etc., as heard a ~, did not recognize his ~, cried out in a loud ~, has lost her (esp. singing) ~, is not in ~ (proper vocal condition for singing or speaking), CHEST², HEAD¹, ~, the ~ of the cuckoo, veiled ~ (due to malformation etc.) see, storm, lifts up the ~, whence -VOICED² (-st) a. **2.** Use of the ~, utterance esp. in spoken or (fig.) written words, opinion so expressed, right to express opinion, as gave ~ to his indignation in a pamphlet, dog gave ~ to his joy, took it (natural phenomenon, calamity, popular outcry, etc.) for the ~ (expression of the will, resentment, etc.) of God, I count on your ~ (spoken or written support), I have no ~ in the matter, refused with one ~ (unanimously); (arch., rhet.) my ~ is for peace. **3.** (phonet.) Sound uttered with resonance of vocal cords, not with mere breath. **4.** (gram.) Set of forms of a verb showing relation of the subject to the action, as ACTIVE, PASSIVE, MIDDLE, ~. **5.** v.t. Give utterance to, express, as was chosen to ~ their grievance, believe I am voicing the general sentiment when I say; (Mus.) regulate tone-quality of (organ pipes); (Phonet.) utter with ~, make sonant, as in p-p.). [vb f. n.) OF vois f. L vocem, nom. vox]

voice'ful (-sf-), a. (poet.). Sonorous. [-FUL]

voice'less (-sl-), a. Speechless, dumb, mute; (Phonet.) not voiced. Hence ~NESS n. [-LESS]

void, a., n., & v.t. **1.** Empty, vacant, as a ~ space, interval; (of office) vacant, as bishopric fell ~; (esp. Law, of deed, promise, contract, etc.) invalid, not binding, as null & ~; (poet., rhet.) ineffectual, useless; ~ of, lacking, free from, as a proposal wholly ~ of sense, his style is ~ of affectation. Hence ~LY² adv., ~NESS n. **2.** n. Empty space, as vanished into the ~, (fig.) the aching ~ of his heart, cannot fill the ~ made by death. **3.** v.t. Render invalid; emit (excrement etc.); (arch.) quit, evacuate. Hence ~ABLE a. [vb f. OF voider) perh. ult. f. L vacuus empty]

void'ance, n. Ejection from benefice; vacancy in benefice; voiding. [OF (prec., -ANCE)]

void'ĕd, a. In vbl senses, also (Her., of bearing) having the central area cut away so as to show the field. [-ED¹]

voile (vwahl, voil), n. A thin semi-transparent cotton, woollen, or silken dress material. [F, = veil]

vŏl'ant, a. (Zool.) flying, able to fly; (Her.) represented as flying; (poet.) nimble, rapid. [F, f. L volare fly, see -ANT]

Volapük' (-ook), n. **Vŏl'apuk** (-ook). Artificial international language invented about 1879 by J. M. Schleyer. Hence ~IST², 3) n. [Volapük (vol world + -a- + pük speech)]

vŏl'ar, a. (anat.). Of the palm or sole. [f. L vola palm, sole + -AR¹]

vŏl'atile, a. Evaporating rapidly, as ~ salts, (= ESSENTIAL) oil; (fig.) lively, gay, changeable, as ~ wit, writer,

disposition. Hence or cogn. ~NESS, vŏla-tĭl′ĭTY, nn. [OF (-il, -ile), f. L *volatilis* (*volare* -at- fly, +ILE)]

vŏlă′tĭliz|e, v.t. & i. (Cause to) evaporate. Hence or cogn. ~ABLE a., ~A′TION n. [-IZE]

vol-au-vent (see Ap.), n. Kind of rich raised pie. [F]

volcā′nō, n. (pl. ~es). Mountain, hill, having opening(s) in earth's crust through which lava, cinders, water, gases, etc., are expelled continuously or at intervals (*active, dormant, extinct, ~; submarine ~*, originating beneath sea & rising above surface by accumulation). Hence **vŏl′canism**(2), **vŏl′canist**(3), **volcanŏl′OGY**, nn., **volcanŏlŏ′gical** a. [It., f. L as VULCAN]

vōle[1], n., & v.i. (In some card-games) winning of all the tricks in a deal; (vb) win all the tricks. [vb f. n.) f. *voler* fly f. L *volare*]

vōle[2], n. Kinds of mouselike rodent; *water~*, large kind. [orig. *~mouse* field-mouse, cf. Icel *völlr*, Norw. *voll*, Sw. *vall*, field]

vŏl′et (-lā), n. Panel, wing, of triptych. [F.]

vŏl′itant a. (zool.) = VOLANT. [f. L *volitare* frequent. of *volare* fly, see -ANT]

vŏli′tion, n. Exercise of the will; power of willing. Hence ~AL, ~ARY[1], ~LESS, (-shǒ-), **vŏli′tĭve**, aa. ~ally[2] adv. [F, f. med. L *volitionem* (*velle* wish, pres. *volo*, see -TION)]

vŏlks′lied (f.., -lēt), n. Folk-song. [G]

vŏlks′raad (f.., -rāht), n. (hist.). Legislative assembly of Transvaal & Orange Free State. [S.-Afr. Du.]

vŏll′ey, n. (pl. ~s), & v.t. & i. 1. Simultaneous discharge of missiles, missiles so discharged; (fig.) noisy emission (of oaths etc.) in quick succession; (Tennis, Lawn tennis) return of ball in play before it touches ground; (Crick.) pitching of ball, ball pitched, right up to batsman or wicket without bouncing; *half~*, (Lawn tennis) return of ball as soon as it touches ground, (Crick.) ball so pitched that batsman may hit it as it bounces, hit so made, (v.t.) return, send, (ball, or abs.) made; *~gun*, machine gun discharging ~ thus; *~gun*, machine gun discharging ~ 2. vb. Discharge (missiles, abuse, etc., or abs.) in ~; (Tennis, Crick.) return, send, (ball, or abs.) in ~; (of missiles) fly in a ~; (of guns etc.) sound together. [(vb f. n.), f. F *volée* flight (as VOLE, cf. -ADE)]

vŏl′plane, n. & v.i. (Of aeroplane or its pilot) descent, descend, by gliding without use of engine. [f. F *vol plané* (*vol* flight, *planer* hover)]

vŏlt[1], v.i., & n. Make a volte; (n., var. of) VOLTE. [VOLTE]

vŏlt[2], n. Unit of electromotive force, the force that would carry one ampere of current against one ohm resistance. Hence ~METER n., instrument for measuring electric currents in ~s. [as VOLTA[1]]

vŏl′ta (f.., (mus.; pl. -te pr. -tā). *Una ~, due etc. volte*, once, twice etc.; *prima etc. ~*, first etc. time. [It.]

vŏl′tage, n. Electromotive force expressed in volts. [-AGE]

vŏltā′ic, a. (chiefly hist.). Of electricity produced by chemical action, galvanic, as *~ battery, cell*, PILE[2]. [f. A. Volta, Italian physicist, d. 1827, +IC]

Vŏltaĭr′ian|ism, nn. Principles of Voltaire, scepticism. [-IAN, -ISM]

vŏltam′ēter, n. Instrument for measuring electric currents by their electrolytic effects. [as VOLTA[1], -METER]

vŏlte, n. (Fenc.) quick movement to escape thrust; circular tread of horse. [F, f. It. *volta* turn]

vŏlte-face (-fahs), n. Turning round, esp. (fig.) complete change of front in argument, politics, etc. [F]

vŏl′ūb|le, a. (Of speech or speaker) fluent, glib, whence or cogn. **vŏlūbĭl′ITY**, ~le-NESS, nn., ~ly[2] adv.: (arch.) revolving, rotating; (Bot., also **vŏlū′bĭlate**[2] (-lō-), ~le, aa.) twisting round a support, twining. [F, f. L *volubilis* (*volvere* roll, see -BLE)]

vŏl′ūme, n. 1. Set of (usu. printed) sheets of paper bound together & forming part or the whole of a work or comprising several works (abbr. *vol.*), as *is now issued in 3 ~s, an odd ~ of Punch, library of 12,000 ~s*, SPEAK ~s (for): (Hist.) scroll of papyrus etc., ancient form of book. 2. (usu. pl.). Wreath, coil, rounded mass, of smoke etc. 3. Solid content, bulk, whence **vŏlu′mĭnal** (-lō-) a.; (Mus.) fullness of tone, Hence (~)**vŏlūmĭned**[2] (-md) a. [OF, f. L *volumen -minis* roll *volvere*, see prec.]

volūmēnŏm′ēter (-lō-), n. Instrument for measuring volume of a solid body by quantity of liquid etc. displaced. Hence ~ŎM′ETRY n. [irreg. f. L as prec. +-o- +METER]

volū′mēter (-lō-), n. Kinds of instrument for measuring volume of gas. Hence **vŏlumĕt′rĭc**(AL) aa., **vŏlumĕt′rĭcally**[2] adv. [irreg. f. VOLUME +-METER]

volū′minous (or -lō-), a. Having coils or convolutions (of snakes, the brain, etc.; now rare); consisting of many volumes, as *a ~ work*; (of writer) producing many books; of great volume, bulky, (of drapery etc.). Hence ample. Hence **volūminŏs′ITY**, ~NESS, nn., ~LY[2] adv. [f. LL *voluminosus* (as VOLUME, see -OUS)]

vŏl′untary, a. & n. 1. Done, acting, able to act, of one's own free will, not constrained, purposed, intentional, as *a ~ gift, there was no ~ mis-statement, was a ~*

agent in the matter, ~ *confession* (opp. to *compulsory*)
service, army, ~ *confession* (of criminal);
not prompted by promise or threat;
brought about, produced, etc., by ~
action, as ‖ ~ *school* (supported by ~
contributions), ~ *waste* (of property by
tenant's deliberate act or order); (of limb,
muscle, movement) controlled by the
will; (Law) (~ *conveyance* (made without
~ conveyance), ~ *partition* (by mutual
agreement, not by judgement of court).
Hence **vŏl'untarĭly** adv., **vŏl'untari-**
NESS n. 2. n. Organ solo played before,
during, or after service; one who holds
that the Church or the schools should be
independent of the State & supported by
~ contributions, whence ~ISM (3) n.,
reliance on ~ subscriptions & not on
State aid for the maintenance of education, reliance on ~ enlisting & not on
compulsion for raising naval & military
forces, ~ISM(2) n.; (in competitions) special
performance left to performer's choice.
[f. F *volontaire* f. L *voluntarius* (*voluntas*
free will f. *velle* will, part. st. *volent-*,
+ -*ant-*, -ARY¹)]

volŭnteer', n., & v.t. & i. 1. Spontaneous
undertaker of task etc.; person who
voluntarily enters military or other service, esp. member of any of the corps of
voluntary soldiers formerly organized in
U.K. & provided with instructors, arms,
etc., by government (often attrib., as ~
corps, manœuvres); (attrib., of vegetation) growing spontaneously. 2. Vb.
Undertake, offer, (one's services, remark,
explanation, etc., *to* do) voluntarily;
make voluntary offer of one's services (*for*
campaign, purpose); be a ~. [(vb f. n.)
as prec., W. assim. to -EER]

volŭp'tuary, a. & n. Concerned with,
(person) given up to, luxury & sensual
gratifications. [f. L *voluptu(a)arius* (as
foll., see -ARY¹)]

volŭp'tuous, a. Of, tending to, occupied
with, sensuous or sensual gratification, as
~ *life, liver, music, beauty*. Hence ~LY²
adv., ~NESS n. [f. L *voluptuosus* (*voluptas*
-atis pleasure, see -OUS; *-u-* as if f. vbl n.
in *-us*; cf. *sensuous*, & VIRTUOUS)]

vŏl'ute, n. & a. 1. Spiral scroll characteristic of Ionic, Corinthian, & Composite
capitals, whence ~ED² a.; kinds of
(chiefly tropical) gasteropod often with
beautiful shell, whence **vŏl'utŏid** a. & n.
2. adj. (bot.). Rolled up. [F, f. L *voluta*
(fig., of volcano, chimney, etc.) eject
(fem. of *volutus* volut-roll)]

volū'tion (-lōō-), n. Spiral turn; whorl(s)
of spiral shell; (Anat.) convolution. [as
prec., -TION]

vŏm'er, n. (anat.). The small thin bone
partitioning the nostrils in man and most
vertebrates. [L, = ploughshare]

vŏm'it, v.t. & i. & n. 1. Eject from
stomach through mouth; puke, spew;

violently, belch forth. 2. n. Matter
vomited from stomach; emetic; *black* ~,
(black substance ~ed in) yellow fever;
~ *-nut*, = NUX VOMICA. [(n. f. L *vomitus*

vŏm'itory, a. & n. 1. Emetic (a. & n.), so
vŏm'itīve a. 2. n. (Rom. ant.). Each of a
series of passages for entrance & exit in
(amphi)theatre. [f. L *vomitorius* a., *-um*
n., (as prec., see -ORY]

vŏmĭturĭ'tion, n. Ineffectual attempt to
vomit, retching; repeated vomiting.
[irreg. f. L *vomere* ~ed from stomach]

vŏō'doo, n., & v.t. 1. Use of, belief in,
witchcraft & the like prevalent among
W.-Ind. & U.S. creoles & Negroes; (also
~ *doctor*, ~ *priest*) person skilled in this.
Hence ~ISM, ~ISM(2, 3), m. 2. v.t. Affect
by ~, bewitch. [(vb f. n.) Afr. *vodu*]

vorā'cious (-shŭs), a. Greedy in eating,
ravenous, (lit. & fig.), as *partly of* ~
trippers, *a* ~ *appetite for scandal*, *a* ~
whirlpool. Hence or cogn. ~LY² adv.,
~NESS, **vorā'city**, nn. [f. L *vorax*
-*acis* (*vorare* devour, see -ACIOUS)]

-vora. See -VOROUS.

-vore. See foll.

-vorous, suf. f. L *-vorus* (*vorare* swallow)
+ -OUS, forming adji. w. sense ' feeding
on ', as *carni-* ~, *omni-* ~; also *-vora*, in L
neut. pl. names of animals classified by
their food, as *herbivora*; also F & E *-vore*
forming name of individual of such class,
as *carnivore*.

vŏr'tex, n. (pl. *-ices*, *-exes*). Mass of
whirling fluid, esp. whirlpool; (Physics)
portion of fluid whose particles have
rotatory motion; any whirling motion
or mass, esp. (fig.) system, pursuit, etc.,
viewed as swallowing up or engrossing
those who approach it, as *the* ~*ex of
society*, ~*ex* (spiral arrangement of fibres
at apex) *of the heart*; ~*ex-ring*, ~*ex* whose
axis is a closed curve, e.g. smoke-ring
puffed from smoker's lips or pipe. Hence
~**iCAL**, ~**iCOSE**, ~**ic'ular**¹ [-UL-], aa.,
~**iCALLy**² adv. [L, var. of VERTEX]

vŏr'ticel, n. Bell-shaped animalcule
found in stagnant water etc. [dim. f.
prec.]

vŏr'ticist, n. (Metaphys.) person regarding the universe, with Descartes, as a
plenum in which motion propagates itself
in circles; (Art) painter of recent school
using vortices as the CUBIST uses cubes
etc. So ~ISM n. [f. *vortic-* st. of L VORTEX
+ -IST]

vor'tiginous, a. Whirling, vortical. [f.
L VERTIGO, *vor-*, + -OUS]

vot'arÿ, n. Person vowed to the service
of (God etc.); ardent follower, devoted
adherent or advocate, (*of* system, pursuit, etc.). Hence ~NESS¹ n. [f. L as foll.
+ -ARY¹]

vote, n., & v.i. & t. 1. Formal expression
of will or opinion in regard to election
of officer etc., sanctioning law, passing

resolution, etc., signified by ballot, show of hands, voice, or otherwise, as *shall give my* ~ *to or for the Labour candidate, passed without a dissentient* ~, CAST[1] ~, SPLIT[1] one's ~, CASTING-VOTE, TRANSFERABLE ~; opinion expressed, money granted, by majority of ~s, as *Government received a* ~ *of confidence, the army* ~; *the collective* ~s *given or to be given by a party etc., as will lose the Labour* ~, *Conservative* ~, *the floating* ~ (of persons not attached to a party; *the right to* ~, *as women now have the* ~; ticket etc, used for recording ~. Hence ~'LESS a. **2.** vb. Give a ~ *(for, against, person or measure)*; enact, resolve, *(that)*, grant *(sum)*, by majority of ~s; *(colloq.)* pronounce, declare, by general consent, as *was* ~d *a failure*; *(colloq.)* propose *(that)*; ~ *down, defeat (measure)* by ~s; ~ *in*, elect by ~s. Hence VO'TABLE a., VO'TER[1] n. [n.f. neut. p.p. as noun = wish) f. L *votīre* vot- vow]

vō'ting, n. [see -ING[1]]

vō'tive, a. Offered, consecrated, in fulfilment of a vow, as ~ *offering, tablet, picture*. [f. L *votīvus* (as VOTE, see -IVE)]

vouch, v.t. & i. Confirm, uphold, *(statement)* by evidence or assertion; answer *for*, be surety for, as *will* ~ *for the truth of this, for him or his honesty, can* ~ *for it that no step was taken.* [f. OF *vocher* f. L *vocāre* call]

vouch'er, n. In vbl senses, esp. document, receipt, etc., establishing the payment of money or the truth of accounts. [AF *(prec.* -ER[4])]

vouchsafe', v.t. Condescend to grant, as ~d *me no answer*, ~ *me a visit*; condescend *(to do).* [VOUCH + SAFE, = guarantee securely]

voussoir (vōō'swär), n. Each of the wedge-shaped stones forming an arch. [f. OF *vossoir*, ult. f. L *volvere* roll]

vow, n., & v.t. **1.** Solemn promise or engagement esp. in the form of an oath to God, as *baptismal* ~s *(given at baptism by baptized person or by sponsors), monastic* ~ *(by which monk binds himself to poverty, celibacy & obedience), lovers'* ~s *(promises of fidelity), am under (have taken) a* ~ *to drink no wine*; action, condition, etc., promised by ~, *as is this your* ~? **2.** v.t. Promise solemnly *(thing, conduct)*, as ~*ed a temple to Apollo, vow'ed obedience; vengeance against the oppressor; (arch.)* utter, make, *a* ~; declare solemnly *(that)* (arch.) declare, as *I* ~ *you are most obliging.* [f. OF *vou, veu*, f. L as VOTE]

vow'el, n. Each of the more open sounds uttered in speaking, sound capable of forming a syllable, *(opp. to* CONSONANT); letter representing this, as *a, e, i, o, u; neutral* ~ *(heard in second syllable of cousin,*

reason, haddock); ~ *gradation*, = ABLAUT; ~ *mutation*, = UMLAUT; ~ *point*, each of a set of marks indicating ~s in Hebrew & other Oriental languages. Hence (~)-l-ED< (-ld), ~LESS, ~LY[2], aa. [f. OF *vouel* f. L *vocālis (littera)* VOCAL (letter)]

vow'elize, v.t. Insert the vowels in (Hebrew etc., shorthand). [-IZE]

vōx, n. ~ *barb'ara* (Anat., Bot., etc.), hybrid or incorrectly formed word; ~ *et praet'ěrěa ně'hil*, a voice & nothing more (i.e., esp. an empty word); ~ *hāma'na* (-mā-, -mah-), organ-stop with tones supposed to resemble human voice; ~ *pŏp'ŭlī*, the people's voice (i.e. public opinion, the general verdict, popular belief, or rumour). [see VOICE]

voy'age, n., & v.i. & t. **1.** Journey, esp. long one, by sea or water; *broken* ~*e, unsuccessful whaling etc.* ~e. **2.** vb. Travel, traverse, by water. Hence ~EABLE (-ĭjo-)a., ~ER[1] n. [(vb f. F *voyager*) f. OF *voiage* f. L VIATICUM]

voyageur (vwahyahzhér'), n. Man employed in transportation of goods & passengers between trading posts in the Hudson's Bay territory; Canadian boatman. [F]

vraisemblance (vrāsahnblahns'), n. Appearance of truth, plausible appearance, verisimilitude. [F]

vril, n. A natural wonder-working force assumed in Lytton's *The Coming Race* to have been discovered. [arbitrary]

Vul'can, n. (Rom. Myth.) god of fire & metal-working; ~ *powder*, an explosive. [f. L *Volcānus, Vu-*]

vulcan'ic etc. See vol-.

vul'canist, n. (geol.). Holder of PLUTONIC theory. [f. F *vulcanisle* (VULCAN, -IST)]

vul'canite, n. Hard vulcanized rubber, ebonite. [-ITE[1]]

vul'caniz|e, v.t. Treat (rubber) with sulphur at high temperature to increase elasticity & strength & yield hard or soft flexible rubber. Hence ~ABLE a., ~A'TION, ~ER[1](1, 2), nn. [-IZE]

vul'gar, a. Of, characteristic of, the common people, plebeian, coarse, low, as *of expressions, mind, tastes, finery, an air of* ~ *prosperity, the* ~ HERD[1], (abs.) *the* ~, the common people; in common use, generally prevalent, as ~ *errors, superstitions, the* ~ (national, esp. formerly as opp. to Latin) *tongue*, ~ FRACTION, *the (Christian) era.* Hence or cogn. ~ISM(4, 2), vulga'rITY, nn., ~LY[2] adv. ff. L *vulgāris*, *vō-* *(vulgus, vo-*, common people, see -AR[1])]

vul'gariz|e, v.t. Make (person, manners, etc.) vulgar, infect with vulgarity; spoil (scene, sentiment, etc.) by making too common or frequented or well known. Hence ~A'TION n. [VULGAR + -IZE (3)]

vul'gar|ian, n. Vulgar (esp. rich) person. [-IAN]

Vul'gate, n. Latin version of the Bible

prepared by Jerome late in the 4th c. [f. L *vulgata* (*editio* edition), fem. p.p. of *vulgare* make public (see VULGAR)] verse-exercise in some schools. [corrupt. of 16th-c. ... passages = vulgar-tongue (i.e. English) passages for rendering into Latin]

vul'nerable, a. That may be wounded (lit. & fig.); susceptible of injury, not proof against weapon, criticism, etc.; (Contract Bridge) having won one game towards rubber & therefore being liable to higher penalties. Hence ~BILITY, ~ABLENESS, nn. [f. LL *vulnerabilis* (*vulnerare* wound f. *vulnus* -*eris* wound, see -BLE]

vul'nerary, a. & n. (Drug, unguent, etc.) useful or used for healing wounds. [f. L *vulnerarius* (*vulnus*, see prec. & -ARY¹)]

vul'pine, a. Of (the nature of) a fox, so ~IDE(1, 2) n.; crafty, cunning. [f. L *vulpinus* (*vulpes* fox, see -INE¹)]

vul'tur|e, n. Kinds of large bird of prey with head & neck more or less bare of feathers feeding chiefly on carrion; (fig.) rapacious person. Hence or cogn. ~INE¹, ~ISH¹, ~OUS, aa., (-cher-), [f. L *vultur*]

vul'va, n. (anat.). Opening, orifice, esp. of female genitals. Hence ~AR¹, ~ATE² aa., ~IFORM, aa., ~ITIS n., ~o- comb. form. [L]

vying. See VIE.

W

W (dŭb'l yōō), letter (pl. Ws, W's).

‖Waac (wăk), n. (colloq.). Member of Women's Army Auxiliary Corps (organized in 1917). [f. initials]

‖Waaf (wăf), n. (colloq.). Member of the Women's Auxiliary Air Force (organized in 1939). [f. initials]

wabble. See WOBBLE.

wäc'ke (-ke), n. Kind of greyish-green or brownish clay resulting from decomposition of volcanic rock. [G, f. MHG *wacke* large stone]

wad (wŏd), n., & v.t. (-dd-). 1. Small lump of soft material used to keep things apart or in place or to stuff up opening, esp. disk of felt etc. keeping powder or shot compact in gun; *(sl.) roll of notes, money. 2. v.t. Press (cotton etc.) into ~ or wadding; line (garment, coverlet), protect (person, walls, etc.), with wadding (also fig., as *well* ~*ded with conceit*); stop up (aperture, gun-barrel), keep (powder etc.) in place, with ~; ram (~)home. [cf. Sw. *vadd* wadding, G *watte*]

wadding (wŏd'-), n. Spongy material used for stuffing, to pack fragile articles in, quilts, etc., or to stuff garments, of cotton or wool used to stuff garments, cotton wool; material from which gun-wads are made. [-ING¹]

waddle (wŏd'l), v.i., & n. 1. Walk with

wa'ffle (wŏ-), n. Small batter cake baked in ~-iron, special utensil. [f. WAFER]

waft (wahft, wŏ-), v.t. & n. 1. Convey (as) through air or over water, sweep smoothly & lightly along. 2. n. Single sweep of bird's wing; whiff of odour; fugitive sensation of peace, joy, etc.; (Naut., also *waft*) distress signal, e.g. ensign rolled or knotted or garment flown in rigging; [back form. f. obs. *wafter* convoying-ship prob. f. Du. *wachter* a guard (*wachten* to wait, watch)]

wag¹, v.t. & i. (-gg-), & n. 1. Shake (t. & i., of thing attached by one end, as tail) to & fro, oscillate, (*dog* ~*s his tail*, in sign of pleasure; *tail was* ~*ging*; *tail* ~*s dog*, least important member of society or section of party has control); ~ *one's finger at*, in reproof etc.; ~ *one's head*, in derision or amusement; *beards, chins, jaws, tongues, are* ~*ging*, talk going on); (arch., of the wind, times, etc., go along with varied fortune or characteristics (*how* ~*s the world?*); ~'*tail*, kinds of small

the rocking motion natural to fat short-legged person or to bird with short legs set far apart as duck or goose; hence ~ing gait. [WADE

wa'ddy (wŏ-), n. Australian war-club. [native]

wade, v.i. & t., & n. 1. Walk through water or other impeding medium as snow, mud, sand (also fig., as ~ *through slaughter* or *blood*, make one's way by massacre etc.; ~ *through book*, read it in spite of dullness etc.; ~ *in*, make vigorous attack on one's opponent); ~ *into*, attack energetically); ford (stream) on foot, whence ~ABLE a.; *wading bird*, long-legged water-bird that ~s (opp. short-legged web-footed swimmers). 2. n. Spell of wading. [OE *wadan* wade, trudge, cf. Du. *waden*, G *waten*; cogn. w. L *vadere* go, *vadum* ford]

wa'der, n. In vbl senses; esp.: wading bird (see prec.); (pl.) high waterproof boots worn in fishing. [-ER¹]

wa'di, -y, (wah-), n. Rocky watercourse dry except in rainy season (chiefly of Eastern countries). [Arab. *wádi*]

Wa'd (-ah-), n. The extreme Nationalist party in Egypt. Hence ~IST a. & n. [Arab.]

wa'fer, n., & v.t. 1. Kind of very thin sweet honeycomb-faced biscuit now chiefly eaten with ices (*thin as a* ~, whence ~Y² a.); thin disk of unleavened bread used in Eucharist; small disk of dried paste formerly used for fastening letters, holding papers together, etc.; disk of red seal. 2. v.t. Attach or seal with ~. [f. ONF *waufre* (cf. GOFER, GOFFER) f. MLG *wâfel* (cf. foll.), perh. cogn. w. G *wabe* honeycomb]

bird (*pied*, *yellow*, etc., ~*tail*) with long tail in constant motion. **2. n.** Single ~*ging* motion (*with a* ~ *of his tail*, *head*, etc.). [ME *wagian* f. root of OE *wagian* rock]

wag², n. Facetious person, one given to jesting or practical jokes; ‖ (sl.) truant (esp. *play* ~ *or the* ~). Hence ~**g'ERY** (4) **n.**, ~**g'ISH³ a.**, ~**g'ISHLY²** adv., ~**g'ISHNESS** **n.** (~*g-*). [prob. for obs. *wag-halter* gallows-bird (prec. yb)]

wāge¹, n. Amount paid periodically, esp. by the day or week or month, for time during which workman or servant is at employer's disposal (usu. pl. exc. in certain phrr.; *gets good* ~*s*; *brings his* ~*s home*; *at a* ~ or ~*s of £5 a week*; *living* ~=that allow earner to live without fear of starvation; *a fair day's work for a fair day's* ~; *the* ~*s of sin is death*); requital (usu. pl.; *the* ~*s of sin is death*); ~(*s*)-*fund* in Pol. Econ., part of community's capital devoted to paying ~*s* & salaries (the ~-*fund theory*, that ~*s* can rise only if either capital increases or population diminishes). [OF, = *guage* GAGE¹]

wāge², v.t. Carry on (war, conflict); (arch.) sense *declare* (*war*) f. ONF *wagier* (prec.)]

wā'ger, n., & v.t. **1.** =BET n. & v.t. (but not now in familiar use). **2.** (hist.). ~ *of battle*, ancient form of trial by personal combat between parties or champions; ~ *of law*, COMPURGATION. [f. OF *wageure* (as prec., -URE)]

wagg'le, v.i. & v.t., & n. =WAG¹ (but in more familiar use); esp. (Golf) of swinging club-head to & fro over ball before playing shot. Hence **wāgg'ly²** a., unsteady. [-LE(3)]

wǎg(g)'on, n. Four-wheeled vehicle for drawing heavy loads, often with removable semicylindrical tilt or cover, usu. drawn by two or more horses (*hitch* one's ~ *to a star*, utilize powers higher than one's own); ‖ open railway truck; ~ -*boiler*, -*ceiling*, -*roof*, -*vault*, shaped like ~ -tilt. [f. Du. *wagen*, cf. OE *wægn* WAIN]

wǎg(g)'oner, n. Driver of wagon; *the* W~, constellation Auriga. [-ER¹]

wǎg(g)onĕtte', n. Four-wheeled open pleasure vehicle (or with removable cover) for one or more horses & with facing side seats. [-ETTE]

wǎgon-lit (văgawnlē'), n. Sleeping-car on continental railway. [F]

Waha'bī, -ee, (-hahbē'), n. One of a sect of Mohammedan puritans following the letter of the Koran. [Abd-el-*Wahhab*, founder c. 1760]

waif, n. Ownerless object or animal, thing cast up by or drifting in sea or brought by unknown agency; homeless & helpless person, esp. unowned or abandoned child; ~*s & strays*, odds & ends, unowned or neglected children. [AF, prob. of Scand. orig., cf. ON *veif* thing flapping about; n. corresp. to WAIVE]

wail, v.i. & t., & n. (Lament, i. & t., with) prolonged plaintive inarticulate usu. high-pitched cry; (fig.) lamentation in words (often *over*); (of wind etc.) sound (v. & n.) like person ~*ing*; ~*ing wall*, *place*, part of the Solomonic wall at Jerusalem where the Jews assemble to bewail the destruction of the Temple. Hence ~**FUL²** a. (poet.), ~**'ing LY²** adv. [cf. ON *væla* (*væ* int., see WOE)]

wain, n. Wagon (chiefly poet. or agricultural); *Charles's*, *Arthur's*, *or the* W~, CHARLES'S WAIN. [f. OE *wægn*, cf. Du. & G *wagen*; cogn. w. L *vehere* carry, Skr. *vahana* vehicle, Gk *okhos* car, & WEIGH]

wain'scot, n., & v.t. **1.** Wooden panelling or boarding on room-wall. **2.** v.t. Line with ~, whence ~**ING⁴**(3) n. [earlier sense *kind of oakwood*, f. MLG *wagenschot* perh. f. *wagen* wagon; for *schot* boarding cf. CAMPSHOT]

waist, n. **1.** Part of human body below ribs & above hips (*large*, *small*, ~, of such circumference; *long*, *short*, ~, of such vertical extent). **2.** Contraction marking this in normal figure (*has no* ~, of stout person); analogous contraction in middle of long object, e.g. fiddle or hour-glass. **3.** Part of ship between forecastle & quarter-deck. **4.** Part of garment encircling ~, band round ~ from which petticoats etc. may be suspended; *bodice*. **5.** ~*-cloth*, = LOIN-*cloth*; ‖ ~*-coat* (wās(t)'kŏt, wĕs'kŏt), garment reaching down to ~ with front showing when coat is open & usu. without sleeves (*sleeved* ~*coat*, with sleeves for extra warmth or for use without coat by workmen); ~*-deep* or -*high* aa. & advv., up to ~. Hence (-)~**ED²** a., **~band** (WAX²), cf. Goth. *vahstus* growth]

wait¹, v.i. & t. **1.** Abstain from action or departure till some expected event occurs, pause, tarry, stay, kick one's heels, be expectant or on the watch, (often *for*, *till*; ~ *a minute*; *shall not* ~ *here any longer*; *kept me* ~*ing* or *made me* ~; *have a month to* ~ *yet*; ~ *till I come*, *for high water* or *a fine day*; *everything comes to those who* ~; *always has to be* ~*ed for*, is unpunctual; *you must* ~ *my convenience*; *am only* ~*ing the signal*). **3.** Act as waiter, as servant shifting plates etc. at table, (*are you accustomed to* ~*ing?*; *often at table*), (*wait at table*). **2.** Await, bide, (*is* ~*ing his opportunity*; *you must* ~ *your time*; ~ *orders*). **4.** Defer (meal) till someone arrives (*don't* ~ *dinner for me*). **5.** ~*-a-bit* (fr. Afrikaans *wag-'n-bietje*), kinds of S.-Afr. shrub with hooked thorns; ~ (*up*)*on*, watch (arch.), await convenience of, serve as attendant esp. at table, pay visit to (person regarded as superior), escort (arch.), (in race) purposely keep close behind (competitor), follow as result; ~*ing-room*, provided for persons to ~ in esp. at railway-station or

house of consultant. [f. OF *guetter* (now *guetter*) f. OHG *wahtên*, to watch (cogn. w. WAKE¹)]

wait² n. 1. pl. Official bands of musicians maintained by a city or town (hist.); street singers of Christmas carols. 2. Act or time of waiting (*had a long ~ for the train*); watching for enemy, ambush, (*lie in* or *lay ~* usu. *for*). [sense 1 f. OF *waite* sentinel f. OF as prec.; sense 2 f. prec.]

wait'er, n. 1. pl. In vbl senses; also or esp. man who takes & executes orders, shifts plates, etc., at hotel or restaurant tables, whence **wait'ress¹** n. fem. ~; [-ER¹] DUMB¹~; TIDE~.] 1 n; tray, salver;

waive, v.t. Forbear to insist on or use, (right, claim, opportunity, legitimate plea, etc.). Hence **waiv'ER¹** n (legal). [AF *weyver* f. OF *gaiver* make into a WAIF]

wake¹, v.i. & t. (past *woke*, ~d; p.p. *woken*, *woke*). 1. Cease to sleep, rouse from sleep, (often *up*; also fig., as *spring ~s all nature, nature ~s*); be awake (arch. exc. in part. or gerund, as *in his waking hours, waking or sleeping; waking dream, day-dream, reverie*); cease or rouse from sloth, torpidity, inactivity, or inattention (usu. *up*; *~ up there!; wants something to rise or rouse from the dead*. 2. (chiefly Ir.) Hold wake over. 3. Disturb (silence, place) with noise, make re-echo. 4. ~*robin*, wild arum or lords-&-ladies, [mixture of OE *wǽcan wōc* arise, be born, & *wacian* wake, watch, cf. Du. *waken*, cogn. w. VIGIL, VEGETABLE]

wake² n. 1. Vigil commemorating church dedication, merry-making or fair on the occasion, (hist.); || annual holiday in northern England. 2. (Ir.) || Watch by corpse before burial, lamentations & merry-making in connexion with it. [perh. f. ON *vaka* vigil, cogn. w. prec.]

wake³, n. Strip of smooth water left behind moving ship (*in the ~ of*, behind, following, after the example of). [f. ON *vaka* opening in ice, cogn. w. Gk *hugros*, L *humidus*, wet]

wake'ful (-kf-), a. Unable to sleep, (of person's night etc.) passed with little or no sleep; vigilant. Hence ~LY² adv., ~NESS n. [WAKE¹, -FUL]

wak'en, v.i. & t. Cause to be, become, awake (usu. = *wake up*, but conveying less of abruptness). [OE *wæcnan* (~-an WAKE¹)]

Walach, Wall-, (wŏl'ak), n. = VLACH. Hence **Wal(l)achian** (wŏlak'ian) a. (of the ~s or of Walachia, a principality now forming part of Rumania) & n. (= ~, also the language of the ~s). [see VLACH]

Walden'ses (wŏ-, -z), n. pl. Puritan sect in valleys of Piedmont, Dauphiné, & Provence, started c. 1170 & much persecuted in 16th & 17th cc. Hence ~IAN a. & n. [Peter *Waldo* of Lyons, founder]

wāle, weal, n., & v.t. 1. Ridge raised on flesh by stroke of rod or whip; || *wale-knot* (in *wale-knot*, made at end of rope by intertwining strands to prevent unravelling or act as stopper. 2. v.t. Raise ~ on; (Mil., *wale*) weave (a hurdle or gabion). Hence **wāl'ING¹** n. hurdlework used as revetment. [OE *walu* stripe, ridge, cf. OFris. *walu*, ON *vǫlr*; rod; also GUNWALE, CHANNEL²]

Wāl'er, n. Horse imported for Indian army from New South Wales. [N.S. Wales]

Wāles (-lz), n. Principally inhabited by the Welsh (*Prince of ~*, title usu. conferred on heir-apparent of Great Britain). [OE *Wealas* pl. of *wealh* see WELSH¹]

Walhalla. See VALHALLA.

walk¹ (wawk), v.i. & t. 1. (Of men) progress by advancing each foot alternately never having both of ground at once (*heel-&-toe ~ing*, in which both heel & toe are used, as required in ~*ing-races*; ~ *backwards, sideways*, go in those directions with analogous motions; ~ *over course* or ~ *over*, have WALK²-over; ~ *away from*, easily out-distance), go with the gait usual except when speed is desired (~*ing DICTIONARY*); (of animals) go with slowest gait corresponding to human walk. 2. Travel or go on foot (~ *into*, eat heartily of; ~ *off*, depart, esp. abruptly); *~ off* or *away with*, carry off, steal.; *~ out on person*, leave him). 3. (arch). Live with or in specified principle or manner, conduct oneself, (~ *in love, humbly, honestly, after the flesh, by faith, with God*, etc.). 4. Perambulate, tread, floor or surface of, (*Him that ~ed the waves*; ~ *the streets*, in gen. sense, also be prostitute; ~ *the boards*, be actor; ~ *the hospitals*, be medical student; ~ *the chalk*, prove sobriety to police etc. by ~*ing* straight between chalked lines), whence ~*ABLE* (wawk-) a. 5. Cause to ~ with one, have ~*ing-race* with, (~ *horse*, when riding or driving or leading it; ~ *policeman ~ed the man off; Smith will ~ Jones for £100 a side; you have ~ed me off my legs, tired out*). 6. (Of farmer etc.) take charge of (hound puppy). 7. ~*ING¹ chair* = go¹-*cart*; ~*ING² delegate*, trade-union official who visits sick members, interviews employers, etc.; ~*ING¹-dress*, for outdoor wear; ~*ING¹-fern*, N.-Amer. kind with slender-tipped fronds that bow down to ground & take root; ~*ING² gentleman, lady*, actor, actress, of part requiring good presence but no skill; ~*ING²-leaf*, insect imitating leaf;

~ING¹-papers or -ticket, sl., dismissal; ||~ING-stick, carried in ~ing; ~ING¹-tour, pleasure journey on foot. [OE wealcan roll, rove, cf. Du. walken press hats, Icel. vŏlka roll, G walken full cloth]

walk² (wawk), n. Walking gait, person's action in walking, (see prec.; *go at, never gets beyond, a ~*; *know him a walk off by his ~*); excursion on foot, stroll, constitutional, (*go for, take, a ~*; *across the hills from X to Z is a good ~*; *~over*, race in which from absence or inferiority of competitors winner can go at a ~ if he chooses, easy victory); person's favourite walking ground, round of hawker etc., place or track intended or suitable for strollers or foot-passengers, promenade, colonnade, footpath, (ROPE-~; SHEEP-~; *~*-out, workmen's strike. [f. prec.]

wa'lker (wawk-), n. In vbl senses: esp.: || SHOP-~; STREET-~; (class-name for) bird such as common fowl that neither flies nor swims, also bird that does not hop but walks on alternate feet. [-ER¹]

Wa'lkyrie. See VALKYRE.

wall (wawl), n., & v.t. **1.** Continuous & usu. vertical & solid structure of stones, bricks, concrete, timber, etc., narrow in proportion to length & height serving to enclose (partly) or protect or divide off town, house, room, field, etc., surface of inner side(s) of room, (*party* or *partition ~*, separating two rooms, houses, fields, etc.; *~ of partition*, fig., line of division, gulf; *blank ~*, without door or gate or window, also without decoration; *run one's head against a ~*, attempt impossibilities; *see through brick ~*, have miraculous insight; *~s have ears*, eavesdroppers are or may be about; *with one's back to the ~*, brought to bay, fighting alone against odds; RETAINING~). **2.** Something resembling ~ in appearance or effect (*mountain~*, line of steep hills; *~ of armed men, fire, bayonets*, protection or obstacle consisting of these; *cell-~, ~s of the chest etc.*, enclosing tissue or framework in Bot. or Anat.; *hanging, foot-*, in mining, upper, lower, rock enclosing lode). **3.** (Position next) ~ as opp. kennel side of street footpath (*give one the ~*, allow him cleaner part in passing; *take the ~ of*, refuse this courtesy to). **4.** Side as opp. centre of road (*the weakest goes to the ~*, is pushed aside, gets the worst in competition). **5.** *~creeper*, kinds of bird; *~cress*, kinds of plant growing in stony places; *~fern*, common polypody; *~flower*, fragrant spring garden-plant with usu. orange or brown clustered flowers, (colloq.) woman sitting out dances for lack of partners; *~fruit*, of trees fastened against ~ for protection & warmth; ||*~game*, an Eton form of football; *~painting*, on ~ usu. of room, esp. fresco; *~paper*, for pasting over room-~s, usu. with decorative printed patterns; *~pepper*, kind of stonecrop; *~plate*, timber laid in or on ~ to distribute pressure of girder etc.; *~rue*, small fern growing on ~s & rocks; *~washer*, plate used with tie-rod in supporting shaky ~; hence ~LESS (wawl-l) a. **6.** v.t. Provide or protect with ~ (esp. in p.p, as *~ed towns*); block up aperture etc. with ~. [OE weal f. L vallum rampart, palisade]

walla(h) (wŏl'a), n. (Anglo-Ind.). Person or thing employed about or concerned with something, -man, (BOX²-~; *competition-~*, Indian civilian appointed by competitive examination; *punkah-~*, servant who works punkah). [f. Hind. -wŏlā suf.=-ER¹(3)]

wa'llaby (wŏ-), n. Kinds of smaller kangaroo; *on the ~* (track), on tramp, unemployed; (pl. colloq.) Australians. [Austral.]

Wallach. See WALLACH.

wallaroo (wŏ-), n. Kinds of larger kangaroo. [Austral.]

wa'llet (wŏ-), n. (Arch.) bag for carrying personal necessaries, food, etc., on journey, esp. pilgrim's or beggar's scrip; small leather case holding repairing tools for bicycle etc., fishing-kit, papers, or other small articles; flat case for holding bank-notes etc. [etym. dub.; perh. by metathesis for WATTLE]

wall-eye (wawl'ī), n. Appearance of whitish opacity of eye caused by injury or disease; (loosely) eye showing abnormal amount of white owing to squint etc., or large & glaring as in some fishes. [back formation f. foll.]

wall-eyed (wawl'īd), a. Having wall-eye. [f. ON vagl-eygr (vagl unexpl., auga eye)]

|| **wall-knot.** See WALE.

Walloon' (wŏ-), n. & a. **1.** Member, language (a French dialect), of people scattered in Belgium & neighbouring parts of France. **2.** adj. Of the ~s or in their language. [f. OF Wallon f. Teut. wadh, cf. VLACH, WELSH]

wa'llop (wŏ-), v.t., & n. (sl.). **1.** Thrash, beat, hide; (part.) big, strapping, thumping. **2.** n. A heavy blow. Hence ~ING¹(1) n. [earlier senses gallop, boil, bubble, flounder; f. ONF as GALLOP]

wallow (wŏl'ō), v.i., & n. **1.** Roll about in mud, sand, water, etc. (*~ in money*, be very rich); take swinish or gross delight (in sensuality etc. **2.** n. Place to which buffaloes etc. resort to ~. [OE wealwian roll, cogn. w. L volvere]

Wa'llsénd (wawlz-), n. Kind of superior house-coal orig. from ~ on Tyne.

Wall Street (wawl), n. (Used for) the American money-market. [street in New York]

wa'lnut (wawl-), n. (Kinds of tree yielding) delicate-flavoured nut in pair of similar boat-shaped shells (*over the ~s*

& the wine, at dessert); timber of ~-tree used in cabinet-making & for gunstocks. [f. OE *wealh* foreign, Gaulish (cf. WELSH¹), NUT]

Walpur'gis-night (vahlpoorgis-nït), n. Eve of 1st May, when witches meet at the Brocken or elsewhere & hold revels with the devil. [*Walpurgis*, female saint of 8th c.; connexion unknown]

wa'lrus (waw-, wŏ-), n. Kinds of large amphibious arctic long-tusked mammal related to seal, morse, sea-horse. [Du., prob. w. metath. f. Scand. (ON *hrosshvalr* kind of whale, *rosmhvalr* walrus)]

waltz (wawls), n., & v.i. **1.** Dance, or music for it, in triple time with graceful flowing melody & one harmony in each bar. **2.** v.i. Dance ~; dance *in*, *out*, *round*, etc., in joy etc.; hence ~'ER¹ (wawls-) n. [f. G *walzer* (*walzen* revolve)]

wampee' (wŏ-), n. (Tree yielding) grape-like fruit grown in China & E. Indies. [Chin. (*hwang* yellow, *pï* skin)]

wa'mpum (wŏ-), n. Beads made from shells & strung for money or decoration by N.-Amer. Indians. [f. N.-Amer. Ind. *wampumpeag* (*wampi* white, *-ompi* string)]

wan (wŏn), a. Pale, colourless, bloodless, looking worn or exhausted, (chiefly of persons or their complexion or look, or of sky or light); (arch., of night, water, etc.) dark, black. Hence ~'LY² adv., ~'NESS (-n-n-) n. [OE *wann*, *wonn*, dark, black, etym. dub.]

wand (wŏ-), n. Slender rod for carrying in hand or setting in ground as temporary mark (chiefly now of conjurer's or music conductor's baton, or of staff symbolizing some officials' authority). [f. ON *vöndr*, perh. cogn. w. WIND³ w. ref. to suppleness]

wa'nder (wŏ-), v.i. & t. **1.** Rove, stroll, go from country to country or from place to place without settled route or destination, (~*ing Jew*, supposed to be still living from when Christ said 'Thou shalt ~ on the earth till I return' as punishment for an insult, also person who never settles down, also kinds of climbing plant; ~*ing cells*, *abscess*, *kidney*, etc., moving about, normally or abnormally attached to place in body; ~*ing sailor*, kinds of climbing plant), whence ~'ER¹ (wŏ-) n. **2.** Stray, diverge from the right way lit. or fig., get lost, depart from home. **3.** Talk or think irrelevantly or disconnectedly or incoherently, stray from subject in hand, be inattentive or delirious. (*his wits are ~'ing*; ~*s in his talk*). **4.** Traverse desultorily (*you may ~ the world*, or usn. *the world through*, & not find such another). Hence ~'ING-(I-) n. (usu. pl.), ~'ingLY² adv. (wŏ-). [OE *wandrian* (WEND, -ER³), cf. G & LG *wandern*]

wa'nderlust (vahn'derlŏŏst), n. Eager desire or fondness for travelling or wandering. [G]

wanderoo' (wŏ-), n. Kind of Ceylon monkey. [Singhalese *wandēru*]

wane, v.i., & n. **1.** Decrease in size or splendour like moon after the full, lose power or vigour or importance or repute, decline. **2.** n. Process of waning (esp. *is on the ~*, declining). [OE *wanian* (*wan*, see WANT¹), & WANTON]

‖ **wangle** (wăng'gl), v.t., & n. (sl.). **1.** Secure (favour, desired result) by plausible means; show in the desired light, cook, fake, (report etc.). **2.** n. Act of ~ing. [etym. dub.; first recorded (1888) as printers' sl.]

‖ **wanion** (wŏn'yon), n. *With a ~ (to)*, imprecation (arch.). [var. of *waniand* part. of WANE (waning moon = unlucky hour)]

want¹ (wŏ-, wah-), n. Lack, absence; deficiency, of (*ship rotting for ~ of paint*; *shows great ~ of thought*, *care*, *sense*, *judgement*); need of, need of sustenance, poverty, (*is in ~ of money*, *a servant*, etc.; *living in the direst ~*; *is a severe but efficient teacher*); desire for thing as necessary to life or happiness or success or completion (whence ~'LESS a.), thing so desired, (*a man of few ~s*; *superfluities soon become ~s*; *its*, *supplies*, *a felt ~*; *can supply your ~s*). [f. ON *vant* neut. of *vanr* lacking, cf. OE *wan* (WANE)]

want² (wŏ-, wah-), v.i. & t. **1.** Be without or deficiency supplied with, fall short of, fall short by (specified amount) of specified limit, (part.) lacking *in* quality or unequal to requirements or absent or deficient or (orig. dial.) lacking in intelligence, (~*s*, *is ~ing in*, *judgement*; *fortunately he ~s the power to do it*; *what was ~ing*, ~*s the power to do it*; *what was wanting*; ~*s something*, or ~*s*, *of perfection*; *be found ~ing*, or ~*ing to the occasion*, one's duty, etc.; *head of statue is ~ing*; *statue ~s the head*; *infinitive ~ing*, *verb has none*; ~*s half a minute of the hour*, *an inch of the regulation measurement*). **2.** Be in want (*for*; *let him ~ for nothing*; *must not be allowed to ~*). **3.** Require (thing, ~*ing*, ~*s*, to be -ed, to do; *boy ~s the whip*, *whipping*, *is careful handling*; *it ~s careful handling*). **4.** Desire, wish for possession or presence of, (to do, thing, person; *don't ~ to go*; *I ~ some sugar*, *it done*, *you to try*; *call me if I am ~ed*; *is ~ed by the police*, *of suspected criminal etc.*; *tell Jones I ~ him*, *send him to me*). [f. ON *vanta* (prec.)]

wa'nting (wŏ-, wah-), prep. Without, minus, less, (~ *common honesty*, *nothing can be done*; *made a century* ~ *one run*). [-ING²; use of part. either abs., cf. NOTWITHSTANDING, or in ordinary agreement]

wa'nton (wŏ-), a., n. & v.i. **1.** Sportive, gambolling, playful, irresponsible, capricious, (~ *child*, *kid*, *wind*, *mood*);

luxuriant, unrestrained, wild, (~ *growth*, *ringlets*, *profusion*); licentious, unchaste, lewd, (*a ~ woman*; ~ *thoughts*); motiveless, serving no purpose, random, arbitrary, (~ *mischief*, *destruction*); hence ~LY² adv., ~NESS n. **2.** n. Unchaste woman or rarely man; (rare) playful child. **3.** v.i Sport, gambol, more capriciously; (rare) act lasciviously. [ME *wantoun*, *-towen* (*wan*, see WANE, used as pref. with sense *un-* as in obs. *wanhope* despair, OE *togen*, p.p. of *teon* draw, educate, cf. G *gezogen*)]

wap. See WHOP.

‖**waˈpentāke** (wŏ-), n. (Old name in Anglian districts for) hundred or division of shire. [OE *wǣpengetæc* f. ON *vápnatak* (*vápn* weapon, *tac* taking f. *taka* TAKE) w. ref. to brandishing of weapons as form of voting]

waˈpiti (wŏ-), n. N.-Amer. stag resembling red deer but larger. [f. Amer.-Ind. *wapitik* white deer]

‖**Wappens(chaw** (wah'penshaw), n.(Sc.) (Hist.) periodical muster & inspection of (men under arms in a particular district; (mod.) rifle-meeting. [f. *wapin* obs. form of *weapon* + *schaw* show n.]

war¹ (wŏr), n. **1** Quarrel usu. between nations conducted by force, state of open hostility & suspension of ordinary international law prevalent during such quarrel, military or naval attack or series of attacks, (fig.) hostility or contention between persons, (*civil ~*, between parts of one nation for supremacy; *cold ~*, unfriendly relations between nations characterized by hostile propaganda & attempted economic sabotage; ~ *of nerves*, attempt to wear down opponent by gradual destruction of morale, opp. SHOOTing ~; *private ~*, *feud ~*, carried on in defiance of laws of murder etc., or armed attack made by members of one State without government sanction upon another; *holy ~*, waged in support of some religious cause; *make* or *wage ~*, begin or carry on hostile operations; *declare ~*, announce that hostilities may be expected, often upon another nation, also fig. *upon institution, party, custom,* etc.; so *declaration of ~*; *drift into ~*; *be at ~*, engaged in hostilities with enemy or abs., also fig.; *roll back tide of ~*, repel invasion; *go to the ~s*, arch., serve as soldier; *carry the ~ into the enemy's country*, (fig.) make counter-accusations etc., not confine oneself to defence; *has been in the ~s*, usu. fig. of person who has been mauled physically or otherwise; *on a ~ footing*, of army, fleet, etc., with full establishment; ~ *to the knife*, struggle to the bitter end usu. between persons; *Secretary of State for War*, also *Secretary for War*, *War Secretary*, ‖ parliamentary head of War Office; *art of ~*, strategy & tactics; *trade of ~*, soldier's profession;

sineus of ~, money etc. for waging ~ or for effecting any object; TUG, CONTRABAND, COUNCIL, HONOUR⁴s, *of ~*; MAN¹-*of-~*; *laws of ~*, those recognized by civilized nations as limiting belligerents' action; *rights of ~*, those similarly permitting to belligerents certain acts illegitimate in peace; *the dogs of ~*, poet., havoc attending ~; ~*s & rumours of ~s*, prevalence of the appeal to force among nations; ~ *of the elements*, storms & catastrophes in nature; *all's* FAIR² *in love & ~*. **2**, = ~ *baby*, illegitimate child attributable to ~ conditions; ~-*cloud*, position of international affairs that threatens ~; ~-*cry*, phrase or name formerly shouted in charging or rallying to attack, party catchword, savages' battle-shout; ~-*dance*, indulged in by savages before ~; ~-*game*, = KRIEGSPIEL; ~-*god*, one worshipped as giving victory in ~, esp. the Greek Ares or Roman Mars; ~-*head*, explosive head of torpedo or similar weapon; ~-*horse*, charger (arch. & poet. exc. in phr. *like an old ~-horse*, of person excited by memories of abandoned pursuit or controversy); ~-*lord* (rhet.), great captain (esp. of William II of Germany, & of Chinese civil-war generals); ‖ *War Office*, State department in charge of army; ~-*paint*, put on body by savages before battle, (fig.) ceremonial costume, full fig; ~-*path*, (route of) warlike expedition of Amer. Indians (*be, go, on the ~-path*, fig., be engaged in, enter upon, any conflict, have taken, take, up the cudgels); ~-*ship*, for use in ~; ~-*song*, sung by savages before battle, also any song on martial theme; ~-*whoop*, yell esp. of Amer. Indians in charging; ~-*worn*, experienced in or damaged or exhausted by ~. [f. OF *werre* (now *guerre*) f. OHG *werra* confusion (*werran* embroil, cf. G *verwirren* confuse); cogn. W. WORSE]

war² (wŏr), v.i. & t.(-rr-). Make war (arch.); bring or beat *down* by war; (part.) rival, competing, inconsistent, (~*ring creeds, principles*), [f. prec.]

warˈble¹ (wŏr-), v.i. & t., & n. **1.** Sing (i. & t.) in gentle continuous trilling manner (esp. of birds, also of person or sound); speak, utter, in manner suggestive of bird's song; relate in verse. **2.** n. ~*ed song* etc.; ~*ing voice* (*spoke in a ~e*). [f. OF *werble(r)* f. OHG *werbel* a rattle etc. (cf. MHG *wirbel* whirlpool, & WHIRL)]

warˈble² (wŏr-), n. Hard lump on horse's back from galling of saddle; (tumour produced by) larva of gadfly. [cf. MSw. *varbulde* boil (*var* pus, *bulde* tumour)]

warˈbler (wŏr-), n. In vbl senses; esp., many kinds of small bird including nightingale, blackcap, robin, redstart, & hedge-sparrow, some not remarkable for song. [-ER¹]

ward¹ (wŏrd), n. **1.** Act of guarding or

defending, place etc. (now only in *keep watch &c.*). **2.** Guard or parry in fencing (arch.). **3.** Confinement, custody, guardian's control, (arch.; *is under ~*; *put him in ~*; *to whom the child is in ~*). **4.** Minor under care of guardian or Court of Chancery. **5.** Administrative division of city. **6.** Separate room or division in prison (*condemned* etc. *~*) or workhouse (*isolation* etc. *~*). **7.** pl. Notches & projections in key and lock designed to prevent opening by wrong key. **8.** *~-mote*, meeting of city ward. [OE *mót* meeting(1); *~room*, meeting-room, in warship for commissioned officers below commanding officer. [OE *weard* watching, cf. OHG *warta*; a doublet of GUARD]

ward[2] (wôrd), v.t. Have in keeping, protect, (chiefly now of God); parry (blow, often off), keep off (danger, poverty, etc.). [OE *weardian* (prec.)]

-ward(s) (-ward, -dz), suf. repr. OE *weard* t. OE *weorthan* become, turn to, past *weard*; cf. L *versus* towards, f. the cogn. *vertere* turn. In OE compds of *-weard* were orig. adjj., the adj. used occas. becoming obs. & being redeveloped in later E f. the adv., as in *forward*. *-ward* formed adv. & prep. by addition of *-ES*, often more or less loc., as *backwards, bedward, Perthwards*. In older E *-ward* could in some cases be separated f. its component, as in *to usward*. Mod. E retains many adjj. & advv. in *-ward* as *backward, forward, northward, homeward*, advv. in *-wards, towards*, & the prep. *towards* (less usu. *-ward*); as living suffixes, *-ward, -wards*, form extempore adjj. & advv., as GUARD]

war'den[1] (wôr-), n. Watchman, sentinel, (arch.); member of civilian organization for assisting the civil population in air raids; guardian, president, governor of (in obs. or existent titles, as *W~ of the Marches, Merton College* etc., *the Cinque Ports*), whence *~SHIP* n. [f. OF *wardein* as GUARDIAN]

war'den[2] (wôr-), n. Kind of cooking pear. [perh. f. AF *warder* to guard, = keeping pear]

war'der (wôr-), n. ||Sentinel (arch.); ||jailor, whence **war'dress**[1] (wôr-), n.; (Hist.) staff of authority carried by king or commander & occas. used to give signals. [AF *wardour* (WARD[2], -OR[2])]

War'dour Street (wôrder), n. A London street noted for antique furniture etc. (*~ English*, affectedly archaic).

ward'robe (wôr-), n. Place where clothes are kept, esp. large cabinet or movable cupboard with pegs, shelves, etc.; person's stock of clothes; *~ dealer*, dealer in second-hand clothes; *~ trunk* (fitted with drawers, coat-hangers, etc., & designed to stand on end, serving as *~*). [f. OF *warderobe* (as GUARD[2] ROBE)]

war'dship (wôr-), n. Tutelage, guardian's care, (*under ~*; *has the ~ of*). [WARD[1], -SHIP]

ware[1], n. **1.** Things manufactured for sale, esp. pottery of any kind (otherwise usu. in comb. as *HARD~, tin~*); (pl.) articles that person etc. has for sale (usu. *his* etc. *~s*); (with distinctive epithet) kind of manufactured material esp. pottery, named from inventor, place of manufacture, or some characteristic (*Wedgwood, Delft, black*, etc. *~*). **2.** *~house* (-s) n., building in which goods are stored, bonded, or displayed for sale, repository, wholesale or large retail store; *~house* (-z) v.t. store (esp. furniture or bonded goods) temporarily in repository; *~houseman*, owner of or repository. [OE *waru*, cf. Du. *waar*, G *waare*, prob. cogn. w. GUARD]

ware[2], pred. a. (poet.). Aware. [OE *wær* heedful, cf. ON *varr*]

ware[3] (-ā-), v.t. (Imperat.) look out for, be cautious about, (*~ hounds, wire, traps!*; esp. in hunting-field); (colloq. usu. imperat.) decline to have anything to do with, bar, avoid, fight shy of. [OE *warian* take heed (prec.)]

war'fare (wôr-), n. State of war, campaigning, being engaged in war, (*after long ~*; *his ~ is over*). [orig. sense military expedition (FARE[2])]

war'like (wôr-), a. Martial, fond of or skilful in war; military, of or for war, (*~ preparations*); bellicose, threatening war. [-LIKE]

war'lock (wôr-), n. (arch.). Sorcerer, wizard. [OE *wærloga* deceiver (*wær* truth, cogn. w. L *verus* true, *loga* liar f. *léogan* LIE[2])]

warm[1] (wôrm), a. & n. **1.** Hottish, of or at rather high temperature, (*hot, ~*; *tepid, cool, cold*; *~ water, weather, countries*; (*a ~ partisan, friend, welcome, RECEPTION*; *~ thanks*). **4.** Animated, heated, exciting or excited, in or resulting from sanguine or offended or unreserved mood, (*when ~ with wine*; *the dispute or disputants grew ~*; *~ work*, keen or dangerous conflict. **5.** (Of position etc.) difficult or dangerous to maintain or meet (*a ~ corner*, hot part of battle etc.; so *~ RECEPTION*; *make it or things ~ for one*; so **6.** (Of feelings etc.) sympathetic, emotional, affectionate, susceptible, (*has a ~ heart, ~-heart-...*

ĕdly² adv., ~heart'edness n.; a ~ temperament, susceptible esp. to amorous impressions; ~ descriptions etc., intended to appeal to amorous feelings, indelicate). **7.** (Of colour) suggestive of ~th, esp. containing rich reds or yellows. **8.** (Of scent in hunting) fresh & strong, indicating recent passage of quarry; (of seeker in children's hiding games) near the object sought, on verge of finding. **9.** (Of person) comfortably off, rich. **10.** (Of official etc.) no longer strange, comfortably established, in office. **11. n.** Something ~, esp. BRITISH ~. Hence ~'LY² adv., ~TH¹ n., (wŏ-). [OE *wearm*, cf. Du. & G *warm*; perh. cogn. w. L *formus*, Gk *thermos*, Skr. *gharmá* heat]

warm² (wŏrm), v.t. & i., & n. **1.** Make warm, excite, (fire ~s room, person, etc.; *wine to* ~ *the heart*; ~ oneself at fire etc.; ~ *person or his jacket*, thrash him, whence ~'ING¹ n., sl.); ~ oneself at fire etc.; become warm or animated or sympathetic (often *up*; *room is* ~*ing up*; *he* ~*ed up* or ~*ed as he got into his subject*; *my heart* ~*s to him*); ~*ing-pan*, flat closed long-handled usu. brass vessel holding live coals formerly used for ~ing inside of bed before it was occupied, (fig.) person holding office temporarily to keep it for another not yet of age etc.; hence (-)~ER¹ (2) n. **2. n.** Act of ~ing oneself or something (*must have, give it, another* ~ *first*). [OE *wirman, wearmian*, (prec.)]

warn (wŏrn), v.t. Give notice to, put on guard, caution, admonish, (person *of* danger or consequences or future or unknown present circumstance, *against* of danger or *doing, that* something impends or must be reckoned with, *that* he is or has neglected to do something, *to* do, or abs.). Hence ~'ingLY² adv. [OE *w(e)arnian*, cf. G *warnen*; cogn. w. WARY, WARE²]

war'ning (wŏ-), n. In vbl senses (*take* ~, have one's caution excited, mentally register danger etc., act on a ~); also or esp.: thing that serves to warn (*palpitation is a* ~ *of heart trouble; let this be a* ~ *to you; give* (master, servant)~, announce that employment is to terminate in specified (e.g. *a month's*) time. [-ING¹]

warp¹ (wŏrp), v.t. & i. **1.** Make or become crooked or perverted, change from straight or right or natural state, bias, (*sun heat* ~*ed the boards; seasoned timber does not* ~; *hardship* ~*ed his disposition; judgement* ~*ed by self-interest*). **2.** (naut.) Haul (ship) in some direction by rope attached to fixed point, progress thus. **3.** Fertilize by inundating with warp. [OE *weorpan* throw, cf. ON *verpa*, Du. *werpen*, G *werfen*]

warp² (wŏrp), n. **1.** Threads stretched lengthwise in loom to be crossed by weft. **2.** Rope used in towing or warping. **3.** Crooked state produced in timber etc. by uneven shrinking or expansion; (fig.) perversion or perverse inclination in mind. **4.** Sediment or alluvial deposit, esp. that left by turbid water kept standing on poor land. [OE *wearp*, cf. ON *varp* cast of net, G *werft* warp; cogn. w. prec.]

warrant¹ (wŏ-), n. **1.** Thing that bears person out in or sanctions action (*have no* ~ *for what you do; his promise or order, our strength, is our* ~; *I will be your* ~; *with the* ~ *of a good conscience*). **2.** Voucher, written authorization to receive money (dividend, TREASURY, ~), carry out arrest or distress (*a* ~ *is out against him*), represent principal in lawsuit (~ *of attorney*), etc. **3.** Certificate from War Office or Admiralty or Air Ministry (cf. COMMISSION) held by ~ officer (between commissioned officers & N.C.O.s, as gunner, boatswain, sergeant-major). [f. OF *warant* f. Teut. (G *gewähren* certify), -ANT]

warrant² (wŏ-), v.t. Serve as warrant for, justify, (*nothing can* ~ *such insolence*), whence ~ABLE a., (also, of a stag) of an age to be hunted (5 or 6 years); = (the now more usual) GUARANTEE v., esp. in sense *answer for genuineness* etc. of (goods; ~*ed pure* etc., *to be so*), & in *I* or *I'll* ~ (*you*) usu. parenthet. =no doubt, assuredly (~ER¹, ~OR², ~EE' (one to whom warranty is given), nn., (wŏ-). [f. OF *warantir* (prec.)]

warranty (wŏ-), n. Authority or justification (usu. *for* doing or saying or supposing); (Law) express or implied undertaking on vendor's part that thing sold is vendor's & is fit for use or fulfils specified conditions. [f. OF *warantie* fem. p.p. of *warantir* WARRANT²]

warren (wŏ-), n. Piece of ground in which rabbits are preserved or abound (*like rabbits in a* ~, of thick population). [f. OF *warenne* (*warir* keep, cogn. w. WARE³)]

warrior (wŏ-), n. Distinguished or veteran soldier (rhet., poet.); member of any of the fighting services (*the Unknown W*~, or *Soldier*, unidentified body of one killed in the 1914–18 war selected for public burial as symbolizing his country's sacrifice); (attrib., of nation etc.) martial; (of savages) fighting man; ~ *ant*, of kinds that make slaves of other species. [f. OF *guerreiur* (*guerreier* make WAR)]

wart (wŏrt), n. Small hardish excrescence on skin caused by abnormal growth of papillae (*paint one with his* ~, without concealment of blemishes), similar lump on stem etc. of plant; ~*grass, -weed, -wort*, kind of spurge with juice used to cure ~s; ~*hog*, kinds of African large-headed swine with ~y lumps on face. Hence ~Y² a. [OE *wearte*, cf. Du. *wrat*, G *warze*]

war'ĭ, a. Given to caution, habitually on the look-out, circumspect; cautious

of doing; showing, done with, caution. Hence ~ily² adv., ~iness n. [as ware² +-y²]

was. See BE.

wash¹ (wŏ̄'), v.t. & i. 1. Cleanse with liquid (~ one's face etc., oneself, or any object; ~ thing out, clean its inside; ~ one's dirty LINEN; ~ one's hands, fig., decline responsibility usu. of), (fig.) purify (~ me throughly from mine iniquity); take (stain, dirt, etc.) out or off or away by washing; ~ up (plates etc., or usu. abs.), clean table utensils after use; (abs.) ~ oneself or one's (face &) hands (must ~ before dinner), ~ clothes (~es for a living). 2. (Of coloured material or dye) bear ~ing without loss of colour (won't ~, fig. of argument etc., stand examination; whence ~'ING² (wŏ̄-) a.; ~ed out, enfeebled, limp, demoralized, esp. as effect of dissipation. 3. Moisten (roses ~ed with dew); (of river, sea, etc.) touch (coast, bank, country) with its waters. 4. (Of moving liquid) carry along in specified direction (chiefly in pass.; a wave ~ed him overboard; was ~ed up by the sea; beef ~ed down with ale); denude (sea—~ed cliffs); scoop out (under had ~ed a channel); go splashing or sweeping over, along, out in, or into. 5. Sift (ore) by action of water. 6. Brush thin coating of watery colour over (paper in water-colour or sepia painting, wall), coat (inferior metal) thinly with gold etc. Hence ~'ABLE (wŏ̄-) a. [OE wæscan, cf. Du. wasschen, G waschen, w. WATER]

wash² (wŏ̄-), n. 1. Washing or being washed (give it a good ~; must get a ~; the ~, treatment at laundry, as send the linen to the ~); quantity of clothes just (to be, being) washed. 2. Visible or audible motion of agitated water, esp. waves caused by passage of vessel. 3. Soil swept off by water, alluvium. 4. Kitchen water & scraps given to pigs. 5. Thin or weak claret, or inferior liquid food (this soup, tea, claret, is mere ~); (fig.) twaddle, wishwash. 6. Liquid for spreading over surface to cleanse or heal or colour, lotion, cosmetic, thin coating of water-colour, wall-colour-

wash— (wŏ̄-), comb. form of WASH¹, ² often = & used as substitute for washing¹: ||~-basin; ~-board, of ribbed wood for use in scrubbing clothes at wash, also board attached to gunwale, port, etc., to prevent water from washing in, also board skirting bottom of room-wall; ~-boiler, apparatus for purifying cauldron; ~-bottle, clothes-washing cauldron; ~-bottle, apparatus for purifying gases etc. by passage through liquid; ~-bout; ~-cloth, piece of linen etc. used in washing dishes or bodies; ~-day, on which clothes are washed; ||~-hand-basin; ||~-hand-stand, piece of furniture with toilet utensils; ~-house, laundry; ~-leather, chamois or similar leather; ~-out, breach in railway or road

track caused by flood, heavy rainfall, etc., (sl.) complete failure esp. to hit target, fiasco, (sl.) useless or inefficient person; ~-pot (arch. exc. of pot with melted tin for final dipping of tinplate); = WASH-stand. ~-hand-stand.; ~-tub, esp. for clothes.

wa'sher (wŏ̄-), n. In vbl senses: also, flat ring or perforated piece of leather, rubber, metal, etc., used to give tightness to joint, nut, fastening, etc.; ||~-woman, laundress. [-ER¹]

wa'shing (wŏ̄-), n. In vbl senses (& see WASH¹); esp. linen etc. sent to the wash; ~ soda, sodium carbonate, used dissolved in water for ~ & cleaning; ~-stand, ton. [-ING¹]

wa'shy (wŏ̄-), a. (Of liquid food etc.) too watery, weak, thin, insipid; (of colour) faded-looking, thin; (of style, sentiment, etc.) diffuse, feeble, lacking vigour or compression. Hence ~ily² adv., ~iness n. [-y¹]

Washing'ton'ia (wŏ̄-), n. Californian palm-tree named after George Washington. [-I¹]

Wa'shington (wŏ̄-), n. (Used for) the U.S. Government, [capital of U.S.]

wasp (wŏ̄-), n. Kinds of hymenopterous social or solitary insect of which the common kind has black & yellow transverse stripes, very slender waist, taste for fruit & sweets, & powerfully venomous sting (has a waist like a ~'s, whence ~-waisted² a.); ~-bee, -beetle, -fly, kinds having some resemblance to ~. [OE wæps, cf. G wespe; for metath. cf. ASK, HASP; cogn. w. WEAVE, w. ref. to nests, & w. L vespa]

wa'spish (wŏ̄-), a. Irritable, petulant, ill-tempered, sharp in retort. Hence ~ly² adv., ~ness n. [-ISH¹]

wassail (wŏ̄'sl, wā'sl), n., & v.i. (arch.). 1. Festive occasion, drinking-bout; kind of liquor drunk on such occasion; ~-bowl, -cup, -horn, etc. 2. v.i. Make merry, hold festivities. [f. OE wes be thou (cf. was see BE), hāl WHOLE, form of salutation]

wast. See BE.

wa'stage, n. Amount wasted or that runs to waste, loss by waste. [-AGE]

waste¹, a. (Of district etc.) desolate, desert, uninhabited, uncultivated, as result of natural barrenness etc. or of ravages or catastrophe (lay ~, ravage); lie ~, be uncultivated; ~ land, not occupied for any purpose); (fig.) monotonous or presenting no features of interest (the ~ periods of history); superfluous, refuse, no longer serving a purpose, left over after use, (~ products, useless by-products of manufacture; ~ energy, steam, etc.; ~ paper, esp. books or documents that fail or are valueless). [f. OE wēst

waste², v.t. & i. Lay WASTE¹; (law) bring (estate) into bad condition by damage

or neglect; expend to no purpose or for inadequate result, use extravagantly, squander, (~e money, time, food, etc., or abs. as ~ not, want not; ~e breath or words, talk uselessly); wear (t. & l.) gradually away, wither, (arch., of time) pass t. & i., (his resources were ~ed, were rapidly ~ing; day ~es, draws to a close; is sorcerer ~ed his arm; a ~ing disease; is ~ing away for lack of food); run to waste (that water is ~ing). [f. OF waster (now gâter) f. L vastare (prec.)]

wāste³, n. 1. Desert, waste region, dreary scene, (a ~ of waters, unbroken expanse of sea). 2. Being used up, diminution by wear & tear, (the ~ of tissue is continuous; ~ & repair balance each other). 3. Waste material or food, useless remains, refuse, scraps, shreds; ~ = COTTON ~. 4. Act of wasting, throwing away or extravagant or inefficient use of time, money, food, etc., (wilful ~ makes woeful want; it is ~ of time to argue further; run to ~, of liquid or fig., of affection etc., be wasted). 5. (law). Injury to estate caused by act or neglect esp. of life-tenant. [as WASTE¹ ¹, ²:]

wāste~, comb. form of WASTE¹ ², ³: ~basket, for waste odds & ends esp. of paper; ||~-book in book-keeping, book in which rough preliminary entries of transactions are made; wāste´FUL (-tf-) a., extravagant, given to or exhibiting waste, whence wāste´fully² adv., wāste´fulNESS n.; wāste´LESS (-tl-) a.; ||~pap'er-basket, receptacle for used papers etc.; ~-pipe, for carrying off used or superfluous water.

wāst´er, n. In vbl senses; also, article spoilt or flawed in manufacture; (sl.) good-for-nothing person. [-ER¹]

wāst´rel, n. Thing spoilt in making; stray child, street arab, waif, good-for-nothing fellow; wasteful person. [f. WASTE² + -REL]

watch¹ (wŏ), n. 1. Wakefulness at night (now rare; in the ~es of the night, while one lies awake; pass as a ~ in the night, be soon forgotten). 2. Alert state, being on the look-out, vigilance, constant observation, attention to what may come, (keep ~, a ~, good or a good ~; ~ & ward, orig. guard by night & day, now emphatic reduplication of ~; on the ~, waiting usu. for expected or desired or feared occurrence), whence ~´FUL adv., ~´fulNESS n. 3. (hist.). Man or body of men charged with patrolling streets at night, guard (BLACK¹ ~, orig. an armed company). 4. (hist.). One of three or of four parts into which night was anciently divided (first etc. or evening etc. ~). 5. Four-hour spell of duty on board ship (DOG~, 2-hr); one of the halves (starboard & port ~ from position of men's bunks) into which ship's crew is divided to take alternate duty. 6. Small timepiece worked by coiled spring for carrying on

person (STOP~). 7. ~-case, outer metal case enclosing ~works; ~-chain, metal ~-guard; ||W~ Committee, committee of a borough council dealing with policing & lighting; ~-dog, employed to give alarm of burglars etc.; ~-fire, at night in camps etc.; ||~-glass, disk covering face of ~; ~-guard, chain or string for securing ~ on person; ~-key, instrument for winding up ~works; ~-maker; ~-man, (formerly, & still poet.) sentinel or member of street patrol, (now) man employed to look after empty building etc. at night; ~-night, last night of year esp. as celebrated by religious services; ~ oil, fine thin kind for lubricating ~works etc.; ~-pocket, in garment esp. waistcoat, or separate for attachment to bed etc., holding ~; ~-spring, kind used in ~ works, also mainspring of ~; ~-stand, small pillar etc. for hanging ~ on; ~-tower, post of observation usu. fortified; ~word, (formerly) military password, (now) phrase expressing briefly the principles of a party etc. (e.g. Equal pay for equal work). [OE wæcce (wæccan, see foll.)]

watch² (wŏ), v.i. & t. Remain awake for a purpose (now rare; ~ed all night by his side; ~ & pray); be on the watch, keep watch, be vigilant, look out for opportunity etc., exercise protecting care over; keep eyes fixed on, keep under observation, follow observantly, (had him ~ed by detectives; if you don't ~ it, colloq., take care or precautions; ~ed pot never boils, strained expectation makes time seem long); look out for, bide, await, (opportunity; ~ one's time, wait for right moment). Hence ~´ER¹ n. [OE wæccan doublet of wacian WAKE¹]

wa´ter¹ (waw-), n. 1. Colourless transparent tasteless scentless compound of oxygen & hydrogen in liquid state convertible by heat into steam & by cold into ice, kinds of liquid consisting chiefly of this seen in sea, lake, stream, spring, rain, tears, sweat, saliva, urine, serum, etc., body of ~ as sea or lake or river, (hot & cold, salt & fresh or sweet, smooth or still & rough or troubled, HARD or SOFT, aerated, saline, chalybeate, thermal, BLUE¹, HEAVY, HOLY, MINERAL, etc., ~; strong ~s, arch., distilled spirits; table ~s, esp. mineral ~s bottled for use at meals; red ~, bloody urine; in smooth ~, going easily, past one's troubles; on the ~, in boat or ship; by ~, using ships, barges, etc., for travel or transport; in deep ~ or ~s, floundering, in great difficulties, in affliction; still ~s run deep, quiet manner may cover depths of emotion, knowledge, or cunning; FISH² in troubled ~s; cup of cold ~, symbol of charitable intent; get into, be in, hot ~, bring or have brought trouble or rebuke on oneself by indiscretion etc.; throw cold ~ on scheme etc.,

discourage or poohpooh it; **written in ~**, of name, achievements, etc., transient; **keep one's head above ~**, chiefly fig., avoid financial ruin; **the ~s**, rhet., the sea, as **cross the ~s**; **cast one's bread upon the ~s**, do good without looking for gratitude or immediate or definite return; **drink the ~s**, attend spa for health; **brings the ~s to one's mouth**, makes it water; **fish out of ~**, arch., symbol of necessities of life not to be supplied to outlaw; HOLD¹ ~; **make, pass, ~**, void urine; **tread ~**, maintain position in deep ~ by action of marking time; **~ on the brain, knee**, etc., morbid accumulation of fluid; **~ be-witched**, very weak tea etc. or spirit-&-~; **~ of life**, spiritual enlightenment; **~s of forgetfulness**, Lethe, oblivion, death). 2. State of tide (**high, low, ~; in low ~**, fig., in depressed condition, esp. badly off for money; **high, low, ~mark**, highest, lowest, point reached by tidal ~, also brilliance of gem esp. diamond (**of the first ~**), of finest quality, often also transf. as **a genius, blunder, of the first ~**). **3.** Solution of specified sub-stance in ~ (*lavender, rose*, etc., ~, scents; *soda, lithia, dill*, etc., ~, bever-ages or medicines). **4.** Transparency & lustre of diamond. **5.** (Finance) amount of nominal capital added by watering. **6.** ~ (in compounds of which those especially that distinguish varieties of plants & animals are too numerous to be given separately), haunt-ing, growing in, used or employed on, etc., the ~; or, for, worked or effected by, made with, containing, using, yielding, etc., ~. **7.** ||~-**anchor**, = DRAG²-anchor; ||~-**bailiff**, customhouse officer at port (hist.), official who prevents poaching of fish in protected ~s; ~**bed**, rubber mattress filled with ~ for invalid to avoid bed-sores; ~**bellows**, blower made by suspension in ~ of inverted valved vessel by raising & lowering of which air is drawn in & expelled; ~**bird**; ~**biscuit**; ~**blister**, containing colourless fluid, not blood; ~**boatman**, kind of aquatic bug; ~**borne**, (of goods) conveyed by ~, (of diseases) communicated or propagated by use of contaminated drinking-~; ~**bottle**, esp. of glass for wash-hand-stand or dining table, also of metal etc. for soldier's kit; ~**brash**, form of indiges-tion with eructation of watery fluid; ~-BREAKER²; ~**buffalo**, the common domestic Indian buffalo; ~**butt**; W~**carrier**, Aquarius; ~**cart**, esp. with ~ for sale or for watering roads; ~**chute**, slope of boards slippery with running ~ for tobogganing down; ~**closet**, place for evacuation of bowels with arrangement

for flushing pan with ~; ~**colour**, pig-ment mixed with ~ & not oil, picture painted with such colours, (pl. or sing.) art of painting such pictures; ~ com-PRESS²; ~**course**, brook, stream; ~**cracker**, kind of biscuit; ~**cress**, creeping ~plant eaten as salad; ~**cure**, hydro-pathy; ~**drinker**, (esp.) abstainer from alcohol; ~**fall**, stream falling over precipice or down steep hillside; ~**fender**, dowser (DOWSING); ~**fowl** (usu. collect. as pl.), birds haunting ~, esp. as objects of sport; ~**gas**, got by decomposing ~ & used after treatment with carbon as illuminant; ~**gate**, flood-gate, also gate giving access to river etc.; ~**gauge**, glass tube etc., indicating height of ~ inside reservoir, boiler, etc.; ~**glass**, tube with glass bottom enabling objects under ~ to be observed, also solution of silicate of soda used as a vehicle for fresco-painting, or used for preserving eggs; ~**gruel**; ~**hammer**, percussion made by ~ in pipe when tap is turned off, or by ~ in steam-pipe when live steam is admitted; ~**hen**, = MOOR¹hen; ~**hole**, shallow depression in cavity in which ~ collects (esp. in the bed of a river otherwise dry); ~**ice**, flavoured & frozen ~ & sugar; ~**inch**, quantity discharged in 24 hrs through 1 in. pipe under least pressure; ~**jacket**, case filled with ~ & enclosing part of machine that is to be kept cool; ~**joint**, proof against leakage; ~**junket**, sandpiper; ~**laid**, (of rope) = CABLE¹-laid; ~**lens**, magnifying lens made of glass-bottomed brass cell filled with ~; ~**level**, surface of ~ in reservoir etc., also plane below which ground is saturated with ~, also levelling-instrument made of glass tube to be held horizontal with two upturned graduated open ends in which the con-tained ~ must be at same height; ~**lily**, kinds of plant with broad leaves & white or like or yellow or red flowers floating on surface of ~; ~**line**, along which surface of ~ touches ship's side (when loaded, **load-~line**, when empty, **light ~line**), also one of the semi-transparent parallel lines formed in some papers in manufacture; ~**logged**, (of wood) so saturated, (of vessel) so filled, with ~ as barely to float; ~**main**, main pipe in ~-supplying system; ~**man**, boatman plying for hire, also oarsman good, bad, etc., at keeping boat truly balanced etc.; ~**manship**(3) n.; ~**mark**, (n.) faint design seen in some paper when held against light indicating maker, size, etc., (v.t.) impress such mark on in making; ~**meadow**, kept fertile by being flooded; ~**melon**, one of two divisions of melon (the other being mush-melon) with ellipse shape, smooth skin, & watery juice; ~**meter**; ~**mill**, worked by ~wheel; ~**monkey**, jar with long narrow neck for ~ used in hot countries; ~**motor**, ~**wheel**,

turbine, small motor using ~ under pressure; ~nymph, naiad; ~ OUZEL; pillar, upright with revolving head for feeding steam-engines etc.; ~pipe; ~plane, plane passing through ship's line; ~plate, with double bottom to hold hot ~ for keeping food warm; ~platter, kind of ~lily with upturned edges to leaves; W~ Poet (the), John Taylor (d. 1653); ~polo, hand-ball game with goals played by swimmers; ~power, mechanical force got from weight or motion of ~, fall in stream capable of being utilized as force; ~proof, (adj.) impervious to ~, (n.) ~proof garment or material, (v.t.) make ~proof with rubber etc., whence ~proofER[1] n.; ~ram, hydraulic ram; ~rat, = ~vole; ~rate, || charge made for use of public ~supply; ~sail, below lower studding-sail close over ~; ~seal, body of ~ used in bent pipe or about mouth of pipe to prevent passage or escape of gas; ~shed, line of separation between ~s flowing to different rivers or basins or seas [cogn. w. SHED[1]], (pop.) slope down which ~ flows, (pop.) river basin; ~shoot, pipe or trough throwing off ~ from house etc.; ~side', margin of sea, lake, or river; ~skin, skin bag for carrying ~; ~soldier, aquatic plant with flowers above surface; ~souchy (soō'shi), fish boiled & served in its own liquor; ~spout, phenomenon in which whirling cloud forms a funnel-shaped pendant, which descends towards sea & draws up corresponding volume of whirling ~, the whole forming a pillar uniting sea & cloud; ~sprite; ~supply, providing & storing of ~, amount of ~ stored, for use of town, house, etc.; ~table, string-course arranged to throw off building, plane below which the soil or rock is saturated with ~; ~tiger, larva of certain ~beetles; ~tight, (of joint, boots, cask, compartment in ship, etc.) tightly enough fastened or fitted to prevent ingress or egress of ~ (~tight compartments, fig., keeping of subjects etc. entirely separate); ~tower, supporting elevated tank to secure pressure for distributing ~supply; ~tube boiler, in which ~ circulates in tubes exposed to flames & hot gases; ~vole, large role haunting ~; ~waggon, sl., abstaining from alcohol); ~wagtail, common pied wagtail; ~wave, wave in the hair produced by ~waving, a method of waving hair with the use of ~; ~way, navigable channel, also thick planks at outer edge of deck along which channel is hollowed for ~ to run off by; ~wheel, kinds of wheel (overshot, undershot, breast, & turbine, wheel) worked by ~ & working machinery; ~wings, floats attached to shoulders of persons learning to swim; ~witch, = ~finder, also kinds of bird; ~withe, W.-Ind. vine so full of sap that branch broken off yields draught of ~; ~works, establishment for managing ~supply, also ornamental fountain (turn on the ~works, sl., shed tears). Hence ~LESS a. [Aryan; OE wæter, cf. Du. water, G wasser, Gk hudōr, L unda wave, Skr. udán; cogn. w. WET]

wa'ter[2] (waw-), v.t. & i. 1. Sprinkle (road, plants, etc.), adulterate (milk, beer, etc.), with water. 2. Give drink of water to (horse etc.), (of animals) go to pool etc. to drink. 3. (Of ship, engine, etc., or persons in charge) take in supply of water. 4. (Of smarting eyes, or of mouth when food is seen or food or pleasure eagerly anticipated) secrete or run with water (makes one's mouth ~, excites desire or envy). 5. (Chiefly in p.p., as ~ed silk) produce irregular wavy damask-like markings on (material) by moistening & pressing in manufacture. 6. (Finance) increase (company's debt or nominal capital) by issue of new shares without corresponding addition to assets. 7. ~ down, make (details of story etc.) less vivid or horrifying; ~ing-cart, with perforated pipe or other device for ~ing road; ~ing-place, pool etc. at which animals ~, also spa, also seaside place frequented at certain seasons by holiday makers & invalids; ~ing-pot, with perforated nozzle for ~ing plants. [OE wæterian f. water, see prec.]

Waterloo' (waw-), n. The battle in which Napoleon was finally defeated; (with a or his) crushing blow, decisive contest, chiefly in phr. meet one's ~.

wa'ter[y] (waw-), a. Containing too much water, over-moist, sodden, (esp. of cooked vegetables or fish); (of eyes or lips) suffused or running with water; (of liquids) too thin, actually or apparently diluted, resembling water, (fig., of expression, talk, style, etc.) vapid, insipid, uninteresting, feeble, (of colour) pale, washed out; indicative of rain (a ~y moon, sky). Hence ~iNESS n. [-Y2]

watt (wot), n. Unit of electric power, rate of working in circuit when electromotive force is one volt & intensity of current one ampere. Hence ~METER n. [J. W~, engineer (d. 1819)]

Watteau (wŏ'tō), n. French painter d. 1721 (~ back, arrangement of woman's dress-back with broad pleat falling from neck to ground without girdle; ~ bodice, with square opening at neck & short ruffled sleeves).

wa'ttle[1] (wŏ-), n., & v.t. 1. Interlaced rods & twigs as material of fences, walls, or roofs (~ & daub, plastered with mud or clay; (sing. or pl.) rods & twigs for such use; kinds of Australian acacia supplying such twigs, having bark used in tanning, & bearing golden flowers adopted as national emblem; (dial.) a wicker hurdle. 2. v.t. Construct of ~; interlace (twigs

etc.); enclose or fill up with ~-work. [OE *watul* etym. dub., cf. *watela* a hand-age]
wattle² (wŏ-), n. Fleshy appendage on head or throat of turkey & other birds; BARB¹ of fish. Hence ~ED² (wŏt'ĭd) a. [perh. f. prec. through the doubtful sense *wicker-basket*; perh.=obs. *wartle* dim. of WART]

waul, v.i. Squall, cry like cat. [imit.]
wāve¹, v.i., v.i. & t. 1. Vibrate or be stirred with sinuous or sweeping motions like those of flag or tree or field of corn in wind, flutter, undulate; impart waving motion to (~ *sword*, brandish it as en-couragement to followers etc.; ~ *one's hand* often *to person*, in greeting or as signal); ~ hand or thing held in it usu. to person, give direction thus to person *to do*, send (person *away* thus, summon (person) *nearer* thus, direct (person) thus *to do*, express *farewell* etc. thus; ~ *aside*, dismiss as intrusive or irrelevant. 2. Give undulating surface or course or appear-ance to (hair of head, lines in drawing, etc.), make wavy, (of hair, line, etc.) have such appearance, be wavy. [OE *wafian* undulate, cf. MHG *waben*]

wāve², n. 1. Ridge of water between two depressions or (also *breaker*) long body of water curling into arched form & break-ing on shore (*the* ~*s* or *the* ~; poet. & rhet., the sea, water; *attack in* ~*s*, Mil., in successive lines advancing like sea-~s). 2. Disturbance of the particles of a fluid medium e.g. water, air, ether, into a ridge-&-trough oscillation by which mo-tion is propagated & heat, light, sound, electricity, etc., conveyed in some direc-tion without corresponding advance of the particles in the same direction; single curve in the course of such motion. 3. Temporary heightening of some influence or condition or feeling (*a* ~ *of enthusiasm, prosperity, depression; heat, cold,* ~; rise or fall of temperature travelling over large area). 4. Undulating line or outline or surface, waviness. 5. Gesture of waving. 6. ~-*length*, distance in any undulation be-tween one crest to the next; corresponding distance between points in the same phase in sound ~s or electromagnetic radiation i.e. the speed of light divided by the frequency. Hence ~LESS a., ~LET¹ n., (-ĭv-). [f. prec.]

wāv'er, v.i. Oscillate unsteadily, flicker, quiver, (rare; chiefly of flame); (of troops) falter, become unsteady, begin to give way; be irresolute or undecided between different courses or opinions, be shaken in resolution or belief. Hence ~ING¹ n. [ME *wa-, we-*]
~ingly² adv. [WAVE¹, -ES¹]
wāv'y¹, a. Undulating, (of line or surface) consisting of or showing alternate con-trary curves, (colloq.). R.N.V.R. (from insignia on sleeve). Hence wāv'ĭir²·age²]

wāv'y²·ey², n. The snow-goose. [f. Amer.-Ind. *wawa*]
wawl = WAUL.
wax¹, n. & v.t. 1. Sticky plastic yellowish substance secreted by bees as material of honeycomb cells, bees~, white trans-lucent scentless tasteless material got from this by bleaching & purifying & used for candles, in modelling, & for other purposes, (*mould one like* ~, form his character on desired lines or induce him to act just as desired); substance resembling ~ in some respect, as the secretion of some other insects esp. *Chinese* ~, *ear*~ or cerumen, *mineral* ~, esp. ozocerite, bee-bread, *paraffin* ~, obtained from shale or petroleum, *vegetable* ~ or exudation of certain plants, SEAL²*ing*~, COBBERS²'~; (attrib., now usu. preferred to *waxen*) made of ~, ~-*bill*, kinds of small bird with trans-lucent bill; ~ *candle*, ~-*chandler*, maker or seller of ~-candles; ~-*cloth*, floor-cloth; ~ *doll*, with face etc. of ~, also person esp. woman with pretty but unexpressive face; ~-*insect*, kinds that secrete ~, esp. that collected as Chinese ~ from which superior candles are made; ~-*light*, taper or candle of ~; ~-*myrtle*, candleberry; ~-*painting*, encaustic; ~-*palm*, S.-Amer. palm with stem coated in mixture of resin & ~; ~-*paper*, waterproofed with layer of ~; ~-*pink*, kind of garden-plant; ~-*pocket*, one of bee's ~-exuding apertures; ~-*pod*, = BUTTER-*bean*; ~-*tree*, kinds exuding ~ or encrusted with it by insects; ~-*wing*, kinds of bird with small horny tips like red sealing-~ to some feathers; ~-*work*, modelling-work, objects modelled, in ~, esp. dummies of persons with face & hands of coloured ~ clothed to look like life & be exhibited. 3. v.t. Smear, polish, encrust, treat sur-face of, with ~. [com.-Teut.; OE *weax*, cf. Du. *was*, G *wachs*]

wax², v.i. (Of moon between new & full) have progressively larger part of surface illuminated (cf. *wane*; ~ *& wane* also transf. of influence etc., undergo alterna-tions of increase & decrease); (with adj. compl.) poet., grow or increase; (with adj. compl.) pass into specified condition or esp. mood or tone (~ *fat, old, merry, facetious, in-dignant, pathetic, angry*). [Aryan; OE *weaxan*, G *wachsen*; Gk *auxanō*, L *augeo*, Skr *vaksh*.]
wax³, n. (sl.). Fit of anger (*is in, got into, put him in, a* ~). [?]
wax'en, a. Made of wax (being ousted by attrib. use of *wax*); presenting surface as of wax (esp. of complexion, used with less of depreciation than *waxy*); impressible as wax, plastic. [-EN³]
wax'y¹, a. Resembling wax in some way, esp. easily moulded or presenting smooth

pale translucent surface; (of tissue) having degenerated into consistency resembling wax (so ~*y tiver* etc.); || (sl.) angry, quick-tempered. Hence ~**ily**³ adv., ~**iness** n. [WAX¹, ³, -Y²]

way, n. **1.** Road or track lit. or fig. provided for passing along (HIGH~; OVER *the* ~; || *permanent* ~, complete piece of regular railroad track; || *six-foot* ~, space left between each pair of rails & the next on railway; *covered* ~, roofed or in Fortif. screened passage: *Appian, Latin,* etc., *Way,* great Roman roads in Italy; MILKY ~; *the* ~ *of the Cross,* series of paintings in church etc., to receive successive attention in certain services, illustrating Christ's progress to Calvary; *to the* ~ *of all the earth, of all flesh, of nature,* die; *pave the* ~ *for,* take steps that will facilitate or prepare people's minds to accept some change); (pl.) structure of timber etc. on which new ship is slid down at launch. **2.** Best route or route taken or contemplated between two places or to place, method or plan for attaining object, person's desired or chosen course of action, (*ask the* or *one's* ~: *farthest* ~ *about is nearest* ~ *home,* short cuts are delusive; *find one's* or *the* ~, reach destination; *lose one's* or *the* ~, *go astray; parting of the* ~*s,* usu. fig., time for momentous decision; *take one's* ~, go in some direction, usu. *to* or *towards*; *go one's* ~ or ~*s, depart; came by* ~ *of London,* via; *lead the* ~, act as guide or leader; show by example how thing can be done; *put oneself out of the* ~, inconvenience oneself to serve another; *is nothing out of the* ~, not uncommon or remarkable; *an out-of-the-*~ *corner,* remote, inaccessible; *go out of the* or *one's* ~ *to be rude,* show wanton rudeness; *right & wrong* ~*s of doing a thing; that is the* ~ *to do it; don't like the* ~ *she smiles; where there's a will there's a* ~; *you will never manage it that* ~; *will find or make a* ~; *will do it one* ~ or *another*; ~*s & means,* methods esp. of providing money as in parliamentary *Committee of Ways & Means; go, take, one's own* ~, act independently esp. against others' advice; *have one's own* or *one's* ~, get what one wants, see one's orders carried out or desires gratified). **3.** Travelling-distance, length of road etc. (to be) traversed, (*India is a long* ~ *off; went a little, a good, a long, some,* ~ *with* or *to meet him;* ONCE *in. a* ~; *is still a long* ~ *off perfection*). **4.** Unimpeded opportunity of advance, room free of obstacles, ground over which advance is desired or would naturally take place, (GIVE¹, MAKE¹, ~; MON *in the* ~; *stand, be, in the* ~ *of, in one's* ~, or *in the* ~, *be obstacle to, be obstacle; get out of, in, the* ~, cease, begin, to be impediment; *get thing out of the* ~, dispose of, get rid of, *settle; put person out of the* ~, confine or

secretly kill him; *clear the* ~, remove obstacles, stand aside; RIGHT *of* ~; *put one in the* ~ *of a good bargain, of doing,* give him opportunity). **5.** Being engaged, time spent, in locomotion lit. or fig. (*with songs to cheer the* ~; *met him on the* ~ *out* or *home; is on the* ~, travelling or approaching; *by the* ~, (during journey, (fig.) incidentally, often used by speaker to introduce more or less irrelevant remark). **6.** Specified direction (usu. in adv. phrr. without prep.: *which* ~ *is he looking, going?: look the other* ~, avoid meeting person's eye, cut him; appended colloq. to names of places, as *lives somewhere London* ~). **7.** Custom, manner of behaving, personal peculiarity, (*the good old* ~*s, old fashions; stand in the ancient* ~*s, avoid what is newfangled; the* ~ *of the world,* conduct no worse than is justified by custom; *it is not my* ~ *to desert people in misfortune; has a little* ~ *of leaving his bills unpaid; it is only his* ~, piece of rudeness. from him has no special significance, so *pretty Fanny's* ~). **8.** Scope, sphere, range, line of occupation, branch of business, (*lumbing is not, does not lie or come or fall, in my* ~; *is in the grocery* ~, a grocer; *want a few things in the stationery* ~). **9.** Advance in some direction, impetus, progress, (*make one's* ~ *home, into a shop,* etc.; *make one's* or *one's own* ~, prosper; *make the best of one's* ~, go as fast as one can; *make* ~, advance lit. or fig.; *gather, lose,* ~, gain or lose speed; *give* ~, of oarsmen, row hard; ~ *enough!,* call to boat's crew to complete their stroke & then cease rowing; *ship has* ~ *on, is under* ~, moves through water). **10.** Respect (*not a bad fellow in some* ~*s; is satisfactory for* or *a* ~; *in a* ~, to a limited extent, not altogether; *no* ~ *inferior,* not at all). **11.** Ordinary course (did it in the ~ *of business*). **12.** Condition, assumption, hypothesis, state, train, degree, (*things are in a bad* ~; *have it* BOTH ~*s; || each* ~, *both* ~*s, in backing horse* etc., to win, to be placed; *any* ~, in either or any case or event; *we are all in the same* ~, *live in a* SMALL ~; *is an author, builds ships, in a small* ~, on small scale; || *be in* ~ *a* or *a great* ~, colloq., be agitated; || *be in the family* ~, with child). **13.** *By* ~ *of, as* substitute for or form of, with intention of, (*carries a stick by* ~ *of weapon; did it by* ~ *of apology, of discovering the truth; is by* ~ *of making an effort,* represents himself to himself or others to be doing so). **14.** ~*-bill,* list of passengers or parcels on conveyance; || ~*-board,* thin layer separating thicker strata; ~*-farer, ~faring,* traveller, travelling, esp. on foot; ~ *faring-tree,* white-flowered shrub common along roadsides; ~*-lay* v.t., lie in wait for, wait about for to rob or interview; ~ *leave,* right ~ *of* ~ rented by mine-

owners etc.; ~-shaft in steam-engine, rocking shaft for working slide-valve from eccentric; ~-side, side of road (esp. attrib., as ~side flowers, inn); ~-worn, tired with travel. [com.-Teut.: cf. Du. & G. weg, cogn. w. WAIN, L vehere carry; Skr. vah carry.]

-ways (-z), suf. forming adv. of position or direction, & often used indifferently with -WISE; length-~, side-~, &c.; etc. [prec., -ES]

way'ward, a. Childishly self-willed or perverse, capricious, unaccountable, freakish. Hence ~LY¹ adv., ~NESS n. [for awayward, cf. froward.]

||ways'goose, n. Printing-house's annual festivity. [earlier wayzgoose (1683: wayz-1731), etym. dub.]

wē, pl. subj. of I² (used, besides the ordinary pron. use, by royal person in proclamations etc. instead of I, by writer in unsigned article of newspaper etc. & as collective name for speaker & all others of the class that context shows him to be representing for the moment). [com.-Teut.: OE wē, cf. Du. wij, G wir, Skr. vay-am]

weak, a. 1. Wanting in strength or power or number, fragile, easily broken or bent or defeated, (~ barrier, rope, etc.; ~ as a cat, water; a ~ eleven, of poor players; offer but a ~ resistance; ~ vessel, usu. fig., unreliable person; a ~ crew, short-handed; ~ hand, deficient in high cards; the ~er sex, women; ~est goes to WALL, ~ knees, usu. fig., inability to stand firm; want of resolution, whence ~-kneed² (-nēd) a.; ~ ending in blank verse, unaccented or proclitic word such as if at end). 2. Wanting in vigour, not acting strongly, sickly, feeble, (~ constitution, stomach, easily upset; ~ eyes, sight, easily tired or not seeing well, whence ~-eyed² (-id), ~-sighted² aa.; ~ heart, acting feebly; ~ mind, head, below average in intelligence, verging on idiocy, whence ~-minded², ~-headed² aa.; so ~ intellect; ~ imagination; ~ voice, easily tired or not reaching far; ~ demand for goods or stocks, slack; so the market was ~). 3. Wanting in resolution or power of resisting temptation, easily led, (~ character, man; person's ~ side or point, at which he is open to temptation; (of action) indicating want of resolution in agent (a ~ surrender, compliance). 4. Unconvincing, logically deficient, (~ logic, evidence; a ~ argument). 5. (Of mixed liquid or solution) watery, thin, (~ tea, brandy-&-water, brine). 6. (Of style etc.) not nervous or well-knit, diffuse, slipshod. 7. (gram.) Inflected by consonantal additions to, not vowel change in, stem (in English esp. of verbs making past & p.p. by addition of -ed, as WEAK). Hence ~EN⁴ v.t. & i., ~ISH² a., ~'LY¹ [-LY²] adv. [f. ON veik-r weak, cogn. w. OE wác pliant]

weak'ling, n. Feeble person etc. [-LING¹]

weak'ly², a. Sickly, not robust, ailing. [-LY¹]

weak'ness, n. In adj. senses; also or esp.: weak point or defect; inability to resist a particular temptation; foolish liking or inclination for. [-NESS]

weal¹, n. Welfare, prosperity, good fortune, (chiefly now in ~ & woe, ~ or woe, in COMMONWEAL, & in for the public or general ~). [OE wela wealth, cogn. w. WELL³]

weal², See WALE.

||weald, n. District including parts of Kent, Surrey, Hants, & Sussex, with geologically interesting characteristics; ~-clay, beds of clay, sandstone, limestone, & iron-stone, forming top of ~ strata, with abundant fossil remains. [OE = forest, cogn. w. WOLD]

||weal'den, a. & n. 1. Of the weald, resembling the weald geologically. 2. n. Series of lower-cretaceous freshwater strata above oolite & below chalk best exemplified in the weald. [-EN⁵]

wealth (wěl-), n. Welfare, prosperity, (arch.: in health & ~ long to live); riches, large possessions, opulence, being rich; the rich abundance, a profusion or great quantity or display, of (a ~ of illustration, wit, fruit; ~ of words is not eloquence). Hence ~Y² a., ~'ILY² adv., ~'INESS n. [WEAL¹ + -TH¹, cf. Du. weelde luxury]

wean¹, v.t. Teach (sucking child or animal) to feed otherwise than from the breast (often from mother or breast); disengage or cure from or rarely of habit, specified company, etc., by enforced abstinence or counter-attractions. [OE wenian, accustom, cf. Du. wennen, G gewöhnen, accustom; cogn. w. WONT¹]

||wean², n. (Sc.) Child. [= wee ane little one]

wean'ling, n. New-weaned chilM etc. [-LING²]

wea'pon (wěp-), n. Material thing designed or used or usable as an instrument for inflicting bodily harm, e.g. gun, rifle, sword, spear, stick, hammer, poker, horn, claw; action or procedure or means used to get the better in a conflict (irony is a double-edged ~; use the ~ of a general strike; tears the woman's ~). Hence ~LESS a. [com.-Teut.: OE wǣpen cf. Du. wapen, G waffe]

wear¹ (wār-), v.t. & i. (wore, worn). 1. Be dressed habitually in, have on, carry or exhibit on one's person or some part of it, (~s green, serge, knickerbockers, etc. as usual colour etc.; ~ing diamonds, on this occasion; worn clothes, that have been put on at least once; ~ the crown, sword, gown, willow, breeches, be a mourner, soldier, lawyer, desolate lover, husband-ruling wife; ~ one's hair long, short, etc.; ~ a face of joy, sour look,

wear**|y̆, a., & v.t. & i. 1.** Tired, with energy abated, dispirited; sick or impatient of; tiring, tedious, irksome; hence ~ir'y² adv., ~iness n. **2.** vb. Make ~y (esp. of or with importunity or monotony), whence ~isome a.., ~isomery² adv., ~isomeness n.; grow ~y (esp. of importunity or importunate person), whence ~iless a.; (chiefly Sc.) long to do or for. [OE wērig, cf. OHG wuarag drunk; cogn. w. OE wōrian go astray; not f. WEAR¹]

weas'and (wēz-), n. (arch.). [slit one's ~, cut his throat). [OE wǣsend, cf. OHG weisunt, etym. dub.]

weas'el (-zl), n. Small nimble reddish-brown white-bellied slender-bodied carnivorous quadruped allied to stoat & ferret (catch a ~ asleep, deceive wide-awake person); ~faced, with thin sharp features. [OE wesle, cf. Du. wezel, G wiesel]

wea'ther¹ (wĕdh-), n. & a. **1.** Atmospheric conditions prevailing at a place & time, combination produced by heat or cold, clearness or cloudiness, dryness or moisture, wind or calm, high or low pressure, & electrical state, of local air & sky, (April ~, showers alternating with sunshine, fig. smiles & tears; FAIR², FOUL¹, DIRTY, FINE, SOFT, ~; || King's or Queen's ~, fine on ceremonial occasion; favourable, seasonable, good, bad, etc., ~; under stress of ~, owing to storms etc.; CLERK of the ~; make good or bad ~. Naut. meet with; make heavy ~ of, fig., find trying; under the ~, sl., indisposed, out of sorts). **2.** ~beaten, seasoned by or bearing the marks of exposure to storms; ~board, (n.) sloping board attached at bottom of door to keep out rain, (vb) supply with ~boarding, -boards, horizontal boards of which each overlaps the next below to throw off rain as protective casing to wall etc.; ~bound, unable to proceed owing to bad ~; ~box, ~indicator with figures of man & woman, one issuing to foreshow rain, the other fine ~; ~bureau, meteorological office ~chart, diagram showing details of ~ over wide area; ~cock, revolving pointer often in shape of cock mounted in high place esp. on church spire to show whence wind blows, (fig.) inconstant person; ~contact or -cross, leakage from one telegraph wire to another due to wet ~; ~forecast, prophecy of the day's ~; ~glass, barometer; ~map, ~chart; ~moulding, dripstone; ~PROOF²; ~prophet, person who foretells ~; ~service, -ship, organization, ship, for meteorological observations; ~stain, discoloration of wall etc. by exposure; so ~stained; ~station, post of observation in connexion with ~service; ~strip, piece of material used to make door or window proof against rain or wind; ~tiles, arranged to overlap like ~boarding;

etc.; ~ HEART on sleeve; ~ person or principle in one's heart, be devoted to; ~ one's years well, remain young-looking, whence ~'ER¹ n.; (of ship) fly (flag). **2.** Injure surface of, partly consume or obliterate, damage, attenuate, or alter, by rubbing or use, suffer such injury or consumption or change, come or bring into specified state by use, rub (t. & i.) off or out or away or down, (step worn with pilgrims' knees; worn clothes, the worse for wear; inscription has been worn, or has worn, away; ~ the freshness, the nap, off; impression soon ~s off; clothes ~ to one's shape, fit better with use; ~ one's trousers, trousers have worn, into holes or bagginess; seams ~ white, ragged, threadbare; is worn to a shadow with care; stick ~s down to a stump; a worn or well-worn joke, stale; ~ out, use or be used till usable no longer). **3.** Exhaust, tire or be tired out, put down by persistence, (worn with travel; a ~ing occupation, companion, etc.; ~ out one's welcome, go too often or stay too long as visitor etc.; his patience wore, or was worn, out at last; succeeded in ~ing down opposition). **4.** Endure continued use well, badly, etc., remain specified time in working order or presentable state, last long, (won't ~, of inferior material, transitory impression, etc.; ~s for years; person ~s well, retains youthful strength or esp. look). **5.** (Of time) go slowly or tediously on, pass (t. & i. of time) gradually away, (winter, time, day, ~s on or away; away or out one's life or time or youth in trifles; ~ through the day, get through it somehow). **6.** Make (hole, groove, channel) by attrition. (usu. of incidental or undesigned action, cf. BORE¹; often of water). **7.** ~ing-apparel, clothes; ~ing-iron or -plate, piece of metal attached to protect surface exposed to friction. Hence ~ABLE a. [Aryan: OE werian, cf. ON verja, Goth. wasjan; cogn. w. L vestis, Gk esthēs, clothes, Skr. vas to dress]

wear² (wār), n. **1.** Wearing or being worn on person, use as clothes, (the best materials for Sunday, working, spring, seaside, etc., ~; serges were in general ~, fashionable; the coat I have in ~, am regularly wearing). **2.** Thing to wear, fashionable or suitable apparel, (in phr., on type of motley's the only ~; also in foot etc. ~ chiefly in trade use as collective for things worn on feet etc.). **3.** Damage sustained as result of ordinary use (esp. ~ & tear; will stand any amount of ~; is the worse for ~, damaged by use). **4.** Capacity for resisting ~ & tear (there is a great deal of, no, ~ in it). [f. prec.]

wear³ (wār), v.t. & i. (naut.; past & p.p. wore). Bring (ship), (of ship) come, about by putting up of helm (cf. tack). [etym. dub.: perh. corrupt. of VEER by confusion w. WEAR¹]

wear⁴.=WEIR.

cast ~, = ~cock; ~-wise, able to forecast ~; ~-worn, marked by storms etc.
3. adj. (naut.). Windward (on the ~
quarter, beam, bow, etc.; have the ~ gage
or gauge of; keep one's ~ eye open, &c.).
be on the look-out); hence ~most a.
[com.-Teut.: cf. Du. weder, G
weller; cogn. w. wind¹, & w. Skr. vā,
ādmi, blow]

wea′ther² (wědh-), v.t. & i. **1.** Expose to
atmospheric changes; (usu. in pass.) discolour or partly disintegrate (rock, stones)
by exposure to air (esp. in Geol.); be discoloured or worn thus. **2.** (Of ship or its
crew) get to windward of (cape etc.);
come safely through (storm lit. or fig.).
3. Make (boards, tiles) overlap downwards, whence ~ing² n. [f. prec.]
wea′therly (wědh-), a. (naut.). (Of ship)
making little leeway, capable of keeping
close to wind. Hence ~iness n. [-ly¹]
weave, v.t. & i. (wove, woven &, chiefly in
some trade phrr., wove), & n. **1.** Form
(thread etc.) into fabric, (fabric) out of
thread etc., by interlacing, make fabric
thus, work at loom; work up (facts etc.),
introduce (details), into a story or connected whole, fashion (tale, poem, etc.);
contrive (plot); (R.A.F. sl.) dodge, take
evasive action; wove(n) paper, with uniform unlined surface given by making in
frame of crossed wire-gauze. **2.** n. Style
of weaving. [com.-Teut.: cogn. w. Gk huphē,
web]

weav′er, n. In vbl senses; esp.: artisan
who lives by weaving (~'s knot, kind
used esp. for joining cords of different
size); (also ~-bird) kinds of bird remarkable for elaborate or dextrously made
textile nests. [-ER¹]

weazen. See wizened.

web, n. **1.** Woven fabric, amount woven
in one piece, (also fig., as a ~ of lies).
2. Cob~ (with help of context only;
often spider's ~), similar product of any
spinning creature, gossamer, etc. **3.**
Membrane filling spaces between toes
esp. of swimming bird or bat; connective
tissue. **4.** Vane of feather. **5.** Large roll
of paper used esp. in newspaper-printing.
6. Thin flat part connecting more solid
parts in machinery etc., e.g. part of railway-carriage wheel between nave & rim.
7. ~-eye, disease of eye with film or
excrescence, whence ~eyed² (-īd) a.;
~fingers, -toes, abnormally or normally
connected ~s, whence ~-fingerd²,
~-toed² (-tōd), aa.; ~-foot, with ~-toes,
whence ~-footed² a.; ~-wheel, with plate
or ~ instead of spokes, or with rim
spokes, & centre, in one piece as in watch-
wheels; ~-worm, kinds of gregarious
larvae spinning large ~s to sleep for or
feed on enclosed foliage in. Hence
~bed² (-bd) a. [OE webb (wefan WEAVE),
cf. Du. web, G gewebe]

web′bing, n. Strong narrow fabric such
as is used for horse-girths, gymnastic
belts, etc.; stronger edging of more delicate fabric. [-ING¹]

wed, v.t. & i. (~ded, ~ded or rarely &
not in adj. use wed). (Of party, priest, (Of
parent etc.) MARRY¹ (t. & i., rhet. exc. in
p.p. ~ded in adj. use, as a ~ded pair);
~ded to (life, bliss, etc., in matrimony);
unite (qualities often separated; ~ efficiency to economy); (p.p.) devoted to
opinions, pursuits, etc., so as to be unable
to abandon them. [OE weddian to pledge
(wed a pledge, cogn. w. L wēs vadis),
cf. Du. wedden, G wetten, wager, & WAGE.
WAGER, GAGE¹]

wed′ding, n. Marriage ceremony (&
festivities); silver, golden, diamond, ~,
25th, 50th, 60th or 75th, anniversary of
~; || penny ~, with money contributions
from guests; ~ break(fast, entertainment
usual between ~ ceremony & departure
for honeymoon; ~-cake, distributed to
~-guests & sent in portions to absent
friends; ~-cards, with names of pair sent
to friends as announcement of ~; ~-day,
day or anniversary of ~; ~-favour, white
rosette or knot of ribbons worn in honour
of ~; ~-garment, qualification for parti-
cipating in something (ref. to Matt. xxii.
11); ~-ring, that put on bride's finger at
~-ceremony & usu. worn constantly as
distinctive mark of married woman.
[-ING¹]

wedge, n. & v.t. **1.** Piece of wood or
metal of which one end is an acute-
angled edge formed by two converging
planes used to split wood or rock or widen
opening or exert force in various ways,
one of the MECHANICAL powers (or a special
application of the INCLINE¹d plane), (thin
end of the ~, change, measure, action, etc.,
that will lead to further changes or
developments & is therefore of more
importance than it seems); anything
resembling a ~ in being chiefly outlined
by two radial planes or lines converging
at acute angle (a ~ of cake etc.; the seats
are disposed in ~s; drew up his men in a
~); ~-shaped, like solid ~, also V-shaped;
~-tailed, of birds having middle tail-
feathers longest; hence ~ WISE adv. **2.**
v.t. Split with ~ (rare); fasten by use of
~; thrust or pack (usu. in, tightly between
other things or persons; push off or away
like a ~. [com.-Teut.: OE weeg, cf. Du.
wegge, G wecke kind of loaf]

Wedg′wood, n. Kind of semi-vitrified
pottery. [J. ~, inventor d. 1795]

wed′lock, n. The married state (born in
lawful ~; legitimately, of married parents). [OE wedlāc (wed pledge, lāc action) marriage vow]

Wednesday (wenz′dī), n. Fourth day of
week (ash² ~). [OE wōdnes dæg day of
Woden or Odin, transl. of LL diēs Mer-
curii]

wee, a. (~er, ~est). Little, very small, (chiefly in nursery or Sc. use); *Wee Frees*, nickname for part of Free Church of Scotland that refused inclusion in the United Free Church in 1900. [f. ME *wei*, *wee*, *we*, bit, usu. in phr. *a little wee*, f. OE *wǣg* weight, balance, cf. WEY]

weed, n., & v.t. & i. 1. Wild herb springing where it is not wanted (*till ~s grow apace*, gibe at tall or fast-growing child); cigar (colloq.); *the* (*Indian*, *soothing*, etc.) ~; tobacco; lanky & weakly horse or person; hence ~'LESS, ~'Y², aa., ~'INESS n. 2. vb. Clear (ground) of ~s (also fig.), cut off or uproot ~s, whence ~'ER¹(1, 2) n.; sort out (inferior parts or members of a quantity or company) for riddance, rid (quantity or company) of inferior members etc. [vb (cf. Du. *wieden*) f. n., OE *wēod*, cf. OSax. *wiod*, etym. dub.]

weeds (z), n. pl. Mourning worn by widow (usu. *widow's ~*). [earlier sense in sing. *garment*, ME *wēde* f. OE *wǣd*, *wǣde*, cf. ON *váđ*]

week, n. 1. Period of seven days reckoned from midnight on Saturday–Sunday (*what day of the ~ is it?*, is it Thursday, Monday, Tuesday, Wednesday, Thursday, Friday, or Saturday?; HOLY, PASSION, EASTER, ~ *of Sundays* or ~s, seven ~s; *feast of ~s*, Jewish PENTECOST; *middle of next* ~, see KNOCK¹). 2. Period of seven days reckoned from any point (*can you come to us for a ~?*; *today* ~, ~'s days hence; *tomorrow*, *yesterday*, *Friday*, etc., ~, day later, earlier, than such future, past, day by a ~; *have not seen you for ~s*; *did it ~s ago*). 3. The six days between Sundays. 4. ~*-day*, any day other than Sunday; ~*-end*, Sunday & parts of Saturday & Monday as time for holiday or visit, (v.i.) make ~*-end* visit etc., whence ~*-*ÉN'DER¹ n. [com.-Teut.: OE *wice*, *wucu*, cf. Du. *week*, OHG *wehha*; also ON *vikja* to turn, G *wechsel* change]

week'ly, a., adv., & n. 1. (Occurring, issuing, done, etc.) once a week, every week; of or for or lasting a week. 2. n. ~ newspaper or periodical. [-LY¹, ²]

ween, v.t. (poet.). Be of opinion (usu. *I ~* abs. & parenthet. also with *that* expressed or omitted); expect to get etc. [com.-Teut.: OE *wēnan*, cf. Du. *wanen*, G *wähnen*, fancy]

weep, v.i. & t. (*wept*). 1. Shed tears (for person; *for* pain, rage, joy, etc.); shed tears for, lament over, bewail. 2. Send forth or be covered with drops, come or send forth in drops, exude, sweat, drip, (~*ing eczema*, with exudation; ~*ing pine*, designed to drip at intervals); *W~ing Cross* (hist.), wayside cross for penitents to pray at (*come home by W~ing Cross*, be made to repent one's conduct etc.). 3. (Of tree) have drooping branches

(chiefly in part. as distinctive epithet of variety, ~*ing birch*, *willow*, etc.). 4. ~ *out*, utter with tears; ~ *oneself out*, ~ one's fill; ~ *away*, consume (time) in ~ing. [com.-Teut.: OE *wēpan* cry aloud (*wōp* outcry), cf. OHG *wuofan*, Goth. *wōpjan*]

weep'er, n. In vbl senses; also or esp.: hired mourner at funeral; crape hat-sash worn by men at funerals; widow's black crape veil; (pl.) widow's white cuffs. [-ER¹]

weev'er, n. Kinds of fish (*Dragon & Lesser W~*) with sharp dorsal spines inflicting wound that often festers. [f. OF *wivre* WIVERN, weever]

weev'il, n. Kinds of beetle with head extended into a proboscis feeding on grain, nuts, fruit, & leaves; any insect damaging stored grain similarly to corn ~. Hence (f grain) ~*'*LED² (-vld), ~*Y²* (-vĭl), aa. [OE *wifel*, cf. MDu. *wevel*, OHG *wibil*; perh. cogn. w. WEAVE]

weft', n. Cross-threads woven into warp to make web; (loosely) web. [OE *vefta*, cf. ON *vipta*, & WEAVE]

weft'¹. Var. of WAFT n. (naut.).

Wehrmacht (vār'mahχt), n. German armed forces. [G.; = defensive force]

weigh (wā), v.t. & i., & n. 1. Find weight of with scales or other machine, whence ~'ABH(4) (wā'ĭj) n., balance in hands (as if) to guess weight of, (~ *sugar*, *luggage*; *meditatively* ~*ed his stick in his hand*; ~ *out*, take definite weight of, take specified weight from larger quantity, distribute in definite quantities, by aid of scales, *as* ~ *out butter*, *portions* or 3 lb. *of butter*); ascertain one's own weight (*when did you* ~ *last?*; ~ *out*, *in*, of jockey before & after race, & transf., ~ *in*, enter an appearance; ~ *in with* argument etc., produce it triumphantly). 2. Estimate relative value or importance of, compare with or against or abs., consider with a view to choice or rejection or preference, (~ *consequences*, *pros & cons*, *oath* or *argument with* or *against* another; ~ *one's words*, select such as express neither more nor less than one means; ~ *the claims*, *merits*, etc., *of rival candidates*). 3. Be equal to or balance (specified weight) in the scales, (fig.) have specified importance, exercise pressure or influence, have weight or importance, be heavy or burdensome, (~*s a ton*, 6 *oz*, *little*, *nothing*, *light*, *heavy*, *heavily*; ~ *heavy* etc., *or abs.*, *upon*, be burdensome or depressing to; *the point that* ~*s with me*). 4. Bring *down* by weight lit. or fig., (of counterweight) force *up*, (*fruit* ~*s down branch*; *one good argument* ~*s down six bad ones*; ~*ed down with cares*; *bucket is* ~*ed up by mass of iron at end of lever*). 5. Raise from below water (~ *anchor*, start for voyage; ~ *ship*, raise, refloat it when sunk). 6. ~*-beam*, portable steel-yard suspended in frame; ~*bridge*,

~ing-machine with plate on to which ~, vehicles etc. can be driven to be ~ed; ~-house, building in which goods can be weighed officially; ~-lock, canal lock with provision for ~ing barges; ~ing-machine, usn. for great weights or of more complicated mechanism than simple balance.

7. n. Process or occasion of ~ing; under ~, corruption of under WAY. [Aryan: OE wegan carry, cf. Du. wegen weigh, Skr. vah carry L vehere carry]

weight (wāt), n. 1. [L.] Force with which body tends to centre of attraction (the ~s of the planets) (of terrestrial things) degree of downward tendency in body produced as resultant of earth's gravitation & centrifugal force (the ~ of a body varies with latitude & altitude, its mass does not). 2. Relative mass or quantity of matter contained, downward force, heaviness, regarded as a property of bodies (superior both in size & in ~; he is twice your ~; DEAD ~; ~ of metal, total amount that can be thrown by ship's guns at one discharge). 3. Body's mass numerically expressed in some recognized scale (what is your ~?; reached the ~ of 12 st.); scale or notation for expressing ~s (TROY, AVOIRDUPOIS, ~); BOX³ing ~s. 4. Heavy body (keep papers down with a ~; clock is worked by ~s; must not lift ~s); piece of metal etc. of known mass used in scales for weighing articles (where is the ounce ~?). 5. Load to be supported (the pillars have a great ~ to bear), heavy burden of care, responsibility, etc. 6. Importance, convincing effect, influence, preponderance, (considerations of no ~; men of ~; has great ~ with me; the ~ of evidence is against him). Hence ~¹LESS a. [OE gewiht (prec.)]

weight² (wāt), v.t. Attach a weight to, hold down with a weight or weights; impede or burden with load lit. or fig.; treat (fabric) with minerals etc. to make it seem stouter. [f. prec.]

weight³y (wāt-), a. Weighing much, heavy; momentous, important; well-weighed, evidencing thought, deserving of consideration; influential, authoritative. Hence ~ILY² adv., ~INESS n. [-Y¹]

weir, wear, (wēr), n. Dam across river to raise level of water above it; enclosure of stakes etc. set in stream as trap for fish. [OE wer (werian defend), cf. G wehr defence]

weird¹ (wērd), n. Fate, destiny, (chiefly Sc.: DREE one's ~). [OE wyrd (weorthan be, happen, see WORTH²)]

weird² (wērd), a. Connected with fate (the ~ sisters, the fates, witches); supernatural, uncanny, unearthly; super- (colloq.) queer, odd, old-fashioned, strange, incomprehensible. Hence ~LY² adv., ~-NESS n. [f. prec. used attrib. in ~ sisters)

Weis'mannism (vīs-), n. A theory of

heredity, in which transmission of acquired characters is denied. [August Weismann, German biologist, +-ISM]

Welch¹, a. Var. of WELSH¹ in names of regiments (~ Regiment, Royal ~ Fusiliers; but Welsh Guards).

Welch²(er). See WELSH².

wel'come, int. n., v.t., & a. 1. Hail, know that your coming gives pleasure (often with adv. addition, as ~ home, to Edinburgh!). 2. n. Saying ~ to person, kind or glad reception or entertainment given one ~, assure him he is ~; WEAR¹ out or outstay one's ~; give warm ~, show great joy at arrival, also make vigorous resistance). 3. v.t. Say ~ to, greet on arrival, receive (guest, arrival, news, opportunity, event) with pleasure or signs of it. 4. adj. Gladly received (a ~ guest, interruption, gift, rest, denial, sight, etc.; ~ as snow in harvest, un~; make one ~, let him feel so); (pred. only) ungrudgingly permitted to do or given right to thing, absolved of thanking or recompensing, (you are ~ to take what steps you please; any one is ~ to my share, to any service I can do; you are ~, or ellipt. ~, no thanks required); hence ~NESS n. [orig. f. OE wilcuma (wil-+ cuma comer) person who comes to please another, changed in sense by confusion with WELL³ COME, cf. ON velkominn a. welcome]

weld¹, n. Dyer's-weed, plant formerly used to dye yellow. [prob. cogn. w. WOLD]

weld² v.t. & i., & n. 1. Unite (pieces of metal, esp. iron) into homogeneous mass by hammering or pressure (usn. when iron is softened by heat but not melted), make (by ~ing, (of iron etc.) admit of being ~ed easily etc.); bring (recruits, parts, arguments etc.) into homogeneous whole (usn. into); hence ~ABLE a. 2. n. ~ed junction. [var. of WELL² in orig. sense boil]

wel'fare, n. Satisfactory state, health & prosperity, well-being, (usn. of person, society, etc., or with my etc.); ~ State, one having national health, insurance, & other social services; ~ work, efforts to make life worth living for employees etc. [WELL³ FARE²]

wel'kin, n. (poet., or arch.). Fade, wither. [ME welken (OHG welk flaccid)]

wel'kin, n. (poet.). Sky. [OE wolcnu clouds, cf. G wolke cloud]

well¹, n. 1. Spring or fountain, (fig.) source, (poet. or arch.: ~ of English undefiled, Chaucer). 2. Shaft sunk in ground & lined with stone or other protection for obtaining subterranean water, oil, etc. (ARTESIAN ~). 3. Enclosed space more or less resembling ~-shaft, space in middle of house from floor to roof containing stairs (also ~ staircase) or lift or surrounded by stairs (also ~-hole) or open

4895   3 A   3

for light & ventilation; ‖ railed space for counsel etc. in court; receptacle for ink in inkstand. **4.** ~-*deck*, space on main deck enclosed by bulwarks & higher decks; ~-*dish*, with hollow for gravy to collect in; ~-*grate*, in which fire burns on hearth, receiving its air supply from below; ~-*head*, source, fountain-head; ~-*room*, where spa water is dispensed; ~-*sinker*, person whose occupation is sinking ~s; ~-*spring*, = ~-*head*, cogn. w. WILL 1, w. sense *agreeably to wish*]

well², v.i. Spring (as) from fountain (often *up, out, forth*). [OE *wellan* causative of *weallan* (prec.)]

well³, adv. (*better, best*), pred. a. (*better, best*), attrib. a. (no comp.), & n. **1.** In good manner or style, satisfactorily, rightly, (*the work is ~ done; that is ~ said; a ~ situated house; ~ begun is half done; ~ done!, rum!,* etc., cry of commendation; *~ met!*, greeting to person one has been wanting to see; *come off ~*, have good luck, distinguish oneself; *wish I was ~ out of it*, without disaster etc.; *you did ~, it was ~ done of you, to come*). **2.** Thoroughly, with care or completeness, sufficiently, to a considerable distance or extent, with margin enough to justify description, quite, (*look ~ to yourself; judge ~ & truly; smack him, polish it, ~; is ~ up in the list, ~ on in life, ~ advanced the leaders of thought; as ~*, in addition, *he is a Christian as ~, he gave me clothes as ~ as food*). **3.** Heartily, kindly, laudatorily, approvingly, on good terms, (*love, like, person ~; treat person ~; think or speak ~ of; it speaks ~ for his discipline that he never punishes*, serves as commendation; *stand ~ with one*, be in his good graces). **4.** Probably, not incredibly, easily, with reason, wisely, advisably, (*it may ~ be that ~ :* can, cannot, *~ manage it; you may ~ ask, say, that; we might ~ make the experiment; as ~*, with equal reason, preferably, without worse consequences, *as you might as ~ throw your money into the sea as lend it to him, as ~ be hanged for a sheep as a lamb, we may as ~ begin at once; that is just as ~*, need not be regretted; *you might as ~*, nursery formula of request). **5.** pred. adj. (often indistinguishable from adv.). In good health (*is she ~ or ill? ; will soon be better; is best in the winter; quite ~, thank you; am perfectly ~*); in satisfactory state or position, satisfactory, advisable, (*am very ~ where I am; all's ~; it is all very ~*, ironical expression of discontent, or rejection of comfort, arguments, etc.; *it is ~ with him; it would have been, were, ~ for him if; it would be ~ to inquire*; enough, tolerably good or good-looking; *as ~*, not unadvisable, *as it may be as*

to explain; *~ & good*, formula of dispassionate acceptance of decision, as *if you choose to take my advice, ~ & good*; VERY ~). **6.** attrib. adj. (rare). In good health (*a ~ man should not be sick*). **7.** n. Good things (*I wish him ~*); what is satisfactory (*let ~ alone*, do not meddle needlessly). [com.-Teut.: OE *wel*, cf. Du. *wel*, G *wohl*, cogn. w. WILL 1, w. sense *agreeably to wish*]

well⁴, int. expressing great astonishment (*~, who would have thought it?; ~!; ~ to be sure!*), relief (*~, here we are at last*), concession (*~, come if you like; ~, perhaps you are right; ~ then, say no more about it*), resumption of talk (*~, who was it? ; ~, he says he must see you*), qualified recognition of point (*~, but what about Jones?*), expectation (*~ then?*), resignation (*~, it can't be helped*), etc. [ellipt. uses of prec. adv.]

well- **1.** In a few words *well-* or *well* is an inseparable pref.: ~-*being*, welfare; ~-*doer*, -*doing*, virtuous person, conduct; ~-*nigh*, rhet., almost; ~-*wisher*, person who wishes well to one. **2.** *Well* may precede any participle or word in -ED², when the combination is used attrib. with n. following, it is usu. hyphened (*he is a ~-known person*; this is done in the pred. use also when the combination ends in -ING² or -ED³, but not usu. when it ends in -ED¹ (*the stroke was well timed*, cf. a ~-*timed stroke*) unless it has acquired a sense or use other or more restricted than that of the separate elements (*my watch is well regulated; I do not think his action was ~-advised*, cf. *he is not well advised by his friends*); a list of the commoner combinations follows with special senses or contexts noted; ~-*advised*, prudent, wise, (chiefly of action taken); ~ *aimed*; ~-*appointed*, having all necessary equipment (esp. of expedition, fleet, etc.); ~ *armed*; ~ *attested*; ~ *authenticated*; ~-*balanced*, sane, sensible, (esp. of mind); ~-*behaved*; ~ *beloved*; ~-*born*, of noble or distinguished family; ~-*bred*, having good breeding or manners; ~ *chosen*, esp. of good or pure stock; ~-*conditioned*, not ~ *conducted*, characterized by good conduct; ~-*connected*, connected by blood etc. with good families; ~ *contented*; ~ *contested*; ~ *defined*; ~ *directed*, esp. of blow or shot; ~-*disposed*, having good disposition or kindly feeling (*towards*); ‖ ~ *done*, of meat cooked through; ~ *dressed*; ~ *drilled*; ~ *earned*; ~ *educated*; ~-*favoured*, good-looking; ~ *fed*; ~ *fought*; ~-*found*, = ~-*appointed*; ~ *founded*, having foundation in fact (of suspicion or other belief or sentiment); ~ *furnished*; ~-*graced*, possessed of attractive qualities; ~ *grounded*; ~ *founded*, also ~ *trained in rudiments*;

~-informed, having ~-stored mind or access to best information; ~-intentioned, aiming or aimed (usu. unsuccessfully) at good results; ~-judged, showing good judgement or tact or good aim (of action taken); ~-knit, compact, not loose-made or sprawling (esp. of person or his frame); ~ known; ||~-liking, with ~-fed prosperous look (usu. fat &~-liking); ~-made, (esp.) of symmetrical bodily make; ~-mannered, with good manners; ~-marked, distinct, easy to detect; ~-meaning, = ~-intentioned (of person or meaning), = ~-intentioned (of attempt); ~ oiled, (fig., of expression) complimentary; ~ ordered, arranged in orderly manner; ~ paid; ~ painted; ~ pleased; ||~-pleasing; ~-proportioned; ~-read, having read much [cf. -ED-(2)], with mind ~ stored by reading; ~ regulated, under proper control, not undisciplined; ~ remembered (of person or of good repute; ~-rounded, complete & symmetrical; ~-seen (arch.), satisfactory or good; ||~-set, compact, firmly knit, (esp.) also ~ set up, of bodily frame); ~ sifted (esp. of facts or of evidence); ~ spent (esp. of time or effort); ~-spoken, refined in speech; ~-timbered; ~ timed, opportune; ~ trained; ~-trod, often tested with good result; ~-trodden (den.), frequented; ~ tuned; ~ turned, happily expressed (of compliment, phrase, verse); ~-worn, (esp.) trite, stale. ~ off, = fortunately situated (does not know when he is ~ off), sufficiently rich, is two words when used pred., but hyphened when attrib. (~-off people); ~-to-do, = sufficiently rich, is hyphened when attrib. & usu. when pred. also.

welladay', -away', int. of grief (arch. or joc.). [OE wella wa, woe, lo! woe]

||Wellingtōn'ia, n. Kinds of sequoia, [named after Duke of Wellington. -IA¹]

||Wěll'ingtons (-z), n. pl. Boots coming up or nearly up to knees. [as prec.]

Wělsh¹ (& see WELCH¹), a. & n. (language, the people) of Wales (~ mutton, from small mountain sheep; ~ rabbit or by pop. etym. rarebit, dish of toasted cheese); ~ man, ~'woman, native of Wales. [OE wælisc foreign (wealh foreigner, Celt., -ISH¹)]

wělsh² , **wělch**, v.t. & i. Decamp without paying (winner of bet on horse-race, or dub.). Hence ~'ER¹ n. [f. 1857; etym. dub.]

wělt¹, n., & v.t. **1.** Strip of leather sewn round edge of boot or shoe uppers to serve as attachment to sole; weal. **2.** v.t. Provide with ~; raise weals on, beat, flog. [ME welte, walt, etym. dub.]

wělt² (v-), n. (German for) world; ~ anschau'ung (-show'ŏŏ), philosophical survey of the world as a whole; ~'politik' (-ēk), foreign policy on the grand scale;

~'schmerz (-shměrts), vague yearning & discontent with regard to the constitution of things. [G]

wěl'ter¹, v.i., & n. **1.** Roll, wallow, be washed about, be soaked or steeped or dabbled in blood etc. **2.** n. General confusion, disorderly mixture or aimless conflict of creeds, policies, vices, etc. [f. MDu. welteren roll, cf. Icel. velta, G wälzen; cogn. w. WALTZ, WALLOW]

wěl'ter² n. **1.** Heavy rider (now rare) (attrib.), ~ race, cup, stakes, handicap, etc., horse-races for heavy-weight riders (also ellipt. ~=race); ~ weight, heavy weight rider, also weight carried apart from weight for age as test, (Boxing) see BOX'ing-weights. **2.** (colloq.). Heavy blow, big person or thing. [prop. (orig. in last sense) f. WELT¹ flog + -ER¹; = big one, cf. WHACKER]

wěn¹, n. More or less permanent tumour of benign character on scalp or other part of body; goitre; (fig.) abnormally large or congested city (the great ~, London). [OE wenn, cf. Du. wen, etym. dub.]

wěn² n. The old English letter p (w). [OE, var. of wynn joy (see WINSOME) used as beginning with the letter, cf. THORN]

wench, n., & v.i. & t. **1.** Girl or young woman, lass, (esp. of rustics or servants, or joc. & colloq.); a strapping, buxom, etc., ~); ||(arch.) strumpet. **2.** v.b. Court (dial.); whore, haunt company of strumpet. [ME wenche(l) f. OE wencel infant (wancol ~), joc. f. G wanken totter)]

wěnd¹, v.t. & i. Direct one's way; (arch.) go. [corr.-Teut.: OE wendan turn t. & i., cf. Du. & G wenden; the past was formerly went (now used to supply past of GO¹)]

Wěnd², n. One of a Slavonic race formerly spread over N. Germany, & now inhabiting E. Saxony. Hence ~'ic, ~'ISH, aa. [f. G Wende, etym. dub.]

~ **Wěns'leydāle** (-zli-), n. Kind of cheese. [~ in Yorks.]

went. See GO¹, WEND¹ etym.

wěn'tletrăp (-tel-), n. Shellfish with spiral shell of many whorls. [f. Du. wenteltrap orig. = winding stairs]

wept. See WEEP.

were. See BE.

were'wolf, **wer'wolf**, (wēr'wŏŏlf), n. (myth.: pl. -ves). Human being turned into wolf. [OE were-wulf (wer man, cf. L vir, WOLF)]

wert. See BE.

Wer'therism (vār'ter-), n. Morbid sentimentality as of Werther in Goethe's Sorrows of Werther. [-ISM(3)]

Wěsleyan (wěz'lian, wěs'-), a. & n. (hist.). (Member) of the denomination founded by John Wesley (d. 1791). Hence ~ISM(3) n. [-AN: the normal form would be Wesleian (see -EAN), whence the doubtful pronunc.]

wěst, adv., n., & a. (abbr. W.). **1.** Towards or in the region in front of observer

on equator at equinox who faces setting sun (~ BY¹ *north* or *south*; ~ *of*, farther than; DUE¹~; *lies* etc. *east & ~*, length-wise along line between east & ~; *go, gone, ~*, sl., die, dead); ~*north*~, ~*south*~, advv., nn., & aa., (regions) mid-way between ~ & *north*~, *south*~ (with uses & derivatives corresponding to those of ~, as ~*north*~*erly*, ~*north*~*ern*, ~*north*~*wardly*; see WESTERLY etc.); hence ~'WARD adv. & n., ~⁴ WARDS adv. & n. 2. n. Cardinal point lying (~) western part of England, Scot-land, Ireland, or Europe, part of U.S. beyond earlier settled States or ~ of Mississippi; ~ WESTERN *Empire*); western part of any country (~ *wind*. 3. adj. Situated, dwelling, in or more towards the ~; ~ *longitude*, ||~*central*, abbr. W.C., London postal district; ||~*country*, part of Eng-land ~ of line from Southampton to mouth of Severn; W~ INDIES, whence W~-*Indian* a.; W~ *End*, richer & more fashionable district in ~ of London; (of wind) coming from the ~; ||~*country*, of or from or characteristic of the ~ country; ~*countryman* (or -*woman*), native of ~ ft; W~-*end*, in or characteristic of W~ End. [com.-Teut.: OE, Du., G, etc.; prob. cogn. w. Gk *hesperos*, L *vesper*, evening]

wes'tering, a. & part. Tending towards the west (usu. of sun). [f. obs. *vester* vb (prec. in vbl use, -ER⁶)]

wes'terly, a. & adv. =foll. (rare); (of direction) towards the west; (of wind) blowing from the west or thereabouts. [f. WEST as EASTERLY]

wes'tern, a. & n. 1. Living or situated in, coming from, the west (W~ *Empire*, one of two parts, with Rome as capital, cf. *Eastern Empire* with Constantinople, into which Theodosius divided Roman Em-pire 395; W~ or *Latin Church*, part of Christian church that continued to ac-knowledge the popes at the Greek schism, see GREEK); =OCCIDENTAl; (of wind) westerly (rare); hence ~ER⁴(4) n., ~IZE(3) v.t., make (oriental people or country) ~er; a film or novel dealing with cowboys, rustlers, sheriffs, etc. [-ERN]

wes'ting, n. Westward progress or devia-tion esp. in sailing (cf. NORTHING). [-ING¹]

West'minster, n. City forming part of London (~ *Abbey*, fig., glorious death such as would entitle one to place among celebrities there buried); (the Houses of) Parliament, the political arena; member of ~ School; STATUTE of ~.

am ~ *to the skin*, with clothes soaked through); *not prohibiting or opposing use of alcohol; ~ BLANKET¹; ~ *bargain*, closed with drink; ~ BOB⁵.; ~ *bulb*, see DRY¹-*bulb thermometer*; ~ *dock*, in which ship can float; ~ *pack*, wrapping of body in ~ cloths enclosed in dry blankets etc.; ~ *plate* in photog, sensitized collodion plate exposed while ~; rainy (~ *day, weather*); ~*nurse*, (n.) woman employed to suckle another's child, (v.t.) act as ~*nurse* to (child); hence ~ NESS n., ~t'ISH¹(2) a. 2. v.t. Make (~ *bargain*, close it with drink; ~*one's whistle*, drink); hence ~t'ING¹(1) n. 3. n. Moisture, liquid that ~s something, rainy weather; (sl.) a drink; *opponent of prohibition. [OE *wæt*, cf. ON *vátr*; cogn. w. WATER]

weth'er (-dh-), n. Castrated ram. [com.-Teut.: OE *wedher*, cf. Du. *veer*, G *widder*; prob. cogn. w. L *vitulus* calf]

wey (wā), n. Unit of weight varying from 2 cwt to 3 cwt with different kinds of goods. [OE *wæge* weight (*wegan* WEIGH]

wh-. In a few of the words beginning thus the w is, as indicated in the pro-nunc. brackets, not sounded; in all others the h is silent in ordinary modern usage, but the earlier sound, = hw, is retained by the Scots, Irish, Welsh, & northern English, & by purists in unfamiliar wds as well as for the nonce in unfamiliar wds or such as might be confused with com-moner wds having no -h- (*whel, whey*).

whack, v.t. & n. 1. Strike heavily with stick etc., thwack, whence ~ING¹(1) n.: (sl.) go shares in, distribute. 2. n. Heavy blow esp. with stick; (sl.) share (*have had may ~ of pleasure*). [imit.]

whack'er, n. (sl.). Thing or person big of its kind. [-ER¹; cf. *thumper, whopper*, etc.]

whack'ing, a. (sl.). Big of its kind. [-ING²; see prec.]

whale, n. & v.i. 1. Kinds of large fishlike marine mammal some of which are hunted for their oil, spermaceti, ~bone, ambergris, etc. (*right, arctic, Greenland,* or *bowhead* ~, kind yielding best ~bone; SPERM², *humpback, bottle-nosed*, etc.; ~ *bull, cow*, ~, adult male, female, ~; *very like a* ~, ironical assent to absurd state-ment, see *Hamlet* III. ii. 399). 2. 4 ~ *of* (colloq.), no end of; *a* ~ *on, at, for*, very good at or keen on (something); ~*boat*, (double-bowed like those) used in whal-ing; ~*bone*, elastic horny substance growing in thin parallel plates in upper jaw of certain ~s, & used in many kinds of manufacture; ~*calf*, young ~; ~*fin*, commerc. name for ~bone; ~*head*, African bird allied to herons & storks; ~*line*, superior rope 2 in. round used in whaling; ~'*man*, seaman engaged in whaling; ~*oil*, train oil or sperm oil got from ~s. 3. v.i. Be engaged in ~-fishing;

For pronunciation of words in *wh*- see WH-.

whaling-gun, for firing harpoon etc. at ~s; **whaling-master**, captain of a whaler. [OE *hwæl*, cf. OHG *wal* (G *walfisch*)]

whal'er, n. Whaling ship or man; kind of clinker-built seaboat with pointed stern, carried by some warships. [-ER¹]

whang, v.t. & i., & n. (colloq.) 1. Strike heavily & loudly, whack; (of drum etc.) sound (as) under blow. 2. n. ~ing sound or blow. [imit.]

whangee' (-ngg-), n. Cane made from a kind of Chinese bamboo. [Chin. *huang*]

wharf (wôrf), n. (pl. ~fs, ~ves), & v.t. 1. Wooden or stone platform beside which ship may be moored for (un)loading etc.; hence ~AGE¹, 4) n. 2. v.t. Moor (ship) at, store (goods) on, ~. [OE *hwearf*, cf. Du. & G *werf*]

wharf'inger (wôrf'njer), n. Wharf-owner. [for *wharfager* (wôrf'njer)]

what (wŏt), a. & pron. interrog., excl., & rel. 1. adj.: (a) interrog., asking for selection from indefinite number (cf. *which* from definite number; *~ books have you read?*; *don't know ~ plan he will try*) or for specification of amount or number or kind (*~ money, men, abilities, has he?*; *~ news?*; *~ matter?*, does it matter?; *~ good, use, is it?*; *~ purpose will it serve?*; *~ manner of man is he?*; *I know ~ difficulties there are*, cf. c); (b) excl., = how great or strange or otherwise remarkable for good or ill (*~ a fool you are!*; *~ impudence!*; *~ an idea!*; *~ genius he has!*) or, before adj. & n. = how (*~ partial judges we are!*); (c) rel. = the — that, any — that, as much or many — as, (*dispose of ~ difficulties there are*, cf. a; *lend me ~ money or men you can*; *will give you ~ help is possible*; *~ time*, arch., when, while). 2. pron.: (a) interrog.; = ~ thing(s)?, with many modifications given by context, & often in ellipt. uses for sentence, some of which are here illustrated (*so ~?*, colloq. freq. implying that one is at a loss ~ to do or think; *~ will people say?*, is it respectable to do it?; *~?*, i.e. did you say?; *~ ho!*, excl. of greeting or hailing; *~ is he?*, i.e. in respect of occupation; *~, do you really mean it?*, i.e. I must have heard wrongly; *~ if we were to try?*, i.e. would result; *~ for?*, for ~ reason or purpose?; *~ for* n. (sl.), severe punishment, reprimand, etc., as *he gave him ~-for*; *~ though we are poor?*, i.e. does it matter; *~ next?*, no absurdity can outdo this; *~ of* or *about —?*, i.e. ~ news?, or how can you dispose of this point?; *well, ~ of it?*, formula admitting fact but not inference etc. from it; *~ is he the better for it?*, in ~ way or to ~ extent; *~ is your name?*; *~ not* usu. without interrog. mark, many other things of the same kind, anything; *~ not*, piece of furniture with shelves for knick-knacks; *~ like is he?*, provincial for ~ is he like? or what sort of man is he?; *~ d'ye-call-him,-her,-it,-'em, ~'s-his*(or-her,-its)-*name*, substitutes for name that has slipped memory; *I wonder ~ you are*; *don't know ~ he said*; *~ followed is doubtful*, cf. c; *cannot guess ~ he was attempting*, cf. c; **~ have you* (sl.), anything else of that sort; *I know ~*, have a new idea; *I'll tell you ~*, i.e. the truth or right thing(s), how much!, etc. (*~ he has suffered!*); (c) rel., = that or those which, the thing(s) that, anything that, a thing that, (*~ followed was unpleasant*, cf. a; *did ~ he was attempting*, cf. a; *~ I have said I have said*; *~ I know not is no ~ knowledge*; *give me ~ you can*; *~ is called the general reader*; *come ~ will or may*, in spite of any results etc.; *tell me ~ you remember of it*; *but, ~ even you must condemn, he was lying*; *will do ~ I can for you*; *use no arguments but ~ you believe in yourself*; so also various more or less incorrect colloq. uses of *but ~* for *but*, as *not a day comes but ~ makes a change, not a man but ~ likes her, not a day but ~ it rains, I never see him but ~ I think, I don't know but ~ I will*, NOT *but ~*, with *~ knowledge*; *— between various causes etc., as ~ with drink & ~ with fright, he did not know much about the facts*). [neut. of WHO]

whatev'er (wŏt-), **whate'er** (poet.: wŏtâr'), a. & pron. indef. rel. used (1) = prec. in rel. uses with addition of or emphasis on indefinite sense (*~ I have is yours*; *do ~ like*); (2) in indef. concessive clauses where *~ what* is not possible, = though any(thing), as *~ results follow, ~ happens, ~ friends we may offend, we shall have done our duty*; (3) ellipt. for ~ it, he, etc., may be, = at all after noun in negative context (never *whate'er*), as *there is no doubt ~, is there any chance ~?, no one ~ would accept, cannot see any one ~*; (4) colloq. for WHAT-EVER. [WHAT + EVER]

What'man (-ŏt-), n. (attrib.). ~ (paper), brand of paper used for drawing, water-colours, engraving, & photography. [maker's name]

what'so (arch.: -ŏt-), **whatsoev'er** (emphatic), **whatsoe'er** (poet.: wŏtsoâr'), aa. & pronn. = WHATEVER (1, 2), & *whatsoever* = also WHATEVER (3). [so]

||**whaup**, n. Curlew (chiefly Sc.). [imit. of cry]

wheal¹, mis-spelling of WALE, WEAL.

||**wheal²**, n. (Cornwall). Mine (esp. tin-mine). [Cornish *huel*]

wheat, n. (Highly nutritious seeds of) kinds of corn-plant bearing dense four-sided spike of grain (esp. *winter* or *unbearded ~, summer* or *bearded ~*, & *German ~* or *spelt*); *~-grass*, couch-grass. Hence ~EN⁵ a. [OE *hwǣte*, cf. Du. *weit*, G *weizen*; cogn. w. WHITE]

wheat′ear, n. Small bird, the stonechat or whitetail. [earlier *wheatears* (WHITE, ARSE)]

Wheat′stone bridge, n. Apparatus for measuring electrical resistances. [C. *Wheatstone*, English physicist]

whee′dle, v.t. Coax *into* doing or *into* good temper etc., persuade by flattery or endearments, cajole, humour for one's own ends; get (thing) by ~*ing out of* person; cheat (person) *out of* thing by ~*ing*. Hence ~ER¹ n., ~ING² a., ~ING**ly** adv. [perh. for *weadle* f. OE *wǽdlian beg* (*wǽdl* poverty)]

wheel¹, n. **1.** Circular frame or disk arranged to revolve on axis & used to facilitate motion of vehicle or for various mechanical purposes, machine etc. of which a ~ is an essential part, object resembling a ~, (BALANCE, CATHERINE, COG¹, FLY³, MILL¹, OVERSHOT, PADDLE, POTTER'S, RATCHET, SPIN*ning*, STEERING, SUN-&-*planed*, UNDERSHOT, ~); *eccentric* ~, turning on axis not at its centre; *fifth* ~, apparatus enabling front ~s etc. of four-wheeled conveyance to be slewed, also see FIFTH ~; ~s *within* ~s, intricate machinery, indirect or secret agencies; *the* ~s *of life*, the vital processes etc.; ~ *of life*, scientific toy converting series of pictures of successive attitudes into semblance of continuous motion; *Fortune's* ~, with which Fortune is depicted as symbol of ups & downs, also fig. vicissitudes; *break on the* ~, maim & kill on medieval instrument of torture that revolved with victim bound on it; BREAK¹ *butterfly on a* FLY¹ *on the* ~; *put* SPOKE¹ *in* one's ~, one's SHOULDER *to the* ~; ~ *&* axle, utilization of leverage given by ~ & its axle, in circumference between ~ & its axle, called one of the MECHANICAL *powers*; *go on* ~s, smoothly; *Fortune's* ~ (*we may be rich at the next turn of the* ~); *steering-*~ (*don't speak to the man at the* ~). **2.** Motion as of ~, circular motion, motion of line as on military evolution; (*street arab turning* ~s *in the gutter*; *the* ~s *&* somersaults *of the gulls*; *right*, *left*, etc., ~, words of command to company etc. in line to swing round on right, left, flank as pivot). **3.** = ¹BARROW², ~*chair*, invalid's on ~s; ~*horse*, wheeler; ~*house*, steersman's shelter; ~*lock*, (gun with) antiquated lock having steel ~ to rub against flint etc.; ~*man*, cyclist; ~*seat*, part of axle fitting into hub; ~*tread*, part of carriage etc. ~ that touches ground; ~*window*, circular with spoke-like tracery; ~*wright*, maker of ~s. Hence (-)~ED² (-ld), ~LESS, aa. [Aryan: OE *hwéol*, cf. Da. *hjul*, Du. *wiel*; cogn. w. Gk *kuklos* circle, wheel, & *polos* axis, L *colus* distaff]

wheel², v.t. & i. Swing (t. & i. of line of

men etc.) round in line on one flank as pivot, (loosely) change direction lit. or fig., face another way, (often *round*); push or pull (wheeled thing esp. wheel-barrow or Bath chair or its load or occupant, or furniture on castors) in some direction; go in circles or curves; ride on bicycle. [f. prec.]

wheel′er, n. In vbl senses; also: pole or shaft horse in four-in-hand, tandem, etc. (cf. LEADER); FOUR-~; ‖ wheelwright. [WHEEL¹,², -ER¹]

wheeze, v.i. & t., & n. **1.** Breathe with audible friction; ~ *out*, utter with ~*ing*. **2.**, n. Sound of ~*ing*, whence ~Y² a., ~*iLY*² adv., ~*iNESS* n.; (Theatr. sl.) joke, anecdote, etc., interpolated by actor during performance. [prob. f. ON *hvæsa* to hiss]

whelk¹, n. Kinds of marine spiral-shelled mollusc, some used as food. [ME *wilk*, OE *wioloc* etym. dub., with *wh-* by assim. to foll.]

whelk², n. Pimple. Hence ~ED² (-kt) a. [OE *hwylca* (*hwelian* suppurate)]

whelm, v.t. (poet., rhet.). Engulf, submerge, overwhelm. [prob. f. obs. *whelve* f. OE *hwylfan* overturn, cogn. w. G *wölben* arch over, Gk *kolpos* bosom]

whelp, n., & v.i. & t. **1.** Young dog, pup; young lion, tiger, bear, wolf, etc., cub; disagreeable or ill-bred child or youth. **2.** vb. Produce pups or cubs or (derog.) child, give birth to (esp. derog. of human mother); originate (evil scheme etc.). [OE *hwelp*, cf. Du. *welp*, G *welf*, etym. dub.]

when, adv. interrog. & rel., pron., & n. **1.** adv. interrog. At what time?, on what occasion?, how soon?, how long ago?, (~ *did*, *shall*, *you see him?*; *don't know*—*it was*; *say* ~, ellipt., i.e. process is to begin or stop; in rhet. questions equivalent to neg. statement, as ~ *shall we see his like again?*, *did I suggest such a thing?*). **2.** adv. rel. (With time etc. as antecedent) at which (*the time* ~ *such things could happen is gone*; *there are occasions*, *conjunctures*, *etc.*, ~); at the or any time that, on the or any occasion that, at whatever time, as soon as, (*he exclaimed* ~ *he saw me*; ~ *Greek meets Greek*; ~ *it rains he stays at home*; *shall have it* ~ *you ask politely*; also ellipt. like WHILE² *as he looked in* ~ *passing*, ~ *found make a note of*; also introducing exclamatory clause with ellipse of apodosis, as ~ *I think what I have done for that man!*); although, considering that, (*walks* ~ *he might ride*; *how could you*, ~ *you knew* ~ *he will not listen?*; *how convince him* ~ *he will not listen?*); after or upon which, but just then, & then, (*the conflict began*, ~ *it soon appeared which was stronger*; *we were just coming to the*

For pronunciation of words in *wh-* see WH-.

point ~ *the bell interrupted us*). **3.** pron. What (interrog.) or which (rel.) time (*till ~ can you stay?, from ~ does it date?*). **4.** n. Time, date, occasion, (*told me the ~ & the how of it*). [OE *hwænne, hwenne*, f. stem of WHO, cf. G *wann* when, *wenn* if, MDu. *wan, wen*]

whence, adv. interrog. & rel., pron., & n. (now poet., literary, etc.). **1.** From what place or source? (being ousted by *where* — *from* in lit. sense & *how, why*, etc., in fig.: *~ comes it that*, how is it that: *no one knows ~ she comes*); (with place etc. as antecedent) from which (*the source ~ these evils spring*; now usu. *from which*; to or rarely at or from the place from which (*return ~ you came; abides ~ he sent me; comes ~ he came*; now usu. *where*) ~whatever place or source. **2.** pron. What (interrog.) or which (rel.) starting-place (*from~ is he?; the source from~ it springs*). **3.** n. Source (*we know neither our ~ nor our ~ whither*). [ME *whennes (whenne)*, f. stem of WHO, OE *hwanon* whence f. WHO, +-ES]

whenev'er, whene'er' (poet.; -âr), **whĕnsŏev'er** (emphatic), adv. rel. indef. (cf. WHEN, EVER). At whatever time, on whatever occasion. As soon as, every time that. [so, EVER]

where (-wâr), adv. interrog. & rel., pron., & n. **1.** adv. interrog. In or to what place or position lit. or fig., in what direction, at what part, in what respect, (*~ is Heaven?; ~ did you read that?*, in what book?; *~ are you going?*, now usu. preferred to *whither*; *showed me ~ they were*; *~ does it touch our interests?; ~ are you looking?, ~ shall we be if prices fall now?*; how situated; *don't know ~ to have him*, said of person or elusive character; often in rhet. questions = neg. statements, as *~ is the sense of it?, ~ is the use of trying?*). **2.** adv. rel. (see also WHERE-). (With place etc. as antecedent) in which (*places ~ they sing*; also with ellipse of noun, as *~ he is weakest is in his facts*); in or to that or any place, in the direction or part or respect, in which (*~ your treasure is; go ~ you like; is, send him, ~ he will be taken care of; ~ the ancients knew nothing we know a little; that's ~ it is*, colloq., that is the real reason for it or point of it). **3.** pron. What (interrog.) or which (rel.) place (*~ do you come from, are you going to?*; vulg. in rel. use, as *the place ~ he comes from*). **4.** n. Place, scene of something, (*the ~s & whens are important*; cf. any~, no~, every~). [OE *hwǣr*, cf. Du. *waar*, G *wer(um)*; cogn. W. WHO, WHEN]

where- (-wâr). **1.** ~ is written in one word with appended prep. as substitute for interrog. *what* or rel. *which* pron. or comb.:— prep. preceding or following *what* inter-rog. pron. or *which* rel. pron. (*~by we know him?; the signs ~by he shall be*

known; *~by I saw that he was angry*), cf. corresp. compounds of *there*; the use is becoming rare exc. either in formal or poet. or in joc. or noted writing or in special uses as noted: **~'about'** (& see 2); **~at'; ~by'; ~'fore** (for what reason?, why?, on what account, on which ac-count; also as n. pl.=reasons, as *the whys & ~fores*); **~from'; ~in'** (also **~inso-ev'er**); **~'into; ~of'; ~on'; ~out'; ~through'** (still common introducing new sentence in narrative); **~'upon'** (still common introducing new sentence in narrative); **~with'** (or **~withal**, the longer form common as n.= money etc. needed for a purpose; *has not the ~withal to do it*, or *the ~withal*). **2.** ~ is added in combination to give, in its proper local use in qualified in sense by additions: **~abouts'** adv. interrog., where within considerable limits or vaguely (*~abouts is he?; don't know even ~abouts to look*), (n., *~abouts*) person's or thing's locality roughly defined; **~as'** conj., taking into consideration or having as premiss the fact that (esp. in legal pre-ambles), in contrast or comparison with the fact that, but in contrast with what has been said; **wherev'er, where'er'** (poet.; -âr), **~soev'er** (emphatic, **where'er'** rel. indef., in or to whatever place etc. (cf. *where* EVER).

whĕ'rry, n. Light shallow rowing-boat usu. for carrying passengers. [?]

whĕt, v.t. (-tt-), & n. **1.** Sharpen by rubbing on or with stone etc.; stimu-late (appetite, stomach, desire); **~stone,** shaped stone for tool-sharpening, thing that sharpens the wits. **2.** n. Sharpening; small quantity taken to create or creating appetite for more; dram. [OE *hwettan* (*hwæt* bold), cf. Du. *wetten*, G *wetzen*]

whether[1] (wĕdh-), a. & pron. interrog. & rel. (arch.). Which of the two. [OE *hwæther* (*hwæth-*), cf. ON *hvárr*, MHG *weder*]

whether[2] (wĕdh-), conj. **1.** Introducing indirect questions of which the direct form would be answerable with *yes* or *no* (*don't know ~ he will be here*); such ques-tions involve an alternative, which may be unexpressed as above, expressed precisely (*~ he is here or ~ he is in London*, or more usu. ellipt. *or in London*), or expressed comprehensively by the negative (*~ he is here or ~ he is not here*, or more usu. ellipt. *or not*); i.e., the alternative if expressed has always *or*, after which *~* is usu. repeated if subj. & vb are expressed; *~* clauses may be appended directly to many adj. & nn. as well as to vbs (*doubt-ful, uncertain, anxious*, etc.; *~; the question* etc.), though up to a point formerly also with direct questions (*~ shall we live or die?*). **2.** Used with follow-ing *or* or *~* (according as second alterna-tive has its subj. & vb expressed, as in 1) to introduce the protasis having alternatives

corresponding to a single conditional apodosis (*~ we stay* or *~ we go*, *~ we go to him or he comes to us*, *~ we go or not, the result will be bad*); *~ or* NO²; formerly also when each alternative had apodosis (*~ we live, we live unto the Lord, & ~ we die, we die*). [f. prec.]

whew (hwū), int. expressing (usu. joc.) consternation.

whey (wā), n. Part of milk that remains liquid when the rest forms curds; *~faced* (arch.), pale esp. with fear. [OE *hwǣg*, cf. Du. *wei*]

which, a. & pron. interrog. & rel. **1.** adj. interrog. Asking for selection from alternatives conceived as limited in number or known (cf. WHAT: *~ way shall we go?*; *say ~ chapter you prefer*). **2.** adj. rel. And, now, although, since, etc., this or these (now rare exc. with n. serving to sum up details of a compound or vague antecedent: *a smile & a sixpence, ~ equipment is within most people's reach, will suffice*; *~ things are an allegory*); *the ~*, arch. for *~*. **3.** pron. interrog. *~* person(s), *~* thing(s), (*~ of you am I to thank for this?*; *say ~ you would like best*; *~ is ~?*; *~* two etc. given persons etc. corresponds to one of given descriptions etc.). **4.** pron. rel. (cf. THAT). Used to convert what would in the simplest grammar be an independent sentence into a subordinate clause by being substituted for a noun expressed in it after being expressed or implied in the sentence to which it is to be subordinated, = *~ person or persons* (arch.), *~ thing(s)*, modified by context, (*Our Father, ~ art in heaven*; *the river ~*, or better *that*, *flows through London*; *the meeting, ~ was held in the Park, was a failure*; *he said he saw me there, ~ was a lie*; occas. in clause preceding antecedent, as *moreover, ~ you will hardly credit, he was not there himself*; *the ~*, arch. for *~*; in the possessive case *whose* is occas. for convenience preferred to the usual *of ~*, as *the only place whose supply of baths is adequate*). [OE *hwilc* (WHO, -LIKE), cf. Du *welk*, G *welch*]

whichev'er, **whichsóev'er** (emphat.), aa. & pron. rel. indef. used correspondingly to WHATEVER, WHATSOEVER, but with the restricted area of choice that distinguishes WHICH from WHAT (cf. *which* EVER). [SO, EVER]

whid'ah-bĭrd (-dǝ), n. Small W.-Afr. bird, male of which has tail-feathers of enormous length. [orig. WIDOW-*bird*, altered f. assoc. w. *Whidah* in Dahomey]

whiff¹, n., & v.i. & t. **1.** Puff of air, smoke, odour, etc. (*~ of grape-shot*, a few discharges; *want a ~ of fresh air*); (Commerc.) small cigar; || light uncovered outrigged sculling-boat. **2.** vb. Blow or puff (t. & i.) lightly. [imit.]

whiff², n. Kind of flatfish. [?]

whiff³, n., v.i. Fish with line towing bait near surface. [?]

whif'fle, v.i. & t., & n. **1.** (Of wind) blow lightly, shift about, drive (ship) in varying directions; (of flame, leaves, & fig. of thought etc.) flicker, flutter, wander; make the sound of a light wind in breathing etc. **2.** n. Slight movement of air. [f. WHIFF¹ + -LE(3)]

whig, n. & a. (Member) of the political party that, after the Revolution of 1688, aimed at subordinating the power of the crown to that of Parliament & the upper classes, passed the Reform Bill, & in the 19th c. was succeeded by the Liberals (opp. TORY; DISH² *the ~s*). Hence ~g'ERY (4), ~g'ISM(3), nn., ~g'ISH¹ a., ~g'ishy² adv., ~g'ishness n., (-g-), [earlier of Scotch covenanters, short for *whiggamor* nickname (perh. f. Sc. *whig* jog, drive, + MARE²) of western Scots who came to Leith for corn]

while¹, n., & v.t. **1.** Space of time, time occupied by or given to some action etc., (*have been waiting all this ~*; *go away for a ~*; *in a little ~*, soon; MEAN²; *once in a ~*, occasionally, at long intervals; *have not seen him for a long ~, this long ~ past*; *happened a long ~ ago*; *that is enough for one ~*, for some time; *worth ~ or nay* etc. *~*, repaying the time spent in doing it etc.; *looked in her eyes the ~* or *whilst*, during some other process; *the ~* or *whilst*, poet., during the time that). **2.** v.t. Pass (time, hour, etc.) *away* in leisurely manner. [Aryan: OE *hwíl*, cf. Sw. *vila* rest, G *weile*; cogn. w. L *quies* QUIET]

while², **whiles** (arch.; wīlz), conj. **1.** During the time that, for as long as, at the same time as, (*please write ~ I dictate*; *Jones got 98 ~ his partner was making 15*; *~ there is life there is hope*; also with ellipse of pronominal subject & *am, is, was*, etc., as *~ reading I fell asleep, we are safe ~ in his care, he retained the consciousness of it ~ asleep*). **2.** In contrast more or less marked with the fact that simultaneously, although, whereas, (chiefly journalistic) and, (*Nero fiddling ~ Rome burns*; *~ I have no money to spend, you have nothing to spend money on*; *~ I admit his good points I can see his bad*; also erron. *~ admitting* etc., cf. the correct ellipses above; *Jones lost an arm, Brown a leg, ~ Robinson had both amputated*). [f. a case of prec.; for *whiles* see -ES & cf. WHILST]

whil'om, adv. & a. **1.** (arch.). Once, formerly. **2.** adj. Quondam (*his ~ friend*). [OE *hwílum* instr. pl. (WHILE¹)]

whilst, conj. & n. =WHILE²; (n.) *the ~*, =*the* WHILE¹. [WHILE¹, ES]

whim, n. Sudden fancy, caprice, crotchet; kind of windlass for raising ore from

For pronunciation of words in *wh-* see WH-.

mine; ~*wham*, arch. [redupl. of ~], plaything, toy. ~; [perh. of Scand. orig.; cf.
ON *hvima* wander with the eyes]

whim'brel, n. Kind of curlew. [*whim*,
imit. of its cry, -REL]

whim'per, v.i. & t. & n. 1. Make feeble
querulous or frightened sounds, cry &
whine softly; utter ~ingly; hence ~ER¹
n., ~ingly² adv. 2. n. Sound of ~ing.
[imit.]

whim'sical (-z-), a. Capricious; odd-
looking, fantastic. Hence ~ITY (-zikăl'-)
n., ~LY² adv. [fol., -ICAL]

whim'sy (-zi), n. Crotchet, whim. [see
WHIM]

whin¹, n. Gorse, furze, (used in pl. also);
~*chat*, kind of small bird. [cf. Norw.
hvine, Sw. *hven*, kinds of grass]

whin², **whin'sill,** **whin'stone,** nn. Kinds
of basaltic rock or hard sandstone. [?]

whin'gle, v.i. & t. & n. (Make) long-drawn
complaining cry (as) of dog; (utter)
querulous talk; utter ~ingly (often *oud*).
Hence ~ER¹ n., ~ingly² adv. [OE
hwinan, cf. ON *hvina* whiz]

¶ **whing'er,** n. Short sword, dirk, or long
knife. [also *whinyard*; etym. dub.]

whin'y¹, v.i. & n. 1. Neigh gently or joy-
fully. 2. n. ~ing sound. [imit., cf. WHINE]

whip¹, v.t. & i. (-pp-). 1. Move (t. & i.)
with sudden motion, snatch, dart, (always
with adv. or prep.; ~ *behind the cupboard*;
~*ped away to France*; ~*ped up her toy
terrier*; ~ *out sword, knife*; ~ *off one's
coat*). 2 Bind (cord, stick) with close
covering of twine, sew (seam) with overhand stitches. 3. Flog, lash, (horse, boy,
etc.; ~ *in, off together*, of managing
hounds with ~, & transf. followers esp. in
Parliament; ~ *stream*, fish it with ~ping
motion; ~ *horses on*, urge with whip; ~
fault out of person; ~ *eggs, cream*, beat
into froth); (sl.) excel, defeat, (~ *creation*,
beat all). 4. Hoist (coal etc.) with rope
passed through pulley. 5. ~*ping-boy*
(hist.), boy educated with & chastised for
young prince; ~*ping-post*, to which persons were tied to be ~ped; ~*ping-top*,
kept spinning by blows of lash. Hence
~PING¹(4) n. [cf. Du. *wippen* skip,
hasten, Sw. *vippa* to wag, G *wippen* move
up & down; perh. cogn. w. L *vibrare*
VIBRATE]

whip³, n. 1. Instrument for urging on or
punishing with lash attached to short or
long stick; *good, poor*, etc., coachman
(esp. of four-in-hand or tandem driver).
2. (Also *whipper-in*,) hunt official subordinate to huntsman charged with man-
agement of hounds; || (transf.) official
appointed to maintain discipline among,
secure attendance of, & give necessary
information to, members of his party in
House of Parliament, also written notice
(variously underscored with number of
lines representing degrees of urgency, as
three-line ~) requesting attendance on

particular occasion. 3. (Also ~-*&-derry*)
rope-&-pulley hoisting apparatus. 4. ~
cord, tightly twisted cord such as is used
for making ~-*crane*, light derrick with
tackle for hoisting; ~-*fish*, kind with
dorsal fin produced into filament like ~
lash; ~-*gin*, tackle-block with hoisting
rope with several ends each to be simultaneously hauled on; ~ *hand*, hand that
holds ~ (esp. in *have the* ~ *hand of*, be
in position to control); ~-*ray*, ray-fish
with long slender tail; ~-*round*, appeal
circulated among friends, members of a
club or society, etc., for contributions
(usu. for some charitable object); ~-*saw*,
narrow saw-blade with ends held by
frame; ~-*snake*, slender kinds. Hence
~p'Y² a., flexible, springy, ~p'iNESS n.
[partly f. prec., partly f. cogn. LG nn.]

whip'per, n. In vbl senses; esp.: ~-*in*,
(now usu. shortened to) whip²: ~-*snap-
per*, small child, young & insignificant
but presuming or intrusive person [perh.
for *whipsnapper*, implying noise & unimportance; but cf. WHIPSTER.] [-ER¹]

whip'pet, n. Cross-bred dog of modified
greyhound type used for racing; (Mil.)
fast light tank. [f. 1610 in sense *small
dog*; cf. obs. vb & n. ~ = frisk]

whip'-poor-will, n. American bird allied
to goatsucker. [imit. of cry]

Whip'snade, n. (Used for) ~ Park, in
the Chilterns, a reserve for the breeding
& exhibition of wild animals. [place]

whip'ster, n. Small child; || trifling frivo-
lous person such as should still be subject
to the whip. [-STER]

whir(r), v.i. (part. *whir'ring*), & n. (Make)
continuous buzzing or softly clicking
sound as of bird's wings quickly flapped
or cogwheels in rapid action. [f. Da.
hvirre whirl, or imit.]

whirl, v.t. & i., & n. 1. Swing (t. & i.)
round & round, revolve (t. & i.) rapidly
(~*ing* DERVISH); send (missile etc.), (of
moving body) travel, swiftly in orbit or
curve; convey or go rapidly *away* etc. In
wheeled conveyance; (of brain, senses,
etc.) be giddy, seem to spin round, (of
thoughts etc.) follow each other in bewildering succession. 2. n. ~ing movement (*my thoughts are in a* ~). 3. ~*pool*,
circular eddy in sea etc.; ~*wind*, mass
of air ~ing rapidly round & round in
cylindrical or funnel shape (*sow wind &
reap* ~*wind*, suffer worse results of bad
action). [l. ON *hvirfla*, cf. G *wirbeln*;
cogn. w. OE *hweorfan* turn]

whir'ligig (-g-), n. Kinds of spinning toy;
(fig.) revolving motion (~ *of time*, changes
of fortune); merry-go-round; kinds of
water beetle that circle about on surface.
[prec., GIG¹]

whisk, n. See WHIST¹.

whisk, n. & v.t. & i. 1. Bunch of grass,
hair, etc., to flap dust off, flies away, etc.,

with: instrument for beating up eggs or cream; quick movement (as) of ~ or of animal's tail. **2.** vb. Flap (dust, fly, etc.) *away or off*; beat up (eggs etc.); take away or off with sudden motion (*waiter ~ed my plate off*); convey or go lightly & quickly esp. out of sight (*was ~ed across channel in aeroplane; mouse ~s into its hole*); brandish lightly or flip or wave about (*went ~ing a cane, her tail*). [earlier *wisk*, prob. of Scand. orig.; cf. Da. *viske* wipe, G *wischen* wipe, ON *visk* & OHG *wisa wisp*, LG *wisk* quick movement]

whis'ker, n. Hair of man's cheek (cf. *moustache, beard*; usu. in pl.); bristle growing from upper lip of cat etc., set of such bristles on one side. Hence (-)~ED² (-erd) a. [prec., -ER¹]

whis'ky¹, -key, n. Spirit distilled from malted barley, other grains, or sugar etc.; *whiskified* (joc.), affected by ~-drinking; ~-*liver*, liver-complaint from alcoholic poisoning. [f. Gael. *uisge(-beatha)* water (of life), cf. USQUEBAUGH]

whis'ky², n. Kind of light gig or chaise. [f. WHISK, w. ref. to lightness of motion]

whis'per, v.i. & t., & n. **1.** Speak without vibration of vocal cords; talk with intention of being audible only close at hand or to confidant; inform or bid (person) thus *that* or *to do*; converse privately, indulge in slander or plotting; put secretly in circulation (tale, *that*; esp. *it is ~ed that*); (of leaves, stream, etc.) rustle; ~*ing-gallery*, gallery, cave, etc., in which some acoustic peculiarity causes least sound made at a particular point to be audible at another far off; hence ~ER¹, ~ING³ (1), nn. ~**ingly¹** adv. **2.** n. ~ing speech (*always talks in a ~ or ~s*); ~ed remark; rumour of unknown origin, mysterious hint; rustling sound. [ONorthumb. *hwisperian*, cf. G *wispern*]

|| **whist¹**, **whisht** (hw-), int. enjoining silence (now rare exc. in representations of Irish talk, *-sht*). [cf. HIST, HUSH]

|| **whist²** a. (arch.). Silent. [f. prec.]

whist³, n. Card game of mingled skill & chance for four or exceptionally three or two persons (*long, short, ~, with ten, five, points to game*; DUMMY, *double* DUMMY; ~; RUBBER² *of* ~; ~ *drive*, PROGRESSIVE ~ *party*. [earlier *whisk* (perh. w. ref. to whisking off of cards from table), afterwards changed w. ref. to the silence usual in the game]

whis'tle (wi'sl), v.i. & t., & n. **1.** Make with the lips or with instrument for the purpose, or (of birds etc.) with the voice, or (of missile, wind, etc.) by rapid motion, the shrill sound of breath forced through small orifice formed with lips (*boy, bird, steam-engine, driver, wind, bullet, ~s; ~e for a wind*, of becalmed sailors, whence *may ~e for it*, vainly wish; *let one go ~e*,

disregard his wishes; ~*ing*, in names of kinds of bird & animal, as ~*ing eagle, marmot*); (obs.) act as informer, peach; summon or give signal to (dog, attendant) by ~*ing* (*~e down the wind*, metaph. f. hawking, let go, abandon); give (tune etc.) by ~*ing*. **2.** n. ~ing sound or note; instrument for producing such sound (*penny ~e*, tin pipe with six holes giving notes; *steam ~e*, sounded by jet of steam; *pay for one's ~e* (of anecdotic orig.), pay high for some caprice; throat WET *one's ~e*). [OE *hwistle* n., *hwistlian* make hissing sound, cf. ON *hvisla* whisper; imit.]

whist'ler (wis'ler), n. In vbl senses; esp.: kind of marmot; kinds of bird. [-ER¹]

whit¹, n. Particle, least possible amount, (usu. in *no ~, not* or *never a ~*, not at all). [OE *wiht* WIGHT, whit]

Whit¹, Whit'|sun, aa. ~ *Sunday*, seventh Sunday after Easter, commemorating day of Pentecost; ~ *Monday, Tuesday*, those following; ~ *week*, that containing, ~ *Sunday*; ~ *suntide*, ~ *Sunday* & following days; ~*sun week*, ~ *week*. [OE *Hwita Sunnandæg*, lit. White Sunday; *Whitsun* short for *Whitsunday's*; *Whit Sunday*=white Sunday, so called because christenings, & therefore white robes, were common on it]

white, a., & v.t. **1.** Resembling a surface reflecting sunlight without absorbing any of the visible rays, of the colour of fresh snow or common salt or the common swan's plumage, having some approach to such colour, pale (*~ as a sheet*), less dark than other things of the same kind (*bleed ~*, fig., drain of wealth etc., w. ref. to hanging of calf to ~n veal), characterized by presence of some white, (~ in many -ED² compounds used esp. in naming animals etc., as ~-*backed, -beaked, -bearded, -bellied, -breasted, -crested, -crowned, -eyed, -faced, -footed, -fronted, -headed, -necked, -rumped, -tailed, -throated, -winged*). **2.** (Of water, air, light) transparent, colourless. **3.** (fig.). Innocent, unstained, of harmless kind. **4.** Of ~ men (see ~ *man* below; ~ *culture, civilization*, etc.). **5.** (pol.). Of royalist or counter-revolutionary or reactionary tendency (opp. RED, & cf. TERROR). **6.** ~ *alloy*, any of the cheap imitations of silver; ANT. ~ *bait*, small fish prob. the fry of several kinds eaten fried in quantities when about 2 in. long; ~ *beam*, small tree with silvery underleaf; ~ *bear*, polar bear; W~ *boy*, member of 18th-c. illegal agrarian association in Ireland wearing ~ frocks at nightly meetings & outrages; ~ *caps*, breakers out at sea; (snowy) *Christmas*; ~ *coffee* (with milk); ~ *corpuscle*, = LEUCOCYTE; ~ CROW¹, CURRANT, W~ *Czar* (hist.), (Asiatic

For pronunciation of words in *wh-* see WH-.

phr. for) Czar of Russia.; ~ ELEPHANT; ||~ ENSIGN, flown by ships of British navy, cf. RED *ensign*.; ~ FEATHER¹; ~*fish*, commerc., other than salmon, also of whiting & haddock in particular.; ~ FLAG⁴, FRIAR, FROST; ||~ *gloves* (presented to assize judge who finds no criminal cases to try); ~ GROUSE¹; ~ *gum*, eruption on infant's neck & arms; ~ *hands*, (lit.) as sign of exemption from labour, (fig.) innocency or integrity; so ~-*handed*; ~ *heart-cherry*, pale heart-shaped kind.; ~ HEAT¹ (lit. & fig. of passion etc.; so ~-*hot*); ~ *horses*, waves with ~ crests at sea; W~ *House*, official residence of U.S. president; ~ LEAD¹, LIE¹; ~ *light*, colourless, e.g. ordinary daylight, also fig. of unprejudiced judgement; ~-*lipped*, esp. with fear; ~-*livered*, cowardly; ~ MAGIC; ~ *man*, member of one of the paler races chiefly inhabiting or having inhabited Europe, & characterized by a certain type of civilization (cf. *black, brown, red, yellow, man.; the* ~ *man's burden*, task of leading the world forward), (colloq.) person of honourable character, good breeding, etc.; ~ *meat*, poultry, veal, rabbits, pork; ~ *metal*, = ~ *alloy*; ~ *mixture*, a hospital aperient; ||~ *paper*, report issued by Government to give information; W~ (western) *Russia(n)*; ~ *sale* (of house- & body-linen); ~ SCOURGE; ~ *sheet*, penitent's garb (usu. *stand in a* ~ *sheet*, confess sin etc.); ~ *slave*, girl entrapped (& exported for purpose of prostitution (the ~-*slave traffic*, ~ *slavery*); ~ *smith*, worker in tin, also polisher or galvanizer of iron; ~ *squall*, sudden tropical storm at sea announced only by line of ~ water approaching; ~*thorn*, hawthorn (cf. BLACK¹-*thorn*); ~-*throat*, kinds of small songbird; ~ *war*, war without bloodshed, economic warfare; ~*wash*, (n.) solution of quicklime or of whiting & size for brushing over walls, ceilings, etc., to give clean appearance, also fig. means employed to clear person or his memory of imputations, ||(colloq.) glass of sherry after other wine, (v.t.) cover with ~*wash*, attempt to clear reputation of, (pass., of insolvent) get fresh start by passage through bankruptcy court; ~*wine*, of amber or golden colour (opp. *red*); ~ *witch*, (using power for beneficent purposes only); hence ~LY² adv., (rare), ~NESS (-tn-) n. [OE *hwit*, cf. Du. *wit*, G *weiss*, Skr. *çvetrá-* whitish]

white², n. White or nearly white colour; kinds of white pigment (Chinese etc. ~); white clothes or material (*dressed in* ~); albuminous part round yolk of egg; visible part round iris of eye; = *white man* (MEAN² ~.); kinds of butterfly; (usu. pl.) = LEUCORRHŒA. [f. prec.]

||**White'chapel** (-t-ch-), n., & v.i. 1. ~ *cart*, light two-wheeled spring-cart used by shopkeepers for sending goods round. 2. (whist). Lead from one-card suit with a view to subsequent trumping. [~ in London]

||**White'hall¹** (-t-hawl), n. (Used for) the Civil Service, the Government offices. [street in London]

white'ning (-tn-), n. = WHITING¹. [(WHITE¹¹), -ING¹]

whith'er (-dh-), adv. interrog. & rel. (chiefly arch.), & n. 1. To what place or point? (now usu. *where²*; *where* ~ *to ?*, *how far ?*, etc., but cf. *I see* ~ *your question tends*), whence ~WARD adv.; (rel., with antecedent *place* etc.) to which (now usu. *to which, where*), (without antecedent) to the or (also ~*soever*) any place to which (now usu. *where*); = & thither. 2. n. Destination (*our whence & our* ~; *no* ~, arch., to no place). [OE *hwider*]

whit'ing¹, n. Chalk prepared by drying, grinding, etc., for use in whitewashing, plate-cleaning, etc. [WHITE¹ vb. -ING¹(4)]

whit'ing², n. Kind of sea-fish much used as food; ~*-out*, fish with some resemblance to ~ & an inflatable membrane over part of head. [WHITE¹ a., -ING³]

whit'leather (-ledh-), n. White leather dressed with alum instead of being tanned. [WHITE¹]

||**Whit'ley Coun'cil**, n. A council of representatives of employers & workers for discussion & settlement of industrial relations & conditions. Hence **Whit'ley**-ISM n., use of such methods for dealing with industrial problems. [J. H. *Whitley*, Speaker 1921–8]

whit'low (-ō), n. Inflammatory tumour on finger esp. about the nail. [earliest form *whitflawe*, perh. = *white flaw*, with *whit* = *white* as in WHIT²]

Whitsun. See WHIT²

Whit'worth thread (-wŏ-, -rĕd), n. Standard screw-thread for metal. [Sir Joseph *Whitworth*, English engineer (d. 1887)]

whit'y, a. Inclining to white (usu. in comb., with other colour-name, esp. ~*brown*). [-Y¹]

whiz, whizz, v.i. (-zz-), & n. (Make) sound given by friction of body moving at great speed through air; ~-*bang* (army sl.), shell from a small-calibre high-velocity German gun. [imit.]

who (hŏŏ), pron. pers. interrog. & rel. (obj. *whom* pr. hŏŏm; poss. WHOSE pr. hŏŏz). 1. interrog. What person(s)?, which

person(s)?, what sort of person(s) in regard to position or authority?, (~ *said so?*; ~*m* or colloq. ~ *do you mean?*; *told him* ~ *they were*, ~*m* or colloq. *to look out for*; ~ *see son is he?*; ~ *would have thought it?*, *no one would*; ~ *are the Joneses, I should like to know?*; ~*m am I that I should object?*; *know* ~*'s*, ~ *or what each person is*; *a* ~*'s who*, list with description of notables). **2.** rel. (Person or persons) that (*the man* ~*m you saw*; *those for* ~*se behalf it was done*; *anyone* ~ *chooses can apply*; *there is no one* ~ *we can believe is competent*, often incorrectly ~*m*; (arch.) the or any person(s) that (~ *breaks pays*; ~*m the gods love die young*; *as* ~ *should say*, like a person ~ *said*; since, if, etc., he, him, they, etc. (*sent it to Jones*, ~ *passed it on to Smith*; *is flirting with Dick*, ~*m she detests*). [Aryan: OE *hwā*, with neut. *hwæt*, gen. *hwæs*, dat. *hwǣm*, instr. *hwī*; cf. Du. *wie* who, *wat* what, *wien* whose, *wien* whom, G *wer* who, *was* what, *wessen* whose, *wen* & *wem* whom, L *quis*, Skr. *ka*; the rel. senses are later than the interrog.]

whoa. See WO.

who'du(n)nit (hoŏ-), n. (sl.). Detective or mystery story. [= *who done* (illiterate for *did*) *it?*]

whoev'er, who'só (arch.), **whosoĕv'er** (emphat.),**whoe'er**) & **whosöe'er** (poet.; -âr), (hoŏ-), pronn. pers. indef. rel. (cases as with WHO; whomsoever or the incorrect whoever is usu. substituted without special emphasis for whomever, & whosesoever occas. for whose-ever), used (1) as mod. equivalent of arch. *who* in indef. rel. sense (*whoever comes will be welcome*; *stopped whomsoever or whoever or whomever he saw*; *return it to whose-ever or whosesoever address is on it*; (2) in indef. concessive clauses = though any one (*who-ever else objects, I do not*; *whose-ever it is, I mean to have it*; *whomsoever or who-ever or whomever I quote, you retain your opinion*); (3) vulg. for *who* in EVER. [WHO, SO, EVER]

whole (hōl), a. & n. **1.** (arch.) In good health, well, (*they that be* ~ *need not a physician*). **2.** In sound condition, uninjured, not broken, intact, (*hope you will come back* ~; *got off with a* ~ *skin*; *there is not a plate left* ~; *has swallowed a raisin* ~). **3.** Integral, consisting of one or more units, without fractions, (~ *numbers*, integers). **4.** Undiminished, without subtraction, (*bread made of* ~ *meal*, not deprived by bolting of some constituents). **5.** (With *a* in sing.) not less than (*spent* ~ *years of misery*; *went up a* ~ *tone*; *lasted three* ~ *days*; ~ *regiments were cut down*; *talked a* ~ *lot of nonsense*; (with *the*, *his*, etc.) all that there is of (*the*

~ *truth, world, duty of man*; *do thing with one's* ~ *heart*, heartily, with concentrated effort etc., without doubts etc., whence ~**hearted**[2] a., ~**heart'edly** adv., ~**heart'edness** n.: *the* ~ *priesthood, city, etc.*, all members or inhabitants of it; COMMITTEE *of the* ~ *House*; *go the* ~ HOG[1], whence ~**hŏgg'er**[1] (-g-) n.). **6.** ~ **coloured**, all of one colour; ~**hoofed**, with undivided hoofs; ~**length**, (portrait) representing person from head to foot; *~ **note**, semi-breve; ~**'sale**, (n., chiefly attrib.) selling of articles in large quantities to be retailed by others (*a* ~*sale dealer*; *sells by* ~*sale*; ~*sale prices*), (adj. & adv.) on the ~*sale* plan, (transf.) on large scale, (*our business is* ~*sale only*; *sells* ~*sale*; *a* ~*sale slaughter took place*; *sends out begging letters* ~*sale*); ~**'saler**, ~*sale* dealer; hence ~'NESS (hōln-) n. **7.** n. Thing complete in itself; all that there is of something (often *of*; *the golden rule contains the* ~ *of morality*; *in* or *upon the* ~, taking into consideration everything that bears on the question, after weighing pros & cons etc.); organic unity, complete system, total made up of parts, (*nature is a* ~; *the* ~ *& the parts*). [OE *hāl* HALE[1], cf. G *heil*, Du. *heel*; cogn. w. HEAL, HOLY]

whole'some (hōls-), a. Promoting physical or moral health, salubrious, salutary, not morbid, (~ *food, air, exercise, advice, neglect, excitement*). Hence ~LY[2] adv., ~NESS n. [prec., -SOME]

wholly (hōl'li), adv. Entirely, without abatement, (*I am* ~ *yours*); exclusively, without admixture, (*a* ~ *bad example*). [WHOLE, -LY[2]]

whom. See WHO.

whoop (hoŏp). Var. of HOOP[2].

*whoo'pee** (woō-), n. (colloq.). *Make* ~, rejoice noisily, have a roaring time. [f. prec.]

whop, v.t. (sl.; -pp-). Thrash, (fig.) defeat, overcome, whence ~**p'ing**[1](1) n.; (part.) very large of its kind (esp. a ~*ping lie*), whence ~**p'er**[1] n. [also *we(h)op*, *wop*; etym. dub.]

whore (hōr), n. & v.i. (not in decent use). **1.** Prostitute, strumpet, (the SCARLET W~); ~**master**, ~**monger**, fornicator; hence ~**tom** (hōrd-) n. **2.** v.i. (Of man) practise fornication; (fig., arch., esp. *go a-whoring after strange gods* etc.) practise idolatry or iniquity. [late OE *hōre* prob. f. ON *hóra* adulteress, cf. Du. *hoer*, G *hure*; cogn. w. L *carus* dear]

whôrl, n. Ring of leaves or other organs round stem etc. of plant; one turn of a spiral; disk on spindle steadying its motion. Hence ~ED[2](-ld) a. [ME *wharuyl*, *whorwhil*, cf. OE *hweorfan* turn, -LE(1); or perh. var. of WHIRL]

whor'tleberry (wôrtelb-), n.=BILBERRY.

[also *whortle, whort, hurtleberry, hurtle, hurt*, perh. f. F *heurté* a rounded azure in heraldry.]

whose (hōōz). Possessive case of who, used also as case of WHICH 4; ~*ever*, ~*soever*, see WHOEVER.

whoso, whosoever. See WHOEVER.

why¹, adv. Interrog. & rel. & n. (pl. ~s).
1. On what ground?, for what reason?, with what purpose?, (~ *did you do it?*; *cannot think* ~ *you came*; often ellipt. as *You are late*; ~?, esp. in ~ *so?*, demand for grounds of statement or view); (rel.) on account of which (*the reasons* ~ *he did it are obscure*). **2.** n. Reason, explanation, (*cannot go into the* ~*s & wherefores now*). [OE *hwī* instr. of WHO, WHAT]

why², int. expr. surprised discovery or recognition (~, *it is surely Jones!*; ~, *what was it*), protest at simplicity of question etc. (~, *of course, that child could answer that*), pause for reflection (*Is it true?* ~, *four.*; ~, *yes, I think so*), introduction of apodosis (*if silver will not do,* ~ *we must try gold*), etc. [ellipt. uses of prec. interrog.]

wick¹, n. (Piece of) fibrous or spongy material by which lamp or candle flame is kept supplied with melted grease or oil; (Surg.) gauze strip inserted in wound to drain it. [OE *wēoce, wēoc,* cf. MDu. *wiecke,* Da. *vœge*]

wick², n. Town, hamlet, district, (rare exc. in place-names as *Hampton W.*~ or other compounds as *baili*~). [OE *wīc* f. L *vīcus*]

wick³, a. Sinful, iniquitous, vicious, (~ given to or involving immorality, (~ *bible,* edition of 1632 with *not* omitted in seventh commandment), offending intentionally against the right; spiteful, ill-tempered, intending or intended to give pain, playfully mischievous, roguish. Hence ~*ly² adv.,* ~*NESS n.* [ME, f. obs. *wick* of same sense (perh. adj. use of OE *wicca* wizard)+-ED¹ as in WRETCHED]

wick'er, n. Plaited twigs or osiers as material of baskets, chairs, mats, protective covers, etc. (usu. attrib., as ~ *chair*), whence ~*ED²* (-ęrd) a.; ~*work,* (things made of) ~. [earlier sense *pliant twig,* f. Scand. (MSw. *viker* osier cf. Sw. *vika* to bend, OE *wīcan* give way): cogn. w. WEAK]

wick'et, n. **1.** Small door or gate, esp. one beside or in the compass of a larger one for use when the latter is not open (also ~*door,* ~*gate*); turnstile entrance; aperture in door or wall usu. closed with sliding panel; door closing only lower half of doorway. **2.** (cricket). One set of three stumps & two bails (*keep* ~, be ~*keeper* or fieldsman stationed close behind batsman's ~; *keep one's* ~ *up,* succeed in not being put out); the ~s as defended

by one batsman (*5* ~*s down,* five men out; *match won by 2* ~*s,* with three of winning side still not out); good etc. state of the pitch (*play began on a perfect* ~); *be on a* ~ (fig.) be in an advantageous, unfavourable, position. [ME & AF *wiket,* mod. F *guichet,* f. uncertain Teut. source; cricket ~ orig. resembled gate, being 2 ft wide by 1 ft]

widd'ershins. Var. of WITHERSHINS.

wide, a., adv., & n. **1.** Measuring much or more than other things of same kind across or from side to side, broad, not narrow, (~ *door, road, river, brim, margin, cloth, interval;* ~ *margin,* fig., a good deal more allowed than is likely to be needed). **2.** (Appended to measurement) in width (*a strip 3 ft* ~). **3.** Extending far, embracing much (*as* ~ *range*; ~ *fame,* known to many; *the* ~ *world,* all the world great as it is; *a* ~ *domain, large; is of* ~ *distribution,* occurs in many places; *a* ~ *generalization,* covering many particulars; *there is a* ~ *difference between,* ~ & esp. *in far &* ~, whence ~*ly² adv.* **4.** Not tight or close or restricted, loose, free, liberal, unprejudiced, general, (~ *takes* ~ *views; hazard a* ~ *guess,* one allowing margin for errors of detail; ~ *berth to,* not go too near, keep clear of, avoid). **5.** Open to full extent (*staring with* ~ *eyes*; also adv. or pred. a., as ~ *yawned* ~, *open your mouth* ~, *window is* ~ *open, person is* ~ *awake*). **6.** At considerable distance from a point or mark, not within reasonable distance of, (~ *ball* in cricket, ball judged by umpire to pass wicket beyond batsman's reach & counting one to his side; *give an answer quite* ~ *of the mark or purpose*; also adv. or pred. a., as *is bowling, shooting,* ~; *arrow fell* ~ *of target*). **7.** n. A ~ *ball; the* ~, *the* ~ *world (broke to ~).* **8.** ~ *awake a.* (colloq.), wary, knowing; ~*awake n.,* soft ~*brimmed felt hat;* ~*spread,* ~*ly disseminated (esp. of beliefs or impressions).* Hence **wid'ish¹** a. [OE *wīd* a.]

wid'geon (wī'jn), n. Kinds of wild duck. [perh. ult. f. L *vīpio vīgeon,* which however are not recorded as early as E ~]

wid'ow (-ō), n. & v.t. **1.** Woman who has lost her husband by death & not married again (GRASS ~; ~*'s cruse,* supply that looks small, but proves inexhaustible, see 1 *Kings* xvii. 10-16; ~*'s mite,* see *Mark* xii. 42; ~*'s peak,* V-shaped growth of hair in centre of forehead; also attrib., as ~ *lady, woman*); the ~ (colloq.) champagne [f. the *Veuve* (F = ~) Cliquot brand]; ~*bird,* black-plumaged African bird of genus *Vidua* (L = ~);

hence ~HOOD (-dŏh-) n. **2.** v.t. Kill husband or mate of, deprive of husband or wife or mate, make into ~ or widower, (usu. in p.p.; *the ~ed father, mother*, etc.); (poet.) bereave of friend etc. [Aryan: OE *widewe*, cf. Du. *weduwe*, G *witwe*; cogn. w. L *viduus* bereft, Gk *éitheos* bachelor, Skr. *vidhávā*]

wid'ower (-ōer), n. Man who has lost his wife by death & not married again. [prec.,-ER¹]

width, n. Distance or measurement from side to side; comprehensiveness or liberality of mind, views, etc.; piece of material of certain ~ (*shall want three ~s of it*). [WIDE, TH¹]

wield, v.t. Control, sway, hold & use, manage with the hands or otherwise, (~ *the sceptre, a kingdom* etc. chiefly poet., *weapon* lit. or fig.). [OE *wieldan, wealdan* rule, cf. ON *valda*, G *walten*; perh. cogn. w. L *valére* be strong]

wife, n. (pl. -ves). **1.** Woman, esp. one who is old & rustic or uneducated (now rare exc. in *old wives' tale*, foolish or superstitious tradition, & in comb. as FISH¹, HOUSEWIFE, MIDWIFE). **2.** Married woman esp. in relation to her husband (usu. *my* etc. ~, *the ~ of*, or with epithet as *will make a good ~; wedded, lawful, ~, take, to ~; as ~*). Hence ~'HOOD (-fh-) **wif'ie** [-Y¹, ³], nn., ~'LESS, ~'LIKE, ~'LY (-fl-), aa. [OE *wīf*, cf. Du. *wijf*, G *weib*, all neut. nn., etym. dub.]

wig¹, n. Artificial head of hair formerly much worn as ornament, & still to conceal baldness or disguise appearance || or as part of official dress esp. of judge or lawyer or of servant's livery (*there will be ~s on the green*, a free fight). Hence (-)~GED² (-gd), ~'LESS, aa. [short for PERIWIG]

wig², v.t. (-gg-). Rebuke sharply, rate, (chiefly in the vbl n.). Hence ~G'ING¹(1) (-g-) n. [perh. w. ref. to bewigged superior reprimanding]

wig'an, n. Stiff canvas-like material used for stiffening. [*Wigan* in Lancashire]

wig'gle, v.t.(colloq. or dial.). Cause (something) to move from side to side; || scull (a boat) with single oar over stern. [cogn. w. or f. (M)LG *wiggelen*; cf. WAG¹ & WAGGLE]

wight (wīt), n. (arch. or joc.), Person, being, (esp. *luckless, wretched*, etc., ~), [OE *wiht* creature, person, thing, cf. Du. *wicht* child, G *wicht* creature; doublet of WHIT¹]

wig'wăm (or -ŏm), n. N-Amer. Indian's tent or hut of skins or mats or bark. [native]

wild, a., adv., & n. **1.** Not domesticated or cultivated (chiefly of animals & plants, & esp. of species allied to others that are not ~; in the commoner combinations ~ & the n. are hyphened, or treated as one wd with accent on ~; ~ *beast, plant; ~ man, savage; ~ ass; ~ boar; ~ duck; ~ fowl; ~ vine; ~ oat* lit., also fig. as a. or attrib. of finance or commercial speculations, reckless, unsound; ~*goose* lit., also in ~*goose chase*, absurdly impossible enterprise; ~ *horse*, also in *be drawn by ~ horses*, form of torture & death; ~ *hyacinth*, bluebell; OATS; ~ *scenery* etc., of conspicuously desolate appearance; *woodnotes ~*, spontaneous & artless poetry). **2.** (Of horses, game-birds, etc.) shy, given to shying, easily startled, hard to get near. **3.** Unrestrained, wayward, disorderly, irregular, out of control, unconventional, (*a ~ fellow; settled down after a ~ youth; ~ work*, lawless doings; *hair hanging in ~ locks; living in ~ times; room is in ~ disorder; run ~*, grow unchecked or untrained). **4.** Tempestuous, violent, (*a ~ wind, night*, etc.). **5.** Intensely eager, excited, frantic, passionate, distracted, mad, (*is ~ with excitement, to try it; the ~ men*, extremists of a party etc.; ~ *about* person or subject, enthusiastically devoted to; ~ *delight, excitement, enthusiasm, grief, rage; ~ looks, appearance*, etc., indicating distraction; *drive ~*, madden). **6.** Haphazard, rash, ill-considered, ill-aimed, disturbed by excitement, (*a ~ guess, shot, blow, venture; ~ opinions, bowling*; also as adv., as *shoot, talk, ~*). **7.** ~'fire, = Greek FIRE¹ (*report spreads like ~fire*, very fast). Hence ~ISH¹(2) a., ~'LY² adv., ~'NESS n. **8.** n. Desert, tract. [com.-Teut.: OE *wilde*, cf. Du. & G *wild*; prob. cogn. w. WILL w. orig. sense *wilful*]

wil'debeest (v-), n. The gnu. [S.-Afr. Du.,(prec., BEAST)]

|| **wil'der**, v.t. (poet.). Bewilder. [prob. shortened f. *wildern* see foll.]

wil'derness, n. Desert, uncultivated & uninhabited tract, (*voice in the ~* etc., unregarded advocate of some reform, w. ref. to *Matt.* iii, 3 etc.; *wandering* etc. *in the ~ of* political party out of office, w. ref. to *Num.* xiv. 33 etc.); part of garden left wild; unlimited number or quantity of. [prob. f. obs. *wildern* savage, f. OE *wild-dēor* wild beast +-EN⁵, +-NESS]

wild'ing, n. Plant sown by natural agency, esp. wild crab-apple, or fruit of such plant (also attrib.). [-ING³]

wile, n., & v.t. **1.** Trick, cunning procedure, artifice, (usu. in pl.). **2.** v.t. Lure, entice, *away, into*, etc. (also incorrectly for WHILE¹ vb). [ME *wil*, perh. f. Scand. (ON *wēl* craft)]

wil'ful, a. For which compulsion or ignorance or accident cannot be pleaded as excuse, intentional, deliberate, due to perversity or self-will, (~ *murder, waste, ignorance, disobedience*); obstinate, self-willed, headstrong; refractory. Hence ~'LY² adv., ~'NESS n. [WILL², -FUL]

Wilhelmstrasse (vil'helmshtrahse), n. (Used for) the German Foreign Office. [Berlin street]

will, v.t. & aux. (pres. I, he, we, you, they; thou wilt or 'lt; past & condit. I, he, we, you, they would or 'd, thou wouldst pr. wŏŏdst or wŏŏldst or 'd; neg. forms ~ not or wouldn't, or 'd not; no other forms or parts used). **1.** (used irrespective of person with more or less of orig. sense of volition). Desire (thing; arch.; what would they?; want of will); desire or choose to (the heaven where I would be; come when you ~); wish that, rarely that (usu. in condit. with optative effect; I often omitted; it shall be as you ~; said it should be as we would; would or I would I were a bird!; would it were otherwise!; would God I had died!, i.e. if only God had wished, or perh. ellipt. for I would to God; I would to heaven I was dead.; would-be, prefixed as adj. or adv. to wd describing character that person vainly aspires to or that thing is meant to have, as a would-be gentleman, smart say-ing); consent or be prevailed on to (~ or would not go any further; wound would not heal; would you pass the salt?; would not do it for £100); refuse to be prevailed on not to (boys ~ be boys'; accidents ~ hap-pen; you ~ have your way; he ~, good, get in my light); be accustomed or ob-served from time to time to (~ sit there for hours; now & then a blackbird would call; ~ succeed once in ten times!); be likely to turn out to (this ~ be Waterloo, I suppose; I don't know who it would be). **2.** As tense & mood auxiliaries ~ & would are used (a) in 2nd & 3rd person (1st having shall, should) to form a plain future or conditional statement or ques-tion (you ~ hear soon enough; they would have been killed if they had let go; ~ or would you, they, be able to hear at such a distance?, but cf. shall 5); (b) in 1st per-son (others having shall, should) to form a future or conditional statement ex-pressing speaker's will or intention (I ~ not be caught again; we would have come if you had given us longer notice); (c) alterna-tively with shall, should, in sentences of type a changed in reporting to 1st from other person (you say I ~, said I would, never manage it, reporting 'You ~ never manage it'; now more usu. shall, should) or from first to other person (he said he would never manage it, reporting 'I shall never ~'); (d) in reporting 1st pers. sentences of type b (you promised you would not be caught again). [Aryan: OE willan, cf. Du. willen, G wollen; cogn. WELL³.]

will², n. **1.** Faculty by which person de-cides or conceives himself as deciding upon & initiating action (mind consists of the understanding & the ~; freedom of the ~, free ~; power of determining one's choice of action independently of causa-tion). **2.** (Also ~-power) control exercised by deliberate purpose over impulse, self-control. (has a strong, weak, etc., ~). **3.** Deliberate or fixed intention (the ~ to live in a patient is the surgeon's best ally; determination to win power etc.; did it against my ~, of my own free ~; where there's a ~ there's a way; may poverty but not my ~ consents). **4.** Energy of inten-tion, power of effecting one's intentions or dominating other persons, (do thing with a ~, energetically; has a ~ that over-bears all opposition). **5.** Contents of the ~, what is desired or ordained by person, (thy ~ be done; what is your ~?, what do you wish done; have one's ~, get thing desired; worked his wicked ~ upon them). **6.** Arbitrary discretion (esp. at ~, when-ever one pleases; tenant at ~, who can be turned out without notice; ~-worship; arch. religion constructed to suit oneself. **7.** Disposition towards others, wishing of good or ill. (good, ill, ~, usu. as compd wds). **8.** Directions written in legal form for disposition to be made of per-son's property & minor children after his death (often last ~ & testament; nuncu-pative ~, see NUNCUPATE; make one's ~. Hence (-)~ED² (-)d), ~LESS aa. [OE willa (prec.)]

will³, v.t. **1.** Have as contents of one's will, intend unconditionally, (God ~s, ~eth, ~ed, that man should be happy; can we ~ what we are told to ~?; he who ~s success is half way to it); (abs.) exercise will-power (has no power to ~); (~ing & wishing not the same). **2.** Instigate or impel or compel by exercise of will-power (you can ~ yourself into contentment; mesmerist ~s patient to think himself well; ~ed the gentle into his presence). **3.** Bequeath by will (shall ~ my money to a hospital). [OE willian, f. prec.]

will'et, n. N.-Amer. snipe. [imit. of cry]

will'ing, a. Not reluctant, cheerfully ready, (to do, or abs.; do not spur a ~ horse); of, given etc. by, ~ person (~ hands, help, etc.). Hence ~LY² adv., ~NESS n. [WILL¹, -ING²]

will-o'-the-wisp'(-dh-), n. **1.** IGNIS FA-TUUS, JACK-'o'-lantern; also, person of uncertain whereabouts or appearances. [abbr. of William; wisp = handful (lighted) tow etc.]

wil'low¹(-ō), n. **1.** Kinds of tree & shrub with pliant branches growing usu. near water in temperate climates, many of which yield osiers & some timber used for cricket bats & other purposes (wear the ~; mourn loss or absence of one's be-loved, formerly indicated by garland of ~ leaves; ~-pattern, conventional de-sign of Chinese type done in blue on white

china etc., introduced in England 1780). 2. Cricket-bat (*handle the ~, bat*). 3. *~herb*, kinds of plant, the commonest with leaves like ~ & pale purple flowers. [OE *welig*, cf. Du. *wilg*]

will'ow² (-ō), v.t. & n., will'ly, n. 1. Clean (fibrous material) by beating, picking, etc., with machinery. 2. n. (Also *~ow*, *~owing*, *-machine*) machine for ~owing. [OE *wilige* n. (prec.)]

will'owy (-ōi), a. Abounding in willows; lithe & slender. [-Y²]

will'y-nill'y. See NILL.

wilt¹. See WILL¹.

wilt², v.t. & i. Wither (t. & i. of plant, leaf, flower), (make) droop. [perh. var. of WELK]

Wil'ton, n. (Also *~ carpet*) kind of Brussels carpet with loops cut open into thick pile made at town of ~ in Wilts.

wil'y, a. Full of wiles, crafty, cunning. Hence ~ILY² adv., ~INESS n. [WILE, -Y²]

Wim'bledon (-ld-) adv., ~INESS n. (Used for the lawn-tennis tournaments with champion-ship matches etc. held at ~.

wim'ple, n., & v.t. & i. 1. Covering of linen etc. worn by nuns & formerly by other women arranged in folds about head, cheeks, chin, & neck; (vb) put ~ upon, veil, arrange in folds. 2. Winding, twist, turn, ripple; (vb) fall in folds, (of stream) twist about, meander, ripple. [OE *wimpel*, cf. Du. & G *wimpel* streamer]

win, v.t. & i. (won pr. wŭn), & n. 1. Secure as result of fighting or competition or (often of person) betting & gaming or of effort (*~ victory, fortress, prize, honour, fame, fortune, one's bread, wife*; ~ one's spurs, be knighted, (fig.) get recognition as expert at something; *won £5 of him at cards*, whence ~n'ings n. pl. see -ING⁴(2); ~ one's way, progress by struggle etc.; ~ one's bread, earn livelihood, chiefly now in BREAD-~ner; ~ ore etc., get it from mine). 2. Be victorious in (*~ battle, game, bet, race*; ~ the field, be victorious in battle or fig.; ~ the TOSS); (abs.) ~ race, CANTER, money, etc. (*~ by a HEAD¹, in a CANTER, HAND¹S down, by two etc. lengths, easily*, etc.; ~NING¹-post, mark-ing end of race; *the ~ning horse, side*, etc.; ~ at cards; *let those laugh who ~*); (part.) determining victory (*the ~ning hit, goal, card*, etc.). 3. Make one's way to (*~ the shore, summit*, etc.). 4. Make one's way, or (with compl.) become by successful effort, (*~ home*; ~ through the day, through all difficulties; *~ free, clear*, etc.). 5. Persuade, induce to do, gain over, (*you have won me; won him to con-sent; soon won his audience over*). 6. Exer-cise increasing attraction upon (*a theory that ~s upon one by degrees*); (part. as adj.) charming, attractive, (*a ~ning smile, ~ning manners, personality*, etc.), whence ~n'ingLY² adv. 7.~ning HAZARD¹. Hence (-)~ner¹ n. 8. n. A success or victory in a

game (*has had three ~s & no defeats*). [com.-Teut.: OE *winnan* fight, toil, cf. Du. *winnen*, G *gewinnen*]

wince, v.i., & n. 1. Show bodily or mental pain or distress by slight start or loss of composure, flinch, (often *under pain, the knife, at allusion*, etc.). 2. n. Act of wincing. [cf. OF *guencir* f. Teut., cf. WINK]

win'cey, n. (pl. ~s). Strong material of wool & cotton or wool used for shirts etc. Hence ~ETTE'(2) (-si-) n. [perh. corrupt. of LINSEY-WOOLSEY]

winch, n. Crank of wheel or axle; hoist-ing-machine, windlass. [OE *wince*, cogn. w. WINK]

Win'chester¹, n. ~ (rifle, type of repeat-ing rifle used esp. by big-game hunters. [O. F., Amer. manuf.]

Win'chester², n. ~ (quart), (bottle hold-ing) half a gallon. [~ in Hants, where standard measures were orig. deposited]

wind¹ (poet. also wī-), n. 1. Air in more or less rapid natural motion, breeze or gale or blast, (*north* etc. ~, coming from N. etc.; *fair, contrary*, helping, hindering, ship's course; *hot, cold, whistling, variable*, etc., ~s: constant ~, that always blows in same direction at same place; *periodical* ~, recurring at known periods; ~ *rises*, begins to blow or gets stronger; ~ *sound, scent, is carried by, comes on, the* ~; CAP-FUL, SLANT, *of* ~; ILL ~; *before, down, the* ~, helped by its force; WHISTLE *down the* ~; BETWEEN ~ & *water*; *sail, be, close to or near the* ~, as nearly against it as is con-sistent with using its force, (fig.) venture very near indecency or dishonesty; *in the* ~'s *eye, in the teeth of the* ~, directly against it; *on a* ~, Naut., sailing against a ~ *on either bow*; *off the* ~, Naut., sailing with the ~ *on either quarter*; *fling or cast prudence* etc. *to the* ~s, aban-don, neglect, take no thought of; PUT *the* ~ *up one*; *have or get the* ~ *up*, sl., be or become frightened; *go like the* ~, swiftly; *there is something in the* ~, there are signs that some step is being secretly prepared; *find out how the* ~ *blows or lies*, what developments are likely or what is the state of public opinion; *take the* ~ *out of one's sails*, frustrate him by anticipat-ing his arguments, using his material, etc.; *sow* ~, & *reap* WHIRL~; *raise the* ~, fig., obtain money needed). 2.~ward position or weather-GAUGE¹ (*take or get the* ~ *of*). 3. pl. The four cardinal points (*came from the four ~s of heaven*). 4. More empty words, unmeaning rhetoric. 5. Artifi-cially produced air-current, air stored for use or used as current, (collect.) part of band consisting of ~-instruments, (*organ stops when the* ~ *is exhausted; was knocked down by the* ~ *of the blow; the strings were drowned by the* ~, *the wood*~, i.e. flutes etc., *by the brass*). 6. Smell conveyed on ~, indication of thing's whereabouts or

existence, commencing publicity, (get ~
rumour of; take or get ~, be rumoured).
7. Gas generated in bowels etc. by
indigestion, flatulence, (break-~, release it
by anus; baby etc. is troubled with ~).
8. Breath as needed in exertion, power of
fetching breath without difficulty while
running or making similar continuous
effort, spot below centre of chest blow on
which temporarily paralyses breathing,
(have lost, let me recover or get, my ~; has
a good, bad, ~; second ~, see BROKEN-
winded; second ~, recovery of ~ in course
of exercise after initial breathlessness;
in the ~; hit him in the ~). **9.** ~bag,
wordy orator; ~bound, unable to sail for
contrary ~s; ~break, fence, shrubs, etc.,
serving to break force of ~; ~chest, box
for compressed air in organ; ~colic, pain
caused by flatulence; ~cutter, upper lip
of mouth of flue-pipe in organ; ~egg,
unfertilized egg incapable of producing
chicken; ~fall, fruit blown down, (fig.)
unexpected good fortune, legacy; ~
instrument, musical instrument in which
sound is produced by current of air, as
organ, flute; ~jammer (sl.), merchant
sailing-ship; ~mill, mill worked by
action of ~ on sails (fight ~mills, tilt at
imaginary foe or grievance, w. ref. to Don
Quixote; ~mill plane, aeroplane supported by vanes revolving horizontally);
~pipe, breathing-tube, trachea; ~row,
line of raked hay, corn-sheaves, peats,
etc., made to allow of drying by ~; ~
sail, canvas funnel conveying air to lower
parts of ship; ||~screen (of glass in front
of motor-car driver); ~sock, canvas
cylinder or cone flying from masthead to
show direction of ~; ~spout, waterspout,
tornado, or whirl~; ~sucker, ~sucking,
(horse with) the vice of noisily drawing in
& swallowing breath; ~swept, exposed;
~TIGHT; ~ward a. & n., (region) lying in
the direction from which the ~ blows,
exposed to the ~, (look to ~ward); the ~
ward side; get to ~ward of, avoid smell of,
also get weather GAUGE[1] of or fig. advantage over). Hence ~LESS a., [ayran: OE,
also Du. & G; cogn. w. L ventus, Skr. vāta,
& see WEATHER[1]]

wind², v.t. **1.** Sound (horn, bugle, blast,
call) by blowing (wi-; winded or by confusion w. foll. wound). **2.** Detect presence
of by scent (wi-; winded, his tobacco half a
mile off). **3.** Breathe, make breathe quick
& deep by exercise, exhaust wind of,

renew wind of by rest, (wi-; winded; give
horse a gallop to ~ him; am quite ~ed by
the climb; rested to ~ the horses). [f. prec.]

wind³, v.i. & t. (wound), & n. **1.** Go in
circular, spiral, curved, or crooked
course, meander, (path, river, ~s; herd
~s o'er the lea; creeper ~s round pole;
~ing staircase, spiral; in ~ing, out of
truth, askew); make one's or its way etc.
circuitously, insinuate oneself into, (brook
~s its way; wound himself or his way into
my affections). **2.** Coil (t. & i.), wrap
closely (t. & i.), surround with coil, embrace, (~ cotton on reel, wool into ball, etc.;
also with off adv. or prep. = unwind; ~
person round one's fingers, exercise complete domination over; wound the blanket
round him, her arms round the child, the
child in her arms; ~ING[1]-sheet, in which
corpse is wound; ~pegtop, coil string
round it; serpent ~s itself or ~s round
victim); hoist or draw by use of windlass
etc. (~ ship out of harbour, are up from
mine). **3.** ~ up (clock etc.). **4.** ~ ship,
reverse positions of bow & stern. **5.** ~ up,
coil the whole of (~ up piece of string),
tighten coiling or coiled spring or fig.
tension or intensity or efficiency of (~ up
strings of fiddle; ~ up clock etc.; is ~ing
himself; ~ up company, arrange its affairs
& dissolve it; company ~s up, ceases
business, goes into liquidation, whence
~ING-UP n.); hence ~ER[1], **2)** n.,
~ingly[2] adv. **6.** n. Bend or turn in
course; single turn in ~ing clock, string,
etc.; ~up, conclusion, finish. [OE
windan, cf. Du. & G winden; cogn. w.
WANDER, WEND[1]]

win'dage, n. Difference between projectile's & gun-bore's diameter allowing
escape of gas; (allowance for) influence of
wind in deflecting missile. [-AGE]

wind'lass, n., & v.t. **1.** Machine for
hauling or hoisting on wheel-&-axle
principle. **2.** v.t. Hoist or haul with ~.
[prob. corrupt. of AF windas f. ON
vindáss (vinda WIND³, áss beam)]

||**win'dlestraw** (-del-), n. **1.** Old stalk of
kinds of grass. [OE windelstréaw]

win'dow (-ō), n. **1.** Opening in wall or
roof of building, ship, carriage, etc., usu.
filled with glass in fixed or sliding or
hinged frames to admit light & sometimes
air to room etc. (look out of ~, be superficial; blank, blind, false, ~, mouldings of
recess as for ~ without aperture; BOW
WINDOW; BAY³, CASEMENT, DORMER, FRENCH,
LATTICE, ORIEL, SASH², ~). **2.** Opening in

envelope to show address written on letter. **3.** ~-box, slide for weights in sash-~, also box on ~-sill in which flowers are grown; ~-dressing, art of arranging goods attractively in shop-~, often fig. of adroit presentation of statistics etc.; ~ envelope (with opening to ~ transparent part allowing address inside to show); ~-shopping, feasting one's eyes on the goods displayed in the shop-~s. Hence (-)~ED² (-ĕd), ~LESS (-ĕ-), aa. [f. ON *vindauga* (WIND¹, EYE¹)]

Wind'sor (-z-), n. Town in Berks. (House of ~, style of British Royal Family assumed 1917; ~ chair, all of wood with curved support for back (& arms); *brown ~ soap*, brown scented kind; ~ *uniform*, blue coat with red collar & cuffs worn at ~ by the royal family, & by others having royal grant).

wind'|y, a. Wind-swept(~*y hill-top, plain, situation*); in which wind is high(~*y night, weather, crossing*); wordy, verbose, empty, (~*y eloquence, logic, speaker*); generating or characterized by flatulence; (arch.) windward (*on the ~y side of the law*, safely out of its reach); (sl.) frightened. Hence ~ILY² adv., ~INESS n. [-Y¹]

wine, n. & v.i. & t. **1.** (Kinds of) fermented grape-juice (*is a sound* ~; DRY¹ *or sweet*, STILL¹ *or sparkling*, WHITE¹ *or red*, ~; *green* ~, in first year; *port* ~; port; COMET ~; *Adam's* ~, water; *good* ~ *needs no* BUSH¹; *new* ~ *in old bottles*, new principle too powerful to be restrained by ancient forms; *take* ~ *with*, pledge & be pledged by at table; SPIRIT *of* ~; TEAR²s *of strong* ~; *over the* WALNUTS *& the* ~; *in* ~, whey, beverage of ~ & curdled milk; *in* ~, exhilarated or drunk with ~). **2.** || (At universities) party for ~-drinking after dinner (~*s have gone out of fashion*). **3.** Fermented drink resembling ~ made from specified fruit etc. (*cowslip, currant, gooseberry, orange, palm,* ~). **4.** Solution of drug in ~ (*quinine* ~; ~ *of opium*). **5.** A dark-red tint. **6.** ~-bag, ~-skin, or ~-bibber, ~bibber, tippler, drunkard; so ~bibbing a. & n.;~bottle, glass bottle for ~, also ~skin;~bowl, lit., also drinking habits etc.;~-carriage, wheeled utensil for circulating ~bottle at table; ~-cooler, vessel in which ~bottles are cooled with ice;~cup, as ~bowl; ||~fat, arch., ~press; ~glass, any glass for drinking ~ from, esp. of size used for sherry, often as measure (also ~-glassful) of medicine to be taken, = four table-spoons; ~MARC; ~palm, kind from which ~ is made; ~press, in which grapes are squeezed; ~sap, large red American winter apple; ~skin, whole skin of goat etc. sewn up & used to hold ~; ~-stone, tartaric deposit in ~ casks; ~vault, cellar in which ~ is kept, also bar etc, where it is retailed; hence ~LESS, **win'y²**, aa. **7.** vb. Drink ~; entertain to ~; often *dine &* ~. [OE *wīn* f. L *vīnum*, cf. G *wein*, Du. *wijn*, Gk *oinos* wine, *oinē* vine]

wing, n. & v.i. & t. & i. **1.** One of the limbs or organs by which the flight of a bird, bat, insect, angel, etc., is effected, part in non-flying bird or insect corresponding to ~, supporting part of flying-machine. (*clip one's* ~*s*, limit his movements or ambitions or expenditure; *come on the* ~*s of the wind*, swiftly; *lend, add,* ~*s to*, accelerate; *take under one's* ~, treat as protégé; *his* ~*s are sprouting* etc., his virtues are too great for a being below the degree of an angel; *money takes to itself* ~*s*, disappears); high-, low-, mid-~, aa., (of monoplane) having the ~s set near the top, near the bottom, in the middle, of the fuselage. **2.** (joc.) (Esp. of wounding) arm. **3.** More or less separate projecting part of something, esp. of building or battle array (*the north* ~ *was added in the 17th century; cavalry were massed on left* ~; ~*s in theatre*, sides of stage, pieces of side scenery). **4.** (Football, Hockey, etc.) forward etc. whose place is either side of the centre (also attrib., as ~ *three-quarter*). **5.** || R.A.F. formation of two or more squadrons. **6.** pl. Pilot's badge in R.A.F. etc. **7.** ~ed flight, ~s, (*on the* ~, flying, travelling, in motion; *take* ~, start flying). **8.** ~-beat, one complete set of motions with ~ in flying; ~-case, horny cover, a modified fore~; protecting some insects' flying ~; ||~-commander, officer of AIR¹-force; ~-covert, one of small feathers covering insertion of bird's flying feathers; ~-footed, poet., swift; ~-sheath, ~-case; ~-spread, measurement across ~s when extended, surface or area of aircraft's ~s; ~-stroke; ~-beat; hence ~ED² (wingd, wing'id), ~LESS, aa., ~LET n. **9.** vb. Equip with ~s, enable to fly or mount, send in flight, lend speed to, (~ *arrow with eagle's feathers or at the mark; vengeance* ~*ed the shaft;* ~*ed words*, going like arrows to mark, significant; *ambition* ~*s his spirit; fear* ~*ed his steps;* ~*ed horse*, Pegasus, poetry; ~*ed god*, Mercury; ~*ed Victory*, statue of goddess of victory with ~s). **10.** Travel, traverse, on ~s (*bird* ~*s its way,* ~*s to its mate,* ~*s the air*). **11.** Wound (bird) in ~, (person) in arm. [ON *vængr*, cf. Da. *vinge*]

wink, v.i. & t., & n. **1.** Close & open eyes, blink, close & open (eyes or eye), (of eye) close & open, (*like* ~*ing*, sl., very quickly or vigorously); momentarily close one eye to awaken attention to or convey private intimation to person (usu. *at* person); (of light, star, etc.) twinkle, shine intermittently; ~ *at*, shut one's eyes to, purposely avoid seeing, affect not to notice, connive at, (abuse, transgression, etc.). **2.** n. Act of ~ing, esp. as signal etc. (*nod is as good as* ~ *to blind horse; tip one the* ~, sl., give him signal

or intimation; could not sleep; ~ all night; forty ~s, nap). [OE *wincian* move sideways; cf. M Du. & G *winken* beckon; cogn. w. WINCE]

winkle (wing'kl), n. 1. Edible sea snail, periwinkle. 2. v.t. ~ *out*, extract or eject (as a ~ from its shell with a pin). [abbr. PERIWINKLE², cf. WIG¹]

winn'ow (-ō), v.t. Fan (grain) free of chaff etc.; fan (chaff etc.) *away* or *out* or *from*; sift, separate, clear of refuse or inferior specimens or falsehood, clear (refuse etc.) *out* or *away*, examine, sort, weed out; stir (hair etc.) (air with wings), flap (wings). [OE *windwian* (WIND¹)]

win'some, a. (Of person or his appearance, manner, smile, etc.) charming, winning, attractive, engaging, bright. Hence ~LY² adv., ~NESS n. [OE *wynsum* (*wynn* joy, cogn. w. WIN, -SOME]

win'ter, n. & v.i. & t. 1. Season between autumn & spring, three or four coldest months of year (in northern latitudes Nov. or Dec. to Jan. or Feb., or, Astron., from Dec. solstice to March equinox; *hard*, *mild*, ~, with, without, much frost); (attrib.) occurring, used, etc., in or lasting for the ~ (*apple, cough, solstice*, etc.); ~ *sleep*, hibernation; ~ *quarters*, esp. to which troops retire for ~; ~ *garden*, glass-covered space with plants etc. used as lounge). 2. (rhet., poet.), Year of life (*a man of 80* ~s, 80 years old). 3. (*a genus of plants green through* ~); ~ *lodge* (Bot.), bud or bulb protecting plant's embryo through ~'; ~*tide* (poet.), the ~ *at, in*, etc.; keep or feed (plants, cattle) during ~. [OE, Du., & G; perh. cogn. w. WET, WATER]

win'try, a. Having the temperature, storminess, or aspect appropriate to winter, cold, windy, cheerless, (~*y weather, day, sun, scene*); (of smile, greeting, etc.) lacking warmth or interest or vivacity. Hence ~INESS n. [-Y²]

wipe, v.t. & i. & n. 1. Clean or dry surface of by rubbing with cloth, paper, hand, etc. (~ *table, dish, face, hands*, etc.; ~ *one's eyes*, dry tears, cease weeping; ~ *one's eye*, sl., steal march on him, get advantage by anticipating him; ~ *out* both or other hollow utensil); get rid of, clear *away* or off, take *up*, wash *out*, by wiping (~ *away* or ~ *your tears*; ~ *up* *slops*; ~ *out stain*, or fig. disgrace, insult, whole *army*, *was* ~*d out*); ~ *the floor with* (sl.), inflict humiliating defeat or correction on (person); (sl.) take or aim sweeping blow or stroke *at* (~*d at me with his stick*). 2. n. Act of wiping (*give this girl a* ~); sweeping blow (*fetched* or *took a* ~ *at* him; *fetched him a* ~); (sl.) handkerchief, etc.). [OE *wīpian*; cogn. w. WHIP]

wire, n. & v.t. & i. 1. (Piece of) metal drawn out into form of thread or slender round or square or tapellie flexible rod (*platinum, silver, copper*, etc., ~; BARB'*ed*, LIVE¹, ~; ~ *telegraph* etc., ~*s*; *private* ~, ~ reserved for person's exclusive use; *was sent for, send congratulations, by* ~, by telegraph; *pull the* ~*s*, control puppets by ~*s* or usu., fig., manage political party or movement by secret influence). 2. Telegraphic message (*sent me a* ~). 3. ~*-cloth*, ~*gauze*, *netting*, etc.; ~*-dancer*, ~*-cutter*, ~*-draw* (metal) out into ~, (fig.) refine or apply or press (argument, point, etc.) with idle or excessive subtlety (esp. in p.p.); ~*-edge*, false edge that turns back when blade is over-sharpened; ~ *entanglement*, arrangement of barbed or other ~ set up to prevent rapid attack of enemy; ~*-gun*, one made by coiling flat ~ round tube; ~*-haired*, with stiff or wiry hair (esp. of dogs); ~*-heel*, disease of horse's foot; ~*-puller*, politician etc., who pulls the ~*s*; ~*-rope*, ends by twisting ~*s* together as strands; ~*-worm*, kinds of destructive larva; ~*-wove*, (of paper) = WOVE (WEAVE). 4. v.b. Provide, fasten, etc., with ~(s); string (beads) on ~; snare (bird) with ~; (Electr.) install circuits for lighting in (a house etc.); (Croquet) obstruct (ball, shot, player) by ~ of hoop (chiefly pass.); telegraph (~*me the result*; ~*d to him*; *was* ~*d for*); ||(sl.) ~ *in*, operate vigorously, put all one's force into some continuous effort. [OE *wīr*, cf. ON *vīrr*, L *vīēre* to plait; cogn. w. WITHE] [-Y²]

wire'less (wīr-), n., a., & v.i. & t. 1. Without wire(s), esp. in TELEGRAPHY. 2. n. ~ *telegraphy* or *telegram*; || ~, receiving set or broadcast or programme, radio, (also attrib.). 3. vb. Send ~ (message) or inform (person) by ~. [-LESS] **wir'y**, a. Made of wire (poet.); tough & flexible as wire, (of persons) sinewy, untiring, whence ~ILY² adv., ~INESS n.

wis, v.i. pres. 1st sing. (pseudo-arch.), I know well (parenth.). [supposed pres. of *wist* (WIT¹), obs. *gwis* certainly, cf. G *gewiss*, being read as *I wis*]

wis'dom (-z-), n. Being wise, (possession of) experience & knowledge together with the power of applying them critically or practically, sagacity, prudence, common sense; wise sayings (*your forth* ~; *W.~ of Solomon*, abbr. *Wisd.*, *W.~ of Jesus the Son of Sirach* or *Ecclesiasticus*, abbr. *Apocrypha*); ~*tooth*, molar usu. cut after 20 years of age (*cut one's* ~*teeth*, gain discretion). [OE *wīsdōm* (WISE¹, -DOM)]

wise¹ (-z), a., & v.t. & i. 1. (Of persons) having, (of action, course, speech, opinion, etc.) dictated by or in harmony with

or showing, experience & knowledge judicially applied, sagacious, prudent, sensible, discreet; having knowledge (~ after the event, of person who has failed to foresee; came away none the ~r or as ~ as he went, knowing no more than before; where ignorance is bliss 'tis folly to be ~); ||(arch.) having occult power or knowledge of mysterious things (~ man, wizard; ||~ woman, witch, fortune-teller, also midwife); suggestive of wisdom, oracular, (with a ~ shake of the head; ~ saw, proverbial saying); *(sl.) be or get ~ to, be or become aware of; *(sl.) put one ~ (to, inform one (of), enlighten one (concerning); *(sl.)~ crack, smart pithy remark (so ~crack v.i.). 2. vb. ~ up (sl.), put or get ~. Hence ~LY² (zi-) adv. [Aryan: OE wīs, cf. Du. wijs, G weis]

wise² (-z), n. Way, manner, guise, (in solemn etc.~, arch.; esp. in some, no, any, ~, on this~). [OE wīse (wīsian show way, orig. make wise, see prec.), cf. Du. wijze, G weise]

-wise (-z), suf. = prec., forming advv. of manner as in clock~ with motion in direction of clock hands, cross~ with cross arrangement, length~ with length arranged in given direction, with regard to length, no~ in no way, not at all.

wise³acre (-zāker), n. Sententious dullard. [corrupt. of MDu. wijsseggher, itself corrupt. (as if = wise sayer) of MHG wīzago (=OE wītiga) seer, cogn. w. WIT¹]

wish, v.t. & i., & n. 1. Have as a desire or aspiration (that-clause with that usu. omitted, or obj. & compl.; ~ I had never been born, were or was a bird, may live to see it; you would be quiet; ~ it is to be ~ed it, is desirable that; I ~ it may not prove, fear it will; could not ~ it better; ~ oneself dead, home, at home, etc.; ~ person happy, away; ~ one at the devil or further, ~ he were away). 2. Want with the kind of desire that tends to affect result (to do, person or thing to do, person or thing ~ed, or rarely with simple obj. esp. pronoun; I ~ to go, you to do it, it finished or to be finished; what do you ~?; they say they ~ peace, an interview) 3. Be well or ill inclined to or to (~es me well, well to all men, ~es nobody ill), whence (~)-ER¹ n. 4. Say one hopes for (joy, luck, pleasant journey, sorrow, etc.) in person's favour or against him (ind. obj. or to; I ~ you joy, ~ success to each & all); ~ person joy of, (iron.) hope he will enjoy; express desire for (has nothing left to ~ for; would not ~ for anything better). 5. ~ing-bone, merrythought (longer part of it when broken between two persons entitling holder to magic fulfilment of any ~); ~ing-cap, magic cap securing to wearer fulfilment of any ~. 6. n. (Expression of) desire or aspiration, request, implied command, (~ is father to

thought, we believe thing because we ~ it true; if ~es were horses beggars might ride; has a great ~ to go to sea, whence ~FUL a., desirous (to do; ~ful thinking, belief founded on ~es rather than facts); good ~es, hopes felt or expressed for another's happiness etc.; cannot grant your ~; he disregarded or disobeyed my ~es); thing desired (have got my ~). [n. f. vb, OE wýscan, cf. Du. wenschen, G wünschen; cogn. w. WINSOME, WEEN]

wish-wash (-osh), n. Washy drink or talk. [redupl. of WASH²]

wish'y-washy (-wŏ-), a. Thin, sloppy, (of soup, tea, talk, etc.). [redupl. of WASHY]

wisp, n. 1. Small bundle or twist of straw etc. 2. Flock (of snipe). [f. 14th c., etym. dub.]

wist. See WIT¹.

wistā'ria, n. Kinds of pale-purple-flowered climbing plant. [C. Wistar, American anatomist, -IA¹]

wist'ful, a. Affected with or betraying vague yearnings or unsatisfied desire to understand (of persons or usu. of eyes, look, voice, mood, etc.). Hence ~LY² adv., ~NESS n. [perh. assim. of obs. wistly adv. intently (cf. WHIST¹, ²) to wishful, w. corresp. change of sense]

wit¹, v.t. & i. (arch.; pres. I, he, wot, thou wottest; past wist; inf. ~, part. ~ting; other parts not used). Know (God wot, knows; I wot, know well; to ~, that is to say, namely; ~ting, not unconscious or unintentional, whence ~t'ingly² adv.). [Aryan: OE witan, cf. Du. weten, G wissen; cogn. w. L vidēre see, Gk eidon I saw, oida know, Skr. veda knowledge]

wit², n. 1. (Sing. or pl.) intelligence, understanding, (has not the ~, the ~s, ~ enough, to see; remedy is past the ~ of man to devise; out of one's ~s, mad, distracted; has his ~s about him, is observant or of lively intelligence; has quick, slow, etc., ~s, a nimble~, whence(-)~TED³ a.; at one's ~'s end, utterly at a loss; live by one's ~s, by ingenious hand-to-mouth shifts; the five ~s, arch., the senses or the mind), whence ~'LESS a.,~'lessly² adv., ~'lessness n. 2. (Power of giving sudden intellectual pleasure by) unexpected combining or contrasting of previously unconnected ideas or expressions (possessed of both ~ & HUMOUR; pages sparkling with ~), whence ~t'Y² a., ~t'ILY² adv., ~t'INESS n. [OE, = understanding (witan WIT¹)]

wit³, n. Wise man (arch.); witty person (see prec.), person who talks wittily, whence ~'ING²(2) n. [uses of prec.; 1st sense f. 15th, 2nd f. 17th, c.]

witch, n., & v.t. 1. Woman or (now rarely) man practising sorcery (white ~, using powers for beneficent purposes only; ~es' SABBATH), (fig.) fascinating or be-

witching woman; ugly old woman, hag;
(local) flat-fish resembling the lemon
sole. **2.** ~'craft, sorcery, use of magic;
~-doctor, = MEDICINE-man; ~-hunt, (fig.)
search for suspected Communists, spies,
etc.; ~-meal, pollen of CLUB¹-moss. **3.** v.t.
Bewitch (the ~*ing* time *of night*, Haml. III.
ii. 406, time when ~es are active, mid-
~ERY4, 5) n., ~ERY4, ~'ING² a., ~'ingry² adv.
[OE *wicca* masc., *wicce* fem. (*wiccian*
practise sorcery, etym. dub.); the mod.
vb prob. aphetic f. *bewitch*]

witch-. See WYCH-.

witenagemot' (-g-), n. (hist.) Anglo-
Saxon national council or parliament.
[OE *witena* gen. pl. of *wita* wise man,
gemōt meeting]

with (-dh, -th), prep. **1.** In antagonism to,
against, (*fight, quarrel, struggle, dispute,
argue, compete, vie,* ~). **2.** In or into company of or relation to, among, beside,
(*come, go, walk, eat, live, spend the day,
mix* t. & i., *meet,* ~; *king is expected* ~ *us
together* ~ *queen & court; numbered* ~ *the
transgressors; compare* ~; *have nothing to
do* ~; *deal* ~; = *God, dead* & *in heaven;
have* ~ *you,* arch., I accept your offer or
challenge; *so done* ~ *you*). **3.** Agreeably
or in harmonious relations to (*I feel,
think, sympathize,* ~ *you*; *also with neg.
wth* in opp. sense, *as I disagree* ~ *you; he
that is not* ~ *me is against me; vote* ~ *the
Liberals; blue does not go* ~ *green; one
that is not* ~ *me is against me; vote* ~ *the
Liberals; blue does not go* ~ *green; one
~, part of same whole as*). **4.** Having,
carrying, possessed of, characterized by,
(*ease* ~ *handles, man* ~ *sinister expression;
walking* ~ *a gun; went out* ~ *no hat on;
~ child or young, pregnant*). **5.** In the
care or charge or possession of (*leave no
money* ~ *me; leave child, parcel,* ~ *nurse,
porter; it rests* ~ *you to decide; the deal,
decanter, next move, is* ~ *you*). **6.** By use
of as instrument or means (*cut it* ~ *a knife;
leave no pen to write* ~; *walks* ~ *a crutch;
damn* ~ *faint praise*). **7.** By addition or
supply or acquisition or possession of as
material (*fill it, overflowing,* ~ *water;
laden* ~ *baggage; blessed* ~ *beauty; adorn
~ frescoes*). **8.** In same way or direction or
degree or at the same time as (*changes* ~
the seasons, ~; *rise* ~ *the sun*; ~ *that,
thereupon, simultaneously; begin* ~, *take
as starting-point*). **9.** Because or by
operation of, owing to, (*trembles* ~ *fear; is
down* ~ *fever; stiff, silent,* ~ *cold, shame*).
10. Displaying or so as to display, under
favourable or unfavourable circumstances of, (*heard it* ~ *calmness; fought
~ courage; won* ~ *ease, difficulty; a good
deal to spare; shot well* ~ *a good, wretched,
light*). **11.** In regard to, concerning, in the
sphere of, in the mind or view of, (*be
patient* ~ *him; bear, do, or put up,* ~,
*tolerate, be indulgent to; my dealings
the natives; what do you want* ~ *me*;

etc.; ~ thee ; *it is holiday time* ~ *us; the
first object* ~ *him is; has great influence* ~
the House). **12.** So as to be separated from
(*part, break, dispense,* ~). **13.** Despite,
notwithstanding, (*~ all his learning, he is
the simplest of men* ; ~ *many
admirable qualities, the best of intentions,
he failed completely*). [OE shortened f.
wither against, cf. G *wider* against, ON
mid with have passed to it]

‖ withal' (-dhawl), adv. & prep. (arch.).
1. With it, in addition, moreover, as well,
at the same time. **2.** prep. (always after
its expressed or omitted obj.). With
(*what shall he fill his belly* ~*?*). [prec.,
ALL]

withdraw' (-dh-), v.t. & i. Pull aside or
back (~ *curtain, one's hand*); take away,
remove, (*boy from school, coins from
circulation, horse from race, troops from
position, favour etc. from person*); retract
(*offer, statement, promise; cries of ‘ , ’
demands that speaker shall unsay something as unparliamentary etc.); retire
from presence or place, go aside or
apart; ‖ ~*ing-room* (arch.), DRAWING-ROOM.
Hence ~AL²(2) n. [*with* in obs. sense for
words (oneself, & so away from others),
DRAW¹]

withe (-dhi, *or* widh), **with'y** (-dhi), n.
(pl. -*thes* pr. -dhiz, *or* -*ths*). Tough flexible
branch esp. of willow or osier used for
binding bundles etc. [OE *withthe, withig,
Gk *itea* willow, L *vimen* twig, *vitis* vine]

with'er (-dh-), v.t. & i. Make or become
dry & shrivelled (often *up*), deprive of or
lose vigour or vitality or freshness or importance (often *away*), decline, languish,
decay, (*has a* ~*ed arm; flowers & beauty
~; age cannot* ~ *her; the* ‖*witheried* ~*s,
ceases to be important*); blight with
scorn etc. (~ *one with a look* usu. joc.),
whence ~*ING³* a., ~*ingry²* adv. [ME
widren expose to WEATHER¹]

with'ers (-dherz), n. pl. Ridge between
horse's shoulder-blades (*my* ~ *are un-
wrung*, imputation etc. does not touch
me). [named as the part that resists or
takes strain of collar f. OE *wither* against,
see WITH]

withhold' (-dh-h-), v.t. (-*held*). Refrain
from putting in action, refuse to grant,
(~ *one's hand*, arch. for *hold*, not take
action; ~ *one's consent, support, the tight

away, down, up, to the devil, etc., ~ *him,
take or send or put him, he may go, away
etc.; can do anything, nothing,* ~ *him, influence or utilize him in any, no, direction; ~ God all things are possible; is it
well* ~

of one's countenance, etc.). [WITH as in WITHDRAW, HOLD]

within' (-dh-), adv., n., & prep. **1.** Inside, to or at or on the inside, indoors, internally, (chiefly arch.: *clean ~ & without: go into house or room; stay ~, not go out of doors: is Mr Jones ~?*, at home; *beauty without & foulness ~; make me pure ~*, in spirit: *Bishopsgate ~*, inside the walls). **2.** n. The inside (*as seen from the walls*). **3.** prep. To or on or in the inside of, enclosed by, (*~ doors*, in or into house; *safe ~ the walls;* WHEEL1s & ~ *wheels*); not beyond, not too far for, not transgressing, so as not to pass or exceed, subject to, (*live, keep, ~ one's income; ~ the meaning of the law*, not illegal; *keep it ~ bounds; a task well ~ his powers; running ~ himself*, without putting forth whole power; *is true ~ limits*); not too far for, near enough to affect or be affected by, not farther off than (of with sense *from*, or abs.), (*is ~ reach, sight, call*, near enough to reach or be reached etc.; often of, as *~ sight of port; is ~ three miles of a station; was ~ an ace of destruction*); in a time no longer than, before expiration or since beginning of, (of with sense *from*, or abs.; *shall have it ~ an hour; ~ a year of his death, ~ a year, all was changed; have seen him ~ these three days*). [OE *withinnan* on the inside (WITH, *innan* adv. in)]

without' (-dh-), adv., n., prep., & conj. **1.** Outside, to or at or on the outside, out-of-doors, externally, (chiefly arch.: *white within & ~; stands desconsolate ~*, outside the house etc.; *listening to the wind ~*). **2.** n. The outside, external sources, (*as seen from ~; the suggestion came from ~*). **3.** prep. Outside of (*met us ~ the gates; negotiations within & ~ the House: is ~ the pale of civilization; things ~ us*, all that is not ourselves); not having, not with, with no, devoid of, lacking, in want of, free from, with freedom from, not feeling or showing, in or with absence of, less, (*came ~ a hat; a rose ~ a thorn; am ~ friends or money; did it ~ difficulty or being discovered; act ~ hesitation; cannot live ~ her, go away ~ thanking you; is absolutely ~ fear, anxiety; cannot make* OMELETTE *~ breaking eggs; ~ health happiness is impossible; do, go, ~*, dispense with, also ellipt. dispense with something implied; COLD ~; *doubt, admittedly, certainly; ~* FAIL1, PREJUDICE, RESERVE4; *~ end*, infinite, eternal; *goes ~ saying*, too well known or obvious to need mention). **4.** conj. (arch., vulg.). Unless. [OE *withūtan* (WITH, *ūtan* adv. out)]

withstand' (-dh-), v.t. & i.(-stood). Resist, oppose, (person, force, hardship, wear, etc.); make opposition (poet.). [OE *withstandan* (WITH, STAND)]

withy. See WITHE.

wit'ness, n., & v.t. & i. **1.** Testimony, evidence, (*bear ~ to* or *of*, state one's belief in, state facts tending to establish), thing stated by way of evidence (*my ~ is not true;* arch.), confirmation (*stands there in ~ of the event; call to ~*, appeal to for confirmation); thing or person whose existence, position, state, etc., serves as testimony to or proof of (*is a living ~ to my clemency*); (also EYE-~) spectator of incident, bystander, person present at event; person giving sworn testimony in lawcourt or for legal purpose (~ often used for *the* ~); person attesting genuineness of signature to document by adding his signature; ||~*box*, enclosure in lawcourt reserved for ~es. **2.** vb. State in evidence (noun, *that*, etc.: arch.); give evidence (*against, for, to;* or as *~ my poverty*, of which let my poverty be the proof); be a ~ or the ~ (arch.: ~ *Heaven!*, I call Heaven to ~); indicate, serve as evidence of, ((*a deathly pallor ~ed his agitation*); see, be spectator of; sign (document) as ~. [OE *witnes* (WIT2, -NESS)]

witt'icism, n. Witty remark, jest, (usu. in disparaging sense). [coined by Dryden f. wit1*ty*, after *criticism*]

||**witt'ol**, n. (arch.). Man who winks at wife's infidelity, acquiescent cuckold. [ME *wetewold*, prob. formed by substitution of WIT1 for first syllable of *cokewold* CUCKOLD]

wive, v.t. & i. (now rare). Provide with, take, wife. [OE *wifian* (WIFE)]

wiv'ern, wyv-, n. (her.). Winged two-legged dragon with barbed tail. [f. OF *wyvre, wivre*, f. L VIPERA; for -n, cf. BITTERN]

wives. See WIFE.

wiz'ard, n. & a. **1.** Magician, sorcerer, male witch; person who effects seeming impossibilities; conjurer: *the W~ of the North*, Sir Walter Scott. **2.** adj. (sl.). Wonderful. Hence ~RY(4, 5) n. [ME *wisard* (WISE1, -ARD)]

wiz'ened (-nd), **wiz'en, weaz'en**, a. Of shrivelled or dried-up appearance (chiefly of person or his face or form). [f. OE *wisnian* become dry, cf. ON *visna* wither (*visana* withered)]

wizier. See VIZIR.

wō, whoa (wō'a), int. Stop (chiefly to horses); GEE-*wo; wo-back'*, int. used in backing horses.

woad, n., & v.t. **1.**(Plant yielding) kind of blue dye. **2.** v.t. Dye with ~. [OE *wād*, cf. Du. *weede*, G *waid*]

wob'ble, wa'bble (wo-), v.i., & n. **1.**(Of top or revolving body) revolve with changing inclinations, rock: (of person, missile, etc.) go unsteadily, vibrate from side to side, swerve, stagger; (fig.) vacillate, waver, act inconsistently, be incon-

stant, whence **wŏbb'ler¹** n.; (of voice or sound) quaver, pulsate. **2.** n. Rocking movement, change of direction or policy, swerve, piece of vacillation. [var. now rare, is the earlier form; cf. MHG *wabbelen* move restlessly, ON *vafla* waver, cogn. w. WAVE¹]

wōe, n. (chiefly poet. or joc.). Affliction, bitter grief, distress, (*weal & ~*, prosperity & adversity; *~ is me*, alas! *~ to the*, curse upon; *~ worth² the day*); (pl.) calamities, troubles; *~begone* (-awn, -ŏn), dismal-looking. [p.-p. of OE *wāwan* (BY, GO) surround). Hence **~FUL**(wōf⁴) a., **~fully²** adv. (often joc., as *~ful ignorance*), **~fulness** n. [OE *wā* int., orig. cry of pain, cf. Du. *wee*, G. *weh*, & nn., L *vae* int.]

woke. See WAKE¹.

wōld, n. Piece of open uncultivated country, down or moor land. [com.-Teut.; cf. WEALD]

wolf (wŏŏ-), n. (pl. *-ves*), & v.t. **1.** Erect-eared straight-tailed harsh-furred tawny-grey wild gregarious carnivorous quadruped allied to dog preying on sheep etc., or combining in packs to hunt larger animals (*cry ~ too often*, raise false alarms till genuine ones are disregarded: *have, hold, ~ by the ears*, be in situation where one can neither retreat, advance, nor stop; *keep ~ from door*, avert starvation; *~ in sheep's clothing*, hypocrite). **2.** Rapacious or greedy person, whence **~ISH** a., **~'ishly²** adv., **~'ishNESS** n. (wŏŏ-). **3.** (mus.) Jarring sound from some notes in a bowed instrument; out-of-tune effect when playing in extremer keys on old organs (before present 'equal temperament' was in use). **4.** *~ cub*, young *~*, junior boy scout; *~-dog*, kinds of dog; *dog-&-~* hybrid; *~-fish*, large voracious kind; *~-hound*, Russian breed of dog, (also) Alsatian breed popular in U.K.; *~'s-bane*, monk's-hood, aconite; *~'s-claws, ~'s-foot*, club-moss; ||*~'s-milk*, kind of spurge; *~ spider*, tarantula, also kinds that chase instead of netting prey; *~-tooth*, supernumerary pre-molar in horse. **5.** v.t. Devour or swallow greedily (often *down*). [Aryan; OE *wulf*, cf. Du. & G *wolf*, Gk *lukos*, L *lupus*, Skr. *vṛkas*]

wo'lfram (wŏŏ-), n. (Also *~ite*) ore yield-ing tungsten, native tungstate of iron & manganese; (now usu. for) tungsten. [G. perh. f. WOLF+*rahm* cream, or MHG *rām* dirt, soot]

wo'lverēne (wŏŏ-), **-ine** (-ēn), n. Ameri-can carnivorous mammal called also GLUTTON & *carcajou*. [irreg. dim. of WOLF, perh. after MHG *vilfrāȝ*]

wolves. See WOLF.

wo'man (wŏŏ-), n. (pl. *women* pr. wim'in), & v.t. **1.** Adult human female (*every ~ is to him a lady; ~'s or women's rights*, posi-tion of legal equality with men demanded for women; *there's a ~ in it*, way of ac-counting for man's inexplicable conduct; *~ with a past*, with some scandal attach-ing to her past life; *~ of the world*, ex-perienced in society, not raw & innocent; *play the ~*, weep or show fear; *make an honest ~ of*, marry after seducing; *tied to ~'s apron-strings*, controlled like child by her; *single ~*, spinster; *the SCARLET ~; WISE¹ ~*). **2.** (Without article) the average or typical *~*, the female sex, any *~*, (*how does ~ differ from man?; man born of ~; mortal man¹ is an excellent thing in ~; ~'s wit*, instinctive insight or resource; *~'s REASON¹; O W~!*, in apostrophes). **3.** Queen's or great lady's female atten-dant, lady in waiting, (arch.; *sent one of her women to ask*). **4.** Man with feminine characteristics (*is a ~ in tenderness; the old women in the Cabinet; all the old women of both sexes*). **5.** The feminine emotions (*all the ~ in her rose in rebellion; stirred the ~ in him; has much of the ~ in his composition*). **6.** attrib. Female (*~ doctor, friend, counsellor, councillor; ~ suffrage*, extension or possession of political suffrage to or by women). **7.** (As suf-fix, chiefly in terms correl. to compounds in *-man*) *~* concerned or dealing or skilful with (*country~, shop~, horse~, church~, chair~, ferry~, apple~, needle~*, etc.; also by close comb. with adj., as *gentle~*). **8.** *~* (one's *~kind*, womenfolk, the women of one's family; **wo'menfolk**, women, one's *~kind*; hence **~HOOD** n., **~manHOOD** n. **9.** v.t. Make behave like a *~*, cause to weep etc.; *~ a man* (not 'lady'). [OE *wīfman* (WIFE, MAN) i.e. woman person]

wo'manish (wŏŏ-), a. (Of man or his feelings, conduct, looks, etc.) like wo-men or their ways etc. (usu. derog.), effeminate. Hence **~LY²** adv., **~NESS** n. [-ISH¹]

wo'manīze (wŏŏ-), v.t. & i. Make woman-ish; (of men) be licentious, frequent pro-stitutes. [-IZE]

wo'manly (wŏŏ-), a. (Of woman or her feelings, conduct, etc.) having or showing the qualities befitting a woman, not mas-culine or girlish, (*a truly ~y woman; ~y modesty, compassion, tact*, etc.). Hence **~lNESS** n. [-LY¹]

womb (wŏŏm), n. Organ in woman & other female mammals in which child or young is conceived & nourished till birth, uterus, (*falling of the ~*, PROLAPSUS; *fruit of the ~*, children; also fig., as *in the ~ of time*, of future events etc.). [com.-Teut.: OE *wamb, womb*, belly, cf. Du. *wam*, G *wamme*]

wom'băt, n. Australian marsupial mammal about size of badger. [f. native womback, -at]

won. See WIN.

women. See WOMAN.

wo'nder¹ (wŭ-), n. 1. Miracle, prodigy, strange or remarkable thing or specimen or performance or event, (signs & ~s, do miracles; work ~s, succeed remarkably; whence ~worKER¹ n.; the child is a ~, marvellously precocious etc.; did ~s, had remarkable success; seven ~s of the world, sights, of which one was the pyramids, so called in antiquity: a nine-days' ~, event of passing interest; for a ~, esp. by way of welcome exception, as you are punctual for a ~; what ~, it is no ~, that, naturally, inevitably, (of course, one cannot be surprised or might have guessed that, that usu. omitted; so he refused, & no ~; is a ~ of delicate workmanship). 2. Emotion excited by what surpasses expectation or experience or seems inexplicable, surprise mingled with admiration or curiosity or bewilderment, (were filled with ~; looked at him in silent or openmouthed ~). 3. ~land, fairyland, a country of surprising fertility etc.; ~struck, -stricken, filled or dumb with ~. [OE wundor portent, cf. Du. wonder, G wunder, etym. dub.]

wo'nder² (wŭ-), v.i. & t. Be filled with wonder, feel surprise, (usu. at, rarely to see etc., or abs.; shall never cease to ~ at it; can you ~ at it?; I ~ at you to child etc.; ~ed to hear your voice; the kind of person that never ~s), whence ~ingLY² adv., ~MENT n. (wŭ-); be surprised to find that (that usu. omitted: I ~ he didn't kill you); becurious, desire, to know (~ why pain exists, who invented gas-lamps, what the time is, how to proceed, etc.). [OE wundrian (prec.)]

wo'nderful (wŭ-), a. Marvellous, surprising, exceeding what was expected, remarkable, admirable. Hence ~LY² adv. [-FUL]

wo'ndrous (wŭ-), a. & adv. (poet., rhet.). 1. Wonderful; hence ~LY² adv., ~NESS n. 2. adv. (qualifying adj. only). Wonderfully (~ kind etc.), [corrupt. on -ous of obs. wonders (genit. of wonder n. used as adj. & adv.) wondrous(ly)]

∥ wŏnk'y, a. (sl.). Shaky, groggy; unreliable. [etym. dub., but cf. G wanken totter]

wont¹ (wō-, wŭ-), pred. a. Accustomed to do (usu. after is, was, are, etc.; as he was ~ to say). [OE gewunod p.p. of gewunian (wunian dwell, cf. G wohnen), ME woned p.p. of wonen]

wont² (wō-, wŭ-), v. aux. (poet.; pres. ind., ~, ~est, ~s or ~, pl. ~; past ind., ~, ~est, ~, pl. ~, or ~ed for ~). Be accustomed (usu. to do). [prop. past, =woned, of ME wonen see prec.]

wont³ (wō-, wŭ-), n. What is customary in general or habitual to a person (use & ~, established custom; according to his ~; it is my ~ to). [perh. a use of the p.p., see WONT¹]

won't. See WILL.

wont'ed (wō-, wŭ-), attrib. a. Habitual to person, (rarely) usual, (heard me with his ~ courtesy; met with the ~ obstacles). If wont = woned p.p. see WONT¹ w. erron. addition of -ED¹]

woo, v.t. (rhet.). Ask in marriage, pay amorous court to, ask the love of, whence ~ER¹ n.; pursue, seek to win, (fame, fortune, etc.); (abs.) go courting, conduct oneself as ~er; coax, importune, try to persuade, (person usu., to do or to compliance etc.). Hence ~'ingLY² adv. [ME wowen, or OE dwógian, etym. dub.]

woo'but, ou'bit (ōō-), n. = WOOLLY-bear. [ME wolbode (WOOL, perh. + OE budda beetle)]

wood, n. 1. Growing trees occupying considerable tract of ground, forest, (also pl. in same sense, as came upon a clearing in the ~s; cannot see ~ for trees, details impede general view; don't halloo till you are out of the ~, assume too soon that difficulties are over), whence (-)~ED² a. 2. Fibrous substance between pith & bark of tree, whether growing or cut for timber or fuel. 3. The cask or unbottled storage of wine etc. (in, from, the ~). 4. (mus.). (Also ~-wind) the wooden wind-instruments of a band etc. 5. (Bowls) a BOWL² (first sense); (Golf) a wooden club. 6. ~agate, showing grain of ~; ~anemone, the wild flowering ANEMONE; ~bine or -bind, wild honeysuckle; ~block, die usn. of box~ from which ~cuts are taken; ~cock, kinds of game bird related to snipe; ~craft, knowledge of forest conditions esp. as applied in hunting etc.; ~cut, (print, usu. as illustration in book or newspaper, taken from) engraving made on ~; ~cutter, man who cuts ~; ~cuts, ~engraver, maker of ~cuts, kinds of boring insect; ~fibre, fibre got from ~ esp. as material for paper; ~gas, carburetted hydrogen got from ~; ~ ibis, kind of N.Amer. stork; ~land, ~ed country, ~s, (often attrib., as ~land scenery; the ~land choir, birds); ~leopard, kind of moth; ~louse, kinds of small land crustacean & wingless many-legged insect; ~man, forester, ~cutter; ~notes, spontaneous poetry; ~nymph, dryad, kinds of humming-bird & moth; ~opal, silicified ~; ~ paper, made of ~-pulp; ~ pavement, wooden blocks used as paving of road; ~pecker, kinds of bird that cling to tree-stems & tap them to discover insects; ~pie, great spotted ~pecker; ~pigeon, ringdove; ~pulp, fibre reduced to pulp as material for paper; ~ruff, kinds of plant, sweet ~ruff grown esp. for fragrance of leaves when dried or crushed; ~s'man, dweller in or

frequenter of ~s; ~ *sorrel*, kinds of acid-juiced plant; ~ *spirit*, crude methyl alcohol got from ~; ~warbler, kinds of bird; ~wasp, kinds that hang nest in fir tree or burrow in rotten; ~wool, fine pine shavings used as surgical dressing or for packing; ~work, things made of ~, esp. the wooden part of a house etc. Hence ~'LESS a. [OE *wudu*, cf. ON *viðr*, OHG *witu*, also Gael. *fiodh*, W *gwydd*]

wood'chuck, n. Kind of N.-Amer. marmot. [corrupt. of Amer.-Ind. *wejack*]

wood'en, a. Made of wood (~ *head*, whence ~-**headed**² a., ~-**head**²-**ED·NESS** (-*hēd*-) n.; ~ *horse*, by use of which Troy was taken; ~ *spoon*, see NIGHTSHADE). Hence ~**NESS** n. [-Y²]

wood'ly, a. (Of region) abounding in woods, well-wooded; of the nature, consisting, of wood (*the* ~*y parts of a plant*); ~*y stem, tissue*; (rare) found in woods (~*y* NIGHTSHADE). Hence ~**INESS** n. [-Y²]

woof, n. 1. Kind of hair distinguished by fineness & wavy structure & scaly surface, forming fleece of sheep, goat, alpaca, etc., & occurring mixed with ordinary hair in coat of some other animals (*carding or short, combing or long*, ~); less, more, than 4 in. long & prepared by different processes for spinning; *dyed in the* ~, dyed before spinning or weaving, (fig.) thorough-going, out-&-out; *much cry & little* ~, disappointing result, fiasco; *go for* ~ *& come home shorn*, have tables turned on one), whence ~ED²-ld)a. 2. Woollen yarn, worsted, (*spent an hour matching* ~s; *fine dyed* ~ for knitting etc.); woollen garments or cloth (*safest to* ~ *wear* ~). 3. Soft short under-fur or down. 4. Negro's hair, (joc.) any person's hair (*lose one's* ~, sl. show anger). 5. Kinds of ~-like substance (COTTON¹-~; LEAD¹-~; ~ *mineral*, made from molten slag subjected to strong blast & used for packing walls etc.). 6. ~-*ball*, esp. lump of contracted ~ occas. formed in stomach of sheep etc.; ~-*carding, -combing*, processes by which short, long, ~ is prepared for spinning; ~-*dyed*, dyed in the ~, see above; ~-*fat, -oil*, lanolin; ~-*fell*, skin of sheep etc. with fleece still on; ~-*gathering*, absent-minded(ness), inatten-tive (mood); ‖~-*hall*, exchange or market; ~-*pack*, (formerly) 240-lb. bale of ~, also fleecy cloud; ‖~-*sack*, ~-stuffed cushion on which Lord Chancellor sits in House of Lords (*reach etc. the* ~*sack*, become Lord Chancellor; *take seat on the* ~*sack*, open proceedings in House of Lords); ~-*sorters' disease*, an-

thrax; ~-*stapler*, one who grades producer's ~ & sells to manufacturer; ~-*work*, embroidery with Berlin ~s imitating tapestry. [Aryan: OE *wull*, cf. Du. *wol*, G *wolle*; cogn. w. Skr. *ūrṇā*, Gk *lēnos*, L *lāna* & *vellus* fleece]

woollen, a. & n. 1. Made of wool. 2. n. ~ *fabric*, as blanket, flannel, cloth; ~ *draper*, retailer of ~s; hence ~**ETTE**²(2) n. [-EN⁵]

wool'ly, a. & n. 1. Bearing or naturally covered with wool or wool-like hair (*the* ~ *flock*; ~-*bear*, kinds of hairy cater-pillar; *a* ~ *puppy, head*); resembling or suggesting wool (~ *hair, clouds*; ~ *voice, husky*); (Paint.) lacking in definition or luminosity or incisiveness (~ *texture, style*, etc.); (fig., of the mind) confused & hazy; (Bot.) downy, pubescent. 2. n. Woollen garment, esp. sweater. Hence **wool'liness** n. [-Y¹]

Wool'wich (-lij) n. (Used for) Arsenal with magazines for naval & military stores; (formerly used for) the Royal Military Academy, ~, for cadets of Royal Engineers & Artillery; ~ *infant* (name given to a 19th-c. pattern of exceptionally heavy gun). [~ in Kent]

woora'li (-ah-), **woora'ra** a. =CURARE. [Wop.

*Wop¹. See WHOP.

*Wop²,** n. (sl.). Mid- or South-European (esp. Italian) immigrant in U.S. (cf. DAGO, SQUAREHEAD). [?]

word⁴ (werd), n. 1. Any sound or combination of sounds (or its written or printed symbol) recognized as a PART¹ of speech, conveying an idea or alternative ideas, & capable of serving as a member of a sentence (*coin, play upon, torture*, ~s; *is not the* ~ *for it*, not an adequate descrip-tion; *have no* ~s *to express my gratitude etc.; takes* ~s *for things*; ~s *are the wise man's counters & the fool's money*; *in a* ~, briefly, to sum up; *translate or repeat* ~ *for* ~, literally or verbatim). 2. Speech (*honest in* ~ *& deed; bold in* ~ *only; by* ~ *of mouth*, orally). 3. Thing said, saying, remark, conversation, (just cited, etc.; *wild & whirling* ~s, not well weighed; *hard* ~s *break no bones, fine* ~s *butter no parsnips*, ~s *are but wind*, deprecations of talk as compared with action; *so* ~s *or things*, ~s *& deeds*; *have* ~s *with*, quarrel with; *they had* ~s, quarrelled; *have a* ~ *with*, converse briefly with; *so a* ~ *with you as* demand for interview; *suit the action to the* ~, do at once what one has threatened etc.; *on or with the* ~, as soon as something has been said; *a* ~ *& a blow*,

impetuous person's procedure; *proceed from ~s to blows; waste ~s,* talk vainly; *a ~ in, out of, season,* well, ill, timed advice or interference; *have the last ~,* not let opponent in altercation speak last; *the last ~* on a subject, pronouncement including latest views & likely to be definitive; *a truer ~ was never spoken; have a ~ to say,* something worth hearing; *man of few ~s,* taciturn; *hasn't a ~ to throw at a dog,* is unsociably or superciliously taciturn; *say a good ~ for,* commend, defend; *give person one's good ~,* recommend him for post etc.; *eat one's ~s,* retract, apologize under compulsion; *~ of command,* ~ or phrase giving direction esp. to soldiers being drilled; *a ~ to the wise,* transl. of VERBUM SAPIENTI; *God's W~,* the scriptures; *so the W~ of God,* & see below). **4.** News, intelligence, a message, (*send ~ of; send ~; ~ came that* or *of*). **5.** One's promise, assurance, or responsible statement (*give person, give, pledge, pass, one's ~,* make promise or rarely statement; *keep, break, one's ~* or *I give you my ~ for it,* promise it shall be or state that it is so; so ellipt. *my ~ upon my ~,* on my honour, also as excl. at something that shocks; *~ of honour,* promise or statement made upon one's HONOUR; *a man of his ~,* a promise-keeper; *he as good as one's ~,* fulfil or exceed what one has promised; *his ~ is as good as his bond,* may be relied on). **6.** Command, order, password, motto, (*this ~ is law; give the ~ to do* or *for; act promptly at the ~; must give the ~ before you can pass; sharp's the ~,* exhortation to hurry). **7.** *The W~* (of God), Christ as mediator or manifestation of God to man. **8.** *~blind, -deaf,* incapacitated by kinds of brain trouble from attaching meaning to ~s seen or heard; *~book,* vocabulary; *~painter, -painting,* graphic or picturesque writer, writing; *~-perfect,* knowing part, piece, etc., by heart; *~picture,* piece of ~-painting; *~-play,* verbal fencing, also play on ~s, pun, etc.; *~-splitter, -splitting,* (maker of) oversubtle verbal distinctions; *~-square,* set of ~s so chosen that when they are written under each other the letters read downward in columns give same ~s, e.g. *rat, ado, too.* Hence ~LESS a. [cf. Du. *woord,* G *wort;* cogn. w. L VERBUM, Gk *eirō* speak]

word² (wĕrd), v.t. Put into words, phrase, select words to express. Hence ~ING¹ n. [f. prec.]

wor'dĭly (wĕr-), a. Verbose, given to or expressed in many words, diffuse; in, consisting of, words (*~y warfare*). Hence ~ILY² adv., ~IVESS n. [-Y²]

wōre. See WEAR¹,³.

work¹ (wĕrk), n. **1.** Expenditure of energy, striving, application of effort to some purpose, (*set to ~,* begin or make begin operations; *has got to, is at, at last; all ~ & no play; never does a stroke of ~; never liked, will do no, ~;* (Physics) exertion of force in overcoming resistance or producing molecular change (*convert heat into~; unit of ~,* lifting of 1 lb. for 1 ft; *internal ~,* exerted on molecules of a body). **2.** Task (to be) undertaken, materials (to be) used in task, (*the ~ of converting the heathen; have one's ~ cut out for one,* no light task, as much as one can do; *all in the day's ~,* normal; *bring your ~ downstairs,* i.e. sewing-materials, lesson-books, etc.). **3.** Thing done, achievement, thing made, book or piece of literary or musical composition, literary or other product of, specimen of, (Theol., usu. in pl.) meritorious act as opposed to faith or grace, (*mighty ~s,* miracles; *a good day's ~,* much accomplished; *the ~s of God,* nature; *honest work the noblest ~ of God; the ~s of Cicero,* his writings; *a learned, historical, ~,* book; *a ~ of art,* fine picture, building, poem, etc.; *is the ~ of the devil; ~s of mercy,* charitable actions; *~ of covenant ~s,* O.-T. dispensation; *~s of* SUPEREROGATION. **4.** Doings or experiences of specified kind (*sharp, bloody, wild, ~; thirsty, dry, ~; make short ~ of,* quickly accomplish or get rid of or overcome). **5.** Employment, esp. the opportunity of earning money by labour, laborious occupation, (*is out of, is in regular, wants, is looking for, ~; many hands make light ~; do you want the ~* or *the wages?; rich men's luxury makes ~ for the poor*). **6.** (Usu. in pl., & in comb. or with adj.) piece of fortification, structure for defence, (*the ~s are impregnable; advanced, detached, defensive, ~s* or *~; out~s, earth-~s*). **7.** pl. Operations in building etc. (*public ~s,* such operations done by or for the State; ‖ *Ministry of W~s;* CLERK *of the ~s*). **8.** pl. Acting or operative part of machine (usu. of; *the ~s of a watch* etc.; *something must be wrong with the ~s*). **9.** pl. (Often with sing. constr., usu. in comb. with attrib. n.) manufactory (*the owner of an iron, a glass, ~; the ~s will be closed from 1st Oct.*). **10.** (Articles having) ornamentation of kind specified by adj. or by usu. hyphened attrib. n., things or parts made of material or with tools etc. so specified, (*covered with elaborate ~; rustic, embossed, beaten, frosted, etc., ~; wood~, iron~, stone~; fancy, needle, stucco, relief, poker, ~;* (Naut.) UPPER ~s. **11.** *~aday,* fit for or used or seen on ~days, ordinary, practical, (now chiefly in *this ~aday world*); *~bag, -basket, -box,* holding materials & implements for, esp. for sewing; *~day,* day other than Sunday or festival; *~house,* ‖ public institution for reception of paupers in parish or union of parishes; *~man,* operative, man hired to do manual labour, person good, bad, skilled, etc., at

work (an ill ~*man* quarrels with his tools;) ~*ship*, characteristic of a good ~*man*; ~*manship*, person's relative skill in doing task, relative finish or execution seen in manufactured article or ~ of art, ... one's job ~; ~*manship* (we are God's or of God's ~*manship*); ~*-people*, ~*men* or ~*women*; ~*-room*, in which ~ is done; ~*shop*, room or building in which manufacture is carried on; ~*shy*, (adj.) disinclined to work, (n.) lazy wastrel; ~*-table*, with drawers for sewing-materials etc.; ~*-woman*, female operative. Hence ~LESS a. [Aryan: OE *weorc*, cf. Du. & G *werk*, Gk *ergon*]

work², (wörk), v.t. & i. (~*ed*; also *wrought* pr. rawt, arch. exc. as specified below). **1.** Engage or be engaged in bodily or mental work, carry on operations, make efforts, be a craftsman in some material, (*men must* ~; ~ *away* or *on*, continue to ~; ~ *double* TIDES; ~ *to rule*, make efficiency impossible by keeping every rule in & out of season, as substitute for open strike; *is* ~*ing at Greek, history, social reform*; ~*s*, ~*ed* or *wrought*, *in brass, leather, oils, distemper*; *person is hard to* ~ *with*, impracticable; *is* ~*ing for, against, the cause*). **2.** (Of machine, plan, etc.) operate, act, do its appointed work, (of person) put or keep (machine etc.) in operation, keep (person, horse, machine, etc.) going or at work, exact toil from, (*charm, drug, pump, scheme,* ~*s or will not* ~; ~ *ship, typewriter;* ~*s his men etc. too hard, to death*); (of wheel etc.) run, revolve, go through regular motions, (*strop, handle, wheel,* ~*s on a wheel, pivot, axle;* ~ *freely, stiffly, etc.*). **3.** Carry on, manage, control, (~ *mine, scheme;* ~*s the coach from London to Brighton*, has charge of it; *my partner* ~*s the Liverpool district; is* ~*ed by wires, electricity, etc.*). **4.** Have influence or effect, exercise influence on, (often *wrought*; *now let it* ~; *leave it to produce its effect;* ~ *upon person or his mind etc.; all these things have* ~*ed together for good; the appeal wrought powerfully upon him;* ~ *the* ORACLE). **5.** Bring about, effect, accomplish, produce as result, (often *wrought*; ~ *wonders, cures, mischief, a change;* ~ *one's will*, accomplish one's purpose often *upon person or thing; will* ~ *it if I can*, bring it about). **6.** Be in motion, be agitated, cause agitation, ferment lit. & fig., (*face, features,* ~*ed violently; waves* ~ *to & fro; thoughts, conscience,* ~*ing within him; yeast began to* ~; *to be wroth with one we love doth* ~ *like madness in the brain*). **7.** Make way or make (*way within one, into,* etc.), or cause to make way slowly or with difficulty or by shifting motions (usn. with adv. or prep.), gradually become (loose, free, tight, etc.) by motion, (*loose, shirt,* ~ *doom, up; needle* ~*ed out eventually from her arm; ferrule has* ~*ed off, loose;* ~ *your knife through the card, your point in; grub* ~*s its way into or out of; wind has* ~*ed round; ship is* ~*ing eastwards; some influences* ~ *upwards, some downwards, in society; angler* ~*s up stream*). **8.** Knead, hammer, fashion, into shape or desired consistence (~ *dough, clay, etc.; butter should be thoroughly* ~*ed; wrought iron*, forged or rolled, not cast). **9.** Artificially & gradually excite into (~*ed his audience, himself, into enthusiasm, a rage*). **10.** Do, make by, needlework or the like (*reads to them while they* ~; ~ *pattern, initials, etc., on linen etc.; is* ~*ing a shawl*). **11.** Solve (sum) by mathematical processes. **12.** Purchase (one's passage) with labour instead of money, also transf. **13.** ~ *in*, find place for (illustration, subject, etc.), admit of being introduced. **14.** ~ *off*, get rid of, get over, find customers etc. for, (~*s off his bad temper on his servants; has* ~*ed off his debauch;* ~ *off 3000 copies;* ~*s off old jokes on us*). **15.** ~ *out*, find (amount etc.) or solve (sum) by calculation, (of amount etc.) be calculated at (~*s out at £6 10s.*), (of sum) give definite result (*will not* ~ *out*), exhaust with work (*person, mine, etc., is quite* ~*ed out*), accomplish or attain with difficulty (~ *out one's salvation*), provide for or plan all details of (*has* ~*ed out a scheme of invasion*); ~*-out* n. (esp. Boxing, Sports, etc.), a practice or test. **16.** ~ *up*, bring gradually to efficient state, elaborate in description (often *wrought*), advance gradually to (climax), excite (persons, expectations, etc.) by degrees (often *wrought; his wrought-up state*, nervous; *in a highly wrought-up state*, hysterical), mingle (materials) into whole, acquire familiarity with (subject) by study. [OE *wircan, wyrcan,* past *worhte* (prec.)]

work|a|ble (wér-), a. That can be worked, that will work, that is worth working, practicable, feasible. Hence ~ABIL'ITY, ~ableNESS, nn., ~ably² adv. [-ABLE]

work'er (wér-), n. In vbl senses: esp. (also ~ *bee, ant,* etc.) undeveloped female of various social insects. [-ER¹]

work'ing¹ (wér-), n. In vbl senses; also or esp.: way thing works or result of its ~ (*the* ~*s of his face, conscience, fancy*); mine, quarry, etc., or part of it in which work is being or has been done (*was found in a disused* ~); ~*-day*, also hours of the twenty-four devoted to work; ~ *capital, expenses,* (serving as guide for building or construction); ~*-out*, calculation of results, elaboration of details; ~ *party*, (esp.) committee appointed to secure efficiency in an industry etc. or to investigate & report on some question. [-ING¹]

wor'king² (wếr-), a. In vbl senses; esp., engaged in manual labour (~ *man*; *the ~ class*). [-ING²]

world (wếr-), n. **1.** Time or state or scene of existence (*the* or *this ~*; *mortal life*; *the other* or *next ~*; *the ~ to come*, *life after death*; *the lower ~*, *hell*, *Earth*; *Prince of this ~*, *the devil*; *we bring nothing into this ~*, *at birth*; *bring child into the ~*, *beget* or *bear it*; *make the best of both ~s*, *reconcile secular & spiritual interests*; *the end of the ~*, *cessation of all mortal life by destruction of universe or otherwise*: ~ *without end*, *for ever*). **2.** Secular interests & occupations (*the ~*, *the flesh, & the devil*, *kinds of temptation*; *forsake the ~*). **3.** The universe, all creation, everything, (*the creation of the ~*; *the best of all possible ~s*; *in the ~*, *at all, that exists, etc., as who, how, what, in the ~ was it?*, *nothing in the ~*; *for all the ~ like*, *precisely like*; *carry the ~ before one*, *have rapid & complete success*). **4.** Everything that exists outside oneself (*the external ~*, *all phenomena*; *the ~ of dreams*, *things as they seem in dreams*; *would not do it for the*, *to gain the whole*, ~; *she is all the ~ to me*; *would give the ~ to know*). **5.** The earth, heavenly body supposed to resemble it, its countries & their inhabitants, all people, the earth as known or in some respect limited, (*go round the ~*; *to the ~'s end*, *to farthest attainable distance*; *a universe of ~s*; *are there other ~s than ours?*; *federation of the ~*, *combination of all peoples in one State*; *citizen of the ~*, *cosmopolitan*; *all the ~'s a stage*; *make a noise in the ~*, *be widely talked of*; *all the ~ knows*, *it is generally known*; *makes the whole ~ kin*; *the wise old ~*, *general experience & custom*; *politics, movement, tendency, affecting or seen among many peoples*; *the Old W~*, Europe, Asia, & Africa, part known by ancients to exist; *the New W~*, America; *the Roman etc. ~*, *as much of the ~ as concerned Rome etc.*; *the Anglo-Saxon, English-speaking, etc.*, ~). **6.** Human affairs, their course & conditions, active life, (*so wags the ~*; *how goes the ~ with you?*; *know, see, the ~*, *have, acquire, experience*; *man of the ~*, *experienced practical tolerant person*; *begin the ~*, *start one's career*; *all's right with the ~ as it is, as one finds it*, *be adaptable*; *let the ~ slide*, *not try to influence events*, also *disregard convention & public opinion*). **7.** Average or respectable or fashionable society or people or their customs or opinions (*the great ~*, *fashionable society*; *all the ~ & his wife*, *all with pretensions to fashion*; *what will the ~ say?*, *dare we defy opinion?*; *live out of the ~*, *avoid society*). **8.** All that concerns or all who belong to specified department or class, sphere, domain, (*the literary, scientific,

sporting, animal, ancient*, ~; *the ~ of letters, art, sport*). **9.** A vast or infinite number or amount or extent (*a ~ of waters*, *expanse of sea*; *a ~ too wide etc., by far*). **10.** To *the ~* (sl.), utterly (*tired, drunk, etc., to the ~*; *perh. by misapplication of dead to the ~*); ~ *language*, that was or will be or is meant to be universal, also spoken in more than one part of ~; ~*-old*, (usu. by exag.) old as creation; ~*-power*, powerful State whose policy etc. may affect the ~ at large; ~*-weary*, tired of existence; ~*-wide*, spread over the ~, known or found everywhere. [comb.: OE *weoruld* (*wer man*, ELD; lit. sense *age of man*), cf. Du. *wereld*, G *welt*] Teut.

wor'lding (wếr-), n. Worldly person. [-LING¹]

wor'ldly (wếr-), a. Temporal, earthly, (~ *goods, property*); exclusively or preponderantly concerned with or devoted to the affairs of this life, esp. to pursuit of wealth or pleasure (~ *wisdom*, esp. prudence in advancing one's own interests; ~ *people, life, etc.*); ~*-minded*, intent on ~ things, whence ~*-mind'edness* n.; ~*-wise*, having ~ wisdom. Hence **wor'ldliness** (wếr-) n. [-LY¹]

worm¹ (wếrm), n. **1.** Kinds of invertebrate limbless or apparently limbless creeping animal, esp. such as are segmented in rings or are parasitic in the intestines or tissues (also in compd names of larvae, insects, lizards, etc., with some resemblance to ~s, as *silk, glow, slow*, ~; *dog, child, has ~s*, *internal parasites*; *food for ~s*, *of person when dead*; *a ~ will turn*, *the meekest will resist or retaliate if pushed too far*; *the ~ of conscience*, *gnawing pain of remorse*; *so where their ~ dieth not*; *am a ~ today*, *out of sorts & spiritless*, W. ref. to Ps. xxii. 6). **2.** Insignificant or contemptible person. **3.** Spiral part of screw, spiral cartridge-extractor, spiral pipe of still in which vapour is cooled & condensed. **4.** Ligament under dog's tongue. **5.** ~*-cast*, tubular mass of earth voided by earth~; ~*-eaten*, gnawn by ~s, full of ~-holes, (fig.) antiquated; ~*-fishing*, with ~ for bait; ~*-gear*, arrangement of toothed wheel worked by revolving spiral; ~*-hole*, left in wood, fruit, etc., by passage of ~; ~*-holed*, ~eaten (lit.); ~*-seed*, (Levantine plant bearing) seed used to expel intestinal ~s; ~*'s-eye view* (loc.), as seen from below (opp. *bird's-eye view*); ~*-wheel*, wheel of ~-gear. Hence ~*Y²* a., ~*'iNESS* n. [OE *wyrm*, cf. Du. *worm*, G *wurm*; cogn. w. L *vermis*, Gk (*h)romos*]

worm² (wếrm), v.t. & i. **1.** Insinuate oneself into (favour, person's confidence, etc.); convey oneself, progress, make one's way, with crawling motion (~*ed himself* or *his way* or ~*ed through the bushes*). **2.** Draw (secret etc.) by crafty persistence out (of

person). 3. Cut worm of (dog's tongue). 4. Rid (garden-bed etc.) of worms. [f. prec.]

wor'mwood (wer-), n. Kinds of perennial herb with bitter, tonic, & stimulating qualities used in preparation of vermouth & absinth & in medicine; bitter mortification or its cause. [OE *wermod*, cf. OHG *wer(i)muota*, etym. dub., w. assim. to *worm, wood*]

worn. See WEAR¹.

wor'rit (wri-), v.t. & i., & n. =foll.(vulg.).

wo'rrly (wri-), v.t. & i., & n. 1. (Of dogs) bite (rat, sheep, dog) repeatedly, shake or pull about with the teeth (*~y problem etc. out*, assail it again & again till it is solved); *~y the sword* in fencing, try to fluster opponent by small movements in quick succession); tease, harass, importune, be continuously or intermittently troublesome to, allow no rest or peace of mind to (*~y oneself*, take needless trouble; *is much ~ied*, full of uneasiness; *wears a ~ied look*, looks anxious or troubled); give way to anxiety, let the mind dwell on troubles, fret; **I should~y* (colloq.), it doesn't trouble me at all; *~y along*, manage to advance in spite of obstacles; hence ~iMENT n. 2. n. ~yingly² adv. 2. n. Hound's *~ying* of quarry; (usu. in pl.) care(s), thing(s) *~ying* person; cares, *~ied state*, over-anxiety; hence ~LESS a. [OE *wyrgan*, cf. Du. *worgen*, G *weirgen*, strangle]

worse (wês), a. & adv. comp., & n. 1. More BAD or BADLY; (as pred. a.) in or Into less good health (*is ~today*), in or ~), in less good condition or circumstances (*is none the ~ for it*). 2. n. *~ thing(s)* (*there ~ to tell; but ~ followed, remains*); *the ~*, defeat in contest (*have, put to, the ~*), be defeated, defeat, ~ condition (*a change for the ~*). Hence wor'sEN⁶ (wêr-) v.t. &i. [OE *wyrs* acc. *wyrsa* adj., cf. OSax. *wirs, wirsa*, Goth. *wairs, wairsiza*, the last retaining the compar suf. & corresponding to E obs. or vulg. *worser*; perh. cogn. w. G *wirren* twist]

wor'ship (wêr-), n., & v.t. & i. (-pp-). 1. (arch.). Worthiness, merit, recognition given or due to these, honour & respect, (*men of ~*, worthies; *win, have, ~ reach, enjoy, high repute*; ∥ so still in *your, his, W~*, used to or of certain magistrates, or to show respect for person of higher station or ironical pretence of this), whence ~FUL a., ~fully² adv., ~fulNESS n. 2. Reverent homage or service paid to God (*public ~, the hours of ~, forms of ~*, etc., church services; *place of ~*, church); adoration or devotion comparable to this felt or shown towards person or principle (*an object of ~; regarding her with ~ in his eyes; the ~ of rank, wealth, intellect, athletics*). 3. vb. Adore as divine, pay religious homage to; idolize, regard with adoration, (*~s the ground she treads on*);

attend ~ public ~ (*where does he ~?*), whence ~PER¹ n.; be full of adoration. [f. OE *weordhscipe* (WORTH¹, -SHIP)]

worst (wêr-), a. & adv. sup., n. & v.t. 1. Most BAD, BADLY. 2. n. ~ part, feature, state, possible assumption, event, possible issue, or action (*the ~ of the storm is over; the ~ of it is that ~; see him at his ~; when things are at the or their ~; at ~, our lives are safe; get the ~ of it, at the ~, have, put to, the ~, be defeated, defeat; the ~ has happened; be prepared for the ~; if the ~ comes to the ~*, if the ~ happens; *do your, let him etc. do his etc. ~*, expression of defiance). 3. v.t. Get the better of, defeat, outdo, best. [OE *wyrst* adv., *wyrsta* adj. (WORSE, -EST), the vb (recorded from 17th c. only) f. the adj.]

wor'sted (wûos-), n. Woollen yarn (often attrib., as *~ sock*). [*Worstedd* in Norfolk]

wort (wêrt), n. 1. Plant, herb, (rare exc. in comb., as *spleen, stitch, ~*). 2. Infusion of malt before it is fermented into beer. [sense 1 f. OE *wyrt*, G *wurz*; cogn. w. ROOT; sense 2 f. OE *wyrt*, cf. G *wûrze* spice, brewer's ~]

worth¹ (wêrth), pred. a. (governing noun like trans. part.), & n. 1. Of value equivalent to (*is ~ much, little, nothing; about 2/6; is little ~*, poet., *~ little*; BIRD *in the hand is ~ two in bush; what is the house ~?; the rarer it is the more it is ~*). 2. Deserving, worthy of, bringing compensation for, (*~ one's salt*, earning one's keep by good service; *~ doing, hearing, notice, the trouble*, WHILE¹; *an effort, trouble; oneself about*, etc.; *~ it*, colloq.; *~ while; to reign is ~ ambition; game not ~ the* CANDLE; *I give you, you must take, this for what it is ~*; I do not guarantee its truth, wisdom, etc.). 3. Possessed of, having property amounting to, (*is died, ~ a million; spend all he was ~ on it; for all one is ~*, sl., with one's utmost efforts, without reserve). 4. *~while*, that is ~ while (*a ~-while experiment*). 5. n. What a person or thing is ~, value, merit, high merit or excellence, (*of great, little, no, ~; persons of ~; true ~*, often goes unrecognized), whence ~LESS a., ~lessly² adv., ~lessNESS n. 6. Coin's equivalent in commodity (*give me a shilling's, half a crown's, ~ of stamps*; also in comb. as *penny-, two-penny~ or -pennorth, three-hat'porth*, etc.). [OE *weorth* a. & n., cf. Du. *waard* a., G *werth* a. & n.]

∥ **worth²** (wêrth), v.t. 3rd sing. subjunct. (arch.). Befall (only in *woe ~ the day* = cursed be). [f. OE *weordhan* become, cf. G *weorden*]

worthy (wêr'dhi), a. & n. 1. Estimable, having some moral worth, of a fair degree of merit, respectable, (*a ~ man; has lived a ~ life*; often with patronizing effect, cf. HONEST, *as I asked the ~ rustic*

whether); deserving of or deserving of or deserving to be or do (is ~ of or rarely ~ remembering or being remembered; is ~ to be remembered, take the lead; also in comb. as praise~, blame~); correspond-ing to the worth of or of, adequate, ap-propriate, of sufficient worth or merit, (in words ~ of or ~ the occasion; is not ~ of or ~ my sword, steel; has found a ~ adversary, received a ~ reward); hence **wor'thily²** adv., **wor'thiness** n., (wȇr'dhi-). **2.** n. ~ person, person of some distinction in his country, time, etc., (esp. in pl., as the Worthies of Eng-land; an Elizabethan etc. ~). [WORTH¹ n. +-Y²]

wot. See WIT¹.

would. See WILL¹.

would-bē (wŏŏd-), a. & adv. prefixed to n. or adj. expressing a quality aspired to or intended (~ gentleman, facetious). [WILL¹, BE]

wound¹ (wōō-), n., & v.t. **1.** Injury done by cut or stab or blow or tear to animal or vegetable tissues including & usu. going beyond the cutting or piercing or break-ing or tearing of the skin or bark or other integument, (fig.) injury done to person's reputation etc. or pain inflicted on his feelings, (poet.) pangs of love, (receive, inflict, make, heal, a ~; incised, punc-tured, confused, lacerated, ~; open, in-curable, festering, mortal, ~); ~-wort, kinds of plant supposed to have healing properties; hence ~'LESS a. **2.** v.t. Inflict ~ on (often fig., esp. ~ed vanity, feelings; willing to ~, spiteful). [com.-Teut.: OE wund, cf. Du. wond, G wunde; vb (OE wundian) f. n.]

wound². See WIND², ³.

woura'li. See CURARE.

wove(n). See WEAVE.

*****wow,** n. (sl.). (Esp. Theatr.) a sensational success. [?]

wows'er (-z-), n. (Austral.). Puritanical fanatic. [?]

wr-. In all words beginning thus w is silent.

wrack, n. Sea-weed cast up & used for manure etc.; wreckage; = RACK¹. [OE wræc (wrecan WREAK) vengeance, damage, w. senses added f. MDu. wrak WRECK]

wraith, n. Person's double or apparition seen shortly before or after his death. [orig. Sc., etym. dub.]

wrangle (rang'gl), v.i., & n. Brawl, (en-gage in) loud or vulgar or confused argu-ment or altercation or quarrel. [cogn. w. WRING, -LE(3)]

wrang'ler (-ngr-), n. In vbl senses; || also, (Camb. Univ.) person placed in first class of mathematical tripos (senior, junior, 3rd, class being called senior, junior, optime; senior ~, first in first class when it was arranged in order of merit), whence

~SHIP n. [-ER¹; spec. sense f. obs. sense of vb dispute publicly on a thesis]

wrap, v.t. & i. (-pp-), & n. **1.** Enfold, enclose or pack or conceal in folded or soft encircling material, (often up; ~ it in paper, cotton wool; ~ up parcel; mountain, affair, is ~ped in mist, mystery; ~ up his meaning in tortuous sentences, allegory) (p.p. with up) engrossed or included (mother, country's prosperity, is ~ped up in her child, its shipping); ~ up, put on ~s (mind you ~ up well if you go out); arrange or draw (pliant covering) round or about person or thing (~ped her shawl closer about her), whence ~p'ING¹(3) n.; **2.** n. (Usu. in pl.) shawl(s), rug(s), cloak(s), neckerchief(s), etc., as addition to ordi-nary clothes. [etym. dub.; cf. obs. wrap-pen in same sense, & LAP²]

wrapp'age, n. Wrapping(s). [-AGE]

wrapp'er, n. In vbl senses; esp.: (gar-ment resembling) dressing-gown; paper enclosing newspaper or similar packet for posting; detachable paper cover of book, outer tobacco-leaf of superior quality enclosing cigar. [-ER²]

wrapt. = RAPT.

wrasse, n. Kinds of thick-lipped strong-toothed bright-coloured rock-haunting sea-fish. [f. Cornish wrach, wrath, cf. W gwrach]

wrath (rawt-), n. Anger, indignation, (poet., rhet., or joc.: vessels, children, of ~, persons destined to divine chastise-ment; slow to ~, not irascible). Hence ~'FUL a., ~'fully adv. [OE wrǣththu (WROTH)]

wreak, v.t. Avenge (wrong, wronged per-son; arch.); give play or satisfaction to, put in operation, (vengeance, rage, etc., usu. upon enemy etc.; rarely desire etc., as ~ one's thoughts upon expression, find adequate words). [com.-Teut.: OE wre-can avenge, cf. Du. wreken, G rächen; orig. sense drive, cogn. w. WRACK, WRECK, L urgēre URGE, Gk eírgō hem in]

wreath, n. (pl. pr. -dhz). Flowers or leaves strung or woven or wound together into ring for wearing on head or for decorating statue, building, coffin, etc., carved imitation of such ~; similar ring of soft twisted material such as silk; curl of smoke, circular or curved band of cloud, (poet.) circle of dancers or specta-tors. [OE wridha fillet cogn. w. WRITHE]

wreathe (-dh), v.t. & i. Encircle as or with or as with a wreath (face ~d in smiles); form (flowers, silk, etc.) into wreath; wind one's arms etc. or (of snake etc.) itself round person etc.; make (gar-land); (of smoke etc.) move in shape of wreaths. [f. prec. & partly f. WRITHE]

wreck, n., & v.t. & i. **1.** Ruin, destruction, disablement, esp. of ship (save ship, one's

In words beginning with wr-, w is silent.

fortunes, from ~; gale caused many ~s; the ~ of the *Hesperus*, of his life); ship that has suffered ~, greatly damaged or disabled building or person, disorganized remains or sorry remnant of, (shores are strewn with ~s; person, building, is a ~; is but a ~ or the ~ of his former self); goods etc. cast up by the sea (~ *of the sea belongs to the Crown*); ~-master, officer appointed to take charge of goods etc. cast up from ~ed ship. **2.** vb. Cause ~ of (ship, train, hopes, undertaking, person or his fortunes), (p.p.) involved in ship-~ (~ed sailors, goods); || ~ing amendment (Pol.), alteration designed to frustrate the whole purpose of a bill; suffer ~ (rare; *this is the obstacle your hopes will ~ on*). [vb f. n., AF *wrec* f. ON (Norw., Icel., *rek*) f. st. of *wrekan* to drive, see WREAK]

wreck'age, n. Wrecked material, remnants, fragments. [-AGE]

wreck'er, n. In vbl senses: also: man who tries from shore to bring about shipwreck with a view to profiting by wreckage or who steals such wreckage; person employed in recovering wrecked ship or its contents. [-ER¹]

wren¹, n. Kinds of very small cock-tailed short-winged European songbird (often *Jenny W~*). [OE *wrenna*, cf. Icel. *rindill*]

|| Wren², n. Member of the Women's Royal Naval Service. [f. initials]

wrench, n., & v.t. **1.** Violent twist or oblique pull or tearing off, (fig.) pain caused by parting, (*gave a ~ to his ankle, at the door-handle; leaving home was a great ~*). **2.** Implement made to grip & turn nuts, bolts, etc. **3.** v.t. Twist or pull violently round or sideways, injure or pull off or away by twisting, (*~ed the door open, his horse's head round, his ankle, foul's head off, opponent's sword from him*); pervert, wrest, (facts etc.). [n. f. vb, OE *wrencan* twist, practise guile, f. n., OHG *renchan*]

wrest, v.t. & n. **1.** Twist, deflect, distort, pervert, (*~s the law to suit himself; ~ the facts, sense or words of a passage*, etc., force or wrench away from person's grasp (*~ed his sword from him*). **2.** n. Key for tuning harp etc.; ~-block, part of piano holding ~-pins, to which strings are attached. [OE *wræstan*, cf. Icel. *reista*, Da. *vriste*; cogn. w. WRITHE, WREST]

wre'stle, (-sl), v.i. & t., & n. **1.** Grapple with & try to throw adversary esp. in sporting contest under code of rules (*with*, or abs.); have ~ing-match with; contend, grapple, do one's utmost to deal, *with* evil, temptation, duty, task, problem, etc.; *~e with God* or *in prayer*, pray fervently; hence ~ER¹, ~ING¹, nn. (WRES'T-). **2.** n. ~ing-match; hard struggle. [prec., -LE(3)]

wretch, n. Very unfortunate or miserable person; despicable person, person without conscience or shame (often as term of playful abuse). [OE *wrecca* outcast (*wrecan* WREAK)]

wretch'ed, a. Miserable, unhappy, afflicted; inferior, of bad quality or no merit, contemptible, unsatisfactory, causing discontent or discomfort or nuisance, confounded, (*~ weather, health, horse, inn, accommodation, poetry, poet*, etc.); (with nn. of condemnation) great, severe, excessive, (*~ insufficiency, stupidity*, etc.). Hence ~LY² adv., ~NESS n. [prec. +ED¹, cf. WICKED]

wrick, rick, v.t., & n. **1.** Slightly sprain or strain (neck, back, joint). **2.** n. Sprain or strain (*have a ~ in my neck; gave my back a ~*). [cf. Du. *wrikken* stir to & fro (also ME *wricken* obs.)]

wrig'gle, v.i. & t., & n. **1.** (Of worm etc.) move body with short twistings, (of animals or persons) make wormlike motions, (fig.) be slippery, practise evasion; make [one's] way along, through, out, in, etc., by ~ing (often fig., as *~e out of a difficulty*); move oneself, one's body, tail, hand, etc., with ~ing motion; make one's way by ~ing. **2.** n. ~ing movement. [f. LG *wriggeln* frequent. of *wriggen*, whence E dial. *wrig* to twist]

wright (rīt), n. Workman, maker, (now rare exc. in comb. as ship, wheel, play, ~, or with help of context as *the wheel must go to the ~ for repair*). [OE *wryhta*, (*wurk-* var. stem of WORK²)]

wring, v.t. (wrûng), & n. **1.** Squeeze, squeeze & twist, twist forcibly, break by twisting, pervert sense of, torture, (~ person's hand, squeeze it with emotion; ~ one's hands, squeeze them together in sign of great distress; ~ out or ~ clothes, press water from them by twisting; ~ing wet, or colloq. ~ing, so wet as to need ~ing; ~ neck of, kill chicken etc.; has wrung the words from their true meaning; soul was wrung with agony); extract by squeezing, get out by pressure or importunity, extort, (~ water, groan, consent, money, from or out of or out); hence (-)~ER²(2) n. **2.** n. Squeeze (gave my hand, give those clothes, a ~). [OE *wringan*, cf. Du. *wringen*, G *ringen*]

wrin'kle¹ (ring'kl), n., & v.t. & i. **1.** Furrow-like crease or depression or ridge in the skin (esp. of the kind produced by age) or other flexible surface; hence wrink'ly² a. **2.** vb. Produce ~s in (often *up*; *he ~d his forehead; ~d with age*); assume ~s, show ~d appearance. [prob. back form. f. OE *gewrinclod* sinuous, etym. dub.]

wrin'kle² (ring'kl), n. Piece of serviceable information not generally known, tip, dodge, (*is full of ~s; gave me, put me up to, a ~ or two*). [perh. a use of prec.; so with pun in Swift]

wrist, n. Joint connecting hand with forearm; (effect got in fencing, ball-games,

sleight-of-hand, etc., by) working of the hand from the ~ alone (*this wonderful* ~; *that was all* ~); (Mech., also ~*pin*) stud projecting from crank etc. as attachment for connecting-rod; ~*band* (riz'band), band usu. of folded & starched linen forming or concealing end of shirt-sleeve, cuff; ~*drop*, paralysis of forearm muscles from lead-poisoning. [OE. cogn. w. WRITHE; orig. *hand-wrist* = hand-turner; cf. ON *rist* instep, G *rist* instep, wrist]

wrist′let, n. Band or ring worn on wrist to strengthen or guard it or as ornament, bracelet, handcuff, etc. (~ *watch*, attached to~). [-LET]

writ¹, n. *Holy, sacred*, ~, the Bible; form of written command in name of sovereign, State, court, etc., issued to official or other person & directing him to act or abstain from acting in some way (~ of *attachment, habeas corpus, subpoena*, etc.; *serve* ~ *on* one, deliver it to him; ~ *runs* in district etc., is theoretically valid or is actually respected). [OE (*gewrit* a writing (WRITE)]

writ². See foll.

write, v.i. & t. (*wrote*, arch. *writ*; *written*, arch. *writ*). 1. Trace symbols representing word(s) esp. with pen or pencil on paper or parchment, trace (such symbols), trace the symbols that represent or constitute (word, special script, etc.), (fig.) stamp marks indicating (quality or conditions) *on* or *in* or over person's face etc., (~ *well, legibly, disgracefully*, etc.; ~ *in ink, in pencil*; ~ *a good, niggling*, etc., *hand*, produces good etc. writing; *cannot read* ~; *can* ~ *his alphabet, the Greek letters, Greek*; ~ *your letters separate*; ~ one's *name*; *has honestly written in his face*; *a paper written all over, covered with writing*; *a notice is written up on the wall*; *what I have written I have written*, of refusal to correct, see John xix. 22; ~ *thing down*, record or take note of it in writing; ~ *off*, ~ & dispatch letter; ~ *out*, ~ the whole of, ~ in full; ~ *out fair*, make fair copy of; *name is written in book of life*, included in the list of the saved; *written in* or *on water*, unrecorded; *writ large*, aggravated, esp. w. ref. to intended remedy that reproduces former evils in greater degree). 2. Full, draw up or fill in with writing (*has written three sheets*; ~ *cheque, certificate, application*, etc.; ~ *up the books, reports*, etc., make entries bringing them up to date). 3. Compose for written or printed reproduction for publication, put into literary form & set down in writing, be engaged temporarily or permanently in such composition, *compose books* etc. *well* etc., *is writing a book, article, his life, poetry, a novel, report, letter*, etc.; ~ *off*, compose with facility;

~*s cleverly, like an angel*; ~*s a little*, in or for the papers, *for a living*, etc.), 4. ~ & send letter (*to* person or abs., also commerc. or colloq. without *to*; ~*s home once a week*; *have written to him*; *we wrote you last week*; *will* ~ *off*, or ~, *for a fresh supply*). 5. Send or convey (person or *to* person news, *that, how*, etc.) by letter (~ *me all the news, the result, how you got home*; *wrote to his mother that he was bullied*). 6. State in writing of print (*Herodotus* ~*s, it is written, that*). 7. Describe, put down, in writing as (~*s himself esquire*; ~ *me down an ass*). 8. ~ *down*, disparage in writing, (also) reduce nominal value of (stock); ~ *off*, cancel, recognize in writing the non-existence or annulment of, (bad debts, sums absorbed by depreciation, etc.); ~ *out*, refl., exhaust by writing (*has written himself out*, has no ideas etc. left); ~ *up*, praise in writing, also elaborate account of (incident etc.), G *reissen* tear; orig. sense *score, cut*]

writ′er, n. In vbl senses; esp. ‖ (clerk in certain offices, whence ~SHIP n.; author; manual teaching how to write specified language (*French* etc.~); ‖ ~ *to the signet*, abbr. W.S., Scots solicitor; ~*'s cramp* or *palsy*, muscular affection incapacitating for writing. [-ER¹]

writhe (riдh), v.i. & t., & n. 1. Twist or roll oneself about (as) in acute pain, squirm; twist (one's *body* etc.) about; shrink mentally, be stung or bitterly annoyed, (*under, at*, insult etc.: *with shame* etc.). 2. n. Act of writhing. [OE *wriдham*, cf. ON *riдha*, OHG *riдam*]

writ′ing, n. In vbl senses; also: written document; piece of literary work done, book, article, etc., (*the* ~*s of Plato*); *put thing in the* ~, write it down; ~*case*, holding ~*materials*; ~*desk, desk*; ~*ink*, opp. printing-ink; *the* ~ *on the wall*, ominously significant event etc. (see Dan. v); ~*paper*, paper for ~ on esp. cut to size usual for letters; ~*table, ~*-hole or other table kept for ~ at. [-ING¹]

written. See WRITE.

wrong, a. (*more, most*), n., adv. (no comp.), & v.t. 1. Out of order, in(to) bad condition, (*something is* ~ *with him*; *my liver is* or *has gone* or *has got* ~; *what's* ~ *with*—?, colloq., surely no substitute is wanted); contrary to law or morality, wicked, (*knows the right from the* ~; *lying is* ~); other than the right or the more or most desirable (*always does the* ~ *thing*; *took the* ~ *way*; *the* ~ *answer, move*; *in the* ~ *box*, awkwardly placed, in a difficulty, at a disadvantage; *is* ~ *side out*, inside out; *has hold of the* ~ *end of the stick*, has inverted a theory, position, etc.; *on the* ~ *side of* 40 etc., older than; ~ *side of the* BLANKET; ~ *found*, abbr.

In words beginning with *wr*-, w is silent.

v.f, notice to compositor that letter or word is not of right FOUNT²); mistaken, in error, (a ~ opinion, guess, decision, hypothesis; I think you are, can prove you, ~); ~-headed, perverse & obstinate; hence ~-lỹ² adv. 2. n. What is morally & ~; can two ~s make a right?; do ~, notice difference between right & ~; action, (the difference between right & ~; can two ~s make a right?; do ~, ~ sin, offend, transgress, whence ~'doer, ~'doing, n., (-dŏŏ-); king can do no ~, maxim expressing principle of ministerial responsibility in constitutional monarchy); injustice, unjust action or treatment, (do ~ to; suffer ~; has done me a great ~; you do me ~; malign me; complains of her ~s); position of or responsibility for having caused quarrel, made the mistake, been the offender, etc. (you were, they are both, in the ~; put one in the ~, show or make it appear that he was the offender); hence (of actions) ~'FUL a., ~'fully² adv., ~'fulness n. 3. adv. (usu. placed last). Amiss, in wrong direction, with incorrect result, (aim, guess, answer, do sum, sort things, ~; you guessed, led, me ~; go ~, take ~ path, esp. fig. of woman failing in chastity); (colloq.) get in ~ with person, incur his dislike, disfavour. 4. v.t. Treat unjustly, do ~ to, (this deeply~ed wife); mistakenly attribute bad motives etc. to (I assure you you ~ me). [OE wrang n. f. ON (Icel. rangr awry, Da. vrang wrong a.); cogn. w. WRING; the adj. use not in OE]

‖wrŏng'ous, a. (Sc. law). Illegal, unjust. [f. ME wrangeus, cf. RIGHTEOUS]

wrote. See WRITE.

‖wrŏth (rō-, rŏ-), pred. a. (rhet., poet., or joc.). Angry. [OE wrāth (WRITHE) = perverted in temper, cf. Du. wreed cruel, OHG reid twisted]

wrought. See WORK².

wrung. See WRING.

wry, a. (-ier, -iest, or -yer, -yest). Distorted, turned to one side, skew, (~ face, mouth, nose); ~'bill, kind of plover; has a ~ mouth, grimace expressing disgust; ~'mouth, kinds of fish; ~'neck, bird allied to woodpeckers able to turn head over shoulder. Hence ~'NESS n. [f. OE wrigian tend, incline, swerve, cf. WRIGGLE]

wy'andôtte, n. American breed of fowl. [name of Amer.-Ind. tribe]

wych-, wich, wych, pref. in names of trees, as ~-alder, -elm, -hazel, f. OE wice, wic; orig. sense pliant, cogn. w. WEAK.

wye, n. Letter Y; thing so shaped.

Wyke'hamist (-kəm-), a. & n. (Past or present member) of Winchester college. [William of Wykeham, founder, -1st]

‖wynd, n. (Sc.), Alley in Scots town. [perh. var. of WIND³ n.]

wyvern. See WIVERN.

X

X (ĕks), letter (pl. Xs, X's). (As Rom. numeral) 10, as IX 9, XV 15, lx 60, XC 90, MX 1010, DXL 540; (Alg.: x) first unknown quantity (cf. A, Y), (transf., incalculable or mysterious factor or influence (X-RAY¹s).

Xanthipp'ê (zănti-), n. Shrewish wife. [wife of Socrates]

xăn'thi(o)- (z-), comb. forms of Gk xanthos yellow; ~ate, a salt of ~ic acid; ~ēin(e), soluble part of Yellow colouring-matter in flowers; ~ic, yellowish (~ic acid, ethyl-disulpho-carbonic acid with yellow salts; ~ic flowers, typically yellow & never passing into blue but only into red or white, opp. cyanic flowers with blue as typical, & red or white as alternative colours); ~ŏch'rŏï (-k-) n. pl. (Ethnol.), blonds or fair whites (cf. MELANOCHROI); ~omĕl'anous (Ethnol.), with black hair & yellow or brown or olive skin; ~ophyll, yellow colouring-matter occurring with chlorophyll in plants; ~ous (Ethnol.), yellow or Mongoloid.

xĕb'ĕc (z-), n. Small three-masted Mediterranean vessel with some square & some lateen sails. [f. F chebec etym. dub., cf. OSp. xabeque, It. sciabecco, Turk. sumbeki]

xĕnĕlăs'ia (z-), n. (Gk hist.). Spartan system of excluding & expelling aliens. [Gk (-nē-), f. xenos stranger, elaunō drive]

xĕn(o)- (z-), comb. forms of Gk xenos strange(r); ~'ial, of hospitality or relations between host & guest; ~ŏg'amy (Bot.), cross-fertilization; ~'ŏlith (Geol.), stone or rock occurring in a system of rocks to which it does not belong; ~ophŏb'ia, morbid dislike of foreigners, so ~'OPHOBE.

xē'n(on) (z-), n. (chem.). Heavy inert gaseous element. [Gk, neut. of xenos strange]

xēr(o)- (z-), comb. forms of Gk xēros dry; ~ăn'sis [Gk, f. xēreinō dry up], desiccation, drying up; ~in'thenam, kinds of annual with everlasting composite flowers; ~ŏph'ilous (Bot.), adapted to hot & dry climate; ~ŏphthăl'mia, ophthalmia without discharge.

Xi, n. Greek letter (Ξ, ξ) = x. [Gk]

xiph(ĭ-, -o)- (z-), comb. forms of Gk xiphos sword; ~'oid, sword-shaped (~oid appendage, cartilage, or process, or ~oid as n., lower end of sternum); ~istern'um, ~oid appendage.

xŏ'anon (z-), n. (Gk Ant.; pl. -ana), Primitive usu. wooden image of deity supposed to have fallen from heaven. [Gk (xoö scrape)]

X-rays, n. pl. (Now usu. term for) Röntgen RAY's; attrib. in sing., as X-ray examining, X-ray photograph. Hence X-ray, v.t., examine or treat or photograph with ~. [see x]

xȳ'lĕm (z-), n. (bot.). Woody tissue (opp. PHLOEM). [Gk, & as phloem]

xyl(o)- (z-), comb. forms of Gk *xulon* wood: ~*obal samum*, (decoction of) dried twigs of balm-of-Gilead tree; ~*ocarp*, (tree with) hard woody fruit, so ~*ocarp'ous* a.; ~*ograph*, a. (esp. 15th-c.) wood-engraving; also a decorative pattern got by mechanical reproduction of wood-grain, so ~*og'raphy*, ~*og'rapher*, ~*ograph'ic*; ~*onite*, = CELLULOID n.; ~*öph'agous*, (of insects) feeding on wood [-PHAGOUS]; ~*ophone*, musical instrument of wooden bars graduated in length & vibrating when struck.

xys'ter (z-), n. (surg.) Instrument for scraping bones. [f. Gk *xuster* (*xuō* scrape)]

xys'tus (z-), n. (pl. -*tī*). Covered portico used by athletes for exercise in classical antiquity; garden walk or terrace. [L, f. Gk *xustos* orig. = polished (prec.)]

Y

Y (wī), letter, (pl. Ys, Y's). (Alg.: *y*) second unknown quantity (cf. x, B); Y-shaped arrangement of lines, piping, roads, etc., forked clamp or support, (often attrib., as Y-*branch*, -*cartilage*, -*joint*, -*ligament*); Y-*cross*, Y-shaped cross esp. on chasubles suggesting figure of crucified Christ; Y-*gun*, gun with two firing-arms for discharging depth-bombs (usu. mounted aft in destroyers); Y-*level*, surveying-level mounted on Y's; Y-*moth*, kind called also gamma with mark like Y or gamma on wings; Y-*track*, Y of railway-line with two branches running into main track enabling engine to reverse direction by running down one branch into store & returning up the other.

Y-, pref. common in ME & still found in a few arch. forms (*yclad*, YCLEPT, *ycis* surely), repr. OE, Du., & G *ge-* as pref. of p.pp. collective nn., & other wds; the same element is seen under different forms in ALIKE, AMONG, AWARE, EITHER, ENOUGH, HANDIWORK.

-y¹, suf. of abstract nn. & of adjj., repr. original L -*ius* -*ia* -*ium*, added directly to stem as *remedium* remedy, *furia* fury, or to another suf. as in wds in -*orius*, -*arius*; also repr. L -*iā* f. Gk -*iā*. The suf. being unaccented in L, -i- was in normal F absorbed into the accented syllable, as in *gloire, péremptoire, victoire, précaire*, or disappeared, as in *remède*; but learned formations also occur in -*ie* & are common in mod. F, as in *furie, centurie*; & L or mod. L wds, whether thr. F or not, have the corresponding -*y*, as *victory, glory, remedy, primary, peremptory*; but many adjj. add a new suf. as -OUS, -AL, (*meritorious, monitorial*).

-y², suf. forming adjj. f. nn., repr. OE -*ig*; used freely as a living suf., w. senses *full of, composed of, having the character of*, as *bony, thorny, milky, slangy*; also appended with sense of -ISH(²) to adj. of colour when it is to be used as comb. form (*whity-brown, pinky-white*, etc.); also forming adjj. chiefly poet. f. other adjj. without change of sense (*paly, steepy, lanky, stilly*). Mute -e is dropped before -y (*icy, stony*); a single final consonant of monosyllables, if preceded by a single vowel, is doubled (*knobby, finny*, but *beery, downy*); in wds of more than one syl. treatment varies, as *scoundrelly, fidgety*; in *clayey, skyey*, -e- is inserted to divide the *ys*. In *tardy* -y is of different origin.

-y³, suf. w. dim. sense added to monosyllabic personal names (*Johnny, Jenny, Annie*) or animal names (*piggy, doggie*) or other nouns (*lassie, cooky*) & occas. forming nn. f. monosyl. adjj. (*darky* nigger, *fatty*), with implication of affection or familiarity; the -y form occas. supplants the parent n. in ordinary use (*baby*); for -*y*, after Sc. -*ie* is common; for treatment of final consonants & mute -e see prec.; a modern development is the colloq. substitution of -y for final syllable of the first syllable of polysyllabic nn. & adjj. (*hanky, mighty, comfy*, for handkerchief, nightdress, comfortable).

-y⁴, suf. in nn. repr. F p.p. termm. -*é* -*ée*, & ult. L -*ātus*, -*āta*, -*ātum*, cf. -ADE(1, 3), -ADO. So *deputy* (F *député*, = -*atus*), *army* (F *armée*, = -*āta*), *assembly* (OF *assemblé*, = -*āto*), *delivery* (AF *delivrée*, = -*āto*), *ditty* (OF *dité* f. L *dictātum*), *treaty* (F *traité* f. L *tractātum*); other wds are formed by anal., as *expiry, entreaty*.

yacht (yŏt), n., & v.i. 1. Light sailing-vessel kept, & usu. specially built & rigged, for racing; vessel propelled by sails, steam, electricity, or motive power other than oars, & used for private pleasure excursions, cruising, travel, etc.; ~*club*, esp. for ~-racing; ~*s'man*, person who ~s. 2. v.i. Race or cruise in ~; hence ~ING¹ (yŏt-) n. [f. Du. *jacht*, *jagt*, cf. *jagen* to hunt; named f. its speed]

||**yăf'fle, yăff'il**, n. The green woodpecker. [imit. of laughing cry]

yăg'er (-gẽr), n. Member of certain German military corps esp. of riflemen. [f. G *jäger* orig. = hunter (*jagen* hunt)]

yah, int. of derision.

yahoo' (-a-h-), n. Brute in human shape (*Gulliver's Travels*): coarse person or bestial passions & habits. [made by Swift]

Yahveh (-vä) n., **Yah'vist** n., **Yahvis'tic** a., = JEHOVAH, JEHOVIST(IC).

yăk, n. Long-haired humped grunting wild or domesticated ox of Tibet; ~*lace*, heavy kind made from ~'s hair. [f. Tibetan *gyak*]

Yāle lŏck, n. Cylinder lock for doors etc. invented by L. Yale. [P]

yăm, n. (Edible tuber of) kinds of tropical climbing plant. [f. Port. *inhame*, etym. dub.]

Ya′ma (yah-), n. Hindu god of departed spirits & judge of the dead. [Skr.]

ya′men, -mun, (yah-), n. Chinese mandarin's official residence (the *Tsung ti ~*, Chinese Foreign Office). [Chin. *ya gen-eral's marquee, mun gate*]

yank¹, v.t. & i., & n. (colloq.). 1. Pull (lever etc., or abs.) with a jerk. 2. n. Sudden hard pull. [?]

Yănk², n. (colloq.). Yankee. [abbr.]

Yănk′ee (-ki), n. Inhabitant of New England ; Federal soldier or inhabitant of northern States in American civil war; Inhabitant of U.S., American ; (attrib.) of or as of the ~s (~ *notions*, American appliances etc.); ~ *Doodle*, American tune & song regarded as a national air; ~ *-fied*, of acquired ~ character [-FY]. Hence ~DOM, ~ISM (2, 4), nn. [prob. f. Du. *Janke* dim. of *Jan* John used derisively; or perh. orig. pl.f. *Yengees* Indian corrupt. of *English*]

yăp, v.i. (-pp-), & n. 1. Bark shrilly or fussily ; (colloq.) chatter, talk idly. 2. n. Shrill or fussy bark. [imit.]

yăp′ŏck, n. S.-American water-opossum, with webbed hind feet. [f. *Oyapok*, S.-Amer. river]

yăpp, n. Kind of book-binding with limp leather cover projecting considerably. [inventor's name]

yăr′ough (-ru), n. Whist or bridge hand with no card above a 9. [f. an Earl of Y~ who betted against its occurrence]

yard¹, n. 1. The unit of long measure, = 3 ft. 36 in., or 1|1760 mile (abbr. *yd.*; 100 ~s, esp. flat-race distance; *square*, *cubic*, ~); ~-length of material (5 ~s, a ~ of cloth). 2. Cylindrical spar tapering to each end slung horizontally (square ~) or slantwise (*lateen ~*) across mast to support sail (*lower, topsail, top-gallant, royal*, ~, according to sail supported; *man the* ~s, place men, stand, along ~s as form of salute). 3. (arch.). Penis. 4. ~-*arm*, either end of sail-~; ~*-measure*, rod, tape, etc., a ~ long & usu. divided into feet, inches, & quarters or fifths; ~*-stick*, *-wand*, rigid ~-measure; ~*-stick*, (fig.) standard of comparison. [OE *gerd* stick, cf. Du. *garde*, G *gerte*, L *hasta* spear]

yard², n., & v.t. 1. Piece of enclosed ground, especially one surrounded by or attached to building(s) or used for some manufacturing or other purpose often specified by combination with another word (CHURCH¹, COURT¹, DOCK¹, FARM¹, KALE, RICK¹, TIMBER, ~, VINEYARD; *brick-~*, where bricks are made; *railway-~*, space near station where rolling-stock is kept, trains made up, etc.; *stock-~*, where cattle are penned; *tan-~*, tanning-ground); || the Y~, SCOTLAND YARD. 2. v.t. Put (cattle) into stock-~, so ~AGE(4) n. [doublet of

GARDEN ; OE *geard*, cf. Du. *gaard*, G *garten*, L *hortus*, Gk *khortos*]

yärn, n., & v.i. 1. Any spun thread esp. of kinds prepared for weaving, knitting, or rope-making (~*beam* or *roll*, on which warp-threads are wound for weaving). 2. (colloq.). Story, traveller's tale, anecdote, rambling discourse, (*spin a ~*, ~, tell ~s). 3. v.i. (colloq.). Tell ~s. [OE *gearn*, cf. Du. *garen*, G *garn*; cogn. w. Gk *khordē* cord]

yă′rrow (-ō), n. Common perennial herb with pungent smell & astringent taste, milfoil. [OE *gæaruwe*, cf. Du. *geru-* G *garbe*, men in public. [Arab.]

yăsh′mak, n. Veil worn by Moslem women in public. [Arab.]

yăt′aghan (-găn), n. Mohammedan sword without guard or cross-piece. [Turk.]

yaw, v.i., & n. (naut., aeron.). 1. (Of ship or aircraft) fail to hold straight course, fall off, go unsteadily. 2. n. Deviation of ship etc. from course. [cf. ON *jaga* swing] || **yawl¹**, v.i., & n. (rare). Howl, yell. [ME *goulen*, imit.]

yawl², n. Kinds of small boat, esp. ship's jolly-boat with four or six oars; two-masted fore-&-aft sailing-boat with mizen-mast stepped abaft the rudder post; kind of fishing-boat. [f. Du. *jol*, cf. Da. *jolle*; *jolly-boat* is perh. of same orig.]

yawn, v.i. & t., & n. 1. (Of chasm etc.) gape, be wide open, (*a ~ing gulf, rent*, etc.; *hell ~s for him*), (of person or animal) open the mouth wide as effect of drowsiness, boredom, etc.; utter or say with a ~ (~*ed goodnight*; '*What is the use?*' *he ~ed*). 2. n. Act of ~ing. Hence ~′ing**ly** adv. [OE *geonian, gīnian*, cf. ON *gīna*,

yaws (-z), n. pl. Framboesia. [?]

ȳclept′, a. (arch., joc.). Called (*so-&-so*). [Aryan: OE *gē*, *ge*, cf. Du. *jū*, G *ihr*, Goth. *jus*, Gk *humeis*, Skr. *yūyūm*]

ye (yē or yī acc. to emphasis), 2nd pers. pron. pl. (cf. THOU, YOU) now only poet., arch., religious, or joc. or colloq. & almost exclusively (after confusion in 15th–18th cc.) as subjective case (*blessed are ye when men shall hate you; ye zephyrs! joc.; go it, ye cripples!, joc. encouragement; also written or spoken for you in some familiar phr., as *How d'ye do?, What d'ye think?, Thank ye, I tell ye*).

yea (yā), particle & n. (arch.; pl. ~s). Yes (*let your communication be ~, ~ nay, may, yes & no without oaths; ~s & nays, arch., ayes & noes, affirmative & negative votes; ~ & moreover*); indeed, nay, (*ready, ~ eager*). [OE *gēa*, cf. Du. & G *ja*]

yean, v.t. & i. (arch.). Bring forth lamb or kid. [perh.—Y—+ OE *ēanian*, perh. cogn. w. EWE]

yean′ling, n. Young lamb or kid. [-LING¹]

year, n. 1. Time occupied by the earth in one revolution round the sun (also

astronomical, equinoctial, natural, solar, tropical, ~; 365d. 5h. 48′ 46″ in length) or (astral or sidereal ~, longer by 20′ 23″) by the sun in recovering its previous apparent relation to the fixed stars or (Platonic or Great or Perfect ~, estimated by ancient astronomers at about 26000 ~s) by the celestial bodies in recovering their relative positions at the Creation. 2. Period of days (esp. common ~ of 365 or leap ~ or bissextile ~ of 366 reckoned from 1st Jan.) used by community for dating or other purposes commencing on a certain day & corresponding more or less exactly in length to the astronomical ~ (also legal, civil, calendar, ~; lunar ~, of 12 lunar months; LUNI-SOLAR ~; NEW¹, OLD, ~; Gregorian, Julian, ~, as fixed by GREGORIAN, JULIAN, calendars; SABBATICAL ~; ~ of GRACE, of our LORD; in the ~ 1950; in the ~ 1, lit., & = very long ago; from ~ to ~, by ~, as ~s go by, each ~; ~ in ~ out, right through the ~, continuously). 3. Period of the same length as a civil ~ commencing at any day (Christian, Church, ecclesiastical ~, round of sacred seasons reckoned from & to Advent; the fiscal ~, reckoned from 1st April for taxing purposes; the school ~; ~'s school terms usu. reckoned from beginning of autumn term; a ~ & a day, period specified in some legal matters; was away for two ~s; it is ~s since we met). 4. pl. Age, time of life, (young for his ~s, bearing age lightly; in ~s, old). 4. ~-book, annual publication bringing information on some subject up to date; ~-long, lasting a ~. [OE gē(a)r, cf. Du. jaar, G jahr, ON ár; cogn. w. Gk hōros, hōra, season]

year'ling, n. & a. 1. Animal more than one & less than two years old; (Racing) colt a year old dating from 1st Jan. of year of foaling. 2. adj. A year old, having existed or been so-&-so for a year, (~ heifer, bride). [-LING¹]

yearn (yĕrn), v.i. & (impers., arch.) t. Be filled with longing or compassion or tenderness (for or after rest, home, affection, etc.; to do; towards or to person etc.); whence ~'ING¹ n., ~'ING² a., ~'ing¹y² adv.; ∥it~s me, arch., I~ or am troubled. [OE giernan, cf. ON girna, G begehren, desire; cogn. w. Du. gist, G gist, G gischt; hortāri exhort]

yeast, n. Yellowish frothy viscous substance consisting of fungous cells developed by germination in contact with saccharine liquids & producing alcoholic fermentation, used in brewing beer, making wine, distilling spirit, & raising bread etc.; ~-powder, substitute for ~ used in bread-making. [OE gist, cf. Du. gist, G gischt; cogn. w. Gk zeō boil]

yeast ! ŷ, a. Frothy like yeast (~y waves etc.); in a ferment, working like yeast, (a ~y conscience, turmoil, imaginings); wordy, superficial, (a ~y fellow; ~y talk, professions). Hence ~INESS n. [-Y²]

*yĕġg, n. (sl.) (Also ~'man) travelling burglar or safe-breaker. [?]

yelk, See YOLK.

yĕll, v.i. & v.t. & n. (Make, utter with) shrill cry of pain or anger or fright, high-pitched shout, or uncontrollable burst of laughter (~ed with pain, fury, delight, laughter; ~ out an oath, orders; ~ed curses, my name, a refusal, defiance; with ~s of horror etc.); (U.S. Univ.) organized cry used by students e.g. in encouraging their representatives in athletic contests. [OE gellan, cf. Du. gillen, G gellen]

yĕll'ow (-ō), a. (~er, ~est) & n. & v.t. & i. 1. Of the colour between green & orange in the spectrum, coloured like buttercup or primrose or lemon or sulphur or gold, (with many names of plants, animals, etc., as ~ rattle, wagtail, ochre, jaundice; often also in comb. with parts of body etc., as ~-bill, -head, -legs, -root, -rump, -seed, -shanks, -tail, -throat, -top, -wood, forming animal & plant names; ∥~ boy, obs. sl., gold coin; ~ cartilage, elastic kind forming artery-walls etc.; ~ fever, or Jack, tropical fever with jaundice & black vomit; ~ jacket, state garment in China for royal persons & subjects selected for high honour; the SERE & ~ leaf; ~ men, races, etc., Chinese, Japanese, Mongols, etc.; ~ metal, brass of 60 parts copper & 40 parts zinc; the ~ peril, the danger that the ~ races may overwhelm the white or overrun the world; the ~ press, sensational newspapers esp. of chauvinistic tendencies, orig. of U.S. newspapers urging war with Spain 1898; ~ spot, point of acutist vision in retina). 2. (fig.). (Of looks, mood, feelings, etc.) jealous, envious, suspicious; (colloq.) cowardly. 3. ∥~-back, cheap novel in ~ paper boards common in mid-19th c., also French novel in ~ paper cover; ~-gum, infants' black jaundice; ~-hammer, bunting with ~ head & neck & breast [hammer prob. not a corruption, but of separate orig.]; hence ~ISH²(2) (-ĭsh), ~Y²(-ŏi), aa., ~NESS (-ōn-) n. 4. n. ~ colour; kinds of ~ pigment; (colloq.) cowardice; kinds of moth & butterfly; the ~s, jaundice, (arch.) jealousy, *a peach-disease. 4. vb. Turn ~ (paper ~ed with age; the ~ing leaves). [OE geolu, cf. Du. geel, G gelb, L helvus; cogn. w. GALL¹]

yĕlp, v.i., & n. (Utter) cry (as) of dog in pain or in eager anticipation. [OE gilpan boast, cf. LG galpen croak]

yĕn, n. (pl. yen). Japanese monetary unit. [Jap., f. Chin. yüan round, dollar]

yeo'man (yō-), n. (pl. -men). 1. (hist.). Person qualified by possessing free land of 40/- annual value to serve on juries;

vote for knight of shire, etc. **2.** ‖ Small landowner, farmer, person of middle class engaged in agriculture; ‖ member of the yeomanry force. **3.** (naut.). ‖ ~ *of signals*, || ~ *of the guard*, petty officer concerned with visual signalling: *petty officer perform-ing clerical duties on board ship.* **4.** ~('s) *service*, help in need; ~ *of the guard*, BEEFeater. Hence ~LY¹ a. [ME *yeman*, prob. = YOUNG+MAN]

yeo(manry (yō-), n. Yeomen; ‖ volunteer cavalry force raised from farmers etc. [-RY]

-yer, suf. seen in *lawyer, sawyer, bowyer,* arising f. the use in ME of the suf. *-ien* in place of *-en* in causal vbs & vbs formed on nn. Thus OE *tacu* n. *tace* gave *tacian* vb & in ME *tacien*, whence *tacier* n. as var. of *tacer. Lawyer, sawyer, bowyer,* are formed on this anal. direct f. the nn. *law* etc.

yer cum. See MUDAR. [Tamil]

yes, particle equivalent to affirmative sen-tence, & n. (pl. ~es). **1.** The answer to your question is affirmative, it is as you say or as I have said, your request or command will be complied with, the statement made or course intended is correct or satisfactory. (~ *&*, ~ *or*, forms for substituting stronger phr., as *I could endure, ~, & enjoy it; he would beat me, ~, or you either*; ~?, indeed?, is that so?); (in answer to summons or address) I am here, I hear or am attending to you. (~?, what more have you to say?). **2.** n. The word or answer ~, consent; *con-fine yourself to ~ & no or ~es & noes!*); weakly acquiescent person. [OE *ġēse, gese*, prob. = *ġēa* ȝea+*si* 3 s. pres. subj. of *bēon* BE]

yes'ter- in comb. (1) in ~**day** n. & adv. (on) the day before today (*he arrived ~day; is but of ~day*, of recent origin; *the day before ~day*, n. & adv.; often attrib. as ~*day morning*); (2) chiefly poet. with sense of ~*day*, in compds serving as nn. & adv. for which ordinary usage prefers ~*day* — or *last* —; so ~*morn(ing)* (usu. ~*day morning*), ~*eve*, ~*even(ing)*, (Sc.) ~*yestreen²* (usu. ~*day evening*),~*night* (usu. *last night*); (3) poet. w. sense *last past* in ~*year* n. & adv. (usu. *last year*). [OE *geostra* usu. in *geostran dæg* yesterday, cf. Du. *gisteren*, G *gestern*; cogn. w. L *hesternus*, Gk *khthes*, Skr. *hyás*; for -ter see -THER]

yet, adv. & conj. **1.** As late as now or then, still, (continuance to this or to that time, (*there is ~ time; is he ~ alive?; there is life in the old dog ~; much ~ remains to be done; there is one ~ missing; his hands were ~ red with blood; his ~ unfinished task; I seem to see him ~; while it was ~ morning*). **2.** (With neg. context) so soon as now or then, by this or by that time, (*it is not so far, in the immediate future,* time ~; *is he dead ~?; they have not ~ heard; I have never ~ lied; the largest ~ found; haven't you learnt ~ that fire burns?; these things are not ~; it will not happen just ~; these things are not ~*). **3.** Again, in addition, (~ *once more* or ~ *once; another & ~ another; ~ again; more & ~ more*); (with *nor*) either (*won't listen to me nor ~ to her*). **4.** Before the matter is done with, before all is over, in the time that still remains, (*he will win, I will be even with you, ~*). **5.** (With compar.) even (*a ~ more difficult, easier, task*). **6.** Neverthe-less, and in spite of that, but for all that, (*though they curse, ~ bless thou; &, having nothing, ~ hath all; it is strange, & ~ it is true; strange & ~ true; the logic seems sound, but ~ it does not convince me*). **7.** As ~, up to now or then (esp. w. suggestion that the statement would not be true of later time; *it has worked well as ~; a conscience as ~ clear*). **8.** conj. But at the same time, & ~, (~ *what is the use of it all?; faint ~ pursuing; a rough ~ ready helper*). [OE *ġiet*, cf. OFris. *ieta*]

yew, n. (Wood of) kinds of slow-growing dark-leaved evergreen tree (also ~-*tree*) often planted in graveyards & used for-merly for making bows & still in cabinet-making. [OE *ĕw*, cf. *ĕ ĕow*]

Yg(g)'drasil (ig-), n. (Scand. myth.). Tree whose roots & branches bind together heaven & earth & hell. [ON *yg(g)drasill* perh. f. *Yggr* name of Odin+*drasill* horse]

Yidd'ish, a. & n. (In) a form of old Ger-man (with words borrowed from many modern languages) spoken by Jews in or from Slavonic countries. [f. G *jüdisch* Jewish]

yield, v.t. & i., & n. **1.** Produce or give or bring as fruit or result (*earth ~s her increase; land ~s good crops; investment ~s 5%; tax ~s a handsome revenue, little; sin ~s bitter fruit*); (abs., of land etc., repay cultivation etc. *well, poorly*, etc. **2.** Give up, deliver over, surrender (trans.), resign (trans.), comply with demand for, concede, (~ *fortress* etc.; ~ *oneself prisoner; ~ possession, one's pride of place; ~ precedence to; ~ the palm, be surpassed; ~ submission, consent, submit, consent; ~ up the ghost, die; ~ the point, concede it in argument*); surrender (intr.), make submission to, give consent or change one's course in deference to, comply with demand (whence ~'ING² a., ~ing-ly² adv.), be inferior or confess inferiority to, (*town ~ed without awaiting assault; ~ to superior force, persuasion; courage never to submit or ~; I ~ to none in appreciation of his merits*). **3.** n. Amount ~ed or produced, output, return. [OE *gĕldan* pay, cf. Du. *gelden*, G *gelten* be worth]

-yl, suf. (chem.) used to form wds denot-ing a RADICAL. [f. Gk *hulē* material, sub-stance]

yl'ang-yl'ang (ēlă, -ēlă), n. Malayan tree from the flowers of which a perfume is distilled: the perfume itself. [Tagalog *álang-ílang*]

yōd'el, v.t. & i. (-ll-), & n. **1.** Sing (t. & i.), make melodious inarticulate sounds, with frequent changes between falsetto & normal voice in the manner of Swiss & Tyrolese mountaineers. **2.** n. ~ling cry, match of ~ling. [f. G dial. *jodeln*]

yōg'a, n. Hindu system of philosophic meditation & asceticism designed to effect the reunion of the devotee's soul with the universal spirit. [Hind. f. Skr. =union]

yogh (yōχ), n. The middle-English letter ʒ used for certain values of g & y. [prob. f. ME ʒoc yoke, as beginning with the sound]

yōg'i (-gē), n. Devotee of yoga. Hence **yōg'ism(3)** (-g-) n. [Hind. (YOGA)]

yō'heave-hō', yoho', intt. used by sailors in heaving together.

yoicks int. & n. **yoick** v.i. & t. Foxhunter's halloo; (vb) cry yoicks, urge (hounds) on etc. with it. [?]

yōke, n... & v.t. & i. **1.** Wooden cross-piece fastened over necks of two oxen etc. & attached to the plough or waggon that they are to (help to) draw; (Rom. Hist.) uplifted ~ or arch of three spears symbolizing it under which defeated enemy was made to march (*send, pass intr., under the ~*); (fig.) sway or dominion or servitude (*submitted to his ~; the heavy ~ of opinion; had never endured the ~*); (fig.) bond of union esp. the marriage tie. **2.** Pair of oxen etc. (|| ~ *of land*, arch., as much as one ~ of oxen can plough in a day). **3.** Piece of timber shaped to fit person's shoulders & support pail etc. at each end. **4.** Separately made shoulder-piece of shirt or coat or blouse, or waist-piece of skirt, from which the rest is suspended. **5.** Cross-bar on which bell swings; cross-bar of rudder to whose ends ropes are fastened; coupling-piece of two pipes discharging into one; kinds of coupling or controlling piece in machinery. **6.** ~*bone*, cheek-bone connecting bones of head & face; ~*'fellow*, ~*mate*, partner in marriage, work, etc.; ~*lines*, ~*ropes*, with which rudder~ is worked. **7.** vb. Put ~ upon; couple or unite (esp. pair) in marriage or otherwise, link (one to another); (intr.) match or work together (*together, with*, or abs.; *do not ~ well*). [Aryan; OE *geoc*, Du. *juk*, G *joch*, L *jugum* (cf. *jungere* join), Gk *zugon*, Skr. *yugá-m*]

yōk'el, n. Rustic, country bumpkin. [f. 19th c., etym. dub.]

yōlk (yōk), (now rare) **yēlk**, n. Yellow part of egg; sebaceous secretion from skin of sheep, wool-oil; ~*bag, -sac*, membrane enclosing ~ of egg. Hence (-)~ED² (yōkt), ~Y² (yō'ki), aa. [OE *geolca* (YELLOW)]

|| **yŏn**, a., adv., & pron. **1.** Yonder (a. & adv.: arch. or poet. or provincial). **2.** pron. (arch. etc.). Yonder person or thing. [OE *geon*, cf. G *jener*, ON *enn*]

yŏn'der, a. & adv. (Situated) over there, in the direction towards which I am looking or pointing, within or conceived as within view but distant. [ME (prec., -THER)]

yōre, n. Old times (now only in *of ~*, formerly, in or of old days). [OE *geāra* long ago, etym. dub.]

York', n. ~ & ~ *Lancaster*, rival royal houses & parties in the Wars of the Roses (~*&-Lancaster rose*, parti-coloured kind; *House of ~*, kings Edw. IV-Rich. III; ~*stone*, kind used in building.

yōrk², v.t. Bowl with yorker. [back form.]

York'er, n. Ball so bowled as to pitch immediately in front of batsman's block (also *tice*). [prob. f. *York*, as introduced in Yorkshire. -ER¹]

York'ist, a. & n. (Adherent) of family descended from Edmund Duke of York son of Edward III, or of the White-rose party fighting for it in Wars of the Roses. [-ISP]

York'shire (-er), n. County (~ *flannel, undyed*; ~ *grit*, stone used in polishing marble; ~ *pudding*, batter baked under & eaten with meat esp. beef; ~ *stone*, kind used in building; ~ *terrier*, small shaggy toy kind).

you (ū or yŏŏ *acc. to emphasis*), 2nd pers. pron. sing. (w. pl. vb) & pl. (arch. etc. subj. pl. YE; arch. etc. sing. THOU, *thee*; possess. YOUR, YOURS). **1.** The person(s) or thing(s) addressed (~ *are mad, an angel, all fools; who sent ~ ?*; *I choose ~ three*; *the rest of ~ can stay here*; *& I or me*; *~'re another*, vulg., retort to one who calls names; occas. expressed w. imperat., as *don't ~ go away, begin ~* or *~ begin*; as voc. w. n. in apposition = exclamatory statement, as ~ *fool!*, ~ *darling!*, occas. w. ~ appended also, as ~ *idiot ~!*; as voc. calling attention, as ~ *there, what is your name?*). **2.** (arch.). Yourself (*get ~ gone, begone*; ~ *should find ~ a wife; sit ~ down*). **3.** (In general statements) one, any one, all concerned, every one, a person, (~ *never can tell; what are ~ to do with a child like this?; it is bad at first, but ~ soon get used to it; there's a shot for ~ '*). [OE *ēow* acc. & dat. of YE, supplanting ye f. more frequent use of obj. case, & *thou & thee* (cf. similar substitutes in F, G, It.) as more courteous form]

young (yŭ-), a. (~*er*, ~*est*, pr. -ngg-), & n. (only in collect. sing.). **1.** Not far advanced in life or growth or development, of recent birth or origin or formation, not yet old, still vigorous, immature, youthful, inexperienced, (a ~ *child, man, animal, plant, nation, institution; a ~ family*, of ~ children; *a ~ person*, ser-

vants' phr. for unknown ~ woman of lower classes; *the ~ person*, those whose innocence must be shielded from the indecent (from it & literature; ~ *people*, esp. the marriageable; *my etc.* ~ *man or woman*, sweetheart; *the night, year, century, ~ is yet* ~, still near its beginning; OLD *head on ~ shoulders*; ~ *& OLD*; *you ~ rascal etc.*, usu. in playful address to child; *a ~ man in a hurry*, esp. ardent reformer; ~ *for his YEARS*; *men are now* (at fifty) *an old man but a ~ convert*; ~ BLOOD¹; ~ *er son*, esp. member of noble family poor owing to primogeniture; ~ *things*, often indulgently etc. of persons; *is ~ in crime*, unpractised; ~ *Jones*, esp. Jones the son; ~ *'un*, youngster, often as *ambition*, etc., felt in or characteristic of youth; *the ~er* before or after name of person to be distinguished from another, as *the ~er Pitt, Tenters the ~er*; so *the* PRETENDER; ~ *England, Ireland, Italy*, etc., especially as names of political parties claiming to speak for the rising generation; I ~ *Turks*, esp. the party that in 1908 forced the Sultan to restore the constitution; ~*ers oceas.* as n. pl. opp. *elders, as is kind to his ~ers*). 2. n. Offspring esp. of animals before or soon after birth (*with ~*, pregnant; *cares for deserts, its* ~). [Aryan: OE *geong*, Du. *jong*, G *jung*. W *ieuanc*, L *iuvenis*, Skr *yúvan-*]

you'nker (yŭ-), n. Child, esp. active or lively boy. [-STER]

you'nker (yŭ-), n. Youngster (arch. or colloq.): = JUNKER. [f. MDu. *jonckher*]

you'nster (yŭ-), n.
(*gone young, hëre lord*)]

your (ûr, yŏŏr, yer, *acc. to emphasis*), attrib. a. Of, belonging to, spoken of by, done to or by, you (~ *danger, hat, expectations; so this is ~ immaculate saint!; ~ dismissal of him, by him; ~ father & mine; ~ & my father, fathers*; cf. foll.) (colloq. & chiefly arch., now usu. w. depreciatory implication) much talked of, well known, familiar, (*no one so fallible as ~ expert in handwriting; ~ facetious bore is the worst of all*). [OE *ēower* genit. pl. of YE]

yours (ûrz, yŏŏrz), pron. & pred. a. 1. The one(s) belonging to or of you (*my father & ~; & my father, erron. for your &; my father is not ~; I like ~ better; ~ is the only way; am no child of ~; you & ~, you & your family, property, etc.; ~ is to hand, your letter has come; so ~ of the 11th etc.*). 2. adj. Belonging to you, at your service, (*it is ~ if you will accept it; ever ~, ~ truly*, FAITHFULLY, OBEDIENTLY, etc., epistolary formulae preceding signature; *~ truly, joc., I, as but ~ truly was not taking any, I refused etc.*); *what's ~?* (colloq.), what will you drink? [prec., -ES, see OURS]

yourse'lf (ûr- etc., *as in* YOUR), pron. (pl.

(*-ves*). (Emphat.) You in person, in particular, in your normal state, & not another or others, or alone (usu. in apposition w. *you except in commands, & either next, after it or later, rarely substituted for it; please see to it ~ or yourselves; you ~ said so or yourselves; you have said it, arch. poet., etc.; by ~, alone, as why are you sitting by ~?, also unaided, as you cannot do it by yourselves; it is ~ I want, not your money; how's ~?, sl., how are you?, esp. after answering similar inquiry; ~ ~, colloq., pull ~ together; you are not quite ~ tonight, are out of humour etc.; (refl.) the person(s) previously described as you, or to whom a command is addressed (have you hurt ~?; you seemed pleased with yourselves; ask ~ whether it is not true*). [YOUR, SELF]

youth (ûth), n. (*pl. pr. ûdhz*). Being young, adolescence, (the vigour or enthusiasm or weakness or inexperience or other characteristic of) the period between childhood & full manhood or womanhood, (*has all the appearance of extreme ~; in my hot, raw, vigorous, etc. ~; from ~ onwards; ~ is a staff will not endure; the secret of perpetual, of keeping one's, ~; the ~ of the world, early times), whence ~*FUL (ûth-) a., ~*fully² adv., ~*fulness n.; *young man (as a ~ of 20; promising, lanky, etc., ~s*); young men & women (*the ~ of the country; loves to be surrounded by ~; our ~ are infected with commercial cynicity*); ~ *hostel*, place where hikers etc. can put up for the night. [OE *geoguth* (YOUNG, -TH²)]

yowl v. & n. Var. of YAWL¹.

ytte'rbium | **yttrium**, n. (chem.). Rare-earth metallic element. Hence ~*io a. [Ytterby in Sweden, -IUM]

yttrium, n. (chem.). Rare-earth metallic element. Hence ~*ic, ~*ious, aa., ~*o-comb. form. [as prec.]

yu'cca, n. Kinds of American white-flowered liliaceous plant. [Carib]

Yugoslav. See JUGOSLAV.

yule (ūl), n. The Christmas festival (also ~*tide; ~*-log, burnt on Christmas Eve). [OE *gēol, cf. ON *jól*, etym. dub.]

Z

Z (zĕd; *zē*), letter (pl. Zs, Z's, *zeds*); (Alg.; 2) third unknown quantity (cf. x, Y).

Zad'kiël, n. (Used for) a popular astrological almanac founded by R. J. Morrison (d. 1874), who adopted this pseudonym.

za'ffre (-er), **zä'ffer**, n. Impure oxide of cobalt used in making cobalt-blue & as blue pigment in enamelling & porcelain-painting. [f. F *zafre*, etym. dub.]

Zäm'bo. Var. of SAMBO (in first sense).

zän'y, n. (Hist.) attendant clown awkwardly mimicking chief clown in shows, merry andrew; (mod.) person given to

buffoonery, foolish jester, half-witted person. [f. F *zanni* f. It. *zanni* abbr. of *Giovanni* John]

Zanzibar'i, n. & a. (Native) of Zanzibar. [f.

zap'tieh (-ă), n. Turkish policeman. [f. Turk. *ḍabṭīyeh* f. Arab. *ḍabṭ* administration]

Zarathustr-. See ZOROASTRIAN.

zari'ba (-rē-), **-rēb'a,** n. Hedged or palisaded enclosure for protection of camp or village in the Sudan etc. [f. Arab. *zarība* pen]

zax. Var. of SAX.

zeal, n. Earnestness or fervour in advancing a cause or rendering service, hearty & persistent endeavour. So ~'ous (zěl-) a.., ~'ously² adv. [ME *zele* f. L f. Gk *zēlos*]

zeal'ot (zěl-), n. Uncompromising or extreme partisan, fanatic, (Z~, one of a Jewish sect resisting the Romans A.D. 6-70). Hence ~RY(4) n. [f. eccl. L f. Gk *zēlōtēs* (prec., -OT²)]

zebec(k). Var. of XEBEC.

zeb'ra, n. Kinds of striped quadruped (true or mountain ~, Burchell's ~, quagga) allied to ass or horse; (attrib., & in comb. w. names of animals etc.) striped like (~ *markings*, ~ *caterpillar*, ~ *woodpecker*, ~*wood*, etc.). Hence **zĕb'rINE¹** a. [Congolese]

zēb'ū, n. The E.-Ind. humped ox. [F (zē-)]

zĕd, n. Letter Z. [f. F *zède* f. L f. Gk *zēta*]

zĕd'oary, n. Kinds (*long, round, ~*) of aromatic gingerlike substance made from rootstock of E.-Ind. plants & used in medicine, perfumery, & dyeing. [f. med. L *zedoarium* f. Arab. *zedwār*]

zeit'geist (tsītgī-), n. Spirit of the times, drift of thought & feeling in a period. [G] [It.]

zĕmin'dar, n. (Anglo-Ind.). (Hist.) district governor & revenue-farmer under Mogul empire; (later) Indian landed proprietor paying land-tax to British government. [Hind., f. Pers. *zamīndār zamīn* earth, *dār* holder]

zĕmst'vŏ, n. (pl. ~s). Local elective assembly regulating affairs of district in Russia. [Russ., f. *zemlyá* land]

zēna'na (-äh), n. Part of house in which women of high-caste families are secluded in India (~ *mission*, of women visiting ~s to spread medical & other reform among inmates); ~ (*cloth*), a light fabric for women's dresses. [Hind., f. Pers. *zanāna* (*zan* woman, cf. Gk *gunē*, & QUEAN)]

Zĕnd, n. Ancient language of the Iranian family, allied to Sanskrit, named from the Zend-Avesta (Avesta or text & Zend or commentary) or Zoroastrian scriptures.

zēn'ith, n. Point of heavens directly above observer (opp. NADIR); (transf.) highest point, time, or place of greatest power or

prosperity or happiness, (*is at his, its, the,* ~); ~*distance,* are intercepted between any body & ~, complement of body's altitude. Hence ~AL a. [f. OF *cenit* f. Arab. *samt (ar-rās)* way (of the head)]

zē'olite, n. Any one of a number of minerals consisting mainly of hydrous silicates of lime, soda, & alumina, commonly found in the cavities of igneous rocks. [f. Gk *zeō* boil + -LITE; from their characteristic swelling & fusing before the blowpipe]

zĕph'yr (-er), n. 1. The west wind personified (Z~); balmy breeze, light wind. 2. Athlete's thin gauzy jersey for running, rowing, boxing, etc. in; kinds of dress-material. [f. L f. Gk *zephuros* west wind]

Zĕpp'elin, n. (colloq. *Zepp*). Large dirigible airship of type built, orig. for military use in Germany. [Count ~, inventor]

zēr'ō, n. (pl. ~s). Figure 0, cipher; no quantity or number, nil; starting-point in scales from which positive & negative quantity is reckoned (~ in thermometers, freezing-point of water or other point selected to reckon from; *absolute* ~ in temperature, point at which the particles whose motion constitutes heat would be at rest, estimated at −273·7° C.); (Mil.) point of time from which the start of each movement in a timed programme is at a specified interval; lowest point, bottom of scale, nullity, nadir; *fly at* ~ (under 1,000 ft). [It., contr. of *zefiro* f. Arab. as CIPHER]

zĕst, n. Piquancy, stimulating flavour, (esp. fig.; *adds a* ~ *to*); keen enjoyment or interest, relish, gusto, (*entered into it with* ~). [earlier sense *shred of lemon-peel*; OF. = skin of walnut-kernel, etym. dub.]

zē'ta, n. Greek letter (Z, ζ) = z. [Gk]

zētĕt'ic, a. (rare). Proceeding by inquiry. [f. Gk *zētētikos* (*zēteō* seek, -IC)]

zeug'ma, n. (gram.). Figure of speech in which a verb or adjective does duty with two nouns to one of which it is strictly applicable while the other is not used (e.g. *kill the boys & sc. destroy the baggage, with weeping eyes & sc. grieving hearts*; cf. SYLLEPSIS). Hence **zeugmāt'ic** a. [Gk (genit. *-atos*), *f. zeugnumi* yoke, -M]

Zeus, n. (Gk Ant.). King of the Olympian gods. [Gk]

zib'ĕt, n. The Asiatic or Indian civet. [f. med. L *zibethum* as CIVET]

zig'zăg, a., n., adv., & v.i.(-gg-). **1.** With abrupt alternate right & left turns, with alternating salient & re-entrant angles, with motion as of tacking ship, (*a* ~ *line, course, road, fence, trench, flash of lightning*). **2.** n. ~ line or (esp. for mounting steep hill) road or (in sieges) set of trenches. **3.** adv. With ~ course. **4.** v.i. Go ~, [F, etym. dub., cf. G *zickzack*]

zill'ah (-ŏ), n. Administrative district in British India. [Hind. *zilah* t. Arab. *dilah*]

zinc, n., & v.t. I. A white metallic element much used in the arts esp. as component of brass & German silver, as coating for sheet iron (cf. GALVANIZE), in electric batteries, & in relief-printing blocks (*flowers of* ~ or ~ *oxide*, powder used as white pigment & in kinds of ointment & cement); hence ~ic, ~IFEROUS, ~OID, aa., ~IFY v.t.; ~IFICA'TION n., ~OUS (esp. of negative pole of voltaic battery), zink'y², aa., with ~. [f. G *zink* etym. dub.]

zinc'ŏ, n. (pl. ~s), & vb. = ZINCOGRAPH. [abbr.]

zinc'ograph (-ahf), n., & v.i. & t. 1. Zinc plate with design etched in relief on it for printing from, picture taken from it. 2. vb. Etch (t. & i.) on zinc, reproduce (design) thus. So ~OG'RAPHY, ~OG'RAPHER, nn., ~OGRAPH'IC a. [ZINCO-, -GRAPH]

zinc'otype, n. = prec. In [as prec. TYPE]

Zing'arŏ (-ngg-), n. (pl. -ri). Gipsy. [It.]

zinn'ia, n. Kinds of composite plant with showy rayed flowers of deep red & other colours. [j. G. *Zinn* German botanist, -IA¹]

Zī'on, n. (Holy hill of) ancient Jerusalem; the Hebrew theocracy; the Christian Church; the Heavenly Jerusalem or king-dom of heaven, whence ~WARDS adv.; ‖(name for) nonconformist chapel. [f. eccl. L *Sion* t. Heb. *Tsiyōn* orig. hill]

Zī'onism, n. A movement resulting in the re-establishment of a Jewish nation in Palestine. So ~IST. [-ISM(3)]

zip, n. Light sharp sound, as of bullet passing through air, the sudden tearing of cloth, etc.; (fig.) energy, 'pep'; ~ fastener. (also zipp'er) fastening device consisting of two flexible stringers operated by means of the constriction of a sliding clip pulled between them. Hence zipp'er n. [imit.]

zīrc'on, n. A silicate of zirconium of which some varieties (HYACINTH, JARGON²) are cut into gems. [f. F *zircone* f. Arab. *zarqūn*]

zirc'onium, n. A metallic element found chiefly in zircon & used to alloy iron. Hence zirc'onia a., zirc'onate¹(3) n. [-IUM]

zith'er(n), n. Simple flat many-stringed instrument placed on table or knees & played partly with fingers of left hand & partly with plectrum in right hand. Hence ~IST(1) n. [G (as CITHER)]

zlŏt'y, n. Polish coin. [Pol.]

Zō'ar, n. Place of refuge, sanctuary. [*Gen.* xix]

zŏd'iac, n. A belt of the heavens limited by lines about 8° from the ecliptic on each side, including all apparent posi-tions of the sun & planets as known to the ancients, & divided into 12 equal parts called *signs of the* ~ (Aries, Taurus, Gemini, Cancer, Leo, Virgo, Libra, Scor-pio, Sagittarius, Capricorn(us), Aquarius, Pisces) each formerly containing the similarly named *zodiacal constellation* but now by precession of equinoxes coincid-ing with the constellation that bears the name of the preceding sign (e.g. the con-stellations Pisces, Aries, are now in the signs Aries, Taurus); (transf., now rare) complete course, circuit, or compass. [f. OF *zodiaque* t. late Gk *zōdiakos* t, *zōd/dion* animal (*zōos* living cf. *zaō* live), -AC]

zŏdī'acal, a. Of, in, the zodiac (~ *light*, luminous tract of sky shaped like tall triangle occas. seen in west after sunrise or in west after sunset esp. in tropics). [-AL]

zō'ètrope, n. WHEEL¹ of life. [irreg. f. Gk *zōē* life, *tropos* turn]

Zŏ'har, n. A cabalistic textbook prob. of 14th c. called Bible of the Mystics. [Heb. = brightness]

zŏ'ic, a. Of animals; (Geol., of rocks etc.) containing fossils, with traces of animal or plant life. [f. Gk *zōïkos* (*zōon* see ZODIAC, -IC)]

Zŏī'aism, n. Absence of reserve, detailed realism, in describing the gross or im-moral. So ~IST(2) n. ~ESQUE' (-ĕsk), ~IS'TIC, aa. [*Zola*, French novelist d. 1902, -ISM]

zŏll'verein (tsŏl'fĕrīn), n. Union of States having a common customs-tariff against outsiders & usu. free trade with each other. [G]

zŏm'bi(e), n. A corpse said to be revived by witchcraft. [?]

zōne, n., & v.t. 1. Belt or girdle worn round the body (chiefly arch. & poet.; *maiden* or *virgin* ~, symbol of virginity; *loose the maiden* ~ *of*, deprive of virginity). 2. Encircling band or stripe distinguish-able in colour or texture or character from the rest of the object encircled. 3. (Geog.) any of five divisions of the earth bounded by circles parallel to the equator (*frigid* ~s, N. of arctic, S. of antarctic, circle; *torrid* ~, between the tropics; *North, South, temperate* ~, be-tween *frigid* & *torrid* ~s); area enclosed between two exact or approximate con-centric circles; part of surface of sphere enclosed between two parallel planes, or of cone or cylinder between such planes cutting it perpendicularly to axis; any well-defined tract of more or less beltlike form; ~ *time*, local time for any longitude as opposed to Greenwich time; hence zōn'AL, zŏn'ARY¹, zŏn'ĬLAR¹ [-UL-], zŏn'ATE²(Bot., Zool.), aa., zŏn'ALY²adv. 4. v.t. Encircle as or with ~; arrange or distribute by ~s. [f. L f. Gk *zōnē* girdle]

Zŏŏ, n. (colloq.). Zoological garden, esp. that in London. [abbr.]

zōō-, comb. form of Gk *zōos* living, *zōon* an animal (see ZODIAC), = of animals, of animal life, (occas. as opp. vegetables & minerals, occas. excluding man also or especially); *zōōg'amy*, sexual reproduction; *~geog'raphy*, zoology dealing with local distribution of animals, so *~geōg'rapher*, *~geograph'ic(al)*; *zōōg'raphy*, descriptive zoology, so *zōōg'rapher*, *~graph'ic(al)*, *zōōg'raphist*; *zōōl'atry*, religious worship of animals; *zō'olite*, fossil animal, fossilized animal substance; *zō'omancy*, divination from appearances or behaviour of animals; *~morph'ic*, dealing with or represented under animal forms, having gods of beastlike form (cf. *anthropomorphic*), so *~morph'ism*; *zō'ophyte*, kinds of plantlike animal, esp. holothurians, starfishes, jelly-fishes, sea anemones, & sponges, so *~phyt'ic*, *~phytol'ogy*, *~phytolo'gical*, *~phytol'ogist*; *zō'osperm*, spermatozoon, also *~spore*; *zō'ospore*, spore capable of motion, so *~spo'ric*; *zōōt'omy*, dissection or anatomy of animals other than man.

zō'oid, a. & n. 1. Of incompletely animal nature. 2. n. Organic body or cell resembling but not being animal or plant; more or less independent organism given by germination or fission; member of compound organism. [prec., -OID]

zōōl'og'y̆, n. Natural history of animals, science of their structure, physiology, classification, habits, & distribution. So **zōōlō'gical** a. (*~ical garden*, public garden or park with collection of animals kept for exhibition), **zōōlō'gically²** adv., *~IST(3)* n. [ZOO-, -LOGY]

zōōm, v.i., & n. (aeron. sl.). 1. Force aeroplane to mount at high speed & steep angle. 2. n. Aeroplane's steep climb. [?]

zō'ril, n. Carnivorous quadruped of Africa & Asia Minor allied to skunk & weasel. [f. F *zorille* f. Sp. *zorrilla* (*zorra* fox)]

Zōrōäs'trĭan, Zărathus'tr- (-thōō-), nn. & aa. (Follower) of Zoroaster, Zarathustra, or Zerdusht; (adherent) of the religious system taught by him & his followers in the Zend-Avesta based on the conflict between Ormuzd god of light & good & Ahriman god of darkness & evil, the religion of the magi & ancient Persia still held by Parsees & occas. called *fire-worship*. Hence **Zŏrōäs'trĭan-ĭsm(3), Zărathus'tr(ĭan)ĭsm**, nn. [f. L.f. Gk *Zoroastrēs* f. Zend *Zarathustra*, -IAN]

zouave (zōō'ahv), n. 1. Member of French light-infantry corps orig. formed of Algerians & retaining Oriental uniform. 2. Woman's short jacket like that of ~ uniform. [name of tribe]

zounds (-z), int. (arch.) of indignation. [= (God)'s *wounds* (i.e. Christ's on the cross)]

zucchetti'a, -ĕtt'ō, (tsŏŏk-), n. R.-C. ecclesiastic's skull-cap, black for priest, purple for bishop, red for cardinal, & white for Pope. [It. (-a), dim. of *zucca* gourd]

Zŭlu (zōōl'ōō), n. 1. Member, language, of a S.-Afr. Kafir tribe. 2. Rough conical straw hat formerly much worn by children in summer. [native]

zwieback (tswēb'ahk), n. Kind of biscuit rusk or sweet cake toasted in slices. [G]

Zwing'lian (tswĭng-), a. & n. (Follower) of the Swiss religious reformer Zwingli (1484–1531). [-IAN]

zўg'al, a. H-shaped (esp. of brain-fissures). [as foll., -AL]

zўg(o)-, comb. forms of Gk *zugon* yoke: *zugapŏph'ysis*, one of the processes on a vertebra serving as articulation with another; *zygodac'tyl* a. & n., *-ylous* a., (bird) with toes disposed in pairs, two toes pointing forward & two backward; *zygomorph'ous*, (of flower) divisible into similar halves only in one plane; *zyg'o-spore*, spore formed by conjugation of two similar gametes.

zўgō'ma, n. (pl. *~ta*). Bony arch of cheek, yoke-bone. Hence **zўgōmăt'ĭc** a. [f. Gk *zugōma, -atos* yoke(bone) f. *zugoō* to yoke (prec.), -M]

zўgō'sĭs, n. (biol.). =CONJUGATION. [f. Gk *zugōsis* joining (prec.)]

zўg'ōte, n. Product of the fusion of two gametes, e.g. zygospore. [f. Gk *zugoō* yoke (*zugon*)]

zўmō'sĭs, n. Fermentation: zymotic disease in general or any form of it. [f. Gk *zumōsis* (*zumoō* ferment f. *zumē* leaven f. *zeō* boil)]

zўmŏt'ĭc, a. Of fermentation (*~ diseases*, epidemic, endemic, contagious, or sporadic diseases regarded as caused by multiplication of germs introduced from without). [f. Gk *zumōtikos* (prec., -OTIC)]

ADDENDA

NOTE

THESE addenda consist of (1) words not recorded in the body of the dictionary, and (2) further senses and constructions of words already treated. Additions of the latter kind, being arranged as appendages to existing articles, are readily distinguished by the absence of pronunciation, grammatical description, and etymology from the independent articles dealing with new words.

An obelus preceding an italicized word indicates a cross reference within the addenda; e.g. †*baby-sitter* s.v. *sit*. All other references are in SMALL CAPITALS.

A-bomb (ā'bòm), n. Atomic bomb. [4 for ATOMIC]

above. (Also, adj.) preceding, previous, as *the ~ statements.*

ăbrēăc′tion, n. (psycho-an.). The remoral by revival & expression of the emotion associated with forgotten or repressed ideas of the event that first caused it. [AB-, REACTION]

ac′cidie (ăks-). **acēd′ia,** nn. Sloth, torpor; despair. [f. OF *accide* f. LL *acedia* f. Gk *akēdia* (a-(7), *kēdos* care)]

accommodation. ~ *unit*, a home.

accredited. Now also used of a grade of milk.

acid.[2] Hence **acid′** ′ia a. (chem.).

ăc′roným, n. Word formed from initial letters of other words (e.g. *Anzac*, *Nato*, *radar*). [ACRO- + Gk *onoma* name]

act[1]. (Also) one of the series of short performances in circus or variety programme.

action (n.). ~ *committee* or *group*, (in Communist use) committee etc. that purges a society etc. of non-Communists; ~ *stations*, positions taken up by troops etc. before going into ~.

adapt. Hence (also) ~.

ad libitum. Ad-lib (ă-), v.i. (colloq.), speak extempore.

advise. (Also) inform, notify.

aero-. ~*biol′ogy*, study of airborne micro-organisms or spores; ~*plank′ton*, collective name for all the forms of minute organic life drifting in the air.

after[1]. Hence ~**s** n. pl.(colloq.), course following main course esp. at midday meal.

afterlight (ahr′terlīt), n. Light of what is known afterwards, hindsight. [AFTER a.]

ā′gēne, n. Nitrogen trichloride, used for whitening flour. [P]

Aglaia (ăgli′ia), n. One of the Graces. [Gk]

agree (v.t.). (Also) consent to or approve of (proposal, terms, etc.).

ahimsa (a-him′sah), n. Non-violence or non-killing acclaimed in Hindu Scriptures as the highest form of duty. [f. Skr. *a* without, *himsa* injury]

---

aid[2]. *What's (all) this in ~ of?* (colloq.), what's your object?

air[1]. ~*bridge*, link between points provided by ~ *transport*; ~ *hostess*, stewardess on ~ *liner*; ~*lift*, transport of supplies etc. by ~; ~*-stop*, helicopter passenger station; ~*-to-*~, from one ~*craft* to another.

alcohol. ~**ic,** (also, n.) person addicted to excessive consumption of ~.

alert. (Also v.t.) make ~; *put on the* ~, put on the ~.

Alexăn′drian (ăl-), a. Relating to the late Greek civilization of Alexandria in Egypt. [-AN]

ăl′ipĕd, a. & n. 1. Wing-footed. 2. n. animal. e.g. bat. [f. L *ala* wing, *pes pedis* foot]

all. *All Blacks* (colloq.), New Zealand rugby football international team; ~ *time high*, (*low*), a record high, (low), level or figure; ~*-up*, (of aircraft) total (weight) of machine, crew, passengers, cargo, etc., when in air.

allē′gle. Hence ~**ed** (-ĕjd) a., ~′**ĕdly**[2] adv., (used in statements for which author disclaims responsibility).

ăll′emände, n. Name of several German dances; country dance figure. [F, = German]

alpha. ~ *plus*, superlatively good.

alternate[1]. ***(Also, awĭ*)[*] n. & a., deputy (representative).

ămeri′cium (-ishi-), n. Radio-active transuranic metallic element. [f. *America*]

‖ amôrce′, n. Priming charge; percussion cap for toy pistol. [F, f. OF *amorche* bite]

amphibian. (Also): (Zool.) member of the Amphibia; (tank or other vehicle) adapted for both land & water, so *amphibious* a.

amplitude. (Also): (Phys.) extent of vibration or oscillation; (Electr.) maximum departure from average of alternating current or wave.

anachronism. (Also) building etc. out of harmony with its surroundings in point of time.

ăn'drŏgĕn, n. Any substance (e.g. a male sex hormone) capable of developing & maintaining many male sexual characteristics. [f. Gk *andro-* male +-GEN]

angel. (Also, sl.) financial backer of enterprise.

annex(e), Also, now usu., pron. ăn'ĕks.

ăn'ŏrăk, n. Jacket of skin or cloth with hood attached, worn esp. in arctic regions. [f. Eskimo *ánoráq*]

ănŏx'ia, n. (med.). Deficiency of oxygen. [f. AN-(5), OX(YGEN), -IA-1]

ăntĭbĭŏt'ĭc, a. & n. (Substance) that destroys or injures living organisms, esp. bacteria. [ANTI-(2), Gk *bios* life, -IC]

An'zŭs (ă-), n. Three-power pact for Pacific security formed 1952 by Australia, New Zealand, & the United States. [f. initial letters]

apar'theid (-t-hāt), n. (S. Afr.). Racial segregation. [Afrikaans (APART, -HOOD)]

appease. (Also) try to conciliate or bribe (a potential aggressor) by making concessions, freq. with implication of sacrifice of principles.

approve. ~*d school,* State school for young offenders.

apron. (Also) hard-surfaced area on airfield, used for handling & (un)loading aircraft.

ā'qualung, n. Portable diving apparatus consisting of cylinders of compressed air strapped on back & feeding air automatically through a valve to diver as he requires it. [f. L *aqua* water +LUNG]

arabesque. (Also) ballet dancer's posture in which body is bent forward on one leg with the other leg extended horizontally backwards.

arrest1. ~*or hook,* hook-like device for catching on cables on deck of aircraft carrier & checking speed of aircraft as they land.

arriviste (ărēvēst'), n. Careerist, parvenu. [F]

arson. Hence *~IST n.,* incendiary. [F]

ăr'thrŏpŏd, n. (zool.). Member of *Arthrópoda,* consisting of animals with jointed body & limbs. [ARTHRO-, Gk *pous podos* foot]

Arthūr'ian (âr-), a. Relating to King Arthur or his knights. [-IAN]

as1. *As for,* with regard to.

ash2. ~*can,* dustbin.

Asian (āsh'ăn), a. & n. (Native) of Asia. [f. L.f. Gk *Asianos* (*Asia,* see -AN)]

aspect. (Also, Gram.) a verbal form expressing action or being in respect of its inception, duration, or completion.

asphyxia. Hence (also) ~A'TION n., suffocation.

assault1. (Also, euphem. for) rape (of woman).

assault2. (Also, euphem. for) rape (woman).

assembly. ~ *line,* group of machines & workers operating on some product to be assembled.

astro-. *As'tronaut,* student or devotee of ~*naut'ics,* science of aerial navigation in space.

atomic. ~ *warfare* (in which ~ *bombs* are used).

aubergine (ōb'ĕrzhēn), n. Purple fruit of egg-plant. [F]

auction. (Also, v.t.) sell by ~.

aur'eate, a. Golden, gold-coloured; resplendent. [f. L *aureatus* f. *aureus* golden f. *aurum* gold, -ATE2]

autarchy1. Hence **autärch'ic**(AL)(-k-) aa.

autarky, autarchy2. Hence **autärk'ic**(AL) aa., **auf'arkist** n.

auto-. *Aut'ism* n., morbid self-admiration, absorption in phantasy; *autis'tie* a. [AUTO-, DIDACTIC]

aut'odidăct, n. Self-taught person. [AUTO-, DIDACTIC]

automā'tion, n. Automatic control of the manufacture of a product through successive stages, (loosely) use of machinery to save manual labour. [irreg. formed f. AUTOMATIC]

autostrad|a (owtostrah'dah), n. (pl. ~e, pr. -ā). Italian arterial road. [It., = motor-car road]

aweigh' (awā), adv. (Of anchor) just lifted from ground in weighing. [A2 prep. +WEIGH]

B

baby. ~-*sitter,* person sitting with or looking after a ~ while its parents are out.

back1 (a.). ~-*drop,* ~-*cloth;* ~-*ground,* (also, fig.) person's cultural knowledge, education, experience, etc.; ~-*log,* reserves, arrears of unfulfilled orders; ~-*room boys* (colloq.), men engaged in (secret) research.

back3. ~-*pedal,* (also, fig.) check a forward movement, reverse one's action; ~-*woodsman,* |(also, fig.) peer who rarely or never attends House of Lords.

baffle. ~-*board, wall,* devices to prevent spread of noise.

bāguette' (-gĕt), n. (archit.). Small moulding like an astragal. [F, f. It. f. L *bacculum* stick]

Bail'ey bridge, n. Emergency bridge designed for rapid construction. [Sir D. Bailey (b. 1901), designer]

băll1. (Also, pl., vulg.): testicles: nonsense; *make a ~s of,* do badly, make a mess of. ~-*point,* (of fountain pen) having a tiny ~ as its writing point.

ballerina. (Now only or esp.) dancer taking one of the five leading classical female roles in ballet.

ballet. Hence **bălletomāne', bălléto-MAN'IA,** nn., enthusiast, enthusiasm, for ~ performances.

balloon1. (Also, colloq.) ~-shaped line

bál'sa (or bawl-), n. American tropical tree yielding light strong wood, cork-wood; raft or float. [Sp.]

band¹. ~ waggon, wagon for ~ of musicians esp. in circus parade, (fig.) imaginary vehicle regarded as carrying a ~ of political leaders likely to be successful (*climb on the* ~ *wagon*, strive to be on the winning side).

bárbitúr'ic, a. (chem.), ~ic acid, an acid from which various hypnotic and sedative drugs are derived. Hence ~ATE³ (3) n. [f. F (-ique) f. G barbitur(säure)]

bard². Hence (Also) ~ÓLATRY n., worship of Shakespeare, the "B~ of Avon".

bash. (Also, n.) heavy blow; *have a* ~ *at it* (sl.), attempt it.

báth'yscaphe (-âf), n. Bathysphere. [f. Gk bathus deep, scaphē boat]

battery. (Also) series of nesting-boxes, cages, &c., in which laying hens are confined for intensive laying or poultry reared & fattened.

***bazook'a,** n. Anti-tank rocket-gun. [?]

bearer. (Also) native carrier.

Beaúf'ort scále (bōf-), n. Scale of wind velocity ranging from 0 (calm) to 12 (hurricane) (75 miles an hour or over). [Sir F. Beaufort, English admiral (d. 1857)]

***bēb'óp,** n. Kind of jazz music. [imit.]

belly. ~-ache, (also, v.i., sl.) complain bitterly.

Bén'élúx, n. Belgium, the Netherlands, & Luxembourg in association as a regional economic group; freq. attrib. as the ~ countries. [f. Belgium, Netherlands, Luxembourg]

berry¹. (Also) grain of wheat etc.

bés'óm² (-z-), n. (Sc.). (Term of abuse for) woman. [?]

best¹ (a.). ~ seller, (also) author of popular novel etc.

beta. ~ plus, rather better than second-class.

bét'atrón, n. (phys.). Apparatus for accelerating speed of electrons. [f. BETA +(ELEC)TRON]

bifocal. (Also, n. pl.) ~ spectacles.

bill'on, n. Alloy of gold or silver with a predominating amount of some base metal. [F, f. bille BILLET³]

biology. Biological warfare (involving use of living organisms esp. disease germs).

bipártisán' (-z-: or -pärt'), a. Of or involving two (political) parties. [BI- (1 a) +PARTISAN¹]

bit². ~-s & pieces (colloq.), odds & ends.

bitch. (Also, derog.) woman, esp. a catty or treacherous one.

biz'óne, n. Economic & political unit constituted by both of two zones, esp. the British & American zones of occupation in Germany after the 1939-45 war. Hence bizón'AL a. [BI- (1 a) +ZONE]

blatant. (Also) flagrant, palpable, as a ~ lie.

bleep, n., & v.i. 1. (Sound of radio signal transmitted from) Russian earth satellite launched in 1957. 2. v.i. Transmit this signal. [imit.]

block¹. (Also) *area in town or suburb.

block². (Also) restrict use or expenditure of (currency or other asset; chiefly in P.P.). Hence ~´AGE (3) n. a ~ed (up) state.

blood¹. ~ bank, place where supply of ~ for transfusion is stored; ~ sports, those involving ~shed or the killing of animals.

blot². ~ one's copybook (colloq.), stain one's character, commit an indiscretion.

blow². ~ up, (also) lose one's temper, enlarge (map, print).

blue¹. ~-chip attrib., (St. Exch., of shares) constituting a fairly reliable investment, though less secure than gilt-edged.

bluff². (Also) act of bluffing (call person's ~, make him show his cards, also fig.).

***bóbb'y-sōx,** n. pl. Short socks covering ankle. Hence ~ER¹ (3) n., girl wearing ~, freq. derog. of girl in early teens who is an ardent follower of film stars esp. crooners. [?]

bŏff'in, n. (sl.), Man engaged in research, scientist. [?]

bŏm'a, n. (Central Africa). Defensible enclosure; police or military post: magistrate's office. [Swahili]

bombard. (Also, Phys.) subject (atoms etc.) to a stream of high-speed particles; insanity.

bone¹. ~-meal, crushed or ground ~s used esp. as fertilizer.

boot¹ (n.). (Also) luggage-receptacle at back of body of motor-car.

border¹. ~ line, line of demarcation; ~(-)line adj., on the ~ line, as a ~-line case, (esp., Psych.) one verging on insanity.

bottom¹ (a.). ~ drawer, drawer in chest of drawers etc. in which a woman stores clothes etc. in preparation for marriage.

bounce¹. (Also, sl., of cheque) be returned to drawer when there are no funds to meet it.

***Bour'bon²** (boor-), n. Reactionary. [f. the ~ family whose descendents founded dynasties in France and Spain]

box³. ~ing-weights (revised 1951; amateur given first, professional in brackets), Heavy-weight over 12 st. 10 (over 12 st. 7), Light Heavy (or Cruiser)-weight (12 st. 6), (12 st. 7), Middle-weight 11 st. 11 (11 st. 6), Light Middle-weight 11 st. 2 (not a professional category), Welter-weight 10 st. 8 (10 st. 7), Light Welter-weight 10 st. (not a professional category), Light-weight 9 st. 7 (9 st. 9), Feather-weight 9 st. (9 st.), Bantam-weight 8 st. 7 (8 st. 6), Fly-weight 8 st. (8 st.). [?]

boxer. (Also) medium-sized smooth-haired kind of dog derived from German bulldog.

bra (-ah), n. (colloq.). Brassiere. [abbr.]

bracket¹. (Also) group bracketed together (*income~, class of tax-payers grouped according to income).

brahmin. *(Also, B~) highly cultured or intellectual person (colloq, usu. derog.).

break¹. ~ down, (also) analyse (cost, total, etc.) into its component items (~down n... such analysis); ~ even, emerge with neither gain nor loss.

breast¹. ~ stroke, stroke made while swimming on the ~ by extending the arms in front and sweeping them back.

breeze². (Also, v.i., sl.) go like a ~, move along in lively manner.

brief³. (Also, n. pl., colloq.) shorts, women's panties.

brother. (Also, Bibl.) kinsman.

buffer². (Also, Nav. sl.) chief boatswain's mate.

bulge¹. (Also) temporary increase in volume or numbers.

bulk¹. ~ buying, purchase by one buyer of all or most of a producer's output.

*bum². (Also, v.t.) obtain by sponging, scrounge.

bummaree. (Also) licensed porter at Smithfield meat-market in London.

Būn'a, n. Synthetic rubber made by the polymerization of butadiene. [f. †buta(diene)+na(trium) sodium]

burlesque. Also: *(vulgar) variety show freq. featuring comic strip-tease.

burn². (Also) utilize nuclear energy of (uranium etc.).

bürp, n., & v.i. (sl.). Belch. [imit.]

bush¹. ~telegraph, rapid spreading of information, rumour, etc.

būtadi'ēne, n. (chem.). Gas used in making synthetic rubber. [f. †buta(ne)+DI²+-ENE]

bit'āne, n. (chem.). Hydrocarbon of the methane series. [f. BUT(YR-)+-ANE]

buy. ~ers' market (in which goods are plentiful & low prices favour ~ers).

bwa'na (-ah-), n. (Africa). Master, sir. [Swahili]

C

caboose. (Also) *guard's van or car on goods train for workmen etc.

*cā'gey (-ji), a. Shrewd; unapproachable, not forthcoming, self-contained. Hence **cā'gīLY²** adv. [?]

caldera (kahldār'a), n. (geol.). Deep cauldron-like cavity on summit of volcano. [Sp. = cauldron]

call². (Also) a ring on or conversation over the telephone; ~girl, prostitute accepting appointments by telephone.

calyp'sō, n. Spontaneous topical W.-Ind. song. [?]

can¹. ~ned music (sl.), music recorded for reproduction esp. on gramophone.

cañās'ta, n. Card game of S.-Amer. origin resembling rummy. [Sp.=basket]

candid. ~ camera, small camera for taking informal pictures of persons freq. without their knowledge.

cannibal. Hence (also) ~IZE (4) v.t., use (one of a number of similar machines) to provide spare parts for the others.

canon. (Also) list of recognized genuine works of a particular author (the Shakespearian~).

capital (a.). ~ goods, goods to be used in producing commodities, opp. consumer goods.

capitalize. (Also) turn to account, make use of to one's advantage.

carbon. (Also)== copy (made with ~ paper).

carcass. ~ meat, raw meat as dist. from corned or tinned meat.

card². (Also) an eccentric person, a character.

career. *~ diplomat, professional diplomat.

carriage. ~way, part of road intended for vehicular traffic.

carrier. ~ wave, continuous electromagnetic wave motion emitted by radio transmitter.

cartel. Hence~IZE (3) v.t. & i., combine to form a (business)~.

cārtŏl'ogŷ, n. Study of maps & charts. So **cārtŏlŏ'gICAL** a. [f. F carte (CARD²)+-OLOGY]

case¹. ~ history, record of person's ancestry, personal history, etc., for use in determining necessary treatment etc.; ~work, social work concerned with the individual.

castle¹. ~nut, one with notched extension for locking pin.

cat¹. ~'s-eye, (also) reflector stud on road.

catabolism. Var. of KATABOLISM.

*cayuse (kī'ūs), n. Indian pony. [Amer. Ind.]

ceilidh (kāl'i), n. (Sc.). Informal gathering for song & story. [Gael.]

celadon. (Also) grey green glaze used on some pottery.

centrifugal. Hence (also) **cĕn'trifŭge** n., ~ machine rotating at very high speed, designed to separate solids from liquids, or liquids from other liquids (e.g. cream from milk).

certify. ~ied milk, guaranteed free from tubercle bacillus.

chaise. ~ longue (longg; F. = long chair), kind of sofa with a rest for the back at one end only.

‖ **chā'r³,** n. (sl.). Tea. [f. Chin. cha TEA]

chee-chee, n. (Anglo-Ind.). The affected English accent attributed to Eurasians; a Eurasian. [f. Hind. chhī-chhī filth, fie!]

Chelsea. ~ bun, kind of rolled currant-bun.

chēmothě'rapŷ (kē-), n. Treatment of disease by chemical means. [f. chem(ical)+-o-+THERAPY]

chichi (shē'shē), a. & n. Frilly (thing), fussy or effeminate (person). [F]

chigg'er (-g-), n. = CHIGOE.

china. ~**man,** n. (Cricket) left-handed bowler's off-break to right-handed bats-man.

chin'dit, n. Member of Brigadier Wingate's commando force in Burma in 1943. [native name]

chinook', n. Warm dry wind which blows on the eastern side of the Rocky Mountains. [native name]

chlóromý'cětin (kl-), n. An antibiotic used in some diseases, e.g. typhus. **-IN** [CHLORO-², Gk *mukēs* fungus, -IN]

cinema. Hence **cinemat'ic** a., relating to, having the qualities characteristic of, the ~.

circle¹. *Run round in* ~s (colloq.), be fussily busy with little result.

clever. *Clever-clever,* excessively ~.

climate. (Also, fig.) trend or attitude of something.

clinic. *(Also)* †seminar (last two meanings)

clione, n. A group of plants produced vegetatively from one original seedling or stock. Hence **clón¹** AL n. [f. Gk *klōn* twig, slip]

clot (n.). (Also, sl.) stupid person.

clobb'er, n. Black paste used to hide cracks in leather; (sl.) clothing, gear. [?]

eloche. (Also) glass cover (orig. bell-shaped) for forcing or protecting outdoor plants.

clip² (vb). (Also) remove small piece from (railway, bus, etc. ticket) to show that it has been used. Hence ~**p'ie** [-Y³] n. (colloq.), bus conductress.

coach (n.). (Also) long-distance bus.

***coc'a-cōl'a,** n. Aerated non-alcoholic drink. [P]

cock¹. ~ *salmon,* male.

cŏd'piece, n. (hist.). Bagged appendage to the front of men's breeches. [f. OE *codd* bag, PIECE¹]

coel'acănth (sēl-), a. & n. (Fish) having a hollow spine. [f. COELO(-, Gk *akantha* spine, thorn]

coexistence. *(Peaceful)* ~, (of peoples with different political & social systems) living in mutual toleration.

collate. (Also) put together.

collect². (Also, colloq.) call for, fetch, as *he went to* ~ *his suitcase.*

colúmb'ium, n. (chem.). = NIOBIUM. [f. *Columbia* United States, -IUM]

comb². (Also) search (place) thoroughly.

comfort (n.). (Also) *eiderdown quilt.

comic (n.). (Also) *paper.

Cŏm'ínförm, n. International Communist organization established in 1947 to carry on the propaganda formerly conducted by the Comintern. [f. first elements of Russ. forms of *Com(munist) Inform(ation Bureau)*]

common¹. ~**sens'icǎl,** possessing, marked by, ~ sense.

communism. (Also, usu. C~): movement or political party advocating ~; party affirming need for a dictatorship of the proletariat, associated with the Comintern (1919–43) & the Cominform (1947–56).

compel. Hence ~**ling** a., rousing strong interest or feeling, of admiration.

compère. (Also, v.t.) act as ~ to.

comprehensive. ~ *school,* large secondary school providing courses of varied kinds & lengths.

condense. Hence (also) ~**ERY** (3) n., factory for ~ed milk.

congruent. (Also, Math., of figures) coinciding exactly when superposed.

conquist'ador, n. Conqueror, esp. one of the Spanish conquerors of Mexico & Peru in 16th c. [Sp.]

consumer. ~ *resistance,* = SALES *resistance.*

contact (n.). ~ *man,* intermediary esp. between a Government department & the public.

contain. Hence (also) ~**MENT** n., (esp.) policy of building up strength against a possible enemy in the hope of eventual agreement with him.

convection. Hence ~**OR²** n., heating apparatus for circulating warm air.

conventional. (Also, of bombs etc.) other than atomic.

copy. ~**-writer,** one who writes or prepares advertising ~ for publication.

cŏr'isōne, n. Drug used for rheumatic diseases. [P]

corny¹. (Also, sl., of jokes etc.) out of date, old-fashioned.

cǒr'onary, a. (anat.). Resembling, encircling like, a crown. [f. L *coronarius* (*corona* crown, -ARY²)]

coroner. (Also) official holding inquiry in cases of treasure trove.

corsair. (Also) a pirate.

cosh. ~**boy,** youth or man armed with ~. [P]

costume (n.). ~ *jewellery,* artificial jewellery worn for decorative purposes.

cŏtěrm'inous, a. Var. of CONTERMINOUS. [co-]

coun'ter-rěvolu'tion (-lŏŏ-, -lū-), n. A revolution opposed to a former one or reversing its results. Hence ~**ARY¹** (-shon-) a., [COUNTER- (1)]

court¹. ∥(Also, in a town) yard surrounded by houses & communicating with street by an entry.

couture (kŏŏtüür'), n. Dressmaking. Hence ~**ier** (kŏŏtüür'ĭā), masc., ~**ière** (kŏŏtüür'yĕā), fem. dressmaker. [F]

cover. Hence (also) ~**AGE** n., area of community reached by a particular advertising medium, risk ~ed by insurance policy.

cover². ∥~ *girl,* girl or woman whose picture illustrates ~ of magazine etc.

crash¹ (n.). ~ *helmet,* protective helmet of motor cyclist etc.

crave. Hence **crāv'ing**[1] n., strong desire, intense longing, *(for)*.

creāte'. (Also, v.i. sl.) make a fuss *(he's always ~ing about nothing)*.

crime passionnel (krēm' pàsyònèl'), n. Crime due to jealousy. [F, =crime of passion]

cross[2]. ~ *one's fingers* or *keep one's fingers ~ed*, crook one finger over another to bring good luck.

cross-. ~*section* (fig.), a comprehensive representative sample.

***crüll'er**, n. A small cake made of dough containing eggs, butter, sugar, etc., twisted or curled & fried in fat. [f. Du. *krullen* curl]

crȳp'tō, n. (colloq.). Person owing secret allegiance to a political creed etc.; esp. short for *~Communist*. [as CRYPT(O)-]

cub (n.). (Also, colloq., short for) *~ reporter*, young or inexperienced newspaper reporter.

cŭr'ium, n. (chem.). Radio-active transuranic element. [f. Marie & Pierre *Curie*), French scientists, +-IUM]

curric'ulum. Hence ~**AR**[1] a.

cwm (koom), n. Var. of COOMB.

cÿbernet'ics, n. Study of system of control & communications in animals & electrically operated devices such as calculating machines. [f. Gk *kubernētēs* steersman, -ICS]

D

dare. (Also, n.) act of daring, challenge.

dāg, n. (Sc.). A day's work; a definite amount of work. [contr. f. *dagwerk* or *dagwark*, day-work]

dark[1]. *The ~ ages*, (also, esp.) the period between the break-up of the Roman Empire (A.D. 395) & the end of the 10th c.

date[2]. *~line*, (also) line in newspaper at head of message, special article, etc., giving ~ & place of dispatch.

datum. (Also, pl.) facts of any kind, notes.

dead (a.). *~ pan* (sl.), expressionless immobile face.

dēbāg', v.t. (sl.; -gg-). Remove the 'bags' (=trousers) from. [DE-, BAG[1]]

deck[1]. (Also, sl.) the ground.

déclass'ify, v.t. Remove from secret list. [DE-]

défatt'ed, a. Deprived of its fat. [DE-]

defence. ~ *in depth*, system of ~ comprising successive areas of resistance.

delegate[2]. ~*d legislation*, delegation to Ministers, by Acts of Parliament, of the power to make orders & regulations which have the force of law.

demob. ~*suit* (issued to soldier etc. when demobilized after the 1939–45 war).

dēna'zifÿ (-ahts-), v.t. Rid of Nazism & its influence. Hence ~**FICA'TION** n. [DE-]

dendr(o)-. Hence (also) **dĕn'drophīl(E)**, **dĕn'drophōbe**, aa. & nn.

denier[2]. (Also, Commerce.) unit of weight by which silk & rayon yarn is weighed & its fineness estimated.

denominator. *Common ~*, (least) common multiple of the ~s of a number of fractions; also fig.

dēra'tion, v.t. Remove (food etc.) from rationed category. [DE-]

derelict (n.). (Also) person abandoned by society.

dērequisi'tion (-z-), v.t. Free (requisitioned property). [DE-]

dě'rris, n. Kinds of tall tropical woody climbers; insecticide made from the powdered tuberous root of some of these. [Gk, =leather covering]

***dēsĕg'rēgāte**, v.t. Abolish racial segregation (in schools etc.). [DE-, SEGREGATE]

dēvăl'ūe, v.t. Reduce the value of. Hence **dēvălūa'TION** n. [DE-]

deviation. Hence ~**IST** (-sho-) n., one who departs from strict Communist doctrine.

Diasp'ora, n. The DISPERSION (of the Jews). [Gk. f. DIA (*spora* f. *speirō* scatter)]

differential (n.). (Also) difference in wage between industries or between skilled & unskilled workers in same industry.

digest[1]. (Also) periodical synopsis of current literature or news.

dim (a.). *Take a ~ view of* (colloq.), regard with pessimism.

dinâr' (dē-), n. Unit of currency in Iraq & Jugoslavia. [Arab. *dīnār* f. L *denarius* (see DENARIUS)]

director. (Also) elaborate gun-sight for co-ordinating fire of several guns.

dirigisme (dērēzhizm'), n. Policy of State direction & control in economic & social matters. [F (*diriger* DIRECT[1])]

dīrn'dl, n. Kind of dress imitating Alpine peasant costume with bodice & full skirt; (also ~ *skirt*) full skirt with tight waistband. [G, dim. of *dirne* girl]

disincen'tive, n. & a. Deterrent. [DIS-]

disinflā'tion, n. (econ.). Deflation. Hence ~**ARY**[1] (-sho-) a. [DIS-]

disk. (Also) gramophone record; *~ jockey* (sl.), compère of radio programme of gramophone records.

distribute. (Also, Print.) separate (type that has been set up) & return each letter to its proper box in the case.

distribution. (Also, Print.) act or process of distributing type.

division. (Also) part of county or borough returning a Member of Parliament.

dollar. In 1949, as result of alteration in exchange value of pound sterling, U.S. ~ became worth about 7s.; ~ *area* (in which currency is linked to U.S. ~).

dope. (Also) drug etc. given to horse or greyhound to try to make it win, (v.t.) give ~ to. (cf. NOBBLE).

double[2]. (Also): (Darts) a throw on the narrow space enclosed by the two outer circles of a dartboard; (Racing) a bet on two horses etc. in different races, the

winnings & stake from one race being
carried forward & bet on the second.

drag[1]. *~* one's *feet*, (fig.) be slow or
reluctant to do something.

drag[2]. *(Also, sl.)* Influence, pull.

dragée. *(Also)*: sugar-coated almond;
small silver ball for decorating cake.

drape. (Also, n.) piece of drapery, curtain.

dress ugg[?] (-zhzh), n. Training of horse in
obedience & deportment. [F, f. *dresser*
train]

drey[2] (drā), n. Squirrel's nest. [?]

dry.[1] *~ up,* (also, Theatr.) forget one's
lines.

dub[2]. (Also, Cinemat.) make another
recording of sound-track of (film) esp. in
a different language.

*dúnk, v.t. & i. Dip (bread, cake, etc.)
into soup or a beverage while eating.
[f. G *tunken* dip]

dust[1]. **~bowl,* area denuded of vegetation by drought & overcropping, & so
reduced to desert.

E

eat. Hence (also)*~'*ER[1] n, one who or that
which *~*s (*he is a big~er, an opium-~er*),
fruit that may be *~*en raw.

echo. *~gram,* record of *~sounder*
(sounding apparatus for determining
depth of sea beneath ship).

edge[1]. *Have the ~ on* (sl.), have the advantage of.

Edward'ian (ĕdwŏ'-), a. & n. 1. Of the
time of any of the Edwards, Kings of
England (esp.) characteristic of Edward
VII's reign (1901–10). 2. n. Person belonging to this period. [-IAN]

égalitā'rian, a. & n. 1. Of, relating to,
holding, the principle of the equality of
mankind. 2. n. person. Hence *~*ISM n.
[f. F *égalitaire* f. *égal* equal]

egg[1]. **~head* (sl.), intellectual.

Elzevir. (Also) a printing type.

'em, pron. (colloq.). Them. [orig. a form
of ME *hem,* dat. & acc. 3rd pers. pl.; now
regarded as abbr. of *them*]

eminence. *éminence grise* (ā'mēnahns
grēz', F, = grey cardinal), confidential
agent esp. one who exercises power un-
officially (applied orig. to Cardinal Riche-
lieu's private secretary).

empire. (Also, attrib., *E~*) denoting a
style of furniture or dress fashionable
during the first (1804–15) or second (1851–
70) French E~.

encôde', v.t. Put (message) into code or
cipher. [EN-]

end[1]. *Go (in) off the deep ~,* (also) lose
one's temper.

ĕn'osĭs, n. Union of Cyprus with Greece.
[Gk *henôsis*]

èpeirŏgĕn'ĕsĭs (-pīr-), n. (geol.). Process
of making continents. [Gk *èpeiros* main-
land, GENESIS]

ĕp'ĭgône, n. One of a later (& less dis-

tinguished) generation. [f. L f. Gk
epigonos (*epi* after, + root of *gignomai* be
born)]

epilogue. *(Also, Radio)* short religious
service towards the end of some B.B.C.
programmes.

equity. *(Also)* net value of mortgaged
property after deduction of charges.

E'rato (ĕ'-), n. Muse of lyric poetry. [Gk]

érica'ceous (-shus), a. Belonging to the
heath genus *Erica* or its family *Ericá-
ceae.* [f. L f. Gk *ereikē* heath, see -ACEOUS]

Erin'ys (ĕ'-), n. (pl. *Erinyes,* pr. ĕrin'iēz),
A Fury. [Gk]

Ern'ie (ĕr-), n. Device for drawing prize-
winning numbers of premium bonds,
[electronic random number indicator
equipment]

Er'ŏs (ĕr'-), n. Love, god of love, Cupid.
[Gk *erôs*]

escape[1]. *~ clause,* one specifying conditions under which contracting party is
free from obligations.

escape[2]. Hence **éscapEE**' n, one who has
*~*d.

ethic. *~al,* (also, of drugs) conforming to a
recognized standard.

ĕth'narch (-k), n. Governor of a people or
province. So *~*Y[1] (-ki) n. [f. Gk *ethnos*
nation + *archō* rule]

Eumĕn'ides (-ēz), n. pl. (Euphemistic
name for) Furies. [Gk, = gracious ones]

euphŏr'ia, euphŏr'y, nn. Feeling of well-
being. Hence **euphŏr'ic** a. [f. Gk EU-
(*phoria f. pherō* bear)

Euphrŏs'ynē (or -z-), n. One of the
Graces. [Gk]

eutĕc'tic, a. (chem.). *~ mixture,* in which
the constituents are in such proportions
as to solidify at one temperature (*~ temperature* or *point*) like a pure substance.
[f. EU- + Gk *tēktos* melt + -IC]

every. *~ so often,* occasionally, at intervals.

existential. Hence *~*ISM (3) (-shǎl) n.,
an anti-intellectualist philosophy of life,
holding that man is free & responsible,
based on the assumption that reality as
existence can only be lived but can never
become the object of thought.

expend. Hence *~*ABLE a, likely to be or
meant to be sacrificed or destroyed.

expertise' (-ēz), n. Expert opinion or
skill or knowledge. [F]

expression|ism. So *~*IST n. & a.

F

façade. (Also, fig.) frontal or outward
appearance.

faculty. **(Also)* staff of university or
college.

fail[1]. (Also) failure, one who falls, in an
examination.

Falán'gist, n. Member of a Spanish
Fascist organization **Falán'ge** (-ghā),
[Sp. *~a f. falange* phalanx]

fall[2]. ~*-out* n., airborne particles of radioactive materials from explosion of atomic or hydrogen bomb.

fascia. (Also, in full, ~ *board*) instrument board of motor-car.

fault (v.t.). (Also) find ~ with, blame.

favour[2]. (Also, Journalism) choose to wear.

feather[1]. ~*-bed* v.t., make things easy for, pamper.

ferrous. (Also, more loosely) containing iron (~ *& non-~ metals*).

fiddle. (Also, sl.): an act of cheating; (v.t.) cheat, swindle.

filibuster. Hence ~ER[1] n., a ~, one who ~s.

final. Hence ~IZE v.t., complete, bring to an end.

fire[1]. *~-bug* (colloq.), incendiary, pyromaniac.

fission. (Also, Chem.) splitting of atomic nuclei (~ *bomb*, atom bomb). Hence ~ABLE (-sho-) a.

fix[1]. (Also) mend, repair.

flamboyant (a.). (Also) florid, ostentatious, showy.

flap (n.). (Also, colloq.) state of excitement (*be in, get into, a ~*).

flat[1]. (Also, Nav.) ship's compartment on to which cabins etc. open (*after cabin, wardroom, ~*).

flicker. Hence **flick** n. (sl.), a cinema film, (pl.) a cinema performance (*he is going to the flicks tonight*).

flog. (Also, sl.) sell.

floor (n.). ~ *show*, entertainment presented not on stage but on ~ of night-club etc.

flush[5]. *Straight ~* (of cards in a regular sequence): *royal ~* (Poker), a straight ~ headed by ace.

fly[2]. *~-over*, (also *~-over bridge, viaduct*) a bridge for carrying vehicles over traffic-congested areas, esp. over main roads.

fly[3]. *~-past* n., ceremonial flight of air-craft past some person or place, cf. MARCH[1] past.

flying. ~ *saucer*, saucer-like object occas. reported as having been seen flying at great speed & height.

forebear (fōr̄ˈbar̄), n. = FORBEAR[1].

fore-. *~name*, first or Christian name.

foundation. ~ *garment*, woman's supporting undergarment, e.g. corset, corset, girdle.

four (a.). *The ~ hundred*, the exclusive social set of any place.

foursome. (Also, colloq.) a company or party of four persons.

frame[2]. (Also) single complete image or picture transmitted in series of lines by television; attrib., as ~ *synchronization*.

franc. (Also) Belgian & Swiss monetary unit.

fraternity. *(Also) students' society in college or university.

free[1]. (Also, adv.) ~*ly*, without cost or

payment, (Naut.) not close-hauled. ~ *house*, public house not tied to a particular brewery.

freeze. (Also) peg or stabilize (prices, wages, etc.); also as n., as *wage ~*.

freighter. (Also) freight-carrying air-craft.

frenetic. Var. of PHRENETIC.

frequency. ~ *modulation* (Radio), varying the ~ of the carrier wave in accordance with speech or music, system of broadcasting using this method of modulation.

frigate. (Also, in recent use) corvette, sloop, small destroyer.

frigid. (Also) sexually irresponsive.

frog[1]. ~*man*, person equipped for underwater operations esp. against enemy shipping.

front (n.). (Also, Meteor.) boundary between cold & warm air masses (*cold, warm, ~*, forward boundary of a mass of advancing cold, warm, air).

fugue. (Also) loss of memory coupled with disappearance from one's usual haunts.

fully. ~ *fashioned*, (of women's stockings) seamed & shaped.

fusion. ~ *bomb*, hydrogen bomb.

fuss (n.). *~-pot* (colloq.), person who is always making a ~.

G

gag (v.i.). (Also) retch, choke.

gaggle, n., & v.i. **1.** Flock (of geese); (derog.) company (of women). **2.** v.i. (Of geese) cackle. [prob. imit.]

galliard, n. (hist.). Quick & lively dance in triple time for two persons. [f. OF *gaillard*, etym. dub.]

gambit. (Also, fig.) opening move in some action etc.

gamma. ~ *plus*, rather better than third-class.

gammy, a. (sl.). = GAME[4]. [?]

*gang. (Also, v.t.) arrange (tools etc.) to work in co-ordination.

gangling (-ngg-), a. Loosely built, straggling. [f. *gangle* frequent. of GANG]

gas (n.). *~holder*, large receptacle for storing ~, gasometer: ~*ification*, (also) underground production of ~ from un-mined coal.

gash[2] a. (naut. sl.). Spare, extra. [?]

*gat, n. (sl.). Gun, revolver. [abbr. of GATLING]

gauss. (Now) unit of magnetic induction.

gear (vb). (Also) make (an industry or factory) subservient or ancillary to another, or to a programme.

Geiger counter (gīˈg-), n. (In full *Geiger-Müller counter*) device for detecting radio-activity consisting of a gas-filled cylindrical cathode having for its anode a thin wire running down the centre, every charged particle entering

cylinder being recorded. [f. *Geiger*, whose invention was improved by *Müller*]

general (a.), ~ *hospital*, (also) one not specializing in any particular disease.

gen'ocide, n. Extermination of a race. [f. Gk *genos* race, -CIDE (2)]

genteel. Hence ~ISM (4) n., word used instead of the ordinary natural word because it is thought to be more ~, e.g. *lady-dog* for *bitch*, *perspire* for *sweat*.

gēomórphŏl'ŏgy, n. Study of the physical features of the (crust of the) earth and its geological structures. [GEO-, MORPHOLOGY]

gēophy̆s'ĭcs (-z-), n. The physics of the earth. Hence ~ICIST n. [GEO-]

gēriăt'rĭc, a. Relating to ~ics n. pl., branch of medical science dealing with old age & its diseases. So **gēriatri'cian** (-shn), ~IST (3), ~Y[1], (jĕrĭ'a-), nn. [f. Gk *gēras* old age, *iātros* physician, -IC]

gēr'mănĭum, n. Brittle white metallic element. [mod. L, f. *Germanus* GERMAN[2]]

gērŏntŏl'ŏgy (g-, j-), n. Scientific study of old age & its diseases. [f. Gk *gerōn -ontos* old man, -LOGY]

get', ~ *together*, (also) unite in discussion, promotion of plan, etc.; ~-*together* n., (social) assembly.

gĭlt³ (g-), n. Young sow. [f. ON *gyltr*]

***gĭmm'ĭck** (g-), n. (sl.). Tricky device. [?]

gĭn², ~ *and* n[2]; *pink* ~, ~ flavoured with angostura bitters.

gĭrl. (Also) female (~ *friend*).

glăss¹, ~ *wool*, ~ in form of fine fibres for packing & insulation.

glēep, n. Kind of atomic pile. [f. initials of graphite low energy experimental pile]

go¹. *Go for*, (also) be applicable to; *go it alone*, act by oneself or without support.

***gŏb'blede̅gook'** (-lĕdĭ-), -dy̆-, n. (sl.). Pompous official jargon. [imit. of turkey-cock]

gŏd¹. *God's (own) country*, alleged description of the U.S. by Americans.

gōld. ~ *bloc* (of countries with currencies tied to ~); *go off* ~, abandon the ~ STANDARD.

gŏng (n.). (Also, sl.) medal.

***goŏn**, n. Person hired by racketeers to terrorize workers; stupid person. [perh. f. *gorilla* & *baboon*; orig. a subhuman creature in a comic strip]

goy, n. (Yiddish for) Gentile. [Heb., = nation]

grade (n.). *(Also) class, form, in school.

gradua̅te². So ~ *and* n., one about to receive an academic degree.

grape. ~-*vine*, (also) rumour, false report.

graph¹. (Also, v.t.) plot or trace on a ~.

grăt'ĭcule, n. Fine lines or fibres incorporated in telescope or other optical instrument as measuring scale or as aid in locating objects; (Surveying) network or lines on paper representing meridians & parallels. [F, f. med. L *graticula* for *craticula* gridiron (L *cratis* hurdle, -ULE)]

green¹ (a.), ~ *light* (colloq.), permission to go ahead with some project.

grey. ~ *eminence*, = *éminence grise* (see *éminence*).

grŏp'er, n. Var. of GROUPER.

ground¹. ~ *nut*, (also) now usual name for PEAnut or monkey-nut.

guide¹. (Also, esp. in Switzerland etc.) professional mountain-climber.

guide². ~d *missiles* (under remote control).

guinea. ~-*pig*, (also) person used as subject for medical experiment.

gun. (Also) insecticide spray.

H

haggadah. (Also) ritual for Passover Eve.

hair. ~-*do* (colloq.), style or process of woman's ~-*dressing*.

half (a.). ~-*time*, time showing that ~ of a game or contest is completed.

ham¹ (~-*fisted*(sl.),heavy-handed,clumsy.

***hăm'burger** (~g-), n. (Also *Hamburg steak*) chopped steak usu. cooked or eaten with onions; kind of sausage. [*Hamburg* in Germany... ~-ER¹]

hammer. ~ *and sickle*, symbol of worker and peasant, emblem on the national flag of the U.S.S.R.

hand². ~-*out*, (also) information ~ed out to the press etc.

hard. ~*board*, stiff type of pasteboard made from wood waste & used as substitute for wood.

have¹. *He has had it*, (also) there's no longer any chance that he'll get it, (also) his fate is sealed.

|| **hăv'er**, v.i. & n. (Sc.). **1.** Talk foolishly, babble. **2.** n. (usu. pl.). Foolish talk, nonsense. [?]

hay², hey² (hā), n. (Figure in) country dance. [?]

H-bomb (āch'bŏm), n. †Hydrogen bomb. [H for HYDROGEN]

head¹. ~-*word*, word forming a heading. Euphem. for HELL in imprecations.

heck², n. (sl.). *(Also) employees.

help². *(Also) employees.

hetero-. ~*cyc'lic*, (of chem. compounds) with molecule of a ring composed of atoms of different kinds.

high (a.). ~ *light*, (also) moment or detail of vivid interest, outstanding feature; ~*light* v.t., bring into prominence.

hind'sight (-sīt), n. Back sight of gun; (joc.) wisdom after the event (opp. *fore-sight*). [HIND³, SIGHT¹]

Hitt'ite, n. & a. **1.** Member, language, of an ancient people of Asia Minor & Syria. **2.** adj. Of the ~s or ~. [f. Heb. *Hittim*]

hive (vb.). ~ *off*, (of firm) assign production of some goods to subsidiary company in order to avoid complete nationalization.

hollow² (a.). ~ *ware*, = articles of metal, china, etc., as pots, kettles, jugs.

hŏl′us-bōl′us, adv. All in a lump, altogether. [app. sham L.]

holy (a.). ~ *Willie*, a hypocritically pious person.

hombre (ŏm′brā), n. Man. [Sp.]

home¹. *~work*, work (to be) done at ~, esp. lessons to be done by a school-child at ~.

home². *Homing device*, mechanism for automatic guiding of missiles.

homogeneous. Hence **homŏ′gēniZE** v.t. make ~, make (milk) more digestible by breaking up the fat droplets into smaller particles.

hood (n.). *(Also)* bonnet of motor-car.

***Hoo′sier** (-zher), n. (Nickname for) inhabitant of State of Indiana. [?]

hospital. Hence ~IZE v.t., admit, confine, so difficult to dispose of.

hot¹ (a.). *(Also, sl.,* of stolen jewellery, bank-notes, etc.) easily identifiable & so difficult to dispose of.

hotel′ier, n. Hotel-keeper. [F *hôtelier*]

hound¹. *(Also)* dogfish (short for ~*fish*).

***hûrding′er**, n. (sl.). Exceptionally good person or thing. [?]

hydrogen. ~ *bomb*, (also *fusion* or *thermonuclear bomb*) bomb charged with a compound, in which nuclear reaction, initiated by an atomic bomb contained in it, turns ~ into helium with an enormous release of energy.

hȳdrŏx′ide, n. (chem.). Compound of element or radical with hydrogen & oxygen, not with water. [HYDRO- +OXIDE]

hypertén′s|ion (-shn), n. Abnormally high blood pressure. So ~IVE a. [HYPER- +TENSION]

hypodermic. *~ needle, syringe,* for ~ injection. (Also, n.) ~ injection, syringe.

hypoten′s|ion (-shn), n. Low blood pressure. So ~IVE a. [HYPO- +TENSION]

I

ice¹. *Dry* ~, frozen carbon dioxide; *~*box*, refrigerator; *~*hockey* (played on skates).

idle (v.i.). (Also, of motor-car, aero, etc., engine) revolve slowly with throttle closed.

impact¹. (Also) effect, influence.

implaus′|ible (-z-), a. Not plausible. Hence or cogn. ~iBIL′ITY n., ~iBLY² adv. [M-²]

impŏnderabil′ia, n. pl. Imponderables. [L]

***incommūnica′dō** (-ah-), a. Without means of communication (of prisoner) in solitary confinement. [Sp. (-*mu-*)]

indŏc′trin|āte, v.t. Teach, instruct; imbue with a doctrine, idea, or opinion. Hence ~A′TION n. [IN-³, DOCTRINE, -ATE³]

infra-. *~structure*, system of airfields, telecommunications, & public services forming a basis for the defence of Europe.

inter-. ~*plan′etary* a., between planets; ~*zōn′al* a., based upon, existing between, two or more zones of occupation in Germany.

intermission. (Also) interval in theatre etc., musical selection during this.

intra-. ~*ven′ous*, in(to) a vein or veins.

invert². ~ *sugar*, mixture of dextrose & laevulose.

iron¹. ~ *curtain*, (esp., recently) barrier to passage of information at (esp. Western) limit of Soviet sphere of influence.

irradiate. (Also) subject to sunlight or ultra-violet rays.

Israel. (Also) the Jewish State established in Palestine in May 1948; also attrib. Hence ~i (izrā′ī) a. & n., (inhabitant) of this State.

Italian. Hence (also) ~ATE² a., having ~ style or appearance.

J

jăcarăn′da, n. Kinds of tropical American hardwood tree with scented wood & trumpet-shaped blue flowers. [Braz.]

***jalŏp(p)′y**, n. A dilapidated motor-car. [?]

jet². (Also, colloq.) ~*propelled* plane.

*jive, n., & v.i. 1. Kind of jazz music. 2. v.i. Play ~, dance to ~. [?]

jockey² *for position*, try to gain an advantageous position esp. by skilful manoeuvring in yacht-racing, (also) try to gain an unfair advantage.

‖ jō′ey², n. (sl.). A threepenny (orig. a fourpenny) bit. [f. *Joseph Hume*]

jŭdd′er, v.i. & n. 1. Shake, wobble. 2. n. Shaking, wobbling. [?]

jū′dō (jōō-), n. (Now usu. name for) JU-JUTSU. [Jap.]

*juke-bŏx (jōōk), n. Machine that automatically plays selected gramophone records when coin is inserted. [?]

K

*kib′itzer, n. (colloq.). Meddlesome person, one who gives advice gratuitously, one who watches a game of cards from behind the players. [Yiddish, f. G *kiebitz* lapwing]

kil′ō (or kē-), n. (pl. ~s). Abbr. for KILOGRAM(ME), KILOMETRE. [F]

kiosk. (Also) structure for public telephone.

kiwi. (Also, colloq., K~) a New Zealander.

Knĕss′et, n. Israeli parliament. [Heb.]

knot¹. (Also) unit of speed equivalent to a nautical mile per hour.

knŏt³, n. Small wading bird of sandpiper family. [?]

Koin′ē, n. The common literary language of the Greeks from the close of classical Attic to the Byzantine era. [f. Gk *koinē* (*dialektos*) common (language)]

kremlin. *The K~,* (used for) the Russian Government. *~'s line* (Naut.), line marked on compass showing direction of ship's head.

Kyrie eleison. Also pron. kǐ'riē.

L

lab, n. (colloq.). Laboratory. [abbr.]

Lāl'an, a. & n. (Sc.). I. Of the Lowland Scots dialect. **2.** n. (Also *~s*) Lowland dialect. [var. of *Low 'land*]

Lambeth. *~ degree,* honorary degree conferred by Archbishop of Canterbury.

land.[2] (Also, of aircraft) come down to ground or surface of water.

Land.[3] (Ger.) n. (pl. *Länder,* pr. lěn'ĕ). Land, country. [G]

Latin. *~ Quarter* (F *Quartier Latin*), educational centre of Paris, where ~ was spoken in the Middle Ages, noted for its unconventional mode of life.

lay.[3] *~-by,* portion of road extended to permit a vehicle to stop there without interfering with traffic; *~out,* (also): (of plans etc.) drawing showing arrangement, make-up of book, newspaper, advertisement, etc.

lean.[2] (vb). *~ over backwards,* go to the other extreme, go to the limit of eagerness (to agree).

left (n.). Hence (also, colloq.) *~'ISM* (3) n., principles or policy of the political *~,*
~'IST (2) n. & a.

leg (n.). (Also, colloq.): one of two games constituting a round; hop or stage of long-distance flight.

Lēn'inism, n. Political theories & practices of Nikolai Lenin (d. 1924). So *~IST*

Lesbian. (Also, n.) a female homosexual.

lethal. Hence **lēthǎl'rry** n.

leucó'tomy, n. (med.). Incision by kind of needle (*leuc'otome*) into frontal lobe of brain to relieve some cases of mental disorder. [f. Gk *leukos* white, *-TOMY*]

liaison. Hence **liaise'** (-z) v.i., establish or maintain *~ with.*

lig'er (-g-), n. Offspring of lion & tigress [portmanteau wd]

line.[2] (Also) one of the very narrow vertical sections in which televised scenes are photographed & reproduced.

live.[2] (Of broadcast) heard during the occurrence of an event, not a recording.

loan[2], loan'ing, nn. (Sc.). Lane; open space where cows are milked. [OE *tone*]
LANE: *-ING[1]*

lobót'omỹ, n. (med.). = †*Leucotomy.* [f. LOBE, *-O-, -TOMY*]

lodging. *~ turn,* spell of duty in railway service during which a train crew sleeps away from home for a night.

logistics. Hence **logis'tic** a.

long[1] (a.). *~-distance,* (of weather forecast) made several days in advance.

lŏrdō'sis, n. (med.). Forward curvature of spine. [Gk, **ə** *lordos* bent back, *-OSIS*]

lubber. *(Also, euphem.)* brothel-keeper.

lunatic (a.). *~ fringe,* the more eccentric or visionary adherents of a political or other movement.

M

madam. *(Also,* euphem.) brothel-keeper.

măg'nētrŏn, n. (phys.). Thermionic tube for generating very high frequency oscillations. [f. MAGNET+(ELEC)TRON]

mahatma. (Also, *M~*) popularly prefixed as title in India to names of exalted personages, esp. Gandhi.

make[1]. *~-up.* (Also): (cosmetics for) woman's facial decoration; person's character & temperament.

major[2]. *(Also) a student's special subject or course; (v.i.) take, or qualify *in,* a.*,

man[1]. *~-hour,* work done by one ~ in one hour.

mania. Hence **mănǐ'rc** a., of or affected by *~(manic-depressive psychosis,* kind of mental disorder alternating between periods of elation & depression, occas. with intermediate periods of sanity).

Marc'an, a. Of St Mark. [f. L *Marcus* Mark, *-AN*]

mǎrge[2]. (Also, n.) Margarine. [abbr.]

marginal. (Also, of land) difficult & expensive to cultivate.

marijuana, -huana, (mahrǐhwah'neh), n. Dried leaves of Indian hemp, used to make doped cigarettes (called *reefers*). Sp. *-hu-*]

marine (n.). (Also) specialist in commando & amphibious operations.

mark[2]. *~-up* n. (commerce.), amount added by shopkeepers to cost price of goods to cover overhead charges & profit.

mass[2] (n.). *~-spectrograph,* apparatus separating isotopes by atomic discharge through electric & magnetic fields.

mastoid. *~ operation,* surgical procedure for relief of disease of tympanum or eardrum.

maximum. (Also, adj.) largest or largest possible.

*McCar'thyism (makǎr-), n. Policy of hunting out (suspected) Communists & removing them esp. from Government departments. Hence *~ISM* a. & n. [f. Joseph *McCartha,* U.S. senator, *-ISM*]

mean.[3]. *~s test,* principle of requiring some proof of need as condition of assistance.

mean.[3] *(Also) uncomfortable, malicious, ill tempered.

median (n.). (Also, Math.) straight line drawn from angular point of triangle to middle of opposite side.

mega-. ~*ton*, 1,000,000 tons.

meiosis. (Also, Biol.) phase of nuclear change in germ cells.

*meld[1], v.t. & i. Merge. [perh. f. *melt* + *weld*]

meld[2], v.t. & i., & n. (In some card games) declare for a score; (n.) act of ~*ing*, group of cards (to be) ~*ed*. [f. G *melden* announce]

melŏd'ic, a. Of or relating to melody. [f. F *mélodique* (as MELODY, see -IC)]

member. || (Also) person admitted to Order of the British Empire, 5th class (M.B.E.), & to Royal Victorian Order, 4th or 5th class (M.V.O.).

mĕs'ŏn, n. (phys.). Fundamental particle intermediate in mass between proton & electron, found in cosmic rays & atomic nuclei. [f. Gk *mesos* middle]

meticulous. (Also, pop.) very careful, accurate.

micro-[1]. ~*film*, (also, v.t. & i.) photograph on ~*film*; ~*organism*, organism of (ultra-) microscopic size; ~*wave*, Hertzian wave of length between 50 cms & 1 cm.

mil'eage (-lĭj), n. Var. of MILAGE.

milk[1], ~*run* (U.S. Air Force), regularly recurring operational flight (with ref. to ~*man's* daily round).

mill[2]. ~*ing machine*, machine tool for cutting grooves or slots in metal sheets.

mine[2]. Hence **mǐn'ING**[4](1) n. (freq. in comb., as *coal*, *gold*, -*mining*; also attrib., as *mining engineer*)

minimum. (Also, adj.) smallest or smallest possible.

mistreat', v.t. Treat badly. Hence ~MENT n. [MIS-[1]]

model[2]. (Also, v.i.) act or pose as an artist's model or a mannequin.

modulate. modulation. (also, Radio) alteration in amplitude or frequency of a wave by a frequency of a different order.

mŏll, n. Prostitute; gangster's mistress. [pet form of *Mary*]

monitor (n.). (Also) detector for induced radio-activity, esp. in workers in an atomic plant.

monolith. ~*ic*, (also) solidly uniform throughout, showing or allowing no variation.

mōp'ĕd, n. Motorized pedal cycle. [f. *motorized pedal*]

morgue[1]. (Also, Journalism) repository where miscellaneous material for reference is kept.

moron. Hence **morŏn'ic** a.

mōtěl', n. Hotel or group of furnished cabins by the roadside where motorists may stay for the night. [f. *motorists' hotel*]

moth. ~*ball*, (also) airtight plastic cover sprayed on & enclosing working parts of gun-mountings, machinery, etc. of ship.

move[1]. (Also) change of residence, business premises, etc.

mugwump. (Also) one who sits on the fence.

multi-. ~*lateral*, (also, of agreement, treaty, etc.) in which more than two sides or states participate; ~*lingʼual* (-nggw-), in many languages.

Mün'ich (-ĭk), n. An act of appeasement between nations. [f. the agreement to dismember Czechoslovakia made with Hitler in 1938 at ~ in S. Germany]

mūsicŏl'ogȳ (-z-), n. All study of music except that directed to proficiency in performance or composition. Hence ~IST n., **mūsicŏlo'gICAL** a., (-z-). [f. MUSIC+-OLOGY]

must[3] *(Also, n.) *a* ~, a thing that cannot or should not be missed.

mystique (-tēk), n. The atmosphere of mystery & veneration investing some creeds, doctrines, arts, professions, etc., or personages; any professional skill or technique which mystifies & impresses the layman. [F, as MYSTIC]

mỹxōm'a, n. (path.; pl. ~*ta*). Tumour of mucous or gelatinous tissue. Hence ~tōs'IS n., virus disease in rabbits. [mod. L, f. Gk *myxa* mucus]

N

nap[3]. (Also, v.t.) name (horse) as probable winner.

năp'alm (-ahm), n. Product of naphthalene & coco-nut oil (~ *bomb*, one containing jellied petrol). [NA(PHTHALENT), PALM[1]]

national (n. pl.). (Also) citizens of a specified country.

năt'ter, v.i. (colloq.). Chatter idly; grumble, talk fretfully. Hence ~**ed** (-erd), ~ỹ, aa., peevish. [var. of dial. *gnatter* be peevish]

needle (v.t.). (Also) incite, irritate, prod into action.

net[1](n.). ~*work*, (also) a number of broadcasting stations connected for simultaneous broadcast of same programme. **never.** *Never-never system* (joc.), hire-purchase system.

new[1]. ~ *look*, modern (1947) fashion in women's dress marked esp. by longer & fuller skirt, (colloq.) up-to-date appearance.

nostalgia. (Also) sentimental yearning for (some period of) the past.

not. ~ *too well*, rather ill, rather badly.

notation. *(Also) note, annotation.

note[1]. ~*case*, pocket wallet for holding bank-notes.

novēn'a, n. (R.-C. Church). Devotion consisting of special prayers or services on nine successive days. [med. L, f. L *novem* nine]

nub. (Also) point or gist (*of* matter or story).

nucle|us. ~*ar fission*, splitting up of a

heavy atom, e.g. of uranium, into two or more new atoms, with an enormous release of energy; ~ar fuel, source of atomic energy; ~ar reactor, atomic PILE².
nun'atak (-tō-), n. Isolated peak of rock projecting above the surface of land ice or snow e.g. in Greenland. [Eskimo]
nutrition. Hence ~AL (-shon-) a., of or relating to ~.

O

O.¹ (Also) symbol for nought, cipher.
ŏbscūr'um per ŏbscūr'ius, n.=IGNOTUM PER IGNOTIUS. [L., = the obscure by the still more obscure.]
occlude. occlusion. (also, Meteor.) closing of the cold *front* on to the warm front in a depression.
odds. ~ *on*, state of betting when ~ are laid.
oer'stèd (ōr-), n. Unit of magnetic force. [O—, Danish physicist (d. 1851)]
oestrum. (Also) sexual heat of animals, rut.
off (prep.)., (Also) with a handicap of, as *he plays* ~ *5*; *~-shore purchases, goods &c.,* purchased by one country in another country, esp. orders placed by the U.S. in other countries for anything connected with the defence programme; ~-*white,* not quite white.
officer. ‖ (Also) member of 4th class of Order of the British Empire (O.B.E.).
official (n.). Hence (also) ~ESE' (-shólēz)
n., ~ jargon.
offset. (Also v.t.) counterbalance, compensate.
-ōma, suf. used to denote tumour or other abnormal growth. [Gk -ōma -ōmatos]
optic (n.). ‖ (Also) device fastened to neck of bottle for measuring out spirits in public houses.
ŏptŏm'ĕter. Hence ~m'ĕtrist n., sight-tester. ~m'ĕtry n.
oral. (Also, colloq., n.) ~ examination.
orbit. (Also, v.i., of satellite &c.) move in an ~.
ŏrogĕn'esis, n. (geol.). Process of making mountains. [Gk *oros* mountain, GENESIS]
orth(o)-. ~*odŏn'tia* (-shiǒ), ~*odŏn'tics,* correction of irregularities in teeth, ~*odŏn'tic* a., ~*odŏn'tist* n.
***Os'car** (ŏs-). n. One of the statuettes awarded by the Motion Picture Academy for excellence in acting, directing, etc. [man's name]
ŏt'ic (*or* ō-). a. Of or relating to the ear. [f. Gk *ous ōtos* ear, -IC]
out-. ~*smart* v.t. (colloq.), be too clever for.
outside (adj.). (Also, of a chance) remote, very unlikely.
~*odŏn'tic* a., ~*odŏn'tist* n.
over-. ~*fulfil'ment* n., completion of a
over (adv.). Hence ~IX² adv. (chiefly U.S. & Sc.), excessively, too.

P

paddock. (Also, Austral.) field, plot of land.
padlock (n.). ~ *law,* one providing for closing & locking up premises.
paed(o)-, ped(o)-. Hence ~*iāt'rics* n. pl., branch of medical science dealing with the study of childhood & diseases of children, so ~*iàtri'cian* (-shn), ~*iàt'rist,* nn. [Gk *iātros* physician]
palimpsest. (Also) monumental brass turned & re-engraved on reverse side.
panel. (Also) team in some radio quiz programmes. Hence ~LIST n., member of this.
papyro-. ~*logist,* ~*logy,* (-ŏl-), student, study, of ancient papyri.
para-¹. (Also, Chem., before a vowel *par-*) denoting modification of substance to which name prefix is attached (*paral-dehyde,* polymer of ALDEHYDE, used as
paranoia. Hence **pàranoi'**AC a. & n.
par avion (pär ávyawn'), n. By airmail. [F, = by aeroplane]
part¹ (n.). ~ *time,* less than full time; ~*-timer* (colloq.), ~*-time* worker.
pāsh, n. (sl.). Passion. [abbr.]
pĕd'icūre, n., & v.t. 1. Chiropody: chiropodist. 2. v.t. Cure or treat (feet) by removing corns etc. [f. F *pédicure* f. L *pes pedis* foot + *cura* care]
pedŏl'ogy, n. Science of soils. Hence **pedŏlŏ'gist** n. [f. Gk *pedon* ground, -LOGY]
pelōr'us, n. Sighting device on ship's compass for taking bearings. [?]
pĕnàm'ūlar, a. Almost ring-like. [f. L *paene* almost, ANNULAR]
pentagon. *The P~,* headquarters of U.S. defence forces, in Washington.
penthouse. *(Also) apartment or flat built on roof.
perimeter. (Also) outer boundary of camp or fortification.
***persona.** ~ *non grāt'a,* unacceptable person.
pervert². (Also, Psych.) person showing sexual perversion.
petit. ~ *four* (foor), small fancy biscuit.
phase. (Also) aspect (of situation or question).
phillum'enist (-loo-, ĭl-), n. Student or collector of match-box labels. [f. PHIL-, L *lumen* light, -IST]

(right column, continuing)
Soviet five-year plan before the appointed time; ~*men,* (also) mining ~*seer,* an underground foreman.
ŏx'idāte, v.t.& i. Oxidize. Hence **ŏxidā'-** TION n., oxidizing or being oxidized, combination with oxygen. [f. F *oxider,* -ATE²]
‖ **ŏx'ter, n., & v.t.** (Sc., Ir.) Armpit; inner side of upper arm. 2. v.t. Support with or by taking the arm, put under the arm; hug. [f. OE *ōxta*]

phōn′ēme, n. (philol.). A unit of significant sound in a given language. Hence **phonēm′ıc** a. [f. F *phonème* f. Gk *phōnēma* sound]

photo. ~*-finish*, close finish of horse-race photographed to enable judge to decide winner.

photo-. ~*syn′thesis*, process by which the energy of sunlight is trapped by the chlorophyll of green plants & used to build up complex materials from carbon dioxide & water.

piece¹. ~ *Go to* ~*s* (fig.), collapse.

pilot (n.). ~ *balloon*, small balloon whose movements are observed as it rises in the air, used to ascertain direction & velocity of currents at various heights; ~ *scheme*, preliminary experimental trial of project on small scale.

pin¹. ~*point* v.t., (also) designate precisely.

pipe¹. ~*line*, (also, fig.) continuous flow of goods in transit from producer to retailer or (industrial) consumer etc.

placate. Hence **plāc′atory** a., propitiatory.

plant¹. (Also) factory.

plastic. Hence (also) ~**izer** n., substance that produces or promotes ~*ity*.

plēd. U.S., Sc., & dial. past & p.p. of PLEAD.

plough². ~ *a lonely furrow*, take one's own solitary course.

point¹. ~ *of no return*, ~ in a long-distance flight over the ocean at which an aircraft has not enough fuel to reach to its starting-place & must continue onwards; also fig.

poin′tillism (pwăn-), n. Method of producing light effects by crowding a surface with small spots of various colours, which are blended by the eye. So ~**ist** n. [f. F *pointillisme* f. *pointiller* mark with dots f. *point* POINT¹, ISM]

pōl′io, n. (colloq.). (Person suffering from) poliomyelitis. [abbr.]

Polyhym′nia, n. The Muse of sacred song. [L. f. Gk *Polumnia* (POLY-, HYMN)]

pomm′y, n. (sl.). British immigrant to Australia or New Zealand. [?]

pontifical. (Also) assuming infallibility, pompously dogmatic.

pontificate. (Also, v.i, pr. -āt) POSTIFY.

pool² (n.). *Football* ~, form of gambling in which a proportion of the entry money for the competition is awarded in prizes to those who correctly forecast the results of certain football matches.

portfolio. (Also) list of investments held by company etc.

Portuguese. ~ *man-of-war*, dangerous (sub-)tropical jellyfish with sail-shaped crest & poisonous sting, travelling rarely to Britain.

post-. ~*-post′script* (abbr. P.P.S.), a second postscript.

postal. *~ card*, postcard with printed stamp sold by the post-office.

post-mortem (n.). (Also, colloq.) subsequent discussion of (esp. card) game.

pot¹. ~*-roast*, (n.) piece of meat cooked by braising, (v.t.) braise; ~*-shot*, (also) random shot.

pot². (Also) abridge, epitomize.

poundage. (Also) charge on postal order etc.

powder (n.). ~*-room*, ladies' cloakroom.

power. (Also, v.t.) supply (vehicle, vessel, etc.) with ~ (esp. of engine).

prēd′ator, n. Predatory animal. [f. L *praedator* (see PREDATORY)]

prēf′ab, n. (colloq.). Prefabricated house. [abbr.]

premature. (Also, n.) ~ explosion of shell.

press². ~*-button war* (carried on by means of guided missiles whose flight is controlled by ~*ing* a button).

pressure. ~*-cooker*, apparatus for cooking under high ~ at high temperature, so ~*-cooking*; ~ *group*, group exerting ~ on a government etc. for their own special purpose.

preventive (a.). ~ *custody*, detention.

price. *At a* ~, at a relatively high cost; ~ *oneself out of the market*, charge a prohibitive ~.

prime³. (Also) inject petrol into (cylinder or carburettor of internal-combustion engine).

procedure. Hence ~AL (-dyer-) a., of or relating to ~*e*.

profile (n.). (Also, Journalism) short biographical or character sketch.

proliferate. (Also) increase rapidly.

prŏp³, n. (colloq.). Aircraft propeller. [abbr.]

prŏp⁴, n. (theatr.) Stage property. [abbr.]

propeller. ~ *turbine* or *prŏp′-jet engine*, aircraft engine having a turbine-driven ~.

prōt′ıum, n. (chem.). Ordinary hydrogen as dist. from heavy hydrogen (DEUTERIUM). [f. PROT(O)-, -IUM]

protocol. (Also) diplomatic etiquette.

proximity. ~ *fuse*, radio device causing projectile to explode when near target.

psēph′ŏl′ogy (or s-), n. Study of elections and voting. Hence ~ol′ogıst n. [f. Gk *psephos* pebble, vote, -LOGY]

psycho-. ~*ŏm′etry*, (also) measurement of mental states or processes, so ~*ŏmet′rics* n. pl.; ~*ŏsomăt′ıc* a., of mind & body, (of bodily disease) caused or made worse by worry.

psychosis. Hence **psychŏt′ıc** (psĭk-, sĭk-) a. & n., of, relating to, (person) suffering from, a ~.

public (a.). ~ *relations*, relations of a department, organization, etc. with the general—(~ *relations officer*, abbr. *P.R.O.*, person who gives out information to the ~ in connexion with some department etc.).

pŭl′chritūde (-kr-), n. Beauty. [f. L *pulchritudo* (*pulcher* beautiful, -TUDE)]

pull¹. ~-*out* n., page or plate in book that unfolds out from front edge of leaves to facilitate reference.

puppet. ~ *state*, country professing to be independent but actually under the control of some greater power, so ~ *king*, ~ *ruler*.

purple (a.). ~ *patch*, ornate passage in literary composition.

purport. Hence ~édly² adv.

pursuit. *~ *plane*, fighter aircraft. *~-*button war*, = †press-button war.

pursy. *~-*foot* v.i., move stealthily, act cautiously.

pyjamas. Also attrib. in sing. form **pyjama** (-ah-), as *pyjama jacket*, *trousers*.

pyrosis, n. (med.). Burning sensation in the stomach with eructation of watery fluid, water-brash. [mod. L f. Gk *purōsis* f. *pur* fire]

Q

quar'tile (kwŏr-), a. & n. (astrol.). **1.** Connected with or relating to an aspect of two heavenly bodies which are 90° distant from each other. **2.** n. A ~ aspect. [f. med. L *quartilis* f. *quartus* fourth]

quite. (Also) rather, to some extent, as *it took ~ a long time*; ~ *a few*, a fair number.

quota. (Also): quantity of goods which under Government controls must be manufactured, exported, imported, etc.; number of yearly immigrants allowed to enter the United States from any one country.

R

radio-. ~*gen'ic* a., produced by ~ activity, suitable for being broadcast by radio; ~*sonde*, miniature radio transmitter, carried aloft in a balloon & descending by parachute, for broadcasting pressure, temperature, & humidity at various levels.

rail¹ (n.). ~(*way*)*man*, ~*way* employee. Hence ~'AGE (4).

rake¹ (n.). (Also) slope of stage or auditorium in theatre.

react. Hence (also) **reac'tor²** n., atomic pile² (also *nuclear ~or*).

reaction. (Also) impression, influence.

reactivate, v.t. Restore to a state of activity. Hence **reactiva'TION** n. [RE- 8]

ready (v.t.). (Also) make ~, prepare.

rebar'bative, a. Repellent, unattractive. [f. F *rébarbatif, -ive,* f. *barbe* beard]

rec'ap. v.t. & n. (colloq.). Recapitulate; (n.) recapitulation. [abbr.]

recess. *(Also, v.i.) take a ~, adjourn.

record¹. (Also, Radio) register & reproduce (item, programme) by RECORDING.

red. ||~-*brick*, (of university) of modern foundation.

redeploy'ment, n. Improved physical arrangements in factories as means of increasing output. [RE- 8]

reefer². n. See †*marijuana.* [?]

ref. n. (colloq.). Football referee. [abbr.]

release¹. (Also) make (information) public.

remand (n.). ~ *home*, temporary institution for young persons.

remembrance. R~ *Day*, day (11th November, ARMISTICE *Day*, or the Sunday immediately preceding it) commemorating those who fell in the wars of 1914-18 & 1939-45.

rep³, n. (sl.). Repertory theatre or company. [abbr.]

rep'aint, n. A repainted golf-ball. [RE- 9]

replacement. (Also) person or thing that replaces another.

report². (Also) periodical statement on a pupil's work, conduct, etc. at school.

resist. Hence (also) ~*or²* n., device offering electrical resistance.

reward. ~*ing* a., (of task, book, etc.) well worth doing, reading, etc.

rhesus. R~ *factor* (abbr. *Rh-factor*), substance occurring in red blood cells of most persons and some animals (as in the ~ *monkey,* in which it was first observed). Subjects in which this substance is present, absent, are said to be *Rh-positive, Rh-negative.*

rocket². Hence ~RY n., study or use of ~s.

rode². v.i. (Of wildfowl) fly landward in the evening. (of woodcock) fly in evening during breeding season. [?]

roman-à-clef (rōmahn' ah klā'), n. Novel in which real persons or events appear in disguise. [F, = novel with a key]

rotary (n.). *(Also) traffic roundabout.

round³ (adv.). ~ *about,* (adj.) approximately (*it will cost ~ about £10*).

row¹. *~*house,* = †*terrace-house.*

run¹. (Also) allow (account, bill) to accumulate for some time before paying.

run². ~ -*down,* reduction in numbers esp. of armed forces, by demobilization. ~ *of the mill* or *mine,* ordinary or average product or specimen, not specially selected or distributed.

rün'cible spoon, n. Kind of fork with three broad prongs, one with a cutting edge, and hollowed out like a spoon. [*runcible,* nonsense word of Edward Lear (d. 1888), SPOON¹]

running. ~ *commentary,* oral description of events in progress.

rush² (n.). (Also, Cinemat.) first print or preliminary showing of film before cutting.

sabbatical. ~ *year*, (also) year's leave granted to university professor for study, travel, etc. [F]

sǎb'oteur (-tőr), n. One who commits sabotage. [F]

sadism. (Also) pleasure derived from inflicting or watching cruelty.

saleable. Var. of SALABLE.

sám'ba, n. Brazilian native dance; ballroom dance imitative of this. [Braz.]

sate² (sát, sāt). Arch. past & p.p. of SIT.

satellite. (Also) artificial body launched from & encircling the earth; ~ *state*, country subservient to or controlled by a greater power; ~ *town*, smaller town dependent on a larger town for short distance away.

scatter. (Also, n.) act of ~ing, extent of distribution esp. of shot.

Schnork'el (shn-), n. (German name for) SNORT²

scooter. (Also) simple kind of motor cycle.

score (n.). (Also) a weight of 20 (or 21) pounds, esp. in weighing pigs or oxen.

scramble (v.t.). (Also) after frequency of transmitted speech of (telephone conversation) so as to make it unintelligible to an eavesdropper.

screen (v.t.). (Also) prevent from causing electrical interference.

scribe (n.). (Also) ancient or medieval copyist of manuscripts.

script. (Also) kind of non-cursive handwriting imitating print.

sculduggery. See †skul(l)duggery.

sea. ~ *food*, edible salt-water (shell)fish; ~ *shell*, shell of any salt-water mollusc.

seed (n.). (Also, colloq.) ~ed competitor.

self-. ~*service* 1, (attrib., of restaurant, shop, etc.) in which customers help themselves to food or goods & afterwards pay a cashier, thereby reducing the need for sales assistants. (n.) this kind of service.

sell (vb). *(Also): advertise or publish merits of; give (person) information on value of something, inspire with desire to possess something; *be sold on*, be enthusiastic about. ~ers' market (in which goods are scarce & high prices favour ~ers).

sémlnar', n. Small class at university for discussion & research; *conference of specialists; short intensive course of study. [G, as seminary]

Sénuss'i (-ōō-), n. (Now usu. form of) SENOUS(S)I.

séra'pe (-áhpā), n. Shawl or blanket worn by Spanish-Americans. [Sp.]

serve (vb). Hence (also) **sérv'ery** (3) n., room from which meals etc. are ~d & in which utensils are kept.

shake¹. (Also, colloq.) upset composure of (person).

Sher'pa, n. One of a Tibetan people living on the Himalayas.

shimmy.² *(Also) vibration of (front) wheels of car, (v.i.) vibrate.

*shinn'ÿ²**, v.i. (colloq.). Shin tree etc., usu. *up*. [SHIN]

shock¹. ~ *stall*, excessive strain produced by air resistance on aircraft when speed approximates to that of sound; ~ *tactics*, (also, fig.) sudden & violent action.

shoe¹. ~*string*, *(also, colloq.) a small or inadequate amount of money; ~*string* *(attrib.), precarious; just adequate, as a ~*string majority*.

shoot¹. ~*ing-stick*, a walking-stick which may be adapted to form a seat.

short (n.). (Also colloq.) a drink of spirits.

shot¹ (n.). ~*firer*, one who fires the ~ in blasting; ~*gun*, smooth-bore gun for firing small ~ at short range.

shoulder (n.). ~*strap*, (also) one of two strips of cloth suspending a garment from the wearer's ~s.

show¹. ~ *up*, (also, colloq.) appear, be present.

sib. (Also, as n. in genetics, usu. pl.) a brother or sister (disregarding sex), Hence ~LING¹ n., one of two or more children having one or both parents in common (usu. pl.), ~SHIP n., the group of children (disregarding sex) from the same two parents.

sign². ~ *off*, (Bridge) indicate by a conventional bid that one is ending the bidding, (Radio) cease transmitting; so ~*off* n.

sit. (Also) undergo, be a candidate at, (an examination); ~ *in* (colloq.), act as ~*ter-in* (=†baby-sitter).

skě'rrÿ, n. Reef, rocky isle. [f. ON *sker*]

skif'fle, n. Kind of music played by a ~ *group* (a band accompanying a single singing guitarist or banjoist on a variety of instruments). [perh. imit.]

skin¹. *Get under one's* ~ (colloq.), take strong hold on one, interest or annoy one intensely.

skittle (n. pl.). (Also, in full, *table*~s) game played with nine pins set up on board to be knocked down by swinging suspended ball.

*skul(l)dugg'erÿ** (-g-), sc-, n. (joc.). Trickery; corrupt behaviour. [?]

sky (n.). ~*way*, airway.

slalom. (Also) obstacle race in canoes.

slate¹ (vb). *(Also) nominate, propose for office etc.

sleazy. (Also, colloq.) slatternly.

sleep². ~ *in* (Sc.), ~ *late*, over~ oneself.

slink¹. Hence ~'ÿ² a.. gracefully slender & flowing, sinuous.

slip¹. ~ *up* (colloq.), make a mistake, fail.

slip-. ~*road*, minor & local by-pass.

slurry. (Also) sticky muddy residue separated from coal at the pithead washing plants.

smash (vb). ~*ing* (sl.), unusually good, superlative.

smôg, n. Mixture of smoke & fog. [portmanteau wd]

smoke¹. ~ (also) Hence (also) **smŏk'ŏ** n.

smoke². *~ *out*, discover by thorough investigation.

snack. ~ *bar* or *counter*, place where ~s are served.

***snăfu'** (-fōō), a. & n. (Service sl.). 1. Chaotic. 2. n. Utter confusion. [f. initial letters of 'situation normal, all fouled up']

snub, n., & v.t. (-bb-; chiefly Sc.). 1. Bolt, fastening, catch, of door, window, etc. 2. v.t. Bolt, fasten. [?]

snout. Hence (also) ~y², like a ~, having a (prominent) ~ (colloq.; also **snoŏt'y**) supercilious, conceited.

snow¹. *Abominable Snowman*, (sub-human animal alleged to have seen), or supposed to leave tracks in the ~, on the higher Himalaya mountains.

social (a.). Hence (also) ~ITE¹ (-shoᵉ-) n., prominent society person.

soft (a.). ~ *wood*, (wood of) coniferous tree.

|| **sōke,** n. A right of local jurisdiction (hist.); district under a particular jurisdiction, as *the S~ of Peterborough*. [f. OE *socn*]

sŏn'ĭc, a. Of or relating to sound or sound-waves (~ *barrier*, excessive resistance offered by air to objects moving at speed near that of sound). [f. L *sonus* sound, -ıc]

sŏn'ŏbuoy (-boi), n. Buoy for detecting submarines, dropped by parachute from aircraft & equipped with hydrophone & radio for transmitting sounds to aircraft & surface vessels. [f. L *sonus* sound & BUOY¹]

south (a.). ~ *paw* a. & n., left-handed (person), esp. in sport.

space¹. ~ *ship*, craft for travelling through interplanetary space.

spanner. *Throw a ~ into the works*, introduce an upsetting element or influence.

spastic. (Also, n.) person suffering from cerebral palsy.

spend. ~ *a penny* (colloq.), evacuate bladder or bowels; *~*ing money*, pocket money.

splash. ~ *headline*, conspicuous, designed to attract attention.

splinter (n.). ~ *party* (Pol.), a party that has broken away from a larger one, esp. when very small in numbers.

spring². ~-*clean* v.t., clean (house, room) thoroughly, esp. in ; ~-*cleaning* n.

sput'nik (-ōōt-), n. Russian earth satellite. [Russ., = travelling companion]

square (vb). ~ *up to difficulties or problems*, face & tackle them resolutely.

squid¹, n. Anti-submarine mortar with several barrels firing depth-charges ahead of ship. [?]

stack (v.t.). (Also) instruct to fly round at different levels (aircraft waiting to land at aerodrome).

staging. ~ *post*, regular stopping place on air route.

stăkhàn'ovĭte (-kahn-), n. A (Russian) worker who increases his output to an exceptional extent; also attrib. [f. *Stakhánov*, a Russian miner, + -ITE¹(1)]

Stăl'inĭsm (-ah-), n. Political theories & practices of Josef V. Stalin (d. 1953). So ~IST n. & a., ~ITE¹ n. & a., [-ISM]

stand. ~ *in*, (also) deputize for. ~-*in* n., deputy, substitute.

star¹. ~*ry-eyed* (colloq.), visionary.

steel (n.). ~ *wool*, fine shavings of massed together, used esp. for cleaning pots & pans.

stein (stīn), n. Beer mug. [G. = stone]

stereo-. ~*phon'ic* a., (of sound reproduced) giving the effect of coming from more than one direction.

sterling (n.). ~ *area*, group of countries keeping their reserves in ~ & not in gold or dollars, & transferring money freely between each other.

stock (n.). ~*piling*, accumulating ~s of commodities etc., orig. purchase by U.S. for ~ of raw materials not (sufficiently) available from its own resources, so ~*pile* n. & v.t.

stŏmatŏl'ogy, n. (med.). Science of (diseases of) the mouth. [f. STOMATO-, -LOGY]

stooge (n.). (Also) subordinate, puppet.

stop. *~ *off*, ~ *over*, break one's journey; ~-*over*, nn., a break in one's journey.

story. (Also, Journalism) any narrative or descriptive article in a newspaper.

straight (a.). ~ *jet*, jet aircraft with no propeller.

strap (n.). Hence (also) ~LESS a., (of dress) without shoulder-~s.

street. *~ *car*, tram-car.

strěptomy'cin, n. An antibiotic produced by the *Streptomyces* group of bacteria, effective against some groups of disease-producing bacteria which are immune to penicillin. [f. Gk *streptos* torque, twisted (*strephō* turn), *mukēs* fungus, -IN]

strike (n.). (Also) attack esp. from the air; ~ (Also) immobilized by ~.

strip². (Also) narrow space in newspaper for small pictures telling a comic or serial story.

strong. ~ *suit*, suit at cards that is able to take tricks, (fig.) thing at which one excels.

strontium. ~ *90*, product of atomic fission, concentrating selectively on the bones.

stub (n.). *(Also) counterfoil.

sub-. ~*liminal advertising*, technique of flashing an advertisement on a screen for a fraction of a second so that the image penetrates to the viewer's subconsciousness though it makes no impression on his conscious mind.

subtŏpī'a, n. (derog.). Term applied to

urban and rural areas disfigured by ill-planned and ugly building development; unsightly suburbs regarded as encroaching upon the natural scene; also fig. Hence ~AN. [f. SUB- +(U)TOPIA]

sun. ~*flower*, (also) plant grown for its seeds which yield an edible oil; ~*glasses*, for protecting the eyes from direct ~*light* or glare.

sup'ersound, n. Vibrations of same type as sound but too rapid to be audible. [SUPER- 1 c]

Swahili (swahhē'lǐ), n. A Bantu people (or one of them) inhabiting Zanzibar & the adjacent coasts; (also *Kiswahili*) their language. [f. Arab. *sawāḥil* pl. of *sāḥil* coast]

swank. Hence~**v²** a. (sl.), marked by ~, ostentatiously smart.

swarf (swörf), n. Chips or filings of wood, metal, etc. [f. ON *swarf* file-dust]

swatch (-ŏ-), n. (chiefly Sc. & north.) Sample of cloth or fabric. [?]

sweater. ~ *girl* (colloq.), girl or woman with well-developed bust.

sweep. *Swept-wing* or *swept-back wing*, (of aircraft) having the outer portion of the wing aft of the inner portion.

switch (vb). (Also) race (horse) under another's name.

swith'er (-dh-), v.i. (Sc.). Hesitate, be uncertain. [?]

swi'zzle, n. Compounded intoxicating drink (~*stick*, red with brushlike end used for frothing or flattening drinks). [?]

syndicate (n.). (Also) group of people who combine to rent a shooting, fishing, etc.

T

tab. (Also, v.t., colloq.; -bb-) tabulate, record.

tail¹ (v.t.). (Also) dock tail of (lamb etc.); (colloq.) follow closely, shadow.

take¹. ~ *care of*, be adequate provision for, be able to deal with; ~*over bid*, an offer to purchase shares which will secure for the bidder control of a company.

tanker. (Also) aircraft for refuelling other aircraft in air.

teens. **Teen-ager*, person between 13 & 20.

tele- (Also) abbr. for TELEVISION; televi-sion broadcast programme or item: *tēl'ēfilm*, cinema film transmitted by television; *telegēn'ic*, suitable for being televised; *telekǐn'ema*, picture-house for showing ~*films*; ~*promp'ter*, electronic device that slowly unrolls speaker's text, in large print, outside the sight of the audience; ~*record'ing*, recorded item or programme (to be) televised.

tell'y, n. (sl.). Television. [abbr.]

temperature. (Also, colloq.) body ~ above normal.

temporar·ly. (Also, n.) person employed ~ly.

term¹. ~*s of trade*, ratio between prices paid for imports & received for exports.

terrace. ~*house*, one of row of houses joined by party-walls.

territorial (a.). ~ *waters*, marginal waters under the jurisdiction of a State, esp. that part of the sea within three miles of the shore measured from low-water mark.

Thalia. (Also) one of the Graces.

thé dansant (tā dahnsahn'), n. Afternoon tea with dancing. [F]

thermo-. ~*nuclear* (hydrogen) *bomb*; ~*setting*, (of plastics) setting when heated.

three. ~*decker*, (also) novel in ~ volumes; ~*lane*, wide enough for ~ lines of traffic.

through. *(Also) up to & including (*from Friday ~ Tuesday*). ~*put*, amount of material put ~ in a manufacturing etc. process.

thumb (n.). *~*tuck*, drawing-pin.

‖ **tidd'ler**, n. (Nursery name for) stickle-back. [?]

tig'on, n. Offspring of tiger & lioness. [portmanteau wd]

tin (n.). ~*pan alley*, (fig.) the world of the composers & publishers of popular music.

title. (Also) a book or publication.

Tit'ōism (tē-), n. Marshal Tito's kind of Communism in Jugoslavia as dist. from that of Russia & her satellite countries. So ~IST (2) n. & a. [-ISM (3)]

tolerance. (Also) permissible variation in dimension, weight, &c.

too (adv.). (Also, colloq.) very (*you are ~ kind; he is not ~ well today*).

tōrc, n. See TORQUE.

trace¹. ~ *elements* (occurring, or required to be present, esp. in soil, in ~s). **tracer**, (also) artificially produced radio-active isotope introduced into human body in food or otherwise & capable of being followed in its course by the radiations it produces.

tractor. (Also) self-propelled vehicle for hauling other vehicles, farm machines, etc.

traffic. *~ *circle*, roundabout. Hence (also)~**ātor** n., movable direction-indica-tor or on motor vehicle.

tranquil. ~*lizer*, (also) sedative drug.

****transceiv'er** (-nsēv-), n. Combined radio transmitter & receiver. [f. *trans-mitter*+*receiver*]

transcribe. (Also, Radio) record for sub-sequent reproduction, broadcast by *transcription* (recorded programme).

transis'tor (-z-), n. Non-vacuum elec-tronic device performing functions usu. performed by the thermionic valve. [f. *transfer*+*tresistor*]

transūrăn'ic, a. (chem.). (Of elements) having a higher atomic number than uranium 238. [TRANS-]

tri-. ~**chlor'ide** (-īd-), compound of element or radical with three atoms of chlorine.

trit'ium, n. (chem.). Heavy isotope of hydrogen with mass about three times that of ordinary hydrogen. [f. +-IUM]

triv'ia, n. pl. Trifles, trivialities. [mod. L, see TRIVIAL]

triz'one, n. The British, American, & French zones of occupation in Germany after the 1939-45 war. Hence **trizōn'al** a. [TRI- +ZONE]

trouble (n.). *~**-shooter** (colloq.), man employed to detect & correct mechanical faults.

turb'o-, comb. form of TURBINE; ~**-jet** engine (having a turbine-driven compressor for supplying compressed air to the combustion chamber); ~**-prop(eller)** engine (having a turbine-driven propeller).

twin (a.). ~ **set,** woman's matching cardigan & jumper.

U

ultra-. ~**són'ic** a., =SUPERSONIC; ~**són'ics** n. pl., =SUPERSONICS.

um'bles (-blz), n. pl. (obs.). Edible offal of deer: attrib. in *umble-pie* (cf. HUMBLE pie. [var. of F *numbles* f. L *tumbulus* dim. of *lumbus* loin]

un-2 (1). *Unget-at-able,* inaccessible.

under-. ~**tíne**1, (also) stress, emphasize; *~*/*poss.* subway.

ûn'derpriv'ileged (-jid), a. Less privileged than others, belonging to the lower classes of society. [UNDER- 3]

uni-. ~**lateral,** (also, of car-parking) restricted to one side of the street.

up (a.). *Up-and-coming,* enterprising, alert.

Uran'ia (ū-), n. The Muse of astronomy. [L, f. Gk *ouranos* heaven]

V

vacuum. (Also, colloq.) ~ cleaner.

val'gus, n. Deformity involving outward bending of distal part of limb; knock-kneed person. [L]

variety. (Also) ~ entertainment or show.

vector. (Also, v.t.) direct (aircraft in flight) to desired point.

venereal. Hence ~**ŏr'ōgist,** ~**ŏr'ogy,** nn.

view (n.). ~**point,** point of ~.

virement (vēr'mahñ), n. Power to transfer items from one account to another. [F]

*****vise,** n. & v.t. =VICE2.

vital. ~ **statistics,** (also, colloq.) feminine measurements of bust, waist, & hips.

vraic (vrāk), n. A seaweed found in the Channel Isles, used for fuel and manure. [F dial.; cf. VAREC]

W

waf'fle2 (wŏ-), v.i. & n. (Indulge in) continual rapid chatter, twaddle. [?]

walk1. ~**-ie-talkie** (wawk'i-tawk'i) n., small transmitting & receiving radio set carried on the person.

walk2. *~**-way,** passage for walking along, esp. one connecting different sections of a building; wide path in garden etc.

war1. ~**-monger,** one who seeks to bring about ~.

Wardour Street. (Now also or esp. used for) the film trade.

water1. *~ **bus,** river craft carrying passengers on regular run; ~**-diviner,** dowser (see DOWSING); ~**-splash,** part of road submerged by stream or pool.

weasel. *(Also, v.i.) equivocate, quibble.

wedge (n.). *~ golf-club with ~-shaped head used for approaching.

weight1. (Also, Statistics) multiply components of (average) by compensating factors. Hence ~ING1 (wāt-) n., extra pay or allowances given in special cases.

welt1 (n.). (Also) border or edging of garment etc., trimming.

wheel1. ~ **base,** distance between front & rear axles of vehicle.

whip1. ~**-ping-boy,** (also, fig.) scapegoat.

white1. ~ **coal,** water power [F *houille blanche*]; ~**-collar worker,** one not engaged in manual labour; ~ **night,** a sleepless night [F *nuit blanche*].

wide (a.). (Also, sl.) crafty, as ~ *boy.*

wind1. ~**-tunnel,** tunnel-like apparatus for producing air-stream of known velocity past model aircraft etc. to investigate effect of ~ pressure on structure.

wing. (Also) mudguard of motor vehicle.

|| **wŏdge,** n. (colloq.). Chunk. [perh. f. WEDGE]

wŏg1, n. (army sl.). Native of a Middle Eastern country, esp. Egypt. [?]

work1. ~**-piece,** thing worked on with tool or machine; ~ **study,** system of measuring jobs so that they can produce the best results for employees & employer.

Y

yaourt (yah'oort), **yog(h)urt** (yŏg'oort), n. A sour fermented liquor made from milk in the Levant. [f. Turk. *yŏghurt*]

*****yĕn**2 (x), n. & v.i. (sl.). 1. Longing, yearning. 2. v.i. Yearn. [Chin., =smoke, opium]

yet'i (yĕ-), n. Native (Sherpa) name for the *Abominable* †*Snowman.*

Z

zebra. ~ *crossing,* striped street-crossing where pedestrians have precedence over other traffic.

APPENDIX I

GENERAL ABBREVIATIONS

(For list of special abbreviations used in text see p. xiv)

ABBREVIATIONS are made chiefly in two ways. (1) The beginning of the word is given, and at any point (after one letter, after all but one letter, or anywhere between) it is cut short with a full stop; so N. = North, Liv. = Livy, syn. = synonym; the full stop serves to announce that it is needless to go further with the word. (The mathematical abbreviations for cosecant, cosine, cotangent, secant, sine, and tangent, namely cosec, cos, cot, sec, sin, and tan, are used without the full stop. Sometimes, as in ENSA and SCAPA, the full stop is omitted between the letters.) (2) Some portion of the middle of the word is dropped out, the first and last letters being retained with or without others between; so wt = weight, hrs = hours, exrx = executrix, Abp = Archbishop; the writing of a full stop at the end of these on the analogy of that in l, though now usual, is to be deprecated; it is not a natural device (as in l), but artificial; it has very rarely the merit of announcing that the letters printed are not a few word, since that is nearly always clear without it (*caps for capitals* is one of the few exceptions); and it has always the demerit of failing to let the reader know that in the riddle he is called upon to read the last as well as the first letter is given him. There is also a mixed class in which the full stop at the end does convey that the end of the word is missing, but without implying (as in l) that all the letters up to that point are present; such are cg. = c(enti)g(ram), cf. = c(on)f(er), avdp. = av(oir)d(u)p(ois); the first two of these consist of the initial letters of their words' etymological elements, the last gives the first letter followed by such of the consonants as may suggest the general sound.

The method adopted in the following list is to omit the otiose full stop in accordance with the view expressed above; it is, however, to be understood that all abbreviations here given without the full stop may also be, and more frequently are, used with it. The U.S. State names and those of British counties should be mentioned; in the former we give the full stop or omit it as explained above (Vt, Va, Ky, for Vermont, Virginia, Kentucky; Mass., O., Oreg., for Massachusetts, Ohio, Oregon); in the latter we write the full stop after the 's' (Yorks., Leics., Berks., etc.) as representing *shire*. Viz and oz are preferred to viz. and oz. on the ground that the z itself represents a written terminal flourish.

A., adult (i.e. for adults only, referring to cinema picture); air; alto; *avancer* (on timepiece regulator, = to accelerate).

A., anti-aircraft; Automobile Association.

A.A.A., *Agricultural Adjustment Administration; Amateur Athletic Association.

A.A.F., Auxiliary Air Force.

A.A.G., Assistant Adjutant-General.

A. and M., Ancient and Modern (Hymns).

A.A.Q.M.G., Assistant Adjutant and Quartermaster-General.

A.B., able-bodied seaman.

A.B.C., the alphabet; alphabetical time-table; Aerated Bread Company('s Shop).

---

ab init., *ab initio* (= from the beginning).

Abp, Archbishop.

A.C., aircraftman; Alpine Club; alternating current; *ante Christum* (= before Christ).

a/c, account.

A.C.A., Associate of the Institute of Chartered Accountants.

acc., account.

A.C.F., Army Cadet Force.

A.C.G.B., Arts Council of Great Britain.

A.C.I., Army Council Instruction.

A.C.I.S., Associate of the Chartered Institute of Secretaries.

A.C.U., Autocycle Union.

A.C.W., aircraftwoman.

A.D., *anno Domini* (= in the year of our Lord). [Club.

A.D.C., aide-de-camp: Amateur Dramatic

ad fin., *ad finem* (= towards the end).

ad init., *ad initium* (= at the beginning).

Adjt, Adjutant.

Adm., Admiral.

advt., advertisement.

Æ (see Æ in dictionary).

A.E.F., Allied Expeditionary Force.

A.E.U., Amalgamated Engineering Union.

A.F., Admiral of the Fleet.

A.F.A., Amateur Football Association.

A.F.A.S., Associate of the Faculty of Architects & Surveyors.

A.F.C., Air Force Cross.

A.F.L., American Federation of Labour.

A.F.M., Air Force Medal.

A.F.O., Admiralty Fleet Order.

A.F.S., Army Fire Service; Auxiliary Fire Service.

A.F.V., Armoured Fighting Vehicle.

A.G., Adjutant-General; air gunner.

A.H., *anno Hegirae* (= in the year of the Hegira).

A.I., Admiralty Instruction.

A.I.A., Associate of the Institute of Actuaries.

A.I.D., A.I.H., artificial insemination by donor, by husband.

a.l., autograph letter.

Ala, Alabama.

Alas., Alaska.

Alban., (Bp) of St Albans (see Cantuar.).

Ald., Alderman.

a.l.s., autograph letter signed.

A.M., Air Ministry; Albert Medal; = M.A.

a.m., *anno mundi* (= in the year of the world); *ante meridiem* (= before noon).

A.M.D.G., *ad majorem Dei gloriam* (= to the greater glory of God).

A.M.G.(O.T.), Allied Military Government (of Occupied Territory).

A.M.I.C.E., A.M.I.E.E., A.M.I.Mech. E., Associate Member of Institution of Civil, Electrical, Mechanical, Engineers.

A.M.S., Army Medical Staff (or Service).

A.M.S.E., Associate Member of the Society of Engineers.

A.M.T.P.I., Associate Member of the Town Planning Institute.

A.O., Army Order. [(in-Chief).

A.O.C. (-in-C.), Air Officer Commanding

A. of F., Admiral of the Fleet.

A.P., Associated Press.

A.P.M., Assistant Provost-Marshal.

Apocr., Apocrypha.

Apr., April.

A.Q.M.G., Assistant Quartermaster-General.

A.R., advice of receipt; annual return.

A.R.A., Associate of the Royal Academy.

A.R.A.D., Associate of the Royal Academy of Dancing.

A.R.A.M., Associate of the Royal Academy of Music.

A.R.C.M., A.R.C.O., A.R.C.S., Associate of the Royal College of Music, of Organists, of Science.

A.R.I.B.A., Associate of the Royal Institute of British Architects.

A.R.I.C., Associate of the Royal Institute of Chemistry.

A.R.I.C.S., Associate of the Royal Institute of Chartered Surveyors.

Ariz., Arizona.

Ark., Arkansas.

A.R.P., air raid precautions.

arr., arrives etc.

A.R.S.H., Associate of the Royal Society for the Promotion of Health.

A.R.W.S., Associate of the Royal Society of Painters in Water Colours.

A.S., Anglo-Saxon.

Asaph., (Bishop) of St Asaph (see Cantuar.).

A.S.C., American Society of Cinematographers.

A.S.E., Amalgamated Society (*or* Associate of the Society) of Engineers.

A.S.L.E.F., Associated Society of Locomotive Engineers & Firemen.

A.S.L.I.B., Association of Special Libraries & Information Bureaux.

A.S.R.S., Amalgamated Society of Railway Servants.

Asst. Assistant.

A.T.A.(S.), Air Transport Auxiliary (Service).

A.T.C., Air Training Corps.

A.T.S., Auxiliary Territorial Service.

A.U., Ångström unit.

A.U.C., *ab urbe condita* or *anno urbis conditae* (= from, in the year of, the founding of the city, i.e. Rome).

Aug., August.

a.u.n., *absque ulla nota* (= unmarked).

A.V., Authorized Version (of the Bible).

avdp., avoirdupois.

A.V.M., Air Vice Marshal.

*A.W.O.L., absent without leave.

B, black (of pencil-lead).

B, *Beatus, -a* (= Blessed).

b., born; (in cricket) bowled, bye.

B.A., Bachelor of Arts; British Academy.

B.Agr(ic)., Bachelor of Agriculture.

B.A.O.R., British Army of the Rhine.

Bart, Baronet.

Bart's, St Bartholomew's Hospital.

Bath. & Well., (Bishop) of Bath & Wells (see Cantuar.).

BB, BBB, double-, treble-, black (of pencil-lead).

B.B.C., British Broadcasting Corporation.

B.C., Battery Commander; before Christ; British Columbia.

B.C.A., Bureau of Current Affairs.

B.Ch., = Ch.B.

B.C.L., Bachelor of Civil Law.

B.Com., Bachelor of Commerce.

B.D., Bachelor of Divinity.

Bdr., Bombardier.
bds., boards (in book-binding).
B.D.S.T., British double summer time.
B.E. (Order of the) British Empire.
B.E.A., British European Airways.
B.Ed., Bachelor of Education.
Beds., Bedfordshire.
B.E.F., British Expeditionary Force.
B.E.M., British Empire Medal.
B.Eng., Bachelor of Engineering.
Berks., Berkshire.
B.F.B.S., British & Foreign Bible Society.
b.h.p., brake horse-power.
B.I.F., British Industries Fair.
B.L., Bachelor of Law.
B.Litt., Bachelor of Letters.
B.M., Bachelor of Medicine.
B.M.A., British Medical Association.
B.Mus., Bachelor of Music.
B.N.C., Brasenose College, Oxford.
B.O., body odour.
B.O.A., British Optical Association.
B.O.A.C., British Overseas Airways Corporation.
B.O.T., Board of Trade.
bot., bought.
B.P., British Pharmacopoeia; British Public.
Bp., Bishop.
B.Q.M.S., Battery Quartermaster-Sergeant.
brev., brevet.
B.R., British Railways.
B.R.C.S., British Red Cross Society.
Brig. (-Gen.), Brigadier(-General).
Brit., Britain; British.
Britt., *Brit*(*t*)*an*(*n*)*orum* (= of the Britains, on coins).
Bros., brothers.
B.S.A., Birmingham Small Arms (Co.); British South Africa.
B.S.A.A.C., British South African Airways Corporation.
B.S.A.P., British South Africa Police.
B.Sc., Bachelor of Science.
b.s.g.d.g., *breveté sans garantie du gouvernement* (= patented without government guarantee).
B.S.M., Battery Sergeant-Major.
B.S.I., British Standards Institution.
B.S.T., British summer time.
Bt., Baronet.
B.T.C., British Transport Commission.
B.Th.U., British thermal unit.
Bucks., Buckinghamshire.
B.U.P., British United Press.
B.V.M., *Beata Virgo Maria* (= the Blessed Virgin Mary).
B.W.I., British West Indies.
B.W.T.A., British Women's Temperance Association.

C, centum (= 100).
C., Centigrade.
c., caught; cent(s); century; chapter; *circa*; *circiter*; colt; cubic.

C.A., chartered accountant (Sc.).
C.A.B., citizens' advice bureau.
Cal.(if.), California.
Cambs., Cambridgeshire.
Can., Canada.
c. & b., caught & bowled.
Cant., Canticles.
Cantab., Cantabrigian.
Cantuar., of Canterbury. (The signature of certain bishops consists of their Christian name(s) or initial(s) followed by an abbreviation of the Latin adj. of place; thus Dr Fisher signs *Geoffrey Cantuar*.).
cap., *caput* (= chapter).
caps., capital letters.
Capt., Captain.
Card., Cardinal.
Carliol., (Bishop) of Carlisle (see *Cantuar*.).
C.B., Companion of the Bath; confinement etc. to barracks; counter bombardment.
C.B.E., Commander of (the Order of) the British Empire.
C.C., County Council(lor); cricket club.
c.c., cubic centimetre.
C.C.C., *Corpus Christi College, Cambridge.*
‖ Corpus Christi College, Cambridge.
C.C.S., casualty clearing station; Ceylon Civil Service.
C.D., Civil Defence; Contagious Diseases (Acts).
c.d., c.div., cum dividend.
c.d.v., *carte de visite* (= visiting card).
C.E., Church of England; Civil Engineer.
C.E.A., Central Electricity Authority.
Cels., Celsius.
C.E.M.A., Council for the Encouragement of Music & the Arts (now Arts Council of Great Britain).
C.E.M.S., Church of England Men's Society.
Cent., Centigrade.
cent., century.
cf., *confer* (= compare).
C.F., Chaplain to the Forces.
cg., centigram.
C.G.M., Conspicuous Gallantry Medal.
C.G.S., centimetre, gramme, second (as elements in a system of scientific measurement); Chief of the General Staff.
C.G.T., *Confédération Générale du Travail* (= General Confederation of Labour; French T.U.C.).
C.H., Companion of Honour.
ch., chap., chapter.
Chas., Charles.
Chir., *Chirurgiae Baccalaureus* (= Bachelor of Surgery).
Ch.B.,
Ch.Ch., Christ Church, Oxford.
C.H.E.L., Cambridge History of English Literature.
Ches., Cheshire.

Ch.M., *Chirurgiae Magister* (= Master of Surgery).

Chron., Chronicles (O.T.).

C.I., Channel Islands; (Order of the) Crown of India.

Cicestr., (Bishop) of Chichester (see Cantuar.).

C.I.D., Committee for Imperial Defence; Criminal Investigation Department.

C.I.E., Companion of (the Order of) the Indian Empire.

c.i.f., cost, insurance, freight.

C.I.G.S., Chief of the Imperial General Staff.

C.-in-C., Commander-in-Chief.

C.I.O., Congress of Industrial Organizations.

circ., *circa; circiter.*

C.J., Chief Justice.

cl., centilitre; class; classical.

Clar., Clarendon (type).

cm., centimetre.   [Society.

C.M.A.S., Clergy Mutual Assurance

C.M.B., (certificated by) Central Midwives' Board; coastal motor-boat.

Cmd, command paper (with series number, as *Cmd 7957*).

Cmdr, Commander.

Cmdre, Commodore.

C.M.F., Central Mediterranean Forces.

C.M.G., Companion of (the Order of) St Michael & St George.

C.M.S., Church Missionary Society.

C.O., Colonial Office; commanding officer; conscientious objector.

Co., company; county.

c/o, care of.

C.O.D., cash on delivery; Concise Oxford Dictionary.

C. of E., Church of England.

Col, Colonel; Colorado; Colossians (N.T.).

col., column.

Coll., College.

Colo., Colorado.

Col.-S(er)gt, Colour-Sergeant.

Conn., Connecticut.

Cons., Conservative; Consul.

Co-op., Co-operative Society.

C.O.P.E.C., COPEC, Conference on Politics, Economics, & Citizenship.

Cor., Corinthians (N.T.).

Corn., Cornwall.

Corp., Corporal.

C.O.S., Charity Organization Society.

cos, cosine.

cosec, cosecant.

cot, cotangent.

Coy, Company.

c.p., candle-power.

cp., compare.

Cpl, Corporal.

C.P.O., Chief Petty Officer.

C.P.R., Canadian Pacific Railway.

C.P.R.E., Council for the Preservation of Rural England.

C.Q.M.S., Company Quartermaster-Sergeant.

Cr, Creditor.

C.R.A., C.R.E., Commander Royal Artillery, Royal Engineers.

cres., crescendo.

crim. con., criminal conversation.

C.S.C., Conspicuous Service Cross.

C.S.C.S., Civil Service Co-operative Stores.

C.S.I., Companion of (the Order of) the Star of India.

C.S.M., Company Sergeant-Major.

C.T.C., Cyclists' Touring Club.

cu, cub, cubic.

C.U.A.C., C.U.A.F.C., Cambridge University Athletic Club, Association Football Club.

C.U.B.C., C.U.C.C., C.U.L.T.C., C.U.G.C., C.U.H.C., C.U.L.T.C., C.U.R.U.F.C., Cambridge University Boat Club, Cricket Club, Dramatic Society, Golf Club, Hockey Club, Lawn Tennis Club.

Cumb., Cumberland.

cum d., cum div., cum dividend.

C.U.P., Cambridge University Press.

C.U.R.U.F.C., Cambridge University Rugby Union Football Club.

C.V.O., Commander of the Royal Victorian Order.

C.W.S., Co-operative Wholesale Society.

cwt, hundredweight.

d, date; daughter; *dele* (= expunge); *denarius* (= penny); departs etc.; died.

d—, damn.

D.A., District Attorney.

D.A.A.G., Deputy Assistant Adjutant-General.

D.A.B., Dictionary of American Biography.

D.A.D.M.S., D.A.D.O.S., Deputy Assistant Director of Medical, Ordnance, Services.

D.A.G., Deputy Adjutant-General.

dag., decagram.

Dak., Dakota.

dal., decalitre.

dam., decametre.

Dan., Daniel.

D.A.Q.M.G., Deputy Assistant Quartermaster-General.

D.B.E., Dame Commander of (the Order of) the British Empire.

D.C., *da capo* (= repeat from the beginning; also **d.c.**); direct current; District of Columbia.

D.C.L., Doctor of Civil Law.

D.C.L.I., Duke of Cornwall's Light Infantry.

D.C.M., Distinguished Conduct Medal; District Court Martial.

D.D., Doctor of Divinity; *dono dedit* (= gave as a gift; also **d.d.**).

d—d, damned.

D.D.D., *dat, dicat, dedicat* (= gives, devotes, & dedicates; also **d.d.d.**).

D.D.S., Doctor of Dental Surgery.

D.D.T., dichlor-diphenyl-trichlorethane (an insecticide).
Dec., December.
deg., degree.
Del., Delaware.
del., *delineavit* (= drew this).
dep., departs etc.
dept., department.
Deut., Deuteronomy (O.T.).
D.F., direction finder (*or* finding).
D.F.C., D.F.M., Distinguished Flying Cross, Medal.
D.G., *Dei gratia* (= by the grace of God); Dragoon Guards.
dg., decigram.
dim., diminuendo; diminutive etc.
dkg., dkl., dkm., decagram, decalitre, decametre.
D.L., Deputy Lieutenant.
dl., decilitre.
D.L.I., Durham Light Infantry.
D.Lit., Doctor of Literature.
D.Litt., Doctor of Letters.
D.M., Doctor of Medicine.
dm., decimetre.
D.M.I., Director of Military Intelligence.
D.Mus., Doctor of Music.
d—n, damn.
D.N.B., Dictionary of National Biography.
do, ditto.
dol., dollar(s).
D.O.M., *Deo optimo maximo* (= to God the best & greatest).
D.O.R.A., Defence of the Realm Act.
doz., dozen.
D.P., displaced person.
D.P.H., Diploma in Public Health.
D.Ph.(il), Doctor of Philosophy.
D.P.I., Director of Public Instruction.
D.R., dead reckoning; despatch rider.
Dr., Debtor; Doctor.
dr., drachm.
dram., *dramatis personae* (= characters of the play).
D.S., *dal segno* (= repeat from the mark).
D.S.C., Distinguished Service Cross.
D.Sc., Doctor of Science.
D.S.M., D.S.O., Distinguished Service Medal, Order.
d.t.(s)., D.T., delirium tremens.
Dunelm., (Bishop) of Durham (see Cantuar.).
D.Th(eol)., Doctor of Theology.
D.V., *Deo volente* (= God willing).
dwt., pennyweight.
dyn(am)., dynamics.

E., East (as compass point, & as London postal district); Egyptian (in £E); Engineering.
E. & O.E., errors & omissions excepted.
E.B., Encyclopaedia Britannica.
E. by N., E by N, east by north.
Ebor., (Archbishop) of York (see Cantuar.).
E. by S., E by S, east by south.

E.C., East Central (London postal district).
E.C.A., Economic Co-operation Administration (now M.S.A.).
Eccles., Ecclesiastes (O.T.).
Ecclus, Ecclesiasticus (Apocr.).
E.C.U., English Church Union.
Ed., Edward.
ed., editor etc.
E.D.C., European Defence Community.
E.D.D., English Dialect Dictionary.
Edin., Edinburgh.
Edm., Edmund.
E.D.S., English Dialect Society.
Edw., Edward.
E.E.T.S., Early English Text Society.
e.g., *exempli gratia* (= for example).
E.I.S., Educational Institute of Scotland
E. long., east longitude.
E.M.F., electromotive force.
E.N.E., ENE, east-north-east.
ENSA, Entertainments National Service Association; also **En'sa.**
ent. Sta. Hall., entered at Stationers' Hall.
E.P., electroplate.
Eph., Ephesians (N.T.).
E.P.N.S., electroplated nickel silver.
E.P.T., excess profits tax.
E.R., *Elizabeth Regina* (= Queen Elizabeth); East Riding (of Yorkshire).
E.R.P., European Recovery Programme.
E.S.E., ESE, east-south-east.
Esq., Esquire.
Esth., Esther (O.T.).
E.T.A., estimated time of arrival.
et seq., et seqq., et sq., et sqq., *et sequentia* (= and what follows).
etc., et cetera.
E.T.U., Electrical Trades Union.
E.W.O., Essential Work Order.
exc., except; *excudit* (= engraved this).
ex div., ex dividend.
Exod., Exodus (O.T.).
Exon., (Bishop) of Exeter (see Cantuar.)
exor(s), executor(s).
exrx, executrix.
Ezek., Ezekiel (O.T.).

F, fine (of pencil-lead); French.
F., Fahrenheit.
f., feet; feminine; filly; foot; franc(s).
f., *forte* (= loud).
F.A., Football Association.
F.A.A., Fleet Air Arm.
f.a.a., free of all average.
Fahr., Fahrenheit.
F.A.N.Y., First Aid Nursing Yeomanry.
F.A.O., Food & Agriculture Organization.
f.a.s., free alongside ship.
F.B.A., Fellow of the British Academy.
F.B.I., *Federal Bureau of Investigation; ‖ Federation of British Industries.
F.B.O.A., Fellow of the British Optical Association.
F.C., Football Club.
F.C.A., Fellow of the Institute of Chartered Accountants.
fcap, fcp, foolscap.

F.C.I.S., Fellow of the Chartered Institute of Secretaries.

F.D., *Fidei Defensor* (= Defender of the [Faith).

Feb., February.

fec., *fecit* or *fecerunt* (= made).

F.E.I.S., Fellow of the Educational Institute of Scotland.

*F.E.R.A., Federal Emergency Relief Administration.

ff., *fortissimo* (= very loud).

F.F.A.S., Fellow of the Faculty of Architects & Surveyors.

f.g.a., free of general average.

F.G.C.M., field general court-martial.

F.G.S., Fellow of the Geological Society.

F.H., fire hydrant.

F.I.A., Fellow of the Institute of Actuaries.

F.I.A.T., *Fabbrica Italiana Automobile Torino* (= Italian automobile factory, Turin)

Fid. Def., = F.D.

fi. fa., *fieri facias* (= see it is done).

fig., figure.

fin., *ad finem* (= towards the end).

f.l., *falsa lectio* (= false reading).

fl., florin(s); *floruit* (= flourished).

Fla., Florida.

flor., floruit (= flourished).

F.L.S., Fellow of the Linnaean Society.

Flt-Lt., -Sgt, Flight-Lieutenant, -Sergeant.

F.M., Field Marshal.

F.M.S., Federated Malay States.

F.O., Flying Officer; Foreign Office.

Fo, folio.

f.o.b., free on board.

fol., folio.

f.o.r., free on rail. [pupil.

F.P., field punishment; fire plug; former

fp., forte-piano (= loud, then soft).

Fr., Father.

Fr., French.

fr., franc(s).

F.R.A.D., Fellow of the Royal Academy of Dancing.

F.R.A.M., Fellow of the Royal Academy of Music.

F.R.A.S., Fellow of the Royal Astronomical Society.

F.R.C.M., F.R.C.O., F.R.C.P.(E.), F.R.C.S.(E.), Fellow of the Royal College of Music, of Organists, of Physicians (of Edinburgh), of Surgeons (of Edinburgh).

F.R.G.S., Fellow of the Royal Geographical Society.

Fri., Friday.

F.R.I.B.A., Fellow of the Royal Institute of British Architects.

F.R.I.C., Fellow of the Royal Institute of Chemistry.

F.R.I.C.S., Fellow of the Royal Institute of Chartered Surveyors.

Frl., *Fräulein* (= Miss).

F.R.P.S., Fellow of the Royal Photographic Society.

F.R.S., Fellow of the Royal Society.

F.R.S.A., F.R.S.E., Fellow of the Royal Society of Arts, of Edinburgh.

F.R.S.G.S., Fellow of the Royal Scottish Geographical Society.

F.R.S.H., Fellow of the Royal Society for the Promotion of Health.

F.R.S.L., F.R.S.S., Fellow of the Royal Society of Literature, of the Royal Statistical Society.

F.S., Fleet Surgeon.

F.S.A., Fellow of the Society of Antiquaries, of Arts.

F.S.E., Fellow of the Society of Engineers.

F.S.M.C., Freeman of the Spectacle Makers' Company.

F.S.R., Field Service Regulations.

F.S.S., Fellow of the Statistical Society.

F.S.S.U., Federated Superannuation System for Universities.

ft, feet; foot.

fur., furlong.

F.W.A., Family Welfare Association.

F.Z.S., Fellow of the Zoological Society.

g., guinea.

Ga, Georgia.

Gal., Galatians (N.T.).

gal., gallon(s).

G.A.T.T., General Agreement on Tariffs & Trade.

G.B., Great Britain.

G.B.E., Knight (*or* Dame) Grand Cross (of the Order) of the British Empire.

G.B.S., George Bernard Shaw.

G.C., George Cross.

G.C.A., ground control(led) approach (of aircraft).

G.C.B., Knight Grand Cross of the Bath.

G.C.E., General Certificate of Education.

G.C.F., greatest common factor.

G.C.I.E., Knight Grand Commander of (the Order) of the Indian Empire.

G.C.M., general court-martial; greatest common measure.

G.C.M.G., Knight Grand Cross (of the Order) of St Michael & St George.

G.C.S.I., Knight Grand Commander (of the Order) of the Star of India.

G.C.V.O., Knight Grand Cross of the (Royal) Victorian Order.

Gen., General; Genesis (O.T.).

Geo., George.

Ger., German.

G.G., Grenadier Guards.

G.H.Q., General Headquarters.

*G.I., government issue; (colloq.) enlisted man.

Gib., Gibraltar.

Glam., Glamorganshire.

Glos., Gloucestershire.

G.M., George Medal.

gm, gramme(s).

G.M.C., General Medical Council.

G.M.T., Greenwich mean time.

G.O.C. (-in-C.), General Officer Commanding (-in-Chief).

G.O.M., grand old man.
G.P., general practitioner (doctor).
G.P.I., general paralysis of the insane.
G.P.O., General Post Office.
G.R., general reserve; *Georgius Rex* (= King George).
gr., grain(s); grammar.
grm., gramme.
G.S., general service.
gs., guineas.
G.S.O., General Staff Officer.
gym., gymnasium; gymnastics.

H, hard (of pencil-lead).
h., hour(s).
H.A.A., heavy anti-aircraft.
Hab., Habakkuk (O.T.).
H.A.C., Honourable Artillery Company.
Hag., Haggai (O.T.).
h. & c., hot & cold (water).
Hants., Hampshire.
HB, hard black (of pencil-lead).
H.B.M., Her (or His) Britannic Majesty.
H.C. (B.), House of Commons (Bill).
H.C.F., highest common factor.
H.C.S., Home Civil Service.
H.E., high explosive; His Excellency.
Heb., Hebrew; Hebrews (N.T.).
hectog., hectol., hectom., hectogram, hectolitre, hectometre.
Herts., Hertfordshire.
hf bd., half-bound.
hf cf., half-calf.
H.G., High German (also HG); His (or Her) Grace; Holy Ghost; Home Guard; Horse Guards.
hg., hectogram.
H.H., His (or Her) Highness; His Holiness (the Pope).
hhd., double hard (of pencil-lead).
hhd., hogshead.
H.I.H., His (or Her) Imperial Highness.
H.I.M., His (or Her) Imperial Majesty.
H.K., House of Keys (Isle of Man).
hl., hectolitre.
H.L., House of Lords.
H.L.I., Highland Light Infantry.
H.M., Her (or His) Majesty.
hm., hectometre.
H.M.A.S., H.M.C.S., Her (or His) Majesty's Australian, Canadian, Ship.
H.M.I.(S.), Her (or His) Majesty's Inspector (of Schools).
H.M.S., H.M.T., Her (or His) Majesty's Ship, Trawler.
H.O., Home Office; hostilities only.
ho., house.
Hon., Honorary; Honourable.
Hon. Sec., Honorary Secretary.
Hos., Hosea (O.T.).
h.p., half-pay; high pressure; hire purchase; horse-power.
H.Q., Headquarters.
hr.,
H.R.H., His (or Her) Royal Highness.
hrs., hours.

H.S.E., *hic sepultus est* (= here is buried).
H.S.H., His (or Her) Serene Highness.
h.t., high tension.
h.w., hit wicket.
Hunts., Huntingdonshire.
H.W.M., high-water mark.
Hy., Henry.

I., Idaho; Island(s).
I.A., Indian Army.
ib., *ibid., ibidem.*
I/c, in charge.
I.C.B.M., inter-continental ballistic missile.
I.C.S., Indian Civil Service.
id., *idem.*
I.D.B., illicit diamond buying.
I.E., (Order of the) Indian Empire.
i.e., *id est.*
i.h.p., indicated horse-power.
IHS (see dictionary).
Ill., Illinois.
I.L.O., International Labour Organization.
I.L.P., Independent Labour Party.
I.M.S., Indian Medical Service.
in., inch (es).
Inc., Incorporated.
incog., incognito.
Ind., India(n); Indiana.
inf., *infra.*
init., *initio.*
int. comb., internal combustion.
internat., international.
inv., *invenit, invenerunt.*
I.N.R.I., *Iesus Nazarenus Rex Iudaeorum* (= Jesus of Nazareth, King of the Jews)
inst., instant (= of the current month)
I. of M., I. of W., Isle of Man, of Wight.
I.O.G.T., International Order of Good Templars.
I.O.M., Isle of Man.
IOU (see dictionary).
I.O.W., Isle of Wight.
I.Q., intelligence quotient.
i.q., *idem quod.*

I.R.A., I.R.B., Irish Republican Army Brotherhood.
I.R.O., International Refugee Organization.
Is., Isaiah (also Isa.); Island.
I.S.O., Imperial Service Order.
I.T.A., Independent Television Authority.
it(al)., italic (type).
I.W., Isle of Wight.
I.W.T.(D.), Inland Water Transport (Department).
I.W.W., Industrial Workers of the World.

J., Judge; Justice.
J.A., Judge Advocate.
J.A.G., Judge Advocate-General.
Jam., Jamaica; James (N.T.).
Jan., January.
Jas., James.
J.C., Justice Clerk.
Jer., Jeremiah.

jn, junction.
Jno., John.
Jon., Jonathan.
Jos., Joseph.
Josh., Joshua (also O.T.).
J.P., Justice of the Peace.
Jr, junior.
J.T.C., Junior Training Corps (in schools).
Jud., Judith (Apocr.).
Judg., Judges (O.T.).
jun., junr, junior.

Kan., Kansas.
K.B., King's Bench.
K.B.E., Knight Commander (of the Order) of the British Empire.
K.C., King's College; King's Counsel; Knight(s) of Columbus.
kc., kilocycle(s).
K.C.B., K.C.I.E., K.C.M.G., K.C.S.I., K.C.V.O., Knight Commander (of the Order) of the Bath, (of the Order) of St Michael & St George, (of the Order) of the Star of India, of the (Royal) Victorian Order.
K.G., Knight (of the Order) of the Garter.
kg., kilogram.
K.H.C., K.H.P., K.H.S., Honorary Chaplain, Physician, Surgeon, to the King.
'K.K.K., Ku Klux Klan
kl., kilolitre.
km., kilometre.
Knt, Knight.
K.O., knock-out.
K.O.S.B., K.O.Y.L.I., King's Own Scottish Borderers, Yorkshire Light Infantry.
K.P., Knight (of the Order) of St Patrick.
K.R., King's Regulations.
K.R.R.C., King's Royal Rifle Corps.
K.S., King's Scholar.
K.S.L.I., King's Shropshire Light Infantry.
K.T., Knight (of the Order) of the Thistle; Knight Templar.
Kt, Knight.
kv., kilovolt.
kw., kilowatt.
Ky, Kentucky.

L, Latin; learner (on motor vehicle); Roman numeral = 50.
L., Liberal.
l, left; *libra(e)* = pound(s); fine; lira; lire; litre(s).
La, Louisiana.
L.A.A., light anti-aircraft.
Lab., Labour; Labrador.
L.A.C., leading aircraftman; London Athletic Club.
Lam., Lamentations (O.T.).
Lancs., Lancashire,
Lat., Latin.
lat., latitude.
l.b., leg-bye.

lb, *libra(e)* = pound(s) in weight.
L.-Bdr, Lance-Bombardier.
l.b.w., leg before wicket.
L.C., left centre (of stage).
l.c., *loco citato*; lower case (of print).
L.C.C., London County Council.
L.C.J., Lord Chief Justice.
L.C.M., lowest common multiple.
L.C.P., Licentiate of the College of Preceptors.
Ld, limited; Lord.
L.D.S., Licentiate in Dental Surgery.
Leics., Leicestershire.
Lev., Leviticus (O.T.).
L.F.A.S., Licentiate of the Faculty of Architects & Surveyors.
L.G., Life Guards.
L.G.U., Ladies' Golf Union.
Lib., Liberal.
Lieut., Lieutenant.
Lieut.-Col., -Gen., -Gov., Lieutenant-Colonel, -General, -Governor.
L.I.F.O., L.I.L.O., last in first out, last in last out (stock valuation).
Lincs., Lincolnshire.
Linn., Linnaeus.
Lit. Hum., *literae humaniores.*
Litt.D., *literarum doctor.*
Liv., Livy.
L.J., Lord Justice.
L.JJ., Lords Justices.
ll., lines.   [Laws).
Ll.B., *legum baccalaureus* (= Bachelor of
Ll.D., *legum doctor* (= Doctor of Laws).
L.M.S., London Missionary Society.
loc. cit., *loco citato.*
log., logarithm; logic.
Londin., London., (Bishop) of London (see Cantuar.).
long., longitude.   [sure.
loq., *loquitur.*
l.p., large paper; long primer; low pressure.
L.P.T.B., London Passenger Transport Board.
L.R.A.D., Licentiate of the Royal Academy of Dancing.
L.R.A.M., Licentiate of the Royal Academy of Music.
L.R.C.P., Leander, London, Rowing Club.
L.R.C.P., L.R.C.S., Licentiate of the Royal College of Physicians, Surgeons.
l.s., *locus sigilli* (= the place of the seal).
L.S.D., = £. s. d.; Lightermen, Stevedores, & Dockers.
L.S.O., London Symphony Orchestra.
Lt, Lieutenant.
l.t., landed terms; low tension.
L.T.A., Lawn Tennis Association; London Teachers' Association.
L.T.C., Lawn Tennis Club.
Lt-Col., Lt-Com(m)., Lieutenant-Colonel, -Commander.
Ltd, Limited.
Lt-Gen., Lt-Gov., Lieutenant-General, -Governor.
L.W.M., low-water mark.

LXX., Septuagint.

M., Monsieur.

m., maiden (over); male; mark(s) (coin); married; masculine; metre(s); mile(s); million(s); minute(s).

£E, *libra*(e) (= pounds sterling).

£E, pounds Egyptian.

£, s. d. (see dictionary).

£T, pounds Turkish.

M.A., Master of Arts; Military Academy.

M.A.B., Metropolitan Asylums Board.

Macc., Maccabees (Apocr.).

Maj.; Maj.-Gen., Major-General.

Mal., Malachi (O.T.).

Man., Manitoba (also Manit.).

Mancun., (Bishop) of Manchester (see Cantuar.).

M. & B., initials of manufacturers (May & Baker) used as name of therapeutic drug (also M. & B. 693).

Mar., March.

Mass., Massachusetts.

matric., matriculation.

Matt., Matthew.

M.B., *medicinae baccalaureus* (= Bachelor of Medicine).

M.B.E., Member (of the Order) of the British Empire.

M.C., Master of Ceremonies; Member of Congress (or Council); Military Cross.

M.C.C., Marylebone Cricket Club.

M.Ch., *magister chirurgiae* (= Master of Surgery).

M.D., *medicinae doctor* (= Doctor of Medicine); mentally deficient.

Md., Maryland.

Me., Maine; *Maître* (French advocate's title).

M.E.L.F., Middle East Land Forces.

mem., *memento* (= remember).

memo., memorandum.

Messrs (see MESSIEURS).

met., meteorology etc.

Met.R., Metropolitan Railway (London).

Metro., Metropolitan Railway (Paris).

mf, *mezzo forte* (= half loud).

M.F.H., Master of Foxhounds.

m.g., machine gun.

mg., milligram(s).

Mgr., Monseigneur; Monsignor (pl. Mgrі).

M.I., Military Intelligence (*M.I.5*, branch dealing with security & counter-espionage in Britain); Mounted Infantry.

Mic., Micah (O.T.).

M.I.C.E. = M.Inst.C.E.

Mich., Michaelmas; Michigan.

Milt., Milton.

M.I.M.E., M.I.Mech.E., Member of the Institution of Mining, Mechanical, Engineers.

Minn., Minnesota.

M.Inst.C.E., Member of the Institution of Civil Engineers.

misc., miscellaneous; miscellany.

Miss., Mississippi.

M.I.T., Massachusetts Institute of Technology.

mk, mark (coin).

ml., millilitre(s).

M.L.N.S., Ministry of Labour & National Service.

M.M., Military Medal.

M.M., Messieurs.

mm., millimetre(s).

Mlle, Mademoiselle (pl. Mlles).

M.L.A., Member of the Legislative Assembly; Modern Languages Association.

Mme, Madame (pl. Mmes).

M.Mus., Master of Music.

M.N., Merchant Navy.

M.N.I., Ministry of National Insurance.

M.O., mass observation; Medical Officer; money order.

Mo., Missouri.

Mods., Moderations (Oxt. Univ.).

M.O.H., Medical Officer of Health; Ministry of Health.

Mon., Monday; Monmouthshire.

Mont., Montana.

M.O.W.B., Ministry of Works & Buildings.

M.P., Member of Parliament; military police.

mp, *mezzo piano* (= half soft).

m.p.g., m.p.h., miles per gallon, per hour.

M.P.S., Member of the Pharmaceutical (or Philological or Physical) Society.

M.R., Master of the Rolls; municipal reform(er).

Mr (see MISTER).

M.R.C.P. (E., I.), Member of the Royal College of Physicians (of Edinburgh, of Ireland).

M.R.C.S. (E., I.), Member of the Royal College of Surgeons (of Edinburgh, of Ireland).

M.R.C.V.S., Member of the Royal College of Veterinary Surgeons.

M.R.G.S., Member of the Royal Geographical Society.

Mrs (see dictionary).

M.R.S.H., Member of the Royal Society for the Promotion of Health.

MS., manuscript.

M.S.A., Mutual Security Agency (replacing E.C.A.).

M.Sc., Master of Science.

M.S.E., Member of the Society of Engineers.

M.S.L., mean sea-level.

M.S.M., Meritorious Service Medal.

MSS., manuscripts.

M.T., Mechanical (or Motor) Transport.

Mt., Mount.

M.T.B., motor torpedo-boat.

M.T.P.I., Member of the Town Planning Institute.

Mus.B(ac)., Mus.D(oc)., Mus.M., *musicae baccalaureus, doctor, magister* (= Bachelor, Doctor, Master, of Music).

M.V., motor vessel; (also m.v.) muzzle velocity.

M.V.O., Member of the (Royal) Victorian Order.

M.W.B., Metropolitan Water Board.

Mx, Middlesex.

N., Nationalist; Navigator; New; North (as compass point, & as London postal district).

n., neuter; nominative; noon; noun.

N.A.A.F.I., Navy, Army, & Air Force Institutes (also **Naafi,** pr. năf'ĭ).

Nah., Nahum (O.T.).

N.A.L.G.O., National & Local Government Officers' Association (also **Năl'gō**).

N.A.S.D., National Amalgamated Stevedores & Dockers.

Nat., Nathaniel; National(ist).

N.A.T.O., North Atlantic Treaty Organization (also **Nāt'ō**).

N.B., New Brunswick; North Britain; *nota bene.*

n.b., no ball (Cricket).

N. by E., N by E, North by East.

N.B.G., n.b.g., no bloody good.

N. by W., N by W, North by West.

N.C., North Carolina.

N.C.B., National Coal Board.

N.C.C.V.D., National Council for Combating Venereal Diseases.

N.C.O., non-commissioned officer.

N.C.U., National Cyclists' Union.

n.d., no date; not dated.

N.Dak., North Dakota.

N.D.C., National Defence Contribution.

N.E., NE, North-east(ern).

N.E. by E., NE by E, N.E. by N., NE by N, North-east by East, by North.

Neb(r)., Nebraska.   [O.E.D.).

N.E.D., New English Dictionary (=

Neh., Nehemiah (O.T.).

nem. con., nem. dis(s)., nemine contra-dicente, dissentiente.

Nev., Nevada.

N.F., Newfoundland; Norman French.

N.F.S., National Fire Service.

N.F.U., National Farmers' Union.

N.H., New Hampshire.

N.H.I., National Health Insurance.

n.h.p., nominal horse-power.

N.H.S., National Health Service.

N.J., New Jersey.

N.L., National Liberal; north latitude (also **N. lat.**).

N.L.C., N.L.F., National Liberal Club, Federation.

N.Mex., New Mexico.

N.N.E., NNE, North-north-east.

N.N.W., NNW, North-north-west.

N.O., natural order.

n.o., not out (Cricket).

Nº *numero* (= in number); number.

N.O.D., Naval Ordnance Department.

N.O.I.C., Naval Officer in charge.

nom., nominal.

non-com., non-commissioned officer.

Northants., Northamptonshire.

Northumb., Northumberland.

Norvic., (Bishop) of Norwich (see Cantuar.).

Nos, nos, numbers.

Notts., Nottinghamshire.

Nov., November.

N.P., Notary Public.

n.p., net personalty; new paragraph.

n.p., or d., no place or date.

N.R., Northern Rhodesia; North Riding (of Yorkshire).

nr, near.

N.R.A., *National Recovery Administra-tion; National Rifle Association.

N.S., new style; Nova Scotia.

n.s., not sufficient (funds to meet cheque).

N.S.A., National Skating Association.

N.S.P.C.C., National Society for the Prevention of Cruelty to Children.

N.S.W., New South Wales.

N.T., New Testament; Northern Territory (Australia).

N.U.G.M.W., National Union of General & Municipal Workers.

N.U.M., National Union of Mineworkers.

Num., Numbers (O.T.).

N.U.R.,   N.U.S.E.C.,   N.U.T.,
N.U.W.T., National Union of Railway-men, of Societies for Equal Citizenship, of Teachers, of Women Teachers.

N.W., NW, North-west; North-western (London postal district).

N.W. by N., NW by N, N.W. by W., NW byW, North-west by North, by West.

N.W. Prov., North-west Provinces (India).

N.W.T., North-west Territories (Canada).

N.Y. (C.), New York (City).

N.Z., New Zealand.

O., observer; Ohio.

O.A.S., on active service.

ob., *obiit.*

Obad., Obadiah (O.T.).

obdt, obedient.

O.B.E., Officer of the (Order of the) British Empire.

ob.s.p., *obiit sine prole* (= died without issue).

O.C., Officer Commanding.

Oct., October.

oct., octavo.

O.C.T.U., Officer Cadets Training Unit (also **Oc'tu**).

O.E.D., Oxford English Dictionary.

O.E.E.C., Organization for European Economic Co-operation.

O.F.C., Overseas Food Corporation.

O.F.M., Order of Friars Minor.

O.F.S., Orange Free State.

O.H.M.S., on Her (or His) Majesty's Service.

O.K., all correct.

Okla., Oklahoma.

Ol., Olympiad.

O.M., Order of Merit.

Ont., Ontario.

O.P., observation post; (also **o.p.**) opposite prompt (side, in theatre); *Ordinis Praedicatorum* (= of the Order of Preachers, i.e. Dominicans).

o.p., out of print; over proof.

op, opus.

op. cit., *opere citato* (= in the work quoted).

opp., opposite.

O.R., other ranks.

ord., ordained; order; ordinary.

Ore(g)., Oregon.

O.S., old style; ordinary seaman; Ordnance Survey; outsize.

O.S.A., O.S.B., O.S.D., O.S.F., of the Order of St Augustine, Benedict, Dominic, Francis.

O.T., Old Testament.

O.T.C., Officers' Training Corps.

O.U.A.C., O.U.A.F.C., O.U.B.C., O.U.C.C., Oxford University Athletic, Association Football, Boat, Cricket, Club.

O.U.D.S., Oxford University Dramatic Society.

O.U.G.C., O.U.H.C., O.U.L.T.C., Oxford University Golf, Hockey, Lawn Tennis, Club.

O.U.P., Oxford University Press.

O.U.R.F.C., Oxford University Rugby Football Club.

Oxf., Oxford.

Oxon. (Bishop) of Oxford (see Cantuar.); Oxfordshire); Oxford University.

oz., ounce(s).

P., (eat) park; pawn (Chess); pedestrian (crossing).

p., page; particle; past; perch.

p., *piano*.

P.A., Press Association.

p.a., *per annum*.

Pa., Pennsylvania.

P. & O., Peninsular & Oriental (Steamship Co.).

par., paragraph.

P.A.Y.E., pay as you earn.

Paym. (-Gen.), Paymaster(-General).

P.B., Prayer Book.

P.B.I., poor bloody infantry.

P.C., police constable; postcard; Privy Council(lor).

p.c., per cent; postcard.

pd., paid.

pdr., -pounder (of fish, gun, etc.).

p.e., personal estate.

P.E.N., (International Association of) Poets, Playwrights, Editors, Essayists, & Novelists.

pen(in)., peninsula.

Penn., Penna, Pennsylvania.

P.E.P., Political & Economic Planning.

per pro., *per procurationem* (= by proxy).

Pet., Peter (N.T.).

Petriburg., (Bishop) of Peterborough (see Cantuar.).

P.F., Procurator Fiscal.

pf, *piano forte* (= soft, then loud).

p.f.c., private first class.

P.G., paying guest.

P.G.A., Professional Golfers' Association.

Ph.B., Ph.D., *philosophiae baccalaureus, doctor* (= Bachelor, Doctor, of Philosophy).

Phil., Philippians (N.T.).

phot., photograph.

pinx., pinxit.

pizz., pizzicato.

pl., place; plate; plural.

P.L.A., Port of London Authority.

P.M., Prime Minister; Provost Marshal.

p.m., *post meridiem; post mortem.*

P.M.G., Paymaster-General; Postmaster-General.

p.m.h., production per man-hour.

P.M.O., Principal Medical Officer.

pnxt., pinxit.

P.O., Petty Officer; Pilot Officer; postal order; Post Office.

pop., population.

P.O.S.B., Post Office Savings Bank.

P.O.W., prisoner of war.

P.P., parcel post; Parish Priest.

p.p., past participle; = *per pro.*

pp., pages.

pp., pianissimo.

P.P.C., *pour prendre congé* (= to take leave).

P.P.S., Parliamentary Private Secretary; *post postscriptum* (= further postscript).

P.R., proportional representation.

pr., pair; -pounder.

P.R.A., President of the Royal Academy.

P.R.B., Pre-Raphaelite Brotherhood.

Pref., Preface.

Preb., Prebendary.

pref., preference etc.; prefix.

prep., preparation; preposition.

Pres., President.

P.R.O., Public Relations Officer.

Prof., Professor.

Prol., Prologue.

prop., proposition.

pro tem., pro tempore (= for the time).

Prov., Proverbs (O.T.).

prox., proximo.

prox. acc., proxime accessit.

P.S., police sergeant; postscript; (also p.s.) prompt side.

Ps., Psalms (O.T.).

P.S.A., Pleasant Sunday Afternoon.

P.T., physical training.

Pte., Private (soldier).

pt., part; pint; port.

P.T.O., please turn over.

pty., proprietary.

P.W.D., Public Works Department.

pxt., pinxit.

Q., Queen.

q., query.

Q.A.I.M.N.S., Queen Alexandra's Imperial Military Nursing Service.

Q.B., Queen's Bench.

Q.B.D., Q.C., Queen's Bench, Counsel.

Q.E.D., Q.E.F., Q.E.I., see quod.

Q.F., quick-firing (gun).

q.l., *quantum libet.*

Q.M., Quartermaster.

Q.M.G., Q.M.S., Quartermaster-General, -Sergeant.

q.p., *quantum placet.*

qr., quarter.

Q.S., Quarter Sessions.

q.s., *quantum sufficit.*

q.t. (sl.), quiet (*on the strict q.t.,* privately, avoiding notice).

qt, quart(s).

qu., quasi; query.

quant. suff., *quantum sufficit.*

Que., Quebec.

quot., quotation etc.

q.v., *quantum vis* (= as much as you wish); QUOD *vide.*

qy, query.

R., Réaumur; *Regina*; *retarder* (on time-piece regulator; = to retard); *Rex*; River.

R., railway; right; run(s); rupee.

R.A., Royal Academy (*or* Academician); Royal Artillery.

R.A.A.F., Royal Australian Air Force; Royal Auxiliary Air Force.

R.A.C., Royal Armoured Corps; Royal Automobile Club.

rad., radical.

R.A.D.A., Royal Academy of Dramatic Art.

R.A.D.C., R.A.E.C., Royal Army Dental, Educational, Corps.

R.A.F.(V.R.), Royal Air Force (Volunteer Reserve).

R.A.G.C., Royal & Ancient Golf Club, St Andrews; also **R. & A.**

rall, *rallentando.*

R.A.M., Royal Academy of Music.

R.A.M.C., Royal Army Medical Corps.

R.A.N., Royal Australian Navy.

R.A.O.C., R.A.P.C., R.A.S.C., Royal Army Ordnance, Pay, Service, Veterinary, Corps.

R.B., Rifle Brigade.

R.B.A., R.B.S., Royal (Society of) British Artists, Sculptors.

R.C., Red Cross; right centre (of stage); Roman Catholic.

R.C.A.F., Royal Canadian Air Force.

R.C.M., Royal College of Music.

R.C.M.P., Royal Canadian Mounted Police.

R.C.N., Royal Canadian Navy; Royal College of Nursing.

R.C.O., Royal College of Organists.

R.C. of Sig., Royal Corps of Signals.

R.C.P., R.C.S., Royal College of Physicians, of Surgeons.

R.D., refer to drawer; Royal (Naval Reserve) Decoration.

rd, road.

R.D.C., Rural District Council.

R.E., Royal Engineers.

recd, received.

regt, regiment.

R.E.M.E., Royal Electrical & Mechanical Engineers.

repr., represent etc.; reprinted.

R. (et I., *Regina (et) Imperatrix* (= Queen & Express); *Rex (et) Imperator* (= King & Emperor).

Rev., Revelation (N.T.); Reverend.

rev., revolution.

Revd, Reverend.

R.F., Royal Fusiliers.

R.F.C., "Reconstruction Finance Corporation: Rugby Football Club.

R.G.S., Royal Geographical Society.

R.H., Royal Highlanders; Royal Highness.

R.H.A., R.H.G., Royal Horse Artillery, Guards.

R.H.S., Royal Horticultural, Humane, Society.

R.I., = R. et I.; Rhode Island; Royal Institute (of Painters in Water-colours); Royal Institution.

R.I.A., Royal Irish Academy.

R.I.B.A., Royal Institute of British Architects.

R.I.C., Royal Irish Constabulary.

R.I.I.A., Royal Institute of International Affairs.

R.I.P., *requiesca(n)t in pace.*

R.M., Resident Magistrate; Royal Mail; Royal Marines.

R.M.A., Royal Military Academy (Sandhurst; formerly Woolwich).

R.M.C., Royal Military College (Sandhurst; now R.M.A.).

R.M.S., Royal Mail Steamer.

R.M.S.P., Royal Mail Steam Packet (Company).

R.N., Royal Navy.

R.N.C., R.N.D., Royal Naval College, Division.

R.N.L.I., Royal National Lifeboat Institution.

R.N.(V.)R., Royal Naval (Volunteer) Reserve.

R.N.Z.A.F., R.N.Z.N., Royal New Zealand Air Force, Navy.

Robt, Robert.

R.O.C., Royal Observer Corps.

Roffen., (Bishop) of Rochester (see Cantuar.).

Rom., Romans (N.T.).

rom., roman (type).

R.P.S., Royal Photographic Society.

R.Q.M.S., Regimental Quartermaster-Sergeant.

R.R.C., (Lady of the) Royal Red Cross.

R.S., Royal Scots; Royal Society.

Rs, rupees.

R.S.A., Royal Scottish Academy; Royal Society of Arts.

R.S.A.A.F., Royal South African Air Force.

R.S.F., Royal Scots Fusiliers.

R.S.M., Regimental Sergeant-Major.

R.S.O., railway sub-office.

R.S.P.C.A., Royal Society for the Prevention of Cruelty to Animals.

R.S.V.P., *répondez s'il vous plaît.*

R.S.W., Royal Scottish Society of Painters in Water-colours.

R.T., R/T, radio-telegraphy, -telephony.

Rt Hon., Right Honourable.

R.T.O., Railway Transport Officer.

R.T.R., Royal Tank Regiment.
Rt Rev., Right Reverend.
R.T.S., Religious Tract Society.
R.U., Rugby Union.
R.U.R., Royal Ulster Rifles.
R.V., Revised Version (of Bible).
R.W.S., Royal Society of Painters in Water-colours.
Rx, tens of rupees.
Ry., railway.
R.Y.S., Royal Yacht Squadron.
R, recipe.
Rs, rupee.
Rs, rupees.
Rx, tens of rupees.

S., Saint; Signor; soprano; South(ern); Submarines.
S., second, shilling; singular; *solidus*; son.
S.A., Salvation Army; South Africa; (also SA.) *Sturmabteilung* (= storm detachment; Nazi party army).
S.A.A., small arms ammunition.
Salop, Shropshire.
Sam., Samuel (O.T.).
S. & M., (Bishop) of Sodor & Man (see Cantuar.).
Sarum., (Bishop) of Salisbury (see Cantuar.).
Sask., Saskatchewan.
Sat., Saturday.
S.A.T.B., soprano, alto, tenor, bass.
S. by E., S by E, S by W, S by W, South by East, by West.
S.C., South Carolina; Special Constable.
sc., *scilicet*; *sculpsit*.
SCAPA, Society for Checking the Abuses of Public Advertising.
s. caps, small capital letters.
S.C.C., Sea Cadet Corps.
sch., scholar; school.
scil., *scilicet*.
S.C.M., State Certified Midwife.
sculps., *sculpsit*.
s.d., several dates.
S.Dak., South Dakota.
S.E., SE, South-east; (London postal district).-
S.E.A.T.O., South-east Asia Treaty Organization (also Seat'o).
S.E. by E., SE by E, S.E. by S, SE by S, South-east by East, by South.
Sec., Secretary.
sec., second.
sect., section.
Sen., Senate; Senator; Senior (also Senr).
Sept., September; Septuagint.
seq(q)., *sequentes*, *sequentia*.
Sergt., Sergeant.
s.f., *sub finem*.
sf., *sforzando*.
S.F.A., Scottish Football Association.
s.g., specific gravity.
s.g.d.g., *sans garantie du gouvernement* (= without government guarantee).
Sgt., Sergeant.
S.H., School House.

sh., shilling(s).
S.H.A.P.E., Supreme Headquarters Allied Powers in Europe (also Shape).
s.h.p., shaft horse-power.
S.I., (Order of the) Star of India.
S.J., Society of Jesus.
S.J.A.A., S.J.A.B., St John Ambulance Association, Brigade.
*S.J.C., Supreme Judicial Court.
S., lat., South latitude.
S.M., Sergeant-Major; short metre.
S.M.O., Senior Medical Officer.
s.m.p., *sine mascula prole* (= without male issue).
S.N.O., Senior Naval Officer.
S.O., Staff Officer; Stationery Office; sub-Office.
Soc., Socialist; Society.
S.O.E.D., Shorter Oxford English Dictionary.
Sol.-Gen., Solicitor-General.
Som., Somerset.
Song of Sol., Song of Solomon (O.T.).
S.O.S., (see dictionary).
sov., sovs, sovereign(s) (coin).
S.P., starting price (Betting); stirrup pump.
s-p., *sine prole* (= without issue).
S.P.C.K., Society for Promoting Christian Knowledge.
S.P.E., Society for Pure English.
S.P.G., Society for the Propagation of the Gospel.
sp. gr., specific gravity.
S.P.Q.R., *senatus populusque Romanus* (= the senate & people of Rome); small profits & quick returns.
S.P.R., Society for Psychical Research.
s.p.s., *sine prole superstite* (= without surviving issue).
sq., square.
sq(s)., *sequentes*, *sequentia*.
Sqd(n). Ldr, Squadron Leader.
S.R., Scottish Rifles; Southern Rhodesia.
Sr., Senior.
S.R.N., State Registered Nurse.
S.R.O., Statutory Rules & Orders.
S.R.U., Scottish Rugby Union.
S.S., Saints.
S.S., *Schutzstaffel* (= protection patrol; Nazi police force; also SS.); steamer (also s.s.) steamship.
S.S.A.F.A., Soldiers', Sailors', & Airmen's Families Association.
S.S.C., Solicitor to the Supreme Court (Scotland).
S.S.E., SSE, South-south-east.
S.S.J.E., Society of St John the Evangelist.
S.S.W., SSW, South-south-west.
St, Saint; Strait; Street.
st., stem; stone (weight); stumped.
Staffs., Staffordshire.
S.T.C., Senior Training Corps (at universities).
St. Ex(ch)., Stock Exchange.
stg, sterling.

S.T.P., *sanctae theologiae professor* (= Professor of 'Sacred Theology').
str., stroke (oar).
S.T.S., Scottish Text Society.
Sts, Saints.
Sun., Sunday.
sup., superlative: *supra* (= above).
suppl., supplement.
Supt, Superintendent.
surg., surgeon; surgery.
s.v., *sub voce.*
S.W., SW, South-west; South-western (London postal district).
S.W. by S., SW by S., S.W. by W., SW by W., South-west by South, by West.
S.Y., steam yacht.

T., tenor; Turkish (pounds).
t., taken (Betting); ton(s).
T.A., Territorial Army.
T. & o., taken & offered.
T.B., torpedo-boat; tubercle bacillus; tuberculosis.
T.B.D., torpedo-boat destroyer.
T.C., Town Council(lor).
T.C.D., Trinity College, Dublin.
T.D., *Teachd Dála* (= Deputy of Dáil); Territorial (Officer's) Decoration.
t.e.g., top edge(s) gilt.
temp. (see dictionary).
Tenn., Tennessee.
Tex., Texas.
T.F., Territorial Force.
T.G.W.U., Transport & General Workers' [Union.
Thess., Thessalonians (N.T.).
Thos, Thomas.
Thurs., Thursday.
T.H.W.M., Trinity high-water mark.
T.I.H., Their Imperial Highnesses.
Tim., Timothy (N.T.).
Tit., Titus (N.T.).
T.N.T., trinitrotoluene.
T.O., Transport Officer; turn over.
Toc H (see dictionary).
T.R.C., Thames Rowing Club.
Treas., Treasurer.
T.R.H., Their Royal Highnesses.
trs., transpose.
Truron., (Bishop) of Truro (see Cantuar.).
T.S.H., Their Serene Highnesses.
T.S.O., town sub-office. [Association.
T.S.S.A., Transport Salaried Staffs
T.T., teetotaller; Tourist Trophy; tuber-culin tested.
T.U., Trade Union.
T.U.C., Trades Union Congress.
Tues., Tuesday.
T.V., T.V., television.
T.V.A., Tennessee Valley Authority.
T.W.A., Trans World Airlines.
12mo, duodecimo.
T.Y.C., Thames Yacht Club.

U., universal (i.e. for everyone, referring to cinema picture).
U.A.B., Unemployment Assistance Board.

u.c., upper case (of print).
U.D.C., Urban District Council.
U.K.(A.), United Kingdom (Alliance).
ult., *ultimo.*
U.N., United Nations.
U.N.E.S.C.O., United Nations Educational, Scientific, & Cultural Organization (also Unes'co).
Univ., University.
U.N.O., United Nations Organization (also Uno).
U.N.R.R.A., United Nations Relief & Rehabilitation Administration (also UNRRA, Unrra, pr. ŭn'rah).
U.P., United Presbyterian; United Press.
u.p., under proof.
U.S., United States (of America).
U.S.A., United States of America; United States Army.
U.S.(A.)A.F., United States (Army) Air Force.
U.S.N., United States Navy.
U.S.S., United States Senate; United States Ship (or Steamer).
U.S.S.C., United States Supreme Court.
U.S.S.R., Union of Soviet Socialist Republics.
Ut., Utah.

V, *Vergeltungswaffe* (= reprisal weapon; V 1, flying bomb; V 2, long-range rocket projectile).
V., verse; versus; *vide;* volt.
V.A., Vice-Admiral; (Order of) Victoria & Albert.
Va, Virginia.
V.A.D., Voluntary Aid Detachment.
V.C., Vice-Chancellor; Victoria Cross.
V.D., venereal disease; Volunteer Decoration.
v.d., various dates.
v. dep., verb deponent.
V.D.H., valvular disease of the heart.
VE, victory in Europe (*VE day,* 8/5/45).
Ven., Venerable.
v.f., very fair.
V.G., Vicar-General.
v.g., very good.
V.H.F., very high frequency.
Vic., Victoria.
V.I.P., very important person.
Vis., Visct, Viscount.
viz, *videlicet.*
VJ, victory in Japan (*VJ day,* 15/8/45 or in U.S. 2/9/45).
v.l., *varia lectio.*
V.O., Victorian Order.
vol., volume.
V.R., *Victoria Regina* (= Queen Victoria); Volunteer Reserve.
V.S., Veterinary Surgeon.
Vt, Vermont.
Vulg., Vulgate.
vv., verses.

W., Welsh; West (as compass point, & as London postal district).

w., watt; wicket; wide; wife; with.

W.A.A.C., Women's Army Auxiliary Corps (in 1914-18 war.)

W.A.A.F., Women's Auxiliary Air Force.

w.a.f., with all faults.

War., Warwickshire.

Wash., Washington.

W. by N., W by N. by S., W by S, W by N. by S., W by S.

W.C., West Central (London postal district).

w.c., water closet.

W.C.A., Women's Christian Association.

W.D., War Department.

W.D.A., W.D.C., War Damage Act, Contribution.

W.E.A., Workers' Educational Association.

Wed., Wednesday.

w.f., wrong fount.

W.F.T.U., World Federation of Trade Unions.

W.I., West Indies; Women's Institute.

Wigorn., (Bishop) of Worcester (see Cantuar.).

Wilts., Wiltshire.

Winton., (Bishop) of Winchester (see Cantuar.).

Wisc., Wisconsin.

Wisd., Wisdom (of Solomon; Apocr.).

W/L., wave length.

W.L.A., Women's Land Army.

W. long., West longitude.

Wm., William.

W.N.W., WNW., West-north-west.

W.O., War Office; Warrant Officer.

Worcs., Worcestershire.

W.P., weather permitting.

W.P.B., waste-paper basket.

W.R., West Riding (of Yorkshire).

W.R.A.C., W.R.A.F., Women's Royal Army Corps, Air Force.

W.R.I., War Risk Insurance; Women's Rural Institute. [vice.

W.R.N.S., Women's Royal Naval Ser-

W.S., Writer to the Signet.

W.S.P.U., Women's Social & Political Union.

W.S.W., WSW, West-south-west.

W/T, wireless telegraphy, telephony.

wt, weight.

W. Va., West Virginia.

W.V.S., Women's Voluntary Service(s).

Wyo., Wyoming.

x-cp., ex coupon.

xd, x-d, x-div., ex dividend.

x-i., ex interest.

Xmas, Christmas.

x-n., ex new shares.

Xt(ian), Christ(ian). (prop. X = Gk letter chi, formed like English X).

Y., Yeomanry.

ye (pr. as the), the (y a survival in corrupt form of obs. þ, symbol for th; still used as archaism).

Yeo(m)., Yeomanry.

Y.H.A., Youth Hostels Association.

Y.L.I., Yorkshire Light Infantry.

Y.M.C.A., Young Men's Christian Association.

Yorks., Yorkshire.

yr(s), year(s); your(s).

yᵗ (pr. as that), that (conj.; as yᵉ).

Y.W.C.A., Young Women's Christian Association.

Zech., Zechariah (O.T.).

Zeph., Zephaniah (O.T.).

APPENDIX II

PRONUNCIATION OF NON-ENGLISH WORDS

THE words in the following Appendix list are those containing sounds that (like the French nasals and the Scotch ch) are non-English and therefore not covered by our notation. In this appendix they are arranged in three lists: the words in their ordinary form; the anglicized pronunciation, denoted by the same symbols as those used throughout the dictionary, but with extra symbols to represent the unEnglish sounds; and the foreign pronunciation in the alphabet of the Société Phonétique Internationale.

CONSONANTS

In the anglicized pronunciation the new symbol to be noted is CH, which is used here to represent a soft guttural sound between sh and k, heard in Scotch words like *loch* and common in German.

In the International Phonetic alphabet the consonants have their usual values, except the following:

ʒ is the sound in Eng. young   ʒ is the sound in Eng. vision
ɲ ,, ,,   Fr. digne   x ,, ,,   Scotch and German loch.
ʃ ,, ,,   Eng. shout

VOWELS

The nasal vowels characteristic of French are pronounced 'through the nose,' that is, with the soft palate at the back of the mouth lowered so that the breath passes through the nasal passages. The nasal vowels are four; and are approximately the nasalized forms of the vowels in English at, ahñ, awñ, ôrñ, earl. In the anglicized pronunciation they are denoted by áñ, ahñ, awñ, ôrñ, in the phonetic alphabet by ɛ̃ ɑ̃ ɔ̃ œ̃. These vowels are all heard in the phrase un bon vin blanc (œ̃ bɔ̃ vɛ̃ blɑ̃).

The vowels in the International Phonetic alphabet are as follows:

a as in Fr. patte	o as in Fr. note				
ɑ ,, pas	ɔ̃ ,, bon (=nasalized aw)				
ɑ̃ ,, ban (= nasalized ah)	ø ,, peu				
e ,, dé	œ ,, seul				
ɛ ,, fait	œ̃ ,, brun (= nasalized ôr)				
ɛ̃ ,, fin (= nasalized ä)	u ,, tout				
ə ,, de (obscure)	y ,, pu				
i ,, ni	ɥ ,, buis				
o ,, beau					

ˑ denotes that the preceding syllable is long.

Ordinary Form.	Anglicized Pronunciation.	Foreign Pronunciation.
abandon	äbahn′dawñ	abɑ̃dɔ̃
abattoir	äbat′wahr	abatwaːr
accouchement	äkōō′shmahn	akuʃmɑ̃
accoucheur	äkōō′shêr	akuʃøːr
accoucheuse	äkōō′shêrz	akuʃøːz
acharnement	äshahrn′mahn	aʃarnəmɑ̃
a deux	ah dêr′	a dø
affaire de cœur	äfär′ de kêr′	afɛːr də kœːr

Ordinary Form.	Anglicized Pronunciation.	Foreign Pronunciation.
à fond	ah fawñ'	a fɔ̃
agent provocateur	ah'zhahñ provŏkahtər'	aʒɑ̃ provokatœ·r
aide-de-camp	ā' de kahñ'	ɛ-dəka
âme damnée	ahm dahn'ā	a·m da·ne
amende honorable	ämahñd' ŏnŏrahr'bl	amɑ̃·d onorabl
ancien régime	ahñ'syañ räzhēm'	ɑ̃sjɛ̃ reʒim
à outrance	ah ŏō'trahns	a utrɑ̃·s
aperçu	ahp'ärsŏo	apɛrsy
aplomb	ahp'lawñ	aplɔ̃
arme blanche	ärm blahñ'sh	arm blɑ̃·ʃ
arrière-pensée	à'rir' pahñ'sā	arjɛ·r pɑ̃se
arrondissement	ärondēs'mahñ	arɔ̃dismɑ̃
atelier	at'elyā	atəlje
au fond	ō fawñ'	o fɔ̃
au grand sérieux	ō grahñ sērēə'	o grɑ̃ serjø
au naturel	ō nätürel'	o natyrɛl
ausgleich	ows'glīch	ausglaix
avion	äv'yawñ	avjɔ̃

B

ballon d'essai	bäl'awñ dĕsā'	balɔ̃ dese
bas bleu	bah blə'	ba blø
battue	bätoō'	baty
beau monde	bō mawnd'	bo mɔ̃·d
lèche-de-mer	bāsh' de mâr	beʃ de me·r
bersaglieri	bärsahlyâr'ē	bersalje·ri
bon	bawñ	bɔ̃
bon-bon	bŏñ'bŏn	bɔ̃bɔ̃
bonne bouche	bon bŏō'sh	bon buʃ
bonnes fortunes	bon fŏr'tŭn'	bon fɔrtyn
bon ton	bawñ tawñ	bɔ̃ tɔ̃
bon vivant	bawñ vē'vahñ	bɔ̃ vi·vɑ̃
bouillon	bŏōl'yawñ	bujɔ̃

C

café chantant	kàf'ā shō'ntahñ	kafe ʃɑ̃·tɑ̃
cancan	kahñ'kahñ	kɑ̃kɑ̃
carte blanche	kärt blahñsh	kart blɑ̃·ʃ
char-à-bancs	shä'rabäng	ʃa·rabɑ̃
charlotte russe	shär'löt rōōs'	ʃarlɔt rys
chartreuse	shärtrərz'	ʃartrø·z
chassé-croisé	shäs'ā krwah'zā	ʃase krwaze
chevalier d'industrie	shĕvàlē' däñ'dŏōstrē	ʃ(ə)valje dɛ̃dystri
chiffon	shif'ŏn	ʃifɔ̃
chignon	shìnŏn', shèn'yŏn	ʃiɲɔ̃
chose jugée	shōz zhŏō'zhā	ʃo·z ʒy·ʒe
chronique scandaleuse	krŏn'ēk skahñdälərz'	kronik skɑ̃dalø·z
ci-devant	sē devahñ'	sidvɑ̃
coiffeur	kwäf'fər	kwafœ·r
coiffure	kwäf'fŭr	kwafy·r
communiqué	komü'nikā	komynike
concierge	kŏñsē'ärzh	kɔ̃sjɛrʒ
confrère	kŏn'frär	kɔ̃frɛ·r
congé	kawñ'zhā	kɔ̃ʒe
consommé	konsō'mā	kɔ̃sɔme
contretemps	kawñ'tretahñ	kɔ̃trətɑ̃
convenances	kawñ'venahñs	kɔ̃vnɑ̃·s
corvée	kŏr'vā	kɔrve
cordon bleu	kŏr'dawñ blə̄'	kɔrdɔ̃ blø
corps de ballet	kŏr de bälā'	ko·r də balɛ
coup-de-main	kŏō' de mäñ	kudmɛ̃
cul-de-sac	kŏōl' de säk	kydsak
curé	kū'rā	kyre

Ordinary Form.	Anglicized Pronunciation.	Foreign Pronunciation.

D

Ordinary Form.	Anglicized Pronunciation.	Foreign Pronunciation.
début	dā'bōō	deby
débutant	dā'bōōtahn	debytā
débutante	dā'bōōtahnt	debytā·t
dégagé	dāgah'zhā	degaзe
de haut en bas	de ōtahn bah'	de ho tā ba
démenti	dāmahn'tē	demā·tĩ
dénouement	dānōō'mahn	denumā
déshabillé	dāzahbē'yā	dezabije
détente	dātŏn't	detā·t
deux-temps	dĕr'tahn	do tā
distingué	distĕn'gā	distĕ·ge
double entendre	dŏōbl ahntahn'dr	dubl ātā·dr
douceur	dōō'sĕr	dusœ·r
doyen	doi'yen	dwajɛ̃
duvet	dōō'vā	dyve

E

Ordinary Form.	Anglicized Pronunciation.	Foreign Pronunciation.
eau sucrée	ō sōō'krā	o sykre
éclaircissement	āklārsēs'mahn	eklɛrsismā
édition de luxe	edish'on de lōōks	edisjɔ̃ d(ə)lyks
élan	ā'lahn	elā
embonpoint	ahnbawn'pwahn'	ābɔ̃pwɛ̃
embouchure	ahnbōōshōōr'	ābuʃy·r
émeute	āmū·t	emø·t
empressement	ahnprĕs'mahn	āprɛsmā
enceinte	ahnsănt'	ãsɛ̃·t
encore	ŏngkŏr'	āko·r
enfant terrible	ahn'fahn tĕrēbl'	āfā teri·bl
en garçon	ahn gär'sawn	ā garsɔ̃
ennui	ŏn'wē	ānɥi
ennuyé	ŏnwē'yā	ānɥije
en passant	ahn pās'ahn	ā posā
ensemble	ahnsahnbl'	āsā·bl
entente cordiale	ōntŏr'ut kŏrdiahl'	ātā·t kordjal
entourage	ŏntōōrah'zh	ātura·ʒ
entr'acte	ŏn'trakt	ā·trakt
entrée	ŏn'trā	ā·tre
entremets	ŏn'tremā	ā·tremɛ
entre nous	ŏn'tre nōō	ā·tre nu
entrepôt	ŏn'trepō	ā·trepo
entresol	ŏn'tresōl	ā·tresɔl
espièglerie	ĕspiā'glerē	ɛspjɛglǝri

F

Ordinary Form.	Anglicized Pronunciation.	Foreign Pronunciation.
faïence	fah'yahns	fajā·s
fainéant	fā'nāahn	feneā
fait accompli	fāt ahkawn'plē	fetakɔ̃pli
fanfare	fan'fār	fāfa·r
fauteuil	fōtĕr'ē	fotœ·j
femme de chambre	fām de shahn'br	fam de ʃā·br
fête champêtre	fāt shahnpātr'	fɛ·t ʃāpɛ·tr
feuilleton	fĕr'yetawn	fœjtɔ̃
fiancé(e)	fēahn'sā	fjā·se
fin-de-siècle	făn de syăkl'	fɛ̃ de sjɛkl
fine champagne	fēn shahnpēn'	fin ʃāpaɲ
franc-tireur	frahn tērœr'	frā tirœ·r

G

Ordinary Form.	Anglicized Pronunciation.	Foreign Pronunciation.
gamin	găm'ăn	gamɛ̃
garçon	găr'sawn	garsɔ̃
gendarme	zhŏn'därm	ʒādarm
gendarmerie	zhŏndärm'erē	ʒādarmǝri

Ordinary Form.	Anglicised Pronunciation.	Foreign Pronunciation.
genre	zhahɪr	ʒɑ̃ːr
gourmand	gŏŏr'mahn̄	gurmɑ̃
gourmandise	gŏŏr'mahndēz	gurmɑ̃diz
grande	grahn̄d	grɑ̃ːd
grand seigneur	grahn̄ sĕnyēr'	grɑ̃ sɛɲœːr
gratin	grăt'ăn̄	gratɛ̃
grisaille	grēzăll'	grizaːj
guilloche	gēyōshĕ'	gijɔʃ
guipure	gē'pŭr	gipyːr

hauteur	ōtēr'	hoːtœːr
hors concours	ōr kawn̄kŏŏr'	hor kɔ̃kuːr
hors de combat	ŏr̄dekawm'bah	hor d(ǝ)kɔ̃ba
hors-d'œuvre	ōrdēr'vr	hɔrdœːvr

Ingénue	ăn̄'zhānŏŏ	ɛ̃ʒeny
Insouciance	ăn̄sŏŏs'yahn̄s	ɛ̃susjɑ̃ːs
Insouciant	ăn̄sŏŏs'yahn̄	ɛ̃susjɑ̃
Instantané	zhŏ̄	ɛ̃stɑ̃tane
jeu	zhŏ̄ despré	ʒǝ
jeu d'esprit	zhŏ̄' nĕs dŏr'ă	ʒǝ despri
jeunesse dorée	zhawn̄'glēr	ʒœnɛs doːre
jongleur	zhōŏlyēn'	ʒɔ̃glœːr
Julienne		ʒyljɛn
kümmel	kŏŏm'el	kümel

langue-d'oc	lahn̄ge dŏk'	lɑ̃ːgdɔk
langue-d'oïl	lahn̄ge dŏïl'	lɑ̃gdɔil
le roi le veut	le rwah le vēŏ̄	lǝ rwa lǝ vǝ
le roi s'avisera	le rwah sahvē'zerah	lǝ rwa savizǝra
liaison	liă'zn	ljɛzɔ̃
lingerie	lă'n̄zherē	lɛ̃ʒri
littérateur	léttrahtēr'	literatœːr
loch	lŏн	lɔx
lough	lŏн	lɔx

mademoiselle	mădemwăzĕl'l	madmwazɛl, mamzɛl
manqué	mahn̄'kă	mɑ̃ːke
mariage de convenance	mä'riahzh de kawn̄'venahn̄s	marja:ʒ dǝ kɔ̃vnɑ̃s
marron glacé	mä'rŏn glah'să	marɔ̃ glase
marseillaise	mårsĕlăz'	masejɛz
masseur	măsēr'	masœːr
masseuse	măsŏ̄z'	masoːz
mauvaise honte	mōvāz ŏn̄t'	movɛːz hɔ̃ːt
mauvais quart d'heure	mō'vă kärdēr'	novɛ kardœːr
mauvais sujet	mō'vă sŏŏ'zhă	novɛ syʒɛ
mêlange	māl'ahn̄zh	melɑ̃ːʒ
menu	mĕnŏŏ', mĕn'ŭ	m(ǝ)ny
mésalliance	māzăl'iahn̄s	mezaljɑ̃ːs
mignon	mē'nyawn̄	miɲɔ̃
milieu	mē'lyēr	miljø
mise en scène	mēzahn̄sān'	miːz ɑ̃ seːn
mitrailleuse	mētrahlyēz'	mitrajøːz
moire antique	mwahr ŏntē'k	mwaːr ɑ̃tik
monseigneur	mawnsĕnyēr'	mɔ̃sɛɲœːr
monsieur	mĕsyēr'	m(ǝ)sjø
morgue anglaise	mŏrg ahnglăz'	morg ɑ̃glɛːz
mot juste	mō zhŏŏst'	mo ʒyst

Ordinary Form.	Anglicized Pronunciation.	Foreign Pronunciation.
N–O		
nom-de-guerre	nŏm de gŭr'	nɔ̃ de gɛ:r
nom-de-plume	nŏm-de plōom'	nɔ̃ de plym
nuance	nū'ăns	nɥɑ:s
och	ŏch	ɔx
ombre	awŏ'br	ɔ̃:br
on dit	ŏn dē'	ɔ̃ di
P		
par excellence	păr ĕ'ksĕlăns	par ɛkselɑ̃:s
parvenu	păr'venōō	parvəny
pas-de-deux	păh de dĕr'	pɑ də dø
passé	pă'sā	pase
passementerie	pás'mentrĭ	pasmɑ̃'tri
pas seul	păh sŭl'	pɑ sœl
pâté	pă'tā	pɑ:te
patois	pă'twah	patwɑ
peignoir	pā'nwăr	pɛɲwa:r
penchant	pähñ'shahñ	pɑ̃:ʃɑ̃
père	păr	pɛ:r
petits soins	pĕtē swăñ'	p(ə)ti swɛ̃
pibroch	pē'brŏch	pibrɔx
pièce-de-résistance	pē'ăs de rāzēs'tahñs	pjɛs de rezistɑ̃:s
pince-nez	păñs'nā	pɛ̃:sne
planchette	plahñshĕt'	plɑ̃:ʃet
poilu	pwah'lōō	pwaly
pompon	pŏm'pŏn	pɔ̃-pɔ̃
poseur	pōzĕr'	po:zœ:r
poste restante	pōst rĕ'stahnt	post restɑ̃:t
prie-dieu	prēdyĕr'	pridjø
Provençal	prŏvahñsah'l	provɑ̃:sal
purée	pūr'ă	py:re
pur sang	pūr sahñ'	pysɑ̃
Q–R		
quand même	kahñ măm'	kɑ̃ mɛ:m
raconteur	răkŏntĕr'	rakɔ̃tœ:r
raconteuse	răkŏntĕ'rz	rakɔ̃tø:z
raison d'être	rā'zawñ dā'tr	rɛzɔ̃ dɛ:tr
ranz des vaches	rahñs dā vahsh'	rɑ̃:s de vaʃ
rapprochement	răprōsh'mahñ	raprɔʃ'mɑ̃
Réaumur	rā'ōmūr	reomyr
réchauffé	răshō'fā	reʃo'fe
recherché	reshăr'shā	reʃɛrʃe
réclame	rā'klahm	rekla:m
renaissance	rĕnā'sahns	rənɛsɑ̃:s
rencontre	rahñkawñ'tr	rɑ̃kɔ̃:tr
répondez s'il vous plaît	rāpawñ'dā sĭl vōō plā	repɔ̃de sil vu plɛ
restaurant	rĕ'storahñ	rɛstɔrɑ̃
résumé	rā'zōōmā	rezyme
robe-de-chambre	rŏb de shahñ'br	rɔb də ʃɑ̃:br
roturier	rōtū'rēā	rotyrje
ruche	rōōsh	ryʃ
ruse	rōōz	ryz
rusé	rōō'zā	ryze
S		
salle-à-manger	săl a mahñ'zhă	salamɑ̃ʒe
salle d'attente	săl dătăñ't	saldatɑ̃:t
salon	săl'awñ	salɔ̃
sang-froid	sahñfrwah'	sɑ̃ frwa

Ordinary Form.	Anglicized Pronunciation.	Foreign Pronunciation.
sans cérémonie	sahñ sĕ″rĕmŏnē	sã seremoni
sansculotte	sahñ′koōlŏt	sã kylŏt
sans façon	sahñ fäs′awñ	sã fasɔ̃
sans gêne	sahñ zhä″n	sã ʒɛ·n
sans peur et sans reproche	sahñ pêr′ ä sahñ rĕprŏsh′	sã pœ·r e sã reprɔʃ
sans phrase	sahñ frahz′	sã fra·z
sans souci	sahñ sōō′sē	sã susi
Sassenach	säs′enăcн	sasənax
savant	säv′ahñ	savã
séance	sā′ahñs	seãs
Sèvres	sā′vr	sɛ·vr
soi-disant	swah dē′zahñ	swadizã
soixante-quinze	swah′zahñt kăñz′	swasã·t kɛ̃·z
soupçon	sōō′psawñ	supsɔ̃
succès d'estime	sŏŏksā dĕstē′m	sykse destim
succès fou	sŏŏksā fōō′	sykse fu

T

tableau vivant	täb′lō vē′vahñ	tablo vivã
tic douloureux	tĭk dŏlerŏŏ′	tik dulurø
timbre	tăm′ber	tɛ̃br
tirailleur	tĕrahyêr′	tirajœ·r
torchon	tŏr′shŏn	tɔrʃɔ̃
tout ensemble	tōōt ahñsahñ′bl	tutãsã·bl
train de luxe	trän de lŏŏks′	trɛ̃ dlyks
trente-et-quarante	trahñt ä kä′rahnt	trã·t e karã·t
trois-temps	trwah tahñ	trwa tã
trouvaille	trōō′vîl	tru·vaj
tulle	tōōl, tŭl	tyl

V

Valenciennes	vălĕnsēnz′	valã·sjen
ventre à terre	vahñ′trah′tĕr	vã·tratɛ·r
vingt-et-un	vän′t ä ŭñ	vɛ̃te œ̃
vin ordinaire	văn ŏrdinâr′	vɛ̃ ordinɛ·r
vol-au-vent	vŏl′ōvahñ	volovã

PRONUNCIATION OF PROPER NAMES

This list is intended as a guide to the pronunciation of some difficult proper names frequently met with. It makes no claim to completeness, and many geographical names in particular have had to be omitted.

One or two general points may perhaps be noted here: Classical names ending in -es are usually pronounced (-ēz). In New Zealand and most newly-colonized countries all native names are pronounced with all vowels sounded (and pronounced as Italian vowels, i.e. a = ah, e = ā or ĕ, i = ē or ĭ, u = oo). The U.S. pronunciation of some American place-names differs from the usual English pronunciation; in the following list such specifically U.S. pronunciations are preceded by an asterisk. There are many proper names (e.g. Kerr, Smyth) the pronunciation of which varies according to the family or individual referred to; such names have usually been employed in indicating pronunciation, in addition to those in the body of the work.

The following symbols have been employed in indicating pronunciation, in addition to those in the body of the work:

x = ch in the Scottish pronunciation of loch.
ğ = 'soft' g in ginger.
ñ indicates that the preceding vowel is nasalized.

Aar′on (ä′-)
Abbeville (ăb′vĕl)
Abéd′nĕgō
A′bel (ā-)
Ab′élärd (ă-)
Abi′jah (-α)
Aboukir (ahbōōkēr′)
About (ah′bōō)
A′braham (ā-)
Abruz′zi (-brōōtsĭ)
Abÿd′ŏs
Accra (ăk′ra or akrah′)
Aceĺ′dama (-k- or -s-)
Ach′erŏn (ăk-)
Achit′ophĕl (αk-)
Ad′élaïde (ă-)
A′den (ä-)
Adirŏn′dăck (ă-)
Adoni′is (ă-)
A′braham (ă-)
Adriăt′ic (ā-)
Æ′olus
En′êĭd
Ænê′ās
ElÍ′ric (ă-)
Æg′na
Æ̆gê′an
Æ̆s′op
Æs′chy̆lus (-k-)
Afghán′istán (ăfg-; or -ahn; or ăfgănistăn′)
A′gāg (ā-)
Agincourt (ăg′ĭnkôrt)
Ag′ra (ah- or ā-)
Aï′da (ah-ē-)
Aix-la-Chapelle (ā′ks-lah-shäpĕl′)
Aix-les-Bains (ā′ks-lā-băn)

Ajmēr′ (ah-)
Alabama (ălabah′ma; *-bă-)
Albani (ălbah′nĭ)
Al′bany (awl-)
Alcan′tara (ălcahn-)
Alcĕs′tĭs (ă-)
Alcĭbi′adēs (ă-; -z)
Aldĕb′aran (ă-)
Algêêĭ′as (ă-)
Algêêr′ia (ă-)
Algiers (ălğēr′z)
Allahabad (ălα-habăd′)
Alleghany (ălĕgăn1; or -ănĭ)
Almeri′a (ă-)
Alsace (ăl′săs; or -ăs)
Amiens [French city] (ăm′ĭăñ)
Amiens [in Shakespeare] (ăm′ĭens)
A′mŏs (ā-)
Anăc′reon
Anani′as (ă-)
An′ám (ă-)
Anchises (ăngkī′sĕz)
Andes (ăn′dēz)
Andrŏm′ache (ă-; -z)
Androm′eda (ă-)
Andrôm′ĭous [in Shakespeare] (ă-)
An′drŏclēs (ă-; -z)
An′ğevin (ă-)
Angoĺ′a (ăngg-; or ăng′gora)
Antæ′us (ă-)
Anthæa (ăn′thĭa)
Antig′onē (ă-)
Antigua (ăntē′gwa)
Antin′ous (ă-)

Antonin'us (ă-)
Apell'ēs (-z)
Aphrōdit'ē (ă-)
Apollinar'is
Appalach'ian (ă-; or -ăch-)
Aquin'as
Arach'nē (-kn-)
Aravalli (arah⌣valī)
Archimedes (ärkimēd'ēz)
Arēōpagit'ica (ā-; or -g-)
Arēthūs'a (ă-; -za)
Ar'gentine (ā-)
Argyll (ārgīl')
Ariad'nē (ā-)
Ar'iel (ā-)
Aristid'ēs (ă-; -z)
Aristoph'anēs (ă-; -z)
A'ristotle (ă-)
Arizōn'a (ă-)
Arkansas (är'kạnsaw)
Artaxerxes (ärtagzêr'ksēz)
Ar'temis (ār-)
Ar'un (ār-)
A'rundel (ă-)
Asia (ā'shạ)
Assi'si (ăsē-)
Assouan (ăsōōän')
Astăr'tē (ă-)
Astrakhan (ăstrakăn')
Atalăn'ta (ă-)
A'tē (ă- or ah-)
Athēn'ē
Ath'ens (ă-; -z)
At'ropos (ă-)
Auch'inlēck (awk-, *Scottish* ŏȳ-)
Augē'as
Aŋgūs'tine
Aurēl'ius
Autōl'ycus
Av'alon (ăv'ĕnyawn)
Avignon (ăv'ĕnyawn)
A'von (ā-)
Azōrēs' (-ōrz)
Az'raēl (ă-)
Bach (bă⍵)
Ba'den (bah-)
Bă'den-Pow'ell (-ðel)
Bagehot (băg'ĕt)
Bahama (ba-hah'mạ)
Baiæ (bī'ē)
Băléa'ric (*or* balēā'ie)
Băll'iol
Bălmō'ral
Bălthazar' [in Shakespeare]
Balu'chistản (-lŏŏk-; *or* balŏŏkistản')
Bantu (bah'ntŏŏ; *or* băn-)
Barăbb'as
Băr'băd'oes (-ōz)
Băr'mēcīde
Barōd'a
Bărōt'sēland
Băs'ăn
Băsh'ăn
Băs'ra (-z-; *or* bŭs-)
Bassan'iō (-ahn-)
Băstille' (-tēl)

Basut'ōlănd (-ōŏ-)
Batăv'ia
Băt'on Rouge (rŏŏzh)
Bar'cis
Bayeux (bă-yŏŏ')
Bayreuth (bī'roit)
Bea'consfield (bē- *or* bĕ-)
Beauchamp (bē'chạm)
Beaulieu (bū'li)
Beaune (bōn)
Bēchua'na (-kɦahnạ; *or* bĕch-)
Bēel'zēbūb (*or* bĕĕl-)
Beethoven (bāt'ōven)
Behr'ing (bē-; *or* bâr-)
Beira (bī'ra)
Beirut (bā'rŏŏt)
Bēl'gium (-vm)
Bĕl'ial
Bēllăgg'iō (-j-)
Belle'rophon
Bĕlli'ni (-lē-)
Belvoir (bēv'er)
Bēnăr'ēs (-z; *or* bĕ-)
Bĕn'tham (-tạm)
Berkeley (bärk'li)
Bĕrk'ley [America]
Berkshire (bärk'sher)
Berlioz (bâr'liōs)
Bērmūd'as (-z)
Berwick (bĕ'rik)
Bethune [English surname] (bĕ'ten)
Bicester (bis'ter)
Biđ'ēford
Big'ēlow (-g-; -ō)
Bihar'
Bīkanir' (-ēr)
Bilbā'ō
Blanc (-ahn)
Bleriot (blē'riō)
Bloem'fontein (-ŏŏ-; -ân)
Blücher (blŏŏk'er)
Bōadicē'a
Bōcca'ciō (-kahch-)
Bōd'iham (-dɦam)
Bōdleian (-lē'ạn)
Bōēth'ius
Bohun (bŏŏn)
Boleyn (bŏŏl'in)
Bom'pas (-ŭm-)
Boötes (bō-ō'tēz)
Bôrdeaux' (-dō)
Bōđōn'ē
Bō'tha (-ta)
Bŏtticĕll'i (-chĕl-)
Boulogne (bŏŏlōn')
Bourchier (bow'cher)
Bow (bō)
Bōz (*or* -ō-)
Braemăr' (brā-)
Brāse'nōse (-zn-; -z)
Breadal'bane (ĕdawl-)
Brougham (brŏŏm *or* brŏŏ'ạm)
Bruges (brŏŏzh)
Buccleuch (bŭklŏŏ')
Būch'arĕst (-ker-)
Būd'apĕst'

Buenos Ayres (bwŏn′ŏzäī′iz; or bŏ′īn-)
Bulawayo (bŏŏlăwī′ō)
Bŭr′leigh (-lī)
Bŷr′on
Bysshe (bĭsh)
Bŷzăn′tĭum
Căb′ot
Căd′īz
Cadog′an (-ŭg-)
Cæd′mon (kăd-)
Caen (kahn)
Cagliostro (kȧlyos′trō)
Cai′aphăs (kī-)
Cairo (kīr′ō)
Caius [Roman name] (kī′ŭs)
Caius [Cambridge college] (kēz)
Căl′ais (-īs or -ā or -ĭ)
Calēdŏn′ĭa
Călĭg′ŭla
Căll′ŏpē
Cămbȳs′ēs (-z)
Cămpa′gna (-ahnya)
Campbell (kăm′bl)
Căn′berra
Cāndĭ̄′cē
Canōp′us
Carăc′tacus
Carew′ (-ōō)
Carew [Thomas, 1589–1639] (kār′ī)
Căr′ey
Cārlisle′ (-līl)
Carmăr′then (-dh-)
Carnăr′von
Cărnĕg′ie (-gĭ; or -ăgĭ)
Cărolin′a
Căssahĭtan′ca
Căssiopē′a (-sĭ-)
Castile′ (-ēl)
Căthay′
Cătr′ŏna (or kătrĕō′na)
Cătŭll′us
Căv′ell
Căv′our′ (-oor)
Cecil (sĕsl or sĭsl)
Cēcil′ia
Cellini (chĕlē′nĭ)
Cencĭ (chĕn′chĭ)
Cĕt′ēs (-z)
Cĕtvān′tēs (-z)
Ceylŏn′ (sĭ-)
Cĕzânne′ (sā-)
Chăl′kĭs (k-)
Chāl′ĭe
Chamonix (shăm′onĭ)
Chapultĕpĕc′ (chahpool-)
Chá′ring Cross (-aˑvs; or chär-)
Charlemagne (shä′lĕmān)
Chăr′teris (-terz)
Chăt′ham (-tam)
Chăttan′qua (shȯ-; -kwa)
Cherbourg (shĕr′boorg)
Cher′well (chär-)
Chĭcago (shĭkah′gŏ, *shĭkaw′gŏ)
Chĭl′ē
Chĭswick (chĭz′ĭk)
Chloe (klō′ī)
Cholmondeley (chŭm′lĭ)
Chopin (shŏp′ăñ or shō-)

Cicero (sĭs′erō)
Cimabu′e (chē-; -ōō-ī)
Cinnaŏs′a (chē-; -z-)
Cincinnati′i (or -ah-)
Cĭr′encĕster (or sĭs′ĭster)
Clăv′erhouse (or klăv′erz)
Clerk′enwell (klär-)
Clough (klŭf, klŏ)
Clovĕll′ȳ
Cŏch′in-Chin′a
Cŏckaigne′ (-kān)
Cœur de Lion (kẽrdelē′awn̄)
Colbourne (kŏb′en)
Cŏl′chis (-k-)
Cologne′ (-ōn)
Colom′bo (-ŭm-)
Colōn′
Cŏlora(dō (-ah-; •-ā-)
Colquhoun (ko-hŏōn′)
Cŏm′ō
Comte (kaunt)
Connect′icut (-nĕt-)
Crĕ̄ton (krē′ōō′za)
Crichton (krīt′om)
Crimē′a
Crō′cē (-ch-)
Cullōd′en
Cȳm′bĕline (-līn)
Cȳn′ēwulf (k-; -ōōlf)
Cȳren′ē
Cȳthēr′a
Czech (chĕk)
Děd′alus
Dahŏm′ey (dȧ-h-)
Dakŏt′a
Dăn′āē (-ī)
Dāph′nē
Dăr′ēs (-z)
Dar′ius
Daudet (dō′dā)
Dâv′entry (or dän′trĭ)
Da′vos (dah-; or dȧvōs′)
Debüss′y (-ē)
De Crespigny (dekrĕp′īnĭ; or -krĕs-)
De gâs (dä-)
Dehra Dun (dā′rȧ-dōōn′)
Dĕlagŏ′a
De la Mare (dĕl′amaā)
Delhi (dĕl′ī)
Dĕl′ius
Dĕl′phī
Dĕmĕt′er
Dĕmĕt′rius (or -mĕt-)
Dĕmŏc′ritus
Dĕmŏs′thenĕs (-z)
Dĕn′bigh (-bĭ)
De Reszke (derĕs′kĭ)
Dĕr′went

Descartes (dắk'ãrt)
Desdemón'a (dēz-)
Des Moines (dĭmoin')
Détroit'
Deutsch'land (doich-)
Diderot (dēd'erō)
Did'ō
Dieppe (dē-ĕp')
Dijon (dē'zhawn)
Diōclē'tian (-shĭαn)
Dĭōg'enēs (-z)
Diomēd'ēs (-z)
Dionȳs'ius
Dionȳs'us
Disrael'i (-zrãl-)
Domĭ'tian (-shĭαn)
Don Glova'mnĭ (gōvah-)
Don Ju'an (jōōαn)
Donne
Donne [John, 1573–1631] (dŭn)
Don Quix'ōte (or kwĭk'set)
Do'theboys (dŏōdhe-)
Doug'las (dŭg-)
Drey'fus (drā-)
Dŭb'lin
Düll'wich (-lĭj)
Dŭ'mas (-mah)
Du Maurier (mo̅r'iā)
Dŭmfries' (-ēs)
Dŭnēd'ĭn
Dŭr'ban
Durham (dŭĭ'rαm)
Dvorak (dvŏr'zhák)
Ebbw (ĕb'ōō)
Ed'ĭnburgh (ĕ;-bure)
Eiff'el-tower (ĭf-)
Einstein (ĭn stĭn)
Eire (ār'ē)
El'ı (ē-)
El'ıa (ē-)
El'y̆ (ē-)
Emped'ocles (ĕ-:-z₁)
Endy̆m'ĭŏn (ĕ-)
Eng'land (ĭngg-)
Entĕbb'ē (ĕf-)
Epĭctē'us (ĕf-)
E'rewhŏn (ē-)
Erie (ēr'ĭ)
Erin (ē'rĭn or ĕr'-)
Es'tē (ĕ-)
Esthōni'a (ĕ-)
Etherege (ĕth'erĭj)
Euboea (ūbī'α)
Euphrāt'ēs (-z)
Euph'ūēs (-z)
Eurĭp'ĭdēs (ūr-:-z)
Europe (ūr'ŏp)
Eurȳd'ĭcē (ūr-)
Evēlĭn'a (ĕ-:-ēnα)
Ev'ely̆n (ĕ- or ē-)
Eyck (ĭk)
Ezēk'ĭel (-ĭ)
Fåg'ĭn (-g-)
Fall'odon
Fåf'quhar (-kwer)
Fåt'ĭma

Fa(u)lk'land (fawk-)
Faust (fowst)
Featherstonehaugh (fãn'shaw)
Fĭde'lĭō (-dā-)
Fiennes (fĭnz)
Fĭe'solē (fē-āz-)
Fĭg'arō
Fĭjĭ (fē'jē)
Fĭnĭsterre' (-āĭ)
Flō̄r'ēs (-z)
Flō'rĭda
Foch (fŏsh)
Fŏlk'estone (fōks-)
Frănçes'ca (or -chēs-)
Freud (froĭd)
Frō'bel (frēr-)
Frō̄b'isher
Froude (froŏd)
Frowde (-owd; or -ōōd)
Gala'pagŏs (gahlah-)
Găl'ēn
Gălĭle'o (-āō)
Galle (gawl)
Galsworthy (gaw'lzwerdhĭ)
Gamāl'ĭel
Gán'gēs (-z)
Gēdd'ēs (g-)
Geoff'rey (gĕf-)
Ghats (gawts)
Ghĭrlándaĭ'o (gēr-; -dĭ'yō)
Gĭaour (gowr)
Gĭbral'tar (ḡ-; -awl-)
Gĭd'ēa (g-)
Gĭl'ēād (g-)
Gĭllēttē' (g-)
Gĭŏngĭō'nē (ḡ-;-ḡ-)
Gĭŏtt'ō (g-)
Gĭovanni (gōvah'nĭ)
Glamĭs (glahmz)
Glăs'gow (-zgō)
Gloucester (glŏs'ter)
Ghuck (-ōōk)
Gō'a
Gōd'almĭng
Gōda'vari (-dah-)
Godĭv'a
Goethe (gĕr'te)
Gounod (gōōn'ō)
Gracchus (grăk'us)
Grātĭa'nō (-shtah-)
Greuse (grērz)
Grieg (grēg)
Grĭn'delwald (-vahld)
Groote Schoor (grŏt'skoor)
Gros'venor (grōv-)
Guadeloupe (gwahdĕlo̅op')
Guatemala (gwätĭmah'lα)
Gudrun (gōōd'rŏōn)
Guelph (gwĕlf)
Guĭana (gĭ-ah'nα)
Gŭsta'vus (-tah-)
Hāg'ãĭ
Hăgg'ãĭ
Hague (hāg)
Haifa (hīf'α)

Hain'ault (-awt)
Haït'í (or hī-)
Hak'luyt (-lŏŏt)
Hare'wŏŏd (hăr-)
Hăr'lech (-k)
Hā'run-al-Rasch'id (-rŏŏ-; or -shĭd)
Harwich (hă'rĭj)
Hausa (hou'za)
Havre (hah'vr)
Hawaï'i (-wī-ē)
Haw'arden (-erd-; or hărd-)
Hay'dn (hī-)
Hēb'ridēs (-z)
Hēe'atē
He'gel (hāg-)
Hei'delbĕrg (hī-)
Heine (hī'ne)
Hell'espont
Hĕm'ans
Hĕn'gist (-ngg-)
Hē'raclēs (-z)
Hĕraclī'tus
Hĕr'culēs (-z)
Hĕr'eward
Hĕr'mǐonē
Hē'rŏd
Hē'rŏd'ias
Hē'rŏd'otus
Hert'ford [England] (hăr'-)
Hĕrt'ford [America]
Herts (hărts)
Hĕspĕ'ridēs (-z)
Hiawăth'a (-wŏ-)
Hil'dĕbrănd
Himalāy'a (or hĭmah'lia)
Hin'du-Kush (-dŏŏ kŏŏsh)
Hippŏc'ratēs (-z)
Hippŏl'ўta
Hŏbb'ēma
Hŏ'hōken
Hŏle'enlin'den (hŏen-)
Hŏl'bein (-bīn)
Hŏl'born (hōben)
Hŏlŏfĕr'nēs (-z)
Hŏl'yrŏŏd
Hŏl'ўwĕll
Hŏm'er
Hŏndūr'ăs
Hŏnolu'lu (-lŏŏlŏŏ)
Hous'ton (hŏŏs-)
Hūd'ibrăs
Hū'on
Hun'yadi (hŏŏn-yah-)
Hūr'on
Hў̆d'erabăd
Hў̆gei'a (-īa)
Hў̆mĕtt'us
Hў̆pā'tia (-shǐa)
Hў̆pĕr'ion
Iago (i-ah'gō)
Iăn'thē (ī-)
Ic'arus (ī-)
Idaho (ī'da-hō)
Iq'ō (ī-)
Idūmē'a (ī-)
Illinois (ĭ-; -noi)

Illў'ria (ĭ-)
Indian'a (ĭ-)
Indianăp'olis (ĭ-)
Inge (ĭng or ĭng)
Ingelow (ĭn'gilō)
In'igō (ĭ-)
I'owa (ī-)
Iphigēnī'a (ĭ-)
Iquique (ĭkē'kē)
Iŏlăn'thē (ī-)
Iŏl'chus (ī-; -k-)
Ī'ran (ĭ-)
I'roquois (ĭ-; -kwoi or -kwah)
Isaac (ĭz'ac)
Isaiah (īzī'a)
Iş'is (ī-)
Is'leworth (īzelw-)
Ismailia (ĭzmah-ē'lia)
Isŏc'ratēs (ī-; -z)
Isolde (ĭzōl'dǎ)
Ispahan (ĭspǎ-hahn')
Ixī'on (ī-)
Jā'el
Jaipur (jīpoor')
Jăïr'us (or jīī'us)
Janeir'ō (-ēr-)
Jăph'ĕt
Jā'ques [in Shakespeare] (-kwiz)
Jăr'va (jäh-)
Je'na (yā-)
Jē'rome (or Jĕrōm')
Jĕr'vaulx (-vō)
Jŏhann'ĕsbŭrg
Jŏï'ĕt
Jō'seph'us
Jungfrau (yŏŏng'frou)
Kaap'stadt (kah-; -t)
Kabul' (-ŏŏl; or kaw'bŏŏl)
Kalahä'rï (kah-; -ee)
Kălamazŏō'
Kăndahăr' (-da-h-)
Kăn'sas [estate] (-nz-)
Kăn'sas [city] (-ns-)
Kara chī (-rah-)
Kăttegăt'
Kē'ble
Kĕd'ā
Kentŏck'ў
Kē'nўa (or kĕn-)
Kĕr'guēlĕn (-gĕl-)
Keswick (kĕz'ĭk)
Keynes (kānz)
Khaŕtum' (k- ; ŏŏm)
Khayyam (ki-ahm')
Khўb'er (k-)
Kieff (kēĕr')
Kiel (kēl)
Kĭl'imanjăr'ō
Kīfkoud'bright (-kŏō'bǔ,?)
Knollys (nōlz)
Kōb'ē
Kreisler (krīs'ler)
Kreutzer (kroit'ser)
Lăbouchère' (-bŏŏshăr')

Lách'esis (-k-)
Laci̅'tés (-z)
Lafitte (lahfét')
Läg'os
La Junta (lah hŏon'ta)
L'Alle'gro (lälä-)
Lancelot (lahn'slĕt)
Läŏc'ŏŏn
Lascelles (läs'els)
Las Pal'mas (lahs pahl-)
Lauren'çŏ Márques' (-sŏ; -ks)
Lausánne' (lŏz-)
Láv'engrŏ
Láv'er̄ȳ (or lä-)
Lávoi'sier (-vwahzyǟ)
Léǎn'der (or lē-)
Lĕd'a
Lĕı̄'ȳ
Le Feuvre (ffĕv'er)
Leicoester (lĕs'ter)
Leigh (lē)
Lein'ster (lĕn-)
Leip'zig (līp-)
Leith (lē-)
Lĕl'and
Lŏn'ĭn
Leominster (lĕm'ster)
Leonard'ŏ (lä-on-)
Le Queux (lekŭ')
Leveson-Gower (lŏŏ'sen-gŏr')
Lhás'a (la-)
Liège (llǟzh')
Li̅'ma (lē-)
Limoges' (-ŏzh)
Liszt (-st)
Llan- [as the first element in Welsh names] (hlän-)
Llewéll'ȳn (lŏŏ-)
Lŏh'engrïn (lŏ-)
Lŏngĭn'us (-nj-)
Lŏr'élei (-i)
Lŏs An'gĕlĕs (-ăngg•, also -anğ•; -z)
Louisiän'a (lŏŏ-ĕáz-)
Lŏŭ'isville (lŏŏ-)
Lourdes (loord)
Luga'nŏ (lŏŏgah-)
Lȳ'cidäs
Lȳ̆cŭr̄'gus
Lȳ̆'lȳ̆
Lȳ'm'ington
Lȳmpne (lĭm)
Lȳ̆'san'der
Má'cĕdon
Mackay (makī')
Macleod (maklowd')
Madrás' (or -ahs)
Madrid'
Mad'ura
Mae'terlinck (mah- or mä-)
Mäf'eking
Mággŏr'e (-j-)
Mahón' (ma-h-; or -ŏŏn)
Mahony (mah'nĭ)
Mainwaring (mäń'erĭng)
Māl'achi (-k-)
ᶜAl'herbe (-lär̄b)

Māl'or̄ȳ
Mal'ta (mawl-)
Mal'vern (mawl-)
Mär'et (-ā)
Mar'ion (or mä-)
Marjoribänks (mär'chb-)
Märque'säs (-kä-)
Mä́r'tıneau (-nŏ)
Mártinique' (-ĕk)
Mä́r'ȳländ (*mĕ-)
Má'rylebone (-elĕbn; or mä'rıben)
Masaí' (-sǐ; or mah'sǐ)
Mássachus'ĕtts (-ŏŏ-)
Mäss'enet (-enä)
Mátabēl'é
Maurī'tius (-shyes)
Mazzini (mädzēn'ı̆)
Mĕch'lĭn (-kl-)
Mĕdé'a
Mĕd'ici (-chi)
Mĕdĭn'a (-ē-)
Mĕdĭn'a [America]
Meis'tersinger (mī-)
Mĕn'ai (-nǐ)
Mĕn'delssohn (-son; or -sŏn)
Mĕnélä'us
Menzies (mĕn'zĭz, mĕng'ĭs, mĭng'ĭs)
Mĕroöd'ĕs (-z)
Mĕr̄oǐ'tiŏ (-shǐ-)
Mĕ'redith (in Wales mĕrĕd'ĭth)
Mĕ'ropé
Mĕssĭn'a (-sē-)
Mĕtt'ernich (-k)
Mey'nell (mĕ- or mä-)
Mĭäm'ĭ
Mich'ĭgan (-shĭ-)
Mĭd'äs
Mĭlǟn' (or mĭl'an)
Mĭll'aïs (-ā)
Mĭlngavie (mĭlgī')
Minneáp'olis
Minnĕsŏt'a
Miràn'da
Missour'ı̄ (-oor-: *mĭz-)
Mithridät'ĕs (-z)
Mĭtylēn'ē (or -ē)
Mŏbĭle' (-ēl)
Mŏh'ican (mŏ-; properly mŏ-hē'-)
Mohun (mŏŏn)
Mŏl'iere (-liǟ)
Mŏna'cŏ (-ah-)
Mŏntaigne' (-än)
Mŏntreál' (-awl)
Mŏrŏn'é
Mŏs'cow (-ŏ)
Moul'main
Mŏzambïque' (-bĕk)
Müller (mĭl'er)
Multan (mŏŏl'tahn)
Mı̄̆nı̄ll'ŏ
Mȳcē'næ
Mȳtilēn'ē (or -ē)
Nairōb'ï (nī̄-)
Nä'omï
Näp'ïer (or nɒpēï')
Natäl'
Näv'ajo (-ɑ-hŏ)

Nepal' (-awl)
Neva'da (-vah-; *-ă-)
Newfoundland (-fend-)
Niag'ara
Nibelung (nēb'ĕloong)
Nietzsche (nē'chĕ)
Ni'ger
Nigē'ria
Nil'giri (-g-)
Nin'eveh (-vĕ)
Norwich (nŏr'rij)
N'yás(s)'a
Ob'an (ō-)
Ober-ämm'ergau (ō-; -gow)
Ob'eron (ō-)
Odys'seus (-ius)
Œnōr'ē (ē-)
Ohī'ō (ō-h-)
Oklahōm'a (ō-)
Omaha (ōmȧ-hah'; •-aw)
Oman (ōmahn')
Ontār'iō (ō-)
Ophēl'ia (ō-)
Orēs'tēs (ō-; -z)
Orī'on (ō-)
Orlé'ans (ō-; -z)
Orleans [America] (ôrlēanz')
Orpheus (ôr'fūs)
Orsino (ôrsēn'ō)
Osīr'is (ō-)
Os'ler (ō-)
Ota'gō (ōtah-)
Othĕll'ō (ō-)
Ottawa (ŏt'a-wa)
Ottinī'wa (ō-)
Ouida (wē'da)
Ouse (ōoz)
Ov'īd (ō-)
Pach'mann (pahk-)
Pâderew'skī (-ĕvskī)
Pagani'nī (-ēn-)
Paglacci (pȧliȧch'ī)
Palæmōd'ēs (-z)
Pāl'amon
Pālestrī'na (-ēn-)
Pall'ās
Pâll Mäll' (or pĕl'mĕll')
Panama (-äh)
Pâph'ōs
Pâ'raguay (-gwä or -gwī)
Parnäss'us
Paroīl'ēs
Pâs'teur (-ĕr)
Patroc'lus
Pau (pō)
Pausān'iäs
Pav'ia
Pekin'
Pēl'eus (-lūs)
Pĕlopōnnēs'us
Pēl'ops
Pĕnnsÿlvān'ia
Pĕnthĕsilē'a
Pepys (pēps or pĕps or pĕp'is)
Pēr'dita
Pêrgole'sē (-läz-)
Pēr'iclēs (-z)

Pê'rrault (-rō)
Pêrsēph'onē
Pêrsēp'olis
Pêr'seus (-ūs)
Peru' (-rōō)
Perug'inō (-ōōgē-)
Peshawar (peshōr')
Pestalozz'ī (-tsī)
Pĕsth (-st)
Pêt'ra
Pĕt'rärch (-k)
Pêtru'chio (-ōōk- or -ōōch-)
Phæd'ra
Phā'ĕthōn
Phārsāl'ia
Philēm'ōn
Phō'cis
Phœb'ē (fē-)
Phœnic'ia (fē-)
Phrÿn'ē
Plâr'tō
Plin'ÿ
Plotīn'us
Piu'tärch (-ōō-; -k)
Pōllaino'lō (-li-ōō-ō-)
Pole Carew (pōōl' kär'ī)
Pōlyb'ius
Pōlyc'ratēs (-z)
Pōlÿphēm'us
Pōlÿx'ēna
Pompeī'ī (-ēī or -āē)
Pom'frĕt (pŭm-)
Pōrt Saïd (-ēd or säd)
Pōsei'dōn (-sī-)
Potōm'äc
Poughkeep'sie (pōkip-)
Poussin (pōō'săn)
Pō'wÿs
Prâxit'elēs (-z)
Prêtōr'ia
Prī'am
Prometh'eus (-ius)
Prōs'erpine
Proust (prōost)
Pû'cini (pōōchē'ni)
Punjab' (-ahb)
Py'ramus
Pÿthāg'orās
Quêbec'
Rāb'elais (-elä)
Rāc'īne (-sēn)
Rae'bûrn (rā-)
Rajputana (rähjpōotah'nȧ)
Raleigh (raw'li or räh- or rä-)
Rām'ēsēs (-z)
Rân'elagh (-le)
Râph'ăel
Ra'walpindI (rah-w-)
Read'ing (rĕd-)
Reger (rāg'er)

Reik'javik (rēkya-)	Sim'on
Reu'ter (roi-)	Simplon (săn'plawn)
Rheims (rēms)	Sī'nai (-nī)
Rhōdé'sia (rō-; -z- or -s-; *also* -zha, sha'	Sis'ŷphus
Ri'ca (rē-)	Sī'va (shē-)
Rich'elieu (-shelū)	Skŭdd'aw (*or* skiddaw')
Rio (rē'ō)	Slough (slow)
Rivier'a (-ēra)	Smēth'wick (-dhik)
Robespierre (rōbz'pyār')	Sōc'ratēs (-z)
Rocke'feller (-kf-, *-kif-)	Sōfi'a
Rōm'ney (*or* rūm-)	Sōma'li (-ah-)
Rōntgen (rĕrn'tyen)	Som'ersēt (sŭm-)
Rōō'sevelt (-sv-, *-siv-)	Sōph'oclēs (-z)
Rossëtt'i (rōz-)	Southey (sow'dhi)
Rōtoru'a (-ōia)	Southwark (sŭdh'ark)
Rouen (rōō'añn)	Sou'za (-ōō-)
Rox'burgh (-bre)	Srĭna gar (-ah-)
Ruy Blas (rwē blahs)	St Al'bans (awl-)
Ság'inaw	Stendhal (stahn'dahl)
Sainte-Beurve (săit bĕrv)	St John (sĭn'jon)
Saint-Saens (săñ sahñs)	St Lou'is (sănt lōō-)
Salis'burŷ (sawlzb-)	St Ma'lō (-ah-)
Salōm'ē	Stōke Pō'gēs
Salōn'ica (*or* sälonē'-)	Strachan (strawn *or* strah'χan)
Săn'chō (-ngk-)	Streath'am (strĕt-)
Săn Diego (dē-ā'gō)	Stuy'vésant (stī-)
Săn Jacin'tō	Sudán' (sōō- *or* sōō-)
Săn Joaquin (wahkēn')	St ĕz (-ōō-)
Săn Jose (hōsā')	Suma'tra (sōōmah-)
Săn Juan' (hwahn)	Sumurun (sōōmōōrōōn')
Săn Re'mō (rā-)	Surát' (sōō-)
Săn'ta Fé (fā)	Süsquehánn'a (-kw-)
Săndia'gō (-ah-)	Swa'zīland (swah-)
Sárasa'tē (-ah-)	Sŷnge (-ng)
Sara'wak (-rah-)	Sŷr'acuse (-z)
Sáskátch'ewan	Sŷr'acuse [America]
Sáskatōōn'	Tăg'us
Sault Sainte Marie (sōō sănt mā̆r'i; *or* sănt)	Tahi'ti (tah-hē-)
Săvonarōl'a	Táj Mahal (tahj mahahl')
Sca'fell' (scaw-)	Tăngányi'ka (-ngg-; -ŷē-)
Scal'iger	Tăngier' (-jēr)
Sohēhēreza'dē (sh-; -ezah-)	Tănnhāu'ser (-hoiz-)
Schénéc'tadŷ (sk-)	Tărragōn'a
Schu'bért (shōō-)	Tchaikovsky (chikōv'skI)
Schuy'ler (ski-)	Tectīm'seh (-sē)
Schuy'lkill (skōōl-)	Teh'erán (tāer-)
Scill'ŷ (s-)	Teignmouth (tĭn'meth)
Scip'iō (s-)	Télém'achus (-kus)
Scri'abīn	Tēnerif(f)e' (-ēf)
Scone (skōōn)	Tĕr'psīch'orē (-k-)
Sédan'	Te'rra del Fuego (fōōā̆'gō)
Séd'bergh [school] (-ber- bŏrg)	Tĕr'till'ian
Séd'bergh [town] (-ber)	Thame (tām)
Seine (sān)	Thames (tĕmz)
Sēm'élē	Thăn'ĕt
Sēmī'ramis	Thēbes (-bz)
Sēn'éca	Thémist'oclēs (-z)
Sēnégal' (-awl)	Thē'obald (-awld; *or* tĭb'ald)
Sēnnách'erīb (-k-)	Thēōd'oric
Sēt'ébos	Thĕrmŏp'ŷlae
Shrews'burŷ (-ōōz- *or* -ōz-)	Thĕrsīt'ēs (-z)
Siăm'	Thōs'eus -tĭsŷ
Sierr'a Léone' (-ār-; -ōn-)	Thĕs'pis
̄in'éon	Thĕssaloni'ca
	Thĕss'alŷ
	Thīs'bē (-z-)
	Thom'as (tŏm-)

Thomas [Ambroise] (tŏ′mah)
Thoẽ′eau (-ō)
Thŏẽ′d′idēs (-z)
Thŏẽ′us
Tibĕt′
Tibŏll′us
Tĭcĩ′nō (-chē-)
Tĭg′rĭs
Tĭm′ŏ ı
Tintăg′el
Tĭtăn′ia
Tĭt′ian (-shı-)
Tĭt′us
Tĭv′olĭ
Tŏbĭ′as
Tŏ′kyō
Tŏlĕ′dō (or -ā′dō)
Tŏ′rnēs
Tŏt′nĕs
Toulon (tŏŏlawn′)
Toulouse (tŏŏlŏŏz′)
Touraine′ (tŏŏ-)
Tours (toor)
Tow′cester (tō′ster)
Trafăl′gar (or trăfalgăr′)
Trăj′an
Trăn′skei (-kı)
Transvaal (trănz′nsvahl)
Trĕvĭ′sa (-vēz-)
Trĭchĭnŏp′olĭ
Trĭĕste′
Trĭnc′ŏmalee′
Trŏll′ope (-ŭp)
Trŏss′achs (-ks)
Trŏut′ville (-ŏŏ-)
Tucson (tŏŏ′sawn; or -ăn)
Tuileries (twēl′erē)
Tūlĭn′ (or tūr′ĭn)
Tŭnĭs
Tŭnkĕstăn′
Tŭskē′gee
Tussaud′s′ (-sŏz)
Tў′chō (-k-)
Tўn′dale (-dĺl)
Tў′rol (or tĭrŏl′ or tīrŏl′)
Tўr′whitt (-rĭt)
Ŭgăn′da (ū- or ŏŏ-)
Ŭh′land (ōō-)
U′ĭst (ū-)
Ŭlўss′ēs (ū-; -z)
Ŭphar′sĭn (ū-)
Ûr′ah (ūr-)
Ur′ĭel (ūr-)
Urquhart (ûr′kert)
Uruguay (ōō′rŏŏgway′; or -ī)
Ush′ant (ŭ-)
Utah (ū′tah, *ū′taw)
Ŭth′er (ū-)
Utrecht (ūtrĕkt′)
U′ĭst (ū-)
Vălkўrie
Văl′ois (-wah)
Vălparăis′ō (-z-)
Văn′burgh (-bre)
Văsă′ı
Văs′cō da Ga′ma (gah-)
Văth′ĕk
Vaughan (vawn)

Vauxhall (vŏks′hawl′)
Vĕlăs′quez (-kwĭz or-kĭz)
Vĕn′ĕzĕ′la
Vĕrde
Vĕr′dĭ (văr-)
Vĕr′dun (or văr-)
Vĕr′gĭl
Verne (vărn)
Vērone′se (-āzĕ)
Vĕr′ulam (-ōō-)
Vēstrў′ius
Vĕry′lus
Vichy (vē′shē)
Vĭĕnn′a
Vĭg′ŏ
Vĭll′iers (lerz)
Vĭn′ci (-chī)
Vĭ′ola
Vĭr′gĭl
Vosges (vōzh)
Wa′bash (waw-)
Wadham (wŏd′am)
Wag′ner (vah-)
Waldegrăve (wawl′g-)
Wantage (won′tĭj)
Wapp′ing (wŏ-)
Wăr′ing
Warwick (wŏ′rĭk)
Watteau (wŏt′ō)
Wazir′istan (-ĕĕ-; -ahn)
Wear [river] (wēr)
Wednes′bury (wĕnzb-)
Weiss′hŏrn (vīs-h-)
Welwyn (wĕl′ĭn)
Wemyss (wēmz)
We′ser (vāz- or wēz-)
Whewell (hūl)
Wies′baden (vēzbah-)
Wĭs′bĕch (-z-)
Wiecŏn′sin
Wŏll′wich (-ĭj)
Wŏŏt′on
Worcester (wŏŏs′ter)
Wōrms (v:-z)
Wrĕk′ĭn (r-)
Wўch′erley
Wўe′lĭf
Wўe′ombe (-om)
Wўk′eham (-kam)
Wymondham [Norfolk] (wĭnd′am)
Wўō′ming
Xăv′ier (z-)
Xĕn′ophon (z-)
Xĕr′xĕs (z-; -z)
Xhosa (kaw′sa)
Yeats (yăts)
Yĕ′men (yă-)
Yeo′vĭl (yō-)
Yŏkŏha′ma (-hah-)
Yŏsĕm′itĕ
Ypres (ēpr, wī′perz)
Ysaye (ēsī′)
Yncatan′ (ū-; -ahn)
Zăcharī′ah (-ä)
Zeiss (zīs)
Zĕlŏt′ĕs (-z)

Zĕn′ō
Zĭmba′bwē (-bah-)
Zō′ē
Zōl′a

Zōrōäs′ter
Zürich (zū′rĭk)
Zuy′der Zee′ (zī-)

APPENDIX IV

WEIGHTS AND MEASURES

(a) ENGLISH AND METRIC EQUIVALENTS

English to Metric.

Linear Measure:

1 inch	= 25·3999 millimetres.
1 foot (12 inches)	= 0·30480 metre.
1 yard (3 feet)	= 0·914399 metre.
1 pole (5½ yards)	= 5·02919 metres.
1 chain (22 yards)	= 20·1168 metres.
1 furlong (220 yards)	= 201·16778 metres.
1 mile (1,760 yards)	= 1·60934 kilometres.

Square Measure:

1 square inch	= 6·45159 sq. centimetres.
1 square foot (144 sq. in.)	= 9·29028 sq. decimetres.
1 square yard (9 sq. ft.)	= 0·836126 sq. metre.
1 perch (30¼ sq. yards)	= 25·29280 sq. metres.
1 rood (40 perches)	= 10·11712 ares.
1 acre (4,840 sq. yards)	= 0·40468 hectare.
1 square mile (640 acres)	= 258·99824 hectares.

Cubic Measure:

1 cubic inch	= 16·3870 cubic centimetres.
1 cubic foot (1,728 cub. in.)	= 0·02832 cubic metre.
1 cubic yard (27 cub. ft.)	= 0·764553 cubic metre.

Measure of Capacity:

1 gill	= 1·42058 decilitres.
1 pint (4 gills)	= 0·56823 litre.
1 quart (2 pints)	= 1·13646 litres.
1 gallon (4 quarts)	= 4·545961 litres.
1 peck (2 gallons)	= 9·0917 litres.
1 bushel (8 gallons)	= 3·6366 dekalitres.
1 quarter (8 bushels)	= 2·90935 hectolitres.

Apothecaries' Measure:

1 fluid drachm (60 minims)	= 3·55145 millilitres.
1 fluid ounce (8 drachms)	= 2·84123 centilitres.
1 gal. (8 pts. or 160 fluid oz.)	= 4·54596 litres.

Avoirdupois Weight:

1 grain	= 0·0648 gramme.
1 dram (27·34 gr.)	= 1·77185 grammes.
1 ounce (16 dr.)	= 28·34953 grammes.
1 pound (16 oz.)	= 0·43359243 kilogram.
1 stone (14 lb.)	= 6·35029 kilograms.
1 quarter (28 lb.)	= 12·70059 kilograms.
1 hundredweight (cwt. 112 lb.)	= 50·80235 kilograms.
1 ton (20 cwt.)	= 1·01604 tonnes.

Troy Weight:

1 pennyweight (24 grains)	= 1·55517 grammes.
1 ounce (480 grs. avoir.)	= 31·10348 grammes.

Apothecaries' Weight:

1 scruple (20 grains) = 1·29598 grammes.
1 drachm (3 scruples) = 3·88794 grammes.
1 ounce (8 drachms) = 31·10348 grammes.

The Apothecaries' ounce is the Troy ounce of 480 Avoirdupois grains.

(b) METRIC AND ENGLISH EQUIVALENTS

Linear Measure:

		Metric to English.
1 millimetre (1/1000 m.)	=	0·03937 inch.
1 centimetre (1/100 m.)	=	0·39370 inch.
1 decimetre (1/10 m.)	=	3·93701 inches.
1 metre (m.)	=	1·0936143 yards.
1 decametre (10 m.)	=	10·93614 yards.
1 hectometre (100 m.)	=	109·3614 yards.
1 kilometre (1,000 m.)	=	0·62137 mile.
1 myriametre (10,000 m.)	=	6·21372 miles.

Square Measure:

1 sq. centimetre	=	0·15500 sq. inch.
1 sq. decimetre (100 sq. centimetres)	=	15·50006 sq. inches.
1 sq. metre or centiare (100 sq. decimetres)	=	{ 10·76393 sq. feet.
1 are (100 sq. metres)		1·19599 sq. yards.
1 hectare (100 ares or 10,000 sq. metres)	=	119·59926 sq. yards.
	=	2·47106 acres.

Cubic Measurement:

1 cubic centimetre (1,000 cub. millimetres)	=	0·06102 cubic inch.
1 cubic decimetre (1,000 cub. centimetres)	=	61·02394 cubic inches.
1 cubic metre or stere (1,000 cub. decimetres)	=	{ 35·31477 cubic feet.
		1·307954 cubic yards.

Measure of Capacity:

1 millilitre (1/1000 litre)	=	0·00704 gill.
1 centilitre (1/100 litre)	=	0·07039 gill.
1 decilitre (1/10 litre)	=	0·17598 pint.
1 litre	=	1·75985 pints.
1 decalitre (10 litres)	=	2·19981 gallons.
1 hectolitre (100 litres)	=	2·74976 bushels.
1 kilolitre (1000 litres)	=	3·43720 quarters.

Weight:

1 milligram (1/1000 grm.)	=	0·01543 grain.
1 centigram (1/100 grm.)	=	0·15432 grain.
1 decigram (1/10 grm.)	=	1·54324 grains.
1 gramme	=	15·43236 grains.
1 decagram (10 grms.)	=	5·64383 drams.
1 hectogram (100 grms.)	=	3·52740 ounces.
1 kilogram (1,000 grms.)	=	2·2046223 lb.
1 myriagram (10 kilog.)	=	22·04622 lb.
1 quintal (100 kilog.)	=	1·96841 cwt.
1 tonne (1,000 kilog.)	=	0·98420 ton.

	Troy	
1 gramme =	{	0·03215 oz.
		15·43236 grains.
"	Apothecaries'	0·25721 drachm.
"		0·77162 scruple.
		15·43236 grains.